ULRICH'S

PERIODICALS DIRECTORY

48th Edition

2010

International Periodicals Information Since 1932

Ulrich's Periodicals Directory
was prepared by Proquest Serials Editorial Department

Editorial
Laurie Kaplan, Director, Serials
Martha David, Quality Control/Technical Manager
Ewa Kowalska, Valerie A. Mahon, Managing Editors
Christopher King, Senior Editor
Shawn Chen, Pappaparvathi Patham, Senior Associate Editors
Kathryn Stewart, Halyna Testerman, Filippo Valli, and Michael Weingardner, Associate Editors
Debra James, Margit Linforth, Maria R. Mucino, Anne Picker, and Leo Weinstock, Contributing Editors

Data Acquisition
O'Sheila Delgado, Editorial Coordinator
Jennifer Williams, Associate Editor

Production & Manufacturing Services
Doreen Gravesande, Senior Director, Data Distribution
Andy Haramasz, Manager, Raw Data and Data Distribution
Lorena Soriano, Gunther Stegmann, Project Managers, Production

Editorial Systems, Information Technology Group
Mark Heinzelman, Chief Data Architect
Steve Gorski, Programmer Analyst
Computer Operations Group
John Nesselt, UNIX Administrator

48th Edition

ULRICH'S™

PERIODICALS DIRECTORY

2010

International Periodicals Information Since 1932

including
Irregular Serials & Annuals

Volume 4

Indexes

Cross-Index to Subjects • Cessation • ISSN • Title • CD-ROM Producers
Online Services • International Organizations

US Newpapers and Indexes

8907-11708

Published by ProQuest
630 Central Avenue, New Providence, NJ 07974

Ulrich's Hotline (U.S. only): 1-800-346-6049
Editorial (Canada only, call collect): 1-908-219-0286
ProQuest Fax (overseas users): (+1) 908-219-0182
ProQuest E-mail: ulrichs@proquest.com
URL: http://www.ulrichsweb.com

Ulrich's and ulrichsweb.com are trademarks of ProQuest

International Standard Book Number
ISBN 13: 978-1-60030-127-8 (4-Volume set)
ISBN 13: 978-1-60030-123-0 (Volume 1)
ISBN 13: 978-1-60030-124-7 (Volume 2)
ISBN 13: 978-1-60030-125-4 (Volume 3)
ISBN 13: 978-1-60030-126-1 (Volume 4)

International Standard Serial Number
0000-2100

Library of Congress Control Number
32-16320

Printed and bound in the United States of America

Contents

Ulrich's
Serials Librarianship Award

Presented by the Serials Section
Association for Library Collections and Technical Services (ALCTS)
Division of the American Library Association (ALA)

Sponsored by ProQuest

Formerly sponsored by R.R. Bowker LLC

This annual award is given in recognition of distinguished and ongoing contributions to serials librarianship. Qualified individuals demonstrate leadership in serials-related activities through their participation in professional associations, groups, and/or library education programs; make significant contributions to serials literature; and, in general, strive to enhance our comprehension of the serials world.

AWARD RECIPIENTS

1985 Marcia Tuttle

1986 Ruth C. Carter

1987 James P. Danky

1988 Marjorie E. Bloss

1989 John E. Merriman

1990 Jean S. Cook

1991 Deana L. Astle/Charles A. Hamaker

1992 Linda K. Bartley

1993 Ann L. Okerson

1994 Tina Feick

1995 Peter Gellatly

1996 Jean L. Hirons

1997 Cindy Hepfer

1998 Crystal Graham

1999 Regina Romano Reynolds

2000 Trisha L. Davis

2001 not awarded

2002 Eric Lease Morgan

2003 Frieda Rosenberg

2004 Pamela Bluh

2005 Dan Tonkery

2006 Karen Hunter

2007 Julia Blixrud

2008 Vicky Reich

2009 Brian Green

Preface

In the 78 years since **Ulrich's™ Periodicals Directory** was first published, technology has substantially transformed both the methods and mission of the library and research center. Access, rather than ownership, has become a key consideration. Resource sharing and networking have become common practices in the effort to maintain the flow of quality information. As promising as these changes in collections and services may be, they generate a new set of questions in nearly every sphere of serials management: acquisition; bibliographic control; conservation and preservation; access; standards; and education and training.

At ProQuest, we have set ourselves the task of addressing these transitions by developing and expanding **Ulrich's™ Periodicals Directory** in a variety of ways. Now in its 48th edition, **Ulrich's** has established itself as the premier serials reference source in the world, providing serials users with essential bibliographic and access information that ranges from subscription rates to the latest web sites. For complete details on these changes, please see the User's Guide on pages ix-xv of the prefatory material of Volumes 1-4.

As libraries, institutions, and researchers shift focus from physical ownership of materials to acquiring individual articles on demand, our coverage of document delivery services now includes 15 different services offering the full text of articles from over 50,171 serials listed in **Ulrich's**. For a brief explanation of such services, please refer to the "Document Suppliers" section in the User's Guide, page xiii of the prefatory material. For contact information for these services, please see the company listings section on page xxvi of the prefatory material.

Though the printed serial is by no means on the wane, the use of electronic research tools, whether online or on CD-ROM, continues unabated. There has been a dramatic increase in the use of the Internet as a publishing medium, resulting in new breeds of serials. Electronic publications, such as e-journals and e-zines, emerge every day and are reflected in **Ulrich's**. This edition includes 68,581 serials available exclusively online or in addition to other media. 7,378 serials are indicated as available on CD-ROM. These serials are indicated by a notation in the main entry and a bullet (•) in the TITLE INDEX.

Regardless of the publication medium, serials remain the key tools for scholarship and the primary source of current information and topical news in all fields of endeavor. In toto, the 48th edition of **Ulrich's** contains information on over 215,880 serials published throughout the world, classified and cross-referenced under 897 subject headings. Additionally, each entry is assigned at minimum one Dewey Decimal Classification number from the 22nd edition. Included are serials that are currently available, issued more frequently than once a year and usually published at regular intervals, as well as publications issued annually or less frequently than once a year, or irregularly. While aiming for maximum title coverage, we have established certain criteria for inclusion. We report all publications that meet the definition of a serial except administrative publications of governmental agencies below state level that can be easily found elsewhere. A limited selection of membership directories, comic books, and puzzle and game books is included.

Entries have been updated to reflect the most current information available and 6,067 serials have been added this year, some of which may have since ceased or suspended publication. Included in this edition is cessation or suspension information that has been recorded in our database during the past three years for 5,954 titles. The ceased or suspended titles are preceded by a dagger (†) in the TITLE INDEX for instant identification.

Users can identify 7,008 newer serials, which are known to have begun publication since January 1, 2007, by an inverted solid triangle (▼) in both the CLASSIFIED LIST

OF SERIALS and the TITLE INDEX. This symbol is also used to highlight the 198 forthcoming serial launches announced for publication in the years 2009-2010. In addition, 26,627 refereed serials notations, approximately 94,688 brief descriptions, over 48,342 LC Classification Numbers, and some 17,952 CODEN appear in this edition.

Further facilitating access to serials are indicators found in over 69,600 titles denoting coverage by some 762 abstracting and indexing services, over 18,830 notations of reprint availability, over 54,780 e-mail addresses and over 56,100 company URLs (Uniform Resource Locators on the World Wide Web).

There are many copyright implications associated with the distribution of published material from the Internet and the delivery and sharing of other documents. We therefore provide Copyright Clearance Center notations for over 30,040 registered titles along with over 18,940 entries with Rights & Permissions contact names. When available, we include telephone contact information as well. These data elements make it easy to comply with the law without interrupting the flow of information.

Beginning with the 34th edition, the publication date of **Ulrich's** moved from August to November. Publication in November enables us to provide thousands of updated prices for 2010 since many publishers establish prices for the upcoming year between May and October. Prices set and received by us later than mid-September were not updated for this print edition. However, data are entered as received, so price changes and other information, such as title changes, cessations, and new releases, received after mid-September will appear in issues of the electronic versions of **Ulrich's**. These include **ulrichsweb.com™**, updated weekly on the Internet at http://www.ulrichsweb.com, providing article-level content and linking to journal full-text; Ulrich's Serials Analysis System™, the collection evaluation and reporting tool for library professionals at http://www.ulrichsweb.com/analysis.

Your purchase and use of **Ulrich's** is complemented by access to the **Ulrich's Hotline**, a toll-free number that subscribers may phone for help in solving particular research problems and questions. Canadian users are asked to call a special number collect, and our overseas users are asked to use a designated fax number. (Please refer to page iv for our mailing address, telephone/fax numbers, and e-mail address.) Publishers are encouraged to e-mail updates as changes to their titles occur, using the e-mail address ulrichs@proquest.com.

As we continue to research, plan, and implement enhancements to the **Ulrich's** database and our database maintenance system, we consider feedback from our users to be essential. Please contact us to let us know your thoughts and suggestions. You may write to us, send us a fax, call us on the telephone, or send us e-mail.

Gratitude is extended to the entire staff of **Ulrich's** for their unflagging dedication and diligent work in updating and maintaining the serials database in preparation of the 48th edition of **Ulrich's**. Appreciation is also extended to all vendors and service suppliers for working with us to produce this directory. Finally, we thank the various information specialists, serialists, national libraries, and serials publishers throughout the world who have aided us in updating **Ulrich's**. We consider their participation and interest in the dissemination of accurate and comprehensive serials information to be of tremendous value to **Ulrich's** and its users.

This directory offers two primary access methods for locating periodicals: by subject in the CLASSIFIED LIST OF SERIALS (Volumes 1-3), and alphabetically in the TITLE INDEX (Volume 4). Ceased serials are listed in a separate CESSATIONS section (Volume 4) and are also accessible by means of the TITLE INDEX. Other indexes provide listings of selected periodicals in specific categories. These indexes, in Volume 4 are PRODUCER LISTING/SERIALS ON CD-ROM, ONLINE SERVICE LISTING/SERIALS ONLINE, PUBLICATIONS OF INTERNATIONAL ORGANIZATIONS, and ISSN INDEX. See the User's Guide in Volume 4 for a content description and use instructions for the U.S. NEWSPAPERS section.

In addition, separate subheadings for "Abstracting, Bibliographies and Statistics" under major subject headings provide convenient access to these types of publications. Page references for these subheadings are given in the "Subject Guide to Abstracting and Indexing" on page I. This listing provides an overview of subjects for which abstracting and indexing publications have been identified.

The "User's Guide" is separated into three divisions for ease of use: (I) Section Descriptions, (II) Full Entry Content Description, and (III) Cataloging Rules for Main Entry Title.

Section Descriptions

CLASSIFIED LIST OF SERIALS

This is the main section of the book, containing bibliographic information for currently published serials classified by subject. Entries are arranged alphabetically by title within each subject heading. Subject cross-references in the text direct the user to the location of subheadings.

Volume 1 contains subjects A - Edu-C, from "Abstracting and Indexing" through "Education-Computer Applications." Volume 2 contains subjects Edu-G - Med-F, "Education-Guides to Schools and Colleges" through "Medical Sciences-Gastroenterology." Volume 3 contains subjects Med-G - Z, from "Medical Sciences - Hematology" through "Zoology."

A complete listing of the "Subjects" used in the CLASSIFIED LIST OF SERIALS appears on p. li. To aid international users, this list is translated into four languages. For additional guidance on the subject classification scheme, the user should also consult the CROSS-INDEX TO SUBJECTS in Volume 4, which contains additional key word references.

Each serial is listed with full bibliographic information only once. If a serial covers several subjects, title cross-references appear under the related headings, directing the user to the heading where the full entry is listed.

New serials beginning publication in the past three years, as well as titles announced for publication in the coming year are highlighted by an inverted triangle symbol ▼ in front of the title.

The "Cataloging Rules for Main Entry Title" section of this "User's Guide" explains the title cataloging rules followed in compiling **Ulrich's**.

CESSATIONS

In this section, entries for serials for which cessation was noted in the past year are listed alphabetically by title. The cessation entry includes: title, Dewey Decimal Classification number, former frequency of publication, publisher name and address, country-of-publication code, and, if available, other information such as ISSN, subtitle, corporate author, year of first issue, and year ceased. Titles which were originally planned as continuing series but which have closed are included in the CESSATIONS section although back issues may still be available.

If a title has "ceased" because a new title is being used, there will not be an entry in the CESSATIONS section. Instead, the entry is maintained in the CLASSIFIED LIST OF SERIALS under the new title, with a **"Formerly"** or **"Former titles"** indication.

ISSN INDEX

The ISSN INDEX lists serials in order by ISSN number. It includes all serials contained in the **Ulrich's** database, whether current, ceased, or inactive, to which an ISSN has been assigned in our file. A dagger symbol (†) indicates that the title is ceased. If an ISSN appears twice, it usually indicates that the serial has split into two or more parts. Titles that have changed and for which new ISSNs have been assigned will show cross-references from one ISSN to the new ISSN. If no new

ISSN has been assigned, the cross-reference is from ISSN to new title. Entries for inactive titles do not appear in the book.

Boldface type indicates the page number where a complete entry can be found for active titles. Titles for which cessation was noted in the last three years have a page reference to the listing in the CESSATIONS INDEX. If no page reference appears for a ceased title, it means that the cessation was noted more than three years ago and is not listed in this edition. ISSNs of inactive titles likewise do not have page references and are not listed in this book.

A full description of the ISSN and its use is provided on p. xvi.

TITLE INDEX

The TITLE INDEX is the second major access point for serials. To locate a serial by its title, the user should be familiar with title cataloging rules as described in the "Cataloging Rules for Main Entry Titles" paragraphs of this "User's Guide."

The TITLE INDEX lists all current and ceased serials included in this directory. **Boldface** type indicates the page number where the complete entry will be found.

For serials with identical titles published within a country, the city of publication is added in parentheses, and sometimes the year of first publication is given to further distinguish the titles.

If a serial title consists of or contains an acronym, a cross-reference is provided from the full name to the acronym form of the title.

Cross-references are provided from former titles and variant titles, and from the alternate language titles of multi-language publications. Recent title changes are noted, with a reference to the current title. The TITLE INDEX also lists the country code for all serials, along with the ISSN, if known.

The inverted triangle symbol (▼) used in the "Classified List of Serials" to indicate new serials also appears in this index, preceding the title. A dagger (†) appears preceding the title if the publication has ceased. The bullet symbol (●) indicates that the title is available in one or more electronic formats, including online, CD-ROM or e-mail, either exclusively or in addition to printed formats. The arrow symbol (➤) indicates that a title is refereed or peer-reviewed by an editorial board. These symbols appear in a new footer at the bottom of every right-hand page.

CROSS-INDEX TO SUBJECTS

This index lists alphabetically all main subject headings in the **Ulrich's** Subject Authority Database, as well as keyword references that direct users to main or subheadings where publications on those topics are likely to be found. The number following each subject term directs users to the page on which the subject begins within the CLASSIFIED LIST OF SERIALS.

A keyword may refer the user to more than one subject category. In this case, the subject references are listed in alphabetical order and are not necessarily listed in hierarchical order.

Main subject headings appear in uppercase, e.g. AGRICULTURE. Subheadings contain the main subject term in uppercase and the specific subheading term in mixed case, e.g. AGRICULTURE—Agricultural Economics. The keywords, except for acronyms, are displayed entirely in mixed case.

PRODUCER LISTING/SERIALS ON CD-ROM

This section is an alphabetical listing of identified producers of serials on CD-ROM. Entries include the producer address, and contact numbers, and an alphabetical listing of all serial titles known to be available.

ONLINE SERVICE LISTING/SERIALS ONLINE

This section is an alphabetical listing of identified providers of online periodicals. Entries include addresses, contact numbers for the provider, and an alphabetical listing of all titles known to be available, with file names or numbers, if known.

INDEX TO PUBLICATIONS OF INTERNATIONAL ORGANIZATIONS

Complexity of corporate author structure, as well as title page variations in multilingual texts, compound the problems in cataloging publications of international organizations. This special index is provided so that the user may have one reference point for these titles. This index consists of four sections:

European Union
International Congress Proceedings
International Organizations
United Nations

The index contains all current titles listed in the **Ulrich's** database. The user must consult the CLASSIFIED LIST OF SERIALS for the full bibliographic information pertaining to these titles. Page references are provided in bold.

Full Entry Content Description

Basic Information
The following elements are mandatory for listing and appear in all entries: main entry title, frequency of publication, publisher address, country code, and Dewey Decimal Classification number.

Certain electronic journals may not have a physical mailing address; the URL and/or e-mail address provide a means of contacting the publication.

Dewey Decimal Classification Number
The Dewey Decimal number is printed at the top left of each entry. More than one Dewey number may have been assigned if a serial covers several subjects.

LC Classification Number

The Library of Congress classification number, if known, appears directly below the Dewey Decimal number. Shelf numbers are not included.

Country Code

The ISO Country Code is printed at the top center of each entry following the Dewey Decimal number. A complete list of country codes used will be found beginning on page xxii.

ISSN

The ISSN for the main entry title is printed to the right of the country code. Not all publications have been assigned an ISSN, and lack of a number does not render a publication ineligible for listing.

CODEN

The CODEN designation, if known, is printed directly below the country code and ISSN. The CODEN is an alphanumeric code, applied uniquely to a specific publication. Devised by the American Society for Testing and Materials, it is used primarily for scientific and technical titles. New CODEN are assigned by Chemical Abstracts Service.

Title Information

The main title is printed in **boldface** and uppercase as the first item in the entry. Titles are catalogued according to rules described below in the "Cataloging Rules for Main Entry Title" section. For multi-language publications, the parallel language title is also printed in uppercase, immediately following the main entry title, and is separated from it by a slash.

An inverted triangle symbol (▼) printed before the title indicates that the title began publishing within the past three years. This symbol also appears before titles announced for publication in the coming year. An asterisk (*) printed after the title indicates that the address in the entry was not verified by the publisher for this edition.

The subtitle is printed in lowercase after the title. Variant titles are given within the entry and are labeled as such. The Key Title, which is assigned at the time of ISSN assignment by the responsible center of the International Serials Data System, is given only if it is different from the main entry title. Former titles are given at the end of the bibliographic data. See the paragraph below.

Language

The language or languages is given, even if a serial is written in the main language of the country of publication. The order of languages is generally alphabetical and does not represent prominence. If a serial includes abstracts, summaries or sections in additional language(s), that information will be provided as well.

Year First Published

The year first published is given if provided by the publisher. If a title has been suspended and later resumed publication, these dates may be provided as well. If volume numbering was restarted, the notation "N.S." denoting new series precedes the date. If information is lacking, a volume number and specific year may be provided to indicate the approximate age of the publication.

Frequency

The frequency of publication is given in abbreviated form, such as "a." for annual, "irreg." for irregular, "m." for monthly, "3/yr." for three times per year. All abbreviations used are listed in the "General Abbreviations and Special Symbols" on page xix.

Price

Unless otherwise indicated, the price given is the annual price for an individual subscription in the currency of the country of origin. The price in U.S. dollars may also be given if it is provided by the publisher. No attempt is made to convert foreign currency to U.S. dollars. Separate postage information is not given, since postal rates vary widely. A complete list of ISO currency codes used will be found beginning on page xx.

Special Features

A listing of special features may include such items as book or other types of reviews, advertising (usually meaning commercial, not classified advertising), charts, illustrations, bibliography section, article abstracts, and an annual index to the periodical's contents.

Reprint Services

If a serial is known to be available from a reprint service, a code referring to the service appears in the entry. More than one code may be listed. For a list of reprint services and a translation of the codes, please refer to page xxx.

Pages Per Issue; Columns Per Page

When known, the number of pages per issue (p./no.:) and/or columns per page (cols./p.:) is/are noted.

Refereed Serial

The manuscript peer review and evaluation system is utilized to protect, maintain and raise the quality of scholarly material published in serials. The arrow symbol (➤) appears before the title if a serial is known to be refereed or juried. This information is generally provided by the serial publisher.

Document Type

Notations are included to indicate type of publication, e.g. Academic/Scholarly, Trade, Newsletter, or Abstract/Index. The words "**Document type**" appear in boldface, followed by the document type description, in entries where this information is known. More than one document type may be listed for a single publication, if applicable.

Brief Description

A brief description of the contents and editorial focus of the publication may be provided, preceded by the word "**Description:**" at the end of the bibliographic data.

These descriptions were submitted by the publisher or were written by editorial staff after examination of sample copies or publisher catalogs.

Former Titles

Title changes are common phenomena in serials publishing. Many entries contain extensive former title information, providing a history of changes which may be useful for bibliographic record-keeping. Previous titles for the serial are given, along with their ISSN, if known. ISSN are assigned to specific titles and therefore change with the title. The former titles are preceded by a description of the type of title change. Simple title changes are noted by the words "Formerly" or "Former titles." Other types may include mergers, incorporations or supersessions. Dates provided are generally the date that the change became effective. For mergers and incorporations, date ranges indicate the years of publication for that previous title.

Media

The primary medium is specified for other than the traditional print on paper, with the exception of the notation "Duplicated." Common media listed include Online, CD-ROM, Diskette, Microfilm and Microfiche. Online - full text denotes that the entire text of all the articles of a serial is available online, while Online - full content denotes that the entire content including graphics is available. If a serial is primarily available in Braille or Large Type, that notation will be found here.

Related Titles

This section provides information on all available formats, editions and related publications. Often the title and ISSN are provided. The diamond symbol (◆¨) indicates that there is a complete listing elsewhere in the CLASSIFIED LIST OF SERIALS. Please refer to the TITLE INDEX for the page number

---

SAMPLE ENTRY

1 641.337   **2** USA   **3** ISSN 1234-5678

4 HD9199.A1   **5** CODEN: COCIEO

6 ➤ **7** CHINESE JOURNAL OF COFFEE RESEARCH; **8** short articles on coffee research. **9** Key title: Coffee Research **10** (In 3 sections.) **11** Text in Chinese, English. **12** 1987. **13** 24/yr. (in 2 vols.) **14** USD 136 in US and Canada; USD 148 elsewhere (effective 2001) **15** bk.rev. abstr. illus. cum. index: 1987-1997; **16** back issues avail.; reprint service avail. from SWZ,UMI **17** 8 cols./p., 20 p./no. **18** Document type: *Academic/scholarly.*

19 Description: Offers articles, coffee news and data analyses to scientists, engineers and research managers.

20 Supersedes in part (in 1989): Acta Scientifica Cafe **21** (0000-8888); Which was formerly: Coffee Research Techniques

22 Media: Online - full text (from Grinder, Inc.) **23** Related titles: CD-ROM ed.: Coffee Research on Disc. 1992. q. USD 32. (from Cafe Institute (File no.42), Platter Corp.); Microfilm ed. (from SMI); Japanese ed.: ISSN 2345-6789. Supplement: Annual Coffee Review. ISSN 6789-1234.

24 Indexed: Food Sci.& Tech.Abstr.

25 --- BLDSC (1234.567890), CISTI, GNLM **26** CCC.

27 Published by: (Coffee Research Institute), **28** Chinese Coffee Inc., **29** 140 US Rte 400, Parsippany, NJ 07974. **30** TEL 908-665-2800, **31** FAX 908-771-7725, **32** Telex 9735 PARV TH, **33** usinfo@coffee.com, **34** http://www.coffeeresearch.com. **35** Eds. Shawn King, Jane Weiner. **36** Pub. Richard Stocker. **37** R&P Ewa Picker TEL 908-665-2875. **38** Adv. contact Sankar Lara **39** adv.: B&W page USD 2,300, color page USD 3,500; trim 7 x 10. **40** circ. 5,000 (paid); 3,200 (controlled) **41** Wire service: SP **42** Subscr. in the Americas to: Science Research Centre, Regional Sales Office, PO Box 435, New York, NY 10159-0945. TEL 212-465-7645, FAX 212-576-4785; **43** Dist. by: Cafe Distributors, 23 Chen Lu, Beijing 100031, People's Republic of China. TEL 86-10-12345, FAX 86-10-34567. **44** Co-sponsors: Chinese Coffee Organization; Chinese Science Society. Affiliate: United States Coffee Research Society.

KEY

1	Dewey Decimal Classification
2	ISO Country Code
3	ISSN
4	LC Classification
5	CODEN
6	Refereed Symbol
7	Main Entry Title
8	Subtitle
9	Key Title
10	Bibliographic Note
11	Language
12	First Published
13	Frequency
14	Price
15	Special Features
16	Back Issues & Reprint
17	Page Format
18	Document Type
19	Brief Description
20	Title Changes
21	Former ISSN
22	Media
23	Related Editions
24	Abstracting & Indexing
25	Document Suppliers
26	Copyright Clearance Center
27	Corporate Author
28	Publishing Company
29	Address
30	Telephone
31	Fax
32	Telex
33	E-mail
34	URL
35	Editor
36	Publisher
37	Rights & Permissions Contact
38	Advertising Contact
39	Advertising Rates
40	Circulation
41	Wire Service
42	Subscription
43	Distributor
44	Co-sponsors and other bodies

of that listing. When no complete record is available, data such as start year, frequency, or price may be provided.

Information on alternate media editions, such as online, CD-ROM or microform editions, is provided here. Online providers and CD-ROM producer names are given if known to be different from the publisher. Complete address and contact information for these companies is provided in the ONLINE SERVICE LISTING and CD-ROM PRODUCER LISTING sections, in Volume 4. For publications available in microform, a three-letter code for the vendor or micropublisher is provided. A list of names, addresses, and contact information begins on page xxviii.

Abstracting and Indexing

The notation **"Indexed"** precedes a list of abbreviations for all abstracting and indexing services known to cover the serial on a regular basis. The complete names of the abstracting and indexing services are listed with their abbreviations on page xxxiii. This section also includes status information and related titles. Consult the TITLE INDEX for page references to entries in the CLASSIFIED LIST OF SERIALS for active services.

Document Suppliers

These notations are preceded by an em-dash (—). The presence of a notation indicates the availability of articles from that serial through the specified service, by permission from the copyright holder. Such permissions are subject to change without notice. Articles may be available in paper and/or electronic format, depending on the service. The full names and complete address and contact information for these companies are listed beginning on page xxvi.

The British Library Document Supply Centre shelfmark number, a unique identifier of each serial, appears in parentheses after that organization's code, ex. "BLDSC (0000.000000)." The format of the shelfmark is four digits, a decimal point, then six digits.

The **Ulrich's** database and the individual databases of document suppliers were matched on the presence of ISSNs. When a match was successful, the appropriate document supplier code was noted. Not all serials titles in general or in these individual databses, have ISSNs. Therefore, the absence of one or any document supplier codes in an **Ulrich's** listing does not necessarily mean the title is not available from one or any of these suppliers.

Copyright Clearance Center, Inc.

Copyright Clearance Center, Inc. (CCC), the largest licenser of text reproduction rights in the world, was formed in 1978 to facilitate compliance with U.S. Copyright law. CCC provides licensing systems for reproduction and distribution of copyrighted materials in print and electronic formats. CCC manages rights for over 1.75 million works and represents over 9,600 publishers and hundreds of thousands of authors and other creators, directly or through their representatives. CCC-licensed customers in the U.S. number over 10,000

corporations and subsidiaries, and thousands of government agencies, law firms, document suppliers, libraries, academic institutions, copy shops and bookstores.

The boldfaced **CCC** notation appears in the entries of titles for which the CCC has been authorized by the publisher to grant photocopy permissions on any of their works.
Contact them at 222 Rosewood Dr., Danvers, MA 01923, USA; tel: 978-750-8400; fax: 978-750-4470;
URL: http://www.copyright.com.

Publishing Company Information

This section begins with the bold phrase "**Published by**" or "**Address**" if the company name is the same as the title.

Many serials are editorially controlled by a sponsoring organization or corporate author and published by a commercial publisher. In these instances, the commercial publishing company's name and address are given, and the name of the corporate author is given in parentheses immediately preceding. In other instances, either a sponsoring organization or a commercial publishing company has sole responsibility, and only one name is given. We avoid listing printers as publishing companies, preferring the name and address of someone with editorial responsibility. For the same reason, we avoid listing distributors as publishing companies.

Telephone, Fax, Telex Numbers, E-mail, and Web Site Addresses

Telephone, fax, telex numbers and e-mail as well as web site addresses (URLs) are given when provided by the publisher. U.S. and Canadian numbers are given in standard North American format. Toll-free numbers within U.S. and Canada are also included, when available. Numbers in other countries are provided in the same format as supplied by the publisher, resulting in some inconsistencies (e.g. sometimes with a country and/or city code, sometimes without). Users are advised to consult an international operator before placing calls.

Editor

Only one or two names are given when known, preceded by the notation "Ed." or "Eds." Advanced degrees and titles are omitted, except for medical, military and religious titles; absence of a title does not mean that the editor has none.

Publisher

Only one or two names are given when known, preceded by the notation "Pub." or "Pubs." Advanced degrees and titles are omitted, except for medical, military and religious titles; absence of a title does not mean that the publisher has none.

If the publisher is also the editor, and no publishing company name is available, the person's name is given in place of company name with the notation "Ed. & Pub."

Rights and Permissions Contact

A name is given when supplied, preceded by the notation "R&P contact." The telephone number information follows, when known and different from the main number.

Advertising Rates and Contact

When provided by the publisher, the name of the advertising contact, as well as full-page advertising rates and sizes are indicated. Most dimensions are listed in millimeters, except for U.S. publications, the dimensions of which are usually in inches.

Circulation

All circulation figures used are approximate. Circulation is given only if provided by the publisher. The notation "controlled" indicates that the publication is available only to qualified persons, usually members of a particular trade or profession. The notation "paid" indicates that subscribers pay to receive the publication, while the notation "free" indicates that the title is freely distributed.

Wire Services

If a newspaper is known to use one or more news or photo wire services, abbreviations or names of the services used are listedin the entry. Such information is preceded by the words "Wire Service(s)." Abbreviations for wire services used are listed on page xxxi of this volume.

Subscription or Distribution Information

A second address is given only if the address for ordering subscriptions is different from the publishing company's address. Distributors are listed only if we have been informed that a particular organization is the exclusive distributor. Additional subscription and/or distribution offices of international publishers are listed, if known. Telephone and fax numbers and e-mail and URL addresses for subscription and/or distribution offices appear if provided by the publisher.

Other related organizations and companies such as co-sponsors, affiliates, or co-publishers may be noted here.

Newspaper Ownership

The name of the owner(s) of a newspaper is listed, usually accompanied by the owner(s) address, and telephone and fax numbers. The owner address may differ from the newspaper location address. Owner information is preceded by the notation "Owner(s):."

Cataloging Rules for Main Entry Title

The majority of titles in the Ulrich's database were cataloged according to *Anglo-American Cataloging Rules* prior to 1978, the date of the new edition of *Anglo-American Cataloging Rules*. The new *AACR II* reflects a trend toward the Key Title concept of cataloging as used by the International Serials Data System (ISDS) and published in its *International Standard Bibliographic Description for Serials* (1974).

Because recataloging such a database was not feasible, our cataloging rules were modified but not radically changed. Cross-references are provided in the TITLE INDEX from variant forms of title, such as Key Title, to aid users searching by other methods.

Whenever possible, main entry title cataloging is done from a sample of the title page of the most recent issue, according to the follwoing rules:

Articles at the beginning of titles are omitted, or are bypassed in filing.

Serials with distinctive titles are usually entered under title. For example:

Annual Bulletin of Historical Literature
Business Week
Milton Studies

If a title consists only of a generic term followed by the name of the issuing body, or if the name of the issuing body clarifies the content of the publication, entry is under the name of the issuing body. For example:

Newsletter of the American Theological Library Association

is entered as

American Theological Library Association. Newsletter

Economic Performance and Prospects, issued by the Private Development Corporation of the Philippines

is entered as

Private Development Corporation of the Philippines. Economic Performance and Prospects

A title which consists of a subject modified generic term followed by the name of the issuing body is considered nondistinctive and is entered under the name of the isssuing body. For example:

Annual Meeting Scientific Proceedings of the American Animal Hospital Association

is entered as

American Animal Hospital Association. Annual Meeting Scientific Proceedings

Government publications with nondistinctive titles are entered under the name of the government jurisdiction of the issuing body, although distinctive titles of government organizations may be entered directly under title. For example:

Great Britain. Economic and Social Research Council. Annual Report

but

Statistical Abstract of Iceland

Titles which begin with the initials of the issuing body are entered under the initials. Cross-references from the full name are provided in the TITLE INDEX.

If a geographic name is part of the name of the issuing body, entry will be under the common form of the name of the body.

For example:

University of the West Indies. Vice-Chancellor's Report

not

West Indies. University. Vice-Chancellor's Report

Note, however, that government publications retain similar cataloging as government jurisdiction.

Canada. Statistics Canada. Field Crop Reporting Series

Multilingual titles are entered under the first title given on the title page, or the first title reported by the publisher if the title page is not available. Titles in other languages are entered directly after the main entry title. Cross-references are provided in the TITLE INDEX for each language title.

FILING RULES

Due to the restrictions imposed by computer filing of titles, the following special filing rules should be noted. The majority of

punctuation marks are treated as spaces. A combination of punctuation and spaces is treated as one space.

Acronyms and initals are treated as such and are listed at the beginning of each letter of the alphabet.

D H Lawrence Review
D.L.A.N.Y. Newsletter
D N R
Dade County Teacher

Hyphenated words are treated as separate words:

Pre-Text

precedes

Preaching

Initial articles may be provided for a title, but do not affect their alphabetization. Articles and prepositions within titles are alphabetized as words:

Journal of the West

precedes

Journal of Theological Studies

Diacritical marks have been omitted. The German and Scandinavian umlaut has been replaced by the letter "e" following the vowels a, e, o, and u. In Danish, Norwegian, and Swedish, the letter å is sequenced as "aa" and the letter ø as "oe."

International Standard Serial Number (ISSN)

1. What is the ISSN?

An internationally accepted, concise, unique, and unambiguous code for the identification of serial publications. One ISSN represents one serial title.

The ISSN consists of seven numbers with an eighth check digit calculated according to Modulus 11 and used to verify the number in computer processing. A hyphen is printed after the fourth digit, as a visual aid, and the acronym, ISSN, precedes the number.

2. How did the ISSN evolve as an international system?

The International Organization for Standardization Technical Committee 46 (ISO/TC 46) is the agency responsible for the development of the ISSN as an international standard. The organization responsible for the administration and coordination of ISSN assignments worldwide is the ISSN International Centre in Paris, which is supported by the French government and UNESCO.

ISSNs are assigned by over 50 national centers worldwide. The National Serials Data Program (NSDP) is the U.S. national center. The centers form a network that is coordinated by the ISSN International Centre located in Paris.

The implementation of the ISSN system started with the numbering of 70,000 titles in the serials database of R.R. Bowker (*Ulrich's International Periodicals Directory* and *Irregular Serials and Annuals*). The next serials database numbering was the *New Serials Titles 1950-70* cumulation listing 220,000 titles, cumulated, converted to magnetic tape, and published by R.R. Bowker in collaboration with the Serials Record Division of the Library of Congress. These two databases were used as the starting base for the implementation of the ISSN.

3. What types of publications are assigned ISSNs?

For assignment of an ISSN, a serial is defined as a publication in print or non-print form, issued in successive parts, usually having numerical or chronological designations, and intended to be continued indefinitely.

4. How is the ISSN used?

The ISSN is employed as a component of bar codes and as a tool for the communication of basic information about a serial title and for such processes as ordering, billing, inventory control, abstracting, and indexing. In library processes, the ISSN is used in operations such as acquisitions, claiming, binding, accessioning, shelving, cooperative cataloging, circulation, interlibrary loans, and retrieval of requests.

5. Can a publication have an International Standard Book Number (ISBN) and an ISSN?

Yes! Monographic series (separate works issued indefinitely under a common title, generally in a uniform format with numeric designations) and annuals or titles planned to be issued indefinitely under the same title may be defined as serials. The ISSN is assigned to the serial title, while an ISBN is assigned to each individual title or monograph in the series.

A new ISBN is assigned to each volume or edition by the publisher, while the ISSN, which is assigned by the ISSN International Centre or national ISSN centers, remains the same for each issue. Both numbers should be printed on the copyright page or other appropriate page of each volume, with their acronyms or words preceding each number for immediate identification. With the availability of both an ISSN and ISBN, the problem of defining the overlap of serials and monographs has been resolved.

SAMPLE TITLE

Advances in the Biosciences
ISSN 0065-3446
Vol. 1 Proceedings: Berlin. Schering
   Symposium of Endocrinology, Berlin. Ed.
   by Gerhard Raspe. 1969. 40.00
   (ISBN 0-08-013395-9). Pergamon.

Vol. 2 Proceedings. Schering Symposium on
   Biodynamics & Mechanisms of Action of
   Steroid Hormones, Berlin. Ed. by Gerhard
   Raspe. 1969. 41.25 (ISBN 0-08-006942-8).
   Pergamon.

Vol. 3 Proceedings. Schering Workshop on Steroid Metabolism "in Vitro Versus in Vivo," Berlin. Ed. by Gerhard Raspe. 1969. 41.25 (ISBN 0-08-017544-9). Pergamon.

Vol. 4 Proceedings. Schering Symposium on Mechanisms Involved in Conception. Berlin. Ed. by Gerhard Raspe. 1970. text ed. 41.25 (ISBN 0-08-017546-5). Pergamon.

Vol. 25 Development of Responsiveness to Steroid Hormones. Alvin M. Kaye & Myra Kaye et al. LC 79-42938. 1980. 66.00 (ISBN 0-08-024949-X). Pergamon.

ISSN International Centre
45, rue de Turbigo
75003 Paris
France
Tel: +33 (0) 1 44 88 22 20
Fax: +33 (0) 1 40 26 32 43
E-mail: issnic@issn.org
URL: http://www.issn.org

The address for the U.S. national ISSN center is:

National Serials Data Program (NSDP)
Library of Congress
Washington, DC 20540-4160
Tel: 202-707-6452
Fax: 202-707-6333
E-mail: ISSN@loc.gov
URL: http://lcweb.loc.gov/issn

6. Where should the ISSN appear on the serial?

In a prominent position on or in each issue of the serial, such as the front cover, back cover, masthead, title, or copyright pages. The international standard recommendation is that the ISSN of a periodical be printed, whenever possible, in the upper right corner of the front cover.

Promotional and descriptive materials about the serial should include the ISSN.

7. When a title changes, is a new ISSN assigned?

In most instances, a new ISSN is assigned when a title changes. However, the determination is made by the ISSN International Centre or the appropriate national ISSN centers. Publishers should report all the title changes to their respective centers.

8. How does a publisher apply for an ISSN?

The publisher should contact the appropriate national ISSN center or the ISSN International Centre. Centers require bibliographic evidence of a serial, including a copy of the title page and cover. There is no charge to publishers for the assignment of ISSNs.

For full information, publishers should contact the national library or bibliographic center in the country where they are publishing. The address of the ISSN International Centre is:

9. What is SISAC?

SISAC stands for the Serials Industry Systems Advisory Committee. SISAC is an industry group formed to develop voluntary standardized formats for electronically transmitting serials business transaction information. SISAC provides a forum where serial (particularly journal) publishers, library system vendors, and librarians can discuss mutual concerns regarding the electronic transmission of serial information and develop cooperative solutions, in the form of standardized formats, to efficiently address these concerns. *(Reprinted with permission from SISAC.)*

10. What is the SISAC Symbol (SICI) and its relationship to the ISSN?

The Serial Item and Contribution Identifier (SICI) is a serial identification code that follows the ISSN and is a string of letters and/or numbers that uniquely identify a particular issue of a serial. Encoded in the SICI are chronological and enumeration data that identify serials by date and volume/issue numbers. According to SISAC, "the ANSI* standard extends the code down to the article level by adding location number and necessary title information, plus a record validation character. Code 128 is the bar code symbology selected by SISAC for displaying this number string in scannable form. When displayed in the Code 128 symbology, the SICI is called the SISAC symbol." The SICI is the ANSI standard; the SISAC symbol is the bar code. *(Reprinted with permission from SISAC.)*

*ANSI American National Standards Institute. Organization that coordinates the voluntary standards system in the United States. U.S. member of the International Standards Organization (ISO).

Abbreviations
General Abbreviations and Special Symbols

a.	annual
abstr.	abstracts
adv.	advertising
approx.	approximately
avail.	available
B&W	Black & White
bi-m.	bimonthly (every two months)
bi-w.	biweekly (every two weeks)
bibl.	bibliographies
bk.rev.	book reviews
CCC	Copyright Clearance Center
c/o	care of
circ.	circulation
cols./p.	columns per page
cum.index	cumulative index
Cy.	County
d.	daily
dance rev.	dance reviews
Dir.	Director
dist.	distributed
ed., eds.	edition(s)
Ed., Eds.	Editor(s)
film rev.	film reviews
fortn.	fortnightly (every two weeks)
ISSN	International Standard Serial Number
illus.	illustrations
irreg.	irregular
m.	monthly, month
mkt.	market prices
mos.	months
music rev.	music reviews
N.S.	New Series
no., nos.	number(s)

pat.	patents
play rev.	play reviews (theater reviews)
p./no.	pages per issue/number
Prof.	Professor
pt.	point type
Pub., Pubs.	Publisher(s)
q.	quarterly
R&P	Rights & Permissions
rec.rev.	record reviews
rev.	reviews
s-a.	semiannually (twice annually)
s-m.	semimonthly (twice monthly)
s-w.	semiweekly (twice weekly)
software rev.	software reviews
stat.	statistics
subscr.	subscription
tel.rev.	television program reviews
3/m.	3 times a month
3/w.	3 times a week
3/yr.	3 times a year
tr.lit.	trade literature (manufacturers' catalogs, reader response cards)
tr.mk.	trade marks
video rev.	video reviews
vol., vols.	volume(s)
w.	weekly, week
yr., yrs.	year(s)
✱	not updated / unverified
●	electronic serial
▼	new serial
†	ceased
◆	complete listing available
➤	refereed

Currency Codes

This list of world currencies and their codes is the International Standards Organization (ISO) set of three-letter currency abbreviations. This is the complete list of ISO codes, though not all currencies may be present in **Ulrich's**. The codes are mnemonic in most cases, with the first two letters representing the country name and the third representing the currency name.

CODE	CURRENCY	CODE	CURRENCY
ADP	Andorran Peseta	EGP	Egyptian Pound
AED	United Arab Emirates Dirham	ERB	Eritrean Birr
AFA	Afghanistan Afghani	ESP	Spanish Peseta
ALL	Albanian Lek	ETB	Ethiopian Birr
AMD	Armenian Dram	EUR	Euro
ANG	Netherlands Antillian Guilder	FIM	Finnish Markka
AON	Angolan New Kwanza	FJD	Fiji Dollar
ARS	Argentinean Peso	FKP	Falkland Islands Pound
ATS	Austrian Schilling	FRF	French Franc
AUD	Australian Dollars	GBP	British Pound
AWG	Aruban Florin	GEL	Georgian Lari
AZM	Azerbaijan Manat	GHC	Ghanaian Cedi
BAD	Bosnian Dinar	GIP	Gibraltar Pound
BAM	Bosnia & Herzegovina Convertible Mark	GMD	Gambian Dalasi
BBD	Barbados Dollar	GNF	Guinea Franc
BDT	Bangladeshi Taka	GNS	Guinea Syli
BEF	Belgian Franc	GRD	Greek Drachma
BGL	Bulgarian Lev	GTQ	Guatemalan Quetzal
BHD	Bahraini Dinar	GWP	Guinea-Bissau Peso
BIF	Burundi Franc	GYD	Guyanan Dollar
BMD	Bermudan Dollar	HKD	Hong Kong Dollar
BND	Brunei Dollar	HNL	Honduran Lempira
BOB	Bolivian Boliviano	HRK	Croatian Kuna
BPS	British Pounds Sterling	HTG	Haitian Gourde
BRL	Brazilian Real	HUF	Hungarian Forint
BSD	Bahamian Dollar	IDR	Indonesian Rupiah
BTN	Bhutan Ngultrum	IEP	Irish Punt
BWP	Botswanan Pula	ILS	Israeli Shekel
BYB	Belarus Ruble	INR	Indian Rupee
BZD	Belize Dollar	IQD	Iraqi Dinar
CHF	Swiss Franc	IRR	Iranian Rial
CLP	Chilean Peso	ISK	Iceland Krona
CND	Canadian Dollars	ITL	Italian Lira
CNY	Yuan (Chinese) Renminbi	JMD	Jamaican Dollar
COP	Colombian Peso	JOD	Jordanian Dinar
CRC	Costa Rican Colon	JPY	Japanese Yen
CSD	Serbian Dinar	KES	Kenyan Schilling
CUP	Cuban Peso	KGS	Kyrgyzstan Som
CVE	Cape Verde Escudo	KHR	Cambodian New Riel
CYP	Cyprus Pound	KMF	Comoros Franc
CZK	Czech Koruna	KPW	North Korean Won
DEM	Deutsche Mark	KRW	South Korean Won
DJF	Djibouti Franc	KWD	Kuwaiti Dinar
DKK	Danish Krone	KYD	Cayman Islands Dollar
DOP	Dominican Peso	KZT	Kazakhstani Tenge
DZD	Algerian Dinar	LAK	Lao Kip
ECS	Ecuador Sucre	LBP	Lebanese Pound
EEK	Estonian Kroon	LKR	Sri Lanka Rupee

LRD	Liberian Dollar		SBD	Solomon Islands Dollar
LSL	Lesotho Loti		SCR	Seychelles Rupee
LTL	Lithuanian Litas		SDP	Sudanese Pound
LUF	Luxembourg Franc		SEK	Swedish Krona
LVL	Latvian Lat		SGD	Singapore Dollar
LYD	Libyan Dinar		SHP	St. Helena Pound
MAD	Moroccan Dirham		SIT	Slovenian Tolar
MDL	Moldova Leu		SKK	Slovakian Koruna
MGF	Malagasy Franc		SLL	Sierra Leone Leone
MKD	Macedonian Denar		SOS	Somali Schilling
MLF	Mali Franc		SRG	Suriname Guilder
MMK	Myanmar Kyat		STD	Sao Tome and Principe Dobra
MNT	Mongolian Tugrik		SVC	El Salvador Colon
MOP	Macao Pataca		SYP	Syrian Pound
MRK	German Marks		SZL	Swaziland Lilangeni
MRO	Mauritanian Ouguiya		THB	Thai Bhat
MTL	Maltese Lira		TJR	Tajikistan Rubl
MUR	Mauritius Rupee		TMM	Turkemenistan Manat
MVR	Maldive Rufiyaa		TND	Tunisian Dinar
MWK	Malawi Kwacha		TOP	Tongan Pa'anga
MXN	Mexican New Peso		TPE	East Timor Escudo
MYR	Malaysian Ringgit		TRL	Turkish Lira
MZM	Mozambique Metical		TTD	Trinidad and Tobago Dollar
NAD	Namibian Dollar		TWD	Taiwan Dollar
NGN	Nigerian Naira		TZS	Tanzanian Schilling
NIC	Nicaraguan Gold Cordoba		UAK	Ukraine Hryvnia
NLG	Dutch Guilder		UGX	Uganda Shilling
NOK	Norwegian Kroner		USD	US Dollars
NPR	Nepalese Rupee		UYP	Peso Uruguayo
NZD	New Zealand Dollar		UZS	Uzbek Som
OMR	Omani Rial		VEB	Venezuelan Bolivar
PAB	Panamanian Balboa		VND	Vietnamese Dong
PEN	Peruvian New Sol		VUV	Vanuatu Vatu
PGK	Papua New Guinea Kina		WST	Somoan Tala
PHP	Philippine Peso		XAF	CFA Franc BEAC
PKR	Pakistan Rupee		XDR	Special Drawing Rights
PLZ	Polish Zloty		XEC	Eastern Caribbean Dollar
PTE	Portuguese Escudo		XOF	CFA Franc BCEAO
PYG	Paraguay Guarani		XPF	French Polynesian Franc
QAR	Qatari Rial		YER	Yemeni Rial
ROL	Romanian Leu		YUN	Yugoslavian New Dinar
RUR	Russian Ruble		ZAR	South African Rand
RWF	Rwanda Franc		ZMK	Zambian Kwacha
SAR	Saudi Arabian Riyal		ZWD	Zimbabwe Dollar

Country of Publication Codes

This list of countries and their codes is the International Standards Organization (ISO) set of three-letter country abbreviations. This is the complete list of ISO codes, though not all countries may be represented in **Ulrich's**. The codes are mnemonic in most cases. The country names listed here may have been shortened to a more common usage form. Country names no longer in use remain on the list to represent any titles that may have ceased while that country name was still in use.

Code Sequence

ABW	Aruba	DJI	Djibouti	KWT	Kuwait
AFG	Afghanistan	DMA	Dominica	LAO	Laos
AGO	Angola	DNK	Denmark	LBN	Lebanon
AIA	Anguilla	DOM	Dominican Republic	LBR	Liberia
ALB	Albania	DZA	Algeria	LBY	Libya
AND	Andorra	ECU	Ecuador	LCA	St. Lucia
ANT	Netherlands Antilles	EGY	Egypt	LIE	Liechtenstein
ARE	United Arab Emirates	ERI	Eritrea	LKA	Sri Lanka
ARG	Argentina	ESH	Western Sahara	LSO	Lesotho
ARM	Armenia	ESP	Spain	LTU	Lithuania
ASM	American Samoa	EST	Estonia	LUX	Luxembourg
ATA	Antarctica	ETH	Ethiopia	LVA	Latvia
ATF	French Southern Territories	FIN	Finland	MAC	Macau
ATG	Antigua & Barbuda	FJI	Fiji	MAR	Morocco
AUS	Australia	FLK	Falkland Islands	MCO	Monaco
AUT	Austria	FRA	France	MDA	Moldova
AZE	Azerbaijan	FRO	Faeroe Islands	MDG	Madagascar
BDI	Burundi	FSM	Fed. States of Micronesia	MDV	Maldive Islands
BEL	Belgium	GAB	Gabon	MEX	Mexico
BEN	Benin	GBR	United Kingdom	MHL	Marshall Islands
BFA	Burkina Faso	GEO	Georgia	MKD	Macedonia
BGD	Bangladesh	GHA	Ghana	MLI	Mali
BGR	Bulgaria	GIB	Gibraltar	MLT	Malta
BHR	Bahrain	GIN	Guinea	MMR	Myanmar
BHS	Bahamas	GLP	Guadeloupe	MNE	Montenegro
BIH	Bosnia & Herzegovina	GMB	Gambia	MNG	Mongolia
BLR	Belarus	GNB	Guinea-Bissau	MNP	Northern Mariana Islands
BLZ	Belize	GNQ	Equatorial Guinea	MOZ	Mozambique
BMU	Bermuda	GRC	Greece	MRT	Mauritania
BOL	Bolivia	GRD	Grenada	MSR	Monteserrat
BRA	Brazil	GRL	Greenland	MTQ	Martinique
BRB	Barbados	GTM	Guatemala	MUS	Mauritius
BRD	West Germany	GUF	French Guiana	MWI	Malawi
BRN	Brunei Darussalam	GUM	Guam	MYS	Malaysia
BTN	Bhutan	GUY	Guyana	MYT	Mayotte
BVT	Bouvet Island	HKG	Hong Kong	NAM	Namibia
BWA	Botswana	HMD	Heard Island & McDonald Islands	NCL	New Caledonia
CAF	Central African Republic	HND	Honduras	NER	Niger
CAN	Canada	HRV	Croatia	NFK	Norfolk Island
CCK	Cocos (Keeling) Islands	HTI	Haiti	NGA	Nigeria
CHE	Switzerland	HUN	Hungary	NIC	Nicaragua
CHL	Chile	IDN	Indonesia	NIU	Niue
CHN	China	IND	India	NLD	Netherlands
CIV	Cote D'Ivoire	IOT	British Indian Ocean Territory	NOR	Norway
CMR	Cameroon	IRL	Ireland	NPL	Nepal
COD	Congo, Democratic Republic of	IRN	Iran	NRU	Nauru
COG	Congo	IRQ	Iraq	NZL	New Zealand
COK	Cook Islands	ISL	Iceland	OMN	Oman
COL	Colombia	ISR	Israel	PAK	Pakistan
COM	Comoros	ITA	Italy	PAN	Panama
CPV	Cape Verde	JAM	Jamaica	PCN	Pitcairn
CRI	Costa Rica	JOR	Jordan	PER	Peru
CSK	Czechoslovakia	JPN	Japan	PHL	Philippines
CUB	Cuba	KAZ	Kazakstan	PLW	Palau
CXR	Christmas Island	KEN	Kenya	PNG	Papua New Guinea
CYN	Cayman Islands	KGZ	Kyrgyzstan	POL	Poland
CYP	Cyprus	KHM	Cambodia	PRI	Puerto Rico
CZE	Czech Republic	KIR	Kiribati	PRK	Korea, Democratic People's Rep. of
DDR	East Germany	KNA	Saint Kitts & Nevis		
DEU	Germany	KOR	Korea, Republic of	PRT	Portugal

PRY	Paraguay	STP	Sao Tome e Principe	TZA	Tanzania
PSE	Occupied Palestinian Territory	SUN	U.S.S.R.	UGA	Uganda
PYF	French Polynesia	SUR	Suriname	UKR	Ukraine
QAT	Qatar	SVK	Slovakia	UMI	US Minor Islands
REU	Reunion	SVN	Slovenia	URY	Uruguay
ROM	Romania	SWE	Sweden	USA	United States
RUS	Russia	SWZ	Swaziland	UZB	Uzbekistan
RWA	Rwanda	SYC	Seychelles	VAT	Vatican City
SAU	Saudi Arabia	SYR	Syrian Arab Republic	VCT	St. Vincent & Grenadines
SCG	Serbia & Montenegro	TCA	Turks & Caicos Islands	VEN	Venezuela
SDN	Sudan	TCD	Chad	VGB	Virgin Islands, British
SEN	Senegal	TGO	Togo	VIR	Virgin Islands, U.S.
SGP	Singapore	THA	Thailand	VNM	Viet Nam
SGS	South Georgia & Sandwich Islands	TJK	Tajikistan	VUT	Vanuatu
SHN	Saint Helena	TKL	Tokelau	WLF	Wallis & Futuna
SJM	Svalbard & Jan Mayen	TKM	Turkmenistan	WSM	Samoa
SLB	Solomon Islands	TNP	East Timor	YEM	Yemen
SLE	Sierra Leone	TON	Tonga	YUG	Yugoslavia
SLV	El Salvador	TTO	Trinidad & Tobago	ZAF	South Africa
SMR	San Marino	TUN	Tunisia	ZAR	Zaire
SOM	Somalia	TUR	Turkey	ZMB	Zambia
SPM	Saint Pierre & Miquelon	TUV	Tuvalu	ZWE	Zimbabwe
SRB	Serbia	TWN	Taiwan		

Country Sequence

Country	Code	Country	Code	Country	Code
AFGHANISTAN	AFG	EAST TIMOR	TMP	MACAO	MAC
ALBANIA	ALB	ECUADOR	ECU	MACEDONIA	MKD
ALGERIA	DZA	EGYPT	EGY	MADAGASCAR	MDG
AMERICAN SAMOA	ASM	EL SALVADOR	SLV	MALAWI	MWI
ANDORRA	AND	EQUATORIAL GUINEA	GNQ	MALAYSIA	MYS
ANGOLA	AGO	ERITREA	ERI	MALDIVE ISLANDS	
ANGUILLA	AIA	ESTONIA	EST	MDV	
ANTARCTICA	ATA	ETHIOPIA	ETH	MALI	MLI
ANTIGUA & BARBUDA	ATG	FAEROE ISLANDS	FRO	MALTA	MLT
ARGENTINA	ARG	FALKLAND ISLANDS	FLK	MARSHALL ISLANDS	MHL
ARMENIA	ARM	FED. STATES OF MICRONESIA	FSM	MARTINIQUE	MTQ
ARUBA	ABW	FIJI	FJI	MAURITANIA	MRT
AUSTRALIA	AUS	FINLAND	FIN	MAURITIUS	MUS
AUSTRIA	AUT	FRANCE	FRA	MAYOTTE	MYT
AZERBAIJAN	AZE	FRENCH GUIANA	GUF	MEXICO	MEX
BAHAMAS	BHS	FRENCH POLYNESIA	PYF	MOLDOVA	MDA
BAHRAIN		FRENCH SOUTHERN TERRITORIES	ATF	MONACO	MCO
BHR		GABON	GAB	MONGOLIA	MNG
BANGLADESH	BGD	GAMBIA	GMB	MONTENEGRO	MNE
BARBADOS	BRB	GEORGIA	GEO	MONTSERRAT	MSR
BELARUS	BLR	GERMANY	DEU	MOROCCO	MAR
BELGIUM	BEL	GHANA	GHA	MOZAMBIQUE	MOZ
BELIZE	BLZ	GIBRALTAR	GIB	MYANMAR	MMR
BENIN	BEN	GREECE	GRC	NAMIBIA	NAM
BERMUDA	BMU	GREENLAND	GRL	NAURU	NRU
BHUTAN	BTN	GRENADA	GRD	NEPAL	NPL
BOLIVIA	BOL	GUADELOUPE	GLP	NETHERLANDS	NLD
BOSNIA & HERZEGOVINA	BIH	GUAM	GUM	NETHERLANDS ANTILLES	ANT
BOTSWANA	BWA	GUATEMALA	GTM	NEW CALEDONIA	NCL
BOUVET ISLAND	BVT	GUINEA	GIN	NEW ZEALAND	NZL
BRAZIL	BRA	GUINEA-BISSAU	GNB	NICARAGUA	NIC
BRITISH INDIAN OCEAN TERRITORY	IOT	GUYANA	GUY	NIGER	NER
BRUNEI DARUSSALAM	BRN	HAITI	HTI	NIGERIA	NGA
BULGARIA	BGR	HEARD ISLAND & MCDONALD		NIUE	NIU
BURKINA FASO	BFA	ISLANDS	HMD	NORFOLK ISLAND	NFK
BURUNDI	BDI	HONDURAS	HND	NORTHERN MARIANA ISLANDS	MNP
CAMBODIA	KHM	HONG KONG	HKG	NORWAY	NOR
CAMEROON	CMR	HUNGARY	HUN	OCCUPIED PALESTINIAN	
CANADA	CAN	ICELAND	ISL	TERRITORY	PSE
CAPE VERDE	CPV	INDIA	IND	OMAN	OMN
CAYMAN ISLANDS	CYM	INDONESIA	IDN	PAKISTAN	PAK
CENTRAL AFRICAN REPUBLIC	CAF	IRAN	IRN	PALAU	PLW
CHAD	TCD	IRAQ	IRQ	PANAMA	PAN
CHILE	CHL	IRELAND	IRL	PAPUA NEW GUINEA	PNG
CHINA	CHN	ISRAEL	ISR	PARAGUAY	PRY
CHRISTMAS ISLAND	CXR	ITALY	ITA	PERU	PER
COCOS (KEELING) ISLANDS	CCK	JAMAICA	JAM	PHILIPPINES	PHL
COLOMBIA		JAPAN	JPN	PITCAIRN	PCN
COL		JORDAN	JOR	POLAND	POL
COMOROS	COM	KAZAKHSTAN	KAZ	PORTUGAL	PRT
CONGO	COG	KENYA	KEN	PUERTO RICO	PRI
CONGO, DEMOCRATIC		KIRIBATI	KIR	QATAR	QAT
REPUBLIC OF	COD	KOREA, DEMOCRATIC PEOPLE'S		REUNION	REU
COOK ISLANDS	COK	REP. OF	PRK	ROMANIA	
COSTA RICA	CRI	KOREA, REPUBLIC OF	KOR	ROM	
COTE D'IVOIRE	CIV	KUWAIT	KWT	RUSSIA	RUS
CROATIA	HRV	KYRGYZSTAN	KGZ	RWANDA	RWA
CUBA	CUB	LAOS	LAO	SAINT HELENA	SHN
CYPRUS	CYP	LATVIA	LVA	SAINT KITTS-NEVIS	KNAI
CZECH REPUBLIC	CZE	LEBANON	LBN	SAINT PIERRE & MIQUELON	SPM
CZECHOSLOVAKIA	CSK	LESOTHO	LSO	SAMOA	WSM
DENMARK	DNK	LIBERIA	LBR	SAN MARINO	SMR
DJIBOUTI	DJI	LIBYA	LBY	SAO TOME E PRINCIPE	STP
DOMINICA	DMA	LIECHTENSTEIN	LIE	SAUDI ARABIA	SAU
DOMINICAN REPUBLIC	DOM	LITHUANIA	LTU	SENEGAL	SEN
EAST GERMANY	DDR	LUXEMBOURG	LUX	SERBIA	SER

SERBIA & MONTENEGRO	SCG	SWEDEN	SWE	UNITED KINGDOM	GBR
SEYCHELLES	SYC	SWITZERLAND	CHE	UNITED STATES	USA
SIERRA LEONE	SLE	SYRIAN ARAB REPUBLIC	SYR	URUGUAY	URY
SINGAPORE	SGP	TAIWAN	TWN	US MINOR ISLANDS	UMI
SLOVAKIA	SVK	TAJIKISTAN	TJK	UZBEKISTAN	UZB
SLOVENIA	SVN	TANZANIA	TZA	VANUATU	VUT
SOLOMON ISLANDS	SLB	THAILAND	THA	VATICAN CITY	VAT
SOMALIA		TOGO	TGO	VENEZUELA	VEN
SOM		TOKELAU	TKL	VIET NAM	VNM
SOUTH AFRICA	ZAF	TONGA	TON	VIRGIN ISLANDS, BRITISH	VGB
SOUTH GEORGIA & SANDWICH		TRINIDAD & TOBAGO	TTO	VIRGIN ISLANDS, U.S.	VIR
ISLAND	SGS	TUNISIA	TUN	WALLIS & FUTUNA	
SPAIN	ESP	TURKEY	TUR	WLF	
SRI LANKA	LKA	TURKMENISTAN	TKM	WEST GERMANY	BRD
ST. LUCIA	LCA	TURKS & CAICOS ISLANDS	TCA	WESTERN SAHARA	ESH
ST. VINCENT & GRENADINES	VCT	TUVALU	TUV	YEMEN	YEM
SUDAN	SDN	U.S.S.R.	SUN	YUGOSLAVIA	YUG
SURINAM	SUR	UGANDA	UGA	ZAIRE	ZAR
SVALBARD & JAN MAYEN	SJM	UKRAINE	UKR	ZAMBIA	ZMB
SWAZILAND	SWZ	UNITED ARAB EMIRATES	ARE	ZIMBABWE	ZWE

Document Suppliers

AskIEEE   **AskIEEE**
10850 Wilshire Blvd, 8th Fl, Los Angeles, CA
90024
TEL 800-422-4633
E-mail askieee@ieee.org
URL http://ieee.org/portal/pages/services/
askieee/index.html

BLDSC   **British Library Document Supply Centre**
Boston Spa, Wetherby, West Yorkshire LS23
7BQ, United Kingdom
TEL 44-1937-546060, FAX 44-1937-546333
E-mail dsc-customer-services@bl.uk
URL
http://www.bl.uk/services/document/sed.html

CASDDS   **Chemical Abstracts Service Document
Detective Service**
2540 Olentangy River Rd, PO Box 3012,
Columbus, OH 43210-0012
TEL 614-447-3670, 800-678-4337, FAX
614-447-3648
E-mail dds@cas.org
URL http://www.cas.org/Support/dds.html

CINDOC   **I E D C Y T Servicio de Acceso al
Documento**
Albasanz, 26-28, Madrid 28037, Spain
TEL 34-91-6022302, FAX 34-91-3045710
Joaquin Costa, 22, Madrid 28002, Spain
TEL 34-91-5635482, FAX 34-91-5642644
E-mail bib-icytfot@cindoc.csic.es
URL http://www.cindoc.csic.es/

CIS   **LexisNexis Academic & Library Solutions**
(Subsidiary of: LexisNexis North America)
7500 Old Georgetown Rd, Ste 1300,
Bethesda, MD 20814-6126
TEL 800-638-8380
E-mail academicinfo@lexisnexis.com
URL
http://academic.lexisnexis.com/cis/cis.aspx

CISTI   **C I S T I**
(Canada Institute for Scientific and Technical
Information)
(Subsidiary of: National Research Council
Canada (N R C))
1200 Montreal Rd, Bldg M-55, Ottawa, ON
K1A 0R6, Canada
TEL 613-993-9251, 800-668-1222, FAX
613-993-7619
E-mail cisti.producthelp@nrc.ca,
info.cisti@nrc-cnrc.gc.ca
URL http://cisti-icist.nrc-cnrc.gc.ca/
docdel/docdel_e.shtml,
http://www.nrc.ca/cisti

East View   **East View Information Services**
10601 Wayzata Blvd, Minneapolis, MN 55305
TEL 952-252-1201, 800-477-1005, FAX
952-252-1202
E-mail info@eastview.com
URL http://www.eastview.com

GNLM   **German National Library of Medicine
/Deutsche Zentralbibliothek fuer
Medizin**
Gleueler Str 60, Cologne 50931, Germany
TEL 49-221-4787070, FAX 49-221-4787062
E-mail auskunft@zbmed.de
URL http://www.zbmed.de

IDS   **Thomson Reuters, Scientific**
(Subsidiary of: Thomson Reuters Corp.)
1500 Spring Garden, 4th Fl, Philadelphia, PA
19130
TEL 215-386-0100, 800-336-4474,
800-603-4367, FAX 215-386-2911,
856-787-1679
E-mail general.info@thomson.com,
service@tsdoc.com
URL http://science.thomsonreuters.com/,
http://scientific.thomson.com/products/ds/

DOCUMENT SUPPLIERS

IE   **Information Express**
565 Middlefield Rd, 2nd, Menlo Park, CA
94025-3443
TEL 650-812-3588, FAX 650-812-3573
E-mail service@ieonline.com
URL http://www.ieonline.com

ingenta   **IngentaConnect**
(Subsidiary of: Publishing Technology Plc.)
875 Massachusetts Ave., 7th Fl., Cambridge,
MA 02139
TEL 617-497-6514, FAX 617-354-6875
E-mail help@ingentaconnect.com,
info@ingenta.com
URL http://www.ingentaconnect.com/

Infotrieve   **Infotrieve**
20 Westport Rd, Ste 105, PO Box 7102,
Wilton, CT 06897
TEL 203-423-2175, 800-422-4633, FAX
203-423-2155
E-mail service@infotrieve.com
URL
http://www4.infotrieve.com/docdelivery.asp

INIST   **Centre National de la Recherche
Scientifique (C N R S), Institut de
l'Information Scientifique et Technique
(INIST)**
8, rue Jean Calvin, Paris 75005, France
TEL 33-1-45350177, FAX 33-1-43370019
2, Allee du Parc de Brabois, CS 10310,
Vandoeuve-les-Nancy 54519, France
TEL 33-3-83504600, FAX 33-3-83504650
URL http://www.inist.fr,
http://international.inist.fr/rubrique3.html

Linda Hall   **Linda Hall Library of Science, Engineering
& Technology, Document Delivery
Services**
5109 Cherry St, Kansas City, MO 64110-2498
TEL 816-363-4600, 800-662-1545, FAX
816-926-8785
E-mail requests@lindahall.org
URL
http://www.lindahall.org/services/document_delivery/

PADDS   **Petroleum Abstracts Document Delivery
System**
Univeristy of Tulsa - McFarlin Library, 2933 E
6th St, Tulsa, OK 74104-3123
TEL 918-631-2231, 800-247-8678, FAX
918-613-3823
URL http://www.pa.utulsa.edu/padds.mhtml

Micropublishers and Distributors

AJP   **American Jewish Periodical Center**
No Longer a Micropublisher

ALP   **Alpha Com**
Sportallee 6, Hamburg 22335, Germany
TEL 49-40-51302123
FAX 49-40-51302111
E-mail info-hamburg@alpha-com.de
URL http://www.alpha-com.de

AMP   **Adam Matthew Publications Ltd.**
Pelham House, London Rd, Marlborough,
Wiltshire SN8 2AA, United Kingdom
TEL 44-1672-511921
FAX 44-1672-511663
E-mail info@ampltd.co.uk
URL http://www.ampltd.co.uk

BHP   **Brookhaven Press**
(Subsidiary of: N M T Corporation)
PO Box 2287, La Crosse, WI 54602-2287
TEL 608-781-0850
FAX 608-781-3883
E-mail brookhaven@nmt.com
URL http://www.brookhavenpress.com

BNB   **British Library National Bibliographic Service**
Boston Spa, Weyherby, W Yorkshire LS23 7BQ,
United Kingdom
TEL 44-1937-546060
FAX 44-1937-546586
E-mail customer-service@bl.uk
URL http://www.bl.uk/

BNQ   **Bibliotheque et Archives Nationales du Quebec**
2275, rue Holt, Montreal, PQ H2G 3H1, Canada
TEL 514-873-1100, 800-363-9028
FAX 514-873-9312
URL http://www.banq.qc.ca/

CIS   **LexisNexis Academic & Library Solutions**
(Subsidiary of: LexisNexis North America)
7500 Old Georgetown Rd, Ste 1300, Bethesda,
MD 20814-6126
TEL 800-638-8380
E-mail academicinfo@lexisnexis.com
URL http://academic.lexisnexis.com/cis/cis.aspx

CML   **Commonwealth Imaging**
200, 1601-9th Ave SE, Calgary, AB T2R 0H4,
Canada
TEL 403-541-5644, 800-267-2555
FAX 403-228-5712
URL http://www.commonwealthimaging.com/

EVP   **East View Information Services**
10601 Wayzata Blvd, Minneapolis, MN 55305
TEL 952-252-1201, 800-477-1005
FAX 952-252-1202
E-mail info@eastview.com
URL http://www.eastview.com

GCS   **Preston Microfilming Services**
2215 Queen St E, Toronto, ON M4E 1E8, Canada
TEL 416-699-7154
FAX 416-699-7155
E-mail prestonmicrofilm@rogers.com
URL http://webhome.idirect.com/~filming/

IDC   **I D C Publishers**
(Subsidiary of: Brill)
PO Box 11205, Leiden 2301 EE, Netherlands
TEL 31-71-5142700
FAX 31-71-5131721
E-mail info@idc.nl
URL http://www.idc.nl

LCP   **The Library of Congress Photoduplication Service**
101 Independence Ave SE, Washington, DC
20540-4570
TEL 202-707-5640
FAX 202-707-1771
E-mail photoduplication@loc.gov
URL http://www.loc.gov/preserv/pds

LIB   **B M I Imaging Systems**
1115 E Arques Ave, Sunnyvale, CA 94805
TEL 408-736-7444, 800-359-3456
FAX 408-736-4397
E-mail info@bmiimaging.com
URL http://www.bmiimaging.com

MICROPUBLISHERS AND DISTRIBUTORS

MIM   **Elsevier**
The Boulevard, Langford Ln., Kidlington, Oxford
OX5 1GB, United Kingdom
TEL 44-1865-843000
E-mail cservice@harcourt.com
URL http://www.elsevierhealth.com

MML   **Micromedia ProQuest**
(Subsidiary of: ProQuest LLC (Ann Arbor))
789 E Eisenhower Pkwy, PO Box 1346, Anne
Arbor, MI 48106-1346
TEL 734-761-4700, 800-521-0600
URL http://il.proquest.com/en-US/products/
    brands/pl_mm.shtml

MMP   **McLaren Micropublishing**
PO Box 972, Sta. F, Toronto, ON M4Y 2N9,
Canada
TEL 416-651-1610
FAX 416-652-9968
E-mail mmicro@interlog.com
URL http://home.interlog.com/~mmicro/home.htm

NAP   **National Archive Publishing Company**
300 N Zeeb Rd, PO Box 998, Ann Arbor, MI
48103-0998
TEL 734-302-6500, 800-420-6272
FAX 734-302-6580
E-mail info@napubco.com
URL http://www.napubco.com

NBI   **Newsbank, Inc.**
4501 Tamiami Trail N., Ste. 316, Naples, FL
34103
TEL 802-875-2910, 800-762-8182
FAX 239-263-3004
E-mail sales@newsbank.com
URL http://www.newsbank.com

NTI   **U.S. Department of Commerce, National
Technical Information Service**
5301 Shawnee Rd, Alexandria, VA 22312
TEL 703-605-6050, 888-584-8332
FAX 703-605-6900
E-mail customerservice@ntis.gov
URL http://www.ntis.gov

PMC   **Princeton Microfilm Corp.**
43 Princeton Hightstown Rd #C, Princeton Jct, NJ
08550-1118
TEL 609-452-2066, 800-257-9502
FAX 609-275-6201

PQC   **ProQuest LLC (Ann Arbor)**
(Subsidiary of: Cambridge Information Group)
789 E Eisenhower Pkwy, PO Box 1346, Ann
Arbor, MI 48106-1346
TEL 734-761-4700, 800-521-0600
FAX 734-997-4040, 800-864-0019
E-mail info@proquest.com
URL http://www.proquest.com

RPI   **Primary Source Media**
(Subsidiary of: Gale)
12 Lunar Dr, Woodbridge, CT 06525-2398
TEL 203-397-2600, 800-444-0799
FAX 203-397-3893
E-mail gale.sales@cengage.com
URL http://www.gale.cengage.com/psm/

SOC   **Societe Canadienne du Microfilm Inc.
/Canadian Microfilming Company Limited**
464, rue Saint-Jean, Ste 110, Montreal, PQ H2Y
2S1, Canada
TEL 514-288-5404
FAX 514-843-4690
E-mail info@socami.qc.ca
URL http://www.socami.qc.ca

SWZ   **Nashuatec Farrington**
No Longer a Micropublisher

WMP   **World Microfilms**
POB 35488, St John's Wood, London NW8 6WD,
United Kingdom
TEL 44-20-75864499
FAX 44-20-77221068
E-mail microworld@ndirect.co.uk
URL http://www.microworld.uk.com/

WSH   **William S. Hein & Co., Inc.**
1285 Main St, Buffalo, NY 14209-1987
TEL 716-882-2600, 800-828-7571
FAX 716-883-8100
E-mail mail@wshein.com
URL http://www.wshein.com

Reprint Services

IRC **International Reprint Corp.**
287 E H St, Benicia, CA 94510
TEL 707-746-8740
FAX 707-746-1643
E-mail irc@intlreprints.com
URL http://www.intlreprints.com

PSC **Periodicals Service Co.**
11 Main St, Germantown, NY 12526
TEL 518-537-4700
FAX 518-537-5899
E-mail psc@periodicals.com
URL http://www.periodicals.com

SCH **Schmidt Periodicals GmbH**
Dettendorf Roemerring 12, Bad Feilnbach D
83075, Germany
TEL 49-8064221
FAX 49-8064557
E-mail schmidt@periodicals.com
URL http://www.periodicals.com

WSH **William S. Hein & Co., Inc.**
1285 Main St, Buffalo, NY 14209-1987
TEL 716-882-2600, 800-828-7571
FAX 716-883-8100
E-mail mail@wshein.com
URL http://www.wshein.com

AAP **Australian Associated Press**
3 Rider Blvd, Rhodes Waterside, Rhodes, NSW 2138, Australia
TEL 61-2-93228000
URL http://aap.com.au

AFP **Agence France-Presse**
11-15 Place de la Bourse, Paris 75002, France
TEL 33-1-40414646
E-mail communication@afp.com
URL http://www.afp.com

AP **Associated Press**
450 W 33rd St, New York, NY 10001-2606
TEL 212-621-1500
E-mail info@ap.org
URL http://www.ap.org

APP **Associated Press of Pakistan**
18, Mauve Area, G-7/1, Islamabad, Pakistan
TEL 92-51-2203064
FAX 92-51-2203069
E-mail news@app.com.pk
URL http://www.app.com.pk

BNS **Baltic News Service**
(Subsidiary of: Alma Media Group)
Toompuiestee 35, Tallinn 15043, Estonia
TEL 372-6108800
FAX 372-6108811
E-mail bns@bns.ee
URL http://www.bns.ee

CNS **Creative News Service**
5777 West Century Blvd, Ste 700, PO Box 120190, Los Angeles, CA 90045
TEL 310-337-7003
FAX 310-337-7625
E-mail info@creators.com
URL http://www.creators.com

CaNS **Catholic News Service**
3211 Fourth St, NE, Washington, DC 20017
TEL 202-541-3250
FAX 202-541-3255
E-mail cns@catholicnews.com
URL http://www.catholicnews.com

CanP **The Canadian Press**
36 King St East, Toronto, ON M5C 2L9, Canada
TEL 416-364-0321, 800-434-7578
FAX 416-364-0207
E-mail info@cp.org
URL http://www.thecanadianpress.com

CiNS **City News Service**
11400 W Olympic Blvd, Ste780, Los Angeles, CA 90064
TEL 310-481-0404
FAX 310-481-0416
E-mail news@socalnews.com
URL http://www.socalnews.com

DJNS **Dow Jones Newswires**
(Subsidiary of: Dow Jones & Company)
Harborside Financial Center, 800 Plaza Two, Jersey City, NJ 07311
TEL 800-223-2274
E-mail newswires@dowjones.com
URL http://solutions.dowjones.com

EFE **Agencia EFE**
C/Espronceda, 32, Madrid 28003, Spain
TEL 34-91-3467400, 34-91-3467100
E-mail comunicacion@efe.es
URL http://www.efe.com/

GNS **Gannett News Service**
7950 Jones Branch Dr, McLean, VA 22107
TEL 703-854-5800
FAX 703-854-2152
URL http://www.gannett.com

JTA **Jewish Telegraphic Agency**
330 Seventh Ave, 17th Fl, New York, NY 10001
TEL 212-643-1890
FAX 212-643-8499
E-mail info@jta.org
URL http://www.jta.org

LAT-WAT **Los Angeles Times-Washington Post News Service**
1150 15th St., NW, Washington, DC 20071
TEL 202-334-6173
FAX 202-334-5096
E-mail latwp@newsservice.com
URL http://www.newsservice.com

MCT **McClatchy-Tribune Information Services**
700 12th St, NW, Ste 1000, Washington, DC 20005
TEL 202-383-6095
URL http://www.mctdirect.com

NYT **New York Times News Service**
620 Eight Ave, 9th Fl, New York, NY 10018
TEL 212-556-1927
E-mail nytns@nytimes.com
URL http://www.nytsyn.com

WIRE SERVICES

PR   **PR Newswire Association LLC**
350 Hudson St, Ste 300, New York, NY 10014
TEL 800-776-8090
FAX 800-793-9313
URL http://www.prnewswire.com

RN   **Reuters**
(Subsidiary of: Thomson Reuters Corp.)
The Thomson Reuters Building, South
Colonnade, Canary Wharf, London E14 5EP,
United Kingdom
TEL 44-20-72501122
URL http://www.reuters.com

SAPA   **South African Press Association**
Cotswold House, Greenacres Office Park, Cnr.
Victory & Rustenburg Rds, Victory Park, PO Box
7766, Johannesburg 2000, South Africa
TEL 27-11-7821600
FAX 27-11-7821587
E-mail comms@sapa.org.za
URL http://www.sapa.org.za

SH   **Scripps Howard News Service**
1090 Vermont Ave., N.W., Ste. 1000,
Washington, DC 20005
TEL 202-408-1484
FAX 202-408-2062
E-mail copelandp@shns.com
URL http://www.shns.com

UPI   **United Press International**
1133 19th St NW, Washington, DC 20036
TEL 202-898-8000
FAX 202-898-8048
E-mail jugo@upi.com
URL http://www.upi.com

Abstracting and Indexing Services

This list contains the full names of all abstracting and indexing services whose abbreviations are used in entries in the CLASSIFIED LIST OF SERIALS. For all currently published abstracting and indexing services, please consult the TITLE INDEX for page references to full entries in the CLASSIFIED LIST OF SERIALS. (Bibliographic information on titles for which cessations were noted more than three years ago are not listed in this book. To view information on such titles, one must refer to Ulrich's™ on Disc, Ulrich's Online, or ulrichsweb.com™

A

A&AAb †Astronomy and Astrophysics Abstracts (Supersedes (in 1969): Astronomischer Jahresbericht)

A&ATA A A T A Online (Art and Archaeology Technical Abstracts) (Former titles (until 2002): Art and Archaeology Technical Abstracts (Print Edition); (until 1966): I I C Abstracts)

AA Art Abstracts (Formerly (until 1997): Wilson Art Abstracts)

AAR Accounting Articles (Formerly: C C H Accounting Articles)

ABC †BioCommerce Abstracts (Formerly (until 1997): Abstracts in Biocommerce)

ABCPolSci C S A Political Science & Government (Cambridge Scientific Abstracts) (Formerly (until vol. 32, no. 6, 2000): A B C Pol Sci)

ABCT †ARTbibliographies Current Titles (Email Edition) (Formerly (until 2003): ARTbibliographies Current Titles (Print Edition))

ABIPC Abstract Bulletin of Paper Science and Technology (Former titles (until 1998): Institute of Paper Science and Technology. Abstract Bulletin; (until July 1989): Institute of Paper Chemistry. Abstract Bulletin; (until 1958): Institute of Paper Chemistry. Bulletin)

ABIX †A B I X: Australasian Business Intelligence (Former titles: A B I X; (until 1995): Australian Business Index)

ABIn A B I - INFORM (American Business Information)

ABM ARTbibliographies Modern

ABRCLP †Abstracts of Book Reviews in Current Legal Periodicals

ABS&EES American Bibliography of Slavic and East European Studies (Formerly (until 1966): American Bibliography of Russian and East European Studies)

ABSML †Abstracts of Bulgarian Scientific Medical Literature (Online Edition) (Former titles (until 1996): Abstracts of Bulgarian Scientific Medical Literature (Print Edition); (until 1968): Abstracts of Bulgarian Scientific Literature. Medicine; (until 1966): Abstracts of Bulgarian Scientific Literature. Medicine and Physical Culture; (until 1963): Abstracts of Bulgarian Scientific Literature. Biology and Medicine)

ABTICS †Abstracts and Book Title Index Card Service (ABTICS)

AC&P †Criminology, Penology & Police Science Abstracts (Formed by the merger of: Police Science Abstracts; Which was formerly: Abstracts on Police Science; Criminology and Penology Abstracts; Abstracts on Criminology and Penology; Excerpta Criminologica)

AD&D †Alcohol, Drugs and Driving (Formerly: Alcohol, Drugs and Driving: Abstracts and Reviews)

ADPA †Accounting & Finance Abstracts (Former titles (until 2001): Anbar Accounting & Finance Abstracts; (until 1991): Accounting & Data Processing Abstracts; Which superseded in part: Anbar Management Services Abstracts)

AEA Agricultural Engineering Abstracts

AEBA Agricultural & Environmental Biotechnology Abstracts (Online)

AEI Australian Education Index (Online)

AES †Abstracts of English Studies

AESIS †A M F Alert (Australian Mineral Foundation) (Formed by the merger of (1976-1998): A E S I S Quarterly; (1995-1998): A M F Reviews; Which was formerly (1973-1995): Earth Science and Related Information)

AFA American Fisheries Abstracts

AFS †Abstracts of Folklore Studies

AGBP †Guide to Botanical Periodicals (Formerly: Asher's Guide to Botanical Periodicals)

AHCI †Abstracts in Human - Computer Interaction (Formerly: H C I Abstracts)

AHCMS †Abstracts of Health Care Management Studies (Formerly: Abstracts of Hospital Management Studies)

AIA †Artificial Intelligence Abstracts (US)

ABSTRACTING AND INDEXING

AIAP	Avery Index to Architectural Periodicals
AICP	Anthropological Index Online
AIDS Ab	†AIDS Abstracts (Formerly (until 1993): AIDS Information)
AIDS&CR	†AIDS & Cancer Research
AIIM	†Abstracts in Medicine and Key Word Index (Formerly: Abstracts in Internal Medicine)
AIM	†Abridged Index Medicus *consists of:* †Cumulated Abridged Index Medicus
AIPP	†Roth's American Poetry Annual (Incorporates (1985-1986): Annual Survey of American Poetry; (1983-1986): American Poetry Index; (1984-1986): Annual Index to Poetry in Periodicals)
AIT	†A I T Reports and Publications on Energy. Abstracts (Asian Institute of Technology) (Formerly: A I T Reports and Publications on Renewable Energy Resources. Abstracts)
AJEE	†Abstract Journal in Earthquake Engineering
ALISA	†A L I S A (Online) (Australian Library and Information Science Abstracts) (Formerly (until 1996): A L I S A (Print))
ALMD	Australian Legal Monthly Digest (Formerly (until 1967): Legal Monthly Digest)
AMB	Abstracts of Military Bibliography (Former titles (until 1976): Resumenes Analiticos sobre Defensa y Seguridad Nacional; (until 1970): Resumenes Analiticos de Bibliografia Militar)
AMED	A M E D (Allied and Complementary Medicine Database)
AMHA	†Adolescent Mental Health Abstracts
AMR	†European Muslims and Christian-Muslim Relations. Abstracts
ANAG	†Abstracts of North American Geology
APA	Advanced Polymers Abstracts
APC	†Abstracts of Popular Culture
APD	†Acid Precipitation Digest
APEL	Asian - Pacific Economic Literature
API	Architectural Publications Index (Formerly (until 1995): Architectural Periodicals Index; Supersedes: R I B A Library Bulletin)
APIAb	Ei EnCompassLit (Formerly: A P I Lit)
APICat	Technical Literature Abstracts: Catalysts - Zeolites (Online)
APIH&E	Technical Literature Abstracts: Health & Environment (Online)
APIOC	Technical Literature Abstracts: Oilfield Chemicals (Online)
APIPR	Technical Literature Abstracts: Petroleum Refining & Petrochemicals (Online)
APIPS	Technical Literature Abstracts: Petroleum Substitutes (Online)
APITS	Technical Literature Abstracts: Transportation & Storage (Online)
APW	Alt-Press Watch
ARDT	†Abstracts on Rural Development in the Tropics
ARG	Abridged Readers' Guide to Periodical Literature
ARI	†Australian Road Index
AS&TA	Applied Science & Technology Abstracts
AS&TI	Applied Science & Technology Index (Supersedes in part (in 1958): Industrial Arts Index)
ASA	†Australian Speleo Abstracts
ASCA	Personal Alert (E-mail) (Former titles: Research Alert (Print); (until 1989): Automatic Subject Citation Alert; A S C A Topics)
ASD	†African Studies Abstracts (Formerly (until 1994): Afrika Studiecentrum. Documentatieblad)
ASEANManA	A S E A N Management Abstracts (Association of Southeast Asian Nations) (Formerly (until 1982): Management Abstracts of Singapore)
ASFA	Aquatic Sciences & Fisheries Abstracts *consists of:* A S F A Aquaculture Abstracts (Online) A S F A Marine Biotechnology Abstracts (Online) Aquatic Sciences & Fisheries Abstracts. Part 1: Biological Sciences and Living Resources Aquatic Sciences & Fisheries Abstracts. Part 2: Ocean Technology, Policy and Non-living Resources Aquatic Sciences & Fisheries Abstracts. Part 3: Aquatic Pollution and Environmental Quality
ASG	Abstracts in Social Gerontology (Former titles (until 1990): Current Literature on Aging; (until 1963): National Council on the Aging. Library Selected Acquisitions; (until 1961): National Committee on the Aging. Library Selected Acquisitions; (until 1958): National Committee on the Aging. Library List)
ASI	†Australian Science Index
ASIP	Access: The Supplementary Index to Periodicals (Incorporates (1978-1979): Monthly Periodical Index)
ASLHA	American Speech - Language - Hearing Abstracts
ASSIA	A S S I A (Applied Social Sciences Index & Abstracts) (Supersedes (in 1999): A S S I A: Applied Social Sciences Index & Abstracts (Print))
ASTIS	†A S T I S Bibliography (Arctic Science & Technology Information System) (Supersedes (in 1995): A S T I S Bibliography (Microfiche))
ATA	†Agriculture and Environment for Developing Regions (Former titles (until 1996): Abstracts on Tropical Agriculture; (until 1975): Tropical Abstracts)
ATI	Accounting and Tax Index (Online Edition)
AUNI	Air University Library Index to Military Periodicals
AbAn	Abstracts in Anthropology

AbHyg	Abstracts on Hygiene and Communicable Diseases (Former titles: Abstracts on Hygiene; Bulletin of Hygiene)
Acal	†Academic Index
AcoustA	†Acoustics Abstracts (Formerly (until 1967): Acoustics and Ultrasonics Abstracts)
AddicA	Addiction Abstracts
AgBio	AgBiotech News and Information
AgeL	AgeLine
Agr	Agricola (Agricultural OnLine Access)
AgrAg	Agro-Agen
AgrForAb	Agroforestry Abstracts (Online)
AgrLib	Agro-Librex
Agrind	†Agrindex
AltPI	Alternative Press Index
AmH&L	America: History and Life (Formed by the merger of: America: History and Life. Part A: Article Abstracts and Citation; America: History and Life. Part B: Index to Book Reviews; America: History and Life. Part C: American History Bibliography; America: History and Life. Part D: Annual Index) *consists of:* America: History and Life. Annual Index
AmHI	Humanities International Index (Formerly (until 2005): American Humanities Index (Online Edition))
AmStI	American Statistics Index
AnBeAb	Animal Behavior Abstracts (Formerly (until 1974): Behavioural Biology Abstracts, Section A: Animal Behaviour)
AnBrAb	Animal Breeding Abstracts
AnalAb	Analytical Abstracts
AnthLit	Anthropological Literature
ApEcolAb	Ecology Abstracts (Bethesda) (Formerly (until 1980): Applied Ecology Abstracts)
ApMecR	Applied Mechanics Reviews
ApicAb	†Apicultural Abstracts
ArcBib	†Arctic Bibliography
ArchI	Architectural Index
ArtHuCI	Arts & Humanities Citation Index (Online)
ArtIAb	†Artificial Intelligence Abstracts (UK)
ArtInd	Art Index
Artemisa	Artemisa
AusPAIS	A P A I S: Australian Public Affairs Information Service (Online)

B

B&AI	Biological & Agricultural Index (Formerly (until 1964): Agricultural Index)
B&BAb	Biotechnology & Bioengineering Abstracts *consists of:* †A S F A Marine Biotechnology Abstracts (Print) Agricultural & Environmental Biotechnology Abstracts (Online) BioEngineering Abstracts (Online) Genetics Abstracts Medical & Pharmaceutical Biotechnology Abstracts (Online) Microbiology Abstracts: Section A. Industrial & Applied Microbiology
BA	Biofuels Abstracts
BAS	Bibliography of Asian Studies (Online Edition)
BBCI	Biochemistry and Biophysics Citation Index
BBO	Bibliografia Brasileira de Odontologia (Online Edition)
BCI	Biotechnology Citation Index
BCIRA	†B C I R A Abstracts of International Literature on Metal Castings Production (British Cast Iron Research Association) (Former titles: B C I R A Abstracts of International Foundry Literature; (until 1978): B C I R A Abstracts of Foundry Literature)
BDM&CN	†Bibliography of Developmental Medicine and Child Neurology. Books and Articles Received
BEL&L	Annual Bibliography of English Language and Literature (Formerly (until 1924): Bibliography of English Language and Literature)
BHA	B H A Bibliography of the History of Art (Formed by the merger of (1975-1996): International Repertory of the Literature of Art / Repertoire International de la Litterature de l'Art (RILA); (19??-1996): Repertoire d'Art et d'Archeologie (CD-ROM))
BIOBASE	BIOBASE *consists of:* Current Advances in Applied Microbiology & Biotechnology Current Advances in Cancer Research Current Advances in Cell & Developmental Biology Current Advances in Clinical Chemistry Current Advances in Ecological & Environmental Sciences Current Advances in Endocrinology & Metabolism Current Advances in Genetics & Molecular Biology Current Advances in Immunology & Infectious Diseases Current Advances in Neuroscience Current Advances in Plant Science Current Advances in Protein Biochemistry Current Advances in Toxicology
BIOSIS Prev	BIOSIS Previews
BLI	Banking Information Source (Former titles: Banking Information Index (Print Edition); (until 1994): Banking Literature Index)

BMT	B M T Abstracts (British Maritime Technology Ltd.) (Former titles (until 1986): B S R A. Journal of Abstracts; (until 1970): British Ship Research Association. Journal of Abstracts; (until 1968): British Ship Research Association. Journal; (until 1962): British Shipbuilding Research Association. Journal)
BNI	†B N I (British Newspaper Index)
BNNA	Bibliography of Native North Americans
BP	Botanical Pesticides Abstracts
BPI	Business Periodicals Index (Supersedes in part (in 1959): Industrial Arts Index)
BPIA	†Business Publications Index and Abstracts
BPRC&P	†Biweekly List of Papers on Radiation Chemistry and Photochemistry (Former titles (until 1978): Biweekly List of Papers on Radiation Chemistry; Weekly List of Papers on Radiation Chemistry; Which incorporated: Index and Cumulative List of Papers on Radiation Chemistry)
BRI	Book Review Index
BRM	†Book Reviews of the Month
BSLBiol	†Abstracts of Bulgarian Scientific Literature. Biology (Formerly: Abstracts of Bulgarian Scientific Literature. Biology and Biochemistry)
BSLEcon	†Abstracts of Bulgarian Scientific Literature. Economics and Law
BSLGeo	†Abstracts of Bulgarian Scientific Literature. Geosciences (Formerly: Abstracts of Bulgarian Scientific Literature. Geology and Geography)
BSLIndus	†Abstracts of Bulgarian Scientific Literature. Industry, Building and Transport
BSLMath	†Abstracts of Bulgarian Scientific Literature. Mathematical and Physical Sciences (Formerly: Abstracts of Bulgarian Scientific Literature. Mathematics, Physics, Astronomy, Geophysics, Geodesy)
BehAb	†Behavioural Abstracts
BibAg	†Bibliography of Agriculture *consists of:* †Bibliography of Agriculture. Annual Cumulative Index
BibCart	Bibliographia Cartographica (Formerly (until 1972): Bibliotheca Cartographica)
BibInd	Bibliographic Index
BibLing	Linguistic Bibliography
BibRep	Human Reproduction Update (Incorporates (1963-1994): Bibliography of Reproduction)
BioCN&I	Biocontrol News and Information
BioDAb	†Biodeterioration Abstracts
BioEngAb	BioEngineering Abstracts (Online)
BiolAb	Biological Abstracts (Formed by the 1926 merger of: Abstracts of Bacteriology; Botanical Abstracts)
BiolDig	Biology Digest (Incorporates: Environmental Quality Abstracts)

Biostat	Biostatistica
BldManAb	Chartered Institute of Building. Construction Information Quarterly (Incorporates: Building Management Abstracts; Former titles (until 1999): Construction Information File - C I F; (until 1992): Technical Information Service - T I S; Which was formed by the merger of (1971-1982): Chartered Institute of Building. Estimating Information Service; (1971-1982): Chartered Institute of Building. Site Management Information Service; (1977-1982): Chartered Institute of Building. Maintenance Information Service; (1979-1982): Chartered Institute of Building. Surveying Information Service)
BrArAb	British & Irish Archaeological Bibliography (Online)
BrCerAb	World Ceramics Abstracts (Formerly (until 1989): British Ceramic Abstracts)
BrEdI	British Education Index
BrGeoL	†British Geological Literature
BrHumI	British Humanities Index
BrNI	British Nursing Index (Former titles (until 1997): Nursing and Midwifery Index; (until Dec. 1995): Nursing Bibliography)
BrRB	†British Railways Board. Monthly Review of Technical Literature
BrTechI	Abstracts in New Technologies and Engineering (Former titles (until 1997): Current Technology Index; British Technology Index)
BullT&T	†Bulletin of Chemical Thermodynamics (Former titles (until 1976): Bulletin of Thermodynamics and Thermochemistry; (until 1961): Bulletin of Chemical Thermodynamics; Which superseded: Thermochemical Bulletin and Bulletin of Unpublished Thermal Material)
BusDate	Business Dateline
BusEdI	†Business Education Index
BusI	†Business Index

C

C&CR	Catalysts & Catalysed Reactions
C&CSA	Computer & Communications Security Abstracts (Formerly (until 1999): Computer & Communications Security Reviews)
C&ISA	Computer and Information Systems Abstracts Journal (Former titles (until 1978): Computer and Information Systems; (until 1969): Information Processing Journal)
CA	Current Abstracts
CA&I	†Children's Authors and Illustrators
CA/WCA	Ceramic Abstracts / World Ceramic Abstracts
CABA	C A B Abstracts (Formerly: C A B Abstracts (Print Edition))
CADCAM	†C A D - C A M Abstracts (Computer Aided Design - Computer Aided Manufacturing)
CALL	†C A L L (Current Awareness - Library Literature)

CANZLLI	†Current Australian and New Zealand Legal Literature Index
CBA	Conservation Biology Abstracts
CBCABus	Canadian Business and Current Affairs Business (Supersedes in part (in 1998): C B C A Fulltext; Which was formerly (until 1997): Canadian Business and Current Affairs Fulltext (CD-ROM))
CBCARef	Canadian Business and Current Affairs Reference (Supersedes in part (in 1998): C B C A Fulltext; Which was formerly (until 1997): Canadian Business and Current Affairs - Fulltext (CD-ROM))
CBNB	Chemical Business NewsBase
CBPI	†Canadian Index (Formed by the merger of: Canadian Magazine Index; Canadian News Index; Which was formerly: Canadian Newspaper Index; Canadian Business Index; Which was formerly: Canadian Business Periodicals Index)
CBRC	†Current Book Review Citations
CBRI	Children's Book Review Index
CBTA	†Current Biotechnology (Incorporates (1985-2000): Biotechnology: Apparatus, Plant, and Equipment; Which was formerly (until 1991): Biotechnologie; Formerly (until 1990): Current Biotechnology Abstracts)
CCA	†Current Contents Africa (Formerly (until 1978): C C A (Current Contents Africa))
CCI	Chemistry Citation Index
CCIOG	Combined Cumulative Index to Obstetrics and Gynecology
CCIP	Combined Cumulative Index to Pediatrics
CCME	Electronic Current Contents of Periodicals on the Middle East (Formerly: Current Contents of Periodicals on the Middle East)
CCMJ	Current Mathematical Publications (Formed by the merger of (1964-1975): American Mathematical Society. New Publications; (1969-1975): Contents of Contemporary Mathematical Journals)
CCR	†Current Thoughts & Trends (Formerly: Current Christian Abstracts)
CDA	†Child Development Abstracts and Bibliography
CDSP	Current Digest of the Post-Soviet Press (Formerly (until 1992): Current Digest of the Soviet Press; Incorporates: Current Abstracts of the Soviet Press)
CEA	Process and Chemical Engineering (Formerly (until 1991): Chemical Engineering Abstracts)
CEABA	Chemical Engineering and Biotechnology Abstracts (Online) consists of: †Current Biotechnology †Environmental and Safety Technology Process and Chemical Engineering Theoretical Chemical Engineering
CEI	Canadian Business and Current Affairs Education (Formerly (until 1998): Canadian Education Index (CD-ROM Edition))
CERDIC	†Universite de Strasbourg. Centre de Recherche et de Documentation des Institutions Chretiennes. Bulletin du CERDIC
CFA	Canadian Fisheries Abstracts
CHI	Chemical Hazards in Industry
CHNI	†Consumer Health and Nutrition Index
CIA	Composites Industry Abstracts
CIJE	†Current Index to Journals in Education
CIN	†Chemical Industry Notes
CINAHL	Cumulative Index to Nursing & Allied Health Literature (Incorporates: Nursing and Allied Health Index; Which was formerly (1956-1976): Nursing Literature Index; (until 1977): Cumulative Index to Nursing Literature)
CIRFAb	†T & D Abstracts (Training & Development) (Supersedes: C I R F Abstracts)
CIS	Current Index to Statistics (Online) (Formerly (until 2001): Current Index to Statistics (Print))
CISA	†Safety and Health at Work (Former titles: C I S Abstracts; Occupational Safety and Health Abstracts)
CISI	C I S Index to Publications of the United States Congress (Congressional Information Service, Inc.)
CJA	Criminal Justice Abstracts (Former titles: Abstracts on Crime and Juvenile Delinquency; Crime and Delinquency Literature; Formed by the merger of: Information Review on Crime and Delinquency; Selected Highlights of Crime and Delinquency)
CJPI	Criminal Justice Periodical Index
CLA	Canon Law Abstracts
CLFP	†Current Literature in Family Planning
CLI	Current Law Index
CLL	Leather Science Abstracts (Formerly (until 1988): Current Leather Literature)
CLOSS	Current Literature on Science of Science (Formerly: Index to Literature on Science of Science)
CLT&T	†Current Literature in Traffic and Transportation
CLitI	†Canadian Literature Index
CMCI	†Compumath Citation Index
CMHR	Journal of Prevention and Intervention in the Community (Former titles (until 1996): Prevention in Human Services; (until 1981): Community Mental Health Review)
CMM	Communication and Mass Media Complete (Formed by the 2003 merger of: CommSearch; Mass Media Articles Index)
CMPI	Canadian Music Periodical Index
CPA	Crop Physiology Abstracts

ABSTRACTING AND INDEXING

CPE	Contents Pages in Education
CPEI	Compendex (COMPuterized ENgineering InDEX)
CPI	Current Physics Index
CPL	The Catholic Periodical and Literature Index (Former titles: Catholic Periodical Index; Guide to Catholic Literature)
CPLI	†Chicago Psychoanalytic Literature Index
CPM	Contents Pages in Management (Formerly (until 1974): Current Contents in Management)
CPerI	C P I. Q (Canadian Periodical Index)
CRCL	†Canadian Review of Comparative Literature
CREJ	Contents of Recent Economics Journals
CRFR	†Current References in Fish Research
CRIA	N C B Abstracts (National Council for Cement and Building Materials) (Formerly (until 2000): C R I Abstracts)
CRICC	N C B Current Contents (National Council for Cement and Building Materials) (Formerly (until 2000): C R I Current Contents)
CSI	†Directory of Statistics in Canada (Formerly: Canadian Statistics Index)
CSNB	Chemical Safety NewsBase *consists of:* Chemical Hazards in Industry Laboratory Hazards Bulletin †Managing Safety & Health at Work
CTA	Calcium and Calcified Tissue Abstracts (Online)
CTD	†Current Titles in Dentistry
CTE	Current Titles in Electrochemistry (Incorporates: Electrochemical News)
CTFA	†Cotton and Tropical Fibres (Formerly (until 1991): Cotton and Tropical Fibres Abstracts)
CTO	†Current Titles in Ocean, Coastal, Lake & Waterway Sciences
CWI	†Contemporary Women's Issues
CWPI	†Canadian Women's Periodicals Index (Former titles: Canadian Women's Periodicals: Title Word Index; Canadian Women's Periodicals: K W I C Index)
CZA	Canadian Zoology Abstracts
Cadscan	Cadscan (Formerly (until Oct. 1986): Cadmium Abstracts)
CalPI	California Periodicals Index
CerAb	Ceramic Abstracts (Supersedes in part (in 1922): American Ceramic Society. Journal; Which was formerly (until 1917): American Ceramic Society. Transactions)
ChLitAb	†Children's Literature Abstracts
ChPerI	†Chicano Index (Formerly (until 1989): Chicano Periodical Index)

ChemAb	Chemical Abstracts *consists of:* Chemical Abstracts - Applied Chemistry and Chemical Engineering Sections Chemical Abstracts - Biochemistry Sections Chemical Abstracts - Macromolecular Sections Chemical Abstracts - Organic Chemistry Sections Chemical Abstracts - Physical, Inorganic and Analytical Chemistry Sections Chemical Abstracts - Section Groupings Chemical Abstracts Service Source Index
ChemInfo	ChemInform (Formerly (until 1987): Chemischer Informationsdienst; Which was formed by the merger of (1970-1972): Chemischer Informationsdienst. Organische Chemie; (1970-1972): Chemischer Informationsdienst. Anorganische und Physikalische Chemie)
ChemTitl	†Chemical Titles
ChemoAb	Chemoreception Abstracts (Online)
Chicano	Chicano Database (Consists of: Chicano Index; Arte Chicano; Chicano Anthology Index; Chicana Studies Index; Hispanic Mental Health Research; Spanish Speaking Mental Health Database)
ChrPI	Christian Periodical Index
ChromAb	Chromatography Abstracts (Former titles (until 1986): Gas and Liquid Chromatography Abstracts; (until 1973): Gas Chromatography Abstracts)
CivEngAb	C S A Civil Engineering Abstracts (Cambridge Scientific Abstracts)
ClinAlert	Clin-Alert
CommAb	Communication Abstracts
CompAb	Computer Abstracts (Incorporates (1960-1980): Computer News; Former titles (until 1960): Computer Bibliography; (until 1959): Bibliography Series. Computers; I O T A Services Ltd. Monthly Bibliographical Series. Computors)
CompB	†Computer Business
CompC	†Computer Contents
CompD	Computer Database
CompI	†Computer Index
CompIU	†Computer Industry Update
CompLI	Computer Science Index (Former titles (until 2002): Computer Literature Index (Print); (until 1980): Quarterly Bibliography of Computers and Data Processing)
CompR	Computing Reviews
ConcrAb	†Concrete Abstracts
ConsI	†Consumers Index
Copeia	Copeia Abstracts (Formerly: ABSEARCH Ichthyology and Herpetology)

CoppAb	†International Copper Information Bulletin (Supersedes: Copper Abstracts; Incorporates: Kupfer - Mitteilungen; Cuivre, Laitons, Alliages - Bibliographie; Rame - Schede Bibliografiche; Cobre - Resumenes Bibliograficos)
CorrAb	Corrosion Abstracts (Incorporates: Corrosion Prevetion Technology; Which was formerly (1978-1995): Corrosion Prevention - Inhibition Digest)
CurCR	Current Chemical Reactions Database
CurCont	Current Contents *consists of:* Current Contents: Agriculture, Biology & Environmental Sciences Current Contents: Arts & Humanities Current Contents: Clinical Medicine Current Contents: Engineering, Computing & Technology †Current Contents: Health Services Administration Current Contents: Life Sciences Current Contents: Physical, Chemical & Earth Sciences Current Contents: Social & Behavioral Sciences
CurPA	†Current Packaging Abstracts (Formerly (until 1973): Packaging Bulletin)
CybAb	†Cybernetics Abstracts (Formerly (until 1965): Theoretical Cybernetics Abstracts)

D

DAAI	Design and Applied Arts Index
DBA	Derwent Biotechnology Abstracts
DIP	Dietrich's Index Philosophicus
DM&T	†Aerospace Defense Markets & Technology (Formerly: Defense Markets and Technology)
DNP	Digest of Neurology & Psychiatry (Online)
DPD	†Data Processing Digest
DRIE	Database of Research on International Education
DSA	Dairy Science Abstracts
DSHAb	†D S H Abstracts (Deafness, Speech and Hearing)
DYW	†Diversity Your World
DentAb	Dental Abstracts
DentInd	†Index to Dental Literature
DiabCont	†Diabetes Contents
Djerelo	Djerelo
DoGi	DoGi Database - Legal Literature
DokArb	†Arbeitsmedizin (Former titles: Beruf und Gesundheit - Occupational Health; (until 1985): Dokumentation Arbeitsmedizin - Documentation Occupational Health)
DokStr	Dokumentation Strasse

E

E&CAJ	Electronics and Communications Abstracts Journal (Former titles (until 1993): Electronics and Communications Abstracts; (until 1992): Electronics and Communications Abstracts Journal; (until 1972): Electronics Abstracts Journal)
E&PHSE	E & P Health, Safety and Environment (Exploration and Production)
E-psyche	†E-psyche
EA	Ecology Abstracts (Moscow) (Formerly: ABSEARCH Ecology & Plant Science)
EAA	Educational Administration Abstracts (Formerly: Educational Abstracts)
ECER	Exceptional Child Education Resources (Online) (Former titles (until 2004): Exceptional Child Education Resources (Print); (until 1977): Exceptional Child Education Abstracts)
ECI	†E C Index (European Communities)
EEA	Earthquake Engineering Abstracts
EFA	†Essential Fisheries Abstracts
EI	E I (Online) (Excerpta Indonesica) (Formerly (until 2002): E I (Print))
EIA	†Energy Information Abstracts
EIP	Ekistic Index of Periodicals
ELJI	†European Legal Journals Index
ELLIS	†E L L I S (European Legal Literature Information Service)
EMA	Engineered Materials Abstracts *consists of:* Advanced Polymers Abstracts Composites Industry Abstracts
EMBASE	EMBASE
ENW	Ethnic NewsWatch (Formerly (until 200?): Ethnic NewsWatch on CD-ROM)
EPB	Environment Index (Former titles (until 2006): Environmental Issues & Policy Index; (until Dec. 2002): Environmental Policy Index; (until 2002): Environmental Knowledge Base (Online); (until 2000): Environmental Periodicals Bibliography (Print); (until 1973): Environmental Periodicals)
ERA	Educational Research Abstracts Online
ERI	Education Research Index
ERIC	E R I C (Education Resource Information Center)
ERO	EdResearch Online
ESPM	Environmental Sciences and Pollution Management
ETA	Educational Technology Abstracts
EZ&PSA	†Essential Ecology, Zoology & Plant Science Abstracts
EdA	Education Abstracts
EduInd	Education Index

EmerIntel	E M X 95 (Former titles (until 2008): Emerald Fulltext; (until 200?): Emerald Intelligence & Fulltext; (until 1999): Emerald)
Emerald	Emerald Management Reviews (Online) (Former titles (until 2002): Emerald Reviews (Online); (until 2001): Anbar International Management Database; (until 1999): Anbar Management Intelligence (CD-ROM)) *consists of:* †Accounting & Finance Abstracts †Human Resource Management Abstracts †Information Management and Technology Abstracts †Management Books and Resources †Management Development Abstracts †Management of Quality Abstracts †Marketing & Logistics Abstracts †Operations & Production Management Abstracts †Top Management Abstracts
EnerInd	†Energy Information Abstracts Annual (Formed by the 1988 merger of: Energy Index; Energy Information Abstracts Annual)
EnerRA	†Energy Research Abstracts (Formerly (until 1977): E R D A Energy Research Abstracts; (until 1976): E R D A Reports Abstracts)
EnerRev	†Energy Review (Santa Barbara)
EngInd	The Engineering Index Monthly (Former titles (until 1984): Engineering Index Monthly and Author Index; (until 1971): Engineering Index Monthly)
EntAb	Entomology Abstracts
EnvAb	Environment Abstracts (Incorporates (1985-1991): Acid Rain Abstracts; Formerly (until 1974): Environment Information Access)
EnvEAb	Environmental Engineering Abstracts (Online Edition)
EnvInd	Environment Abstracts Annual (Incorporates (in 1990): Acid Rain Abstracts Annual; Which was formerly (until 1988): Acid Rain Annual Index; Incorporates (in 1988): Environment Index)
ErgAb	Ergonomics Abstracts Online
ExcerpMed	Excerpta Medica. Abstract Journals *consists of:* Excerpta Medica. Section 1: Anatomy, Anthropology, Embryology & Histology Excerpta Medica. Section 2: Physiology Excerpta Medica. Section 3: Endocrinology Excerpta Medica. Section 4: Microbiology: Bacteriology, Mycology, Parasitology and Virology Excerpta Medica. Section 5: General Pathology and Pathological Anatomy Excerpta Medica. Section 6: Internal Medicine Excerpta Medica. Section 7: Pediatrics and Pediatric Surgery Excerpta Medica. Section 8: Neurology and Neurosurgery Excerpta Medica. Section 9: Surgery

Excerpta Medica. Section 10: Obstetrics and Gynecology
Excerpta Medica. Section 11: Otorhinolaryngology
Excerpta Medica. Section 12: Ophthalmology
Excerpta Medica. Section 13: Dermatology and Venereology
Excerpta Medica. Section 14: Radiology
Excerpta Medica. Section 15: Chest Diseases, Thoracic Surgery and Tuberculosis
Excerpta Medica. Section 16: Cancer
Excerpta Medica. Section 17: Public Health, Social Medicine and Epidemiology
Excerpta Medica. Section 18: Cardiovascular Diseases and Cardiovascular Surgery
Excerpta Medica. Section 19: Rehabilitation and Physical Medicine
Excerpta Medica. Section 20: Gerontology and Geriatrics
Excerpta Medica. Section 21: Developmental Biology and Teratology
Excerpta Medica. Section 22: Human Genetics
Excerpta Medica. Section 23: Nuclear Medicine
Excerpta Medica. Section 24: Anesthesiology
Excerpta Medica. Section 25: Hematology
Excerpta Medica. Section 26: Immunology, Serology and Transplantation
Excerpta Medica. Section 27: Biophysics, Bio-Engineering and Medical Instrumentation
Excerpta Medica. Section 28: Urology and Nephrology
Excerpta Medica. Section 29: Clinical and Experimental Biochemistry
Excerpta Medica. Section 30: Clinical and Experimental Pharmacology
Excerpta Medica. Section 31: Arthritis and Rheumatism
Excerpta Medica. Section 32: Psychiatry
Excerpta Medica. Section 33: Orthopedic Surgery
†Excerpta Medica. Section 34: Plastic Surgery
Excerpta Medica. Section 35: Occupational Health and Industrial Medicine
Excerpta Medica. Section 36: Health Policy, Economics and Management
†Excerpta Medica. Section 37: Drug Literature Index
Excerpta Medica. Section 38: Adverse Reactions Titles
Excerpta Medica. Section 40: Drug Dependence, Alcohol Abuse and Alcoholism
Excerpta Medica. Section 46: Environmental Health and Pollution Control
Excerpta Medica. Section 48: Gastroenterology
Excerpta Medica. Section 49: Forensic Science Abstracts
Excerpta Medica. Section 50: Epilepsy Abstracts
†Excerpta Medica. Section 51: Mycobacterial Diseases: Leprosy, Tuberculosis and Related Subjects
Excerpta Medica. Section 52: Toxicology
†Excerpta Medica. Section 54: AIDS
†Excerpta Medica. Section 130: Clinical Pharmacology

ExtraMED	ExtraMED

F

F&EA	Fuel and Energy Abstracts (Former titles (until 1978): Fuel Abstracts and Current Titles; (until 1960): Fuel Abstracts)
F&GI	†Farm and Garden Index
F&WA	†Essential Forestry & Wildfire Abstracts
FAMLI	†F A M L I (Family Medicine Literature Index)
FCA	Field Crop Abstracts
FLI	Film Literature Index
FLP	Index to Foreign Legal Periodicals
FLUIDEX	FLUIDEX 　consists of: 　†Current Fluid Engineering Titles 　Fluid Abstracts: Civil Engineering 　Fluid Abstracts: Process Engineering 　†Industrial Jetting Report 　†Pumps and Turbines 　†River and Flood Control Abstracts 　†Tribology & Corrosion Abstracts 　†World Ports and Harbours News
FPA	Forest Products Abstracts
FPRD	†H T F S Digest (Incorporates (1979-1992): Fouling Prevention Research Digest; Former titles (until 1986): Heat Transfer and Fluid Flow Digest; (until 1976): H T F S Digest)
FR	F R A N C I S
FS&TA	Food Science and Technology Abstracts
FaBeAb	†Faba Bean Abstracts
FamI	Family Index
FemPer	Feminist Periodicals
FiP	Fed in Print (Online) (Formerly (until 2000): Fed in Print (Print))
FoMM	†Focus On: Molecular Medicine
FoP	†Focus On: Psychopharmacology
FoSS&M	Focus On: Sports Science and Medicine
FoVS&M	Focus On: Veterinary Science and Medicine
ForAb	Forestry Abstracts
FutSurv	Future Survey (Formerly: Public Policy Book Forecast)

G

GALA	†Institute of Paper Science and Technology. Graphic Arts Bulletin (Former titles (until 1992): Graphic Arts Literature Abstracts; (until 1953): Graphic Arts Progress; Which incorporated (1951-1953): Graphic Arts Index; Which superseded: P I A Management Reports)
GEOBASE	GEOBASE 　consists of: 　Ecological Abstracts 　Geographical Abstracts: Human Geography 　Geographical Abstracts: Physical Geography 　Geological Abstracts 　Geomechanics Abstracts 　International Development Abstracts 　Oceanographic Literature Review

GH	Global Health
GIPL	Guide to Indian Periodical Literature
GJP	European Psychologist (Formerly (until 1995): German Journal of Psychology)
GP&P	†Gas Processing and Pipelining
GPAA	†General Physics Advance Abstracts
GPAI	†Genealogical Periodical Annual Index
GSA	General Science Abstracts
GSI	General Science Index
GSS&RPL	Guide to Social Science and Religion (Former titles (until 1988): Guide to Social Science and Religion in Periodical Literature; (until 1970): Guide to Religious and Semi-religious Periodicals)
GSW	GeoScienceWorld
GW	GenderWatch (Former titles (until 200?): GenderWatch CD-ROM; (until 1999): Women 'R')
GardL	Garden, Landscape & Horticulture Index (Former titles (until 2006): Garden Literature Index (Online); (until 2001): Garden Literature (Print))
GasAb	†Gas Abstracts
GdIns	†Guidelines
GenetAb	Genetics Abstracts
GeoRef	GeoRef
GeophysAb	†Geophysical Abstracts
GeosDoc	Geoscience Documentation
GeotechAb	†Geotechnical Abstracts

H

H&SSA	Health and Safety Science Abstracts (Online)
H&TI	Hospitality & Tourism Index (Incorporates (1998-2003): Articles in Hospitality and Tourism; Former titles (until 2003): Lodging, Restaurant and Tourism Index; (until 1995): Lodging and Restaurant Index)
HAPI	Hispanic American Periodicals Index
HAb	Humanities Abstracts
HBB	†Hungarian Building Bulletin
HDA	Health Devices Alerts
HEA	Higher Education Abstracts (Formerly (until 1984): College Student Personnel Abstracts)
HECAB	†Higher Education Current Awareness Bulletin (Formerly (until 1973): Higher Education)
HGA	†Human Genome Abstracts
HL&ISA	Hungarian Library and Information Science Abstracts
HPNRM	C S A Human Population & Natural Resource Management
HRA	Human Resources Abstracts (Former titles (until 1975): Poverty and Human Resources Abstracts; (until 1971): Poverty and Human Resources; (until 1970): Poverty and Human Resources Abstracts)

HRIR	†Human Rights Internet Reporter (Formerly: Human Rights Internet Newsletter)
HRIS	T R I S Electronic Bibliographic Data Base (Transportation Research Information Services) (Incorporates (in 1996): Highway Research Abstracts; Which was formerly (1968-1990): H R I S Abstracts)
HelmAb	Helminthological Abstracts (Formerly (until 1989): Helminthological Abstracts. Series A: Animal and Human Helminthology; Which superseded in part (in 1970): Helminthological Abstracts)
HerbAb	Grasslands and Forage Abstracts (Formerly: Herbage Abstracts)
HistAb	Historical Abstracts (Formed by the merger of (1971-2003): Historical Abstracts: Part A: Modern History Abstracts, 1450-1914; (1971-2003): Historical Abstracts: Part B: Twentieth Century Abstracts, 1914 to the Present; Both of which superseded in part (1955-1971): Historical Abstracts)
HlthInd	†Health Index
HongKongiana	†HongKongiana
HortAb	Horticultural Science Abstracts (Formerly (until 2004): Horticultural Abstracts)
HospAb	†Health & Social Care Abstracts (Formerly (until 2003): Health Service Abstracts; Incorporates (1961-1985): Hospital Abstracts; (1974-1985): Current Literature on Health Services; Current Literature on General Medical Practice)
HospI	†International Hospitality and Tourism Database CD-ROM (Formerly (until 1995): Hospitality Index)
HospLI	†Hospital and Health Administration Index (Former titles (until 1995): Hospital Literature Index; Hospital Periodical Literature Index)
HumInd	Humanities Index (Supersedes in part (in 1975): Social Sciences and Humanities Index; Which was formerly (until 1966): International Index; (until 1958): International Index to Periodicals; (until 1923): Readers' Guide to Periodical Literature. Supplement)

I

I&DA	Irrigation and Drainage Abstracts
I-WA	Ibis - Wildfowl Abstracts
IAA	International Aerospace Abstracts
IAALC	†Indice Agricola de America Latina y el Caribe (Formerly: Bibliografia Agricola Latinoamericana y del Caribe)
IAB	†Humans & Other Species (Former titles (until 1997): InterActions Bibliography; (until vol.3, 1992): Interactions of Man and Animals)

IABS	Current Awareness in Biological Sciences (Former titles (until 1983): International Abstracts of Biological Sciences; (until 1956): British Abstracts of Medical Sciences; (until 1954): British Abstracts. A3: Physiology, Biochemistry, Anatomy, Pharmacology, Experimental Medicine; (until 1945): British Chemical and Physiological Abstracts. A3: Physiology and Biochemistry; (until 1937): British Chemical Abstracts. AIII: Biochemistry; Which superseded in part (in 1936): British Chemical Abstracts. A: Pure Chemistry; Which was formerly (until 1926): Journal of the Chemical Society. Abstracts; Which superseded in part (in 1877): Journal of the Chemical Society)
IAJS	Index of Articles on Jewish Studies (Online) (Formerly (until 2000): Index of Articles on Jewish Studies (Print))
IAOP	International Abstracts in Operations Research
IAPV	†Index of American Periodical Verse
IBR	Internationale Bibliographie der Rezensionen Geistes- und Sozialwissenschaftlicher Literatur (Former titles (until 1997): I B R. Internationale Bibliographie der Rezensionen Wissenschaftlicher Literatur; (until 1984): Internationale Bibliographie der Rezensionen Wissenschaftlicher Literatur)
IBRH	†Index to Book Reviews in the Humanities
IBSS	International Bibliography of the Social Sciences _consists of:_ International Bibliography of Political Science International Bibliography of the Social Sciences. Anthropology International Bibliography of the Social Sciences. Economics International Bibliography of the Social Sciences. Sociology
IBT&D	International Bibliography of Theatre & Dance (Formerly (until 1999): International Bibliography of Theatre (Print))
IBZ	I B Z - Internationale Bibliographie der Geistes- und Sozialwissenschaftlichen Zeitschriftenliteratur (Former titles (until 2000): I B Z - Internationale Bibliographie der Zeitschriftenliteratur aus Allen Gebieten des Wissens; (until 1984): Internationale Bibliographie der Zeitschriftenliteratur aus Allen Gebieten des Wissens)
IBibSS	†International Bibliography of the Social Sciences: Anthropology, Political Science, Economics, Sociology
IBuildSA	International Building Services Abstracts (E-Mail Edition)
ICEA	International Civil Engineering Abstracts (Former titles (until 1982): I C E Abstracts; (until 1975): European Civil Engineering Abstracts)
ICLPL	Index to Canadian Legal Periodical Literature
ICM	Children's Magazine Guide (Formerly (until 1981): Subject Index to Children's Magazines)

ICUIS	†I C U I S Justice Ministries (Institute on the Church in Urban-Industrial Society) (Supersedes (1970-1978): I C U I S Abstract Service)
IDIS	I D I S (Iowa Drug Information Service)
IDP	†Index to Dance Periodicals
IECT	Bibliografia Espanola de Revistas Cientificas de Ciencia y Tecnologia (Formerly (until 1998): Indice Espanol de Ciencia y Tecnologia)
IFP	†Index to Free Periodicals
IGCS	†International Guide to Classical Studies
IHD	†Industrial Hygiene Digest
IHP	Mapfte'ah L'khit've 'Et B'ivrit
IHTDI	Index to How to Do It Information (Online)
IIBP	International Index to Black Periodicals Full Text
IIFP	International Index to Film Periodicals
IIL	†R S N A Index to Imaging Literature (Radiological Society of North America)
IIMP	International Index to Music Periodicals
IIPA	International Index to the Performing Arts
IIPL	†Index to Indian Periodical Literature
IIS	Index to International Statistics
IITV	†International Index to Television Periodicals
IJCS	†Index to Journals in Communication Studies
IJP	Index to Jewish Periodicals
ILD	†International Labour Documentation
ILM	†Index to Little Magazines
ILP	Index to Legal Periodicals & Books (Formerly (until 1994): Index to Legal Periodicals)
ILSA	Indian Library Science Abstracts
IME	†Indice Medico Espanol (Online)
IMFL	Family & Society Studies Worldwide (Former titles: Family Studies Database; Family Resources; Supersedes: Inventory of Marriage and Family Literature; Which was formerly: International Bibliography of Research in Marriage and the Family)
IMI	†International Management Information Business Digest
IMMAb	I M M Abstracts (Institution of Mining and Metallurgy)
INI	†International Nursing Index
INIS AtomInd	I N I S Atomindex (Online Edition) (International Nuclear Information System) (Formerly (until no.24, vol.28, 1997): I N I S Atomindex (Print); Incorporates (1948-1976): Nuclear Science Abstracts (United States Energy Research and Development Administration); Formerly (until 1968): List of References on Nuclear Energy)
INZP	†Te Puna CD-ROM (Former titles: Index New Zealand; (until 1986): Index to New Zealand Periodicals)
IPA	International Pharmaceutical Abstracts
IPARL	Index to Periodical Articles Related to Law
IPB	Repertoire Bibliographique de la Philosophie (Former titles (until 1949): Revue Philosophique de Louvain. Supplement. Repertoire Bibliographique; (until 1946): Revue Neoscolastique de Philosophie. Repertoire Bibliographique)
IPI	Insurance Periodicals Index
IPP	Index to Philippine Periodicals (Formerly (until 1960): Index to Philippine Periodical Literature)
IPSA	International Political Science Abstracts
IPackAb	Packaging Month (Formerly (until 2001): International Packaging Abstracts; Which was formed by the merger of (1944-1981): Packaging Abstracts; (1976-1981): Referatedienst Verpackung)
IPsyAb	†Indian Psychological Abstracts and Reviews (Formerly (until 1994): Indian Psychological Abstracts)
ISA	Indian Science Abstracts
ISAP	Index to South African Periodicals
ISMEC	Mechanical Engineering Abstracts from C S A (Former titles (until 1993): I S M E C - Mechanical Engineering Abstracts; (until 1988): I S M E C Bulletin)
ISR	Index to Scientific Reviews
ISRS	†International Science Review Series
ISTA	Information Science & Technology Abstracts (Online)
IUSGP	U.S. Government Periodicals Index (Online)
IZBG	International Review of Biblical Studies
ImmunAb	Immunology Abstracts (Online)
IndBusRep	†Index to Business Reports
IndChem	Index Chemicus (Online)
IndIndia	Index India
IndIslam	Index Islamicus (Former titles (until 1995): Quarterly Index Islamicus; (until 1976): Index Islamicus)
IndMed	†Index Medicus
IndVet	Index Veterinarius
Inpharma	†Inpharma Weekly (Formerly (until 1990): Inpharma)
Inspec	Inspec *consists of:* Computer & Control Abstracts †Current Papers in Electrical & Electronics Engineering Current Papers in Physics †Current Papers on Computers & Control Electrical & Electronics Abstracts Key Abstracts - Advanced Materials Key Abstracts - Antennas & Propagation Key Abstracts - Artificial Intelligence Key Abstracts - Business Automation Key Abstracts - Computer Communications and Storage

ABSTRACTING AND INDEXING

Key Abstracts - Computing in Electronics & Power
Key Abstracts - Electronic Circuits
Key Abstracts - Electronic Instrumentation
Key Abstracts - Factory Automation
Key Abstracts - High-Temperature Superconductors
Key Abstracts - Human-Computer Interaction
Key Abstracts - Machine Vision
Key Abstracts - Measurements in Physics
Key Abstracts - Microelectronics & Printed Circuits
Key Abstracts - Microwave Technology
Key Abstracts - Neural Networks
Key Abstracts - Optoelectronics
Key Abstracts - Power Systems & Applications
Key Abstracts - Robotics & Control
Key Abstracts - Semiconductor Devices
Key Abstracts - Software Engineering
Key Abstracts - Telecommunications Physics Abstracts

J

JAIE	†Journal of Abstracts in International Education
JCLA	†Journal of Current Laser Abstracts
JCQM	†Journal Contents in Quantitative Methods
JCR-S	J C R Web Science Edition
JCR-SS	J C R Web Social Science Edition
JCT	†Japan Computer Technology and Applications Abstracts
JEL	Journal of Economic Literature (Formerly (until 1968): Journal of Economic Abstracts)
JHMA	†Junior High Magazine Abstracts
JOF	Journal of Ferrocement (Former titles: N Z F C M A Bulletin; N Z F C M A Newsletter)
JPI	Kokuritsu Kokkai toshokan Zasshi Kiji Sakuin CD-ROM Karento-Ban (Formerly (until 2002): N D L CD-ROM - Line Zasshi Kiji Sakuin. Karento-Ban; Which was formed by the merger of (1948-1996): Zasshi Kiji Sakuin. Jinbun Shakai-Hen - Japanese Periodicals Index. Humanities and Social Science; (1950-1996): Zasshi Kiji Sakuin. Gijutsu-Hen - Japanese Periodicals Index. Science and Technology)
JTA	†Japan Technology Series (Formerly (until 1988): Japanese Technical Abstracts)
JW	Journal Watch General Medicine (Formerly (until 2009): Journal Watch)
JW-C	Journal Watch Cardiology
JW-D	Journal Watch Dermatology
JW-EM	Journal Watch Emergency Medicine
JW-G	Journal Watch Gastroenterology
JW-ID	Journal Watch Infectious Diseases
JW-N	Journal Watch Neurology
JW-P	Journal Watch Psychiatry
JW-WH	Journal Watch Women's Health
JewAb	†Jewish Abstracts

K

KES	†Key to Economic Science (Formerly: Economic Abstracts)
KWIST	Keyword Index to Serial Titles
KWIWR	†Key Word Index of Wildlife Research
Kidney	Kidney (New York, 1992)

L

L&LBA	Linguistics and Language Behavior Abstracts (Incorporates (in 1989, vol.12): Reading Abstracts; Formerly (until 1985): Language and Language Behavior Abstracts)
LAMP	L A M P (Literature Analysis of Microcomputer Publications)
LCR	†Literary Criticism Register
LHB	Laboratory Hazards Bulletin
LHTB	†Library Hi Tech Bibliography
LID&ISL	Lancaster Index to Defence & International Security Literature
LIFT	Literary Journals Index Full Text
LII	†Life Insurance Index
LIMI	Legal Information Management Index
LISA	L I S A: Library & Information Science Abstracts (Supersedes (in 1969): Library Science Abstracts)
LISTA	Library, Information Science & Technology Abstracts
LJI	†Legal Journals Index
LOIS	Law Office Information Service
LRI	LegalTrac (Online) (Former titles: LegalTrac (Print); Legal Resource Index)
LT&LA	Language Teaching (Former titles (until 1982): Language Teaching and Linguistics Abstracts; (until 1975): Language-Teaching Abstracts; (until 1968): English Teaching Abstracts)
LeadAb	†Leadscan (Formerly: Lead Abstracts)
LeftInd	Left Index (Online)
LegCont	†Legal Contents (Former titles (until 1980): C C L P: Contents of Current Legal Periodicals; (until 1976: Contents of Current Legal Periodicals; Incorporates: Survey of Law Reviews)
LibLit	Library Literature & Information Science (Formerly (until 1999): Library Literature)
LingAb	Linguistics Abstracts
LogistBibl	Online Logistics Bibliography (Formerly: Bibliography of Logistics Management. Supplement (Print))

M

M&GPA	Meteorological and Geoastrophysical Abstracts (Formerly (until 1960): Meteorological Abstracts and Bibliography)
M&MA	Management and Marketing Abstracts (Formerly (until 1976): Marketing Abstracts)
M&PBA	Medical & Pharmaceutical Biotechnology Abstracts (Online)
M&TEA	C S A Mechanical & Transportation Engineering Abstracts (Cambridge Scientific Abstracts)
MA	Mammalogy Abstracts
MAB	†Marine Affairs Bibliography
MAG	†Music Article Guide
MASUSE	M A S Ultra - School Edition
MBA	Microbiology Abstracts *consists of:* Microbiology Abstracts: Section A. Industrial & Applied Microbiology Microbiology Abstracts: Section B. Bacteriology Microbiology Abstracts: Section C. Algology, Mycology and Protozoology
MBF	Materials Business File *consists of:* †Nonferrous Metals Alert †Polymers, Ceramics, Composites Alert †Steels Alert
MCIU	†Microcomputer Industry Update
MCR	Medical Care Research and Review (Former titles (until Mar. 1995): Medical Care Review; Public Health Economics and Medical Care Abstracts)
MEA	Multicultural Education Abstracts (Print)
MEA&I	Middle East: Abstracts and Index
MEDLINE	MEDLINE
MEDOC	†Medoc: Index to U S Government Publications in the Medical and Health Sciences
MEDSOC	†Medical Socioeconomic Research Sources (Formerly: Index to the Literature of Medical Socioeconomics)
MELSA	†M E L S A Messenger (Metropolitan Library Service Agency)
METADEX	METADEX *consists of:* Alloys Index Metals Abstracts Metals Abstracts Index
MFA	Surface Finishing Abstracts (Online)
MLA	†M L A Abstracts of Articles in Scholarly Journals
MLA-IB	M L A International Bibliography (Modern Language Association of America) (Former titles (until 1968): M L A International Bibliography of Books and Articles on the Modern Languages and Literatures; (until 1956): M L A American Bibliography of Books and Articles on the Modern Languages and Literatures)

MMI	†Michigan Magazine Index
MOS	Methods in Organic Synthesis
MPI	†United Methodist Periodical Index (Formerly: Methodist Periodical Index)
MRD	†Media Review Digest (Formerly (until 1974): Multi Media Reviews Index)
MRefA	†Developmental Disabilities Abstracts (Former titles: Mental Retardation and Developmental Disabilities Abstracts; Mental Retardation Abstracts)
MResA	Market Research Abstracts (Online) (Formerly (until 2000): Market Research Abstracts (Print))
MS&D	Medical & Surgical Dermatology
MSB	Mass Spectrometry Bulletin
MSCI	Materials Science Citation Index
MSCT	†Marine Science Contents Tables
MSF	Mystery Short Fiction
MSN	MathSciNet *consists of:* Current Mathematical Publications Mathematical Reviews
MagInd	†Magazine Index Plus (Formerly: Magazine Index)
MaizeAb	Maize Abstracts Online
ManagAb	Indian Management Abstracts (Incorporates (1972-1989): Management Abstracts)
ManagCont	†Management Contents
MathR	Mathematical Reviews
MedAb	†Medical Abstract Service
MicrocompInd	Internet & Personal Computing Abstracts (Online)
MinerAb	†MinAbs Online (Formerly (until 2004): Mineralogical Abstracts (Print))
MusicInd	The Music Index (Print)
MycolAb	Abstracts of Mycology

N

NAA	Nordic Archaeological Abstracts
NAmW	North American Wildlife & Natural Resources Abstracts
NBA	†Notiziario Bibliografico di Audiologia O R L e Foniatria (Formerly: Notiziario Bibliografico di Audiologia)
NPI	†New Periodicals Index
NPPA	†Noise Pollution Publications Abstracts
NPU	Natural Product Updates
NRN	Nutrition Research Newsletter (Incorporates (1981-1998): Food Safety Notebook)
NSA	C S A Neurosciences Abstracts (Online) (Cambridge Scientific Abstracts)
NSCI	Neuroscience Citation Index
NTA	New Testament Abstracts

NemAb	Nematological Abstracts (Supersedes: Helminthological Abstracts. Series B: Plant Nematology; Which was Superseded in part (in 1970): Helminthological Abstracts)
NewsAb	Newspaper Abstracts
NucAcAb	Nucleic Acids Abstracts (Online)
NumL	Numismatic Literature
NurAb	†Nursing Abstracts
NutrAb	Nutrition Abstracts and Reviews *consists of:* Nutrition Abstracts and Reviews. Series A: Human and Experimental Nutrition Abstracts and Reviews. Series B: Livestock Feeds and Feeding

O

OGFA	C S A Oncogenes and Growth Factors Abstracts
OR	Organic Research Database
ORA	†Oral Research Abstracts
ORMS	Operations Research - Management Science
OTA	Old Testament Abstracts
OceAb	Oceanic Abstracts (Former titles (until 1984): Oceanic Abstracts with Indexes; (until 1972): Oceanic Index; Oceanic Citation Index)
OffTech	†Offshore Technology
OphLit	†Ophthalmic Literature
OrnA	Ornithology Abstracts
OrnHort	Ornamental Horticulture
OrnithAb	†Essential Ornithological Abstracts

P

P&BA	Paperbase Abstracts (Incorporates (1989-2001): Nonwovens Abstracts; Formerly (until 1995): Paper and Board Abstracts)
PAA&I	Documentation in Public Administration (Supersedes: Public Administration Abstracts and Index of Articles)
PABMI	†Performing Arts Biography Master Index (Formerly: Theatre, Film, and Television Biographies Master Index)
PADDI	Planning Architecture Design Database Ireland
PAIS	P A I S International in Print (Annual) (Public Affairs Information Service) (Former titles (until 1991): P A I S Bulletin; (until 1985): Public Affairs Information Service Bulletin; (until 1967): Public Affairs Information Service. Bulletin)
PBA	Plant Breeding Abstracts
PC&CA	†Abstracts of Research in Pastoral Care and Counseling (Formerly: Pastoral Care and Counseling Abstracts)
PCAb	†P C Abstracts
PCI	Periodicals Index Online (Formerly (until 2006): Periodicals Contents Index)

PCR2	P C R 2 (Personal Computer Review - Squared)
PE&ON	Pharmacoeconomics and Outcomes News (Formerly (until 1996): PharmacoResources)
PEBNI	†Petroleum - Energy Business News Index
PEI	Physical Education Index
PGegResA	Plant Genetic Resources Abstracts
PGrRegA	Plant Growth Regulator Abstracts
PHN&I	Postharvest News and Information
PLESA	Quarterly Index to Africana Periodical Literature (Formerly (until 2000): Quarterly Index to Periodical Literature, Eastern and Southern Africa)
PLII	†Property & Liability Insurance Index
PMA	International Abstracts of Human Resources (Formerly (until 2003): Personnel Management Abstracts)
PMI	†Photography Magazine Index
PMPI	†Popular Music Periodicals Index
PMR	†Magazine Article Summaries (Formerly (until 1987): Popular Magazine Review)
PN&I	Pig News & Information
PNI	Pharmaceutical News Index
PPI	†Popular Periodical Index
PQC	ProQuest Central
PRA	Peace Research Abstracts Journal
PROMT	†Predicasts Overview of Markets and Technology (Formed by the merger of: Chemical Market Abstracts; Equipment Market Abstracts; Which was formerly titled: Electronics Market Abstracts; Electronics and Equipment Market Abstracts)
PSA	C S A Worldwide Political Science Abstracts (Cambridge Scientific Abstracts) (Formed by the 2000 merger of: A B C Pol Sci (Online); (1984-2000): Political Science Abstracts (Online); Which superseded: Political Science Abstracts. Annual Supplement (Print); (1967-1980): Political Science, Government, and Public Policy Series. Annual Supplement)
PSI	†Philanthropic Studies Index
PST	†Packaging Science and Technology Abstracts
PdeR	Repere (Online) (Former titles: Repere (Print); (until 1993): Point de Repere; Which was formed by the merger of (1972-1983): Periodex; (1972-1983): Radar (Montreal))
PerIslam	†Periodica Islamica
PersLit	†Personnel Literature
PetrolAb	Petroleum Abstracts
PhilInd	Philosopher's Index
PhilipAb	Philippine Science and Technology Abstracts (Formerly: Philippine Science and Technology Abstracts Bibliography; Formed by the merger of: Philippine Abstracts; Philippine Science Index)

PhotoAb	Imaging Abstracts (Formerly: Photographic Abstracts)
PhotoInd	Photography Index
PhysBer	†Physics Briefs - Physikalische Berichte (Formerly (until 1980): Physikalische Berichte; Which was formed by the merger of (1877-1920): Beiblaetter zu den Annalen der Physik; (1845-1920): Halbmonatliches Literaturverzeichnis der Fortschritte der Physik)
Pinpoint	†Pinpointer
PlantSci	†Plant Science
PollutAb	Pollution Abstracts
PopulInd	†Population Index (Formerly (until 1937): Population Literature)
PotatoAb	Potato Abstracts
PoultAb	Poultry Abstracts
Press	Press (Formed by the merger of (1946-2001): Printing Abstracts; (1983-2001): World Publishing Monitor; Which was formerly (until 1991): Electronic Publishing Abstracts)
ProtozoAb	Protozoological Abstracts
PsycInfo	PsycINFO
PsycholAb	†Psychological Abstracts
PsycholRG	†Psychological Reader's Guide
PsychopharAb	†Psychopharmacology Abstracts

Q

QAb	†Quality Abstracts
QC&AS	Quality Control and Applied Statistics

R

R&TA	Religious & Theological Abstracts
RA&MP	Review of Aromatic and Medicinal Plants
RAE	Review of Agricultural Entomology & Review of Medical and Veterinary Entomology *consists of:* Review of Agricultural Entomology Review of Medical and Veterinary Entomology
RAPRA	R A P R A Abstracts (Rubber and Plastics Research Association)
RASB	Russian Academy of Sciences Bibliographies
RCI	Reaction Citation Index
RDA	Rural Development Abstracts
REE&TA	†Rural Extension, Education and Training Abstracts
RGAb	Readers' Guide Abstracts - Full Text (Online)
RGPR	Readers' Guide to Periodical Literature
RGYP	†Reader's Guide for Young People
RHEA	Research into Higher Education Abstracts
RI-1	Religion Index One: Periodicals (Formerly: Index to Religious Periodical Literature)
RI-2	†Religion Index Two: Multi-Author Works

RICS	Isurv Knowledge Alert (Formed by the merger of (1965-2005): R I C S Abstracts and Reviews; (1965-2005): R I C S Weekly Briefing)
RILM	R I L M Abstracts of Music Literature (Repertoire International de Litterature Musicale)
RM&VM	Review of Medical and Veterinary Mycology
RPFIA	Reference Point: Food Industry Abstracts (Former titles: F M I Monthly Index Service; S M I Monthly Index Service (Super Market Institute))
RPP	Review of Plant Pathology (Formerly (until 1970): Review of Applied Mycology)
RRTA	Leisure, Recreation and Tourism Abstracts (Formerly: Rural Recreation and Tourism Abstracts)
Reac	Reactions Weekly (Formerly (until 1990): Reactions)
RefSour	†Reference Sources (Supersedes (in 1979): Reference Book Review Index)
RefZh	Referativnyi Zhurnal
RefugAb	Refugee Survey Quarterly (Formerly (until 1994): Refugee Abstracts)
RehabLit	†Rehabilitation Literature (Formerly (until 195?): Bulletin on Current Literature)
Repind	Repindex
ResCtrInd	Resource Center Index (Formerly: Micrographics Index)
RiceAb	Rice Abstracts
RiskAb	Risk Abstracts (Online)
RoboAb	†Robotics Abstracts (Formerly (until 1989): Robomatix Reporter)

S

S&F	Soils and Fertilizers
S&MA	†Sorghum and Millets (Supersedes (in 1994): Sorghum and Millets Abstracts)
S&VD	The Shock and Vibration Digest
SAA	†Small Animals (Formerly (until 1991): Small Animal Abstracts)
SASA	State Academies of Science Abstracts
SBPI	Southern Baptist Periodical Index
SCI	Science Citation Index
SCIMP	†S C I M P (Selective Cooperative Index of Management Periodicals)
SCOPUS	SCOPUS
SD	SportDiscus
SEA	Sociology of Education Abstracts
SEJI	State Education Journal Index and Educators' Guide to Periodicals Research Strategies (Formerly (until 1985): State Education Journal Index)
SENA	Special Educational Needs Abstracts

SFA	†Fisheries Review (Formerly (until 1985): Sport Fishery Abstracts; Incorporates (1972-1985): Fish Health News)
SFSA	Family Studies Abstracts (Formerly (until 2008): SAGE Family Studies Abstracts)
SIA	Sugar Industry Abstracts (Former titles: Tate and Lyle's Sugar Industry Abstracts; Sugar Industry Abstracts)
SJI	Stamp Journals Index
SJW	†Selected Journals on Water
SLSI	†Sri Lanka Science Index
SOMA	Educational Management Abstracts (Formerly (until 2000): School Organisation and Management Abstracts)
SOPODA	†Social Planning - Policy & Development Abstracts (Formerly: Social Welfare, Social Planning, Policy and Social Development)
SPAA	Public Administration Abstracts (Formerly (until 2008): Sage Public Administration Abstracts)
SPI	†Sports Periodicals Index
SPPI	South Pacific Periodicals Index (Formerly (until 1978): Bibliography of Periodical Articles Relating to the South Pacific)
SRI	Statistical Reference Index
SRRA	Race Relations Abstracts (Former titles (until 2008): Sage Race Relations Abstracts; (until 1975): Race Relations Abstracts)
SSA	Social Services Abstracts
SSAI	Social Sciences Full Text (WilsonWeb) *consists of:* Social Sciences Abstracts (WilsonWeb) Social Sciences Index (WilsonWeb)
SSAb	Social Sciences Abstracts (WilsonDisc) (Formerly (until 1997): Wilson Social Sciences Abstracts)
SSCI	Social Sciences Citation Index
SSI	Social Sciences Index (Supersedes in part (in 1974): Social Sciences and Humanities Index; Which was formerly (until 1966): International Index; (until 1958): International Index to Periodicals; (until 1923): Readers' Guide to Periodical Literature. Supplement)
SSciA	C S A Sustainability Science Abstracts (Cambridge Scientific Abstracts)
ST&MA	†Statistical Theory and Method Abstracts (CD-ROM) (Former titles (until vol.42, 2002): Statistical Theory and Method Abstracts (Print); (until 1964): International Journal of Abstracts)
SUSA	Urban Studies Abstracts (Formerly (until 2008): Sage Urban Studies Abstracts)
SWA	Studies on Women and Gender Abstracts (Formerly (until 2000): Studies on Women Abstracts)
SWR&A	Social Work Abstracts (Supersedes in part (in 1994): Social Work Research and Abstracts; Which was formerly (until 1977): Abstracts for Social Workers)

SWRA	Water Resources Abstracts (Online, Bethesda) (Formerly (until 1993): Selected Water Resources Abstracts)
Search	†Search (Devon)
SeedAb	Seed Abstracts
SociolAb	Sociological Abstracts
SoftAbEng	†Software Abstracts for Engineers
SoftBase	SoftBase
SolStAb	Solid State and Superconductivity Abstracts (Former titles: Solid State Abstracts Journal; Solid State Abstracts; Incorporates: Science Research Abstracts Journal. Laser and Electro-Optic Reviews, Quantum Electronics, Unconventional Energy Sources; Science Research Abstracts Journal. Superconductivity, Magnetohydrodynamics and Plasma, Theoretical Physics; Which was formerly: Science Research Abstracts, Part A. MHD and Plasma, Superconductivity and Research, and Theoretical Physics; Which incorporated: Theoretical Physics Journal)
SoyAb	Soybean Abstracts (Online)
SpeleolAb	Speleological Abstracts
SportS	†SportSearch (Former titles (until 1985): Sport and Fitness Index; (until 1984): Sport and Recreation Index - Index de la Litterature des Sports et des Loisirs; (until 1977): Sport Articles)

T

T&DA	†Training and Development Alert
T&II	†Trade & Industry Index
TAR	TropAg & Rural
TCEA	Theoretical Chemical Engineering (Formerly (until 1991): Theoretical Chemical Engineering Abstracts)
TDB	Tropical Diseases Bulletin (Formed by the merger of (1911-1912): Kala Azar Bulletin; (1908-1912): Sleeping Sickness Bulletin)
TEA	Vocational Education & Training Abstracts (Former titles (until 2009): Technical Education & Training Abstracts; (until 1993): Technical Education Abstracts; (until 1980): Technical Education Abstracts from British Sources)
THA	†Tobacco & Health Abstracts (Formerly: Tobacco and Health)
TM	TEMA - Technology and Management
TMA	†Top Management Abstracts (Supersedes in part: Anbar Management Services Abstracts)
TOM	†T O M (Text on Microfilm)
TOSA	†Tropical Oil Seeds (Formerly (until 1991): Tropical Oil Seeds Abstracts)
TRA	†Transportation Research Abstracts (Formerly: Highway Research Abstracts)
TTI	Textile Technology Index (Formerly: Textile Technology Digest)

TelAb	†Telecommunications Abstracts
Telegen	†Telegen Abstracts (Formerly: Telegen Reporter)
TobAb	Tobacco Abstracts
ToxAb	Toxicology Abstracts
TriticAb	Wheat, Barley and Triticale Abstracts (Formerly: Triticale Abstracts)

U

UAA	†Urban Affairs Abstracts

V

V&AA	Violence & Abuse Abstracts
VB	Veterinary Bulletin
VITIS	Vitis - Viticulture and Oenology Abstracts (Online) (Formerly (until 2003): Vitis - Viticulture and Oenology Abstracts (Print))
VirolAbstr	Virology and AIDS Abstracts (Formerly (until 1988): Virology Abstracts)

W

W&CBA	Essential Wildlife & Conservation Biology Abstracts
WAA	Aluminum Industry Abstracts (Formerly (until 1991): World Aluminum Abstracts)
WAE&RSA	World Agricultural Economics and Rural Sociology Abstracts (Supersedes: Digest of Agricultural Economics and Marketing)
WBA	World Banking Abstracts
WBSS	†World Bibliography of Social Security
WLA	Wildlife Abstracts
WLR	†Wildlife Review
WMB	†World Magazine Bank
WRCInf	Aqualine Abstracts (Formerly (until 1985): W R C Information; Supersedes: Water Pollution Abstracts)

WSA	Women Studies Abstracts
WSCA	World Surface Coating Abstracts (Formerly (until 1969): Review of Current Literature on the Paint and Allied Industries)
WSI	†G. K. Hall's Women's Studies Index (Formerly (until 1999): Women's Studies Index (Year))
WTA	World Textile Abstracts (Former titles (until 1969): Textile Abstracts; (until 1967): Journal of the Textile Institute. Abstracts; (until 1956): Journal of the Textile Institute. Proceedings and Abstracts; Which superseded in part (in 1949): Textile Institute. Journal)
WasteInfo	WasteInfo
WatResAb	Hydro-Abstracts (Formerly (until 1980): Water Resources Abstracts)
WeedAb	Weed Abstracts
Weldasearch	Weldasearch Select (Formerly: Weldalert)
WildRev	Wildlife Review Abstracts (Formerly (until 1996): Wildlife Review (Fort Collins, Print Edition))
WorkRelAb	†Work Related Abstracts (Formerly: Employment Relations Abstracts)

Y

YAE&RB	†Association for Education and Rehabilitation of the Blind and Visually Impaired. Yearbook (Incorporates (in 1982): Blindness, Visual Impairment, Deaf-Blindness; Which was formerly: Blindness)

Z

ZentMath	Zentralblatt MATH (Formerly (until 1999): Zentralblatt fuer Mathematik und Ihre Grenzgebiete)
Zincscan	Zincscan (Former titles (until 1986): Zinc Abstracts; (until 1961): Z D A Abstracts)
ZooRec	Zoological Record

Subject Guide to Abstracting and Indexing

The 130 subject headings listed below are major subjects which contain a sub-category headed "Abstracting, Bibliographies, Statistics." This sub-category, which follows the major subject headings in the CLASSIFIED LIST OF SERIALS, identifies publications which abstract and/or index publications in the relevant subject. Bibliographies and statistical publications pertaining to the subject are also included in this sub-category. This guide will enable users to quickly locate subject areas of interest for which abstracting and indexing publications have been identified and to build profiles by combination of relevant subject areas. Page numbers refer to the first page on which the sub-category appears.

Subjects

English	Francais	Deutsch	Español
Abstracting and Indexing Services	Services d'Analyse et d'Indexage	Referate- und Indexdienste	Servicio de Análisis e Indización
Advertising and Public Relations	Publicité et Relations Publiques	Reklamewesen und Public Relations	Relaciones Públicas y Publicidad
Aeronautics and Space Flight	Aéronautique et Astronautique	Luft- und Raumfahrt	Aeronáutica y Vuelo Espacial
Computer Applications	Applications Informatiques	Computer Anwendung	Aplicaciones para Computadoras
Agriculture	Agriculture	Landwirtschaft	Agricultura
Agricultural Economics	Agriculture Économique	Agrarökonomie	Economía Agrícola
Agricultural Equipment	Outillage Agricole	Landwirtschaftsgeräte	Equipo para la Agricultura
Computer Applications	Applications Informatiques	Computer Anwendung	Aplicaciones para Computadoras
Crop Production and Soil	Production Végétale et Terrain	Ernte und Acker	Producción de Cosecha, Tierra
Dairying and Dairy Products	Production Laitière	Milchwirtschaft	Lechería y Productos Lácteos
Feed, Flour and Grain	Pature, Farine et Grain	Futter, Mehl und Getreide	Forraje, Granos y Harina
Poultry and Livestock	Élevage	Geflügel- und Viehwirtschaft	Aves de Corral y Ganadería
Alternative Medicine	Médecine Alternative	Alternative Heilkunde	Medicina Alternativa
Animal Welfare	Protection des Animaux	Tierschutz	Protección a los Animales
Anthropology	Anthropologie	Anthropologie	Antropología
Antiques	Antiquités	Antiquitäten	Antigüedades
Archaeology	Archeologie	Archaeologie	Arqueología
Computer Applications	Applications Informatiques	Computer Anwendung	Aplicaciones para Computadoras
Architecture	Architecture	Architektur	Arquitectura
Computer Applications	Applications Informatiques	Computer Anwendung	Aplicaciones para Computadoras
Art	Art	Kunst	Arte
Computer Applications	Applications Informatiques	Computer Anwendung	Aplicaciones para Computadoras
Arts and Handicrafts	Arts et Métiers	Kunst und Handwerk	Artesanías y Obras Manuales
Asian Studies	Études Asiatiques	Asiatische Studien	Asiatische Studien
Astrology	Astrologie	Astrologie	Astrología
Astronomy	Astronomie	Astronomie	Astronomía
Computer Applications	Applications Informatiques	Computer Anwendung	Aplicaciones para Computadoras
Beauty Culture	Soins de Beauté	Schönheitspflege	Belleza Personal
Perfumes and Cosmetics	Parfums et Cosmétiques	Kosmetik und Parfüme	Perfumes y Cosméticos
Beverages	Boissons	Getränke	Bebidas
Bibliographies	Bibliographies	Bibliographien	Bibliografías
Biography	Biographie	Biographie	Biografía
Biology	Biologie	Biologie	Biología
Biochemistry	Biochimie	Biochemie	Bio-química
Bioengineering	Biogénie	Bioingenieurwesen	Bio-ingeniería
Biophysics	Biophysique	Biophysik	Biofísica
Biotechnology	Biotechnologie	Biotechnologie	Biotecnología
Botany	Botanique	Botanik	Botánica
Computer Applications	Applications Informatiques	Computer Anwendung	Aplicaciones para Computadoras
Cytology and Histology	Cytologie et Histologie	Zytologie und Histologie	Citología e Histología
Entomology	Entomologie	Entomologie	Entomología
Genetics	Génétique	Genetik	Genética
Microbiology	Microbiologie	Mikrobiologie	Microbiología
Microscopy	Microscopie	Mikroskopie	Microscopía
Ornithology	Ornithologie	Ornithologie	Ornitología
Physiology	Physiologie	Physiologie	Fisiología
Zoology	Zoologie	Zoologie	Zoología
Birth Control	Limitation des Naissances	Geburtenregelung	Control de Natalidad
Building and Construction	Bâtiment et Construction	Bauwesen	Edificios y Construcción
Carpentry and Woodwork	Charpenterie et Menuiserie	Zimmerhandwerk und Holzbau	Carpintería y Ebanistería
Hardware	Quincaillerie	Metallbaustoffe	Ferretería
Business and Economics	Affaires et Économie	Wirtschaft und Handel	Economía y Negocios
Accounting	Comptabilité	Rechnungswesen	Contabilidad
Banking and Finance	Banque et Finance	Bank- und Finanzwesen	Bancos y Finanzas
Banking and Finance-Computer Applications	Banque et Finance-Applications Informatiques	Bank- und Finanzwesen-Computer Anwendung	Bancos y Finanzas-Aplicaciones para Computadoras
Chamber of Commerce Publications	Publications des Chambres de Commerce	Veröffentlichungen von Handelskammern	Publicaciones de las Cámaras de Comercio
Computer Applications	Applications Informatiques	Computer Anwendung	Aplicaciones para Computadoras
Cooperatives	Coopératives	Genossenschaften	Cooperativas
Domestic Commerce	Commerce Interieur	Binnenhandel	Comercio Interno
Economic Situation and Conditions	Situations et Conditions Économiques	Wirtschaftliche Situation und Verhältnisse	Condiciones y Situaciones Económicas
Economic Systems and Theories, Economic History	Systèmes et Théories Économiques, Histoire Économique	Ökonomische Systeme und Theorien, Wirtschaftsgeschichte	Sistemas y Teorías Economicos, Historia de la Economia
International Commerce	Commerce International	Aussenhandel	Comercio Internacional
International Development and Assistance	Aide et Développement Internationaux	Internationale Entwicklungshilfe	Desarrollo y Asistencia Internacional
Investments	Investissements	Investitionen	Inversiones
Labor and Industrial Relations	Travail et Relations Industrielles	Arbeits und Industrielle Beziehungen	Trabajo y Relaciones Industriales
Macroeconomics	Macroéconomie	Makroökonomie	Macroeconomía
Management	Gestion	Betriebsführung	Gerencia
Marketing and Purchasing	Marketing et Achats	Marketing und Kauf	Ventas y Mercadeo
Office Equipment and Services	Matériel et Entretien de Bureaux	Büroeinrichtung und Service	Equipo y Servicios de Oficinas
Personnel Management	Gestion du Personnel	Personal Führung	Administración de Personal
Production of Goods and Services	Production de Biens et Services	Produktion	Producción de Bienes y Servicios
Public Finance, Taxation	Tresor Publique, Fiscalité	Staatsfinanzen, Steuerwesen	Finanzas Públicas e Impuestos
Small Business	Petites et Moyennes Entreprises	Kleinbetrieb	Pequeños Negocios
Trade and Industrial Directories	Annuaires de Commerce et d'Industrie	Firmenverzeichnisse	Directorios de la Industria y el Comercio

SUBJECTS

English	French	German	Spanish
Ceramics, Glass and Pottery	Céramique, Verrerie et Poterie	Keramik, Glas und Töpferei	Cerámica, Vidrio y Porcelana
Chemistry	Chimie	Chemie	Química
Analytical Chemistry	Chimie Analytique	Analytische Chemie	Química Analítica
Computer Applications	Applications Informatiques	Computer Anwendung	Aplicaciones para Computadoras
Crystallography	Cristallographie	Kristallographie	Cristalografía
Electrochemistry	Electrochimie	Elektrochemie	Electroquímica
Inorganic Chemistry	Chimie Inorganique	Anorganische Chemie	Química Inorgánica
Organic Chemistry	Chimie Organique	Organische Chemie	Química Orgánica
Physical Chemistry	Physicochimie	Physikalische Chemie	Química Física
Children and Youth	Enfants et Adolescents	Kinder und Jugend	Niños y Jóvenes
About	Au Sujet des	Über	Acerca
For	Pour	Für	Para
Civil Defense	Defense Civile	Ziviler Bevölkerungsschutz	Defensa Civil
Classical Studies	Études Classiques	Klassische Studien	Estudios Clásicos
Cleaning and Dyeing	Nettoyage et Teinturerie	Reinigen und Färben	Limpieza y Tintura
Clothing Trade	Vêtement	Bekleidungsgewerbe	Industria del Vestido
Fashions	Mode	Moden	Modas
Clubs	Clubs	Klubs	Clubes
College and Alumni	Université et Diplomés	Universitäten und Hochschul-absolventen	Universidades y Exalumnos
Communications	Communications	Nachrichtentechnik	Comunicaciones
Computer Applications	Applications Informatiques	Computer Anwendung	Aplicaciones para Computadoras
Postal Affairs	Courrier	Postwesen	Correo
Radio	Radio	Rundfunk	Radio
Telephone and Telegraph	Téléphone et Télégraphe	Telephon und Telegraph	Teléfono y Telégrafo
Television and Cable	Télévision	Fernsehen und Bildfrequenzkanal	Cable y Televisión
Video	Vidéo	Video	Video
Computers	Ordinateurs	Computer	Computadoras
Artificial Intelligence	Intelligence Artificielle	Künstliche Intelligenz	Inteligencia Artificial
Automation	Automation	Automatisierung	Automatización
Calculating Machines	Calculateurs	Rechenmaschine	Calculadoras
Circuits	Circuits	Schaltungen	Circuitos
Computer Architecture	Architecture de la Machine	Computer Architektur	Arquitectura de las Computadoras
Computer-Assisted Instruction	Enseignement Assisté par Ordinateur	Computerunterstützter Unterricht	Enseñanza con la Ayuda de las Computadoras
Computer Engineering	Technique Informatique	Computerentwicklung	Ingeniería de las Computadoras
Computer Games	Jeux sur Ordinateurs	Computer Spiele	Juegos para Computadoras
Computer Graphics	Conception Assistée par Ordinateur	Computergraphik	Diseño a través de Computadoras
Computer Industry	Industrie Informatique	Computerbetrieb	Industria de las Computadoras
Computer Industry Directories	Annuaire de l'Industrie Informatique	Computerbetriebverzeichnisse	Directorios de la Industria de las Computadoras
Computer Industry, Vocational Guidance	Industrie Informatique, Orientation Professionnelle	Computerbetrieb Berufsberatung	Guía para la Industria de las Computadoras
Computer Music	Musique sur Ordinateur	Computer Musik	Música a través de Computadoras
Computer Networks	Réseaux d'Ordinateurs	Rechnernetz	Redes de Computadoras
Computer Programming	Programmation Informatique	Computerprogrammierung	Programación de Computadoras
Computer Sales	Ventes d'Ordinateurs	Computervertrieb	Ventas de Computadoras
Computer Security	Sécurité Informatique	Computersicherheit	Seguridad en Computadoras
Computer Simulation	Simulation sur Ordinateurs	Computersimulation	Simulación a través de Computadoras
Computer Systems	Systèmes Informatiques	Computersystemen	Sistemas de Computadoras
Cybernetics	Cybernétique	Kybernetik	Cibernética
Data Base Management	Gestion de Base de Données	Datenbankverwaltung	Bases de Datos
Data Communications, Data Transmission Systems	Communication de Données	Datenübertragung, Datenübertragungssystem	Comunicación y Transmisión de Datos
Electronic Data Processing	Traitement de l'Information Electronique	Elektronische Datenverarbeitung	Procesamiento Electrónico de Datos
Hardware	Matériel	Hardware	Equipo Físico
Information Science, Information Theory	Théorie de l'Information	Informationstheorie	Ciencia y Teoría de la Información
Internet	Internet	Internet	Internet
Machine Theory	Théorie de Machine	Maschinetheorie	Teoría de las Máquinas
Microcomputers	Micro-Ordinateurs	Mikrocomputer	Microcomputadoras
Minicomputers	Mini-Ordinateurs	Minicomputer	Minicomputadoras
Personal Computers	Ordinateurs Personnels	Persönlichecomputer	Computadoras Personales
Robotics	Robotique	Robotersysteme	Robótica
Software	Logiciel	Software	Aplicaciones de Computadora
Theory of Computing	Théorie de Traitement	Computertheorie	Teoría de Cálculo
Word Processing	Traitement de Textes	Textverarbeitung	Procesador de Textos
Conservation	Conservation	Landschaftsschutz	Conservación
Consumer Education and Protection	Protection du Consommateur	Verbraucherswirtschaftsschutz	Protección al Consumidor
Criminology and Law Enforcement	Criminologie et Police	Kriminologie und Strafvollzug	Criminología y Acción Policial
Computer Applications	Applications Informatiques	Computer Anwendung	Aplicaciones para Computadoras
Security	Securité	Sicherheit	Seguridad
Dance	Danse	Tanz	Baile
Drug Abuse and Alcoholism	Toxicomanie et Alcoolisme	Rauschgiftsucht und Alkoholismus	Alcoholismo y Drogadicción
Earth Sciences	Sciences Géologiques	Wissenschaften der Erde	Ciencias Geológicas
Computer Applications	Applications Informatiques	Computer Anwendung	Aplicaciones para Computadoras
Geology	Géologie	Geologie	Geología
Geophysics	Géophysique	Geophysik	Geofísica
Hydrology	Hydrologie	Hydrologie	Hidrología
Oceanography	Océanographie	Ozeanographie	Oceanografía
Education	Education	Bildungswesen	Educación
Adult Education	Enseignement des Adultes	Erwachsenenbildung	Educación para Adultos
Computer Applications	Applications Informatiques	Computer Anwendung	Aplicaciones para Computadoras
Guides to Schools and Colleges	Guides des Écoles et Colleges	Führer zur Schulen und Universitäten	Guías de Escuelas y Colegios
Higher Education	Enseignement Supérieur	Hochschulwesen	Educación Superior
International Education Programs	Programmes d'Éducation Internationale	Internationale Erziehungs-programme	Programas Internacionales de Educación
School Organization and Administration	Organisation et Administration de l'École	Organisation und Verwaltung von dem Schule	Administración y Dirección de Escuelas
Special Education and Rehabilitation	Enseignement Special et Réhabilitation	Fachunterricht und Rehabilitierung	Educación Especial y Rehabilitación
Teaching Methods and Curriculum	Méthodes Pédagogiques et Programmes Scolaires	Lehrmethoden und Lehrplan	Métodos y Planes de Estudio

Electronics	Electronique	Elektronik	Electrónica
Computer Applications	Applications Informatiques	Computer Anwendung	Aplicaciones para Computadoras
Encyclopedias and General Almanacs	Encyclopédies et Almanachs Générales	Enzyklopädien und Allgemeine Nachschlagewerke	Enciclopedias y Almanaques Generales
Energy	Énergie	Energie	Energía
Computer Applications	Applications Informatiques	Computer Anwendung	Aplicaciones para Computadoras
Electrical Energy	Énergie Électrique	Elektrizitätsenergie	Energía Eléctrica
Geothermal Energy	Énergie Géothermique	Thermalenergie	Energía Geotérmica
Hydroelectrical Energy	Énergie Hydraulique	Hydroelektroenergie	Energía Hidroeléctrica
Nuclear Energy	Énergie Nucléaire	Kernenergie	Energía Nuclear
Solar Energy	Énergie Solaire	Sonnenenergie	Energía Solar
Wind Energy	Énergie Éolienne	Windenergie	Energía de Viento
Engineering	Ingénierie	Ingenieurwesen	Ingeniería
Chemical Engineering	Génie Chimique	Chemieingenieurwesen	Ingeniería Química
Civil Engineering	Génie Civil	Bauingenieurwesen	Ingeniería Civil
Computer Applications	Applications Informatiques	Computer Anwendung	Aplicaciones para Computadoras
Electrical Engineering	Génie Électrique	Elektrotechnik	Ingeniería Eléctrica
Engineering Mechanics and Materials	Méchanique et Materiels	Ingenieurwesen Mechanik und Materialien	Ingeniería Mecanica y de Materiales
Hydraulic Engineering	Génie Hydraulique	Wasserbau	Ingeniería Hidráulica
Industrial Engineering	Génie Industriel	Industrieingenieurwesen	Ingeniería Industrial
Mechanical Engineering	Génie Mécanique	Maschinenbau	Ingeniería Mecánica
Environmental Studies	Science de l'Environnement	Umweltschutz	Estudios Ambientales
Computer Applications	Applications Informatiques	Computer Anwendung	Aplicaciones para Computadoras
Pollution	Pollution	Umweltverschmutzung	Contaminación
Toxicology and Environmental Safety	Toxicologie et Sécurité de l'Environnement	Toxokologie und Umweltsicherheit	Toxicología y Seguridad Ambiental
Waste Management	Gestion de Déchets	Abfallwirtschaft	Administración de Desperdicios
Ethnic Interests	Ethnologie	Allgemeine Völkerkunde	Publicaciones de Temas Etnicos
Fire Prevention	Prévention d'Incendie	Brandbekämpfung	Prevención del Fuego
Fish and Fisheries	Poisson et Pêche	Fische und Fischerei	Pesca y Pesquerías
Folklore	Folklore	Volkskunde	Folklore
Food and Food Industries	Alimentation et Industries Alimentaires	Nahrungsmittel und Lebensmittel-industrie	Alimentos e Industrias de Alimentos
Bakers and Confectioners	Boulangerie et Confiserie	Bäcker- und Konditorgewerbe	Panaderías y Dulcerías
Grocery Trade	Épicerie	Kolonialwarenhandel	Abacerías
Forest and Forestry	Forêts et Exploitation Forestière	Forstwesen und Waldwirtschaft	Bosques y Selvicultura
Lumber and Wood	Bois	Holz	Maderas
Funerals	Funérailles	Beerdigungen	Funerales
Gardening and Horticulture	Jardinage et Horticulture	Gartenpflege und Gartenbau	Jardinería y Horticultura
Florist Trade	Commerce des Fleurs	Blumenhandel	Comercio de Flores
Genealogy and Heraldry	Généalogie et Science Héraldique	Genealogie und Wappenkunde	Genealogía y Heráldica
Computer Applications	Applications Informatiques	Computer Anwendung	Aplicaciones para Computadoras
General Interest Periodicals (Subdivided by country)	Publications d'Intérêt Général (Selon pays)	Allgemeine Zeitschriften (nach Land)	Periódicos de Interés General (por país)
Geography	Géographie	Geographie	Geografía
Computer Applications	Applications Informatiques	Computer Anwendung	Aplicaciones para Computadoras
Gerontology and Geriatrics	Gérontologie	Gerontologie	Gerontología y Geriátrica
Giftware and Toys	Cadeaux et Jouets	Geschenkartikel und Spielwaren	Juguetes y Regalos
Handicapped	Handicapés	Behinderung	Minusválido
Computer Applications	Applications Informatiques	Computer Anwendung	Aplicaciones para Computadoras
Hearing Impaired	Sourds	Schwerhörigkeit	Discapacitado del Oído
Physically Impaired	Handicapés Physiques	Körperbehinderung	Discapacitado Físicamente
Visually Impaired	Aveugles	Blindheit	Discapacitado Visualmente
Health Facilities and Administration	Établissements de Santé et Administration	Gesundheitsanlagen und –verwaltung	Salud Pública y Administración
Heating, Plumbing, and Refrigeration	Chauffage, Plomberie et Réfrigeration	Heizung, Kühlung und Installation	Calefacción, Plomería y Refrigeración
History	Histoire	Geschichte	Historia
Computer Applications	Applications Informatiques	Computer Anwendung	Aplicaciones para Computadoras
History of Africa	Histoire de l'Afrique	Geschichte-Afrika	Historia de Africa
History of Asia	Histoire de l'Asie	Geschichte-Asien	Historia de Asia
History of Australasia and Other Areas	Histoire de l'Australasie et Autres Pays	Geschichte-Australasien und Andere Gebieten	Historia de Australasia y Otras Areas
History of Europe	Histoire de l'Europe	Geschichte-Europa	Historia de la Europa
History of North and South America	Histoire de l'Amérique du Nord et du Sud	Geschichte-Nord- und Südamerika	Historia de América del Norte y del Sur
History of Near East	Histoire du Proche-Orient	Geschichte-Nahe Osten	Historia del Cercano Oriente
Hobbies	Passe-Temps	Hobbies	Pasatiempos
Home Economics	Gestion Domestique	Hauswirtschaft	Economía Doméstica
Homosexuality	Homosexualité	Homosexualität	Homosexualidad
Hotels and Restaurants	Hôtels et Restaurants	Hotels und Restaurants	Restaurantes y Hoteles
Computer Applications	Applications Informatiques	Computer Anwendung	Aplicaciones para Computadoras
Housing and Urban Planning	Logement et Urbanisme	Wohnungswesen und Stadtplanung	Planificación Urbana y Vivienda
Computer Applications	Applications Informatiques	Computer Anwendung	Aplicaciones para Computadoras
How-To and Do-It-Yourself	Bricolage	Selbstanfertigung	Cómo Hacerlo Usted Mismo
Humanities: Comprehensive Works	Humanités: Oeuvres d'Ensemble	Klassische Philologie	Humanidades: Obras Completas
Computer Applications	Applications Informatiques	Computer Anwendung	Aplicaciones para Computadoras
Instruments	Instruments	Instrumente	Instrumentos
Insurance	Assurances	Versicherungswesen	Seguros
Computer Applications	Applications Informatiques	Computer Anwendung	Aplicaciones para Computadoras
Interior Design and Decoration	Agencements Intérieurs et Décoration	Innenarchitektur und Innenausstattung	Diseño Interior y Ornamentación
Furniture and House Furnishings	Meubles et Articles pour la Maison	Möbel und Wohnungseinrichtung	Muebles y Articulos para el Hogar
Jewelry, Clocks and Watches	Bijouterie et Horlogerie	Schmuck und Uhren	Joyería y Relojería
Journalism	Journalisme	Journalismus	Periodismo

SUBJECTS

Labor Unions	Syndicalisme	Gewerkschaften	Sindicatos
Law	Droit	Rechtswissenschaft	Derecho
Civil Law	Droit Civil	Zivilrecht	Derecho Civil
Computer Applications	Applications Informatiques	Computer Anwendung	Aplicaciones para Computadoras
Constitutional Law	Droit Constitutionel	Verfassungsrecht	Derecho Constitucional
Corporate Law	Droit Commercial	Handelsrecht	Derecho Corporativo
Criminal Law	Droit Pénal	Strafrecht	Derecho Criminal
Estate Planning	Succession	Mobiliarvermögensrecht	Planificación de Bienes Raíces
Family and Matrimonial Law	Droit Familial et Matrimonial	Ehegesetz und Familienrecht	Derecho Familial y Matrimonial
International Law	Droit International	Völkerrecht	Derecho Internacional
Judicial Systems	Système Judiciaire	Gerichtswesen	Sistemas Judiciales
Legal Aid	Assistance Judiciaire	Rechtshilfe	Ayuda Legal
Maritime Law	Droit Maritime	Seerecht	Derecho Marítimo
Military Law	Droit Militaire	Kriegsrecht	Derecho Militar
Leather and Fur Industries	Maroquinerie et Fourrure	Leder und Pelz	Pieles y Cuero
Leisure and Recreation	Loisirs et Récréation	Freizeit und Unterhaltung	Tiempo Libre y Recreación
Library and Information Science	Bibliothéconomie et Informatique	Bibliothek- und Informations- wissenschaft	Bibliotecología y Ciencias de la Información
Computer Applications	Applications Informatiques	Computer Anwendung	Aplicaciones para Computadoras
Lifestyle	Divertissement	Lebensstil	Entretenimiento
Linguistics	Linguistique	Sprachwissenschaft	Lingüística
Computer Applications	Applications Informatiques	Computer Anwendung	Aplicaciones para Computadoras
Literary and Political Reviews	Revues Littéraires et Politiques	Literarische und Politische Zeitschriften	Revistas Literarias y Políticas
Literature	Littérature	Literatur	Literatura
Adventure and Romance	Aventure et Romance	Abenteuer und Romantik	Aventura y Romance
Mystery and Detective	Mystère et Policier	Geheimnis und Detektivroman	Misterio y Novela Policiaca
Poetry	Poésie	Poesie	Poesía
Science Fiction, Fantasy, Horror	Science-Fiction, Fantastisque, Horreur	Zukunftsroman, Phantasiegebilde, Grausen	Ciencia Ficción, Fantasía, Horror
Machinery	Machines	Maschinenwesen	Maquinaria
Computer Applications	Applications Informatiques	Computer Anwendung	Aplicaciones para Computadoras
Mathematics	Mathématiques	Mathematik	Matemáticas
Computer Applications	Applications Informatiques	Computer Anwendung	Aplicaciones para Computadoras
Matrimony	Mariage	Ehestand	Matrimonio
Computer Applications	Applications Informatiques	Computer Anwendung	Aplicaciones para Computadoras
Medical Sciences	Médecine	Medizinische Wissenschaften	Ciencias Médicas
Allergology and Immunology	Allergologie et Immunologie	Allergie und Immunologie	Alergología e Imunología
Anaesthesiology	Anesthésiologie	Anaesthesiologie	Anestesiología
Cardiovascular Diseases	Maladies Cardiovasculaires	Kreislauferkrankungen	Enfermedades Cardiovasculares
Chiropractic, Homeopathy, Osteopathy	Chiropraxie, Homéopathie, Ostéopathie	Chiropraktik, Homöopathie, Osteopathie	Quiropráctica, Homeopatía, Osteopatía
Communicable Diseases	Maladies Contagieuses	Infektiöse Krankheiten	Enfermedades Contagiosas
Computer Applications	Applications Informatiques	Computer Anwendung	Aplicaciones para Computadoras
Dentistry	Dentisterie	Zahnmedizin	Odontología
Dermatology and Venereology	Dermatologie et Maladies Vénériennes	Dermatologie und Geschlechtskrankheiten	Dermatología y Venereología
Endocrinology	Endocrinologie	Endokrinologie	Endocrinología
Experimental Medicine, Laboratory Technique	Médecine Expérimentale, Techniques de Laboratoire	Versuchsmedizin, Laboratoriumstechnik	Medicina Experimental, Técnicas del Laboratorio
Forensic Sciences	Médecine Légale	Gerichtliche Medizin	Ciencias Forenses
Gastroenterology	Gastroentérologie	Gastroenterologie	Gastroenterología
Hematology	Hématologie	Hämatologie	Hematología
Hypnosis	Hypnose	Hypnose	Hipnotismo
Internal Medicine	Médecine Interne	Innere Medizin	Medicina Interna
Nurses and Nursing	Personnel et Soins Infirmiers	Krankenpflege	Enfermeros y Enfermería
Obstetrics and Gynecology	Obstétrique et Gynécologie	Gynäkologie und Geburtshilfe	Obstetricia y Ginecología
Oncology	Cancer	Onkologie	Oncología
Ophthalmology and Optometry	Ophtalmologie et Optométrie	Opthalmologie und Optometrie	Oftalmología y Optometría
Orthopedics and Traumatology	Orthopédie et Traumatologie	Orthopädie und Traumatologie	Ortopedia y Traumatología
Otorhinolaryngology	Otorhinolaryngologie	Otorhinolaryngologie	Otorinolaringología
Pediatrics	Pédiatrie	Pädiatrie	Pediatría
Physical Medicine and Rehabilitation	Médecine Physique et Réhabilitation	Physikalische Heilkunde und Rehabilitation	Medicina Física y de Rehabilitación
Psychiatry and Neurology	Psychiatrie et Neurologie	Psychiatrie und Neurologie	Psiquiatría y Neurología
Radiology and Nuclear Medicine	Radiologie et Médecine Nucléaire	Radiologie und Nuklearmedizin	Radiología y Medicina Nuclear
Respiratory Diseases	Maladies Respiratoires	Atmungskrankheiten	Enfermedades Respiratorias
Rheumatology	Rhumatologie	Rheumatologie	Reumatología
Sports Medicine	Médecine du Sport	Sportmedizin	Medicina del Deporte
Surgery	Chirurgie	Chirurgie	Cirugía
Urology and Nephrology	Urologie et Néphrologie	Urologie und Nephrologie	Urología y Nefrología
Meetings and Congresses	Réunions et Congrès	Tagungen und Kongresse	Conferencias y Congresos
Men's Health	Santé de l'Homme	Gesundheit von Männern	Salud de los Hombres
Men's Interests	Publications d'Intérêt Masculin	Männer Interessen	Intereses Masculinos
Men's Studies	Études de l'Homme	Männerstudien	Estudios de los Hombres
Metallurgy	Métallurgie	Metallurgie	Metalurgia
Computer Applications	Applications Informatiques	Computer Anwendung	Aplicaciones para Computadoras
Welding	Soudure	Schweissen	Soldadura
Meteorology	Météorologie	Meteorologie	Meteorología
Computer Applications	Applications Informatiques	Computer Anwendung	Aplicaciones para Computadoras
Metrology and Standardization	Métrologie et Standardisation	Mass- und Gewichtskunde, Normung	Metrología y Normalización
Computer Applications	Applications Informatiques	Computer Anwendung	Aplicaciones para Computadoras
Military	Militaires	Militärwesen	Militares
Mines and Mining Industry	Mines et Resources Minières	Bergwesen und Bergbauindustrie	Minas e Industria Minera
Computer Applications	Applications Informatiques	Computer Anwendung	Aplicaciones para Computadoras
Motion Pictures	Cinéma	Film und Kino	Películas
Museums and Art Galleries	Musées et Galleries	Museen und Kunstgalerien	Museos y Galerías del Arte
Music	Musique	Musik	Música
Computer Applications	Applications Informatiques	Computer Anwendung	Aplicaciones para Computadoras
Native American Studies	Études des Amérindiens	Studienfach Eingeborenen Amerikaner	Estudios de los Americanos Nativos
Needlework	Travaux de Couture	Näherei	Bordado
New Age	New Age	New Age	Nueva Epoca
Numismatics	Numismatique	Numismatik	Numismática
Nutrition and Dietetics	Nutrition et Diététique	Ernährung und Diätetik	Dietas y Nutrición
Occupational Health and Safety	Médecine du Travail et Prévention	Berufsgesundheitspflege und Sicherheit	Sanidad y Seguridad en el Trabajo
Occupations and Careers	Emplois et Carrières	Berufe	Empleos y Ocupaciones

Packaging	Emballage	Verpackung	Empaque
Computer Applications	Applications Informatiques	Computer Anwendung	Aplicaciones para Computadoras
Paints and Protective Coatings	Couleurs et Peintures	Farben und Beläge	Pinturas y Revestimientos Protectores
Paleontology	Paléontologie	Paleontologie	Paleontología
Computer Applications	Applications Informatiques	Computer Anwendung	Aplicaciones para Computadoras
Paper and Pulp	Papier et Pulpe	Papier und Papierstoff	Papel y Pulpa
Parapsychology and Occultism	Parapsychologie et Occultisme	Parapsychologie und Okkultismus	Parapsicología y Ocultismo
Patents, Trademarks and Copyrights	Brevets, Marques Commerciales et Droits d'Auteur	Patente, Schutzmarken und Urheberrechte	Patentes, Marcas Registradas y Derechos de Autor
Petroleum and Gas	Pétrole et Gas Naturel	Petroleum und Gas	Petróleo y Gas Natural
Computer Applications	Applications Informatiques	Computer Anwendung	Aplicaciones para Computadoras
Pets	Animaux Familiers	Haustiere	Mascotas
Pharmacy and Pharmacology	Pharmacie et Pharmacologie	Pharmazie und Pharmakologie	Farmacia y Farmacología
Computer Applications	Applications Informatiques	Computer Anwendung	Aplicaciones para Computadoras
Philately	Philatélie	Briefmarkenkunde	Filatelia
Philosophy	Philosophie	Philosophie	Filosofía
Photography	Photographie	Photographie	Fotografía
Computer Applications	Applications Informatiques	Computer Anwendung	Aplicaciones para Computadoras
Physical Fitness and Hygiene	Santé Physique et Hygiène	Gesundheitszustand und Hygiene	Salud Física e Higiene
Physics	Physique	Physik	Física
Computer Applications	Applications Informatiques	Computer Anwendung	Aplicaciones para Computadoras
Electricity	Electricité	Élektrizität	Electricidad
Heat	Chaleur	Wärme	Calor
Mechanics	Mécanique	Mechanik	Mecánica
Nuclear Physics	Physique Nucléaire	Kernphysik	Física Nuclear
Optics	Optique	Optik	Optica
Sound	Son	Schall	Sonido
Plastics	Plastiques	Kunststoffe	Plásticos
Computer Applications	Applications Informatiques	Computer Anwendung	Aplicaciones para Computadoras
Political Science	Sciences Politiques	Politische Wissenschafte	Ciencias Políticas
Civil Rights	Droits Civiques	Bürgerrechte	Derechos Civiles
International Relations	Relations Internationales	Internationale Beziehungen	Relaciones Internacionales
Population Studies	Démographie	Bevölkerungswissenschaft	Demografía
Printing	Imprimerie	Druck	Imprenta
Computer Applications	Applications Informatiques	Computer Anwendung	Aplicaciones para Computadoras
Psychology	Psychologie	Psychologie	Psicología
Public Administration	Administration Publique	Öffentliche Verwaltung	Administración Pública
Computer Applications	Applications Informatiques	Computer Anwendung	Aplicaciones para Computadoras
Municipal Government	Gouvernement Municipal	Kommunalverwaltung	Gobierno Municipal
Public Health and Safety	Santé Publique et Prévention	Öffentliche Gesundheitspflege	Salud y Seguridad Pública
Publishing and Book Trade	Édition et Commerce du Livre	Verlagswesen und Buchhandel	Editoriales y Ferias de Libros
Computer Applications	Applications Informatiques	Computer Anwendung	Aplicaciones para Computadoras
Real Estate	Immobiliers	Grundbesitz und Immobilien	Bienes Raíces
Computer Applications	Applications Informatiques	Computer Anwendung	Aplicaciones para Computadoras
Religions and Theology	Religions et Théologie	Religion und Theologie	Religión y Teología
Buddhist	Bouddhisme	Buddhist	Budismo
Eastern Orthodox	Églises Orthodoxes	Orthodox	Inglesias Ortodoxas
Hindu	Hindouisme	Hindu	Hinduísmo
Islamic	Islam	Islamische	Islamísmo
Judaic	Judaisme	Jüdäistische	Judaísmo
Protestant	Protestantisme	Evangelische	Iglesia Protestante
Roman Catholic	Catholicisme Romain	Römisch-katholische	Católico Romano
Other Denominations and Sects	Autres	Andere Bekenntnisse und Sekte	Otras Denominaciones y Sectas
Rubber	Caoutchouc	Gummi	Caucho
Computer Applications	Applications Informatiques	Computer Anwendung	Aplicaciones para Computadoras
Sciences: Comprehensive Works	Sciences: Oeuvres d'Ensemble	Wissenschaften: Umfassende Werke	Ciencias: Obras Completas
Computer Applications	Applications Informatiques	Computer Anwendung	Aplicaciones para Computadoras
Shoes and Boots	Chaussures et Bottes	Schuhe und Stiefel	Zapatos y Botas
Singles' Interests and Lifestyles	Intérêts et Style de Vie Célibataire	Ledigenstandinteressen	Intereses y Estilos de Vida de Solteros
Social Sciences: Comprehensive Works	Sciences Sociales: Oeuvres d'Ensemble	Sozialwissenschaften: Umfassende Werke	Ciencias Sociales: Obras Completas
Social Service and Welfare	Service Social et Protection Sociale	Sozialpflege und Fürsorge	Asistencia y Bienestar Social
Sociology	Sociologie	Soziologie	Sociología
Computer Applications	Applications Informatiques	Computer Anwendung	Aplicaciones para Computadoras
Sound Recording and Reproduction	Enregistrement et Reproduction du Son	Tonaufnahme und Tonwiedergabe	Grabaciones y Reproducciones Sonoras
Computer Applications	Applications Informatiques	Computer Anwendung	Aplicaciones para Computadoras
Sports and Games	Sports et Jeux	Sport und Spiele	Deportes y Juegos
Ball Games	Jeux de Balle	Ballspiele	Juegos de Pelota
Bicycles and Motorcycles	Bicyclettes et Motocyclettes	Fahrräder und Motorräder	Bicicletas y Motocicletas
Boats and Boating	Bateaux et Canotage	Boote und Bootfahren	Barcos y Canotaje
Horses and Horsemanship	Equitation	Pferde und Reitsport	Caballos y Equitación
Outdoor Life	Vie en Plein Air	Im Freien	Vida de Campo
Statistics	Statistiques	Statistik	Estadísticas
Technology: Comprehensive Works	Technologie: Oeuvres d'Ensemble	Technologie: Umfassende Werke	Tecnología: Obras Completas
Textile Industries and Fabrics	Textiles	Textil	Telas e Industria Textil
Computer Applications	Applications Informatiques	Computer Anwendung	Aplicaciones para Computadoras
Theater	Théâtre	Theater	Teatro
Tobacco	Tabac	Tabak	Tabaco
Transportation	Transports	Transport	Transporte
Air Transport	Transport Aérien	Luftverkehr	Transporte Aéreo
Automobiles	Automobiles	Kraftfahrzeugen	Automóviles
Computer Applications	Applications Informatiques	Computer Anwendung	Aplicaciones para Computadoras
Railroads	Chemins de Fer	Eisenbahnen	Ferrocarriles
Roads and Traffic	Routes et Circulation	Strassen und Strassenverkehr	Caminos y Tráfico
Ships and Shipping	Navires et Transport Maritimes	Schiffe und Schiffahrt	Barcos y Embarques
Trucks and Trucking	Transports Routiers	Lastkraftwagen	Camiones
Travel and Tourism	Voyages et Tourisme	Reisen und Tourismus	Viaje y Turismo
Airline Inflight and Hotel Inroom	Revues pour Vol de Lignes Aériennes et pour Chambres d'Hôtels	Fluggesellschaft und Hotel Veröffentlichungen	Vuelo en Aerolínea y Cuarto de Hotel
Veterinary Sciences	Science Vétérinaire	Tierheilkunde	Veterinaria
Computer Applications	Applications Informatiques	Computer Anwendung	Aplicaciones para Computadoras
Water Resources	Ressources en Eau	Wasserwirtschaft	Recursos del Agua
Computer Applications	Applications Informatiques	Computer Anwendung	Aplicaciones de los Computadoras
Women's Health	Santé de la Femme	Gesundheit von Frauen	Salud de las Mujeres
Women's Interests	Publications d'Intérêt Féminin	Fraueninteresse	Intereses Femininos
Women's Studies	Études de la Femme	Frauenstudien	Estudios de las Mujeres

Cross-Index to Subjects

This index lists alphabetically all subjects headings in the Ulrich's Subject Authority Database, as well as keyword references that direct users to main or subheadings where publications on those topics are likely to be found. Page references in bold indicate the first page where serials classified under that subject appear in the CLASSIFIED LIST OF SERIALS.

Abortions *see* BIRTH CONTROL **971**; MEDICAL SCIENCES—Obstetrics And Gynecology **5984**

Abrasives *see* MACHINERY **5449**; METALLURGY **6303**

ABSTRACTING AND INDEXING SERVICES **1** *see* also BIBLIOGRAPHIES **614**; and also Abstracting, Bibliographies, Statistics subheadings under specific subjects

Acarology *see* BIOLOGY—Entomology **837**

Accessories *see* CLOTHING TRADE—Fashions **2251**

Accident Prevention *see* OCCUPATIONAL HEALTH AND SAFETY **6672**; TRANSPORTATION—Roads And Traffic **8628**

Accountancy *see* BUSINESS AND ECONOMICS—Accounting **1275**

ACCOUNTING *see* BUSINESS AND ECONOMICS—Accounting **1275**

Acid Rain *see* ENVIRONMENTAL STUDIES—Pollution **3482**

Acoustics *see* PHYSICS—Sound **7085**; SOUND RECORDING AND REPRODUCTION **8151**

Acquired Immunodeficiency Syndrome *see* MEDICAL SCIENCES—Communicable Diseases **5807**

Acting *see* COMMUNICATIONS—Television And Cable **2374**; MOTION PICTURES **6488**; THEATER **8464**

Activation Analysis *see* PHYSICS—Nuclear Physics **7064**

Actuarial Science *see* INSURANCE **4490**; MATHEMATICS **5463**

Acupressure *see* ALTERNATIVE MEDICINE **305**

Acupuncture *see* ALTERNATIVE MEDICINE **305**

Addictions *see* DRUG ABUSE AND ALCOHOLISM **2689**

Adhesives *see* ENGINEERING—Chemical Engineering **3234**

Administrative Law *see* LAW—Constitutional Law **4845**

Adolescence *see* CHILDREN AND YOUTH—About **2142**; CHILDREN AND YOUTH—For **2174**

Adolescent Medicine *see* MEDICAL SCIENCES—Pediatrics **6086**

Adoption and Fostering *see* CHILDREN AND YOUTH—About **2142**; LAW—Family And Matrimonial Law **4906**; SOCIAL SERVICES AND WELFARE **8022**

Ads *see* ADVERTISING AND PUBLIC RELATIONS **18**

ADULT EDUCATION *see* EDUCATION—Adult Education **2937**

Adventism *see* RELIGIONS AND THEOLOGY—Protestant **7743**

ADVENTURE AND ROMANCE *see* LITERATURE—Adventure And Romance **5408**

Advertisers *see* ADVERTISING AND PUBLIC RELATIONS **18**

ADVERTISING AND PUBLIC RELATIONS **18** *see* also BUSINESS AND ECONOMICS—Marketing And Purchasing **1803**

ADVERTISING AND PUBLIC RELATIONS—Abstracting, Bibliographies, Statistics **37**

Advertising Art *see* ADVERTISING AND PUBLIC RELATIONS **18**

Aerobics *see* PHYSICAL FITNESS AND HYGIENE **6980**; SPORTS AND GAMES **8156**

Aerodynamics *see* AERONAUTICS AND SPACE FLIGHT **40**; ENGINEERING—Mechanical Engineering **3372**; PHYSICS—Mechanics **7057**

AERONAUTICS AND SPACE FLIGHT **40** *see* also ENGINEERING—Mechanical Engineering **3372**; TRANSPORTATION—Air Transport **8533**

AERONAUTICS AND SPACE FLIGHT—Abstracting, Bibliographies, Statistics **76**

AERONAUTICS AND SPACE FLIGHT—Computer Applications **77**

Aerophysics *see* PHYSICS—Mechanics **7057**

Aerosol Containers *see* ENVIRONMENTAL STUDIES—Pollution **3482**; PACKAGING **6708**

Aerospace Engineering *see* AERONAUTICS AND SPACE FLIGHT **40**

Aerospace Medicine *see* MEDICAL SCIENCES **5563**

Aesthetics *see* ART **462**; PHILOSOPHY **6901**

African American History *see* HISTORY—History Of North And South America **4281**

African History *see* HISTORY—History Of Africa **4172**

African Studies *see* HISTORY—History Of Africa **4172**

Aging *see* GERONTOLOGY AND GERIATRICS **4037**

Agnosticism *see* PHILOSOPHY **6901**; RELIGIONS AND THEOLOGY **7619**

Agribusiness *see* AGRICULTURE—Agricultural Economics **190**

Agricultural Aviation *see* AERONAUTICS AND SPACE FLIGHT **40**

Agricultural Chemistry *see* AGRICULTURE **77**; CHEMISTRY **2047**

AGRICULTURAL ECONOMICS *see* AGRICULTURE—Agricultural Economics **190**

Agricultural Engineering *see* AGRICULTURE **77**; ENGINEERING **3179**

AGRICULTURAL EQUIPMENT *see* AGRICULTURE—Agricultural Equipment **209**

Agricultural Machinery *see* AGRICULTURE—Agricultural Equipment **209**

Agricultural Marketing *see* AGRICULTURE—Agricultural Economics **190**; FOOD AND FOOD INDUSTRIES—Grocery Trade **3676**

AGRICULTURE **77** *see* also AGRICULTURE—Agricultural Economics **190**; AGRICULTURE—Agricultural Equipment **209**; AGRICULTURE—Computer Applications **215**; AGRICULTURE—Crop Production And Soil **215**; AGRICULTURE—Dairying And Dairy Products **261**; AGRICULTURE—Feed, Flour And Grain **270**; AGRICULTURE—Poultry And Livestock **276**; FOOD AND FOOD INDUSTRIES **3624**; FORESTS AND FORESTRY **3682**; GARDENING AND HORTICULTURE **3721**

AGRICULTURE—Abstracting, Bibliographies, Statistics **173**

AGRICULTURE—Agricultural Economics **190**

AGRICULTURE—Agricultural Equipment **209**

AGRICULTURE—Computer Applications **215**

AGRICULTURE—Crop Production And Soil **215** *see* also AGRICULTURE—Feed, Flour And Grain **270**; GARDENING AND HORTICULTURE **3721**; RUBBER **7824**; TOBACCO **8485**

AGRICULTURE—Dairying And Dairy Products **261** *see* also AGRICULTURE—Poultry And Livestock **276**

AGRICULTURE—Feed, Flour And Grain **270**

AGRICULTURE—Poultry And Livestock **276** *see* also AGRICULTURE—Dairying And Dairy Products **261**; LEATHER AND FUR INDUSTRIES **4972**; VETERINARY SCIENCE **8790**

Agronomy *see* AGRICULTURE **77**

AIDS (Acquired Immune Deficiency Syndrome) *see* MEDICAL SCIENCES—Communicable Diseases **5807**

Air Conditioning *see* HEATING, PLUMBING AND REFRIGERATION **4115**

Air Defense *see* MILITARY **6408**

Air Force *see* MILITARY **6408**

Air Law *see* AERONAUTICS AND SPACE FLIGHT **40**; LAW **4606**; TRANSPORTATION—Air Transport **8533**

Air Navigation *see* AERONAUTICS AND SPACE FLIGHT **40**

Air Pollution *see* ENVIRONMENTAL STUDIES—Pollution **3482**

Air Traffic Control *see* AERONAUTICS AND SPACE FLIGHT—Computer Applications **77**

AIR TRANSPORT *see* TRANSPORTATION—Air Transport **8533**

Aircraft *see* AERONAUTICS AND SPACE FLIGHT **40**; TRANSPORTATION—Air Transport **8533**

AIRLINE INFLIGHT AND HOTEL INROOM *see* TRAVEL AND TOURISM—Airline Inflight And Hotel Inroom **8781**

Airplanes *see* AERONAUTICS AND SPACE FLIGHT **40**; TRANSPORTATION—Air Transport **8533**

Airports *see* AERONAUTICS AND SPACE FLIGHT **40**; TRANSPORTATION—Air Transport **8533**

Alarms *see* CRIMINOLOGY AND LAW ENFORCEMENT—Security **2676**; ELECTRONICS **3089**; ENGINEERING—Electrical Engineering **3293**

Alcoholic Beverages *see* BEVERAGES **596**

Alcoholism *see* DRUG ABUSE AND ALCOHOLISM **2689**

Algae *see* BIOLOGY—Botany **771**

Algebra *see* MATHEMATICS **5463**

Alimentary System *see* MEDICAL SCIENCES—Gastroenterology **5919**

ALLERGOLOGY AND IMMUNOLOGY *see* MEDICAL SCIENCES—Allergology And Immunology **5752**

Alloys *see* METALLURGY **6303**

Almanacs, General *see* ENCYCLOPEDIAS AND GENERAL ALMANACS **3117**

Link to your serials resources and content with ulrichsweb.com

BUSINESS AND ECONOMICS—Small Business **1956**
BUSINESS AND ECONOMICS—Trade And Industrial Directories **1970**
Business Education *see* BUSINESS AND ECONOMICS **1055**; EDUCATION **2821**
Business Law *see* LAW—Corporate Law **4853**
Butane *see* PETROLEUM AND GAS **6761**
Cabinetry *see* BUILDING AND CONSTRUCTION—Carpentry And Woodwork **1049**
Cable Television *see* COMMUNICATIONS—Television And Cable **2374**
Cables *see* COMMUNICATIONS—Telephone And Telegraph **2365**; ENGINEERING—Electrical Engineering **3293**
CAD-CAM *see* COMPUTERS—Computer Graphics **2482**
CAE (Computer Aided Engineering) *see* COMPUTERS—Computer Graphics **2482**; ENGINEERING—Computer Applications **3288**
Cafeterias *see* HOTELS AND RESTAURANTS **4380**
Calculus *see* MATHEMATICS **5463**
Calendars of Events *see* MEETINGS AND CONGRESSES **6277**; TRAVEL AND TOURISM **8679**
Calligraphy *see* ART **462**
Calvinism *see* RELIGIONS AND THEOLOGY—Protestant **7743**
Cameras *see* COMMUNICATIONS—Television And Cable **2374**; COMMUNICATIONS—Video **2399**; MOTION PICTURES **6488**; PHOTOGRAPHY **6963**
Camping *see* LEISURE AND RECREATION **4975**; SPORTS AND GAMES—Outdoor Life **8300**; TRAVEL AND TOURISM **8679**
Canals *see* TRANSPORTATION—Ships And Shipping **8638**
Cancer *see* MEDICAL SCIENCES—Oncology **6007**
Candy *see* FOOD AND FOOD INDUSTRIES—Bakers And Confectioners **3670**
Canning and Preserving *see* FOOD AND FOOD INDUSTRIES **3624**; HOME ECONOMICS **4351**
Canoeing *see* SPORTS AND GAMES—Boats And Boating **8270**
Canon Law *see* RELIGIONS AND THEOLOGY **7619**
Cans *see* ENVIRONMENTAL STUDIES—Waste Management **3503**; PACKAGING **6708**
Canvas *see* TEXTILE INDUSTRIES AND FABRICS **8447**
Capital Punishment *see* LAW **4606**
Capitalism *see* BUSINESS AND ECONOMICS **1055**; BUSINESS AND ECONOMICS—Economic Systems And Theories, Economic History **1535**; POLITICAL SCIENCE **7101**
Car *see* TRANSPORTATION—Automobiles **8553**
Carbohydrates *see* CHEMISTRY—Organic Chemistry **2119**; NUTRITION AND DIETETICS **6654**
Carboniferous Geology *see* EARTH SCIENCES—Geophysics **2776**
Card Games *see* SPORTS AND GAMES **8156**
Cardboard *see* PACKAGING **6708**; PAPER AND PULP **6731**
Cardiology *see* MEDICAL SCIENCES—Cardiovascular Diseases **5775**
CARDIOVASCULAR DISEASES *see* MEDICAL SCIENCES—Cardiovascular Diseases **5775**
Cardiovascular Surgery *see* MEDICAL SCIENCES—Surgery **6234**
Careers *see* OCCUPATIONS AND CAREERS **6691**
Cargo Handling *see* TRANSPORTATION—Ships And Shipping **8638**
Caribbean History *see* HISTORY—History Of North And South America **4281**
Carpal Tunnel Syndrome *see* OCCUPATIONAL HEALTH AND SAFETY **6672**
CARPENTRY AND WOODWORK *see* BUILDING AND CONSTRUCTION—Carpentry And Woodwork **1049**
Carpets and Rugs *see* INTERIOR DESIGN AND DECORATION—Furniture And House Furnishings **4553**
Cartography *see* GEOGRAPHY **3996**
Cartons *see* PACKAGING **6708**
Cartoons *see* ART **462**
Castings *see* METALLURGY **6303**
CAT Scan *see* MEDICAL SCIENCES—Radiology And Nuclear Medicine **6191**
Catamarans *see* SPORTS AND GAMES—Boats And Boating **8270**
Cataracts *see* MEDICAL SCIENCES—Ophthalmology And Optometry **6037**
Catechesis *see* RELIGIONS AND THEOLOGY **7619**
Catering *see* HOTELS AND RESTAURANTS **4380**
Catholicism *see* RELIGIONS AND THEOLOGY—Roman Catholic **7781**
Cats *see* PETS **6802**
Cattle *see* AGRICULTURE—Poultry And Livestock **276**
Cavalry *see* MILITARY **6408**
Caves *see* EARTH SCIENCES—Geology **2722**
CD-ROM *see* COMMUNICATIONS—Computer Applications **2349**; COMPUTERS—Software **2587**
Cell Biology *see* BIOLOGY—Cytology And Histology **826**
Cement *see* BUILDING AND CONSTRUCTION **974**
Cemeteries *see* FUNERALS **3719**
Censorship *see* JOURNALISM **4570**; MOTION PICTURES **6488**; POLITICAL SCIENCE—Civil Rights **7201**; PUBLISHING AND BOOK TRADE **7550**
Census *see* POPULATION STUDIES—Abstracting, Bibliographies, Statistics **7296**
Central American History *see* HISTORY—History Of North And South America **4281**
Central Heating *see* HEATING, PLUMBING AND REFRIGERATION **4115**
CERAMICS, GLASS AND POTTERY **2037** *see also* ART **462**; ARTS AND HANDICRAFTS **530**
CERAMICS, GLASS AND POTTERY—Abstracting, Bibliographies, Statistics **2047**
Cereals *see* AGRICULTURE—Feed, Flour And Grain **270**; FOOD AND FOOD INDUSTRIES **3624**
Cerebellum *see* MEDICAL SCIENCES—Psychiatry And Neurology **6117**
Cerebral Palsy *see* MEDICAL SCIENCES—Psychiatry And Neurology **6117**
Cerebrum *see* MEDICAL SCIENCES—Psychiatry And Neurology **6117**
CHAMBER OF COMMERCE PUBLICATIONS *see* BUSINESS AND ECONOMICS—Chamber Of Commerce Publications **1394**
Chaplains *see* MILITARY **6408**; RELIGIONS AND THEOLOGY **7619**
Charities *see* SOCIAL SERVICES AND WELFARE **8022**
Cheese *see* AGRICULTURE—Dairying And Dairy Products **261**
CHEMICAL ENGINEERING *see* ENGINEERING—Chemical Engineering **3234**
Chemical Warfare *see* MILITARY **6408**
Chemical Wastes *see* ENVIRONMENTAL STUDIES—Pollution **3482**; ENVIRONMENTAL STUDIES—Waste Management **3503**
CHEMISTRY **2047** *see also* CHEMISTRY—Analytical Chemistry **2096**; CHEMISTRY—Computer Applications **2107**; CHEMISTRY—Crystallography **2108**; CHEMISTRY—Electrochemistry **2112**; CHEMISTRY—Inorganic Chemistry **2115**; CHEMISTRY—Organic Chemistry **2119**; CHEMISTRY—Physical Chemistry **2132**

CHEMISTRY—Abstracting, Bibliographies, Statistics **2085**
CHEMISTRY—Analytical Chemistry **2096**
CHEMISTRY—Computer Applications **2107**
CHEMISTRY—Crystallography **2108**
CHEMISTRY—Electrochemistry **2112**
CHEMISTRY—Inorganic Chemistry **2115**
CHEMISTRY—Organic Chemistry **2119**
CHEMISTRY—Physical Chemistry **2132**
Chemotherapy *see* BIOLOGY—Biochemistry **721**; MEDICAL SCIENCES—Oncology **6007**; PHARMACY AND PHARMACOLOGY **6817**
Chess *see* SPORTS AND GAMES **8156**
Chest Diseases *see* MEDICAL SCIENCES—Respiratory Diseases **6211**
Child Abuse *see* CHILDREN AND YOUTH—About **2142**; LAW—Family And Matrimonial Law **4906**; SOCIAL SERVICES AND WELFARE **8022**
Child Care *see* CHILDREN AND YOUTH—About **2142**; LAW—Family And Matrimonial Law **4906**; SOCIAL SERVICES AND WELFARE **8022**
Child Psychology *see* PSYCHOLOGY **7329**
Child Welfare *see* CHILDREN AND YOUTH—About **2142**; SOCIAL SERVICES AND WELFARE **8022**
Childbirth *see* MEDICAL SCIENCES—Obstetrics And Gynecology **5984**
Childhood Diseases *see* MEDICAL SCIENCES—Pediatrics **6086**
CHILDREN AND YOUTH—About **2142** *see also* EDUCATION **2821**; MEDICAL SCIENCES—Pediatrics **6086**
CHILDREN AND YOUTH—Abstracting, Bibliographies, Statistics **2173**
CHILDREN AND YOUTH—For **2174**
Chinese Traditional Medicine *see* ALTERNATIVE MEDICINE **305**
Chiropody *see* MEDICAL SCIENCES—Orthopedics And Traumatology **6054**
CHIROPRACTIC, HOMEOPATHY, OSTEOPATHY *see* MEDICAL SCIENCES—Chiropractic, Homeopathy, Osteopathy **5803**
Chlorofluorocarbons *see* ENGINEERING—Chemical Engineering **3234**; ENVIRONMENTAL STUDIES—Pollution **3482**
Chocolate *see* FOOD AND FOOD INDUSTRIES—Bakers And Confectioners **3670**
Cholesterol *see* CHEMISTRY—Organic Chemistry **2119**; MEDICAL SCIENCES **5563**; NUTRITION AND DIETETICS **6654**
Christianity *see* RELIGIONS AND THEOLOGY **7619**; RELIGIONS AND THEOLOGY—Eastern Orthodox **7703**; RELIGIONS AND THEOLOGY—Other Denominations And Sects **7732**; RELIGIONS AND THEOLOGY—Protestant **7743**; RELIGIONS AND THEOLOGY—Roman Catholic **7781**
Chromatography *see* CHEMISTRY—Analytical Chemistry **2096**
Chromosomes *see* BIOLOGY—Genetics **861**
Church History *see* RELIGIONS AND THEOLOGY **7619**
Cigarettes, Cigars *see* TOBACCO **8485**
CIM (Computer Integrated Manufacturing) *see* ENGINEERING—Computer Applications **3288**
Cinematography *see* MOTION PICTURES **6488**; PHOTOGRAPHY **6963**
CIRCUITS *see* COMPUTERS—Circuits **2465**
Circulatory System *see* MEDICAL SCIENCES—Cardiovascular Diseases **5775**
Circus *see* THEATER **8464**
Cities and Towns *see* HOUSING AND URBAN PLANNING **4402**; PUBLIC ADMINISTRATION—Municipal Government **7486**
Citizenship *see* POLITICAL SCIENCE **7101**
Citrus Fruits *see* AGRICULTURE—Crop Production And Soil **215**; FOOD AND FOOD INDUSTRIES **3624**; GARDENING AND HORTICULTURE **3721**
City Planning *see* HOUSING AND URBAN PLANNING **4402**
Civil Aeronautics *see* TRANSPORTATION—Air Transport **8533**
CIVIL DEFENSE **2225** *see also* MILITARY **6408**
CIVIL DEFENSE—Abstracting, Bibliographies, Statistics **2229**
CIVIL ENGINEERING *see* ENGINEERING—Civil Engineering **3258**
CIVIL LAW *see* LAW—Civil Law **4826**
Civil Liberties *see* LAW—Constitutional Law **4845**; POLITICAL SCIENCE—Civil Rights **7201**
CIVIL RIGHTS *see* POLITICAL SCIENCE—Civil Rights **7201**
Civil Service *see* OCCUPATIONS AND CAREERS **6691**; PUBLIC ADMINISTRATION **7417**
Civilizations *see* ANTHROPOLOGY **322**; HISTORY **4128**; SOCIOLOGY **8084**
Clairvoyance *see* NEW AGE PUBLICATIONS **6643**; PARAPSYCHOLOGY AND OCCULTISM **6740**
Classical Music *see* MUSIC **6541**
CLASSICAL STUDIES **2229** *see also* ARCHAEOLOGY **370**; HISTORY **4128**; LINGUISTICS **5088**; LITERATURE **5247**; MUSEUMS AND ART GALLERIES **6518**
CLASSICAL STUDIES—Abstracting, Bibliographies, Statistics **2242**
Classified Advertising *see* ADVERTISING AND PUBLIC RELATIONS **18**
Clay *see* BUILDING AND CONSTRUCTION **974**; CERAMICS, GLASS AND POTTERY **2037**; EARTH SCIENCES—Geology **2722**; MINES AND MINING INDUSTRY **6456**
CLEANING AND DYEING **2242** *see also* TEXTILE INDUSTRIES AND FABRICS **8447**
CLEANING AND DYEING—Abstracting, Bibliographies, Statistics **2244**
Climacteric *see* MEDICAL SCIENCES—Obstetrics And Gynecology **5984**
Climate Control *see* HEATING, PLUMBING AND REFRIGERATION **4115**
Climatology *see* METEOROLOGY **6345**
Clinical Medicine *see* MEDICAL SCIENCES **5563**
Clinics *see* HEALTH FACILITIES AND ADMINISTRATION **4086**
Clocks *see* JEWELRY, CLOCKS AND WATCHES **4564**
Cloning *see* BIOLOGY—Bioengineering **746**; BIOLOGY—Biotechnology **755**; BIOLOGY—Genetics **861**
CLOTHING TRADE **2244** *see also* CLOTHING TRADE—Fashions **2251**; LEATHER AND FUR INDUSTRIES **4972**; SHOES AND BOOTS **7940**; TEXTILE INDUSTRIES AND FABRICS **8447**
CLOTHING TRADE—Abstracting, Bibliographies, Statistics **2250**
CLOTHING TRADE—Fashions **2251**
CLUBS **2264** *see also* COLLEGE AND ALUMNI **2271**
Co-op Apartments *see* REAL ESTATE **7581**
Coaching *see* SPORTS AND GAMES **8156**
Coal *see* ENERGY **3123**; MINES AND MINING INDUSTRY **6456**
Coast Guard *see* MILITARY **6408**
Coastal Engineering *see* ENGINEERING—Hydraulic Engineering **3360**
Coastal Waters *see* EARTH SCIENCES—Oceanography **2799**
Coats of Arms *see* GENEALOGY AND HERALDRY **3757**

ELECTRICAL ENERGY *see* ENERGY—Electrical Energy 3155

ELECTRICAL ENGINEERING *see* ENGINEERING—Electrical Engineering 3293

ELECTRICITY *see* PHYSICS—Electricity 7051

Electrocardiogram *see* MEDICAL SCIENCES—Cardiovascular Diseases 5775

ELECTROCHEMISTRY *see* CHEMISTRY—Electrochemistry 2112

ELECTRONIC DATA PROCESSING *see* COMPUTERS—Electronic Data Processing 2535

Electronic Funds Transfer *see* BUSINESS AND ECONOMICS—Banking And Finance—Computer Applications 1392

ELECTRONICS 3089

ELECTRONICS—Abstracting, Bibliographies, Statistics 3116

ELECTRONICS—Computer Applications 3117

Electrophysics *see* PHYSICS—Electricity 7051

Electroplating *see* ENGINEERING—Electrical Engineering 3293; METALLURGY 6303

Electrotherapy *see* MEDICAL SCIENCES—Psychiatry And Neurology 6117; MEDICAL SCIENCES—Radiology And Nuclear Medicine 6191

Embroidery *see* NEEDLEWORK 6636

Embryology *see* BIOLOGY 648; MEDICAL SCIENCES 5563

Emergency management *see* CIVIL DEFENSE 2225

Emergency Medicine *see* MEDICAL SCIENCES—Orthopedics And Traumatology 6054

Emergency preparedness *see* CIVIL DEFENSE 2225

Emigration *see* POPULATION STUDIES 7276

Emission Control *see* ENVIRONMENTAL STUDIES—Pollution 3482

Emotional Disorders *see* MEDICAL SCIENCES—Psychiatry And Neurology 6117

Emotionally Disturbed Children *see* CHILDREN AND YOUTH—About 2142; EDUCATION—Special Education And Rehabilitation 3035

Emphysema *see* MEDICAL SCIENCES—Respiratory Diseases 6211

Empiricism *see* PHILOSOPHY 6901

Employee Benefits *see* BUSINESS AND ECONOMICS—Personnel Management 1855

Employment *see* BUSINESS AND ECONOMICS—Labor And Industrial Relations 1661; OCCUPATIONS AND CAREERS 6691

Encephalitis *see* MEDICAL SCIENCES—Psychiatry And Neurology 6117

ENCYCLOPEDIAS AND GENERAL ALMANACS 3117

ENDOCRINOLOGY *see* MEDICAL SCIENCES—Endocrinology 5883

Enduro Racing *see* SPORTS AND GAMES—Bicycles And Motorcycles 8252

ENERGY 3123 *see also* ENERGY—Computer Applications 3155; ENERGY—Electrical Energy 3155; ENERGY—Geothermal Energy 3162; ENERGY—Hydroelectrical Energy 3162; ENERGY—Nuclear Energy 3164; ENERGY—Solar Energy 3176; ENERGY—Wind Energy 3178

ENERGY—Abstracting, Bibliographies, Statistics 3150

ENERGY—Computer Applications 3155

ENERGY—Electrical Energy 3155

ENERGY—Geothermal Energy 3162

ENERGY—Hydroelectrical Energy 3162

ENERGY—Nuclear Energy 3164

ENERGY—Solar Energy 3176

ENERGY—Wind Energy 3178

ENGINEERING 3179 *see also* ENGINEERING—Chemical Engineering 3234; ENGINEERING—Civil Engineering 3258; ENGINEERING—Computer Applications 3288; ENGINEERING—Electrical Engineering 3293; ENGINEERING—Engineering Mechanics And Materials 3335; ENGINEERING—Hydraulic Engineering 3360; ENGINEERING—Industrial Engineering 3365; ENGINEERING—Mechanical Engineering 3372

ENGINEERING—Abstracting, Bibliographies, Statistics 3228

ENGINEERING—Chemical Engineering 3234 *see also* PLASTICS 7090

ENGINEERING—Civil Engineering 3258 *see also* BUILDING AND CONSTRUCTION 974; TRANSPORTATION—Roads And Traffic 8628

ENGINEERING—Computer Applications 3288

ENGINEERING—Electrical Engineering 3293

ENGINEERING—Engineering Mechanics And Materials 3335

ENGINEERING—Hydraulic Engineering 3360

ENGINEERING—Industrial Engineering 3365

ENGINEERING—Mechanical Engineering 3372

Engines *see* ENGINEERING—Mechanical Engineering 3372; TRANSPORTATION 8489

English Language - Study and Teaching *see* LINGUISTICS 5088

Engraving *see* ART 462; PRINTING 7318

Enterology *see* MEDICAL SCIENCES—Gastroenterology 5919

Entertainment *see* COMMUNICATIONS—Radio 2356; COMMUNICATIONS—Television And Cable 2374; COMMUNICATIONS—Video 2399; DANCE 2682; MOTION PICTURES 6488; MUSIC 6541; SPORTS AND GAMES 8156; THEATER 8464; TRAVEL AND TOURISM 8679

ENTOMOLOGY *see* BIOLOGY—Entomology 837

Entrepreneurship *see* BUSINESS AND ECONOMICS—Small Business 1956

Environmental Health *see* ENVIRONMENTAL STUDIES 3400; PUBLIC HEALTH AND SAFETY 7505

ENVIRONMENTAL STUDIES 3400 *see also* BIOLOGY 648; CONSERVATION 2601; ENVIRONMENTAL STUDIES—Computer Applications 3481; ENVIRONMENTAL STUDIES—Pollution 3482; ENVIRONMENTAL STUDIES—Toxicology And Environmental Safety 3493; ENVIRONMENTAL STUDIES—Waste Management 3503; PUBLIC HEALTH AND SAFETY 7505; WATER RESOURCES 8817

ENVIRONMENTAL STUDIES—Abstracting, Bibliographies, Statistics 3477

ENVIRONMENTAL STUDIES—Computer Applications 3481

ENVIRONMENTAL STUDIES—Pollution 3482

ENVIRONMENTAL STUDIES—Toxicology And Environmental Safety 3493

ENVIRONMENTAL STUDIES—Waste Management 3503

Enzymes *see* BIOLOGY—Biochemistry 721; MEDICAL SCIENCES 5563

Ephemerides *see* ASTRONOMY 567

Epidemiology *see* PUBLIC HEALTH AND SAFETY 7505

Epilepsy *see* MEDICAL SCIENCES—Psychiatry And Neurology 6117

Episcopalianism *see* RELIGIONS AND THEOLOGY—Protestant 7743

Epistemology *see* PHILOSOPHY 6901

Equal Opportunity *see* BUSINESS AND ECONOMICS—Labor And Industrial Relations 1661; LAW 4606; POLITICAL SCIENCE—Civil Rights 7201

Equal Rights Amendment *see* POLITICAL SCIENCE—Civil Rights 7201; WOMEN'S STUDIES 8893

Equestrianism *see* SPORTS AND GAMES—Horses And Horsemanship 8286

Equipment *see* AGRICULTURE—Agricultural Equipment 209; MACHINERY 5449

Ergonomics *see* BUSINESS AND ECONOMICS—Labor And Industrial Relations 1661; PSYCHOLOGY 7329

Erosion *see* AGRICULTURE—Crop Production And Soil 215; CONSERVATION 2601

ESP (Extrasensory Perception) *see* PARAPSYCHOLOGY AND OCCULTISM 6740

Esperanto *see* LINGUISTICS 5088

Espionage *see* CRIMINOLOGY AND LAW ENFORCEMENT—Security 2676; MILITARY 6408; POLITICAL SCIENCE—International Relations 7219

ESTATE PLANNING LAW *see* LAW—Estate Planning 4900

Esthetics *see* ART 462; PHILOSOPHY 6901

Ethics *see* PHILOSOPHY 6901; RELIGIONS AND THEOLOGY 7619

ETHNIC INTERESTS 3514

ETHNIC INTERESTS—Abstracting, Bibliographies, Statistics 3574

Ethnography *see* ANTHROPOLOGY 322; SOCIOLOGY 8084

Ethnology *see* ANTHROPOLOGY 322

Ethnopharmacology *see* ANTHROPOLOGY 322; PHARMACY AND PHARMACOLOGY 6817

Ethology *see* BIOLOGY—Zoology 929

Eugenics *see* BIOLOGY—Genetics 861

European History *see* HISTORY—History Of Europe 4194

Euthanasia *see* MEDICAL SCIENCES 5563; PHILOSOPHY 6901; RELIGIONS AND THEOLOGY 7619

Evangelism *see* RELIGIONS AND THEOLOGY—Protestant 7743

Evangelization *see* RELIGIONS AND THEOLOGY 7619

Evolution *see* BIOLOGY 648; SCIENCES: COMPREHENSIVE WORKS 7829

Exceptional Children, Education *see* EDUCATION—Special Education And Rehabilitation 3035

Exchange Students *see* EDUCATION 2821; EDUCATION—International Education Programs 3011

Excursion *see* SPORTS AND GAMES—Outdoor Life 8300; TRAVEL AND TOURISM 8679

Exercise *see* PHYSICAL FITNESS AND HYGIENE 6980

Exhibitions *see* MEETINGS AND CONGRESSES 6277; MUSEUMS AND ART GALLERIES 6518

Existentialism *see* LITERATURE 5247; PHILOSOPHY 6901

Exorcism *see* PARAPSYCHOLOGY AND OCCULTISM 6740; RELIGIONS AND THEOLOGY 7619

EXPERIMENTAL MEDICINE, LABORATORY TECHNIQUE *see* MEDICAL SCIENCES—Experimental Medicine, Laboratory Technique 5901

Exports and Imports *see* BUSINESS AND ECONOMICS—International Commerce 1551

Expositions *see* MEETINGS AND CONGRESSES 6277; MUSEUMS AND ART GALLERIES 6518

Extinction *see* BIOLOGY 648; CONSERVATION 2601; PALEONTOLOGY 6722

Extrasensory Perception *see* PARAPSYCHOLOGY AND OCCULTISM 6740

Extraterrestrials *see* AERONAUTICS AND SPACE FLIGHT 40; PARAPSYCHOLOGY AND OCCULTISM 6740

Eye Care *see* MEDICAL SCIENCES—Ophthalmology And Optometry 6037

Fables *see* FOLKLORE 3614; LITERATURE 5247

Fabrics *see* TEXTILE INDUSTRIES AND FABRICS 8447

Facilities Maintenance *see* BUSINESS AND ECONOMICS—Management 1722; BUSINESS AND ECONOMICS—Office Equipment And Services 1849

Facsimile Transmission *see* COMMUNICATIONS—Computer Applications 2349

Fairy Tales *see* FOLKLORE 3614; LITERATURE 5247

Family *see* SOCIOLOGY 8084

FAMILY AND MATRIMONIAL LAW *see* LAW—Family And Matrimonial Law 4906

Family History *see* GENEALOGY AND HERALDRY 3757

Family Planning *see* BIRTH CONTROL 971

Family Therapy *see* MATRIMONY 5556

Famine *see* SOCIAL SERVICES AND WELFARE 8022

Fantasy *see* LITERATURE—Science Fiction, Fantasy, Horror 5439

Farm Equipment *see* AGRICULTURE—Agricultural Equipment 209; MACHINERY 5449

Farm Management *see* AGRICULTURE 77

Farm Marketing *see* AGRICULTURE—Agricultural Economics 190

Farm Mechanization *see* AGRICULTURE—Agricultural Equipment 209

Farming *see* AGRICULTURE 77

FASHIONS *see* CLOTHING TRADE—Fashions 2251

Fate *see* PARAPSYCHOLOGY AND OCCULTISM 6740; PHILOSOPHY 6901; RELIGIONS AND THEOLOGY 7619

Fatherhood *see* LAW—Family And Matrimonial Law 4906; MEN'S INTERESTS 6285; MEN'S STUDIES 6302

Fauna *see* BIOLOGY—Zoology 929; CONSERVATION 2601

Fax *see* COMMUNICATIONS—Computer Applications 2349

Federalism *see* POLITICAL SCIENCE 7101

FEED, FLOUR AND GRAIN *see* AGRICULTURE—Feed, Flour And Grain 270

Fellowships *see* EDUCATION—Higher Education 2963

Feminist Movement *see* POLITICAL SCIENCE—Civil Rights 7201; WOMEN'S INTERESTS 8850; WOMEN'S STUDIES 8893

Fencing *see* SPORTS AND GAMES 8156

Fertility *see* MEDICAL SCIENCES—Obstetrics And Gynecology 5984; MEN'S HEALTH 6283; WOMEN'S HEALTH 8843

Fertilizers *see* AGRICULTURE—Crop Production And Soil 215

Fiber Optics *see* COMMUNICATIONS—Computer Applications 2349; PHYSICS—Optics 7073

Fiction *see* LITERATURE 5247

Field Crops *see* AGRICULTURE—Crop Production And Soil 215

Film Processing *see* PHOTOGRAPHY 6963

Filmmaking *see* MOTION PICTURES 6488

Finance *see* BUSINESS AND ECONOMICS—Banking And Finance 1304; BUSINESS AND ECONOMICS—Investments 1608

Financial Aid (College) *see* EDUCATION—Higher Education 2963

Finishing *see* PAINTS AND PROTECTIVE COATINGS 6715

FIRE PREVENTION 3575

FIRE PREVENTION—Abstracting, Bibliographies, Statistics 3582

Firearms *see* HOBBIES 4326; SPORTS AND GAMES 8156

Fireworks *see* ENGINEERING—Chemical Engineering 3234; FIRE PREVENTION 3575

Link to your serials resources and content with ulrichsweb.com

Greenhouse Effect see ENVIRONMENTAL STUDIES 3400; METEOROLOGY 6345

Greenhouses see GARDENING AND HORTICULTURE 3721

Greeting Cards see GIFTWARE AND TOYS 4059

Grieving see PSYCHOLOGY 7329; SOCIAL SERVICES AND WELFARE 8022

GROCERY TRADE see FOOD AND FOOD INDUSTRIES—Grocery Trade 3676

Guerrilla Warfare see MILITARY 6408

GUIDES TO SCHOOLS AND COLLEGES see EDUCATION—Guides To Schools And Colleges 2953

Gum Disease see MEDICAL SCIENCES—Dentistry 5832

Gun Control see CRIMINOLOGY AND LAW ENFORCEMENT 2642

Guns see MILITARY 6408; SPORTS AND GAMES 8156

Gymnastics see SPORTS AND GAMES 8156

Gyms see PHYSICAL FITNESS AND HYGIENE 6980

Gynecology see MEDICAL SCIENCES—Obstetrics And Gynecology 5984

Habitat Protection see CONSERVATION 2601; ENVIRONMENTAL STUDIES 3400

Hair Removal see BEAUTY CULTURE 585

Hairdressing see BEAUTY CULTURE 545

Handbags see CLOTHING TRADE 2244; LEATHER AND FUR INDUSTRIES 4972

HANDICAPPED 4063 see also EDUCATION—Special Education And Rehabilitation 3035; HANDICAPPED—Computer Applications 4071; HANDICAPPED—Hearing Impaired 4071; HANDICAPPED—Physically Impaired 4077; HANDICAPPED—Visually Impaired 4078; SOCIAL SERVICES AND WELFARE 8022

HANDICAPPED—Abstracting, Bibliographies, Statistics 4070

HANDICAPPED—Computer Applications 4071

HANDICAPPED—Hearing Impaired 4071

HANDICAPPED—Physically Impaired 4077

HANDICAPPED—Visually Impaired 4078

Handicrafts see ARTS AND HANDICRAFTS 530

Harbors see TRANSPORTATION—Ships And Shipping 8638

HARDWARE see BUILDING AND CONSTRUCTION—Hardware 1053

HARDWARE (COMPUTER) Includes: Analog Computers, Digital Computers. Disk Drives, Input-Output Systems, Laser Printers, Memory Structures, Modems, Monitors, Peripherals, Printers, Tape Decks, Terminals see COMPUTERS—Hardware 2538

Hare Krishna see RELIGIONS AND THEOLOGY—Hindu 7707

Harijan see RELIGIONS AND THEOLOGY—Hindu 7707

Harnesses see LEATHER AND FUR INDUSTRIES 4972

Hashish see DRUG ABUSE AND ALCOHOLISM 2689

Hasidim, Hasidism see RELIGIONS AND THEOLOGY—Judaic 7717

Hay Fever see MEDICAL SCIENCES—Allergology And Immunology 5752

Hazardous Substances see ENVIRONMENTAL STUDIES—Waste Management 3503

Headhunters see OCCUPATIONS AND CAREERS 6691

Health Clubs see PHYSICAL FITNESS AND HYGIENE 6980

HEALTH FACILITIES AND ADMINISTRATION 4086 see also MEDICAL SCIENCES 5563; NUTRITION AND DIETETICS 6654

HEALTH FACILITIES AND ADMINISTRATION—Abstracting, Bibliographies, Statistics 4113

HEALTH FACILITIES AND ADMINISTRATION—Computer Applications 4114

Health Foods see FOOD AND FOOD INDUSTRIES 3624; NUTRITION AND DIETETICS 6654; PHYSICAL FITNESS AND HYGIENE 6980

Health Insurance see INSURANCE 4490

Health Maintenance Organization see HEALTH FACILITIES AND ADMINISTRATION 4086; INSURANCE 4490

Healthcare Administration see HEALTH FACILITIES AND ADMINISTRATION 4086

Hearing see MEDICAL SCIENCES—Otorhinolaryngology 6076

HEARING IMPAIRED see HANDICAPPED—Hearing Impaired 4071

Heart Diseases see MEDICAL SCIENCES—Cardiovascular Diseases 5775

HEAT see PHYSICS—Heat 7053

HEATING, PLUMBING AND REFRIGERATION 4115 see also BUILDING AND CONSTRUCTION 974; ENGINEERING—Mechanical Engineering 3372

HEATING, PLUMBING AND REFRIGERATION—Abstracting, Bibliographies, Statistics 4128

Helicopters see AERONAUTICS AND SPACE FLIGHT 40

HEMATOLOGY see MEDICAL SCIENCES—Hematology 5933

Hemophilia see MEDICAL SCIENCES—Hematology 5933

Hepatology see MEDICAL SCIENCES—Gastroenterology 5919

Heraldry see GENEALOGY AND HERALDRY 3757

Herbal Medicine see ALTERNATIVE MEDICINE 305; BIOLOGY—Botany 771

Herbariums see BIOLOGY—Botany 771; GARDENING AND HORTICULTURE 3721

Herbs see AGRICULTURE 77; BIOLOGY—Botany 771; GARDENING AND HORTICULTURE 3721

Heredity see BIOLOGY—Genetics 861

Heroin see DRUG ABUSE AND ALCOHOLISM 2689

Herpetology see BIOLOGY—Zoology 929

Hi-Fi see SOUND RECORDING AND REPRODUCTION 8151

Hides see LEATHER AND FUR INDUSTRIES 4972

HIGHER EDUCATION see EDUCATION—Higher Education 2963

Highways see ENGINEERING—Civil Engineering 3258; TRANSPORTATION—Roads And Traffic 8628

Hinayana see RELIGIONS AND THEOLOGY—Buddhist 7700

HINDUISM see RELIGIONS AND THEOLOGY—Hindu 7707

Histochemistry see BIOLOGY—Cytology And Histology 826

Histology see BIOLOGY—Cytology And Histology 826

Historic Sites see HISTORY 4128; TRAVEL AND TOURISM 8679

HISTORY 4128 see also ANTHROPOLOGY 322; ARCHAEOLOGY 370; BIOGRAPHY 639; CLASSICAL STUDIES 2229; FOLKLORE 3614; HISTORY—Computer Applications 4171; HISTORY—History Of Africa 4172; HISTORY—History Of Asia 4179; HISTORY—History Of Australasia And Other Areas 4191; HISTORY—History Of Europe 4194; HISTORY—History Of North And South America 4281; HISTORY—History Of The Near East 4319; and also specific subjects

HISTORY—Abstracting, Bibliographies, Statistics 4168

HISTORY—Computer Applications 4171

HISTORY—History Of Africa 4172

HISTORY—History Of Asia 4179 see also ASIAN STUDIES 541

HISTORY—History Of Australasia And Other Areas 4191

HISTORY—History Of Europe 4194 see also CLASSICAL STUDIES 2229

HISTORY—History Of North And South America 4281

HISTORY—History Of The Near East 4319

HIV (Human Immunodeficiency Virus) see MEDICAL SCIENCES—Allergology And Immunology 5752; MEDICAL SCIENCES—Communicable Diseases 5807

HMO see HEALTH FACILITIES AND ADMINISTRATION 4086; INSURANCE 4490

HOBBIES 4326 see also ANTIQUES 362; NEEDLEWORK 6636; NUMISMATICS 6648; PHILATELY 6891; SPORTS AND GAMES 8156

HOBBIES—Abstracting, Bibliographies, Statistics 4351

Hockey see SPORTS AND GAMES 8156

Holidays see FOLKLORE 3614; TRAVEL AND TOURISM 8679

Holistic Medicine see ALTERNATIVE MEDICINE 305

Holocaust see ETHNIC INTERESTS 3514; HISTORY—History Of Europe 4194

Home Appliances see ELECTRONICS 3089; INTERIOR DESIGN AND DECORATION—Furniture And House Furnishings 4553

Home Care see GERONTOLOGY AND GERIATRICS 4037; HANDICAPPED 4063; MEDICAL SCIENCES—Nurses And Nursing 5949; SOCIAL SERVICES AND WELFARE 8022

HOME ECONOMICS 4351 see also INTERIOR DESIGN AND DECORATION 4531; NUTRITION AND DIETETICS 6654

HOME ECONOMICS—Abstracting, Bibliographies, Statistics 4370

Home Improvement see BUILDING AND CONSTRUCTION 974; HOW-TO AND DO-IT-YOURSELF 4437

Home Remodeling and Repairs see BUILDING AND CONSTRUCTION 974; HOW-TO AND DO-IT-YOURSELF 4437

Homelessness see SOCIAL SERVICES AND WELFARE 8022

Homeopathy see MEDICAL SCIENCES—Chiropractic, Homeopathy, Osteopathy 5803

Homophobia see HOMOSEXUALITY 4370

HOMOSEXUALITY 4370

HOMOSEXUALITY—Abstracting, Bibliographies, Statistics 4380

Hormones see MEDICAL SCIENCES—Endocrinology 5883

Horology see JEWELRY, CLOCKS AND WATCHES 4564

Horoscopy see ASTROLOGY 564

Horror see LITERATURE—Science Fiction, Fantasy, Horror 5439

HORSES AND HORSEMANSHIP see SPORTS AND GAMES—Horses And Horsemanship 8286

Horticulture see GARDENING AND HORTICULTURE 3721

Hosiery see CLOTHING TRADE 2244

Hospices see HEALTH FACILITIES AND ADMINISTRATION 4086

Hospital Supplies see HEALTH FACILITIES AND ADMINISTRATION 4086; PHARMACY AND PHARMACOLOGY 6817

Hospitals see HEALTH FACILITIES AND ADMINISTRATION 4086

HOTELS AND RESTAURANTS 4380 see also NUTRITION AND DIETETICS 6654; TRAVEL AND TOURISM 8679

HOTELS AND RESTAURANTS—Abstracting, Bibliographies, Statistics 4401

House Furnishings see INTERIOR DESIGN AND DECORATION—Furniture And House Furnishings 4553

Household Management see HOME ECONOMICS 4351

Houses see BUILDING AND CONSTRUCTION 974; REAL ESTATE 7581

Housewares see CERAMICS, GLASS AND POTTERY 2037; INTERIOR DESIGN AND DECORATION—Furniture And House Furnishings 4553

HOUSING AND URBAN PLANNING 4402 see also BUILDING AND CONSTRUCTION 974; PUBLIC ADMINISTRATION 7417; REAL ESTATE 7581

HOUSING AND URBAN PLANNING—Abstracting, Bibliographies, Statistics 4432

HOW-TO AND DO-IT-YOURSELF 4437

HOW-TO AND DO-IT-YOURSELF—Abstracting, Bibliographies, Statistics 4439

Human Ecology see SOCIOLOGY 8084

Human Geography see GEOGRAPHY 3996; POPULATION STUDIES 7276

Human Immunodeficiency Virus see MEDICAL SCIENCES—Allergology And Immunology 5752; MEDICAL SCIENCES—Communicable Diseases 5807

Human Physiology see BIOLOGY—Physiology 917; MEDICAL SCIENCES 5563

Human Resources see BUSINESS AND ECONOMICS—Personnel Management 1855

Human Rights see POLITICAL SCIENCE—Civil Rights 7201

Humanism see PHILOSOPHY 6901

HUMANITIES: COMPREHENSIVE WORKS 4439

HUMANITIES: COMPREHENSIVE WORKS—Abstracting, Bibliographies, Statistics 4483

HUMANITIES: COMPREHENSIVE WORKS—Computer Applications 4485

Humor see LITERARY AND POLITICAL REVIEWS 5204

Hunger see SOCIAL SERVICES AND WELFARE 8022

Hunting see SPORTS AND GAMES—Outdoor Life 8300

Hurricanes see METEOROLOGY 6345

HYDRAULIC ENGINEERING see ENGINEERING—Hydraulic Engineering 3360

Hydrodynamics see PHYSICS 7002

Hydroelectric Engineering see ENGINEERING—Electrical Engineering 3293

HYDROELECTRICAL ENERGY see ENERGY—Hydroelectrical Energy 3162

Hydrography see WATER RESOURCES 8817

HYDROLOGY see EARTH SCIENCES—Hydrology 2792

Hydroponics see AGRICULTURE—Crop Production And Soil 215

Hydrotherapy see ALTERNATIVE MEDICINE 305

Hygiene see OCCUPATIONAL HEALTH AND SAFETY 6672; PHYSICAL FITNESS AND HYGIENE 6980; PUBLIC HEALTH AND SAFETY 7505

Hyperglycemia see MEDICAL SCIENCES—Endocrinology 5883; NUTRITION AND DIETETICS 6654

Hypertension see MEDICAL SCIENCES—Cardiovascular Diseases 5775

HYPNOSIS see MEDICAL SCIENCES—Hypnosis 5942

Hypochondria see MEDICAL SCIENCES—Psychiatry And Neurology 6117

Hypoglycemia see MEDICAL SCIENCES—Endocrinology 5883; NUTRITION AND DIETETICS 6654

Ichthyology see BIOLOGY—Zoology 929

Iconography see ART 462

Idealism see PHILOSOPHY 6901

Illumination see ENGINEERING—Electrical Engineering 3293; PHYSICS—Electricity 7051

Imaging see COMPUTERS—Computer Graphics 2482

Immigration see POPULATION STUDIES 7276

MEDICAL SCIENCES—Internal Medicine 5943 see also MEDICAL SCIENCES—Cardiovascular Diseases 5775; MEDICAL SCIENCES—Communicable Diseases 5807; MEDICAL SCIENCES—Endocrinology 5883; MEDICAL SCIENCES—Gastroenterology 5919; MEDICAL SCIENCES—Hematology 5933; MEDICAL SCIENCES—Oncology 6007; MEDICAL SCIENCES—Respiratory Diseases 6211; MEDICAL SCIENCES—Rheumatology 6221; MEDICAL SCIENCES—Urology And Nephrology 6264

MEDICAL SCIENCES—Nurses And Nursing 5949 see also GERONTOLOGY AND GERIATRICS 4037; HEALTH FACILITIES AND ADMINISTRATION 4086

MEDICAL SCIENCES—Obstetrics And Gynecology 5984 see also WOMEN'S HEALTH 8843

MEDICAL SCIENCES—Oncology 6007 see also MEDICAL SCIENCES—Radiology And Nuclear Medicine 6191

MEDICAL SCIENCES—Ophthalmology And Optometry 6037

MEDICAL SCIENCES—Orthopedics And Traumatology 6054

MEDICAL SCIENCES—Otorhinolaryngology 6076

MEDICAL SCIENCES—Pediatrics 6086

MEDICAL SCIENCES—Physical Medicine And Rehabilitation 6105

MEDICAL SCIENCES—Psychiatry And Neurology 6117

MEDICAL SCIENCES—Radiology And Nuclear Medicine 6191

MEDICAL SCIENCES—Respiratory Diseases 6211

MEDICAL SCIENCES—Rheumatology 6221

MEDICAL SCIENCES—Sports Medicine 6228

MEDICAL SCIENCES—Surgery 6234

MEDICAL SCIENCES—Urology And Nephrology 6264

Medical Technicians see MEDICAL SCIENCES 5563

Medieval Studies see HISTORY—History Of Europe 4194; LITERATURE 5247; PHILOSOPHY 6901

Meditation see PHILOSOPHY 6901; RELIGIONS AND THEOLOGY 7619

MEETINGS AND CONGRESSES 6277

MEETINGS AND CONGRESSES—Abstracting, Bibliographies, Statistics 6283

Melkite Rite see RELIGIONS AND THEOLOGY—Roman Catholic 7781

Memory Structures see COMPUTERS—Hardware 2538

MEN'S HEALTH 6283

MEN'S INTERESTS 6285

MEN'S STUDIES 6302

Mennonite see RELIGIONS AND THEOLOGY—Other Denominations And Sects 7732

Menopause see MEDICAL SCIENCES—Obstetrics And Gynecology 5984; WOMEN'S HEALTH 8843

Menswear see CLOTHING TRADE 2244

Mental Health see PSYCHOLOGY 7329

Mental Hygiene see PUBLIC HEALTH AND SAFETY 7505

Mental Illness see MEDICAL SCIENCES—Psychiatry And Neurology 6117; PSYCHOLOGY 7329

Mental Retardation see EDUCATION—Special Education And Rehabilitation 3035; MEDICAL SCIENCES—Psychiatry And Neurology 6117; PSYCHOLOGY 7329

Merchandising see BUSINESS AND ECONOMICS—Marketing And Purchasing 1803

Mergers and Acquisitions see BUSINESS AND ECONOMICS 1055; LAW—Corporate Law 4853

Messianism see RELIGIONS AND THEOLOGY—Judaic 7717

Metabolism see BIOLOGY—Physiology 917; MEDICAL SCIENCES—Endocrinology 5883

Metal Industries see METALLURGY 6303

METALLURGY 6303 see also METALLURGY—Welding 6342; MINES AND MINING INDUSTRY 6456

METALLURGY—Abstracting, Bibliographies, Statistics 6338

METALLURGY—Welding 6342

Metaphysics see PHILOSOPHY 6901

METEOROLOGY 6345

METEOROLOGY—Abstracting, Bibliographies, Statistics 6400

Methodism see RELIGIONS AND THEOLOGY—Protestant 7743

Metric System see METROLOGY AND STANDARDIZATION 6400

METROLOGY AND STANDARDIZATION 6400

METROLOGY AND STANDARDIZATION—Abstracting, Bibliographies, Statistics 6407

Microbes see BIOLOGY—Microbiology 879; MEDICAL SCIENCES—Communicable Diseases 5807

Microbial Biology see BIOLOGY—Microbiology 879

MICROBIOLOGY see BIOLOGY—Microbiology 879

MICROCOMPUTERS see COMPUTERS—Microcomputers 2570

Microelectronics see ELECTRONICS 3089

Microfilming see PHOTOGRAPHY 6963

Micrographic Analysis see BIOLOGY—Microscopy 898

Microorganisms see BIOLOGY—Microbiology 879

Micropaleontology see PALEONTOLOGY 6722

Microphotography see PHOTOGRAPHY 6963

Microscopic Anatomy see BIOLOGY—Cytology And Histology 826

MICROSCOPY see BIOLOGY—Microscopy 898

Microwaves see ELECTRONICS 3089

Midwifery see MEDICAL SCIENCES—Obstetrics And Gynecology 5984

Migration see POPULATION STUDIES 7276

MILITARY 6408 see also CIVIL DEFENSE 2225

Military Engineering see ENGINEERING 3179

MILITARY LAW see LAW—Military Law 4971

Military Medicine see MEDICAL SCIENCES 5563

MILITARY—Abstracting, Bibliographies, Statistics 6455

Milk see AGRICULTURE—Dairying And Dairy Products 261

Millinery see CLOTHING TRADE 2244

Milling see AGRICULTURE—Feed, Flour And Grain 270

Millwork see BUILDING AND CONSTRUCTION—Carpentry And Woodwork 1049

Mineral Resources see EARTH SCIENCES—Geology 2722; MINES AND MINING INDUSTRY 6455

Mineralogy see MINES AND MINING INDUSTRY 6456

MINES AND MINING INDUSTRY 6456 see also METALLURGY 6303

MINES AND MINING INDUSTRY—Abstracting, Bibliographies, Statistics 6484

MINES AND MINING INDUSTRY—Computer Applications 6488

MINICOMPUTERS see COMPUTERS—Minicomputers 2573

Minorities see ETHNIC INTERESTS 3514; POLITICAL SCIENCE—Civil Rights 7201

Minting see NUMISMATICS 6648

Miscarriage see MEDICAL SCIENCES—Obstetrics And Gynecology 5984

Missiles see AERONAUTICS AND SPACE FLIGHT 40

Missionaries and Missions see RELIGIONS AND THEOLOGY 7619

Mobile Homes see HOUSING AND URBAN PLANNING 4402; TRANSPORTATION 8489

Modeling see CLOTHING TRADE—Fashions 2251; OCCUPATIONS AND CAREERS 6691

Models and Model Building see HOBBIES 4326

Modems see COMPUTERS—Hardware 2538

Molecular Physics see PHYSICS—Nuclear Physics 7064

Mollusca see BIOLOGY—Zoology 929

Monarchy see POLITICAL SCIENCE 7101

Mongoloidism see EDUCATION—Special Education And Rehabilitation 3035; MEDICAL SCIENCES—Psychiatry And Neurology 6117

Monitors see COMPUTERS—Hardware 2538

Monotheism see RELIGIONS AND THEOLOGY 7619

Moravian Church see RELIGIONS AND THEOLOGY—Protestant 7743

Mormonism see RELIGIONS AND THEOLOGY—Other Denominations And Sects 7732

Morphology see BIOLOGY 648; MEDICAL SCIENCES 5563

Mortality Rate see POPULATION STUDIES—Abstracting, Bibliographies, Statistics 7296

Mortuaries see FUNERALS 3719

Mosses see BIOLOGY—Botany 771

Motels see HOTELS AND RESTAURANTS 4380

Motherhood see LAW—Family And Matrimonial Law 4906; WOMEN'S INTERESTS 8850; WOMEN'S STUDIES 8893

MOTION PICTURES 6488

MOTION PICTURES—Abstracting, Bibliographies, Statistics 6517

Motocross see SPORTS AND GAMES—Bicycles And Motorcycles 8252

Motor Scooters see SPORTS AND GAMES—Bicycles And Motorcycles 8252

Motorcycles see SPORTS AND GAMES—Bicycles And Motorcycles 8252

Mountaineering see SPORTS AND GAMES—Outdoor Life 8300

Movies see MOTION PICTURES 6488

MRI (Magnetic Resonance Imaging) see MEDICAL SCIENCES—Radiology And Nuclear Medicine 6191

Multimedia Computing see COMPUTERS—Computer Networks 2495; COMPUTERS—Personal Computers 2574; COMPUTERS—Software 2587

Multiple Sclerosis see MEDICAL SCIENCES—Psychiatry And Neurology 6117

MUNICIPAL GOVERNMENT see PUBLIC ADMINISTRATION—Municipal Government 7486

Municipal Law see LAW 4606; PUBLIC ADMINISTRATION—Municipal Government 7486

Municipal Transportation see TRANSPORTATION 8489

Murder see CRIMINOLOGY AND LAW ENFORCEMENT 2642

Muscular Dystrophy see MEDICAL SCIENCES—Rheumatology 6221

Musculoskeletal System see MEDICAL SCIENCES—Orthopedics And Traumatology 6054

MUSEUMS AND ART GALLERIES 6518

MUSEUMS AND ART GALLERIES—Abstracting, Bibliographies, Statistics 6541

Mushrooms see AGRICULTURE—Crop Production And Soil 215; BIOLOGY—Botany 771; GARDENING AND HORTICULTURE 3721

MUSIC 6541 see also DANCE 2682; SOUND RECORDING AND REPRODUCTION 8151

Music Therapy see EDUCATION—Special Education And Rehabilitation 3035; MUSIC 6541

MUSIC—Abstracting, Bibliographies, Statistics 6631

MUSIC—Computer Applications 6632 see also COMPUTERS—Computer Music 2495

Musical Instruments see MUSIC 6541

Muslim see RELIGIONS AND THEOLOGY—Islamic 7708

Mutation see BIOLOGY—Biochemistry 721; BIOLOGY—Genetics 861

Mutual Funds see BUSINESS AND ECONOMICS—Investments 1608

Mycology see BIOLOGY—Botany 771

MYSTERY AND DETECTIVE see LITERATURE—Mystery And Detective 5413

Mysticism see NEW AGE PUBLICATIONS 6643; PARAPSYCHOLOGY AND OCCULTISM 6740; RELIGIONS AND THEOLOGY 7619

Mythology see FOLKLORE 3614; LITERATURE 5247

Narcotics see DRUG ABUSE AND ALCOHOLISM 2689; PHARMACY AND PHARMACOLOGY 6817

National Government see PUBLIC ADMINISTRATION 7417

National Guard see MILITARY 6408

National Security see MILITARY 6408; POLITICAL SCIENCE 7101

Nationalism see POLITICAL SCIENCE 7101

Native American History see HISTORY—History Of North And South America 4281

NATIVE AMERICAN STUDIES 6634 see also HISTORY—History Of North And South America 4281

Native Medical Sciences see ALTERNATIVE MEDICINE 305

Natural Foods see AGRICULTURE—Crop Production And Soil 215; FOOD AND FOOD INDUSTRIES 3624; NUTRITION AND DIETETICS 6654

Natural Gas see PETROLEUM AND GAS 6761

Natural History see SCIENCES: COMPREHENSIVE WORKS 7829

Natural Resources see CONSERVATION 2601; ENVIRONMENTAL STUDIES 3400

Naturalization see POLITICAL SCIENCE 7101

Naturopathy see ALTERNATIVE MEDICINE 305

Nautical Arts and Sciences see TRANSPORTATION—Ships And Shipping 8638

Naval Architecture see TRANSPORTATION—Ships And Shipping 8638

Naval Engineering see TRANSPORTATION—Ships And Shipping 8638

Naval Law see LAW—Maritime Law 4969; LAW—Military Law 4971

Naval Medicine see MEDICAL SCIENCES 5563

Navigation see AERONAUTICS AND SPACE FLIGHT 40; TRANSPORTATION—Air Transport 8533; TRANSPORTATION—Ships And Shipping 8638

Navy see MILITARY 6408

Nazarene see RELIGIONS AND THEOLOGY—Other Denominations And Sects 7732

Needlepoint see NEEDLEWORK 6636

NEEDLEWORK 6636 see also ARTS AND HANDICRAFTS 530; HOBBIES 4326

Nematology see BIOLOGY—Zoology 929

Neonatal Care and Medicine see MEDICAL SCIENCES—Obstetrics And Gynecology 5984

Neoplasms see MEDICAL SCIENCES—Oncology 6007

Nephrology see MEDICAL SCIENCES—Urology And Nephrology 6264

Nerves, Nervous System see MEDICAL SCIENCES—Psychiatry And Neurology 6117

Neurology see MEDICAL SCIENCES—Psychiatry And Neurology 6117

Neurophysiology see MEDICAL SCIENCES—Psychiatry And Neurology 6117

Neuropsychology see PSYCHOLOGY 7329

Neuroradiology see MEDICAL SCIENCES—Radiology And Nuclear Medicine 6191

Neurosurgery see MEDICAL SCIENCES—Psychiatry And Neurology 6117; MEDICAL SCIENCES—Surgery 6234

NEW AGE PUBLICATIONS 6643 see also ASTROLOGY 564; PARAPSYCHOLOGY AND OCCULTISM 6740

New Testament see RELIGIONS AND THEOLOGY 7619

Newspaper Business see JOURNALISM 4570; PUBLISHING AND BOOK TRADE 7550

Nickel see METALLURGY 6303; MINES AND MINING INDUSTRY 6456

Nightclubs see HOTELS AND RESTAURANTS 4380

NMRI (Nuclear Magnetic Resonance Imaging) see MEDICAL SCIENCES—Radiology And Nuclear Medicine 6191

Noise Control see ENGINEERING—Mechanical Engineering 3372

Noise Pollution see ENVIRONMENTAL STUDIES—Pollution 3482

North American History see HISTORY—History Of North And South America 4281

NUCLEAR ENERGY see ENERGY—Nuclear Energy 3164

Nuclear Magnetic Resonance Imaging see MEDICAL SCIENCES—Radiology And Nuclear Medicine 6191

Nuclear Medicine see MEDICAL SCIENCES—Radiology And Nuclear Medicine 6191

NUCLEAR PHYSICS see PHYSICS—Nuclear Physics 7064

Nuclear Warfare see MILITARY 6408

Nudism see PHYSICAL FITNESS AND HYGIENE 6980

NUMISMATICS 6648 see also HOBBIES 4326

NUMISMATICS—Abstracting, Bibliographies, Statistics 6653

Nurseries see GARDENING AND HORTICULTURE—Florist Trade 3755

NURSES AND NURSING see MEDICAL SCIENCES—Nurses And Nursing 5949

Nursing Homes see GERONTOLOGY AND GERIATRICS 4037; HEALTH FACILITIES AND ADMINISTRATION 4086; SOCIAL SERVICES AND WELFARE 8022

NUTRITION AND DIETETICS 6654 see also FOOD AND FOOD INDUSTRIES 3624; HEALTH FACILITIES AND ADMINISTRATION 4086; PHARMACY AND PHARMACOLOGY 6817; PHYSICAL FITNESS AND HYGIENE 6980

NUTRITION AND DIETETICS—Abstracting, Bibliographies, Statistics 6671

Nuts see AGRICULTURE—Crop Production And Soil 215; GARDENING AND HORTICULTURE 3721

Obesity see NUTRITION AND DIETETICS 6654; PHYSICAL FITNESS AND HYGIENE 6980

OBSTETRICS AND GYNECOLOGY see MEDICAL SCIENCES—Obstetrics And Gynecology 5984

Occultism see PARAPSYCHOLOGY AND OCCULTISM 6740

OCCUPATIONAL HEALTH AND SAFETY 6672

OCCUPATIONAL HEALTH AND SAFETY—Abstracting, Bibliographies, Statistics 6689

Occupational Therapy see EDUCATION—Special Education And Rehabilitation 3035; MEDICAL SCIENCES 5563

OCCUPATIONS AND CAREERS 6691 see also BUSINESS AND ECONOMICS—Labor And Industrial Relations 1661

OCCUPATIONS AND CAREERS—Abstracting, Bibliographies, Statistics 6706

Ocean Dumping see ENVIRONMENTAL STUDIES—Pollution 3482

OCEANOGRAPHY see EARTH SCIENCES—Oceanography 2799

Ocular Disorders see MEDICAL SCIENCES—Ophthalmology And Optometry 6037

Odontology see MEDICAL SCIENCES—Dentistry 5832

OFFICE EQUIPMENT AND SERVICES see BUSINESS AND ECONOMICS—Office Equipment And Services 1849

Oil Spills see ENVIRONMENTAL STUDIES—Pollution 3482

Oil Wells see PETROLEUM AND GAS 6761

Oils and Fats see CHEMISTRY—Organic Chemistry 2119

Old Age see GERONTOLOGY AND GERIATRICS 4037

Old Testament see RELIGIONS AND THEOLOGY 7619; RELIGIONS AND THEOLOGY—Judaic 7717

Olfactory System see MEDICAL SCIENCES—Otorhinolaryngology 6076

ONCOLOGY see MEDICAL SCIENCES—Oncology 6007

Online Systems see COMPUTERS—Computer Networks 2495

Onomastics see LINGUISTICS 5088

Ontology see PHILOSOPHY 6901

Opera see MUSIC 6541

Operating Systems see COMPUTERS—Software 2587

Operations Research see BUSINESS AND ECONOMICS—Management 1722; COMPUTERS 2404

OPHTHALMOLOGY AND OPTOMETRY see MEDICAL SCIENCES—Ophthalmology And Optometry 6037

Opium see DRUG ABUSE AND ALCOHOLISM 2689

OPTICS see PHYSICS—Optics 7073

Optimization see MATHEMATICS—Computer Applications 5549

Optometry see MEDICAL SCIENCES—Ophthalmology And Optometry 6037

Oral Surgery see MEDICAL SCIENCES—Dentistry 5832

Orchards see AGRICULTURE—Crop Production And Soil 215; GARDENING AND HORTICULTURE 3721

Ore see EARTH SCIENCES—Geology 2722; MINES AND MINING INDUSTRY 6456

ORGANIC CHEMISTRY see CHEMISTRY—Organic Chemistry 2119

Organic Farming see AGRICULTURE—Crop Production And Soil 215

Organic Foods see NUTRITION AND DIETETICS 6654

Organized Crime see CRIMINOLOGY AND LAW ENFORCEMENT 2642

Oriental Medicine see ALTERNATIVE MEDICINE 305

ORIENTAL STUDIES see ASIAN STUDIES 541

ORNITHOLOGY see BIOLOGY—Ornithology 900

Orphanages see SOCIAL SERVICES AND WELFARE 8022

Orthodontics see MEDICAL SCIENCES—Dentistry 5832

ORTHOPEDICS AND TRAUMATOLOGY see MEDICAL SCIENCES—Orthopedics And Traumatology 6054

Orthotics see MEDICAL SCIENCES—Orthopedics And Traumatology 6054

Osteopathy see MEDICAL SCIENCES—Chiropractic, Homeopathy, Osteopathy 5803

Osteoporosis see MEDICAL SCIENCES 5563

Otology see MEDICAL SCIENCES—Otorhinolaryngology 6076

OTORHINOLARYNGOLOGY see MEDICAL SCIENCES—Otorhinolaryngology 6076

OUTDOOR LIFE see SPORTS AND GAMES—Outdoor Life 8300

Ozone Depletion see ENVIRONMENTAL STUDIES 3400; METEOROLOGY 6345

PACKAGING 6708

PACKAGING—Abstracting, Bibliographies, Statistics 6715

Paganism see RELIGIONS AND THEOLOGY—Other Denominations And Sects 7732

PAINTS AND PROTECTIVE COATINGS 6715

PAINTS AND PROTECTIVE COATINGS—Abstracting, Bibliographies, Statistics 6722

Paleobotany see BIOLOGY—Botany 771

PALEONTOLOGY 6722

PALEONTOLOGY—Abstracting, Bibliographies, Statistics 6731

Paleozoology see PALEONTOLOGY 6722

Palmistry see PARAPSYCHOLOGY AND OCCULTISM 6740

PAPER AND PULP 6731 see also FORESTS AND FORESTRY—Lumber And Wood 3709; PACKAGING 6708

PAPER AND PULP—Abstracting, Bibliographies, Statistics 6740

Paper Money see NUMISMATICS 6648; PRINTING 7318

Papyrus see PAPER AND PULP 6731

Parachuting see SPORTS AND GAMES 8156

Parakeets see PETS 6802

Paramedics see MEDICAL SCIENCES—Orthopedics And Traumatology 6054

Paramilitary see MILITARY 6408

Paraplegia see MEDICAL SCIENCES—Psychiatry And Neurology 6117

PARAPSYCHOLOGY AND OCCULTISM 6740 see also NEW AGE PUBLICATIONS 6643

PARAPSYCHOLOGY AND OCCULTISM—Abstracting, Bibliographies, Statistics 6744

Parasitology see BIOLOGY 648; MEDICAL SCIENCES—Communicable Diseases 5807; PUBLIC HEALTH AND SAFETY 7505

Parent Teacher Associations see EDUCATION—School Organization And Administration 3016

Parenting see CHILDREN AND YOUTH—About 2142

Parkinson's Disease see MEDICAL SCIENCES—Psychiatry And Neurology 6117

Parks and Recreation Areas see CONSERVATION 2601; SPORTS AND GAMES—Outdoor Life 8300; TRAVEL AND TOURISM 8679

PATENTS, TRADEMARKS AND COPYRIGHTS 6744

PATENTS, TRADEMARKS AND COPYRIGHTS—Abstracting, Bibliographies, Statistics 6760

Pathology see BIOLOGY 648; MEDICAL SCIENCES 5563

Paving see ENGINEERING—Civil Engineering 3258; TRANSPORTATION—Roads And Traffic 8628

Payroll see BUSINESS AND ECONOMICS—Accounting 1275; BUSINESS AND ECONOMICS—Public Finance, Taxation 1909

Peacekeeping see MILITARY 6408; POLITICAL SCIENCE—International Relations 7219

Pedagogy see EDUCATION 2821; EDUCATION—Teaching Methods And Curriculum 3049

PEDIATRICS see MEDICAL SCIENCES—Pediatrics 6086

Penal Law see LAW—Criminal Law 4883

Penology see CRIMINOLOGY AND LAW ENFORCEMENT 2642

Pensions see BUSINESS AND ECONOMICS—Labor And Industrial Relations 1661; INSURANCE 4490; SOCIAL SERVICES AND WELFARE 8022

Pentecostalism see RELIGIONS AND THEOLOGY—Other Denominations And Sects 7732

Percussion Instruments see MUSIC 6541

Performing Arts see DANCE 2682; MOTION PICTURES 6488; MUSIC 6541; THEATER 8464

PERFUMES AND COSMETICS see BEAUTY CULTURE—Perfumes And Cosmetics 592

Perinatal Care and Medicine see MEDICAL SCIENCES—Obstetrics And Gynecology 5984

Periodontics see MEDICAL SCIENCES—Dentistry 5832

Peripherals see COMPUTERS—Hardware 2538

PERSONAL COMPUTERS see COMPUTERS—Personal Computers 2574

Personal Growth see NEW AGE PUBLICATIONS 6643; PSYCHOLOGY 7329

PERSONNEL MANAGEMENT see BUSINESS AND ECONOMICS—Personnel Management 1855

Pest Control see AGRICULTURE 77; BIOLOGY—Entomology 837; PUBLIC HEALTH AND SAFETY 7505

Pesticides see AGRICULTURE—Crop Production And Soil 215; ENGINEERING—Chemical Engineering 3234; ENVIRONMENTAL STUDIES—Toxicology And Environmental Safety 3493

PETROLEUM AND GAS 6761

PETROLEUM AND GAS—Abstracting, Bibliographies, Statistics 6799

PETROLEUM AND GAS—Computer Applications 6802

Petrology see EARTH SCIENCES—Geology 2722

PETS 6802 see also ANIMAL WELFARE 316

Pewter see METALLURGY 6303

PHARMACY AND PHARMACOLOGY 6817 see also DRUG ABUSE AND ALCOHOLISM 2689; MEDICAL SCIENCES 5563

PHARMACY AND PHARMACOLOGY—Abstracting, Bibliographies, Statistics 6888

PHARMACY AND PHARMACOLOGY—Computer Applications 6890

Phenomenology see PHILOSOPHY 6901

Philanthropy see SOCIAL SERVICES AND WELFARE 8022

PHILATELY 6891 see also HOBBIES 4326

PHILATELY—Abstracting, Bibliographies, Statistics 6901

Philology see CLASSICAL STUDIES 2229; LINGUISTICS 5088

PHILOSOPHY 6901 see also RELIGIONS AND THEOLOGY 7619

PHILOSOPHY—Abstracting, Bibliographies, Statistics 6962

Phobias see MEDICAL SCIENCES—Psychiatry And Neurology 6117

Phonetics see LINGUISTICS 5088

Phonographs see MUSIC 6541; SOUND RECORDING AND REPRODUCTION 8151

Photogrammetry see GEOGRAPHY 3996; PHOTOGRAPHY 6963

Photographic Surveying see ENGINEERING—Civil Engineering 3258

PHOTOGRAPHY 6963 see also MOTION PICTURES 6488

PHOTOGRAPHY—Abstracting, Bibliographies, Statistics 6979

PHOTOGRAPHY—Computer Applications 6979

Photomechanical Processing see PRINTING 7318

Phrenology see PARAPSYCHOLOGY AND OCCULTISM 6740

Physiatry see MEDICAL SCIENCES—Physical Medicine And Rehabilitation 6105

Physical Anthropology see ANTHROPOLOGY 322

PHYSICAL CHEMISTRY see CHEMISTRY—Physical Chemistry 2132

Physical Education see EDUCATION—Teaching Methods And Curriculum 3049; PHYSICAL FITNESS AND HYGIENE 6980; SPORTS AND GAMES 8156

PHYSICAL FITNESS AND HYGIENE 6980 see also MEDICAL SCIENCES 5563; NUTRITION AND DIETETICS 6654; PUBLIC HEALTH AND SAFETY 7505; SPORTS AND GAMES 8156

PHYSICAL FITNESS AND HYGIENE—Abstracting, Bibliographies, Statistics 7001

PHYSICAL MEDICINE AND REHABILITATION see MEDICAL SCIENCES—Physical Medicine And Rehabilitation 6105

Physical Rehabilitation see MEDICAL SCIENCES—Physical Medicine And Rehabilitation 6105

Physical Therapy see MEDICAL SCIENCES—Physical Medicine And Rehabilitation 6105

PHYSICALLY IMPAIRED see HANDICAPPED—Physically Impaired 4077

Physician Assistants see MEDICAL SCIENCES 5563

Physicians see MEDICAL SCIENCES 5563

PHYSICS 7002 see also PHYSICS—Computer Applications 7050; PHYSICS—Electricity 7051; PHYSICS—Heat 7053; PHYSICS—Mechanics 7057; PHYSICS—Nuclear Physics 7064; PHYSICS—Optics 7073; PHYSICS—Sound 7085

PHYSICS—Abstracting, Bibliographies, Statistics 7047

PHYSICS—Computer Applications 7050

PHYSICS—Electricity 7051

PHYSICS—Heat 7053

PHYSICS—Mechanics 7057

PHYSICS—Nuclear Physics 7064

PHYSICS—Optics 7073

PHYSICS—Sound 7085 see also SOUND RECORDING AND REPRODUCTION 8151

PHYSIOLOGY see BIOLOGY—Physiology 917

Phytology see BIOLOGY—Botany 771

Phytopathology see BIOLOGY—Botany 771

Piano see MUSIC 6541

Pigeons see PETS 6802

Piloting see AERONAUTICS AND SPACE FLIGHT 40; TRANSPORTATION—Air Transport 8533

Pituitary Disorders see MEDICAL SCIENCES—Endocrinology 5883

Planned Parenthood see BIRTH CONTROL 971

Plant Breeding see AGRICULTURE—Crop Production And Soil 215; BIOLOGY—Botany 771; GARDENING AND HORTICULTURE 3721

Plant Physiology see BIOLOGY—Botany 771

Plasma see MEDICAL SCIENCES—Hematology 5933

Plasma Physics see PHYSICS 7002

Plastic Surgery see MEDICAL SCIENCES—Surgery 6234

PLASTICS 7090 see also CHEMISTRY—Physical Chemistry 2132; ENGINEERING—Chemical Engineering 3234

PLASTICS—Abstracting, Bibliographies, Statistics 7100

Platinum see JEWELRY, CLOCKS AND WATCHES 4564; METALLURGY 6303

Platonism see PHILOSOPHY 6901

Plays see LITERATURE 5247; THEATER 8464

Pleurisy see MEDICAL SCIENCES—Respiratory Diseases 6211

Plumbing see HEATING, PLUMBING AND REFRIGERATION 4115

Pneumonia see MEDICAL SCIENCES—Respiratory Diseases 6211

Podiatry see MEDICAL SCIENCES—Orthopedics And Traumatology 6054

POETRY see LITERATURE—Poetry 5415

Polar Regions see EARTH SCIENCES 2701; GEOGRAPHY 3996; SCIENCES: COMPREHENSIVE WORKS 7829

Police see CRIMINOLOGY AND LAW ENFORCEMENT 2642

Poliomyelitis see MEDICAL SCIENCES—Psychiatry And Neurology 6117

Political Asylum see POLITICAL SCIENCE—Civil Rights 7201; POLITICAL SCIENCE—International Relations 7219

Political Reviews see LITERARY AND POLITICAL REVIEWS 5204

POLITICAL SCIENCE 7101 see also LITERARY AND POLITICAL REVIEWS 5204; POLITICAL SCIENCE—Civil Rights 7201; POLITICAL SCIENCE—International Relations 7219; PUBLIC ADMINISTRATION 7417

POLITICAL SCIENCE—Abstracting, Bibliographies, Statistics 7198

POLITICAL SCIENCE—Civil Rights 7201

POLITICAL SCIENCE—International Relations 7219 see also LAW—International Law 4915

POLLUTION see ENVIRONMENTAL STUDIES—Pollution 3482

Polo see SPORTS AND GAMES—Horses And Horsemanship 8286

Polyandry see ANTHROPOLOGY 322; MATRIMONY 5556

Polygamy see ANTHROPOLOGY 322; MATRIMONY 5556

Polymers see CHEMISTRY 2047; ENGINEERING—Chemical Engineering 3234

Polynesian History see HISTORY—History Of Australasia And Other Areas 4191

Polyurethane see PAINTS AND PROTECTIVE COATINGS 6715; PLASTICS 7090

Ponies see SPORTS AND GAMES—Horses And Horsemanship 8286

Popular Culture see COMMUNICATIONS—Television And Cable 2374; COMMUNICATIONS—Video 2399; LIFESTYLE 5064; LITERATURE 5247; MOTION PICTURES 6488; MUSIC 6541; SOCIOLOGY 8084

Popular Music see MUSIC 6541

Population Control see BIRTH CONTROL 971; POPULATION STUDIES 7276

POPULATION STUDIES 7276 see also BIRTH CONTROL 971

POPULATION STUDIES—Abstracting, Bibliographies, Statistics 7296

Ports see TRANSPORTATION—Ships And Shipping 8638

Portuguese Language - Study and Teaching see LINGUISTICS 5088

Positivism see PHILOSOPHY 6901

Post-Colonial History see HISTORY—History Of Africa 4172; HISTORY—History Of Asia 4179; HISTORY—History Of Australasia And Other Areas 4191; HISTORY—History Of North And South America 4281

Postage Stamps see COMMUNICATIONS—Postal Affairs 2353; PHILATELY 6891

POSTAL AFFAIRS see COMMUNICATIONS—Postal Affairs 2353

Postcards see PHILATELY 6891

Postmarks see COMMUNICATIONS—Postal Affairs 2353; PHILATELY 6891

Potables see BEVERAGES 596

Potatoes see AGRICULTURE—Crop Production And Soil 215

Pottery see CERAMICS, GLASS AND POTTERY 2037

POULTRY AND LIVESTOCK see AGRICULTURE—Poultry And Livestock 276

Poverty see BUSINESS AND ECONOMICS—International Development And Assistance 1589; SOCIAL SERVICES AND WELFARE 8022; SOCIOLOGY 8084

Power Plants see ENERGY 3123

Pragmatism see PHILOSOPHY 6901

Prayer see RELIGIONS AND THEOLOGY 7619

Preaching see RELIGIONS AND THEOLOGY 7619

Precipitation see METEOROLOGY 6345

Precision Farming see AGRICULTURE—Crop Production And Soil 215

Precision Mechanics see INSTRUMENTS 4486

Prefabricated Houses see BUILDING AND CONSTRUCTION 974

Pregnancy see MEDICAL SCIENCES—Obstetrics And Gynecology 5984

Pregnancy Prevention see BIRTH CONTROL 971; MEDICAL SCIENCES—Obstetrics And Gynecology 5984

Prenatal Care and Medicine see MEDICAL SCIENCES—Obstetrics And Gynecology 5984

Presbyterianism see RELIGIONS AND THEOLOGY—Protestant 7743

Preschool Education see EDUCATION 2821

Presents see GIFTWARE AND TOYS 4059

Preservation and Conservation see ARCHITECTURE 425; ART 462

Preventive Medicine see PUBLIC HEALTH AND SAFETY 7505

Primary Education see EDUCATION 2821

Primatology see BIOLOGY—Zoology 929

PRINTING 7318

PRINTING—Abstracting, Bibliographies, Statistics 7329

PRINTING—Computer Applications 7329 see also COMPUTERS—Computer Graphics 2482

Prisons see CRIMINOLOGY AND LAW ENFORCEMENT 2642

Private Law see LAW—Civil Law 4826

Private Schools see EDUCATION—Guides To Schools And Colleges 0; EDUCATION—School Organization And Administration 3016

Pro-Choice see BIRTH CONTROL 971; POLITICAL SCIENCE—Civil Rights 7201

Pro-Life see BIRTH CONTROL 971; POLITICAL SCIENCE—Civil Rights 7201

Probability see MATHEMATICS 5463

Probate see LAW—Estate Planning 4900

Probation and Parole see CRIMINOLOGY AND LAW ENFORCEMENT 2642

Proctology see MEDICAL SCIENCES—Gastroenterology 5919

Produce see FOOD AND FOOD INDUSTRIES 3624

Produce Marketing see AGRICULTURE—Agricultural Economics 190

Product Finishing see PAINTS AND PROTECTIVE COATINGS 6715

Production Economics see AGRICULTURE—Agricultural Economics 190

PRODUCTION OF GOODS AND SERVICES see BUSINESS AND ECONOMICS—Production Of Goods And Services 1878

Professional Recruiting see OCCUPATIONS AND CAREERS 6691

Programmed Instruction see EDUCATION—Teaching Methods And Curriculum 3049

Programming, Automatic see COMPUTERS—Computer Programming 2504

Proofreading see JOURNALISM 4570; PRINTING 7318

Prose see LITERARY AND POLITICAL REVIEWS 5204; LITERATURE 5247

Prospecting see EARTH SCIENCES—Geology 2722; MINES AND MINING INDUSTRY 6456

Prostate see MEDICAL SCIENCES—Urology And Nephrology 6264

Prosthetics see MEDICAL SCIENCES—Orthopedics And Traumatology 6054

Protective Coatings see PAINTS AND PROTECTIVE COATINGS 6715

PROTESTANTISM see RELIGIONS AND THEOLOGY—Protestant 7743

Protozoology see BIOLOGY—Zoology 929

Psoriasis see MEDICAL SCIENCES—Dermatology And Venereology 5870

PSYCHIATRY AND NEUROLOGY see MEDICAL SCIENCES—Psychiatry And Neurology 6117

Psychic Phenomena see PARAPSYCHOLOGY AND OCCULTISM 6740

Psychical Research see PARAPSYCHOLOGY AND OCCULTISM 6740

Psychoanalysis see PSYCHOLOGY 7329

Psychological Testing see PSYCHOLOGY 7329

PSYCHOLOGY 7329 see also MEDICAL SCIENCES—Psychiatry And Neurology 6117

PSYCHOLOGY—Abstracting, Bibliographies, Statistics 7416

Psychopathology see MEDICAL SCIENCES—Psychiatry And Neurology 6117; PSYCHOLOGY 7329

Psychosomatic Medicine see MEDICAL SCIENCES 5563

Psychotherapy see MEDICAL SCIENCES—Psychiatry And Neurology 6117

PUBLIC ADMINISTRATION 7417 see also HOUSING AND URBAN PLANNING 4402; POLITICAL SCIENCE 7101; PUBLIC ADMINISTRATION—Computer Applications 7485; PUBLIC ADMINISTRATION—Municipal Government 7486; SOCIAL SERVICES AND WELFARE 8022

PUBLIC ADMINISTRATION—Abstracting, Bibliographies, Statistics 7478

PUBLIC ADMINISTRATION—Computer Applications 7485

PUBLIC ADMINISTRATION—Municipal Government 7486 see also HOUSING AND URBAN PLANNING 4402; SOCIAL SERVICES AND WELFARE 8022

Public Affairs see POLITICAL SCIENCE 7101; PUBLIC ADMINISTRATION 7417; SOCIAL SCIENCES: COMPREHENSIVE WORKS 7944

PUBLIC FINANCE, TAXATION see BUSINESS AND ECONOMICS—Public Finance, Taxation 1909

PUBLIC HEALTH AND SAFETY 7505 see also BIRTH CONTROL 971; DRUG ABUSE AND ALCOHOLISM 2689; ENVIRONMENTAL STUDIES 3400; FIRE PREVENTION 3575; FUNERALS 3719; HEALTH FACILITIES AND ADMINISTRATION 4086; MEDICAL SCIENCES 5563; OCCUPATIONAL HEALTH AND SAFETY 6672

PUBLIC HEALTH AND SAFETY—Abstracting, Bibliographies, Statistics 7547

Public Law see LAW—Constitutional Law 4845

Public Opinion see SOCIOLOGY 8084

Public Relations see ADVERTISING AND PUBLIC RELATIONS 18

Public Transportation see TRANSPORTATION 8489

Public Utilities see PETROLEUM AND GAS 6761; PUBLIC ADMINISTRATION 7417

Public Welfare see SOCIAL SERVICES AND WELFARE 8022

Public Works see BUILDING AND CONSTRUCTION 974; ENGINEERING—Civil Engineering 3258; HOUSING AND URBAN PLANNING 4402; PUBLIC ADMINISTRATION 7417

Publicity see ADVERTISING AND PUBLIC RELATIONS 18

Link to your serials resources and content with ulrichsweb.com

PUBLISHING AND BOOK TRADE 7550 see also BIBLIOGRAPHIES 614; JOURNALISM 4570; LIBRARY AND INFORMATION SCIENCES 4984; PATENTS, TRADEMARKS AND COPYRIGHTS 6744; PRINTING 7318

PUBLISHING AND BOOK TRADE—Abstracting, Bibliographies, Statistics 7577

PUBLISHING AND BOOK TRADE—Computer Applications 7579

Pulmonary Diseases see MEDICAL SCIENCES—Respiratory Diseases 6211

Pulp see PAPER AND PULP 6731

Puppets see HOBBIES 4326; THEATER 8464

Puzzles see SPORTS AND GAMES 8156

Pyrotechnics see ENGINEERING—Chemical Engineering 3234; FIRE PREVENTION 3575

Quakers see RELIGIONS AND THEOLOGY—Other Denominations And Sects 7732

Quality Control see BUSINESS AND ECONOMICS—Management 1722; METROLOGY AND STANDARDIZATION 6400

Quantum Chemistry see CHEMISTRY—Physical Chemistry 2132

Quantum Mechanics see PHYSICS 7002

Quarries see MINES AND MINING INDUSTRY 6456

Quaternary see EARTH SCIENCES—Geology 2722; PALEONTOLOGY 6722

Quilting see NEEDLEWORK 6636

Qur'an see RELIGIONS AND THEOLOGY—Islamic 7708

Race Relations see POLITICAL SCIENCE—Civil Rights 7201; SOCIOLOGY 8084

Racing see SPORTS AND GAMES—Horses And Horsemanship 8286; TRANSPORTATION—Automobiles 8553

Racism see POLITICAL SCIENCE—Civil Rights 7201

Racquetball see SPORTS AND GAMES—Ball Games 8219

Radar see COMMUNICATIONS 2310

Radiation see ASTRONOMY 567; BIOLOGY—Biophysics 751; CHEMISTRY—Physical Chemistry 2132; MEDICAL SCIENCES—Radiology And Nuclear Medicine 6191; PHYSICS—Nuclear Physics 7064

Radiation Chemistry see CHEMISTRY 2047

RADIO see COMMUNICATIONS—Radio 2356

Radio Advertising see ADVERTISING AND PUBLIC RELATIONS 18; COMMUNICATIONS—Radio 2356

Radioactive Waste see ENERGY—Nuclear Energy 3164; ENVIRONMENTAL STUDIES—Waste Management 3503

Radiobiology see BIOLOGY 648

Radiocarbon see PHYSICS—Nuclear Physics 7064

Radiological Contamination see ENERGY—Nuclear Energy 3164; ENVIRONMENTAL STUDIES—Waste Management 3503

RADIOLOGY AND NUCLEAR MEDICINE see MEDICAL SCIENCES—Radiology And Nuclear Medicine 6191

Railroad Engineering see TRANSPORTATION—Railroads 8614

RAILROADS see TRANSPORTATION—Railroads 8614

Railway Ties see FORESTS AND FORESTRY—Lumber And Wood 3709; TRANSPORTATION—Railroads 8614

Rainfall see METEOROLOGY 6345

Rainforest see CONSERVATION 2601; ENVIRONMENTAL STUDIES 3400; FORESTS AND FORESTRY 3682

Ramakrishna see RELIGIONS AND THEOLOGY—Hindu 7707

Rape see CRIMINOLOGY AND LAW ENFORCEMENT 2642; MEDICAL SCIENCES—Psychiatry And Neurology 6117

Rare Earths see CHEMISTRY—Inorganic Chemistry 2115

Rationalism see PHILOSOPHY 6901

Reading Guides and Aids see ABSTRACTING AND INDEXING SERVICES 5919; BIBLIOGRAPHIES 614; EDUCATION—Teaching Methods And Curriculum 3049; LIBRARY AND INFORMATION SCIENCES 4984

REAL ESTATE 7581 see also ARCHITECTURE 425; BUILDING AND CONSTRUCTION 974; BUSINESS AND ECONOMICS 1055; BUSINESS AND ECONOMICS—Investments 1608; HOUSING AND URBAN PLANNING 4402; LAW 4606

REAL ESTATE—Abstracting, Bibliographies, Statistics 7616

REAL ESTATE—Computer Applications 7619

Realism see ART 462; LITERATURE 5247; PHILOSOPHY 6901

Recipes see HOME ECONOMICS 4351

Recorded Music see MUSIC 6541; SOUND RECORDING AND REPRODUCTION 8151

Recreation see DANCE 2682; HOBBIES 4326; LEISURE AND RECREATION 4975; SPORTS AND GAMES 8156

Recreation Areas see CONSERVATION 2601; TRAVEL AND TOURISM 8679

Recreational Vehicles see TRANSPORTATION—Automobiles 8553

Recycling see ENVIRONMENTAL STUDIES—Waste Management 3503

Red Cross see SOCIAL SERVICES AND WELFARE 8022

Reed Instruments see MUSIC 6541

Reference Books see ENCYCLOPEDIAS AND GENERAL ALMANACS 3117

Refineries see PETROLEUM AND GAS 6761

Refinishing see HOW-TO AND DO-IT-YOURSELF 4437; PAINTS AND PROTECTIVE COATINGS 6715

Reforestation see FORESTS AND FORESTRY 3682

Reformed Church see RELIGIONS AND THEOLOGY—Protestant 7743

Refractories see CERAMICS, GLASS AND POTTERY 2037

Refrigeration see HEATING, PLUMBING AND REFRIGERATION 4115; PHYSICS—Heat 7053

Refugees see POLITICAL SCIENCE 7101; POLITICAL SCIENCE—International Relations 7219

Refuse see ENVIRONMENTAL STUDIES—Waste Management 3503

Regional Planning see HOUSING AND URBAN PLANNING 4402

Rehabilitation see EDUCATION—Special Education And Rehabilitation 3035; MEDICAL SCIENCES—Physical Medicine And Rehabilitation 6105; SOCIAL SERVICES AND WELFARE 8022

Reincarnation see NEW AGE PUBLICATIONS 6643; PARAPSYCHOLOGY AND OCCULTISM 6740; RELIGIONS AND THEOLOGY 7619

RELIGIONS AND THEOLOGY 7619 see also RELIGIONS AND THEOLOGY—Buddhist 7700; RELIGIONS AND THEOLOGY—Eastern Orthodox 7703; RELIGIONS AND THEOLOGY—Hindu 7707; RELIGIONS AND THEOLOGY—Islamic 7708; RELIGIONS AND THEOLOGY—Judaic 7717; RELIGIONS AND THEOLOGY—Other Denominations And Sects 7732; RELIGIONS AND THEOLOGY—Protestant 7743; RELIGIONS AND THEOLOGY—Roman Catholic 7781

RELIGIONS AND THEOLOGY—Abstracting, Bibliographies, Statistics 7697

RELIGIONS AND THEOLOGY—Buddhist 7700 see also ASIAN STUDIES 541

RELIGIONS AND THEOLOGY—Eastern Orthodox 7703

RELIGIONS AND THEOLOGY—Hindu 7707 see also ASIAN STUDIES 541

RELIGIONS AND THEOLOGY—Islamic 7708

RELIGIONS AND THEOLOGY—Judaic 7717 see also ETHNIC INTERESTS 3514

RELIGIONS AND THEOLOGY—Other Denominations And Sects 7732

RELIGIONS AND THEOLOGY—Protestant 7743

RELIGIONS AND THEOLOGY—Roman Catholic 7781

Religious Freedom see POLITICAL SCIENCE 7101

Religious History see RELIGIONS AND THEOLOGY 7619

Renal Disease see MEDICAL SCIENCES—Urology And Nephrology 6264

Repairs see HOW-TO AND DO-IT-YOURSELF 4437

Reproduction and Fertility see BIOLOGY 648

Reproductive System see MEDICAL SCIENCES—Obstetrics And Gynecology 5984; MEDICAL SCIENCES—Urology And Nephrology 6264

Reprography see PHOTOGRAPHY 6963

Reptiles see BIOLOGY—Zoology 929

Research and Development see TECHNOLOGY: COMPREHENSIVE WORKS 8415

Reservoirs see WATER RESOURCES 8817

Resins see PLASTICS 7090

Resorts see HOTELS AND RESTAURANTS 4380; TRAVEL AND TOURISM 8679

RESPIRATORY DISEASES see MEDICAL SCIENCES—Respiratory Diseases 6211

Restaurants see HOTELS AND RESTAURANTS 4380

Retailing see BUSINESS AND ECONOMICS—Marketing And Purchasing 1803

Retardation (Retarded) see EDUCATION—Special Education And Rehabilitation 3035; MEDICAL SCIENCES—Psychiatry And Neurology 6117

Retirement see BUSINESS AND ECONOMICS—Banking And Finance 1304; BUSINESS AND ECONOMICS—Labor And Industrial Relations 1661; GERONTOLOGY AND GERIATRICS 4037

Rheology see PHYSICS—Mechanics 7057

RHEUMATOLOGY see MEDICAL SCIENCES—Rheumatology 6221

Rhinology see MEDICAL SCIENCES—Otorhinolaryngology 6076

Rice see AGRICULTURE—Crop Production And Soil 215; AGRICULTURE—Feed, Flour And Grain 270

Right-to-Life Movement see BIRTH CONTROL 971; POLITICAL SCIENCE—Civil Rights 7201

ROADS AND TRAFFIC see TRANSPORTATION—Roads And Traffic 8628

Robbery see CRIMINOLOGY AND LAW ENFORCEMENT 2642

ROBOTICS see COMPUTERS—Artificial Intelligence 2444; COMPUTERS—Robotics 2584

Rock see EARTH SCIENCES—Geology 2722; MINES AND MINING INDUSTRY 6456

Rock and Roll see MUSIC 6541

Rock Climbing see SPORTS AND GAMES—Outdoor Life 8300

Rockets see AERONAUTICS AND SPACE FLIGHT 40

Rodeo see SPORTS AND GAMES—Horses And Horsemanship 8286

Roentgenology see MEDICAL SCIENCES—Radiology And Nuclear Medicine 6191

Roller Skating see SPORTS AND GAMES 8156

ROMAN CATHOLICISM see RELIGIONS AND THEOLOGY—Roman Catholic 7781

Roofing see BUILDING AND CONSTRUCTION 974

RUBBER 7824 see also ENGINEERING—Chemical Engineering 3234; PLASTICS 7090

RUBBER—Abstracting, Bibliographies, Statistics 7827

Rugby see SPORTS AND GAMES—Ball Games 8219

Running see PHYSICAL FITNESS AND HYGIENE 6980; SPORTS AND GAMES 8156

Safety Education see BUSINESS AND ECONOMICS—Labor And Industrial Relations 1661; FIRE PREVENTION 3575; OCCUPATIONAL HEALTH AND SAFETY 6672; PUBLIC HEALTH AND SAFETY 7505; TRANSPORTATION—Roads And Traffic 8628

Sailboarding see SPORTS AND GAMES—Outdoor Life 8300

Sailing see SPORTS AND GAMES—Boats And Boating 8270

Salaries see BUSINESS AND ECONOMICS—Labor And Industrial Relations 1661; BUSINESS AND ECONOMICS—Personnel Management 1855

Sales Promotion see ADVERTISING AND PUBLIC RELATIONS 18

Salesmanship see BUSINESS AND ECONOMICS—Marketing And Purchasing 1803

Salvation Army see RELIGIONS AND THEOLOGY—Other Denominations And Sects 7732; SOCIAL SERVICES AND WELFARE 8022

Samsara see RELIGIONS AND THEOLOGY—Buddhist 7700; RELIGIONS AND THEOLOGY—Hindu 7707

Sanitary Engineering see PUBLIC HEALTH AND SAFETY 7505

Sanitation see ENGINEERING—Civil Engineering 3258; ENVIRONMENTAL STUDIES—Waste Management 3503; PHYSICAL FITNESS AND HYGIENE 6980; PUBLIC HEALTH AND SAFETY 7505

Satanism see PARAPSYCHOLOGY AND OCCULTISM 6740; RELIGIONS AND THEOLOGY—Other Denominations And Sects 7732

Satellite Communications see COMMUNICATIONS 2310; COMMUNICATIONS—Computer Applications 2349; COMMUNICATIONS—Television And Cable 2374

Satire see LITERARY AND POLITICAL REVIEWS 5204

Savings and Loan see BUSINESS AND ECONOMICS—Banking And Finance 1304

Scales see INSTRUMENTS 4486; METROLOGY AND STANDARDIZATION 6400

Schizophrenia see MEDICAL SCIENCES—Psychiatry And Neurology 6117

Scholarships see EDUCATION—Higher Education 2963

Scholasticism see PHILOSOPHY 6901

SCHOOL ORGANIZATION AND ADMINISTRATION see EDUCATION—School Organization And Administration 3016

SCIENCE FICTION, FANTASY, HORROR see LITERATURE—Science Fiction, Fantasy, Horror 5439

SCIENCES: COMPREHENSIVE WORKS 7829

SCIENCES: COMPREHENSIVE WORKS—Abstracting, Bibliographies, Statistics 7935

SCIENCES: COMPREHENSIVE WORKS—Computer Applications 7939

Scientific Jurisprudence see MEDICAL SCIENCES—Forensic Sciences 5912

Scientology see RELIGIONS AND THEOLOGY—Other Denominations And Sects 7732

Scooters see SPORTS AND GAMES—Bicycles And Motorcycles 8252

Scouting see CHILDREN AND YOUTH—About 2142; CHILDREN AND YOUTH—For 2174

Screen Printing see PRINTING 7318

Scuba Diving see LEISURE AND RECREATION 4975; SPORTS AND GAMES—Outdoor Life 8300

Sculpture see ART 462

Seafood see FISH AND FISHERIES 3582; FOOD AND FOOD INDUSTRIES 3624; HOME ECONOMICS 4351

Sealants see PAINTS AND PROTECTIVE COATINGS 6715

Seaweed see BIOLOGY—Botany 771; EARTH SCIENCES—Oceanography 2799

Secondary Education *see* EDUCATION **2821**

Securities *see* BUSINESS AND ECONOMICS—Investments **1608**

SECURITY *see* CRIMINOLOGY AND LAW ENFORCEMENT—Security **2676**

Sediment Data *see* ENGINEERING—Hydraulic Engineering **3360**

Sedimentology *see* EARTH SCIENCES—Geophysics **2776**

Seed Crops *see* AGRICULTURE—Feed, Flour And Grain **270**

Seeds *see* AGRICULTURE—Crop Production And Soil **215**

Segregation *see* POLITICAL SCIENCE—Civil Rights **7201**

Seismology *see* EARTH SCIENCES—Geophysics **2776**

Self-help *see* NEW AGE PUBLICATIONS **6643**; PSYCHOLOGY **7329**

Self-instruction *see* EDUCATION—Adult Education **2937**

Selling *see* ADVERTISING AND PUBLIC RELATIONS **18**; BUSINESS AND ECONOMICS—Marketing And Purchasing **1803**

Semantics *see* LINGUISTICS **5088**

Semiconductors *see* PHYSICS—Electricity **7051**

Seminaries *see* EDUCATION—Higher Education **2963**; RELIGIONS AND THEOLOGY **7619**

Semiotics *see* HUMANITIES: COMPREHENSIVE WORKS **4439**; LINGUISTICS **5088**; PHILOSOPHY **6901**

Senior Citizens *see* GERONTOLOGY AND GERIATRICS **4037**

Separatist Movement *see* POLITICAL SCIENCE—International Relations **7219**

Sephardim *see* ETHNIC INTERESTS **3514**; RELIGIONS AND THEOLOGY—Judaic **7717**

Serology *see* MEDICAL SCIENCES—Allergology And Immunology **5752**

Service Stations *see* TRANSPORTATION—Automobiles **8553**

Sewage and Waste Treatment *see* ENVIRONMENTAL STUDIES—Waste Management **3503**; PUBLIC ADMINISTRATION **7417**; PUBLIC HEALTH AND SAFETY **7505**; WATER RESOURCES **8817**

Sewing *see* CLOTHING TRADE—Fashions **2251**; NEEDLEWORK **6636**

Sex Education *see* MEDICAL SCIENCES—Communicable Diseases **5807**; PHYSICAL FITNESS AND HYGIENE **6980**

Sexology *see* MEDICAL SCIENCES **5563**; PSYCHOLOGY **7329**; SOCIAL SCIENCES: COMPREHENSIVE WORKS **7944**

Sexual Dysfunctions *see* MEDICAL SCIENCES—Psychiatry And Neurology **6117**

Sexual Harassment *see* BUSINESS AND ECONOMICS—Labor And Industrial Relations **1661**; LAW **4606**; POLITICAL SCIENCE—Civil Rights **7201**

Sexually Transmitted Diseases *see* MEDICAL SCIENCES—Communicable Diseases **5807**; MEDICAL SCIENCES—Dermatology And Venereology **5870**

Shamanism *see* ANTHROPOLOGY **322**; RELIGIONS AND THEOLOGY—Other Denominations And Sects **7732**

Shareware *see* COMPUTERS—Computer Networks **2495**

Shari'ah *see* LAW **4606**; RELIGIONS AND THEOLOGY—Islamic **7708**

Sheet Metal *see* METALLURGY **6303**

Shellac *see* PAINTS AND PROTECTIVE COATINGS **6715**

Shi'ism *see* RELIGIONS AND THEOLOGY—Islamic **7708**

Shintoism *see* RELIGIONS AND THEOLOGY—Other Denominations And Sects **7732**

Shipbuilding *see* TRANSPORTATION—Ships And Shipping **8638**

Shipping *see* COMMUNICATIONS—Postal Affairs **2353**; TRANSPORTATION **8489**

SHIPS AND SHIPPING *see* TRANSPORTATION—Ships And Shipping **8638**

Shivism *see* RELIGIONS AND THEOLOGY—Hindu **7707**

SHOES AND BOOTS **7940** *see also* LEATHER AND FUR INDUSTRIES **4972**

SHOES AND BOOTS—Abstracting, Bibliographies, Statistics **7942**

Shooting *see* SPORTS AND GAMES—Outdoor Life **8300**

Shorthand *see* BUSINESS AND ECONOMICS—Office Equipment And Services **1849**

Shortwave *see* COMMUNICATIONS—Radio **2356**

Shortwave Electronics *see* ELECTRONICS **3089**

Sick Building Syndrome *see* OCCUPATIONAL HEALTH AND SAFETY **6672**

Sickle-cell Anemia *see* MEDICAL SCIENCES—Hematology **5933**

Siding *see* BUILDING AND CONSTRUCTION **974**

Sign Language *see* HANDICAPPED—Hearing Impaired **4071**; LINGUISTICS **5088**

Sign Manufacturing *see* ADVERTISING AND PUBLIC RELATIONS **18**

Sikhism *see* RELIGIONS AND THEOLOGY—Other Denominations And Sects **7732**

Silicates *see* CERAMICS, GLASS AND POTTERY **2037**

Silicosis *see* MEDICAL SCIENCES **5563**

Silk *see* CLOTHING TRADE **2244**; TEXTILE INDUSTRIES AND FABRICS **8447**

Silver *see* JEWELRY, CLOCKS AND WATCHES **4564**; METALLURGY **6303**; MINES AND MINING INDUSTRY **6456**

Silviculture *see* FORESTS AND FORESTRY **3682**

SINGLES' INTERESTS AND LIFESTYLES **7942**

Site Selection *see* HOUSING AND URBAN PLANNING **4402**; REAL ESTATE **7581**

Skating *see* SPORTS AND GAMES **8156**

Skeet Skooting *see* SPORTS AND GAMES—Outdoor Life **8300**

Skepticism *see* PHILOSOPHY **6901**

Skiing *see* SPORTS AND GAMES—Outdoor Life **8300**

Skin Care *see* BEAUTY CULTURE **585**

Skin Disorders *see* MEDICAL SCIENCES—Dermatology And Venereology **5870**

Slang *see* LINGUISTICS **5088**

Slavery *see* HISTORY **4128**; POLITICAL SCIENCE—Civil Rights **7201**; SOCIOLOGY **8084**

Slavonic Languages - Study and Teaching *see* LINGUISTICS **5088**

SMALL BUSINESS *see* BUSINESS AND ECONOMICS—Small Business **1956**

Smoking *see* DRUG ABUSE AND ALCOHOLISM **2689**; PHYSICAL FITNESS AND HYGIENE **6980**; PUBLIC HEALTH AND SAFETY **7505**; TOBACCO **8485**

Snack Foods *see* FOOD AND FOOD INDUSTRIES—Bakers And Confectioners **3670**

Snowmobiles *see* SPORTS AND GAMES—Outdoor Life **8300**

Soap *see* BEAUTY CULTURE—Perfumes And Cosmetics **592**

Soccer *see* SPORTS AND GAMES—Ball Games **8219**

Social Insurance *see* INSURANCE **4490**; SOCIAL SERVICES AND WELFARE **8022**

Social Medicine *see* PUBLIC HEALTH AND SAFETY **7505**

Social Psychology *see* PSYCHOLOGY **7329**; SOCIOLOGY **8084**

SOCIAL SCIENCES: COMPREHENSIVE WORKS **7944**

SOCIAL SCIENCES: COMPREHENSIVE WORKS—Abstracting, Bibliographies, Statistics **8019**

Social Security *see* INSURANCE **4490**; SOCIAL SERVICES AND WELFARE **8022**

SOCIAL SERVICES AND WELFARE **8022** *see also* DRUG ABUSE AND ALCOHOLISM **2689**; HANDICAPPED **4063**; PUBLIC HEALTH AND SAFETY **7505**

SOCIAL SERVICES AND WELFARE—Abstracting, Bibliographies, Statistics **8079**

Socialism *see* BUSINESS AND ECONOMICS—Economic Systems And Theories, Economic History **1535**; POLITICAL SCIENCE **7101**

Society of Friends *see* RELIGIONS AND THEOLOGY—Other Denominations And Sects **7732**

SOCIOLOGY **8084** *see also* FOLKLORE **3614**; POPULATION STUDIES **7276**; SOCIAL SCIENCES: COMPREHENSIVE WORKS **7944**; SOCIAL SERVICES AND WELFARE **8022**

SOCIOLOGY—Abstracting, Bibliographies, Statistics **8148**

SOCIOLOGY—Computer Applications **8151**

Soft Drinks *see* BEVERAGES **596**

Softball *see* SPORTS AND GAMES—Ball Games **8219**

SOFTWARE *see* COMPUTERS—Software **2587**

Soil *see* AGRICULTURE—Crop Production And Soil **215**; CONSERVATION **2601**; ENGINEERING—Civil Engineering **3258**

Soil Pollution *see* ENVIRONMENTAL STUDIES—Pollution **3482**

SOLAR ENERGY *see* ENERGY—Solar Energy **3176**

Soldering *see* METALLURGY—Welding **6342**

Soldiers *see* MILITARY **6408**

Solid Waste *see* ENVIRONMENTAL STUDIES—Waste Management **3503**

Somatology *see* ANTHROPOLOGY **322**

Sonography *see* MEDICAL SCIENCES—Radiology And Nuclear Medicine **6191**; PHYSICS—Sound **7085**

Sophism *see* PHILOSOPHY **6901**

Sororities *see* COLLEGE AND ALUMNI **2271**

SOUND *see* PHYSICS—Sound **7085**

SOUND RECORDING AND REPRODUCTION **8151** *see also* MUSIC **6541**

SOUND RECORDING AND REPRODUCTION—Abstracting, Bibliographies, Statistics **8156**

SOUND RECORDING AND REPRODUCTION—Computer Applications **8156**

South American History *see* HISTORY—History Of North And South America **4281**

Souvenirs *see* GIFTWARE AND TOYS **4059**

Space Flight *see* AERONAUTICS AND SPACE FLIGHT **40**

Space Sciences *see* AERONAUTICS AND SPACE FLIGHT **40**; ASTRONOMY **567**

Spacecraft *see* AERONAUTICS AND SPACE FLIGHT **40**

Spanish Language - Study and Teaching *see* LINGUISTICS **5088**

Spearfishing *see* SPORTS AND GAMES—Outdoor Life **8300**

SPECIAL EDUCATION AND REHABILITATION *see* EDUCATION—Special Education And Rehabilitation **3035**

Spectrometry *see* CHEMISTRY—Analytical Chemistry **2096**; PHYSICS—Optics **7073**

Spectroscopy *see* CHEMISTRY—Analytical Chemistry **2096**; PHYSICS—Optics **7073**

Spectrum *see* PHYSICS—Optics **7073**

Speech - Study and Teaching *see* LINGUISTICS **5088**

Speech and Hearing Disorders *see* EDUCATION—Special Education And Rehabilitation **3035**; HANDICAPPED—Hearing Impaired **4071**; MEDICAL SCIENCES—Psychiatry And Neurology **6117**

Speech Study and Teaching *see* EDUCATION—Special Education And Rehabilitation **3035**

Speleology *see* EARTH SCIENCES—Geology **2722**

Spices *see* FOOD AND FOOD INDUSTRIES **3624**

Spina Bifida *see* MEDICAL SCIENCES **5563**

Spinal Cord *see* MEDICAL SCIENCES—Psychiatry And Neurology **6117**

Spinning *see* NEEDLEWORK **6636**

Spiritualism *see* NEW AGE PUBLICATIONS **6643**; PARAPSYCHOLOGY AND OCCULTISM **6740**

Spleen *see* MEDICAL SCIENCES—Hematology **5933**

Spontaneous Abortion *see* MEDICAL SCIENCES—Obstetrics And Gynecology **5984**

Sport Utility Vehicles *see* TRANSPORTATION—Automobiles **8553**

Sporting Goods *see* SPORTS AND GAMES **8156**

SPORTS AND GAMES **8156** *see also* MEDICAL SCIENCES—Sports Medicine **6228**; SPORTS AND GAMES—Ball Games **8219**; SPORTS AND GAMES—Bicycles And Motorcycles **8252**; SPORTS AND GAMES—Boats And Boating **8270**; SPORTS AND GAMES—Horses And Horsemanship **8286**; SPORTS AND GAMES—Outdoor Life **8300**

SPORTS AND GAMES—Abstracting, Bibliographies, Statistics **8217**

SPORTS AND GAMES—Ball Games **8219**

SPORTS AND GAMES—Bicycles And Motorcycles **8252**

SPORTS AND GAMES—Boats And Boating **8270**

SPORTS AND GAMES—Horses And Horsemanship **8286**

SPORTS AND GAMES—Outdoor Life **8300**

Sports Cards *see* HOBBIES **4326**

Sports Cars *see* TRANSPORTATION—Automobiles **8553**

SPORTS MEDICINE *see* MEDICAL SCIENCES—Sports Medicine **6228**

Sportswear *see* CLOTHING TRADE **2244**

Spreadsheets *see* COMPUTERS—Data Base Management **2528**; COMPUTERS—Software **2587**

Stage *see* THEATER **8464**

Stained Glass *see* ART **462**; ARTS AND HANDICRAFTS **530**; CERAMICS, GLASS AND POTTERY **2037**

Stainless Steel *see* METALLURGY **6303**

Stamps *see* COMMUNICATIONS—Postal Affairs **2353**; PHILATELY **6891**

Standards *see* METROLOGY AND STANDARDIZATION **6400**

Stationery and Office Equipment *see* BUSINESS AND ECONOMICS—Office Equipment And Services **1849**

STATISTICS **8343** *see also* MATHEMATICS **5463**; POPULATION STUDIES **7276**; and also Abstracting, Bibliographies, Statistics subheadings under specific subjects

STD (Sexually Transmitted Diseases) *see* MEDICAL SCIENCES—Communicable Diseases **5807**; MEDICAL SCIENCES—Dermatology And Venereology **5870**

Steel *see* METALLURGY **6303**

Stenography *see* BUSINESS AND ECONOMICS—Office Equipment And Services **1849**

Stereo Equipment *see* ELECTRONICS **3089**; SOUND RECORDING AND REPRODUCTION **8151**

Sterility *see* MEDICAL SCIENCES—Obstetrics And Gynecology **5984**; MEDICAL SCIENCES—Urology And Nephrology **6264**; MEN'S HEALTH **6283**; WOMEN'S HEALTH **8843**

Sterilization *see* BIRTH CONTROL **971**

Steroids *see* BIOLOGY—Biochemistry **721**; MEDICAL SCIENCES—Endocrinology **5883**; PHARMACY AND PHARMACOLOGY **6817**

Stock and Stock-Breeding *see* AGRICULTURE—Poultry And Livestock **276**

Stocks and Bonds see BUSINESS AND ECONOMICS—Investments 1608

Stoicism see PHILOSOPHY 6901

Stomach Disorders see MEDICAL SCIENCES—Gastroenterology 5919

Stomatology see MEDICAL SCIENCES—Dentistry 5832

Stone see EARTH SCIENCES—Geology 2722; MINES AND MINING INDUSTRY 6456

Store Display and Promotion see ADVERTISING AND PUBLIC RELATIONS 18

Storms see METEOROLOGY 6345

Stress see PSYCHOLOGY 7329

Stringed Instruments see MUSIC 6541

Structural Design see BUILDING AND CONSTRUCTION 974; ENGINEERING—Civil Engineering 3258

Structural Engineering see BUILDING AND CONSTRUCTION 974; ENGINEERING—Civil Engineering 3258

Student Aid see EDUCATION 2821

Student Exchange Programs see EDUCATION—International Education Programs 3011

Substance Abuse see DRUG ABUSE AND ALCOHOLISM 2689

Suffrage see POLITICAL SCIENCE—Civil Rights 7201

Sufism see RELIGIONS AND THEOLOGY—Islamic 7708

Sugar see AGRICULTURE—Crop Production And Soil 215; FOOD AND FOOD INDUSTRIES 3624; FOOD AND FOOD INDUSTRIES—Bakers And Confectioners 3670

Suicide Prevention see MEDICAL SCIENCES—Psychiatry And Neurology 6117; SOCIAL SERVICES AND WELFARE 8022

Sunnis see RELIGIONS AND THEOLOGY—Islamic 7708

Superconductors see ENGINEERING—Electrical Engineering 3293; PHYSICS 7002

Supermarkets see FOOD AND FOOD INDUSTRIES—Grocery Trade 3676

Supernatural see PARAPSYCHOLOGY AND OCCULTISM 6740

Supersonic Transport see AERONAUTICS AND SPACE FLIGHT 40; TRANSPORTATION—Air Transport 8533

Surfing see SPORTS AND GAMES—Outdoor Life 8300

SURGERY see MEDICAL SCIENCES—Surgery 6234

Surgical Instruments see MEDICAL SCIENCES—Surgery 6234

Surrogate Motherhood see LAW—Family And Matrimonial Law 4906; MEDICAL SCIENCES—Obstetrics And Gynecology 5984

Surveying see ENGINEERING—Civil Engineering 3258; GEOGRAPHY 3996

Swimming see SPORTS AND GAMES 8156

Synagogue see RELIGIONS AND THEOLOGY—Judaic 7717

Synthetic Fabrics see TEXTILE INDUSTRIES AND FABRICS 8447

Table Tennis see SPORTS AND GAMES—Ball Games 8219

Tailoring see CLOTHING TRADE 2244

Talking Books see HANDICAPPED—Visually Impaired 4078

Talmud see RELIGIONS AND THEOLOGY—Judaic 7717

Taoism see PHILOSOPHY 6901; RELIGIONS AND THEOLOGY—Other Denominations And Sects 7732

Tape Drives see COMPUTERS—Hardware 2538

Tape Recording see SOUND RECORDING AND REPRODUCTION 8151

Tapestry see NEEDLEWORK 6636

Tariffs see BUSINESS AND ECONOMICS—International Commerce 1551; BUSINESS AND ECONOMICS—Public Finance, Taxation 1909

Tatting see NEEDLEWORK 6636

Taverns see HOTELS AND RESTAURANTS 4380

TAXATION see BUSINESS AND ECONOMICS—Public Finance, Taxation 1909

Taxicabs see TRANSPORTATION—Automobiles 8553

Tea see BEVERAGES 596

TEACHING METHODS AND CURRICULUM see EDUCATION—Teaching Methods And Curriculum 3049

TECHNOLOGY: COMPREHENSIVE WORKS 8415

TECHNOLOGY: COMPREHENSIVE WORKS—Abstracting, Bibliographies, Statistics 8446

Teenagers see CHILDREN AND YOUTH—About 2142; CHILDREN AND YOUTH—For 2174; MEDICAL SCIENCES—Psychiatry And Neurology 6117

Teeth see MEDICAL SCIENCES—Dentistry 5832

Telecommunications see COMMUNICATIONS 2310; ENGINEERING—Electrical Engineering 3293

Telefacsimile see COMMUNICATIONS—Computer Applications 2349

Telegraph see COMMUNICATIONS—Telephone And Telegraph 2365

Telepathy see NEW AGE PUBLICATIONS 6643; PARAPSYCHOLOGY AND OCCULTISM 6740

TELEPHONE AND TELEGRAPH see COMMUNICATIONS—Telephone And Telegraph 2365

TELEVISION AND CABLE see COMMUNICATIONS—Television And Cable 2374

Tendinitis see MEDICAL SCIENCES—Rheumatology 6221

Tennis see SPORTS AND GAMES—Ball Games 8219

Teratology see BIOLOGY 648

Terminals see COMPUTERS—Hardware 2538

Terrorism see CRIMINOLOGY AND LAW ENFORCEMENT 2642; POLITICAL SCIENCE—International Relations 7219

Textbooks see EDUCATION—Teaching Methods And Curriculum 3049; PUBLISHING AND BOOK TRADE 7550

TEXTILE INDUSTRIES AND FABRICS 8447 see also CLEANING AND DYEING 2242; CLOTHING TRADE 2244

TEXTILE INDUSTRIES AND FABRICS—Abstracting, Bibliographies, Statistics 8463

TEXTILE INDUSTRIES AND FABRICS—Computer Applications 8464

Thanatology see MEDICAL SCIENCES—Psychiatry And Neurology 6117; PSYCHOLOGY 7329

THEATER 8464 see also DANCE 2682

THEATER—Abstracting, Bibliographies, Statistics 8485

Theology see RELIGIONS AND THEOLOGY 7619

THEORY OF COMPUTING see COMPUTERS—Theory Of Computing 2600

Theosophy see PHILOSOPHY 6901; RELIGIONS AND THEOLOGY 7619

Therapeutic Systems see ALTERNATIVE MEDICINE 305

Theraphy see MEDICAL SCIENCES—Physical Medicine And Rehabilitation 6105

Theravada see RELIGIONS AND THEOLOGY—Buddhist 7700

Thermodynamics see CHEMISTRY—Physical Chemistry 2132; PHYSICS—Heat 7053

Thermometers see INSTRUMENTS 4486; METROLOGY AND STANDARDIZATION 6400

Thermophysics see PHYSICS—Heat 7053

Thoracic Surgery see MEDICAL SCIENCES—Surgery 6234

Thoroughfares see TRANSPORTATION—Roads And Traffic 8628

Thrombosis see MEDICAL SCIENCES—Cardiovascular Diseases 5775

Tiles see BUILDING AND CONSTRUCTION 974; CERAMICS, GLASS AND POTTERY 2037; INTERIOR DESIGN AND DECORATION 4531

Timber see FORESTS AND FORESTRY—Lumber And Wood 3709

Timetables see TRANSPORTATION 8489

Tin see METALLURGY 6303; MINES AND MINING INDUSTRY 6456

Tires see RUBBER 7824; TRANSPORTATION—Automobiles 8553

TOBACCO 8485 see also AGRICULTURE—Crop Production And Soil 215

TOBACCO—Abstracting, Bibliographies, Statistics 8489

Toiletries see BEAUTY CULTURE 585

Tools see MACHINERY 5449

Topology see MATHEMATICS 5463

Toponyms see GEOGRAPHY 3996; LINGUISTICS 5088

Torah see RELIGIONS AND THEOLOGY—Judaic 7717

Tornados see METEOROLOGY 6345

Totalitarianism see POLITICAL SCIENCE 7101

Touring see TRAVEL AND TOURISM 8679

Tourist Camps see HOTELS AND RESTAURANTS 4380; TRAVEL AND TOURISM 8679

Town Planning see HOUSING AND URBAN PLANNING 4402

Toxicology see ENVIRONMENTAL STUDIES—Toxicology And Environmental Safety 3493; MEDICAL SCIENCES 5563; PHARMACY AND PHARMACOLOGY 6817

TOXICOLOGY AND ENVIRONMENTAL SAFETY see ENVIRONMENTAL STUDIES—Toxicology And Environmental Safety 3493

Toys see GIFTWARE AND TOYS 4059

Track and Field see SPORTS AND GAMES—Outdoor Life 8300

Tractors see AGRICULTURE—Agricultural Equipment 209

Trade see BUSINESS AND ECONOMICS—Domestic Commerce 1425; BUSINESS AND ECONOMICS—International Commerce 1551

TRADE AND INDUSTRIAL DIRECTORIES see BUSINESS AND ECONOMICS—Trade And Industrial Directories 1970

Trade Shows see MEETINGS AND CONGRESSES 6277

Trade Unions see LABOR UNIONS 4589

Trademarks see PATENTS, TRADEMARKS AND COPYRIGHTS 6744

Traditions see ETHNIC INTERESTS 3514; FOLKLORE 3614

Traffic see TRANSPORTATION—Roads And Traffic 8628

Trailers see TRANSPORTATION 8489

Transistors see COMMUNICATIONS—Radio 2356; ELECTRONICS 3089

Translation Services see LINGUISTICS 5088

Transmittable Diseases see MEDICAL SCIENCES—Communicable Diseases 5807

TRANSPORTATION 8489 see also TRANSPORTATION—Air Transport 8533; TRANSPORTATION—Automobiles 8553; TRANSPORTATION—Computer Applications 8614; TRANSPORTATION—Railroads 8614; TRANSPORTATION—Roads And Traffic 8628; TRANSPORTATION—Ships And Shipping 8638; TRANSPORTATION—Trucks And Trucking 8666

Transportation Law see LAW 4606

TRANSPORTATION—Abstracting, Bibliographies, Statistics 8520

TRANSPORTATION—Air Transport 8533

TRANSPORTATION—Automobiles 8553

TRANSPORTATION—Computer Applications 8614

TRANSPORTATION—Railroads 8614

TRANSPORTATION—Roads And Traffic 8628 see also ENGINEERING—Civil Engineering 3258

TRANSPORTATION—Ships And Shipping 8638

TRANSPORTATION—Trucks And Trucking 8666

Trapping see LEATHER AND FUR INDUSTRIES 4972

Trapshooting see SPORTS AND GAMES—Outdoor Life 8300

Traumatology see MEDICAL SCIENCES—Orthopedics And Traumatology 6054

TRAVEL AND TOURISM 8679 see also GEOGRAPHY 3996; HOTELS AND RESTAURANTS 4380; TRAVEL AND TOURISM—Airline Inflight And Hotel Inroom 8781

TRAVEL AND TOURISM—Abstracting, Bibliographies, Statistics 8777

TRAVEL AND TOURISM—Airline Inflight And Hotel Inroom 8781

Treaties see LAW—International Law 4915

Trees see FORESTS AND FORESTRY 3682; GARDENING AND HORTICULTURE 3721

Triage see MEDICAL SCIENCES—Orthopedics And Traumatology 6054

Trial Law see LAW—Criminal Law 4883

Tribology see ENGINEERING—Mechanical Engineering 3372

Trigonometry see MATHEMATICS 5463

Trimurti see RELIGIONS AND THEOLOGY—Hindu 7707

Troops see MILITARY 6408

Tropical Diseases see MEDICAL SCIENCES—Communicable Diseases 5807

Tropical Fish see BIOLOGY—Zoology 929; PETS 6802

TRUCKS AND TRUCKING see TRANSPORTATION—Trucks And Trucking 8666

Tsunami see EARTH SCIENCES—Geophysics 2776; METEOROLOGY 6345

Tuberculosis see MEDICAL SCIENCES—Respiratory Diseases 6211

Tumors see MEDICAL SCIENCES—Oncology 6007

Turning see BUILDING AND CONSTRUCTION—Carpentry And Woodwork 1049

Tutoring see EDUCATION—Teaching Methods And Curriculum 3049

Typewriters see BUSINESS AND ECONOMICS—Office Equipment And Services 1849

Typography see PRINTING 7318

U.S. Armed Forces see MILITARY 6408

UFO see AERONAUTICS AND SPACE FLIGHT 40; PARAPSYCHOLOGY AND OCCULTISM 6740

Ulcers see MEDICAL SCIENCES—Gastroenterology 5919

Ultrasonics see PHYSICS—Sound 7085

Ultrasonography see MEDICAL SCIENCES—Radiology And Nuclear Medicine 6191

Ultrasound see MEDICAL SCIENCES—Radiology And Nuclear Medicine 6191

Ultraviolet see PHYSICS—Optics 7073

Underground Organizations see POLITICAL SCIENCE 7101

Underground Periodicals see LITERARY AND POLITICAL REVIEWS 5204; POLITICAL SCIENCE 7101

Cessations

This section includes abbreviated entries for serials for which cessation was noted in the Ulrich's database during the previous year. They are listed alphabetically by title.

500   USA   ISSN 1062-2195
A A A S HANDBOOK. 19??-199?. a. American Association for the Advancement of Science, 1200 New York Ave, NW, Washington, DC 20005.

687   USA
A A M A COMMITTEE MANUAL. 19??-1996. a. American Apparel & Footwear Association, 1601 N Kent St, Ste. 1200, Arlington, VA 22209.

792 362.7   USA
A A T E NEWSLETTER. (American Alliance for Theatre & Education) 1987-2008 (Dec.). q. American Alliance for Theatre & Education, 7475 Wisconsin Ave, Ste 300A, Bethesda, MD 20814.

332.1   USA   ISSN 1530-1125
A B A BANKERS NEWS. 1981-200?. bi-w. American Bankers Association, 1120 Connecticut Ave N W, Washington, DC 20036.

028   NLD   ISSN 1871-6202
A B C'S BETWEEN THE COVERS. 1998-2007. q. American Book Center, Spul 12, Amsterdam, 1012 XA, Netherlands.

690 346   DNK   ISSN 1603-4546
A B L O NYT; andels- og ejerboligbladet. (Andelsbolighavernes Lands-Organisation) 1987-2002. 5/yr. Landsforeningen af Private Andels- & Ejerboligforeninger i Danmark, Ringstedvej 503, Bjaeverskov, 4632, Denmark.

616.1   USA   ISSN 1556-8571   CODEN: ACJREE
A C C CARDIOSOURCE REVIEW JOURNAL. 1992-2008. m. Elsevier Inc., 360 Park Ave S, New York, NY 10010.

381.33   AUS   ISSN 1832-9470
A C M A CONSUMER BULLETIN. 1997-2005. q. Australian Communications and Media Authority (A C M A), Box 78, Belconnen, ACT 2616, Australia.

540   USA   ISSN 0065-7719   CODEN: ACMOAG
A C S MONOGRAPH SERIES. 19??-1998 (vol.191). irreg. Oxford University Press, 2001 Evans Rd, Cary, NC 27513.

796.332   AUS
A C T A F L PROGRAMME. (Australian Capital Territory Australian Football League) 1946-1991. w. A C T Australian Football League, PO Box 364, Woden, ACT 2606, Australia.

617.96   FRA   ISSN 1168-1128
A C T U A R. (Actualites en Anesthesie Reanimation) 1975-199?. a. Arnette, 1 rue Eugene et Armand Peugeot, Rueil-Malmaison, 92500, France.

370.96   FRA   ISSN 1770-0124
A D E A. LETTRE. (Association pour le Developpement de l'Education en Afrique) 199?-2006. q. Association pour le Developpement de l'Education en Afrique (A D E A), 7-9 Rue Eugene-Delacroix, Paris, 75116, France.

331.89143   USA
A D R CURRENTS; the newsletter of dispute resolution law and practice. (Alternative Dispute Resolution) 1996-2002. q. American Arbitration Association, 1633 Broadway, 10th Fl, New York, NY 10019.

720   ITA   ISSN 1123-9255
A & C INTERNATIONAL. (Archi e Colonne) 1995-200?. q. Gangemi Editore, Piazza San Pantaleo 4, Rome, Italy.

629.892   FRA
A F R I LIAISON. 1982-198?. q. Association Francaise de Robotique Industrielle, 4 Place Jussieu, Tour 66, Paris, Cedex 5 75252, France.

657   USA   ISSN 1047-5079
THE A I C P A'S UNIFORM C P A EXAM. (American Institute of Certified Public Accountants) 1988-1999. a. American Institute of Certified Public Accountants, Harborside Financial Ctr, 201 Plaza Three, 3rd Fl, Jersey City, NJ 07311-9801.

700   ITA   ISSN 0001-1584
A I L A. 1960-ceased. w. Francesco Boneschi Ed. & Pub., Via Giovanni Giolitti, 202, Rome, RM 00185, Italy.

006.3   GBR   ISSN 1476-3036
A I S B J. (Artificial Intelligence and Simulation of Behaviour Journal) 2002-2005. s-a. Society for the Study of Artificial Intelligence and Simulation of Behaviour, Chichester C1-209, School of Science and Technology, University of Sussex, Falmer, Brighton, BN1 9QH, United Kingdom.

296   USA   ISSN 0899-2150
A J C JOURNAL. 1978-1993. bi-m. American Jewish Committee, 165 E 56th St, New York, NY 10022.

664   ITA   ISSN 1593-3334
A L. FOOD & GROCERY. 1966-200?. m. (11/yr.). Gruppo Editoriale A G E P E Srl, Via G Patecchio 2, Milan, MI 20141, Italy.

016.02   AUS
A L I S A (ONLINE). (Australian Library and Information Science Abstracts) 1982-2005. q. R M I T, Publishing, A'Beckett St, PO Box 12058, Melbourne, VIC 8006, Australia.

950   USA
A M S ASIAN STUDIES SERIES. (Abrahams Magazine Service) 197?-19??. irreg. A M S Press, Inc., Brooklyn Navy Yard, 63 Flushing Ave, Bldg 292, Unit #221, Brooklyn, NY 11205.

900   USA   ISSN 0270-6253
A M S STUDIES IN SOCIAL HISTORY. (Abrahams Magazine Service) 1976-199?. irreg. A M S Press, Inc., Brooklyn Navy Yard, 63 Flushing Ave, Bldg 292, Unit #221, Brooklyn, NY 11205.

621.9   ITA   ISSN 0393-0483
A M U. (Annuario Italiano Macchine Utensili e Complementari) 1966-ceased. a. Tecniche Nuove SpA, Via Eritrea 21, Milan, MI 201, Italy.

500 919.8 550   AUS   ISSN 1038-2135   CODEN: ANRPEN
A N A R E REPORTS. (Australian National Antarctic Research Expeditions) 1950-2002. irreg. Department of the Environment, Water, Heritage and the Arts, Antarctic Division, 203 Channel Hwy, Kingston, TAS 7050, Australia.

500   USA   ISSN 0729-6533   CODEN: ANRNDG
A N A R E RESEARCH NOTES. (Australian National Antarctic Research Expeditions) 1982-19??. irreg. Department of the Environment, Water, Heritage & the Arts, Antarctic Division, 203 Channel Hwy, Kingston, TAS 7050, Australia.

500   AUS   ISSN 0312-8059   CODEN: PANSDH
A N Z A A S CONGRESS PAPERS. 1925-1997. a. University of New South Wales, Library, PO Box 1, Kensington, NSW 2033, Australia.

004.16   USA
A P H TECHNOLOGY UPDATE; technology for people who are visually impaired. (American Printing House) 1985-2000. s-a. American Printing House for the Blind, Inc., 1839 Frankfort Ave, PO Box 6085, Louisville, KY 40206.

621.3   USA   ISSN 1084-600X
A P P R. (Asian Power Projects Review) 1994-1998. m. (diskettes q.). PennWell Corporation, 1421 S Sheridan Rd, Tulsa, OK 74112.

658   USA
A P R. (Accessory & Performance Retailer) 2002 (Sep.)-ceased. bi-m. National Business Media, Inc., PO Box 1416, Broomfield, CO 80038.

669.722   DEU
A P T INTERNATIONAL. 200?-2009. 2/yr. Giesel Verlag GmbH, Rehkamp 3, Isernhagen, 30916, Germany.

629.13   CZE
A R T I REPORTS. (Aeronautical Research and Test Institute) 1960-200?. irreg. (2-3/yr.). Vyzkumny a Zkusebni Letecky Ustav, Beranovych 130, Letnany, Prague 9, 19905, Czech Republic.

331.1   USA   ISSN 0194-3642
A S A EMPLOYMENT BULLETIN. 1976-2005. m. American Sociological Association, 1307 New York Ave, N W, Ste 700, Washington, DC 20005-4701.

333.91   USA   ISSN 0273-3218
A W W A MAINSTREAM. 19??-2008. q. American Water Works Association, 6666 W Quincy Ave, Denver, CO 80235.

387.029   GBR   ISSN 0267-7377
ABERDEEN PORT HANDBOOK. 1985-200?. a. Aberdeen Harbour Board, 16 Regent Quay, Aberdeen, AB11 5SS, United Kingdom.

911   DEU   ISSN 0940-7685
ABHANDLUNGEN ANTHROPOGEOGRAPHIE. 1953-2003 (vol.64). irreg. Dietrich Reimer Verlag GmbH, Berliner Str 53, Berlin, 10713, Germany.

700 800 780   DEU   ISSN 0567-4999
ABHANDLUNGEN ZUR KUNST-, MUSIK- UND LITERATURWISSENSCHAFT. 1958 (no.3)-1999. irreg. Bouvier Verlag, Fuerstenstr 3, Bonn, 53111, Germany.

370.1   DEU   ISSN 0065-0366
ABHANDLUNGEN ZUR PHILOSOPHIE, PSYCHOLOGIE UND PAEDAGOGIK. 1954-1999. irreg. Bouvier Verlag, Fuerstenstr 3, Bonn, 53111, Germany.

328   ITA   ISSN 0391-3317
ABRUZZO NOTIZIE; notiziario sull'attivita legislativa del Consiglio Regionale. 1975-ceased. s-m. Consiglio Regionale dell'Abruzzo, Via Michele Jacobucci 4, L'Aquila, 67100, Italy.

700   ESP   ISSN 1130-3565
ABSIDE; boletin de la asociacion de amigos de la catedral. 1987-2000. 3/yr. Asociacion de Amigos de la Catedral de Siguenza, Plaza Obispo de Bernando, s-n, Siguenza, Comunidad de Castilla La Mancha 19250, Spain.

808.838   USA
ABSOLUTE MAGNITUDE; science fiction adventures. 1993-2006. q. D N A Publications, Inc., 1380 East 17th St, Ste 210, Brooklyn, NY 11230.

610 011   USA   ISSN 1042-4423
ABSTRACTS OF CLINICAL CARE GUIDELINES. 1989-1998. 10/yr. Joint Commission on Accreditation of Healthcare Organizations, 1 Renaissance Blvd, Oakbrook Terrace, IL 60181.

378.107   USA
ACADEME THIS WEEK. 1994-199?. w. Chronicle of Higher Education, Inc., 1255 23rd St, NW, Ste 700, 7th Fl, Washington, DC 20037.

610   CZE   ISSN 1801-0466
ACADEMIA MEDICA PRAGENSIS. BULLETIN. 2004-2006. s-a. Medical Tribune CZ, s.r.o., Na Morani 5, Prague 2, 12800, Czech Republic.

370.117   GBR   ISSN 1369-8257
ACADEMIC FREEDOM. 1990-1996. irreg. ZedBooks Ltd., 7 Cynthia St, London, N1 9JF, United Kingdom.

500 NLD ISSN 1163-5657
ACADEMIE INTERNATIONALE D'HISTOIRE DES SCIENCES. COLLECTION DES TRAVAUX. 1948-1996 (vol.37). irreg. Brill, PO Box 9000, Leiden, 2300 PA, Netherlands.

790.13 ITA ISSN 1970-7215
ACCADEMIA CREATIVA. 2006-200?. m. Sprea Editori Srl, Via Torino 51, Cernusco sul Naviglio, MI 20063, Italy.

780 ITA
ACCADEMIA NAZIONALE DI SANTA CECILIA. ARCHIVI DI ETNOMUSICOLOGIA. ANNUARIO. 1915; N.S. 1992-1994. irreg. LIM Editrice Srl, Via di Arsina 296/f, Lucca, LU 55100, Italy.

616.9792 AUS ISSN 1033-9035
ACCENT. 1988-2006. q. A I D S Council of South Australia Inc., PO Box 907, Kent Town, SA 5071, Australia.

306.766 AUS
ACCEPTANCE; a monthly newsletter for Catholic homosexuals. 1974 (Apr.)-1976 (May). m. Acceptance Melbourne Inc., PO Box 4214, Hoppers Crossing, VIC 3029, Australia.

340 USA ISSN 1057-4212
ACCESS (CHICAGO, 1990). 1990-1994. biennial. American Bar Association, 321 N Clark St, Chicago, IL 60610.

919.4 AUS ISSN 1030-0406
ACCOMMODATION DIRECTORY. 1961-1996. s-a. N R M A Ltd., 151 Clarence St, Sydney, NSW 2000, Australia.

618.2 618.12 FRA ISSN 1956-7561
ACCOUCHER. 2007-2007. q. Republic Press International, 176 Bd Vincent-Auriol, B P 99, Paris, Cedex 13 75622, France.

336 BEL ISSN 0773-2163
ACCOUNTANCY THEMA'S; veertiendaagse nieuwsbrief voor bedrijfsrevisoren, accountants, en administratieve en financiele managers. 1981-1986. s-m. C E D Samsom, Kouterveld 14, Diegem, 1831, Belgium.

657 NLD ISSN 1572-4603
ACCOUNTANTSPRAKTIJK. 2004-2007. 8/yr. SDU Fiscale en Financiele Uitgevers, Maanlander 45, Amersfoort, 3824 MN, Netherlands.

658 NLD ISSN 1570-4688
ACCOUNTING. 1894-2005. 10/yr. Reed Business bv, Postbus 152, Amsterdam, 1000 AD, Netherlands.

799 ITA ISSN 0392-3061
ACQUASPORT. 1978-ceased. m. Federazione Italiana Pesca Sportiva ed Attivita Subacquee (F I P S A S), Viale Tiziano 70, Rome, 00196, Italy.

940 NLD ISSN 0169-7293
ACTA COLLEGII HISTORIAE URBANAE. 1967-1992 (vol.4). irreg. Brill, PO Box 9000, Leiden, 2300 PA, Netherlands.

500.9 DEU ISSN 0232-8615
ACTA HISTORICA LEOPOLDINA. SUPPLEMENT. 1977-1993. irreg. Johann Ambrosius Barth Verlag in Medizinverlage Heidelberg GmbH & Co. KG, Ruedigerstr 14, Stuttgart, 70469, Germany.

616.4 618.2 610.73 ITA ISSN 0001-6004 CODEN: AMAXBK
ACTA MEDICA AUXOLOGICA. 1969-ceased. 3/yr. Istituto Auxologico Italiano, Via Lodovico Ariosto, 13, Milan, MI 20145, Italy.

610 CZE ISSN 1211-247X CODEN: SVKSA9
ACTA MEDICA. SUPPLEMENTUM. 1958-2005 (vol.48). a. Nakladatelstvi Karolinum, Ovocny trh 3/5, Prague 1, 11636, Czech Republic.

255.4 ITA ISSN 0001-642X
ACTA ORDINIS SANCTI AUGUSTINI; commentarium officiale. 1956-200?. a. Istituto Patristico Augustinianum, Via Paolo VI 25, Rome, 00193, Italy.

618.92 ITA ISSN 0365-5504
ACTA PAEDIATRICA LATINA. 1948-ceased. q. Artigianato Grafico Editoriale s.n.c., Via Casorati, 29, Reggio Emilia, RE 42100, Italy.

541 NLD ISSN 1872-1508
ACTA PHYSICO - CHIMICA SINICA. 200?-2009. m. Elsevier BV, Radarweg 29, P O Box 211, Amsterdam, 1000 AE, Netherlands.

571 GBR ISSN 0302-2994 CODEN: APSSAD
ACTA PHYSIOLOGICA SCANDINAVICA. SUPPLEMENTUM. 1925-2002. irreg. Wiley-Blackwell Publishing Ltd., 9600 Garsington Rd, Oxford, OX4 2DQ, United Kingdom.

636.089 DNK ISSN 0044-605X CODEN: AVSCA7
ACTA VETERINARIA SCANDINAVICA (PRINT). 1959-2006. q. Den Danske Dyrlaegeforening, Rosenlunds Alle 8, Vanloese, 2720, Denmark.

620 AUS
ACTION (POTTS POINT). 1988-2002. bi-w. Asea Brown Boveri, 166 William St, Potts Point, NSW 2011, Australia.

280.4 GBR ISSN 1033-1913
ACTION AFRICA. 1986-1988. q. Africa Evangelical Fellowship, Hambridge Rd, Africa Evangelical Fellowship, 35 Kingfisher Court, Newbury, Berks RG14 5SJ, United Kingdom.

600 658 AUS ISSN 1445-6125
ACTION RESEARCH INTERNATIONAL. 1998-2004; suspended. s-a. Southern Cross Institute of Action Research, Southern Cross University, Graduate College of Management, Military Rd, P.O. Box 157, Lismore, NSW 2480, Australia.

790 NZL ISSN 1177-4169
ACTIVE COMMUNITIES UPDATE. 2005-2006. irreg. SPARC ihi Aotearoa, PO Box 2251, Wellington, New Zealand.

646.7 CAN ISSN 1705-2688
ACTIVE WOMAN CANADA. 2003-2004. bi-m. Mill Pond Publishing Inc., 30 Mill Pond Dr, Georgetown, ON L7G 4S6, Canada.

381 FRA ISSN 1141-7102
ACTUALITES COMMERCE. 1964-199?. 3/yr. Ecole des Cadres, La Defense 1, 70 Galerie des Damiers, Courbevoie, 92400, France.

621.3125 FRA ISSN 1951-4247
ACTUALITES & ENVIRONNEMENT. 200?-2007. m. Electricite de France, Centre Nucleaire de Production d'Electricite (Golfech, Tarn-et-Garonne), BP 24, Valence d'Agen, 82401 Cedex , France.

284 NLD ISSN 1871-8515
AD INTERIM. 1995-2007. 10/yr. Uitgeverij Damon, Postbus 2014, Budel, 6020 AA, Netherlands.

700 GBR ISSN 0001-8015
ADAM INTERNATIONAL REVIEW. 1932-1988. q. Adam International Review, 28 Emperors Gate, London, SW7 4HZ, United Kingdom.

371.42 USA ISSN 1099-0216
ADAMS EXECUTIVE RECRUITERS ALMANAC; the ultimate guide to employment services for all major industries nationwide. 1998-2000 (2nd ed.). irreg. Adams Media, 4700 E Galbraith Rd, Cincinnati, OH 45236.

331.1 USA
ADAMS INTERNET JOB SEARCH ALMANAC. 1997-2002 (Sep.). irreg. Adams Media, 4700 E Galbraith Rd, Cincinnati, OH 45236.

384 DEU
ADEQUATE INFORMATION MANAGEMENT IN EUROPE. WORKING PAPERS. 200?-2007 (vol.2). irreg. Projekt Verlag GbR, Konrad-Zuse-Str 16, Bochum, 44801, Germany.

055.1 ITA
ADESSONAPOLI; periodico di relazioni culturali. 1995-ceased. m.?. Informedia s.r.l., Viale Villa Santa Maria, 14, Naples, NA 80122, Italy.

668.4 USA ISSN 1025-9287
ADHESION COMMUNICATIONS. 1997-199?. 6/yr. Taylor & Francis Inc., 325 Chestnut St, Ste 800, Philadelphia, PA 19106.

616.992 NLD ISSN 1040-5089
ADJUVANT THERAPY OF CANCER. 1977-1987. irreg. Elsevier BV, North-Holland, Sara Burgerhartstraat 25, Amsterdam, 1055 KV, Netherlands.

614.19 TUR ISSN 1018-5275 CODEN: ATDEE
ADLI TIP DERGISI. 1985-2003. 3/yr. Council of Forensic Medicine of Turkey, Cerrahpasa Medical Faculty, Istanbul, 34303, Turkey.

613 USA ISSN 1533-9890
ADOLESCENT & FAMILY HEALTH. 2000-2004; suspended. q. Institute for Youth Development, PO Box 16560, Washington, DC 20041.

346.0166 USA ISSN 1932-7188
ADVANCED ISSUES & PRACTICAL APPLICATION OF THE (YEAR) DIVORCE CODE AMENDMENTS. 199?-2005 (Sep.). irreg. Pennsylvania Bar Institute, 5080 Ritter Rd, Mechanicsburg, PA 17055.

500 GBR ISSN 0308-3241
ADVANCEMENT OF SCIENCE. 1831-1916; resumed 1939-1971; resumed 1975-1976. irreg. The British Science Association, Welcome Wolfson Bldg, 165 Queen's Gate, London, SW7 5HE, United Kingdom.

630 EGY ISSN 1110-6425
ADVANCES IN AGRICULTURAL RESEARCH IN EGYPT. 1998-ceased. s-a. The Agricultural Research Center, Central Agricultural Pesticides Laboratory, Giza, Egypt.

620.00420285 NLD ISSN 0921-934X CODEN: ACVLEM
ADVANCES IN COMPUTER-AIDED DESIGN FOR VERY LARGE SCALE INTEGRATION CIRCUITS. 1986-1994 (vol.8). irreg. Elsevier BV, North-Holland, Sara Burgerhartstraat 25, Amsterdam, 1055 KV, Netherlands.

610.7365 USA ISSN 1083-8708
ADVANCES IN GERONTOLOGICAL NURSING. 1996-200?. irreg. Springer Publishing Company, 11 W 42nd St, 15th Fl, New York, NY 10036.

616.842 DEU ISSN 1437-1472
ADVANCES IN LASER MEDICINE. 1988-2006. irreg. Ecomed Verlagsgesellschaft AG & Co. KG, Justus-von-Liebig-Str 1, Landsberg, 86899, Germany.

362.1 USA ISSN 1053-0606
ADVANCES IN LONG-TERM CARE. 1992-200?. irreg. Springer Publishing Company, 11 W 42nd St, 15th Fl, New York, NY 10036.

636 GBR ISSN 0885-2405
ADVANCES IN MEAT RESEARCH SERIES. 1985-1997. irreg. Pergamon, The Blvd, Langford Ln, East Park, Kidlington, Oxford OX5 1GB, United Kingdom.

613.7 USA ISSN 0888-9287
ADVANCES IN MOTOR DEVELOPMENT RESEARCH. 1987-1990. a. A M S Press, Inc., Brooklyn Navy Yard, 63 Flushing Ave, Bldg 292, Unit #221, Brooklyn, NY 11205.

613.62 615.82 ITA ISSN 1123-8364
ADVANCES IN OCCUPATIONAL MEDICINE & REHABILITATION/ AGGIORNAMENTI IN MEDICINA OCCUPAZIONALE E RIABILITAZIONE. 1995-ceased. 3/yr. PI-ME Editrice, Via Vigentina 136, Pavia, 27100, Italy.

550 EGY
ADVANCES IN SOIL AND WATER RESEARCH IN ALEXANDRIA. 1981-1987. a. A.M. Balba Group for Soil and Water Research, College of Agriculture, University of Alexandria, El-Shatby, Alexandria, 21545, Egypt.

371.2 NZL ISSN 1177-2093
ADVISER. 1992 (Mar.)-2006 (Jul.). irreg. Christchurch College of Education, Support Services, PO Box 31-065, Ilam, Christchurch, New Zealand.

005.5 USA ISSN 1524-6388
ADVISOR EXPERT: LOTUS NOTES AND DOMINO ADMINISTRATION. 1999-2001. 6/yr. Advisor Media, Inc., 12463 Rancho Bernardo Rd, Ste 509, PO Box 503350, San Diego, CA 92128.

005.5 USA ISSN 1524-6396
ADVISOR EXPERT: LOTUS NOTES & DOMINO R5. 1999-2001. m. Advisor Media, Inc., 12463 Rancho Bernardo Rd, Ste 509, PO Box 503350, San Diego, CA 92128.

005.5 USA ISSN 1524-8887
ADVISOR EXPERT: MICROSOFT S Q L SERVER. 1999-2001. 6/yr. Advisor Media, Inc., 12463 Rancho Bernardo Rd, Ste 509, PO Box 503350, San Diego, CA 92128.

344.01 AUS ISSN 1832-9373
THE ADVOCATE. 2000-2005. q. Australia. Office of the Employment Advocate, 477 Pitt St, 30th Floor, Tower, Sydney, NSW 2000, Australia.

930.1 770 GBR ISSN 0140-9220
AERIAL ARCHAEOLOGY. 1977-1991. irreg. Aerial Archaeology Publications, Lansdown, 3 Breton Close, E. Dereham, Norfolk NR19 1JH, United Kingdom.

629.1 CHN ISSN 1004-9711 CODEN: ACEECG
AEROSPACE CHINA. 1992-1998. s-a. Hangtian Gongye Zong Gongsi, Xinxi Yanjiu-suo, 1 Binhe Lu, Hepingli, PO Box 1408, Beijing, 100013, China.

629.13 GBR ISSN 1369-3522
AEROSPACE EUROPE. 1947-2002. a. C M P Information Ltd., Sovereign House, Sovereign Way, Tonbridge, Kent TN9 1RW, United Kingdom.

380 332 FRA ISSN 0065-3799
AFFAIRES ET GENS D'AFFAIRES. 1952-1973. irreg. College de France, Ecole des Hautes Etudes en Sciences Sociales (E H E S S), 54 Boulevard Raspail, Paris, 75006, France.

781.64 FRA ISSN 0995-6972
L'AFFICHE; le magazine des autres musiques. 1989-2002. m. Editions Lariviere, 6 Rue Olof Palme, Clichy, 92587 , France.

330 GBR ISSN 0144-8234
AFRICA ECONOMIC DIGEST; weekly business news, analysis and forecast. 1980-1999. w. Concord Press of Nigeria, 26-32 Whistler St, London, N5 1NJ, United Kingdom.

016.96 USA ISSN 0749-2308
AFRICAN SPECIAL BIBLIOGRAPHIC SERIES. 1963-2004. irreg. Greenwood Publishing Group Inc., 88 Post Rd W, PO Box 5007, Westport, CT 06881.

950 960 EGY ISSN 0065-4191
AFRO-ASIAN PEOPLES' CONFERENCE. PROCEEDINGS. 1957-198?. irreg. Afro-Asian Peoples' Solidarity Organization, 89 Abdel Aziz Al Saoud St., Manial, Cairo, Egypt.

282 ITA
AGENDA. 1959-ceased. m. Azione Cattolica Italiana (A C I), Via Aurelia 481, Rome, 00165, Italy.

352.7 GBR ISSN 1745-3127
AGENDA FOR LOCAL ECONOMIC DEVELOPMENT. 1984-200?. m. Cobwb Information Ltd., Northumbria House, 5 Delta Bank Rd, Metro Riverside Park, Gateshead, NE11 9DJ, United Kingdom.

332 USA
AGGREGATE SUMMARIES OF ANNUAL SURVEYS OF SECURITIES CREDIT EXTENSION. 1976-1999. a. U.S. Federal Reserve System, Board of Governors, Publications Services, Rm MS 138, Washington, DC 20551.

301.01 ITA
AGORA (RAVENNA). 1972-2002 (no.21). irreg. Angelo Longo Editore, Via Paolo Costa 33, Ravenna, 48121, Italy.

331 DEU ISSN 0941-9888
AGPLAN-HANDBUCH ZUR UNTERNEHMENSPLANUNG. GESAMTAUSGABE. 1970-2004. irreg. Erich Schmidt Verlag GmbH & Co. (Berlin), Genthiner Str 30 G, Berlin, 10785, Germany.

331 DEU ISSN 0941-9837
AGPLAN-HANDBUCH ZUR UNTERNEHMENSPLANUNG. KURZAUSGABE. 1985-2004. irreg. Erich Schmidt Verlag GmbH & Co. (Berlin), Genthiner Str 30 G, Berlin, 10785, Germany.

332.3 DEU ISSN 0941-8741
AGRARFINANZ. 1992-2005. m. Deutscher Sparkassenverlag GmbH, Am Wallgraben 115, Stuttgart, 70565, Germany.

631 551.6 DEU ISSN 0172-9403
AGRARMETEOROLOGISCHER MONATSBERICHT FUER NORDRHEIN-WESTFALEN. 1979-2000. m. Deutscher Wetterdienst, Kaiserleistr 29-35, Offenbach, 63067, Germany.

631 DEU ISSN 0172-293X
AGRARMETEOROLOGISCHER WOCHENBERICHT FUER NORDRHEIN-WESTFALEN. 1979-2001. w. Deutscher Wetterdienst, Kaiserleistr 29-35, Offenbach, 63067, Germany.

630 ITA
AGRICOLTORE (MILAN). 1919-ceased. s-m. Unione Provinciale Agricoltori di Milano, Via Giuseppe Ripamonti, 35, Milan, MI 20136, Italy.

630 ITA ISSN 0400-7719
AGRICOLTORE DI TERRA DI LAVORO. 1955-ceased. m. Unione Provinciale Agricoltori di Caserta, Via Nazario Sauro 22, Caserta, CE 81100, Italy.

630 ITA ISSN 0002-1245
AGRICOLTURA ARETINA. 1945-ceased. m. Unione Provinciale Agricoltori di Arezzo, Corso Italia, 205, Arezzo, AR 52100, Italy.

630 ITA ISSN 0002-127X CODEN: AGITD8
AGRICOLTURA D'ITALIA. 1954-ceased. m. (11/yr.). Gruppo Editoriale Gesualdi, Via Quattro Novembre, 152, Rome, RM 00187, Italy.

630 ITA
AGRICOLTURA MANTOVANA. 1946-ceased. 48/yr. Unione Provinciale degli Agricoltori di Mantova, Via Luca Fancelli 4, Mantova, MN 46100, Italy.

630 USA ISSN 0002-1350
AGRICULTURA DE LAS AMERICAS. 1952-19??. bi-m. Keller International Publishing Corp., 150 Great Neck Rd, Great Neck, NY 11021.

630 AUS ISSN 1449-7352
AGRICULTURAL MEMO. 1981-2004. q. Western Australia, Department of Agriculture, PO Box 483, Northam, W.A. 6401, Australia.

338.1 USA ISSN 1011-3363
AGRICULTURAL REVIEW FOR EUROPE. 1984-1995. irreg. United Nations Publications, 2 United Nations Plaza, Rm DC2-853, New York, NY 10017.

639.2 ESP
AGRIPESCA; revista tecnica de informacion agraria. 1985-1992. q. Delegacion Provincial de Agricultura y Pesca de la Junta de Andalucia, Avda Ana de Viya, 3-3, Cadiz, 11009, Spain.

338.1 FRA ISSN 0989-2648
AGRO PERFORMANCES. 1987-2006. bi-m. Sepco, 83 Avenue de la Grande Armee, Paris, 75782, France.

630 668.6 SVK ISSN 0002-1830 CODEN: AGROB2
AGROCHEMIA/AGRICULTURAL CHEMICALS. 1961-1995. m. V U C H T a.s., Novelova 34, Bratislava, 83603, Slovakia.

371.22 USA ISSN 1058-1324
AID FOR EDUCATION REPORT. 1991-199?. s-m. C D Publications, Inc., 8204 Fenton St, Silver Spring, MD 20910.

616.9 GBR ISSN 0953-0096
AIDS ACTION. 1987-1999. q. Healthlink Worldwide, 56-64 Leonard St, London, EC2A 4LT, United Kingdom.

616.9 GBR ISSN 1465-5470
THE AIDS INFORMER. 1999-2000. m. Modus Operandi, PO Box HP346, Leeds, LS6 1UL, United Kingdom.

616 USA
AIDS WEEKLY PLUS. 1985-1999. m. NewsRx, 2727 Paces Ferry Rd SE, Ste 2-440, Atlanta, GA 30339.

616.9 USA ISSN 1546-279X
AIDSCIENCE. 2001 (Jun.)-2003. bi-w. American Association for the Advancement of Science, 1200 New York Ave, NW, Washington, DC 20005.

629.13 FRA ISSN 1166-0422
AILES MAGAZINE. 1984-2003. m. ConceptAir, 44 rue de Groussay, Rambouillet, 78120, France.

800 EGY
AIN SHAMS UNIVERSITY. FACULTY OF EDUCATION. JOURNAL. LITERARY SECTION/MAGALLAT KOLLIYAT AL-TARBIYAT. AL-QESM AL-ADABI. 198?-2007. irreg. Ain Shams University, Faculty of Education, Heliopolis, Cairo, Egypt.

628.4 USA ISSN 1052-6102 CODEN: PAMEE5
AIR & WASTE MANAGEMENT ASSOCIATION. MEETING PROCEEDINGS. 1979-1996. a. Air & Waste Management Association, One Gateway Ctr 3rd Fl, 420 Fort Duquesne Blvd, Pittsburgh, PA 15222.

621.5 FRA ISSN 0002-225X
AIR COMPRIME. 1955-ceased. q. Atlas Copco France S.A., 326 rue du General-Leclerc, Franconville, 95130, France.

074 FRA ISSN 1288-1201
AIR FRANCE RENDEZ-VOUS. 1998-2004. m. Regie Club International, 136 av. Charles de Gaulle, Neilly sur Seine, 92200, France.

629.13 ITA
AIR PRESS. 1959-ceased. w. Editoriale Aeronautica s.r.l., Via Appia Nuova, 96, Rome, RM 00183, Italy.

796.15 GBR
AIRCRAFT IN MINIATURE MAGAZINE. 2000-2001. q. Aircraft In Miniature Ltd, 19 Watling St, Nuneaton, Warks CV11 6JJ, United Kingdom.

387.7 GBR ISSN 0966-0348
AIRCRAFT VALUE JOURNAL. 1992-200?. m. Aircraft Value Analysis Co., 23 Cherry Ln, Bearley, Startford-upon-Avon, CV37 OSX, United Kingdom.

616.238 GBR ISSN 1479-7313
AIRWAYS JOURNAL. 2003-2006. q. Asthma UK, Providence House, Providence Pl, London, N1 0NT, United Kingdom.

526.3 631.3 POL ISSN 0209-0511
AKADEMIA ROLNICZA WE WROCLAWIU. ZESZYTY NAUKOWE. GEODEZJA I URZADZENIA ROLNE. 1980-2006. irreg. Wydawnictwo Uniwersytetu Przyrodniczego we Wroclawiu

363.7 POL ISSN 1230-4484
AKADEMIA ROLNICZA WE WROCLAWIU. ZESZYTY NAUKOWE. INZYNIERIA SRODOWISKA. 1992-2006. irreg. Wydawnictwo Uniwersytetu Przyrodniczego we Wroclawiu

631.3 621 POL ISSN 0867-3756
AKADEMIA ROLNICZA WE WROCLAWIU. ZESZYTY NAUKOWE. MECHANIZACJA ROLNICTWA. 1990-2006. irreg. Wydawnictwo Uniwersytetu Przyrodniczego we Wroclawiu

631.587 POL ISSN 0137-1967 CODEN: ZNAMDX
AKADEMIA ROLNICZA WE WROCLAWIU. ZESZYTY NAUKOWE. MELIORACJA. 1956-2006. irreg. Wydawnictwo Uniwersytetu Przyrodniczego we Wroclawiu

301.18 POL ISSN 1234-8333
AKADEMIA ROLNICZA WE WROCLAWIU. ZESZYTY NAUKOWE. NAUKI HUMANISTYCZNE. 1983-2006. irreg. Wydawnictwo Uniwersytetu Przyrodniczego we Wroclawiu

664 POL ISSN 0209-0503
AKADEMIA ROLNICZA WE WROCLAWIU. ZESZYTY NAUKOWE. TECHNOLOGIA ZYWNOSCI. 1979-2006. irreg. Wydawnictwo Uniwersytetu Przyrodniczego we Wroclawiu

636.089 POL ISSN 0137-1975 CODEN: ZNRWA9
AKADEMIA ROLNICZA WE WROCLAWIU. ZESZYTY NAUKOWE. WETERYNARIA. 1955-2006. irreg. Wydawnictwo Uniwersytetu Przyrodniczego we Wroclawiu

332.62 DEU ISSN 1618-7768
AKTIEN & CO.; Alles ueber Boersen, Renten, Steuern, Zinsen. 2000-2002. w. Axel Springer Verlag AG, Axel-Springer-Platz 1, Hamburg, 20350, Germany.

349.442 CZE ISSN 1801-7770
AKTUALNI PRIRUCKA SE VZORY PRO STAVEBNI PRAXI. 2001-2005. q. Verlag Dashoefer s.r.o., Na Prikope 18, PO Box 756, Prague 1, 11121, Czech Republic.

930.1 DNK ISSN 1603-2861
AKTUEL ARKAEOLOGI; nyt fra vores fortid. 1994-2005. q. Dahls Forlag, Ny Vordingborgvej 37, Kalvehale, 4771, Denmark.

597 CZE ISSN 1802-2286
AKVA FORUM. 2004-2007. m. Mimoza s.r.o., Americka 2399, Kladno, 272 01, Czech Republic.

220 ISR ISSN 0334-9659
AL HAPEREQ. 1984-2005. s-a. Pedagological Secretariat, 2 Deborah Haneviah St, Jerusalem, 91911, Israel.

388.3 ITA
AL VOLANTE. 1999-ceased. m. Unimedia Srl, Corso di Porta Nuova 3A, Milan, 20121, Italy.

344.046 USA ISSN 1066-1131
ALABAMA ENVIRONMENTAL COMPLIANCE UPDATE. 1993-1997. m. Business & Legal Reports, Inc., 141 Mill Rock Rd E, Old Saybrook, CT 06475.

650 USA ISSN 0002-4392
ALAM ATTIJARAT; the business magazine of the Arab world. 1966-19??. 12/yr. Keller International Publishing Corp., 150 Great Neck Rd, Great Neck, NY 11021.

345 388.1 USA
ALASKA CRIMINAL LAW, MOTOR VEHICLES AND RELATED STATUTES. 1997-200?. a. Gould Publications, Inc., 1333 North US Hwy 17-92, Longwood, FL 32750.

340 USA
ALBANY LAW SCHOOL. ANNUAL CONFERENCE ON INTELLECTUAL PROPERTY. 1987-1989. irreg. Albany Law School, 80 New Scotland Ave, Albany, NY 12208.

869 FRA ISSN 0984-8983
ALBATROZ; literatura de aguarras. 1987-2005. q. Association Albatroz, BP 404, Paris Cedex 20, 75969, France.

153 FRA ISSN 1950-1765
ALBERT. 2006-2006. bi-m. Rocaille Editions, c/o Mlle. Melli, 68 rue Henri Barbusse, Vaires Sur Marne, 77360, France.

370 ISR ISSN 0793-1344
'ALE HINNUKH. 1958-2000. q. Ha-Kibbutz ha-Artzi, Department of Education, Rehov Leonardo de Vinci 13, Tel Aviv, 61400, Israel.

630 ISR
ALEI ESEV. 1979-1986. q. Weed Science Society of Israel, Department of Ornamental Horticulture, Volcani Centre, P O Box 6, Bet Dagan, 50250, Israel.

059.92 ISR
ALEI MERCHAVIM. 1967-1970. m. Merchavim Regional Municipal Council, D N Negev, 85400, Israel.

610.9 GBR ISSN 1743-6745
THE ALEXANDRIA JOURNAL OF THE HISTORY OF MEDICINE. 2005-200?. bi-m. Conquest Hospital, Rosewell Library, Educational Centre, The Ridge, St Leonards-on-Sea, E Sussex TN37 7RD, United Kingdom.

615 BRD ISSN 0721-5193
ALGESIE UND ANALGESIE. 1981-1982. irreg. P M I Verlagsgruppe GmbH, August-Schanz-Str 8-II, Frankfurt Am Main, 60433, Germany.

769.56 ESP ISSN 0401-3689
ALHAMBRA; revista filatelica internacional. 1950-1976. m. Club International Alhambra, PO Box 109, Granada, 18070, Spain.

370 ISR ISSN 0334-5084
ALIM. (Not published from 1956-1970) 1938-1989. a. Jewish Agency, Department of Child and Youth Immigration, P O Box 92, Jerusalem, Israel.

746 USA
ALL TIME FAVORITE CROCHET. 1985-ceased. a. Harris Publications, Inc., 800 Kennesaw Ave, Ste 220, Marietta, GA 30060.

053.1 DEU ISSN 0948-6488
ALLEGRA. 1995-2004. m. Axel Springer Verlag AG, Axel-Springer-Platz 1, Hamburg, 20350, Germany.

616.97 USA ISSN 1097-1424
ALLERGY AND CLINICAL IMMUNOLOGY INTERNATIONAL; journal of the World Allergy Organization. 1989-2007. bi-m. Hogrefe Publishing Corp., 875 Massachusetts Ave, 7th Fl, Cambridge, MA 02139.

368.382 616.97 USA ISSN 1536-8297
ALLERGY CODING ALERT. 2001-200?. q. The Coding Institute, 2272 Airport Rd S, Naples, FL 34112.

368.2 DEU ISSN 0933-2081
ALLGEMEINE BEDINGUNGEN FUER DIE KRAFTFAHRTVERSICHERUNG. 1976-1997. irreg. Erich Schmidt Verlag GmbH & Co. (Berlin), Genthiner Str 30 G, Berlin, 10785, Germany.

344.046 NLD ISSN 0928-1894
ALLIANCE ENVIRONMENTAL LAW NEWSLETTER. 1992-199?. 3/yr. De Brauw Blackstone Westbroek, Postbus 90851, The Hague, 2509 LW, Netherlands.

580 ITA ISSN 0065-6429 CODEN: ALLIAM
ALLIONIA. 1952-ceased. a. Universita degli Studi di Torino, Dipartimento di Biologia Vegetale, Viale Pierandrea Mattioli, 25, Turin, TO 10125, Italy.

646.72 ITA ISSN 1121-9580
ALLURE CLUB. 1993-ceased. bi-m. Edizioni Esav, Via Cavour 50, Turin, 10123, Italy.

614 BRD ISSN 0065-6518
ALMANACH FUER DIE AERZTLICHE FORTBILDUNG. 1956-1973. irreg. J.F. Lehmann, Agnes-Bernauer-Platz 8, Munich, 80687, Germany.

332.6 USA ISSN 1930-8434
ALPHA (NEW YORK). 2003 (Jun.)-2009 (Jul./Aug.). 10/yr. Institutional Investor, Inc., 225 Park Ave, S, 7th Fl., New York, NY 10003-1605.

796.7 DNK ISSN 1395-6515
ALT OM MOTORCYKLER. 1979-2001. 5/yr. Henrik G. Lind, PO Box 365, Aarhus C, 8100, Denmark.

296 FRA ISSN 0240-902X
ALTA NIZZA. 1974-198?. q. Association Traditionnelle Israelite Sefarade, 1 bis Boissy d'Anglas, Nice, 06000, France.

055.1 ITA
ALTA VAL TANARO. 1945-ceased. w. Tipografia Odello, Via Marenco, 95, Ceva, CN 12073, Italy.

056 ESP ISSN 1579-9867
ALTERNATIVAS SUR. 2002-2004. s-a. Fundacion Hogar del Empleado, Centro de Investigacion para la Paz, Duque de Sesto, 40, Madrid, 28009, Spain.

333.79 USA ISSN 0273-8163
ALTERNATIVE ENERGY RETAILER. 1980-2008 (June). m. Zackin Publications Inc., 100 Willenbrock Rd, Oxford, CT 06478.

320.5 ITA ISSN 1594-5812
ALTERNATIVE/I. 1997-200?. bi-m. (5/yr.). Associazione Culturale Altreuropa, Viale Zara 119, Milan, MI 20159, Italy.

133.5 ITA
ALTRA; rivista trimestrale di astrologia, psicologia, spiritualita. 1992-ceased. q. Jupiter Edizioni, Casella Postale 25, San Benedetto, PI 56026, Italy.

850 AUS ISSN 0727-0046
ALTRO POLO. 1978-1996. irreg. University of Sydney Italian Studies Association, Department of Italian Studies, Institute Building, H03, Sydney, NSW 2006, Australia.

340 600 USA ISSN 1087-8823
AM LAW TECH. 1996-2005. a. A L M, 345 Park Ave, S, New York, NY 10010.

620 GBR
AMALGAMATED ENGINEERING AND ELECTRICAL UNION. JOURNAL. 1897-1993. m. Amalgamated Union of Engineering Workers, Engineering Section, 110 Peckham Rd, London, SE15 5EL, United Kingdom.

798 636.13 NLD ISSN 1574-3578
AMAZONE; plezier met paarden. 1999-2008. bi-m. Media Primair, Anthonie Fokkerstraat 2, Barneveld, 3772 MR, Netherlands.

069 ESP
AMBAR. 1994-2002. s-a. Asociacion de Amigos del Museo de Bellas Artes de Alava, Paseo Fray Francisco, 8, Victoria-Gasteiz, 01007, Spain.

344.046 ITA ISSN 1590-1254
AMBIENTE E SVILUPPO (MILAN). 1999-ceased. bi-m. Istituto per l'Ambiente, Via Libero Tremolo, 4, Milan, 20126, Italy.

616.8 USA ISSN 0895-8033
AMERICAN ASSOCIATION ON MENTAL RETARDATION. NEWS AND NOTES. 1988-200?. bi-m. American Association on Intellectual and Developmental Disabilities, 501 3rd St, NW, Ste 200, Washington, DC 20001.

133.5 USA ISSN 0002-7529
AMERICAN ASTROLOGY. 1933-200?. m. Starlog Communications, 1372 Broadway, 2nd Fl, New York, NY 10018.

796.7 USA
AMERICAN BIG TWIN DEALER. 1989-2006. m. Advanstar Communications, Inc., One Park Ave, 2nd Fl, New York, NY 10016.

645 790.132 USA ISSN 1072-6268
AMERICAN COUNTRY COLLECTIBLES. 1991-2000. q. Goodman Media Group, Inc., 250 W 57th St, Ste 710, New York, NY 10107.

617.6 USA ISSN 0065-8073
AMERICAN DENTAL DIRECTORY. 1947-2001. a. American Dental Association, 211 E Chicago Ave, Lower Level, Chicago, IL 60611.

929 USA ISSN 1049-6696
AMERICAN GENEALOGY MAGAZINE. 1986-200?. bi-m. Datatrace Systems, 378 S Baxter, Box 1587, Stephenville, TX 76401.

635 USA
AMERICAN HORTICULTURIST NEWS EDITION. 1957-ceased. 6/yr. American Horticultural Society, 7931 E Boulevard Dr, Alexandria, VA 22308.

657.029 USA ISSN 0743-3948
AMERICAN INSTITUTE OF CERTIFIED PUBLIC ACCOUNTANTS. DIRECTORY OF MEMBER FIRMS. ceased. a. American Institute of Certified Public Accountants, Harborside Financial Ctr, 201 Plaza Three, 3rd Fl, Jersey City, NJ 07311-9801.

613.7 USA ISSN 1090-0500
AMERICAN JOURNAL OF HEALTH STUDIES (PRINT). 1984-2009 (Jan.). q. Texas A & M University, Department of Health & Kinesiology, PO Box 4243, College Station, TX 77843-4243.

340 USA ISSN 0002-9319
AMERICAN JOURNAL OF LEGAL HISTORY. 1957-2003; suspended. q. Temple University, Beasley School of Law, 1719 N Broad St, Philadelphia, PA 19122.

622.338 338.2 USA ISSN 1045-4020
AMERICAN PETROLEUM INSTITUTE. QUARTERLY COMPLETION REPORT. 1967-19??. q. American Petroleum Institute, Publications Section, 1220 L St, NW, Washington, DC 20005.

917.13 USA ISSN 1097-6108
AMERICAN SOUTHWEST TRAVEL-SMART. 1988-ceased. biennial. Avalon Travel Publishing, 1700 4th St, Berkeley, CA 94710.

388.324 ITA ISSN 1826-0578
AMERICAN TRUCKS. 2005-200?. a. Sprea Editori Srl, Via Torino 51, Cernusco sul Naviglio, MI 20063, Italy.

690 USA
AMERICA'S BEST-SELLING HOME PLANS. 1999-2009 (Jan.). q. HomePlans.com, 901 N 3rd St, Ste 216, Minneapolis, MN 55401.

636 ITA ISSN 0394-5987
AMICI MIEI. 1987-ceased. m. Edigamma Publishing, Via Sambuca Pistoiese 70A, Rome, 00138, Italy.

798 ITA ISSN 1121-4139
AMICO CAVALLO (ROME). 1991-ceased. m. Ediset s.r.l., Via Riccardo Zandonai, 61, Rome, RM 00194, Italy.

331.8 621.3 GBR
AMICUS UNION NEWS. 1952-2003. q. Amalgamated Engineering and Electrical Union, Hayes Ct, W Common Rd, Hayes, Bromley, Kent BR2 7AU, United Kingdom.

283 GBR
THE AMPLEFORTH REVIEW. 1895-1980. s-a. Ampleforth Abbey, c/o Rev J Felix Stephens, Ed, York, YO6 4ER, United Kingdom.

370 DEU ISSN 0003-2190
AMTLICHES SCHULBLATT FUER DEN REGIERUNGSBEZIRK DUESSELDORF. 1909-2008. m. Bezirksregierung Duesseldorf, Cecilienallee 2, Duesseldorf, 40474, Germany.

617.96 DEU ISSN 0323-4983 CODEN: ANREDN
ANAESTHESIOLOGIE UND REANIMATION; Zeitschrift fuer Anaesthesiologie, Intensivtherapie, Notfallmedizin und Schmerztherapie. 1976-2004. bi-m. Georg Thieme Verlag, Ruedigerstr 14, Stuttgart, 70469, Germany.

Cessations

351 NLD ISSN 1875-4058
ANALYSE MONITOR SPREIDINGSPLANNEN. ZEEUWS-VLAANDEREN. 2006-2006. a. Scoop, Zeeuws Instituut voor Sociale en Culturele Ontwikkeling, Achter de Houttuinen 8, Postbus 407, Middelburg, 4330 AK, Netherlands.

335.83 ITA ISSN 0390-0886
ANARCHISMO. 1975-19??. m. Edizioni Anarchismo, Casella Postale 61, Catania, CT 95100, Italy.

284.1 AUS
ANCHOR. 1973-200?. bi-m. Redeemer Lutheran Church Waverley, 25 Cypress Ave, Glen Waverley, VIC 3150, Australia.

957 951.73 FRA ISSN 1166-3235
ANDA; L'Allie. 1991-2003. q. Association Anda, Anda/CEMS, UMR 7535, M.A.E., Universite de Paris X, Nanterre, Cedex 92023, France.

346.07 USA
ANDERSON'S (YEAR) OHIO COMMERCIAL LAW HANDBOOK. 1998-199?. a. Anderson Publishing Co., 9443 Springboro Pike, Miamisburg, OH 45342.

340 USA ISSN 1534-4746
ANDERSON'S OHIO LAW ON DISC. 1993-199?. q. Anderson Publishing Co., 9443 Springboro Pike, Miamisburg, OH 45342.

343 USA ISSN 1555-5941
ANDREWS LITIGATION REPORTER: E-BUSINESS LAW BULLETIN. 1999-2006. m. Andrews Publications, 175 Strafford Ave, Bldg 4, Ste 140, Wayne, PA 19087.

800 ITA ISSN 1722-5884
ANGELO DI FUOCO. 2002-2004. s-a. Carocci Editore, Via Sardegna 50, Rome, 00187, Italy.

940 820 410 DEU ISSN 0170-8163
ANGLO-AMERICAN FORUM. 1975-1991 (vol.21). irreg. Peter Lang GmbH Europaeischer Verlag der Wissenschaften, Eschborner Landstr 42-50, Frankfurt Am Main, 60489, Germany.

336 CHN ISSN 1005-6181
ANHUI SHUIWU. 1985-2003. m. Anhui Sheng Guojia Shuiwuju, 11, Yonghong Lu, Hefei, 230061, China.

628.92 CHN ISSN 1003-756X
ANHUI XIAOFANG/ANHUI FIRE PROTECTION. 1981-2004. m. Anhui Sheng Xiaofang Xiehui, 315, Changjiang Xi Lu, Hefei, 230061, China.

894 FRA ISSN 0992-0285
ANKA; revue d'art et de litterature de Turquie. 1986-199?. q. Anka, 13 rue Santeuil, Paris, Cedex 5 75231, France.

746 CZE
ANNA; rucni prace pro radost a poteseni. 1997-2007. m. Burda Praha spol. s.r.o., Premyslovska 2845/43, Prague 2, 13000, Czech Republic.

944 840 FRA ISSN 0399-0826
ANNALES DE BRETAGNE ET DES PAYS DE L'OUEST. 1886-2003. a. Presses Universitaires de Rennes, Campus de la Harpe, 2 Rue du Doyen Denis-Leroy, Rennes, Cedex 35044, France.

617 FRA ISSN 0398-7701
ANNALES DE MEDECINE ET DE CHIRURGIE. 1927-1929. irreg. Arnette, 1 rue Eugene et Armand Peugeot, Rueil-Malmaison, 92500, France.

950 FRA ISSN 0980-5842
ANNALES DU LEVANT. 1985-199?. a. Presses Universitaires de Rennes, Campus de la Harpe, 2 Rue du Doyen Denis-Leroy, Rennes, Cedex 35044, France.

679.7 FRA ISSN 0399-0206 CODEN: ATBCAA
ANNALES DU TABAC. SECTION 1. 1963-1997. a. ALTADIS - Centre de Recherche, 4 rue Andre Dessaux, Fleury-les-Aubrais, Cedex 45401, France.

679.7 FRA ISSN 0399-0354 CODEN: ATSED2
ANNALES DU TABAC. SECTION 2. 1964-1999. a. ALTADIS - Centre de Recherche, 4 rue Andre Dessaux, Fleury-les-Aubrais, Cedex 45401, France.

616.6 FRA ISSN 0003-4401
ANNALES D'UROLOGIE. 1966-2007. 6/yr. Elsevier France, Editions Scientifiques et Medicales, 23 Rue Linois, Paris, 75724, France.

618 ITA ISSN 0300-0087 CODEN: AOGMAU
ANNALI DI OSTETRICIA, GINECOLOGIA E MEDICINA PERINATALE. 1879-1998. q. Mattioli 1885 SpA, Via Coduro 1, Fidenza, PR 43036, Italy.

617.7 ITA ISSN 0003-4665 CODEN: AOCOAG
ANNALI DI OTTALMOLOGIA E CLINICA OCULISTICA. 1874-2001. bi-m. Maccari Editore Srl, Via Palermo 44, Parma, 43100, Italy.

910 ITA ISSN 0392-8713
ANNALI DI RICERCHE E STUDI DI GEOGRAFIA. 1944-ceased. s-a. Patron Editore, Via Badini 12, Quarto Inferiore, BO 40050, Italy.

616.5 ITA ISSN 1592-6826
ANNALI ITALIANI DI DERMATOLOGIA ALLERGOLOGICA CLINICA E SPERIMENTALE. 1945-2007. q. Il Pensiero Scientifico Editore, Via Bradano 3-C, Rome, 00199, Italy.

945 ITA ISSN 1970-5980
ANNALI QUERINIANI. 2001-2005. irreg. Grafo SpA, Via Maiera 27, Brescia, Italy.

745.5 USA ISSN 1556-8113
ANNIE'S PLASTIC CANVAS; creative designs for home & holiday. 2004-2008. bi-m. Dynamic Resource Group (D R G), 306 E Parr Rd, Berne, IN 46711.

336.2 GBR ISSN 0141-6766
ANNOTATED TAX CASES. 1922-1976. irreg. Gee Publishing Ltd., 100 Avenue Rd, Swiss Cottage, London, NW3 3PG, United Kingdom.

651 FRA ISSN 0998-6723
ANNUAIRE DE LA BUREAUTIQUE, INFORMATIQUE, MATERIEL ET MOBILIER DE BUREAU, MECANOGRAPHIE. 1962-1996. a. Editions Louis Johanet, 38 bd Henri Sellier, Suresnes, 92156, France.

338.4762382 FRA ISSN 0396-0269
ANNUAIRE DE LA CONSTRUCTION ET DE LA REPARATION NAVALES. 1933-1980. a. Chambre Syndicale des Constructeurs de Navires, 47 rue de Monceau, Paris, 75008, France.

610 FRA ISSN 1157-4135
ANNUAIRE DE LA RECHERCHE BIO-MEDICALE. 1989-1995. a. Elsevier France, Editions Scientifiques et Medicales, 23 Rue Linois, Paris, 75724, France.

639 FRA ISSN 0066-2623
ANNUAIRE DE L'ARMEMENT A LA PECHE; guide de la peche professionelle francaise. 1957-1992. a. Editions Maritimes, 190 bd. Haussmann, Paris, 75008, France.

621.32 FRA ISSN 0066-264X
ANNUAIRE DE L'ECLAIRAGE. 1987-199?. s-a. Association Francaise de l'Eclairage, 52 bd. Malesherbes, Paris, 75008, France.

631.584 FRA ISSN 1772-4058
L'ANNUAIRE DES ACTEURS DE LA BIO. 2004-2004. a. Centre National de Ressources en Agriculture Biologique (A Bio Doc - C N R A B), Enita - Site de Marmilhat, BP 35, Lempdes, 63370, France.

780 793 FRA ISSN 1244-2267
ANNUAIRE MUSIQUE ET DANSE. 1988-199?. a. Association Departementale pour le Developpement des Arts Haute-Garonne, 5 rue Jules Chalande, Toulouse, 31000, France.

629.1 USA ISSN 1093-9288 CODEN: PBAAE8
ANNUAL BATTERY CONFERENCE ON APPLICATIONS AND ADVANCES. 1986-2002. a. I E E E, 3 Park Ave, 17th Fl, New York, NY 10016-5997.

792 USA
ANNUAL GUIDE FOR THE ARTS - BOSTON. 1995-2007 (May). a. Annual Guides for the Arts, 1801 Bush St, Ste 131-F, San Francisco, CA 94109.

792 USA
ANNUAL GUIDE FOR THE ARTS - CHICAGO. 2004-2007 (May). a. Annual Guides for the Arts, 1801 Bush St, Ste 131-F, San Francisco, CA 94109.

792 USA
ANNUAL GUIDE FOR THE ARTS - METROPOLITAN WASHINGTON, DC. 19??-2007 (May). a. Annual Guides for the Arts, 1801 Bush St, Ste 131-F, San Francisco, CA 94109.

347 GBR ISSN 1360-0257
THE ANNUAL PRACTICE. 1995-1999. a. Sweet & Maxwell Ltd., 100 Avenue Rd, London, NW3 3PF, United Kingdom.

610.73 USA ISSN 1542-412X
ANNUAL REVIEW OF NURSING EDUCATION. 2003-200?. a. Springer Publishing Company, 11 W 42nd St, 15th Fl, New York, NY 10036.

330 USA
ANNUAL SURVEY OF MANUFACTURES. GEOGRAPHIC AREA STATISTICS (PRINT). 19??-ceased. a. U.S. Census Bureau, 4600 Silver Hill Rd, Washington, DC 20233.

026 GBR ISSN 0958-4560
ANNUAL SURVEY OF MUSIC LIBRARIES. 1984-1999. a. International Association of Music Libraries Archives & Documentation Centres (U.K. Branch), The President, Enfield Libraries, Palmers Green Library,, Broomfield Ln, London, N13 4EY, United Kingdom.

388.3 ITA ISSN 1124-5182
ANNUARIO ACCESSORI AUTO. 1991-ceased. a. Edigest s.r.l., Via Brenta, 13, Rome, RM 00198, Italy.

666 ITA ISSN 0066-4472
ANNUARIO CERAMICA. 1970-ceased. a. Casa Editrice Palazzo Vecchio, Via Vittorio Emanuele II, 155, Florence, FI 50134, Italy.

378 ITA ISSN 0393-6368
ANNUARIO D E A DELLE UNIVERSITA E ISTITUTI DI STUDIO E RICERCA IN ITALIA/D E A DIRECTORY OF UNIVERSITIES, SCIENTIFIC AND CULTURAL INSTITUTIONS IN ITALY. 1983-2002. a. D E A Editrice, Via Lima, 28, Rome, RM 00198, Italy.

665.7 ITA
ANNUARIO DEL METANO/NATURAL GAS DIRECTORY. 1985-ceased. biennial. R E S Editrice, Casella Postale 12053, Milan, 20120, Italy.

333.79 ITA ISSN 1972-7003
ANNUARIO ITALIA ENERGIA. 1979-ceased. 2/yr. L' Annuario s.r.l., Via Giulia, 4, Nizza Monferrato, AT 14049, Italy.

621.382 ESP
ANTENA DE TELECOMUNICACION. 1965-2003. bi-m. Asociacion Espanola de Ingenieros de Telecomunicacion, General Arrando, 38, Madrid, 28010, Spain.

621.388 ITA ISSN 0392-470X
L'ANTENNA; rassegna mensile di tecnica elettronica. 1928-ceased. m. Editrice Il Rostro, Via B Buozzi 5, Segrate, MI 20090, Italy.

930 DEU ISSN 0174-8246
DIE ANTIKE. 1925-1944. q. Walter de Gruyter GmbH & Co. KG, Genthiner Str 13, Berlin, 10785, Germany.

628.5 ITA ISSN 1123-3370
ANTINQUINAMENTO. 1994-ceased. bi-m. Tecniche Nuove SpA, Via Eritrea 21, Milan, MI 201, Italy.

070.5 381.45 USA ISSN 1522-2985
ANTIQUARIAN, SPECIALTY AND USED BOOK SELLERS; a subject guide and directory. 1993-1997 (2nd ed.). irreg. Omnigraphics, Inc., 615 Griswold St, Detroit, MI 48226.

745.1 CAN ISSN 1708-6469
ANTIQUE & COLLECTIBLES SHOWCASE. 2003-2008. 6/yr. Trajan Publishing Corp., 103 Lakeshore Rd, Ste 202, St Catharines, ON L2N 2T6, Canada.

745.1 USA
ANTIQUE JOURNAL FOR THE NORTHWEST. 1993-ceased. m. Krause Publications, Inc., 700 E State St, Iola, WI 54990.

745.1 USA
ANTIQUES & COLLECTIBLES JOURNAL. 2007 (Mar.)-2007 (Dec.). m. Krause Publications, Inc., 700 E State St, Iola, WI 54990.

572 615 616.9 GBR ISSN 0956-3202 CODEN: ACCHEH
ANTIVIRAL CHEMISTRY AND CHEMOTHERAPY (PRINT). 1990-2008. bi-m. International Medical Press, 36 St Mary at Hill, London, EC3R 8DU, United Kingdom.

301 ITA ISSN 0392-9035
ANTROPOLOGIA CONTEMPORANEA. 1978-ceased. q. Editrice Il Sedicesimo, Via Mannelli 29, Florence, FI 50136, Italy.

305.8 ESP
ANUARIO ETNOLOGICO DE ANDALUCIA. 198?-2001. a. Consejeria de Cultura y Medio Ambiente, c/o Director of International Programs, c/ San Jose, 3, Seville, 411071, Spain.

346.066 DEU ISSN 1613-0006
ANWALTSPRAXIS WIRTSCHAFTSRECHT. 2004 (Jan.)-2004. bi-m. Deutscher Anwaltverlag GmbH, Wachsbleiche 7, Bonn, 53111, Germany.

004.6 GBR
APACHE WEEK. 1996-2004. w. Apache Week, Red Hat Europe, 10 Alan Turing Way, Guildford, GU2 7YF, United Kingdom.

615.19 DEU ISSN 0177-9591 CODEN: CITOEH
APOTHEKE UND KRANKENHAUS. 1985-2004. q. Deutscher Apotheker Verlag, Postfach 101061, Stuttgart, 70009, Germany.

615.109 FRA ISSN 1774-489X
APOZEME; la revue scientifique de l'ANPPH. 200?-2005. irreg. Association Nationale des Preparateurs en Pharmacie Hospitaliere, B.P. 48, Grezieu-la-Varenne, 69290, France.

687 USA ISSN 0746-889X
APPAREL MERCHANDISING. 1982-1996. 8/yr. Lebhar-Friedman, Inc., 425 Park Ave, New York, NY 10022.

004.16 AUS ISSN 1328-3049
APPLESAUCE. 1980-2000. m. (except Jan.). South Australian Apple Users Club, PO Box 3129, Unley, SA 5061, Australia.

660.6 NZL ISSN 1175-9534
APPLIED BIOTECHNOLOGY, FOOD SCIENCE AND POLICY. 2003 (Mar.)-2003 (no.4). q. Open Mind Journals Ltd., PO Box 300-729, Albany, Auckland, 1311, New Zealand.

616.98 NZL ISSN 1175-9542
APPLIED ENVIRONMENTAL SCIENCE AND PUBLIC HEALTH. 2003 (Mar.)-2004 (no.2). q. Open Mind Journals Ltd., PO Box 300-729, Albany, Auckland, 1311, New Zealand.

597.9 NLD ISSN 1570-7539
APPLIED HERPETOLOGY. 2003-2009 (Vol. 6). q. Brill, PO Box 9000, Leiden, 2300 PA, Netherlands.

401 AUS ISSN 0314-3937
APPLIED LINGUISTICS ASSOCIATION OF AUSTRALIA. OCCASIONAL PAPERS. 1977-200?. irreg. Applied Linguistics Association of Australia, c/o Dr Rachel Burke, ALAA Business Manager, School of Cultural and Language Studies in Education, Queensland University of Technology (Kelvin Grove Campus), Brisbane, QLD 4059, Australia.

530 621.3 NZL ISSN 1176-2314
APPLIED NANOSCIENCE. 2003 (Oct.)-2004. q. Open Mind Journals Ltd., PO Box 300-729, Albany, Auckland, 1311, New Zealand.

304.6 NZL ISSN 1175-9550
APPLIED POPULATION AND POLICY. 2003-2004 (vol.1, no.2). q. Open Mind Journals Ltd., PO Box 300-729, Albany, Auckland, 1311, New Zealand.

702 DEU ISSN 0944-0380
APPLY. 1993-199?. 3/yr. Apply Design Group, Krausenstr 16, Hannover, 30171, Germany.

330.19 BGD ISSN 0422-1311
APPROVED DEVELOPMENT PROGRAMME OF EAST PAKISTAN GOVERNMENT. 19??-19??. a. Bangladesh Government Press, Bangladesh, Bangladesh.

635 ESP
APUNTES DE JARDINERIA. 1986-suspended. q. Glosa, S.A., Ronda San Pedro 22, pral. 2, Barcelona, 08010, Spain.

614 ESP ISSN 1134-055X
APUNTES DE SALUD PUBLICA. 1993-2000. irreg. Asociacion de Alumnos e Masteres en Saude Publica de Galicia, Apartado de Correos 543, Santiago de Compostela, 15780, Spain.

551 551.46 ITA ISSN 0394-6568
AQUA; mensile di acqua, natura, vita. 1986-ceased. m. (11/yr.). Editrice Portoria Srl, Via Chiossetto, 1, Milan, MI 20122, Italy.

639 597 FRA ISSN 1270-3893
AQUA PLAISIR. 1996-2008. m. Aqua Media, 1492 Bd de Bigorre, Z.E. Ma Campagne, Angouleme, 16000, France.

636 FRA ISSN 0769-6361
AQUARIUM MAGAZINE. 1985-2006. m. Editions du Garou, 38 avenue Franklin Roosevelt, Avon, 77215, France.

340.59 NLD ISSN 1574-3446
ARAB AND ISLAMIC LAW SERIES. 1990-2004 (vol.27). irreg. Brill, PO Box 9000, Leiden, 2300 PA, Netherlands.

810 ITA ISSN 1123-9328
ARACHNION. 1995-1996. q. Universita degli Studi di Torino, Via Sant Ottavio 20, Tornino, 10124, Italy.

282 ITA ISSN 0003-7559
ARALDO DI S. ANTONIO; incontri con Papa Giovanni. 1949-ceased. fortn. Orfanotrofio Antoniano dei PP. Rogazionisti, Viale Motta, 54, Desenzano Del Garda, BS 25015, Italy.

296 NLD ISSN 0169-7390
ARBEITEN ZUR LITERATUR UND GESCHICHTE DES HELLENISTISCHEN JUDENTUMS. 1968-1991. irreg. Brill, PO Box 9000, Leiden, 2300 PA, Netherlands.

550 DEU ISSN 0949-1546
ARBEITSHEFTE DEPONIEN. 1995-200?. irreg. E. Schweizerbart'sche Verlagsbuchhandlung, Johannesstr 3A, Stuttgart, 70176, Germany.

550 DEU ISSN 0949-1554
ARBEITSHEFTE GEOLOGIE. 1995-200?. irreg. E. Schweizerbart'sche Verlagsbuchhandlung, Johannesstr 3A, Stuttgart, 70176, Germany.

330.9 388 DEU ISSN 0939-8872
ARBEITSPLAETZE IN UMSCHLAG- UND LAGERANLAGEN VON SPEDITIONSUNTERNEHMEN. 1991-2002. irreg. Erich Schmidt Verlag GmbH & Co. (Berlin), Genthiner Str 30 G, Berlin, 10785, Germany.

004 GBR ISSN 0952-3332
ARCHAEOLOGICAL COMPUTING NEWSLETTER. 1984-2002. q. Staffordshire University, School of Computing, Trent Bldg, College Rd, Stoke on Trent, Staffordshire ST4 2DE, United Kingdom.

591.9561 FRA ISSN 0299-3600 CODEN: ARZOEK
ARCHAEOZOOLOGIA; revue international d'archeozoologie. 1987-2001. 2/yr. Editions La Pensee Sauvage, 12 Place Notre Dame, Grenoble, 38002, France.

624 NLD ISSN 1574-2202
DE ARCHITECT - DETAIL. 1999-2005. 3/yr. Sdu Uitgevers bv, Postbus 20025, The Hague, 2500 EA, Netherlands.

720 DEU
ARCHITECTURE + COMPETITIONS. 1939-2008. irreg. Karl Kraemer Verlag, Schulze-Delitzsch-Str 15, Stuttgart, 70565, Germany.

720 DEU ISSN 0944-4718
ARCHITECTURE AND DETAIL. 1993-2008. s-a. Karl Kraemer Verlag, Schulze-Delitzsch-Str 15, Stuttgart, 70565, Germany.

720 CZE ISSN 0862-7002
ARCHITEKTURA. 1938-1992. a. Obec Architektu, Mikulandska 6, Prague, 11000, Czech Republic.

720 ITA ISSN 0003-8830
L'ARCHITETTURA (MILAN); cronache e storia. 1945-2005. m. Mancosu Editore, Via Alfredo Fusco 71, Rome, 00136, Italy.

720 ITA ISSN 1123-2803
ARCHITETTURA. STORIA E DOCUMENTI. 1975-ceased. s-a. Gangemi Editore, Piazza San Pantaleo 4, Rome, Italy.

578.77 DEU ISSN 0342-1066
ARCHIV FUER HYDROBIOLOGIE. SUPPLEMENT-BAND: UNTERSUCHUNGEN DES ELBE-AESTUARS. 1961-ceased. irreg. E. Schweizerbart'sche Verlagsbuchhandlung, Johannesstr 3A, Stuttgart, 70176, Germany.

616.1 FRA ISSN 1623-9083
ARCHIVES DES MALADIES DU COEUR ET DES VAISSEAUX - INFIRMIERE PRATIQUE. 2000-2002. q. Elsevier Masson, 62 Rue Camille Desmoulins, Issy les Moulineaux, Cedex 92442, France.

930.1 301 ITA ISSN 1828-3039
ARCHIVI REALI DI EBLA. TESTI. 1981-ceased. irreg. Universita degli Studi di Roma "La Sapienza", Dipartimento di Scienze Archeologiche e Antropologiche dell'Antichita, Piazzale Aldo Moro 5, Rome, 00185, Italy.

551.46 551.48 ITA ISSN 0066-667X CODEN: AOLVAE
ARCHIVIO DI OCEANOGRAFIA E LIMONOLOGIA. 1941-2003. irreg. Consiglio Nazionale delle Ricerche (C N R), Istituto di Scienze Marine, Castello 1364-A, Venice, 30122, Italy.

613.62 ITA ISSN 0394-2953
ARCHIVIO DI SCIENZE DEL LAVORO. 1983 (vol.9, no.1)-1995 (vol.11, no.4). q. Istituto Poligrafico e Zecca dello Stato, Piazza Verdi 10, Rome, 00198, Italy.

325.2 ITA ISSN 1128-4382
ARCHIVIO DOCUMENTAZIONE E RICERCA SULL'EMIGRAZIONE VENETA. QUADERNI. 1996-2001 (no.7). irreg. Angelo Longo Editore, Via Paolo Costa 33, Ravenna, 48121, Italy.

305.8 ITA ISSN 0373-3009
ARCHIVIO PER L'ANTROPOLOGIA E LA ETNOLOGIA. 1871-ceased. a. Societa Italiana di Antropologia e Etnologia, Palazzo Nonfinito, Via del Proconsolo, 12, Florence, FI 50122, Italy.

945 ITA
ARCHIVIO STORICO BERGAMASCO; rassegna semestre di storia e cultura. 1981-1995. s-a. Lubrina Editore Srl, Via Cesare Correnti 50, Bergamo, BG 24124, Italy.

945 ITA ISSN 0392-0283
ARCHIVIO STORICO PER LE PROVINCE PARMENSI. 1892-1944. a. Deputazione di Storia Patria per le Antiche Provincie Modenesi, Via Pomposa, 1, Modena, MO 41100, Italy.

945 ITA ISSN 0391-2337
ARCHIVIO STORICO SARDO. 1905-ceased. a. Mondadori - Libreria Dessi, Largo Carlo Felice 17, Sassari, SS 07100, Italy.

960 ESP ISSN 0214-4883
ARCHIVO MUNICIPAL DE CEUTA. CUADERNOS. 1988-1997. q. Ayuntamiento de Ceuta, Ave de Africa s-n, Ceuta, 11700, Spain.

946 ESP ISSN 0004-0630
ARCHIVOS LEONESES; estudios y documentacion de los reinos hispano-occidentales. 1947-1996. s-a. Centro de Estudios e Investigacion "San Isidoro", Plaza de la Regla 6, Leon, 24070, Spain.

354.35 ESP ISSN 1136-5951
AREA; revista de debats territorials. 1994-2000. irreg. Diputacio de Barcelona, Rambla de Catalunya 126, Barcelona, 08008, Spain.

058.1 DNK ISSN 0809-800X
ARENA; stil til maend. 2006-2009. 11/yr. Benjamin Media A/S, Finsensvej 6 D, Frederiksberg, 2000, Denmark.

636 ITA ISSN 1125-1123
ARGOS TREND. 1996-200?. m. Sprea Editori Srl, Via Torino 51, Cernusco sul Naviglio, MI 20063, Italy.

623.82 FRA ISSN 0395-1804
ARGUS DU BATEAU ET DE TOUT LE MATERIEL NAUTIQUE. 1966-199?. 4/yr. Editions Kerfan, 97-103 av. Semeria, BP 18, St Jean Cap Ferrat, 06230, France.

379.8 FRA ISSN 1779-2533
L'ARGUS DU CAMPING-CAR. 1999-2007. bi-m. Editions Lariviere, 6 Rue Olof Palme, Clichy, 92587 , France.

700 800 ISR ISSN 0004-1343
ARIEL (ENGLISH EDITION); the Israel review of arts and letters. 1962-2003. q. Youval Tal Ltd., P O Box 2160, Jerusalem, 91021, Israel.

914 DNK ISSN 0901-0815
ARKAEOLOGISKE UDGRAVNINGER I DANMARK. 1985-2002. a. Kulturministeriet, Kulturarvsstyrelsen, H.C. Andersens Boulevard 2, Copenhagen V, 1553, Denmark.

230 DNK ISSN 0107-4520
ARKEN-TRYK. 1981-2001. irreg. Forlaget Arken, c/o Det Teologiske Facultet, Koebenhavns Universitet, Koebmagergade 44-46, Copenhagen K, 1150, Denmark.

720 690 ITA
ARKOS; scienza e restauro dell'architettura. 2000-2007; suspended. q. Nardini Editore, Piazza della Repubblica 2, Florence, 50123, Italy.

355.31 AUS ISSN 1034-3695
ARMY MAGAZINE. 1989-2002. q. Department of Defence, Army Newspaper Unit, NBH Annex G-6, QVT, PO Box E 33, Canberra, ACT 2600, Australia.

355.31 GBR ISSN 0004-2552
ARMY QUARTERLY AND DEFENCE JOURNAL. 1829-1999. q. AQ & DJ Publications, 1 West St, Tavistock, Devon PL19 8DS, United Kingdom.

361.6 AUS ISSN 1449-9843
AROUND C Y F S. (Child, Youth and Family Services) 19??-2004 (Dec.). bi-m. South Australia, Department for Families and Communities, GPO Box 292, Adelaide, SA 5001, Australia.

690 720 ITA ISSN 0394-5944
ARREDO URBANO. 1980-ceased. bi-m. Istituto Nazionale dell'Arredo Urbano delle Strutture Ambientali, Via dell' Acqua Traversa 255, Rome, 00135, Italy.

690 720 ITA ISSN 0394-5952
ARREDO URBANO BIS; supplemento tecnico. 1980-ceased. q. Istituto Nazionale dell'Arredo Urbano delle Strutture Ambientali, Via dell' Acqua Traversa 255, Rome, 00135, Italy.

800 851 ITA ISSN 0393-8263
ARSENALE; trimestrale di letteratura. 1984-1987. q. Edizioni Il Labirinto, Via Aristide Leonori, 67, Rome, RM 00147, Italy.

700 FRA ISSN 0571-1509
ART DE BASSE NORMANDIE. 1956-200?. q. Art de Basse-Normandie, c/o Jacques Pougheol, 49 rue Canchy, Caen, 14000, France.

910.4 FRA ISSN 1622-874X
L'ART DE VOYAGER; le mensuel pratique du voyage. 1990-2006. m. Editions de Demain, 19 rue Ernest Laval, Vanves, 92170, France.

747 TUR ISSN 1300-5936
ART DECOR. 1993-2005. m. D B R - Dogan Burda Rizzoli Dergi Yayyncylyk ve Pazarlama A.S., Hurriyet Medya Towers, Gunesli - Istanbul, 34212, Turkey.

708 FRA ISSN 0994-7957
L'ART ET LA MER. 1974-199?. q. Association des Peintres Officiels de la Marine, Musee de la Marine, Palais de Chaillot, 2 rue Royale, Paris Nava, 75200I, France.

028.5 ITA ISSN 1721-2227
ART KID'S. 2002-200?. m. Edigamma Publishing, Via Sambuca Pistoiese 70A, Rome, 00138, Italy.

776.6 DNK ISSN 1395-5829
ART-LAND INTERNATIONAL. 1994-2001. s-a. Art-Land International, Gothergade 163,3, Copenhagen K, 1123, Denmark.

760 FRA ISSN 1763-6876
ART PRICE ANNUAL. 1991-2004. plus a. updates. Artprice.com, BP 69, St Romain-au-Mont d'Or, 69270, France.

700 ITA
ART WORLD. 1988-ceased. 3/yr. Michelangelo s.r.l., Via Domenico Cimarosa, 4, Milan, MI 20144, Italy.

700 780 ITA ISSN 1124-0229
ARTE A BOLOGNA; bollettino dei musei civici d'arte antica. 1990-1995. a. Nuova Alfa, Via Trentacoste 7, Milano, 20134, Italy.

700 ITA
ARTE & CORNICE. 1984-ceased. q. Rima Editrice, Viale Sarca 243, Milan, 20126, Italy.

687.3 ITA ISSN 1129-0218
ARTE FEMMINILE. 1996-2005. m. Edizioni Mimosa, Piazza E de Angeli 9, Milan, 20146, Italy.

641.5 ITA ISSN 1128-6121
ARTE IN CUCINA. RICETTE PER LA SALUTE. 1998-ceased. bi-m. Edizioni Mimosa, Piazza E de Angeli 9, Milan, 20146, Italy.

700 ITA ISSN 0390-1319
ARTE NAIVE. 1974-2002. s-a. Artigianato Grafico Editoriale s.n.c., Via Casorati, 29, Reggio Emilia, RE 42100, Italy.

950 ITA
ARTE ORIENTALE IN ITALIA. 1971-ceased. irreg. Museo Nazionale d'Arte Orientale, Via Merulana, 248, Rome, RM 00185, Italy.

700 ITA ISSN 1591-3694
ARTE STAMPA. 1950-ceased. 3/yr. Editrice Liguria, Via de Mari 4, Savona, SV 17100, Italy.

346.94013505 AUS ISSN 1447-2651
ARTICLE 13; law & policy journal of the National Children's and Youth Law Centre. 1993-2002 (Dec.). q. University of New South Wales, National Children's and Youth Centre, 32 Botany St, Randwick, NSW 2031, Australia.

330 ITA
ARTIGIANATO DI SICILIA. 1965-ceased. m. Associazione Artigiani Provincia di Palermo, Artigianato di Sicilia, Via Roma, 391, Palermo, PA 90133, Italy.

745.5 ITA ISSN 0391-707X
ARTIGIANATO OGGI. 1977-1986. m. Confederazione Nazionale Artigianato, Via G A Guattani 13, Rome, 00161, Italy.

650 ITA ISSN 0004-3737
ARTIGIANO MODENESE. 1960-ceased. m. Libero Artigianato e Piccole Aziende Modenesi, Via Emilia Ouest, 101, Modena, MO 41100, Italy.

750 USA
ARTIST'S SKETCHBOOK; your personal guide to discovering the artist within. 2000 (Aug.)-2006. bi-m. F + W Media Inc., 4700 E Galbraith Rd, Cincinnati, OH 45236.

745 USA
ARTS & CRAFTS. 1992-200?. 6/yr. Krause Publications, Inc., 700 E State St, Iola, WI 54990.

700 FRA ISSN 0337-1603
ARTS D'AFRIQUE NOIRE. 1972-2004. q. Arts d'Afrique Noire, B.P. 24, Arnouville-les-Gonesse, 95400, France.

760 FRA ISSN 0984-9602
ARTS GRAPHIQUES MAGAZINE. 1987-1992. 4/yr. C N F S, 15 rue Massena, Maisons Alfort, 94700, France.

700 NZL ISSN 1170-5256
ARTS HORIZON. 1975-200?. s-a. New Zealand Guild of Artist Trust, P.O. Box 20170, Glen Eden, Auckland 7, New Zealand.

700 069 NZL ISSN 1175-0790
ARTSCAPE; a regional arts review. 1994-2002. m. Gallery Books & Crafts, P.O. Box 99, Carterton, New Zealand.

615.1 DEU ISSN 1861-289X
ARZNEIMITTEL IN DER PIPELINE. 2005-200?. q. Deutscher Apotheker Verlag, Postfach 101061, Stuttgart, 70009, Germany.

956 ISR ISSN 0793-0879
ASAKIM & KALKALA. 1973-2005. q. Iggud Lishkot Hamischar Be-Yisrael, P O Box 20027, Tel Aviv, 61200, Israel.

294.54 CAN ISSN 0315-8179
ASCENT MAGAZINE; yoga for an inspired life. 1970-2009 (Mar.). q. Ascent, 837 rue Gilford, Montreal, PQ H2J 1P1, Canada.

340 AUS ISSN 1323-0425
ASIA - PACIFIC CONSTITUTIONAL YEARBOOK. 1993-1997. irreg. University of Melbourne, Centre for Comparative Constitutional Studies, 723 Swanston St, 2nd fl, Melbourne, VIC 3010, Australia.

950.4305 GBR ISSN 1756-7114
ASIAINT SOUTH ASIA REVIEW. 2001-2009. m. Asia Intelligence Ltd., 61 Old St, London, EC1V 9HW, United Kingdom.

345.067 GBR ISSN 1360-8223
ASIAN COMMERCIAL LAW REVIEW. 1996-1998. bi-m. Sweet & Maxwell Ltd., 100 Avenue Rd, London, NW3 3PF, United Kingdom.

340 GBR ISSN 1560-2494
ASIAN LEGAL JOURNALS INDEX. 1996-1998. m. Sweet & Maxwell Ltd., 100 Avenue Rd, London, NW3 3PF, United Kingdom.

500 ESP ISSN 1888-9271
ASOCIACION ESPANOLA DE ENSAYOS NON-DESTRUCTIVOS. BOLETIN INFORMATIVO. 1989-199?. 4/yr. Asociacion Espanola de Ensayos Non-Destructivos, Isal de Saipan 47, Madrid, 28035, Spain.

621.8 FRA ISSN 0750-1269 CODEN: ADHFB6
ASSEMBLAGES; soudage, colles et adhesifs, fixations mecaniques. 1977-2004. bi-m. (5/yr.). Promotion Presse Internationale, 7 Cour des Petites-Ecuries, Paris, 75010, France.

354 FRA ISSN 1277-1856
ASSEMBLEE NATIONALE. DELEGATION POUR L'UNION EUROPEENNE. BULLETIN. 1996-2006. irreg. Assemblee Nationale, Delegation pour l'Union Europeenne, 126 rue de l'Universite, Paris, 75355, France.

340 NLD ISSN 0929-6573
ASSER ACTUEEL. 1993-2005. 3/yr. Kluwer B.V., Postbus 23, Deventer, 7400 GA, Netherlands.

332.6 330.9 GBR ISSN 1367-8086
ASSET FINANCE INTERNATIONAL. 1976-200?. 11/yr. Euromoney Institutional Investor Plc., Nestor House, Playhouse Yard, London, EC4V 5EX, United Kingdom.

360 ITA ISSN 0392-1026
L'ASSISTENZA SOCIALE. 1947-2003. q. Ediesse srl, Via dei Frentani 4A, Rome, 00185, Italy.

027 FRA ISSN 1142-2815
ASSOCIATION DES AMIS DE LA BIBLIOTHEQUE DE FRANCE. RESEAUX. 1989-1993. bi-m. Association des Amis de la Bibliotheque de France, 1 Place Valhubert, Paris, 75013, France.

200 060 FRA ISSN 0066-8907
ASSOCIATION DES AMIS DE PIERRE TEILHARD DE CHARDIN. BULLETIN. 1966-198?. a. Association des Amis de Pierre Teilhard de Chardin, B P 90.001, Paris, Cedex 05 75221, France.

610 FRA ISSN 0571-5415
ASSOCIATION DES MEDECINS DE LANGUE FRANCAISE. REVUE. 1953-1969. q. Expansion Scientifique Francaise, 15 Rue Saint-Benoit, Paris, 75278 Cedex 06, France.

375 USA ISSN 0272-5282
ASSOCIATION FOR SUPERVISION AND CURRICULUM DEVELOPMENT. ANNUAL CONFERENCE. 19??-1974. a. Association for Supervision and Curriculum Development, 1703 N Beauregard St, Alexandria, VA 22311.

366.009 FRA ISSN 1775-2892
ASSOCIATION LE FAUBOURG. BANQUE DE PROJETS. 2005-2006. bi-m. Association Le Faubourg, 7 rue de l'Abreuvoir, Strasbourg, 67000, France.

370 FRA ISSN 0245-5668
ASSOCIATION NATIONALE DES COMMUNAUTES EDUCATIVES. BULLETIN MENSUEL D'INFORMATIONS. 1978-2002. m. Association Nationale des Communautes Educatives, 145 bd. de Magenta, Paris, 75010, France.

327 FRA ISSN 0153-3657
ASSOCIATION POUR L'ETUDE DES PROBLEMES D'OUTRE MER. DOCUMENTATION-DEVELOPPEMENT. 1947-2007. 8/yr. Association pour l'Etude des Problemes d'Outre Mer, 190 bd. Haussmann, Paris, 75008, France.

622.33 FRA
ASSOCIATION TECHNIQUE DE L'IMPORTATION CHARBONNIERE. ANNUAL REPORT. ceased. a. Association Technique de l'Importation Charbonniere, 149 rue de Longchamp, Paris, 75116, France.

622.33 338.2 FRA
ASSOCIATION TECHNIQUE DE L'IMPORTATION CHARBONNIERE. MONTHLY STATISTICS. ceased. m. Association Technique de l'Importation Charbonniere, 149 rue de Longchamp, Paris, 75116, France.

005.1 ITA
ASSOCIAZIONE LAICA. 1979-ceased. q. E N D A S Regionale Lazio, Sede Nazionale, Via Merulana 48, Rome, 00185, Italy.

677 ITA
ASSOCIAZIONE NOBILITAZIONE TESSILE. NOTIZIARIO. 1945-ceased. w. Istituto per l'Assistenza e Servizi alle Aziende Tessili s.r.l., Viale Sarca, 223, Milan, MI 20126, Italy.

352 ITA ISSN 0004-606X
ASTE GIUDIZIARIE. 1949-ceased. w. Istituto Vendite Giudiziarie di Roma, Via Aurelia 1311A, km 13, Rome, 00166, Italy.

133.5 FRA ISSN 1955-9135
ASTRO (YEAR). 2007-2007. a. Editions France Loisirs, 123 Bd de Grenelle, Paris, 75015, France.

Cessations

520 FRA ISSN 0398-074X
ASTROLAB. 1976-198?. q. Philippe Bury Ed. & Pub., 185 rue de Solignac, Limoges, 87000, France.

520 FRA ISSN 0764-2997
ASTROLETTRE. 1984-198?. irreg. (approx. 5/yr.). Philippe Bury Ed. & Pub., 185 rue de Solignac, Limoges, 87000, France.

520 ESP ISSN 1699-7751
ASTRONOMIA. 1985-1999. m. Equipo Sirius, Antequera 2, Madrid, 28041, Spain.

351.93 NZL ISSN 1177-0430
@ M C H. 2001-2005 (Dec.). s-a. Ministry for Culture and Heritage, PO Box 5364, Wellington, New Zealand.

796.4 NZL ISSN 1177-5254
ATHLETICS IN ACTION (PRINT). 1984-2007 (Mar.). q. Executive Publishing Network New Zealand Limited, PO Box 741, Wellington, 6140, New Zealand.

371.42 USA ISSN 1098-9730
THE ATLANTA JOBBANK; the job hunter's guide to Georgia. (Includes: Albany, Columbus, Macon, Savannah and many others.) 1983-2003 (15th ed.). irreg. Adams Media, 57 Littlefield St, Avon, MA 02322.

778.53 DEU
ATLAS FILMSZENE. 1985-1994. q. Atlas Film & Medien AG, Wilhelmshoehe 12, Duisburg, 47058, Germany.

790.1 ITA
ATTIVITA DOPOLAVORISTICHE. 1956-ceased. m. Dopolavoro Ferroviario di Torino, Via Paolo Sacchi, 63, Turin, TO 10125, Italy.

910 ITA ISSN 0394-414X
ATTRAVERSO IL MONDO. 1986-ceased. q. Touring Editore, Corso Italia 10, Milan, 20122, Italy.

821 GBR ISSN 1366-056X
AUDEN STUDIES. 1990-1995. irreg. Oxford University Press, Great Clarendon St, Oxford, OX2 6DP, United Kingdom.

384.55 FRA ISSN 1253-5559
AUDIO VIDEO ECHOS. 19??-200?. 21/yr. Editions du Gaillard, 5 av. de la Republique, Paris, Cedex 75130, France.

621.381 ITA
AUDIONEWS. 1981-199?. 20/yr. Edizioni Publitrade News, Corso Vittorio Emanuele II, 187, Rome, RM 00186, Italy.

003 USA ISSN 0735-9985
AUERBACH SYSTEMS DEVELOPMENT MANAGEMENT. 1976-199?. bi-m. Auerbach Publications, 2000 Corporate Blvd, N W, Boca Raton, FL 33431.

342 DEU ISSN 0937-3071
AUSLAENDER IN DER BUNDESREPUBLIK DEUTSCHLAND. 1967-2005. 8/yr. Deutscher Wirtschaftsdienst, Luxemburger Str 449, Cologne, 50939, Germany.

336 DEU
AUSLANDS - STEUER - TELEX; Spezialdienst mit Kennziffen Service. 1987-2004. s-m. Deubner Verlag GmbH & Co. KG, Oststr 11, Cologne, 50996, Germany.

330 DEU ISSN 0949-0396
AUSLANDSKURIER. 1979-2004. 10/yr. Eppinger-Verlag OHG, Stauffenbergstr 18-20, Schwaebisch Hall, 74523, Germany.

382 DEU ISSN 0171-8126
AUSSENHANDELSBLAETTER. 1949-2003. bi-m. Commerzbank AG, Kaiserplatz, Frankfurt Am Main, 60311, Germany.

336 BRD ISSN 0004-8224
DIE AUSSENWIRTSCHAFT. 1957-1971. w. Deutscher Wirtschaftsdienst, Luxemburger Str 449, Cologne, 50939, Germany.

382 DEU ISSN 0178-8876
AUSSENWIRTSCHAFTSBRIEF; Information fuer das Auslandsgeschaeft. 1985-2003. bi-m. Deutscher Wirtschaftsdienst, Luxemburger Str 449, Cologne, 50939, Germany.

332.6 DEU ISSN 0933-2723
AUSSENWIRTSCHAFTSRECHT; Ergaenzbare Sammlung der fuer die Aussenwirtschaft massgeblichen Bestimmungen der Bundesrepublik Deutschland und der Europaeischen Union. 1961-2003. irreg. Erich Schmidt Verlag GmbH & Co. (Berlin), Genthiner Str 30 G, Berlin, 10785, Germany.

382 DEU ISSN 0937-3438
AUSSENWIRTSCHAFTSRECHT (YEAR); Einfuehrung - Fundstellen - Vorschriftentexte. 1970-2001. plus q. updates. Deutscher Wirtschaftsdienst, Luxemburger Str 449, Cologne, 50939, Germany.

371.42 USA ISSN 1098-9749
THE AUSTIN - SAN ANTONIO JOBBANK; the job hunter's guide to Southern and Western Texas. (Includes: Abilene, Amarillo, Corpus Christi, El Paso, Lubbock, and many others.) 1996-2004 (4th ed.). irreg. Adams Media, 57 Littlefield St, Avon, MA 02322.

793 AUS
AUSTRALASIAN GAMING MAGAZINE. 1989-2003. irreg. (approx. 3-4/yr.). KinLoba Pty. Ltd., c/o Jim Henry, Pub., PO Box 404, Cammeray, NSW 2062, Australia.

387.7 310 AUS ISSN 1320-744X
AUSTRALIA. AIR TRANSPORT STATISTICS. DIGEST OF STATISTICS. 1992-2005; suspended. 2/yr. Bureau of Infrastructure, Transport and Regional Economics, GPO Box 501, Canberra City, ACT 2600, Australia.

387.7 AUS ISSN 1324-5074
AUSTRALIA. AIR TRANSPORT STATISTICS. INTERNATIONAL SCHEDULED AIR TRANSPORT. 1934-2001. a. Bureau of Infrastructure, Transport and Regional Economics, GPO Box 501, Canberra City, ACT 2600, Australia.

387.7 AUS ISSN 1038-0361
AUSTRALIA. AIR TRANSPORT STATISTICS. REGIONAL AIRLINES ANNUAL. 1968-1998. irreg. Bureau of Infrastructure, Transport and Regional Economics, GPO Box 501, Canberra City, ACT 2600, Australia.

630 639.2 AUS
AUSTRALIA BUREAU OF RURAL SCIENCES. WORK PROGRAM. 1990-2000. irreg. Department of Agriculture, Fisheries and Forestry, Bureau of Rural Sciences, Edmund Barton Bldg, Broughton St, Barton, GPO Box 858, Canberra, ACT 2601, Australia.

371.3021 AUS
AUSTRALIA. BUREAU OF STATISTICS. A DIRECTORY OF EDUCATION AND TRAINING STATISTICS (PRINT). 1995-200?. irreg. Australian Bureau of Statistics, Locked Bag 10, Belconnen, ACT 2616, Australia.

319.4 AUS
AUSTRALIA. BUREAU OF STATISTICS. A GUIDE TO A B S SUBSCRIPTIONS: PUBLICATIONS AVAILABLE FOR SUBSCRIPTION IN (YEAR) (ONLINE). 1982-200?. a. Australian Bureau of Statistics, Locked Bag 10, Belconnen, ACT 2616, Australia.

630.021 AUS
AUSTRALIA. BUREAU OF STATISTICS. AGRICULTURAL INDUSTRIES, FINANCIAL STATISTICS, AUSTRALIA, PRELIMINARY. 1989-1992. a. Australian Bureau of Statistics, Locked Bag 10, Belconnen, ACT 2616, Australia.

338.021 AUS
AUSTRALIA. BUREAU OF STATISTICS. AUSTRALIAN AND NEW ZEALAND STANDARD PRODUCT CLASSIFICATION - WEBSITE VERSION. 1990-2001. irreg. Australian Bureau of Statistics, Locked Bag 10, Belconnen, ACT 2616, Australia.

345.021 AUS ISSN 0819-1158
AUSTRALIA. BUREAU OF STATISTICS. AUSTRALIAN CAPITAL TERRITORY COURTS. 1985-1986. a. Australian Bureau of Statistics, Locked Bag 10, Belconnen, ACT 2616, Australia.

363.5021 AUS ISSN 1321-1617
AUSTRALIA. BUREAU OF STATISTICS. AUSTRALIAN HOUSING IN BRIEF. 1995-1998. irreg. Australian Bureau of Statistics, Locked Bag 10, Belconnen, ACT 2616, Australia.

614 AUS ISSN 1032-6138
AUSTRALIA. BUREAU OF STATISTICS. AUSTRALIA'S HEALTH. 1988-2006. biennial. Australian Bureau of Statistics, Locked Bag 10, Belconnen, ACT 2616, Australia.

361.021 AUS ISSN 1321-1455
AUSTRALIA. BUREAU OF STATISTICS. AUSTRALIA'S WELFARE. 1997-2005. biennial. Australian Bureau of Statistics, Locked Bag 10, Belconnen, ACT 2616, Australia.

331.21021 AUS ISSN 1031-0584
AUSTRALIA. BUREAU OF STATISTICS. AVERAGE WEEKLY EARNINGS, AUSTRALIA, PRELIMINARY. 1977-2000. q. Australian Bureau of Statistics, Locked Bag 10, Belconnen, ACT 2616, Australia.

304.6021 363.5021 AUS
AUSTRALIA. BUREAU OF STATISTICS. CENSUS OF POPULATION AND HOUSING: SOCIO-ECONOMIC INDEXES FOR AREAS, AUSTRALIAN CAPITAL TERRITORY. 1996-2001. quinquennial. Australian Bureau of Statistics, Locked Bag 10, Belconnen, ACT 2616, Australia.

338.021 AUS ISSN 1034-4748
AUSTRALIA. BUREAU OF STATISTICS. CONSTANT PRICE ESTIMATES OF MANUFACTURING PRODUCTION, AUSTRALIA. 1949-1986. a. Australian Bureau of Statistics, Locked Bag 10, Belconnen, ACT 2616, Australia.

304.6021 AUS
AUSTRALIA. BUREAU OF STATISTICS. DEMOGRAPHY, AUSTRALIAN CAPITAL TERRITORY (ONLINE). 1990-2004. a. Australian Bureau of Statistics, Locked Bag 10, Belconnen, ACT 2616, Australia.

388.021 AUS
AUSTRALIA. BUREAU OF STATISTICS. DIRECTORY OF TRANSPORT STATISTICS (PRINT). 1994-2000. irreg. Australian Bureau of Statistics, Locked Bag 10, Belconnen, ACT 2616, Australia.

628.021 AUS
AUSTRALIA. BUREAU OF STATISTICS. ENVIRONMENT PROTECTION EXPENDITURE, AUSTRALIA. 1991-2001. biennial. Australian Bureau of Statistics, Locked Bag 10, Belconnen, ACT 2616, Australia.

363.70221 AUS
AUSTRALIA. BUREAU OF STATISTICS. ENVIRONMENTAL ISSUES: PEOPLE'S VIEWS AND PRACTICES (ONLINE). 1992-2007. biennial. Australian Bureau of Statistics, Locked Bag 10, Belconnen, ACT 2616, Australia.

622.021 AUS ISSN 0312-1585
AUSTRALIA. BUREAU OF STATISTICS. FOREIGN OWNERSHIP AND CONTROL OF THE MINING INDUSTRY, AUSTRALIA. 1963-1985. irreg. Australian Bureau of Statistics, Locked Bag 10, Belconnen, ACT 2616, Australia.

339.021 AUS
AUSTRALIA. BUREAU OF STATISTICS. HOUSEHOLD EXPENDITURE SURVEY, AUSTRALIA: CONFIDENTIALISED UNIT RECORD FILE ON FLOPPY DISK. 1994-1996. irreg. Australian Bureau of Statistics, Locked Bag 10, Belconnen, ACT 2616, Australia.

363.5021 AUS
AUSTRALIA. BUREAU OF STATISTICS. HOUSING, AUSTRALIA: A STATISTICAL OVERVIEW. 1992-1996. irreg. Australian Bureau of Statistics, Locked Bag 10, Belconnen, ACT 2616, Australia.

382.021 AUS
AUSTRALIA. BUREAU OF STATISTICS. INFORMATION PAPER: INTERNATIONAL MERCHANDISE TRADE AND SHIPPING STATISTICS, AUSTRALIA: DATA CONFIDENTIALITY. 1994-1999. irreg. Australian Bureau of Statistics, Locked Bag 10, Belconnen, ACT 2616, Australia.

382.021 AUS
AUSTRALIA. BUREAU OF STATISTICS. INTERNATIONAL MERCHANDISE EXPORTS, AUSTRALIA - ELECTRONIC DELIVERY. 2000-2003. m. Australian Bureau of Statistics, Locked Bag 10, Belconnen, ACT 2616, Australia.

332.6021 AUS ISSN 1321-3512
AUSTRALIA. BUREAU OF STATISTICS. INTERNATIONAL MERCHANDISE TRADE, AUSTRALIA. 1978-2003. q. Australian Bureau of Statistics, Locked Bag 10, Belconnen, ACT 2616, Australia.

371.42021 AUS
AUSTRALIA. BUREAU OF STATISTICS. JOB VACANCIES, AUSTRALIA (ONLINE). 1989-2008. q. Australian Bureau of Statistics, Locked Bag 10, Belconnen, ACT 2616, Australia.

331.021 AUS ISSN 1031-038X
AUSTRALIA. BUREAU OF STATISTICS. LABOUR FORCE, AUSTRALIA, PRELIMINARY. 1972-2003. m. Australian Bureau of Statistics, Locked Bag 10, Belconnen, ACT 2616, Australia.

331.11021 AUS
AUSTRALIA. BUREAU OF STATISTICS. LABOUR FORCE, AUSTRALIA - STANDARD TABLES ON MICROFICHE. 1966-1997. irreg. Australian Bureau of Statistics, Locked Bag 10, Belconnen, ACT 2616, Australia.

338.0021 AUS ISSN 1329-4741
AUSTRALIA. BUREAU OF STATISTICS. MANUFACTURING, AUSTRALIA. 1997-2002. a. Australian Bureau of Statistics, Locked Bag 10, Belconnen, ACT 2616, Australia.

339.021 AUS ISSN 1031-2641
AUSTRALIA. BUREAU OF STATISTICS. N I F - 10S MODEL DATA BASE MANUAL. (National Income Forecasting) 1989-1997. q. Australian Bureau of Statistics, Locked Bag 10, Belconnen, ACT 2616, Australia.

362.1021 AUS
AUSTRALIA. BUREAU OF STATISTICS. NATIONAL HEALTH SURVEY: INJURIES, AUSTRALIA (PRINT). 1990-200?. irreg. Australian Bureau of Statistics, Locked Bag 10, Belconnen, ACT 2616, Australia.

362.1021 AUS
AUSTRALIA. BUREAU OF STATISTICS. NATIONAL HEALTH SURVEY: SUMMARY OF RESULTS (PRINT). 1990-19??. irreg. Australian Bureau of Statistics, Locked Bag 10, Belconnen, ACT 2616, Australia.

383.021 AUS
AUSTRALIA. BUREAU OF STATISTICS. NATIONAL LOCALITIES INDEX, AUSTRALIA (ONLINE EDITION). 2003-2007. a. Australian Bureau of Statistics, Locked Bag 10, Belconnen, ACT 2616, Australia.

304.6021 363.5021 AUS
AUSTRALIA. BUREAU OF STATISTICS. NEW SOUTH WALES OFFICE. CENSUS OF POPULATION AND HOUSING: CDATA2001, NEW SOUTH WALES - FULL GIS. 1996-200?. quinquennial. Australian Bureau of Statistics, New South Wales Office, St. Andrews House, 5th Fl., Sydney Sq., Sydney, NSW 2000, Australia.

304.6021 363.5021 AUS
AUSTRALIA. BUREAU OF STATISTICS. NEW SOUTH WALES OFFICE. CENSUS OF POPULATION AND HOUSING: CDATA2001 - QUICKBUILD, NEW SOUTH WALES. 2001-2002. quinquennial. Australian Bureau of Statistics, New South Wales Office, St. Andrews House, 5th Fl., Sydney Sq., Sydney, NSW 2000, Australia.

304.6021 363.5021 AUS
AUSTRALIA. BUREAU OF STATISTICS. NEW SOUTH WALES OFFICE. CENSUS OF POPULATION AND HOUSING: SELECTED SOCIAL AND HOUSING CHARACTERISTICS FOR STATISTICAL LOCAL AREAS, NEW SOUTH WALES AND JERVIS BAY. 1996-2001. quinquennial. Australian Bureau of Statistics, New South Wales Office, GPO Box 796, Sydney, NSW 2001, Australia.

304.6021 363.5021 AUS
AUSTRALIA. BUREAU OF STATISTICS. NEW SOUTH WALES OFFICE. CENSUS OF POPULATION AND HOUSING: SOCIO-ECONOMIC INDEXES FOR AREAS, NEW SOUTH WALES. 1998-200?. quinquennial. Australian Bureau of Statistics, New South Wales Office, GPO Box 796, Sydney, NSW 2001, Australia.

304.6021 AUS
AUSTRALIA. BUREAU OF STATISTICS. NEW SOUTH WALES OFFICE. DEMOGRAPHY, NEW SOUTH WALES (ONLINE). 1990-2006. a. Australian Bureau of Statistics, New South Wales Office, GPO Box 796, Sydney, NSW 2001, Australia.

304.6021 AUS
AUSTRALIA. BUREAU OF STATISTICS. NEW SOUTH WALES OFFICE. POPULATION BY AGE AND SEX, NEW SOUTH WALES - ELECTRONIC DELIVERY. 1994-2005. a. Australian Bureau of Statistics, New South Wales Office, St. Andrews House, 5th Fl., Sydney Sq., Sydney, NSW 2000, Australia.

304.6021 363.5021 AUS
AUSTRALIA. BUREAU OF STATISTICS. NORTHERN TERRITORY OFFICE. CENSUS OF POPULATION AND HOUSING: CDATA2001, NORTHERN TERRITORY - FULL GIS. 1996-2002. every 5 yrs. Australian Bureau of Statistics, Northern Territory Office, 5th Fl., 81 Smith St, Darwin, N.T. 0800, Australia.

304.6021 AUS
AUSTRALIA. BUREAU OF STATISTICS. NORTHERN TERRITORY OFFICE. CENSUS OF POPULATION AND HOUSING: CDATA2001 - QUICKBUILD, NORTHERN TERRITORY. 2001-2001. quinquennial. Australian Bureau of Statistics, Northern Territory Office, 5th Fl., 81 Smith St, Darwin, N.T. 0800, Australia.

304.6021 363.5021 AUS
AUSTRALIA. BUREAU OF STATISTICS. NORTHERN TERRITORY OFFICE. CENSUS OF POPULATION AND HOUSING: POPULATION SUMMARY, NORTHERN TERRITORY (ONLINE). 1996-2002. quinquennial. Australian Bureau of Statistics, Northern Territory Office, 5th Fl., 81 Smith St, Darwin, N.T. 0800, Australia.

304.6021 AUS
AUSTRALIA. BUREAU OF STATISTICS. NORTHERN TERRITORY OFFICE. DEMOGRAPHY, NORTHERN TERRITORY (ONLINE). 1993-2004. a. Australian Bureau of Statistics, Northern Territory Office, 5th Fl., 81 Smith St, Darwin, N.T. 0800, Australia.

647.021 AUS
AUSTRALIA. BUREAU OF STATISTICS. OCCASIONAL PAPER: RECENT CHANGES IN UNPAID WORK. 1992-1995. irreg. Australian Bureau of Statistics, Locked Bag 10, Belconnen, ACT 2616, Australia.

304.6021 AUS
AUSTRALIA. BUREAU OF STATISTICS. QUEENSLAND OFFICE. DEMOGRAPHY, QUEENSLAND (ONLINE). 1990-2004. a. Australian Bureau of Statistics, Queensland Office, 313 Adelaide St, Brisbane, QLD 4000, Australia.

304.6021 AUS ISSN 1031-6264
AUSTRALIA. BUREAU OF STATISTICS. QUEENSLAND OFFICE. ESTIMATED RESIDENT POPULATION: COMPONENTS OF CHANGE, QUEENSLAND. 1966-198?. irreg. Australian Bureau of Statistics, Queensland Office, 313 Adelaide St, Brisbane, QLD 4000, Australia.

319.4 AUS
AUSTRALIA. BUREAU OF STATISTICS. QUEENSLAND OFFICE. REGIONAL STATISTICS, QUEENSLAND (ONLINE). 1994-2004. a. Australian Bureau of Statistics, Queensland Office, 313 Adelaide St, Brisbane, QLD 4000, Australia.

319.4 AUS ISSN 0818-3856
AUSTRALIA. BUREAU OF STATISTICS. REGISTER OF COMMONWEALTH STATISTICAL COLLECTIONS. 1985-1989. triennial. Australian Bureau of Statistics, Locked Bag 10, Belconnen, ACT 2616, Australia.

330.021 AUS ISSN 0819-9876
AUSTRALIA. BUREAU OF STATISTICS. RESEARCH AND EXPERIMENTAL DEVELOPMENT, ALL SECTOR SUMMARY (INTER-YEAR SURVEY), AUSTRALIA. 1985-1988. biennial. Australian Bureau of Statistics, Locked Bag 10, Belconnen, ACT 2616, Australia.

330.021 AUS ISSN 0159-1584
AUSTRALIA. BUREAU OF STATISTICS. RESEARCH AND EXPERIMENTAL DEVELOPMENT, BUSINESS ENTERPRISES, AUSTRALIA, PRELIMINARY. 1978-1987. biennial. Australian Bureau of Statistics, Locked Bag 10, Belconnen, ACT 2616, Australia.

658.021 AUS ISSN 1031-8046
AUSTRALIA. BUREAU OF STATISTICS. RETAIL TRADE, AUSTRALIA: COMMODITY DETAILS. 1988-1990. irreg. Australian Bureau of Statistics, Locked Bag 10, Belconnen, ACT 2616, Australia.

658.021 AUS
AUSTRALIA. BUREAU OF STATISTICS. RETAIL TRADE SPECIAL DATA SERVICES: PERFORMANCE REPORTS - DATA REPORT. 1992-1995. irreg. Australian Bureau of Statistics, Locked Bag 10, Belconnen, ACT 2616, Australia.

658.021 AUS
AUSTRALIA. BUREAU OF STATISTICS. RETAIL TRADE SPECIAL DATA SERVICES: SELF COMPARISON REPORTS - DATA REPORT. 19??-1996. irreg. Australian Bureau of Statistics, Locked Bag 10, Belconnen, ACT 2616, Australia.

388.3021 AUS
AUSTRALIA. BUREAU OF STATISTICS. SALES OF NEW MOTOR VEHICLES, ELECTRONIC DELIVERY. 2002-2007. m. Australian Bureau of Statistics, Locked Bag 10, Belconnen, ACT 2616, Australia.

314.021 AUS
AUSTRALIA. BUREAU OF STATISTICS. SIENA GROUP PAPERS: FAMILIES AT THE END OF THE 20TH CENTURY - VOL 1. 1998-1999. irreg. Australian Bureau of Statistics, Locked Bag 10, Belconnen, ACT 2616, Australia.

314.021 AUS
AUSTRALIA. BUREAU OF STATISTICS. SIENA GROUP PAPERS: FAMILY STATISTICS COUNTRY PAPERS - VOL 2. 1998-1999. irreg. Australian Bureau of Statistics, Locked Bag 10, Belconnen, ACT 2616, Australia.

314.021 AUS
AUSTRALIA. BUREAU OF STATISTICS. SIENA GROUP PAPERS: FUTURE DIRECTIONS FOR THE SIENA GROUP - VOL 3. 1998-1999. irreg. Australian Bureau of Statistics, Locked Bag 10, Belconnen, ACT 2616, Australia.

304.6 AUS
AUSTRALIA. BUREAU OF STATISTICS. SOCIAL INDICATORS, AUSTRALIA. 1976-1992. irreg. Australian Bureau of Statistics, Locked Bag 10, Belconnen, ACT 2616, Australia.

304.6021 363.5021 AUS
AUSTRALIA. BUREAU OF STATISTICS. SOUTH AUSTRALIAN OFFICE. CENSUS OF POPULATION AND HOUSING: SOCIO-ECONOMIC INDEXES FOR AREAS, SOUTH AUSTRALIA. 1996-2001. quinquennial. Australian Bureau of Statistics, South Australian Office, GPO Box 2272, Adelaide, SA 5001, Australia.

362.2021 AUS
AUSTRALIA. BUREAU OF STATISTICS. SUICIDES, AUSTRALIA. 1982-2005. irreg. Australian Bureau of Statistics, Locked Bag 10, Belconnen, ACT 2616, Australia.

304.6021 363.5021 AUS
AUSTRALIA. BUREAU OF STATISTICS. TASMANIAN OFFICE. CENSUS OF POPULATION AND HOUSING: CDATA2001, TASMANIA - FULL GIS. 1996-2002. quinquennial. Australian Bureau of Statistics, Tasmanian Office, GPO Box 66A, Hobart, TAS 7001, Australia.

301.021 AUS
AUSTRALIA. BUREAU OF STATISTICS. TASMANIAN OFFICE. DEMOGRAPHY, TASMANIA (ONLINE). 1990-2004. a. Australian Bureau of Statistics, Tasmanian Office, GPO Box 66A, Hobart, TAS 7001, Australia.

319.4 AUS
AUSTRALIA. BUREAU OF STATISTICS. TASMANIAN OFFICE. REGIONAL STATISTICS, TASMANIA (ONLINE). 1999-2007. irreg. Australian Bureau of Statistics, Tasmanian Office, GPO Box 66A, Hobart, TAS 7001, Australia.

319.4 AUS ISSN 1031-9573
AUSTRALIA. BUREAU OF STATISTICS. TASMANIAN OFFICE. TASMANIAN POCKET YEARBOOK. 1913-2002. a. Australian Bureau of Statistics, Tasmanian Office, GPO Box 66A, Hobart, TAS 7001, Australia.

319.4 AUS ISSN 1034-1803
AUSTRALIA. BUREAU OF STATISTICS. TASMANIAN OFFICE. TASMANIAN STATISTICAL INDICATORS. 1945-2004. m. Australian Bureau of Statistics, Tasmanian Office, GPO Box 66A, Hobart, TAS 7001, Australia.

994.021 AUS ISSN 0082-2116
AUSTRALIA. BUREAU OF STATISTICS. TASMANIAN OFFICE. TASMANIAN YEAR BOOK. 1967-2000. biennial. Australian Bureau of Statistics, Tasmanian Office, GPO Box 66A, Hobart, TAS 7001, Australia.

304.6021 363.5021 AUS
AUSTRALIA. BUREAU OF STATISTICS. VICTORIAN OFFICE. CENSUS OF POPULATION AND HOUSING: CDATA2001, VICTORIA - FULL GIS. 1996-2001. quinquennial. Australian Bureau of Statistics, Victorian Office, GPO Box 2796Y, Melbourne, VIC 3001, Australia.

304.6021 363.5021 AUS
AUSTRALIA. BUREAU OF STATISTICS. VICTORIAN OFFICE. CENSUS OF POPULATION AND HOUSING: SOCIO-ECONOMIC INDEXES FOR AREAS, VICTORIA. 1996-2001. quinquennial. Australian Bureau of Statistics, Victorian Office, GPO Box 2796Y, Melbourne, VIC 3001, Australia.

364.021 AUS ISSN 1325-0477
AUSTRALIA. BUREAU OF STATISTICS. VICTORIAN OFFICE. CRIME AND SAFETY, VICTORIA. 1994-1995. irreg. Australian Bureau of Statistics, Victorian Office, GPO Box 2796Y, Melbourne, VIC 3001, Australia.

304.6021 AUS
AUSTRALIA. BUREAU OF STATISTICS. VICTORIAN OFFICE. DEMOGRAPHY, VICTORIA (ONLINE). 1990-2004. irreg. Australian Bureau of Statistics, Victorian Office, GPO Box 2796Y, Melbourne, VIC 3001, Australia.

304.6021 AUS
AUSTRALIA. BUREAU OF STATISTICS. VICTORIAN OFFICE. ESTIMATED RESIDENT POPULATION BY AGE AND SEX IN STATISTICAL LOCAL AREAS, VICTORIA: DATA ON FLOPPY DISK. 1994-1999. a. Australian Bureau of Statistics, Victorian Office, GPO Box 2796Y, Melbourne, VIC 3001, Australia.

304.6021 AUS
AUSTRALIA. BUREAU OF STATISTICS. VICTORIAN OFFICE. VICTORIA IN FUTURE - THE VICTORIAN GOVERNMENT'S POPULATION PROJECTIONS FOR THE STATE'S LOCAL GOVERNMENT AREAS. 199?-1997. irreg. Australian Bureau of Statistics, Victorian Office, GPO Box 2796Y, Melbourne, VIC 3001, Australia.

994 319 AUS ISSN 0067-1223
AUSTRALIA. BUREAU OF STATISTICS. VICTORIAN OFFICE. VICTORIAN YEAR BOOK. 1873-2002. a. Australian Bureau of Statistics, Victorian Office, GPO Box 2796Y, Melbourne, VIC 3001, Australia.

331.2021 AUS
AUSTRALIA. BUREAU OF STATISTICS. WAGE AND SALARY EARNERS, PUBLIC SECTOR, AUSTRALIA (ONLINE). 1983-2007. q. Australian Bureau of Statistics, Locked Bag 10, Belconnen, ACT 2616, Australia.

304.6021 363.5021 AUS
AUSTRALIA. BUREAU OF STATISTICS. WESTERN AUSTRALIAN OFFICE. CENSUS OF POPULATION AND HOUSING: ABORIGINAL AND TORRES STRAIT ISLANDER PEOPLE, WESTERN AUSTRALIA. 1996-1998. quinquennial. Australian Bureau of Statistics, Western Australian Office, GPO Box K881, Perth, W.A. 6842, Australia.

304.6021 363.5021 AUS
AUSTRALIA. BUREAU OF STATISTICS. WESTERN AUSTRALIAN OFFICE. CENSUS OF POPULATION AND HOUSING: CDATA2001, WESTERN AUSTRALIA - FULL GIS. 1996-2001. quinquennial. Australian Bureau of Statistics, Western Australian Office, GPO Box K881, Perth, W.A. 6842, Australia.

304.6021 363.5021 AUS
AUSTRALIA. BUREAU OF STATISTICS. WESTERN AUSTRALIAN OFFICE. CENSUS OF POPULATION AND HOUSING: SOCIO-ECONOMIC INDEXES FOR AREAS, WESTERN AUSTRALIA. 1996-2001. quinquennial. Australian Bureau of Statistics, Western Australian Office, GPO Box K881, Perth, W.A. 6842, Australia.

304.6021 AUS ISSN 1036-2665
AUSTRALIA. BUREAU OF STATISTICS. WESTERN AUSTRALIAN OFFICE. DEMOGRAPHY, WESTERN AUSTRALIA. 1990-2004. a. Australian Bureau of Statistics, Western Australian Office, GPO Box K881, Perth, W.A. 6842, Australia.

690.021 AUS ISSN 1445-3789
AUSTRALIA. BUREAU OF STATISTICS. WESTERN AUSTRALIAN OFFICE. ESTIMATED STOCKS OF DWELLINGS, WESTERN AUSTRALIA. 1986-1996. a. Australian Bureau of Statistics, Western Australian Office, GPO Box K881, Perth, W.A. 6842, Australia.

005.1021 AUS
AUSTRALIA. BUREAU OF STATISTICS. YEAR 2000 PROBLEM, AUSTRALIA. 1998-2000. irreg. Australian Bureau of Statistics, Locked Bag 10, Belconnen, ACT 2616, Australia.

005.1021 AUS
AUSTRALIA. BUREAU OF STATISTICS. YEAR 2000 PROBLEM, AUSTRALIA, PRELIMINARY. 1998-2000. irreg. Australian Bureau of Statistics, Locked Bag 10, Belconnen, ACT 2616, Australia.

330.9 AUS
AUSTRALIA. DEPARTMENT OF THE TREASURY. NATIONAL FISCAL OUTLOOK. 1993-1998. a. AusInfo, Parliament House, Canberra Mc, ACT 2600, Australia.

330.9 AUS
AUSTRALIA. DEPARTMENT OF THE TREASURY. TREASURY ECONOMIC PAPERS. 1972-1994. irreg. AusInfo, Parliament House, Canberra Mc, ACT 2600, Australia.

004.16 AUS
AUSTRALIAN AMIGA REVIEW. 1984-1996. m. Gareth Powell Pty Ltd., 21 Darley Rd, Randwick, NSW 2031, Australia.

708.994 AUS
AUSTRALIAN ART MUSEUMS AND PUBLIC GALLERIES DIRECTORY. 1990-1994. biennial. Museums Australia Inc., PO Box K346, Haymarket, NSW 1238, Australia.

574.05 AUS ISSN 1030-6234
AUSTRALIAN BIOLOGIST. 1988-2004. 2/yr. Australian Institute of Biology, c/o The Royal Geographical Society of Queensland, 237 Milton Rd, Milton, QLD 4064, Australia.

011 AUS ISSN 0067-172X
AUSTRALIAN BOOKS IN PRINT; including information on book trade associations. 1956-2009. a. Thorpe-Bowker, St Kilda Rd, PO Box 6509, Melbourne, VIC 8008, Australia.

794.1 AUS ISSN 0159-4958
AUSTRALIAN CHESS MAGAZINE. 1966-199?. 6/yr. Peter Parr Ed. & Pub., Haymarket, PO Box K 1022, Sydney, NSW 2000, Australia.

691 AUS ISSN 1035-4611
AUSTRALIAN CLAY JOURNAL & CERAMIC NEWS. 1933-2002. bi-m. Hamilton Press Pty. Ltd., PO Box 386, Manly, NSW 1655, Australia.

355 378 AUS ISSN 1832-0554
AUSTRALIAN DEFENCE FORCE ACADEMY . ALUMNI NEWSLETTER. 2001-2005. a. Australian Defence Force Academy, University of New South Wales, Northcott Dr, Campbell, ACT 2600, Australia.

355 AUS ISSN 1034-6023
AUSTRALIAN DEFENCE REPORT; incorporating aerospace, electronics and defence manufacturing. 1990-2002. bi-w. T M H Enterprises Pty. Ltd., PO Box 4775, Kingston, ACT 2604, Australia.

632.1 AUS
AUSTRALIAN DEPARTMENT OF HEALTH & AGED CARE. HEALTH FINANCING SERIES OCCASIONAL PAPERS. 1999-2001. irreg. Australian Prescriber, GPO Box 9848, Canberra City, ACT 2601, Australia.

610.73 AUS ISSN 1322-8676
THE AUSTRALIAN ELECTRONIC JOURNAL OF NURSING EDUCATION. 1995-2002; suspended. q. Southern Cross University, School of Nursing & Health Care Practices, Box 157, Lismore, NSW 2480, Australia.

333.79 621.042 AUS
AUSTRALIAN ENERGY NEWS (MELBOURNE). 1984-2002. q. Department of Primary Industries and Energy, GPO Box 858, Canberra, ACT 2600, Australia.

794.8 AUS ISSN 1448-8825
AUSTRALIAN GAMEPRO. 2004-2007. bi-m. I D G Communications Pty. Ltd., PO Box 295, St Leonards, NSW 1590, Australia.

629.13 AUS ISSN 0084-7364
AUSTRALIAN GLIDING YEARBOOK. 1969-200?. a. Gliding Federation of Australia, Level 1/34 Somerton Rd, Somerton, VIC 3062, Australia.

351 658 AUS ISSN 1832-3731
AUSTRALIAN GOVERNMENT INFORMATION MANAGEMENT OFFICE. ANNUAL REPORT. 1998-200?. a. Australian Government Information Management Office, John Gorton Bldg, King Edward Terr, Parkes, ACT 2600, Australia.

600 500 AUS ISSN 1444-5026
AUSTRALIAN INNOVATION MAGAZINE. 1991-2002. q. Australia. Department of Industry, Science and Resources, GPO Box 9839, Canberra, ACT 2601, Australia.

338.0029 USA ISSN 0067-1959
AUSTRALIAN MARKET GUIDE. 1964-1980. biennial. Dun's Marketing Services, 3 Sylvan Way, Parsippany, NJ 07054-3896.

352.14 AUS ISSN 0004-9808
AUSTRALIAN MUNICIPAL JOURNAL. 1921-1998. m. Municipal Association of Victoria, GPO Box 4326, Melbourne, VIC 3001, Australia.

790.13 AUS
AUSTRALIAN NATIONAL AVONS COLLECTORS CLUB. NEWSLETTER. 1977-2006. q. Australian National Avons Collectors Club, PO Box 342, Kilmore, VIC 3704, Australia.

333.72 AUS ISSN 1320-9736
AUSTRALIAN NATURE CONSERVATION AGENCY. ANNUAL REPORT. 1980-ceased. a. AusInfo, Parliament House, Canberra Mc, ACT 2600, Australia.

658.31244 AUS ISSN 1329-430X
AUSTRALIAN OCCUPATIONAL HEALTH & SAFETY YEARBOOK. 1993-2007. a. I H S Australian Pty. Ltd., Level 3, 33 Rowe St, Locked Bag 7, Eastwood, NSW 2122, Australia.

004.16 AUS ISSN 0813-1384
AUSTRALIAN P C WORLD (PRINT). 1984-2008. m. I D G Communications Pty. Ltd., PO Box 295, St Leonards, NSW 1590, Australia.

388.3 AUS ISSN 1036-3254
AUSTRALIAN ROAD AND TRACK. 1986-1997. 6/yr. Stop Press Publishing Pty. Ltd., 51 Jackson St, Balgowlah, NSW 2093, Australia.

369.4 AUS ISSN 0815-4627
AUSTRALIAN SCOUT. 1912-2003. 11/yr. Scout Association of Australia, Victoria Branch, PO Box 190, Carlton, VIC 3053, Australia.

590 551.46 AUS ISSN 1832-7273
AUSTRALIAN SEACHANGE. 2005-2006. q. SeaChange Magazine, PO Box 253, Newcastle, NSW 2300, Australia.

663.2 AUS ISSN 1832-5726
AUSTRALIAN SOMMELIER. 2005-200?. q. Edge Publishing Group Pty. Ltd., 51 Whistler St, Manly, NSW 2095, Australia.

614 AUS ISSN 0067-2165
AUSTRALIAN STUDIES IN HEALTH SERVICE ADMINISTRATION. 1968-2002. irreg. University Of New South Wales, School of Public Health and Community Medicine, Level 3, Samuels Bldg, Gate 11, Botany St, Randwick, Sydney, NSW 2052, Australia.

Cessations

079.94 AUS ISSN 1038-6130
AUSTRALIAN STUDIES IN JOURNALISM. 1992-2001; suspended. a. University of Queensland, School of Journalism and Communication, Bldg 91, St Lucia campus, Brisbane, QLD 4072, Australia.

796.172 AUS ISSN 1321-2036
AUSTRALIAN SURF LIFESAVER. 1994-1999. bi-m. Surf Life Saving Australia Ltd., Locked Bag 2, Bondi Beach, NSW 2026, Australia.

384.558 AUS ISSN 1327-0338
AUSTRALIAN VIDEOCAMERA AND DESKTOP VIDEO. 1991-2007. m. VideoCamera Publications Pty. Ltd., PO Box 473, Dee Why, NSW 2099, Australia.

820 GBR
AUSTRALIAN WRITERS SERIES. 1993-ceased. irreg. Oxford University Press, Great Clarendon St, Oxford, OX2 6DP, United Kingdom.

327 AUS
AUSTRALIA'S OVERSEAS AID PROGRAM. 1973-2000. a. AusInfo, Parliament House, Canberra Mc, ACT 2600, Australia.

658 AUS ISSN 0817-3192
AUSTRALIA'S TOP 500 COMPANIES. 1986-2000. a. Dun & Bradstreet Marketing Pty. Ltd., 19 Havilah St, Chatswood, NSW 2067, Australia.

327 DEU
AUSTRALIEN AKTUELL. 1976-2003. m. Australian Embassy, Public Affairs Section, Friedrichstr 200, Berlin, 10117, Germany.

053.1 919.406 AUS ISSN 0728-7399
AUSTRALIEN KURIER/AUSTRALISCHE MONATSZEITUNG. 1984-2002. m. Euro Media Pty. Ltd., 1-3 Seddon St, Bankstown, NSW 2200, Australia.

388 CZE ISSN 1210-4019
AUTO (YEAR) (PRAGUE). 1993-2002. a. Motor-Presse Bohemia, U Krcskeho Nadrazi 36, Prague 4, 14000, Czech Republic.

790.13 FRA ISSN 0766-169X
AUTO 8; le magazine de la voiture radiocommandee. 1985-1999. m. Editions Lariviere, 6 Rue Olof Palme, Clichy, 92587 , France.

920 GBR ISSN 0967-5507
AUTO-BIOGRAPHY; an international & interdisciplinary journal. 1992-2006. 3/yr. Sage Publications Ltd., 1 Oliver's Yard, 55 City Rd, London, EC1Y 1SP, United Kingdom.

055.1 ITA ISSN 1128-630X
AUTO DOC. 1993-ceased. m. Edizioni Juvenis, Viale Lunigiana 7, Milan, 20125, Italy.

355 DEU
AUTO MAGAZINE. 1982-1995. bi-m. Miltrends Verlags GmbH, Postfach 640260, Frankfurt am Main, 60356, Germany.

796.72 USA ISSN 0090-8029
AUTO RACING DIGEST. 1973-2004. bi-m. Century Publishing Inc., 990 Grove St, Evanston, IL 60201-4370.

388.3 ITA
AUTO SPECIAL. 1990-ceased. 3/yr. Ediauto s.r.l., Via Solferino, 31, Guidizzolo, MN 46040, Italy.

620.004 CZE ISSN 1212-3501
AUTODESK NEWS. 1994-2001. q. Computer Press a.s., Pod Vinici 23, Modrany, Prague 4, 143 00, Czech Republic.

388.342 NZL
AUTOFILE NEW AND USED ANNUAL. 1997-ceased. a. G C L Publishing, Ltd., 15 Bath St, 1st Fl., Parnell, PO Box 37-745, Auckland, New Zealand.

629.2 NZL
AUTOFILE QUARTERLY REPORT. 1993-2007. q. G C L Publishing, Ltd., 15 Bath St, 1st Fl., Parnell, PO Box 37-745, Auckland, New Zealand.

750 USA ISSN 1523-6277
AUTOGRAPHICS. 1995-1999; resumed 2004-2006. bi-m. National Business Media, Inc., PO Box 1416, Broomfield, CO 80038.

380.5 GBR ISSN 1469-204X
AUTOINDUSTRY. 1979-2001. m. C M P Information Ltd., Ludgate House, 245 Blackfriars Rd., London, SE1 9UR, United Kingdom.

656.38 DEU ISSN 1611-7085
AUTOMOBILE LUXUS UND LEBEN. 2002-2006. q. Der Heisse Draht Verlag GmbH und Co., Drostestr 14-16, Hannover, 30161, Germany.

388.321 FRA ISSN 1292-0371
AUTOMOBILES GAZ DE PETROLE LIQUEFIE MAGAZINE. 1999-200?. bi-m. Editions Lariviere, 6 Rue Olof Palme, Clichy, 92587 , France.

698 388 USA
AUTOMOTIVE FINISHING. 1998-2004. q. Gardner Publications, Inc., 6915 Valley Ave, Cincinnati, OH 45244.

388.3 629.2 GBR
AUTOMOTIVE NEWS EUROPE (PRINT). 1996-2009. fortn. Crain Communications, Ltd., 3rd Fl, 21 St Thomas St, London, SE1 9RY, United Kingdom.

351 ITA
AUTONOMIE E DIRITTO. 198?-199?. 3/yr. Editrice Ila Palma, Via Isidoro La Lumia, 5-7, Palermo, PA 90139, Italy.

796.77 NLD
AUTOPODIUM. ceased 2005. m. Audax Publishing B.V., Joan Muyskenweg 6-6a, Amsterdam, 1096 CJ, Netherlands.

028.1 ESP ISSN 1699-468X
LOS AUTORES. 199?-200?. irreg. Sociedad General de Autores y Editores, Fernando VI, 4, Madrid, 28004, Spain.

015 ESP ISSN 1136-8217
AUTORIDADES DE LA BIBLIOTECA NACIONAL DE ESPANA EN CD-ROM. 1996-2007. s-a. Biblioteca Nacional de Espana, Paseo Recoletos 20-22, Madrid, 28071, Spain.

796.77 ITA
AUTOSPORT. 1975-ceased. m. Edicentro S.r.l., Via Giuseppe Mantellini, 18, Rome, RM 00179, Italy.

636 ESP ISSN 0005-1896
AVANCES EN ALIMENTACION Y MEJORA ANIMAL. 1960-2000. bi-m. Avances en Alimentacion y Mejora Animal, Juan Vigon, 32o D., Madrid, 28003, Spain.

613.7 CAN ISSN 1201-6144
AVANTE. 1995-ceased. 3/yr. Canadian Association for Health, Physical Education, Recreation and Dance, 2197 Riverside Dr, Ste 403, Ottawa, ON K1H 7X3, Canada.

331.21021 USA ISSN 1934-0974
AVERAGE ANNUAL PAY BY STATE AND INDUSTRY. 1992-2001. a. U.S. Department of Labor, Bureau of Labor Statistics, Postal Square Bldg., 2 Massachusetts Ave, NE, Washington, DC 20212-0001.

330.9 USA
AVERAGE ANNUAL PAY LEVELS IN METROPOLITAN AREAS (YEAR). 1992-2001. a.?. U.S. Department of Labor, Bureau of Labor Statistics, Postal Square Bldg., 2 Massachusetts Ave, NE, Washington, DC 20212-0001.

343.097 GBR ISSN 1352-4003
AVIATION & SPACE LAW REPORTS. 1994-1996. m. (plus a. cumulation). Lloyds of London Press Ltd., Sheepen Pl, Cochester, Essex C03 3LP, United Kingdom.

629.1325 FRA ISSN 1951-9583
AVIATION FRANCAISE MAGAZINE. 2004-2007. bi-m. Avia Editions, 21 Place de la Poste, Rochemaure, 07400, France.

629.73 ITA ISSN 1124-5433
AVIOFLAP. 1993-199?. m. Coop CELI, Via Salaria 825, Rome, 00138, Italy.

636.752 DNK ISSN 0905-7080
AVLS- OG AARBOG FOR LANGHAARET HOENSEHUND. 1982-1999. a. Klubben for den Langhaarede Hoensehund, c/o Peter Werther, Strandvejen 136, Frederiksvaerk, 3300, Denmark.

387.71 GBR ISSN 0961-2513
THE AVMARK AVIATION ECONOMIST. 1984-2003. 10/yr. Avmark Inc., 26 Eccleston Sq, London, W13 0RL, United Kingdom.

610 ITA ISSN 0392-6877
L'AVVENIRE MEDICO. 1961-ceased. a. Fabrizio Serra Editore, c/o Accademia Editoriale, Via Santa Bibbiana 28, Pisa, 56127, Italy.

363.5 GBR ISSN 1467-9086
AXIS. 1964-2006. bi-m. Haymarket Publishing Ltd., 174 Hammersmith Rd, London, W6 7JP, United Kingdom.

913 GBR
AYRSHIRE MONOGRAPHS. 1877; N.S. 1950-200?. s-a. Ayrshire Archaeological & Natural History Society, c/o Ronald W. Brash, Publication Mgr., 10 Robsland Ave, Ayr, Ayrshire KA7 2RW, United Kingdom.

685.31 ITA ISSN 0392-2324
AZETA. 1975-ceased. bi-m. C.E.G., Via del Bosco, 125, Santa Croce Sull'Arno, PI 56029, Italy.

617.6 EGY ISSN 1110-6751
AL AZHAR JOURNAL OF DENTAL SCIENCE. 1988-1994. bi-m. Al-Azhar University, Faculty of Dentistry, Al-Nasr Rd, Nasr City, Cairo, Egypt.

579 EGY ISSN 1110-1601
AL AZHAR JOURNAL OF MICROBIOLOGY. 1987-1999. q. Al-Azhar University, Faculty of Pharmacy, Department of Microbiology, Boys, Nasr City, Cairo, Egypt.

611 EGY ISSN 1110-0400
AL AZHAR MEDICAL JOURNAL/MAGALLAT TIB AL-AZHAR. 1972-1999. s-a. Al-Azhar University, Faculty of Medicine, Department of Anatomy, Madinet Nasr, Cairo, Egypt.

330.9 DEU
B A W - MONATSBERICHT. (Bremer Ausschuss fuer Wirtschaftsforschung) 1978-2004. m. B A W Institut fuer Wirtschaftsforschung, Wilhelm-Herbst-Str 5, Bremen, 28359, Germany.

658 DEU
B B E DATA KOMPAKT. 1996-2006. w. B B E Media GmbH & Co. KG, Am Hammergraben 14, Neuwied, 56567, Germany.

341 ESP ISSN 0213-6945
B C E. BOLETIN DE DERECHO DE LAS COMUNIDADES EUROPEAS. 1986-1992. irreg. Spain. Congreso de los Diputados, Depto. de Publicaciones, Carrera de San Jeronimo s-n, Madrid, 28071, Spain.

741 ITA ISSN 1124-8971
B.D. BODY BOOK. 1996-ceased. bi-m. Edizioni Trentini & C, Via Pier Luigi Nervi 1/B, Argenta, FE 44011, Italy.

020 330 USA ISSN 1048-5376
B F BULLETIN. (Business & Finance) 1962-2006. 3/yr. Special Libraries Association, 331 S Patrick St, Alexandria, VA 22314.

371.42 DEU
B F Z - INFO. 1986-1998. q. Berufsfoerderungszentrum Essen e.V., Karolingerstr 93, Essen, 45141, Germany.

340.5 DEU ISSN 1865-2107
B G H - C D. (Bundesgerichtshof) 1997-200?. a. (plus q. updates). Verlag C.H. Beck oHG, Wilhelmstr 9, Munich, 80801, Germany.

384.55 USA
B I B CHANNELS; what's new in domestic and international television programming and syndication. 1981-199?. q. North American Publishing Co., 1500 Spring Garden St., Ste 1200, Philadelphia, PA 19130.

574.09989 GBR ISSN 0957-4638
B I O T A S NEWSLETTER. (Biological Investigations of Terrestrial Antarctic Systems) 1987-1999. irreg. British Antarctic Survey, High Cross, Madingley Rd, Cambridge, CBE OET, United Kingdom.

780.6 DEU
B M R - CORRESPONDENZ; Informationen - Berichte - Kommentare. 1979-2004. bi-m. Bayerischer Musikrat e.V., Sollner Str 42, Munich, 81479, Germany.

331.255 USA ISSN 1094-7809
B N A'S EMPLOYEE BENEFITS LIBRARY ON CD. (Bureau of National Affairs) 1995-2003. m. The Bureau of National Affairs, Inc., 1801 S Bell St, Arlington, VA 22202.

344.046 USA
B N A'S ENVIRONMENT & SAFETY COMPLIANCE CALENDAR. (Bureau of National Affairs) 1993-2001. q. The Bureau of National Affairs, Inc., 1801 S Bell St, Arlington, VA 22202.

384.5452 310 USA ISSN 1094-4494
B - STATS. (Broadcast) 1997-199?. m. S N L Financial LC, One SNL Plz, PO Box 2124, Charlottesville, VA 22902.

332 DEU
B V - EUROLETTER; E G-Binnenmarkt: Tips, Trends, Termine. (Bayerische Vereinsbank) 1989-1998. m. Bayerische Vereinsbank AG, Zentralbereich Kommunikation und Volkwirtschaft, Kardinal-Faulhaber-Str 1, Munich, 80333, Germany.

330 USA ISSN 1940-8951
B W CHICAGO. (Business Week) 2007 (Nov.)-2008. w. McGraw-Hill Companies, Inc., One Prudential Plaza, Ste 2900, 130 E. Randolph St, Chicago, IL 60601-6213.

663.2 ITA
BACCHUS. 1978-ceased. s-a. Editoriale Lariana s.r.l., Via Ciro Menotti 11-D, Milan, MI 20129, Italy.

332 GBR ISSN 1354-8247
BACK OFFICE FOCUS. 1994-2006. 10/yr. Informa Professional, Informa House, 30-32 Mortimer St, London, W1W 7RE, United Kingdom.

398 ITA
E BAFION. 1974-ceased. s-a. Bafion, Via Galilei, 12, Conselice, RA 48017, Italy.

747 ITA ISSN 1591-7193
BAGNO & CUCINA. 1999-200?. q. Tecniche Nuove SpA, Via Eritrea 21, Milan, MI 201, Italy.

070.48374 CZE ISSN 1214-9624
BAJECNA NEDELE. 2003-2009 (Jan.). w. Sanoma Magazines Praha s.r.o., Lomnickeho 7, Prague 4, 12079, Czech Republic.

338.91 GBR ISSN 1360-9335
BALTIMORE STUDIES IN NATIONALISM AND INTERNATIONALISM. 1996-1999. a. Berg Publishers, Angel Court, 1st Fl, 81 St Clements St, Oxford, Berks OX4 1AW, United Kingdom.

028.5 ISR
BAMA'ALEH. 1926-1997. m. Tenuat Hanoar Haoved Vehalomed, 120 Kibbutz Galuyot St, Tel Aviv, 66877, Israel.

746 649 FRA ISSN 1636-4651
BAMBINO. 2002-2008. q. Editions DIPA Burda, 26 Avenue de l'Europe, Strasbourg, 67013, France.

746.43 DEU
BAMBINO-BABY. 1989-2003. q. Martin Kelter Verlag, Muehlenstieg 16-22, Hamburg, 22041, Germany.

747.7 ESP ISSN 1576-1444
BAN Y COC. 1993-2003. q. E T D Prensa Profesional, SA, Sicilia 95, Atico, Barcelona, 08013, Spain.

070.5 ITA ISSN 1124-2825
BANANA BOOK. 1994-ceased. q. Logos Publishing, Via Curtatona 5/2, Modena, MO 41100, Italy.

332.1 ESP ISSN 1135-8289
BANCO DE BILBAO. AGENDA FINANCIERA. 1949-1988. a. Banco de Bilbao, Gran via, 12, Bilbao, Spain.

330.9 ESP ISSN 0522-1307
BANCO DE BILBAO. ECONOMIC REPORT. 196?-198?. a. Banco de Bilbao, Gran via, 12, Bilbao, Spain.

330.9 ESP ISSN 0214-2724
BANCO DE BILBAO - VIZCAYA . INFORME ECONOMICO. 1942-199?. a. Banco de Bilbao, Servicio de Estudios, Apartado 21, Bilbao, Vizcaya 48070, Spain.

332 ESP ISSN 0005-4798
BANCO DE ESPANA. BOLETIN ESTADISTICO (PRINT). 1960-2007. m. Banco de Espana, C Alcala, 48, Madrid, 28027, Spain.

791.43 ESP ISSN 1138-1981
BANDA APARTE. 1994-2001. q. Ediciones de la Mirada, Rosario 76, Valencia, 46001, Spain.

610 GBR ISSN 1353-9906
BANDOLIER; evidence-based health care. 1994-2007. m. Bandolier Ltd, Pain Research, The Churchill, Oxford, Oxon OX3 7LJ, United Kingdom.

332 659.1 USA ISSN 0274-7111
BANK ADVERTISING NEWS; the independent national newspaper of financial marketing. 19??-2000. bi-w. Thomson Financial, 195 Broadway, New York, NY 10007.

332 USA ISSN 1941-3238
BANK ADVISOR; helping advisors break through the silos. 2007-2009 (Jan.). bi-m. Wiesner Media, LLC, 7009 S Potomac St, Ste 200, Centennial, CO 80112.

332.1 GBR ISSN 0263-6123
BANK OF ENGLAND. TECHNICAL SERIES DISCUSSION PAPERS. 1982-1991. irreg. Bank of England, Publications Group, Threadneedle St, London, EC2R 8AH, United Kingdom.

332.1 USA ISSN 1091-6385 CODEN: BASTFT
BANKING STRATEGIES (PRINT). 1925-2009. bi-m. Bank Administration Institute, One N Franklin, Ste. 1000, Chicago, IL 60606-3421.

332.7 USA ISSN 1549-747X
BANKRUPTCY INSIDER (PRINT); an absolute priority for bankruptcy profesionals. 2004 (Apr.)-2008. w. The Deal, LLC, 105 Madison Ave, New York, NY 10016.

332.1 FRA ISSN 1250-5846 CODEN: EJCRF5
BANQUE DE FRANCE. BULLETIN. SUPPLEMENT STATISTIQUES. 1994-2002. q. Banque de France, 48 rue Croix-des-Petits-Champs, Paris, 75049, France.

332.1 FRA ISSN 1161-3785
BANQUE DE FRANCE. CAHIER DES TITRES DE CREANCES NEGOCIABLES. 1991-2006. m. Banque de France, 48 rue Croix-des-Petits-Champs, Paris, 75049, France.

332 FRA ISSN 1169-8489
BANQUE DE FRANCE. COMITE CONSULTATIF. RAPPORT. 1987-2003. a. Banque de France, 48 rue Croix-des-Petits-Champs, Paris, 75049, France.

332 FRA ISSN 1169-8462
BANQUE DE FRANCE. COMITE DE LA REGLEMENTATION BANCAIRE ET FINANCIERE. RAPPORT. 1989-2004. a. Banque de France, 48 rue Croix-des-Petits-Champs, Paris, 75049, France.

332.1 FRA ISSN 1142-2858
BANQUE DE FRANCE. COMMISSION BANCAIRE. BULLETIN. 1989-2004. s-a. Banque de France, 48 rue Croix-des-Petits-Champs, Paris, 75049, France.

332.1 FRA ISSN 0767-9505
BANQUE DE FRANCE. COMPTES ANNUELS DES ETABLISSEMENTS DE CREDIT. 1949-2003. a. Banque de France, 48 rue Croix-des-Petits-Champs, Paris, 75049, France.

332.1 FRA ISSN 0242-5866
BANQUE DE FRANCE. LA MONNAIE EN... 1970-1999. a. Banque de France, 48 rue Croix-des-Petits-Champs, Paris, 75049, France.

332 FRA ISSN 1624-5709
BANQUE DE FRANCE. LA SITUATION DES ENTREPRISES INDUSTRIELLES. 19??-2005. a. Banque de France, 48 rue Croix-des-Petits-Champs, Paris, 75049, France.

330.9 FRA ISSN 0014-2042
BANQUE SUDAMERIS. ETUDES ECONOMIQUES. forthcoming 1954-2000. irreg. (2-3/yr.). Banque SudAmeris, 4 rue Meyerbeer, Paris, Cedex 9 75429, France.

352.14 FRA
BANQUES DE DONNEES UTILES AUX COLLECTIVITES LOCALES ET TERRITORIALES. 1989-ceased. irreg. Editions F L A Consultants, 27 rue de la Vistule, Paris, 75013, France.

851 ITA
BAOBAB; informazioni fonetiche di poesia. 1978-19??. irreg. (2-3/yr.). Elytra Edizioni s.r.l., Via Mari, 1-A, Reggio Emilia, RE 42100, Italy.

745.5922 USA ISSN 1935-8016
BARBIE COLLECTOR MAGAZINE. 2007 (May)-200?; suspended. q. Jones Publishing, Inc., N 7450 Aanstad Rd, PO Box 5000, Iola, WI 54945.

797.1 ITA ISSN 1124-3732
BARCHE ENTRO E FUORIBORDO; il mensile della nautica a motore. 1994-ceased. m. Editoriale Quadra Srl, Via Tartini 13 c, Milano, 20185, Italy.

820 GBR ISSN 0307-3408
BARD. 193?-1984. s-a. Shakespearean Authorship Trust, Lincoln's Inn, 11 Old Square, London, WC2A 3TS, United Kingdom.

636.7 051 AUS ISSN 1832-7621
BARK!; a lifestyle magazine for dog lovers and owners. 2005-2007. bi-m. The Good Life Publishing Company Pty Ltd, PO Box 993, Double Bay, NSW 1360, Australia.

296 ISR ISSN 0334-1380
BARKAI. 1984-1991. a. Mifal Rabanim Ubnei Torah, c/o Mr. S.R. Sachs, P O Box 7720, Jerusalem, Israel.

340 ESP ISSN 1135-8246
BASE DE DATOS ARANZADI. JURISPRUDENCIA SOCIAL. 1995-2006. q. Editorial Aranzadi S.A., Camino de Galar 15, Cizur Menor, Navarra 31190, Spain.

796.357 USA
BASEBALL GUIDE. 1942-2007. a. American City Business Journals, Inc., 120 W Morehead St, Charlotte, NC 28202.

796.357 USA
BASEBALL REGISTER. 1940-2007. a. American City Business Journals, Inc., 120 W Morehead St, Charlotte, NC 28202.

373 NLD ISSN 1874-4680
BASISSCHOOL IN BEDRIJF. 2005-ceased. 8/yr. Sdu Uitgevers bv, Postbus 20025, The Hague, 2500 EA, Netherlands.

796.323 DEU
BASKETBALL MAGAZIN. 1960-2006. m. D S V Deutscher Sportverlag GmbH, Im Mediapark 8, Cologne, 50670, Germany.

796.323 DEU ISSN 0178-9279
BASKETBALL NEWS. 1955-2003. w. D S V Deutscher Sportverlag GmbH, Im Mediapark 8, Cologne, 50670, Germany.

381 ESP
BASQUE ENTERPRISE. 19??-ceased. 4/yr. Spri S.A., Gran Via 35, 3o, Bilbao, 48009, Spain.

787.87 USA ISSN 1543-3528
BASS GUITAR. 2003-2007. 8/yr. Future U S, Inc., 4000 Shoreline Ct, Ste 400, South San Francisco, CA 94080.

087.5 DEU
BASTELINO. 2003-2005. a. Egmont Ehapa Verlag GmbH, Wallstr 59, Berlin, 10179, Germany.

303 305.8924 ISR
BATEFUTZOT; quarterly newsletter on news from the Jewish world. 1978-2005. q. World Jewish Congress, P O Box 4293, Jerusalem, 91042, Israel.

796.95 FRA ISSN 0984-4899
BATO LOC INTERNATIONAL. 1964-198?. 4/yr. Editions Kerfan, 97-103 av. Semeria, BP 18, St Jean Cap Ferrat, 06230, France.

500 600 DEU ISSN 0932-7541
BATTELLE INFORMATION. 1967-1993. 3/yr. Battelle Europe, Am Roemerhof 35, Frankfurt Am Main, 60486, Germany.

690 DEU ISSN 0933-3924
BAUAUFSICHTLICHE ZULASSUNGEN. 1967-200?. plus irreg. updates. Erich Schmidt Verlag GmbH & Co. (Berlin), Genthiner Str 30 G, Berlin, 10785, Germany.

720 DEU ISSN 1433-5735 CODEN: WZAWA9
BAUHAUS UNIVERSITAET WEIMAR. THESIS. 1994-2004. 6/yr. Bauhaus Universitaet Weimar, Weimar, 99421, Germany.

343.078624 DEU ISSN 1611-9622
BAURECHT UND BAUPRAXIS. 2003-2005. m. Deutscher Anwaltverlag GmbH, Wachsbleiche 7, Bonn, 53111, Germany.

324.3 DEU ISSN 1433-3090
BAUSTEINE FUER FRAUENGRUPPEN. 1998-2001. q. Bergmoser und Hoeller Verlag GmbH, Karl-Friedrich-Str 76, Aachen, 52072, Germany.

016 940 DEU
BAYERISCHE STAATSBIBLIOTHEK. OSTEUROPA-KATALOG AUF CD-ROM. 1972-1999. s-a. Bayerische Staatsbibliothek, Ludwigstr 16, Munich, 80539, Germany.

551 DEU ISSN 0176-4217 CODEN: IBLAFL
BAYERISCHES LANDESAMT FUER WASSERWIRTSCHAFT. INFORMATIONSBERICHTE. 1975-2005. 5/yr. Bayerisches Landesamt fuer Wasserwirtschaft, Lazarettstr 67, Munich, 80636, Germany.

551 DEU ISSN 0172-665X CODEN: SBLWEQ
BAYERISCHES LANDESAMTES FUER WASSERWIRTSCHAFT. SCHRIFTENREIHE. 1975-1996. irreg. Bayerisches Landesamt fuer Wasserwirtschaft, Lazarettstr 67, Munich, 80636, Germany.

720 747 USA ISSN 1046-6312
BEAUTIFUL HOMES. 1988-1994. a. Meredith Corporation, 1716 Locust St, Des Moines, IA 50309.

305.4 ITA ISSN 1124-173X
BEAUTIFUL MAGAZINE. 1990-ceased. w. Casa Editrice Universo SpA, Via Cusani 4, Milan, 20121, Italy.

747 USA ISSN 1935-4444
BEAUTIFUL SOUTHERN HOMES. 2006-2008. s-a. Meredith Corporation, 1716 Locust St, Des Moines, IA 50309.

668.5 NLD ISSN 1574-1273
BEAUTY XPERT. 1987-2008. 6/yr. It's Amazing Business Communication bv, Postbus 7104, Zoetermeer, 2701 AC, Netherlands.

795.4 USA ISSN 1556-2778
BECKETT MAGIC THE GATHERING. 2005 (Aug.-Sept.)-200?. bi-m. Beckett Media LP, 4635 McEwen Rd, Dallas, TX 75244.

690 720 DNK ISSN 1903-0096
BEDRE BOLIG; maanedsmagasinet for aktive boligejere. 2005-2008. 10/yr. Forlaget Fundament, Hovedgaden 11, Fakse Ladeplads, 4654, Denmark.

058.81 DNK ISSN 0906-6349
DET BEDSTE. 1946-2005. m. Det Bedste fra Reader's Digest A-S, Forlaget Det Bedste ApS, Jagtvej 169 B, PO Box 810, Copenhagen Oe, 2100, Denmark.

780.92 USA ISSN 1059-5031
BEETHOVEN FORUM. 1992-2007. biennial. University of Illinois Press, 1325 S Oak St, Champaign, IL 61820.

338 DEU
BEIERSDORF JOURNAL. 1960-2006. q. Beiersdorf AG, Unnastr 48, Hamburg, 20253, Germany.

372 510 DEU ISSN 0522-6090
BEIHEFTE FUER DEN MATHEMATISCHEN UNTERRICHT. 1953-19??. irreg. Vieweg und Sohn Verlagsgesellschaft mbH, Abraham-Lincoln-Str 46, Wiesbaden, 65189, Germany.

613.7 BRD ISSN 0408-7917
BEIHEFTE FUER DEN PHYSIKALISCHEN UNTERRICHT. 1954-1968. irreg. Vieweg und Sohn Verlagsgesellschaft mbH, Abraham-Lincoln-Str 46, Wiesbaden, 65189, Germany.

374 CHN ISSN 1002-414X
BEIJING CHENGREN JIAOYU/BEIJING ADULT EDUCATION. 1982-2001. m. Beijing Chengren Jiaoyu Zazhishe, Beijing, 100088, China.

677 CHN ISSN 1002-3348
BEIJING FANGZHI/BEIJING TEXTILE. 1979-2005. bi-m. Beijing Fangzhi Gongcheng Xuehui, Chaoyangmenwai, 2 Shilipu, Beijing, 100025, China.

547 DEU ISSN 0067-4915
BEILSTEINS HANDBUCH DER ORGANISCHEN CHEMIE. SUPPLEMENT. (The main work was published: 1918-1937; First Supplement: 1928-1938; Second Supplement: 1941-1957; Third Supplement: 1930-1949; Fourth Supplement: 1950-1959; Fifth Supplement: 1960-1979) 1972-1997. irreg. Springer, Tiergartenstr 17, Heidelberg, 69121, Germany.

610 DDR ISSN 0300-4872
BEITRAEGE ZUR KRYOMEDIZIN. 1973-19??. irreg. Verlag Theodor Steinkopff, Loschwitzer Str. 32, Dresden, 01309, East Germany.

310 351.21 DEU ISSN 0340-2517
BEITRAEGE ZUR STATISTIK DES LANDES NORDRHEIN-WESTFALEN. 1948-2000. irreg. Information und Technik Nordrhein-Westfalen, Mauerstr 51, Duesseldorf, 40476, Germany.

571.2 DEU ISSN 0948-5538
BEITRAEGE ZUR ZUECHTUNGSFORSCHUNG. 1995-2002. irreg. Bundesanstalt fuer Zuechtungsforschung an Kulturpflanzen, Erwin-Baur-Str 27, Quedlinburg, 06484, Germany.

304.6 BEL ISSN 0772-764X
BELGIUM. NEDERLANDS INTERUNIVERSITAIR DEMOGRAFISCH INSTITUUT. BEVOLKING EN GEZIN. 1962-2004. 3/yr. Nederlands Interuniversitair Demografisch Instituut, c/o Gerard Godijn, Markiesstraat 1, Brussels, 1000, Belgium.

305.42 ITA ISSN 1970-6898
BELLA. 1944-200?. w. Edizioni Mimosa, Piazza E de Angeli 9, Milan, 20146, Italy.

908 DEU ISSN 1439-2046
BELLEVUE GUIDE MARBELLA, COSTA DEL SOL. 2000-200?. irreg. Bellevue and More AG, Dorotheenstr 64, Hamburg, 22301, Germany.

595.7 DEU ISSN 0946-6193
BEMBIX. 1993-2004 (no.19). irreg. Bembix, Kirchstr 1, Herrsching, 82211, Germany.

150 649 ESP ISSN 1136-3649
BENESTAR Y PROTECCION INFANTIL. 1995-2005. 3/yr. Federacion de Asociaciones para la Prevencion del Maltrato Infantil (F A P M I), Calle Delicias 8, Entreplanta, Madrid, 28045, Spain.

746.9 ITA ISSN 1121-175X
BENISSIMO. 1982-ceased. m. Fabbri Editori, Via Mecenate 91, Milan, 20138, Italy.

028.5 CZE ISSN 1801-6049
BENJAMIN KVITKO. 2006-2006 (ceased same year). m. Egmont CR s.r.o., Zirovnicka 3124, Prague 10, 10600, Czech Republic.

792 USA
BENSON & HEDGES BRITISH THEATRE YEARBOOK. 1989-1992. a. St. Martin's Press, LLC, 175 Fifth Ave, New York, NY 10010.

551.46 DEU ISSN 0940-8096
BEOBACHTUNGEN AUF DEN DEUTSCHEN MESSSTATIONEN DER NORD- UND OSTSEE. 1953-1997. a. Bundesamt fuer Seeschifffahrt und Hydrographie, Bernhard-Nocht-Str 78, Hamburg, 20359, Germany.

641.5 641.22 ITA ISSN 1593-9847
BERE DOLCE. 2001-200?. a. Alexandra Editrice, Largo Lanciani 1, Roma, 00162, Italy.

808.8385 053.1 DEU
BERG-ROMAN; neuer Roman in grosser Schrift. 1971-2005. w. Bastei Verlag Gustav H. Luebbe GmbH und Co., Scheidtbachstr 23-31, Bergisch Gladbach, 51469, Germany.

796 DEU ISSN 0947-5958
BERGE; wo Freizeit zum Erlebnis wird. 1983-2008. bi-m. Olympia Verlag GmbH, Badstr 4-6, Nuernberg, 90402, Germany.

622 DEU ISSN 0935-123X
BERICHTE DER DEUTSCHEN MINERALOGISCHEN GESELLSCHAFT; Beihefte zum European Journal of Mineralogy. 1989-200?. a. E. Schweizerbart'sche Verlagsbuchhandlung, Johannesstr 3A, Stuttgart, 70176, Germany.

940 DEU ISSN 0943-8386
BERICHTE ZU STAAT UND GESELLSCHAFT IN DER TSCHECHISCHEN UND IN DER SLOWAKISCHEN REPUBLIK. 1993-2005. q. Collegium Carolinum e.V., Hochstr 8, Munich, 81669, Germany.

300 DEU
BERLIN FORSCHUNG. 1982-1996. irreg. B W V - Berliner Wissenschafts Verlag GmbH, Axel-Springer-Str 54a, Berlin, 10117, Germany.

332.6 DEU ISSN 0172-0236
BERLINER BANK. BOERSENBRIEF. 1950-1998. fortn. Berliner Bank Aktiengesellschaft, Hardenbergstr 32, Berlin, 10623, Germany.

526.8 DEU ISSN 0172-8784 CODEN: BGAADO
BERLINER GEOWISSENSCHAFTLICHE ABHANDLUNGEN. REIHE A, GEOLOGIE UND PALAEONTOLOGIE. 1977-2002 (vol.215). irreg. Dietrich Reimer Verlag GmbH, Berliner Str 53, Berlin, 10713, Germany.

551 DEU ISSN 0722-687X
BERLINER GEOWISSENSCHAFTLICHE ABHANDLUNGEN. REIHE B, GEOPHYSIK. 1965-2002 (vol.39). irreg. Dietrich Reimer Verlag GmbH, Berliner Str 53, Berlin, 10713, Germany.

526.8 DEU ISSN 0722-6888
BERLINER GEOWISSENSCHAFTLICHE ABHANDLUNGEN. REIHE C, KARTOGRAPHIE. 1980-2002 (vol.18). irreg. Dietrich Reimer Verlag GmbH, Berliner Str 53, Berlin, 10713, Germany.

330.9 DEU
BERNHARD-HARMS-VORLESUNGEN. 1964-2004. irreg. Universitaet Kiel, Institut fuer Weltwirtschaft, Duesternbrooker Weg 120, Kiel, 24105, Germany.

790.1 USA ISSN 0732-5630
BERT SUGAR'S FIGHT GAME; the voice of boxing. 1998-200?. bi-m. Starlog Communications, 250 W 49th St, 3rd Fl Ste 304, New York, NY 10019.

070.5 DEU ISSN 0005-9455
BERTELSMANN BRIEFE. 1960-2001. 2/yr. Bauverlag BV GmbH, Avenwedderstr 55, Guetersloh, 33311, Germany.

055.1 ITA ISSN 0392-2561
BEST BOOMERANG. 1977-ceased. m. Editrice Sopi s.r.l., Vicolo Dei Serpenti, 164, Rome, RM 00184, Italy.

053.1 DEU ISSN 1860-1669
BEST LIFE. 2002-2008. 6/yr. Rodale Motor Presse GmbH und Co. KG, Leuschnerstr 1, Stuttgart, 70174, Germany.

642.5 FRA ISSN 1771-7353
BEST MENUS IN PARIS. 200?-2006. s-a. Best Restaurants in Paris, 102 Av. des Champs-Elysees, Paris, 75008, France.

779.28 CZE ISSN 1212-6136
BEST OF SUPER EXTAZIS. 1999-200?. q. PK 62, a.s., Bohdalecka 6, Prague 10, 101 00, Czech Republic.

658.8 DEU ISSN 1613-236X
BESTSELLER. 1998-2006. bi-m. Deutscher Fachverlag GmbH, Mainzer Landstr 251, Frankfurt Am Main, 60326, Germany.

351 DEU ISSN 0932-5492
BETREFF; Magazin fuer junge Leute im oeffentlichen Dienst. 1957-2002. bi-m. Deutsche Beamtenbund Jugend, Friedrichstr 169-170, Berlin, 10117, Germany.

747 USA ISSN 1530-5015
BETTER HOMES AND GARDENS LIVING ROOM. 2000-200?. a. Meredith Corporation, 1716 Locust St, Des Moines, IA 50309.

613.2 FRA ISSN 1954-9199
BETTER LIFE MAGAZINE. 2006-2007. q. Editions Better Life, 15 Rue de la Crabe, Toulouse, 31300, France.

616.99 305.4 USA ISSN 1935-4541
BEYOND (NEW YORK); live & thrive after breast cancer. 2006-2007. s-a. Meredith Corporation, 1716 Locust St, Des Moines, IA 50309.

808.8385 053.1 DEU ISSN 1439-9512
BIANCA ARZTROMAN. 1999-2006. 9/yr. Cora Verlag GmbH und Co. KG, Valentinskamp 24, Hamburg, 20350, Germany.

910.202 ITA
BIBIONE VACANZE. 1968-ceased. w. (during summer). Pubblistudio de Zorzi Casa Editrice s.a.s., Via Marinoni, 53, Udine, UD 33100, Italy.

220 ESP ISSN 0210-5209
BIBLIA Y FE. 1975-2003. 3/yr. Ediciones Escurialenses, Real Monasterio del Escorial, San Lorenzo del Escorial, Madrid, 28200, Spain.

097 016 DNK
BIBLIOGRAFI OVER EUROPAEISKE KUNSTNERES EX LIBRIS/EUROPAEISCHE EX LIBRIS/EUROPEAN BOOK PLATES/EX LIBRIS D'EUROPE. 1969-1977. a. Klaus Roedel Ed. & Pub., PO Box 109, Frederikshavn, 9900, Denmark.

Cessations

016.809   ITA
BIBLIOGRAFIA E STORIA DELLA CRITICA. 1975-1996 (no.12). irreg. Angelo Longo Editore, Via Paolo Costa 33, Ravenna, 48121, Italy.

011   ITA   ISSN 1970-5891
BIBLIOGRAFIA E STORIE DEL LIBRO E DELLA STAMPA. MONUMENTA. 2003-200?. irreg. Arnaldo Forni Editore, Via Antonio Gramsci 164, Sala Bolognese, BO 40010, Italy.

011   ESP   ISSN 1133-9519
BIBLIOGRAFIA ESPANOLA. CARTOGRAFIA. 1980-2005. a. Biblioteca Nacional de Espana, Paseo Recoletos 20-22, Madrid, 28071, Spain.

011   ESP   ISSN 1133-8563
BIBLIOGRAFIA ESPANOLA. MONOGRAFIAS. INDICES ACUMULATIVOS. 1958-2006. a. Biblioteca Nacional de Espana, Paseo Recoletos 20-22, Madrid, 28071, Spain.

011   ESP
BIBLIOGRAFIA ESPANOLA. MUSICA IMPRESA. 1985-2007. a. Biblioteca Nacional de Espana, Paseo Recoletos 20-22, Madrid, 28071, Spain.

011   ESP   ISSN 1134-6620
BIBLIOGRAFIA ESPANOLA. PUBLICACIONES PERIODICAS. 1971-2005. a. Biblioteca Nacional de Espana, Paseo Recoletos 20-22, Madrid, 28071, Spain.

100   ITA   ISSN 0409-3372
BIBLIOGRAFIA FILOSOFICA ITALIANA. 1949-2001. irreg. Casa Editrice Leo S. Olschki, Viuzzo del Pozzetto 8, Florence, 50126, Italy.

500   ITA   ISSN 1721-5757
BIBLIOGRAFIA ITALIANA DI STORIA DELLA SCIENZA. 1982-1996 (vol.14-15). irreg. Casa Editrice Leo S. Olschki, Viuzzo del Pozzetto 8, Florence, 50126, Italy.

015   ESP   ISSN 1136-9698
BIBLIOGRAFIA NACIONAL ESPANOLA. 1992-2007. q. Biblioteca Nacional de Espana, Paseo Recoletos 20-22, Madrid, 28071, Spain.

020   DEU   ISSN 0723-3590
BIBLIOGRAPHIE DER BUCH- UND BIBLIOTHEKSGESCHICHTE. 1982-2004. a. Bibliographischer Verlag Dr. Horst Meyer, Muehlenstr 47, Bad Iburg, 49186, Germany.

003   DEU   ISSN 0935-8757
BIBLIOGRAPHIE INFORMATIK, DIDAKTIK UND ELEMENTARE COMPUTERANWENDUNGEN FUER SCHULE, HOCHSCHULE UND WEITERBILDUNG. 1987-2005. bi-m. Fachinformationszentrum Karlsruhe, Gesellschaft fuer Wissenschaftlich-Technische Information mbH, Hermann-von-Helmholtz-Platz 1, Eggenstein Leopoldshafen, 76344, Germany.

011   FRA   ISSN 1626-0082
BIBLIOGRAPHIE NATIONALE FRANCAISE. LIVRES, PUBLICATIONS EN SERIE ET DOCUMENTS ELECTRONIQUES. 1989-2003. bi-m. Bibliotheque Nationale de France, Site Francois Mitterand, Quai Francois Mauriac, Paris, 75706, France.

830   DEU   ISSN 0523-2767
BIBLIOGRAPHIEN ZUR DEUTSCHEN LITERATUR DES MITTELALTERS. 1966-1992 (vol.11). irreg. Erich Schmidt Verlag GmbH & Co. (Berlin), Genthiner Str 30 G, Berlin, 10785, Germany.

016.81   USA   ISSN 0742-6860
BIBLIOGRAPHIES AND INDEXES IN AMERICAN LITERATURE. 1984-200?. irreg. Greenwood Publishing Group Inc., 88 Post Rd W, PO Box 5007, Westport, CT 06881.

016.301   USA   ISSN 0742-6844
BIBLIOGRAPHIES AND INDEXES IN ANTHROPOLOGY. 1984-200?. irreg. Greenwood Publishing Group Inc., 88 Post Rd W, PO Box 5007, Westport, CT 06881.

016.33   USA   ISSN 0749-1786
BIBLIOGRAPHIES AND INDEXES IN ECONOMICS AND ECONOMIC HISTORY. 1984-200?. irreg. Greenwood Publishing Group Inc., 88 Post Rd W, PO Box 5007, Westport, CT 06881.

016.3058   USA   ISSN 1046-7882
BIBLIOGRAPHIES AND INDEXES IN ETHNIC STUDIES. 1990-200?. irreg. Greenwood Publishing Group Inc., 88 Post Rd W, PO Box 5007, Westport, CT 06881.

016.91002   USA   ISSN 1044-8349
BIBLIOGRAPHIES AND INDEXES IN GEOGRAPHY. 1989-19??. irreg. Greenwood Publishing Group Inc., 88 Post Rd W, PO Box 5007, Westport, CT 06881.

016.98 016.3   USA   ISSN 1054-9102
BIBLIOGRAPHIES AND INDEXES IN LATIN AMERICAN AND CARIBBEAN STUDIES. 1991-19??. irreg. Greenwood Publishing Group Inc., 88 Post Rd W, PO Box 5007, Westport, CT 06881.

016.32   USA   ISSN 0742-6909
BIBLIOGRAPHIES AND INDEXES IN LAW AND POLITICAL SCIENCE. 1984-200?. irreg. Greenwood Publishing Group Inc., 88 Post Rd W, PO Box 5007, Westport, CT 06881.

016.02   USA   ISSN 0742-6879
BIBLIOGRAPHIES AND INDEXES IN LIBRARY AND INFORMATION SCIENCE. 1987-200?. irreg. Greenwood Publishing Group Inc., 88 Post Rd W, PO Box 5007, Westport, CT 06881.

011.61   USA   ISSN 0896-6591
BIBLIOGRAPHIES AND INDEXES IN MEDICAL STUDIES. 1988-200?. irreg. Greenwood Publishing Group Inc., 88 Post Rd W, PO Box 5007, Westport, CT 06881.

016.1   USA   ISSN 0742-6887
BIBLIOGRAPHIES AND INDEXES IN PHILOSOPHY. 1985-19??. irreg. Greenwood Publishing Group Inc., 88 Post Rd W, PO Box 5007, Westport, CT 06881.

016.5   USA   ISSN 0888-7551   CODEN: BSTEEC
BIBLIOGRAPHIES AND INDEXES IN SCIENCE AND TECHNOLOGY. 1987-19??. irreg. Greenwood Publishing Group Inc., 88 Post Rd W, PO Box 5007, Westport, CT 06881.

016.808338   USA   ISSN 1053-4636
BIBLIOGRAPHIES AND INDEXES IN SCIENCE FICTION, FANTASY, AND HORROR. 1987-19??. irreg. Greenwood Publishing Group Inc., 88 Post Rd W, PO Box 5007, Westport, CT 06881.

016.301   USA   ISSN 0742-6895
BIBLIOGRAPHIES AND INDEXES IN SOCIOLOGY. 1984-200?. irreg. Greenwood Publishing Group Inc., 88 Post Rd W, PO Box 5007, Westport, CT 06881.

016.7928   USA   ISSN 0742-6933
BIBLIOGRAPHIES AND INDEXES IN THE PERFORMING ARTS. 1984-200?. irreg. Greenwood Publishing Group Inc., 88 Post Rd W, PO Box 5007, Westport, CT 06881.

016.305412   USA   ISSN 0742-6941
BIBLIOGRAPHIES AND INDEXES IN WOMEN'S STUDIES. 1984-2003. irreg. Greenwood Publishing Group Inc., 88 Post Rd W, PO Box 5007, Westport, CT 06881.

016.808   USA   ISSN 0742-6801
BIBLIOGRAPHIES AND INDEXES IN WORLD LITERATURE. 1984-2003. irreg. Greenwood Publishing Group Inc., 88 Post Rd W, PO Box 5007, Westport, CT 06881.

016.3048   DEU
BIBLIOGRAPHISCHE INFORMATIONEN ZU MIGRATION UND ETHNIZITAET. 1986-2002. 4/yr. Edition Parabolis, Schliemannstr 23, Berlin, 10437, Germany.

016.56   USA
BIBLIOGRAPHY AND INDEX OF MICROPALEONTOLOGY (ONLINE). suspended 2004. m. Micropaleontology Press, 256 Fifth Ave, New York, NY 10001.

016.56   USA   ISSN 0272-8869
BIBLIOGRAPHY OF FOSSIL VERTEBRATES. 1902-1993. a. Society of Vertebrate Paleontology, 60 Revere Dr, Ste 500, Northbrook, IL 60062.

016.899   ISR   ISSN 0334-309X
BIBLIOGRAPHY OF MODERN HEBREW LITERATURE IN TRANSLATION. 1979-1995. a. Institute for the Translation of Hebrew Literature, P O Box 10051, Ramat Gan, 52001, Israel.

387   GBR   ISSN 1360-8487
BIBLIOGRAPHY OF NAUTICAL BOOKS. 1985-2000. a. Warsash Nautical Books, 6 Dibles Rd, Warsash, Southampton SO31 9HZ, United Kingdom.

001.3   ITA
BIBLIOTECA COMUNALE DI FUSIGNANO. QUADERNI; arte, letteratura, storia. 1989-199?. irreg. Angelo Longo Editore, Via Paolo Costa 33, Ravenna, 48121, Italy.

460 375.4   ESP   ISSN 1988-5393
BIBLIOTECA DE LINGUISTICA. 1982-198?. irreg. Editorial Anagrama S.A., Pedro de la Creu, 58, Barcelona, 08034, Spain.

850   ITA   ISSN 1827-2584
BIBLIOTECA DI LETTERATURE. TESTI UNIVERSITARI. 1979-ceased. irreg. Universita degli Studi di Genova, Istituto di Lingue e Letterature Straniere, Via Balbi 5, Genoa, 16126, Italy.

410   ESP
BIBLIOTECA FILOLOGICA. ENSAYOS. ceased. irreg. Editorial Bello, Barcas, 5, Valencia, 46002, Spain.

410   ESP
BIBLIOTECA FILOLOGICA. MANUALES. 1977 (no.4)-ceased. irreg. Editorial Bello, Barcas, 5, Valencia, 46002, Spain.

839.6 439.6   DNK   ISSN 0067-7841
BIBLIOTHECA ARNAMAGNAEANA; a Jon Helgason condita, auspiciis praesidii Arnamagnaeani. 1941-1999. irreg. Den Arnamagnaeanske Samling, Njalsgade 136, Copenhagen S, 2300, Denmark.

839.6 439.6   DNK   ISSN 0067-785X
BIBLIOTHECA ARNAMAGNAEANA. SUPPLEMENTUM. 1956-1968; resumed 1999-2000. irreg. Den Arnamagnaeanske Samling, Njalsgade 136, Copenhagen S, 2300, Denmark.

028.5   FRA   ISSN 0005-335X
BIBLIOTHEQUE DE TRAVAIL. 1932-2006. 10/yr. Ecole Moderne Francaise - Pedagogie Freinet (P E M F), Mouans-Sartoux, 06376, France.

373 027.626   FRA   ISSN 0005-3414
BIBLIOTHEQUE DE TRAVAIL 2EME DEGRE. 1968-2006. 10/yr. Ecole Moderne Francaise - Pedagogie Freinet (P E M F), Mouans-Sartoux, 06376, France.

372 027.625   FRA   ISSN 0005-3120
BIBLIOTHEQUE DE TRAVAIL JUNIOR. 1965-2006. 10/yr. Ecole Moderne Francaise - Pedagogie Freinet (P E M F), Mouans-Sartoux, 06376, France.

025.2 808.8   NLD   ISSN 1567-8962
BIEB; magazine voor nieuwsgierige mensen. 2000 (June)-2001. bi-m. Biblion Uitgeverij, Postbus 437, Leidschendam, 2260 AK, Netherlands.

054.1   FRA
BIEN DANS MA VIE. 2002 (May)-ceased. m. Axel Springer France, 68 Rue Marjolin, Levallois Perret, 92300, France.

053.1   DEU
BIG BREMEN. 1999-2008. m. Bremer Blatt Verlags GmbH, Humboldtstr 56, Bremen, 28203, Germany.

053.1   DEU
BIG OLDENBURG. 1999-2008. m. Bremer Blatt Verlags GmbH, Humboldtstr 56, Bremen, 28203, Germany.

778.53 790.13   USA   ISSN 0744-723X
BIG REEL; movie, video and Hollywood collectibles. 1974-2008. bi-m. Krause Publications, Inc., 700 E State St, Iola, WI 54990.

796.7   USA
BIG TWIN DEALER; custom building big ideas. 1990-2006 (Nov.). 5/yr. Advanstar Communications, Inc., 201 Sandpointe Ave, Ste 600, Santa Ana, CA 92707-8700.

794   DEU
BIKE-, TOUR-, TREKKINGBIKE-MARKT. 1993-2004. a. Delius Klasing Verlag GmbH, Siekerwall 21, Bielefeld, 33602, Germany.

305.6 371.82   NZL   ISSN 1176-9270
BILINGUAL MAGAZINE. 2004-2005. bi-m. West-East Link, PO Box 13 709, Christchurch, New Zealand.

780.42   USA
BILLBOARD HISTORY OF ROCK 'N ROLL. 1992-199?. irreg. Nielsen Business Publications, 770 Broadway, New York, NY 10003.

929   USA   ISSN 1071-2356
BILYEU BY YOU. 1993-1996. irreg. (2-4/yr). Family Publications, 5628 60th Dr, NE, Marysville, WA 98270.

016.305896   USA   ISSN 0882-7044
BIO-BIBLIOGRAPHIES IN AFRO-AMERICAN AND AFRICAN STUDIES. 1985-19??. irreg. Greenwood Publishing Group Inc., 88 Post Rd W, PO Box 5007, Westport, CT 06881.

016.81   USA   ISSN 0742-695X
BIO-BIBLIOGRAPHIES IN AMERICAN LITERATURE. 1984-19??. irreg. Greenwood Publishing Group Inc., 88 Post Rd W, PO Box 5007, Westport, CT 06881.

016.72   USA   ISSN 1055-6826
BIO-BIBLIOGRAPHIES IN ART AND ARCHITECTURE. 1991-200?. irreg. Greenwood Publishing Group Inc., 88 Post Rd W, PO Box 5007, Westport, CT 06881.

016.332   USA   ISSN 1063-3197
BIO-BIBLIOGRAPHIES IN ECONOMICS. 1992-19??. irreg. Greenwood Publishing Group Inc., 88 Post Rd W, PO Box 5007, Westport, CT 06881.

016.34   USA   ISSN 0882-7052
BIO-BIBLIOGRAPHIES IN LAW AND POLITICAL SCIENCE. 1985-19??. irreg. Greenwood Publishing Group Inc., 88 Post Rd W, PO Box 5007, Westport, CT 06881.

016.78   USA   ISSN 0742-6968
BIO-BIBLIOGRAPHIES IN MUSIC. 1985-200?. irreg. Greenwood Publishing Group Inc., 88 Post Rd W, PO Box 5007, Westport, CT 06881.

016.301   USA   ISSN 0893-8504
BIO-BIBLIOGRAPHIES IN SOCIOLOGY. 1987-19??. irreg. Greenwood Publishing Group Inc., 88 Post Rd W, PO Box 5007, Westport, CT 06881.

016.808   USA   ISSN 0894-2323   CODEN: BDMAEU
BIO-BIBLIOGRAPHIES IN WORLD LITERATURE. 1987-19??. irreg. Greenwood Publishing Group Inc., 88 Post Rd W, PO Box 5007, Westport, CT 06881.

570   GBR   ISSN 1479-0505
BIOFILMS. 2003-2006 (vol.3, no.1). q. Cambridge University Press, The Edinburgh Bldg, Shaftesbury Rd, Cambridge, CB2 8RU, United Kingdom.

570   EGY   ISSN 1110-5747
BIOLOGICAL CURRENT CONTENT OF EGYPT. 1996-2000. biennial. Union of Arab Biologists, Faculty of Science, Cairo University, Orman, Giza, PO Box 144, Cairo, Egypt.

615   NZL   ISSN 1177-5475
BIOLOGICS (PRINT); targets & therapy. 2007-2008. q. Dove Medical Press Ltd., 17/44 William Pickering Dr, Albany, PO Box 300-008, Auckland, 1311, New Zealand.

551.46   DEU   ISSN 0930-8148
BIOLOGISCHE ANSTALT HELGOLAND. BERICHTE. 1986-1997. irreg. Biologische Anstalt Helgoland, Postfach 180, Helgoland, 27483, Germany.

616   DEU   ISSN 0177-3143
BIOMEDICAL JOURNAL. 1982-2001. q. C M S Biomedical Verlag GmbH, Daphnestr 19, Munich, 81925, Germany.

305.23   DEU
BIONICLE. 2003-2009 (Jan.). bi-m. Panini Verlags GmbH, Ravensstr 48, Nettetal, 41334, Germany.

330   DEU   ISSN 1619-5965
BIOTECH-REPORT. 1999-2008. m. Boersenmedien AG, Am Eulenhof 14, Kulmbach, 95326, Germany.

570 600 658   USA
BIOTECHNOLOGY MANAGEMENT PRACTICES. 2003-200?. a. Windhover Information, Inc., 10 Hoyt St, Norwalk, CT 06851.

660.6   GBR
BIOTECHNOLOGY RESEARCH SERIES. 1992-2005 (Sep.). irreg. Cambridge University Press, The Edinburgh Bldg, Shaftesbury Rd, Cambridge, CB2 8RU, United Kingdom.

598.07234   USA   ISSN 1541-5309
BIRD WATCHER. 2001-2003 (Mar.). bi-m. National Geographic Society, PO Box 98199, Washington, DC 20090.

690   ISR   ISSN 0334-0430
BISDEH HABNIYA. 1953-1975. a. Technion - Israel Institute of Technology, National Building Research Institute, Technion City, Haifa, 32000, Israel.

370   ISR   ISSN 0523-1469
BISDEH HEMED. 1957-2006. m. Organizations of Religious Teachers in Israel, 8 Ben Saruk, Tel Aviv, 62969, Israel.

320.52   NLD   ISSN 1873-3670
BITTERLEMON. 2007-2007 (Dec.). bi-m. Bitterlemon Magazine, Postbus 1325, Zwolle, 8001 BH, Netherlands.

690   ISR
BITUMAN. 1958-1993. m. Paz Co. Ltd., P O Box 434, Haifa, 31003, Israel.

330   AUS   ISSN 1444-7134
BIZREVIEW.COM.AU. 1990-2001. bi-m. Publishing Services (Australia) Pty Ltd., 244 St Pauls Terr, Fortitude Valley, Brisbane, QLD 4000, Australia.

917.309   AUS   ISSN 0812-8405
BLACK VOICES. 1984-1989. irreg. James Cook University, Faculty of Arts, Education and Social Sciences, Dept of Social and Cultural Studies, Townsville, QLD 4811, Australia.

305.48 305.8   USA   ISSN 1935-2743
BLACK WOMEN, GENDER & FAMILIES. 2007-2010. s-a. University of Illinois Press, 1325 S Oak St, Champaign, IL 61820.

070.5   GBR   ISSN 0006-436X
BLACKWOOD'S MAGAZINE. 1817-1980. s-a. William Blackwood & Sons Ltd., 106 Queen Street 1844-47, Edinburgh, United Kingdom.

646.72   USA   ISSN 1058-0956
BLACTRESS. 19??-ceased. bi-m. Harris Publications, Inc., 800 Kennesaw Ave, Ste 220, Marietta, GA 30060.

790.13   USA
BLADE MAGAZINE PRESENTS: KNIVES OF EUROPE. 2000-ceased. a. Krause Publications, Inc., 700 E State St, Iola, WI 54990.

781.64 USA ISSN 1534-0554
BLENDER (NEW YORK, 1994); the ultimate guide to music and more. 1994-1997; resumed 2001-2009 (Apr.). 11/yr. Dennis Publishing, Inc., 1040 Ave of the Americas, 23rd Fl, New York, NY 10018.

280.4 DEU ISSN 1431-1992
BLICKPUNKT GEMEINDE; das Magazin fuer Mitarbeiter. 1977-200?. irreg. Oncken Verlag GmbH, Muendener Str 13, Kassel, 34123, Germany.

053.1 DEU
BLOND MAGAZIN. 1998-2008. m. b&d Media Network GmbH, Osterfeldstr 12-14, Hamburg, 22529, Germany.

910 GBR ISSN 0067-9232
BLOOMSBURY GEOGRAPHER. 1968-1996. a. University College London, Department of Geography, University College London, 26 Bedford Way, London, WC1H 0AP, United Kingdom.

051 USA ISSN 1932-6378
BLUEPRINT (NEW YORK, 2006). 2006-200?. 6/yr. Martha Stewart Living Omnimedia LLC, 11 W 42nd St, 25th Fl, New York, NY 10036.

150 USA ISSN 1535-8364
BLUES BUSTER. 2001-2004. 10/yr. Sussex Publishers Inc., 115 E 23rd St, 9th Fl, New York, NY 10010.

781.573 GBR ISSN 0006-5153
BLUES UNLIMITED. 1963-1987. 4/yr. B U Publications Ltd., 36 Belmont Park, Lewisham, London, SE13 5DB, United Kingdom.

635.9 DEU ISSN 1439-9962
BLUMEN WORLDWIDE; The business magazine for the international flower market. 1948-2001. 8/yr. Donau Verlag GmbH & Co. KG, Muensterstr 111, Muenster, 48155, Germany.

790.1 DEU
BOARDSTEIN. 2000-2008. bi-m. Boardstein Verlags- und Handels GmbH, Paderborner Str 15, Dortmund, 44143, Germany.

410 800 NLD ISSN 0523-7971
BOCHUMER ARBEITEN ZUR SPRACH- UND LITERATURWISSENSCHAFT. 1967-1983 (vol.13). irreg. John Benjamins Publishing Co., PO Box 36224, Amsterdam, 1020 ME, Netherlands.

230 NLD ISSN 1573-479X
BODE. 1858-2007. 10/yr. Uitgeverij H. Medema, Postbus 113, Vaassen, 8170 AC, Netherlands.

616 NLD ISSN 1569-7436
BODYMAGAZINE. 2006-2007. 10/yr. Bohn Stafleu van Loghum B.V., Postbus 246, Houten, 3990 GA, Netherlands.

362.7 DNK ISSN 0909-0509
BOERN I TIDEN. 1988-2005. 4/yr. (22/yr.). Boernesagens Faellesraad, Vesterbrogade 24B, Copenhagen V, 1620, Denmark.

362.7 DNK ISSN 1602-8074
BOERN OG UNGE; dag- og doegninstitutioner i Danmark. 1984-2002. a. Kroghs Forlag A-S, Chr. Hansens Vej 3, Vejle, 7100, Denmark.

344.03 372.1 DNK ISSN 1902-1690
BOERN, UNGE, FAMILIER. 1993-2007. 12/yr. Jurainformation, Vesterbrogade 10, Copenhagen V, 1620, Denmark.

674 FRA ISSN 0753-4159
BOIS DU SUD. 1982-199?. 6/yr. Bois du Sud, 8 rue Pierre Rameil, Perpignan, 66000, France.

914 ESP ISSN 0213-6090
BOLETIN DE ARQUEOLOGIA MEDIEVAL. 1987-2005; suspended. a. Asociacion Espanola de Arqueologia Medieval, Parque Arqueologico Alarcos-Calatrava, Apartado Correos 201, Coiudad Real, 13080, Spain.

380 ESP ISSN 0211-1268
BOLETIN DE COYUNTURA Y ESTADISTICA DEL PAIS VASCO. 1969. q. Camara Oficial de Comercio e Industria de Alava, Dato 38, Vitoria, 01005, Spain.

304.6 ESP ISSN 1138-221X
BOLETIN MENSUAL DE COYUNTURA. 1986-1996. m. Comunidad de Madrid, Instituto de Estadistica, Principe de Vargara 108, Madrid, 28002, Spain.

460 ESP ISSN 0211-2140
BOLETIN MILLARES CARLO. 1980-200?. a. Universidad Nacional de Educacion a Distancia (U N E D), Centro Asociado de las Palmas de Gran Canaria, Luis Doreste Silva 101, Las Palmas de Gran Canaria, 35004, Spain.

347 ESP
BOLETIN OFICIAL DE LAS CORTES ESPANOLAS. 19??-ceased. s-w. Spain. Congreso de los Diputados, Depto. de Publicaciones, Carrera de San Jeronimo s-n, Madrid, 28071, Spain.

351.4652 ESP ISSN 1130-5894
BOLETIN OFICIAL DE NAVARRA/NAFARROAKO ALDIZKARI. 1838-suspended. 3/w. Gobierno de Navarra, Fondo de Publicaciones, Calle de la Navas de Tolosa 21, Pamplona, Navarra 31002, Spain.

615.1 ITA ISSN 0006-6648 CODEN: BCFAAI
BOLLETTINO CHIMICO FARMACEUTICO. 1861-ceased. m. Societa Editoriale Farmaceutica (S E F), Via Ausonio 12, Milan, MI 20123, Italy.

615.19 ITA ISSN 1120-8678
BOLLETTINO DI FARMACOSORVEGLIANZA. 1990-2003. 6/yr. Elsevier Masson, Via Paleocapa 7, Milan, 20121, Italy.

617.7 ITA ISSN 0006-677X CODEN: BOOCAH
BOLLETTINO D'OCULISTICA. 1930-ceased. q. Cappelli Editore, Via Farini 14, Bologna, 40124, Italy.

665.5 ITA
BOLLETTINO PETROLIFERO. 1987 (vol.30)-ceased. q.?. Ministero dello Sviluppo Economico, Via Veneto 33, Rome, 00187, Italy.

305.86 FRA
BOMDIA LUSITANO. 2006-2007. m. (11/yr.). Club Bomdia Lusitano, 55 Boulevard Lannes, Paris, 75016, France.

054 FRA ISSN 1951-9486
BON WEEK. 2006-2007. w. Editions Bauer France, 30-32 Rue de Chabrol, Paris, 75010, France.

640 FRA ISSN 1271-545X
BONHEUR; la revue de la famille. 1928-1995. m. E S F Editeur, 2 rue Maurice Hartmann, Issy-les-Moulineaux, 92133 Cedex, France.

053.1 DEU ISSN 0949-0078
BONNER ILLUSTRIERTE. 1979-2004. m. Bouvier Verlag, Fuerstenstr 3, Bonn, 53111, Germany.

310 DEU
BONNER MONATSZAHLEN; Statistik aktuell. 1981-2007. m. Bundesstadt Bonn, Statistikstelle, Bottlerplatz 1, Amt 61-4, Bonn, 53103, Germany.

002 ITA
BOOK BOSS. 1995-ceased. m. Panini SpA, Viale Emilio Po 380, Modena, 41100, Italy.

769.52 GBR ISSN 1353-8128
BOOKPLATE INTERNATIONAL. 1994-200?. s-a. Primrose Academy Ltd., Stratton Audley Park, Bicester, Oxon OX27 9AB, United Kingdom.

808.8 USA
BOOKS ARE EVERYTHING. 1988-1995. q. R.C. Holland, Ed. & Pub., 302 Martin Dr, Richmond, KY 40475.

028.1 CAN ISSN 0045-2564
BOOKS IN CANADA; the Canadian review of books. 1971-2008 (Jan./Feb.). m. (9/yr.). Canadian Review of Books Ltd., 427 Mount Pleasant Rd, Toronto, ON M4S 2L8, Canada.

796.346 DNK ISSN 1604-7591
BORDTENNISGUIDEN. 1982-2007. a. Dansk Bordtennis Union, Idraettens Hus, Brondby, 2605, Denmark.

338.47004 USA ISSN 1533-5674
BOSTON COMPUTERUSER. 1987-199?. m. ComputerUser.com, Inc., PO Box 7738, Hicksville, NY 11791.

371.42 USA ISSN 1098-9757
THE BOSTON JOBBANK; the job hunter's guide to the Bay State. (Includes: all of Massachusetts.) 1980-2005 (20th ed.). biennial. Adams Media, 57 Littlefield St, Avon, MA 02322.

580 DEU ISSN 0938-1759
BOTANICUS BRIEF; info for plant lovers around the world. 1977-2007. m. Botanicus Brief, Gartenweg 9 a, Landau, 76829, Germany.

332 FRA ISSN 1161-9430
BOTTIN DE LA FINANCE. 1991-1992. a. Coface SCRL - Bottin Entreprise, 31 Rue Anatole France, Levallois, Cedex 92685, France.

381 FRA ISSN 0988-9590
BOULOGNE INFORMATIONS. 1951-2002. 2/m. Chambre de Commerce et d'Industrie de Boulogne, 98 quai Leon Gambetta, BP 269, Boulogne-sur-Mer, Cedex 62204, France.

781.64 DEU
BOUNCE. 200?-2007 (Feb.). bi-m. J.L. King Publishing Europe, Koenigstr 60, Landau, 76829, Germany.

332.6 FRA ISSN 1168-3155
BOURSE DE PARIS. ACTIONS. 1967-2004. m. Bourse de Paris, 39 rue Cambon, Paris, 75001, France.

800 FRA ISSN 0339-3801
LA BOUTEILLE A LA MER. 1975-1995. irreg. Bouteille a la Mer, c/o Ed. Marc Beigbeder, 8 rue Theo-Renaudot, Paris, 75015, France.

011 USA ISSN 0000-1775
THE BOWKER BUYER'S GUIDE. 2003-2007. s-a. R.R. Bowker LLC, 630 Central Ave, New Providence, NJ 07974.

070.5 020 USA
BOWKER LIBRARY BULLETIN. 2003 (Oct.)-2006 (Jun.). q. R.R. Bowker LLC, 630 Central Ave, New Providence, NJ 07974.

070 USA ISSN 0000-1783
BOWKER'S NEWS MEDIA DIRECTORY. (Vol.1: Newspaper Directory; Vol.2: Magazine and Newsletter Directory; Vol.3: TV and Radio Directory) 1949-2009. a. ProQuest LLC (Bethesda), 7200 Wisconsin Ave, Ste 715, Bethesda, MD 20814.

794.6 ITA
BOWLING OPEN; international amusement magazine. 1990-ceased. q. Editrice Bowling Open S.n.c., Via Giacomo Camozzi, 130, Bergamo, BG 24121, Italy.

781.65 GBR ISSN 1357-4612
BOZ. 1982-2001. m. Peter Boizot Group, 29 Romilly St, London, W1V 6HP, United Kingdom.

370.993 NZL ISSN 1177-5122
BRAIN WAVE. 2004-2007. q. New Zealand Trade and Enterprise, PO Box 8680, Symonds Street, Auckland, New Zealand.

028.5 NLD ISSN 1874-7760
BRATZ MAGAZINE. 2006-ceased. Juniorpress Magazines B.V., Zwarteweg 6c, Naarden, 1412 GD, Netherlands.

663.3 DEU ISSN 0172-0589
BRAUEREI JOURNAL. 1882-2003. m. Dreistern Verlag GmbH, Andreas-Hofer-Str 1, Munich, 81547, Germany.

641.5 ITA ISSN 1592-9213
BRAVISSIMA IN CUCINA. 2001-200?. m. Ulysse Network, Viale Bianca Maria 19, Milan, Italy.

330.9 USA ISSN 1540-0794
BRAZIL COUNTRY REPORT. 1995-ceased. a. Orbis Publications, LLC, 1924 47th St NW, Washington, DC 20007-1901.

001.3 AUT ISSN 1021-5972
BRENNER-STUDIEN. 1969-2000 (vol.17). irreg. Universitaet Innsbruck, Forschungsinstitut Brenner-Archiv, Josef-Hirn-Str 5, Innsbruck, 6020, Austria.

610 331.88 DEU ISSN 1619-8956
BRENNPUNKT GESUNDHEIT. 1991-2007. q. Gewerkschaft fuer Beschaeftigte im Gesundheitswesen, Hoellturm-Passage 5-6, Radolfzell, 78315, Germany.

796.172 DEU
BRETT; Magazin fuer den Alltag am Strand, auf der Strasse und in den Bergen. 2000-2007. q. Terra Oceanis Verlag, Braunstr 32, Kiel, 24145, Germany.

790.1 GBR ISSN 0968-3372
BRIDGE PLUS. 1989-2009. m. Mr. Bridge, PO Box 384, Reading, Berks RG1 5YP, United Kingdom.

150 616.8 GBR ISSN 1474-3310
BRIEF TREATMENT AND CRISIS INTERVENTION; a journal of evidence-based practice. 2001-2008. q. Oxford University Press, Great Clarendon St, Oxford, OX2 6DP, United Kingdom.

270.092 GBR ISSN 0308-0544
BRIEFING. 1970-2004. m. Catholic Media Trust, 39 Eccleston Sq, London, W13 0RA, United Kingdom.

320.9 TUR
BRIEFING. 1974-ceased. w. Turkish Ekonomik Basin Ajansi (T E B A), Suleyman Haci Abdullahoglu Cad. No:5 D:3, Balgat, Ankara, 06680, Turkey.

769.56 DEU ISSN 0933-968X
BRIEFMARKEN MAGAZIN. 1984-1997. bi-m. E M S Verlag GmbH, Bientzlestr 3, Stuttgart, 70599, Germany.

150 616.8 NLD ISSN 0924-0314
BRILL'S STUDIES IN EPISTEMOLOGY, PSYCHOLOGY AND PSYCHIATRY. 1989-1993 (vol.3). irreg. Brill, PO Box 9000, Leiden, 2300 PA, Netherlands.

028.5 250 USA ISSN 1048-2873
BRIO. 1990-2009. m. Focus on the Family, 8605 Explorer Dr, Colorado Springs, CO 80920.

028.5 USA
BRIO & BEYOND. 2001-2009. m. Focus on the Family, 8605 Explorer Dr, Colorado Springs, CO 80920.

940 NLD ISSN 0066-1821
BRITAIN AND THE NETHERLANDS. 1960-1997. a. Uitgeversmaatschappij Walburg Pers BV, Postbus 4159, Zutphen, 7200 BD, Netherlands.

800 GBR
BRITISH AND IRISH AUTHORS. 1967-1992. irreg. Cambridge University Press, The Edinburgh Bldg, Shaftesbury Rd, Cambridge, CB2 8RU, United Kingdom.

666 GBR ISSN 0268-4373 CODEN: BCPREL
BRITISH CERAMIC PROCEEDINGS. 1964-2003. a. Maney Publishing, Ste 1C, Joseph's Well, Hanover Walk, Leeds, W Yorks LS3 1AB, United Kingdom.

382 TUR ISSN 0007-0416
BRITISH CHAMBER OF COMMERCE OF TURKEY. TRADE JOURNAL. 1908-ceased. m. The British Chamber of Commerce of Turkey, Mesrutiyet Caddesi, 18, Asli Han, Kat 6, Galatasaray, Istanbul, 80050, Turkey.

004 GBR
BRITISH COMPUTER SOCIETY WORKSHOP SERIES. 1981-2009 (May.). irreg. Cambridge University Press, The Edinburgh Bldg, Shaftesbury Rd, Cambridge, CB2 8RU, United Kingdom.

620 370 GBR ISSN 1470-4692
BRITISH JOURNAL OF ENGINEERING EDUCATION. 2000-2006. 3/yr. Sheffield Hallam University, School of Engineering, City Campus, Sheffield, S1 1WB, United Kingdom.

598 GBR ISSN 1363-2965
BRITISH ORNITHOLOGISTS' CLUB. OCCASIONAL PUBLICATIONS. 1994-1999. irreg. British Ornithologists' Club, c/o BOU, British Museum, Tring, Herts HP23 6AP, United Kingdom.

571.6 GBR
BRITISH SOCIETY FOR CELL BIOLOGY. SYMPOSIA. 1976-19??. irreg. Cambridge University Press, The Edinburgh Bldg, Shaftesbury Rd, Cambridge, CB2 8RU, United Kingdom.

571.5 571.6 GBR
BRITISH SOCIETY FOR DEVELOPMENTAL BIOLOGY. SYMPOSIA. 1973-19??. irreg. Cambridge University Press, The Edinburgh Bldg, Shaftesbury Rd, Cambridge, CB2 8RU, United Kingdom.

808.838 ITA ISSN 1828-938X
BRIVIDI COLLECTION. 2006-200?. m. Edigamma Publishing, Via Sambuca Pistoiese 70A, Rome, 00138, Italy.

384.55 USA
BROADCAST AND PRODUCTION. BRASIL EDITION. 2002-200?. bi-m. I M A S Publishing Group, 5827 Columbia Pike, Ste 310, Falls Church, VA 22041.

384.5452 USA
BROADCASTING & CABLE'S TELEVISION INTERNATIONAL. 1983-2001. bi-m. Reed Business Information, 360 Park Ave S, New York, NY 10010.

338 664.6 NLD ISSN 1871-4803
BROOD- EN BANKETZAKEN. 1995-2005. a. Hoofdbedrijfschap Detailhandel, Postbus 90703, The Hague, 2509 LS, Netherlands.

746.9 AUS ISSN 1449-6267
BRUSH (NEWTOWN); Australian make-up artist. 2004-2005. bi-m. Infovea, PO Box 688, Newtown, NSW 2042, Australia.

908 ITA ISSN 0392-3894
BRUTIUM. 1922-2002. 3/yr. Gangemi Editore, Piazza San Pantaleo 4, Rome, Italy.

796.812 DNK ISSN 0903-5524
BRYDNING/WRESTLING. 1972-2002. 4/yr. Danmarks Brydeforbund, Idraettens Hus, Broendby Stadion 20, Broendby, 2605, Denmark.

621 CHE ISSN 0176-926X
BUEHLER. NACHRICHTEN. 19??-1984. irreg. Buehler AG, Uzwil, 9240, Switzerland.

346 USA ISSN 1523-5491
BUFFALO WOMEN'S LAW JOURNAL. 1992-2008. a. State University of New York at Buffalo, School of Law, 404 O'Brien Hall, North Campus, Buffalo, NY 14260-1100.

028.5 TUR ISSN 1301-031X
BUGS BUNNY. 1996-2009. m. Dogan Egmont Yayincilik ve Yapimcilik A.S., 19 Mayis Mahallesi, Golden Plaza No 1, Kat 10, Posta Kodu 34360, Istanbul, Turkey.

690 GBR ISSN 0969-675X
BUILDING & CONSTRUCTION INDEX. 1923-1999. a. C M P Information Ltd., Sovereign House, Sovereign Way, Tonbridge, Kent TN9 1RW, United Kingdom.

690 352.9 USA
BUILDING STANDARDS TODAY. 1933-2002. bi-m. International Conference of Building Officials, 5360 Workman Mill Rd, Whittier, CA 90601.

Cessations

636.7 FRA ISSN 1958-7627
BULL & DOGUE NEWS. 2007-2008. bi-m. CophiPresse SARL, 4 Rue de l'Eglise, B P 40004, Peronne, Cedex 80208, France.

340 FRA ISSN 0242-6781
LE BULLETIN DES ANNONCES LEGALES OBLIGATOIRES. 1912-2005. w. Direction des Journaux Officiels, 26 rue Desaix, Paris, 75727 Cedex 15 , France.

338.642 FRA ISSN 0755-1541
BULLETIN DES METIERS ET DE L'ARTISANAT. 1940-2006. 11/yr. Bulletin des Metiers et de l'Artisanat, 62 rue la Boetie, Paris, 75008, France.

382 FRA ISSN 1154-0842
BULLETIN DES OPPORTUNITES D'ALSACE. 1980-199?. q. Chambre Regionale de Commerce et d'Industrie d'Alsace, 42 rue Schweighaeuser, Strasbourg, 67000, France.

944 FRA ISSN 0766-4516
BULLETIN D'HISTOIRE DE LA REVOLUTION FRANCAISE. 1961-199?. a. Editions du C T H S, 1 rue Descartes, Paris, 75005, France.

615.009 CAN ISSN 0829-5557
BULLETIN D'INFORMATION TOXICOLOGIQUE. 1986-2002. q. Institut National de Sante Publique du Quebec, 945 Av Wolfe, Quebec, PQ G1V 5B3, Canada.

330 FRA ISSN 1777-9553
BULLETIN D'INFORMATIONS ECONOMIQUES ET COMMERCIALES. 2005-2008. bi-m. Comite France Chine, 55 avenue Bosquet, Paris Cedex 07, 75330, France.

340.023 FRA ISSN 1774-7570
BULLETIN DU BATONNIER. 199?-2005. a. Ordre des Avocats de Montpellier, 14 rue Marcel-de-Serres, CS 49503, Montpellier, 34961 Cedex 2, France.

658 341 FRA ISSN 1264-9120
BULLETIN EUROPEEN ET INTERNATIONAL. 1995-2005. bi-m. Editions Francis Lefebvre, 42 rue de Villiers, Levallois-Perret, 92300, France.

639.2 ITA ISSN 1014-1189
BULLETIN OF FISHERY STATISTICS/BOLETIN ESTADISTICO DE PESCA/BULLETIN STATISTIQUE DES PECHES. 1963-19??. irreg. Food and Agriculture Organization of the United Nations (F A O), Via delle Terme di Caracalla, Rome, RM 00100, Italy.

610 174.2 GBR ISSN 0962-9564
BULLETIN OF MEDICAL ETHICS. 1985-2006 (No. 214). 10/yr. Royal Society of Medicine Press Ltd., 1 Wimpole St, London, W1G 0AE, United Kingdom.

611.01816 ITA ISSN 0391-481X CODEN: BMBMD5
BULLETIN OF MOLECULAR BIOLOGY AND MEDICINE; a journal for the rapid publication of reports in the field of biochemical sciences. 1975-1995 (Vol. 20). q. Casa Editrice Idelson Gnocchi, Via Michele Pietravalle 85, Naples, NA 80131, Italy.

330 FRA ISSN 0298-511X
LE BULLETIN OFFICIEL DE LA CONCURRENCE, DE LA CONSOMMATION ET DE LA REPRESSION DES FRAUDES. 1941-2008. m. Direction des Journaux Officiels, 26 rue Desaix, Paris, 75727 Cedex 15 , France.

798.209 FRA ISSN 1274-5626
BULLETIN OFFICIEL DES COMPETITIONS EQUESTRES ET DES EPREUVES D'ELEVAGE. 1997-2007. w. Editions Charles Lavauzelle, Le Prouet, BP 8, Panazol, 87350, France.

340 FRA ISSN 0750-0416
LE BULLETIN OFFICIEL DU MINISTERE DE LA JUSTICE. -2005. q. Direction des Journaux Officiels, 26 rue Desaix, Paris, 75727 Cedex 15 , France.

052 AUS ISSN 1440-7485
THE BULLETIN WITH NEWSWEEK. 1880-2008 (Jan.). w. A C P Magazines Ltd., 54-58 Park St, Sydney, NSW 2000, Australia.

658 GBR ISSN 1350-3197
BULLETPOINT. 1993-2008. 10/yr. Bulletpoint Communications Ltd., Betchworth House, 57-65 Station Rd, Redhill, Surrey RH1 1DL, United Kingdom.

028.5 DEU ISSN 0721-183X
DER BUNTE HUND; Magazin fuer Kinder in den besten Jahren. 1981-2008. 3/yr. Julius Beltz GmbH & Co. KG, Werderstr 10, Weinheim, 69469, Germany.

910.09 ITA ISSN 1121-2969
BUON VIAGGIO. 1991-ceased. m. Editrice Portoria Srl, Via Chiossetto, 1, Milan, MI 20122, Italy.

641.5 ITA
BUONA CUCINA DI PRATICA. 1994-ceased. m. Fabbri Editori, Via Mecenate 91, Milan, 20138, Italy.

641.5 ITA ISSN 1827-8469
LA BUONA CUCINA GOLOSA. 2006-200?. m. Ulysse Network, Viale Bianca Maria 19, Milan, Italy.

641 ITA ISSN 1722-4322
BUONGUSTO ITALIANO. 2003-2004. m. Edizioni Mimosa, Piazza E de Angeli 9, Milan, 20146, Italy.

746.9 FRA ISSN 1772-4112
BURDA L'ESSENTIEL DE LA COUTURE. 2005-2005. q. Editions DIPA Burda, 26 Avenue de l'Europe, Strasbourg, 67013, France.

745.5 790.13 FRA ISSN 1633-7115
BURDA LOISIRS CREATIFS. 200?-2006. irreg. Editions DIPA Burda, 26 Avenue de l'Europe, Strasbourg, 67013, France.

551 FRA ISSN 0369-9382
BUREAU D'ETUDES GEOLOGIQUES ET MINIERES COLONIALES. PUBLICATIONS. 1932-1960. irreg. Editions B R G M, 3, ave Claude-Guillemin, BP 36009, Orleans, Cedex 2 45060, France.

384 USA
BURRELLE'S MEDIA DIRECTORY (CD-ROM EDITION). 1994-2004. a. (plus 3/yr updates). BurrellesLuce, 75 E Northfield Rd, Livingston, NJ 07039.

384 USA
BURRELLE'S MEDIA DIRECTORY. MAGAZINES & NEWSLETTERS. 1994-2004. a. (plus s-a updates). BurrellesLuce, 75 E Northfield Rd, Livingston, NJ 07039.

384 USA ISSN 1074-9446
BURRELLE'S MEDIA DIRECTORY. VOL 1, NEWSPAPERS & RELATED MEDIA. 1994-2004. a. BurrellesLuce, 75 E Northfield Rd, Livingston, NJ 07039.

384 USA ISSN 1074-9462
BURRELLE'S MEDIA DIRECTORY. VOL 3, BROADCAST & RELATED MEDIA. 1994-2004. a. BurrellesLuce, 75 E Northfield Rd, Livingston, NJ 07039.

659.1029 USA ISSN 0883-9999
BURRELLE'S NEW ENGLAND MEDIA DIRECTORY (YEAR). 1975-2004. a. BurrellesLuce, 75 E Northfield Rd, Livingston, NJ 07039.

302.23 USA
BURRELLE'S TEXAS MEDIA DIRECTORY (YEAR). 19??-2004. a. BurrellesLuce, 75 E Northfield Rd, Livingston, NJ 07039.

796.77 AUS ISSN 0155-0535
BUSHDRIVER. 1977-2001. bi-m. Ric Williams and Associates Pty. Ltd., 25 Valley Park Cres, Turramurra, NSW 2074, Australia.

657 346 USA ISSN 0885-1034
BUSINESS ACCOUNTING FOR LAWYERS NEWSLETTER; summary, analysis, and application of current accounting concepts in the practice of law. 1984-19??. 8/yr. Practising Law Institute, 810 Seventh Ave, 21st Fl, New York, NY 10019.

384 USA ISSN 0162-3885 CODEN: BCORBD
BUSINESS COMMUNICATIONS REVIEW. 1971-2007. m. C M P Media LLC, 600 Community Dr, Manhasset, NY 11030.

330 FRA ISSN 0982-0418
BUSINESS - ENTREPRISE. 1986-198?. 6/yr. Business - Entreprise, 23 rue des Apennins, Paris, 75017, France.

338.0029 DEU ISSN 0966-2138
BUSINESS INFORMATION FROM GOVERNMENT. 1992-1999. irreg. K.G. Saur Verlag, Mies-van-der-Rohe-Str 1, Munich, 80807, Germany.

368.094 GBR
BUSINESS INSURANCE EUROPE. 2006-2009. bi-w. Crain Communications, Ltd., 3rd Fl, 21 St Thomas St, London, SE1 9RY, United Kingdom.

346.066 USA
BUSINESS LAW OF THE EUROPEAN UNION; a practice guide. 1996-200?. irreg. Matthew Bender & Co., Inc., 1275 Broadway, Albany, NY 12204.

791.43 USA ISSN 1933-7566
THE BUSINESS OF MOVIE PRODUCTION & DISTRIBUTION. 19??-2006 (13th ed.). irreg. S N L Financial LC, One SNL Plz, PO Box 2124, Charlottesville, VA 22902.

380.1029 USA ISSN 0888-1413
BUSINESS ORGANIZATIONS, AGENCIES, AND PUBLICATIONS DIRECTORY. 1980-2006. irreg. Gale, 27500 Drake Rd, Farmington Hills, MI 48331.

330 USA
BUSINESS RUSSIA (NEW YORK). 1994-200?. m. Economist Intelligence Unit Ltd., 111 W 57th St, New York, NY 10019 .

382 NLD ISSN 1023-9340
BUSINESS T I P S ON CUBA. (Technological Information Promotion System) 1992-ceased. m. Cuba T I P S International, Weena 290 NL-3012, Rotterdam, Netherlands.

658 AUS ISSN 1031-1343
THE BUSINESS WHO'S WHO AUSTRALIAN PRODUCTS AND TRADENAMES GUIDE. 1968-2001. a. Dun & Bradstreet Marketing Pty. Ltd., St. Kilda Rd, PO Box 7405, Melbourne, VIC 3000, Australia.

616.15 GBR ISSN 0260-0129
BUTTERWORTHS INTERNATIONAL MEDICAL REVIEWS: HEMATOLOGY. 1984-199?. irreg. Butterworth & Co. (Publishers) Ltd., 88 Kingsway, London, WC2B 6AB, United Kingdom.

382 ITA ISSN 0007-7380
BUYERS' GUIDE. 1962-ceased. m. Ente Italiano per lo Sviluppo dell'Esportazione, Piazzale Giotto, 8, Perugia, PG 06121, Italy.

770 GBR ISSN 0961-0863
BUYING CAMERAS. 1990-1999. m. Emap Active Ltd. (Apex House), Apex House, Oundle Rd, Peterborough, PE2 9NP, United Kingdom.

942 GBR ISSN 0262-5342
BYGONE KENT; a monthly journal on all aspects of Kent local history. 1979-2006. m. Meresborough Books, Meresborough Books Ltd, 17 Station Rd, Rainham, Gillingham, Kent ME8 7RS, United Kingdom.

004.16 USA
BYTE.COM. 1975-200?. w. C M P Media LLC, 600 Community Dr, Manhasset, NY 11030.

020 ITA ISSN 1593-151X
C A B NEWSLETTER. (Conservazione negli Archivi e nelle Biblioteche) 1992-2004. bi-m. Istituto Centrale di Patologia del Libro, Via Milano 76, Rome, 00184, Italy.

333.80 NLD ISSN 0925-0085
C A D D E T ANALYSIS SERIES. (Centre for the Analysis and Dissemination of Demonstrated Energy Technologies) 1989-2001. irreg. C A D D E T, c/o Mr Boudewijn Huenges Wajer, Novem bv, P.O. Box 17, Sittard, 6130, Netherlands.

580 NLD ISSN 0169-6289
C B S NEWSLETTER. 1983-2000. s-a. Centraalbureau voor Schimmelcultures, Uppsalalaan 8, Utrecht, 3584 CT, Netherlands.

280.4 NLD ISSN 1873-4952
C C, CHRISTENEN IN CONTACT. 2006-2008. bi-w. Evangelische Omroep, Postbus 21000, Hilversum, 1202 BA, Netherlands.

780 USA ISSN 1524-7848
C C M MAGAZINE. (Christ. Community. Music.) 1978-2008. m. Salem Publishing, 104 Woodmont Blvd, Ste 300, Nashville, TN 37205.

369.4 DNK ISSN 0109-2979
C C ORIENTERING. 1983-1986. q. Coordination Committee for Polish - Jewish Youth in Denmark, PO Box 77, Copenhagen K, 1000, Denmark.

304.6 EGY
C D C MONOGRAPHS. STUDIES IN AFRICAN AND ASIAN DEMOGRAPHY. 1970-1992. a. Cairo Demographic Centre, No. 78 St. No. 4, Hadhaba el-Olya, Mokattam, Cairo, 11571, Egypt.

780 GBR ISSN 0967-4411
C D CLASSICS. 1992-ceased. m. Northern & Shell Plc, The Northern & Shell Bldg, Number 10 Lower Thames St, London, EC3R 6EN, United Kingdom.

333.792 FRA ISSN 1276-2776 CODEN: CEAJFG
C E A SACLAY. LE JOURNAL. (Commissariat a l'Energie Atomique) 1997-2002. q. Commissariat a l'Energie Atomique, Centre de Saclay, Gif-sur-Yvette, 91191, France.

639.2 ITA ISSN 1014-9228
C E C A F/E C A F SERIES. 1975-ceased. irreg. Food and Agriculture Organization of the United Nations (F A O), Via delle Terme di Caracalla, Rome, RM 00100, Italy.

305.8 CAN
C E S A. BULLETIN/SOCIETE CANADIENNE D'ETUDES ETHNIQUES. BULLETIN. 1974-1995. irreg. Canadian Ethnic Studies Association, c/o Dept. of History, University of Calgary, 2500 University Dr, N W, Calgary, AB T2N 1N4, Canada.

320 323.5 FRA ISSN 1270-1343
C F D T EN DIRECT. (Confederation Francaise Democratique du Travail) 1996-200?. m. Confederation Francaise Democratique du Travail, 4 bd. de la Villette, Paris, Cedex 19 75955, France.

500 DEU ISSN 0341-4116 CODEN: CFSEDS
C F S; Courier Forschungsergebnisse Senckenberg. (Courier Forschungsinstitut Senckenberg) 1972-2009. irreg. E. Schweizerbart'sche Verlagsbuchhandlung, Johannesstr 3A, Stuttgart, 70176, Germany.

658.152 FRA ISSN 1774-5004
C G A'S NEWS REPORT. 200?-2006. irreg. Compagnie Generale d'Affacturage, 70 rue de Villiers, Levallois-Perret, 92532 Cedex, France.

384 DNK ISSN 1901-8398
C I O; raastof til it-direktoerer og andre it-ansvarlige. 2006-2007. 8/yr. I D G Danmark A/S, Carl Jacobsens Vej 25, Valby, 2500, Denmark.

327.172 ESP ISSN 1139-5222
C I P. ANUARIO. (Centro de Investigacion para la Paz) 1986-2005. a. Fundacion Hogar del Empleado, Centro de Investigacion para la Paz, Duque de Sesto, 40, Madrid, 28009, Spain.

363.7 ISR CODEN: EPRFEH
C I S ENVIRONMENT AND DISARMAMENT YEARBOOK. (Commonwealth of Independent States) 1987-2004. a. Hebrew University of Jerusalem, Marjorie Mayrock Center for Russian, Eurasian and East European Research, c/o Faculty of Social Sciences, Mount Scopus, Jerusalem, 91905, Israel.

352.14 ITA
C I S P E L NOTIZIE. 1974-ceased. s-m. Confederazione Nazionale dei Servizi (Confservizi), Via Cavour 179/a, Rome, 00184, Italy.

500 600 CAN ISSN 0715-8661 CODEN: CSTNDF
C I S T I NEWS (PRINT). 1968-2008 (Dec.). q. National Research Council Canada (N R C), NRC Communications & Corporate Relations, 1200 Montreal Rd, Bldg M-58, Ottawa, ON K1A 0R6, Canada.

690 FRA ISSN 1761-7340
C M S METAL. 1972-2005. bi-m. Edial Editions, 126 rue du Temple, Paris, 75003, France.

341.2 NLD ISSN 1573-2053
C N F QUARTERLY JOURNAL. 1994-2007. q. Co-operating Netherlands Foundations for Central and Eastern Europe, PO Box 156, Hilversum, 1200 AD, Netherlands.

615.9 CAN ISSN 1201-1770
C N T C NEWS. 1993-2003. s-a. Canadian Network of Toxicology Centres, 2nd Fl, Bovey Bldg, Gordon St, University of Guelph, Guelph, ON N1G 2W1, Canada.

382 USA
C O M E C O N FOREIGN TRADE DATA. (Council for Mutual Economic Assistance) 1980-19??. plus biennial updates. Greenwood Publishing Group Inc., 88 Post Rd W, PO Box 5007, Westport, CT 06881.

610 USA
C O R HEALTHCARE LEADERSHIP REVIEW. 1982-200?. m. C O R Health, LLC, PO Box 40959, Santa Barbara, CA 93140.

362 USA
C O R HEALTHCARE STAFFING TREND WATCH. ceased 200?. w. C O R Health, LLC, PO Box 40959, Santa Barbara, CA 93140.

344.1042 GBR
C P A G'S INCOME - RELATED BENEFITS: THE LEGISLATION. 19??-200?. plus a. updates. Sweet & Maxwell Ltd., 100 Avenue Rd, London, NW3 3PF, United Kingdom.

657 USA ISSN 0094-792X
THE C P A LETTER (PRINT); a news report to members. 1920-2008. s-m. (except July-Aug. & Feb.-Mar. combined). American Institute of Certified Public Accountants, 1211 Ave of the Americas, New York, NY 10036.

328 USA ISSN 1936-4547
C P A NEWS (WASHINGTON, D.C., ONLINE). (Center for Policy Alternatives) 1993-ceased. m. Center for Policy Alternatives, 1875 Connecticut Ave, N W, Ste 710, Washington, DC 20009-5728.

351 USA ISSN 0196-612X
C Q GUIDE TO CURRENT AMERICAN GOVERNMENT; a survey of recent significant developments in national government and politics. (Congressional Quarterly) 1961-2008 (Spring). s-a. C Q Press, Inc., 2300 N St, NW, Ste 800, Washington, DC 20037.

657 USA
C S A SENTINEL. (Control Self-Assessment) 1996-2007. 3/yr. Institute of Internal Auditors, Inc., 247 Maitland Ave, Altamonte Springs, FL 32701.

633.63 NLD ISSN 0165-9375
C S M INFORMATIE. 1946-2007. bi-m. C S M Suiker BV, Postbus 349, Amsterdam, 1000 AH, Netherlands.

674 694 FRA ISSN 0984-2438
C T B A INFO. 1985-2007. bi-m. Centre Technique du Bois et de l'Ameublement, 10 av. Saint-Mande, Paris, 75012, France.

658 AUS ISSN 1325-6114
C T C NEWSLETTER. (Competitive Tendering and Contracting Research) 1992-1996. s-a. University of Sydney, Graduate School of Business., C37, Sydney, NSW 2006, Australia.

381.45687 ITA
C T M NEWS. (Commercio Tessuti Moda) 1987-ceased. bi-m. Editrice La Martesana Srl, Via Brescia 22, Cernusco sul Naviglio, MI 20063, Italy.

510 NLD
C W I TRACTS. 1963-2007 (vol.135). irreg. Centrum voor Wiskunde en Informatica, PO Box 94079, Amsterdam, 1090 GB, Netherlands.

343.09946 USA ISSN 0749-7652
CABLE T V LAW REPORTER. 1984-19??. m. S N L Financial LC, One SNL Plz, PO Box 2124, Charlottesville, VA 22902.

799.2 ITA ISSN 1123-413X
CACCIA E CANI. 1967-ceased. m. Silvio Basile Editore, Lungo Bisagno Istria, 34 c, Genoa, GE 16141, Italy.

629.118 ITA ISSN 1127-1329
CAFE RACER. 1998-ceased. m. (11/yr.). Ixo Publishing Italia, Via Vittor Pisani 22, Milan, 20124, Italy.

617 TUR ISSN 1016-5118
CAGDAS CERRAHI DERGISI/JOURNAL OF CURRENT SURGERY. 1987-ceased. q. Logos Yayincilik Ticaret A.S., Yildiz Posta Cad., Sinan Apt. No.36 D 66-67, Gayrettepe, Istanbul, 34349, Turkey.

649 FRA ISSN 1776-3231
CAHIER EVEIL. 2005-2006. irreg. Elsevier France, Editions Scientifiques et Medicales, 23 Rue Linois, Paris, 75724, France.

054.1 FRA ISSN 0222-5956
CAHIERS CONFRONTATION. 1979-1989. s-a. Editions Aubier Montaigne, 13 quai de Conti, Paris, 75006, France.

379 FRA ISSN 0180-9881
LES CAHIERS DE DIRECT. 1976-198?. irreg. Centre d'Information et d'Echanges Television, 39, bid Magenta, Paris, 75010, France.

200 FRA ISSN 1167-1114
CAHIERS DE LA FORMATION. 1992-199?. q. Armee du Salut, 60 rue des Freres Flavien, Paris, Cedex 20 75976, France.

770 FRA ISSN 0294-4081
CAHIERS DE LA PHOTOGRAPHIE. 1981-199?. q. Association de Critique Contemporaire en Photographie, c/o Gilles Mora, Lascledes Brax, Laplume, 47310, France.

800 FRA ISSN 0293-9282
CAHIERS DE L'ENERGUMENE. 1973-1984. 2/yr. Editions Gerard-Julien Salvy, 14 rue du Mail, Paris, 75002, France.

100 FRA ISSN 0752-6903
LES CAHIERS DE PHILOSOPHIE. 19??-199?. irreg. Universite Charles-de-Gaulle Lille 3, Unite de Formation et de Recherche de Philosophie, rue du Barreau, BP 60149, Villeneuve d'Ascq Cedex, 59653, France.

306.4 FRA ISSN 1270-1505
CAHIERS DU FRANCAIS CONTEMPORAIN. 1985-2005. a. E N S Editions, 15 Pavis Rene Descartes, B P 7000, Lyon, Cedex 07 69342, France.

388 FRA ISSN 1773-3464
LES CAHIERS DU MONITEUR AUTOMOBILE. 2005-2007. q. Editions France Auto, 12 Rue de la Bruyere, Paris, 75009, France.

551 FRA ISSN 0008-0241
CAHIERS GEOLOGIQUES. 1950-2003. s-a. Association des Amis et Anciens Eleves du Laboratoire de Geologie, I, Universite Paris VI Tour 14-15-16, 4 place Jussieu, 4e Etage, Paris, 75005, France.

150.19 FRA ISSN 0980-5508
CAHIERS POUR LA RECHERCHE FREUDIENNE. 1986-1989. irreg. Publidix, 200 av. de la Republique, Nanterre, Cedex 92001, France.

850 851 398 ITA ISSN 0008-0551
CALABRIA LETTERARIA; rivista di storia arte cultura. 1952-200?. m. Rubbettino Editore, Viale Rosario Rubbettino 10, Soveria Mannelli, CZ 88049, Italy.

572 USA ISSN 1554-8643
CALCIUM BINDING PROTEINS. 2006 (Jan.)-2008. q. Landes Bioscience, 810 S Church St, Georgetown, TX 78626.

800 USA
CALENDAR OF LITERARY FACTS. 1990-199?. irreg. Gale, 27500 Drake Rd, Farmington Hills, MI 48331.

282 FRA ISSN 0181-1096
CALENDRIER LITURGIQUE. CENTRE. BOURGES. 1969-199?. irreg. Association Diocesaine de Bourges, Archeveche de Bourges, 4 avenue du 95e de Ligne, BP 95, Bourges, Cedex 18020, France.

581.464 634.5 USA ISSN 1538-201X
CALIFORNIA NUTS. 2002-200?. s-m. Vance Publishing Corp., 10901 W 84th Terrace, Lexena, KS 66214.

380 ESP ISSN 0008-1930
CAMARA OFICIAL DE COMERCIO, INDUSTRIA Y NAVEGACION DE BARCELONA. BOLETIN/CAMBRA OFICIAL DE COMERC, INDUSTRIA I NAVEGACIO DE BARCELONA. BUTLLETI. 1967-1991. 4/yr. Cambra Oficial de Comerc Industria i Navegacio de Barcelona, Avinguda Diagonal, 452, Barcelona, 08006, Spain.

942 GBR ISSN 0068-659X
CAMBRIDGE AIR SURVEYS. 1952-2009 (Jun.). irreg. Cambridge University Press, The Edinburgh Bldg, Shaftesbury Rd, Cambridge, CB2 8RU, United Kingdom.

004 GBR ISSN 0266-3236
CAMBRIDGE COMPUTER SCIENCE TEXTS. 1972-1994 (Sep.). irreg. Cambridge University Press, The Edinburgh Bldg, Shaftesbury Rd, Cambridge, CB2 8RU, United Kingdom.

800 GBR ISSN 1754-2022
THE CAMBRIDGE EDITION OF THE WORKS OF JANE AUSTIN. 2005-2009 (Feb.). irreg. Cambridge University Press, The Edinburgh Bldg, Shaftesbury Rd, Cambridge, CB2 8RU, United Kingdom.

892 GBR
CAMBRIDGE HISTORY OF ARABIC LITERATURE. 1990-2006 (Apr.). irreg. Cambridge University Press, The Edinburgh Bldg, Shaftesbury Rd, Cambridge, CB2 8RU, United Kingdom.

341 GBR ISSN 1362-7627
CAMBRIDGE INTERNATIONAL DOCUMENTS SERIES. 1991-2009 (Aug.). irreg. Cambridge University Press, The Edinburgh Bldg, Shaftesbury Rd, Cambridge, CB2 8RU, United Kingdom.

616.8 GBR ISSN 1350-1461
CAMBRIDGE MEDICAL REVIEWS. NEUROLOGY AND PSYCHIATRY. 1991-1995. irreg. Cambridge University Press, The Edinburgh Bldg, Shaftesbury Rd, Cambridge, CB2 8RU, United Kingdom.

956 327 297 GBR ISSN 0961-1398
CAMBRIDGE MIDDLE EAST LIBRARY. 1983-2009 (Apr.). irreg. Cambridge University Press, The Edinburgh Bldg, Shaftesbury Rd, Cambridge, CB2 8RU, United Kingdom.

621.3694 GBR ISSN 0963-7141
CAMBRIDGE NONLINEAR SCIENCE SERIES. 1991-2005 (Sep.). irreg. Cambridge University Press, The Edinburgh Bldg, Shaftesbury Rd, Cambridge, CB2 8RU, United Kingdom.

954 GBR ISSN 0575-6863
CAMBRIDGE SOUTH ASIAN STUDIES. 1966-2008 (Oct.). irreg. Cambridge University Press, The Edinburgh Bldg, Shaftesbury Rd, Cambridge, CB2 8RU, United Kingdom.

951 GBR
CAMBRIDGE STUDIES IN CHINESE HISTORY, LITERATURE AND INSTITUTIONS. 1970-2009 (Mar.). irreg. Cambridge University Press, The Edinburgh Bldg, Shaftesbury Rd, Cambridge, CB2 8RU, United Kingdom.

301 GBR
CAMBRIDGE STUDIES IN CULTURAL SYSTEMS. 1977-2009 (Jul.). irreg. Cambridge University Press, The Edinburgh Bldg, Shaftesbury Rd, Cambridge, CB2 8RU, United Kingdom.

809 100 GBR ISSN 0958-6547
CAMBRIDGE STUDIES IN EIGHTEENTH-CENTURY ENGLISH LITERATURE AND THOUGHT. 1988-2008 (Aug.). irreg. Cambridge University Press, The Edinburgh Bldg, Shaftesbury Rd, Cambridge, CB2 8RU, United Kingdom.

440 840 GBR ISSN 0950-6322
CAMBRIDGE STUDIES IN FRENCH. 1982-2009 (Jul.). irreg. Cambridge University Press, The Edinburgh Bldg, Shaftesbury Rd, Cambridge, CB2 8RU, United Kingdom.

056.1 980 GBR
CAMBRIDGE STUDIES IN LATIN AMERICAN AND IBERIAN LITERATURE. 1990-2009 (Jun.). irreg. Cambridge University Press, The Edinburgh Bldg, Shaftesbury Rd, Cambridge, CB2 8RU, United Kingdom.

536 GBR ISSN 0963-1623
CAMBRIDGE STUDIES IN LOW-TEMPERATURE PHYSICS. 1989-2009 (Sep.). irreg. Cambridge University Press, The Edinburgh Bldg, Shaftesbury Rd, Cambridge, CB2 8RU, United Kingdom.

538 GBR ISSN 0964-0312
CAMBRIDGE STUDIES IN MAGNETISM. 1991-2005 (Oct.). irreg. Cambridge University Press, The Edinburgh Bldg, Shaftesbury Rd, Cambridge, CB2 8RU, United Kingdom.

658 GBR
CAMBRIDGE STUDIES IN MANAGEMENT. 1983-2009 (Jul.). irreg. Cambridge University Press, The Edinburgh Bldg, Shaftesbury Rd, Cambridge, CB2 8RU, United Kingdom.

942 GBR ISSN 0950-6314
CAMBRIDGE STUDIES IN MEDIEVAL LIFE AND THOUGHT; fourth series. 1920; N.S. 1967-19??. irreg. Cambridge University Press, The Edinburgh Bldg, Shaftesbury Rd, Cambridge, CB2 8RU, United Kingdom.

330 GBR ISSN 1462-4877
CAMBRIDGE STUDIES IN MODERN ECONOMIC HISTORY. 1995-2009 (Mar.). irreg. Cambridge University Press, The Edinburgh Bldg, Shaftesbury Rd, Cambridge, CB2 8RU, United Kingdom.

780.01 GBR
CAMBRIDGE STUDIES IN PERFORMANCE PRACTICE. 1992-2009 (Apr.). irreg. Cambridge University Press, The Edinburgh Bldg, Shaftesbury Rd, Cambridge, CB2 8RU, United Kingdom.

304.6 301 GBR ISSN 0954-0547
CAMBRIDGE STUDIES IN POPULATION, ECONOMY AND SOCIETY IN PAST TIME. 1984-2007 (Oct.). irreg. Cambridge University Press, The Edinburgh Bldg, Shaftesbury Rd, Cambridge, CB2 8RU, United Kingdom.

291 GBR
CAMBRIDGE STUDIES IN RELIGIOUS TRADITIONS. 1992-2008 (Dec.). irreg. Cambridge University Press, The Edinburgh Bldg, Shaftesbury Rd, Cambridge, CB2 8RU, United Kingdom.

890 GBR ISSN 0950-6292
CAMBRIDGE STUDIES IN RUSSIAN LITERATURE. 1981-2009 (Sep.). irreg. Cambridge University Press, The Edinburgh Bldg, Shaftesbury Rd, Cambridge, CB2 8RU, United Kingdom.

306 GBR
CAMBRIDGE STUDIES IN SOCIAL AND CULTURAL ANTHROPOLOGY. 1967-2009 (Jan.). irreg. Cambridge University Press, The Edinburgh Bldg, Shaftesbury Rd, Cambridge, CB2 8RU, United Kingdom.

320 GBR ISSN 0575-6871
CAMBRIDGE STUDIES IN THE HISTORY AND THEORY OF POLITICS. 1967-2009 (Jun.). irreg. Cambridge University Press, The Edinburgh Bldg, Shaftesbury Rd, Cambridge, CB2 8RU, United Kingdom.

306.38 NLD ISSN 1871-2193
CAME MAGAZINE. 1999-2007. 8/yr. TOPpers Media BV, Driezeeg 4, Berlicum, 5258 LE, Netherlands.

330.1 ITA ISSN 1125-8306
CAMERA DI COMMERCIO, INDUSTRIA, E AGRICOLTURA DI GENOVA. REGESTI EMEROGRAFICI. 1948-ceased. q. Istituto di Economia Internazionale, Via Garibaldi, 4, Genoa, GE 16124, Italy.

330.1 ITA ISSN 1125-8292
CAMERA DI COMMERCIO, INDUSTRIA, E AGRICOLTURA DI GENOVA. SEGNALAZIONI BIBLIOGRAFICHE. 1948-ceased. q. Istituto di Economia Internazionale, Via Garibaldi, 4, Genoa, GE 16124, Italy.

330 ITA ISSN 1125-8284
CAMERA DI COMMERCIO, INDUSTRIA, E AGRICOLTURA DI GENOVA. SEGNALAZIONI EMEROGRAFICHE. 1948-ceased. q. Istituto di Economia Internazionale, Via Garibaldi, 4, Genoa, GE 16124, Italy.

778.53 FRA ISSN 0248-8868
CAMERA - STYLO. 1981-198?. irreg. Camera - Stylo, 18 rue des Fosses Saint- Jacques, Paris, 75005, France.

388.324 ITA ISSN 1828-3616
CAMION ANNUAL. 1999-200?. a. Sprea Editori Srl, Via Torino 51, Cernusco sul Naviglio, MI 20063, Italy.

945 ITA
CAMPANIA DOCUMENTI. 1974-ceased. bi-m. Societa Editrice Napoletana s.r.l., Corso Umberto I, 1-34, Naples, NA 80138, Italy.

630 332 ESP ISSN 0212-2146
CAMPO; boletin de informacion agraria. 1967-1996. q. Banco de Bilbao - Vizcaya, Servicio de Estudios, Gran Via 1, Bilbao, 48001, Spain.

658 378 USA ISSN 1556-2999
CAMPUS FACILITY MAINTENANCE; promoting a healthy and productive learning environment. 2004-2008. bi-m. Cygnus Business Media, Inc.

781.62 793.3 ESP ISSN 1135-2779
LA CANA DE FLAMENCO. 1991-2000. q. Asociacion Cultural Espana Abierta, Quintana, 20, Madrid, 28008, Spain.

610 CAN ISSN 1481-028X
CANADIAN JOURNAL OF CLINICAL MEDICINE. 1994-1999. m. Medical Scope Publishing Corp., 10012 Jasper Ave, NW, Edmonton, AB T5J 1R2, Canada.

665.5 CAN ISSN 0844-532X
CANADIAN LUBRICATION JOURNAL. 1980-1986. irreg. Shell Canada Ltd., 400 4th Ave S W, Calgary, AB T2P 0J4, Canada.

420 375.4 AUS ISSN 0311-4627
CANBERRA LINGUIST. 1974-19??. s-a. Modern Language Teachers Association of the A.C.T., GPO Box 989, Canberra, ACT 2601, Australia.

374.8 AUS ISSN 0310-1649
CANBERRA PAPERS IN CONTINUING EDUCATION. 1972; N.S. 1981-1985. irreg. Australian National University, Centre for Continuing Education, c/o The Director, Canberra, ACT 0200, Australia.

616.99 NLD ISSN 0921-4410 CODEN: CCBAED
CANCER CHEMOTHERAPY AND BIOLOGICAL RESPONSE MODIFIERS. 1979-2005 (vol.21). a. Elsevier BV, Radarweg 29, P O Box 211, Amsterdam, 1000 AE, Netherlands.

616.99 USA ISSN 0193-1415
CANCER MANAGEMENT. 1978-198?. a. Masson Publishing U.S.A. Inc., 16 E 34th St, 14th Fl, New York, NY 10016.

616.99 EGY ISSN 1110-5313
CANCER MOLECULAR BIOLOGY; international journal of cancer molecular biology research. 1994-2004. 6/yr. Ain Shams Medical Faculty, Oncology Diagnostic Unit, Abbassia, Cairo, Egypt.

616.99 NLD ISSN 0920-7848 CODEN: CPANE2
CANCER PHARMACOLOGY ANNUAL. 1983-1986 (vol.4). a. Elsevier BV, Radarweg 29, P O Box 211, Amsterdam, 1000 AE, Netherlands.

616.99 USA ISSN 0892-0001 CODEN: CREMEX
CANCER RESEARCH MONOGRAPHS. 1983-19??. irreg. Greenwood Publishing Group Inc., 88 Post Rd W, PO Box 5007, Westport, CT 06881.

616.99 USA ISSN 0261-2429 CODEN: CASUD7
CANCER SURVEYS; advances and prospects in clinical, epidemiological, and laboratory oncology. 1982-1999. irreg. Cold Spring Harbor Laboratory Press, 500 Sunnyside Blvd, Woodbury, NY 11797.

636.7 ITA ISSN 1720-1969
IL CANE. 2002-200?. bi-m. Edigamma Publishing, Via Sambuca Pistoiese 70A, Rome, 00138, Italy.

394.14 DEU
CANNABIS KULTUR; das Marijuana Magazin. 2002-2004. bi-m. Cannabis Kultur Magazin, Postfach 120238, Muelheim, 45438, Germany.

330 ESP
CAPITAL. 2000-suspended. m. G y J Espana Ediciones S.L., Albasanz, 15 Edificio A, Madrid, 28037, Spain.

340 USA
CAPITAL DEFENSE JOURNAL. 1988-2005. s-a. Washington and Lee University, School of Law, Virginia Capital Case Clearinghouse, Lexington, VA 24450.

635.64 ITA ISSN 1122-5548
CAPSICUM & EGGPLANT NEWSLETTER. 1982-2004. a. Universita degli Studi di Torino, Facolta di Agraria, Via Leonardo Da Vinci, 44, Grugliasco, TO 10095, Italy.

629.2 GBR ISSN 0961-9372 CODEN: CAPRFJ
CAR DESIGN & TECHNOLOGY. 1991-1992. m. Car Design & Technology, Brackland House, Church St, Saffron Waldon, Saffron Walden, Essex CB10 1LB, United Kingdom.

616.1 DEU ISSN 0947-0522
CARDIOLOGY. 1982-1998. irreg. Schwarz Pharma AG, Alfred-Nobel-Str 10, Monheim, 40789, Germany.

616.12 USA ISSN 1092-6607
CARDIOLOGY REVIEW; bridging the gap between research and practice. 1984-2009 (Feb.). m. Intellisphere, LLC, Office Center at Princeton Meadows, 666 Plainsboro Rd, Bldg 300, Plainsboro, NJ 08536.

616.1 DEU ISSN 1432-9077
CARDIOVASCULAR ENGINEERING; journal for extracorporeal circulation, assist devices, transplantation and artificial organs. 1996-2005. q. Pabst Science Publishers, Am Eichengrund 28, Lengerich, 49525, Germany.

Cessations

378.0025 USA ISSN 1065-9935
CAREERS & COLLEGES (PRINT). 1981-2007. q. Alloy Education, 2 LAN Dr, Ste 100, Westford, MA 01886.

371.42 USA ISSN 1089-7186
CAREERS AND THE COLLEGE GRAD. 1987-1996. a. Crimson & Brown Associates, 170 High St, Waltham, MA 02453.

371.42 USA ISSN 1523-9705
CAREERS AND THE INTERNATIONAL M B A. 1996-1998. a. Crimson & Brown Associates, 170 High St, Waltham, MA 02453.

371.42 330 USA
CAREERS AND THE M B A. (Masters of Business Administration) 1969-199?. 2/yr. Crimson & Brown Associates, 170 High St, Waltham, MA 02453.

371.42 USA
CAREERS AND THE MINORITY LAWYER. 1996-2000. a. Crimson & Brown Associates, 170 High St, Waltham, MA 02453.

371.42 USA
CAREERS AND THE MINORITY M B A. 1992-199?. a. Crimson & Brown Associates, 170 High St, Waltham, MA 02453.

371.42 USA
CAREERS AND THE MINORITY UNDERGRADUATE. 1988-199?. a. Crimson & Brown Associates, 170 High St, Waltham, MA 02453.

371.42 USA
CAREERS AND THE WOMAN M B A. 1994-199?. a. Crimson & Brown Associates, 170 High St, Waltham, MA 02453.

338 GBR ISSN 0142-4742
CARIBBEAN INSIGHT. 19??-2000. w. West India Committee, One Birdcage Walk, London, SW1H 9JJ, United Kingdom.

360 GBR ISSN 0265-7821
CARING TODAY. 1983-1997. bi-m. Vivien Shepherd, Ed. & Pub., 1 Ewood Ct, Hebden Bridge, W Yorks HX7 5QX, United Kingdom.

664.9 ITA
CARNE; dalla produzione al consumo. 1977-ceased. m. Editoriale C.I.M., Via Aureliana, 25, Rome, RM 00187, Italy.

910.202 FRA ISSN 1283-6222
CARNETS DE VOYAGE. 1997-199?. bi-m. Editions Freeway, 1 rue Jean-Richepin, BP 271, Clermont-Ferrand, Cedex 1 63008, France.

371.42 USA ISSN 1072-5741
THE CAROLINA JOBBANK; the job hunter's guide to North and South Carolina. 1992-2004 (7th ed.). irreg. Adams Media, 4700 E Galbraith Rd, Cincinnati, OH 45236.

799.1 GBR ISSN 1359-2637
CARP FISHER. 1981-2008; suspended. bi-m. Carp Society, Horsehoe Lake, Burford Rd, Lechlade, Glos GL9 3QQ, United Kingdom.

799.1 FRA ISSN 1958-1025
CARPE CHALLENGE. 2007-2008. bi-m. Euro Services Internet, 60 rue Vitruve, Paris, 75020, France.

690 AUS
CARPENTER AND JOINER. 1960-1979. irreg. Industrial Printing and Publicity Co. Ltd., 122 Dover St, Richmond, VIC 3121, Australia.

700 ITA ISSN 0392-3347
IL CARROBBIO. 1975-ceased. a. Patron Editore, Via Badini 12, Quarto Inferiore, BO 40050, Italy.

747 ITA ISSN 1591-6944
CASA DECO. 2001-200?. q. Edigamma Publishing, Via Sambuca Pistoiese 70A, Rome, 00138, Italy.

747 ITA ISSN 1721-6869
CASA DECO. SERIE ORO. 2002-200?. s-a. Edigamma Publishing, Via Sambuca Pistoiese 70A, Rome, 00138, Italy.

645 ESP
LA CASA MARIE CLAIRE. 1988-ceased. m. G y J Espana Ediciones S.L., Albasanz, 15 Edificio A, Madrid, 28037, Spain.

809 GBR
CASEBOOKS IN CONTEMPORARY FICTION. 1999-200?. irreg. Oxford University Press, Great Clarendon St, Oxford, OX2 6DP, United Kingdom.

384 621.381 NLD ISSN 1871-7799
CASEMAGAZINE. 200?-2007. q. Casema B.V., Postbus 16192, The Hague, Netherlands.

658 USA ISSN 1526-5927
CASES IN CORPORATE ACQUISITIONS, BUYOUTS, MERGERS & TAKEOVERS. 1999-200?. biennial. Gale, 27500 Drake Rd, Farmington Hills, MI 48331.

330 ITA ISSN 1593-9626
CASSAMARCA; rivista trimestrale di politica economica finanziaria istituzionale e sociale. 1987-2001. q. Cassamarca SpA, Piazza S Leonardo, 1, Treviso, TV 31100, Italy.

230.2 USA ISSN 1087-4038
THE CATHOLIC FAITH. 1995-2002. bi-m. Ignatius Press, 2515 McAllister St, San Francisco, CA 94118.

282 USA ISSN 1057-929X
CATHOLIC HERITAGE. 1991-2000. bi-m. Our Sunday Visitor, Inc., 200 Noll Plz, Huntington, IN 46750.

636.8 USA ISSN 1548-6419
CATS MAGAZINE (IRVINE). 2005-2007. a. BowTie, Inc., 2401 Beverly Blvd, PO Box 57900, Los Angeles, CA 90057.

861 FRA ISSN 1626-1437
CAUCES; revue d'etudes hispaniques. 2000-2005. a. Presses Universitaires de Valenciennes, Le Mont Houy, Valenciennes, Cedex 59313, France.

790.2 USA ISSN 1521-1290
CAVALCADE OF ACTS & ATTRACTIONS. 1973-19??. a. Nielsen Business Publications, 770 Broadway, New York, NY 10003.

070.5 FRA ISSN 1626-0163
CD-ROM ELECTRE. 1989-2007. m. Electre - Editions du Cercle de la Librairie, 35 rue Gregoire de Tours, Paris, 75006, France.

526 CHN ISSN 1006-9712
CEHUI RUANKEXUE YANJIU/RESEARCH ON SOFT SCIENCE OF SURVEYING AND MAPPING. 1995-2002. q. Cehui Ruankexue Yanjiu, Baojian Lu Tie 3 Jie 2 Hao, Ha'erbin, 150086, China.

791.43 NLD ISSN 1569-9587
CELEBRITY. 2001-2008. m. Sanoma Uitgevers B.V., Postbus 1900, Hoofddorp, 2130 JH, Netherlands.

936.4 ITA ISSN 1129-4035
CELTICA. 1999-200?. bi-m. Edizioni Trentini & C, Via Pier Luigi Nervi 1/B, Argenta, FE 44011, Italy.

363.7 USA ISSN 1071-8729
CEMETERIES OF THE U S. 1994-ceased. every 6 yrs. Gale, 27500 Drake Rd, Farmington Hills, MI 48331.

945 ITA ISSN 0392-1409
CENACOLO (TARANTO); rivista storica di Taranto. 1971-2001. a. Mandese Editore s.r.l., Viale Liguria, 82, Taranto, TA 74100, Italy.

001.4 USA ISSN 1057-9656
CENSUS AND YOU; monthly news from the U.S. Bureau of the Census. 1966-1999. m. U.S. Census Bureau, Public Information Office, 4700 Silver Hill Rd., Washington, DC 20233.

351.021 USA ISSN 0082-9358
CENSUS OF GOVERNMENTS (FINAL REPORTS) (PRINT). 1850-2003. quinquennial. U.S. Census Bureau, 4600 Silver Hill Rd, Washington, DC 20233.

363.5021 USA ISSN 0082-9366
CENSUS OF HOUSING. 1940-2000. decennial. U.S. Census Bureau, 4600 Silver Hill Rd, Washington, DC 20233.

330.9 USA
CENSUS OF SERVICE INDUSTRIES: FINAL REPORTS. (Issued in 3 series: Geographic Area Series, Industry Series, and Subject Series) 1933-199?. quinquennial. U.S. Census Bureau, Customer Services, Washington, DC 20233.

371.8 FRA ISSN 1774-4717
CENT POUR CENT ETUDIANT; les news de ta vie d'etudiant. 2005-2006. m. Com.com Universal, 9 bd des Minimes, Toulouse, 31200, France.

932 EGY ISSN 1110-2055
CENTER PAPYROLOGICAL STUDIES. BULLETIN/MAGALLAT MARKAZ AL-DIRASAT AL-BARDIYAT. 1985-2007. irreg. Ain Shams University, Center of Papyrological Studies, Qasr El-Zaefarana, Abbasia, Cairo, Egypt.

629.114 ITA ISSN 1827-8418
CENTO PER CENTO FUORISTRADA. 2006-200?. bi-m. Tattilo Editrice SpA, Via degli Olmetti 18, Rome, 00060, Italy.

351 657 NLD ISSN 1385-1845
CENTRAAL BUREAU VOOR DE STATISTIEK. OCCASIONAL PAPER. NATIONAL ACCOUNTS. 1983-2007. irreg. Centraal Bureau voor de Statistiek, Prinses Beatrixlaan 428, PO Box 4000, Voorburg, 2270 JM, Netherlands.

332 TUR
CENTRAL BANK OF THE REPUBLIC OF TURKEY. MONTHLY STATISTICAL AND EVALUATION BULLETIN. 1986-1989. m. Central Bank of the Republic of Turkey, Istiklal Cad.10 Ulus, Ankara, 06100, Turkey.

929 970 FRA ISSN 0751-3860
CENTRE DE GENEALOGIE ET D'HISTOIRE DES ILES D'AMERIQUE. CAHIERS. 1982-2002. q. Centre de Genealogie et d'Histoire des Iles d'Amerique, 30 rue Boissiere, Paris, 75116, France.

307.1 FRA ISSN 0760-6079
CENTRE DE RECHERCHES ET D'ETUDES SUR PARIS ET L'ILE-DE-FRANCE. CAHIERS. 1983-199?. 4/yr. Documentation Francaise, 29-31 Quai Voltaire, Paris, Cedex 7 75344, France.

330.944 FRA ISSN 1774-0444
CENTRE D'ETUDES ET DE RECHERCHES ECONOMIQUES ET SOCIALES DE PICARDIE. CAHIERS. 199?-2005. q. Centre d'Etudes et de Recherches Economiques et Sociales de Picardie, 24 rue Frederic Petit, Amiens, 80036, France.

551.4 FRA ISSN 1624-7396
CENTRE D'ETUDES TECHNIQUES MARITIME ET FLUVIALES. REVUE TECHNIQUE. 1966-200?. q. Centre d'Etudes Techniques Maritimes et Fluviales, 2, boulevard Gambetta, BP 60039, Compiegne, 60321, France.

332 AUS ISSN 1832-2840
CENTRE FOR APPLIED FINANCE. WORKING PAPER SERIES. 2004-2005. q. University of Western Sydney, Centre for Applied Finance, Locked Bag 1797, Penrith South DC, NSW 1797, Australia.

331 DNK ISSN 0908-8962
CENTRE FOR LABOUR MARKET AND SOCIAL RESEARCH. WORKING PAPERS. 1981-2002. irreg. Centre for Labour Market and Social Research, Building 350, University of Aarhus, Aarhus C, 8000, Denmark.

363.7 DNK ISSN 1396-5581
CENTRE FOR RESEARCH ON THE CULTURAL AND BIOLOGICAL DIVERSITY OF ANDEAN RAINFORESTS. TECHNICAL REPORT. 1996-1999. irreg. Center for Forskning i Kulturel og Biologisk Diversitet i Andesbjergenes Regnskove, National Environmental Research Institute, Dept of Landscape Ecology, Grenavej 14, Kalo, Ronde, DK-8410, Denmark.

990 AUS ISSN 1030-245X
CENTRE FOR SOUTH PACIFIC STUDIES. NEWSLETTER. 1987-2000. irreg. University of New South Wales, Centre for South Pacific Studies, UNSW, Sydney, NSW 2052, Australia.

008 FRA ISSN 0996-4274
CENTRE NATIONAL D'ART ET DE CULTURE GEORGES POMPIDOU. MAGAZINE. 1981-1997. bi-m. Centre National d'Art et de Culture Georges Pompidou, Place Georges Pompidou, Paris, 75004, France.

051 CAN ISSN 1719-9328
CENTRE OF THE CITY. 2001-2009; suspended. bi-m. Metroland Media Group Ltd., 100 Tempo Ave, Toronto, ON M2H 3S5 , Canada.

380.1029 GBR ISSN 0958-7322
CENTRE RANKINGS. 1990-199?. a. Chas E. Goad Ltd., 8-12 Salisbury Sq, Old Hatfield, Herts AL9 5BJ, United Kingdom.

001.3 ESP ISSN 0211-5247
CENTRO DE ALBACETE. ANALES. 1979-1998. irreg. Centro de Albacete, Isaac Peral, 11, Albacete, 02001, Spain.

940 330.1 NLD ISSN 0929-9785
CENTRUM VOOR BEDRIJFSGESCHIEDENIS. CAHIERS. 1986-2002. irreg. Centrum voor Bedrijfsgeschiedenis, Burgemeester Oudlaan 50, Rotterdam, 3000 DR, Netherlands.

720 643.7 666 FRA ISSN 1259-0657
CERAMAGAZINE; le magazine des professionnels du carreau et de la pierre naturelle. 19??-2005. m. Edial Editions, 126 rue du Temple, Paris, 75003, France.

666 ITA ISSN 0366-5801 CODEN: CERMA3
CERAMICA. 1938-1986. bi-m. Casa Editrice Palazzo Vecchio, Via Vittorio Emanuele II, 155, Florence, FI 50134, Italy.

633 664 ITA
CEREAL POLICIES REVIEW. 1991-1999. a. Food and Agriculture Organization of the United Nations (F A O), Via delle Terme di Caracalla, Rome, RM 00100, Italy.

057.86 015 CZE
CESKA NARODNI BIBLIOGRAFIE. CLANKY V NOVINACH A CASOPISECH (CD-ROM EDITION). 1953-2008 (Dec.). q. Narodni Knihovna Ceske Republiky, Klementinum 190, Prague, 11001, Czech Republic.

057.86 015 CZE
CESKA NARODNI BIBLIOGRAFIE. GRAFIKA (CD-ROM EDITION). 1958-2008 (Dec.). a. Narodni Knihovna Ceske Republiky, Klementinum 190, Prague, 11001, Czech Republic.

016.78 CZE
CESKA NARODNI BIBLIOGRAFIE. HUDEBNINY (CD-ROM EDITION). 1937-2008 (Dec.). a. Narodni Knihovna Ceske Republiky, Klementinum 190, Prague, 11001, Czech Republic.

057.86 015 CZE
CESKA NARODNI BIBLIOGRAFIE. KNIHY (CD-ROM EDITION). 1922-2008 (Dec.). q. Narodni Knihovna Ceske Republiky, Klementinum 190, Prague, 11001, Czech Republic.

015 CZE
CESKA NARODNI BIBLIOGRAFIE. ZAHRANICNI BOHEMIKA (CD-ROM EDITION). 1956-2008 (Dec.). a. Narodni Knihovna Ceske Republiky, Klementinum 190, Prague, 11001, Czech Republic.

016.78 CZE
CESKA NARODNI BIBLIOGRAFIE. ZVUKOVE DOKUMENTY (CD-ROM EDITION). 1937-2008 (Dec.). a. Narodni Knihovna Ceske Republiky, Klementinum 190, Prague, 11001, Czech Republic.

370.1 CZE ISSN 1213-6018
CESKA SKOLA. 1999-200?. d. Computer Press a.s., Spielberk Office Centre, Holandska 8, Brno, 639 00, Czech Republic.

330 CZE
CESKY SPOTR EBITEL. ceased 2001. a. Strategie Praha s.r.o., Drtinova 8, Prague 5, 150 00, Czech Republic.

054.108 FRA ISSN 1779-207X
C'EST MA VIE. 2006-2007. bi-m. Editions DIPA Burda, 26 Avenue de l'Europe, Strasbourg, 67013, France.

665.7 333.8 ITA ISSN 1972-6376
CH4 ENERGIA GAS. 1984-ceased. bi-m. Mediafriends srl, Via De Amicis 35, Milan, 20123, Italy.

944 FRA
CHAMBRE DE COMMERCE ET D'INDUSTRIE DE MEAUX. REVUE. ceased. 4/yr. Chambre de Commerce et d'Industrie de Seine et Marne, 12 bd. Jean Rose, BP 216, Meaux, Cedex 77104, France.

944 FRA ISSN 0987-6421
CHAMBRE DE COMMERCE ET D'INDUSTRIE. LA LETTRE. 1987-199?. m. Chambre de Commerce et Industrie (Chartres), 1 rue de l'Etroit Degre, BP 62, Chartres, Cedex 28002, France.

382 FRA ISSN 0396-5945
CHAMBRE FRANCO ALLEMANDE DE COMMERCE ET D'INDUSTRIE. LISTE DES MEMBRES. 1966-1980. a. Chambre Franco Allemande de Commerce et d'Industrie, 18 rue Balard, Paris, 75015, France.

944 FRA ISSN 0220-9241
CHAMBRE REGIONALE DE COMMERCE ET D'INDUSTRIE PROVENCE - ALPES - COTE D'AZUR - CORSE. CONJONCTURE. 1973-2004. s-a. Chambre Regionale de Commerce et d'Industrie Provence - Alpes - Cote d'Azur - Corse, 8 rue Neuve Saint Martin, BP 1880, Marseille, Cedex 1 13222, France.

382 FRA ISSN 1265-230X
CHAMPAGNE - ARDENNE GUIDE DE L'EXPORTATEUR. 198?-1995. a. Chambre Regionale de Commerce et d'Industrie Champagne - Ardenne, Direction de la Communication, 10 rue de Chastillon, B.P. 537, Chalons-sur-Marne, Cedex 51011, France.

769.55 FRA ISSN 0754-4200
CHANGE. 1979-2004. q. S E P S, 12 rue Raymond Poincare, Revigny-sur-Ornain, 55800, France.

370 AUS ISSN 1441-9319
CHANGE. TRANSFORMATIONS IN EDUCATION. 1942-2006. s-a. University of Sydney, Faculty of Education and Social Work, Education Bldg A35, Sydney, NSW 2006, Australia.

370 AUS ISSN 1322-0187
CHANGING EDUCATION (GEELONG). 1994-2002. q. Flinders University, School of Education, PO Box 2100, Adelaide, SA 5001, Australia.

004.16 AUS ISSN 1444-738X
CHANNEL X AUSTRALIA. 2000 (Dec.)-2002 (Aug.). m. I D G Communications Pty. Ltd., PO Box 295, St Leonards, NSW 1590, Australia.

782.42 FRA ISSN 1778-0551
CHANSON MAG. 2005-2006. bi-m. CophiPresse SARL, 4 Rue de l'Eglise, B P 40004, Peronne, Cedex 80208, France.

800 USA
CHARACTERS IN 20TH-CENTURY LITERATURE. 1990-199?. irreg. Gale, 27500 Drake Rd, Farmington Hills, MI 48331.

361.7 GBR ISSN 1472-9016
CHARITIES MANAGEMENT OUTLOOK. 2000-suspended. s-a. Mitre House Publishing Ltd., PO Box 29, South Petherton, TA13 5WE, United Kingdom.

381.45687 ITA
CHARME MODA. 1986-ceased. 6/yr. I G O s.r.l., Via Cappuccini, 14-16, Milan, MI 20122, Italy.

694 FRA ISSN 1282-4887
CHARPENTE - MENUISERIE - PARQUETS; le magazine des metiers du bois. 1910-2005. m. (10/yr.). Editions Bernard Begassat, 17 rue du Louvre, Paris, 75001, France.

657 AUS
CHARTAC TAX PLANNING NEWS. 1982-1998. m. Professional Information Pty. Ltd., 196 Drummond St, Carlton, VIC 3053, Australia.

657 GBR
CHARTERED INSTITUTE OF MANAGEMENT ACCOUNTANTS. ADVANCED MANAGEMENT ACCOUNTING & FINANCE SERIES. 1992-199?. irreg. Academic Press, 32 Jamestown Rd, Camden, London, NW1 7BY, United Kingdom.

792 FRA ISSN 1158-1905
CHATELET. 1990-2006. bi-m. Chatelet - Theatre Musical de Paris, 2 Rue Edouard Colonne, Paris, 75001, France.

697 FRA ISSN 1141-8184
CHAUFFAGE MAGAZINE. 1989-1993. 4/yr. Chauffage Magazine, 61 boulevard Bessieres, Paris, 75017, France.

657 332 USA ISSN 1056-0580
CHECKLISTS AND ILLUSTRATIVE FINANCIAL STATEMENTS FOR FINANCE COMPANIES. 1990-1995. a. American Institute of Certified Public Accountants, 1211 Ave of the Americas, New York, NY 10036.

780 GBR ISSN 0952-8407
CHELYS. 1969-2004. a. The Viola Da Gamba Society, 56 Hunters Way, Dringhouses, York, Y024 1JJ, United Kingdom.

660.029 GBR ISSN 0960-2992
CHEMICAL INDUSTRY EUROPE. 1923-2002. a. C M P Information Ltd., Ludgate House, 245 Blackfriars Rd., London, SE1 9UR, United Kingdom.

615.1029 GBR ISSN 0262-5881
CHEMIST & DRUGGIST DIRECTORY. 1868-2004. a. C M P Information Ltd., Ludgate House, 245 Blackfriars Rd., London, SE1 9UR, United Kingdom.

646 ITA ISSN 0009-3203
CHERIE MODA/CHERIE MODE. 1955-ceased. q. Edizioni Moderne Internazionali, Via Gadames 123, Milan, 20123, Italy.

004 ITA
IL CHI E DELL'I C T. (Information & Communication Technology) 1992-ceased. a. Editrice il Crogiolo S.r.l., Piazza Sant' Agostino 22, Milan, MI 20123, Italy.

053.1 DEU
CHICA. 2003 (Jul.)-2009 (Jan.). m. Egmont Cultfish Media GmbH, Hansastr 32, Munich, 80686, Germany.

371.42 USA ISSN 1072-575X
THE CHICAGO JOBBANK; the job hunter's guide to Metro Chicago. (Includes: Aurora, Peoria, Rockford, Springfield and many others.) 1982-2005 (19th ed.). irreg. Adams Media, 4700 E Galbraith Rd, Cincinnati, OH 45236.

305.4 AUS ISSN 1441-0419
CHICK; the mini-mag for girls who surf. 1998-2006. m. Morrison Media Services, PO Box 823, Burleigh Heads, QLD 4220, Australia.

613.043 GBR ISSN 1363-2094
CHILD HEALTH DIALOGUE. 1995-2000. q. Healthlink Worldwide, 56-64 Leonard St, London, EC2A 4LT, United Kingdom.

345.944 AUS ISSN 1031-6590
CHILDREN'S COURT OF NEW SOUTH WALES INFORMATION BULLETIN. 1978-2000. s-a. Judicial Commission of New South Wales, Level 5, 201 George St, Sydney, NSW 2000, Australia.

028.5 USA ISSN 0272-7145
CHILDREN'S DIGEST. 19??-2009. bi-m. Children's Better Health Institute, 1100 Waterway Blvd, Indianapolis, IN 46202.

330.9 USA
CHINA COUNTRY REPORT. 1999-ceased. a. Orbis Publications, LLC, 1924 47th St NW, Washington, DC 20007-1901.

341 GBR ISSN 1745-7238
CHINA LAW REVIEW. 2005-2008. s-a. Routledge, 4 Park Sq, Milton Park, Abingdon, Oxon OX14 4RN, United Kingdom.

330.9 USA ISSN 1093-5126
CHINA WATCH. 1998-ceased. m. Orbis Publications, LLC, 1924 47th St NW, Washington, DC 20007-1901.

363.7 CHN ISSN 1003-1189 CODEN: CEVSEB
CHINESE ENVIRONMENTAL SCIENCE. 1990-2000. q. Zhongguo Huanjing Kexue Xuehui, 115, Xizhimennei Nan Xiaojie, Beijing, 100035, China.

004 BRD ISSN 0176-2923
CHIPS UND KABEL. 1983-1986. irreg. Kommedia Buchhandlung GmbH, Marheinekeplatz 15, Berlin, 10961, Germany.

615 USA ISSN 1051-4244
CHIROPRACTIC RESEARCH ABSTRACTS COLLECTION. 197?-1990. a. Lippincott Williams & Wilkins, 351 W Camden St, Baltimore, MD 21201.

664.15 DNK ISSN 1601-863X
CHOKOLADE OG KONFEKTURE. 1915-2001. m. Bladforlaget Nygaard ApS, Naestvedvej 12, PO Box 12, Herlufmagle, 4160, Denmark.

079.93 NZL ISSN 1170-1277
CHRISTCHURCH MAIL. 1985-2001. w. Christchurch Mail, 146 Gloucester St, Christchurch, Canterbury, New Zealand.

270 USA ISSN 1548-1956
CHRISTIAN HISTORY AND BIOGRAPHY. 1982-2008. q. Christianity Today International, 465 Gundersen Dr, Carol Stream, IL 60188.

200 ISR ISSN 0009-5532
CHRISTIAN NEWS FROM ISRAEL. 1949-1989. s-a. Ministry of Religious Services, 30 Jaffa St., P O Box 1167, Jerusalem, Israel.

280.4 AUS ISSN 0728-0351
CHRISTOPHANY; Christ displayed. 1950-ceased. q. Perth Bible College, 1 College Ct, Karrinyup, W.A. 6018, Australia.

575.105 GBR ISSN 0961-0901
CHROMATIN. 1991-1992. irreg. University of Cambridge, Faculty Press, 88 Regent St, Cambridge, CB2 1DP, United Kingdom.

330 CHN ISSN 1004-4582
CHUANGYEZHE/ENTREPRENEUR. 1986-2006. m. Guangdong Sheng Laodonghe, Shehui Baozhang Ting, 316, Huanshi Zhonglu, 6F, Jinying Dasha, Guangzhou, 510060, China.

895.1 CHN ISSN 1001-621X
CHUN FENG/SPRING BREEZE. 1979-1986. m. Changchun Shi Wenlian, 11 Jianhe Jie, Changchun, Jilin 130061, China.

791.43 FRA ISSN 1957-4576
CINE HEROS. 2007-2008. bi-m. Editions Tournon, 45 rue Broca, Paris, 75005, France.

791.43 ITA ISSN 1123-0584
IL CINESCOPIO. 1989-ceased. m. (11/yr.). Il Sole 24 Ore Business Media, Divisione J C E, Via Patecchio 2, Milan, 20141, Italy.

910.4 ITA
CIOCIARIA; ieri, oggi, domani. 1987 (vol.7)-ceased. bi-m. Ente Provinciale per il Turismo di Frosinone, Piazzale de Matthaeis, Grattacielo L'Edera, Frosinone, Italy.

621.381 USA ISSN 1070-4779
CIRCUITS ASSEMBLY ASIA. 1993-199?. 6/yr. C M P Media LLC, 600 Community Dr, Manhasset, NY 11030.

658 ESP ISSN 0211-1535
CIRCULO DE EMPRESARIOS. BOLETIN. 1979-2001. 3/yr. Circulo de Empresarios, Paseo de la Castellana, 15 6a Planta, Madrid, 28046, Spain.

056.1 ESP
CITIZEN K. 2005-2009. q. Focus Ediciones SL, Paseo de la Castellana 129, 1o, Madrid, 28046, Spain.

055.1 ITA
CITTA (LATINA); quindicinale di informazione, sport, cultura e spettacolo. 1981-ceased. s-m. La Citta S.r.l., c/o Ardetti, Casella Postale, 128, Latina, LT 04100, Italy.

320 ITA ISSN 0393-6449
LA CITTA NUOVA (NAPLES); rivista di cultura politica. 1986-ceased. m. Gaetano Macchiaroli Editore, Via Michetti 11, Naples, NA 80127, Italy.

635 NZL ISSN 0009-7705
CITY BEAUTIFUL. 1928-1983. 11/yr. Canterbury Horticultural Society, Inc., PO Box 369, Christchurch, New Zealand.

331.1 USA
CITY EMPLOYMENT (ONLINE). 1948-ceased. a. U.S. Census Bureau, c/o Donna Hirsch, Governments Division, 4700 Silver Hill Rd., Washington, DC 20233.

336.73 USA ISSN 0082-9439
CITY GOVERNMENT FINANCES. 1965-1992. a. U.S. Census Bureau, c/o Donna Hirsch, Governments Division, 4700 Silver Hill Rd., Washington, DC 20233.

917 USA
CITY-SMART: CALGARY. 1998-2000. biennial. Avalon Travel Publishing, 1700 4th St, Berkeley, CA 94710.

917.95 USA ISSN 1530-8375
CITY-SMART: PORTLAND. 1996-2000. biennial. Avalon Travel Publishing, 1700 4th St, Berkeley, CA 94710.

917 USA
CITY-SMART: SAN ANTONIO. 1998-2000. biennial. Avalon Travel Publishing, 1700 4th St, Berkeley, CA 94710.

079.93 NZL ISSN 1172-4390
CITY WEEKEND. 1992-200?. w. Waikato Times Ltd, Foreman Rd, Hamilton, Waikato, New Zealand.

351 DEU ISSN 1614-0389
CITYPARTNER; oeffentliche Projekte entwickeln, finanzieren, betreiben. 2004-2008. 4/yr. Deutscher Fachverlag GmbH, Mainzer Landstr 251, Frankfurt Am Main, 60326, Germany.

700 ITA
LA CIVETTA. 1974-1990. irreg. Fabrizio Serra Editore, c/o Accademia Editoriale, Via Santa Bibbiana 28, Pisa, 56127, Italy.

780 ITA ISSN 1971-5315
CIVICA SCUOLA DI MUSICA. QUADERNI. 1980-2000. irreg. Civica Scuola di Musica, Via Stilicone, 36, Milan, MI 20154, Italy.

624 EGY ISSN 1110-0990
CIVIL ENGINEERING RESEARCH MAGAZINE. 1979-199?. q. Al-Azhar University, Faculty of Engineering, Civil Engineering Department, Al-Nasr Rd, Nasr City, Cairo, Egypt.

624 AUS ISSN 0156-2126
CIVIL ENGINEERING WORKING PAPERS. 1978-19??. irreg. Monash University, Department of Civil Engineering, Wellington Rd, Clayton, VIC 3168, Australia.

347.075 USA
CIVIL EVIDENCE TRIAL MANUAL FOR TEXAS LAWYERS. 1991-1997. plus irreg. updates. LexisNexis, PO Box 7587, Charlottesville, VA 22906.

641 ITA ISSN 0390-1572
CIVILTA DEL BERE; mensile di informazione, documentazione e difesa della qualita. 1974-ceased. m. (11/yr.). Editoriale Lariana s.r.l., Via Ciro Menotti 11-D, Milan, MI 20129, Italy.

747 690 USA
CLASSIC HOUSE PLANS. 2001-2009 (Jan.). m. HomePlans.com, 901 N 3rd St, Ste 216, Minneapolis, MN 55401.

385 790.13 GBR ISSN 1464-0317
CLASSIC RAILWAYS. 1990-1998. m. Ebony Media Ltd., c/o Stray Cat Publishing, Ltd., PO Box 36, Liskeard, Cornwall PL14 4YT, United Kingdom.

870 930 GBR ISSN 0069-4460
CLASSICAL ASSOCIATION. PROCEEDINGS. 1904-1999. a. Classical Association, St John's College, Cambridge, CB2 1TP, United Kingdom.

371.33 AUS ISSN 1039-4982
THE CLASSROOM CONNECTION; practical activities for the primary classroom. 1993-2003. q. Research Publications Pty Ltd., 27 A Boronia Rd, Vermont, VIC 3133, Australia.

371.3 USA
CLASSROOM LEADERSHIP; the companion newsletter to ASCD's Educational Leadership magazine. 1997-2005. 9/yr. Association for Supervision and Curriculum Development, 1703 N Beauregard St, Alexandria, VA 22311.

370 FRA ISSN 1243-4450
CLE...S A VENIR; l'innovation on sait faire. 1992-199?. 3/yr. Centre National de Documentation Pedagogique, 4 Av du Futuroscope, Teleport 1, B P 80158, Futuroscope, Cedex 86961, France.

370 362.7 AUS ISSN 1321-8697
CLEARING HOUSE. 1991-2005. q. Free Kindergarten Association of Victoria Inc., 1st Flr., 9-11 Stewart St, Richmond, VIC 3121, Australia.

747 FRA ISSN 1952-8809
LES CLEFS DE LA MAISON. 2006-2008. bi-m. Serum Presse, 5 Rue Hector Berlioz, Tournefeuille, 31170, France.

610 AUS ISSN 1328-3359
CLICK IT @ R A C P. 1996-2000. m. Royal Australasian College of Physicians, 145 Macquarie St, Sydney, NSW 2000, Australia.

636.089 FRA ISSN 1291-2301
CLIENTELE ET CLINIQUES; gestion et developpement veterinaires. 1996-2003. 10/yr. Point Veterinaire S.A., 9 rue Alexandre, BP 233, Maisons-Alfort, Cedex 94702, France.

690 697 ITA ISSN 1124-2612
CLIMA CASA; piu comfort alla vita di ogni giorno. 1995-ceased. m. Tecniche Nuove SpA, Via Eritrea 21, Milan, MI 201, Italy.

610 CAN ISSN 0147-958X CODEN: CNVMDL
CLINICAL AND INVESTIGATIVE MEDICINE (PRINT)/MEDECINE CLINIQUE ET EXPERIMENTALE. 1977-2006. bi-m. Canadian Medical Association, 1867 Alta Vista Dr, Ottawa, ON K1G 3Y6, Canada.

616.15 GBR ISSN 0960-3964
CLINICAL AND LABORATORY HAEMATOLOGY. SUPPLEMENT. 1990-2007. s-a. Wiley-Blackwell Publishing Ltd., 9600 Garsington Rd, Oxford, OX4 2DQ, United Kingdom.

616.8 GBR
CLINICAL AND NEUROBIOLOGICAL ADVANCES IN PSYCHIATRY. 1995-1998 (vol.5). irreg. John Wiley & Sons Ltd., 1-7 Oldlands Way, PO Box 808, Bognor Regis, West Sussex PO21 9FF, United Kingdom.

610.73 GBR ISSN 1361-9004
CLINICAL EFFECTIVENESS IN NURSING. 1997-2007. 4/yr. W.B. Saunders Co. Ltd., 32 Jamestown Rd, Camden, London, NW1 7BY, United Kingdom.

610 GBR ISSN 1462-3846
CLINICAL EVIDENCE (PRINT). 1999-2006. s-a. B M J Group, B M A House, Tavistock Sq, London, WC1H 9JR, United Kingdom.

573.84 GBR ISSN 0885-7431
CLINICAL NEUROCHEMISTRY. 1986-1987 (vol.2). irreg. Academic Press, 32 Jamestown Rd, Camden, London, NW1 7BY, United Kingdom.

616.8 NLD ISSN 1566-2772 CODEN: CNRLBU
CLINICAL NEUROSCIENCE RESEARCH. 2000-2007. 6/yr. Elsevier BV, Radarweg 29, P O Box 211, Amsterdam, 1000 AE, Netherlands.

617.7 NZL ISSN 1177-5467
CLINICAL OPHTHALMOLOGY (PRINT). 2007-2008. q. Dove Medical Press Ltd., 17/44 William Pickering Dr, Albany, PO Box 300-008, Auckland, 1311, New Zealand.

616.07 NLD ISSN 1477-6804
CLINICAL RADIOLOGY EXTRA. 2002-2005. m. Elsevier BV, Radarweg 29, P O Box 211, Amsterdam, 1000 AE, Netherlands.

610 USA ISSN 1077-9914
CLINICIAN NEWS. 1997-200?. 10/yr. Jobson Medical Group, One Meadowlands Plaza, 10th Fl, East Rutherford, NJ 07073.

006 FRA
CLONE. 1994-199?. q. Alpha du Centaure, France.

629.283 DEU ISSN 0933-7075
CLUB MAGAZIN; Aktuelle Informationen des ADAC Nordbaden. 1988-1993. q. D W S Werbeagentur und Verlag GmbH, Kriegsstr 160, Karlsruhe, 76133, Germany.

691 NLD ISSN 1871-5540
COBOUW TOTAAL. VAKBLAD OVER BOUWMATERIALEN. 2005-ceased. bi-m. Sdu Uitgevers bv, Postbus 20025, The Hague, 2500 EA, Netherlands.

004 690 NLD ISSN 1871-5567
COBOUW TOTAAL. VAKBLAD OVER INFORMATIE COMMUNICATIE TECHNOLOGIE EN BOUW. 2005-ceased. bi-m. Sdu Uitgevers bv, Postbus 20025, The Hague, 2500 EA, Netherlands.

306 FRA ISSN 0999-9140
LE COCHONGLIER. 1998-2006. s-a. Association d'Histoire des Societes Rurales, Maison de la Recherche en Sciences Humaines, Universite de Caen, Esplanade de la Paix, Caen, 14032, France.

028.5 DEU ISSN 0942-4997
COCKTAIL (FRANKFURT). 1988-1994. q. Deutsche Jungsozialisten (JUSOS), Fischerfeldstr 7-11, Frankfurt Am Main, 60311, Germany.

010 NLD ISSN 0169-8672
CODICES MANUSCRIPTI BIBLIOTHECAE UNIVERSITATIS LEIDENSIS. 1910-1988 (vol.26). irreg. Brill, PO Box 9000, Leiden, 2300 PA, Netherlands.

613.7 616.12 FRA ISSN 0335-5306
COEUR ET SANTE. 1974-2007. bi-m. Edicardio, 50 rue du Rocher, Paris, 75008, France.

778.53 ESP
COLECCION DIRECTORES DE CINE. ceased 1994. q. Ediciones J C, Monteleon, 35, Madrid, 28010, Spain.

340 ESP ISSN 1699-4469
COLECCION GARRIGUES & ANDERSEN. 1999-2000. irreg. Garrigues y Andersen, Jose Abascal, 45, Madrid, 28003, Spain.

320 ESP
COLECCION IBERICA. 1976-198?. irreg. Editorial Anagrama S.A., Pedro de la Creu, 58, Barcelona, 08034, Spain.

Cessations

791.43 ESP ISSN 1579-9093
COLECCION IMAGENES. 1987-1993. irreg. Ediciones J C, Monteleon, 35, Madrid, 28010, Spain.

296 ESP
COLECCION SENDA ABIERTA. SERIE 2 (AZUL): JUDAISMO. 1974-ceased. irreg. Studium Ediciones, Bailen, 19, Madrid, 28013, Spain.

851 ITA
COLLANA DI POESIA. 1974; N.S. 1977-198?. irreg. Societa Editrice Napoletana s.r.l., Corso Umberto I, 1-34, Naples, NA 80138, Italy.

282 ITA ISSN 0069-5254
COLLANA RICCIANA. FONTI. 1963-1975. irreg. Casa Editrice Leo S. Olschki, Viuzzo del Pozzetto 8, Florence, 50126, Italy.

200 AUS
COLLECTIONS OF RELIGION AND THEOLOGY IN AUSTRALIA AND NEW ZEALAND. 1992-ceased. irreg. (4-5/yr.). Auslib Press Pty Ltd, PO Box 622, Blackwood, SA 5051, Australia.

741.67 746.92 700 FRA ISSN 1152-8885
COLLECTOR (PARIS). 1990-199?. q. Editions du Triangle Rose, 45 rue Sedaine, Paris, Cedex 11 75557, France.

641.5 ITA ISSN 1125-6826
COLLEZIONE DI CUCINA CREATIVA. 1997-200?. q. Ulysse Network, Viale Bianca Maria 19, Milan, Italy.

805 AUS ISSN 1325-9490
COLLOQUY (PRINT); text theory critique. 1994-2005. a. Monash University, School of Literary, Visual and Performance Studies, PO Box 11A, Clayton, VIC 3800, Australia.

917.273 USA ISSN 1095-8878
COLONIAL MEXICO HANDBOOK. 1998-ceased. triennial. Avalon Travel Publishing, 1700 4th St, Berkeley, CA 94710.

749 684.1 NLD ISSN 1389-5699
COLONIAL NEWS. 1999-1999. q. Uitgeverij Lakerveld BV, Mangaanstraat 50, Postbus 43250, The Hague, 2504 AG, Netherlands.

747 USA ISSN 1936-2765
COLOR SCHEMES. 2002-2008. irreg. Meredith Corporation, 1716 Locust St, Des Moines, IA 50309.

331.1 USA
THE COLORADO JOBBANK. 1987-2006 (14th ed.). irreg. Adams Media, 4700 E Galbraith Rd, Cincinnati, OH 45236.

747 USA ISSN 1936-2617
COLORFUL KITCHENS. 2007 (May)-2008. a. Meredith Corporation, 1716 Locust St, Des Moines, IA 50309.

741 ITA ISSN 1129-1745
COLOUR TATTOO. 1999-200?. bi-m. Edizioni Trentini & C, Via Pier Luigi Nervi 1/B, Argenta, FE 44011, Italy.

630 ITA
COLTIVATORE ENNESE. 1951-ceased. bi-m. Federazione Provinciale Coltivatori Diretti di Enna, Via Roma, 429, Enna, EN 94100, Italy.

630 ITA
COLTIVATORE REGGIANO. 1953-ceased. s-m. Federazione Provinciale Coltivatori Diretti di Reggio Emilia, Via B Ricasoli, 4, Reggio Emilia, RE 42100, Italy.

384.6 DEU
COM.UNIQUE; DeTeWe Kundenmagazin. 2000-2004. q. corps - Corporate Publishing Services GmbH, Kasernenstr 69, Duesseldorf, 40213, Germany.

003.3 DNK ISSN 0106-357X
COMBINEDSIMULATION. 1978-1979. irreg. Roskilde Universitetscenter, Datalogi, Roskilde, 4000, Denmark.

681.3 ITA ISSN 1591-0237
COME FARE. 2000-200?. q. Sprea Editori Srl, Via Torino 51, Cernusco sul Naviglio, MI 20063, Italy.

381 ESP ISSN 1885-0391
COMERCIO 45. 1987-1992. 6/yr. Comercio 45, Alameda Recalde, 50, Bilbao, Vizcaya 48008, Spain.

382.025 ESP ISSN 1139-6318
COMERCIO EXTERIOR DE LA COMUNIDAD DE MADRID. 1990-2005. a. Comunidad de Madrid, Instituto de Estadistica, Principe de Vargara 108, Madrid, 28002, Spain.

946.9 ESP ISSN 1138-6428
COMERCIO EXTERIOR DE LA COMUNIDAD VALENCIANA. 1973-199?. a. Camara Oficial de Comercio Industria y Navegacion de Valencia, Jesus 19, Valencia, 46007, Spain.

338.642 741.5 USA ISSN 1534-4606
COMICS & GAMES RETAILER. 1992-2007. m. Krause Publications, Inc., 700 E State St, Iola, WI 54990.

910 ITA
COMITATO DEI GEOGRAFI ITALIANI. COMMISSIONE PER LA GEOGRAFIA STORICA DELLE SEDI UMANE IN ITALIA. (PUBBLICAZIONI NO.). 1974-1980 (no.5). irreg. Casa Editrice Leo S. Olschki, Viuzzo del Pozzetto 8, Florence, 50126, Italy.

389.1 FRA ISSN 1016-3778
COMITE CONSULTATIF POUR LA MASSE ET LES GRANDEURS APPARENTEES/CONSULTATIVE COMMITTEE FOR MASS AND RELATED QUANTITIES. 1981-2003. irreg. Bureau International des Poids et Mesures, Pavillon de Breteuil, Sevres, Cedex 92312, France.

621.389 FRA ISSN 1606-3759
COMITE INTERNATIONAL DES POIDS ET MESURES. COMITE CONSULTATIF DE L'ACOUSTIQUE, DES ULTRASONS ET DES VIBRATIONS/CONSULTATIVE COMMITTEE FOR ACOUSTICS, ULTRASOUND AND VIBRATION. 2000-2003. irreg. Bureau International des Poids et Mesures, Pavillon de Breteuil, Sevres, Cedex 92312, France.

530.8 FRA ISSN 0253-2166
COMITE INTERNATIONAL DES POIDS ET MESURES. COMITE CONSULTATIF DE PHOTOMETRIE ET RADIOMETRIE. (RAPPORT ET ANNEXES)/CONSULTATIVE COMMITTEE FOR PHOTOMETRY AND RADIOMETRY. 1962-2003. irreg. Bureau International des Poids et Mesures, Pavillon de Breteuil, Sevres, Cedex 92312, France.

530.8 FRA ISSN 0069-6463 CODEN: CCTMCZ
COMITE INTERNATIONAL DES POIDS ET MESURES. COMITE CONSULTATIF DE THERMOMETRIE. RAPPORTS ET ANNEXES/CONSULTATIVE COMMITTEE FOR THERMOMETRY. 1950-2003. irreg. Bureau International des Poids et Mesures, Pavillon de Breteuil, Sevres, Cedex 92312, France.

530.8 FRA ISSN 1608-4055
COMITE INTERNATIONAL DES POIDS ET MESURES. COMITE CONSULTATIF D'ELECTRICITE ET MAGNETISME. (RAPPORT ET ANNEXES)/CONSULTATIVE COMMITTEE FOR ELECTRICITY AND MAGNETISM. 1961 (9th ed.)-2003. irreg. Bureau International des Poids et Mesures, Pavillon de Breteuil, Sevres, Cedex 92312, France.

530.8 FRA ISSN 1684-8845
COMITE INTERNATIONAL DES POIDS ET MESURES. COMITE CONSULTATIF DES LONGUEURS (RAPPORT ET ANNEXES)/CONSULTATIVE COMMITTEE FOR LENGTH. 1962 (vol.3)-2003. irreg. Bureau International des Poids et Mesures, Pavillon de Breteuil, Sevres, Cedex 92312, France.

530.8 FRA ISSN 1608-4047
COMITE INTERNATIONAL DES POIDS ET MESURES. COMITE CONSULTATIF DES RAYONNEMENTS IONISANTS (RAPPORT ET ANNEXES)/CONSULTATIVE COMMITTEE FOR IONIZING RADIATION. 1988-2003. irreg. Bureau International des Poids et Mesures, Pavillon de Breteuil, Sevres, Cedex 92312, France.

530.8 FRA ISSN 0373-3181
COMITE INTERNATIONAL DES POIDS ET MESURES. COMITE CONSULTATIF DES UNITES (RAPPORT ET ANNEXES)/ CONSULTATIVE COMMITTEE FOR UNITS. 1967-2003. irreg. Bureau International des Poids et Mesures, Pavillon de Breteuil, Sevres, Cedex 92312, France.

389.1 FRA ISSN 1025-0034
COMITE INTERNATIONAL DES POIDS ET MESURES. COMITE CONSULTATIF POUR LA QUANTITE DE MATIERE. (RAPPORT ET ANNEXES)/CONSULTATIVE COMMITTEE FOR AMOUNT OF SUBSTANCE. 1995-2003. irreg. Bureau International des Poids et Mesures, Pavillon de Breteuil, Sevres, Cedex 92312, France.

382 FRA
COMMERCE EXTERIEUR DES REGIONS PROVENCE, COTE D'AZUR ET CORSE. 1968-ceased. a. Chambre de Commerce et d'Industrie de Marseille, Immeuble CMCI, 2 rue Henri Barbusse, Marseille, Cedex 1 13241, France.

320 330 AUS ISSN 0810-7947
COMMON SENSE. 1981-ceased. irreg. Common Sense Publications, 1 Schneider Rd, Rosevale, QLD 4340, Australia.

330.9 AUS
COMMONWEALTH LEGISLATION REVIEW ANNUAL REPORT. 1996-1997. a. AusInfo, Parliament House, Canberra Mc, ACT 2600, Australia.

371.0025 FRA ISSN 0291-8242
COMMUNAUTES EDUCATIVES. 1972-2003. q. Association Nationale des Communautes Educatives, 145 bd. de Magenta, Paris, 75010, France.

384 USA ISSN 1555-3426
COMMUNICATIONS BUSINESS DAILY. 2005-200?. d. (Mon.-Fri.). Warren Communications News, Inc., 2115 Ward Ct, NW, Washington, DC 20037.

600 DEU
COMMUNICATIONS BY SIEMENS. 1999-2006. q. BurdaYukom Publishing GmbH, Konrad-Zuse-Platz 11, Munich, 81829, Germany.

384.0285 USA ISSN 1534-2840
COMMUNICATIONS CONVERGENCE. 1993-2004 (Oct.). m. C M P Media LLC, 600 Community Dr, Manhasset, NY 11030.

500 EGY ISSN 1110-0028
COMMUNICATIONS IN SCIENCE AND DEVELOPMENT RESEARCH. 1971-1996. 4/yr. Balba Group for Soil and Water Research, College of Agriculture, University of Alexandria, El-Shatby, Alexandria, 21545, Egypt.

383 FRA ISSN 0753-759X
COMMUNIQUER. 1951-1978; resumed 1979-198?. q. Ecole Nationale Superieure des Postes et Telecommunications, Association des Eleves et Anciens Eleves, 46 rue Barrault, Paris, Cedex 13 75634, France.

374 DEU
COMMUNITY EDUCATION INTERNATIONAL. 1984-2003. s-a. International Community Education Association, c/o Prof. Dr. Juergen Zimmer, Pres. & Pub., International Academy, International Center of ICEA, Koenigin-Luise-Strasse 24-26, Berlin, 14195, Germany.

300 ITA
COMO; cultura, turismo, commercio, industria. 1955-ceased. q. Domenico Discacciati, Via Carloni, 8, Como, CO 22100, Italy.

940 NLD ISSN 0922-9744
COMPARATIVE STUDIES IN OVERSEAS HISTORY. 1978-1989 (vol.8). irreg. Brill, PO Box 9000, Leiden, 2300 PA, Netherlands.

338.1 AUS ISSN 0314-0164
COMPLAN HANDBOOK. 1977-1989. a. University of New England, Agricultural Business Research Institute, Armidale, NSW 2351, Australia.

332.6 AUS ISSN 1442-0422
COMPLETE RETIREMENT PLANNER. 1990-ceased. s-a. Universal Magazines Pty. Ltd., Unit 5, 6-8 Byfield St, North Ryde, NSW 2113, Australia.

621.38 DEU ISSN 0945-1145
COMPONENTS (ENGLISH EDITION). 1992-1999. bi-m. Siemens AG, Henkestr 127, Erlangen, 91052, Germany.

621.38 DEU ISSN 0945-1137
COMPONENTS (GERMAN EDITION). 1906-1999. 6/yr. Siemens AG, Henkestr 127, Erlangen, 91052, Germany.

530 NLD ISSN 0927-6440 CODEN: CMNTEU
COMPOSITE INTERFACES (PRINT). 1992-2009. 6/yr. V S P, Brill Academic Publishers, PO Box 9000, Leiden, 2300 PA, Netherlands.

620.1 USA ISSN 1544-9483
COMPOSITES IN MANUFACTURING. 1985-2008. q. Society of Manufacturing Engineers, One SME Dr, PO Box 930, Dearborn, MI 48121.

539 GBR ISSN 1096-598X CODEN: COSEFP
COMPOUND SEMICONDUCTOR. 1995-2009 (Jul.). m. Institute of Physics Publishing Ltd., Dirac House, Temple Back, Bristol, BS1 6BE, United Kingdom.

658.7 ITA
COMPRARE OGGI; rivista di management degli approvvigionamenti. 1987-ceased. 6/yr. Societa Editoriale Farmaceutica (S E F), Via Ausonio 12, Milan, MI 20123, Italy.

617.7 USA ISSN 1527-7313
COMPREHENSIVE OPHTHALMOLOGY UPDATE. 2000 (Jan.)-2007 (Nov.). bi-m. Comprehensive Ophthamology Update LLC, 7 Kent Street, Brookline, MA 02445g.

300 100 FRA ISSN 1626-4207
COMPRENDRE. 2000-2006. s-a. Presses Universitaires de France, 6 Avenue Reille, Paris, 75685 Cedex 14, France.

410.285 651.8 006.3 USA ISSN 0891-2017 CODEN: AJCLD9
COMPUTATIONAL LINGUISTICS. 1974-2008. q. M I T Press, 238 Main St, Ste 500, Cambridge, MA 02142.

551.22 500 USA CODEN: CEPEE7
COMPUTATIONAL SEISMOLOGY AND GEODYNAMICS. 1979-1992; resumed 1994-2007. irreg. American Geophysical Union, 2000 Florida Ave, NW, Washington, DC 20009.

745.5 AUS ISSN 1444-9552
COMPUTER CRAFT. 2001-2004. bi-m. Creative Living Publications Pty. Ltd., PO Box 645, Rozelle, NSW 2039, Australia.

330 USA ISSN 1095-1377
COMPUTER CURRENTS. ATLANTA. 1989-199?. m. ComputerUser.com, Inc., PO Box 7738, Hicksville, NY 11791.

338.47004 USA ISSN 1097-847X
COMPUTER CURRENTS. DALLAS - FT. WORTH. 1987-199?. m. ComputerUser.com, Inc.

338.47004 USA
COMPUTER CURRENTS. NORTHERN CALIFORNIA. 198?-199?. bi-w. ComputerUser.com, Inc., PO Box 7738, Hicksville, NY 11791.

004.22 USA
COMPUTER DESIGN AND ARCHITECTURE SERIES. 1976-ceased. irreg. Elsevier Inc., 360 Park Ave S, New York, NY 10010.

004 ITA ISSN 1126-5159
COMPUTER FACILE. 1998-200?. m. Techno Publishing S.r.l., Via Tacito 5, Corsico, MI 20094, Italy.

004.16 ITA ISSN 1970-4666
COMPUTER GENIUS. 2006-200?. m. Sprea Editori Srl, Via Torino 51, Cernusco sul Naviglio, MI 20063, Italy.

338 USA ISSN 1524-7910
COMPUTER GRANTS ALERT. 1998-2001. m. Aspen Publishers, Inc., 111 Eighth Ave., 7th Fl, New York, NY 10011.

004.16 DEU ISSN 1612-4952
COMPUTER-GUIDE. 1993-2004. m. Vogel IT-Medien GmbH, Gutermannstr 25, Augsburg, 86154, Germany.

004.16 USA ISSN 0748-8610
COMPUTER RETAILERS' GUIDE. 1984-ceased. q. C M P Media LLC, 600 Community Dr, Manhasset, NY 11030.

004 GBR ISSN 0953-3710 CODEN: CMSTEL
COMPUTER SCIENCE TEXTS. 1983-199?. irreg. Wiley-Blackwell Publishing Ltd., 9600 Garsington Rd, Oxford, OX4 2DQ, United Kingdom.

004 GBR ISSN 1361-4339
COMPUTER SERVICES AND SOFTWARE ASSOCIATION. REFERENCE BOOK AND BUYERS' GUIDE. 1985-1997. a. Computer Services and Software Association, Hanover House, 73-74 High Holborn, London, WC1V 6LE, United Kingdom.

384.0285 GBR ISSN 1748-5266
COMPUTER VIDEO EDITING. 1997-2004 (Dec.). bi-m. Highbury - WV, 53-79 Highgate Rd, London, NW5 1TW, United Kingdom.

005.1 ITA ISSN 1825-4551
COMPUTER WEEK SOFTWARE. 2005-200?. m. Sprea Editori Srl, Via Torino 51, Cernusco sul Naviglio, MI 20063, Italy.

004 ITA ISSN 1825-4632
COMPUTER WEEK SPECIALE. 2005-ceased. m. Sprea Editori Srl, Via Torino 51, Cernusco sul Naviglio, MI 20063, Italy.

004 ITA ISSN 1825-4535
COMPUTER WEEK TEST. 2005-200?. m. Sprea Editori Srl, Via Torino 51, Cernusco sul Naviglio, MI 20063, Italy.

004.678 ITA ISSN 1825-4624
COMPUTER WEEK WEB. 2005-200?. m. Sprea Editori Srl, Via Torino 51, Cernusco sul Naviglio, MI 20063, Italy.

004.16 ITA ISSN 1825-4640
COMPUTER WEEKWINDOWS. 2005-200?. m. Sprea Editori Srl, Via Torino 51, Cernusco sul Naviglio, MI 20063, Italy.

929 GBR ISSN 0263-3248 CODEN: CGENER
COMPUTERS IN GENEALOGY. 1982-2005. q. Society of Genealogists, 14 Charterhouse Bldgs, Goswell Rd, London, EC1M 7BA, United Kingdom.

370.285 NZL ISSN 0114-4081
COMPUTERS IN NEW ZEALAND SCHOOLS. 1989-2007 (Jul.). 3/yr. University of Otago Press, Level 1, 398 Cumberland St, PO Box 56, Dunedin, New Zealand.

338.47004 USA ISSN 1533-5615
COMPUTERUSER. CHICAGO. 1997-2006. m. ComputerUser.com, Inc., PO Box 7738, Hicksville, NY 11791.

338.47004 USA ISSN 1533-5550
COMPUTERUSER. HOUSTON. 1989-2006. m. ComputerUser.com, Inc., PO Box 7738, Hicksville, NY 11791.

338.47004 USA
COMPUTERUSER. LOS ANGELES. 1986-2006. m. ComputerUser.com, Inc., PO Box 7738, Hicksville, NY 11791.

330 025.04 USA ISSN 1533-5720
COMPUTERUSER. NEW YORK; for business & IT professionals. 1995-2006. m. ComputerUser.com, Inc., PO Box 7738, Hicksville, NY 11791.

338.47004 USA ISSN 1533-5585
COMPUTERUSER TWIN CITIES. (Regional editions avail.: Atlanta, Boston, Chicago, Dallas-Ft. Worth, Houston, Los Angeles, San Francisco, New York, Philadelphia, Baltimore, Washington D.C., Minneapolis, Detroit, Columbus, Kansas City) 1983-2006. m. ComputerUser.com, Inc., 220 S. 6th St, Ste 500, Minneapolis, MN 55402.

368.00285 GBR ISSN 1363-1942
COMPUTING FOR INSURANCE. 1996-200?; suspended. s-a. Mitre House Publishing Ltd., PO Box 29, South Petherton, TA13 5WE, United Kingdom.

352.14 ITA ISSN 0010-4930
IL COMUNE DEMOCRATICO; rivista delle autonomie locali. 1945-1987. bi-m. Lega per le Autonomie ed i Poteri Locali, Via Cesare Balbo 43, Rome, 00184, Italy.

352 ITA ISSN 1590-4733
COMUNI IN RETE. 1997-2001. bi-w. Maggioli Editore, Via del Carpino 8/10, Santarcangelo di Romagna, RN 47822, Italy.

302.3 ESP ISSN 1132-127X
COMUNICACION Y ESTUDIOS UNIVERSITARIOS. 1990-2002. s-a. Centro Universitario de Ciencias de la Information, Ave. Seminario s-n, Moncada, Valencia 46113, Spain.

384.6 ESP ISSN 1130-4693
COMUNICACIONES DE TELEFONICA I & D. (Investigacion y Desarrollo) 1990-ceased. w. Telefonica, Emilio Vargas 6, Madrid, 28043, Spain.

002 932 ITA ISSN 1970-0253
COMUNICAZIONI. 1995-ceased. irreg. Universita degli Studi di Firenze, Istituto Papirologico "Girolamo Vitelli", Borgo degli Albizi 12-14, Florence, Italy.

297 ITA
COMUNITA ISLAMICA; Jihad periodico Islamico. 1980; N.S. 1990 (Dec.)-19??. bi-m. Edizioni Arktos, Via Gardezzana, 57, Carmagnola, TO 10022, Italy.

630 ESP ISSN 1138-2775
COMUNITAT VALENCIANA AGRARIA. 1994-2005. q. Generalitat Valenciana, Conselleria de Agricultura, Pesa y Alimentacion. Secretaria General, C. Amadeo de Saboya, 2, Valencia, 46010, Spain.

304 ESP ISSN 0214-6681
CON DADOS DE NIEBLA. 1984-1999. s-a. Diputacion Provincial de Huelva, Ave. Martin A. Pinzon, 9, Huelva, 21003, Spain.

658.3 NLD ISSN 1384-6639
CONCEPTS AND TRANSFORMATION; international journal of action research and organizational renewal. 1996-2004. 3/yr. John Benjamins Publishing Co., PO Box 36224, Amsterdam, 1020 ME, Netherlands.

594.1477 ITA ISSN 0394-0152
LA CONCHIGLIA/SHELL; international shell magazine. 1969-2004. q. Evolver S.r.l., Via Cesare Federici, 1, Rome, RM 00147, Italy.

200 FRA ISSN 1140-7654
CONCILIUM; revue international de theologie. 1965-2002. 6/yr. Association Centre Sevres, Faculte Jesuites de Paris, 35 bis rue de Sevres, Paris, 75006, France.

330 USA ISSN 1936-0916
CONDE NAST PORTFOLIO. 2007 (May)-2009. m. Conde Nast Publications, Inc., 4 Times Sq, 6th Fl, New York, NY 10036.

666 FRA ISSN 1265-616X
CONFEDERATION DES INDUSTRIES CERAMIQUES DE FRANCE. ANNUAIRE. 1953-199?. irreg. Septima, 14 rue Falguiere, Paris, 75015, France.

800 940 700 USA ISSN 0891-1908
CONFERENCE ON EDITORIAL PROBLEMS: UNIVERSITY OF TORONTO. 1966-1993. a. A M S Press, Inc., Brooklyn Navy Yard, 63 Flushing Ave, Bldg 292, Unit #221, Brooklyn, NY 11205.

355 341 GBR ISSN 1475-2174
CONFLICT ASSESSMENTS. 2001 (July)-2001. irreg. The Conflict, Security & Development Group, King's College London, Strand, London, WC2R 2LS, United Kingdom.

327 DEU ISSN 1430-8576
CONFLICTS, OPTIONS, STRATEGIES IN A THREATENED WORLD. 1996-1999 (vol.3). irreg. Peter Lang GmbH Europaeischer Verlag der Wissenschaften, Eschborner Landstr 42-50, Frankfurt Am Main, 60489, Germany.

644 FRA ISSN 0761-5779
CONFORT MENAGER. 1983-200?. 10/yr. S.E.P., 9 Place du General Catroux, Paris, 75017, France.

301 ITA ISSN 1129-2229
CONFRONTO (PISA); riflessioni sui modelli di sviluppo. 1995-2007. s-a. Fabrizio Serra Editore, c/o Accademia Editoriale, Via Santa Bibbiana 28, Pisa, 56127, Italy.

328 USA ISSN 0193-4627
CONGRESS IN PRINT; the weekly catalog of congressional documents. 1969-1998. 48/yr. C Q Press, Inc., 2300 N St, NW, Ste 800, Washington, DC 20037.

347 USA ISSN 1079-8129
THE CONGRESSIONAL YEARBOOK. 1993-1996. a. C Q Press, Inc., 2300 N St, NW, Ste 800, Washington, DC 20037.

306.766 FRA ISSN 1951-2708
CONJUGAISON. 1997-2007. m. Association Homonyme, Centre LGBT Lorraine Sud, 7 Rue de Serre, Nancy, 54000, France.

291 FRA ISSN 0296-1288
CONNAISSANCE DES RELIGIONS. 1985-2006. s-a. Editions Dervy, 204 Boulevard Raspail, Paris, 75014, France.

914.406 FRA ISSN 0336-9455
CONNAISSANCE DU PAYS D'OC. 1973-1983; N.S. 1984-198?. bi-m. Editions de la Source, B.P. 1034, Montpellier, Cedex 34006, France.

004 NZL ISSN 1171-1426
CONNECT (CHRISTCHURCH). 1991-2006. m. Christchurch City Libraries, P.O. Box 1466, Christchurch, New Zealand.

371.3 USA ISSN 1554-4583
CONNECTED NEWSLETTER. 1994-2008. 9/yr. Classroom Connect, Inc., 8000 Marina Blvd., Ste. 400, Brisbane, CA 94005-1885.

331.1 USA ISSN 1521-8724
THE CONNECTICUT JOBBANK; the job hunter's guide to Connecticut. (Includes: Hartford, New Haven, Stamford, Waterbury and many more) 1998-2004 (3rd ed.). biennial. Adams Media, 57 Littlefield St, Avon, MA 02322.

333.72025 USA ISSN 0069-911X
CONSERVATION DIRECTORY; a listing of organizations, agencies and officials concerned with natural resource use and management. 1955-2005. a. National Wildlife Federation, 11100 Wildlife Ctr Dr, Reston, VA 20190.

320.52 AUS ISSN 1833-2188
THE CONSERVATIVE. 2005-2006. q. Conservative Publications Pty. Ltd., GPO Box 1600, Sydney, NSW 2001, Australia.

780 ITA ISSN 1724-2533
CONSERVATORIO DI MUSICA GIUSEPPE VERDI DI MILANO. ANNUARIO. 1962-19??. a. Conservatorio di Musica "Giuseppe Verdi" (Conservatorio di Milano), Via Conservatorio 12, Milan, 20122, Italy.

580 ISR
CONSPECTUS FLORAE ORIENTALIS. 1980-1994 (no.9). irreg. Israel Academy of Sciences and Humanities, 43 Jabotinski St, P O Box 4040, Jerusalem, 91040, Israel.

133 NLD ISSN 1574-079X
CONSTANTE. 2004-2006. 3/yr. Uitgeverij Omnicum, Hollandhof 73, Helmond, 5709 DG, Netherlands.

690 FRA ISSN 0010-6682
CONSTRUCTION (PARIS). 1946-1980. m. Dunod, 5 rue Laromiguiere, Paris, 75005, France.

330 USA ISSN 1526-159X
CONSTRUCTION LAW AND BUSINESS. 1999-2002. bi-m. Aspen Publishers, Inc., 111 Eighth Ave., 7th Fl, New York, NY 10011.

332.6 DEU
CONSULT. 1998-2003. q. BurdaYukom Publishing GmbH, Konrad-Zuse-Platz 11, Munich, 81829, Germany.

620 GBR ISSN 1366-5189
CONSULTING ENGINEER. 1995-1998. q. Association for Consultancy and Engineering, Alliance House, 12 Caxton St, London, SW1H 0QL, United Kingdom.

331.1 USA
CONSUMER EXPENDITURE SURVEY: QUARTERLY DATA FROM THE INTERVIEW SURVEY. 1987-1998. q. U.S. Department of Labor, Bureau of Labor Statistics, Postal Square Bldg., 2 Massachusetts Ave, NE, Washington, DC 20212-0001.

635 643.7 NZL ISSN 1175-8376
CONSUMER GARDENING. 1988-2002 (no.72, Nov./Dec.). bi-m. Consumers' Institute, Private Bag 6996, Wellington, 6035, New Zealand.

340.5 GBR ISSN 0967-1978
CONSUMER LAW JOURNAL. 1993-2000. bi-m. Sweet & Maxwell Ltd., 100 Avenue Rd, London, NW3 3PF, United Kingdom.

640.73 GBR ISSN 0961-1134
CONSUMER POLICY REVIEW. 1991-2008 (Sep.). bi-m. Which? Ltd., 2 Marylebone Rd, London, NW1 4DF, United Kingdom.

910.202 640.73 USA ISSN 0887-8439 CODEN: CRTLE3
CONSUMER REPORTS TRAVEL LETTER. 1985-2003. m. Consumers Union of the United States, Inc., 101 Truman Ave, Yonkers, NY 10703.

629.222 USA ISSN 1530-3721
CONSUMER REPORTS USED CAR YEARBOOK. 2000-200?. a. Consumers Union of the United States, Inc., 101 Truman Ave, Yonkers, NY 10703.

640 GBR ISSN 1470-8159
CONSUMER SCIENCES TODAY. 1981-2006. q. Institute of Consumer Sciences Incorporating Home Economics, 21 Portland Pl, London, WIN 1PY, United Kingdom.

330 FRA ISSN 1166-4231
CONTACTS A V A. (Assurances Vieillesse des Artisans) 1963-2005. 6/yr. Magazine Institution d'Assurances Vieillesse des Artisans, 28 boulevard de Grenelle, Paris, Cedex 15 75737, France.

363.7 615 USA ISSN 1556-1410
CONTAMINATION CONTROL; for the life sciences. 2005-2008. q. John Wiley & Sons, Inc., 111 River St, Hoboken, NJ 07030.

951 GBR ISSN 0085-2856
CONTEMPORARY CHINA INSTITUTE PUBLICATIONS. 1970-2009 (Jul.). irreg. Cambridge University Press, The Edinburgh Bldg, Shaftesbury Rd, Cambridge, CB2 8RU, United Kingdom.

616.5 USA ISSN 1541-5791
CONTEMPORARY DERMATOLOGY; a monthly publication for continuing medical education in dermatology. 2003 (Mar.)-2004 (Dec.). m. Lippincott Williams & Wilkins, 530 Walnut St, Philadelphia, PA 19106-3621.

618.97 USA ISSN 1069-0840 CODEN: CPGTFH
CONTEMPORARY GERONTOLOGY; a journal of reviews and critical discourse. 1994-200?. 4/yr. Springer Publishing Company, 11 W 42nd St, 15th Fl, New York, NY 10036.

616.992 USA ISSN 1538-5183
CONTEMPORARY ONCOLOGY. 2002-200?. s-m. Lippincott Williams & Wilkins, 530 Walnut St, Philadelphia, PA 19106-3621.

617.6 USA ISSN 1538-3083
CONTEMPORARY ORAL HYGIENE. 2001 (Aug.)-2007. m. Ascend Media, 7015 College Blvd, Ste 600, Overland Park, KS 66211.

016.30542 USA
CONTEMPORARY WOMEN'S ISSUES. 1997-ceased. w. Gale, 27500 Drake Rd, Farmington Hills, MI 48331.

016.5 GBR
CONTENTSDIRECT. 19??-2006. m. Elsevier Ltd, The Blvd, Langford Ln, Kidlington, Oxford, OX5 1GB, United Kingdom.

550 CHN ISSN 1006-7825 CODEN: CODYFA
CONTINENTAL DYNAMICS. 1996-2001. s-a. Chinese Academy of Geological Sciences, Institute of Geology, 26 Baiwanzhuang Rd, Xicheng District, Beijing, 100037, China.

610.715 USA ISSN 1077-209X
CONTINUING MEDICAL EDUCATION DIRECTORY. 1993-1997. biennial. American Medical Association, 515 N State St, Chicago, IL 60610.

711.4 690 NLD ISSN 1872-2911
DE CONTOUREN. 2005-2006. q. BMC, Postbus 308, Leusden, 3830 AJ, Netherlands.

280.4 DEU
CONTRAPUNKT (ONLINE); christliche Themenzeitschfrift fuer junge Leute. 1999-2005. 10/yr. M B K - Evangelisches Jugend- und Missionswerk e.V., Hermann-Loens-Str 9-14, Bad Salzuflen, 32105, Germany.

973 USA ISSN 0084-9219
CONTRIBUTIONS IN AMERICAN HISTORY. 1970-200?. irreg. Greenwood Publishing Group Inc., 88 Post Rd W, PO Box 5007, Westport, CT 06881.

973 USA ISSN 0084-9227
CONTRIBUTIONS IN AMERICAN STUDIES. 1969-200?. irreg. Greenwood Publishing Group Inc., 88 Post Rd W, PO Box 5007, Westport, CT 06881.

950 USA ISSN 1053-1866 CODEN: PPTRDD
CONTRIBUTIONS IN ASIAN STUDIES. 1991-200?. irreg. Greenwood Publishing Group Inc., 88 Post Rd W, PO Box 5007, Westport, CT 06881.

970 USA ISSN 0163-3813
CONTRIBUTIONS IN COMPARATIVE COLONIAL STUDIES. 1979-2003. irreg. Greenwood Publishing Group Inc., 88 Post Rd W, PO Box 5007, Westport, CT 06881.

364 USA ISSN 0732-4464
CONTRIBUTIONS IN CRIMINOLOGY AND PENOLOGY. 1983-200?. irreg. Greenwood Publishing Group Inc., 88 Post Rd W, PO Box 5007, Westport, CT 06881.

330.1 USA ISSN 0084-9235
CONTRIBUTIONS IN ECONOMICS AND ECONOMIC HISTORY. 1970-200?. irreg. Greenwood Publishing Group Inc., 88 Post Rd W, PO Box 5007, Westport, CT 06881.

305.8 USA ISSN 0196-7088
CONTRIBUTIONS IN ETHNIC STUDIES. 1980-200?. irreg. Greenwood Publishing Group Inc., 88 Post Rd W, PO Box 5007, Westport, CT 06881.

306.85 USA ISSN 0147-1023
CONTRIBUTIONS IN FAMILY STUDIES. 1977-2004. irreg. Greenwood Publishing Group Inc., 88 Post Rd W, PO Box 5007, Westport, CT 06881.

303.842 USA ISSN 0147-1031
CONTRIBUTIONS IN INTERCULTURAL AND COMPARATIVE STUDIES. 1976-19??. irreg. Greenwood Publishing Group Inc., 88 Post Rd W, PO Box 5007, Westport, CT 06881.

340 USA ISSN 0147-1074
CONTRIBUTIONS IN LEGAL STUDIES. 1978-2002. irreg. Greenwood Publishing Group Inc., 88 Post Rd W, PO Box 5007, Westport, CT 06881.

320 USA ISSN 0147-1066
CONTRIBUTIONS IN POLITICAL SCIENCE. 1978-2004. irreg. Greenwood Publishing Group Inc., 88 Post Rd W, PO Box 5007, Westport, CT 06881.

301 USA ISSN 0084-9278
CONTRIBUTIONS IN SOCIOLOGY. 1970-2004. irreg. Greenwood Publishing Group Inc., 88 Post Rd W, PO Box 5007, Westport, CT 06881.

320.5 306 NLD ISSN 1807-9326
CONTRIBUTIONS TO THE HISTORY OF CONCEPTS. 2005-2009 (Vol. 5). s-a. Brill, PO Box 9000, Leiden, 2300 PA, Netherlands.

331.8 NLD ISSN 0921-500X
CONTRIBUTIONS TO THE HISTORY OF LABOUR AND SOCIETY. 1988-1992 (vol.4). irreg. Brill, PO Box 9000, Leiden, 2300 PA, Netherlands.

492.4 NLD ISSN 0169-7846
CONTRIBUTIONS TO THE SOCIOLOGY OF JEWISH LANGUAGES. 1985-1988 (vol.3). irreg. Brill, PO Box 9000, Leiden, 2300 PA, Netherlands.

306.38 USA ISSN 0732-085X
CONTRIBUTIONS TO THE STUDY OF AGING. 1982-200?. irreg. Greenwood Publishing Group Inc., 88 Post Rd W, PO Box 5007, Westport, CT 06881.

301 USA ISSN 0890-9377
CONTRIBUTIONS TO THE STUDY OF ANTHROPOLOGY. 1987-200?. irreg. Greenwood Publishing Group Inc., 88 Post Rd W, PO Box 5007, Westport, CT 06881.

004 USA ISSN 0734-757X CODEN: PCTNDC
CONTRIBUTIONS TO THE STUDY OF COMPUTER SCIENCE. 1983-19??. irreg. Greenwood Publishing Group Inc., 88 Post Rd W, PO Box 5007, Westport, CT 06881.

302.23 USA ISSN 0732-4456
CONTRIBUTIONS TO THE STUDY OF MASS MEDIA AND COMMUNICATIONS. 1983-2003. irreg. Greenwood Publishing Group Inc., 88 Post Rd W, PO Box 5007, Westport, CT 06881.

780 USA ISSN 0193-9041
CONTRIBUTIONS TO THE STUDY OF MUSIC AND DANCE. 1981-2003. irreg. Greenwood Publishing Group Inc., 88 Post Rd W, PO Box 5007, Westport, CT 06881.

200 USA ISSN 0196-7053
CONTRIBUTIONS TO THE STUDY OF RELIGION. 1981-2004. irreg. Greenwood Publishing Group Inc., 88 Post Rd W, PO Box 5007, Westport, CT 06881.

808.838 USA ISSN 0193-6875
CONTRIBUTIONS TO THE STUDY OF SCIENCE FICTION AND FANTASY. 1982-2005. irreg. Greenwood Publishing Group Inc., 88 Post Rd W, PO Box 5007, Westport, CT 06881.

629.8312 GBR ISSN 0010-8022 CODEN: CTLIAW
CONTROL AND INSTRUMENTATION. 1958-2001. m. Centaur Communications Ltd., St Giles House, 50 Poland St, London, W1F 7AX, United Kingdom.

629.13 GBR
CONTROL COLUMN. 1967-19??. 8/yr. Control Column Publications, 127 Hawton Rd, Newark, Notts NG24 4QG, United Kingdom.

001.3 AUS ISSN 1322-7971
CONVIVIO; journal of ideas in Italian studies. 1995-2002. s-a. (Apr. & Oct.). Minerva E & S, PO Box 98, St Lucia, QLD 4067, Australia.

851 ITA
COOPERATIVA ANTIGRUPPO SICILIANO. 1968-ceased. 3/yr. Cooperativa Editrice Antigruppo Siciliano, Via Argenteria Km, 4, Trapani, TP 91100, Italy.

333.9 AUS ISSN 1446-7852
COOPERATIVE RESEARCH CENTRE FOR FRESHWATER ECOLOGY. IDENTIFICATION AND ECOLOGY GUIDE. 1994-2004. irreg. Cooperative Research Centre for Freshwater Ecology, University of Canberra, Canberra, ACT, Australia.

330 DNK ISSN 1398-7461
COPENHAGEN BUSINESS SCHOOL. DEPARTMENT OF INDUSTRIAL ECONOMICS AND STRATEGY. WORKING PAPERS. 1999-2004. irreg. Handelshoejskolen i Koebenhavn, Institut for Industrioekonomi og Virksomhedsstrategi, Kilevej 14 A, Frederiksberg, 2000, Denmark.

327.172 DNK ISSN 1397-0895
COPENHAGEN PEACE RESEARCH INSTITUTE. WORKING PAPERS. 1985-2002. irreg. Copenhagen Peace Research Institute, Fredericiagade 18, Copenhagen V, 1310, Denmark.

410 DNK ISSN 1396-1888
COPENHAGEN WORKING PAPERS IN L S P. (Language for Special Purposes) 1979-2004. irreg. Handelshoejskolen i Koebenhavn, Fakultetet for Sprog, Kommunikation og Kultur, Dalgas Have 15, Frederiksberg, 2000, Denmark.

651.2 ITA
COPIER - DUPLICATOR GUIDE (YEAR). 1990-ceased. a. Editoriale Directa, Viale Sondrio 7, Milan, 20124, Italy.

929 USA ISSN 1097-7236
COPPER STATE JOURNAL. 1965-ceased. q. Arizona State Genealogical Society, PO Box 42075, Tucson, AZ 85733-2075.

015 ITA
COPTIC BIBLIOGRAPHY. 1982-1993. a. Centro Italiano Microfiches, Piazzale Di Ponte Milvio, 28, Rome, RM 00191, Italy.

281.7 NLD ISSN 0167-5818
COPTIC STUDIES. 1978-1993 (vol.2). irreg. Brill, PO Box 9000, Leiden, 2300 PA, Netherlands.

361.73 362.5 338.91 NLD ISSN 1388-4891
CORDAID BULLETIN. 1998-2003. s-a. Cordaid (Mensen in Nood - Caritas Nederland - Bilance - Memisa), Rhijngeesterstraatweg 40, Oegstgeest, 2341 BV, Netherlands.

410 NLD ISSN 0169-779X
CORNELL LINGUISTIC CONTRIBUTIONS. 1977-1986 (vol.5). irreg. Brill, PO Box 9000, Leiden, 2300 PA, Netherlands.

055 ITA
CORPO. N.S. 1993-ceased. q. Corpo, Via della Stazione di San Pietro 40, Rome, 00165, Italy.

687 USA ISSN 1941-3548
CORPORATE APPAREL MAGAZINE. 2007-2008. m. Wiesner Media, LLC, 7009 S Potomac St, Ste 200, Centennial, CO 80112.

346.066 USA
CORPORATE COMPLIANCE & REGULATORY NEWSLETTER. 2003-2006. m. Law Journal Newsletters, 1617 JFK Blvd, Ste 1750, Philadelphia, PA 19103.

025.04 346 USA ISSN 1534-4568
CORPORATE COUNSEL'S WEB SITE REVIEW. 1999-2002. m. Business Laws, Inc., 11630 Chillicothe Rd, PO Box 185, Chesterland, OH 44026.

361.73 USA ISSN 1058-689X
CORPORATE GIVING YELLOW PAGES; guide to corporate giving contacts. 1983-200?. irreg. Gale, 27500 Drake Rd, Farmington Hills, MI 48331.

346 NZL ISSN 1177-6110
CORPORATE GOVERNANCE. 2005-2007. irreg. Minter Ellison Rudd Watts, PO Box 3798, Auckland, New Zealand.

330 USA ISSN 1939-8085
CORPORATE LEADER. 2007 (Nov.)-2009. q. Doubledown Media, LLC, 240 W 35th St, Fl 11, New York, NY 10001.

020 USA ISSN 1558-6049
CORPORATE LIBRARY UPDATE ONLINE. 1992-2002. m. Reed Business Information, 360 Park Ave S, New York, NY 10010.

364.4 USA ISSN 1040-4201
CORPORATE SECURITY. 1975-2008. bi-w. Strafford Publications, Inc., 590 Dutch Valley Rd, N E, P O Drawer 13729, Atlanta, GA 30324.

658.403 GBR ISSN 1360-5739
CORPORATE SYSTEMS. 1995-2000; suspended. q. Mitre House Publishing Ltd., PO Box 29, South Petherton, TA13 5WE, United Kingdom.

918 ITA
CORPUS ANTIQUITATUM AMERICANENSIUM ITALIA. 1981-ceased. irreg. Bonsignori Editore s.r.l., Viale dei Quattro Venti 47, Rome, RM 00152, Italy.

616.7 FRA ISSN 1627-2757
CORRESPONDANCES EN PELVI-PERINEOLOGIE. 2001-2005. q. DaTeBe Editions, 62-64 rue Jean Jaures, Puteaux, 92800, France.

368 USA ISSN 0740-6452
CORRESPONDENT (APPLETON). 1904-2002. bi-m. Thrivent Financial for Lutherans, 625 Fourth Ave S, Minneapolis, MN 55415.

799 ITA ISSN 1590-900X
CORRIERE DELLA PESCA E DELL'ACQUACOLTURA. 1927-2002. m. Federazione Nazionale Cooperativa della Pesca, Via Torino 146, Rome, 00184, Italy.

616.97 ITA ISSN 1722-9995
CORRIERE DELL'ALLERGIA. 2003-2009. q. Ariesdue srl, Via Airoldi 11, Carimate, CO 22060, Italy.

055.1 ITA ISSN 0391-6774
IL CORRIERE DI ROMA. 1948-ceased. bi-w. Gruppo Editoriale Gesualdi, Via Quattro Novembre, 152, Rome, RM 00187, Italy.

653 ITA ISSN 0010-9290
CORRIERE STENOGRAFICO. 1912-199?. q. Unione Stenografica Italiana, Sala Stampa, Via Vittorio Alfieri, 10, Turin, TO 10121, Italy.

700 913 ITA
CORSI INTERNAZIONALI DI CULTURA SULL'ARTE RAVENNATE E BIZANTINA. ATTI. 1953-1977 (no.24). irreg. Angelo Longo Editore, Via Paolo Costa 33, Ravenna, 48121, Italy.

055.1 ITA
CORTINA. 1933-ceased. s-a. Giovanna Mariotti Ed. & Pub., Via Ria de Zeto, 7-9, Cortina D'ampezzo, BL 32043, Italy.

388.3 USA ISSN 0897-4179
CORVETTE QUARTERLY. 1958-2009; suspended. q. C - E Publishing, Aegis Group, 30400 Van Dyke Ave, P O Box 2119, Warren, MI 48093.

322.4 ITA
COSCIENZA DEL CITTADINO. ceased. w. Coscienza del Cittadino, Via Madonna di Loreto, 4, Monterotondo, RM 00015, Italy.

790.13 ITA ISSN 1970-4674
COSE DA FARE. 2006-200?. m. Sprea Editori Srl, Via Torino 51, Cernusco sul Naviglio, MI 20063, Italy.

668.55 ITA
COSMESI. 1969-ceased. 2/yr. Schwegler Editore s.n.c., Via Senato, 18, Milan, MI 20121, Italy.

668.5 GBR ISSN 0305-0319 CODEN: CSWNAR
COSMETIC WORLD NEWS; the international news magazine of the perfumery, cosmetics and toiletries industry. 1950-1992. 6/yr. World News Publications, 130 Wigmore St, London, W1H 0AT, United Kingdom.

028.5 305.4 USA ISSN 1528-4824
COSMOGIRL!. 1999-2008 (Dec.). 10/yr. Hearst Magazines, 300 W 57th St, 12th Fl, New York, NY 10019.

646.4 NLD ISSN 1872-3543
COSMOPOLITAN SHOPPING. 2006-2008. q. Sanoma Uitgevers B.V., Postbus 1900, Hoofddorp, 2130 JH, Netherlands.

391 ITA ISSN 1593-1498
COSTUME. 2001-200?. bi-m. Edizioni Trentini & C, Via Pier Luigi Nervi 1/B, Argenta, FE 44011, Italy.

388 NLD ISSN 1568-3184
COSUN IN BUSINESS. 199?-2002. m. Cosun, Postbus 3411, Breda, 4800 MG, Netherlands.

054.1 FRA ISSN 1299-3573
COTE FEMME. 1972-2006. m. (Plus 6 extras). Bayard Presse, 3-5 rue Bayard, Paris, 75393 Cedex 08, France.

332.6 FRA ISSN 0220-6358
COTE OFFICIELLE. 1967-2005. d. Bourse de Paris, 39 rue Cambon, Paris, 75001, France.

640 USA ISSN 1550-2562
COTTAGE LIVING; life just right. 2001-2008 (Dec.). 8/yr. Southern Progress Corp., 2100 Lakeshore Dr, Birmingham, AL 35209.

635 AUS ISSN 1032-9609
COTTAGER. 1986-199?. q. Wild Woodbine Studio, Lot 35, Bowen Mountain Rd, Bowen Mountain, NSW 2753, Australia.

745.1 USA ISSN 1540-059X
COTTON & QUAIL ANTIQUE GAZETTE. 1988-ceased. m. Krause Publications, Inc., 700 E State St, Iola, WI 54990.

747 FRA ISSN 1959-0040
COULEUR MAISON. 2007-2008. bi-m. Editions Lariviere, 6 Rue Olof Palme, Clichy, 92587 , France.

746.96 FRA ISSN 1775-0040
COULISSES; le mag qui devoile tous les dessous. 2005-2005. bi-m. D F P Production, 48 rue Franklin, Lyon, 69002, France.

352.14 AUS ISSN 0728-5582
COUNCIL AND COMMUNITY. 1981-1996. bi-m. Local Government Association of South Australia, GPO Box 2693, Adelaide, SA 5001, Australia.

332.1 AUS ISSN 1443-6345
COUNCIL OF FINANCIAL REGULATORS. ANNUAL REPORT. 1993-2003. a. Reserve Bank of Australia, PO Box 3947, Sydney, NSW 2001, Australia.

781.642 DEU
COUNTRY CIRCLE. 1988-2004. m. Country Circle Verlag, Soodersteige 4a, Wiesbaden, 65193, Germany.

640 AUS ISSN 1448-7519
COUNTRY COLLECTIONS HOME SERIES. 2004-ceased. q. Universal Magazines Pty. Ltd., Private Bag 154, North Ryde, NSW 2113, Australia.

312 USA ISSN 0360-8514
COUNTRY DEMOGRAPHIC PROFILES. 1973-19??. irreg. U.S. Census Bureau, 4600 Silver Hill Rd, Washington, DC 20233.

910.91 USA ISSN 1531-1767
COUNTRY DISCOVERIES; guiding you to great backroads travel. 2000-2006. bi-m. Reiman Media Group, Inc., PO Box 991, Greendale, WI 53129.

747 USA ISSN 0737-3740
COUNTRY HOME; a more modern country. 1979-2009 (Feb.). 10/yr. Meredith Corporation, 1716 Locust St, Des Moines, IA 50309.

635 USA ISSN 1086-3753
COUNTRY LIVING GARDENER. 1993-2004. s-a. Hearst Magazines, 300 W 57th St, 12th Fl, New York, NY 10019.

658 USA ISSN 1097-7848
COUNTRY MARKETPLACE. 19??-2006. bi-m. Emmis Publishing LP, 707 Kautz Rd, St. Charles, IL 60174.

784 AUS
COUNTRY MUSIC NEWSLETTER. 1970-ceased. 3/yr. Earl Heywood Fan Club, PO Box 186, Murwillumbah, NSW 2484, Australia.

320.94965 320 330.9 USA ISSN 1366-4174
COUNTRY PROFILE. ALBANIA; annual survey of political and economic background. 1952-2009 (Feb.). a. Economist Intelligence Unit Ltd., 111 W 57th St, New York, NY 10019 .

320.965 330.9 USA ISSN 0269-6053
COUNTRY PROFILE. ALGERIA; annual survey of political and economic background. 195?-2009 (Feb.). a. Economist Intelligence Unit Ltd., 111 W 57th St, New York, NY 10019 .

320.9673 330.9 USA ISSN 1352-0830
COUNTRY PROFILE. ANGOLA; annual survey of political and economic background. 195?-2009 (Feb.). a. Economist Intelligence Unit Ltd., 111 W 57th St, New York, NY 10019 .

320.982 330.9 USA ISSN 0269-4468
COUNTRY PROFILE. ARGENTINA. 1952-2009 (Feb.). a. Economist Intelligence Unit Ltd., 111 W 57th St, New York, NY 10019 .

320.9479 USA ISSN 1741-0010
COUNTRY PROFILE. ARMENIA; annual survey of political and economic background. 1952-2009 (Feb.). a. Economist Intelligence Unit Ltd., 111 W 57th St, New York, NY 10019 .

320.994 330.9 USA ISSN 0269-4476
COUNTRY PROFILE. AUSTRALIA. 195?-2009 (Feb.). a. Economist Intelligence Unit Ltd., 111 W 57th St, New York, NY 10019 .

320.9436 330.9 USA ISSN 0269-4484
COUNTRY PROFILE. AUSTRIA. 1952-2009 (Feb.). a. Economist Intelligence Unit Ltd., 111 W 57th St, New York, NY 10019 .

320.94754 USA ISSN 1366-4239
COUNTRY PROFILE. AZERBAIJAN; annual survey of political and economic background. 1952-2009 (Feb.). a. Economist Intelligence Unit Ltd., 111 W 57th St, New York, NY 10019 .

320.95365 330.9 USA ISSN 1473-9100
COUNTRY PROFILE. BAHRAIN. 195?-2009 (Feb.). a. Economist Intelligence Unit Ltd., 111 W 57th St, New York, NY 10019 .

320.95492 330.9 USA ISSN 0269-8145
COUNTRY PROFILE. BANGLADESH. 1952-2009 (Feb.). a. Economist Intelligence Unit Ltd., 111 W 57th St, New York, NY 10019 .

320.947 USA ISSN 1740-9667
COUNTRY PROFILE. BELARUS; annual survey of political and economic background. 1952-2009 (Feb.). a. Economist Intelligence Unit Ltd., 111 W 57th St, New York, NY 10019 .

320.9493 330.9 USA ISSN 0264-6099
COUNTRY PROFILE. BELGIUM; annual survey of political and economic background. 1952-2009 (Feb.). a. Economist Intelligence Unit Ltd., 111 W 57th St, New York, NY 10019 .

320.9728 330.9 USA ISSN 1749-9321
COUNTRY PROFILE. BELIZE; annual survey of political and economic background. 1952-2009 (Feb.). a. Economist Intelligence Unit Ltd., 111 W 57th St, New York, NY 10019 .

320.9479 USA ISSN 1740-8423
COUNTRY PROFILE. BENIN; annual survey of political and economic background. 195?-2009 (Feb.). a. Economist Intelligence Unit Ltd., 111 W 57th St, New York, NY 10019 .

320.9479 USA
COUNTRY PROFILE. BERMUDA; annual survey of political and economic background. 195?-2009 (Feb.). a. Economist Intelligence Unit Ltd., 111 W 57th St, New York, NY 10019 .

330 320 USA ISSN 1741-0355
COUNTRY PROFILE. BHUTAN. 195?-2009 (Feb.). a. Economist Intelligence Unit Ltd., 111 W 57th St, New York, NY 10019 .

320.984 330.9 USA ISSN 0269-5952
COUNTRY PROFILE. BOLIVIA. 1952-2009 (Feb.). a. Economist Intelligence Unit Ltd., 111 W 57th St, New York, NY 10019 .

320.949742 USA ISSN 1462-6829
COUNTRY PROFILE. BOSNIA-HERCEGOVINA; annual survey of political and economic background. 1952-2009 (Feb.). a. Economist Intelligence Unit Ltd., 111 W 57th St, New York, NY 10019 .

320.96883 USA ISSN 1741-0290
COUNTRY PROFILE. BOTSWANA; annual survey of political and economic background. 195?-2009 (Feb.). a. Economist Intelligence Unit Ltd., 111 W 57th St, New York, NY 10019 .

320.981 330.9 USA ISSN 0269-4492
COUNTRY PROFILE. BRAZIL. 1952-2009 (Feb.). a. Economist Intelligence Unit Ltd., 111 W 57th St, New York, NY 10019 .

320.9499 330.9 USA ISSN 1366-4166
COUNTRY PROFILE. BULGARIA. 1971-2009 (Feb.). a. Economist Intelligence Unit Ltd., 111 W 57th St, New York, NY 10019 .

320.9479 330.9 USA ISSN 1741-041X
COUNTRY PROFILE. BURKINA FASO. 195?-2009 (Feb.). a. Economist Intelligence Unit Ltd., 111 W 57th St, New York, NY 10019 .

320.9479 USA ISSN 1740-8407
COUNTRY PROFILE. BURUNDI; annual survey of political and economic background. 195?-2009 (Feb.). a. Economist Intelligence Unit Ltd., 111 W 57th St, New York, NY 10019 .

320.959 330.9 USA ISSN 1740-8326
COUNTRY PROFILE. CAMBODIA; annual survey of political and economic background. 1952-2009 (Feb.). a. Economist Intelligence Unit Ltd., 111 W 57th St, New York, NY 10019 .

320.967 330.9 USA ISSN 1741-0169
COUNTRY PROFILE. CAMEROON. 1952-2009 (Feb.). a. Economist Intelligence Unit Ltd., 111 W 57th St, New York, NY 10019 .

320.971 330.9 USA ISSN 0269-4379
COUNTRY PROFILE. CANADA. 1952-2009 (Feb.). a. Economist Intelligence Unit Ltd., 111 W 57th St, New York, NY 10019 .

320.9479 330.9 USA ISSN 1741-0282
COUNTRY PROFILE. CAPE VERDE; annual survey of political and economic background. 195?-2009 (Feb.). a. Economist Intelligence Unit Ltd., 111 W 57th St, New York, NY 10019 .

320.9479 USA
COUNTRY PROFILE. CAYMAN ISLANDS; annual survey of political and economic background. 195?-2009 (Feb.). a. Economist Intelligence Unit Ltd., 111 W 57th St, New York, NY 10019 .

330.9549 320 USA ISSN 1741-0177
COUNTRY PROFILE. CENTRAL AFRICAN REPUBLIC. 195?-2009 (Feb.). a. Economist Intelligence Unit Ltd., 111 W 57th St, New York, NY 10019 .

320.9479 330.9 USA ISSN 1741-0185
COUNTRY PROFILE. CHAD; annual survey of political and economic background. 2003-2009 (Feb.). a. Economist Intelligence Unit Ltd., 111 W 57th St, New York, NY 10019 .

320.983 330.9 USA ISSN 0269-5081
COUNTRY PROFILE. CHILE. 1952-2009 (Feb.). a. Economist Intelligence Unit Ltd., 111 W 57th St, New York, NY 10019 .

320.951 330.9 USA ISSN 1473-9143
COUNTRY PROFILE. CHINA; annual survey of political and economic background. 1952-2009 (Feb.). a. Economist Intelligence Unit Ltd., 111 W 57th St, New York, NY 10019 .

320.9861 330.9 USA ISSN 0269-5103
COUNTRY PROFILE. COLOMBIA; annual survey of political and economic background. 1952-2009 (Feb.). a. Economist Intelligence Unit Ltd., 111 W 57th St, New York, NY 10019 .

320.9479 USA ISSN 1741-0207
COUNTRY PROFILE. COMOROS; annual survey of political and economic background. 195?-2009 (Feb.). a. Economist Intelligence Unit Ltd., 111 W 57th St, New York, NY 10019 .

320.96724 320 330.9 USA ISSN 1369-4863
COUNTRY PROFILE. CONGO (BRAZZAVILLE); annual survey of political and economic background. 1952-2009 (Feb.). a. Economist Intelligence Unit Ltd., 111 W 57th St, New York, NY 10019 .

320.97286 USA ISSN 1366-4182
COUNTRY PROFILE. COSTA RICA; annual survey of political and economic background. 1952-2009 (Feb.). a. Economist Intelligence Unit Ltd., 111 W 57th St, New York, NY 10019 .

320.966 330.9 USA ISSN 1475-0104
COUNTRY PROFILE. COTE D'IVOIRE; annual survey of political and economic background. 1952-2009 (Feb.). a. Economist Intelligence Unit Ltd., 111 W 57th St, New York, NY 10019 .

320.949742 USA ISSN 1462-6837
COUNTRY PROFILE. CROATIA; annual survey of political and economic background. 1952-2009 (Feb.). a. Economist Intelligence Unit Ltd., 111 W 57th St, New York, NY 10019 .

320.97291 330.9 USA ISSN 0269-5111
COUNTRY PROFILE. CUBA. 1952-2009. a. Economist Intelligence Unit Ltd., 111 W 57th St, New York, NY 10019 .

320.9569 330.9 USA ISSN 1741-007X
COUNTRY PROFILE. CYPRUS; annual survey of political and economic background. 1993-2009 (Feb.). a. Economist Intelligence Unit Ltd., 111 W 57th St, New York, NY 10019 .

320.94371 330.9 USA ISSN 1366-4204
COUNTRY PROFILE. CZECH REPUBLIC; annual survey of political and economic background. 1952-2009 (Feb.). a. Economist Intelligence Unit Ltd., 111 W 57th St, New York, NY 10019 .

320.96751 USA ISSN 1369-4847
COUNTRY PROFILE. DEMOCRATIC REPUBLIC OF CONGO. 195?-2009 (Feb.). a. Economist Intelligence Unit Ltd., 111 W 57th St, New York, NY 10019 .

320.9489 330.9 USA ISSN 0264-486X
COUNTRY PROFILE. DENMARK; annual survey of political and economic background. 1952-2009 (Feb.). a. Economist Intelligence Unit Ltd., 111 W 57th St, New York, NY 10019 .

320.9479 USA ISSN 1740-8369
COUNTRY PROFILE. DJIBOUTI; annual survey of political and economic background. 195?-2009 (Feb.). a. Economist Intelligence Unit Ltd., 111 W 57th St, New York, NY 10019 .

320.9729 USA ISSN 1740-9683
COUNTRY PROFILE. DOMINICAN REPUBLIC; annual survey of political and economic background. 195?-2009 (Feb.). a. Economist Intelligence Unit Ltd., 111 W 57th St, New York, NY 10019 .

320.9866 330.9 USA ISSN 0269-7971
COUNTRY PROFILE. ECUADOR. 1952-2009 (Feb.). a. Economist Intelligence Unit Ltd., 111 W 57th St, New York, NY 10019 .

320.962 330.9 USA ISSN 0269-5227
COUNTRY PROFILE. EGYPT; annual survey of political and economic background. 1952-2009 (Feb.). a. Economist Intelligence Unit Ltd., 111 W 57th St, New York, NY 10019 .

320.9479 330.9 USA ISSN 1473-9208
COUNTRY PROFILE. EL SALVADOR; annual survey of political and economic background. 195?-2009 (Feb.). a. Economist Intelligence Unit Ltd., 111 W 57th St, New York, NY 10019 .

320.9479 330.9 USA ISSN 1741-0320
COUNTRY PROFILE. EQUATORIAL GUINEA; annual survey of political and economic background. 195?-2009 (Feb.). a. Economist Intelligence Unit Ltd., 111 W 57th St, New York, NY 10019 .

320.9479 330.9 USA ISSN 1740-8342
COUNTRY PROFILE. ERITREA; annual survey of political and economic background. 195?-2009 (Feb.). a. Economist Intelligence Unit Ltd., 111 W 57th St, New York, NY 10019 .

320.9479 330.9 USA ISSN 1462-6799
COUNTRY PROFILE. ESTONIA. 195?-2009 (Feb.). a. Economist Intelligence Unit Ltd., 111 W 57th St, New York, NY 10019 .

320.963 330.9 USA ISSN 1364-7369
COUNTRY PROFILE. ETHIOPIA; annual survey of political and economic background. 1952-2009 (Feb.). a. Economist Intelligence Unit Ltd., 111 W 57th St, New York, NY 10019 .

320.94 USA ISSN 1368-4477
COUNTRY PROFILE. EUROPEAN UNION; annual survey of political and economic background. 1998-2009 (Feb.). a. Economist Intelligence Unit Ltd., 111 W 57th St, New York, NY 10019 .

330 USA
COUNTRY PROFILE. FIJI. 195?-2009 (Feb.). a. Economist Intelligence Unit Ltd., 111 W 57th St, New York, NY 10019 .

320.94897 330.9 USA ISSN 0269-5332
COUNTRY PROFILE. FINLAND. 1952-2009 (Feb.). a. Economist Intelligence Unit Ltd., 111 W 57th St, New York, NY 10019 .

320.944 330.9 USA ISSN 0269-5340
COUNTRY PROFILE. FRANCE. 195?-2009 (Feb.). a. Economist Intelligence Unit Ltd., 111 W 57th St, New York, NY 10019 .

320.9672 330.9 USA ISSN 1741-0312
COUNTRY PROFILE. GABON. 1952-2009 (Feb.). a. Economist Intelligence Unit Ltd., 111 W 57th St, New York, NY 10019 .

320.9475 330.9 USA ISSN 1741-0002
COUNTRY PROFILE. GEORGIA; annual survey of political and economic background. 1952-2009 (Feb.). a. Economist Intelligence Unit Ltd., 111 W 57th St, New York, NY 10019 .

320.943 USA ISSN 0968-7858
COUNTRY PROFILE. GERMANY; annual survey of political and economic background. 1992-2009 (Feb.). a. Economist Intelligence Unit Ltd., 111 W 57th St, New York, NY 10019 .

320.9667 330.9 USA ISSN 0269-4549
COUNTRY PROFILE. GHANA. 1986-2009 (Feb.). a. Economist Intelligence Unit Ltd., 111 W 57th St, New York, NY 10019 .

320.9495 330.9 USA ISSN 0269-5367
COUNTRY PROFILE. GREECE. 1952-2009 (Feb.). a. Economist Intelligence Unit Ltd., 111 W 57th St, New York, NY 10019 .

320.97281 330.9 USA ISSN 1473-9194
COUNTRY PROFILE. GUATEMALA; annual survey of political and economic background. 1952-2009 (Feb.). a. Economist Intelligence Unit Ltd., 111 W 57th St, New York, NY 10019 .

320.9665 330.9 USA ISSN 1741-0215
COUNTRY PROFILE. GUINEA; annual survey of political and economic background. 1952-2009 (Feb.). a. Economist Intelligence Unit Ltd., 111 W 57th St, New York, NY 10019 .

320.9479 330.9 USA ISSN 1741-0274
COUNTRY PROFILE. GUINEA-BISSAU; annual survey of political and economic background. 1993-2009 (Feb.). a. Economist Intelligence Unit Ltd., 111 W 57th St, New York, NY 10019 .

320.9881 330.9 USA ISSN 1741-0053
COUNTRY PROFILE. GUYANA; annual survey of political and economic background. 1952-2009 (Feb.). a. Economist Intelligence Unit Ltd., 111 W 57th St, New York, NY 10019 .

320.9479 USA ISSN 1740-9691
COUNTRY PROFILE. HAITI; annual survey of political and economic background. 195?-2009 (Feb.). a. Economist Intelligence Unit Ltd., 111 W 57th St, New York, NY 10019 .

330.9549 USA ISSN 1473-9186
COUNTRY PROFILE. HONDURAS; annual survey of political and economic background. 195?-2009 (Feb.). a. Economist Intelligence Unit Ltd., 111 W 57th St, New York, NY 10019 .

320.9512 330.9 USA ISSN 1741-024X
COUNTRY PROFILE. HONG KONG; annual survey of political and economic background. 1952-2009 (Feb.). a. Economist Intelligence Unit Ltd., 111 W 57th St, New York, NY 10019 .

320.9439 USA ISSN 0269-6061
COUNTRY PROFILE. HUNGARY. 1952-2009 (Feb.). a. Economist Intelligence Unit Ltd., 111 W 57th St, New York, NY 10019 .

320.9479 330.9 USA ISSN 0264-6102
COUNTRY PROFILE. ICELAND; annual survey of political and economic background. 195?-2009 (Feb.). a. Economist Intelligence Unit Ltd., 111 W 57th St, New York, NY 10019 .

320.954 330.9 USA ISSN 1473-9127
COUNTRY PROFILE. INDIA; annual survey of political and economic background. 1952-2009 (Feb.). a. Economist Intelligence Unit Ltd., 111 W 57th St, New York, NY 10019 .

320.9598 330.9 USA ISSN 0269-5375
COUNTRY PROFILE. INDONESIA; annual survey of political and economic background. 1952-2009. a. Economist Intelligence Unit Ltd., 111 W 57th St, New York, NY 10019 .

320.955 330.9 USA ISSN 0269-5960
COUNTRY PROFILE. IRAN; annual survey of political and economic background. 1952-2009 (Feb.). a. Economist Intelligence Unit Ltd., 111 W 57th St, New York, NY 10019 .

320.9567 330.9 USA ISSN 0269-4395
COUNTRY PROFILE. IRAQ; annual survey of political and economic background. 1952-2009 (Feb.). a. Economist Intelligence Unit Ltd., 111 W 57th St, New York, NY 10019 .

320.9417 330.9 USA ISSN 0269-5324
COUNTRY PROFILE. IRELAND; annual survey of political and economic background. 1952-2009 (Feb.). a. Economist Intelligence Unit Ltd., 111 W 57th St, New York, NY 10019 .

320.95694 USA ISSN 1740-9624
COUNTRY PROFILE. ISRAEL. 1952-2009 (Feb.). a. Economist Intelligence Unit Ltd., 111 W 57th St, New York, NY 10019 .

320.945 320 330.9 USA ISSN 0269-5391
COUNTRY PROFILE. ITALY; annual survey of political and economic background. 1952-2009 (Feb.). a. Economist Intelligence Unit Ltd., 111 W 57th St, New York, NY 10019 .

320.952 330.9 USA ISSN 0269-5405
COUNTRY PROFILE. JAPAN; annual survey of political and economic background. 1952-2009 (Feb.). a. Economist Intelligence Unit Ltd., 111 W 57th St, New York, NY 10019 .

320.95695 320 320.9 USA ISSN 0269-8072
COUNTRY PROFILE. JORDAN; annual survey of political and economic background. 1952-2009 (Feb.). a. Economist Intelligence Unit Ltd., 111 W 57th St, New York, NY 10019 .

320.994345 320 330.9 USA ISSN 1364-3541
COUNTRY PROFILE. KAZAKHSTAN; annual survey of political and economic background. 1952-2009 (Feb.). a. Economist Intelligence Unit Ltd., 111 W 57th St, New York, NY 10019 .

320.96762 330.9 USA ISSN 0269-4530
COUNTRY PROFILE. KENYA; annual survey of political and economic background. 1986-2009 (Feb.). a. Economist Intelligence Unit Ltd., 111 W 57th St, New York, NY 10019 .

320.95367 320 330.9 USA ISSN 0269-7327
COUNTRY PROFILE. KUWAIT; annual survey of political and economic background. 1952-2009 (Feb.). a. Economist Intelligence Unit Ltd., 111 W 57th St, New York, NY 10019 .

320.958 USA ISSN 1741-0029
COUNTRY PROFILE. KYRGYZ REPUBLIC; annual survey of political and economic background. 1952-2009 (Feb.). a. Economist Intelligence Unit Ltd., 111 W 57th St, New York, NY 10019 .

320.9479 330.9 USA ISSN 1740-8334
COUNTRY PROFILE. LAOS; annual survey of political and economic background. 195?-2009 (Feb.). a. Economist Intelligence Unit Ltd., 111 W 57th St, New York, NY 10019 .

330.9 USA ISSN 1462-6802
COUNTRY PROFILE. LATVIA; annual survey of political and economic background. 195?-2009 (Feb.). a. Economist Intelligence Unit Ltd., 111 W 57th St, New York, NY 10019 .

320.95692 330.9 USA ISSN 1352-0962
COUNTRY PROFILE. LEBANON; annual survey of political and economic background. 1952-2009 (Feb.). a. Economist Intelligence Unit Ltd., 111 W 57th St, New York, NY 10019 .

320.9479 USA ISSN 1741-0304
COUNTRY PROFILE. LESOTHO; annual survey of political and economic background. 195?-2009 (Feb.). a. Economist Intelligence Unit Ltd., 111 W 57th St, New York, NY 10019 .

320.9479 330.9 USA ISSN 1741-0231
COUNTRY PROFILE. LIBERIA; annual survey of political and economic background. 1992-2009 (Feb.). a. Economist Intelligence Unit Ltd., 111 W 57th St, New York, NY 10019 .

320.9612 330.9 USA ISSN 0269-6347
COUNTRY PROFILE. LIBYA; annual survey of political and economic background. 1952-2009 (Feb.). a. Economist Intelligence Unit Ltd., 111 W 57th St, New York, NY 10019 .

320.9479 USA ISSN 1462-6810
COUNTRY PROFILE. LITHUANIA; annual survey of political and economic background. 1952-2009 (Feb.). a. Economist Intelligence Unit Ltd., 111 W 57th St, New York, NY 10019 .

320.9479 330.9 USA ISSN 0264-6129
COUNTRY PROFILE. LUXEMBOURG; annual survey of political and economic background. 195?-2009 (Feb.). a. Economist Intelligence Unit Ltd., 111 W 57th St, New York, NY 10019 .

320.9479 330.9 USA ISSN 1741-0258
COUNTRY PROFILE. MACAU; annual survey of political and economic background. 195?-2009 (Feb.). a. Economist Intelligence Unit Ltd., 111 W 57th St, New York, NY 10019 .

320.9497 USA ISSN 1462-6780
COUNTRY PROFILE. MACEDONIA; annual survey of political and economic background. 195?-2009 (Feb.). a. Economist Intelligence Unit Ltd., 111 W 57th St, New York, NY 10019 .

320.9691 USA ISSN 1351-8747
COUNTRY PROFILE. MADAGASCAR; annual survey of political and economic background. 195?-2009 (Feb.). a. Economist Intelligence Unit Ltd., 111 W 57th St, New York, NY 10019 .

320.96897 330.9 USA ISSN 0269-4522
COUNTRY PROFILE. MALAWI; annual survey of political and economic background. 1986-2009 (Feb.). a. Economist Intelligence Unit Ltd., 111 W 57th St, New York, NY 10019 .

320.9595 330.9 USA ISSN 1741-0096
COUNTRY PROFILE. MALAYSIA; annual survey of political and economic background. 1952-2009 (Feb.). a. Economist Intelligence Unit Ltd., 111 W 57th St, New York, NY 10019 .

320.9479 330.9 USA ISSN 1741-0436
COUNTRY PROFILE. MALI; annual survey of political and economic background. 2003-2009 (Feb.). a. Economist Intelligence Unit Ltd., 111 W 57th St, New York, NY 10019 .

320.9479 USA ISSN 1741-0088
COUNTRY PROFILE. MALTA; annual survey of political and economic background. 195?-2009 (Feb.). a. Economist Intelligence Unit Ltd., 111 W 57th St, New York, NY 10019 .

320.9479 USA ISSN 1741-0371
COUNTRY PROFILE. MAURITANIA; annual survey of political and economic background. 1993-2009 (Feb.). a. Economist Intelligence Unit Ltd., 111 W 57th St, New York, NY 10019 .

320.9698 330.9 USA ISSN 1740-9640
COUNTRY PROFILE. MAURITIUS; annual survey of political and economic background. 1986-2009 (Feb.). a. Economist Intelligence Unit Ltd., 111 W 57th St, New York, NY 10019 .

320.972 330.9 USA ISSN 0269-5596
COUNTRY PROFILE. MEXICO; annual survey of political and economic background. 1952-2009 (Feb.). a. Economist Intelligence Unit Ltd., 111 W 57th St, New York, NY 10019 .

320.9479 USA ISSN 1740-9675
COUNTRY PROFILE. MOLDOVA; annual survey of political and economic background. 195?-2009 (Feb.). a. Economist Intelligence Unit Ltd., 111 W 57th St, New York, NY 10019 .

320.9479 330.9 USA ISSN 1741-0347
COUNTRY PROFILE. MONGOLIA; annual survey of political and economic background. 195?-2009 (Feb.). a. Economist Intelligence Unit Ltd., 111 W 57th St, New York, NY 10019 .

330.949745 USA ISSN 1756-4344
COUNTRY PROFILE. MONTENEGRO. 199?-2009 (Feb.). a. Economist Intelligence Unit Ltd., 111 W 57th St, New York, NY 10019 .

320.964 330.9 USA ISSN 0269-6614
COUNTRY PROFILE. MOROCCO; annual survey of political and economic background. 1952-2009 (Feb.). a. Economist Intelligence Unit Ltd., 111 W 57th St, New York, NY 10019 .

320.9679 USA ISSN 0269-7017
COUNTRY PROFILE. MOZAMBIQUE; annual survey of political and economic background. 195?-2009 (Feb.). a. Economist Intelligence Unit Ltd., 111 W 57th St, New York, NY 10019 .

320.9591 320 330.9 USA ISSN 1364-3533
COUNTRY PROFILE. MYANMAR; annual survey of political and economic background. 1952-2009 (Feb.). a. Economist Intelligence Unit Ltd., 111 W 57th St, New York, NY 10019 .

320.9688 330.9 USA ISSN 1740-8377
COUNTRY PROFILE. NAMIBIA; annual survey of political and economic background. 195?-2009 (Feb.). a. Economist Intelligence Unit Ltd., 111 W 57th St, New York, NY 10019 .

Cessations

320.9479 330.9 USA ISSN 1741-0339
COUNTRY PROFILE. NEPAL; annual survey of political and economic background. 195?-2009 (Feb.). a. Economist Intelligence Unit Ltd., 111 W 57th St, New York, NY 10019 .

320.9492 330.9 USA ISSN 0264-4886
COUNTRY PROFILE. NETHERLANDS; annual survey of political and economic background. 1981-2009 (Feb.). a. Economist Intelligence Unit Ltd., 111 W 57th St, New York, NY 10019 .

320.993 330.9 USA ISSN 0269-5618
COUNTRY PROFILE. NEW ZEALAND; annual survey of political and economic background. 1952-2009 (Feb.). a. Economist Intelligence Unit Ltd., 111 W 57th St, New York, NY 10019 .

320.9728 330.9 USA ISSN 1473-9178
COUNTRY PROFILE. NICARAGUA; annual survey of political and economic background. 1993-2009 (Feb.). a. Economist Intelligence Unit Ltd., 111 W 57th St, New York, NY 10019 .

320.9662 330.9 USA ISSN 1741-0428
COUNTRY PROFILE. NIGER; annual survey of political and economic background. 1952-2009 (Feb.). a. Economist Intelligence Unit Ltd., 111 W 57th St, New York, NY 10019 .

320.9669 330.9 USA ISSN 0269-6339
COUNTRY PROFILE. NIGERIA; annual survey of political and economic background. 1952-2009 (Feb.). a. Economist Intelligence Unit Ltd., 111 W 57th St, New York, NY 10019 .

330.9549 320 USA ISSN 1740-9489
COUNTRY PROFILE. NORTH KOREA; annual survey of political and economic background. 1993-2009 (Feb.). a. Economist Intelligence Unit Ltd., 111 W 57th St, New York, NY 10019 .

320.9481 330.9 USA ISSN 0269-5626
COUNTRY PROFILE. NORWAY; annual survey of political and economic background. 1952-2009 (Feb.). a. Economist Intelligence Unit Ltd., 111 W 57th St, New York, NY 10019 .

320.95353 330.9 USA ISSN 1367-6148
COUNTRY PROFILE. OMAN; annual survey of political and economic background. 1952-2009 (Feb.). a. Economist Intelligence Unit Ltd., 111 W 57th St, New York, NY 10019 .

320.9965 USA
COUNTRY PROFILE. PACIFIC ISLANDS: FIJI, SOLOMON ISLANDS, TONGA; annual survey of political and economic background. 1952-2009 (Feb.). a. Economist Intelligence Unit Ltd., 111 W 57th St, New York, NY 10019 .

320.9549 330.9 USA ISSN 1741-0142
COUNTRY PROFILE. PAKISTAN; annual survey of political and economic background. 1952-2009 (Feb.). a. Economist Intelligence Unit Ltd., 111 W 57th St, New York, NY 10019 .

320.97287 330.9 USA ISSN 1366-4190
COUNTRY PROFILE. PANAMA; annual survey of political and economic background. 1952-2009 (Feb.). a. Economist Intelligence Unit Ltd., 111 W 57th St, New York, NY 10019 .

320.9479 USA ISSN 1473-916X
COUNTRY PROFILE. PARAGUAY; annual survey of political and economic background. 195?-2009 (Feb.). a. Economist Intelligence Unit Ltd., 111 W 57th St, New York, NY 10019 .

320.985 USA ISSN 0269-5944
COUNTRY PROFILE. PERU; annual survey of political and economic background. 195?-2009 (Feb.). a. Economist Intelligence Unit Ltd., 111 W 57th St, New York, NY 10019 .

320.9599 USA ISSN 0269-5979
COUNTRY PROFILE. PHILIPPINES; annual survey of political and economic background. 1952-2009 (Feb.). a. Economist Intelligence Unit Ltd., 111 W 57th St, New York, NY 10019 .

320.9438 USA ISSN 0269-5219
COUNTRY PROFILE. POLAND; annual survey of political and economic background. 1952-2009 (Feb.). a. Economist Intelligence Unit Ltd., 111 W 57th St, New York, NY 10019 .

320.9469 USA ISSN 0269-5987
COUNTRY PROFILE. PORTUGAL; annual survey of political and economic background. 1952-2009 (Feb.). a. Economist Intelligence Unit Ltd., 111 W 57th St, New York, NY 10019 .

320.9479 330.9 USA ISSN 1473-9119
COUNTRY PROFILE. QATAR; annual survey of political and economic background. 195?-2009 (Feb.). a. Economist Intelligence Unit Ltd., 111 W 57th St, New York, NY 10019 .

320.9498 USA ISSN 0269-638X
COUNTRY PROFILE. ROMANIA; annual survey of political and economic background. 195?-2009 (Feb.). a. Economist Intelligence Unit Ltd., 111 W 57th St, New York, NY 10019 .

320.947 USA ISSN 0969-627X
COUNTRY PROFILE. RUSSIA; annual survey of political and economic background. 195?-2009 (Feb.). a. Economist Intelligence Unit Ltd., 111 W 57th St, New York, NY 10019 .

320.96757 USA ISSN 1740-8393
COUNTRY PROFILE. RWANDA; annual survey of political and economic background. 1952-2009 (Feb.). a. Economist Intelligence Unit Ltd., 111 W 57th St, New York, NY 10019 .

320.9671 330.9 USA ISSN 1741-0266
COUNTRY PROFILE. SAO TOME AND PRINCIPE; annual survey of political and economic background. 1993-2009 (Feb.). a. Economist Intelligence Unit Ltd., 111 W 57th St, New York, NY 10019 .

320.9538 USA ISSN 0269-6355
COUNTRY PROFILE. SAUDI ARABIA; annual survey of political and economic background. 1952-2009 (Feb.). a. Economist Intelligence Unit Ltd., 111 W 57th St, New York, NY 10019 .

320.9479 USA ISSN 1756-4352
COUNTRY PROFILE. SERBIA. 199?-2009 (Feb.). a. Economist Intelligence Unit Ltd., 111 W 57th St, New York, NY 10019 .

320.9479 330.9 USA ISSN 1740-9659
COUNTRY PROFILE. SEYCHELLES; annual survey of political and economic background. 195?-2009 (Feb.). a. Economist Intelligence Unit Ltd., 111 W 57th St, New York, NY 10019 .

320.9479 330.9 USA ISSN 1741-0223
COUNTRY PROFILE. SIERRA LEONE; annual survey of political and economic background. 199?-2009 (Feb.). a. Economist Intelligence Unit Ltd., 111 W 57th St, New York, NY 10019 .

320.95957 USA ISSN 0269-7041
COUNTRY PROFILE. SINGAPORE; annual survey of political and economic background. 1952-2009 (Feb.). a. Economist Intelligence Unit Ltd., 111 W 57th St, New York, NY 10019 .

320.94373 USA ISSN 1366-4212
COUNTRY PROFILE. SLOVAKIA; annual survey of political and economic background. 1952-2009 (Feb.). a. Economist Intelligence Unit Ltd., 111 W 57th St, New York, NY 10019 .

320.94973 320 330.9 USA ISSN 1366-4255
COUNTRY PROFILE. SLOVENIA; annual survey of political and economic background. 1952-2009 (Feb.). a. Economist Intelligence Unit Ltd., 111 W 57th St, New York, NY 10019 .

320.9479 330.9 USA ISSN 1740-8350
COUNTRY PROFILE. SOMALIA; annual survey of political and economic background. 2004-195? (Feb.). a. Economist Intelligence Unit Ltd., 111 W 57th St, New York, NY 10019 .

320.968 USA ISSN 0269-8153
COUNTRY PROFILE. SOUTH AFRICA; annual survey of political and economic background. 1952-2009 (Feb.). a. Economist Intelligence Unit Ltd., 111 W 57th St, New York, NY 10019 .

320.9519 USA ISSN 1740-9470
COUNTRY PROFILE. SOUTH KOREA; annual survey of political and economic background. 1952-2009 (Feb.). a. Economist Intelligence Unit Ltd., 111 W 57th St, New York, NY 10019 .

320.946 USA ISSN 0269-5995
COUNTRY PROFILE. SPAIN; annual survey of political and economic background. 1952-2009 (Feb.). a. Economist Intelligence Unit Ltd., 111 W 57th St, New York, NY 10019 .

320.95493 USA ISSN 0269-5073
COUNTRY PROFILE. SRI LANKA; annual survey of political and economic background. 1952-2009 (Feb.). a. Economist Intelligence Unit Ltd., 111 W 57th St, New York, NY 10019 .

320.9624 USA ISSN 0269-705X
COUNTRY PROFILE. SUDAN; annual survey of political and economic background. 1952-2009 (Feb.). a. Economist Intelligence Unit Ltd., 111 W 57th St, New York, NY 10019 .

320.9479 USA ISSN 1741-0061
COUNTRY PROFILE. SURINAME; annual survey of political and economic background. 199?-2009 (Feb.). a. Economist Intelligence Unit Ltd., 111 W 57th St, New York, NY 10019 .

320.9479 USA ISSN 1740-8385
COUNTRY PROFILE. SWAZILAND; annual survey of political and economic background. 195?-2009 (Feb.). a. Economist Intelligence Unit Ltd., 111 W 57th St, New York, NY 10019 .

320.9485 USA ISSN 0269-6002
COUNTRY PROFILE. SWEDEN; annual survey of political and economic background. 1952-2009 (Feb.). a. Economist Intelligence Unit Ltd., 111 W 57th St, New York, NY 10019 .

320.9494 USA ISSN 0269-6010
COUNTRY PROFILE. SWITZERLAND; annual survey of political and economic background. 1952-2009. a. Economist Intelligence Unit Ltd., 111 W 57th St, New York, NY 10019 .

320.95691 USA ISSN 0269-6045
COUNTRY PROFILE. SYRIA; annual survey of political and economic background. 1952-2009 (Feb.). a. Economist Intelligence Unit Ltd., 111 W 57th St, New York, NY 10019 .

320.967 USA ISSN 1741-0193
COUNTRY PROFILE. TANZANIA; annual survey of political and economic background. 195?-2009 (Feb.). a. Economist Intelligence Unit Ltd., 111 W 57th St, New York, NY 10019 .

320.9593 USA ISSN 1364-9604
COUNTRY PROFILE. THAILAND; annual survey of political and economic background. 1952-2009 (Feb.). a. Economist Intelligence Unit Ltd., 111 W 57th St, New York, NY 10019 .

320.9665 USA ISSN 1741-0363
COUNTRY PROFILE. THE GAMBIA; annual survey of political and economic background. 2003-2009 (Feb.). a. Economist Intelligence Unit Ltd., 111 W 57th St, New York, NY 10019 .

320.9479 330.9 USA ISSN 1740-9632
COUNTRY PROFILE. THE PALESTINIAN TERRITORIES; annual survey of political and economic background. 195?-2009 (Feb.). a. Economist Intelligence Unit Ltd., 111 W 57th St, New York, NY 10019 .

320.9668 USA ISSN 1740-8415
COUNTRY PROFILE. TOGO; annual survey of political and economic background. 1987-2009 (Feb.). a. Economist Intelligence Unit Ltd., 111 W 57th St, New York, NY 10019 .

320.9729 USA ISSN 1741-0045
COUNTRY PROFILE. TRINIDAD AND TOBAGO; annual survey of political and economic background. 1994-2009 (Feb.). a. Economist Intelligence Unit Ltd., 111 W 57th St, New York, NY 10019 .

320.9561 USA ISSN 0269-6029
COUNTRY PROFILE. TURKEY; annual survey of political and economic background. 195?-2009 (Feb.). a. Economist Intelligence Unit Ltd., 111 W 57th St, New York, NY 10019 .

320.9479 USA ISSN 1462-6853
COUNTRY PROFILE. TURKMENISTAN; annual survey of political and economic background. 195?-2009 (Feb.). a. Economist Intelligence Unit Ltd., 111 W 57th St, New York, NY 10019 .

320.9479 USA
COUNTRY PROFILE. TURKS AND CAICOS ISLANDS; annual survey of political and economic background. 195?-2009 (Feb.). a. Economist Intelligence Unit Ltd., 111 W 57th St, New York, NY 10019 .

320.96761 USA ISSN 0269-7076
COUNTRY PROFILE. UGANDA; annual survey of political and economic background. 1952-2009 (Feb.). a. Economist Intelligence Unit Ltd., 111 W 57th St, New York, NY 10019 .

320.9477 USA ISSN 1356-4196
COUNTRY PROFILE. UKRAINE; annual survey of political and economic background. 195?-2009 (Feb.). a. Economist Intelligence Unit Ltd., 111 W 57th St, New York, NY 10019 .

320.95357 USA ISSN 0269-6606
COUNTRY PROFILE. UNITED ARAB EMIRATES; annual survey of political and economic background. 1952-2009 (Feb.). a. Economist Intelligence Unit Ltd., 111 W 57th St, New York, NY 10019 .

320.941 USA ISSN 0269-798X
COUNTRY PROFILE. UNITED KINGDOM; annual survey of political and economic background. 1952-2009 (Feb.). a. Economist Intelligence Unit Ltd., 111 W 57th St, New York, NY 10019 .

320.973 USA ISSN 0269-8005
COUNTRY PROFILE. UNITED STATES OF AMERICA; annual survey of political and economic background. 1952-2009 (Feb.). a. Economist Intelligence Unit Ltd., 111 W 57th St, New York, NY 10019 .

320.9479 USA ISSN 1366-4271
COUNTRY PROFILE. UZBEKISTAN; annual survey of political and economic background. 195?-2009 (Feb.). a. Economist Intelligence Unit Ltd., 111 W 57th St, New York, NY 10019 .

320.987 USA ISSN 1352-0954
COUNTRY PROFILE. VENEZUELA; annual survey of political and economic background. 1952-2009 (Feb.). a. Economist Intelligence Unit Ltd., 111 W 57th St, New York, NY 10019 .

320.9597 USA ISSN 1356-4145
COUNTRY PROFILE. VIETNAM; annual survey of political and economic background. 195?-2009 (Feb.). a. Economist Intelligence Unit Ltd., 111 W 57th St, New York, NY 10019 .

320.9479 USA
COUNTRY PROFILE. WINDWARD AND LEEWARD ISLANDS; annual survey of political and economic background. ceased 2009 (Feb.). a. Economist Intelligence Unit Ltd., 111 W 57th St, New York, NY 10019 .

320.9533 320 330.9 USA ISSN 1367-6156
COUNTRY PROFILE. YEMEN; annual survey of political and economic background. 1952-2009 (Feb.). a. Economist Intelligence Unit Ltd., 111 W 57th St, New York, NY 10019 .

320.96894 USA ISSN 0269-7300
COUNTRY PROFILE. ZAMBIA; annual survey of political and economic background. 1952-2009 (Feb.). a. Economist Intelligence Unit Ltd., 111 W 57th St, New York, NY 10019 .

320.96891 USA ISSN 0269-4360
COUNTRY PROFILE. ZIMBABWE; annual survey of political and economic background. 1952-2009 (Feb.). a. Economist Intelligence Unit Ltd., 111 W 57th St, New York, NY 10019 .

747 729 745.5 USA ISSN 1066-5102
COUNTRY SAMPLER'S DECORATING IDEAS. 1993-2006. bi-m. Emmis Publishing LP, 707 Kautz Rd, St. Charles, IL 60174.

728 USA ISSN 1538-3911
COUNTRY STYLE HOMES, PLANS AND DESIGNS. 1991-2009 (Jan.). q. HomePlans.com, 901 N 3rd St, Ste 216, Minneapolis, MN 55401.

690 720 USA
COUNTRYPOLITAN HOMES & PLANS. 1992-2009 (Jan.). q. HomePlans.com, 213 E. 4th St., 4th Fl., St. Paul, MN 55101-1603.

650 USA ISSN 1064-539X
COUNTY BUSINESS PATTERNS (CD-ROM). (Consists of 1 report per state and a U.S. summary) 1987-200?. a. U.S. Census Bureau, 4600 Silver Hill Rd, Washington, DC 20233.

336 USA ISSN 0098-678X
COUNTY GOVERNMENT FINANCES. 1973-1992. a. U.S. Census Bureau, c/o Donna Hirsch, Governments Division, 4700 Silver Hill Rd., Washington, DC 20233.

387.15029 GBR ISSN 0260-7093
COUNTY GUIDE TO MARINE COMPANIES. 1980-ceased. a. C M P Information Ltd., Sovereign House, Sovereign Way, Tonbridge, Kent TN9 1RW, United Kingdom.

796.77 ITA ISSN 1591-0288
COUPE & CABRIO. 2000-ceased. a. Sprea Editori Srl, Via Torino 51, Cernusco sul Naviglio, MI 20063, Italy.

325 FRA ISSN 1163-5568
COUPLES D'AUJOURD'HUI. 1956-1973. q. Mouvement Francais pour le Planning Familial, 4 square Saint Irenee, Paris, 75011, France.

794.1 FRA ISSN 1272-5005
LE COURRIER DES ECHECS; revue mensuelle d'echecs par correspondance. 1947-200?. m. Association des Joueurs d'Echecs Par Correspondance, Chantalouette, Eygurande, 24700, France.

332 947 FRA ISSN 0590-0239
COURRIER DES PAYS DE L'EST. 1964-2008. bi-m. Documentation Francaise, 29-31 Quai Voltaire, Paris, Cedex 7 75344, France.

340 611 USA
COURTROOM MEDICINE: ABDOMINAL INJURIES. 1973-200?. plus a. updates. Matthew Bender & Co., Inc., 1275 Broadway, Albany, NY 12204.

340 611 USA
COURTROOM MEDICINE: SHOULDER AND ELBOW. 1970-200?. plus a. updates. Matthew Bender & Co., Inc., 1275 Broadway, Albany, NY 12204.

028.5 FRA ISSN 1267-1053
COUSTEAU JUNIOR. 1995-200?. m. Publications des Generations Futures, 10 rue Thierry-le-Luron, Levallois-Perret, Cedex 92592, France.

790 USA ISSN 1082-1376
CRAFTING TRADITIONS. 1983-2004. bi-m. Reiman Media Group, Inc., 5400 S 60th St, Greendale, WI 53129.

745 USA
CRAFTRENDS (ONLINE). 1982-2008 (Nov.). bi-w. C K Media LLC, 741 Corporate Circle, Ste A, Golden, CO 80401.

617 USA ISSN 1050-009X
CRANIO CLINICS INTERNATIONAL. 1991-1991 (vol.1, no.2). 3/yr. Lippincott Williams & Wilkins, 351 W Camden St, Baltimore, MD 21201.

747 FRA ISSN 1291-3138
CREATION PASSION. 1998-200?. bi-m. Publications Bonnier Hachette, 20 Rue de Billancourt, Boulogne-Billancourt, 92100, France.

700 FRA ISSN 0293-0196
CREATIONS. 1959-2006. q. Ecole Moderne Francaise - Pedagogie Freinet (P E M F), Mouans-Sartoux, 06376, France.

745.5 DEU
CREATIV TRENDS. 2004-2007 (Apr.). 16/yr. OZ Verlag GmbH, Roemerstr 90, Rheinfelden, 79618, Germany.

770 ITA
CREATIVE FOTOSTAMPA. 1988-ceased. m. E C I Italia S.r.l., Via Rucellai, 7, Milano, MI 20126, Italy.

746.4 DEU ISSN 1863-4222
CREATIVE HANDARBEITEN. 1991-2006 (Apr.). bi-m. OZ Verlag GmbH, Roemerstr 90, Rheinfelden, 79618, Germany.

641 USA ISSN 1532-5407
CREATIVE HOME. 1995-ceased. q. Meredith Corporation, 1716 Locust St, Des Moines, IA 50309.

690 NZL ISSN 1176-9084
CREATIVE IDEAS. 2006-2007. m. Hot Tin Roof, PO Box 105 301, Auckland, New Zealand.

745.5 USA ISSN 1936-8674
CREATIVE TECHNIQUES. 2006-ceased. q. All American Crafts, Inc., 7 Waterloo Rd, Stanhope, NJ 07874-2621.

746.9 FRA ISSN 1770-8753
CREATOP. 2004-2007. s-a. Creatop, 24 Rue d'Orsel, Paris, 75018, France.

330.9 ITA
CREDIT AND FINANCE IN ITALY. QUARTERLY BULLETIN. 1970 (no.16)-199?. q. Cassa di Risparmio delle Provincie Lombarde (Cariplo), Via Monte Di Pieta', 8, Milan, MI 20121, Italy.

346 332.7 NLD ISSN 1572-123X
CREDIT MANAGEMENT MAGAZINE. 1992-2008. q. Intrum Justitia, Postbus 84096, The Hague, 2508 AB, Netherlands.

690 ESP
CREMI DE CONSTRUCTORS D' OBRES. 1978-2008. 11/yr. Editorial Interpress' S.L., Apdo de Correos 14035, Barcelona, 08080, Spain.

796.358 AUS ISSN 0310-9356
CRICKET QUADRANT. 1973-1976. irreg. Australian Cricket Society, A.C.T. Branch, 91 Gouger St, Torrens, ACT 2607, Australia.

790.1 GBR ISSN 0266-7401
CRICKETER QUARTERLY FACTS AND FIGURES. 1973-2002. q. Sporting Magazines and Publishing Ltd, Ridge Farm, The Down, Lamberhurst, Tunbridge Wells, Kent TN3 8ER, United Kingdom.

364.12 USA ISSN 1089-8476
CRIME & DELINQUENCY NEWS. 19??-19??. m. Washington Council on Crime and Delinquency, 1305 4th Ave, Ste 602, Seattle, WA 98101-2401.

808.8 AUS ISSN 1444-5379
CRIME FACTORY; the Australian crime fiction magazine. 2001-2003. q. Express Media, Meat Market Art House, 42 Courtney St, North Melbourne, VIC 35051, Australia.

363.5021 USA ISSN 1088-4491
CRIME IN AMERICA'S TOP-RATED CITIES (YEARS); a statistical profile. 1995-2000. biennial. Grey House Publishing, 185 Millerton Rd, PO Box 860, Millerton, NY 12546.

364.9 USA ISSN 0194-0953
CRIMINAL JUSTICE HISTORY; an international annual. 1980-2003. irreg. Greenwood Publishing Group Inc., 88 Post Rd W, PO Box 5007, Westport, CT 06881.

345 AUS ISSN 1327-1636
CRIMINAL LAW LIBRARY ON CD-ROM. 1996-2003. m. Lawbook Co., PO Box 3502, Rozelle, NSW 2039, Australia.

800 700 ITA ISSN 0011-1406
CRISI E LETTERATURA; periodico di lettere filosofia arti. 1961-ceased. a. Gaetano Salveti Ed.& Pub., Via Bu Meliana, 12, Rome, RM 00195, Italy.

320 ITA ISSN 0390-0657
CRITICA DEL DIRITTO; stato e conflitto di classe. 1974-ceased. 3/yr. Sapere 2000 S.r.l., Via Filippo Turati, 48, Rome, RM 00185, Italy.

899 900 100 AUS ISSN 0070-1548
CRITICAL REVIEW. 1958-2002. a. James Cook University, PO Box 6811, Cairns, QLD 4870, Australia.

746 USA
CROCHET. 1981-ceased. q. Harris Publications, Inc., 800 Kennesaw Ave, Ste 220, Marietta, GA 30060.

282 FRA ISSN 1778-994X
CROIRE JEUNES. 1996-2007. bi-m. Bayard Presse, 3-5 rue Bayard, Paris, 75393 Cedex 08, France.

363.377 FRA ISSN 1774-9581
LA CROISADE D'ALICE; le mensuel de la prevention durable en pays provencaux. 2005-2005. m. Editions La Belugue, Quartier Saint Esprit, La Celle, 83170, France.

621.388 ITA
CRONACHE; per il personale de Gruppo Philips. 1959-ceased. bi-m. Philips SpA, Piazza Quattro Novembre, 3, Milan, MI 20124, Italy.

630 ITA
CRONACHE DELL'AGRICOLTURA. 1949-ceased. m. Unione Provinciale Agricoltori di Torino, Corso V. Emanuele 58, Turin, TO 10121, Italy.

388.324 ITA ISSN 1824-9582
CRONACHE E TRASPORTI DI PROFESSIONE CAMIONISTA. 2004-200?. m. Sprea Editori Srl, Via Torino 51, Cernusco sul Naviglio, MI 20063, Italy.

630 635 FRA ISSN 0263-9459 CODEN: CRUNDD
CRUCIFERAE NEWSLETTER. 1976-1991; resumed 1993-2004. a. European Association for Research on Plant Breeding, INRA - Station d'Amelioration des Plantes, Domaine de la Motte, BP 29, Le Rheu, 35653, France.

940 ESP ISSN 1132-7553
CUADERNOS DE ESTUDIOS MEDIEVALES Y CIENCIAS Y TECNICAS HISTORIOGRAFICAS. 1973-1995. a. Editorial Universidad de Granada, Antiguo Colegio Maximo, Campus de Cartuja, Granada, 18071, Spain.

610 ESP ISSN 1135-4127
CUADERNOS DE GESTION PARA EL PROFESIONAL DE ATENCION PRIMARIA. 1995-2005. q. Elsevier Doyma, Traversa de Gracia 17-21, Barcelona, 08021, Spain.

913.031 ESP ISSN 0211-3228
CUADERNOS DE PREHISTORIA. 1976-1992. a. Editorial Universidad de Granada, Antiguo Colegio Maximo, Campus de Cartuja, Granada, 18071, Spain.

910 ESP ISSN 1130-8079
CUADERNOS DE TOPONIMIA. 1985-1998. a. Instituto Alaves de Arqueologia, Plaza de la Provincia, s-n, Vitoria-Gasteiz, 01001, Spain.

551.46 ESP ISSN 0213-7208
CUADERNOS MARISQUEROS. PUBLICACION TECNICA. 1978-1991. irreg. Centro Experimental de Vilaxoan, Apartado 208, Vilagarcia De Arousa, Pontevedra 36600, Spain.

641.5 ITA ISSN 1827-7438
CUCINA (MILAN). 2006-200?. m. Ulysse Network, Viale Bianca Maria 19, Milan, Italy.

641.5 ITA ISSN 1591-1160
CUCINA CREATIVA. 2000-200?. m. Ulysse Network, Viale Bianca Maria 19, Milan, Italy.

640 ITA ISSN 1827-8485
LA CUCINA DELIZIOSA. 2006-ceased. m. Ulysse Network, Viale Bianca Maria 19, Milan, Italy.

641.5 ITA ISSN 1827-7446
CUCINA DOLCI. 2006-200?. m. Ulysse Network, Viale Bianca Maria 19, Milan, Italy.

641.5 641.22 ITA ISSN 1128-5486
CUCINA & VINI. 1999-200?. m. (11/yr.). Alexandra Editrice, Largo Lanciani 1, Roma, 00162, Italy.

641.5 ITA ISSN 1723-4026
CUCINA POPOLARE ITALIANA. 2003-200?. m. Edizioni Mimosa, Piazza E de Angeli 9, Milan, 20146, Italy.

641.5 ITA ISSN 1825-9316
CUCINA VEGETARIANA. 2005-200?. m. Edigamma Publishing, Via Sambuca Pistoiese 70A, Rome, 00138, Italy.

351 ESP ISSN 1577-855X
CUENTAS DE LAS ADMINISTRACIONES PUBLICAS DE MADRID. 1984-1996. a. Comunidad de Madrid, Instituto de Estadistica, Principe de Vargara 108, Madrid, 28002, Spain.

641.5 FRA ISSN 1760-0057
CUISINE CREATIVE. 2003-2006. q. Editions DIPA Burda, 26 Avenue de l'Europe, Strasbourg, 67013, France.

641.5 FRA ISSN 1620-1566
CUISINE ET TERROIRS. 2000-2008. q. Rustica S.A., 15-27 rue Moussorgski, Paris, 75895 Cedex 18, France.

641.5 FRA ISSN 1957-4622
CUISINONS SANTE. 2007-2007. q. Republic Press International, 19 Av. d'Italie, Paris, 75013, France.

641.5 NLD ISSN 1574-3918
CULINAIR JAARBOEK. 2004-2004. a. Uitgeverij Bas Lubberhuizen, Singel 389, Amsterdam, 1012 WN, Netherlands.

306.44 GBR
CULTURAL MARGINS. 1994-2002 (Jul.). irreg. Cambridge University Press, The Edinburgh Bldg, Shaftesbury Rd, Cambridge, CB2 8RU, United Kingdom.

001.3 AUS ISSN 1033-8713
CULTURE AND POLICY. 1989-1997. s-a. Griffith University, School of Humanities, PO Box 3370, South Brisbane, QLD 4101, Australia.

001.3 FRA ISSN 1245-2440
CULTURE - CULTURES. 1995-199?. a. Publidix, 200 av. de la Republique, Nanterre, Cedex 92001, France.

327 AUS ISSN 1322-6916
CULTURE MANDALA (PRINT). 1994-2005. irreg. Bond University, Faculty of Humanities and Social Sciences, University Dr., Robina, QLD 4226, Australia.

720 690 CHN ISSN 1002-8439
CUNZHEN JIANSHE/TOWN OR VILLAGE DEVELOPMENT. 1983-1999. bi-m. Zhongguo Jianzhu Jishu Fazhan Zhongxin, 19 Chegongzhuang Dajie, Beijing, 100044, China.

016.6606 DEU ISSN 0960-5037 CODEN: CUBIER
CURRENT BIOTECHNOLOGY. 1983-2005. m. D E C H E M A e.V., Theodor-Heuss-Allee 25, Frankfurt Am Main, 60486, Germany.

330 USA
CURRENT BUSINESS REPORTS. ANNUAL BENCHMARK REPORT FOR WHOLESALE TRADE (PRINT). 1992-ceased. a. U.S. Census Bureau, c/o John Trimble, Service Sector Statistics Division, 4700 Silver Hill Rd., Washington, DC 20233.

658.8 381 USA ISSN 0363-8553
CURRENT BUSINESS REPORTS: MONTHLY WHOLESALE TRADE, SALES AND INVENTORIES (PRINT). 1936-1999. m. U.S. Census Bureau, Customer Services, Washington, DC 20233.

330 USA ISSN 1933-2203
CURRENT BUSINESS REPORTS. SERVICE ANNUAL SURVEY (PRINT). 1966-ceased. a. U.S. Census Bureau, Customer Services, Washington, DC 20233.

690 USA
CURRENT CONSTRUCTION REPORTS. C50, EXPENDITURES FOR RESIDENTIAL IMPROVEMENTS AND REPAIRS. 1961-2007. q. U.S. Census Bureau, 4600 Silver Hill Rd, Washington, DC 20233.

382 380.1029 NZL ISSN 1175-0200
CURRENT DIRECTORY OF INTERNATIONAL CHAMBERS OF COMMERCE AND INDUSTRY. 1999-2002. irreg. Current Pacific Ltd., PO Box 36-536, Northcote, Auckland, 0627, New Zealand.

352.63 USA ISSN 0196-4437
CURRENT GOVERNMENTS REPORTS: PUBLIC EMPLOYMENT. 1940-1992. a. U.S. Census Bureau, c/o Donna Hirsch, Governments Division, 4700 Silver Hill Rd., Washington, DC 20233.

336.2 USA
CURRENT GOVERNMENTS REPORTS: STATE AND LOCAL GOVERNMENT SPECIAL STUDIES. 1936-ceased. irreg. U.S. Census Bureau, 4600 Silver Hill Rd, Washington, DC 20233.

353.55 USA ISSN 0883-8763
CURRENT HOUSING REPORTS. SERIES H-121, HOMEOWNERSHIP TRENDS. 1955-198?. irreg. U.S. Census Bureau, Customer Services, Washington, DC 20233.

616.12 USA ISSN 1523-3839
CURRENT INTERVENTIONAL CARDIOLOGY REPORTS. 1999-2001. 4/yr. Current Science Inc., 400 Market St, Ste 700, Philadelphia, PA 19106-2514.

618 ITA ISSN 1123-8178
CURRENT OBSTETRICS AND GYNAECOLOGY (ITALIAN EDITION). 1992-ceased. 3/yr. Gruppo Editoriale Faenza Editrice SpA, Via Pier de Crescenzi 44, Faenza, RA 48018, Italy.

616 USA ISSN 1535-5942
CURRENT OPINION IN INTERNAL MEDICINE. 2002-2008. bi-m. Lippincott Williams & Wilkins, 530 Walnut St, Philadelphia, PA 19106-3621.

Cessations

304.6 USA
CURRENT POPULATION REPORTS: BLACK POPULATION IN THE UNITED STATES. (Series P-20) 1964-200?. irreg. U.S. Census Bureau, 4700 Silver Hill Rd., Washington, DC 20233.

304.6 USA
CURRENT POPULATION REPORTS. HISPANIC POPULATION IN THE UNITED STATES. 1969-2002. irreg. U.S. Census Bureau, c/o Chief, Population Division, 4700 Silver Hill Rd., Washington, DC 20233.

304.6 USA
CURRENT POPULATION REPORTS. POPULATION CHARACTERISTICS. RESIDENTS OF FARMS AND RURAL AREAS. 1947-1991. a. U.S. Census Bureau, Customer Services, Washington, DC 20233.

618 616.6 616.9 USA ISSN 1548-3584
CURRENT SEXUAL HEALTH REPORTS. 2004 (Mar.)-2008. q. Current Science Inc., 400 Market St, Ste 700, Philadelphia, PA 19106-2514.

617.54 616.21 NLD ISSN 1063-2581
CURRENT TOPICS IN GENERAL THORACIC SURGERY. 1985; N.S. 1991-1995 (vol.3). irreg. Elsevier BV, Radarweg 29, P O Box 211, Amsterdam, 1000 AE, Netherlands.

615.842 GBR
CURRENT TOPICS IN RADIOGRAPHY. 1995-1997 (no.3). irreg. W.B. Saunders Co. Ltd., 32 Jamestown Rd, Camden, London, NW1 7BY, United Kingdom.

616.33 USA ISSN 1092-8472 CODEN: CTOGA7
CURRENT TREATMENT OPTIONS IN GASTROENTEROLOGY (PRINT). 1998-2008. 2/yr. Current Science Inc., 400 Market St, Ste 700, Philadelphia, PA 19106-2514.

370 NZL ISSN 1174-9385
CURRICULUM UPDATE/KORERO MARAUTANGA. 1921-2005. q. Legislation Direct, PO Box 12357, Wellington, 6144, New Zealand.

676.282 658 USA ISSN 1544-0745
CUSTOM GIFT RETAILER. 2002-ceased. bi-m. National Business Media, Inc., PO Box 1416, Broomfield, CO 80038.

796.72 USA ISSN 1076-3678
CUSTOM RODDER. 1990-2007. bi-m. Source Interlink Companies, 774 S Placentia Ave, Placentia, CA 92870.

658 USA
CUSTOMER MANAGEMENT INSIGHT (PRINT). 1988-2008. m. I C M I, Customer Care Center, 102 S Tejon St, Ste 1200, Colorado Springs, CO 80903.

658.8 DEU ISSN 1439-6610
CYBIZ; das Fachmagazin fuer Erfolg mit E-Commerce. 1999-2004. 10/yr. Deutscher Fachverlag GmbH, Mainzer Landstr 251, Frankfurt Am Main, 60326, Germany.

796.6 DNK ISSN 0107-7805
CYKLE-JUL. 1936-1999. a. Joergen Beyerholm, Ed. & Pub., Vestervang 35, Blovstroed, 3450, Denmark.

616.2 GBR ISSN 1355-428X
CYSTIC FIBROSIS. CURRENT TOPICS. 1993-1996 (vol.3). irreg. John Wiley & Sons Ltd., 1-7 Oldlands Way, PO Box 808, Bognor Regis, West Sussex PO21 9FF, United Kingdom.

380 658 AUS ISSN 1445-7660
THE D & B GAZETTE. NEW SOUTH WALES. (In 5 state editions: N.S.W., Vic., S.A., W.A., Qld.) 1887-2001. w. Dun & Bradstreet Information Services, 479 St. Kilda Rd, Melbourne, VIC 3004, Australia.

354.85 DEU
D ANG VERS. (Die Angestelltenversicherung) 1954-2005. m. Bundesversicherungsanstalt fuer Angestellte, Ruhrstr 2, Berlin, 10709, Germany.

331.8 DEU ISSN 0945-0424
D B B MAGAZIN - AUSGABE HAMBURG. 1949-1998. 10/yr. D B B Verlag GmbH, Friedrichstr 165, Berlin, 10117, Germany.

006.42 DEU
D B S IMAGE PROCESSING NEWSLETTER. 1998-200?. m. D B S GmbH, Kohlhoekerstr 61, Bremen, 28203, Germany.

384.5 332 USA ISSN 1054-0814
THE D B S REPORT. (Direct Broadcast Satellite) 1990-2005. m. S N L Financial LC, One SNL Plz, PO Box 2124, Charlottesville, VA 22902.

382 DNK ISSN 1397-7229
D D NEWSLETTER; informationen der Deutsch- Daenischen handelskammer. (Deutsch Daenischen) 1996-2003. irreg. Det Tysk-Danske Handelskammer, Boersen, Copenhagen K, 1217, Denmark.

663 DEU ISSN 0944-4645 CODEN: WEWIAW
D D W - DIE WEINWISSENSCHAFT; viticultural and enological sciences. 1946-2000. 4/yr. Fachverlag Dr. Fraund GmbH, Weberstr 9, Mainz, 55130, Germany.

534 DNK ISSN 1397-6508
DELTA AKUSTIK & VIBRATION. (Dansk Elektronik, Lys og Akustik) 1975-1994. irreg. D E L T A Akustik & Vibration, Akademivej, Building 356, Lyngby, 2800, Denmark.

053.1 DEU
D E S G INFORM. 1985-2001. 10/yr. Deutsch-Europaeischen Studiengesellschaft, Postfach 111927, Hamburg, 20419, Germany.

340 USA ISSN 0276-5675
D E S LITIGATION REPORTER; the national journal of record of diethylstilbestrol litigation. (Diethylstilbestrol) 1981-200?. m. Andrews Publications, 175 Strafford Ave, Bldg 4, Ste 140, Wayne, PA 19087.

615.1 USA ISSN 1540-6539
D I A FORUM. 19??-2009. irreg. Drug Information Association, 800 Enterprise Rd, Ste 200, Horsham, PA 19044.

643 ITA ISSN 1121-8746
D I N. (Dealers International News) 1991-200?. m. (10/yr.). Il Sole 24 Ore Business Media, Divisione J C E, Via Patecchio 2, Milan, 20141, Italy.

389.1 DEU ISSN 0936-0530
D I N CATALOGUE OF TECHNICAL RULES. SUPPLEMENT. (Deutsches Institut fuer Normung) 196?-1992. a. Beuth Verlag GmbH, Burggrafenstr 6, Berlin, 10787, Germany.

683 GBR ISSN 0967-2257
D I Y TRADE BUYERS' GUIDE; the year book for the D I Y, hardware trades, housewares and garden equipment industries. (Do It Yourself) 1908-1997. a. C M P Information Ltd., Ludgate House, 245 Blackfriars Rd., London, SE1 9UR, United Kingdom.

384.55 DEU ISSN 0344-3108
D L F JAHRBUCH. (Deutschlandfunk) 1962-1986. biennial. Deutschlandfunk, Raderbergguertel 40, Cologne, 50968, Germany.

720 FRA ISSN 1167-0991
D L R MAGAZINE. (Distributeurs Loueurs Reparateurs) 198?-1993. 4/yr. S.E.D.L., 28 rue Chapsal, Joinville-le-Pont, 94340, France.

658 025.04 DEU
D M M V SPECIAL. (Deutscher Multimedia Verband) 199?-2004. irreg. Verlag Werben und Verkaufen GmbH, Hultschiner Str 8, Munich, 81677, Germany.

780.7060489 DNK ISSN 0108-9188
D M P F MEDLEMMER. 1975-1987. a. Dansk Musikpaedagogisk Forening, Noerrebrogade 45 A, Copenhagen N, 2200, Denmark.

616.462 616.12 616.398 USA ISSN 1552-2024
D O C NEWS; practical insights on preventing and treating diabetes, obesity and cariovascular disease. (Diabetes, Obesity, Cardiovascular Disease) 2004-2008. m. American Diabetes Association, 1701 N Beauregard St, Alexandria, VA 22311.

385.065489 DNK ISSN 0900-3665
D S B BLADET. (Danske Statsbaner) 1892-1996. D S B, Soelvgade 40, Copenhagen K, 1349, Denmark.

621.38 CZE ISSN 1214-6692
D V. (Digital Video) 2004-2004 (ceased same year). q. Burda Praha, spol. s r.o., Premyslovska 2845/43, Luxembourg Plaza, Prague 3, 13000, Czech Republic.

629.2 DNK ISSN 0901-6945
D V BOGEN. (Danske Vognmaend) 1960-1997. a. Dansk Transport og Logistik, Groenningen 7, PO Box 2250, Copenhagen K, 1019, Denmark.

384.558 NLD ISSN 1872-6402
D V D BRANDEN. (Digital Versatile Disc) 2006-2007. s-a. HUB Uitgevers, Postbus 3389, Haarlem, 2001 DJ, Netherlands.

791 DEU ISSN 1610-7330
D V D PREMIERE. (Digital Video Disc) 1998-2009 (May). 10/yr. Entertainment Media Verlag GmbH und Co. oHG, Einsteinring 24, Dornach, 85609, Germany.

791 CZE ISSN 1213-8703
D V DMAG (ONLINE). (Digital Video Disc) 2002-2007. d. Trade & Leisure Publications, s.r.o., Pernerova 35a, Prague 8, 186 00, Czech Republic.

778.5 CZE ISSN 1214-5467
D V DMAG (PRINT). (Digital Video Disc) 2004-2008. m. Trade & Leisure Publications, s.r.o., Pernerova 35a, Prague 8, 186 00, Czech Republic.

677.3 DEU ISSN 0942-301X CODEN: DWIREC
D W I REPORTS. (Deutsches Wollforschungsinstitut) 1952-2006. a. Deutsches Wollforschungsinstitut, R W T H, Pauwelsstr 8, Aachen, 52056, Germany.

668.5 ESP ISSN 1695-7210
D & P. DROGUERIA & PERFUMERIA; revista professional del sector de la drogueria y perfumeria. 1985-200?. m. Tecnipublicaciones Espana, S.L., Avda de Manoteras 44, 3a Planta, Madrid, 28050, Spain.

666 ITA ISSN 1120-5822
D'A; artigianato tra arte e design. 1990-2003. q. Edizioni Imago, Via Lago dei Tartari 73, Guidonia Montecelio, RM 00012, Italy.

330 FRA ISSN 1258-6900
DAFSA DES ADMINISTRATEURS. 1978 (vol.62)-199?. a. Dafsaliens, 1 Rue de l'Union, Rueil Malmaison, Cedex, France.

332 DNK ISSN 0109-7644
DAGENS DANMARK. 1984-2002. q. Kreditforeningen Danmark, Jarmers Plads 2, Copenhagen V, 1590, Denmark.

340 GBR ISSN 0955-0798
DAILY LAW REPORTS INDEX. 1988-199?. w. Sweet & Maxwell Ltd., 100 Avenue Rd, London, NW3 3PF, United Kingdom.

621 JPN
DAINAMIKKUSU NI KANSARU ODIO BIJUARU SHINPOJIUMU/ AUDIO VISUAL SYMPOSIUM ON DYNAMICS. 1992-1994. irreg. Nihon Kikai Gakkai, Shinanomachi-Rengakan Bldg, Shinanomachi 35, Shinjuku-ku, Tokyo, 160, Japan.

333.72 ITA
DAL COMUNE-NOTIZIE. 1970-ceased. m. Comune di Parma, Via Repubblica 1, Parma, PR 43100, Italy.

371.42 USA ISSN 1069-5435
THE DALLAS - FORT WORTH JOBBANK; the job hunter's guide to the Dallas - Fort Worth Metroplex. (Includes: Abilene, Amarillo, Arlington, Garland, Irving, Lubbock, Plano and many others.) 1988-2003 (14th ed.). irreg. Adams Media, 4700 E Galbraith Rd, Cincinnati, OH 45236.

028 NLD ISSN 1574-1389
DAMON BOEKENMAGAZINE. 2004-2007. q. Uitgeverij Damon, Postbus 2014, Budel, 6020 AA, Netherlands.

850 ITA
DANAE. 1989-ceased. q. Editrice Danae, Via Lucrezio, 3, Carpi, MO 41012, Italy.

793.3 GBR ISSN 0966-6346
DANCE NOW. 1992-2008 (vo.17, no.4). q. Dance Books Ltd., The Old Bakery, 4 Lenten St, Alton, Hamps GU34 1HG, United Kingdom.

336.22 CZE ISSN 1214-6560
DANE V PODNIKANI AKTUALNE. 2004-2007. m. Verlag Dashoefer s.r.o., Na Prikope 18, PO Box 756, Prague 1, 11121, Czech Republic.

629.8 DNK
THE DANFOSS JOURNAL (ONLINE); automatic controls design and practice. 1943-2001. q. Danfoss A-S, Nordborgvej 81, Nordborg, 6430, Denmark.

363.2 CHN ISSN 1003-9325
DANGDAI JINGCHA/POLICE TODAY. 1990-2004. m. Dangdai Jingcha Zazhishe, 192, Ba-Yi Lu, Changsha, 410001, China.

330 CHN ISSN 1003-2126
DANGDAI QIYE/CONTEMPORARY ENTERPRISE. 1985-1997. m. Liaoning Shehui Kexueyuan, 86, Taishan Lu, Huanggu-qu, Shenyang, Liaoning 110031, China.

895.1 CHN
DANGDAI WENTAN BAO. 1983-1997. m. Zhongguo Zuojia Xiehui, Guangdong Fenhui, No 75, Wende Lu, Guangzhou, Guangdong 510030, China.

895.1 CHN ISSN 1005-9083
DANGDAI ZUOJIA/MODERN WRITERS. 1986-1999. bi-m. Changjiang Wenyi Chubanshe, 268, Xiongchu Dajie, Wuhan, Hubei 430070, China.

839.8109 028.5 DNK ISSN 0908-5025
DANISH CHILDREN'S LITERATURE. 1992-2003. a. Danish Literature Information Center, Christians Brygge 1, Copenhagen K, 1219, Denmark.

794 DNK ISSN 1901-7375
THE DANISH COMPUTER GAMES INDUSTRY; annual mapping. 2005-2005. a. Handelshoejskolen i Koebenhavn, Imagine. Creative Industries Research, Kilevej 14 A, Frederiksberg, 2000, Denmark.

740 760 DNK ISSN 1901-7103
THE DANISH DESIGN INDUSTRY; annual mapping. 2005-2005. a. Handelshoejskolen i Koebenhavn, Imagine. Creative Industries Research, Kilevej 14 A, Frederiksberg, 2000, Denmark.

687 DNK ISSN 1901-7359
THE DANISH FASHION INDUSTRY; annual mapping. 2005-2005. a. Handelshoejskolen i Koebenhavn, Imagine. Creative Industries Research, Kilevej 14 A, Frederiksberg, 2000, Denmark.

791.43 DNK ISSN 1901-7367
THE DANISH FILM INDUSTRY; annual mapping. 2005-2005. a. Handelshoejskolen i Koebenhavn, Imagine. Creative Industries Research, Kilevej 14 A, Frederiksberg, 2000, Denmark.

839.810 DNK ISSN 0906-5369
DANISH LITERARY MAGAZINE. 1991-2003. s-a. Danish Literature Information Center, Christians Brygge 1, Copenhagen K, 1219, Denmark.

780 DNK ISSN 1901-7340
THE DANISH RECORDED MUSIC INDUSTRY; annual mapping. 2005-2005. a. Handelshoejskolen i Koebenhavn, Imagine. Creative Industries Research, Kilevej 14 A, Frederiksberg, 2000, Denmark.

595.7 DNK ISSN 0109-7164
DANMARKS DYRELIV/ANIMAL LIFE OF DENMARK. 1984-2000. irreg. Apollo Books, Kirkeby Sand 19, Stenstrup, 5771, Denmark.

910 DNK ISSN 0105-4856
DANMARKS LAERERHOEJSKOLE. GEOGRAFISK INSTITUT. SKRIFTER. 1978-1992. irreg. Danmarks Laererhoejskole, Geografisk Institut, Emdrupvej 101, Copenhagen Nv, 2400, Denmark.

624.17 DNK ISSN 1600-2350
DANMARKS TEKNISKE UNIVERSITET. INSTITUT FOR BAERENDE KONSTRUKTIONER OG MATERIALER. SERIE. 1999-200?. irreg. Danmarks Tekniske Universitet, Institut for Baerende Konstruktioner og Materialer, Bygning 118, Lyngby, 2800, Denmark.

624.17 DNK ISSN 1396-2183
DANMARKS TEKNISKE UNIVERSITET. INSTITUT FOR BAERENDE KONSTRUKTIONER OG MATERIALER. SERIE F. 1969-1999. irreg. Danmarks Tekniske Universitet, Institut for Baerende Konstruktioner og Materialer, Bygning 118, Lyngby, 2800, Denmark.

624.17 DNK ISSN 1396-2175
DANMARKS TEKNISKE UNIVERSITET. INSTITUT FOR BAERENDE KONSTRUKTIONER OG MATERIALER. SERIE I. 1970-1999. irreg. Danmarks Tekniske Universitet, Institut for Baerende Konstruktioner og Materialer, Bygning 118, Lyngby, 2800, Denmark.

526.982 DNK ISSN 0105-5194
DANMARKS TEKNISKE UNIVERSITET. INSTITUTTET FOR LANDMAALING OG FOTOGRAMMETRI. MEDDELELSE. 1941-1990. irreg. Danmarks Tekniske Universitet, Instituttet for Landmaaling og Fotogrammetri, Landmaalervej 7, Lyngby, 2800, Denmark.

914.8 DNK ISSN 0109-6125
DANMARKS TURIST VEJVISER. 1984-1995. a. Glumsoe Bogtrykkeri, Noeddevej 10, Glumso, 4171, Denmark.

015.489 DNK ISSN 0106-2743
DANSK BOGFORTEGNELSE. AARSKATALOG/DANISH NATIONAL BIBLIOGRAPHY, BOOKS. ANNUAL LIST. 1851-2005. a. D B C A/S, Tempovej 7-11, Ballerup, 2750, Denmark.

790.1 DNK ISSN 0902-4042
DANSK DRAGESPORT. 1976-2004. bi-m. Dansk Hanggliding og Paragliding Union, K D A Huset, Lufthavnsvej 28, Roskilde, 4000, Denmark.

914.8 DNK ISSN 0109-6486
DANSK FAELLESREJSE FORENING. MEDLEMSBLAD. 1982-1992. 3/yr. Dansk Faellerejse Forening, c/o Knud Noerr, Sct Laurentiivej 114, Skagen, 9990, Denmark.

595.7 DNK ISSN 0108-1551
DANSK FAUNISTISK BIBLIOTEK. 1981-1983. irreg. Apollo Books, Kirkeby Sand 19, Stenstrup, 5771, Denmark.

770 DNK ISSN 0901-1668
DANSK FOTOGRAFISK TIDSSKRIFT. 1879-2003. 4/yr. Dansk Fotografisk Forening, H. C. Oerstedvej 10 C, Frederiksberg C, 1879, Denmark.

382 DNK ISSN 0109-2669
DANSK-FRANSK HANDELSUNION. BULLETIN/CHAMBRE DE COMMERCE FRANCO-DANOISE. BULLETIN. 1983-1991. q. Dansk-Fransk Handelsunion, c/o P.R. Meurs-Gerken, Advokaterne, Amaliegade 42, Copenhagen K, 1256, Denmark.

796 DNK ISSN 1600-4558
DANSK KARATE FORBUND. 1980-2006. q. Dansk Karate Forbund, Idraettens Hus, Broenby Stadion 20, Brondby, 2605, Denmark.

636.2 DNK ISSN 1601-9644
DANSK LANDBRUGSRAADGIVNING. DANSK KVAEG. KOEDKVAEG. 1991-2003. a. Dansk Landbrugsraadgivning, Dansk Kvaeg, Udkaersvej 15, Skejby, Aarhus N, 8200, Denmark.

636.2 DNK ISSN 1603-9491
DANSK LANDBRUGSRAADGIVNING. DANSK KVAEG. RAPPORT, DANSK KVAEG. 1992-2003. a. Dansk Landbrugsraadgivning, Dansk Kvaeg, Udkaersvej 15, Skejby, Aarhus N, 8200, Denmark.

658 DNK ISSN 1397-3266
DANSK MANAGEMENT FORUM. 1995-2002. 3/yr. Dansk Management Forum, Folke Bernadottes Alle 45, Copenhagen Oe, 2100, Denmark.

786.5 DNK ISSN 0107-4857
DANSK ORGELAARBOG/DAENISCHES ORGELJAHRBUCH/DANISH ORGAN YEARBOOK. 1982-1991. a. Det Danske Orgelselskab, c/o Hans Joergen Oestergaard, PO Box 78, Maribo, 4930, Denmark.

078.9 658.8 DNK ISSN 0106-5343
DANSK PRESSE. 1918-2006. m. Danske Dagblades Forening, Pressens Hus, Skindergade 7, Copenhagen K, 1159, Denmark.

658.4 DNK ISSN 0907-5437
DANSK SECURITY. 199?-2005. 5/yr. Dansk Security, Vedelsgade 46, Vejle, 7100, Denmark.

796.342 DNK ISSN 0909-0282
DANSK SQUASH. 1974-1997. q. Dansk Squash Forbund, Idraettens Hus, Broendby Stadion 20, Brondby, 2605, Denmark.

796.342 DNK ISSN 1901-7871
DANSK TENNIS. 199?-2006. bi-m. Dansk Tennis Forbund, Idraettens Hus, Broendby Stadion 20, Broendby, 2605, Denmark.

388.3409489 DNK ISSN 1397-4122
DANSKE BILIMPORTOERER. MAANEDSSTATISTIK. 1965-2006. m. Danske Bilimportoerer, Lyngbyvej 24, Copenhagen OE, 2100, Denmark.

303.3809489 DNK ISSN 1397-341X
DANSKERNE. 1995-2008. a. Catinet- I F K A, Aabenraa 29, Copenhagen K, 1124, Denmark.

658 USA ISSN 1525-0911
DARTNELL'S FIRST LINE SUPERVISOR. 1967-2007. bi-w. (26/yr.). Dartnell Corp., 360 Hiatt Dr, Palm Beach Garden, FL 33418.

004 USA ISSN 0744-1673 CODEN: DASODY
DATA SOURCES; the comprehensive guide to the data processing industry: hardware, data communications products, software, company profiles. 1981-2001. 2/yr. Gale, 27500 Drake Rd, Farmington Hills, MI 48331.

004.6 DEU ISSN 0176-3288
DATACOM. 1984-2003. m. Datacom Zeitschriften Verlag GmbH, Elbestr 7, Krefeld, 47800, Germany.

684.1 ITA ISSN 0393-330X
DATALIGNUM. 1982-ceased. m. (10/yr.). Milla International S.r.l., Via Stefano Ussi, 4, Milan, MI 20125, Italy.

370.285 DNK ISSN 0108-3708
DATALOGI O. 1973-2003. irreg. Koebenhavns Universitet, Datalogisk Institut, Universitetsparken 1, Copenhagen OE, 2100, Denmark.

677.0029 USA ISSN 0363-5252
DAVISON'S SALESMAN'S BOOK. 1916-ceased. a. Davison Publishing Co., LLC, 3452 Lake Lynda Dr, Ste 363, Orlando, FL 32817.

052 AUS ISSN 1324-7573
DAWN; the magazine for women who want an alternative. 1994-2004. q. Live and Learn - with Class, 203 Great Ocean Rd, Anglesea, VIC 3230, Australia.

917.759 USA ISSN 1541-8960
DAY TRIPS FROM MILWAUKEE; getaways less than two hours away. 2000-2006. biennial (Every 2-3 yrs.). The Globe Pequot Press, Inc., 246 Goose Ln, PO Box 480, Guilford, CT 06437.

917.4 USA ISSN 1536-6200
DAYTRIPS AND GETAWAY WEEKENDS IN CONNECTICUT, RHODE ISLAND, AND MASSACHUSETTS. 2002-ceased. irreg. The Globe Pequot Press, Inc., 246 Goose Ln, PO Box 480, Guilford, CT 06437.

780 NZL
DEAD WEIGHT; putting the sieve back in civilization. 1999-200?. irreg. Dead Weight, c/o Earwig Studios, P.O. Box 34 705, Birkenhead, Auckland, New Zealand.

362.42 USA
DEAF MAGAZINE. 1994-199?. 3/yr. Deaf Magazine

691 USA ISSN 1092-7395
DEALER & APPLICATOR. 1971-2005. 9/yr. Vance Publishing Corp., 400 Knightsbridge Pkwy, Lincolnshire, IL 60069.

631.8 USA ISSN 1043-3104 CODEN: DEPREN
DEALER PROGRESS; how smart agribusiness is growing. 1970-200?. bi-m. The Fertilizer Institute, 501 Second St, N E, Washington, DC 20002.

332.6 USA ISSN 1937-304X
DEALMAKER. 2006-2008. 10/yr. Doubledown Media, LLC, 240 W 35th St, Fl 11, New York, NY 10001.

330 USA ISSN 1941-2614
DEALMAKER EUROPE. 2008 (Mar.)-2009. bi-m. Doubledown Media, LLC, 240 W 35th St, Fl 11, New York, NY 10001.

332 USA ISSN 0731-0536
DEBITS AND DEPOSIT TURNOVER AT COMMERCIAL BANKS. 1969-1996. m. U.S. Federal Reserve System, Board of Governors, Publications Services, Rm MS 138, Washington, DC 20551.

363.728 FRA ISSN 1271-0318
DECHETS SCIENCES ET TECHNIQUES. 1996-2008. q. Groupe D P E - S A P, 9 Rue de l'Arbre Sec, Lyon, Cedex 01 69281, France.

363.728 FRA ISSN 1774-508X
DECH'INFOS. 2004-2005. a. Communaute de Communes La Porte Normande, 8 rue des Epinoches, B.P. 3, Saint-Andre-de-l'Eure, France.

747 DEU ISSN 0938-1635
DECORATION. 1989-2007. bi-m. Gruner und Jahr AG & Co., Am Baumwall 11, Hamburg, 20459, Germany.

747 FRA ISSN 1772-7022
DECORATION DE REVE. 2005-2008. q. Editions DIPA Burda, 26 Avenue de l'Europe, Strasbourg, 67013, France.

745.5 USA ISSN 0893-1097
DECORATIVE ARTIST'S WORKBOOK. 1987-2006. bi-m. F + W Media Inc., 4700 E Galbraith Rd, Cincinnati, OH 45236.

745.5 FRA ISSN 0994-2114
DECORATIVE CROCHET. 1988-199?. bi-m. Editions de Saxe, 20 Rue Croix Barret, Lyon, 69358 Cedex 7, France.

745.5 ITA ISSN 1828-1869
DECOUPAGE CASA. 2006-200?. bi-m. Tattilo Editrice SpA, Via degli Olmetti 18, Rome, 00060, Italy.

351 659.2 NLD ISSN 1871-3866
DEELNAME AAN BUITENLANDSE KANSSPELEN IN NEDERLAND. 199?-2004. biennial. TNS NIPO Consult, Postbus 247, Amsterdam, 1000 AE, Netherlands.

574.92 DNK ISSN 0903-2533
DEEP-SEA NEWSLETTER. 1978-2005. s-a. Deep-Sea Newsletter, c/0 Torben Wolff, Zoological Museum, University of Copenhagen, Copenhagen Oe, 2100, Denmark.

330 FRA ISSN 0759-089X
DEFIS; premier magazine pratique de l'entreprise. 1983-2006. 11/yr. Defis, c/o Free Lance S.A., 204 bd. Raspail, Paris, 75006, France.

641.5 ITA ISSN 1828-9592
DELIZIOSE RICETTE. 2006-200?. m. Ulysse Network, Viale Bianca Maria 19, Milan, Italy.

053.1 DEU ISSN 1861-5961
DELUXE MAGAZIN. 2005-2008. q. Deluxe Premium Magazin Verlag, Georgstr 38, Hannover, 30159, Germany.

369.4 FRA ISSN 0751-5812
DEMAIN. 1920-2004. m. (7/yr.). Editions Scouts de France, 54 av. Jean Jaures, Paris, 75019, France.

720 ITA ISSN 1826-364X
DEMETRA. 1991-ceased. s-a. Ordine Architetti, Pianificatori, Paesaggisti e Conservatori della Provincia di Enna, Via L Da Vinci 9/A, Enna, EN 94100, Italy.

070 CZE ISSN 0011-8214
DEMOCRATIC JOURNALIST. 1953-1991. m. Mezinarodni Organizace Novinaru, Manesova 79, Prague 2, 120 00, Czech Republic.

610.21 ESP ISSN 1138-0489
DEMOGRAFIA Y SALUD. 1988-2007. q. Comunidad de Madrid, Instituto de Estadistica, Principe de Vargara 108, Madrid, 28002, Spain.

599.0188 GBR ISSN 0961-0898
DENDRON; an international biomedical journal for research in neuroscience. 1992-1992. irreg. University of Cambridge, Faculty Press, 88 Regent St, Cambridge, CB2 1DP, United Kingdom.

331 DNK ISSN 1396-7525
DENMARK. ARBEJDSTILSYNET. AARSBERETNING. 1975-1997. a. Arbejdstilsynet, Tryksagsafdelningen, Landskronagade 33-35, Copenhagen Oe, 2100, Denmark.

304.4 DNK ISSN 0108-8076
DENMARK. DANMARKS STATISTIK. BEFOLKNINGEN I KOMMUNERNE/POPULATION IN MUNICIPALITIES. 1971-2001. a. Danmarks Statistik, Sejroegade 11, Copenhagen OE, 2100, Denmark.

352.021 DNK ISSN 0106-9802
DENMARK. DANMARKS STATISTIK. KOMMUNALE FINANSER. 1981-1991. a. Danmarks Statistik, Sejroegade 11, Copenhagen OE, 2100, Denmark.

339.47021 DNK ISSN 0900-2499
DENMARK. DANMARKS STATISTIK. LEVEVILKAAR I DANMARK/DENMARK. STATISTICS DENMARK. LIVING CONDITIONS IN DENMARK; statistisk oversigt. 1976-1997. quadrennial. Danmarks Statistik, Sejroegade 11, Copenhagen OE, 2100, Denmark.

339.3489 DNK ISSN 0107-8771
DENMARK. DANMARKS STATISTIK. LOEN- OG INDKOMSTATISTIK/ STATISTICS OF EARNINGS AND INCOMES. 1982-2002. irreg. (4-6/yr.). Danmarks Statistik, Sejroegade 11, Copenhagen OE, 2100, Denmark.

331.09489 DNK ISSN 0105-1083
DENMARK. DANMARKS STATISTIK. MAANEDLIG BESKAEFTIGELSES- OG LOENSTATISTIK FOR INDUSTRI/DENMARK. STATISTICS DENMARK. MONTHLY STATISTICS OF INDUSTRIAL EMPLOYMENT AND LABOUR COSTS. 1975-1994. m. Danmarks Statistik, Sejroegade 11, Copenhagen OE, 2100, Denmark.

338.09489 DNK ISSN 0105-0877
DENMARK. DANMARKS STATISTIK. MAANEDLIG ORDRE- OG OMSAETNINGSSTATISTIK FOR INDUSTRI/DENMAR. STATISTICS DENMARK. MONTHLY STATISTICS OF INDUSTRIAL SALES AND ORDER BOOKS. 1975-1998. m. Danmarks Statistik, Sejroegade 11, Copenhagen OE, 2100, Denmark.

016.31489 DNK ISSN 1601-1279
DENMARK. DANMARKS STATISTIK. PUBLICERINGSOVERSIGT. 1984-2004. s-a. Danmarks Statistik, Sejroegade 11, Copenhagen OE, 2100, Denmark.

338.09489 DNK ISSN 0108-738X
DENMARK. DANMARKS STATISTIK. REGNSKABSSTATISTIK FOR INDUSTRI/DENMARK. DANMARKS STATISTIK. INDUSTRIAL ACCOUNTS STATISTICS. 1981-1995. a. Danmarks Statistik, Sejroegade 11, Copenhagen OE, 2100, Denmark.

314.89 DNK ISSN 0106-6439
DENMARK. DANMARKS STATISTIK. STATISTISKE MEDDELELSER. 1852-1982. irreg. Danmarks Statistik, Sejroegade 11, Copenhagen OE, 2100, Denmark.

382.09489 DNK ISSN 1902-8512
DENMARK. DANMARKS STATISTIK. UDENRIGSHANDEL, DETALJERET VAREHANDEL (PRINT)/DENMARK. STATISTICS DENMARK. EXTERNAL TRADE OF DENMARK, DETAILED STATISTICS ON TRADE IN GOODS. 1969-2007. a. Danmarks Statistik, Sejroegade 11, Copenhagen OE, 2100, Denmark.

338.476 DNK ISSN 0107-0967
DENMARK. DANMARKS STATISTIK. VARESTATISTIK FOR INDUSTRI. SERIES A. 1970-2006. q. Danmarks Statistik, Sejroegade 11, Copenhagen OE, 2100, Denmark.

338.476 DNK ISSN 0107-0975
DENMARK. DANMARKS STATISTIK. VARESTATISTIK FOR INDUSTRI. SERIES B. 1970-2006. q. Danmarks Statistik, Sejroegade 11, Copenhagen OE, 2100, Denmark.

338.476 DNK ISSN 0107-0983
DENMARK. DANMARKS STATISTIK. VARESTATISTIK FOR INDUSTRI. SERIES C. 1970-2006. q. Danmarks Statistik, Sejroegade 11, Copenhagen OE, 2100, Denmark.

338.476 DNK ISSN 0107-0991
DENMARK. DANMARKS STATISTIK. VARESTATISTIK FOR INDUSTRI. SERIES D. 1970-2005. q. Danmarks Statistik, Sejroegade 11, Copenhagen OE, 2100, Denmark.

016.31489 DNK ISSN 0109-8314
DENMARK. DANMARKS STATISTIK. VEJVISER I STATISTIKKEN. 1978-2001. irreg. Danmarks Statistik, Sejroegade 11, Copenhagen OE, 2100, Denmark.

332 DNK ISSN 1397-5536
DENMARK. FINANSTILSYNET. BOERSOMRAADET, FONDSMAEGLERSELSKABER OG INVESTERINGSFORENINGER (PRINT). 1997-1997. a. Finanstilsynet, Aarhusgade 110, Copenhagen K, 2100, Denmark.

332.6 DNK ISSN 1397-7830
DENMARK. FINANSTILSYNET. FORSIKRINGSSELSKABER, BIND 1, LIVSFORSIKRINGSSELSKABER M.V. 1989-1997. a. Finanstilsynet, Aarhusgade 110, Copenhagen K, 2100, Denmark.

368.109489 DNK ISSN 1397-7857
DENMARK. FINANSTILSYNET. FORSIKRINGSSELSKABER, BIND 2, SKADEFORSIKRINGSSELSKABER (PRINT). 1989-1997. a. Finanstilsynet, Aarhusgade 110, Copenhagen K, 2100, Denmark.

332.3 DNK ISSN 0906-5563
DENMARK. FINANSTILSYNET. TILSYNET MED REALKREDITINSTITUTTER. BERETNING. 1983-1996. a. Finanstilsynet, Aarhusgade 110, Copenhagen K, 2100, Denmark.

640.73 DNK ISSN 1399-2112
DENMARK. FORBRUGERSTYRELSEN. REN BESKED. 1936-2005. 6/yr. Forbrugerstyrelsen, Amagerfaelledvej 56, Copenhagen S, 2300, Denmark.

355 DNK ISSN 0109-5757
DENMARK. FORSVARSMINISTERIET. AARLIGE REDEGOERELSE. 1982-2007. a. Forsvarsministeriet, Holmens Kanal 42, Copenhagen K, 1060, Denmark.

351 DNK ISSN 1602-8589
DENMARK. INDENRIGS- OG SUNDHEDSMINISTERIET. INDENRIGS- OG SUNDHEDSMINISTERIETS AFGOERELSER OG UDTALELSER OM KOMMUNALE FORHOLD. 1981-2003. a. Indenrigs- og Sundhedsministeriet, Slotholmsgade 10-12, Copenhagen K, 1216, Denmark.

344.046 DNK ISSN 1396-4852
DENMARK. MILJOEMINISTERIET. MILJOE- OG ENERGIMINISTERIETS LOVREGISTER; retsinformation, lovregister, stikordsregister. 1984-1997. a. Miljoe- og Energiministeriet, Strandgade 29, Copenhagen K, 1401, Denmark.

620 DNK ISSN 0906-1797
DENMARK. RISOE NATIONAL LABORATORY. OPTICS AND FLUID DYNAMICS DEPARTMENT. ANNUAL PROGRESS REPORT. 1991-2003. a. Risoe D T U, Frederiksborgvej 399, Roskilde, 4000, Denmark.

570 DNK ISSN 1602-0103
DENMARK. RISOE NATIONAL LABORATORY. PLANT RESEARCH DEPARTMENT. ANNUAL REPORT. 1991-2004. a. Risoe D T U, Frederiksborgvej 399, Roskilde, 4000, Denmark.

620 DNK ISSN 1603-2586
DENMARK. RISOE NATIONAL LABORATORY. RADIATION RESEARCH DEPARTMENT. ANNUAL REPORT. 1992-2004. a. Risoe D T U, Frederiksborgvej 399, Roskilde, 4000, Denmark.

338.1060489 DNK ISSN 1395-511X
DENMARK. STATENS JORDBRUGS- OG FISKERIOEKONOMISKE INSTITUT. AARSBERETNING/DANISH INSTITUTE OF AGRICULTURAL AND FISHERIES ECONOMICS. ANNUAL REPORT. 1979-2001. a. Foedevareoekonomisk Institut, University of Copenhagen, Det Biovidenskabelige Facultet, Rolighedsvej 25, Frederiksberg C, 1958, Denmark.

200 USA ISSN 0193-6883
DENOMINATIONS IN AMERICA. 1985-2003. irreg. Greenwood Publishing Group Inc., 88 Post Rd W, PO Box 5007, Westport, CT 06881.

617.6 330 ESP ISSN 1135-4534
DENTAL ECONOMICS; revista de la gestion de la clinica dental. 1995-2005. bi-m. Dental Economics, Ganduxer 5, 5o - 10a A, Barcelona, 08021, Spain.

370.941 GBR ISSN 0141-2825
DEPARTMENT OF EDUCATION AND SCIENCE. DESIGN NOTE. 1968-1992. irreg. Department of Education and Science, Sanctuary Bldg, Great Smith St, London, SW1P 3BT, United Kingdom.

334.46 ESP ISSN 1575-8362
DERECHO Y MEDIO AMBIENTE. 1999-2002; suspended. q. Exlibris Ediciones, S.L., C. Infanta Mercedes, 92-bajo, Madrid, 28020, Spain.

616.5 CZE ISSN 1802-1719
DERMATOLOGIE. 2007-2007 (ceased same year). bi-m. Medakta s.r.o., Evropska 57, Prague 6, 160 00, Czech Republic.

745 DNK ISSN 1602-785X
DESIGN; helt enkelt. 2002-2004. q. Dansk Design Center, HC Andersens Boulevard 27, Copenhagen V, 1553, Denmark.

745 GBR ISSN 1756-1671
DESIGN ARTS. 1987-2008. bi-m. Barrington Publications, 54 Uxbridge Rd, London, W12 8LP, United Kingdom.

628.5 DEU
DESIGN AUSWAHL (YEAR)/DESIGN SELECTION (YEAR). ceased 1994. a. Design Center Stuttgart, Willi-Bleicher-Str 19, Stuttgart, 70174, Germany.

668.9 NLD ISSN 1385-772X CODEN: DMPOF3
DESIGNED MONOMERS AND POLYMERS (PRINT); an international journal on monomer and macromolecular synthesis. 1998-2009. bi-m. V S P, Brill Academic Publishers, PO Box 9000, Leiden, 2300 PA, Netherlands.

793 FRA ISSN 1961-0823
DESSILOGIQUE EXPERT. 2005-2008. irreg. Euro Services Internet, 60 rue Vitruve, Paris, 75020, France.

380.1 381.1 DNK ISSN 0109-1751
DETAILBLADET. 1983-2007. 23/yr. Erhvervs-Bladet A-S, Pilestraede 34, Copenhagen K, 1147, Denmark.

381 NLD ISSN 0168-0021
DETAILHANDEL MAGAZINE. 1971-2004. w. Hoofdbedrijfschap Detailhandel, Postbus 90703, The Hague, 2509 LS, Netherlands.

658.8 ESP
DETALLISTA. -ceased. 12/yr. Union de Detallistas de Alimentacion, Jorge Juan, 19, 1a planta, Madrid, 28001, Spain.

430 NLD ISSN 1386-1115
DEUTSCH; studien zum sprachunterricht und zur interkulturellen didaktik. 1996-2004 (vol.6). irreg. Editions Rodopi B.V., Tijnmuiden 7, Amsterdam, 1046 AK, Netherlands.

332 DEU ISSN 0944-730X
DEUTSCHE BANK RESEARCH. BULLETIN; current economic and monetary issues. 1982-2001. q. Deutsche Bank, Taunusanlage 12, Frankfurt Am Main, 60325, Germany.

597 DEU ISSN 1437-1731
DEUTSCHE CICHLIDEN-GESELLSCHAFT. REGION BERLIN. JAHRESBERICHT. 1995-2001. a. Deutsche Cichliden-Gesellschaft, Region Berlin, Niederneuendorfer Allee 9, Berlin, 13587, Germany.

616.15 DEU ISSN 1439-9156
DEUTSCHE GESELLSCHAFT FUER ANGIOLOGIE, GESELLSCHAFT FUER GEFAESSMEDIZIN. MITTEILUNGEN. 1985-2006. q. Demeter Verlag GmbH und Co. KG, Ammonitenstr 1, Balingen, 72336, Germany.

363.11 613.62 BRD ISSN 0070-4350
DEUTSCHE GESELLSCHAFT FUER ARBEITSSCHUTZ. VERHANDLUNGEN. 1953-1969. irreg. Dr. Dietrich Steinkopff Verlag, Tiergartenstr 17, Heidelberg, 69121, Germany.

612.67 BRD ISSN 0374-048X
DEUTSCHE GESELLSCHAFT FUER GERONTOLOGIE. VEROEFFENTLICHUNGEN. 1968-1970. irreg. Dr. Dietrich Steinkopff Verlag, Tiergartenstr 17, Heidelberg, 69121, Germany.

551.46 DEU ISSN 0946-2015
DEUTSCHE HYDROGRAPHISCHE ZEITSCHRIFT. ERGAENZUNGSHEFT/GERMAN JOURNAL OF HYDROGRAPHY. SUPPLEMENT. 1994-2000 (vol.11). irreg. Bundesamt fuer Seeschifffahrt und Hydrographie, Bernhard-Nocht-Str 78, Hamburg, 20359, Germany.

016.351 DEU ISSN 1434-2502
DEUTSCHE NOTAR CD-ROM. 1997-200?. plus s-a. updates. Verlag C.H. Beck oHG, Wilhelmstr 9, Munich, 80801, Germany.

782.1 DEU
DEUTSCHE OPER BERLIN. BEITRAEGE ZUM MUSIKTHEATER. 1982-2001. a. Deutsche Oper Berlin, Bismarckstr 35, Berlin, 10627, Germany.

613 DEU ISSN 0179-9967
DEUTSCHE ZEITSCHRIFT FUER OEFFENTLICHE GESUNDHEITSPFLEGE. 1869-1933. irreg. Urban und Schwarzenberg, Pettenkoferstr. 18, Munich, 80336, West Germany.

500 DEU ISSN 0722-5318
DEUTSCHER FORSCHUNGSDIENST. BERICHTE AUS DER WISSENSCHAFT. 1954-1996. 51/yr. Deutscher Forschungsdienst, Postfach 205006, Bonn, 53170, Germany.

500 DEU ISSN 0722-5229
DEUTSCHER FORSCHUNGSDIENST. SONDERDIENST ANGEWANDTE WISSENSCHAFT. 1956-1996. 25/yr. Deutscher Forschungsdienst, Postfach 205006, Bonn, 53170, Germany.

371.0025 DEU ISSN 0070-4385
DEUTSCHER HOCHSCHULFUEHRER. 1929-2004 (vol.57). irreg. Dr. Josef Raabe Verlags GmbH, Rotebuehlstr 77, Stuttgart, 70178, Germany.

616.99 DEU ISSN 0932-6235
DEUTSCHES KREBSFORSCHUNGSZENTRUM. RESEARCH REPORT. 1986-2003. biennial. Deutsches Krebsforschungszentrum, Im Neuenheimer Feld 280, Heidelberg, 69120, Germany.

616.9 DEU ISSN 0070-4229
DEUTSCHES KREBSFORSCHUNGSZENTRUM. VEROEFFENTLICHUNGEN. 1965-2003. a. Deutsches Krebsforschungszentrum, Im Neuenheimer Feld 280, Heidelberg, 69120, Germany.

330 DEU
DEUTSCHLAND IM GLOBALEN WETTBEWERB/INTERNATIONAL ECONOMIC INDICATORS. 1980-2003. a. Deutscher Instituts Verlag GmbH, Gustav-Heinemann-Ufer 84-88, Cologne, 50968, Germany.

330 EGY
DEVELOPMENT & SOCIO-ECONOMIC PROGRESS. 1977-ceased. q. Afro-Asian Peoples' Solidarity Organization, 89 Abdel Aziz Al Saoud St., Manial, Cairo, Egypt.

571.6 GBR ISSN 0951-0818 CODEN: DVCBAP
DEVELOPMENTAL AND CELL BIOLOGY SERIES. 1973-2007 (Jul.). irreg. Cambridge University Press, The Edinburgh Bldg, Shaftesbury Rd, Cambridge, CB2 8RU, United Kingdom.

641.13 GBR ISSN 0260-4345
DEVELOPMENTS IN FOOD CARBOHYDRATE. 1977-1982. irreg. Pergamon, The Blvd, Langford Ln, East Park, Kidlington, Oxford OX5 1GB, United Kingdom.

664 GBR ISSN 0263-4376
DEVELOPMENTS IN FOOD PRESERVATION. 1981-1989 (vol.5). irreg. Pergamon, The Blvd, Langford Ln, East Park, Kidlington, Oxford OX5 1GB, United Kingdom.

664 GBR ISSN 0263-4708 CODEN: DVFPDH
DEVELOPMENTS IN FOOD PROTEINS. 1982-1991. irreg. Pergamon, The Blvd, Langford Ln, East Park, Kidlington, Oxford OX5 1GB, United Kingdom.

547.84 GBR ISSN 0264-3022 CODEN: DOPODF
DEVELOPMENTS IN ORIENTED POLYMERS. 1982-1987. irreg. Pergamon, The Blvd, Langford Ln, East Park, Kidlington, Oxford OX5 1GB, United Kingdom.

678.2 GBR ISSN 0262-1584 CODEN: DERTD4
DEVELOPMENTS IN RUBBER TECHNOLOGY. 1979-1987. irreg. Pergamon, The Blvd, Langford Ln, East Park, Kidlington, Oxford OX5 1GB, United Kingdom.

371.42 FRA ISSN 1291-6307
DEVENIR FONCTIONNAIRE; tout ce que vous devez savoir pour devenir fonctionnaire. 1998-2008. q. Editions d'Alleray, 18 Rue Ernest et Henri Rousselle, Paris, 75013, France.

294.307 GBR
DHARMA LIFE. 199?-2005. q. Windhorse Publications, Madhamyaloka, 30 Chantry Rd, Birmingham, B13 8DH, United Kingdom.

616.4 NLD ISSN 0168-9282 CODEN: DIANEW
THE DIABETES ANNUAL. 1985-2002 (vol.13). a. Elsevier BV, Radarweg 29, P O Box 211, Amsterdam, 1000 AE, Netherlands.

616.4 BRD ISSN 0720-0749
DIABETES-REPORT. 1978-1983. irreg. P M I Verlagsgruppe GmbH, August-Schanz-Str 8-II, Frankfurt Am Main, 60433, Germany.

616.0754 USA
DIAGNOSTIC IMAGING SCAN (ONLINE). 1987-200?. s-m. C M P Media LLC, PO Box 16595, North Hollywood, CA 91615-6595.

284.2 DEU ISSN 0173-9077
DIAKONIE IM RHEINLAND. 1963-2005. 6/yr. Diakonisches Werk der Evangelischen Kirche im Rheinland, Lenaustr 41, Duesseldorf, 40470, Germany.

658 DEU
DIALOG & WANDEL. 1997-2000. q. BurdaYukom Publishing GmbH, Konrad-Zuse-Platz 11, Munich, 81829, Germany.

001.3 FRA ISSN 1164-8147
DIALOGUE (GUERNES)/DIALOG/DIALOGOS/DIALOGUS. 1992-199?. q. Association Dialogue, 17 chemin du Pont d'Herville, Guernes, 78520, France.

658.3 NLD ISSN 1384-6671
DIALOGUES ON WORK AND INNOVATION. 1996-2004 (vol.15). irreg. John Benjamins Publishing Co., PO Box 36224, Amsterdam, 1020 ME, Netherlands.

791.43 CHN
DIAN JIANG YING SHI/T V AND FILM LITERATURE. 1981-2006. bi-m. Dianshi Dianying Wenxue Zazhishe, 238 Yan an Xilu, Shanghai, 200040, China.

746.4 DEU ISSN 1434-0534
DIANA BABY. 198?-2007 (Oct.). q. OZ Verlag GmbH, Roemerstr 90, Rheinfelden, 79618, Germany.

746.9 CZE ISSN 1613-3218
DIANA - DETSKA SITA MODA. 2004-2005. 2/yr. Rolino, spol. s.r.o., Bratri Capku 10, Prague 10, 101 00, Czech Republic.

746.4 CZE ISSN 1860-2983
DIANA - HACKOVANA MODA PRO DETI. 2005-2007. 2/yr. Rolino, spol. s.r.o., Bratri Capku 10, Prague 10, 101 00, Czech Republic.

649 CZE ISSN 1614-3736
DIANA - PRO DETI. 2004-2006. 3/yr. Rolino, spol. s.r.o., Bratri Capku 10, Prague 10, 101 00, Czech Republic.

791.43 CHN ISSN 1003-5834
DIANYING YUEBAO/FILM MONTHLY. 1989-1995. bi-m. Guangxi Dianying Zhipian Chang, 26 You'ai Beilu, Nanning, Guangxi 530001, China.

791.43 CHN ISSN 1006-4478
DIANYING ZHI YOU/FILM'S FRIENDS. 1979-2002. m. Fujian Sheng Dianying Faxing Fangying Gongsi, 229 Baima Lu, Fuzhou, Fujian 350001, China.

780 780.7 ITA ISSN 1122-3200
DIASTEMA; rivista di cultura e informazione musicale. 1991-ceased. s-a. Fabrizio Serra Editore, c/o Accademia Editoriale, Via Santa Bibbiana 28, Pisa, 56127, Italy.

230 300 GBR ISSN 1756-0586
THE DIFFERENCE. 2007-200?; suspended. bi-m. RoperPenberthy Publishing Ltd., PO Box 545, Horsham, W Sussex RH12 4QW, United Kingdom.

028.5 DEU
DIGIMON. 1999-2005. fortn. Panini Verlags GmbH, Ravensstr 48, Nettetal, 41334, Germany.

028.5 ITA ISSN 1591-4941
DIGIMON MAGAZINE. 2000-2006. m. Panini SpA, Viale Emilio Po 380, Modena, 41100, Italy.

791.43 770 NLD ISSN 1871-9260
DIGITAAL FILMEN EN FOTOGRAFEREN. 2005-2006. s-a. HUB Uitgevers, Postbus 3389, Haarlem, 2001 DJ, Netherlands.

770.285 ITA ISSN 1824-8152
DIGITAL CAMERA SHOPPING. 2004-200?. bi-m. Sprea Editori Srl, Via Torino 51, Cernusco sul Naviglio, MI 20063, Italy.

770 GBR ISSN 1742-7398
DIGITAL PHOTOGRAPHY USER. 1998-200?. m. Highbury - WV, 53-79 Highgate Rd, London, NW5 1TW, United Kingdom.

621.388 GBR ISSN 1744-8034
DIGITAL SATELLITE CHOICE. 1993-2005. q. Highbury - WV, 53-79 Highgate Rd, London, NW5 1TW, United Kingdom.

790.13 USA ISSN 1553-1996
DIGITAL SCRAPBOOKING MAGAZINE. 2005-2009 (Mar.). bi-m. C K Media LLC, 1450 Pony Express Rd, Bluffdale, UT 84065.

621.388 GBR ISSN 1478-8691
DIGITAL T V TESTS. 2003-2004. a. Highbury - WV, 53-79 Highgate Rd, London, NW5 1TW, United Kingdom.

004 DEU ISSN 1612-4847
DIGITAL WORLD; Technik, die Spass macht. 2003-2007 (Mar.). q. I D G Communications Verlag AG, Lyonel-Feininger-Str 26, Munich, 80807, Germany.

384.55 ITA
DIGITALE TV SAT. 1998-200?. m. Il Sole 24 Ore Business Media, Divisione J C E, Via Patecchio 2, Milan, 20141, Italy.

613.2 ITA ISSN 1826-9338
DIMAGRIRE FACILE. 2005-200?. m. Edigamma Publishing, Via Sambuca Pistoiese 70A, Rome, 00138, Italy.

331.88 ITA ISSN 1720-7495
DIMENSIONE LAVORO. 1980-ceased. fortn. Editrice Dimensione Lavoro, Via Cavour, 108, Rome, RM 00184, Italy.

055.1 ITA ISSN 0012-2904
DIMENSIONI; rivista abruzzese di cultura e d'arte. 1957-1974. bi-m. Dimensioni, Via Bendetto Croce, 172, Pescara Colli, PE 65100, Italy.

621.381 USA ISSN 1040-0249
DIODE D.A.T.A. DIGEST. 1957-2000. a. D.A.T.A. Business Publishing, 15 Inverness Way E, Box 6510, Englewood, CO 80155-6510.

327.2 NZL ISSN 1173-9452
DIPLOMATIC AND CONSULAR LIST. 1943-2007. s-a. Ministry of Foreign Affairs and Trade, c/o Publication Officer, Private Bag 18-901, Wellington, New Zealand.

595.7 DEU ISSN 1436-5596
DIPTERON. 1998-2001. irreg. Dipteron, c/o Christian Kassebeer, Olshausenstr 40, Kiel, 24118, Germany.

379 FRA ISSN 0339-3313
DIRECT (PARIS). 1974-198?. m. Centre d'Information et d'Echanges Television, 39, bld Magenta, Paris, 75010, France.

368 FRA ISSN 0766-7078
DIRECTIONS. 1987-2005. 4/yr. Directions, 4 bd. Poissonniere, Paris, 75009, France.

330.9025 ESP ISSN 1577-1342
DIRECTORIO DE UNIDADES DE ACTIVIDAD ECONOMICA DE LA COMUNIDAD DE MADRID. 1999-2006. a. Comunidad de Madrid, Instituto de Estadistica, Principe de Vargara 108, Madrid, 28002, Spain.

330.9025 ESP ISSN 1579-3907
DIRECTORIO DE UNIDADES DE ACTIVIDAD ECONOMICA DE LA COMUNIDAD DE MADRID (ABRIDGE EDITION). 2001-2004. a. Comunidad de Madrid, Instituto de Estadistica, Principe de Vargara 108, Madrid, 28002, Spain.

378.0025 USA ISSN 1546-7759
DIRECTORY OF COLLEGE & UNIVERSITY ADMINISTRATORS. 1988-2005. a. Thomson Peterson's, Princeton Pike Corporate Center, 2000 Lenox Dr, 3rd Fl, PO Box 67005, Lawrenceville, NJ 08648.

304.6 FRA ISSN 0152-9757
DIRECTORY OF DEMOGRAPHIC RESEARCH CENTERS/ANNUAIRE DES CENTRES DE RECHERCHE DEMOGRAPHIQUE. 1974-1985. irreg. Committee for International Cooperation in National Research in Demography, 133 Boulevard Davout, Paris, 75980 Cedex 20 , France.

745.2025 GBR ISSN 0959-1710
DIRECTORY OF DESIGNERS. 1990-1991. a. Design Council, 34 Bow St, London, WC2E 7DL, United Kingdom.

780.79 DNK ISSN 1397-1999
DIRECTORY OF EUROPEAN JAZZ FESTIVALS AND RELATED MAJOR JAZZ EVENTS. 1982-1996. biennial. Danish Jazz Center, Borupvej 66 B, Ronnede, 4683, Denmark.

790 USA ISSN 1094-3005
DIRECTORY OF FUNPARKS & ATTRACTIONS; international guide to amusement parks, family entertainment centers, waterparks, and attractions. 1961-2006. a. (Mar.). Nielsen Business Publications, 770 Broadway, New York, NY 10003.

340 333.33 USA ISSN 1064-0355
DIRECTORY OF INTELLECTUAL PROPERTY ATTORNEYS. 1989-1995. a. Aspen Law & Business, 1185 Ave of the Americas, 37th Fl, New York, NY 10036.

658 371.42 AUS ISSN 1448-1332
DIRECTORY OF INTERNSHIPS AVAILABLE IN VICTORIAN HOSPITALS. (Victorian Medical Postgraduate Foundation) 1964-2005. a. Victorian Medical Postgraduate Foundation Inc., Level 8, 27 Victoria Parade, Fitzroy, VIC 3065, Australia.

340 USA ISSN 1932-1910
DIRECTORY OF LAW REVIEWS (PRINT). 1999-2005. irreg. LexisNexis, PO Box 7587, Charlottesville, VA 22906.

381.029 USA ISSN 1521-1304
DIRECTORY OF NORTH AMERICAN FAIRS, FESTIVALS AND EXPOSITIONS. 1888-19??. a. (Jan.). Nielsen Business Publications, 770 Broadway, New York, NY 10003.

025.04 USA ISSN 1081-2024
DIRECTORY OF ONLINE SERVICES. 1994-200?. a. LexisNexis, PO Box 7587, Charlottesville, VA 22906.

629.1 FRA
DIRECTORY OF RUSSIAN SPACE INDUSTRY. 1993-ceased. biennial. Sevig Press Publishing, 6 rue Bellart, Paris, 75015, France.

020 DEU
DIRECTORY OF SPECIAL COLLECTIONS IN WESTERN EUROPE. 1993-2001. irreg. K.G. Saur Verlag, Mies-van-der-Rohe-Str 1, Munich, 80807, Germany.

780 USA ISSN 0893-3065
DIRECTORY OF TRADITIONAL MUSIC. 1974-2005. biennial. International Council for Traditional Music, U C L A Department of Ethnomusicology, 2539 Schoenberg Music Bldg., Box 957178, Los Angeles, CA 90095-7178.

372 ITA ISSN 0012-3382
DIRITTI DELLA SCUOLA; mensile per la scuola primaria. 1899-2008; suspended. 10/yr. De Agostini Editore, Via G da Verrazzano 15, Novara, 28100, Italy.

347.9 ITA ISSN 0012-3404
DIRITTO DEL LAVORO; rivista di dottrina e di giurisprudenza. 1927-2006. bi-m. Fondazione Diritto del Lavoro, Via Antonio Gramsci 14, Rome, 00197, Italy.

340 330 ITA ISSN 0394-8366
DIRITTO ED ECONOMIA; rivista-dibattito interdisciplinare quadrimestrale. 1988-ceased. 3/yr. Maggioli Editore, Via del Carpino 8/10, Santarcangelo di Romagna, RN 47822, Italy.

658 614.8 ITA ISSN 0416-024X
IL DIRITTO SANITARIO MODERNO. 1953-19??. q. Edizioni Luigi Pozzi s.r.l., Via Panama 68, Rome, 00198, Italy.

362 USA ISSN 1538-2060
DISABILITY, CULTURE AND EDUCATION. 2002-200?. s-a. Information Age Publishing, Inc., PO Box 79049, Charlotte, NC 28271-7047.

362.4 340 USA ISSN 1083-625X
DISABILITY LAW REPORT. 1995-2006. m. Center for Education and Employment Law, PO BOX 3008, Malvern, PA 19355 .

368.382 362.4 GBR ISSN 0260-4108
DISABILITY RIGHTS BULLETIN. 1979-2006. 3/yr. Disability Alliance, Universal House, 88-94 Wentworth St, London, E1 7SA, United Kingdom.

790.1 DNK ISSN 0107-9042
DISCINFORM. 1982-1982. q. Dansk Frisbee Disc Forbund, PO Box 140, Farum, 3520, Denmark.

287.6 USA ISSN 1052-3804
DISCIPULOS RESPONSABLES. 1987-19??. q. United Methodist Publishing House, 201 8th Ave S, PO Box 801, Nashville, TN 37202.

919.3005 NZL ISSN 1177-1135
DISCOVER DOWNUNDER NEW ZEALAND; ein vierteljahrliches Magazin fur Besucher in Neuseeland. 2005-2005. q. Discover Downunder New Zealand Ltd., Level 7, 2 Woodward St, Wellington, New Zealand.

621.38 USA ISSN 1040-0214
DISCRETE SEMICONDUCTORS. POWER SEMICONDUCTORS. 1974-2000. a. D.A.T.A. Business Publishing, 15 Inverness Way E, Box 6510, Englewood, CO 80155-6510.

621.38 USA ISSN 1040-0222
DISCRETE SEMICONDUCTORS. THYRISTORS. 1973-2000. a. D.A.T.A. Business Publishing, 15 Inverness Way E, Box 6510, Englewood, CO 80155-6510.

800 ITA ISSN 0012-3668
DISCRETIO. 1962-ceased. irreg. Discretio, Via F. M. Penna 20, Sicily 97018, Italy.

636.089 590 FRA ISSN 1608-0610
DISEASE INFORMATION (ONLINE EDITION). 1999-2006. w. Organisation Mondiale de la Sante Animale (O I E), 12 rue de Prony, Paris, 75017, France.

745.2 ITA ISSN 1594-8528
DISEGNO INDUSTRIALE INDUSTRIAL DESIGN. 2002-200? (vol.8). q. Gangemi Editore, Piazza San Pantaleo 4, Rome, Italy.

004.678 DEU
DISINFOJOURNAL; the first international e-journal of disinformation on the net. 2003-2003 (ceased same year). irreg. Institute for the Examination of Information Behavior at the Internet

362.7 DEU ISSN 0937-9614
DISKURS; Studien zu Kindheit, Jugend, Familie und Gesellschaft. 1990-2005. 3/yr. Deutsches Jugendinstitut e.V., Nockherstr 2, Munich, 81541, Germany.

028.5 USA ISSN 1050-2491
DISNEY ADVENTURES. 1990-2007. 10/yr. Disney Publishing Worldwide, 114 Fifth Ave, 16th Fl, New York, NY 10011-5690.

028.5 DEU
DISNEY FAMILY. 2004-2005. q. Egmont Ehapa Verlag GmbH, Wallstr 59, Berlin, 10179, Germany.

028.5 DEU
DISNEY FLUCH DER KARIBIK; das Magazin zum Film. 2007-2008 (Sep.). q. Egmont Ehapa Verlag GmbH, Wallstr 59, Berlin, 10179, Germany.

028.5 DEU
DISNEY FUN; raetseln, malen, lachen. 2007-2008 (Jun.). q. Egmont Ehapa Verlag GmbH, Wallstr 59, Berlin, 10179, Germany.

028.5 DEU
DISNEY KLEINE KOECHE. 2004-2006 (Jun.). bi-m. Egmont Ehapa Verlag GmbH, Wallstr 59, Berlin, 10179, Germany.

028.5 DEU
DISNEY'S PRINZESSIN SPEZIAL. 2001-200?. 2/yr. Egmont Ehapa Verlag GmbH, Wallstr 59, Berlin, 10179, Germany.

746.9 GBR ISSN 1755-7208
DISTILL. 2008 (Sep.)-2009. 6/yr. Distill Magazine, 800 Guillat Ave, Kent Science Park, Sittingbourne, ME9 8GU, United Kingdom.

690 USA ISSN 0897-6236
DISTINGUISHED HOME PLANS. 1985-2009 (Jan.). q. HomePlans.com, 901 N 3rd St, Ste 216, Minneapolis, MN 55401.

388.3 FRA ISSN 0153-3142
DISTRIBUTEUR AUTOMOBILE. 1977-2005. 10/yr. Distributeur Automobile, 194 rue Marcadet, Paris, 75018, France.

340 AUS
DISTRICT COURTS JUDGMENTS INDEXES. 1997-2007. m. Supreme Court Library Committee, Queensland, PO Box 19, Brisbane, Albert St., QLD 4002, Australia.

658.8 NLD ISSN 1871-2959
DISTRIFOOD INSTORE. 2005-2005. biennial. Reed Business bv, Hanzestraat 1, Doetinchem, 7006 RH, Netherlands.

300 GBR ISSN 0263-3221
DITCHLEY CONFERENCE REPORTS. 1981-2000. 15/yr. Ditchley Foundation, Ditchley Foundation Ltd, Ditchley Park, Enstone, Chipping Norton, Oxon OX7 4ER, United Kingdom.

300 340 GBR ISSN 0262-8015
DITCHLEY NEWSLETTER. 1981-2003. 3/yr. Ditchley Foundation, Ditchley Foundation Ltd, Ditchley Park, Enstone, Chipping Norton, Oxon OX7 4ER, United Kingdom.

840 FRA ISSN 1262-3598
DIX-NEUF-VINGT; revue de litteraire moderne. 1996-199?. s-a. Dix-Neuf-Vingt, 816 av. du Marechal Foch, Mont-de-Marsan, 40000, France.

072.1 GBR ISSN 0264-9691
DOCKLANDS NEWS. 1983-2005. m. Docklands Media, The Custom House, King George V Lock, Woodwich Manor Way, London, E16 2NJ, United Kingdom.

320.9 FRA ISSN 1958-8143
DOCUMENT BRUT. 2007-2007. m. Editions Independantes, 144 rue de Rivoli, Paris, 75001, France.

621.388 AUS ISSN 1442-844X
DOCUMENTER. 1988-2001. q. Documenter Journals Inc, 288 Brunswick St, Fitzroy, ACT 3065, Australia.

410 FRA ISSN 0085-4786
DOCUMENTS DE LINGUISTIQUE QUANTITATIVE. 1969-1980. irreg. Editions Jean Favard, 37 rue du Four A Chaux, St Sulpice de Favieres, 91910, France.

900 USA ISSN 0749-4831
DOCUMENTS IN IMPERIAL HISTORY. 1985-200?. irreg. Greenwood Publishing Group Inc., 88 Post Rd W, PO Box 5007, Westport, CT 06881.

639.2 GBR ISSN 0958-5648 CODEN: DONREF
DOCUMENTS OF THE N R P B. (National Radiological Protection Board) 1990-2005. irreg. Health Protection Agency, Radiation Protection Division, Centre for Radiation, Chemical and Environmental Hazards, Chilton, Didcot, Oxon OX11 0RQ, United Kingdom.

333.95416 GBR ISSN 0265-5640 CODEN: DODODN
DODO; journal of the wildlife conservation trusts. 1977-2002. a. Currell Wildlife Preservation Trust, Les Augres Manor, Trinity, Jersey Channel Isl JE3 5BP, United Kingdom.

362.4 DNK ISSN 1604-6110
DOEVBLEVNE.INFO. 1992-2006. irreg. Landsforeningen for Bedre Hoerelse, Doevblevneafdelingen, c/o Landsforeningen for Bedre Hoerelse, Kloeverprisvej 10 B, Hvidovre, 2650, Denmark.

917.97772 636.7 USA ISSN 1534-6722
THE DOG LOVER'S COMPANION TO SEATTLE. 1996-ceased. irreg. Avalon Travel Publishing, 1700 4th St, Berkeley, CA 94710.

053.1 DEU
DOIN' FINE. 1999-200?. bi-m. CapCom Media GmbH, Marsstr 13, Munich, 80335, Germany.

306 390 FRA ISSN 1951-4964
DOKIDOKI MAGAZINE. 2006-2006. a. Association Japon et Culture, 100 Rue Brule-Maison, Lille, 59000, France.

016.3276 DEU ISSN 0342-040X
DOKUMENTATIONSDIENST AFRIKA. AUSGEWAEHLTE NEUERE LITERATUR. 1973-2005. q. Deutsches Uebersee-Institut, Uebersee-Dokumentation, Neuer Jungfernstieg 21, Hamburg, 20354, Germany.

016.3276 DEU ISSN 0720-2032
DOKUMENTATIONSDIENST AFRIKA. KURZBIBLIOGRAPHIE. 1980-2005. irreg. Deutsches Uebersee-Institut, Uebersee-Dokumentation, Neuer Jungfernstieg 21, Hamburg, 20354, Germany.

327.6 DEU ISSN 0342-0442
DOKUMENTATIONSDIENST AFRIKA. REIHE A. 1973-1999. irreg. Deutsches Uebersee-Institut, Uebersee-Dokumentation, Neuer Jungfernstieg 21, Hamburg, 20354, Germany.

016.3275 DEU ISSN 0936-9171
DOKUMENTATIONSDIENST ASIEN UND SUEDPAZIFIK. AUSGEWAEHLTE NEUERE LITERATUR. 1975-2005. q. Deutsches Uebersee-Institut, Uebersee-Dokumentation, Neuer Jungfernstieg 21, Hamburg, 20354, Germany.

016.3275 DEU ISSN 0938-3638
DOKUMENTATIONSDIENST ASIEN UND SUEDPAZIFIK. KURZBIBLIOGRAPHIE. 1978-2005. irreg. Deutsches Uebersee-Institut, Uebersee-Dokumentation, Neuer Jungfernstieg 21, Hamburg, 20354, Germany.

016.3275 DEU ISSN 0937-5929
DOKUMENTATIONSDIENST ASIEN UND SUEDPAZIFIK. REIHE A. 1971-2003. irreg. Deutsches Uebersee-Institut, Uebersee-Dokumentation, Neuer Jungfernstieg 21, Hamburg, 20354, Germany.

016.3278 DEU ISSN 0342-037X
DOKUMENTATIONSDIENST LATEINAMERIKA. AUSGEWAEHLTE NEUERE LITERATUR/DOCUMENTACION LATINOAMERICANA. BOLETIN BIBLIOGRAFICO. 1971-2005. q. Deutsches Uebersee-Institut, Uebersee-Dokumentation, Neuer Jungfernstieg 21, Hamburg, 20354, Germany.

327 DEU ISSN 0937-5937
DOKUMENTATIONSDIENST VORDERER ORIENT. AUSGEWAEHLTE NEUERE LITERATUR. 1970-2005. q. Deutsches Uebersee-Institut, Uebersee-Dokumentation, Neuer Jungfernstieg 21, Hamburg, 20354, Germany.

016.327 DEU ISSN 0938-2666
DOKUMENTATIONSDIENST VORDERER ORIENT. KURZBIBLIOGRAPHIE. 1978-2005. irreg. Deutsches Uebersee-Institut, Uebersee-Dokumentation, Neuer Jungfernstieg 21, Hamburg, 20354, Germany.

016.3275 DEU ISSN 0937-5945
DOKUMENTATIONSDIENST VORDERER ORIENT. REIHE A. 1973-2005. irreg. Deutsches Uebersee-Institut, Uebersee-Dokumentation, Neuer Jungfernstieg 21, Hamburg, 20354, Germany.

629.1 DEU ISSN 0948-7050
DOKUMENTE DER LUFT- UND RAUMFAHRTINDUSTRIE. 1994-1996 (vol.15). irreg. Daimler-Benz Aerospace AG, Postfach 801109, Munich, 81663, Germany.

618 613.04244 ITA ISSN 1721-5579
DOLCE ATTESA; nove mesi per diventare mamma. 2002-ceased. q. Sfera Editore SpA, Via Angelo Rizzoli 2, Milan, MI 20132, Italy.

790.13 GBR ISSN 1358-3506
DOLL MAGAZINE; the international doll collector's magazine. 1992-2008. bi-m. Ashdown Publishing Ltd., Ancient Lights, 19 River Rd, Arundel, W Sussex RH13 8RY, United Kingdom.

282 BRD
DER DOM. 1895-1990. a. Bernward Mediengesellschaft mbH, Domhof 24, Hildesheim, 31134, Germany.

055.1 ITA ISSN 1121-7847
IL DOMANI DI NOI RAGAZZI. 1960-ceased. q. Editrice Luigi Pellegrini, Via de Rada 67c, Cosenza, CS 87100, Italy.

747 ITA ISSN 1129-0498
DOMINA. 1984-ceased. m. Domina Srl, Piazza Castello 9, Milan, 20121, Italy.

659.152 ITA ISSN 1125-4629
DOMINA SPOSA. 1988-ceased. s-a. Domina Srl, Piazza Castello 9, Milan, 20121, Italy.

747 640 USA ISSN 1554-7361
DOMINO; the shopping magazine for you home. 2005-2009. 10/yr. Conde Nast Publications, Inc., 4 Times Sq, 6th Fl, New York, NY 10036.

720 ITA ISSN 1122-8938
DOMUS DOSSIER. 1993-199?. s-a. Editoriale Domus, Via Gianni Mazzocchi 1/3, Rozzano, MI 20089, Italy.

959.152 ITA ISSN 0393-795X
DONNA; international fashion magazine. 1979-ceased. m. Hachette Rusconi SpA, Viale Sarca 235, Milan, 20126, Italy.

620 NLD ISSN 0012-5482
DOORKIJK. 1965-2005. 6/yr. Katholiek Vrouwengilde Nederland, Bisonspoor 1204, Maarssen, 3605 KZ, Netherlands.

780.42 DEU
DOORS QUARTERLY MAGAZINE. 1983-2000. q. Doors Quarterly Magazine, Muelheimer Str 132, Duisburg, 47057, Germany.

320 ITA
DOSSIER EUROPA. 1955-ceased. s-a. Commissione Europea, Rappresentanza in Italia, Via IV Novembre 149, Rome, 00187, Italy.

371.335 027.8 NLD ISSN 1569-9633
DOSSIER KENNIS EN MEDIA. 1983-2005. bi-m. Biblion Uitgeverij, Veursestraatweg 280, Leidschendam, 2265 CL, Netherlands.

336.2 NLD ISSN 1872-6496
DOSSIER V P B 2007. (Vennootschapsbelasting Tweeduizendzeven) 2006-2007. bi-m. SDU Fiscale en Financiele Uitgevers, Maanlander 45, Amersfoort, 3824 MN, Netherlands.

305.42 LUX ISSN 1012-1935
DOSSIER WOMEN OF EUROPE. 1977-1998. irreg. European Commission, Office for Official Publications of the European Union, 2 Rue Mercier, Luxembourg, L-2985, Luxembourg.

700 FRA ISSN 0756-5860
LES DOSSIERS DE L'ART PUBLIC. 1983-199?. irreg. Association pour la Promotion de l'Art Public (A.P.A.P.), 71 rue d'Hautpoul, Paris, 75019, France.

658 FRA ISSN 0769-5918
DOSSIERS DU MARKETING DIRECT. 1984-199?. 11/yr. Centre Francais pour la Promotion du Marketing Direct, 4 rue de Commaille, Paris, 75007, France.

339.543 382 NLD ISSN 1872-4132
DOUANEBESPAARBRIEF. 2006-ceased. bi-m. Sdu Uitgevers bv, Postbus 20025, The Hague, 2500 EA, Netherlands.

796 ITA ISSN 1825-7186
DOVE PESCARE DOLCE. 2005-200?. a. Sprea Editori Srl, Via Torino 51, Cernusco sul Naviglio, MI 20063, Italy.

808.8385 053.1 DEU
DR. MONIKA LINDT; die Kinderaerztin mit dem Guten Herzen. 1980-2003. w. Bastei Verlag Gustav H. Luebbe GmbH und Co., Scheidtbachstr 23-31, Bergisch Gladbach, 51469, Germany.

346.052 USA ISSN 1559-5188
DRAFTING FUNDAMENTAL ESTATE PLANNING DOCUMENTS. 19??-2005 (Apr.). biennial. Pennsylvania Bar Institute, 5080 Ritter Rd, Mechanicsburg, PA 17055.

794.8 GBR ISSN 1466-2388
DREAMCAST. 1999-2001. bi-m. Dennis Publishing Ltd., 30 Cleveland St, London, W1T 4JD, United Kingdom.

796.7 DEU
DRIFT; Das Supermoto Magazin. 2003-2008 (Oct.). 6/yr. Mo Medien Verlag GmbH, Schrempfstr 8, Stuttgart, 70597, Germany.

658.507 DNK ISSN 0108-6707
DRIFTSTEKNIKERBOGEN. 1974-1998. a. Danmarks Tekniske Universitet, Institut for Produktions- og Virksomhedsledelse, Bygn 423, Lyngby, 2800, Denmark.

663 GBR ISSN 0951-7723
THE DRINK FORECAST. 1994-2001. q. N T C Publications Ltd., PO Box 69, Henley-on-Thames, Oxon RG9 1GB, United Kingdom.

663 GBR ISSN 0965-5360
DRINK POCKET BOOK (YEAR). 1989-2006. a. N T C Publications Ltd., Farm Rd, Henley-on-Thames, Oxon RG9 1EJ, United Kingdom.

531.64 621.3 DEU ISSN 0939-8007 CODEN: DCONEQ
DRIVE AND CONTROL. 1981-1998. 4/yr. Siemens AG, Henkestr 127, Erlangen, 91052, Germany.

531.64 621.3 DEU ISSN 0939-7663
DRIVE UND CONTROL. 1981-1998. q. Siemens AG, Henkestr 127, Erlangen, 91052, Germany.

001.3 FRA ISSN 1954-9083
DROIT DE CITES. 2006-2007. q. Presses Universitaires de France, 6 Avenue Reille, Paris, 75685 Cedex 14, France.

622 340 FRA ISSN 0999-9353 CODEN: REAIE7
DROIT DU SOUS-SOL. 1989-1995. 2/yr. Editions ESKA, 12 Rue du Quatre-Septembre, Paris, 75002, France.

686.2 DEU
DRUCK-SACHEN; Informationsdienst der deutschen Druckindustrie. 1978-1999. irreg. Bundesverband Druck und Medien e.V., Biebricher Allee 79, Wiesbaden, 65187, Germany.

686.2 DEU ISSN 0933-663X
DRUCKBEHAELTERVERORDNUNG. 1981-200?. irreg. Erich Schmidt Verlag GmbH & Co. (Berlin), Genthiner Str 30 G, Berlin, 10785, Germany.

686.2 DEU
DRUCKSPIEGEL SPECIAL. 1994-2003. 5/yr. Druckspiegel Verlagsgesellschaft mbH und Co., Borsigstr 1-3, Heusenstamm, 63150, Germany.

615.1 USA ISSN 1098-9986
DRUG FACTS AND COMPARISONS NEWS. 1998-200?. m. Facts and Comparisons, 77 West Port Plz, Ste 450, St. Louis, MO 63146.

615 USA ISSN 1072-6047
DRUG INFORMATION ASSOCIATION. NEWSLETTER. 1965-200?. q. Drug Information Association, 800 Enterprise Rd, Ste 200, Horsham, PA 19044.

615 USA ISSN 0146-4051
DRUG THERAPY REVIEWS. 1977-1979. irreg. Masson Publishing U.S.A. Inc., 16 E 34th St, 14th Fl, New York, NY 10016.

362.29 AUS ISSN 1036-9864
DRUGS IN SOCIETY. 1986-2004. q. Alcohol and Drug Foundation, PO Box 332, Spring Hill, QLD 4004, Australia.

615.1 GBR ISSN 1368-8529
DRUGS QUARTERLY. 1997-2002. q. Pillar Publications Ltd., 45 Woodland Grove, Weybridge, Surrey KT13 9EQ, United Kingdom.

786.9 NZL ISSN 1176-6816
DRUM CONNEXIONS. 2004-2006. q. Drum Connexions, PO Box 42044, Homedale, Wellington, New Zealand.

796.7 ITA ISSN 1121-5534
DUE RUOTE. 1990-ceased. bi-m. Editoriale Domus, Via Gianni Mazzocchi 1/3, Rozzano, MI 20089, Italy.

028.5 SWE ISSN 1652-9758
DUEL MASTERS. 2005-2005. bi-m. Egmont Serieforlaget AB, Stora Varvsgatan 19A, Malmo, 20507, Sweden.

305.23 DEU
DUEL MASTERS MAGAZIN. 2004-2005 (Jun.). 4/yr. Panini Verlags GmbH, Ravensstr 48, Nettetal, 41334, Germany.

305.42 ESP ISSN 1130-409X
DUNIA. 1976-2003. m. G y J Espana Ediciones S.L., Albasanz, 15 Edificio A, Madrid, 28037, Spain.

700 CHN ISSN 1000-6028
DUO YUN/ART CLOUDS. 1981-1997. s-a. Shanghai Shuhua Chubanshe, 81 Qinzhou Nanlu, Shanghai, 200233, China.

616.8 TUR ISSN 1018-8681
DUSUNEN ADAM/JOURNAL OF PSYCHIATRY AND NEUROLOGICAL SCIENCES; psikiyatri ve norolojik bilimler dergisi. 1987-ceased. q. Logos Yayincilik Ticaret A.S., Yildiz Posta Cad., Sinan Apt. No.36 D 66-67, Gayrettepe, Istanbul, 34349, Turkey.

780.42 NLD
THE DUTCH GO DURAN INTERNATIONAL; the independent fanzine. 1988-2006 (no.73). q. Dutch Go Duran International, Waldeck Pyrmontsingel 71, Nijmegen, 6524 BA, Netherlands.

053.931 AUS ISSN 1320-9450
DUTCH WEEKLY; the national Dutch language newspaper for Australia, New Zealand & Indonesia. 1951-2004. fortn. Dutch Weekly Pty. Ltd., Ste. 301, 541 George St1, Sydney, NSW 2000, Australia.

690 352.9 USA ISSN 1055-4505
DWELLING CONSTRUCTION UNDER THE UNIFORM MECHANICAL CODE. 1991-199?. triennial. International Conference of Building Officials, 5360 Workman Mill Rd, Whittier, CA 90601.

006.6 USA ISSN 1094-2548
DYNAMIC GRAPHICS MAGAZINE; quick, cool, creative ideas for Mac & PC. 1996-ceased. bi-m. Dynamic Graphics Group, PO Box 9007, Maple Shade, NJ 08052.

531 NLD ISSN 1874-5628
DYNAMICAL PROPERTIES OF SOLIDS. 1974-1995 (vol.7). irreg. Elsevier BV, North-Holland, Sara Burgerhartstraat 25, Amsterdam, 1055 KV, Netherlands.

179 DNK ISSN 1397-1379
DYRENES RET. 1977-1998. q. Landsforeningen Komiteen mod Dyreforsoeg, Valdemarsgade 67, 5 tv, PO Box 59, Charlottenlund, 2920, Denmark.

658 GBR ISSN 1744-3547
E-BUSINESS PROCESS. 1993-200?. 10/yr. SODAN, 20 Mead Rd, Uxbridge, Mddx UB8 1AU, United Kingdom.

Cessations

336 NLD
E C CORPORATE TAX LAW. (European Commission) ceased 2009. plus s-a. updates. International Bureau of Fiscal Documentation (I B F D), H J E Wenckebachweg 210, Amsterdam, 1096 AS, Netherlands.

354.762114 GBR ISSN 1366-9788
E C INFORM TRANSPORT. (European Commission) 1997-2002 (Dec.). m. E C Inform, Russet House, Red House Ln, Elstead, Godalming, Surrey GU8 6DR, United Kingdom.

658 FRA ISSN 1952-3955
E-COMMERCE & V A D. LA LETTRE. (Vente a Distance) 2005-2006. bi-w. Editialis, 13 Rue Louis Pasteur, Boulogne Billancourt, Cedex 92513, France.

658 FRA ISSN 1952-3947
E-COMMERCE & V A D. LE MAGAZINE. (Vente a Distance) 2006-2008. bi-m. Editialis, 13 Rue Louis Pasteur, Boulogne Billancourt, Cedex 92513, France.

330.9 KOR ISSN 1329-1149
E D A P JOINT POLICY STUDIES. (Economic Development Management in Asia and the Pacific) 1997-1998 (no.9). q. Asia Pacific Press, The Crawford Bldg, Ellery Circuit, The Australian National University, Canberra, ACT 0200, Australia.

620 370 NLD ISSN 1682-8941
E D U NEWS. (Education News) 2002-2004. irreg. European Space Agency, Communication Production Office, Keplerlaan 1, Noordwijk, 2200 AG, Netherlands.

363.19 GBR ISSN 1360-399X
E E C S NEWSLETTER. (Electrical Equipment Certification Service) 1984-2001. s-a. Health and Safety Executive, Rose Court, 2 Southwark Bridge, London, SE1 9HS, United Kingdom.

323.445 AUS ISSN 1329-6906
E F A NEWS. 1995-1999 (Aug.). q. Electronic Frontiers Australia Inc., PO Box 382, North Adelaide, SA 5006, Australia.

338 AUS
E F I C ASSIST NEWS. 1992-2002. q. Export Finance and Insurance Corporation, Level 10, Export House, 22 Pitts St, Sydney, NSW 2000, Australia.

382.63060489 DNK ISSN 0902-2236
E F R - AARSBERETNING. (Erhvervsfremme) 1982-1988. a. E F R - Erhvervsfremme Styrelsen, Tagensvej 137, Copenhagen N, 2200, Denmark.

332.66 DEU ISSN 0937-2369
E G WIRTSCHAFTSRECHT AUSSENWIRTSCHAFT. (Europaische Gemeinschaft) 1989-2005. 12/yr. Deutscher Wirtschaftsdienst, Luxemburger Str 449, Cologne, 50939, Germany.

004 DEU
E-GUIDE. 2000-2001. q. BurdaYukom Publishing GmbH, Konrad-Zuse-Platz 11, Munich, 81829, Germany.

643 ITA
E I - ELETTRORADIO INFORMAZIONI; the magazine for manufacturers, retailers, dealers and technicians of consumer electronic goods. 1960-ceased. every 15 days. Publiedim s.r.l., Via Matteo Civitali, 51, Milan, MI 20148, Italy.

643 ITA
E I - ELETTRORADIO INFORMAZIONI INTERNATIONAL. 1989-ceased. m. Publiedim s.r.l., Via Matteo Civitali, 51, Milan, MI 20148, Italy.

338.7 NLD ISSN 0169-6297
E I M JAARVERSLAG. 1961-1988. a. Economisch Instituut voor het Midden- en Kleinbedrijf, Postbus 7001, Zoetermeer, 2701 AA, Netherlands.

330.95 USA
E I U COUNTRY FORECASTS ON DISC: ASIA-PACIFIC. (Economist Intelligence Unit) 1994-2003. m. SilverPlatter Information, Incorporated, 333 Seventh Ave, 20th Fl, New York, NY 10001.

320.947 USA
E I U COUNTRY FORECASTS ON DISC: EASTERN EUROPE. (Economist Intelligence Unit) 1994-2003. m. SilverPlatter Information, Incorporated, 333 Seventh Ave, 20th Fl, New York, NY 10001.

320.96 USA
E I U COUNTRY FORECASTS ON DISC: MIDDLE EAST-AFRICA. (Economist Intelligence Unit) 1994-2003. m. SilverPlatter Information, Incorporated, 333 Seventh Ave, 20th Fl, New York, NY 10001.

330.98 USA
E I U COUNTRY FORECASTS ON DISC: THE AMERICAS. (Economist Intelligence Unit) 1994-2003. m. SilverPlatter Information, Incorporated, 333 Seventh Ave, 20th Fl, New York, NY 10001.

320.94 USA
E I U COUNTRY FORECASTS ON DISC: WESTERN EUROPE. (Economist Intelligence Unit) 1994-2003. m. SilverPlatter Information, Incorporated, 333 Seventh Ave, 20th Fl, New York, NY 10001.

330.95 USA
E I U COUNTRY REPORTS ON DISC: ASIA-PACIFIC. (Economist Intelligence Unit) 1993-2003. m. SilverPlatter Information, Incorporated, 333 Seventh Ave, 20th Fl, New York, NY 10001.

330.947 USA
E I U COUNTRY REPORTS ON DISC: EASTERN EUROPE. (Economist Intelligence Unit) 1993-2003. m. SilverPlatter Information, Incorporated, 333 Seventh Ave, 20th Fl, New York, NY 10001.

330.956 USA
E I U COUNTRY REPORTS ON DISC: MIDDLE EAST - NORTH AFRICA. (Economist Intelligence Unit) 1993-2003. m. SilverPlatter Information, Incorporated, 333 Seventh Ave, 20th Fl, New York, NY 10001.

330.967 USA
E I U COUNTRY REPORTS ON DISC: SUB-SAHARAN AFRICA. (Economist Intelligence Unit) 1993-2003. m. SilverPlatter Information, Incorporated, 333 Seventh Ave, 20th Fl, New York, NY 10001.

330.98 USA
E I U COUNTRY REPORTS ON DISC: THE AMERICAS. (Economist Intelligence Unit) 1993-2003. m. SilverPlatter Information, Incorporated, 333 Seventh Ave, 20th Fl, New York, NY 10001.

320.94 USA
E I U COUNTRY RISK SERVICE ON DISC: ASIA-PACIFIC. 199?-2003. m. SilverPlatter Information, Incorporated, 333 Seventh Ave, 20th Fl, New York, NY 10001.

330.9 332 USA
E I U COUNTRY RISK SERVICE ON DISC: EUROPE. (Economist Intelligence Unit) 1997-2003. m. SilverPlatter Information, Incorporated, 333 Seventh Ave, 20th Fl, New York, NY 10001.

330.9 332 USA
E I U COUNTRY RISK SERVICE ON DISC: MIDDLE EAST-NORTH AFRICA. (Economist Intelligence Unit) 1997-2003. m. SilverPlatter Information, Incorporated, 333 Seventh Ave, 20th Fl, New York, NY 10001.

330.9 332 USA
E I U COUNTRY RISK SERVICE ON DISC: SUB-SAHARAN AFRICA. (Economist Intelligence Unit) 1997-2003. m. SilverPlatter Information, Incorporated, 333 Seventh Ave, 20th Fl, New York, NY 10001.

382 338 USA
E I U INTERNATIONAL BUSINESS NEWSLETTERS ON DISC. (Economist Intelligence Unit) 1993-2003. m. SilverPlatter Information, Incorporated, 333 Seventh Ave, 20th Fl, New York, NY 10001.

322.6 USA
E I U INVESTING, LICENSING AND TRADING. (Economist Intelligence Unit) 1995-2003. m. SilverPlatter Information, Incorporated, 333 Seventh Ave, 20th Fl, New York, NY 10001.

336.71 CZE ISSN 1801-268X
E-MAIL NOVINY BANKOVNI AKTUALITY. 2005-2006. m. Verlag Dashoefer s.r.o., Na Prikope 18, PO Box 756, Prague 1, 11121, Czech Republic.

380.1 NZL ISSN 1175-1932
E.OFFICE (YEAR); NZ Office Products News annual buyers guide to products & services. 1993-2000. a. Profile Publishing Ltd., Wellesley St, PO Box 5544, Auckland, New Zealand.

616.8 GBR ISSN 1726-0620
E P D A FOCUS. (European Parkinson's Disease Association) 1993-2004. 3/yr. European Parkinson's Disease Association, 4 Golding Rd, Sevenoaks, Kent TN13 3NJ, United Kingdom.

020 AUS ISSN 1833-0711
E - PERMANENCE BULLETIN. 2003-2006. irreg. Australia. National Archives, Government Recordkeeping Branch, PO Box 7425, Parkes, ACT 2600, Australia.

340 658.3 USA ISSN 1068-3542
E R I S A AND BENEFITS LAW JOURNAL. (Employee Retirement Income Security Act) 1992-1999. 4/yr. LexisNexis, PO Box 7587, Charlottesville, VA 22906.

300 NLD ISSN 1387-0904
E S H H S. EUROPEAN SOCIETY FOR THE HISTORY OF THE HUMAN SCIENCES. 1973-2005. s-a. International Society for History of the Behavioral and Social Sciences, c/o Ruud Abma, Ed., Interdisciplinary Social Science, Universiteit Utrecht, PO Box 80140, Utrecht, 3508, Netherlands.

384.33 AUS ISSN 1447-0896
E-TRADING AND E-SERVICES MARKET. 1984-2003. a. Paul Budde Communication Pty. Ltd., 5385 George Downes Dr, Bucketty, NSW 2250, Australia.

330 CZE ISSN 1214-7346
E U TIP. (Evropska Unie) 2004-2006. fortn. Verlag Dashoefer s.r.o., Na Prikope 18, PO Box 756, Prague 1, 11121, Czech Republic.

388 NLD
E W SPECIAL; transport en verpakking. 1976 (no.2)-1988. irreg. Reed Business bv, Van de Sande, Bakhuyzenstraat 4, Amsterdam, 1061 AG, Netherlands.

700 800 USA ISSN 1059-1168
EARLY DRAMA, ART, AND MUSIC REFERENCE SERIES. 1978-2002. irreg. Medieval Institute Press, Western Michigan University, Walwood Hall, 1903 W Michigan, Kalamazoo, MI 49008.

370 AUS ISSN 1832-1364
EARLY LEARNINGS. 2004-2006. a. Telstra Foundation, Locked Bag 5680, Melbourne, VIC 3001, Australia.

052 NZL
EARWIG. 1969-1972. s-a. Earwig Graphics, 10 Norfolk St, Auckland 2, New Zealand.

015 GBR ISSN 0046-0958
EAST ANGLIAN BIBLIOGRAPHY. 1960-2003. q. East Anglian Librarian's Consultative Committee, Central Library, St Andrews St N, Bury St Edmunds, Suffolk IP33 1TZ, United Kingdom.

950 GBR
EAST ASIAN SOCIAL SCIENCE MONOGRAPHS. 1973-198?. irreg. Oxford University Press, Great Clarendon St, Oxford, OX2 6DP, United Kingdom.

342 USA ISSN 1075-8402
EAST EUROPEAN CONSTITUTIONAL REVIEW. 1992-2003. q. New York University School of Law, 161 Ave of the Americas, 12th Fl, New York, NY 10013.

940 947 USA ISSN 0012-8449
EAST EUROPEAN QUARTERLY. 1967-2008. q. East European Quarterly, c/o Stephen Fischer-Galati, Box 945, Taylor, TX 76574.

641.5 USA ISSN 1526-0275
EASY HOME COOKING. 1997-2008 (Feb.). bi-m. Publications International Ltd., 7373 North, Cicero, IL 60646.

641.5 USA ISSN 1559-8500
EAT (DES MOINES). 2006-2007. q. Meredith Corporation, 1716 Locust St, Des Moines, IA 50309.

637 FRA ISSN 1143-4376
ECHO DE LA CREMERIE. 1989-199?. 4/yr. Echo de la Cremerie, 29 rue Violet, Paris, 75015, France.

382 FRA ISSN 1148-1757
ECHOS DE L'EXPORTATION. 1984-199?. 48/yr. Echos de l'Exportation, 46 rue la Boetie, Paris, Cedex 8 75381, France.

262.3 ITA
L'ECO DI SAN GERMANO. 1957-ceased. m. Tipolitografia San. Lorenzo Tortona, Largo Paolo Savini, 1, Varzi, PV 27057, Italy.

613.1 GBR ISSN 0968-5693
ECO DIRECTORY OF ENVIRONMENTAL DATABASES IN THE UNITED KINGDOM. 1992-1996. a. Eco Environmental Information Trust, 10-12 Picton St, Montpelier, Bristol BS6 5QA, United Kingdom.

629.2 ITA ISSN 0422-2628
ECO MOTORI. 1958-ceased. m. (10/yr.). Editrice Cicerone s.r.l., Piazza Aldo Moro, 33-A, Bari, BA 70122, Italy.

370 FRA ISSN 0759-2914
L'ECOLE ET LA NATION-ACTUALITES. 1975-1983. q. Parti Communiste Francais, 2 place du Colonel Fabien, Paris, 75019, France.

720 FRA ISSN 1951-2694
ECOLE NATIONALE SUPERIEURE D'ARCHITECTURE (PARIS-VAL-DE-SEINE). JOURNAL. 2005-2006. q. Ecole Nationale Superieure d'Architecture de Paris-Val-de-Seine, 14 Rue Bonaparte, Paris, 75006, France.

028.1 FRA ISSN 1259-1130
ECOLE NATIONALE SUPERIEURE DES SCIENCES DE L'INFORMATION ET DES BIBLIOTHEQUES. REVUE DES SOMMAIRES. 1992-2001. 11/yr. Ecole Nationale Superieure des Sciences de l'Information et des Bibliotheques (E N S S I B), 17-21 bd. du 11 Novembre 1918, Villeurbanne, Cedex 69623, France.

371.3 FRA ISSN 0765-6017
ECOLES DES LETTRES. SECOND CYCLE. 1908-2006. 14/yr. Ecole des Loisirs, 11 Rue de Sevres, Paris, Cedex 6 75278, France.

158 ITA ISSN 0394-1310
ECOLOGIA DELLA MENTE. 1986-ceased. s-a. Il Pensiero Scientifico Editore, Via Bradano 3-C, Rome, 00199, Italy.

577 USA ISSN 0012-9623 CODEN: BECLAG
ECOLOGICAL SOCIETY OF AMERICA. BULLETIN (PRINT). 1917-2002. q. Ecological Society of America, 1707 H St, N W, Ste 400, Washington, DC 20006.

363.7 GBR ISSN 0261-3131 CODEN: ECLGEZ
THE ECOLOGIST (PRINT). 1970-2009 (Jul.). 10/yr. Ecosystems Ltd., 18 Chelsea Wharf, 15 Lots Rd, London, SW10 0JZ, United Kingdom.

330.1 AUS ISSN 0816-6838
ECONOMETRICS DISCUSSION PAPERS. 1985-1999. irreg. University of Sydney, Faculty of Economics and Business, Rm 384, Merewether Bldg, Corner City Rd and Butlin Ave, Sydney, NSW 2006, Australia.

330.9 ITA
ECONOMIA EMILIA-ROMAGNA. 1994-ceased. m. Unione delle Camere di Commercio dell'Emilia-Romagna, Via Aldo Moro 62, Bologna, BO 40127, Italy.

330 ESP ISSN 0211-4763
ECONOMIA GUIPUZCOANA. 1965-198?. 4/yr. Camara Oficial de Comercio Industria y Navegacion de Guipuzcoa, Ramon Maria Lili, 6, San Sebastian, Spain.

330 ESP ISSN 0012-9801
ECONOMIA INTERNACIONAL. 1956-1984. m. Economia Internacional, Balmes, 213, Barcelona, 08001, Spain.

330 DEU ISSN 0343-754X
ECONOMIC BULLETIN. 1963-2004. m. Deutsches Institut fuer Wirtschaftsforschung, Koenigin-Luise-Str 5, Berlin, 14195, Germany.

330.9 DEU ISSN 0431-6045
ECONOMIC SITUATION IN THE FEDERAL REPUBLIC OF GERMANY. 1993-2001. m. Bundesministerium der Finanzen, Adenauerallee 99-103, Bonn, 53105, Germany.

300 330 FRA ISSN 1637-9802
ECONOMIE ET HUMANISME. 1952-2007. q. Economie et Humanisme, 14 rue Antoine Dumont, Lyon, Cedex 8 69372, France.

780 FRA ISSN 1142-2491
ECOUTER VOIR. 1989-2003. m. Association pour la Cooperation de l'Interprofession Musicale, Mediatheque Musicale de Paris, Forum des Halles, 8 Porte Saint-Eustache, Paris, 75001, France.

840 FRA ISSN 1257-1512
ECRIVAIN MAGAZINE. 1995-1997. bi-m. Alpha Presse, 5 rue de l'Echelle, Paris, 75001, France.

200 NZL
ECUSTICS; newsletter of the conference of churches in Aotearoa New Zealand. 1987-2001 (Oct.). m. Conference of Churches in Aotearoa New Zealand, P.O. Box 13 171, Christchurch, New Zealand.

900 ESP ISSN 1138-8560
EDADES. 1997-2005. s-a. Asociacion de Jovenes Historiadores de Cantabria, Edif. Interfacultativo, Ave. los Castros, s-n, Santander, Comunidad de Cantabria 39080, Spain.

794.8 DEU
EDGE. 2005-2007 (May). bi-m. Computec Media AG, Dr-Mack-Str 77, Fuerth, 90762, Germany.

794.8 AUS ISSN 1449-9215
EDGE. 2004-2005. m. Derwent Howard Media Pty Ltd., PO Box 1037, Bondi Junction, NSW 1355, Australia.

300 ESP
EDICIONES PENINSULA. SERIE UNIVERSITARIA. HISTORIA, CIENCIA, SOCIEDAD. 1966-2001. irreg. Edicions 62 S.A., Peu de la Creu, 4, Barcelona, 08001, Spain.

551 GBR ISSN 0265-7244
EDINBURGH GEOLOGIST. 1977-2005. irreg. Edinburgh Geological Society, c/o Caroline Paterson, Editor, 4 South Sq, Fittie, Aberdeen, AB11 5DT, United Kingdom.

015.44 FRA ISSN 0245-1875
LES EDITEURS ET DIFFUSEURS DE LANGUE FRANCAISE. 1975-2004. a. Electre - Editions du Cercle de la Librairie, 35 rue Gregoire de Tours, Paris, 75006, France.

839.608 439 DNK ISSN 0070-9077
EDITIONES ARNAMAGNAEANAE. SERIES B. 1960-1998. irreg. Den Arnamagnaeanske Samling, Njalsgade 136, Copenhagen S, 2300, Denmark.

839.6 DNK ISSN 0070-9085
EDITIONES ARNAMAGNAEANAE. SUPPLEMENTUM. 1963-1964. irreg. Den Arnamagnaeanske Samling, Njalsgade 136, Copenhagen S, 2300, Denmark.

070.4 659.2 USA
EDITOR & PUBLISHER - FREE PAPER PUBLISHER COMMUNITY PUBLICATIONS YEAR BOOK; a media buyers guide. 1996-ceased. a. Editor & Publisher Co., Inc., 770 Broadway, New York, NY 10003-9595.

370 GBR
EDUCATION COMPASS. announced never published 2008. bi-m. Wiley-Blackwell Publishing Ltd., 9600 Garsington Rd, Oxford, OX4 2DQ, United Kingdom.

370 FRA ISSN 1634-359X
EDUQUER. 2002-2007. q. L' Harmattan, 5 rue de l'Ecole Polytechnique, Paris, 75005, France.

641.5 NLD ISSN 1572-4263
EEN JAAR LANG KOKEN!. 2003-2005. a. Uitgeverij Becht, Postbus 317, Haarlem, 2000 AH, Netherlands.

658.45 ISR
EFFECTIVE COMMUNICATION. 1998-ceased. bi-w. Hodu Winning Documents, Aish Kodesh 11-6, Betar Illit, 99879, Israel.

362.1 613 ITA ISSN 1722-7690
EFFECTIVE HEALTH CARE (ITALIAN EDITION). 1996-2003. bi-m. Zadig s.r.l., Via Calzecchi 10, Milan, 20133, Italy.

794.8 DEU
EGAMES. 2006-2007 (Oct.). m. Inter Content KG, Karlsruher Str 31, Rastatt, 76437, Germany.

370 TUR
EGITIM BULTENI/EDUCATION BULLETIN. 1972-ceased. m. Turkey. Ministry of National Education & Culture, Lefkosa - Nicosia, Mersin, Turkey.

500 EGY ISSN 1110-0532
THE EGYPTIAN ACADEMY OF SCIENCES. PROCEEDINGS. 192?-19??. a. Egyptian Academy of Sciences, Dar El-Hekma, 42 Qasr El-Aini Str, Cairo, Egypt.

362 EGY ISSN 1110-6573
THE EGYPTIAN HOSPITALS ASSOCIATION. BULLETIN. 1949-ceased. a. Association of the Egyptian Hospitals, Dar El-Hekma, 42 Qasr El-Aini St, Cairo, Egypt.

639.9 634.9 EGY ISSN 1110-113X
EGYPTIAN JOURNAL OF WILDLIFE AND NATURAL RESOURCES. 1979-1987. a. Egyptian Association for Conservation of Natural Resources, 22 Murad Str, Giza Zoo, Giza, Egypt.

616.07 EGY ISSN 1110-7669
EGYPTIAN SOCIETY OF ULTRASONICS IN MEDICINE. JOURNAL. 198?-ceased. a. Egyptian Society of Ultrasonics in Medicine, Dar El-Hekma, 42 Qasr El-Aini Str, Cairo, Egypt.

808.838 AUS ISSN 1038-5657
EIDOLON; the journal of Australian science fiction and fantasy. 1990-2000. q. Eidolon Publications, PO Box 225, North Perth, W.A. 6906, Australia.

658.5 NLD ISSN 0929-8479
EINDHOVEN UNIVERSITY OF TECHNOLOGY. DEPARTMENT OF TECHNOLOGY MANAGEMENT. RESEARCH REPORT. 1983-2000 (no.94). irreg. Eindhoven University of Technology, Department of Technology Management, PO Box 90159, Eindhoven RM, 5600, Netherlands.

305.4 DEU
EINFACH FRAU; Hier fuehle Ich mich wohl!. 2008 (Jan.)-2008 (Sep.). m. Gube Verlagsgesellschaft mbH, Osterstr 128, Hamburg, 20255, Germany.

658 DEU ISSN 0722-4850
EINZELHANDELS BERATER. 1958-2003. m. B B E Media GmbH & Co. KG, Am Hammergraben 14, Neuwied, 56567, Germany.

385 DEU
EISENBAHN-BEFOERDERUNGSRECHT. 1939-2001. irreg. Erich Schmidt Verlag GmbH & Co. (Berlin), Genthiner Str 30 G, Berlin, 10785, Germany.

796.962 DEU
EISHOCKEY LIVE. 1998-2001. m. D S V Deutscher Sportverlag GmbH, Im Mediapark 8, Cologne, 50670, Germany.

340 CZE ISSN 1801-6324
EKOLOGIE V PODNIKOVE PRAXI. 2006-2007. m. Verlag Dashoefer s.r.o., Na Prikope 18, PO Box 756, Prague 1, 11121, Czech Republic.

956.1 TUR
EKONOMI/ECONOMY. 1978-ceased. w. Turkish Cypriot Chamber of Commerce, Bedrettin Demirel Caddesi No.90, Lefkosa, TRNC-via Mersi, P O Box 718, Mersin, 10, Turkey.

618.97 362.6 USA ISSN 1550-9745
ELDERCARE REPORTER. 198?-2005. m. Freiberg Press Inc., 2302 W 1st St, PO Box 612, Cedar Falls, IA 50613.

621.3 NZL ISSN 0110-3539
ELECTRICAL INDUSTRY DIRECTORY YEARBOOK. 1963-1983. m. (11/yr.). Ward Publishing (1988) Ltd., 568 Anglesea St, PO Box 9323, Hamilton North, New Zealand.

621.3 629.286 FRA ISSN 1247-0015
L'ELECTRICITE AUTOMOBILE. 1946-2002. bi-m. Electricite Automobile, 59 rue du Faubourg Poissonniere, Paris, 75009, France.

338 537 011 FRA ISSN 1249-4208
ELECTRICITE DE FRANCE. RESULTATS TECHNIQUES D'EXPLOITATION/ELECTRICITY OF FRANCE. OPERATION TECHNICAL RESULTS. 1959-1999. a. Electricite de France, Direction de la Production et du Transport, Observatoire Statistique du Systeme Electrique, Cap Ampere, Saint-Denis, Cedex 93282, France.

547 GBR ISSN 0963-5637 CODEN: ESTPEA
ELECTROCHEMICAL SCIENCE AND TECHNOLOGY OF POLYMERS. 1987-1990. irreg. Pergamon, The Blvd, Langford Ln, East Park, Kidlington, Oxford OX5 1GB, United Kingdom.

343.73 347.3 621.3 USA ISSN 1069-6695
ELECTROMAGNETIC FIELD LITIGATION REPORTER. 1986-2000 (Jun.). m. Andrews Publications, 175 Strafford Ave, Bldg 4, Ste 140, Wayne, PA 19087.

332 FRA ISSN 1630-9553
ELECTRONIC BANKING NEWS. 1998-2005. m. (11/yr). Publi-News, 47 rue Aristide Briand, Levallois-Perret, 92300, France.

794.8 USA ISSN 1058-918X
ELECTRONIC GAMING MONTHLY. 1986-2009 (Jan.). m. Ziff Davis Media Inc., 28 E 28th St, New York, NY 10016.

621.381029 USA ISSN 0422-9053
ELECTRONIC INDUSTRY TELEPHONE DIRECTORY (YEAR). 1963-2006. a. Advantage Business Media, 100 Enterprise Dr, Ste 600, PO Box 912, Rockaway, NJ 07886.

659.1 ITA ISSN 0393-9170
ELECTRONIC MASS MEDIA AGE. 1985-ceased. m. Systems Comunicazioni, Via Olanda 6, Vigano di Gaggiano, MI 20083, Italy.

327 CZE
THE ELECTRONIC NEW PRESENCE; Central European weekly. 1998-200?. w. Electronic New Presence, Narodni tr 11, Prague 1, 110 00, Czech Republic.

351.0258 NLD ISSN 1385-7495
ELECTRONIC SERIES ON INTEGRATED ASSESSMENT MODELING. 1998-ceased. irreg. Baltzer Science Publishers B.V., Hooftlaan 51, Bussum, 1401 EC, Netherlands.

643 USA ISSN 1045-6627 CODEN: EWNEE9
ELECTRONIC WORLD NEWS. 1989-1993 (Mar.). m. C M P Media LLC, 600 Community Dr, Manhasset, NY 11030.

621.3029 GBR
ELECTRONICS 150. 1979; N.S. 1995-200?. a. Pergamon, The Blvd, Langford Ln, East Park, Kidlington, Oxford OX5 1GB, United Kingdom.

621.381 USA ISSN 1544-9459
ELECTRONICS MANUFACTURING ENGINEERING. 1986-2006. q. Society of Manufacturing Engineers, One SME Dr, PO Box 930, Dearborn, MI 48121.

659.152 646.7 ITA ISSN 1121-8312
ELEGANTISSIMA. 1945-ceased. q. IBI s.r.l., Via Camillo Finocchiaro Aprile, 5, Milan, MI 20124, Italy.

621.381 ITA ISSN 1591-7185
ELETTRONICA INDUSTRIALE. 1991-ceased. bi-m. Tecniche Nuove SpA, Via Eritrea 21, Milan, MI 201, Italy.

621.381 ITA ISSN 1121-8835
ELETTRONICA PROFESSIONALE. 1992-ceased. 9/yr. Il Sole 24 Ore Business Media, Divisione J C E, Via Patecchio 2, Milan, 20141, Italy.

551 665.5 FRA ISSN 1279-8215 CODEN: BCRPFQ
ELF EXPLORATION PRODUCTION. CENTRES DE RECHERCHES. BULLETIN. 1967-1998. s-a. Elf Edition Exploration, Avenue Larribau, Pau, Cedex 64018, France.

700 ITA ISSN 1972-2613
ELITE. 1966-ceased. irreg. Fabbri Editori, Via Mecenate 91, Milan, 20138, Italy.

053.1 DEU ISSN 1614-9726
ELLE GIRL. 2003-2005. m. Elle Verlag GmbH, Arabellastr 23, Munich, 81925, Germany.

664 NLD ISSN 1568-4008
ELSEVIER FOOD INTERNATIONAL. 1998-2009. q. Reed Business bv, Hanzestraat 1, Doetinchem, 7006 RH, Netherlands.

781.542 GBR ISSN 0013-6484
ELVIS MONTHLY. 1958-2000. m. Heanor Record Centre Ltd., 6 Empire Rd, Leicester, LE3 5HE, United Kingdom.

005.1 USA ISSN 1074-4916
EMBEDDED SYSTEMS PROGRAMMING PRODUCT NEWS. 1994-199?. q. C M P Media LLC, 600 Harrison St, 6th Fl., San Francisco, CA 94107.

363.34 AUS ISSN 1329-8755
EMERGENCY SUPPORT. 1995-2003. 3/yr. Emergency Support Network Pty Ltd., PO Box 106, Palmyra, W.A. 6957, Australia.

330.9 GBR ISSN 1029-8681
EMERGING MARKET TRENDS. 1977-1998. q. L G T Asset Management plc, Economic Research Unit, Alban Gate 14th Fl, 125 London Wall, London, EC2Y 5AS, United Kingdom.

332.6 USA ISSN 1093-2666
EMERGING MARKETS QUARTERLY. 1993-2001. q. Institutional Investor, Journals, 225 Park Ave S, 8th Fl, New York, NY 10003.

371.42 USA ISSN 0882-3316
EMERGING PATTERNS OF WORK AND COMMUNICATIONS IN AN INFORMATION AGE. 1985-19??. irreg. Greenwood Publishing Group Inc., 88 Post Rd W, PO Box 5007, Westport, CT 06881.

945 ITA ISSN 1124-9218
EMEROTECA STORICA ITALIANA; rassegna bibliografica annuale degli articoli di argomento storico pubblicati in Italia su riviste e atti di convegni. 1994-1998. a. Emeroteca Storica Italiana S.N.C., Casella Postale 255, Verona, VR 37100, Italy.

051 USA ISSN 1553-4049
EMPIRE (NEW YORK, 2000). 2000 (Spr.)-200?. q. H X Media, LLC, 230 W 17th St, 8th Fl, New York, NY 10011.

331.255 USA ISSN 1090-4220
EMPLOYEE BENEFITS AND EXECUTIVE COMPENSATION COUNSELOR. 1993-1999. m. Business Laws, Inc., 11630 Chillicothe Rd, PO Box 185, Chesterland, OH 44026.

331.255 USA ISSN 1048-2814
EMPLOYEE BENEFITS ISSUES: THE MULTIEMPLOYER PERSPECTIVE. 1956-2005. a. International Foundation of Employee Benefit Plans, 18700 W Bluemound Rd, Brookfield, WI 53008-0069.

658 NZL ISSN 0046-1903
EMPLOYER. 1971-2001 (no.202). 11/yr. New Zealand Employers Federation, PO Box 1786, Wellington, New Zealand.

331 USA
EMPLOYMENT COST INDEXES. 1975-1999. irreg. U.S. Department of Labor, Bureau of Labor Statistics, Postal Square Bldg., 2 Massachusetts Ave, NE, Washington, DC 20212-0001.

331.125 USA
EMPLOYMENT, HOURS, AND EARNINGS: STATES AND AREAS. 1939-1994. a. U.S. Department of Labor, Bureau of Labor Statistics, Postal Square Bldg., 2 Massachusetts Ave, NE, Washington, DC 20212-0001.

331.11 USA
EMPLOYMENT IN PERSPECTIVE: MINORITY WORKERS. 1979-1994. q. U.S. Department of Labor, Bureau of Labor Statistics, Postal Square Bldg., 2 Massachusetts Ave, NE, Washington, DC 20212-0001.

331.4 USA
EMPLOYMENT IN PERSPECTIVE: WOMEN IN THE LABOR FORCE. 198?-1994. q. U.S. Department of Labor, Bureau of Labor Statistics, Postal Square Bldg., 2 Massachusetts Ave, NE, Washington, DC 20212-0001.

914.499 FRA ISSN 1774-7473
EN ARRIVANT. 200?-2005. irreg. Dajaloo Editions, Chemin des Heyrauds, Menerbes, 84560, France.

287.96 FRA ISSN 0013-6921
EN AVANT. 1882-2002. w. Armee du Salut, 60 rue des Freres Flavien, Paris, Cedex 20 75976, France.

054 FRA ISSN 1251-0483
ENCRES VAGABONDES; creation litteraire et magazine de l'ecrit. 1994-2003. 3/yr. Encres Vagabondes, 23 rue des Trianons, Rueil-Malmaison, 92500, France.

296.03 ISR ISSN 0303-7819
ENCYCLOPAEDIA JUDAICA YEAR BOOK. 1973-1993. a. Keter Publishing House Ltd., P O Box 7145, Jerusalem, 91071, Israel.

010 USA
ENCYCLOPEDIA OF ASSOCIATIONS SUPPLEMENT. (Encyclopedia of Associations) 1964-200?. s-a. Gale, 27500 Drake Rd, Farmington Hills, MI 48331.

338.0029 USA ISSN 1086-4768
ENCYCLOPEDIA OF BUSINESS. 1995-19??. triennial. Gale, 27500 Drake Rd, Farmington Hills, MI 48331.

616 FRA ISSN 1283-0836
ENCYCLOPEDIE MEDICO-CHIRURGICALE. TRATADO DE PRAXIS MEDICA. 1998-2002. plus q. updates. Elsevier France, Editions Scientifiques et Medicales, 23 Rue Linois, Paris, 75724, France.

301 USA ISSN 1525-1233
ENDANGERED PEOPLES OF THE WORLD. 2000-200?. irreg. Greenwood Publishing Group Inc., 88 Post Rd W, PO Box 5007, Westport, CT 06881.

059.956 ITA
ENDAS PIEMONTE; organo di informazione dell'Endas Piemontese. 1979-ceased. bi-m. E N D A S Piemonte, Via Giovanni Giolitti, 19, Turin, TO 10123, Italy.

333.79 ITA ISSN 0392-7911
ENERGIA; rivista trimestrale sui problemi dell'energia. 1980-ceased. q. A C I Mondadori SpA, Via Cassanese 224, Segrate, MI 20090, Italy.

333.79 ISR ISSN 0792-0288
ENERGIA. 1987-1989. bi-m. R B S Ltd., P O Box 3039, Herziliyah B, 46103, Israel.

665.5 DNK ISSN 1604-0597
ENERGIBLADET. 1989-2006. biennial. Dansk Olie og Naturgas, Kraftvaerksvej 53, Fredericia, 7000, Denmark.

690 DEU ISSN 1611-8642
ENERGIEEFFIZIENTES BAUEN. 2000-2005. q. EnergieEffizientes Bauen Verlags GmbH, Kernerweg 18, Urbach, 73660, Germany.

333.79 USA
ENERGY INSIGHT; news from the Sierra Club Legislative Office in Sacramento. 19??-198?. d. Platts, 2 Penn Plz, 25th Fl, New York, NY 10121.

333.79 USA ISSN 0149-9386 CODEN: ENGYD4
ENERGY MAGAZINE. 1975 (Mar.)-19??. q. Business Communications Co., Inc., 25 Van Zant St, Ste 13, Norwalk, CT 06855-1781.

333 USA ISSN 1531-3891
ENERGY NETWORK. 2000-200?. bi-w. Energy Intelligence Group, Inc., 5 E 37th St, 5th Fl, New York, NY 10016.

616.27 USA ISSN 0360-7577
ENGINEERING IN MEDICINE. 1975-1976 (vol.2). irreg. Springer New York LLC, 233 Spring St, New York, NY 10013.

620.0029 NZL ISSN 0110-3571
ENGINEERING REFERENCE HANDBOOK. 1976-1995. irreg. (approx. 18/yr). Engineering Handbook Ltd., P.O. Box 26-269, Epsom, Auckland, New Zealand.

418 ISR ISSN 0333-533X
ENGLISH TEACHERS' JOURNAL (ISRAEL)/'ALON L'MORIM L'ANGLIT. 1968-2003. s-a. Ministry of Education, 34 Shivtei Israel St., P O Box 292, Jerusalem, 91911, Israel.

663.2 ITA ISSN 0390-2048
ENOHOBBY. 1974-ceased. m. Enohobby, Via di San Tarcisio, 5, Rome, RM 00178, Italy.

333.330 FRA ISSN 1770-1791
ENQUETE FONCIERE ET IMMOBILIERE AUPRES DES ETUDES NOTARIALES DE LA REGION NORD PAS-DE-CALAIS. 1990-2005. a. Observatoire Regional de l'Habitat et de l'Amenagement, 17 rue Jeanne d'Arc, Lille, 59000, France.

616.21 616.3 ITA
ENTERON & PHARYNGOS. 1999-200?. bi-m. Ariesdue srl, Via Airoldi 11, Carimate, CO 22060, Italy.

Cessations

621.8 FRA ISSN 0765-006X
ENTRAINEMENTS & SYSTEMES; transmissions mecaniques, hydrauliques, pneumatiques, commandes et assertissements. 1967-2004. 7/yr. Promotion Presse Internationale, 7 Cour des Petites-Ecuries, Paris, 75010, France.

536.7 621.4 FRA ISSN 0013-9084 CODEN: ENTPA5
ENTROPIE; revue internationale d'energetique, genie chimique, genie biologique. 1965-2003. 7/yr. Association Entropie, B.P. 63, Creteil, Cedex 940022, France.

347.779 DEU ISSN 0255-3430
ENTSCHEIDUNGEN DER BESCHWERDEKAMMERN DES EUROPAEISCHEN PATENTAMTS/DECISIONS DES CHAMBRES DE RECOURS DE L'OFFICE EUROPEEN DES BREVETS/DECISIONS OF THE BOARDS OF APPEAL OF THE EUROPEAN PATENT OFFICE. 1983-2005. irreg. European Patent Office, Munich, 80298, Germany.

053.1 BRD ISSN 0936-1243
ENTWURFBOTE; literarische Korrespondenzen. 1987-1989. 10/yr. Entwurfbote, Sportplatzstr 19, Goldbach, 63773, West Germany.

333.72 AUS ISSN 1037-9010
ENVIRONMENT SOUTH AUSTRALIA. 1971-2004. q. Conservation Council of South Australia, Conservation Centre, 120 Wakefield St, Adelaide, SA 5000, Australia.

363.728 GBR ISSN 1460-5147
ENVIRONMENTAL & WASTE MANAGEMENT. 1997-2002. q. E P P Publications, 52 Kings Rd, Richmond, Surrey TW10 6EP, United Kingdom.

363.7 USA ISSN 1072-5083
ENVIRONMENTAL ENCYCLOPEDIA. 1994-2003. triennial. Gale, 27500 Drake Rd, Farmington Hills, MI 48331.

628.4 USA ISSN 1092-8758 CODEN: EESCF5
ENVIRONMENTAL ENGINEERING SCIENCE (PRINT). 1984-2009. bi-m. Mary Ann Liebert, Inc. Publishers, 140 Huguenot St, 3rd Fl, New Rochelle, NY 10801-5215.

344.046 AUS
ENVIRONMENTAL LAW QUEENSLAND. 1996-2003. plus q. updates. Lawbook Co., PO Box 3502, Rozelle, NSW 2039, Australia.

333.77 363.7 ISR ISSN 0333-6735
ENVIRONMENTAL PLANNING/TIKHNUN S'VIVATI. 1965-1999. q. Israeli Association for Environmental Planning, 5 Gazit St, Tel Aviv, 69417, Israel.

363.7 GBR
ENVIRONMENTAL PROTECTION YEARBOOK. 1950-2003. a. Environmental Protection UK, 44 Grand Parade, Brighton, E Sussex BN2 9QA, United Kingdom.

628 USA ISSN 1089-232X
ENVIRONMENTAL TECHNOLOGY. 1991-2000. 7/yr. Adams Business Media, 2101 S Arlington Heights Rd, 150, Arlington, IL 60005.

711.4 GBR ISSN 1352-8564
ENVIRONMENTS BY DESIGN. 1996-2003. s-a. Kingston University Press, Eagle Chambers, 16-18 Eden St, Kingston Upon Thames, Surrey KT1 2QJ, United Kingdom.

262.9 ITA ISSN 0013-9491
EPHEMERIDES IURIS CANONICI. 1945-1993. q. Officium Libri Catholici, Via Dei Lucchesi, 20, Rome, RM 00187, Italy.

610 ITA
EPIDEMIOLOGIA E PREVENZIONE (ONLINE). 1977-2004. bi-m. Associazione Italiana di Epidemiologia, Via Giusti 4, Castellanza, VA 21053, Italy.

913 ITA ISSN 0013-9572
EPIGRAPHICA; periodico internazionale di epigrafia. 1939-200?. s-a. Fratelli Lega Editori, Corso Mazzini 33, Faenza, RA 48018, Italy.

616.853 NLD ISSN 0922-9833 CODEN: ERSUED
EPILEPSY RESEARCH SUPPLEMENTS. 1988-1996 (no.11). irreg. Elsevier BV, Radarweg 29, P O Box 211, Amsterdam, 1000 AE, Netherlands.

616.853 CZE ISSN 1801-6375
EPILEPTOLOGICKE LISTY. 2001-2007. s-a. Solen s.r.o., Lazecka 297/51, Olomouc 51, 779 00, Czech Republic.

617.6 ITA ISSN 1593-9952
EQUIPE ODONTOIATRICA. 2002-2009. 3/yr. Ariesdue srl, Via Airoldi 11, Carimate, CO 22060, Italy.

664 658 USA
EQUIPMENT SOLUTIONS. 19??-2005. bi-m. Talcott Communications Corporation, 20 W Kinzie St, Ste 1200, Chicago, IL 60654.

100 ESP ISSN 0213-1668
ER; revista de filosofia. 1985-2005. 3/yr. Ediciones de Intervencion Cultural, C. Sant Antoni 86 Local 9, Mataro, Barcelona, 08301, Spain.

330.9489 DNK ISSN 1602-1819
ERHVERVS POSTEN. 1998-2002. d. E P Erhverv, Media Huset ApS, Jyllingevej 57, PO Box 1670, Vanloese, 2720, Denmark.

016.37 DNK ISSN 0901-9316
ERHVERVSUDDANNELSERNE. 1979-2006. a. Fonden Undervisnings Information, Siljangade 6, Copenhagen S, 2300, Denmark.

535 ESP ISSN 0210-9891 CODEN: EOCTDA
ESCUELA DE OPTICA CUANTICA. CURSOS. 1978-ceased. a. Sociedad Espanola de Optica, Serrano, 121, Madrid, 28006, Spain.

002 ITA ISSN 0392-9752
L'ESOPO; rivista trimestrale di bibliofilia. 1979-199?. q. Edizioni Rovello, Piazza Castello, 11, Milan, MI 20121, Italy.

056 ESP ISSN 1136-1581
ESPAI DE LLIBERTAT. 1996-2007. q. Fundacio Francesc Ferrer i Guardia, C/ Avinyo 44, Barcelona, 08002, Spain.

745.1 ITA ISSN 1590-0266
L'ESPERTO RISPONDE. 1985-ceased. m. Edi Marketing s.r.l., Via Pacini, 41, Milan, MI 20131, Italy.

382 ITA ISSN 0014-0740
ESPORTAZIONE; mensile per gli esportatori. 1961-ceased. 11/yr. Ente Italiano per lo Sviluppo dell'Esportazione, Piazzale Giotto, 8, Perugia, PG 06121, Italy.

240 FRA ISSN 0396-969X
ESPRIT SAINT; revue de spiritualite. 1952-2008. q. Congregation du Saint-Esprit, Fraternites du Saint-Esprit, 30 rue Lhomond, Paris, 75005, France.

101 AUS
ESSAYS IN SOUND. 1992-1995. a. Essays in Sound, 64 Newman St, Newtown, NSW 2042, Australia.

641.5 ITA ISSN 1720-1845
ESSERE & BENESSERE. 1996-200?. m. Gruppo Editoriale Futura, Via XXV Aprile 39, Bresso, MI 20091, Italy.

631 580 ESP ISSN 0365-1800
ESTACION EXPERIMENTAL DE AULA DEI. ANALES. 1948-1996. a. Estacion Experimental de Aula Dei, Apdo. de Correos 202, C. Montanana 177, Zaragoza, 50081, Spain.

304.6021 ESP ISSN 1696-0440
ESTADISTICAS DEL MOVIMIENTO NATURAL DE LA POBLACION DE LA COMUNIDAD DE MADRID. MATRIMONIOS. 1990-2006. a. Comunidad de Madrid, Instituto de Estadistica, Principe de Vargara 108, Madrid, 28002, Spain.

304.6021 ESP ISSN 1696-0467
ESTADISTICAS DEL MOVIMIENTO NATURAL DE LA POBLACION DE LA COMUNIDAD DE MADRID. MORTALIDAD SEGUN CAUSAS MULTIPLES. 1996-2007. a. Comunidad de Madrid, Instituto de Estadistica, Principe de Vargara 108, Madrid, 28002, Spain.

304.6021 ESP ISSN 1696-0432
ESTADISTICAS DEL MOVIMIENTO NATURAL DE LA POBLACION DE LA COMUNIDAD DE MADRID. NACIMIENTOS. 1990-2007. a. Comunidad de Madrid, Instituto de Estadistica, Principe de Vargara 108, Madrid, 28002, Spain.

668.5 FRA ISSN 1146-5794
ESTHETICA PROFESSIONNEL. 1985-199?. 10/yr. Esthetica Professionnel, 58 rue Saint Georges, Paris, 75009, France.

646.72 FRA ISSN 0220-1941
ESTHETIQUE. 1969-200?. 11/yr. Esthetique, 8 rue Fort Notre Dame, Marseille, 13007, France.

960 ESP ISSN 1130-8788
ESTUDIS CASTELLONENCS. 1983-2005. a. Diputacio Provincial de Castello, Placa Aules, 1, Castello, Comunidad Valenciana 12001, Spain.

330 381 382 DEU ISSN 0721-7072
ETAGE; Chef-Informationen. 1981-200?. q. Dr. Horst Kerlikowsky Verlag, Brauhofstr 5, Berlin, 10587, Germany.

647.95 NLD ISSN 1872-0013
ETEN IN DE NEDERLANDSE HORECA. 1998-2006. irreg. Bedrijfschap Horeca en Catering, Postbus 121, Zoetermeer, 2700 AC, Netherlands.

360 917.306 USA ISSN 0737-1411
ETHNIC AMERICAN VOLUNTARY ORGANIZATIONS. 1983-19??. irreg. Greenwood Publishing Group Inc., 88 Post Rd W, PO Box 5007, Westport, CT 06881.

100 200 FRA ISSN 1155-2239
ETUDES SCHWEITZERIENNES; revue annuelle d'ethique, de theologie et de philosophie. 1990-199?. a. Editions Oberlin, 19 rue des Francs-Bourgeois, Strasbourg, 67000, France.

384.5 FRA ISSN 0999-582X
ETUDES TELECOM. 1989-2000. 10/yr. Attis Communications, 14 rue des Reculettes, Paris, 75013, France.

028.5 363.7 FRA ISSN 1951-1698
EUREKA (PARIS). 2005-2007. q. Bayard Presse, 3-5 rue Bayard, Paris, 75393 Cedex 08, France.

330 DEU ISSN 0939-2734
EURO BRIEF. 1991-2004. m. Deutscher Wirtschaftsdienst, Luxemburger Str 449, Cologne, 50939, Germany.

057.87 SVK ISSN 1337-6772
EURO DOMINO. 1998-2008 (Aug.). w. Fons Domino n.o., Hviezdoslavovo nam 14, Bratislava, 810 01, Slovakia.

410 ITA
EUROASIATICA; journal of neohistorical linguistics. 1970-1980. irreg. Fabrizio Serra Editore, c/o Accademia Editoriale, Via Santa Bibbiana 28, Pisa, 56127, Italy.

004 DNK
EUROCOMPUTER; Nordens edb-avis. 1995-2002. 6/yr. Media-Huset ApS, Jyllingevej 57, PO Box 1670, Vanlose, 2720, Denmark.

305.90664 DEU ISSN 1439-653X
EUROGAY. 1999-2003. m. Eurogay Media AG, Baumeisterstr 2, Hamburg, 20099, Germany.

341.7 DEU
EUROLEX. 1990-2005. s-a. Bundesanzeiger Verlagsgesellschaft mbH, Amsterdamer Str 192, Cologne, 50735, Germany.

330.94 ITA
EUROMEDIA. 1997-ceased. d. Mare s.r.l. Editrice, Centro Direzionale Is. X G1, Naples, NA 80143, Italy.

004 GBR
EUROMILCOMP (YEAR); military computers, systems and software. ceased 1997. a. Nexus Media Ltd., Nexus House, Azalea Dr, Swanley, Kent BR8 8HU, United Kingdom.

340 DEU ISSN 1435-3253
EUROPA BLAETTER. 1992-2006. bi-m. Bundesanzeiger Verlagsgesellschaft mbH, Amsterdamer Str 192, Cologne, 50735, Germany.

341 ITA
L'EUROPA DELLA C E E. (Comunita Economica Europea) 1988-ceased. m. Pirola Editore SpA, Via Parabiago 19, Milan, MI 20151, Italy.

327 ITA
EUROPA EUROPE. 1992-2001. q. Bollati Boringhieri Editore, Corso Vittorio Emanuele II, 86, Turin, TO 10121, Italy.

327 NLD ISSN 0165-7070
EUROPA VAN MORGEN. 1970-2003. s-m. European Commission, Netherlands Office, Postbus 30465, The Hague, 2500 GL, Netherlands.

346 DEU ISSN 0933-8314
EUROPAEISCHE GESETZE GEGEN WETTBEWERBSBESCHRAENKUNGEN. 1969-1992. irreg. Erich Schmidt Verlag GmbH & Co. (Berlin), Genthiner Str 30 G, Berlin, 10785, Germany.

327 DEU
EUROPAEISCHE ZEITUNG. 1949-2003. 10/yr. Europa Union Verlag GmbH, Holtorfer Str 35, Bonn, 53229, Germany.

674 DEU
EUROPAEISCHER WIRTSCHAFTSDIENST. INFORMATIONSBRIEF HOLZ - ZELLSTOFF - PAPIER. 1969-2008. m. E U W I D - Europaeischer Wirtschaftsdienst GmbH, Bleichstr 20-22, Gernsbach, 76593, Germany.

674 DEU
EUROPAEISCHER WIRTSCHAFTSDIENST. TIMBER. 1926-2000. w. E U W I D - Europaeischer Wirtschaftsdienst GmbH, Bleichstr 20-22, Gernsbach, 76593, Germany.

608.7 DEU ISSN 0170-9305 CODEN: EPATE8
EUROPAEISCHES PATENTBLATT (PRINT)/BULLETIN EUROPEEN DES BREVETS/EUROPEAN PATENT BULLETIN. 1978-2004. w. European Patent Office, Munich, 80298, Germany.

382.029 FRA ISSN 0762-4468
EUROPAGES. 1982-2007. a. Euredit S.A., 47 rue Louis Blanc, Paris La Defense, Cedex 92984, France.

054.1 FRA ISSN 1164-7957
EUROPE ET LIBERTE MAGAZINE. 1988-2004. q. Europe et Liberte, 32 rue du Paradis, Paris, 75010, France.

400 FRA ISSN 1161-8884
EUROPE PLURILINGUE. 1991-2002. s-a. Association pour le Rayonnement des Langues Europeenes, BP 43, Neuilly-sur-Seine, 92200, France.

658.31244 ESP ISSN 1029-7022
EUROPEAN AGENCY FOR SAFETY AND HEALTH AT WORK. NEWSLETTER. 1998-2003 (no.16). q. European Agency for Safety and Health at Work, Gran Via 33, Bilbao, E-48009, Spain.

639.2 338 DNK ISSN 0967-5795
EUROPEAN ASSOCIATION OF FISHERIES ECONOMISTS. BULLETIN. 1991-2001 (latest issue: 17, 2001); suspended. s-a. European Association of Fisheries Economists, c/o Hans Frost, Rolighedsvej 25, Frederiksberg, 1958, Denmark.

663.3 DEU ISSN 0367-018X
EUROPEAN BREWERY CONVENTION. PROCEEDINGS OF THE CONGRESS. 1947-1999. biennial. Fachverlag Hans Carl, Andernacher Str 33A, Nuernberg, 90411, Germany.

332 DEU
EUROPEAN CENTRAL BANK. COMPENDIUM: COLLECTION OF LEGAL INSTRUMENTS. ceased 2002. bi-m. European Central Bank, Kaiserstr 23, Frankfurt am Main, 60311, Germany.

551.5 GBR ISSN 1012-6899
EUROPEAN CENTRE FOR MEDIUM-RANGE WEATHER FORECASTS. TECHNICAL REPORT. 1976-1995. irreg. European Centre for Medium-Range Weather Forecasts, Research Department, Shinfield Park, Reading, Berks RG2 9AX, United Kingdom.

616.027 GBR ISSN 1047-5354
EUROPEAN CLINICAL LABORATORY. 1982-2006. 6/yr. International Scientific Communications, Ltd., ISC House, 12 Bridge Ave, Maidenhead, Berkshire GB-SL6 1RR, United Kingdom.

016.6161 GBR ISSN 0421-7527
EUROPEAN CONGRESS OF CARDIOLOGY. ABSTRACTS OF PAPERS. 1952-200?. a. Academic Press, 32 Jamestown Rd, Camden, London, NW1 7BY, United Kingdom.

792.8 USA
EUROPEAN DANCE NEWS. 2004-2006. 8/yr. Macfadden Performing Arts Media, LLC., 110 William St, 23rd Fl, New York, NY 10038.

629.8 USA
EUROPEAN DESIGN AUTOMATION CONFERENCE. PROCEEDINGS. 1990-199?. biennial. I E E E, 3 Park Ave, 17th Fl, New York, NY 10016-5997.

620 551.22 ITA ISSN 0394-5103 CODEN: EEENEZ
EUROPEAN EARTHQUAKE ENGINEERING; international journal of earthquake engineering and engineering seismology. 1987-2007 (No.3). 3/yr. Patron Editore, Via Badini 12, Quarto Inferiore, BO 40050, Italy.

551.4 NLD ISSN 0928-9542
EUROPEAN GEOPHYSICAL SOCIETY SERIES ON HYDROLOGICAL SCIENCES. 1992-ceased. irreg. Elsevier BV, Radarweg 29, P O Box 211, Amsterdam, 1000 AE, Netherlands.

020.6 GBR ISSN 0261-2747
EUROPEAN INFORMATION SERVICE. 1978-2007. 10/yr. Local Government International Bureau, Local Government House, Smith Sq, London, SW1P 3H2, United Kingdom.

004 DEU ISSN 0947-4862
EUROPEAN INFORMATION TECHNOLOGY OBSERVATORY (YEAR). 1993-2007. a. European Information Technology Observatory, Hahnstr 70, Frankfurt am Main, W 60528, Germany.

340.0711 344.07 GBR ISSN 1684-1360
EUROPEAN JOURNAL OF LEGAL EDUCATION. 2001-2009. s-a. Routledge, 4 Park Sq, Milton Park, Abingdon, Oxon OX14 4RN, United Kingdom.

910 NLD ISSN 1571-473X
EUROPEAN JOURNAL OF NAVIGATION. 2003-2008. q. Reed Business - Geo, PO Box 112, Lemmer, 8530 AC, Netherlands.

384 GBR ISSN 0966-7458
THE EUROPEAN JOURNAL OF TELEWORKING. 1993-2003. q. Addico Cornix Ltd., 70 Causewayhead, Penzance, Cornwall TR18 2SR, United Kingdom.

616.7 617 ITA ISSN 1828-440X
THE EUROPEAN JOURNAL OF TRAUMA AND EMERGENCY SURGERY. 1975-2007. q. Elsevier Masson, Via Paleocapa 7, Milan, 20121, Italy.

610 797.23 DEU ISSN 1605-9204
EUROPEAN JOURNAL OF UNDERWATER AND HYPERBARIC MEDICINE. 2000-2007. q. European Underwater and Baromedical Society, c/o Dr. Peter Mueller, Speyerer Str 91-93, Mannheim, 68163, Germany.

959 NLD ISSN 0929-6727
EUROPEAN NEWSLETTER OF SOUTHEAST ASIAN STUDIES. 1988-2004. 2/yr. K I T L V Press, PO Box 9515, Leiden, 2300 RA, Netherlands.

338.7 NLD
EUROPEAN OBSERVATORY FOR S M ES. ANNUAL REPORT. (Small to Medium Enterprises) 1993-2004. a. E I M, PO Box 7001, Zoetermeer, 2701 AA, Netherlands.

385.09405 USA ISSN 1746-5427
EUROPEAN RAIL OUTLOOK. 2004 (May.)-2007 (Oct.). q. Simmons-Boardman Publishing Corp., 345 Hudson St, 12th Fl, New York, NY 10014.

307.1 GBR ISSN 0960-6130
EUROPEAN RESEARCH IN REGIONAL SCIENCE. 1990-2003. a. Pion Ltd., 207 Brondesbury Park, London, NW2 5JN, United Kingdom.

384.51 USA ISSN 1052-5068
EUROPEAN TELEVISION. 1989-2003. m. S N L Financial LC, One SNL Plz, PO Box 2124, Charlottesville, VA 22902.

636.089 NLD ISSN 1569-0229
EUROPEAN VETERINARY DISSERTATIONS. 199?-2001. q. Euroscience, PO Box 408, Bilthoven, 3720 AK, Netherlands.

056.1 ESP ISSN 1135-0482
EL EUROPEO DE LAS CUATRO ESTACIONES. 1988-1993. m. Ediciones Deturse, Serrano, 6 2o izda, Madrid, 28001, Spain.

341 NLD ISSN 1572-3593
EUROPESE MONOGRAFIEEN. 1964-2006 (vol.83). irreg. Kluwer B.V., Postbus 23, Deventer, 7400 GA, Netherlands.

796.3 CHE ISSN 1661-822X
EUROSOCCER. 2006-2008. m. Sportverlag Europa Medien AG, Seestr 473, Zurich, 8038, Switzerland.

056 FRA ISSN 1276-7816
EUROSTAR. 1995-200?. m. B C Editions, au Capital de 12 240 00F, 43 rue de Villiers, Nevilly-Sur-Sein, 92523, France.

746.9 NLD ISSN 1387-0076
EUROSTITCH MAGAZINE. 1994-2008. bi-m. Eurostitch Magazine, De Huchstr 43, Almeer, 1327, Netherlands.

053.1 DEU
EUROWINGS MAGAZIN. 1973-2005. q. C.O.M.B.O. Communications Medienagentur Verlag GmbH, Romanstr 64, Munich, 80639, Germany.

930.1 ITA ISSN 1121-1628
EUTOPIA; commentarii novi de antiqvitatibvs totivs evropae. 1967-2003. 3/yr. Edizioni Quasar, Via Ajaccio 41-43, Rome, 00198, Italy.

460 300 ESP ISSN 0213-246X
EUTOPIAS. DOCUMENTOS DE TRABAJO. 1985-2007. irreg. Episteme, S.L., Ave de Suecia 17-4a, Valencia, 46010, Spain.

791.43 USA
EV; entertainment and the digital economy. 2000-2001; suspended. m. Reed Business Information, 5900 Wilshire Blvd, Ste 3100, Los Angeles, CA 90036.

320.9 USA ISSN 0014-3650
EVANS-NOVAK POLITICAL REPORT; what's happening...who's ahead...in politics today. 1967-2009 (Feb.). bi-w. Phillips International, Inc., 1 Massachusetts Ave, NW, Ste 610, Washington, DC 20001.

052 GBR ISSN 1471-5023
EVE; the original woman. 2000 (Nov.)-2008 (Sep.). m. Haymarket Publishing Ltd., 174 Hammersmith Rd, London, W6 7JP, United Kingdom.

072.3 GBR ISSN 0307-2711
EVENING ECHO, BOURNEMOUTH. 1900-1997. d. (except Sun.). Evening Echo Bournemouth, Richmond Hill, Bournemouth, Dorset BH2 6HH, United Kingdom.

300 ITA
EVENTI. 1993-ceased. bi-m. Presidenza del Consiglio dei Ministri, Dipartimento per l'Informazione e l'Editoria, Via Po 14, Rome, 00198, Italy.

700 800 ITA
EVENTI E INTERVENTI. 198?-2002 (no.9). irreg. Angelo Longo Editore, Via Paolo Costa 33, Ravenna, 48121, Italy.

380.1029 NLD
EVENTLINE; an international database of conferences, symposia, trade fairs & exhibitions. 1990-2003. plus m. updates. Elsevier BV, Radarweg 29, P O Box 211, Amsterdam, 1000 AE, Netherlands.

616.02 USA ISSN 1525-1667
EVERY SECOND COUNTS. 1999-2003. bi-m. National Safety Council, 1121 Spring Lake Dr, Itasca, IL 60143.

327 USA ISSN 0251-690X
EVERYONE'S UNITED NATIONS; a handbook on the work of the United Nations. 1948-1995. irreg. United Nations Publications, 2 United Nations Plaza, Rm DC2-853, New York, NY 10017.

663 USA ISSN 1527-8557 CODEN: EGVAAN
EVIDENCE - BASED GASTROENTEROLOGY. 2000-2008. q. Lippincott Williams & Wilkins, 530 Walnut St, Philadelphia, PA 19106-3621.

610 NZL ISSN 1176-2349
EVIDENCE - BASED PREVENTIVE MEDICINE. 2003 (Oct.)-2004. q. Open Mind Journals Ltd., PO Box 300-729, Albany, Auckland, 1311, New Zealand.

641.5 FRA ISSN 1776-2081
EWA RECETTES DE NOS GRAND-MERES. 2005-2007. q. Editions de la Rose, 37 Rue de Lauterbourg, Schiltigheim, 67300, France.

004.4 CZE ISSN 1801-5670
EXCEL PRI RUCE. 2006-2007. fortn. Verlag Dashoefer s.r.o., Na Prikope 18, PO Box 756, Prague 1, 11121, Czech Republic.

500 600 GBR
EXCELLENCE IN SCIENCE. 1980-200?. bi-m. The Royal Society Publishing, Publishing Section, 6-9 Carlton House Terr, London, SW1Y 5AG, United Kingdom.

004.6 USA
EXCHANGE & OUTLOOK PRO V I P. 1998-2008. w. Penton Technology Media, 221 E 29th St, Loveland, CO 80538.

352.160 FRA ISSN 1773-424X
L'EXECUTIF DES GRANDES VILLES DE FRANCE. 2005-2005. irreg. Compagnie Europeenne d'Editions et Publications Periodiques, 120 av des Champs-Elysees, Paris, 75008, France.

658 AUS ISSN 1327-5534
EXECUTIVE EXCELLENCE. 1996-2004. m. Prospect Media Pty. Ltd., 71-73 Lithgow St, St Leonards, NSW 2065, Australia.

330 USA ISSN 1051-2829
THE EXECUTIVE MEMO (PRINT). 19??-2008 (Dec.). bi-w. The Illinois Manufacturers Association, 1211 W 22nd St, Ste 620, Oak Brook, IL 60523.

658.8 NLD ISSN 1568-8925
EXECUTIVE OUTLOOK. 196?-2007. q. Reed Business bv, Postbus 4, Doetinchem, 7000 BA, Netherlands.

340 FRA ISSN 0981-8685
EXPERTS. 1986-199?. 4/yr. Cap Gemini Sogeti, 6-8 Rue Duret, Paris, 75784, France.

510.285 CZE ISSN 0231-8393
EXPLIZITE BESCHREIBUNG DER SPRACHE UND AUTOMATISCHE TEXTBEARBEITUNG/EKSPLITSITNOE OPISANIE YAZYKA I AVTOMATICHESKAYA OBRABOTKA TEKSTOV. 1975-1990. irreg. Matfyzpress, Ke Karlovu 3, Prague, 12116, Czech Republic.

382.6 USA ISSN 8755-013X
EXPORTERS' ENCYCLOPAEDIA. 1904-200?. a. (plus s-m. updates). Dun & Bradstreet, 103 JFK Parkway, Short Hills, NJ 07078.

363.7 DEU ISSN 0948-8251
EXPRESSDIENST UMWELTRECHT. 1995-2003. 10/yr. Erich Schmidt Verlag GmbH & Co. (Berlin), Genthiner Str 30 G, Berlin, 10785, Germany.

796.72 GBR ISSN 1476-8739
F 1 NEWS INTERNATIONAL. (Formula 1) 1992-2002. fortn. Peakcourt Ltd., 116-118 Liscombe, Birch Hill, Bracknell, Berks RG12 7DE, United Kingdom.

385.324 ITA
F A I. (Federazione Autotraportatori Italiani) 1964-ceased. m. Federazione Autotraportatori Italiani (F A I), Via Bacchiglione 16, Milan, 20139, Italy.

338.1 ITA ISSN 1011-5366
F A O INVESTMENT CENTRE TECHNICAL PAPER. (Food and Agriculture Organization) 1985-2003. irreg. Food and Agriculture Organization of the United Nations (F A O), Via delle Terme di Caracalla, Rome, RM 00100, Italy.

630 ITA ISSN 0259-2533
F A O TRAINING SERIES. (Food and Agriculture Organization) 19??-ceased. irreg. Food and Agriculture Organization of the United Nations (F A O), Via delle Terme di Caracalla, Rome, RM 00100, Italy.

052 DEU
F A Z WEEKLY. (Frankfurter Allgemeine Zeitung) 2002 (Jul.)-2005. w. Frankfurter Allgemeine Zeitung GmbH, Hellerhofstr 2-4, Frankfurt Am Main, 60327, Germany.

579.072 GBR ISSN 0921-8254
F E M S MICROBIOLOGY. 1977-1992. 62/yr. Wiley-Blackwell Publishing Ltd., 9600 Garsington Rd, Oxford, OX4 2DQ, United Kingdom.

370 DEU ISSN 1613-2009
F F. (Fremdsprachen Fruehbeginn) 1998-2004. bi-m. Domino Verlag, Menzinger Str 13, Munich, 80638, Germany.

058.81 DNK ISSN 1603-3736
F H M (DENMARK). (For Him Magazine) 2003-2009. m. Benjamin Media A/S, Finsensvej 6 D, Frederiksberg, 2000, Denmark.

052 AUS ISSN 1448-2452
F H M COLLECTIONS. (For Him Magazine) 1998-2007. s-a. Emap Australia Pty. Ltd., 187 Thomas St, Level 6, Haymarket, NSW 2000, Australia.

020.621 NLD ISSN 0168-6224
F I D PUBLICATION/FEDERATION INTERNATIONAL DE DOCUMENTATION. PUBLICATION/INTERNATIONALEN VERBANDES FUER DOKUMENTATION. VEROEFFENTLICHUNGEN. 1895-ceased. irreg. International Federation for Information and Documentation, FID Secretariat, PO Box 90402, The Hague, 2509 LK, Netherlands.

746.334 DEU
F I F A MAGAZINE. 1983-2008. m. Medienfabrik Guetersloh GmbH, Carl-Bertelsmann-Str 33, Guetersloh, 33311, Germany.

621 FRA ISSN 1639-0431
F I M EN LIGNE. (Federation des Industries Mecaniques) 1926-2006. 21/yr. Editions Sedom, 10 av. Hoche, Paris, Cedex 8 75382, France.

331.88 NLD ISSN 1380-7579
F N V NEWS. 1977-1999. 3/yr. Federatie Nederlandse Vakbeweging, Postbus 8456, Amsterdam, 1005 AL, Netherlands.

746.92 DEU ISSN 1614-4872
F - THE FASHION BUSINESS. 1983-2007. 2/yr. Deutscher Fachverlag GmbH, Mainzer Landstr 251, Frankfurt Am Main, 60326, Germany.

720 DEU ISSN 0340-2967
F UND I-BAU; Bauen mit Systemen. 1970-1992. q. Element Verlag GmbH, Ernst-Heinkel-Str 4/2, Fellbach, 70734, Germany.

948.94 DNK ISSN 0106-8822
FAABORG-AARBOGEN. 1979 (vol.5)-1983. a. Edvard Andersen, Oesterbro 42, Faaborg, 5600, Denmark.

595.7 DEU ISSN 0940-8150
FACETTA. 1990-2005. a. Entomologische Gesellschaft Ingolstadt e.V., c/o Dieter Jungwirth, Anatomiestr 2, Ingolstadt, 85049, Germany.

360 DEU ISSN 0944-825X
FACHDIENST DER LEBENSHILFE. 1984-2008. q. Bundesvereinigung Lebenshilfe fuer Menschen mit Geistiger Behinderung e.V., Raiffeisenstr 18, Marburg, 35043, Germany.

658 NLD ISSN 1872-5848
FACILITY AND FINANCE SELECT. 2006-2007. bi-m. Kluwer B.V., Postbus 4, Alphen aan den Rijn, 2400 MA, Netherlands.

363.72 USA ISSN 1079-5049
FACING THE GLOBAL ENVIRONMENT CHALLENGE. 1994-1995. bi-m. World Bank Group, 1818 H St, NW, Washington, DC 20433.

610 310 USA ISSN 1074-8849
FACTS ABOUT FAMILY PRACTICE. 1987-200?. a. American Academy of Family Physicians, 11400 Tomahawk Creek Pkwy, Leawood, KS 66211-2672.

612.67 FRA ISSN 1295-2109
FACTS, RESEARCH AND INTERVENTION IN GERIATRICS. NEWSLETTER: NUTRITION. 1992-199?. 3/yr. Editions S E R D I, 320 Rue Saint-Honore, Paris, 75001, France.

340 900 FRA ISSN 0989-7925
FACULTES DE DROIT ET DE LA SCIENCE JURIDIQUE. REVUE D'HISTOIRE. 1984-2007. s-a. Association pour l'Histoire des Facultes de Droit et de la Science Juridique, Universite de Paris V, 10 av. Pierre Larousse, Malakoff, Cedex 92241, France.

330 CZE ISSN 1212-5598
FACULTY OF AGRICULTURE IN CESKE BUDEJOVICE. COLLECTION OF SCIENTIFIC PAPERS. SERIES FOR ECONOMICS, MANAGEMENT AND TRADE. 1986-2006. s-a. Jihoceska Univerzita v Ceskych Budejovicich, Zemedelska Fakulta, Studentska 13, Ceske Budejovice, 37005, Czech Republic.

636.9322 DNK ISSN 0900-288X
FAELLESUDVALGET TIL KANINAVLENS FREMME. BERETNING. 1965-1984. biennial. Faellesudvalget til Kaninavlens Fremme, Birkevaenget 74, Vejen, 6600, Denmark.

331 USA ISSN 1545-4460
FAIR EMPLOYMENT PRACTICES SUMMARY OF LATEST DEVELOPMENTS. 1965-2003. bi-w. The Bureau of National Affairs, Inc., 1801 S Bell St, Arlington, VA 22202.

333.33 323.4 USA ISSN 1095-2926
FAIR HOUSING - FAIR LENDING. 1997-200?. m. Aspen Publishers, Inc., 111 Eighth Ave., 7th Fl, New York, NY 10011.

053.1 DEU ISSN 1613-6837
FAKTOR.F. 2004-2006. 4/yr. Audimax Verlag GmbH, Hauptmarkt 6-8, Nuernberg, 90403, Germany.

790.1 910.91 NLD ISSN 1573-2142
FAMILIEFEEST!. 2004-2006. a. Toeristisch Nederland BV, Postbus 5443, Haarlem, 2000 GK, Netherlands.

286.132 USA ISSN 1079-526X
FAMILY BIBLE SERIES: ADULTS. 19??-2000. q. LifeWay Christian Resources, 1 Lifeway Plz, Nashville, TN 37234.

635 USA ISSN 1549-7259
FAMILY CIRCLE EASY GARDENING. 1992-200?. 3/yr. Family Circle, Inc., 375 Lexington Ave, New York, NY 10017-5514.

643 USA
FAMILY CIRCLE HOME SWEET HOME. 2000-ceased. bi-m. Family Circle, Inc., 375 Lexington Ave, New York, NY 10017-5514.

929 AUS ISSN 0812-3136
FAMILY LOCAL HISTORY SOURCES IN VICTORIA. 1983-1996. biennial. Custodians of Records, PO Box 30, Blackburn, VIC 3130, Australia.

610 USA
FAMILY MEDICINE NET GUIDE; your guide to the internet. 2000-200?. 4/yr. Intellisphere, LLC, Office Center at Princeton Meadows, 666 Plainsboro Rd, Bldg 300, Plainsboro, NJ 08536.

610 USA
FAMILY MEDICINE NET GUIDE ENEWSLETTER. 2000-200?. bi-m. Intellisphere, LLC, Office Center at Princeton Meadows, 666 Plainsboro Rd, Bldg 300, Plainsboro, NJ 08536.

690 USA
FAMILY STYLE HOME PLANS; homes to fit your family. 1994-2009 (Jan.). q. HomePlans.com, 901 N 3rd St, Ste 216, Minneapolis, MN 55401.

929 USA ISSN 1556-8024
FAMILY TREE MAGAZINE: YEARBOOK (YEAR). 2000-2004. a. F + W Media Inc., 4700 E Galbraith Rd, Cincinnati, OH 45236.

640 ITA ISSN 1724-9244
FANTASIA IN CUCINA. 2004-200?. bi-m. Edigamma Publishing, Via Sambuca Pistoiese 70A, Rome, 00138, Italy.

535 DEU ISSN 0014-7680
DIE FARBE; Zeitschrift fuer alle Zweige der Farbenlehre und ihre Anwendung. 1952-2003. irreg. Muster-Schmidt Verlag, Schuhstr, Sudheim, 37154, Germany.

747 ITA ISSN 1970-4682
FARE E DECORARE. 2006-200?. m. Sprea Editori Srl, Via Torino 51, Cernusco sul Naviglio, MI 20063, Italy.

657 GBR
FARM BUSINESS ACCOUNTS. SUMMARY OF RESULTS (YEAR). 1999-2001. a. Promar International, Northcroft House, Newbury, Berks RG14 1HD, United Kingdom.

615 ITA ISSN 0393-9693
FARMACI & TERAPIA. 1984-ceased. 3/yr. Editrice Il Sedicesimo, Via Mannelli 29, Florence, FI 50136, Italy.

636.089 ITA ISSN 1825-3237
FARMACIA VETERINARIA. 1997-ceased. 10/yr. Point Veterinaire Italie Srl, Via Medardo Rosso 11, Milan, 20159, Italy.

615.1 FRA ISSN 0014-827X CODEN: FRMCE8
IL FARMACO. 1988-2005. m. Elsevier France, Editions Scientifiques et Medicales, 23 Rue Linois, Paris, 75724, France.

677 ITA
FASHION; il settimanale italiano della moda. 1970-ceased. w. Fashion Edizioni Ecomarket SpA, Corso Venezia 26, Milan, 20121, Italy.

Cessations

666 ITA ISSN 1123-8135
FASHION CERAMIC TILES. 1983-ceased. s-a. Gruppo Editoriale Faenza Editrice SpA, Via Pier de Crescenzi 44, Faenza, RA 48018, Italy.

646.724 ITA ISSN 1125-6214
FASHION PARADE. 1979-ceased. q. Tecniche Nuove SpA, Via Eritrea 21, Milan, MI 201, Italy.

629.3 GBR ISSN 0969-2630
FAST FERRY OPERATORS DIRECTORY. 1991-1999. a. Fast Ferry Information Ltd., 14 Marston Gate, Winshester, SO23 7DS, United Kingdom.

591.945 ITA ISSN 0430-1226 CODEN: FIITA
FAUNA D'ITALIA; repertorio generale delle specie animali esistenti in Italia. 1956-199?. s-a. Il Sole 24 Ore Business Media, Via Monterosa 91, Milan, 20149, Italy.

590 AUS
FAUNA OF AUSTRALIA. 1987-200?. irreg. Australian Biological Resources Study, GPO Box 787, Canberra, ACT 2601, Australia.

571.2 DEU ISSN 0344-7227
FAUNISTISCH-FLORISTISCHE NOTIZEN AUS DEM SAARLAND. 1968-2000. irreg. Delattinia - Arbeitsgemeinschaft fuer Tier- und Pflanzengeographische Heimatforschung im Saarland, c/o Harald Schreiber, Am Bergwerk 10, Landsweiler-Reden, 66578, Germany.

280.4 ITA
FEDELTA; mensile di in-formazione. 1976-ceased. m. Fedelta, Via Vespucci, 3-19, Prato, FI 59100, Italy.

348.041 AUS ISSN 1443-5527
FEDERAL CASES (DISK 1). 1996-200?. m. Lawbook Co., PO Box 3502, Rozelle, NSW 2039, Australia.

340 AUS ISSN 1443-5535
FEDERAL CASES (DISK 2). 1995-200?. irreg. Lawbook Co., PO Box 3502, Rozelle, NSW 2039, Australia.

354.9 AUS ISSN 0812-0838
FEDERAL POLICE DISCIPLINARY TRIBUNAL. ANNUAL REPORT. 1982-2006. a. Federal Police Disciplinary Tribunal, Law Courts Bldg, Level 16, Queens Square, NSW 2000, Australia.

332 USA ISSN 1547-6863
FEDERAL RESERVE BULLETIN. STATISTICAL SUPPLEMENT. 1915-2008. m. U.S. Federal Reserve System, Board of Governors, Publications Services, Rm MS 138, Washington, DC 20551.

332.1 USA ISSN 1932-4200
FEDERAL RESERVE SYSTEM. BOARD OF GOVERNORS. STATISTICAL DIGEST. 1981-19??. irreg. U.S. Federal Reserve System, Board of Governors, Publications Services, Rm MS 138, Washington, DC 20551.

320.9 ITA ISSN 0393-1358
THE FEDERALIST; a political review. 1959-ceased. q. E D I F, Via Porta Pertusi, 6, Pavia, PV 27100, Italy.

610.6 060 ITA
FEDERAZIONE DELLE SOCIETA MEDICO - SCIENTIFICHE ITALIANE. CONGRESSI (YEAR). 1978-ceased. a. Federazione delle Societa Medico - Scientifiche Italiane (F I S M), Corso di Porta Vittoria 29, Milan, 20122, Italy.

615 ITA
FEDERFARMA NOTIZIE; organo d'informazione settimanale dei titolari di farmacia. 1986-ceased. w. Editoriale Giornalidea, Piazza della Repubblica 19, Milan, 20124, Italy.

790.1 USA
FEELING SPORTS MAGAZINE. 1975-2007. bi-m. Braille Sports Foundation, 4601 Excelsior Ave., S, St. Louis Park, MN 55416.

793 DEU
FEIERABEND-RAETSEL. 1977-200?. w. Deutscher Raetselverlag GmbH & Co. KG, Muenchener Str 101-09, Ismaning, 85737, Germany.

940 NLD ISSN 0929-2411
FEIT & FICTIE. 1993-2006. q. Historische Uitgeverij, Westersingel 37, Groningen, 9718 CC, Netherlands.

700 913 ITA ISSN 0391-7517
FELIX RAVENNA; rivista di antichita ravennati, cristiane e bizantine. 1911-2004. a. Edizioni del Girasole s.r.l., Via P Costa, 10, Ravenna, RA 48100, Italy.

570 DNK ISSN 0109-856X
FELTUNDERSOEGELSER; noter og meddelelser. 1967-1989. irreg. Midtsjaellands Naturhistoriske Forening, Dronning Margarethesvej 33, Ringsted, 4100, Denmark.

305.4 USA ISSN 1550-736X
FEMINISTA!. 1997-200?. irreg. Feminista!, 1388 Haight St, PMB 30, San Francisco, CA 94117.

690 USA ISSN 0895-450X
FENESTRATION; a magazine for manufacturers & distributors of windows, doors, & other fenestration products. 1987-199?. 10/yr. Ashlee Publishing Co., Inc., 18 E 41st St, 20th Fl, New York, NY 10017.

057.86 CZE ISSN 1212-5490
FENIX. 1999-2004. q. Czech Press Group a.s., Klisska 1432-18, Usti nad Labem, 400 01, Czech Republic.

683 ESP ISSN 0212-8276
FERRETICA. 1980-198?. 9/yr. Ferretica, Mazustegui, 21 4o planta, Bilbao, Vizcaya 48006, Spain.

530 GBR ISSN 1025-9260
FERROELECTRICS COMMUNICATIONS. 1996-1997. bi-m. Taylor & Francis Ltd., 4 Park Sq, Milton Park, Abingdon, OX14 4RN, United Kingdom.

385 ITA ISSN 1120-0251
IL FERROVIERE. 1981-ceased. m. Giorgio Bellini, 7 via Judrio, Udine, 33100, Italy.

798.2 DEU ISSN 1618-4505
FEST IM SATTEL; Das unabhaengige Reitermagazin. 2002-2008 (Jan.). 4/yr. Minerva Verlag GmbH, Hocksteiner Weg 38, Moenchengladbach, 41189, Germany.

668.4 ESP
FETRAPLAST. 1992-2002. q. E T D Prensa Profesional, SA, Sicilia 95, Atico, Barcelona, 08013, Spain.

618 618.92 GBR ISSN 1369-4588
FETUS AND NEONATE; physiology and clinical applications. 1993-1995 (Oct.). irreg. Cambridge University Press, The Edinburgh Bldg, Shaftesbury Rd, Cambridge, CB2 8RU, United Kingdom.

790.094 FRA ISSN 1775-8289
FICHENN DEKNIKEL/FICHE TECHNIQUE - ADDAV 56. 200?-2004. irreg. Association Departementale pour le Developpement des Arts Vivants dans le Morbihan, 12 bis rue Richemont, Vannes, 56000, France.

820 NZL ISSN 1175-3862
FICTION-PLUS; creating opportunities for writers. 1994-2001 (Jul.). bi-m. Write Now Magazine, 76 Saxby Road, Hamilton, 99838, New Zealand.

363.7 GBR ISSN 0428-304X CODEN: FSTUBX
FIELD STUDIES. 1959-2003. a. Field Studies Council, Central Services, Preston Montford, Montford Bridge, Shrewsbury, Shrops SY4 1HW, United Kingdom.

690 381 ITA ISSN 0393-8050
LE FIERE; rassegna periodica tecnica di documentazione e informazione. 1968-ceased. irreg. Casa Editrice la Fiaccola, Via Conca del Naviglio 37, Milan, MI 20123, Italy.

739.27 051 ITA
FILES LUXURY INTERNATIONAL. 2003-ceased. q. Sothis Editrice srl, Via Pietro Maestri 3, Rome, 00191, Italy.

677 FRA ISSN 1146-0733
FILIERE MAILLE. 1982-2004. q. Editions de l' Industrie Textile, 16 rue Ballu, Paris, 75311 Cedex 9 , France.

028.5 CZE ISSN 1210-6801
FILIPS; film - literatura - pisnicky - sport. 1953-1995. m. Mlada Fronta, Mezi Vodami 1952/9, Prague 4, 14300, Czech Republic.

791.43 GBR ISSN 1367-5141
FILM AND TELEVISION IN EDUCATION. 1991-1995. biennial. British Universities Film and Video Council, 77 Wells St., London, W1T 3QJ, United Kingdom.

778.53 USA
FILM & TV GRAPHICS; an international survey of the art of film animation. 1967-1976. a. Graphis Inc., 307 Fifth Ave, 10th Fl, New York, NY 10016.

791.43 SVK ISSN 0862-8130
FILM FAN. 1991-1995. m. Ringier Slovakia a. s., Prievozska 14, PO Box 46, Bratislava 24, 82004, Slovakia.

778.53 DNK ISSN 0108-772X
FILM MAGASINET. 1982-1982. bi-m. Film Magasinet, Ulshoejvej 16, Kalundborg, 4400, Denmark.

791.43 CZE ISSN 1801-6553
FILM NA SOBOTU. 2006-2006 (ceased same year). w. Trade & Leisure Publications, s.r.o., Pernerova 35a, Prague 8, 186 00, Czech Republic.

791.433 DNK ISSN 0909-0002
FILM & VIDEO. 1942-2004. 6/yr. Danmarks Film- og Videoamatoerer, c/o Henning Volder, Bastebjerg 57, Karlslunde, 2690, Denmark.

778.53029 USA ISSN 1058-2630
FILM PRODUCERS, STUDIOS, AGENTS AND CASTING DIRECTORS GUIDE. 1989-2000. a. IFILM, 1024 N Orange Dr, Hollywood, CA 90038.

781.542 USA ISSN 1527-7291
FILM SCORE GUIDES. 2000-200?. irreg. Greenwood Publishing Group Inc., 88 Post Rd W, PO Box 5007, Westport, CT 06881.

011.37 DNK ISSN 0107-0940
FILMATISEREDE BOEGER. 1974-2004. a. D B C A/S, Tempovej 7-11, Ballerup, 2750, Denmark.

200 ITA
FILOSOFIA DELLA RELIGIONE. TESTI E STUDI. 1977-1980 (no.3). irreg. Paideia Editrice, Via Corsica 130, Brescia, BS 25125, Italy.

332.1 GBR ISSN 1367-0832
FINANCE FOR SMALL FIRMS. 1994-2004. a. Bank of England, Publications Group, Threadneedle St, London, EC2R 8AH, United Kingdom.

332.6 ISR ISSN 0334-6595
FINANCIAL DATA OF T A - 100 COMPANIES - QUARTERLY. 1981-199?. q. Tel Aviv Stock Exchange, 54 Ahad Ha am St, Tel Aviv, 65202, Israel.

332.0285516 GBR ISSN 1462-1991
FINANCIAL SECTOR PREPARATIONS FOR THE YEAR 2000. 1998-1999. irreg. Bank of England, Publications Group, Threadneedle St, London, EC2R 8AH, United Kingdom.

332 USA ISSN 1934-2888
FINANCIALWEEK. 2006-2008 (Dec.). w. Crain Communications, Inc., 711 Third Ave, New York, NY 10017.

332 NLD ISSN 1383-7656
FINANCIELE & MONETAIRE STUDIES. 1982-2006. q. Uitgeverij Lemma BV, Postbus 3320, Utrecht, 3502 GH, Netherlands.

331.25 NLD ISSN 1570-3894
FINANCIELE GEGEVENS VAN DE PENSIOENFONDSEN. 1984-2004. a. De Nederlandsche Bank, Divisie Statistiek en Informatie, Postbus 98, Amsterdam, 1000 AB, Netherlands.

352 CZE ISSN 1801-8386
FINANCNI ZDROJE PRO OBCE. 2004-2007. plus q. updates. Nakladatelstvi Dr. Josef Raabe, s.r.o., Sokolovska 155/31, Prague 8, 180 00, Czech Republic.

330 ESP ISSN 0210-4997
FINANZAS. 1956-198?. 12/yr. Finanzas, Alcala, 20, Apartado 14776, Madrid, 28014, Spain.

747 USA ISSN 1938-4424
FIND IT! (CHICAGO); kitchen & bath sourcebook. 2006-2008. a. Meredith Corporation, 1716 Locust St, Des Moines, IA 50309.

301 USA ISSN 0891-1835
FINDING THE SOURCE. 1987-19??. irreg. Greenwood Publishing Group Inc., 88 Post Rd W, PO Box 5007, Westport, CT 06881.

700 AUS
FINEART FORUM; art and technology network news service. 1987-2004. m. FineArt Forum, Art Science and Technology Network, PO Box 3603, South Brisbane, QLD 4101, Australia.

340 USA
FINE'S WISCONSIN EVIDENCE; a quick guide to courtroom evidence. 1988-ceased. plus irreg. updates. LexisNexis, PO Box 7587, Charlottesville, VA 22906.

667.6 531 011 USA ISSN 1544-9440
THE FINISHING LINE. 1984-2006. q. Society of Manufacturing Engineers, One SME Dr, PO Box 930, Dearborn, MI 48121.

698 USA ISSN 1934-3477 CODEN: IPPOEA
FINISHING TODAY; evolution of industrial paint & powder. 1924-2008. m. B N P Media, 2401 W Big Beaver Rd, Ste 700, Troy, MI 48084.

635 ITA ISSN 1724-9279
FIORI E PIANTE SPECIAL. 2004-200?. q. Edigamma Publishing, Via Sambuca Pistoiese 70A, Rome, 00138, Italy.

330 ITA ISSN 0391-6405
FIORINO; quotidiano del mattino di finanza economia e attualita. 1969-ceased. d. Societa Editrice Esedra s.r.l., Via Parigi, 11, Rome, RM 00185, Italy.

628.92 ITA
FIRE. 1998-ceased. 8/yr. Il Sole 24 Ore Business Media, Divisione J C E, Via Patecchio 2, Milan, 20141, Italy.

628.92 362.18 USA ISSN 1549-0742
FIRE E M S. (Emergency Medical Services) 2003 (May/Jun.)-200?. 10/yr. PennWell Corporation, 1421 S Sheridan Rd, Tulsa, OK 74112.

799.1 ITA ISSN 1970-5573
FISH BOATS. 2006-200?. m. Sprea Editori Srl, Via Torino 51, Cernusco sul Naviglio, MI 20063, Italy.

639.2 310 USA
FISHERIES MARKET NEWS REPORT. 1981-2003. 3/w. Urner Barry Publications, Inc., PO Box 389, Toms River, NJ 08754.

920 USA ISSN 1087-3996
FIVE HUNDRED LEADERS OF INFLUENCE. 1993-2003. a. American Biographical Institute, Inc., Governing Board of Editors, 5126 Bur Oak Cir, Raleigh, NC 27612.

920 USA ISSN 1087-3953
FIVE THOUSAND PERSONALITIES OF THE WORLD. 1986-1998. biennial. American Biographical Institute, Inc., Governing Board of Editors, 5126 Bur Oak Cir, Raleigh, NC 27612.

600 USA ISSN 1058-0948
FLAME RETARDANCY NEWS. 1991 (Jan.)-2006. m. Business Communications Co., Inc., 25 Van Zant St, Ste 13, Norwalk, CT 06855-1781.

398 914.603 ESP
FLAMENCO; boletin de informacion. 1975 (vol.5)-ceased. irreg. (2-3/yr.). Tertulia Flamenca de Ceuta, PO Box 344, Ceuta, Cadiz 11700, Spain.

724 ITA
FLARE; architectural lighting magazine. 1989-ceased. 3/yr. Editore Lupetti & Co., Via Hayez 12, Milan, MI 20129, Italy.

636.082 FRA ISSN 1774-7341
FLASH (PACE). 2005-2005. irreg. Sersia France, 19 bd Nominoe, Pace, 35740, France.

617.3 616.8 FRA ISSN 1276-356X
FLASH-INFORMATIONS HANDICAP. 1978-2004. w. Centre Technique National d'Etudes et de Recherches sur les Handicaps et les Inadaptations, 236 bis rue de Tolbiac, Paris, 75013, France.

371.5 NLD ISSN 1871-8477
FLAUWEKUL VOOR KIDS. 1999-2006. s-a. Uitgeverij Intermed, Postbus 2306, Groningen, 9704 CH, Netherlands.

664.9 DEU ISSN 1615-9829
FLEISCHER-SERVICE; das Feinkostmagazin der AFZ. 1997-2002. 6/yr. Deutscher Fachverlag GmbH, Mainzer Landstr 251, Frankfurt Am Main, 60326, Germany.

332 AUS
FLINDERS UNIVERSITY. SCHOOL OF COMMERCE. RESEARCH PAPER SERIES (PRINT). 199?-2002. irreg. (9 issues in 2002; 11 issues in 2003, 7 issues in 2004). Flinders University, School of Commerce, PO Box 2100, Adelaide, SA 1001, Australia.

677 DEU ISSN 0933-2316
FLOCK; international trade journal for the flock industry. 1984-2004. q. Flock Verlag, Auf der Obersten Beunde 28, Buedingen, 63654, Germany.

340.5 USA
FLORIDA CIVIL PRACTICE GUIDE. 1992-200?. irreg. Matthew Bender & Co., Inc., 1275 Broadway, Albany, NY 12204.

340.5 346.07 USA
FLORIDA CIVIL PROCEDURE LITIGATION MANUAL. 1998-199?. a. Anderson Publishing Co., 9443 Springboro Pike, Miamisburg, OH 45342.

690 USA ISSN 1084-9548
FLORIDA CONSTRUCTION NEWS WEEKLY COVERING MIAMI & VICINITY. 1995-199?. w. McGraw-Hill Construction Dodge, 148 Princeton-Hightstown Rd. N1, Hightstown, NJ 08520.

371.42 USA ISSN 1069-8981
THE FLORIDA JOBBANK; the job hunter's guide to the Sunshine State. (Includes: Fort Lauderdale, Jacksonville, Miami, Orlando, Tampa and many others.) 1996-2005 (16th ed.). irreg. Adams Media, 4700 E Galbraith Rd, Cincinnati, OH 45236.

346.046 USA
FLORIDA LAND USE AND GROWTH MANAGEMENT LAW. 1976-199?. plus irreg. updates. LexisNexis, PO Box 7587, Charlottesville, VA 22906.

340 USA
FLORIDA REAL ESTATE CLOSINGS. 1990-1999. plus irreg. updates. LexisNexis, PO Box 7587, Charlottesville, VA 22906.

332 USA
FLOW OF FUNDS SUMMARY STATISTICS. 19??-1996. q. U.S. Federal Reserve System, Board of Governors, Publications Services, Rm MS 138, Washington, DC 20551.

635.9 NZL ISSN 1170-1749
FLOWERS NEW ZEALAND. 1990-2004 (May). bi-m. Magus Media, 4 Leamington Rd, Mt. Eden, P.O. Box 10-276, Auckland, New Zealand.

387.736 DEU ISSN 0937-8758
FLUGMAGAZIN N R W. (Nordrhein-Westfalen) 1967-2006. m. BarthelsTeam Werbeagentur und verlag, Am Wiedenhof 1, Lindlar, 51789, Germany.

788.32 AUS
FLUTE AUSTRALASIA. 1995-2003. s-a. Flute Australasia, PO Box 236, Croydon, NSW 2132, Australia.

791.43 FRA ISSN 1242-1898
FOCALES; revue d'histoire et de theorie du cinema et de la television. 1992-1996. biennial. Presses Universitaires de Nancy, 42-44 av. de la Liberation, Nancy, 54000, France.

378.56946 ISR
FOCUS. 1983-2007. 3/yr. University of Haifa, Department of External Relations and Resource Development, Mt. Carmel, Haifa, 31905, Israel.

338.47687 USA ISSN 0749-8357
FOCUS: AN ECONOMIC PROFILE OF THE APPAREL INDUSTRY. 1962-2000. a. American Apparel & Footwear Association, 1601 N Kent St, Ste. 1200, Arlington, VA 22209.

363.7 USA ISSN 1062-3086
FOCUS ON: GLOBAL CHANGE. 1990-1993. fortn. Thomson Reuters, Scientific, 1500 Spring Garden, 4th Fl, Philadelphia, PA 19130.

917.904 USA ISSN 1525-5026
FODOR'S ARIZONA. 1985-2005. a. Fodor's Travel Publications, Inc., 1745 Broadway, 15th Fl, New York, NY 10019.

306.766 USA ISSN 1094-0057
FODOR'S GAY GUIDE TO THE USA. 1996-2001. a. Fodor's Travel Publications, Inc., 1745 Broadway, 15th Fl, New York, NY 10019.

915.104 USA
FODOR'S KOREA. 19??-1993. a. Fodor's Travel Publications, Inc., 1745 Broadway, 15th Fl, New York, NY 10019.

917.304 USA ISSN 1043-0253
FODOR'S UNITED STATES OF AMERICA. 1976-1989. a. Fodor's Travel Publications, Inc., 1745 Broadway, 15th Fl, New York, NY 10019.

059.9162 IRL ISSN 1393-3701
FOINSE; priomhnuachtan naisiunta na gaeilge. 1996-2009. w. Foinse, An Cheathru Rua, Co. Gaillimhe, Ireland.

306 384 378 DNK ISSN 1901-5569
FOKUS; et internationalt netwaerk for kultur, medier og kommunikationsteknologi. 2006-2006. irreg. Crossroads Copenhagen, Rued Langgaards Vej 7, Copenhagen S, 2300, Denmark.

610 ITA ISSN 1124-8270 CODEN: AMSNAB
FOLIA DERMATOLOGICA. 1959-19??. a. Fabrizio Serra Editore, c/o Accademia Editoriale, Via Santa Bibbiana 28, Pisa, 56127, Italy.

540 CZE ISSN 1211-2070
FOLIA FACULTATIS SCIENTIARUM NATURALIUM UNIVERSITATIS MASARYKIANAE BRUNENSIS: CHEMIA. 1960-1994. a. Masarykova Universita, Prirodovedecka Fakulta, Kotlarska 2, Brno, 61137, Czech Republic.

550 CZE ISSN 1211-3670
FOLIA FACULTATIS SCIENTIARUM NATURALIUM UNIVERSITATIS MASARYKIANAE BRUNENSIS: GEOLOGIA. 1960-2002 (vol.39). a. Masarykova Universita, Prirodovedecka Fakulta, Kotlarska 2, Brno, 61137, Czech Republic.

530 CZE ISSN 1210-9614 CODEN: FFSPER
FOLIA FACULTATIS SCIENTIARUM NATURALIUM UNIVERSITATIS MASARYKIANAE BRUNENSIS: PHYSICA. 1960-1992. a. Masarykova Universita, Prirodovedecka Fakulta, Kotlarska 2, Brno, 61137, Czech Republic.

580 CZE ISSN 0139-9667
FOLIA MUSEI RERUM NATURALIUM BOHEMIAE OCCIDENTALIS. BOTANICA. 1972-2005 (vol.43). s-a. Zapadoceske Muzeum v Plzni, Kopeckeho sady 2, Plzen, 30135, Czech Republic.

550 CZE ISSN 0139-9764 CODEN: FMBOAI
FOLIA MUSEI RERUM NATURALIUM BOHEMIAE OCCIDENTALIS. GEOLOGICA. 1971-2001 (vol.44). irreg. Zapadoceske Muzeum v Plzni, Kopeckeho sady 2, Plzen, 30135, Czech Republic.

590 CZE ISSN 0139-9713 CODEN: FMRZEX
FOLIA MUSEI RERUM NATURALIUM BOHEMIAE OCCIDENTALIS. ZOOLOGICA. 1971-2001 (vol.41). s-a. Zapadoceske Muzeum v Plzni, Kopeckeho sady 2, Plzen, 30135, Czech Republic.

305.8 DNK ISSN 0085-0756
FOLK; journal of the Danish Ethnographic Society. 1959-2006. a. Dansk Etnografisk Forening, c/o Institute of Anthropology, University of Copenhagen, Frederiksholms Kanal 4, Copenhagen K, 1220, Denmark.

016.37 DNK ISSN 0909-6477
FOLKESKOLEN. KATALOG. 1979-2006. a. Fonden Undervisnings Information, Siljangade 6, Copenhagen S, 2300, Denmark.

930.1 ESP ISSN 0210-2366
FONAMENTS; prehistoria i mon antic als paisos catalans. 1978-1996. a. Curial Edicions Catalan, C. de Bruc, 144, Barcelona, Catalunya 08037, Spain.

800 ITA ISSN 1122-102X
FONDAMENTI. 1985-1986. q. Fabrizio Serra Editore, c/o Accademia Editoriale, Via Santa Bibbiana 28, Pisa, 56127, Italy.

055.1 ITA ISSN 1721-2812
FONDAZIONE LIBERAL. 1995-2007. w. Fondazione Liberal, Via della Panetteria 10, Rome, 00187, Italy.

945 ITA ISSN 0071-6901
FONTI SUI COMUNI RURALI TOSCANI. 1961-1984 (no.9). irreg. Casa Editrice Leo S. Olschki, Viuzzo del Pozzetto 8, Florence, 50126, Italy.

382 TUR
FOOD & PACKAGING EXPORTS - TURKEY. ceased. q. Iletisim Magazin Gazetecilik San. ve Tic. A.S., Ihlas Holding Merkez Binasi, 29 Ekim Cad. 23, P.K. 34197, Yenibosna - Istanbul, 34197, Turkey.

664 USA
FOOD CREATION. 200?-2005. q. Putman Media, 555 W Pierce Rd, Ste 301, Itasca, IL 60143.

664 USA ISSN 1070-1788
FOOD INGREDIENT NEWS. 1994 (Jan.)-2006. m. Business Communications Co., Inc., 25 Van Zant St, Ste 13, Norwalk, CT 06855-1781.

664 663 NLD ISSN 0168-325X
FOOD MANAGEMENT; vakblad voor de voedings- en genotmiddelenindustrie. 1983-2004. m. (11/yr.). Keesing Noordervliet BV, De Molen 82, Houten, 3995 AX, Netherlands.

664 621.9 GBR ISSN 0268-1196
FOOD MANUFACTURE. INGREDIENT AND MACHINERY SURVEY. 1967-1998. a. C M P Information Ltd., Ludgate House, 245 Blackfriars Rd., London, SE1 9UR, United Kingdom.

664 DEU ISSN 0944-6850
FOOD P P P. 1993-2002. 3/yr. Dr. Harnisch Verlagsgesellschaft GmbH, Blumenstr 15, Nuernberg, 90402, Germany.

664 ITA
FOOD PLANTS & TECHNOLOGY. 1981-ceased. a. Zeus International Srl, Viale Lunigiana 14, Milan, MI 20125, Italy.

664 ITA
FOOD PROCESSING. 1984-ceased. bi-m. Zeus International Srl, Viale Lunigiana 14, Milan, MI 20125, Italy.

362.1 664 NLD ISSN 1875-1911
FOOD SAFETY ONLINE (DUTCH EDITION). 2007-2009. m. Food Doctors, Kievitstr 11, Woerden, 3443 BD, Netherlands.

362.1 664 NLD ISSN 1875-192X
FOOD SAFETY ONLINE (ENGLISH EDITION). 2007-2009. m. Food Doctors, Kievitstr 11, Woerden, 3443 BD, Netherlands.

664 346.006 USA ISSN 1523-4533
FOOD SAFETY REPORT. 1999-2002. w. The Bureau of National Affairs, Inc., 1801 S Bell St, Arlington, VA 22202.

796.332 USA ISSN 1526-8179
FOOTBALL PLAYER. 1998-2000. bi-m. L C Clark Publishing Inc, 840 US Hwy 1, Ste 330, North Palm Beach, FL 33408-3834.

320 DNK ISSN 0907-1296
FOQUS. 1984-2000. bi-m. Kristeligt Folkeparti, Bernhard Bangs Alle 23, Frederiksberg, 2000, Denmark.

616.6 USA ISSN 1525-9471
FOR PATIENTS ONLY. 1988-200?. bi-m. Ashlee Publishing Co., Inc., 18 E 41st St, 20th Fl, New York, NY 10017.

392.509 GBR ISSN 1367-6776
FOR THE BRIDE. 1993-2007. q. Montrose Publishing Ltd., 12 Eton St, Richmond-upon-Thames, Surrey TW9 1EE, United Kingdom.

621.381 DNK ISSN 1901-760X
FORBRUGERELEKTRONIK MAGASINET; magasin for branchens professionelle aktoerer. 1974-2008. 10/yr. Horisont Gruppen A/S, Center Boulevard 5, Copenhagen S, 2300, Denmark.

640.73 DNK ISSN 0105-9122
FORBRUGERINDEKS. 1978-2006. a. D B C A/S, Tempovej 7-11, Ballerup, 2750, Denmark.

365.64 ITA
FORCESICUREZZA. 1986-ceased. m. Publi & Consult SpA, Via Tagliamento, 29, Rome, RM 00198, Italy.

327 AUS ISSN 1329-9549 CODEN: INSIFS
FOREIGN AFFAIRS AND TRADE RECORD. 1992-2000. q. Department of Foreign Affairs and Trade, Overseas Information Branch, RG Casey Bldg, John McEwen Crescent, Barton, ACT 0221, Australia.

382 USA ISSN 0732-0418
FOREIGN DIRECT INVESTMENT IN THE UNITED STATES; operations of U.S. affiliates of foreign companies. 1977-1994. a. U.S. Department of Commerce, Bureau of Economic Analysis, 1441 L St NW, Washington, DC 20230.

398 DNK ISSN 1396-0660
FORENINGEN DANMARKS FOLKEMINDER. SKRIFTER. 1908-1997. irreg. Foreningen Danmarks Folkeminder, Christians Brygge 3, Copenhagen K, 1219, Denmark.

674 AUS
FOREST LOGGER & SAWMILLER MONTHLY. 1992-2006. m. Australasian Forest Logger & Sawmiller, PO Box 1507, Mornington, TAS 7018, Australia.

070.5025 DNK ISSN 0109-405X
FORLAGSVEJVISER. 1984-2004. a. D B C A/S, Tempovej 7-11, Ballerup, 2750, Denmark.

643 ITA
FORME. 1962-ceased. bi-m. Luigi Massoni Editore, Via G Cermenate 37, Como, CO 22072, Italy.

658.8029 GBR ISSN 1352-2485
FORMER SOVIET UNION MARKETING, MEDIA & ADVERTISING DIRECTORY. 1993-ceased. a. Hughes Publishing Ltd., 43 Lower Belgrave St, London, SW1W 0LS, United Kingdom.

621.9 FRA ISSN 1252-7505
FORMES, LA MAITRISE DU VOLUME. 1964-200?. q. Centre d'Etudes de la Productivite dans les Industries du Moule Modele et Maquette, 39-41 rue Louis Blanc, Courbevoie, 92400, France.

937 ITA
FORMIANUM. 1993-1998. a. Armando Caramanica Editore, Via Appia, 762, Marina Di Minturno, LT 04020, Italy.

640 DNK ISSN 1604-5858
FORMIDL. 1930-2006. 12/yr. Forening for Formidlere af Viden om Husholdning, Ernaering og Sundhed, Vandkunsten 12, Copenhagen K, 1467, Denmark.

628.5 USA ISSN 1075-3699
FORMING AND FABRICATING. 1994-2004. m. Society of Manufacturing Engineers, One SME Dr, PO Box 930, Dearborn, MI 48121.

796.72 NLD ISSN 1566-5364
FORMULA 1 CHAMPIONSHIP YEARBOOK (DUTCH EDITION). 1998-2006. a. Uitgeverij Ars Scribendi b.v., Postbus 65, Harmelen, 3480 DB , Netherlands.

860 ESP ISSN 0211-8629
FORO DE LAS CIENCIAS Y DE LAS LETRAS. 1981-199?. q. Colegio Oficial de Doctores y Licenciados en Ciencias y Letras. Granada, General Narvaez, 1-1o., Granada, 18002, Spain.

331.120715 DEU ISSN 0340-8973
FORSCHUNGSDOKUMENTATION ZUR ARBEITSMARKT- UND BERUFSFORSCHUNG. 1970-2003. 3/yr. Bundesagentur fuer Arbeit, Institut fuer Arbeitsmarkt- und Berufsforschung, Regensburger Str 104, Nuernberg, 90478, Germany.

333.79 DEU ISSN 1433-5522
FORSCHUNGSZENTRUM JUELICH. SCHRIFTEN. REIHE ENERGIETECHNIK. 1998-2007 (vol.70). irreg. Forschungszentrum Juelich GmbH, Leo-Brandt-Str, Juelich, 52428, Germany.

610 DEU ISSN 1433-5549
FORSCHUNGSZENTRUM JUELICH. SCHRIFTEN. REIHE LEBENSWISSENSCHAFTEN. 1998-2007 (vol.41). irreg. Forschungszentrum Juelich GmbH, Leo-Brandt-Str, Juelich, 52428, Germany.

530 DEU ISSN 1433-5506
FORSCHUNGSZENTRUM JUELICH. SCHRIFTEN. REIHE MATERIE UND MATERIAL. 1998-2007 (vol.41). irreg. Forschungszentrum Juelich GmbH, Leo-Brandt-Str, Juelich, 52428, Germany.

610.7 DNK ISSN 1601-6688
FORSKNING OG UDVIKLINGSARBEJDE I SUNDHEDSSEKTOREN; forskningsstatistik. 1999-2004. irreg. Dansk Center for Forskningsanalyse, Aarhus Universitet, Finlandsgade 4, Aarhus N, 8200, Denmark.

616.2 BRD ISSN 0071-7967
FORTSCHRITTE DER STAUBLUNGENFORSCHUNG. 1950-1967. irreg. Niederrheinische Druckerei, Ostermayerstr 54, Emmerich, 46446, Germany.

660 BRD ISSN 0340-501X
FORTSCHRITTE DER VERFAHRENSTECHNIK. ABTEILUNG B: MECHANISCHE VERFAHRENSTECHNIK. 1954-1985. irreg. V D I Verlag GmbH, Graf-Recke-Str. 84, Duesseldorf, 40239, West Germany.

660 BRD ISSN 0340-5036
FORTSCHRITTE DER VERFAHRENSTECHNIK. ABTEILUNG C: THERMISCHE VERFAHRENSTECHNIK. 1954-1985. irreg. V D I Verlag GmbH, Graf-Recke-Str. 84, Duesseldorf, 40239, West Germany.

660 BRD ISSN 0340-5052
FORTSCHRITTE DER VERFAHRENSTECHNIK. ABTEILUNG D: REAKTIONSTECHNIK. 1954-1985. irreg. V D I Verlag GmbH, Graf-Recke-Str. 84, Duesseldorf, 40239, West Germany.

660 BRD ISSN 0340-4048
FORTSCHRITTE DER VERFAHRENSTECHNIK. ABTEILUNG E: PLANUNG UND BETRIEB VON ANLAGEN. 1954-1985. irreg. V D I Verlag GmbH, Graf-Recke-Str. 84, Duesseldorf, 40239, West Germany.

660 BRD ISSN 0340-4064
FORTSCHRITTE DER VERFAHRENSTECHNIK. ABTEILUNG F: SPEZIELLE TECHNOLOGIEN. 1954-1985. irreg. V D I Verlag GmbH, Graf-Recke-Str. 84, Duesseldorf, 40239, West Germany.

330 USA
FORTUNE C N E T TECHNOLOGY REVIEW. 19??-2001. s-a. Time Inc., Time & Life Bldg, Rockefeller Center, 29th Fl, 1271 Ave of the Americas, New York, NY 10020-1393.

371.14 DNK ISSN 0902-3518
FORTVIVL-IKKE. 1980-1993. irreg. (5-6/yr.). Invandrerlaererforeningen, c/o Dan Saederup, Danmarksgade 16, Odense C, 5000, Denmark.

374 DEU ISSN 0176-3687
DAS FORUM (MUNICH, 1961). 1961-2002. s-a. Bayerischer Volkshochschulverband, Faeustlestr 5a, Munich, 80339, Germany.

320.94 FRA ISSN 1775-0008
FORUM (PARIS, 2005). 2005-2005. irreg. Editions Publia, 2 bis rue Dupont-de-l'Eure, Paris, 75020, France.

341 NLD ISSN 0924-8153
FORUM INTERNATIONALE; lectures on commercial law and arbitration. 1983-2000 (no.26). irreg. Kluwer Law International, PO Box 316, Alphen aan den Rijn, 2400 AH, Netherlands.

372.862 BRD ISSN 0170-1479
FORUM TECHNISCHE BILDUNG. AUSGABE PRIMARSTUFE. 1973-1981. s-a. Vieweg und Teubner Verlag, Abraham-Lincoln-Str 46, Wiesbaden, 65189, Germany.

372.862 BRD ISSN 0170-1487
FORUM TECHNISCHE BILDUNG. AUSGABE SEKUNDARSTUFE. 1973-1981. s-a. Vieweg und Teubner Verlag, Abraham-Lincoln-Str 46, Wiesbaden, 65189, Germany.

770 ITA ISSN 1129-0145
FOTOCOMPUTER. 1997-ceased. 11/yr. Il Sole 24 Ore Business Media, Divisione J C E, Via Patecchio 2, Milan, 20141, Italy.

770 TUR ISSN 1018-7901
FOTOGRAF. 1978-1993. 6/yr. Ankara Fotograf Sanatcilari Dernigli, Kizilay, P K 649, Ankara, 06425, Turkey.

770 DNK ISSN 1399-445X
FOTOGUIDEN. 1955-2000. s-a. Forlaget Fotoinformation ApS, Bredgade 111, Broenderslev, 9700, Denmark.

770 DEU ISSN 1436-381X
FOTOHEFT. 1981-2008 (Jan.). m. Vereinigte Verlagsanstalten GmbH, Hoeherweg 278, Duesseldorf, 40231, Germany.

948.95 DNK ISSN 0107-2757
FRA BJERRINGBRO KOMMUNE. 1980-2006. a. Bjerringbro Kommunes Lokalhistoriske Arkiv, Bjerringbro Bibliotek, Realskolevej 12, Bjerringbro, 8850, Denmark.

595.7 ITA ISSN 0429-288X
FRAGMENTA ENTOMOLOGICA. 1951-ceased. s-a. Universita degli Studi di Roma "La Sapienza", 5 Piazzale Aldo Moro, Rome, 00185, Italy.

333.792 FRA ISSN 0029-3997
FRANCE. COMMISSARIAT A L'ENERGIE ATOMIQUE. NOTES D'INFORMATION. 1962-1992. 2/yr. Commissariat a l'Energie Atomique, Batiment Le Ponant D, 25 rue Leblanc, Paris, 75015, France.

Cessations

336.2 FRA ISSN 0997-4768
FRANCE. CONSEIL DES IMPOTS. RAPPORT AU PRESIDENT DE LA REPUBLIQUE. 1972-2005. irreg. Direction des Journaux Officiels, 26 rue Desaix, Paris, 75727 Cedex 15 , France.

614 FRA ISSN 1768-0611
FRANCE. MINISTERE DE L'EMPLOI, DU TRAVAIL, ET DE LA COHESION SOCIALE. BULLETIN OFFICIEL. 1971-2007. w. Direction des Journaux Officiels, 26 rue Desaix, Paris, 75727 Cedex 15 , France.

331.1 314 FRA ISSN 1161-8205
FRANCE. MINISTERE DE L'EMPLOI ET DE LA SOLIDARITE. BULLETIN MENSUEL DES STATISTIQUES DU TRAVAIL. 1972-2002. m. Documentation Francaise, 29-31 Quai Voltaire, Paris, Cedex 7 75344, France.

690.021 FRA ISSN 1274-8668
FRANCE. MINISTERE DE L'EQUIPEMENT, DES TRANSPORTS, DU LOGEMENT, DU TOURISME ET DE LA MER. STATISTIQUES DE LA CONSTRUCTION. 1979-2002. 4/yr. Documentation Francaise, 29-31 Quai Voltaire, Paris, Cedex 7 75344, France.

355 FRA ISSN 0755-2289
FRANCE. MINISTERE DES ARMEES. BULLETIN OFFICIEL DES ARMEES. EDITION CHRONOLOGIQUE. 1974-2006. w. Editions Charles Lavauzelle, Le Prouet, BP 8, Panazol, 87350, France.

355 FRA ISSN 0755-2270
FRANCE. MINISTERE DES ARMEES. BULLETIN OFFICIEL DES ARMEES. EDITION CHRONOLOGIQUE. PARTIE PRINCIPALE. 1974-2006. w. Editions Charles Lavauzelle, Le Prouet, BP 8, Panazol, 87350, France.

333.642 DEU ISSN 1614-3868
FRANCHISE UND KOOPERATION. 1990-2007. a. Deutscher Fachverlag GmbH, Mainzer Landstr 251, Frankfurt Am Main, 60326, Germany.

971 973 CAN ISSN 1183-2487
FRANCOPHONIES D'AMERIQUE. 1991-2005. s-a. University of Ottawa Press, 542 King Edward, Ottawa, ON K1N 6N5, Canada.

557 560 DEU ISSN 0173-1742
FRANKFURTER GEOWISSENSCHAFTEN ARBEITEN. SERIE A. GEOLOGIE PALAEONTOLOGIE. 1982-2002. irreg. Johann Wolfgang Goethe Universitaet Frankfurt am Main, Fachbereich Geowissenschaften, Bockenheimer Landstr. 133, 6, OG, Frankfurt am Main, 60054, Germany.

944 DNK ISSN 0900-2995
FRANKRIG INFORMATION; nyhedsbrev. 1985-1991. 8/yr. Frankrig Information, PO Box 260, Roskilde, 4000, Denmark.

053.1 DEU
FRAU IM SPIEGEL LEGENDEN. 2003-2006 (Sep.). q. Verlag Ehrlich und Sohn GmbH & Co. KG, Griegstr 75, Hamburg, 22763, Germany.

616.89 GBR ISSN 0267-0887
FREE ASSOCIATIONS; psychoanalysis, groups, politics, culture. 1984-2004. q. Process Press, 26 Freegrove Rd, London, N7 9RQ, United Kingdom.

327 AUS ISSN 0157-3845
FREE PALESTINE. 1979-1990. bi-m. P L O Office, c/o A. Kazak, Pub., PO Box 4646, Kingston, ACT 2604, Australia.

340 AUS ISSN 0817-3532
FREEDOM OF INFORMATION REVIEW. 1986 (Feb)-2004. bi-m. Legal Service Bulletin Co-Operative Ltd., Law Faculty, Monash University, VIC 3800, Australia.

519 DEU ISSN 1616-7155
FREENET.DE. 2000-2006 (Mar.). q. T V und Mehr Zeitschriftenverlag GmbH, Bavariafilmplatz 7, Gebaeude 033/206, Gruenwald - Geiselgasteig, 82031, Germany.

053.1 DEU ISSN 1864-3256
FREI-LITERARISCH ORIENTIERTE BEITRAEGE. 2007-2006 (Nov.). irreg. Frei-literarisch Orientierte Beitraege, Kochstr 26, Leipzig, 04275, Germany.

370 DNK ISSN 0109-9108
FREINET NYT. 1980-2000. q. Arbejdsgruppen af Freinetpaedagoger, c/o Michael Cain, Vestervangen 13, Esbjerg N, 8715, Denmark.

910.202 DEU
FREIZEIT UND REISEN. 1987-1991. m. E R Medien GmbH, Falkstr 45-47, Duisburg, 47058, Germany.

079.94 AUS
FREMANTLE HERALD. 1989-2005. w. Herald Publishing Co. Pty. Ltd., 41 Cliff St, Fremantle, W.A. 6160, Australia.

016.37 DNK ISSN 0901-4578
FREMMEDSPROG. 1985-2006. a. Fonden Undervisnings Information, Siljangade 6, Copenhagen S, 2300, Denmark.

054.1 FRA ISSN 1761-7138
FRENCH NEWS; France's English language newspaper. 1987-2008. m. SARL Brussac, 225 Route d'Angouleme, Perigueux Cedex, 24004, France.

051 FRA ISSN 1632-4293
FRENCH TIMES. 2001-2005. bi-m. SARL Brussac, 225 Route d'Angouleme, Perigueux Cedex, 24004, France.

787.87 USA ISSN 1552-8359
FRETS. 2004-2006. q. NewBay Media, LLC, 810 Seventh Ave, 27th Fl, New York, NY 10019.

796 NZL ISSN 1173-9223
FRIDAY FLASH. 1989-2006. w. Fairfax Media, 155 New North Rd, Eden Terrace, PO Box 1327, Auckland, New Zealand.

305.4 ITA ISSN 1825-0459
FRIENDLY. 2004-ceased. m. Unialfa Srl, Corso di Porta Nuova 3A, Milan, 20121, Italy.

368.121 USA ISSN 0279-6856
FRIENDLY EXCHANGE. 1980-ceased. q. C - E Publishing, Aegis Group, 30400 Van Dyke Ave, P O Box 2119, Warren, MI 48093.

797.1 DNK ISSN 0905-9741
FRITID TIL SOES. 1974-1994. m. Fogeds Forlag, Asgaard 11, PO Box 265, Frederikssund, 3600, Denmark.

597.8 AUS ISSN 1327-8592
FROG CENSUS. 1998-2002. irreg. Southern Australia, Environment Protection Agency, GPO Box 2607, Adelaide, SA 5001, Australia.

133 AUS ISSN 1832-9888
FROM MY DESK. 2005-2006. m. Michaela/ Scherr, Brisbane, QLD, Australia.

362.1 613 USA ISSN 1096-231X
FRONTIERS IN HEALTH POLICY RESEARCH (PRINT). 1986-2004. a. M I T Press, 55 Hayward St, Cambridge, MA 02142-1493.

382.414 DNK ISSN 0106-4207
FRUGT, GROENT, BLOMSTER & GARTNER NYT. 1979-2003. m. Danmarks Frugthandlere, Groentorvet 34, Valby, 2500, Denmark.

614.84 ESP ISSN 0212-8284
FUEGO. 1965-1982. bi-m. Asociacion Espanola de Lucha Contra el Fuego, Jacometrezo, 4 Planta 8, Madrid, 28013, Spain.

630 DEU ISSN 1615-9373
FUEHRUNGSKRAEFTE UND MANAGEMENT. 2000-2004. q. B A I Verlag GmbH, Konrad Adenauer Str 18, Habichtswald, 34317, Germany.

614 BRD ISSN 0721-1473
FUER DIE PRAXIS. 1981-1981. q. P M I Verlagsgruppe GmbH, August-Schanz-Str 8-II, Frankfurt Am Main, 60433, Germany.

320.9 ESP ISSN 0016-2477
FUERZA NUEVA. 1966-199?. w. Fuerza Nueva, Nunez de Balboa, 31, Madrid, 28001, Spain.

917.61 USA ISSN 1535-5713
FUN WITH THE FAMILY IN ALABAMA; hundreds of ideas for day trips with the kids. 2000-200?. irreg. The Globe Pequot Press, Inc., 246 Goose Ln, PO Box 480, Guilford, CT 06437.

352.14 ESP ISSN 0210-1807
FUNCIONARIO MUNICIPAL. 1960-199?. 11/yr. Funcionario Municipal, Doctor Sanchis Sivera, 19 6o, Valencia, 46008, Spain.

371.3 AUS ISSN 0313-6825
FUNCTION. 1977-2004. 5/yr. Monash University, Department of Mathematics, PO Box 197, Caulfield East, VIC 3145, Australia.

510.712 CAN ISSN 0821-2708
FUNCTIONS. 197?-1996. m. New Brunswick Teachers' Association, PO Box 752, Fredericton, NB E3B 5B4, Canada.

330 370 ESP ISSN 0211-2388
FUNDACION UNIVERSIDAD - EMPRESA. BOLETIN. 1974-2004. q. Fundacion Universidad - Empresa, Calle Serrano Jover 5, Madrid, 28015, Spain.

900 ESP ISSN 0532-8578
FUNDACION UNIVERSITARIA ESPANOLA. PUBLICACIONES. 1958-ceased. irreg. Fundacion Universitaria Espanola, Alcala, 93, Madrid, 28009, Spain.

930.1 ESP ISSN 1132-1717
FUNDAMENTOS DE ANTROPOLOGIA. 1992-2001. a. Centro de Investigaciones Etnologicas "Angel Ganivet", Palacio Condes de Gabia, Plaza Girones, 1, Granada, Andalucia 18009, Spain.

352.73 GBR ISSN 1479-330X
FUNDING FOR CHANGE. 2003-2005. q. Directory of Social Change, 24 Stephenson Way, London, NW1 2DP, United Kingdom.

900 DEU ISSN 1438-0307
FUNDUS (GOETTINGEN); Forum fuer Geschichte und ihre Quellen. 1998-2003 (vol.5). irreg. Duehrkohp & Radicke, Hannah-Vogt-Str. 1, Goettingen, D-37085, Germany.

790 DEU
FUNPARK GUIDE. 2002-2004. a. EuroTransportMedia Verlags- und Veranstaltungs-GmbH, Handwerkstr 15, Stuttgart, 70565, Germany.

055.1 ITA ISSN 0016-2876
FUOCO; rassegna di cultura e d'arte. 1953-19??. bi-m. Edizioni Il Fuoco, Via Giacinto Carini, 28, Rome, RM 00152, Italy.

500 FRA ISSN 0293-5880
FUSION; la science passionnement!. 1981-2006. 5/yr. Editions Alcuin, 53 rue d'Hauteville, Paris, 75010, France.

796.322 DEU ISSN 0934-4586
FUSSBALL-JAHRBUCH. 1904-1990. a. Deutscher Fussball-Bund, Otto-Fleck-Schneise 6, Frankfurt Am Main, 60528, Germany.

681.3 ITA ISSN 1825-4810
FUTURE MUSIC. 2005-200?. q. Sprea Editori Srl, Via Torino 51, Cernusco sul Naviglio, MI 20063, Italy.

681.3 ITA ISSN 1826-3585
FUTURE TECH. 2005-200?. q. Sprea Editori Srl, Via Torino 51, Cernusco sul Naviglio, MI 20063, Italy.

553.2809982 DNK ISSN 0909-0630
G H E X I S NEWSLETTER. (Greenland Hydrocarbon Exploration Information Service) 1990-2004. irreg. (1-2/yr). De Nationale Geologiske Undersoegelser for Danmark og Groenland, Oester Voldgade 10, Copenhagen K, 1350, Denmark.

004 DEU ISSN 0724-4339
G M D - SPIEGEL. 1971-2000. q. G M D - Forschungszentrum Informationstechnik GmbH, Schloss Birlinghoven, Sankt Augustin, 53754, Germany.

796.7 DEU ISSN 1862-4561
G Q CARS. (Gentlemen's Quarterly) 2004-2007. 2/yr. Conde Nast Verlag GmbH, Karlstr 23, Munich, 80333, Germany.

388 NLD
G V B NIEUWS. 1979-2008. s-a. Gementevervoerbedryf Amsterdam, Prins Hendrikkade 108-114, Amsterdam, 1011 AK, Netherlands.

686.2 AUS
G X REPORT. 1998-2004. bi-m. M P C Media - Pileport Pty. Ltd., PO Box 813, Tewantin, QLD 4565, Australia.

383.4 ITA ISSN 1121-2624
IL GABBIANO. 1991-ceased. bi-m. Emmeffe Srl, Via della Cavona 2, Casal Morena, RM 00040, Italy.

300 ESP ISSN 0210-6116
GADES. 1978-1999. a. Diputacion Provincial de Cadiz, Plaza de Espana s/n, Cadiz, Andalucia 11006, Spain.

058.81 299 DNK ISSN 1603-6670
THE GAIA GUARDIAN; unfolding new visions of science, education, lifestyle and politics. 2003-2003. irreg. Gaia Consciousness Institute in Denmark, Skodsborgvej 189, Naerum, 2850, Denmark.

051 USA
GAINESVILLE LIFE. 2004-2005. 4/yr. Morris Multimedia, Inc., 725 Broad St, Augusta, GA 30901.

053.931 NLD ISSN 1876-1992
GALA. 2007-2008. w. Gruner und Jahr - R B A Publishing C.V., Gebouw Stede, Dalsteindreef 82 t/m 92, Diemen, 1112 XC, Netherlands.

056.1 ESP ISSN 1698-4749
GALA (MADRID). 2004-suspended. w. G y J Espana Ediciones S.L., Albasanz, 15 Edificio A, Madrid, 28037, Spain.

520 028.5 NZL ISSN 1175-1576
GALAXY. 1999-2004. q. Royal Astronomical Society of New Zealand, Education Section, Box 24 187, Auckland, New Zealand.

500 ITA
GALILEO (ROME); giornale di scienza e problemi globali. 1996-ceased. w. Tribunale di Roma, Corso Trieste, 95, Rome, RM 00198, Italy.

798 DEU ISSN 1611-6178
GALOPP. 2003-2004. bi-m. Huddle Verlags GmbH, Laubacher Str 10, Berlin, 14197, Germany.

053.1 DEU
GALORE; Kultur. Gesellschaft. Menschen. 2003-2009 (Jun.). bi-m. Dialog GmbH, Maerkische Str 115-117, Dortmund, 44141, Germany.

794.1 DEU ISSN 0937-5457
GAMBIT REVUE. 1989-2002. 4/yr. Schachverlag Manfred Maedler, Waegnerstr 5, Dresden, 01309, Germany.

794.8 USA ISSN 1523-7516
GAMES BUSINESS. 1998-2000. s-m. Future U S, Inc., 4000 Shoreline Ct, Ste 400, South San Francisco, CA 94080.

004.565 795 NLD ISSN 1872-2903
GAMES & D V D. 2005-2007 (no.1). bi-m. iMediate, Postbus 2227, Hilversum, 1200 CE, Netherlands.

794.8 USA ISSN 1933-6160
GAMES FOR WINDOWS. 1981-200?. m. Ziff Davis Media Inc., 28 E 28th St, New York, NY 10016.

794.8 CZE ISSN 1212-3331
GAMESTAR CZECH REPUBLIC. 1998-2006. m. I D G Czech, a.s., Seydlerova 2451-11, Prague 5, 158 00, Czech Republic.

070 USA ISSN 0433-163X
GANNETTEER. 1955-2008. bi-m. Gannett Company, Inc., 7950 Jones Branch Dr., McLean, VA 22107-0001.

635 AUS ISSN 1030-0392
GARDEN PESKEM; the Australian directory of garden pesticides. 1987-2000. irreg. University of Queensland, Gatton College, Lawes (via Gatton), QLD 4343, Australia.

635 USA
GARDEN STYLE. 1998-2005. q. F + W Media Inc., 4700 E Galbraith Rd, Cincinnati, OH 45236.

665.7029 GBR ISSN 0954-853X
GAS INDUSTRY DIRECTORY (YEAR). 1896-2002. a. C M P Information Ltd., Sovereign House, Sovereign Way, Tonbridge, Kent TN9 1RW, United Kingdom.

004 ESP
GASP. 1998-2004. bi-w. Gasp, Spain.

665.5 USA ISSN 1078-3954 CODEN: GASTCD
GASTIPS; technology, information, and products for supply. 1994-2007. 3/yr. Hart Energy Publishing, LP, 1616 S Voss Rd, Ste 1000, Houston, TX 77057.

616.3 ITA ISSN 1120-3757
GASTROENTEROLOGIA CLINICA. 1972-2003. q. Il Pensiero Scientifico Editore, Via Bradano 3-C, Rome, 00199, Italy.

780.904 NLD ISSN 0923-6244
GAUDEAMUS INFORMATION (ENGLISH EDITION). 1966-1984. 6/m. Gaudeamus Foundation, Swammerdamstraat 38, Amsterdam, 1091 RV, Netherlands.

647.94 DEU
GAULT MILLAU. 2006-2008. 6/yr. CapCom Media GmbH, Marsstr 13, Munich, 80335, Germany.

630 ITA
GAZZETTA AGRICOLA. 1945-19??. 28/yr. Gazzetta Agricola, Via Guidelli, 10, Reggio Emilia, RE 42100, Italy.

770 ITA ISSN 0393-0785
LA GAZZETTA DELLA FOTOGRAFIA. 1923-19??. m. Gazzetta della Fotografia, Via Principe Di Granatelli, 96, Palermo, PA 90139, Italy.

001.3 ITA
GAZZETTA DI GAETA. 1973-ceased. m. Gaetano Andrisani Ed. & Pub., Via Bologna, 15, Gaeta, LT 04024, Italy.

630 ITA
GAZZETTINO AGRICOLO DI PARMA. 1947-ceased. w. Unione Provinciale Agricoltori di Parma, Viale Gramsci 26b, Parma, PR 43100, Italy.

647.9 DEU ISSN 1430-2748
GEBAEUDE MANAGEMENT; Immobilien Facilities Services. 1996-2004. 10/yr. Deutscher Fachverlag GmbH, Mainzer Landstr 251, Frankfurt Am Main, 60326, Germany.

351.43 DEU ISSN 0942-1653
GEMEINDEORDNUNG UND AMTSORDNUNG FUER DAS LAND BRANDENBURG. 1992-199?. irreg. Erich Schmidt Verlag GmbH & Co. (Berlin), Genthiner Str 30 G, Berlin, 10785, Germany.

929 001.6 USA ISSN 0277-5913
GENEALOGICAL COMPUTING. 1981-2006. q. MyFamily.com Inc., 360 West 4800 N, Provo, UT 84604.

368.941 GBR ISSN 1361-9756
GENERAL INSURANCE OUTLOOK. 1996-200?; suspended. m. Mitre House Publishing Ltd., PO Box 29, South Petherton, TA13 5WE, United Kingdom.

073 DEU
GENERALANZEIGER. 1971-2003. 4/yr. Zeitungs- und Zeitschriftenverlag Heinrichs, Brueggekamp 1, Barsinghausen, 30890, Germany.

368 DEU
GENERALI-LLOYD-VERSICHERUNGEN. NEWS. 1999-2002. bi-m. Generali-Lloyd-Versicherungen, Tunisstr 19-23, Cologne, 50667, Germany.

340 ESP ISSN 0213-3539
GENERALITAT DE CATALUNYA. DIARI OFICIAL (CATALAN EDITION). 1931-200?. 3/w. Generalitat de Catalunya, Carrer Sant Honorat 1-3, Barcelona, 08002, Spain.

371.334 FRA ISSN 1162-6496
GENIE EDUCATIF. 1991-199?. 6/yr. E C 2, 269 rue de la Garenne, Nanterre, 92000, France.

006.32 FRA ISSN 1265-1397 CODEN: GLSEED
GENIE LOGICIEL. 1985-199?. q. E C 2, 269 rue de la Garenne, Nanterre, 92000, France.

572.8 171.7 GBR ISSN 1474-7596
GENOME BIOLOGY (PRINT); biology for the post-genomic era. 2000-2006. m. BioMed Central Ltd., Middlesex House, 34-42 Cleveland St, London, W1T 4LB, United Kingdom.

615.842 535 USA ISSN 1544-6778 CODEN: AGTMC7
GENOMIC PROTEOMIC TECHNOLOGY. 2001-2003. bi-m. International Scientific Communications, Inc., 30 Controls Dr, PO Box 670, Shelton, CT 06484.

051 USA ISSN 1074-5246
GENRE MAGAZINE. 1991-2009. 12/yr. Genre Media Llc., 333 Seventh Ave., 4th Fl, New York, NY 10001.

320 ITA ISSN 0393-7941
GENTE MESE; mensile di politica, attualita, cultura. 1986-ceased. m. Hachette Rusconi SpA, Viale Sarca 235, Milan, 20126, Italy.

055.1 ITA ISSN 0393-7925
GENTE MONEY; mensile di economia attualita, cultura e politica. 1984-ceased. m. Hachette Rusconi SpA, Viale Sarca 235, Milan, 20126, Italy.

910.285 ITA ISSN 1128-8132
GEO MEDIA; la newsletter italiana di geomatica. 1996-ceased. irreg. Maggioli Editore, Via del Carpino 8/10, Santarcangelo di Romagna, RN 47822, Italy.

551 USA ISSN 0277-6669
GEODYNAMICS SERIES. 1980-2003 (vol.31). irreg. American Geophysical Union, 2000 Florida Ave, NW, Washington, DC 20009.

911.3 DEU ISSN 0933-0356
GEOGRAPHIA RELIGIONUM. 1985-1996 (vol.10). irreg. Dietrich Reimer Verlag GmbH, Berliner Str 53, Berlin, 10713, Germany.

528 CZE ISSN 1212-4311
GEOINFO. 1998-2005. q. Computer Press a.s., Spielberk Office Centre, Holandska 8, Brno, 639 00, Czech Republic.

551 624 ITA ISSN 0435-3870 CODEN: GAIDBG
GEOLOGIA APPLICATA E IDROGEOLOGIA. 1986-ceased. a. Universita degli Studi di Bari, Istituto di Geologia Applicata e Geotecnica, Facolta di Ingegneria, Via Re David 200, Bari, 70125, Italy.

551 USA ISSN 0096-4271
GEOLOGICAL SOCIETY OF AMERICA, INC. PROCEEDINGS VOLUME. 1933-19??. a. Geological Society of America, 3300 Penrose Pl, PO Box 9140, Boulder, CO 80301.

554 FRA ISSN 0397-2844 CODEN: AUPGDY
GEOLOGIE MEDITERRANEENNE. 1891-2001. q. Universite de Provence (Aix-Marseille I), U.F.R. Sciences de la Vie, de la Terre et de l'Environnement, Centre Saint-Charles Place Victor Hugo, Marseille, Cedex 3 13331, France.

690 ITA
GEOMETRI INFORMAZIONE. 1979-199?. m. Chiandetti Editore s.r.l., Via Vittorio Veneto, 106, Reana Del Roiale, UD 33010, Italy.

516 ESP ISSN 0213-4780
GEOMETRIA. 1986-2001. 2/yr. Geometria, Olmos, 5, Malaga, 29018, Spain.

363.7 306 GBR ISSN 1472-6300
GEOPHILOS. 2000-2003. s-a. Land Research Trust, 7 Kings Rd, Teddington, TW11 0QB, United Kingdom.

796.334 GBR ISSN 1461-6335
GEORGE BEST'S UNITED MONTHLY. 1998-200?. m. Northern & Shell Plc, The Northern & Shell Bldg, Number 10 Lower Thames St, London, EC3R 6EN, United Kingdom.

346 USA
GEORGIA CORPORATIONS, PARTNERSHIPS AND ASSOCIATIONS LAW ANNOTATED. 1994-ceased. irreg. LexisNexis, PO Box 7587, Charlottesville, VA 22906.

344.046 USA ISSN 1044-2324
GEORGIA ENVIRONMENTAL LAW LETTER. 1989-2005. m. M. Lee Smith Publishers LLC, 5201 Virginia Way, PO Box 5094, Brentwood, TN 37024.

551 GBR ISSN 0278-7091
GEOSCIENCE TEXTS. 1980-1985. irreg. Wiley-Blackwell Publishing Ltd., 9600 Garsington Rd, Oxford, OX4 2DQ, United Kingdom.

910 USA ISSN 1529-7403
GEOSPATIAL SOLUTIONS; applications of GIS and related spatial information technologies. 1990-2007. m. (12/yr.). Questex Media Group Inc., 275 Grove St, Bldg 2, Ste 130, Newton, MA 02466.

677.028 GBR ISSN 1072-6349 CODEN: GINTFD
GEOSYNTHETICS INTERNATIONAL. 1994-200?. bi-m. Thomas Telford Ltd., 2nd Fl, 40 Marsh Wall, London, E14 9TP, United Kingdom.

690 ITA
GEOTEC. 1988-ceased. 9/yr. Professional Press s.r.l., Piazzale Francesco Baracca, 10, Milan, MI 20123, Italy.

280.4 NLD ISSN 0016-8610
GEREFORMEERD THEOLOGISCH TIJDSCHRIFT. 1900-2003. q. Uitgeversmaatschappij J.H. Kok B.V., Postbus 5018, Kampen, 8260 GA, Netherlands.

615.851 BRD ISSN 0934-5086
GERIATRIE UND REHABILITATION. 1985-1988. q. Vless Verlag GmbH, Valentingasse 7-9, Ebersberg, 85560, Germany.

351.43 DEU ISSN 1616-0940
GERMAN BRIEF. 1989-2004. w. Frankfurter Allgemeine Zeitung GmbH, Postfach 200163, Frankfurt Am Main, 60605, Germany.

629.2 DEU ISSN 1860-1111
GERMAN MOTOR DIRECTORY. 1951-2007. a. Messe Frankfurt Medien und Service GmbH, Ludwig-Erhard-Anlage 1, Frankfurt am Main, 60327, Germany.

500 DEU ISSN 0949-7811
GERMAN RESEARCH SERVICE. SPECIAL SCIENCE REPORTS. 1985-1996. m. Deutscher Forschungsdienst, Postfach 205006, Bonn, 53170, Germany.

331.11 314 DEU
GERMANY. BUNDESAGENTUR FUER ARBEIT. BERUFSBERATUNG. 1953-2005. a. Bundesagentur fuer Arbeit, Regensburger Str 104, Nuernberg, 90478, Germany.

388 DEU
GERMANY. BUNDESMINISTERIUM FUER VERKEHR. STRASSENBAUBERICHT. 1971-2004. a. Bundesanzeiger Verlagsgesellschaft mbH, Amsterdamer Str 192, Cologne, 50735, Germany.

327 DEU ISSN 0344-9130
GERMANY. DEUTSCHER BUNDESTAG. WISSENSCHAFTLICHE DIENSTE. MATERIALIEN. 1965-2002. irreg. Deutscher Bundestag, Abteilung Wissenschaftliche Dienste, Platz der Republik 1, Berlin, 11011, Germany.

338.0029 332.1 DEU
GERMANY'S TOP 500; a handbook of Germany's largest corporations. 1991-2003. a. Frankfurter Allgemeine Zeitung GmbH, Postfach 200163, Frankfurt Am Main, 60605, Germany.

016 DEU
GESAMTVERZEICHNIS (YEAR). 1936-ceased. a. Boehlau Verlag GmbH & Cie, Ursulaplatz 1, Cologne, 50668, Germany.

616.026 BRD ISSN 0371-6910
GESELLSCHAFT FUER INNERE MEDIZIN DER DEUTSCHEN DEMOKRATISCHEN REPUBLIK. TAGUNGSBERICHT. 1964-1983. irreg. Georg Thieme Verlag, Ruedigerstr 14, Stuttgart, 70469, Germany.

320.532 DEU ISSN 0945-4403
GESELLSCHAFTSREFORM JETZT!; Monatszeitung fuer Wissenschaft, Kultur und Politik. 1969-2005. m. Edition Wissenschaft Kultur und Politik, Postfach 919110, Berlin, 12413, Germany.

808.838 DEU
GESPENSTER GESCHICHTEN. 1974-2006. w. Bastei Verlag Gustav H. Luebbe GmbH und Co., Scheidtbachstr 23-31, Bergisch Gladbach, 51469, Germany.

808.838 DEU
GESPENSTER SPEZIAL. 197?-2006. m. Bastei Verlag Gustav H. Luebbe GmbH und Co., Scheidtbachstr 23-31, Bergisch Gladbach, 51469, Germany.

613.7 DEU
GESUNDHEITS BILD. 2003-2006. bi-m. Axel Springer Verlag AG, Axel-Springer-Platz 1, Hamburg, 20350, Germany.

614 DEU
GESUNDHEITSNACHRICHTEN. 2005-2008. m. Biermann Verlag GmbH, Otto-Hahn-Str 7, Cologne, 50997, Germany.

690 USA
GETAWAY CABINS & COTTAGES. 1998-2009 (Jan.). q. HomePlans.com, 901 N 3rd St, Ste 216, Minneapolis, MN 55401.

333.91 DEU ISSN 0931-2498
GEWASSERBESCHAFFENHEIT IN BAYERN. 1986-2003. a. Bayerisches Landesamt fuer Wasserwirtschaft, Lazarettstr 67, Munich, 80636, Germany.

373.246 DEU
GEWERKSCHAFTLICHE BILDUNGSPOLITIK; Stellungnahmen - Analysen - Informationen. 1950-2004. m. Deutscher Gewerkschaftsbund, Bundesvorstand, Henriette-Herz-Platz 2, Berlin, 10178, Germany.

320 ITA ISSN 1124-9021
GIANO; ricerche per la pace. 1989-2007; suspended. 3/yr. Odradek Edizioni, via dei Banchi Vecchi, 57, Rome, 00186, Italy.

746 USA ISSN 1935-7443
GIFTMAKER; paper crafting, stamping, embellishing & more. 19??-200?. bi-m. Dynamic Resource Group (D R G), 306 E Parr Rd, Berne, IN 46711.

781.66 USA ISSN 1093-5657
GIG MAGAZINE; for professional bands and musicians. 1997-200?. m. C M P Information, Inc., 2800 Campus Dr, San Mateo, CA 94403.

340 USA
GILBERT LAW SUMMARIES. INCOME TAX 1 (INDIVIDUAL). ceased 2002. irreg. Gilbert Law Summaries, 610 Opperman Dr, Eagan, MN 55123.

340 USA
GILBERT LAW SUMMARIES. REVIEW FOR THE MULTISTATE BAR EXAMINATION. 1982-1984. irreg. Gilbert Law Summaries, 610 Opperman Dr, Eagan, MN 55123.

350 GBR ISSN 0340-6369
GIORGIO LEVI DELLA VIDA CONFERENCES. REPORTS OF THE CONFERENCE. 1970-19??. biennial. Cambridge University Press, The Edinburgh Bldg, Shaftesbury Rd, Cambridge, CB2 8RU, United Kingdom.

799.2 ITA
GIORNALE DEL CACCIATORE. 1951-200?. bi-m. Federazione Italiana della Caccia, Associazione Cacciatori Alto Adige, Via Rosmini, 51, Bolzano, BZ 39100, Italy.

669 ITA ISSN 1590-9611
IL GIORNALE DEL SERRAMENTISTA E DELLE COSTRUZIONI IN ALLUMINIO. 1983-200?. 12/yr. Edimet SpA, Via Corfu 102, Brescia, BS 25124, Italy.

577 ITA ISSN 1121-8487
GIORNALE DELLA NATURA; mensile delle alternative del vivere ecologico. 1986-ceased. m. Stampa Natura Solidarieta SpA, Via Antonio Bazzini, 40, Milan, MI 20131, Italy.

631 ITA ISSN 0393-9200
GIORNALE DELLA SOIA. 1985-199?. 5/yr. Giornale della Soia, Via Savorgnana, 26, Udine, UD 33100, Italy.

647.94 ITA ISSN 1593-7941
IL GIORNALE DELL'ALBERGATORE. 2001-200?. q. Tecniche Nuove SpA, Via Eritrea 21, Milan, MI 201, Italy.

660 ITA ISSN 0393-4608
GIORNALE DELL'INDUSTRIA. 1979-1985. m. Societa Chimica Italiana, Viale Liegi 48c, Rome, RM 00198, Italy.

770 ITA
GIORNALE DI FOTOLOGIA. 1994-199?. q. Fratelli Alinari SpA, Largo Fratelli Alinari 15, Florence, FI 50123, Italy.

615.89 ITA ISSN 1120-3560
GIORNALE ITALIANO DI RIFLESSOTERAPIA ED AGOPUNTURA. 1989-2000. s-a. Societa Italiana di Riflessoterapia Agopuntura Auricoloterapia, C.so Galileo Ferraris 164, Torino, 10134, Italy.

850 ITA ISSN 0017-0496
GIORNALE STORICO DELLA LETTERATURA ITALIANA. 1883-2000. q. Loescher Editore, Via Vittorio Amedeo II, 18, Turin, 10121, Italy.

055.1 ITA ISSN 0017-0526
GIOVANE CRITICA. 1963 (no.19)-1973. irreg. (5-6/yr.). Giovane Critica, Via Della Trinita' Dei Pellegrini, 19, Rome, RM 00186, Italy.

028.5 ITA ISSN 1120-2564
GIOVANI AMICI. 1966-ceased. m. Universita Cattolica del Sacro Cuore, Largo Gemelli 1, Milan, MI 20123, Italy.

271 ITA ISSN 0072-4548
GIOVENTU PASSIONISTA/PASSIONIST YOUTH; rivista di formazione e d'informazione passionista. 1955-ceased. irreg. Edizioni E C O, San Gabriele Dell'addolorata, TE 64048, Italy.

028.5 DEU
GIRL'S CLUB; das magazin fuer echte Maedchen. 2000-2000; N.S. 2002-2004. m. Panini Verlags GmbH, Ravensstr 48, Nettetal, 41334, Germany.

720 GBR ISSN 1476-0517
GLASS AGE. 1958-2007 (Jan.). m. C M P Information Ltd., City Reach, 5 Greenwich View Pl, Millharbour, London, E14 9NN, United Kingdom.

666.1029 GBR
GLASS AGE DIRECTORY. 1986-2007. a. C M P Information Ltd., City Reach, 5 Greenwich View Pl, Millharbour, London, E14 9NN, United Kingdom.

666 380.1 USA ISSN 0017-1018 CODEN: GLDIAE
GLASS DIGEST; trade magazine serving the flat glass, architectural metal and allied products industry. 1922-199?. 13/yr. Ashlee Publishing Co., Inc., 18 E 41st St, 20th Fl, New York, NY 10017.

666 669 USA
GLASS DIGEST BUYER'S GUIDE. 1958-199?. a. Ashlee Publishing Co., Inc., 18 E 41st St, 20th Fl, New York, NY 10017.

666.1 ITA ISSN 1129-3950
GLASS STYLE. 1998-2008. s-a. Artech Publishing Srl, Via Gramsci 63, Cormano, MI 20032, Italy.

450 CAN ISSN 1201-821X
GLENNGOULD. 1995-2008. s-a. University of Toronto Press, Journals Division, 5201 Dufferin St, Toronto, ON M3H 5T8, Canada.

641.36209411 GBR ISSN 1747-5996
GLEN'S GUIDE. 2004-2006. a. Quality Meat Scotland, Rural Centre, West Mains, Ingliston, Newbridge, EH28 8NZ, United Kingdom.

659.1 658.8 ITA
GLOBAL. 1988-ceased. 4/yr. Media Key s.r.l., Via Lippi Filippino, 33 C, Milan, MI 20131, Italy.

330 GBR ISSN 1479-0289
GLOBAL AGENDA. 2003-2006. irreg. The Economist Newspaper Ltd., 25 St James's St, London, SW1A 1HG, United Kingdom.

346.08 GBR ISSN 1743-6036
GLOBAL FINANCIAL SERVICES REGULATORS. ASIA PACIFIC. 2004-2006. s-a. Oxford University Press, Great Clarendon St, Oxford, OX2 6DP, United Kingdom.

346.08 GBR ISSN 1743-601X
GLOBAL FINANCIAL SERVICES REGULATORS. MIDDLE EAST AND AFRICA. 2004-2006. s-a. Oxford University Press, Great Clarendon St, Oxford, OX2 6DP, United Kingdom.

658 TWN
GLOBAL INNOVATION RESEARCH. 2008-2009. 2/yr. Business Essay Consultancy Center, 4F, No 20, Lane 22, WenZhou St, Taipei, Taiwan.

340 NLD
GLOBAL LAW ASSOCIATION. SELECTED DOCUMENTS. 1994-1998 (vol.2). irreg. Global Law Association, PO Box 9001, Tilburg, 5000 HA, Netherlands.

384.6 AUS
GLOBAL MOBILE COMMUNICATIONS MARKET. 1984-2005. a. Paul Budde Communication Pty. Ltd., 5385 George Downes Dr, Bucketty, NSW 2250, Australia.

304.6 USA
GLOBAL POPULATION PROFILE. 1985-2002. biennial. U.S. Census Bureau, Customer Services, Washington, DC 20233.

600 GBR ISSN 1473-9518
GLOBAL WATCH. 2000-2007. m. Pera Business Connection, Melton Mowbray, Leicester LE13 0PB, United Kingdom.

052 AUS ISSN 1328-7435
GLOBE. 1996-2003. q. A C P Custom Media, 54 Park St, Sydney, NSW 2000, Australia.

639.2 ITA
GLOBEFISH. SPECIAL SERIES. 1997-ceased. irreg. Food and Agriculture Organization of the United Nations (F A O), Globefish, Fisheries Industries Division, Viale delle Terme di Caracalla, Rome, 00100, Italy.

Cessations

794.8 NLD ISSN 1874-5458
GMR. 2006-2008. bi-m. HUB Uitgevers, Postbus 3389, Haarlem, 2001 DJ, Netherlands.

796.334 ITA
GOAL. 1995-ceased. w. Panini SpA, Viale Emilio Po 380, Modena, 41100, Italy.

636.39 NZL ISSN 1174-0434
THE GOAT FARMER. 1986-2002. bi-m. Capricorn Publications Ltd., P.O. Box 641, 130 Maunu Rd, Whangarei, New Zealand.

640.73 NLD
GOEDE WAAR. 1982-2007. 6/yr. Goede Waar en Co., Postbus 61236, Amsterdam, 1005 HE, Netherlands.

382 314 NLD ISSN 1383-5777
GOEDERENNAALIJST. 1969-2005. a. Centraal Bureau voor de Statistiek, Prinses Beatrixlaan 428, PO Box 4000, Voorburg, 2270 JM, Netherlands.

330 DEU ISSN 1610-0247
DER GOLD-REPORT; Edelmetall-Aktien. 2002-2003. m. Boersenmedien AG, Am Eulenhof 14, Kulmbach, 95326, Germany.

331.88 ISR ISSN 0017-1638
DI GOLDENE KEYT. 1949-1996. q. Histadrut, Beit Hamlin, 30 Weizmann St., Tel Aviv, Israel.

780 USA
GOLDMINE (YEAR) ANNUAL; the standard reference for music collectors. 1996-200?. a. Krause Publications, Inc., 700 E State St, Iola, WI 54990.

796.352 USA ISSN 0898-4719
GOLF FOR WOMEN. 1988-2008. bi-m. The Golf Digest Companies, 20 Westport Rd, Wilton, CT 06897.

796.352 AUS ISSN 1175-0693
GOLF LEISURE & LIFESTYLE. 1999-2003. s-a. Pacific Client Publishing, 35-51 Mitchell St, McMahons Point, NSW 2060, Australia.

796.352 FRA ISSN 1953-0919
GOLF MEDITERRANEE. 2006-2007. q. Reference Sud, 6 Rue Jean Daumas, Cannes, 06400, France.

796.352 DNK ISSN 0906-1851
GOLFHAANDBOGEN. 1984-2003. a. Dansk Golf Union, c/o Idraettens Hus, Broendby Stadion 20, Broendby, 2605, Denmark.

641.5 ITA ISSN 1827-7454
GOLOSE IN CUCINA. 2006-ceased. m. Ulysse Network, Viale Bianca Maria 19, Milan, Italy.

641.5 ITA ISSN 1828-5392
GOLOSITA. 2006-200?. m. Ulysse Network, Viale Bianca Maria 19, Milan, Italy.

677 ITA ISSN 0017-1964
GOMITOLO. CHERIE MODA. 1963-ceased. 5/yr. Edizioni Moderne Internazionali, Via Gadames 123, Milan, 20123, Italy.

053.931 NLD ISSN 1874-544X
GOODIES. 2006-2008. q. Goodies Media en Awareness, Postbus 2720, Rotterdam, 3000 CS, Netherlands.

664 DEU ISSN 0017-2243 CODEN: GORDAM
GORDIAN; Internationale Zeitschrift fuer Lebensmittel und Lebensmittel-technologie. 1895-2003. 10/yr. Nahrungs- und Genussmittel-Fachverlag A. Gordian GmbH & Co. KG, Postfach 605128, Hamburg, 22246, Germany.

330 USA
GOVERNMENT ENTERPRISE. 2003-200?. bi-m. C M P Media LLC, 600 Community Dr, Manhasset, NY 11030.

633 AUS
GRAINLINE. 1967-1999. biennial. GrainCorp Operations Ltd., Level 10, 51 Druitt St, Sydney, NSW 2000, Australia.

796.333 ITA ISSN 1826-7076
IL GRANDE RUGBY. 2005-200?. m. Sprea Editori Srl, Via Torino 51, Cernusco sul Naviglio, MI 20063, Italy.

686 FRA ISSN 1252-4522
GRAPH ECHOS. 19??-200?. 21/yr. Editions du Gaillard, 5 av. de la Republique, Paris, Cedex 75130, France.

006.68 USA
GRAPHING AND CHARTING, SIMPLIFIED. 1976-200?. irreg. Gould Publications, Inc., 1333 North US Hwy 17-92, Longwood, FL 32750.

970 USA ISSN 0148-771X
GRASS ROOTS PERSPECTIVES ON AMERICAN HISTORY. 1978-1985. irreg. Greenwood Publishing Group Inc., 88 Post Rd W, PO Box 5007, Westport, CT 06881.

340 USA ISSN 1078-3547
GRAVEN IMAGES; a journal of culture, law, and the sacred. 1994-2002. a. University of Wisconsin at Madison, Law School, 975 Bascom Mall, Madison, WI 53706.

551.46 AUS ISSN 0810-6983
GREAT BARRIER REEF MARINE PARK AUTHORITY. SPECIAL PUBLICATION SERIES. 1983-19??. irreg. Great Barrier Reef Marine Park Authority, 2-68 Flinders St, PO Box 1379, Townsville, QLD 4810, Australia.

375 GBR ISSN 0072-7113
GREAT BRITAIN. SCHOOLS COUNCIL PUBLICATIONS. CURRICULUM BULLETINS. 1965-ceased. irreg. Routledge, 2 Park Sq, Milton Park, Abingdon, Oxon OX14 4RN, United Kingdom.

370.941 GBR ISSN 0072-7121
GREAT BRITAIN. SCHOOLS COUNCIL PUBLICATIONS. EXAMINATIONS BULLETINS. 1963-1984. irreg. Routledge, 4 Park Square, Milton Park, Abingdon, Oxon OX14 4RN, United Kingdom.

371.42 USA ISSN 1098-982X
THE GREATER PHILADELPHIA JOBBANK; the job hunter's guide to Greater Philadelphia. 1988-2002 (14th ed.). irreg. Adams Media, 4700 E Galbraith Rd, Cincinnati, OH 45236.

712 796.352 FRA ISSN 0993-3093
GREEN KEEPER. 1986-200?. 4/yr. Egerie Golf, 13 rue des Harias, BP 5, Mareil-sur-Mauldre, 78124, France.

324.4 USA ISSN 1062-9726
GREENWOOD HISTORICAL ENCYCLOPEDIA OF THE WORLD'S POLITICAL PARTIES. 1982-19??. irreg. Greenwood Publishing Group Inc., 88 Post Rd W, PO Box 5007, Westport, CT 06881.

055.1 ITA
LA GRINTA; rivista mensile di attualita, politica, cultura, turismo e sport. 1971-19??. m. Edizioni La Grinta s.r.l., Via A. Pacinotti, 16, Vercelli, 13100, Italy.

796.6 GBR ISSN 1465-0207
GRIP DIRT BIKE. 1998-1999. bi-m. Air Publications Ltd., 2-4 Trinity St, Worcester, Worcs WR1 2PW, United Kingdom.

551 910 ITA ISSN 0373-7500
GROTTE D'ITALIA. 1927-ceased. a. Societa Speleologica Italiana, Via Zamboni 67, Bologna, BO 40126, Italy.

620.0029 GBR ISSN 0959-9959
GROUND ENGINEERING YEARBOOK. 1990-2003. a. Emap Construct Ltd., Greater London House, Hampstead Rd, London, NW1 7EJ, United Kingdom.

700 AUS ISSN 1832-6986
GROUNDWORK. 2005-2008. s-a. Regional Arts Victoria, PO Box 600, Port Melbourne, VIC 3207, Australia.

612.67 USA ISSN 1041-1232 CODEN: GDAGE9
GROWTH, DEVELOPMENT & AGING. 1937-2008. s-a. Growth Publishing Co., Inc., PO Box 205, Hulls Cove, ME 04644-0205.

028.5 DEU
GRUENBUCH DER KINDER- UND JUGENDMEDIEN. 1997-2000. a. Eulenhof Verlag, Sartoriusstr 22, Hamburg, 20257, Germany.

820 BRD ISSN 0174-0679
GRUNDRISS DER LITERATURGESCHICHTEN NACH GATTUNGEN. 1973-1987. irreg. Wissenschaftliche Buchgesellschaft, Hindenburgstr 40, Darmstadt, 64295, Germany.

551.4 DNK ISSN 1395-248X
GRUNDVANDSOVERVAAGNING. 1992-2004. a. De Nationale Geologiske Undersoegelser for Danmark og Groenland, Oester Voldgade 10, Copenhagen K, 1350, Denmark.

363.7 DEU ISSN 1433-5328
GRUNDZUEGE DES UMWELTRECHTS. 1997-1998. irreg. Erich Schmidt Verlag GmbH & Co. (Berlin), Genthiner Str 30 G, Berlin, 10785, Germany.

641.5 CHN ISSN 1005-5657
GUANGDONG SHIPIN/GUANGDONG FOOD. 1985-2002. bi-m. Guangdong Shipin Zazhshe, Guangdong Sheng Kewei Xinxi Dalou, Room 301, 171 Lianxin Lu, Guangzhou, Guangdong 510033, China.

330 CHN ISSN 1008-1712
GUANGXI JINGMAO/GUANGXI ECONOMIC & TRADE. 1984-2003. m. Guangxi Jingmao, 1, Minsheng Lu, Quzhengfu Dalou, 627, Nanning, 530012, China.

500 600 CHN ISSN 1007-2268
GUANLI YU XINXI/MANAGEMENT & INFORMATION. 1996-1997. w. Zhongguo Kexue Jishu Xinxi Yanjiusuo, 15, Fuxing Lu, Beijing, 100038, China.

070.5 ESP ISSN 0212-5242
LA GUIA DE EDITORES DE ESPANA. 1950-1976. irreg. Federacion de Gremios de Editores de Espana, c/o Juan Ramon Jimenez, 45-9 Iz., Madrid, 28036, Spain.

384.5 ESP
GUIA DE LA RADIOAFICION Y C B. -200?. a. Tecnipublicaciones Espana, S.L., Avda de Manoteras 44, 3a Planta, Madrid, 28050, Spain.

344.01 ESP ISSN 1135-660X
GUIA DEUSTO LABORAL. 1991-2008. a. Ediciones Deusto S.A., Alameda Recalde 27, Bilbao, Vizcaya 48009, Spain.

388.3 ITA ISSN 1827-837X
LA GUIDA AI FUORISTRADA. 2006-200?. bi-m. Tattilo Editrice SpA, Via degli Olmetti 18, Rome, 00060, Italy.

663.2 ITA
GUIDA AI VINI DEL MONDO. 1992-ceased. biennial. Arcigola Slow Food Editore, Via Mendicita Istruita 14, Bra, CN 12042, Italy.

005.5 ITA
GUIDA ALLE APPLICAZIONI OS-2 WARP. 1996-ceased. s-a. Il Sole 24 Ore Business Media, Divisione J C E, Via Patecchio 2, Milan, 20141, Italy.

771 ITA ISSN 1828-2679
LA GUIDA PHOTOCAMERE DIGITALI. 2006-ceased. bi-m. Tattilo Editrice SpA, Via degli Olmetti 18, Rome, 00060, Italy.

428.24025 ITA
GUIDA RAGIONATA ALLE SCUOLE D'INGLESE IN ITALIA. 1992-ceased. biennial. Edizioni Linguistic Club, Via Principe Amedeo, 15, Frascati, RM 00044, Italy.

388.3 ITA ISSN 1824-2235
GUIDA UFFICIALE MONOVOLUME. 2004-200?. a. Sprea Editori Srl, Via Torino 51, Cernusco sul Naviglio, MI 20063, Italy.

388.3 ITA ISSN 1824-7628
GUIDA UFFICIALE S U V. (Sports Utility Vehicle) 2004-200?. a. Sprea Editori Srl, Via Torino 51, Cernusco sul Naviglio, MI 20063, Italy.

658.3 FRA ISSN 1773-4142
GUIDE DE L'ADJOINT DES RESSOURCES HUMAINES; gestion - contrats - remuneration. 2005-2006. irreg. Editions Dalian, 1 Rue Eugene et Armand Peugeot, B P 720, Rueil Malmaison, 92856 Cedex, France.

629.286 FRA ISSN 1157-1888
GUIDE DE L'EQUIPEMENT ET DE L'OUTILLAGE. 1989-1994. a. Editions Techniques pour l'Automobile et l'Industrie (E T A I), 20-22 rue de la Saussiere, Boulogne Billancourt, 92100, France.

620 011 FRA
GUIDE DES BANQUES DE DONNEES FACTUELLES FRANCAISES SUR LES MATERIAUX. 1989-ceased. irreg. Editions F L A Consultants, 27 rue de la Vistule, Paris, 75013, France.

005.74 FRA
GUIDE INTERNATIONAL DES BANQUES DE DONNEES SUR LES BREVETS ET LES MARQUES. 1993-ceased. irreg. Editions F L A Consultants, 27 rue de la Vistule, Paris, 75013, France.

668.55029 FRA ISSN 1766-2826
GUIDE INTERNATIONAL DES FOURNISSEURS DE LA BEAUTE/GENERAL DIRECTORY OF THE PERFUME AND COSMETIC INDUSTRY. 1948-2004. biennial. Editions Publi-Guid, 195 quai de la Gourdine, Lagny, 77400, France.

658 FRA ISSN 1961-5272
LE GUIDE JURIDIQUE ET FISCAL DE L'ENTREPRISE. 1992-2008. plus updates 4/yr. Editions Dalian, 1 Rue Eugene et Armand Peugeot, B P 720, Rueil Malmaison, 92856 Cedex, France.

676 FRA ISSN 1764-6499
GUIDE P N P. (Profession Nouveau Papetier) 1995-2003. a. Editions Litteraires Techniques et Artistiques (ELTA), 16 rue Saint Fiacre, Paris, 75002, France.

798 ITA ISSN 1827-9597
LE GUIDE PRATICHE DEI NOSTRI AMICI CAVALLI. 2006-200?. bi-m. Sprea Editori Srl, Via Torino 51, Cernusco sul Naviglio, MI 20063, Italy.

336.2 USA
GUIDE TO AUDITING HEALTH CARE BILLING PRACTICES. 1999-200?. plus updates 12/yr. Atlantic Information Services, Inc., 1100 17th St, NW, Ste 300, Washington, DC 20036.

340.0711 NLD ISSN 1374-478X
GUIDE TO LEGAL STUDIES IN EUROPE (YEAR). 1993-2001. a. Kluwer Law International, PO Box 316, Alphen aan den Rijn, 2400 AH, Netherlands.

910 381 USA
GUIDE TO SPRINGFIELD; an encyclopedia of facts and figures on the queen city of the Ozarks. 1987-2008. a. Springfield Communications, Inc., 520 S Union, Springfield, MO 65802.

917.08 USA ISSN 1537-3339
GUIDE TO THE NATIONAL PARK AREAS: WESTERN STATES. 1999-200?. biennial. The Globe Pequot Press, Inc., 246 Goose Ln, PO Box 480, Guilford, CT 06437.

640.73 USA
GUIDE TO WASHINGTON AREA RESTAURANTS. 1988-2000. irreg. (approx. triennial). Center for the Study of Services, 1625 K St NW, 8th Fl, Washington, DC 20006.

933 ISR
GUIDES TO ANTIQUITY SITES. 1992-suspended. irreg. Israel Antiquities Authority, P O Box 586, Jerusalem, 91004, Israel.

787 USA ISSN 1525-3562
GUITAR ONE; the magazine you can play. 1983-2007. m. Future U S, Inc., 4000 Shoreline Ct, Ste 400, South San Francisco, CA 94080.

787.87 USA ISSN 1549-6376
GUITAR WORLD ACOUSTIC. 1995-2007. bi-m. Future U S, Inc., 4000 Shoreline Ct, Ste 400, South San Francisco, CA 94080.

930.1 ESP
GUIZE. 1994-1999. a. Asociacion Canaria de Antropologia, Facultad de Geografia e Historia, Campus de Guajara, La Laguna-Tenerife, 38205, Spain.

338.7409489 DNK ISSN 0905-5878
GULDNUMMERET. 1974-2002. a. A-S Boersen Magasiner, Moentergade 19, Copenhagen K, 1140, Denmark.

623.4 USA ISSN 0894-8119
GUN LIST; the indexed firearms paper. 1984-200?. bi-w. Krause Publications, Inc., 700 E State St, Iola, WI 54990.

610 CHN ISSN 1003-0387
GUOWAI KEJI ZILIAO MULU (YIYAO WEISHENG)/FOREIGN SCIENCE AND TECHNOLOGY CATALOGUE (MEDICAL HEALTH). 1977-2002. m. Zhongguo Yixue Kexueyuan, Zhaoyang-qu, 3, Yabao Lu, Beijing, 100020, China.

895.1 CHN ISSN 1002-6401
GUSHI DAGUAN/KINGDOM OF THE STORIES. 1984-2003. m. Gushi Daguan Zazhishe, 19, Huanbichuan Lu, Jining, 272000, China.

790.13 DEU
GUTE ZEITEN - SCHLECHTE ZEITEN RAETSELSPASS. 1997-2006. m. Panini Verlags GmbH, Ravensstr 48, Nettetal, 41334, Germany.

304.6 330 KOR ISSN 1228-8160
GYEONGJE HWALDONG INGU WOLBO/KOREA (REPUBLIC). NATIONAL STATISTICAL OFFICE. MONTHLY REPORT ON THE ECONOMICALLY ACTIVE POPULATION SURVEY. 1998-2008. m. Tong'gyecheong, Government Complex Daejeon, 139 Seonsaro (920 Dunsan 2-dong), Seo-gu, Daejeon, 302-701, Korea, S.

016.37 DNK ISSN 0901-9308
GYMNASIET OG HF. 1973-2006. a. Fonden Undervisnings Information, Siljangade 6, Copenhagen S, 2300, Denmark.

796.41 ITA
GYMNICA. 1987 (vol.4)-ceased. m. Federazione Ginnastica d'Italia, Palazzo delle Federazioni Sportive Nazionali, Viale Tiziano 70, Rome, 00196, Italy.

618 FRA ISSN 0240-172X
GYN OBS - LA MEDECINE ET LA FEMME. 1979-2007. 12/yr. Elsevier France, Editions Scientifiques et Medicales, 23 Rue Linois, Paris, 75724, France.

378 NLD ISSN 0167-0468
H B O JOURNAAL. (Hoger Beroepsonderwijs) 1978-2004. 9/yr. Koninklijke Van Gorcum BV, PO Box 43, Assen, 9400 AA, Netherlands.

378 AUS ISSN 1323-4021
H E R D S A GOLD GUIDE SERIES. 1994-1998. irreg. Higher Education Research and Development Society of Australasia, PO Box 27, Milperra, NSW 2214, Australia.

378.9 AUS ISSN 0813-524X
H E R D S A GREEN GUIDE SERIES. 1984-1997. irreg. Higher Education Research and Development Society of Australasia, PO Box 27, Milperra, NSW 2214, Australia.

362 FRA ISSN 1276-2172
H M H. HYGIENE EN MILIEU HOSPITALIER. 1997-suspended. bi-m. Editions Lamarre, 1 Rue Eugene et Armand Peugeot, Rueil Malmaison, 92500, France.

004.14 USA ISSN 1065-6189
THE H P PALMTOP PAPER. (Hewlett-Packard) 1986-2000. bi-m. Thaddeus Computing, Inc., c/o Wayne Kneeskern, Controller, Box 869, Fairfield, IA 52556-0869.

664 636 USA
H R I - BUYERS GUIDE (PRINT). (Hotels, Restaurants, Institutions) 1970-2003. w. Urner Barry Publications, Inc., PO Box 389, Toms River, NJ 08754.

316.628 CZE ISSN 1801-6669
H R TIP. 2006-2007. m. Verlag Dashoefer s.r.o., Na Prikope 18, PO Box 756, Prague 1, 11121, Czech Republic.

362.1 GBR ISSN 1368-6828
H S E CONTRACT RESEARCH REPORT. 1987-2002. irreg. Health and Safety Executive, Rose Court, 2 Southwark Bridge, London, SE1 9HS, United Kingdom.

800 GBR
H U. (Honest Ulsterman) 1968-2003. irreg. (3-4/yr.). Ulsterman Publications, 49 Main St, Greyabbey, Newtownards, BT22 2NF, United Kingdom.

305.90664 051 USA ISSN 1524-0339
H X MAGAZINE. (Homo Xtra) 1996-2009 (Jul.); suspended. w. H X Media, LLC, 230 W 17th St, 8th Fl, New York, NY 10011.

051 USA
H XTRA; the totally biased politically incorrect party paper. 1991-2009. w. H X Media, LLC, 230 W 17th St, 8th Fl, New York, NY 10011.

387 ISR
HA-SAPANUT HA-YISRE'ELIT/ISRAEL SHIPPING. 1975-2007. a. Haifa University, Wydra Institute of Shipping and Aviation Research, University of Haifa, Eshkol Tower, Haifa, 31905, Israel.

690 DNK ISSN 0105-9416
HAANDVAERKET & MASKINEN. 1975-1981. 6/yr. Haandvaerket og Maskinen, PO Box 92, Hellerup, 2900, Denmark.

745 DNK ISSN 0109-4564
HAANDVAERKSHISTORISK TIDSSKRIFT. 1983-198?. q. Haandvaerkshistorisk Selskab, c/o Birgit C Villumsen, Foerlev, Illerupvej 2, Skanderborg, 8660, Denmark.

690 DNK ISSN 1902-7788
HAANDVAERKSRAADET. BYGGEANALYSE (ONLINE). 199?-2007; suspended. s-a. Haandvaerksraadet, Islands Brygge 26, PO Box 1990, Copenhagen S, 2300, Denmark.

059.943 TUR
HABER. 1949 (Aug.)-ceased. d. Haber, Lefkosa - Nicosia, Mersin 10, Turkey.

500.9 GBR ISSN 0028-9043
HABITAT (LONDON). 1959-2000. 10/yr. Environment Council, 212 High Holborn, London, WC1V 7BW, United Kingdom.

551.5 ITA
HABITAT - CALABRIA. 1965-ceased. m. Habitat-Calabria s.r.l., Via Parco Fiamma, 8, Reggio Calabria, RC 89126, Italy.

933 ISR ISSN 1565-043X
HADASHOT ARKHEOLOGIYOT; excavations and surveys in Israel. 2000-2005. irreg. Israel Antiquities Authority, P O Box 586, Jerusalem, 91004, Israel.

330 ISR
HAD'SHOT PENSIA UVITTU'AH SOTSIALI. 1968-2007. m. Kaliah Ltd., Rehov Ben-Yeduha 165, Tel Aviv, 63471, Israel.

058.691 DNK ISSN 1604-2344
HAFNARPOSTURINN. 1980-1982; resumed 1983-2005. 6/yr. Islendingafelagid i Kaupmannahoefn, Oester Voldgade 12, Copenhagen K, 1350, Denmark.

320.54095694 ISR
AL-HAHOMA. 1913-1986. m. Hashomer Hatzair Israel, 7 Bezalel Yaffe St, Tel Aviv, 65204, Israel.

646.724 AUS
HAIR +; every day is a good hair day. 2003-2005. m. Derwent Howard Media Pty Ltd., PO Box 1037, Bondi Junction, NSW 1355, Australia.

895.1 CHN ISSN 1005-7536
HAISHANG WENTAN/HAI SHANG CULTURE WORLD. 1991-2006. m. Haishang Wentan Zazhishe, 675, Julu Lu, Shanghai, 200040, China.

900 DEU
HALBGRAUE REIHE ZUR HISTORISCHEN FACHINFORMATIK. SERIE A: HISTORISCHE QUELLENKUNDEN/HALF-GRAY SERIES ON HISTORICAL INFORMATION TECHNOLOGY. SERIES A: STUDY OF HISTORICAL SOURCES. 1989-1997 (vol.31). irreg. Max-Planck-Institut fuer Geschichte, Hermann-Foege-Weg 11, Goettingen, 37073, Germany.

900 DEU
HALBGRAUE REIHE ZUR HISTORISCHEN FACHINFORMATIK. SERIE B: SOFTWAREBESCHREIBUNGEN/HALF-GRAY SERIES ON HISTORICAL INFORMATION TECHNOLOGY. SERIES B: SOFTWARE DESCRIPTIONS. 1989-1993 (vol.11). irreg. Max-Planck-Institut fuer Geschichte, Hermann-Foege-Weg 11, Goettingen, 37073, Germany.

320.96 DEU ISSN 0947-4900
HAMBURG AFRICAN STUDIES/ETUDES AFRICAINES HAMBOURGEOISES. 1993-2005 (vol.14). irreg. G I G A Institute of African Affairs, Neuer Jungfernstieg 21, Hamburg, 20354, Germany.

796.334 GBR ISSN 1353-7431
HAMMERS NEWS MAGAZINE. 1987-2008 (Jun.). m. Hammers News Magazine, Unit 4, Ashton Gate, Harold Hill, Romford, RM3 8UF, United Kingdom.

610 CHN ISSN 1008-3073
HANDAN YIXUE GAODENG ZHUANKE XUEXIAO XUEBAO/HANDAN MEDICAL COLLEGE. JOURNAL. 1986-2006. bi-m. Handan Yixue Gaodeng Zhuanke Xuexiao, 42, Congtai Lu Jia, Handan, 056029, China.

330.1 USA ISSN 1054-7681
HANDBOOK OF COMPARATIVE ECONOMIC POLICIES. 1991-19??. irreg. Greenwood Publishing Group Inc., 88 Post Rd W, PO Box 5007, Westport, CT 06881.

336.2 NLD
HANDBOOK ON THE 1989 DOUBLE TAXATION CONVENTION BETWEEN THE FEDERAL REPUBLIC OF GERMANY AND THE UNITED STATES OF AMERICA. 1966-2008. plus a. updates. International Bureau of Fiscal Documentation (I B F D), H J E Wenckebachweg 210, Amsterdam, 1096 AS, Netherlands.

332.6 DEU ISSN 0947-5931
HANDBUCH FUER DAS ERFOLGREICHE OSTGESCHAEFT. 1977-2003. irreg. (6-8/yr.). Deutscher Wirtschaftsdienst, Luxemburger Str 449, Cologne, 50939, Germany.

658 DEU ISSN 0942-2609
HANDBUCH KULTURMANAGEMENT. 1992-2006. irreg. Dr. Josef Raabe Verlags GmbH, Rotebuehlstr 77, Stuttgart, 70178, Germany.

330 DNK ISSN 0106-4363
HANDELSHOEJSKOLEN I AARHUS. INSTITUT FOR ERHVERVS- OG SAMFUNDSBESKRIVELSE. SKRIFTSERIE C. 1974-1995. irreg. Handelshoejskolen i Aarhus, Institut for Erhvervs- og Samfundsbeskrivelse, Fuglesange Alle 20, Aarhus V, 8210, Denmark.

332 DNK ISSN 0105-4058
HANDELSHOEJSKOLEN I AARHUS. INSTITUT FOR FINANSIERING OG KREDITVAESEN. KOMPENDIUM D. 1971 (no.8)-1983. irreg. Handelshoejskolen i Aarhus, Institut for Finansiering og Kreditvaesen, Aarhus, Denmark.

658.8 380 DEU ISSN 1616-1483
HANDELSMAGAZIN B A G. 1961-2002. m. Bundesarbeitsgemeinschaft der Mittel- und Grossbetriebe des Einzelhandels e.V., Atrium Friedrichstr 60, Berlin, 10117, Germany.

362.4 FRA ISSN 1295-2362
HANDICAP; revue de sciences humaines et sociales. 1978-2005. q. Centre Technique National d'Etudes et de Recherches sur les Handicaps et les Inadaptations, 236 bis rue de Tolbiac, Paris, 75013, France.

362.4 362.6 DNK ISSN 1902-1704
HANDICAPPEDE, SINDSLIDENDE, AELDRE. 1986-2007. 12/yr. Jurainformation, Vesterbrogade 10, Copenhagen V, 1620, Denmark.

358 USA
HANDLOADER'S DIGEST. 1961-2003 (18th Ed.). irreg. Krause Publications, Inc., 700 E State St, Iola, WI 54990.

004.14 DEU
HANDY UND NOTEBOOK PRAXIS; Tipps, Workshops, Kaufberatung. 2005-2006. 2/yr. Data Becker GmbH & Co. KG, Merowingerstr 30, Duesseldorf, 40223, Germany.

331.8 694 DNK ISSN 1902-9691
HANDYMAG. 2005-2008. irreg. (3-4/yr). Forbundet Trae-Industri-Byg i Danmark, Landsungdomsudvalget, Mimersgade 41, Copenhagen N, Denmark.

629.1325 CHN ISSN 1004-6518
HANGKONG ZHOUKAN/AVIATION NEWS WEEKLY. 1963-2005. w. Zhongguo Hangkong Gongye Fazhan Yanjiu Zhongxin, 14, Anwai Xiaoguan Dongli, Beijing, 100029, China.

720 NLD ISSN 1871-4056
HANZEHOGESCHOOL GRONINGEN. ACADEMIE VAN BOUWKUNST. JAARBOEK. 2004-2006. a. Hanzelhogeschool Groningen, Academie van Bouwkunst, Zuiderkuipen 19, Groningen, 9711 HR, Netherlands.

380.1029 KOR ISSN 0073-0335
HAPDONG YONGAM. 1963-ceased. a. Yonhap News Agency, 85-1 Susong-dong, Jongro-gu, Seoul, Korea, S.

005.117 USA ISSN 1543-1282
HARDCORE DELPHI. 1995-2004. m. Eli Journals, 700 Metro Park, Rochester, NY 14623.

779.28 CZE ISSN 1214-8636
HARDCORE INTERNATIONAL. 2004-2006. 2/yr. PK 62, a.s., Bohdalecka 6, Prague 10, 101 00, Czech Republic.

005.1 USA ISSN 1543-222X
HARDCORE WEB SERVICES. 2002-200?. m. Eli Journals, 700 Metro Park, Rochester, NY 14623.

055.1 ITA ISSN 1594-283X
HARMONY COMEDY. 2002-ceased. 2/m. Harlequin Mondadori, Concordia 7, Milan, 20129, Italy.

055.1 ITA ISSN 1123-8437
HARMONY DESIRE. 1995-ceased. w. Harlequin Mondadori, Concordia 7, Milan, 20129, Italy.

055.1 ITA ISSN 1722-070X
HARMONY INTRIGUE. 2003-ceased. 3/m. Harlequin Mondadori, Concordia 7, Milan, 20129, Italy.

055.1 ITA ISSN 1721-369X
HARMONY OASI DONNA. 2003-ceased. m. Harlequin Mondadori, Concordia 7, Milan, 20129, Italy.

055.1 ITA ISSN 1122-5394
HARMONY. SERIE JOLLY. 1982-ceased. 8/m. Harlequin Mondadori, Concordia 7, Milan, 20129, Italy.

330 ISR ISSN 0334-8121
HAROSHET; monthly review for the Israeli producer. 1986-1992. m. Kalia Press Ltd., Rehov Ben-Yehuda 165, Tel Aviv, 63471, Israel.

659.152 ITA ISSN 1121-7375
HARPER'S BAZAAR ITALIA. 1970-ceased. 8/yr. Edizioni S Y D S Italia s.r.l., Viale Stelvio, 57, Milan, MI 20159, Italy.

659.152 ITA ISSN 1121-7251
HARPER'S BAZAAR ITALIA UOMO; bimestrale moda uomo. 1979-ceased. bi-m. Edizioni S Y D S Italia s.r.l., Viale Stelvio, 57, Milan, MI 20159, Italy.

645 ITA ISSN 0394-1132
HARPER'S GRAN BAZAAR. 1978-ceased. 6/yr. Edizioni S Y D S Italia s.r.l., Viale Stelvio, 57, Milan, MI 20159, Italy.

808.839 USA ISSN 1556-9241
HARRINGTON GAY MEN'S LITERARY QUARTERLY. 1998-200?. q. Harrington Park Press, 10 Alice St, Binghamton, NY 13904.

800 700 306.489 USA ISSN 1556-9225
HARRINGTON LESBIAN LITERARY QUARTERLY. 2000 (Spring)-2007. q. Alice Street Editions, 10 Alice St, Binghamton, NY 13904.

670.29 USA
HARRIS DIRECTORY. VERMONT MANUFACTURING. 2000-2008. a. Harris InfoSource, 2057 E Aurora Rd, Twinsburg, OH 44087.

665.7 333.79 USA ISSN 1090-8706
HART'S ENERGY MARKETS. 1993-2005. 12/yr. Hart Energy Publishing, LP, 1616 S Voss Rd, Ste 1000, Houston, TX 77057.

070.4 658.8 USA ISSN 1524-5519
HARVARD MANAGEMENT COMMUNICATION LETTER. 1998-2006. q. Harvard Business School Publishing, 60 Harvard Way, Boston, MA 02163.

658 USA ISSN 1525-9595
HARVARD MANAGEMENT UPDATE. 1996-2009. m. Harvard Business School Publishing, 60 Harvard Way, Boston, MA 02163.

640 DEU
HAUSHALTS JOURNAL. 1986-2006. m. D S H - Verlag, Osterbrooksweg 35-45, Schenefeld, 22867, Germany.

616.5 DEU ISSN 0938-7196
HAUTNAH. MYKOLOGIE. 1991-1993. irreg. M M V Medien und Medizin Verlagsgesellschaft mbH Muenchen, Neumarkter Str 18, Munich, 81673, Germany.

363.5021 USA ISSN 1080-4161
HEALTH & ENVIRONMENT IN AMERICA'S TOP-RATED CITIES: A STATISTICAL PROFILE (YEARS). 1994-1997. biennial. Grey House Publishing, 185 Millerton Rd, PO Box 860, Millerton, NY 12546.

658.31244 GBR ISSN 1356-1928
HEALTH AND SAFETY AT WORK DIRECTORY. 199?-1998. a. Croner.C C H Group Ltd., 145 London Rd, Kingston, Surrey KT2 6SR, United Kingdom.

344 USA ISSN 1537-3592
HEALTH CARE EMPLOYMENT LAW LETTER. 2002 (Jan.)-2004. m. M. Lee Smith Publishers LLC, 5201 Virginia Way, PO Box 5094, Brentwood, TN 37024.

658 664 USA ISSN 1090-2260
HEALTH CARE FOOD & NUTRITION FOCUS. 1984-2006. m. Lippincott Williams & Wilkins, 530 Walnut St, Philadelphia, PA 19106-3621.

610 AUS ISSN 1445-6842
HEALTH COMMUNICATION WEEKLY. 2001 (Apr.)-2001 (Jun.). w. Health Communication Network, Level 4, 39-41 Chandos St, P O Box 67, St Leonards, NSW 2065, Australia.

362.1068 GBR ISSN 1473-124X
HEALTH DEVELOPMENT TODAY. 2001-2004. bi-m. National Institute for Health and Clinical Excellence, MidCity Pl, 71 High Holborn, London, WC1V 6NA, United Kingdom.

613.7 USA
HEALTH FAMILY. 2004 (May)-200?. bi-m. Navigator Publishing LLC., 58 Fore St, Portland, ME 04101-4842.

360 362 AUS ISSN 1832-0031
HEALTH INEQUALITIES MONITORING SERIES. 2004-ceased. a. Australian Institute of Health and Welfare, GPO Box 570, Canberra, ACT 2601, Australia.

610 USA
HEALTH NETWORKING NEWS. 1993-200?. 8/yr. C M P Media LLC, 600 Community Dr, Manhasset, NY 11030.

362.1 USA
HEALTHCARE ENTERPRISE. 2003 (Nov.)-200?. q. C M P Media LLC, 600 Community Dr, Manhasset, NY 11030.

362 GBR ISSN 1472-5401
HEALTHCARE EQUIPMENT SUPPLIES INTERNATIONAL. 2000-2002. bi-m. Wilmington Media & Entertainment, Maidstone Rd, Footscray, Sidcup, Kent DA14 5HZ, United Kingdom.

610 USA ISSN 1048-8103
HEALTHCARE STANDARDS UPDATE. 1990-2002. q. Emergency Care Research Institute, 5200 Butler Pike, Plymouth Meeting, PA 19462.

780 AUS
HEARD MAGAZINE. 1994-suspended. m. hEARd, 28 Lake Rd, Swansea, NSW 2281, Australia.

347 AUS ISSN 0725-6108
HEARSAY. 1980-2001. q. Legal Aid Commission of Western Australia, 105 St George's Terrace, Perth, W.A. 6000, Australia.

616.1 USA ISSN 1521-737X
HEART DISEASE; a journal of cardiovascular medicine. 1999-2003. bi-m. Lippincott Williams & Wilkins, 530 Walnut St, Philadelphia, PA 19106-3621.

780 DEU
HEARTBEAT!. 1984-199?. q. Hans-Juergen Klitsch Ed. & Pub., Moselstr 2, Schortens, 26419, Germany.

370 FRA ISSN 1276-9290
L'HEBDO. 1983-2003. w. Association Nationale des Communautes Educatives, 145 bd. de Magenta, Paris, 75010, France.

610 300 ISR ISSN 0333-6964
HEBREW UNIVERSITY OF JERUSALEM. AUTHORITY FOR RESEARCH AND DEVELOPMENT. RESEARCH. 1964-1995. a. Hebrew University of Jerusalem, Authority for Research and Development, Jerusalem, 91904, Israel.

374 ISR ISSN 0333-9076
HED HA-ULPAN. 1974-1997. 3/yr. Ministry of Education, 34 Shivtei Israel St., P O Box 292, Jerusalem, 91911, Israel.

610 DEU ISSN 0945-1382 CODEN: HUFHAR
HEFTE ZUR ZEITSCHRIFT DER UNFALLCHIRURG. 1929-2002 (vol.284). irreg. Springer, Tiergartenstr 17, Heidelberg, 69121, Germany.

944 FRA ISSN 0336-030X
HEIMDAL; revue d'heritage Norois. 1971-198?. q. Editions Heimdal, Chateau de Damigny, B P 61350, Bayeux, Cedex 14406, France.

Cessations

280.4 DEU
HELFENDE HAENDE; Zeitschrift des diakonischen Werkes Westfalen. 1950-2005. q. Diakonisches Werk der Evangelischen Kirche von Westfalen, Friesenring 32-34, Muenster, 48147, Germany.

796.93 USA
HELISKI CATSKI JOURNAL. 2007-200?. q. Skinner Media, Box 121, Kitty Hawk, NC 27949.

361.8 362.7 GBR ISSN 1751-0937
HELPING CHILDREN LOCALLY INFORMATION BOOK. ceased 2006. q. Helping Children Locally, Star Chambers, 7 Sirocco Close, Moulton Park, Northampton, NN3 6AP, United Kingdom.

658 GBR ISSN 1745-7866
HENLEY MANAGER UPDATE. 1973-2007. q. Braybrooke Press Ltd., Remenham House, Remenham Hill, Henley-on-Thames, Oxon RG9 3EP, United Kingdom.

747 NOR ISSN 1500-6034
HENNE INTERIOR. 1997-2001. 4/yr. Aller Forlag AS, Stenersgaten 2, Sentrum, Oslo, 0189, Norway.

289.5 USA ISSN 0146-7174
THE HERALD OF CHRISTIAN SCIENCE. 1903-1996. m. (French, German, Spanish and Portuguese eds.; q. , other eds. and English-Braille). The Christian Science Publishing Society, One Norway St, Boston, MA 02115.

808.87 FRA
HERISSON. 1936-ceased. w. Publications Georges Ventillard, 12 rue de Bellevue, 2A, Paris, 75019, France.

920 820 AUS ISSN 0729-2449
HERMIT PRESS PAMPHLETS. 1982-ceased. irreg. Pioneer Books, PO Box 57, Oaklands Park, SA 5046, Australia.

616.1 DEU ISSN 0720-0730
HERZ UND GEFAESSE; Zeitschrift fuer praktische Kardioangiologie. 1981-1993; resumed 199?-1998. bi-m. Demeter Verlag GmbH und Co. KG, Ruedigerstr 14, Stuttgart, 70469, Germany.

305.23 DEU
HEY! GIRLS. 2006-2008 (Jan.). m. Panini Verlags GmbH, Ravensstr 48, Nettetal, 41334, Germany.

371.9 DEU
HHHHOLTER-DDIE-PPPOLTER. 1993-2005. 2/yr. Bundesvereinigung Stotterer-Selbsthilfe e.V., Zuelpicher Str 58, Cologne, 50674, Germany.

340 AUS ISSN 1323-3289
HIGH COURT AND FEDERAL COURT DECISIONS. 1998-2004. m. Computer Law Services, PO Box 1993, Canberra, ACT 2600, Australia.

666 USA ISSN 1045-2397
HIGH TECH CERAMICS NEWS. 1989 (Jan.)-2006. m. Business Communications Co., Inc., 25 Van Zant St, Ste 13, Norwalk, CT 06855-1781.

294.5 AUS
HINDU MISSION'S JOURNAL OF STUDIES IN THE BHAGAVADGITA. 1981-1996. irreg. University of Sydney, Department of Religious Studies, c/o Ms.Patricia Ricketts, Sydney, NSW 2006, Australia.

917.106 031 USA
HISPANIC - AMERICAN ALMANAC. 1992-2003. irreg. Gale, 27500 Drake Rd, Farmington Hills, MI 48331.

359.009 FRA ISSN 1774-0401
L'HISTOIRE DE LA MARINE; la marine du present, du passe, du futur. 2005-2008. q. Editions Orphee, 74 rue du Gros-Chene, Laneuveville-devant-Nancy, France.

500.9 FRA ISSN 1141-4588
HISTOIRE DES SCIENCES ET DES TECHNIQUES. 1969-1991. irreg. College de France, Ecole des Hautes Etudes en Sciences Sociales (E H E S S), 54 Boulevard Raspail, Paris, 75006, France.

900 020 FRA ISSN 1278-382X
HISTOIRE ET ARCHIVES. 1997-2007. s-a. Honore Champion, 3 Rue Corneille, Paris, 75006, France.

500.9 FRA ISSN 0396-9681
HISTOIRE ET NATURE. 1968-1993. s-a. Association pour l'Histoire des Sciences de la Nature, BP 402, Bagneres de Bigorre, Cedex 65204, France.

946 ESP
HISTORIA GRAFICA DE CATALUNYA DIA A DIA. 1978-2001. a. Edicions 62 S.A., Peu de la Creu, 4, Barcelona, 08001, Spain.

910.03 USA
HISTORIC LANDMARKS OF BLACK AMERICA. 1991-ceased. irreg. Gale, 27500 Drake Rd, Farmington Hills, MI 48331.

900 ITA ISSN 0018-2427
HISTORICA; rivista di cultura. 1948-ceased. q. Historica Rivista di Cultura, Via Domenico Muratore, 25, Reggio Calabria, RC 89127, Italy.

069 AUS ISSN 1448-3319
HISTORY MATTERS (ADELAIDE). 1979-2008. 4/yr. History Trust of South Australia, GPO Box 1836, Adelaide, SA 5001, Australia.

990 NZL ISSN 1173-3438
HISTORY NOW; te pae tawito o te wa. 1960; N.S. 1995-2005 (Nov.). 4/yr. (until 2001 2/yr.). University of Canterbury, Department of History, Private Bag, Christchurch, 4800, New Zealand.

384.55 DEU
HITSHOP; das Magazin fuer Home Entertainment. 1997-2003. 10/yr. Entertainment Media Verlag GmbH und Co. oHG, Einsteinring 24, Dornach, 85609, Germany.

790.13 016 DNK ISSN 0105-9939
HOBBYINDEKS FOR BOERNEBIBLIOTEKER. 1974-2004. a. D B C A/S, Tempovej 7-11, Ballerup, 2750, Denmark.

790.1 DEU
HOCH HINAUS. 1985-2005. q. Drachen Club Deutschland e.V., Martinistr 87, Osnabrueck, 49080, Germany.

338.91 DDR ISSN 0232-4660
HOCHSCHULE FUER OEKONOMIE "BRUNO LEUSCHNER" BERLIN. INSTITUT OEKONOMIK DER ENTWICKLUNGSLAENDER. WISSENSCHAFTLICHE BEITRAEGE. 1978-1990. q. Hochschule fuer Oekonomie "Bruno Leuschner" Berlin, Hermann-Duncker-Str 8, Berlin, 1157, Germany.

796.962 NLD ISSN 0920-5888
HOCKEY MAGAZINE. 1934-2008. fortn. Koninklijke Nederlandse Hockey Bond, Postbus 85396, Utrecht, 3508 AJ, Netherlands.

796.3 GBR ISSN 1363-4321
HOCKEY SPORT. 1975-2005. m. P B Publications, 29 Romilly St, London, W1V 6HP, United Kingdom.

002.2 DEU ISSN 1993-7636
HOERBUCH REPORT; Deutschlands grosses Hoerbuch-Magazin. 2007-2007 (Dec.). m. Infosat Verlag und Werbe GmbH, Julius-Saxler-Str 3, Daun, 54550, Germany.

384.54 DEU ISSN 0179-1869
HOERUEBERSICHT INTERNATIONAL; aktuelle Programmzeitschrift des Deutschsprachigen internationalen Rundfunks. 1978-1990. q. DX Listeners Service, Postfach 1122, Homberg, 34576, Germany.

636 USA ISSN 1056-1374
HOGS TODAY. 1985-1999. m. (10/yr..). Farm Journal Media, 1818 Market St., 31st Fl, Philadelphia, PA 19103.

910.2 FRA ISSN 1959-0857
HOLIDAY'S; l'esprit des voyages. 2007-2007. m. European Magazine Group, 5 Rue Chazelles, Paris, 75017, France.

728 USA ISSN 0278-2839
HOME; the remodeling and decorating resource. 1955-2008. 8/yr. Hachette Filipacchi Media U.S., Inc., 1633 Broadway, New York, NY 10019.

690 USA ISSN 1550-5715
HOME BUILDING. 2000-200?. a. Hachette Filipacchi Media U.S., Inc., 1633 Broadway, New York, NY 10019.

791.5 CZE ISSN 1801-5441
HOME CINEMA. 2005-2007. m. Computer Press a.s., Spielberk Office Centre, Holandska 8, Brno, 639 00, Czech Republic.

640 USA ISSN 1071-4782
HOME COOKING. 1973-2008. m. Dynamic Resource Group (D R G), 306 E Parr Rd, Berne, IN 46711.

690 USA ISSN 0897-621X
HOMESTYLES HOME PLANS. 1986-2009 (Jan.). q. HomePlans.com, 901 N 3rd St, Ste 216, Minneapolis, MN 55401.

284.1 USA ISSN 0738-0534 CODEN: JMEDDD
HOMILETIC (PRINT). 1976-2009. s-a. Religious Speech Communication Association, Perkins School of Theology, Dallas, TX 75275.

900 FRA ISSN 0073-3202
HOMMES ET LA TERRE. 1956-1992. irreg. College de France, Ecole des Hautes Etudes en Sciences Sociales (E H E S S), 54 Boulevard Raspail, Paris, 75006, France.

301 FRA ISSN 0563-9743
HOMO; psychologie, education, culture, societe. 1953-2002. a. Presses Universitaires du Mirail, Universite de Toulouse II (Le Mirail), 5, Allee Antonio Machado, Toulouse, 31058, France.

331 ITA ISSN 0439-4291
HOMO FABER; rassegna internazionale de lavoro e dell'istruzione. 1950-ceased. m. Mario Pantaleo Ed. & Pub., Via Dei Gracchi, 181-185, Rome, RM 00192, Italy.

301 ESP
HOMO SOCIOLOGICUS. 1974-2001. irreg. Edicions 62 S.A., Peu de la Creu, 4, Barcelona, 08001, Spain.

808.803538 USA ISSN 0733-5865
HONCHO. 1989 (vol.12, no.5)-2009. m. Mavety Media Group, 225 Broadway, Ste 2801, New York, NY 10007-3079.

332.6 DEU ISSN 0933-3169
HOPPENSTEDT STOCK GUIDE GERMANY. 1987-2002. q. Hoppenstedt Publishing GmbH, Havelstr 9, Darmstadt, 64295, Germany.

780.01 ITA ISSN 1129-4965
HORTUS MUSICUS. 2000-2005 (No.24). q. Ut Orpheus Edizioni S.r.l., Piazza di Porta Ravegnana 1, Bologna, 40126, Italy.

610 GBR ISSN 0262-3145
HOSPITAL DOCTOR. 1967-2007 (Dec.). 48/yr. Reed Business Information, Healthcare, Quadrant House, The Quadrant, Brighton Rd, Sutton, Surrey SM2 5AS, United Kingdom.

362.11 NZL ISSN 1177-8652
HOSPITAL THROUGHPUT (ONLINE). 1996-2005. a. New Zealand Ministry of Health, Box 5013, Wellington, New Zealand.

647.9 910.202 ESP ISSN 1988-9674
HOSTELSERVICE DIGITAL. 1998-200?. m. Tecnipublicaciones Espana, S.L., Avda de Manoteras 44, 3a Planta, Madrid, 28050, Spain.

028.5 DEU
HOT WHEELS. 2004-2006. m. Egmont Ehapa Verlag GmbH, Wallstr 59, Berlin, 10179, Germany.

336.2 USA ISSN 1536-6847
HOUSING BOND REPORT; a monthly publication on the low-income housing tax-exempt bond industry. 1998-ceased. m. Novogradac & Co. LLP, 246 1st St, 5th Fl, San Francisco, CA 94105.

371.42 USA ISSN 1070-8634
THE HOUSTON JOBBANK; the job hunter's guide to Houston. (Includes: Baytown, Beaumont, Galveston, Pasadena and many others.) 1996-2003 (12th Ed.). irreg. Adams Media, 4700 E Galbraith Rd, Cincinnati, OH 45236.

365 GBR ISSN 1368-4124
HOWARD LEAGUE HANDBOOKS. 1994-1996. irreg. Howard League for Penal Reform, 1 Ardleigh Rd, London, N1 4HS, United Kingdom.

540 662.6 CHN ISSN 1004-0862
HUAGONG ZHI YOU/FRIEND OF CHEMICAL INDUSTRY. 1981-2007. q. Hebei Shiyou Huagong Guihua Shejiyuan, 11 Jichang Lu, Shijiazhuang, Hebei 050071, China.

780 CZE ISSN 1211-6408
HUDEBNI UDALOSTI V CESKE REPUBLICE/MUSICAL EVENTS IN THE CZECH REPUBLIC. 1995-2002. a. Hudebni Informacni Stredisko, Besedni 3, Prague 1, 118 00, Czech Republic.

025.04 610 NLD ISSN 1871-708X
DE HUISARTS, SPECIALIST EN HET ELEKTRONISCHE MEDISCH DOSSIER. 199?-2006. a. Erasmus Universiteit, Afdeling Medische Informatica, Erasmus MC, kamer Ee2100, Dr Molewaterplein 50, Postbus 1738, Rotterdam, 3000 DR, Netherlands.

332.63 339 NLD ISSN 1573-6253
HUIZEN AAN DE SPAANSE COSTA'S!. 2003-2008. s-a. Uitgeverij Interdijk BV, Postbus 10, Uithoorn, 1420 AA, Netherlands.

616 NLD ISSN 1872-0501
HULPMIDDELEN KOMPAS. 2004-2004. biennial. College voor Zorgverzekeringen, Postbus 320, Diemen, 1110 AH, Netherlands.

910.02 GBR
HUMAN GEOGRAPHY UPDATE. 2001-200?. s-a. Elsevier Ltd, The Blvd, Langford Ln, Kidlington, Oxford, OX5 1GB, United Kingdom.

323.4 NLD ISSN 0965-934X CODEN: HRCDFI
HUMAN RIGHTS CASE DIGEST; the European convention system. 1990-2009 (Vol. 18). bi-m. Martinus Nijhoff, PO Box 9000, Leiden, 2300 PA, Netherlands.

342.085 NZL ISSN 1173-5252
HUMAN RIGHTS LAW AND PRACTICE. 1995-2003 (Feb.). q. Thomson Brookers, Level 1 - Guardian Trust House, 15 Willeston St, PO Box 43, Wellington, New Zealand.

323.096 USA
HUMAN RIGHTS WATCH. A. 1989-2008. irreg. Human Rights Watch, 350 Fifth Ave, 34th Fl, New York, NY 10118.

323.4 USA
HUMAN RIGHTS WATCH. B. 1989-2008. irreg. Human Rights Watch, 350 Fifth Ave, 34th Fl, New York, NY 10118.

323.4 USA
HUMAN RIGHTS WATCH. C. 1985-2008. irreg. Human Rights Watch, 350 Fifth Ave, 34th Fl, New York, NY 10118.

323 USA ISSN 1552-7042
HUMAN RIGHTS WATCH. D. 1997-2008. irreg. Human Rights Watch, 350 Fifth Ave, 34th Fl, New York, NY 10118.

323.4 USA
HUMAN RIGHTS WATCH. E. 1989-2008. irreg. Human Rights Watch, 350 Fifth Ave, 34th Fl, New York, NY 10118.

323.4 DEU ISSN 1015-5945
HUMAN RIGHTS WORLDWIDE. 1990-2000. 4/yr. Internationale Gesellschaft fuer Menschenrechte, Borsigallee 9, Frankfurt Am Main, 60388, Germany.

808.87 ITA
HUMOR GRAPHIC. 1960-ceased. a. Museo Internazionale dell'Umorismo, Via Arzaga, 28, Milan, MI 20146, Italy.

378 CHN ISSN 1001-6074 CODEN: HJUUEY
HUNAN JIAOYU XUEYUAN XUEBAO/HUNAN EDUCATIONAL INSTITUTE. JOURNAL. (Issues 1, 3, 4 and 6 cover social sciences; issues 2 and 5 cover natural sciences) 1983-2001. bi-m. Hunan Jiaoyu Xueyuan, Xuebao Bianjibu, Zuojialong, Changsha, Hunan 410012, China.

914.2654 GBR ISSN 1752-3206
HUNTS LIFE. 2006-2006. q. Archant Herts and Cambs, Bank House, Primett Rd, Stevenage, SG1 3EE, United Kingdom.

779.28 CZE ISSN 1212-2548
HUSTLER. 1998-2007. m. Geronia Czech Republic, s.r.o., Narodni 10/138, Prague 1, 110 00, Czech Republic.

523.8 CZE ISSN 0862-173X
HVEZDARNA A PLANETARIUM MIKULASE KOPERNIKA V BRNE. PRACE/NICHOLAS COPERNICUS OBSERVATORY AND PLANETARIUM IN BRNO. CONTRIBUTIONS. 1964-2002. irreg. Hvezdarna a Planetarium Mikulase Kopernika v Brne, Kravi Hora 2, Brno, 61600, Czech Republic.

572.8 USA ISSN 1554-0014 CODEN: HHYYBF
HYBRIDOMA (PRINT); a journal of molecular immunology and experimental and clinical immunotherapy. 1981-2009. bi-m. Mary Ann Liebert, Inc. Publishers, 140 Huguenot St, 3rd Fl, New Rochelle, NY 10801-5215.

627 NLD ISSN 0166-2112
HYDRO DELFT. 1965-2007. q. Delft Hydraulics, Rotterdamseweg 185, PO Box 177, Delft, 2600 MH, Netherlands.

529 DEU ISSN 1433-3988
HYGIENE UND MIKROBIOLOGIE. 1996-2004. q. Deutsche Gesellschaft fuer Hygiene und Mikrobiologie, c/o Institut fuer Hygiene und Mikrobiologie, Universitaet Wuerzburg, Josef-Schneider-Str 2, Wuerzburg, 97080, Germany.

121 540 DEU ISSN 1433-5158 CODEN: HYLEFD
HYLE; international journal for philosophy of chemistry. 1995-2006. a. Hyle Publications, Morgenstr 2, Karlsruhe, 76137, Germany.

616.132005 GBR ISSN 1754-8004
HYPERTENSION CLINIC. 2007 (Jul.)-2007 (Dec.). m. Stanford Publishing Ltd., 24 Chapel Rd, Stanford in the Vale, Faringdon, SN7 8LE, United Kingdom.

300 ITA ISSN 0393-9367
HYRIA; cultura e societa della nuova Europa. 1972-ceased. q. Hyria, Via Tansillo 4, Nola, NA 80035, Italy.

933 ISR
I A A REPORTS. 1996-1983. irreg. Israel Antiquities Authority, P O Box 586, Jerusalem, 91004, Israel.

330.9 JPN
I B J MONTHLY REPORT; economic & industrial trends in Japan. 1969-2000. m. Industrial Bank of Japan, 3-3, Marunouchi 1-chome, Chiyoda-ku, Tokyo, 100-8210, Japan.

621.381 001.6 USA ISSN 0018-8646 CODEN: IBMJAE
I B M JOURNAL OF RESEARCH AND DEVELOPMENT (PRINT). 1957-2008. bi-m. I B M Corp., 1133 Westchester Ave, White Plains, NY 10604.

629.8 NLD ISSN 0169-4693
I B M NIEUWS. (International Business Machines) 1964-1995. 4/yr. I B M Nederland N.V., Johan Huizingalaan 765, PO Box 9999, Amsterdam, 1000 AG, Netherlands.

003 USA ISSN 0018-8670 CODEN: IBMSA7
I B M SYSTEMS JOURNAL (PRINT). (International Business Machines) 1962-2008. q. I B M Corp., 1101 Kitchawan Rd, Yorktown Heights, NY 10598-0218.

658 USA ISSN 1058-5036
I C 2 MANAGEMENT AND MANAGEMENT SCIENCE SERIES. 1991-19??. irreg. Greenwood Publishing Group Inc., 88 Post Rd W, PO Box 5007, Westport, CT 06881.

332.1 GBR ISSN 1355-8447
I C B NEWSLETTER. (International Correspondent Banker) 1988-1996. m. Euromoney Institutional Investor Plc., Nestor House, Playhouse Yard, London, EC4V 5EX, United Kingdom.

621.381 ESP ISSN 1136-2065
I C E REVISTA DE INSTRUMENTACION, COMPONENTES Y EQUIPOS ELECTRONICOS. 1998-2005. 11/yr. Extra Editorial S.L., C/ Francisco Silvela, 77- Bis 4o, Madrid, 28028, Spain.

004 GBR ISSN 1364-310X CODEN: ISJOF2
I C L SYSTEMS JOURNAL. 1978-2001. s-a. International Computers Ltd., Lovelace Rd, Bracknell, Berks RG12 4SN, United Kingdom.

300 ITA ISSN 0250-7641
I D O C INTERNAZIONALE. 1970-ceased. q. International Documentation and Communication Center, Via di Santa Maria dell'Anima 30, Rome, 00186, Italy.

006.6 USA
I E E E JOURNAL OF TECHNOLOGY COMPUTER AIDED DESIGN. (Institute of Electrical and Electronics Engineers) 1996-2001. irreg. I E E E, 3 Park Ave, 17th Fl, New York, NY 10016-5997.

621.3 USA
I E E E POWER ENGINEERING SOCIETY. SUMMER MEETING. PREPRINTS. (Institute of Electrical and Electronics Engineers) 19??-2002. a. I E E E, 3 Park Ave, 17th Fl, New York, NY 10016-5997.

621.3 USA ISSN 0073-9154
I E E E POWER ENGINEERING SOCIETY. WINTER MEETING. PREPRINTS. (Institute of Electrical and Electronics Engineers) 19??-2002. a. I E E E, 3 Park Ave, 17th Fl, New York, NY 10016-5997.

384.33 USA ISSN 1559-9272
I E E E WORKSHOP ON I P OPERATIONS AND MANAGEMENT/ INSTITUTE OF ELECTRICAL AND ELECTRONICS ENGINEERS WORKSHOP ON INTERNET PROTOCOL OPERATIONS AND MANAGEMENT. 200?-2004. a. I E E E, 445 Hoes Ln, Piscataway, NJ 08854-1331.

628.53 690 USA ISSN 1094-2769
I E Q STRATEGIES; a guide to the practical control of indoor air problems. (Indoor Environmental Quality) 1988-200?. m. Aspen Law & Business, 1185 Ave of the Americas, 37th Fl, New York, NY 10036.

539 DEU ISSN 0340-0743
I F F BULLETIN. (Institut fuer Festkoerperforschung) 1972-1998. s-a. Institut fuer Festkoerperforschung, Kernforschungsanlage Juelich, Forschungszentrum Juelich GmbH, Juelich, 52425, Germany.

344.046 ITA ISSN 1022-3878
I J O NEWSLETTER. 1988-ceased. q. International Juridical Organization for Environment and Development, Via Barberini, 3, Rome, RM 00187, Italy.

026 GBR ISSN 0965-3554
I N T A M E L METRO; giving the global view. 1992-2002. s-a. International Association of Metropolitan City Libraries, 36 Highbury, Jesmond, Newcastle upon Tyne, NE2 3EA, United Kingdom.

658 USA ISSN 1538-4934
I O M A'S REPORT ON CUSTOMER RELATIONSHIP MANAGEMENT. (Institute of Management & Administration) 1997-200?. m. Institute of Management & Administration, Inc.(I O M A), One Washington Park, Ste 1300, Newark, NJ 07102.

614.8 658 USA
I O M A'S SAFETY DIRECTOR'S REPORT. (Institute of Management & Administration) 1999-2004. m. Institute of Management & Administration, Inc.(I O M A), One Washington Park, Ste 1300, Newark, NJ 07102.

053.1 DEU
I Q STYLE. 1998-2008 (Mar.). m. I Q Verlagsgesellschaft mbH, Schlesische Str 29-30, Berlin, 10997, Germany.

371.025 371.9 GBR ISSN 1749-5458
I S B I SCHOOLS. (Independent Schools of the British Isles) 1987-2007. s-a. Which School Ltd., Tilshead House, Tilshead, Salisbury, Wilts SP3 4RX, United Kingdom.

020 DEU ISSN 1015-9991
I S B N NEWSLETTER. (International Standard Book Number) 1990-2006. irreg. International I S B N Agency, Staatsbibliothek zu Berlin, Preussischer Kulturbesitz, Potsdamer Str 33, Berlin, 10772, Germany.

025.3 DEU ISSN 0342-4634
I S B N REVIEW. (International Standard Book Number) 1977-1998. a. International I S B N Agency, Staatsbibliothek zu Berlin, Preussischer Kulturbesitz, Potsdamer Str 33, Berlin, 10772, Germany.

297 NLD ISSN 1871-4374
I S I M REVIEW. (International Institute for the Study of Islam in the Modern World) 1998-2008. s-a. International Institute for the Study of Islam in the Modern World, PO Box 11089, Leiden, 2301 EB, Netherlands.

016.05 FRA ISSN 1018-4783 CODEN: ILSAEN
I S S N COMPACT; CD-ROM edition of the ISSN Register. (International Standard Serial Number) 1992-2006. q. International Centre for the Registration of Serials, I S S N International Centre, 20 rue Bachaumont, Paris, 75002, France.

011 FRA ISSN 1021-500X
I S S N REGISTER (TAPE)/REGISTRE DE L'I S S N (EDITION SUR BANDE MAGNETIQUE). (International Standard Serial Number) 1974-2004. q. International Centre for the Registration of Serials, I S S N International Centre, 20 rue Bachaumont, Paris, 75002, France.

628.4 DNK ISSN 0906-1436
I S W A TIMES. 1990-2001. q. International Solid Waste Association, Overgaden Oven Vandet 48 E, Copenhagen K, 1415, Denmark.

004.6 DNK ISSN 1600-3616
I T BRANCHEN. (Information Technology) 1999-2002. 18/yr. I D G Danmark A/S, Carl Jacobsens Vej 25, Valby, 2500, Denmark.

338 NZL
I T CONTRACTORS HANDBOOK. (Information Technology) 2000-2001. a. I D G Communications Ltd., Wellesley St, PO Box 6813, Auckland, 1036, New Zealand.

338.47004 DEU
I T DIALOG. (Information Technology) 2000-2000. q. BurdaYukom Publishing GmbH, Konrad-Zuse-Platz 11, Munich, 81829, Germany.

362.11068 USA ISSN 1520-8591
I T HEALTH CARE STRATEGIST. 1999-2002. m. Aspen Publishers, Inc., 111 Eighth Ave., 7th Fl, New York, NY 10011.

681.3 CZE ISSN 1212-6780
I T - NET. (Information Technology) 1999-2003. m. Burda Praha, spol. s r.o., Premyslovska 2845/43, Luxembourg Plaza, Prague 3, 13000, Czech Republic.

004.16 DNK
I T PARTNER DENMARK. (Information Technology) ceased. 18/yr. I D G Danmark A/S, Carl Jacobsens Vej 25, Valby, 2500, Denmark.

892.76 EGY
IBDA'/INNOVATION. 1983-ceased. irreg. Magallat Ibda', 27 Sharia Abd al-Khaliq Tharwat, P O Box 626, Cairo, Egypt.

946 300 GBR ISSN 0307-3262
IBERIAN STUDIES. 1972-1991. s-a. University of Keele, School of Earth Sciences & Geography, University Of Keele, Keele, Newcastle, Staffs ST5 5BG, United Kingdom.

616.1 ESP ISSN 1136-5943
IBEROAMERICAN JOURNAL OF HYPERTENSION. 1993-ceased. 9/yr. Sociedad Espanola de Hipertension - Liga Espanola para la Lucha contra la Hipertension Arterial (S E H - L E L H A), Paseo de la Castellana 201, 6o, Madrid, 28046, Spain.

808.838 AUS ISSN 1326-1452
IBN QIRTAIBA. 1993-2003. irreg. Terminus Network Services, 208/112 Mounts Bay Road, West Perth, W.A. 6005, Australia.

704.948 DNK ISSN 0106-1348
ICONOGRAPHISK POST; nordisk tidsskrift for ikonografi - Nordic iconographic review. 1970-2001. q. Koebenhavns Universitet, Institut for Kirkehistorie. Center for Kunst og Kristendom, Koebmagergade 44-46, PO Box 2164, Copenhagen K, 1150, Denmark.

755 NLD ISSN 0169-9822
ICONOGRAPHY OF RELIGIONS. SECTION 17, GREECE AND ROME. 1976-1988. irreg. Brill, PO Box 9000, Leiden, 2300 PA, Netherlands.

755 NLD ISSN 0169-8435
ICONOGRAPHY OF RELIGIONS. SECTION 20, MANICHAEISM. 1982-1982 (vol.1). irreg. Brill, PO Box 9000, Leiden, 2300 PA, Netherlands.

755 NLD ISSN 0169-9776
ICONOGRAPHY OF RELIGIONS. SECTION 21, MANDAEISM. 1978-1978 (vol.1). irreg. Brill, PO Box 9000, Leiden, 2300 PA, Netherlands.

755 NLD ISSN 0169-8087
ICONOGRAPHY OF RELIGIONS. SECTION 5, AUSTRALIAN ABORIGINAL RELIGION. 1974-1974 (vol.4). irreg. Brill, PO Box 9000, Leiden, 2300 PA, Netherlands.

320 DNK ISSN 0107-1149
IDE POLITIK. 1971-2007. 40/yr. Kristeligt Folkeparti, Bernhard Bangs Alle 23, Frederiksberg, 2000, Denmark.

910 ITA ISSN 1826-9265
IDEA VIAGGI. 2005-200?. bi-m. Edizioni Trentini & C, Via Pier Luigi Nervi 1/B, Argenta, FE 44011, Italy.

746.4 FRA ISSN 1628-0695
IDEAL BRODERIE. 2001-2008. q. Editions de la Rose, 37 Rue de Lauterbourg, Schiltigheim, 67300, France.

371.3 USA ISSN 1042-5330
IDEAS PLUS. 1984-2002. irreg. National Council of Teachers of English, 1111 W Kenyon Rd, Urbana, IL 61801.

747 ITA ISSN 1591-6928
IDEE PER LA CASA. 1990-200?. m. Edigamma Publishing, Via Sambuca Pistoiese 70A, Rome, 00138, Italy.

659.1 DEU ISSN 0176-859X
IDEEN ARCHIV. 1979-ceased. m. Bergmoser und Hoeller Verlag GmbH, Karl-Friedrich-Str 76, Aachen, 52072, Germany.

745.582 FRA ISSN 1773-9837
IDEES CREATIONS BIJOUX ET PERLES. 2005-2007. bi-m. Euro Services Internet, 60 rue Vitruve, Paris, 75020, France.

363.7 FRA ISSN 1953-6720
IDEO MAG; le premier magazine de l'eco-citoyen. 2007-2008. s-a. Pressimedia, 63 Rue Hoche, Montreuil, 93100, France.

623 CZE ISSN 1211-8702
IDET NEWS. 1997-2005. biennial. Military System Line s.r.o., PO Box 11, Kounice, 289 15, Czech Republic.

910.4 FRA ISSN 1012-8107
ILES; le magazine de toutes les iles. 1988-2003. 6/yr. Chloe Communications, 77 rue du Cardinal Lemoine, Paris, 75005, France.

347.06 USA
ILLINOIS EVIDENTIARY FOUNDATIONS. 1991-1997 (2nd ed.). w/ current supplement) plus irreg. updates. Michie Company, 701 E Water St, Charlottesville, VA 22902.

020 USA ISSN 0019-2104
ILLINOIS LIBRARIES. 1919-2001. q. Office of the Secretary of State, Illinois State Library, 300 S Second St, Springfield, IL 62701.

340 USA
ILLINOIS LIMITATIONS MANUAL. 1989-199?. plus a. updates. LexisNexis, PO Box 7587, Charlottesville, VA 22906.

791.43 GBR ISSN 0950-2114 CODEN: IMATEV
IMAGE TECHNOLOGY; technology of motion picture film, sound, television, audio, visual. 1936-200?. 10/yr. B K S T S - The Moving Image Society, Pinewood Studios, Pinewood Rd, Iver Heath, Buckinghamshire SL0 0NH, United Kingdom.

668.54 ITA
IMAGINE. 1975-ceased. bi-w. Sfera Editore SpA, Via Angelo Rizzoli 2, Milan, MI 20132, Italy.

791.068 ITA ISSN 1593-9286
IMMAGINIFICO; trimestrale di spettacolo popolare - culture materiali - mestieri - nomadismi. 1992-2002. q. Pretini & C. s.r.l. - Trapezio Libri, Morena Torre 2, Reana del Rojale, UD, Italy.

207.2 ISR ISSN 0302-8127
IMMANUEL; religious thought and research in Israel. 1972-1995. s-a. Ecumenical Theological Research Fraternity in Israel, P O Box 249, Jerusalem, 91002, Israel.

333.5 DEU
IMMOBILIEN & AMBIENTE. 2002-2003. m. Der Heisse Draht Verlag GmbH und Co., Drostestr 14-16, Hannover, 30161, Germany.

333.33 FRA ISSN 1961-6988
IMMOBILIER MAGAZINE (PARIS, 2008). 2008-2008. m. Les Editions Neressis, 40 Rue du Docteur-Roux, Paris, 75015, France.

576 GBR ISSN 0953-4954
IMMUNOLOGY. SUPPLEMENT. 1988-1989. irreg. Wiley-Blackwell Publishing Ltd., 9600 Garsington Rd, Oxford, OX4 2DQ, United Kingdom.

135 USA
IMPACT (ATLANTA); turning your dreams into reality. 2000-200?. m. Impact, Inc., 1100 Spring St, Ste 640, Atlanta, GA 30309.

371.3 ITA ISSN 1126-0270
IMPARO SUBITO. 1997-200?. m. Gruppo Editoriale Futura, Via XXV Aprile 39, Bresso, MI 20091, Italy.

615.47 FRA ISSN 1158-1336
IMPLANTODONTIE. 1991-2005. 4/yr. Elsevier Masson

617.6 ITA ISSN 1827-3742
IMPLANTOLOGIA ORALE. 1997-ceased. bi-m. Tecniche Nuove SpA, Via Eritrea 21, Milan, MI 201, Italy.

338 ITA ISSN 1125-2529
L'IMPRENDITORE. 1948-ceased. m. Confederazione Generale dell'Industria Italiana (Confindustria), Centro Studi, Viale dell'Astronomia 30, Rome, 00144, Italy.

658.2 BRD ISSN 0344-4546
IMPULS (COLOGNE); Zeitung fuer Sicherheit im Betrieb. 1968-1989. m. Gothaer Versicherungsbank VVaG, Arnoldiplatz 1, Cologne, 50969, Germany.

658 GBR ISSN 1363-1063
IN BRIEF. 1981-2004. q. Institute for Employment Studies, Mantell Bldg, University of Sussex Campus, Brighton, BN1 9RF, United Kingdom.

338.642 USA ISSN 0190-2458 CODEN: INBSD5
IN BUSINESS (EMMAUS); the magazine for environmental entrepreneuring. 1979-2007. bi-m. J G Press, Inc., 419 State Ave, Emmaus, PA 18049.

340 GBR ISSN 0965-3597
IN COMPETITION. 1993-1997. m. Sweet & Maxwell Ltd., 100 Avenue Rd, London, NW3 3PF, United Kingdom.

641.5 ITA ISSN 1824-0232
IN CUCINA; pasta, amore e fantasia. 2004-200?. m. Ulysse Network, Viale Bianca Maria 19, Milan, Italy.

331.255 USA
IN FOCUS (BROOKFIELD). 2001-2004. q. International Foundation of Employee Benefit Plans, 18700 W Bluemound Rd, Brookfield, WI 53008-0069.

850 ITA ISSN 1120-3382
IN OLTRE; letterature e materiali. 1988-ceased. s-a. Schena Editore, Viale Stazione 177, Fasano, BR 72015, Italy.

914.504 914.503 ITA
IN SARDEGNA; periodico di turismo ambiente e cultura. 1992-1995. a. Edizioni Sole, Via Capitanata, 24, Cagliari, CA 09121, Italy.

780 FRA ISSN 1286-2312
IN SIT'. 1997-2005. q. Editions Henry Lemoine, 41 Rue Bayen, Paris, 75017, France.

621.38 USA ISSN 0888-9406
IN-STAT ELECTRONICS REPORT. 198?-2006. m. Reed Business Information, 6909 E. Greenway Pkwy, Ste. 250, Scottsdale, AZ 85254.

333.33 GBR ISSN 0966-6680
IN THE STICKS; the national property magazine for the countrylover. 1989-2009. q. In the Sticks, Market House, Market Place, Alston, Cumbria CA9 3HS, United Kingdom.

384.55 GBR
IN THE VILLAGE. 1977; N.S. 1994-ceased. q. Six of One - Prisoner Appreciation Society, Six Of One, PO Box 66, Ipswich, IP2 9TZ, United Kingdom.

615 570 USA ISSN 1539-4921
IN VIVO EUROPE RX. 2002-200?. m. Windhover Information, Inc., 10 Hoyt St, Norwalk, CT 06851.

051 USA ISSN 8756-6338
INCHES. 1985-2009. m. Mavety Media Group, 225 Broadway, Ste 2801, New York, NY 10007-3079.

327 ITA ISSN 0019-3496
L'INCONTRO; pacifist periodical independent. 1949-ceased. m. L' Incontro, Via Consolata, 11, Turin, TO 10122, Italy.

300 ESP ISSN 1695-730X
INDAGA; revista internacional de ciencias sociales y humanas. 2003-2006. a. Foro de Investigaciones Sociales, San Martin 75, 7a izq., Santa Cruz de Tenerife, Islas Canarias 38001, Spain.

Cessations

016 USA ISSN 1041-1321
INDEX AND ABSTRACT DIRECTORY; an international guide to services and serials coverage. 1989-1993. biennial. EBSCO Publishing, 10 Estes St, Ipswich, MA 01938.

016 USA ISSN 0090-9130
INDEX OF AMERICAN PERIODICAL VERSE. 1971-2006. a. Scarecrow Press, Inc., 4501 Forbes Blvd, Ste 200, Lanham, MD 20706.

344.0424 USA
INDEX TO CHEMICAL REGULATIONS. 1980 (Jan.)-2005. m. The Bureau of National Affairs, Inc., 1801 S Bell St, Arlington, VA 22202.

016.327 USA ISSN 0193-905X
INDEX TO INTERNATIONAL PUBLIC OPINION. 1980-200?. a. Greenwood Publishing Group Inc., 88 Post Rd W, PO Box 5007, Westport, CT 06881.

340 DEU
INDEX TO LEGAL CITATIONS AND ABBREVIATIONS. 1981-1999. irreg. K.G. Saur Verlag, Mies-van-der-Rohe-Str 1, Munich, 80807, Germany.

010 USA ISSN 0884-8440
INDEX TO SCIENTIFIC BOOK CONTENTS. 1985-2006. q. (plus a. cumulation). Thomson Reuters, Scientific, 1500 Spring Garden, 4th Fl, Philadelphia, PA 19130.

320 AUS ISSN 1031-2331
INDIAN OCEAN REVIEW. 1980-2000. q. Indian Ocean Centre, Curtin University of Technology, PO Box U 1987, Perth, W.A. 6845, Australia.

181.4 NLD ISSN 0924-8986
INDIAN THOUGHT. 1990-1993 (vol.5). irreg. Brill, PO Box 9000, Leiden, 2300 PA, Netherlands.

030 317.72 USA ISSN 0886-330X
INDIANA FACTBOOK. 1985-1999. irreg. Indiana University Press, 601 N Morton St, Bloomington, IN 47404.

340.56 346.05 USA
INDIANA TRIAL PROCEDURE CIVIL LITIGATION MANUAL. 1998-199?. a. Anderson Publishing Co., 9443 Springboro Pike, Miamisburg, OH 45342.

333.33 FRA ISSN 1622-1303
INDICATEUR BERTRAND. MEDITERRANEE MIDI-PYRENEES. 1976-2003. m. Editions Indicateur Bertrand, 43 bd. Barbes, Paris, 75018, France.

333.33 FRA ISSN 0980-8744
INDICATEUR BERTRAND. RHONE-ALPES. 1986-2003. m. Editions Indicateur Bertrand, 43 bd. Barbes, Paris, 75018, France.

300 ZAF
INDICATOR S A REPORT. 1983-2003. s-a. Indicator Project S A, Centre for Social and Development Studies, Private Bag X10, Dalbridge, 4014, South Africa.

300 ZAF ISSN 0259-188X
INDICATOR SOUTH AFRICA; the barometer of social trends. 1983-2003. q. Indicator Project S A, Centre for Social and Development Studies, Private Bag X10, Dalbridge, 4014, South Africa.

001.422 190 DNK ISSN 1901-628X
INDIKATORER FOR DANSK FORSKNING OG INNOVATION. 2005-2005 (same year). irreg. Dansk Center for Forskningsanalyse, Aarhus Universitet, Finlandsgade 4, Aarhus N, 8200, Denmark.

331 USA ISSN 1085-0058
INDIVIDUAL EMPLOYMENT RIGHTS. 1986-2003. irreg. The Bureau of National Affairs, Inc., 1801 S Bell St, Arlington, VA 22202.

665.5 ITA ISSN 1126-2923
INDUSTRIA DEL PETROLIO E BILANCIO ENERGETICO. 1958-ceased. a. Ministero dello Sviluppo Economico, Via Veneto 33, Rome, 00187, Italy.

658.8 ITA ISSN 1591-6243
INDUSTRIA & DISTRIBUZIONE; rivista di economia e gestione dei rapporti di canale. 1999-2003. q. Franco Angeli Edizioni, Viale Monza 106, Milan, 20127, Italy.

677.21 ITA ISSN 1825-7127
INDUSTRIA TESSILE COTONIERA, LINIERA E DELLA NOBILITAZIONE. 1965-2004. 6/yr. Associazione Tessile Italiana, Viale Sarca 223, Milan, 20126, Italy.

330.9 338.91 ITA ISSN 1460-6682
INDUSTRIAL DEVELOPMENT POLICY DISCUSSION PAPER. 1997-ceased. irreg. Universita degli Studi di Ferrara, Facolta di Economia, Via del Gregorio 13, Ferrara, 44100, Italy.

331 AUS ISSN 1324-3276
INDUSTRIAL RELATIONS AND MANAGEMENT LETTER. 1979-2005. m. Ian Huntley Pty. Ltd., PO Box 99, Cremorne, NSW 2090, Australia.

363.7 ITA ISSN 1120-172X
LE INDUSTRIE ITALIANE PER LA PROTEZIONE CIVILE E ECOLOGIA. ANNUARIO. 1988-ceased. a. Publi & Consult SpA, Via Tagliamento, 29, Rome, RM 00198, Italy.

363.7 FRA ISSN 0378-9993 CODEN: IENVDB
INDUSTRY AND ENVIRONMENT. 1978-2004. q. United Nations Environment Programme, Division of Technology, Industry and Economics, Tour Mirabeau, 39-43 quai Andre Citroen, Paris, Cedex 15 75739, France.

331.125 USA ISSN 0148-9208
INDUSTRY WAGE SURVEYS. CORRUGATED AND SOLID FIBER BOXES. 1976-1987. irreg. U.S. Department of Labor, Bureau of Labor Statistics, Postal Square Bldg., 2 Massachusetts Ave, NE, Washington, DC 20212-0001.

004.678 AUS
INFO. 1985-2001. q. University of Tasmania, Information Services Division, GPO Box 252-69, Hobart, TAS 7109, Australia.

616.8 CAN ISSN 0715-3120
INFO A L S. (Amyotrophic Lateral Sclerosis) 1980-199?. a. Amyotrophic Lateral Sclerosis Society of Canada, 220 6 Adelaide St, East, Toronto, ON M5C 1H6, Canada.

355 FRA ISSN 0299-8459
INFO D G A. (Delegation Generale pour l'Armement) suspended 1986. m. (10/yr.). Etablissement de Communication et de Production Audiovisuelle de la Defense - E C P A D, 2 - 8 Route du Fort d'Ivry, Ivry-sur-Seine Cedex, 94205, France.

333.79 GBR ISSN 1741-2188
INFO POINT. 1988-2004. q. C A D D E T, ETSU, 168 Harwell, Didcot, Oxon OX11 0QJ, United Kingdom.

360 AUS ISSN 0725-5489
INFOCAB. 1979-ceased. m. Community Information Victoria, Level 2, 343 Lt Collins St, Ste 209, Melbourne, VIC 3000, Australia.

362.8 AUS ISSN 0815-6905
INFOCUS NEWS MAGAZINE. 1975-2000. q. Ethnic Communities' Council of N.S.W., 221 Cope St, Waterloo Dc, NSW 2017, Australia.

621.388 DEU
INFODIGITAL. 2005-2007 (Nov.). m. Infosat Verlag und Werbe GmbH, Julius-Saxler-Str 3, Daun, 54550, Germany.

028.5 SVN ISSN 1318-3877
INFORMACIJE Z P M S. (Zveza Prijateljev Mladine Slovenije) 1959-200?. bi-m. Zveza Prijateljev Mladine Slovenije, Miklosiceva 16, Ljubljana, 61000, Slovenia.

387.5 ITA
INFORMARE. 1984-ceased. 10/yr. Media Angle S.r.l., Via Giovanni Pacini, 36, Milan, MI 20131, Italy.

944 FRA ISSN 1764-6510
L'INFORMATEUR ECONOMIQUE DU CHOLETAIS. 1956-2007. a. Chambre de Commerce et Industrie (Cholet), 34 rue Nationale, BP 2116, Cholet, Cedex 49321, France.

001.6 ITA ISSN 0393-0572
INFORMATICA 70; la rivista italiana dell'information & communication technology. 1972-ceased. bi-m. Editrice il Crogiolo S.r.l., Piazza Sant' Agostino 22, Milan, MI 20123, Italy.

610.285 AUS ISSN 1323-4382
INFORMATICS IN HEATHCARE AUSTRALIA. 1991-2000. 2/yr. Health Informatics Society of Australia (H I S A) Ltd., 413 Lygon St, Brunswick East, VIC 3057, Australia.

004 DEU ISSN 0934-4721
INFORMATIK BETRIFFT UNS. 1988-2000. q. Bergmoser und Hoeller Verlag GmbH, Karl-Friedrich-Str 76, Aachen, 52072, Germany.

363.728 USA ISSN 1538-6651
INFORMATION PLUS REFERENCE SERIES. GARBAGE AND OTHER POLLUTION. 1994-2004. biennial. Gale, 27500 Drake Rd, Farmington Hills, MI 48331.

150 362.2 616.89 USA ISSN 1548-8039
INFORMATION PLUS REFERENCE SERIES. MENTAL HEALTH. 2004-200?. biennial. Gale, 27500 Drake Rd, Farmington Hills, MI 48331.

301 USA ISSN 1538-6627
INFORMATION PLUS REFERENCE SERIES. PROFILE OF THE NATION; an American portrait. 1996-2004. biennial. Gale, 27500 Drake Rd, Farmington Hills, MI 48331.

306.85 USA ISSN 1534-164X
INFORMATION PLUS REFERENCE SERIES. THE AMERICAN FAMILY; reflecting a changing nation. 1999-2005. biennial. Gale, 27500 Drake Rd, Farmington Hills, MI 48331.

388 USA ISSN 1536-5247
INFORMATION PLUS REFERENCE SERIES. TRANSPORTATION; America's lifeline. 1981-2003. biennial. Gale, 27500 Drake Rd, Farmington Hills, MI 48331.

364.36 303.60835 USA ISSN 1548-8020
INFORMATION PLUS REFERENCE SERIES. YOUTH VIOLENCE, CRIME, AND GANGS; children at risk. 2004-200?. biennial. Gale, 27500 Drake Rd, Farmington Hills, MI 48331.

651.8 ISR ISSN 0073-7879
INFORMATION PROCESSING ASSOCIATION OF ISRAEL. NATIONAL CONFERENCE ON DATA PROCESSING. PROCEEDINGS. 1964-1970 (#2). a. Information Processing Association of Israel, Kfar Hamakabia, Ramat Gan, 52109, Israel.

629.8 016 DEU ISSN 0179-0811
INFORMATIONSDIENST F I Z TECHNIK. REGELUNGSTECHNIK. 1970-2002. m. Fachinformationszentrum Technik e.V., Hanauer Landstr 151-153, Frankfurt Am Main, 60314, Germany.

025.04 DNK ISSN 1601-9172
INFORMATIONSPORTALEN. 1982-2002. 10/yr. I N F O S C A N, Statens Information, Kigkurren 10, Copenhagen, 2300, Denmark.

910.09 340 ITA ISSN 0394-8900
INFORMATORE GIURIDICO DELL'OPERATORE TURISTICO. 1988-ceased. 3/yr. Informatore Giuridico dell'Operatore Turistico, Via Emilia Ovest, 21 A, Rubiera, RE 42048, Italy.

340 ITA ISSN 0390-9379
L'INFORMATORE LEGISLATIVO. 1966-ceased. m. Presidenza del Consiglio dei Ministri, Dipartimento per l'Informazione e l'Editoria, Via Po 14, Rome, 00198, Italy.

658.3 336 ITA
INFORMATORE PIROLA. 1964-ceased. w. (48/yr.). Il Sole 24 Ore Business Media, Via Monterosa 91, Milan, 20149, Italy.

687 ITA
INFORMATORE TESSILE. 1978-ceased. 9/yr. Beta Editoriale s.a.s., Via Duomo 305, Naples, NA 80133, Italy.

016.36534 RUS
INFORMATSIONNYI BYULLETEN'. INOSTRANNAYA PECHAT' O TEKHNICHESKOM OSNASHCHENII POLITSII ZARUBEZHNYKH GOSUDARSTV. 1996-2008 (Dec.). m. Vserossiiskii Institut Nauchnoi i Tekhnicheskoi Informatsii (VINITI), Ul Usievicha 20, Moscow, 125190, Russian Federation.

537.5 ITA ISSN 0390-2455
INFORMAZIONE ELETTRONICA. 1973-ceased. m. Editrice Il Rostro, Via B Buozzi 5, Segrate, MI 20090, Italy.

338 ITA ISSN 0020-0786
INFORMAZIONE INDUSTRIALE. 1920-ceased. s-m. Unione Industriale Torino, Via Manfredo Fanti 17, Turin, TO 10128, Italy.

330 ITA ISSN 0020-0794
INFORMAZIONE MEDITERRANEA. 1958-ceased. w. Carlo de Leva Ed. & Pub., Via Giovanni Campolo, 49, Palermo, PA 90145, Italy.

384.5 ITA ISSN 0300-3973
INFORMAZIONE RADIO TV; studi documenti e notizie. 1970-ceased. s-a. R A I - Radiotelevisione Italiana, Viale Giuseppe Mazzini 14, Rome, 00195, Italy.

658 ITA ISSN 1128-1928
INFORMAZIONI AZIENDALI E PROFESSIONALI. QUADERNI. 1976-2004. irreg. De Lillo Editore s.r.l., Via Mecenate 76/3, Milan, 20138, Italy.

711.4 ITA
INFORMAZIONI S U N I A. (Sindacato Unitario Nazionale Inquilini Assegnatari) 1978-ceased. q. Sindacato Unitario Nazionale Inquilini ed Assegnatari, Via Monzermone, 14, Reggio Emilia, RE 42100, Italy.

658 USA ISSN 1096-4126
THE INFORMED OUTLOOK. 1996-2004. m. American Society for Quality, 600 North Plankinton Ave, P O Box 3005, Milwaukee, WI 53203.

003 NZL ISSN 1173-3764
INFOSYS; the electronic newsletter for information systems. 1994-ceased. w. Massey University, Information Systems Department, Albany, New Zealand.

615.9 CAN ISSN 1208-669X
INFOTOX. 1995-2001. s-a. Canadian Network of Toxicology Centres, 2nd Fl, Bovey Bldg, Gordon St, University of Guelph, Guelph, ON N1G 2W1, Canada.

004 NLD ISSN 1387-1005
INFOWORLD NETHERLANDS (PRINT EDITION). 1996-2002. bi-w. I D G Communications Nederland BV, Postbus 5446, Haarlem, 2000 GK, Netherlands.

686.2 USA ISSN 1545-813X CODEN: AMIKAK
INK MAKER; for manufacturers of printing inks and related graphic arts specialty colors. 1922-2007. m. (10/yr.). Cygnus Business Media, Inc., 3 Huntington Quadrangle, Ste 301 N, Melville, NY 11747.

378 GBR
INKING. 1929-199?. 3/yr. University of Sheffield, Union of Students, Media Hub, Level 4, Sheffield, S10 2TG, United Kingdom.

790.1 DEU ISSN 1612-1627
INLINE MAGAZIN. 2001-2005. bi-m. b&d Media Network GmbH, Osterfeldstr 12-14, Hamburg, 22529, Germany.

001.3 KOR ISSN 1229-6201
INMUN GWAHAG/JOURNAL OF HUMANITIES. 1957-2004. 2/yr. Yonsei University Press, Seodaemoon-ku, 134 Sinchon Dong, Seoul, 120749, Korea, S.

600 DEU
INNOVATIONSFOERDERUNG. 1985-2003. a. Bundesministerium fuer Bildung und Forschung, Hannoversche Str 28-30, Berlin, 10115, Germany.

016.6151 NZL ISSN 1173-8324
INPHARMA WEEKLY; rapid alerts to news on drugs and drug therapy. 1975-2008 (Dec.). 50/yr. Adis International Ltd., 41 Centorian Dr, Mairangi Bay, Private Bag 65901, Auckland, 1311, New Zealand.

299.93 NZL ISSN 1177-2131
INPUT (TAURANGA). ceased 2007 (Feb.). m. New Page Ltd., PO Box 6152, Brookfield, Tauranga, New Zealand.

794.8 USA ISSN 1938-4459
INQUEST GAMER. 1995-2007. m. Wizard Entertainment, 151 Wells Ave, Congers, NY 10920.

153 USA ISSN 1093-1082
INQUIRY (UPPER MONTCLAIR); critical thinking across the disciplines. 1988-2005. q. Philosophy Documentation Center, PO Box 7147, Charlottesville, VA 22906.

059 NLD ISSN 0167-3696
INS AND OUTS; a magazine of awareness. 1978-1980. irreg. Ins & Outs Press, Box 3759, Amsterdam, Netherlands.

610 USA
INSIDE DISEASE MANAGEMENT. 2005-200?. 24/yr. Atlantic Information Services, Inc., 1100 17th St, NW, Ste 300, Washington, DC 20036.

344.01 USA ISSN 1088-9922
INSIDE EMPLOYEE RIGHTS LITIGATION. 1996-2000. m. Aspen Law & Business, 1185 Ave of the Americas, 37th Fl, New York, NY 10036.

327 AUS ISSN 0814-1185
INSIDE INDONESIA (PRINT). 1983-2007. q. Indonesia Resources & Information Programme, 124 Napier St, Fitzroy Vic, Melbourne, VIC 3065, Australia.

790.1 658 USA
INSIDE SPORTING GOODS. 19??-ceased. 5/w. SportsOneSource Group, PO Box 480156, Charlotte, NC 28269.

917.5 973.7 USA ISSN 1544-2640
INSIDERS' GUIDE TO CIVIL WAR SITES IN THE SOUTHERN STATES. 2000-2006. triennial. The Globe Pequot Press, Inc., 246 Goose Ln, PO Box 480, Guilford, CT 06437.

917.9 910.2 USA ISSN 1542-1635
INSIDERS' GUIDE TO IDAHO PANHANDLE; including Spokane and Coeur d'Alene. 2001-suspended. biennial. The Globe Pequot Press, Inc., 246 Goose Ln, PO Box 480, Guilford, CT 06437.

917.6944 917.72 USA ISSN 1543-0219
THE INSIDERS' GUIDE TO LOUISVILLE AND SOUTHERN INDIANA. 1997-suspended. biennial. The Globe Pequot Press, Inc., 246 Goose Ln, PO Box 480, Guilford, CT 06437.

917.44 USA ISSN 1549-7291
INSIDERS' GUIDE TO THE BERKSHIRES. 2004-ceased. biennial (Every 2-3 yrs). The Globe Pequot Press, Inc., 246 Goose Ln, PO Box 480, Guilford, CT 06437.

796.72 USA ISSN 1547-8769
INSIDERS' GUIDE TO THE N A S C A R TRACKS. (National Association for Stock Car Auto Racing) 2004-2006. biennial (every 2-3/yrs.). The Globe Pequot Press, Inc., 246 Goose Ln, PO Box 480, Guilford, CT 06437.

952 GBR ISSN 0966-8071
INSIGHT JAPAN. 1992-2003. q. Insight Japan, 19 Hugh St, London, SW1V 1QJ, United Kingdom.

051 USA ISSN 1051-4880
INSIGHT ON THE NEWS. 1985-2004. bi-w. Washington Times Corporation, 3600 New York Ave, N E, Washington, DC 20002-1947.

347 NLD ISSN 1573-2096
INSOLVENTIERECHT. 2004-2004. biennial. Kluwer B.V., Postbus 23, Deventer, 7400 GA, Netherlands.

371.4 GBR ISSN 0263-9696
INSPECTION AND ADVICE. 1974-198?. s-a. National Association of Inspectors and Educational Advisors, New Inn, Nebo House, Devauden, Chepstow, Gwent NP6 6NW, United Kingdom.

747 NZL ISSN 1177-4096
INSPIRATIONS @ HOME. 2006-2007. q. Marketplace Press Ltd, Remuera, PO Box 28-372, Auckland, New Zealand.

617.96 FRA ISSN 0301-8113
INSTITUT D'ANESTHESIOLOGIE. ACTA. 1953-1970. q. Arnette, 1 rue Eugene et Armand Peugeot, Rueil-Malmaison, 92500, France.

331.8 DEU ISSN 0949-703X
INSTITUT DER DEUTSCHEN WIRTSCHAFT. GEWERKSCHAFTSREPORT. 1993-2000. 4/yr. Deutscher Instituts Verlag GmbH, Gustav-Heinemann-Ufer 84-88, Cologne, 50968, Germany.

320.5322 FRA ISSN 0222-7762
INSTITUT DES RECHERCHES MARXISTES. ISSUES. 1979-2001. 4/yr. Espaces Marx, 6 Av. Mathurin Moreau, Paris, Cedex 19 75167, France.

362.11 DDR ISSN 0323-4738
INSTITUT FUER TECHNOLOGIE DER GESUNDHEITSBAUTEN BERLIN. MITTEILUNGEN. 1965-19??. a. Institut fuer Technologie und Grundfondsoekonomie im Gesundheits- und Sozialwesen, Ackerstr 76, Berlin, 133, East Germany.

677 DEU ISSN 0515-0582
INSTITUT FUER TEXTILTECHNIK DER RHEINISCH-WESTFAELISCHEN TECHNISCHEN HOCHSCHULE AACHEN. MITTEILUNGEN. 1953-2000. a. Institut fuer Textiltechnik der Rheinisch-Westfaelischen Technischen Hochschule Aachen, Eilfschornsteinstr 18, Aachen, 52062, Germany.

336.2 GBR ISSN 1369-4685
INSTITUTE FOR FISCAL STUDIES. WORKING PAPERS (PRINT). 1979-2002. irreg. Institute for Fiscal Studies, 7 Ridgmount St, 3rd Fl, London, WC1E 7AE, United Kingdom.

657 AUS
INSTITUTE OF CHARTERED ACCOUNTANTS IN AUSTRALIA. ANNUAL REPORT AND ACCOUNTS. 19??-1986. a. The Institute of Chartered Accountants in Australia, GPO Box 3921, Sydney, NSW 2001, Australia.

628.5 USA ISSN 1069-367X
INSTITUTE OF INDUSTRIAL ENGINEERS. INTEGRATED SYSTEMS CONFERENCE. PROCEEDINGS. 1978-1990. s-a. Institute of Industrial Engineers, 3577 Pky Ln, Ste 200, Norcross, GA 30092.

510 GBR ISSN 0960-2526 CODEN: IMACFF
INSTITUTE OF MATHEMATICS AND ITS APPLICATIONS. CONFERENCE SERIES. N.S. 1984-2002. irreg. Oxford University Press, Great Clarendon St, Oxford, OX2 6DP, United Kingdom.

344.01 USA ISSN 1065-7835
INSTITUTE ON LABOR LAW DEVELOPMENTS. ANNUAL PROCEEDINGS. 1984-1998. a. Matthew Bender & Co., Inc., 1275 Broadway, Albany, NY 12204.

621 GBR ISSN 1357-9193 CODEN: ISEME4
INSTITUTION OF MECHANICAL ENGINEERS SEMINAR PUBLICATION. 1995-200?. irreg. John Wiley & Sons Ltd., 1-7 Oldlands Way, PO Box 808, Bognor Regis, West Sussex PO21 9FF, United Kingdom.

622 669 GBR ISSN 0262-527X
INSTITUTION OF MINING AND METALLURGY. OCCASIONAL PAPERS. 1982-1983. irreg. Institution of Mining and Metallurgy, Danum House, South Parade, Doncaster, DN1 2DY, United Kingdom.

621.3 660 NZL ISSN 0111-946X CODEN: TPESDJ
INSTITUTION OF PROFESSIONAL ENGINEERS NEW ZEALAND. ELECTRICAL, MECHANICAL AND CHEMICAL ENGINEERING SECTION. TRANSACTIONS. 1980-2000. a. Institution of Professional Engineers New Zealand, Electrical, Mechanical and Chemical Engineering Section, 101 Molesworth St, PO Box 12-241, Wellington, New Zealand.

620 NZL
INSTITUTION OF PROFESSIONAL ENGINEERS NEW ZEALAND. GENERAL ENGINEERING SECTION. TRANSACTIONS. 1988-2000. a. Institution of Professional Engineers New Zealand, General Engineering Section, 101 Molesworth St., P.O. Box 12-241, Wellington, New Zealand.

001.3 ESP ISSN 0584-6374
INSTITUTO DE ESTUDIOS MADRILENOS. ANALES. 1966-1997. irreg. Consejo Superior de Investigaciones Cientificas, Instituto de Estudios Madrilenos, Vitruvio, 8, Madrid, 28001, Spain.

570 ESP ISSN 0214-0861
INSTITUTO PIRENAICO DE ECOLOGIA. MONOGRAFIAS. 1987-1992. irreg. Consejo Superior de Investigaciones Cientificas, Instituto Pirenaico de Ecologia, Avda. Regimento de Galicia, s-n, Jaca, Huesca 22700, Spain.

632.9 NLD ISSN 0074-0446
INSTITUUT VOOR PLANTEZIEKTENKUNDIG ONDERZOEK. JAARVERSLAG/RESEARCH INSTITUTE FOR PLANT PROTECTION. ANNUAL REPORT. 1950-1991. a. Instituut voor Planteziektenkundig Onderzoek, PO Box 9060, Wageningen, 6700 GW, Netherlands.

384.5 POL ISSN 0032-6259 CODEN: PITRAT
INSTYTUT TELE- I RADIOTECHNICZNY. PRACE. 1957-1991. q. Instytut Tele-i Radiotechniczny, Ratuszowa 11, Warsaw, 03450, Poland.

368.323 USA ISSN 1054-2892
INSURANCE COLLISION REPORT PASSENGER CARS, CARGO VANS, PICKUPS, AND UTILITY VEHICLES. 1976-1989. a. Highway Loss Data Institute, 1005 N Glebe Rd, Ste 700, Arlington, VA 22201.

368.99 AUS
INSURANCE IN AUSTRALIA AND NEW ZEALAND. 1966-1996. a. Craftsman Publishing Pty. Ltd., 125 Highbury Rd, Burwood, VIC 3125, Australia.

268 GBR ISSN 1366-0853
INSURANCE INTERNATIONAL OUTLOOK. 1996-suspended. q. Mitre House Publishing Ltd., PO Box 29, South Petherton, TA13 5WE, United Kingdom.

368.994 AUS ISSN 0725-4644
INSURANCE RECORD OF AUSTRALIA & NEW ZEALAND; journal of insurance, banking and finance. 1877-1996. m. (except Jan.). Craftsman Publishing Pty. Ltd., 125 Highbury Rd, Burwood, VIC 3125, Australia.

363.728 628.4458 ESP ISSN 1133-2298
INTEC URBE. 1989-2004. bi-m. Tecnipublicaciones Espana, S.L., Avda de Manoteras 44, 3a Planta, Madrid, 28050, Spain.

363.7 DEU ISSN 1389-5176
INTEGRATED ASSESSMENT; an international journal. 2000-200?. q. Integrated Assessment Society (TIAS), c/o Hadi Dowlatabadi, Editor, University of British Columbia, 422, 2202 Main Mall, V6T 1Z4, Vancouver, BC, Canada.

621.381 USA ISSN 1057-4530
INTEGRATED CIRCUITS. DIGITAL. 1969-2000. a. D.A.T.A. Business Publishing, 15 Inverness Way E, Box 6510, Englewood, CO 80155-6510.

621 USA
INTEGRATED MANUFACTURING TECHNOLOGY. 1988-199?. q. A S M E International, Three Park Ave, New York, NY 10016.

590 GBR ISSN 1749-4869
INTEGRATIVE ZOOLOGY. 2006-200?. q. Wiley-Blackwell Publishing Ltd., 9600 Garsington Rd, Oxford, OX4 2DQ, United Kingdom.

004.678 USA
INTELLIGENT E A I. (Enterprise Application Integration) 2000-ceased. bi-m. C M P Media LLC, 600 Harrison St, 6th Fl., San Francisco, CA 94107.

300 FRA ISSN 0335-3265
INTERACTION. 1974-1977. irreg. Editions Mouton et Cie, 7 rue Dupuytren, Paris, 75006, France.

617 FRA ISSN 1778-3739
INTERACTIVE SURGERY. 2006-2008. 4/yr. Springer France, 22 Rue de Palestro, Paris, 75002, France.

571.6 GBR ISSN 0957-0799 CODEN: IINCEH
INTERCELLULAR AND INTRACELLULAR COMMUNICATIONS. 1986-2009 (Jul.). irreg. Cambridge University Press, The Edinburgh Bldg, Shaftesbury Rd, Cambridge, CB2 8RU, United Kingdom.

940 950 NLD ISSN 0165-2850
INTERCONTINENTA. 1978-2005 (vol.25). irreg. Leiden University, Institute for the History of European Expansion, History Department, PO Box 9515, Leiden, 2300 RA, Netherlands.

800 649 AUS ISSN 1832-0996
INTERFACE (SYDNEY). 2004-200?. a. Vibewire Youth Inc., 525 Harris St, Ultimo, NSW 2007, Australia.

305.8 RUS
INTERFAX. BELARUS NEWS. 200?-200?. d. Interfax Ltd., 1-ya Tverskaya-Yamskaya, dom 2, stroenie 1, Moscow, 127006, Russian Federation.

330 RUS
INTERFAX. BUSINESS WOCHE. 200?-200?. w. Interfax Ltd.

330 RUS
INTERFAX. CHINA BUSINESS REPORT. 200?-200?. w. Interfax Ltd., 1-ya Tverskaya-Yamskaya, dom 2, stroenie 1, Moscow, 127006, Russian Federation.

330 RUS
INTERFAX. CZECH REPUBLIC BUSINESS NEWS. 200?-200?. w. Interfax Ltd., 1-ya Tverskaya-Yamskaya, dom 2, stroenie 1, Moscow, 127006, Russian Federation.

330 RUS
INTERFAX. RUSSIAN COMPANY NEWS. 19??-200?. w. Interfax Ltd., 1-ya Tverskaya-Yamskaya, dom 2, stroenie 1, Moscow, 127006, Russian Federation.

057.1 330 RUS
INTERFAX VREMYA; politiko-ekonomicheskii ezhenedel'nik. 1995-2000. m. Interfax Ltd., 1-ya Tverskaya-Yamskaya, dom 2, stroenie 1, Moscow, 127006, Russian Federation.

535 DEU ISSN 0940-0117
INTERFERENZEN. 1990-1997. q. Deutsche Gesellschaft fuer Holografie e.V., Salinenstr 26, Bad Salzdetfurth, 31162, Germany.

330.9 FRA ISSN 1267-0669
INTERIEUR SYSTEMES; la construction seche en action. 1995-2005. bi-m. Edial Editions, 126 rue du Temple, Paris, 75003, France.

747 GBR ISSN 0956-988X
INTERIOR DESIGN HANDBOOK. 1981-2005. a. Cheerman Ltd., 3-6 Kenrick Pl, London, W1H 3FF, United Kingdom.

747 USA
INTERIOR DESIGN MARKET. 1986-ceased. s-a. Reed Business Information, 360 Park Ave S, New York, NY 10010.

790.1 USA ISSN 1083-9399
INTERNATIONAL AMUSEMENT INDUSTRY BUYERS GUIDE. 1972-ceased. a. Nielsen Business Publications, 5055 Wilshire Blvd, 7th Fl., Los Angeles, CA 90036.

900 USA ISSN 1047-3408
INTERNATIONAL ANNUAL OF ORAL HISTORY. 1980-19??. a. Greenwood Publishing Group Inc., 88 Post Rd W, PO Box 5007, Westport, CT 06881.

616.89 GBR ISSN 0085-2007
INTERNATIONAL ASSOCIATION FOR SCIENTIFIC STUDY OF MENTAL DEFICIENCY. PROCEEDINGS OF INTERNATIONAL CONGRESS. 1967-ceased. triennial. Routledge, 2 Park Sq, Milton Park, Abingdon, Oxon OX14 4RN, United Kingdom.

551.48 DEU ISSN 0538-4680 CODEN: IVTMAS
INTERNATIONAL ASSOCIATION OF THEORETICAL AND APPLIED LIMNOLOGY. COMMUNICATIONS/INTERNATIONALE VEREINIGUNG FUER THEORETISCHE UND ANGEWANDTE LIMNOLOGIE. MITTEILUNGEN. 1953-1996. irreg. E. Schweizerbart'sche Verlagsbuchhandlung, Johannesstr 3A, Stuttgart, 70176, Germany.

387.7 GBR ISSN 0443-7365
INTERNATIONAL AVIATION NEWS. 1948-200?. m. Airtimed Group, 12 Nymans Court, Forestfield, Crawley, W Sussex RH10 6PP, United Kingdom.

660.6 GBR ISSN 0888-7225
INTERNATIONAL BIOTECHNOLOGY LABORATORY. 1983-2006. 6/yr. International Scientific Communications, Ltd., ISC House, 12 Bridge Ave, Maidenhead, Berkshire GB-SL6 1RR, United Kingdom.

920 USA ISSN 1087-397X
INTERNATIONAL BOOK OF HONOR. 1985-1999. biennial. American Biographical Institute, Inc., Governing Board of Editors, 5126 Bur Oak Cir, Raleigh, NC 27612.

336 NLD ISSN 0074-2104
INTERNATIONAL BUREAU OF FISCAL DOCUMENTATION. ANNUAL REPORT. 1953-ceased. a. International Bureau of Fiscal Documentation (I B F D), H J E Wenckebachweg 210, Amsterdam, 1096 AS, Netherlands.

790.1 USA ISSN 1078-1390
INTERNATIONAL CALCULATOR COLLECTOR. 1993-ceased. q. International Association of Calculator Collectors, 14561 Livingston St, Tustin, CA 92780.

613.2 AUS ISSN 0813-9008 CODEN: ICNRDJ
INTERNATIONAL CLINICAL NUTRITION REVIEW. 1981-2002. q. Integrated Therapies Pty. Ltd., PO Box 370, Manly, NSW 2095, Australia.

690 352.9 USA ISSN 0896-9752
INTERNATIONAL CONFERENCE OF BUILDING OFFICIALS. ANALYSIS OF REVISIONS TO THE (YEAR) UNIFORM CODES. 19??-ceased. triennial. International Conference of Building Officials, 5360 Workman Mill Rd, Whittier, CA 90601.

690 352.9 USA ISSN 0896-9728
INTERNATIONAL CONFERENCE OF BUILDING OFFICIALS. DWELLING CONSTRUCTION UNDER THE UNIFORM BUILDING CODE. 19??-200?. triennial. International Conference of Building Officials, 5360 Workman Mill Rd, Whittier, CA 90601.

690 352.9 USA ISSN 0501-1213
INTERNATIONAL CONFERENCE OF BUILDING OFFICIALS. UNIFORM HOUSING CODE. 1955-200?. triennial. International Conference of Building Officials, 5360 Workman Mill Rd, Whittier, CA 90601.

690 352.9 USA ISSN 0896-9671
INTERNATIONAL CONFERENCE OF BUILDING OFFICIALS. UNIFORM MECHANICAL CODE. 1967-19??. triennial. International Conference of Building Officials, 5360 Workman Mill Rd, Whittier, CA 90601.

800 NLD ISSN 1574-1214
INTERNATIONAL CONFERENCE ON GREY LITERATURE. CONFERENCE MEMORANDUM. 2004-2008. m. Greynet - Grey Literature Network Service, Javastraat 194-HS, Amsterdam, 1095 CP, Netherlands.

005.12 USA ISSN 1523-4479
INTERNATIONAL CONFERENCE ON SOFTWARE ENGINEERING: EDUCATION AND PRACTICE. PROCEEDINGS. 199?-1998. a. I E E E, 3 Park Ave, 17th Fl, New York, NY 10016-5997.

629.8021 310 EGY ISSN 1110-7707
INTERNATIONAL CONGRESS FOR STATISTICS, COMPUTER SCIENCE. 198?-ceased. a. Ain Shams University, Scientific Computer Center, Abbasia, Cairo, Egypt.

500 NLD ISSN 0531-5131 CODEN: EXMDA4
INTERNATIONAL CONGRESS SERIES. 1952-2006 (vol.1304). 14/yr. Elsevier BV, Radarweg 29, P O Box 211, Amsterdam, 1000 AE, Netherlands.

676.2 USA
INTERNATIONAL CONTAINER DIRECTORY. 19??-2004. a. Advanstar Communications, Inc., 7500 Old Oak Blvd, Cleveland, OH 44130.

341 332.6 NLD
INTERNATIONAL CONTRACT MANUAL. (Consists of: Guide to Practical Applications of the U.N. Convention on Contracts for International Sale of Goods; Contract Checklists; Country Handbooks; Compliance Checklists) 1990-1994. plus updates 8/yr. Kluwer Law International, PO Box 316, Alphen aan den Rijn, 2400 AH, Netherlands.

330.9 USA ISSN 0738-1425
INTERNATIONAL DEVELOPMENT RESOURCE BOOKS. 1984-19??. irreg. Greenwood Publishing Group Inc., 88 Post Rd W, PO Box 5007, Westport, CT 06881.

012 USA ISSN 1087-3988
INTERNATIONAL DIRECTORY OF DISTINGUISHED LEADERSHIP. 1968-2003. a. American Biographical Institute, Inc., Governing Board of Editors, 5126 Bur Oak Cir, Raleigh, NC 27612.

358.4 AUS
INTERNATIONAL DIRECTORY OF MILITARY AIRCRAFT (YEAR). 1995-2003 (Jan.). biennial. Aerospace Publications Pty. Ltd., PO Box 1777, Fyshwick, ACT 2609, Australia.

333.794029 GBR ISSN 0255-0059
INTERNATIONAL DIRECTORY OF NEW AND RENEWABLE ENERGY INFORMATION SOURCES AND RESEARCH CENTRES. 1982-1993 (vol.3). irreg. Earthscan Ltd., Dunstan House, 14a St Cross St, London, EC1N 8XA, United Kingdom.

920 020 USA
INTERNATIONAL DIRECTORY OF SERIALS SPECIALISTS. 1995-199?. irreg. Haworth Press, Inc., 325 Chestnut St, Ste 800, Philadelphia, PA 19106.

020.621 NLD
INTERNATIONAL FEDERATION FOR INFORMATION AND DOCUMENTATION. CONFERENCE AND CONGRESS PROCEEDINGS. 1895-ceased. biennial. Elsevier BV, Radarweg 29, P O Box 211, Amsterdam, 1000 AE, Netherlands.

614.84 GBR ISSN 0961-3730
INTERNATIONAL FIRE & SECURITY PRODUCT NEWS. 1975-2004. bi-m. C M P Information Ltd., Ludgate House, 245 Blackfriars Rd., London, SE1 9UR, United Kingdom.

382 AUS
INTERNATIONAL FOCUS. 1969-200?. s-a. Australian Industry Group, PO Box 289, North Sydney, NSW 2059, Australia.

760 DNK ISSN 0020-6830
INTERNATIONAL GRAFIK; original graphics review. 1969-1975; resumed 1976-1977. s-a. International Grafik, PO Box 109, Frederikshavn, 9900, Denmark.

336.2 NLD
THE INTERNATIONAL GUIDE TO ADVANCE RULINGS. 1997-suspended. plus a. updates. International Bureau of Fiscal Documentation (I B F D), H J E Wenckebachweg 210, Amsterdam, 1096 AS, Netherlands.

336.2 332.63 346.04 NLD
THE INTERNATIONAL GUIDE TO THE TAXATION OF REAL ESTATE. 1999-ceased. plus a. updates. International Bureau of Fiscal Documentation (I B F D), H J E Wenckebachweg 210, Amsterdam, 1096 AS, Netherlands.

336 NLD
THE INTERNATIONAL GUIDE TO THE TAXATION OF SPORTSMEN AND SPORTSWOMEN. 2001-ceased. plus s-a. updates. International Bureau of Fiscal Documentation (I B F D), H J E Wenckebachweg 210, Amsterdam, 1096 AS, Netherlands.

336 NLD
THE INTERNATIONAL GUIDE TO THE TAXATION OF TRANSFERS OF TECHNOLOGY. 2001-ceased. plus a. updates. International Bureau of Fiscal Documentation (I B F D), H J E Wenckebachweg 210, Amsterdam, 1096 AS, Netherlands.

331 DNK ISSN 0109-2650
INTERNATIONAL HORISONT. 1982-2006. q. Arbejderbevaegelsens Internationale Forum, Nyropsgade 14, 1, Copenhagen V, 1602, Denmark.

361.77 USA ISSN 1098-3333
INTERNATIONAL INFORMATION DIRECTORY. 1998-2001. irreg. C Q Press, Inc., 2300 N St, NW, Ste 800, Washington, DC 20037.

631.6 NLD ISSN 0165-1803 CODEN: AILRAS
INTERNATIONAL INSTITUTE FOR LAND RECLAMATION AND IMPROVEMENT. ANNUAL REPORT. 1960-2000. a. International Institute for Land Reclamation and Improvement, PO Box 45, Wageningen, 6700 AA, Netherlands.

016.6316 NLD ISSN 0074-6436 CODEN: BIIIDY
INTERNATIONAL INSTITUTE FOR LAND RECLAMATION AND IMPROVEMENT. BIBLIOGRAPHY. 1960-1984 (no.18). irreg. International Institute for Land Reclamation and Improvement, PO Box 45, Wageningen, 6700 AA, Netherlands.

346.086 GBR ISSN 0968-2090
INTERNATIONAL INSURANCE LAW REVIEW. 1993-1998. m. Sweet & Maxwell Ltd., 100 Avenue Rd, London, NW3 3PF, United Kingdom.

671.5 DNK ISSN 0905-6866 CODEN: IJJMEY
INTERNATIONAL JOURNAL FOR THE JOINING OF MATERIALS. 1989-2006. 4/yr. J O M Institute, Strandvej 28, Gilleleje, 3250, Denmark.

720 GBR ISSN 1026-3454
THE INTERNATIONAL JOURNAL OF ARCHITECTURAL MANAGEMENT PRACTICE & RESEARCH. 1996-1999. S A A M, The Chief Executive, Alverton Grange, Nottinghamshire NG13 9PB, United Kingdom.

616.2 NZL ISSN 1176-9106
THE INTERNATIONAL JOURNAL OF CHRONIC OBSTRUCTIVE PULMONARY DISEASE (PRINT). 2006-2008. q. Dove Medical Press Ltd., 17/44 William Pickering Dr, Albany, PO Box 300-008, Auckland, 1311, New Zealand.

343.099405 GBR ISSN 1468-9685
INTERNATIONAL JOURNAL OF ELECTRONIC COMMERCE LAW & PRACTICE. 2000-2002. q. E M I S Professional Publishing, Fulford Grange, Micklefield Ln, Rawdon, Leeds, W Yorks LS19 6BA, United Kingdom.

620 GBR ISSN 1029-6646
INTERNATIONAL JOURNAL OF ELEVATOR ENGINEERING. 1996-1998. a. I A E E Publications, Hallmark House, 25 Downham Rd, Ramsden Heath, Essex CM11 1PU, United Kingdom.

616.025 USA ISSN 1865-1372
INTERNATIONAL JOURNAL OF EMERGENCY MEDICINE (PRINT). 2008-2009. q. Springer New York LLC, 233 Spring St, New York, NY 10013.

616.994061 CHE ISSN 0933-0453
INTERNATIONAL JOURNAL OF EXPERIMENTAL AND CLINICAL CHEMOTHERAPY. 1988-1993 (vol.6). irreg. Ecomed Verlagsgesellschaft AG & Co. KG, Justus-von-Liebig-Str 1, Landsberg, 86899, Germany.

020 FRA ISSN 1290-2942
INTERNATIONAL JOURNAL OF INFORMATION SCIENCES FOR DECISION MAKING (PRINT). 1997-200?. irreg. Centre de Recherche Retrospective de Marseille, Faculte des Sciences et Techniques de St. Jerome, Marseille, Cedex 20 13397, France.

610.28 NZL ISSN 1176-9114
INTERNATIONAL JOURNAL OF NANOMEDICINE (PRINT). 2006-2008. q. Dove Medical Press Ltd., 17/44 William Pickering Dr, Albany, PO Box 300-008, Auckland, 1311, New Zealand.

616.8 GBR ISSN 0968-0624 CODEN: DEPPEH
THE INTERNATIONAL JOURNAL OF PSYCHIATRIC NURSING RESEARCH. 1994 (Aug.)-2008. 3/yr. International Journal of Psychiatric Nursing Research, PO Box 1062, Southampton, Hamps SO17 1BJ, United Kingdom.

643 USA ISSN 0010-2164 CODEN: ILBYA6
INTERNATIONAL LABORATORY. 1971-2006. 6/yr. International Scientific Communications, Inc., 30 Controls Dr, PO Box 670, Shelton, CT 06484.

660.6 USA
INTERNATIONAL LABORATORY BUYERS' GUIDE. 1972-200?. a. International Scientific Communications, Inc., 30 Controls Dr, PO Box 670, Shelton, CT 06484.

643 USA
INTERNATIONAL LABORATORY NEWS. 1993-2006. m. International Scientific Communications, Inc., 30 Controls Dr, PO Box 670, Shelton, CT 06484.

330 GBR ISSN 1368-6917
INTERNATIONAL LIBRARY OF MACROECONOMIC AND FINANCIAL HISTORY. 1991-1996. irreg. Edward Elgar Publishing Ltd, The Lypiatts, 15 Lansdown Rd, Cheltenham, Glos GL50 2JA, United Kingdom.

690 352.9 USA
INTERNATIONAL ONE- AND TWO-FAMILY DWELLING CODE. 1971-2000. a. International Conference of Building Officials, 5360 Workman Mill Rd, Whittier, CA 90601.

341.7 NLD ISSN 0920-7767
INTERNATIONAL ORGANIZATIONS AND THE LAW OF THE SEA (YEAR); documentary yearbook. 1987-2005 (vol.18). a. Martinus Nijhoff, PO Box 9000, Leiden, 2300 PA, Netherlands.

615 FRA ISSN 1289-0146
INTERNATIONAL PHARMA NEWS. 1998-2004. 11/yr. Droit & Pharmacie, 12 rue de Lorraine, Levallois-Perret Cedex, 92309, France.

665.54 USA ISSN 0272-1090
INTERNATIONAL PIPE LINE INDUSTRY. 1971-200?. m. Gulf Publishing Co., PO Box 2608, Houston, TX 77252.

150 GBR
INTERNATIONAL REVIEW OF HEALTH PSYCHOLOGY. 1992-1994. irreg. John Wiley & Sons Ltd., The Atrium, Southern Gate, Chichester, West Sussex PO19 8SQ, United Kingdom.

658 GBR ISSN 1067-9987
INTERNATIONAL REVIEW OF PROFESSIONAL ISSUES IN SELECTION AND ASSESSMENT. 1993-1996 (vol.2). a. John Wiley & Sons Ltd., 1-7 Oldlands Way, PO Box 808, Bognor Regis, West Sussex PO21 9FF, United Kingdom.

796.9 FRA ISSN 1778-8242
INTERNATIONAL SKATING MAGAZINE. 2006-2006. bi-m. Skating France SARL, 12 bis av. Becquerel, Pessac Cedex, 33608, France.

651 ITA
INTERNATIONAL STATIONERY; events in the world of stationery. 1988-ceased. q. Raddicchi Editore S.R.L., Via San Giovanni B. De La Salle, 4, Milan, MI 20132, Italy.

599.2 CZE
INTERNATIONAL STUDBOOK EQUUS PRZEWALSKI. 1960-1997. a. Zoologicka Zahrada v Praze, U Trojskeho Zamku 3/120, Prague 7, 17100, Czech Republic.

342.085 NLD ISSN 0903-9961
INTERNATIONAL STUDIES. NORDIC SEMINAR ON HUMAN RIGHTS. PROCEEDINGS. -1997. irreg. Martinus Nijhoff, PO Box 9000, Leiden, 2300 PA, Netherlands.

347.016 ITA ISSN 0074-9435
INTERNATIONAL UNION OF LATIN NOTARIES. PROCEEDINGS OF CONGRESS. 1948-ceased. triennial. International Union of Latin Notaries., Notaio Emanuele Ferrari, Via Antonio Locatelli, 5, Milan, MI 20124, Italy.

671.52 DEU ISSN 0930-9241
INTERNATIONAL WELDING ENGINEERING. 1987-1999. a. D V S Verlag GmbH, Aachener Str 172, Duesseldorf, 40223, Germany.

920 USA ISSN 1073-9734
INTERNATIONAL WHO'S WHO OF CONTEMPORARY ACHIEVEMENT. 1989-1999. biennial. American Biographical Institute, Inc., Governing Board of Editors, 5126 Bur Oak Cir, Raleigh, NC 27612.

025.04 USA ISSN 1530-1354
INTERNATIONAL WORKSHOP ON ADVANCE ISSUES OF E-COMMERCE AND WEB-BASED INFORMATION SYSTEMS. PROCEEDINGS. 1999-2002. a. I E E E, 3 Park Ave, 17th Fl, New York, NY 10016-5997.

333.77 GBR ISSN 0952-3847
INTERNATIONAL YEARBOOK OF RURAL PLANNING. 1980-1988. irreg. Pergamon, The Blvd, Langford Ln, East Park, Kidlington, Oxford OX5 1GB, United Kingdom.

614.85 BRD ISSN 0379-7473
INTERNATIONALE SEKTION DER I V S S FUER DIE VERHUETUNG VON ARBEITSUNFAELLEN UND BERUFSKRANKHEITEN DURCH ELEKTRIZITAET. BULLETIN/COMITE INTERNATIONAL DE L'A I S S POUR LA PREVENTION DES RISQUES PROFESSIONNELS DUS A L'ELECTRICITE. BULLETIN/ INTERNATIONAL SECTION OF THE I S S A FOR THE PREVENTION OF OCCUPATIONAL RISKS DUE TO ELECTRICITY. BULLETIN. 1970-1987. irreg. Berufsgenossenschaft der Feinmechanik und Elektrotechnik, Gustav-Heinemann Ufer 130, Cologne, 50968, Germany.

681.3 CZE ISSN 1211-6351
INTERNET. 1996-2003. m. Trade & Leisure Publications, s.r.o., Pernerova 35a, Prague 8, 186 00, Czech Republic.

025.4 DEU
INTERNET FUER EINSTEIGER. 2000-2003. a. Data Becker GmbH & Co. KG, Merowingerstr 30, Duesseldorf, 40223, Germany.

025.04 ITA ISSN 1828-7840
INTERNET GENIUS. 2006-200?. m. Sprea Editori Srl, Via Torino 51, Cernusco sul Naviglio, MI 20063, Italy.

610.25 IND
INTERNET HE@LTH; the journal on medical internet research applications, communication and ethics. 2003-2004. s-a. Center for Cybermedicine and Internet Research, Perumcheril 33-4711, Malaparamba, Calicut, Kerala, 673009, India.

572 GBR ISSN 1462-2149
INTERNET JOURNAL OF SCIENCE - BIOLOGICAL CHEMISTRY. 1997-1997 (vol.4); suspended. irreg. Emedia Science Ltd, P O Box 92, New Ferry, CH63 9WA, United Kingdom.

025.4 NZL ISSN 1175-3811
INTERNET MAGAZINE. 2000-2002 (Nov.). 11/yr. I D G Communications Ltd., Wellesley St, PO Box 6813, Auckland, 1036, New Zealand.

681.3 ITA ISSN 1591-6995
INTERNET PRATICO. 1999-200?. bi-m. Gruppo Editoriale Futura, Via XXV Aprile 39, Bresso, MI 20091, Italy.

004.678 ITA ISSN 1824-8403
INTERNET.PRO. 1995-2006. m. Tecniche Nuove SpA, Via Eritrea 21, Milan, MI 201, Italy.

025.04 DEU ISSN 1619-6481
INTERNET PROFESSIONELL. 1997-2007. m. Nielsen Business Publications Deutschland GmbH, Riesstr 25, Munich, 80992, Germany.

004.678 NLD ISSN 1570-9175
INTERNET TIPS & TRUCS. 2001-2004. m. I D G Communications Nederland BV, Richard Holkade 8, Haarlem, 2033 PZ, Netherlands.

850 ITA
INTERPRETAZIONI TENDENZIOSE. 1995-ceased. s-a. Ediesse srl, Via dei Frentani 4A, Rome, 00185, Italy.

058.7 SWE ISSN 0349-5574
INVANDRARTIDNINGEN PA FRANSKA INFORMATION. 1972-1990. m. Stiftelsen Invandrartidningen, Fack 1352, Stockholm, 11183, Sweden.

616.1 ESP ISSN 1139-2096 CODEN: ICNACZ
INVESTIGACION CARDIOVASCULAR. 1998-2006; suspended. s-a. Fundacion Mapfre, Paseo de Recoletos, 23, Madrid, 28004, Spain.

930.1 ESP ISSN 1132-2446
INVESTIGACIONES ARQUEOLOGICAS. 1988-2003. a. Gobierno de Canarias, Consejeria de Educacion, Cultura y Deportes, Direccion General del Patrimonio Historico, Edificio Quegles, Las Palmas de Gran Canaria, Spain.

336.2 NLD
INVESTMENT FUNDS (PRINT EDITION). 1996-ceased. plus a. updates. International Bureau of Fiscal Documentation (I B F D), H J E Wenckebachweg 210, Amsterdam, 1096 AS, Netherlands.

649 ITA
IO E MIO FIGLIO. 1978-ceased. m. Publibaby Srl, Via Enrico Fermi, 18, Cusago, MI 20090, Italy.

340 USA
IOWA PLEADING AND CAUSES OF ACTION. 1989-199?. (2-3 updates/yr)) plus irreg. updates. LexisNexis, PO Box 7587, Charlottesville, VA 22906.

929 AUS ISSN 0814-5482
IRISH LINK; Irish family history magazine. 1984-1999. 3/yr. Irish Link, PO Box 242, Yarram, VIC 3971, Australia.

305.4 FRA ISSN 1620-9621
ISA. 2000-2008. m. Hachette Filipacchi Medias S.A., 149/151 Rue Anatole France, Levallois-Perret, 925340, France.

910.09 ITA
ISCHIA MONDO. 1972-ceased. fortn. Lubranopublicitas, Via Roma, 139 T, Ischia, AP, Italy.

704.94897 956 USA ISSN 0739-3261
ISLAMIC ART. 1981-2001. irreg. Oxford University Press, 198 Madison Ave, New York, NY 10016.

025.4 USA
ISOURCE BUSINESS. 2000-2003. m. Grand View Media Group, Inc., 200 Croft St, Ste 1, Birmingham, AL 35242.

500 ISR ISSN 0333-6190
ISRAEL ACADEMY OF SCIENCES AND HUMANITIES. SECTION OF SCIENCES. PROCEEDINGS. 1963-1984. irreg. Israel Academy of Sciences and Humanities, 43 Jabotinski St, P O Box 4040, Jerusalem, 91040, Israel.

352.88 ISR ISSN 0302-8976
ISRAEL. COMMISSIONER FOR COMPLAINTS FROM THE PUBLIC (OMBUDSMAN). ANNUAL REPORT. 1972-1995. a. State Comptroller and Ombudsman Office, 669, Jerusalem, 91006, Israel.

382.029 ISR ISSN 0793-4947
ISRAEL CONVENTIONS, TRADE SHOWS, FESTIVALS & SPECIAL EVENTS. 1992-1997. a. Pick Communications Ltd., P O Box 57500, Tel Aviv, 61574, Israel.

793.31 ISR
ISRAEL DANCE QUARTERLY. 1993-1999. q. Zoom Hafakot, 39 Shoham St., Haifa, 34679, Israel.

791.43 ISR ISSN 0792-8610
ISRAEL FILM CENTRE INFORMATION BULLETIN. 1969-1993. a. Ministry of Trade and Industry, Israel Film Centre, P O Box 299, Jerusalem, Israel.

327 DNK
ISRAEL INFORMATION. 1980-198?. irreg. Israelske Ambassade, SK, Lundevangsvej 4, Hellerup, 2900, Denmark.

301 ISR ISSN 0075-1227
ISRAEL INSTITUTE OF APPLIED SOCIAL RESEARCH. RESEARCH REPORT. 1963-1994. biennial. Israel Institute of Applied Social Research, 19 Washington St., P O Box 7150, Jerusalem, Israel.

361 ISR
ISRAEL. MINISTRY OF LABOUR AND SOCIAL AFFAIRS. DEPARTMENT OF INTERNATIONAL RELATIONS. THE PRESS ON WELFARE; a selection of articles on welfare from the Israeli press. 1970-1978. s-a. Ministry of Labour and Social Affairs, 10 Yad Harutzim St., Talpiot, Jerusalem, 91000, Israel.

334 ISR ISSN 0080-1313
ISRAEL. MINISTRY OF LABOUR. REGISTRAR OF COOPERATIVE SOCIETIES. REPORT ON THE COOPERATIVE MOVEMENT IN ISRAEL. 1964-1988. a. Ministry of Labour and Social Affairs, 10 Yad Harutzim St., Talpiot, Jerusalem, 91000, Israel.

553.28 ISR ISSN 0047-1585
ISRAEL OIL NEWS. 1972-1983. s-a. Israel Institute of Petroleum & Energy, Ramat Aviv, 26 Chaim Levanon St, Tel Aviv, 61170, Israel.

530 ISR ISSN 0309-8710 CODEN: AIPSDK
ISRAEL PHYSICAL SOCIETY. ANNALS; conference proceedings. 1977-2001. a. Israel Physical Society, c/o Department of Physics, Technion, Haifa, 32000, Israel.

320 ISR
ISRAEL STUDIES. 1981-1993. s-a. Jerusalem Institute for Israel Studies, 20 A Radak St, Jerusalem, 92186, Israel.

790 ISR
ISRAEL TOURIST NEWS. 1962-1978. m. Ministry of Tourism, Information Centre, P O Box 1018, Jerusalem, 91009, Israel.

323.4 ISR
ISRAEL UPDATE. 1989-1998. bi-m. Society for the Protection of Personal Rights for Lesbians Gay Men & Bisexual in Israel, P O Box 37604, Tel Aviv, 61375, Israel.

052 956 ISR
ISRAELI ACADEMIC CENTER IN CAIRO. BULLETIN. 1982-2004. irreg. Israel Academy of Sciences and Humanities, 43 Jabotinski St, P O Box 4040, Jerusalem, 91040, Israel.

382 ISR
ISRAEL'S FOREIGN TRADE. 1974-ceased. a. Pick Communications Ltd., P O Box 57500, Tel Aviv, 61574, Israel.

020 AUS ISSN 0814-303X
ISSUES (TOOWONG); for serials librarians. 1984-2001. irreg. (2-3/yr.). International Subscription Agencies Australia, PO Box 709, Toowong, QLD 4066, Australia.

338 USA ISSN 1096-9446
ISSUES AND ANSWERS IN SALES MANAGEMENT. 1997-2005. bi-w. Clement Communications, Inc., 10 LaCrue Ave, PO Box 36, Concordville, PA 19331.

510 TUR ISSN 1300-0713
ISTANBUL UNIVERSITESI. FEN FAKULTESI. MATEMATIK DERGISI/UNIVERSITY OF ISTANBUL. FACULTY OF SCIENCE. THE JOURNAL OF MATHEMATICS. 1989-2003. a. Istanbul Universitesi, Fen Fakultesi, Dergi Editor Kurulu, Vezneciler - Istanbul, 34459, Turkey.

551.4 ITA ISSN 1120-3080
ISTITUTO DI IDROBIOLOGIA E ACQUACOLTURA G. BRUNELLI. QUADERNI. 1980-ceased. irreg. Istituto di Idrobiologia e Acquacoltura G. Brunelli, Casali di Paola, Sabaudia, LT, Italy.

367 ITA ISSN 0080-3928
ISTITUTO GIAPPONESE DI CULTURA, ROME. NOTIZIARIO. 1965-ceased. a. Istituto Giapponese di Cultura, Via Antonio Gramsci 74, Rome, 00197, Italy.

330 ITA ISSN 0075-1529
ISTITUTO MOBILIARE ITALIANO. ANNUAL REPORT. 1932-1994. a. Istituto Mobiliare Italiano, Viale Dell' Arte, 25, Rome, RM 00144, Italy.

639.3 551.46 ITA ISSN 0393-3571 CODEN: QIRMEJ
ISTITUTO RICERCHE PESCA MARITTIMA. QUADERNI. 1970-ceased. irreg. Istituto Ricerche sulla Pesca Marittima, Largo Fiera della Pesca, Ancona, AN 60125, Italy.

579 ITA ISSN 0021-2547 CODEN: BISMAP
ISTITUTO SIEROTERAPICO MILANESE. BOLLETTINO. 1917-1992. bi-m. Istituto Sieroterapico Milanese, Via Darwin 22, Milan, 20100, Italy.

355.31 ITA
ISTITUTO STORICO E DI CULTURA DELL'ARMA DEL GENIO. BOLLETTINO. 1935-ceased. s-a. Ministero della Difesa, Istituto Storico e di Cultura dell'Arma del Genio, Lungotevere della Vittoria 31, Rome, 00195, Italy.

792 ITA
ISTITUZIONI CULTURALI PIEMONTESI. PUBBLICAZIONI. 1976-ceased. irreg. Cassa di Risparmio di Torino, Via Venti Settembre, 31, Turin, TO 10121, Italy.

320 ITA ISSN 1724-1316
ISTITUZIONI E SOCIETA. 1994-ceased. irreg. Edizioni Scientifiche Italiane SpA, Via Chiatamone 7, Naples, NA 80121, Italy.

001.3 ITA ISSN 0535-9031
ITALIA; rivista di documentazione fotografica. 1953-ceased. s-a. Presidenza del Consiglio dei Ministri, Dipartimento per l'Informazione e l'Editoria, Via Po 14, Rome, 00198, Italy.

910.2 910.91 ITA ISSN 1828-2881
ITALIA MERAVIGLIOSA. 1971-ceased. irreg. Touring Editore, Corso Italia 10, Milan, 20122, Italy.

363.35 ITA
ITALIA NOSTRA. SEZIONE DI TRENTO. BOLLETTINO. 1972-ceased. s-a. Italia Nostra, Sezione di Trento, Via Oss Mazzurana 54, Trento, TN 38100, Italy.

914 ITA ISSN 1972-6074
ITALIA TURISTICA; rivista di cultura e turismo delle regioni italiane. 1962-2008; suspended. bi-m. Editrice Italia Turistica, Via C Anti 9, Padua, PD 35124, Italy.

320 ITA
ITALIA VIVA; mensile politico. 1971-ceased. m. Italia Viva, Via Milano, 37, Pasian Di Prato, UD 33037, Italy.

617.6 ITA ISSN 1593-4977
ITALIAN DENTAL ECONOMIST. 2001-200?. bi-m. (5/yr.). Elsevier Masson, Via Paleocapa 7, Milan, 20121, Italy.

664 621.9 ITA
ITALIAN FOOD MACHINES. 1989-ceased. 3/yr. Zeus International Srl, Viale Lunigiana 14, Milan, MI 20125, Italy.

618.92 ITA ISSN 1720-8424
THE ITALIAN JOURNAL OF PEDIATRICS (PRINT). 1964-200?. bi-m. Pacini Editore SpA, Via A Gherardesca 1, Ospedaletto, PI 56121, Italy.

616.8 ITA ISSN 1122-2247
THE ITALIAN JOURNAL OF PSYCHIATRY AND BEHAVIOURAL SCIENCES. 1991-ceased. 3/yr. Elsevier Masson, Via Paleocapa 7, Milan, 20121, Italy.

055.1 ITA ISSN 1122-4029
ITALIAN LIFE. 1991-ceased. 6/yr. Edizioni Calderara, Via Marzocchi, 4, Calderara Di Reno, BO 40012, Italy.

663.2 ITA
ITALIAN WINES & SPIRITS (UK EDITION). 1979-ceased. q. Editoriale Lariana s.r.l., Via Ciro Menotti 11-D, Milan, MI 20129, Italy.

663.2 ITA
ITALIAN WINES & SPIRITS (US AND CANADA EDITION). 1977-ceased. q. Editoriale Lariana s.r.l., Via Ciro Menotti 11-D, Milan, MI 20129, Italy.

314 ITA ISSN 0390-6620
ITALY. ISTITUTO NAZIONALE DI STATISTICA. INDICATORI MENSILI. 1950-1971. m. Istituto Nazionale di Statistica (I S T A T), Via Cesare Balbo 16, Rome, 00184, Italy.

382 314 ITA ISSN 1129-6496
ITALY. ISTITUTO NAZIONALE DI STATISTICA. NOTIZIARIO. 1948-ceased. m. Istituto Nazionale di Statistica (I S T A T), Via Cesare Balbo 16, Rome, 00184, Italy.

360 314 ITA ISSN 1971-4629
ITALY. ISTITUTO NAZIONALE DI STATISTICA. STATISTICHE DELLA PREVIDENZA, DELLA SANITA E DELL'ASSISTENZA SOCIALE. 1951-1995. a. Istituto Nazionale di Statistica (I S T A T), Via Cesare Balbo 16, Rome, 00184, Italy.

372.021 ITA
ITALY. ISTITUTO NAZIONALE DI STATISTICA. STATISTICHE DELLA SCUOLA MATERNA ED ELEMENTARE. 1992-ceased. a. Istituto Nazionale di Statistica (I S T A T), Via Cesare Balbo 16, Rome, 00184, Italy.

372.021 ITA
ITALY. ISTITUTO NAZIONALE DI STATISTICA. STATISTICHE DELLA SCUOLA MEDIA INFERIORE. 1992-ceased. a. Istituto Nazionale di Statistica (I S T A T), Via Cesare Balbo 16, Rome, 00184, Italy.

373.021 ITA
ITALY. ISTITUTO NAZIONALE DI STATISTICA. STATISTICHE DELLE SCUOLE SECONDARIE SUPERIORI. 1992-ceased. a. Istituto Nazionale di Statistica (I S T A T), Via Cesare Balbo 16, Rome, 00184, Italy.

634.9 ITA ISSN 1126-2958
ITALY. ISTITUTO NAZIONALE DI STATISTICA. STATISTICHE FORESTALI. 1955-ceased. a. Istituto Nazionale di Statistica (I S T A T), Via Cesare Balbo 16, Rome, 00184, Italy.

330 ITA
ITALY. MINISTERO DEL BILANCIO E DELLA PROGRAMMAZIONE ECONOMICA. RELAZIONE GENERALE SULLA SITUAZIONE ECONOMICA DEL PAESE. 1951-ceased. a. Ministero del Bilancio, Via 20 Settembre, 97, Rome, RM, Italy.

330.9 ITA
ITALY. MINISTERO DEL BILANCIO E DELLA PROGRAMMAZIONE ECONOMICA. RELAZIONE PREVISIONALE E PROGRAMMATICA. 1965-ceased. a. Ministero del Bilancio e della Programmazione Economica, Via Venti Settembre, 97, Rome, RM 00187, Italy.

355 ITA ISSN 0036-9845
ITALY. SCUOLA DI GUERRA. BIBLIOTECA. BOLLETTINO. 1952-ceased. bi-m. Scuola di Guerra, Biblioteca, Civitavecchia, RM 00053, Italy.

629.1 ESP ISSN 0213-1250
ITAVIA. 1973-2003. 3/yr. Asociacion y Colegio de Ingenieros Tecnicos Aeronauticos, Hortaleza, 61, Madrid, 2804, Spain.

306.766 NLD ISSN 0928-6527
ITCH. 1979-2008. 3/yr. Itch, Kanaaldijk Noord 11, Eindhoven, 5613 DH, Netherlands.

100 ITA ISSN 1121-2772
ITINERARI FILOSOFICI. 1991-ceased. 3/yr. Societa Italiana per la Ricerca Filosofica, Via Carlo Crivelli 20, Milan, MI 20122, Italy.

338.0029 EGY ISSN 1110-1199
ITTIHAD AL-SINAAT AL-MISRIYAH. YEAR BOOK/FEDERATION OF EGYPTIAN INDUSTRIES. YEAR BOOK. 1949-19??. a. Federation of Egyptian Industries, 26A Sharia Sherif Pasha, P O Box 251, Cairo, Egypt.

343.097 NLD
J A R AMENDMENT SERVICE TO REGULATORY DOCUMENTS. ceased 2003. irreg. Joint Aviation Authorities, JAA Headquarters, Saturnusstraat 8-10, PO Box 3000, Hoofddorp, 2130 KA, Netherlands.

617.7 ITA ISSN 0393-800X
J D; rivista d'informazione dentale. (Junior Dental) 1986-ceased. q. Imadent s.n.c., Via Locana, 14-A, Turin, TO 10143, Italy.

354.3 ISR ISSN 0021-3705
J N F ILLUSTRATED; journal of land reclamation, afforestation and environmental improvement in Israel. 1927-2000. a. Jewish National Fund, P O Box 283, Jerusalem, Israel.

028.5 DEU
J P I - JUGEND PRESSE INFORMATIONEN. 1978-2003. 8/yr. Communications Consulting Network GmbH, Kottenforststr 20, Meckenheim, 53340, Germany.

438 DEU ISSN 0940-4961
J U M A. 1974-2006. q. Tiefdruck Schwann Bagel GmbH, Frankfurter Str 40, Cologne, 51065, Germany.

700 720 741.672 NLD ISSN 1574-3888
JAARBOEK NEDERLANDSE VORMGEVING. 2004-2005. a. Episode Publishers, Marconistr 52, Rotterdam, 3029 AK, Netherlands.

052 GBR
JACK. 2002-2004 (Aug.). m. Dennis Publishing Ltd., 30 Cleveland St, London, W1T 4JD, United Kingdom.

306.7660993205 NZL ISSN 1177-410X
JACK; a magazine for men. 2005-2007. q. Goode Press, PO Box 68868, Auckland, New Zealand.

379.2 ITA
JAEGERZEITUNG. 1951-ceased. q. Suedtiroler Jagdverband, Via Rosmini, 51, Bolzano, BZ 39100, Italy.

659.8 DEU ISSN 0021-3985
JAHRBUCH DER ABSATZ- UND VERBRAUCHSFORSCHUNG. 1955-2008. q. Duncker und Humblot GmbH, Carl-Heinrich-Becker-Weg 9, Berlin, 12165, Germany.

621.3 DEU ISSN 0722-0340
JAHRBUCH ELEKTROTECHNIK. 1982-2006. a. Beuth Verlag GmbH, Burggrafenstr 6, Berlin, 10787, Germany.

678 BRD ISSN 0171-5054
JAHRBUCH FUER VULKANISATION UND REIFENTECHNIK. 1952-1989. a. B V A Bielefelder Verlag GmbH & Co. KG, Ravensberger Str 10F, Bielefeld, 33602, Germany.

510 DEU ISSN 0179-2849
JAHRBUCH UEBER DIE FORTSCHRITTE DER MATHEMATIK. 1871-1944. irreg. Walter de Gruyter GmbH & Co. KG, Genthiner Str 13, Berlin, 10785, Germany.

613.62 DEU ISSN 0721-829X
JAHRESBERICHT DER GEWERBEAUFSICHT DES FREISTAATES BAYERN. 19??-2004. a. Bayerisches Staatsministerium fuer Gesundheit, Ernaehrung und Verbraucherschutz, Schellingstr 155, Munich, 80797, Germany.

615 DEU ISSN 0368-1521
JAHRESBERICHT DER PHARMAZIE. 1842-1943. a. Deutscher Apotheker Verlag, Postfach 101061, Stuttgart, 70009, Germany.

639 DEU ISSN 0075-2851
JAHRESBERICHT UEBER DIE DEUTSCHE FISCHWIRTSCHAFT. 1949-2006. a. Bundesministerium fuer Ernaehrung, Landwirtschaft und Verbraucherschutz, Rochusstr 1, Bonn, 53123, Germany.

975 320 USA ISSN 0361-6169
THE JAMES SPRUNT STUDIES IN HISTORY AND POLITICAL SCIENCE. 1900-2000. irreg. University of North Carolina Press, 116 S Boundary St, Chapel Hill, NC 27514.

305.42 USA ISSN 1093-8737
JANE. 1997-2007. 10/yr. Fairchild Publications, Inc., 7 W 34th St, New York, NY 10001-8191.

320.952 DEU ISSN 1436-3518
JAPAN AKTUELL (HAMBURG); journal of current Japanese affairs. 1991-2008. bi-m. G I G A Institute of Asian Studies, Rothenbaumchaussee 32, Hamburg, 20148, Germany.

332 338 JPN ISSN 0385-2369
JAPANESE FINANCE AND INDUSTRY: QUARTERLY SURVEY. 1949-1997. q. Industrial Bank of Japan, 3-3, Marunouchi 1-chome, Chiyoda-ku, Tokyo, 100-8210, Japan.

620.11 GBR ISSN 0954-3503
JAPANESE NEW MATERIALS YEARBOOK. 1987-198?. a. Elsevier International Bulletins, Mayfield House, 256 Banbury Rd, Oxford, OX2 7DH, United Kingdom.

635.9 ESP
JARDINAL. 1988-ceased. bi-m. Tecnipublicaciones Espana, S.L., Avda de Manoteras 44, 3a Planta, Madrid, 28050, Spain.

005.117 USA ISSN 1531-1228
JAVA ENTERPRISE DEVELOPER. 2000-200?. m. Eli Journals, 700 Metro Park, Rochester, NY 14623.

780.7 USA ISSN 1540-2886
JAZZ EDUCATION JOURNAL. 1968-2008. bi-m. International Association of Jazz Educators, PO Box 724, Manhattan, KS 66505-0724.

781.65 AUS ISSN 1039-7795
JAZZCHORD. 1993-2002. bi-m. Jazz Co-Ordination Association of New South Wales, PO Box 124, French Forest, NSW 2086, Australia.

929 DNK ISSN 0105-8347
JEG ARBEJDER MED; dansk slaegtsforskerfortegnelse. 1978-1996. a. Dansk Historisk Haandbogsforlag ApS, Buddingevej 87 A, Lyngby, 2800, Denmark.

002.074 ISR
JERFAIR NEWS; the Jerusalem International Book Fair newsletter. 1975-2000. irreg. Jerusalem International Book Fair, P O Box 775, Jerusalem, 91007, Israel.

657 ISR
JERUSALEM CONFERENCE ON ACCOUNTANCY. 1971-ceased. triennial. Institute of Certified Public Accountants in Israel, 1 Montefiore St., P O Box 29281, Tel Aviv, Israel.

070.5 ISR
JERUSALEM FELLOW. 1989-ceased. irreg. Jerusalem International Book Fair, P O Box 775, Jerusalem, 91007, Israel.

798.2 DNK ISSN 1901-6875
JESSY. 2006-200?. m. Egmont Serieforlaget A/S, Vognmagergade 11, Copenhagen, 1148, Denmark.

053.1 BRD ISSN 0720-6623
JET TALES. 1973-1981. bi-m. Sueddeutscher Verlag GmbH, Sendlinger Str 80, Munich, 80331, Germany.

745.594 AUS ISSN 1449-020X
JEWELLERY MAKING IDEAS. 2004-ceased. a. Universal Magazines Pty. Ltd., Private Bag 154, North Ryde, NSW 2113, Australia.

700.48296 ISR ISSN 0792-0660
JEWISH ART. 1974-1998. a. Hebrew University of Jerusalem, Center for Jewish Art, Mount Scopus Humanities Bldg., Jerusalem, 91905, Israel.

296.05 USA ISSN 0075-3726
JEWISH BOOK ANNUAL. 1942-1999. a. Jewish Book Council, 520 8th Avenue, 4th Fl, New York, NY 10018.

296 ISR ISSN 0792-8467
JEWISH STUDIES. 1967-2001. biennial. Jerusalem Academy of Jewish Studies, P O Box 5454, Jerusalem, Israel.

296 ISR ISSN 0792-6111
JEWISH WORLD; yearbook for Jewish communities and organizations. 1970-2005. a. Jewish World, P O Box 5086, Ramat Gon, 52150, Israel.

305.6296047 ISR ISSN 0334-4487
JEWS AND THE JEWISH PEOPLE - PETITIONS, LETTERS AND APPEALS FROM SOVIET JEWS/EVREI I EVREISKI NAROD - PETICII PIS'MA I OBRASENI EVREEV S S S R. 1970-199?. irreg. Hebrew University of Jerusalem, Center for Research and Documentation of East European Jewry, Givat Ram, Jerusalem, 91904, Israel.

Cessations

600 CHN ISSN 1001-3687
JIANGSU KEJI CHENGGUO TONGBAO. 1985-2001. m. Jiangsu-sheng Keji Qingbaosuo, 77, Suojin-Cun, Nanjing, 210042, China.

370 CHN ISSN 0254-8682
JIAOYU ZHANWANG/EDUCATIONAL PROSPECTS. 1984-2002. q. Zhongguo Duiwai Fanyi Chuban Gongsi, 4 Taipingqiao Dajie, Beijing, 100810, China.

618 TUR ISSN 1300-0438
JINEKOLOJI VE OBSTETRIK BULTENI. 1992-ceased. q. Hekimler Yayin Birligi, Bilkent Plaza, A3 Blok 21-24, Bilkent, Ankara, 06533, Turkey.

920 CHN ISSN 1005-3786
JINRI MINGLIU/CONTEMPORARY CELEBRITIES. 1994-2001. m. Jinri Mingliu, Wuchang-qu, 417, Donghu Lu, Wuhan, 430077, China.

600 CHN ISSN 1002-283X
JISHU KAIFA YU YINJIN/TECHNOLOGY DEVELOPMENT AND INTRODUCTION. 1985-1999. bi-m. Fujiansheng Keji Xinxi Yanjiusuo, 11 Hudong Lu, Fuzhou, Fujian 350003, China.

332.63 AUS
JOBSON'S ONLINE. 2000-2008. a. Dun & Bradstreet Marketing Pty. Ltd., St. Kilda Rd, PO Box 7405, Melbourne, VIC 3000, Australia.

780 GBR ISSN 1360-5798
JOCKEY SLUT. 1993-2004. bi-m. Jockey Slut Publishing Ltd., Unit 4C, Beehive Mill, Jersey St, Manchester, Lancs M4 6JG, United Kingdom.

387.7 629.13 NLD
JOINT AVIATION AUTHORITIES. CERTIFICATION INFORMATION - PROCEDURES. ceased 2003. plus q. updates. Joint Aviation Authorities, JAA Headquarters, Saturnusstraat 8-10, PO Box 3000, Hoofddorp, 2130 KA, Netherlands.

387.7 NLD
JOINT AVIATION AUTHORITIES. GENERAL INFORMATION - PROCEDURES. INFORMATION LEAFLETS. ceased 2003. plus q. updates. Joint Aviation Authorities, JAA Headquarters, Saturnusstraat 8-10, PO Box 3000, Hoofddorp, 2130 KA, Netherlands.

387.7 629.13 NLD
JOINT AVIATION AUTHORITIES. MAINTENANCE INFORMATION - PROCEDURES. ceased 2003. plus q. updates. Joint Aviation Authorities, JAA Headquarters, Saturnusstraat 8-10, PO Box 3000, Hoofddorp, 2130 KA, Netherlands.

387.7 NLD
JOINT AVIATION AUTHORITIES. NOTICE OF PROPOSED AMENDMENT SCHEME. ceased 2003. irreg. Joint Aviation Authorities, JAA Headquarters, Saturnusstraat 8-10, PO Box 3000, Hoofddorp, 2130 KA, Netherlands.

343.097 NLD
JOINT AVIATION AUTHORITIES. REGULATORY DOCUMENTS. ceased 2003. irreg. Joint Aviation Authorities, JAA Headquarters, Saturnusstraat 8-10, PO Box 3000, Hoofddorp, 2130 KA, Netherlands.

658 352.8 USA ISSN 1542-8680
JOINT COMMISSION INTERNATIONAL NEWSLETTER. 2003 (Jan./Feb.)-200?. bi-m. Joint Commission on Accreditation of Healthcare Organizations, 1 Renaissance Blvd, Oakbrook Terrace, IL 60181.

346.066 USA
JOINT VENTURES WITH THE SOVIET REPUBLICS; law and practice. 1990-199?. plus a. updates. LexisNexis, PO Box 7587, Charlottesville, VA 22906.

910.09 ITA
JONATHAN DIMENSIONE AVVENTURA. 1984-ceased. m. Systems Comunicazioni, Via Olanda 6, Vigano di Gaggiano, MI 20083, Italy.

630 634.9 DNK ISSN 0107-6108
JORDBRUG OESTJYLLAND; tidsskrift for landbrug, skovbrug og gartneri. 1980-1997. fortn. Jordbrug Oestjylland (Midt), c/o Bo Eriksson, Fussingsvej 21, Horsens, 8700, Denmark.

369 NLD ISSN 1871-7470
JOURNAAL ZORGVERZEKERINGEN. 2005-ceased. bi-m. Sdu Uitgevers bv, Postbus 20025, The Hague, 2500 EA, Netherlands.

594 AUS ISSN 0021-7719 CODEN: JCNYAE
JOURNAL DE CONCHYLIOLOGIE. 1850-1979. q. Journal de Conchyliologie, Ed. Dr. P.H. Fischer, 18/55 Prince Albert St, Mosman, NSW 2088, Australia.

034 FRA ISSN 0449-4733
JOURNAL DE L'ANNEE. 1966-2004. a. Editions Larousse, 21 rue du Montparnasse, Paris, 75283 Cedex 06, France.

510 FRA
LE JOURNAL DE MATHS DES ELEVES. 1994-199?. irreg. Ecole Normale Superieure de Lyon, Department de Mathematiques et Informatique, 46 Allee d'Italie, Lyon, Cedex 7 69364, France.

306.4 USA ISSN 0891-7124
JOURNAL FOR THE ANTHROPOLOGICAL STUDY OF HUMAN MOVEMENT (PRINT). 1980-2009. s-a. University of Illinois Press, 1325 S Oak St, Champaign, IL 61820.

615.7 USA ISSN 1540-5303 CODEN: JGDTEF
JOURNAL OF AGING & PHARMACOTHERAPY. 1986-2008. irreg. Routledge, 270 Madison Ave, New York, NY 10016.

331 USA ISSN 1525-7088
JOURNAL OF ALTERNATIVE DISPUTE RESOLUTION IN EMPLOYMENT. 1999-2001. q. C C H Inc., 2700 Lake Cook Rd, Riverwoods, IL 60015.

616.5 ITA ISSN 0392-8543 CODEN: JACOEL
JOURNAL OF APPLIED COSMETOLOGY; quarterly review of cosmetic dermatology. 1983-ceased. q. International Ediemme, Via Innocenzo XI, 41, Rome, RM 00165, Italy.

150 301 300 AUS ISSN 1442-0872
JOURNAL OF APPLIED HEALTH BEHAVIOUR. 1995-2002. s-a. University of Sydney, School of Behavioural and Community Health, PO Box 170, Lidcombe, NSW 2141, Australia.

956 AUS ISSN 1320-7199
JOURNAL OF ARABIC, ISLAMIC AND MIDDLE EASTERN STUDIES. 1993-1999. s-a. Deakin University, Faculty of Arts and Education (Burwood), 221 Burwood Hwy, Burwood, VIC 3125, Australia.

614 USA ISSN 1093-0019
JOURNAL OF BORDER HEALTH/REVISTA DE SALUD FRONTERIZA. 1984-2001; suspended. q. United States - Mexico Border Health Association, 5400 Suncrest Dr, Ste C-5, El Paso, TX 79912.

615.8 USA ISSN 1533-2098
JOURNAL OF BRIEF THERAPY. 2001-200?. 3/yr. Springer Publishing Company, 11 W 42nd St, 15th Fl, New York, NY 10036.

616.994 USA ISSN 1543-7671
JOURNAL OF CANCER PAIN & SYMPTOM PALLIATION. 2005-2008. q. The Haworth Medical Press, 10 Alice St, Binghamton, NY 13904.

572 USA ISSN 1946-4940 CODEN: JCELF3
JOURNAL OF CAPILLARY ELECTROPHORESIS AND MICROCHIP TECHNOLOGY. 1994-2008. bi-m. International Scientific Communications, Inc., 30 Controls Dr, PO Box 670, Shelton, CT 06484.

610.7362 GBR ISSN 1753-1594
JOURNAL OF CHILDREN'S AND YOUNG PEOPLE'S NURSING. 2007 (May)-2008 (Mar.); suspended. m. M A Healthcare Ltd., St. Jude's Church, Dulwich Rd, London, SE24 0PB, United Kingdom.

610 USA ISSN 1057-3321 CODEN: JFSYEU
JOURNAL OF CHRONIC FATIGUE SYNDROME; multidisciplinary innovations in research, theory & clinical practice. 1995-2008. q. The Haworth Medical Press, 10 Alice St, Binghamton, NY 13904.

612 USA ISSN 0892-5070
JOURNAL OF CLINICAL ELECTROPHYSIOLOGY. 1989-1999. s-a. American Physical Therapy Association, 1111 N Fairfax St, Alexandria, VA 22314.

570.285 USA ISSN 1066-5277 CODEN: JCOBEM
JOURNAL OF COMPUTATIONAL BIOLOGY (PRINT); a journal of computational molecular cell biology. 1994-2010 ( ). bi-m. (10/yr.). Mary Ann Liebert, Inc. Publishers, 140 Huguenot St, 3rd Fl, New Rochelle, NY 10801-5215.

930.1 NLD ISSN 1574-0773
JOURNAL OF CONFLICT ARCHAEOLOGY. 2005-2009 (Vol. 5). a. Brill, PO Box 9000, Leiden, 2300 PA, Netherlands.

610 362 USA ISSN 1530-1060
JOURNAL OF CONTROVERSIAL MEDICAL CLAIMS. 1991-2009. q. Aspen Publishers, Inc., 111 Eighth Ave., 7th Fl, New York, NY 10011.

025.06 USA ISSN 1540-7284
JOURNAL OF DIGITAL & ELECTRONIC ACQUISITIONS. 2006 (Spring)-200?. q. Haworth Information Press, 10 Alice St, Binghamton, NY 13904.

780 GBR ISSN 1355-7726
JOURNAL OF ELECTROACOUSTIC MUSIC. 1984-2002. a. Sonic Arts Network, The Jerwood Space, 171 Union St, London, SE1 0LN, United Kingdom.

331 USA ISSN 1528-1337
JOURNAL OF EMPLOYMENT DISCRIMINATION LAW. 1999-2001. q. C C H Inc., 2700 Lake Cook Rd, Riverwoods, IL 60015.

628.05 CAN ISSN 1496-2551
JOURNAL OF ENVIRONMENTAL ENGINEERING AND SCIENCE (PRINT). 2002-200?. bi-m. N R C Research Press, 1200 Montreal Rd, Bldg M-55, Ottawa, ON K1A 0R6, Canada.

616.8 USA ISSN 1521-1029 CODEN: JFNEFE
JOURNAL OF FORENSIC NEUROPSYCHOLOGY. 1998-2007. q. Taylor & Francis Inc., 325 Chestnut St, Ste 800, Philadelphia, PA 19106.

610 ITA ISSN 1591-0989
JOURNAL OF FUNCTIONAL SYNDROMES. 1998-ceased. 3/yr. Mattioli 1885 SpA, Via Coduro 1, Fidenza, PR 43036, Italy.

230.208968 USA ISSN 1077-7989
JOURNAL OF HISPANIC - LATINO THEOLOGY. 1993-2003. q. Liturgical Press, St John's Abbey, PO Box 7500, Collegeville, MN 56321.

633.53 USA ISSN 1537-7881 CODEN: JIHOAU
JOURNAL OF INDUSTRIAL HEMP; production, processing and products. 1994 (Spr.)-2008 (vol.13, no.2). s-a. Haworth Press, Inc., 325 Chestnut St, Ste 800, Philadelphia, PA 19106.

305.4 AUS ISSN 1325-1848
JOURNAL OF INTERDISCIPLINARY GENDER STUDIES. 1995-2006. s-a. University of Newcastle, Faculty of Education and Arts, Faculty of Arts and Social Sciences, Newcastle, NSW 2308, Australia.

300 USA ISSN 0363-2873
JOURNAL OF LIBERTARIAN STUDIES; an interdisciplinary review. 1977-2008. s-a. Ludwig von Mises Institute, 518 W Magnolia Ave, Auburn, AL 36832.

617.6 GBR ISSN 1464-3294
JOURNAL OF LINGUAL ORTHODONTICS. 1999-2003. q. Decker Europe Ltd., 36 Rochester Pl, London, NW1 9JJ, United Kingdom.

621.9 USA ISSN 1532-4435 CODEN: JMLRAJ
JOURNAL OF MACHINE LEARNING RESEARCH (PRINT). 2001-2004. 8/yr. M I T Press, 55 Hayward St, Cambridge, MA 02142-1493.

495.1 GBR ISSN 0967-1927
JOURNAL OF MACROLINGUISTICS. 1992-1996. q. Household World Ltd., 1 Ben Rhydding Rd, Ilkley, LS29 8RJ, United Kingdom.

616.863 USA ISSN 1091-1332
JOURNAL OF MAINTENANCE IN THE ADDICTIONS; innovations in research, theory, & practice. 1996-2008. q. Taylor & Francis Inc., 325 Chestnut St, Ste 800, Philadelphia, PA 19106.

610.73 USA ISSN 1526-8233
JOURNAL OF MULTICULTURAL NURSING AND HEALTH. 1994-2007. 3/yr. Riley Publications, Inc., Chautauqua Institution, PO Box 1107, Chautauqua, NY 14722.

516 GBR ISSN 0963-2654
JOURNAL OF NATURAL GEOMETRY. 1992-2003. q. Jnan Bhawan, 15 Queens Rd, London, W5 2SA, United Kingdom.

616.8 TUR ISSN 1302-1664
JOURNAL OF NEUROLOGICAL SCIENCES (PRINT)/NOROLOJIK BILIMLER DERGISI. 1998-ceased. q. Ege University Press, c/o Prof. Nezih Oktar, Ege University Hospital, Faculty of Medicine, Department of Neurosurgery, Bornova, Izmir, 35100, Turkey.

616.8 USA ISSN 1543-7698
JOURNAL OF NEUROPATHIC PAIN & SYMPTOM PALLIATION. 2005 (Spring)-2008. q. The Haworth Medical Press, 10 Alice St, Binghamton, NY 13904.

150 331.252 155.946 GBR ISSN 1740-4193
JOURNAL OF OCCUPATIONAL PSYCHOLOGY, EMPLOYMENT AND DISABILITY (PRINT). 2002-2008. s-a. Department for Work and Pensions, Psychology Division, B3 Porterbrook House, 7 Pear St, Sheffield, S11 8JF, United Kingdom.

346.066 USA ISSN 1930-5176
JOURNAL OF PAYMENT SYSTEMS LAW. 2005 (Feb.)-200?. 8/yr. Sheshunoff Information Services Inc., 807 Las Cimas Pky, Ste 300, Austin, TX 78746.

615 USA ISSN 1538-5396 CODEN: JPFEA5
JOURNAL OF PHARMACEUTICAL FINANCE, ECONOMICS & POLICY. 2003-2008. q. Pharmaceutical Products Press, 10 Alice St, Binghamton, NY 13904.

615.19 658 USA ISSN 0883-7597 CODEN: JPMMEY
JOURNAL OF PHARMACEUTICAL MARKETING AND MANAGEMENT. 1986-2008. q. Pharmaceutical Products Press, 10 Alice St, Binghamton, NY 13904.

615.071 USA ISSN 1044-0054 CODEN: JOPTET
JOURNAL OF PHARMACY TEACHING. 1990-2008. s-a. Pharmaceutical Products Press, 10 Alice St, Binghamton, NY 13904.

547.13 KOR ISSN 1225-8555
JOURNAL OF PHOTOSCIENCE. 1994-2005. q. Korean Society of Photoscience, Chungnam National University, Department of Chemistry, 220 Gung-dong, Yuseong-gu, Daejeon, 305-764, Korea, S.

370 AUS ISSN 1443-1483
JOURNAL OF POSTCOLONIAL EDUCATION. 2002-200?. s-a. James Nicholas Publishers, Pty. Ltd., PO Box 5179, South Melbourne, VIC 3205, Australia.

371 GBR ISSN 1355-3097
JOURNAL OF PRACTICE IN EDUCATION FOR DEVELOPMENT. 1995-2000. 3/yr. University of Manchester, School of Education, Humanities - Devas St, Oxford Rd, Manchester, M13 9PL, United Kingdom.

340 378.155 AUS ISSN 0810-9729
JOURNAL OF PROFESSIONAL LEGAL EDUCATION. 1983-1998. s-a. The College of Law Pty. Ltd., 2 Chandos St, St Leonards, NSW 2065, Australia.

340 USA ISSN 1053-8445
JOURNAL OF PROGRESSIVE LEGAL THOUGHT. 1989-1993. s-a. Florida State University, College of Law, 425 W Jefferson St, Tallahassee, FL 32306.

500 TUR ISSN 0022-4057 CODEN: JPASBN
JOURNAL OF PURE AND APPLIED SCIENCES/TEMEL VE UYGULAMALI BILMLER DERGISI. 1968-1990 (vol.3, no.2). irreg. (approx. 3/yr.). Middle East Technical University, Public Relations and Publications Office, Ismet Inonu Bulvari, Ankara, 06531, Turkey.

574 USA ISSN 1082-9695
JOURNAL OF RARE DISEASES. 1995-1998. bi-m. Dowden Health Media, Inc, 110 Summit Ave, Montvale, NJ 07645.

360 USA ISSN 1521-1037
JOURNAL OF RELIGION & ABUSE; advocacy, pastoral care and prevention. 1999-2008. q. Routledge, 325 Chestnut St, Ste 800, Philadelphia, PA 19106.

301 AUS ISSN 1443-2161
JOURNAL OF SOCIAL CHANGE AND CRITICAL INQUIRY. 1999-2000. 3/yr. Institute of Social Change and Critical Inquiry, Faculty of Arts, University of Wollongong, Northfields Ave, Wollongong, NSW 2522 , Australia.

658.8 USA ISSN 1554-5393
JOURNAL OF STRATEGIC E-COMMERCE. 2003 (Fall)-200?. s-a. Allied Academies, 145 Travis Rd, PO Box 2689, Cullowhee, NC 28723.

540 NLD ISSN 1472-7862 CODEN: JSCOC9
JOURNAL OF SUPRAMOLECULAR CHEMISTRY. 2001-2002 (vol.2, no.6). bi-m. Elsevier BV, Radarweg 29, P O Box 211, Amsterdam, 1000 AE, Netherlands.

617.6 NZL ISSN 1174-3913
JOURNAL OF TE AO MARAMA. 1996-2000. a. New Zealand Maori Dental Association, c/o John Broughton, Dept of Preventive and Social Medicine, Dunedin School of Medicine, Univ of Otago, PO Box 913, Dunedin, New Zealand.

347.006 USA ISSN 1533-2608
JOURNAL OF THREAT ASSESSMENT. 2001-2003. q. Haworth Press, Inc., 325 Chestnut St, Ste 800, Philadelphia, PA 19106.

910.202 AUS ISSN 1035-4662
THE JOURNAL OF TOURISM STUDIES. 1990-2005. s-a. James Cook University, School of Business, Tourism Program, Townsville, QLD 4810, Australia.

631 614.7 GBR ISSN 1478-548X
JOURNAL OF TURFGRASS AND SPORTS SURFACE SCIENCE. 1929-2008. a. Sports Turf Research Institute, St Ives Estate, Bingley, W Yorks BD16 1AU, United Kingdom.

025.04 USA ISSN 1553-3611
JOURNAL OF WEBSITE PROMOTION; innovations in internet business research, theory, and practice. 2005-2009. q. Internet Practice Press, 10 Alice St, Binghamton, NY 13904.

617.375 USA ISSN 1533-2888 CODEN: JWRDA9
JOURNAL OF WHIPLASH & RELATED DISORDERS. 2002 (Spring)-2008. s-a. The Haworth Medical Press, 10 Alice St, Binghamton, NY 13904.

616.0754 USA ISSN 1084-824X CODEN: JWIOAV
JOURNAL OF WOMEN'S IMAGING. 1997-200?. q. Lippincott Williams & Wilkins, 530 Walnut St, Philadelphia, PA 19106-3621.

338.4791 AUS ISSN 1449-0927
JOURNEYS. 2004-2009. q. Tourism Western Australia, GPO Box X2261, Perth, W.A. 6847, Australia.

362.7 DEU ISSN 0342-0175
JUGEND BERUF GESELLSCHAFT; Zeitschrift fuer Jugendsozialarbeit. 1949-2007. q. Bundesarbeitsgemeinschaft Jugendsozialarbeit, Chausseestr 128/129, Berlin, 10115, Germany.

028.5 DEU ISSN 1431-4800
JUGENDROTKREUZ. 1952-2007. bi-m. Deutsches Rotes Kreuz, Jugendrotkreuz, Carstennstr 58, Berlin, 12205, Germany.

808.8 GBR
JUICED. 1998-200?. w. Telegraph Group Ltd, One Canada Sq, Canary Wharf, London, E14 5DT, United Kingdom.

370 DNK ISSN 0107-8887
JULEHILSEN. 1962-2000. a. Elevforeningen for Hoven Ungdomsskole, Tarm, 6880, Denmark.

808.8385 053.1 DEU ISSN 1435-3695
JULIA SPECIAL. 1997-2005. irreg. Cora Verlag GmbH und Co. KG, Valentinskamp 24, Hamburg, 20350, Germany.

613 DEU
JUMPIN. 1994-2008. 4/yr. BurdaYukom Publishing GmbH, Konrad-Zuse-Platz 11, Munich, 81829, Germany.

280.4 AUS ISSN 1030-0287
JUNIOR CLUBHOUSE. 1975-2001. bi-m. Mission Publications of Australia, 19 Cascade St, PO Box 21, Lawson, NSW 2785, Australia.

808.8 028.5 895.1 CHN ISSN 1006-4818
JUREN/GIANT. 1981-2002. bi-m. Shaonian Ertong Chubanshe, 1538 Yan an Xilu, Shanghai, 200052, China.

340 DEU
JURFIX. 2002-2006. bi-m. D A T E V eG, Paumgartnerstr 6-14, Nuernberg, 90429, Germany.

340 FRA ISSN 0981-356X
JURIS LIBERAL. 1985-2004. bi-m. Editions Juris-Service, 12 quai Andre Lassagne, Lyon, 69001, France.

368.4 NLD ISSN 1572-4336
JURISPRUDENTIE WET WERK EN BIJSTAND (PRINT). 2004-ceased. s-m. Kluwer B.V., Postbus 23, Deventer, 7400 GA, Netherlands.

347 365.34 CAN ISSN 1715-0558
JUST LIVING. 1976-200?. s-a. Canadian Friends Service Committee, 60 Lowther Ave, Toronto, ON M5R 1C7, Canada.

345 NZL ISSN 1173-7573
JUSTICE MATTERS. 1992-2004. s-a. Ministry of Justice, P.O Box 12-418, Thorndon, Wellington, New Zealand.

340 CZE ISSN 1214-276X
JUSTICNI PRAXE; casopis pro pravni praxi. 1952-2003. 10/yr. Ministerstvo Spravedlnosti Ceske Republiky, Vysehradska 16, Prague, 12810, Czech Republic.

340 ESP ISSN 1134-3923
JUSTIFORUM; papers d'estudis i formacio. 1986-2000. 3/yr. Generalitat de Catalunya, Centre d'Estudis Juridics i Formacio Especialitzada, Roger de Flor, 196, Barcelona, 08013, Spain.

330 KOR ISSN 1225-0295
K B W. 1985-1994. m. Korea Businessworld Ltd., 107-6 Banpo-dong, Seocho-ku, 4-F Suhgun Bldg, Seoul, 137040, Korea, S.

951.9 KOR
K C C I BUSINESS JOURNAL. 1986-2000. q. Korea Chamber of Commerce and Industry, 45 Namdaemunno 4 ga Chung gu, PO Box 25, Seoul, 100743, Korea, S.

330 332 339 KOR
K D B ECONOMIC & INDUSTRIAL FOCUS. 1977-2003. m. Korea Development Bank, 16-3, Yeouido-dong, Yeongdeungpo-gu, Seoul, 150-973, Korea, S.

338.91 NLD ISSN 1380-1643
K I T NEWSLETTER. 1991-2000. s-a. K I T Publishers, Mauritskade 63, PO Box 95001, Amsterdam, 1090 HA, Netherlands.

004 332.1 GBR
K M NEWS. (Knowledge Management) 1998-2008. 10/yr. Bizmedia, Royal Station Court, Station Rd, Twyford, Reading, Berks RG10 9NF, United Kingdom.

796.332 NLD ISSN 1871-4978
K N V B JAARBOEK. -2000; resumed 2004-2005. a. Koninklijke Nederlandse Voetbalbond, Postbus 515, Zeist, 3700 AM, Netherlands.

331 DNK ISSN 1602-7094
K R I F A A-KASSE. 1985-2004. q. Kristelig Arbejdsloeshedskasse, PO Box 239, Randers, 8900, Denmark.

362.4 362.7 NLD ISSN 1572-400X
K2.BRABANT. 2003-2007. q. K2, Brabants Kenniscentrum Jeugd, Postbus 2347, 's-Hertogenbosch, 5202 CH, Netherlands.

028.5 DEU
KAEPT'N BLAUBAER; das fantastische Luegenmagazin. 2002 (Jul.)-2008 (Nov.). bi-m. Panini Verlags GmbH, Ravensstr 48, Nettetal, 41334, Germany.

384.5 USA ISSN 1098-0989
KAGAN'S RADIO FINANCIAL DATABOOK. 1998-199?. a. S N L Financial LC, One SNL Plz, PO Box 2124, Charlottesville, VA 22902.

331.88 SVK
KALENDAR ODBORARA. 1961-1993. a. Praca spol. s r.o., Odborarske nam 3, Bratislava, 81271, Slovakia.

700 ESP ISSN 0214-6762
KALIAS; revista de arte. 1989-2001. s-a. Generalitat Valenciana, Conselleria de Cultura i Educacio, Plaza de Manise, 3, Valencia, 46003, Spain.

371.42 CZE ISSN 1801-8300
KANCELARSKA ABECEDA. 2002-2007. q. Nakladatelstvi Dr. Josef Raabe, s.r.o., Sokolovska 155/31, Prague 8, 180 00, Czech Republic.

800 AUS ISSN 1036-3262
KANGAROO. 1980-1994. a. University of New England, Armidale Students' Association, Armidale, NSW 2351, Australia.

613.7 CHN ISSN 1005-314X
KANGLE SHIJIE/HEALTH AND HAPPINESS. 1994-2000. bi-m. Zhongguo Zhongyiyao Baoshe, 7, Xindong Lu, Beijing, 100027, China.

610.73 USA
KANSAS STATE BOARD OF NURSING. NEWSLETTER. 1987-19??. q. Arthur L. Davis Publishing Agency, Inc., 517 Washington St, PO Box 216, Cedar Falls, IA 50613.

332.1 DNK ISSN 1603-9947
KAPITAL. 1900-2006. s-a. Finansraadet, Finansraadets Hus, Amaliegade 7, Copenhagen K, 1256, Denmark.

616.1 DEU ISSN 0938-7293
KARDIOLOGIE ASSISTENZ. 1989-2007. q. Dr. Dietrich Steinkopff Verlag, Tiergartenstr 17, Heidelberg, 69121, Germany.

510 DDR ISSN 0300-0540
KARL-MARX-UNIVERSITAET LEIPZIG. MATHEMATISCH-NATURWISSENSCHAFTLICHE REIHE. WISSENSCHAFTLICHE ZEITSCHRIFT. 1952-1990. irreg. Universitaet Leipzig

016.37 DNK ISSN 0904-1893
KATALOG FOR SKOLEBIBLIOTEKER. ELEVERNE. 1986-2005. a. D B C A/S, Tempovej 7-11, Ballerup, 2750, Denmark.

016.37 DNK ISSN 0904-1907
KATALOG FOR SKOLEBIBLIOTEKER. SKOLEBIBLIOTEKAREN. 1975-2000. a. D B C A/S, Tempovej 7-11, Ballerup, 2750, Denmark.

362.18 BRD ISSN 0455-0250
KATASTROPHENMEDIZIN. 1963-1970. irreg. Wehr und Wissen Verlagsgesellschaft mbH, Heilsbachstr 26, Bonn, 53123, Germany.

026.282 NLD ISSN 0168-602X
KATHOLIEK DOCUMENTATIE CENTRUM. JAARBOEK. 1971-1999. a. Katholiek Documentatie Centrum, Erasmuslaan 36, Nijmegen, 6525 GG, Netherlands.

620 GBR ISSN 0075-5400
KEMPE'S ENGINEERS YEAR-BOOK. 1894-2002. a. C M P Information Ltd., Sovereign House, Sovereign Way, Tonbridge, Kent TN9 1RW, United Kingdom.

334 DEU ISSN 0721-4596
KERAMIK UND GLAS. 1970-2008. q. Berufsgenossenschaft der Keramischen und Glas-Industrie, Deelboegenkamp 4, Hamburg, 22297, Germany.

781.64 AUS
KERRANG!; life is loud. 2001-2004. m. Emap Australia Pty. Ltd., 187 Thomas St, Level 6, Haymarket, NSW 2000, Australia.

354.75 ISR
KESHER, ELEKTRONIKA, MACHSHEVIM. 1985-1992. q. Ministry of Defense Publishing House, 25 David Eleazer St., Hakirya, Tel Aviv, Israel.

378 410 NLD ISSN 1874-8163
KEUZEGIDS HOGER ONDERWIJS. DEEL B: TAAL EN COMMUNICATIE. 2006-2006. a. Hoger Onderwijs Persbureau, Postbus 2054, Leiden, 2301 CB, Netherlands.

500 600 CHN ISSN 1002-7076
KEXUE JISHU YANJIU CHENGGUO GONGBAO/BULLETIN OF SCIENTIFIC AND TECHNOLOGICAL ACHIEVEMENTS. 1981-2004. m. Guojia Kewei, Chengguo Guanli Bangongshi, No 15 Fuxing Lu, Beijing, 100038, China.

334 ISR ISSN 0792-7290
KIBBUTZ TRENDS. 1974-2005. s-a. Yad Tabenkin, C/o Ruth Sobol, Efal, 52960, Israel.

796.334 DEU
KICK CLUB. 2005-2008. m. Egmont Cultfish Media GmbH, Hansastr 32, Munich, 80686, Germany.

640 USA ISSN 1938-4963
KIDS' PARTIES. 200?-2008. a. Meredith Corporation, 1716 Locust St, Des Moines, IA 50309.

028.5 NLD ISSN 1871-2622
KIDSLIVE!. 2005-ceased. bi-m. KidsLive Foundation, Abby of Rolduc, Heyendallaan 64, Kerkrade, 6464 EP, Netherlands.

028.5 USA ISSN 1547-2019
KIDZONE. 2000-2008 (Nov.). bi-m. Scott Publications, 30595 Eight Mile, Livonia, MI 48152-1798.

330.9 DEU ISSN 0340-6970
KIELER VORTRAEGE. 1921-2004. a. Universitaet Kiel, Institut fuer Weltwirtschaft, Duesternbrooker Weg 120, Kiel, 24105, Germany.

820 NLD ISSN 1871-3211
KINBOTE. 2005-2007. 3/yr. Uitgeverij Prometheus B.V., Postbus 1662, Amsterdam, 1000 BR, Netherlands.

016.791 DDR ISSN 0233-2116
KINO FUER KINDER. 1983-1989. irreg. Progress Film-Verleih, Immanuelkirchstr 14 b, Berlin, 10405, Germany.

016.296 ISR ISSN 0023-1851
KIRYAT SEFER; bibliographical quarterly. 1924-2004. q. Jewish National and University Library, Jewish National and University Library, PO Box 34165, Jerusalem, Israel.

746 DEU ISSN 1619-5566
KIT FIGUREN-MODELL JOURNAL. 2001-2008. bi-m. N M C Nuernberger Modell-Literatur GmbH, Breitscheidstr 56, Nuernberg, 90459, Germany.

648 USA ISSN 1933-6241
KITCHEN STYLE & STORAGE. 2006-200?. a. Meredith Corporation, 1716 Locust St, Des Moines, IA 50309.

820 NZL
KITE. 1991-2001. s-a. University of Otago, Department of English, PO Box 56, Dunedin, New Zealand.

658 KOR
KIYUP KYUNGYUNG/BUSINESS MANAGEMENT. 1958-1998. m. Han-gug Saeng-san-seong Bonbu, 1676, Sangyeok 2-dong, Buk-gu, 1st Fl, Daegu Exhibition and Convention Center, Daegu, 702-845, Korea, S.

890 375.4 FRA ISSN 1142-3056
KLASK. 1989-2004. a. Presses Universitaires de Rennes, Campus de la Harpe, 2 Rue du Doyen Denis-Leroy, Rennes, Cedex 35044, France.

371.383 DEU
KLASSENZIELE. 2003-2006. 2/yr. corps - Corporate Publishing Services GmbH, Kasernenstr 69, Duesseldorf, 40213, Germany.

629.2 NLD ISSN 1574-2164
DE KLASSIEKEN REEKS. 2004-ceased. irreg. Uitgeverij Elmar, Delftweg 147, Rijswijk, 2289 BD, Netherlands.

057.86 CZE ISSN 1212-6586
KLEOPATRA. 1999-2004. q. Czech Press Group a.s., Klisska 1432-18, Usti nad Labem, 400 01, Czech Republic.

572.4 CZE ISSN 1210-7921 CODEN: KBMEF
KLINICKA BIOCHEMIE A METABOLISMUS. 1972-2007. q. Nakladatelske Stredisko C L S J.E. Purkyne, Sokolska 31, Prague, 12026, Czech Republic.

617 AUT ISSN 0368-6132
KLINISCHE MEDIZIN. 1946-1967. irreg. Oesterreichische Gesellschaft fuer Chirurgie, Frankgasse 8, Billroth-Haus, Vienna, 1096, Austria.

617.6 DNK ISSN 0109-2294
KLINISKE TANDTEKNIKERE. 1935-2004. m. Landsforeningen af Kliniske Tandteknikere, Vester Farimagsgade 6, 1, Copenhagen V, 1606, Denmark.

354.75 NLD ISSN 1872-0056
KLINK; het vakblad voor overheidscommunicatie. 1980-2006. 10/yr. Sdu Uitgevers bv, Postbus 20025, The Hague, 2500 EA, Netherlands.

613.66 621.932 USA
KNIFE DEFENSE. 1994-200?. irreg. Gould Publications, Inc., 1333 North US Hwy 17-92, Longwood, FL 32750.

028.5 370 USA ISSN 0163-4844
KNOW YOUR WORLD EXTRA. 1967-2008. bi-m. Weekly Reader Corporation, 3001 Cindel Dr, PO Box 8037, Delran, NJ 08075.

305.23 DEU
KOALA BRUEDER. 2005-2006. 4/yr. Panini Verlags GmbH, Ravensstr 48, Nettetal, 41334, Germany.

314.891 DNK ISSN 1399-8870
KOBENHAVNS STATISTISKE AARBOG. 1919-2005. a. Center for Raadgivning og Udvikling, Statistik, Vester Voldgade 87, Copenhagen V, 1552, Denmark.

700 ESP ISSN 0214-7955
KOBIE, REVISTA DE BELLAS ARTES Y CIENCIAS: SERIE BELLAS ARTES. 1969-2000. a. Diputacion Foral de Bizkaia, Departamento de Cultura, C Diputacion No. 7, PO Box 97, Bilbao, 48070, Spain.

384.5532 DEU
KOCHDUELL. 2000-2001. m. Egmont Cultfish Media GmbH, Hansastr 32, Munich, 80686, Germany.

353.55 DNK ISSN 0573-9799
KOEBENHAVNS BOLIGKOMMISSION. AARSBERETNING. 1940-2001. a. Koebenhavns Boligkommission, Ottiliavej 3, Valby, 2500, Denmark.

948 DNK ISSN 0105-936X
KOEBENHAVNS BYMUSEUM. 1978-1982. a. Koebenhavns Bymuseum, Absalonsgade 3, PO Box 3004, Copenhagen V, 1507, Denmark.

410 DNK ISSN 0908-0627
KOEBENHAVNS UNIVERSITET. OESTEUROPAINSTITUT. RAPPORTER. 1980-1995. irreg. Koebenhavns Universitet, Oesteuropainstitut, Snorresgade 17-19, Copenhagen K, 2300, Denmark.

630.24 668.6 NLD ISSN 0169-7625
KOERIER AGRO CHEMIE. 1959-2002. irreg. (2-3/yr.). Bayer Nederland B.V., Postbus 80, Mijdrecht, 3640 AB, Netherlands.

333.783 ISR
KOL ATAR/EVERY PLACE; bulletin of the National Park Authority. 1973-1990. s-a. National Park Authority, P O Box 7028, Tel Aviv, 61070, Israel.

541.345 BRD ISSN 0340-1480
KOLLOID-GESELLSCHAFT. MITTEILUNGEN. 19??-1976. irreg. Dr. Dietrich Steinkopff Verlag, Saalbaustr. 12, Darmstadt, 64283, West Germany.

352 DEU ISSN 1437-2444
KOMMUNALPRAXIS. AUSGABE BRANDENBURG, MECKLENBURG-VORPOMMERN, SACHSEN, SACHSEN-ANHALT, THUERINGEN, BERLIN. 1992-2004. 11/yr. Carl Link Verlag, Adolf-Kolping-Str 10, Kronach, 96317, Germany.

341.750614 DNK ISSN 1398-1420
KOMMUNERNE & EUROPA. 1989-2006. bi-m. Kommuneinformation A/S, Sommerstedgade 5, Copenhagen V, 1718, Denmark.

616.7 DEU
KOMPAKT RHEUMATOLOGIE UND OSTEOPOROSE. 2003-2004. 6/yr. Biermann Verlag GmbH, Otto-Hahn-Str 7, Cologne, 50997, Germany.

640 642.4 NLD ISSN 1871-4951
KOMPAS VOOR BELEID. HORECA. 1997-2002. a. Bedrijfschap Horeca en Catering, Postbus 121, Zoetermeer, 2700 AC, Netherlands.

670.29 DEU ISSN 0945-1900
KOMPASS DEUTSCHLAND. BAND 1. PRODUKTE/SERVICE/ KOMPASS GERMANY; informationswerk ueber ausgewaehlte Deutsche firmen/register of selected German industry and commerce. 1972-2000. a. Kompass Deutschland Verlags- und Vertriebsgesellschaft mbH, Jechtinger Str 13, Freiburg Im Breisgau, 79111, Germany.

670.29 NLD ISSN 0075-6660
KOMPASS HOLLAND; informatiewerk over het Nederlandse Bedrijfsleven. 1964-ceased. a. Kompass Nederland, Perkinsbaan 12E, Nieuwegein, 3439 ND, Netherlands.

200 DEU ISSN 1436-946X
KONFERNORMAL; die Arbeitshilfer fuer den KU. 1996-2003. m. Guetersloher Verlagshaus, Carl-Miele-Str 214, Guetersloh, 33311, Germany.

028.5 DEU ISSN 0942-1343
KONFETTI. 1964-2002. q. Deutscher Genossenschafts-Verlag eG, Leipziger Str 35, Wiesbaden, 65191, Germany.

570 DNK ISSN 0366-3612 CODEN: BSVSAQ
DET KONGELIGE DANSKE VIDENSKABERNES SELSKAB. BIOLOGISKE SKRIFTER. 1801-2001. irreg. Det Kongelige Danske Videnskabernes Selskab, H C Andersens Blvd 35, Copenhagen V, 1553, Denmark.

630.711 636.07 DNK ISSN 1600-2490
KONGELIGE VETERINAER- OG LANDBOHOEJSKOLE. DE STUDERENDES RAAD. TVAERFAGLIGT RUSUDVALG. BRUGSANVISNING I KVL. 1981-2001. a. Kongelige Veterinaer- og Landbohoejskole, Studerendes Raad, Dyrlaegevej 9, Frederiksberg, 1870, Denmark.

330 634 710 DNK ISSN 0909-0703
KONGELIGE VETERINAER- OG LANDBOHOEJSKOLE. INSTITUT FOR OEKONOMI, SKOV OG LANDSKAB. SAMFUNDSVIDENSKABELIG MEMO-SERIE/SOCIAL SCIENCE RESEARCH PAPERS. 1994-1994. irreg. Kongelige Veterinaer- og Landbohoejskole, Institut for Oekonomi, Skov og Landskab, Rolighedsvej 23, Frederiksberg C, 1958, Denmark.

630 DNK ISSN 0906-9550
KONGELIGE VETERINAER- OG LANDBOHOEJSKOLE. JORDBRUGSTEKNISK INSTITUT. RAPPORT. 1959-1992. irreg. Kongelige Veterinaer- og Landbohoejskole, Institut for Jordbrugsvidenskab, Thorvaldsensvej 40, Frederiksberg C, 1871, Denmark.

300 NLD ISSN 0923-5418
KONINKLIJK INSTITUUT VOOR TAAL-, LAND- EN VOLKENKUNDE. WORKING PAPERS SERIES. 1988-1999 (no.14). irreg. K I T L V Press, PO Box 9515, Leiden, 2300 RA, Netherlands.

551 622 NLD ISSN 0075-6741 CODEN: VGMGAD
KONINKLIJK NEDERLANDS GEOLOGISCH MIJNBOUWKUNDIG GENOOTSCHAP. VERHANDELINGEN. 1912-1980 (no.32). irreg. Koninklijk Nederlands Geologisch Mijnbouwkundig Genootschap, PO Box 6012, Delft, 2600, Netherlands.

948 NLD ISSN 1386-8969
KONINKLIJK NEDERLANDS HISTORISCH GENOOTSCHAP. KRONIEK; lijst van de voornaamste in...verschenen boeken en artikelen op het van de Nederlandse geschiedenis. 1995-2003. a. Koninklijk Nederlands Historisch Genootschap, Postbus 90406, The Hague, 2509 LK, Netherlands.

327 DNK ISSN 0105-0982
KONTAKT. 1946-2005. 6/yr. Mellemfolkeligt Samvirke, Faelledvej 12, Copenhagen N, 2200, Denmark.

380.1029 KOR ISSN 1225-0147
KOREA ANNUAL; comprehensive handbook on Korea. 1963-2004. a. Yonhap News Agency, 85-1 Susong-dong, Jongro-gu, Seoul, Korea, S.

380.1029 KOR ISSN 1225-4401
KOREA DIRECTORY. 1967-200?. a. Korea Directory Corp., 2nd Fl, KD Center, 8-15, Sinsa 1 Dong, Eunpyeong-gu, Seoul, 122-879, Korea, S.

016.9519 KOR
KOREA INSTITUTE FOR NATIONAL UNIFICATION. K I N U RESEARCH ABSTRACTS. 1997-2002. irreg. Korea Institute for National Unification, Suyu 6(yuk)-dong Gangbuk-gu, Seoul, 142-728, Korea, S.

052 KOR
KOREA NOW. 1972-2005. bi-w. Herald Media Inc., 3rd-5th Fl., 1-17, Jeong-dong, Jung-gu, CPO Box 6479, Seoul, 100-120, Korea, S.

327 KOR ISSN 0377-0451
KOREAN JOURNAL OF INTERNATIONAL STUDIES. 1970-2004. q. Korean Institute of International Studies, PO Box 426, Seoul, 110604, Korea, S.

369.463 NZL ISSN 1177-3111
HE KORERO MAHIRI. 2006-2007. m. Guides New Zealand, PO Box 13-143, Christchurch, New Zealand.

380.15 DEU ISSN 1437-5559
KRAFTVERKEHRSRECHT VON A-Z. 1950-2003. irreg. Erich Schmidt Verlag GmbH & Co. (Berlin), Genthiner Str 30 G, Berlin, 10785, Germany.

380.524 DNK ISSN 1603-7812
KRAKS TRANSPORT OG EMBALLAGE. 1973-2006. a. Kraks Forlag AS, Virumsgaardvej 21, Virum, 2830, Denmark.

914.891 DNK ISSN 0900-2243
KRAKS VEJVISER. 1901-1994. a. Kraks Forlag AS, Virumsgaardvej 21, Virum, 2830, Denmark.

368 DEU ISSN 0939-8104
KRANKENVERSICHERUNG UND UNFALLVERSICHERUNG IN RECHTSPRECHUNG UND SCHRIFTTUM. 1959-1998. irreg. Erich Schmidt Verlag GmbH & Co. (Berlin), Genthiner Str 30 G, Berlin, 10785, Germany.

745.5 NLD ISSN 1382-368X
KREAPLUS; hobby magazine. 1995-2007. q. E P N International N.V., Nieuwstr 20, Son, 5691 AC, Netherlands.

745.5 DEU
KREATIV: DEKORIEREN, BASTELN & NAEHEN. 1997-2008. q. Dollami Verlag GmbH, Hundsrueckstr 6, Wehretal-Langenhain, 37287, Germany.

345 DNK ISSN 1397-355X
KRIMINALFORSORGEN. 1997-2000. a. Direktoratet for Kriminalforsorgen, Strandgade 100, Copenhagen K, 1401, Denmark.

100 NLD ISSN 0168-275X
KRISIS (PRINT); tijdschrift voor empirische filosofie. 1980-2007. s-a. Boom Uitgevers Amsterdam, Prinsengracht 747-751, Amsterdam, 1017 JX, Netherlands.

529 NLD ISSN 1567-715X
KRONOSCOPE (PRINT); journal for the study of time. 2001-2009. 2/yr. Brill, PO Box 9000, Leiden, 2300 PA, Netherlands.

552 CZE ISSN 0454-5524 CODEN: KRYSAV
KRYSTALINIKUM; studies in geology, mineralogy, petrography. 1962-2006. a. Moravske Zemske Muzeum, Zelny trh 6, Brno, 65937, Czech Republic.

643 DEU
DIE KUECHEN-ZEITUNG. 2001-2005. 2/yr. Die Planung Verlagsgesellschaft mbH, Holzhofallee 25-31, Darmstadt, 64295, Germany.

747 DEU ISSN 1435-103X
KUECHENWELT; das Magazin fuer moderne Kuechengestaltung. 1998-2006. s-a. Die Planung Verlagsgesellschaft mbH, Holzhofallee 25-31, Darmstadt, 64295, Germany.

028.5 ISR ISSN 0334-648X
KULANU. 1985-2001. fortn. Z.Z. Printing & Productions, Derech Ben-Zvi 84, Tel Aviv, 68104, Israel.

028.5 ISR ISSN 0792-8149
KULANU - PILON; semi-monthly magazine for children. 1976-2000. 26/yr. Z.Z. Printing & Productions, Derech Ben-Zvi 84, Tel Aviv, 68104, Israel.

794 FIN ISSN 1459-1618
KULTARISTIKOT. 1980-2004. m. Sanoma Magazines Finland Corporation, Lapinmaentie 1, Helsinki, 00350, Finland.

910 300 DNK ISSN 0106-5866
KULTURGEOGRAFISKE HAEFTER. 1974-1998. 3/yr. Kulturgeografiske Haefter, Oestervoldgade 10, Copenhagen K, 1350, Denmark.

910 DNK ISSN 0108-3945
KULTURGEOGRAFISKE HAEFTERS SKRIFTSERIE. 1981-1992. irreg. Kulturgeografiske Haefter, Oestervoldgade 10, Copenhagen K, 1350, Denmark.

351 DNK ISSN 0907-1156
KULTURKONTAKTEN. 1992-2000; resumed 2002-2007. q. Kulturministeriet, Nybrogade 2, Copenhagen K, 1015, Denmark.

700 DNK ISSN 1901-144X
KULTURMAGASINET SKOPET. 1993-2006. bi-m. Kulturmagasinet Skopet, Kattesundet 10, Aalborg, 9000, Denmark.

306.7663 DNK ISSN 0108-1888
KVINDER, KVINDER. 1972-1981. a. Lesbisk Bevaegelse, Kvindehuset, Gothersgade 37, Copenhagen K, 1153, Denmark.

600 KOR
KWAHAK KISUL YORAM/HANDBOOK OF SCIENCE AND TECHNOLOGY. 1970-ceased. a. Korea, Republic of. Ministry of Science and Technology, Seoul, Korea, S.

027.44895 DNK ISSN 0108-7711
L A N A NYT. 1982-2004. q. Lokalhistoriske Arkiver i Nordjyllands Amt, c/o Aalborg Stadsarkiv, Arkivstraede 1, PO Box 1353, Aalborg, 9100, Denmark.

004.68 NLD
L A N INTERNETWORKING BUYERS GUIDE. (Local Area Network) 1998-1998. 3/yr. I D G Communications Nederland BV, Postbus 5446, Haarlem, 2000 GK, Netherlands.

658 332 USA
L I M R A'S VISION; effective strategy for tomorrow's leaders. (Life Insurance Marketing and Research Association) 1996-200?. bi-m. L I M R A International, Inc., 300 Day Hill Rd, Windsor, CT 06095.

428.24 GBR ISSN 0952-7206
L T U. (Language Testing Update) 1985-2004. s-a. Lancaster University, Centre for Research in Language Education, Bowland College, Department of Linguistics, Lancaster, LA1 4YT, United Kingdom.

331 ITA ISSN 0023-6489
LABOR. 1960-ceased. q. Labor, Via Tunisi, 4, Palermo, PA 90138, Italy.

320.994 AUS ISSN 0158-9245
LABOR ESSAYS. 1980-2004. a. Pluto Press, Locked Bag 199, Annandale, NSW 2038, Australia.

324.2 AUS ISSN 1441-7707
LABOR HERALD. 1894-2004. q. John Curtin Ltd., PO Box E 1, Kingston, ACT 2604, Australia.

331 USA ISSN 1041-5904
LABOR'S HERITAGE. 1989-2004. q. George Meany Center for Labor Studies, 10000 New Hampshire Ave, Silver Spring, MD 20903.

331 ISR
LABOUR AND SOCIAL AFFAIRS AND NATIONAL INSURANCE/'AVODA UR'WAHA UVITTU-AH L'UMMI. 1949-1997. m. Ministry of Labour and Social Affairs, 10 Yad Harutzim St., Talpiot, Jerusalem, 91000, Israel.

331.8 ISR ISSN 0023-6969
LABOUR IN ISRAEL. 1947-1994. irreg. (3-4/yr.). Histadrut, 93 Arlozoroff St., Tel Aviv, Israel.

344.01 NLD ISSN 1387-0777
LABOUR LAWS OF EUROPE. 1998-ceased. irreg. Global Law Association, PO Box 9001, Tilburg, 5000 HA, Netherlands.

200 ITA
LABRYS; annuario dell'Istituto di Studi Tradizionali. 1980-ceased. a. Istituto di Studi Tradizionali, Via del Roscetto, 22, Perugia, 06122, Italy.

374.8025 DNK ISSN 1397-1824
LAERERHEFTE TIL VI UNDERSOEGER OG MIN VEJ. 1996-2003. a. Raadet for Uddannelses- og Erhvervsvejledning (R.U.E.), Vester Voldgade 123, Copenhagen V, 1552, Denmark.

323.4 AUS ISSN 1329-7236
LAND RIGHTS QUEENSLAND. 1994-2002. m. Faira Aboriginal Corporation, PO Box 8402, Woolloongabba, QLD 4102, Australia.

388.1 NZL ISSN 1177-6285
LAND TRANSPORT ROAD ASSETS. 200?-2008. a. New Zealand Transport Agency, Lambton Quay, PO Box 5084, Wellington, 6145, New Zealand.

631.302 DNK ISSN 0107-461X
LANDBRUGETS MASKINOVERSIGT. 1972-2005. a. Landskontoret for Bygninger og Maskiner, Skejby, Udkaersvej 15, Aarhus N, 8200, Denmark.

630.60489 DNK ISSN 0302-4946
LANDBRUGSAARBOG; noeglen til dansk landbrug. 1899-2006. a. Det Kongelige Danske Landhusholdningsselskab, Axeltorvet 3, Copenhagen V, 1609, Denmark.

550 DEU ISSN 1617-1330 CODEN: JGLBAV
LANDESAMT FUER GEOLOGIE, ROHSTOFFE UND BERGBAU BADEN-WUERTTEMBERG. JAHRESHEFTE. 1955-2004. a. Landesamt fuer Geologie Rohstoffe und Bergbau Baden-Wuerttemberg, Albertstr 5, Freiburg Im Breisgau, 79104, Germany.

616.07 USA ISSN 1529-7780
LANGE SMART CHARTS: PATHOLOGY. 2000-200?. triennial. McGraw-Hill Companies, Inc., 2 Penn Plaza, New York, NY 10121.

028.5 FRA ISSN 1956-2713
LAPINPIN. 2006-2006. bi-m. Editions Balisier, 13 Rue Gounod, Saint-Cloud, 92210, France.

330 ISR ISSN 0792-075X
LATA'ASYAN. 1987-1988. m. Manufacturers Association of Israel, 29 Hamered St, Tel Aviv, 68125, Israel.

336.2 NLD
LATIN AMERICAN TAXATION DATA BASE ON CD-ROM. ceased. 4/yr. International Bureau of Fiscal Documentation (I B F D), H J E Wenckebachweg 210, Amsterdam, 1096 AS, Netherlands.

920 980 NLD ISSN 1384-5799
LATINOAMERICANISTAS EN EUROPA (YEAR); registro bio-bibliografico. 1973-2002. irreg. Centrum voor Studie en Documentatie van Latijns Amerika, Keizersgracht 395-397, Amsterdam, 1016 EK, Netherlands.

331.8 ITA
IL LAVORO. 1946-ceased. a. Camera Confederale del Lavoro UIL, Via Ugo Polonio, 5, Trieste, TS 34125, Italy.

658.31244 ITA ISSN 0390-2528
LAVORO SICURO; uomo, ambiente, macchine. 1973-ceased. m. (9/yr.). Il Sole 24 Ore Business Media, Divisione J C E, Via Patecchio 2, Milan, 20141, Italy.

346.013 USA
LAW ENFORCEMENT VOLUNTEERS. 198?-1989. q. American Association of Retired Persons (A A R P), 601 E St, NW, Washington, DC 20049.

340.0711 USA ISSN 0529-097X
LAW SCHOOL RECORD. 1951-19??. s-a. University of Chicago, Law School, 1111 E 60th St, Chicago, IL 60637.

712 GBR
LAWN & GARDEN EQUIPMENT. 1988-2005. m. Nelson Communications Ltd., 25a New St, Salisbury, Wilts SP1 2PH, United Kingdom.

658.3 USA ISSN 0739-1706
LAWYER HIRING & TRAINING REPORT. 1980-1995. m. Aspen Law & Business, 1185 Ave of the Americas, 37th Fl, New York, NY 10036.

709 NZL ISSN 1176-8487
LEAD. 2004-2005 (no.2). s-a. Lead Magazine, 10 Don St, Invercargill, New Zealand.

287.6 371.2 USA ISSN 1931-8200
LEADER IN CHRISTIAN EDUCATION MINISTRIES. 1988-2008. q. United Methodist Publishing House, 201 8th Ave S, PO Box 801, Nashville, TN 37202.

352.14 NZL ISSN 1173-5058
LEADERS (AUCKLAND). 1975-2001 (May). q. T P L. Media (Trade Publications), Newmarket, PO Box 9596, Auckland, 1149, New Zealand.

303 USA ISSN 1073-5631
THE LEADERSHIP ADVANTAGE. 1994-2001. m. Rutherford Publishing, 1600 Lake Air Dr, Waco, TX 76710.

155.67 USA ISSN 1072-0502 CODEN: LEMEFO
LEARNING & MEMORY (PRINT). 1994-2008. bi-m. Cold Spring Harbor Laboratory Press, 500 Sunnyside Blvd, Woodbury, NY 11797.

664 DEU ISSN 0945-9391
LEBENSMITTEL VERPACKEN. 1994-1996. m. Buecker Fachverlag GmbH & Co. KG, Postfach 1363, Bad Breisig, 53492, Germany.

664 DEU ISSN 0945-2907
LEBENSMITTELHANDEL IM SPIEGEL DER STATISTIK (YEAR). 1955-2003. a. Bundesverband des Deutschen Lebensmittelhandels e.V., Am Weidendamm 1A, Berlin, 10117, Germany.

340 640 DEU ISSN 1615-0996
LEBENSMITTELRECHT RECHTSPRECHUNG CD-ROM. 2000-2007. plus updates 2/yr. Verlag C.H. Beck oHG, Wilhelmstr 9, Munich, 80801, Germany.

530 DEU ISSN 1616-6361 CODEN: LNPHA4
LECTURE NOTES IN PHYSICS. MONOGRAPHS. 1969-2003 (vol.73). irreg. Springer, Tiergartenstr 17, Heidelberg, 69121, Germany.

658 DNK ISSN 0905-8966
LEDELSE I DAG. 1990-2005. q. Ledernes Hovedorganisation, Vermlandsgade 63, Copenhagen S, 2300, Denmark.

374.013 DNK ISSN 0109-9299
LEDER-KURSUSKATALOG. 1984-1985. a. Koebenhavns Universitet, Noerregade 10, Copenhagen, 1017, Denmark.

900 800 GBR ISSN 0024-0281
LEEDS PHILOSOPHICAL AND LITERARY SOCIETY. PROCEEDINGS. LITERARY AND HISTORICAL SECTION. 1925-1999. irreg. (1-4/yr.). Leeds Philosophical and Literary Society, Dr John Lydon, The Secretary, The City Museum, c/o The Town Hall, Leeds, LS1 3AD, United Kingdom.

639.2 799.1 ITA
LEGA PESCA NEWS. 1975-200?. 24/yr. Lega Pesca, Via Nazionale 243, Rome, RM 00184, Italy.

362.58 AUS ISSN 1030-2913
LEGAL AID NEWS. 1986-2005. s-a. Legal Aid Commission of New South Wales, 323 Castlereagh St, Sydney, NSW 2000, Australia.

346.05 USA
LEGALINES: ESTATE AND GIFT TAX KEYED TO THE SURREY CASEBOOK. ceased 200?. irreg. Gilbert Law Summaries, 610 Opperman Dr, Eagan, MN 55123.

808.83874 CZE ISSN 1801-6421
LEGENDY DIVOKEHO ZAPADU. 2006-2007. m. Moravska Bastei MOBA, s.r.o., Kotlarska 53, Brno, 602 00, Czech Republic.

349 ITA ISSN 0024-0400
LE LEGGI. 1961-ceased. 2/m. Zanichelli Editore SpA, Via Irnerio 34, Bologna, BO 40126, Italy.

830 NLD ISSN 0169-8559
LEIDSE GERMANISTISCHE EN ANGLISTISCHE REEKS. 1962-1983 (vol.21). irreg. Brill, PO Box 9000, Leiden, 2300 PA, Netherlands.

340 NLD ISSN 0169-8605
LEIDSE JURIDISCHE REEKS/JURIDICAL STUDIES OF THE UNIVERSITY OF LEIDEN. 1954-1981. irreg. Brill, PO Box 9000, Leiden, 2300 PA, Netherlands.

479 879 NLD ISSN 0169-8656
LEIDSE ROMANISTISCHE REEKS. 1954-1990 (vol.24). irreg. Brill, PO Box 9000, Leiden, 2300 PA, Netherlands.

659.1 DEU
LEIPZIGER MESSEJOURNAL. 1967-1990. a. Leipziger Messeamt, Markt 11-15, Leipzig, 04109, Germany.

798 ITA ISSN 1827-9589
L'ENCICLOPEDIA DEL CAVALLO E DEL CAVALIERE. 2006-200?. s-m. Sprea Editori Srl, Via Torino 51, Cernusco sul Naviglio, MI 20063, Italy.

779.28 CZE ISSN 1211-4529
LEO ALBUM. 1994-2008. q. PK 62, a.s., Bohdalecka 6, Prague 10, 101 00, Czech Republic.

378.1 GBR ISSN 0024-0923
LEODIENSIAN. 1886-2008 (Oct.). a. Leeds Grammar School, Alwoodley Gates, Harrogate Rd, Leeds, LS17 8GS, United Kingdom.

910.202 USA ISSN 1530-8278
LET'S GO: SOUTHEAST ASIA (YEAR). 1996-2004. a. Let's Go Publications, Inc., c/o Relevant Guidebook, 67 Mt Auburn St, Cambridge, MA 02138.

613.7 USA ISSN 0024-1288 CODEN: JNMDAN
LET'S LIVE; America's foremost health & preventive medicine magazine. 1933-2007. m. Franklin Publications, 11050 Santa Monica Blvd, Los Angeles, CA 90025.

100 ITA ISSN 1970-6197
LETTERE FILOSOFICHE. 2000-200?. irreg. Poligrafo Casa Editrice, Via Cassan Carlo 34, Padua, PD 35121, Italy.

944 FRA ISSN 1150-4706
LA LETTRE D'ACTIVITES EN PAYS BASQUE. 1950-2003. q. Bayonne and Basque country's Chamber of Commerce, 50-51 allees Marines, B.P. 215, Bayonne, Cedex 64102, France.

004 FRA ISSN 1163-3867
LETTRE DE LA SURETE DE FONCTIONNEMENT. 1987-199?. bi-m. E C 2, 269 rue de la Garenne, Nanterre, 92000, France.

006.3 FRA ISSN 0767-4910
LETTRE DE L'INTELLIGENCE ARTIFICIELLE. 1985-1998. 11/yr. E C 2, 269 rue de la Garenne, Nanterre, 92000, France.

780 FRA ISSN 1259-542X
LA LETTRE DU DISQUE. 1994-2004. w. Bandiagara Editions, 36 rue de Romainville, Paris, 75019, France.

338.642 FRA ISSN 1143-8894
LA LETTRE SOCIALE DE NOTE D'INFOS FISCALES, SOCIALES ET JURIDIQUES. 1989-2004. m. S I D Communications, BP 1119, Poitiers 9, Cedex 86061, France.

668.802 DNK ISSN 0902-4905
LEVERANDOERHAANDBOGEN. 1979-1993. biennial. Emballage- og Transportinstituttet, Gregersensvej, PO Box 141, Taastrup, 2630, Denmark.

056 ESP ISSN 0210-6337
LEVIATAN; revista de hechos e ideas. 1934-2001. q. Editorial Pablo Iglesias, Monte Esquinza 30, 3o. D, Madrid, 28010, Spain.

336.1 CZE ISSN 1801-7932
LEXIKON DANOVYCH USPOR. 2002-2007. plus q. updates. Verlag Dashoefer s.r.o., Na Prikope 18, PO Box 756, Prague 1, 11121, Czech Republic.

338 CZE ISSN 1801-769X
LEXIKON TECHNICKYCH MATERIALU SE ZAHRANICNIMI EKVIVALENTY. 1998-2006. q. Verlag Dashoefer s.r.o., Na Prikope 18, PO Box 756, Prague 1, 11121, Czech Republic.

551 CHN ISSN 1000-6273
LIAONING DIZHI/LIAONING GEOLOGY. 1984-2001. q. Liaoning Dizhi Bianjibu, No 29, Beiling Dajie, Shenyang, Liaoning 110032, China.

059.951 CHN ISSN 0457-6306
LIAONING HUABAO/LIAONING PICTORIAL. 1945-1998. m. Liaoning Huabao She, No 29, Minzu Beijie, Heping-qu, Shenyang, Liaoning, China.

198.9 DNK ISSN 0109-5978
LIBER ACADEMIAE KIERKEGAARDIENSIS. 1980-1992. a. C.A. Reitzels Boghandel & Forlag A/S, Noerregade 20, Copenhagen K, 1165, Denmark.

340 051 USA ISSN 1078-3555
LIBERTY, LIFE AND FAMILY. 1994-2000. s-a. Regent University, School of Law, 1000 Regent University Dr, Virginia Beach, VA 23464.

020 GBR
LIBRARY AND INFORMATION ACTIVISTS RECORD. 1987-1988. 4/yr. Hector & Ruffle Ltd., Eaton Court, 11 Eaton Rd, Sutton, Surrey SM2 5DZ, United Kingdom.

020 GBR
LIBRARY AND INFORMATION RESEARCH (PRINT). 1978-2007. 3/yr. Library and Information Research Group, c/o Elizabeth Gadd, Pilkington Library, Loughborough University, Loughborough, Leicestershire LE11 3TU, United Kingdom.

230 USA ISSN 0075-9090
LIBRARY OF CHRISTIAN CLASSICS. 1953-1966. irreg. Westminster John Knox Press, Rm 2047, 100 Witherspoon St, Louisville, KY 40202.

794.8 ITA ISSN 1824-4491
IL LIBRO DEI CODICI. 2004-200?. bi-m. Tattilo Editrice SpA, Via degli Olmetti 18, Rome, 00060, Italy.

011 800 GBR ISSN 1741-7880
LIGHT'S LIST OF LITERARY MAGAZINES. 1986-2007; suspended. a. Photon Press, 37 The Meadows, Berwick-upon-Tweed, Northd TD15 1NY, United Kingdom.

055.1 ITA
LIGURIA. 1933-ceased. m. Editrice Liguria, Via de Mari 4, Savona, SV 17100, Italy.

700 AUS ISSN 1327-5445
LIKE, ART MAGAZINE. 1988-2001. 3/yr. Royal Melbourne Institute of Technology, Faculty of Art, Design & Communication, GPO Box 2476 V, Melbourne, VIC 3001, Australia.

373 DNK ISSN 1902-6501
LILLESKOLEN. 2001-2008. a. Lilleskolerne, Ny Kongensgade 10, Copenhagen K, 1472, Denmark.

323 NLD ISSN 1574-0943
DE LIMIT. 2003-2005. q. Fractie Leefbaar Rotterdam, Postbus 8734, Rotterdam, 3009 AS, Netherlands.

338.1 NZL ISSN 1170-7607
LINCOLN UNIVERSITY. AGRIBUSINESS AND ECONOMICS RESEARCH UNIT. DISCUSSION PAPER. 1968-2005. irreg. Lincoln University, Agribusiness and Economics Research Unit, PO Box 84, Canterbury, 7647, New Zealand.

686.2 ITA ISSN 0024-3744
LINEAGRAFICA/INTERNATIONAL REVIEW OF GRAPHIC DESIGN AND VISUAL COMMUNICATIONS; rivista di grafica e communicazione visiva. 1946-ceased. bi-m. Progetto Editrice Srl, Corso Giuseppe Garibaldi 64, Milan, MI 20121, Italy.

700 ITA
LINEAVERDE; periodico di arte attualita e cultura. 1973-ceased. bi-m. Rossieditore, Via L. Giordano 56, Casella Postale 1008, Vomero, NA 80100, Italy.

410.151 ITA ISSN 0392-6907
LINGUISTICA COMPUTAZIONALE. 1981-2006. s-a. Fabrizio Serra Editore, c/o Accademia Editoriale, Via Santa Bibbiana 28, Pisa, 56127, Italy.

450 ITA
LINGUISTICA E DIALETTI. 1974-1988 (no.12). irreg. Angelo Longo Editore, Via Paolo Costa 33, Ravenna, 48121, Italy.

382 338.95694 ISR ISSN 0792-9765
LINK; Israel's international business magazine. 1991-2001. m. Pick Communications Ltd., P O Box 57500, Tel Aviv, 61574, Israel.

004 USA ISSN 1544-4511
LINUXWORLD (PRINT); the leading linux resource in the world !. 2003 (Sept./Oct.)-2009. bi-m. SYS-CON Media, Inc., 135 Chestnut Ridge Rd, Montvale, NJ 07645.

369.1 ITA
THE LION. 1953-ceased. m. (10/yr.). Lions Clubs International, Italy - Distretto 108 IB1, Via Giacomo Leopardi 5, Milan, 20015, Italy.

369.5 ITA
LIONISMO. 1974-ceased. bi-m. Lions Clubs International, Italy - Distretto 108 L, Piazza G Frua 22, Rome, Italy.

615 BRD ISSN 0720-0714
LIPID-SPIEGEL. 1978-1981. irreg. P M I Verlagsgruppe GmbH, August-Schanz-Str 8-II, Frankfurt Am Main, 60433, Germany.

610 GBR
LIPIDS AND ATHEROSCLEROSIS ANNUAL. 2001-2003. a. Taylor & Francis Ltd., 4 Park Sq, Milton Park, Abingdon, OX14 4RN, United Kingdom.

663.1 AUS ISSN 1323-5869
LIQUOR RETAILING HANDBOOK. 1987-1995. a. Reed Business Information Pty Ltd., Tower 2, 475 Victoria Ave, Locked Bag 2999, Chatswood, NSW 2067, Australia.

332.63 330.9 ITA
LIST OF ITALIAN STOCKS. 1950-ceased. m. Banca Commerciale Italiana, Piazza Della Scala, 6, Milan, MI 20121, Italy.

551.48 ESP
LISTA FAUNISTICA Y BIBLIOGRAFICAS. 1984-2002. a. Asociacion Iberoamericana de Limnologia, Apdo de Correcos 644, Bilbao, 48080, Spain.

668.5 ITA
LISTINO DI IMAGINE. 1959-ceased. 5/yr. Sfera Editore SpA, Via Angelo Rizzoli 2, Milan, MI 20132, Italy.

780 GBR ISSN 0459-5084
THE LISZT SOCIETY. NEWSLETTER. 1965-197?. q. The Liszt Society, 9 Burnside Close, Twickenham, Mddx TW1 1ET, United Kingdom.

331 016 DEU ISSN 0342-0922
LITERATURDOKUMENTATION ZUR ARBEITSMARKT- UND BERUFSFORSCHUNG. 1972-2003. 2/yr. Bundesagentur fuer Arbeit, Institut fuer Arbeitsmarkt- und Berufsforschung, Regensburger Str 104, Nuernberg, 90478, Germany.

011 DEU
LITERATURSCHAU: ZERSTOERUNGSFREIE PRUEFUNG/BULLETIN OF ABSTRACTS: NON-DESTRUCTIVE TESTING. 1973-2007. 12/yr. Fachinformationszentrum Technik e.V., Hanauer Landstr 151-153, Frankfurt Am Main, 60314, Germany.

620.11 012 DEU ISSN 1433-2221
LITERATURSCHAU ZERSTOERUNGSFREIE PRUEFUNG/ABSTRACT JOURNAL: NON-DESTRUCTIVE TESTING. 1976-2007. 12/yr. Deutsche Gesellschaft fuer Zerstoerungsfreie Pruefung, Max-Planck-Str 6, Berlin, 12489, Germany.

070.5 DEU
LITFASS. 1976-1995. bi-m. BurdaYukom Publishing GmbH, Konrad-Zuse-Platz 11, Munich, 81829, Germany.

340.5 GBR ISSN 1355-610X
THE LITIGATOR. 1994-1997. q. Sweet & Maxwell Ltd., 100 Avenue Rd, London, NW3 3PF, United Kingdom.

017.1 DNK ISSN 0108-7215
LITTERATUR PAA INDVANDRERSPROG I DANSKE FOLKEBIBLIOTEKER. 1983-2004. a. D B C A/S, Tempovej 7-11, Ballerup, 2750, Denmark.

800 CHN ISSN 1000-9132
LITTERATURE CHINOISE. 1964-2000. q. Zhongguo Wenxue Chubanshe, 24 Baiwanzhuang Lu, Beijing, 100037, China.

800 FRA ISSN 1279-7367
LITTERATURE LORRAINE. 1992-1998. a. Presses Universitaires de Nancy, 42-44 av. de la Liberation, Nancy, 54000, France.

746.9 668.5 USA
LITTLE BROWN BOOK; the magazine for Bloomingdale's insiders. 2006-200?. bi-m. Rodale, Inc., 33 E Minor St, Emmaus, PA 18098.

747 ESP
LIVING AT HOME. 2004-suspended. s-a. G y J Espana Ediciones S.L., Albasanz, 15 Edificio A, Madrid, 28037, Spain.

001.3 ESP ISSN 0213-9936
LLETRA DE CANVI. 1988-1998. q. Ediciones de Intervencion Cultural, C. Sant Antoni 86 Local 9, Mataro, Barcelona, 08301, Spain.

332 GBR
LLOYDS TSB. ECONOMIC BULLETIN. 1979-2003. q. Lloyds TSB, 71 Lombard St, London, EC3P 3BS, United Kingdom.

940.53 ISR ISSN 0334-9470
LO NISHKACH. 1985-1998. a. Second Generation For Perpetuation of Greek Jewish Holocaust, 68 Levinsky St, Tel Aviv, 66855, Israel.

551.5 USA ISSN 0198-2885
LOCAL CLIMATOLOGICAL DATA. SAINT JOSEPH, MISSOURI. ANNUAL SUMMARY WITH COMPARATIVE DATA. 19??-1981. a. National Oceanic and Atmospheric Administration (N O A A), National Climatic Data Center, Federal Bldg, 151 Patton Ave, Asheville, NC 28801.

384.6 USA ISSN 1087-8998
LOCAL COMPETITION REPORT. 1992-2003. bi-w. (26/yr.). Warren Communications News, Inc., 2115 Ward Ct, NW, Washington, DC 20037.

657 USA ISSN 1042-0231
LOCAL GOVERNMENTAL ACCOUNTING TRENDS AND TECHNIQUES. 1988-1993. a. American Institute of Certified Public Accountants, Harborside Financial Ctr, 201 Plaza Three, 3rd Fl, Jersey City, NJ 07311-9801.

700 CAN ISSN 1718-5017
LOCUS SUSPECTUS. 2006-2009. 3/yr. Locus Suspectus, 36 rue Faillon Est, Montreal, PQ H2R 1K6, Canada.

948.9 DNK ISSN 0106-0430
LOEGUMKLOSTER-STUDIER. 1978-1992. irreg. Historisk Forening for Loegumkloster Kommune, Museet Holmen Loegumkloster, Logumkloster, 6240, Denmark.

378 DNK ISSN 1398-6244
LOENMAGASIN. 198?-2000. a. Dansk Magisterforening, Nimbusparken, Peter Bangs Vej 32, Frederiksberg, 2000, Denmark.

690 USA ISSN 1536-3252
LOG & TIMBER STYLE. 2001-2007 (Jan.). bi-m. Wiesner Media, LLC, 7009 S Potomac St, Ste 200, Centennial, CO 80112.

709.9305 NZL ISSN 1174-2216
LOG ILLUSTRATED. 1992-2002 (no.15). 3/yr. Physics Room, P.O. Box 22-351, Christchurch, New Zealand.

004.0688 FRA ISSN 1630-9782
LOGICIELS & SERVICES. 1986-2004. 10/yr. Publications G R D, 85, rue du Dessous des Berges, Paris, 75013, France.

621.3 FRA ISSN 1295-4152
LOGIN. 1993-2005. m. Posse Press, BP 1121, Toulouse, 31036, France.

621.3 FRA ISSN 1299-6599
LOGIN. HORS-SERIE. 2000-2004. quadrennial. Posse Press, BP 1121, Toulouse, 31036, France.

382 DEU ISSN 1864-094X
LOGISTIK UND LAGER. 2006-2007. m. Forum Verlag Herkert GmbH, Mandichostr 18, Merching, 86504, Germany.

629 CZE ISSN 1801-8009
LOGISTIKA V PRAXI. 2003-2008. s-a. Verlag Dashoefer s.r.o., Na Prikope 18, PO Box 756, Prague 1, 11121, Czech Republic.

401 DEU ISSN 1439-9849
LOGOS AND LANGUAGE; journal of general linguistics and language. 2000-2005. s-a. Gunter Narr Verlag, Postfach 2567, Tuebingen, 72015, Germany.

948.9 DNK ISSN 0109-002X
LOKALHISTORIE: HADSUND KOMMUNE. 1982-1985. 10/yr. Jysk Lokalhistorisk Forlag, Jyllandsgade 43 B, Skorping, 9520, Denmark.

792 USA ISSN 1043-6650
LONDON STAGE 1800-1900: A DOCUMENTARY RECORD AND CALENDAR OF PERFORMANCES. 1990-19??. irreg. Greenwood Publishing Group Inc., 88 Post Rd W, PO Box 5007, Westport, CT 06881.

072.1 GBR ISSN 0958-9600
LONDON WEEKLY ADVERTISER. 1987-1990. w. Brittain Publications, 137 George Ln, S Woodford, London, E18 1AJ, United Kingdom.

362 USA ISSN 1536-7517
LONG TERM CARE LITIGATION. 2001-2002. m. Aspen Publishers, Inc., 111 Eighth Ave., 7th Fl, New York, NY 10011.

053.1 DEU
LOOK; das neue People-Magazin. 2006-2007 (Jan.). w. Verlag Ehrlich und Sohn GmbH & Co. KG, Griegstr 75, Hamburg, 22763, Germany.

200.7 GBR ISSN 0954-5611
LOOK! HEAR!; the magazine for preachers, teachers, and families. 1988-1998. 3/yr. A V A Magazine Ltd., c/o Subscriptions Secretary, 1 Briarswood, Springfield, Chelmsford, Essex CM1 6UH, United Kingdom.

324.2 AUS ISSN 1832-9071
LOOKING FORWARD. 2005-2006. irreg. Andrew Southcott, Pub., 760 Marion Rd, Marion, SA 5043, Australia.

Cessations

371.42 USA ISSN 1098-9765
THE LOS ANGELES JOBBANK; the job hunter's guide to Southern California. (Includes: Orange, Riverside, San Bernardino, San Diego, Santa Barbara, Ventura Counties and others.) 1981-2003 (17th ed.). irreg. Adams Media, 57 Littlefield St, Avon, MA 02322.

369.4 FRA ISSN 0751-5685
LOUVETEAU. 1924-2004. bi-m. Editions Scouts de France, 54 av. Jean Jaures, Paris, 75019, France.

340 DNK ISSN 0106-8458
LOVTIDENDE FOR KONGERIGET DANMARK. AFDELING A. 1871-2007. s-w. Justisministeriet, Civilstyrelsen. Retsinformation, Gyldenloevesgade 11,2, Copenhagen V, 1600, Denmark.

341 DNK ISSN 0106-8474
LOVTIDENDE FOR KONGERIGET DANMARK. AFDELING C. 1936-2007. irreg. Justisministeriet, Civilstyrelsen. Retsinformation, Gyldenloevesgade 11,2, Copenhagen V, 1600, Denmark.

747 ITA ISSN 1720-8017
LUCE INTERNATIONAL. 2002-200?. s-a. Design Diffusion Edizioni, Via Lucano 3, Milan, 20135, Italy.

053.1 DEU ISSN 1862-460X
LUCKY. 2004-2008. 2/yr. Conde Nast Verlag GmbH, Karlstr 23, Munich, 80333, Germany.

684.1 FRA ISSN 1251-4012
LUMINAIRE. 1994-1994. a. Editions du Tigre, 23 rue Joubert, Paris, 75009, France.

327 401 NLD ISSN 1257-0273 CODEN: LUSOEP
LUSOTOPIE. 1994-2009 (Vol. 16). s-a. Brill, PO Box 9000, Leiden, 2300 PA, Netherlands.

284.1 USA
LUTHERAN HOUR MESSAGES. 1930-2008. w. International Lutheran Laymen's League, Lutheran Hour Ministries, 660 Mason Ridge Center, St. Louis, MO 63141-8557.

780 ITA ISSN 1124-7355
LYRICA. 1993-ceased. m. Ermitage, Piazza Trento e Trieste 1, Bologna, BO 40137, Italy.

620 DEU ISSN 0173-9646
M A N FORSCHEN, PLANEN, BAUEN; das Technik-Magazin der MAN Gruppe. 1970-2003. a. M A N Aktiengesellschaft, Stabsabteilung Information und Marktbeobachtung, Ungererstr 69, Munich, 80805, Germany.

621.9 DEU
M A N ROLAND REVUE; technology and trends in sheet-fed offset. 1970-1998. s-a. M A N Roland Druckmaschinen Aktiengesellschaft, Muehlheimer Str 341, Offenbach Am Main, 63075, Germany.

531 ITA ISSN 1126-4284
M & A. (Meccanica e Automazione) 1995-200?. 11/yr. Gruppo Editoriale Futura, Via XXV Aprile 39, Bresso, MI 20091, Italy.

780.65 GBR
M B I ASIAN REPORT. (Music Business International) 1996-1996. a. C M P Information Ltd., 8 Montague Close, 4th Fl, London, SE1 9UR, United Kingdom.

025.04 USA ISSN 1532-3137
M-BUSINESS; the voice of the next mobile economy. 2000-2002. m. C M P Media LLC, 600 Harrison St, 6th Fl., San Francisco, CA 94107.

781.64 USA ISSN 1533-3019
M C 2 (SAN MATEO). (Music Computer Culture) 2000-200?. 8/yr. C M P Information, Inc., 2800 Campus Dr, San Mateo, CA 94403.

005.5 ITA ISSN 1123-2722
M C - MICROCOMPUTER SOFTWARE. 1990-ceased. m. (11/yr.). Technipress Srl, Via Olindo Guerrini 20 D, Rome, 00139, Italy.

610 USA
M D N G ENEWSLETTER. (Medical Doctor Net Guide) 1999-2001. bi-w. Intellisphere, LLC, Office Center at Princeton Meadows, 666 Plainsboro Rd, Bldg 300, Plainsboro, NJ 08536.

610 ITA ISSN 1122-1909
M E D I C. METODOLOGIA E DIDATTICA CLINICA/CLINICAL METHODOLOGY AND DIDACTICS. 1993-ceased. q. Il Pensiero Scientifico Editore, Via Bradano 3-C, Rome, 00199, Italy.

664.9 NZL ISSN 0465-4390
M I R I N Z. (Meat Industry Research Institute of New Zealand) 1957-2000. irreg. Meat Industry Research Institute of New Zealand, Ruakura Research Centre, 5th Fl Tower Block, East St, Hamilton, New Zealand.

341.45 AUS ISSN 0811-4293
M L A A N Z JOURNAL. 1978-2006. a. Maritime Law Association of Australia and New Zealand, c/o TC Beirne School of Law, University of Queensland, Brisbane, QLD 4072, Australia.

005.43 POL ISSN 1896-4745
M S CODER. (Microsoft) 2006-2007. bi-m. Software - Wydawnictwo Sp. z o.o., ul Bokserska 1, Warsaw, 02-682, Poland.

373 NZL ISSN 1178-5454
M S R YOUTH. (Middle School Review) ceased 2008 (Sep.). q. New Zealand Association of Intermediate and Middle Schools, Fairfield Intermediate School, 216 Clarkin Rd, Hamilton, 2001, New Zealand.

796.525 AUS ISSN 1035-4697
M U C G - RAKER. 1977-1997. a. Macquarie University, Caving Group, c/o Macquarie University Sports Association, Macquarie University, NSW 2109, Australia.

796.75 USA ISSN 1531-1198
M X RACER. (Motocross) 1997-2004. bi-m. Source Interlink Companies, 27500 Riverview Center Blvd, Bonita Springs, FL 34134.

384 DEU
M-ZONE; mobile music - movies - games. 2004-2007. 4/yr. Entertainment Media Verlag GmbH und Co. oHG, Einsteinring 24, Dornach, 85609, Germany.

640.73 ISR ISSN 0334-0902
MA K'DAI; a monthly guide for consumers. 1975-1995. m. Israel Consumer Board, 28 Albert Mendeler St., Hakirya, Tel Aviv, Israel.

334 ISR
MA'ANIT. 1946-1959. q. Union of Moshavim of Hapoal Hamizrachi, 166 Even Giverol St., Tel Aviv, Israel.

004 ISR ISSN 0303-142X
MA'ASEH HOSHEV. 1972-2001. bi-m. Information Processing Association of Israel, Kfar Hamakabia, Ramat Gan, 52109, Israel.

004.16 FRA ISSN 1950-1773
MAC & CO. 200?-2006. bi-m. Bleucom Editions, 12-14 Rue de l'Eglise, Paris, 75015, France.

796 ISR
MACCABI WORLD UNION. NEWSLETTER. 1951-1984. m. Maccabi World Union, Kfar Hamaccabiah, Israel.

070 659.1 GBR ISSN 0262-2297
MACCLESFIELD EXPRESS ADVERTISER. 1981-1997. w. Lancashire and Cheshire County Newspapers Ltd., 37 Chestergate, Macclesfield, Ches, United Kingdom.

841 FRA ISSN 1251-1153
MACHE-LAURIER; revue de poesie de langue francaise. 1994-2008. s-a. Editions Obsidiane, 11 rue Andre Gateau, Sens, 89100, France.

621.8 GBR ISSN 1369-992X
MACHINE PLANT & SYSTEMS MONITOR. 1997-2000. bi-m. Coxmoor Publishing Co., PO Box 72, Chipping Norton, Oxford OX7 6JU, United Kingdom.

382 TUR ISSN 1301-4609
MACHINERY EXPORTS - TURKEY. 1997-ceased. q. Iletisim Magazin Gazetecilik San. ve Tic. A.S., Ihlas Holding Merkez Binasi, 29 Ekim Cad. 23, P.K. 34197, Yenibosna - Istanbul, 34197, Turkey.

621.9 USA ISSN 1544-9467
MACHINING TECHNOLOGY. 1990-2008. q. Society of Manufacturing Engineers, One SME Dr, PO Box 930, Dearborn, MI 48121.

004 ISR ISSN 0333-7413
MACHSHEVIM P C. 1980-2000. m. Merav - Koren Publishing Ltd., 11 Haavoda St, Rosh Haayin, 48017, Israel.

004 005 ITA ISSN 1120-8465
MACINTOSH MAGAZINE. 1989-ceased. m. M G E Communications, Via Cola di Rienzo, 163, Roma, 00192, Italy.

378 AUS ISSN 1327-7774
MACQUARIE UNIVERSITY NEWS. 1967-19??. 10/yr. Macquarie University, Balaclava Rd, North Ryde, NSW 2109, Australia.

636.7 GBR ISSN 1464-553X
MAD ABOUT DOGS. 1997-200?. m. HiHo Publishing Ltd., Techno Trading Estate, 25a Bramble Rd, Swindon, Wilts SN2 6DS, United Kingdom.

051 USA
MADISON RELOCATION GUIDE. ceased 2008. a. Nei-Turner Media Group, 93 W Geneva St, PO Box 1080, Williams Bay, WI 53191.

282 ITA ISSN 0391-7169
MADONNA. 1954-ceased. bi-m. Opera Madonna del Divino Amore, Km 12, Via Ardeatina, Rome, 00179, Italy.

990 AUS ISSN 0811-1197
MAFFRA & DISTRICT HISTORICAL SOCIETY. BULLETIN. 1973-2004. q. Maffra & District Historical Society Inc., PO Box 321, Maffra, VIC 3860, Australia.

069 AUS ISSN 1449-9347
THE MAG. 1999-2008. bi-m. Museums and Galleries N S W, 43-51 Cowper Wharf Rd, Woolloomooloo, NSW 2011, Australia.

666 688 ITA
MAGAZINE PREMIERE. 1987-ceased. 4/yr. Eva Rutter Editore s.r.l., Via Emilia, 98, Santa Giuletta, PV 27046, Italy.

028.5 790.1 NLD ISSN 1871-3874
MAGIC. 2005-2005. Scripta Media, Nieuwe Herengracht 47, Amsterdam, 1011 RN, Netherlands.

913 ITA ISSN 0024-9955
MAGNA GRAECIA; rassegna di archeologia storia arte attualita. 1966-ceased. bi-m. Editoriale Magna Graecia, Viale della Repubblica, 293-C, Cosenza, CS 87100, Italy.

913 HUN ISSN 0076-2504
MAGYARORSZAG REGESZETI TOPOGRAFIAJA/ARCHEOLOGICAL TOPOGRAPHY OF HUNGARY. 1967-1998 (vol.10). irreg. Akademiai Kiado Rt., Prielle Kornelia U. 19, Budapest, 1117, Hungary.

800 FRA ISSN 1163-7307
MAIN DE SINGE. 1991-2005. 6/yr. Editions Act Mem - Fonds Comp'Act, 173 Carre Curial, Chambery, 73000, France.

338.47004 USA
MAINFRAME MARKET MONITOR. 1991-199?. q. Xephon, 9330 Lyndon B Johnson Fwy., Ste. 800, Dallas, TX 75243-4310.

747 635 FRA ISSN 1630-487X
MAISON & JARDIN PASSION. 1999-2007. bi-m. Editions DIPA Burda, 26 Avenue de l'Europe, Strasbourg, 67013, France.

747 745.5 FRA ISSN 1629-2472
MAISON PASSION CREATION. 2001-2006. bi-m. Editions DIPA Burda, 26 Avenue de l'Europe, Strasbourg, 67013, France.

331.89 USA
MAJOR COLLECTIVE BARGAINING SETTLEMENTS IN PRIVATE INDUSTRY. 19??-1995. q. U.S. Department of Labor, Bureau of Labor Statistics, Postal Square Bldg., 2 Massachusetts Ave, NE, Washington, DC 20212-0001.

331.89 USA
MAJOR COLLECTIVE BARGAINING SETTLEMENTS IN STATE AND LOCAL GOVERNMENT. ceased 1995. s-a. U.S. Department of Labor, Bureau of Labor Statistics, Postal Square Bldg., 2 Massachusetts Ave, NE, Washington, DC 20212-0001.

800 GBR
MAJOR EUROPEAN AUTHOR SERIES. 1967-2009 (Jul.). irreg. Cambridge University Press, The Edinburgh Bldg, Shaftesbury Rd, Cambridge, CB2 8RU, United Kingdom.

599 USA ISSN 0076-3519 CODEN: MLNSBP
MAMMALIAN SPECIES (PRINT). 1969-2005. irreg. American Society of Mammalogists, PO Box 1897, Lawrence, KS 66044.

301 NLD ISSN 0165-4578
MAN. 1972-2005. 8/yr. De Telegraaf Tijdschriftengroep, Postbus 127, Amsterdam, 1000 AC, Netherlands.

615 USA ISSN 1075-2358
MANAGED PHARMACEUTICAL REPORT. 1994-2003. m. Lippincott Williams & Wilkins, 16522 Hunters Green Pkwy, Hagerstown, MD 21740.

658 GBR
MANAGEMENT AND INDUSTRIAL RELATIONS SERIES. 1982-19??. irreg. Cambridge University Press, The Edinburgh Bldg, Shaftesbury Rd, Cambridge, CB2 8RU, United Kingdom.

658 CZE ISSN 1801-7738
MANAGEMENT JAKOSTI S PODPOROU NOREM ISO 9000:2000. 2000-2006. q. Verlag Dashoefer s.r.o., Na Prikope 18, PO Box 756, Prague 1, 11121, Czech Republic.

306.766 USA ISSN 0360-1005
MANDATE; the international magazine of entertainment & eros. 1974-2009. m. Mandate Publications, Ltd., 225 Broadway, Ste 2801, New York, NY 10007.

055.1 ITA
MANI-FESTA; il diverso della scrittura. 1988-ceased. q. Mani-festa, Via Francesco Giordani, 23, Naples, NA 80122, Italy.

378 NZL ISSN 1176-3590
MANU MATAURANGA. 2001-2006. bi-m. Tertiary Education Commission, PO Box 27-048, Wellington, New Zealand.

690 NLD ISSN 1872-1052
MANURENBOEK BURGERWERK. 2000-ceased. a. Sdu Uitgevers bv, Postbus 20025, The Hague, 2500 EA, Netherlands.

690 NLD ISSN 1872-1044
MANURENBOEK WONING- EN UTILITEITSBOUW. 2005-ceased. a. Sdu Uitgevers bv, Postbus 20025, The Hague, 2500 EA, Netherlands.

800 ESP ISSN 1136-3703
MANUSCRT.CAO. 1988-200?. irreg. Universidad Autonoma de Madrid, Departamento de Filologia Espanola, Carretera de Colmenar, km 15,000, Cr Canto Blanco, Madrid, 28049, Spain.

930.1 945 ITA
LE MARCHE ARCHEOLOGIA, STORIA, TERRITORIO. 1987-ceased. s-a. Istituto Regionale per la Pre-Protostoria nelle Marche, Vicolo Lazzarini, 2, Sassoferrato, AN 60041, Italy.

945 ITA ISSN 1126-9022
MARCHE CONTEMPORANEE. 1984-2000. irreg. Istituto Internazionale di Studi Piceni, Palazzo Oliva, Sassoferrato, AN 60041, Italy.

800 700 GBR ISSN 0950-5091
MARGIN; at the edge of literature & ideas. 1986-1990. q. Common Margins Ltd., Square Inch, Lower Granco St, Dunning, Perth PH2 0SQ, United Kingdom.

387 ITA ISSN 0025-309X
LA MARINA ITALIANA; rassegna delle industrie del mare. 1902-ceased. bi-m. Silvio Basile Editore, Lungo Bisagno Istria, 34 c, Genoa, GE 16141, Italy.

387.5 ITA ISSN 0025-3103
LA MARINA MERCANTILE. 1947-ceased. m. Silvio Basile Editore, Lungo Bisagno Istria, 34 c, Genoa, GE 16141, Italy.

347.75 USA
MARITIME LAW REPORTER. 1987-1999. bi-m. LexisNexis, PO Box 7587, Charlottesville, VA 22906.

629.1 USA
MARKET INTELLIGENCE REPORTS: WORLD AIRLINE MAINTENANCE FORECAST. 1996-200?. plus q. updates. Forecast International Inc., 22 Commerce Rd, Newtown, CT 06470.

658.8 ITA
MARKETING & MANAGERS. 1988-ceased. 11/yr. Multispe s.r.l., Piazza Della Conciliazione, 2, Milan, MI 20123, Italy.

658.8 GBR ISSN 0952-2581
MARKETSEARCH. 1976-2004. a. (plus q. updates). Arlington Management Publications Ltd., 1 Hay Hill, Berkeley Sq, London, WIJ 6DH, United Kingdom.

617.6 TUR ISSN 1018-5992
MARMARA UNIVERSITY. FACULTY OF DENTISTRY. JOURNAL. 1990-2001. a. Marmara Universitesi, Faculty of Dentistry, Buyukciftlik Sok. No. 6, Nisantasi - Istanbul, 80200, Turkey.

301.412 USA ISSN 0897-5469
MARRIAGE PARTNERSHIP (PRINT). 1984-2008. q. Christianity Today International, 465 Gundersen Dr, Carol Stream, IL 60188.

649 USA
MARTHA STEWART BABY. 2000-200?. s-a. (Mar. & Sep.). Martha Stewart Living Omnimedia LLC, 11 W 42nd St, 25th Fl, New York, NY 10036.

649 USA ISSN 1546-4709
MARTHA STEWART KIDS. 2001 (June)-200?. q. Martha Stewart Living Omnimedia LLC, 11 W 42nd St, 25th Fl, New York, NY 10036.

340.021 USA ISSN 1099-7881
MARTINDALE-HUBBELL CORPORATE LAW DIRECTORY. 1868-2003. a. Martindale-Hubbell, 121 Chanlon Rd, New Providence, NJ 07974.

340.029 USA ISSN 1071-7455
MARTINDALE-HUBBELL LAW DIRECTORY ON CD-ROM. 1990-2003. irreg. Martindale-Hubbell, 121 Chanlon Rd, New Providence, NJ 07974.

570 CZE ISSN 1211-2836
MASARYK UNIVERSITY. FACULTY OF SCIENCES. SCRIPTA BIOLOGY/SCRIPTA FACULTATIS SCIENTIARIUM NATURALIUM UNIVERSITATIS MASARYKIANAE BRUNENSIS. BIOLOGY. 1971-2004 (vol.29). irreg. Masarykova Universita, Prirodovedecka Fakulta, Kotlarska 2, Brno, 61137, Czech Republic.

540 CZE ISSN 1211-2828
MASARYK UNIVERSITY. FACULTY OF SCIENCES. SCRIPTA CHEMIA/SCRIPTA FACULTATIS SCIENTIARUM NATURALIUM UNIVERSITATIS MASARYKIANAE BRUNENSIS. CHEMIA. ceased 1998. a. Masarykova Universita, Prirodovedecka Fakulta, Kotlarska 2, Brno, 61137, Czech Republic.

510 CZE ISSN 1211-4723
MASARYK UNIVERSITY. FACULTY OF SCIENCES. SCRIPTA COMPUTER SCIENCE AND APPLIED MATHEMATICS/SCRIPTA FACULTATIS SCIENTIARUM NATURALIUM UNIVERSITATIS MASARYKIANAE BRUNENSIS. MATHEMATICA. 1971-1993. a. Masarykova Universita, Prirodovedecka Fakulta, Kotlarska 2, Brno, 61137, Czech Republic.

910 CZE ISSN 1211-2844
MASARYK UNIVERSITY. FACULTY OF SCIENCES. SCRIPTA GEOGRAPHY/SCRIPTA FACULTATIS SCIENTIARUM NATURALIUM UNIVERSITATIS MASARYKIANAE BRUNENSIS. GEOGRAPHIA. ceased 1998. a. Masarykova Universita, Prirodovedecka Fakulta, Kotlarska 2, Brno, 61137, Czech Republic.

150 CZE ISSN 1211-3522
MASARYKOVA UNIVERZITA. FILOZOFICKA FAKULTA. SBORNIK PRACI. P: RADA PSYCHOLOGICKA. 1996-2006. a. Masarykova Univerzita, Filozoficka Fakulta, Arna Novaka 1, Brno, 60200, Czech Republic.

320 CZE ISSN 1211-7013
MASARYKOVA UNIVERZITA. FILOZOFICKA FAKULTA. SBORNIK PRACI. T: RADA POLITOLOGICKA. 1997-1997 (ceased same year). a. Masarykova Univerzita, Fakulta Socialnich Studii, Jostova 10, Brno, 602 00, Czech Republic.

346.01 USA
MASSACHUSETTS FAMILY LAW GUIDEBOOK; a view from the Bench. 1984-1992. plus a. updates. LexisNexis, PO Box 7587, Charlottesville, VA 22906.

346.03 USA
MASSACHUSETTS TORT LAW. 1994-ceased. irreg. Michie Company, 701 E Water St, Charlottesville, VA 22902.

338.1 NZL ISSN 0110-5558
MASSEY UNIVERSITY. CENTRE FOR APPLIED ECONOMICS AND POLICY STUDIES. AGRICULTURAL POLICY PAPER. 1978-1998. irreg. Massey University, Centre for Applied Economics and Policy Studies, Palmerston North, New Zealand.

338.1 NZL ISSN 0111-6339
MASSEY UNIVERSITY. CENTRE FOR APPLIED ECONOMICS AND POLICY STUDIES. AGRICULTURAL POLICY PROCEEDINGS. 1976-1997 (no.19). irreg. Massey University, Centre for Applied Economics and Policy Studies, Palmerston North, New Zealand.

020 NZL ISSN 1175-1738
MASSEY UNIVERSITY. DEPARTMENT OF INFORMATION SYSTEMS. TECHNICAL REPORT. ceased 2007. irreg. Massey University, Department of Information Systems, Private Bag 11222, Palmerston North, New Zealand.

070.5 CAN ISSN 0832-512X
MASTHEAD; the magazine about magazines. 1987-2008 (Nov./Dec.). bi-m. North Island Publishing, 1606 Sedlescomb Dr, Unit 8, Mississauga, ON L4X 1M6, Canada.

053.1 DEU ISSN 1862-0876
MATADOR; Maenner wollen's wissen. 2004-2008 (May). m. Heinrich Bauer Smaragd KG, Charles-de-Gaulle-Str 8, Munich, 81737, Germany.

306 USA ISSN 0743-7528
MATERIAL CULTURE DIRECTORIES. 1988-19??. irreg. Greenwood Publishing Group Inc., 88 Post Rd W, PO Box 5007, Westport, CT 06881.

950 ITA
MATERIALI PER IL VOCABOLARIO NEOSUMERICO. 1974-ceased. a. Bonsignori Editore s.r.l., Viale dei Quattro Venti 47, Rome, RM 00152, Italy.

346 USA
MATERIALS ON CORPORATE POLITICAL ACTIVITY. 1981-1999. a. Business Laws, Inc., 11630 Chillicothe Rd, PO Box 185, Chesterland, OH 44026.

670 GBR ISSN 1462-0138
MATERIALS PROCESSING NEWS. 1998-200?. q. Institute of Materials, 1 Carlton House Terr, London, SW1Y 5DB, United Kingdom.

540 510 GBR ISSN 1049-2801 CODEN: MCHEET
MATHEMATICAL CHEMISTRY. 1991-2003 (vol.7). irreg. Taylor & Francis Ltd., 4 Park Sq, Milton Park, Abingdon, OX14 4RN, United Kingdom.

808.81 800 AUS ISSN 0810-2740
MATILDA MAGAZINE: LITERARY AND ART MAGAZINE. 1980-1985. q. Matilda Publications, 7 Mountfield St, Brunswick, VIC 3056, Australia.

327 GBR ISSN 0265-444X
MAURITIAN INTERNATIONAL. 1964-2002. q. Nautilus Publishing Co., Nautilus Publishing Co, PO Box 4100, London, SW20 0XN, United Kingdom.

028.5 DEU
DIE MAUS (BERLIN). 1997-2008 (Jan.). m. Egmont Ehapa Verlag GmbH, Wallstr 59, Berlin, 10179, Germany.

746.92 DEU ISSN 1617-5530
MAX; Das Magazin fuer Popkultur und Style. 1991-2008 (Jan.). m. Verlagsgruppe Milchstrasse, Mittelweg 177, Hamburg, 22786, Germany.

669 DEU ISSN 0585-783X
MAX-PLANCK-INSTITUT FUER METALLFORSCHUNG. MITTEILUNGEN. 1966-2001. 3/yr. Max-Planck-Institut fuer Metallforschung, Seestr 92, Stuttgart, 70174, Germany.

305.31 ITA ISSN 1127-1108
MAXIM. 1998-200?. m. Gruppo Editoriale Futura, Via XXV Aprile 39, Bresso, MI 20091, Italy.

305.31 SGP
MAXIM SINGAPORE. 2004-2008. m. S P H Magazines Pte Ltd., 82 Genting Ln Level 7, Media Centre, Singapore, 349567, Singapore.

332.6 DEU
MAXIMIZE; das Anlegermagazin von maxblue. 2001-2002. q. corps - Corporate Publishing Services GmbH, Kasernenstr 69, Duesseldorf, 40213, Germany.

787 780.7 USA
MAXIMUM GUITAR. 1989-1998. bi-m. Harris Publications, Inc., 1115 Broadway, New York, NY 10010.

796.6 GBR ISSN 1461-1619
MAXIMUM MOUNTAIN BIKE. 1998-2000. m. Cabal Communications Ltd., 374 Euston Rd, London, NW1 3BL, United Kingdom.

004.16 ITA ISSN 1824-5706
MAXIMUM P C. 2004-200?. bi-m. Sprea Editori Srl, Via Torino 51, Cernusco sul Naviglio, MI 20063, Italy.

305.8 ISR ISSN 0543-1786
MA'YANOT. 1952-1986. irreg. World Zionist Organization, P O Box 92, Jerusalem, Israel.

330 DEU ISSN 1611-1400
MAYDORN-REPORT; der Boersenbrief fuer Technologie- und Wachstumsaktien. 199?-2006. m. Boersenmedien AG, Am Eulenhof 14, Kulmbach, 95326, Germany.

054 FRA ISSN 0754-4766
M'BOLO. 1980-200?. s-a. Berger-Levrault Editions

330 DEU ISSN 1619-9138
MCK WISSEN. 2002-2007. 4/yr. Brand Eins Verlag GmbH, Schauenburger Str 21, Hamburg, 20095, Germany.

340 615 USA ISSN 1543-2149
MEALEY'S LITIGATION REPORT: EPHEDRA & P P A. 2001 (May)-2008. m. Mealey Publications & Conferences Group, 217 W Church Rd, King of Prussia, PA 19406-0230.

808.83 AUS ISSN 1035-9761
MEAN STREETS. 1990-1996. q. What Goes On Pty. Ltd., 214 Hat Hill Rd, Blackheath, NSW 2785, Australia.

636 338.1 NZL ISSN 0112-739X
MEAT AND WOOL BOARDS' ECONOMIC SERVICE. ANNUAL REVIEW OF THE NEW ZEALAND SHEEP & BEEF INDUSTRY; review of physical and economic conditions in sheepfarming in New Zealand. 1952-2003. a. Meat and Wool New Zealand Economic Service, PO Box 121, Wellington, 6140, New Zealand.

664.9 658.8 NLD ISSN 1572-0748
MEATBUSINESS. 2001-2005. bi-w. Reed Business bv, Hanzestraat 1, Doetinchem, 7006 RH, Netherlands.

410.285 USA ISSN 0543-2073
MECHANICAL TRANSLATION AND COMPUTATIONAL LINGUISTICS. 1954-1970. irreg. Association for Computational Linguistics, 209 N Eighth St, East Stroudsburg, PA 18360.

620.11233 GBR ISSN 0959-5864
MECHANICS OF CREEP BRITTLE MATERIALS. 1989-1991. irreg. Pergamon, The Blvd, Langford Ln, East Park, Kidlington, Oxford OX5 1GB, United Kingdom.

618.92 FRA ISSN 1639-6758
MEDECINE CLINIQUE POUR LES PEDIATRES. 2002-2004. bi-m. Elsevier Masson, 62 Rue Camille Desmoulins, Issy les Moulineaux, Cedex 92442, France.

610 FRA ISSN 0183-5734
MEDECINS DU VAL-DE-MARNE. 1977-2007. 4/yr. Association Medicale du Val de Marne, 4 Rue Octave Dumesnil, Creteil, 94000, France.

371.33 USA ISSN 0025-6897
MEDIA & METHODS; educational products, technologies & programs for schools & universities. 1964-2006. 5/yr. American Society of Educators, 1429 Walnut St, Philadelphia, PA 19102.

659.111 DEU ISSN 1430-1474
MEDIA FACTS. 1995-2001. m. Deutscher Fachverlag GmbH, Mainzer Landstr 251, Frankfurt Am Main, 60326, Germany.

282 DEU ISSN 1433-6472
MEDIA FORUM. 1972-2006. q. Catholic Media Council, Publizistische Medienplanung fuer Entwicklungslaender e.V., Anton-Kurze-Allee 2, Aachen, 52074, Germany.

659.1 ITA ISSN 0394-9575
MEDIAFORUM. 1970-ceased. w. Ediforum srl, Via Pietrasanta 14, Edificio 7, Milan, 20141, Italy.

658.8 ITA
MEDIA KEY; mensile professionale di comunicazione, media e marketing. 1982-ceased. m. (10/yr.). Media Key s.r.l., Via Lippi Filippino, 33 C, Milan, MI 20131, Italy.

343.09946 AUS
MEDIA LAW AND PRACTICE. 1987-ceased. 5-6 updates/yr.) plus bi-m. updates. Lawbook Co., PO Box 3502, Rozelle, NSW 2039, Australia.

621.388 DEU ISSN 0267-4467
MEDIA MONOGRAPH. 1984-1995. irreg. Europaeisches Medieninstitut e.V., Zollhof 2A, Duesseldorf, 40221, Germany.

070.449796 310 USA ISSN 0889-0951
MEDIA SPORTS BUSINESS. 1982-19??. m. S N L Financial LC, One SNL Plz, PO Box 2124, Charlottesville, VA 22902.

659.1 CZE ISSN 1210-8294
MEDIA TARIF. 1993-2001. 2/yr. Strategie Praha s.r.o., Drtinova 8, Prague 5, 150 00, Czech Republic.

900 GBR ISSN 0268-8638
MEDIAEVAL AND RENAISSANCE STUDIES. 1941-1968. irreg. Warburg Institute, University of London, Woburn Sq, London, WC1H 0AB, United Kingdom.

658.45 NLD ISSN 1873-3662
MEDIAMENSEN. 2006-2006. bi-m. Media Business Press BV, Postbus 8632, Rotterdam, 3009 AP, Netherlands.

600 ITA ISSN 1120-1932
MEDIAPLUSNEWS; monthly of information, culture, technological actualities. 1987-ceased. m. Media Plus s.r.l., Via Ausonio, 5, Milan, MI 20123, Italy.

610.28 USA ISSN 1096-1801
MEDICAL DESIGN TECHNOLOGY (PRINT); new products, materials & components for medical device designers. 1997-2008. m. Advantage Business Media, 100 Enterprise Dr, Ste 600, PO Box 912, Rockaway, NJ 07886.

610 340 USA ISSN 1532-9224
THE MEDICAL INFORMATION TECHNOLOGY LAW REPORT. 1999-200?. m. Civic Research Insitute, 4478 US Rte 27, PO Box 585, Kingston, NJ 08528.

368.382 657.832 USA ISSN 1558-6391
MEDICAL OFFICE H I P A A ALERT; the essential guide to health information compliance. (Health Insurance Portability and Accountability Act) 2003-2006. m. The Coding Institute, 2272 Airport Rd S, Naples, FL 34112.

610.73 USA ISSN 1553-4383
MEDICAL OFFICE NURSE. 200?-2006. m. The Coding Institute, 2272 Airport Rd S, Naples, FL 34112.

615 USA ISSN 1559-8160
MEDICARE DRUG FOCUS. 2005-2007. w. F-D-C Reports, Inc., 5635 Fishers Ln, Ste 6000, Rockville, MD 20852.

368.4 USA ISSN 1558-5530
MEDICARE DRUG REIMBURSEMENT GUIDE. 2005-2007. m. F-D-C Reports, Inc., 5550 Friendship Blvd, Ste One, Chevy Chase, MD 20815-7278.

615.842 ESP ISSN 1134-9913
MEDICINA AEROSPACIAL Y AMBIENTAL. 1994-ceased. s-a. Sociedad Espanola de Medicina Aeroespacial, Apdo 46269, Madrid, 28080, Spain.

610 ITA ISSN 0392-4548
MEDICINA OGGI; periodico di attualita in medicina e chirurgia. 1980-1998 (Vol. 18). q. Casa Editrice Idelson Gnocchi, Via Michele Pietravalle 85, Naples, NA 80131, Italy.

616.2 ITA ISSN 0393-8506
MEDICINA TORACICA. 1978-2001. 4/yr. Elsevier Masson, Via Paleocapa 7, Milan, 20121, Italy.

571.2 CAN ISSN 1430-953X
MEDICINAL PLANT CONSERVATION. 1995-2007 (vol.13); suspended. irreg. I U C N Species Survival Commission, Medicinal Plant Specialist Group, c/o Dr Danna J Leaman, 98 Russell Ave, Ottawa, ON K1N 7X1, Canada.

616.8 150.5 ITA ISSN 1126-7127
MEDICINE, MIND AND ADOLESCENCE/MEDICINA, PSICHE E ADOLESCENZA; semestrale di psicologia medica e di filosofia della medicina - semi-annual journal of philosophy of medicine, medical psychology and adolescentology. 1983-2003. s-a. Fabrizio Serra Editore, c/o Accademia Editoriale, Via Santa Bibbiana 28, Pisa, 56127, Italy.

384 DEU ISSN 0179-5724
MEDIENSPIEGEL. 1975-2008. m. Deutscher Instituts Verlag GmbH, Gustav-Heinemann-Ufer 84-88, Cologne, 50968, Germany.

610 ITA ISSN 1121-2810
MEDIFAX; la rivista del medico che legge. 1991-ceased. q. Il Pensiero Scientifico Editore, Via Bradano 3-C, Rome, 00199, Italy.

615 615.329 614.8 DEU ISSN 0171-3876
MEDIKAMENT & MEINUNG; Zeitschrift fuer Arzneimittel- und Gesundheitswesen. 1978-2001. m. Bundesverband der Pharmazeutischen Industrie e.V., Friedrichstr 148, Berlin, 10117, Germany.

610 NLD ISSN 1385-6103
MEDISCH NIEUWS. 1981-2006. 11/yr. Elsevier Gezondheidszorg bv, Planetenbaan 80-99, Maarssen, 3606 AK, Netherlands.

613 DEU ISSN 0179-0404
MEDIZIN HEUTE; die gesunden Seiten des Lebens. 1950-2005. m. Deutscher Aerzte-Verlag GmbH, Dieselstr 2, Cologne, 50859, Germany.

610 DEU
MEDIZINISCH JURISTISCHE NACHRICHTEN. 1999-2004. q. Dr. Schilke Medizinischer Verlag GmbH, Hainichener Str 21, Braeunsdorf, 09603, Germany.

610 011 DEU
MEDIZINISCHER LITERATUR ANZEIGER; bibliographische Zeitschrift fuer medizinische Neuerscheinungen. 1950-2005. m. Dustri-Verlag Dr. Karl Feistle, Bajuwarenring 4, Oberhaching, 82041, Germany.

551.46 DEU ISSN 0433-7670
MEERESKUNDLICHE BEOBACHTUNGEN UND ERGEBNISSE. 1953-1997. irreg. Bundesamt fuer Seeschifffahrt und Hydrographie, Bernhard-Nocht-Str 78, Hamburg, 20359, Germany.

302 150 ISR ISSN 0025-8679
MEGAMOT; behavioural sciences journal. 1949-2004. q. Henrietta Szold Institute, Kiryat Menachem, 9 Columbia St, Jerusalem, 96583, Israel.

028.5 DEU
MEGAPHON. 1983-2004. bi-m. Schuelerzeitung Megaphon, Gymnasium Burgdorf, Berliner Ring 27, Burgdorf, 31303, Germany.

779.28 CZE ISSN 1213-7642
MEGASEX. 2002-2003. 2/yr. PK 62, a.s., Bohdalecka 6, Prague 10, 101 00, Czech Republic.

055.1 ITA ISSN 0025-8717
MEGLIO. 1959-ceased. bi-m. Meglio, Viale Giuseppe di Vittorio, 205-C, Foggia, FG 71100, Italy.

636.7 ITA ISSN 1825-3008
IL MEGLIO DEL CANE. 2005-200?. q. Edigamma Publishing, Via Sambuca Pistoiese 70A, Rome, 00138, Italy.

641.5 ITA ISSN 1825-3016
IL MEGLIO DI FANTASIA IN CUCINA. 2005-200?. bi-m. Edigamma Publishing, Via Sambuca Pistoiese 70A, Rome, 00138, Italy.

915.69 ISR ISSN 0081-8585
MEHKARIM BAGEOGRAFIYA SHEL ERETZ YISRAEL/STUDIES IN THE GEOGRAPHY OF ISRAEL. 1964-2003. irreg. Israel Exploration Society, P O Box 7041, Jerusalem, 91070, Israel.

617.7 CHN ISSN 1000-0348
MEIGUO YIXUEHUI YANKE ZAZHI (ZHONGWEN BAN)/ARCHIVES OF OPHTHALMOLOGY (CHINESE EDITION). 1988-2006. q. Zhonghua Yixuehui, Haidian District, Xueyuan Road, Beiyi Sanyuan, Beijing, 100083, China.

808.8385 DEU
MEIN GESTAENDNIS. 2002-2005. bi-m. Bastei Verlag Gustav H. Luebbe GmbH und Co., Scheidtbachstr 23-31, Bergisch Gladbach, 51469, Germany.

Cessations

028.5 DEU
MEIN KLEINES PONY. 1986-1991. m. Egmont Ehapa Verlag GmbH, Wallstr 59, Berlin, 10179, Germany.

636 DEU
MEIN TIER UND ICH. 2006-2007 (Nov.). bi-m. Panini Verlags GmbH, Ravensstr 48, Nettetal, 41334, Germany.

305.4 DEU
MEINE BUNTE WOCHE. 2008-2008 (May). m. Heinrich Bauer Verlag, Burchardstr 11, Hamburg, 20077, Germany.

808.8385 DEU
MEINE LEIDENSCHAFT. 2002-2003. bi-m. Bastei Verlag Gustav H. Luebbe GmbH und Co., Scheidtbachstr 23-31, Bergisch Gladbach, 51469, Germany.

808.8385 DEU
MEINE VERSUCHUNG. 200?-2004. bi-m. Bastei Verlag Gustav H. Luebbe GmbH und Co., Scheidtbachstr 23-31, Bergisch Gladbach, 51469, Germany.

700 CHN ISSN 1007-4805
MEISHU QIMENG. 1989-2002. m. Zhejiang Renmin Meishu Chubanshe, 347, Tiyuchang Lu, 18F, Chuban Dasha, Hangzhou, 310006, China.

623 ESP ISSN 0211-4488
MEMORIAL DE INGENIERIA DE ARMAMENTO. 1965-1997. q. Colegio Oficial de Ingenieros de Armamento, Avenida de Betanzos 79, Madrid, 28034, Spain.

301 CAN ISSN 1207-0998
MEMORIAL UNIVERSITY OF NEWFOUNDLAND. INSTITUTE OF SOCIAL AND ECONOMIC RESEARCH. BIBLIOGRAPHY. 1971-199?. irreg. Memorial University of Newfoundland, Institute of Social and Economic Research, Arts and Administration Bldg, St. John's, NF A1C 5S7, Canada.

621.38 USA ISSN 1048-2598
MEMORY I CS D.A.T.A. DIGEST. 1971-2000. a. D.A.T.A. Business Publishing, 15 Inverness Way E, Box 6510, Englewood, CO 80155-6510.

610.73 USA ISSN 1558-6243
MEN IN NURSING. 2006 (Jan./Feb.)-2008. bi-m. Lippincott Williams & Wilkins, 530 Walnut St, Philadelphia, PA 19106-3621.

613.081 CZE ISSN 1213-5143
MEN'S HEALTH. 2001-2006 (Dec.). m. Sanoma Magazines Praha s.r.o., Lomnickeho 7, Prague 4, 12079, Czech Republic.

613.088041 DNK ISSN 1500-6964
MEN'S HEALTH (NORWEGIAN EDITION). 1998-2001. m. Bonnier Publications AS, Strandboulevarden 130, Copenhagen OE, 2100, Denmark.

053.1 DEU
MEN'S MAGAZINE. 2006-2007 (Sep.). bi-m. Grafik Studio Teichmann, Karl-Franz-Str 66, Buehl, 77815, Germany.

664 ITA ISSN 1127-0489
MENU. 1992-ceased. q. Editoriale Moda Srl, Via Giardini 476, Modena, MO 41100, Italy.

658.8 ESP ISSN 1137-7615
MERCADOCONTINUO. 1992-2000. m. Ediciones 9, C. Mendez Nunez, 59, Villagarcia de Arosa, Pontevedra 36600, Spain.

796.95 ITA ISSN 1123-9867
MERCATO NAUTICO; giornale della nautica da diporto. 1987-ceased. m. Tortuga Srl

330 USA ISSN 1076-3600
THE MERGER YEARBOOK. 1980-2000. a. Thomson Financial, 195 Broadway, New York, NY 10007.

301.451 USA
MERRICK - WASHINGTON MAGAZINE FOR THE BLIND. 1952-2007. s-a. Brown Enterprises, PO Box 11447, Durham, NC 27703.

790.13 FRA ISSN 0396-4914
MES PREMIERES GRILLES. 1976-2005. bi-m. Publications Guy Hachette, La Petite Motte Senille, Chatellerault, 86100, France.

450 ITA ISSN 0461-9080
MESSANA; rassegna di studi filologici linguistici e storici. N.S. 1950-ceased. 3/yr. Editrice Sicania, Via Catania 62, Messina, ME 98124, Italy.

200 FRA ISSN 0026-0401
MESSIDOR; la tribune de Dieu-revue de la vie totale. 1951-1997. q. Alliance Universelle, La Prefete, BP 27, Montfavet, 84140, France.

671 NLD ISSN 1873-9466
METAAL KRANT. 2006-2007. m. Reed Business bv, Postbus 4, Doetinchem, 7000 BA, Netherlands.

781.64 USA ISSN 1559-4297
METAL MANIACS; the voice of the underground. 1984-2009. 10/yr. Zenbu Media, Llc., 104 W 29th St, 11th Fl, New York, NY 10001.

693 USA
METAL MARKETPLACE; for the metal building & metal roofing industries. 2003-2009. bi-m. ERAN Media, Inc., PO Box 2144, Highland Park, IL 60035.

669 DEU ISSN 0369-2345
METALLGESELLSCHAFT AKTIENGESELLSCHAFT. REVIEW OF THE ACTIVITIES. 1929; N.S. 1959-1981. a. Metallgesellschaft AG, Reuterweg 14, Frankfurt Am Main, 60271, Germany.

658.5 FRA ISSN 0153-9035 CODEN: TMDEDJ
METAUX DEFORMATION. 1969-1988. bi-m. Revue Francaise des Metallurgistes, 32 rue Saint-Marc, Paris, 75002, France.

551.5 DEU ISSN 0342-4332
METEOROLOGISCHE ABHANDLUNGEN. SERIE B, GRUNDLAGENMATERIAL. 1975-1998. irreg. Dietrich Reimer Verlag GmbH, Berliner Str 53, Berlin, 10713, Germany.

500 NLD ISSN 0377-9025 CODEN: MPTTDK
METHODS AND PHENOMENA; their applications in science and technology. 1975-1984 (vol.7). irreg. Elsevier BV, Radarweg 29, P O Box 211, Amsterdam, 1000 AE, Netherlands.

305.4 DEU ISSN 0939-5970
METIS. 1992-2003. s-a. Edition Ebersbach, Droysenstr 8, Berlin, 10629, Germany.

401 ITA
METODOLOGIA DELLE SCIENZE E FILOSOFIA DEL LINGUAGGIO. 197?-200?. irreg. Armando Editore Srl, Viale Trastevere 236, Rome, 00153, Italy.

020 ESP ISSN 1134-2838
METODOS DE INFORMACION. 1994-2002. bi-m. Associacio Valenciana d'Especialistes en Informacio, Apdo. de Correos 1321, Valencia, 46080, Spain.

639.2 ITA
METROPOLITAN MARKET SERIES. 1998-ceased. irreg. Food and Agriculture Organization of the United Nations (F A O), Globefish, Fisheries Industries Division, Viale delle Terme di Caracalla, Rome, 00100, Italy.

371.42 USA ISSN 1098-979X
THE METROPOLITAN NEW YORK JOBBANK; the job hunter's guide to Metro New York. 1984-2005 (19th ed.). irreg. Adams Media, 4700 E Galbraith Rd, Cincinnati, OH 45236.

330.9 USA
MEXICO COUNTRY REPORT. 1996-ceased. a. Orbis Publications, LLC, 1924 47th St NW, Washington, DC 20007-1901.

610 NLD ISSN 0167-5885 CODEN: MPDID9
MEYLER AND PECK'S DRUG-INDUCED DISEASES. 1962-1980 (vol.5). irreg. Elsevier BV, Radarweg 29, P O Box 211, Amsterdam, 1000 AE, Netherlands.

747 ITA ISSN 1970-9455
LA MIA CASA (FORMELLO). 2006-200?. bi-m. Tattilo Editrice SpA, Via degli Olmetti 18, Rome, 00060, Italy.

004.16 FRA ISSN 0765-2887
MICRO P C. 1987-198?. m. Editions Verona, 69 rue de Rome, Paris, 75008, France.

621.381 ITA ISSN 0394-1361
MICROELETTRONICA E IMPRESE. 1986-ceased. 6/yr. Microelettronica e Imprese, Via Alghero, 20, Milan, MI 20128, Italy.

004.678 USA
MICROSOFT VISUAL J++ INFORMANT. 1996-200?. m. Informant Communications Group, 5105 Florin Perkins Rd., Sacramento, CA 95826-4817.

341 346 GBR ISSN 1357-0005
MIDDLE EAST COMMERCIAL LAW REVIEW. 1995-1996. bi-m. Sweet & Maxwell Ltd., 100 Avenue Rd, London, NW3 3PF, United Kingdom.

956 ISR ISSN 0076-8529
MIDDLE EAST RECORD. 1960-1977. irreg. Keter Publishing House Ltd., P O Box 7145, Jerusalem, 91071, Israel.

053.931 NLD ISSN 1566-6891
MIDI. 1999-2008. m. Sanoma Uitgevers B.V., Postbus 1900, Hoofddorp, 2130 JH, Netherlands.

782.42 ITA ISSN 1826-4174
LE MIE CANZONI. 2005-200?. m. Edigamma Publishing, Via Sambuca Pistoiese 70A, Rome, 00138, Italy.

635.9 ITA ISSN 1825-4160
LE MIE ROSE. 2005-200?. m. Sprea Editori Srl, Via Torino 51, Cernusco sul Naviglio, MI 20063, Italy.

800 ISR ISSN 0792-3414
MIFGASH/LIQA'; majallah fasliyyah adabiyyah 'ibriyyah - 'arabiyyah. 1964-1997. 4/yr. Histadrut Jewish-Arab Institute, Beit Berl, Kfar Sabba, 44905, Israel.

632.9 ITA ISSN 1014-2193
MIGRANT PEST NEWSLETTER. 1961-19??. a. Food and Agriculture Organization of the United Nations (F A O), Via delle Terme di Caracalla, Rome, RM 00100, Italy.

304.8 DEU ISSN 0721-2887
MIGRATION; a European journal of international migration and ethnic relations. 1987-2005. 6/yr. Edition Parabolis, Schliemannstr 23, Berlin, 10437, Germany.

681.322 BRD ISSN 0174-6073
MIKROCOMPUTER-JAHRBUCH. 1979-1984. a. Vieweg und Teubner Verlag, Abraham-Lincoln-Str 46, Wiesbaden, 65189, Germany.

781.64 AUS ISSN 1327-256X
MIKROPOLYPHONIE. 1996-200?. irreg. La Trobe University, Music Department

637.1 DEU ISSN 0933-0682
MILCHSTRASSE; die Kundenzeitschrift fuer Kaese, Butter und Milchfrischprodukte. 1987-2000. bi-m. Buecker Fachverlag GmbH & Co. KG, Postfach 1363, Bad Breisig, 53492, Germany.

629 355 USA ISSN 1540-3149
MILITARY AEROSPACE TECHNOLOGY. 2002-2006. 8/yr. Kerrigan Media International, Inc., 1300 Piccard Dr, Ste 200, Rockville, MD 20850.

355 USA ISSN 1074-3286
MILITARY SOURCES, QUERIES AND REVIEWS. 1994-1995. irreg. (2-4/yr.). Family Publications, 5628 60th Dr, NE, Marysville, WA 98270.

810 USA ISSN 1536-9064
MILLER'S POND; poetry magazine. 1998-2003. a. H & H Press, R.R. 2, Box 241, Middlebury Center, PA 16935.

659.1 ITA ISSN 0392-5498
IL MILLIMETRO; periodico di informazioni aziendali di marketing e di pubblicita. 1964-ceased. q. St. Paul's International, Via Giotto, 36, Milan, MI 20145, Italy.

374.8025 DNK ISSN 1396-9684
MIN VEJ. 1996-2003. a. Raadet for Uddannelses- og Erhvervsvejledning (R.U.E.), Vester Voldgade 123, Copenhagen V, 1552, Denmark.

615.842 ITA ISSN 1125-1778
MINERVA RIFLESSOTERAPEUTICA E LASERTERAPEUTICA. 1976-199?. s-a. Edizioni Minerva Medica, Corso Bramante 83-85, Turin, 10126, Italy.

700 ITA
MINIATURA E ARTI MINORI IN CAMPANIA. 1967-1981 (no.16). irreg. Edizioni Scientifiche Italiane SpA, Via Chiatamone 7, Naples, NA 80121, Italy.

549 AUS
MINING AND THE ENVIRONMENT. 1976-1998. irreg. Minerals Council of Australia, PO Box 363, Dickson, ACT 2602, Australia.

351 DNK ISSN 0085-3461
MINISTERIALTIDENDE FOR KONGERIGET DANMARK. 1871-2007. w. Justisministeriet, Civilstyrelsen. Retsinformation, Gyldenloevesgade 11,2, Copenhagen V, 1600, Denmark.

344.046 USA ISSN 1072-916X
MINNESOTA ENVIRONMENTAL COMPLIANCE UPDATE. 1994-1997. m. Business & Legal Reports, Inc., 141 Mill Rock Rd E, Old Saybrook, CT 06475.

340 USA ISSN 0278-7628
MINNESOTA REAL ESTATE LAW JOURNAL. 1981-2005. bi-m. Michie Company, 701 E Water St, Charlottesville, VA 22902.

649 ITA ISSN 0026-5756
IL MIO BEBE. CHERIE MODA. 1966-ceased. s-a. Edizioni Moderne Internazionali, Via Gadames 123, Milan, 20123, Italy.

635 ITA ISSN 1825-4144
IL MIO ORTO. 2005-200?. a. Sprea Editori Srl, Via Torino 51, Cernusco sul Naviglio, MI 20063, Italy.

728 ITA ISSN 1824-2227
IL MIO TERRAZZO. 2004-200?. a. Sprea Editori Srl, Via Torino 51, Cernusco sul Naviglio, MI 20063, Italy.

946 ESP ISSN 0213-2257
MISCEL.LANIA DE TEXTOS MEDIEVALS. 1972-1996. irreg. Consejo Superior de Investigaciones Cientificas, Instituto de Estudios Madrilenos, Vitruvio, 8, Madrid, 28001, Spain.

690 FRA ISSN 1951-8641
MISE AUX NORMES ET SECURITE DES BATIMENTS. 1998-2007. plus q. updates. Editions Weka, 249 Rue de Crimee, Paris, 75935 Cedex 19, France.

615 572 FRA ISSN 0294-0671
MISES AU POINT DE BIOCHIMIE PHARMACOLOGIQUE. 1977-198?. irreg. Elsevier Masson, 62 Rue Camille Desmoulins, Issy les Moulineaux, Cedex 92442, France.

700 ISR ISSN 0334-9810
MISHKAFAYIM. 1987-2001. q. Israel Museum, Youth Department, P O Box 71117, Jerusalem, 91710, Israel.

363.7 NLD ISSN 1380-2070
MISSET'S MILIEUHANDBOEK. 1993-1995. a. Reed Business bv, Hanzestraat 1, Doetinchem, 7006 RH, Netherlands.

207.2 DNK ISSN 0106-5610
MISSION; nordisk missionstidsskrift. 1889-1998. a. Dansk Missionsraad, Skt Lukas Vej 13, Hellerup, 2900, Denmark.

929 USA ISSN 1075-6191
MISSOURI SOURCES, QUERIES AND REVIEWS. 1994-1995. irreg. (2-4/yr.). Family Publications, 5628 60th Dr, NE, Marysville, WA 98270.

616 BRD ISSN 0172-4258
MITTEILUNGEN DER DEUTSCHEN UND DER OESTERRICHISCHEN GESELLSCHAFT FUER INTERNISTISCHE INTENSIVMEDIZIN. 19??-1988. irreg. Dr. Dietrich Steinkopff Verlag, Tiergartenstr 17, Heidelberg, 69121, Germany.

520 DEU ISSN 0944-1999
MITTEILUNGEN ZUR ASTRONOMIEGESCHICHTE. 1992-2005. s-a. Astronomische Gesellschaft, Arbeitskreis Astronomiegeschichte, c/o Wolfgang R. Dick, Otterkiez 14, Potsdam, 14478, Germany.

610 DDR ISSN 0368-9913
MITTEILUNGEN ZUR GESCHICHTE DER MEDIZIN DER NATURWISSENSCHAFTEN UND TECHNIK. 1902-1964. irreg. Johann Ambrosius Barth Verlag, Salomonstr. 18B, Leipzig, 04103, East Germany.

808.83872 DEU
MITTERNACHTS-ROMAN; unheimliches zur Geisterstunde. 1985-2001. w. Bastei Verlag Gustav H. Luebbe GmbH und Co., Scheidtbachstr 23-31, Bergisch Gladbach, 51469, Germany.

646.72 659.152 ITA
MIXART NEWS. 1998-ceased. s-a.?. SEPEM s.r.l., Via Grado 9, Milan, MI 20125, Italy.

663 ITA
MIXER. 1976-ceased. 10/yr. Gruppo E.S. s.r.l., Via Andrea Solari, 19, Milan, MI 20144, Italy.

305.8918 ITA ISSN 1124-657X
MLADIKA. 1957-ceased. m. Mladika S.c.a.r.l., Via Donizetti, 3, Trieste, 34133, Italy.

681.3 CZE ISSN 1801-7037
MOBIL. 1996-2007. m. Trade & Leisure Publications, s.r.o., Pernerova 35a, Prague 8, 186 00, Czech Republic.

621.385 AUS ISSN 1036-014X
MOBILES. 1990-2004. m. (11/yr.). Teleresources Engineering (Aust) Pty. Ltd., PO Box 693, Brookvale, NSW 2100, Australia.

646.724 ITA ISSN 1124-2086
MODA CAPELLI. 1994-200?. q. Edigamma Publishing, Via Sambuca Pistoiese 70A, Rome, 00138, Italy.

646.4 NLD ISSN 1574-6186
MODEJOLI. 2005-2007. 4/yr. Uitgeverij Rielies Timmer, Tuinbouwweg 23, Maarssen, 3602 AT, Netherlands.

790.13 DEU ISSN 1862-7498
MODELLCOLLECTOR. 2006-2007 (Mar.). bi-m. Carl Ed. Schuenemann KG, Zweite Schlachpforte 7, Bremen, 28195, Germany.

659.152 ITA ISSN 1121-8290
MODELLINA. 1946-ceased. q. IBI s.r.l., Via Camillo Finocchiaro Aprile, 5, Milan, MI 20124, Italy.

615 610.73 USA ISSN 1044-0704
MODELL'S DRUGS IN CURRENT USE AND NEW DRUGS. 1955-200?. a. Springer Publishing Company, 11 W 42nd St, 15th Fl, New York, NY 10036.

625.19 DNK ISSN 0107-6310
MODELTOGET. 1979-2005. bi-m. Foreningen Toget, c/o Arne Wagenschwarz, Magleparken 49, Ballerup, 2750, Denmark.

943 830 GBR ISSN 0268-5930
MODERN GERMAN STUDIES. 1985-2000. irreg. Association for Modern German Studies, c/o Ingrid Williams, 2 Nicholas Gardens, London, W5 5HY, United Kingdom.

615.3205 AUS ISSN 1322-2775
MODERN PHYTOTHERAPIST. 1994-2003. q. MediHerb Pty Ltd, PO Box 714, Warwick, QLD 4370, Australia.

615 GBR ISSN 0544-6910
MODERN TRENDS IN PHARMACOLOGY AND THERAPEUTICS. 1967-19??. irreg. Butterworth & Co. (Publishers) Ltd., 88 Kingsway, London, WC2B 6AB, United Kingdom.

391 USA ISSN 1548-3258
MODERN UNIFORMS. 2004 (Feb.)-2007. bi-m. Advertising Specialty Institute, 4800 Street Rd, Trevose, PA 19053.

687 FRA ISSN 0248-0034
MODES ET TECHNIQUES. 1957-2002. bi-m. Editions Vauclair, 41 bd. General Martial Valin, Paris, 75015, France.

808 GBR
MOMENTUM. 1985-1992. 3/yr. Wrexham Writers' Workshop, Almere Farm, Rossett, Wrexham, Clwyd LL12 0BY, United Kingdom.

639.34 FRA ISSN 1771-3129
MON PREMIER AQUARIUM. 2004-2008. bi-m. Aqua Media, 1492 Bd de Bigorre, Z.E. Ma Campagne, Angouleme, 16000, France.

330 AUS ISSN 1832-8490
MONASH BUSINESS REVIEW. 2005 (Aug.)-2008 (Dec.). 3/yr. Monash University ePress, Bldg 4, Monash University, Wellington Rd, Clayton, VIC 3800, Australia.

910 AUS
MONASH PUBLICATIONS IN GEOGRAPHY AND ENVIRONMENTAL SCIENCE. 1996-2002. irreg. Monash University, School of Geography & Environmental Science, Bldg 11, Monash University, Monash, VIC 3800, Australia.

950 AUS ISSN 1323-2649
MONASH UNIVERSITY. DEVELOPMENT STUDIES CENTRE. OCCASIONAL PAPERS. 1989-1999. irreg. Monash University, Development Studies Centre, c/o Publications Officer, Monash Asia Institute, Clayton, VIC 3168, Australia.

282 ITA
MONASTICA. 1960-ceased. q. Monastero di Santa Scolastica, Civitella San Paolo, RM 00060, Italy.

301 FRA ISSN 0758-4431
MONDE ALPIN ET RHODANIEN; revue regionale d'ethnologie. 1973-2006. q. Centre Alpin et Rhodanien d'Ethnologie, Musee Dauphinois, 30 rue Maurice Gignoux, Grenoble, Cedex 1 38031, France.

332.1 ITA ISSN 0026-9506
MONDO BANCARIO; rassegna bimestrale illustrata di cultura, di studi e di documentazione. 1959-ceased. bi-m. Futura 2000 SpA, Via Jacopo Sannazzaro, 6-8, Rome, RM 00141, Italy.

620.00420285 ITA
MONDO C A D. (Computer-Aided Design) 1989-ceased. 5/yr. Franco Ziviani Editore Srl, Via Melchiorre Gioia, 168, Milan, MI 20125, Italy.

951 ITA ISSN 0390-2811
MONDO CINESE. 1973-199?. q. Istituto Italo Cinese per gli Scambi Economici e Culturali, Via Giosue' Carducci, 18, Milan, MI 20123, Italy.

685.31 ITA
MONDO DELLA CALZATURA: TECNOLOGIE E MATERIE. 1983-ceased. m. Servizi Editoriali Riuniti, Viale Espinasse 141, Milan, 20156, Italy.

685 ITA ISSN 1127-1876
IL MONDO DELLA PELLETTERIA. 1986-ceased. q. Servizi Editoriali Riuniti, Viale Espinasse 141, Milan, 20156, Italy.

320 ITA
MONDO PADANO. 1981-ceased. fortn. Societa Servizi Editoriali, Via delle Industrie 2, Cremona, CR 26100, Italy.

398 ITA
MONDO POPOLARE. 1990-2001 (no.16). irreg. Angelo Longo Editore, Via Paolo Costa 33, Ravenna, 48121, Italy.

332 NLD ISSN 0925-4129 CODEN: IJATB7
MONEY. 1990-2005. 10/yr. Reed Business bv, Hanzestraat 1, Doetinchem, 7006 RH, Netherlands.

388 FRA ISSN 0762-9184
LE MONITEUR AUTOMOBILE. 1984-2008. bi-w. Editions France Auto, 12 Rue de la Bruyere, Paris, 75009, France.

362 657.832 NLD ISSN 1871-0433
MONITORING BEHEERSKOSTEN ALGEMENE WET BIJZONDERE ZIEKTEKOSTEN. 2001-2005. a. College voor Zorgverzekeringen, Postbus 320, Diemen, 1110 AH, Netherlands.

330.1 FRA ISSN 0767-7480
MONNAIE, PRIX, CONJONCTURE. 1952-1973. irreg. College de France, Ecole des Hautes Etudes en Sciences Sociales (E H E S S), 54 Boulevard Raspail, Paris, 75006, France.

610 USA ISSN 1535-2706
MONOCLONAL ANTIBODIES WEEKLY. 2000-ceased. w. NewsRx, 2727 Paces Ferry Rd SE, Ste 2-440, Atlanta, GA 30339.

345 364 NLD ISSN 0169-1384
MONOGRAFIEEN STRAFRECHT. 1983-2001 (vol.19,1994). irreg. Kluwer B.V., Postbus 23, Deventer, 7400 GA, Netherlands.

720.92 NLD
MONOGRAFIEEN VAN NEDERLANDSE ARCHITECTEN/ MONOGRAPHS OF DUTCH ARCHITECTS. 1989-1998 (vol.10,1996). irreg. Uitgeverij 010 Publishers, Watertorenweg 180, Rotterdam, 3063 HA, Netherlands.

616.97 CHE ISSN 0077-0760 CODEN: MOALAR
MONOGRAPHS IN ALLERGY. 1966-1996 (vol.33). irreg. S. Karger AG, Allschwilerstr 10, Basel, 4055, Switzerland.

304.6 GBR ISSN 0964-5942
MONOGRAPHS IN ETHNIC RELATIONS. NEW SERIES. 1983-1996. irreg. University of Warwick, Centre for Research in Ethnic Relations, Ramphal Bldg, Coventry, CV4 7AL, United Kingdom.

510 GBR
MONOGRAPHS ON NUMERICAL ANALYSIS. 1957-200?. irreg. Oxford University Press, Great Clarendon St, Oxford, OX2 6DP, United Kingdom.

780 ESP ISSN 0210-4083
MONSALVAT. 1973-1992. m. Ediciones de Nuevo Arte Thor, Placa De Gal.La Placidia, 1-16, Barcelona, 08006, Spain.

796.7 DEU ISSN 1860-0662
MOPPED; die etwas andere Motorrad-Zeitschrift. 1993-2008 (Sep.). m. Motor-Presse Stuttgart GmbH und Co. KG, Leuschnerstr 1, Stuttgart, 70174, Germany.

332.72 GBR ISSN 1753-5638
MORTGAGE DISTRIBUTOR. 2007-2008. m. Centaur Media PLC, 50 Poland St, London, W1F 7AX, United Kingdom.

332.3 USA ISSN 1070-5708
MORTGAGE ORIGINATOR. 1991-2009 (Jun.). m. Summit Business Media LLC, 1801 Park 270 Dr, Ste 550, Maryland Heights, MO 63146.

920.02 USA ISSN 1073-788X
MOST ADMIRED MEN AND WOMEN OF THE YEAR. 1993-1996. a. American Biographical Institute, Inc., Governing Board of Editors, 5126 Bur Oak Cir, Raleigh, NC 27612.

700 ITA
MOSTRE E MUSEI. 1975-1984 (no.8). irreg. Societa Editrice Napoletana s.r.l., Corso Umberto I, 1-34, Naples, NA 80138, Italy.

388 DEU ISSN 0027-1462
MOT; die Autozeitschrift. 1955-2006. fortn. Vereinigte Motor-Verlage GmbH & Co. KG, Leuschnerstr 1, Stuttgart, 70174, Germany.

388.347 796.7 ITA ISSN 0390-0304
LA MOTO. 1976-200?. m. Edigamma Publishing, Via Sambuca Pistoiese 70A, Rome, 00138, Italy.

796.7 ITA ISSN 1121-6263
LA MOTO JUNIOR. 1991-200?. m. Edigamma Publishing, Via Sambuca Pistoiese 70A, Rome, 00138, Italy.

796.7 AUS ISSN 1449-0684
MOTO MANUAL. 2004-ceased. a. Universal Magazines Pty. Ltd., Private Bag 154, North Ryde, NSW 2113, Australia.

388 USA ISSN 1359-4532
MOTOR BUSINESS ASIA PACIFIC. 1994-200?. q. Economist Intelligence Unit Ltd., 111 W 57th St, New York, NY 10019 .

388.3 ITA ISSN 0391-6456
MOTOR ITALIA. EUROMOTOR. 1926-ceased. a. Motor Italia S.r.l., c/o Stamperia Artistica Nazionale, Corso Siracusa, 37, Turin, TO 10136, Italy.

388.3 GBR ISSN 0306-6274
MOTOR REPORT INTERNATIONAL. 1979-1993. fortn. Circlemartin Ltd., Circlemartin Ltd, Box 87, Dorking, Surrey RH4 2YS, United Kingdom.

388 ITA ISSN 0393-7666
MOTORI. 1950-ceased. bi-m. Torino Motori s.r.l., Corso Galileo Ferraris, 162, Turin, TO 10134, Italy.

388 DEU ISSN 1861-6143
MOTORS. 1970-2006 (Feb.). m. Motor-Presse Stuttgart GmbH und Co. KG, Leuschnerstr 1, Stuttgart, 70174, Germany.

053.931 808.8 NLD
MOUSEBIT; een dynamisch webmagazine dat groeit en vloeit op het Web - a dynamic webmagazine that grows and flows on the Web. ceased 200?. irreg. Frans Tooten, Ed. & Pub., Netherlands.

791.43 GBR ISSN 0027-268X
MOVIE. 1962-200?. irreg. Movie, c/o Ian Cameron, Ed & Pub., PO Box 1, Moffat, Dumfriesshire DG10 9SU, United Kingdom.

791.43 AUS ISSN 0314-0326
MOVIE. 1973-2000. bi-m. Greater Union Organization, 49 Market St, Sydney, NSW 2000, Australia.

388.324 USA ISSN 1064-4253
THE MOVING WORLD. 1991-199?. s-m. American Moving and Storage Association, 1611 Duke St, Alexandria, VA 22314.

658 USA
MR. CHEAP'S CHICAGO; shopping, bargains, factory outlets, off-price stores, cheap eats, cheapplaces to stay and much more. 1994-2000 (2nd ed.). irreg. Adams Media, 4700 E Galbraith Rd, Cincinnati, OH 45236.

658 USA ISSN 1529-1170
MR. CHEAP'S NEW YORK; shopping, bargains, factory outlets, off-price stores, cheapeats, cheapplaces to stay and much more. 1993-2000. irreg. Adams Media, 4700 E Galbraith Rd, Cincinnati, OH 45236.

658 USA
MR. CHEAP'S WASHINGTON D.C.; shopping, bargains, factory outlets, off-price stores, cheap eats, cheapplaces to stay and much more. 1996-1997 (Jan.). irreg. Adams Media, 4700 E Galbraith Rd, Cincinnati, OH 45236.

610 BRD ISSN 0303-4593
MUENSTERSCHE BEITRAEGE ZUR GESCHICHTE UND THEORIE DER MEDIZIN. 1970-1985 (vol.26). irreg. Burgverlag, Am Steinkamp 20, Tecklenburg, 49545, Germany.

025.1 994 AUS ISSN 1448-4129
MULTICULTURAL LIBRARIES. 1980-2002. 2/yr. Working Group on Multicultural Library Services (Victoria), 313 Racecourse Rd, Flamington, VIC 3031, Australia.

570 NLD ISSN 1573-6105
MULTIDISCIPLINE MODELING IN MATERIALS AND STRUCTURES. 2005-2009 (Vol. 5). q. V S P, Brill Academic Publishers, PO Box 9000, Leiden, 2300 PA, Netherlands.

004.6 USA ISSN 1076-2442 CODEN: ECCOEE
MULTIMEDIA WIRE. 1993-199?. d. Warren Communications News, Inc., 2115 Ward Ct, NW, Washington, DC 20037.

708 ITA
MUSEO NAZIONALE D'ARTE ORIENTALE. SCHEDE. 1974 (no.6)-ceased. irreg. Museo Nazionale d'Arte Orientale, Via Merulana, 248, Rome, RM 00185, Italy.

069 USA ISSN 0196-0237
MUSEOLOGY. 1975-19??. irreg. Texas Tech University Press, 2903 4th St, Ste 201, PO Box 41037, Lubbock, TX 79409.

069.7 NLD ISSN 1872-3160
MUSEUM CATHARIJNECONVENT MAGAZINE. 2005-2007. a. Uitgeverij Intermed, Postbus 2306, Groningen, 9704 CH, Netherlands.

809 ITA ISSN 0392-6931
MUSEUM CRITICUM. 1975 (vol.10)-1989. irreg. Fabrizio Serra Editore, c/o Accademia Editoriale, Via Santa Bibbiana 28, Pisa, 56127, Italy.

069 USA ISSN 1094-009X
MUSEUMS BOSTON. 1997-2006. 4/yr. Art Knowledge Corp., 56 W 22nd St, 5th Fl, New York, NY 10010.

780 ITA ISSN 1123-4016
MUSIC CITY; l'ipermercato dell'informazione musicale. 1994-ceased. m. Edizioni Milano Publishing s.r.l., Via Marconi, 28, Bresso, MI 20091, Italy.

780 ITA ISSN 1824-7350
MUSIC COMPILATION. 2004-200?. irreg. Edigamma Publishing, Via Sambuca Pistoiese 70A, Rome, 00138, Italy.

780 ITA
MUSICA D'OGGI; periodico di cultura musica spettacolo. 1975-ceased. m. Musica d'Oggi, Via Romolo Balzani, 64-6, Rome, RM 00177, Italy.

780.7 USA ISSN 0737-0032
MUSICAL WOMAN. 1983-199?. irreg. Greenwood Publishing Group Inc., 88 Post Rd W, PO Box 5007, Westport, CT 06881.

780 ITA ISSN 0027-4674
MUSICALBRANDE; arvista piemonteisa. 1959-1994. q. Musicalbrande, Corso Palermo, 11, Turin, TO 10152, Italy.

681.81 FRA ISSN 1629-9213
MUSICIENS MAGAZINE. 2001-2001. bi-m. Editions Lariviere, 6 Rue Olof Palme, Clichy, 92587 , France.

781.64 DEU
MUSIKER JAHRBUCH. 1985-2000. biennial. Deutsche Rock- und Pop Musikerverband, Kulturelles Jugendbildungswerk, Kolberger Str 30, Lueneburg, 21339, Germany.

001.3 FRA ISSN 1241-3623
MUSIQUE ET SCIENCES HUMAINES. DOCUMENTS DE RECHERCHES. 1993-199?. irreg. Publidix, 200 av. de la Republique, Nanterre, Cedex 92001, France.

330 FRA ISSN 0985-2433
MUTATIONS. 1987-2001. a. Novespace, 15 rue des Halles, Paris, 75001, France.

378.44 FRA ISSN 0247-6355
LA MUTU. 1981-198?. s-a. Mutuelle Nationale des Etudiants de France, 16 av. Raspail, Gentilly, 94250, France.

332.6327 USA ISSN 0897-5108
MUTUAL FUND PROFILES. 1987-1997. q. Standard & Poor's, 55 Water St, New York, NY 10041.

630.21 FRA ISSN 0989-0025
MUTUALITE SOCIALE AGRICOLE. ANNUAIRE STATISTIQUE. 19??-199?. a. Mutualite Sociale Agricole, Les Mercuriales, 40 rue Jean Jaures, Bagnolet, Cedex 93547, France.

943.7 708.371 CZE ISSN 0505-8228
MUZEUM VYSOCINY. ODDELENI VED PRIPODNICH. VLASTIVEDNY SBORNIK VYSOCINY. 1957-2003. biennial. Muzeum Vysociny, Oddeleni Ved Pripodnich, Masarykovo nam 55, Jihlava, 58601, Czech Republic.

658.8 781.91 789.91 NLD ISSN 1873-944X
MUZIEK EN BEELD JAARBOEK. 2003-2006. a. iMediate, Postbus 2227, Hilversum, 1200 CE, Netherlands.

690 USA ISSN 1555-2500
MY HOUSE IN THE MOUNTAIN STATES. 2005 (Jan./Feb.)-2006. bi-m. McGraw-Hill Companies, Inc., 1221 Ave of the Americas, 43rd fl, New York, NY 10020.

808.8385 DEU ISSN 1615-6471
MY LADY DUETT. 2000-2005. 4/yr. Cora Verlag GmbH und Co. KG, Valentinskamp 24, Hamburg, 20350, Germany.

384.6 DEU
MYHANDY. 2001-2003. bi-m. Der Heisse Draht Verlag GmbH und Co., Drostestr 14-16, Hannover, 30161, Germany.

330 DEU
MYJOB; das Qualifizierungsmagazin. 2006-2007. 5/yr. Data Becker GmbH & Co. KG, Merowingerstr 30, Duesseldorf, 40223, Germany.

610 BRD ISSN 0720-0692
MYKOLOGISCHE PRAXIS. 1980-1982. irreg. P M I Verlagsgruppe GmbH, August-Schanz-Str 8-II, Frankfurt Am Main, 60433, Germany.

796.323 USA ISSN 1067-5159
N B A INSIDE STUFF. (National Basketball Association) 1992-2008. bi-m. Professional Sports Publications (P S P), 519 8th Ave, Ste 2500, New York, NY 10018.

797.1 USA ISSN 1545-8733
N C BOATING LIFESTYLE; the lifestyle magazine for North Carolina power boat owners. (North Carolina) 2003-2009; suspended. m. Ballantyne Publishing, PO Box 29585, Greensboro, NC 27429.

540 ITA ISSN 1592-2286
N C F INTERNATIONAL. (Notiziario Chimico Farmaceutico) 1997-2004. q. Tecniche Nuove SpA, Via Eritrea 21, Milan, MI 201, Italy.

615.1029 USA ISSN 0890-6610
THE N D A PIPELINE. (New Drug Approval) 1981-2006. a. F-D-C Reports, Inc., 5550 Friendship Blvd, Ste One, Chevy Chase, MD 20815-7278.

621.3 JPN ISSN 0547-051X CODEN: NECRAU
N E C RESEARCH AND DEVELOPMENT. (Nippon Electric Company) 1960-2003. q. N E C Media Products Ltd., 1-23, Heiwajima 4-Chome, Octa-ku, Tokyo, 143-0006, Japan.

614.84 USA ISSN 1097-1505
N F P A UPDATE. (National Fire Protection Association) 1916-200?. m. National Fire Protection Association, 1 Batterymarch Park, Quincy, MA 02169.

Cessations

665.7 388 NZL ISSN 1175-2807
N G V WORLDWIDE. (Natural Gas Vehicles) 2000-2004. q. Sigma Group Partnership, PO Box 33-212, Takapuna, New Zealand.

347 USA ISSN 1555-2179
N I J RESEARCH REVIEW. 2000-2004. q. U.S. Department of Justice. National Institute of Justice, 810 Seventh St, NW, Washington, DC 20531.

015 USA ISSN 1041-5327
N I O S H PUBLICATIONS CATALOG. (National Institute for Occupational Safety and Health) 1980-1997. a. Centers for Disease Control & Prevention, National Institute for Occupational Safety and Health, 1600 Clifton Rd, Atlanta, GA 30333.

001.3 500 ITA ISSN 1970-5484
N I S STUDI SUPERIORI. (Nuova Italia Scientifica) 1993-ceased. irreg. La Nuova Italia Scientifica (N I S), Via Sardegna 50, Rome, 00187, Italy.

658.8 USA ISSN 1090-1906
N P N INTERNATIONAL. (National Petroleum News) 1996-2006. 6/yr. Adams Business Media, 2101 S Arlington Heights Rd, Ste 150, Arlington Heights, IL 60005-4142.

336.2 USA
N T A FORUM. 19??-1999. q. National Tax Association, 725 15th St, N W, Ste 600, Washington, DC 20005.

005.43 USA
N T UPDATE. ceased. m. Xephon, 9330 Lyndon B Johnson Fwy., Ste. 800, Dallas, TX 75243-4310.

658 DEU ISSN 1864-5151
NACHGEFRAGT. 2007-2007 (no.3). irreg. Christoph Busch Unternehmensberatung GmbH, Mainzer Landstr 176, Frankfurt am Main, 60327, Germany.

280.042 DEU
NACHRICHTEN AUS DER BASLER MISSION. 1908-2001. bi-m. Basler Mission Deutscher Zweig, Vogelsangstr 62, Stuttgart, 70197, Germany.

330 DEU ISSN 1611-7611
NANOTECH-REPORT; Deutschlands erster Boersenbrief ueber Nanotechnologie. 2003-2008. m. Boersenmedien AG, Am Eulenhof 14, Kulmbach, 95326, Germany.

073.7 SVK ISSN 1335-4671
NARODNA OBRODA; dennik o hospodarstve a spolocnosti. 1990-2005. 6/w. (except Sun.). Pegas 2 Slovakia s.r.o., Nevadzova 5, PO Box 40, Bratislava, 82007, Slovakia.

016.912 CZE
NARODNI BIBLIOGRAFIE CESKE REPUBLIKY. MAPY (CD-ROM EDITION). 1958-2008. a. Narodni Knihovna Ceske Republiky, Klementinum 190, Prague, 11001, Czech Republic.

600 016 CZE
NARODNI TECHNICKE MUZEUM. BIBLIOGRAFIE A PRAMENY. 1970-2003 (vol.27). irreg. Narodni Technicke Muzeum, Kostelni 42, Prague 7, 17078, Czech Republic.

330 AUS ISSN 1036-4145
NATIONAL BUSINESS BULLETIN. 1992-2004. m. National Business Magazine, PO Box 687, Darlinghurst, NSW 2010, Australia.

338 NZL ISSN 1176-2977
NATIONAL BUSINESS REVIEW DESK COMPANION. 1999-2003. a. Liberty Holdings, PO Box 1734, Auckland, New Zealand.

304.6 USA ISSN 0744-1010
NATIONAL CLEARINGHOUSE FOR CENSUS DATA SERVICES. ADDRESS LIST. 1979-1981. irreg. U.S. Census Bureau, 4700 Silver Hill Rd., Washington, DC 20233.

370.285 USA ISSN 0743-2364
NATIONAL EDUCATIONAL COMPUTING CONFERENCE. PROCEEDINGS. 1979-1983. a. International Society for Technology in Education, 1710 Rhode Island Ave NW, Ste 900, Washington, DC 20036.

339.373 USA ISSN 0361-3895
NATIONAL INCOME AND PRODUCT ACCOUNTS OF THE UNITED STATES: STATISTICAL TABLES. 1929-19??. quinquennial. U.S. Department of Commerce, Bureau of Economic Analysis, 1441 L St NW, Washington, DC 20230.

330 GBR ISSN 0077-4928
NATIONAL INSTITUTE OF ECONOMIC AND SOCIAL RESEARCH, LONDON. OCCASIONAL PAPERS. 1946-1996 (Mar.). irreg. Cambridge University Press, The Edinburgh Bldg, Shaftesbury Rd, Cambridge, CB2 8RU, United Kingdom.

368.01 ISR
NATIONAL INSURANCE INSTITUTE, JERUSALEM. FULL ACTUARIAL REPORT. 1959-1996. triennial. National Insurance Institute, 13 Sderot Weizman, Jerusalem, Israel.

020 AUS ISSN 1039-3498
NATIONAL LIBRARY OF AUSTRALIA GATEWAYS (PRINT). 1979-2003. bi-m. National Library of Australia, Services to Libraries, Canberra, ACT 2600, Australia.

333.95416 AUS ISSN 1442-5505
NATIONAL PARK AND WILDLIFE JOURNAL. 1997-2002. q. National Parks and Wildlife South Australia, GPO Box 1047, Adelaide, SA 5001, Australia.

384.5 EGY ISSN 1110-6972
NATIONAL RADIO SCIENCE CONFERENCE. PROCEEDINGS/AL-MU'TAMAR AL-QAWMI LI-'ILM AL-RADYU. 1983-200?. a. Academy of Scientific Research and Technology, Ain Shams University, Faculty of Engineering, Abbasia, Cairo, Egypt.

797.25 AUS ISSN 1323-1197
NATIONAL WATER POLO NEWS. 1985-2007. q. McKinnon Media Pty. Ltd., PO Box 89, Bull Creek, W.A. 6149, Australia.

330.9 DEU
NATIONALEINKOMMEN UND EINKOMMENSKREISLAUF. 1973-2005. q. Deutsches Institut fuer Wirtschaftsforschung, Koenigin-Luise-Str 5, Berlin, 14195, Germany.

970.1 USA ISSN 1063-9632
NATIVE AMERICANS INFORMATION DIRECTORY. 1992-1998. irreg. Gale, 27500 Drake Rd, Farmington Hills, MI 48331.

613 AUS
NATURAL HEALTH REVIEW. 1998-2002. bi-m. Publishing Services (Australia) Pty Ltd., 244 St Pauls Terr, Fortitude Valley, Brisbane, QLD 4000, Australia.

500 ITA ISSN 1128-6334
NATURALMENTE; bollettino di informazione degli insegnanti di scienze naturali. 1989-2007. quadrennial. Fabrizio Serra Editore, c/o Accademia Editoriale, Via Santa Bibbiana 28, Pisa, 56127, Italy.

613.194 ITA ISSN 0392-4173
NATURISMO; rivista naturista e umanitaria. 1972-199?. s-a. Unione Naturisti Italiani, Galleria Subalpina 30, Turin, TO 10123, Italy.

615.535 USA ISSN 1559-0399
NATUROPATHY DIGEST (PRINT). 2006-2008. m. M P A Media, PO Box 4139, Huntington Beach, CA 92605-4139.

387.2 797.1 USA ISSN 1094-0170
NAUTICAL WORLD. 1994-1999. bi-m. Source Interlink Companies, 27500 Riverview Center Blvd, Bonita Springs, FL 34134.

051 ITA
NAUTILUS. 1996-2003. m. Nautilus, Italy.

387 ITA ISSN 0390-2927
NAVIGAZIONE INTERNA. 1974-ceased. q. Unione di Navigazione Interna Italiana (U N I I), Via Banchina dell'Azoto 15D, Marghera, VE 30175, Italy.

355 GBR ISSN 0955-7261
NAVINT; the international naval newsletter. 1989-2002. fortn. Tileprint Ltd., 145A Putney High St, London, SW15 1SU, United Kingdom.

305.8924 USA ISSN 0028-176X
NEAR EAST REPORT (PRINT); a Washington newsletter on American Middle East policy. 1957-2008. bi-w. Near East Research, Inc., 440 First St, N W, Ste 607, Washington, DC 20001.

053 NLD ISSN 0166-0586
HET NEDERLANDSE BOEK. 1852-2005. bi-m. Het Nederlandse Boek, Postbus 10576, Amsterdam, 1001 EN, Netherlands.

948 NLD ISSN 0920-4032
NEDERLANDSE HISTORISCHE BRONNEN. 1979-1995 (no.11). irreg. Koninklijk Nederlands Historisch Genootschap, Postbus 90406, The Hague, 2509 LK, Netherlands.

336.2 NLD
NEDERLANDSE JURISPRUDENTIE INZAKE INTERNATIONAAL BELASTINGRECHT; directe belastingen van internationaal opererende ondernemingen. 1993-ceased. plus irreg. updates. International Bureau of Fiscal Documentation (I B F D), H J E Wenckebachweg 210, Amsterdam, 1096 AS, Netherlands.

747 ITA
NEGOZIO MODERNO. 1981-ceased. 8/yr. EDIBA Editrice Bagnasco, Via Ponte Rotto, Induno Olona, VA 21056, Italy.

201.6 AUS ISSN 0726-0458
NELEN YUBU. 1978-2002. 3/yr. Nelen Yubu Missiological Unit, 1 Roma Ave, PO Box 156, Hensington, NSW 2033, Australia.

340 NLD ISSN 0922-0801
NEMESIS; tijdschrift voor vrouwen en recht. 1984-2003. bi-m. Kluwer B.V., Postbus 23, Deventer, 7400 GA, Netherlands.

666 DEU
NEMO. 1981-2002. a. Verlag Schmid GmbH, Postfach 6609, Freiburg Im Breisgau, 79042, Germany.

700 DEU
NEOX. 2004-2008 (Apr.). bi-m. Pabel-Moewig Verlag KG, Karlsruherstr 31, Rastatt, 76437, Germany.

004.678 ISR ISSN 1565-4621
NET MAGAZIN. 2000-2007. m. S B C Group, 8 Shefa Tal St., Tel Aviv, 67013, Israel.

004.6 NLD ISSN 1569-4356
NET PROFESSIONAL. 1994-2003. 11/yr. I D G Communications Nederland BV, Postbus 5446, Haarlem, 2000 GK, Netherlands.

304.621 NLD ISSN 1389-5133
NETHERLANDS. CENTRAAL BUREAU VOOR DE STATISTIEK. JEUGD: FEITEN EN CIJFERS. 1999-2003. biennial. Centraal Bureau voor de Statistiek, Prinses Beatrixlaan 428, PO Box 4000, Voorburg, 2270 JM, Netherlands.

314 NLD ISSN 1384-6981
NETHERLANDS. CENTRAAL BUREAU VOOR DE STATISTIEK. MAANDSTATISTIEK VAN DE INTERNATIONALE HANDEL. 1989-2002. m. Centraal Bureau voor de Statistiek, Prinses Beatrixlaan 428, PO Box 4000, Voorburg, 2270 JM, Netherlands.

932 962 NLD ISSN 0922-5234
NETHERLANDS INSTITUTE OF ARCHAEOLOGY AND ARABIC STUDIES IN CAIRO. PUBLICATIONS. 1973-1981 (vol.4). irreg. Brill, PO Box 9000, Leiden, 2300 PA, Netherlands.

301 NLD ISSN 0924-1477
THE NETHERLANDS JOURNAL OF SOCIAL SCIENCES. 1963-2004. 3/yr. Koninklijke Van Gorcum BV, PO Box 43, Assen, 9400 AA, Netherlands.

001.422 310 NLD ISSN 0920-2048
NETHERLANDS OFFICIAL STATISTICS. 1986-2000. q. Centraal Bureau voor de Statistiek, Prinses Beatrixlaan 428, PO Box 4000, Voorburg, 2270 JM, Netherlands.

025.04 781.64 DEU
NETSPOTTING; das Magazin fuer Musik und Popkultur im Internet. 2000-2001. m. Netspotting Verlag GmbH, Im Bruehl 1-5, Duesseldorf, 40625, Germany.

613.9 618 616.95 USA ISSN 0270-3637
NETWORK (DURHAM). 1979-2007. q. Family Health International, International Fertility Research Program, PO Box 13950, Research Triangle Park, NC 27709.

551.5 USA ISSN 1948-2558
NETWORK NEWSLETTER AND E N S O SIGNAL. (Environmental Societal Impacts Group) 1995-2005. 4/yr. University Corporation for Atmospheric Research, PO Box 3000, Boulder, CO 80307.

305.42 ISR
NETWORKING FOR WOMEN. 1986-2000. q. Israel Women's Network, P O Box 53186, Jerusalem, 91531, Israel.

378.1 AUS ISSN 1036-4587
NEUCLEUS; U.N.E. student newspaper. 1947-2005. 8/yr. University of New England, Armidale Students' Association, Armidale, NSW 2351, Australia.

630 DEU ISSN 0937-9851
DIE NEUE D L. 1955-2001. bi-m. Bund der Deutschen Landjugend im Deutschen Bauernverband e.V., Reinhardtstr 18, Berlin, 10117, Germany.

613 DEU ISSN 1436-915X
NEUE GESUNDHEIT. 1974-2007 (Nov.). m. Klambt Verlag GmbH, Im Neudeck 1, Speyer, 67346, Germany.

053.1 DEU
NEUE NACHRICHT; Das Magazin. 1970-2007. 4/yr. Criticon Verlag GmbH, Kurfuerstenstr 40, Bonn, 53115, Germany.

370 DEU ISSN 0028-3355
NEUE SAMMLUNG; Vierteljahres-Zeitschrift fuer Erziehung und Gesellschaft. 1945-2005. q. Erhard Friedrich Verlag GmbH, Im Brande 17, Seelze, 30926, Germany.

616.8 DEU ISSN 1439-491X
NEURO-PSYCHIATRISCHE NACHRICHTEN. 1999-2007. m. Biermann Verlag GmbH, Otto-Hahn-Str 7, Cologne, 50997, Germany.

616.83 NLD ISSN 1387-683X
NEUROLOGEN VADEMECUM. 1998-2005. bi-m. Bohn Stafleu van Loghum B.V., Postbus 246, Houten, 3990 GA, Netherlands.

616.8 GBR ISSN 1740-925X
NEURON GLIA BIOLOGY. 2003-2008. q. Cambridge University Press, The Edinburgh Bldg, Shaftesbury Rd, Cambridge, CB2 8RU, United Kingdom.

616.89 NZL ISSN 1176-6328
NEUROPSYCHIATRIC DISEASE AND TREATMENT (PRINT). 2004-2008. bi-m. Dove Medical Press Ltd., 17/44 William Pickering Dr, Albany, PO Box 300-008, Auckland, 1311, New Zealand.

616.8 GBR ISSN 0893-6609 CODEN: NRCOEE
NEUROSCIENCE RESEARCH COMMUNICATIONS. 1987-2005. bi-m. John Wiley & Sons Ltd., 1-7 Oldlands Way, PO Box 808, Bognor Regis, West Sussex PO21 9FF, United Kingdom.

400 DEU ISSN 0028-3983
NEUSPRACHLICHE MITTEILUNGEN AUS WISSENSCHAFT UND PRAXIS. 1948-2006. q. Paedagogischer Zeitschriftenverlag GmbH & Co. KG, Axel-Springer-Str. 54b, Berlin, 10117, Germany.

796.93 ITA ISSN 0028-4114
NEVE INTERNATIONAL. 1959-ceased. q. PubliTec Srl, Via Passo Pordoi 10, Milan, MI 20139, Italy.

320.5 USA
NEW DIRECTIONS (CHICAGO); life skills for the new millenium. 1976-1999. m. Live Free, Inc., 11123 St Lawrence Ave, Chicago, IL 60628.

917.404 USA ISSN 1099-4114
NEW ENGLAND'S BEST BED AND BREAKFASTS. 1992-1998 (4th ed.). irreg. Fodor's Travel Publications, Inc., 1745 Broadway, 15th Fl, New York, NY 10019.

340.5 USA
NEW HAMPSHIRE ACTIONS AND PROCEEDINGS (YEAR). 1992-ceased. a. LexisNexis, PO Box 7587, Charlottesville, VA 22906.

305.89185 USA ISSN 0364-8184
NEW HORIZON - POLISH AMERICAN CULTURAL REVIEW. 1975-2001 (vol.26, no.8). m. Bicentennial Publishing Corp., 333 W 38th St, New York, NY 10018-2914.

370 AUS ISSN 0028-5382
NEW HORIZONS IN EDUCATION. 1937-2006. s-a. World Education Fellowship (Australia), 21 Ridgway Dr, Flagstaff Hill, SA 5159, Australia.

646.724 USA ISSN 1058-0964
NEW IDEAS FOR HAIR STYLING. 19??-2007. bi-m. Harris Publications, Inc., 800 Kennesaw Ave, Ste 220, Marietta, GA 30060.

974.9 USA ISSN 0028-5757
NEW JERSEY HISTORY; a magazine of New Jersey history. 1845-200?. s-a. New Jersey Historical Society, 52 Park Pl, Newark, NJ 07102-4302.

331.1 USA ISSN 1524-8011
THE NEW JERSEY JOBBANK; the job hunter's guide to New Jersey. (Includes all counties in northern, central and southern New Jersey) 1999-2007 (4th ed.). biennial. Adams Media, 4700 E Galbraith Rd, Cincinnati, OH 45236.

349.749 USA ISSN 1069-689X CODEN: JBROF2
NEW JERSEY LAWYER (EDISON). 1992-2009. w. New Jersey Lawyer, Inc., 1 Cragwood Rd, South Plainfield, NJ 07080-2448.

349.789 USA
NEW MEXICO CREDITOR - DEBTOR LAW, REVISED EDITION. 1989-ceased. 1-2/yr.) plus irreg. updates. LexisNexis, PO Box 7587, Charlottesville, VA 22906.

349.789 USA
NEW MEXICO PROBATE MANUAL. 1978-ceased. plus irreg. updates. LexisNexis, PO Box 7587, Charlottesville, VA 22906.

348.789 USA
NEW MEXICO RULES OF EVIDENCE. 1983-2004. plus irreg. updates. LexisNexis, PO Box 7587, Charlottesville, VA 22906.

200 NZL ISSN 1171-591X
NEW SLANT; an initiative for region and cultures. 1991-2002. 3/yr. The DeepSight Trust, PO Box 87362, Auckland, New Zealand.

690 USA
NEW SMALL HOMES; home plans under 2,000 square feet. 2000-2009 (Jan.). q. HomePlans.com, 901 N 3rd St, Ste 216, Minneapolis, MN 55401.

364.021 AUS
NEW SOUTH WALES. ATTORNEY GENERAL'S DEPARTMENT. BUREAU OF CRIME STATISTICS AND RESEARCH. RESEARCH STUDY. 1982-1986. irreg. New South Wales. Attorney General's Department, Bureau of Crime Statistics and Research, GPO Box 6, Sydney, NSW 2001, Australia.

622.33 310 AUS
NEW SOUTH WALES COAL STATISTICS. 1989-2005. a. Joint Coal Board, GPO Box 3842, Sydney, NSW 2001, Australia.

913 GBR
NEW STUDIES IN ARCHAEOLOGY. 1976-2009 (Jun.). irreg. Cambridge University Press, The Edinburgh Bldg, Shaftesbury Rd, Cambridge, CB2 8RU, United Kingdom.

301 621.381 GBR ISSN 0959-0684
NEW TECHNOLOGY IN THE HUMAN SERVICES. 1985-2003. q. Centre for Human Service Technology, University of Southampton, Department of Social Work Studies, Southampton, Hants S017 1BJ, United Kingdom.

305.42 GBR ISSN 0955-6907
NEW WOMAN. 1988-2008. m. Emap Consumer Media, Endeavour House, 189 Shaftesbury Ave, London, WC2H 8JG, United Kingdom.

600 DEU ISSN 1435-1730
NEW WORLD; the Siemens magazine. 1996-2002. q. Siemens AG, Wittelsbacher Platz 2, Munich, 80333, Germany.

306.766 USA
THE NEW YORK BLADE (PRINT). 1997-2009. w. H X Media, LLC, 230 W 17th St, 8th Fl, New York, NY 10011.

340 352.3 USA
NEW YORK CITY FIRE LAW HANDBOOK. 1988-2007. a. Gould Publications, Inc., 1333 North US Hwy 17-92, Longwood, FL 32750.

346.065 USA ISSN 1527-7372
NEW YORK EMPLOYMENT LAW & PRACTICE. 1999-2006. m. Law Journal Newsletters, 1617 JFK Blvd, Ste 1750, Philadelphia, PA 19103.

340 USA
NEW YORK LEGAL FORMS & PROCEDURES HANDBOOK. 1989-200?. irreg. Gould Publications, Inc., 1333 North US Hwy 17-92, Longwood, FL 32750.

791.43 USA ISSN 0362-3688
NEW YORK TIMES FILM REVIEWS. 1913-2000. biennial. Times Books, 201 E 50th St, New York, NY 10022-7703.

798.4 NZL ISSN 0113-7859
NEW ZEALAND BLOODHORSE; the magazine for the thoroughbred industry. 1975-2008. m. Bloodhorse Ltd, PO Box 595, Orewa, 0946, New Zealand.

526.8 NZL ISSN 1171-1337 CODEN: NZCJDK
NEW ZEALAND CARTOGRAPHY AND GEOGRAPHIC INFORMATION SYSTEMS. 1970-1994 (vol.24, no.2). 2/yr. New Zealand Cartographic Society Inc., PO 12454, Thorndon, New Zealand.

792.8 NZL ISSN 1177-1127
NEW ZEALAND DANCER. 2006-2008. s-a. New Zealand Dancer Magazine, PO Box 89006, Torbay, Auckland, 0742, New Zealand.

363.7 NZL ISSN 0110-6287
NEW ZEALAND ENVIRONMENT. 1971-1992. q. Environmental Publications Trust, 34 Norana Ave, Remuera, Auckland, 1105, New Zealand.

610 NZL ISSN 0110-022X CODEN: NZFPDJ
NEW ZEALAND FAMILY PHYSICIAN. 1974 (Mar.)-2008 (Dec.). s-m. Royal New Zealand College of General Practitioners, PO Box 10440, Wellington, New Zealand.

327 NZL ISSN 1172-7195
NEW ZEALAND FOREIGN AFFAIRS AND TRADE RECORD. 1992-2006 (Dec.). 11/yr. Ministry of Foreign Affairs and Trade, c/o Publication Officer, Private Bag 18-901, Wellington, New Zealand.

635 NZL
NEW ZEALAND FUCHSIA SOCIETY. NEWS LETTER. 195?-ceased. bi-m. New Zealand Fuchsia Society, Ellerslie, P.O. Box 11-082, Auckland 6, New Zealand.

919.31 NZL ISSN 0078-0030 CODEN: PGECAV
NEW ZEALAND GEOGRAPHY CONFERENCE PROCEEDINGS SERIES. 1955-2003 (no.22). s-a. New Zealand Geographical Society Inc., Dept. of Geography, Univ. of Waikato, Private Bag 3105, Hamilton, New Zealand.

330 NZL ISSN 0078-0049
NEW ZEALAND INSTITUTE OF ECONOMIC RESEARCH. DISCUSSION PAPER. 1961-199?. irreg. New Zealand Institute of Economic Research, PO Box 3479, Wellington 1, New Zealand.

327 NZL ISSN 0113-1044
NEW ZEALAND INSTITUTE OF INTERNATIONAL AFFAIRS. OCCASIONAL PAPER (NO.). 1986-1990. irreg. New Zealand Institute of International Affairs, c/o Victoria University of Wellington, PO Box 600, Wellington, 6140, New Zealand.

615.53 NZL ISSN 1177-3499
NEW ZEALAND INTOUCH. 1990-2007. bi-m. Szuson Wong, Ed. & Pub., PO Box 188, Te Aroha, New Zealand.

510 NZL ISSN 1171-6096 CODEN: MTHCB3
NEW ZEALAND JOURNAL OF MATHEMATICS. 1969-2006 (Oct.). s-a. University of Auckland, Department of Mathematics, Private Bag 92019, Auckland Mail Centre, Auckland, 1142, New Zealand.

388.1 NZL ISSN 1176-841X
NEW ZEALAND. LAND TRANSPORT NZ. NEWS. 2004-2008 (Jul.). m. New Zealand Transport Agency, Lambton Quay, PO Box 5084, Wellington, 6145, New Zealand.

027 NZL ISSN 0110-1803
NEW ZEALAND LIBRARY SYMBOLS. 1964-2007. a. National Library of New Zealand, PO Box 1467, Wellington, 6140, New Zealand.

005 NZL ISSN 1176-5690
NEW ZEALAND MACGUIDE. 2002-2007. bi-m. Parkside Media, Herne Bay, PO Box 46-020, Auckland, New Zealand.

333.79 658 NZL ISSN 1171-5375
NEW ZEALAND MANUFACTURER. 1949-2001. 11/yr. New Zealand Manufacturers Federation, 3 Church St, PO Box 11-543, Wellington 1, New Zealand.

797.10993 NZL ISSN 1173-5880
NEW ZEALAND MARINE SCENE. 1995-2003. m. New Zealand Marine Scene, Symonds St., PO Box 8688, Auckland, New Zealand.

327.93 NZL ISSN 1173-0315
NEW ZEALAND. MINISTRY OF FOREIGN AFFAIRS AND TRADE. INFORMATION BULLETIN. 1982-2000 (no.62). irreg. Ministry of Foreign Affairs and Trade, c/o Publication Officer, Private Bag 18-901, Wellington, New Zealand.

327 NZL ISSN 0114-6971
NEW ZEALAND. MINISTRY OF FOREIGN AFFAIRS AND TRADE. OVERSEAS POSTS; a list of New Zealand representative abroad. ceased 2003 (Oct.). s-a. Ministry of Foreign Affairs and Trade, c/o Publication Officer, Private Bag 18-901, Wellington, New Zealand.

796 NZL ISSN 0110-5248
NEW ZEALAND RUNNER. 1978-2005. bi-m. Dunmore Press Magazines, PO Box 55008, Mission Bay, New Zealand.

796.79 790.1 NZL ISSN 1177-7036
NEW ZEALAND RV LIFESTYLE. 2001-2008 (Jan./Feb.). bi-m. Media North, PO Box 522, Whangarei, New Zealand.

664.94 NZL ISSN 1173-0161
NEW ZEALAND SEAFOOD INDUSTRY ECONOMIC REVIEW. 1993-2001. irreg. New Zealand Seafood Industry Council, Seafood Industry House, 74 Cambridge Terrace, Private Bag 24-901, Wellington, New Zealand.

330 NZL
NEW ZEALAND. STATISTICS NEW ZEALAND. BUSINESS ACTIVITY (G S T) INDICATOR. (Goods and Services Tax) 1998-2002. q. Statistics New Zealand, PO Box 2922, Wellington, New Zealand.

330 NZL ISSN 1171-2163
NEW ZEALAND. STATISTICS NEW ZEALAND. BUSINESS ACTIVITY STATISTICS. 1986-2000. a. Statistics New Zealand, PO Box 2922, Wellington, New Zealand.

330 NZL
NEW ZEALAND. STATISTICS NEW ZEALAND. CROWN ACCOUNTS ANALYSIS. 199?-2005. a. Statistics New Zealand, PO Box 2922, Wellington, New Zealand.

352.7 310 NZL
NEW ZEALAND. STATISTICS NEW ZEALAND. ESTIMATE OF NEW DWELLING UNITS. 1987-2000. m. Statistics New Zealand, PO Box 2922, Wellington, New Zealand.

382 310 NZL
NEW ZEALAND. STATISTICS NEW ZEALAND. INTERNATIONAL INVESTMENT POSITION. 1990-200?. a. Statistics New Zealand, PO Box 2922, Wellington, New Zealand.

382 310 NZL ISSN 1179-1160
NEW ZEALAND. STATISTICS NEW ZEALAND. OVERSEAS CARGO STATISTICS (12 MONTHS). 1987 (Sept.)-2007 (Sept.). a. Statistics New Zealand, PO Box 2922, Wellington, New Zealand.

354.93068 NZL ISSN 1171-6673
NEW ZEALAND. TE PUNI KOKIRI. NEWSLETTER. 1992-2001. irreg. New Zealand. Te Puni Kokiri, PO Box 3943, Wellington, New Zealand.

351 NZL
NEW ZEALAND. TOTALISATOR AGENCY BOARD. T A B HALF YEAR REPORT. 1951-2000. s-a. Totalisator Agency Board, 106-110 Jackson St, Petone, New Zealand.

381.029 NZL ISSN 1175-0219
NEW ZEALAND TRADE DIRECTORY. 1994-2001. a. Current Pacific Ltd., PO Box 36-536, Northcote, Auckland, 0627, New Zealand.

797.33 NZL ISSN 0114-3344
NEW ZEALAND WINDSURFER. 1988-2000. 3/yr. Pirate Publishing Ltd., P.O. Box 105-207, Queen St, Auckland, New Zealand.

388.325 USA ISSN 1523-5971
NEWPORT'S ROADSTAR. 1999-2008. m. Newport Communications (Irvine), 38 Executive Pk, Ste 300, Irvine, CA 92614.

617.6 ITA ISSN 1592-9574
NEWS DENTOSAN. 2001-2005. q. Ariesdue srl, Via Airoldi 11, Carimate, CO 22060, Italy.

378 USA ISSN 0028-923X
NEWS, NOTES, AND QUOTES. 1956-2002. q. Phi Delta Kappa International, 408 N Union St, PO Box 789, Bloomington, IN 47402-0789.

052 AUS ISSN 1329-3052
NEWS OF THE DAY. 1995-2000. d. Global Web Builders, PO Box 11, Mt Crosby News, QLD 4306, Australia.

011 USA ISSN 0899-0425
NEWSLETTERS IN PRINT. 1966-2006. a. Gale, 27500 Drake Rd, Farmington Hills, MI 48331.

070 332.6 USA ISSN 1042-4326
NEWSPAPER INVESTOR. 1989-2002. m. S N L Financial LC, One SNL Plz, PO Box 2124, Charlottesville, VA 22902.

700 ITA ISSN 0394-6428 CODEN: IKNEE3
NEXT. 1985-ceased. q. Joyce & Co. - Associazione Culturale, Via Natale Del Grande, 51, Rome, RM 00153, Italy.

051 USA
THE NEXT 50; central Virginia's lifestyle magazine for the 50+ generation. 2008 (Apr.)-2008 (Nov.); suspended. bi-m. Target Media, Inc., 2525 Wind River Rd, Charlottesville, VA 22901.

794.8 ITA ISSN 1129-0412
NEXT STATION. 1999-ceased. m. Next Publishing S.r.l., Via Niccolini, 30, Milano, 20154, Italy.

305.8 DEU
NICARAGUA HEUTE. 1982-1995. s-a. Christliche Initiative Romero, Frauenstr 3-7, Muenster, 48143, Germany.

051 USA ISSN 1540-9333
NICK JR. FAMILY. 1999-200?. 9/yr. Nickelodeon Magazine, Inc., 1515 Broadway, New York, NY 10036.

051 USA ISSN 1073-7510
NICKELODEON MAGAZINE. 1993-2009. 10/yr. Nickelodeon Magazine, Inc., 1515 Broadway, New York, NY 10036.

280.4 028.5 DEU
NICKI. 1925-2005. 4/yr. Born-Verlag, Leuschnerstr 74, Kassel, 34134, Germany.

358.8 DNK ISSN 0902-8242
NIELSEN MARKETING RESEARCH. NEWS. 1960-1987. q. Markeds Data, Ahlefeldtsgade 16, Copenhagen K, 1359, Denmark.

004 NLD ISSN 0920-1319
NIEUWS BERICHTEN INFORMATIE. 1981-2009 (no.205). 8/yr. Cobidoc B.V., J P Coengebouw, Kabelweg 37, Amsterdam, 1014 BA, Netherlands.

636.089 636.2 NLD ISSN 1872-3586
NIEUWSBRIEF GEZONDHEIDSDIENST VOOR DIEREN UIERGEZONDHEIDSCOACH. 2005-2007. q. Gezondheidsdienst voor Dieren, Postbus 9, Deventer, 7400 AA, Netherlands.

373 371.2 NLD ISSN 1574-3594
NIEUWSBRIEF ONDERBOUW. 2003-2007. q. Schoolmanagers Voortgezet Onderwijs, Postbus 8282, Utrecht, 3503 RG, Netherlands.

333.95416 CZE ISSN 0862-514X
NIKA. 1980-2007. q. Obcanske Sdruzeni Nika, Libanska 2337/8, Horni Pocernice, Prague 9, 19000, Czech Republic.

200 NLD ISSN 0169-930X
NISABA; religious texts translation series. 1973-1989 (vol.17). irreg. Brill, PO Box 9000, Leiden, 2300 PA, Netherlands.

808 DEU ISSN 1433-1896
NODE9; an e-journal of writing and technology. 1997-1999. irreg. Freiburg University, Institute for Northamerican Studies, Rempartstr 15, Freiburg, 79085, Germany.

153 AUS ISSN 1324-6038
NOETICA; a cognitive science forum. 1995-1998. irreg. University of Queensland, School of Psychology, McElwain Building, St Lucia, QLD 4072, Australia.

305.42 ISR ISSN 0333-6387
NOGA; a woman's magazine. 1980-2006. 3/yr. Lilit, P O Box 21376, Tel Aviv, 61213, Israel.

808.838 ITA
NOI DUE. 1976-ceased. m. Lancio SpA, Via Roccagiovine 267, Rome, 00156, Italy.

059.9435 TUR
NOKTA. 1983-2007 (Mar.). w. Nokta Basin A.S., Buyukdere Cad. Ali Kaya Sok. 8, Levent - Istanbul, 34394, Turkey.

510 KOR ISSN 1229-1595
NONLINEAR FUNCTIONAL ANALYSIS AND APPLICATIONS. 1996-2007. q. Kyungnam University Press, 449 Wolyong-dong, Habpo-gu, Masan, Kyungnam 631-701, Korea, S.

519 DEU CODEN: NSTOE4
NONLINEAR SCIENCE TODAY (ONLINE); an electronic adjunct to Journal of Nonlinear Science. 1991-200?. irreg. Springer, Tiergartenstr 17, Heidelberg, 69121, Germany.

327 DEU ISSN 0933-1743
NORD - SUED AKTUELL. 1987-2005. q. Deutsches Uebersee-Institut, Uebersee-Dokumentation, Neuer Jungfernstieg 21, Hamburg, 20354, Germany.

305.395 AUS ISSN 1327-905X
NORDIC NOTES. 1996-199?. a. Flinders University, Centre for Scandinavian Studies, GPO Box 2100, Adelaide, SA 5001, Australia.

796 DEU ISSN 1860-5966
NORDIC WALKER. 2005-2007 (Oct.). bi-m. Jahr Top Special Verlag, Troplowitzstr 5, Hamburg, 22529, Germany.

351 DNK ISSN 0029-1285
NORDISK ADMINISTRATIVT TIDSSKRIFT. 1919-2007; suspended. q. Jurist- og Oekonomforbundets Forlag A/S, Lyngbyvej 17, PO Box 2702, Copenhagen OE, 2100, Denmark.

808.81 ITA
NORDSEE; poesia in forma di manifesto. 1977-ceased. q. Maurizio Maldini Ed. & Pub., Via Augusto Romagnoli, 39, Bologna, BO 40137, Italy.

929 GBR ISSN 0309-8486
NORTHAMPTONIANA. 1977-1979. q. Northampton Family History Society, 294 Birchfield Rd E., Northampton, NN3 2SY, United Kingdom.

381.147 USA
NORTHEAST C-STORE JOURNAL. 2004-2008. m. Kevin B. Griffin, 201 Oak St, Ste A, Pembroke, MA 02359.

346.04 USA
NORTHERN CALIFORNIA REAL ESTATE LEGAL REVIEW. 2006-2007. m. Law Journal Newsletters, 1617 JFK Blvd, Ste 1750, Philadelphia, PA 19103.

791.43 384 DNK ISSN 1601-829X
NORTHERN LIGHTS; film and media studies yearbook. 1973-2006. a. Museum Tusculanum Press, c/o University of Copenhagen, Njalsgade 126, Copenhagen S, 2300, Denmark.

079.93 NZL
NORTHLAND TIMES AND RODNEY REPORTER. 1904-2000. d. (except Sun.). North Auckland Times Co. (1982) Ltd., 45 Normanhy St, Northland, Dargaville, 0300, New Zealand.

791.43 ESP ISSN 1131-9372
NOSFERATU (SPANISH EDITION). 1989-2007. q. Ayuntamiento de San Sebastian, Donostia Kultura, Plaza de la Constitucion 1, Donostia, San Sebastian, 20003, Spain.

640 ITA ISSN 1721-8187
I NOSTRI DOLCI. 2003-200?. m. Edigamma Publishing, Via Sambuca Pistoiese 70A, Rome, 00138, Italy.

635.9 ITA ISSN 1826-1019
I NOSTRI FIORI. 2005-200?. bi-m. Edigamma Publishing, Via Sambuca Pistoiese 70A, Rome, 00138, Italy.

370 ITA ISSN 0029-3792
NOSTRI RAGAZZI; incontri tra scuola elementare e famiglia. 1958-19??. 7/yr. Associazione Genitori, P.O. Box 217, Bologna, BO 40100, Italy.

001.3 ITA ISSN 0550-0877
NOTE E DISCUSSIONI ERUDITE. 1951-1997 (no.21). irreg. Edizioni di Storia e Letteratura, Via delle Fornaci 24, Rome, 00165, Italy.

945 ITA
NOTIZIARIO COMMERCIO ESTERO. 1960-ceased. m. Camera di Commercio Industria Artigianato e Agricoltura di Vicenza, Corso Antonio Fogazzaro, 37, Vicenza, VI 36100, Italy.

055.1 ITA
NOTIZIARIO CULTURALE. 1955-ceased. m. Universita Popolare Sestrese, Ptta. dell'Universita Popolare, Genoa Sestri, GE 16154, Italy.

700 ITA ISSN 0029-4322
NOTIZIARIO D'ARTE. 1949-19??. bi-m. Ennio Francia Ed. & Pub., Via del Babuino 197, Rome, RM, Italy.

571.6 ITA
NOTIZIARIO DI CITOLOGIA. 1980-ceased. 3/yr. Pacini Editore SpA, Via A Gherardesca 1, Ospedaletto, PI 56121, Italy.

330 ITA
NOTIZIE DELL'ECONOMIA. 1945-ceased. m. Camera di Commercio Industria Artigianato e Agricoltura di Teramo, Via Savini 48-50, Teramo, TE 64100, Italy.

540 ITA
NOTIZIE DOW. 1967-ceased. bi-m. Dow Italia, Via Gioacchino Murat, 23, Milan, MI 20159, Italy.

282 FRA ISSN 0761-8638
NOTRE HISTOIRE; la memoire religieuse de l'humanite. 1983-2006. 11/yr. Publications Historiques, 12 rue Ampere, Paris, 75017, France.

630 FRA ISSN 0299-3635
NOTRE TERROIR. 1987-198?. 24/yr. Notre Terroir, 1 rue du Chateau, Chambery, 73000, France.

384 FRA ISSN 1769-101X
LES NOUVEAUX DOSSIERS DE L'AUDIOVISUEL. 1981-2006. bi-m. Documentation Francaise, 29-31 Quai Voltaire, Paris, Cedex 7 75344, France.

944 FRA ISSN 0029-4799
NOUVELLE REVUE FRANC-COMTOISE. 1946-199?. q. Nouvelle Revue Franc-Comtoise, c/o Dir. B. Chazelle, Ed., 13 rue Pasteur, Dole, Cedex 39102, France.

551.46 570 ITA ISSN 0369-5271
NOVA THALASSIA. 1948-ceased. irreg. Edizioni Lint Trieste, Viale Ortles 54a, Milan, 20139, Italy.

400 ITA
NOVANTIQUA; biblioteca di filologia, curiosita e dialettologia. 1977-1984. irreg. Societa Editrice Napoletana s.r.l., Corso Umberto I, 1-34, Naples, NA 80138, Italy.

621.381 ESP ISSN 1138-1477
NOVEDADES ELECTRONICAS. 1997-200?. 10/yr. Editorial Alcion Ingenieria Quimica, S.A., Medea, 4, Madrid, 28037, Spain.

610 016 CZE ISSN 1212-3862
NOVINKY LITERATURY. ZDRAVOTNICTVI-PRIRUSTKY FONDU NARODNI LEKARSKE KNIHOVNY. 1955-2003. 4/yr. Narodni Lekarska Knihovna, Sokolska 54, Prague, 12132, Czech Republic.

379.8 SVK ISSN 1336-7781
NOVY CAS L'UDIA. 2005-2008 (Sep.). w. Ringier Slovakia a. s., Prievozska 14, PO Box 46, Bratislava 24, 82004, Slovakia.

636 ESP ISSN 0210-5659
NUESTRA CABANA; revista de la nueva ganaderia espanola. 1972-ceased. m. Tecnipublicaciones Espana, S.L., Avda de Manoteras 44, 3a Planta, Madrid, 28050, Spain.

615 ESP ISSN 1579-5829
NUESTRA FARMACIA ACTUAL. 2002-200?. m. (11x yr.). Tecnipublicaciones Espana, S.L., Avda de Manoteras 44, 3a Planta, Madrid, 28050, Spain.

305.868 USA
EL NUEVO HUDSON. 1995-2009 (Feb.). w. (Thu.). Evening Journal Association, 30 Journal Sq., Jersey City, NJ 07306.

304.6 TUR ISSN 0259-6334
NUFUSBILIM DERGISI/TURKISH JOURNAL OF POPULATION STUDIES. 1979-2002. a. Hacettepe Universitesi, Nufus Etutleri Enstitusu, Merkez Kampusu, Sihhiye, Ankara, 06100, Turkey.

780 ITA ISSN 0391-3724
NUOVA RASSEGNA DI STUDI MUSICALI. 1977-1978. 2/yr. Fabrizio Serra Editore, c/o Accademia Editoriale, Via Santa Bibbiana 28, Pisa, 56127, Italy.

616.8 ITA ISSN 1122-035X
NUOVA RIVISTA DI NEUROLOGIA. 1928-2003. bi-m. Il Pensiero Scientifico Editore, Via Bradano 3-C, Rome, 00199, Italy.

300 ITA ISSN 1121-774X
NUOVE RICERCHE METODOLOGICHE; interventi e contributi per la lotta di classe nella cultura. 1965-ceased. 3/yr. Edizioi di Nuove Ricerche Metodologiche, Casella Postale 2297, Naples, NA 80100, Italy.

320 ITA ISSN 1122-6900
NUOVO ARCHIVIO TRIMESTRALE; rassegna storica di studi sul movimento republicano. 1975-ceased. q. Istituto di Studi per la Storia del Movimento Repubblicano, Via Tomacelli, 146, Rome, RM 00186, Italy.

663.1 ITA ISSN 0017-0119
NUOVO GIORNALE DEI DISTILLATORI; alcoli - acquaviti - liquori. 1962-ceased. m. Guido Scialpi Editore, Via Ugo De Carolis, 7, Rome, RM 00136, Italy.

658 ITA
IL NUOVO MANAGEMENT. 1999-200?. 3/yr. Franco Angeli Edizioni, Viale Monza 106, Milan, 20127, Italy.

330 ITA ISSN 0029-6376
NUOVO MEZZOGIORNO. 1958-1999. m. Edizioni Nuovo Mezzogiorno, Corso Vittorio Emanuele II, 154, Rome, RM 00186, Italy.

297.57 TUR
NUR - THE LIGHT. 1986-ceased. m. Nur - The Light, Nuruosmaniye Cad. Sorkun Han No. 28-2, Cagaloglu - Istanbul, 34410, Turkey.

610.73 GBR ISSN 1467-1158
NURSE PRESCRIBER. 2004-2005. irreg. Cambridge University Press, The Edinburgh Bldg, Shaftesbury Rd, Cambridge, CB2 8RU, United Kingdom.

610.73 USA ISSN 1076-1632 CODEN: NLFOFM
NURSING LEADERSHIP FORUM. 1995-200?. 4/school-academic yr. Springer Publishing Company, 11 W 42nd St, 15th Fl, New York, NY 10036.

613.2 EGY ISSN 1110-0974
THE NUTRITION INSTITUTE OF THE ARAB REPUBLIC OF EGYPT. BULLETIN. 1981-ceased. a. The Nutrition Institute, 16A Qasr El-Aini Str, Cairo, Egypt.

850 ITA ISSN 1592-2308
NUVOLE. 1990-ceased. bi-m. Edizioni Sonda, Corso Indipendenza 63, Casale Monferrato, AL, Italy.

615.89 DNK ISSN 1901-6360
NY MEDICIN; livskvalitet og helbredelse uden piller. 2004-2005. s-a. Forskningscenter for Livskvalitet, Teglgaardsstraede 4-8, Copenhagen K, 1452, Denmark.

629.2 DNK ISSN 1603-3744
NYT OM BILER; autocar. 2003-2008. m. Aller Press A/S, Vigerslev Alle 18, Valby, 2500, Denmark.

327 341.2422 DNK ISSN 1397-4289
NYT SYN PAA EUROPA. 1993-2006. bi-w. Den Danske Europabevaegelse, Bremerholm 6, Copenhagen K, 1069, Denmark.

840 FRA ISSN 0982-4677
NYX. 1987-199?. q. Nyx, 4 square Saint-Irenee, Paris, 75011, France.

747 USA ISSN 1549-1994
O AT HOME. 2003-2008 (Nov.). q. Hearst Magazines, 300 W 57th St, 12th Fl, New York, NY 10019.

330.021 FRA ISSN 1026-1877
O E C D HISTORICAL STATISTICS (PRINT). (Organisation for Economic Cooperation and Development) 1982-2001. irreg. Organisation for Economic Cooperation and Development (O E C D), 2 Rue Andre Pascal, Paris, 75775 Cedex 16, France.

384.0285 USA ISSN 1071-8990
O E M MAGAZINE. (Original Equipment Manufacturer) 1993-1997. 8/yr. C M P Media LLC, 600 Community Dr, Manhasset, NY 11030.

054.1 FRA ISSN 1248-0452
O K! PODIUM. 1993-2001. s-m. Hachette Filipacchi Medias S.A., 149/151 Rue Anatole France, Levallois-Perret, 925340, France.

340 DEU ISSN 0945-2176
O L G - RECHTSPRECHUNG NEUE LAENDER; fuer Brandenburg, Mecklenburg-Vorpommern, Sachsen, Sachsen-Anhalt, Thueringen. (Oberlandesgerichte) 1994-2007. m. Verlag C.H. Beck oHG, Wilhelmstr 9, Munich, 80801, Germany.

370 NLD ISSN 1567-5599
O N - W I J S. (Online Onderwijs) 1997-2008 (Apr.). w. Jan Bult, Ed. & Pub.

621.48 DNK ISSN 0105-4899
O O A - SAERTRYK. (Organisationen til Oplysning om Atomkraft) 1974-1985. irreg. Energibevaegelsen O O A, Ryesgade 19, Copenhagen N, 2200, Denmark.

304.609 GBR ISSN 0953-3435
O P C S MONITOR. PP3. 1976-1998. irreg. Office of Population Censuses and Surveys, 1 Myddelton St, London, EC1R 1UW, United Kingdom.

314.2 GBR ISSN 0951-4287
O P C S MONITOR. WEEKLY RETURN. 19??-1991. w. Office of Population Censuses and Surveys, 1 Myddelton St, London, EC1R 1UW, United Kingdom.

338.2 665.5 AUT ISSN 1015-6224
O P E C PAPERS. (Organization of the Petroleum Exporting Countries) 1980-198?. irreg. Organization of the Petroleum Exporting Countries, PR and Information Department, Obere Donaustrasse 93, Vienna, W 1020, Austria.

331 NLD ISSN 1874-4052
O R IN DE OVERHEID. (Ondernemingsraad) 1993-2008. bi-m. Kluwer B.V., Postbus 23, Deventer, 7400 GA, Netherlands.

255.4 ITA
O S A INTERNATIONALIA. 1972-ceased. q. Istituto Patristico Augustinianum, Via Paolo VI 25, Rome, 00193, Italy.

001.94 GBR ISSN 0262-7795
O S E A P CENTRE UPDATE. 1982-198?. irreg. Organisation for Scientific Evaluation of Aerial Phenomena, 2 Acer Ave, Crewe, Ches, United Kingdom.

001.94 GBR ISSN 0262-5954
O S E A P JOURNAL. 1982-198?. irreg. Organisation for Scientific Evaluation of Aerial Phenomena, 2 Acer Ave, Crewe, Ches, United Kingdom.

782.1 DEU
O-TON. 1981-2003. m. Deutsche Oper Berlin, Bismarckstr 35, Berlin, 10627, Germany.

355 DEU ISSN 0029-7402
DIE OASE. 1951-2005. bi-m. Deutsches Afrika-Korps e.V., Paderbornerstr 42, Paderborn-Elsen, 33104, Germany.

577 ITA ISSN 1591-2736
OASIS; natura, ecologia, fotografia e viaggi. 1985-ceased. bi-m. Industrie Grafiche Editoriali Musumeci SpA, Loc Amerique 99, Quart, AO 11020, Italy.

618 340 USA ISSN 1077-8888
OB-GYN MALPRACTICE PREVENTION. 1994-2004. m. Lippincott Williams & Wilkins, 530 Walnut St, Philadelphia, PA 19106-3621.

323 USA ISSN 0029-7593
OBJECTIVE: JUSTICE. 1971-199?. s-a. United Nations Publications, 2 United Nations Plaza, Rm DC2-853, New York, NY 10017.

520 FRA ISSN 0769-0878
OBSERVATIONS ET TRAVAUX. 1982-1996. q. Societe Astronomique de France, 3 rue Beethoven, Paris, 75016, France.

610 GBR ISSN 1362-6337
OBSTETRIC ULTRASOUND. 1993-1994. irreg. Oxford University Press, Great Clarendon St, Oxford, OX2 6DP, United Kingdom.

331 USA
OCCUPATIONAL COMPENSATION SURVEYS. 1992-1996. a. U.S. Department of Labor, Bureau of Labor Statistics, Postal Square Bldg., 2 Massachusetts Ave, NE, Washington, DC 20212-0001.

659.1029 USA ISSN 0191-0051
O'DWYER'S DIRECTORY OF PUBLIC RELATIONS EXECUTIVES. 1979-2000. triennial. J.R. O'Dwyer Co., Inc., 271 Madison Ave, Ste 600, New York, NY 10016.

362.718 FRA ISSN 1257-8002
L'ODYSSEE DU SANG. 197?-1997. q. Centre Regional de Transfusion Sanguine et de Genetique Humaine, 609 Chemin de la Breteque, BP 58, Bois-Guillaume, 76232, France.

551.46 ITA ISSN 0392-6613 CODEN: OEBAEN
OEBALIA. 1975-ceased. 3/w. Istituto Sperimentale Talassografico Attilio Cerruti, Via Roma 3, Taranto, 74100, Italy.

028.5 NLD ISSN 1574-7638
OEK!. 1946-2008. 5/yr. Kok Tijdschriften, Postbus 5018, Kampen, 8260 GA, Netherlands.

631 DEU ISSN 0935-6258
OEKOLOGIE IN FORSCHUNG UND ANWENDUNG. 1988-1995. irreg. Margraf Publishers, Kanalstr 21, Weikersheim, 97990, Germany.

616.86 364.3 USA ISSN 1533-0133
OFFENDER SUBSTANCE ABUSE REPORT. 2001 (Jan./Feb.)-200?. bi-m. Civic Research Insitute, 4478 US Rte 27, PO Box 585, Kingston, NJ 08528.

314.205 GBR ISSN 0262-8392
OFFICE OF POPULATION CENSUSES AND SURVEYS. MONITOR: SOCIAL SURVEYS. 1981-1994. irreg. Office of Population Censuses and Surveys, 1 Myddelton St, London, EC1R 1UW, United Kingdom.

304.609 GBR ISSN 1367-3130
OFFICE OF POPULATION CENSUSES AND SURVEYS. OCCASIONAL PAPER. 1977-1996. irreg. Office of Population Censuses and Surveys, 1 Myddelton St, London, EC1R 1UW, United Kingdom.

519 DEU ISSN 1863-4109
OFFICE SECURITY TICKER. 2006-2008. fortn. V N R Verlag fuer die Deutsche Wirtschaft AG, Theodor-Heuss-Str 2-4, Bonn, 53095, Germany.

387.742 USA
THE OFFICIAL FREQUENT FLYER GUIDE; the essential frequent traveler program guide. 1990-2000. a. FlightPlan, Inc., 1930 Frequent Flyer Point, Colorado Springs, CO 80915.

929.9 719.13 USA
THE OFFICIAL LICENSE PLATE BOOK. 1997-200?. a. Gould Publications, Inc., 1333 North US Hwy 17-92, Longwood, FL 32750.

796.71 NLD ISSN 1872-0668
HET OFFICIELE F1 JAARBOEK. 2005-2006. a. Uitgeverij de Alk bv, Postbus 9006, Alkmaar, 1800 GA, Netherlands.

371.42 FRA ISSN 1953-5775
LES OFFRES COURRIER CADRES. 2006-2007. w. Association pour l'Emploi des Cadres (A P E C), 51 Bd. Brune, Paris, Cedex 14 75689, France.

331.1 USA ISSN 1099-0186
THE OHIO JOBBANK; includes: Cincinnati, Cleveland, Columbus, Toledo, and many more. (Includes: Cincinnati, Cleveland, Columbus, Toledo and many others) 1988-2007 (12th ed.). irreg. Adams Media, 4700 E Galbraith Rd, Cincinnati, OH 45236.

028.5 CZE ISSN 0030-1272
OHNICEK; zabava do kapsy. 1950-2001. fortn. Mlada Fronta, Mezi Vodami 1952/9, Prague 4, 14300, Czech Republic.

553.28 665.5 AUS ISSN 1038-118X
OIL AND GAS RESOURCES OF AUSTRALIA. 1991-2004. a. Geoscience Australia, GPO Box 378, Canberra, ACT 2601, Australia.

340 USA
OKLAHOMA DISCOVERY PRACTICE MANUAL. 1987-ceased. plus a. updates. LexisNexis, PO Box 7587, Charlottesville, VA 22906.

362.6 GBR ISSN 1367-1065
OLD AGE: A REGISTER OF SOCIAL RESEARCH. 1955-1991. a. Centre for Policy on Ageing, 25-31 Ironmonger Row, London, EC1V 3QP, United Kingdom.

388.342 GBR ISSN 1361-3766
OLDER CAR PRICE GUIDE; Parker's prices (year). 1995-1999. bi-m. Emap Active Ltd. (Angel House), Angel House, 338-346 Goswell Rd, London, EC1V 7QP, United Kingdom.

629.222 NLD ISSN 1871-4986
OLDTIMER CATALOGUS. 1994-ceased. a. Uitgeverij Elmar, Delftweg 147, Rijswijk, 2289 BD, Netherlands.

547 FRA ISSN 1258-8210 CODEN: RFCGAE
OLEAGINEUX CORPS GRAS LIPIDES (PRINT). 1954; N.S. 1994-2008. bi-m. John Libbey Eurotext, 127 Avenue de la Republique, Montrouge, 92120, France.

665 FIN ISSN 1237-5608
OLJYHUOLTO. 1969-2003. q. Sanoma Magazines Finland Corporation, Lapinmaentie 1, Helsinki, 00350, Finland.

001.9 001.942 ITA ISSN 1124-3708
OLTRE; la conoscenza. 1996-ceased. bi-m. Sprea Editori Srl, Via Torino 51, Cernusco sul Naviglio, MI 20063, Italy.

850 ITA
OLTRE ...; rivista italiana di letteratura di genere fantastico. 1991-ceased. q. Edizioni Il Borghetto, Borgo Buio, 11, Montepulciano, SI 53045, Italy.

796.9 ITA ISSN 1124-5514
ON BOARD; Italian snowboarding culture. 1995-ceased. m. N Y N Pubblicita & Marketing, Via Vitruvio, 43, Milan, MI 20124, Italy.

629.13 NLD ISSN 1562-8019
ON STATION. 1999-2004. q. European Space Agency, Communication Production Office, Keplerlaan 1, Noordwijk, 2200 AG, Netherlands.

621.389 AUS
ON THE WIRE. 1984-2005. 3/yr. National Film & Sound Archive, McCoy Circuit, Acton, ACT 2601, Australia.

796.7 GBR ISSN 0309-5584
ON TWO WHEELS. 1976-198?. w. Orbis Publishing Ltd., Griffin House, 161 Hammersmith Rd, London, W6 8SD, United Kingdom.

621.381 ITA ISSN 0390-3087
ONDA QUADRA. 1973-ceased. m. GRAM 2, Via Fondoripa 6, Brivio (LC), I-23883, Italy.

332 NLD ISSN 1381-4427
ONDERNEMINGSANALYSES. TRENDS BIJ BANKEN. 1993-2004. a. Reed Business bv, Postbus 16400, Den Haag, 2500 BK, Netherlands.

368 NLD ISSN 1381-4435
ONDERNEMINGSANALYSES. TRENDS BIJ VERZEKERINGSMAATSCHAPPIJEN. 1993-2004. a. Reed Business bv, Postbus 16400, Den Haag, 2500 BK, Netherlands.

660 NLD ISSN 1381-4478
ONDERNEMINGSANALYSES. TRENDS IN DE CHEMIE. 1993-2004. a. Reed Business bv, Postbus 16400, Den Haag, 2500 BK, Netherlands.

669 NLD ISSN 1381-4443
ONDERNEMINGSANALYSES. TRENDS IN DE METAAL- EN ELEKTRO-INDUSTRIE. 1993-2004. a. Reed Business bv, Postbus 16400, Den Haag, 2500 BK, Netherlands.

664 NLD ISSN 1381-446X
ONDERNEMINGSANALYSES. TRENDS IN DE VOEDINGS- EN GENOTMIDDELENINDUSTRIE. 1993-2004. a. Reed Business bv, Postbus 16400, Den Haag, 2500 BK, Netherlands.

380 NLD ISSN 1381-4486
ONDERNEMINGSANALYSES. TRENDS IN TRANSPORT. 1990-2004. a. Reed Business bv, Postbus 16400, Den Haag, 2500 BK, Netherlands.

336.2 CAN ISSN 1189-9131
ONTARIO INCOME TAX WITH RELATED TAXES. 1960-2000 (28th ed.). irreg. C C H Canadian Ltd., 90 Sheppard Ave E, Ste 300, North York, ON M2N 6X1, Canada.

700 USA ISSN 0316-4055
ONTARIO REVIEW. 1974-2008 (Spring issue). s-a. Ontario Review, Inc., 9 Honey Brook Dr, Princeton, NJ 08540.

025.8 ESP ISSN 1698-0298
OOOH!. 2004-200?. m. Bayard Revistas, Alcala, 261-265, Edif. 4 Planta 1a, Madrid, 28027, Spain.

028.5 ITA ISSN 1124-2906
OP LA. 1995-ceased. m. Logos Publishing, Via Curtatona 5/2, Modena, MO 41100, Italy.

370 AUS
OPEN BOOK. 1972-1975. irreg. Open Book, 21 Smith St, Thornbury, VIC 3071, Australia.

069 AUS ISSN 1443-5144
OPEN MUSEUM JOURNAL. 1999-2006. a. Australian Museums & Galleries Online, PO Box K346, Haymarker, NSW 1238, Australia.

004.678 ITA ISSN 1723-7041
OPEN SOURCE. 1995-ceased. m. Systems Comunicazioni, Via Olanda 6, Vigano di Gaggiano, MI 20083, Italy.

305.26 NLD ISSN 0030-3453
OPEN VENSTERS; maandblad voor ouderen. 1957-2005. m. Boekencentrum Uitgevers, Goudstraat 50, Postbus 29, Zoetermeer, 2700 AA, Netherlands.

782.1 ITA ISSN 1121-4112
L'OPERA (MILAN). 1987-ceased. m. Edizioni di Sabino Lenoci, Via Carlo Botta, 4, Milan, MI 20135, Italy.

782.1 AUS ISSN 1328-214X
OPERA - OPERA. 1978-2007. m. Pellinor Pty. Ltd., PO Box R 361, Royal Exchange, NSW 1225, Australia.

782.1 AUS
OPERA - OPERA LIBRETTO SERIES. 1978-2007. irreg. Pellinor Pty. Ltd., PO Box R 361, Royal Exchange, NSW 1225, Australia.

610.73 ITA ISSN 0392-5153
L'OPERATORE SANITARIO. 1981-ceased. q. Mattioli 1885 SpA, Via Coduro 1, Fidenza, PR 43036, Italy.

336 DNK ISSN 0906-8643
OPGAVESAMLING I SKATTERET 1. 1980-1994. a. Alternativ Revisions Forlag, Riddergade 7, Naestved, 4700, Denmark.

336 DNK ISSN 0908-8237
OPGAVESAMLING I SKATTERET 2. 1980-1994. a. Alternativ Revisions Forlag, Riddergade 7, Naestved, 4700, Denmark.

800 NLD ISSN 0168-5899
OPTIMA. 1982-2004. 4/yr. Uitgeverij Prometheus B.V., Postbus 1662, Amsterdam, 1000 BR, Netherlands.

368 DEU ISSN 1861-5104
OPTIMAL VERSICHERT. 2005-2008. m. Voxpop Verlag fuer Nutzwertkommunikation, Stresemannstr 14, Duesseldorf, 40210, Germany.

621.381 535 ESP ISSN 1136-2057
OPTO. 1990-2005. bi-m. Extra Editorial S.L., C/ Francisco Silvela, 77-Bis 4o, Madrid, 28028, Spain.

621.38 USA ISSN 1040-0907
OPTOELECTRONICS D.A.T.A. DIGEST. 1975-2000. a. D.A.T.A. Business Publishing, 15 Inverness Way E, Box 6510, Englewood, CO 80155-6510.

005.5 USA ISSN 1080-0654
ORACLE INFORMANT; the independent monthly guide to Oracle development. 1996-1997. m. Informant Communications Group, 5105 Florin Perkins Rd., Sacramento, CA 95826-4817.

005.74 USA
ORACLE UPDATE. ceased. m. Xephon, 9330 Lyndon B Johnson Fwy., Ste. 800, Dallas, TX 75243-4310.

055 ITA ISSN 0393-4012
GLI ORATORI DEL GIORNO. 1927-ceased. bi-m. Oratori del Giorno, Via Dei Colli Della Farnesina, 144, Rome, RM 00194, Italy.

780.01 ISR ISSN 0303-3937
ORBIS MUSICAE. 1971-2003. irreg. Tel Aviv University, Department of Musicology, Ramat Aviv, 69978, Israel.

808 410 DNK ISSN 0908-715X
ORD & TEKST. 1994-1994. irreg. Det Danske Sprog- og Litteraturselskab, Christians Brygge 1, Copenhagen K, 1219, Denmark.

929 USA ISSN 1069-7454
OREGON TRAIL SOURCES, QUERIES AND REVIEWS. 1993-1995. irreg. (2-4/yr.). Family Publications, 5628 60th Dr, NE, Marysville, WA 98270.

631.8 AUS ISSN 0816-6668
ORGANIC GROWING (ULVERSTONE). 1976-1994. q. Organic Gardening and Farming Society of Tasmania Inc., PO Box 228, Ulverstone, TAS 7315, Australia.

658 ITA ISSN 0474-635X
ORGANIZZARSI. 1962-ceased. q. ORGA Srl, Via Vitruvio 3, Milan, 20124, Italy.

371.4 ITA
ORIENTAMENTO SCOLASTICO PROFESSIONALE. 1976 (vol.16)-1999. q. Associazione Italiana di Orientamento Scolastico e Professionale, Via Leopoldo Serra, 5, Rome, RM 00153, Italy.

055.1 ITA
ORIENTE E OCCIDENTE. 1978-ceased. 3/yr. Oriente e Occidente, Via Sappusi, 12, Marsala, TP 91025, Italy.

020 BRD
ORIENTIERUNGSHILFEN. 1974-1988 (vol.32). irreg. B W V - Berliner Wissenschafts Verlag GmbH, Axel-Springer-Str 54a, Berlin, 10117, Germany.

610 ITA ISSN 0394-2678
ORIS MEDICINA; monthly of cultural, scientific and technical information. 1987-1993. m. Diade s.r.l., Via Ausonio, 5, Milan, MI 20123, Italy.

383 ITA ISSN 0030-5634
ORIZZONTI PROFESSIONALI; rivista bimestrale di tecnica, cultura ed informazioni. 1960-ceased. bi-m. Istituto Professionale di Stato per l'Industria e l'Artigianato "E. Ascione" Palermo, Via Leonardo Da Vinci, 364, Palermo, PA 90135, Italy.

681.114 ITA ISSN 1594-5936
OROLOGI & MARKET; la rivista internazionale del mercato dell'orologio. 1997-ceased. m. Edizioni Sondep S.r.l., Via Del Fagutale, 2, Rome, RM 00184, Italy.

616.7 ITA ISSN 1721-2588
ORTOPEDIA E TRAUMATOLOGIA. 1998-ceased. s-a. Mattioli 1885 SpA, Via Coduro 1, Fidenza, PR 43036, Italy.

362 ITA ISSN 0390-0746
GLI OSPEDALI DELLA VITA. 1974-2007. q. Zadig s.r.l., Via Calzecchi 10, Milan, 20133, Italy.

301 ITA ISSN 1122-2581
OSSIMORI; periodico di antropologia e scienze umane. 1992-1997. s-a. Protagon Editori Toscani, Strada di Ficareto, Siena, SI 53100, Italy.

281 DEU ISSN 0030-6487
OSTKIRCHLICHE STUDIEN. 1952-2002. q. Augustinus Verlag, Grabenberg 2, Wuerzburg, 97070, Germany.

004 USA
OTHER VOICES; viewpoints on technology. 1998-200?. irreg. Other Voices

320.947 RUS ISSN 1029-8223
OTKRYTAYA POLITIKA; zhurnal rossiiskoi politicheskoi zhizni. 1994-2000. bi-m. Evraziya, Tverskaya ul 20, Moscow, 103789, Russian Federation.

305.90664 DEU
OUR MUNICH; Muenchens Stadtmagazin fuer Schwule und Lesben. 1996-2007. m. CityHeat! Verlag, Grafinger Str 6, Munich, 81671, Germany.

231.76 USA
OUR SUNDAY VISITOR'S NEW COVENANT. 1969-2002. m. Our Sunday Visitor, Inc., 200 Noll Plz, Huntington, IN 46750.

306.766 NZL ISSN 0110-4454
OUT!. 1976-2009. m. Lawrence Publishing Co. N.Z. Ltd., Private Bag 92126, Auckland 1, New Zealand.

020 DNK ISSN 0904-3853
OVER BROEN; bibliotekarstuderendes blad. 1970-1999. 4/yr. Danmarks Biblioteksskole, Birketinget 6, Copenhagen S, 2300, Denmark.

333.33 AUS ISSN 1449-6526
OWNERS OWN; homes - farms - business. 198?-2006. m. A C P Action, 73 Atherton Rd, Oakleigh, VIC 3166, Australia.

540 GBR ISSN 0302-4199
OXFORD CHEMISTRY SERIES. 1972-1990. irreg. Oxford University Press, Great Clarendon St, Oxford, OX2 6DP, United Kingdom.

616.89 GBR ISSN 1362-9980
OXFORD PSYCHIATRY SERIES. 1993-1994. irreg. Oxford University Press, Great Clarendon St, Oxford, OX2 6DP, United Kingdom.

576.8 GBR ISSN 0265-072X CODEN: OSEBE3
OXFORD SURVEYS IN EVOLUTIONARY BIOLOGY. 1984-1993. a. Oxford University Press, Great Clarendon St, Oxford, OX2 6DP, United Kingdom.

910.2 GBR ISSN 0265-2692
P A T A FACTFINDER. (Pacific Area Travel Association) 19??-199?. a. Maclean Hunter Ltd., 30 Old Burlington St, London, W1X 1RL, United Kingdom.

004.16 005.36 ITA ISSN 1127-1248
P C ACTION; guida alla civilta del personal computer. 1992-ceased. 11/yr. Xenia Edizioni Srl, Via Dell' Annunciata, 31, Milan, MI 20121, Italy.

621.381 ITA
P C B INTERNATIONAL. 1995-ceased. 4/yr. Il Sole 24 Ore Business Media, Divisione J C E, Via Patecchio 2, Milan, 20141, Italy.

004 CZE ISSN 1212-3110
P C DEALER. (Personal Computer) 1998-2000. m. Burda Praha, spol. s r.o., Premyslovska 2845/43, Luxembourg Plaza, Prague 3, 13000, Czech Republic.

004.16 FRA ISSN 1164-6977
P C DIRECT. 1992-2007. m. (11/yr.). Nielsen Business Publications (France), 2-6 Rue Bourets, Le Ventose, Suresnes, 92154, France.

004.16 DEU ISSN 0943-4038
P C DIREKT; the up-to-date buyer's magazine. (Personal Computer) 1991-2005. m. Nielsen Business Publications Deutschland GmbH, Riesstr 25, Munich, 80992, Germany.

794.8 AUS ISSN 1447-0470
P C GAMES ADDICT. 2002-2006. m. Derwent Howard Media Pty Ltd., PO Box 1037, Bondi Junction, NSW 1355, Australia.

794.8 DNK ISSN 1603-3620
P C GAMING WORLD. 1999-2005. m. Bonnier Publications A/S, Strandboulevarden 130, Copenhagen OE, 2100, Denmark.

004.16 DEU ISSN 0949-2461
P C INTERN. (Personal Computer) 1995-2007 (Apr.). q. Data Becker GmbH & Co. KG, Merowingerstr 30, Duesseldorf, 40223, Germany.

004.165 USA ISSN 0888-8507
P C MAGAZINE (PRINT); the independent guide to personal computing and the Internet. 1982-2009. m. Ziff Davis Media Inc., 28 E 28th St, New York, NY 10016.

004.16 ITA ISSN 1126-5132
P C MARKET; la prima grande guida all'acquisto dei prodotti informatici. 1998-200?. m. Techno Publishing S.r.l., Via Tacito 5, Corsico, MI 20094, Italy.

794.805 DEU
P C POWERPLAY. (Personal Computer) 2004-2007 (Sep.). m. CyPress GmbH, Max-Planck-Str 13, Hoechberg, 97204, Germany.

004.16 005.36 ITA ISSN 1826-5375
P C PRATICO MAGAZINE. 1994-200?. m. Gruppo Editoriale Futura, Via XXV Aprile 39, Bresso, MI 20091, Italy.

681.3 ITA ISSN 1720-7649
P C SOLUZIONI. 2002-200?. m. Gruppo Editoriale Futura, Via XXV Aprile 39, Bresso, MI 20091, Italy.

004 FRA ISSN 1264-935X
P C TEAM. 1995-2005. m. Posse Press, BP 1121, Toulouse, 31036, France.

005.43 ITA
P C WINDOWS. 1991-ceased. m. G R Edizioni s.r.l., Viale Carlo Espinasse, 93, Milan, MI 20156, Italy.

004.16 DNK ISSN 1600-2822
P C WORLD. (Personal Computer) 1983-2006. 22/yr. I D G Danmark A/S, Carl Jacobsens Vej 25, Valby, 2500, Denmark.

004.16 CZE ISSN 1210-1079
P C WORLD (PRINT). (Personal Computer) 1991-200?. m. I D G Czech, a.s., Seydlerova 2451-11, Prague 5, 158 00, Czech Republic.

615.1 USA ISSN 1537-9892
P D R MONTHLY PRESCRIBING GUIDE. (Physicians' Desk Reference) 2002-2007. m. Thomson P D R, Five Paragon Dr, Montvale, NJ 07645.

051 USA
P D X MAGAZINE. 2005 (Oct.)-2009 (Jun.). m. P D X Magazine, 5200 SW Macadam, Ste. 370, Portland, OR 97239.

342.082 USA ISSN 1559-2073
THE P E R M QUARTERLY. 2006-200?. q. I L W.com, PO Box 1830, New York, NY 10156.

621 ITA ISSN 1129-0188
P M. PROGETTAZIONE MACCHINE; panorama internazionale della progettazione. 1999-200?. 9/yr. Gruppo Editoriale Futura, Via XXV Aprile 39, Bresso, MI 20091, Italy.

793 DEU
P.M. RHETORIK-TRAINER. 2003-2007 (Jan.). bi-m. Gruner und Jahr AG & Co., Weihenstephaner Str 7, Munich, 81673, Germany.

794.8 ITA ISSN 1591-3775
P S 2. (PlayStation) 2000-2007. m. Future Media Italy SpA, Via Asiago 45, Milano, MI 20128, Italy.

351.94 AUS ISSN 0157-6178
P S B BULLETIN. 1978-1987. bi-m. AusInfo, Parliament House, Canberra Mc, ACT 2600, Australia.

794.8 ITA ISSN 1126-490X
P S M; 100% indipendente PlayStation magazine. (Play Station Magazine) 1996-ceased. m. Sprea Editori Srl, Via Torino 51, Cernusco sul Naviglio, MI 20063, Italy.

681.3 HRV ISSN 1331-7849
P S X. 1999-2002. m. Janus Press, Cakovecka 17, Zagreb, 10000, Croatia.

605.31 DEU
P WIE PAPI; das Vaeter-Magazin. 2001-2003. 2/yr. Buettner Medien GmbH, Sigmund-Freud-Str 77a, Frankfurt Am Main, 60435, Germany.

255.3 ITA
PACE E BENE, ASSISI; rivista Francescana missionaria TOR. 1947-ceased. bi-m. Editrice Franciscanum, Via Tor dei Conti 31a, Rome, 00184, Italy.

910.029 AUS ISSN 0311-0826
PACIFIC TRAVEL DIRECTORY. 1973-1975. a. Pacific Travel Directory, c/o Pacific Airlines News, PO Box 1, Surfers Paradise, QLD 4217, Australia.

797.124 NZL ISSN 1175-7213
PACIFIC YACHTING; New Zealand's luxury sailing magazine. 2002-2004. 2/yr. D & B Publishing Ltd., PO Box 91134, Auckland Mail Centre, Auckland, New Zealand.

688.8 ITA ISSN 1123-3273
PACK; tecnologie e prodotti per l'imballaggio e il confezionamento. 1994-ceased. m. Tecniche Nuove SpA, Via Eritrea 21, Milan, MI 201, Italy.

300 ITA
PADANIA (MILAN); societa ambiente economia tradizioni. 1992-ceased. m. (11/yr.). Editoriale Padania s.r.l., Viale Elvezia, 12, Milan, MI 20154, Italy.

797.122 AUS
PADDLER. 1976-2000. q. Victorian Canoe Association, 332 Banyle Rd, View Bank, VIC 3084, Australia.

618.92 DEU ISSN 1439-488X
PAEDIATRISCHE NACHRICHTEN. 1998-2007. bi-m. Biermann Verlag GmbH, Otto-Hahn-Str 7, Cologne, 50997, Germany.

617.96 ITA
THE PAIN CLINIC. PROCEEDINGS. 1985-ceased. irreg. World Society of Pain Clinicians, Corso Dante, 1, Cuneo, 12100, Italy.

368.382 617.96 USA ISSN 1536-8270
PAIN MANAGEMENT CODING ALERT. 2001-2006. q. The Coding Institute, 2272 Airport Rd S, Naples, FL 34112.

Cessations

700 ITA ISSN 0031-0255
PALAESTRA. 1962-1968. bi-m. Palaestra, Via Tiglio S Biagio, Maddaloni, CE 81024, Italy.

344.10 GBR ISSN 0267-5951
PALMER'S COMPANY CASES. 1985-1989. bi-m. Sweet & Maxwell Ltd., 100 Avenue Rd, London, NW3 3PF, United Kingdom.

306.766 DNK ISSN 1604-0023
PANBLADET. 1954-2007. 10/yr. Landsforeningen for Boesser og Lesbiske, Teglgaardstraede 13, PO Box 1023, Copenhagen K, 1007, Denmark.

052 NZL ISSN 1174-4030
THE PANDER. 1997-199?. q. The Pander, Wellesley St., PO Box 6153, Auckland, 1036, New Zealand.

300 ITA ISSN 1824-6516
IL PANE E LA STORIA. 2000-200?. irreg. Silva Editore, Via Nazionale 23, Collecchio, Parma 43044, Italy.

613.04244 CZE
PANI DOMU EXTRA. 2002-2008 (Mar.). q. R F Hobby s.r.o., Bohdalecka 6, Prague 10, 110 00, Czech Republic.

641.5 CZE
PANI DOMU SPECIAL. 2002-2005. bi-m. R F Hobby s.r.o., Bohdalecka 6, Prague 10, 110 00, Czech Republic.

301 FRA ISSN 1162-1915
PANORAMIQUES. 1991-2005. q. Editions Arlea, 106 bd. Saint Denis, Courbevoie, 92400, France.

338.9 GBR ISSN 0951-8819
PANOSCOPE (LONDON). 1987-1994. bi-m. Panos Institute, 9 White Lion St, London, N1 9PD, United Kingdom.

053.931 NLD ISSN 1874-7353
PAPARAZZI. 2006-2007. bi-m. Just Entertainment, PO Box 134, Hilversum, 1200 AC, Netherlands.

676 FRA ISSN 1284-9235
PAPER & BOARD NEWS. 1997-2006. s-m. Editions Litteraires Techniques et Artistiques (ELTA), 16 rue Saint Fiacre, Paris, 75002, France.

676 GBR ISSN 1471-5090
PAPER & PRINT FOCUS. 1986-2006. m. Paper Trail Trading Ltd., Apsley Mills Cottage, London Rd, Hemel Hempstead, Herts HP3 9RY, United Kingdom.

676 AUS ISSN 1832-3030
PAPER2PAPER EDGE. 2004-2005. bi-m. IndustryEdge, GPO Box 77, Hobart, TAS, Australia.

658 910.202 GBR ISSN 0960-6629
PAPERS IN LEISURE AND TOURISM STUDIES. 1990-1995. irreg. U N L Press, University Of North London, 277-281 Holloway Rd, London, N7 8HN, United Kingdom.

302 DNK ISSN 0906-0510
PAPERS IN ORGANIZATION. 1991-2004. irreg. (3-5 per year). Handelshoejskolen i Koebenhavn, Institut for Organisation og Arbejdssociologi, Solbjerg Plads 3, Frederiksberg, 2000, Denmark.

674 USA ISSN 1180-9175
PAPERTREE LETTER; independent analysis of forest products economics. 1981-2007 (Dec.). m. R I S I, Inc., 4 Alfred Cir, Bedford, MA 01730.

913 ITA
PAPYROLOGICA CASTROCTAVIANA. 1967-1988 (no.12). irreg. Pontificio Istituto Biblico, Via della Pilotta 25, Rome, 00187, Italy.

020 ESP ISSN 1133-9756
PARABIBLOS. 1988-2000. a. Asociacion Canaria de Archiveros, Bibliotecarios y Documentalistas, Obispo Rabadan, 22, Las Palmas de Gran Canaria, 35003, Spain.

282 FRA ISSN 0031-1561
PARABOLES. 1949-1993. 4/yr. Communautes Chretiennes Universitaires, 5 rue de l'Abbaye, Paris, 75006, France.

910.2 ESP ISSN 0210-3796
PARALELO 37; revista de estudios geograficos. 1977-2003. a. Diputacion Provincial de Almeria, C. Navarro Rodrigo, 17, Almeria, 04071, Spain.

940 ITA ISSN 1121-5542
PARALLELI. 1991-ceased. bi-m. Editoriale Domus, Via Gianni Mazzocchi 1/3, Rozzano, MI 20089, Italy.

055.1 ITA
PARENTESI; panorama di politica economia cultura attualita. 1989-ceased. bi-m. Associazione Culturale Parentesi, S.S. 114 Pal Iles, Messina, ME 98125, Italy.

690 FRA ISSN 1296-2902
PARIS LE JOURNAL. 1977-2002. m. Association pour l'Information Municipale, Hotel de Ville, Paris R.p., 75196, France.

810 DEU
PARK AND READ. 1995-200?. s-a. Park and Read

053.1 DEU
PARK AVENUE. 2005-2009 (Jan.). m. Park Avenue GmbH, Am Baumwall 11, Hamburg, 20459, Germany.

343.093 USA ISSN 1530-2857
PARKER'S CALIFORNIA VEHICLE CODE. 1988-ceased. a. LexisNexis, PO Box 7587, Charlottesville, VA 22906.

388.342 GBR ISSN 1466-9528
PARKER'S USED & NEW CAR CHOOSER; your guide to the right used car. 1998-2003. m. Emap Active Ltd. (Angel House), Angel House, 338-346 Goswell Rd, London, EC1V 7QP, United Kingdom.

320.1 351.1 ITA ISSN 1720-2337
PARLAMENTI REGIONALI. 2001-2005. 3/yr. Franco Angeli Edizioni, Viale Monza 106, Milan, 20127, Italy.

054.1 FRA ISSN 0258-4751
PARLEMENTS ET FRANCOPHONIE. 1969-2003. q. Assemblee Internationale des Parlementaires de Langue Francaise, 235 bd. Saint-Germain, Paris, 75007, France.

282 ITA ISSN 0031-2428
PARROCCHIA. 1947-ceased. m. Opera Madonna del Divino Amore, Km 12, Via Ardeatina, Rome, 00179, Italy.

320.531 ESP
PARTIDO SOCIALISTA POPULAR. CONGRESO. (ACTAS). 1976 (no.3)-1978. irreg. Tucar Ediciones S.A., Paseo Eduardo Dato, 21, Madrid, 28010, Spain.

780.43 DEU ISSN 1860-7659
PARTITUREN; Das Magazin fuer klassische Musik. 2005-2008 (Aug.). bi-m. Friedrich Berlin Verlagsgesellschaft mbH, Reinhardtstr 29, Berlin, 10117, Germany.

700 860 ESP ISSN 1130-0388
EL PASEANTE. 1985-2001. q. Ediciones Siruela S.A., El Pabellon, Plaza Manuel Becerra, 15, Madrid, 28028, Spain.

333.72 ISR ISSN 0334-3022
PASHOSH. 1974-2005. m. Society for the Protection of Nature in Israel, 4 Hashefela St, Tel Aviv, 66183, Israel.

780 ITA
PASQUINO MUSICALE. 1991-ceased. m. (10/yr.). Saturnia Diffusione, Villa Il Parnaso, Via Carizia 25, Sezze Romano, LT 04018, Italy.

745.5 FRA ISSN 1767-9567
PASSION DU PATCHWORK. 2004-2007. bi-m. Editions de Saxe, 20 Rue Croix Barret, Lyon, 69358 Cedex 7, France.

351 AUS ISSN 1833-2307
PATHWAYS. 2004 (Oct.)-2006. q. South Australia, Department for Administrative and Information Services, State Records of South Australia, GPO Box 1072, Adelaide, SA 5001, Australia.

616.5 USA
PATIENT CARE: PRIMARY CARE TOPICS IN DERMATOLOGY. 1967-2007. bi-m. Advanstar Communications, Inc., 123 Tice Blvd, Ste 300, Woodcliff Lake, NJ 07677.

362.10285 GBR ISSN 1464-9543
PATIENT I T. (Information Technology) 1998-2005. fortn. Informed Publications Ltd., PO Box 2087, Shoreham-by-Sea, West Sussex BN43 5RH, United Kingdom.

327 DEU
PATRIKA. 1993-1999. q. Indische Botschaft, Adenauerallee 262-264, Bonn, 53113, Germany.

057.86 CZE ISSN 1213-1229
PAUZA. 2000-2005. d. Computer Press a.s., Spielberk Office Centre, Holandska 8, Brno, 639 00, Czech Republic.

940 DEU ISSN 1617-6219
PAX ET GAUDIUM. 2000-2008 (Jun.). q. Ludwig Fischer Verlag, Severinusweg 2, Mechernich-Kommern, 53894, Germany.

332 FRA ISSN 1636-6891
PAYMENT SYSTEMS NEWS. 1999-2005. m. (11/yr). Publi-News, 47 rue Aristide Briand, Levallois-Perret, 92300, France.

914.4 FRA ISSN 1266-4081
PAYS DE BRETAGNE; le magazine du patrimoine, de l'histoire et de l'art de vivre. 1995-200?. 6/yr. Editions Freeway, 1 rue Jean-Richepin, BP 271, Clermont-Ferrand, Cedex 1 63008, France.

327.172 AUS
PEACE PLANS. 1964-2002 (no.1779). irreg. (approx. 70/yr.). Libertarian Microfiche Publishing, 35 Oxley St, Berrima, NSW 2577, Australia.

327.172 NZL
THE PEACEMAKER. 1936-2002. q. New Zealand Christian Pacifist Society, 3 Muir Ave, Aotearoa, Christchurch 3, New Zealand.

618.92238 GBR
THE PEDIATRIC ASTHMA VIRTUAL JOURNAL. 2002-200?. m. B M J Group, B M A House, Tavistock Sq, London, WC1H 9JR, United Kingdom.

618.92 USA ISSN 1532-9798
PEDIATRIC CASE REVIEWS; cost-effective, evidence-based diagnosis and management. 2002-2004. q. Lippincott Williams & Wilkins, 530 Walnut St, Philadelphia, PA 19106-3621.

347 USA
PENNSYLVANIA JUDICIARY AND JUDICIAL PROCEDURE. 1983-200?. a. Gould Publications, Inc., 1333 North US Hwy 17-92, Longwood, FL 32750.

320.531 ITA
PENSARE FAENZA/THINKING ABOUT FAENZA. 1904-1924; resumed 1946-1958; resumed 1966-ceased. s-m. Unione Comunale Partito Socialista Italiano di Faenza, Via 20 Settembre, 29, Faenza, RA 48018, Italy.

340 USA ISSN 1052-9640
PENSION FUND LITIGATION REPORTER. 1990-ceased. s-m. Andrews Publications, 175 Strafford Ave, Bldg 4, Ste 140, Wayne, PA 19087.

305.31 ESP
PENTHOUSE. 1978-2000. m. Blue Sky Ediciones S.A., Londres, 2-4, Esc. A 1o 4e, Barcelona, 08029, Spain.

296 USA ISSN 0735-455X
THE PEOPLE TAKE THE LEAD. 19??-ceased. a. American Jewish Committee, 165 E 56th St, New York, NY 10022.

305.8 USA
PEOPLES OF THE WORLD. (Regional volumes each updated quinquennially) 1989-ceased. irreg. Gale, 27500 Drake Rd, Farmington Hills, MI 48331.

028.5 NLD ISSN 1873-9490
PEPPA BIG MAGAZINE. 2006-2006. 4/yr. Big Balloon Publishers, Postbus 136, Heemstede, 2100 AC, Netherlands.

945.092 ITA
PER IL SESSANTOTTO. 1991-2000. 6/m. Associazione Centro Documentazione di Pistoia, Via Pertini, Pistoia, PT 51100, Italy.

779.28 CZE ISSN 1801-500X
PERFECT GIRLS. 2006-2007. 2/yr. PK 62, a.s., Bohdalecka 6, Prague 10, 101 00, Czech Republic.

782 USA ISSN 1068-9664
PERFORMING SONGWRITER. 1993-2009. 8/yr. Desktop Communications, PO Box 40931, Nashville, TN 37204.

668.54 GBR ISSN 1462-043X
PERFUME COLLECTION; discover the world's most enduring fragrances. 1998-199?. bi-w. Orbis Publishing Ltd., Griffin House, 161 Hammersmith Rd, London, W6 8SD, United Kingdom.

070.5 USA ISSN 0737-7843
PERIODICAL TITLE ABBREVIATIONS. 1969-2006 (17th ed.). irreg. Gale, 27500 Drake Rd, Farmington Hills, MI 48331.

538 541.37 GBR ISSN 0374-406X
PERKIN-ELMER N M R QUARTERLY. (Nuclear Magnetic Resonance) 1971-1976. q. Perkin-Elmer Ltd., Post Office Lane, Beaconsfield, Bucks CF72 8YW, United Kingdom.

808.83876 DEU
PERRY RHODAN 3. AUFLAGE. 1973-2007. fortn. Pabel-Moewig Verlag KG, Karlsruherstr 31, Rastatt, 76437, Germany.

004.16 GBR ISSN 0142-0232 CODEN: PCWODU
PERSONAL COMPUTER WORLD. 1978-2009. m. V N U Business Publications Ltd., 32-34 Broadwick St, London, W1A 2HG, United Kingdom.

332 USA ISSN 1535-413X
PERSONAL FINANCIAL PLANNING MONTHLY. 2001 (June)-200?. m. Aspen Publishers, Inc., 111 Eighth Ave., 7th Fl, New York, NY 10011.

346.0323 USA
PERSONAL INJURY DEFENSE REPORTER. 1985-200?. plus s-a. updates. Matthew Bender & Co., Inc., 1275 Broadway, Albany, NY 12204.

368.51 USA ISSN 1047-8566
PERSONAL INJURY NEWSLETTER. 1958-2004. fortn. Matthew Bender & Co., Inc., 1275 Broadway, Albany, NY 12204.

020 GBR ISSN 0960-1619
PERSONNEL TRAINING AND EDUCATION; a journal for library and information workers. 1972-2004. 3/yr. Library Association Personnel Training and Education Group, 14 Aireville Ave, Bradford, BD9 4HH, United Kingdom.

369.5 ESP
PERSPECTIVA ROTARIA. 1991-2002. q. Asociacion Editorial Rotaria, PDG Vicente Carmenati Francia, Ed., Urb. los Girasoles 2, Girona, 17248, Spain.

341.758 GBR
PERSPECTIVES ON INTELLECTUAL PROPERTY LAW AND POLICY. 1997-2005. irreg. Sweet & Maxwell Ltd., 100 Avenue Rd, London, NW3 3PF, United Kingdom.

616.994 ITA ISSN 0069-8520 CODEN: PPQCDL
PERUGIA QUADRENNIAL INTERNATIONAL CONFERENCES ON CANCER. PROCEEDINGS. 1957-ceased. quadrennial. Universita degli Studi di Perugia, Division of Cancer Research, P O Box 327, Monteluce, PG 06100, Italy.

796 ITA ISSN 1720-3988
PESCI & PESCA MARE. 2002-200?. a. Sprea Editori Srl, Via Torino 51, Cernusco sul Naviglio, MI 20063, Italy.

910 DEU ISSN 0031-6229 CODEN: PGGMA3
PETERMANNS GEOGRAPHISCHE MITTEILUNGEN; Zeitschrift fuer Geo- und Umweltwissenschaften. 1855-2004. 6/yr. Justus Perthes Verlag Gotha GmbH, Justus Perthes Str 3-5, Gotha, 99867, Germany.

770 USA ISSN 0199-4913
PETERSEN'S PHOTOGRAPHIC. 1972-2005. m. Source Interlink Companies, 6420 Wilshire Blvd, 10th Fl, Los Angeles, CA 90048.

507.1 USA ISSN 1086-2226
PETERSON'S TOP COLLEGES FOR SCIENCE. 1996-200?. biennial. Thomson Peterson's, Princeton Pike Corporate Center, 2000 Lenox Dr, 3rd Fl, PO Box 67005, Lawrenceville, NJ 08648.

665.5 ITA ISSN 0031-6563
PETROLIERI D'ITALIA. 1954-ceased. m. Interpetrol, Viale Andrea Doria, 3, Milan, MI 20124, Italy.

800 FRA ISSN 0181-4087
PEUPLES NOIRS, PEUPLES AFRICAINS. 1978-199?. q. Editions des Peuples Noirs, 82 av. de la Porte des Champs, Rouen, 76000, France.

580 DEU ISSN 0079-1342 CODEN: PFZNAQ
PFLANZENSCHUTZ-NACHRICHTEN. 1962-ceased. 3/yr. Bayer CropScience AG, Alfred-Nobel-Str 50, Monheim am Rhein, 40789, Germany.

053.1 BRD ISSN 0931-7791
PFLASTERSTRAND. KASSEL - NORDHESSEN. 1986-1987. fortn. Pflasterstrand-GmbH, Ludwigstr 33-37, Frankfurt am Main, 60327, Germany.

610 DEU ISSN 1862-6912
PFLEGE, BETREUUNG UND THERAPIE AKTUELL. 2006-2008. m. Forum Verlag Herkert GmbH, Mandichostr 18, Merching, 86504, Germany.

615 USA ISSN 1932-1953
PHARMA D D. (Discovery & Development) 2001-2007. bi-m. Cambridge Healthtech Institute, 250 1st Ave, Ste 300, Needham, MA 02494.

615.1 GBR ISSN 1753-7878
PHARMACEUTICAL EXECUTIVE EUROPE (PRINT). 2003-2008. 6/yr. Advanstar Communications (UK) Ltd., Chiswick High Rd, London, W4 5RG, United Kingdom.

615 DEU
PHARMACOLOGY OF CEREBRAL ISCHEMIA. 1994-2004. biennial. Medpharm GmbH Scientific Publishers, Postfach 101061, Stuttgart, 70009, Germany.

615.19 658.8 GBR ISSN 1751-0902
PHARMACY TODAY. 1980-2007. m. C M P Information Ltd., Ludgate House, 245 Blackfriars Rd., London, SE1 9UR, United Kingdom.

530 GBR ISSN 1062-7901 CODEN: PTCPEJ
PHASE TRANSITIONS AND CRITICAL PHENOMENA. 1972-2001. irreg. Academic Press, 32 Jamestown Rd, Camden, London, NW1 7BY, United Kingdom.

676.029 GBR ISSN 0954-8521
PHILLIPS' INTERNATIONAL PAPER DIRECTORY. 1904-2003. a. C M P Information Ltd., Sovereign House, Sovereign Way, Tonbridge, Kent TN9 1RW, United Kingdom.

200 NLD ISSN 0166-5030
PHILOSOPHIA PATRUM; interpretations of patristic texts. 1971-1984 (vol.7). irreg. Brill, PO Box 9000, Leiden, 2300 PA, Netherlands.

100 305.4 DEU ISSN 0936-7586
DIE PHILOSOPHIN; Forum fuer feministische Theorie und Philosophie. 1990-2005. s-a. Edition Diskord, Scheidswaldstr 22, Frankfurt am Main, 60385, Germany.

371.42 USA ISSN 1072-5946
THE PHOENIX JOBBANK; the job hunter's guide to Arizona. (Includes: Flagstaff, Metro Phoenix, Tucso, Yuma and many others.) 1990-2004 (9th ed.). irreg. Adams Media, 4700 E Galbraith Rd, Cincinnati, OH 45236.

820 821 AUS ISSN 0819-3606
PHOENIX REVIEW. 1973-1992. 4/yr. Victoria College, 119 Maltravers Rd, Ivanhoe, VIC 3079, Australia.

780.65 DEU
PHONO PRESS; Jahresheft fuer den Tontraegermarkt. 1973-2000. a. Bundesverband Musikindustrie e.V., Oranienburger Str 67-68, Berlin, 10117, Germany.

770 ITA ISSN 1125-1131
PHOTO. 1996-ceased. 10/yr. Hachette Rusconi SpA, Viale Sarca 235, Milan, 20126, Italy.

770 FRA ISSN 1161-0824
PHOTO ECHOS. 198?-200?. 21/yr. Editions du Gaillard, 5 av. de la Republique, Paris, Cedex 75130, France.

770 FRA ISSN 1299-006X
PHOTO PLUS. 1965-200?. 10/yr. Editions V.M., 100 av. des Ternes, Paris, 75017, France.

770 FRA ISSN 0152-4119
PHOTO WORK. 1978-198?. 4/yr. Edira Editions, 126 rue des 3 Epis, Katzenthal, 68230, France.

770.29 AUS ISSN 1327-0710
PHOTOGRAPHERS DIRECTORY. 1995-1998. a. Yaffa Publishing Group Pty Ltd., 17-21 Bellevue St, Surry Hills, NSW 2010, Australia.

976.07 ISR ISSN 0333-5259
PHYSICAL EDUCATION AND SPORT. 1966-2004. bi-m. Wingate Institute, Wingate Post, 42902, Israel.

541 GBR
PHYSICAL ORGANOMETALLIC CHEMISTRY. 1996-2004 (vol.4). irreg. John Wiley & Sons Ltd., 1-7 Oldlands Way, PO Box 808, Bognor Regis, West Sussex PO21 9FF, United Kingdom.

332.6 USA ISSN 1089-1404
THE PHYSICIAN MEDICAL GROUP ACQUISITION REPORT. 1996-200?. a. Irving Levin Associates, Inc., 268-1/2 Main Ave, Norwalk, CT 06851.

581 USA ISSN 0898-3437
PHYTOCHEMICAL BULLETIN. 19??-19??. irreg. Botanical Society of America, Inc., PO Box 299, St. Louis, MO 63166-0299.

028.5 530 ISR ISSN 0333-6948
PI HA'ATOM; popular physics magazine. 1981-1998. 3/yr. Weizmann Institute of Science, Youth Activities Section, P O Box 26, Rehovot, 76100, Israel.

571.2 635 ITA ISSN 1825-4187
LE PIANTE AROMATICHE. 2005-200?. m. Sprea Editori Srl, Via Torino 51, Cernusco sul Naviglio, MI 20063, Italy.

635 ITA ISSN 1825-4179
PIANTE DA INTERNO. 2005-200?. m. Sprea Editori Srl, Via Torino 51, Cernusco sul Naviglio, MI 20063, Italy.

571.2 615.85 ITA ISSN 1825-4209
PIANTE DELLA SALUTE. 2005-200?. m. Sprea Editori Srl, Via Torino 51, Cernusco sul Naviglio, MI 20063, Italy.

635 ITA ISSN 1722-5345
PIANTE DI CASA. 2003-200?. m. Edigamma Publishing, Via Sambuca Pistoiese 70A, Rome, 00138, Italy.

381 ITA ISSN 0393-9448
PIAZZA MERCATO. 1983-ceased. m. Promodis Italia Editrice s.r.l., Via Creta, 56, Brescia, BS 25124, Italy.

338.642 ITA ISSN 0394-7947
PICCOLA IMPRESA/SMALL BUSINESS. 1988-ceased. 3/yr. Ins-Edit, Viale Sauli, 49, Genoa, GE 16121, Italy.

630 330.9 ITA ISSN 0392-5056
IL PICENTINO. 1845-ceased. q. Societa Economica della Provincia di Salerno, Biblioteca Provinciale di Salerno, Via Valerio Laspro, Salerno, SA 84100, Italy.

910.91 KOR ISSN 1738-2491
PICTORIAL KOREA. 19??-2006. m. Korean Overseas Information Service, 82-1, Sejongno, Jongno-gu, Seoul, 110050, Korea, S.

724 ITA ISSN 1123-993X
PIETRANTICA. 1996-200?. bi-m. Edizioni Trentini & C, Via Pier Luigi Nervi 1/B, Argenta, FE 44011, Italy.

945 850 ITA ISSN 1122-1399
PIETRASERENA; ricerca storica e creativita letteraria. 1989-ceased. q. Nova Arti Grafiche srl, Via Cavalcanti 9D, Signa, FI 50058, Italy.

028.5 FRA ISSN 1954-4790
PILOUNE. 2006-2006. bi-m. Editions Balisier, 13 Rue Gounod, Saint-Cloud, 92210, France.

028.5 NLD ISSN 1873-5630
PINGU. 2006-2007. irreg. Juniorpress Magazines B.V., Zwarteweg 6c, Naarden, 1412 GD, Netherlands.

028.5 GBR ISSN 1353-3355
PINGU STICKER FUN. 1994-ceased. m. B B C Magazines Ltd., Woodlands, 80 Wood Ln, London, W12 0TT, United Kingdom.

667.6 ESP ISSN 0031-9953 CODEN: PACIDY
PINTURAS Y ACABADOS INDUSTRIALES; recubrimientos organicos y metalicos. 1958-2006. 8/yr. Ediciones CEDEL, Mallorca 257, Barcelona, 08008, Spain.

828.009 AUS ISSN 0313-7546
PIONEER BOOKS MONOGRAPHS LITERARY SERIES. 1977-199?. irreg. Pioneer Books, PO Box 57, Oaklands Park, SA 5046, Australia.

053.1 DEU ISSN 1433-4720
PIPE & CIGAR; Spass am Geniessen. 1997-2005. q. Ebner Verlag GmbH, Karlstr 41, Ulm, 89073, Germany.

780 NLD ISSN 1873-3247
DE PIRAAT DER LAGE LANDEN. 2006-2007. bi-m. De Piraat der Lage Landen, Twentepoort O28, Almelo, 7609 RG, Netherlands.

598 FRA ISSN 0999-4637
LE PISTRAC; bulletin de l' A R O M P. 1979-2002. a. Association Regionale Ornithologique du Midi et des Pyrenees, Museum d'Histoire Naturelle, 35, allees Jules-Guesde, Toulouse, 31000, France.

639.2 FRA ISSN 0986-5675
PLAISANCE MER ET PECHE; en Mediterranee. 1987-198?. 4/yr. Editions Kerfan, 97-103 av. Semeria, BP 18, St Jean Cap Ferrat, 06230, France.

799.1 FRA ISSN 0398-2041
PLAISIRS DE LA PECHE. 1953-1987; resumed 1989-2005. bi-m. Editions du Cameleon, 11 rue Vauthier, Boulogne-Billancourt, 92100, France.

332.63 DEU
PLAN; das Immobilienjournal von IVG. 1999-2008. 3/yr. Facts & Figures GmbH, Stubbenhuk 3, Hamburg, 20459, Germany.

782.42 GBR ISSN 1744-2435
PLAN B MAGAZINE. 2002-2009 (Jun.). m. Plan B Publishing Ltd., 156-158 Grays Inn Rd, London, WC1X 8ED, United Kingdom.

629.13 DEU ISSN 1616-7872
PLANET AEROSPACE (FRENCH EDITION); mensuel d'information aeronautique et spatiale. 1970-2008. q. GeraMond Verlag GmbH, Innsbrucker Ring 15, Munich, 81673, Germany.

387.7 DEU ISSN 1616-7848
PLANET AEROSPACE (GERMAN EDITION); aeronautics - space defence. 1995-2008. 4/yr. European Aeronautic Defence and Space Company, Willy-Messerschmittstr, Ottobrunn, 85521, Germany.

020 USA
PLANET I T; the community of I T professionals. 1998-ceased. d. C M P Media LLC, 600 Community Dr, Manhasset, NY 11030.

791.4375 DEU
PLANET MOVIE. 2002-2003. m. CyPress GmbH, Max-Planck-Str 13, Hoechberg, 97204, Germany.

354.35 NLD ISSN 0304-176X
PLANNING AND ADMINISTRATION. 1967-1989. s-m. International Union of Local Authorities, Laan Copes van Cattenburch 60A, The Hague, 2585 GC, Netherlands.

346 USA ISSN 1067-2257
PLANNING FOR AGING OR INCAPACITY. 1993-1994. a. Practising Law Institute, 810 Seventh Ave, 21st Fl, New York, NY 10019.

690.028 GBR
PLANT & EQUIPMENT GUIDE; the standard reference for new and used construction equipment values. 1969-1999. m. Emap Construct Ltd., Greater London House, Hampstead Rd, London, NW1 7EJ, United Kingdom.

668.4 GBR ISSN 1477-7398
PLASTICS BOARD INDUSTRIES FEDERATION MAGAZINE. 1987-2008. bi-m. Plastics & Board Industries Federation, Rock House, Maddacombe Rd, Kingskerswell, Newton Abbot, Devon TQ12 5LF, United Kingdom.

668.4 338 USA ISSN 1544-9475
PLASTICS INSIGHTS. 2001-2006. q. Society of Manufacturing Engineers, One SME Dr, PO Box 930, Dearborn, MI 48121.

794.8 ITA ISSN 1594-9230
PLAY NATION 2 MAGAZINE. 2002-2007. m. Future Media Italy SpA, Via Asiago 45, Milano, MI 20128, Italy.

794.8 DEU ISSN 0946-6320
PLAY TIME. 1991-1995. m. Computec Media AG, Dr-Mack-Str 77, Fuerth, 90762, Germany.

794.8 DEU
PLAY VANILLA. 2007-2008. bi-m. Computec Media AG, Dr-Mack-Str 77, Fuerth, 90762, Germany.

387 ESP ISSN 0210-9956
PLAYAMAR; revista tecnica de actualidad nautica. 1978-1981. m. Editorial Borrmart S.A., C. Don Ramon de la Cruz, 68 6o, Madrid, 28001, Spain.

796.025 FRA ISSN 1626-715X
PLAYBOX. 2000-2002. m. Posse Press, BP 1121, Toulouse, 31036, France.

305.3 CZE ISSN 1212-5520
PLAYBOY (SLOVAK EDITION). 1998-2003. m. Millennium a.s., Tesnov 1, Prague, 110 00, Czech Republic.

796.332 DEU
PLAYER. 2005-2007. m. b&d Media Network GmbH, Osterfeldstr 12-14, Hamburg, 22529, Germany.

306.766 USA ISSN 0733-5695
PLAYGUY. 1989 (vol.13)-2009. m. Mavety Media Group, 225 Broadway, Ste 2801, New York, NY 10007-3079.

794 ITA ISSN 1594-2473
PLAYPOWER STATION. 1996-2007. m. Future Media Italy SpA, Via Asiago 45, Milano, MI 20128, Italy.

794.8 CZE ISSN 1213-7545
PLAYSTATION 2; oficialni magazin cz. 2002-2008. m. Burda Praha, spol. s r.o., Premyslovska 2845/43, Luxembourg Plaza, Prague 3, 13000, Czech Republic.

794.8 ITA
PLAYSTATION NATION. 1999-ceased. m. Xenia Edizioni Srl, Via Carducci, 31, Milano, 20123, Italy.

794.8 ITA ISSN 1127-4956
PLAYSTATION PLUS. 1998-2007. m. Future Media Italy SpA, Via Asiago 45, Milano, MI 20128, Italy.

794.8 ITA ISSN 1127-3518
PLAYSTATION TIPS. 1998-2007. m. Future Media Italy SpA, Via Asiago 45, Milano, MI 20128, Italy.

794.8 DEU
PLAYZONE. 1998-2008. m. Computec Media AG, Dr-Mack-Str 77, Fuerth, 90762, Germany.

800 ITA ISSN 0037-3478
PLEIADI. 1976-2001 (no.53). irreg. Angelo Longo Editore, Via Paolo Costa 33, Ravenna, 48121, Italy.

363.7 333.72 USA ISSN 1553-2321
PLENTY; the world in green. 2004-2009 (Jan.). bi-m. Plenty, 250 W 49th St, Ste 403, New York, NY 10019.

796.352 DEU
PLOCK!. 2005-2007 (Jan.). 6/yr. Delius Klasing Verlag GmbH, Siekerwall 21, Bielefeld, 33602, Germany.

352.63 USA
PLUNKETT'S EMPLOYERS' INTERNET SITES WITH CAREERS INFORMATION. 1999-2005. a. Plunkett Research, Ltd, PO Drawer 541737, Houston, TX 77254.

301 FRA ISSN 1247-4592
PLURIEL RECHERCHES. 1993-200?. irreg. L' Harmattan, 5 rue de l'Ecole Polytechnique, Paris, 75005, France.

910.09 ITA
POCKET TRAVEL AGENZIE DI VIAGGIO. 1992-ceased. a. Turismo & Attualita Srl, Via di Santa Prisca 16, Rome, 00153, Italy.

808.83 USA ISSN 1947-4644
POE STUDIES. 1968-2009. a. (s-a. until vol.35). Wiley-Blackwell Publishing, Inc., Commerce Pl, 350 Main St, Malden, MA 02148.

841 FRA ISSN 0752-272X
POESIE. 1939-2005. 5/yr. Pierre Seghers, 161 bis rue Saint Martin, Paris, 75003, France.

830 ITA ISSN 0079-2500
POETI E PROSATORI TEDESCHI. 1962-1982. irreg. Fabrizio Serra Editore, c/o Accademia Editoriale, Via Santa Bibbiana 28, Pisa, 56127, Italy.

016.61 CZE ISSN 1212-4575 CODEN: POUSE
POHYBOVE USTROJI; pokroky ve vyzkumu diagnostice a terapii. 1957-1999. q. Ortotika s.r.o., Truhlarska 8, Prague 8, 11000, Czech Republic.

791.43 FRA ISSN 0079-2535
POINTS. FILMS. 1971-1972. irreg. Editions du Seuil, 27 Rue Jacob, Paris, 75006, France.

345 USA ISSN 0092-8933
POLICE AND LAW ENFORCEMENT. 1973-1988. a. A M S Press, Inc., Brooklyn Navy Yard, 63 Flushing Ave, Bldg 292, Unit #221, Brooklyn, NY 11205.

364 USA
POLICE SCIENCE FUNDAMENTALS. 1973-200?. irreg. Gould Publications, Inc., 1333 North US Hwy 17-92, Longwood, FL 32750.

362.6 GBR ISSN 1367-1162
POLICY STUDIES IN AGEING. 1982-1989. irreg. Centre for Policy on Ageing, 25-31 Ironmonger Row, London, EC1V 3QP, United Kingdom.

379 ITA
POLITICA DELLA SCUOLA. 1972-ceased. s-a. Associazione Nazionale per Il Progresso della Scuola Italiana, Piazza SS, Apostoli N. 80, Rome, RM, Italy.

320.9 ITA ISSN 0391-2264
POLITICA ED ECONOMIA/POLITICS AND ECONOMICS. 1970-198?. bi-m. Donzelli Editori, Via Mentana 2, Rome, 00185, Italy.

055 ITA
POLITICA POPOLARE; rassegna di ispirazione sturziana. 1954-ceased. m. Politica Popolare, Via Costantinopoli, 84, Naples, NA 80138, Italy.

320.5322 USA ISSN 0032-3128
POLITICAL AFFAIRS (PRINT); journal of Marxist thought. 1922-2008 (Jul.). bi-m. (m. until 2008). Political Affairs, 235 W. 23rd St., New York, NY 10011.

331 ITA ISSN 1970-6030
POLITICHE DEL LAVORO. 1986-199?. irreg. Franco Angeli Edizioni, Viale Monza 106, Milan, 20127, Italy.

320.6 TUR
POLITIK EKONOMIK BULTEN GAZETESI. 1986-ceased. w. Politik Ekonomik Bulten Gazetesi, Buyukdere Cad. 81-16, Mecidiyekoy - Istanbul, 80300, Turkey.

440 375.4 FRA ISSN 1145-1742
LE POLYGLOTTE. 1990-2007. q. Association des Professeurs de Langues Vivantes de l'Enseignement Public, 19 rue de la Glaciere, Paris, 75013, France.

686 DEU ISSN 0943-0083
POLYGRAPH INTERNATIONAL; magazine for the printing industry and communication technology. 1952-2002. 6/yr. Polygraph Press Medien GmbH, Eckendorfer Str 91, Bielefeld, 33609, Germany.

800 FRA ISSN 1287-3047
LA POLYGRAPHE. 1998 (Jan.)-2005. q. Editions Act Mem - Fonds Comp'Act, 173 Carre Curial, Chambery, 73000, France.

798 FRA ISSN 1268-9696
PONEY SCOPE. 1995-199?. m. Editions du Poney, 8 rue du Faubourg Poissonniere, Paris, 75010, France.

200 ITA
PONTE D'ORO. 1966-ceased. m. Opera Missionaria della Santa Infanzia, Segretariato Generale dell'Infanzia Missionaria, Piazza di Spagna 48, Rome, RM 00187, Italy.

970 USA ISSN 0193-6891
POPULAR CULTURE BIO-BIBLIOGRAPHIES. 1982-1999. irreg. Greenwood Publishing Group Inc., 88 Post Rd W, PO Box 5007, Westport, CT 06881.

694 USA
POPULAR WOODWORKING: TOOL BUYING GUIDE (YEAR). 2000-200?. a. F + W Media Inc., 4700 E Galbraith Rd, Cincinnati, OH 45236.

387 FRA ISSN 0396-4388
PORT AUTONOME DU HAVRE. BULLETIN ANALYTIQUE DE DOCUMENTATION GENERALE. 1971-199?. m. Port Autonome du Havre, Centre de Documentation, BP 1413, Le Havre, Cedex 76067, France.

387 FRA ISSN 0396-4396
PORT AUTONOME DU HAVRE. BULLETIN ANALYTIQUE DE DOCUMENTATION TECHNIQUE. 1966-198?. m. Port Autonome du Havre, Centre de Documentation, BP 1413, Le Havre, Cedex 76067, France.

Cessations

004.6 ITA ISSN 1722-8891
PORTATILE & WIRELESS. 1998-ceased. m. Sprea Editori Srl, Via Torino 51, Cernusco sul Naviglio, MI 20063, Italy.

330.1 FRA ISSN 0079-4074
PORTS - ROUTES - TRAFICS. 1951-1988. irreg. College de France, Ecole des Hautes Etudes en Sciences Sociales (E H E S S), 54 Boulevard Raspail, Paris, 75006, France.

289.9 USA ISSN 1545-276X
POSITIVE THINKING. 1945-2008 (July). 6/yr. Peale Center for Christian Living, Guideposts, 66 E Main St, Pawling, NY 12564.

795.4 USA ISSN 0746-6102
POSTCARD COLLECTOR; the marketplace for postcard and paper collectibles. 1982-2008. bi-m. Krause Publications, Inc., 700 E State St, Iola, WI 54990.

664 CZE ISSN 1213-693X
POTRAVINARSKE AKTUALITY. 1958-2004. 10/yr. Ustav Zemedelskych a Potravinarskych Informaci, Potravinarske Aktuality, Slezska 7, Prague 2, 120 56, Czech Republic.

664.028 CZE ISSN 0862-2116
POTRAVINARSKE AKTUALITY. LIHOVARSKO-KONZERVARENSKY PRUMYSL. 1958-2000. 5/yr. Ustav Zemedelskych a Potravinarskych Informaci, Potravinarske Aktuality, Slezska 7, Prague 2, 120 56, Czech Republic.

664.9 CZE ISSN 1212-5113
POTRAVINARSKE AKTUALITY. MASNY A DRUBEZARSKY PRUMYSL. 1998-2000. 5/yr. Ustav Zemedelskych a Potravinarskych Informaci, Potravinarske Aktuality, Slezska 7, Prague 2, 120 56, Czech Republic.

637 CZE ISSN 0862-2132
POTRAVINARSKE AKTUALITY. MLEKARENSKY PRUMYSL. 1958-2000. 5/yr. Ustav Zemedelskych a Potravinarskych Informaci, Potravinarske Aktuality, Slezska 7, Prague 2, 120 56, Czech Republic.

664.752 CZE ISSN 0862-2140
POTRAVINARSKE AKTUALITY. MLYNSKY, PEKARENSKY A CUKRARENSKY PRUMYSL. 1958-2000. 5/yr. Ustav Zemedelskych a Potravinarskych Informaci, Potravinarske Aktuality, Slezska 7, Prague 2, 120 56, Czech Republic.

663 CZE ISSN 0862-2159
POTRAVINARSKE AKTUALITY. NAPOJOVY PRUMYSL. 1958-2000. 10/yr. Ustav Zemedelskych a Potravinarskych Informaci, Potravinarske Aktuality, Slezska 7, Prague 2, 120 56, Czech Republic.

664 CZE ISSN 1211-7633
POTRAVINARSKE AKTUALITY. VYZIVA A LEGISLATIVA. 1991-2000. 5/yr. Ustav Zemedelskych a Potravinarskych Informaci, Potravinarske Aktuality, Slezska 7, Prague 2, 120 56, Czech Republic.

305.4 DEU ISSN 1433-7444
POTSDAMER STUDIEN ZUR FRAUEN- UND GESCHLECHTERFORSCHUNG. 1997-2006. irreg. Potsdamer Studien zur Frauen- und Geschlechterforschung e.V., Postfach 601553, Potsdam, 14415, Germany.

333.79 GBR ISSN 0950-1487 CODEN: PIHEE2
POWER INTERNATIONAL. 1955-1999. 6/yr. Lincoln Publications, 28 Centre Point House, St Giles High St, London, WC2H 8LW, United Kingdom.

796.7 ITA ISSN 1828-8472
POWER MOTO. 2006-200?. m. Sprea Editori Srl, Via Torino 51, Cernusco sul Naviglio, MI 20063, Italy.

537 GBR ISSN 0743-7137
POWER SOURCES. N.S. 1962-2003. biennial. Academic Press, 32 Jamestown Rd, Camden, London, NW1 7BY, United Kingdom.

616.4 USA ISSN 0730-3491
PRACTICAL DIABETOLOGY. 1982-2008. q. R.A. Rapaport Publishing, Inc., 150 W 22nd St, Ste 800, New York, NY 10011.

420 372 DNK ISSN 1901-5550
PRACTICAL ENGLISH. 2005-2006. q. Malling Beck, Laehegnet 71, Albertslund, 2620, Denmark.

610 GBR ISSN 0956-9588
PRACTICAL GUIDES FOR GENERAL PRACTICE. 198?-1994. irreg. Oxford University Press, Great Clarendon St, Oxford, OX2 6DP, United Kingdom.

364 USA
PRACTICAL TIPS FOR NEW YORK LAW ENFORCEMENT. 1994-200?. irreg. Gould Publications, Inc., 1333 North US Hwy 17-92, Longwood, FL 32750.

330 CZE ISSN 1211-3514
PRAGUE BUSINESS JOURNAL. 1996-2003. s-m. New World Publishing Inc., Sokolska 22, Prague 2, 120 00, Czech Republic.

914.37 CZE ISSN 1213-2128
PRAGUE IN YOUR POCKET. 2000-2002. 5/yr. Prague In Your Pocket, Vodickova 41, Prague 1, 11209, Czech Republic.

410 NLD ISSN 1383-7583
PRAGUE LINGUISTIC CIRCLE PAPERS/TRAVAUX DU CERCLE LINGUISTIQUE DE PRAGUE. 1995-2002 (vol.4). irreg. John Benjamins Publishing Co., PO Box 36224, Amsterdam, 1020 ME, Netherlands.

340.5 NLD
PRAKTIJKSERIE SOCIAAL RECHT. 1976; N.S. 1994-1997 (vol.3). irreg. Kluwer B.V., Postbus 23, Deventer, 7400 GA, Netherlands.

305.42 ITA ISSN 1120-4575
PRATICA. 1988-ceased. m. Fabbri Editori, Via Mecenate 91, Milan, 20138, Italy.

610.72 FRA ISSN 1764-9137
PRATIQUES DU SOIGNANT. 2004-2007. 4/yr. Elsevier France, Editions Scientifiques et Medicales, 23 Rue Linois, Paris, 75724, France.

352 CZE ISSN 1801-8319
PRAVNI RAADCE STAROSTY. 2002-2007. plus q. updates. Nakladatelstvi Dr. Josef Raabe, s.r.o., Sokolovska 155/31, Prague 8, 180 00, Czech Republic.

280.4 AUS
PRAYERS AND PROJECTS. 1930-2000. 3/yr. Uniting Church in Australia, 222 Pitt St, 8th Fl, Sydney S, NSW 1235, Australia.

660.6 USA ISSN 1542-9431 CODEN: PRECC8
PRECLINICA. 2003 (Mar./Apr.)-2004 (Nov.). bi-m. Eaton Publishing Co., One Research Dr, Suite 400A, PO Box 1070, Westboro, MA 01581.

016.37 CZE ISSN 1211-8079
PREHLED PEDAGOGICKE LITERATURY. RADA A. 1949-2004. bi-m. Ustav pro Informace ve Vzdelavani, Statni Pedagogicka Knihovna Komenskeho, Mikulandska 5, Prague 1, Czech Republic.

016.37 CZE ISSN 1211-8087
PREHLED PEDAGOGICKE LITERATURY. RADA B. 1949-2004. bi-m. Ustav pro Informace ve Vzdelavani, Statni Pedagogicka Knihovna Komenskeho, Mikulandska 5, Prague 1, Czech Republic.

760 ESP
PRENSA DE LA INDUSTRIA GRAFICA. 1989-ceased. 11/yr. Trebol Comunicacion S.A., Doctor Esquerdo, 105, Madrid, 28007, Spain.

372 373 DNK ISSN 1603-9106
PRENT; avisen i undervisningen. 2003-2008 (Dec.). 3/yr. Danske Dagblades Forening, Avisen i Undervisningen, c/o Pressens Hus, Skindergade 7, Copenhagen K, 1159, Denmark.

629.13 NLD ISSN 1018-8657 CODEN: PRFUEZ
PREPARING FOR THE FUTURE: E S A TECHNOLOGY QUARTERLY. 1991-2002 (vol.12, no.2). q. European Space Agency, Communication Production Office, Keplerlaan 1, Noordwijk, 2200 AG, Netherlands.

686.2244416 NLD ISSN 1386-2596
PREPRESS. 1990-2007. bi-m. ManagementMedia B.V., PO Box 1932, Hilversum, 1200 BX, Netherlands.

378 ITA ISSN 0478-1376
PRESENZA. 1969-ceased. q. Universita Cattolica del Sacro Cuore, Largo Gemelli 1, Milan, MI 20123, Italy.

055.1 ITA ISSN 1122-4320
PRESTIGE; motori, moda, costume. 1984-ceased. m. Ediauto S.r.l., Via Giovanni Battista Cassinis, 23, Milan, MI 20139, Italy.

340 USA ISSN 0734-1660
PREVENTIVE LAW REPORTER. 1965-2004. q. University of Denver, College of Law, 2255 E Evans Ave, Denver, CO 80208.

338.476 USA ISSN 1528-3496
PREVENTIVE MEDICINE IN MANAGED CARE. 2000-200?. q. Ascend Media, 7015 College Blvd, Ste 600, Overland Park, KS 66211.

332.6 ITA ISSN 0394-5367
PREVISIONI DELL'ECONOMIA ITALIANA. 1987-2000. s-a. Confederazione Generale dell'Industria Italiana (Confindustria), Centro Studi, Viale dell'Astronomia 30, Rome, 00144, Italy.

332.63 USA ISSN 1013-7440
PRICE PROSPECTS FOR MAJOR PRIMARY COMMODITIES. 1989-2005. biennial. World Bank Group, 1818 H St, NW, Washington, DC 20433.

338.1 USA
PRICES OF AGRICULTURAL PRODUCTS AND SELECTED INPUTS IN EUROPE AND NORTH AMERICA. 1950-1996. biennial. United Nations Publications, 2 United Nations Plaza, Rm DC2-853, New York, NY 10017.

610 362.1 USA ISSN 1096-8954 CODEN: PCRVFS
PRIMARY CARE CASE REVIEWS. 1998-2003. q. Lippincott Williams & Wilkins, 530 Walnut St, Philadelphia, PA 19106-3621.

330 DEU ISSN 1611-2741
PRIME REPORT; Deutschlands erster Boersenbrief fuer den Prime Standard. 1998-2004. w. Boersenmedien AG, Am Eulenhof 14, Kulmbach, 95326, Germany.

780 700 500 ITA
PRIMI PIANI; mensile d'arte, costume, cultura, scienza, spettacolo e turismo. 1964-ceased. m. Primi Piani, Via Bolzano, 32, Rome, RM 00198, Italy.

640 ITA ISSN 1593-4136
PRIMI PIATTI. 2001-ceased. m. Edigamma Publishing, Via Sambuca Pistoiese 70A, Rome, 00138, Italy.

300 ESP ISSN 1138-2759
PRINCIPE DE VIANA. SUPLEMENTO DE CIENCIAS SOCIALES. 1981-1999. a. Gobierno de Navarra, Fondo de Publicaciones, Calle de la Navas de Tolosa 21, Pamplona, Navarra 31002, Spain.

028.5 NLD ISSN 1574-7107
PRINSES. 2004-2008. m. Sanoma Uitgevers B.V., Postbus 1900, Hoofddorp, 2130 JH, Netherlands.

004 GBR ISSN 1466-0458
PRINT IT MAGAZINE; regular updates on PC and Mac driven printers. 1999-2001. q. Paper Trail Trading Ltd., Apsley Mills Cottage, London Rd, Hemel Hempstead, Herts HP3 9RY, United Kingdom.

686.22 AUS
PRINTING INDUSTRIES ASSOCIATION OF AUSTRALIA. NATIONAL BULLETIN. 1979-2001. bi-m. Printing Industries Association of Australia, Level 10, 99 York St, Sydney, NSW 2000, Australia.

686.2 USA ISSN 1084-1369
(YEAR) PRINTING INDUSTRY GOLD BOOK. 1995-2001. a. North American Publishing Co., 1500 Spring Garden St., Ste 1200, Philadelphia, PA 19130.

686.209 GBR ISSN 0079-5372
PRINTING TRADES DIRECTORY. 1960-2003. a. C M P Information Ltd., Sovereign House, Sovereign Way, Tonbridge, Kent TN9 1RW, United Kingdom.

371.3 USA
PRIORITIES IN PRACTICE. 1991-2007. irreg. Association for Supervision and Curriculum Development, 1703 N Beauregard St, Alexandria, VA 22311.

342 USA ISSN 1533-4597
PRIVACY LAW ADVISER. 2000-2002. bi-w. Pike & Fischer, Inc., 1010 Wayne Ave, Ste 1400, Silver Spring, MD 20910.

910.91 387.7 USA ISSN 1541-7913
PRIVATE AIR. 2002-2009. bi-m. Doubledown Media, LLC, 240 W 35th St, Fl 11, New York, NY 10001.

363.7 ITA
PRO NATURA GENOVA; periodico di informazione ai soci. 197?-ceased. q. Pro Natura Genova, c/o Museo di Storia Naturale, Via Brigata Liguria 9, Genoa, GE 16121, Italy.

330.9 BRD ISSN 0722-5792
PRO NORD. 1982-1982. m. Media-Mail Verlagsgesellschaft, Postfach 2453, Coburg, 96413, Germany.

629.118 DEU ISSN 0177-7661
PRO VELO. 1984-2002. s-a. Allgemeiner Deutscher Fahrrad-Club e.V., Gruenenstr 120, Bremen, 28199, Germany.

133 GBR ISSN 0260-8189
PROBE REPORT. 198?-1983. q. Probe, 16 Marigold Walk, Ashton, Bristol, BS3 2PD, United Kingdom.

794.1 ESP ISSN 0032-9223
PROBLEMAS. 1935; N.S. 1978 (3rd series)-ceased. q. Sociedad Espanola de Problemistas de Ajedrez, Avinguda Princep D'Asturies, 35 4 2a, Barcelona, 08012, Spain.

572 FRA ISSN 0555-2354
PROBLEMES ACTUELS DE BIOCHIMIE APPLIQUEE. 1967-1980. irreg. Elsevier Masson, 62 Rue Camille Desmoulins, Issy les Moulineaux, Cedex 92442, France.

100 055 ITA ISSN 0032-9339
PROBLEMI; periodico quadrimestrale di cultura. 1967-2001. 3/yr. G.B. Palumbo & C. Editore SpA, Via Ricasoli 59, Palermo, 90139, Italy.

370 ITA ISSN 0032-9347
I PROBLEMI DELLA PEDAGOGIA. 1955-ceased. bi-m. Marzorati Editore, Via Pordoi, 8, Settimo Milanese, MI 20019, Italy.

300 ITA
PROBLEMI DI CIVILTA. 1978-ceased. bi-m. Societa Editrice Napoletana s.r.l., Corso Umberto I, 1-34, Naples, NA 80138, Italy.

617 USA ISSN 0739-8328
PROBLEMS IN GENERAL SURGERY. 1984-2003 (vol.20, no.4). q. Lippincott Williams & Wilkins, 530 Walnut St, Philadelphia, PA 19106-3621.

055 ITA ISSN 0552-2323
LA PROCELLARIA. 1953-ceased. q. Procellaria Editrice, Via de Nova, 21c, Reggio Calabria, RC, Italy.

004 FRA ISSN 1141-9636
PROCESSEURS. 1989-199?. 42/yr. Porcedit, 182 rue du Faubourg Saint-Denis, Paris, 75010, France.

664.09 USA
PRODUCE SERVICES SOURCEBOOK. 1980-2004. a. Vance Publishing Corp., 10901 W 84th Terrace, Lexena, KS 66214.

333.7932 FRA ISSN 0429-4858
PRODUCTION DISTRIBUTION DE L'ENERGIE ELECTRIQUE EN FRANCE. 1955-1999. a. Direction du Gaz, de l'Electricite et du Charbon, 97-99 rue de Grenelle, Paris, Cedex 75700, France.

330.9 USA
PRODUCTIVITY BY INDUSTRY (YEAR). 1995-2000. a. U.S. Department of Labor, Bureau of Labor Statistics, Postal Square Bldg., 2 Massachusetts Ave, NE, Washington, DC 20212-0001.

651.2 DEU
PRODUKTUEBERSICHT: SEITEN - LASERDRUCKER. 1989-2005. s-a. Broetzmann e.K., Buedericher Str 14, Willich, 47877, Germany.

636 ITA ISSN 0033-0000
PRODUZIONE ANIMALE. 1962-ceased. q. Istituto della Produzione Animale, Facolta di Agraria, Portici, NA 80055, Italy.

808.8385 CZE ISSN 1801-9854
PROFESOR ZAMORRA. 2006-2006 (ceased same year). m. Moravska Bastei MOBA, s.r.o., Kotlarska 53, Brno, 602 00, Czech Republic.

331.5 FRA ISSN 1269-3790
PROFESSION FONCTIONNAIRE. 1996-2004. m. P.G.P. Rebondir, B.P. 101, Puteaux Cedex, 92803, France.

690 USA
PROFESSIONAL BUILDER'S HOME PLAN DATABASE CD-ROM. 19??-200?. a. HomePlans.com, 213 E. 4th St., 4th Fl., St. Paul, MN 55101-1603.

620 GBR ISSN 1468-3938
PROFESSIONAL ENGINEERING PUBLISHING. ENGINEERING RESEARCH SERIES. 1999-2004. q. Professional Engineering Publishing Ltd., 1 Birdcage Walk, London, SW1H 9JJ , United Kingdom.

338.1 AUS ISSN 0312-889X
PROFESSIONAL FARM MANAGEMENT GUIDEBOOK. 1965-1976. irreg. (approx. 1/yr.). University of New England, Agricultural Business Research Institute, Armidale, NSW 2351, Australia.

686.2 GBR ISSN 0308-4205
PROFESSIONAL PRINTER. 1968-2003. bi-m. Institute of Printing, The Mews, Hill House, Clanricarde Rd, Tunbridge Wells, Kent TN1 1PJ, United Kingdom.

331.21 USA ISSN 1042-4482
PROFESSIONAL, SALES & TECHNICAL REMUNERATION, CANADA. 1986-1987. a. Watson Wyatt Data Services, 218 Rte 17 N, Rochelle Park, NJ 07662.

635 ITA ISSN 1825-4152
PROGETTI FIORITI. 2005-200?. a. Sprea Editori Srl, Via Torino 51, Cernusco sul Naviglio, MI 20063, Italy.

687 ITA
PROGETTI MODA SHOES. 1990-ceased. 2/yr. Muggiani Giampiero Editore, Via IV Novembre 54, Settimo Milanese, MI 20019, Italy.

643.7 ITA ISSN 1970-9463
PROGETTO CASA. 2006-ceased. bi-m. Tattilo Editrice SpA, Via degli Olmetti 18, Rome, 00060, Italy.

327 NZL ISSN 1171-2031
PROGRAMME PROFILES - NEW ZEALAND OFFICIAL DEVELOPMENT ASSISTANCE. 1980-2002. a. Ministry of Foreign Affairs and Trade, c/o Publication Officer, Private Bag 18-901, Wellington, New Zealand.

610.28 DEU ISSN 1431-8202
PROGRESS IN BIOMEDICAL RESEARCH. 1996-2004. bi-m. Friedrich-Alexander University Erlangen-Nuremberg, Department of Biomedical Engineering, Henkestr 91, Erlangen, 91052, Germany.

571.6 NLD ISSN 0924-8315 CODEN: PRCREB
PROGRESS IN CELL RESEARCH. 1990-1997 (vol.7). irreg. Elsevier BV, Radarweg 29, P O Box 211, Amsterdam, 1000 AE, Netherlands.

615.9 GBR ISSN 0887-6142 CODEN: PPBTDV
PROGRESS IN PESTICIDE BIOCHEMISTRY AND TOXICOLOGY. 1981-1995. irreg. John Wiley & Sons Ltd., The Atrium, Southern Gate, Chichester, West Sussex PO19 8SQ, United Kingdom.

572.57 NLD ISSN 0168-9614 CODEN: PPLIEF
PROGRESS IN PROTEIN - LIPID INTERACTIONS. 1985-1986 (vol.2). irreg. Elsevier BV, Radarweg 29, P O Box 211, Amsterdam, 1000 AE, Netherlands.

616.7 ITA ISSN 1129-8758
PROGRESSI IN REUMATOLOGIA. 1999-2005. q. Mattioli 1885 SpA, Via Coduro 1, Fidenza, PR 43036, Italy.

352.91 NLD ISSN 1874-0014
PROJECTEN ABCDELFLAND. 2004-ceased. a. Hoogheemraadschap van Delfland, Postbus 3061, Delft, 2601 DB, Netherlands.

616.3 DEU ISSN 1615-8733
PROKTO. 2000-2002. bi-m. Edition Nymphenburg GmbH & Co. KG, Jakob-Endl-Str. 10, Passau, 94032, Germany.

358.4 DNK ISSN 0033-1279
PROPEL; tidsskrift for civil og militaer flyvning. 1943-2003. m. Luft- og Rumfartsforlaget, Kastanievej 4, Gudme, 5884, Denmark.

621.389 DEU ISSN 0945-750X
PROSOUND; Beschallungstechnik - Elektroakustik - PA-Systeme. 1993-2007 (Nov.). bi-m. Verlag Michel und Wedell GbR, Industriestr 59, Bochum, 44894, Germany.

363.7 ITA ISSN 1120-1681
PROTEC; il progresso e l'ambiente. 1986-ceased. 8/yr. Publi & Consult SpA, Via Tagliamento, 29, Rome, RM 00198, Italy.

820 GBR ISSN 0141-0334
PROTEUS (MILTON KEYNES). 1977-1978. irreg. Open University, Walton Hall, Milton Keynes, Bucks MK7 6AA, United Kingdom.

054 FRA ISSN 1951-1175
PROVENCE LIFE. 2006-2008. m. Provence Life, 13 ch. de Bellevue, Sainte-Anastasie-sur-Issole, 83136, France.

382 ITA ISSN 0033-1902
PROVINCIA DI FORLI IN CIFRE. 1959-1997; resumed 1999-ceased. w. Camera di Commercio Industria Artigianato e Agricoltura di Forli-Cesena, Corso della Repubblica 5, Forli', FC 47100, Italy.

305.235 NZL ISSN 1176-9408
PROVOKE NEWSLETTER. 2005-2006. 3/yr. Ministry of Youth Development, Level 1, Charles Fergusson West Block, Bowen St, PO Box 1556, Wellington, 6001, New Zealand.

800 700 ISR ISSN 0334-4975
PROZA; literary and art magazine. 1976-1993. m. Proza, P O Box 969, Ramat Gon, 52109, Israel.

664 CZE ISSN 0033-1988 CODEN: PPOTAP
PRUMYSL POTRAVIN/FOOD INDUSTRY; technika a ekonomika prumyslove vyroby potravin. 1950-1989. m. M K Press, Nam Jana Husa 83, Komarno, 26762, Czech Republic.

158 ESP ISSN 0213-0092
PSICOMOTRICIDAD. 1981-2002. irreg. Centro de Investigaciones de Tecnicas Aplicadas de Psicomotricidad, Jose Celestino Mutis 13-15, Madrid, 28028, Spain.

158.1 CZE ISSN 1213-3159
PSYCHE ET NATURA. 2000-2000 (ceased same year). s-a. Nakladatelstvi Tomase Janecka, Svatopluka Cecha 97, Brno, 612 00, Czech Republic.

616.8 USA
PSYCHIATRY IN PROGRESS. 1994-1996 (vol.3). irreg. Hogrefe Publishing Corp., 875 Massachusetts Ave, 7th Fl, Cambridge, MA 02139.

616.89 EGY ISSN 1110-760X
PSYCHIATRY UPDATE. 1998-200?. s-a. Ain Shams University, University Hospital, Abbassia, Cairo, Egypt.

110 054 FRA ISSN 1779-2525
PSYCHIC; la sagesse rencontre l'elegance. 2006-2007. m. Psychic Sarl, 65 Rue d'Amsterdam, Paris, 75008, France.

616.89 GBR ISSN 0264-1801
PSYCHOLOGICAL MEDICINE. MONOGRAPH SUPPLEMENT. 1982-1994 (vol.23). irreg. Cambridge University Press, The Edinburgh Bldg, Shaftesbury Rd, Cambridge, CB2 8RU, United Kingdom.

616.89 DEU ISSN 0935-2937
PSYCHOMED. 1989-2005. q. Ernst Reinhardt Verlag, Kemnatenstr 46, Munich, 80639, Germany.

370.15 150 DNK ISSN 0906-690X
PSYKOLOGISK PAEDAGOGISK RAADGIVNING. MONOGRAFI. 1969-1997. irreg. Forlaget Skolepsykologi, Havrevaenget 9, Herfoelge, 4681, Denmark.

028.5 FRA ISSN 0997-3745
P'TIT LOUP. 1989-2002. m. Disney Hachette Presse, 10 rue Thierry le Luron, Levallois Perret, Cedex 92592, France.

614 ISR ISSN 0301-0422 CODEN: PBHRAM
PUBLIC HEALTH REVIEWS; an international quarterly. 1972-2005. q. Technosdar Ltd., P O Box 31684, Tel Aviv, 61316, Israel.

020 AUS ISSN 0729-199X
PUBLIC LIBRARIES IN WESTERN AUSTRALIA. STATISTICAL BULLETIN. 1981-1998. a. Library and Information Service of Western Australia, Alexander Library Bldg., Perth Cultural Centre, Perth, W.A. 6000, Australia.

621.38 GBR ISSN 0963-5084
PUBLIC NETWORK EUROPE. 1990-2003. 10/yr. Public Network Europe, Axe and Bottle Ct, 70 Newcomen St, London, SE1 1YT, United Kingdom.

510 GBR ISSN 1366-2651
PUBLICATIONS OF THE NEWTON INSTITUTE. 1994-2009 (Aug.). irreg. Cambridge University Press, The Edinburgh Bldg, Shaftesbury Rd, Cambridge, CB2 8RU, United Kingdom.

352 NLD ISSN 1871-9384
PUBLIEKE DIENSTVERLENING: VAN VANDAAG NAAR MORGEN. 2005-ceased. irreg. Sdu Uitgevers bv, Postbus 20025, The Hague, 2500 EA, Netherlands.

659.1 ITA ISSN 0033-3999
PUBLITRANSPORT. 1961-ceased. q. Impresa Generale Pubblicita, Piazza Cavour, 1, Milan, MI 20121, Italy.

676 AUS ISSN 1449-9703
PULP & PAPER EDGE. 2004-2007. m. IndustryEdge, GPO Box 77, Hobart, TAS, Australia.

676.2 USA ISSN 1370-754X CODEN: PPEUFH
PULP & PAPER EUROPE. 1879; N.S. 1996-2002. bi-m. R I S I, Inc., 55 Hawthorne, Ste 510, San Francisco, CA 94105.

332.6 ESP
PULSO BURSATIL. ceased 1996. m. Banco Hispano Americano, Division de Banca Corporativa y Mercado de Capitales, Plaza Canalejas, 1, Madrid, 28014, Spain.

330 DEU ISSN 1439-0019
PUNCTO!. 1996-2005. 5/yr. Deutscher Sparkassenverlag GmbH, Am Wallgraben 115, Stuttgart, 70565, Germany.

780 USA ISSN 1047-4528
PUNCTURE; a magazine of music and the arts. 1982-199?. q. Puncture Magazine, PO Box 14806, Portland, OR 97293-0806.

028.5 364.4 ITA
PUNGOLO; periodico dei giovani. 1982-ceased. m. European Information Service, Via Col Romej, 7, Trapani, TP 91100, Italy.

055.1 ITA ISSN 0033-4294
PUNGOLO VERDE; arti-science e lettere. 1947-ceased. m. Pungolo Verde, PO Box 54, Campobasso, CB 86100, Italy.

330.9 ITA ISSN 0391-3082
PUNTO; rivista di economia di Como, Lecco, Varese, Alto Milanese e Canton Ticino. 1980-ceased. bi-m. Fratelli Pini Editori s.r.l., Via L. Battista Alberti 10, Milan, MI 20149, Italy.

001.3 ITA
PUNTO D'INCONTRO; rivista di attualita politica, di economia, cultura, costume. 1978-ceased. q. Punto d'Incontro, Via V Veneto, 5, Lanciano, CH 66034, Italy.

820 FRA ISSN 1169-2111
Q - W - E - R - T - Y; arts, litteratures & civilisations du monde anglophone. 1991-2002. a. Publications de l'Universite de Pau (PUP), Bibliotheque Sciences, Avenue de l'Universite, Pau, 64000, France.

301 401 780 ITA ISSN 1126-8441
QUADERNI DE L'UOMO. 1977-ceased. irreg. Universita degli Studi di Roma "La Sapienza", 5 Piazzale Aldo Moro, Rome, 00185, Italy.

945 850 ITA ISSN 1125-3916
I QUADERNI DEL CARDELLO. 1990-2001 (no.11). a. Angelo Longo Editore, Via Paolo Costa 33, Ravenna, 48121, Italy.

616.8 ITA ISSN 0515-2976
QUADERNI DI ACTA NEUROLOGICA. 1950-ceased. irreg. Istituto di Clinica delle Malattie Nervose e Mentali, Policlinico USL BA4, Piazza G. Cesare, Bari, 70124 , Italy.

640 ITA ISSN 1724-157X
I QUADERNI DI CONFESSIONE DONNA. I LAVORI DI CASA. 2003-200?. bi-m. Edizioni Mimosa, Piazza E de Angeli 9, Milan, 20146, Italy.

746 ITA ISSN 1724-1545
I QUADERNI DI CONFESSIONE DONNA. IL PUNTO CROCE. 2002-200?. bi-m. Edizioni Mimosa, Piazza E de Angeli 9, Milan, 20146, Italy.

746 ITA ISSN 1724-1553
I QUADERNI DI CONFESSIONE DONNA. LA MAGLIA. 1998-200?. bi-m. Edizioni Mimosa, Piazza E de Angeli 9, Milan, 20146, Italy.

700 ITA
QUADERNI DI STORIA DELL'ARTE. 1966-2002 (no.21). irreg. Universita degli Studi di Parma, Via Universita 12, Parma, PR 43100, Italy.

913 526 ITA ISSN 1122-0953
QUADERNI DI TOPOGRAFIA ANTICA. 1961-1988. irreg. Casa Editrice Leo S. Olschki, Viuzzo del Pozzetto 8, Florence, 50126, Italy.

945 ITA ISSN 0392-1875
QUADERNI MEDIEVALI. 1976-2005. s-a. Edizioni Dedalo, Viale Luigi Jacobini 5, Bari, BA 70123, Italy.

780 ITA ISSN 1128-1715
QUADERNI PUCCINIANI. 1982-199?. irreg. Istituto di Studi Pucciniani, Fondazione Simonetta Puccini, Viale Puccini 266, Torre del Lago, Lucca 55048, Italy.

320 ITA ISSN 1971-419X
QUADERNI ROMANI; rivista di discussione e proposta politica. 1992-1993. bi-m. Sapere 2000 S.r.l., Via Filippo Turati, 48, Rome, RM 00185, Italy.

144 300 ITA ISSN 1593-5272
QUADERNI SARDI DI FILOSOFIA, LETTERATURA E SCIENZE UMANE. 1977-200?. s-a. Mondadori - Libreria Dessi, Largo Cavallotti 17, Sassari, SS 07100, Italy.

945 ITA ISSN 1125-1824
QUADERNI SARDI DI STORIA. 1980-198?. irreg. Mondadori - Libreria Dessi, Largo Cavallotti 17, Sassari, SS 07100, Italy.

340 ESP ISSN 1695-8438
QUADERNS DE DRET LOCAL. 2002-2005. 3/yr. Diputacio de Barcelona, Rambla de Catalunya 126, Barcelona, 08008, Spain.

055.1 ITA
QUADRILATERO. 1990-ceased. q. Multimedia s.a.s., Corso de Michetti, 80, Teramo, TE 64100, Italy.

808.87 USA
QUAGMIRE; livellafotoorehtsitnemnrevog. 1981-2006. biennial. N O T - S A F E, PO Box 5743 PD, Santa Barbara, CA 93150-5743.

362 USA ISSN 1047-5311
THE QUALITY LETTER FOR HEALTHCARE LEADERS. 1989-2005. m. Lippincott Williams & Wilkins, 530 Walnut St, Philadelphia, PA 19106-3621.

649 AUS ISSN 1320-1867
QUALITY TIME; the free magazine for parents. 1993-2003. bi-m. Telling Words Company Pty Ltd., 161 Barkly Ave, Richmond, VIC 3121, Australia.

658.3 USA ISSN 1072-9135
THE QUALITY YEARBOOK. 1994-2002. a. McGraw-Hill Companies, Inc., 1221 Ave of the Americas, 43rd fl, New York, NY 10020.

330 CHN ISSN 1002-6584
QUANGUO QINGGONG XINXI/CHINA LIGHT INDUSTRIES NEWS. 1986-2001. w. Zhonguo Qinggongye Jingji Keji Xinxi Zhongxin, 22 B Fuwai Dajie, Beijing, 100833, China.

500 610 ITA ISSN 1592-5021
QUARK. 2001-2006. m. Hachette Rusconi SpA, Viale Sarca 235, Milan, 20126, Italy.

331.11 FRA ISSN 0255-3627
QUARTERLY LABOUR FORCE STATISTICS/O C D E STATISTIQUES TRIMESTRIELLES DE LA POPULATION ACTIVE. 1983-2004. q. Organisation for Economic Cooperation and Development (O E C D), 2 Rue Andre Pascal, Paris, 75775 Cedex 16, France.

305.42 ITA ISSN 0048-6205
QUARTO MONDO. 1971-ceased. m. Fronte Italiano di Liberazione Femminile, Piazza Santi Apostoli, 49, Rome, RM 00187, Italy.

633.1 AUS ISSN 1321-1986
QUEENSLAND GRAINGROWER. 1969-1995. w. Western Publishers Pty. Ltd., 10 Joseph St, PO Box 188, Toowoomba, QLD 4350, Australia.

325 ITA ISSN 1825-2583
QUELLI DI FUORI; dall'emigrazione all'immigrazione: il caso italiano. 2002-2002. irreg. Franco Angeli Edizioni, Viale Monza 106, Milan, 20127, Italy.

282 FRA ISSN 1276-5910
QUESTIONS ACTUELLES. 1998-2004. bi-m. Bayard Presse, 3-5 rue Bayard, Paris, 75393 Cedex 08, France.

384.5 ITA
QUI RAI. N.S. 1995-ceased. q. Rai International, Casella Postale 320, Rome, RM 00100, Italy.

640 USA ISSN 1556-7397
QUICK & SIMPLE. 2005 (Aug.)-2008. w. Hearst Magazines, 300 W 57th St, 12th Fl, New York, NY 10019.

917.59 USA ISSN 1535-5705
QUICK ESCAPES: FLORIDA; 29 weekend escapes in and around the sunshine state. 1998-2006. biennial (Every 2-3 yrs.). The Globe Pequot Press, Inc., 246 Goose Ln, PO Box 480, Guilford, CT 06437.

917.4 338.4791 USA ISSN 1551-6830
QUICK ESCAPES: PITTSBURGH; 26 weekend getaways from the Steel City. 2001-200?. irreg. The Globe Pequot Press, Inc., 246 Goose Ln, PO Box 480, Guilford, CT 06437.

746 USA ISSN 1059-0684
QUILT. 19??-ceased. q. Harris Publications, Inc., 800 Kennesaw Ave, Ste 220, Marietta, GA 30060.

410 800 GBR ISSN 0140-3397
QUINQUEREME; new studies in modern languages. 1977-1990. s-a. Claverton Down Bath Quinquereme, School of Modern Languages, The University, Bath, Avon BA2 7AY, United Kingdom.

054.1 FRA ISSN 1274-3526
QUO; les cles de la vie quotidienne. 1996-2000. m. Hachette Filipacchi Medias S.A., 149/151 Rue Anatole France, Levallois-Perret, 925340, France.

646 CZE ISSN 1211-7129
QUO. 1997-2003. m. Hachette Filipacchi 2000 s.r.o., Na Zatorce 3, Prague 6, 160 00, Czech Republic.

005.8 USA
R A C F UPDATE. (Resource Access Control Facility) ceased. q. Xephon, 9330 Lyndon B Johnson Fwy., Ste. 800, Dallas, TX 75243-4310.

500 USA ISSN 0033-6793
R & D CONTRACTS MONTHLY; a continuously up-dated sales and R & D tool for all research organizations and manufacturers. (Research & Development) 1962-1994. m. Government Data Publications, Inc., 2300 M St, NW, Washington, DC 20037.

781.546 USA ISSN 1076-6502
R & R. 1973-2009. w. (Fri.). Radio & Records, Inc., 2049 Century Park East, 41st Fl, Los Angeles, CA 90067.

747 AUS ISSN 1832-116X
R + B HOME. (Renovate + Build) 2004-2006. 3/yr. Prestige Publications, PO Box 8337, Woolloongabba, QLD 4102, Australia.

780 GBR ISSN 0965-190X
R C D. (Rock Compact Disc Magazine) 1992-1993. m. Northern & Shell Plc, The Northern & Shell Bldg, Number 10 Lower Thames St, London, EC3R 6EN, United Kingdom.

384.5 USA ISSN 1533-0796
R C R WIRELESS NEWS. 1981-2009 (Mar.). w. Crain Communications, Inc., 1746 Cole Blvd, Ste 150, Golden, CO 80401.

630 KOR
R D A JOURNAL OF AGRICULTURAL SCIENCE. (Rural Development Administration) 1958-1996. s-a. Rural Development Administration, Research Support Division, Suwon, 441707, Korea, S.

374.4 ESP ISSN 1131-8783
R E D. (Revista de Educacion a Distancia) 1991-2001. 3/yr. C I D E A D, C. Argumosa, 43, Madrid, 28012, Spain.

150 FRA ISSN 1025-3807
R E I R P R. CAHIERS. (Reseau Europeen Interdisciplinaire de Recherche sur Psychologie et Reanimation) 1992-2005. irreg. Reseau Europeen Interdisciplinaire de Recherche sur Psychologie et Reanimation, 4, Rue de Provence, Ostwald, 67540, France.

371.911 USA ISSN 0899-1510
R E: VIEW; rehabilitation and education for blindness and visual impairment. (Rehabilitation and Education) 1969-2008 (Aug.). q. Heldref Publications, 1319 18th St, NW, Washington, DC 20036-1802.

Cessations

327   CZE
R F E - R L NEWSLINE. (Radio Free Europe - Radio Liberty) 1990-2008 (May). 5/w. Radio Free Europe - Radio Liberty Inc., Publications Department, Vinohradska 1, Prague 1, 110 00, Czech Republic.

352   FRA   ISSN 1958-1254
R H PUBLIQUES. 1999-2008. m. Editions Weka, 249 Rue de Crimee, Paris, 75935 Cedex 19, France.

380.5   DEU   ISSN 0935-915X
R K W HANDBUCH FUEHRUNGSTECHNIK UND ORGANISATION. (Rationalisierungs Kuratorium der Deutschen Wirtschaft) 1978-2008. plus updates 2/yr. Erich Schmidt Verlag GmbH & Co. (Berlin), Genthiner Str 30 G, Berlin, 10785, Germany.

059.918   CZE   ISSN 0862-6375
R O K. (Revue Otevrene Kultury) 1990-1993. 6/yr. Spolecnost Jana Skacela, Gorkeho 16, Brno, 60200, Czech Republic.

016.65   AUS   ISSN 1440-9127
R S P A S PRINT NEWS. 1998-2004. irreg. Coombs Academic Publishing, Canberra, ACT 0200, Australia.

658.7   USA   ISSN 0887-3003
R T W REVIEW. (Ready To Wear) 1985-200?. bi-m. Creative Concepts Group, 1970 Norhardt Dr., Unit D, Brookfield, WI 53045-5086.

642   CZE   ISSN 1801-8335
RAADCE GASTRONOMICKEHO PROVOZU. 2002-2005. plus irreg. updates. Nakladatelstvi Dr. Josef Raabe, s.r.o., Sokolovska 155/31, Prague 8, 180 00, Czech Republic.

296.0711   USA
RABBINICAL ASSEMBLY. PROCEEDINGS. 1927-1970; N.S. 1973-2004. a. Rabbinical Assembly, 3080 Broadway, New York, NY 10027.

296.0711   USA   ISSN 1042-1807
RABBINICAL COUNCIL OF AMERICA. SERMON ANTHOLOGY. 1943-19??. a. Rabbinical Council of America, 305 Seventh Ave, 12th Fl, New York, NY 10001.

794.8   ITA   ISSN 1825-1315
RACCOLTA CODICI. 2005-200?. bi-m. Tattilo Editrice SpA, Via degli Olmetti 18, Rome, 00060, Italy.

851   ITA   ISSN 1824-6311
RACCONTARE LA POESIA. 1998-ceased. irreg. Silva Editore, Via Nazionale 23, Collecchio, Parma 43044, Italy.

305.8   GBR   ISSN 0033-7358
RACE TODAY. 1960-198?. bi-m. Race Today Collective, Brixton, 165 Railton Rd, London, SE24 0LU, United Kingdom.

700 800 851   ITA
RADAR - SEI; rivista mensile di attualita-arte-cultura. 1973-ceased. m. Organizzazione "X" di Armando Rositani, Corso Cavour, 113, Bari, BA 70121, Italy.

796.156   USA   ISSN 1529-8361
RADIO CONTROL NITRO. 2000-2005. 8/yr. Air Age Media, 100 E Ridge, Ridgefield, CT 06877-4606.

616.07   USA   ISSN 1069-1286   CODEN: RIOLEC
THE RADIOLOGIST. 1994-2004. bi-m. Lippincott Williams & Wilkins, 351 W Camden St, Baltimore, MD 21201.

385   NZL   ISSN 1176-9564
RAIL NEWSLETTER. 2003-2006. irreg. New Zealand Transport Agency, Lambton Quay, PO Box 5084, Wellington, 6145, New Zealand.

790.133   USA   ISSN 1043-5441
RAILMODEL JOURNAL; modeling from the prototype. 1989-2008. m. Golden Bell Press Inc., 2403 Champa St, Denver, CO 80205.

385   NZL   ISSN 0110-6155
RAILS. 1971-2003. m. Southern Press Ltd., R.D. 1, Porirua, Wellington, New Zealand.

028.5   CZE
RAINBOW & RAINDROPS. 1949-199?. 10/yr. Publishing House R & R, Preslickova 2886, Prague, 10600, Czech Republic.

746   ITA   ISSN 1825-8034
RAKAM COLLEZIONE. 1992-ceased. s-a. Hachette Rusconi SpA, Viale Sarca 235, Milan, 20126, Italy.

796.72   ITA   ISSN 1124-5409
RALLY & MOTORI. 1993-200?. m. Barbero Editori Srl, Via Galileo Galilei 3, Chieri, TO 10023, Italy.

910.202   USA   ISSN 1057-9834
RAND MCNALLY WORLD FACTS & MAPS. 19??-2000. irreg. Rand McNally & Co., PO Box 7600, Chicago, IL 60680.

371.20021   USA   ISSN 1931-4809
RANKINGS & ESTIMATES: RANKINGS OF THE STATES AND ESTIMATES OF SCHOOL STATISTICS. 1999-200?. a. National Education Association of the United States, 1201 16th St, N W, Washington, DC 20036.

621   USA   ISSN 1544-9491
RAPID PROTOTYPING. 1995-2008. q. Society of Manufacturing Engineers, One SME Dr, PO Box 930, Dearborn, MI 48121.

016.669   GBR   ISSN 0307-8531
RARE EARTH BULLETIN. 1973-2006. bi-m. Multi-Science Publishing Co. Ltd., 5 Wates Way, Brentwood, Essex CM15 9TB, United Kingdom.

664   ITA
RASSEGNA ALIMENTARE. 1981-ceased. 6/yr. Zeus International Srl, Viale Lunigiana 14, Milan, MI 20125, Italy.

327   ITA
RASSEGNA DEL MONDO ARABO. N.S. 1976-ceased. m. Lega degli Stati Arabi a Roma, Piazzale delle Belle Arti 6, Rome, RM, Italy.

333.33 340   ITA   ISSN 1128-1820
RASSEGNA DELLE LOCAZIONI E DEL CONDOMINIO. 1979-2006. 3/yr. C E D A M, Via Giuseppe Jappelli 5-6, Padua, PD 35121, Italy.

382   ITA   ISSN 0483-9722
RASSEGNA DI DIRITTO E TECNICA DOGANALE E DELLE IMPOSTE DI FABBRICAZIONE. 1952-ceased. m. Rassegna di Diritto e Tecnica Doganale e delle Imposte di Fabbricazione, Via Conca D'Oro, 348, Rome, RM 00141, Italy.

340   ITA   ISSN 0033-9512
RASSEGNA DI DIRITTO PUBBLICO. 1945-ceased. q. Edizioni Scientifiche Italiane SpA, Via Chiatamone 7, Naples, NA 80121, Italy.

615.53   ITA   ISSN 0481-780X
RASSEGNA DI MEDICINA OMEOPATICA. 1953-199?. q. Palombi Editore, Via Gregorio VII 224, Rome, 00165, Italy.

700   ITA
RASSEGNA DI STUDI E DI NOTIZIE. 1973-2006 (vol.30, no.33). a. Settore Cultura e Musei, Civiche Raccolte d'Arte Applicata ed Incisioni, Castello Sforzesco, Milan, 20121, Italy.

945   ITA
RASSEGNA ECONOMICA DELLA PROVINCIA DI SONDRIO. 1948-ceased. bi-m. Camera di Commercio Industria Artigianato e Agricoltura di Sondrio, Via Giuseppe Piazzi 23, Sondrio, SO 23100, Italy.

618.92   ITA   ISSN 0390-0495
RASSEGNA ITALIANA DI CHIRURGIA PEDIATRICA. 1959-ceased. q. Il Pensiero Scientifico Editore, Via Bradano 3-C, Rome, 00199, Italy.

636.089   ITA   ISSN 1724-8892
RASSEGNA MEDICA FELINA. 1992-ceased. q. Mattioli 1885 SpA, Via Coduro 1, Fidenza, PR 43036, Italy.

610   ITA   ISSN 1123-9166
RASSEGNA MEDICO-CHIRURGICA. 1978-2004. q. M & S S Management and Scientific Service, Viale Mellusi, 134, Benevento, BN 82100, Italy.

782.1   ITA   ISSN 0033-9784
RASSEGNA MELODRAMMATICA; corriere di musica. 1890-ceased. s-m. Rassegna Melodrammatica, Via Alfredo Oriani, 4, Milan, MI 20122, Italy.

336   ITA   ISSN 0393-4098
RASSEGNA MENSILE DELLA IMPOSTE DIRETTE. 1952-ceased. m. Rassegna Mensile della Imposte Dirette, c/o Antonino La Mattina, Ed., Via Fregene, 14, Rome, RM 00183, Italy.

945   ITA
RASSEGNA STORICA PONTINA; quadrimestrale di studi risorgimentali. 1993-ceased. 3/yr. Istituto per la Storia del Risorgimento Italiano, Comitato di Latina, Via Ovidio, 57, Latina, LT 04100, Italy.

800   NLD   ISSN 0924-0934
RASTER. 1977-2009. q. Uitgeverij De Bezige Bij, Postbus 75184, Amsterdam, 1070 AD, Netherlands.

700   NLD   ISSN 1871-3432
READER. 2004-2005. s-a. De Appel, Nieuwe Spiegelstraat 10, Amsterdam, 1017 DE, Netherlands.

687   DEU   ISSN 0935-6452
READYWEAR. 1972-1994. 2/yr. Fachpresse-Verlag Michael Steinert, An der Alster 21, Hamburg, 20099, Germany.

006.6   GBR   ISSN 1077-2014   CODEN: REIMFQ
REAL-TIME IMAGING. 1995-2005. bi-m. Academic Press, 32 Jamestown Rd, Camden, London, NW1 7BY, United Kingdom.

616.6   GBR   ISSN 1464-2883
RECENT ADVANCES IN UROLOGY. 1957-200?. irreg. W.B. Saunders Co. Ltd., 32 Jamestown Rd, Camden, London, NW1 7BY, United Kingdom.

307.14   FRA   ISSN 1283-0712
RECHERCHE URBAINE. 1973-1978. irreg. College de France, Ecole des Hautes Etudes en Sciences Sociales (E H E S S), 54 Boulevard Raspail, Paris, 75006, France.

347 362.5   NLD   ISSN 0920-0568
RECHTSHULP. 1977-2004. 10/yr. Paris Legal Publishers, Postbus 4083, Zutphen, 7200 BB, Netherlands.

340 341   DEU
RECHTSSTAAT IN DER BEWAEHRUNG. 1975-2002 (vol.36). irreg. C.F. Mueller Verlag Huethig GmbH & Co. KG, Im Weiher 10, Heidelberg, 69121, Germany.

306.4   USA   ISSN 1554-4389
RECREATION; having a good time in America. 1999-2007. biennial. Gale, 27500 Drake Rd, Farmington Hills, MI 48331.

301   USA   ISSN 0894-4830
RECREATION: CURRENT SELECTED RESEARCH. 1988-1991. a. A M S Press, Inc., Brooklyn Navy Yard, 63 Flushing Ave, Bldg 292, Unit #221, Brooklyn, NY 11205.

790.1   USA   ISSN 1046-316X
RECREATION RESOURCES; new products, services & ideas for planning tomorrow's facilities. 1981-2002. 9/yr. Adams Business Media, 2101 S Arlington Heights Rd, 150, Arlington, IL 60005.

341 327   FRA   ISSN 0994-8554
LE RECUEIL DES TRAITES ET ACCORDS DE LA FRANCE. 1994-2004. m. Direction des Journaux Officiels, 26 rue Desaix, Paris, 75727 Cedex 15 , France.

015   ESP   ISSN 1132-6840
RED DE BIBLIOTECAS UNIVERSITARIAS; catalogo colectivo. 1992-ceased. s-a. D O C 6 S.A., Mallorca, 272, Barcelona, 08015, Spain.

057.86   CZE   ISSN 1213-273X
REDHOT. 2001-2008. w. Stratosfera s.r.o., Drtinova 8, Prague 5, 150 00, Czech Republic.

929   USA   ISSN 1076-2957
REED READ REID ROOTS. 1994-1996. irreg. (2-4/yr.). Family Publications, 5628 60th Dr, NE, Marysville, WA 98270.

599   ISR   ISSN 0334-1461
RE'EM. 1982-1988. a. Society for the Protection of Nature in Israel, 4 Hashefela St, Tel Aviv, 66183, Israel.

016.3071   DEU   ISSN 0341-2512
REFERATEBLATT ZUR RAUMENTWICKLUNG. 1968-2001. q. Bundesamt fuer Bauwesen und Raumordnung, Deichmanns Aue 31-37, Bonn, 53179, Germany.

016.572   RUS
REFERATIVNYI ZHURNAL. BIOORGANICHESKAYA KHIMIYA. MAKROMOLEKULY; vypusk razdela-toma. 1982-2007. m. Vserossiiskii Institut Nauchnoi i Tekhnicheskoi Informatsii (VINITI), Ul Usievicha 20, Moscow, 125190, Russian Federation.

016.33 016.664   RUS
REFERATIVNYI ZHURNAL. EKONOMIKA OTRASLEI PISHCHEVOI I LEGKOI PROMYSHLENNOSTI; vypusk svodnogo toma. 1960-2008 (Dec.). m. Vserossiiskii Institut Nauchnoi i Tekhnicheskoi Informatsii (VINITI), Ul Usievicha 20, Moscow, 125190, Russian Federation.

016.6151 016.58   RUS
REFERATIVNYI ZHURNAL. LEKARSTVENNYE RASTENIYA; vypusk razdela-toma. 1991-2008 (Dec.). m. Vserossiiskii Institut Nauchnoi i Tekhnicheskoi Informatsii (VINITI), Ul Usievicha 20, Moscow, 125190, Russian Federation.

016.669   RUS   ISSN 0202-9685
REFERATIVNYI ZHURNAL. TEKHNICHESKII ANALIZ V METALURGII; vypusk svodnogo toma. 1961-2008 (Dec.). m. Vserossiiskii Institut Nauchnoi i Tekhnicheskoi Informatsii (VINITI), Ul Usievicha 20, Moscow, 125190, Russian Federation.

016.62148   RUS   ISSN 0034-2653
REFERATIVNYI ZHURNAL. YADERNYE REAKTORY; otdel'nyi vypusk. 1958-2008 (Dec.). m. Vserossiiskii Institut Nauchnoi i Tekhnicheskoi Informatsii (VINITI), Ul Usievicha 20, Moscow, 125190, Russian Federation.

616.6   CZE   ISSN 1212-320X
REFERATOVY VYBER A AKTUALITY Z UROLOGIE/ABSTRACTS OF UROLOGY. 1979-2005. q. Narodni Lekarska Knihovna, Sokolska 54, Prague, 12132, Czech Republic.

900   USA   ISSN 1054-9110
REFERENCE GUIDES TO ARCHIVAL AND MANUSCRIPT SOURCES IN WORLD HISTORY. 1991-19??. irreg. Greenwood Publishing Group Inc., 88 Post Rd W, PO Box 5007, Westport, CT 06881.

900   USA   ISSN 0885-7555
REFERENCE GUIDES TO ARCHIVES AND MANUSCRIPT COLLECTIONS ON IMMIGRANT CULTURE. 1986-19??. irreg. Greenwood Publishing Group Inc., 88 Post Rd W, PO Box 5007, Westport, CT 06881.

900   USA
REFERENCE GUIDES TO STATE HISTORY AND RESEARCH. 1982-19??. irreg. Greenwood Publishing Group Inc., 88 Post Rd W, PO Box 5007, Westport, CT 06881.

300   USA   ISSN 0730-3335
REFERENCE SOURCES FOR THE SOCIAL SCIENCES AND HUMANITIES. 1982-19??. irreg. Greenwood Publishing Group Inc., 88 Post Rd W, PO Box 5007, Westport, CT 06881.

331.88   DNK   ISSN 1604-5076
REFLEKS. 1901-2007. q. HK Trafik og Jernbane, Weidekampsgade 8, PO Box 470, Copenhagen C, 0900, Denmark.

797.1   ITA
REFOLADE. 1985-ceased. 3/yr. Societa Velica Barcola Grignano, Viale Miramare 32, Trieste, TS 34134, Italy.

630   AUS   ISSN 1329-184X
REFORM (KINGSTON). 1997-2002. q. National Farmers Federation, PO Box E10, Kingston, ACT 2604, Australia.

280.4   GBR   ISSN 0034-3080
REFORMER. 1930-19??. bi-m. Protestant Alliance, 77 Ampthill Rd, Flitwick, Bedford, Beds MK45 1BD, United Kingdom.

621.56   ESP   ISSN 1133-7761
REFRIGERACION - FRIAL. 1987-2001. q. El Instalador, S.A., C/Navaleno, 9, Madrid, 28033, Spain.

629.136   FRA   ISSN 1141-5304
REGARDS. 1966-199?. q. Comite d'Etablissement Air France-Orly Sud, Extension Est, Batiment CRP, Aerogare d'Orly Sud, France.

314.021   GBR   ISSN 1740-6013
REGION IN FIGURES. EAST. 1999-2005. s-a. Office for National Statistics, Rm 1015, Government Bldgs, Newport, NP10 8XG, United Kingdom.

314.021   GBR   ISSN 1740-6021
REGION IN FIGURES. EAST MIDLANDS. 1999-2005. s-a. Office for National Statistics, Rm 1015, Government Bldgs, Newport, NP10 8XG, United Kingdom.

314.021   GBR   ISSN 1740-6048
REGION IN FIGURES. NORTH EAST. 1999-2005. s-a. Office for National Statistics, Rm 1015, Government Bldgs, Newport, NP10 8XG, United Kingdom.

314.021   GBR   ISSN 1740-6080
REGION IN FIGURES. NORTH WEST. 1999-2005. s-a. Office for National Statistics, Rm 1015, Government Bldgs, Newport, NP10 8XG, United Kingdom.

314.021   GBR   ISSN 1740-6056
REGION IN FIGURES. SOUTH EAST. 1999-2005. s-a. Office for National Statistics, Rm 1015, Government Bldgs, Newport, NP10 8XG, United Kingdom.

314.021   GBR   ISSN 1740-6072
REGION IN FIGURES. WEST MIDLANDS. 1999-2005. s-a. Office for National Statistics, Rm 1015, Government Bldgs, Newport, NP10 8XG, United Kingdom.

314.021   GBR   ISSN 1740-6099
REGION IN FIGURES. YORKSHIRE AND THE HUMBER. 1999-2005. s-a. Office for National Statistics, Rm 1015, Government Bldgs, Newport, NP10 8XG, United Kingdom.

664   AUS   ISSN 1832-6781
REGIONAL FOOD AUSTRALIA. 2005-2008; suspended. q. Regional Food Communications, PO Box 1113, Glebe Point, NSW 2037, Australia.

330.9   ITA
REGIONE ABRUZZO. 1972-ceased. m. Consiglio Regionale dell'Abruzzo, Via Michele Jacobucci 4, L'Aquila, 67100, Italy.

338.642   NLD   ISSN 1873-9504
REGIOPINIE (ED. BRABANT/ZEELAND). 2004-2007. bi-m. Uitgever De Status Magazine, Kuiperbergweg 2, Amsterdam, 1101 AG, Netherlands.

338.642 NLD ISSN 1872-4825
REGIOPINIE (NORTHWEST NETHERLANDS EDITION). 2004-2007. q. Uitgever De Status Magazine, Kuiperbergweg 2, Amsterdam, 1101 AG, Netherlands.

338.642 NLD ISSN 1872-4817
REGIOPINIE (RHINE EDITION). 2004-2007. q. Uitgever De Status Magazine, Kuiperbergweg 2, Amsterdam, 1101 AG, Netherlands.

200 DEU ISSN 0174-0091
REGULAE BENEDICTI STUDIA. ANNUARIUM INTERNATIONALE. 1972-2001 (vol.20). irreg. E O S Verlag, Erzabtei St. Ottilien, St.Ottilien, 86941, Germany.

800 AUS ISSN 1832-4681
REID'S MAGAZINE; the short fiction & poetry magazine. 2005-2006. m. Attalanta Press, PO Box 513, Rosny, TAS 7018, Australia.

910.91 DEU ISSN 1611-6569
REISE BILD. 2003 (Mar.)-2006. 2/yr. Axel Springer Verlag AG, Axel-Springer-Platz 1, Hamburg, 20350, Germany.

268 ITA ISSN 1125-7156
RELIGIONE E SCUOLA; rivista dell'insegnante di religione. 1972-2006. 5/yr. Editrice Queriniana, Via Enrico Ferri 75, Brescia, BS 25123, Italy.

200 USA ISSN 1057-2961
RELIGIOUS LEADERS OF AMERICA. 1991-ceased. triennial. Gale, 27500 Drake Rd, Farmington Hills, MI 48331.

296.68 ISR
RELIGIOUS ZIONISM IN ACTION - ESSAYS/MESILOT. 1984-2001. a. Mizrachi Hapoel Hamizrachi World Organization, 54 King George St., Jerusalem, Israel.

057.86 CZE ISSN 1214-617X
RELOAD. 2004-2007. fortn. Stratosfera s.r.o., Drtinova 8, Prague 5, 150 00, Czech Republic.

070.50688 ITA ISSN 0034-4176
REMAINDERS' BOOK ITALIANO; il servizio internazionale per l'acquisto del libro a meta del prezzo di copertina. 1967 (no.3)-ceased. q. Libreria Internazionale Guida, Via Port'Alba, 20-21-24, Naples, NA 80134, Italy.

332 ESP ISSN 0034-4184
REMANSO. 1958-197?. bi-m. Caja de Ahorros y Monte de Piedad de Zaragoza, Aragon y Rioja, San Jorge, 8, Zaragoza, 50001, Spain.

325.1 FRA ISSN 0766-6500
REMISIS. 1985-1999. q. REMISIS URMIS, Rack 7027, 2 Jussieu Place, Paris, 75251, France.

526.982 AUS ISSN 1441-7723
REMOTE SENSING AND PHOTOGRAMMETRY NEWS. 1992-2002. 3/yr. Remote Sensing & Photogrammetry Association of Australia, PO Box 471, Wembley, W.A. 6014, Australia.

809 GBR ISSN 1362-1149
RENAISSANCE FORUM; an electronic journal of early-modern literary and historical studies. 1996-2004. 2/yr. University of Hull, Department of History, University Of Hull, Cottingham Rd, Hull, HU6 7RX, United Kingdom.

333.79 GBR ISSN 0306-364X
RENEWABLE ENERGY BULLETIN. 1974-2005 (Dec.). bi-m. Multi-Science Publishing Co. Ltd., 5 Wates Way, Brentwood, Essex CM15 9TB, United Kingdom.

304.6 CHN ISSN 1003-8426
RENKOU YU FAZHAN (CHENGDU)/POPULATION AND DEVELOPMENT. 1987-199?. q. Sichuan University, Renkou Yanjiusuo, Jiugenqiao, Sichuan Daxue Xiaonei, Chengdu, Sichuan 610064, China.

355.4 FRA ISSN 1295-4896
RENSEIGNEMENTS ET OPERATIONS SPECIALES. 1999-2002. irreg. L' Harmattan, 5 rue de l'Ecole Polytechnique, Paris, 75005, France.

778.1 NLD ISSN 0168-6542
REPEAT. 1972-1997. q. Drukkerij Veldwijk, Waddinxveen, Netherlands.

492.7 EGY
REPERTOIRE CHRONOLOGIQUE D'EPIGRAPHIE ARABE. 1931-1991 (no.18). irreg. Institut Francais d'Archeologie Orientale du Caire, Kasr el-Aini, 37 Sharia Sheikh Aly Youssef, Mounira, P O Box 11562, Cairo, Egypt.

025.04 FRA ISSN 1147-7814
REPERTOIRE DES BANQUES DE DONNEES PROFESSIONNELLES/ PROFESSIONAL DATABASES DIRECTORY. ceased 1998. irreg. Association des Professionnels de l'Information et de la Documentation (A D B S), 25 rue Claude Tillier, Paris, 75012, France.

332.1 658 FRA ISSN 0982-3085
REPERTOIRE INTERNATIONAL DES BANQUES DE DONNEES POUR LE MARKETING ET LES ETUDES. 1987-1994. irreg. Editions F L A Consultants, 27 rue de la Vistule, Paris, 75013, France.

070 ITA
IL REPERTORIO DEL GIORNALISMO ITALIANO. 199?-199?. irreg. Olgiata Editrice, Largo Dell' Olgiata, 15 bis 106-I-f, Rome, RM 00123, Italy.

340 613.62 USA ISSN 1067-0483
REPETITIVE STRESS INJURY LITIGATION REPORTER. 1992-2001. m. Andrews Publications, 175 Strafford Ave, Bldg 4, Ste 140, Wayne, PA 19087.

374 GBR ISSN 1351-086X
REPORTBACK. 1969-199?. s-a. Workers' Educational Association, 70 Clifton St, 3rd Fl, London, EC2A 4HB, United Kingdom.

076 ESP ISSN 1139-3823
THE REPORTER (FUENGIROLA); the Spanish connection. 1992-ceased. m. Sun Print Publications S.L., Avda. Alcalde Clemente Diaz Ruiz, 37, Pueblo Lopez, Fuengirola, Malaga 29640, Spain.

320.9 KOR
THE REPUBLIC OF KOREA POLICY SERIES. 1973 (no.16)-199?. irreg. Korean Overseas Information Service, 82-1, Sejongno, Jongno-gu, Seoul, 110050, Korea, S.

364 USA ISSN 1042-4636
RESEARCH AND BIBLIOGRAPHICAL GUIDES IN CRIMINAL JUSTICE. 1989-19??. irreg. Greenwood Publishing Group Inc., 88 Post Rd W, PO Box 5007, Westport, CT 06881.

355 USA ISSN 0899-0166
RESEARCH GUIDES IN MILITARY STUDIES. 1988-19??. irreg. Greenwood Publishing Group Inc., 88 Post Rd W, PO Box 5007, Westport, CT 06881.

541 USA ISSN 1380-6777 CODEN: RCKIE9
RESEARCH IN CHEMICAL KINETICS. 1993-1997 (vol.4). irreg. Blackwell Scientific Publications, Inc., 238 Main St, Ste 501, Cambridge, MA 02142-1413.

020 GBR ISSN 0734-3310
RESEARCH STRATEGIES. 1983-2007. 4/yr. Pergamon, The Blvd, Langford Ln, East Park, Kidlington, Oxford OX5 1GB, United Kingdom.

620 GBR ISSN 0277-7045
RESEARCH TECHNIQUES IN NONDESTRUCTIVE TESTING. 1970-1987. irreg. Academic Press, 24-28 Oval Rd, London, NW1 7DX, United Kingdom.

700 800 ESP ISSN 1578-9926
RESENA. 1964-2004. 11/yr. Compania de Jesus, Centro Loyola de Estudios y Comunicacion Social, Pablo Aranda 3, Madrid, 28006, Spain.

660.6 GBR ISSN 1358-2283 CODEN: REBIFD
RESOURCE AND ENVIRONMENTAL BIOTECHNOLOGY. 1988-2002. 4/yr. A B Academic Publishers, PO Box 42, Bicester, Oxon OX26 7NW, United Kingdom.

333.7 AUS ISSN 1039-5423
RESOURCE SCIENCES INTERFACE. 1993-1995. 3/yr. Department of Agriculture, Fisheries and Forestry, Bureau of Rural Sciences, Edmund Barton Bldg, Broughton St, Barton, GPO Box 858, Canberra, ACT 2601, Australia.

780 GBR
RESOURCES OF MUSIC SERIES. 1969-19??. irreg. Cambridge University Press, The Edinburgh Bldg, Shaftesbury Rd, Cambridge, CB2 8RU, United Kingdom.

658 381 GBR ISSN 1465-9409
RETAIL DETAILS. 1999-2000. bi-w. Corporate Intelligence Group, 48 Bedford Sq, London, WC1B 3DP, United Kingdom.

336 346.066 USA
RETIREMENT AND BENEFIT PLANNING; strategy and design for businesses and tax-exempt organizations. 1991-199?. plus a. updates. LexisNexis, PO Box 7587, Charlottesville, VA 22906.

320 AUS ISSN 0310-9143
RETRIEVAL. 1971-1977. m. Retrieval, PO Box 51, Fitzroy, VIC 3065, Australia.

628.4458 GBR ISSN 0048-7457
REUSE - RECYCLE. 1971-2004. m. Sage Science Press (UK), 1 Oliver's Yard, 55 City Rd, London, EC1Y 1SP, United Kingdom.

629.22 NZL ISSN 1177-0643
REV. 2003 (Jan.)-2006 (Jul.). m. Delta Publishing Limited, PO Box 38 675, Howick, Auckland, New Zealand.

330 USA ISSN 1475-3685
REVIEW OF MIDDLE EAST ECONOMICS AND FINANCE (PRINT). 2003 (Apr.)-2005. 3/yr. Berkeley Electronic Press, 2809 Telegraph Ave, Ste 202, Berkeley, CA 94705.

301 HUN ISSN 1417-8648
REVIEW OF SOCIOLOGY. 1992-2009 (Jan.). s-a. Akademiai Kiado Rt., Prielle Kornelia U. 19, Budapest, 1117, Hungary.

330.9 371.42 GBR ISSN 0265-9387
REVIEW OF THE ECONOMY AND EMPLOYMENT. 1981-19??. irreg. Institute for Employment Research, University Of Warwick, Gibbet Hill Rd, Coventry, Warks CV4 7AL, United Kingdom.

330.9 ESP ISSN 1134-8291
REVISTA ASTURIANA DE ECONOMIA. 1994-2005; suspended. 3/yr. Asociacion Asturiana de Estudios Economicos, Apdo. de Correos 1693, Oviedo, 33080, Spain.

658 651 BRA ISSN 1518-6776
REVISTA DE ADMINISTRACAO MACKENZIE (PRINT). 2000-2008. bi-m. Universidade Presbiteriana Mackenzie, Rua da Consolacao 896, Pr.2, Sao Paulo-SP, SP 01302-907, Brazil.

158 ESP ISSN 1139-1170
REVISTA DE ATENCION TEMPRANA. 1997-2004. s-a. Asociacion de Atencion Temprana de la Region de Murcia, Alameda de Cervantes, Resd. Las Palmeras Fase II B, Lorca, Murcia 30800, Spain.

344.046 ESP ISSN 0214-4042
REVISTA DE DERECHO AMBIENTAL; la publicacion de la ecologia juridica. 1988-2002. s-a. Asociacion de Derecho Ambiental Espanol, Apdo. de Correos 4234, Murcia, 30080, Spain.

346.066 332 336 ESP ISSN 0484-6885
REVISTA DE DERECHO FINANCIERO Y DE HACIENDA PUBLICA. 1951-2004. bi-m. Editoriales de Derecho Reunidas S.A., Valverde, 32, 1o izda., Madrid, 28004, Spain.

336 ESP ISSN 1137-5051
REVISTA DE HACIENDA LOCAL. 1971-2000. 3/yr. Editoriales de Derecho Reunidas S.A., Valverde, 32, 1o izda., Madrid, 28004, Spain.

363.1 ESP ISSN 0214-8102
REVISTA DE PROTECCION CIVIL. 1984-2003. bi-m. Direccion General de Proteccion Civil, Quintiliano, 21, Madrid, 28002, Spain.

616.8 ESP ISSN 1130-5142
REVISTA DE PSICOTERAPIA. 1981-ceased. q. Sociedad Espanola para la Integracion de la Psicoterapia, Apdo. de Correos 90097, Barcelona, 08080, Spain.

614.1 ESP ISSN 1137-1145
REVISTA ESPANOLA DE PSIQUIATRIA FORENSE, PSICOLOGIA FORENSE Y CRIMINOLOGIA. 1996-1999. 3/yr. Diaz de Santos S.A., Libreria Cientifico-Tecnica, Lagasca, 95, Madrid, 28006, Spain.

003 ESP ISSN 1576-4745
REVISTA ESPANOLA DE SISTEMAS. 2000-200?. a. Sociedad Espanola de Sistemas Generales, Edificio Facultad de Medicina, Esc B, 1 A, Avenida Blasco Ibanez 15, Valencia, Spain.

351 ESP ISSN 1139-3750
REVISTA IBEROAMERICANA DE ADMINISTRACION PUBLICA. 1998-2003. s-a. Instituto Nacional de Administracion Publica, Atocha 106, Madrid, 28012, Spain.

616.1 ESP ISSN 0214-3941
REVISTA IBEROAMERICANA DE TROMBOSIS Y HEMOSTASIA. 1988-2002. q. Elsevier Doyma, Traversa de Gracia 17-21, Barcelona, 08021, Spain.

616.1 ESP ISSN 0214-395X
REVISTA IBEROAMERICANA DE TROMBOSIS Y HEMOSTASIA. SUPLEMENTO. 1988-199?. irreg. Elsevier Doyma, Traversa de Gracia 17-21, Barcelona, 08021, Spain.

794.1 ESP ISSN 0214-8900
REVISTA INTERNACIONAL DE AJEDREZ. 1987-ceased. 12/yr. Ediciones Eseuve S.A., c/o Oficina de Justificacion de la Difusion (OJD), Plaza Marques de Salamanca, 9-4D, Madrid, 28006, Spain.

616.12 ESP ISSN 1578-2700 CODEN: RLCEEK
REVISTA LATINA DE CARDIOLOGIA. 1980-2002. bi-m. Elsevier Doyma, Traversa de Gracia 17-21, Barcelona, 08021, Spain.

338.4 ROM ISSN 1222-5428
REVISTA ROMANA DE TURISM. 1994-1996. bi-m. Ministerul Turismului, Institutul de Cercetari pentru Turism, Str. Apolodor 17, Bucharest, 70663, Romania.

053.1 DEU ISSN 1862-295X
REVUE. 1966-2008. w. (Thu.). Heinrich Bauer Verlag, Burchardstr 11, Hamburg, 20077, Germany.

806 910.03 FRA ISSN 1277-6408
REVUE AFRAM/AFRAM REVIEW. 1975-2004. s-a. Cercle d'Etudes Afro-Americaines, 12 square de Montsouris, Paris, 75014, France.

610 FRA ISSN 0557-8582
REVUE DE MEDECINE FONCTIONELLE. 1967-1997. a. Societe de Medecine Fonctionnelle, 33, ave Arouet, Antony, 92160, France.

382 FRA ISSN 0753-3098
REVUE DE PRESSE ET DE DOCUMENTATION ALLEMANDE. 19??-1999. m. Chambre Regionale de Commerce et d'Industrie d'Alsace, 42 rue Schweighaeuser, Strasbourg, 67000, France.

338 FRA ISSN 1282-5247
LA REVUE DES ENTREPRISES. 1956 (no.142)-2002. m. Conseil National du Patronat Francais, 31 av. Pierre 1er de Serbie, Paris, Cedex 16 75784, France.

910 FRA ISSN 0035-3213 CODEN: RGGEB2
REVUE GEOGRAPHIQUE DE L'EST. 1960-2007. q. Association de Geographes de l'Est, Universite de Nancy 2, Departement de Geographie, 23 Boulevard Albert 1er, BP 3397, Nancy, 54015, France.

647.94 FRA ISSN 1637-2808
LA REVUE H R C. (Hotels, Restaurants, Collectivites) 1949-2004. m. Nouvelles du Monde, 25 rue de la Plaine, Paris, 75020, France.

929 FRA ISSN 0338-1978
LA REVUE LORRAINE POPULAIRE. 1974-2009. bi-m. Revue Lorraine Populaire, Les Tremblois, Laneuvelotte, 54280, France.

840 FRA ISSN 1156-296X
REVUE MARIVAUX. 1990-199?. irreg. Honore Champion, 3 Rue Corneille, Paris, 75006, France.

355 FRA ISSN 0035-3671
REVUE MILITAIRE GENERALE. 1956-1973. m. Berger-Levrault Editions, 525 Rue Andre Ampere, Logistique Est, B P 79, Champigneulles, 54250, France.

700 960 FRA ISSN 1157-4127
REVUE NOIRE; art contemporain africain - African contemporary art. 1991-2002. q. Revue Noire, 8 rue Cels, Paris, 75014, France.

747 FRA ISSN 0754-9172
REVUE PROFESSIONNELLE DES METIERS DE L'AMEUBLEMENT ET DE LA DECORATION. 1982-199?. q. Revue Professionnelle des Metiers de l'Ameublement et de la Decoration, 38 rue Pascal, Paris, 75013, France.

355.4 FRA ISSN 0994-155X
REVUE SCIENTIFIQUE ET TECHNIQUE DE LA DEFENSE. 1922-2004. q. Etablissement de Communication et de Production Audiovisuelle de la Defense - E C P A D, 2 - 8 Route du Fort d'Ivry, Ivry-sur-Seine Cedex, 94205, France.

697 621.56 FRA ISSN 1254-2075 CODEN: APAVBZ
REVUE TECHNIQUE A P A V E. (Associations de Proprietaires d'Appareils a Vapeur et Electriques) 1920-2007. q. S A D A V E, 191 rue de Vaugirard, Paris, 75015, France.

615.82 ITA ISSN 0557-9430
LA RIABILITAZIONE; rivista di medicina fisica e riabilitazione. 1968-ceased. 4/yr. Massimo De Vecchi Editore, Via Eustachi 45, Milan, Italy.

646.724 ITA ISSN 1129-0463
RICCI E CAPRICCI. 1999-200?. m. Edigamma Publishing, Via Sambuca Pistoiese 70A, Rome, 00138, Italy.

450 ITA
RICERCHE DI STORIA DELLE LINGUE CLASSICHE. 1967-ceased. irreg. Fabrizio Serra Editore, c/o Accademia Editoriale, Via Santa Bibbiana 28, Pisa, 56127, Italy.

370 ITA ISSN 0035-5046
RICERCHE DIDATTICHE. 1951-ceased. m. Movimento Circoli della Didattica, Via Crescenzio, 25, Rome, RM 00193, Italy.

796.9 FRA ISSN 1287-6747
RIDER. 1997-2003. q. Concerto Vertical, 55 bd. des Alpes, Meylan, 38240, France.

320.9 ITA ISSN 0035-5380
RINASCITA; rassegna politica di attualita, economia, e cultura. 1944-1991. w. Nuova Iniziativa Editoriale SpA, Via dei Due Macelli 23/13, Rome, 00187, Italy.

790.1 USA ISSN 1089-618X CODEN: SMRAFY
RINGSIDE WRESTLING. 1991-200?. bi-m. Starlog Communications, 250 W 49th St, 3rd Fl Ste 304, New York, NY 10019.

Cessations

306.405 AUS ISSN 1832-9594
RIOT. 2005-ceased (no.6). bi-m. Arc Media & Entertainment, 28 Paternoster Row, Pyrmont, NSW 2007, Australia.

658 FRA ISSN 1760-2009
RISQUES & MANAGEMENT INTERNATIONAL. 2003-2005. s-a. L' Harmattan, 5 rue de l'Ecole Polytechnique, Paris, 75005, France.

300 ITA ISSN 0035-5623
RISVEGLIO DEL MOLISE E DEL MEZZOGIORNO; attualita, cultura, economia, politica e problemi meridionali. 1961-ceased. m. Editrice Rismol s.r.l., Via Luigi Arati, 25, Rome, RM 00151, Italy.

054.1 FRA ISSN 1141-4073
RIVE GAUCHE MAGAZINE. 1961-1970. m. Editions Municipales S.A.R.L., 38 rue Croix-des-Petits-Champs, Paris, 75001, France.

363.73 363.728 AUS
RIVER POST. 1994-2001. bi-m. Hawkesbury-Nepean Catchment Management Trust, 68 Mileham St, Windsor, NSW 2756, Australia.

052 NZL ISSN 1170-0424
THE RIVERSIDER. 1990-1998. m. The Riversider, PO Box 1547, Hamilton, New Zealand.

910 ITA
RIVIERA ECO. 1962-ceased. w. Riviera Eco, Viale dei Mille, 14, Riccione, FO 47036, Italy.

808.838 ITA ISSN 1724-4900
LA RIVISTA DEI MAGHI E DELLE STREGHE. 2004-200?. m. Sprea Editori Srl, Via Torino 51, Cernusco sul Naviglio, MI 20063, Italy.

387 ITA ISSN 0035-5925
RIVISTA DEL PORTO DI NAPOLI. 1927-19??. bi-m. Consorzio Autonomo del Porto, Molo Pisacane, Naples, NA 80133, Italy.

055 ITA
RIVISTA DELLA DONNA. 1971-ceased. q. Editoriale Publiaci, Via Tribuna di Tor de' Specchi 18a, Rome, Italy.

410 ITA
RIVISTA DELLE LINGUE; il mondo delle lingue e della comunicazione multimedia. 1992-ceased. bi-m. Edizioni Linguistic Club, Via Principe Amedeo, 15, Frascati, RM 00044, Italy.

480 ITA ISSN 0035-6220
RIVISTA DI FILOLOGIA E DI ISTRUZIONE CLASSICA. 1872-2000. q. Loescher Editore, Via Vittorio Amedeo II, 18, Turin, 10121, Italy.

798 ITA ISSN 1720-8564
RIVISTA DI IPPIATRIA E IPPOLOGIA. 1995-200?. q. Societa Italiana di Ippologia (S I D I), Corso Svizzera 185, Turin, 10149, Italy.

610 616 ITA
RIVISTA DI MEDICINA E CHIRURGIA. 1979-ceased. q. Fabrizio Serra Editore, c/o Accademia Editoriale, Via Santa Bibbiana 28, Pisa, 56127, Italy.

618 ITA ISSN 0394-977X
RIVISTA DI OSTETRICIA E GINECOLOGIA. 1945-2001. bi-m. Edizioni Riviste Scientifiche, Via R Giuliani 419, Florence, 50141, Italy.

616.07 ITA ISSN 0035-6417
RIVISTA DI PATOLOGIA E CLINICA. 1946-1999. bi-m. Maccari Editore Srl, Via Palermo 44, Parma, 43100, Italy.

330 ITA ISSN 0391-6170
RIVISTA DI POLITICA ECONOMICA. SELECTED PAPERS. 1946-1988. bi-m. Confederazione Generale dell'Industria Italiana (Confindustria), Centro Studi, Viale dell'Astronomia 30, Rome, 00144, Italy.

363.2 ITA ISSN 0035-6476
RIVISTA DI POLIZIA; rassegna di dottrina tecnica e legislazione. 1947-ceased. m. Rivista di Polizia, Via Mazzocchi, 175, Santa Maria Capua Vetere, CE 81055, Italy.

616.8 ITA ISSN 1122-2298
RIVISTA DI RIABILITAZIONE PSICHIATRICA E PSICOSOCIALE. SUPPLEMENTO. 1992-199?. 3/yr. Casa Editrice Idelson Gnocchi, Via Michele Pietravalle 85, Naples, NA 80131, Italy.

001.3 971 ITA ISSN 1120-3420
RIVISTA DI STUDI CANADESI. 1988-ceased. a. Schena Editore, Viale Stazione 177, Fasano, BR 72015, Italy.

945 ITA ISSN 0035-6603
RIVISTA DI STUDI LIGURI/REVUE D'ETUDES LIGURES. 1942-199?. q. Istituto Internazionale di Studi Liguri, Via Romana 39, Bordighera, IM 18012, Italy.

634.8 663.2 ITA ISSN 0370-7865 CODEN: RVENAL
RIVISTA DI VITICOLTURA E DI ENOLOGIA. 1948-ceased. q. Rivista di Viticoltura e di Enologia, Via XXVIII Aprile, 26, Conegliano Veneto, TV 31015, Italy.

262.3 ITA ISSN 0035-6654
RIVISTA DIOCESANA DEL PATRIARCATO DI VENEZIA. 1918-ceased. m. Patriarcato di Venezia, Castello 5660, Venice, VE 30122, Italy.

617 ITA ISSN 0035-6689
RIVISTA GENERALE ITALIANA DI CHIRURGIA. 1960-2000. bi-m. Maccari Editore Srl, Via Palermo 44, Parma, 43100, Italy.

820 ITA ISSN 1590-7953
RIVISTA ITALIANA DI LETTERATURA COMPARATA. 1990-1999. a. Besa Editrice, Via Duca degli Abruzzi, 13/15, Nardo, 73048, Italy.

668.5 664.5 ITA ISSN 0392-0445 CODEN: RIEPD7
RIVISTA ITALIANA E P P O S. (Essenze Profumi Piante Officianali Saponi) 1939-2007. s-a. Istituto Tetrahedron, Via Capitani di Mozzo, 12, Mozzo, BG 24030, Italy.

330 ITA
RIVISTA MILANESE DI ECONOMIA. 1972 (vol.7)-199?. q. Cassa di Risparmio delle Provincie Lombarde (Cariplo), Via Monte Di Pieta', 8, Milan, MI 20121, Italy.

778.53 ITA ISSN 0035-7081
RIVISTA TECNICA DI CINEMATOGRAFIA. 1950-1978. s-a. Edizione Cinemeccanica SpA, Viale Campania, 23, Milan, MI 20133, Italy.

900 ITA ISSN 1722-344X
RIVIVERE LA STORIA. 2003-200?. bi-m. Edizioni Trentini & C, Via Pier Luigi Nervi 1/B, Argenta, FE 44011, Italy.

338.1 ISR ISSN 0792-0806
RIV'ON KUTNA. 1987-1990. q. Heshev, P O Box 40021, Tel Aviv, 61400, Israel.

747 USA ISSN 1550-5006
ROBB REPORT LUXURY HOME. 2004-2007. q. CurtCo Media LLC., 29160 Heathercliff Rd, Ste 200, Malibu, CA 90265.

629.892 USA CODEN: ROTODJ
ROBOTICS TODAY. 1979-2008. q. Society of Manufacturing Engineers, One SME Dr, PO Box 930, Dearborn, MI 48121.

790.1 ITA
ROMAGNA PUNTO SPORT. 1979-ceased. m. Romagna Sera, Via Paolo Bonoli, 32, Forli', FO 47100, Italy.

340.54 USA ISSN 1551-1375
ROMAN LEGAL TRADITION (PRINT); a journal of ancient medieval and modern civil law. 2002-2008. biennial. University of Kansas, School of Law, 1535 W 15th St, Lawrence, KS 66045.

808.8385 DEU
ROMAN REVUE. 1999-2008. bi-m. Bastei Verlag Gustav H. Luebbe GmbH und Co., Scheidtbachstr 23-31, Bergisch Gladbach, 51469, Germany.

808.83 ITA ISSN 0161-682X
THE ROMANTIST. 1977-1986. irreg. Genius Loci, Centro Studie Ricerche, Francis Marion Crawford, Via Angri 64, Sant' Agnello do Sorrento, 80065, Italy.

808.8385 DEU
ROMANWOCHE - SCHICKSALE HAUTNAH. 2005-2007. bi-m. Pabel-Moewig Verlag KG, Karlsruherstr 31, Rastatt, 76437, Germany.

055.1 ITA ISSN 1722-7984
I ROMANZI D'AMORE DI CONFESSIONI DONNA. 1999-200?. m. Edizioni Mimosa, Piazza E de Angeli 9, Milan, 20146, Italy.

055.1 ITA ISSN 1721-5714
I ROMANZI PROIBITI DI CONFESSIONI DONNA. 1999-200?. bi-m. Edizioni Mimosa, Piazza E de Angeli 9, Milan, 20146, Italy.

796.7 AUS
ROOST. 2001-2004. q. Emap Australia Pty. Ltd., 187 Thomas St, Level 6, Haymarket, NSW 2000, Australia.

781.623981 DNK ISSN 1902-8539
ROOTS ZONE (PRINT). 1980-2009. 3/yr. Folkemusikkens Faelles Sekretariat, Saltholmsgade 22, Aarhus C, 8000, Denmark.

011 AUS
ROSTRUM. 1976-1996. a. Rank Publishing Co., 66 Chandos St, St Leonards, NSW 2065, Australia.

580.095694 ISR ISSN 0333-9904
ROTEM. 1981-1990. q. Society for the Protection of Nature in Israel, 4 Hashefela St, Tel Aviv, 66183, Israel.

333.33 NLD ISSN 1871-5605
ROTTERDAM REAL ESTATE CITY BOOK; assets - locations - market - players. 2005-2005. s-a. Europe Real Estate Publishers B.V., North Sea Bldg, Gevers Deynootweg 93R, The Hague, 2586 BK, Netherlands.

342 AUS ISSN 1328-5335
ROUNDTABLE. 1992-2000. q. Constitutional Centenary Foundation, Level 2, 723 Swanston St, Carlton, VIC 3053, Australia.

942 GBR ISSN 0080-4398
ROYAL HISTORICAL SOCIETY. GUIDES AND HANDBOOKS. 1938; N.S. 1974-2000 (Apr.). irreg. Cambridge University Press, The Edinburgh Bldg, Shaftesbury Rd, Cambridge, CB2 8RU, United Kingdom.

500 GBR ISSN 0035-8959 CODEN: PIGBAI
ROYAL INSTITUTION OF GREAT BRITAIN. PROCEEDINGS. 1851-2001. a. Oxford University Press, Great Clarendon St, Oxford, OX2 6DP, United Kingdom.

808.838 ITA ISSN 1124-1381
RUBACUORI. 1996-ceased. m.?. Sisted s.r.l., S P Turanese km, 44,500, Carsoli, AQ 67061, Italy.

796.333 AUS
RUGBY LEAGUE COACHING MANUALS. 1998-2004. bi-m. Shamrock Books, 3 Andrews St, Southport, QLD 4215, Australia.

796.333 FRA ISSN 1953-6216
RUGBY MAGAZINE. 2006-2008. m. Editions Leo, 7 Rue Aristide Berges, Mas Guerido, Cabestany, 66330, France.

796.333 FRA ISSN 1959-1527
RUGBY SELECTION. 2007-2007. bi-m. Euro Services Internet, 60 rue Vitruve, Paris, 75020, France.

796.334 DEU
RUND; das Fussballmagazin. 2005-2007 (May). m. Olympia Verlag GmbH, Badstr 4-6, Nuernberg, 90402, Germany.

794 DEU
RUNNING WOMAN. 2004-2006. bi-m. Sportagentur WAG's, Badenweiler Str 2-4, Freiburg, 79117, Germany.

678.32 ITA ISSN 0393-7526
RUOTASPRING; tyre-rubber fortnightly journal. 1970-ceased. bi-m. Minuti Luisa, Via Alatri, 30, Rome, RM 00171, Italy.

384.0285 USA ISSN 1077-4653
RUSSIA ONLINE AND WIRELESS. 1994-2005. m. Gist, Inc., 2200 Wilson Blvd, Ste 102G, Arlington, VA 22201.

621.382 USA
RUSSIAN TELECOMMUNICATIONS INVESTOR'S GUIDE. 1996-2005. a. Gist, Inc., 2200 Wilson Blvd, Ste 102G, Arlington, VA 22201.

636.3 AUS
S A C S O S NEWSLETTER. 1974-ceased. m. South Australian Coloured Sheep Owners' Society Inc., PO Box 110, Fullarton, SA 5063, Australia.

700 AUS ISSN 0819-2936
S.A. CRAFTS. (South Australia) 1985-2001. q. Craftsouth, Centre for Contemporary Craft & Design Inc., PO Box 8067, Station Arcade, SA 5000, Australia.

020 011 GBR ISSN 0307-1456
S A L G NEWSLETTER. 1973-2009. a. South Asia Library Group, c/o Oriental and India Office Collections, British Library, 96 Euston Rd, London, NW1 2DB, United Kingdom.

058.81 DNK ISSN 1399-6444
S A S MAGASINET. 1983-2001. m. Mediacenter Denmark A-S, Soenderhoej 12, Viby J, 8260, Denmark.

003 USA ISSN 1060-1074
S C O MAGAZINE. (Santa Cruz Operation) 1991-ceased. bi-m. C M P Media LLC, 600 Community Dr, Manhasset, NY 11030.

320.531 DNK ISSN 0902-1612
S F STATUS; SF's officielle dokumenter og vedtagelser. (Socialistisk Folkeparti) 1975-1999. a. Forlaget Axel, c/o Socialistisk Folkeoplysningsforbund, Blegdamsvej 24 A, Copenhagen, 2200, Denmark.

200 ITA ISSN 1017-0324
S I D I C; review information. 1968-2009. 3/yr. Service International de Documentation Judeo-Chretienne, Via Garibaldi 28, Rome, 00153, Italy.

016.31 AUS ISSN 1031-5020
S I L - A A I B BIBLIOGRAPHY. (In 4 sections: Academic Works, Vernacular-Secular Works, Vernacular-Religious Works Audiography) 1972-1996. irreg. Summer Institute of Linguistics, Australian Aborigines and Islanders Branch, Berrimah, N.T. 0828, Australia.

378.1012 ITA ISSN 0391-8599
S I P E. (Service International de Presse Etudiante) 1969-ceased. m. Istituto per la Cooperazione Universitaria, Viale Gioacchino Rossini 26, Rome, 00198, Italy.

378 ITA ISSN 0391-8572
S I P E-FAMIGLIA. (Service International de Presse Etudiante) 1977-199?. bi-m. Palombi Editore, Via Gregorio VII 224, Rome, 00165, Italy.

615 ITA ISSN 0081-0703
S I S F DOCUMENTI. 1965-ceased. irreg. Societa Italiana di Scienze Farmaceutiche (S I S F), Viale Abruzzi 32, Milan, 20131, Italy.

122 GBR ISSN 1362-7686
S I S INTERNET DIGEST. 1996-2002. s-a. Society for Interdisciplinary Studies, 10 Witley Green, Darley Heights, Stopsley, Beds LU2 8TR, United Kingdom.

004.6 ITA
S M A U NEWS. 1994-ceased. 7/yr. Il Sole 24 Ore Business Media, Divisione J C E, Via Patecchio 2, Milan, 20141, Italy.

005 NOR ISSN 1504-0631
S M B - DATA; loesninger, produkter, nytte. 2004-2005. bi-m. I D G Magazines Norge AS, PO Box 9090, Groenland, Oslo, 0133, Norway.

780 ITA ISSN 1591-7045
S M. STRUMENTI MUSICALI. 1979-ceased. m. (11/yr.). Mixxnow Publishing srl, Via Cumabue, 39, Lissone, Milano 20035, Italy.

660 GBR
S P S BULLETIN. 1974-1998. q. Separation Processes Service, Bldg 404, Harwell Laboratory, Didcot, Oxon OX11 0RA, United Kingdom.

659.1021 USA ISSN 1067-1641 CODEN: BULLE7
S R D S THE BULLET; the latest in list activity. (Standard Rate and Data Service) 1991-2000. bi-m. S R D S, 1700 Higgins Rd, Des Plaines, IL 60018.

300 ISR ISSN 0334-5971
S S D A YEDI'ON - NEWSLETTER. (Social Science Data Archives) 1983-1998. s-a. Hebrew University of Jerusalem, Faculty of Social Sciences, Mount Scopus, Jerusalem, 91905, Israel.

057.86 CZE ISSN 1214-8970
S TEBOU...ME BAVI ZIVOT. 2004-2009 (Jan.). w. Sanoma Magazines Praha s.r.o., Lomnickeho 7, Prague 4, 12079, Czech Republic.

746.4 CZE ISSN 1613-0685
SABRINA - FILETOVE HACKOVANI. 2004-2004 (ceased same year). s-a. Rolino, spol. s.r.o., Bratri Capku 10, Prague 10, 101 00, Czech Republic.

381 FRA ISSN 1165-5224
SACHEZ-LE ENVIRONNEMENT. 1993-200?. m. Chambre Regionale de Commerce et d'Industrie Champagne - Ardenne, Direction de la Communication, 10 rue de Chastillon, B.P. 537, Chalons-sur-Marne, Cedex 51011, France.

664 362.1 AUS
SAFEFOOD NEWS. 1972-2002. a. SafeFood New South Wales, PO Box A2613, Sydney South, NSW 1235, Australia.

398 USA ISSN 1086-1769
SAGA. 1996-2001. a. White Cloud Press, PO Box 3400, Ashland, OR 97520.

340 USA ISSN 1085-2425
SAINT LOUIS - WARSAW TRANSATLANTIC LAW JOURNAL. 1995-2002. a. Saint Louis University, School of Law, 3700 Lindell Blvd, Saint Louis, MO 63108.

658.8 310 USA ISSN 0361-1329
SALES & MARKETING MANAGEMENT SURVEY OF BUYING POWER. 1995-2005. a. Nielsen Business Publications, 770 Broadway, New York, NY 10003.

338.642 USA ISSN 0278-5048
SALES REP'S ADVISOR. 1981-19??. m. Alexander Communications Group, Inc., 712 Main St, Ste 187B, Boonton, NJ 07005.

320.5322 DNK ISSN 0907-0974
SALT. 1992-2007. bi-m. Mediefabrikken, St Kongensgade 40 D, Copenhagen K, 1264, Denmark.

614 ESP ISSN 1578-858X
SALUD PUBLICA Y EDUCACION PARA LA SALUD. 2001-2006. s-a. Asociacion de Alumnos e Masteres en Saude Publica de Galicia, Apartado de Correos 543, Santiago de Compostela, 15780, Spain.

613 ESP ISSN 1575-5371
SALUD TOTAL DE LA MUJER. 1999-2002. 3/yr. Elsevier Doyma, Traversa de Gracia 17-21, Barcelona, 08021, Spain.

664.9 ITA
SALUMAIO E IL GASTRONOMO. 1988-ceased. 12/yr. Valentini Editore s.r.l., Via Fabio Filzi, 19, Milan, MI 20124, Italy.

028.5 FRA ISSN 0397-7854
SALUT. 1962-2006. bi-w. Salut, 13 rue de la Cerisaie, Paris, 75004, France.

613.7 ITA ISSN 1594-6193
SALUTE & BENESSERE. 2001-ceased. m. Ulysse Network, Viale Bianca Maria 19, Milan, Italy.

613.7 649 ITA ISSN 1722-0416
SALUTE E BENESSERE. IL TUO BAMBINO. 2003-ceased. m. Ulysse Network, Viale Bianca Maria 19, Milan, Italy.

500 ISR ISSN 0792-1896
SAMUEL NEAMAN INSTITUTE FOR ADVANCED STUDIES IN SCIENCE AND TECHNOLOGY. ANNUAL REPORT. 1978-1997. a. Technion - Israel Institute of Technology, Samuel Neaman Institute for Advanced Studies in Science and Technology, Technion City, Haifa, 32000, Israel.

371.42 USA ISSN 1098-9889
THE SAN FRANCISCO BAY AREA JOBBANK; the job hunter's guide to Northern California. (Includes: the Bay Area, Oakland, Sacramento, San Jose, Silicon Valley and many others.) 1982-2007 (18th ed.). irreg. Adams Media, 4700 E Galbraith Rd, Cincinnati, OH 45236.

800 400 ITA ISSN 0392-5099
SANDALION; quaderni di cultura classica, cristiana e medievale. 1978-ceased. a. Universita degli Studi di Sassari, Via Universita, 40, Sassari, SS 07100, Italy.

615 CHE ISSN 1422-6472
SANDORAMA (GERMAN-FRENCH EDITION). 1990-1994. q. Sandoz Pharma AG, Hinterbergstr 24, Cham 2, 6330, Switzerland.

613.2 ITA ISSN 1722-5825
SANE E BELLE. 2003-200?. m. Edigamma Publishing, Via Sambuca Pistoiese 70A, Rome, 00138, Italy.

616.1 ESP ISSN 0036-4355 CODEN: SNGRAW
SANGRE; trabajos de hematologia y hemoterapia. 1956-1999. bi-m. Asociacion Espanola de Hematologia y Hemoterapia, C Balcells, 21-25 Bajos, Barcelona, 08024, Spain.

362 FRA ISSN 1270-850X
SANTE PAYS DE LA LOIRE. 1993-2005. irreg. Observatoire Regional de la Sante des Pays de la Loire, Hotel de la Region, 1 Rue de la Loire, Nantes, 44266, France.

282 ITA ISSN 1970-6006
I SANTI. 2006-200?. q. Tattilo Editrice SpA, Via degli Olmetti 18, Rome, 00060, Italy.

282 ITA ISSN 0036-4606
IL SANTO DEI VOLI. 1946-ceased. bi-m. Santuario S. Giuseppe da Copertino, Via Piave, 8, Copertino, LE 73043, Italy.

630 ITA ISSN 0391-8726
SARDEGNA AGRICOLTURA. 1970-ceased. bi-m. Sardegna Agricoltura, Piazza Annunziata, 4, Cagliari, CA 09123, Italy.

384.51 ITA ISSN 1126-5140
SAT & CO. 1998-200?. m. Techno Publishing S.r.l., Via Tacito 5, Corsico, MI 20094, Italy.

384.55 ITA ISSN 1122-9284
SATELLITE EUROSAT; tecnologia della televisione via satellite. 1986-ceased. m. Il Sole 24 Ore Business Media, Divisione J C E, Via Patecchio 2, Milan, 20141, Italy.

330 CZE ISSN 1802-176X
SATISFACTION. 2006-2007. s-a. Economia a.s., Dobrovskeho 25, Prague 7, 170 55, Czech Republic.

597 FRA ISSN 0220-1429
SAUMONS. 1977-2002. q. Association Nationale de Defense des Rivieres a Saumons, 1 place Edouard Renard, Paris, 75012, France.

052 NZL ISSN 1177-4584
SAVVY. 2004-2006. bi-m. Warwick Finn Publishers Ltd., PO Box 65226, Mairangi Bay, Auckland, New Zealand.

629.221 USA ISSN 0199-7327
SCALE R - C MODELER. (Radio-Controlled) 19??-1999. bi-m. Challenge Publications, Inc., 9509 Vassar Ave, Unit A, Chatsworth, CA 91311.

779.28 NZL
SCANDALS; adult entertainment and contacts. 1997-2008. m. Impressions, PO Box 91763, Auckland, New Zealand.

794.1 NLD ISSN 1384-9174
SCHAAKNIEUWS. 1986-2008. 24/yr. Schaaknieuws, Visserstraat 16 B, Eindhoven, 5612 BT, Netherlands.

028.1 ITA ISSN 0036-5955
SCHEDARIO; periodico di letteratura giovanile. 1970 (vol.17)-1998. q. Giunti Gruppo Editoriale SpA, Via Bolognese 165, Florence, 50139, Italy.

150 NLD ISSN 1574-5570
DE SCHEURKALENDER VOOR HOOG SENSITIEVE PERSONEN. 2004-2004. a. Uitgeverij Archipel, Postbus 2877, Amsterdam, 1000 CW, Netherlands.

700 500 390 DEU ISSN 0036-6153
SCHLESIEN; arts, science, folklore. 1956-1996. q. Bergstadtverlag, Hermann-Herder-Str 4, Freiburg, 79104, Germany.

053.1 DEU
SCHLOSS EINSTEIN MAGAZIN. 2000-2003. m. Egmont Cultfish Media GmbH, Hansastr 32, Munich, 80686, Germany.

940 USA ISSN 1059-9185
SCHOLARS OF EARLY MODERN STUDIES. 1966-2000. a. Sixteenth Century Journal Publishers, Inc., Truman State University, 100 E Normal St, Kirksville, MO 63501.

648 NLD ISSN 1573-3130
SCHOONMAAK TOTAAL. 2003-2003. a. Kluwer B.V., Postbus 4, Alphen aan den Rijn, 2400 MA, Netherlands.

500 DEU ISSN 1433-5581
SCHRIFTEN DES FORSCHUNGSZENTRUMS JUELICH. 1990-2003 (vol.33). irreg. Forschungszentrum Juelich GmbH, Leo-Brandt-Str, Juelich, 52428, Germany.

172.2 DEU ISSN 0944-1611
SCHRIFTEN ZUR POLITISCHEN ETHIK. 1993-1998 (vol.8). irreg. Verlag fuer Entwicklungspolitik Saarbruecken GmbH, Auf der Adt 14, Saarbruecken, 66130, Germany.

613.62 DEU ISSN 0945-1064
SCHRIFTENREIHE ZENTRALBLATT FUER ARBEITSMEDIZIN. 1976-2000 (vol.19). irreg. Dr. Curt Haefner Verlag GmbH, Dischingerstr 8, Heidelberg, 69123, Germany.

685.31 DEU
SCHUH - SERVICE - POST. 1972-2001. 3/yr. C. Maurer Druck und Verlag, Schubartstr 21, Geislingen, 73312, Germany.

780 016 USA ISSN 1080-6970
SCHWANN ARTIST; America's guide to classical performers. 1975-2001. a. Schwann Publications, 1280 Santa Anita Ct, Woodland, CA 95776.

791.436 FRA ISSN 1777-8042
SCI FI MAGAZINE. 2006-2008. bi-m. N B C Universal Global Networks France, 46 Quai le Gallo, Boulogne-Billancourt, 92100, France.

384.55 808.838 USA
SCI-FI TV. 1998-200?. bi-m. Starlog Communications, 250 W 49th St, 3rd Fl Ste 304, New York, NY 10019.

500 600 USA
SCIENCE AND TECHNOLOGY (PITTSBURGH, 1960) (ONLINE); a purchase guide for libraries. 1960-200?. a. Carnegie Library of Pittsburgh, Science and Technology Department, 4400 Forbes Ave, Pittsburgh, PA 15213.

500 USA
SCIENCE@BERKELEY LAB. 1999-2008. irreg. Ernest Orlando Lawrence Berkeley National Laboratory, Public Information Department, 1 Cyclotron Rd MS-65, Berkeley, CA 94720.

500 GBR ISSN 0300-3361
SCIENCE CHELSEA. 1966-1980. irreg. Chelsea College, Students Union, Manresa Rd, London, SW3 6LX, United Kingdom.

751.6 FRA ISSN 0988-3789
SCIENCE ET TECHNOLOGIE DE LA CONSERVATION ET DE LA RESTORATION DES OEUVRES D'ART ET DU PATRIMOINE. 1988-199?. s-a. E R E C, 68 rue Jean Jaures, Puteaux, 92800, France.

808.838 NLD ISSN 1385-1616
SCIENCE FICTION & FANTASY WARP; over science fiction, fantasy en andere speculatieve zaken. 1996-2005. s-a. Uitgeverij M, Herengracht 540, Amsterdam, 1017 BV, Netherlands.

362.13 USA ISSN 1539-6150
SCIENCE OF AGING KNOWLEDGE ENVIRONMENT. 2001-2006. w. American Association for the Advancement of Science, 1200 New York Ave, NW, Washington, DC 20005.

500 AUS ISSN 1446-6430
SCIENCEMAX. 2002-2004. q. Heinemann Interactive, 22 Samon St, Port Melbourne, VIC 3207, Australia.

616.8 GBR ISSN 0952-2255
SCIENTIFIC BASIS OF PSYCHIATRY. 1985-2009 (Jul.). irreg. Cambridge University Press, The Edinburgh Bldg, Shaftesbury Rd, Cambridge, CB2 8RU, United Kingdom.

500 DEU ISSN 0938-7676
SCIENTIFIC SERIES OF THE INTERNATIONAL BUREAU. 1990-2001 (vol.45). irreg. Forschungszentrum Juelich GmbH, Leo-Brandt-Str, Juelich, 52428, Germany.

930 301 930.1 ITA ISSN 1123-5713
SCIENZE DELL'ANTICHITA. 1987-ceased. irreg. Universita degli Studi di Roma "La Sapienza", 5 Piazzale Aldo Moro, Rome, 00185, Italy.

360 GBR ISSN 0144-0462
SCOPE (BELFAST); a review of social policy & voluntary action in Northern Ireland. 1975-2007. m. Northern Ireland Council for Voluntary Action, 61 Duncairn Gardens, Belfast, N Ireland BT15 2GB, United Kingdom.

028.5 ITA ISSN 1124-2922
SCOPERTE DOC/DISCOVER. 1996-ceased. m. (10/yr.). Logos Publishing, Via Curtatona 5/2, Modena, MO 41100, Italy.

929 AUS ISSN 1030-7788
SCOTS LINK; the Scottish family history magazine Australia and New Zealand. 1987-2004. q. (May, Aug., Nov. & Feb.). Scots Link, PO Box 477, Melton, VIC 3337, Australia.

100 GBR ISSN 0144-3062
SCOTS PHILOSOPHICAL MONOGRAPHS. 1980-1986. irreg. Scots Philosophical Club, University of St Andrews, c/o Department of Philosophy, University of Aberdeen, Old Brewery, High St, Aberdeen, AB24 3UB, United Kingdom.

664 GBR
SCOTTISH ASSOCIATION OF MASTER BAKERS. YEAR BOOK. 1902-1984. a. Scottish Association of Master Bakers, Atholl House, 4 Torphichen St, Edinburgh, EH3 8JQ, United Kingdom.

032 CAN ISSN 1491-7998
SCOTT'S CANADIAN SOURCEBOOK. 1966-2004. a. (in Nov.). Business Information Group, 12 Concorde Pl, Ste 800, Toronto, ON M3C 4J2, Canada.

369.4 FRA ISSN 0751-5731
SCOUTS. 1924-2004. q. Editions Scouts de France, 54 av. Jean Jaures, Paris, 75019, France.

369.4 FRA ISSN 1151-3365
SCOUTS AVENIR. 1924-2004. q. Editions Scouts de France, 54 av. Jean Jaures, Paris, 75019, France.

686.2 USA ISSN 1538-1862
SCREEN & DISPLAY GRAPHICS. 199?-2003. bi-m. National Business Media, Inc., PO Box 1416, Broomfield, CO 80038.

800 ITA
LA SCRITTURA SCENICA. 1971-19??. q. Bulzoni Editore, Via dei Liburni 14, Rome, 00185, Italy.

351 ITA ISSN 1120-7159
SCUOLA SUPERIORE DELLA PUBBLICA AMMINISTRAZIONE. BOLLETTINO. DOCUMENTI E INFORMAZIONI. 1989-ceased. 3/yr. Presidenza del Consiglio dei Ministri, Dipartimento per l'Informazione e l'Editoria, Via Po 14, Rome, 00198, Italy.

370 ITA ISSN 0036-9926
SCUOLA VIVA; mensile per educatori. 1964-ceased. q. Societa Editrice Internazionale, Corso R. Margherita 176, Turin, TO 10152, Italy.

364 345 NLD ISSN 1871-5478
SDU WETTENVERZAMELING. JEUGDRECHT. 2005-ceased. a. Sdu Uitgevers bv, Postbus 20025, The Hague, 2500 EA, Netherlands.

344.046 NLD ISSN 1871-5362
SDU WETTENVERZAMELING. MILIEURECHT. 2005-ceased. a. Sdu Uitgevers bv, Postbus 20025, The Hague, 2500 EA, Netherlands.

342.066 NLD ISSN 1871-546X
SDU WETTENVERZAMELING. RUIMTELIJK BESTUURSRECHT. 2005-ceased. a. Sdu Uitgevers bv, Postbus 20025, The Hague, 2500 EA, Netherlands.

368 NLD ISSN 1874-7299
SDU WETTENVERZAMELING VERZEKERINGSRECHT. 2006-ceased. a. Sdu Uitgevers bv, Postbus 20025, The Hague, 2500 EA, Netherlands.

664 USA ISSN 0270-417X
SEAFOOD PRICE-CURRENT. 1973-200?. s-w. Urner Barry Publications, Inc., PO Box 389, Toms River, NJ 08754.

914.2 NLD ISSN 1871-8124
SEASONS ENGELAND. 2005-2007. a. Sanoma Uitgevers B.V., Postbus 1900, Hoofddorp, 2130 JH, Netherlands.

641.5 NLD ISSN 1871-8116
SEASONS KOKEN & ETEN. 2005-2007. s-a. Sanoma Uitgevers B.V., Postbus 1900, Hoofddorp, 2130 JH, Netherlands.

371.42 USA ISSN 1098-9897
THE SEATTLE JOBBANK; the job hunter's guide to Washington. (Includes: Bellevue, Spokane, Tacoma and many others) 1989-2003 (13th ed.). irreg. Adams Media, 4700 E Galbraith Rd, Cincinnati, OH 45236.

052 GBR ISSN 1351-3591
SECOND SHIFT. 1993-199?. q. Second Shift, 11 Petworth St, Cambridge, Cambs CB1 2LY, United Kingdom.

365.34 FRA ISSN 1957-231X
SECULIVE MAGAZINE. 2007-2008. q. Seculive, 4 Rue du General Leclerc, Corbeil-Essonnes, 91100, France.

621.389 FRA ISSN 1151-4787
SECURITE ECHOS. 19??-200?. 21/yr. Editions du Gaillard, 5 av. de la Republique, Paris, Cedex 75130, France.

005.8 FRA ISSN 0297-9101
SECURITE INFORMATIQUE. 1986-2005. m. (11/yr.). Publi-News, 47 rue Aristide Briand, Levallois-Perret, 92300, France.

332.6 USA ISSN 0149-3582
SECURITIES WEEK. 1973-2006. w. Standard & Poor's, 55 Water St, New York, NY 10041.

851 ITA ISSN 0393-9464
IL SEGNALE; percorsi di ricerca letteraria - pathways of literary research. 1981-ceased. 3/yr. I Dispari, Via Fratelli Bronzetti 17, Milan, MI 20129, Italy.

796 ITA ISSN 1828-3608
I SEGRETI DEI PESCATORI. 2006-200?. m. Sprea Editori Srl, Via Torino 51, Cernusco sul Naviglio, MI 20063, Italy.

796 ITA ISSN 1825-7178
I SEGRETI DELLA PESCA DOLCE. 2005-200?. m. Sprea Editori Srl, Via Torino 51, Cernusco sul Naviglio, MI 20063, Italy.

796 ITA ISSN 1825-716X
I SEGRETI DELLA PESCA MARE. 2005-200?. m. Sprea Editori Srl, Via Torino 51, Cernusco sul Naviglio, MI 20063, Italy.

747 DEU
SELBER PLANEN; Neubau - Umbau - Renovierung. 2006-2007. 3/yr. Data Becker GmbH & Co. KG, Merowingerstr 30, Duesseldorf, 40223, Germany.

100 DEU ISSN 0939-0952
SELBSTORGANISATION. JAHRBUCH FUER KOMPLEXITAET IN DEN NATUR-, SOZIAL- UND GEISTESWISSENSCHAFTEN. 1990-2001. a. Duncker und Humblot GmbH, Carl-Heinrich-Becker-Weg 9, Berlin, 12165, Germany.

016.9489 DNK ISSN 0105-9475
SELECT BIBLIOGRAPHY OF DANISH WORKS ON THE HISTORY OF TOWNS PUBLISHED. (Forms also part of: Byhistoriske Hjaelpemidler) 1973-1996. irreg. Dansk Komite for Byhistorie, c/o Tore Nyberg, Institute of History, University of Odense, Campusvej 55, Odense M, 5230, Denmark.

332 USA
SELECTED BORROWINGS IN IMMEDIATELY AVAILABLE FUNDS OF LARGE COMMERCIAL BANKS. 1964-1997. w. U.S. Federal Reserve System, Board of Governors, Publications Services, Rm MS 138, Washington, DC 20551.

781.57 DNK ISSN 1396-0911
SELECTIVE AND PRELIMINARY LIST OF DANISH JAZZ CLUBS. 1972-1993. a. Danske Jazzcenter, Borupvej 66, Ronnede, 4683, Denmark.

384.1 ITA
SELEZIONANDO S I P; giornale aziendale. 1950-1994. bi-m. Societa Italiana per l'Esercizio delle Telecomunicazioni P.A., Via Flaminia, 189, Rome, RM 00196, Italy.

055.1 ITA ISSN 0037-1483
SELEZIONE DAL READER'S DIGEST (ITALIAN EDITION). 1948-ceased. m. Selezione dal Reader's Digest SpA, Via Lorenzini 4, Milan, MI 20139, Italy.

332 658 GBR ISSN 1462-3552
SELLING FINANCIAL SERVICES. 1998-2006. q. Quest Media, 9 The Leather Market, Weston St, London, SE1 3ER, United Kingdom.

387.15029 GBR ISSN 1362-7783
SELL'S MARINE INDUSTRY BUYERS' GUIDE. 1978-1999. a. C M P Information Ltd., Sovereign House, Sovereign Way, Tonbridge, Kent TN9 1RW, United Kingdom.

338.0029 GBR ISSN 0957-8889
SELL'S PRODUCTS & SERVICES DIRECTORY. 1885-2002. a. C M P Information Ltd., Sovereign House, Sovereign Way, Tonbridge, Kent TN9 1RW, United Kingdom.

338 DNK ISSN 1399-8935
DE SELVSTAENDIGE. 1995-2007. 5/yr. Haandvaerksraadet, Islands Brygge 26, PO Box 1990, Copenhagen S, 2300, Denmark.

499.992 DNK ISSN 0108-3759
SEMAJNA BULTENO; Europa semajna Esperanto gazeto. 1976-1989. irreg. (20-25/yr.). Esperanto Domo, Haslevangsvej 30, Aarhus V, 8210, Denmark.

621.381 USA ISSN 1523-7184
SEMICONDUCTOR BUSINESS NEWS. 1997-ceased. s-m. (22/yr.). C M P Media LLC, 600 Community Dr, Manhasset, NY 11030.

Cessations

616.5 ITA ISSN 1121-1881
SEMINARI IN DERMATOLOGIA. 1992-ceased. q. Il Pensiero Scientifico Editore, Via Bradano 3-C, Rome, 00199, Italy.

302 ESP ISSN 1134-3974
SEMIOSFERA; humanidades - tecnologias. 1994-1998. s-a. Universidad Carlos III de Madrid, Instituto de Cultura y Tecnologia "Miguel de Unamuno", Calle Madrid 126, Madrid, 28903, Spain.

850 ITA
SEMPLICE; almanacco delle prose. 1995-ceased. irreg. Fondazione San Carlo, Via San Carlo, 5, Modena, MO 41100, Italy.

590 DEU ISSN 0037-2102 CODEN: SBBOAG
SENCKENBERGIANA BIOLOGICA; international journal on biodiversity. 1919-2009. s-a. E. Schweizerbart'sche Verlagsbuchhandlung, Johannesstr 3A, Stuttgart, 70176, Germany.

580 DEU ISSN 0944-0178 CODEN: SNDTER
SENDTNERA. 1950-2002. irreg. (1-2/yr.). Botanische Staatssammlung Muenchen, Menzinger Str 67, Munich, 80638, Germany.

613.04244 DEU ISSN 1616-6582
SENSES. 1999-2004. 2/yr. Lady International Verlag, Salzmannweg 17, Stuttgart, 70192, Germany.

621.389 780 USA ISSN 0199-4654
THE SENSIBLE SOUND; helping audiophiles and music lovers to spend less and get more. 1977-2008 (Mar-Apr); suspended. bi-m. Sensible Sound, Inc., 403 Darwin Dr., Snyder, NY 14226.

006.3 USA ISSN 0746-9462
SENSORS (PRINT); your resource for sensing, communications, and control. 1984-2006 (Dec.). m. Questex Media Group Inc., 275 Grove St, Bldg 2, Ste 130, Newton, MA 02466.

150.18 GBR ISSN 1741-4725
SENSORY FORMATIONS. 2003 (Dec.)-200?. irreg. Berg Publishers, Angel Court, 1st Fl, 81 St Clements St, Oxford, Berks OX4 1AW, United Kingdom.

630 KOR ISSN 1013-4077 CODEN: SNYOEF
SEOUL DAEHAG'GYO NONGHAG YEON'GU/SEOUL NATIONAL UNIVERSITY JOURNAL OF AGRICULTURAL SCIENCES. 1973; N.S. 1976-1997. s-a. Seoul Daehag'gyo Nong'gwa Daehag, Seoul Daehag'gyo Nong'eob Gae'bal Yeon'guso, 103 Seodoon-dong, Suwon, 170, Korea, S.

500 600 KOR
SEOUL NATIONAL UNIVERSITY. FACULTY PAPERS. C & D, SCIENCE AND TECHNOLOGY SERIES, MEDICINE AND PHARMACY SERIES. 1971-1975. biennial. Seoul National University, San 56-1 Sinlim-dong, Kwanak-ku, Seoul, 151742, Korea, S.

570 KOR CODEN: SNBAAO
SEOUL NATIONAL UNIVERSITY. FACULTY PAPERS. E, BIOLOGY AND AGRICULTURE SERIES. 1971-1975 (vol.4). a. Seoul National University, San 56-1 Sinlim-dong, Kwanak-ku, Seoul, 151742, Korea, S.

200 ITA
SER SIMILIA SANTINI; iconografia, devozione, collezionismo di immaginette sacre. 1995-ceased. q. Barbieri Ediitore, Via Santa Lucia 1, Manduria, TA 74024, Italy.

282 ITA
IL SERAFICO. 1955-ceased. m. Frati Cappuccini della Provincia Basilicata - Salerno, Via Lungomare 162, Salerno, SA 84100, Italy.

613.8 CZE ISSN 1213-9548
SERGEI. 2002-2002 (ceased same year). m. Sdruzeni Marcus Group, Uvoz 24, Brno, 602 00, Czech Republic.

760 FRA ISSN 0999-7903
SERI MAGAZINE. 1989-199?. bi-m. Ediscreen, 14 av. Henry Dunant, BP 38, Villemomble, 93250, France.

296.092 ISR ISSN 0333-6174
SERIDIM. 1982-2004. a. Standing Committee of the Conference of European Rabbis, P O Box 5324, Jerusalem, 91052, Israel.

016.80883 DNK ISSN 1601-135X
SERIEKATALOG, SKOENLITTERATUR. 1967-2001. a. D B C A/S, Tempovej 7-11, Ballerup, 2750, Denmark.

962 932 EGY ISSN 1687-1510
SERVICE DES ANTIQUITES DE L'EGYPTE. ANNALES. 1900-19??. a. Service des Antiquites de l'Egypte, c/o Egyptian National Museum, Midan al-Tahrir, Kasr el-Nil, Cairo, Egypt.

647 FRA ISSN 1150-1502
SERVICE TRAITEUR. 1990-199?. 5/yr. Service Traiteur, 4 rue Santerre, Paris, 75012, France.

282 ITA ISSN 1123-931X
SERVITIUM; quaderni di ricerca spirituale. 1967-ceased. bi-m. Iniziative Culturali SRL, Via Ticino 2, Gorle (BG), 24020, Italy.

352.14 ITA
SERVIZI PUBBLICI LOCALI. 1972-ceased. 11/yr. Confederazione Nazionale dei Servizi (Confservizi), Via Cavour 179/a, Rome, 00184, Italy.

551 ITA ISSN 0366-2241
SERVIZIO GEOLOGICO D'ITALIA. BOLLETTINO. 1870-ceased. a. Istituto Superiore per la Protezione e la Ricerca Ambientale (I S P R A), Servizio Geologico d'Italia, Largo di Santa Susanna 13, Rome, Italy.

595.7 ESP ISSN 1134-7783
SESSIO CONJUNTA D'ENTOMOLOGIA. 1980-ceased. biennial. Societat Catalana de Lepidopterologia, Apartat de Correus 35049, Barcelona, 08080, Spain.

342.029 USA
SETON HALL CONSTITUTIONAL LAW JOURNAL. 1989-2002. s-a. Seton Hall University, School of Law, One Newark Center, Newark, NJ 07102.

340 ITA ISSN 0392-7253
SETTIMANA GIURIDICA. 1960-2004. w. Casa Editrice Italedi, Piazza Cavour 19, Rome, 00193, Italy.

779.28 CZE ISSN 1213-7634
SEXRANDE. 2002-2007. m. PK 62, a.s., Bohdalecka 6, Prague 10, 101 00, Czech Republic.

610 DEU
SEXUALMEDIZIN FUER DEN ARZT. 1997-2003. q. Dr. Schilke Medizinischer Verlag GmbH, Hainichener Str 21, Braeunsdorf, 09603, Germany.

808.838 AUS ISSN 1832-0651
SHADOWED REALMS. 2004-2006 (Oct.). bi-m. Angela Challis

387 387.7 ISR
SHAI MARITIME MAGAZINE. 1978-2007. fortn. Haifa University, Wydra Institute of Shipping and Aviation Research, University of Haifa, Eshkol Tower, Haifa, 31905, Israel.

822.33 USA ISSN 0914-1677
SHAKESPEARE WORLDWIDE. 1974-1995. a. A M S Press, Inc., Brooklyn Navy Yard, 63 Flushing Ave, Bldg 292, Unit #221, Brooklyn, NY 11205.

808.83872 FRA ISSN 1951-1108
SHANGHAI EXPRESS; feuilletons crimes et recits noirs. 2006-2006. 8/yr. Shanghai Express, 37 Rue Rousselet, Paris, 75007, France.

334 ISR
HA-SHAVU'A. 1951-1989. w. Ha-Kibbutz ha-Artzi, P O Box 40009, Tel Aviv, 61400, Israel.

796 646.4 NLD ISSN 1873-9261
SHE. 2006-2008. bi-m. Maruba b.v., Winthontlaan 200, Utrecht, 3526 KV, Netherlands.

020 AUS ISSN 1325-7919
SHELF LIFE. 1995-2004. q. University of New England, Dixson Library, Armidale, NSW 2351, Australia.

362.1 GBR ISSN 0144-2104
SHELLFISH INFORMATION LEAFLET. 1965-1975. irreg. Ministry of Agriculture Fisheries and Food, Huntingdon Rd, Ministry Of Agriculture Fisheries & Food, Whitehouse Ln, Cambridge, CB3 0LF, United Kingdom.

015.51 CHN ISSN 1000-0097
SHIJIE TUSHU/WORLD BOOKS. 1956-1994. m. China National Publications Import and Export Corporation, PO Box 88, Beijing, 100020, China.

054 FRA ISSN 1951-2910
SHINE. 2006-2006. q. Editions Shine, 38 Avenue des Mathurins, Paris, 75008, France.

305.31 CHN ISSN 1672-3112
SHISHANG CAIFU/HIS. 2003-2005. m. Zhongha Aiguo Gongcheng Lianhehui, 8, Dongtucheng Lu, Linda Dasha B-ceng, Beijing, 100013 , China.

028.5 305.4 CHN
SHISHANG - COSMOGIRL!. 2001-2007. m. Trends Communication Co. Ltd., 9, Guanghua Rd., Beijing, 100020, China.

054.1 FRA ISSN 1774-8488
SHOPPING MAGAZINE. 2003-2005. q. Prisma Presse, 73-75 Rue La Condamine, Paris, 75854 Cedex 17, France.

055.1 ITA ISSN 1720-7959
SHOPPING MILANO. 1988-ceased. q.?. Studio Uno s.a.s. di Annamaria Repellini & C., Via Carlo Pisacane, 18, Milan, MI 20129, Italy.

749.63 ITA
SHOWCASE. 1989-ceased. 2/yr. Editore Lupetti & Co., Via Hayez 12, Milan, MI 20129, Italy.

795.412 DEU
SHOWDOWN. 2007-2008 (May). bi-m. W E K A Media Publishing GmbH, Gruberstr 46a, Poing, 85586, Germany.

387.736 GBR
SHOWNOTES. 1989-2002. fortn. Airport Exhibitions Ltd., 4 Roumelia Ln, Bournemouth, Hants BH5 1ET, United Kingdom.

745.61 CHN ISSN 1000-6044
SHUFA YANJIU/STUDIES IN CALLIGRAPHY. 1979-2004. bi-m. Shanghai Shuhua Chubanshe, 81 Qinzhou Nanlu, Shanghai, 200233, China.

687 GBR ISSN 1361-3499
SHUTTLE PLUS. 1979-1999. q. Sewing Machine Trade Association, 24 Fairlawn Grove, London, W4 5EH, United Kingdom.

327 DEU ISSN 1611-907X
SICHERHEIT UND STABILITAET; Zeitschrift fuer den erweiterten Sicherheitsbegriff. 2003-2006. 2/yr. B W V - Berliner Wissenschafts Verlag GmbH, Axel-Springer-Str 54a, Berlin, 10117, Germany.

059.951 CHN ISSN 1005-2097
SICHUAN TODAY/JINRI SICHUAN. 1984-2000. q. Jinri Sichuan Zazhishe, 16 Shangye St, Chengdu, Sichuan 610012, China.

384 363.22 ITA ISSN 1723-5065
SICUREZZA DIGITALE. 2003-2004. bi-m. Tecniche Nuove SpA, Via Eritrea 21, Milan, MI 201, Italy.

001.3 ESP ISSN 0214-3216
EL SIGLO QUE VIENE. 1987-2003. q. Ayuntamiento de Sevilla, Area de Cultura, C. Almirante Apodaca 6A, Sevilla, 41001, Spain.

005.115 USA
SIGMAPASCAL. 1997-2005. m. Sigmapascal

150.195 FRA ISSN 1778-7793
SIGNES & SENS. 2000-2007. bi-m. Psychanalyse Magazine, 195 Allee Louis Montagnat, ZA Chalancon 1, Vedene, 84270, France.

659 CZE ISSN 1212-0588
SIGNMAKING. 1997-2005. q. Strategie Praha s.r.o., Drtinova 8, Prague 5, 150 00, Czech Republic.

004.6 USA ISSN 0896-4068
SILVERPLATTER EXCHANGE. 1988-2000. irreg. SilverPlatter Information, Incorporated, 333 Seventh Ave, 20th Fl, New York, NY 10001.

838.8385 CZE ISSN 1212-9240
SILVIA. 1991-2006. m. Moravska Bastei MOBA, s.r.o., Kotlarska 53, Brno, 602 00, Czech Republic.

363.7 AUS ISSN 0314-3155
SIMPLY LIVING. 1983-1996. q. Simply Living, 78 Renwick St, Redfern, NSW 2016, Australia.

940 NLD ISSN 0920-5551
SIR THOMAS BROWNE INSTITUTE. PUBLICATIONS. NEW SERIES. 1962; N.S. 1982-1995 (vol.13). irreg. Brill, PO Box 9000, Leiden, 2300 PA, Netherlands.

808.838 AUS
SIRIUS. 1993-ceased. q. Sirius, PO Box 188, Curtin, ACT 2605, Australia.

330 ITA ISSN 1825-0742
SISTEMA ITALIA. 1948-ceased. a. Franco Angeli Edizioni, Viale Monza 106, Milan, 20127, Italy.

651.2 ITA
SISTEMI UOMINI MACCHINE ORGANIZZAZIONE. 1958-ceased. 5/yr. Il Sole 24 Ore Business Media, Divisione J C E, Via Patecchio 2, Milan, 20141, Italy.

382 ESP ISSN 0213-2273
SITUACION; review of the Spanish economy. 1973-1996. q. Banco de Bilbao - Vizcaya, Servicio de Estudios, Gran Via 1, Bilbao, 48001, Spain.

328 ESP ISSN 1130-9466
SITUACION LATINOAMERICANA. 1990-1999. bi-m. Fundacion Centro Espanol de Estudios de America Latina, Sagasta, 15 6a Derecha, Madrid, 28004, Spain.

382 ESP ISSN 0213-229X
SITUACION. SUPLEMENTO DE COYUNTURA. 1978-199?. m. Banco de Bilbao - Vizcaya, Servicio de Estudios, Gran Via 1, Bilbao, 48001, Spain.

796.93 DEU ISSN 0930-1194
SKILAEUFER. 1948-2000. 7/yr. Brinkmann Henrich Medien GmbH, Heerstr 5, Meinerzhagen, 58540, Germany.

331.88 USA ISSN 0279-2028
SKILL; the UAW's international magazine for skilled trades members. 1981-2003. q. International Union, United Automobile, Aerospace and Agricultural Implement Workers of America, 8000 E Jefferson Ave, Detroit, MI 48214.

616.5 USA ISSN 1540-9740
SKINMED; dermatology for the clinician. 2002 (Sept.)-2008; suspended. bi-m. Le Jacq Communications, Inc., 3 Enterprise Dr, Ste 401, Shelton, CT 06484-4694.

747 DNK ISSN 0106-8679
SKOENNE HJEM. 1980-1984. q. Fogtdals Blade A-S, Farimagsgade 49, Copenhagen K, 1364, Denmark.

388 NLD
SKOOP. 1994-ceased. a. RAI Langfords bv, Postbus 10099, Amsterdam, 1001 EB, Netherlands.

387 DEU ISSN 1430-4201
SKYWEEK. 1988-2006. w. Daniel Fischer, Im Kottsiefen 10, Koenigswinter, 53639, Germany.

582.16 CZE ISSN 0323-0724
SLEZSKE ZEMSKE MUZEUM. CASOPIS. SERIE C. DENDROLOGIE. 1952-1979. s-a. Slezske Zemske Muzeum, Tyrsova 1, Opava, 74601, Czech Republic.

016 SVK ISSN 1335-2202
SLOVENSKA NARODNA BIBLIOGRAFIA. 1997-2004 (Dec.). q. Slovenska Narodna Kniznica, Martin, Nam J C Hronskeho 1, Martin, 03601, Slovakia.

070.5 GBR
SMALL PRESS LISTINGS. 1995-2000. q. National Small Press Centre, BM Bozo, London, WC1N 3XX, United Kingdom.

005.74 USA ISSN 1066-7911
SMART ACCESS. 1993-200?. m. Pinnacle Publishing, Inc., 1000 Holcomb Woods Pkwy, Bldg 200, Ste 280, Roswell, GA 30076.

051 USA ISSN 1536-5328
SMART HOMEOWNER (PRINT); innovative solutions for creating efficient, healthy, eco-friendly homes. 2001-2009; suspended. bi-m. Navigator Publishing LLC., 58 Fore St, Portland, ME 04101-4842.

005.117 USA ISSN 1544-1660
SMART SOLUTIONS. 1997-200?. m. Informant Communications Group, 5105 Florin Perkins Rd., Sacramento, CA 95826-4817.

004.16 USA ISSN 1930-6369
SMARTPHONE & POCKET P C. (Personal Computer) 1997-2008. bi-m. Thaddeus Computing, Inc., 110 N. Court, Fairfield, IA 52556.

654.1 ITA ISSN 1826-5790
SMARTPHONE E PALMARI. 2005-200?. bi-m. Sprea Editori Srl, Via Torino 51, Cernusco sul Naviglio, MI 20063, Italy.

642.57 DEU ISSN 1435-9898
SNACK BISTRO. 1968-2006. 11/yr. B & L MedienGesellschaft mbH & Co. KG, Max-Volmer-Str 28, Hilden, 40724, Germany.

328.94 338.7 AUS ISSN 1039-0537
SNOWY MOUNTAINS COUNCIL. ANNUAL REPORT. 1974-2002. a. AusInfo, Parliament House, Canberra Mc, ACT 2600, Australia.

282 ITA ISSN 0037-7562
SOCCORSO PERPETUO DI MARIA. 1946-ceased. m. Santuario della Madonna del Perpetuo Soccorso, Padri Redentoristi di Bussolengo, Via Ospedale 12, Bussolengo, VR 37012, Italy.

616.8 302 GBR ISSN 1749-5016
SOCIAL COGNITIVE AND AFFECTIVE NEUROSCIENCE (PRINT). 2006 (Summer)-2008. a. Oxford University Press, Great Clarendon St, Oxford, OX2 6DP, United Kingdom.

368.4 362 AUS ISSN 0817-3524
SOCIAL SECURITY REPORTER. 1981-2004. bi-m. Legal Service Bulletin Co-Operative Ltd., Law Faculty, Monash University, VIC 3800, Australia.

361.30941 GBR ISSN 0957-3623
SOCIAL WORK AND SOCIAL WELFARE YEARBOOK. 1989-1991. a. Open University Press, Shoppenhangers Rd, Maidenhead, Berks MK7 6AA, United Kingdom.

361.30711 USA ISSN 0037-8062
SOCIAL WORK EDUCATION REPORTER. 1953-2006. 3/yr. Council on Social Work Education, 1725 Duke St, Ste 500, Alexandria, VA 22314.

300 NLD ISSN 0037-8097
SOCIALE WETENSCHAPPEN. 1957-2005. q. Universiteit van Tilburg, Faculteit Sociale Wetenschappen, Postbus 90153, Tilburg, 5000 LE, Netherlands.

635 ESP
SOCIEDAD ESPANOLA DE HORTICULTURA. REVISTA. 1935-19??. m. Sociedad Espanola de Horticultura, Arrieta, 7-5, Madrid, 28013, Spain.

780 ESP ISSN 0210-1440
SOCIEDAD ESPANOLA DE MUSICOLOGIA. BOLETIN. 1978-ceased. s-a. Sociedad Espanola de Musicologia, Carretas 14, 7o. Desp. B-3, Madrid, 28012, Spain.

660 ITA ISSN 0393-4594
SOCIETA CHIMICA ITALIANA. BOLLETTINO. 1979-ceased. m. Societa Chimica Italiana, Viale Liegi 48c, Rome, RM 00198, Italy.

001.3 ITA
SOCIETA LETTERARIA DI VERONA. BOLLETTINO. 18??-ceased. a. Societa Letteraria di Verona, Piazzetta Scalette Rubiani 1, Verona, 37121, Italy.

617 ITA ISSN 1121-1342
SOCIETA MEDICO-CHIRURGICA DELLA PROVINCIA DI CREMONA. BOLLETTINO. 1946-1974. s-a. Societa Medico-Chirurgica di Cremona, Ordine dei Medici, Via Palestro, 66, Cremona, CR 26100, Italy.

930.1 700 ITA
SOCIETA PIEMONTESE DI ARCHEOLOGIA E BELLE ARTI. BOLLETTINO. 1874-ceased. a. Societa Piemontese di Archeologia e Belle Arti, Via Giovanni Francesco Napione, 2, Turin, TO 10124, Italy.

945 ITA ISSN 0583-8002
SOCIETA STORICA MAREMMANA. BOLLETTINO. 1923-1936; resumed 1960-1997. s-a. Societa Storica Maremmana, Piazza del Popolo 3, Grosseto, 58100, Italy.

340 ESP ISSN 1578-3804
SOCIETAS & LEX. 2001-2002. bi-m. Dykinson, S.L., C Melendez Valdes, 61, Madrid, 28015, Spain.

500 ESP ISSN 1130-4758 CODEN: BSCMDI
SOCIETATS CATALANES DE FISICA, QUIMICA, MATEMATIQUES I TECNOLOGIA. BUTLLETI. 1934-199?. s-a. Institut d'Estudis Catalans, Carrer del Carme 47, Barcelona, 08001, Spain.

301 FRA ISSN 1629-825X
SOCIETES BRESILIENNES/SOCIEDADES BRASILEIRAS. 2001-2003. s-a. L' Harmattan, 5 rue de l'Ecole Polytechnique, Paris, 75005, France.

327 NLD ISSN 1871-8868
SOCIETIES WITHOUT BORDERS; human rights and the social sciences. 2006-2009 (Vol.4). s-a. Brill, PO Box 9000, Leiden, 2300 PA, Netherlands.

579.3 GBR ISSN 1467-4734
SOCIETY FOR APPLIED MICROBIOLOGY. SYMPOSIUM SERIES. 1971-2003. a. Wiley-Blackwell Publishing Ltd., 9600 Garsington Rd, Oxford, OX4 2DQ, United Kingdom.

579 GBR ISSN 0081-1394 CODEN: SSGMAI
SOCIETY FOR GENERAL MICROBIOLOGY. SYMPOSIUM. 1961-2006 (Apr.). a. Cambridge University Press, The Edinburgh Bldg, Shaftesbury Rd, Cambridge, CB2 8RU, United Kingdom.

301 150 GBR ISSN 1367-4102
SOCIETY FOR PSYCHOLOGICAL ANTHROPOLOGY. PUBLICATIONS. 1992-2008 (Jun.). irreg. Cambridge University Press, The Edinburgh Bldg, Shaftesbury Rd, Cambridge, CB2 8RU, United Kingdom.

551.3 USA ISSN 1547-3090
SOCIETY OF ECONOMIC GEOLOGISTS. GUIDEBOOK SERIES (PRINT). (no.35 (2001) also published in print & CD-ROM edition) 1987-1999 (no.31). irreg. Society of Economic Geologists, Inc., 7811 Shaffer Pkwy, Littleton, CO 80127.

301 ITA
SOCIOLOGIA (NAPLES). 1975 (no.4)-ceased. irreg. Societa Editrice Napoletana s.r.l., Corso Umberto I, 1-34, Naples, NA 80138, Italy.

301 DEU ISSN 0942-4482 CODEN: POISEN
SOCIOLOGIA INTERNATIONALIS. BEIHEFT. 1992-1992 (ceased same year). irreg. Duncker und Humblot GmbH, Carl-Heinrich-Becker-Weg 9, Berlin, 12165, Germany.

301 DNK ISSN 0106-536X
SOCIOLOGICAL MICROJOURNAL. 1967-1985. a. Erik Manniche and Kaare Svalastoga Eds. & Pubs., Linnegade 22, Copenhagen K, 1361, Denmark.

301 AUS ISSN 0156-4943
SOCIOLOGY OCCASIONAL PUBLICATIONS. 1978-1980. irreg. University of New England, School of Social Science, Armidale, NSW 2351, Australia.

330 DNK ISSN 0109-2863
SOENDERJYLLANDS ERHVERVSORIENTERING: PRODUKTION, HANDEL, KONTAKT. 1983-1987. q. Langenberg Trykkeri, Falstersgade 2, Sonderborg, 6400, Denmark.

005.5 GBR ISSN 0964-6841
SOFTWARE DEVELOPMENT MONITOR. 19??-1994. 12/yr. Pergamon, The Blvd, Langford Ln, East Park, Kidlington, Oxford OX5 1GB, United Kingdom.

005.36 USA ISSN 0000-006X
SOFTWARE ENCYCLOPEDIA; a guide for personal, professional, and business users. 1985-2009. a. R.R. Bowker LLC, 630 Central Ave, New Providence, NJ 07974.

005.5 USA ISSN 0897-8085 CODEN: SMWMEQ
SOFTWARE MAGAZINE. 1981-2002. bi-m. King Content Co., 233 Needham St, Ste 300, Newton, MA 02464.

016.55 551 NLD ISSN 1380-7838
SOIL SCIENCE ALERT; an alerting service covering current articles in Elsevier soil science journals. 1994-200?. 6/yr. Elsevier BV, Radarweg 29, P O Box 211, Amsterdam, 1000 AE, Netherlands.

910.202 NZL ISSN 1175-5253
SOJOURNEY. 2001-2004. s-a. Limelight Media, Seventh Ave., PO Box 148, Tauranga, New Zealand.

687.2 ITA
SOLOINTIMO INTERNATIONAL. 1987-ceased. 5/yr. Editrice Acalifa s.r.l., Via San Rocco 17, Milan, 20135, Italy.

338.9 315 KOR ISSN 1976-8370
SOMAE PANMAE-AEG TONGGYE/KOREA (REPUBLIC). NATIONAL STATISTICAL OFFICE. ANNUAL REPORT ON THE CONSUMER PRICE INDEX. 1967-2008. a. Tong'gyecheong, Government Complex Daejeon, 139 Seonsaro (920 Dunsan 2-dong), Seo-gu, Daejeon, 302-701, Korea, S.

282 DEU ISSN 0176-862X
SONNTAGSDIENSTE. 1972-2001. m. Bergmoser und Hoeller Verlag GmbH, Karl-Friedrich-Str 76, Aachen, 52072, Germany.

055 ITA
IL SOSPIRO DEL TIFOSO; periodico vicentino di sport e cultura. 1964-2002. bi-w. Pino Dato, Piazza Biade, 19, Vicenza, VI 36100, Italy.

333.5 USA ISSN 1521-2459
SOTHEBY'S INTERNATIONAL REALTY DOMAIN. 1998-2007. q. The Pohly Co., 99 Bedford St, Fl 5, Boston, MA 02111.

786.74 ITA
SOUNDSCAPES RELAXING MUSIC. 1996-ceased. m. Novaera Edizioni s.a.s., Casella Postale 88, Pesaro, PS 61100, Italy.

025 CZE ISSN 1212-3870
SOUPIS ZAHRANICNICH CASOPISU DOCHAZEJICICH DO C R A S R V ROCE.../LIST OF FOREIGN PERIODICALS ACQUIRED IN CZECH AND SLOVAK LIBRARIES IN (YEAR). 1997-2003. a. Narodni Lekarska Knihovna, Sokolska 54, Prague, 12132, Czech Republic.

025 CZE ISSN 1212-3889
SOUPIS ZAHRANICNICH CASOPISU OBJEDNANYCH DO C R A S R V ROCE (...)/LIST OF FOREIGN PERIODICALS ORDERED IN CZECH AND SLOVAK LIBRARIES IN (YEAR). 1998-2004. a. Narodni Lekarska Knihovna, Sokolska 54, Prague, 12132, Czech Republic.

332.6 FRA ISSN 1608-1072
SOURCE O E C D. INSTITUTIONAL INVESTORS STATISTICS. (Organisation for Economic Cooperation and Development) 2000-2005. irreg. Organisation for Economic Cooperation and Development (O E C D), 2 Rue Andre Pascal, Paris, 75775 Cedex 16, France.

382 FRA ISSN 1608-1145
SOURCE O E C D. INTERNATIONAL TRADE AND COMPETITIVENESS STATISTICS/SOURCE O C D E INDICATEURS DU COMMERCE INTERNATIONAL ET DE LA COMPETITIVITE. (Organisation for Economic Cooperation and Development) 2000-200?. irreg. Organisation for Economic Cooperation and Development (O E C D), 2 Rue Andre Pascal, Paris, 75775 Cedex 16, France.

296.1 ISR ISSN 0082-4585
SOURCES OF CONTEMPORARY JEWISH THOUGHT/MEKEVOT. 1970-1979. irreg. World Zionist Organization, Department for Torah Education and Culture in the Diaspora, P O Box 92, Jerusalem, 91920, Israel.

930.1 NLD
SOUTH ASIAN ARCHAEOLOGY; proceedings of the international conference. 1971-1999. biennial. International Institute for Asian Studies, PO Box 9515, Leiden, 2300 RA, Netherlands.

621.3 AUS ISSN 0038-2892
SOUTH AUSTRALIAN ELECTRICAL CONTRACTOR. 1956-1983. bi-m. Electrical Contractors Association of S.A. Inc., PO Box 47, Eastwood, SA 5063, Australia.

354.35 388 GBR ISSN 1366-8978
SOUTH GLOUCESTERSHIRE COUNCIL. TRANSPORT POLICIES AND PROGRAMME. SUBMISSION. 1998-1999. a. South Gloucestershire Council, Planning, Transportation and Environmental Services, Castle St, Thornbury, S Glos BS12 1HF, United Kingdom.

658.8 USA
SOUTHEAST C-$TORE JOURNAL. 2006-2008. m. Kevin B. Griffin, 201 Oak St, Ste A, Pembroke, MA 02359.

747 635 USA ISSN 0149-516X
SOUTHERN ACCENTS; the magazine of fine Southern interiors and gardens. 1977-2009 (Aug.). bi-m. Southern Progress Corp., 2100 Lakeshore Dr, Birmingham, AL 35209.

690 USA
SOUTHERN HOME PLANS. 1998-2009 (Jan.). q. HomePlans.com, 901 N 3rd St, Ste 216, Minneapolis, MN 55401.

820 NZL ISSN 1178-8607
SOUTHERN OCEAN REVIEW; international on-line magazine of the arts. 1996-2009 (no. 50, Jan.). q. Square One Books, P.O. Box 2143, Dunedin, New Zealand.

370 DEU CODEN: SINFEY
SOWI. 1972-2005. q. Erhard Friedrich Verlag GmbH, Im Brande 17, Seelze, 30926, Germany.

629.1 AUS ISSN 1329-4857
SPACE INDUSTRY NEWS. 1985-2003. q. Cooperative Research Centre for Satellite Systems, GPO Box 1483, Canberra, ACT 2601, Australia.

383 ESP
SPAIN. DIRECCION GENERAL DE CORREOS Y TELECOMUNICACION. BOLETIN OFICIAL DE CORREOS Y TELECOMUNICACION. 1975-2002. s-w. Direccion General de Correos y Telecomunicacion, Madrid, Spain.

639.2 ESP
SPAIN. DIRECCION GENERAL DE PESCA MARITIMA. PUBLICACIONES TECNICAS. 197?-2002. irreg. Direccion General de Pesca Maritima, Madrid, Spain.

351 ESP
SPAIN. SENADO. TEMAS. 19??-ceased. irreg. Spain. El Senado de Espana, Plaza de la Marina Espanola 8, Madrid, 28071, Spain.

351 ESP
SPAIN. SENADO. TEXTOS NORMATIVOS. (Contains 2 subseries: Constitucion Espanola - Reglamento del Senado (Year); Standing Orders of the Senate (Year)) 19??-ceased. irreg. Spain. El Senado de Espana, Plaza de la Marina Espanola 8, Madrid, 28071, Spain.

658.8 GBR
SPAR NETWORK. 1973-2007. 12/yr. Spar Today, 32-40 Headstone Dr., Harrow, Mddx HA3 5QT, United Kingdom.

658.86 ESP
SPARCO; revista tecnica mensual de la distribucion. 1960-ceased. m. SPAR Espanola, Gran Via 46, 1o, Madrid, 28013, Spain.

330 DEU ISSN 1435-8379
SPARKASSEN-MAGAZIN. 1976-2003. m. Deutscher Sparkassenverlag GmbH, Am Wallgraben 115, Stuttgart, 70565, Germany.

674 ITA ISSN 1120-4788
SPAZIOLEGNO. 1999-ceased. 6/yr. Milla International S.r.l., Via Stefano Ussi, 4, Milan, MI 20125, Italy.

361 NZL ISSN 1176-161X
SPEAR BULLETIN. 2003-2007. q. SPEaR Secretariat, Center for Social Research and Evaluation, Ministry of Social Development, Bowen State Bldg, Bowen St, PO Box 1556, Wellington, 6140, New Zealand.

371.97 USA ISSN 1080-1375
SPECIAL EDUCATION TODAY. 1995-2008. q. LifeWay Christian Resources, 1 Lifeway Plz, Nashville, TN 37234.

747 ITA ISSN 1825-7933
SPECIALE CASA. 2005-200?. bi-m. Tattilo Editrice SpA, Via degli Olmetti 18, Rome, 00060, Italy.

636.7 ITA ISSN 1128-5389
SPECIALE TUTTE LE RAZZE. 1997-ceased. a. Sprea Editori Srl, Via Torino 51, Cernusco sul Naviglio, MI 20063, Italy.

621.38 USA ISSN 1059-3772
SPECIALTY REFERENCES. APPLICATION NOTES. 1972-1999. a. D.A.T.A. Business Publishing, 15 Inverness Way E, Box 6510, Englewood, CO 80155-6510.

371.9 DNK ISSN 0907-6069
SPECIALUNDERVISNING. 1976-2005. biennial. Landsforeningen for Laesepaedagoger, Strandstien 18, Thorupstrand, Fjerritslev, 9690, Denmark.

792 FRA ISSN 0295-6047
SPECTACLES INFOS. 1985-199?. 4/yr. Promoscience, 97 rue Reaumur, Paris, 75002, France.

800 ITA
SPECULUM ARTIUM. 1977-1997 (no.21). irreg. Angelo Longo Editore, Via Paolo Costa 33, Ravenna, 48121, Italy.

796.77 796.72 AUS ISSN 1449-6984
SPEED. 2002-2005. bi-m. A C P Magazines Ltd., 54-58 Park St, Sydney, NSW 2000, Australia.

690.028 688.76 NLD ISSN 1871-949X
SPEELTUIN. 200?-2008. q. Reed Business bv, Van Bylandthuis, Benoordenhoutseweg 46, Den Haag, 2596 BC, Netherlands.

550 398 910 ITA ISSN 0394-5057
SPELEO. 1978-ceased. q. Speleo Club Firenze, Via Torre del Gallo, 30, Florence, FI 50125, Italy.

306 ITA ISSN 0038-738X
SPETTACOLO; rassegna economica e sociale degli spettacoli e delle attivita artistiche e culturali. 1951-2002. q. Societa Italiana degli Autori ed Editori (S I A E), Viale della Letteratura 30, Rome, 00144, Italy.

314.5 ITA ISSN 1126-8581
LO SPETTACOLO IN ITALIA; annuario statistico. 1936-ceased. a. Societa Italiana degli Autori ed Editori (S I A E), Viale della Letteratura 30, Rome, 00144, Italy.

363.7382 GBR ISSN 1353-2561 CODEN: SSTBEK
SPILL SCIENCE & TECHNOLOGY BULLETIN; oils - chemicals - land - marine. 1994-2004. bi-m. Pergamon, The Blvd, Langford Ln, East Park, Kidlington, Oxford OX5 1GB, United Kingdom.

617.375 DEU ISSN 1613-7140
SPINEART; a spine arthroplasty magazine. 2004-2005. q. Springer, Tiergartenstr 17, Heidelberg, 69121, Germany.

615.535 299 GBR ISSN 1743-1867
SPIRITUALITY AND HEALTH INTERNATIONAL. 2004-2008. q. John Wiley & Sons Ltd., The Atrium, Southern Gate, Chichester, West Sussex PO19 8SQ, United Kingdom.

617.1 TUR ISSN 1300-5278
SPOR VE TIP. 1993-ceased. 6/yr. Lodos Yayincilik Ticaret A.S., Yildiz Posta Cad., Sinan Apt.no. 36 D 66-67, Gayrettepe - Instanbul, 80280, Turkey.

796 FRA ISSN 1764-1756
SPORT. 2003-2009 (Apr.). w. Sports Medias et Strategie, 16-18 rue Rivay, Levallois Perret, 92300, France.

388 DEU
SPORT AND TUNING MARKT. 1991-2008 (Mar.). q. A M O Verlag GmbH, Sattlerstr 7, Luebeck, 23556, Germany.

790.1 DEU
SPORT IM SPIEGEL. 1955-2007. m. Deutscher Olympischer Sportbund, Otto-Fleck-Schneise 12, Frankfurt Am Main, 60528, Germany.

794 DEU
SPORT JOURNAL. 2007-2008. m. Pferdesport Verlag Rolf Ehlers GmbH, Rockwinkeler Landstr 20, Bremen-Oberneuland, 28355, Germany.

790.1 DEU
SPORT & CO. 2000-2002. 2/yr. Martin Kelter Verlag, Muehlenstieg 16-22, Hamburg, 22041, Germany.

617.1 ESP ISSN 1130-0183
SPORT & MEDICINA. 1990-1994. bi-m. Ediciones Eseuve S.A., c/o Oficina de Justificacion de la Difusion (OJD), Plaza Marques de Salamanca, 9-4D, Madrid, 28006, Spain.

790.1 DNK ISSN 0109-9787
SPORTEN. 1952-2002. a. Forlaget Carlsen A-S, Krogshoejvej 32, Bagsvaerd, 2880, Denmark.

621.8 USA ISSN 1930-479X
SPORTING KNIVES. 2002-2006. a. Krause Publications, Inc., 700 E State St, Iola, WI 54990.

796.334 FRA ISSN 1638-7031
SPORTMAG. LANGUEDOC-ROUSSILLON. 2003-2008. bi-m. Even'dia, 15 Av. Charles Cros, Jacou, 34830, France.

796.334 FRA ISSN 1777-7275
SPORTMAG. MIDI-PYRENEES. 2006-2008. bi-m. Even'dia, 15 Av. Charles Cros, Jacou, 34830, France.

796 FRA ISSN 1956-3280
SPORTMAG. RHONE-ALPES. 2007-2008. bi-m. Even'dia, 15 Av. Charles Cros, Jacou, 34830, France.

796.41 ITA ISSN 1123-721X
SPORTMAN & FITNESS. 1973-ceased. bi-m. Edizioni Sportman, Strada Francesca, 42, Zingonia, BG 24040, Italy.

790.1 NLD
SPORTS DESK QUARTERLY. 2000-ceased. q. Infostrada BV, Binnenwal 2, Nieuwegein, 3432 GH, Netherlands.

016.6137 GBR ISSN 0142-1794
SPORTS DOCUMENTATION MONTHLY BULLETIN. 1971-2002. m. Centre for Sports Science and History, Main Library, University of Birmingham, Edgbaston, Birmingham B15 2TT, United Kingdom.

796.0688 GBR ISSN 1460-8359
SPORTS MARKETING. 1997-200?. m. Centaur Communications Ltd., St Giles House, 50 Poland St, London, W1F 7AX, United Kingdom.

658.8 DEU ISSN 1269-3626
SPORTS RETAIL EUROPE; the only European trade magazine for sporting goods retailers. 1996-200?. s-a. S A Z Verlag GmbH, Rumfordstr 42, Munich, 80469, Germany.

796 USA ISSN 1545-309X
SPORTS TV PRODUCTION. 2003-2000. bi-m. NewBay Media, LLC, 810 Seventh Ave, 27th Fl, New York, NY 10019.

799 USA ISSN 1549-4969
SPORTSMEN'S ATLAS. 2002-2005. bi-m. Outdoor Empire Publishing, Inc., 21415 87th St, Woodinville, WA 98072.

629.45 FRA ISSN 1273-8476
SPOUTNIK MAGAZINE; histoires de la conquete spatiale. 1997-199?. q. Editions Explorer France, Le Prologue 1 voie no. 1, Labege, Cedex 31312, France.

809 DEU ISSN 0948-7417
SPRACHKONTAKT IN AFRIKA/LANGUAGE CONTACT IN AFRICA. 1995-2000 (vol.4). irreg. Ruediger Koeppe Verlag, Wendelinstr 73-75, Cologne, 50933, Germany.

618.082 155.3 USA ISSN 0272-202X
SPRINGER SERIES: FOCUS ON WOMEN. 1980-200?. irreg. Springer Publishing Company, 11 W 42nd St, 15th Fl, New York, NY 10036.

616.8 USA ISSN 0740-4212
SPRINGER SERIES IN PSYCHIATRY. 1982-ceased. irreg. Springer Publishing Company, 11 W 42nd St, 15th Fl, New York, NY 10036.

610.73 USA
SPRINGER SERIES ON ADVANCED PRACTICE NURSING. 1993-200?. irreg. Springer Publishing Company, 11 W 42nd St, 15th Fl, New York, NY 10036.

158 616.8 USA ISSN 0278-6729
SPRINGER SERIES ON BEHAVIOR THERAPY AND BEHAVIORAL MEDICINE. 1976-ceased. irreg. Springer Publishing Company, 11 W 42nd St, 15th Fl, New York, NY 10036.

155.937 USA ISSN 0271-1192
SPRINGER SERIES ON DEATH AND SUICIDE. 1979-200?. irreg. Springer Publishing Company, 11 W 42nd St, 15th Fl, New York, NY 10036.

362.6 USA
SPRINGER SERIES ON ETHICS, LAW, AND AGING. 1994-200?. irreg. Springer Publishing Company, 11 W 42nd St, 15th Fl, New York, NY 10036.

362.82 USA
SPRINGER SERIES ON FAMILY VIOLENCE. 1998-200?. irreg. Springer Publishing Company, 11 W 42nd St, 15th Fl, New York, NY 10036.

610.7365 USA
SPRINGER SERIES ON GERIATRIC NURSING. 1991-200?. irreg. Springer Publishing Company, 11 W 42nd St, 15th Fl, New York, NY 10036.

362.1 USA ISSN 0748-0334
SPRINGER SERIES ON HEALTH CARE AND SOCIETY. 1977-ceased. irreg. Springer Publishing Company, 11 W 42nd St, 15th Fl, New York, NY 10036.

612.67 USA
SPRINGER SERIES ON LIFE STYLES & ISSUES ON AGING. 1978-200?. irreg. Springer Publishing Company, 11 W 42nd St, 15th Fl, New York, NY 10036.

610.711 USA ISSN 0277-4186
SPRINGER SERIES ON MEDICAL EDUCATION. 1977-200?. irreg. Springer Publishing Company, 11 W 42nd St, 15th Fl, New York, NY 10036.

615.82 362.4 USA ISSN 0734-6522
SPRINGER SERIES ON REHABILITATION. 1981-200?. irreg. Springer Publishing Company, 11 W 42nd St, 15th Fl, New York, NY 10036.

360 USA ISSN 0891-9720
SPRINGER SERIES ON SOCIAL WORK. 1984-200?. irreg. Springer Publishing Company, 11 W 42nd St, 15th Fl, New York, NY 10036.

051 USA ISSN 0195-0894
SPRINGFIELD! MAGAZINE (SPRINGFIELD, 1979). 1979-2008. m. Springfield Communications, Inc., 520 S Union, Springfield, MO 65802.

410 DNK ISSN 0107-8895
SPROGFORENINGENS ALMANAK. 1893-1992. a. Dy-Po Bogforlag, Soenderborg, Denmark.

255.3 ITA ISSN 0038-8750
LA SQUILLA DEI FRATINI MISSIONARI DI RECCO. 1924-ceased. bi-m. Francescani di Recco, Via S Francesco, 4, Recco, GE 16036, Italy.

792.071 USA ISSN 1080-7268
STAGE OF THE ART. 1988-2008 (Spr.). 4/yr. American Alliance for Theatre & Education, 7475 Wisconsin Ave, Ste 300A, Bethesda, MD 20814.

636.160948 DNK ISSN 0900-5846
STAMBOG OVER SHETLAND PONYER. 1969-1991. a. Avlsforeningen for Shetlandsponyer, c/o Else Enemark, Riisvej 24, Faarevejle, 4540, Denmark.

620.1 ITA ISSN 1592-3541
STAMPI E DESIGN. 1999-2006. m. Tecniche Nuove SpA, Via Eritrea 21, Milan, MI 201, Italy.

079.94 AUS ISSN 0812-9762
THE STANDARD (WARRNAMBOOL). 18??-1949. 6/w. (Mon.-Sat.). Standard (Warrnambool), 170-176 Koroit St, Warrnambool, VIC 3280, Australia.

332 USA
STANDARD & POOR'S BANKRATINGS SERVICE. 19??-1999. q. Standard & Poor's, 55 Water St, New York, NY 10041.

330 USA ISSN 0196-4674
STANDARD & POOR'S CORPORATION RECORDS. CURRENT NEWS EDITION. 1923-2008. d. (5/wk.). Standard & Poor's, 55 Water St, New York, NY 10041.

332.6 USA ISSN 1062-5607
STANDARD & POOR'S DIRECTORY OF DIVIDEND REINVESTMENT PLANS. 1991-2000. a. Standard & Poor's, 55 Water St, New York, NY 10041.

332.6 USA ISSN 1088-2847
STANDARD & POOR'S INDUSTRY REPORTS. 1990-1996. m. Standard & Poor's, 55 Water St, New York, NY 10041.

332.6 USA ISSN 1085-6927
STANDARD & POOR'S SMALLCAP 600 GUIDE. 1995-2003. irreg. McGraw-Hill Companies, Inc., 1221 Ave of the Americas, 43rd fl, New York, NY 10020.

659.1029 USA ISSN 1048-2415
STANDARD DIRECTORY OF ADVERTISERS (BUSINESS CLASSIFICATIONS EDITION). 1964-2002. a. Marquis Who's Who LLC., 890 Mountain Ave, Ste 300, PO Box 10, New Providence, NJ 07974.

028.5 DEU
STAR HITS!. 2005-2007. q. Egmont Cultfish Media GmbH, Hansastr 32, Munich, 80686, Germany.

780 ITA ISSN 1828-1893
STAR MUSIC. 2006-200?. m. Edigamma Publishing, Via Sambuca Pistoiese 70A, Rome, 00138, Italy.

791.43 DEU
STAR TREK (RHEINFELDEN). 1998-2007 (Jun.). q. OZ Verlag GmbH, Roemerstr 90, Rheinfelden, 79618, Germany.

791.45 DEU
STAR TREK (STUTTGART). 2000-2001. bi-m. Panini Verlags GmbH, Ravensstr 48, Nettetal, 41334, Germany.

028.5 DEU ISSN 1612-9571
STARFLASH. 2002 (Sep.)-2008. m. Axel Springer Mediahouse Muenchen GmbH, Leonrodstr 52, Munich, 80636, Germany.

940 NLD
HET STARING INSTITUUT. WERKEN. 1980-1984. a. Het Staring Instituut, Postbus 686, Doetinchem, 7000 AR, Netherlands.

352 CZE ISSN 1801-8327
STAROSTA A OBCANE. 2002-2007. plus q. updates. Nakladatelstvi Dr. Josef Raabe, s.r.o., Sokolovska 155/31, Prague 8, 180 00, Czech Republic.

791.456 DEU
STARS ON T V. 2007 (Aug.)-2008 (Feb.). m. Klambt Verlag GmbH, Im Neudeck 1, Speyer, 67346, Germany.

629.286 ITA ISSN 1124-2418
STARTER. 1984-ceased. m. Casa Editrice Universo SpA, Via Cusani 4, Milan, 20121, Italy.

368.382 USA ISSN 1522-5348
STATE HEALTH MONITOR. 1993-2002. 12/yr. Atlantic Information Services, Inc., 1100 17th St, NW, Ste 300, Washington, DC 20036.

351 USA ISSN 1530-0188
STATE INFORMATION DIRECTORY (YEAR). 2001-2003. irreg. C Q Press, Inc., 2300 N St, NW, Ste 800, Washington, DC 20037.

310 USA ISSN 1020-0991
STATISTICAL HANDBOOK. 1993-1996. a. World Bank Group, 1818 H St, NW, Washington, DC 20433.

330.9 USA ISSN 0251-0073
STATISTICAL INDICATORS OF SHORT TERM ECONOMIC CHANGES IN E.C.E. COUNTRIES. 1959-1991. m. United Nations Publications, 2 United Nations Plaza, Rm DC2-853, New York, NY 10017.

304.6 USA ISSN 1051-8002
STATISTICAL RECORD OF BLACK AMERICA. 1990-ceased. biennial. Gale, 27500 Drake Rd, Farmington Hills, MI 48331.

314.8 DNK ISSN 1600-3020
STATISTICS ACROSS BORDERS/HAGTOEL UM LANDAMAK/ HAGTOELUR AN LANDAMAERA/KISITSISTIGUT NAATSORSUEQQISSAARNEQ KILLIQARFEQANNGITSUMIK/ STATISTIK UDEN GRAENSER/STATISTIK UTEN GRAENSER/STATISTIKK UTEN GRENSER/TILASTO YLI RAJOJEN; Nordic regional statistics. 1992-2004. a. Danmarks Statistik, Sejroegade 11, Copenhagen OE, 2100, Denmark.

630.21 DNK ISSN 1604-8555
STATISTIK NYT FRA DANSK LANDBRUG. 197?-2008. 10/yr. Dansk Landbrug, Axelborg, Vesterbrogade 4 A, Copenhagen V, 1620, Denmark.

338.4 FRA ISSN 1776-1247
STATISTIQUES TECHNIQUES DE L'INDUSTRIE GAZIERE EN FRANCE. ceased 2000. a. Direction du Gaz, de l'Electricite et du Charbon, 97-99 rue de Grenelle, Paris, Cedex 75700, France.

314.891 DNK ISSN 0906-2211
STATISTISK AARBOG FOR HOVEDSTADSREGIONEN/STATISTICAL YEARBOOK FOR THE COPENHAGEN REGION. 1977-2004. a. Hovedstadsregionens Statistikkontor, Vester Voldgade 87 4, Copenhagen V, 1552, Denmark.

352.021 DNK ISSN 0107-6744
STATISTISK TIAARS-OVERSIGT FOR KOEBENHAVNS KOMMUNE. 1981-2005. biennial. Center for Raadgivning og Udvikling, Statistik, Vester Voldgade 87, Copenhagen V, 1552, Denmark.

625.19 621.8 USA
STEAM TRACTION; continuing the tradition of iron-men album. 1946-19??. bi-m. Ogden Publications, 1503 S W 42nd St, Topeka, KS 66609.

385 GBR ISSN 0959-0897
STEAM WORLD. (02/09: Cessation as per telecalling on (5/21/2009). - JA) 1990-199?. m. Emap Active Ltd. (Apex House), Apex House, Oundle Rd, Peterborough, PE2 9NP, United Kingdom.

669.1 USA ISSN 1020-8887
THE STEEL MARKET AND PROSPECTS. 1953-2001. biennial. United Nations Publications, 2 United Nations Plaza, Rm DC2-853, New York, NY 10017.

338.476 669.142 AUS ISSN 0726-0865
STEEL PROFILE. 1981-2001. q. Broken Hill Proprietary Co. Ltd, 140 William St, Melbourne, VIC 3001, Australia.

388.324 USA ISSN 0039-1298
THE STEERING WHEEL. 1936-1992; resumed 2004-2006. s-a. Naylor Publications, Inc., 5950 NW 1st Pl, Gainesville, FL 32607.

370 GBR ISSN 1361-7400
STEINER EDUCATION. 1931-19??. s-a. Steiner Waldorf Schools Fellowship, Kidbrooke Park, Forest Row, Sussex, RH18 5JB, United Kingdom.

778.53 ITA
STELLE FILANTI. 1978-ceased. irreg. Gremese Editore S.r.l., Via Virginia Agnelli, 88, Rome, RM 00151, Italy.

796.334 ITA
STELLE ROSSONERE. 1996-ceased. w. E.P.I. s.r.l., Via Pietro Magistretti, 10, Milan, MI 20128, Italy.

914 ITA ISSN 0039-1131
STELUTIS ALPINIS. 1955-ceased. m. Unione Operaia Escursionisti Italiani, Sezione di Udine, Viale Europa Unita, 117, Udine, UD 33100, Italy.

001.942 ESP
STENDEK. 1970-1981. 4/yr. Centro de Estudios Interplanetarios de Barcelona, Apto. 282, Barcelona, Spain.

686 USA ISSN 1540-2436 CODEN: SSGRE3
STEP INSIDE DESIGN; the world of design from the inside out. 1985-ceased. bi-m. Jupitermedia Corp., 23 Old Kings Hwy South, Darien, CT 06820.

280.4 AUS
STEPPING UP. 1999-ceased. 3/yr. Perth Bible College, 1 College Ct, Karrinyup, W.A. 6018, Australia.

621.39 CZE ISSN 1210-7026
STEREO & VIDEO. 1993-2007. m. Trade & Leisure Publications, s.r.o., Pernerova 35a, Prague 8, 186 00, Czech Republic.

621.389 AUS ISSN 0819-0208
STEREO BUYER'S GUIDE. C D PLAYERS, TURNTABLES AND CASSETTES DECKS. 1971-1992. a. Words Words Words, PO Box 209, Church Point, NSW 2105, Australia.

621.389 ESP ISSN 0211-7045
STEREOFONIA. 1980-ceased. 11/yr. Stereofonia, Cardenal Herrera Oria 171, Ciudad de los Periodistas, Edif. Azorin Torre 2, Madrid, 28034, Spain.

370.116 DEU
STERN SPEZIAL OSKAR'S. 1990-2003. 2/yr. Gruner und Jahr AG & Co., Am Baumwall 11, Hamburg, 20459, Germany.

028.5 DEU
STERNENTAENZER. 2007-2008 (Aug.). bi-m. Panini Verlags GmbH, Ravensstr 48, Nettetal, 41334, Germany.

620 336.2 DEU ISSN 0949-2860
STEUER-BRIEF FUER ARCHITEKTEN UND INGENIEURE. 1995-2003. m. Deubner Verlag GmbH & Co. KG, Oststr 11, Cologne, 50996, Germany.

368 DEU ISSN 0942-4431
STEUER-BRIEF FUER HANDELS- UND VERSICHERUNGSVERTRETER. 1992-2003. m. Deubner Verlag GmbH & Co. KG, Oststr 11, Cologne, 50996, Germany.

367 336.2 DEU ISSN 0948-4248
STEUER-BRIEF FUER PERSONENGESELLSCHAFTEN. 1995-2003. m. Deubner Verlag GmbH & Co. KG, Oststr 11, Cologne, 50996, Germany.

028.5 796 CZE ISSN 0862-6553
STEZKA; mesicnik pro sport, turistiku, brannost. 1970-1990. m. Mlada Fronta, Mezi Vodami 1952/9, Prague 4, 14300, Czech Republic.

280.4 DEU
STIFTSKIRCHE; Protestantisches Gemeindeblatt fuer das Dekanat Landau. 1930-2000. m. Bezirkskircherat des Kirchenbezirks Landau, Westring 3, Landau In Der Pfalz, 76829, Germany.

598.9 DNK ISSN 0109-274X
STIGSNAES; rapport. 1981-1995. a. Dansk Ornitologisk Forening i Vestsjaelland, Stigsnaes Fuglestation, Lille Valmosevej 1, Herlufmagle, 4160, Denmark.

620 ITA ISSN 1123-430X
STILE INDUSTRIA; rivista di ricerca del progetto - design research journal. 1995-ceased. q. Editoriale Domus, Via Gianni Mazzocchi 1/3, Rozzano, MI 20089, Italy.

230 DEU ISSN 0938-541X
STIMME DER BEFREITEN KIRCHE. 1971-2003. q. News Service Informationsdienst, Graf-Gottfried-Str 7, Schmallenberg, 57392, Germany.

796.72 USA ISSN 1540-2193
STOCK CAR REV. 2002 (Oct.)-200?. bi-m. Starlog Communications, 250 W 49th St, 3rd Fl Ste 304, New York, NY 10019.

770 DEU
STOCK PHOTO FEES AND TERMS OF BUSINESS IN EUROPE. 1993-2002. a. Presse Informations Agentur GmbH, Lothar-von-Kuebel Str 18, Sinzheim, 76547, Germany.

690 USA ISSN 1525-4909
STONE MAGAZINE; the trade magazine for specifiers, fabricators, and suppliers of dimensional stone. 1985-199?. 12/yr. Ashlee Publishing Co., Inc., 18 E 41st St, 20th Fl, New York, NY 10017.

004 USA ISSN 1524-6558
STORAGE INC. 1997-2004. q. West World Productions, Inc., 420 N Camden Dr, Beverly Hills, CA 90210.

910.2 338.4 ITA ISSN 1825-6848
STORIA DEL TURISMO. ANNALE (YEAR). 1999-200?. a. Franco Angeli Edizioni, Viale Monza 106, Milan, 20127, Italy.

945 ITA
STORIA E SOCIETA. 1976-ceased. irreg. Ricardo F. Levi Editore SpA, Via Vaciglio, 1085-2, Modena, MO 41100, Italy.

055 ITA
LO STRADONE; il giornale di Corato. 1979-2008. m. Civitas Societa Editoriale per Lo Stradone, Viale Vittorio Veneto 122, Corato, BA 70033, Italy.

914 DEU
STRAND & BERGE; Das Reisetipp-Magazin fuer Deutschland und Europa. 2003-2004. 4/yr. Bruckmann Verlag GmbH, Infanteriestr 11a, Munich, 80797, Germany.

659.1 ITA
STRATEGIA. 1973-ceased. m. (11/yr.). Media Consultants Editrice, Via A Salaino 7, Milan, 20144, Italy.

355 AUS
STRATEGIC AND DEFENCE STUDIES CENTRE. NEWSLETTER. 1981-2007. s-a. Strategic and Defence Studies Centre, Australian National University, Coombs Bldg # 9, Fellows Rd, Canberra, ACT 0200, Australia.

028.5 340 360 AUS
STREETWIZE COMMUNICATIONS; youth rights comics. 1984-2007. irreg. Streetwize Comics Ltd., Ste 7, 24 S Chalmer St, Redfern, NSW 2016, Australia.

779.28 CZE ISSN 1211-8842
STRIP. 1997-2000. m. PK 62, a.s., Bohdalecka 6, Prague 10, 101 00, Czech Republic.

370 ITA ISSN 1970-5859
STRUMENTI PER LE SCIENZE DELLA FORMAZIONE. TEORIE DELL'EDUCAZIONE. 200?-200?. irreg. U T E T SpA, Via Montefeltro 6/a, Milan, 20156, Italy.

610 DNK ISSN 0039-2634
STUD MED. 1936-2004. s-a. Foreningen af Danske Laegestuderende, c/o FADL, Blegdamsvej 3, Copenhagen N, 2200, Denmark.

384 792 ITA ISSN 1970-5840
STUDI BOMPIANI. 1993-ceased. irreg. U T E T SpA, Via Montefeltro 6/a, Milan, 20156, Italy.

930 950 ITA ISSN 0081-6124
STUDI CLASSICI E ORIENTALI; rivista dei Dipartimenti di Filologia Classica, Linguistica, Scienze Archeologiche, Scienze Storiche del Mondo Antico dell'Universita degli Studi di Pisa. 1951-2001. a. Fabrizio Serra Editore, c/o Accademia Editoriale, Via Santa Bibbiana 28, Pisa, 56127, Italy.

900 ITA ISSN 1824-677X
STUDI DI STORIA E STORIOGRAFIA. 1989-ceased. irreg. Edizioni Scientifiche Italiane SpA, Via Chiatamone 7, Naples, NA 80121, Italy.

800 ITA ISSN 1593-0750
STUDI DUEMILLESCHI. 2001-2002. a. Fabrizio Serra Editore, c/o Accademia Editoriale, Via Santa Bibbiana 28, Pisa, 56127, Italy.

720 ITA ISSN 0301-6455
STUDI E DOCUMENTI DI ARCHITETTURA. 19?? (no.2)-ceased. q. Universita degli Studi di Firenze, Istituto di Composizione Architettonica, Florence, FI, Italy.

809 ITA
STUDI E TESTI DELL'ANTICHITA. 1975-1987 (no.19). irreg. Societa Editrice Napoletana s.r.l., Corso Umberto I, 1-34, Naples, NA 80138, Italy.

809 850 ITA
STUDI E TESTI DI LETTERATURA ITALIANA. 1974-1987 (no.24). irreg. Societa Editrice Napoletana s.r.l., Corso Umberto I, 1-34, Naples, NA 80138, Italy.

709 701.18 ITA
STUDI E TESTI DI STORIA E CRITICA DELL'ARTE. 1975-1984 (no.19). irreg. Societa Editrice Napoletana s.r.l., Corso Umberto I, 1-34, Naples, NA 80138, Italy.

913 956.91 ITA ISSN 0393-0246
STUDI EBLAITI. 1979-ceased. irreg. Universita degli Studi di Roma "La Sapienza", 5 Piazzale Aldo Moro, Rome, 00185, Italy.

800 330 ITA ISSN 1971-5692
STUDI ECONOMICO - GIURIDICI. 1909-ceased. a. Mondadori - Libreria Dessi, Largo Cavallotti 17, Sassari, SS 07100, Italy.

387 343.09 ITA ISSN 0392-5021
STUDI MARITTIMI; economia, diritto e tecnica della navigazione dei porti. 1978-1996. q. Consorzio Autonomo del Porto, Molo Pisacane, Naples, NA 80133, Italy.

382 ITA
STUDI RICERCHE DOCUMENTAZIONE. 1975-1993. 3/yr. Unione delle Camere di Commercio dell'Emilia-Romagna, Via Aldo Moro 62, Bologna, BO 40127, Italy.

270 ITA ISSN 1122-5564
STUDI STORICI E RELIGIOSI. 1992-ceased. s-a. Edizioni Scientifiche Italiane SpA, Via Chiatamone 7, Naples, NA 80121, Italy.

945 ITA
STUDI SUL FASCISMO REPUBBLICANO. 1987-199?. q. Studi sul Fascismo Repubblicano, Viale Premuda, 2, Milan, MI 20129, Italy.

225 NLD ISSN 0169-801X
STUDIA AD CORPUS HELLENISTICUM NOVI TESTAMENTI. 1970-1978 (vol.4). irreg. Brill, PO Box 9000, Leiden, 2300 PA, Netherlands.

221 NLD ISSN 0169-9954
STUDIA BIBLICA. 1983-1990. irreg. Brill, PO Box 9000, Leiden, 2300 PA, Netherlands.

540 ESP ISSN 0370-923X CODEN: SCUSAS
STUDIA CHEMICA. 1965-1992. a. Ediciones Universidad de Salamanca, Apartado 325, Salamanca, 37080, Spain.

400 ITA ISSN 0391-4143
STUDIA HISTORICA ET PHILOLOGICA: SECTIO ROMANICA. 1974-ceased. irreg. Licosa SpA, Via Duca di Calabria 1-1, Florence, FI 50125, Italy.

400 ITA ISSN 0390-4393
STUDIA HISTORICA ET PHILOLOGICA: SECTIO SLAVICA. 1973-ceased. irreg. Licosa SpA, Via Duca di Calabria 1-1, Florence, FI 50125, Italy.

400 ITA ISSN 0391-416X
STUDIA HISTORICA ET PHILOLOGICA: SECTIO SLAVO-ROMANICA. 1973-ceased. irreg. Licosa SpA, Via Duca di Calabria 1-1, Florence, FI 50125, Italy.

200 DEU ISSN 0081-6663
STUDIA IRENICA. 1968-1998 (vol.37). irreg. Peter Lang GmbH Europaeischer Verlag der Wissenschaften, Eschborner Landstr 42-50, Frankfurt Am Main, 60489, Germany.

577 ESP ISSN 0211-4623 CODEN: STOEEB
STUDIA OECOLOGICA. 1981-1995. a. Ediciones Universidad de Salamanca, Apartado 325, Salamanca, 37080, Spain.

100 NLD ISSN 0921-9129
STUDIEN ZUR ANTIKEN PHILOSOPHIE. 1971-1987 (vol.14). irreg. John Benjamins Publishing Co., PO Box 36224, Amsterdam, 1020 ME, Netherlands.

800 DEU ISSN 0340-9023
STUDIEN ZUR LITERATUR DER MODERNE. 1976-2002 (vol.28). irreg. Bouvier Verlag, Fuerstenstr 3, Bonn, 53111, Germany.

189 940.1 NLD ISSN 0169-9857
STUDIEN ZUR PROBLEMGESCHICHTE DER ANTIKEN UND MITTELALTERLICHEN PHILOSOPHIE. 1966-1973 (vol.7). irreg. Brill, PO Box 9000, Leiden, 2300 PA, Netherlands.

346.066 NLD ISSN 1566-0435
STUDIES IN COMPARATIVE CORPORATE AND FINANCIAL LAW. 1998-ceased. irreg. Kluwer Law International, PO Box 316, Alphen aan den Rijn, 2400 AH, Netherlands.

809 USA ISSN 0081-7775
STUDIES IN COMPARATIVE LITERATURE. 1950-19??. irreg. University of North Carolina Press, 116 S Boundary St, Chapel Hill, NC 27514.

336 USA ISSN 0081-7929
STUDIES IN FEDERAL TAXATION. 1969-1990. irreg. American Institute of Certified Public Accountants, 1211 Ave of the Americas, New York, NY 10036.

323 USA ISSN 0273-1231
STUDIES IN FREEDOM. 1981-19??. irreg. Greenwood Publishing Group Inc., 88 Post Rd W, PO Box 5007, Westport, CT 06881.

900 USA ISSN 1046-526X
STUDIES IN HISTORIOGRAPHY. 1990-200?. irreg. Greenwood Publishing Group Inc., 88 Post Rd W, PO Box 5007, Westport, CT 06881.

610 IND ISSN 0970-5562
STUDIES IN HISTORY OF MEDICINE AND SCIENCE. 1977-200?. s-a. Jamia Hamdard, Hamdard Nagar, New Delhi, 110 062, India.

323.4 USA ISSN 0146-3586
STUDIES IN HUMAN RIGHTS. 1975-19??. irreg. Greenwood Publishing Group Inc., 88 Post Rd W, PO Box 5007, Westport, CT 06881.

296.09 NLD ISSN 0169-961X
STUDIES IN JUDAISM IN LATE ANTIQUITY. 1973-1989 (vol.39). irreg. Brill, PO Box 9000, Leiden, 2300 PA, Netherlands.

994.38 AUS ISSN 0155-381X
STUDIES IN NORTH QUEENSLAND HISTORY. 1977-1997. irreg. James Cook University, Department of History and Politics, Townsville, QLD 4810, Australia.

304.6 USA ISSN 0147-1104
STUDIES IN POPULATION AND URBAN DEMOGRAPHY. 1975-2001. irreg. Greenwood Publishing Group Inc., 88 Post Rd W, PO Box 5007, Westport, CT 06881.

360 USA ISSN 8755-5360
STUDIES IN SOCIAL WELFARE POLICIES AND PROGRAMS. 1985-199?. irreg. Greenwood Publishing Group Inc., 88 Post Rd W, PO Box 5007, Westport, CT 06881.

531 NLD ISSN 0081-8542 CODEN: SSTMBG
STUDIES IN STATISTICAL MECHANICS. 1962-1988 (vol.14). irreg. Elsevier BV, North-Holland, Sara Burgerhartstraat 25, Amsterdam, 1055 KV, Netherlands.

430.82 USA ISSN 0081-8593
STUDIES IN THE GERMANIC LANGUAGES AND LITERATURES. 1949-2004. irreg. University of North Carolina Press, 116 S Boundary St, Chapel Hill, NC 27514.

949.2 NLD ISSN 0923-8956
STUDIES IN THE HISTORY OF LEIDEN UNIVERSITY. 1983-1989 (vol.6). irreg. Brill, PO Box 9000, Leiden, 2300 PA, Netherlands.

339 GBR ISSN 0081-864X
STUDIES IN THE NATIONAL INCOME AND EXPENDITURE OF THE UNITED KINGDOM. 1966-1996 (Jan.). irreg. Cambridge University Press, The Edinburgh Bldg, Shaftesbury Rd, Cambridge, CB2 8RU, United Kingdom.

658 USA ISSN 1014-1472
STUDIES IN THE PROCESSING, MARKETING AND DISTRIBUTION OF COMMODITIES. 1984-1989. irreg. United Nations Publications, 2 United Nations Plaza, Rm DC2-853, New York, NY 10017.

300 USA
STUDIES IN THE SOCIAL SCIENCES. 1899-1943. irreg. University of Iowa Press, 100 Kuhl House, Iowa City, IA 52242-1000.

620.2 GBR ISSN 1361-4746
STUDIO SOUND. 1959-2001. m. C M P Information Ltd., Ludgate House, 245 Blackfriars Rd., London, SE1 9UR, United Kingdom.

780 ITA ISSN 1128-9252
SUBSIDIA MUSICA VENETA. 1980-ceased. irreg. Arnaldo Forni Editore, Via Antonio Gramsci 164, Sala Bolognese, BO 40010, Italy.

340 GBR ISSN 1362-3710
SUDEBNIK. 1996-2009. q. Wildy, Simmonds and Hill Publishing, Lincoln's Inn Archway, 58 Carey St, London, WC2A 2JD, United Kingdom.

053.1 DEU ISSN 1860-0042
SUGAR. 1998-2008 (Sep.). m. Egmont Cultfish Media GmbH, Hansastr 32, Munich, 80686, Germany.

687 ITA
SUGGESTIONS SHOE MODELS FOR MAN. 1990-ceased. 2/yr. Muggiani Giampiero Editore, Via IV Novembre 54, Settimo Milanese, MI 20019, Italy.

687 ITA
SUGGESTIONS SHOE MODELS FOR WOMAN. 1990-ceased. 2/yr. Muggiani Giampiero Editore, Via IV Novembre 54, Settimo Milanese, MI 20019, Italy.

338 ESP
SUMINISTROS INDUSTRIALES. 19??-ceased. 6/yr. Suministros Industriales, Via Augusta, 59, 8o Of. 812, Barcelona, 08006, Spain.

361.30711 USA ISSN 0145-7314
SUMMARY INFORMATION ON MASTER OF SOCIAL WORK PROGRAMS. 19??-2004. a. Council on Social Work Education, 1725 Duke St, Ste 500, Alexandria, VA 22314.

613.2 DNK ISSN 1901-1288
SUND OG SLANK; lev livet let. 2003-2006. 10/yr. Egmont Magasiner A/S, Hellerupvej 51, Hellerup, 2900, Denmark.

794.8 ITA ISSN 1594-2511
SUPER CONSOLE. 1994-200?. 11/yr. Gruppo Editoriale Futura, Via XXV Aprile 39, Bresso, MI 20091, Italy.

793.7 DEU
SUPER T V RAETSEL MAGAZIN. 2006-2008. bi-m. Deutscher Raetselverlag GmbH & Co. KG, Muenchener Str 101-09, Ismaning, 85737, Germany.

629.2 NLD ISSN 1875-4317
SUPERCAR. 2007-2008. bi-m. F & L Automotive Publications B.V., Meijhorst 60-10, Postbus 31331, Nijmegen, 6503 CH, Netherlands.

654.197 CZE ISSN 1802-3169
SUPERSPY T V. 2007-2007 (ceased same year). w. Stratosfera s.r.o., Drtinova 8, Prague 5, 150 00, Czech Republic.

790 USA ISSN 0887-1035
SUPERSTAR WRESTLERS. 1986-200?. 8/yr. Starlog Communications, 250 W 49th St, 3rd Fl Ste 304, New York, NY 10019.

658.31244 USA ISSN 1549-7348
SUPERVISOR'S GUIDE TO ERGONOMICS. 2000-2006. m. Clement Communications, Inc., 10 LaCrue Ave, PO Box 36, Concordville, PA 19331.

336.2 NLD ISSN 0039-5927
SUPPLEMENTARY SERVICE TO EUROPEAN TAXATION. 1963-2006. plus m. updates. International Bureau of Fiscal Documentation (I B F D), H J E Wenckebachweg 210, Amsterdam, 1096 AS, Netherlands.

347 USA ISSN 1054-2701
SUPREME COURT YEARBOOK. 1990-2000. a. C Q Press, Inc., 2300 N St, NW, Ste 800, Washington, DC 20037.

796.172 ITA ISSN 1123-914X
SURFERS. 1995-ceased. 6/yr. Life Edizioni, Via Stazione 2, Baveno, VB 28831, Italy.

796.172 ITA ISSN 1120-0227
SURFING. 1988-ceased. a. Hi Promotion s.r.l., Via San Marco, 48, Milan, MI 20121, Italy.

526.8 ISR ISSN 0333-5623
SURVEY OF ISRAEL. CARTOGRAPHIC PAPERS. 1965-1996. irreg. Survey of Israel, P O Box 14171, Tel Aviv, 61141, Israel.

526.8 ISR ISSN 0333-5720
SURVEY OF ISRAEL. PHOTOGRAMMETRIC PAPERS. 1976-ceased. irreg. Survey of Israel, P O Box 14171, Tel Aviv, 61141, Israel.

338 ISR ISSN 0081-9743
SURVEYS AND DEVELOPMENT PLANS OF INDUSTRY IN ISRAEL/HATA'ASIYAH BE-YISRAEL. 1964-ceased. a. Ministry of Industry, Trade and Labour, Jerusalem, Israel.

639.2 KOR ISSN 1226-1858
SU'SAN GWAHAG YEON'GU/FISHERIES SCIENCE RESEARCH. 1985-2000. a. Kunsan Daehaggyo, Su'san Gwahag Yeon'guso, 1170 Deahak-Ro, Kunsan, Chollabuk-do 573-701, Korea, S.

636 AUS ISSN 1832-0937
SUSTAINABLE GRAZING ON SALINE LANDS NETWORK NEWS. 2004-2005. q. Australia. Land & Water Australia, Sustainable Grazing on Saline Lands, GPO Box 2182, Canberra, ACT 2601, Australia.

940 DNK ISSN 0106-5378
SVANTEVIT; dansk tidsskrift for slavistik. 1975-2001. s-a. Dansk Slavistforbund, c/o Hans Kristian Mikkelsen, Det Kongelige Bibliotek, Postboks 2149, Copenhagen, 1016, Denmark.

296 USA ISSN 1044-0011
S'VARA. 1990-1993. s-a. Columbia University, School of Law, 435 W 116th St, New York, NY 10027.

839.7 SWE ISSN 0348-3940
SVENSKA SERIER. 1979-1996. q. Egmont Seriefoerlaget AB, Stora Varvsgatan 19A, Malmo, 20507, Sweden.

791 CZE ISSN 1214-1275
SVET D V D. (Digital Video Disc) 2002-2008 (Jan.). m. Burda Praha, spol. s r.o., Premyslovska 2845/43, Luxembourg Plaza, Prague 3, 13000, Czech Republic.

590 CZE ISSN 1211-5606
SVETEM ZVIRAT. 1993-2008. m. Profi Press s.r.o., Drtinova 8, Prague 5, 150 00, Czech Republic.

891.86 CZE ISSN 0039-7075
SVETOVA LITERATURA; revue. 1956-1996. irreg. Spolecnost pro Svetovou Literaturu, Masarykovo nabr 26, Prague 1, 110 00, Czech Republic.

Cessations

340 GBR ISSN 0308-8928
SWEET AND MAXWELL'S STUDENTS' LAW REPORTER. 1970-19??. 3/yr. Sweet & Maxwell Ltd., 100 Avenue Rd, London, NW3 3PF, United Kingdom.

610 DNK
SYDDANSKE LAEGER. 2006-2008. bi-m. Laegekredsforeningen for Syddanmark, Worsaaesgade 10, Vejle, 7100, Denmark.

028.5 AUS ISSN 1034-0084
SYDNEY FOR PARENTS. 1982-ceased. a. Universal Magazines Pty. Ltd., Unit 5, 6-8 Byfield St, North Ryde, NSW 2113, Australia.

820 375.4 AUS ISSN 0156-5419
SYDNEY STUDIES IN ENGLISH. 1975-2006. a. University of Sydney, Department of English, Sydney, NSW 2006, Australia.

700 NLD ISSN 0923-9073
SYMBOLA ET EMBLEMATA. 1989-2000 (vol.10). irreg. Brill, PO Box 9000, Leiden, 2300 PA, Netherlands.

780 ITA ISSN 1120-9909
SYMPHONIA. 1990-ceased. m. Ermitage, Piazza Trento e Trieste 1, Bologna, BO 40137, Italy.

332.67 341 USA
SYMPOSIUM ON PRIVATE INVESTMENTS ABROAD. 1967-2004. a. Matthew Bender & Co., Inc., 1275 Broadway, Albany, NY 12204.

332 FRA ISSN 1261-7733
SYSTEMES DE PAIEMENT. 1995-2005. m. Publi-News, 47 rue Aristide Briand, Levallois-Perret, 92300, France.

629.13 ISR ISSN 0072-9302 CODEN: TIDRAR
T.A.E. REPORT. 1959-2001. irreg. Technion - Israel Institute of Technology, Department of Aeronautical Engineering, Haifa, Israel.

331 NLD ISSN 1388-1558
T A P. TIJDSCHRIFT VOOR ARBEID EN PARTICIPATIE. 1977-ceased. q. Arkel, Uitgeverij Jan van, Postbus 13094, Utrecht, 3507, Netherlands.

651.3 DEU ISSN 0341-2024
T B REPORT; Archivierung und Datensicherung im Technischen Buero. (Technische Buero) 1970-2002. q. B I T Verlag Weinbrenner GmbH & Co. KG, Fasanenweg 18, Leinfelden-Echterdingen, 70771, Germany.

660 ITA ISSN 1724-3971 CODEN: TECCDK
T C NEWS. (Tecnologie Chimiche) 1981-ceased. 6/yr. Reed Business Information Spa, Viale G. Richard 1/A, Milan, 20143, Italy.

740 ESP ISSN 0210-3761
T G; revista de las artes decorativas. 1968-ceased. bi-m. Tapicerias Gancedo, Velazquez 21, Madrid, 28001, Spain.

613 GBR ISSN 0266-9056
T H S HEALTH SUMMARY. (Times Health Supplement) 1981-2005. w. Times Newspapers Ltd., Priory House, St Jonh's Ln, London, EC1M 4BX, United Kingdom.

799.1 USA ISSN 1531-6335
T N N OUTDOORS. 2000-2001. bi-m. Grand View Media Group, Inc., 200 Croft St, Ste 1, Birmingham, AL 35242.

005.1 USA
T S O / I S P F UPDATE. (Time Sharing Option / Interactive System Productivity Facility) ceased. q. Xephon, 9330 Lyndon B Johnson Fwy., Ste. 800, Dallas, TX 75243-4310.

380 910.2 GBR
T T G DIRECTORY. (Travel Trade Gazette) 1958-2002. a. C M P Information Ltd., Sovereign House, Sovereign Way, Tonbridge, Kent TN9 1RW, United Kingdom.

384.55 ITA
T V KEY; mensile professionale di communicazione televisiva. 1982-ceased. m. (9/yr.). Media Key s.r.l., Via Lippi Filippino, 33 C, Milan, MI 20131, Italy.

384.5532 DEU
T V LIFE; Fernsehen erleben. 2007-2008 (Jul.). fortn. Heinrich Bauer Programmzeitschriftenverlag KG, Burchardstr 11, Hamburg, 20077, Germany.

671.388 DEU
T V MOVIE MULTIMEDIA. 2006-2007 (Nov.). m. Heinrich Bauer Verlag, Burchardstr 11, Hamburg, 20077, Germany.

381.1 USA ISSN 0885-2340
T V PROGRAM INVESTOR. 1985-2006. m. S N L Financial LC, One SNL Plz, PO Box 2124, Charlottesville, VA 22902.

384.55 DEU
T V WORLD. 2004-2006. fortn. Heinrich Bauer Programmzeitschriftenverlag KG, Burchardstr 11, Hamburg, 20077, Germany.

790.1 USA ISSN 1053-041X
T V WRESTLERS. 1989-200?. q. Starlog Communications, 250 W 49th St, 3rd Fl Ste 304, New York, NY 10019.

401 NLD ISSN 1871-7322
TAAL EN ARBEIDSMARKT. 1995-2008. q. Instituut voor Taalonderzoek en Taalonderwijs Anderstaligen, Spuistraat 210, Amsterdam, 1012 VT, Netherlands.

633.71 ITA ISSN 1124-3791 CODEN: AISTD4
IL TABACCO. 1897-2003. a. Istituto Sperimentale per il Tabacco, Via P Vitiello 66, Scafati, SA 84018, Italy.

282.93 NZL ISSN 0110-4853
TABLET. 1873-1996. w. New Zealand Tablet Co. Ltd., 39 Crawford St, Dunedin, New Zealand.

580.74 DEU ISSN 0171-3558 CODEN: CJHPBW
TAECKKOLMIA. 1968-19??. a. Koeltz Scientific Books, PO Box 1360, Koenigstein, 61453, Germany.

056.1 ESP ISSN 0214-0527
TAIFA. 1988-1997. m. Editorial Lumen, Rocafort 219, Barcelona, 08029, Spain.

388.324 USA ISSN 1529-4021
TAILGATE. 2000-200?. bi-m. Paisano Publications, Inc., 28210 Dorothy Dr, Box 3075, Agoura Hills, CA 91301.

793.73 GBR ISSN 1466-7703
TAKE A BREAK'S KIDS' STUFF. 1999-2004. q. H. Bauer Publishing Ltd., Academic House, 24-28 Oval Rd, London, NW1 7DT, United Kingdom.

314.891 DNK ISSN 1397-6567
TAL FRA KOEBENHAVNS KOMMUNE, STATISTISK KONTOR. 1972-2005. a. Center for Raadgivning og Udvikling, Statistik, Vester Voldgade 87, Copenhagen V, 1552, Denmark.

320 GBR ISSN 0955-8780
TALKING POLITICS. 1988-2007. 3/yr. Politics Association, Old Hall Ln, Manchester, Lancs M13 0XT, United Kingdom.

110 GBR ISSN 1464-2042
TALKING STICK MAGICKAL JOURNAL. 1989-ceased. s-a. Talking Stick Magazine, PO Box 3719, London, SW17 8X7, United Kingdom.

946 ESP ISSN 1133-4959
TALLER D'HISTORIA. 1993-1995. s-a. Diputacion Provincial de Valencia, Centro de Estudios de Historia, Carrer Corona, 36, Valencia, 46003, Spain.

508 NZL ISSN 0496-8026 CODEN: TJACA8
TANE. 1948-1999. biennial. Offshore Islands Research Group, c/o Auckland Museum, Private Bag 921018, Auckland, New Zealand.

746 ITA ISSN 1826-1035
TANTE IDEE. 2003-200?. m. Edizioni Mimosa, Piazza E de Angeli 9, Milan, 20146, Italy.

330 HUN ISSN 1588-9734
TARSADALOM ES GAZDASAG/SOCIETY AND ECONOMY. 1994-2009. s-a. Akademiai Kiado Rt., Prielle Kornelia U. 19, Budapest, 1117, Hungary.

004.6 USA
TASTY BITS FROM THE TECHNOLOGY FRONT. 1994-2000. w. Tasty Bits from the Technology Front

323.4 ISR ISSN 0793-5439
TAT-TARBUT. 1995-1997. a. Society for the Protection of Personal Rights for Lesbians Gay Men & Bisexual in Israel, P O Box 37604, Tel Aviv, 61375, Israel.

336 USA
TAX ANALYST MICROFICHE DATABASE. 1981-1996. w. Tax Analysts, 400 S Maple Ave, Ste 400, Falls Church, VA 22046.

336.2 640.75 USA ISSN 0279-4446 CODEN: THAOAU
TAX HOTLINE; the inside report for people who need to be on top of every tax break the law allows. 1981-2008. m. Boardroom, Inc., 281 Tresser Blvd, 8th Fl, Stamford, CT 06901.

336.2 USA ISSN 1087-2922
TAX MANAGEMENT FINANCIAL PRODUCTS REPORT. 1996-2000. s-m. Tax Management Inc., 1801 S Bell St, Arlington, VA 22202.

336 USA
TAX MANAGEMENT I R S PRACTICE AND POLICY. 1990-200?. m. Tax Management Inc., 1801 S Bell St, Arlington, VA 22202.

336.2 NLD ISSN 0040-0076
TAX NEWS SERVICE (PRINT). 1965-ceased. w. International Bureau of Fiscal Documentation (I B F D), H J E Wenckebachweg 210, Amsterdam, 1096 AS, Netherlands.

336.2 USA ISSN 1058-3971
TAX NOTES INTERNATIONAL WEEKLY NEWS. 1991 (Sep.)-1991 (Dec.). w. Tax Analysts, 400 S Maple Ave, Ste 400, Falls Church, VA 22046.

336 NLD
TAX TREATMENT OF CROSS-BORDER DONATIONS; including the tax status of charities and foundations. 1994-2003. plus a. updates. International Bureau of Fiscal Documentation (I B F D), H J E Wenckebachweg 210, Amsterdam, 1096 AS, Netherlands.

336 NLD
THE TAX TREATMENT OF TRANSFER PRICING. 1987-2009. plus s-a. updates. International Bureau of Fiscal Documentation (I B F D), H J E Wenckebachweg 210, Amsterdam, 1096 AS, Netherlands.

336 NLD
TAXATION & INVESTMENT IN MEXICO. 1994-2003. plus s-a. updates. International Bureau of Fiscal Documentation (I B F D), H J E Wenckebachweg 210, Amsterdam, 1096 AS, Netherlands.

336.2 332.6 NLD
TAXATION & INVESTMENT IN SOUTH AFRICA. 1994-2003. plus a. updates. International Bureau of Fiscal Documentation (I B F D), H J E Wenckebachweg 210, Amsterdam, 1096 AS, Netherlands.

053.1 DEU
TCHIBO CLUB-MAGAZIN. 1952-1996. m. BurdaYukom Publishing GmbH, Konrad-Zuse-Platz 11, Munich, 81829, Germany.

792.029 DNK ISSN 1397-9426
TEATERMAGASINET ARTE NYT. (Arbejdernes Teaterorganisation) 1971-2001. 4/yr. (plus a. special issue). Arte Kulturformidling, Hvidkildevej 64, Copenhagen Nv, 2400, Denmark.

792 ITA
TEATRO ARCHIVIO; bollettino del Civico Museo Biblioteca dell'Attore. 1970-19??. 3/yr. Bulzoni Editore, Via dei Liburni 14, Rome, 00185, Italy.

004 AUS ISSN 1038-5231
TECHNICAL COMPUTING. 1968-1994. q. National Publications Pty. Ltd., PO Box 197, Cronulla, NSW 2230, Australia.

004 DNK ISSN 0900-3762
TECHNICAL PRODUCT UPDATE. 198?-1989. m. Digital Equipment Corporation A-S, Aadalsvej 99, Horsholm, 2970, Denmark.

016.378 ISR ISSN 0792-7355
TECHNION - ISRAEL INSTITUTE OF TECHNOLOGY. ABSTRACTS OF RESEARCH THESES. 1983-1998. a. Technion - Israel Institute of Technology, Graduate School, Technion City, Haifa, 32000, Israel.

620 ISR ISSN 0040-1188 CODEN: TCNNAN
TECHNION MAGAZINE. 1965-1984. s-a. Technion - Israel Institute of Technology, Public Affairs Division, Technion City, Haifa, 32000, Israel.

669 DEU ISSN 0368-9530
TECHNISCHE HOCHSCHULE AACHEN. EISENHUETTENMAENNISCHE INSTITUT. MITTEILUNGEN. 1906-1925. irreg. R W T H, Institut fuer Eisenhuettenkunde, Intzestr 1, Aachen, 52072, Germany.

332 FRA ISSN 0765-3069
TECHNOLOGIES BANCAIRES. 1984-2004. m. Publi-News, 47 rue Aristide Briand, Levallois-Perret, 92300, France.

004.16 AUS ISSN 1445-8675
TECHNOLOGY & BUSINESS. 1994-2006. m. ZDNet Australia, Level 4, 45 Murray St, Pyrmont, NSW 2009, Australia.

328 USA ISSN 1936-6981
TECHNOLOGY DAILY. 19??-2008. d. National Journal Group, Inc., 600 New Hampshire Ave, N W, Washington, DC 20037.

607.1 AUS ISSN 1034-6902
TECHNOLOGY DESIGN EDUCATION. 1960-2000. q. Institute of Industrial Arts Technology Education, PO Box 52, Forestville, NSW 2087, Australia.

608.7 ESP ISSN 0040-179X
TECNICA E INVENCION. 1954-1984. m. Tecnica e Invencion, Princesa, 14, Madrid, 28008, Spain.

688.8 658.788 664 ESP
TECNIENVASE. 2002-200?. bi-m. Tecnipublicaciones Espana, S.L., Avda de Manoteras 44, 3a Planta, Madrid, 28050, Spain.

674 ESP
TECNIMADERA CONSTRUCCION. 2000-200?. 3/yr. Tecnipublicaciones Espana, S.L., Avda de Manoteras 44, 3a Planta, Madrid, 28050, Spain.

674 ESP
TECNIMADERA FORESTAL. 2000-200?. 3/yr. Tecnipublicaciones Espana, S.L., Avda de Manoteras 44, 3a Planta, Madrid, 28050, Spain.

051 USA ISSN 1527-6775
TEEN NEWSWEEK. 1999-2006. 13/yr. Weekly Reader Corporation, 3001 Cindel Dr, PO Box 8037, Delran, NJ 08075.

100 600 FRA ISSN 1251-0777
TEKHNEMA; journal of philosophy and technology. 1993-2000. a. American University of Paris, 31 av. Bosquet, Paris, 75007, France.

340 NLD ISSN 1871-0980
TEKST EN TOELICHTING WET GELUIDHINDER. 2004-ceased. a. Sdu Uitgevers bv, Postbus 20025, The Hague, 2500 EA, Netherlands.

342.492 NLD ISSN 1574-9436
TEKSTEN AMBTENARENRECHT. 2001-ceased. a. Sdu Uitgevers bv, Postbus 20025, The Hague, 2500 EA, Netherlands.

327 ISR ISSN 0333-6611
TEL AVIV UNIVERSITY. DAVID HOROWITZ INSTITUTE FOR THE RESEARCH OF DEVELOPING COUNTRIES. ANNUAL REPORT. 1970-1981. a. Tel Aviv University, David Horowitz Institute for the Research of Developing Countries, Tel Aviv, Israel.

327 ISR
TEL AVIV UNIVERSITY. DAVID HOROWITZ INSTITUTE FOR THE RESEARCH OF DEVELOPING COUNTRIES. RESEARCH REPORTS AND PAPERS. 1972-ceased. irreg. Tel Aviv University, David Horowitz Institute for the Research of Developing Countries, Tel Aviv, Israel.

770.285 ITA ISSN 1721-2154
TELECAMERE DIGITALI. 2002-200?. m. Play Media Company, Via di Santa Cornelia 5A, Formello, RM 00060, Italy.

621.382 ESP
TELECAST & BROADCAST. -ceased. 12/yr. Telecast & Broadcast, Ciudad de los Periodistas, Efc. Azorin Torre 2, Avda Cardenal Herrera Oria, 171, Madrid, 28034, Spain.

621.38 AUS
TELECOMMUNICATIONS PERFORMANCE MONITORING BULLETIN. 1996-2005. q. Australian Communications and Media Authority (A C M A), PO Box 13112, Melbourne, VIC 8010, Australia.

343.09943 AUS
TELECOMMUNICATIONS REPORTER. 1990-2003. plus irreg. updates. Lawbook Co., PO Box 3502, Rozelle, NSW 2039, Australia.

384.041 USA ISSN 1467-5234
TELECOMS DEAL REPORT. 1999-2000. fortn. Access Intelligence, LLC, 1201 Seven Locks Rd, Ste 300, Potomac, MD 20854.

621.382 AUS
TELECOMS IN ASIA. 1996-2003. a. Paul Budde Communication Pty. Ltd., 5385 George Downes Dr, Bucketty, NSW 2250, Australia.

384.1 USA ISSN 0740-9354
TELECONNECT. 1983-2001. m. C M P Media LLC, 11 W 19th St, New York, NY 10011-4280.

383 DEU
TELEFAXBUCH DER DEUTSCHEN TELEKOM AG. 1984-2000. a. Deutsche Telekom AG, Friedrich-Ebert-Allee 140, Bonn, 53113, Germany.

384.6 ITA
TELEFONI CELLULARI MAGAZINE. 1994-200?. bi-m. Gruppo Editoriale Futura, Via XXV Aprile 39, Bresso, MI 20091, Italy.

621.385 ITA ISSN 1122-2735
IL TELEFONO. 1991-ceased. bi-m. Studio Zeta S.r.l., Via S Fruttuoso, 10, Monza, MI 20052, Italy.

616.027 USA ISSN 1559-484X
TELEHEALTH PRACTICE REPORT. 1996-2005. bi-m. Civic Research Insitute, 4478 US Rte 27, PO Box 585, Kingston, NJ 08528.

621.388 USA ISSN 0497-1515
TELEVISION DIGEST WITH CONSUMER ELECTRONICS. 1945-2003. w. Warren Communications News, Inc., 2115 Ward Ct, NW, Washington, DC 20037.

384.5 USA ISSN 1544-0516
TELEVISION WEEK (PRINT). 1982; N.S. 2003 (Mar.)-2009. w. Crain Communications, Inc., 1155 Gratiot Ave, Detroit, MI 48207.

946 ESP
TEMAS DE HISTORIA Y POLITICA CONTEMPORANEAS. 1977-2001. irreg. Edicions 62 S.A., Peu de la Creu, 4, Barcelona, 08001, Spain.

850.9 ITA
TEMI E PROFILI DEL NOVECENTO. 1997-2001 (no.5). irreg. Angelo Longo Editore, Via Paolo Costa 33, Ravenna, 48121, Italy.

759.152 ITA
TEMI - TENDENZE MODA ITALIA. 1984-ceased. bi-m. Temi, Via Alfonso Lamarmora, 22, Milan, MI 20122, Italy.

630 FRA ISSN 0338-1811
TEMPE INFORMATIONS. 1972-199?. m. Cooperative Laiti, 420 av. de Monclar, Montauban, Cedex 82017, France.

929.712 ITA ISSN 1592-7997
TEMPLARI. 2001-200?. bi-m. Edizioni Trentini & C, Via Pier Luigi Nervi 1/B, Argenta, FE 44011, Italy.

796.77 CZE ISSN 1212-6454
TEMPO!; magazin o nejrychlejsich kalech. 1999-2002. bi-m. Club 91, 5 Kvetna 1323/9, Prague 4, 140 00, Czech Republic.

720 ITA
TEMPO MATERIA ARCHITETTURA; rivista trimestrale di restauro. 1993-2001. q. U T E T SpA, Via Montefeltro 6/a, Milan, 20156, Italy.

055 ITA ISSN 1128-2967
TEMPO NUOVO. 1937-1946. w. R C S Periodici, Via San Marco 21, Milan, 20121, Italy.

055.1 ITA
TEMPO POLLINO; mensile politico-culturale e d'informazione. 1978-ceased. m. Tempo Pollino, Via Telesio, 12, Castrovillari, CS 87012, Italy.

647.9 ESP ISSN 0213-2982
TENEDORES Y ESTRELLAS. 1983-ceased. bi-m. Tenedores y Estrellas, Mazustegui, 21, 4a planta, Bilbao, Vizcaya 48006, Spain.

796.342 DEU
TENNIS-JAHRBUCH. 1952-2000. a. Deutscher Tennis Bund e.V., Hallerstr 89, Hamburg, 20149, Germany.

796.342 DNK ISSN 1602-8740
TENNISMAGASINET. 1920-200?. irreg. Dansk Tennis Forbund, Idraettens Hus, Broendby Stadion 20, Broendby, 2605, Denmark.

330 CHN ISSN 1008-3286
TEQU JINGJI YU KONGGAOTAI JINGJI/ECONOMY IN S E Z AND HONG KONG, MACAO AND TAIWAN. 1984-2004. m. Zhongguo Renmin Daxue Shubao Zilio Zhongxin, Dongcheng-qu, 3, Zhangzizhong Lu, Beijing, 100007, China.

596 CZE ISSN 1802-2294
TERA FORUM. 2004-2007. m. Mimoza s.r.o., Americka 2399, Kladno, 272 01, Czech Republic.

551 011 GBR ISSN 0954-4887
TERRA ABSTRACTS. 1981-1999. irreg. Wiley-Blackwell Publishing Ltd., 9600 Garsington Rd, Oxford, OX4 2DQ, United Kingdom.

630 ITA ISSN 0040-3768
TERRA E SOLE; agricoltura pratica e meccanica agraria. 1945-ceased. m. Iacico Srl, Via Angelo Poliziano 80, Rome, 00184, Italy.

747 635 ITA ISSN 1825-7666
TERRAZZI E BALCONI. 2005-200?. q. Sprea Editori Srl, Via Torino 51, Cernusco sul Naviglio, MI 20063, Italy.

929 USA ISSN 1076-9854
TERRY TRACINGS. 1994-1995. irreg. (2-4/yr). Family Publications, 5628 60th Dr, NE, Marysville, WA 98270.

055.1 ITA
TERZA PAGINA; antigruppo siciliano. 1950-ceased. w. Cooperativa Editrice Antigruppo Siciliano, Via Argenteria Km, 4, Trapani, TP 91100, Italy.

055.1 ITA ISSN 1126-8069
TERZO MILLENNIO VERSO L'ANTROPOCRAZIA. 1998-ceased. m. Nonsiamosoli Video, 1824 via Molino 1, S. Elpidio a Mare, AP 63019, Italy.

381 ESP ISSN 1130-8338
TESON. 1953-ceased. m. Fidelitas Asesores, Alonso Quintanilla 3, 2o H, Oviedo, Asturias 33002, Spain.

144 ITA
TESTI E STUDI UMANISTICI. 1981-1996 (no.4). irreg. Angelo Longo Editore, Via Paolo Costa 33, Ravenna, 48121, Italy.

347 USA ISSN 1071-7595
TESTIFYING EXPERT. 1993-2005. m. L R P Publications, Inc., 747 Dresher Rd, Ste 500, PO Box 980, Horsham, PA 19044.

570 GBR ISSN 0951-4309
TESTS OF AGROCHEMICALS AND CULTIVARS. 1980-2006. a. Association of Applied Biologists, Horticultural Research International, Warwick Enterprise Park, Wellesbourne, Warwick, CV35 9EF, United Kingdom.

910.09 KOR ISSN 1225-8075
TEURAEBEUL TEUREIDEU JEONEOL/TRAVEL TRADE JOURNAL. 1986-2004. m. Travel Trade Journal, 3/F, Christian Women's Mission Center, 1-1, Yeonji-dong, Chongno-gu, Seoul, 110-470, Korea, S.

630 USA ISSN 0162-3001
TEXAS AGRICULTURE. WEST TEXAS REGIONAL EDITION. 1935-19??. 20/yr. Texas Farm Bureau, PO Box 2689, Waco, TX 76702.

344.046 USA ISSN 1075-2595
TEXAS ENVIRONMENTAL COMPLIANCE UPDATE. 1991-ceased. m. M. Lee Smith Publishers LLC, 5201 Virginia Way, PO Box 5094, Brentwood, TN 37024.

388.3 USA
TEXAS VEHICLE LAWS FLIP CODE. 1996-200?. biennial. Gould Publications, Inc., 1333 North US Hwy 17-92, Longwood, FL 32750.

332.6 USA
TEXAS WEALTH MANAGEMENT BUSINESS (PRINT). 2008 (Apr.)-2009 (Feb/Mar.); suspended. m. France Publications, Inc., 3500 Piedmont Rd, Ste 415, Atlanta, GA 30305.

368.41 USA
TEXAS WORKERS' COMPENSATION LAW: A GUIDE TO PRACTICE BEFORE COMMISSION AND COURTS. 1990-200?. plus irreg. updates. Matthew Bender & Co., Inc., 1275 Broadway, Albany, NY 12204.

340 FRA ISSN 0429-4769
TEXTES D'INTERET GENERAL. 1952-2003. irreg. Direction des Journaux Officiels, 26 rue Desaix, Paris, 75727 Cedex 15 , France.

297 EGY ISSN 1110-001X
TEXTES ET TRADUCTIONS D'AUTEURS ORIENTAUX. 1937-ceased. irreg. Institut Francais d'Archeologie Orientale du Caire, Kasr el-Aini, 37 Sharia Sheikh Aly Youssef, Mounira, P O Box 11562, Cairo, Egypt.

054 FRA ISSN 1278-4362
TEXTO. 1994-199?. bi-m. Editions Freeway, 1 rue Jean-Richepin, BP 271, Clermont-Ferrand, Cedex 1 63008, France.

677 DNK ISSN 1603-8967
TEXTUELT MONTHLY. 1943-2004. m. Dansk Textil og Beklaedningsindustri, Birk Centerpark 38, PO Box 507, Herning, 7400, Denmark.

572.8 GBR ISSN 1472-9288 CODEN: TRSHBY
THALAMUS AND RELATED SYSTEMS. 2001-2008 (vol.4, no.1). q. Cambridge University Press, The Edinburgh Bldg, Shaftesbury Rd, Cambridge, CB2 8RU, United Kingdom.

658 DEU ISSN 1615-9535
THEMENBRIEF MITARBEITERFUEHRUNG. 2000-2008. m. Forum Verlag Herkert GmbH, Mandichostr 18, Merching, 86504, Germany.

296 NLD ISSN 0169-8370
THEOKRATIA: JAHRBUCH DER FRANZ DELITZSCH - ARBEITSGEMEINSCHAFT. 1967-1979 (vol.3). irreg. Brill, PO Box 9000, Leiden, 2300 PA, Netherlands.

615.7 NZL ISSN 1176-6336
THERAPEUTICS AND CLINICAL RISK MANAGEMENT (PRINT). 2004-2008. bi-m. Dove Medical Press Ltd., 17/44 William Pickering Dr, Albany, PO Box 300-008, Auckland, 1311, New Zealand.

662 333.7915 GBR ISSN 1750-8363
THERMALNET. 2006-2008. s-a. Aston University, Bio-Energy Research Group, Aston Triangle, Birmingham, B4 7ET, United Kingdom.

330 AUS ISSN 1833-363X
THINKING BUSINESS. 1947-200?. bi-m. S A I Global, GPO Box 5420, Sydney, NSW 2001, Australia.

658.0029 USA
THOMAS REGISTER. 1908-2006. irreg. Thomas Publishing Company (New York), Five Penn Plz, New York, NY 10001.

346.066 AUS ISSN 1834-6103
THOMSON'S CORPORATIONS LAW ACADEMIC ALERT. 2005-2007. bi-m. Thomson Legal & Regulatory Ltd., Level 5, 100 Harris St, Pyrmont, NSW 2009 , Australia.

011 AUS ISSN 1038-3395
THORPE - R O M; Australian & New Zealand books in print, plus annotations, on CD-ROM. 1993-200?. m. Thorpe-Bowker, St Kilda Rd, PO Box 6509, Melbourne, VIC 8008, Australia.

613.7 CHN ISSN 1006-6845
TIANRAN BAOJIAN PIN/NATURAL HEALTH PRODUCTS. 1995-2001. m. Neimenggu Yaoxuehui, PO Box 35, Xincheng Youzheng, Hohhot, 010010, Mongolia.

950 GBR ISSN 0735-1364
TIBET SOCIETY JOURNAL. 1981-1988. q. Tibet Society, 114 Tottenham Court Rd, London, Mddx W1P 9HL, United Kingdom.

070.5 DNK ISSN 1397-9272
TIDNINGSTEKNIK (COPENHAGEN). 1967-1999; resumed 2000-2003. 6/yr. MediaMind A/S, PO Box 1419, Glostrup, 2600, Denmark.

590 DEU ISSN 1610-7160
TIER BILD. 2002-2006. 6/yr. Axel Springer Verlag AG, Axel-Springer-Platz 1, Hamburg, 20350, Germany.

590 DEU
TIERE UNSERE BESTEN FREUNDE. 1982-2007 (Oct.). q. OZ Verlag GmbH, Roemerstr 90, Rheinfelden, 79618, Germany.

808.8385 053.1 DEU ISSN 0949-5525
TIFFANY. 1983-2006. w. Cora Verlag GmbH und Co. KG, Valentinskamp 24, Hamburg, 20350, Germany.

808.8385 053.1 DEU ISSN 0949-5533
TIFFANY DUO. 1984-2006. 13/yr. Cora Verlag GmbH und Co. KG, Valentinskamp 24, Hamburg, 20350, Germany.

577.51 363.7 NLD ISSN 1871-9252
TIJ SCHRIFT TIENGEMETEN. 1999-2007. 3/yr. Deltanatuur, Postbus 800, Rotterdam, 3000 AV, Netherlands.

360 NLD ISSN 0921-2116
TIJDSCHRIFT VOOR DE SOCIALE SECTOR. 1977-2007. 11/yr. Nederlands Instituut voor Zorg en Welzijn, Postbus 19 152, Utrecht, 3501 DD, Netherlands.

666 691.4 USA ISSN 0192-9550
TILE & DECORATIVE SURFACES; the voice of America's tile market. 1950-199?. m. Ashlee Publishing Co., Inc., 18 E 41st St, 20th Fl, New York, NY 10017.

645.4029 ITA
TILE BRICKS REFRACTORIES SUPPLIERS BOOK. 1976-ceased. a. Gruppo Editoriale Faenza Editrice SpA, Via Pier de Crescenzi 44, Faenza, RA 48018, Italy.

769.56 FRA ISSN 1772-3434
TIMBRES & VOUS. 2005-2008. bi-m. Phil@poste, 28 Rue de la Redoute, Fontenay aux Roses, 92266, France.

659.13 ITA ISSN 1594-9168
TIMER MAGAZINE. 2002-200?. 9/yr. Gruppo Editoriale Futura, Via XXV Aprile 39, Bresso, MI 20091, Italy.

821 AUS
TIMESTREAM. 1971-1975. bi-m. Timestream, c/o Richard Coady, Ed., PO Box a360, Sydney South, NSW 2000, Australia.

028.5 NLD ISSN 1877-3397
TINKELBEL. 2006-2007. m. Sanoma Uitgevers B.V., Postbus 1900, Hoofddorp, 2130 JH, Netherlands.

338.47004 DEU
TIPS & TRENDS. 1982-1997. 4/yr. Deutsches Video Institut e.V., Budapester Str 44, Berlin, 10787, Germany.

331.1 NZL
TODAY. 1966-2001. m. Wellington Regional Employers Association (Inc.), Federation House, 6th Floor, Box 1087, 95-99 Molesworth St, Wellington, New Zealand.

659.1 658.8 ITA
TODAY FAX. 1989-ceased. d. Marketing Finanza Italia s.r.l., Via Alessandro Stradella, 3, Milan, MI 20129, Italy.

305.42 USA ISSN 0163-1799
TODAY'S CHRISTIAN WOMAN. 1978-2009. bi-m. Christianity Today International, 465 Gundersen Dr, Carol Stream, IL 60188.

639.34 GBR ISSN 1475-8709 CODEN: AQPOAR
TODAY'S FISHKEEPER. 1924-2005. m. T R M G Ltd, Winchester Court, 1 Forum Place, Hatfield, Herts, AL10 0RN, United Kingdom.

690 USA
TODAY'S LIFESTYLES HOME PLANS. 1994-2009 (Jan.). q. HomePlans.com, 901 N 3rd St, Ste 216, Minneapolis, MN 55401.

371.07 NLD ISSN 1568-8763
TOER; impulsen voor inspirerend kerk-zijn. 1959-2007. 6/yr. Boekencentrum Uitgevers, Goudstraat 50, Postbus 29, Zoetermeer, 2700 AA, Netherlands.

028.5 LTU ISSN 1392-2645
TOM & JERRY. 1997-2000. m. Egmont Lietuva, Algirdo 51A, Vilnius, 03609, Lithuania.

025.04 053.1 DEU ISSN 1436-9192
TOMORROW; Das Internet-Magazin. 1998-2009 (Feb.). m. Verlagsgruppe Milchstrasse, Mittelweg 177, Hamburg, 22786, Germany.

054.1 FRA ISSN 1298-0013
TOP FAMILLE MAGAZINE. 2000-2007. m. Hachette Filipacchi Medias S.A., 149/151 Rue Anatole France, Levallois-Perret, 925340, France.

283 AUS ISSN 1037-1664
TOP GEAR; discipleship studies for youth. 1991-1993. s-a. Joint Board of Christian Education, 65 Oxford St, PO Box 1245, Collingwood, VIC 3066, Australia.

779.28 GBR ISSN 1363-6073
TOP HEAVY VIDEO SPECIAL. 1996-1997. m. Northern & Shell Plc, The Northern & Shell Bldg, Number 10 Lower Thames St, London, EC3R 6EN, United Kingdom.

914 ITA
TOP NEWS. 1984-ceased. bi-m. Ideatour s.r.l., Via Mario Pagano, 39, Milan, MI 20145, Italy.

780 DEU
TOP OF THE POPS QUIZMAG. 2001-200?. irreg. Egmont Ehapa Verlag GmbH, Wallstr 59, Berlin, 10179, Germany.

613.7 NLD ISSN 1381-1770
TOP SANTE; gesond & lekker leven. 1994-2008. m. Sanoma Uitgevers B.V., Postbus 1900, Hoofddorp, 2130 JH, Netherlands.

541 DEU ISSN 0941-2646 CODEN: TPCHFC
TOPICS IN PHYSICAL CHEMISTRY. 1991-1999. irreg. Deutsche Bunsen Gesellschaft fuer Physikalische Chemie, Theodor-Heuss-Allee 25, Frankfurt am Main, 60486, Germany.

296.68 ISR
TORAH EDUCATION. 1969-1981. q. World Zionist Organization, Department for Torah Education and Culture in the Diaspora, P O Box 92, Jerusalem, 91920, Israel.

306.766 USA ISSN 0733-5873
TORSO. 1981-2009. m. Mavety Media Group, 225 Broadway, Ste 2801, New York, NY 10007-3079.

369.5 ITA
TOSCANA LIONS. 1972-ceased. m. Lions Clubs International, Italy - Distretto 108 LA, Via Gioberti 3, Montecatini Terme, PI 51016, Italy.

914 ITA ISSN 1591-2701
TOSCANA QUI. 1980-ceased. bi-m. Editrice Bonechi, Via dei Cairoli, 18BB, Florence, FI 50131, Italy.

791.33 DNK ISSN 1901-5208
TOTAL FILM. 2006-2007. m. Audio Media A-S, Sejroegade 7-9, Copenhagen OE, 2100, Denmark.

646.72 FRA ISSN 1950-3172
TOTAL RELOOK. 2006-2007. bi-m. Bleucom Editions, 12-14 Rue de l'Eglise, Paris, 75015, France.

796.812 GBR ISSN 1478-1859
TOTAL WRESTLING. 2002-2004. bi-m. Highbury - WV, 53-79 Highgate Rd, London, NW5 1TW, United Kingdom.

796 ITA ISSN 1123-2919
TOTOCORRIERE. 1979-ceased. w. Nemod Srl, Via Sardegna, 50, Rome, RM 00187, Italy.

664 FRA ISSN 0758-5055
TOUTE L'ALIMENTATION. 1958-2006. 11/yr. S E D I P A L, 15 rue de Rome, Paris, 75008, France.

647.94 FRA ISSN 0150-7540
TOUTES LES NOUVELLES DE L'HOTELLERIE ET DU TOURISME. 1971-ceased. m. Sedotourmovico, 4 rue Barye, Paris, 75017, France.

354.35 NLD ISSN 1387-4888
TOWARDS UNDIVIDED CITIES IN WESTERN EUROPE; new challenges for urban policy. 1997-1998. irreg. Delft University Press, Nieuwe Hemweg 6B, Amsterdam, 1013 BG, Netherlands.

052 659.1 AUS
TOWN AND COUNTRY MAGAZINE. 1976-1996. w. Queanbeyan Publishing Co., 210 Crawford St, Queanbeyan, NSW 2620, Australia.

363.1791094105 GBR ISSN 0953-7414
TOXIC SUBSTANCES BULLETIN. 1984-2003. irreg. Health and Safety Executive, Rose Court, 2 Southwark Bridge, London, SE1 9HS, United Kingdom.

790.132 USA ISSN 1533-6913
TOY CARS AND MODELS. 1974-2008. m. Krause Publications, Inc., 700 E State St, Iola, WI 54990.

745.592 USA ISSN 0898-5650
TOY SHOP. 1988-1999. bi-w. Krause Publications, Inc., 700 E State St, Iola, WI 54990.

028.5 NLD ISSN 1872-1583
TRACTOR TOM. 2006-2007. irreg. Juniorpress Magazines B.V., Zwarteweg 6c, Naarden, 1412 GD, Netherlands.

380.1029 USA ISSN 1093-8885
TRADE AND CUSTOMS WORLD DIRECTORY. 2003-2004. a. C Q Press, Inc., 2300 N St, NW, Ste 800, Washington, DC 20037.

Cessations

380.1029 DNK ISSN 0109-467X
TRADE DIRECTORY FOR DENMARK/ANNUAIRE DE L'EXPORTATION DU DANEMARK/ANUARIO DE LA EXPORTACION DE DINAMARCA/DAENISCHER HANDELSKALENDER. 1956-2004. biennial. Information Office of the Danish Foreign Trade, Hellerupvej 78, Hellerup, 2900, Denmark.

790.1 USA ISSN 1086-7341
TRADE FAX. 1995-200?. s-w. Krause Publications, Inc., 700 E State St, Iola, WI 54990.

621.39 ITA
TRADE NEWS; news magazine per dealer, VAR, superstore e system integrator. 1995-ceased. m. (10/yr.). Il Sole 24 Ore Business Media, Divisione J C E, Via Patecchio 2, Milan, 20141, Italy.

380.1029 USA
TRADE SHOWS & EXHIBITS SCHEDULE. 1925-2001. s-a. Nielsen Business Publications, 770 Broadway, New York, NY 10003.

642.5 ITA ISSN 1122-3510
TRADIZIONE NELLA RISTORAZIONE ITALIANA. 1992-ceased. a. Ordine Ristoratori Professionisti Italiani (O R P I), Via Quarto 12, Genoa, GE 16148, Italy.

410 ITA
TRADUZIONE, SOCIETA E CULTURA. 1991-ceased. irreg. Campanotto Editore, Via Marano 46, Pasian di Prato, UD 33037, Italy.

800 CZE ISSN 1210-6488 CODEN: IPGEE3
TRAFIKA; an international literary review. 1993-1994. 3/yr. Trafika Press Inc., Finska 9, Prague 10, 11000, Czech Republic.

796.5 DNK ISSN 0108-6758
TRAILER. 1983-1986. m. Fut og Fart, Vejlevej 49, Brande, 7330, Denmark.

631.3 DNK ISSN 1601-877X
TRAKTOR AARBOGEN. 2000-2006. a. Dansk Landbrugs Medier, Vester Farimagsgade 6, Copenhagen V, 1606, Denmark.

006.6 USA ISSN 1534-2832 CODEN: TMRAB7
TRANSFORM; reinventing business with content and collaboration technologies. 1992-2004. m. C M P Media LLC, 11 W 19th St, New York, NY 10011-4280.

621.38 USA ISSN 1040-0230
TRANSISTOR D.A.T.A. DIGEST. 1956-2000. a. D.A.T.A. Business Publishing, 15 Inverness Way E, Box 6510, Englewood, CO 80155-6510.

200.19 AUS ISSN 1324-9878
TRANSNATIONAL NETWORK FOR THE STUDY OF PHYSICAL, PSYCHOLOGICAL & SPIRITUAL WELL-BEING. NEWSLETTER. 1989-1997. s-a. Linking Publications, 16 Campbell Rd, Kenthurst, NSW 2156, Australia.

617 USA ISSN 1535-2684
TRANSPLANT & TISSUE WEEKLY. 1998-ceased. w. NewsRx, 2727 Paces Ferry Rd SE, Ste 2-440, Atlanta, GA 30339.

380.5 AUS
TRANSPORT AND COMMUNICATIONS INDICATORS (ONLINE). 1976-199?. q. AusInfo, Parliament House, Canberra Mc, ACT 2600, Australia.

387 DNK ISSN 0109-128X
TRANSPORTNYT; orientering for transportkoebere om transport og kommunikation. 1982-2002. m. Erhvervenes Transportudvalg, Vesterbrogade 6 D 4, Copenhagen V, 1620, Denmark.

025 FRA ISSN 0988-8705
TRANSVERSALES. 1988-2005. 6/yr. Association des Directeurs de Bibliotheques Departementales de Pret, B.P. 216, Mont-saint-Aignan, 76136, France.

621 ITA ISSN 1122-5025
TRASMISSIONI DI POTENZA; guida italiana dei fornitori. 1960-ceased. a. Tecniche Nuove SpA, Via Eritrea 21, Milan, MI 201, Italy.

720 ITA ISSN 0082-6006
TRATTATI DI ARCHITETTURA. 1966-1998. irreg. Edizioni Il Polifilo, Via Borgonuovo, 2, Milan, MI 20121, Italy.

617.1 340 USA ISSN 0564-1470
TRAUMA; personal injury, medicine, and surgery. 1959-2005. bi-m. Matthew Bender & Co., Inc., 1275 Broadway, Albany, NY 12204.

919.6904 USA ISSN 1531-7390
TRAVEL-SMART. HAWAII. 1988-ceased. biennial. Avalon Travel Publishing, 1700 4th St, Berkeley, CA 94710.

914 GBR ISSN 0262-5709
TRAVEL TRADE GAZETTE EUROPA. 1968-199?. fortn. C M P Information Ltd., Sovereign House, Sovereign Way, Tonbridge, Kent TN9 1RW, United Kingdom.

910.202 USA ISSN 1068-2554
TRAVELAMERICA. 1985-2005. bi-m. World Publishing Co., 990 Grove St, Evanston, IL 60201.

799 USA ISSN 1942-0129
TRAVELING SPORTSMAN. 2008 (Jun.)-2009 (Jan.); suspended. q. Fish Publications, PO Box 271161, Tampa, FL 33688.

700 FRA ISSN 0336-9730
TRAVERSES. 1975-1994. 3/yr. Edition du Centre Pompidou, Paris, Cedex 4 75191, France.

798.4 DNK ISSN 0109-2308
TRAVSPORT FOR FAGFOLK. 1983-1993. q. Bent Kim Jepsen Ed. & Pub., Faarupvej 102, Mundelstrup, 8381, Denmark.

549 GBR ISSN 1354-1528
TREASURES OF THE EARTH; the minerals and gemstones collection. 1994-1998. bi-w. Orbis Publishing Ltd., Griffin House, 161 Hammersmith Rd, London, W6 8SD, United Kingdom.

860 ESP ISSN 1133-0287
TREBO. 1982-1995. a. Asociacion Cultural Colectivo Trebo, Blanco Amor, 2, Orense, 32004, Spain.

615 FRA ISSN 0246-8476
LE TREBUCHET; la revue des professionnels de l'officine. 1980-2004. 10/yr. Elsevier France, Editions Scientifiques et Medicales, 23 Rue Linois, Paris, 75724, France.

333.75 AUS ISSN 0814-4680
TREES AND NATURAL RESOURCES. 1959-2003. q. Natural Resources Conservation League of Victoria, 593 Springvale Rd, Springvale South, VIC 3172, Australia.

369.4 DNK ISSN 0109-0003
TREKLANGEN; hjem, hjemstavn, faedreland. 1951-1998. m. Dansk Ungdomssekretariat, Moltkesgade 20 A, Flensborg, 2390, Denmark.

780.42 028.5 ITA ISSN 1129-4264
TREND DISCOTEC. 1989-ceased. m. Edizioni Juvenis, Viale Lunigiana 7, Milan, 20125, Italy.

330 DEU ISSN 0942-1300
TRENDS (FRANKFURT). 1948-2002. q. Dresdner Bank AG, Volkswirtschaftliche Abteilung, Frankfurt Am Main, 60301, Germany.

371.3 USA ISSN 1527-4241
TRENDS AND ISSUES IN POSTSECONDARY ENGLISH STUDIES. 1999-2000. a. National Council of Teachers of English, 1111 W Kenyon Rd, Urbana, IL 61801.

385 ESP
TRENET. -ceased. 4/yr. Trenet, Amadeu Vies s/n, Cornella de Llobregat, Barcelona 08940, Spain.

796.172 ESP
TRES 60 BODYBOARD. 1991-ceased. a. 3sesenta, Iparraguirre 59, 2o, Santurzi, Vizcaya 48980, Spain.

340 USA
TRESPASS TO TRY TITLE. 1988-ceased. plus a. updates. LexisNexis, PO Box 7587, Charlottesville, VA 22906.

630 ESP ISSN 0210-5616
TRIA; una revista para el campo. 1964-1986. fortn. Estructura S.A., Grupo de Estudios Economicos, Gran Via, 32, Madrid, 28013, Spain.

347.91 USA ISSN 1530-0390
THE TRIAL LAWYER; journal of strategy, technique and case management. 1978-2001. bi-m. Aspen Law & Business, 1185 Ave of the Americas, 37th Fl, New York, NY 10036.

346.07 USA ISSN 1559-551X
TRIAL TACTICS, TIPS & TECHNIQUES. 1995-2008 (Jun.). biennial. Pennsylvania Bar Institute, 5080 Ritter Rd, Mechanicsburg, PA 17055.

006.7 NLD ISSN 1876-2301
TRIB MAGAZINE. 1988-2008. bi-m. Broadcast Press Hilversum BV, Postbus 576, Hilversum, 1200 AN, Netherlands.

055.1 ITA
TRIBUNA DELL'IRPINIA; settimanale di attualita. 1967-ceased. w. Editrice Periodici Settimanali, Via Touro, 13, Avellino, AV 83100, Italy.

345 NLD ISSN 1020-3745
TRIBUNAL PENAL INTERNATIONAL POUR L'EX-YOUGOSLAVIE. DOCUMENTS DE REFERENCE/INTERNATIONAL CRIMINAL TRIBUNAL FOR THE FORMER YUGOSLAVIA. BASIC DOCUMENTS. 1995-2001. irreg. International Criminal Tribunal for the Former Yugoslavia, PO Box 13888, The Hague, 2501 EW, Netherlands.

746 FRA ISSN 0397-9075
TRICOT - SELECTION. 1967-2006. 10/yr. Editions de Saxe, 20 Rue Croix Barret, Lyon, 69358 Cedex 7, France.

133.5 DNK ISSN 0108-2450
TRIGON; magazine for professional astrology. 1981-1987. 3/yr. Forlaget Stjernerne, Irene Christensen Instituttet, Farimagsgade 63-1, Copenhagen K, 1364, Denmark.

255.42 GBR ISSN 0049-4712
TRINITARIAN BIBLE SOCIETY. QUARTERLY RECORD. 1859-19??. q. Trinitarian Bible Society, Tyndale House, Dorset Rd, London, SW19 3NN, United Kingdom.

028.5 DEU
TRIXI PFERDESPASS; Comics, Pferde. Spass. 2008 (Jan.)-2008 (Aug.). bi-m. Panini Verlags GmbH, Ravensstr 48, Nettetal, 41334, Germany.

909.09 NLD ISSN 0167-708X
TROPENINSTITUUT. 1980-1983. 10/yr. Koninklijk Instituut voor de Tropen, Mauritskade 63, Amsterdam, 1092 AD, Netherlands.

631.091 GBR ISSN 0041-3291 CODEN: TROSAC
TROPICAL SCIENCE. 1959-2008. q. John Wiley & Sons Ltd., The Atrium, Southern Gate, Chichester, West Sussex PO19 8SQ, United Kingdom.

388.324 AUS ISSN 0041-3380
TRUCK AND BUS; Australia's leading national road transport fleetowner monthly. 1940-2003. m. Shennen Publishing & Publicity Co. Pty. Ltd., 64 Kippax St, Surry Hills, NSW 2010, Australia.

380.5 DEU
TRUCK RACE BOOK. 1998-2001. a. EuroTransportMedia Verlags- und Veranstaltungs-GmbH, Handwerkstr 15, Stuttgart, 70565, Germany.

388.324 DEU
TRUCK TRIAL GUIDE. 2002-2003. a. EuroTransportMedia Verlags- und Veranstaltungs-GmbH, Handwerkstr 15, Stuttgart, 70565, Germany.

770 ISR ISSN 0334-7826
TSILLUM MIKTSO'I/PROFESSIONAL PHOTOGRAPHY. 1985-1999. q. Studio 19 Productions Ltd., P O Box 26177, Tel Aviv, 61261, Israel.

795.4 796.3 USA
TUFF STUFF PRESENTS: FLEER TRADING CARDS. 2001-ceased. a. Krause Publications, Inc., 700 E State St, Iola, WI 54990.

629.286 ITA ISSN 1970-4992
TUNED CARS. 2006-200?. s-a. Sprea Editori Srl, Via Torino 51, Cernusco sul Naviglio, MI 20063, Italy.

624.1 GBR ISSN 1463-242X
TUNNEL MANAGEMENT INTERNATIONAL. 1998-2006. q. Tunnel Management International Ltd., Kempston, PO Box 452, Bedford, MK43 9PL, United Kingdom.

910.202 BRA ISSN 1415-6393
TURISMO (PRINT); visao e acao. 1998-2007. s-a. Universidade do Vale do Itajai, Rua Uruguai, 458, Itajai, SC 88302-202, Brazil.

910.202 ITA
TURISMO GRADESE. 1960-ceased. w. (during summer). Pubblistudio de Zorzi Casa Editrice s.a.s., Via Marinoni, 53, Udine, UD 33100, Italy.

338.48 ESP ISSN 1135-0067
TURISMO RURAL Y AGROTURISMO EN LA COMUNIDAD VALENCIANA. 1994-1994. irreg. C I R I E C - Espana, Ave de los Naranjos, s-n, Edif. Dep. Oriental 2P21, Valencia, 46022, Spain.

930.1 TUR ISSN 0564-5042
TURK ARKEOLOJI DERGISI/TURKISH REVIEW OF ARCHAEOLOGY. 1956-1997. a. Ministry of Culture, General Directorate of Monuments and Museums, Ulus, Ankara, 06100, Turkey.

305.8 TUR ISSN 0082-6898
TURK ETNOGRAFYA DERGISI/TURKISH REVIEW OF ETHNOGRAPHY. 1956-1998 (vol.21). a. Ministry of Culture, General Directorate of Monuments and Museums, Ulus, Ankara, 06100, Turkey.

315.61 TUR ISSN 0041-4263
TURKEY. DEVLET ISTATISTIK ENSTITUSU. AYLIK ISTATISTIK BULTENI/TURKEY. TURKISH STATISTICAL INSTITUTE. MONTHLY BULLETIN OF STATISTICS. 1952-2003. m. T.C. Basbakanlik, Turkiye Istatistik Kurumu, Yucetepe Mah. Necatibey Cad No.114, Cankaya, Ankara, 06100, Turkey.

647 TUR
TURKEY: HOTELS - CAMPING. 1964-ceased. a. Ministry of Culture and Tourism, Gazi Mustafa Kemal Bulvari 33, Ankara, Turkey.

315.61 TUR
TURKEY. TURKISH STATISTICAL INSITUTE. CENSUS OF INDUSTRY AND BUSINESS ESTABLISHMENTS - 2ND STAGE RESULTS, TRADE. 1974-1992. irreg. T.C. Basbakanlik, Turkiye Istatistik Kurumu, Yucetepe Mah. Necatibey Cad No.114, Cankaya, Ankara, 06100, Turkey.

315.61 TUR ISSN 1300-7173
TURKEY. TURKISH STATISTICAL INSTITUTE. CENSUS OF INDUSTRY AND BUSINESS ESTABLISHMENTS - 1ST STAGE RESULTS. 1974-1992. irreg. T.C. Basbakanlik, Turkiye Istatistik Kurumu, Yucetepe Mah. Necatibey Cad No.114, Cankaya, Ankara, 06100, Turkey.

315.61 TUR
TURKEY. TURKISH STATISTICAL INSTITUTE. CENSUS OF INDUSTRY AND BUSINESS ESTABLISHMENTS - 2ND STAGE RESULTS, LARGE SCALE MANUFACTURING INDUSTRIES. 1976-1992. irreg. T.C. Basbakanlik, Turkiye Istatistik Kurumu, Yucetepe Mah. Necatibey Cad No.114, Cankaya, Ankara, 06100, Turkey.

315.61 TUR
TURKEY. TURKISH STATISTICAL INSTITUTE. CENSUS OF INDUSTRY AND BUSINESS ESTABLISHMENTS - 2ND STAGE RESULTS, SERVICE, HOTEL, RESTAURANT, GUEST HOUSE, CAFE. 1974-1992. irreg. T.C. Basbakanlik, Turkiye Istatistik Kurumu, Yucetepe Mah. Necatibey Cad No.114, Cankaya, Ankara, 06100, Turkey.

315.61 TUR
TURKEY. TURKISH STATISTICAL INSTITUTE. CENSUS OF INDUSTRY AND BUSINESS ESTABLISHMENTS - 2ND STAGE RESULTS, SMALL-SCALE MANUFACTURING INDUSTRIES. 1975-1992. irreg. T.C. Basbakanlik, Turkiye Istatistik Kurumu, Yucetepe Mah. Necatibey Cad No.114, Cankaya, Ankara, 06100, Turkey.

315.61 TUR ISSN 1300-0802
TURKEY. TURKIYE ISTATISTIK KURUMU. AYLIK DIS TICARET OZETI/TURKEY. TURKISH STATISTICAL INSTITUTE. MONTHLY SUMMARY OF FOREIGN TRADE. 1964-1994. m. T.C. Basbakanlik, Turkiye Istatistik Kurumu, Yucetepe Mah. Necatibey Cad No.114, Cankaya, Ankara, 06100, Turkey.

690.021 TUR ISSN 1013-5529
TURKEY. TURKIYE ISTATISTIK KURUMU. BINA INSAAT ISTATISTIKLERI/TURKEY. TURKISH STATISTICAL INSTITUTE. BUILDING CONSTRUCTION STATISTICS. 1969-2003. a. T.C. Basbakanlik, Turkiye Istatistik Kurumu, Yucetepe Mah. Necatibey Cad No.114, Cankaya, Ankara, 06100, Turkey.

630.21 TUR ISSN 1300-123X
TURKEY. TURKIYE ISTATISTIK KURUMU. CIFTCININ ELINE GECEN FIYATLAR/TURKEY. TURKISH STATISTICAL INSTITUTE. PRICES RECEIVED BY FARMERS. 1977-1993. a. T.C. Basbakanlik, Turkiye Istatistik Kurumu, Yucetepe Mah. Necatibey Cad No.114, Cankaya, Ankara, 06100, Turkey.

315.61 TUR ISSN 1300-6746
TURKEY. TURKIYE ISTATISTIK KURUMU. GAP IL ISTATISTIKLERI/TURKEY. TURKISH STATISTICAL INSTITUTE. S E A P PROVINCIAL STATISTICS. 1993-1998. a. T.C. Basbakanlik, Turkiye Istatistik Kurumu, Yucetepe Mah. Necatibey Cad No.114, Cankaya, Ankara, 06100, Turkey.

315.61 TUR ISSN 1300-1116
TURKEY. TURKIYE ISTATISTIK KURUMU. GAZ VE SU ISTATISTIKLERI/TURKEY. TURKISH STATISTICAL INSTITUTE. GAS AND WATER STATISTICS. 1986-1999. a. T.C. Basbakanlik, Turkiye Istatistik Kurumu, Yucetepe Mah. Necatibey Cad No.114, Cankaya, Ankara, 06100, Turkey.

363.73021 TUR ISSN 1300-1108
TURKEY. TURKIYE ISTATISTIK KURUMU. GEVRE ISTATISTIKLERI - HAVA KIRLILIGI/TURKEY. TURKISH STATISTICAL INSTITUTE. ENVIRONMENTAL STATISTICS - AIR POLLUTION. 1991-1993. a. T.C. Basbakanlik, Turkiye Istatistik Kurumu, Yucetepe Mah. Necatibey Cad No.114, Cankaya, Ankara, 06100, Turkey.

315.61 TUR ISSN 1300-8838
TURKEY. TURKIYE ISTATISTIK KURUMU. IL VE BOLGE ISTATIKLERI/TURKEY. TURKISH STATISTICAL INSTITUTE. PROVINCIAL AND REGIONAL STATISTICS. 1993-1994. a. T.C. Basbakanlik, Turkiye Istatistik Kurumu, Yucetepe Mah. Necatibey Cad No.114, Cankaya, Ankara, 06100, Turkey.

387.021 TUR ISSN 1300-1000
TURKEY. TURKIYE ISTATISTIK KURUMU. KABOTAJ VE ULUSLARARASI DENIZ TASIMASI ISTATISTIKLERI/TURKEY. TURKISH STATISTICAL INSTITUTE. STATISTICS OF COASTAL AND INTERNATIONAL SEA TRANSPORTATION. 1959-1993. a. T.C. Basbakanlik, Turkiye Istatistik Kurumu, Yucetepe Mah. Necatibey Cad No.114, Cankaya, Ankara, 06100, Turkey.

370.21 TUR ISSN 1300-1043
TURKEY. TURKIYE ISTATISTIK KURUMU. KAMU KURUMU VE KURULUSLARI HIZMET ONCESI VE HIZMET ICI EGITIM ISTATISTIKLERI/TURKEY. TURKISH STATISTICAL INSTITUTE. STATISTICS ON TRAINING IN STATE INSTITUTIONS. 1987-1999. a. T.C. Basbakanlik, Turkiye Istatistik Kurumu, Yucetepe Mah. Necatibey Cad No.114, Cankaya, Ankara, 06100, Turkey.

315.61 TUR ISSN 1300-1094
TURKEY. TURKIYE ISTATISTIK KURUMU. MADEN ISTATISTIKLERI/TURKEY. TURKISH STATISTICAL INSTITUTE. MINING STATISTICS. 1967-2001. a. T.C. Basbakanlik, Turkiye Istatistik Kurumu, Yucetepe Mah. Necatibey Cad No.114, Cankaya, Ankara, 06100, Turkey.

370.21 TUR
TURKEY. TURKIYE ISTATISTIK KURUMU. MILLI EGITIM ISTATISTIKLERI OGRETIM YILI BASI. 1933-1974. a. T.C. Basbakanlik, Turkiye Istatistik Kurumu, Yucetepe Mah. Necatibey Cad No.114, Cankaya, Ankara, 06100, Turkey.

338.528 TUR ISSN 1300-1035
TURKEY. TURKIYE ISTATISTIK KURUMU. PERAKENDE FIYAT ISTATISTIKLERI/TURKEY. TURKISH STATISTICAL INSTITUTE. RETAIL PRICE STATISTICS. 1972-2004. a. T.C. Basbakanlik, Turkiye Istatistik Kurumu, Yucetepe Mah. Necatibey Cad No.114, Cankaya, Ankara, 06100, Turkey.

315.61 TUR
TURKEY. TURKIYE ISTATISTIK KURUMU. SANAYI URETIM INDEKSI (DONEMLER ITIBARIYLE)/TURKEY. TURKISH STATISTICAL INSTITUTE. INDUSTRIAL PRODUCTION INDEXES (QUARTERLY). 1984-1990. q. T.C. Basbakanlik, Turkiye Istatistik Kurumu, Yucetepe Mah. Necatibey Cad No.114, Cankaya, Ankara, 06100, Turkey.

315.61 TUR
TURKEY. TURKIYE ISTATISTIK KURUMU. SPOR KULUPLERI/TURKEY. TURKISH STATISTICAL INSTITUTE. SPORTS CLUBS. 1972-1997. a. T.C. Basbakanlik, Turkiye Istatistik Kurumu, Yucetepe Mah. Necatibey Cad No.114, Cankaya, Ankara, 06100, Turkey.

381 TUR ISSN 1300-3992
TURKEY. TURKIYE ISTATISTIK KURUMU. TASIMACILIK ACISINDAN TURKIYE'NIN DIS TICAETI/TURKEY. TURKISH STATISTICAL INSTITUTE. FOREIGN TRADE BY TRANSPORT SYSTEM. 1994-1996. a. T.C. Basbakanlik, Turkiye Istatistik Kurumu, Yucetepe Mah. Necatibey Cad No.114, Cankaya, Ankara, 06100, Turkey.

315.61 TUR ISSN 1013-6185
TURKEY. TURKIYE ISTATISTIK KURUMU. TICARET, OTEL, LOKANTA VE HIZMET ISTATISTIKLERI/TURKEY. TURKISH STATISTICAL INSTITUTE. STATISTICS OF TRADE, HOTELS, RESTAURANTS AND SERVICES. 1991-2001. a. T.C. Basbakanlik, Turkiye Istatistik Kurumu, Yucetepe Mah. Necatibey Cad No.114, Cankaya, Ankara, 06100, Turkey.

315.61 TUR ISSN 1012-6376
TURKEY. TURKIYE ISTATISTIK KURUMU. TOPTAN ESYA VE TUKETICI FIYATLARI AYLIK INDEKS BULTENI/TURKEY. TURKISH STATISTICAL INSTITUTE. WHOLESALE AND CONSUMER PRICE INDEXES MONTHLY BULLETIN. 1963-1994. m. T.C. Basbakanlik, Turkiye Istatistik Kurumu, Yucetepe Mah. Necatibey Cad No.114, Cankaya, Ankara, 06100, Turkey.

315.61 TUR ISSN 1300-1264
TURKEY. TURKIYE ISTATISTIK KURUMU. TURKIYE EKONOMISI ISTATISTIK VE YORUMLAR/TURKEY. TURKISH STATISTICAL INSTITUTE. TURKISH ECONOMY STATISTICS AND EVALUATIONS. 1990-2002. m. T.C. Basbakanlik, Turkiye Istatistik Kurumu, Yucetepe Mah. Necatibey Cad No.114, Cankaya, Ankara, 06100, Turkey.

315.61 TUR ISSN 0259-5141
TURKEY. TURKIYE ISTATISTIK KURUMU. YILLIK IMALAT SANAYI ISTATISTIKLERI/TURKEY. TURKISH STATISTICAL INSTITUTE. ANNUAL MANUFACTURING INDUSTRY STATISTICS. 1974-2001. a. T.C. Basbakanlik, Turkiye Istatistik Kurumu, Yucetepe Mah. Necatibey Cad No.114, Cankaya, Ankara, 06100, Turkey.

358.4 TUR ISSN 1300-5030
TURKISH DEFENCE & AEROSPACE UPDATE. 1990-ceased. m. Monch Turkiye Yayincilik, Hosdere Caddesi, Halit Ziya Sokak, No 26/9, Cankaya / Ankara, 06540, Turkey.

052 TUR ISSN 1010-8874
TURKISH REVIEW; quarterly digest. 1985-1994. q. Republic of Turkey. Directorate General of Press and Information, Office of the Prime Minister, Citations Ceyhun Kansu Caddesi No.122, Balgat, Ankara, 06688, Turkey.

956 TUR ISSN 0085-7432
TURKIYAT MECMUASI. 1925-1996 (Vol.20). irreg. Istanbul University, Institute of Turkish Researches, Kavalah sokagi 5-4, Horhor, Fstih-istanbul, Turkey.

015.561 TUR ISSN 0041-4328
TURKIYE BIBLIYOGRAFYASI/TURKISH NATIONAL BIBLIOGRAPHY. 1928-2002. m. Milli Kutuphane Baskanligi, Bibliografya Hazirlama Sube Mudurlugu, Bahcelievler, Ankara, 06490, Turkey.

330 TUR ISSN 0034-6500
TURKIYE IS BANKASI. REVIEW OF ECONOMIC CONDITIONS. 1954-2002. q. Turkiye Is Bankasi, Musteri Iliskileri Isbank, P K 134, Levent - Istanbul, 34330, Turkey.

015.561 TUR ISSN 0041-4344
TURKIYE MAKALELER BIBLIYOGRAFYASI/BIBLIOGRAPHY OF ARTICLES IN TURKISH PERIODICALS. 1952-2002. m. Milli Kutuphane Baskanligi, Bibliografya Hazirlama Sube Mudurlugu, Bahcelievler, Ankara, 06490, Turkey.

794.8 ITA
TUTTO CODICI; bimestrale a carattere di informazioni programmi e giochi per computer. 1999-200?. bi-m. Tattilo Editrice SpA, Via degli Olmetti 18, Rome, 00060, Italy.

794.8 ITA
TUTTO PLAYSTATION; mensile a carattere di informazioni programmi e giochi per computer. 1999-200?. m. Tattilo Editrice SpA, Via degli Olmetti 18, Rome, 00060, Italy.

796 ITA ISSN 1121-3884
TUTTOCICLISMO. 1974-199?. w. Cooperativa di Giornalisti I S I D E, Via Ovidio, 10, Rome, RM 00193, Italy.

796.72 ITA ISSN 1124-5395
TUTTOPISTA. 1994-200?. m. Barbero Editori Srl, Via Galileo Galilei 3, Chieri, TO 10023, Italy.

711.4 ISR ISSN 0041-4549
TVAI; periodical for architecture, town planning, industrial design & the plastic arts. 1966-1993. a. Tvai, 27, Shlomo Hamelech St., Tel Aviv, Israel.

808.838 NLD ISSN 1387-229X
TWILIGHT WORLD. 1993-2004. irreg. Twilight World, PO Box 67, Utrecht, 3500 AB, Netherlands.

133.5 DNK ISSN 1902-083X
TYCHO; the information quarterly from the Museum of Astrology. 2007-2007 (vol. 2, 2007); suspended. q. Astrologisk Museum, Noerrebrogade 66 D, Copenhagen N, 2200, Denmark.

658.8 ESP
U D A PRESS. (Union de Detallistas de Alimentacion) -200?. 26/yr. Union de Detallistas de Alimentacion, Departamento de Publicaciones, Jorge Juan, 19, 1a planta, Madrid, 28001, Spain.

001.942 ITA ISSN 1128-6709
U F O NETWORK. 1999-200?. m. Futuro, Via Appia Nuova 59, Roma, 00183, Italy.

304.6094105 GBR ISSN 1749-5733
THE U K CONSUMER MARKETPLACE (YEAR). 200?-2006. a. World Advertising Research Center Ltd., Farm Rd, Henley-on-Thames, Oxon RG9 1EJ, United Kingdom.

643 USA ISSN 1460-3055
U K LABORATORY. 1997-2000. bi-m. International Scientific Communications, Inc., 30 Controls Dr, PO Box 670, Shelton, CT 06484.

327 NZL ISSN 1173-3543
U N A NEW Z; quarterly news magazine. 1945-1998. 3/yr. United Nations Association of New Zealand, PO Box 12324, Wellington, New Zealand.

382 338.91 USA ISSN 1014-370X
U N C T A D REVIEW. (United Nations Conference on Trade and Development) 1979-1996. s-a. United Nations Publications, 2 United Nations Plaza, Rm DC2-853, New York, NY 10017.

304.6 USA ISSN 1559-789X
U.S.A. STATISTICS IN BRIEF (PRINT). 1972-ceased. a. U.S. Census Bureau, 4600 Silver Hill Rd, Washington, DC 20233.

330.9021 USA ISSN 0095-926X
U.S. BUREAU OF LABOR STATISTICS. C P I DETAILED REPORT (PRINT). (Consumer Price Index) 1919-2007. m. U.S. Department of Labor, Bureau of Labor Statistics, Postal Square Bldg., 2 Massachusetts Ave, NE, Washington, DC 20212-0001.

331.11 USA ISSN 0098-1818
U.S. BUREAU OF LABOR STATISTICS. MONTHLY LABOR REVIEW. 1915-2008; suspended. m. U.S. Department of Labor, Bureau of Labor Statistics, Postal Square Bldg., 2 Massachusetts Ave, NE, Washington, DC 20212-0001.

331 USA ISSN 1543-3145
U.S. BUREAU OF LABOR STATISTICS. P P I DETAILED REPORT. 1972-2006. a. U.S. Department of Labor, Bureau of Labor Statistics, Postal Square Bldg., 2 Massachusetts Ave, NE, Washington, DC 20212-0001.

650.021 USA
U.S. BUREAU OF THE CENSUS. (YEAR) ECONOMIC CENSUS. CENSUS OF RETAIL TRADE (PRINT). (Issued in 3 series: Geographic Area Series, Industry Series, and Subject Series) 1929-ceased. quinquennial. U.S. Census Bureau, 4600 Silver Hill Rd, Washington, DC 20233.

690.021 USA
U.S. BUREAU OF THE CENSUS. (YEAR) ECONOMIC CENSUS. CONSTRUCTION (PRINT). (Issued in 3 series: Geographic Area Series, Industry Series, and Special Report Series.) 1930-ceased. quinquennial. U.S. Census Bureau, 4600 Silver Hill Rd, Washington, DC 20233.

338.0021 USA
U.S. BUREAU OF THE CENSUS. (YEAR) ECONOMIC CENSUS. MANUFACTURING (PRINT). (Issued in 3 series: Geographic Area Series, Industry Series, and Subject Series) 1810-ceased. quinquennial. U.S. Census Bureau, Customer Services, Washington, DC 20233.

622.00021 USA
U.S. BUREAU OF THE CENSUS. (YEAR) ECONOMIC CENSUS. MINING (PRINT). (Issued in 3 series: Geographic Area Series, Industry Series, and Subject Series) 1840-ceased. quinquennial. U.S. Census Bureau, Customer Services, Washington, DC 20233.

380.521 USA
U.S. BUREAU OF THE CENSUS. (YEAR) ECONOMIC CENSUS. TRANSPORTATION AND WAREHOUSING (PRINT). 1963-ceased. quinquennial. U.S. Census Bureau, Customer Services, Washington, DC 20233.

304.6 USA
U.S. BUREAU OF THE CENSUS. CURRENT POPULATION REPORTS. POPULATION CHARACTERISTICS. GEOGRAPHICAL MOBILITY. 1948-200?. a. U.S. Census Bureau, Customer Services, Washington, DC 20233.

304.6 USA
U.S. CENSUS BUREAU. CENSUS CATALOG AND GUIDE. 1946-1998. a. U.S. Census Bureau, Customer Services, Washington, DC 20233.

637.1021 USA ISSN 0093-1446
U.S. DEPARTMENT OF AGRICULTURE. NATIONAL AGRICULTURAL STATISTICS SERVICE. DAIRY PRODUCTS (PRINT). 1972-200?. 13/yr. U.S. Department of Agriculture, National Agricultural Statistics Service, 1400 Independence Ave, SW, Washington, DC 20250.

331.1193 USA ISSN 0363-8545
U.S. DEPARTMENT OF AGRICULTURE. NATIONAL AGRICULTURAL STATISTICS SERVICE. FARM LABOR (PRINT). 1943-2006. q. U.S. Department of Agriculture, National Agricultural Statistics Service, 1400 Independence Ave, SW, Washington, DC 20250.

633 USA
U.S. DEPARTMENT OF AGRICULTURE. NATIONAL AGRICULTURAL STATISTICS SERVICE. HOP STOCKS (PRINT). ceased 19??. s-a. U.S. Department of Agriculture, National Agricultural Statistics Service, 1400 Independence Ave, SW, Washington, DC 20250.

636.6 USA ISSN 0094-3851
U.S. DEPARTMENT OF AGRICULTURE. NATIONAL AGRICULTURAL STATISTICS SERVICE. SHEEP AND GOATS (PRINT). 1972-200?. 3/yr. U.S. Department of Agriculture, National Agricultural Statistics Service, 1400 Independence Ave, SW, Washington, DC 20250.

382 USA ISSN 1057-8773
U.S. EXPORTS OF MERCHANDISE (CD-ROM). 1989-2002. m. U.S. Census Bureau, 4600 Silver Hill Rd, Washington, DC 20233.

332.1 USA ISSN 0364-8370
U.S. FEDERAL RESERVE SYSTEM. SELECTED INTEREST AND EXCHANGE RATES. WEEKLY SERIES OF CHARTS. 19??-2003. w. U.S. Federal Reserve System, Board of Governors, Publications Services, Rm MS 138, Washington, DC 20551.

382 USA ISSN 1057-8765
U.S. IMPORTS OF MERCHANDISE (CD-ROM). 1989-2002. m. U.S. Census Bureau, 4600 Silver Hill Rd, Washington, DC 20233.

382 USA ISSN 1057-9680
U.S. MERCHANDISE TRADE. F T 925, EXPORTS, GENERAL IMPORTS, AND IMPORTS FOR CONSUMPTION - STANDARD INTERNATIONAL TRADE CLASSIFICATION REVISION 3 - COMMODITY BY COUNTRY. 1943-1996. m. U.S. Census Bureau, 4700 Silver Hill Rd., Washington, DC 20233.

615 USA ISSN 0740-4174 CODEN: USPIE9
U S P - D I. VOL. 1. DRUG INFORMATION FOR THE HEALTH CARE PROFESSIONAL. (United States Pharmacopeia) 1980-2007. a. (plus m. update). Micromedex, 6200 South Syracuse Way, Suite 300, Greenwood Village, CO 80111-4740.

333.72 DEU ISSN 1431-1062
U T A INTERNATIONAL. (Umwelt Technologie Aktuell) 1995-2000. 4/yr. G I T Verlag GmbH, Roesslerstr 90, Darmstadt, 64293, Germany.

340 AUS ISSN 1442-4959
THE U T S LAW REVIEW. (University of Technology, Sydney) 1999-2005 (vol.9). a. University of Technology, Sydney, Faculty of Law, PO Box 123, Broadway, NSW 2007, Australia.

636.2142 DNK ISSN 1397-3010
UGENYT FRA MEJERIFORENINGEN. 1973-2004. w. Mejeriforeningen, Frederiks Alle 22, Aarhus C, 8000, Denmark.

690 NLD ISSN 1567-6110
UGO KRANT. 1990-2007. q. F N V Bouw, Postbus 520, Woerden, 3440 AM, Netherlands.

811 HUN ISSN 0082-7312
UJ MAGYAR NEPKOLTESI GYUJTEMENY/NEW HUNGARIAN COLLECTION OF POPULAR POETRY. 1955-2002 (vol.26). irreg. Akademiai Kiado Rt., Prielle Kornelia U. 19, Budapest, 1117, Hungary.

690 GBR
ULSTER BUILDER AND ALLIED TRADES JOURNAL. 1946-1981. m. Ulster Builder and Allied Trades Journal, c/o William H. Guilfoyle, 27 Dunlambert Park, Belfast, BT15 3NJ, United Kingdom.

650 AUS ISSN 1443-7023
ULTIBASE JOURNAL. 1996-2003. m. Royal Melbourne Institute of Technology, Faculty of Education, Language and Community Services, PO Box 2476V, Melbourne, VIC 3001, Australia.

700 USA ISSN 0160-0699
UMBRELLA. 1978-2005. irreg. Umbrella Associates, PO Box 3640, Santa Monica, CA 90408.

363.7 DEU
UMWELT-SERVICE. 1988-2005. q. Deutscher Instituts Verlag GmbH, Gustav-Heinemann-Ufer 84-88, Cologne, 50968, Germany.

614.7 BRD ISSN 0343-1312
UMWELTBRIEF (BERLIN). 1973-1987. irreg. Bundesministerium des Innern, Alt-Moabit 101D, Berlin, 10559, Germany.

628 DEU ISSN 1616-5829 CODEN: EGFGDW
UMWELTPRAXIS; ein Bertelsmann Fachmagazin fuer Umwelttechnik in Industrie und Kommunalwirtschaft. 2001-2003. 10/yr. Deutscher Fachverlag GmbH, Mainzer Landstr 251, Frankfurt Am Main, 60326, Germany.

700 AUS ISSN 1449-6747
UN MAGAZINE. 2004-2005. q. Lily Hubberd, PO Box 2016, North Melbourne, VIC 3051, Australia.

778.53 GBR ISSN 0267-8497
UNDERCUT. 1981-1990. s-a. Undercut, c/o 17 West Grove, London, SE10 8QT, United Kingdom.

331.137941 GBR ISSN 1350-6455
UNEMPLOYED CLAIMANTS. SUMMARY STATISTICS. 1992-1997. irreg. Government Statistical Service, 1 Myddelton St, London, EC1R 1UW, United Kingdom.

551.4 DEU ISSN 1863-5555
UNESCO INTERNATIONALES HYDROLOGISCHES PROGRAMM: OPERATIONELLES HYDROLOGISCHES PROGRAMM: JAHRBUCH BUNDESREPUBLIK DEUTSCHLAND/UNESCO. INTERNATIONAL HYDROLOGICAL PROGRAMME: OPERATIONAL HYDROLOGY PROGRAMME: YEARBOOK FEDERAL REPUBLIC OF GERMANY. 1965; N.S. 1968-2005. a. Bundesanstalt fuer Gewaesserkunde, Am Mainzer Tor 1, Koblenz, 56068, Germany.

Cessations

016.37 DNK ISSN 0901-9294
UNGDOMS- OG VOKSENUNDERVISNING. 1979-2006. a. Fonden Undervisnings Information, Siljangade 6, Copenhagen S, 2300, Denmark.

005.5 USA ISSN 1537-0305
UNICENTER ADVISOR. 1995-2004. q. Advisor Media, Inc., 12463 Rancho Bernardo Rd, Ste 509, PO Box 503350, San Diego, CA 92128.

500 600 AUS ISSN 1329-7724
UNISERVE SCIENCE NEWS. 1995-2000. 3/yr. UniServe Science, Carslaw Bldg F07, University of Sydney, Sydney, NSW 2006, Australia.

321.92 ITA ISSN 0390-038X
UNITA PROLETARIA. 1975-1984. m. Unita Proletaria, Via Tomacelli, 146, Rome, RM 00186, Italy.

347 341 NLD ISSN 1385-173X
UNITED KINGDOM LAW REVIEW. 1993-ceased. s-a. Global Law Association, PO Box 9001, Tilburg, 5000 HA, Netherlands.

364 USA ISSN 0082-8025
UNITED NATIONS CONGRESS ON THE PREVENTION OF CRIME AND THE TREATMENT OF OFFENDERS. REPORT. 1956-2000. irreg. United Nations Publications, 2 United Nations Plaza, Rm DC2-853, New York, NY 10017.

690.021 USA ISSN 0257-9073
UNITED NATIONS. DEPARTMENT OF INTERNATIONAL ECONOMIC AND SOCIAL AFFAIRS. STATISTICAL OFFICE. CONSTRUCTION STATISTIC YEARBOOK. 1974-1988. a. United Nations Publications, 2 United Nations Plaza, Rm DC2-853, New York, NY 10017.

327 AUS ISSN 0814-1967
UNITED NATIONS GENERAL ASSEMBLY: REPORT OF THE AUSTRALIAN DELEGATION. 1946-1996. a. Australia. Department of Foreign Affairs and Trade, R G Casey Bldg, John McEwen Cresc, Barton, ACT 0221, Australia.

364 ITA
UNITED NATIONS INTERREGIONAL CRIME AND JUSTICE RESEARCH INSTITUTE. PUBLICATION. 1969-ceased. irreg. United Nations Interregional Crime and Justice Research Institute, Piazza San Marco 50, Rome, 00186, Italy.

339 USA ISSN 0259-3009
UNITED NATIONS. NATIONAL ACCOUNTS STATISTICS. GOVERNMENT ACCOUNTS AND TABLES. 1958-1986. a. United Nations Publications, 2 United Nations Plaza, Rm DC2-853, New York, NY 10017.

341 332.6 USA
UNITED STATES IMPORT TRADE LAW. 1992-ceased. plus irreg. updates. LexisNexis, PO Box 7587, Charlottesville, VA 22906.

341 USA ISSN 1089-8948
UNITED STATES-MEXICO LAW JOURNAL. 1993-199?. a. University of New Mexico, School of Law, MSC11 6070, 1 University of New Mexico, Albuquerque, NM 87131.

004 FRA ISSN 1767-4085
UNIVERS MAC. 1992-2007. m. (11/yr.). Editions Pressimage, 5-7 rue Raspail, Montreuil, Cedex 93108, France.

635.96 AUS ISSN 1039-8279
UNIVERSAL'S POPULAR PLANTS AND FLOWERS SERIES. COTTAGE GARDEN AND FRAGRANT PLANTS. 1992-ceased. a. Universal Magazines Pty. Ltd., Unit 5, 6-8 Byfield St, North Ryde, NSW 2113, Australia.

635.96 AUS ISSN 1039-9526
UNIVERSAL'S POPULAR PLANTS AND FLOWERS SERIES. FRUITS, VEGETABLES AND HERBS. 1992-ceased. a. Universal Magazines Pty. Ltd., Unit 5, 6-8 Byfield St, North Ryde, NSW 2113, Australia.

635.98 AUS ISSN 1039-9534
UNIVERSAL'S POPULAR PLANTS AND FLOWERS SERIES. PLANTS FOR CONTAINERS AND COURTYARDS. 1992-ceased. a. Universal Magazines Pty. Ltd., Unit 5, 6-8 Byfield St, North Ryde, NSW 2113, Australia.

635.96 AUS ISSN 1039-9542
UNIVERSAL'S POPULAR PLANTS AND FLOWERS SERIES. PLANTS FOR SHADE AND WATERGARDENS. 1992-ceased. a. Universal Magazines Pty. Ltd., Unit 5, 6-8 Byfield St, North Ryde, NSW 2113, Australia.

635 AUS ISSN 1039-8260
UNIVERSAL'S POPULAR PLANTS AND FLOWERS SERIES. TREES, SHRUBS AND GROUND COVERS. 1992-ceased. a. Universal Magazines Pty. Ltd., Unit 5, 6-8 Byfield St, North Ryde, NSW 2113, Australia.

945 ITA
UNIVERSITA CATTOLICA DEL SACRO CUORE. ISTITUTO DI STORIA ANTICA. CONTRIBUTI. 1972-199?. irreg. Universita Cattolica del Sacro Cuore, Largo Gemelli 1, Milan, MI 20123, Italy.

060 ITA
UNIVERSITA DEGLI STUDI DI CAGLIARI. FACOLTA DI MAGISTERO. ANNALI. 1976-ceased. irreg. Universita degli Studi di Cagliari, Facolta di Magistero, Cagliari, CA 09100, Italy.

554 560 ITA
UNIVERSITA DEGLI STUDI DI FERRARA. ISTITUTO DI GEOLOGIA. PUBBLICAZIONI. 1950-ceased. a. Universita degli Studi di Ferrara, Istituto di Geologia, C.So Ercole 1 d'Este 32, Ferrara, Italy.

549 ITA
UNIVERSITA DEGLI STUDI DI FERRARA. ISTITUTO DI MINERALOGIA. ANNALI. NUOVA SERIE. SEZIONE: SCIENZE DELLA TERRA. 1973 (vol.1, no.7)-ceased. irreg. Universita degli Studi di Ferrara, Istituto di Mineralogia, C.so Ercole 1o d'Este 32, Ferrara, FE 44100, Italy.

363.5021 ITA ISSN 0041-896X
UNIVERSITA DEGLI STUDI DI FIRENZE. ISTITUTO DI STATISTICA. DOCUMENTAZIONE; ricerca sul problema delle abitazioni in Italia. 1965-ceased. irreg. Universita degli Studi di Firenze, Istituto di Statistica, Via Curtatone, 1, Florence, FI 50123, Italy.

900 ITA
UNIVERSITA DEGLI STUDI DI GENOVA. ISTITUTO DI MEDIEVISTICA. COLLANA STORICA DI FONTI E STUDI. 1958-ceased. irreg. Libreria Bozzi, via Cairoli 2, Genoa, GE 16124, Italy.

100 ITA ISSN 0390-0614
UNIVERSITA DEGLI STUDI DI LECCE. BOLLETTINO DI STORIA DELLA FILOSOFIA. 1973-2002. a. Universita degli Studi di Lecce, Dipartimento di Filosofia, Via V M Stampacchia, Lecce, LE 73100, Italy.

378 ITA
UNIVERSITA DEGLI STUDI DI MILANO. ANNUARIO. 1924-ceased. a. Universita degli Studi di Milano, Piazza S. Alessandro I, Milan, 20123, Italy.

900 300 ITA ISSN 0469-5461
UNIVERSITA DEGLI STUDI DI NAPOLI. FACOLTA DI LETTERE E FILOSOFIA. ANNALI. 1950-1988. a. Universita degli Studi di Napoli "Federico II", Facolta di Lettere e Filosofia, Via Porta di Massa 1, Naples, 80133, Italy.

384 ITA
UNIVERSITA DEGLI STUDI DI PARMA. CENTRO STUDI E ARCHIVIO DELLA COMUNICAZIONE. ARCHIVI DEL PROGRETTO - COLLANA. 1989-ceased. a. Universita degli Studi di Parma, Via Universita 12, Parma, PR 43100, Italy.

384 ITA
UNIVERSITA DEGLI STUDI DI PARMA. CENTRO STUDI E ARCHIVIO DELLA COMUNICAZIONE. CATALOGHI. 1976-ceased. irreg. Universita degli Studi di Parma, Via Universita 12, Parma, PR 43100, Italy.

330 ITA
UNIVERSITA DEGLI STUDI DI PARMA. FACOLTA DI ECONOMIA E COMMERCIO. STUDI E RICERCHE. 1964-ceased. a. Universita degli Studi di Parma, Via Universita 12, Parma, PR 43100, Italy.

630 ITA ISSN 0374-4981 CODEN: AASPAZ
UNIVERSITA DEGLI STUDI DI PERUGIA. FACOLTA DI AGRARIA. ANNALI. 1942-ceased. a. Universita degli Studi di Perugia, Facolta di Agraria, Piazza dell'Universita 1, Perugia, 06100, Italy.

617 ITA ISSN 0365-2270
UNIVERSITA DEGLI STUDI DI PERUGIA. FACOLTA DI MEDICINA E CHIRURGIA. ANNALI. 1885-199?. q. Universita degli Studi di Perugia, Facolta di Medicina e Chirurgia, Perugia, PG, Italy.

338.1 ITA
UNIVERSITA DEGLI STUDI DI TRIESTE. ISTITUTO DI RICERCHE ECONOMICO AGRARIE. PUBBLICAZIONE. 1971-ceased. irreg. Universita degli Studi di Trieste, Istituto di Ricerche Economico-Agrarie, Trieste, TS, Italy.

500 ITA ISSN 0037-8860
UNIVERSITA DI MESSINA. SOCIETA PELORITANA DI SCIENZE FISICHE MATEMATICHE E NATURALI. ATTI. 1955-ceased. q. Universita degli Studi di Messina, Societa Peloritana di Scienze Fisiche Matematiche e Naturali, Via dei Verdi, Messina, 98122, Italy.

491.7 891.7 CZE ISSN 0231-9268
UNIVERSITA PALACKEHO. PEDAGOGICKA FAKULTA. SBORNIK PRACI: RUSKY JAZYK A LITERATURA. 1972-1989. irreg. Univerzita Palackeho v Olomouci, Pedagogicka Fakulta, Krizkovskeho 10, Olomouc, 77147, Czech Republic.

305.8 FRA ISSN 0249-5635
UNIVERSITE DE BORDEAUX II. CAHIERS ETHNOLOGIQUES. 1972-2000. s-a. Presses Universitaires de Bordeaux, 3 Place de la Victoire, Bordeaux, 33000, France.

305.8 FRA ISSN 0985-9837
UNIVERSITE DE BORDEAUX II. CAHIERS ETHNOLOGIQUES. MEMOIRES. 1986-ceased. Presses Universitaires de Bordeaux, 3 Place de la Victoire, Bordeaux, 33000, France.

551 FRA ISSN 1162-9584 CODEN: ASBGEJ
UNIVERSITE DE FRANCHE-COMTE. ANNALES SCIENTIFIQUES. GEOLOGIE. 1946-199?. irreg. Presses Universitaires Franche-Comte, Place St Jacques, Besancon, 25030, France.

330 NZL ISSN 0112-9759
UNIVERSITY OF AUCKLAND. DEPARTMENT OF ECONOMICS. POLICY DISCUSSION PAPERS. 1985-2004. irreg. University of Auckland, Department of Economics, Owen G Glenn Bldg, 12 Grafton Rd, Auckland, New Zealand.

301 NZL ISSN 1173-2636
UNIVERSITY OF AUCKLAND. DEPARTMENT OF SOCIOLOGY. WORKING PAPERS IN SOCIOLOGY. 1974-1997. irreg. University of Auckland, Department of Sociology, Private Bag 92019, Auckland, New Zealand.

620.82 USA ISSN 0096-9311
UNIVERSITY OF CALIFORNIA PUBLICATIONS IN ENGINEERING. 1907-1962. irreg. University of California Press, Book Series, 2120 Berkeley Way, Berkeley, CA 94720.

330 NZL ISSN 1171-0705
UNIVERSITY OF CANTERBURY. DEPARTMENT OF ECONOMICS. DISCUSSION PAPER. 1984-2001. irreg. University of Canterbury, Department of Economics, Private Bag 4800, Christchurch, New Zealand.

790 USA ISSN 1051-2225
UNIVERSITY OF MIAMI ENTERTAINMENT & SPORTS LAW REVIEW. 1983-1997. s-a. University of Miami, School of Law, 1311 Miller Dr, Rm C 423, P O Box 248087, Coral Gables, FL 33124.

628.1 AUS ISSN 1038-3859
UNIVERSITY OF NEW ENGLAND. CENTRE FOR WATER POLICY RESEARCH. DISCUSSION PAPERS (NO.). 1991-1993. irreg. University of New England, Centre for Ecological Economics & Water Policy Research, Armidale, NSW 2351, Australia.

378.74 AUS ISSN 1443-3435
UNIVERSITY OF NEW ENGLAND. TEACHING & LEARNING CENTRE. UPDATES. 1956-2004. s-a. University of New England, Teaching & Learning Centre, Armidale, NSW 2351, Australia.

344 USA ISSN 1940-8064
UNIVERSITY OF PENNSYLVANIA JOURNAL OF BUSINESS AND EMPLOYMENT LAW. 1998-2008. q. University of Pennsylvania, Law School, 3400 Chestnut St, Philadelphia, PA 19104.

107.11 AUS
UNIVERSITY OF QUEENSLAND. DOCTOR OF PHILOSOPHY HANDBOOK (ONLINE). 1996-2002. a. University of Queensland, Calendar and Handbooks Office, St. Lucia, QLD 4072, Australia.

330 AUS ISSN 1833-1076
UNIVERSITY OF QUEENSLAND. EAST ASIAN ECONOMIC RESEARCH GROUP. DISCUSSION PAPER SERIES. 2005-200?. irreg. University of Queensland, School of Economics, East Asia Economic Research Group, Level 6, Colin Clark Bldg (39), St Lucia, QLD 4072, Australia.

650 AUS ISSN 1443-2943
UNIVERSITY OF SOUTH AUSTRALIA. CENTRE OF BUSINESS ANALYSIS AND RESEARCH. WORKING PAPER (ONLINE). 1999-2002. irreg. University of South Australia, Division of Business and Enterprise/Centre of Business Analysis and Research, GPO Box 2471, Adelaide, SA 5001, Australia.

636 CZE ISSN 1212-558X
UNIVERSITY OF SOUTH BOHEMIA IN CESKE BUDEJOVICE. FACULTY OF AGRICULTURE. COLLECTION OF SCIENTIFIC PAPERS. SERIES FOR ANIMAL SCIENCES. 1984-2006. s-a. Jihoceska Univerzita v Ceskych Budejovicich, Zemedelska Fakulta, Studentska 13, Ceske Budejovice, 37005, Czech Republic.

378 AUS ISSN 1037-1818
UNIVERSITY OF SOUTHERN QUEENSLAND. HANDBOOK. 1979-2003. a. University of Southern Queensland, Toowoomba, QLD 4350, Australia.

338.1 AUS ISSN 0817-8771
UNIVERSITY OF SYDNEY. DEPARTMENT OF AGRICULTURAL ECONOMICS. RESEARCH REPORT. 1957-199?. irreg. University of Sydney, Department of Agricultural Economics, R D Watt Bldg, Syndey, NSW 2006, Australia.

333.72 AUS ISSN 0313-5780
UNIVERSITY OF TASMANIA. CENTRE FOR ENVIRONMENTAL STUDIES. WORKING PAPERS. 1976-199?. irreg. University of Tasmania, Centre for Environmental Studies, Private Bag 86, Hobart, TAS 7001, Australia.

343.096 NLD ISSN 1052-1216
UNIVERSITY OF VIRGINIA. CENTER FOR OCEANS LAW AND POLICY. ANNUAL SEMINAR. 1977-1993 (vol.17). a. Martinus Nijhoff, PO Box 9000, Leiden, 2300 PA, Netherlands.

610 CZE ISSN 0457-4206
UNIVERZITA KARLOVA. LEKARSKA FAKULTA HRADEC KRALOVE. LEKARSKE ZPRAVY. 1956-2007. q. Nakladatelstvi Karolinum, Ovocny trh 3/5, Prague 1, 11636, Czech Republic.

622 DEU ISSN 0343-8198
UNSER BETRIEB. 1968-2004. 2/yr. Deilmann - Haniel GmbH, Haustenbecke 1, Dortmund, 44319, Germany.

658 DEU ISSN 1435-5418
UNTERNEHMENSBERATER. 1997-2005. bi-m. Dr. Curt Haefner Verlag GmbH, Dischingerstr 8, Heidelberg, 69123, Germany.

055.1 ITA ISSN 1591-7177
UOMO. 2001-200?. q. Gruppo Editoriale Futura, Via XXV Aprile 39, Bresso, MI 20091, Italy.

351.93 362.7 NZL ISSN 1176-6964
UPDATE; youth development programmes. 2004-2005. q. Ministry of Youth Development, Level 1, Charles Fergusson West Block, Bowen St, PO Box 1556, Wellington, 6001, New Zealand.

323.4 USA
UPDATE (NEW YORK). 1982-200?. q. Human Rights Watch, 350 Fifth Ave, 34th Fl, New York, NY 10118.

616.99481 GBR ISSN 1744-196X
UPDATES IN LYMPHOMATOUS MENINGITIS. 2004-2004. s-a. Darwin Grey Communications, Sterling House, Oxford Rd, Kingston Bagpuize, Oxon OX13 5AP, United Kingdom.

307.1416 FRA ISSN 1770-9970
URBAINE. 2004-2007. m. Devorateurs d'Espaces, 7 Rue de l'Arbalete, Paris, 75005, France.

782.421 AUS
URBAN HITZ. 2004-2006. bi-m. Derwent Howard Media Pty Ltd., PO Box 1037, Bondi Junction, NSW 1355, Australia.

307.1 ESP ISSN 0213-9391
URBANISMO. 1987-1998. 3/yr. Colegio Oficial de Arquitectos de Madrid, Barquillo, 12, Madrid, 28004, Spain.

616.02 USA ISSN 1933-1193
URGENT CARE; the official journal of the american academy of urgent care medicine. 2006-2007. m. ((bi-m. until 2007)). Quadrant HealthCom, 7 Century Dr, Ste 302, Parsippany, NJ 07054.

629.23 NZL ISSN 1176-9890
USED CAR SAFETY RATINGS. 2004-2007. a. New Zealand Transport Agency, Lambton Quay, PO Box 5084, Wellington, 6145, New Zealand.

940 NLD ISSN 0929-984X
UTRECHTSE BIJDRAGEN TOT DE MEDIEVISTIEK. 1983-2004 (vol.20). a. Uitgeverij Verloren, Torenlaan 25, Hilversum, 1211 JA, Netherlands.

371.911 USA
V C S RESOURCE UPDATE. (Vision Community Services) 1988-2005. bi-m. M A B Community News, 200 Ivy St, Brookline, MA 02446.

778.53 ITA ISSN 0394-2384
V R; mensile di videoregistrazione creativa. (Video Registrare) 1985-ceased. m. Systems Comunicazioni, Via Olanda 6, Vigano di Gaggiano, MI 20083, Italy.

005.13 USA
V S A M UPDATE. (Virtual Storage Access Method) 1991-19??. q. Xephon, 9330 Lyndon B Johnson Fwy., Ste. 800, Dallas, TX 75243-4310.

371.334 USA
V S T E JOURNAL. 2001-2008. irreg. Virginia Society for Technology in Education, 9702 Gayton Rd, PO Box 149, Richmond, VA 23238.

796.77 DEU ISSN 1611-0374
V W GOLF & CO. SCENE. 2000-2007 (Apr.). bi-m. T V Trend Verlag GmbH, Hertener Markt 7, Herten, 45699, Germany.

363 USA ISSN 1541-2474
THE VALUATION REPORT; a monthly publication of the low-income housing tax credit industry. 2002-ceased. m. Novogradac & Co. LLP, 246 1st St, 5th Fl, San Francisco, CA 94105.

658 USA ISSN 1559-3576
VALUE ENGINEERING TODAY. 1960-200?. m. Business Publishers, Inc., PO Box 17592, Baltimore, MD 21297.

070.48374 CZE ISSN 1214-9845
VANESSA. 2004-2005. w. Sanoma Magazines Praha s.r.o., Lomnickeho 7, Prague 4, 12079, Czech Republic.

053.1 DEU ISSN 1864-7774
VANITY FAIR. 2007 (Feb.)-2009 (Feb.). w. Conde Nast Verlag GmbH, Karlstr 23, Munich, 80333, Germany.

613.125 NZL ISSN 1176-6344
VASCULAR HEALTH AND RISK MANAGEMENT (PRINT). 2004-2008. bi-m. Dove Medical Press Ltd., 17/44 William Pickering Dr, Albany, PO Box 300-008, Auckland, 1311, New Zealand.

658 333.5 NLD ISSN 1574-1729
DE VASTGOEDBEHEERDER. 2005-2008. m. (11/yr.). Sdu Uitgevers bv, Postbus 20025, The Hague, 2500 EA, Netherlands.

056.1 ESP ISSN 1131-7736
VEINTIUNO; thought and culture review. 1989-2003. q. Fundacion Canovas del Castillo, Marques de la Ensenada 14, Madrid, 28004, Spain.

027.402 DNK ISSN 0902-6533
VEJVISER OVER FOLKEBIBLIOTEKER I STORKOEBENHAVN. 1973-1997. a. Gentofte Bibliotekerne Centralbibliotek for Koebenhavns Amt, Ahlmanns alle 6, Hellerup, 2900, Denmark.

370 ESP ISSN 1136-0313
VELA MAJOR. 1994-1999. 3/yr. Editorial Barcanova, Plaza Lesseps, 33 Entre Sol 1a., Barcelona, 08023, Spain.

944 FRA ISSN 0994-1258
VENDEE MAGAZINE. 1988-199?. 11/yr. P A M, 4 rue Marechal-Foch, La Roche-sur-Yon, 85000, France.

949.2 NLD ISSN 1871-7527
VENLOSE KATERNEN. 2005-2008. irreg. Gemeentearchief Venlo, Doktor Blumenkampstraat 1, Venlo, 5914 PV, Netherlands.

668.5 ESP ISSN 1136-1433
VENTAS DE PERFUMERIA Y COSMETICA. 1980-199?. 12/yr. Ediciones 4 Mas 4, C. Portala 27-6, Barcelona, 08023, Spain.

327 ITA
VENTO DEL SUD; periodico di lotta meridionale. 1973-ceased. bi-m. Vento del Sud, Casella Postale 188, Reggio Calabria, RC 89100, Italy.

332.6 USA
VENTURE CAPITAL YEARBOOK. 1983-1998. a. Thomson Financial, 195 Broadway, New York, NY 10007.

621.38 DEU ISSN 0946-7777
VERBINDUNGSTECHNIK IN DER ELEKTRONIK UND FEINWERKTECHNIK. 1989-2003. bi-m. D V S Verlag GmbH, Aachener Str 172, Duesseldorf, 40223, Germany.

807.34 HUN ISSN 1585-079X
VERBUM; analecta neolatina. 1999-2009 (Jan.). s-a. Akademiai Kiado Rt., Prielle Kornelia U. 19, Budapest, 1117, Hungary.

347 USA ISSN 1931-4310
VERDICTSEARCH ILLINOIS. 2004-200?. m. VerdictSearch, 120 Broadway, New York, NY 10271.

347 USA
VERDICTSEARCH TEXAS EVALUATOR. ceased. a. VerdictSearch, 120 Broadway, New York, NY 10271.

001.3 ITA
VERIFICHE E PROPOSTE. 1975-ceased. irreg. Tringale Editore, Via Vecchia Ognina 90, Catania, CT 95129, Italy.

282 FRA ISSN 1625-7464
VERMEIL. 1984-2007. 10/yr. Bayard Presse, 3-5 rue Bayard, Paris, 75393 Cedex 08, France.

368.382 NLD ISSN 1874-6403
VERMOGENSRAPPORTAGE ZIEKENFONDSEN. 2003-2005. a. College voor Zorgverzekeringen, Postbus 320, Diemen, 1110 AH, Netherlands.

362.1 GBR
VERNON COLEMAN'S NEWSLETTER. 1996-2002. m. Dr. Vernon Coleman's Health Letter, Publishing House, Trinity Pl, Barnstaple, Devon EX32 9HJ, United Kingdom.

520 BRD ISSN 0340-9821
VEROEFFENTLICHUNGEN DER ASTRONOMISCHEN INSTITUT DER UNIVERSITAET BONN. 1930-1984. irreg. Astronomische Institute der Universitaet Bonn - Sternwarte, Auf dem Huegel 71, Bonn, 53121, Germany.

330 DEU ISSN 1610-8019
VERSICHERUNG UND ALLFINANZ. 2002-2002. bi-m. BAUVE AG i.G., Kirchdorfer Str 87, Bad Woerishofen, 86825, Germany.

630 DEU ISSN 0342-6769
DAS VERTRIEBENE LANDVOLK. 1957-2006. m. Bauernverband der Vertriebenen e.V., Marktstr 4, Lippstadt, 59555, Germany.

380.1029 DEU ISSN 1432-9700
VERZEICHNIS LIEFERBARER KAUFMEDIEN. 1988-2006. s-a. Entertainment Media Verlag GmbH und Co. oHG, Einsteinring 24, Dornach, 85609, Germany.

700 800 ITA ISSN 0393-6147
IL VESUVIO. 1964-ceased. d. Fiaccola Ercolanese, Via Liberta, San Sebastiano Al Vesuvio, NA 80040, Italy.

320.9 ITA
LA VETTA D'ITALIA; mensile di politica e di cultura dell'Alto Adige. 1960-ceased. m. Tipografia Presel, Via Roma, 69, Bolzano, BZ 39100, Italy.

850 ITA
VIA LATTEA; rivista di letteratura. 1988-ceased. s-a. Via Lattea, Via Piave, 2, Catania, CT 95129, Italy.

910.09 ITA
VIAGGIARE. 1988-ceased. m. Editrice Portoria Srl, Via Chiossetto, 1, Milan, MI 20122, Italy.

790.18 ITA ISSN 1826-1000
VIAGGIARE E SOGNARE. 2002-200?. bi-m. Edigamma Publishing, Via Sambuca Pistoiese 70A, Rome, 00138, Italy.

910.09 ITA ISSN 1592-1913
VIAGGIO IN ITALIA. 1983-ceased. 4/yr. Edizioni Scientifiche Tecniche Europee (E S T E), Via A. Vassallo 31, Milan, 20125, Italy.

780 315.4 746.9 051 USA ISSN 1556-2581
VIBE VIXEN. 2005-2007 (Aug./Sep.). q. Vibe / Spin Ventures, 215 Lexington Ave, 6th Fl, New York, NY 10016.

051 USA ISSN 1941-9104
VIBE VIXEN PRESENTS TEEN DREAMZ. 2008-2009. q. Vibe Media Group, LLC., 120 Wall St., 21st. Fl., New York, NY 10005.

930.1 DNK ISSN 0907-6824
VIBORG STIFTSMUSEUMS RAEKKE. 1991-1998. irreg. Jysk Arkaeologisk Selskab, c/o Moesgaard, Hojbjerg, 8270, Denmark.

360 GBR ISSN 0083-601X
VICTORIA LEAGUE FOR COMMONWEALTH FRIENDSHIP. ANNUAL REPORT. 1901-2002. a. Victoria League, 55 Leinster Sq, London, W2 4PW, United Kingdom.

658 NZL ISSN 1173-4523
VICTORIA UNIVERSITY OF WELLINGTON. G S B G M WORKING PAPER SERIES. (Graduate School of Business and Government Management) 1990-2000 (no.5). irreg. Victoria University of Wellington, Graduate School of Business & Government Management, P.O. Box 600, Wellington, New Zealand.

331.2592 AUS ISSN 1327-4724
VICTORIAN COURSES DIRECTORY 2: SHORT COURSES FOR JOB SKILLS. 1992-199?. s-a. Department of Education, Level 1, Central Wing, 2 Treasury Place, East Melbourne, VIC 3002, Australia.

016 800 AUS ISSN 0158-3921
VICTORIAN FICTION RESEARCH GUIDES. 1979-2004. irreg. (3-4/yr.). University of Queensland, Media and Cultural Studies Centre, School of E M S A H, St Lucia, QLD 4072, Australia.

011 AUS
VICTORIAN GOVERNMENT PUBLICATIONS INDEX. 1976-2008 (May.). m. Government Publications Librarian, State Library of Victoria, 328 Swanston St, Melbourne, VIC 3000, Australia.

798.46 AUS
THE VICTORIAN, SOUTH AUSTRALIAN & TASMANIAN HARNESS RACER. 1948-2008. m. Harness Racing Board, 740 Mt Alexander Rd, Moonee Ponds, VIC 3039, Australia.

794.8 ITA ISSN 1723-3348
VIDEOGIOCHI (MILAN, 2003). 2003-200?. m. Sprea Editori Srl, Via Torino 51, Cernusco sul Naviglio, MI 20063, Italy.

384.55 ITA ISSN 1120-7647
VIDEOTECNICA. 1989-200?. m. Vidigest Srl, Via Brenta 13, Rome, 00198, Italy.

658 NLD ISSN 1382-7936
VIEW. 1995-1995. q. Benelux Periodieken B.V., Postbus 397, Veenendaal, 3900 AJ, Netherlands.

154.6 ESP ISSN 1132-9572
VIGILIA SUENO. 1992-2007. 3/yr. Fundacion Sueno Vigilia, General Alvarez de Castro 41, Oficina 10, Madrid, 28010, Spain.

663.2 FRA ISSN 0221-301X
VINETEC. 1978-198?. m. S.F.P. Vinitec, 79 rue Raymond Poincare, Le Bouscat, 33110, France.

663.2 641.2021 AUS ISSN 1442-780X
VINTAGE; the Australian wine industry statistical yearbook. 1998-2002. a. Wine Publishers Pty Ltd, PO Box 6015, Halifax St, SA 5000, Australia.

388.3 FRA ISSN 1150-4919
VIRAGES. 1952-200?. 6/yr. Renault Vehicles Industriels, 129 rue Servient, Lyon, 69003, France.

929 USA ISSN 0300-645X
VIRGINIA GENEALOGIST. 1957-2006. q. Virginia Genealogist, PO Box 5860, Falmouth, VA 22403-5860.

371.42 USA ISSN 1098-9900
THE VIRGINIA JOBBANK; the job hunter's guide to Virginia. 1997-2004 (4th ed.). irreg. Adams Media, 4700 E Galbraith Rd, Cincinnati, OH 45236.

344.01 USA
VIRGINIA WORKERS' COMPENSATION CASE FINDER. 1990-2003 (3rd ed.). irreg. Matthew Bender & Co., Inc., 1275 Broadway, Albany, NY 12204.

808.066791 ESP ISSN 1132-9041
VIRIDIANA. 1991-1998. q. Fundacion Viridiana, Almirante, 15, Madrid, 28004, Spain.

610.73 NZL ISSN 1174-9784
VISION; journal of nursing. 1995 (Nov.)-2006 (Nov.). s-a. Eastern Institute of Technology, Faculty of Health & Sport Science, Taradale, Private Bag 1201, Hawke's Bay, New Zealand.

621.8 USA ISSN 1544-3531
VISION (DEARBORN). 1985-2006. q. Society of Manufacturing Engineers, One SME Dr, PO Box 930, Dearborn, MI 48121.

005.13 USA ISSN 1552-5341
VISUAL BASIC DEVELOPER. 1994-200?. m. Eli Journals, 700 Metro Park, Rochester, NY 14623.

005.13 USA ISSN 1079-0608
VISUAL C++ DEVELOPER. 1994-2000. m. Eli Journals, 700 Metro Park, Rochester, NY 14623.

005.117 USA
VISUAL J PLUS PLUS INFORMANT. 1997-200?. m. Informant Communications Group, 5105 Florin Perkins Rd., Sacramento, CA 95826-4817.

004.6 DEU
VISUAL-X. 2003-2007 (May). q. Software & Support Verlag GmbH, Geleitsstr 14, Frankfurt am Main, 60599, Germany.

613.7 028.5 ITA
VITA E SALUTE JUNIOR; rivista mensile per ragazzi che vogliono crescere e capire. 1994-ceased. m. Edizioni A D V, Via Chiantigiana, 30, Falciani, Impruneta, FI 50023, Italy.

282 DEU
VITA FRATRUM. 1964-1995. 3/yr. Bayerische Franziskanerprovinz, Sankt-Anna-Str 19, Munich, 80538, Germany.

910.202 ITA ISSN 0504-5010
VITA ITALIANA (ROME)/ITALY' LIFE/LEBEN IN ITALIEN/VIE ITALIENNE. 1953-ceased. irreg. Ente Nazionale Industrie Turistiche, Via Marghera 2, Rome, 00185, Italy.

001.3 500 ITA ISSN 0394-6940
VITA ITALIANA. CULTURA E SCIENZA. 1986-199?. q. Presidenza del Consiglio dei Ministri, Dipartimento per l'Informazione e l'Editoria, Via Po 14, Rome, 00198, Italy.

300 ITA ISSN 0507-1712
VITA ITALIANA. DOCUMENTI E INFORMAZIONI. 1951-1998. m. Presidenza del Consiglio dei Ministri, Dipartimento per l'Informazione e l'Editoria, Via Po 14, Rome, 00198, Italy.

300 ITA ISSN 1125-3355
VITA ITALIANA. QUADERNI. 1967-199?. irreg. Presidenza del Consiglio dei Ministri, Dipartimento per l'Informazione e l'Editoria, Via Po 14, Rome, 00198, Italy.

351.45 ITA ISSN 1120-5520
VITA ITALIANA. SPECIALE. 1987-199?. bi-m. Presidenza del Consiglio dei Ministri, Dipartimento per l'Informazione e l'Editoria, Via Po 14, Rome, 00198, Italy.

384 ITA ISSN 1120-5512
VITA ITALIANA. SPECIALE. ISTITUZIONI E COMUNICAZIONE. 1987-ceased. q. Presidenza del Consiglio dei Ministri, Dipartimento per l'Informazione e l'Editoria, Via Po 14, Rome, 00198, Italy.

300 ITA ISSN 1120-5504
VITA ITALIANA. TEMI. 1986-199?. s-a. Presidenza del Consiglio dei Ministri, Dipartimento per l'Informazione e l'Editoria, Via Po 14, Rome, 00198, Italy.

331.8 ITA ISSN 0042-7357
VITA SINDACALE BERGAMASCA. 1960-ceased. fortn. Unione Sindacale Provinciale, Via Carnovale 88, Bergamo, BG 24100, Italy.

664 DEU ISSN 1862-152X
VIVA!. 1985-2008 (Jun.). m. Gruner und Jahr AG & Co., Am Baumwall 11, Hamburg, 20459, Germany.

646.724 305.89607305 USA ISSN 1946-6471
VIVACIOUS; the urban guide to health and natural hair care. 2009-suspended. m. Lenaj Publishing, 4108-A Townhouse Rd, Richmond, VA 23228.

305.4 AUS ISSN 1832-2298
VIVE +; working woman's directory. 2005-2006. a. POL Publications, 125-127 Little Eveleigh St, Redfern, NSW 2016, Australia.

055.1 ITA ISSN 1121-8673
VIVERE. 1992-ceased. 21/yr. Pierangelo Repanati, Ed. & Pub., Via Roma 52, Corte Palasio, LO 26834, Italy.

746.9 646.72 FRA ISSN 1634-8028
VIVRE AU FEMININ. 2002-2007. m. Editions DIPA Burda, 26 Avenue de l'Europe, Strasbourg, 67013, France.

613.262 FRA ISSN 0042-7608
VIVRE EN HARMONIE. 1952-200?. m. Editions Vivre en Harmonie, 26 rue Remy, Auvers sur Oise, 95430, France.

943.7 CZE
VLASTIVEDNY ZPRAVODAJ PODBRDSKA. 1966-199?. irreg. Okresni Archiv Pribram, Dlouha 142, Pribram, 26101, Czech Republic.

636 328.37 NLD ISSN 1874-7736
VLEESWETGEVING COMPACT. 1999-ceased. a. Sdu Uitgevers bv, Postbus 20025, The Hague, 2500 EA, Netherlands.

055.1 ITA ISSN 0042-7802
VOCE BRUZIA; indipendente politico letterario. 1961-ceased. m. (14/yr.). Voce Bruzia, c/o Ed. Ruggiero Magliocchi, Via Nicola Serra, 80, Cosenza, CS 87100, Italy.

658.8 ITA ISSN 0042-7837
VOCE DELLA FIERA; bisettimanale di economia e problemi di mercato. 1964-ceased. s-w. Organizzazione "X" di Armando Rositani, Corso Cavour, 113, Bari, BA 70121, Italy.

055.1 ITA
VOCE DELLA REGIONE. 1968-ceased. m. Silvio Panaro Editore, Via Giovanni Gentile, 53-C, Bari, BA 70126, Italy.

055.1 ITA
VOCE DI MONASTEROLO. 1968-1987. s-a. Voce di Monasterolo, Via Divisione Tridentina, 5, Bergamo, BG 24121, Italy.

282 ITA
VOCI AMICHE; bollettino parrocchiale. 1951-ceased. bi-m. Tipografia Pistoiese, Corso Gramsci, 49, Pistoia, PT 51100, Italy.

639.2 CZE ISSN 1214-6625
VODNI REVUE. 2004-2006. q. Unipress, spol. s r.o., Svobodova 1, Prague 2, 12817, Czech Republic.

330 DEU ISSN 1615-1860
VOGUE BUSINESS. 2000-2005. 4/yr. Conde Nast Verlag GmbH, Karlstr 23, Munich, 80333, Germany.

614.8 NLD
VOICE OF THE PEDESTRIAN. 1963-1983. s-a. International Federation of Pedestrians, Wassenaarseweg 43, The Hague, 2596 CG, Netherlands.

331.87 GBR ISSN 0042-8248
VOICE OF THE UNIONS. 1925-197?. m. Voice of the Union Ltd., 11 Brambledown Rd, South Croydon, Surrey CR2 0BN, United Kingdom.

384.6 USA
VOIP LINE. 2006-2007. 2/w. (Tues./Th.). C M P Media LLC, 600 Community Dr, Manhasset, NY 11030.

614 361 DNK ISSN 1902-1682
VOKSNE. 1984-2007. 12/yr. Jurainformation, Vesterbrogade 10, Copenhagen V, 1620, Denmark.

629.1 ESP
VOLAR. 1988-ceased. 12/yr. Trade Zap, S.L., C. las Llamas, 5, S. Sebastian De Los Reyes, (Madrid) 28707, Spain.

Cessations

354.35 NLD ISSN 0926-6291
VOLKSHUISVESTING IN THEORIE EN PRAKTIJK. 1983-1999 (vol.40). irreg. Delft University Press, Nieuwe Hemweg 6B, Amsterdam, 1013 BG, Netherlands.

398 DEU ISSN 0083-6877
VOLKSTUM DER SCHWEIZ. 1941-1979 (vol.12). irreg. Dr. Rudolf Habelt GmbH, Am Buchenhang 1, Bonn, 53115, Germany.

362 GBR ISSN 1465-4067
VOLUNTARY ACTION. 1998-2006. 3/yr. Institute for Volunteering Research, Regent's Wharf, 8 All Saints St, London, N1 9RL, United Kingdom.

956.940 296 ISR ISSN 0042-8671
VOLUNTEER. 1967-1969. s-m. Pedagogic Center, Department for Jewish Zionist Education, Kiryat Moriah, 3 HaAskan St., Jerusalem, Israel.

303.4 NLD ISSN 1574-6038
VOORTSCHRIJDENDE INZICHTEN. 2001-2009 (no.22). 4/yr. Uitgeverij Tinsentiep, Bovencamp 57, Houten, 3992 RX, Netherlands.

700 NLD ISSN 0169-6858
VORM EN INDUSTRIE IN NEDERLAND. 1984-1986 (vol.7). irreg. Uitgeverij 010 Publishers, Watertorenweg 180, Rotterdam, 3063 HA, Netherlands.

621.31 ITA
IL VORTICE; rivista tecnica e di informazione per settore - materiale elettrico. 1989-ceased. 6/yr. Il Sole 24 Ore Business Media, Divisione J C E, Via Patecchio 2, Milan, 20141, Italy.

636.7 FRA ISSN 1952-7470
VOS CHIENS JUNIOR. 2006-2007. q. Editions d' Anglon, 735 Route de Jarcieu, Lapeyrouse, 26210, France.

794.8 NLD ISSN 1872-2938
VPLAY. 2005-2005. s-a. Kidsweek BV, Postbus 3564, Amsterdam, 1001 AJ, Netherlands.

053.931 NLD ISSN 1574-0854
HET VRIJE WOORD. 2004-2006. Jonge Fortuynisten, Postbus 68, Voorburg, 2270 AB, Netherlands.

027.44891 DNK ISSN 0108-691X
VULKANEN. 1982-2006. irreg. (2-3/yr.). Lokalhistoriske Arkiver i Vestsjaellands Amt, c/o Slagelse Centralbibliotek, Stenstuegade 3, Slagelse, 4200, Denmark.

551 CZE ISSN 0474-8476 CODEN: SRHSAY
VYSOKA SKOLA BANSKA - TECHNICKA UNIVERZITA OSTRAVA. SBORNIK VEDECKYCH PRACI: RADA HORNICKO-GEOLOGICKA. 1955-2006. irreg. Vysoka Skola Banska, Technicka Univerzita Ostrava, 17 listopadu 15, Ostrava, 70833, Czech Republic.

613.2 CZE ISSN 1212-0022
VYZIVA A SPOTREBA POTRAVIN V CISLECH. 1968-1998. a. Spolecnost pro Vyzivu, Slezska 32, Prague 2, 12000, Czech Republic.

380.3 CZE ISSN 0231-6951
VYZKUMNY USTAV SPOJU. SBORNIK PRACI. 1974-1991. irreg. (2-3/yr.). Nakladatelstvi Dopravy a Turistiky Nadatur Ltd. Co., Hybernska 5, Prague 1, 110 00, Czech Republic.

340 DEU ISSN 0042-9678
W G O - MONATSHEFTE FUER OSTEUROPAEISCHES RECHT; die wichtigsten Gesetzgebungsakten in den Laendern Ost- und Suedosteuropas. 1959-2007. bi-m. Lit Verlag, Grindelberg 15a, Hamburg, 20144, Germany.

300 330 AUS ISSN 1321-3067
W I S E R. 1993-1998. q. Whitlam Institute for Social and Economic Research, PO Box 9, Everton Park, QLD 4053, Australia.

028.5 NLD ISSN 1571-1870
W.I.T.C.H. 2001-2008. m. Sanoma Uitgevers B.V., Postbus 1900, Hoofddorp, 2130 JH, Netherlands.

994 AUS ISSN 0085-7858
WAGGA WAGGA AND DISTRICT HISTORICAL SOCIETY. JOURNAL. 1968-1996. irreg. Wagga Wagga & District Historical Society, PO Box 90, Wagga Wagga, NSW 2650, Australia.

305.8 AUS ISSN 1326-4869
WALKING TOGETHER. 1992-2001. q. Council of Aboriginal Reconciliation, Locked Bag 14, Kingston, ACT 2604, Australia.

338.47665 GBR ISSN 0309-4758
WALTER SKINNER'S NORTH SEA AND EUROPE OFFSHORE YEARBOOK AND BUYERS' GUIDE. 1975-1978. a. Financial Times Business Ltd., One Southwark Bridge, London, SE1 9HL, United Kingdom.

709 USA ISSN 0083-7148
WALTER W.S. COOK ALUMNI LECTURE. 1960-19??. irreg. J.J. Augustin, Inc., PO Box 311, Locust Valley, NY 11560.

796.552 CZE
WAMPUM NESKENONU; pro skauty a woodcraftery. 1980-2006. q. Obcanske Sdruzeni Nika, Libanska 2337/8, Horni Pocernice, Prague 9, 19000, Czech Republic.

384 CHN ISSN 1673-5730
WANGKUAN SHIDAI/BROAD TIMES. 1984-2007. q. Beijing Shi Dianxin Kexue Yanjiusuo, 18 Taipinghu dong Li, Xicheng-qu, Beijing, 100031, China.

355 DEU ISSN 0344-3086
WAR AND SOCIETY NEWSLETTER. 1973-2002. a. Oldenbourg Wissenschaftsverlag GmbH, Rosenheimer Str 145, Munich, 81671, Germany.

790.13 796.357 USA ISSN 1931-020X
WARMAN'S BASEBALL CARD FIELD GUIDE. 2004-200?. irreg. Krause Publications, Inc., 700 E State St, Iola, WI 54990.

355 USA ISSN 1540-2207
WARZONES. 2002-200?. bi-m. Starlog Communications, 250 W 49th St, 3rd Fl Ste 304, New York, NY 10019.

336 346 USA
WASHINGTON TAXES; a taxpayer's manual for practice before the Department of Revenue. 1992-ceased. plus irreg. updates. LexisNexis, PO Box 7587, Charlottesville, VA 22906.

351.0285 USA ISSN 1528-7815
WASHINGTON TECHWAY. 2000-2002. bi-w. Post Newsweek Tech Media, 10 G St, N E, Ste 500, Washington, DC 20002-4228.

628.1 333.7 DEU ISSN 0511-3520 CODEN: WAKADP
WASSER - KALENDER; Jahrbuch fuer das gesamte Wasserfach. 1966-2001. a. Erich Schmidt Verlag GmbH & Co. (Berlin), Genthiner Str 30 G, Berlin, 10785, Germany.

628.1 AUS ISSN 1328-3464
WATER AND THE ENVIRONMENT. 1959-200?. bi-m. Water Research Foundation of Australia, c/o Centre for Resource and Environmental Studies, Canberra A C T, Australian National University, NSW 0200, Australia.

333.91 AUS
WATER RESEARCH IN AUSTRALIA: CURRENT PROJECTS. 19??-1989. a. Department of Primary Industries and Energy, GPO Box 858, Canberra, ACT 2600, Australia.

628.1 GBR
WATER RESOURCES MANAGEMENT SERIES. 1995-1997. irreg. Oxford University Press, Great Clarendon St, Oxford, OX2 6DP, United Kingdom.

628 NLD ISSN 0169-2577
WATER SUPPLY AND WASTEWATER DISPOSAL - INTERNATIONAL ALMANAC. 1976-1993. a. International Institute for Water Supply and Wastewater Disposal, Gooiland 11, Zoetermeer, 2716 BP, Netherlands.

551.6 USA ISSN 0731-5627
WEATHER ALMANAC. 1974-2004. irreg. Gale, 27500 Drake Rd, Farmington Hills, MI 48331.

004.678 FRA ISSN 1295-697X
WEB MAGAZINE. 1999-2002. m. Prisma Presse, 73-75 Rue La Condamine, Paris, 75854 Cedex 17, France.

078.9 DNK ISSN 1601-6270
WEEKEND NU. 1871-2001. 6/w. Fri Aktuelt, Raadhuspladsen 45-47, Copenhagen V, 1595, Denmark.

070.5 AUS ISSN 1449-2407
WEEKLY BOOK NEWLSETTER MEDIA EXTRA. 2004-200?. w. Thorpe-Bowker, St Kilda Rd, PO Box 6509, Melbourne, VIC 8008, Australia.

381.45002 AUS ISSN 0812-7042
WEEKLY BOOK NEWSLETTER. 1984-2004. w. Thorpe-Bowker, Bldg C3, 85 Turner St, Port Melbourne, VIC 3207, Australia.

332 USA
WEEKLY CONSOLIDATED CONDITION REPORT OF LARGE COMMERCIAL BANKS AND DOMESTIC SUBSIDIARIES. 19??-1996. w. U.S. Federal Reserve System, Board of Governors, Publications Services, Rm MS 138, Washington, DC 20551.

636.2142 USA ISSN 0270-4153
WEEKLY INSIDERS DAIRY & EGG LETTER. 1974-2003. w. Urner Barry Publications, Inc., PO Box 389, Toms River, NJ 08754.

664 636 USA ISSN 0160-4872
WEEKLY INSIDERS POULTRY REPORT (PRINT). 1972-2002. w. Urner Barry Publications, Inc., PO Box 389, Toms River, NJ 08754.

694 DEU
WEINIG INFO. 1960-1989. s-a. Michael Weinig AG, Weinigstrasse 2/4, Tauberbischofsheim, 97941, Germany.

671.52 GBR ISSN 0043-2237
THE WELDER. 1929-1979. q. Esab Group (UK) Ltd., Hertford Rd, Waltham Cross, ., Waltham Cross, Herts EN8 7RP, United Kingdom.

330 613.7 USA ISSN 1931-5430
WELLNESS & FITNESS ENTREPRENEUR. 2004-2007. m. R B Publishing, Inc., 2901 International Ln, Ste 200, Madison, WI 53704.

360 GBR
WELSH OFFICE. SOCIAL SERVICES INSPECTORATE. TRAINING SUPPORT PROGRAMME FOR THE PERSONAL SOCIAL SERVICES. PROGRESS REPORT. ceased 199?. a. Welsh Office, Social Services Inspectorate, New Crown Bldg, Cathays Park, Cardiff, CF1 3NQ, United Kingdom.

053.1 DEU
WELT DER FRAU. 2001-2007 (Mar.). w. Klambt Verlag GmbH, Im Neudeck 1, Speyer, 67346, Germany.

385.264 BRD ISSN 0175-3061
WERKVERKEHR UND VERLADER. 1955-1984. q. Bundesverband Werkverkehr und Verlader, Lengsdorfer Hauptstr 75, Bonn, 53127, Germany.

658.562 USA ISSN 0083-8217
WEST COAST RELIABILITY SYMPOSIUM. 1964 (5th)-1971. irreg. American Society for Quality, 600 North Plankinton Ave, P O Box 3005, Milwaukee, WI 53203.

798.2 DEU
WESTERN PFERDE JOURNAL; Freizeit Reiter. 1988-2004. bi-m. Deutscher Bauernverlag GmbH, Wilhelmsaue 37, Berlin, 10713, Germany.

944 USA ISSN 0099-0329
WESTERN SOCIETY FOR FRENCH HISTORY. PROCEEDINGS OF THE ANNUAL MEETING. 1974-2005. a. University Press of Colorado, 5589 Arapahoe Ave., Ste. 206C, Boulder, CO 80303-8153.

781.642 CZE ISSN 1213-5119
WESTERN WORLD. 2001-2008. m. Profi Press s.r.o., Drtinova 8, Prague 5, 150 00, Czech Republic.

333.72 363.7 AUS
WETLANDS ALIVE. 1993-2003. q. Wetland Care Australia, P.O. Box 437, Berri, SA 5343, Australia.

690 GBR ISSN 0142-9094
WHAT'S NEW IN BUILDING. 1978-200?. m. C M P Information Ltd., Ludgate House, 245 Blackfriars Rd., London, SE1 9UR, United Kingdom.

663.52 NLD ISSN 1873-359X
WHISKY SCHEURKALENDER. 2006-2006. a. Uitgeverij Het Spectrum B.V., Postbus 97, Houten, 3990 DB, Netherlands.

327.092 DEU
WHO'S WHO IN EUROPEAN INTEGRATION STUDIES. 1989-2000. irreg. Nomos Verlagsgesellschaft mbH und Co. KG, Waldseestr 3-5, Baden-Baden, 76530, Germany.

026 USA ISSN 0278-842X
WHO'S WHO IN SPECIAL LIBRARIES. 1981-2001. a. Special Libraries Association, 331 S Patrick St, Alexandria, VA 22314.

351.025 USA ISSN 1069-6946
WHO'S WHO IN THE FEDERAL EXECUTIVE BRANCH. 1993-1997. a. C Q Press, Inc., 2300 N St, NW, Ste 800, Washington, DC 20037.

658.31 920 USA ISSN 0092-4598
WHO'S WHO IN TRAINING AND DEVELOPMENT. 1970-19??. a. American Society for Training & Development, 1640 King St, PO Box 1443, Alexandria, VA 22313.

920 360 USA ISSN 1076-4755
WHO'S WHO IN WASHINGTON NONPROFIT GROUPS. 1994-1996. a. C Q Press, Inc., 2300 N St, NW, Ste 800, Washington, DC 20037.

630 DEU ISSN 0939-9445
WILDHALTUNG. 1990-2001. bi-m. Bundesverband fuer Landwirtschaftliche Wildhaltung e.V., Godesberger Allee 142-148, Bonn, 53175, Germany.

500 DEU
WILLI WILLS WISSEN. 2006-2007 (Oct.). bi-m. Gruner und Jahr AG & Co., Weihenstephaner Str 7, Munich, 81673, Germany.

745.5 DEU
WINDOW COLOR; Gestalten und Dekorieren mit abziehbaren Fensterfarben. 2000-2007. q. OZ Verlag GmbH, Roemerstr 90, Rheinfelden, 79618, Germany.

005.43 USA ISSN 1543-6454 CODEN: WDJOFH
WINDOWS DEVELOPER NETWORK; application development from windows to web. 1990-2003. m. C M P Media LLC, 1601 W 23rd St, Ste 200, Lawrence, KS 66046.

005.446 DEU
WINDOWS VISTA. 2007-2008. m. Computec Media AG, Dr-Mack-Str 77, Fuerth, 90762, Germany.

005.446 ITA ISSN 1970-464X
WINDOWS VISTA UFFICIALE. 2006-200?. m. Sprea Editori Srl, Via Torino 51, Cernusco sul Naviglio, MI 20063, Italy.

663.2 USA ISSN 1544-8576
WINE SPECTATOR MAGAZINE'S ULTIMATE GUIDE TO BUYING WINE. 1992-1993. biennial. Marvin R. Shanken Communications, Inc., 387 Park Ave S, New York, NY 10016.

663.2 AUS ISSN 1442-8415
WINEDARK SEA. 2000-2000. q. Winedark Sea Pty Ltd, Southgate, PO Box 367, Sylvania, NSW 2224, Australia.

028.5 NLD ISSN 1574-6402
WINNIE DE POEH. 1989-2007. m. Sanoma Uitgevers B.V., Postbus 1900, Hoofddorp, 2130 JH, Netherlands.

631.4 DEU ISSN 0049-7711 CODEN: WIFUAB
DAS WIRTSCHAFTSEIGENE FUTTER; Erzeugung-Konservierung-Verwertung. 1955-1997. 3/yr. D L G Verlags GmbH, Eschborner Landstr 122, Frankfurt Am Main, 60489, Germany.

344.775 347.75044605 USA ISSN 1077-9299
WISCONSIN ENVIRONMENTAL LAW JOURNAL. 1992-2002. a. University of Wisconsin at Madison, Law School, 975 Bascom Mall, Madison, WI 53706.

796 USA ISSN 0893-5769
WISCONSIN OUTDOOR JOURNAL; Wisconsin's hunting & fishing authority. 1987-200?. 8/yr. Krause Publications, Inc., 700 E State St, Iola, WI 54990.

384.0285 DEU ISSN 0863-0798
WISSENSCHAFTLICHE BEITRAEGE ZUR INFORMATIK. 1971-1997. irreg. Technische Universitaet Dresden, Fakultaet Informatik, Hans-Grundig-Str 25, Dresden, 01307, Germany.

616.99 DEU ISSN 0931-8364
WISSENSCHAFTLICHER ERGEBNISBERICHT. 1982-2004. biennial. Deutsches Krebsforschungszentrum, Im Neuenheimer Feld 280, Heidelberg, 69120, Germany.

280.4 USA ISSN 1554-2459
THE WITTENBURG DOOR. 1971-2008; suspended. bi-m. Trinity Foundation, Inc., PO Box 1444, Waco, TX 76703-1444.

551.6 DEU ISSN 1436-6797
WITTERUNGS-REPORT. DATEN. 1999-2005. m. Deutscher Wetterdienst, Bibliothek, Kaiserleistr 29-35, Offenbach Am Main, 63067, Germany.

551.6 DEU ISSN 1863-3757
WITTERUNGS-REPORT. EXPRESS (ONLINE). 1999-2006. m. Deutscher Wetterdienst, Bibliothek, Kaiserleistr 29-35, Offenbach Am Main, 63067, Germany.

190 DEU ISSN 1439-765X
WITTGENSTEIN-JAHRBUCH. 2001-2007. a. Peter Lang GmbH Europaeischer Verlag der Wissenschaften, Eschborner Landstr 42-50, Frankfurt Am Main, 60489, Germany.

053.1 DEU ISSN 1610-9457
WOMAN; das Frauen- und Lifestylemagazin. 2002 (Oct.)-2007 (Apr.). fortn. Gruner und Jahr AG & Co., Am Baumwall 11, Hamburg, 20459, Germany.

392.4 DNK ISSN 1601-4073
WOMAN WEDDING. 2001-2005. s-a. Benjamin Media A/S, Finsensvej 6 D, Frederiksberg, 2000, Denmark.

683.4075 799.2 305.4 USA ISSN 1546-7651
WOMAN'S OUTLOOK. 2003 (Jan.)-2006. m. National Rifle Association of America, 11250 Waples Mill Rd, Fairfax, VA 22030.

331 AUS ISSN 0311-5119
WOMEN & WORK. 1977-1998. q. Department of Employment, Education, Training and Youth Affairs, GPO Box 9880, Canberra, ACT 2601, Australia.

200 305.4 AUS ISSN 1030-0139
WOMEN - CHURCH; an Australian journal of feminist studies in religion. 1987-2007. s-a. Women - Church Journal Collective Inc., GPO Box 2134, Sydney, NSW 1043, Australia.

305.42 BEL ISSN 1025-871X
WOMEN OF EUROPE NEWSLETTER. 1990-2000. m. European Commission, Directorate General X - Women's Information Section, Rue de la Loi - Wetstraat 2000, Brussels, 1049, Belgium.

305.42 NZL ISSN 0112-4099
WOMEN'S STUDIES JOURNAL. 1984-2007 (vol.21, no.2). 2/yr. University of Otago Press, Level 1, 398 Cumberland St, PO Box 56, Dunedin, New Zealand.

677.3 NZL ISSN 0112-2851
WOOL RESEARCH ORGANISATION OF NEW ZEALAND REPORTS. 1970-2002. irreg. Wool Research Organisation of New Zealand Inc., Private Bag 4749, Christchurch, New Zealand.

614.85 FIN ISSN 0783-6899
WORK HEALTH SAFETY. 1982-2002. a. Tyoterveyslaitos, Topeliuksenkatu 41a A, Helsinki, 00250, Finland.

331 NZL ISSN 1177-343X
WORKERS' CHARTER. 2006-2008 (Jun.). m. Workers' Charter Editorial Group, PO Box 13-157, Auckland, New Zealand.

368.382 USA ISSN 1066-2669
WORKERS' COMP MANAGED CARE. 1992-200?. m. Aspen Publishers, Inc., 111 Eighth Ave., 7th Fl, New York, NY 10011.

368.4 USA ISSN 1096-7850
WORKERS' COMPENSATION MONITOR. 1988-2006. 12/yr. L R P Publications, Inc., 747 Dresher Rd, Ste 500, PO Box 980, Horsham, PA 19044.

005.369 USA ISSN 1530-4345
WORKING SMARTER WITH MICROSOFT POWERPOINT. (Avail. in 2 versions: Powerpoint 2000 and PowerPoint 2002) 1999-200?. bi-w. OneOnOne Computer Training, 751 Roosevelt Rd, Ste 108, Glen Ellyn, IL 60137-5905.

929 USA ISSN 1071-1554
WORKMAN BRANCHES; including Woertman and Wortman. 1993-1994. irreg. (2-4/yr.). Family Publications, 5628 60th Dr, NE, Marysville, WA 98270.

331 AUS
WORKPLACE INTELLIGENCE. 1992-2005. m. Newsletter Information Services, PO Box 2095, Manly, NSW 2095, Australia.

616.863 362.29 USA ISSN 1091-823X
WORKPLACE SUBSTANCE ABUSE ADVISOR. 1986-2007. 22/yr. L R P Publications, Inc., 747 Dresher Rd, Ste 500, PO Box 980, Horsham, PA 19044.

785.16 FRA ISSN 1287-406X
WORLD. 1998-1999. bi-m. Editions Freeway, 1 rue Jean-Richepin, BP 271, Clermont-Ferrand, Cedex 1 63008, France.

616.9792 GBR ISSN 0954-6510
WORLDAIDS. 1988-1995. bi-m. Panos Institute, 9 White Lion St, London, N1 9PD, United Kingdom.

342.37 USA ISSN 0960-0949
WORLD ARBITRATION & MEDIATION REPORT. 1990-2006. m. Juris Publishing, Inc., 71 New St, Huntington, NY 11743.

330 USA ISSN 1020-0525
WORLD BANK. POLICY RESEARCH WORKING PAPERS (PRINT). 1988-2007. irreg. World Bank Group, 1818 H St, NW, Washington, DC 20433.

332.1 016 USA ISSN 1014-5842
WORLD BANK. PUBLICATIONS UPDATE. 1973-19??. bi-m. World Bank Group, PO Box 960, Herndon, VA 20172.

330 GBR ISSN 1749-9275
WORLD BUSINESS. 2006 (Apr.)-2007. m. Haymarket Publishing Ltd., 174 Hammersmith Rd, London, W6 7JP, United Kingdom.

526 USA ISSN 0084-1471 CODEN: WCARB4
WORLD CARTOGRAPHY. 1951-1993. irreg. United Nations Publications, 2 United Nations Plaza, Rm DC2-853, New York, NY 10017.

621.042 GBR ISSN 1361-7524
WORLD DIRECTORY OF RENEWABLE ENERGY SUPPLIERS AND SERVICES. 1983-200?. a. Earthscan Ltd., Dunstan House, 14a St Cross St, London, EC1N 8XA, United Kingdom.

304.6 NLD
WORLD FERTILITY SURVEY. SUMMARY OF COUNTRY REPORTS (CD-ROM EDITION). 1977-1985. irreg. International Statistical Institute, Princes Beatrixlaan 428, PO Box 950, Voorburg, 2270 AZ, Netherlands.

384.55 USA ISSN 1084-9475
(YEAR) WORLD GUIDE TO TELEVISION. 1990-1999. a. North American Publishing Co., 1500 Spring Garden St., Ste 1200, Philadelphia, PA 19130.

796.355 GBR
WORLD HOCKEY (ONLINE). 1969-2006. m. P B Publications, 29 Romilly St, London, W1V 6HP, United Kingdom.

325.1 AUS ISSN 1445-677X
WORLD IMMIGRATION POLICY REPORT. 2001 (Jul.)-2001 (Sep.). bi-m. Moonstrong Productions, PO Box 481, Edgecliff, NSW 2027, Australia.

370.025 378.0025 GBR
WORLD LIST OF UNIVERSITIES AND OTHER INSTITUTIONS OF HIGHER EDUCATION/LISTE MONDIALE DES UNIVERSITES. 1952-2006. triennial. Palgrave Macmillan Ltd., Houndmills, Basingstoke, Hants RG21 6XS, United Kingdom.

016 USA ISSN 1080-7950
WORLD MAGAZINE BANK. 1995-19??. m. EBSCO Publishing, 10 Estes St, Ipswich, MA 01938.

011 USA ISSN 0043-8677 CODEN: WMUCB
WORLD MEETINGS: OUTSIDE UNITED STATES AND CANADA. 1968-2003. 3/yr. Gale, 27500 Drake Rd, Farmington Hills, MI 48331.

300.6 USA ISSN 0194-6161
WORLD MEETINGS: SOCIAL & BEHAVIORAL SCIENCES, HUMAN SERVICES AND MANAGEMENT. 1971-2003. 3/yr. Gale, 27500 Drake Rd, Farmington Hills, MI 48331.

011 USA ISSN 0043-8693 CODEN: WMUCA
WORLD MEETINGS: UNITED STATES AND CANADA. 1963-2003. 3/yr. Gale, 27500 Drake Rd, Farmington Hills, MI 48331.

700 ISR ISSN 0333-9718
WORLD OF ART/OLAM HAOMANUT. 1977-1995. s-a. World of Art Inc., 190 Ben Yehuda St, Tel Aviv, 63471, Israel.

794.72 NLD ISSN 1388-9834
WORLD REPORT THREE CUSHION. 1993-2005. m. (11/yr.). Francis Productions B.V., Beursplein 37, Postbus 30166, Rotterdam, 3001 DD, Netherlands.

296 ISR ISSN 0333-9068
WORLD UNION OF JEWISH STUDIES. PROCEEDINGS/DIVRE HAKONGRESS HA-OLAMI LEMADDA'E HAYAHADUT. 1977-2001. irreg. Magnes Press, Hebrew University, Jerusalem, The Sherman Building for Research Management, PO Box 39099, Jerusalem, 91390, Israel.

051 296 ISR
WORLD ZIONIST PRESS SERVICE. 1980-2001. m. World Zionist Organization, Department for Zionist Activity, PO Box 92, Jerusalem, 91000, Israel.

665.5 USA ISSN 1073-8037
WORLDWIDE OFFSHORE RIG OWNERS & PERSONNEL DIRECTORY; including worldwide marine rig register. 1989-2008; suspended. a. O D S - Petrodata, 3200 Wilcrest Dr, Ste 170, Houston, TX 77042.

790.1 USA ISSN 0885-8551
WRESTLING ALL STARS HEROES AND VILLAINS. 1982-200?. 8/yr. Starlog Communications, 250 W 49th St, 3rd Fl Ste 304, New York, NY 10019.

796 ITA ISSN 1826-4344
WRESTLING POWER. 2005-2007. m. Future Media Italy SpA, Via Asiago 45, Milano, MI 20128, Italy.

808.42 USA ISSN 1057-0756
WRITER'S FORUM (CINCINNATI). 19??-2007. 3/yr. F + W Media Inc., 4700 E Galbraith Rd, Cincinnati, OH 45236.

810 USA ISSN 0163-9072
WRITERS' FORUM (NIWOT). 1974-2002. a. University Press of Colorado, 5589 Arapahoe Ave., Ste. 206C, Boulder, CO 80303-8153.

371.33 USA ISSN 0279-7208
WRITING; the magazine of effective communication. 1974-2008. 6/yr. (m., during the school year). Weekly Reader Corporation, 3001 Cindel Dr, PO Box 8037, Delran, NJ 08075.

320 DEU ISSN 0930-9306
WUQUF; Beitraege zur Entwicklung von Staat und Gesellschaft in Nordafrika. 1986-2003. irreg. Edition Wuquf, Postfach 130662, Hamburg, 20106, Germany.

016.387 ISR
WYDRA INSTITUTE OF SHIPPING AND AVIATION RESEARCH. SPECIAL BIBLIOGRAPHIES. 1995-2006. irreg. Haifa University, Wydra Institute of Shipping and Aviation Research, University of Haifa, Eshkol Tower, Haifa, 31905, Israel.

794.8 DEU
X BOX ZONE; das unabhaengige XBox-Magazin. 2002-2006. bi-m. Computec Media AG, Dr-Mack-Str 77, Fuerth, 90762, Germany.

005.117 USA ISSN 1537-2421
X M L DEVELOPER. 2000-200?. m. Eli Journals, 700 Metro Park, Rochester, NY 14623.

028.5 SWE ISSN 1101-4601
X-MEN. 1989-2006. 6/yr. Egmont Seriefoerlaget AB, Stora Varvsgatan 19A, Malmo, 20507, Sweden.

800 CHN ISSN 1003-0581
XIAOSHUO/SHORT STORIES. 1985-1998. q. Zhongguo Qingnian Chubanshe, Qikan Bu, 21 Dongsi 12 Tiao, Beijing, 100708, China.

800 CHN ISSN 1005-6939
XIAOSHUOJIA/STORY WRITER. 1983-2002. bi-m. Baihua Wenyi Chubanshe, Heping Qu, 35, Xikang Lu, Kangyue Dasha, Tianjin, 300053, China.

028.5 CHN ISSN 1671-2188
XIAOXUE SHIDAI/ELEMENTARY SCHOOL YEARS. 1984-2004. m. Beifang Funu Ertong Chubanshe, 4646, Renmin Dajie, Changchun, Jilin 130021, China.

360 FRA ISSN 1256-9941
XOANA; images et sciences sociales. 1993-199?. s-a. Editions Jean-Michel Place, 3 rue Lhomond, Paris, 75005, France.

384.558 USA ISSN 1546-9557
XTREME VIDEO. 2003 (Fall)-200?. q. NewBay Media, LLC, 810 Seventh Ave, 27th Fl, New York, NY 10019.

296 ISR ISSN 0333-7596
YAD L'ACHIM WALL CALENDAR/LU'AH HA-HODESH - YAD LA'ACHIM. 1975-ceased. bi-m. Yad L'achim, 8 Nahum St., P O Box 5195, Jerusalem, Israel.

340 TUR ISSN 1300-2481
YAKLASIM. 1993-ceased. m. Yaklasin Yayincilik San. ve Tic. A.S., Bukulm Sk. No. 117-3, Kavaklidere - Ankara, Turkey.

677 687 ISR ISSN 0793-2065 CODEN: YLTUAM
YALQUT L'TEQSTIL/YALKUT FOR FIBRES AND TEXTILE TECHNOLOGY. 1952-2006. q. Israel Textile and Fashion Association, 12 Anna Frank St, P O Box 243, Ramat Gon, 52526, Israel.

741.58 ITA ISSN 1824-372X
YATTA!. 2004-200?. m. Play Media Company, Via di Santa Cornelia 5A, Formello, RM 00060, Italy.

781.64 USA
YEAH YEAH YEAH; a rock & roll magazine. 1996-2003. q. Yeah Yeah Yeah, PO Box 208, Boonton, NJ 07005-0208.

314 NLD ISSN 1386-2421
THE YEAR IN FIGURES. 1989-2003. a. Centraal Bureau voor de Statistiek, Prinses Beatrixlaan 428, PO Box 4000, Voorburg, 2270 JM, Netherlands.

700 720 741.672 NLD ISSN 1574-3896
YEARBOOK DUTCH DESIGN. 2004-2005. a. Episode Publishers, Marconistr 52, Rotterdam, 3029 AK, Netherlands.

343.099 346.048 GBR
THE YEARBOOK OF COPYRIGHT AND MEDIA LAW. 1995-2002. a. Oxford University Press, Great Clarendon St, Oxford, OX2 6DP, United Kingdom.

382 387 ISR ISSN 0084-3830
YEARBOOK OF ISRAEL PORTS STATISTICS/SHENATON STATISTI LE-NIMELE YISRA'EL. 1963-ceased. a. Israel Ports Authority, P O Box 20121, Tel-aviv, Israel.

850 ITA ISSN 1122-1542
YEARBOOK OF ITALIAN STUDIES. 1971-1995. irreg. Edizioni Cadmo, Via Benedetto da Maiano 3, Fiesole, FI 50014, Italy.

323 USA ISSN 0251-6519
YEARBOOK ON HUMAN RIGHTS. 1946-1988. irreg. United Nations Publications, 2 United Nations Plaza, Rm DC2-853, New York, NY 10017.

333.72 ISR ISSN 0334-0600
YEDI'ON; rashut shmurat hateva. 1975-1998. 3/yr. Israel Nature and National Parks Protection Authority, 3 Am VeOlamo St, Giv'at Sha'ul, Jerusalem, 95463, Israel.

636 USA ISSN 1066-8195
THE YELLOW SHEET (PRINT). 1892-2007. d. (Mon-Fri). Urner Barry Publications, Inc., PO Box 389, Toms River, NJ 08754.

296 830 ISR ISSN 0334-9594
YERUSHOLAIMER ALMANAKH. 1973-1999. a. Yidishe Shrayber Grupe in Yerusholaim, Shederot Eshkol 12-6, Jerusalem, Israel.

304.6 ISR
YIDI'OT HAMERCAZ LE-DEMOGRAFIA. 1981-1991. s-a. Ministry of Employment and Welfare, Demography Center, P O Box 915, Jerusalem, 91008, Israel.

332.6 382 CHN ISSN 1002-3879
YINJIN YU ZIXUN/IMPORTING AND CONSULTING. 1985-2006. q. Fujian Sheng Keji Zixun Zhongxin, Gaoqiao Dasha, 7th Fl, Wuyi Zhonglu, Fuzhou, Fujian 350005, China.

613.704 181.45 USA
YOGALIFE. 2006 (Sum.)-2007. s-a. Rodale, Inc., 33 E Minor St, Emmaus, PA 18098.

610 KOR ISSN 0375-5207 CODEN: YRTMA6
YONSEI REPORTS ON TROPICAL MEDICINE. 1970-199?. a. Yonsei University, Institute of Tropical Medicine, PO Box 8044, Seoul, 120752, Korea, S.

410 GBR ISSN 0954-6316
YORKSHIRE DIALECT SOCIETY. TRANSACTIONS. 1897-19??. a. Yorkshire Dialect Society, c/o Librarian, School of English, University of Leeds, Leeds, W Yorks LS2 9JT, United Kingdom.

053.1 DEU
YOUNG; woman's magazine. 2002-2009 (Feb.). m. Medien Innovation GmbH, Am Kestendamm 1, Offenburg, 77652, Germany.

613.7 USA ISSN 0279-9324
YOUR HEALTH & FITNESS. 1980-2001. q. General Learning Communications, 900 Skokie Blvd, Ste 200, Northbrook, IL 60062.

027.5 DEU
YUKIKO. 2004-2008 (Jan.). m. Panini Verlags GmbH, Ravensstr 48, Nettetal, 41334, Germany.

780 ISR ISSN 0084-439X
YUVAL; studies of the Jewish Music Research Centre. 1968-2003. irreg. Magnes Press, Hebrew University, Jerusalem, The Sherman Building for Research Management, PO Box 39099, Jerusalem, 91390, Israel.

780 296 ISR ISSN 0334-3758
YUVAL MONOGRAPH SERIES. 1974-1996 (vol.11). irreg. Magnes Press, Hebrew University, Jerusalem, The Sherman Building for Research Management, PO Box 39099, Jerusalem, 91390, Israel.

053.1 DEU ISSN 0945-781X
Z D F - W I S O MAGAZIN. (Zweites Deutsches Fernsehen - Wirtschaft und Sozialwissenschaft) 1993-2007. m. BAUVE AG i.G., Kirchdorfer Str 87, Bad Woerishofen, 86825, Germany.

808.87 CZE ISSN 1214-911X
ZABAVENO. 1945-1995. fortn. Star Production, s.r.o., Hybernska 20, Prague 1, 110 00, Czech Republic.

657 NLD ISSN 1872-4213
ZAKBOEKJE JAARREKENING KLEINBEDRIJF. 2006-2006. a. Reed Business bv, Postbus 4, Doetinchem, 7000 BA, Netherlands.

268 ISR ISSN 0792-9307
ZAV-ZAV. 1989-1999. m. Select Publishing House, P O Box 28110, Tel Aviv, 61280, Israel.

614 CZE ISSN 1214-2883
ZDRAVOTNICKE PRAVO V PRAXI. 2003-2006. q. Solen s.r.o., Lazecka 297/51, Olomouc 51, 779 00, Czech Republic.

646.72 ITA
ZEFFIRO CAPELLI. ceased. 6/yr. Zeffiro Capelli & Company, Via Cavour 46, Turin, TO 10123, Italy.

610 DEU ISSN 0937-6801
ZEITSCHRIFT FUER ALLGEMEINMEDIZIN. AUSGABE B. 1925-2003. m. Deutscher Aerzte-Verlag GmbH, Dieselstr 2, Cologne, 50859, Germany.

610 DEU ISSN 1434-4203
ZEITSCHRIFT FUER ALLGEMEINMEDIZIN. AUSGABE C. 1987-2003. m. Deutscher Aerzte-Verlag GmbH, Dieselstr 2, Cologne, 50859, Germany.

550 DEU ISSN 0044-2259 CODEN: ZANGAK
ZEITSCHRIFT FUER ANGEWANDTE GEOLOGIE. 1955-200?. 2/yr. E. Schweizerbart'sche Verlagsbuchhandlung, Johannesstr 3A, Stuttgart, 70176, Germany.

570 DEU ISSN 1619-1749
ZEITSCHRIFT FUER BIOPOLITIK. 2002-2005. q. Biocom AG, Stralsunder Str 58-59, Berlin, 13355, Germany.

830 BRD ISSN 0044-250X
ZEITSCHRIFT FUER DEUTSCHE SPRACHE. 1964-1971. 3/yr. Walter de Gruyter GmbH & Co. KG, Genthiner Str 13, Berlin, 10785, Germany.

Cessations

300   DEU   ISSN 0930-9381
ZEITSCHRIFT FUER INTERNATIONALE ERZIEHUNGS- UND SOZIALWISSENSCHAFTLICHE FORSCHUNG. 1966-1999. 2/yr. Boehlau Verlag GmbH & Cie, Ursulaplatz 1, Cologne, 50668, Germany.

200   NLD   ISSN 0514-650X
ZEITSCHRIFT FUER RELIGIONS- UND GEISTESGESCHICHTE. BEIHEFTE. 1955-1989 (vol.31). irreg. Brill, PO Box 9000, Leiden, 2300 PA, Netherlands.

073.71   CZE   ISSN 1210-9665
ZEME KORUNY CESKE. 1994-1997. bi-m. Zeme Koruny Ceske, c/o J Pondelicek, Vinohradska 46, Vinohrady, Prague 2, 120 41, Czech Republic.

305.42   CHN   ISSN 1671-2382
ZHIYE NUXING/WOMEN. 1992-2008. m. Zhiye Nuxing Zazhishe, Dongcheng-qu, Andingmein Nei, 3, Huayuanhutong, Beijing, 100009, China.

760   CHN   ISSN 1005-0787
ZHONGGUO BANHUA. 1993-2004. q. Renmin Meishu Chubanshe, 32, Beizongbu Hutong, Beijing, 100735, China.

616.075   CHN   ISSN 1009-8380
ZHONGGUO CHAOSHENG ZHENDUAN ZAZHI/CHINESE JOURNAL OF ULTRASOUND DIAGNOSIS. 1999-2006. m. Zhongguo Chaosheng Zhenduan Zazhi, 9, Xiaoying Lu, Yayunhaoting A-Zuo 1-E, Beijing 9770 Xinxiang, Beijing, 100101, China.

079.51   CHN
ZHONGGUO YINJIN SHIBAO/CHINESE INTERNATIONAL TIMES. 1998-1999. s-w. Zhonghua Renmin Gongheguo Guojia Waiguo Zhuanjia Ju, 1-50307, Zhongguancun Nan Dajie, Beijing, 100873, China.

330   TWN   ISSN 1017-9631
ZHONGUA MINGUO TAIWAN DIQU JINGJI TONGJI TUBIAO/GRAPHICAL SURVEY OF THE ECONOMY OF TAIWAN DISTRICT, REPUBLIC OF CHINA. 1972-1991. a. Zhongyang Yinhang, 2 Roosevelt Rd, Sec 1, Taipei, 10066, Taiwan.

384.55   CHN   ISSN 1005-0965
ZHONGWAI DIANSHI YUEKAN/CHINESE & OVERSEAS T V MONTHLY. 1985-2001. m. Zhongwai Dianshi Zazhishe, 76, Dongshui Lu, Fuzhou, 100866, China.

808.03 895.1   CHN   ISSN 1004-7972
ZHONGWAI GUSHI CHUANQI. 1988-1998. bi-m. Baihuazhou Wenyi Chubanshe, 310, Yangming Lu, Nanchang, Jiangxi 330008, China.

351   CHN   ISSN 1007-7618
ZHONGWAI KEJI XINXI/SCIENCE & TECHNOLOGY INTERNATIONAL. 1986-2003. m. Zhongguo Kexueyuan, Wenxian Qingbao Zhongxin, 8 Kexueyuan Nanlu, Zhongguancun, Beijing, 100080, China.

510   CHN   ISSN 1003-3750
ZHUSUAN/ABACUS. 1986-2002. bi-m. Zhusuan Bianjibu, Zhongyang Caijin Xueyuan Nei, Sidaokou Xizhimenwai, Beijing, 100081, China.

300   ESP   ISSN 1130-7617
ZIENTZIARTEKOA; revista especializada en ciencias sociales. 1986-ceased. 3/yr. Solokoetxe Argitarapenak, Fika, 45 2o. Izq., Bilbao, 48006, Spain.

781.46   CZE   ISSN 1212-5644
ZIVEL. 1995-2005. q. iMedia s.r.o., U Zvonarky 16, Prague 2, 120 00, Czech Republic.

700   FRA   ISSN 0044-4952
ZODIAQUE. 1951-2003. s-a. Editions Zodiaque, Abbaye de la Pierre-Qui-Vire, St Leger Vauban, 89630, France.

300   ESP   ISSN 0210-2692
ZONA ABIERTA. 1974-200?. q. Editorial Pablo Iglesias, Monte Esquinza 30, 3o. D, Madrid, 28010, Spain.

590   GBR   ISSN 0084-5612   CODEN: SZSLAM
ZOOLOGICAL SOCIETY OF LONDON. SYMPOSIA. 1960-1999. irreg. Oxford University Press, Great Clarendon St, Oxford, OX2 6DP, United Kingdom.

808.2   DNK   ISSN 1396-3783
ZOOTROP. 1984-1997. m. Statens Filmcentral, Vestergade 27, Copenhagen K, 1456, Denmark.

362.61   NLD   ISSN 0924-8161
ZORG EN ONDERNEMEN; vaktijdschrift ouderenzorg. 1989-2006. 10/yr. Bohn Stafleu van Loghum B.V., Postbus 246, Houten, 3990 GA, Netherlands.

618.92   NLD   ISSN 1572-5049
ZORG ROND DE PASGEBORENE. 197?-2004. a. Uitgeverij Kloosterhof Acquisitie Services, Napoleonsweg 128a, Neer, 6086 AJ, Netherlands.

378   NLD   ISSN 1874-9054
ZOWEL-KRANT. 2004-ceased. 10/yr. Eenvoudig Communiceren, Postbus 10208, Amsterdam, 1001 EE, Netherlands.

340.5   DEU
ZUSAMMENSTELLUNG DER JAHRESABSCHLUESSE. 1974-2004. m. Bundesanzeiger Verlagsgesellschaft mbH, Amsterdamer Str 192, Cologne, 50735, Germany.

740   NLD   ISSN 0169-0469
ZWART EN WIT. 1951-1982. 3/yr. Ravenberg Pers, Paasberg 26, Oosterbeek, 6862 CC, Netherlands.

141   NLD   ISSN 1574-308X
DE ZWARTE HAND. 2004-2004. irreg. Uitgeverij Aspekt, Amersfoortsestr 27, Soesterberg, 3769 AD, Netherlands.

378   USA   ISSN 1933-2378
02138 MAGAZINE; the world of Harvard. 2006-2008. bi-m. Manhattan Media, LLC, 63 W 38th St, Ste 206, New York, NY 10018.

323.4   DEU   ISSN 0176-8662
4-3 FACHZEITSCHRIFT ZU KRIEGSDIENSTVERWEIGERUNG, WEHRDIENST UND ZIVILDIENST. 1982-2003. q. Deutsche Friedensgesellschaft - Vereinigte Kriegsdienstgegnerinnen, Kasseler Str 1a, Frankfurt am Main, 60486, Germany.

388.324   AUS   ISSN 1444-531X
4 W D AUSTRALIA. 1988-ceased. irreg. Universal Magazines Pty. Ltd., Unit 5, 6-8 Byfield St, North Ryde, NSW 2113, Australia.

629.22   AUS   ISSN 1441-9408
4 W D OFF-ROAD TIPS. 2001-ceased. irreg. Universal Magazines Pty. Ltd., Unit 5, 6-8 Byfield St, North Ryde, NSW 2113, Australia.

075   ITA   ISSN 1120-5261
7. 1987-2004. s-w. R C S Quotidiani, Via San Marco 21, Milan, 20121, Italy.

388   DNK   ISSN 1902-3502
7DOEGN. 2007-2008. 34/yr. H T S Handel, Transport og Service, Sundkrogskaj 20, Copenhagen OE, 2100, Denmark.

055.1   ITA   ISSN 1129-017X
20 ANNI. 1999-200?. m. Gruppo Editoriale Futura, Via XXV Aprile 39, Bresso, MI 20091, Italy.

793.732   FRA   ISSN 1775-8394
60 GRILLES DE MOTS FLECHES. 2005-2008. bi-m. Euro Services Internet, 60 rue Vitruve, Paris, 75020, France.

320   ITA   ISSN 1720-4240
1989. RIVISTA DI DIRITTO PUBBLICO E SCIENZE POLITICHE. 1991-2002. s-a. Giannini Editore, Via Cisterna dell'Olio 6B, Naples, NA 80134, Italy.

ISSN Index

This index lists serials in order by ISSN. It includes all serials that contain an ISSN in the Ulrich's database, whether the title is active, ceased or has an inactive listing. For title changes, a reference is given to the ISSN of the new title. If a title has changed and a new ISSN has not been assigned (or has not been entered in the Ulrich's database) a reference to the new title will be given. The ISSN assigned to editions of serials listed in Ulrich's are given with reference to the main title's ISSN. Duplicate ISSN entries with references to new titles and/or new ISSN, indicate that the serial has split. Ceased titles are identified by the dagger symbol (†).

Page numbers in bold refer to the location of main entries for active titles and cessation entries for titles for which cessation was noted in the Ulrich's database during the previous three years. If no page reference appears for ceased titles, it means that the title's cessation was noted more than three years ago and is not listed in this edition. Titles from inactive listings do not have page references and are not included in this book.

ISSN

0001-6799 Shokubutsu Bunrui, Chiri *changed to* 1346-7565 **773**
0001-6810 Acta Politica **7101**
0001-6829 Acta Poloniae Historica **4196**
0001-6837 Acta Poloniae Pharmaceutica **6818**
0001-6845 Acta Polytechnica Scandinavica. E L. Electrical Engineering Series **3294**
0001-687X Acta Polytechnica Scandinavica. M E. Mechanical Engineering Series **3372**
0001-6896 Acta Psiquiatrica y Psicologica de America Latina **6119**
0001-690X Acta Psychiatrica Scandinavica **6119**
0001-6918 Acta Psychologica **7330**
0001-6942 Acta Sagittariana **6542**
0001-6950 Acta Scholae Medicinalis Universitatis in Kioto†
0001-6969 Acta Universitatis Szegediensis. Acta Scientiarum Mathematicarum **5465**
0001-6977 Acta Societatis Botanicorum Poloniae **773**
0001-6993 Acta Sociologica **8085**
0001-7000 Acta Stomatologica Belgica†
0001-7019 Acta Stomatologica Croatica **5833**
0001-7043 Acta Technica C S A V **3179**
0001-7051 Acta Theriologica **930**
0001-706X Acta Tropica **5808**
0001-7094 Drug Therapy†
0001-7108 Current Literature on Blood†
0001-7116 Acta Universitatis Carolinae. Medica **5567**
0001-7124 Acta Universitatis Carolinae. Biologica **650**
0001-7132 Acta Universitatis Carolinae. Geologica **2723**
0001-7140 Acta Universitatis Carolinae. Mathematica et Physica **5465**
0001-7159 Acta Universitatis Lundensis Sectio: Medica, Mathematica, Scientiae Rerum Naturalium†
0001-7175 Acta Universitatis Szegediensis. Acta Bibliothecaria†
0001-7183 Acta Urologica Belgica†
0001-7213 Acta Veterinaria Brno **8790**
0001-7221 Acta Veterinaria Japonica†
0001-723X Acta Virologica **880**
0001-7272 Acta Zoologica **930**
0001-7280 Acta Zoologica et Pathologica Antverpiensia†
0001-7299 Acta Zoologica Fennica **930**
0001-7310 Actas Dermo-Sifiliograficas **5871**
0001-7345 Actes Pontificaux†
0001-7353 Actinides and Lanthanides Reviews†
0001-7396 Action (Rensselaerville)†
0001-740X Action†
0001-7426 Action et Pensee†
0001-7442 Action Line (Annapolis) **2965**
0001-7469 Action Nationale **7102**
0001-7477 Action Poetique **5415**
0001-7507 Action Sociale **7102**
0001-7523 Action Veterinaire†
0001-754X Active Handicapped†
0001-7558 Active Service
0001-7566 Actividade Economica de Angola
0001-7574 C E E D. Actividades†
0001-7582 Actividades Petroleras†
0001-7590 Activist†
0001-7612 Activities of the Communist World Organizations†
0001-7620 ACTivity **2824**
0001-7655 Actualidad Economica **1435**
0001-7671 Actualidad Pediatrica†
0001-768X Actualidades de Japon
0001-7701 General Relativity and Gravitation **7014**
0001-771X Actualite Economique **1056**
0001-7728 L'Actualite Juridique. Droit Administratif **4609**
0001-7744 Actualite Missionnaire†
0001-7752 Actualite Pedagogique a l'Etranger†
0001-7760 Actualite Publicitaire
0001-7779 Actualite Terminologique *changed to* 1712-0063 **5091**
0001-7795 Actualites et Culture Veterinaires†
0001-7809 Actualites Marines†
0001-7817 Actualites Odonto-Stomatologiques **5833**
0001-7825 The Actuary **4491**
0001-7833 Actuel†
0001-7868 Aktuelle Urologie **6264**
0001-7892 Ad
0001-7906 AD-Cards†
0001-7914 Ad Change†
0001-7930 Ad Fontes
0001-7949 Ad Lib
0001-7957 Ad Libs†
0001-7965 Ad Marginem **6542**
0001-7973 Ad Rem†
0001-7981 Behavioral Science in Progress†
0001-799X Adalbert-Stifter-Institut des Landes Oberoesterreich. Vierteljahresschrift†
0001-8007 Adam (Los Angeles)†
0001-8015 Adam International Review† **8928**
0001-8023 Adam Magazine†
0001-8066 Adcrafter **19**
0001-8082 Addictions†
0001-8090 Adding Life to Years†
0001-8112 A D E G - Kaufmann **3676**
0001-8120 A D E G - Kurier
0001-8139 Adelaar **2271**
0001-8171 Adem **6542**
0001-821X Adhesives Age†
0001-8228 Adhuna Sahitya†
0001-8236 Adirondac **8301**
0001-8244 Behavior Genetics **863**
0001-8252 Adirondack Life **8301**
0001-8260 Adler **3758**
0001-8279 Der Adler **41**
0001-8295 Admap **19**
0001-8317 Administratieve Arbeid†
0001-8325 Administration **7418**
0001-8333 Quarterly Journal of Administration†
0001-8368 Administrative Law Review (Chicago) **4610**
0001-8392 Administrative Science Quarterly **7419**
0001-8414 Administrator Quarterly
0001-8430 Administrators Notebook†
0001-8449 Adolescence **2143**
0001-8473 Adult & Continuing Education Today†
0001-849X Adult Education†
0001-8511 Adult Education in Nova Scotia†
0001-852X Adult Education in the Public Schools†
0001-8546 Adult Jewish Education†
0001-8600 Advance Abstracts of Contributions on Fisheries and Aquatic Sciences in India†
0001-8619 Advance Australia†
0001-8627 Advanced Battery Technology **3294**
0001-8635 Advanced Documentation List†
0001-8651 Advanced Publications†
0001-8678 Advances in Applied Probability **5466**
0001-8686 Advances in Colloid and Interface Science **2132**
0001-8694 Advances in Education **2824**
0001-8708 Advances in Mathematics **5466**
0001-8724 Shinkei Kenkyu No Shimpo/Advances in Neurological Sciences *changed to* 1881-6096 **6127**
0001-8732 Advances in Physics **7004**
0001-8740 Adveniat
0001-8759 Advent Christian Missions†
0001-8775 Adventure†
0001-8783 Adventure (Nashville) **2175**
0001-8791 Journal of Vocational Behavior **7381**
0001-8813 Adventure Time†
0001-883X Adventures in Western New York History†
0001-8856 Advertentieblad
0001-8864 Advertisement Parade
0001-8880 Adweek†
0001-8899 Advertising Age **20**
0001-8902 Advertising & Marketing for Manufactures†
0001-8988 Advertlink†
0001-8996 The Advocate (Los Angeles, 1967) **4370**
0001-9003 Advocate (New York)†
0001-9011 Adyar
0001-902X Brahmavidya **7733**
0001-9038 Aegir **3583**
0001-9046 Aegyptus **371**
0001-9054 Aequationes Mathematicae **5467**
0001-9062 Aerial†
0001-9070 Aerial Applicator
0001-9089 Sardegna-Agricoltura (Varese)
0001-9097 Aero†
0001-9100 Aero†
0001-9127 Aeroespacio **42**
0001-9135 Aero Field†
0001-916X Aero Mundial
0001-9178 Aero Philatelist Annals†
0001-9194 Aerograph Research Notes†
0001-9224 Aerologische Berichte†
0001-9232 Aeromodeller *changed to* 1360-5526 **4328**
0001-9240 The Aeronautical Journal **42**
0001-9267 Aeronautical Society of India. Journal *changed to* 0972-950X **63**
0001-9321 Aerospace (Washington)†
0001-9372 Aerospace International†
0001-9410 Aerospace Medicine and Biology†
0001-9445 Flieger-Revue **55**
0001-9461 Aerovoz
0001-9488 Aerzteblatt Rheinland-Pfalz **5569**
0001-9496 Aerztliche Forschung†
0001-950X Aerztliche Fortbildung†
0001-9518 Aerztliche Jugendkunde†
0001-9534 Aerztliche Praxis **5569**
0001-9542 Aerztliche Tonbandzeitung†
0001-9550 Aersceala **43**
0001-9569 Aesculape†
0001-9585 Aetnalzer†
0001-9593 Aevum **5091**
0001-9615 Affaires†
0001-9623 Affairs of State†
0001-964X Affari Esteri **7219**
0001-9666 Affiches d'Alsace et de Lorraine - Moniteur des Soumissions et des Ventes de Bois de l'Est **975**
0001-9674 Affirmation†
0001-9682 Afghanistan
0001-9690 Aficion Espanola†
0001-9704 Afinidad **2049**
0001-9720 Africa **4172**
0001-9739 Africa†
0001-9747 Africa **4172**
0001-9763 Africa†
0001-978X Africa Diary
0001-9828 Africa Quarterly **7102**
0001-9836 Africa Report†
0001-9844 Africa Research Bulletin. Political, Social and Cultural Series **7102**
0001-9852 Africa Research Bulletin. Economic, Financial and Technical Series **1435**
0001-9860 Africa Samachar
0001-9879 Africa Tervuren†
0001-9887 Africa Today **7102**
0001-9909 African Affairs **7103**
0001-9925 African Aquarist†
0001-9933 African Arts **464**
0001-9941 African Books Newsletter **615**
0001-9976 African Communist **7103**
0002-0036 African Journal of Tropical Hydrobiology and Fisheries **3583**
0002-0044 African Labour News
0002-0052 African Law Digest **4611**
0002-0087 African Notes **3516**
0002-0109 Behind the News†
0002-0133 African Recorder **7103**
0002-0168 African Social Research **7945**
0002-0184 African Studies **323**
0002-0206 African Studies Review **3516**
0002-0222 African Succulent Plant Society. Bulletin†
0002-0230 African Target†
0002-0249 African Trader†
0002-0265 African Violet Magazine **3721**
0002-029X Africana Bulletin **7945**
0002-0311 Africana Marburgensia **4173**
0002-032X Africana Notes and News†
0002-0346 Afrika†
0002-0389 Afrika-Post **3517**
0002-0397 Afrika Spectrum **7103**
0002-0400 Afrika-Spiegel†
0002-0427 Afrika und Uebersee **5091**
0002-0443 The Journal of Nursing Administration **5965**
0002-046X Afrique & Culture†
0002-0478 Afrique Contemporaine **7220**
0002-0516 Afrique Medicale
0002-0524 Afrique Mon Pays
0002-0532 Afrique Nouvelle†
0002-0559 Afrique Urbaine†
0002-0591 Afro-Asia **4441**
0002-0605 Afro-Asian and World Affairs†
0002-0613 Afro Asian Economic Review
0002-0621 Afro-Asian Journalist
0002-0664 Lotus
0002-0699 After Beat†
0002-0710 Agrarische Rundschau **81**
0002-0729 Age and Ageing **4038**
0002-0737 Age de la Science†
0002-0745 Age of Achievement†
0002-0753 Age of Tomorrow **3899**
0002-0761 Agence d'Informations Europeennes. Bulletin
0002-077X Revue Parlementaire†
0002-0796 Agenda (London) **5416**
0002-080X Agenor **7220**
0002-0826 Agent Commercial†
0002-0834 Agente
0002-0869 Agenzia di Viaggi **8682**
0002-0877 Agenzia Economica Finanziaria
0002-0893 Agenzia Nazionale Informazioni Turistiche
0002-0923 Aggiornamenti in Ematologia†
0002-094X Aggiornamenti Sociali **7946**
0002-0958 Aggiornamento Pediatrico
0002-0966 Aging (Washington)†
0002-0982 Aging in the News†
0002-0990 A G M A Zine **6541**
0002-1024 Agra Europe **191**
0002-1032 Agra University Journal of Research (Science) **7833**
0002-1040 Agradoot **2143**
0002-1067 Agrarirodalmi Szemle†
0002-1075 Agrarisch Weekoverzicht†
0002-1105 Agrartorteneti Szemle **81**
0002-1121 Agrarwirtschaft **81**
0002-1148 Agressologie†
0002-1172 Agri Hortique Genetica†
0002-1180 AgriMarketing **193**
0002-1199 Agri-Pick-Up
0002-1202 L'Agricoltore (Perugia) **82**
0002-1210 L'Agricoltore Ferrarese
0002-1229 Agricoltore Trevisano
0002-1237 Agricoltura (Rome)
0002-1245 Agricoltura Aretina† **8928**
0002-1253 Agricoltura Bergamasca†
0002-127X Agricoltura d'Italia† **8928**
0002-1288 Agricoltura Nostra
0002-1296 Agricoltura Romagnola†
0002-130X Agriculteur du Sud-Est Magazine†
0002-1318 Agricultor†
0002-1326 Agricultor Venezolano
0002-1334 Agricultura **82**
0002-1342 Agricultura al Dia†
0002-1350 Agricultura de las Americas† **8928**
0002-1407 Nippon Nogeikagaku Kaishi/Agricultural Chemical Society of Japan. Journal *changed to* 0453-073X **737**
0002-1415 Agricultural Co-Operative Bulletin†
0002-1431 Agricultural Economist
0002-1466 Agricultural Finance Review **192**
0002-1474 Agricultural Gazette of New South Wales†
0002-1482 Agricultural History **83**
0002-1490 Agricultural History Review **84**
0002-1520 Agricultural Literature of Czechoslovakia†
0002-1539 Agricultural Machinery Journal†
0002-1547 Agricultural Marketing†
0002-1555 Agricultural Marketing **84**
0002-158X Agricultural News (LaFayette) **84**
0002-1601 U.S. Department of Agriculture. National Agricultural Statistics Service. Agricultural Prices **187**
0002-161X Agricultural Research **217**
0002-1679 Agricultural Situation in India **85**
0002-1687 Agriculture†
0002-1695 Agriculture†
0002-1717 Agriculture Abroad†
0002-1725 Agriculture and Agro-Industries Journal **85**
0002-1733 Agriculture Checklist **174**
0002-1741 Agriculture Decisions **4611**
0002-1784 Agrisul†
0002-1792 Agro-Industrialist†
0002-1814 Agro-Service **86**
0002-1822 Agroborealis **87**
0002-1830 Agrochemia† **8929**
0002-1849 Agrochemia *changed to* 1732-2634 **88**
0002-1857 Agrochimica **87**
0002-1865 Agrohemija†
0002-1873 Agrokemia es Talajtan **87**
0002-1881 Agrokhimiya **87**
0002-1903 Agronomia†
0002-1911 Agronomia Lusitana **217**
0002-192X Agronomia Tropical **217**
0002-1938 Agronomics†
0002-1946 Agronomie Tropicale†
0002-1954 Agronomski Glasnik **88**
0002-1962 Agronomy Journal **88**
0002-1970 Agros **88**
0002-1989 Agrotehnicar **88**
0002-1997 Agrotis **88**
0002-2004 Agua†
0002-2012 Agway Cooperator†
0002-2039 Ahijuna
0002-2047 Ahora **3835**
0002-2055 Ahorro†

0002-211X Aikyat†
0002-2136 L'Ain Agricole 89
0002-2144 Ain Shams Medical Journal 5570
0002-2152 Air Actualites 6408
0002-2179 Air and Space Age†
0002-2195 Air B P†
0002-2225 Air Carrier Financial Statistics 8521
0002-2241 Air Classics 44
0002-225X Air Comprime† 8929
0002-2268 Air Conditioning & Refrigeration in India
0002-2276 Air Conditioning, Heating & Refrigeration News 4116
0002-2306 Air-Cushion Vehicles†
0002-2314 Air Europa
0002-2365 Air Force Comptroller 6409
0002-2403 Air Force Times (U.S. Edition) 6409
0002-2411 Air Line Employee 4589
0002-242X Air Line Pilot 44
0002-2446 Air Mail
0002-2454 Air Navigation Radio Aids†
0002-2497 Air Pollution Titles†
0002-2543 Air Transport World 45
0002-2586 Air University Library Index to Military Periodicals 6455
0002-2624 Airadio News†
0002-2675 Aircraft Illustrated 45
0002-2683 Aircraft Industry Record
0002-2691 A O P A Magazine changed to A O P A Pilot 41
0002-2705 Airfix†
0002-2721 Airline Fleet Record
0002-2748 Airline Newsletter†
0002-2756 Airman 6409
0002-2772 Airman's Information Manual. Part 2: Airport Directory†
0002-2802 Airport Forum†
0002-2837 Airport Times
0002-2888 Airways International†
0002-2918 Ajastan Kensabanakan Handes 651
0002-2926 Aiton Review†
0002-2942 Asian Economies 1591
0002-2977 Akademie der Wissenschaften und der Literatur. Geistes- und Sozialwissenschaftliche Klasse. Abhandlungen 4441
0002-2985 Akademie der Wissenschaften und der Literatur, Mainz. Klasse der Literatur. Abhandlungen 5250
0002-2993 Akademie der Wissenschaften und der Literatur, Mainz. Mathematisch - Naturwissenschaftliche Klasse. Abhandlungen 7833
0002-3000 Akademische Monatsblaetter 7782
0002-3019 Akademischer Dienst changed to 0930-2093
0002-3299 Akademiya Nauk S.S.S.R. Institut Geologii Rudnykh Mestorozhdenii, Petrografii, Mineralogii i Geokhimii. Trudy†
0002-3302 Institut Teoreticheskoi Astronomii. Byulleten'†
0002-3612 Akaroa Mail 3916
0002-3620 Akashi 2356
0002-3639 Akhand Anand 3878
0002-3655 Akher Sa'a 3835
0002-3663 Akis
0002-368X Akitaken Noson Igakkai Zasshi 5570
0002-3698 Akrides
0002-3701 Akron Dental Society. Bulletin 5833
0002-371X Akron Law Review 4612
0002-3728 Akros†
0002-3752 Die Aktiengesellschaft 1879
0002-3760 Aktion†
0002-3787 Aktualne Problemy Informacji i Dokumentacji†
0002-3809 Aktuelle Freie Praxis†
0002-3825 Aktuelle Kulturpolitik†
0002-3892 Akuntansi & Administrasi†
0002-3922 Akvariet†
0002-3930 Akvarium, Terarium†
0002-3949 Akwesasne Notes†
0002-3957 Akzente 5416
0002-3965 Al-Ousbou' al-Arabi 5232
0002-3981 Ahad
0002-399X Al-Dirasat al-Islamiyyah 4658
0002-4015 Al-Ma'arif 7713
0002-4023 Al-Machriq†
0002-4058 Al-Maskukat
0002-4066 Ai Nostri Amici
0002-4074 Ta'awun
0002-4082 Turath al-Sha'bi
0002-4090 A L A 5415
0002-4112 Alabama Academy of Science. Journal 7834
0002-4139 Alabama Association of Secondary School Principals. Bulletin†
0002-4147 The Alabama Baptist Historian 7744
0002-4155 Alabama Builder 975
0002-418X Alabama Contractor 4116
0002-4198 Alabama Dental Association. Journal†
0002-421X Alabama Food Merchants Journal
0002-4236 Alabama Historical Quarterly
0002-4252 Alabama Journal of Medical Sciences†
0002-4279 Alabama Law Review 4612
0002-4287 The Alabama Lawyer 4612
0002-4295 Alabama Librarian 4988
0002-4309 Alabama Municipal Journal 7487
0002-4317 Alabama Nurse 5950
0002-4325 Alabama Purchasor 1804
0002-4341 The Alabama Review 4282
0002-435X Alabama School Journal 2825
0002-4368 Alabama Social Welfare†
0002-4384 Alabama Trucker†
0002-4392 Alam Attijarat† 8929
0002-4406 Alambre
0002-4414 Alameda-Contra Costa Medical Association. Bulletin 5570
0002-4422 Alamo†
0002-4430 Alan Watts Journal†
9004-4465 Alaska Conservation Review†
0002-4503 Alaska Journal†
0002-4538 Alaska Medicine 5570
0002-4546 Alaska Nurse 5950
0002-4562 Alaska 3969

0002-4570 Sourdough†
0002-4600 Alata Internazionale†
0002-4619 Alauda 901
0002-4627 Alba†
0002-4643 Albania Oggi†
0002-4651 Albania Report†
0002-4686 Albany Regional Medical Program. Report†
0002-4708 Albert Einstein Medical Center.Journal†
0002-4740 Alberta Calls
0002-4759 Alberta Conservative†
0002-4767 Alberta Farm Economist†
0002-4775 Alberta Gazette 3806
0002-4805 Alberta Journal of Educational Research 2825
0002-4813 Alberta Labour†
0002-4821 Alberta Law Review 4613
0002-483X Library Association of Alberta. Bulletin†
0002-4848 Alberta Medical Bulletin†
0002-4902 Alberta Transport Reporter
0002-4910 Albertina Studien†
0002-4937 Album
0002-4953 Albuquerque Archaeological Society Newsletter 372
0002-4961 Albus†
0002-4988 Alcan Magazine†
0002-4996 Alcan News†
0002-5011 Alchimist†
0002-502X Alcoholism 2691
0002-5038 Alcoholism Review†
0002-5054 Alcool ou Sante changed to 1762-1097 2690
0002-5062 Alcor
0002-5070 Alcuinus
0002-5089 Aldebaran Review†
0002-5097 Alderley and Wilmslow and Knutsford Advertiser
0002-5100 Aldrichimica Acta 2119
0002-5119 Aldus†
0002-5127 Aleh†
0002-5135 Alemanha Internacional†
0002-5143 Alemas
0002-5151 Alergia changed to Revista Alergia Mexico 5765
0002-5178 Alerta†
0002-5186 Alerte Atomique†
0002-5208 Alexanor 838
0002-5216 Alfa 5092
0002-5224 Alfred Hitchcock's Mystery Magazine (Print Edition) 5413
0002-5232 Algebra and Logic 5467
0002-5240 Algebra Universalis 5468
0002-5259 N R C - Handelsblad 3915
0002-5267 Algemeen Maconniek Tijdschrift changed to 1573-5699 7658
0002-5275 Algemeen Nederlands Tijdschrift voor Wijsbegeerte 6903
0002-5283 Algemeen Politieblad van het Koninkrijk der Nederlanden changed to 1871-4307 4630
0002-5291 Algeria. Institut Pedagogique National. Bureau de Documentation et d'Information Scolaires Universitaires et Professionnelles. Informations et Documents†
0002-5313 Algerien en Europe†
0002-5321 Universite d'Alger. Publications Scientifiques. Serie A: Mathematiques†
0002-533X Universite d'Alger. Publications Scientifiques. Serie B: Sciences Physiques†
0002-5372 Al-Hikmat
0002-5380 Ali Nuove†
0002-5399 Alieia
0002-5402 Alimenta 3626
0002-5410 L'Alimentation au Quebec 3676
0002-5453 Alive†
0002-5461 Alive (St. Louis)†
0002-547X Alive (Harrisonburg)†
0002-5488 Alkahest†
0002-5496 Alkohol-Industrie 597
0002-5534 All-Africa Church Music Association. Journal†
0002-5542 All-Church Press Newspapers
0002-5550 All Clear†
0002-5569 All England Law Reports 4946
0002-5577 All Hands 6410
0002-5585 All-India Anglo-Indian Association. Review 7220
0002-5593 All India Reporter 4613
0002-5607 All Outdoors
0002-5623 All the World 7745
0002-5631 Alla Bottega 5251
0002-564X Allam- es Jogtudomany 4613
0002-5658 Allattani Kozlemenyek 931
0002-5674 Alle Hens 6410
0002-5682 Alle Kvinner†
0002-5690 Allegheny County Pharmacist†
0002-5704 Allegro 4589
0002-5712 Allemagne d'Aujourd'hui 5205
0002-5720 Allemagne Internationale†
0002-5739 Allen Memorial Art Museum. Bulletin†
0002-5747 Allergia 5753
0002-578X Allers 3954
0002-5798 Allgemeine Bauzeitung
0002-5801 Allgemeine Bauzeitung 975
0002-581X Allgemeine Deutsche Gesellen-Zeitung†
0002-5828 Allgemeine Deutsche Imkerzeitung 90
0002-5852 Allgemeine Forst- und Jagdzeitung 3683
0002-5895 Allgemeine Hotel- und Gaststaetten-Zeitung 4381
0002-5917 A P R 6731
0002-5925 Allgemeine Schweizerische Militaerzeitschrift 6410
0002-5968 Allgemeine Vermessungs-Nachrichten 3259
0002-5976 Allgemeine Waermetechnik†
0002-5992 Allgemeiner Muehlen-Markt
0002-600X Allgemeiner Samen- und Pflanzen Anzeiger†
0002-6018 Allgemeines Statistisches Archiv changed to 1863-8171 8343
0002-6050 Alliance Israelite Universelle en France. Cahiers 7717
0002-6069 Alliance Journal†
0002-6085 Alliance News 7104
0002-6093 Alliance Review 2825
0002-6107 Allied Industrial Worker†
0002-6123 Allis-Chalmers Engineering Review†

0002-614X Alloy Digest 6304
0002-6158 Allpress - F F A Korrespondenz†
0002-6166 Allround-Collector Address-List†
0002-6190 Allt om Hobby 4327
0002-6204 Allt om Mat & Vin 3626
0002-6247 Alma Mater†
0002-6271 Almanaque Aeronautico†
0002-628X Almas 7620
0002-6298 Der Almbauer 90
0002-6301 Aloe 774
0002-631X Aloft†
0002-6328 Along the Boardwalk†
0002-6336 Die Alpen 8302
0002-6344 Alpengarten†
0002-6352 Alpenlaendische Bienenzeitung 90
0002-6387 Kappan
0002-6395 Alpha
0002-6417 Alpha Omegan 5834
0002-6425 Alphabet†
0002-6433 Alphabet††
0002-6468 Le Alpi Venete 8302
0002-6492 Alpino 3896
0002-6506 Alt for Damerne 8851
0002-6514 Altkatholische Kirchenzeitung 7745
0002-6549 Alta Direccion 1725
0002-6565 Alte und Moderne Kunst†
0002-6573 Altenheim 5951
0002-659X Alternative
0002-6611 Alternative†
0002-662X Alternative Press Index 4571
0002-6646 Das Altertum†
0002-6662 Altra Italia
0002-6670 Der Altsprachliche Unterricht 5092
0002-6689 Aluminium changed to International Aluminium Journal 6316
0002-6778 Amaru†
0002-6786 Amaterska Scena 8465
0002-6808 Amateur Athlete 8157
0002-6816 Amateur Baseball News 8220
0002-6840 Amateur Photographer 6963
0002-6859 Amateur Radio 2356
0002-6867 Amateur Stage 8465
0002-6875 Amateurtuinder changed to 1871-8388 3752
0002-6883 Amateur Winemaker†
0002-6905 Ambassade van de U.S.S.R. in Nederland. Informatie-Bulletin†
0002-6913 Ambassador†
0002-693X Amber-Hi-Lites†
0002-6948 Ambiance de Paris†
0002-6956 Ambience†
0002-6964 Ambienti†
0002-6972 Ambit 5252
0002-6980 Ambix 2049
0002-7014 Ameghiniana 6723
0002-7049 America 7782
0002-7065 America: History and Life 4168
0002-709X America Latina
0002-712X American Academy of Arts and Sciences. Bulletin 4442
0002-7162 American Academy of Political and Social Science. Annals 7104
0002-7189 American Academy of Religion. Journal 7620
0002-7197 Independent Agent 4506
0002-7200 American Agent and Broker 4492
0002-7227 American Aircraft Modeler†
0002-7243 American Analgesia Society. Journal
0002-726X American Annals of the Deaf 4071
0002-7278 American Anthropological Association. Bulletin 324
0002-7294 American Anthropologist 324
0002-7316 American Antiquity 372
0002-7324 American Archives of Rehabilitation Therapy†
0002-7359 American Art Journal†
0002-7367 American Artisan†
0002-7375 American Artist 465
0002-7421 American Association of Dental Examiners. Board Bulletin 5834
0002-7499 American Association of Teachers of Esperanto Quarterly Bulletin 3050
0002-7502 American Association of Workers for the Blind. Dictionary Catalogue†
0002-7529 American Astrology† 8929
0002-7537 American Astronomical Society. Bulletin 568
0002-7561 American Banker 1307
0002-760X American Bar News†
0002-7618 American Bard†
0002-7626 American Bee Journal 90
0002-7634 American Beef Producer†
0002-7642 American Behavioral Scientist 7946
0002-7650 The American Benedictine Review 7782
0002-7669 American Bibliography of Agricultural Economics†
0002-7685 The American Biology Teacher 652
0002-7707 American Book Publishing Record 7551
0002-7715 American Breeds Magazine†
0002-7723 American Brewer†
0002-7731 American Building Supplies†
0002-7766 American Business Law Journal 4854
0002-7790 American Catholic Society of Philadelphia. Records changed to American Catholic Studies 7782
0002-7804 American Cemetery 3719
0002-7812 American Ceramic Society. Bulletin 2037
0002-7820 American Ceramic Society. Journal 2037
0002-7839 American Chamber of Commerce Executives. Journal†
0002-7847 American Chamber of Commerce in Japan. Journal 1395
0002-7863 American Chemical Society. Journal 2049
0002-788X American Choral Foundation. Research Memorandum Series 6543
0002-7898 American Choral Review 6543
0002-7928 American Cinematographer 6489
0002-7952 A C H A Action 6980
0002-7979 American College of Dentists. Journal 5834
0002-7995 American College of Neuropsychiatrists. Bulletin†
0002-8045 American College of Surgeons. Bulletin 6235

0002-807X American Cooner 8303
0002-8126 American Criminologist†
0002-8142 American Dachshund†
0002-8150 American Dahlia Society. Bulletin 3722
0002-8177 American Dental Association. Journal 5834
0002-8193 American Dialect Society. Newsletter 5092
0002-8207 Publications of the American Dialect Society 5163
0002-8215 American Dialog†
0002-8223 American Dietetic Association. Journal 6654
0002-8258 American Drycleaner 2242
0002-8282 The American Economic Review 1436
0002-8304 American Education†
0002-8312 American Educational Research Journal 2825
0002-8320 American Entomological Society. Transactions 838
0002-8339 American Esperanto Magazine†
0002-838X American Family Physician 5571
0002-8401 American Farm Youth†
0002-8436 American Fencing 8158
0002-8444 American Fern Journal 774
0002-8452 American Field 8303
0002-8460 American Film Institute. Education Membership Newsletter†
0002-8487 American Fisheries Society. Transactions 3584
0002-8525 American Flint†
0002-8541 American Forests 3683
0002-8568 American Fruit Grower 3722
0002-8576 American Funeral Director 3719
0002-8592 The American Genealogist 3758
0002-8614 American Geriatrics Society. Journal 4040
0002-8622 American-German Review†
0002-8630 American Girl (Inkprint Edition)†
0002-8649 American Glass Review†
0002-8665 American Grocer†
0002-869X American Harp Journal 6543
0002-8703 American Heart Journal 5776
0002-8711 American Helicopter Society. Journal 46
0002-8738 American Heritage 4282
0002-8754 American Histadrut Cultural Exchange Institute. Bulletin†
0002-8762 American Historical Review 4129
0002-8835 American Hungarian Review†
0002-8843 American Idea†
0002-8886 American Indian Law Newsletter†
0002-8908 American Industry 1879
0002-8967 American Institute of Homeopathy. Journal changed to 1934-2454 5803
0002-8975 American Institute of Hypnosis. Journal
0002-8983 American Institute of Landscape Architects. Journal†
0002-9033 American-Israel Economic Horizons†
0002-905X American Jewish Archives Journal (Print Edition) changed to 1537-7989 7717
0002-9076 American Jewish Times Outlook 7718
0002-9084 American Jewish World 3518
0002-9092 American Journal of Agricultural Economics 193
0002-9114 American Journal of Archaeology 372
0002-9122 American Journal of Botany 774
0002-9149 The American Journal of Cardiology 5776
0002-9157 American Journal of Clinical Hypnosis 5942
0002-9165 American Journal of Clinical Nutrition 6655
0002-9173 American Journal of Clinical Pathology 5572
0002-919X American Journal of Comparative Law 4916
0002-9246 American Journal of Economics and Sociology 1059
0002-9254 American Journal of Enology and Viticulture 597
0002-9262 American Journal of Epidemiology 5572
0002-9270 American Journal of Gastroenterology 5920
0002-9297 American Journal of Human Genetics 862
0002-9300 American Journal of International Law 4916
0002-9319 American Journal of Legal History† 8929
0002-9327 American Journal of Mathematics 5468
0002-9343 The American Journal of Medicine 5572
0002-936X American Journal of Nursing 5951
0002-9378 American Journal of Obstetrics and Gynecology 5985
0002-9394 American Journal of Ophthalmology 6038
0002-9432 American Journal of Orthopsychiatry 7333
0002-9440 The American Journal of Pathology 5573
0002-9459 American Journal of Pharmaceutical Education 6820
0002-9475 American Journal of Philology 5092
0002-9483 American Journal of Physical Anthropology 324
0002-9505 American Journal of Physics 7004
0002-9513 American Journal of Physiology (Consolidated) 918
0002-953X American Journal of Psychiatry 6122
0002-9548 The American Journal of Psychoanalysis 7333
0002-9556 American Journal of Psychology 7333
0002-9564 American Journal of Psychotherapy 6122
0002-9599 American Journal of Science 2701
0002-9602 American Journal of Sociology 8087
0002-9610 The American Journal of Surgery 6235
0002-9629 American Journal of the Medical Sciences 5573
0002-9637 American Journal of Tropical Medicine and Hygiene 5810
0002-9645 American Journal of Veterinary Research 8791
0002-9653 Dimensions in American Judaism†
0002-9661 American Judoman
0002-967X American Killifish Association. Journal 3584
0002-9688 American Labor†
0002-9718 American Laundry Digest†
0002-9726 American Leather Chemists Association. Journal 4972
0002-9742 American Legion Press Association News-Letter 4571
0002-9750 American Legislator†
0002-9769 American Libraries 4988
0002-9777 American Library Association. Adult Services Division Newsletter†
0002-9785 American Library Association. Library Education Division. Newsletter†
0002-9793 American Library Directory Updating Service†
0002-9815 American Literary Accents†
0002-9831 American Literature 5252
0002-9882 American Maritime Officer 4589
0002-9890 American Mathematical Monthly 5468
0002-9920 American Mathematical Society. Notices 5469
0002-9939 American Mathematical Society. Proceedings 5469
0002-9947 American Mathematical Society. Transactions 5469
0002-998X American Mercury†

0002-9998 American Metal Market 1805
0003-0007 American Meteorological Society. Bulletin 6346
0003-0015 American-Mexican Medical Association. Journal
0003-0031 American Midland Naturalist 7834
0003-004X The American Mineralogist (Print) 6456
0003-0066 American Motor Carrier†
0003-0082 American Museum Novitates 931
0003-0090 American Museum of Natural History. Bulletin 931
0003-0104 American Music Center. Newsletter†
0003-0112 American Music Teacher 6544
0003-0139 American Musicological Society. Journal 6544
0003-0147 The American Naturalist 652
0003-0155 The American Neptune†
0003-018X American Nuclear Society. Transactions 3164
0003-0198 American Nurseryman 3722
0003-021X J A O C S 2124
0003-0279 American Oriental Society. Journal 542
0003-0295 American Oxonian 5205
0003-0325 American Painting Contractor 6716
0003-0341 Paper, Paperboard, & Wood Pulp 6740
0003-0376 American Pen†
0003-0406 Abstracts of Air and Water Conservation Literature†
0003-0473 American Philatelist 6891
0003-0481 American Philosophical Quarterly 6903
0003-049X American Philosophical Society. Proceedings 4442
0003-0503 American Physical Society. Bulletin changed to 1058-8132 7002
0003-0503 American Physical Society. Bulletin 7005
0003-0511 American Pigeon Journal
0003-052X American Place Theatre. News†
0003-0546 American Poet
0003-0554 American Political Science Review 7105
0003-0627 Pharmacy Times 6874
0003-0651 American Psychoanalytic Association. Journal 7333
0003-066X American Psychologist 7333
0003-0678 American Quarterly 4442
0003-0686 American Racing Pigeon News 8158
0003-0694 American Railway Engineering Association Bulletin†
0003-0708 American Rationalist 6903
0003-0716 American Record Guide 6544
0003-0724 American Recorder 6544
0003-0732 American Red Cross Youth Journal†
0003-0775 American Report†
0003-0791 American Review of Eastern Orthodoxy
0003-0813 American Review of World Health†
0003-083X American Rifleman 8158
0003-0848 American Risk and Insurance Association. Commission on Insurance Terminology. Bulletin†
0003-0872 American Rodding†
0003-0880 American Roofer and Building Improvement Contractor
0003-0902 American Salesman 1805
0003-0937 American Scholar 5206
0003-0945 American School & University 3017
0003-0953 American School Board Journal 3017
0003-0961 American School News†
0003-097X American Schools of Oriental Research. Bulletin 542
0003-0996 American Scientist 7835
0003-1003 American Secondary Education 3017
0003-1011 American Security Council Washington Report†
0003-102X American Sephardi 7718
0003-1038 American Shoemaking changed to Shoemaking International 7942
0003-1046 American Small Stock Farmer†
0003-1062 American Society for Horticultural Science. Journal 3722
0003-1070 American Society for Psychical Research. Journal 6741
0003-1089 American Society for the Study of Orthodontics. Journal†
0003-1100 American Society of Civil Engineers. Engineering Mechanics Division. Newsletter†
0003-1135 American Society of Civil Engineers. Structural Division. Newsletter†
0003-1143 American Society of Civil Engineers. Surveying & Mapping Division. Newsletter†
0003-1151 American Society of Civil Engineers. Waterways & Harbors Division. Newsletter†
0003-116X American Society of Farm Managers and Rural Appraisers. Journal 91
0003-1186 American Society of Papyrologists. Bulletin 372
0003-1224 American Sociological Review 8087
0003-1232 The American Sociologist 8087
0003-1240 American Soft Drink Journal†
0003-1259 American Sokol 6982
0003-1275 Soybean Profits†
0003-1283 American Speech 5092
0003-1305 The American Statistician 8344
0003-1313 American String Teacher 6544
0003-1348 American Surgeon 6236
0003-1356 American Surgical Dealer†
0003-1380 American Teacher 4589
0003-1399 American Theological Library Association. Newsletter 4989
0003-1429 American Translator†
0003-1445 American Turf Monthly 8286
0003-1453 American University Law Review 4615
0003-147X American Vegetarian-Hygienist†
0003-1488 American Veterinary Medical Association. Journal 8791
0003-150X American Water Works Association. Journal 8817
0003-1518 American Way 8782
0003-1534 American West†
0003-1550 American Zionist†
0003-1593 America's Future 7105
0003-1615 The Americas 4283
0003-1623 Amerikanischer Wirtschaftsbrief
0003-1631 Amerikas Latvietis†
0003-1682 Amgueddfa†
0003-1704 Ami du Peuple 3840
0003-1747 Amico dell'Arte Cristiana 466
0003-1755 Amiga 8851
0003-1763 Aminco Laboratory News†
0003-178X Amis de Han Ryner. Cahiers†
0003-1798 Amis de la Radiesthesie†

0003-181X Association Les Amis de Milosz. Cahiers 5258
0003-1844 Amis des Roses 3723
0003-1852 Amis du Chateau de Pau. Bulletin 466
0003-1879 Amistad†
0003-1917 Amministrazione Socialista†
0003-195X Among Friends†
0003-1984 Amor Artis Bulletin†
0003-1992 Amperland 4197
0003-200X Amphora 7551
0003-2026 A M P O 5204
0003-2034 Amposta†
0003-2042 Ampul
0003-2050 Amro Beursnieuws†
0003-2069 Amsterdam in de Markt†
0003-2077 Amsterdam-Rotterdam Bank. Economic Quarterly Review†
0003-2107 Amtliche Veterinaernachrichten†
0003-2115 Amtlicher Anzeiger 7420
0003-2131 Amtliches Kreisblatt fuer den Kreis Herzogtum Lauenburg 7487
0003-2166 Wiener Warenboerse. Amtliches Kursblatt. Holz 1659
0003-2174 Wiener Warenboerse. Amtliches Kursblatt. Rohhaeute und Felle, Leder Treibriemen und Technische Lederartikel 1659
0003-2190 Amtliches Schulblatt fuer den Regierungsbezirk Duesseldorf† 8929
0003-2204 Amtliches Schulblatt fuer die Volks-, Real- und Berufsschulen fuer den Bezirksregierung Trier†
0003-2220 Amtsblatt der Oesterreichischen Justizverwaltung 4615
0003-2247 Wels, Stadt. Amtsblatt
0003-2271 Amtsblatt fuer das Land Vorarlberg 7487
0003-228X Amtsblatt fuer den Regierungsbezirk Aurich†
0003-2344 Amusement Business†
0003-2360 An Lef Kernewek†
0003-2409 Anaesthesia (Oxford) 5768
0003-2417 Der Anaesthesist 5769
0003-2425 Anais Azevedos†
0003-2441 Anais de Farmacia e Quimica de Sao Paulo
0003-245X Anais Paulistas de Medicina e Cirurgia
0003-2468 Analecta Bollandiana 7783
0003-2476 Analecta Cisterciensia†
0003-2484 Anales Cientificos 7835
0003-2492 Anales de Bromatologia†
0003-2506 Anales de Mecanica y Electricidad 3373
0003-2522 Anales de Sociologia
0003-2530 Anales del Instituto Corachan†
0003-2549 Anales del Servicio de Psiquiatria
0003-2557 Anales Espanoles de Odontoestomatologia†
0003-2565 Univerzitet u Beogradu. Pravni Fakultet. Anali 4805
0003-2573 Analise Social 8087
0003-2581 Analisis - Confirmado 3790
0003-259X Analisis de Actualidades Societicas†
0003-2638 Analysis 6904
0003-2654 The Analyst 2097
0003-2662 Anarisuto†
0003-2670 Analytica Chimica Acta 2097
0003-2689 Analytical Abstracts 2085
0003-2697 Analytical Biochemistry 722
0003-2700 Analytical Chemistry 2098
0003-2719 Analytical Letters 2098
0003-2727 Anaqueles†
0003-2751 Anarchy†
0003-2778 Anatomical Society of India. Journal 653
0003-2824 Anblick 8303
0003-2840 Anchor
0003-2883 Ancora†
0003-2905 Andean Air Mail and Peruvian Times†
0003-2913 Andelsbladet changed to 1604-9764 1423
0003-2948 Andes
0003-2956 Andhra Agricultural Journal 91
0003-2964 Andhra Pradesh Productivity Council. Target 91
0003-2972 Andover Newton Quarterly†
0003-2980 Andrews University Seminary Studies 7621
0003-2999 Anesthesia and Analgesia 5769
0003-3006 Anesthesia Progress 5834
0003-3022 Anesthesiology 5769
0003-3049 Angeiologie 5777
0003-3057 Angel Hair†
0003-3103 Angels†
0003-3154 Angewandte Ornithologie†
0003-3170 Angiologia 5777
0003-3197 Angiology 5777
0003-3200 Angiopatias
0003-3219 Angle Orthodontist 5834
0003-3235 Anglers' Digest
0003-3243 Angler's Mail 8303
0003-326X Anglica†
0003-3278 Anglican Digest 7745
0003-3286 Anglican Theological Review 7746
0003-3294 Angling†
0003-3308 Angling Times 8303
0003-3332 Anglo-German Medical Review†
0003-3340 Anglo-German Review
0003-3367 Anglo-Jewish Art and History†
0003-3375 Anglo-Norwegian Trade Journal
0003-3383 Anglo-Spanish Quarterly Review 7221
0003-3391 Anglo Swiss Times†
0003-3405 Anglo-Welsh Review†
0003-3413 Angola. Direccao dos Servicos de Estatistica. Boletim Mensal 8345
0003-343X Instituto de Investigacao Cientifica de Angola. Relatorios e Comunicacoes 7866
0003-3448 Laboratorio de Engenharia de Angola. Boletim Informativo†
0003-3456 Angola. Direccao Provincial dos Servicos de Geologia e Minas. Boletim 2724
0003-3464 Angora Goat & Mohair Journal 278
0003-3472 Animal Behaviour 932
0003-3499 Animal Breeding Abstracts 174
0003-3510 Animal Health Age†
0003-3545 Animal Life†
0003-360X Animaldom 6803

0003-9683 Archives des Maladies du Coeur et des Vaisseaux *changed to* 1875-2136 **5777**
0003-9756 Archives Europeennes de Sociologie **8088**
0003-9810 Archives Internationales d'Histoire des Sciences **7836**
0003-9829 Archives Italiennes de Biologie **6123**
0003-9837 Archives Juives **7718**
0003-9853 Archives of American Art Journal **467**
0003-9861 Archives of Biochemistry and Biophysics **723**
0003-987X Archives of Dermatology **5872**
0003-9888 Archives of Disease in Childhood **6088**
0003-9896 Archives of Environmental Health *changed to* 1933-8244 **3404**
0003-990X Archives of General Psychiatry **6124**
0003-9918 Archives of Hygiene†
0003-9926 Archives of Internal Medicine **5944**
0003-9934 Archives of Medical Hydrology†
0003-9942 Archives of Neurology **6124**
0003-9950 Archives of Ophthalmology **6038**
0003-9969 Archives of Oral Biology **934**
0003-9993 Archives of Physical Medicine and Rehabilitation **6106**
0004-0002 Archives of Sexual Behavior **5577**
0004-0010 Archives of Surgery **6237**
0004-0029 Archives of Traditional Music. Trimester Report†
0004-0045 Archivi e Cultura **4990**
0004-0061 Archivio de Vecchi†
0004-007X Archivio di Chirurgia Toracica e Cardiovascolare†
0004-0088 Archivio di Filosofia **6905**
0004-0096 Archivio di Fisiologia†
0004-010X Archivio di Medicina Interna†
0004-0126 Archivio di Ostetricia e Ginecologia†
0004-0142 Archivio di Patologia e Clinica Medica†
0004-0150 Archivio di Psicologia, Neurologia e Psichiatria†
0004-0169 Archivio di Scienze Biologiche†
0004-0177 Archivio di Studi Urbani e Regionali **4403**
0004-0193 Archivio E. Maragliano di Patologia e Clinica†
0004-0207 Archivio Glottologico Italiano **5096**
0004-0215 Archivio Italiano delle Malattie dell'Apparato Digerente†
0004-0231 Archivio Italiano di Anatomia e Istologia Patologica†
0004-024X Archivio Italiano di Chirurgia†
0004-0266 Archivio Italiano di Patologia e Clinica dei Tumori†
0004-0274 Archivio Italiano di Pediatria e Puericoltura†
0004-0304 Archivio Penale†
0004-0320 Archivio Stomatologico
0004-0347 Archivio Storico Lodigiano **4200**
0004-0355 Archivio Storico per la Calabria e la Lucania **4200**
0004-0371 Archivio Storico Ticinese **4200**
0004-038X Archivmitteilungen†
0004-0398 Archivni Casopis **4990**
0004-0401 Archivo de Ciencias Biologicas y Naturales, Teoricas y Aplicadas†
0004-041X Archivio di Medicina Mutualistica†
0004-0428 Archivo Espanol de Arte **467**
0004-0436 Archivo Espanol de Morfologia **654**
0004-0452 Archivo Ibero-Americano **4200**
0004-0479 Archivio Veterinario Italiano†
0004-0495 Archivos Argentinos de Reumatologia†
0004-0509 Archivos Argentinos de Tisiologia y Neumonologia†
0004-0517 Archivos Argentinos de Enfermedades del Aparato Digestivo **5920**
0004-0525 Archivos Bolivianos de Medicina **5577**
0004-0541 Archivos de Criminologia, Neuro-Psiquiatria y Disciplinas Conexas
0004-055X Archivos de Historia Potosina **4284**
0004-0568 Archivos de Medicina Experimental†
0004-0584 Archivos de Pediatria del Uruguay **6088**
0004-0592 Archivos de Zootecnia **279**
0004-0606 Archivos Dominicanos de Pediatria **6088**
0004-0614 Archivos Espanoles de Urologia **6265**
0004-0622 Archivos Latinoamericanos de Nutricion **6655**
0004-0630 Archivos Leoneses† **8931**
0004-0649 Archivos Venezolanos de Puericultura y Pediatria **6088**
0004-0665 Archivum Franciscanum Historicum **7784**
0004-069X Archivum Immunologiae et Therapiae Experimentalis **5754**
0004-0703 Archivum Linguisticum **4990**
0004-0738 Archiwum Budowy Maszyn **3374**
0004-0819 Arcispedale S. Anna di Ferrara†
0004-0835 Arcoscenico
0004-0843 Arctic **7836**
0004-086X Arctic Circular†
0004-0894 Area **3999**
0004-0916 Area Trends in Employment and Unemployment†
0004-0959 Arena†
0004-0967 Arepo†
0004-0975 Arethusa **2230**
0004-0991 Argentina Automotriz
0004-1025 Argentina. Direccion Nacional de Asistencia Nacional. DAS
0004-1033 Pergamino, Argentine Republic. Estacion Experimental Agropecuario. Boletin de Divulgacion†
0004-1041 Argentina Futuro
0004-105X Argentina Grafica **7318**
0004-1076 Argentina. Servicio de Hidrografia Naval. Boletin†
0004-1084 Argentine Science Fiction Review **5439**
0004-1092 Argentino
0004-1106 Argentinos Lietuviu Balsas **3519**
0004-1114 Argosy†
0004-1130 Argot†
0004-1149 Argument foer Frihet och Raett†
0004-1157 Das Argument **7948**
0004-1165 The Argus (Thunder Bay) **2273**
0004-1181 Argus (Bloomington) **2273**
0004-119X Argus des Collectivites†
0004-1254 Arhiv za Higijenu Rada i Toksikologiju **3494**
0004-1297 Arhivski Pregled†
0004-1300 Aria Compressa†
0004-1319 Arid Lands Research Newsletter†
0004-1327 A R I E L **5248**
0004-1335 Ariel **2375**
0004-1343 Ariel (English Edition)† **8931**
0004-1386 Arizona Advocate†
0004-1394 Arizona Alumnus **2273**
0004-1459 Arizona Dental Journal†
0004-1467 Arizona Economic Indicators†
0004-1483 Arizona English Bulletin **5096**
0004-1521 Arizona Highways **8683**
0004-153X Arizona Law Review **4621**
0004-1548 Arizona Librarian†
0004-1564 Arizona Mobile Citizen†
0004-1599 Arizona Nurse **5952**
0004-1610 Arizona Quarterly **5207**
0004-1637 Arizona Roadrunner†
0004-167X The Ark **318**
0004-170X Ark/Ozark
0004-1718 Arkansas Archeologist **380**
0004-1726 Arkansas Banker **1308**
0004-1742 Arkansas Business and Economic Review **1061**
0004-1750 Arkansas Cattle Business **279**
0004-1785 Arkansas Farm Research†
0004-1815 Arkansas Grocer†
0004-1823 Arkansas Historical Quarterly **4284**
0004-1831 Arkansas Law Review **4621**
0004-184X Arkansas Libraries **4991**
0004-1858 Arkansas Medical Society. Journal **5577**
0004-1874 Arkansas Oil and Gas Statistical Bulletin **6799**
0004-1882 Arka-Tech **2273**
0004-1904 Arkham Collector†
0004-1920 Arkhimedes **5473**
0004-1939 Arkhitektura S.S.S.R.†
0004-1955 Arkhiv Patologii **5578**
0004-1963 Arhiv za Farmaciju **6822**
0004-1971 Arkitekt
0004-198X Arkitekten **433**
0004-1998 Arkitektnytt **433**
0004-2005 A T - Arkitekttidningen *changed to* 0347-058X **433**
0004-2013 Arkitektur DK **433**
0004-2021 Arkitektur **433**
0004-203X Arkiv **4131**
0004-2048 Arkiv for Astronomi†
0004-2056 Chemica Scripta†
0004-2064 Arkiv for Geofysik†
0004-2080 Arkiv foer Matematik **5473**
0004-2099 Arkiv for Mineralogi och Geologi†
0004-2102 Arkiv for Sjoerett†
0004-2145 Arma
0004-2153 Armament Data Sheets
0004-2161 Armas y Tiro
0004-217X The Armchair Detective†
0004-2188 Armed Forces Comptroller **6410**
0004-2277 Armee-Rundschau†
0004-2293 Armenya Segodnya†
0004-2323 Armenian Digest
0004-2331 Armenian Guardian†
0004-234X Armenian Mirror - Spectator **3519**
0004-2366 Armenian Review **5207**
0004-2374 Armenian Weekly **3519**
0004-2382 Armenian Welfare Association of New York News
0004-2390 Armenopoulos
0004-2404 Armenytt *changed to* 1652-3571 **6425**
0004-2420 Armor **6411**
0004-2439 Arms and Armour Society Journal **364**
0004-2447 Arms Control and National Security†
0004-2455 Army **6411**
0004-2463 Army, Air Force & Naval Air Statistical Record
0004-2471 United States Army Aviation Digest†
0004-248X Army Aviation **6411**
0004-2528 Army Logistician **6412**
0004-2536 Army Museum Newsletter†
0004-2544 Army Orders†
0004-2552 Army Quarterly and Defence Journal† **8931**
0004-2579 Army Reserve Magazine **6412**
0004-2595 Army Times **6412**
0004-2617 Arnold Air Letter **47**
0004-2633 Arnoldia **3723**
0004-265X Ars Sutoria **7940**
0004-2676 Arquitecto Peruano
0004-2684 Arquitectura Mexico†
0004-2706 Arquitectura **433**
0004-2714 Arquivo de Patologia†
0004-2722 Arquivo do Distrito de Aveiro†
0004-2730 Arquivos Brasileiros de Endocrinologia e Metabologia **5884**
0004-2749 Arquivos Brasileiros de Oftalmologia **6038**
0004-2765 Arquivos Brasileiros de Tuberculose e Doencas do Torax†
0004-2773 Arquivos Catarinenses de Medicina **5578**
0004-2781 Arquivos de Angola **4173**
0004-279X Arquivos de Biologia†
0004-2803 Arquivos de Gastroenterologia **5920**
0004-2811 Arquivos de Higiene e Saude Publica†
0004-282X Arquivos de Neuro-Psiquiatria **6124**
0004-2846 Arredare la Casa†
0004-2854 Arredorama†
0004-2870 Ars Aequi **4621**
0004-2889 Bukkyo Geijutsu **480**
0004-2897 Ars Medici **5578**
0004-2900 Ars Medici et Nouveautes Medicales
0004-2919 Ars Organi **6546**
0004-2927 Ars Pharmaceutica **6822**
0004-296X Art Alliance Bulletin **468**
0004-2986 Art and Archaeology Newsletter
0004-2994 Art and Archaeology Technical Abstracts (Print Edition) *changed to* A A T A Online **529**
0004-301X Art and Australia **468**
0004-3044 Art and Life†
0004-3079 The Art Bulletin **468**
0004-3087 Art Chretien†
0004-3095 Art d'Eglise†
0004-3109 Art Direction†
0004-3125 Art Education **469**
0004-315X Art et Curiosite†
0004-3168 Art et Decoration **4531**
0004-3184 Art Gallery†
0004-3206 Art Gallery of South Australia. Bulletin†
0004-3214 Art in America **469**
0004-3222 Art Index **529**
0004-3230 Art International†
0004-3249 Art Journal **470**
0004-3273 Artnews **474**
0004-329X Art of the Americas. Bulletin†
0004-3303 Art Quarterly†
0004-3389 De Arte **471**
0004-3397 Qui Arte Contemporanea†
0004-3400 Arte Cristiana **472**
0004-3419 Arte e Poesia†
0004-3443 Arte Lombarda
0004-3451 Arterama†
0004-3486 Artes
0004-3508 Artes Graficas en Mexico†
0004-3516 Artes Hispanicas†
0004-3524 Artes/Letras
0004-3540 Artha†
0004-3559 Artha Vijnana **1061**
0004-3567 Artha-Vikas **1880**
0004-3575 Arthaniti **1061**
0004-3583 Arthritis and Rheumatic Diseases Abstracts†
0004-3591 Arthritis & Rheumatism **6222**
0004-3613 Arthur Young Journal†
0004-363X Art e Mercature **1395**
0004-3648 Artibus Asiae **473**
0004-3680 Artifact **381**
0004-3702 Artificial Intelligence **2446**
0004-3729 Artificial Limbs†
0004-3737 Artigiano Modenese† **8931**
0004-3745 Artigliere
0004-3753 Artigos Selecionados†
0004-377X Artikkelindeks Foer Bygg†
0004-3788 Artilleri-Tidskrift **6412**
0004-380X Artillerie Rundschau†
0004-3818 Artilleriiskii Zhurnal†
0004-3826 Artillery Journal **6412**
0004-3842 Artis **473**
0004-3877 The Artist **473**
0004-3907 Artistes et Varietes†
0004-3915 Artlook†
0004-3931 Arts and Activities **3051**
0004-3958 Arts Asiatiques **474**
0004-3966 Arts en Auto **8556**
0004-3982 Arts et Industries **3182**
0004-4024 Arts in Society†
0004-4032 Arts in Virginia†
0004-4059 Arts Magazine†
0004-4067 Arts Management **8465**
0004-4083 Arts of Asia **475**
0004-4121 Artweek **476**
0004-413X Arunodayam†
0004-4148 Arx†
0004-4156 Aryan Path†
0004-4164 Aryana
0004-4172 Arzneimittel-Forschung **6823**
0004-4180 Arzt in Niederoesterreich **5578**
0004-4202 As We Are†
0004-4210 Asahi Garasu Kenkyu Hokoku **2037**
0004-4229 Asbarez **5207**
0004-4237 Asbestos†
0004-4245 Asbestos Worker†
0004-427X Ascent†
0004-4288 Aschehougs Leksikonservice†
0004-4296 A S E C O L D A†
0004-430X Aseguradores **4493**
0004-4318 Asfalt **3259**
0004-4326 Ashanti Times†
0004-4342 Achkhar†
0004-4350 Ashland Dealer†
0004-4377 Ashtree Echo **3759**
0004-4385 Asi†
0004-4423 Asia Bulletin†
0004-4431 Asia Calling†
0004-444X Asia Christian Colleges Association. Bulletin†
0004-4458 Asia Foundation Program Quarterly†
0004-4466 Asia Letter **1437**
0004-4474 Asia Magazine†
0004-4482 Asia Major **543**
0004-4520 Asian Almanac **7198**
0004-4547 Asian Books Newsletter **616**
0004-4555 Asian Economic Review **1062**
0004-4636 Asian Printer†
0004-4644 Asian Recorder **3879**
0004-4660 Asian Student†
0004-4679 Asian Studies **543**
0004-4687 Asian Survey **7107**
0004-4695 Asiatic Research Bulletin†
0004-4709 Asiatic Society of Bombay. Journal **544**
0004-4717 Asiatische Studien **544**
0004-4725 Asie Nouvelle†
0004-4733 Asien-Bibliographie†
0004-4741 Asociacion Argentina Criadores de Cerdos. Revista **279**
0004-4776 Asociacion Colombiana de Facultades de Medicina. Cronica†
0004-4784 Asociacion Costarricense de Bibliotecarios. Boletin **4991**
0004-4792 Asociacion Cultural Humboldt. Boletin†
0004-4806 Asociacion de Ex-Alumnos de la Escuela Nacional de Bibliotecarios. Boletin **4992**
0004-4814 Asociacion Franco-Mexicana de Ingenieros y Tecnicos. Boletin **3182**
0004-4822 Asociacion Geologica Argentina. Revista **2725**
0004-4830 Asociacion Medica Argentina. Revista **5579**
0004-4849 Asociacion Medica de Puerto Rico. Boletin **5579**
0004-4857 Asociacion Mexicana de Facultades y Escuelas de Medicina. Boletin
0004-4873 Asociacion Numismatica Argentina. Revista
0004-4881 Asociacion Odontologica Argentina. Revista **5835**
0004-4911 Aspect (Somerville)†
0004-4946 Aspetti Letterari
0004-4962 Aspire†

9008 0004-4970 ULRICH'S PERIODICALS

0004-4970 Asprenas 7784
0004-4989 Assam Information 3879
0004-4997 Assam Review and Tea News 3627
0004-5012 Assayad 7107
0004-5020 Assegai†
0004-5098 Assicurazione
0004-511X Assicurazioni 4493
0004-5128 Assignment Children†
0004-5187 Associacao Bahiana de Bibliotecarios. Informa
0004-5195 Associacao Brasileira de Pesquisas sobre Plantas Aromaticas e Oleos Essenciais. Boletim
0004-5209 Associacao Comercial de Lourenco Marques. Boletim†
0004-5217 Associacao Comercial do Amazonas. Boletim
0004-5225 Associacao Medica Brasileira. Boletim†
0004-5233 Associacao Medica Brasileira. Jornal 5580
0004-525X Associacao Medica de Minas Gerais. Revista†
0004-5292 Association and Society Manager†
0004-5306 Association Canadienne d'Education. Bulletin 2827
0004-5322 Association de Geographes Francais. Bulletin 3999
0004-5411 Association for Computing Machinery. Journal 2407
0004-542X Association for Psychoanalytic Medicine. Bulletin 7337
0004-5438 A R S C Journal 8151
0004-5454 Association for the Study of Perception. Journal†
0004-5470 Revue de l'Association Francaise des Techniciens du Petrole *changed to* 1622-1036 6786
0004-5527 Association Guillaume Bude. Bulletin 5097
0004-5535 Art *changed to* Art Albums Series 468
0004-5551 Association Internationale d'Etudes du Sud-Est Europeen. Bulletin 4201
0004-5578 Association Management *changed to* 1557-7562 1726
0004-5608 Association of American Geographers. Annals 3999
0004-5616 Association of American Medical Colleges. Bulletin†
0004-5632 Annals of Clinical Biochemistry 722
0004-5659 Association of College Unions - International. Bulletin 2967
0004-5667 Association of College Unions - International. Union Wire 2967
0004-5675 Association of Collegiate Schools of Planning. Bulletin†
0004-5683 Association of Economic Geographers. Annals 1063
0004-5772 Association of Physicians of India. Journal 5580
0004-5780 Association of Public Analysts. Journal†
0004-5799 Association of Public Passenger Transport Operators. Journal†
0004-5837 Association of the Bar of the City of New York. Record 4622
0004-5853 Association of Urban Universities Newsletter†
0004-590X Associazione degli Africanisti Italiani. Bollettino
0004-5918 Associazione degli Industriali di Arezzo. Notiziario
0004-5977 Associazione Italiana Veterinari per Piccoli Animali. Bollettino 8793
0004-5985 Associazione Nazionale Ex Internati. Bollettino Ufficiale
0004-5993 Associazione Nazionale Mutilati e Invalidi di Guerra. Sezione di Roma. Notiziario
0004-6000 Associazione Romana di Entomologia. Bollettino 840
0004-6019 L'Assurance Francaise†
0004-6027 Assurances *changed to* 1705-7299 4493
0004-6035 Assurances Banques Transports†
0004-6051 Assyrian Star 3520
0004-606X Aste Giudiziarie† 8931
0004-6116 Astrado 5258
0004-6124 Astral Projection†
0004-6140 The Astrological Magazine 565
0004-6167 Astrologische Gids†
0004-6175 Astrologischer Auskunftsbogen†
0004-6191 Astrology Guide
0004-6221 Astronautik†
0004-623X Astronautyka 47
0004-6256 The Astronomical Journal 569
0004-6264 Publications of Astronomical Society of Japan 580
0004-6272 Astronomical Society of the Pacific. Leaflet†
0004-6280 Astronomical Society of the Pacific. Publications 570
0004-6299 Astronomicheskii Zhurnal 570
0004-6302 L'Astronomie 570
0004-6337 Astronomische Nachrichten 570
0004-6353 Astronomy
0004-6361 Astronomy & Astrophysics 570
0004-637X The Astrophysical Journal 571
0004-640X Astrophysics and Space Science 572
0004-6434 At Cooper Union 2273
0004-6450 At Home with the South African Permanent†
0004-6485 Atemschutz-Informationen†
0004-6493 Atene e Roma 2230
0004-6558 Ateneo Veneto 7837
0004-6566 Athenaeum 2273
0004-6574 Athenaeum 2231
0004-6582 Athene†
0004-6590 L'Athenee†
0004-6604 Athens Annals of Archaeology 382
0004-6620 Institut Pasteur Hellenique. Archives
0004-6647 Athletic Director†
0004-6671 Athletics Weekly 8159
0004-668X Atletiekwereld†
0004-6698 Athletik†
0004-6701 Atlanta Magazine 3969
0004-6736 Atlante†
0004-6744 Atlantic Advocate†
0004-6752 The Atlantic Baptist 7746
0004-6760 Atlantic Community Quarterly†
0004-6787 Atlantic Mirror†
0004-6809 Atlantic Naturalist†
0004-6817 Atlantic Observer - Knickerbocker International†
0004-6825 Atlantic Provinces Inter-University Committee on the Sciences. Newsletter
0004-6833 Atlantic Psychologist†
0004-6841 Atlantic Report 1438
0004-6876 Atlantida 7949
0004-6914 Marine/Atlantische Welt†
0004-6965 Atmanirvrithi†
0004-699X Air Pollution Abstracts†
0004-7007 Atoka 5258
0004-7015 Atom 3164
0004-7023 Atom†
0004-704X Atom Mind 5207
0004-7066 Atom und Strom†
0004-7104 Atomic Energy Law Journal
0004-7112 Atomic Energy Review†
0004-7120 Nippon Genshiryoku Gakkaishi/Atomic Energy Society of Japan. Journal *changed to* Atomos 3165
0004-7155 A T O M K I Kozlemenyek†
0004-7163 Atomnaya Energiya 3165
0004-718X Atomo Petrolio Elettricita†
0004-7244 Att Bo†
0004-7279 Atterraggio Forzato
0004-7287 Societa degli Ingegneri e degli Architetti in Torino. Atti e Rassegna Tecnica 3283
0004-7309 Attualita di Laboratorio†
0004-7317 Attualita di Ostetricia e Ginecologia†
0004-7325 Attualita Mediche
0004-7368 Actualides Pernambucanas†
0004-7376 Au Fil du Rail
0004-7384 Au Grand Air
0004-7392 Auberge de la Jeunesse†
0004-7414 Auburn Pharmacist†
0004-7422 Auckland City Art Gallery Quarterly†
0004-7449 Auckland Star†
0004-7465 The Auctioneer 1805
0004-7481 Audenshaw Papers 7623
0004-749X Audience†
0004-7503 Audience (Print Edition)†
0004-752X Audio (New York)†
0004-7554 Audio Engineering Society. Journal *changed to* 1549-4950 8151
0004-7570 Audio Visual Journal
0004-7619 Audiotecnica
0004-7627 Audiovisivi
0004-7643 Audit-Poetry
0004-7651 Auditor 7733
0004-7716 Auerbach Computer Notebook International†
0004-7732 Auerbach Data Handling Reports†
0004-7740 Auerbach Graphic Processing Reports†
0004-7783 Auerbach Standard E D P Reports†
0004-7791 Auerbach Time Sharing Reports†
0004-7813 Aufbau†
0004-7821 Aufbau†
0004-7856 Der Aufschluss 2725
0004-7864 Der Aufstieg†
0004-7872 Der Auftrag
0004-7880 Auftrag 7746
0004-7899 Ran 7176
0004-7902 Der Augenarzt 6038
0004-7910 Augenoptik†
0004-7929 Der Augenoptiker 6039
0004-7937 Der Augenspiegel 6039
0004-7945 Augsburg Echo 2273
0004-7953 Augsburg in Zahlen†
0004-7961 Augsburger Kulturnachrichten 8684
0004-7988 The Augustan 3759
0004-7996 Augustana College Bulletin†
0004-8003 Augustiniana 7785
0004-8011 Augustinianum 7785
0004-802X Augustinus 7785
0004-8038 The Auk 901
0004-8054 Aural News
0004-8062 Aurea Parma
0004-8089 Aurora 3999
0004-8100 Der Ausbilder 2938
0004-8119 Ausblick (Duesseldorf) 4590
0004-8143 Avsonia
0004-8186 Der Aussenhandelskaufmann†
0004-8194 Aussenpolitik†
0004-8208 Aussenpolitische Korrespondenz†
0004-8216 Aussenwirtschaft 1552
0004-8224 Die Aussenwirtschaft† 8932
0004-8283 Australian Citrus News 3723
0004-8313 Australasian Beekeeper 93
0004-833X Australasian Corrosion Engineering
0004-8380 Australasian Journal of Dermatology 5872
0004-8402 Australasian Journal of Philosophy 6906
0004-8410 Australasian Manufacturer
0004-8461 Australasian Radiology *changed to* 1754-9477 6200
0004-8496 Australasian Stamp Collector
0004-8585 Australia. Bureau of Statistics. Western Australian Office. Quarterly Statistical Abstract†
0004-8607 Australia International†
0004-8615 Australia Newsletter†
0004-8623 Australian Academic & Research Libraries 4993
0004-8658 Australian and New Zealand Journal of Criminology 2644
0004-8666 The Australian and New Zealand Journal of Obstetrics and Gynecology 5986
0004-8674 Australian & New Zealand Journal of Psychiatry 6125
0004-8739 Australian Baptist†
0004-8763 Australian Bookseller and Publisher *changed to* 1833-5403 7555
0004-8798 Australian Building Science and Technology
0004-8801 Australian Business Communications†
0004-8828 Australian Chemical Engineering
0004-8852 Australian Christian (Print) *changed to* Australian Christian (Online) 7624
0004-8992 Australian Economic History Review 1536
0004-900X Australian Economic Papers 1064
0004-9018 The Australian Economic Review 1064
0004-9026 Australian Education Index (Print)†
0004-9042 Australian Electronics Engineering†
0004-9069 Australian External Territories†
0004-9077 Australian Family Safety†
0004-9093 Australian Economic News†
0004-9107 Australian Fish Trades Review
0004-9123 Australian Flying 47
0004-9131 Australian Food Manufacturer and Distributor†
0004-914X Australian Forest Research†
0004-9158 Australian Forestry 3684
0004-9174 The Australian Gemmologist 4564
0004-9182 Australian Geographer 3999
0004-9190 Australian Geographical Studies *changed to* 1745-5863 4011
0004-9255 Australian Hardware Journal 1053
0004-9263 Australian Harness Sport
0004-928X Australian Home Beautiful 5065
0004-9298 Australian Home Journal†
0004-9301 Australian Hot Rodding Review†
0004-931X Australian House & Garden 4532
0004-9328 Australian Humanist†
0004-9409 Australian Journal of Agricultural Research *changed to* 1836-0947 103
0004-9425 Australian Journal of Chemistry 2051
0004-9433 Australian Journal of Dairy Technology 261
0004-9441 Australian Journal of Education 2829
0004-9468 Australian Journal of French Studies 5259
0004-9484 Australian Journal of Music Education *see* 0255-7614 6577
0004-9506 Australian Journal of Physics†
0004-9514 Australian Journal of Physiotherapy 6107
0004-9522 Australian Journal of Politics and History 7108
0004-9530 Australian Journal of Psychology 7338
0004-9573 Australian Journal of Soil Research 220
0004-959X Australian Journal of Zoology 934
0004-9603 Australian Lapidary Magazine
0004-9611 Australian Law Journal 4946
0004-9638 Australian Left Review†
0004-9646 Australian Legal Monthly Digest 4821
0004-9654 Australian Liberal†
0004-9662 Communion 7634
0004-9670 The Australian Library Journal 4993
0004-9689 Australian Library News†
0004-9697 Australian Literary Studies 5259
0004-9727 Australian Mathematical Society. Bulletin 5474
0004-9743 Australian Meteorological Magazine 6347
0004-976X Australian Mining 6457
0004-9808 Australian Municipal Journal† 8933
0004-9816 Australian National Bibliography†
0004-9832 Australian National University News†
0004-9875 Australian Numismatic Journal 6649
0004-9883 Australian Numismatic Society. Report
0004-9964 Australian Photography 6964
0004-9980 Australian Pistol Shooters' Bulletin
0005-0008 Australian Plants 777
0005-0016 Australian Plastics and Rubber Journal†
0005-0024 Australian Police Journal 2644
0005-0067 Australian Psychologist 7338
0005-0229 Australian Science Index†
0005-0237 Australian Seacraft†
0005-0261 Australian Society of Accountants. Bulletin†
0005-030X Australian Student†
0005-0318 Australian Sugar Journal†
0005-0350 Australian Thoroughbreds†
0005-0377 Australian Tradition†
0005-0385 Australian Transport†
0005-0393 Australian Traveller†
0005-0415 Australian University†
0005-0423 Australian Veterinary Journal 8793
0005-044X Australian Wine, Brewing & Spirit Review†
0005-0458 The Australian Women's Weekly 8852
0005-0482 Australijas Latvietis 3521
0005-0490 Austria Export 1553
0005-0504 I F E F Austria Sekcio. Bulteno 8618
0005-0512 Austria-Philatelist 6892
0005-0520 Austrian Information 7222
0005-0539 Austro-Motor†
0005-0555 Austroflug†
0005-0563 Austropack 6708
0005-0571 Auszuege aus den Gebrauchsmustern 6746
0005-0598 Auszuege aus Presseartikeln 1211
0005-0601 Aut Aut 6906
0005-0628 The Author 5259
0005-0652 Authority in Crisis†
0005-0695 Autospark 8566
0005-0709 Auto Age 8557
0005-0717 Auto and Flat Glass Journal 2037
0005-0768 L'Auto-Journal 8558
0005-0776 Auto Laundry News 8558
0005-0792 Auto-Motor 8559
0005-0806 Auto Motor und Sport 8559
0005-0814 Auto Noticias
0005-0822 Auto Racing†
0005-0830 Autorevue 8491
0005-0857 Auto-Technik
0005-0873 Autovisie 8567
0005-0903 Auto Accessorio
0005-0911 Autobody and the Reconditioned Car†
0005-0938 Autocar et Cargo Routier†
0005-0946 Autoclub 8562
0005-0989 Autohaus 8562
0005-0997 Autokampioen 8562
0005-1004 Autolinea†
0005-1012 Automat 2457
0005-1020 Automated Education Letter†
0005-1039 Automaten-Markt 1806
0005-1055 Automatic Documentation and Mathematical Linguistics 5202
0005-1071 Automatic Machining 5449
0005-1098 Automatica 2458
0005-111X Avtomaticheskaya Svarka 6342
0005-1128 Automatie 2458
0005-1144 Automatika 2458
0005-1179 Automation and Remote Control 2458
0005-1187 Automation Council News
0005-1233 Automatisch-Verkaufen†
0005-125X Automatizace 2458
0005-1268 Automatizacija Poslovanja
0005-1284 Automazione e Strumentazione 2459
0005-1306 Automobil-Industrie 8563
0005-1314 Automobil - Revue *see* 0035-0761 8510
0005-1330 Automobile *changed to* 1711-7526 8563
0005-1349 Automobile 8563
0005-1373 Automobile Club di Milano. Notiziario Economico†

0005-1403 Automobile India
0005-142X Automobile News
0005-1438 Automobile Quarterly **8563**
0005-1489 Automotive Chain Store†
0005-1497 Automotive Cooling Journal **8564**
0005-1519 Automotive Fleet **8565**
0005-1551 Automotive News **8565**
0005-156X Automotive News of the Pacific Northwest **8565**
0005-1608 Automotor
0005-1616 Automovil de Venezuela **8566**
0005-1632 Automovilismo en Espana **8566**
0005-1659 Autoparade†
0005-1683 Autorama **8566**
0005-1691 Auto Revista **8560**
0005-1713 Autorevue†
0005-173X Autosport†
0005-1748 Autosprint **8160**
0005-1756 Autostrade
0005-1764 Autotechnisch Tijdschrift.
0005-1772 Autotoerist†
0005-1780 Autotransportes "Tres Estrellas de Oro"
0005-1799 Autoveteranen
0005-1810 Autowelt†
0005-1845 Auvergne Litteraire†
0005-1861 Volunteer Leader†
0005-1888 Avalanche†
0005-1896 Avances en Alimentacion y Mejora Animal† **8934**
0005-190X L'Avant-Garde†
0005-1918 Avant Garde†
0005-1926 The Avant Gardener **3724**
0005-1942 A. D. Correspondence†
0005-1950 Avedik
0005-1969 Avenirs†
0005-1985 Avenue†
0005-1993 Aves **902**
0005-2000 Aves & Ovos
0005-2035 Avia†
0005-2043 Avia Aeroespacial
0005-2078 Aviacion **6413**
0005-2086 Avian Diseases **8794**
0005-2094 Aviasport†
0005-2140 Aviation Mechanics Bulletin *changed to* 1934-4015 **8533**
0005-2159 Aviation Reports
0005-2167 Aviation Studies International. Official Price List
0005-2175 Aviation Week & Space Technology **49**
0005-2213 Rivista di Avicoltura **299**
0005-2221 Aviculteur Quebecois
0005-2248 Avicultura Brasileira
0005-2256 Avicultural Magazine **902**
0005-2272 Avion†
0005-2310 Avtomatika i Telemekhanika **2459**
0005-2337 Avtomobil'naya Promyshlennost' **8568**
0005-2345 Avtomobil'nyi Transport **8568**
0005-2353 Avtomobil'nye Dorogi **3260**
0005-2361 L'Avvenire Agricolo **94**
0005-237X Awake! **7733**
0005-2388 Awakener
0005-2426 Axial
0005-2442 Ayrshire Cattle Society's Journal **261**
0005-2450 Ayrshire Digest **261**
0005-2469 Ayu
0005-2477 Ayurved Vikas†
0005-2485 Ayurveda-Bharati†
0005-2493 Ayurveda Doot†
0005-2515 Azad Mazdur **7108**
0005-2523 Azerbaidzhanskii Meditsinskii Zhurnal **5582**
0005-2531 Azerbaidzhanskii Khimicheskii Zhurnal†
0005-254X Azimut
0005-2558 Azione
0005-2566 L'Azione Cooperativa
0005-2574 Aziya i Afrika Segodnya **7222**
0005-2590 Aztec Engineer†
0005-2604 Aztlan **3521**
0005-2655 B A S F Review†
0005-2698 B-U Nachrichten
0005-2701 B & Z†
0005-2728 B B A - Bioenergetics **778**
0005-2736 B B A - Biomembranes **827**
0005-2744 B B A - Enzymology†
0005-2779 B.B.A. Nieuws†
0005-2833 Bokrevy†
0005-2841 B C A News **1064**
0005-2892 B C Power Engineer†
0005-2949 B C Studies **7949**
0005-2957 B C Teacher
0005-2981 B D K Mitteilungen **3052**
0005-299X B D V-Dienst Niedersachsen†
0005-3015 B. E. A. Bulletin†
0005-304X B E M A Bulletin **3182**
0005-3058 B E N E L U X International†
0005-3066 B H P Review
0005-3074 B H P Technical Bulletin
0005-3082 B I B - Liner
0005-3090 B I C C Bulletin†
0005-3112 B I I L†
0005-3120 Bibliotheque de Travail Junior† **8936**
0005-3155 Bios **661**
0005-318X B I T S **1212**
0005-3198 Bonniers Litteraera Magasin **5209**
0005-321X B M G
0005-3228 B N A Policy and Practice Series **1856**
0005-3236 Revista do B N D E†
0005-335X Bibliotheque de Travail† **8936**
0005-3392 B T O News **902**
0005-3414 Bibliotheque de Travail 2eme Degret† **8936**
0005-3430 The B V A Bulletin **4079**
0005-3449 B V E A Reporter
0005-3457 B V N. Boletin Informativo
0005-3503 Babel **3052**
0005-3546 Babson's Washington Service†
0005-3554 Baby & Junior **2245**
0005-3562 Baby & Tiener†
0005-3570 Baby Care†
0005-3600 Bach **6547**
0005-3643 Back to Godhead **7707**
0005-366X Backstretch†
0005-3686 Bad und Kueche†
0005-3759 Badger History†
0005-3767 Badger Legionnaire **6413**
0005-3775 Badger Sportsman **8305**
0005-3783 Badia Greca di Grottaferrata. Bollettino **7785**
0005-3791 Badminton†
0005-383X Baecker und Konditor†
0005-3848 Baender, Bleche, Rohre **6306**
0005-3856 Baessler Archiv **330**
0005-3872 Baeuerlicher Ratgeber†
0005-3880 Bagdala **5208**
0005-3902 Baghdad Observer
0005-3910 Bagin
0005-3937 Bagvertising Weekly
0005-3953 Bahamas
0005-397X Bahamian Review **1440**
0005-3988 Bahana **5259**
0005-3996 Hadshot Hahistadrut†
0005-4003 Baileya†
0005-402X Bakelite Review†
0005-4070 Baker Street Journal **5413**
0005-4097 Bakers Journal **3671**
0005-4100 Bakers' Review *changed to* 1475-4363 **3671**
0005-4127 Bakery Production and Marketing†
0005-416X Baking Industry†
0005-4194 Bal Bharati **2177**
0005-4208 Bal Sandesh†
0005-4216 Balance **5884**
0005-4224 Balance of Payments Reports†
0005-4232 The Balance Sheet *changed to* College Challenges & Changes
0005-4240 Banque Populaire Suisse. Balance Sheet Prospectus **1320**
0005-4259 Balans **2645**
0005-4275 Balde Branco **261**
0005-4283 Bulgarski Ezik **5101**
0005-4291 Baljivan **2177**
0005-4313 Balkan Studies **4202**
0005-4380 Ballroom Dancing Times *changed to* 1475-2336 **2685**
0005-4399 Ballsout†
0005-4402 Balneologia Polska **6107**
0005-4410 Balon **8222**
0005-4429 Balthazar
0005-4437 Baltic Exchange
0005-4453 Baltimore Magazine **5065**
0005-447X Baltimore Bulletin of Education†
0005-4496 Baltimore Engineer **3182**
0005-450X Baltimore Jewish Times **7718**
0005-4518 Baltimore Museum of Art Record†
0005-4526 Baltische Briefe **7109**
0005-4534 Baltische Hefte†
0005-4542 Bama'arakha†
0005-4569 Bamat Hatzarkhan†
0005-4585 Banas
0005-4607 Banca Nazionale del Lavoro. Quarterly Review **1310**
0005-4615 Banca y Comercio **1310**
0005-4623 Bancaria **1310**
0005-4631 Bancni Vestnik **1311**
0005-4658 Banco Central de Costa Rica. Revista†
0005-4666 Banco Central de Honduras. Revista Trimestral†
0005-4674 Banco Central de la Republica Argentina. Boletin Estadistico **1212**
0005-4712 Banco Central de Reserva del Peru. Boletin **1311**
0005-4720 Banco Central de Venezuela. Revista **1311**
0005-4739 Banco Central del Ecuador. Boletin **1311**
0005-478X Banco de Angola. Boletim Trimestral†
0005-4798 Banco de Espana. Boletin Estadistico (Print)† **8934**
0005-4801 Banco de Fomento Nacional. Boletim de Informacao†
0005-481X Banco de Guatemala. Boletin Estadistico **1312**
0005-4828 Banco de la Republica. Revista **1312**
0005-4844 Economia y Finanzas
0005-4852 Banco de Vizcaya. Noticiario Economico†
0005-4860 Banco di Sicilia. Informazioni Sulla Congiuntura
0005-4879 Banco do Brasil. Boletim†
0005-4887 Banco Nacional Ultramarino. Boletim Trimestral†
0005-4917 Band†
0005-4933 Band Journal **6547**
0005-495X Toon en Beeld
0005-4968 Bandwagon **8466**
0005-4992 Banif's Investment Bulletin **1611**
0005-500X Banijya Barta
0005-5018 Bank- en Effectenbedrijf **1313**
0005-5026 Bank and Quotation Record†
0005-5042 Bank Board Letter **1312**
0005-5077 Bank Karamchari **4590**
0005-5115 Bank Negara Malaysia. Bulletin Ekonomi Suku Tahunan **1441**
0005-5123 Bank News **1313**
0005-5158 Bank of Canada. Weekly Financial Statistics **1213**
0005-5166 Bank of England Quarterly Bulletin **1441**
0005-5212 Bank of India. Bulletin **1441**
0005-5239 Bank of Jamaica. Bulletin†
0005-5247 Bank of Japan. Economic Statistics Monthly **1213**
0005-5271 Bank of Libya. Economic Research Division. Economic Bulletin
0005-528X Bank of London & South America. Revista Mensual†
0005-5298 Bank of London and South America Review†
0005-5301 Bank of Mauritius. Monthly Bulletin **1315**
0005-531X Bank of Montreal Business Review†
0005-5328 Bank of Nova Scotia. Monthly Review†
0005-5344 Bank of Taiwan Quarterly **1441**
0005-5387 Bank One
0005-5395 The Banker **1316**
0005-5409 Banker & Tradesman **7583**
0005-5425 Bankers Digest **1317**
0005-5433 The Banker's Letter of the Law **1317**
0005-5506 The Banking Law Journal **1317**
0005-5522 Bankinsurance News **1318**
0005-5530 Bankruptcy Law Reports **4857**
0005-5557 Banner (Grand Rapids) **7746**
0005-5565 Banneret†
0005-5573 Bano†
0005-559X Banque Centrale des Etats de l'Afrique de l'Ouest. Notes d'Information et Statistiques **1319**
0005-5603 Banque de Port-Said. Revue Economique Trimestrielle
0005-5611 Banque Nationale de Belgique. Bulletin *changed to* 1372-3162 **1320**
0005-562X Banque Nationale de Paris. Revue†
0005-5670 Banyaszati es Kohaszati Lapok - Kohaszat **6306**
0005-5689 Baptist Bulletin **7747**
0005-5700 Baptist Herald†
0005-5719 Baptist History and Heritage **7747**
0005-5727 Baptist Leader†
0005-5751 Baptist Progress (Waxahachie) **7747**
0005-576X Baptist Quarterly **7747**
0005-5778 Baptist Record **7747**
0005-5786 Baptist Times **7747**
0005-5808 Baptist World **7747**
0005-5816 N A B E News†
0005-5824 The Bar Examiner **4627**
0005-5840 Bar-Server†
0005-5859 Barat Review†
0005-5867 Baratz'ba
0005-5883 Barba
0005-5891 Barbados Museum and Historical Society. Journal **4285**
0005-5921 Barco Pesquero†
0005-5948 Bardic Echoes†
0005-5956 Barid Hollanda
0005-5964 Barkai†
0005-5999 Barmherzigkeit **8027**
0005-6006 Barn i Hem, Skola, Samhaelle **2830**
0005-6014 Barnard Bulletin **2274**
0005-609X Baseball Digest **8222**
0005-6103 Basic Journal Abstracts†
0005-6111 Basilicata
0005-6138 Basis **477**
0005-6146 Basis†
0005-6170 Basketball Weekly **8223**
0005-6189 Basler Predigten
0005-6197 Basse Normandie Automobile
0005-6219 Basteria **935**
0005-6227 Bat Research News **935**
0005-6278 Batiment†
0005-6308 Baatnytt **8272**
0005-6332 Battaglia Letteraria
0005-6340 Battaglie Postelegrafoniche
0005-6359 The Battery Man **8569**
0005-6367 Batting the Breeze
0005-6375 Battleacts†
0005-6383 Bau†
0005-643X Bau und Baustoff **979**
0005-6448 Baustoffmarkt **981**
0005-6456 Bauindustrie
0005-6480 Baubeschlag Magazin **1053**
0005-6499 Bingo **3789**
0005-6545 Bauen mit Holz **1049**
0005-6553 Bauen und Siedeln **4404**
0005-6561 Der Bauer **94**
0005-657X Bauern und Gaertner†
0005-6596 Bauforum
0005-6618 Das Baugeruest **7624**
0005-6626 Baugeschaeft und Bauunternehmer **979**
0005-6634 Baugewerbe **3260**
0005-6650 Bauingenieur **980**
0005-6677 Baum Bugle **5260**
0005-6707 Baumaschinen und Baugeraette Revue†
0005-6715 Baumaschinen- und Baugeraete-Handel **980**
0005-674X Baumeister **435**
0005-6758 Bauplanung - Bautechnik†
0005-6804 Baustoff- und Baubedarfsgrosshandel **981**
0005-6855 Bauwelt **435**
0005-6863 Bauwirtschaft. Ausgabe B†
0005-6952 Bayavaya Uskalos†
0005-6987 Bayer-Mitteilungen fuer die Gummi-Industrie†
0005-6995 Bayerische Akademie der Wissenschaften. Mathematisch-Naturwissenschaftliche Klasse. Abhandlungen **7839**
0005-7002 Bayerische Beamtenzeitung†
0005-7010 Bayerische Blaetter fuer Stenographie **1849**
0005-7029 Bayerische Boerse in Muenchen. Amtliches Kursblatt **1612**
0005-7045 Bayerische Gemeindezeitung **3844**
0005-7053 Bayerische Kleingaertner†
0005-7061 Das Bayerische Kraftfahrzeughandwerk†
0005-707X Der Bayerische Krippenfreund **7624**
0005-7088 Der Metzgermeister **3656**
0005-710X Bayerische Akademie der Wissenschaften. Philosophisch-Historische Klasse. Abhandlungen, N.F. **4444**
0005-7118 Bayerischer Landesverein fuer Familienkunde. Blaetter **3760**
0005-7126 Bayerisches Aerzteblatt **5583**
0005-7142 Bayerisches Justizministerialblatt **4628**
0005-7169 Bayerisches Landwirtschaftliches Wochenblatt **95**
0005-7231 Bayernturner **8161**
0005-7258 Baylor Dental Journal **5836**
0005-7266 Baylor Geological Studies Bulletin **2726**
0005-7274 Baylor Law Review **4628**
0005-7312 De Bazuin *changed to* 1571-4004 **7693**
0005-7339 The Beacon (New York, 1922) **6907**
0005-7347 The Beacon **5098**
0005-7363 Beaconette **5098**
0005-7371 Be'ad Ve- Neged†
0005-738X Beaken **5098**
0005-7398 Beam
0005-7428 Bearing Engineer†
0005-7436 Beato Angelo
0005-7460 Beautiful British Columbia *changed to* 1709-4623 **8688**
0005-7487 Beauty Fashion **592**

ISSN

0005-7495	Beauty Tips†	
0005-7517	The Beaver 4285	
0005-7525	Beaver 2274	
0005-7533	Bebidas 598	
0005-755X	Beckman Report 4486	
0005-7576	Bedford Stuyvesant Youth in Action Monthly Newsletter	
0005-7584	Bedford Transport†	
0005-7592	Bedfordshire Magazine†	
0005-7614	Bedrijf en Techniek†	
0005-7630	Bedrijfsjournalist†	
0005-7673	Bedsitter†	
0005-769X	Beduin 5261	
0005-7703	Bee Craft 95	
0005-772X	Bee World changed to 1751-2891 127	
0005-7738	Beef 280	
0005-7754	Beekeeping 95	
0005-7789	Beet†	
0005-7800	Begegnung (Berlin)†	
0005-7819	Begegnung mit Polen†	
0005-786X	Behavioral Research in Highway Safety†	
0005-7894	Behavior Therapy 7339	
0005-7916	Journal of Behavior Therapy and Experimental Psychiatry 6149	
0005-7932	Behavioral Neuropsychiatry†	
0005-7959	Behaviour 935	
0005-7967	Behaviour Research and Therapy 7340	
0005-7983	Behind the Headlines 7223	
0005-8009	Bei Uns	
0005-8041	Beitraege zur Biologie der Pflanzen†	
0005-805X	Beitraege zur Entomologie 840	
0005-8076	Beitraege zur Geschichte der Deutschen Sprache und Literatur 5099	
0005-8084	Beitraege zur Linguistic und Informationsverarbeitung†	
0005-8092	Literaturkunde. Beitraege†	
0005-8106	Beitraege zur Musikwissenschaft†	
0005-8114	Beitraege zur Namenforschung 5099	
0005-8149	Beitraege zur Orthopaedie und Traumatologie†	
0005-8157	Beitraege Paedagogischer Arbeit 6907	
0005-8181	Romanische Philologie. Beitraege†	
0005-8254	Bekhan Wa Bedan	
0005-8297	Beku Nyusu	
0005-8300	Bela Abela	
0005-8327	Belaruskaya Carkva†	
0005-8335	Maandblad Belasting Beschouwingen 1934	
0005-8343	Financieel Economisch Weekblad Beleggers Belangen 1346	
0005-8351	Belfagor 5208	
0005-8386	Het Beste uit Reader's Digest (Dutch Edition) 3801	
0005-8416	Belgique Hoteliere†	
0005-8459	Belgische Duivensport	
0005-8467	Belgische Fruitrevue†	
0005-8483	Belgische Tuinbouw	
0005-853X	Belgium. Ministere des Finances. Administration des Contributions. Bulletin des Contributions 1912	
0005-8572	Bell Ringer	
0005-8610	Bellamy - Nieuws	
0005-8629	Belleza y Moda†	
0005-8637	Bellezza	
0005-8645	Bellona†	
0005-8661	Beloit Poetry Journal 5417	
0005-867X	Belora†	
0005-8696	Benavides	
0005-8726	Benedictines 7785	
0005-8734	Benedictijns Tijdschrift 7785	
0005-8742	Benediktusbote	
0005-8750	U.S. Unemployment Insurance Service. Benefit Series Service, Unemployment Insurance†	
0005-8777	Benelux Publikatieblad 7423	
0005-8785	Benfica 8161	
0005-8793	Bengal Medical Journal†	
0005-8807	Bengal: Past and Present 4180	
0005-8815	Bengali Literature	
0005-884X	Bent of Tau Beta Pi 3183	
0005-8866	Beratende Ingenieure 3183	
0005-8874	Berea Alumnus 2274	
0005-8890	The Berean Searchlight 7624	
0005-8912	B H M 6458	
0005-8920	Bergbauwissenschaften und Verfahrenstechnik†	
0005-8947	Das Bergmann-Echo 6964	
0005-8955	Bergomum†	
0005-8971	Bergverks-Nytt 6458	
0005-9013	Berichte Biochemie und Biologie†	
0005-9048	Berichte Physiologie, Physiologische Chemie und Pharmakologie†	
0005-9080	Berichte ueber Landwirtschaft 95	
0005-9099	Berichte zur Deutschen Landeskunde 4000	
0005-9102	Berichte zur Raumforschung und Raumplanung	
0005-9110	Berichten van de Afdeling Volkskredietwezen†	
0005-9145	Berita Selulosa 3684	
0005-9153	Berita Shell 6764	
0005-9161	Berkeley Barb†	
0005-9188	Berkeley Tribe†	
0005-920X	Berkshire Review†	
0005-9226	Berlin	
0005-9250	Berlin Programm 8686	
0005-9269	Berliner Baer†	
0005-9307	Berliner Liberale Zeitung†	
0005-9323	Berliner Sozialversicherungs Beamte und Angestellte†	
0005-934X	Berliner Studentenzeitung†	
0005-9358	Berliner Turnzeitung	
0005-9366	Berliner und Muenchener Tieraerztliche Wochenschrift 8794	
0005-9382	The Bermudian 3802	
0005-9404	Berner Briefmarken-Zeitung 6892	
0005-9420	Berner Zeitschrift fuer Geschichte und Heimatkunde 4204	
0005-9455	Bertelsmann Briefe† 8935	
0005-9471	Beruf und Gesinnung 2830	
0005-951X	Die Berufsbildende Schule 2939	
0005-9528	Berufsbildende Schule Oesterreichs†	
0005-9536	Berufsbildung 2830	
0005-9560	Berufstaetige Frau Oesterreichs†	

0005-9579	Besco News†	
0005-9587	Besier's Hauswirtschaftliche†	
0005-9609	Besseres Obst 3724	
0005-9617	Best in Documents†	
0005-9625	Best Sellers†	
0005-9641	Best Songs†	
0005-965X	Best Wishes 2145	
0005-9676	Das Beste aus Reader's Digest (Swiss-German Edition) 3957	
0005-9684	Det Beste Fra Reader's Digest (Norwegian Edition) 3921	
0005-9749	Bet ha-Talmud†	
0005-9773	Betar Jagat 2357	
0005-9781	Betelgeuse†	
0005-979X	Beit-Miqra 7719	
0005-9803	Bethany Guide†	
0005-9811	Bethany Nazarene College Today†	
0005-982X	Bethel College Bulletin changed to Context (North Newton) 2279	
0005-9838	Bethlehem Express†	
0005-9846	Beton 981	
0005-9854	Beton Arme	
0005-9889	Beton i Zhelezobeton 982	
0005-9900	Beton- und Stahlbetonbau 982	
0005-9935	Der Betrieb 4858	
0005-9943	Betrieb und Absatz†	
0005-9951	Betriebliche Altersversorgung 4496	
0006-0062	Better Business†	
0006-0070	Better Camping†	
0006-0089	Better Crops with Plant Food 221	
0006-0100	Better Driving†	
0006-0119	Better Editing†	
0006-0127	Better Education	
0006-0151	Better Homes and Gardens 4533	
0006-016X	Better Investing 1612	
0006-0178	Better Letters	
0006-0194	Better Radio and Television 2357	
0006-0208	Better Roads 3260	
0006-0216	Better Supervision†	
0006-0224	Better Times†	
0006-0232	Better Tomorrows†	
0006-0313	Beursbengel 4496	
0006-033X	Bevar†	
0006-0348	Beverage Alcohol Reporter†	
0006-0356	Beverage Bulletin	
0006-0372	Beverage Media 599	
0006-0399	Beverages†	
0006-0429	Bewusster Leben 6983	
0006-0453	Bezpecnost a Hygiena Prace 6674	
0006-0461	Bhagirath 8818	
0006-047X	Bharat Medical Journal†	
0006-0488	Bharat Sevak†	
0006-0496	Bharatha Darshana 6907	
0006-050X	Bharati Te Videshi Sahita 5262	
0006-0518	Bhavan's Journal 5262	
0006-0526	Bhopal Regional College of Education. Journal†	
0006-0534	Bhubaneswar Review	
0006-0542	Bhushan's World Trade Enquiries 1553	
0006-0569	Biafra Time†	
0006-0585	Bibbia e Oriente 7625	
0006-0593	Bibel Heute 7785	
0006-0607	Bibel-Journalen†	
0006-0615	Bibel und Gemeinde 7748	
0006-0623	Bibel und Kirche 7785	
0006-064X	Bibel und Liturgie 7625	
0006-0690	Bible Collector†	
0006-0720	Bible et Vie Chretienne†	
0006-0739	Bible Friend 7625	
0006-0763	Bible Lands 7748	
0006-078X	Bible Searchers†	
0006-0798	Bible Searchers. Teacher†	
0006-0801	American Bible Society Record 7621	
0006-081X	Bible Standard and Herald of Christ's Kingdom changed to 1556-8555 7625	
0006-0828	Bible-Time	
0006-0836	The Bible Today 7627	
0006-0860	Biblia 5057	
0006-0879	Biblia Revuo†	
0006-0887	Biblica 7786	
0006-0909	Biblical Missions 7748	
0006-0917	Biblical Theology 7627	
0006-0925	Biblical Viewpoint†	
0006-0941	La Bibliofilia 7553	
0006-0968	Bibliografia Argentina de Artes y Letras†	
0006-0992	Bibliografia Classificada	
0006-1018	Bibliografia Elettrotecnica†	
0006-1034	Bibliografia Internazionale di Scienze ed Arti†	
0006-1042	Bibliografia Italiana di Idraulica†	
0006-1050	Bibliografia Medica Internacional†	
0006-1069	Bibliografia Mexicana 617	
0006-1093	Bibliografia Zawartosci Czasopism 617	
0006-1107	Statni Knihovna C S R. Bibliograficky Casopis†	
0006-1166	Bibliografija Prispelih Knjiga Clanaka iz Strucnih Casopisa i Drugih Dokumenata†	
0006-1174	Bibliograma†	
0006-1190	Bibliographia Africana 618	
0006-1212	Bibliographia Asiatica 564	
0006-1239	Bibliographia Geodaetica†	
0006-1247	Bibliographia Neuroendocrinologica†	
0006-1255	Bibliographic Index 618	
0006-1271	Bibliographical Bulletin for Welding and Allied Processes†	
0006-128X	Bibliographical Society of America. Papers 7553	
0006-1298	Bibliographie Africaine†	
0006-1301	Bibliographie Agricole Courante Roumaine†	
0006-1328	Centre Technique du Cuir. Bibliographie Analytique et Signaletique†	
0006-1336	Bibliographie de Belgique 618	
0006-1352	Bibliographie de la Philosophie 6962	
0006-1379	Bibliographie der Kunstblaetter†	
0006-1387	Bibliographie der Pflanzenschutzliteratur†	
0006-1417	Bibliographie der Wirtschaftspresse 1215	

0006-1433	Bibliographie, Documentation, Terminologie†	
0006-1441	Bibliographie du Quebec 618	
0006-1468	Bibliographie Staat und Recht der Deutschen Demokratischen Republik (Vierteljahresbibliographie)†	
0006-1476	World Bibliography of Social Security†	
0006-1484	Bibliographies of Atomic Energy Literature†	
0006-1506	Bibliographische Berichte†	
0006-1514	Bibliographische Zeitschrift fuer Aesthetik†	
0006-1530	Bibliography of Agriculture†	
0006-1573	Bibliography of Systematic Mycology 713	
0006-1581	Shu Mo Chi Kan 5059	
0006-159X	Biblion†	
0006-1611	Biblioteca (Buenos Aires, 1968)	
0006-162X	Biblioteca Americana de Autores. Boletin†	
0006-1646	Biblioteca de Menendez Pelayo. Boletin 5262	
0006-1654	Biblioteca della Liberta 7109	
0006-1662	Biblioteca do Sejur. Boletim 4821	
0006-1697	Biblioteca "Jose Artigas". Boletin - Junta de Vecinos 619	
0006-1700	Biblioteca Labronica Notiziario†	
0006-1719	Universidad Nacional Autonoma de Mexico. Instituto de Investigaciones Bibliograficas. Boletin 638	
0006-1727	Biblioteca Nacional Jose Marti. Revista 4445	
0006-176X	Bibliotecas 4995	
0006-1816	Bibliotekar 4995	
0006-1832	Bibliotekarstvo 4995	
0006-1840	Biblioteket Presenterar Nya Boecker†	
0006-1859	Biblioteki Z.N.E.P.A.N. Biuletyn Informacyjny†	
0006-1867	BBL: Biblioteksbladet changed to 1651-5447 4995	
0006-1913	Bibliotheca Orientalis 4169	
0006-1921	Bibliotheca Sacra 7748	
0006-193X	The Bibliotheck 619	
0006-1964	Der Bibliothekar†	
0006-1972	Bibliotheksdienst 4996	
0006-1999	Bibliotheque d'Humanisme et Renaissance 4205	
0006-2006	Bibliotheques de France. Bulletin 4997	
0006-2014	Biblische Zeitschrift 7628	
0006-2022	Biblos 4997	
0006-2057	Bichitra†	
0006-2073	Bicycling 8254	
0006-2081	Biddend Nazareth	
0006-209X	Bielarus 3522	
0006-212X	Die Biene 96	
0006-2146	Bienenvater 96	
0006-2154	Bienenwelt 96	
0006-2219	Bihar Industries 1957	
0006-2235	Bijbellessen voor de Kinderen†	
0006-2243	Bijbellessen voor de Sabbatschool	
0006-2251	Bijblad bij de Industriele Eigendom changed to Bijblad 6746	
0006-2278	Bijdragen 6907	
0006-2286	Bijdragen tot de Geschiedenis 4133	
0006-2294	Bijdragen tot de Taal-, Land- en Volkenkunde 330	
0006-2308	Bijeen†	
0006-2316	Bijou Magazine†	
0006-2324	Biken Journal†	
0006-2340	Bilanz	
0006-2367	Bilbransjen - Bilteknisk Fagblad 8569	
0006-2375	Bild der Wissenschaft 7841	
0006-2383	Bild und Ton†	
0006-2405	Bildermaerchen†	
0006-2413	Bildlexikon der Nutzhoelzer	
0006-2456	Bildung und Erziehung 2831	
0006-2499	The Bill of Rights Journal†	
0006-2510	Billboard (New York) 6549	
0006-2529	Bille-Anzeigen-Rundschau	
0006-2537	Billedbladet 3833	
0006-2545	Billiards & Snooker†	
0006-2553	Billiken 2179	
0006-2596	Bilten Dokumentacije. Goriva i Maziva†	
0006-2626	Bilten Dokumentacije. Industrija Tekstila i Papira†	
0006-2642	Bilten Dokumentacije. Metalurgija†	
0006-2715	Bilten Dokumentacije. Sumarstvo i Drvna Industrija†	
0006-2731	Bilten Pravne Sluzbe J N A 4630	
0006-2758	Zavod za Osnovno Obrazovanje i Obrazovanje Nastavnika Sr Srbije. Bilten†	
0006-2766	Bim	
0006-2774	Iranian Journal of Plant Pathology 795	
0006-2790	Bimestre†	
0006-2804	Binario 435	
0006-2812	Binden en Bouwen	
0006-2863	BioDynamics 221	
0006-2871	Bio-Graphic Quarterly†	
0006-2901	Bioastronautics Report†	
0006-291X	Biochemical and Biophysical Research Communications 724	
0006-2928	Biochemical Genetics 863	
0006-2952	Biochemical Pharmacology 6825	
0006-2960	Biochemistry 725	
0006-2979	Biochemistry (Moscow) 725	
0006-3002	Biochimica et Biophysica Acta 726	
0006-3029	Biofizika 752	
0006-3045	Biograf-Bladet†	
0006-3053	Biography Index 648	
0006-3088	Biologia 657	
0006-3096	Biologia 657	
0006-310X	Biologia Culturale†	
0006-3118	Biologia Gabonica†	
0006-3126	Biology of the Neonate changed to 1661-7800 5999	
0006-3134	Biologia Plantarum 779	
0006-3150	Biologica Latina†	
0006-3169	Biological Abstracts 713	
0006-3177	Biological & Agricultural Index 713	
0006-3185	Biological Bulletin 658	
0006-3193	Shengwuxue Tongbao 704	
0006-3207	Biological Conservation 2604	
0006-3223	Biological Psychiatry 6126	
0006-324X	Biological Society of Washington. Proceedings 659	
0006-3266	Biologie Medicale†	
0006-3282	Biologische Abhandlungen†	
0006-3290	Biologische Rundschau†	
0006-3339	Biologist††	

ISSN

0006-8667 Brackety - Ack **2275**
0006-8675 Bradfield College Chronicle **2275**
0006-8705 Bragantia **97**
0006-8721 Brahmavadin†
0006-873X Braille Book Review **4080**
0006-8756 Braille Chess Magazine **8163**
0006-8764 Braille Digest†
0006-8772 The Braille Forum **4080**
0006-8780 Braille Journal of Physiotherapy **4080**
0006-8810 Braille Mirror†
0006-8829 Braille Monitor **4080**
0006-8837 Braille Music Magazine **4080**
0006-8853 Braille News Summary†
0006-887X Braille Radio Times **4080**
0006-8896 Braille Science Journal **4080**
0006-890X Braille Sporting Record **4080**
0006-8918 Braille Star Theosophist **7733**
0006-8926 Braille Sunday School Quarterly†
0006-8942 Braille Variety News†
0006-8950 Brain **6127**
0006-8969 No To Shinkei/Brain and Nerve *changed to* 1881-6096 **6127**
0006-8977 Brain, Behavior and Evolution **6127**
0006-8985 Brain News†
0006-8993 Brain Research **6128**
0006-9000 Brainstorms†
0006-9035 BrandAus **3575**
0006-9043 Brandeis University Bulletin†
0006-906X Die Brandhilfe. Ausgabe Baden-Wuerttemberg **3575**
0006-9078 Branding Iron **4286**
0006-9094 Brandschutz **3575**
0006-9116 Brandwacht **3575**
0006-9124 Brandweer†
0006-9132 Brangus Journal **281**
0006-9140 Branicevo **5209**
0006-9159 Die Branntweinwirtschaft **600**
0006-9167 Brazil Acucareiro
0006-9191 Brasil Jovem†
0006-9205 Brasil-Medico†
0006-9248 Bratislavske Lekarske Listy **5588**
0006-9256 Bratrsky Vestnik **4496**
0006-937X Brazil. Conselho Nacional de Economia. Revista†
0006-9388 Brazil. Departamento de Agricultura. Boletim†
0006-9442 Brazil. Ministerio da Saude. Departamento Nacional de Endemias Rurais. Divisao de Cooperacao e Divulgacao. Boletim Bibliografico†
0006-9469 Pernambuco. Secretaria do Saneamento, Habitacao e Obras. Boletim Tecnico **7460**
0006-9477 Brazila Esperantisto
0006-9485 Brazilian Bulletin†
0006-9493 Brazilian Business†
0006-9515 Bread of Life†
0006-9523 Break-In **2357**
0006-9531 Breakthru
0006-954X Brecon and Radnor Farmer†
0006-9566 Bref Rhone - Alpes **1443**
0006-9574 Bremer Missionsschiff†
0006-9582 Bremer Schulblatt **3018**
0006-9604 Brennpunkt†
0006-9647 Bretagne Reelle **7110**
0006-9655 Brethren Journal **7628**
0006-9663 Brethren Life and Thought **7749**
0006-968X Breve, il Gruppo, la Cultura, l'Idee
0006-9698 Breviora **936**
0006-9701 Brewers Bulletin
0006-971X Brewers Digest **600**
0006-9728 Brewers' Guardian **600**
0006-9779 Brickbats & Bouquets†
0006-9787 Brides & Setting Up Home *changed to* 1475-6293 **5557**
0006-9817 Bridge†
0006-9825 Bridge **8163**
0006-985X Bridge d'Italia **8163**
0006-9892 Bridgeport News†
0006-9906 Bridge Tidningen **8163**
0006-9914 Le Bridgeur **8163**
0006-9949 Brief aus Wahlwies
0006-9965 Southern Methodist University School of Law. Brief **4786**
0006-9973 Briefe an den Chef†
0006-9981 Briefe an den Mitarbeiter†
0006-999X Briefe an den Mitmenschen†
0007-0017 Briefed†
0007-0025 Briefing Papers **4631**
0007-0033 Briefmarke **6892**
0007-0041 Briefmarken-Spiegel **6892**
0007-005X Briefmarken Post **6892**
0007-0068 Briefs†
0007-0076 Brieven Aan de Chef†
0007-0084 Brigade Leader
0007-0122 Brighton Head and Freak Magazine
0007-0157 Brightonian **2275**
0007-0173 Brio **4998**
0007-019X Bristol Medico-Chirurgical Journal†
0007-0203 Britannia†
0007-0238 British Amateur Journalist†
0007-0262 British Antarctic Survey. Bulletin†
0007-0289 British Archer†
0007-0297 British Astronomical Association. Journal **572**
0007-0300 British Baker **3672**
0007-0319 The British Bandsman **6551**
0007-0327 British Bee Journal **97**
0007-0335 British Birds **904**
0007-0343 British Book News†
0007-0416 British Chamber of Commerce of Turkey. Trade Journal† **8937**
0007-0432 British Chemist†
0007-0440 British Chess Magazine **8163**
0007-0459 British Citizen†
0007-0467 British Clothing Manufacturer†
0007-0475 B C U R A Monthly Bulletin†
0007-0483 B C Catholic **7785**
0007-0505 The British Columbia Gazette, Part I **4632**
0007-053X British Columbia Library Quarterly†
0007-0548 British Columbia Lumberman†
0007-0556 British Columbia Medical Journal **5588**
0007-0572 British Columbia Orchardist **3726**
0007-0580 British Columbia School Trustee†
0007-0602 British Deaf News *changed to* British Deaf News **4072**
0007-0610 British Dental Journal **5836**
0007-0637 British Education Index **2931**
0007-0661 British Engineer†
0007-067X La Brita Esperantisto **5101**
0007-070X British Food Journal **3628**
0007-0777 British Homing World **8163**
0007-0815 British Humanities Index **4484**
0007-0823 British Industry and Engineering†
0007-084X British Interplanetary Society Journal **50**
0007-0858 British Italian Trade Review
0007-0866 British Jeweller & Watch Buyer†
0007-0874 British Journal for the History of Science **7842**
0007-0882 The British Journal for the Philosophy of Science **7842**
0007-0904 British Journal of Aesthetics **6908**
0007-0912 British Journal of Anaesthesia **5770**
0007-0920 British Journal of Cancer **6010**
0007-0939 British Journal of Chiropody†
0007-0955 The British Journal of Criminology **2645**
0007-0963 British Journal of Dermatology **5872**
0007-0998 British Journal of Educational Psychology **7341**
0007-1005 British Journal of Educational Studies **2832**
0007-1013 British Journal of Educational Technology **3053**
0007-1048 British Journal of Haematology **5935**
0007-1080 British Journal of Industrial Relations **1668**
0007-1102 British Journal of Mathematical and Statistical Psychology **7342**
0007-1145 The British Journal of Nutrition **6656**
0007-1161 British Journal of Ophthalmology **6039**
0007-1188 British Journal of Pharmacology **6826**
0007-1196 British Journal of Photography **6965**
0007-1226 British Journal of Plastic Surgery (Print Edition) *changed to* 1748-6815 **6249**
0007-1234 British Journal of Political Science **7110**
0007-1250 British Journal of Psychiatry **6128**
0007-1269 British Journal of Psychology **7342**
0007-1285 British Journal of Radiology **6193**
0007-1307 British Journal of Social Psychiatry†
0007-1315 British Journal of Sociology **8091**
0007-1323 British Journal of Surgery **6238**
0007-1404 British Medical Abstracts†
0007-1420 British Medical Bulletin **5589**
0007-1455 British Medical Register of Holiday Accommodation†
0007-1463 British Mouthpiece **6552**
0007-1544 British National Bibliography **621**
0007-1595 British Ornithologists' Club. Bulletin **904**
0007-1609 British Patents Abstracts†
0007-1633 British Polio Fellowship. Bulletin **6129**
0007-1668 British Poultry Science **281**
0007-1676 British Practice in International Law†
0007-1714 British Railways Board. Monthly Review of Technical Literature†
0007-1722 British Record†
0007-1757 British Road Federation. Bulletin†
0007-1773 British Society for Phenomenology. Journal **6908**
0007-1803 British-Soviet Friendship
0007-1846 British Studies Monitor†
0007-1854 British Sugar Beet Review **223**
0007-1862 British Tax Guide†
0007-1870 British Tax Review **1913**
0007-1900 British Travel News†
0007-196X Brittonia **782**
0007-1986 Public Health†
0007-1994 Broadcast Engineering **2376**
0007-2001 Broadcast Journal†
0007-201X Broadcasters Bulletin
0007-2044 Broadsheet
0007-2052 China Policy Study Group. Broadsheet†
0007-2109 Broadside and the Free Press†
0007-2125 Broadside Series
0007-2133 Broadway†
0007-2141 Broderskap **7111**
0007-215X Brodogradnja **8640**
0007-2192 Bromides in Agriculture
0007-2206 Bromley Weekly Review
0007-2214 Bron†
0007-2249 Bronx County Historical Society Journal **4286**
0007-2273 Bronxboro†
0007-2281 Bronze
0007-2303 Brookings Papers on Economic Activity **1536**
0007-232X Brooklyn Barrister **4632**
0007-2346 Brooklyn Heights Press **3971**
0007-2362 Brooklyn Law Review **4632**
0007-2397 Brooklyn Public Library Bulletin†
0007-2451 Brothers Newsletter†
0007-2494 Brown Gold **7628**
0007-2516 Brown Swiss Bulletin **262**
0007-2524 Brownie **2146**
0007-2559 Browser†
0007-2583 Bruecke
0007-2605 Bruecke (Neustadt)†
0007-2613 Die Bruecke (Munich)†
0007-2621 Bruel & Kjaer Technical Review **7087**
0007-2648 Brug
0007-2656 Brug†
0007-2664 Bruehl
0007-2672 Brulot†
0007-2699 Brunswickan **2275**
0007-2710 Brushware **1053**
0007-2729 B. B. B. Agenda†
0007-2745 Bryologist **782**
0007-2753 B't
0007-2761 Buch der Zeit†
0007-277X Buch und Bildung
0007-2788 Druck und Verarbeitung†
0007-2796 Buchhaendler Heute **7556**
0007-280X Landesmuseum fuer Kaernten. Buchreihe **6527**
0007-2818 Buck Investment Letter†
0007-2834 Buckeye Farm News **98**
0007-2842 A D A C Motorwelt **8554**
0007-2869 Bucknell Review†
0007-2893 Budapester Rundschau†
0007-2907 Budavox Telecommunication Review†
0007-294X Budget
0007-3040 Buecherschau **4998**
0007-3059 Buecherschiff†
0007-3067 Der Buechsenmacher - Messer und Schere **4331**
0007-3075 Buehne **8467**
0007-3083 Buehnengenossenschaft **8467**
0007-3091 Buehnentechnische Rundschau **8467**
0007-3121 Der Buerger im Staat **7111**
0007-3148 Bueromarkt†
0007-3164 Burotechnische Praxis†
0007-3210 Bugantics
0007-3261 Builder (Columbus) **4496**
0007-330X Builders' Weekly Guide†
0007-3318 Building **435**
0007-3326 Building Abstracts Service C I B†
0007-3334 Building Alaska†
0007-3342 Building & Construction
0007-3350 Building & Contract Journal
0007-3377 Building & Heating Product Guide
0007-3393 Building & Realty Record†
0007-3407 Building Design + Construction **985**
0007-3415 Building Construction in Texas†
0007-3423 Building Design **436**
0007-3431 The Building Economist **985**
0007-3466 Building Forum
0007-3490 Building Operating Management **986**
0007-3504 Building Materials†
0007-3555 Building Permit Activity in Florida **7425**
0007-3563 Building Permit Values†
0007-3571 Building Practice†
0007-3598 Building Progress†
0007-3601 Building Research†
0007-361X Building Research News†
0007-3636 Building Science Abstracts†
0007-3717 Building Tradesman **4591**
0007-3725 Buildings **987**
0007-3733 Asian Regional Institute for School Building Research. Newsletter
0007-3741 Buitenlandse Boek
0007-375X Nieuwsbrief†
0007-3768 Buitenspoor **8307**
0007-3806 Buletin de Informare Stiintifica Biologie†
0007-3822 Buletin de Informare Stiintifica. Fizica†
0007-3830 Istorie-Arheologie†
0007-3849 Buletin de Informare Stiintifica. Matematica, Mecanica, Astronomie†
0007-3857 Psihologie; Buletin de Informare Stiintifica†
0007-3865 Sociologie; Buletin de Informare Stiintifica†
0007-3873 Stiinte Economice†
0007-3881 Stiinte Juridice†
0007-389X Vyzkumny Ustav Rybarsky a Hydrobiologicky. Bulletin†
0007-3938 Bulgarsko Geologichesko Druzhestvo. Spisanie **2727**
0007-3946 Bulgarian Review†
0007-3954 Bulgarian Trade Unions
0007-3989 Bulgarska Akademiia na Naukite. Spisanie **7842**
0007-4012 Bulgarsko Foto†
0007-4047 The Bulletin **3801**
0007-4055 Bulletin Agricole des Hautes Pyrenees **98**
0007-4063 Centre de Documentation Siderurgique. Bulletin Analytique†
0007-4071 Bulletin Analytique de Documentation Politique, Economique et Sociale Contemporaine†
0007-408X Bulletin Analytique de Linguistique Francaise **5101**
0007-4098 Bulletin Analytique d'Entomologie Medicale et Veterinaire†
0007-4101 Bulletin Analytique Petrolier†
0007-411X Bulletin Annote des Lois et Decrets **4633**
0007-4128 Bulletin Baudelairien **5266**
0007-4136 Bulletin Belge de Metrologie†
0007-4144 Bulletin Bi-Mensuel des Tirages†
0007-4160 Bulletin Bibliographique International du Machinisme Agricole†
0007-4187 Bulletin Biologique de la France et de la Belgique†
0007-4209 Bulletin Critique du Livre en Francais **7577**
0007-4217 Bulletin de Correspondance Hellenique **2231**
0007-4225 Belgium. Ministere des Communications. Bulletin de Documentation†
0007-4284 Bulletin de Geophysique†
0007-4292 Bulletin de la Librairie Ancienne et Moderne†
0007-4306 Belgium. L'Administration Penitentiaire. Bulletin
0007-4322 Bulletin de Litterature Ecclesiastique **7786**
0007-4330 Bulletin de l'Oeuvre Apostolique
0007-4357 Bulletin de Madagascar†
0007-4381 Bulletin de Paris
0007-4403 Bulletin de Psychologie **7342**
0007-4411 Bulletin de Psychologie Scolaire et d'Orientation
0007-4446 Le Bulletin des Agriculteurs **98**
0007-4489 Bulletin des Lettres†
0007-4497 Bulletin des Sciences Mathematiques **5476**
0007-4535 Bulletin d'Information des Centrales Electriques†
0007-4543 France. Commissariat a l'Energie Atomique. Bulletin d'Informations Scientifiques et Techniques.†
0007-4551 Bulletin du Cancer (Print) **6010**
0007-4594 E G U Bulletin†
0007-4624 Bulletin for International Fiscal Documentation *changed to* 1819-5490 **1913**
0007-4640 Bulletin Hispanique **4207**
0007-4705 Bulletin Medical Franco-Japonais
0007-4713 France. Institut National de la Statistique et des Etudes Economiques. Bulletin Mensuel de Statistique **8373**
0007-473X Bulletin Monumental **385**
0007-4756 Bulletin of Applied Linguistics†
0007-4764 American Journal of Art Therapy *changed to* 0742-1656 **6106**
0007-4799 Bulletin of Business Research†
0007-4802 Canadian Petroleum Geology. Bulletin **6765**

0007-4837 Bulletin of Dental Education **5837**
0007-4845 Bulletin of Endemic Diseases
0007-4853 Bulletin of Entomological Research **841**
0007-4861 Bulletin of Environmental Contamination and Toxicology **3494**
0007-4888 Bulletin of Experimental Biology and Medicine **663**
0007-4896 Bulletin of Grain Technology **98**
0007-4918 Bulletin of Indonesian Economic Studies **1443**
0007-4926 Bulletin of Information on Current Research on Human Sciences Concerning Africa
0007-4950 Bulletin of Labour Statistics **1215**
0007-4969 Bulletin of Legal Developments **4633**
0007-4977 Bulletin of Marine Science **2801**
0007-5000 Bulletin of Mechanical Engineering Education†
0007-5019 Bulletin of Paedagogical Research
0007-5027 Laboratory Medicine **5908**
0007-5043 Bulletin of Physical Education **3053**
0007-5108 Bulletin of the Comediantes **5267**
0007-5140 Bulletin of the History of Medicine **5589**
0007-5167 Bulletin of Zoological Nomenclature **937**
0007-5191 Sport en Roumanie†
0007-523X United Nations. Bulletin on Narcotics **2700**
0007-5248 Bulletin on the Rheumatic Diseases†
0007-5256 Bulletin Ornithologique **904**
0007-5272 Bulletin Quotidien d'Informations Textiles†
0007-5280 Institut Royal Meteorologique de Belgique. Bulletin Quotidien du Temps **6357**
0007-5302 Bulletin Signaletique des Telecommunications†
0007-5736 Bulletin Technique *see* Fachhefte Bulletin Technique **7320**
0007-5752 Bureau Veritas. Bulletin Technique†
0007-5779 Bulletins of American Paleontology **6723**
0007-5787 Bullettino delle Scienze Mediche **5589**
0007-5795 Bullettino Storico Empolese **4207**
0007-5809 Bullettino Storico Pistoiese **4207**
0007-5817 Bumazhnaya Promyshlennost'†
0007-5868 Bundesarbeitsblatt **1668**
0007-5884 Bundesbaublatt **4405**
0007-5949 Die Bundeswehr **6414**
0007-5957 Bundeswehrverwaltung **4634**
0007-5965 Das Bunte Blatt†
0007-6007 The Bur†
0007-6015 Burbujas **4080**
0007-6023 Burda Bunte Bild Rezepte†
0007-604X Le Bureau†
0007-6066 Bureau Briefs (Trenton, NJ)†
0007-6155 Philippines. Bureau of Agricultural Economics. Bureau of Agricultural Economics Reporter†
0007-6163 Bureau of Government Research Bulletin†
0007-6201 Burgen und Schloesser **4207**
0007-621X Burgenlaendische Forschungen **4207**
0007-6228 Burgenlaendische Gemeinschaft **3797**
0007-6244 Burgenlaendische Landwirtschaftskammer. Mitteilungsblatt **98**
0007-6252 Burgenlaendisches Leben
0007-6260 Buried History **385**
0007-6279 Burlington County Times Advertiser†
0007-6287 Burlington Magazine **480**
0007-6295 Burma Medical Journal†
0007-6309 The Burning Bush **7629**
0007-6333 Burroughs Bulletin **5440**
0007-6341 Burroughs Clearing House†
0007-6376 Busara
0007-6392 Buses **8492**
0007-6406 Business Abroad†
0007-6422 Business Advertising†
0007-6457 Business and Economic Dimensions†
0007-6465 Business & Economic Review **1070**
0007-6473 Business and Finance **1322**
0007-6481 Business and Financial Indicators†
0007-6503 Business & Society **1070**
0007-652X Business and Technology Sources†
0007-6538 Business Archives **1071**
0007-6554 Northern Trust Business Comment **1372**
0007-6562 Business Comments†
0007-6600 Business Conditions in Argentina†
0007-6627 Business Credit and Hire Purchase Journal
0007-6643 Zrak'or
0007-666X Business Economics **1071**
0007-6678 Business Education Forum **1071**
0007-6686 Business Education Journal†
0007-6694 Business Education World†
0007-6708 Business Equipment Digest **1850**
0007-6716 Business Equipment Guide†
0007-6724 Business Europe **1444**
0007-6732 Business Systems & Equipment†
0007-6740 U B S Business Facts and Figures†
0007-6775 Business Graphics†
0007-6783 Business Herald **1730**
0007-6791 Business History **1072**
0007-6805 Business History Review **1072**
0007-6813 Business Horizons **1072**
0007-683X Business in Nebraska **1444**
0007-6856 Business Inquiry†
0007-6864 Business Insurance **4496**
0007-6872 Business International†
0007-6880 Business Latin America **1444**
0007-6899 The Business Lawyer **4859**
0007-6937 Business Management†
0007-6945 Business Memo from Belgium **1397**
0007-6953 Business Opportunities Digest
0007-6961 Business Periodicals Index **1216**
0007-7011 Federal Reserve Bank of Philadelphia. Business Review **1486**
0007-7038 Business Review and Economic News from Israel†
0007-7062 Business Service Checklist†
0007-7097 Business Systems & Equipment†
0007-7100 Business Today (Princeton) **2275**
0007-7127 Business Trends in New York State†
0007-7135 BusinessWeek **1077**
0007-7151 Businessman
0007-7216 Bustan†
0007-7232 Busy Bees' News†
0007-7240 Butane Propane†
0007-7259 Butane - Propane News **6764**
0007-7275 Butter-Fat†
0007-7291 Butterfly†
0007-7313 Butterley Foundry News†
0007-733X Buttons†
0007-7364 Buxom Belle Courier†
0007-7372 Buyer†
0007-7380 Buyers' Guide† **8938**
0007-7402 Buyers Purchasing Digest
0007-7429 Byarozka **2181**
0007-7437 Byelorussian-American Union. Bulletin†
0007-7445 Bygd†
0007-747X Bygge Fagene†
0007-7488 Bygge Nyt†
0007-750X Byggeindustrien **988**
0007-7518 Byggekunst *changed to* 1504-7628 **433**
0007-7542 Bygglitteratur†
0007-7550 Byggmaestaren†
0007-7569 Byggnadsarbetaren **1049**
0007-7607 Byggnadstidningen†
0007-7615 Byggnadsvaerlden†
0007-7623 Bygmesteren†
0007-7631 Byminner **4208**
0007-764X Byoin Setsubi **4089**
0007-7658 Byplan **4405**
0007-7690 Byulleten' Stroitel'noi Tekhniki **988**
0007-7704 Byzantinische Zeitschrift **545**
0007-7712 Byzantinoslavica **545**
0007-7720 Canadian Review of American Studies **4287**
0007-7739 C A E News†
0007-778X Cal†
0007-7798 Calf News *changed to* Calf News **318**
0007-7801 C A M†
0007-7836 C A R D A N. Fiches Analytiques†
0007-7844 Council for the Advancement of Small Colleges. Newsletter†
0007-7852 C. A. S. I. Transactions†
0007-7860 C A T C A Journal†
0007-7925 Select†
0007-7941 C B M News **3296**
0007-795X C B Magazine†
0007-7968 C.B.R.I. Abstracts†
0007-7984 C C B Outlook (Large Print Edition)†
0007-7992 Accounting Articles **1199**
0007-800X C C I T U Labour Bulletin†
0007-8050 C E A Advisor **2833**
0007-8069 C E A Critic **5267**
0007-8093 C E A P Bulletin†
0007-8131 C E C Update†
0007-814X C E D A G Informativo†
0007-8158 C E D A M Notiziario Bibliografico†
0007-8166 C. E. D. Contact†
0007-8174 C. E. D. Dokumentoj†
0007-8204 English Education **3060**
0007-828X C E N T O Newsletter†
0007-8301 C E R I L H Bulletin Analytique†
0007-8328 C E R N Reports **7065**
0007-8336 C E S I N News
0007-8352 C G D Betriebstraete-Mitteilungen
0007-8425 Central Institute of Education. Newsletter
0007-845X C I M Notes **6552**
0007-8468 C. I. M. Notiziario
0007-8506 C I R P Annals **3375**
0007-8514 C I S Index to Publications of the United States Congress **7479**
0007-8530 Catholic Knights of America Journal **2265**
0007-8549 C L A Journal **5102**
0007-8565 Cumann Leabharlannaithe Scoile. C L S Bulletin†
0007-8581 C. M. A. A. Newsletter†
0007-8603 C M A S Bulletin d'Information **2801**
0007-8611 C M B Newsletter **1809**
0007-862X C M D†
0007-8670 C M R†
0007-8700 C. N. A. P. T. Bulletin†
0007-8794 C O N E S C A L†
0007-8808 C O P H Bulletin†
0007-8816 C O P N I P List†
0007-8859 C O T A L **8690**
0007-8875 C. P. C. Monthly Report†
0007-8883 C P C U News **4497**
0007-8891 C P E C Taxpayers News†
0007-8921 C P S Reporter†
0007-8948 C Q Elettronica & Computer
0007-8964 C Q Ham Radio **2357**
0007-8972 Foodservice and Hospitality **4386**
0007-9057 C R V Newsletter†
0007-9065 C S A Quarterly Review†
0007-9073 C S C Newsletter **7749**
0007-9111 C S I R Library Information & Accessions†
0007-9154 C S I R Recorder†
0007-9219 C T V D: Cinema - T V - Digest†
0007-9227 C W A News (Washington) **4591**
0007-9235 C A **6010**
0007-9243 Ca Va **5103**
0007-926X Cabellian†
0007-9294 Cablecasting-Cable TV Engineering†
0007-9316 Cabore
0007-9332 Cacaos, Cafes, Sucres†
0007-9340 Cacau Atualidades†
0007-9359 Cacciatore Siciliano
0007-9367 Cactus and Succulent Journal **782**
0007-9391 Cad†
0007-9405 Cadenza **6553**
0007-9421 Cadernos de Biblioteconomia, Arquivistica e Documentacao **4999**
0007-943X Cadernos de Jornalismo e Comunicacao†
0007-9456 Cadet Journal and Gazette
0007-9464 Les Dossiers CADRECO†
0007-9480 Caducee†
0007-9502 Caesaraugusta **385**
0007-9553 Caffe†
0007-9561 Cage & Aviary Birds **904**
0007-957X Civilisation Libertaire†
0007-9588 African Administrative Studies **7419**
0007-9596 Cahiers Astrologiques
0007-9618 Cahiers Bourbonnais **5268**
0007-9626 Cahiers Bruxellois **4208**
0007-9650 Cahiers d'Action Litteraire†
0007-9685 Cahiers d'Anesthesiologie†
0007-9693 Cahiers d'Archeologie et d'Histoire du Berry
0007-9715 Cahiers de Bibliographie Therapeutique Francaise. Edition Medicale†
0007-9723 Cahiers de Biologie Marine **664**
0007-9731 Cahiers de Civilisation Medievale **4133**
0007-974X Les Cahiers de Droit **4636**
0007-9758 Cahiers de Droit Europeen **4919**
0007-9766 Cahiers de Geographie du Quebec **4001**
0007-9790 Cahiers de la Ceramique, du Verre et des Arts du Feu *changed to* 1169-2537 **539**
0007-9804 Association Belge de Documentation. Cahiers de la Documentation **4992**
0007-9820 Cahiers de la Puericultrice **2146**
0007-9839 Les Cahiers de la Reconciliation **7112**
0007-9847 Cahiers de la Renaissance Vaudoise **5268**
0007-9863 Cahiers de l'Enfance Inadaptee†
0007-9871 Cahiers de Lexicologie **5103**
0007-988X Cahiers de Linguistique Theorique et Appliquee **5103**
0007-9898 Cahiers de l'Iroise **4208**
0007-9901 Cahiers de l'Optique de Contact†
0007-991X Cahiers de l'Oronte
0007-9936 Cahiers de Medecine Interprofessionnelle (Print) *changed to* Cahiers de Medecine Interprofessionnelle (Online) **5591**
0007-9944 Cahiers de Medecine Veterinaire
0007-9952 Cahiers de Notes Documentaires **6675**
0007-9960 Cahiers de Nutrition et de Dietetique **6656**
0007-9979 Cahiers de Reeducation & de Readaptation Fonctionnelles†
0007-9995 Cahiers de Sociologie et de Demographie Medicales **7278**
0008-0012 Cahiers de Tunisie **4446**
0008-0039 Cahiers des Naturalistes **7843**
0008-0047 Cahiers des Religions Africaines **7787**
0008-0055 Cahiers d'Etudes Africaines **332**
0008-0063 Cahiers d'Etudes Cathares **7629**
0008-008X Cahiers d'Histoire (Lyon) **4134**
0008-0101 Cahiers du Chemin†
0008-011X Les Cahiers du Cinema **6491**
0008-0128 Club de la Grammaire. Cahiers†
0008-0136 Cahiers du Communisme†
0008-0144 Cahiers du Medecin Specialiste
0008-0195 Cahiers Economiques de Bruxelles **1536**
0008-0209 Cahiers Economiques et Sociaux **1078**
0008-0217 Cahiers Francais **3840**
0008-0225 Cahiers Franco-Anglais
0008-0241 Cahiers Geologiques† **8939**
0008-025X Cahiers Haut-Marnais **4134**
0008-0268 Cahiers Integres de Medecine†
0008-0276 Cahiers Internationaux de Sociologie **8092**
0008-0284 Cahiers Internationaux de Symbolisme **6909**
0008-0306 Cahiers Jean Tousseul†
0008-0314 Cahiers Laennec†
0008-0322 Cahiers Libres de Leon Emery†
0008-0330 Cahiers Lyonnais d'Histoire de la Medecine†
0008-0365 Les Cahiers Naturalistes **5269**
0008-0373 Cahiers Numismatiques **6649**
0008-0411 Cahiers Oceanographiques†
0008-042X Cahiers Pedagogiques **2834**
0008-0438 Cahiers Pierre Loti†
0008-0446 Cahiers pour l'Analyse†
0008-0454 Cahiers Raciniens†
0008-0462 Cahiers Rationalistes **7843**
0008-0470 Cahiers Renaud Barrault†
0008-0519 Caiet de Documentare Cinematografica†
0008-0527 Caiet pentru Literatura si Istoriografie
0008-0535 Cake and Cockhorse **4208**
0008-0551 Calabria Letteraria† **8939**
0008-056X Calabria Nobilissima
0008-0616 Calcoin News†
0008-0624 Calcolo **5477**
0008-0632 Calculi†
0008-0659 Calcutta Mathematical Society. Bulletin **5477**
0008-0667 Calcutta Medical Journal†
0008-0675 Calcutta Municipal Gazette **7489**
0008-0683 Calcutta Statistical Association. Bulletin **8359**
0008-0705 University of Calcutta. University College of Medicine. Bulletin†
0008-073X Calendar of Coming Meetings of Interest to Historians†
0008-0772 Calendar of Sports Events†
0008-0845 California Agriculture **99**
0008-0853 California Agriculture Department Biennial Report†
0008-0861 California Air Environment†
0008-087X California Air Quality Data **3484**
0008-0896 California Apparel News **2246**
0008-0926 California Business *changed to* 1079-3445
0008-0942 California Cattleman **282**
0008-0950 California Courier **3524**
0008-0985 California Dental Association. Newsletter†
0008-1000 California. Division of Mines and Geology. Bulletin†
0008-1019 California Elementary Administrator†
0008-1027 California Engineer **3184**
0008-1051 California Farmer **99**
0008-106X Western Financial Journal†
0008-1078 California Fish and Game **937**
0008-1094 California Forestry and Forest Products **3710**
0008-1108 California Future Farmer†
0008-1116 California Garden **3726**
0008-1124 California Grange News **99**
0008-1140 California Highway Patrolman†
0008-1191 California Industrial Relations Reports†
0008-1205 California Journal†
0008-1221 California Law Review **4636**

ISSN

0008-7017 Carte Blanche†
0008-7033 Carthusian **2276**
0008-7041 The Cartographic Journal **4037**
0008-7068 Cartoonist Profiles **481**
0008-7076 Cartophilic Notes & News **4331**
0008-7092 Carwash Journal†
0008-7114 Caryologia **828**
0008-7122 Casa
0008-7149 Casa de la Cultura Ecuatoriana. Revista†
0008-7157 Casa de las Americas **5271**
0008-7165 Casa do Douro Boletim†
0008-7173 Casa Vogue†
0008-7181 Casabella **436**
0008-719X La Casana **3896**
0008-7203 Casas y Jardines
0008-7211 Cascade Caver†
0008-722X Cascades†
0008-7238 Case and Comment Magazine (Rochester)†
0008-7246 Case & Counsel†
0008-7254 Case Western Reserve Journal of International Law **4920**
0008-7262 Case Western Reserve Law Review **4641**
0008-7289 Cash Box†
0008-7297 Ontario Corn Producer **244**
0008-7300 Cashew Bulletin **3630**
0008-7319 Cashier
0008-7327 C & S†
0008-7335 Casopis Lekaru Ceskych **5592**
0008-736X Casopis pro Mezinarodni Pravo†
0008-7386 Casopis pro Moderni Filologii **5105**
0008-7416 Cassa di Soccorso e Malattia per i Dipendenti dell'Azienda Trasporti Municipali di Milano. Bollettino d'Informazione
0008-7475 Castanea **783**
0008-7483 Casteel†
0008-7491 Il Castello
0008-7505 Castillos de Espana
0008-753X Castoro†
0008-7548 Burmah International†
0008-7556 Castrum Peregrini **5210**
0008-7580 Casualty Simulation **7512**
0008-7629 Catalogue & Index **5057**
0008-7661 Catalyst (Amherst) **7953**
0008-767X Catalyst (Philadelphia) **2053**
0008-770X Catch Society of America. Journal†
0008-7726 Catechist **7787**
0008-7750 Universidad de Granada. Catedra Francisco Suarez. Anales **6958**
0008-7769 Catena **7787**
0008-7777 Caterer & Hotelkeeper **4383**
0008-7807 Catering Executive†
0008-7815 Catering Industry Employee **4591**
0008-7823 Catering Quarterly†
0008-7866 Cathcart Chronicle†
0008-7874 Cathedral Age **7750**
0008-7882 Cathode Press†
0008-7904 Catholic Advance **7787**
0008-7912 Catholic Biblical Quarterly **7788**
0008-7947 Catholic Business Education Review†
0008-7971 Catholic Chronicle **7788**
0008-7998 Catholic Digest **7788**
0008-8005 Catholic Documentation†
0008-8013 Catholic Education Today†
0008-803X Catholic Fireside
0008-8048 Catholic Forester **3971**
0008-8056 Catholic Free Press **7788**
0008-8064 Catholic Gazette†
0008-8072 The Catholic Herald **7788**
0008-8080 The Catholic Historical Review **7789**
0008-8110 Catholic Institutional Management†
0008-8129 The Catholic Journalist **4573**
0008-8145 The Catholic Leader **7789**
0008-8161 Catholic Library Association. Northern Illinois Chapter. Newsletter
0008-820X Catholic Library World **5001**
0008-8226 Catholic Medical Quarterly **7789**
0008-8234 Catholic Messenger **7789**
0008-8242 Catholic Mind†
0008-8250 Catholic News†
0008-8269 Catholic Nurse†
0008-8277 Catholic Peace Fellowship Bulletin **7789**
0008-8285 The Catholic Periodical and Literature Index **7698**
0008-8293 Catholic Pictorial **7789**
0008-8307 Catholic Press Directory **622**
0008-8315 Catholic Review (Baltimore) **7789**
0008-834X Catholic School Editor†
0008-8366 Catholic Standard **7790**
0008-8382 Catholic Trustee
0008-8404 Catholic Virginian **7790**
0008-8412 Catholic Voice **7790**
0008-8420 Catholic Weekly **7791**
0008-8439 Catholic Weekly **7791**
0008-8447 Catholic Witness **7791**
0008-8455 Catholic Woman's Journal†
0008-8463 Catholic Worker **7791**
0008-8471 Catholic Workman **7791**
0008-8498 Catholica†
0008-8501 Catholica **7791**
0008-851X Catholica Unio†
0008-8528 Catolicismo†
0008-8536 Catonsville Roadrunner†
0008-8552 Cattleman **283**
0008-8579 Caustic **2053**
0008-8609 The Cavalier Daily **2277**
0008-8625 Caves and Karst†
0008-8641 Caxtonian†
0008-8668 Cebu y Derivados
0008-8676 Cecidologia Internationale **842**
0008-8692 Ceiba **100**
0008-8706 Celebriamo **6554**
0008-8722 Celik†
0008-8749 Cellular Immunology **5755**
0008-8757 Cellule†
0008-8765 Cellulosa e Carta†
0008-8781 Celuloide†
0008-8803 Cement†
0008-8811 Cement **990**
0008-882X Cement **990**
0008-8838 Cement & Concrete†
0008-8846 Cement and Concrete Research **990**
0008-8889 Cement Special **990**
0008-8919 Cemento - Hormigon **991**
0008-8927 Cemento Portland†
0008-8935 Cenacolo (Turin)
0008-8943 Cenhadwr†
0008-896X Cenobio **5210**
0008-8978 Centaur†
0008-8986 Centauros
0008-8994 Centaurus (Copenhagen) **7844**
0008-9001 Centenary College Conglomerate **2277**
0008-9036 Center for Children's Books. Bulletin **2147**
0008-9044 Center for Chinese Research Materials. Newsletter **564**
0008-9052 University of Michigan. Center for Coordination of Ancient and Modern Studies. Newsletter†
0008-9079 Center for Law Enforcement Research Information†
0008-9117 Center Forum†
0008-9141 Cento **2277**
0008-9168 Centraal Orgaan voor de Handel in Aardappelen, Groenten en Fruit†
0008-9176 Central African Journal of Medicine **5593**
0008-9184 Central African Zionist Digest **7114**
0008-9192 Central Asiatic Journal **546**
0008-9206 Central Bank News†
0008-9249 Central Bank of Egypt. Economic Review **1446**
0008-9257 Central Bank of Iraq. Quarterly Bulletin
0008-9273 Central Bank of Malta. Quarterly Review **1325**
0008-9281 Central Bank of Nigeria. Economic and Financial Review **1446**
0008-929X Central Bank of Nigeria. Monthly Report **1325**
0008-9303 Philippine Financial Statistics†
0008-9311 Central Bible Quarterly†
0008-9346 Central Constructor†
0008-9362 Central Europe Journal†
0008-9389 Central European History **4209**
0008-9397 Central Glass and Ceramic Research Institute. Bulletin **2038**
0008-9400 Central Ideas†
0008-9443 Chubu Nippon Seikei Geka Saigai Geka Gakkai Zasshi **6057**
0008-9451 Central Michigan Life **2277**
0008-946X Central New York Academy of Medicine. Bulletin
0008-9478 Central New York Regional Medical Program. Bulletin†
0008-9494 Central News†
0008-9508 Central Opera Service Bulletin†
0008-9524 Central Pennsylvania Labor News
0008-9532 Central Railway Chronicle **8616**
0008-9559 Central States Archaeological Journal **386**
0008-9583 Centralblatt fuer das Gesamte Forstwesen **3686**
0008-9613 Centre d'Amitie Internationale. Revue d'Art-Tourisme-Culture
0008-9648 Centre de Formation des Journalistes. Feuillets†
0008-9664 Centre de Recherche et d'Information Socio-Politiques. Etudes Africaines†
0008-9680 Centre de Recherches et d'Etudes Oceanographiques. Travaux†
0008-9702 Centre d'Etude des Matieres Plastiques. Bulletin de Documentation†
0008-9710 Shikshak†
0008-9729 Cotton: Review of the World Situation **8449**
0008-9737 Universite Libre de Bruxelles. Centre d'Etudes de Recherche Operationnelle. Cahiers **1799**
0008-9761 Centre d'Etudes Socialistes. Cahiers†
0008-9788 Centre d'Information Civique, Paris. Etudes†
0008-9826 Centre Medical†
0008-9850 Centre Scientifique et Technique du Batiment. Cahiers†
0008-9907 Centro America Odontologica
0008-9915 Instituto de Investigacao Cientifica de Mocambique. Centro de Documentacao Cientifica. Boletim†
0008-9931 Portugal. Ministerio do Ultramar. Centro de Documentacao Tecnico-Economica. Boletim Bibliografico
0008-994X Sindicato Espanol Universitario. Comisaria. Centro de Documentacion. Boletin†
0008-9990 Centro de Historia del Estado Falcon. Boletin
0009-0034 Centro Interamericano de Vivienda y Planeamiento. Lista de Nuevas Adquisiciones†
0009-0050 Centro Latino-Americano de Fisica Noticia†
0009-0069 Centro Latino-Americano de Pesquisas em Ciencias Sociais. Boletim Bibliografia
0009-0085 Centro Nacional de Informacion de Ciencias Medicas. Revista de Resumenes. Cuaderno 2. Cirugia†
0009-0093 Centro Nacional de Informacion de Ciencias Medicas. Revista de Resumenes. Cuaderno 4. Higiene, Epidemiologia, Medios de Diagnostico y Otros†
0009-0107 Centro Nacional de Informacion de Ciencias Medicas. Revista de Resumenes. Cuaderno 1. Medicina†
0009-0115 Centro Nacional de Informacion de Ciencias Medicas. Revista de Resumenes. Cuaderno 3. Pediatria†
0009-0123 Centro Naval. Boletin **6415**
0009-0131 Centro Pan-Americano de Fiebre Aftosa. Boletin **7512**
0009-014X Centro Regional de Pesquisas Educacionais Jaoa Pinheiro. Boletim Informativo†
0009-0158 Century
0009-0166 Century†
0009-0174 Ceol†
0009-0204 Ceramic Awareness Bulletin†
0009-0212 Ceramic Forum†
0009-0220 Ceramic Industry **2038**
0009-0247 Ceramic Scope†
0009-0271 Ceramica Informazione **2039**
0009-031X Ceramics Japan **2039**
0009-0328 Ceramics Monthly **2039**
0009-0336 La Ceramique Moderne. Edition Technique **2040**
0009-0344 Cercle d'Etudes Numismatiques. Bulletin **6649**
0009-0352 Cereal Chemistry **3630**
0009-0379 Ceres†
0009-0387 Cerkev v Sedanjem Svetu **7791**
0009-0433 Certified Milk†
0009-0441 Cerveny Kvet
0009-0468 Ceska Literatura **5272**
0009-0484 Ceske Listy†
0009-0492 Ceskoslovenska Akademie Ved. Vestnik†
0009-0506 Ceskoslovenska Armada†
0009-0514 Cesko-Slovenska Dermatologie **5873**
0009-062X Ceskoslovenska Psychologie **7344**
0009-0646 Ceskoslovenska Spolecnost Mikrobiologicka. Bulletin **883**
0009-0689 Ceskoslovenske Zdravotnictvi†
0009-0700 Ceskoslovensky Casopis pro Fyziku **7008**
0009-0719 Ceskoslovensky Hornik a Energetik†
0009-0727 Ceskoslovensky Kolorista†
0009-0735 Ceskoslovensky Rozhlas a Televize†
0009-0743 Ceskoslovensky Sach†
0009-0786 Cesky Jazyk a Literatura **2835**
0009-0794 Cesky Lid **333**
0009-0832 Sri Lanka Journal of Historical and Social Studies **4162**
0009-0875 Ceylon Medical Journal **5593**
0009-0905 Avicultura Industrial **280**
0009-0921 Chain Merchandiser†
0009-0948 Chain Saw Industry & Power Equipment Dealer†
0009-0972 Chalkmarks†
0009-1006 Challenge (London, 1960) **2182**
0009-1014 Challenge (Sandbach) **7791**
0009-1049 Challenge (New York) **7115**
0009-1057 Challenge†
0009-1065 New Stationer†
0009-1073 Challenge (Richmond)†
0009-1103 Chalmers†
0009-112X Chalmers Tekniska Hoegskola. Institutionen foer Skeppshydromekanik. Rapport†
0009-1154 Chamber of Commerce of the U.S. Association Letter†
0009-1162 Chamber of Mines Journal **6460**
0009-1200 Chambre de Commerce et d'Industrie de Marseille. Cahiers de Documentation†
0009-1227 Bulletin Economique *changed to* 0986-2013 **1399**
0009-1235 Chambre de Commerce Francaise du Japon. Bulletin†
0009-126X Chambre Syndicale des Mines de Fer de France. Bulletin Technique†
0009-1294 Champagne News
0009-1308 Der Champignon **224**
0009-1316 De Champignoncultuur†
0009-1332 Champak **2182**
0009-1359 Chandrabhaga **5272**
0009-1383 Change **2971**
0009-1413 Changing Education†
0009-1421 Changing Schools†
0009-1464 Channel (New Paltz)†
0009-1480 Gambit†
0009-1502 Channels (Omaha)†
0009-1510 Channels (Exeter)†
0009-1529 Channels of Blessing **7750**
0009-1537 Chanoyu Quarterly†
0009-1553 Chantecoq†
0009-1561 The Chanticleer **2277**
0009-1588 Chantiers†
0009-1596 Chantiers Cooperatifs **991**
0009-160X Les Chantiers du Cardinal **991**
0009-1618 Chantiers Pedagogiques†
0009-1626 Children's Book Review†
0009-1650 Chappaqua Speculator†
0009-1669 Character Potential†
0009-1723 Charity and Children **2147**
0009-1731 Charivari†
0009-174X Charlatan: Interdisciplinary Journal†
0009-1766 Charles C. Adams Center for Ecological Studies. Occasional Papers
0009-1774 Charles S. Peirce Society. Transactions **6910**
0009-1790 Charlotte-Mecklenburg School Report†
0009-1812 Charm†
0009-1839 Charme†
0009-1847 Charolais Banner
0009-188X Chartered Accountant **1284**
0009-1901 Chartered Engineer†
0009-1944 Chartotheca Translationum Alphabetica†
0009-1952 The Chase **8309**
0009-1960 Chasovoi
0009-1987 The Chat **905**
0009-1995 Chatelaine (English Edition) **8855**
0009-2002 Chaucer Review **5272**
0009-2037 Chauffage-Plomberie†
0009-2045 Chauffeur
0009-2061 Chavhata Weekly
0009-2118 Checkpoint
0009-2126 Cheering Words **7750**
0009-2142 Cheese Reporter **262**
0009-2177 Chefs
0009-2185 Chelsea **5272**
0009-2207 Chemexcil Export Bulletin **1555**
0009-2223 Chemia Analityczna **2099**
0009-2258 Chemical Abstracts **2093**
0009-2274 Chemical Abstracts - Macromolecular Sections **2093**
0009-2282 Chemical Abstracts - Organic Chemistry Sections **2093**
0009-2304 Chemical Abstracts - Biochemistry Sections **714**
0009-2320 Chemical Age of India **2053**
0009-2347 Chemical & Engineering News **3237**
0009-2355 Chemical and Petroleum Engineering **3238**
0009-2363 Chemical & Pharmaceutical Bulletin **2053**
0009-238X Chemical-Biological Activities (CBAC)†
0009-2398 Chemical Bond **2053**
0009-2401 Chemical Bulletin **2053**
0009-2436 Chemical Economy and Engineering Review†
0009-2460 Chemical Engineering **3238**
0009-2479 Chemical Engineering Education **3238**
0009-2509 Chemical Engineering Science **3239**
0009-2517 Chemical Engineering World **3239**
0009-2525 Chemical Equipment *changed to* 1931-9924 **3237**
0009-2533 Chemical Era **2054**

ISSN

0009-2541 Chemical Geology 2703
0009-255X Chemical Highlights†
0009-2576 Chemical Industry News 3239
0009-2584 Chemical Industry Report††
0009-2614 Chemical Physics Letters 2133
0009-2630 Chemical Processing 3239
0009-2665 Chemical Reviews 2054
0009-2673 The Chemical Society of Japan. Bulletin 2055
0009-269X Chemical Substructure Index†
0009-2711 Chemical Titles†
0009-272X Chemical Week 3240
0009-2738 Chemicals & Allied Products Export News
0009-2746 Chemicals - International 2055
0009-2754 Chemicals, Quarterly Industry Report†
0009-2770 Chemicke Listy 2055
0009-2789 Chemicky Prumysl†
0009-2797 Chemico-Biological Interactions 3495
0009-2800 Chemie-Anlagen und Verfahren 3240
0009-2819 Chemie der Erde / Geochemistry 2728
0009-2827 Chemie en Techniek†
0009-2851 Chemie in Unserer Zeit 2055
0009-286X Chemie-Ingenieur-Technik 3240
0009-2886 Chemik 2056
0009-2908 Chemins†
0009-2959 Chemische Industrie†
0009-2967 Chemische Industrie International†
0009-2983 Chemische Rundschau 2056
0009-3025 The Chemist 2056
0009-3033 Chemist & Druggist 6828
0009-3041 Chemist & Drugstore News†
0009-3068 Chemistry & Industry 2057
0009-3084 Chemistry and Physics of Lipids 728
0009-3092 Chemistry and Technology of Fuels and Oils 6765
0009-3122 Chemistry of Heterocyclic Compounds (New York, 1965) 2121
0009-3130 Chemistry of Natural Compounds 2121
0009-3149 Chemists Review 6828
0009-3157 Chemotherapy 6828
0009-3173 Chempress changed to Safety! Magazine 3255
0009-3203 Cherie Moda† 8941
0009-3289 Cheshire Life 3862
0009-3300 Chesopiean 387
0009-3327 Chess Correspondent 8166
0009-3335 Chess Digest†
0009-3424 Chez Nous 5105
0009-3432 Chhandita 5273
0009-3467 Chibaken Kisho Geppo 6349
0009-3483 Chic†
0009-3491 Chicago Academy of Sciences. Bulletin 7845
0009-3521 Chicago Daily Hide and Tallow Bulletin 4972
0009-3548 Chicago Fire Fighter†
0009-3556 Chicago Genealogist 3762
0009-3564 Chicago Herpetological Society. Bulletin 938
0009-3572 Chicago Illini†
0009-3580 Chicago Journalism Review†
0009-3599 Chicago - Kent Law Review 4642
0009-3602 Chicago Magazine†
0009-3610 Chicago Maroon 2277
0009-3629 Chicago Medical School Quarterly†
0009-3637 Chicago Medicine 5594
0009-3653 Chicago Police Star†
0009-3661 Chicago Psychoanalytic Literature Index†
0009-367X Chicago Purchasor 1810
0009-3696 Chicago Review 5273
0009-370X The Chicago Shimpo 3526
0009-3718 Chicago Studies 7791
0009-3742 Chicagoland Food News
0009-3793 Chicory (Baltimore)†
0009-3823 Jiefangjun Huabao 6428
0009-3831 Education of Earth Science 2706
0009-384X Chiiki Fukushi†
0009-3858 Chikitsak Samaj
0009-3866 Chikudenchi 3297
0009-3874 Chikusan no Kenkyu 284
0009-3882 Child and Family
0009-3904 Child Care†
0009-3920 Child Development 2147
0009-3939 Child Development Abstracts and Bibliography†
0009-3947 Child Education 2836
0009-3963 Child Health Investigation†
0009-3971 Child Life†
0009-398X Child Psychiatry and Human Development 6131
0009-3998 Child Psychiatry Quarterly†
0009-4005 Child Study Journal 2836
0009-4013 Child Wear†
0009-4021 Child Welfare 8032
0009-403X Childbirth Education†
0009-4056 Childhood Education 3054
0009-4080 Children's Digest†
0009-4102 Friend 7736
0009-4110 Children's Hospital Notes†
0009-4153 Children's Own 2182
0009-417X Children's Styles†
0009-4196 Children's Theatre Review changed to 0892-9092 8485
0009-420X Children's World 2182
0009-4226 Chile - Economic Notes†
0009-4234 Chile-Economic Background Information†
0009-4242 Chile. Ejercito. Anexo Historico. Memorial
0009-4277 Chiltern Life†
0009-4285 Chimes (Notre Dame) 5273
0009-4293 Chimia 2058
0009-4315 La Chimica e l'Industria 3241
0009-4366 Chimie et Technique
0009-4382 China Glass & Tableware†
0009-4404 China News Analysis 3823
0009-4412 China Notes†
0009-4420 China Pictorial 3823
0009-4455 China Report 7226
0009-4471 China Today†
0009-448X China Trade Report 1555
0009-4498 China's Foreign Trade 1555
0009-4501 Chinatown News†

0009-451X Chinchilla-Zucht†
0009-4536 Chinese Chemical Society. Journal 2058
0009-4544 Chinese Culture†
0009-4579 Chinese Journal of Administration 7430
0009-4595 Chinese Language Teachers Association. Journal 5105
0009-4609 Chinese Law and Government 4642
0009-4617 Chinese Literature†
0009-4625 Chinese Sociology and Anthropology 8093
0009-4633 Chinese Studies in History 4135
0009-4641 Chinese Voice
0009-465X Ch'ing Documents†
0009-4668 Ching Feng 7631
0009-4684 Chirimo
0009-4692 Chirogram†
0009-4714 Chiropody Review changed to 1756-3291 6255
0009-4722 Der Chirurg 6238
0009-4749 La Chirurgia degli Organi di Movimento changed to 2035-5106 6252
0009-4757 Chirurgia e Patologia Sperimentale†
0009-4765 Chirurgia Gastroenterologica
0009-4773 Chirurgia Italiana
0009-4781 Chirurgia Maxillofacialis et Plastica†
0009-479X Chirurgia Narzadow Ruchu i Ortopedia Polska 6057
0009-4811 Chirurgia Triveneta†
0009-482X Chirurgia Veterinaria†
0009-4838 Chirurgien-Dentiste de France 5837
0009-4846 Chirurgische Praxis 6239
0009-4854 Chishitsu Nyusu 2729
0009-4870 Chitrali 3799
0009-4897 Chizu 4002
0009-4919 Chlodnictwo 4117
0009-4935 Choc-Talk†
0009-496X Choice 2635
0009-4978 Choice 7558
0009-4986 Choice†
0009-4994 Choisir 7631
0009-5001 Choix Artistique et Litteraire†
0009-5028 Choral Journal 6555
0009-5036 Der Chordirigent†
0009-5044 Chorleiter†
0009-5060 Der Christ im Zwanzigsten Jahrhundert
0009-5087 Christ und Buch†
0009-5117 The Christadelphian 7631
0009-5133 Christelijk-Historisch Tijdschrift†
0009-515X Onze Vacatures†
0009-5184 Die Christengemeinschaft 7631
0009-5214 Christian Adventurer†
0009-5265 Christian Beacon†
0009-5281 The Christian Century 7631
0009-5303 Christian Communications
0009-5311 Christian Cynosure†
0009-5338 The Christian Endeavor World†
0009-5346 Christian Family†
0009-5354 Christian Herald (Chappaqua)†
0009-5362 Christian Heritage†
0009-5370 Christian Home†
0009-5389 Christian Home & School 2149
0009-5400 Christian Labor Herald†
0009-5419 Christian Leader 7733
0009-5435 Christian Living 7632
0009-5451 Christian Medical College Vellore Alumni Journal 5595
0009-5478 Christian Messenger 7751
0009-5486 Christian Minister†
0009-5494 Christian Monthly 7751
0009-5516 Christian News 7751
0009-5524 Christian News Bulletin†
0009-5532 Christian News from Israel† 8941
0009-5540 Christian Nurse†
0009-5559 Christian Order 7734
0009-5567 Christian Peace Conference†
0009-5575 Christian Record 7632
0009-5583 Christian Record Talking Magazine 7632
0009-5591 Christian Recorder†
0009-5605 Christian Rural Fellowship. Bulletin†
0009-5613 The Christian Science Journal 7734
0009-563X Christian Science Sentinel 7734
0009-5648 Christian Socialist 7116
0009-5656 Christian Standard 7632
0009-5664 The Christian Statesman 7632
0009-5672 Christian Teacher†
0009-5680 Vanguard (Toronto)
0009-5699 Christian Voice 7734
0009-5702 Christian Woman 7632
0009-5710 Christiane†
0009-5729 Christianisme au Vingtieme Siecle 7632
0009-5745 Christianity and Crisis†
0009-5753 Christianity Today 7632
0009-5761 Christlich-Paedagogische Blaetter
0009-5788 Christliche Frau changed to 1612-9407 7796
0009-5796 Christliche Innerlichkeit 7792
0009-5818 Christophorus (Frankenthal) 7792
0009-5834 Christus 7633
0009-5850 Christus en Israel†
0009-5869 Die Christus Post 7633
0009-5885 Christusruf†
0009-5893 Chromatographia 2099
0009-5915 Chromosoma 864
0009-5931 Chronica 4210
0009-5958 Chronicle†
0009-5974 Chronicle†
0009-5982 The Chronicle of Higher Education 2972
0009-5990 The Chronicle of the Horse 8289
0009-6008 Chronicle of U S Classic Postal Issues 6893
0009-6024 Chronicles of Oklahoma 4288
0009-6032 La Chronique 991
0009-6040 Chronique de l'I R S A C 7846
0009-6067 Chronique d'Egypte 5274
0009-6148 Chroniques de l'Art Vivant†
0009-6172 Chronmy Przyrode Ojczysta 2606
0009-6180 Chronos†
0009-6199 Chrysalis†

0009-6237 Chugoku Electric Power Co. Technical Laboratory. Report
0009-6253 Chung-Ang Herald
0009-6261 Chung Chi Bulletin 2277
0009-6296 Chuo Law Review 4642
0009-630X Church Advocate 7734
0009-6318 Church and Community†
0009-6334 Church & State 7633
0009-6342 Church and Synagogue Libraries changed to 1934-2292 5003
0009-6393 Church Herald 7751
0009-6407 Church History 7633
0009-6415 Church Labor Letter†
0009-6474 Church News†
0009-6482 The Church Observer 7751
0009-6504 Church of God Missions 7751
0009-6512 The Church of Ireland Gazette 7751
0009-6520 Church of Light Quarterly 6644
0009-6539 Church Panorama†
0009-6547 Church Quarterly†
0009-6555 Church Renewal†
0009-6563 Church Scene
0009-658X Church Times 7751
0009-6598 Churchwoman 7752
0009-6601 Church World 7633
0009-661X Churchman 7751
0009-6679 Cibles 4331
0009-6687 Ciceroniana 5274
0009-6709 Ciel et Terre 573
0009-6717 Ciencia Aeronautica
0009-6725 Ciencia e Cultura 7846
0009-6733 Ciencia e Investigacion 7846
0009-675X Ciencia Interamericana†
0009-6768 Ciencia y Naturaleza 7847
0009-6784 Ciencias Administrativas†
0009-6792 Ciencias Neurologicas†
0009-6806 Ciencias Sociales†
0009-6814 Cigar Makers' Official Journal†
0009-6830 Cimaise 529
0009-6849 Cimarron Review 5274
0009-6865 Cimone
0009-6881 University of Cincinnati Law Review 4803
0009-6903 Cincinnati Purchasor†
0009-6911 Cinderella Philatelist†
0009-6946 Cine Cubano 6492
0009-6954 Cine News 6965
0009-6997 Cine World
0009-7004 Cineaste 6493
0009-7020 Cinecronache
0009-7039 Cineforum 6493
0009-7047 Cinema†
0009-7063 Cinema†
0009-7071 Cinema - Canada†
0009-708X Cinema de Amadores
0009-7101 Cinema Journal 6493
0009-711X Cinema Nuovo†
0009-7128 Cinema Pratique†
0009-7144 Cinema Rangam†
0009-7152 Cinema Societa
0009-7160 Cinemasud
0009-7179 Cinematografia in Presa†
0009-7187 La Cinematografia Italiana
0009-7195 Cines d'Orient†
0009-7209 Cinesiologie 5742
0009-7217 Cinestudio
0009-7225 Cinque Foil
0009-7241 Circolo Letterario†
0009-725X Circolo Matematico di Palermo. Rendiconti 5478
0009-7268 Circolo Speleologico Romano. Notiziario 2729
0009-7284 Circuit Magazine†
0009-7314 Colegio Oficial de Farmaceutico. Circular Farmaceutica 6829
0009-7322 Circulation (Baltimore) 5782
0009-7330 Circulation Research 5782
0009-7349 Circulo 4447
0009-7357 Circulo Odontologico de Rosario. Revista†
0009-7365 Circus†
0009-7381 Cirugia del Uruguay 6239
0009-739X Cirugia Espanola 6239
0009-7411 Cirugia y Cirujanos 6239
0009-7438 Citatel†
0009-7446 Citation†
0009-7497 Citeaux 7792
0009-7500 Cites et Villes†
0009-7527 Cithara 7633
0009-7535 Cities and Villages 4407
0009-7551 Citizen and Week End Review
0009-756X Citizens' Business 7489
0009-7578 Citrograph†
0009-7586 Citrus & Vegetable 225
0009-7594 Citrus Industry Magazine 3631
0009-7608 Citrus World†
0009-7624 Patavium†
0009-7632 Citta di Vita 7633
0009-7640 Citta e Societa†
0009-7667 Cittadino Canadese 3527
0009-7675 City†
0009-7683 City Almanac†
0009-7691 St. Louis Art Museum. Bulletin 6536
0009-7705 City Beautiful† 8941
0009-7713 City Business Courier†
0009-7748 City Press†
0009-7756 La Ciudad de Dios 7792
0009-7772 Civic Affairs 7490
0009-7780 Civic Forum
0009-7799 Civic Leader†
0009-7810 Civil Air Patrol News 2225
0009-787X Civil Engineering, Construction & Public Works Journal†
0009-790X Civil Liberties (New York)†
0009-7918 Civil Liberties Bulletin†
0009-7934 Civil Liberties Reporter 4828
0009-7942 Rights, Opportunities, Action Reporter†

DIRECTORY 2010 0010-3632 9017

0009-7950 Civil Rights Court Digest
0009-8000 Civil Service Leader
0009-8051 Civil Service Sports Quarterly†
0009-806X Civil Transport Data Sheets
0009-8078 Civil War History **4288**
0009-8086 Civil War Round Table Digest **4288**
0009-8108 Civil War Token Society. Journal
0009-8140 Civilisations **8093**
0009-8167 Civilta Cattolica **7792**
0009-8175 Civilta della Strada†
0009-8191 Civitas **7116**
0009-8213 Clan McLaren Society, U S A. Quarterly **3762**
0009-8221 Clare Market Review†
0009-823X Claridad **3994**
0009-8256 Clarin Economico **1447**
0009-8272 Clark Now†
0009-8280 C L A S S: Reading†
0009-8299 Classe e Stato†
0009-8310 Classic Car†
0009-8337 Classical Bulletin **2232**
0009-8345 Classical Folia†
0009-8353 Classical Journal **2232**
0009-8361 Classical Outlook **2232**
0009-837X Classical Philology **2232**
0009-8388 Classical Quarterly **2232**
0009-840X Classical Review **2233**
0009-8418 Classical World **2233**
0009-8426 I Classici del Giallo
0009-8434 Classification Management **1733**
0009-8450 Classified Abstract Archive of the Alcohol Literature†
0009-8493 Claudia **8855**
0009-8507 Claudia **8855**
0009-8515 Claudia **8855**
0009-8523 Clausthaler Geologische Abhandlungen†
0009-854X Clavier *changed to* Clavier Companion **6557**
0009-8558 Clay Minerals **2704**
0009-8574 Clay Science **6460**
0009-8604 Clays and Clay Minerals **6460**
0009-8620 Clean Water Report **3484**
0009-8655 The Clearing House **2837**
0009-8663 Clearinghouse Announcements in Science & Technology†
0009-8671 Clearinghouse on Self-Instructional Materials for Health Care Facilities. Bulletin†
0009-868X Clearinghouse Review **4643**
0009-8698 Clearway **8630**
0009-8728 Cleo en la Moda **4973**
0009-8752 La Clessidra **4565**
0009-8779 Cleveland Citizen **991**
0009-8817 Cleveland Food Dealer **3677**
0009-8825 Cleveland Jewish News **3527**
0009-8833 Cleveland Medical Library. Bulletin†
0009-8841 Cleveland Museum of Art. Bulletin†
0009-885X Cleveland Public Library Staff Association. News and Views†
0009-8876 Cleveland State Law Review **4643**
0009-8884 Business Bulletin†
0009-8892 Clevelander **1447**
0009-8906 Clic Fotografiamo
0009-8930 Climate Control†
0009-8957 Climatological Data for Jakarta Observatory **6350**
0009-8965 Climb†
0009-8981 Clinica Chimica Acta **5595**
0009-899X Clinica de Endocrinologia y Metabolismo. Boletin†
0009-9007 Clinica Europea†
0009-9015 Clinica Geral†
0009-9023 Clinica Ortopedica†
0009-9058 Clinica Pediatrica†
0009-9066 Clinica Psichiatrica
0009-9074 La Clinica Terapeutica **5595**
0009-9082 Clinica Veterinaria†
0009-9104 Clinical and Experimental Immunology **5756**
0009-9112 Clinical Anesthesia†
0009-9120 Clinical Biochemistry **729**
0009-9139 Quarterly Literature Reports. Clinical Biochemistry†
0009-9147 Clinical Chemistry (Washington, DC) **5904**
0009-9155 Clinical Electroencephalography *changed to* Clinical Electroencephalography and Neuroscience **6131**
0009-9163 Clinical Genetics **864**
0009-918X Rinsho Shinkeigaku **6183**
0009-9201 Clinical Obstetrics and Gynecology **5988**
0009-921X Clinical Orthopaedics and Related Research **6057**
0009-9228 Clinical Pediatrics **6090**
0009-9236 Clinical Pharmacology and Therapeutics **6829**
0009-9244 The Clinical Psychologist **7345**
0009-9252 Rinsho Hoshasen **6207**
0009-9260 Clinical Radiology **6194**
0009-9295 Clinical Symposia†
0009-9317 Clinical Trends in Rheumatology†
0009-9333 Clinicas Obstetricas y Ginecologicas de Norteamerica
0009-9341 Clinician†
0009-935X Clinique†
0009-9368 La Clinique Ophtalmologique†
0009-9376 Clio **4135**
0009-9384 Clio: Devoted to Commercials
0009-9414 Clipsheet†
0009-9422 Clique†
0009-9430 Clocktower **2278**
0009-9538 Club Committee & Northern Free Trade News†
0009-9546 Club du Griffon d'Arret a Poil Dur Korthal. Bulletin†
0009-9562 Club Folk†
0009-9570 Club Francais de la Medaille
0009-9589 Club Management **2265**
0009-9600 Fussball Club Pforzheim. Club-Nachrichten **8229**
0009-9627 Club Operations†
0009-9635 Club Secretary†
0009-9651 Clube Filatelico de Portugal. Boletim **6893**
0009-966X Clube Militar Naval. Anais **6416**
0009-9740 Co-Op Highlights
0009-9759 Co-Op Maandblad†
0009-9767 Co-Op Report†
0009-9821 Co-Operative News **1422**
0009-9848 Co-operative Review†
0009-9880 Coaching Clinic†
0009-9899 Coaching Journal and Bus Review†
0009-9929 Coal and Steel†
0009-9945 Coal Miner†
0009-9988 Coal Research†
0010-0005 Coast†
0010-003X The Coat of Arms **3762**
0010-0056 Cobbers†
0010-0064 Cobouw **992**
0010-0072 Sonntagsblatt - Coburger Heimatglocken
0010-0080 Cock†
0010-0110 Cockpit†
0010-0137 Cocoa Statistics†
0010-0161 Cocuk Sagligi ve Hastaliklari Dergisi **6090**
0010-0188 Codes Larcier **4644**
0010-0196 Codex†
0010-020X Codicillus **4644**
0010-0226 Coeur†
0010-0250 Coffee Mazdoor Sahakari **3631**
0010-0277 Cognition **7346**
0010-0285 Cognitive Psychology **7347**
0010-0293 Cogwheel†
0010-0307 Cohesion†
0010-0358 Coiffure et Beaute†
0010-0366 Coimbra Medica†
0010-0374 Coin Dealer†
0010-0412 Coin Prices **6650**
0010-0447 Coin World **6650**
0010-0455 Coinage **6650**
0010-0463 Coinamatic Age†
0010-0471 Coins **6650**
0010-0544 Colada†
0010-0579 Colegio de Abogados de Puerto Rico. Revista **4644**
0010-0587 Colegio de Abogados. Revista
0010-0595 Colegio de Bibliotecarios Colombianos.(Revista)†
0010-0609 Colegio de Ingenieros Arquitectos y Agrimensores de Puerto Rico. Revista
0010-0617 Colegio de Ingenieros de Caminos, Canales y Puertos. Boletin de Informacion **3263**
0010-0625 Colegio de Ingenieros de Venezuela. Boletin Informativo
0010-0633 Colegio de Profesores de Venezuela. Seccional No.1. Boletin Informativo
0010-0641 Colegio Medico de El Salvador. Archivos **5598**
0010-065X The Coleopterists Bulletin **842**
0010-0676 Colfeian **2278**
0010-0692 Collage†
0010-0706 Collage
0010-0722 Collana di Monografie Turistiche†
0010-0730 Collectanea Botanica **784**
0010-0749 Collectanea Franciscana **7792**
0010-0757 Collectanea Mathematica **5478**
0010-0765 Collection of Czechoslovak Chemical Communications **2058**
0010-0781 Collections Baur. Bulletin **6522**
0010-079X Collective Bargaining Negotiations and Contracts **4592**
0010-082X Collector **1327**
0010-0838 Collectors Club Philatelist **6893**
0010-0854 Collector's World†
0010-0870 College & Research Libraries **5002**
0010-0889 College and University **2972**
0010-0951 College Board Review **2972**
0010-096X College Composition and Communication **3055**
0010-0986 College Echoes†
0010-0994 College English **3055**
0010-1001 Education et Societe†
0010-101X College Law Bulletin†
0010-1028 College Library Notes†
0010-1060 College of Emporia Compass†
0010-1087 College of Physicians of Philadelphia. Transactions & Studies†
0010-1125 College Press Service **2973**
0010-1133 Journal of College Radio **2359**
0010-1141 College Store Executive **1811**
0010-1176 College Student Personnel Institute. Newsletter†
0010-1192 College Voice (Trenton)†
0010-1206 Collegian (Elyria) **2278**
0010-1214 Collegiate Journalist†
0010-1222 Collegiate News and Views†
0010-1230 Collegiate Scene†
0010-1249 Collegio **2278**
0010-129X Collins Signal Magazine†
0010-1311 Colloquium†
0010-132X Colloqui Cremonese†
0010-1338 Colloquia Germanica **5107**
0010-1346 Colloquium†
0010-1354 Colloquium Mathematicum **5479**
0010-1389 Colombia. Ministerio de Defensa. Boletin†
0010-1397 Colombia Today†
0010-1419 Colombo Plan Newsletter **1592**
0010-1435 Colonial Courier **3762**
0010-1443 C N L **6649**
0010-1451 Coloquio: Letras **5276**
0010-146X Color Engineering†
0010-1478 Color Engineering†
0010-1516 Colorado Beverage Analyst **601**
0010-1524 Colorado Business Review†
0010-1532 Colorado C P A Report†
0010-1559 Colorado Dental Association. Journal **5838**
0010-1567 Colorado Editor **4573**
0010-1583 Colorado Engineer Magazine **3185**
0010-1605 Colorado F.P.†
0010-1613 Colorado Genealogist **3762**
0010-163X Colorado Journal of Pharmacy
0010-1664 Colorado Municipalities **7490**
0010-1672 Colorado Music Educator
0010-1699 Colorado Outdoors **8309**
0010-1702 Colorado Prospector **4289**
0010-1710 Colorado Quarterly†
0010-1788 Colores y Pinturas†
0010-1796 Colorado-Rocky Mountain West†
0010-180X Shikizai Kyokaishi **6721**
0010-1818 Colour Review†
0010-1826 Colourage **2243**
0010-1834 Cols Bleus **6416**
0010-1842 Colstonian **2837**
0010-1850 Coltivatore e Giornale Vinicolo Italiano†
0010-1869 Columbia (New Haven) **7793**
0010-1877 The Columbia Basin Farmer **102**
0010-1885 Columbia College Pre-Med†
0010-1893 Columbia Daily Spectator **2278**
0010-1907 Columbia Forum†
0010-1915 Columbia Jester†
0010-1923 Columbia Journal of Law and Social Problems **4645**
0010-1931 Columbia Journal of Transnational Law **4921**
0010-194X Columbia Journalism Review **4573**
0010-1958 Columbia Law Review **4645**
0010-1966 Columbia Library Columns **5003**
0010-1982 Columbia Review **5276**
0010-1990 C.S.P.A.A. Bulletin†
0010-2024 Columbian (Chicago)†
0010-2059 Columbus Business Forum†
0010-2091 The Columns (Fairmont) **2279**
0010-2113 Combat†
0010-2121 Combat **7117**
0010-213X Combat Crew†
0010-2148 Combattente della Liberta
0010-2156 Toesj/Combo†
0010-2164 International Laboratory† **8966**
0010-2172 Combustion†
0010-2180 Combustion and Flame **3185**
0010-2199 Combustion Institute. Western States Section. Papers **3242**
0010-2202 Combustion Science and Technology **2134**
0010-2237 Comentarios Bibliograficos Americanos†
0010-2245 Comercio **1400**
0010-2253 Comercio **1426**
0010-227X Comercio & Mercados†
0010-2288 Comercio Colombo Americano†
0010-2296 Comercio Ecuatoriano **1400**
0010-2326 Comercio Hispano Britanico **1400**
0010-2342 Comercio y Produccion **1400**
0010-2350 Comercio y Produccion **1400**
0010-2369 Comhar
0010-2385 Comino†
0010-2393 Mexico. Comision Nacional de Valores. Boletin Bimestral
0010-2407 Comissao de Desenvolvimento Economico do Estado do Amazonas. Boletim Informativo
0010-244X Comites de Prevention du Batiment et des Travaux Publics. Cahiers†
0010-2474 Command **6416**
0010-2520 Comme les Autres†
0010-2539 Comment†
0010-2555 Comment†
0010-2571 Commentarii Mathematici Helvetici **5479**
0010-258X Commentarii Mathematici Universitatis Sancti Pauli **5479**
0010-2598 Commentarium pro Religiosis et Missionariis
0010-2601 Commentary **7720**
0010-2628 Commentationes Mathematicae Universitatis Carolinae **5479**
0010-2644 Commentator†
0010-2652 Commentator **2279**
0010-2660 Comments on Argentine Trade **1400**
0010-2741 Commerce†
0010-275X Commerce
0010-2768 Commerce†
0010-2776 Commerce†
0010-2784 Commerce & Industry†
0010-2792 Commerce & Industry Monthly Journal
0010-2814 Commerce du Levant **1426**
0010-2830 Commerce Franco-Suisse **1400**
0010-2849 Commerce in France†
0010-2857 Commerce in Germany **1084**
0010-2865 Commerce Industrial and Mining Review
0010-2881 Australia. Perth Chamber of Commerce. Commerce News†
0010-2911 Commercial Bulletin
0010-2938 Commercial Courier **1400**
0010-2997 Australian Commercial Fishing & Marketing
0010-3012 Commercial Herald **1426**
0010-3039 Commercial Journal **1426**
0010-3063 Commercial Motor **8669**
0010-3071 Allied Trades Association. Commercial News
0010-3098 Commercial Record (New York)†
0010-3101 Commercial Review **271**
0010-3136 Commercial Vehicles†
0010-3160 Commercium **1426**
0010-3179 Commission **7752**
0010-3217 Commitment†
0010-3233 Commodity Trade Statistics **1222**
0010-325X Common Ground **7634**
0010-3276 Common Life†
0010-3314 Commonplace Book†
0010-3330 Commonweal **5211**
0010-3349 The Commonwealth **7431**
0010-3357 Commonwealth **7117**
0010-3365 Commonwealth Magazine†
0010-3373 Commonwealth Education Liaison Committee Newsletter†
0010-3411 Commonwealth†
0010-342X Commonwealth Producer
0010-3438 Commonwealth Secretariat Rice Bulletin†
0010-3446 Communaute Autogestion†
0010-3497 Communicatio Socialis **7793**
0010-3500 Communication Arts International
0010-3519 Communication Arts **23**
0010-3527 Communication Disorders†
0010-3543 Communication Reports†
0010-356X Communications†
0010-3616 Communications in Mathematical Physics **7008**
0010-3624 Communications in Soil Science and Plant Analysis **225**
0010-3632 Communications News **2316**

ISSN

9018 0010-3640 ULRICH'S PERIODICALS

0010-3640 Communications on Pure and Applied Mathematics **5480**
0010-3683 Communicator†
0010-3691 Comunidades†
0010-3705 Communio **7793**
0010-3713 Communio Viatorum **7752**
0010-3756 Communist Viewpoint†
0010-3772 Community (Chicago)
0010-3802 Community Development Journal **8034**
0010-3829 Community Development Society. Journal *changed to* 1557-5330 **8034**
0010-3837 Community Health†
0010-3853 Community Mental Health Journal **8035**
0010-387X Community Planning Review *changed to* 0315-4920
0010-3888 Community School and Its Administration†
0010-3918 Community Teamwork†
0010-3942 Compact†
0010-3969 Companheiros **8309**
0010-3985 Companion†
0010-3993 Companion†
0010-4019 Company Law Journal†
0010-4027 Company News and Notes **1883**
0010-4043 Comparative and International Education Society. Newsletter **2838**
0010-4051 Comparative and International Law Journal of Southern Africa **4921**
0010-4078 Comparative Drama **5277**
0010-4086 Comparative Education Review **2838**
0010-4116 Comparative Law Review **4647**
0010-4124 Comparative Literature **5277**
0010-4132 Comparative Literature Studies **5277**
0010-4140 Comparative Political Studies **7117**
0010-4159 Comparative Politics **7117**
0010-4167 Comparative Romance Linguistics Newsletter **5107**
0010-4175 Comparative Studies in Society and History **8095**
0010-4221 Compendio Medico
0010-423X Compendio Pediatrico
0010-4310 Component Technology†
0010-4329 Comportamiento Humano
0010-4337 Composer†
0010-4353 Composers, Authors and Artists of America
0010-437X Compositio Mathematica **5480**
0010-440X Comprehensive Psychiatry **6133**
0010-4418 Comprendre
0010-4426 Compressed Air†
0010-4469 Computer Abstracts **2442**
0010-4485 Computer-Aided Design **3289**
0010-4523 Computer Applications Service†
0010-4582 Computer Display Review†
0010-4590 Computer Education **2948**
0010-4620 The Computer Journal **2412**
0010-4639 Computer Management†
0010-4655 Computer Physics Communications **7050**
0010-4736 Computer Services†
0010-4752 Computer Studies in the Humanities and Verbal Behavior†
0010-4760 Computer Survey **2570**
0010-4787 Computer Weekly **2413**
0010-4817 Computers and the Humanities *changed to* 1574-020X **4485**
0010-4825 Computers in Biology and Medicine **825**
0010-4833 Computers in Medicine Abstracts†
0010-4841 Computerworld **2570**
0010-485X Computing **2415**
0010-4868 Computing Newsletter for Schools of Business†
0010-4884 Computing Reviews **2415**
0010-4906 Konpyutopia†
0010-4922 Comune (Rome)
0010-4930 Il Comune Democratico† **8943**
0010-4957 Comune di Roma. Ufficio di Statistica e Censimento. Bollettino Statistico†
0010-4965 Comune di Roma. Ufficio di Statistica e Censimento. Notiziario Statistico Mensile
0010-4973 Comuni d'Europa **7490**
0010-5007 Instituto de Ciencias da Informacao Comunicacoes & Problemas
0010-5015 Comunicacoes Bioquimicas
0010-5023 Comunidad†
0010-504X Comunita
0010-5066 La Comunita Internazionale **7227**
0010-5082 Combustion, Explosion and Shock Waves **3241**
0010-5090 Con Edison Library Bulletin†
0010-5104 Con Safos
0010-5112 Concept
0010-5120 Concept of Pakistan
0010-5147 Conceptos de Matematica **5481**
0010-5155 Conceptus **6911**
0010-5163 Concern (New York)†
0010-5171 Concern†
0010-5198 Concerning Food & Nutrition†
0010-5201 Concerning Poetry†
0010-521X Conch†
0010-5228 Conciliatore
0010-5236 Concilium **7634**
0010-5244 Concord†
0010-5252 Concordia
0010-5260 Concordia Historical Institute Quarterly **7752**
0010-5287 Concordia Torch **4499**
0010-5309 Concours Medical **5600**
0010-5317 Concrete (London) **992**
0010-5341 Concrete Construction and Architecture **993**
0010-535X Concrete Industry Bulletin **993**
0010-5368 Concrete Products **993**
0010-5376 Concrete Quarterly **993**
0010-5414 Condor†
0010-5422 The Condor **905**
0010-5473 Confectionery Production **3673**
0010-549X Confederacion de Camaras Nacionales de Comercio. Carta Semanal†
0010-5511 Confederate Historical Society. Journal†
0010-5554 Conference Board Statistical Bulletin†
0010-5570 Conference on Latin American History Newsletter **4289**
0010-5589 Conferences du Cenacle†
0010-5600 Conferencias
0010-5627 Confit†
0010-5635 Confidencias†
0010-5651 Confidential Confessions†
0010-566X Confidential Detective Cases†
0010-5686 Confinia Psychiatrica†
0010-5708 Confort
0010-5716 Confrontation **5277**
0010-5732 Confronto†
0010-5740 Congiuntura Estera
0010-5759 Congiuntura Italiana
0010-5775 Congo Disque
0010-5805 Congo. Centre National de la Statistique et des Etudes Economiques. Bulletin Mensuel de la Statistique **8364**
0010-5821 Congregational Library. Bulletin **5003**
0010-5848 Christian Leader†
0010-5856 Congregationalist **7752**
0010-5880 Congress Bulletin†
0010-5899 Congressional Digest **7118**
0010-5902 Congressional Monitor
0010-5929 Rivista di Coniglicoltura **299**
0010-5937 Conjunto **8468**
0010-5945 Conjuntura Economica **1448**
0010-5953 Connaissance de la Campagne†
0010-5961 Connaissance de la Mer†
0010-5996 Connaissance des Hommes *changed to* 1168-2957
0010-6003 Connaissance des Plastiques†
0010-602X Connaitre la Wallonie†
0010-6038 Connchord
0010-6046 Connecticut Action†
0010-6070 Connecticut Bar Journal **4648**
0010-6097 Connecticut Conference Missioner†
0010-6100 Connecticut Conservation Reporter†
0010-6119 Connecticut Government **7432**
0010-6127 Connecticut Health Bulletin†
0010-6143 Connecticut. Labor Department. Bulletin†
0010-6151 Connecticut Law Review **4648**
0010-616X Connecticut Libraries **5003**
0010-6178 Connecticut Medicine **5600**
0010-6216 Connecticut Review†
0010-6232 Connecticut State Dental Association. Journal **5838**
0010-6240 Connecticut Teacher†
0010-6259 Connecticut Woodlands **3686**
0010-6267 Connection†
0010-6283 Connoisseur's Guide†
0010-6291 Conocimiento de la Nueva Era **6741**
0010-6305 Conoscenza
0010-6313 Conparlist†
0010-6348 Conquiste del Lavoro **3896**
0010-6356 Conradiana **5278**
0010-6364 Consejo Nacional de Investigaciones Cientificas y Tecnicas. Informaciones†
0010-6410 Conselho Estadual de Educacao de Sao Paulo. Acta
0010-6445 Conservacionista†
0010-647X Conservation News†
0010-6542 Conservative Judaism **7720**
0010-6550 Conservatoire de Musique de Geneve. Bulletin **6558**
0010-6569 Il Consiglio di Stato *changed to* 1828-4418 **4681**
0010-6577 Consol News **6461**
0010-6593 Consommation†
0010-6607 Constabulary Gazette **2647**
0010-6623 Constitutional and Parliamentary Information *see* 0251-3617 **7142**
0010-6631 Construcao Sao Paulo **994**
0010-6658 De Constructeur **3263**
0010-6682 Construction (Paris)† **8943**
0010-6690 Construction in Southern Africa†
0010-6704 Construction (Norcross) **994**
0010-6712 Construction Advisor†
0010-6720 Construction Bulletin (Norcross) **995**
0010-6755 Construction Equipment Distribution **995**
0010-6771 Construction Equipment Operation and Maintenance†
0010-6836 Construction Labor Report **1673**
0010-6852 Construction Moderne
0010-6860 Construction News **997**
0010-6895 Construction Products & Technology†
0010-6917 Construction Review **1045**
0010-6925 The Construction Specifier **998**
0010-6941 Construction West†
0010-695X Constructional Review†
0010-6968 Constructioneer **1049**
0010-6976 Constructions Equipements pour les Loisirs **998**
0010-7018 Constructor **998**
0010-7034 Construire **999**
0010-7042 Consudel **3673**
0010-7050 Consulente Immobiliare **7587**
0010-7069 Consultant (Greenwich) **5600**
0010-7077 Consultant (Midland)†
0010-7085 Consultant (Columbia) **3686**
0010-7158 Consumer Education Forum†
0010-7174 Consumer Reports **2636**
0010-7182 Consumers Digest **2637**
0010-7190 Consumers Voice†
0010-7220 Austria Contact
0010-7239 Contact†
0010-7263 Contact†
0010-7301 Contact Point **5839**
0010-7328 O A A G Bulletin†
0010-7379 Containerisation International **8641**
0010-7387 Containers and Packaging†
0010-7409 Contamination Newsletter†
0010-7417 Contante y Sonante
0010-7468 Contemporary Authors **641**
0010-7476 Contemporary Education†
0010-7484 Contemporary Literature **5278**
0010-7492 Contemporary Literature in Translation†
0010-7514 Contemporary Physics **7009**
0010-7522 Contemporary Poland†
0010-7530 Contemporary Psychoanalysis **7349**
0010-7549 Contemporary Psychology: A P A Review of Books (Print) *changed to* 1554-0138 **7394**
0010-7565 The Contemporary Review **5212**
0010-7573 Contemporary Writers in Christian Perspective†
0010-7581 Contenido **3908**
0010-7603 Contents Pages: Electronics and Electricity†
0010-7611 Contents Pages of Iranian Science and Social Science Journals†
0010-762X Contenuti **5278**
0010-7646 Jaybee
0010-7654 Contigo†
0010-7697 Continental Bulletin
0010-7719 Continental Iron and Steel Trade Reports
0010-7727 Continental Magazine (Dearborn)†
0010-776X Continuing Education Report†
0010-7778 Continuous Learning†
0010-7824 Contraception **971**
0010-7875 Contracting in the Carolinas
0010-7883 Contractor and Plant Manager†
0010-7891 Contractor
0010-7948 Contrast†
0010-7956 Contratista
0010-7964 Contrepoint†
0010-7972 Instituto Ecuatoriano de Ciencias Naturales. Contribuciones **7866**
0010-7999 Contributions to Mineralogy and Petrology **2730**
0010-8014 Controcorrente
0010-8022 Control and Instrumentation† **8944**
0010-8030 Control and Science Record†
0010-8049 Control Engineering **2459**
0010-8065 Control Systems
0010-8073 The Controller **52**
0010-809X Controspazio **438**
0010-8103 Controvento
0010-8111 Convegno Musicale
0010-812X Convegno
0010-8138 Convenience Store Journal†
0010-8146 Convergence **2940**
0010-8154 Convergence†
0010-8170 Conversation et Traduction†
0010-8189 Converter **6732**
0010-8200 Conveyancer and Property Lawyer **7587**
0010-8227 Convivium†
0010-8235 Convivium **6912**
0010-8243 Convorbiri Literare **5279**
0010-8251 Cook County Highway News†
0010-826X Cookbook Digest **4354**
0010-8308 Coop-Habitat†
0010-8316 Cooperacion Libre
0010-8359 Cooperation Agricole†
0010-8367 Cooperation and Conflict **7228**
0010-8391 The Cooperative Accountant **1286**
0010-843X Cooperative Education Association Newsletter (Print Edition) *changed to* Cooperative Education Association Newsletter (Online Edition) **2839**
0010-8448 Cooperative Farmer†
0010-8456 Cooperativismo & Nordeste†
0010-8464 Cooperator **1423**
0010-8472 Cooperator†
0010-8480 Cooperazione di Credito **1423**
0010-8499 Cooperazione e Societa†
0010-8502 Cooperazione Educativa **2839**
0010-8510 Cooperazione Italiana†
0010-8529 Coopercotia
0010-8537 Cooper's Hero-Hobby†
0010-8545 Coordination Chemistry Reviews **2059**
0010-857X Copper†
0010-8650 Cor et Vasa **5783**
0010-8669 Coranto†
0010-8677 Corcoran Gallery of Art Bulletin†
0010-8685 Cord **7793**
0010-8707 Corduroy†
0010-8731 Cork Historical and Archaeological Society. Journal **388**
0010-8758 Cormoran†
0010-8766 Cormoran y Delfin **5420**
0010-8782 Cornell Countryman†
0010-8804 The Cornell Hotel & Restaurant Administration Quarterly *changed to* 1938-9655 **4384**
0010-8812 Cornell International Law Journal **4922**
0010-8820 Cornell Journal of Social Relations†
0010-8839 Cornell Law Forum **4651**
0010-8847 Cornell Law Review **4651**
0010-8855 Cornell Newsletter, Chemicals-Pesticides Program†
0010-8863 Cornell Plantations Magazine **2279**
0010-8901 Cornell Veterinarian†
0010-8936 Coronet†
0010-8952 Corporate Communications Report†
0010-8987 Corporate Planning: Formation, Operation and Management†
0010-8995 Corporate Practice Commentator **4864**
0010-9029 Correction Sidelights†
0010-9045 Corrections Digest **2647**
0010-9088 Correio Serrano
0010-9096 Correo del Delta
0010-910X Correo del Sur **3908**
0010-9118 Correo Economico **1448**
0010-9150 Corriere Nucleare†
0010-9169 Il Corriere dei Ciechi **4081**
0010-9177 Corriere dei Congressi†
0010-9193 Corriere dei Trasporti **8642**
0010-9207 Corriere del Farmacista†
0010-9215 Corriere del Teatro
0010-9223 Corriere dell'Aviatore
0010-9231 Corriere di Caracas
0010-924X Corriere d'Italia **3528**
0010-9258 Corriere Fitopatologico **784**
0010-9266 Corriere Internazionale del Teatro
0010-9274 Corriere Italiano
0010-9282 Corriere Sindacale†
0010-9290 Corriere Stenografico† **8944**
0010-9304 Corrispondenza Socialista
0010-9312 Corrosion **3375**
0010-9320 Corrosion Abstracts†
0010-9339 Corrosion Abstracts **3229**

0011-5185 D W I - Berichte†
0011-5193 D W V - Mitteilungen
0011-5207 Da-a - U dela
0011-5231 Der Dachshund **6806**
0011-5258 Dados **7958**
0011-5266 Daedalus **4449**
0011-5290 The Daffodil Journal **3728**
0011-5320 Daheim bei der W A G **4409**
0011-5339 Dahl, Dunn & Hargitt's Moving Average Commodity Service†
0011-5347 Dai Damu
0011-5355 Daiichi Kogyo Seiyaku. Shaho **2122**
0011-5371 The Daily Athenaeum **2280**
0011-538X Daily Blessing **7753**
0011-5398 Daily Cardinal **2280**
0011-5401 Daily Construction Service **1001**
0011-541X Daily Gleaner - Farmers Weekly†
0011-5428 Daily Gleaner - Food Supplement **3633**
0011-5436 Hebrew Journal†
0011-5444 Daily Kent Stater **2280**
0011-5479 Flygvapennytt *changed to* 1652-3571 **6425**
0011-5487 The Daily Reporter (Columbus) **4654**
0011-5509 Daily Variety (Los Angeles) **2379**
0011-5517 South Africa. Weather Bureau. Daily Weather Bulletin **6395**
0011-5525 Daily Word **7753**
0011-5568 Dairy Council Digest **6657**
0011-5592 Dairy Goat Journal **284**
0011-5614 Dairy Herd Management **263**
0011-5630 Dairy Industry Journal of Southern Africa†
0011-5681 Dairy Science Abstracts **179**
0011-5738 Dairynews†
0011-5762 Dak Tar **2354**
0011-5800 Dalesman **3864**
0011-5819 Dalhousie Gazette **2281**
0011-5827 The Dalhousie Review **5213**
0011-586X Dallas Medical Journal **5603**
0011-5894 Daltons Weekly **7588**
0011-5908 Damals **4137**
0011-5916 Damernas Vaerld **3955**
0011-5940 Damn You
0011-5959 Het Dampsel **8168**
0011-5967 Damu Nippon **3264**
0011-5975 Dan Smoot Report†
0011-5983 Dance & Dancers†
0011-6009 Dance Magazine **2684**
0011-6017 Dance News†
0011-6025 Dance News and Recall
0011-6033 Dance Perspectives†
0011-6041 Dance Scope†
0011-605X Dancing Times **2685**
0011-6068 Dandy
0011-6084 Danish Journal†
0011-6149 Danmarks Nationalbank. Monetary Review **1334**
0011-6157 Danmarksposten **3529**
0011-6173 Danses†
0011-6203 Dansk Artilleri-Tidsskrift **6417**
0011-6238 Dansk Bridge **8168**
0011-6297 Geological Society of Denmark. Bulletin **2739**
0011-6335 Dansk Kemi **2059**
0011-6351 Nye Dansk Landbrug†
0011-636X Dansk Mejeritidende†
0011-6394 Dansk Ornitologisk Forenings Tidsskrift **906**
0011-6416 Dansk Patenttidende **6748**
0011-6424 Dansk Pelsdyravl **4973**
0011-6548 Dansk Vejtidsskrift *changed to* Trafik & Veje **3285**
0011-6610 Danske Oekonomer *changed to* 0107-699X **4707**
0011-6637 Darbininkas **7794**
0011-6645 Daring Confessions
0011-667X Dark Horse†
0011-6688 Dark Shadows†
0011-6718 Darpon†
0011-6726 D'Ars **485**
0011-6734 Darshana International†
0011-6750 Dartmouth College Library Bulletin **5005**
0011-6769 Dartnell Office Administration Service†
0011-6777 Dartnell Sales and Marketing Service†
0011-6793 Darwiniana **785**
0011-6831 Data Management†
0011-6858 Data Processing Digest†
0011-6882 Data Processing Practitioner†
0011-6890 Data Processor†
0011-6971 Dataweek†
0011-698X Dateline Delhi
0011-7005 Datenjournal†
0011-703X Davar **5213**
0011-7048 Davka†
0011-7064 Dawn†
0011-7080 Day by Day **5213**
0011-7102 Daybreak
0011-7110 Dayig u-Midgeh be-Yisrael **3590**
0011-7129 Daytime TV†
0011-7145 Db **8152**
0011-7161 Echo (De Aar)†
0011-7188 DePaul Law Review **4656**
0011-7196 Deadwood†
0011-7242 Debates Sociais **8036**
0011-7250 Decalogue Journal†
0011-7269 The Deccan Geographer **4003**
0011-7293 Decimal Currency and Metrication News†
0011-7307 Decision **7754**
0011-7315 Decision Sciences **1738**
0011-7323 United States Government Accountability Office. Decisions of the Comptroller General of the United States **7474**
0011-7331 U.S. Department of the Interior. Decisions **7472**
0011-734X Deco Trefoil†
0011-7358 Decor (Maryland Heights) **4555**
0011-7412 Decorating Your First Home†
0011-7420 Decoration - Ameublement
0011-748X Defence Science Journal **6418**
0011-7501 Defender (Defiance) **2281**
0011-7552 Defense de l'Occident†
0011-7560 Defense des Distillateurs Ambulants et des Bouilleurs de Cru†
0011-7587 Defense Law Journal **4830**
0011-7595 Defense Management Journal†
0011-7625 Defense Transportation Journal **6419**
0011-7641 A Defesa Nacional†
0011-765X Anuario Estadistico da Defensa Nacional **6410**
0011-7676 Definition†
0011-7684 Dein Freund†
0011-7706 Deirdre†
0011-7714 Dekalb Literary Arts Journal†
0011-7722 Delavska Enotnost **4593**
0011-7730 Delaware Archaeology†
0011-7749 Delaware Geological Survey. Reports of Investigations **2730**
0011-7765 Delaware History **4290**
0011-7773 Delaware Library Association Bulletin **5005**
0011-7781 Delaware Medical Journal **5603**
0011-782X Delfts Bouwkundig Studenten Gezelschap Styles. Mededelingen
0011-7846 Delhi Law Times **4656**
0011-7854 Delhi Medical Journal†
0011-7862 Deli News **3677**
0011-7870 Delinquency and Society†
0011-7889 Delirante†
0011-7927 Delmarva Report†
0011-7935 Delo†
0011-7951 Delos **5283**
0011-7978 Delta **104**
0011-7986 Delta (Plymouth)
0011-7994 Delta†
0011-8036 Delta Farm Press **104**
0011-8044 Delta Kappa Gamma Bulletin **2977**
0011-8052 Delta Pi Epsilon Journal **2977**
0011-8060 The Paper Book **4755**
0011-8087 Deltion Diikiseos Epichiriseon **1738**
0011-8095 Deltion Dimotikis Vivliothikis Hermoupoleos†
0011-8141 DeLuxe General Rewind†
0011-8184 D E Mly†
0011-8192 Democrat (Washington)†
0011-8206 Democratic German Report†
0011-8214 Democratic Journalist† **8949**
0011-8222 Democratie Moderne **7129**
0011-8249 Demografia **7281**
0011-8265 Demografie **7305**
0011-8281 Demography and Development Digest†
0011-829X Demokraat†
0011-832X Demos (Amsterdam)†
0011-8338 Demosta†
0011-8346 Radio Waves and Examination†
0011-8370 Denken en Doen
0011-8389 Denki Seiko **6310**
0011-8397 Denkisha no Kagaku†
0011-8419 Denmark. Civilforsvarsstyrelsen. Orientation†
0011-8435 Radio, TV, HiFi & Electronics†
0011-8451 Densei Technical Journal
0011-8486 Dental Abstracts **5744**
0011-8524 Dental Cadmos **5839**
0011-8532 Dental Clinics of North America **5839**
0011-8540 Dental Concepts†
0011-8559 Dental-Dienst†
0011-8575 Dental Echo†
0011-8583 Dental Economics **5840**
0011-8605 Dental Health **5840**
0011-863X Dental Industry Newsletter†
0011-8656 Das Dental-Labor **5840**
0011-8672 Dental Laboratory Review†
0011-8680 Dental Management†
0011-8699 Dental Mirror
0011-8702 Shikai Tenbo **5865**
0011-8710 Dental Practice **5840**
0011-8737 Dental Products Report **5841**
0011-8788 Dental Survey†
0011-8796 Dental Technician **5841**
0011-8818 Dentists Marketplace
0011-8826 Denver Art Museum. Quarterly†
0011-8869 Denver Quarterly **4449**
0011-8885 Department Store Employees Union. Local Twenty One Guide†
0011-8915 Department Store Workers' Union. Local 1-S News **4593**
0011-8990 Derbyshire Life and Countryside **3864**
0011-9008 Derevoobrabatyvayushchaya Promyshlennost' **3711**
0011-9016 Dergi†
0011-9032 Dermatologia†
0011-9059 International Journal of Dermatology **5877**
0011-9156 Des Moines. Public Library. Monthly Memo†
0011-9164 Desalination **8820**
0011-9172 Desalination Abstracts†
0011-9199 Desarrollo†
0011-9202 Desarrollo Administrativo†
0011-9210 Descant **5283**
0011-9229 Desert Call
0011-9245 Design†
0011-9261 Design†
0011-927X Design†
0011-9288 Design & Components in Engineering†
0011-9296 Design & Development†
0011-9318 Design Australia†
0011-9342 Design Engineering **3186**
0011-9385 Design Industrie
0011-9407 Design News **8420**
0011-9415 Design Quarterly†
0011-9423 Designer (London)†
0011-944X Designscape†
0011-9474 Desmos
0011-9490 Dessa Mina Minsta†
0011-9547 Destellos Evangelicos†
0011-9563 Destino†
0011-9571 Detail (German Edition) **440**
0011-9601 Detroit Dental Bulletin†
0011-9636 Detroit Institute of Arts. Bulletin **486**
0011-9644 Detroit Jewish News **7720**
0011-9652 The Detroit Lawyer†
0011-9687 The Detroit Society for Genealogical Research. Magazine **3764**
0011-9695 Detroit Teacher **2841**
0011-9709 Detroiter **1401**
0011-9725 Dettaglio Tessile e dell'Abbigliamento†
0011-9741 Deutsch als Fremdsprache **5110**
0011-975X Die Deutsche Buehne **8469**
0011-9822 Deutsche Akademie fuer Staedtebau und Landesplanung. Mitteilungen **4409**
0011-9857 Deutsche Apotheker Zeitung **6832**
0011-9881 Deutsche Aussenpolitik†
0011-989X Deutsche Automobil Revue†
0011-9911 Deutsche Baumeister†
0011-992X Deutsche Baumschule **3728**
0011-9954 Deutsche Bibliographie. Das Deutsche Buch†
0011-9989 Deutsche Buecherschau†
0011-9997 Deutsche Bundesbank. Mitteilungen **1335**
0012-0006 Deutsche Bundesbank. Monatsberichte **1335**
0012-0030 Dokumentationszentrale Wasser Schriftenreihe
0012-0081 Der Deutsche Fallschirmjaeger†
0012-009X Defazet†
0012-0189 Deutsche Geologische Gesellschaft. Zeitschrift *changed to* 1860-1804 **2730**
0012-0197 Deutsche Gesellschaft fuer Geologische Wissenschaften. Berichte. Reihe A: Geologie und Palaeontologie, Reihe B: Mineralogie und Lagerstaettenforschung†
0012-0200 Deutsche Gesellschaft fuer Versicherungsmathematik. Blaetter *changed to* 1864-0281 **4496**
0012-026X Deutsche Hebammen-Zeitschrift **5989**
0012-0332 Deutsche Jugend **2150**
0012-0413 Deutsche Lebensmittel-Rundschau **3633**
0012-0421 Deutsche Lehrerzeitung
0012-043X Deutsche Literaturzeitung†
0012-0456 Deutsche Mathematiker Vereinigung. Jahresbericht **5482**
0012-0464 Deutsche Mechaniker Zeitung†
0012-0472 Deutsche Medizinische Wochenschrift **5604**
0012-0480 Deutsche Milchwirtschaft **264**
0012-0553 Der Deutsche Pelztierzuechter†
0012-057X Deutsche Polizei **2650**
0012-0588 Deutsche Post (Berlin)†
0012-0618 Deutsche Rentenversicherung **4501**
0012-0693 Die Deutsche Schrift **486**
0012-0707 Deutsche Schuetzenzeitung **8169**
0012-0731 Die Deutsche Schule **2841**
0012-0812 Deutsche Studien†
0012-0820 Der Deutsche Tabakbau **8486**
0012-091X Deutsche Versicherungszeitschrift†
0012-0936 Deutsche Vierteljahrsschrift fuer Literaturwissenschaft und Geistesgeschichte **4449**
0012-0944 Neue Volkskunst†
0012-1029 Deutsche Zahnaerztliche Zeitschrift **5842**
0012-1045 Deutsche Zeitschrift fuer Philosophie **6913**
0012-1096 Deutscher Drucker **7319**
0012-110X Der Fass- und Weinkuefer†
0012-1134 Deutscher Lebensmittelgrosshandel **3633**
0012-1142 Deutscher Lebensmittelhandel **3633**
0012-1169 Deutscher Palaestina-Verein. Zeitschrift **548**
0012-1177 Deutscher Studenten-Anzeiger†
0012-1185 Deutscher Verein fuer Oeffentliche und Private Fuersorge. Nachrichtendienst **8037**
0012-1193 Deutsches Adelsblatt **3764**
0012-1207 Deutsches Aerzteblatt. Ausgabe A **5604**
0012-1215 Deutsches Architektenblatt **440**
0012-1223 Deutsches Archiv fuer Erforschung des Mittelalters **4137**
0012-1231 D A R **4654**
0012-1304 Deutsches Institut fuer Wirtschaftsforschung. Wochenbericht **1476**
0012-1320 Deutsches Medizinisches Journal†
0012-1339 Deutsches Museum. Abhandlungen und Berichte **6523**
0012-1363 Deutsches Verwaltungsblatt **4657**
0012-1401 Deutschland - Frankreich†
0012-141X Deutschland-Magazin **7129**
0012-1428 Deutschland Archiv **7958**
0012-1436 Deutschland-Berichte
0012-1444 Deutschland-Informationen†
0012-1452 Der Deutschland-Sammler†
0012-1460 Der Deutschunterricht **3057**
0012-1509 Deux Mille†
0012-1525 Developer
0012-1533 Developing Economies **1593**
0012-155X Development and Change **1593**
0012-1576 Development Digest†
0012-1592 Development, Growth and Differentiation **668**
0012-1606 Developmental Biology **668**
0012-1622 Developmental Medicine and Child Neurology **6091**
0012-1630 Developmental Psychobiology **668**
0012-1649 Developmental Psychology **7351**
0012-1665 Devenir Historico
0012-1673 Devil's Advocate†
0012-1681 Devon and Cornwall Notes and Queries **4214**
0012-169X Devon Farmer **105**
0012-1703 Devon Life **3864**
0012-172X Dewey Newsletter†
0012-1738 Dhara
0012-1746 Dharma **7637**
0012-1762 Dia Medico†
0012-1789 Diabete et Nutrition†
0012-1797 Diabetes **5886**
0012-1819 Diabetes Literature Index†
0012-186X Diabetologia **5890**
0012-1878 Diafora
0012-1886 Diaghonios†
0012-1894 Diagnosi - Laboratorio e Clinica†
0012-1916 Diagnostica†
0012-1924 Diagnostica **7352**
0012-1959 Diakonia†

DIRECTORY 2010 0013-9130 9023

0013-3167 Ekonomisk Revy†
0013-3183 Ekonomiska Samfundets Tidskrift **1103**
0013-3205 Ekonomista **1103**
0013-323X Ekonomska Misao
0013-3248 Ekonomska Politika **1482**
0013-3264 Ekonomski Anali **1104**
0013-3272 Ekonomski Glasnik†
0013-3302 Ekran **6497**
0013-3353 Ekspress-Informatsiya. Automobilestroenie†
0013-3361 Ekspress-Informatsiya. Avtomobil'nyi Transport†
0013-3396 Ekspress-Informatsiya. Elektricheskie Mashiny i Apparaty†
0013-340X Ekspress-Informatsiya. Elektricheskie Stantsii, Seti i Sistemy†
0013-3426 Ekspress-Informatsiya. Fotokinoapparatura. Nauchnaya i Prikladnaya Fotografiya†
0013-3434 Ekspress-Informatsiya. Garazhi i Garazhnoe Oborudovanie†
0013-3442 Ekspress-Informatsiya. Gidroenergetika†
0013-3450 Ekspress-Informatsiya. Gornorudnaya Promyshlennost'†
0013-3477 Ekspress-Informatsiya. Iskusstvennye Sooruzheniya na Avtomobil'nykh Dorogakh†
0013-3493 Ekspress-Informatsiya. Khimicheskaya Tekhnologiya Pererabotki Vysokopolimernykh Materialov†
0013-3507 Ekspress-Informatsiya. Khimiya i Pererabotka Nefti i Gaza†
0013-3515 Ekspress-Informatsiya. Khimia i Tekhnologiya Neorganicheskikh Veshchestv†
0013-3558 Ekspress Informatsiya. Lokomotivostroenie i Vagonostroenie†
0013-3574 Ekspress-Informatsiya. Myasnaya i Molochnaya Promyshlennost'†
0013-3582 Ekspress-Informatsiya. Nefte- i Gazodobyvayushchaya Promyshlennost'†
0013-3590 Ekspress-Informatsiya. Obogashchenie Poleznykh Iskopaemykh†
0013-3612 Ekspress-Informatsiya. Pishchevaya Promyshlennost'†
0013-3620 Ekspress-Informatsiya. Pod'emno-Transportnoe Mashinostroenie†
0013-3701 Ekspress-Informatsiya. Radiolokatsiya, Televidenie, Radiosvyaz'†
0013-3736 Ekspress-Informatsiya. Rybnaya Promyshlennost'†
0013-3744 Ekspress-Informatsiya. Sel'skokhozyaistvennye Mashiny i Orudiya. Mekhanizatsiya Sel'skokhozyaistvennykh Rabot†
0013-3752 Ekspress-Informatsiya. Silikatnye Stroitel'nye Materialy†
0013-3787 Ekspress-Informatsiya. Steklo, Keramika i Ogneupory†
0013-3795 Ekspress-Informatsiya. Stroitel'stvo i Ekspluatatsiya Avtomobilnykh Dorog†
0013-3809 Ekspress-Informatsiya. Sudostroenie†
0013-3833 Ekspress-Informatsiya. Tekhnicheskaya Ekspluatatsiya Podvizhnogo Sostava i Tyaga Poezdov†
0013-3884 Ekspress-Informatsiya. Tekstil'naya Promyshlennost'†
0013-3892 Ekspress-Informatsiya. Teoriya i Praktika Nauchnoi Informatsii†
0013-3906 Ekspress-Informatsiya. Teploenergetika†
0013-3914 Ekspress-Informatsiya. Traktorostroenie†
0013-3922 Ekspress-Informatsiya. Transport i Khranenie Nefti i Gaza†
0013-3930 Ekspress-Informatsiya. Tsellyulozno-Bumazhnaya Promyshlennost'†
0013-3957 Ekspress-Informatsiya. Ugol'naya Promyshlennost'†
0013-3965 Ekspress-Informatsiya. Vodnyi Transport†
0013-3973 Ekspress-Informatsiya. Vozdushnyi Transport†
0013-3981 Ekspress-Informatsiya. Vychislitel'naya Tekhnika†
0013-4007 Elbranschen **3302**
0013-4023 El Paso Archaeology **392**
0013-404X El Salvador. Direccion General de Estadistica y Censos. Boletin Estadistico **8367**
0013-4058 Elam
0013-4082 Elders
0013-4120 Electric Light and Power **3302**
0013-4139 Electric Power Statistics (Washington)†
0013-4244 Electrical Business **3302**
0013-4279 Electrical Contractor (Sydney)
0013-4317 Electrical Equipment *changed to* 1472-1287 **3297**
0013-435X Electrical India **3303**
0013-4384 Electrical Review **3303**
0013-4414 Electrical Times **3304**
0013-4422 Electrical Wholesaler **3304**
0013-4430 Electrical Wholesaling **1815**
0013-4481 Electricite
0013-4538 Electricity and Electronics **3095**
0013-4589 Electro Optics **7075**
0013-4635 Electro-Technology†
0013-4643 Electro-Technology **3304**
0013-4651 Electrochemical Society. Journal **2113**
0013-466X Electrochemical Society of India. Journal **2113**
0013-4686 Electrochimica Acta **2113**
0013-4708 Electrolysis Digest†
0013-4716 Electromechanical Design†
0013-4740 Electron†
0013-4767 Electron **2358**
0013-4775 Electroanalytical Abstracts†
0013-4783 Electronic Age†
0013-4791 Electronic & Appliance Specialist†
0013-4813 Electronic Application News **3095**
0013-4848 Electronic Capabilities†
0013-4872 Electronic Design **3095**
0013-4929 Electronic Instrument Digest†
0013-4953 Electronic Products **3096**
0013-4961 Electronic Progress†
0013-5011 Electronic Trends: International†
0013-502X Electronica†
0013-5046 Elternblatt†
0013-5054 Electronica y Fisica Aplicada†
0013-5062 Electronicien
0013-5100 Electronics and Communications†
0013-5119 Electronics and Communications Abstracts†
0013-5143 Electronics Digest†
0013-516X Electronics for You **3096**
0013-5194 Electronics Letters **3097**
0013-5208 Electronics Record†
0013-5224 Electronics Weekly **3097**
0013-5267 Electronique Medicale†
0013-5283 Electronique Professionnelle Belge
0013-5313 Electrotecnia Popular†
0013-5348 Eleftherotypia
0013-5372 Elektricheskie Stantsii (Moscow, 1929)†
0013-5380 Elektrichestvo **3157**
0013-5399 Elektrie
0013-5402 Elektrik Muhendisligi **3305**
0013-5429 Elektrische Ausruestung fuer Maschine und Betrieb
0013-5437 Elektrische Bahnen **8617**
0013-5445 E M A - Elektrische Maschinen **3301**
0013-5453 I T T Elektrisches Nachrichtenwesen
0013-5488 Elektrizitaetsverwertung†
0013-550X Elektro *changed to* 1502-4911 **3307**
0013-5534 Elektro-Heizung
0013-5542 E H - Elektro Handel†
0013-5550 Elektro Nachrichten†
0013-5569 Elektropraktiker **3306**
0013-5577 Elektromarkt **3097**
0013-5585 Biomedizinische Technik **5587**
0013-5615 Electronaut†
0013-5658 Elektronik **3098**
0013-5674 Elektronik Journal **3098**
0013-5690 Elektronikk **3098**
0013-5739 Elektronnaya Obrabotka Materialov **5008**
0013-5763 Elektropromishlenost i Priborostroene
0013-5771 Elektrosvyaz' **2358**
0013-5828 Elektrotehnicar†
0013-5836 Elektrotehnika **3306**
0013-5844 Elektrotehnika **3306**
0013-5852 Elektrotehniski Vestnik **3306**
0013-5860 Elektrotekhnika **3306**
0013-5887 Elektrowirtschaft **3306**
0013-5895 Elektuur **3099**
0013-5909 Elelmezesi Ipar **3634**
0013-5933 Elementa†
0013-5984 The Elementary School Journal **2852**
0013-600X Elemente†
0013-6018 Elemente der Mathematik **5486**
0013-6026 Elements, Produits, Services†
0013-6042 Elenco dei Quotidiani e Periodici Italiani†
0013-6050 Elenco Ufficiale dei Protesti Cambiari Levati nella Provincia di Torino
0013-6069 Elepaio **906**
0013-6077 Elet es Tudomany **7852**
0013-6093 Elettrificazione **3158**
0013-6107 Elettrodomestica†
0013-6115 Elettrodomus†
0013-6123 Elettronica e Telecomunicazioni **3099**
0013-614X Elevator Constructor **1006**
0013-6158 Elevator World **1006**
0013-6190 Elinstallatoeren **3306**
0013-6212 Elisabethbode **7640**
0013-6220 Elisha Mitchell Scientific Society. Journal *changed to* North Carolina Academy of Science. Journal **7893**
0013-6247 Elizabeth†
0013-6255 Elizabethan†
0013-6263 The Elks Magazine **2265**
0013-6298 Elle (Paris) **8860**
0013-6301 Ellery Queen's Anthology†
0013-631X Ellery Queen's Mystery Magazine. Braille Edition†
0013-6336 Ellinika **2234**
0013-6352 Eloquenza
0013-6360 Eloquenza Siciliana
0013-6409 Elsevier Select†
0013-6417 Elta†
0013-6468 Eltheto†
0013-6484 Elvis Monthly† **8953**
0013-6492 Eiyo Nippon **6658**
0013-6522 Emantalehti **4357**
0013-6530 Embalagem
0013-6557 Emballage Digest **6709**
0013-6581 Emballering **6709**
0013-662X Ementario da Legislacao do Petroleo **4822**
0013-6638 Ementario Forense
0013-6646 Emergency Health Services Newsletter†
0013-6654 Emergency Medicine **6059**
0013-6662 Emerita **5114**
0013-6697 Emigrato Italiano
0013-6700 Emigrazione†
0013-6719 Emmanuel **7796**
0013-6727 Emory Magazine **2282**
0013-6743 The Forum (Syracuse) **4503**
0013-676X Empire State Geogram **2733**
0013-6786 Empire State Iris Society Newsletter†
0013-6794 Empire State Mason **2266**
0013-6808 Employee Benefit Plan Review **1860**
0013-6824 Employee Relations in Action **1677**
0013-6883 Employment Review (Albany) **1680**
0013-6891 Empoli
0013-6913 Emuna†
0013-6921 En Avant† **8953**
0013-693X En Concreto
0013-6956 En Haa†
0013-6964 En Marche **6985**
0013-6972 En Viaje†
0013-6980 Enact **8470**
0013-6999 Enamelling Newsletter†
0013-7006 L'Encephale **6137**
0013-7057 Encore: a Quarterly of Verse & Poetic Arts†
0013-7065 Encounter†
0013-7073 Encounter (London, 1953)†
0013-7081 Encounter (Indianapolis) **7640**
0013-709X Encounter Today†
0013-7103 Encres Vives **5421**
0013-7111 Encuentro†
0013-712X Encyclopaedia Africana. Information Report **4174**
0013-7138 Encyclopaedia Moderna†
0013-7146 Encyclopedie Politique Arabe. Documents et Notes
0013-7154 Trends in End-Use Markets for Plastics†
0013-7170 Endeavour
0013-7227 Endocrinology **5891**
0013-7235 Endocrinology Index†
0013-7243 Endocrinologya y Terapeutica†
0013-726X Endoscopy **5923**
0013-7278 Energetik **3128**
0013-7294 Energetyka **3128**
0013-7316 Energia es Atomtechnika **3167**
0013-7324 Energia Nuclear†
0013-7332 Energia Nucleare†
0013-7340 Energie†
0013-7359 Energie†
0013-7413 Energiestatistiek
0013-7448 Energija **3129**
0013-7472 Energy and Character
0013-7502 Energy Developments†
0013-7510 Energy Info†
0013-7545 Enfance **2151**
0013-7553 L'Enfant†
0013-7561 Enfant en Milieu Tropical†
0013-757X Enfants du Monde **8038**
0013-7596 Enfys **3532**
0013-7626 Engei Gakkai Zasshi *changed to* 1882-3351 **3739**
0013-7642 Engelhard Industries Technical Bulletin†
0013-7669 Engenharia†
0013-7723 Engenheiro Moderno†
0013-774X Engine Data Sheets
0013-7758 The Engineer **3188**
0013-7782 Engineering **3188**
0013-7812 Engineering & Science **3189**
0013-7847 Engineering Capacity and Export Review
0013-7898 Engineering Designer **3189**
0013-7901 Engineering Digest†
0013-791X The Engineering Economist **3189**
0013-7928 Facts from Gatorland†
0013-7936 Engineering Forum **3189**
0013-7944 Engineering Fracture Mechanics **3344**
0013-7952 Engineering Geology **3266**
0013-7979 Engineering Index Card-A-Lert†
0013-7987 Engineering Industries & Trade Journal
0013-8029 Engineering Journal **3266**
0013-8053 Engineering Production†
0013-810X Engineering Research News†
0013-8134 Engineering Times
0013-8142 Engineers and Engines Magazine **8617**
0013-8169 Engineers' Digest **3190**
0013-8177 Coast Guard Engineer's Digest **3184**
0013-8185 Englisch **5114**
0013-8215 English **5289**
0013-8231 English Dance and Song **6565**
0013-824X English for Immigrants†
0013-8266 The English Historical Review **4217**
0013-8274 English Journal **3061**
0013-8282 English Language Notes **5290**
0013-8304 E L H **5286**
0013-8312 English Literary Renaissance **5290**
0013-8339 English Literature in Transition, 1880-1920 **5290**
0013-8355 English Quarterly *changed to* English Quarterly Canada **3061**
0013-8363 English Record **5290**
0013-8398 English Studies in Africa **4451**
0013-8401 English Westerners' Society. Brand Book **4292**
0013-841X English Westerners' Tally Sheet **4292**
0013-8444 Enjiniasu **3191**
0013-8460 Enbi to Porima **2122**
0013-8479 Enlightenment Essays
0013-8487 Enlite†
0013-8495 Enoch Pratt Free Library. Staff Reporter **5008**
0013-8509 Enquiry†
0013-8517 Enquiry **7133**
0013-8533 Ensanian Physicochemical Institute. Journal **7010**
0013-855X Ensayo†
0013-8584 L'Enseignement Mathematique **5486**
0013-8592 Ensemble†
0013-8614 Ensino Secundario
0013-8622 Ente Provinciale per il Turismo di Nuoro. Notiziario†
0013-8630 Entente Africaine **3532**
0013-8657 Enterprise (Ontario) **3809**
0013-8665 Enterprise†
0013-8673 Enterprise **1959**
0013-8681 Enterprise
0013-8703 Entomologia Experimentalis et Applicata **844**
0013-872X Entomological News **844**
0013-8738 Entomological Review **845**
0013-8746 Entomological Society of America. Annals **845**
0013-8762 Entomological Society of India. Bulletin of Entomology **845**
0013-8797 Entomological Society of Washington. Proceedings **846**
0013-8819 Entomologische Arbeiten aus dem Museum G. Frey, Tutzing-Bei Muenchen†
0013-8827 Entomologische Berichten **846**
0013-8835 Entomologische Blaetter fuer Biologie und Systematik der Kaefer **846**
0013-8843 Entomologische Zeitschrift **846**
0013-8851 Entomologiske Meddelelser **846**
0013-886X Entomologisk Tidskrift **846**
0013-8878 The Entomologist†
0013-8886 L'Entomologiste **846**
0013-8894 Entomologist's Gazette **846**
0013-8908 Entomologist's Monthly Magazine **846**
0013-8916 Entomologist's Record and Journal of Variation **846**
0013-8924 Entomology Abstracts **715**
0013-8932 Florida. Department of Agriculture and Consumer Services. Entomology Circular **847**
0013-8967 Entomops†
0013-8975 Entr'acte†
0013-9041 Entrepreneur Menuisier
0013-9084 Entropie† **8954**
0013-9092 Entscheidung (Holzgerlingen) **7755**
0013-9106 Entscheidungen des Bundesverwaltungsgerichts (Cologne) **4666**
0013-9130 Environnement

ISSN

ISSN

DIRECTORY 2010 0017-3916 9029

0016-7975 Geominas **2708**
0016-7983 Geophysical Abstracts†
0016-8017 Geophysical Magazine†
0016-8025 Geophysical Prospecting **2782**
0016-8033 Geophysics **2782**
0016-8076 George Washington Law Review **4679**
0016-8092 Georgetown Law Journal **4680**
0016-8106 Georgetown Medical Bulletin
0016-8122 Georgia Agricultural Research†
0016-8130 Georgia Alumni Record **2285**
0016-8149 Georgia AnchorAge **8644**
0016-8157 Georgia Augusta **2982**
0016-8181 Georgia C. P. A†
0016-819X Georgia Dental Association. Journal
0016-822X Georgia Engineer†
0016-8262 Georgia Future Farmer **115**
0016-8297 Georgia Historical Quarterly **4293**
0016-8300 Georgia Law Review **4680**
0016-8335 Georgia Nursing **5959**
0016-8378 Georgia Rehabilitation News†
0016-8386 The Georgia Review **5300**
0016-8394 Georgia School Boards Bulletin
0016-8408 Georgia Social Science Journal†
0016-8424 Georgia State University Signal **2285**
0016-8483 Geoscience Documentation **2720**
0016-8505 Geotechnique **3268**
0016-8521 Geotectonics **2782**
0016-853X Geotektonika **2744**
0016-8556 Geotimes *changed to* 1943-345X **2706**
0016-8572 Gep **5452**
0016-8599 Geraniums Around the World **3733**
0016-8610 Gereformeerd Theologisch Tijdschrift† **8959**
0016-8629 Gereformeerde Kerken in Noord-Brabant en Limburg. Kerkblad†
0016-8637 Gerencia
0016-867X Geriatrics **4045**
0016-8688 Geriatrics Digest†
0016-8696 Gerlands Beitraege zur Geophysik†
0016-870X Gerling-Informationen fuer Geschaeftsfreunde†
0016-8726 German Constructions†
0016-8769 German International†
0016-8777 German Life and Letters **5300**
0016-8793 German News **1488**
0016-8807 German Patents Abstracts†
0016-8823 German Postal Specialist **6895**
0016-8831 The German Quarterly **5122**
0016-884X Philosophy and History†
0016-8858 German Tribune†
0016-8866 Germana Esperanta Fervojista Asocio. Bulteno **8617**
0016-8874 Germania **395**
0016-8890 The Germanic Review **5122**
0016-8904 Germanisch-Romanische Monatsschrift **5300**
0016-8912 Germanistik (Tuebingen) **5407**
0016-8920 Germantown Courier
0016-8963 Germany Stamp News†
0016-9005 Gerontologie
0016-9013 The Gerontologist **4046**
0016-9021 Geschaeftsmann und Christ **7759**
0016-903X Geschaeftsmappe fuer Gemeinden und Standesaemter†
0016-9056 Geschichte in Wissenschaft und Unterricht **4140**
0016-9080 Gesellschaft fuer Natur- und Voelkerkunde Ostasiens. Nachrichten **549**
0016-9099 Gesellschaft und Politik **7138**
0016-9102 Gesellschaftspolitische Kommentare **7138**
0016-9129 Gesetz- und Verordnungsblatt fuer Schleswig-Holstein **7493**
0016-9145 Gesher **7721**
0016-9153 Gesichertes Leben *changed to* Zukunft Jetzt **8079**
0016-9161 Gesnerus **5619**
0016-920X Gesta **491**
0016-9218 Gestions Hospitalieres **4094**
0016-9226 Gesund durch Sauna†
0016-9234 Gesund Leben **6986**
0016-9242 Gesunde Mensch†
0016-9250 Gesundes Leben *changed to* 1613-3943 **6993**
0016-9285 Gesundheitsnachrichten **6987**
0016-9293 Gesundheitspolitik†
0016-9307 Gesundheitspolitische Umschau†
0016-9323 Getraenkelndustrie **604**
0016-9331 Der Getraenkehandel **604**
0016-9374 Geuzen Penning†
0016-9390 Gewaltfreie Aktion **7237**
0016-9404 Gewerbearchiv **4868**
0016-9420 Gewerblicher Rechtsschutz und Urheberrecht **6750**
0016-9447 Gewerkschaftliche Monatshefte†
0016-9455 Gewerkschaftliche Rundschau†
0016-9463 Gewerkschafts Presse†
0016-9471 Das Gewissen†
0016-9498 Gezinsblad
0016-9501 Gezond Limburg†
0016-951X Gezondheid en Ziekenfonds†
0016-9536 Ghana Geographical Association. Bulletin **4013**
0016-9544 Ghana Journal of Science **7858**
0016-9552 Ghana Library Journal
0016-9560 Ghana Medical Journal **5619**
0016-9579 Ghana News **7138**
0016-9587 Ghana Review **3861**
0016-9633 Ghost Dance†
0016-965X Il Giardino Fiorito†
0016-9668 Gib Acht†
0016-9684 Gibson Report
0016-9706 Gidroliznaya i Lesokhimicheskaya Promyshlennost'†
0016-9714 Gidrotekhnicheskoe Stroitel'stvo **3361**
0016-9730 De Gids **5218**
0016-9757 Giervalk-Gerfaut†
0016-9765 Giesserei **6313**
0016-9773 Giesserei - Erfahrungsaustausch **6313**
0016-9781 Giesserei-Praxis **6313**
0016-979X Giesserei Rundschau **6313**
0016-9854 Gift Buyer International
0016-9862 Gifted Child Quarterly **3040**
0016-9900 Gigiena i Sanitariya **6987**
0016-9935 Technology and Industries†
0016-9943 Gil Vicente†
0016-9951 Gilbert and Sullivan Journal†
0016-9978 Gildenfreund†
0016-9986 Gildenweg **2266**
0016-9994 Giligia†
0017-0003 Gimlaoth†
0017-0011 Ginekologia Polska **5991**
0017-0054 Giocattoli†
0017-0062 Gioia **8865**
0017-0089 Giornale Critico della Filosofia Italiana **6921**
0017-0097 Giornale degli Economisti e Annali di Economia **1113**
0017-0100 Giornale degli Uccelli
0017-0119 Nuovo Giornale dei Distillatori† **8978**
0017-0127 Giornale dei Genitori†
0017-0135 Giornale degli Allevatori
0017-016X Giornale del Genio Civile **3268**
0017-0186 Giornale del Mezzogiorno
0017-0208 Giornale della Cogne
0017-0224 Giornale della Arteriosclerosi
0017-0232 Giornale dello Spettacolo **2686**
0017-0259 Giornale di Barga **3897**
0017-0283 Giornale di Fisica **7014**
0017-0305 Giornale di Gerontologia **4047**
0017-033X Giornale di Mathematiche di Battaglini
0017-0364 Giornale di Medicina Militare **5619**
0017-0372 Giornale di Metafisica **6921**
0017-0380 Giornale di Microbiologia†
0017-0399 Giornale di Psichiatria e di Neuropatologia†
0017-0429 Giornale Economico **1403**
0017-0445 Giornale Italiano di Chemioterapia†
0017-0453 Giornale Italiano di Chirurgia†
0017-0461 Giornale Italiano di Filologia **5122**
0017-047X Giornale Italiano di Patologia e Scienze Affini†
0017-0496 Giornale Storico della Letteratura Italiana† **8959**
0017-050X Giornale Storico della Lunigiana e del Territorio Lucense **4224**
0017-0518 Giornalismo Europeo†
0017-0526 Giovane Critica† **8959**
0017-0534 Giovane Montagna
0017-0542 Gioventu Evangelica
0017-0569 Girl Crusader†
0017-0577 Girl Scout Leader **2153**
0017-0631 Giustizia Civile **4831**
0017-064X Giustizia Nuova†
0017-0682 Gjuteriet **6314**
0017-0690 Glaces et Verres†
0017-0720 Glad Tidings **7759**
0017-0739 Glad Tidings of Good Things
0017-0747 Glamour (New York) **8865**
0017-0763 Glas-Email-Keramo-Technik†
0017-0771 Glas Istre **5218**
0017-078X Glas och Porslin **2041**
0017-0798 Glas Omladine†
0017-0801 Glas Podravine **5218**
0017-081X Glas Podrinja **3945**
0017-0828 Glas Trebinja†
0017-0836 Glasblaeser†
0017-0852 Glasforum **443**
0017-0860 Glasgow Chamber of Commerce. Journal **1403**
0017-0879 Glasgow Herald Trade Review†
0017-0887 Glasgow Illustrated
0017-0895 Glasgow Mathematical Journal **5490**
0017-0917 Glasgow University Guardian **2285**
0017-0925 Srpska Pravoslavna Crkva. Glasnik
0017-0933 Advokatska Komora Vojvodine. Glasnik **4611**
0017-095X Glasnik Matematicki **5490**
0017-0976 Glasnik Poljoprivredne Proizvodnje, Prerade i Plasmana **115**
0017-0984 Glass (Redhill) **2041**
0017-1018 Glass Digest† **8959**
0017-1026 Glass Industry†
0017-1050 Glass Technology *changed to* 1753-3546 **2040**
0017-1069 Glass Workers News†
0017-1077 Glass Workshop
0017-1093 Glasteknisk Tidskrift†
0017-1107 Glaswelt **2042**
0017-1131 The Gleaner (Camden)
0017-1166 Gledista **4454**
0017-1204 Globe and Laurel **6422**
0017-1212 Globe and Mail Report on Business **1488**
0017-1220 Globen†
0017-1239 Glocke†
0017-1263 Glos Nauczycielski **2860**
0017-1271 Glossa†
0017-1298 Glotta **2234**
0017-1301 Gloucester Diocesan Gazette
0017-1336 Giovani in Dialogo
0017-1352 The Gloxinian *changed to* Gesneriads **791**
0017-1360 Glucose Informatie†
0017-1387 Glueckauf-Forschungshefte **6463**
0017-1409 Gnade und Herrlichkeit **7645**
0017-1417 Gnomon **2234**
0017-1425 Gnosis†
0017-145X Go Boating
0017-1476 Go Greyhound†
0017-1484 Goa Today **3882**
0017-1506 Gobbles **287**
0017-1522 Goetheana Periodico Literario
0017-1549 Goettingische Gelehrte Anzeigen **5123**
0017-1565 Gold Cross **6061**
0017-1581 Golden Eye†
0017-162X Golden West Purchasor
0017-1638 Di Goldene Keyt† **8960**
0017-1654 Die Sphinx†
0017-1670 Goldmanns Mitteilungen fuer den Buchhandel†
0017-1700 Goleuad **7759**
0017-1735 Golfmagazin **8233**
0017-1751 Golf Canada
0017-176X Golf Digest **8231**
0017-1794 Golf Journal†
0017-1816 Golf Monthly **8232**
0017-1832 Golf Singapore Review
0017-1867 Golf/U.S.A†
0017-1883 Golf World **8233**
0017-1891 Golf World **8233**
0017-1913 Golfer†
0017-1948 Golas Radzimy **3800**
0017-1956 Goltdammer's Archiv fuer Strafrecht **2653**
0017-1964 Gomitolo. Cherie Moda† **8960**
0017-1980 Gong
0017-1999 Gong **2381**
0017-2022 Good Counsel†
0017-2049 Good Farming†
0017-2065 Good Government†
0017-2081 Good Housekeeping **8866**
0017-209X Good Housekeeping **4359**
0017-2111 Good Motoring **8582**
0017-212X Good News†
0017-2146 Good News **7645**
0017-2154 Confident Living†
0017-2197 Good Times†
0017-2219 Goodyear Revue†
0017-2235 Gopher Music Notes **6570**
0017-2243 Gordian† **8960**
0017-2251 Christian Scholar's Review **7632**
0017-226X Gornik†
0017-2278 Gornyi Zhurnal **6464**
0017-2294 Gorteria **791**
0017-2308 Goshen College Bulletin **2285**
0017-2332 Gospel Carrier†
0017-2359 The Gospel Messenger **4081**
0017-2367 Gospel Standard **7759**
0017-2413 Gospodarka Paliwami i Energia **3136**
0017-243X Gospodarka Rybna†
0017-2448 Gospodarka Wodna **8824**
0017-2456 Gospodarstvo
0017-2472 Gothique
0017-2480 Gottes Wort im Kirchenjahr **7646**
0017-2499 Gottesdienst und Kirchenmusik **6570**
0017-2529 Gouden Sleutels
0017-2537 Gouden Uren
0017-2553 Gourmet **3645**
0017-2561 Gourmet Club
0017-257X Government and Opposition **7138**
0017-2596 Government Contractor **4682**
0017-260X Government Employee Relations Report **1684**
0017-2626 Government Executive **7440**
0017-2642 Government Product News **7440**
0017-2693 Gown **2285**
0017-2707 Gownsman†
0017-2715 Goya **491**
0017-2723 Gozdarski Vestnik **3692**
0017-2774 Gradbeni Vestnik
0017-2790 Roots
0017-2804 Graduate Careers†
0017-2812 Graduate Careers in Science and Technology†
0017-2863 Graffitti†
0017-2898 Grafica†
0017-2901 Graficas **7321**
0017-291X El Grafico **8175**
0017-2928 Grafico
0017-2936 Graficus **7321**
0017-2952 Grafische Literatuur Centrale†
0017-2960 Grafiscope
0017-2995 De Grafiske Fag **7321**
0017-3029 Grain Age†
0017-3053 Grain Bulletin†
0017-307X Revue Technique Automobile **8601**
0017-3088 Gralswelt†
0017-310X Gramophone **6570**
0017-3118 Gran Pavese†
0017-3126 Gran Tiramolla
0017-3134 Grana **791**
0017-3142 Grande Hotel
0017-3185 Grani†
0017-3207 Granite Cutters Journal†
0017-3223 Granma Diario **3831**
0017-3231 Granta **5218**
0017-324X Granthagar **5011**
0017-3258 Grapevine†
0017-3266 Graphia
0017-3274 Graphic Antiquarian†
0017-3304 Graphic Arts Buyer†
0017-3320 Graphic Arts Patent Abstracts†
0017-3339 Graphic Arts Product News†
0017-341X Graphic Trends†
0017-3436 Graphicus **7322**
0017-3452 Graphis *changed to* Graphis Photography Annual **6969**
0017-3452 Graphis *changed to* Graphis Design Annual **492**
0017-3452 Graphis *changed to* Graphis Advertising Annual **25**
0017-3479 Graphische Revue Oesterreichs **7322**
0017-3495 Grasas y Aceites **2123**
0017-3517 Grass Roots Forum†
0017-3541 Grassroots Editor **4576**
0017-3592 Graybar Outlook **3309**
0017-3606 Grazhdanskaya Aviatsiya **8542**
0017-3630 Great Britain. Central Statistical Office. Statistical News **8374**
0017-3665 Great Lakes News Letter†
0017-3673 Great Plains Journal **3976**
0017-369X Great Speckled Bird†
0017-3703 Greater Amusements and International Projectionist
0017-3762 Delaware Valley Business Fortnight†
0017-3770 Greater Pittsburgh†
0017-3797 Greater Rochester Commerce†
0017-3819 Grecia de Ayer, de Hoy y de Siempre†
0017-3835 Greece and Rome **2234**
0017-3851 Greek Bibliography†
0017-386X Greek Gazette†
0017-3886 Greek Observer
0017-3894 Greek Orthodox Theological Review **7704**
0017-3908 Greek Report
0017-3916 Greek, Roman and Byzantine Studies **2234**

ISSN

0017-3924　Green and White 2285
0017-3940　Green Cross†
0017-3967　Green Island 5423
0017-3975　Green Pyne Leaf†
0017-3983　Green Revolution 6922
0017-3991　Green River Current 2285
0017-4009　Green River Review†
0017-4017　Green Tree†
0017-4041　Greenfield Review†
0017-4068　Greenleaf†
0017-4084　Greensboro Review 5302
0017-4092　Greensward 116
0017-4114　Gregorianum 7799
0017-4122　Gregoriusblad 6571
0017-4149　Grenoble Universite. Faculte des Lettres et Sciences Humaines. Centre de Documentation et de Recherches Bibliographiques. Bulletin d'Information†
0017-4157　Greyhound 8176
0017-4165　Greyhound Owner & Breeder 6809
0017-4181　Grial 4454
0017-419X　Gridley Wave 5443
0017-4254　Grille†
0017-4289　Grit 3977
0017-4297　Grit and Steel 8176
0017-4300　Grito†
0017-4319　Grits and Grinds†
0017-4327　Grits and Grinds (Swedish edition)†
0017-4335　Grive
0017-4343　Grlica†
0017-4351　The Grocer 3679
0017-436X　Grocer Management/Western†
0017-4378　Grocers' and Storekeepers' Journal of Western Australia
0017-4386　Grocers Gazette
0017-4416　Grocery Communications†
0017-4440　Grocery Review changed to Retail News 1840
0017-4459　Groei†
0017-4475　Groei en Bloei 3734
0017-4483　De Groene Amsterdammer 5218
0017-4505　Grondboor en Hamer 2745
0017-453X　Gronk†
0017-4548　Groenkoepings Veckoblad 5218
0017-4556　Groenland (Charlottenlund) 4013
0017-4599　Gross Wartenberger Heimatblatt 625
0017-4610　Grosse Pointe Public Library. Newsletter†
0017-4629　The Grosse Pointer 8276
0017-4637　Grosseteste Review
0017-4645　Grosswetterlagen Europas†
0017-4653　Ground Engineering 3268
0017-467X　Ground Water 2794
0017-4688　Grounds Maintenance†
0017-4696　Groundsman 8316
0017-4718　Group Leader's Workshop
0017-4742　Group Research Report†
0017-4750　Group Travel†
0017-4777　The Grower 233
0017-4785　Grower changed to 0269-9478 3737
0017-4807　Growth and Acquisition Guide†
0017-4815　Growth and Change 1887
0017-4831　Growth Fund Guide 1628
0017-484X　Growth Stock Digest†
0017-4874　Die Waage 3859
0017-4882　Das Grundeigentum 4411
0017-4904　Grundfoerbaettring†
0017-4912　Grundig Technische Informationen†
0017-4947　Gruppenpsychotherapie und Gruppendynamik 6143
0017-4971　Guaira†
0017-498X　Guajana
0017-4998　Guanabara Industrial†
0017-5005　Guardia Nacional
0017-5013　Guardian†
0017-5021　Guardian (New York)†
0017-503X　The Guards Magazine 6423
0017-5048　Guatemala. Instituto Nacional de Estadistica. Boletin Estadistico†
0017-5056　Guatemala Indigena†
0017-5064　Guatemala Pediatrica
0017-5080　Guepes†
0017-5110　Guernsey Breeders' Journal 264
0017-5137　Gueterverkehr 8671
0017-5145　Guia Aeronautico 8543
0017-5153　Guia Guarani
0017-5161　Guia para Maestros de Ninos†
0017-5218　Guidance Report†
0017-5226　Guide (Hagerstown) 7760
0017-5250　Guide des Parents d'Eleves†
0017-5269　Guide Post†
0017-5285　Guide to Indian Periodical Literature 8020
0017-5331　Guideposts 7646
0017-5366　Guild Gardener. Newsletter†
0017-5390　The Guild Practitioner 4832
0017-5404　Guild Reporter 4595
0017-5412　Guilde du Livre
0017-5455　Guion†
0017-5463　Guitar Player 6571
0017-5471　Guitar Review 6571
0017-548X　Guitare et Musique Chansons Poesie†
0017-5501　Gujarat Labour Gazette 1684
0017-551X　Gujarat Law Reporter 4683
0017-5528　Gujarat Law Times 4683
0017-5536　Gujarat Revenue Tribunal Law Reporter 4683
0017-5552　Gulf Coast Cattleman 288
0017-5587　Gulf Review†
0017-5609　Gummibereifung 7824
0017-5617　The Gun Report 4336
0017-5641　Gun World 8176
0017-5668　Gunma Daigaku Kyoikugakubu Kiyo. Shizen Kagaku Hen 7859
0017-5684　Guns & Ammo 8316
0017-5692　Guns Review 4336
0017-5706　Gurukul Kangri Vishwavidyalaya†
0017-5714　Gurukula Prakashana†
0017-5730　Gustav-Adolf-Blatt 7760

0017-5749　Gut 5925
0017-5757　Gut Wohnen
0017-5765　Gute Fahrt 8583
0017-5781　Gute Nachrichten 3797
0017-579X　Gute Reise†
0017-5811　Le Gutenberg 4595
0017-582X　Guter Rat! 4359
0017-5846　Guy†
0017-5854　Guyana Business†
0017-5897　Y Gwyddonydd†
0017-5900　Gyermekgyogyaszat 6092
0017-5927　Gymnasieskolen 2861
0017-5935　Das Gymnasion†
0017-5951　Gymnasium Helveticum 2861
0017-596X　Gymnastikk og Turn 8176
0017-5994　Der Gynaekologe 5992
0017-6036　Gyogyszereszet 6845
0017-6095　Gypsies for Christ
0017-6109　H A Bulletin†
0017-6117　H & S Reports†
0017-6125　H & W†
0017-6176　H E A News Flash†
0017-6192　H N O (Berlin) 6080
0017-6206　H. P†
0017-6249　H S U Brand 2286
0017-6273　H T A Horizon†
0017-629X　HTS'er†
0017-6311　H U D Newsletter†
0017-632X　Haagse Jazz Club
0017-6346　Habinjan 7721
0017-6354　Habinyan†
0017-6362　Habit 2256
0017-6370　Habitat†
0017-6397　Habitat†
0017-6419　Habitation 444
0017-6443　Haboneh†
0017-646X　Hinukh†
0017-6478　Hacia la Luz 4081
0017-6486　Hacienda
0017-6508　Hadashot Mehachaim Hadatiyim Beisrael†
0017-6516　Hadassah Magazine 3536
0017-6524　Hadoar†
0017-6532　Hadorom 7721
0017-6540　Hadtortenelmi Kozlemenyek 6423
0017-6559　Haematologia†
0017-6575　Haematologica Latina†
0017-6605　Hagemi 4078
0017-6613　Kir - Ou - Kirk†
0017-6621　Hahnemannian
0017-6680　Addis Ababa University. College of Technology. Library Bulletin 4987
0017-6699　Hailer†
0017-6702　Hair & Beauty†
0017-6710　Hair and Makeup Trends†
0017-6729　Hair Beauty Magazine†
0017-6737　Hair Magic†
0017-6753　Hairdressers' Guide
0017-677X　Hairenik Weekly 5219
0017-6788　Haiti. Institut Haitien de Statistique. Bulletin Trimestriel de Statistique 8375
0017-6796　Hakku 6423
0017-6818　I D†
0017-6834　De Halve Maen 4294
0017-6850　Ha-Maapil 7153
0017-6869　Hamburg Air†
0017-6877　Hamburg in Zahlen 7481
0017-6885　Hamburg Journal†
0017-6915　Hamburger Aerzteblatt 5623
0017-6931　Hamburger Export-Woche†
0017-6982　Hamburger Sport - Mitteilungen 8176
0017-6990　Hamburger Vorschau 1568
0017-7032　Hamdden†
0017-7040　Hamevaser 7721
0017-7059　Ha-Mifal†
0017-7067　Hamilton Alumni Review 2286
0017-7075　Hamilton County Pharmacist
0017-7083　Ham-mizrah He-Hadash 550
0017-7091　Mlonai
0017-7113　Hampshire
0017-7121　Hampshire Farmer 117
0017-7148　Hand Vol Pluis
0017-7156　Handarbeit†
0017-7199　Handbook of Basic Economic Statistics†
0017-7210　Handbuch des Hausbesitzers†
0017-7229　Der Handel 1428
0017-7237　Handel en Nywerheid†
0017-7245　Handel Zagraniczny 1568
0017-7253　Handelingen der Staten-Generaal
0017-7288　Handelsbelangen†
0017-7296　Handelsblatt 1428
0017-7326　Handelsnytt 4595
0017-7334　Revue Commerciale†
0017-7377　Handes Amsorya 5124
0017-7393　Handloader changed to 1933-2750 8330
0017-7407　Handweaver and Craftsman†
0017-7423　Handy Shipping Guide†
0017-744X　Korea Development Bank. Monthly Economic Review 1496
0017-7458　Hannibal Labor Press†
0017-7482　Hanover News
0017-7504　Hansa 8645
0017-7520　Animal Reproduction Techniques 278
0017-7539　Hanson's Latin America Letter†
0017-7547　Hanzai Shinrigaku Kenkyu 7360
0017-7555　Ha-Olam Hazeh†
0017-7563　Happening in New York†
0017-7571　Praklit
0017-758X　Harangue†
0017-761X　Harbinger (Crystal City)
0017-7636　Harbour and Shipping 8645
0017-7644　Hard Fibres†
0017-7652　Hardlines Wholesaling†

0017-7709　Hardware Merchandiser†
0017-7768　Ha-Refuah 5622
0017-7806　Harmonica Accordeon et Musique†
0017-7830　Die Harmonika†
0017-7849　Harmonizer 6572
0017-7857　Harness Horse†
0017-7873　Harper's Bazaar 2256
0017-789X　Harper's 5219
0017-7911　Harpoen 2286
0017-7938　Harris-Report†
0017-7970　Hartford Hospital Bulletin†
0017-8004　Harvard Advocate 5303
0017-8012　Harvard Business Review 1117
0017-8020　Harvard Business School. Bulletin changed to 1553-1546 1117
0017-8039　Harvard Civil Rights - Civil Liberties Law Review 4832
0017-8055　Harvard Educational Review 2862
0017-8063　Harvard International Law Journal 4927
0017-808X　Harvard Journal on Legislation 4685
0017-8098　Harvard Lampoon 2286
0017-8101　Harvard Law Record 4685
0017-811X　Harvard Law Review 4685
0017-8136　Harvard Library Bulletin 5011
0017-8144　Harvard Project Physics. Newsletter†
0017-8160　Harvard Theological Review 7646
0017-8179　Harvard Today†
0017-8195　Fengnian 113
0017-8225　Harvester 117
0017-8233　Haryana Cooperation 1423
0017-8241　Haryana Health Journal 7520
0017-825X　Haryana Journal of Education
0017-8268　Haryou-Act News†
0017-8284　Ha-Sifrut†
0017-8292　Hask
0017-8314　Hassadeh
0017-8322　Hastings Law Journal 4685
0017-8330　Hat Worker†
0017-8381　Hatvertising Weekly
0017-8403　Haus und Grund 1011
0017-8454　Hauswirtschaft und Wissenschaft 4360
0017-8470　Der Hautarzt 5877
0017-8497　Havebladet 3736
0017-8500　Haven 3736
0017-8519　Havenloods
0017-8527　Hawadess
0017-8543　Hawaii Beverage Guide 604
0017-8594　Hawaii Medical Journal 5623
0017-8624　Hawaiian Shell News 945
0017-8640　Hay Guetron
0017-8691　Yatsiv
0017-8713　Head, Heart, Hands & Health in Virginia†
0017-8721　Head Start Newsletter†
0017-873X　Head Teachers Review 2862
0017-8748　Headache 6144
0017-8764　Headlight
0017-8780　Foreign Policy Association. Headline Series 7235
0017-8799　Heads Up†
0017-8810　Healdsburg Tribune-Enterprise and Scimitar
0017-8829　Healing Hand 7646
0017-8853　Health†
0017-8861　Health†
0017-887X　Health†
0017-8888　Health and Efficiency 6987
0017-8926　Ofakim 5345
0017-8969　Health Education Journal 7522
0017-8977　Health Foods Retailing†
0017-8993　Health Information Digest†
0017-9019　Health Insurance Underwriter 4505
0017-9035　Health Laboratory Science†
0017-9043　Health News†
0017-9051　Health - P A C Bulletin†
0017-9078　Health Physics 5626
0017-9124　Health Services Research 4096
0017-9132　Health Trends†
0017-9159　Healthways Magazine†
0017-9167　Healthy Living
0017-9175　Hear This 2286
0017-9183　Hearing†
0017-9248　Heart Bulletin†
0017-9256　Heart of America Purchaser
0017-9280　Hearth and Home†
0017-9299　Hearthstone†
0017-9302　Hearts of Oak Journal†
0017-9310　International Journal of Heat and Mass Transfer 3382
0017-9329　Heat Engineering changed to Foster Wheeler Review 3193
0017-9353　Heating, Air Conditioning & Refrigeration†
0017-9396　Heating and Ventilating Review 4120
0017-9418　Heating, Plumbing, Air Conditioning 4120
0017-9426　Heavy Construction News changed to 1910-118X 1028
0017-9442　Hebezeuge und Foerdermittel 3268
0017-9485　Hechos y Dichos†
0017-9493　Hed Hachinuch 2863
0017-9515　Heemschut 444
0017-9523　Heer en Mode†
0017-9566　Heghapoghagan Albom
0017-9590　The Heights (Chestnut Hill) 2286
0017-9612　Heilberufe 5627
0017-9612　Das Heilige Band 3536
0017-9620　Heiliger Dienst 7646
0017-9639　Heilkunst†
0017-9647　Heilpaedagogische Forschung 6144
0017-9655　Vierteljahresschrift fuer Heilpaedagogik und Ihre Nachbargebiete 3049
0017-9663　Heilsbanier
0017-9698　Heima er Bezt 3877
0017-9701　Die Heimat changed to 1611-3829 4247
0017-9728　Heimat und Kirche†
0017-9736　Heimat und Staat†
0017-9752　Heimat - Zeitung Roemerstaedter Laendchen 4226
0017-9787　Heimatland Lippe 3850
0017-9809　Das Heimatmuseum Alsergrund 4226

0017-9817 Heimatschutz **2613**
0017-9841 Heimen **4226**
0017-985X Heimevernsbladet **6423**
0017-9884 Heirs†
0017-9914 Hejnal Mariacki **7799**
0017-9922 Helan Medical Magazine†
0017-9965 Helicopter World†
0017-9973 Helictite **2746**
0017-9981 Helikon **2235**
0017-999X Helikon **5304**
0018-0009 Helinium†
0018-0025 Hellenic-American Chamber of Commerce. Newsletter†
0018-0041 Hellenic Review
0018-005X Hellenic Shipping International
0018-0068 Elliniki Ktiniatriki
0018-0076 Hellenicos Erythros Stavros Neotitos
0018-0084 Hellenika **5304**
0018-0092 Hellenike Cheirougike *changed to* Hellenic Journal of Surgery **6245**
0018-0114 Helmantica **4455**
0018-0149 Helse **6988**
0018-0149 Helse *changed to* 1903-8461 **6988**
0018-019X Helvetica Chimica Acta **2063**
0018-0254 Hem och Samhaelle **4360**
0018-0270 Hemecht **4141**
0018-0300 Hemisphere†
0018-0319 Hemispherica†
0018-0327 Hemmets Journal **3955**
0018-0335 Hemmets Vaen **7647**
0018-0343 Hemtraedgaarden **3736**
0018-0351 Hemvaernet **6423**
0018-0386 Hennepin Reporter†
0018-0416 Henry Ford Hospital Medical Journal†
0018-0467 Herald **3926**
0018-0483 Herald of Freedom†
0018-0491 Herald of Health **6988**
0018-0505 Herald of Health†
0018-0521 Herald of Library Science **5012**
0018-0548 Heraldo Mercantil Internacional
0018-0572 Herb Grower Magazine†
0018-0599 Herba Polonica **792**
0018-0629 Hercules Chemist†
0018-0637 Hercynia **7861**
0018-0645 Herder - Korrespondenz **7800**
0018-0661 Hereditas **871**
0018-067X Heredity **871**
0018-0688 Herefordshire Farmer **118**
0018-0696 Here's Health **6988**
0018-070X Black Music Review†
0018-0718 Heritage of Vermilion County **4295**
0018-0734 Herkenning (The Hague, 1948)†
0018-0742 Hermanus News†
0018-0750 Hermathena **4455**
0018-0777 Hermes **2235**
0018-0785 Hermes Exchange†
0018-0793 Herold (Berlin) **3770**
0018-0815 Herold des Kostbaren Blutes
0018-0823 Heroldo de Esperanto **5124**
0018-0831 Herpetologica **946**
0018-084X Herpetological Review **946**
0018-0858 Der Herr†
0018-0874 Herrenjournal†
0018-0890 Herst†
0018-0912 Hertha **8867**
0018-0920 Hervormd Arnhem†
0018-0947 Hervormd Wageningen
0018-0955 Hervormde Gemeente Musselkanaal. Kerkblad
0018-0971 Herzogia†
0018-098X Hesperia **396**
0018-0998 Hesperide†
0018-1005 Hesperis - Tamuda†
0018-1013 Hesperus†
0018-1021 Hessische Kreiszahlen **8376**
0018-103X Hessische Blaetter fuer Volksbildung **2942**
0018-1056 Hessische Erzieher†
0018-1064 Hessische Familienkunde **3770**
0018-1072 Hessischer Gaertner†
0018-1099 Hessische Jugend **2192**
0018-1102 Hessische Standesbeamte†
0018-1110 Hestesport†
0018-1137 Heterofonia **6573**
0018-1145 Heuristics†
0018-1153 Hewlett-Packard Journal†
0018-1188 Hey Lady†
0018-1196 The Heythrop Journal **7647**
0018-1218 Hi-Fi - Stereo Buyers' Guide†
0018-1285 Hidalguia **3770**
0018-1307 Hides and Skins Quarterly†
0018-1315 Hidro Mecanica en la Construccion Mexicana
0018-1323 Hidrologiai Kozlony **8824**
0018-1331 Hidrologija i Meteorologija **6353**
0018-1358 Hidrotehnicka Bibliografija†
0018-1404 Hifuka no Rinsho **5877**
0018-1412 High Change & Unitholder†
0018-1420 High Country†
0018-1439 High Energy Chemistry **2135**
0018-1447 High Energy Physics Index†
0018-1471 High Plains Journal **118**
0018-148X High Points†
0018-1498 The High School Journal **2863**
0018-151X High Temperature **7054**
0018-1544 High Temperatures - High Pressures **7054**
0018-1552 High Voltage Engineering Corporation Newsletter†
0018-1560 Higher Education **2984**
0018-1579 Higher Education and National Affairs **2984**
0018-1609 Higher Education Review **2985**
0018-1617 Highland Hotelkeeper & Touristmaker
0018-1625 Highlights†
0018-165X Highlights for Children **2192**
0018-1668 Highlights of Agricultural Research **118**
0018-1676 Highway†
0018-1684 Highway **7760**
0018-1692 Highway Builder **3269**
0018-1706 Highway Common Carrier Newsletter
0018-1722 Highway Mail **3948**
0018-1757 Highway Transport†
0018-179X Hika **5423**
0018-1803 Leather Technology **4974**
0018-1811 Leather Chemistry **4974**
0018-182X Hikone Ronso†
0018-1854 Hillbilly†
0018-1862 Hillel Gate **3537**
0018-1889 Himachal Agricultural Newsletter **118**
0018-1897 Himavanta **8317**
0018-1900 Himmat
0018-1927 Hinduism
0018-1935 Hindustan Antibiotics Bulletin **6846**
0018-1951 Hinshitsu Kanri *changed to* 1347-0213 **1771**
0018-1986 Hints to Potato Growers **234**
0018-1994 Hinyokika Kiyo **6268**
0018-2001 Hippokrates†
0018-2028 Hiradastechnika **2322**
0018-2079 Hiroshima Mathematical Journal **5491**
0018-2087 Hiroshima Daigaku Igaku Zasshi **5628**
0018-2117 Hisairdec News†
0018-2125 Hispalis Medica†
0018-2133 Hispania **5124**
0018-2141 Hispania **4227**
0018-215X Hispania Sacra **7647**
0018-2168 Hispanic American Historical Review **4295**
0018-2176 Hispanic Review **5125**
0018-2192 Hispano Americano†
0018-2206 Hispanofila **5306**
0018-2214 The Histochemical Journal *changed to* 1567-2379 **834**
0018-2230 Histoire de la Medecine†
0018-2257 Histoire Sociale **8105**
0018-229X Historia **4142**
0018-2311 Historia **2235**
0018-2346 Historia Natural y Pro Natura†
0018-2354 Historia y Vida **4142**
0018-2362 Historiallinen Aikakauskirja **4142**
0018-2370 The Historian (East Lansing) **4143**
0018-2389 Historic Aviation†
0018-2397 Historic Kern **4296**
0018-2427 Historica† **8962**
0018-2443 Historical Aviation Album
0018-2451 Historical Firearms Society of South Africa. Journal **366**
0018-246X Historical Journal **4143**
0018-2478 Historical Journal of Japan **4183**
0018-2508 Historical New Hampshire **4296**
0018-2516 Historical Review **4192**
0018-2524 Historical Review of Berks County **4296**
0018-2532 Historical Society of Haddonfield. Bulletin **4296**
0018-2540 Historical Society of Nigeria. Journal **4144**
0018-2567 Historical Wyoming†
0018-2575 Historicky Casopis **4144**
0018-2583 Historie a Vojenstvi **6424**
0018-2591 Historiographer†
0018-2605 Das Historisch-Politische Buch **4144**
0018-2613 Historische Zeitschrift **4144**
0018-2621 Historisches Jahrbuch **4144**
0018-263X Historisk Tidsskrift **4144**
0018-2648 History **4145**
0018-2656 History and Theory **4145**
0018-2664 History Book Club Review **7562**
0018-2672 Wyoming History News **4319**
0018-2680 History of Education Quarterly **2864**
0018-2702 History of Political Economy **1542**
0018-2710 History of Religions **7647**
0018-2737 History of the Twentieth Century†
0018-2745 The History Teacher **4145**
0018-2753 History Today **4230**
0018-2761 Hit†
0018-277X Hitachi Review **3100**
0018-2796 Hitotsubashi Journal of Commerce and Management **1750**
0018-280X Hitotsubashi Journal of Economics **1118**
0018-2818 Hitotsubashi Review **1118**
0018-2842 Hjemmet **3923**
0018-2869 Hlas L'udu **3945**
0018-2877 Hoads Readout
0018-2885 Hoard's Dairyman **264**
0018-2893 Hobart Weldworld†
0018-2974 Das Hochschulwesen **2864**
0018-2990 Hockey e Pattinaggio†
0018-3016 The Hockey News **8177**
0018-3059 Hoechstrichterliche Finanzrechtsprechung **4687**
0018-3067 Hoeden & Boetiek†
0018-3091 Die Hoehle **2746**
0018-3105 Hoehlenpost **2746**
0018-3113 Hoerzu **2382**
0018-3121 Hoergeschaedigte Kinder *changed to* Hoergeschaedigte Kinder - Erwachsene Hoergeschaedigte **4074**
0018-3164 Hoffheimer Nachrichten†
0018-3199 Hog Guide†
0018-3210 Hogar **8867**
0018-3229 Hogar Cristiano **7760**
0018-3237 Hogar y Arquitectura
0018-3245 Hohe Bruecke
0018-3253 Hohenzollerische Heimat **4230**
0018-327X Hoiku No Tomo **8044**
0018-3288 Hoja de Informacion Economica
0018-3296 Hoja del Lunes de Lugo†
0018-330X Hoja del Lunes de Orense
0018-3326 Hoja Tisiologica
0018-3334 Hoejskolebladet **2942**
0018-3342 Hoken no Kagaku **6988**
0018-3350 Health and Physical Education **2862**
0018-3369 Hokenfu no Kekkaku Tenbo **5960**
0018-3385 Hokkaido Veterinary Medical Association. Journal **8798**
0018-3423 Meteorological Data of Hokkaido **6391**
0018-3431 Hokkaido Toshokan Kenkyukai. Kaiho **5012**
0018-344X Hokkaido University. Faculty of Agriculture. Journal *changed to* 1345-6601 **119**
0018-3474 Hokkaido University. Faculty of Science. Journal. Series 4: Geology and Mineralogy†
0018-3490 Agriculture in Hokkaido **86**
0018-3512 Holectechniek†
0018-3555 Holidays in Romania†
0018-3563 Holland Herald **8784**
0018-3598 Hollandia Varia†
0018-3601 Hollands Maandblad **5219**
0018-361X Hollandse Huis†
0018-3628 Hollar†
0018-3636 Hollingsworth Register†
0018-3644 Hollins Critic **5219**
0018-3652 Hollins Symposium†
0018-3660 The Hollywood Reporter **6502**
0018-3741 Holy Name Monthly†
0018-3768 Holz als Roh- und Werkstoff *changed to* European Journal of Wood and Wood Industries (Print) **3711**
0018-3784 Holz Kurier **3712**
0018-3792 Holz-Zentralblatt **3712**
0018-3806 Holzarbeiter-Zeitung
0018-3822 H O B - Die Holzbearbeitung **3712**
0018-3830 Holzforschung **3712**
0018-3849 Holzforschung und Holzverwertung†
0018-3857 Holzindustrie†
0018-3865 Die Holzschwelle†
0018-3881 Holztechnologie **3712**
0018-3938 Home & Country **8867**
0018-3946 Home and Family **8867**
0018-3970 Home Builder News†
0018-4004 Home Ec News
0018-4020 Home Economics Research Abstracts†
0018-4039 Home Finders Directory
0018-4071 HomeLife **7760**
0018-411X Home Office Report†
0018-4128 Home Rule†
0018-4152 Homecare
0018-4160 Homefinder†
0018-4179 Homefront I A D†
0018-4195 Perspectives-In Long Term Care†
0018-4217 Homemakers Guide†
0018-4233 Homes and Gardens **4542**
0018-4241 Homes Overseas **7593**
0018-425X Homesewing Trade News†
0018-4268 Homiletic and Pastoral Review **7800**
0018-4276 Homiletische Monatshefte **7648**
0018-4284 Homin Ukrainy **3538**
0018-4292 Homine†
0018-4306 L'Homme et la Societe (Paris, 1966) **8105**
0018-4314 L'Homme Libre
0018-4322 L'Homme Nouveau **7648**
0018-4357 Hommes et Fonderie **6314**
0018-439X Hommes et Terres du Nord *changed to* 1954-4863 **4031**
0018-4403 Hommes Libres†
0018-4411 Hommes Volants†
0018-442X HOMO **341**
0018-4446 Homeopathic Sandesh†
0018-4454 Homoeopathic Science Quarterly†
0018-4462 Homoeopathic Vikas†
0018-4500 Hon & Han†
0018-4519 Art & Architecture
0018-4527 Hondenwereld **6809**
0018-4535 Honduras Pediatrica
0018-456X Honeyguide **908**
0018-4594 Hong Kong Manager **1750**
0018-4616 Hong Kong Travel Bulletin†
0018-4632 Honnold Library Record†
0018-4659 Honolulu Weekly Snooper†
0018-4675 Honourable Company of Master Mariners. Journal **8646**
0018-4683 Hoof Beats **8292**
0018-4691 Dimensie†
0018-4705 Hoofdlijnen **6145**
0018-4721 Hoosharar†
0018-473X Hoosier Banker **1351**
0018-4748 Hoosier Farmer **119**
0018-4772 Hoosier Legionnaire **6424**
0018-4780 Hoosier Outdoors†
0018-4799 Hoosier Purchasor†
0018-4829 Hooyce†
0018-4845 Hopfen-Rundschau **234**
0018-4861 Hopital a Paris†
0018-487X Hopitaux Civils et Militaires. Gazette†
0018-4934 Hoerelsen **4074**
0018-4942 Die Horen **5306**
0018-4977 Horizon (Tuscaloosa)†
0018-5000 Horizons in Leisure†
0018-5019 Horizons Unlimited **2864**
0018-5027 Horizontes **4455**
0018-5043 Hormone and Metabolic Research **5893**
0018-506X Hormones and Behavior **5894**
0018-5078 The Horn Book Magazine **7562**
0018-5086 Hornet **2286**
0018-5108 Horological Journal **4566**
0018-5132 Hors Cote†
0018-5140 Horse and Hound **8292**
0018-5159 Horse & Rider **8292**
0018-5167 Horse and Show Inc†
0018-5191 Horse World **8293**
0018-5213 Horseless Carriage Gazette **366**
0018-5221 Horseman†
0018-523X Horseman and Fair World **8293**
0018-5256 Horsemen's Journal **8293**
0018-5264 The Horsetrader **8293**
0018-5280 Horticultural Abstracts *changed to* Horticultural Science Abstracts **3755**
0018-5302 Horticultural Society of New York. Bulletin†
0018-5329 Horticulture **3737**
0018-5337 Hortikultura
0018-5345 HortScience **3738**
0018-5388 Hosiery and Textile Journal **2247**
0018-5442 Arquivos dos Hospitais e da Faculdade de Ciencias Medicas da Santa Casa de Sao Paulo **4088**

0019-1558 Ifju Zenebarat†
0019-1574 Igaku Hyoron **5632**
0019-1582 Igaku to Fukuin **5632**
0019-1590 Gekkan Igaku to Iryo
0019-1604 Igaku to Seibutsugaku **5632**
0019-1612 Igakushi Kenkyu **5632**
0019-1639 Igiene e Sanita Pubblica **7524**
0019-1647 Igiene Mentale†
0019-1655 L'Igiene Moderna
0019-1663 Igitur Revista Literaria **5308**
0019-1671 Iglesia Evangelica del Rio de la Plata. Revista Parroquial†
0019-1701 Ihre Brigitte†
0019-1728 Ikai Jiho
0019-1744 Ikon **2325**
0019-1752 Ikon†
0019-1779 Ilanga **3948**
0019-1795 Iliff Review†
0019-1809 Illiana Genealogist **3771**
0019-1817 Illiana Research Report†
0019-1833 Illinois Agricultural Economics†
0019-185X Illinois Banker **1352**
0019-1868 Illinois Baptist **7761**
0019-1876 Illinois Bar Journal **4690**
0019-1906 Illinois Braille Messenger **4082**
0019-1922 Illinois Business Review†
0019-1957 Illinois Courts Bulletin **4690**
0019-2015 Illinois Engineer **3197**
0019-2023 Illinois English Bulletin **3064**
0019-2031 Illinois Geographical Society. Bulletin **4015**
0019-204X Illinois Health Messenger†
0019-2082 Illinois Journal of Mathematics **5492**
0019-2090 Illinois Labor Bulletin†
0019-2104 Illinois Libraries† **8963**
0019-2112 Illinois Master Plumber Magazine **4120**
0019-2139 Illinois Municipal Review **7494**
0019-2147 Illinois Music Educator **6575**
0019-2155 Illinois Parks & Recreation **8318**
0019-2171 Illinois Police Association. Official Journal **2654**
0019-2201 Illinois Research†
0019-221X Illinois School Board Journal **3024**
0019-2236 Illinois Schools Journal **2865**
0019-2252 Illinois State Academy of Science. Transactions **7864**
0019-2295 Illinois Quarterly†
0019-2309 Illinois Truck News **8671**
0019-2317 Illinois Wildlife
0019-2325 Illovo Digest†
0019-2341 Shomei Gakkai Shi **3331**
0019-2384 Illuminotecnica **3318**
0019-2392 Illustrated Bristol News
0019-2422 Illustrated London News†
0019-2430 Illustrated Weekly of India **3883**
0019-2465 Illustrator **495**
0019-2473 Illustrazione Pubblicitaria†
0019-2481 Illustre Protestant†
0019-252X Ilmailu **59**
0019-2538 Ilocos Review **4183**
0019-2546 I L T A M Newsletter
0019-2562 Ilusion y Aventura†
0019-2570 Ilustrovana Politika **3945**
0019-2597 Im Lande der Bibel **7649**
0019-2619 Image
0019-2651 Image Technology†
0019-2694 Imago†
0019-2708 Imballaggio†
0019-2716 Imbongi†
0019-2724 Imfama (Inkprint Edition) **4082**
0019-2732 Imkerfreund **120**
0019-2767 Immex†
0019-2805 Immunology **5760**
0019-2813 Casting Digest **6308**
0019-2821 Impact (Littleton) **7761**
0019-2848 Impact (Valley Forge)†
0019-2856 Impact (Columbia)†
0019-2864 Impact - Africa†
0019-2872 Impact of Science on Society†
0019-2880 Impacto *changed to* Impacto El Diario **3909**
0019-2899 Impacts
0019-2902 Imparcial
0019-2929 Impermeabile Europeo†
0019-2945 Impianti Industriali†
0019-2953 Implement & Tractor **211**
0019-2961 Import†
0019-3003 Impresa Pubblica†
0019-3011 Impressions
0019-302X Imprimerie Nouvelle†
0019-3038 Imprint (Bristol)
0019-3046 Imprint†
0019-3054 Imprint†
0019-3062 Imprint (New York) **5961**
0019-3097 Impuls†
0019-3100 In†
0019-3127 Animaland†
0019-3135 In Brief†
0019-3143 inBritain **8720**
0019-3151 In de Rechte Straat **7800**
0019-316X In de Waagschaal
0019-3178 In- en Uitvoer Nieuws **1569**
0019-3186 In Famiglia
0019-3216 In Particular†
0019-3224 Printing Industry†
0019-3240 In-Plant Reprographics†
0019-3259 In Review†
0019-3283 In Touch (Pinner) **7649**
0019-3291 In Transit **4596**
0019-3321 In Your Hands†
0019-333X Newspaper Techniques *changed to* W A N - I F R A Magazine **7329**
0019-3399 Inchieste di Urbanistica e Architettura†
0019-3410 Incidenza
0019-3437 Income-Tax Journal†
0019-3453 Income Tax Reports **1929**
0019-3461 I D S Report *changed to* 1745-3739 **1686**
0019-347X Incontri Culturali†
0019-3488 Incontri Meridionali†
0019-3496 L'Incontro† **8963**
0019-3518 Weekly Law Reports **4811**
0019-3526 Incorporated Law Society of Northern Ireland. Gazette†
0019-3542 Incredible Idaho†
0019-3550 Incunable†
0019-3569 I N D A C Magazine **2266**
0019-3577 Indagationes Mathematicae **5492**
0019-3585 Yugoslavia. Savezni Zavod za Statistiku. Indeks *changed to* Srbija i Crna Gora Zavod za Statistiku. Indeks **8402**
0019-3615 Independant-Chaussures
0019-3658 Independent Adjuster†
0019-3666 Independent American
0019-3674 Independent Banker **1353**
0019-3690 Independent College Funds of America Bulletin†
0019-3720 Independent Formosa†
0019-3747 Independent School†
0019-3763 Independent Shavian **5308**
0019-378X Index Analytique†
0019-3798 Index Bibliographique de Botanique Tropicale†
0019-3801 Index Bibliographique du Vide - Vacuum Index†
0019-3828 Index Chemicus Registry System†
0019-3836 Index de la Litterature Nucleaire Francaise†
0019-3844 Index India **564**
0019-3852 Index Indo-Asiaticus **564**
0019-3860 Index: Industrial Extension for the Forest Products Industry†
0019-3879 Index Medicus†
0019-3887 Index Medicus Danicus†
0019-3895 Index of Fungi **716**
0019-3917 Index of Mathematical Papers **5548**
0019-3925 Index of New Products†
0019-3941 Index of Veterinary Specialities†
0019-3968 Index to Australian Book Reviews†
0019-3984 Index to Current Malaysian, Singapore, and Brunei Periodicals†
0019-3992 Index to Dental Literature†
0019-400X Index to Foreign Legal Periodicals **4822**
0019-4018 Index to Forthcoming Russian Books†
0019-4026 Index to Indian Economic Journals **1241**
0019-4034 Index to Indian Legal Periodicals **4822**
0019-4042 Index to Indian Medical Periodicals†
0019-4050 Index to Jewish Periodicals **7698**
0019-4069 Index to Latin American Periodicals†
0019-4093 Index to Periodical Articles Related to Law **4823**
0019-4115 Index to the Literature of Magnetism†
0019-4123 Index Veterinarius **8816**
0019-4131 The Indexer **5015**
0019-414X India Book House News†
0019-4158 India Calling†
0019-4174 India. Central Statistical Organization. Monthly Abstract of Statistics
0019-4182 India in Industries†
0019-4204 India. Ministry of Finance. Finance Library. Weekly Bulletin **1353**
0019-4239 India Today and Tomorrow **1569**
0019-4247 Indian Academy of Applied Psychology. Journal **7362**
0019-4255 Indian Academy of Dentistry. Journal†
0019-4271 Indian Academy of Philosophy. Journal **6925**
0019-4301 Indian Advocate **4691**
0019-4328 Indian Agricultural News Digest†
0019-4336 Indian Agriculturist **120**
0019-4344 Journal of Indian and Buddhist Studies **7701**
0019-4360 Indian & Eastern Pharmacy†
0019-4379 Indian and Foreign Review†
0019-4387 Indian Anthropological Society. Journal **342**
0019-4395 Indian Antiquary†
0019-4409 Indian Architect†
0019-4417 Indian Aviation
0019-4425 Indian Bee Journal **120**
0019-4433 Indian Book Industry **7563**
0019-4441 Indian Book Review Supplement **7563**
0019-445X Indian Books **7578**
0019-4476 Indian Business Review†
0019-4484 Indian Cashew Journal **3646**
0019-4492 Indian Ceramics **2043**
0019-4506 Indian Chemical Engineer **3246**
0019-4514 Indian Chemical Journal†
0019-4522 Indian Chemical Society. Journal **2064**
0019-4530 Indian Church History Review **7649**
0019-4549 Indian Coffee **3646**
0019-4557 Indian Communist†
0019-4565 Indian Concrete Journal **3269**
0019-4573 Indian Construction News
0019-4581 Indian Cooperative Review **1423**
0019-459X Indian Cotton Mills Federation Journal
0019-4603 Indian Dairyman **265**
0019-4611 Indian Dental Association. Journal **5847**
0019-462X Indian Drugs **6847**
0019-4638 Indian Drugs and Pharmaceuticals Industry†
0019-4646 Indian Economic and Social History Review **7972**
0019-4654 Indian Economic Diary
0019-4662 Indian Economic Journal **1122**
0019-4670 Indian Economic Review **1122**
0019-4689 Indian Education
0019-4697 Indian Education Abstracts **2934**
0019-4700 Indian Educational Review **2866**
0019-4719 Indian Engineering Exporter **3197**
0019-4735 Indian Export Trade Journal
0019-4743 Indian Exporter and Importer
0019-4751 Indian Exporter Quarterly†
0019-476X Indian Factories Journal
0019-4778 Indian Farm Mechanization†
0019-4786 Indian Farming **120**
0019-4794 Indian Finance
0019-4808 Indian Food Packer **3647**
0019-4816 Indian Forester **3693**
0019-4824 Indian Geographical Journal **4015**
0019-4832 Indian Heart Journal **5790**
0019-4867 Indian Homoeopathic Gazette
0019-4875 Indian Horticulture **3738**
0019-4883 Indian Hotelier and Caterer†
0019-4913 Indian Institute of Architects. Journal†
0019-493X Indian Institute of Metals. Transactions **6315**
0019-4948 Indian Institute of Public Opinion. Quarterly Economic Report **1490**
0019-4956 Indian Institute of Road Transport. Monthly Bulletin **8498**
0019-4972 Indian Institute of World Culture. Transactions **4456**
0019-4980 I I T C Bulletin **1568**
0019-4999 Indian Investment Centre. Monthly Newsletter **1490**
0019-5006 Indian Journal of Adult Education **2942**
0019-5014 Indian Journal of Agricultural Economics **200**
0019-5022 Indian Journal of Agricultural Sciences **120**
0019-5030 Indian Journal of American Studies **4297**
0019-5049 Indian Journal of Anaesthesia **5771**
0019-5057 Indian Journal of Animal Health **8798**
0019-5073 Indian Journal of Applied Psychology **7362**
0019-509X Indian Journal of Cancer **6022**
0019-512X Indian Journal of Commerce **1429**
0019-5138 Journal of Communicable Diseases **5820**
0019-5146 Indian Journal of Dairy Science **265**
0019-5154 Indian Journal of Dermatology **5877**
0019-5170 Indian Journal of Economics **1122**
0019-5189 Indian Journal of Experimental Biology **678**
0019-5197 Indian Journal of Experimental Psychology†
0019-5200 Indian Journal of Genetics and Plant Breeding **793**
0019-5227 Indian Journal of Helminthology†
0019-5235 Indian Journal of History of Science **7865**
0019-5243 Indian Journal of Homoeopathic Medicine **5805**
0019-5251 Indian Journal of Horticulture **3738**
0019-526X Indian Journal of Hospital Pharmacy **6847**
0019-5286 Indian Journal of Industrial Relations **1687**
0019-5294 Indian Journal of International Law **4928**
0019-5308 Indian Journal of Labour Economics **1687**
0019-5316 Indian Journal of Marketing **1820**
0019-5324 Indian Journal of Mathematics **5493**
0019-5359 Indian Journal of Medical Sciences **5634**
0019-5367 Indian Journal of Medicine & Surgery
0019-5375 Indian Journal of Mental Retardation
0019-5391 Indian Journal of Occupational Health
0019-5413 Indian Journal of Orthopaedics **6061**
0019-5456 Indian Journal of Pediatrics **6092**
0019-5464 Indian Journal of Pharmaceutical Education *changed to* Indian Journal of Pharmaceutical Education & Research **6848**
0019-5499 Indian Journal of Physiology and Pharmacology **923**
0019-5502 Indian Journal of Plant Physiology **794**
0019-5510 Indian Journal of Political Science **7142**
0019-5529 Indian Journal of Poultry Science **289**
0019-5537 Indian Journal of Power and River Valley Development **8825**
0019-5545 Indian Journal of Psychiatry **6145**
0019-5561 Indian Journal of Public Administration **7445**
0019-557X Indian Journal of Public Health **7525**
0019-5588 Indian Journal of Pure and Applied Mathematics **5493**
0019-5596 Indian Journal of Pure & Applied Physics **7016**
0019-5626 Indian Journal of Social Research **7972**
0019-5634 Indian Journal of Social Work **8046**
0019-5642 Indian Journal of Sociology
0019-5650 Indian Journal of Surgery **6245**
0019-5685 Indian Journal of Theology **7649**
0019-5693 Indian Journal of Theoretical Physics **7016**
0019-5707 Indian Journal of Tuberculosis **6215**
0019-5723 Indian Labour Journal **1687**
0019-5731 Indian Law Institute. Journal **4691**
0019-574X Indian Leather **4973**
0019-5758 Indian Leather Technologists' Association. Journal **4973**
0019-5766 Indian Libertarian†
0019-5774 Indian Librarian
0019-5782 Indian Library Association. Bulletin **5015**
0019-5790 Indian Library Science Abstracts **5058**
0019-5804 Indian Literature **5308**
0019-5812 Indian Management **1752**
0019-5820 Indian Management Abstracts **1242**
0019-5839 Indian Mathematical Society. Journal **5493**
0019-5847 Indian Medical Association. Journal **5634**
0019-5855 Indian Medical Forum
0019-5863 Indian Medical Gazette **6246**
0019-5898 Indian Medical Record†
0019-5901 Indian Merchants' Chamber. Journal **1429**
0019-591X Indian Military Academy Journal
0019-5928 Indian Mineralogist **6464**
0019-5936 Indian Minerals **6464**
0019-5944 Indian Mining & Engineering Journal **6464**
0019-5952 Indian Modeller
0019-5979 Indian Movie News
0019-5987 Indian Museum Bulletin **6526**
0019-5995 Indian Music Journal
0019-6002 Indian National Bibliography **627**
0019-6029 Indian News†
0019-6037 Indian News Index†
0019-6045 Indian Oil and Soap Journal†
0019-6053 The Indian P.E.N. **5308**
0019-6061 Indian Pediatrics **6093**
0019-607X Indian Perfumer **594**
0019-6096 Indian Philosophy & Culture†
0019-610X Indian Plastics Review†
0019-6126 Indian Political Science Review†
0019-6134 Indian Ports
0019-6150 Indian Poultry Review **289**
0019-6169 The Indian Practitioner **5634**
0019-6177 Indian Press Index **4587**
0019-6185 Indian Print & Paper
0019-6193 Indian Progress
0019-6207 Indian Promenade†
0019-6215 Indian Psychological Review **7362**
0019-6223 Indian Publisher and Bookseller†
0019-6231 Indian Pulp and Paper **6734**
0019-624X Indian Radio Amateur
0019-6258 Indian Railway Gazette

ISSN

ISSN

0020-8752 International Society of Barristers. Quarterly **4696**
0020-8817 International Studies **7245**
0020-8825 International Studies of Management and Organization **1762**
0020-8833 International Studies Quarterly **7245**
0020-8841 International Sugar Journal **3649**
0020-885X International Sugar Organization. Statistical Bulletin **3670**
0020-8868 International Surgery **6246**
0020-8876 International Swimmer†
0020-8884 World Federation of Teachers' Unions. Information Letter
0020-8914 International Textiles **8453**
0020-8930 International Theatre†
0020-8957 International Trade Forum **1571**
0020-8981 International Trade Review **1572**
0020-899X International Trade Union News†
0020-9007 International Transport Workers' Journal†
0020-9066 International Union for Vacuum Science, Technique and Applications. News Bulletin (Print Edition)†
0020-9090 International Whaling Statistics†
0020-9104 Wheelspin News
0020-9120 International Women's News **8868**
0020-9139 International Woodworker *changed to* 0894-7481
0020-9155 International Zoo News **948**
0020-9163 Internationale - A.M.R.†
0020-9198 Internationale Bibliographie der Versicherungsliteratur†
0020-921X I B N **8276**
0020-9252 Internationale Kirchliche Zeitschrift **7651**
0020-9287 Das Internationale Podium
0020-9317 Internationale Spectator **4932**
0020-9341 Internationale Transport Zeitschrift **8500**
0020-935X Internationale Wirtschaft
0020-9368 Internationale Wirtschafts-Briefe **1931**
0020-9384 Gaswaerme International **4119**
0020-9422 Internationaler Holzmarkt **1051**
0020-9430 Internationales Afrikaforum†
0020-9449 Internationales Asienforum **552**
0020-9503 Internationales Recht und Diplomatie†
0020-9511 Internationales Verkehrswesen **8632**
0020-952X Internationella Studier **7246**
0020-9554 Der Internist **5946**
0020-9562 Internist Observer†
0020-9570 Internistische Praxis **5946**
0020-9597 Interplanetary News **61**
0020-9635 Interpretation (Flushing) **7144**
0020-9643 Interpretation (Richmond) **7651**
0020-9651 The Interpreter (Durham) **4510**
0020-966X Buffalo and Erie County Public Library Bulletin **4998**
0020-9678 Interpreter (Nashville) **7762**
0020-9686 Interpreter Releases **4696**
0020-9694 Quarterly Report on Public Welfare in Arkansas†
0020-9716 Interstages†
0020-9724 Interstampa della Capitale†
0020-9759 Intervalo†
0020-9783 Interwing Weekly Review
0020-9805 Intimate Confessions
0020-9813 Intimate Story†
0020-9864 Intrepid
0020-9872 Inuktitut **4298**
0020-9910 Inventiones Mathematicae **5498**
0020-9929 Inverness Courier **3867**
0020-9937 Investicni Vystavba†
0020-9961 Investigaciones en Sociologia **8111**
0020-9996 Investigative Radiology **6199**
0021-0013 Investigator **4192**
0021-0021 Investimenti e Prospettive
0021-0064 Investment & Marketing **1823**
0021-0080 Investment Dealers' Digest **1632**
0021-0110 Investment Quality Trends **1633**
0021-0153 Investor **1633**
0021-0218 Investors League Bulletin†
0021-0250 Inward Light†
0021-0269 Inyala News†
0021-0285 Inzhenerno-Fizicheskii Zhurnal **3203**
0021-0307 Inzicht **2871**
0021-0315 Inzynieria i Budownictwo **3273**
0021-0331 Io **497**
0021-034X Ion†
0021-0358 Ionian **2288**
0021-0366 Ionospheric Bulletin of Pakistan
0021-0382 Ionospheric Data in Japan **6358**
0021-0390 Ionospheric Predictions†
0021-0404 Ios†
0021-0439 Iowa Architect **446**
0021-0455 Iowa Bird Life **909**
0021-0463 Business & Industry
0021-0471 Iowa Conservationist *changed to* 1936-2080 **2615**
0021-0498 Iowa Dental Journal **5849**
0021-0501 Iowa Engineer†
0021-051X Iowa Farm Bureau Spokesman **123**
0021-0528 Iowa Food Dealer†
0021-0552 Iowa Law Review **4696**
0021-0560 Iowa Legionnaire **2267**
0021-0579 Iowa Library Quarterly†
0021-0609 The Iowa Music Educator **6578**
0021-0625 Iowa Plumbing, Heating, Cooling Contractor
0021-0633 Iowa Police Journal **2656**
0021-065X The Iowa Review **5310**
0021-0668 Iowa School Board Dialogue
0021-0676 Iowa Science Teachers Journal†
0021-0714 Iowa Veterinarian†
0021-0722 The Iowan **3979**
0021-0730 Iowa's People†
0021-0749 Ipargazdasag†
0021-0757 Energiagazdalkodas
0021-0773 Iqbal Review **6927**
0021-0781 Iran News
0021-079X Iran Oil Journal **6775**
0021-0803 Iran Trade and Industry
0021-082X Iranian Journal of Dermatology
0021-0846 Iranian Library Association Bulletin†
0021-0854 Iranian Petroleum Institute. Bulletin
0021-0862 Iranian Studies **552**
0021-0870 Iranica Antiqua **399**
0021-0889 Iraq **399**
0021-0900 Iraq. Central Statistical Organization. Summary of Foreign Trade Statistics
0021-0919 Iraq. Statistics Bureau. Quarterly Bulletin of Foreign Trade Statistics†
0021-0927 Iraqi Medical Professions' Association. Journal†
0021-0943 Ireland of the Welcomes **8724**
0021-0951 Ireland's Own **3893**
0021-096X Ireland's Press and Print†
0021-0978 Irenikon **7651**
0021-1001 The Iris **2288**
0021-1028 Irish Accountant and Secretary†
0021-1052 The Irish Astronomical Journal†
0021-1060 Irish Banking Review **1359**
0021-1079 The Irish Beekeeper **124**
0021-1117 Irish Contracts Weekly
0021-1133 Irish Dental Association. Journal **5850**
0021-1168 Irish Farmers' Journal **124**
0021-1176 Irish Farming News†
0021-1184 Irish Field **8293**
0021-1192 Irish Forestry **3694**
0021-1206 Irish Georgian Society. Bulletin **446**
0021-1214 Irish Historical Studies **4232**
0021-1222 The Irish Independent **3893**
0021-1257 Irish Journal of Education **2871**
0021-1265 Irish Journal of Medical Science **5641**
0021-1273 Irish Jurist **4697**
0021-1311 The Irish Naturalists' Journal **7868**
0021-132X Irish Numismatics†
0021-1389 The Irish Sword **6425**
0021-1400 Irish Theological Quarterly **7651**
0021-1419 Irish Travel Trade News **8724**
0021-1427 Irish University Review **5311**
0021-1443 Irish World and Gaelic American
0021-1486 Irodalomtorteneti Kozlemenyek **5311**
0021-1494 Irohin Yoruba **3920**
0021-1575 Tetsu to Hagane **6335**
0021-1613 Iron & Steel Journal of India **6317**
0021-1621 Iron Worker†
0021-163X Ironworker **4596**
0021-1656 Irrigation Age†
0021-1699 Iryo (Tokyo, 1946)
0021-1710 Iscani†
0021-1753 Isis **7868**
0021-1761 Iskra **7704**
0021-1796 Isla Literaria†
0021-180X Al-Islaam
0021-1818 Der Islam **7711**
0021-1826 Islam and the Modern Age **7712**
0021-1834 Islamic Culture **7712**
0021-1842 The Islamic Quarterly **7712**
0021-1850 Islamic Review and Arab Affairs†
0021-1893 Isotope†
0021-1907 Isotope and Radiation Research **6199**
0021-1923 Isotopes and Radiation Technology†
0021-1931 Isotopics†
0021-194X Israel **7144**
0021-1982 Israel. Central Bureau of Statistics. Monthly Bulletin of Statistics **8381**
0021-2008 Israel. Central Bureau of Statistics. Price Statistics Monthly **1245**
0021-2040 Israel Economist
0021-2059 Israel Exploration Journal **399**
0021-2075 Israel Financial Review
0021-2083 Israel Horizons **7246**
0021-2148 Israel Journal of Chemistry **2066**
0021-2164 Israel Journal of Earth Sciences **2711**
0021-2172 Israel Journal of Mathematics **5498**
0021-2199 Israel Journal of Physiotherapy†
0021-2202 Israel Journal of Technology†
0021-2210 Israel Journal of Zoology *changed to* 1565-9801 **949**
0021-2229 Israel Labour Party Bulletin†
0021-2237 Israel Law Review **4697**
0021-2245 Israel†
0021-2261 Israel. Meteorological Service. Series B: Observational Data. Monthly Weather Report†
0021-2288 Israel Numismatic Journal *changed to* Israel Numismatic Research **6651**
0021-230X Israel Seaman†
0021-2334 Die Gemeinde **7721**
0021-2369 Issue (Albany)†
0021-2423 Istina **7652**
0021-2490 Istituto Italiano di Cultura. Newsletter†
0021-2512 Istituto Mobiliare Italiano. Quarterly Economic Review†
0021-2520 Istituto Nazionale della Previdenza Sociale. Atti Ufficiali **4510**
0021-2547 Istituto Sieroterapico Milanese. Bollettino† **8967**
0021-2571 Istituto Superiore di Sanita. Annali **7527**
0021-258X Istituto Tecnico
0021-2598 Istituto Vaccinogeno e dei Consorzi Provinciali Antitubercolari. Rivista†
0021-2644 Istorijski Glasnik
0021-2652 Istorijski Zapisi **4233**
0021-2725 It-Torca **4596**
0021-2733 Italdoc†
0021-2741 Italia (Rome, 1953)†
0021-2768 Italia che Scrive
0021-2776 Italia Forestale e Montana **3694**
0021-2784 Italia Grafica **7324**
0021-2806 Italia Missionaria **2194**
0021-2822 Italia Nostra **6526**
0021-2830 Italia Numismatica
0021-2849 L'Italia Scacchistica **8181**
0021-2857 Italia sul Mare
0021-2865 Italia Vinicola ed Agraria†
0021-2873 Italian American Business†
0021-2881 Italian Books and Periodicals *see* 0024-2683 **7566**
0021-289X Italian Business†
0021-2903 Italian American Chamber of Commerce of Chicago. Bulletin **1405**
0021-2911 Italian Economic Survey†
0021-292X Italian General Review of Dermatology
0021-2938 Italian Journal of Biochemistry **734**
0021-2946 Italian Production
0021-2954 Italian Quarterly
0021-2970 Italiana Stil Maglia
0021-2989 Italian Stock Market†
0021-2997 Italian Trade Topics†
0021-3020 Italica **5311**
0021-3063 Italy - Documents and Notes†
0021-3071 Annali della Sanita Pubblica **7507**
0021-308X Italy and Nigeria†
0021-3098 Italy Canada Trade **1405**
0021-3101 Italy. Centro per la Statistica Aziendale. Index†
0021-3128 Ferrovie dello Stato. Informazioni Doc
0021-3136 Italy. Istituto Nazionale di Statistica. Bollettino Mensile di Statistica **8381**
0021-3152 Italy. Ministero delle Poste e delle Telecomunicazioni. Comunicazioni Postali Con l'Estero. Bollettino Mensile†
0021-3187 Itineraires†
0021-3195 Itinerario-Guia del Viajero†
0021-3209 Itinerarium **7801**
0021-3217 It's Good Psychology
0021-3225 Acta Biologica Iugoslavica. Serija C: Iugoslavica Physiologica et Pharmacologica Acta *changed to* Acta Physiologica et Pharmacologica Serbica
0021-3241 Ivra **4698**
0021-325X Ius Canonicum **7652**
0021-3268 Iustitia **7652**
0021-3276 Ivy Leaf **2288**
0021-3284 Iwate Igaku Zasshi **5642**
0021-3292 Iyo Denshi to Seitai Kogaku *changed to* 1347-443X
0021-3306 Iyyun **6927**
0021-3314 Outdoor America **2624**
0021-3357 Izmir Ticaret Odasi Dergisi
0021-339X Izumi
0021-3411 Izvestiya Vysshikh Uchebnykh Zavedenii. Fizika **7018**
0021-342X Timiryazevskaya Sel'skokhozyaistvennaya Akademiya. Izvestiya **162**
0021-3438 Izvestiya Vysshikh Uchebnykh Zavedenii. Tsvetnaya Metallurgiya **6318**
0021-3446 Izvestiya Vysshikh Uchebnykh Zavedenii. Matematika **5499**
0021-3454 Izvestiya Vysshikh Uchebnykh Zavedenii. Priborostroyeniye **3383**
0021-3462 Izvestiya Vysshikh Uchebnykh Zavedenii. Radiofizika **7018**
0021-3470 Izvestiya Vysshikh Uchebnykh Zavedenii. Radioelektronika **2359**
0021-3489 Izvestiya Vysshikh Uchebnykh Zavedenii. Tekhnologiya Legkoi Promyshlennosti†
0021-3497 Izvestiya Vysshikh Uchebnykh Zavedenii. Tekhnologiya Tekstil'noi Promyshlennosti **8453**
0021-3500 J A F News Letter†
0021-3551 Japan Agricultural Research Quarterly **125**
0021-356X J.B. Speed Art Museum Bulletin†
0021-3624 J E I **1543**
0021-3632 J E M F Quarterly†
0021-3640 J E T P Letters **7019**
0021-3659 J E T S Journal†
0021-3667 Journal of General Education **2876**
0021-3683 J M
0021-3705 J N F Illustrated† **8967**
0021-3713 J N K V V News **124**
0021-3721 J N K V V Research Journal **124**
0021-3799 J W V A Bulletin **7722**
0021-3802 Formule 1†
0021-3810 Jacetania **8725**
0021-3829 Jack and Jill (Inkprint Edition) **2194**
0021-3845 Jack-Pine Warbler **909**
0021-387X Jacobsen's Fats & Oils Bulletin **3649**
0021-3888 Jadeed Science **7869**
0021-3896 Jaegerblatt **62**
0021-390X Jag†
0021-3918 Jagawani
0021-3926 Jagd und Jaeger in Rheinland-Pfalz **8319**
0021-3942 Der Jagdgebrauchshund **8319**
0021-3950 Der Jagdspaniel **6810**
0021-3969 Jagriti
0021-3985 Jahrbuch der Absatz- und Verbrauchsforschung† **8967**
0021-4019 Jahrbuecher fuer Geschichte Osteuropas **4234**
0021-4027 Jahrbuecher fuer Nationaloekonomie und Statistik **1246**
0021-4035 Jain Jagran
0021-4043 Jain Journal **7737**
0021-406X Jaktmarker och Fiskevatten **8320**
0021-4078 Jalkine **7941**
0021-4086 Jamaica and West Indian Review
0021-4094 Jamaica Chamber of Commerce Journal **1405**
0021-4116 News Review†
0021-4124 Jamaica Journal **3995**
0021-4132 Jamaica Public Health†
0021-4140 Jamaican Nurse **5963**
0021-4167 Missionland†
0021-4183 James Joyce Quarterly **5313**
0021-4191 Jamia Educational Quarterly†
0021-4205 Jana Sangh Patrika†
0021-4213 Janaman **7145**
0021-4221 Janata **7145**
0021-423X Jantantra
0021-4248 Janus†
0021-4256 Janus†
0021-4264 Janus†
0021-4272 Janus & S C T H
0021-4329 Japan Automotive News **8586**
0021-4337 Japan Book News†
0021-4345 Japan Camera Trade News **6970**
0021-4353 Japan Christian Activity News **7652**
0021-437X Tonyobyo **5900**
0021-440X Japan Harvest **7762**
0021-4418 Japan Illustrated†

0021-4442 Japan Interior Design†
0021-4450 Japan Interpreter†
0021-4469 Japan Labour Bulletin **1690**
0021-4477 Japan Lumber Journal **3713**
0021-4485 Kaijo Hoancho Suirobu Suiro Yoho†
0021-4493 Nihon Ishikai Zasshi **5687**
0021-4507 Japan Medical Gazette†
0021-4515 Japan Medical News†
0021-4523 Japan Metal Bulletin (Print Edition) *changed to* Japan Metal Bulletin (Online Edition) **6318**
0021-4531 Fukyo *changed to* 1344-7297 **7652**
0021-4574 Japan Plastics†
0021-4582 Japan Plastics Age†
0021-4590 Japan Quarterly†
0021-4620 Nihonkaiku Suisan Kenkyusho Kenkyu Hokoku†
0021-4639 Gesuido Kyokaishi **7518**
0021-4647 Japan Shipbuilding & Marine Engineering
0021-4655 Japan Socialist Review†
0021-468X Doboku Gakkaishi **3265**
0021-471X Japan Society of Mathematical Education. Journal
0021-4728 Japan Society of Mechanical Engineers. Journal **3384**
0021-4736 Japan Stock Journal
0021-4779 Japan Welding News†
0021-4787 Japan Welding Society. Journal **6343**
0021-4809 Japanese Archives of Internal Medicine†
0021-4833 Economic Survey of Japan†
0021-4868 Japanese Heart Journal (Print) *changed to* 1349-2365 **5790**
0021-4876 Nippon Kinzoku Gakkaishi **6327**
0021-4884 Arerugi **5754**
0021-4892 Masui **5772**
0021-4914 Nihon Oyo Dobutsu Konchu Gakkaishi **856**
0021-4922 Japanese Journal of Applied Physics: Part 1. Regular Papers & Short Notes *changed to* Japanese Journal of Applied Physics **7019**
0021-4922 Japanese Journal of Applied Physics. Part 2, Letters & Express Lettres *changed to* 1882-0778 **7006**
0021-4930 Nihon Saikingaku Zasshi **5823**
0021-4949 Gan No Rinsho **6020**
0021-4965 Rinsho to Kenkyu **5910**
0021-4973 Rinsho Hifuka **5881**
0021-499X Nihon Hifuka Gakkai Zasshi **5880**
0021-5007 Nippon Seitai Gakkaishi **3456**
0021-5015 Kyoiku Shinrigaku Kenkyu **7382**
0021-5023 Japanese Journal of Ethnology **344**
0021-5066 Japanese Journal of Geophysics†
0021-5082 Nihon Eiseigaku Zasshi **6994**
0021-5104 Rikusui Gaku Zasshi **2798**
0021-5147 Eiyogaku Zasshi **6658**
0021-5155 Japanese Journal of Ophthalmology **6044**
0021-5163 Nippon Koku Geka Gakkai Zasshi **5857**
0021-518X Shonika Rinsho **6104**
0021-5198 The Japanese Journal of Pharmacology (Print Edition) *changed to* 1347-8613 **6855**
0021-5201 Japanese Weekly on Pharmacy and Chemistry
0021-5228 Japanese Journal of Plastic & Reconstructive Surgery **6247**
0021-5236 Shinrigaku Kenkyu **7408**
0021-5252 Kyobu Geka **6251**
0021-5260 Nettai Nogyo **139**
0021-5279 Japanese Journal of Tuberculosis and Chest Diseases†
0021-5287 Nihon Hinyokika Gakkai Zasshi **6272**
0021-5325 Nippon Seikei Geka Gakkai Zasshi **6068**
0021-535X Japanese Poetry in English†
0021-5368 Japanese Psychological Research **7367**
0021-5384 Nihon Naika Gakkai Zasshi **5948**
0021-5392 Nippon Suisan Gakkaishi **3603**
0021-5414 Japanese Sociological Review **8111**
0021-5457 Jardin des Modes†
0021-5481 Jardins de France **3739**
0021-5546 Jaernvaegteknik†
0021-5554 La Jaune et la Rouge **8428**
0021-5597 Jazykovedny Casopis **5132**
0021-5627 Jazz & Pop†
0021-5643 Jazz Hot **6578**
0021-566X Jazz Magazine **6578**
0021-5678 Jazz Monthly†
0021-5686 Jazz Podium **6579**
0021-5694 Jazz Report†
0021-5708 Musikrevue†
0021-5716 Jazz Times **6579**
0021-5724 Der Jazzfreund
0021-5740 Je Crois†
0021-5775 Jedinstvo†
0021-5783 Jedleseе†
0021-5791 Jednota **3542**
0021-5805 Jednotna Skola†
0021-5813 Jeevan Jauban
0021-5821 Jefferson Medical College Alumni Bulletin **5643**
0021-583X J.E.M.†
0021-5856 Jenaer Jahrbuch†
0021-5880 Jeopardy **5313**
0021-5899 Jernindustri†
0021-5929 The Jersey **290**
0021-5945 Jersey Concrete†
0021-5953 Jersey Journal **290**
0021-597X The Jerusalem Post (Weekly Overseas Edition)†
0021-5996 Jet **3979**
0021-602X Jetline Schedules
0021-6038 Jeugd†
0021-6062 Jeugdnatuurwachter†
0021-6070 J N†
0021-6119 Jeune (S)†
0021-6127 Quebec Science **7901**
0021-6135 Les Jeunes **8182**
0021-6143 Jeunes Annees **2195**
0021-6151 Jeunes Avocats *changed to* Guide du Jeune Avocat **4683**
0021-616X Jeunes des Auberges
0021-6194 Jeunesse an Deux Mille†
0021-6208 Jeunesse et Orgue†
0021-6232 Revue Internationale des Jeux et Jouets†
0021-6240 Jevrejski Pregled†
0021-6259 Jewel of Africa†
0021-6291 Jewelry Workers' Bulletin†
0021-6305 Jewish Affairs **7722**
0021-6313 Jewish Affairs **3542**
0021-6321 Jewish Braille Review **4082**
0021-633X Jewish Chronicle **3542**
0021-6348 Jewish Civic Press **7722**
0021-6372 Jewish Community Center Program Aids†
0021-6380 Jewish Current Events
0021-6399 Jewish Currents **3542**
0021-6410 Jewish Digest†
0021-6437 Jewish Exponent **7722**
0021-6453 Jewish Frontier†
0021-6488 Jewish Herald-Voice **7723**
0021-6534 Jewish Journal of Sociology
0021-6542 Jewish Labor Movement. Bund Archives. Bulletin†
0021-6550 The Jewish Ledger **7723**
0021-6569 Jewish Liberation Journal†
0021-6577 Jewish Life†
0021-6585 Jewish Memorial Hospital Bulletin†
0021-6615 Jewish Observer (New York) **7723**
0021-6623 Jewish Observer and Middle East Review†
0021-6631 Jewish Parent†
0021-6666 Jewish Press (Omaha) **7723**
0021-6674 Jewish Press (Brooklyn) **7723**
0021-6682 The Jewish Quarterly Review **7723**
0021-6704 Jewish Social Studies **7724**
0021-6720 Jewish Spectator†
0021-6739 Jewish Standard **7724**
0021-6747 Jewish Standard **4577**
0021-6755 Jewish Telegraph (Manchester Edition) **3543**
0021-6763 J T A Weekly News Digest **7722**
0021-678X The Jewish Transcript *changed to* J T News **7722**
0021-6801 Jewish Vanguard **7724**
0021-681X Jewish Vegetarian **6661**
0021-6828 The Jewish Voice (Wilmington) **7724**
0021-6879 Jewish Western Bulletin *changed to* 1910-9377 **7723**
0021-6925 Jezik **5132**
0021-6933 Jezik in Slovstvo **5132**
0021-6941 Jezyk Polski **5132**
0021-695X Jicarilla Chieftain **3543**
0021-6968 Jikeikai Medical Journal **5644**
0021-6976 Jiwan Dhara **4577**
0021-6984 Free World
0021-700X Jnanadhara **5313**
0021-7026 Job
0021-7050 Jobber News **8587**
0021-7077 Joblinglass†
0021-7115 Jockey Club†
0021-7131 Joedisk Orientering **7724**
0021-714X Joel†
0021-7166 Jogtudomanyi Kozlony **4699**
0021-7174 Johann Wilhelm Klein **4082**
0021-7182 Johannesburg Stock Exchange Monthly Bulletin **1634**
0021-7190 John Herling's Labor Letter†
0021-7204 The John Liner Letter **4510**
0021-7255 Johns Hopkins Magazine **2288**
0021-7263 Johns Hopkins Medical Journal†
0021-7271 Johnson Drillers Journal†
0021-728X Johnsonian News Letter **5314**
0021-7298 Joho Kanri **2548**
0021-7301 Desfile **4356**
0021-731X Joint Acquisitions List of Africana†
0021-7336 National Defence College Gazette
0021-7344 Jok†
0021-7395 Jonge Kerk†
0021-7409 Jonge Muziek
0021-7417 Stakkato†
0021-7441 Jordbruksekonomiska Meddelanden†
0021-7468 Jordemodern **5994**
0021-7476 Jorden Runt†
0021-7484 Jordens Folk **344**
0021-7522 Jornal de Estomatologia†
0021-7530 Jornal de Letras e Artes
0021-7557 Jornal de Pediatria **6094**
0021-7565 Jornal de Poesia
0021-7573 Jornal do Medico
0021-7603 Josephite Harvest **7653**
0021-762X Journal Asiatique **553**
0021-7638 Journal Bandeirante†
0021-7670 Journal d'Analyse Mathematique **5499**
0021-7697 Journal de Chirurgie **6247**
0021-7700 Journal de Compton News
0021-7719 Journal de Conchyliologie† **8968**
0021-7735 Journal de France des Appellations d'Origine†
0021-776X Journal de la Construction de la Suisse Romande **1018**
0021-7778 Journal de la Corse Agricole **125**
0021-7794 Le Journal de la Paix **7802**
0021-7824 Journal de Mathematiques Pures et Appliquees **5499**
0021-7859 Journal de Medecine de Besancon†
0021-7875 Journal de Medecine de Caen†
0021-7883 Journal de Medecine de Lyon†
0021-7905 Journal de Medecine de Strasbourg†
0021-7913 Journal de Medecine et de Chirurgie Pratiques†
0021-793X Journal de Pharmacologie†
0021-7956 Journal de Psychologie Normale et Pathologique†
0021-7980 Journal de Semiologie Medicale†
0021-8006 Journal Historique des Bernier **3772**
0021-8014 Journal des Combattants **6429**
0021-8030 Journal des Communes **7494**
0021-8049 Journal des Finances **1360**
0021-8065 Le Journal des Ingenieurs *changed to* 1378-6652 **3204**
0021-8081 Journal des Medecins du Nord & de l'Est†
0021-8103 Journal des Savants **5314**
0021-8111 Journal des Sciences Medicales de Lille†
0021-812X Journal des Tribunaux **4699**
0021-8138 Journal d'Hotel
0021-8170 Journal du Droit International†
0021-8197 Journal du Textile **8454**
0021-8227 Journal Export†
0021-8235 Journal for Anthroposophy **7737**
0021-8251 Journal for Research in Mathematics Education **3066**
0021-8286 Journal for the History of Astronomy **576**
0021-8294 Journal for the Scientific Study of Religion **7653**
0021-8308 Journal for the Theory of Social Behaviour **7367**
0021-8324 Journal Francais de Medecine et Chirurgie Thoraciques†
0021-8340 Journal Francais Langenscheidt†
0021-8367 Journal fuer Marktforschung†
0021-8375 Journal fuer Ornithologie *changed to* Journal of Ornithology **909**
0021-8391 Journal Magazine
0021-8405 Journal Mondial de Pharmacie†
0021-8413 Journal Musical Francais-Musica Disques†
0021-843X Journal of Abnormal Psychology **7368**
0021-8448 Journal of Accountancy **1293**
0021-8456 Journal of Accounting Research **1294**
0021-8464 Journal of Adhesion **7019**
0021-8480 Journal of Adventist Education **7762**
0021-8499 Journal of Advertising Research **27**
0021-8502 Journal of Aerosol Science **6711**
0021-8510 Journal of Aesthetic Education **2874**
0021-8529 Journal of Aesthetics and Art Criticism **498**
0021-8537 The Journal of African History **4176**
0021-8553 Journal of African Law **4700**
0021-8561 Journal of Agricultural and Food Chemistry **238**
0021-857X Journal of Agricultural Economics **202**
0021-8588 Nogyo Kisho/Journal of Agricultural Meteorology *changed to* 1346-5368 **6395**
0021-8596 The Journal of Agricultural Science **126**
0021-860X Journal of Agriculture†
0021-8626 Journal of Agriculture-South Australia†
0021-8642 Journal of Air Law and Commerce **4700**
0021-8650 Journal of Air Traffic Control **63**
0021-8669 Journal of Aircraft **63**
0021-8693 Journal of Algebra **5500**
0021-8715 Journal of American Folklore **3619**
0021-8723 Journal of American History **4298**
0021-8731 Journal of American Indian Education **6635**
0021-874X Journal of American Insurance†
0021-8758 Journal of American Studies **4299**
0021-8774 Journal of Analytical Psychology **7368**
0021-8782 Journal of Anatomy **680**
0021-8790 Journal of Animal Ecology **680**
0021-8804 Journal of Animal Morphology and Physiology **680**
0021-8812 Journal of Animal Science **291**
0021-8820 Journal of Antibiotics **5645**
0021-8839 Journal of Apicultural Research *changed to* 1751-2891 **127**
0021-8855 Journal of Applied Behavior Analysis **7368**
0021-8863 The Journal of Applied Behavioral Science **7368**
0021-8898 Journal of Applied Crystallography **2111**
0021-8901 Journal of Applied Ecology **680**
0021-891X Journal of Applied Electrochemistry **2114**
0021-8928 Journal of Applied Mathematics and Mechanics **3349**
0021-8936 Journal of Applied Mechanics **3385**
0021-8944 Journal of Applied Mechanics and Technical Physics **3349**
0021-8960 Journal of Applied Nutrition
0021-8979 Journal of Applied Physics **7019**
0021-8995 Journal of Applied Polymer Science **3248**
0021-9002 Journal of Applied Probability **5501**
0021-9010 Journal of Applied Psychology **7369**
0021-9029 Journal of Applied Social Psychology **7369**
0021-9037 Journal of Applied Spectroscopy **7077**
0021-9045 Journal of Approximation Theory **5501**
0021-9053 Journal of Arizona History **4299**
0021-907X Journal of Art History **498**
0021-9088 Bijutsu Kenkyu **478**
0021-9096 Journal of Asian and African Studies **8112**
0021-910X Journal of Asian History **4184**
0021-9118 Journal of Asian Studies **553**
0021-9142 Journal of the Astronautical Sciences **64**
0021-9150 Atherosclerosis **5778**
0021-9177 Journal of Auditory Research†
0021-9193 Journal of Bacteriology **888**
0021-9207 Journal of Band Research **6580**
0021-9215 Journal of Bank Research†
0021-9231 Journal of Biblical Literature **7654**
0021-924X Journal of Biochemistry **735**
0021-9258 Journal of Biological Chemistry **735**
0021-9266 Journal of Biological Education **681**
0021-9274 Journal of Biological Psychology-Worm Runner's Digest†
0021-9282 Journal of Biological Sciences
0021-9290 Journal of Biomechanics **5646**
0021-9304 Journal of Biomedical Materials Research *changed to* 1549-3296 **766**
0021-9304 Journal of Biomedical Materials Research *changed to* 1552-4973 **766**
0021-9320 Journal of Biosocial Science **8112**
0021-9347 Journal of Black Studies **7978**
0021-9355 Journal of Bone and Joint Surgery: American Volume **6063**
0021-9371 Journal of British Studies **4235**
0021-9398 The Journal of Business (Chicago)†
0021-9428 Journal of Business & Social Studies **1133**
0021-9436 Journal of Business Communication **1764**
0021-9460 Journal of Business Law **4872**
0021-9487 Journal of Canadian Petroleum Technology **6775**
0021-9495 Journal of Canadian Studies **4460**
0021-9509 The Journal of Cardiovascular Surgery **5792**
0021-9517 Journal of Catalysis **2136**
0021-9525 The Journal of Cell Biology **833**
0021-9533 Journal of Cell Science **833**
0021-9541 Journal of Cellular Physiology **923**
0021-955X Journal of Cellular Plastics **7093**
0021-9568 Journal of Chemical and Engineering Data **2067**
0021-9584 Journal of Chemical Education **2067**
0021-9592 Journal of Chemical Engineering of Japan **3248**
0021-9606 Journal of Chemical Physics **7019**
0021-9614 The Journal of Chemical Thermodynamics **2136**
0021-9622 Journal of Chemicals and Allied Industries **2067**

ISSN

DIRECTORY 2010 0023-0324 9039

0022-4634 Journal of Southeast Asian Studies **4185**
0022-4642 Journal of Southern History **4300**
0022-4650 Journal of Spacecraft and Rockets **64**
0022-4669 Journal of Special Education **3043**
0022-4693 Journal of Spelean History **2751**
0022-4707 The Journal of Sports Medicine and Physical Fitness **6231**
0022-4715 Journal of Statistical Physics **7022**
0022-4723 Journal of Steel Castings Research†
0022-474X Journal of Stored Products Research **853**
0022-4766 Journal of Structural Chemistry **2069**
0022-4790 Journal of Surgical Oncology **6250**
0022-4804 Journal of Surgical Research **6250**
0022-4812 The Journal of Symbolic Logic **5507**
0022-4839 Journal of Systems Management†
0022-4847 Taiwan Nongye Yanjiu **160**
0022-4855 Journal of Tamil Studies **5136**
0022-4863 Journal of Taxation **1932**
0022-4871 Journal of Teacher Education **2878**
0022-4898 Journal of Terramechanics **8501**
0022-4901 Journal of Texture Studies **3652**
0022-4928 Journal of the Atmospheric Sciences **6359**
0022-4979 Karnatak University. College of Education. Journal **2880**
0022-4995 Journal of the Economic and Social History of the Orient **4322**
0022-5002 Journal of the Experimental Analysis of Behavior **7381**
0022-5010 Journal of the History of Biology **685**
0022-5029 Bukkyo Shigaku *changed to* 0288-6472 **7700**
0022-5037 Journal of the History of Ideas **4461**
0022-5045 Journal of the History of Medicine and Allied Sciences **5655**
0022-5053 Journal of the History of Philosophy **6930**
0022-5061 Journal of the History of the Behavioral Sciences **7381**
0022-5096 Journal of the Mechanics and Physics of Solids **7060**
0022-510X Journal of the Neurological Sciences **6157**
0022-5118 Journal of the New African Literature and the Arts†
0022-5134 Journal of the Royal Artillery **6430**
0022-5142 Journal of the Science of Food and Agriculture **128**
0022-5169 Journal of the West **4300**
0022-5177 Journal of the West Australian Nurses†
0022-5185 Journal of Theological Studies **7657**
0022-5193 Journal of Theoretical Biology **685**
0022-5207 Journal of Therapy **5655**
0022-5223 The Journal of Thoracic and Cardiovascular Surgery **6250**
0022-5231 Journal of Thought **7980**
0022-524X Journal of Transpersonal Psychology **7381**
0022-5258 Journal of Transport Economics and Policy **8501**
0022-5266 The Journal of Transport History **8501**
0022-5274 Kotsu Igaku **6066**
0022-5282 Journal of Trauma **6066**
0022-5339 Journal of Undergraduate Mathematics **5507**
0022-5347 The Journal of Urology **6270**
0022-5363 The Journal of Value Inquiry **6930**
0022-538X Journal of Virology **890**
0022-5401 Journal of West African Languages **5136**
0022-541X The Journal of Wildlife Management **2616**
0022-5436 Journal of World History†
0022-5452 Journal of Yugoslav Foreign Trade†
0022-5509 Journalism†
0022-5541 Journalist **4578**
0022-555X De Journalist **4578**
0022-5576 Journalist **4578**
0022-5584 Journalist
0022-5592 Journalisten **4578**
0022-5630 Journee du Batiment†
0022-5681 Jours de France†
0022-569X Joy†
0022-5711 Jucunda Laudatio†
0022-572X Judaica **7725**
0022-5738 Judaica Bohemiae **7725**
0022-5746 Judaica Book Guide†
0022-5754 Judaica Book News†
0022-5762 Judaism **7725**
0022-5770 Judean
0022-5789 Judge **4704**
0022-5800 Judicature **4953**
0022-5819 Judo **8183**
0022-5843 Judo Kokokan†
0022-5908 Jugend Kurier†
0022-5916 Jugend und Buch†
0022-5940 Jugendhilfe **8052**
0022-6017 Jugoslavenska Advokatura†
0022-6033 Jugoslavija†
0022-6041 Yugoslavskie Profsoyuzy†
0022-605X Jugoslawische Touristenzeitung†
0022-6084 Jugoslovenska Revija za Medjunarodno Pravo *changed to* 1820-2039 **4943**
0022-6114 Jugoslovenski Pregled *changed to* 1451-4761 **3945**
0022-6130 Jugoslovensko Vinogradarstvo i Vinarstvo†
0022-6149 Jugovinil
0022-6157 Juguetes y Juegos de Espana **4060**
0022-6165 Juillard†
0022-6181 Juke Box†
0022-6203 Juncture - Where Ideas Meet†
0022-6254 Europaeer†
0022-6262 Der Junge Florist†
0022-6270 Junge Gaertner†
0022-6289 Junge Gemeinde **7763**
0022-6297 Junge Generation†
0022-6319 Junge Kirche **7657**
0022-6343 Junge Sammler **6896**
0022-636X Junge Stimme†
0022-6394 Junger Tischler†
0022-6424 Jungfreiheitliche†
0022-6440 Eisenhardt-Post
0022-6475 Junior **2196**
0022-6483 Junior Age†
0022-6505 Junior Bookshelf†
0022-6521 Junior Church Paper†
0022-6602 Texas Historian **4314**
0022-6629 Junior Keynotes **6581**
0022-667X Junior News†
0022-6688 Junior Scholastic **3069**
0022-670X Junior Student†
0022-6726 Quest (New York)†
0022-6769 Juntendo Medical Journal **5656**
0022-6777 Juridica†
0022-6785 Juridical Review **4705**
0022-6807 Juris **4706**
0022-6815 Hogaku Kyokai Zasshi **4687**
0022-6831 Jurisprudence du Port d'Anvers **4970**
0022-684X Jurisprudencia e Doutrina
0022-6858 Jurist **7802**
0022-6882 Juristenzeitung **4707**
0022-6890 Juristische Analysen†
0022-6912 Juristische Blaetter **4707**
0022-6920 Juristische Rundschau **4707**
0022-6939 Juristische Schulung **4707**
0022-6955 Jus **4708**
0022-6963 Jus Gentium
0022-6971 Jussens Venner **4708**
0022-7048 Justice Weekly
0022-7064 Justiz-Ministerial-Blatt fuer Hessen **4708**
0022-7102 Jute and Synthetics Review†
0022-7129 Jute Markets and Prices
0022-7137 Jutro Polski†
0022-7145 Juvenile Braille Monthly†
0022-7161 Juvenile Merchandising†
0022-717X Juvenile Rechabite†
0022-7196 Juventud†
0022-720X Juventud en Accion†
0022-7218 Juventud Panadera **3674**
0022-7226 Juzen Igakkai Zasshi **5656**
0022-7234 Jyotish Kalp†
0022-7242 K A C B Auto Revue **8587**
0022-7277 K & C†
0022-7366 K L M Literatuuroverzicht†
0022-7374 K L M News†
0022-7412 K U L S A A Newsletter
0022-7439 K V P News **6201**
0022-7463 De Kaarsvlam **566**
0022-7471 Kachiku to Eiyo†
0022-748X Kadima
0022-7498 Kadmos **2236**
0022-7536 Der Kaelte und Klima-Fachmann†
0022-7552 Kaerntner Gemeindeblatt **7494**
0022-7560 Kaerntner Heimatleben **3619**
0022-7579 Kaerntner Landes-Zeitung **7494**
0022-7587 Kaerntner Museumsschriften **6527**
0022-7595 Kaerntner Naturschutzblaetter†
0022-7609 Kaffee und Tee Markt†
0022-7625 Kagaku **7873**
0022-7633 Kagaku Gijutsu Bunken Sabisu†
0022-7641 Kagaku Gijutsu Bunken Sokuho. Doboku, Kenchiku Kogaku Hen **3232**
0022-765X Kagaku Gijutsu Bunken Toyama†
0022-7668 Kagaku Kisoron Kenkyu **7874**
0022-7684 Kagaku to Kogyo (Tokyo) **2069**
0022-7692 Kagakushi Kenkyu **7874**
0022-7706 Kagoshimaken Nogyo Kisho Geppo
0022-7730 Kaigai Gijutsu Hairaito†
0022-7757 Kairos†
0022-7765 Kairos†
0022-779X Kaiserswerther Mitteilungen **7657**
0022-7803 Kaiun **8649**
0022-7811 Maizuru Kaiyo Kishodai. Kaiyo Sokuho **2811**
0022-7846 Kakteen und Andere Sukkulenten **799**
0022-7854 Kaku Igaku **6202**
0022-7862 Kakyevole†
0022-7870 Kalaikathir **7874**
0022-7889 Kalakeli
0022-7919 Kaleidoscope (Springfield)
0022-7927 Kaleidoscope†
0022-7943 Kali†
0022-796X Kalibreur
0022-7978 Kalimat Al-Mar'ah†
0022-7994 Kalki†
0022-8001 Kalksburger Korrespondenz
0022-8028 Kalyan **7657**
0022-8036 Kalyan Kalpataru†
0022-8052 Kamakoti Vani
0022-8087 Kamer van Koophandel en Nijverheid van Antwerpen. Bulletin **1406**
0022-8117 Kamerad Tier **6810**
0022-8133 Kameralehti **6970**
0022-8141 University of Leiden. Kamerlingh Onnes Laboratory. Communications
0022-815X Kami Pa Gikyoshi **6734**
0022-8176 Kamm und Schere†
0022-8184 Kammer Nachrichten **1406**
0022-8206 Campana **3525**
0022-8214 Kampanje! **1827**
0022-8230 Kampf dem Krieg
0022-8265 Kampioen **8727**
0022-8273 Kamratposten **2196**
0022-8281 Kanadai Magyarsag
0022-829X Kanadski Srbobran **3545**
0022-8311 Kanazawa Irigaku Sosho†
0022-832X Kanazawa Daigaku Kogakubu Kiyo†
0022-8338 Kanazawa University. Science Reports **7874**
0022-8354 Kandelaar†
0022-8362 Kango **5968**
0022-8370 Kango Kenkyu **5968**
0022-8397 Kanot-Nytt *changed to* 1653-2503 **8280**
0022-8400 Kansai Ika Daigaku. Zasshi **5656**
0022-8419 Kansallis-Osake-Pankki. Economic Review†
0022-8427 Kansantaloudellinen Aikakauskirja **1139**
0022-8435 Kansas! **3979**
0022-8443 Kansas Academy of Science. Transactions (Print) **7874**
0022-8478 The Kansas Banker **1363**
0022-8486 Kansas Bar Association. Journal **4709**
0022-8494 Kansas Beverage News **605**
0022-8516 Kansas City Grocer†
0022-8524 Kansas City Jewish Chronicle **3545**
0022-8532 Kansas Economic Development Report†
0022-8559 Kansas Engineer **3207**
0022-8567 Kansas Entomological Society. Journal **853**
0022-8575 Kansas Farm Bureau News†
0022-8605 Kansas Food Dealers Bulletin
0022-8613 Kansas Government Journal **7495**
0022-863X Kansas Job Opportunities†
0022-8656 Kansas Judicial Council Bulletin
0022-8702 Kansas Music Review **6582**
0022-8710 Kansas Nurse **5968**
0022-8729 Kansas Ornithological Society. Bulletin **909**
0022-8737 Kansas Publisher†
0022-8753 Kansas Restaurant **4392**
0022-8761 Kansas School Board Journal†
0022-877X Kansas School Naturalist **7874**
0022-880X Kansas. State Department of Education. Special Education Section. Typical Report†
0022-8826 Kansas Stockman **291**
0022-8869 Kansas Water News†
0022-8877 Kant Studien **6930**
0022-8885 Kantinen **4597**
0022-8893 Kantoor en Efficiency **1852**
0022-8907 Kantoor - School - Huis†
0022-8923 Kanu Sport **8277**
0022-894X Kappa Delta Epsilon Current **2289**
0022-8958 Kappa Delta Pi Record **3069**
0022-8966 Karachi Commerce Weekly
0022-8974 Karachi University Gazette†
0022-8990 Karamu **5317**
0022-9008 Karate and Oriental Arts†
0022-9024 Karayollari Teknik Bulteni
0022-9032 Kardiologia Polska **5794**
0022-9040 Kardiologiya **5794**
0022-9059 Karlovacki Tjednik **5222**
0022-9075 Karma Album Review†
0022-9083 Karnatak Granthalaya
0022-9091 Karnataka Law Journal **4709**
0022-9105 Die Karpatenpost **3545**
0022-9113 Kartei der Praktischen Medizin
0022-913X Karting Magazine **8587**
0022-9148 Kartofel' i Ovoshchi **240**
0022-9156 Der Kartoffelbau **240**
0022-9164 Kartographische Nachrichten **4018**
0022-9172 Karty Dokumentacyjne†
0022-9199 Karys **6430**
0022-9202 Kaseki **6726**
0022-9210 Kashmir Affairs **554**
0022-9237 Kasr-el-Aini Journal of Surgery
0022-9245 Kasseler Sonntagsblatt **7658**
0022-9253 Kastner & Oehler Firmen Zeitung **1890**
0022-9261 Kasturi **3884**
0022-927X Kasvatus **2880**
0022-9288 Katallagete†
0022-9296 Katedra **2289**
0022-9318 Katha-Sahitya **5317**
0022-9326 Kathakali†
0022-9334 Katholieke Kleuterschool†
0022-9350 Metamedica†
0022-9377 Katholische Frauenbewegung Oesterreichs. Fuehrungsblatt **7803**
0022-9415 Katilolehti **5997**
0022-9466 Kauchuk i Rezina **7825**
0022-9474 Kaufhaus und Warenhaus **1430**
0022-9539 Kaviamuthu **3884**
0022-9547 Kavita **5425**
0022-9555 Kayak†
0022-9571 Kaytannon Maamies **130**
0022-9598 Kazak†
0022-961X Keen Teen
0022-9644 Keeping Posted with N C S Y†
0022-9652 Keeping the Record Straight†
0022-9687 Kehilwenyane **7803**
0022-9695 Keidanren Review **1139**
0022-9709 Keio Economic Studies **1139**
0022-9717 Keio Journal of Medicine **5657**
0022-9725 Keizai Kagaku **1139**
0022-9733 Keizai Kenkyu **1140**
0022-9741 Keizai Shirin **1140**
0022-975X Keizaigaku Kenkyu (Tokyo) **1140**
0022-9768 Keizaigaku Ronshu **1140**
0022-9776 Kekkaku **6215**
0022-9784 Kelderblom
0022-9792 Keltia **6930**
0022-9806 Keltner Commodity Letter†
0022-9830 Kemija u Industriji **3249**
0022-9857 Kemio Internacia†
0022-9865 Kemisti *changed to* 1457-9936 **2072**
0022-9873 Kemixon Reporter†
0022-9881 Kemphaan
0022-989X Kenpo Nyusu **4511**
0022-9903 Kempton Park Parade†
0022-9938 Kenko Kyoiku
0022-9946 Kenko na Kurashi
0022-9962 Kennel Gazette **6810**
0022-9997 Kensetsu Kogyo Bukka Chingin Geppo
0023-0014 Kent Archaeological Review **402**
0023-0022 Kent Farmer **130**
0023-0030 Kent Life **3867**
0023-0057 Kentaur **6430**
0023-0065 Kentering†
0023-0073 Kentuckiana Purchasor†
0023-0103 Kentucky Ancestors **3772**
0023-0111 Kentucky Banker **1363**
0023-0138 Kentucky Beverage Journal **605**
0023-0146 Kentucky Civil War Round Table. Bulletin **4300**
0023-0197 Kentucky English Bulletin **5136**
0023-0243 Kentucky Historical Society. Register **4300**
0023-0251 Kentucky Labor News
0023-026X Kentucky Law Journal **4709**
0023-0294 Kentucky Medical Association. Journal **5657**
0023-0324 Kentucky Press **4578**

ISSN

0023-5938 Kwartalnik Pedagogiczny **2881**
0023-5954 Kybernetika **5508**
0023-5962 Kyklos **8117**
0023-5989 Kymppi *changed to* 0789-9726
0023-5997 Kyoiku Hyoron **2881**
0023-6004 Kyokuchi **7878**
0023-6012 Kyoto Prefectural University of Medicine. Medical Society. Journal **5659**
0023-6020 Kyoto Shobo **3579**
0023-6039 Kyoto University. Bulletin of Stomatology†
0023-6063 Kyoto University. Faculty of Engineering. Memoirs†
0023-6071 Kyoto University. Institute for Chemical Research. Bulletin†
0023-608X Kyoto University. Journal of Mathematics **5508**
0023-6098 Kyoto University. Misaki Marine Biological Institute. Bulletin†
0023-6101 Kyoto Kyoiku Daigaku Kiyo. B: Shizen Kagaku/Kyoto University of Education. Bulletin. Series B, Mathematics and Natural Science *changed to* Kyoto Kyoiku Daigaku Kiyou **7878**
0023-611X Kypros **3832**
0023-6128 Kyrios†
0023-6136 Kyrkofoerfattningar†
0023-6144 Kyushu Neuro-Psychiatry **6158**
0023-6152 Kyushu University. Faculty of Agriculture. Journal **132**
0023-6217 L A M Y A Revista Mensual
0023-6225 L A R C Reports†
0023-625X L B I News **4150**
0023-6268 L G A Rundschau *changed to* 1611-8243 **1897**
0023-6276 L G M Mededelingen†
0023-6292 L I D News Bulletin†
0023-6306 L K A B-Tidningen†
0023-6330 L M S - Lingua **5138**
0023-6349 L O G A†
0023-6357 L P A News
0023-6365 L S A Bulletin (Print) *changed to* L S A Bulletin (Online) **5138**
0023-6373 L S C R R C Newsletter†
0023-6381 Laurence Scott Engineering Bulletin†
0023-639X L S E Magazine **2289**
0023-6411 L S U Engineering News **2289**
0023-6438 Lebensmittel - Wissenschaft und Technologie *changed to* L W T- Food Science and Technology **3653**
0023-6446 La-Ya'aran†
0023-6454 Lab World†
0023-6462 Labeo **4711**
0023-6489 Labor† **8970**
0023-6497 Labor†
0023-6500 Labor Arbitration Awards **4597**
0023-6519 Labor Chronicle†
0023-6527 Labor Developments Abroad†
0023-6543 Labor Education Viewpoints†
0023-656X Labor History **1692**
0023-6578 Labor in Print†
0023-6586 Labor Law Journal **4711**
0023-6594 Labor Leader **4597**
0023-6616 Labor Record
0023-6640 Labor Today
0023-6667 The Labor World **4597**
0023-6683 Laboratoires Squibb. Recueil de Nouvelles†
0023-6691 Laboratorio†
0023-6721 Laboratoriums-Praxis†
0023-6772 Laboratory Animals **953**
0023-6799 Laboratory Digest†
0023-6810 Laboratory Equipment **5908**
0023-6829 Laboratory Equipment Digest†
0023-6837 Laboratory Investigation **5908**
0023-6853 Laboratory Practice†
0023-6861 Laboratory Primate Newsletter **5909**
0023-6888 The Laborer **4597**
0023-6896 Labour and Employment Gazette†
0023-690X Labour Arbitration Cases **1694**
0023-6934 Labour Gazette **1694**
0023-6942 Labour History **1694**
0023-6950 Labour in Exile
0023-6969 Labour in Israel† **8970**
0023-6977 Labour Law Journal **4711**
0023-6985 Labour Monthly†
0023-6993 Labour Organiser†
0023-7000 Labour Research **1695**
0023-7027 Labour Woman†
0023-7035 Labour World
0023-7051 Lacerta **953**
0023-706X Lach-Manoeuvre
0023-7078 Lackawanna Jurist **4711**
0023-7086 Lacrossetalk **8237**
0023-7094 Lada'at†
0023-7108 Ladder†
0023-7124 Ladies' Home Journal **8871**
0023-7140 Ladue Public Schools Bulletin *changed to* Link (Conway) **2883**
0023-7159 Ladugaardsfoermannen **292**
0023-7167 The Lady **3867**
0023-7191 Lady's Circle†
0023-7205 Laekartidningen **5659**
0023-7213 Laeknabladid **5659**
0023-7256 Lagena†
0023-7272 Lagos Weekend†
0023-7280 Lagrimal Trifurca **5319**
0023-7299 Lahey Clinic Foundation Bulletin†
0023-7302 Le Lait (Print) *changed to* 1958-5586 **884**
0023-7329 Lake Carriers' Association. Bulletin†
0023-7353 Lakimies **4711**
0023-7361 Lakimiesuutiset **4712**
0023-7388 Lal-Baugh **3741**
0023-7396 Lalit Kala Contemporary **502**
0023-7418 The Lamp **6776**
0023-7450 Lana Moda
0023-7469 Lancashire Life **3867**
0023-7477 Lancaster County Historical Society. Journal **4301**
0023-7485 Lancaster Farming **132**
0023-7493 Lance **2289**
0023-7515 Lanciana **8588**
0023-7523 The Land **132**
0023-7531 Land **3956**
0023-754X Landscape Architecture News Digest **448**
0023-7558 Der Land- und Forstwirtschaftlicher Betrieb
0023-7574 Land and Liberty **7597**
0023-7604 Land and Water International **241**
0023-7639 Land Economics **202**
0023-7655 Land Pollution Reporter
0023-7663 Land und Garten
0023-768X Land Use Digest **4418**
0023-7698 Land van Valkenburg†
0023-7744 Landbote
0023-7752 Landbouw en Plantenziekten†
0023-7779 Landbouweekblad **133**
0023-7795 Landbouwmechanisatie **212**
0023-7825 Landbouwwereldnieuws†
0023-7833 Landbrukstidende **133**
0023-7876 Landesamtsblatt fuer das Burgenland **7450**
0023-7884 Landesgesetzblatt fuer das Land Salzburg **7495**
0023-7922 Landesversicherungsanstalt Hessen. Nachrichten **4512**
0023-7930 Landfall **5223**
0023-7949 Landis und Gyr Mitteilungen†
0023-7957 Landjugend **2199**
0023-7973 Landmaschinen - Handwerk - Handel **212**
0023-799X Landowning in Scotland
0023-8007 Die Landpost **133**
0023-8015 Landsbygdens Folk **133**
0023-8023 Landscape†
0023-8031 Landscape Architecture **448**
0023-8066 Landskab **3742**
0023-8082 Landtechnik (Muenster) **241**
0023-8228 Langage Total†
0023-8244 Langenscheidt's English Monthly†
0023-8252 Langenscheidts Sprach-Illustrierte†
0023-8287 Language and Automation†
0023-8309 Language and Speech **5139**
0023-8317 Language and Style **5140**
0023-8333 Language Learning **5141**
0023-8341 Language Sciences†
0023-8368 Langue Francaise **5142**
0023-8376 Langues Modernes **5142**
0023-8384 Lansing Labor News **4598**
0023-8406 Lantern
0023-8414 Lantern
0023-8422 Lantern **2882**
0023-8430 Lantmaestaren **134**
0023-8449 Lantmannen **134**
0023-8457 Lapidary Journal *changed to* 1936-5942 **4568**
0023-8473 Laputa Gazette and Faculty News†
0023-8481 Lara Lamont
0023-8503 Lares **3619**
0023-8511 Larvae du Golden Gate
0023-852X The Laryngoscope **6082**
0023-8538 Las Polski **3695**
0023-8546 Las Vegas Voice
0023-8597 Laser Journal†
0023-8635 Last Day Messenger†
0023-8651 Last Post
0023-866X Lastauto Omnibus **8588**
0023-8686 Lastebilen *changed to* 1504-4017 **8669**
0023-8694 Lastechniek **6343**
0023-8716 Lather†
0023-8740 Latin American Books Newsletter **7578**
0023-8759 Latin American Calendar†
0023-8767 Latin American Digest†
0023-8791 Latin American Research Review **7982**
0023-8813 Latin American Theatre Review **8473**
0023-883X Latinitas **5142**
0023-8856 Latomus **2237**
0023-8872 Laettbetong†
0023-8899 Latvija **3547**
0023-8902 Latvija Amerika **3547**
0023-8937 Laufende Mitteilungen Zum Stand der Politischen Bildung in der Bundesrepublik Deutschland†
0023-8988 Laurel Messenger **3773**
0023-8996 The Laurel of Phi Kappa Tau **2289**
0023-9003 The Laurel Review **5320**
0023-9011 Laurentian University Review†
0023-902X Laurentianum
0023-9038 Laval Administration **1772**
0023-9054 Laval Theologique et Philosophique **6931**
0023-9062 Lavender Band†
0023-9070 Lavoro e Medicina†
0023-9097 Il Lavoro Neuropsichiatrico
0023-9119 Lavoro Sud†
0023-9135 Lavoura **134**
0023-9143 Lavoura Arrozeira **274**
0023-9186 Law and Contemporary Problems **4713**
0023-9194 Law and Order Magazine **2659**
0023-9216 Law & Society Review **4714**
0023-9240 Law Books Published **4823**
0023-9267 Law Institute Journal **4715**
0023-9283 Law Library Journal **5024**
0023-9321 Law Officer†
0023-933X The Law Quarterly Review **4716**
0023-9356 Buffalo Law Review **4633**
0023-9364 Law Society of Upper Canada **4717**
0023-9399 Law Thesaurus **4717**
0023-9402 Lawn Care†
0023-9453 Lawyer's Association. Journal
0023-9461 Lawyers Marketplace
0023-947X Lawyer's Medical Journal†
0023-9488 Lawyers' Recreation†
0023-9526 Lazio
0023-9542 An Leabharlann **5025**
0023-9550 Lead†
0023-9577 Lead and Zinc Statistics **6340**
0023-9585 Leader†
0023-9593 Leader†
0023-9607 Leader
0023-964X Leaflet (Assonet) **5142**
0023-9666 Leaguer
0023-9674 Lealtad
0023-9682 Learn†
0023-9690 Learning and Motivation **2882**
0023-9712 Learning Resources†
0023-9747 Leather and Shoes†
0023-9763 The Leather Manufacturer **4974**
0023-9771 Leather Science **4974**
0023-978X Leather Titles Service†
0023-9801 Leathergoods Buyer†
0023-981X Leatherneck **6431**
0023-9828 Leathers **4974**
0023-9836 Leaves of Twin Oaks **8118**
0023-9852 Lebanese Medical Journal **5660**
0023-9879 Lebe Dich Gesund
0023-9909 Lebende Sprachen **5143**
0023-9917 Lebendige Erde **134**
0023-9933 Lebendige Schule†
0023-9941 Lebendiges Zeugnis **7804**
0023-9992 Lebensmittel Praxis **3680**
0024-0052 Lebensweiser†
0024-0079 Lecciones y Ensayos **4719**
0024-0087 Lectura†
0024-0095 Lectura†
0024-0109 Lectura para Todos†
0024-0125 Lecture et Tradition
0024-0133 Lectures Francaises
0024-015X Ledarforum **1424**
0024-0184 Leder Echo†
0024-0192 L S L†
0024-0214 Lederwaren-Report **4974**
0024-0222 Ledger†
0024-0230 Lediga Platser **6700**
0024-0249 Leeds African Studies Bulletin **3547**
0024-0265 Leeds Dental Journal **5855**
0024-0281 Leeds Philosophical and Literary Society. Proceedings. Literary and Historical Section† **8970**
0024-029X Communist News
0024-0303 Left†
0024-032X Lega Navale **8649**
0024-0362 Legal Executive **4719**
0024-0370 Legal Record†
0024-0389 Legerkoerier *changed to* 1572-1248 **6431**
0024-0397 Legetoejs-Tidende†
0024-0400 Le Leggi† **8971**
0024-0419 Leggi delle Comunita Europee†
0024-0435 Legion Magazine
0024-0451 Legionair†
0024-0494 Legislative Roundup†
0024-0508 Legislator
0024-0524 La Legislazione Italiana†
0024-0532 Il Legno **3713**
0024-0540 Legon Observer
0024-0567 Lehigh Valley Safety News†
0024-0575 Ligstraal - Lehlasedi†
0024-0583 Lehrbogen fuer Leibesuebungen
0024-0591 Spark (New York) **7741**
0024-063X Leica Photography†
0024-0664 Leicestershire Historian **4151**
0024-0672 Nationaal Natuurhistorisch Museum. Zoologische Mededelingen **957**
0024-0699 Leipuri **3674**
0024-0702 Leistung†
0024-0710 Leisure Painter **502**
0024-0729 Leisure Time†
0024-0745 Lekarz Wojskowy **5661**
0024-0761 Lemouzi **4240**
0024-0796 Lenguaje y Ciencias **5143**
0024-0885 Lentaja†
0024-0893 Lente (Inkprint Edition)†
0024-0907 Lenzinger Berichte
0024-0915 Leo Baeck Institut. Bulletin†
0024-0923 Leodiensian† **8971**
0024-094X Leonardo: Art Science and Technology **502**
0024-0958 Il Leone **2267**
0024-0966 Lepidopterists' Society. Journal **854**
0024-0974 Cho to ga **842**
0024-1016 Leprologia†
0024-1040 Lerindustrien†
0024-1067 Les **3713**
0024-1075 Leserzeitschrift†
0024-1083 Lesestunde mit dem Grossen Freizeit-Programm
0024-1091 Leshonenu La'am **5143**
0024-1113 Lesnoe Khozyaistvo **3696**
0024-1121 Lesotho-Canada†
0024-1148 Lesovedenie **3696**
0024-1156 Letectvi a Kosmonautika **65**
0024-1164 Lethaia **6726**
0024-1172 Letopis' Gazetnykh Statei **629**
0024-1202 Letopis' Zhurnal'nykh Statei **629**
0024-1210 Letras†
0024-1229 Letras de Ayer y de Hoy†
0024-1245 Letras Potosinas **5321**
0024-1253 Let's Dance **2686**
0024-1261 Scholastic Let's Find Out **3080**
0024-1288 Let's Live† **8971**
0024-130X Letterato **5224**
0024-1326 Lettere d'Affari
0024-1334 Lettere Italiane **5321**
0024-1350 Il Lettore di Provincia **5322**
0024-1369 Lettres **5322**
0024-1377 Lettres et Medecins†
0024-1385 Lettres et Poesie
0024-1393 Lettres Francaises†
0024-1407 Lettres Nouvelles†
0024-1415 Les Lettres Romanes **5322**
0024-1423 Lettrisme†
0024-1431 Lettura Stenografica
0024-144X Letture **8118**
0024-1458 Cineschedario - Letture Drammatiche
0024-1466 Leukemia Abstracts†
0024-1482 Leuvense Bijdragen **5144**

9042 0024-1504 ULRICH'S PERIODICALS

0024-1504 Levante **7251**
0024-1512 Leveltari Kozlemenyek **4151**
0024-1520 Levende Natuur **2617**
0024-1547 Levend Woord
0024-158X Legislacao Federal e Marginalia
0024-1598 Lex **4723**
0024-1628 Lexington Theological Quarterly **7659**
0024-1636 Ley **4723**
0024-1644 Ley†
0024-1660 Leyland Journal†
0024-1679 Leyte-Samar Studies†
0024-1687 Liaison†
0024-1709 Federation Nationale des Anciens Combattants et Coalets des Transmissions. Liaison des Transmissions†
0024-1717 Liaisons†
0024-1733 Al Liamm **5322**
0024-1741 Liaudies Balsas†
0024-175X Libelle **8871**
0024-1784 Liberal†
0024-1792 Liberal Catholic **7764**
0024-1806 Liberal Context†
0024-1814 Liberal Debatt **7151**
0024-1822 Liberal Education **2992**
0024-1830 Liberal Opinion†
0024-1857 Liberal Ungdom **7151**
0024-1873 Liberation **7212**
0024-1881 Liberation **7151**
0024-189X Liberation†
0024-1903 Liberation News Service†
0024-1911 Liberation News Service
0024-1954 Liberia
0024-1962 Liberian Age
0024-1970 Liberian Law Journal†
0024-1989 Liberian Studies Journal **7983**
0024-1997 La Liberta **7804**
0024-2020 Liberte **5425**
0024-2047 Libertijn†
0024-2055 Liberty (Hagerstown) **7660**
0024-2101 Libra†
0024-2144 Libraries in International Development. Newsletter†
0024-2152 Librarium **7566**
0024-2160 The Library **5026**
0024-2179 L I S A: Library & Information Science Abstracts **5058**
0024-2187 Library Associate†
0024-2217 The Library Bookseller **7566**
0024-2225 State University of New York. Upstate Medical Center. Library Bulletin†
0024-2233 Library Chronicle (Philadelphia)†
0024-2241 Library Chronicle†
0024-2276 Library Counselor†
0024-2284 Library for the Blind and Physically Handicapped. Newsletter†
0024-2292 Library Herald **5027**
0024-2306 Library History *changed to* 1758-3489 **5026**
0024-2330 Library Keynotes†
0024-2349 Library Leaves†
0024-2357 Library Lines†
0024-2365 Contra Costa County Library Link†
0024-2411 Library Notes†
0024-2438 Library Notes†
0024-2446 North Dakota Library Notes†
0024-2462 Library Opinion†
0024-2489 Library Periodicals Directory†
0024-2497 Library Progress†
0024-2500 Library Publicity Clippings†
0024-2519 The Library Quarterly **5029**
0024-2535 Library Review **5029**
0024-2551 Library Service News
0024-2578 Library System†
0024-2586 Library Technology Reports **5029**
0024-2594 Library Trends **5029**
0024-2608 Library World†
0024-2632 L S A **1829**
0024-2640 Libreria†
0024-2667 Libri **5029**
0024-2683 Libri e Riviste d'Italia **7566**
0024-273X Libro Espanol†
0024-2756 Libros†
0024-2764 Licensed Beverage Journal
0024-2772 Licensed Bookmaker & Betting Office Proprietor
0024-2780 Licensed Retailer
0024-2810 Lichamelijke Opvoeding **3070**
0024-2829 The Lichenologist **800**
0024-2845 Lichtbogen **2071**
0024-287X Licitationen **1020**
0024-2896 Lide a Zeme **4018**
0024-2918 Lien†
0024-2942 Liens†
0024-2950 Lietuviu Dienos **3548**
0024-3019 Life†
0024-3043 Life and Health†
0024-306X Life & Work **7764**
0024-3086 Lifeboat **8277**
0024-3094 Life Boy Link†
0024-3132 Life Insurance Planning†
0024-3140 Life Insurance Selling **4513**
0024-3159 Life International†
0024-3167 Life Lines†
0024-3205 Life Sciences **7880**
0024-3221 New York City Association of Life Underwriters. Bulletin **4516**
0024-3299 Light and Life **7764**
0024-3310 Light Aviation
0024-3345 Light Metal Age **6320**
0024-3353 Light of New York†
0024-3361 Light of the Moon **4082**
0024-3396 Lightbearer
0024-340X Lighter†
0024-3418 Lighting Equipment News *changed to* Lighting **4560**
0024-3434 Ligne de Communication†
0024-3442 Ligstraal - Umsebe - Umtha†
0024-3450 Liguorian **7804**
0024-3469 Liiketaloudellinen Aikakauskirja **1144**
0024-3477 Lijecnicki Vjesnik **5661**
0024-3485 Lillabulero†
0024-3493 Lille Chirurgical†
0024-3523 Limba Romana **5144**
0024-354X Limen
0024-3558 Limit†
0024-3566 Limiar
0024-3590 Limnology and Oceanography **2797**
0024-3620 Limosa **910**
0024-3639 Linacre Quarterly **5661**
0024-3647 Linage†
0024-3663 Lincoln Business†
0024-3671 Lincoln Herald **4301**
0024-368X Lincoln Law Review **4724**
0024-3698 Lincoln Library Bulletin **5030**
0024-3701 Lincolnian†
0024-371X Lincolnshire Life **3867**
0024-3744 Lineagrafica† **8971**
0024-3752 Linea Italiana†
0024-3760 Linea Maschile e Femminile†
0024-3779 Linea Z†
0024-3787 Lineamaglia†
0024-3795 Linear Algebra and Its Applications **5509**
0024-3817 Lineastruttura†
0024-3841 Lingua **5144**
0024-385X Lingua e Stile **5145**
0024-3868 Lingua Nostra **5145**
0024-3876 Lingue del Mondo *changed to* Le Lingue del Mondo
0024-3892 Linguistic Inquiry **5145**
0024-3906 Linguistic Reporter†
0024-3914 Linguistic Society of Japan. Journal **5146**
0024-3922 Linguistica **5146**
0024-3930 Linguistische Berichte **5147**
0024-3949 Linguistics **5147**
0024-3965 Lingvologia Revuo†
0024-3973 Linieofficeren†
0024-399X Link†
0024-4007 Link (New York, 1967) **7251**
0024-4015 Link-Up†
0024-4023 Linking Ring **4338**
0024-404X Links†
0024-4066 Linnean Society. Biological Journal **687**
0024-4074 Linnean Society. Botanical Journal **800**
0024-4082 Linnean Society. Zoological Journal **953**
0024-4090 Linneana Belgica **854**
0024-4112 Linoticias†
0024-4139 Linzer Theaterzeitung **8473**
0024-4155 Legkaya Atletika **8185**
0024-4163 The Lion (Oak Brook) **2267**
0024-4171 The Lion en Espanol **2267**
0024-4198 Lion **3956**
0024-4201 Lipids **738**
0024-4228 Liquified Natural Gas†
0024-4244 Lira **6585**
0024-4260 Lisbon. Instituto Gulbenkian de Ciencia. Arquivo. Section A. Estudos Matematicos e Fisico-Matematicos†
0024-4309 List-O-Tapes†
0024-4341 List of Technical Studies and Experimental Housing Projects†
0024-435X Listen **2696**
0024-4384 Listen†
0024-4392 Listener†
0024-4414 Listening **8118**
0024-4430 Listino Ufficiale della Borsa Valori di Torino†
0024-4457 Listy Filologicke **2237**
0024-4465 Listy Sv. Frantiska†
0024-449X Liteinoe Proizvodstvo **6321**
0024-4503 Literacy Discussion†
0024-4511 Literary Cavalcade†
0024-452X Literary Criterion **5224**
0024-4546 Literary Guild Newsletter†
0024-4554 Literary Half-Yearly **5324**
0024-4562 Literary Herald†
0024-4570 Literary Quarterly of the Yugoslav Pen-Centre†
0024-4589 The Literary Review **5324**
0024-4597 Literary Sketches†
0024-4600 Literary Studies
0024-4627 Der Literat **5324**
0024-4643 Literatur in Wissenschaft und Unterricht **5225**
0024-466X Literatur und Kritik **5324**
0024-4678 Literatur zum Bibliothekswesen†
0024-4686 Literatura i Mastatstva **5325**
0024-4694 Literatura Kajero
0024-4708 Literatura Ludowa **5225**
0024-4759 Literature and Psychology†
0024-4767 Literature East and West **5326**
0024-4775 Literature, Music, Fine Arts†
0024-4783 Literature on Economic Development and Planning - a Select Bibliography†
0024-4791 Literaturen Zbor **5326**
0024-4805 Rat fuer Formgebung. Literaturhinweise
0024-4821 Literaturna Ukraina **5225**
0024-4872 Literaturrundschau†
0024-4902 Lithology and Mineral Resources **2752**
0024-4910 Lithopinion†
0024-4937 Lithos **2752**
0024-4953 Litmus
0024-4961 Litografia Oggi
0024-497X Litologiya i Poleznye Iskopaemye **6468**
0024-4988 Litterair Paspoort†
0024-4996 Litterature de Jeunesse†
0024-5011 Little Bronzed Angel†
0024-502X Little Flower†
0024-5054 Little Review **5327**
0024-5062 The Little Ship **8277**
0024-5070 Little Square Review†
0024-5089 Lituanus **4240**
0024-5100 Liturgisches Jahrbuch **7660**
0024-5127 Liv og Helse†
0024-5135 Livarski Vestnik **6321**
0024-5143 Live Lines†
0024-5151 Liverpool Bulletin†
0024-5208 Livestock Market Digest **292**
0024-5232 Living Blues **6585**
0024-5240 Living Church **7765**
0024-5259 Living Health Newsletter†
0024-5275 The Living Light†
0024-5283 The Living Museum **503**
0024-5291 Living Tapes†
0024-5313 Livingston County Agricultural News **134**
0024-533X Le Livre et l'Estampe **7566**
0024-5372 Livrustkammaren **4240**
0024-5380 Livs†
0024-5399 Livsmedelsteknik *changed to* Livsmedel i Fokus **3654**
0024-5429 Ljuskultur **3324**
0024-5437 Llais Llyfrau†
0024-5445 Y Llan
0024-5453 Llangollen Broadsheet
0024-5488 Lloyd's Law Reports **4724**
0024-5526 Local Government Bulletin **7496**
0024-5534 Local Government Chronicle **7496**
0024-5569 Local Government Journal of Western Australia†
0024-5585 The Local Historian **4240**
0024-5607 Local Preachers Magazine **7765**
0024-5615 Local Self-Government†
0024-5623 All India Institute of Local Self Government. Quarterly Journal **7487**
0024-5631 Local Taxation†
0024-5704 Lockheed Orion Service Digest†
0024-5739 Loco Revue **4338**
0024-5763 Lodigiano Sudmilano†
0024-5771 Lodzki Numizmatyk **6651**
0024-578X Loefgrenia
0024-5798 Log **65**
0024-5828 Log of Mystic Seaport **6528**
0024-5836 Logique et Analyse **6932**
0024-5852 Logistics Spectrum **8431**
0024-5887 Logos
0024-5895 Logos **7805**
0024-5917 Lok Rajya **2884**
0024-5925 Lok Udyog†
0024-5941 Lokomotivtechnik†
0024-595X Loktantra Samiksha **7152**
0024-5984 London Archaeologist **404**
0024-6018 London Clinic Medical Journal†
0024-6026 London Corn Circular
0024-6034 London Diary of Social Events†
0024-6069 London Information
0024-6077 London Letter†
0024-6085 London Magazine (London, 1954)†
0024-6093 London Mathematical Society. Bulletin **5509**
0024-6107 London Mathematical Society. Journal **5509**
0024-6115 London Mathematical Society. Proceedings **5510**
0024-6131 London Philatelist **6896**
0024-614X London Review†
0024-6166 London Times Index†
0024-6174 London Town†
0024-6190 London Weekly Diary of Social Events†
0024-6204 Cymro Llundain **5213**
0024-6220 Long Cane News Letter
0024-6255 Long Island Catholic **7805**
0024-6263 Long Island Courant†
0024-628X Long Island Forum **4302**
0024-6298 Long Island University Magazine†
0024-6301 Long Range Planning **1773**
0024-631X Long Room **5059**
0024-6328 Longitude **8651**
0024-6336 Look†
0024-6344 Look and Learn†
0024-6352 Look & Listen **2384**
0024-6360 Look Around†
0024-6379 Look at Finland†
0024-6417 Looking Back
0024-6425 Lookout (New York) **8054**
0024-6433 Lookout
0024-645X The Loon **910**
0024-6476 Looys **7705**
0024-6484 Lorain Labor Leader†
0024-6492 Lore **6528**
0024-6514 Loris **2617**
0024-6557 Los Angeles County Museum of Art. Bulletin†
0024-6573 Los Angeles Free Press†
0024-6581 Image†
0024-6603 Eisenwaren Allgemeine†
0024-6611 Loshen und Leben
0024-662X Loteria
0024-6646 Lotta Operaia
0024-6654 Lottery Gazette
0024-6662 Lottoroscopo **8186**
0024-6670 Lotus Bleu **6933**
0024-6689 Intergroup Relations Newsletter†
0024-6697 Lou Pais†
0024-6735 Louisiana Agriculture **134**
0024-6743 Louisiana Baptist Builder **7765**
0024-6751 Louisiana Business Review†
0024-6778 Louisiana Conservationist **2617**
0024-6816 Louisiana History **4302**
0024-6840 Louisiana L P-Gas News
0024-6859 Louisiana Law Review **4725**
0024-6875 Louisiana Methodist†
0024-6891 Louisiana Revy **503**
0024-6913 Louisiana Senior Citizen†
0024-6921 Louisiana State Medical Society. Journal **5662**
0024-6956 Louvain Medical **5662**
0024-6964 Louvain Studies **7805**
0024-6980 Lov og Rett **4725**
0024-6999 Lovacki Vjesnik **8186**
0024-7014 Lovec **8321**
0024-7022 Lovejoy's Guidance Digest
0024-7030 Low Bidder **8632**
0024-7049 Low Cost Automation Review†
0024-7057 Lowell Observatory Bulletin
0024-7065 Lowry-Cocroft's Review of the Food Service Literature†

DIRECTORY 2010 0025-2999 9043

0024-7081 Loyola University Chicago Law Journal **4726**
0024-709X Liquefied Petroleum Gas **6777**
0024-7103 L P - Gas **6776**
0024-7146 Lubrication **6777**
0024-7154 Lubrication Engineering *changed to* 1545-858X **3398**
0024-7170 Lucas Engineering Review†
0024-7200 Luci sulla Via†
0024-7219 Lucknow Librarian **5030**
0024-7235 Lucy Moda†
0024-7243 Lufkin Line†
0024-7286 Luister **6585**
0024-7294 Lumber Co-Operator **3713**
0024-7324 Lumen Vitae **7805**
0024-7332 Lumiere†
0024-7359 Lumiere et Vie **7661**
0024-7383 Luonnon Tutkija **687**
0024-7391 Luscinia **910**
0024-7413 Luso - Brazilian Review **5225**
0024-7421 Lustrum **2237**
0024-743X The Lutheran **7765**
0024-7448 Lutheran Education **7765**
0024-7456 Lutheran Forum **7765**
0024-7464 Lutheran Layman **7766**
0024-7472 Lutheran Libraries **5030**
0024-7480 Lutheran Messenger for the Blind **4083**
0024-7510 Lutheran Sentinel **7766**
0024-7537 Lutheran Spokesman **7766**
0024-7553 Lutheran Theological Journal **7766**
0024-757X The Lutheran Witness **7766**
0024-7588 Lutheran Witness-Reporter Edition†
0024-7626 Die Lutherkirche **7766**
0024-7634 Lutra **954**
0024-7650 Lutte Ouvriere **7152**
0024-7669 Lux **3324**
0024-7685 Lux Vera **4083**
0024-7693 Luz **7726**
0024-7715 Luz Apostolica†
0024-7723 Luz del Cosmos†
0024-7731 Luz Y Verdad†
0024-774X Lyd & Tone†
0024-7758 Journal of Reproductive Medicine **5997**
0024-7766 Lymphology **5896**
0024-7774 Lynx **954**
0024-7782 Lyon Chirurgical†
0024-7790 Lyon Medical†
0024-7820 Lyric **5426**
0024-7839 Lyric Opera News **6585**
0024-7847 Lyrica Germanica†
0024-7863 Lys Mykyta†
0024-7898 M A C Gopher†
0024-7928 M A S T Newsletter
0024-7944 M & B Laboratory Bulletin†
0024-7952 M B A†
0024-7979 M B - Der Arzt in Krankenhaus und Gesundheitswesen
0024-7995 M C - Nytt **8260**
0024-8002 M D en Espanol
0024-8045 M D S **6859**
0024-8118 M E N Economic Weekly
0024-8134 M F C News†
0024-8169 M G Conquest†
0024-8185 M H S Miscellany. N **4302**
0024-8231 M L B Log†
0024-824X M' - le Magazine de Madame†
0024-8266 Astronomical Society of Southern Africa. Monthly Notes **570**
0024-8282 M O N Y News
0024-8355 M Report†
0024-8398 M S H A†
0024-8444 M S S C Exchange†
0024-8452 M S S P A Bugle†
0024-8460 M S U Business Topics†
0024-8487 M T A News†
0024-8495 Weekly Bulletin **3877**
0024-8509 M T M Journal of Methods-Time Measurement†
0024-8517 M T T†
0024-8525 M T Z **8589**
0024-8533 Meridiano Dodici†
0024-8541 Maailma ja Me†
0024-855X Maal og Minne **5149**
0024-8568 Maalarilehti *changed to* 1459-4994 **6721**
0024-8576 M G V **6159**
0024-8665 Nederduitse Gereformeerde Kerk van Natal Gemeente Vryheid. Maandbrief **7768**
0024-8738 Netherlands. Centraal Bureau voor de Statistiek. Maandstatistiek van de Buitenlandse Handel per Goederensoort†
0024-8746 Netherlands. Centraal Bureau voor de Statistiek. Maandstatistiek van de Buitenlandse Handel per Land†
0024-8754 Netherlands. Centraal Bureau voor de Statistiek. Maandstatistiek van de Landbouw†
0024-8770 Netherlands. Centraal Bureau voor de Statistiek. Maandstatistiek Verkeer en Vervoer†
0024-8819 Maarakennus ja Kuljetus†
0024-8843 Maatschappijbelangen **1897**
0024-8851 Maatstaf†
0024-8886 Macabre†
0024-8894 Macaroni Journal†
0024-8940 McCall's Fabrics Plus†
0024-8975 McCormick Quarterly†
0024-8991 McDonnell Douglas Spirit
0024-9009 Macedonian Tribune **2267**
0024-9017 Macelleria Italiana
0024-9025 McGill Dental Review
0024-9033 McGill Journal of Education **2885**
0024-9041 McGill Law Journal **4730**
0024-905X McGill Medical Journal†
0024-9068 McGill News **2291**
0024-9076 McGill University, Montreal. Industrial Relations Centre. Review†
0024-9092 Machine and Machinery **5455**
0024-9106 Machine and Tool Blue Book†
0024-9114 Machine Design **3388**
0024-9157 Machine Shop and Engineering Manufacture†
0024-9165 Machine Tool Engineering†
0024-9173 Machine-Tool Review†
0024-9211 Machinery Market **5456**
0024-9238 Machines Francaises†
0024-9246 Machinisme Agricole Tropical†
0024-9262 Maclean's **3812**
0024-9270 McMaster University Library Research News†
0024-9289 Macomb County Legal News **4726**
0024-9297 Macromolecules **2126**
0024-9300 Mad†
0024-9319 Mad **5226**
0024-9327 Mad og Gaester†
0024-9335 Mada†
0024-9343 Madam†
0024-9351 Madam **4083**
0024-936X Madame **8872**
0024-9386 Made in Poland†
0024-9416 Madencilik **6469**
0024-9432 Madhuri **6506**
0024-9459 Madhya Pradesh Law Journal **4726**
0024-9467 Madhya Pradesh Medical Journal†
0024-9475 Laboratory Enquiry Service
0024-9483 Madison Avenue†
0024-9521 Indonesian Journal of Geography **4015**
0024-953X Madjalah Manager†
0024-9556 Madjalah Pertanian
0024-9580 Madonna di Barbana†
0024-9599 Madonna di Castelmonte
0024-9602 The Madras Agricultural Journal **135**
0024-9637 Madrono **800**
0024-9645 Maelkeritidende **266**
0024-9653 Maelstrom†
0024-9661 Der Maerker **4241**
0024-967X Maerkische Zeitung
0024-9688 Maerklin-Magazin **4339**
0024-9696 Il Maestro **7805**
0024-9726 Magadh University Journal†
0024-9750 Magazin fuer Fortschrittliche Haustechnik und Wohnkultur†
0024-9793 Media Industry Newsletter **29**
0024-9807 Magazine Litteraire **5329**
0024-9831 Magazine of Concrete Research **1021**
0024-9866 Magazyn Polski†
0024-9904 Magic Cauldron **4339**
0024-9920 The Magistrate **4955**
0024-9955 Magna Graecia† **8972**
0024-9963 Magneet-Revue†
0024-9971 The Magistrate
0024-998X Magnetohydrodynamics **3324**
0025-0007 Magnificat **7805**
0025-0015 Magnitnaya Gidrodinamika†
0025-0031 Maguey†
0025-004X Magyar Allatorvosok Lapja **8802**
0025-0074 Magyar Epitoipar **1021**
0025-0090 Magyar Filozofiai Szemle **6933**
0025-0104 Magyar Fizikai Folyoirat†
0025-0120 Magyar Geofizika†
0025-0147 Magyar Jog **4727**
0025-0163 Magyar Kemikusok Lapja **2072**
0025-0171 Magyar Konyvszemle
0025-018X Magyar Mezogazdasag **135**
0025-0198 Magyar Mezogazdasagi Bibliografia **183**
0025-021X Magyar Noorvosok Lapja **5997**
0025-0228 Magyar Nyelv **5149**
0025-0236 Magyar Nyelvor **5149**
0025-0244 Magyar Onkologia **6027**
0025-0252 Magyar Orvosi Bibliografia†
0025-0260 Magyar Pedagogia **2884**
0025-0279 Magyar Pszichologiai Szemle **7384**
0025-0287 Magyar Radiologia **6202**
0025-0295 Magyar Sebeszet **6251**
0025-0325 Magyar Tudomany **7881**
0025-0333 Magyar Tudomanyos Akademia. Biologiai Tudomanyok Osztalya. Kozlemenyek†
0025-0368 Magyar Tudomanyos Akademia. Nyelv- es Irodalomtudomanyi Osztaly. Kozlemenyek†
0025-0376 Magyar Tudomanyos Akademia. Filozofiai es Tortenettudomanyi Osztaly. Kozlemenyek†
0025-0384 Magyar Zene
0025-0392 Maharashtra
0025-0406 Maha Bodhi **7701**
0025-0414 Mahajanmer Lagna **6933**
0025-0422 Maharaja Sayajirao University of Baroda. Journal **7881**
0025-0430 The Maharashtra Co-Operative Quarterly **1424**
0025-0449 Maharashtra, India. Directorate of Industries. Industrial Bulletin†
0025-0465 Maharashtra Law Journal **4727**
0025-0473 Maharashtra Parichaya†
0025-0481 Maharashtra Quarterly Bulletin of Economics and Statistics **1250**
0025-049X Mahenjodaro **5329**
0025-0511 Die Mahnung **7212**
0025-052X Maehrisch-Schlesische Heimat†
0025-0538 Maia **2237**
0025-0562 Mail Trade†
0025-0570 Main Currents in Modern Thought†
0025-0597 Main Roads†
0025-0600 Main Sheet
0025-0619 Maine Business Indicators **1497**
0025-0651 Maine Law Review **4727**
0025-0694 Maine Medical Association. Journal†
0025-0708 Maine Nature†
0025-0767 The Maine Nurse **5969**
0025-0791 Maine Townsman **7497**
0025-0805 Maine Water Utilities Association. Journal **8828**
0025-0813 Mainichi Graphic **3900**
0025-0848 Mainly†
0025-0899 Maintenance Engineering†
0025-0910 Maintenance News†
0025-0929 Maintenance Supplies **1021**
0025-0937 La Maison - Dieu **7661**
0025-0945 Maison et Jardin†
0025-0953 Maison Francaise **4546**
0025-0996 Le Maitre Imprimeur **7324**
0025-1003 International Phonetic Association. Journal **5130**
0025-102X Majallah†
0025-1046 Majallat Shi'r
0025-1089 Makedonski Jazik **5149**
0025-1097 Makedonski Medicinski Pregled **5664**
0025-1119 Makerere Medical Journal **5664**
0025-1127 Matekon†
0025-1151 Making Music†
0025-1178 Mala Ukrstenica†
0025-1186 Malabar Herald†
0025-1208 Maladosts' **5226**
0025-1216 The Malahat Review **5426**
0025-1224 Malamalama†
0025-1267 Malawi Patent Journal and Trade Marks Journal **6754**
0025-1283 Malayan Law Journal **4727**
0025-1291 Malayan Nature Journal
0025-1305 Malaysia†
0025-1313 Quarterly Bulletin of Statistics Relating to the Mining Industry of Malaysia **6486**
0025-1321 Malaysian Agricultural Journal **135**
0025-1348 Malaysian Management Review **1774**
0025-1399 Mallige **3885**
0025-1410 Malmoe Museum. Aktuellt†
0025-1429 Studia Historyczne **4269**
0025-1437 Malta. Central Office of Statistics. Quarterly Digest of Statistics **8387**
0025-1453 Malyatko **2201**
0025-1461 Mammalia **954**
0025-147X Mamme e Bimbi
0025-150X Man and His Music†
0025-1518 Man and Metal†
0025-1526 Man and Society†
0025-1542 Man-Environment-Communication Center Report†
0025-1550 Man - Environment Systems **3451**
0025-1569 Man in India **347**
0025-1615 Manab Mon **7384**
0025-164X Management†
0025-1674 The Management Accountant **1296**
0025-1704 Management & Operations†
0025-1712 Management Australia†
0025-1720 Management Consultant†
0025-1747 Management Decision **1775**
0025-1771 Management Ideas **1775**
0025-178X Management in Nigeria **1775**
0025-1798 Management Index†
0025-1828 Management Japan†
0025-1836 Management Horizons†
0025-1860 Management Quarterly **1776**
0025-1895 Management Review **1776**
0025-1909 Management Science **1776**
0025-1925 Management Today **1777**
0025-1933 Management's Bibliographic Data†
0025-195X Manager's Letter†
0025-1968 Manager's Magazine†
0025-1976 Manas†
0025-1984 Manas
0025-1992 Manchester Chamber of Commerce. Record **1407**
0025-2026 Manchester Review†
0025-2077 Manequim **2258**
0025-2093 Manhattan College Engineer†
0025-2107 Manhattan East
0025-2123 Manhattan Review†
0025-2131 Mani di Fata **4363**
0025-214X Manicomio Judiciario Heitor Carrilho. Arquivos
0025-2158 Il Manifesto **3897**
0025-2166 Manifold **5426**
0025-2174 Manion Forum†
0025-2239 Manitoba Co-operator **136**
0025-2255 Manitoba Medical Review†
0025-2271 Manitoba Professional Engineer
0025-228X Manitoba Teacher **2885**
0025-2298 Manitoban **2291**
0025-2336 Mankind†
0025-2344 Mankind Quarterly **347**
0025-2387 Manovella†
0025-2409 Manpower and Applied Psychology
0025-2441 ManRoot†
0025-245X Man's Conquest†
0025-2468 Man's Illustrated†
0025-2476 Man's Magazine
0025-2484 Manse Mail†
0025-2492 Manteia†
0025-2506 Mantova
0025-2514 Manuelle Medizin **6112**
0025-2530 Manufacturers' Monthly **1898**
0025-2603 Manuscripta **5330**
0025-2611 Manuscripta Mathematica **5510**
0025-262X Manuscripts **7567**
0025-2638 Manuskripte **5330**
0025-2646 Manutencion y Almacenaje **8503**
0025-2662 Manutention, Mecanique et Automation†
0025-2689 Mapocho†
0025-2697 Die Mappe **6719**
0025-2700 Maquinas & Metais **5456**
0025-2735 Mar y Pesca **3601**
0025-2751 Marathwada University Journal
0025-2778 Marburger Umschau†
0025-2808 March of Education†
0025-2859 Marches Tropicaux et Mediterraneens **1577**
0025-2867 Marcolian **2291**
0025-2891 Marechal†
0025-2913 Marg (Mumbai) **449**
0025-2921 Margin **1147**
0025-293X Marginales **5330**
0025-2948 Marginalien **5226**
0025-2956 Margriet **8873**
0025-2972 Maria **7806**
0025-2980 Mariages
0025-2999 Mariahilfer Pfarrbote **7806**

ISSN

9044 0025-3006 ULRICH'S PERIODICALS

0025-3006 Marian†
0025-3014 Marianist
0025-3022 Mariannhill **7661**
0025-3049 Marie Claire **2258**
0025-3065 Regard de Foi†
0025-3073 Marien Report†
0025-309X La Marina Italiana† **8972**
0025-3103 La Marina Mercantile† **8972**
0025-312X Marine & Recreation News
0025-3138 Marine and Air Catering†
0025-3146 Marine Biological Association of India. Journal **688**
0025-3154 Marine Biological Association of the United Kingdom. Journal **688**
0025-3162 Marine Biology **688**
0025-3170 Marine Corps Gazette **6432**
0025-3227 Marine Geology **2812**
0025-3235 Marine Geophysical Researches **2812**
0025-3243 Marine News **8651**
0025-3251 Marine Observer **6390**
0025-326X Marine Pollution Bulletin **3488**
0025-3286 Marine Resources Digest/Marine Biology Digest†
0025-3308 Marine Science Contents Tables†
0025-3324 Marine Technology Society Journal **2812**
0025-3332 Marine Equipment News
0025-3340 Marineblad **6432**
0025-3359 Mariner's Mirror **4152**
0025-3367 Mariners Weather Log **6390**
0025-3375 Marinnytt *changed to* 1652-3571 **6425**
0025-3413 Maritime Command Trident **6432**
0025-343X Maritime Farmer and Co-Operative Dairyman
0025-3448 Maritime Reporter and Engineering News **8653**
0025-3472 Maritimes **2812**
0025-3480 Marjolaine
0025-3499 Mark Twain Journal **5331**
0025-3510 Markedskommunikasjon†
0025-3537 Market†
0025-3545 West Virginia. Department of Agriculture. Market Bulletin **170**
0025-3553 Market Frontier News†
0025-3561 Market Industries News
0025-357X Market Place†
0025-360X Market Research Facts and Trends†
0025-3634 Marketing
0025-3650 Marketing **1831**
0025-3685 Marketing/Communications†
0025-3707 Marketing Image
0025-3715 Marketing Horizons†
0025-374X Marketing Information Guide†
0025-3774 Marketing Journal *changed to* 1866-5438 **1830**
0025-3782 Marketing Mix Digest *changed to* 1570-8799 **1832**
0025-3790 Marketing News **1832**
0025-3812 Marketing World†
0025-3820 Markham Review†
0025-3863 Der Markt **1834**
0025-388X Maroc-Medical†
0025-3898 Maroquinerie-Voyage-Parapluie-Chaussure†
0025-3901 Maroquinerie, Sellerie et Bagages de France†
0025-3928 Marquee (Elmhurst) **449**
0025-3944 Marquetarian **4339**
0025-3952 Marquette Business Review†
0025-3960 Marquette Engineer†
0025-3979 Marquette Journal **5331**
0025-3987 Marquette Law Review **4728**
0025-3995 Marquette Tribune (Milwaukee) **2291**
0025-4061 Mart†
0025-4096 Maruee **3885**
0025-4118 Marxism Today†
0025-4126 Marxist Studies
0025-4134 Marxist Veekshanam **7153**
0025-4142 Maryknoll Magazine **7806**
0025-4150 Maryland and Delaware Genealogist†
0025-4177 Maryland Bar Journal **4728**
0025-4185 Maryland C.P.A. Quarterly†
0025-4193 Maryland Conservationist†
0025-4223 Maryland Fruit Grower **3742**
0025-4231 Maryland Herpetological Society. Bulletin **955**
0025-424X Maryland Historian **4152**
0025-4258 Maryland Historical Magazine **4303**
0025-4274 The Maryland Horse **8294**
0025-4282 Maryland Law Review **4728**
0025-4312 Maryland Music Educator **6586**
0025-4339 Maryland P T A Bulletin **2885**
0025-4347 Maryland Pharmacist **6860**
0025-4355 Maryland State Dental Association. Journal *changed to* M S D A Journal **5855**
0025-4371 Maryland Teacher†
0025-4398 Maryland Veterinarian†
0025-441X Mas Chistes†
0025-4428 Masada†
0025-4436 Masalah Bangunan†
0025-4479 Maschinenbau†
0025-4487 Maschinenbau und Fertigungstechnik der U d S S R
0025-4495 Maschinenbau Technik†
0025-4533 Maschinenwelt - Elektrotechnik†
0025-4541 MascuLines†
0025-455X Mashinostroene
0025-4568 Mashinostroitel' **5456**
0025-4584 Mashriq **3549**
0025-4606 Maske und Kothurn **8473**
0025-4649 Maslozhirovaya Promyshlennost' **3655**
0025-4665 Masonic Record
0025-4681 Masonry **1022**
0025-469X Masque
0025-4703 Masque
0025-4711 Masque†
0025-4738 Mass Spectrometry Bulletin **2094**
0025-4770 Massachusetts C P A Review†
0025-4789 Massachusetts College of Pharmacy. Bulletin **6860**
0025-4800 Massachusetts Dental Society. Journal **5855**
0025-4819 Massachusetts Heritage†
0025-4878 Massachusetts Review **5227**
0025-4894 Massachusetts State Labor Council A F L - C I O Newsletter **4598**
0025-4908 Massachusetts Teacher†
0025-4924 Massachusetts Wildlife **2618**
0025-4932 Massimario del Foro Italiano **4730**
0025-4940 Massimario della Giurisprudenza Italiana **4730**
0025-4959 Massimario di Giurisprudenza del Lavoro **1697**
0025-4975 Massis **7705**
0025-4991 Master Builders' Journal **1022**
0025-5017 Master Detective†
0025-5025 Master Drawings **504**
0025-5033 Master, Mate & Pilot **4598**
0025-505X Master Plumber and Heating Contractor†
0025-5068 Master Plumber of South Australia
0025-5114 Master's Thesis Abstracts Bulletin†
0025-5122 The Masthead (Harrisburg) **4579**
0025-5165 Matematicki Vesnik **5511**
0025-519X Matematikai Lapok **5511**
0025-5238 Materia Medica Nordmark†
0025-5246 Materia Medica Polona†
0025-5270 Material und Organismen†
0025-5289 Materiale Plastice **7095**
0025-5300 Materialpruefung *changed to* Materials Testing **3354**
0025-5319 Materials Engineering†
0025-5327 Materials Evaluation **3353**
0025-5335 Materials Handling and Management†
0025-5343 Materials Management & Distribution **8503**
0025-5351 Materials Handling News **5457**
0025-5408 Materials Research Bulletin **2111**
0025-5440 Materidouska **2201**
0025-5459 Materie Plastiche ed Elastomeri **7095**
0025-5475 Maternal and Child Care†
0025-5491 Maternidade e Infancia†
0025-5521 Mathematica Scandinavica **5512**
0025-553X Mathematicae Notae **5512**
0025-5548 Mathematical Algorithms†
0025-5556 Mathematical Association of India. Bulletin
0025-5564 Mathematical Biosciences **5512**
0025-5572 Mathematical Gazette **5513**
0025-5580 Mathematical Log **5513**
0025-5602 Mathematical Pie **5514**
0025-5610 Mathematical Programming **5554**
0025-5629 Mathematical Reviews **5548**
0025-5637 Mathematical Sciences Employment Register†
0025-5645 Mathematical Society of Japan. Journal **5514**
0025-5653 Mathematical Spectrum **5515**
0025-567X Matematicheskie Zametki **5511**
0025-5696 Mathematics Flyer
0025-570X Mathematics Magazine **5515**
0025-5718 Mathematics of Computation **5516**
0025-5742 Mathematics Student **5516**
0025-5769 Mathematics Teacher **3072**
0025-5785 Mathematics Teaching **5516**
0025-5793 Mathematika **5516**
0025-5807 Der Mathematikunterricht **5516**
0025-5831 Mathematische Annalen **5516**
0025-584X Mathematische Nachrichten **5517**
0025-5858 Universitaet Hamburg. Mathematisches Seminar. Abhandlungen **5544**
0025-5866 Der Mathematische und Naturwissenschaftliche Unterricht **5517**
0025-5874 Mathematische Zeitschrift **5517**
0025-5904 Mathitiki Estia **2201**
0025-5912 Mati
0025-5939 Letopis Matice Srpske **5321**
0025-5947 Matieland **2291**
0025-5955 Matilda Ziegler Magazine for the Blind
0025-5998 Matrix and Tensor Quarterly†
0025-6021 Mature Years **7766**
0025-603X Mature Years-New Directions†
0025-6048 Mauricien Medical
0025-6064 Mauritius Times **3789**
0025-6072 Mausolee *changed to* 1628-9595 **6476**
0025-6110 Maxwell Review **2885**
0025-6129 May Day Pictorial News†
0025-6137 May Trends **1963**
0025-6153 Maydica **242**
0025-6161 Mayfair **6295**
0025-6188 Mayibuye **7212**
0025-6196 Mayo Clinic Proceedings **5665**
0025-620X Mazdaznan - Blatt
0025-6218 Mazputnins†
0025-6234 Mbioni **7984**
0025-6269 Me **1424**
0025-6277 Me Naiset **8874**
0025-6285 Meander **2237**
0025-6331 Measuring for Medicine & the Life Sciences†
0025-634X Meat†
0025-6358 Meat Board Reports†
0025-6374 Meat Industry†
0025-6390 Meat Processing *changed to* 0892-6077 **3655**
0025-6412 Meat Trades Journal **3656**
0025-6420 Mecanica Popular *changed to* 1544-5216 **8435**
0025-6455 Meccanica **7060**
0025-6463 Meccano Magazine†
0025-6501 Mechanical Engineering **3389**
0025-651X Mechanical Engineering News†
0025-6544 Mechanics of Solids **7061**
0025-6552 Mechanik **3389**
0025-6595 Mechanizacia†
0025-6609 Mecman - Technique
0025-6625 Medailles **4339**
0025-6641 MedBooks†
0025-665X Medborgaren **7154**
0025-6692 Le Medecin du Quebec **5666**
0025-6714 Etudes Medicales
0025-6730 Medecine et Gastronomie†
0025-6749 Medecine et Hygiene *changed to* 1660-9379 **5706**
0025-6757 Medecine et Travail *changed to* 1775-0318 **6679**
0025-6765 Medecine Hospitaliere†
0025-6773 Medecine Infantile†
0025-6781 Medecine Interne†
0025-6811 Medecine Practicienne†
0025-682X Medecine Tropicale **5822**
0025-6897 Media & Methods† **8973**
0025-6927 Medianite **3743**
0025-6943 Medical Abstract Service†
0025-6986 Medical Annals of the District of Columbia†
0025-7001 Medical Aspects of Human Sexuality†
0025-7028 Medical Association of Georgia. Journal **5667**
0025-7036 Medical Association of Thailand. Journal. Supplement **5667**
0025-7060 Medical Book News **5749**
0025-7079 Medical Care **5667**
0025-7095 Medical Centre Journal†
0025-7109 Medical Checklist **5749**
0025-7117 Medical Chronicle
0025-7125 Medical Clinics of North America **5667**
0025-7133 Medical College and Hospital, Calcutta. Bulletin†
0025-7141 Medical College of Virginia Quarterly†
0025-715X Medical Counterpoint†
0025-7168 Medical Digest†
0025-7184 Medical Digest
0025-7192 Medical Ecology and Clinical Research†
0025-7206 Medical Economics **5668**
0025-7222 Medical Electronics & Communications Abstracts†
0025-7273 Medical History **5669**
0025-729X Medical Journal of Australia **5669**
0025-732X The Medical Letter on Drugs and Therapeutics (English Edition) **6860**
0025-7346 National Library of Medicine. Current Catalog Proofsheets†
0025-7354 Medical Marketing & Media **6860**
0025-7370 Medical Missionary News
0025-7397 Medical - Moral Newsletter†
0025-7427 Medical Pharmacy **6860**
0025-7435 The Medical Post **5670**
0025-746X Medical Radiography and Photography†
0025-7494 Medical Research Bulletin†
0025-7508 Medical Research Engineering†
0025-7540 Medical Socioeconomic Research Sources†
0025-7559 Medical Staff in Action†
0025-7567 Medical-Surgical Review†
0025-7583 Medical Times†
0025-7591 Medical Trial Technique Quarterly **4837**
0025-7621 Medical World
0025-763X Medical World News†
0025-7648 Medicamenta†
0025-7664 Medicamundi **6203**
0025-7672 Medicare Report
0025-7680 Medicina **5673**
0025-7699 Medicina **5947**
0025-7702 Medicina
0025-7729 Medicina **5673**
0025-7753 Medicina Clinica **5673**
0025-7761 Medicina Clinica e Sperimentale†
0025-777X Medicina Contemporanea†
0025-7796 Medicina Danas†
0025-780X Medicina de Madrid
0025-7818 La Medicina del Lavoro **6681**
0025-7826 Medicina dello Sport **6231**
0025-7834 Medicina e Morale **5673**
0025-7842 Medicina Espanola†
0025-7850 Journal of Medicine†
0025-7893 Medicina Psicosomatica **6159**
0025-7907 Medicina Rural†
0025-7923 Medicina Tedesca†
0025-7931 Respiration **6218**
0025-7958 Medicina Tropical†
0025-7966 Medicinar **5855**
0025-7974 Medicine (Baltimore) **5674**
0025-7982 Medicine and Medicaments Courier
0025-8008 Medicine & Surgery
0025-8016 Medecine Europeene†
0025-8024 Medicine, Science and the Law **5915**
0025-8032 Medicine Today†
0025-8067 Medicinska Revija†
0025-8075 Meditsinskaya Tekhnika **5676**
0025-8105 Medicinski Pregled **5675**
0025-8113 Medicinski Radnik†
0025-8121 Medicinski Razgledi
0025-813X Medico†
0025-8148 Il Medico d'Italia
0025-8164 Medico-Legal Bulletin†
0025-8172 Medico-Legal Journal **5915**
0025-8180 Medico Moderno†
0025-8202 Medicos†
0025-8210 Medicus†
0025-8229 Medjimurje **5227**
0025-8237 Medion†
0025-8245 Medisch Contact **5676**
0025-8253 Mediscope†
0025-827X Mediterranean Diplomatic Observer
0025-8296 Mediterranee (Aix-en-Provence) **4019**
0025-830X Meditsinskii Zhurnal Uzbekistana **5676**
0025-8318 Meditsinskaya Gazeta **5676**
0025-8326 Meditsinskaya Parazitologiya i Parazitarnye Bolezni **5822**
0025-8350 Medium†
0025-8377 The Medium **5032**
0025-8385 Medium Aevum **5332**
0025-8393 Medizin in Bild und Ton†
0025-8407 Medizin und Ernaehrung†
0025-8431 Medizinhistorisches Journal **5677**
0025-844X Medizinische Bild†
0025-8482 Medizinische Neuerscheinungen†
0025-8490 Der Medizinische Sachverstaendige **5677**
0025-8512 Die Medizinische Welt **5677**
0025-8539 Nordisk Numismatisk Unions Medlemsblad **6652**
0025-8547 Foerfattaren **5297**
0025-8555 Medjunarodni Problemi **7252**
0025-8601 Medycyna Doswiadczalna i Mikrobiologia **891**
0025-8628 Medycyna Weterynaryjna **8803**
0025-8636 Medycyna Wiejska *changed to* Medycyna Ogolna **5678**

Link to your serials resources and content with ulrichsweb.com

0027-0482 Monthly Radiation Summary (Microfiche Edition)†
0027-0490 The Radiation Observatory Radiation Yearbook†
0027-0504 Monthly Railway Statistics 8527
0027-0520 Monthly Review 7155
0027-0547 Monthly Statistics of Foreign Trade of India 1252
0027-0563 Han' Guk T'onggye Wolbo changed to 1228-8101 8376
0027-058X Monthly Summary of Business Conditions in Southern California†
0027-0598 Monthly Summary of Jute and Gunny Statistics 8464
0027-061X Monthly Technical Review†
0027-0636 Great Britain. Meteorological Office. Monthly Weather Report†
0027-0644 Monthly Weather Review 6391
0027-0717 Quebec Medical
0027-0725 Montreal. Museum of Fine Arts. Quarterly Review†
0027-0733 Monument in Cantos and Essays†
0027-0741 Monumenta Nipponica 556
0027-0776 Monumentum†
0027-0814 Moody's Bank and Finance News Reports
0027-0822 Moody's Bond Survey changed to Moody's Credit Perspectives 1640
0027-0865 Moody's O T C Industrial News Reports 1641
0027-0873 Moody's Public Utility News Reports 1641
0027-0881 Moody's Stock Survey†
0027-089X Moody's Transportation News Reports 1641
0027-0911 Moon Magazine†
0027-092X Moonshine Can
0027-0989 Mopac News†
0027-1055 Moreland News and Views
0027-1071 Morgagni
0027-108X Morgan Guaranty Survey†
0027-1098 The Morgan Horse 8294
0027-1136 Mornaricki Glasnik 6437
0027-1144 Morning Rays†
0027-1160 Morocco Tourism
0027-1179 Morokami
0027-1187 Morris Arboretum Bulletin†
0027-1195 Morsingboen 3834
0027-1209 Morsko Ribarstvo 3602
0027-125X Morton Arboretum Quarterly†
0027-1268 Mortuary Management 3720
0027-1276 Mosaic (Winnipeg, 1967) 5336
0027-1284 Mosaic (Washington)†
0027-1306 Moscow News†
0027-1314 Moscow University Chemistry Bulletin 2073
0027-1322 Moscow University Mathematics Bulletin 5519
0027-1330 Moscow University Mechanics Bulletin 7061
0027-1349 Moscow University Physics Bulletin 7026
0027-1365 Moskovskii Gosudarstvennyi Universitet. Vestnik. Seriya 6: Ekonomika 1150
0027-1403 Moskovskoe Obshchestvo Ispytatelei Prirody. Biologicheskii Otdel. Byulleten 690
0027-1446 Mosul University. College of Medicine. Annals 5681
0027-1454 Mosupa - Tsela†
0027-1462 Mot† 8975
0027-1470 Mot - Bau 3278
0027-1500 Mother†
0027-1527 Mother Cabrini Messenger
0027-1535 Mother Earth News 3982
0027-1543 Mother India 6935
0027-1594 Motion Picture Daily†
0027-1624 Motion Picture Magazine†
0027-1632 Motion Pictures Technical Bulletin 6507
0027-1667 Motive†
0027-1675 Moto†
0027-1683 Moto Revija†
0027-1691 Motociclismo 8262
0027-1713 Motor 8591
0027-1721 Motor 8262
0027-173X Motor 8592
0027-1748 MOTOR 8591
0027-1756 Motor†
0027-1764 Motor 8591
0027-1780 Motor Boat & Yachting 8278
0027-1837 Motor Cycle†
0027-1853 Motorcycle News 8263
0027-190X Motor in Canada†
0027-1969 Motor Revue†
0027-2000 Motor Ship 8654
0027-2019 Motor Sport 8592
0027-2035 Motor Trade Journal 8593
0027-2043 Motor Trader 8593
0027-2051 Motor Trader and Fleet Operator 8593
0027-206X Motor Transport 8673
0027-2094 Motor Trend 8593
0027-2108 Motor Truck 8673
0027-2124 Motor West†
0027-2140 Motorbranschen 8593
0027-2167 Enthusiast 8258
0027-2205 Motorcyclist 8263
0027-2213 Motorfoereren 8593
0027-223X Motorindia 8594
0027-2248 Motoring 8594
0027-2256 Motoring Life 8594
0027-2264 Motoring News
0027-2299 Motorist
0027-2302 Motorists Guide to New & Used Car Prices
0027-2337 Motorliv†
0027-2361 Motorpraxis†
0027-237X Das Motorrad 8263
0027-2388 Motortidningen Kart†
0027-2396 Motrix†
0027-2485 Mount Allison Record 2293
0027-2493 Mount Holyoke Alumnae Quarterly 2293
0027-2507 Mount Sinai Journal of Medicine 5681
0027-254X Mountain Geologist 2756
0027-2558 Mountain Life and Work†
0027-2566 Mountain†
0027-2574 Mountain Path 6935
0027-2612 Mountain Visitor†
0027-2620 Mountaineer (Seattle) 8323
0027-2639 Mousaion 5032

0027-2655 Mouthpiece
0027-2663 Mouvement†
0027-2671 Le Mouvement Social 4154
0027-268X Moviet 8975
0027-2698 Movie Life†
0027-271X Movie Mirror 6508
0027-2736 Movie News†
0027-2744 Movie Stars†
0027-2779 Movie World†
0027-2833 Movoznavstvo 5153
0027-2841 Le Moyen Age 4246
0027-2892 Moznayim 5336
0027-2906 M.S. for Medical Secretaries†
0027-2914 Muanyag es Gumi 7095
0027-2930 El Mueble 4547
0027-2957 Muell und Abfall 7532
0027-2965 Mueller Clipper 3325
0027-2981 Muenchner Woche
0027-299X Das Muenster 506
0027-3007 Muenzen und Medaillen 6651
0027-3015 Muszaki Egyetemi Konyvtaros†
0027-3066 Mujer de America
0027-3104 Mukta 5228
0027-3120 Il Mulino 5228
0027-3147 Multi†
0027-3155 Multihull International†
0027-3171 Multivariate Behavioral Research 7386
0027-3198 Zahnaerztlicher Anzeiger 5870
0027-321X Office International de Bibliographie. Communications Mundaneum
0027-3228 Mundartfreunde Oesterreichs. Mitteilungen 5153
0027-3244 Mundo Cristao†
0027-3252 Mundo Cristiano 3953
0027-3287 Mundo Economico
0027-3295 Mundo Eletrico
0027-3309 Mundo Hispanico†
0027-3317 Mundo Hospitalario†
0027-3325 Mundo Madereru
0027-3333 Mundo Nuevo
0027-335X Mundo Social†
0027-3376 Mundo Textil Argentino 8455
0027-3384 Mundus
0027-3392 Mundus†
0027-3406 Mundus Artium†
0027-3465 Municipal Engineers Journal 3279
0027-3554 New York Municipal Reference & Research Center Notes†
0027-3570 Municipal South†
0027-3589 Municipal World 7498
0027-3597 The Municipality 7498
0027-3600 Munka†
0027-3627 Munson-Williams-Proctor Institute. Bulletin 6529
0027-366X Murimi†
0027-3678 Murmesteren 1025
0027-3686 Murray Hill News 3982
0027-3767 Musee Carnavalet. Bulletin†
0027-3775 Musee du Soir†
0027-3791 Musee National de Varsovie. Bulletin 6529
0027-3821 Musees de Geneve†
0027-383X Musees et Collections Publiques de France 6530
0027-3856 Musees Royaux des Beaux-Arts de Belgique. Bulletin 6530
0027-3872 Musei e Gallerie d'Italia†
0027-3880 Museo Argentino de Ciencias Naturales "Bernardino Rivadavia." Instituto Nacional de Investigacion de las Ciencias Naturales. Revista. Geologia†
0027-3899 Museo de Ciencias Naturales. Boletin†
0027-3910 Museo Nacional de Historia Natural. Boletin 7884
0027-3953 Museo Nazionale del Cinema. Notiziario†
0027-397X Museologist†
0027-4003 Museum
0027-4038 Museum Boymans-van Beuningen. Bulletin†
0027-4046 Museum Graphic†
0027-4054 Museum Helveticum 2238
0027-4089 Museum News changed to 1938-3940 6531
0027-4097 Museum Notes (Providence) 507
0027-4100 Museum of Comparative Zoology. Bulletin 956
0027-4127 Museum of Modern Art. Members Newsletter†
0027-4135 Museum of the Fur Trade Quarterly 4304
0027-416X Museums Journal 6532
0027-4178 Museumskunde 6532
0027-4194 Courrier Roumain†
0027-4216 Music & Artists†
0027-4224 Music and Letters 6589
0027-4240 Music Article Guide†
0027-4259 Music at Georgia†
0027-4275 The Music Box 6590
0027-4291 Music City News†
0027-4321 Music Educators Journal 6590
0027-433X Music in Education†
0027-4348 The Music Index (Print) 6632
0027-4356 Music Industry
0027-4364 Music Journal†
0027-4372 The Music Leader†
0027-4380 Music Library Association. Notes 5033
0027-4399 Music Maker†
0027-4402 Music Ministry†
0027-4437 Music Now 6591
0027-4445 Music Review changed to 1479-4098 6599
0027-4461 Music Teacher 3073
0027-447X Music Tempo†
0027-4488 The Music Trades 6592
0027-4496 Music World†
0027-4518 Musica†
0027-4526 Musica e Dischi 6592
0027-4542 Musica Jazz 6593
0027-4550 Musica Universita†
0027-4569 Musicae Sacrae Ministerium
0027-4585 Musical Denmark†
0027-4615 Musical Merchandise Review 6593
0027-4623 Musical Opinion 6593
0027-4631 The Musical Quarterly 6594

0027-4658 Musical Show 8474
0027-4666 Musical Times 6594
0027-4674 Musicalbrandet 8975
0027-4682 Musicasia†
0027-4690 Impulse 3883
0027-4704 Musik in der Schule 6595
0027-4720 Musik & LjudTeknik 6595
0027-4739 Musik og Handel†
0027-4747 Musik und Bildung 6595
0027-4755 Musik und Gesellschaft†
0027-4771 Musik und Kirche 6595
0027-478X Musikern 6596
0027-4798 Musikerziehung 6596
0027-4801 Die Musikforschung 6596
0027-481X Musikhandel 6596
0027-4828 Das Musikinstrument 6596
0027-4844 Musikrevy†
0027-4852 Musique et Instruments†
0027-4860 Muslim Africa 7714
0027-4887 Muslim Digest 7714
0027-4895 Muslim Review 7714
0027-4909 Muslim World 7715
0027-4917 Mustang Review†
0027-4976 Muszaki Lapszemle. Elelmiszeripar†
0027-5085 Muszaki Tudomany†
0027-5093 Mut 7253
0027-5115 Mutech Chemical Engineering Journal†
0027-5123 Mutisia 802
0027-5131 Mutter
0027-514X Muttersprache 5153
0027-5158 Mutual Benefit Estate and Tax Letter†
0027-5182 Mutual Funds Guide 1641
0027-5220 Mutualita' Democratica
0027-5239 Mutualite 4515
0027-5247 Muveszettorteneti Ertesito 507
0027-5255 Muzejni a Vlastivedna Prace changed to 1803-0386 6533
0027-5263 Muzeum 6533
0027-5271 Muzicka Omladina
0027-528X Muziek Express†
0027-5301 Muziekhandel 6597
0027-531X Muzika†
0027-5328 Muzilo†
0027-5336 Muzsika 6597
0027-5344 Muzyka 6598
0027-5352 Muzykal'naya Zhizn' 6598
0027-5360 Muzzle Blasts 8323
0027-5379 My Baby†
0027-5387 My Devotions 7768
0027-5395 Canadian Golden West†
0027-5417 My i Svit†
0027-5425 My Career 6701
0027-5433 My Magazine of India
0027-545X My Story 5411
0027-5468 My Volk†
0027-5506 Myasthenia Gravis Foundation. Newsletter
0027-5514 Mycologia 802
0027-5522 Mycological Papers 802
0027-5549 Mycophile 803
0027-5565 Mylpaal†
0027-5573 Mysindia†
0027-5581 Mysl Polska
0027-559X Mysore Commerce 1407
0027-5603 Mysore Economic Review
0027-5611 Mysore Industrial Diary†
0027-5638 Mysterium 7664
0027-5662 N A A F I News 6437
0027-5670 A D A S Quarterly Review†
0027-5719 N A C†
0027-576X N A C W P I Journal 6598
0027-5794 N A D A Official Used Car Guide 8594
0027-5859 N A I I News Memo†
0027-5867 N A I I Press Samplings†
0027-5875 N A I L M News 2243
0027-5883 N A I S Report†
0027-5891 Two Wheeler Dealer†
0027-593X N A N T I S News†
0027-5956 Air Pollution Abstracts†
0027-5964 N A P I A Bulletin 4515
0027-5980 N A R G U S Bulletin†
0027-6006 N A S C Quarterly 6651
0027-6014 N A S P A Journal (Print)†
0027-6022 N A S W News 8056
0027-6103 N A W G A Management and Controller's Bulletin†
0027-6111 N & M†
0027-6138 N B O Abstracts 1048
0027-6154 N B O. Building Information Bulletin†
0027-6162 N B R I Information Sheet†
0027-6170 The N C A A News 8189
0027-6189 N C A E News Bulletin 2888
0027-6219 N C A Today†
0027-6227 N C A W E News†
0027-6235 N C C D News†
0027-6278 N C D C Bulletin 1424
0027-6316 N C I Newsletter†
0027-6359 N C Scene
0027-6367 N C W News 8876
0027-6383 Prosecutor 4897
0027-6413 N E A Research Bulletin†
0027-6421 N E C News 2432
0027-643X N E D A Journal - Electronic Merchandising†
0027-6448 N E P P C O News†
0027-6499 N F A Reports†
0027-6537 Conservation Commission News 2607
0027-6545 N H D S Newsletter 5856
0027-657X N H K Laboratories Note 2386
0027-6642 N I F Weekly
0027-6650 N I H Publications List 5682
0027-6669 N I M Abstracts†
0027-6685 N I N 3945
0027-6723 N I R. Nordiskt Immateriellt Raettsskydd 6755
0027-674X N J E A Reporter 3028

9048 0027-6758 ULRICH'S PERIODICALS

0027-6758 N J E A Review **2888**
0027-6782 N L G I Spokesman **6778**
0027-6855 N M U Pilot†
0027-6898 N P L Technical Bulletin **7027**
0027-6901 N P N Bulletin†
0027-6952 N R I Journal†
0027-6979 N R T A Journal†
0027-7010 N S S News **2757**
0027-7029 New South Wales Contract Reporter†
0027-7045 N T D R A Dealer News†
0027-7053 N T L Institute News and Reports†
0027-7126 Nya Argus **5232**
0027-7134 N Y L A Bulletin **5033**
0027-7142 N Y L I C Review **4516**
0027-7150 N Y P M A Bulletin
0027-7177 The New Zealand Baptist *changed to* 1176-8711 **7747**
0027-7193 N.Z.H. Maandblad†
0027-7231 N. Z. Meat Trades Journal
0027-724X New Zealand Shipping Gazette **8655**
0027-7266 N Z T C A Journal†
0027-7274 N.Z. Truth
0027-7320 Na Vijvent†
0027-7339 Naaimachine - Nieuws†
0027-7363 Nach der Arbeit **2944**
0027-7371 Nachal'naya Shkola (Moscow, 1933) **2889**
0027-7401 Oesterreichisches Chemiefaser-Institut. Nachrichten†
0027-741X Nachrichten fuer Aussenhandel **1642**
0027-7428 Nachrichten fuer die Zivile Luftfahrt, Deutsche Demokratische Republik†
0027-7444 Nachrichten fuer Seefahrer **8654**
0027-7452 Nachrichtenblatt der Bayerischen Entomologen **855**
0027-7460 Deutsche Gesellschaft fuer Geschichte der Medizin, Naturwissenschaft und Technik. Nachrichtenblatt **5604**
0027-7479 Nachrichtenblatt des Deutschen Pflanzenschutzdienstes *changed to* 1867-0911 **238**
0027-7509 Nacion **7156**
0027-7525 Nadel Faden Fingerhut†
0027-7533 Naeringsrevyen†
0027-755X Nafta **6779**
0027-7568 Nagaoka College of Technology. Research Reports **3211**
0027-7576 Nagarjun†
0027-7584 Nagarlok **7499**
0027-7606 Nagoya Shiritsu Daigaku Igakkai Zasshi **5682**
0027-7622 Nagoya Journal of Medical Science **5682**
0027-7630 Nagoya Mathematical Journal **5519**
0027-7649 Nagoya Medical Journal **5682**
0027-7665 Nagoya University. Institute of Plasma Physics. Research Report
0027-7681 Naho†
0027-7711 Nailaer Zeitung†
0027-772X Namari to Aen **6327**
0027-7738 Names **5154**
0027-7746 Namib Times **3913**
0027-7762 Namrugram†
0027-7770 Nanak Prakash Patrika **7707**
0027-7827 Napoleon **4247**
0027-7835 Napoli Nobilissima **508**
0027-7843 Napred **3945**
0027-7851 Narciso
0027-7886 Narod†
0027-7894 Narod Polski **3552**
0027-7916 Narodna Odbrana
0027-7932 Narodne Novine **5229**
0027-7959 Narodni Borac
0027-7975 Narodni List **5229**
0027-7983 Narodni Sumar
0027-8009 Narodni Vybory†
0027-8017 Narodno Stvaralastvo - Folklor
0027-8025 Narodno Zdravlje†
0027-8033 Narodnoe Obrazovanie **2889**
0027-805X Narragansett Naturalist†
0027-8068 Nas Chov **294**
0027-8084 Nas Jezik **5154**
0027-8106 Nas Svijet†
0027-8114 Nas Vesnik†
0027-8122 Nasa Rec **3945**
0027-8130 Nasa Riject†
0027-8149 Nasa Stampa
0027-8157 Nasa Strucna Skola†
0027-8203 Nase Rec **5154**
0027-8211 Nase Vojsko†
0027-8238 Nash Sovremennik **5229**
0027-8246 Nash Swit
0027-8254 Nashe Slovo **3552**
0027-8262 Nasi Dani†
0027-8270 Nasi Zbori **6598**
0027-8319 Nasza Droga†
0027-8335 Natal University News†
0027-8378 The Nation **5229**
0027-8394 The Nation†
0027-8408 Nation Europa **5229**
0027-8424 National Academy of Sciences. Proceedings **7886**
0027-8505 National Agricultural Library Catalog†
0027-8513 National Alliance (Washington) **4599**
0027-8521 National Amateur **4580**
0027-853X National AMVET **6438**
0027-8556 National Antiques Review†
0027-8572 Kukhoe Tosogwanbo **5024**
0027-8645 National Association of Regulatory Utility Commissioners. Bulletin **7454**
0027-8688 National Association of Watch and Clock Collectors. Bulletin **4568**
0027-8726 National Auricula & Primula Society (Northern) Year Book **3744**
0027-8750 National Bank of Ethiopia. Quarterly Bulletin **1370**
0027-8769 National Beauty School Journal *changed to* 1052-4169
0027-8777 National Bibliography of Botswana **7578**
0027-8807 National Builder *changed to* Insite (Macclesfield)
0027-8815 National Buildings Organisation. Journal **1025**
0027-884X National Button Bulletin **4342**
0027-8866 Cancer Care and the National Cancer Foundation. Report about the Services Your Contributions Support†
0027-8874 National Cancer Institute. Journal (Print) **6028**
0027-8890 National Capital Pharmacist
0027-8920 National Catholic Register **7808**
0027-8939 National Catholic Reporter **7808**
0027-8963 National Chinchilla Breeders of Canada. Bulletin **4974**
0027-898X National Chronicle
0027-9013 National Civic Review **7499**
0027-9048 American Bankruptcy Law Journal **4614**
0027-9056 National Conference on Social Welfare. Conference Bulletin
0027-9110 National Defence Academy. Journal†
0027-9145 National Diary
0027-9153 Kokuritsu Kokkai Toshokan Geppo **5023**
0027-917X N.D.T.I. Review†
0027-9218 National Engineer **3390**
0027-9250 National Fisherman **3602**
0027-9269 National Fluoridation News†
0027-9293 National Franchise Reports†
0027-9331 National Gardener **3744**
0027-934X National Genealogical Society Quarterly **3776**
0027-9358 National Geographic **4020**
0027-9374 National Geographical Journal of India **4021**
0027-9447 National Hog Farmer **294**
0027-9455 The National Horseman **8295**
0027-9501 National Institute Economic Review **1152**
0027-951X Japan. National Institute of Animal Health Quarterly†
0027-9544 National Jeweler **4568**
0027-9587 National Lampoon†
0027-9609 National Leaders Magazine†
0027-9668 National Live Stock Producer†
0027-9676 National Medical and Dental Association. Bulletin **5683**
0027-9684 National Medical Association. Journal **5683**
0027-9706 National Merchandiser†
0027-9722 National Model Railroad Association. Bulletin *changed to* 1934-5720 **4346**
0027-9749 National Music Council Bulletin†
0027-9765 National News†
0027-9773 British Association of Colliery Management. National News Letter†
0027-9781 National News of the Blind†
0027-9803 National Observer†
0027-9811 National Oceanographic Data Center. Newsletter†
0027-9838 National P T A Bulletin†
0027-9897 National Pharmaceutical Association. Journal†
0027-9927 National Press Club Record **4580**
0027-9951 National Prospector's Gazette & Treasure Hunter's News†
0027-996X The National Provisioner *changed to* 1943-1929 **3646**
0027-9994 National Real Estate Investor **7601**
0028-0003 National Renaissance Bulletin
0028-0011 National Research Council of Thailand. Journal **7887**
0028-0038 National Review **7156**
0028-0054 National Review of Criminal Sciences
0028-0062 Al-Magallat al-Igtima'iyyat al-Qawmiyyat
0028-0070 N R A Journal **8323**
0028-0089 The National Rural Letter Carrier **2354**
0028-0097 National Safety *changed to* National Safety & Occupational Hygiene **7533**
0028-0151 National Service to Regional Councils. Regional Review†
0028-0186 National Society for Medical Research. Bulletin†
0028-0208 National Speed Sport News **8190**
0028-0232 National Stamp News†
0028-0240 Greece. National Statistical Service. Monthly Statistical Bulletin **8375**
0028-0267 National Stock Dog **6811**
0028-0275 Guoli Taiwan Daxue Yixueyuan Yanjiu Lunwen Zhaiyaoji†
0028-0283 National Tax Journal **1936**
0028-0321 National U. Weekly†
0028-0364 National Voice of Salesmen
0028-0372 National Voter **7156**
0028-0380 National Waterways Conference Newsletter
0028-0399 National Westminster Bank Quarterly Review†
0028-0402 National Wildlife **2620**
0028-0437 Der Nationale Demokrat†
0028-0453 Nationaloekonomisk Tidsskrift **7987**
0028-047X Nation's Business†
0028-0496 The Nation's Health **7533**
0028-050X Nations Nouvelles
0028-0518 Nation's Restaurant News **4394**
0028-0534 Native Nevadan†
0028-0542 Native Voice **3602**
0028-0550 Natturufraedingurinn **7887**
0028-0585 Natur og Museum **7887**
0028-0593 Natur und Heimat **7887**
0028-0607 Natur und Land **7887**
0028-0615 Natur und Landschaft **2620**
0028-0623 Natur- und Nationalparke†
0028-0631 Natura **7888**
0028-064X Natura **7888**
0028-0658 Natura & Montagna **692**
0028-0666 Natura Mosana **855**
0028-0682 Natural and Applied Science Bulletin†
0028-0704 Natural Health World
0028-0712 Natural History **7888**
0028-0739 The Natural Resources Journal **2621**
0028-0755 Natural Rubber News†
0028-0771 The Naturalist **692**
0028-0798 Naturaliste Canadien†
0028-0801 Les Naturalistes Belges **692**
0028-0836 Nature **7889**
0028-0844 Nature and Resources†
0028-0860 Nature Study **3455**
0028-0887 Naturen **7889**
0028-0895 Naturens Verden **7889**
0028-0909 Nature's Path†
0028-0917 Naturforschende Gesellschaft zu Freiburg. Berichte **7889**
0028-0925 Naturfreund **8740**
0028-095X Naturhistorisches Museum in Wien. Monatsprogramm **6534**
0028-0968 Naturisme *changed to* 1874-0197 **6999**
0028-0976 Naturist und Welt†
0028-0984 Naturkautschuk
0028-100X Naturopath†
0028-1018 Naturschutz- und Naturparke
0028-1026 Naturstein **1026**
0028-1042 Naturwissenschaften **7890**
0028-1050 Naturwissenschaftliche Rundschau **7890**
0028-1093 Natuur en Techniek *changed to* 1573-6083 **7890**
0028-1107 Natuurhistorisch Maandblad **7890**
0028-1115 Natya
0028-1123 Nauchen Zhivot
0028-1239 Nauka i Religiya **7665**
0028-1263 Nauka i Zhizn' **7890**
0028-128X N A U N L U **138**
0028-1298 Naunyn-Schmiedeberg's Archives of Pharmacology **6863**
0028-1301 Natur und Museum **7887**
0028-1336 Nautical Magazine **8654**
0028-1344 Nautilus (Sanibel) **957**
0028-1352 Nautilus†
0028-1379 Nautisk Tidskrift **8654**
0028-1409 Naval Affairs **6438**
0028-1417 Naval Aviation News **67**
0028-1425 Naval Engineers Journal **3212**
0028-1433 Naval Record
0028-145X Naval Research Reviews†
0028-1484 Naval War College Review **6438**
0028-1492 Navalkatha†
0028-1506 Navbharat Times **3886**
0028-1522 Navigation (Washington) **67**
0028-1530 Navigation **8654**
0028-1557 Navigator (Washington, D.C.)
0028-1581 Navioneers **67**
0028-159X Navires Ports & Chantiers†
0028-1603 Navis **8279**
0028-162X Navnirman **3212**
0028-1662 Navy News†
0028-1670 Navy News **6439**
0028-1697 Navy Times **6439**
0028-1700 Nazareth
0028-1727 Nea Agrotiki Epitheoresis **139**
0028-1735 Nea Hestia **5338**
0028-1743 Middle East Council of Churches. News Bulletin†
0028-1751 Near East Foundation News†
0028-176X Near East Report (Print)† **8976**
0028-1778 Near North News
0028-1786 Nebelspalter **5229**
0028-1808 Nebraska Beverage Analyst **608**
0028-1816 The Nebraska Bird Review **911**
0028-1832 Nebraska Dental Association. Journal†
0028-1859 Nebraska History **4304**
0028-1875 Nebraska Legionnaire **2268**
0028-1883 Nebraska Library Association. Quarterly **5035**
0028-1891 Nebraska Mortar and Pestle **6863**
0028-1905 Nebraska Municipal Review **7499**
0028-1913 Nebraska Newspaper
0028-1921 Nebraska Nurse **5970**
0028-193X Nebraska on the March†
0028-1964 Nebraskaland Magazine **2622**
0028-1972 Nedele†
0028-1980 Nedeljne Novine **3945**
0028-1999 Nedeljne Novosti†
0028-2030 Nederlandsch Archief voor Kerkgeschiedenis *changed to* 1871-241X **7633**
0028-2073 Nederlands Korfbalblad *changed to* 1871-6792 **8184**
0028-2103 Nederlands Militair Geneeskundig Tijdschrift **5684**
0028-2111 Nederlands Tandartsenblad **5856**
0028-212X Nederlands Theologisch Tijdschrift **7665**
0028-2162 Nederlands Tijdschrift voor Geneeskunde **5684**
0028-2170 Nederlands Tijdschrift voor Medische Studenten†
0028-2200 Nederlands Tijdschrift voor Tandheelkunde **5856**
0028-2227 Nederlands Weekblad voor de Groothandel in Levensmiddelen†
0028-2235 Nederlands Tijdschrift voor de Psychologie en haar Grensgebieden *changed to* 1872-552X **7386**
0028-2251 Nederlandsch-Turksche Vereeniging. Berichten†
0028-226X De Nederlandsche Leeuw **3776**
0028-2278 Nederlandse Gedachten†
0028-2324 Nederlandse Vereniging van Huisvrouwen Afdeling Amsterdam. Maandbericht†
0028-2375 Neen†
0028-2383 Neerlandia **5229**
0028-2391 Neerlands Postduiven Orgaan **8190**
0028-2413 Nef†
0028-2421 Neftekhimiya **6780**
0028-243X Neftyanik (Moscow, 1956)†
0028-2448 Neftyanoe Khozyaistvo **6780**
0028-2456 Negocios y Bancos **1370**
0028-2464 Negotiation Research Digest†
0028-2561 Neirofiziologiya **925**
0028-260X Nemuno Krastas†
0028-2626 Nemzetor
0028-2642 Neo Aftokinito†
0028-2669 Neo Scholio
0028-2677 Neophilologus **5339**
0028-2685 Neoplasma **6029**
0028-2715 Nepal Medical Association. Journal **5685**
0028-2723 Nepal Press Digest **3914**
0028-2731 Nepal Press Report **3914**
0028-274X Nepal Rastra Bank. Quarterly Economic Bulletin **1501**
0028-2758 Nepal Review Monthly†
0028-2790 Neptunus **8655**
0028-2804 Der Nervenarzt **6163**
0028-2812 Nestor **425**
0028-2820 Net (Cambridge)†
0028-2847 Netherhall News†
0028-2871 Amsterdam. Bureau van Statistiek. Maandbericht†
0028-2960 Netherlands Journal of Zoology *changed to* 1570-7555 **932**

0028-2979 Netherlands. Ministerie van Cultuur, Recreatie en Maatschappelijk Werk. Centrale Afdeling Internationale Betrekkingen. Informatie Bulletin†
0028-2995 Netherlands Patents Report†
0028-3045 Networks (New York) **5555**
0028-3053 Neue Technik und Wirtschaft†
0028-3061 Neue Alternative **7157**
0028-3088 Neue Betriebswirtschaft und Betriebwirtschaftliche Datenverarbeitung†
0028-3134 Der Neue Bund†
0028-3142 Neue Deutsche Hefte†
0028-3150 Neue Deutsche Literatur†
0028-3169 Das Neue Erlangen†
0028-3207 Neue Huette†
0028-3223 Neue Illustrierte Wochenschau
0028-3231 Neue Justiz **4740**
0028-324X Der Neue Kaufmann
0028-3258 Neue Kommentare†
0028-3274 Der Neue Mahnruf
0028-3282 Neue Museumskunde†
0028-3312 Neue Physik
0028-3320 Neue Politische Literatur **7157**
0028-3339 Neue Produkte **1579**
0028-3347 Neue Rundschau **5229**
0028-3355 Neue Sammlung† **8976**
0028-3371 Neue Stenographische Praxis
0028-338X Neue Steuerpraxis **1936**
0028-3398 Neue Technik **2432**
0028-3401 Neue Technik im Buero†
0028-3444 Neue Wege *changed to* Beamer **2178**
0028-3460 Neue Wirtschafts-Briefe **1936**
0028-3479 Zeitschrift fuer Parapsychologie und Grenzgebiete der Psychologie **6744**
0028-3495 Neue Zeitschrift fuer Missionswissenschaft†
0028-3517 Neue Zeitschrift fuer Systematische Theologie und Religionsphilosophie **7665**
0028-3525 Neue Zeitschrift fuer Wehrrecht **4972**
0028-3533 Die Neuen Buecher **631**
0028-3568 Zions Freund **7697**
0028-3630 Neues Jahrbuch fuer Geologie und Palaeontology. Monatshefte *changed to* 0077-7749 **2757**
0028-3649 Neues Jahrbuch fuer Mineralogie. Monatshefte *changed to* 0077-7757 **6474**
0028-3657 Neues Leben
0028-3665 Neues Leben **7665**
0028-3673 Neues Optikerjournal
0028-3681 Neues Polizeiarchiv **2662**
0028-3738 Neukirchenblatt Berlin/Wien/Zurich
0028-3754 Neuphilologischer Verein in Helsinki. Mitteilungen **5155**
0028-3770 Neurochirurgie **6252**
0028-3800 Neurobiologia **6163**
0028-3827 Neuroendocrine Control Mechanism†
0028-3835 Neuroendocrinology **5898**
0028-3843 Neurologia i Neurochirurgia Polska **6165**
0028-3851 Neurologia, Neurocirugia y Psiquiatria **6165**
0028-3878 Neurology **6166**
0028-3886 Neurology India **6166**
0028-3908 Neuropharmacology **6863**
0028-3916 Neuropsichiatria
0028-3932 Neuropsychologia **6168**
0028-3940 Neuroradiology **6204**
0028-3967 Neurosciences Research Program Bulletin†
0028-3983 Neusprachliche Mitteilungen aus Wissenschaft und Praxis† **8976**
0028-4033 Nevada Education Journal
0028-4041 Nevada Highway News†
0028-4084 Nevada Outdoors and Wildlife Review†
0028-4114 Neve International† **8976**
0028-4122 Nevesport Illustrato
0028-4130 New†
0028-4149 New Magazine†
0028-4165 New African†
0028-4181 New Amberola Graphic
0028-4203 New American & Canadian Poetry†
0028-4246 New Atlantis†
0028-4254 New Aurora
0028-4262 Green Mountain Post
0028-4289 New Blackfriars **7809**
0028-4297 New Book Review†
0028-4300 New Books†
0028-4327 New Books on Family Planning†
0028-4351 New Brunswick Economic Statistics†
0028-4378 New Business Incorporations **1899**
0028-4386 New Canada
0028-4408 New Captain George's Whizzbang†
0028-4416 New Christian
0028-4467 New Collage Magazine **5339**
0028-4491 New Construction†
0028-4505 New Cornwall†
0028-4513 New Dawn†
0028-453X The New Day†
0028-4548 New Day†
0028-4572 New Democrat†
0028-4599 New Dimensions†
0028-4610 New Directions
0028-4637 New Driver†
0028-470X New England Construction **1026**
0028-4734 New England Electrical News†
0028-4742 New England Furniture News†
0028-4750 New-England Galaxy†
0028-4785 New England Historical and Genealogical Register **3776**
0028-4793 New England Journal of Medicine **5685**
0028-4807 New England Journal of Optometry†
0028-4823 New England Law Review **4741**
0028-4866 The New England Quarterly **5340**
0028-4874 New England Railroad Club. Official Proceedings
0028-4882 New England Reading Association. Journal **2890**
0028-4890 New England Real Estate Journal **7601**
0028-4939 New England Water Works Association. Journal **8830**
0028-4955 New Entomologist **856**
0028-4963 New Equipment Digest **8433**
0028-4971 New Equipment News
0028-498X New Equipment News **8433**
0028-4998 New Era
0028-5013 New Era†
0028-5021 New Era (Ely) **2268**
0028-5072 New Factory Report†
0028-5080 New Forerunner†
0028-5102 New Generation†
0028-5110 New Geographical Literature and Maps†
0028-5129 New Germany Reports†
0028-5137 New Guard
0028-5145 New Guinea and Australia, the Pacific and South-East Asia†
0028-5153 New Guinea Bulletin†
0028-5161 New Guinea Periodical Index†
0028-517X New Guinea Psychologist†
0028-5188 New Guinea Research Bulletin†
0028-5242 New Hampshire Highways **8633**
0028-5250 New Hampshire Horizons†
0028-5269 N H L A Newsletter **5033**
0028-5277 New Hampshire Motor Transport†
0028-5293 New Hampshire Polyglot
0028-5307 New Hampshire Profiles
0028-5315 New Hampshire Quarter Notes
0028-5331 New Haven I N F O Magazine
0028-5366 New Horizon
0028-5374 New Horizons (New York)†
0028-5382 New Horizons in Education† **8976**
0028-5404 New Idea **4365**
0028-5420 New in Dentistry†
0028-5439 New Individualist Review†
0028-5455 New Jersey Academy of Science. Bulletin **7891**
0028-5463 New Jersey Academy of Science. Newsletter **7891**
0028-5536 New Jersey Banker†
0028-5552 New Jersey Beverage Journal **608**
0028-5560 New Jersey Business **1899**
0028-5587 New Jersey Club Woman and Even'tide†
0028-5595 New Jersey Correction News†
0028-5617 New Jersey County Government†
0028-5633 New Jersey Days†
0028-5676 New Jersey Economic Review†
0028-5706 New Jersey Equine Industry News†
0028-5714 New Jersey Federation of Planning Officials. Federation Planner
0028-5722 New Jersey Federation of Planning Officials. Federation Planning Information Reports
0028-5757 New Jersey History† **8976**
0028-5765 New Jersey Journal of Optometry†
0028-5773 New Jersey Journal of Pharmacy **6863**
0028-5781 New Jersey Labor Herald
0028-579X New Jersey Landings†
0028-5803 New Jersey Law Journal **4743**
0028-5811 New Jersey Libraries†
0028-5846 New Jersey Municipalities **7499**
0028-5854 New Jersey Music and Arts†
0028-5889 New Jersey Outdoors†
0028-5897 New Jersey Parent Teacher **2891**
0028-5919 New Jersey Realtor **7602**
0028-5927 N J S D C Research Bulletin†
0028-5935 New Jersey Speech and Hearing Association. Journal†
0028-6001 New Journal **2293**
0028-601X New Journal of Statistics and Operational Research
0028-6044 The New Leader†
0028-6060 New Left Review **5229**
0028-6087 New Literary History **5340**
0028-6125 New Messenger (Braille Edition)†
0028-6176 New Mexico Dental Journal **5856**
0028-6184 New Mexico Extension News†
0028-6192 New Mexico Farm & Ranch **140**
0028-6206 The New Mexico Historical Review **4305**
0028-6214 New Mexico Law Review **4744**
0028-6222 New Mexico Libraries†
0028-6249 New Mexico Magazine **8741**
0028-6257 New Mexico Municipal League. Municipal Reporter **7499**
0028-6265 New Mexico Musician **6599**
0028-6273 New Mexico Nurse
0028-6303 New Mexico School Review†
0028-6338 New Mexico Wildlife **2622**
0028-6354 New Morality
0028-6362 New Musical Express **6599**
0028-6389 Tidewater Virginian†
0028-6400 New Orleans Review **5340**
0028-6419 New Outlook
0028-6427 New Outlook
0028-6443 The New Philosophy **6936**
0028-6451 The New Physician **5685**
0028-646X New Phytologist **804**
0028-6494 New Politics **7158**
0028-6532 New Race†
0028-6540 The New Rambler **5340**
0028-6559 New Records
0028-6567 New Reference Books at U C L A†
0028-6575 The New Renaissance **5340**
0028-6583 The New Republic **5230**
0028-6591 New Research Centers **7891**
0028-6613 New Scholar†
0028-663X New School Bulletin†
0028-6656 New Schools Exchange Newsletter†
0028-6680 U.S. Library of Congress. New Serial Titles†
0028-6699 New Serial Titles-Classed Subject Arrangement
0028-6737 New Solidarity
0028-677X New South Wales Industrial Gazette **1699**
0028-6788 New South Wales Library Bulletin†
0028-6826 New South Wales Statistical Bulletin†
0028-6869 New Technical Books **7938**
0028-6877 New Testament Abstracts **7699**
0028-6885 New Testament Studies **7666**
0028-6907 New Trail **2293**
0028-6966 New Window†
0028-6974 New Woman†
0028-6990 New World **7255**
0028-7008 New World **7158**
0028-7032 New World
0028-7075 New Worlds†
0028-7083 New Writing from Zambia
0028-7105 New York Academy of Medicine. News Notes†
0028-7113 New York Academy of Sciences. Transactions **7892**
0028-713X New York Auto Repair News **8595**
0028-7180 New York Column†
0028-7199 New York Entomological Society. Journal *changed to* 1947-5136 **844**
0028-7210 New York Fish and Game Journal†
0028-7237 New York Genealogical and Biographical Record **3776**
0028-7245 New York Generator **4599**
0028-7296 New York Journal of Dentistry†
0028-7326 New York Law Journal **4745**
0028-7342 New York Letter Carriers' Outlook
0028-7369 New York Magazine **3983**
0028-7431 New York Podiatrist†
0028-7458 New York Professional Engineer **3212**
0028-7482 New York Quarterly **5428**
0028-7490 New York Retailer†
0028-7504 New York Review of Books **7568**
0028-7539 New York State Banker
0028-7563 New York State Conference of Mayors and Other Municipal Officials. Legal Bulletin†
0028-7571 The New York State Dental Journal **5857**
0028-7598 New York State Education†
0028-761X New York State Housing and Community Renewal Reporter†
0028-7628 New York State Journal of Medicine†
0028-7636 New York State Law Digest **4745**
0028-7644 New York State Nurses Association. Journal **5971**
0028-7652 New York State Nurses Association. Report **5971**
0028-7687 N Y S Psychologist **7386**
0028-7741 New York State Society of Dentistry for Children. Bulletin
0028-7768 New York State Statistical Reporter†
0028-7806 New York Times Book Review **7568**
0028-7822 New York Times Magazine **3983**
0028-7830 New York Times School Weekly†
0028-7849 New York Times Student Weekly†
0028-7857 New York University. Center for International Studies. Policy Papers†
0028-7865 New York University Journal of Dentistry†
0028-7873 New York University Journal of International Law and Politics **4936**
0028-7881 New York University Law Review (New York, 1950) **4746**
0028-789X New York University Medical Center News†
0028-792X The New Yorker **5230**
0028-7989 New Zealand Camellia Bulletin **3745**
0028-8004 New Zealand Coal†
0028-8012 New Zealand Commerce†
0028-8047 New Zealand Dental Journal **5857**
0028-8098 New Zealand Farmer†
0028-811X New Zealand. Forest Service. Forest Research Institute. Research Leaflet†
0028-8128 New Zealand Furnishing and Appliance World†
0028-8136 New Zealand Gardener **3745**
0028-8144 New Zealand Geographer **4022**
0028-8160 New Zealand Hardware Journal (Auckland, 1955)†
0028-8179 New Zealand Holiday†
0028-8187 New Zealand Home Journal†
0028-8209 New Zealand Horse & Pony **8295**
0028-8233 New Zealand Journal of Agricultural Research **140**
0028-8241 New Zealand Journal of Agriculture†
0028-825X New Zealand Journal of Botany **805**
0028-8276 New Zealand Journal of Educational Studies **2891**
0028-8292 New Zealand Journal of Geography *changed to* 0028-8144 **4022**
0028-8306 New Zealand Journal of Geology and Geophysics **2758**
0028-8322 New Zealand Journal of History **4193**
0028-8330 New Zealand Journal of Marine and Freshwater Research **2813**
0028-8373 New Zealand Law Journal **4746**
0028-8381 New Zealand Libraries *changed to* 1177-3308 **5035**
0028-8403 New Zealand Local Government **7499**
0028-8438 New Zealand Meat Producer†
0028-8454 New Zealand Medical Record†
0028-8470 New Zealand Model Railway Journal **4342**
0028-8489 New Zealand Monthly Review†
0028-8500 New Zealand News U.K. **3918**
0028-8527 New Zealand Numismatic Journal **6652**
0028-8594 New Zealand Plumbing, Heating and Ventilation Review†
0028-8616 New Zealand Poultry World†
0028-8624 New Zealand Railway Observer **8621**
0028-8632 New Zealand Rationalist and Humanist *changed to* 1175-8619 **6937**
0028-8640 New Zealand Export Review†
0028-8667 New Zealand Science Review **7892**
0028-8683 New Zealand Slavonic Journal **4466**
0028-8721 New Zealand Stamp Monthly†
0028-873X New Zealand Stock Market Review†
0028-8829 New Zealand Woman's Weekly **8877**
0028-8845 Newark Beth Israel Medical Center. Journal†
0028-8861 Newberry Library Bulletin†
0028-887X Newcastle Medical Journal†
0028-8888 Newfoundland Gazette **3813**
0028-8918 Newport History **4305**
0028-8926 Newport Newstory†
0028-8969 News & Letters **7159**
0028-9043 Habitat (London)† **8961**
0028-9094 News from Pondy†
0028-9108 News from Rohde & Schwarz *see* 0548-3093 **2335**
0028-9132 News from South Africa†
0028-9140 News from the Center†
0028-9175 News from the Library†
0028-9183 News from the Vineyards†
0028-9205 News in Engineering **3212**
0028-9221 News 'n Views†
0028-923X News, Notes, and Quotes† **8977**

ISSN

0029-5086 Nova Scotia Farm News†
0029-5116 Novas de Alegria **7739**
0029-5124 Novaya i Noveishaya Istoriya **4154**
0029-5132 Novel: A Forum on Fiction **5344**
0029-5167 Novinar†
0029-5175 Novinarstvo†
0029-5264 Novitur†
0029-5302 Novy Orient **557**
0029-5310 Novy Shliakh **3555**
0029-5337 Novyi Zhurnal **3555**
0029-5345 Now **3886**
0029-5361 Now and Then (Muncy) **4306**
0029-537X Nowa Szkola **2892**
0029-5388 Nowe Drogi†
0029-5396 Nowe Rolnictwo†
0029-540X Nowotwory **6029**
0029-5418 Nowy Casnik **3555**
0029-5426 Ag-Chem Age **80**
0029-5434 Nozzle **8596**
0029-5442 Nsanja Ya Olonda
0029-5450 Nuclear Technology **7070**
0029-5469 Nuclear Canada†
0029-5493 Nuclear Engineering and Design **3355**
0029-5507 Nuclear Engineering International **3171**
0029-5515 Nuclear Fusion **7069**
0029-5523 Nuclear India **3171**
0029-5566 Nuklearmedizin **6204**
0029-5574 Nuclear News **3172**
0029-5604 Nuclear Safety†
0029-5639 Nuclear Science and Engineering **3172**
0029-5647 Hezi Kexue **7066**
0029-5655 Nuclear Standards News **3172**
0029-5663 Nuclelec†
0029-5671 La Recherche **7902**
0029-568X Nucleus **835**
0029-5698 Nucleus **3172**
0029-5701 Nuestra Arquitectura **451**
0029-571X Nuestra Historia†
0029-5728 Nuestra Industria. Revista Economica†
0029-5752 Nuestro Amigo **7769**
0029-5760 Nuestro Anhelo
0029-5787 Nuestro Holando
0029-5795 Nuestro Tiempo **5231**
0029-5809 Nuestros Ninos (Student Edition)†
0029-5817 Nueva Educacion
0029-5825 Nueva Forma†
0029-585X Nueva Pompeya **7810**
0029-5922 Nukleonika **3173**
0029-5965 Number Three St. James' Street
0029-5973 Numen **7667**
0029-5981 International Journal for Numerical Methods in Engineering **3200**
0029-599X Numerische Mathematik **5555**
0029-6007 Numero Economique du Vendredi†
0029-6015 Nvmisma **6652**
0029-6023 Numismatic Circular **6652**
0029-6031 Numismatic Literature **6652**
0029-604X Numismatic News **6652**
0029-6066 Numismatic Society of India. Journal **6652**
0029-6074 Numismaticke Listy **6652**
0029-6090 Numismatist **6652**
0029-6112 Nuntempa Bulgario†
0029-6120 Nuntius Radiologicus†
0029-6139 Nuorten Sarka *changed to* 1459-4463 **173**
0029-6147 Nuova Antologia **5231**
0029-6155 Nuova Corrente **5344**
0029-6163 Nuova Critica
0029-618X Nuova Era†
0029-6198 Nuova Gazzetta di Calabria
0029-6201 Nuova Rassegna **5231**
0029-621X Nuova Rivista Internazionale†
0029-6228 Nuova Rivista Musicale Italiana **6600**
0029-6236 Nuova Rivista Storica **4154**
0029-6244 Nuova Rivista Tributaria
0029-6260 Nuova Venezia
0029-6279 Nuova Veterinaria†
0029-6295 Nuovi Argomenti **5344**
0029-6309 Nuovo Agora Omaggio
0029-6317 Nuovo Bollettino Bibliografico Sardo
0029-6325 Il Nuovo Cantiere **1027**
0029-6333 Nuovo Chirone
0029-635X Nuovo Didaskaleion†
0029-6368 Il Nuovo Diritto **4750**
0029-6376 Nuovo Mezzogiorno† **8978**
0029-6384 Nuovo Osservatore
0029-6392 Nuovo Pensiero Militare
0029-6422 Nursery World **2163**
0029-6457 Nursing†
0029-6465 Nursing Clinics of North America **5973**
0029-6473 Nursing Forum **5973**
0029-6503 Nursing Journal of India **5974**
0029-6538 Nursing News (Concord) **5974**
0029-6546 Nursing News (Floral Park) **5974**
0029-6554 Nursing Outlook **5974**
0029-6562 Nursing Research **5975**
0029-6570 Nursing Standard **5975**
0029-6643 Nutrition Reviews **6666**
0029-6651 Nutrition Society. Proceedings **6667**
0029-666X Nutrition Today **6667**
0029-6694 Nuus Oor Afrika†
0029-6708 Nuwe Protestant†
0029-6716 Nux **2294**
0029-6724 Ny Boky No Loharanom-Pandrosoana†
0029-6759 Ny Politik†
0029-6775 Den Ny Verden **1602**
0029-6791 Nyelvtudomanyi Kozlemenyek **5157**
0029-6848 Nyt fra Historien **4155**
0029-6910 O A S Chronicle *changed to* 1945-4708
0029-6937 O & M†
0029-6961 O C L A E Revista **5232**
0029-7038 O E C D Liaison Bulletin Between Research and Training Institutes†
0029-7054 O E C D Observer **1504**
0029-7089 O G B-Bildungsfunktionaer†
0029-7097 O I R T Information†
0029-7127 Office International de la Vigne et du Vin. Bulletin **608**
0029-7143 O L O G O S **7705**
0029-7151 O L W†
0029-716X O M I Farm News†
0029-7178 O.M.I. Missions†
0029-7216 O R M P Newsletter†
0029-7224 Office de la Recherche Scientifique et Technique Outre-Mer. Cahiers. Serie Entomologie Medicale et Parasitologie†
0029-7283 O S U Research Review†
0029-7321 O T Kaner **143**
0029-733X O T O†
0029-7356 Oak Leaf†
0029-7372 Oak Ridge Associated Universities. Newsletter†
0029-7380 Oakhamian **2294**
0029-7399 Aomoriken Kisho Geppo **6346**
0029-7402 Die Oase† **8978**
0029-7410 Oasis (London, 1969) **5344**
0029-7437 Ob-Gyn News **6000**
0029-7445 Ob-Gyn Observer†
0029-747X Obcan†
0029-7496 Oberfraenkische Wirtschaft **1408**
0029-7518 Oberlin Alumni Magazine **2294**
0029-7526 Oberlin Review **2294**
0029-7534 Oberoesterreichische F P O - Nachrichten fuer Freiheit und Recht†
0029-7542 Oberoesterreichische Gemeindezeitung
0029-7550 Oberoesterreichische Heimatblaetter **4250**
0029-7585 Obiter Dicta **4750**
0029-7593 Objective: Justice† **8978**
0029-7615 Objets et Mondes†
0029-7658 Obrero Ferroviario
0029-7682 Institut Royal Meteorologique de Belgique. Bulletin Mensuel: Observations Climatologiques **6357**
0029-7704 The Observatory **579**
0029-7712 The Observer **3869**
0029-7720 Observer†
0029-7739 The Observer (Rockford) **7810**
0029-7763 Obshchestvennye Nauki v Uzbekistane **7990**
0029-778X Obst-Gemuese
0029-7798 Obst und Garten **3745**
0029-7828 Obstetrical & Gynecological Survey **6000**
0029-7836 Obstetricia y Ginecologia Latino Americana
0029-7844 Obstetrics and Gynecology **6001**
0029-7852 Obzor†
0029-7879 Occident†
0029-7909 Occupational Hazards *changed to* 1945-9599 **6676**
0029-7917 Occupational Health **5976**
0029-7941 Occupational Health Review†
0029-8018 Ocean Engineering **2814**
0029-8026 Ocean Industry†
0029-8042 Ocean Oil Weekly Report (Print) *changed to* Ocean Oil Weekly Report (Online)
0029-8069 Ocean Science News
0029-8077 Oceania **350**
0029-8115 Oceanic Linguistics **5157**
0029-8123 Oceanite **8656**
0029-814X Haiyang yu Huzhao **2805**
0029-8158 Oceanology†
0029-8174 Oceans†
0029-8182 Oceanus **2815**
0029-8190 Ochanomizu Joshi Daigaku Shizen Kagaku Hokoku **7894**
0029-8239 Ochrona Roslin **143**
0029-8247 Ochrona Zabytkow **509**
0029-8271 The Octagon **2075**
0029-8328 Oculus **6047**
0029-8336 Odbrana†
0029-8344 Odbrana i Zastita **2227**
0029-8360 Der Odenwald **3854**
0029-8387 Odjek
0029-8395 Odontoiatria†
0029-8417 Odontologia Chilena **5858**
0029-8476 Odontologiste des Hopitaux†
0029-8484 Shigaku *changed to* 1618-1247 **5858**
0029-8492 Odontoprotesi†
0029-8506 Odontostomatological Progress **5858**
0029-8514 Odrodzenie i Reformacja w Polsce **4250**
0029-8522 Odu **4177**
0029-8530 Odvjetnik **4751**
0029-8549 Oecologia **695**
0029-8565 Der Oeffentliche Dienst **4751**
0029-8581 Das Oeffentliches Haushaltswesen in Oesterreich
0029-859X Die Oeffentliche Verwaltung **4751**
0029-862X L'Oeil **509**
0029-8638 Oekonomik Gartenbau†
0029-8646 Oekonomisk Kronik†
0029-8654 Oekumenische Rundschau **7667**
0029-8689 Oel†
0029-8700 Oil World Weekly **204**
0029-8719 Oertliche Raumheizung†
0029-8727 Oes†
0029-8735 Oeste†
0029-8751 Oesterreich-Nederland **1408**
0029-876X Oesterreichische Krankenhaus Zeitung
0029-8786 Oesterreichische Aerztezeitung **5689**
0029-8832 Oesterreichische Akademie der Wissenschaften. Philosophisch-Historische Klasse. Sitzungsberichte **4250**
0029-8840 Oesterreichischer Alpenverein. Akademische Sektion Graz. Mitteilungen **8325**
0029-8859 Oesterreichische Apotheker-Zeitung **6865**
0029-8867 Oesterreichische Arbeitsgemeinschaft fuer Rehabilitation. Information†
0029-8875 Der Oesterreichische Arzt
0029-8891 Oesterreichische Bauzeitung **1028**
0029-8905 Oesterreichische Bauernzeitung
0029-8921 Oesterreichische Blaetter fuer Gewerblichen Rechtsschutz und Urheberrecht **6755**
0029-8956 Brandverhuetung **3575**
0029-8964 Oesterreichische Buchbinder, Kartonage-, Etui-, Kassetten- und Papierwarenerzeuger
0029-9022 Oesterreichische Eisen- und Metallbranche
0029-9030 Die Oesterreichische Feuerwehr
0029-9057 Der Oesterreichischer Filmamateur **6509**
0029-9065 Der Oesterreichische Friseur **590**
0029-9073 Strassengueterverkehr **8511**
0029-9081 Oesterreichische Fussbodenzeitung
0029-9111 Oesterreichische Gefluegelwirtschaft
0029-912X Oesterreichische Gemeinde-Zeitung **7500**
0029-9138 Oesterreichische Geographische Gesellschaft. Mitteilungen **4023**
0029-9154 Oesterreichische Gesellschaft fuer Holzforschung. Schrifttumskarteidienst - Card Index Service **3714**
0029-9170 Das Oesterreichische Graphische Gewerbe **7325**
0029-9189 Oesterreichische Hausbesitz **7602**
0029-9197 Oesterreichische Hochschulzeitung
0029-9200 Die Oesterreichische Hoehere Schule **2996**
0029-9227 Der Oesterreichische Installateur **4124**
0029-9235 Oesterreichische Installateurzeitung
0029-9243 Der Oesterreichische Jungarbeiter **2205**
0029-9251 Oesterreichische Juristen - Zeitung **4751**
0029-9286 Oesterreichische Leder- und Haeutewirtschaft†
0029-9308 Oesterreichische Monatshefte **7160**
0029-9340 Oesterreichische Notariats-Zeitung **4751**
0029-9359 Oesterreichische Numismatische Gesellschaft. Mitteilungen **6652**
0029-9375 Oesterreichische Osthefte **7160**
0029-9405 Oesterreichische Raumausstatterzeitung
0029-9421 Oesterreichische Schachzeitung†
0029-943X Oesterreichische Schlosser-und Maschinenbauerzeitung†
0029-9448 Oesterreichische Schmiede-Zeitung†
0029-9499 Der Oesterreichische Spengler und Kupferschmied **1028**
0029-9502 Oesterreichische Foerster Zeitung
0029-9529 Oesterreichische Steuerzeitung **1937**
0029-9537 Austria Tabakwerke A. G. Fachliche Mitteilungen†
0029-9545 Oesterreichische Textil-Mitteilungen
0029-9561 Oesterreichische Trafikanten-Zeitung **8486**
0029-957X Der Oesterreichische Volkswirt
0029-9596 Oesterreichische Zahnaerztezeitung **5858**
0029-9626 Oesterreichische Zeitschrift fuer Kunst und Denkmalpflege **509**
0029-9669 Oesterreichische Zeitschrift fuer Volkskunde **3621**
0029-9685 Oesterreichische Zoll und Steuer Nachrichten **1937**
0029-9707 Oesterreichisches Institut fuer Raumplanung. Mitteilungen†
0029-9715 Oesterreichischer Alpenverein. Mitteilungen **8325**
0029-9731 Oesterreichischer Brieftaubensport
0029-974X Kameradschaft der Wiener Panzer-Division. Mitteilungsblatt **6430**
0029-9758 Der Oesterreichischer Kleingaertner
0029-9766 Oesterreichischer Kleintierzuechter **8804**
0029-9782 Oesterreichischer Markenanzeiger **6755**
0029-9790 Oesterreichischer Personenverkehr **8507**
0029-9804 Oesterreichischer Wohnungs- Geschaefts- und Realitaeten-Anzeiger
0029-9812 Oesterreichischer Yachtsport
0029-9847 Oesterreichisches Cafe Journal **4395**
0029-9898 Oesterreichisches Institut fuer Wirtschaftsforschung. Monatsberichte **1505**
0029-9901 Oesterreichisches Jugendrotkreuz. Arbeitsblaetter **8060**
0029-991X Oesterreichisches Klerus Blatt†
0029-9944 Oesterreichisches Patentblatt **6755**
0029-9952 Oesterreichs Standesamt
0029-9987 Oesterreichs Fischerei **3604**
0030-0047 Of Consuming Interest†
0030-0055 Of Sea and Shore **959**
0030-0063 Off-Licence Journal
0030-0071 Off Our Backs **8902**
0030-0098 Offene Kreis†
0030-0101 Offene Tore **7739**
0030-011X Offene Tueren **7667**
0030-0128 Office†
0030-0187 Office Equipment News **1853**
0030-0233 Office Products Dealer†
0030-0268 The Officer **6440**
0030-0284 Official Board Markets **6712**
0030-0314 Official Gazette of Guyana **7458**
0030-0330 Official Journal (Patents)
0030-0373 Official Railway Equipment Register **8621**
0030-0381 Official Steamship Guide
0030-039X Officiel de la Couleur†
0030-0403 Officiel de la Couture et de la Mode de Paris **2259**
0030-0411 Officiel de la Droguerie†
0030-042X Officiel de la Librairie†
0030-0438 Officiel de la Photographie et du Cinema†
0030-0454 Officiel de l'Automobile†
0030-0462 Officiel des Plastiques et du Caoutchouc†
0030-0489 Vetir†
0030-0500 Officiel des Spectacles **8745**
0030-0586 Offizieller Salzburger Wochenspiegel
0030-0608 Offshore (Tulsa) **6782**
0030-0624 Oficina Moderna **1853**
0030-0640 Oficinas **1853**
0030-0675 Oftal'mologicheskii Zhurnal **6047**
0030-0691 Ogam†
0030-0705 Oggi **3898**
0030-0713 Oglas za Pomorce **8656**
0030-0756 Ogrodnictwo *changed to* 1730-2803 **3749**
0030-0802 Ohio Banker *changed to* Ohio Record **1373**
0030-0861 Ohio Contractor **8633**
0030-087X Ohio Dental Journal†
0030-0896 Ohio Farmer **143**
0030-090X Ohio Florists Association. Bulletin
0030-0918 Ohio Forestry Association. Bulletin†
0030-0942 Ohio Jewish Chronicle **7727**
0030-0950 The Ohio Journal of Science **7895**
0030-0985 The Ohio Motorist **8745**
0030-0993 Ohio Nurses Review **5976**

ISSN

9052 0030-1035 ULRICH'S PERIODICALS

0030-1035 Ohio Reading Teacher 3075
0030-1051 Ohio Researcher†
0030-1086 Ohio Schools 2893
0030-1116 Ohio State Lantern 2294
0030-1140 Ohio State University. Institute of Polar Studies. Newsletter†
0030-1159 Ohio State University Libraries Notes†
0030-1183 Ohio Tavern News 608
0030-1221 Ohio Wesleyan Magazine 2294
0030-123X Ohio Woodlands†
0030-1248 Ohioana Quarterly 5345
0030-1256 Ohio's Health†
0030-1264 Ohmio†
0030-1272 Ohnicek† 8978
0030-1280 Oiga
0030-1299 Oikos 3458
0030-1302 Oikoumenikon†
0030-1329 Oil & Chemical Worker 4600
0030-1345 Oil & Gas Discoveries†
0030-1388 Oil & Gas Journal 6783
0030-1442 Oil Mill Gazetteer 274
0030-1450 Oil News 6784
0030-1493 Oilgas 6785
0030-1507 Oils and Oilseeds Journal†
0030-1523 L'Oise Agricole 143
0030-1531 Oiseau et la Revue Francaise d'Ornithologie†
0030-154X Okajima's Folia Anatomica Japonica 695
0030-1558 Okayama Igakkai Zasshi†
0030-1566 Okayama University. Mathematical Journal 5523
0030-1574 Rossiiskaya Akademiya Nauk. Okeanologiya 2817
0030-1612 Okki *changed to* 1572-431X 2205
0030-1612 Okki *changed to* 1872-0293 2195
0030-1647 Oklahoma Banker 1373
0030-1663 Oklahoma Beverage News 608
0030-1671 Oklahoma Business Bulletin 1257
0030-168X Oklahoma C.P.A†
0030-1698 Oklahoma Cowman 295
0030-171X Oklahoma Daily 2294
0030-1728 Oklahoma Register (Oklahoma City) 4958
0030-1736 Oklahoma Geology Notes 2760
0030-1744 Oklahoma Labor Market†
0030-1752 Oklahoma Law Review 4752
0030-1760 Oklahoma Librarian 5038
0030-1779 Oklahoma Mason 2268
0030-1787 Oklahoma Nurse 5976
0030-1795 Oklahoma Observer 7161
0030-1809 Oklahoma Odd Fellow 2268
0030-1833 Oklahoma Reader 3075
0030-1841 Oklahoma Retailer 1836
0030-185X Oklahoma School Board Journal 3029
0030-1876 Oklahoma State Medical Association. Journal 5689
0030-1892 Oklahoma Today 3984
0030-1906 Oekonomi og Politik 1156
0030-1949 Oktobar†
0030-1973 Old English Newsletter 5345
0030-199X The Old Lady 3869
0030-2007 Old Man 2387
0030-2031 Old-Time New England 368
0030-2058 Old West Journal†
0030-2074 Oldenburgische Familienkunde 3778
0030-2090 Olearia
0030-2139 Olomeinu 7727
0030-2147 Oltre il Cielo
0030-2155 Oltremare†
0030-2163 Olympian (San Francisco)
0030-218X Oma
0030-2201 Omaha District Dental Society. Chronicle†
0030-2228 Omega: Journal of Death and Dying 7388
0030-2260 Omnia Medica et Therapeutica†
0030-2287 Omnipraticien Francais†
0030-2317 Instytut Metali Niezelaznych. Biuletyn†
0030-2325 On Course†
0030-2333 On Dit 2295
0030-2341 On Target†
0030-2368 On the Road (Cape Town) 1836
0030-2376 On the Sound†
0030-2384 On the Track†
0030-2392 On Watch 3392
0030-2414 Oncology 6030
0030-2422 Ondas†
0030-2457 Onder de Vlam
0030-2465 Onderstepoort Journal of Veterinary Research 8804
0030-2473 Onderwijs en Media†
0030-2503 One Church†
0030-252X One in Christ 7810
0030-2546 1001 Custom & Rod Ideas†
0030-2562 One/Two†
0030-2597 Ongakugaku 6601
0030-2600 Ongaku Geijutsu†
0030-2619 Onlooker 3886
0030-2627 Onomastica†
0030-2651 Ons Erfdeel 3801
0030-2686 Ons Huis†
0030-2694 Ons Jeugt†
0030-2708 Ons Jonge Platteland†
0030-2732 Ons Platteland†
0030-2767 Ons Trekpaard†
0030-2775 Ons Vee
0030-2783 Ons Wapen†
0030-2805 Ons Ziekenhuis†
0030-2813 Onsei Gengo Igaku 6083
0030-2821 Onsen Kagaku 2760
0030-283X Ontario Association of Children's Aid Societies. Journal 8060
0030-2856 Ontario College of Pharmacy. Bulletin†
0030-2929 Ontario Fish and Wildlife Review†
0030-2937 Ontario Gazette 3815
0030-2945 Families 3765
0030-2953 Ontario History 4307
0030-2988 Ontario Hydro Research Quarterly†
0030-2996 Ontario Library Review†
0030-3011 Ontario Mathematics Gazette 5523
0030-302X Ontario Medical Review 5690
0030-3038 Ontario Milk Producer 268
0030-3054 Ontario Psychologist†
0030-3062 O P A L
0030-3070 Ontario Register†
0030-3089 Ontario Reports 4753
0030-3127 Ontario Statute Citator 4753
0030-316X Ontwaak!
0030-3194 Onze Eigen Tuin 3746
0030-3208 Onze Luchtmacht 6440
0030-3224 Onze Vogels 912
0030-3232 Onze Wereld 7256
0030-3259 Oomoto 7667
0030-3275 Oost en West†
0030-3283 Civis Mundi 7116
0030-3305 Op Cit
0030-3321 Op de Rails 8621
0030-3348 Opakowanie 6712
0030-3356 Opbouw 7769
0030-3399 Open Deur†
0030-3410 Open Door†
0030-3429 Open Forum (Los Angeles) 4753
0030-3437 Open Road and the Professional Driver†
0030-3445 Open Shelf†
0030-3453 Open Vensters† 8979
0030-3488 Openbare Uitgaven *changed to* 1875-8401 1905
0030-350X Openings†
0030-3518 Oper und Konzert *changed to* 1436-5529 6560
0030-3526 Opera 6601
0030-3542 Opera
0030-3577 Opera - Canada 6601
0030-3585 Opera Journal 6602
0030-3593 European Intelligence 1484
0030-3607 Opera News 6602
0030-3615 Operation L A P L†
0030-3631 Operations Forestieres et de Scierie 3714
0030-364X Operations Research 2433
0030-3658 Operations Research - Management Science 1257
0030-3674 Opereshonzu Risachi 1783
0030-3690 Opernwelt 6602
0030-3720 Ophthalmic Literature†
0030-3747 Ophthalmic Research 6048
0030-3755 Ophthalmologica 6048
0030-3763 Ophthalmologist†
0030-3798 Opinion†
0030-3836 Klank en Weerklank *changed to* 1569-9420 6582
0030-3852 Opportunities 7458
0030-3879 Opsaal†
0030-3887 Opsearch 1783
0030-3895 Opstina†
0030-3917 Optica Pura y Aplicada 7081
0030-3968 Optician 6049
0030-3976 Opticien Belge†
0030-3984 Opticien-Lunetier†
0030-3992 Optics & Laser Technology 7082
0030-400X Optics and Spectroscopy 7083
0030-4018 Optics Communications 7083
0030-4026 Optik 7083
0030-4034 Optika i Spektroskopiya 7083
0030-4050 Optima 6475
0030-4069 Optimist (Abilene) 2295
0030-4085 Optometric Management 6049
0030-4107 Optometric World
0030-4123 Optometrie 6049
0030-4131 Opus†
0030-414X Opuscula Medica†
0030-4166 Or Hamizrach†
0030-4174 Ora et Labora 7810
0030-4182 Orafo Orologiaio
0030-4204 Oral Health Magazine 5859
0030-4212 Oral Research Abstracts†
0030-4239 Orang Peladang 144
0030-428X Orange County Illustrated†
0030-4298 Orange County Jewish Heritage 3556
0030-431X Orangeburg Historical and Genealogical Record
0030-4328 Oranje-Nassau Post†
0030-4336 Orante†
0030-4352 Oratoriana†
0030-4360 Orbanismo†
0030-4379 Orbis 5158
0030-4387 Orbis (Kidlington) 7256
0030-4425 Orbis (Nuneaton) 5428
0030-4433 Orbit 2894
0030-445X Orbita†
0030-4468 Das Orchester 6602
0030-4476 The Orchid Review 3746
0030-4484 Orchideeen 806
0030-4492 Ord & Bild 5232
0030-4506 Ordem dos Medicos. Boletim
0030-4514 Order of Scottish Clans Lion Rampant†
0030-4549 Ordinismo†
0030-4565 Ordre des Medecins. Bulletin 5690
0030-4581 Ordu Dergisi
0030-459X Ore†
0030-4611 Oregon Agriculture†
0030-462X Oregon Beverage Analyst†
0030-4638 Oregon Business Review†
0030-4662 Oregon Daily Emerald 2295
0030-4697 Oregon Grange Bulletin 144
0030-4727 Oregon Historical Quarterly 4307
0030-4743 Oregon Music Educator
0030-4751 Oregon Nurse 5977
0030-4786 Oregon Purchasor
0030-4794 Oregon Science Teacher 7896
0030-4816 Oregon State Bar Bulletin 4754
0030-4832 Oregon State University. Forest Research Laboratory. Index†
0030-4840 Oregon Teamster 4600
0030-4859 Oregon Voter Digest
0030-4875 Orfeo
0030-4883 The Organ 6602
0030-4891 Organ Show-Business
0030-4905 Organi di Trasmissione 3214
0030-4948 Organic Preparations and Procedures International 2128
0030-4964 Organisation Gestion des Enterprises
0030-5006 Organische Land -und Gartenkultur†
0030-5014 Organiser 3886
0030-5081 Organizer†
0030-509X Organizzazione Ferroviaria
0030-5103 Organizzazione Industriale†
0030-5138 Organometallic Compounds
0030-5154 Organon†
0030-5162 Organometallics in Chemical Synthesis†
0030-5170 L'Orgue 6603
0030-5189 Oriens Antiquus†
0030-5197 Oriens Extremus 558
0030-5227 Orient 558
0030-5251 Orientacion Docente
0030-526X Orientacion Economica†
0030-5278 Oriental Art 558
0030-5308 Oriental Geographer 4023
0030-5316 Oriental Insects 857
0030-5324 Oriental Institute. Journal 558
0030-5332 Oriental Rug
0030-5340 Journal of Oriental Society of Australia 553
0030-5359 Oriental Tide
0030-5367 Orientalia 558
0030-5375 Orientalia Christiana Periodica 7739
0030-5383 Orientalistische Literaturzeitung 558
0030-5391 Orientamenti Pedagogici 2894
0030-5405 Orientamenti Sociali†
0030-543X Orientations 1870
0030-5448 Orientations 510
0030-5464 Oriente Europeo†
0030-5472 Oriente Moderno 558
0030-5502 Orientierung 7810
0030-5510 Origin†
0030-5529 The Original Art Report 510
0030-5537 University of Victoria. Department of Hispanic and Italian Studies. Original Works†
0030-5545 Original Works; Art, Poetry, Fiction†
0030-5553 The Oriole 912
0030-557X Orion 579
0030-5588 Orissa Education
0030-5596 Orita 7668
0030-560X Orizont 5346
0030-5618 Orizzonti Aperti
0030-5634 Orizzonti Professionali† 8979
0030-5650 Orkestra
0030-5669 Orleans Parish Medical Society. Bulletin†
0030-5677 Ormanci Gazetesi
0030-5685 Ornis Fennica 912
0030-5707 Der Ornithologische Beobachter 912
0030-5723 Ornithologische Mitteilungen 912
0030-5804 Orphic Lute
0030-5812 Orta Dogu†
0030-5820 Orthodox Life 7705
0030-5839 Orthodox Word 7705
0030-5863 Orthopaedics - Oxford†
0030-588X Orthopaedische Praxis 6069
0030-5898 Orthopedic Clinics of North America 6069
0030-5901 Seikei Geka 6072
0030-591X Orthopod†
0030-5936 Ortodoncia 5860
0030-5944 Ortodontia 5860
0030-5979 Ortopedici e Sanitari 6070
0030-6002 Orvosi Hetilap 5691
0030-6010 Orvosi Konyvtaros†
0030-6029 Orvosi Szemle†
0030-6037 Orvoskepzes 5691
0030-6045 Orvostudomany†
0030-6053 Oryx 959
0030-607X Orzel Bialy†
0030-6088 Oosakafu Kisho Geppo 6393
0030-6096 Osaka City Medical Journal 5691
0030-6118 Oosaka Ika Daigaku Zasshi 5690
0030-6126 Osaka Journal of Mathematics 5523
0030-6134 Oosaka Kogyo Daigaku Kiyo. Jinbun Shakai Hen 4467
0030-6150 Shika Igaku 5865
0030-6169 Medical Journal of Osaka University†
0030-6177 Osaka University. Faculty of Engineering. Technology Reports†
0030-6185 Osgoode Hall Law Journal 4754
0030-6207 Journal of the Oslo City Hospitals†
0030-6223 Osnovaniya, Fundamenty i Mekhanika Gruntov 3280
0030-6231 Ospedale 4108
0030-624X Ospedale al Mare. Archivio
0030-6258 Ospedali d'Italia†
0030-6266 Ospedali d'Italia - Chirurgia†
0030-6274 Ospedali Italiani - Pediatria e Specialita Chirurgiche†
0030-6290 Osservatore Legale†
0030-6304 Osservatore Politico Letterario
0030-6320 Osservatore Tributario e Rassegna Tributaria†
0030-6339 Ostdeutscher Literatur-Anzeiger†
0030-6347 Ost-West-Kurier
0030-6363 Osten 5232
0030-6371 Osteopathic Physician†
0030-638X Osteroder Zeitung
0030-6398 Oesterreich - Polen, Austria - Polska
0030-6428 Osteuropa 7161
0030-6436 Osteuropa-Naturwissenschaft und Technik†
0030-6444 Osteuropa-Recht 4754
0030-6452 Osteuropaeische Rundschau†
0030-6460 Osteuropa-Wirtschaft 1157
0030-6479 Ostfriesland†
0030-6487 Ostkirchliche Studien† 8979
0030-6517 Ostomy Quarterly†
0030-6525 Ostrich 913
0030-655X Otazky Miru a Socialismu†
0030-6584 Otia
0030-6592 Oto†
0030-6622 Journal of Otolaryngology of Japan 6082
0030-6657 Otolaryngologia Polska 6083

ISSN

0031-7640	Philippine Journal of Nutrition†
0031-7659	Philippine Journal of Ophthalmology 6050
0031-7667	Philippine Journal of Pediatrics 6102
0031-7675	Philippine Journal of Public Administration 7460
0031-7683	Philippine Journal of Science 7898
0031-7691	Philippine Journal of Surgical Specialities 6255
0031-7705	Philippine Journal of Veterinary Medicine 8804
0031-7713	Philippine Junior Red Cross Magazine†
0031-7721	Philippine Law Journal 4758
0031-773X	Philippine Manager
0031-7748	Philippine Medical Association. Journal
0031-7764	Philippine Progress†
0031-7799	Philippine Scientific Journal 5695
0031-7810	Philippine Sociological Review 8125
0031-7829	Philippine Statistician
0031-7837	Philippine Studies 4469
0031-7845	Philippine Tax Journal
0031-7853	Philippine Women's University Administrative News 2296
0031-787X	Philippines Labor Relations Journal†
0031-7888	Philippines Transportation
0031-790X	Philips Music Herald†
0031-7926	Philips Technical Review†
0031-7969	Philobiblon†
0031-7977	Philological Quarterly 5160
0031-7985	Philologus 2239
0031-7993	Philosopher's Index 6962
0031-8000	Philosophia 6940
0031-8019	Philosophia Mathematica 6940
0031-8027	Philosophia Naturalis 6940
0031-8035	Philosophia Reformata 6940
0031-8043	Philosophical Association. Journal†
0031-8051	Philosophical Books 6963
0031-806X	Philosophical Forum 6940
0031-8078	Philosophical Journal†
0031-8094	The Philosophical Quarterly 6941
0031-8108	Philosophical Review 6941
0031-8116	Philosophical Studies 6941
0031-8159	Philosophische Rundschau 6942
0031-8167	Philosophische Zeitspiegel
0031-8175	Philosophischer Literaturanzeiger 6942
0031-8183	Philosophisches Jahrbuch 6942
0031-8191	Philosophy 6942
0031-8205	Philosophy and Phenomenological Research 6942
0031-8213	Philosophy and Rhetoric 6943
0031-8221	Philosophy East and West 6943
0031-8248	Philosophy of Science 7898
0031-8256	Philosophy Today 6944
0031-8264	Philotelia 6898
0031-8272	Philwomenian 2296
0031-8299	Phoenix (Toronto, 1946) 2239
0031-8310	Phoenix†
0031-8329	Phoenix 411
0031-8337	Phoenix†
0031-8388	Phonetica 5161
0031-8396	Phoni tou Evangeliou 7669
0031-8442	Photo†
0031-8485	Photo Dealer†
0031-8515	Photographic Processor†
0031-8523	Photo Interpretation 4023
0031-8531	P M A Magazine 6972
0031-8566	Photo Screen
0031-8574	Photo-Technik und -Wirtschaft†
0031-8604	Photo Trade of Japan†
0031-8639	Photo Typesetting
0031-8655	Photochemistry and Photobiology 2139
0031-868X	The Photogrammetric Record 4024
0031-8698	Photographer 6974
0031-8744	Photographic Processing changed to 1554-6888
0031-8833	Photon
0031-885X	Photoplay†
0031-8868	Phronesis 6944
0031-8876	Phytiatrie-Phythopharmacie†
0031-8884	Phycologia 808
0031-8906	Phylon 8125
0031-8949	Physica Scripta 7031
0031-8973	Physical Education Newsletter†
0031-8981	Physical Educator 3076
0031-9007	Physical Review Letters 7032
0031-9015	Physical Society of Japan. Journal 7032
0031-9023	Physical Therapy 6113
0031-9031	Physicians' Association of Madras. Journal
0031-904X	Physicians' Basic Index†
0031-9058	Physicians' Drug Manual†
0031-9066	Physician's Management†
0031-9074	Physicians Market Place
0031-9082	Seibutsu Butsuri Kagaku 745
0031-9090	Physics and Chemistry of Glasses changed to 1753-3562 2041
0031-9104	Physics and Chemistry of Liquids 7062
0031-9120	Physics Education 7033
0031-9147	Physics in Canada 7033
0031-9155	Physics in Medicine and Biology 7033
0031-918X	Physics of Metals and Metallography 6328
0031-9201	Physics of the Earth and Planetary Interiors 2787
0031-921X	The Physics Teacher 7034
0031-9228	Physics Today 7034
0031-9252	Physik in Unserer Zeit 7034
0031-9317	Physiologia Plantarum 808
0031-9333	Physiological Reviews 926
0031-9341	Nihon Seirigaku Zasshi 926
0031-9376	The Physiologist 926
0031-9384	Physiology & Behavior 927
0031-9392	Physiotherapie†
0031-9406	Physiotherapy 6114
0031-9414	Physis 7898
0031-9422	Phytochemistry 808
0031-9430	Phytologia
0031-9449	Phytomorphology 809
0031-9457	Phyton 809
0031-9465	Phytopathologia Mediterranea 809
0031-949X	Phytopathology 809

0031-9511	Phytoprotection 809
0031-952X	Pi Mu Epsilon Journal 5524
0031-9538	Pianeta
0031-9546	Piano Guild Notes 6605
0031-9562	Piano Technicians Journal 6605
0031-9570	La Pianura 1408
0031-9589	Picchiarello†
0031-9597	A.P.I†
0031-9600	Il Piccolo Missonario 7670
0031-9627	Pick'n' and Sing'n' Gather'n'. Newsletter
0031-9635	Pictorial†
0031-9651	Pictorial News Review 7165
0031-966X	Picturegoer†
0031-9678	Pictures & Prints†
0031-9686	Pictures on Exhibit†
0031-9694	Picturescope†
0031-9708	Pie†
0031-9716	Pierian Spring†
0031-9732	Pig Breeders Gazette†
0031-9775	Pig Progress†
0031-9783	Pigeon News†
0031-9791	Piggin String
0031-9805	Pilgrim 7670
0031-983X	Pin High†
0031-9856	Pine Cone
0031-9864	Rap†
0031-9880	Pingrin†
0031-9899	Pinheiros Farmaceutico†
0031-9902	Pinkster Protestant†
0031-9910	Pinpointer†
0031-9929	Pins and Needles†
0031-9945	Pintores 6720
0031-9953	Pinturas y Acabados Industriales† 8981
0031-9961	Rivista degli Infermieri†
0031-9988	Pioneer†
0032-0013	Pioneer America Society. Newsletter 4308
0032-0048	Pionerskaya Pravda 2207
0032-0056	Pionier 7770
0032-0099	Pionir-Kekec†
0032-0102	Pioneriya†
0032-0137	Pipeline†
0032-0161	The Pipe Smoker's Ephemeris 8486
0032-017X	Pipe World
0032-0188	Pipeline & Gas Journal 6788
0032-020X	Pipes & Pipelines International changed to 1471-3101 6789
0032-0234	Piraiki-Patraiki 8456
0032-0242	Pirkka 1837
0032-0277	Piscator†
0032-0293	Pit & Quarry 6476
0032-0315	Pittsburgh Business Review†
0032-0323	Pittsburgh Catholic 7812
0032-0331	Pittsburgh Legal Journal (Daily Edition)†
0032-034X	Pittsburgh Musician 6606
0032-0358	Pittsburgh Symphony Orchestra Program 6606
0032-0382	Pivot (Philadelphia)†
0032-0404	Pjichk
0032-0420	The Plain Truth 6944
0032-0439	Plain Truth†
0032-0447	Plains Anthropologist 351
0032-0498	Plaisir de la Maison†
0032-051X	Plaisirs Equestre†
0032-0528	Plamuk 5233
0032-0536	Plan 3215
0032-0544	Plan Canada 4423
0032-0560	Plan 4422
0032-0579	Plan
0032-0587	Plan Ahead†
0032-0617	Plane and Pilot 68
0032-0633	Planetary and Space Science 579
0032-065X	Planned Parenthood Report†
0032-0668	Planned Savings†
0032-0684	Planning & Changing 3029
0032-0692	Planning and Development in the Netherlands†
0032-0706	Planning Comment†
0032-0765	Planseeberichte fuer Pulvermetallurgie†
0032-0781	Plant and Cell Physiology 835
0032-079X	Plant and Soil 810
0032-0803	Plant Breeding Abstracts 185
0032-082X	Plant Engineering 3215
0032-0838	Plant Engineer 3215
0032-0854	Plant Operating Management†
0032-0862	Plant Pathology 811
0032-0870	Florida. Department of Agriculture and Consumer Services. Plant Pathology Circular 789
0032-0889	Plant Physiology 812
0032-0897	Plant Protection Abstracts†
0032-0919	Plant Science Bulletin 812
0032-0935	Planta 813
0032-0943	Planta Medica 6875
0032-096X	Malaysian Rubber Board. Planters Bulletin 7825
0032-0978	Planters' Chronicle 3660
0032-0986	Planters Journal and Agriculturist
0032-0994	Plantes Medicinales et Phytotherapie†
0032-1036	Plasterer and Cement Mason 4600
0032-1052	Plastic and Reconstructive Surgery 6255
0032-1060	Plastic Industry Notes†
0032-1079	Plastic Laminating†
0032-1087	Plastic-Revue Edition Schweiz†
0032-1133	Plasticos em Revista 7096
0032-1141	Plasticos y Resinas†
0032-115X	Plastics Abstracts†
0032-1176	Plastics Design & Processing†
0032-1192	Plastics in Engineering†
0032-1206	Plastics Industry News Japan†
0032-1214	Plastics Industry Notes†
0032-1249	Plastics, Rubber and Leather Industries Journal
0032-1257	Plastics Technology 7098
0032-1265	Plastics Trends†
0032-1338	Plastverarbeiter 7098
0032-1346	Plateau†
0032-1354	Plateau†

0032-1400	Platinum Metals Review (Print)†
0032-1435	Plavi Vjesnik†
0032-1443	Play Schools Newsletter
0032-1451	Playback†
0032-146X	Playbill (Theatre Edition) 8476
0032-1478	Playboy (Chicago) 6297
0032-1486	Players (De Kalb)†
0032-1508	Playhour
0032-1516	Playing Fields†
0032-1532	Playmen†
0032-1540	Plays 8476
0032-1567	Playthings 4061
0032-1583	Psychologies 8881
0032-1591	Plomberie Chauffage et Climatisation†
0032-163X	Plumb Line 2269
0032-1656	Plumbing 4124
0032-1680	The Wholesaler 4127
0032-1699	Plumbing and Heating Journal
0032-1737	Plymouth Bulletin 368
0032-1753	Plymouth Traveler†
0032-1761	Plyn 6789
0032-1796	Pobeda
0032-180X	Pochvovedenie 248
0032-1826	Pocket List of Railroad Officials 8621
0032-1869	Podnikova Organizace†
0032-1885	Poem 5430
0032-1893	Poesia de Venezuela 5430
0032-1907	Poesia en la Calle
0032-1915	Poesia-Poesia
0032-1923	Poesie
0032-1931	Poesie Vivante
0032-194X	Poet 5430
0032-1966	Poet Lore 5430
0032-1974	Cahiers de Litterature et de Poesie: Poetes et Leurs Amis†
0032-1990	Poeti Italiani Contemporanei†
0032-2024	Poetique 5234
0032-2032	Poetry (Chicago) 5430
0032-2040	Poetry & Audience 5431
0032-2059	Poetry Australia†
0032-2075	Poetry India†
0032-2083	Poetry Market
0032-2105	Poetry Nippon
0032-2113	Poetry Northwest 5431
0032-2156	Poetry Review 5431
0032-2164	Poetry Singapore†
0032-2199	Poetry Venture†
0032-2202	Poetry Wales 5432
0032-2237	Poezja†
0032-2245	Pogledi (Skopje)
0032-2253	Pogledi i Iskustva u Odgoju i Obrazovanju†
0032-227X	Poids Lourd†
0032-2288	Poilu Lorrain
0032-230X	Point of View
0032-2318	Point of View
0032-2326	Point 3 4469
0032-2342	Pointer (London)†
0032-2350	The Pointer (West Point) 2297
0032-2377	Poirieria 960
0032-2385	Poissonnier Belge
0032-2393	Pojistny Obzor 4519
0032-2407	Pokret†
0032-2415	Pokrof 7705
0032-2423	Pokroky Matematiky, Fyziky a Astronomie 7898
0032-2431	Pola Esperantisto†
0032-244X	Poland†
0032-2458	Poland and Germany (East & West)†
0032-2474	Polar Record 4024
0032-2482	Polar Times 4024
0032-2490	Polarforschung 2715
0032-2504	Pole et Tropiques
0032-2520	Polet†
0032-2547	Poletarac†
0032-2555	Police 2663
0032-2563	Police†
0032-2571	Police Chief 2663
0032-258X	The Police Journal 2663
0032-2598	Police Life 2663
0032-261X	Police World
0032-2628	Policia Portuguesa Revista Ilustrada†
0032-2636	Il Policlinico. Sezione Chirurgica
0032-2644	Il Policlinico. Sezione Pratica
0032-2687	Policy Sciences 7166
0032-2709	Poligrafico Italiano
0032-2717	Poligrafiya 7325
0032-2725	Polimery 2129
0032-2784	Polish Affairs†
0032-2792	Polish American Journal 3558
0032-2806	Polish American Studies
0032-2814	Polish Building Abstracts†
0032-2822	Polish Co-Operative Review†
0032-2857	Polish Endocrinology see 0423-104X 5892
0032-2873	Polish Facts and Figures†
0032-2881	Polish Foreign Trade†
0032-289X	Polish Literature†
0032-2903	Polish Machinery News†
0032-2911	Polish Maritime News†
0032-2938	Polish Medical Journal†
0032-2946	Polish Music 6606
0032-2954	Polish News
0032-2962	Polish Perspectives†
0032-2970	Polish Review 3930
0032-2989	Polish Scientific Periodicals-Contents†
0032-3004	Polish Technical and Economic Abstracts†
0032-3012	Polish Technical Review†
0032-3020	Polish Weekly†
0032-3039	Polish Western Affairs†
0032-3047	Polish Western Association of America. Quarterly
0032-3055	Politecnica 3215
0032-3063	Politica del Diritto 4759
0032-3071	Politica e Mezzogiorno†
0032-3101	Politica Internazionale 7260

ISSN

DIRECTORY 2010 0034-4834 9059

0033-9423 La Rassegna della Letteratura Italiana **5357**
0033-9431 Rassegna della Letteratura Odontoiatrica
0033-944X Rassegna della Letteratura sui Cicli Economici
0033-9458 Rassegna della Stampa†
0033-9482 Rassegna di Cultura e Vita Scolastica†
0033-9490 Rassegna di Dermatologia e Sifilografia†
0033-9504 Rassegna di Diritto Cinematografico, Teatrale e della Radiotelevisione
0033-9512 Rassegna di Diritto Pubblico† **8984**
0033-9547 Rassegna di Legislazione Italiana Nei Rapporti Internazionali†
0033-9555 Rassegna di Medicina Sperimentale†
0033-9563 Rassegna di Patologia dell'Apparato Respiratorio **6218**
0033-9571 Rassegna di Pedagogia **2903**
0033-958X Rassegna di Politica e di Storia
0033-9598 Rassegna di Scienze Filosofiche†
0033-9601 Rassegna di Servizio Sociale **8064**
0033-961X Rassegna di Statistiche del Lavoro†
0033-9636 Rassegna di Studi Psichiatrici†
0033-9644 Rassegna di Teologia
0033-9652 Rassegna ed Archivio di Chirurgia†
0033-9679 Rassegna Giuridica ed Economica sui Danni di Guerra†
0033-9687 Rassegna Grafica **7327**
0033-9695 Rassegna Internazionale di Clinica e Terapia†
0033-9725 Rassegna Italiana di Linguistica Applicata **5165**
0033-9733 Rassegna Italiana di Ricerca Psichica
0033-975X Rassegna Lucchese†
0033-9768 Rassegna Medica e Culturale†
0033-9776 Rassegna Medica Sarda†
0033-9784 Rassegna Melodrammatica† **8984**
0033-9792 Rassegna Mensile di Israel **7728**
0033-9806 Rassegna Musicale Curci
0033-9822 Rassegna Petrolifera†
0033-9857 Rassegna Sovietica
0033-9865 Rassegna Speleologica Italiana†
0033-9873 Rassegna Storica del Risorgimento **4256**
0033-9881 Rassegna Storica Toscana **4256**
0033-9911 Rassegna Trimestrale di Odontoiatria†
0033-992X Rassegna di Urologia e Nefrologia†
0033-9938 Raster†
0033-9946 Rastitel'nye Resursy **814**
0033-9989 Der Ratgeber†
0034-0006 Ratio **6946**
0034-0030 Individualist†
0034-009X Raumausstattung Report†
0034-0111 Raumforschung und Raumordnung **4436**
0034-0138 Rave†
0034-0146 The Raven (Lynchburg) **913**
0034-0162 Ray Palmer's Forum†
0034-0170 Rayito (Counselor's Edition)†
0034-0197 Rayons
0034-0219 La Raza Newspaper **3560**
0034-0227 Razgledi **5358**
0034-0235 Razon y Fe **4471**
0034-0243 Razonoda Miliona†
0034-026X Razvedka i Okhrana Nedr **6477**
0034-0278 Razvitak **5236**
0034-0294 Re: Search†
0034-0316 Reach Out†
0034-0332 Reactor Technology†
0034-0359 Read Magazine **3078**
0034-0375 Reader's Digest **3986**
0034-0383 Reader's Digest (Asian Edition) **3875**
0034-0391 Reader's Digest (Australian Edition) **3796**
0034-0405 Reader's Digest (British Edition) **3870**
0034-0413 Reader's Digest†
0034-0421 Reader's Digest (Indian Edition) **3888**
0034-043X Reader's Digest (Japanese Edition)†
0034-0448 Reader's Digest (New Zealand Edition) **3919**
0034-0456 Reader's Digest (South African Edition) **3949**
0034-0464 Readers' Guide to Periodical Literature **13**
0034-0502 Reading Horizons **3045**
0034-0510 Reading Improvement **3045**
0034-0537 Reading Newsreport†
0034-0545 Reading Quarterly†
0034-0553 Reading Research Quarterly **2903**
0034-0561 The Reading Teacher **2903**
0034-057X Reaktorn†
0034-0588 Real†
0034-060X Real Academia de Cordoba de Ciencias, Bellas Letras y Nobles Artes. Boletin **5358**
0034-0626 Real Academia de la Historia. Boletin **4158**
0034-0634 Real Academia Nacional de Medicina. Anales **5702**
0034-0642 Real Confessions Magazine
0034-0693 Real Estate Investment Planning Checklist and Forms†
0034-0707 Real Estate Forum **7608**
0034-0723 Real Estate Investment Ideas†
0034-0731 Real Estate Investment Planning†
0034-0758 Real Estate Law Brief Case†
0034-0766 Real Estate News (New York)†
0034-0790 Real Estate Review **7609**
0034-0839 Real Life Confessions
0034-0847 Real Living†
0034-0855 Real Property, Probate and Trust Journal *changed to* Real Property, Trust and Estate Law Journal **4905**
0034-0863 Real Sociedad Arqueologica. Boletin Arqueologico *changed to* 1695-5862 **413**
0034-0898 Real West†
0034-091X The Realist†
0034-0936 Realites Libyennes
0034-0944 Realites
0034-0960 Reality **7814**
0034-0979 Reality†
0034-0987 Reality (Alexandria)
0034-0995 Realta†
0034-1029 Realta Sovietica†
0034-1037 Realtor Headlines†
0034-1045 Realty and Building **7610**
0034-1061 Realty Review†
0034-1118 Rebe und Wein **609**
0034-1142 Rec Naroda **5236**
0034-1150 Recall†
0034-1185 Recent Publications on Governmental Problems†
0034-1193 Recenti Progressi in Medicina **5702**
0034-1207 Recenzija†
0034-1231 C A R D A N. Bulletin d'Information et de Liaison†
0034-124X Recherche Sociale **7995**
0034-1258 Recherches de Science Religieuse **7814**
0034-1282 Recherches Sociographiques **8127**
0034-1290 Rechnoi Transport **8658**
0034-1312 Recht der Jugend und des Bildungswesens **2166**
0034-1320 Recht der Schiffahrt
0034-1339 Recht im Amt **7465**
0034-1363 Rechtspflegerblatt **4766**
0034-138X Rechtsprechung in Strafsachen **2667**
0034-1398 Rechtstheorie **4767**
0034-1479 Reconciliation Quarterly **7772**
0034-1487 Reconstruction **7728**
0034-1495 Reconstructionist **7728**
0034-1509 Rencontre Orient Occident†
0034-1517 Record (San Francisco)†
0034-1525 Lancashire Authors' Association. Record
0034-1541 The Record (New York, 1940) **4601**
0034-155X Record Collector (Leicester)
0034-1568 The Record Collector (Broomfield) **6610**
0034-1592 Record Research†
0034-1614 Record Stockman **298**
0034-1622 Record World
0034-1630 Recorded Sound†
0034-1649 Recorder
0034-1657 Recorder†
0034-1703 Records and Statistics†
0034-1711 Records Management Journal†
0034-1738 Records of Huntingdonshire **4256**
0034-1746 Records of the Month†
0034-1843 Recueil de Medecine Veterinaire d'Alfort†
0034-1851 Recueil des Brevets d'Invention **6757**
0034-1878 Recueil Juridique de l'Est Securite Sociale **4520**
0034-1886 Recueil Officiel des Marques de Fabrique et de Commerce†
0034-1932 Recusant History **7814**
0034-1940 Red and Black (Washington) **2298**
0034-1959 Red and Green **2298**
0034-1967 Red Cedar Review **5236**
0034-1975 Red Clay Reader†
0034-1991 Panorama†
0034-2025 Red Notes
0034-2068 Red Star Weekly†
0034-2106 Redbook **8882**
0034-2122 Redeemer's Voice†
0034-2165 Redstart **7902**
0034-219X Reed's Aircraft & Equipment News†
0034-222X Reeducation Orthophonique **6084**
0034-2238 Reel
0034-2254 Referatekartei Korrosion-Korrosionsschutz†
0034-2262 Bibliographie Philosophie†
0034-2297 Referativnyi Zhurnal. Avtomobil'nyi i Gorodskoi Transport **8528**
0034-2300 Referativnyi Zhurnal. Biologiya **718**
0034-2343 Referativnyi Zhurnal. Fizika **7049**
0034-236X Referativnyi Zhurnal. Geofizika **2720**
0034-2378 Referativnyi Zhurnal. Geografiya **4036**
0034-2386 Referativnyi Zhurnal. Gornoe Delo **6486**
0034-2408 Referativnyi Zhurnal. Issledovanie Kosmicheskogo Prostranstva **76**
0034-2432 Referativnyi Zhurnal. Legkaya Promyshlennost'. Tekhnologiya i Oborudovaniye. Otdel'nyi Vypusk **1260**
0034-2440 Referativnyi Zhurnal. Lesovedenie i Lesovodstvo **3709**
0034-2459 Referativnyi Zhurnal. Mashinostroitel'nye Materialy, Konstruktsii i Raschet Detalei Mashin. Gidroprivod **3233**
0034-2467 Referativnyi Zhurnal. Matematika **5548**
0034-2475 Referativnyi Zhurnal. Meditsinskaya Geografiya **5750**
0034-2483 Referativnyi Zhurnal. Mekhanika **3233**
0034-2491 Referativnyi Zhurnal. Metallurgiya **6341**
0034-2505 Referativnyi Zhurnal. Metrologiya i Izmeritel'naya Tekhnika **6408**
0034-2513 Referativnyi Zhurnal. Nasosostroenie i Kompressorostroenie. Kholodil'noe Mashinostroenie **4128**
0034-2521 Referativnyi Zhurnal. Oborudovanie Pishchevoi Promyshlennosti **5462**
0034-2548 Referativnyi Zhurnal. Pochvovedenie i Agrokhimiya **185**
0034-2556 Referativnyi Zhurnal. Promyshlennyi Transport **8529**
0034-2580 Referativnyi Zhurnal. Tekhnologiya i Oborudovanie Tsellyulozno-vumazhnogo i Poligraficheskogo Proizvodstva†
0034-2599 Referativnyi Zhurnal. Tekhnologiya Mashinostroeniya **3234**
0034-2602 Referativnyi Zhurnal. Traktory i Sel'skokhozyaistvennye Mashiny i Orudiya **185**
0034-2610 Referativnyi Zhurnal. Truboprovodnyi Transport **3234**
0034-2629 Referativnyi Zhurnal. Turbostroenie. Kotlostroenie **3234**
0034-2637 Referativnyi Zhurnal. Voprosy Tekhnicheskogo Progressa i Organizatsii Proizvodstva v Mashinostroenii **3234**
0034-2645 Referativnyi Zhurnal. Vzaimodeistvie Raznykh Vidov Transporta i Konteinernye Perevozki **8529**
0034-2653 Referativnyi Zhurnal. Yadernye Reaktory† **8984**
0034-267X Referativnyi Zhurnal. Radiotekhnika **3117**
0034-2696 Referatovy Vyber z Chirurgie†
0034-270X Referatovy Vyber z Chorob Infekcnich†
0034-2726 Referatovy Vyber z Endokrinologie†
0034-2734 Referatovy Vyber z Fysiologie†
0034-2742 Referatovy Vyber z Gastroenterologie†
0034-2750 Referatovy Vyber z Gerontologie a Geriatrie†
0034-2777 Referatovy Vyber z Lekarenstvi†
0034-2785 Referatovy Vyber z Lekarskeho Tisku o Vychove a Doskolovani Zdravotnickych Pracovniku†
0034-2793 Referatovy Vyber z Neurologie†
0034-2807 Referatovy Vyber z Oftalmologie†
0034-2815 Referatovy Vyber z Onkologie†
0034-2831 Referatovy Vyber z Otorhinolaryngologie a Foniatrie†
0034-284X Referatovy Vyber z Patologicke Anatomie†
0034-2858 Referatovy Vyber z Pediatrie†
0034-2866 Referatovy Vyber z Porodnictvi a Gynekologie†
0034-2882 Referatovy Vyber z Revmatologie (Print) *changed to* 1214-5076 **5750**
0034-2890 Referatovy Vyber z Pneumologie a Tuberkulosy†
0034-2912 Refarensu **4767**
0034-2947 Reflector (Amersfoort) **4520**
0034-2963 The Reflector Newsletter **580**
0034-2971 Reflets et Perspectives de la Vie Economique **1164**
0034-298X Reflets Guildiens†
0034-303X Reformation Review†
0034-3048 Reformation Today **7772**
0034-3056 Reformed World **7772**
0034-3072 Reformed Theological Review **7673**
0034-3080 Reformer† **8984**
0034-3129 Refrigerated Transporter **8675**
0034-3137 Refrigeration†
0034-3218 Regelrecht **34**
0034-3250 Regensburger Bistumsblatt **7673**
0034-3269 Der Reggeboge **3560**
0034-3293 Regio Basiliensis **4026**
0034-3315 Region Six Sentinel†
0034-3323 Regional Action†
0034-334X International Seismological Centre. Regional Catalogue of Earthquakes **2784**
0034-3358 Regional Cultural Institute. Journal
0034-3390 Regional Spotlight†
0034-3404 Regional Studies **4425**
0034-3412 Regione e Potere Locale†
0034-3439 Regionwide†
0034-3471 Regmaker
0034-348X Regmi Research Series **4187**
0034-3498 Il Regno **7814**
0034-3501 Rehabilitation in South Africa†
0034-351X Rihabiriteshon Igaku **6116**
0034-3528 Rehabilitation†
0034-3536 Die Rehabilitation **6115**
0034-3552 Rehabilitation Counseling Bulletin **4069**
0034-3579 Rehabilitation Literature†
0034-3609 Rehovot†
0034-3617 Reinforced Plastics **7099**
0034-3633 Reino†
0034-3641 Reinsurance Reporter **4520**
0034-365X Reinwardtia **815**
0034-3668 Deutsche Reisebuero-Zeitung†
0034-3684 Reiss-Davis Clinic Bulletin†
0034-3692 Reiter Revue International **8297**
0034-3714 Reito **4126**
0034-3765 Relacoes Humanas†
0034-3781 Relations **8065**
0034-379X Relations Industrielles **1705**
0034-3803 Relations Latines
0034-3811 Relations Publiques Informations **34**
0034-3838 Relazioni†
0034-3846 Relazioni Internazionali†
0034-3862 Relazioni Sociali†
0034-3897 Relics **4310**
0034-3900 Relics†
0034-3935 Religioese Graphik
0034-3943 Religion and Church in the Communist Orbit†
0034-3951 Religion and Society
0034-401X Religion Teacher's Journal **7675**
0034-4036 Religiose nell'Apostolato Diretto†
0034-4052 Religious and Theological Resources†
0034-4060 Religious Book Review Index **7699**
0034-4087 Religious Education **7676**
0034-4095 Religious Humanism **7676**
0034-4109 R N A Newsletter **4582**
0034-4117 Religious Periodicals Index†
0034-4125 Religious Studies **7676**
0034-4168 Remag
0034-4176 Remainders' Book Italiano† **8985**
0034-4184 Remanso† **8985**
0034-4230 Reminder†
0034-4249 Remodeling Contractor (Arlington)†
0034-4257 Remote Sensing of Environment **4026**
0034-4265 Removals and Storage **8509**
0034-4273 Rempart
0034-429X Renaissance and Reformation **5359**
0034-4338 Renaissance Quarterly **5359**
0034-4346 Renascence **5359**
0034-4354 Rencontres Sous le Signe de la Langue Francaise†
0034-4370 Rendez-Vous†
0034-4389 Rendez Vous
0034-4397 Rendez-Vous de la Mode†
0034-4400 Rendezvous **4471**
0034-4419 Rendiconti†
0034-4451 Renfro Valley Bugle **6610**
0034-446X Renovacion
0034-4478 Renovacion
0034-4486 Renovatio†
0034-4508 Rensselaer Engineer **8436**
0034-4516 Rent-All Magazine†
0034-4524 Rental Equipment Register **1839**
0034-4567 Repertoire Bibliographique de la Philosophie **6963**
0034-4575 Repertoire des Voyages†
0034-4591 Repertorio Analitico della Stampa Italiana. Quotidiani e Periodici†
0034-4613 Repertorio Centroamericano†
0034-4648 Repertuar Khudozhestvennoi Samodeyatel'nosti†
0034-4656 Varta Report
0034-4664 Report from Germany†
0034-4680 Report on Education of the Disadvantaged†
0034-4737 Report on World Affairs **7177**
0034-4745 Reportage **5236**
0034-4753 Reporter
0034-4761 Reporter (Newcastle)
0034-4788 Reporter
0034-4796 Reporter for Conscience' Sake
0034-4818 Reportero Industrial **5459**
0034-4826 I A B C Notebook†
0034-4834 Reporting on Governments

ISSN

9060 0034-4842 ULRICH'S PERIODICALS

0034-4842 Union of Japanese Scientists and Engineers. Reports of Statistical Application Research **5543**
0034-4877 Reports on Mathematical Physics **7037**
0034-4885 Reports on Progress in Physics **7037**
0034-4893 Representation **7177**
0034-4907 Representative Research in Social Psychology†
0034-4915 Representor
0034-4931 Reprints from the Soviet Press
0034-4982 Reprographics†
0034-5016 National Central Library Newsletter **5034**
0034-5032 Republic Weekly with Newsday
0034-5040 Republica Argentina. Transporte Aereo. Noticiero
0034-5059 Republican†
0034-5083 Res
0034-5091 Res Gestae†
0034-5105 Resale Weekly **1032**
0034-5113 Research†
0034-513X Research and Industry **8436**
0034-5202 Research Film†
0034-5210 Research in African Literatures **5360**
0034-5237 Research in Education (Manchester) **2904**
0034-5245 Research in Librarianship†
0034-5253 Research in Reproduction†
0034-5261 Research in the Life Sciences†
0034-527X Research in the Teaching of English **3078**
0034-5288 Research in Veterinary Science **8805**
0034-5296 Research Index
0034-530X Hokkaido University. Research Institute for Catalysis. Journal†
0034-5318 Research Institute for Mathematical Sciences. Publications **5529**
0034-5326 Research into Higher Education Abstracts **2935**
0034-5342 Research News†
0034-5393 California University Center for Research and Development in Higher Education. Research Reporter†
0034-5407 American Institute for Economic Research. Research Reports **1059**
0034-5415 Research Reports in Social Science†
0034-5431 Research Society of Pakistan. Journal **4187**
0034-5458 Researcher†
0034-5474 Resena de Hispanoamerica†
0034-5512 Reserve Bank of India. Bulletin **1378**
0034-5547 Reserve Marine
0034-5555 Resident and Staff Physician†
0034-5571 Resin Review†
0034-5598 Resistenza†
0034-5628 Resort & Motel Administration
0034-5652 Resource†
0034-5695 Respond†
0034-5709 Response (New York, 1967)
0034-5725 Response (New York, 1969) **7773**
0034-575X Ressorgiment†
0034-5792 Restaurante
0034-5806 Restaurator **5043**
0034-5814 Restauratoeren **4397**
0034-5822 Restoration & Eighteenth Century Theatre Research
0034-5830 Restoration Herald **7676**
0034-5865 Resument†
0034-5946 Mozambique. Servico Meteorologico. Resumos Meteorologicas para a Aeronautica†
0034-5962 Resurgam
0034-5970 Resurgence **7177**
0034-5989 Retail Ad News†
0034-6136 Retail World **3681**
0034-6152 Retarded
0034-6187 Rettens Gang **4769**
0034-6195 Rjettur†
0034-6233 Reumatologia **6226**
0034-6241 Reus Avicola y Agricola†
0034-625X Revealing Confession
0034-6268 Revealing Romances†
0034-6284 Reveil Missionnaire **7814**
0034-6292 Reveil Socialiste de Lannemezan†
0034-6306 Reveille **6443**
0034-6314 Revetements Sols et Murs†
0034-6330 Review (London)†
0034-6349 The Review **4521**
0034-6373 Review and Expositor **7773**
0034-639X Review for Religious **7814**
0034-6403 Review of Agricultural Economics Malaysia†
0034-6438 Review of Plant Pathology **720**
0034-6446 The Review of Black Political Economy **1165**
0034-6454 Review of Business **1165**
0034-6489 Review of Communist Scientific and Political Publications (Soviet Union)†
0034-6500 Turkiye Is Bankasi. Review of Economic Conditions† **8995**
0034-6527 The Review of Economic Studies **1166**
0034-6535 The Review of Economics and Statistics **1166**
0034-6543 Review of Educational Research **2905**
0034-6551 The Review of English Studies **5360**
0034-6578 Review of Ghana Law **4769**
0034-6586 Review of Income and Wealth **1721**
0034-6608 Review of International Cooperation **7262**
0034-6624 Review of Medical and Veterinary Mycology **720**
0034-6632 The Review of Metaphysics **6948**
0034-6659 Nutrition & Food Science **6665**
0034-6667 Review of Palaeobotany and Palynology **6730**
0034-6675 Review of Physical Chemistry of Japan†
0034-6691 Review of Polarography **2105**
0034-6705 The Review of Politics **7178**
0034-6713 Review of Popular Astronomy†
0034-6721 Review of Religions **7715**
0034-673X Review of Religious Research **7677**
0034-6748 Review of Scientific Instruments **4489**
0034-6764 Review of Social Economy **1166**
0034-6772 Review of Soviet Medical Sciences†
0034-6799 Review of Economic Conditions in Italy†
0034-6810 Review of the River Plate **1514**
0034-6861 Reviews of Modern Physics **7037**
0034-687X Reviews of Pure and Applied Chemistry†
0034-690X Revija za Kriminalistiko in Kriminologijo **2667**
0034-6918 Revision & Regnskabsvaesen **1300**
0034-6926 Asociacion de Prensa Hondurena. Revista
0034-6942 Revista Aeronautica **68**
0034-6950 Revista Aguas e Energia Eletrica de Sao Paulo†
0034-6969 Revista Alamar†
0034-6977 Revista Alentejana *changed to* Revista Alentejo **5236**
0034-6985 Anales de la Legislacion Argentina **4615**
0034-7000 Revista Argentina de Cardiologia **5798**
0034-7043 Revista Arhivelor **4257**
0034-706X Revista Bancaria Brasileira **1380**
0034-7078 Revista Biblica†
0034-7086 Revista Bibliotecilor†
0034-7094 Revista Brasileira de Anestesiologia **5773**
0034-7116 Revista Brasileira de Cancerologia **6033**
0034-7124 Revista Brasileira de Cirurgia†
0034-7140 Revista Brasileira de Economia **1166**
0034-7159 Revista Brasileira de Energia Eletrica†
0034-7167 Revista Brasileira de Enfermagem **5980**
0034-7175 Revista Brasileira de Estatistica **8396**
0034-7183 Revista Brasileira de Estudos Pedagogicos **2905**
0034-7191 Revista Brasileira de Estudos Politicos **7178**
0034-7205 Revista Brasileira de Filosofia†
0034-7213 Revista Brasileira de Folclore†
0034-723X Revista Brasileira de Geografia **4026**
0034-7256 Revista Brasileira de Malariologia e Doencas Tropicais†
0034-7264 Revista Brasileira de Medicina **5704**
0034-7272 Revista Brasileira de Odontologia **5863**
0034-7280 Revista Brasileira de Oftalmologia **6051**
0034-7299 Revista Brasileira de Otorrinolaringologia **6084**
0034-7329 Revista Brasileira de Politica Internacional **7262**
0034-7337 Revista Brasileira de Saude Mental†
0034-7353 Revista Campinense de Cultura
0034-7361 C E C Revista
0034-737X Revista Ceres **151**
0034-7388 Revista Chilena de Neuropsiquiatria **6181**
0034-740X Revista Chilena de Entomologia **858**
0034-7418 Revista Colombiana de Ciencias Quimico Farmaceuticas **6878**
0034-7426 Revista Colombiana de Matematicas **5529**
0034-7434 Revista Colombiana de Obstetricia y Ginecologia **6003**
0034-7450 Revista Colombiana de Psiquiatria **6181**
0034-7469 Revista Comercial de Nicaragua
0034-7485 Revista Cubana de Ciencia Agricola **151**
0034-7493 Revista Cubana de Cirugia **6256**
0034-7507 Revista Cubana de Estomatologia **5863**
0034-7515 Revista Cubana de Farmacia **6878**
0034-7523 Revista Cubana de Medicina **5704**
0034-7531 Revista Cubana de Pediatria **6103**
0034-754X Revista Cultului Mozaic **7729**
0034-7558 Bolsa de Valores de Sao Paulo. Revista†
0034-7566 Revista da Construcao Civil†
0034-7582 Revista da Madeira **3715**
0034-7590 R A E **1788**
0034-7604 Revista de Administracao Municipal **7501**
0034-7612 Revista de Administracao Publica **7466**
0034-7620 Revista de Administracion Publica **7466**
0034-7639 Revista de Administracion Publica **7466**
0034-7647 Revista de Aeronautica y Astronautica **68**
0034-7655 Revista de Agricultura **151**
0034-7701 Revista de Antropologia **353**
0034-771X Revista de Archivos, Bibliotecas y Museos†
0034-7728 Revista de Bellas Artes†
0034-7736 Revista de Biologia **700**
0034-7744 Revista de Biologia Tropical **701**
0034-7752 Revista de Chimie **2078**
0034-7787 Revista de Ciencias Juridicas†
0034-7817 Revista de Ciencias Sociales **7996**
0034-7825 Revista de Compendios de Articulos de Economia **1261**
0034-7833 Revista de Conservatorio†
0034-7841 Revista de Criminalistica do Rio Grande do Sul†
0034-785X Revista de Cultura Brasilena†
0034-7868 Revista de Derecho†
0034-7884 Revista de Derecho Deportivo **8196**
0034-7892 Revista de Derecho Internacional y Ciencias Diplomaticas
0034-7906 Revista de Derecho, Jurisprudencia y Administracion **4770**
0034-7914 Revista de Derecho Penal y Criminologia†
0034-7922 Revista de Derecho Privado **4771**
0034-7930 Revista de Derecho Puertorriqueno **4771**
0034-7949 Revista de Derecho y Ciencias Politicas **4771**
0034-7965 Revista de Derecho y Legislacion†
0034-7973 Revista de Diagnostico Biologico *changed to* 1888-4008 **5705**
0034-7981 Revista de Dialectologia y Tradiciones Populares **5167**
0034-8007 Revista de Direito Administrativo†
0034-8015 Revista de Direito Publico†
0034-804X Revista de Economia Latinoamericana†
0034-8066 Revista de Economia y Estadistica **1167**
0034-8082 Revista de Educacion (Madrid) **2906**
0034-8090 Revista de Enfermagem†
0034-8104 Revista de Engenharia do Estado da Guanabara
0034-8112 Revista de Engenharia Mackenzie†
0034-8139 Revista de Entomologia de Mocambique†
0034-8147 Revista de Espiritualidad **7677**
0034-818X Revista de Estudios Hispanicos **5361**
0034-8198 Revista de Etnografie si Folclor **353**
0034-821X Revista de Ferreteria y Ramos Generales
0034-8236 Revista de Filosofia (Santiago, 1949) **6948**
0034-8244 Revista de Filosofia **6948**
0034-8252 Revista de Filosofia **6948**
0034-8260 Revista de Filosofie **6948**
0034-8279 Revista de Geofisica†
0034-8287 Revista de Ginecologia e d'Obstetricia†
0034-8309 Revista de Historia **4310**
0034-8317 Revista de Historia†
0034-8325 Revista de Historia de America **4310**
0034-8333 Revista de Ideas Esteticas†
0034-8341 Revista de Indias **4311**
0034-835X Revista de Informacao Legislativa
0034-8368 Revista de Intendencia
0034-8376 Revista de Investigacion Clinica **5705**
0034-8384 Revista de Investigacion en Salud Publica†
0034-8392 Revista de Istorie si Teorie Literara **5361**
0034-8406 Revista de la Defensa Nacional†
0034-8457 Revista de las Fuerzas Armadas
0034-8473 Revista de las Fuerzas Armadas
0034-8481 Revista de Legislacion Argentina **4771**
0034-8511 Revista de Marina **6443**
0034-852X Revista de Marina
0034-8538 Revista de Marina del Peru **6443**
0034-8546 Revista de Marinha **8659**
0034-8562 Revista de Medicina Social y del Trabajo
0034-8570 Revista de Metalurgia **6330**
0034-8597 Revista de Neuro-Psiquiatria **6181**
0034-8600 Revista de Nutricion y Aterosclerosis
0034-8619 Revista de Obras Publicas **3282**
0034-8635 Revista de Occidente **5236**
0034-8651 Revista de Pedagogia†
0034-866X Revista de Tecnologia Educativa **2950**
0034-8678 Revista de Pedagogie **2906**
0034-8686 Revista de Planeacion y Desarrollo **1903**
0034-8694 Revista de Planificacion†
0034-8708 Revista de Plasticos Modernos **7099**
0034-8724 Revista de Politica Social†
0034-8732 Prevencion **7536**
0034-8740 Revista de Psicoanalisis **7403**
0034-8759 Revista de Psihologie **7404**
0034-8767 Revista de Psiquiatria Dinamica†
0034-8775 Revista de Publicaciones Navales **6455**
0034-8791 Filosofie-Logica; Revista de Referate, Recenzii si Sinteze†
0034-8805 Istorie- Etnografie Revista de Referate, Recenzii si Sinteze†
0034-8813 Lingvistica-Filologie; Revista de Referate, Recenzii si Sinzeze†
0034-8821 Psihologie; Revista de Referate Recenzii si Sinteze†
0034-883X Sociologie; Revista de Referate Recenzii si Sinteze†
0034-8848 Stiinte Economice; Revista de Referate, Recenzii si Sinteze†
0034-8856 Stiinte Juridice; Revista de Referate, Recenzii si Sinteze†
0034-8864 Teoria si Istoria Literaturii si Artei; Revista de Referate, Recenzii si Sinteze†
0034-8872 Revista de Resumenes†
0034-8880 Revista de Revistas
0034-8902 Revista de Santander
0034-8910 Revista de Saude Publica **7539**
0034-8937 Revista de Servicio Social
0034-8961 Revista de Telecomunicacion†
0034-8988 Revista de Trabajo **1705**
0034-8996 Revista de Urologia†
0034-9003 Costa Rica. Archivo Nacional. Revista **4136**
0034-9011 Revista del Cafe†
0034-902X Circulo Odontologico del Sur. Revista†
0034-9046 Revista del Ejercito **6443**
0034-9054 Revista del Ejercito y Armada
0034-9070 Revista del Hogar
0034-9089 I D I E M Revista†
0034-9097 Revista del Mexico Agrario **151**
0034-9100 Revista del Pacifico†
0034-9135 Rivista dell'Informazione†
0034-9178 Revista Diesel†
0034-9186 Diners
0034-9194 Revista Diplomatica e Internacional
0034-9208 Revista do Ar **69**
0034-9216 Sao Paulo (City) Arquivo Municipal. Revista **4312**
0034-9224 Revista do Comercio de Cafe **3662**
0034-9240 Revista do Servico Publico
0034-9259 Revista dos Criadores
0034-9267 Revista dos Transportes†
0034-9275 Revista dos Tribunais **4772**
0034-9291 Revista Economica†
0034-9305 Revista Ecuatoriana de Educacion†
0034-9313 Revista Ecuatoriana de Medicina y Ciencias Biologicas **5705**
0034-933X El Sol **2913**
0034-9356 Revista Espanola de Anestesiologia y Reanimacion **5774**
0034-9372 Revista Espanola de Derecho Canonico **7814**
0034-9380 Revista Espanola de Derecho Internacional **4939**
0034-9399 Revista Espanola de Derecho Militar **4972**
0034-9453 Revista Espanola de Oto-Neuro-Oftalmologia y Neurocirugia†
0034-9461 Revista Espanola de Pedagogia **2906**
0034-947X Revista Espanola de Pediatria **6103**
0034-9488 Revista Espanola de Seguros **4521**
0034-9496 Revista Farmaceutica **6879**
0034-950X Revista Ferroviaria **8624**
0034-9518 Revista Financiera
0034-9526 Revista Finlay†
0034-9534 Revista Fiscal e de Legislacao de Fazenda†
0034-9550 Revista Genealogica Latina **3780**
0034-9569 Revista General de Marina **6443**
0034-9585 Revista Goiana de Medicina†
0034-9593 Revista Hispanica Moderna **5361**
0034-9631 Revista Iberoamericana **5361**
0034-964X Revista Iberoamericana de Seguridad Social†
0034-9658 Revista I B Y S†
0034-9666 Revista Imposto Fiscal
0034-9690 Interamerican Journal of Psychology **7363**
0034-9704 Revista Interamericana de Radiologia†
0034-9712 Revista Internacional de Sociologia **8129**
0034-9720 Revista Internacional y Diplomatica
0034-9739 Revista Juridica (Rio de Janeiro)†
0034-9801 Revista Latinoamericana de Sociologia†
0034-981X Revista Literaria Azor
0034-9828 Cenit
0034-9844 Manana (Mexico, D.F.) **3909**
0034-9852 Revista Manizales **5237**
0034-9860 Revista Maritima Brasileira **6443**
0034-9887 Revista Medica de Chile **5706**
0034-9895 Revista Medica de Corrientes
0034-9917 Revista Medica de Valparaiso†

0034-9933 Revista Medica del Paraguay
0034-9984 Revista Mexicana de Cirugia, Ginecologia y Cancer†
0035-0001 Revista Mexicana de Urologia **6274**
0035-001X Revista Mexicana de Fisica **7038**
0035-0028 Revista Mexicana de Ingenieria y Arquitectura†
0035-0036 Revista Mexicana de la Construccion
0035-0044 Revista Mexicana de la Propiedad Industrial y Artistica **6758**
0035-0079 Revista Mexicana de Psicologia†
0035-0095 Revista Mexicana del Trabajo
0035-0109 Revista Militar†
0035-0117 Revista Militar
0035-0133 Revista Militar
0035-0141 Revista Militar del Peru
0035-015X Revista Militar y Naval†
0035-0176 Revista Minería, Geologia y Mineralogia
0035-0184 Revista Municipal†
0035-0214 Revista Nacional da Pesca
0035-0222 Revista Nacional de Agricultura **151**
0035-0230 Revista Nacional de Cultura
0035-0265 Revista Odontologica de Concepcion†
0035-0281 Revista Odontologica de Puerto Rico
0035-0303 Revista para Parvulos y Principiantes†
0035-0346 Revista para Uniones de Primarios†
0035-0354 Revista Paraguaya de Sociologia **8129**
0035-0370 Revista Peruana de Derecho Internacional **4939**
0035-0389 Revista Portuguesa de Ciencias Veterinarias **8806**
0035-0397 Revista Portuguesa de Estomatologia e Cirurgia Maxilo-Facial **5864**
0035-0400 Revista Portuguesa de Filosofia. Suplemento Bibliografico *see* 0870-5283 **6949**
0035-0443 Revista Rotaria†
0035-0451 Revista Signos **5361**
0035-046X Revista Sindical de Estadistica†
0035-0478 Sur†
0035-0486 Revista Tamaulipas **3911**
0035-0494 Revista Tecnica Iem
0035-0524 Revista Textil **8456**
0035-0540 Revista Trimestral de Jurisprudencia **4773**
0035-0567 Rivista Veneta†
0035-0575 Revista Venezolana de Folklore†
0035-0583 Revista Venezolana de Sanidad y Asistencia Social†
0035-0591 Revista Venezolana de Urologia **6274**
0035-0605 Revista do Livro (Rio de Janeiro)†
0035-0621 Revolution Africaine
0035-0672 La Revue Administrative **7466**
0035-0710 Revue Analytique d'Education Physique et de Sport†
0035-0729 Revue **8752**
0035-0737 Revue Archeologique **414**
0035-0761 Revue Automobile **8510**
0035-077X Revue Belge d'Archeologie et d'Histoire de l'Art **515**
0035-0788 Revue Belge de Droit International **4939**
0035-0818 Revue Belge de Philologie et d'Histoire **4159**
0035-0834 Revue Belge de Securite Sociale **7466**
0035-0850 Revue Belge des Vins & Spiritueux
0035-0869 Revue Belge d'Histoire Contemporaine **4159**
0035-0877 Revue Belge d'Histoire Militaire **6443**
0035-0885 Revue Belge d'Homoeopathie **5807**
0035-0893 Revue Benedictine **7815**
0035-0907 Revue Biblique **7677**
0035-0931 Revue Congolaise des Sciences Humaines†
0035-0958 Revue Critique de Droit International Prive **4939**
0035-0966 Revue Critique de Jurisprudence Belge **4773**
0035-1008 Revue d'Auvergne **4258**
0035-1016 La Revue de Belles-Lettres **5237**
0035-1040 Revue de Chirurgie Orthopedique et Reparatrice de l'Appareil Moteur *changed to* 1877-0517 **6072**
0035-1059 Revue de Comminges **4258**
0035-1083 Revue de Droit Intellectuel l'Ingenieur-Conseil **4774**
0035-1091 Revue de Droit International de Sciences Diplomatiques et Politiques **7263**
0035-1113 Revue de Droit Social **4774**
0035-1156 Revue de Geographie du Maroc **4027**
0035-1199 Revue de la Cooperation Scolaire†
0035-1210 Revue de la France Libre *changed to* 1630-5078 **6421**
0035-1237 Revue de la Police Nationale†
0035-1245 Revue de la Presse Arabe†
0035-127X Revue de la Soudure
0035-1288 Revue de l'Agenais
0035-130X Revue de l'Alcoolisme†
0035-1318 Revue de l'Aluminium†
0035-1326 Revue de l'Art **515**
0035-1334 Revue de Laryngologie - Otologie - Rhinologie **6085**
0035-1342 Revue de l'Avranchin et du Pays de Granville **414**
0035-1350 Revue de l'Economie du Centre-Est†
0035-1407 Revue de l'Enseignement Superieur *changed to* 0068-5119
0035-1423 Revue de l'Histoire des Religions **7677**
0035-1458 Revue de Linguistique Romane **5168**
0035-1466 Revue de Litterature Comparee **5362**
0035-1482 Revue de Madagascar†
0035-1512 Revue de Medecine†
0035-1555 Revue de Medecine Veterinaire **8806**
0035-1563 Revue de Metallurgie **6330**
0035-1571 Revue de Metaphysique et de Morale **6949**
0035-1598 Revue de Micropaleontologie **6730**
0035-1601 Revue de Musicologie **6611**
0035-161X Revue de Neuropsychiatrie de l'Ouest†
0035-1644 Revue de Pediatrie†
0035-1652 Revue de Philologie, de Litterature et d'Histoire Anciennes **2239**
0035-1679 Revue de Physiologie Subaquatique et Medecine Hyperbare†
0035-1725 Revue de Qumran **7677**
0035-1733 Revue de Science Criminelle et de Droit Penal Compare **2667**
0035-1741 Revue de Science Financiere†
0035-1768 Revue de Stomatologie et de Chirurgie Maxillo-Faciale **6257**
0035-1776 Revue de Synthese **6949**
0035-1784 Revue de Theologie et de Philosophie **7677**
0035-1806 Revue de Zoologie Agricole et de Pathologie Vegetale†
0035-1849 Revue d'Egyptologie **414**
0035-1865 Revue d'Elevage et de Medecine Veterinaire des Pays Tropicaux **8806**
0035-1873 Lebanese Dental Journal†
0035-1938 Revue des Caisses d'Epargne et de Prevoyance *changed to* 0751-1809
0035-1997 Revue des Ecoles **2907**
0035-2004 Revue des Etudes Anciennes **2239**
0035-2012 Revue des Etudes Augustiniennes *changed to* 1768-9260 **7677**
0035-2039 Revue des Etudes Grecques **2239**
0035-2047 Revue des Etudes Italiennes **5362**
0035-2063 Revue des Etudes Sud-Est Europeennes **4473**
0035-2098 Revue des Hotesses†
0035-211X Revue des Langues Vivantes†
0035-2136 Revue des Lettres Modernes†
0035-2160 Revue des Questions Scientifiques **7903**
0035-2187 Revue des Sciences Economiques†
0035-2209 Revue des Sciences Philosophiques et Theologiques **6949**
0035-2217 Revue des Sciences Religieuses **7815**
0035-2241 Revue des Societes Savantes de Haute Normandie **7903**
0035-2284 Revue Desjardins **1380**
0035-2292 Revue d'Esthetique *changed to* 1969-2269 **6937**
0035-2306 Revue d'Etudes Militaires, Aeriennes et Navales†
0035-2330 Revue d'Histoire de la Medecine Hebraique†
0035-2349 Revue d'Histoire de la Pharmacie **6879**
0035-2357 Revue d'Histoire de l'Amerique Francaise **4311**
0035-2365 Revue d'Histoire Diplomatique **4159**
0035-2381 Revue d'Histoire Ecclesiastique **7678**
0035-2403 Revue d'Histoire et de Philosophie Religieuses **7678**
0035-2411 Revue d'Histoire Litteraire de la France **5362**
0035-242X Revue d'Hygiene du Travail†
0035-2446 Revue d'Hygiene et Medecine Scolaire et Universitaire†
0035-2462 Revue d'Informatique Medicale†
0035-2470 Revue d'Odonto-Stomatologie du Midi de la France†
0035-2497 Revue d'Oto-Neuro-Ophtalmologie†
0035-2500 Revue du Bois Detail†
0035-2527 Revue du Bouton†
0035-2543 Revue du Cinema International & TV†
0035-2551 Revue du Clerge Africain†
0035-256X Revue du Droit du Travail†
0035-2578 Revue du Droit Public et de la Science Politique en France et a l'Etranger **7179**
0035-2594 Revue du Jouet **4061**
0035-2608 La Revue du Louvre et des Musees de France *changed to* 1962-4271 **6536**
0035-2616 Revue du Marche Commun **1581**
0035-2632 Revue du Notariat **4774**
0035-2640 La Revue du Praticien **5706**
0035-2667 Revue du Rouergue†
0035-2683 Asia Quarterly†
0035-2705 Revue du Travail **1705**
0035-2713 La Revue du Tresor *changed to* 1969-1009 **1289**
0035-2748 Revue du Vivarais **4159**
0035-2756 Revue E (Supplement)†
0035-2764 Revue Economique **1168**
0035-2772 Revue Economique et Sociale **1168**
0035-2780 Revue Economique Francaise **1168**
0035-2802 Revue Europeenne des Papiers Cartons-Complexes†
0035-2829 Revue Forestiere Francaise **3701**
0035-2861 Revue Francaise de Bridge†
0035-2888 Revue Francaise de Gastro-Enterologie†
0035-290X Revue Francaise de Gynecologie et d'Obstetrique†
0035-2918 Revue Francaise de l'Agriculture†
0035-2926 Revue Francaise de l'Electricite†
0035-2942 Revue Francaise de Psychanalyse **7405**
0035-2950 Revue Francaise de Science Politique **7179**
0035-2969 Revue Francaise de Sociologie **8129**
0035-2985 Revue Francaise des Affaires Sociales **8130**
0035-3051 Revue Francaise du Marketing **1841**
0035-3086 Revue Generale de Droit **4774**
0035-3094 Publication de la Revue Generale de Droit International Public **4938**
0035-3108 Revue Generale de l'Air et de l'Espace†
0035-3124 Revue Generale de l'Enseignement des Deficients Auditifs†
0035-3132 Revue Generale de l'Etancheite et de l'Isolation†
0035-3140 Revue Generale de l'Hotellerie, de la Gastronomie et du Tourisme†
0035-3183 Revue Generale des Chemins de Fer†
0035-3213 Revue Geographique de l'Est† **8985**
0035-323X Revue Graphique-Imprivaria
0035-3248 Acta Technica Belgica. Revue H F: Electricite Courants Faibles. Electronique Telecommunications
0035-3256 Revue Hellenique de Droit International **4939**
0035-3264 Revue Historique **4159**
0035-3272 Revue Historique Ardennaise **414**
0035-3280 Revue Historique de Droit Francais et Etranger **4774**
0035-3299 Revue Historique des Armees **6444**
0035-3310 Revue Independante **5237**
0035-3337 Revue Internationale de Droit Compare **4939**
0035-3388 Revue Internationale de l'Eclairage *see* 1871-3661 **1016**
0035-3396 Revue Internationale de Police Criminelle *changed to* 1562-8434
0035-3418 Comptabilite Economique Universelle-Scientifique†
0035-3426 Revue Internationale des Fleuristes†
0035-3434 Revue Internationale des Hautes Temperatures et des Refractaires†
0035-3442 Revue Internationale des Industries Agricoles. Bulletin Analytique†
0035-3450 Revue Internationale des Produits Tropicaux†
0035-3477 Revue Internationale des Tabacs†
0035-3485 Revue Internationale d'Ethnopsychologie Normale et Pathologique†
0035-3493 Revue Internationale d'Oceanographie Medicale†
0035-3515 Revue Internationale du Droit d'Auteur **6758**
0035-354X International Review for Business Education **1129**
0035-3574 Revue Juridique et Politique Independance et Cooperation **4959**
0035-3582 Revue de l'Air Liquide†
0035-3590 Revue Laitiere Francaise **269**
0035-3604 Revue Legale
0035-3620 Revue Mabillon **7815**
0035-3639 Revue Medicale de Bruxelles **5706**
0035-3655 Revue Medicale de la Suisse Romande *changed to* 1660-9379 **5706**
0035-3663 Revue Medicale de Liege. Supplement *see* 0370-629X **5706**
0035-3671 Revue Militaire Generale† **8985**
0035-368X Revue Militaire Suisse **6444**
0035-3698 Revue Moderne
0035-3728 Revue Municipale **4425**
0035-3744 Revue Musicale de Suisse Romande **6611**
0035-3787 Revue Neurologique **6182**
0035-3795 R N D **7813**
0035-3809 Revue Nouvelle
0035-3825 Revue Penitentiaire et de Droit Penal **4775**
0035-3833 Revue Philosophique de la France et de l'Etranger **6949**
0035-3841 Revue Philosophique de Louvain **6949**
0035-385X Revue Politique et Parlementaire **7179**
0035-3876 Revue Pratique des Questions Commerciales et Economiques†
0035-3884 Societe Calviniste de France. Revue Reformee **7775**
0035-3906 Revue Romane **5168**
0035-3930 Revue Roumaine de Chimie **2079**
0035-3957 Revue Roumaine de Linguistique **5168**
0035-3965 Revue Roumaine de Mathematiques Pures et Appliquees **5530**
0035-4066 Revue Roumaine des Sciences Techniques. Serie Electrotechnique et Energetique **3329**
0035-4074 Revue Roumaine des Sciences Techniques. Serie de Mecanique Appliquee **3394**
0035-4104 Revue Scolaire†
0035-4112 Revue Senegalaise de Droit
0035-4147 Revue Stomato-Odontologique du Nord de la France†
0035-4163 Revue Suisse de Numismatique **6653**
0035-418X Revue Suisse de Zoologie **962**
0035-4201 Revue Suisse du Trafic Routier†
0035-421X Revue Syndicale Suisse†
0035-4244 R I A. Revue Economique et Technique de l'Industrie Alimentaire Europeenne **3661**
0035-4260 Revue Technique Luxembourgeoise **8437**
0035-4279 Revue Technique Thomson - C S F†
0035-4287 Revue Textile Melliand†
0035-4295 Revue Thomiste **7678**
0035-4317 Revue Trimestrielle de Droit Europeen **4775**
0035-4333 Revue Tunisienne des Sciences Sociales **7998**
0035-4341 Revue Universelle des Mines, de la Metallurgie, de la Mecanique, des Travaux Publics, des Sciences et des Arts Appliques a l'Industrie†
0035-4368 Revue Vinicole Internationale†
0035-4376 Revues Medicales Normandes†
0035-4384 Revue de Droit Penal et de Criminologie **4897**
0035-4406 La Revuo Orienta **5168**
0035-4422 Rexevents
0035-4457 Rheinisch-Westfaelische Boerse zu Duesseldorf. Amtliches Kursblatt **1648**
0035-4473 Rheinische Vierteljahrsblaetter **4258**
0035-4481 Rheinisches Aerzteblatt **5706**
0035-449X Rheinisches Museum fuer Philologie **5168**
0035-4503 Rheinisches Zahnaerzteblatt **5864**
0035-4511 Rheologica Acta **7062**
0035-452X Rheology Abstracts **7050**
0035-4538 Rheology Bulletin **7062**
0035-4546 Rheumatism **6226**
0035-4562 Rhode Island Beverage Journal **609**
0035-4619 Rhode Island History **4311**
0035-4635 Rhode Island Resources†
0035-466X Rhodeo†
0035-4694 Rhodesia and World Report
0035-4716 Zimbabwe. National Archives. Occasional Papers†
0035-4791 Rhodesian Industrialist
0035-4864 Rhodesian Property & Finance
0035-4899 Rhodesian Viewpoint†
0035-4902 Rhodora **815**
0035-4937 Rhythm†
0035-4953 Ribarski List
0035-4961 Rice Journal†
0035-4988 Rice University Review†
0035-4996 Rice University Studies†
0035-5011 Ricerca Scientifica†
0035-502X Ricerche Bibliche e Religiose†
0035-5038 Ricerche di Matematica **5530**
0035-5046 Ricerche Didattiche† **8985**
0035-5062 Ricerche Filosofiche†
0035-5070 Ricerche Storiche (Reggio Emilia) **4258**
0035-5089 Richard Cotten's Conservative Viewpoint
0035-5097 Richesses de France†
0035-5100 Greater Richmond Chamber of Commerce. Research Bulletin†
0035-5119 Richmond County History†
0035-5143 Ridge News†
0035-516X Riding
0035-5186 Ridotto **8477**
0035-5224 Rifleman **8197**
0035-5240 Riforma della Scuola†
0035-5259 La Riforma Medica†
0035-5267 Rig **354**
0035-5275 Right of Way **7611**
0035-5283 Rights†
0035-5291 Rights & Reviews†
0035-5305 Rihabiriteshon **8066**
0035-5313 Het Rijk der Vrouw
0035-5321 Rijkstuinbouwconsulentschap. Mededelingen
0035-5364 Sweden. Kungliga Biblioteket. Notiser fraan Riksbibliotekarien†
0035-5372 Rimba Indonesia
0035-5380 Rinascita† **8985**
0035-5410 The Ring **8197**
0035-5429 The Ring **913**

ISSN

0035-5437 Ring-Rund†
0035-5453 Ringing World **6612**
0035-5488 Rinsho Shika
0035-5496 Rinshou Shinrigaku Kenkyuu **7405**
0035-550X Journal of Clinical Pediatrics **6094**
0035-5518 Ripley's Believe It or Not†
0035-5534 Ripresa Nazionale
0035-5550 Rise Hvezd†
0035-5593 Risk Management **4521**
0035-5607 Il Risorgimento **4258**
0035-5615 Il Risparmio **1380**
0035-5623 Risveglio del Molise e del Mezzogiorno† **8986**
0035-5658 Ritmo **6612**
0035-5666 Rivarol **7998**
0035-5720 Riviere†
0035-5739 Rivista Abruzzese **4473**
0035-5755 Rivista Agricola dell'O C D E†
0035-5763 Rivista Amministrativa della Repubblica Italiana **7467**
0035-5771 Rivista Araldica **3780**
0035-578X Rivista Bancaria - Minerva Bancaria **1380**
0035-5798 Rivista Biblica **7678**
0035-5836 Rivista degli Infortuni e delle Malattie Professionali **6685**
0035-5844 Rivista degli Ospedali†
0035-5887 Rivista del Diritto Commerciale e del Diritto Generale delle Obbligazioni **4776**
0035-5895 Rivista del Diritto della Navigazione†
0035-5925 Rivista del Porto di Napoli† **8986**
0035-595X Guardia di Finanza. Rivista **1927**
0035-5976 Rivista della Proprieta' Industriale e della Concorrenza†
0035-5984 Rivista della Proprieta Intellettuale ed Industriale†
0035-600X Consacrazione e Servizio **7635**
0035-6018 Rivista delle Societa **4852**
0035-6042 Rivista di Archeologia Cristiana **414**
0035-6050 Rivista di Biologia **701**
0035-6069 Rivista di Chirurgia Pediatrica†
0035-6085 Rivista di Cultura Classica e Medioevale **2240**
0035-6093 Rivista di Diritto Civile **4841**
0035-6115 Rivista della Pesca†
0035-6123 Rivista di Diritto Europeo
0035-6131 Rivista di Diritto Finanziario e Scienza delle Finanze **1380**
0035-614X Rivista di Diritto Industriale **6758**
0035-6158 Rivista di Diritto Internazionale **4940**
0035-6166 Rivista di Diritto Internazionale e Comparato del Lavoro†
0035-6174 Rivista di Diritto Internazionale Privato e Processuale **4940**
0035-6182 Rivista di Diritto Processuale **4841**
0035-6190 Rivista di Economia Agraria **206**
0035-6204 Rivista di Emoterapia ed Immunoematologia†
0035-6212 Rivista di Estetica **6949**
0035-6220 Rivista di Filologia e di Istruzione Classica† **8986**
0035-6239 Rivista di Filosofia **6949**
0035-6247 Rivista di Filosofia Neo-Scolastica **6950**
0035-6255 Rivista di Gastroenterologia†
0035-6263 Ingegneria†
0035-6271 Rivista di Legislazione Scolastica Comparata†
0035-628X Rivista di Lugano **3959**
0035-6298 Universita degli Studi di Parma. Rivista di Matematica **5543**
0035-631X Rivista di Medicina Aeronautica e Spaziale **5707**
0035-6328 Rivista di Meteorologia Aeronautica
0035-6352 Rivista di Neuropsichiatria e Scienze Affini†
0035-6360 Rivista di Organizzazione Aziendale†
0035-6387 Rivista di Parassitologia
0035-6395 Rivista di Pastorale Liturgica **7678**
0035-6417 Rivista di Patologia e Clinica† **8986**
0035-6468 Rivista di Politica Economica **1168**
0035-6476 Rivista di Polizia† **8986**
0035-6484 Rivista di Psichiatria **6183**
0035-6492 Rivista di Psicoanalisi **7405**
0035-6514 Rivista di Scienze Preistoriche **415**
0035-6522 Rivista di Servizio Sociale **8066**
0035-6530 Rivista di Sociologia†
0035-6557 Rivista di Storia della Chiesa in Italia **7678**
0035-6565 Rivista di Storia della Medicina†
0035-6573 Rivista di Storia e Letteratura Religiosa **7678**
0035-6581 Rivista di Studi Classici†
0035-659X Rivista di Studi Crociani
0035-6603 Rivista di Studi Liguri† **8986**
0035-6611 Rivista di Studi Politici Internazionali **7263**
0035-662X Rivista di Suinicoltura **299**
0035-6638 Rivista di Vita Spirituale **7678**
0035-6654 Rivista Diocesana del Patriarcato di Venezia† **8986**
0035-6662 Rivista Diocesana Rimini†
0035-6689 Rivista Generale Italiana di Chirurgia† **8986**
0035-6697 Rivista Geografica Italiana **4027**
0035-6719 Rivista Internazionale di Dialogo†
0035-6727 Rivista Internazionale di Filosofia del Diritto **4776**
0035-6735 Rivista Internazionale di Filosofia Politica e Sociale e Diritto Comparato†
0035-6743 Rivista Internazionale di Psicologia e Ipnosi†
0035-6751 Rivista Internazionale di Scienze Economiche e Commerciali *changed to* 1865-1704 **1130**
0035-676X Rivista Internazionale di Scienze Sociali **1381**
0035-6786 Rivista Italiana del Tracoma e di Patologia Oculare Virale Ed Esotica†
0035-6794 Rivista Italiana della Saldatura **6343**
0035-6808 Rivista Italiana delle Sostanze Grasse **2130**
0035-6816 Impresa†
0035-6824 Rivista Italiana di Diritto Sociale†
0035-6832 Rivista Italiana di Economia Demografia e Statistica **7314**
0035-6840 Rivista Italiana di Ginecologia†
0035-6867 Rivista Italiana di Musicologia **6612**
0035-6875 Rivista Italiana di Ornitologia **914**
0035-6883 Rivista Italiana di Paleontologia e Stratigrafia **6730**
0035-6891 Rivista Italiana di Previdenza Sociale†
0035-6913 Rivista Italiana di Studi Napoleonici **4259**
0035-6921 Rivista Italiana d'Igiene
0035-693X Rivista Italiana di Ortopedia e Traumatologia†
0035-6956 Rivista Liturgica **7815**
0035-6964 Rivista Marittima **6444**
0035-6972 Rivista della Citta di Trieste†
0035-6980 Rivista Militare **6444**
0035-6999 Rivista Militare della Svizzera Italiana **6444**
0035-7006 Rivista Mineraria Siciliana
0035-7022 Rivista Penale **4898**
0035-7030 Rivista Rosminiana di Filosofia e di Cultura **6950**
0035-7049 Rivista Siciliana della Tubercolosi e delle Malattie Respiratorie†
0035-7065 Rivista Storica del Mezzogiorno
0035-7073 Rivista Storica Italiana **4259**
0035-7081 Rivista Tecnica di Cinematografia† **8986**
0035-709X Rivista Tributaria
0035-7103 Rivista Trimestrale†
0035-7111 Rivista Trimestrale di Scienza Politica e dell' Amministrazione
0035-7154 R L C's Museum Gazette
0035-7170 Road Ahead **8601**
0035-7189 Road & Track **8601**
0035-7200 Road Apple Review
0035-7219 Road International†
0035-7235 Raad & Roen **3944**
0035-7251 Road Tar†
0035-726X Road Test - Dune Buggy†
0035-7316 Road Way **8675**
0035-7332 Roads and Road Construction
0035-7367 Roanoke Review **5363**
0035-7383 Robert Dumm Piano Review†
0035-7391 Robot **8602**
0035-7405 Rochester Engineer **3218**
0035-7413 Rochester History **4311**
0035-7480 Rocket†
0035-7510 Rockhurst Hawk **2299**
0035-7529 Rocks and Minerals **6478**
0035-7537 Rocks & Minerals in Canada
0035-7596 Rocky Mountain Journal of Mathematics
0035-7642 Western Association of Africanists. Newsletter†
0035-7650 Rocky Mountain Union Farmer *changed to* Rocky Mountain Farmers Union **152**
0035-7685 Roczniki Filozoficzne **6950**
0035-7707 Roczniki Humanistyczne **4473**
0035-7715 Panstwowy Zaklad Higieny. Roczniki **7535**
0035-7766 Rodina a Škola **2908**
0035-7774 Rodo no Kagaku **6685**
0035-7782 Roedovre Avis†
0035-7790 Roeh Hacheshbon **1301**
0035-7812 Roemische Quartalschrift fuer Christliche Altertumskunde und Kirchengeschichte **7815**
0035-7820 Roentgenpraxis **6208**
0035-7847 Rohm and Haas Reporter†
0035-7871 Rolandino†
0035-788X Roll Call **7180**
0035-7898 Roll Sign **8510**
0035-791X Rolling Stone **6613**
0035-7928 Rolling Stone of Tampa†
0035-7936 Rollins Sandspur **2299**
0035-7944 Rolls-Royce News†
0035-7952 Rolls Royce Owner
0035-7960 Roma e Provincia Attraverso la Statistica **8397**
0035-7979 Roman-Zeitung†
0035-7995 Romance Notes **5363**
0035-8002 Romance Philology **5169**
0035-8029 Romania **5169**
0035-8045 Romanian Books†
0035-8053 Romanian Bulletin†
0035-8061 Romanian Engineering†
0035-807X Romanian Foreign Trade†
0035-8088 Romanian Review **5237**
0035-8096 Rumanian Scientific Abstracts†
0035-810X Romanian Scientific Abstracts. Social Sciences†
0035-8118 Romanic Review **5364**
0035-8126 Romanische Forschungen **5169**
0035-8142 Romantikk†
0035-8169 Rond de Tafel *changed to* 1571-4942 **7692**
0035-8177 Rondom het Boek†
0035-8185 Ronzatore
0035-8207 Rooi Rose **8882**
0035-8215 Roopa - Lekha **539**
0035-8266 El Rosacruz **6950**
0035-8274 Rosario de Maria **7815**
0035-8282 Il Rosario e la Nuova Pompei **7815**
0035-8290 Rosebank Record†
0035-8304 Roseburg Woodsman†
0035-8312 Rosenberg Library Bulletin†
0035-8320 Roses and Gold from Our Lady of the Ozarks†
0035-8339 Rosicrucian Digest **6950**
0035-8363 Rossica Society of Russian Philately Journal **6899**
0035-838X The Rotarian **2269**
0035-8444 Rothwell Advertiser†
0035-8495 Rotunda **515**
0035-8525 Rough Notes **4522**
0035-8533 The Round Table **7263**
0035-8541 Round-up - Children's Services†
0035-8568 Route **8602**
0035-8606 Royal Air Force College Journal†
0035-8614 R A F News **6442**
0035-8630 Royal Air Forces Quarterly†
0035-8649 Royal Arch Mason **2269**
0035-8665 Royal Army Medical Corps. Journal
0035-8673 Royal Army Pay Corps Journal†
0035-8681 Royal Army Veterinary Corps. Journal†
0035-8711 Royal Astronomical Society. Monthly Notices **580**
0035-872X Royal Astronomical Society of Canada. Journal **580**
0035-8762 Royal Australian Historical Society. Journal **4194**
0035-8800 Royal College of Physicians and Surgeons of Canada. Annals†
0035-8835 Royal College of Surgeons of Edinburgh. Journal *changed to* 1479-666X **6259**
0035-8843 Royal College of Surgeons of England. Annals **6257**
0035-8851 Royal Commonwealth Society Library Notes†
0035-8878 Royal Engineers Journal **6444**
0035-8908 Royal Gazette (Charlottetown) **3817**
0035-8916 Royal Historical Society of Queensland. Bulletin **4194**
0035-8959 Royal Institution of Great Britain. Proceedings† **8986**
0035-8991 Royal Irish Academy. Proceedings. Section C: Archaeology, Celtic Studies, History, Linguistics and Literature **415**
0035-9009 Royal Meteorological Society. Quarterly Journal **6394**
0035-9025 Royal Military Police Journal **6444**
0035-9033 Royal Naval Medical Service. Journal **5707**
0035-9041 Royal Naval Sailing Association Journal **8281**
0035-905X Royal Neighbor **2269**
0035-9068 Royal Nepal Economist†
0035-9076 Royal Pioneer
0035-9092 Royal Society International Scientific Information Services. Bulletin†
0035-9106 Royal Society of Antiquaries of Ireland. Journal **415**
0035-9122 Royal Society of Canada. Transactions **7904**
0035-9149 Royal Society of London. Notes and Records **7904**
0035-9165 Royal Society of Medicine. Section of Odontology Proceedings†
0035-9173 Royal Society of New South Wales. Journal and Proceedings **7905**
0035-919X Royal Society of South Africa. Transactions **7905**
0035-9203 Royal Society of Tropical Medicine and Hygiene. Transactions **5825**
0035-9211 Royal Society of Victoria. Proceedings **7905**
0035-922X Royal Society of Western Australia. Journal **7905**
0035-9254 Royal Statistical Society. Journal. Series C: Applied Statistics **8397**
0035-9262 Royal Tehran Hilton
0035-9297 University of Malta. Faculty of Arts. Journal†
0035-9300 Royalauto **8602**
0035-9327 Rozhl'ady†
0035-9335 Rozhlasova Prace
0035-9343 Rozhledy Matematicko-Fyzikalni **5530**
0035-9351 Rozhledy v Chirurgii **6257**
0035-9378 Narodni Technicke Muzeum. Rozpravy†
0035-9394 Rozprawy Hydrotechniczne†
0035-9416 Rozvoj Mistniho Hospodarstvi†
0035-9424 Rtam **5170**
0035-9432 Rub-Off†
0035-9467 Rubber Chem Lines†
0035-9475 Rubber Chemistry and Technology **7826**
0035-9483 Rubber Developments **7826**
0035-9491 Rubber India **7826**
0035-9513 Rubber News **7826**
0035-9548 Rubber Statistical Bulletin **7828**
0035-9556 Rubber Statistical News Sheet†
0035-9564 Rubber Trends†
0035-9572 Rubber World **7827**
0035-9580 Ruby Magazine
0035-9599 Ruch Filozoficzny **6950**
0035-9602 Ruch Literacki **5365**
0035-9610 Ruch Muzyczny **6614**
0035-9629 Ruch Prawniczy, Ekonomiczny i Socjologiczny†
0035-9637 Rudarski Glasnik†
0035-9661 Ruedo†
0035-9696 Rudy i Metale Niezelazne **6331**
0035-970X La Rue†
0035-9726 Rugby†
0035-9793 Rukovet **5237**
0035-9831 Ruminskii Biuleten Naucinoi Informatii. Obscestvennie Nauki†
0035-9882 Rundfunkjournalistik in Theorie und Praxis†
0035-9920 Hotel und Gastgewerbe **4390**
0035-9955 Ruota Diorama
0035-9963 Rupambara **5365**
0035-998X Ruperto-Carola **2299**
0036-0007 The Rural Councillor **206**
0036-0023 National Rural Education News **2890**
0036-0058 Rural India **206**
0036-0074 Rural Life†
0036-0104 Rural Roundup **299**
0036-0112 Rural Sociology **8130**
0036-0120 Rural Youth
0036-0139 Ruralista
0036-0147 Ruritan **2269**
0036-0155 Rusky Jazyk†
0036-0163 Russell **6950**
0036-0171 Russell's Official National Motor Coach Guide **8753**
0036-0201 Russian Castings Production†
0036-021X Russian Chemical Reviews **2079**
0036-0236 Russian Journal of Inorganic Chemistry **2118**
0036-0244 Russian Journal of Physical Chemistry A **2141**
0036-0252 Russian Language Journal†
0036-0260 Russian Language Monthly†
0036-0279 Russian Mathematical Surveys **5530**
0036-0295 Russian Metallurgy **6331**
0036-0309 Russian Oil and Gas Bulletin†
0036-0317 Russian Orthodox Journal **7706**
0036-0325 Russian Pharmacology and Toxicology
0036-0341 The Russian Review **4260**
0036-0384 Russkii Yazyk za Rubezhom **5170**
0036-0406 Russky Golos **3562**
0036-0414 Russland und Wir
0036-0422 Ruta Dominicana
0036-0430 Rutas de Pasion **5412**
0036-0465 Rutgers Law Review **4777**
0036-0473 Rutgers University Libraries. Journal **5044**
0036-0503 Rybovodstvo i Rybolovstvo **3606**
0036-052X Rynki Zagraniczne **1582**
0036-0538 Ryoiku **3046**
0036-0546 Rythmes du Monde†
0036-0570 South African Banking†
0036-0600 South African Cerebral Palsy Journal†
0036-0643 South African Draughtsman **8439**
0036-0678 Transactions S A E S T **2115**
0036-0708 S A F E - Nachrichten **3329**
0036-0767 S A I P A†
0036-0775 S A I S Review **7264**
0036-0813 S A M P E Journal†
0036-0848 South African Machine Tool Review **5459**

0036-0864 South African National Bibliography (Print)†
0036-0899 S. A. News for the Deaf†
0036-0953 SASSAR†
0036-097X S A T I S†
0036-1003 Texnews
0036-1011 S A Worker **4601**
0036-102X S B **1034**
0036-1054 S B S-Werkszeitung der Schoeller-Bleckmann Stahlwerke
0036-1062 Bibliotheque de Travail avec Supplement†
0036-1089 S C A A Viewpoint†
0036-1135 S C J
0036-1143 S C L A Data†
0036-116X Il Messaggio della Santa Casa **7806**
0036-1178 S D C Bulletin†
0036-1186 S D L Newsletter†
0036-1267 S E D O C **7679**
0036-1275 S E H A Newsletter and Proceedings
0036-1380 S H E N†
0036-1399 S I A M Journal on Applied Mathematics **5531**
0036-1410 S I A M Journal on Mathematical Analysis **5531**
0036-1429 S I A M Journal on Numerical Analysis **5531**
0036-1445 S I A M Review **5532**
0036-147X S I G L A S H Newsletter†
0036-1488 Sida: Contributions to Botany *changed to* 1934-5259 **781**
0036-1526 S I G S P A C†
0036-1542 S I L B I Bollettino
0036-1585 S Z
0036-1607 Special Libraries Association. Geography and Map Division. Bulletin†
0036-1615 S L F Tidningen†
0036-1682 S M P T E Journal *changed to* 1545-0279 **6511**
0036-1771 S. O. L. A. I. A. T
0036-1798 S. O. S. Soviet Jewry†
0036-1801 S.O.S., U.S.A. Ship of State
0036-181X S P A Journal†
0036-1852 Spic **8757**
0036-1879 Sweden. Sjukvaardens och Socialvaardens Planerings- och Rationaliseringsinstitut. S P R I Litteraturtjaenst†
0036-1887 Resume **34**
0036-1933 S & T A-Scienza e Tecnologia degli Alimenti†
0036-1941 S T A Educator†
0036-1976 S T E L C O - Scope†
0036-1992 S U D A M Biblioteca. Informa
0036-200X S U D E NE. Boletim da Biblioteca†
0036-2034 Society of St. Vincent de Paul. Bulletin for Southern Africa†
0036-2050 Zpravy S V U **3573**
0036-2085 S.W.L.A. Newsletter†
0036-2115 Saarbruecker Hefte **5237**
0036-2123 Saastopankki
0036-2131 Sabah Society. Journal **7729**
0036-214X Sabbath Recorder **7773**
0036-2158 Sabena Revue†
0036-2204 Sacramento Business†
0036-2212 Sacramento Observer **3562**
0036-2239 Sacramento Teacher†
0036-2247 Sacramento Valley Union Labor Bulletin **4601**
0036-2255 Sacred Music **6614**
0036-2263 The Sacred Organ Journal **6614**
0036-2271 Saddle & Bridle **8298**
0036-231X Holzindustrie†
0036-2328 Saenger- und Musikantenzeitung **6614**
0036-2336 Saenger-Zeitung
0036-2344 Saeugetierkundliche Mitteilungen†
0036-2352 Safari†
0036-2360 Safe and Security News†
0036-2379 The Safe Deposit Bulletin **1381**
0036-2387 Safe Driver†
0036-2395 Safe Engineering†
0036-2409 SAFECO Agent **4522**
0036-2433 Safety†
0036-245X Safety Briefs **7540**
0036-2476 Safety Energizer†
0036-2514 Environmental Control & Safety Management†
0036-2549 Safety Review†
0036-2565 Saga†
0036-2573 Sagan-Sprottauer Heimatbriefe
0036-2581 Saguenay Medical†
0036-2611 Sahakari Jagat
0036-262X Sahamies†
0036-2638 Sahara†
0036-2654 Sahifat Al-Tarbiya
0036-2700 Sail **8281**
0036-2719 Sailing **8281**
0036-2727 Sailing Industry News†
0036-2735 Sailplane and Gliding **69**
0036-2743 Sainik Samachar **6444**
0036-276X Saint Anthony Messenger **7816**
0036-2786 St. Caecilia *changed to* 1571-6791 **6590**
0036-2794 Triomphe Saint-Cyr
0036-2808 St. Dunstan's Review
0036-2832 St. Gallen **8754**
0036-2840 Saint George's Hospital Gazette *changed to* The Saint George's Gazette **4111**
0036-2859 St. Hallvard **4261**
0036-2867 Saint Hubert†
0036-2875 St. Hubertus **8332**
0036-2905 Saint John's Law Review **4778**
0036-2921 St. Jude's Magazine†
0036-293X St. Louis Commerce Magazine **1410**
0036-2948 St. Louis Countian **4778**
0036-2956 St. Louis Genealogical Society Quarterly **3781**
0036-2964 St. Louis Jewish Light **7729**
0036-2972 The St. Louis Journalism Review **4584**
0036-2999 St. Louis Pharmacists' Association Magazine
0036-3006 Saint Louis Purchaser†
0036-3014 Saint Louis University Research Journal **4474**
0036-3022 St. Louis Review **7816**
0036-3030 Saint Louis University. Law Journal **4778**
0036-3081 St. Luke's Hospital Gazette†
0036-3103 St. Mark's Review **7679**
0036-3111 St. Martin's Review **7816**
0036-312X St. Mary's Hospital Gazette†
0036-3146 Saint Paul Area Chamber of Commerce Action†
0036-3154 St. Paul News
0036-3162 St. Poeltner Dioezesanblatt **7679**
0036-3197 Saint Thomas More Political Science Journal
0036-3227 St. Vladimir's Theological Quarterly **7706**
0036-326X Sairaala **4111**
0036-3286 Collecting and Breeding†
0036-3294 Saison†
0036-3308 Saitenspiel **6614**
0036-3316 Saiva Siddhanta **6950**
0036-3332 Wine, Spirits and Provisions Monthly Statistics
0036-3367 Salt†
0036-3375 Salamandra **962**
0036-3391 Sales†
0036-3405 Sales Executive†
0036-3464 Sales/Slants†
0036-3472 Sales Tax Advices **1942**
0036-3480 Salesian **7816**
0036-3502 Salesianum **7816**
0036-3529 Salmagundi **4474**
0036-3537 Salmanticensis **7816**
0036-3545 Salmon and Trout Magazine†
0036-3561 Salotto Culturale
0036-357X Salpisma **7773**
0036-360X Salt Lick
0036-3618 Salt Water Sportsman **8331**
0036-3634 Salud Publica de Mexico **7540**
0036-3642 Salus Militiae
0036-3669 Salvage Bids **4522**
0036-3677 Salzburger Wirtschaft **1409**
0036-3693 Samaj Kalyan
0036-3715 Samarbete **1424**
0036-374X Samatat Prakashan
0036-3790 Samlarnytt **2269**
0036-3804 Sammelwerk Bauzentrumring†
0036-3839 Samoa Times†
0036-3847 Samostiina Ukrayina†
0036-3855 Samouprava Zavarovancev†
0036-3863 Samoupravljanje
0036-3871 Sampada **1516**
0036-388X Samphire†
0036-3898 Sample Case **2269**
0036-391X Samson Technology Trends†
0036-3928 Samtiden **5238**
0036-3944 Samvirke **3834**
0036-3960 San Antonio Monthly
0036-3987 San Beda Review
0036-3995 San Bernardino County Library Newsletter†
0036-4002 San Diego Business†
0036-4029 Door
0036-4037 San Diego Law Review **4778**
0036-4053 San Diego Numismatic Society. Bulletin **6653**
0036-4061 San Diego Physician **5709**
0036-407X San Diego Sound Post **4602**
0036-410X San Francisco Business†
0036-4118 San Francisco Camera
0036-4126 San Francisco Earthquake†
0036-4169 San Francisco Unified School District Newsletter†
0036-4185 San Jose Post-Record **4778**
0036-4215 San Luis Valley Historian **4312**
0036-4223 San Marino (Repubblica) Bollettino Ufficiale **7467**
0036-424X San Salvatore da Horta
0036-4258 Sanatorio Sao Lucas. Boletim†
0036-4266 Sand Castles†
0036-4282 Sandal Prints†
0036-4312 Saneamento
0036-4339 Sangeet Natak **6614**
0036-4355 Sangre† **8987**
0036-4363 Sangue della Redenzione†
0036-4371 Sangyo Gijutsu Joho Yokkaichi **8437**
0036-438X Industrial Training **1752**
0036-4398 Sangyo Sharyo **8603**
0036-4401 Sanitaer- und Heizungstechnik **4126**
0036-4428 University of California. Sanitary Engineering and Environmental Health Research Laboratory. News Quarterly†
0036-4436 Sanitary Maintenance **1842**
0036-4444 Sanity†
0036-4460 Sannio Elegante
0036-4495 Sanshi Kenkyu†
0036-4525 Santa Clara County in Action†
0036-4541 Santa Fe Magazine†
0036-455X Santa Gertrudis Journal†
0036-4568 La Sante de l'Abeille **154**
0036-4576 Sante et Sport†
0036-4584 Sante, Liberte et Vaccinations†
0036-4606 Il Santo dei Voli† **8987**
0036-4614 Santuario de Aparecida **7679**
0036-4622 Il Santuario della Madonna delle Rocche **7816**
0036-4649 Sanyo Kasei News **2080**
0036-4657 Sao Paulo **3804**
0036-4665 Instituto de Medicina Tropical de Sao Paulo. Revista **5818**
0036-4681 Sapere **7907**
0036-469X Sapeur-Pompier **3581**
0036-4703 Sapientia **6951**
0036-4711 Sapienza **6951**
0036-472X Sapporo Igaku Zasshi **5709**
0036-4738 Sarah Lawrence Journal†
0036-4754 Sarasvat **3889**
0036-4762 Sarawak Gazette **3907**
0036-4770 Sardegna Economica **1409**
0036-4789 Sardegna Informazioni
0036-4797 Sarika **5367**
0036-4827 Sarsia *changed to* 1745-1000 **688**
0036-4835 Sarvodaya **8067**
0036-4843 Sash†
0036-4851 SaskTel News **2371**
0036-4886 Saskatchewan Bulletin **2909**
0036-4894 The Saskatchewan Gazette **4779**
0036-4908 Saskatchewan History **4312**
0036-4916 Saskatchewan Law Review **4779**
0036-4924 Saskatchewan Library†
0036-4975 Saturday Night†
0036-4991 Satya Prakash **3889**
0036-5009 Sau og Geit **299**
0036-5025 Saucers, Space & Science†
0036-5041 Sauvegarde de l'Enfance†
0036-505X Sauvegarde des Chantiers†
0036-5068 Savacou **516**
0036-5092 Savez Omladine†
0036-5149 Savita
0036-5157 Savoia
0036-5173 Savremena Praksa **4779**
0036-5203 Savremeno Domacinstvo
0036-522X Sbirka Soudnich Rozhodnuti a Stanovisek **4779**
0036-5246 Sbornik Archivnich Praci **5045**
0036-5270 Sbornik Geologickych Ved: Antropozoikum **2766**
0036-5289 Sbornik Geologickych Ved: Hydrogeologie, Inzenyrska Geologie **2798**
0036-5297 Sbornik Geologickych Ved: Paleontologie **6730**
0036-5300 Sbornik Geologickych Ved: Technologie, Geochemie†
0036-5327 Sbornik Lekarsky *changed to* 1214-6994 **5698**
0036-5335 Narodni Muzeum v Praze. Sbornik. Rada A: Historie **6533**
0036-5343 Narodni Muzeum v Praze. Sbornik. Rada B: Prirodni Vedy **6533**
0036-5351 Narodni Muzeum v Praze. Sbornik. Rada C: Literarni Historie **6533**
0036-536X V S D a V u D Sobornik Praci†
0036-5408 Scabbard and Blade Journal **6445**
0036-5424 Scale Modeler†
0036-5467 Scan (New York) **3562**
0036-5483 Scandia (Lund) **4160**
0036-5513 Scandinavian Journal of Clinical & Laboratory Investigation **5910**
0036-5521 Scandinavian Journal of Gastroenterology **5930**
0036-5548 Scandinavian Journal of Infectious Diseases **5826**
0036-5564 Scandinavian Journal of Psychology **7406**
0036-5599 Scandinavian Journal of Urology and Nephrology **6274**
0036-5602 Scandinavian Public Library Quarterly **5045**
0036-5610 Scandinavian Research Information Notes†
0036-5629 Scandinavian Shipping Gazette†
0036-5637 Scandinavian Studies (Provo) **5367**
0036-5653 Scandinavica **5367**
0036-5661 Scanlan's Monthly†
0036-5696 Scautismo
0036-5726 Scena
0036-5734 Scena **8478**
0036-5742 Scena Illustrata **5238**
0036-5777 Scene from Oceana†
0036-5815 Scenografie†
0036-5858 Schakel
0036-5882 Schakels†
0036-5904 Schaktbladet
0036-5920 Scharnhorst Auslese
0036-5955 Schedario† **8987**
0036-6005 La Scherma **8199**
0036-6013 Schiedamse Gemeenschap†
0036-6056 Schiffbauforschung **8660**
0036-6110 Schism, a Journal of Divergent American Opinion†
0036-6137 Schlager fuer Dich
0036-6145 Der Schlern **516**
0036-6153 Schlesien† **8987**
0036-617X Der Schluessel†
0036-6188 Der Schluessel†
0036-6226 Schmierungstechnik†
0036-6250 Schoeffe†
0036-6269 Schoen - Visie **7941**
0036-6307 Schoenwereld *changed to* 1570-520X **7942**
0036-6315 Schoevers Koerier
0036-6331 Scholarly Books in America†
0036-6358 Scholars' Choice **7699**
0036-6374 Scholarships for Foreign Students and Postgraduates at Austrian Universities and Art Academies†
0036-6412 Scholastic Scope **3080**
0036-6439 School Administrator **3031**
0036-6447 School and Community **2909**
0036-6463 School Arts **3080**
0036-6471 School Board†
0036-6501 School Bus Fleet **8510**
0036-651X School Business Affairs **3031**
0036-6544 School en Godsdienst†
0036-6587 School Law Review†
0036-6595 School Librarian **5045**
0036-6668 School Music News
0036-6676 School Musician Director and Teacher†
0036-6684 School News
0036-6706 Michigan State University. School of Labor and Industrial Relations. Newsletter **1697**
0036-679X School Science **7907**
0036-6803 School Science and Mathematics **3081**
0036-6811 School Science Review **7907**
0036-6846 School Times†
0036-6854 School Trustee *changed to* 1711-9405 **3031**
0036-6862 School Yarn Magazine†
0036-6897 Schoolgirl Story Magazine†
0036-6900 Schools in Action†
0036-6943 Evangelischer Bund in Oesterreich. Schriftenreihe **7757**
0036-6978 N T M International Journal of History and Ethics of Natural Sciences, Technology and Medicine *changed to* N T M Journal of History of Sciences, Technology, and Medicine **7885**
0036-6986 Das Schrifttum der Agrarwirtschaft†
0036-7036 Schuh im Bild
0036-7044 Schuh-Kurier **7941**
0036-7060 Schuh-Zeitung
0036-7087 Schuhwirtschaft†
0036-7109 Schule und Europa†
0036-7117 Schule und Gesellschaft†
0036-7125 Schulfernsehen (Munich) **2910**

ISSN

0036-7133	Schutz und Wehr†
0036-7184	Schweissen und Schneiden **6343**
0036-7206	Schweisstechnik **6344**
0036-7257	Schweizer Aluminium Rundschau†
0036-7281	Schweizer Archiv fuer Tierheilkunde **8807**
0036-729X	Schweizer Auto-Verkehr†
0036-7303	Schweizer Baublatt *changed to* 1660-4504 **979**
0036-732X	Schweizer Buch **7573**
0036-7338	Schweizer Buchhandel **7573**
0036-7362	Schweizer Illustrierte **3959**
0036-7370	Schweizer Journal **456**
0036-7397	Schweizer Maschinenmarkt **5459**
0036-7400	Schweizer Monatshefte **5238**
0036-7419	Schweizer Musiker-Revue
0036-7443	Schweizer Schule **2910**
0036-746X	Der Schweizer Treuhaender **1301**
0036-7486	Schweizerische Aerztezeitung **5710**
0036-7532	Beobachter **3957**
0036-7540	Schweizerische Bienen-Zeitung **154**
0036-7575	Schweizerische Entomologische Gesellschaft. Mitteilungen **858**
0036-7613	Schweizerische Juristen-Zeitung **4780**
0036-7699	Schweizerische Mineralogische und Petrographische Mitteilungen **6479**
0036-7737	Schweizerische Photorundschau
0036-7745	Schweizerische Schachzeitung **8199**
0036-7753	Schweizerische Schreinerzeitung **1051**
0036-7796	Schweizerische Weinzeitung **610**
0036-7818	Schweizerische Zeitschrift fuer Forstwesen **3701**
0036-7834	Schweizerische Zeitschrift fuer Geschichte **4160**
0036-7850	Schweizerische Zeitschrift fuer Musik-Handel und Industrie†
0036-7893	Schweizerische Zeitschrift fuer Strafrecht **2668**
0036-794X	Schweizerisches Archiv fuer Volkskunde **3622**
0036-7958	Schweizerisches Gutenbergmuseum†
0036-8016	Schweizer Jaeger **8332**
0036-8032	Schwenkfeldian **7774**
0036-8040	Sci **8332**
0036-8059	Sci-Tech News **7938**
0036-8067	Sci/Tech Quarterly Index†
0036-8075	Science **7908**
0036-8083	Le Scienze **7913**
0036-8091	Physics Abstracts **7048**
0036-8105	Electrical & Electronics Abstracts **3229**
0036-8113	Computer & Control Abstracts **2442**
0036-8121	Science Activities **7908**
0036-813X	Science Affairs†
0036-8148	Science and Children **7908**
0036-8156	Science and Culture **7908**
0036-8164	Science and Engineering **3219**
0036-8172	Doshisha Daigaku Rikogaku Kenkyu Hokoku **3187**
0036-8180	Science and Industry†
0036-8237	Science & Society **7182**
0036-8245	Science and Technology (New York)†
0036-8261	Science Bulletin
0036-827X	Science Citation Index **7938**
0036-8288	Science Curriculum Improvement Study Newsletter†
0036-8326	Science Education **7909**
0036-8334	Science Education News
0036-8342	Science et Nature†
0036-8369	Science & Vie **7909**
0036-8377	Science Fiction Review†
0036-8385	Science for Schools
0036-8407	Science in Parliament **7910**
0036-8423	Science News **7910**
0036-8458	Science of Mind Magazine **7741**
0036-8466	Science of the Soul **7680**
0036-8482	Science Policy Reviews†
0036-8504	Science Progress **7910**
0036-8512	Science Reporter **7910**
0036-8520	Science Review†
0036-8555	The Science Teacher **3081**
0036-858X	Science Today **7911**
0036-8598	Science Tools†
0036-861X	The Sciences†
0036-8628	Sciences & l'Enseignement des Sciences†
0036-8636	Sciences et Avenir **7912**
0036-8679	Scientia **7912**
0036-8687	Scientia†
0036-8695	Scientia Electrica†
0036-8709	Scientia Pharmaceutica **6880**
0036-8725	Scientiarum Historia†
0036-8733	Scientific American **7912**
0036-8792	Industrial Lubrication & Tribology **3379**
0036-8857	Scientific World†
0036-8881	Scienza e Tecnica Agraria
0036-892X	Scierie & Charpente†
0036-8946	Scintilla
0036-8954	Scooter World†
0036-8962	Scopcraeft†
0036-8970	Scope†
0036-9012	Scope†
0036-9039	Score†
0036-9063	Scotland's Magazine†
0036-9071	Scots Independent **7182**
0036-908X	Scots Law Times **4780**
0036-911X	Scottish Art Review
0036-9136	Scottish Baptist Magazine†
0036-9144	Scottish Birds **914**
0036-9160	Scottish Curler **8199**
0036-9179	Scottish Educational Journal **2910**
0036-9195	The Scottish Farmer **155**
0036-9209	Scottish Field **3870**
0036-9217	Scottish Forestry **3701**
0036-9233	Scottish Grocer **3681**
0036-9241	The Scottish Historical Review **4160**
0036-925X	Scottish Home and Country **8883**
0036-9276	Scottish Journal of Geology **2766**
0036-9284	Scottish Journal of Occupational Therapy†
0036-9292	Scottish Journal of Political Economy **1172**
0036-9306	Scottish Journal of Theology **7680**
0036-9314	Scottish Law Gazette **4781**
0036-9322	Scottish Licensed Trade News **610**
0036-9330	Scottish Medical Journal **5711**
0036-9349	Scottish Miner
0036-9357	Scottish Pharmacist†
0036-9373	Scottish Primary Quarterly†
0036-939X	Scottish Schoolmaster†
0036-9411	Scottish Studies **4262**
0036-942X	Scottish Sunday School Teacher†
0036-9446	Scottish Women's Temperance News
0036-9489	Scouting **2212**
0036-9500	Scouting **2168**
0036-9535	Scraper†
0036-9543	Screen (Oxford) **2390**
0036-9551	Screen (Mumbai) **6512**
0036-9594	Screen Printing **7327**
0036-9608	Screen Stories†
0036-9616	Screenland†
0036-9624	Screw†
0036-9632	Scribblings†
0036-973X	Scripta Mercaturae **1549**
0036-9764	Scripta Theologica **7680**
0036-9772	Scriptorium **4474**
0036-9780	Scripture Bulletin **7817**
0036-9799	Scroll of Phi Delta Theta **2300**
0036-9802	Scugnizzo†
0036-9810	Scuola Cattolica **7817**
0036-9837	Scuola di Base†
0036-9845	Italy. Scuola di Guerra. Biblioteca. Bollettino† **8967**
0036-9853	Scuola & Citta **2910**
0036-9861	Scuola e Didattica **2911**
0036-987X	La Scuola e l'Uomo **2911**
0036-9888	Scuola Italiana Moderna **2911**
0036-9896	Scuola Media†
0036-9926	Scuola Viva† **8987**
0036-9942	Sdelovaci Technika **2371**
0036-9950	Se Vuoi **7680**
0036-9977	Sea Breezes **8660**
0037-007X	The Seafarer **8660**
0037-010X	Seafood Export Journal **3607**
0037-0118	Seahorse†
0037-0126	Seal†
0037-0142	Seaman†
0037-0169	Seara Medica Neurocirurgica†
0037-0193	Search and Seizure Bulletin **2668**
0037-0207	Search: Chemical Materials & Products Division†
0037-0215	Search: Coal, Coke & Mineral Tars Division†
0037-0223	Search: CPI Marketing & Statistics Division†
0037-0231	Search: Drugs Division†
0037-024X	Search: Dyes, Pigments & Coatings Division†
0037-0258	Search: Essential Oils, Soaps & Toiletries Division†
0037-0266	Search: Fertilizers Division†
0037-0274	Search: Foodstuffs Division†
0037-0282	Search: Inorganic Chemicals Division†
0037-0304	Search: Metals Division†
0037-0312	Search: Non-Metallic Minerals Division†
0037-0320	Search: Oils, Fats & Waxes Division†
0037-0339	Search: Organic Chemicals Division†
0037-0347	Search: Pesticides Division†
0037-0355	Search: Petroleum Division†
0037-0363	Search: Plastics & Resins Division†
0037-0371	Search: Pulp & Paper Division†
0037-038X	Search: Rubber Division†
0037-0398	Search: Textiles Division†
0037-0401	Searcher (Burbank) **3782**
0037-041X	Searcher **4602**
0037-0460	Seattle Folklore Society Newsletter **3622**
0037-0495	Adhesion and Adhesives **7090**
0037-0509	Sechaba†
0037-0517	Secolul 20 **5369**
0037-055X	Second District Dental Society. Bulletin **5865**
0037-0576	Second Line **6615**
0037-0592	Secret Confessions
0037-0606	The Secret Place **7774**
0037-0657	Securitas†
0037-0665	Securities Regulation & Law Report **4781**
0037-0673	Securities Regulation and Transfer Report†
0037-0711	Sedia e Il Mobile†
0037-0738	Sedimentary Geology **2766**
0037-0746	Sedimentology **2766**
0037-0762	See India **8755**
0037-0789	Seed Trade News†
0037-0797	Seed World **252**
0037-0819	The Seeing Eye Guide **4085**
0037-0827	Seek†
0037-0851	Seer(Inkprint Edition)†
0037-0878	Der Seewart†
0037-0894	Sefarad **4325**
0037-0916	Seglarbladet **8282**
0037-0932	Segnalazioni Cinematografiche
0037-0940	Camera di Commercio Italiana per la Gran Bretagna e il Commonwealth. Segnalazioni
0037-0967	Segretario del Comune e della Provincia†
0037-0991	Seihin News†
0037-1009	Seihonkai
0037-1017	Seikagaku **745**
0037-1025	Seikatsu to Kankyo **3465**
0037-1033	Seikei Geka to Saigai Geka **6072**
0037-1041	Seine et Paris†
0037-105X	Seisan Kenkyu **8438**
0037-1076	Seishin Bunseki†
0037-1084	Seishin Studies **4474**
0037-1092	Seishonen Sekijuji†
0037-1106	Seismological Society of America. Bulletin **2789**
0037-1114	Jishin **2784**
0037-1122	Seiva **155**
0037-1157	Selbst ist der Mann **4439**
0037-1173	Sele Arte†
0037-119X	Selecciones de Teologia **7680**
0037-1203	Selecciones del Reader's Digest (Chilean Edition) **3822**
0037-1246	Selecciones del Reader's Digest (Iberian Edition)
0037-1262	Selecoes Zootecnicas†
0037-1297	Selected Abstracts of Non-U.S. Literature on Production and Industrial Uses of Radioisotopes†
0037-1300	University of California, Berkeley. Library School Library. Selected Additions to the Library School Library Collection†
0037-1335	Selected Philippine Periodical Index†
0037-1343	Selected Rand Abstracts **7939**
0037-1351	Princeton University. Industrial Relations Section. Selected References **1259**
0037-1378	Reader's Digest, Selection **3816**
0037-1386	Selection du Reader's Digest (French Edition) **3842**
0037-1394	Selection du Reader's Digest (Swiss-French Edition) **3959**
0037-1408	Selection du Reader's Digest (Belgian-French Edition) **3801**
0037-1424	Selection of International Railway Documentation†
0037-1459	Selektsiya i Semenovodstvo **252**
0037-1483	Selezione dal Reader's Digest (Italian Edition)† **8987**
0037-1505	Selezione per l'Avicoltore
0037-1521	La Selezione Veterinaria
0037-153X	Self†
0037-1556	Self-Knowledge **6951**
0037-1564	Self-Realization **7741**
0037-1602	Selling Christmas Decorations **4061**
0037-1629	Selling Today
0037-1637	Selmer Bandwagon†
0037-1661	Sel'skoe Khozyaistvo
0037-1718	Selskostopanska Tekhnika **214**
0037-1734	Semailles†
0037-1750	Semaine Commerciale
0037-1777	La Semaine des Hopitaux†
0037-1793	Semana **3953**
0037-1815	Semana Medica de Centroamerica y Panama
0037-184X	Semana Vitivinicola **252**
0037-1858	Semanario Israelita
0037-1866	Sembrador
0037-1874	Semeador Baptista **7774**
0037-1882	Gemengo Textiel†
0037-1890	Sementi Elette *changed to* dal Seme **227**
0037-1912	Semigroup Forum **5533**
0037-1939	Seminar **5369**
0037-1947	Seminar†
0037-1963	Seminars in Hematology **5941**
0037-198X	Seminars in Roentgenology **6208**
0037-1998	Semiotica **5173**
0037-2005	Seema†
0037-203X	Sempre Pronto **2911**
0037-2064	Sen-i Kogyo Zasshi†
0037-2072	Sen'i Seihin Shohi Kagaku **8457**
0037-2102	Senckenbergiana Biologica† **8988**
0037-2110	Senckenbergiana Lethaea *changed to* 1867-1594 **6727**
0037-2129	Sendbote des Herzens Jesu
0037-2137	Sendingnuus
0037-2145	Seneca Review **5434**
0037-2161	Senftenegger Monatsblatt fuer Genealogie und Heraldik†
0037-217X	Sen'i Kako†
0037-2218	The Senior Golfer†
0037-2250	Seniorscope†
0037-2277	Sentai Chii Zappo†
0037-2307	Sentinel (Dollard des Ormeaux)†
0037-2315	Sentinel (Ottawa)†
0037-234X	Sentinella Agricola **155**
0037-2374	Sepia†
0037-2404	Sept Jours de l'Economie Francaise†
0037-2412	Sequences **6512**
0037-2420	Sequoia (Stanford)†
0037-2447	Serials Bulletin†
0037-2455	Nihon Sanshigaku Zasshi/Journal of Sericultural Science of Japan *changed to* 1881-0551 **858**
0037-2463	Series Haematologica†
0037-248X	Sermon Builder†
0037-2498	Serpe†
0037-2501	Serra d'Or **5238**
0037-251X	Serra-Post†
0037-2536	Serviam
0037-2544	Service†
0037-2552	Service and Indemnity†
0037-2579	Revue Technique Diesel **8601**
0037-2595	Service Economique & Financier "Secofi" **1382**
0037-2633	Service Social†
0037-265X	Service Station
0037-2692	Servicio Nacional Tecnico del Carton Ondulado. Revista†
0037-2757	Servir Mieux†
0037-2765	Servire **2212**
0037-2773	Servizio della Parola **7681**
0037-2781	Rassegna degli Archivi di Stato **4256**
0037-279X	Servizio Informazioni Avio†
0037-2803	Servizio Migranti **7182**
0037-2811	Sesenta
0037-282X	Scottish Council of Law Reporting. Session Cases **4780**
0037-2846	Sestina Sveta v Obrazecht†
0037-2862	Setimo Ceu†
0037-2870	Seto Marine Biological Laboratory. Publications **704**
0037-2889	Square Dancing†
0037-2897	Settanta Anni di Calcio†
0037-2900	Settegiorni
0037-2927	Settimana Medica†
0037-2935	Settimanale di Diritto e Legislazione del Lavoro†
0037-2951	Seva-Bharati
0037-2986	Seven Arts†
0037-2994	Seven Arts Digest†
0037-3001	Seven Arts Guide†
0037-301X	Seventeen **8883**
0037-3028	Seventeenth - Century News **5369**
0037-3052	The Sewanee Review **5370**
0037-3095	Sexual Behavior†
0037-3125	Shabistan Urdu Digest†
0037-3133	Shade Tree **3750**
0037-3176	Shaheen
0037-3184	Shahpar†

0037-3214 Shakespeare Newsletter **5370**
0037-3222 Shakespeare Quarterly **5370**
0037-3257 Shale Shaker **2767**
0037-3265 Shalom **7729**
0037-3273 Shama **3889**
0037-3281 Shankar's Weekly†
0037-329X Shantih†
0037-3311 Shareholder†
0037-332X Sharkara
0037-3346 Shavian **5371**
0037-3362 Shawcover†
0037-3370 She **8883**
0037-3389 She†
0037-3400 Sheep Breeder and Sheepman **300**
0037-3419 Sheera Udyog†
0037-3435 Sheet Metal Industries†
0037-3478 Pleiadi† **8981**
0037-3494 Shelfmark **635**
0037-3508 Shell Aviation News†
0037-3516 Shell Bitumen Review†
0037-3559 Shell Revue†
0037-3583 Shenandoah **5238**
0037-3605 Shepherd's Call†
0037-3613 Shepherd's Magazine
0037-3621 Sherlock Holmes Journal **5415**
0037-3648 Shetkari
0037-3656 Sheviley Hahinuch†
0037-3664 Shichokaku Kyoiku **2912**
0037-3672 Shield
0037-3699 Shikoku Igaku Zasshi **5713**
0037-3710 Shika Gakuho **5865**
0037-3729 Shilo Stag **6446**
0037-3737 Shin Kaki†
0037-3745 Shin Nippon Denki Giho†
0037-3761 Shin Toshi **4427**
0037-3788 Shinkan News for Readers **7573**
0037-3796 Shinkei Kagaku **6185**
0037-380X Shinryo to Shinyaku **5714**
0037-3818 Shinshu University. Faculty of Engineering. Journal **3219**
0037-3826 Shinshu Medical Journal **5714**
0037-3834 Ship & Boat International **8661**
0037-3842 Ship-Shape†
0037-3885 Shipping and Port Review†
0037-3893 Shipping Digest **8661**
0037-3907 Shipping Executive
0037-3915 Shipping Gazette **8661**
0037-3931 Shipping World & Shipbuilder **8661**
0037-394X Ships Monthly **8662**
0037-3958 Shipyard Review
0037-3966 Shire & Municipal Record†
0037-3982 Shiryo Gaido†
0037-3990 Shitai Fujiyu Kyoiku **3046**
0037-4008 Shituf
0037-4016 Purchasing and Materials Management
0037-4024 Shkola i Proizvodstvo **2912**
0037-4040 Shoe and Leather News†
0037-4067 Shoe Service Wholesaler†
0037-4075 Shoe Workers' Journal†
0037-4091 Shokubutsu Boeki **252**
0037-4105 Shokuhin To Kagaku **3663**
0037-4113 Shoni Hoken Kenkyu **6996**
0037-4121 Shonika **6104**
0037-4148 Shooting Industry **8200**
0037-4164 Shooting Times and Country Magazine **8200**
0037-4172 S E N: Shop Equipment & Shopfitting News *changed to* 1470-9600
0037-4180 Shop Fitting and Equipment Monitor†
0037-4199 Shop Property†
0037-4237 Shore & Beach **2627**
0037-4245 Short's Story
0037-4261 Short Wave Magazine *changed to* 1748-8117 **2363**
0037-427X Shorthorn News **300**
0037-4288 Shorthorn World†
0037-430X Show-Business†
0037-4318 Show Business **8478**
0037-4334 Show-Me Missouri Legionnaire
0037-4342 Showa Medical Association. Journal
0037-4350 Showcase
0037-4393 Shropshire Magazine
0037-4407 Shubyo to Engei **3750**
0037-4415 Shui Hsing Tsa Chih
0037-4423 Shujutsu **6258**
0037-444X Si De Ka Magazine†
0037-4466 Siberian Mathematical Journal **5536**
0037-4474 Sibirskii Matematicheskii Zhurnal **5536**
0037-4482 Sibylle†
0037-4512 Sichere Arbeit **6687**
0037-4539 Sicherheit Zuerst **8625**
0037-4547 Sicherheitstechniker-Korrespondenz†
0037-4563 Sicilia
0037-4571 Sicilia Archeologica **416**
0037-458X Siculorum Gymnasium **4475**
0037-4598 Sicurezza Sociale†
0037-4601 Sidemount Reporter **4347**
0037-461X 7 Tage **3861**
0037-4628 Siecle a Mains
0037-4687 Elektrodienst†
0037-4733 Sierra Leone
0037-4741 Sierra Leone. Central Statistics Office. Quarterly Statistical Bulletin†
0037-475X Sierra Leone Studies†
0037-4768 Sierra Leone Trade Journal **1433**
0037-4784 Siete Dias Ilustrados **3792**
0037-4792 Sifriya Laam **5372**
0037-4806 Sight and Sound **6513**
0037-4814 Sight & Sound Marketing
0037-4830 Sightlines (Niles)†
0037-4849 Sigma†
0037-4857 Sigma **4523**
0037-4873 Sign (Union City)†
0037-4903 Signa†

0037-4911 Signal†
0037-492X Signal†
0037-4938 Signal Magazine (Fairfax) **2338**
0037-4946 Signal (Upminster)†
0037-4954 Signal†
0037-4970 Signal International **4347**
0037-4997 Signal und Draht **8625**
0037-5012 Signal 8-2 **2668**
0037-5020 Signalman's Journal **4602**
0037-5055 Signs of the Times **7681**
0037-5063 Signs of the Times **35**
0037-5071 Signs of the Times†
0037-5101 Sika **300**
0037-5128 Sikh Review **7681**
0037-5144 Sikkim†
0037-5152 Sikorsky News
0037-5160 Siksha - O - Sahitya **2912**
0037-5179 Silarus **5239**
0037-5187 The Silent Advocate **4076**
0037-5209 Silent Picture†
0037-5225 Silicates Industriels **2045**
0037-5233 Silikattechnik†
0037-5268 Silk Screen *changed to* 1871-6741 **7328**
0037-5276 Silliman Christian Leader†
0037-5284 Silliman Journal **7916**
0037-5306 Silo†
0037-5314 Silpakon
0037-5322 Sil's'ke Budivnytstvo **156**
0037-5330 Silva Fennica **3702**
0037-5349 Silvae Genetica **817**
0037-5365 Silver Screen†
0037-5373 Silvicultura†
0037-539X Simian **6815**
0037-5403 Simiente **156**
0037-5411 Simiolus **517**
0037-542X Simmenthal Club†
0037-5446 Simon Fraser University. Library. Information Bulletin†
0037-5462 Restorica **455**
0037-5470 Simon's Town Historical Society Bulletin **4178**
0037-5497 Simulation **3220**
0037-5527 Sin Nombre†
0037-5535 Sinai Hospital of Detroit. Bulletin†
0037-5543 Sindacato Moderno
0037-556X Sindicato Nacional de la Pesca. Boletin de Informacion **3608**
0037-5578 Sindicato Nacional Textil. Boletin de Informacion†
0037-5608 Sinfonie Scacchistiche
0037-5616 Sinformation
0037-5624 Sing Out! **6616**
0037-5640 Singapore. Department of Statistics. Monthly Digest of Statistics **8399**
0037-5659 Singapore International Chamber of Commerce. Economic Bulletin **1409**
0037-5675 Singapore Medical Journal **5715**
0037-5721 Singende Kirche **6616**
0037-5748 Single Parent†
0037-5756 Sinn und Form **5373**
0037-5764 Sino Azul
0037-5780 Sintesi Economica†
0037-5799 Sintesis Informativa Economica y Financiera **1517**
0037-5810 Sion
0037-5829 Sioux City Journal Farm Weekly†
0037-5837 Sipapu†
0037-5845 Sir
0037-5853 Siren†
0037-5888 Sistematica **6952**
0037-590X Sisters Today
0037-5934 Situation in Argentina†
0037-5942 Gesellschaft Naturforschender Freunde zu Berlin. Sitzungsberichte. Neue Folge **7857**
0037-5950 Sivam **7708**
0037-5985 S J - Nytt **8624**
0037-6000 Sjoesport†
0037-6019 Sjukgymnasten *changed to* 1653-5804 **5617**
0037-6043 Skakbladet **8201**
0037-6078 Skandinavisk Emballage- och Transport-Tidskrift†
0037-6124 Skate†
0037-6132 Skating **8201**
0037-6140 Skeet Shooting Review **8201**
0037-6159 Ski **8333**
0037-6167 Ski
0037-6175 Ski Area Management **8333**
0037-6213 Ski Racing **8201**
0037-6221 Ski Runner
0037-6248 Skier (Brattleboro)†
0037-6264 Skiing Magazine **8333**
0037-6310 Ringsport **8197**
0037-6329 Skillings' Mining Review **6479**
0037-6337 Skin & Allergy News **5882**
0037-6345 Skin Diver†
0037-637X Sklar a Keramik **2045**
0037-6396 Skogeieren **3702**
0037-640X Skogen **3702**
0037-6418 S L A-Tidskriften†
0037-6434 Skogsbruket **3702**
0037-6450 Skola Danas
0037-6469 Skolans Artikelservice **635**
0037-6477 Barn & Kultur†
0037-6485 Skolefilm†
0037-6515 Skolledaren **2913**
0037-6523 Skolska Televizija†
0037-6531 Skolske Novine **2913**
0037-654X Skolski Vjesnik
0037-6558 Skolta Mondo†
0037-6566 Skolvaerlden **2913**
0037-6582 Skov og Soe†
0037-6604 Sky & Telescope **581**
0037-6620 Skylights†
0037-6663 Skyttebladet **8201**
0037-6671 Skyways†
0037-668X Slaboproudy Obzor
0037-6736 Slavia **5174**

0037-6744 Slavia Orientalis **5174**
0037-6752 Slavic and East European Journal **5174**
0037-6779 Slavic Review **8002**
0037-6787 Slavica Slovaca **5175**
0037-6795 Slavonic and East European Review **5373**
0037-6817 Sleep-Learning Association. Journal†
0037-6825 Slevarenstvi
0037-6833 Slezsky Sbornik **8132**
0037-685X Slingervel **7775**
0037-6868 Sloboda
0037-6876 Sloboda†
0037-6884 Slobodna Rec†
0037-6892 Sloejd och Ton†
0037-6914 Slovak Press Digest **3564**
0037-6922 Slovansky Prehled **7183**
0037-6930 Slovenska Akademia Vied. Biologicke Prace†
0037-6957 Slovenska Drzava **7183**
0037-6973 Slovenska Literatura **5373**
0037-6981 Slovenska Rec **5175**
0037-699X Slovenske Divadlo **8478**
0037-7007 Slovenske Pohlady na Literaturu a Umenie **5373**
0037-7015 Slovensky Hlas†
0037-7031 Slovo a Slovesnost **5175**
0037-7058 Slowakei†
0037-7074 Sluzba Bozja **7681**
0037-7090 Sojuzot za Fizicka Kultura na Makedonija. Sluzben Glasnik
0037-7104 Sluzbene Novine Opcine Karlovac
0037-7112 Opcina Podravska Slatina. Sluzbeni Glasnik
0037-7120 Sluzbeni Glasnik Opcine Rovinj **7502**
0037-7155 Sluzbeni Vjesnik Opcine Buje, Novigrad i Umag
0037-721X Small Pond Magazine of Literature **5374**
0037-7228 Small Press Review (Print) *changed to* 1949-2731 **7574**
0037-7260 Small World†
0037-7295 Holecpost (Dutch Edition)†
0037-7317 Smith College Studies in Social Work **8068**
0037-7333 Smithsonian **8002**
0037-735X Smog
0037-7376 Smuffeltje†
0037-7449 Sneha Sandesh†
0037-7457 Snips **4126**
0037-7473 Snowy Egret **5374**
0037-749X Soap, Perfumery & Cosmetics **596**
0037-7503 Soaring **70**
0037-7511 Slaski Kwartalnik Historyczny "Sobotka" **4161**
0037-752X Sobre Educacion Superior†
0037-7538 Soccer News†
0037-7554 Soccer World
0037-7562 Soccorso Perpetuo di Maria† **8988**
0037-7627 Social Action **8002**
0037-7651 Social and Economic Studies **8002**
0037-766X Social Biology *changed to* 1948-5565 **864**
0037-7686 Social Compass **8132**
0037-7694 The Social Crediter **7183**
0037-7716 Social Defence **2668**
0037-7724 Social Education **3082**
0037-7732 Social Forces **8133**
0037-7767 Social Justice Review **7817**
0037-7783 Social Policy **8003**
0037-7791 Social Problems **8134**
0037-7805 Church & Society **7751**
0037-783X Social Research **8003**
0037-7872 Social Science Record
0037-7880 Social Science Reporter and Public Relations Research Review†
0037-7902 Social Security Abstracts†
0037-7910 Social Security Bulletin **4523**
0037-7937 Social Service†
0037-7945 Social Service Outlook†
0037-7953 Social Service Quarterly†
0037-7961 Social Service Review **8069**
0037-797X Social Services in Wisconsin†
0037-7996 The Social Studies **8005**
0037-8003 Social Studies Teacher†
0037-8011 Social Survey†
0037-802X Social Theory and Practice **6952**
0037-8038 Social Welfare **8070**
0037-8046 Social Work **8070**
0037-8054 Social Work **8070**
0037-8062 Social Work Education Reporter† **8988**
0037-8097 Sociale Wetenschappen† **8989**
0037-8100 Socialfoerfattningar **8071**
0037-8119 Socialism and Health **7542**
0037-8127 Socialisme *changed to* 1371-676X **7176**
0037-8135 Socialisme en Democratie **7183**
0037-8151 Socialismo Settanta†
0037-816X Socialist Action†
0037-8178 Socialist Commentary†
0037-8186 Socialist Digest
0037-8194 Socialist Forum **7183**
0037-8208 Socialist India **7183**
0037-8216 Sotsialisticheskii Trud†
0037-8232 Socialist Monitor†
0037-8259 Socialist Standard **7183**
0037-8283 Socialista†
0037-8291 Socialisticka Skola†
0037-8313 Socialisticke Zemedelstvi†
0037-8321 Socialisticky Obchod†
0037-833X Socialmedicinsk Tidskrift **5715**
0037-8356 Socialt Tidskrift†
0037-8364 Sociedad Americana de Oftalmologia y Optometria. Archivos **6051**
0037-8380 Sociedad Argentina de Biologia. Revista†
0037-8402 Sociedad Bolivariana de Venezuela. Revista **4312**
0037-8437 Sociedad Cientifica Argentina. Anales **7917**
0037-8453 Sociedad Colombiana de Ortodoncia. Revista
0037-8461 Sociedad Colombiana de Quimicos Farmaceuticos. Boletin
0037-847X Sociedad Cubana de Historia de la Medicina. Revista†
0037-8488 Sociedad Cubana de Ingenieros. Revista†
0037-8496 Sociedad de Bibliotecarios de Puerto Rico. Boletin†
0037-850X Sociedad de Biologia de Concepcion. Boletin **705**

9066 0037-8518 ULRICH'S PERIODICALS

0037-8518 Sociedad de Ciencias Naturales la Salle. Memoria 7917
0037-8526 Sociedad de Cirugia de Rosario. Boletines†
0037-8534 Sociedad de Medicina Veterinaria de Chile. Revista
0037-8542 Sociedad de Obstetricia y Ginecologia de Buenos Aires. Revista 6005
0037-8569 Sociedad Espanola de Socorros Mutuos y Beneficencia. Boletin
0037-8577 Sociedad Geografica de Colombia. Boletin 4029
0037-8585 Sociedad Geografica de Lima, Peru. Boletin 4029
0037-8607 Sociedad Malacologica del Uruguay. Comunicaciones 963
0037-8615 Sociedad Matematica Mexicana. Boletin 5536
0037-8623 Sociedad Quimica del Peru. Boletin *changed to* 1810-634X 2080
0037-8631 Sociedad Rural Argentina. Anales 301
0037-864X Sociedad Rural Argentina. Boletin 157
0037-8658 Sociedad Vasco-Navarra de Pediatria. Boletin 6104
0037-8666 Sociedade Brasileira de Estudos sobre Discos Voadores. Boletim 70
0037-8674 Sociedade Brasileira de Geografia. Boletim 4029
0037-8682 Sociedade Brasileira de Medicina Tropical. Revista 5826
0037-8690 Sociedade de Geografia de Lisboa. Boletim 4029
0037-8712 Sociedade Paranaense de Matematica. Boletim 5537
0037-8720 Societa Astronomica Italiana. Memorie 581
0037-8739 Societa di Studi Valdesi. Bollettino 4264
0037-8747 Societa Entomologica Italiana. Memorie 859
0037-8755 Societa Geografica Italiana. Bollettino 4029
0037-8763 Societa Geologica Italiana. Bollettino 2767
0037-8771 Societa Italiana di Biologia Sperimentale. Bollettino†
0037-8798 Societa Italiana di Farmacia Ospedaliera. Bollettino 6881
0037-8844 Societa Italiana di Scienze Naturali e del Museo Civico di Storia Naturale. Atti 7917
0037-8860 Universita di Messina. Societa Peloritana di Scienze Fisiche Matematiche e Naturali. Atti† 8996
0037-8879 Societas†
0037-8887 Archivum Historicum Societatis Iesu 7784
0037-8895 Societe Archeologique, Historique, Litteraire et Scientifique du Gers. Bulletin Trimestriel 417
0037-8933 Societe Belge d'Etudes Napoleoniennes. Bulletin†
0037-895X Societe Centrale d'Education et d'Assistance pour les Sourds-Muets en France. Bulletin d'Information†
0037-8984 Societe d'Anthropologie de Paris. Bulletins & Memoires 355
0037-9034 Societe de Botanique du Nord de la France. Bulletin 818
0037-9050 Societe de l'Histoire du Protestantisme Francais. Bulletin 7775
0037-9069 Societe de Linguistique de Paris. Bulletin 5175
0037-9085 Societe de Pathologie Exotique. Bulletin 5716
0037-9093 Societe de Pharmacie de Bordeaux. Bulletin 6881
0037-9107 Societe de Pharmacie de Lyon. Bulletin des Travaux†
0037-9115 Societe de Pharmacie de Montpellier. Travaux†
0037-9131 Societe de Pharmacie de Strasbourg. Bulletin†
0037-9158 Societe d'Emulation du Bourbonnais. Bulletin 417
0037-9174 Societe des Americanistes. Journal 356
0037-9182 Societe Internationale des Amis de Montaigne. Nuveau Bulletin 5374
0037-9190 Societe des Antiquaires de l'Ouest. Bulletin *changed to* 1767-6320 4258
0037-9204 Societe des Antiquaires de Picardie. Bulletin Trimestriel 4265
0037-9212 Revue Francaise d'Histoire du Livre 7572
0037-9220 Societe des Chirurgiens de Paris. Bulletin et Memoires†
0037-9247 Societe des Sciences Medicales du Grand-Duche de Luxembourg. Bulletin 5716
0037-9271 Societe Entomologique de France. Annales 859
0037-928X Societe Entomologique de France. Bulletin 859
0037-9344 Societe Francaise de Numismatique. Bulletin 6653
0037-9352 Societe Francaise de Philosophie. Bulletin 6953
0037-9360 Societe Francaise de Physique. Bulletin *changed to* 1953-793X 7037
0037-9379 Societe Francaise d'Egyptologie. Bulletin 417
0037-9387 Societe Genealogique Canadienne-Francaise. Memoires 3783
0037-9409 Societe Geologique de France. Bulletin 2767
0037-9441 Societe Industrielle de Mulhouse. Bulletin 8439
0037-9484 Societe Mathematique de France. Bulletin 5537
0037-9492 Societe Medico-Chirurgicale des Hopitaux et Formations Sanitaires des Armees. Bulletin†
0037-9506 Societe Paul Claudel. Bulletin†
0037-9522 Societe Royale Belge de Gynecologie et d'Obstetrique. Bulletin†
0037-9549 Societe Royale Belge des Ingenieurs et des Industriels. Revue†
0037-9565 Societe Royale des Sciences de Liege. Bulletin 7918
0037-9581 Societe Scientifique de Bretagne. Bulletin 7918
0037-959X Societe Scientifique de Bruxelles. Annales. Sciences Mathematiques, Astronomiques et Physiques†
0037-9603 Societe Vaudoise des Sciences Naturelles. Bulletin 7918
0037-9611 Societe Vaudoise des Sciences Naturelles. Memoires 7918
0037-962X Societe Zoologique de France. Bulletin 963
0037-9662 Society and Culture
0037-9670 Society and Leisure†
0037-9700 Society for Army Historical Research. Journal 6446
0037-9735 Society for Historical Archaeology Newsletter 417
0037-9751 Society for Psychical Research. Journal 6743
0037-976X Society for Research in Child Development. Monographs 7409
0037-9786 Society for the Study of State Governments. Journal
0037-9794 Society of Actuaries. Transactions (General)†
0037-9808 Society of Architectural Historians. Journal 457
0037-9816 Society of Archivists. Journal 5048
0037-9875 Sen'i Gakkaishi 8457
0037-9883 Society of Film & Television Arts. Journal†
0037-9905 Society of Health of Nigeria. Journal†
0037-9913 Society of Independent Professional Earth Scientists. Newsletter 2717
0037-993X Society of Malawi Journal 7918
0037-9948 Society of Medalists. News Bulletin†
0037-9956 Society of Medical Friends of Wine. Bulletin
0037-9980 Yuki Gosei Kagaku Kyokaishi 2132
0038-0008 Society of Professional Investigators. Bulletin
0038-0075 Society Page†
0038-0091 Socijalna Politika†
0038-0105 Socijalni Rad
0038-0113 Socio-Economic History 1549
0038-0121 Socio-Economic Planning Sciences 7468
0038-013X Sociocom Directory of Positions†
0038-0148 Sociologia†
0038-0156 Sociologia (Rome) 8135
0038-0164 Sociologia Internationalis 8072
0038-0180 Sociologia Religiosa†
0038-0199 Sociologia Ruralis 8136
0038-0202 Sociological Abstracts 8150
0038-0229 Sociological Bulletin 8136
0038-0237 Sociological Focus 8136
0038-0245 Sociological Inquiry 8136
0038-0253 The Sociological Quarterly 8137
0038-0261 The Sociological Review 8137
0038-0288 Sociologicky Casopis 8138
0038-0296 Sociologie du Travail 1707
0038-030X Sociologie et Societes 8138
0038-0318 Sociologija 8138
0038-0326 Sociologija Sela 8138
0038-0334 Sociologische Gids *changed to* 1574-3314 8138
0038-0342 Sociologisk Forskning 8138
0038-0369 Sociologist
0038-0377 Sociologus 8138
0038-0385 Sociology 8138
0038-0393 Sociology and Social Research†
0038-0407 Sociology of Education 2913
0038-0415 Sociology of Education Abstracts 2935
0038-0466 Socker Handlingar†
0038-0474 Sodobna Pedagogika 2913
0038-0482 Sodobnost 5374
0038-0504 Soekaren 6744
0038-0520 Soefart 8662
0038-0598 Soft Serve & Drive-in Field†
0038-061X Software Age†
0038-0628 Software Central†
0038-0644 Software: Practice and Experience 2598
0038-0652 Software World 2598
0038-0660 Sogo Kango 5981
0038-0679 Social Democracy
0038-0687 Soil & Health Journal *changed to* 1175-5970 245
0038-0695 Soil and Water†
0038-0717 Soil Biology & Biochemistry 745
0038-0741 Soil Mechanics and Foundation Engineering 3283
0038-075X Soil Science 253
0038-0768 Soil Science and Plant Nutrition 253
0038-0784 Soil Sense†
0038-0792 Soils and Fertilizers 186
0038-0806 Soils & Foundations 3283
0038-0814 Soins 5981
0038-0822 Sokol Polski 3565
0038-0830 Sokuchi Gakkaishi 4029
0038-0849 El Sol 5176
0038-0857 Sol de Uruapan
0038-0903 Solanus 7574
0038-092X Solar Energy 3177
0038-0938 Solar Physics 581
0038-0946 Solar System Research 581
0038-0954 Soldado Argentino 6446
0038-0962 Der Soldat 6446
0038-0970 Soldat im Volk 6446
0038-0989 Soldat und Technik *changed to* 1860-5311 6448
0038-0997 Soldaten Kurier†
0038-1004 Soldier 6446
0038-1012 Soleil†
0038-1039 Solia - The Herald 7706
0038-1047 Solicitors' Journal 4784
0038-1055 Solid Fuel†
0038-1098 Solid State Communications 7040
0038-1101 Solid-State Electronics 3114
0038-111X Solid State Technology 3114
0038-1128 Solid Waste Report 3512
0038-1160 Solidarity 3928
0038-1187 Solon†
0038-1195 Solothurner Zeitung 3959
0038-1209 Sols Africains 254
0038-1217 Sols-Soils†
0038-125X Solvent Extraction Reviews†
0038-1276 Somborske Novine 3945
0038-1284 Some/Thing†
0038-1292 Someni†
0038-1314 Somerset Farmer 157
0038-1322 Somerset Gazette†
0038-1349 Something Else Newsletter†
0038-1373 Songwriter's Review†
0038-1381 Sonjog
0038-139X Sonntagspost
0038-1446 Sons of Italy News 2270
0038-1454 Sons of Italy Times 3565
0038-1462 Sons of Norway Viking *changed to* 1944-3366 3571
0038-1489 Gosudarstvennyi Astronomicheskii Institut im. P.K. Shternberga. Soobshcheniya†
0038-1500 Sooner L P G Times 6793
0038-1519 Sooner State Press†
0038-1527 Sophia 7682
0038-1551 Sorby Natural History Society. Newsletter 7919
0038-156X T V Sorrisi e Canzoni 2394
0038-1586 Sosei to Kako 8439
0038-1640 Sosiologia 8139
0038-1659 Sot la Nape 5239
0038-1675 Sotilasaikakauslehti 6447
0038-1705 Sotsialistychna Kul'tura†
0038-1713 Sotsial'noe Obespechenie†
0038-1756 Soul (Washington, New Jersey) 7817
0038-1764 Soul Force†
0038-1802 Sound & Image†
0038-1845 Sound & Communications 8155
0038-1853 Soundings (Santa Barbara)†
0038-1861 Soundings (Portland) 4475
0038-187X Sounds of Truth and Tradition 7817
0038-1896 Source†
0038-190X SourceBook for Interior Planning and Design
0038-1969 South African Archaeological Bulletin 418
0038-1985 South African Association for the Advancement of Science. Newsletter†
0038-1993 South African Bakery and Confectionery Review 3675
0038-2000 S A Banker 1381
0038-2019 South African Bee Journal 157
0038-2027 S A Builder 1034
0038-2043 South African Cancer Bulletin†
0038-2094 South African Chessplayer†
0038-2132 South African Digest†
0038-2159 South African Fire Services Institute. Quarterly†
0038-2183 South African Garden & Home 3750
0038-2191 South African Hardware†
0038-2221 South African Institute of Electrical Engineers. Transactions *changed to* 1991-1696 3294
0038-223X South African Institute of Mining and Metallurgy. Journal 6332
0038-2256 South African Insurance Magazine†
0038-2264 South African Jersey†
0038-2272 S. A. Jewellery & Gifts†
0038-2280 South African Journal of Economics 1177
0038-2302 South African Journal of Medical Laboratory Technology†
0038-2310 South African Journal of Medical Sciences†
0038-2329 South African Journal of Obstetrics and Gynaecology 6005
0038-2337 South African Journal of Occupational Therapy
0038-2353 South African Journal of Science 7919
0038-2361 South African Journal of Surgery 6259
0038-237X South African Lapidary Magazine 2717
0038-2388 South African Law Journal 4785
0038-2396 The South African Law Reports 4785
0038-2418 South African Library. Quarterly Bulletin *changed to* 1562-9392 5034
0038-2442 South African Mechanical Engineer 3395
0038-2485 South African Motor-Cyclist
0038-2493 South African Music Teacher 6618
0038-2515 South African Observer 7184
0038-2523 New South African Outlook 7665
0038-2566 South African Philatelist 6899
0038-2612 South African Refractionist†
0038-2620 South African Reserve Bank. Quarterly Bulletin 1383
0038-2647 South African Review†
0038-2655 South African Rider†
0038-2671 South African Shipping News and Fishing Industry Review *changed to* Southern African Shipping News 8662
0038-2698 South African Bureau of Standards. Bulletin 6406
0038-271X South African Statistical Journal 8402
0038-2728 South African Sugar Journal 3664
0038-2744 South African Table Tennis News†
0038-2760 South African Transport 8511
0038-2779 South African Treasurer
0038-2787 South African Typographical Journal 4602
0038-2833 South & West
0038-2841 South Asian Review†
0038-285X South Asian Studies 561
0038-2876 S A Q: The South Atlantic Quarterly 5237
0038-2892 South Australian Electrical Contractor† 8989
0038-2906 The South Australian Government Gazette 7469
0038-2922 South Australian Institute of Architects' Monthly Bulletin
0038-2965 South Australian Naturalist 7919
0038-2973 South Australian Ornithologist 914
0038-3007 South Australian Storekeepers' Journal
0038-3023 South Australiana†
0038-304X South Carolina Economic Indicators 1519
0038-3058 South Carolina Education Journal†
0038-3074 South Carolina Farmer-Grower†
0038-3082 The South Carolina Historical Magazine 4313
0038-3090 South Carolina History Illustrated†
0038-3104 South Carolina Law Review 4785
0038-3120 South Carolina Magazine†
0038-3139 South Carolina Medical Association. Journal 5717
0038-3155 South Carolina Nursing†
0038-3163 South Carolina Review 5375
0038-3171 South Carolina Schools†
0038-318X South Carolina. State Department of Education. Office of General Education Media Services Newsletter†
0038-3198 South Carolina Wildlife 2628
0038-3228 South Coast Herald 3950
0038-3236 South Dakota
0038-3244 South Dakota Bar Journal 4785
0038-3252 South Dakota Bird Notes 914
0038-3260 South Dakota Business Review 1177
0038-3279 South Dakota Conservation Digest 2628
0038-3317 South Dakota Journal of Medicine *changed to* South Dakota Medicine 5717
0038-3325 South Dakota Law Review 4785
0038-3341 South Dakota Musician 6618
0038-335X South Dakota Nurse 5982
0038-3368 South Dakota Review 5375
0038-3376 South Dakota State Library Commission Bulletin†
0038-3384 South Dakota Stockgrower 301
0038-3414 South-East Asia Treaty Organization. Economic Bulletin†
0038-3430 The South End 2301
0038-3465 South India Churchman 7708
0038-3473 South Indian Horticulture 3750
0038-3481 South Indian Teacher
0038-349X South Pacific Bulletin†
0038-3562 South Wales Institute of Architects. Journal†
0038-3600 Southeast Asia Journal 2914
0038-3627 Southeast Furniture & Appliance News†
0038-366X Southeastern Geographer 4029
0038-3678 Southeastern Geology 2769
0038-3686 Southeastern Librarian 5048

0038-3694 Southeastern Peanut Farmer **254**
0038-3716 Southeasterner **4584**
0038-3732 Southerly **5375**
0038-3775 Southern Africa†
0038-3791 Southern Africa Textiles†
0038-3805 Southern and Southwestern Railway Club. Proceedings
0038-3813 Southern Association of Colleges and Schools. Proceedings **3002**
0038-3821 Southern Automotive Journal†
0038-383X Southern Banker†
0038-3848 Southern Baptist Educator **7775**
0038-3856 Southern Bell Views **2371**
0038-3872 Southern California Academy of Sciences. Bulletin **7919**
0038-3899 Southern California Dental Hygienists' Association. Journal†
0038-3902 Southern California Guide **8757**
0038-3910 Southern California Law Review **4786**
0038-3929 Southern California Quarterly **4313**
0038-3937 Southern California Rancher†
0038-3945 Southern California Dental Laboratory Association. Bulletin†
0038-3953 Southern California Teamster **4602**
0038-4003 Southern Cooperator
0038-4011 Southern Cross **7818**
0038-402X Southern Dairy Products Journal†
0038-4038 Southern Economic Journal **1178**
0038-4046 Southern Economist **1178**
0038-4054 Southern Engineer **3220**
0038-4070 Southern Exposure (Talladega) **6977**
0038-4135 Southern Funeral Director†
0038-4143 Southern Gardens
0038-416X Southern Hardware†
0038-4178 Southern Hospitals Magazine†
0038-4186 Southern Humanities Review **4475**
0038-4208 Southern Industrial Supplier†
0038-4216 Southern Insurance†
0038-4275 Southern Journal of Optometry†
0038-4283 The Southern Journal of Philosophy **6953**
0038-4291 Southern Literary Journal **5375**
0038-4305 Southern Living **3988**
0038-4313 Southern Lumberman **3716**
0038-4348 Southern Medical Journal **5717**
0038-4364 Southern Methodist University. Industrial Information Services. Newsletter†
0038-4372 Southern Motor Cargo†
0038-4380 Southern News and Views **2301**
0038-4461 Southern Plumbing, Heating, Cooling *changed to* Southern P H C Magazine **4127**
0038-447X Southern Poetry Review **5435**
0038-4496 Southern Quarterly **4476**
0038-450X Southern Railways **8625**
0038-4518 Southern Research Institute Bulletin†
0038-4526 Southern Review **8140**
0038-4534 The Southern Review **5375**
0038-4542 Southern Sawdust†
0038-4577 Southern Sociologist **8140**
0038-4607 Southern Textile News **8457**
0038-464X Southern Wings
0038-4674 Southwest Jewish Chronicle†
0038-4690 Southwest Kansas Register **7818**
0038-4712 The Southwest Review **5240**
0038-4747 Southwestern Association on Indian Affairs. Quarterly†
0038-4763 Southwestern Collegian†
0038-478X Southwestern Historical Quarterly **4313**
0038-4828 Southwestern Journal of Theology **7682**
0038-4844 Southwestern Lore **418**
0038-4852 Southwestern (Georgetown) **2301**
0038-4860 Southwestern Medicine†
0038-4887 Southwestern Minnesota Education Association Bulletin†
0038-4909 Southwestern Naturalist **7919**
0038-4917 Southwestern News **7775**
0038-4941 Social Science Quarterly **8004**
0038-495X Southwestern Veterinarian†
0038-4984 Sou'wester (South Bend) **4314**
0038-5271 Soviet Antarctic Expedition Information Bulletin†
0038-5425 Soviet Hydrology: Selected Papers†
0038-5468 Soviet Jewry Action Newsletter†
0038-5522 Soviet Land†
0038-5603 Soviet News†
0038-5727 Soviet Plastics†
0038-5786 Soviet Review†
0038-5816 Soviet Science Review†
0038-5891 Soviet Technology Bulletin†
0038-5905 Soviet Weekly†
0038-5921 Sovietica†
0038-5948 Sovremennik†
0038-5956 Sovremennoye Pol'skoye Pravo†
0038-5972 Sovremenost
0038-5980 The Sower **7682**
0038-5999 Sowjetstudien†
0038-6014 Soybean Digest *changed to* 1544-1644 **225**
0038-6049 Soziale Berufe
0038-6057 Soziale Selbstverwaltung **4524**
0038-6065 Soziale Sicherheit **4524**
0038-6073 Soziale Welt **8140**
0038-609X Sozialer Fortschritt **8006**
0038-6103 Der Sozialistische Akademiker†
0038-6111 Sozialistische Arbeitswissenschaft††
0038-612X Sozialistische Aussenhandel†
0038-6138 Sozialistische Demokratie†
0038-6146 Sozialistische Erziehung **2914**
0038-6162 Der Sozialistische Kaempfer **7185**
0038-6170 Sozialkunde Heute†
0038-6189 Sozialpaedagogik†
0038-6197 Sozialpolitik und Arbeitsrecht
0038-6200 Sozial Versicherung - Arbeitsschutz†
0038-6219 Space (London)
0038-6227 Space†
0038-6235 Space Age Market Research
0038-6251 Space Business Week†
0038-6278 Space Letter†
0038-6308 Space Science Reviews **582**

0038-6324 Space-Wise
0038-6332 Space World (Amherst)†
0038-6340 Spaceflight **72**
0038-6367 Spafaswap†
0038-6375 Spain. Departamento de Fomento y Difusion Internacional. Documentacion†
0038-6456 Spanish Cultural Index
0038-6464 Spanish Newsletter†
0038-6499 Spare Time **1652**
0038-6502 Sparebankbladet **1384**
0038-6537 Sparer Magazin†
0038-6553 Spark
0038-6561 Sparkasse **1384**
0038-657X Sparkling Gems†
0038-6596 Spartacist **7185**
0038-6618 Frosch†
0038-6626 Speaking of "Columbias" **301**
0038-6634 Spear **3921**
0038-6650 Spearhead†
0038-6677 Spear's Special Situation Reports†
0038-6685 Specchio del Libro per Ragazzi†
0038-6693 Special
0038-6715 Special Events in Georgia†
0038-6731 Special Libraries Association. Biological Sciences Division. Reminder†
0038-6782 Special Libraries Association. Publishing Division. Bulletin†
0038-6804 Special Papers in Palaeontology **6730**
0038-6855 Specialities†
0038-6863 Specializzazione
0038-688X Specialty Baker's Voice
0038-6898 Specialty Foods Magazine†
0038-6952 The Spectator **5240**
0038-6960 Spectator (Radnor)†
0038-6995 Spectroscopia Molecular†
0038-7002 Bunko Kenkyu **7074**
0038-7010 Spectroscopy Letters **7085**
0038-7061 Spectrum (Amherst)
0038-707X Spectrum (New York)†
0038-7088 Spectrum (Richmond)†
0038-710X Spectrum International
0038-7126 Speculator†
0038-7134 Speculum **4266**
0038-7142 Speech and Drama *changed to* 1757-9384 **8484**
0038-7150 Speech and Hearing Association of Virginia. Journal†
0038-7185 Speed Age†
0038-7215 Speed and Supercar†
0038-7223 Speed Mechanics†
0038-7231 Speedway Post†
0038-724X Speedway Star
0038-7258 D O E†
0038-7266 Spejlet **591**
0038-7274 Spektrum†
0038-7282 S P E L D Information†
0038-7290 Speleologia Emiliana
0038-7304 Speleologist
0038-7312 Spelewei†
0038-7320 Speling **7682**
0038-7339 Spelling Progress Bulletin†
0038-7355 Sperimentale†
0038-738X Spettacolo† **8989**
0038-7398 Spettatore Internazionale†
0038-741X Sphincter
0038-7428 Sphinx **5240**
0038-7436 Sphinx-Magazin
0038-7444 Spica
0038-7452 Der Spiegel **3857**
0038-7460 Spiegel der Historie†
0038-7479 Spiegel der Letteren **5376**
0038-7487 Spiegel Historiael *changed to* 1872-0625 **4140**
0038-7509 Spiel und Theater **8479**
0038-7517 Der Spielplan **8479**
0038-7525 Das Spielzeug **4061**
0038-7533 Spin†
0038-755X Spinning Wheel†
0038-7584 Spirit (South Orange)†
0038-7592 Spirit & Life **7818**
0038-7606 Spiritual Book News **7574**
0038-7614 Spiritual Frontiers†
0038-7622 The Spiritual Healer **7683**
0038-7630 Spiritual Life **7683**
0038-7649 Spiritualita (Casorezzo)†
0038-7657 Der Spirituosen- und Weinhandel **610**
0038-7665 Spiritus **7683**
0038-7711 Spokane, Washington. Official Gazette **7502**
0038-7738 Spokeswoman†
0038-7746 Spolem **1944**
0038-7754 Spoljnopoliticka Dokumentacija†
0038-7770 Sport **8202**
0038-7789 International Union of Students. Sport Bulletin†
0038-7797 Sport†
0038-7800 Sport Age†
0038-7835 Sport Aviation **72**
0038-7851 Sport en Spel†
0038-7878 Sport Flying†
0038-7894 Sport in de Pers
0038-7916 Sport Italia
0038-7932 Sport und Technik†
0038-7940 Sport World†
0038-7967 Sportdykaren **8205**
0038-7991 Sportimes†
0038-8017 The Sporting Goods Dealer **8206**
0038-805X The Sporting News **8206**
0038-8084 Shooting Times **8200**
0038-8092 Sportivnaya Zhizn' Rossii **8206**
0038-8106 Sportivnye Igry **8206**
0038-8122 Sportowiec†
0038-8149 Sports Afield **8335**
0038-8173 Sports Car World†
0038-8181 Sports and Recreation Equipment†
0038-8203 Sports-Famille
0038-8211 Sportsfiskeren **3609**

0038-822X Sports Illustrated **8207**
0038-8238 Sports Loisirs, Education Physique†
0038-8270 Sportshelf News†
0038-8297 Sportswear on Parade
0038-8300 Sportyvna Hazeta **8209**
0038-8319 La Sposa **5561**
0038-8343 Spot News from Abroad†
0038-8351 Spotlight††
0038-8408 Spotlight on South Africa†
0038-8440 Spraakvaard **5376**
0038-8459 Der Sprachdienst **5177**
0038-8475 Sprache im Technischen Zeitalter **5377**
0038-8483 Sprachkunst **5377**
0038-8491 Sprachlabor†
0038-8505 Der Sprachmittler†
0038-8513 Sprachspiegel **5177**
0038-8521 Spraak og Spraakundervisning†
0038-853X Sprawy Miedzynarodowe **7266**
0038-8556 Sprig of Shillelagh†
0038-8572 Spring 3100 **2669**
0038-8580 Springfield-Illinois-Review of Business & Economic Conditions†
0038-8599 Springfield. Massachusetts. City Library Bulletin†
0038-8602 Springfield Public Schools. News and Views†
0038-8610 Concordia Theological Quarterly **7635**
0038-8629 Springs & Brakpan Advertiser **3950**
0038-8637 Sprinkler Bulletin **4524**
0038-8645 Sprog og Kultur†
0038-8661 Spudman **254**
0038-8696 Spurk
0038-870X Der Spurkranz
0038-8726 Sputnik Junior†
0038-8742 Squash Rackets News
0038-8750 La Squilla dei Fratini Missionari di Recco† **8990**
0038-8769 Squilla di S. Gerardo
0038-8807 Sruth†
0038-8815 St. Paul's Printer **7679**
0038-884X Der Staat **7185**
0038-8858 Staat und Recht†
0038-8874 Staatsbuerger†
0038-8882 Staatspensioenen
0038-8890 Stacks†
0038-8904 Stad Gods **7818**
0038-8912 Stadio Club†
0038-8920 Stadion†
0038-8939 Stadlinger Post **7503**
0038-8947 Stads og Havneingenioeren *changed to* 1902-2654 **3222**
0038-8963 Stadsbyggnad **7503**
0038-8971 Amtsblatt der Landeshauptstadt Linz **7487**
0038-8998 Stadtbau-Informationen†
0038-9013 Stadtverkehr **8511**
0038-9021 S I N Information†
0038-9048 Der Staedtetag **7503**
0038-9056 Starch **2130**
0038-9072 Staff Spectator†
0038-9110 Stage in Canada†
0038-9145 Stahlbau **3283**
0038-917X Stainless Steel **6332**
0038-9196 Stal†
0038-920X Stal' **6333**
0038-9226 Stalactite **2769**
0038-9277 Stamp Lover **6900**
0038-9307 Stamp Weekly†
0038-9323 Stampa Medica†
0038-934X Stamping/Diemaking†
0038-9358 Stamps **6900**
0038-9374 Standard **7818**
0038-9390 The Standard (Boston) **4524**
0038-9420 Standard & Poor's Stock Summary†
0038-9447 Standard Bearer (Sacramento) **7775**
0038-9498 Canadian Advertising Rates and Data **38**
0038-9501 Dati e Tariffe Pubblicitarie **24**
0038-9536 Standard Rate and Data Service. Network Rates and Data†
0038-9579 Tarif Media **36**
0038-9609 Standard Rate and Data Service. Transit Advertising Rates and Data†
0038-9625 Standardisering†
0038-9633 Standards Action **6406**
0038-9668 Standards Engineering **6406**
0038-9676 A N S I Reporter **6400**
0038-9684 Standards: Monthly Additions **6406**
0038-9692 Standardy i Kachestvo **6407**
0038-9706 Stander **8283**
0038-9730 Standpunte†
0038-9749 Stanford Alumni Almanac†
0038-9757 Stanford Chaparral **2301**
0038-9765 Stanford Law Review **4787**
0038-9781 Stanford M.D.†
0038-979X The Stanford Observer†
0038-9811 S T I N **2586**
0038-982X Stanovnistvo **7294**
0038-9846 Star and Garter Magazine†
0038-9854 Star & Lamp of Pi Kappa Phi
0038-9862 Star & Style **6514**
0038-9870 Star of Zion **7776**
0038-9889 Star Serviceman
0038-9900 Star West
0038-9919 Stardock
0038-9927 Starlights **8283**
0038-9943 Start & Speed†
0038-9951 Start und Aufstieg
0038-996X Startling Detective†
0038-9978 Stash Capsules†
0038-9986 Stat (Madison) **5982**
0039-0003 State Bank of India. Monthly Review **1519**
0039-0011 State Bank of Pakistan. Bulletin **1384**
0039-0054 State Engineer†
0039-0070 New Jersey School Boards Association. School Board Notes **3028**
0039-0089 State Geologists Journal **2769**

0039-5587 Suomen Lehdisto **4584**
0039-5595 Suomen Maataloustieteellisen Seuran Julkaisuja†
0039-5625 Suomen Silta **3839**
0039-5633 Suomi Merella
0039-565X Super Omnia Charitas†
0039-5668 Super Power Publications†
0039-5684 Super Sports†
0039-5706 Superba **8210**
0039-5714 Superconducting Devices and Materials†
0039-5765 Superlove†
0039-5773 Supermachos†
0039-5781 Supermarket *changed to* 1654-4544 **1830**
0039-579X Supermarket Management†
0039-5803 Supermarket News **3681**
0039-5838 Supernovelas†
0039-5846 Supertiendas†
0039-5854 Supervision **1709**
0039-5889 Supervisor's Bulletin†
0039-5927 Supplementary Service to European Taxation† **8991**
0039-5935 Supply House Times **4127**
0039-5951 Supreme Court Cases **4965**
0039-596X Supreme Court Notes†
0039-6028 Surface Science **7042**
0039-6036 Surfer **8336**
0039-6052 Surfing East†
0039-6060 Surgery **6259**
0039-6109 Surgical Clinics of North America **6259**
0039-6117 Surgical Journal of Delhi
0039-6125 Surgo
0039-6133 Surinaamse Landbouw **159**
0039-615X Surplus Record **5460**
0039-6168 Surrealist Transformaction
0039-6184 Sursum Corda†
0039-6192 Survey†
0039-6206 Survey of Anesthesiology **5751**
0039-6222 Survey of Current Business **1521**
0039-6230 Survey of International Development†
0039-6257 Survey of Ophthalmology **5751**
0039-6265 Survey Review **3284**
0039-6338 Survival (Abingdon) **7268**
0039-6362 Sus Hijos†
0039-6370 Sushama **5383**
0039-6397 Sussex Life **3872**
0039-6419 Svedectvi†
0039-6435 Svensk Bergs- & Brukstidning **6480**
0039-6443 Svensk Bokfoerteckning (Print edition) *changed to* Nationalbibliografin - Boecker **631**
0039-6451 Svensk Bokhandel **7574**
0039-646X Svensk Botanisk Tidskrift **819**
0039-6486 Svensk Damtidning **8885**
0039-6494 Nord-Emballage **6712**
0039-6575 Svensk Handelstidning Justitia **1946**
0039-6583 Svensk Jakt **8336**
0039-6591 Svensk Juristtidning **4965**
0039-6621 Svensk Leksaksrevy **4061**
0039-663X Svensk Litteraturtidskrift†
0039-6699 S P T: Svensk Pastoraltidskrift **7679**
0039-6702 Svensk Sjoefartstidning **8663**
0039-6753 Svensk Tapetserar Tidning **4563**
0039-6761 Svensk Teologisk Kvartalskrift **7686**
0039-677X Svensk Tidskrift **5241**
0039-6788 Svensk Tidskrift for Industriellt Rattsskydd†
0039-6796 Svensk Traevaru- och Pappersmassetidning†
0039-6818 Svensk Valltidskrift†
0039-6834 Gasnytt *changed to* 1653-5367 **6767**
0039-6842 Svenska Litteratursaellskapet i Finland. Skrifter **5436**
0039-6869 Svenska Mejeriernas Riksfoerening. Meddelande†
0039-6885 Svenska Museer†
0039-6893 Meddelanden fraan Svenska Riksarkivet†
0039-6907 Svenska Tidningsartiklar†
0039-6915 Svenska Tidskriftsartiklar†
0039-6931 Svenska Kraftverksfoereningens Publikationer†
0039-6958 Sverige - Nytt†
0039-6974 Sveriges Natur **2628**
0039-6982 Tandlaekartidningen **5867**
0039-6990 Sveriges Utsaedesfoerenings Tidskrift **255**
0039-7008 Svet†
0039-7016 Svet Motoru **8606**
0039-7032 Svet v Obrazech†
0039-7059 Svetlost **5241**
0039-7067 Svetotekhnika **3331**
0039-7075 Svetova Literatura† **8991**
0039-7091 Svetsen **6344**
0039-7113 Svijet (Zagreb) **5241**
0039-7121 Svijet (Sarajevo)†
0039-713X Svinovodstvo **301**
0039-7156 Svit†
0039-7164 Svitlo **7819**
0039-7199 Swarajya†
0039-7202 Swatantra in Parliament†
0039-7210 Swatantra Newsletter†
0039-7229 Swaziland Recorder†
0039-7245 Sweden Now†
0039-7253 Sweden. Statistiska Centralbyraan. Allmaen Maanadsstatistik **8408**
0039-727X Sweden. Statistiska Centralbyraan. Utrikeshandel. Kvartalsstatistik **8408**
0039-7296 The Swedish Economy **1905**
0039-7431 Swimming World and Junior Swimmer *changed to* Swimming World Magazine **8210**
0039-744X Swing Journal **6621**
0039-7474 Swiss Journal **3567**
0039-7482 Swiss Observer†
0039-7490 Swiss Review of World Affairs†
0039-7504 Swiss Technics†
0039-7547 Sword of the Lord **7687**
0039-7563 Sybarite Review
0039-7571 Sydan **5800**
0039-7601 Sydney Tourist Guide
0039-761X Sydney Water Board Journal†
0039-7660 Sylwan **3704**
0039-7679 Symbolae Osloenses **2241**
0039-7695 Symposium **4477**
0039-7709 Symposium **5384**
0039-7717 Syn og Segn **5241**
0039-7733 Synagogue Service†
0039-7741 Syndicalisme Hebdo **4603**
0039-7776 Syndicat des Critiques Litteraires. Bulletin†
0039-7784 Syndicat National des Officers de la Marine Marchande C.F.D.T. Bulletin de Liaison†
0039-7830 Synopsis Revue†
0039-7849 Synpunkt†
0039-7857 Synthese **6956**
0039-7881 Synthesis **2131**
0039-7903 Synthesis Microbiologica†
0039-7911 Synthetic Communications **2131**
0039-792X Syracuse Chemist **2082**
0039-7938 Syracuse Law Review **4792**
0039-7946 Syria **420**
0039-7962 Syrie et Monde Arabe **7268**
0039-8020 Systems & Communications
0039-8039 Systems Education Forum†
0039-8047 Systems Technology†
0039-8071 Szabadalmi Kozlony es Vedjegyertesito **6758**
0039-8098 Szazadok **4163**
0039-8101 Szemeszet **6052**
0039-811X Szene†
0039-8128 Szigma†
0039-8136 Szinhaz
0039-8144 Szklo i Ceramika **2046**
0039-8152 Szpilki†
0039-8160 T.I.T. Journal of Life Sciences
0039-8195 T A C Quarterly Circular
0039-8209 T A I C H News†
0039-8217 T.A. Informations *changed to* 1248-9433 **5204**
0039-8225 T A L B Talks†
0039-8233 T A M S Journal **6653**
0039-8276 Transportation and Distribution Management†
0039-8292 T E A News *changed to* 1538-2907 **2917**
0039-8306 T E A Newsletter **2917**
0039-8314 T E C Report
0039-8322 T E S O L Quarterly **5185**
0039-8330 T F C Nieuws†
0039-839X T. I. P. Informatie†
0039-8403 T I P R O Reporter†
0039-8411 T I S C O Technical Journal
0039-842X T N A News
0039-8438 T N C - Aktuellt†
0039-8454 T.P.A. Travelers
0039-8462 T P Annales *changed to* 1254-5678 **7471**
0039-8470 T.P.L. News **5049**
0039-8497 T T A†
0039-8527 T V Comic†
0039-8543 T V Guide **2392**
0039-8551 T V Hebdo **2392**
0039-8608 T V Times†
0039-8632 T W A Ambassador†
0039-8640 T W A U News†
0039-8659 T W U Express **4603**
0039-8675 Ta Kung Pao **3875**
0039-8683 Taag **8625**
0039-8691 Taal en Tongval **5185**
0039-8705 Die Taalgenoot **5241**
0039-8721 Tabak **8487**
0039-8756 Der Tabakpflanzer Oesterreichs†
0039-8780 Table et Cadeau **4563**
0039-8799 Table Tennis News **8248**
0039-8802 Tableaux de l'Economie Francaise†
0039-8837 The Tablet **7687**
0039-8845 The Tablet (New York) **7819**
0039-8861 Tabor
0039-8888 Tachydromos†
0039-8896 Tactics†
0039-8934 Wiener Tagebuch†
0039-8950 Tagus
0039-8969 Tahqiqat-i Iqtisadi (Chap-i Farsi) *see* 1010-657X **1181**
0039-8977 Taide **521**
0039-8985 Taiiku no Kagaku **3083**
0039-8993 Taikabutsu **6334**
0039-9019 Air Pollution News†
0039-9027 Tail-Wagger and Family Magazine†
0039-9051 Taipei Hua K'an **3960**
0039-906X Tairyoku Kagaku **6998**
0039-9078 Taiwan†
0039-9094 Taiwan Chenglian
0039-9108 Taiwan Industrial Panorama **1905**
0039-9124 Taiwan Trade Monthly†
0039-9140 Talanta **2106**
0039-9159 Talespinner†
0039-9175 Talim-O-Tarbiat **2216**
0039-9183 Talking Book Topics **4085**
0039-9213 Talks and Tales†
0039-9221 Taller **5385**
0039-9248 Talon†
0039-9256 Tamarack Review†
0039-9264 Tamarind Fact Sheets†
0039-9280 Tamil Arasu **3890**
0039-9299 Tamil Culture
0039-9302 Tamil Nadu Electricity Board. Journal
0039-9310 Tamil Nadu Information **7471**
0039-9329 Tamil Nadu Police Journal **2669**
0039-9353 Tandlaegebladet **5867**
0039-9361 Tandteknikern **5867**
0039-937X Tanecni Listy†
0039-9388 Tangent†
0039-940X Tangerine
0039-9418 Tank (Wareham) **6448**
0039-9434 Report of Coal Mine Safety†
0039-9442 Tanner
0039-9450 Tanpakushitsu Kakusan Koso **746**
0039-9469 Tanzania. National Bureau of Statistics. Quarterly Statistical Bulletin **8408**
0039-9477 Tanzania Education Journal **2917**
0039-9485 Tanzania Notes & Records **3961**
0039-9507 Tanzania Zamani **4163**
0039-9574 Tapetsereren†
0039-9582 Tapissier Decorateur
0039-9590 Taproots†
0039-9604 Taptoe **2216**
0039-9620 Tar Heel Nurse **5982**
0039-9655 Lengo†
0039-968X Tarheel Wheels†
0039-9698 Tarikh†
0039-971X Tarsadalmi Szemle†
0039-9728 Tartarino
0039-9736 Wijk en Speeltuinvereniging Tarwewijk. Mededelingenblad†
0039-9787 Tasmanian Fruitgrower & Farmer†
0039-9795 Tasmanian Government Gazette **7471**
0039-9809 Tasmanian Historical Research Association. Papers and Proceedings **4194**
0039-9817 Tasmanian Journal of Agriculture†
0039-985X Tasmanian Motor Trader
0039-9892 Tatka
0039-9906 Tatler & Bystander
0039-9914 Tatrzanski Orzel **3568**
0039-9922 Finland. Patentti- ja Rekisterihallitus. Tavaramerkkilehti **6750**
0039-9930 Tawow†
0039-9949 Tax Administrators News (Print) *changed to* Tax Administrators News (Online) **1946**
0039-9957 The Tax Adviser **1947**
0039-9965 Tax Affairs
0039-9973 Tax Alert†
0040-0017 United States Tax Court Reports **1954**
0040-0025 The Tax Executive **1947**
0040-0041 Tax Law Review **4792**
0040-005X The Tax Lawyer **4792**
0040-0068 Philippines. National Tax Research Center. Tax Monthly†
0040-0076 Tax News Service (Print)† **8992**
0040-0084 Tax Planning†
0040-0092 Tax Planning Ideas†
0040-0106 Tax Policy†
0040-0122 Tax Times **1950**
0040-0149 Taxation **1950**
0040-0157 Taxation **1950**
0040-0173 Taxation Record Journal
0040-0203 Taxes Interpreted†
0040-0211 Taxi News Digest†
0040-0246 Taxicab Management†
0040-0254 Taxinews **8512**
0040-0262 Taxon **819**
0040-0270 Taxpayer **1951**
0040-0289 Taxpayer
0040-0297 Tchahert **7706**
0040-0300 Te Ao Hou†
0040-0327 Te-ve Guia
0040-0343 Tea and Coffee Trade Journal **3665**
0040-0386 Tea Room, Restaurant and Catering Journal†
0040-0394 Teach†
0040-0408 The Teacher **2917**
0040-0424 Teacher Education in New Countries†
0040-0467 Teacher Paper†
0040-0505 Message of the Teacher **2993**
0040-0521 Teacher's World **2918**
0040-053X Teaching†
0040-0548 Teaching Adults†
0040-0572 Teaching & Training†
0040-0599 Teaching Exceptional Children **3048**
0040-0602 Teaching History **3085**
0040-0610 Teaching History **3085**
0040-0645 Teaching Pictures for Bible Searchers†
0040-0696 Team
0040-0734 Teashi no Fujiyuuna Kodomotachi†
0040-0750 Teatern†
0040-0769 Teatr **8481**
0040-0793 Teatro
0040-0807 Teatro e Cinema†
0040-084X Tech Engineering News†
0040-0866 Technica **8440**
0040-0890 Technical Book Review Index†
0040-0904 Technical Co-operation†
0040-0912 Education & Training **2940**
0040-0955 T.I.†
0040-098X Technical Progress in Israel†
0040-1021 Technicien Belge en Prothese Dentaire†
0040-1056 Technicka Praca†
0040-1064 Technicky Tydenik **5460**
0040-1072 Technicuir†
0040-1099 Die Technik†
0040-1102 Technik und Betrieb†
0040-1110 Technika **636**
0040-117X Technikgeschichte **8441**
0040-1188 Technion Magazine† **8992**
0040-1250 Technique Moderne†
0040-1285 Techniques†
0040-1293 Techniques C E M
0040-1307 Techniques de l'Air Comprime†
0040-1315 Techniques de l'Habillement†
0040-1382 Techniques Nouvelles†
0040-1420 Technische Information Armaturen†
0040-1439 Technische Mitteilungen†
0040-1455 R F Z Technische Mitteilungen†
0040-1501 Technische Universitaet Clausthal. Mitteilungsblatt **6480**
0040-1536 Technischer Ansporn†
0040-1544 Technischer Fortschritt (Duesseldorf)†
0040-1552 Technischer Handel **8441**
0040-1560 Technisches Journal†
0040-1587 Technocracy Digest **8009**
0040-1595 Technocrat†
0040-1617 Technocratic Trendevents†
0040-1625 Technological Forecasting and Social Change **8441**
0040-165X Technology and Culture **8442**
0040-1676 Technology Ireland **8442**
0040-1706 Technometrics **3222**

ISSN

ISSN

0041-3127 Triumph†
0041-3135 Triveni
0041-3143 Trivsel†
0041-3186 Der Tropenlandwirt *changed to* 1612-9830 **126**
0041-3216 Tropical Agriculture **163**
0041-3224 Tropical Agriculturist **163**
0041-3240 Tropical Diseases Bulletin **5751**
0041-3259 Tropical Fish Hobbyist **4349**
0041-3267 Tropical Medicine **5827**
0041-3275 Tropical Medicine and Hygiene News **5827**
0041-3283 Tropical Products Quarterly†
0041-3291 Tropical Science† **8994**
0041-333X Trottingbred†
0041-3348 Trotwaer *changed to* 1571-4020 **5335**
0041-3356 Trotzdem **7189**
0041-3364 Trout **2629**
0041-3372 Trout and Salmon **8338**
0041-3380 Truck and Bus† **8994**
0041-3429 Trucking News†
0041-3437 Trudbenik **4603**
0041-3445 Trudov Invalid
0041-3453 Gosudarstvennyi Astronomicheskii Institut im. P.K. Shternberga. Trudy†
0041-3461 True†
0041-347X True Confessions†
0041-3488 True Confessions **5415**
0041-3496 True Confidential Confessions
0041-350X True Detective†
0041-3518 True Experience†
0041-3534 True Life Secrets
0041-3542 True Love†
0041-3550 True Love **5412**
0041-3569 True Modern Romances
0041-3585 True Romance†
0041-3593 True Story†
0041-3615 True West **4315**
0041-3658 Truppendienst **6449**
0041-3674 Trustee **4112**
0041-3682 Trusts & Estates **1656**
0041-3690 The Truth (Philadelphia) **4526**
0041-3704 Truth about Communism†
0041-3712 Truth Seeker **6958**
0041-3720 Trybuna Spoldzielcza†
0041-3739 Tryckluft†
0041-3747 Trziste Povrca i Voca†
0041-3755 Trziste Stoke i Stochih Proizoda
0041-3771 Tsitologiya†
0041-378X Tsopano News **3996**
0041-3798 Tsuchi to Kiso **3286**
0041-3801 Tsukumo Earth Science†
0041-381X Tsushin Kogyo **2373**
0041-3844 Tu Sei Me
0041-3852 Tuatara†
0041-3860 Tuatara†
0041-3895 Tuberkulozis es Tudogyogyaszat Referalo Szemle†
0041-3909 Tubular Structures†
0041-3917 Tudomanyos es Muszaki Tajekoztatas **5060**
0041-3925 Turk Idare Dergisi **7472**
0041-3933 Tuesday
0041-3941 Tufts Dental Outlook†
0041-3992 Tulane Law Review **4798**
0041-4018 Tulane Studies in Geology and Paleontology†
0041-4026 Tulanian **2304**
0041-4034 Tulimuld **5243**
0041-4042 Tulsa†
0041-4069 Tulsa Lawyer **4798**
0041-4085 Tummelplatz
0041-4093 Tumor Research: Experimental and Clinical **6035**
0041-4107 Tungsram Technische Mitteilungen†
0041-4115 Tunisia. Institut National de la Statistique. Bulletin Mensuel de Statistique **8409**
0041-4123 Tunisie Economique
0041-4131 La Tunisie Medicale **5724**
0041-4158 Turf and Sport Digest†
0041-4190 Turist **8769**
0041-4204 Turisticke Novine **8770**
0041-4247 Turk Tarih Kurumu. Belgeler **4325**
0041-4255 Turk Tarih Kurumu. Belleten **4325**
0041-4263 Turkey. Devlet Istatistik Enstitusu. Aylik Istatistik Bulteni† **8994**
0041-428X Turkeys†
0041-4298 Turkish Digest†
0041-4301 Turkish Journal of Pediatrics **6105**
0041-4328 Turkiye Bibliyografyasi† **8995**
0041-4344 Turkiye Makaleler Bibliyografyasi† **8995**
0041-4360 Turrialba†
0041-4395 Tutti Fotografi **6978**
0041-4409 Tuttitalia†
0041-4417 Tutto Cucciolo
0041-4441 Tuttosport **8213**
0041-445X Tuttoville
0041-4484 T V and Movie Play†
0041-4530 T V Star Parade†
0041-4549 Tvai† **8995**
0041-4573 Twainian **5391**
0041-4581 Twee N
0041-459X Twentieth Century†
0041-462X Twentieth Century Literature **5391**
0041-4638 Twentieth Century Studies†
0041-4662 Two Bridges News†
0041-4670 Two Rivers†
0041-4697 Two Wheeler†
0041-4700 Two Wheels **8269**
0041-4719 Two Worlds
0041-4727 Tworczosc **5243**
0041-4735 Tijdschrift voor het Middelbaar Technisch Onderwijs
0041-4751 Tydskrif vir Geesteswetenskappe **4479**
0041-476X Tydskrif vir Letterkunde **5391**
0041-4778 Journal for Secondary Education†
0041-4786 Tydskrif vir Natuurwetenskappe†
0041-4794 Tydskrif vir Rasse-Aangeleenthede **3569**
0041-4808 Tygodnik Powszechny **5243**
0041-4816 Tyo, Terveys, Turvallisuus **6688**
0041-4824 Typetalks Magazine†
0041-4832 Typographical Journal
0041-4840 Typografische Monatsblaetter **7328**
0041-4859 Tyres and Accessories **7827**
0041-4905 Tsvetovodstvo **3752**
0041-4921 U. A. L. Economic and Financial Review†
0041-493X U A M P T†
0041-4948 Egypt. Ministry of Tourism. Statistical Bulletin
0041-4972 U A W Fair Practices Fact Sheet†
0041-4980 U A W Washington Report **4603**
0041-5006 U B N†
0041-5014 U C L A Graduate Journal†
0041-5030 U E C Journal†
0041-5065 U E News **4603**
0041-5073 U F O Investigator†
0041-5081 U F O - Nachrichten†
0041-5103 U.I.A.M.S. Informations
0041-5162 U.I.U. Journal†
0041-5170 Press Gazette **4582**
0041-5189 U L L I C O Bulletin **4526**
0041-5251 Unesco Oficina Regional de Educacion para America Latina y el Caribe. Boletin de Educacion†
0041-5278 UNESCO Courier (Print)†
0041-5286 UNESCO Features†
0041-5294 UNESCO Philippines **2922**
0041-5375 U N U C I. Rivista **6449**
0041-5383 U.P.A. Journal†
0041-5391 U P College of Dentistry Journal
0041-5405 U P E N **2305**
0041-5421 University Review†
0041-5456 U S A F Instructors Journal†
0041-5464 U S A Record **4604**
0041-5472 U S B W A Tip-Off **8250**
0041-5480 U S C O L D Newsletter **8833**
0041-5502 U S G A Green Section Record **3753**
0041-5537 U S News & World Report **3991**
0041-5642 Ubulum†
0041-5650 U C L A Law Review **4799**
0041-5677 Udenrigs Handel og Industri Information†
0041-5707 Uebersee Rundschau†
0041-5715 Ufahamu (Print) *changed to* 2150-5802 **3569**
0041-574X The Uganda Journal **4178**
0041-5758 Uganda. Ministry of Planning and Economic Development. Statistics Division. Quarterly Economic and Statistical Bulletin†
0041-5766 Uganda Teacher†
0041-5782 Ugeskrift for Laeger **5725**
0041-5790 Ugol' **6482**
0041-5804 Ugol' Ukrainy **6482**
0041-5839 Uhren Juwelen **4570**
0041-588X Uit Europoortkringen *changed to* 1568-881X **8643**
0041-5898 Uit in Utrecht
0041-5901 Uit Ons Werk†
0041-591X Uitgelezen†
0041-5928 Uitgever†
0041-5936 Uitlotings-Archief
0041-5944 Uitzicht
0041-5952 Uj Iras†
0041-5979 Ukiyoe Geijutsu **523**
0041-5987 Ukrainian Bulletin†
0041-5995 Ukrainian Mathematical Journal **5543**
0041-6002 Ukrainian News **3569**
0041-6010 The Ukrainian Quarterly **7270**
0041-6029 Ukrainian Review†
0041-6037 Ukrainian Voice **3569**
0041-6045 Ukrainskii Khimicheskii Zhurnal **2083**
0041-6053 Ukrains'kyi Matematychnyi Zhurnal **5543**
0041-6061 Ukrains'kyi Istoryk **4165**
0041-607X Ukrainian Medical Association of North America. Journal **5725**
0041-610X Ukrains'kyi Biokhimichnyi Zhurnal **746**
0041-6142 Ukrains'kyi Samostijnyk†
0041-6185 Ulster Commentary†
0041-6193 The Ulster Medical Journal **5725**
0041-6207 Ulster Motorist
0041-6215 Ulster Young Farmer
0041-6223 Ultima Moda **2262**
0041-624X Ultrasonics **7089**
0041-6258 Ultreya **7821**
0041-6266 Ulysses S. Grant Association. Newsletter†
0041-6274 Umafrika **7691**
0041-6282 Umana†
0041-6290 Umanesimo†
0041-6312 Umbria Agricola
0041-6320 Umetnost†
0041-6339 Umpqua Trapper **4315**
0041-6355 Umwelt **3491**
0041-641X U N A Nursing Journal†
0041-6428 Una Sancta†
0041-6436 Unasylva **3706**
0041-6444 Unausforschlicher Reichtum **7691**
0041-6452 Unauthorized Practice News†
0041-6460 Under Glass†
0041-6479 Under the Sign of Pisces: Anais Nin and Her Circle†
0041-6487 Undergraduate Journal of Philosophy†
0041-6525 Underground Official†
0041-6541 Underseas Cable World†
0041-655X Understanding
0041-6576 Understanding Japan **3901**
0041-6584 Undervisning og Velferd
0041-6592 Underwater Letter†
0041-6606 Underwater Naturalist **2819**
0041-6622 Underwriters' Report†
0041-6649 Unzer Weg†
0041-6681 Unicorn Folio†
0041-669X Unicorn Journal
0041-6703 Unidad†
0041-6711 Unidad Cristiana-Oriente Cristiano†
0041-672X Uniform Commercial Code Law Journal **4825**
0041-6738 Uniforms and Accessories Review†
0041-6754 Unijapan Film Quarterly†
0041-6762 Unilit **5392**
0041-6770 Union **5392**
0041-6800 Union Agricultural Cooperative of Syra. Bulletin†
0041-6819 Union Agriculture†
0041-6827 Assembly of Western European Union. Monthly Information Bulletin†
0041-686X Electrical Union World **4593**
0041-6878 Union Farmer **164**
0041-6924 Union Labor News **4604**
0041-6932 Union Matematica Argentina. Revista **5543**
0041-6959 Union Medicale du Canada†
0041-6975 Leeds Student **2290**
0041-7009 Union Postale **2355**
0041-7017 Union Recorder **2305**
0041-7033 Union Signal **2700**
0041-7041 Union Sociale **8075**
0041-7076 Unione degli Industriali della Provincia di Imperia. Notiziario†
0041-7092 Unionist (New York) **4604**
0041-7130 Unitas†
0041-7149 Unitas **523**
0041-7173 United Asia†
0041-7181 United Association Journal **4604**
0041-719X United Bible Societies. Bulletin **7691**
0041-7211 Journal of Current Social Issues†
0041-7238 The United Church Observer **7778**
0041-7246 United Church Review†
0041-7270 United Evangelical Action†
0041-7289 United Kingdom Atomic Energy Authority. List of Publications Available to the Public†
0041-7319 United Methodist Periodical Index†
0041-7327 United Mine Workers Journal **4604**
0041-7343 United Nations. Dag Hammarskjold Library. Current Bibliographical Information†
0041-7378 Quarterly Bulletin of Steel Statistics for Europe†
0041-7386 International Social Development Review†
0041-7432 United Nations Statistical Office. Monthly Bulletin of Statistics **8412**
0041-7440 United Neighborhood Houses. News†
0041-7483 U S A (New York)†
0041-7548 U S Catholic **7821**
0041-7556 U. S. Chemical Patents†
0041-7637 U S Farm News†
0041-7661 U.S. Glass, Metal & Glazing **1041**
0041-770X U S I Journal **6450**
0041-7726 L C Card Number Index to the National Union Catalog
0041-7734 U.S. Library of Congress. Accessions List: India†
0041-7769 U.S. Library of Congress. Accessions List: Middle East†
0041-7904 U.S. Library of Congress. Information Bulletin **5052**
0041-7912 U.S. Library of Congress. Classification - Additions and Changes†
0041-7939 U.S. Library of Congress. Quarterly Journal†
0041-798X U S Naval Institute. Proceedings **6450**
0041-8013 U S P Boletim Informativo†
0041-803X United States Patents Quarterly **6759**
0041-8048 U S Piper **6336**
0041-8056 United States Review†
0041-8072 Gosudarstvennaya Biblioteka S.S.S.R. im. V.I. Lenina. Informatsionnyi Byulleten' Novykh Inostrannykh Knig, Postupivshikh v Biblioteku. Seriya 1: Fiziko-Matematicheskie i Khimicheskie Nauki; Nauki o Zemle; Tekhnika i Tekhnicheskie Nauk†
0041-8080 Gosudarstvennaya Biblioteka S.S.S.R. im. V.I. Lenina. Informatsionnyi Byulleten' Novykh Inostrannykh Knig, Postupivshikh v Biblioteku. Seriya 3: Obshchestvennye Nauki; Khudozhestvennaya Literatura; Iskusstvo†
0041-8099 United States Ski News†
0041-8153 United Synagogue Review *changed to* 1945-2659 **7719**
0041-817X Uniter **2306**
0041-8218 Universalist
0041-8226 The Universe **7821**
0041-8234 Universidad
0041-8242 Universidad†
0041-8250 Universidad Argentina de la Empresa. Revista†
0041-8277 Universidad Autonoma de Santo Domingo. Biblioteca Central. Boletin de Adquisiciones
0041-8285 Universidad Central de Venezuela. Facultad de Agronomia. Revista **165**
0041-8307 Universidad Central de Venezuela. Facultad de Farmacia. Revista **6884**
0041-8331 Universidad de Buenos Aires. Facultad de Filosofia y Letras. Gaceta†
0041-834X Universidad de Buenos Aires. Instituto Bibliotecologico. Boletin Informativo†
0041-8374 Universidad de Chile. Boletin
0041-8390 Universidad de Cuenca. Anales **5243**
0041-8412 Universidad de Guayaquil. Facultad de Ciencias Medicas. Revista
0041-8420 Universidad de la Habana. Departamento de Actividades Culturales. Revista
0041-8439 Universidad de la Republica. Facultad de Ciencias Economicas y de Administracion. Instituto de Estadistica. Indice de Precios al Consumidor **8413**
0041-8447 Universidad de la Republica. Facultad de Humanidades y Ciencias. Publicaciones†
0041-8455 Universidad de la Republica. Hospital de Clinicas. Informe Estatistico
0041-848X Universidad de Narino. Biblioteca Central. Boletin Informativo y Bibliografico†
0041-8498 Universidad Autonoma de Nuevo Leon. Centro de Investigaciones Economicas. Boletin Bimestral **1187**
0041-851X Universidad Interamericana de Puerto Rico. Revista Juridica **4802**
0041-8528 Universidad de Puerto Rico. Servicio de Extension Agricola. Boletin Ganadero†
0041-8579 Universidad Industrial de Santander. Boletin Informativo†
0041-8609 Universidad Mayor de San Andres. Gaceta Universitaria
0041-8625 Universidad Nacional de la Plata. Revista **4479**
0041-8633 Boletin Mexicano de Derecho Comparado **4631**
0041-8641 Noticias de la Biblioteca†

0042-3920 Vergleichende Paedagogik†
0042-3939 Verhuetet Unfaelle changed to 1611-2393 6737
0042-3947 Veritas
0042-3955 Veritas 3804
0042-398X Verkeersrecht†
0042-4013 Verkehrsblatt 8637
0042-4021 Verkehrsmedizin und ihre Grenzgebiete†
0042-4048 Verkehrspsychologischer Informationsdienst 8637
0042-4064 Verladen†
0042-4099 Der Vermessungsingenieur changed to V D V Magazin 3287
0042-4102 Vermessungstechnik
0042-4129 Vermissa Herald
0042-4145 Vermont Catholic Tribune 7821
0042-4161 Vermont History 4316
0042-417X Vermont Life 3992
0042-420X Vero Dialogo
0042-4242 Verona Fedele 7821
0042-4250 Wiener Boersekammer. Verordnungsblatt
0042-4277 Die Verpackung 6715
0042-4293 Verpackungs-Berater†
0042-434X Vers Demain 7821
0042-4358 Versicherungswirtschaft 4527
0042-4366 Versiones†
0042-4374 Verso l'Azzurro
0042-4382 Versorgungswirtschaft 3334
0042-4412 Vertegenwoordiger†
0042-4420 Vertex 8339
0042-4439 Vertical File Index 17
0042-4447 Vertice 5244
0042-4455 Vertiflite 74
0042-4471 Vertriko Visie†
0042-4498 Die Verwaltung 7475
0042-4501 Verwaltungsarchiv 4808
0042-451X Verwarming en Ventilatie 4127
0042-4528 Verzekerings-Archief 4527
0042-4536 Veseli Svet†
0042-4544 Vesmir 4033
0042-4552 Udruzenje Pravoslavnog Svestenstva S.F.R. Jugoslavije. Glavni Savez. Vesnik
0042-4587 Vestnik†
0042-4609 Vestnik Dermatologii i Venerologii 5882
0042-4625 Vestnik Khirurgii im. I.I. Grekova 6262
0042-4633 Vestnik Mashinostroeniya 3359
0042-465X Vestnik Oftal'mologii 6052
0042-4668 Vestnik Otorinolaringologii 6086
0042-4676 Vestnik Rentgenologii i Radiologii 6210
0042-4684 Vestnik Sel'skokhozyaistvennoi Nauki Kazakhstana
0042-4765 Veteran 6452
0042-4781 Veteran Car 8610
0042-481X Veterantics†
0042-482X Veterinaria Mocambicana†
0042-4838 Veterinario y la Industria†
0042-4846 Veterinariya 8811
0042-4854 Veterinary Bulletin 8816
0042-4862 Veterinary Economics 1969
0042-4870 Veterinary Institute, Pulawy. Bulletin 8812
0042-4897 Veterinary Practice 8813
0042-4900 The Veterinary Record 8814
0042-4935 Vetus Testamentum 7731
0042-4951 Vi Menn 6301
0042-496X Vi Unge 2219
0042-4986 Via Libera
0042-4994 Via Migliore (Middle School Edition)†
0042-5028 Vialidad†
0042-5060 Vibrations†
0042-5079 Vichiana 5193
0042-5087 Vickers Voice†
0042-5109 Victoria Reports†
0042-5125 Victorian 2308
0042-5141 Victorian Dry Cleaner†
0042-5184 The Victorian Naturalist 2631
0042-5192 Victorian Newsletter 5395
0042-5206 Victorian Poetry 5437
0042-5214 Victorian Reports 4808
0042-5222 Victorian Studies 4481
0042-529X Vidici 5244
0042-5303 Vidura 3890
0042-5346 Vie Canine†
0042-5362 Vie Catholique du Berry 7822
0042-5370 Vie Collective†
0042-5400 Vie Communale et Departementale 7476
0042-5419 Vie de la Douane†
0042-5435 Vie des Arts 524
0042-5451 Vie des Transports†
0042-546X Qui Touring 3898
0042-5478 La Vie du Rail 8627
0042-5524 Vie et Sante†
0042-5532 Vie et Travail†
0042-5567 Vie Judiciaire†
0042-5583 Vie Medicale†
0042-5591 Vie Musicale†
0042-5605 Vie Sociale 8146
0042-5613 Vie Spirituelle 7692
0042-563X Vie Urbaine†
0042-5648 Vie Wallonne
0042-5656 Vient de Paraitre†
0042-5672 Naturforschende Gesellschaft in Zuerich. Vierteljahresschrift†
0042-5680 Vierteljahresschrift Wirtschaft und Verwaltung†
0042-5702 Vierteljahrshefte fuer Zeitgeschichte 4166
0042-5710 Vietnam 3994
0042-5788 Vietnambulletinen†
0042-5818 Viewpoints 3570
0042-5834 Viewpoint (London, 1965) 7192
0042-5842 Viewpoint (London, 1970) 1052
0042-5850 Viewpoint†
0042-5869 Viewpoint (Indianapolis)†
0042-5893 Views†
0042-5907 Views and Ideas on Mankind†
0042-5915 Views & Reviews (New York, 1937) 36
0042-5931 Viga en el Ojo

0042-594X Vigencia 4482
0042-5958 Vigilance 3226
0042-5966 Vigilance†
0042-5974 Vigilancia
0042-5982 Vigilia 7822
0042-6024 Vigiliae Christianae 7692
0042-6040 Vignes & Raisins†
0042-6059 Vigo County Public Library Staff Bulletin†
0042-6075 Vigyan Pragati 7928
0042-6083 Vijesti Muzealaca i Konzervatora Hrvatske 6539
0042-6105 Vikan 3878
0042-6113 Viikkosanomat††
0042-6121 Vikram
0042-613X Vikrant
0042-6148 Vilaggazdasag 1524
0042-6156 Villa & Hem i Sverige†
0042-6164 Villa de Madrid†
0042-6199 Villager 3992
0042-6229 Villanova Law Review 4808
0042-6237 VilleGiardini 460
0042-6253 Viltis†
0042-6288 Vinduet 5395
0042-630X Vini d'Italia†
0042-6326 Vinohrad
0042-6334 Vins d'Alsace 612
0042-6350 The Vintage Ford 369
0042-6385 Vinyl Technology Newsletter†
0042-6407 Viola 3753
0042-6474 Virginia Cavalcade†
0042-6490 Virginia Economic Indicators 1524
0042-6504 Virginia Forward†
0042-6512 Virginia Geographer†
0042-6571 Virginia Journal of International Law 4944
0042-658X Virginia Journal of Science 7928
0042-6601 Virginia Law Review 4809
0042-661X Virginia Law Weekly 4809
0042-6636 Virginia Magazine of History and Biography 4317
0042-6652 Virginia Minerals 6483
0042-6709 Virginia P T A Bulletin 2924
0042-6717 The Virginia Pharmacist 6885
0042-6725 Virginia Polytechnic Institute and State University. Extension News†
0042-6733 Virginia Poultryman
0042-675X Virginia Quarterly Review 5244
0042-6768 Virginia Record
0042-6776 Virginia School Boards Association Newsletter 3035
0042-6784 Virginia Town & City 7505
0042-6792 Virginia Wildlife 2631
0042-6806 Virittaaja 5194
0042-6822 Virology 897
0042-6849 Viroviticki List
0042-6857 Uirusu 897
0042-6865 Visages de l'Ain†
0042-6873 Visao
0042-6881 Vishwakarma 3226
0042-6911 Vision
0042-692X Vision Magazine 524
0042-6946 Vision and Voice†
0042-6954 Vision - Europe†
0042-6962 Vision Letter†
0042-6970 Vision of India†
0042-6989 Vision Research 6053
0042-7004 Visnyk 5244
0042-7020 Visnyk Sil's'kogospodar'skoi Nauki†
0042-7039 Vispera†
0042-7047 Visserij†
0042-7101 Vista†
0042-7128 Vistazo 3835
0042-7136 Visti Ukrayins'kykh Inzheneriv 3226
0042-7144 Image Dynamics in Science & Medicine†
0042-7152 Visual Education†
0042-7160 Visual Medicine†
0042-7179 Visva - Bharati Patrika 5395
0042-7187 Visva - Bharati Journal of Philosophy 6960
0042-7195 Visva - Bharati Quarterly 5244
0042-7209 Viswa Rachana 5395
0042-7217 Viswasilp†
0042-7233 Vita Cattolica 7822
0042-7241 Vita dell'Infanzia 2925
0042-725X Vita e Pensiero 5244
0042-7268 Vita e Salute 6999
0042-7276 Vita Giuseppina 7822
0042-7284 La Vita in Cristo e nella Chiesa 7822
0042-7292 Vida Italiana†
0042-7330 Vita Consacrata 7693
0042-7349 La Vita Scolastica 2925
0042-7357 Vita Sindacale Bergamasca† 8997
0042-7365 Vita Sociale†
0042-7411 Vital Notes on Medical Periodicals†
0042-742X Vital Speeches of the Day 4585
0042-7438 Vital Statistics Monthly Report†
0042-7470 Vitchyzna 5244
0042-7489 Vitesse - Speed†
0042-7497 Vitezna Kridla
0042-7500 Vitis 258
0042-7519 Vitreous Enameller 2046
0042-7527 Vivant Univers changed to 1379-4205 7232
0042-7543 Vivarium 4277
0042-7551 Viviamo
0042-756X Vivienda†
0042-7586 La Rivista del Clero Italiano 7815
0042-7594 Vivliothiki Ghoneon
0042-7608 Vivre en Harmonie† 8997
0042-7616 Vizugyi Kozlemenyek 3399
0042-7632 Vjesnik Rada 1714
0042-7640 Vjesnik U Srijedu†
0042-7659 Splitsko-Makarska Nadbiskupija. Vjesnik 7683
0042-7675 De Vlaamse Gids 5244
0042-7683 Vlaanderen 525
0042-7705 Vliegende Hollander 6452
Voz de Mocambique
0042-773X Vnitrni Lekarstvi 5728

0042-7756 Vocation†
0042-7780 La Voce 3899
0042-7802 Voce Bruzia† 8997
0042-7810 La Voce degli Italiani 3571
0042-7829 La Voce del Tabaccaio 8488
0042-7837 Voce della Fiera† 8997
0042-7845 Voce della Madonna delle Grazie†
0042-7861 Voce di Siracusa
0042-7888 Voci Fraterne
0042-790X Vodohospodarsky Casopis 2799
0042-7934 Voedingsmiddelentechnologie 3667
0042-7942 Voeest-Alpine Betriebskurier
0042-7977 Voetbal International 8250
0042-7985 Het Vogeljaar 916
0042-7993 Die Vogelwelt 916
0042-8000 Vogue 2262
0042-8019 Vogue Australia 2263
0042-8027 Vogue Italia 2263
0042-8035 Vogue Living 4563
0042-8078 Voice of A G S 303
0042-8086 Voice of Ahinsa 7743
0042-8094 Voice of Buddhism 7703
0042-8108 Voice of Business†
0042-8116 Voice of Freedom†
0042-8132 Voice of Islam 7716
0042-8140 Voice of Jamaica
0042-8159 Voice of Liberty†
0042-8167 Voice of Methodism†
0042-8175 Voice of Missions
0042-8183 Voice of the Black Community 3571
0042-8191 Voice of the Cement, Lime, Gypsum and Allied Workers†
0042-8213 Voice of the Nazarene
0042-8221 Voice of the People
0042-8248 Voice of the Unions† 8997
0042-8256 Voice of Youth 2220
0042-8264 Full Gospel Business Men's Voice 7644
0042-8272 Voices (New Bern) 7414
0042-8280 Voices International†
0042-8299 Voicespondent 8155
0042-8302 Phase Zero†
0042-8329 Voie de la Paix†
0042-8337 Volk auf dem Weg 7272
0042-8345 Voix de l'Edition de la Presse et de l'Audiovision†
0042-8353 Voix Dentaire
0042-8396 Voix et Visages†
0042-840X Vojni Glasnik 6453
0042-8426 Vojno Delo 6453
0042-8442 Vojnoistorijski Glasnik 6453
0042-8450 Vojnosanitetski Pregled 6453
0042-8469 Vojnotehnicki Glasnik 6453
0042-8507 Volkshochschule Brigittenau. Mitteilungsblatt†
0042-8531 Volkskunde in Oesterreich 3624
0042-8574 Volkstuin 3753
0042-8582 Wirtschaftswoche 1525
0042-8620 Volt
0042-8639 The Volta Review 4076
0042-8647 Voluntary Action 8146
0042-8671 Volunteer† 8998
0042-8701 Volunteer's Digest†
0042-8736 Voprosy Ekonomiki 1192
0042-8744 Voprosy Filosofii 6960
0042-8752 Voprosy Ikhtiologii 967
0042-8779 Voprosy Istorii 4166
0042-8787 Voprosy Kurortologii, Fizioterapii i Lechebnoi Fizicheskoi Kul'tury 6117
0042-8795 Voprosy Literatury 5396
0042-8809 Voprosy Meditsinskoi Khimii changed to Biomeditsinskaya Khimiya 727
0042-8817 Zhurnal Voprosy Neirokhirurgii im. N.N. Burdenko 6264
0042-8833 Voprosy Pitaniya 6671
0042-8841 Voprosy Psikhologii 7414
0042-8922 Vorschriften fuer die Veterinaerverwaltung†
0042-8930 Vorwaerts 4605
0042-8965 Votre Beaute 592
0042-8981 Vou†
0042-899X Vox Romanica 5194
0042-9007 Vox Sanguinis 5767
0042-9015 Vox Theologica†
0042-9031 Voyages†
0042-9058 Voenno-Istoricheskii Zhurnal 6452
0042-9066 Voennyi Vestnik 6453
0042-9082 Voz de la Biblioteca Universitaria†
0042-9090 Voz del Pueblo
0042-9112 Vredesactie†
0042-9139 Vriend changed to 1874-1010 4076
0042-9147 Vriend der Kinderen†
0042-9155 Vriend van Oud en Jong
0042-9198 Vrishchik
0042-9228 Free State Educational News 2858
0042-9287 Vu Par les Belges†
0042-9309 Vukovarske Novine
0042-9317 Vuoriteollisuus changed to 1459-9694 6469
0042-9325 Vyapar (Gujarati Edition) 1192
0042-9376 Vystavba a Architektura†
0042-9384 Vytis 2270
0042-9392 Vytvarnictvo, Fotografia, Film 525
0042-9406 Vyziva a Zdravie†
0042-9422 Vyzvol'nyi Shlyakh 5244
0042-9465 W.A. Grower 169
0042-952X W & L Magazine 2308
0042-9538 W & V 37
0042-9562 W B F O 4431
0042-9589 W D†
0042-9635 W E M Newsletter†
0042-966X W G A Geschaeftsbericht 1586
0042-9678 W G O - Monatshefte fuer Osteuropaeisches Recht† 8998
0042-9686 World Health Organization. Bulletin 5731
0042-9694 W H O Chronicle†
0042-9732 W I Z O Review 7731
0042-9740 Indo-Iran Journal 7241

0042-9767 W M O Bulletin **6397**
0042-9775 W N Y F **3582**
0042-9864 Women Strike for Peace†
0042-9902 Wacht te Kooi
0042-9945 Waffen- und Kostuemkunde†
0042-9953 Wagenbouwnieuws†
0042-9961 Waggoner†
0042-997X Karosseriebauer und Wagner†
0042-9988 Wagtail
0042-9996 Die Wahrheit **7192**
0043-0005 Waiblinger Anzeigenblatt†
0043-0013 Wakayama Medicine **5729**
0043-0021 Wakayamaken Kisho Geppo **6398**
0043-003X Wake Forest Law Review **4810**
0043-0048 Die Waldarbeit†
0043-0056 Wales
0043-0064 Walkabout†
0043-0072 Walker Watchword†
0043-0099 Wall Street Reports
0043-0102 The Wall Street Transcript **1658**
0043-0129 Wallaces Farmer **169**
0043-0137 Wallerstein Laboratories Communications†
0043-0161 Walls & Ceilings **1042**
0043-0196 Wanasan **3707**
0043-020X War Communiques†
0043-0218 War Cry *changed to* 1718-5769 **7741**
0043-0226 War Cry **7779**
0043-0234 The War Cry **7779**
0043-0242 War Cry **7779**
0043-0250 War Cry **7779**
0043-0307 Waratah†
0043-0315 Ward's AutoWorld **8611**
0043-0323 Ward's Bulletin
0043-0358 Warmte†
0043-0374 Warship International **6453**
0043-0382 Balai Penyelidikan Perusahaan Perkebunan Gula. Warta Bulanan†
0043-0390 Warwickshire and Worcestershire Life†
0043-0412 Wascana Review **5397**
0043-0420 Washburn Law Journal **4810**
0043-0439 Washington Academy of Sciences. Journal **7928**
0043-0455 Washington and Jefferson Literary Journal†
0043-0463 Washington and Lee Law Review **4810**
0043-0501 Washington Coach
0043-051X Washington County Education News†
0043-0536 Washington Dental Service Newsletter
0043-0544 Washington Diocese *changed to* Washington Window **7779**
0043-0552 Washington Education†
0043-0560 Washington Food Dealer Magazine†
0043-0595 Washington Insurance Newsletter†
0043-0609 Washington International Arts Letter
0043-0617 Washington Law Review **4811**
0043-0633 The Washington Monthly **7193**
0043-0684 Washington Newspaper **4585**
0043-0692 Washington Plumbing and Heating Contractor
0043-0706 Washington Purchaser†
0043-0749 Science Trends†
0043-0773 Washington State Entomological Society. Proceedings†
0043-0781 Washington State Journal of Nursing†
0043-082X Washington State University. Mathematics Notes **5546**
0043-0838 Washington State University. Research Studies†
0043-0846 Washington State Voter
0043-0897 Washingtonian **3992**
0043-0927 Wasmann Journal of Biology†
0043-0978 Wasserwirtschaft **8836**
0043-0994 Wasserwirtschaftliche Mitteilungen **8836**
0043-1001 Waste Age **3513**
0043-1036 Wat Kan Ons Opvoer'†
0043-1079 Watchmaker, Jeweller & Silversmith†
0043-1087 Watchtower **7743**
0043-1141 Water & Wastes Digest **3514**
0043-1192 Water Conditions in Wisconsin†
0043-1206 Water Desalination Report **8837**
0043-1222 Water in the News†
0043-1257 Water Management Bulletin†
0043-1265 Water News **8837**
0043-1273 Water Newsletter†
0043-1354 Water Research **8838**
0043-1397 Water Resources Research **8840**
0043-1427 Water Skier
0043-1435 Water Spectrum†
0043-1443 Water Well Journal **8841**
0043-1451 Waterkampioen **8284**
0043-1494 Watershed News
0043-1508 Watersheds†
0043-1516 Watersport†
0043-1524 Waterways Journal **8665**
0043-1532 Watsonia **822**
0043-1559 Wave Hill News†
0043-1567 Wavriensia **4278**
0043-1575 The Way **7694**
0043-1583 The Way (Philadelphia) **7822**
0043-1605 Way of Life **7694**
0043-1621 The Wayne Law Review **4811**
0043-163X Wayne State University Alumni News **2309**
0043-1648 Wear **3399**
0043-1656 Weather **6398**
0043-1672 Weatherwise **6398**
0043-1680 Webb Society Quarterly Journal *changed to* 0967-6139 **574**
0043-1710 Wee Wisdom†
0043-1729 Weed Abstracts **190**
0043-1737 Weed Research **258**
0043-1745 Weed Science **258**
0043-1761 Week-End†
0043-177X Weekblad Cinema
0043-1796 Weekblad voor Fiscaal Recht **4811**
0043-1818 Weekend†
0043-1834 Weekly Letter Commentary†
0043-1842 Weekly Livestock Reporter **304**
0043-1850 Weekly Market Bulletin **208**
0043-1869 National Braille Press. Weekly News†
0043-1907 National Promotion Audit†
0043-1923 Weekly Statistical Sugar Trade Journal
0043-1966 Weekly Underwriter†
0043-1974 Weekly Weather and Crop Bulletin **258**
0043-1982 Weekly Weather Report of Pakistan & Kashmir
0043-2016 Weg en Waterbouw†
0043-2024 Weg und Ziel†
0043-2032 Weg zur Gesundheit **6999**
0043-2040 Wege zum Menschen **7694**
0043-2059 Wege zur Sozialversicherung **8078**
0043-2067 Wegen *changed to* 1872-0129 **3261**
0043-2075 Gornictwo Odkrywkowe **6463**
0043-2091 Wegwijs in de Sportliteratuur†
0043-2105 Wegwijzer
0043-2148 Wehrmedizin und Wehrpharmazie **5729**
0043-2156 Wehrmedizinische Monatsschrift **5729**
0043-2164 Wehrpolitische Information†
0043-2172 Wehrtechnik **75**
0043-2180 Weight Watchers Magazine **6671**
0043-2199 Weimarer Beitraege **5397**
0043-2202 Weiss - Blaue Rundschau
0043-2229 Welcome to Singapore†
0043-2237 The Welder† **8998**
0043-2245 Welding and Metal Fabrication **6344**
0043-2253 Welding Design & Fabrication *changed to* 1935-5572 **6343**
0043-2288 Welding in the World **6345**
0043-2296 Welding Journal **6345**
0043-2318 Welding Research Abroad **6345**
0043-2326 Welding Research Council Bulletin **6345**
0043-2369 Welfare Reporter (Trenton)†
0043-2385 Welfarer†
0043-2393 Well Servicing **6797**
0043-2407 Welldoer†
0043-2431 Welsh History Review **4166**
0043-244X Welsh Music **6628**
0043-2466 Welsh Rugby
0043-2474 Welsh Secondary Schools Review†
0043-2482 Welt der Arbeit†
0043-2490 Die Welt der Buecher†
0043-2512 Die Molkerei-Zeitung Welt der Milch **267**
0043-2520 Die Welt der Slaven **5195**
0043-2539 Die Welt des Islams **7717**
0043-2547 Die Welt des Orients **4167**
0043-2563 Welt und Sport†
0043-258X Weltblick†
0043-2598 Die Weltbuehne†
0043-2601 Weltgewerkschaftsbewegung†
0043-261X Weltkunst **369**
0043-2636 Weltwirtschaftliches Archiv *changed to* 1610-2878 **1166**
0043-2652 Die Weltwirtschaft†
0043-2660 Die Weltwoche **3959**
0043-2679 Die Wende†
0043-2687 Wendepunkt†
0043-2725 Werbung in Oesterreich
0043-275X Wereldwijzer†
0043-2784 Werkpaedagogische Hefte†
0043-2792 Werkstatt und Betrieb **5461**
0043-2849 Die Weser†
0043-2873 Wesley Historical Society. Proceedings **7780**
0043-289X Wesleyan Advocate *changed to* Wesleyan Life **7780**
0043-2911 Wesleyan News†
0043-292X Wessex Life†
0043-2954 West-Ost-Journal
0043-2962 West Africa†
0043-2970 West African Builder and Architect
0043-2989 West African Journal of Biological and Applied Chemistry **746**
0043-2997 West African Journal of Education **2925**
0043-3004 West African Medical Journal
0043-3020 West African Science Association. Journal **7929**
0043-3047 West & East **7273**
0043-3055 West Australian Craftsman
0043-3071 West Bengal Labour Gazette **1714**
0043-3098 West Cameroon Monthly Digest of Statistics†
0043-3136 West Georgia College Review†
0043-3144 West Indian Medical Journal **5730**
0043-3195 West Virginia Agriculture & Forestry†
0043-3209 West Virginia Archaeologist†
0043-3217 West Virginia C.P.A. **1303**
0043-3225 West Virginia Dental Journal†
0043-325X West Virginia History **4317**
0043-3268 West Virginia Law Review **4812**
0043-3276 West Virginia Libraries **5054**
0043-3284 West Virginia Medical Journal **5730**
0043-3292 West Virginia Pharmacist†
0043-3306 West Virginia Progress†
0043-3357 WestArt†
0043-3365 Wenatchee Business Journal **1193**
0043-3373 Westchester County Press
0043-339X Westchester Realtor **7615**
0043-342X Westerly **5398**
0043-3454 Western†
0043-3462 Western American Literature **5398**
0043-3489 Western Australia. Government Gazette **7476**
0043-3519 Western Banker†
0043-3527 Western Buddhist†
0043-3535 Western Builder **1043**
0043-3551 Western Carolina University Journal of Education†
0043-3691 Western Farm Equipment
0043-3721 Western Fisheries†
0043-373X Western Folklore **3624**
0043-3799 Western Grower and Shipper **259**
0043-3802 Western Heart
0043-3810 The Western Historical Quarterly **4317**
0043-3829 Western Horizons **6885**
0043-3837 Western Horseman **8300**
0043-3845 Western Humanities Review **5398**
0043-3853 Western Illinois University Bulletin†
0043-3934 Western Miner†
0043-3942 Western Mobile News†
0043-3950 Western Motor Fleet†
0043-3977 Western New York Motorist **8611**
0043-3993 Western Ontario History Nuggets†
0043-4000 Western Outdoors **8341**
0043-4051 Western Plains Library System Newsletter
0043-4086 Western Printer & Lithographer†
0043-4094 Western Producer **170**
0043-4124 Western Real Estate News **7616**
0043-4132 Western Recorder **7780**
0043-4175 Western School Law Review†
0043-4191 Western Socialist†
0043-4256 Western Underwriter†
0043-4299 Western World Review†
0043-4329 Western's World†
0043-4345 Westhoek†
0043-4361 Westinghouse Engineer†
0043-4388 Westminster Theological Journal **7694**
0043-440X Westport Historical Quarterly†
0043-4418 Der Westpreusse **3860**
0043-4434 Westways **8774**
0043-4450 Wetter und Leben†
0043-4477 Whaley-Eaton Foreign Letter†
0043-4493 What†
0043-4523 What's Happening†
0043-4558 What's New in Advertising and Marketing **40**
0043-4574 What's New in Co-Op Information†
0043-4582 What's New in Food and Drug Research†
0043-4612 What's News in Reinsurance†
0043-4620 What's on for Young People†
0043-4647 What's on in Calcutta **8774**
0043-4655 What's on in Glasgow
0043-4663 What's On in Jersey
0043-4701 Wheat Life **259**
0043-4728 Wheat Scoop†
0043-4744 Wheel Clicks **8627**
0043-4752 The WHEEL of Delta Omicron **6628**
0043-4760 Wheeled Sportsman†
0043-4779 Wheels **8612**
0043-4825 Whereas†
0043-4841 Which? **2642**
0043-4868 Whitaker's Books of the Month and Books to Come†
0043-4876 White Collar **4605**
0043-4906 White County Heritage **4318**
0043-4922 White Fathers†
0043-4965 White Ribbon Bulletin **2700**
0043-4973 The White Ribbon **2700**
0043-499X White Tops **8484**
0043-5007 White Wing Messenger **7694**
0043-504X Wholesale Commodity Prices†
0043-5058 Wholesale Food Prices†
0043-5074 Wiadomosci
0043-5082 Wiadomosci Archeologiczne **423**
0043-5090 Wiadomosci Botaniczne **822**
0043-5104 Wiadomosci Chemiczne **2084**
0043-5112 Wiadomosci Elektrotechniczne **3334**
0043-5120 Wiadomosci Gornicze **6483**
0043-5147 Wiadomosci Lekarskie **5730**
0043-5155 Wiadomosci Numizmatyczne **6653**
0043-5163 Wiadomosci Parazytologiczne **711**
0043-518X Poland. Glowny Urzad Statystyczny. Wiadomosci Statystyczne **8394**
0043-5201 Poland. Urzad Patentowy. Wiadomosci **6757**
0043-5244 Widnokregi†
0043-5260 De Wielewaal **917**
0043-5295 Wiener Buecherbriefe
0043-5309 Wiener Entomologische Gesellschaft. Zeitschrift
0043-5317 Wiener Geschichtsblaetter **4278**
0043-5325 Wiener Klinische Wochenschrift **5730**
0043-5333 Wiener Library Bulletin†
0043-5341 Wiener Medizinische Wochenschrift **5730**
0043-5384 Wiener Zeitschrift fuer Nervenheilkunde und deren Grenzgebiete†
0043-5406 Wigs & Hairpieces†
0043-5414 Wijsgerig Perspectief op Maatschappij en Wetenschap **6961**
0043-5422 Wild und Hund **8341**
0043-5449 Wilderness Travel Magazine†
0043-5481 Wildlife Australia **2632**
0043-549X Wildlife in North Carolina **2632**
0043-5538 Wildlife Views†
0043-5554 Willamette Bridge†
0043-5570 Der Wille zur Form **526**
0043-5589 William and Mary Law Review **4814**
0043-5597 William and Mary Quarterly **4318**
0043-5600 William and Mary Review **5399**
0043-5627 Williams' Family Bulletin†
0043-5635 Wilmington Public Schools. Profile†
0043-5643 Wilson Bulletin *changed to* 1559-4491 **917**
0043-5651 Wilson Library Bulletin†
0043-566X Wiltshire Farmer **170**
0043-5678 Wimpel†
0043-5694 W I N B A N News†
0043-5708 Wind Bell **7703**
0043-5716 Windless Orchard†
0043-5724 Windowt†
0043-5759 House & Garden (London) **4542**
0043-5775 Off Licence News **608**
0043-5791 Wine Magazine†
0043-5805 Wine Review†
0043-5813 Wine, Spirit & Malt†
0043-5821 Wineletter†
0043-583X Wines and Vines **613**
0043-5848 Winged Arrow†
0043-5856 The Winged Foot **7000**
0043-5864 Winged Head **2271**
0043-5880 Wings **75**
0043-5937 Winner **2700**
0043-5953 Der Winzer **259**
0043-5961 Wir Blenden Auf†
0043-5996 Wire **6336**
0043-6011 Wire Industry **6336**
0043-6135 Wirtschaft und Recht†

ISSN

Link to your serials resources and content with ulrichsweb.com

0044-2194 Zeitschrift fuer Agrargeschichte und Agrarsoziologie **171**
0044-2224 Zeitschrift fuer Alternsforschung†
0044-2259 Zeitschrift fuer Angewandte Geologie† **8999**
0044-2267 Zeitschrift fuer Angewandte Mathematik und Mechanik **5547**
0044-2275 Zeitschrift fuer Angewandte Mathematik und Physik **5547**
0044-2291 Zeitschrift fuer Angewandte Zoologie†
0044-2305 Zeitschrift fuer Anglistik und Amerikanistik **5404**
0044-2313 Zeitschrift fuer Anorganische und Allgemeine Chemie **2084**
0044-2321 Zeitschrift fuer Arbeitsrecht und Sozialrecht **4818**
0044-233X Zeitschrift fuer Archaeologie†
0044-2348 Zeitschrift fuer Auslaendisches Oeffentliches Recht und Voelkerrecht **4945**
0044-2356 Zeitschrift fuer Balkanologie **4280**
0044-2364 Zeitschrift fuer Bayerische Landesgeschichte **4168**
0044-2372 Z f B **1802**
0044-2380 Zeitschrift fuer Bibliothekswesen und Bibliographie **5056**
0044-2410 Zeitschrift fuer das Gesamte Familienrecht **4818**
0044-2429 Zeitschrift fuer das Gesamte Genossenschaftswesen **8018**
0044-2437 Zeitschrift fuer das Gesamte Handelsrecht und Wirtschaftsrecht **4818**
0044-247X Zeitschrift fuer den Lastenausgleich†
0044-2496 Zeitschrift fuer Deutsche Philologie **5198**
0044-250X Zeitschrift fuer Deutsche Sprache† **8999**
0044-2518 Zeitschrift fuer Deutsches Altertum und Deutsche Literatur **5198**
0044-2526 Zeitschrift fuer die Alttestamentliche Wissenschaft **7696**
0044-2542 Zeitschrift fuer die Gesamte Innere Medizin und Ihre Grenzgebiete†
0044-2585 Zeitschrift fuer die Gesamte Versicherungswissenschaft **4529**
0044-2593 Zeitschrift fuer die Geschichte der Juden†
0044-2607 Zeitschrift fuer die Geschichte des Oberrheins **4280**
0044-2615 Zeitschrift fuer die Neutestamentliche Wissenschaft und die Kunde der Aelteren Kirche **7696**
0044-2658 Erzmetall *changed to* 1613-2394 **6337**
0044-2666 Zeitschrift fuer Ethnologie **361**
0044-2674 Zeitschrift fuer Evangelische Ethik **7696**
0044-2690 Zeitschrift fuer Evangelisches Kirchenrecht **7781**
0044-2720 Zeitschrift fuer Fischerei und deren Hilfswissenschaften†
0044-2747 Zeitschrift fuer Franzoesische Sprache und Literatur **5198**
0044-2763 Zeitschrift fuer Ganzheitsforschung **6962**
0044-2771 Zeitschrift fuer Gastroenterologie **5932**
0044-2798 Zeitschrift fuer Geomorphologie, Supplementbaende *changed to* 0372-8854 **2776**
0044-2828 Zeitschrift fuer Geschichtswissenschaft **4168**
0044-2836 Zeitschrift fuer Gletscherkunde und Glazialgeologie **2776**
0044-2852 Zeitschrift fuer Heereskunde **6455**
0044-2887 Zeitschrift fuer Jagdwissenschaft *changed to* 1612-4642 **319**
0044-2895 Zeitschrift fuer Katholische Theologie **7823**
0044-2925 Zeitschrift fuer Kirchengeschichte **7696**
0044-2968 Zeitschrift fuer Kristallographie **2112**
0044-2976 Zeitschrift fuer KulturAustausch **7276**
0044-2992 Zeitschrift fuer Kunstgeschichte **528**
0044-300X Zeitschrift fuer Landeskultur†
0044-3093 Zeitschrift fuer Metallkunde *changed to* 1862-5282 **6316**
0044-3107 Zeitschrift fuer Mikroskopisch-Anatomische Forschung†
0044-3123 Zeitschrift fuer Missionswissenschaft und Religionswissenschaft **7696**
0044-3182 Zeitschrift fuer Naturheilkunde **316**
0044-3220 Zeitschrift fuer Orthopaedie und Ihre Grenzgebiete *changed to* 1864-6697 **6075**
0044-3247 Zeitschrift fuer Paedagogik **2928**
0044-3301 Zeitschrift fuer Philosophische Forschung **6962**
0044-3344 Zeitschrift fuer Physikalische Medizin†
0044-3360 Zeitschrift fuer Politik **7197**
0044-3409 Zeitschrift fuer Psychologie mit Zeitschrift fuer Angewandte Psychologie *changed to* Zeitschrift fuer Psychologie - Journal of Psychology **7416**
0044-3441 Zeitschrift fuer Religions- und Geistesgeschichte **7697**
0044-3476 Zeitschrift fuer Schweizerische Archaeologie und Kunstgeschichte **425**
0044-3484 Zeitschrift fuer Schweizerische Kirchengeschichte *changed to* 1661-3880 **7679**
0044-3492 Zeitschrift fuer Slavische Philologie **5199**
0044-3506 Zeitschrift fuer Slawistik **5199**
0044-3514 Zeitschrift fuer Sozialpsychologie *changed to* 1864-9335 **7409**
0044-3522 Zeitschrift fuer Sozialberatung†
0044-3549 Zeitschrift fuer Theologie und Kirche **7781**
0044-3638 Zeitschrift fuer Vergleichende Rechtswissenschaft **4945**
0044-3654 Zeitschrift fuer Verkehrssicherheit **8637**
0044-3662 Zeitschrift fuer Verkehrsrecht **4819**
0044-3670 Zeitschrift fuer Verkehrswissenschaft **8637**
0044-3700 Zeitschrift fuer Volkskunde **3624**
0044-3751 Zeitschrift fuer Wirtschaftsgeographie **4035**
0044-3778 Zeitschrift fuer Wissenschaftliche Zoologie. Abteilung A†
0044-3786 Zeitschrift fuer Wuerttembergische Landesgeschichte **4280**
0044-3816 Zeitschrift Interne Revision **1304**
0044-3824 Zeitschriftendienst Musik†
0044-3867 Zellstoff und Papier†
0044-3875 Zemedelska Skola†
0044-3913 Zemledelie **172**
0044-3921 Zemlja Sovjeta†
0044-3948 Zemlya i Vselennaya **584**
0044-3980 Zenit†
0044-3999 Zenit†
0044-4006 Zenken Journal **1044**
0044-4022 Zentralblatt fuer Aero- und Astronautik†
0044-409X Zentralblatt fuer Chirurgie **6263**
0044-4103 Zentralblatt fuer Didaktik der Mathematik *changed to* 1863-9690 **5547**
0044-4189 Zentralblatt fuer Geologie und Palaeontologie. Teil II: Palaeontologie **6731**
0044-4197 Zentralblatt fuer Gynaekologie **6006**
0044-4251 Zentralblatt fuer Neurochirurgie *changed to* 1868-4904 **6130**
0044-4278 Zentralblatt fuer Sozialversicherung, Sozialhilfe und Versorgung†
0044-4286 Zentralblatt fuer Verkehrs-Medizin, Verkehrs-Psychologie, Luft- und Raumfahrt-Medizin†
0044-4324 Zentralverein der Wiener Lehrerschaft. Mitteilungen
0044-4340 Zero One **3873**
0044-4383 Zeszyty Problemowe Gornictwa†
0044-4391 Zeszyty Historyczne **4168**
0044-4405 Katolicki Uniwersytet Lubelski. Zeszyty Naukowe **7803**
0044-4413 Fasciculi Mathematici **5487**
0044-4448 Zheleznodorozhnyi Transport **8628**
0044-4456 Zhenshchiny Mira†
0044-4464 Zhilishchnoe i Kommunal'noe Khozyaistvo **1909**
0044-4472 Zhilishchnoe Stroitel'stvo **1044**
0044-4502 Zhurnal Analiticheskoi Khimii **2107**
0044-4510 Zhurnal Eksperimental'noi i Teoreticheskoi Fiziki **7047**
0044-4529 Zhurnal Evolyutsionnoi Biokhimii i Fiziologii **746**
0044-4537 Zhurnal Fizicheskoi Khimii **2142**
0044-457X Zhurnal Neorganicheskoi Khimii **2119**
0044-4588 Zhurnal Nevropatologii i Psikhiatrii im. S.S. Korsakova **6191**
0044-4596 Zhurnal Obshchei Biologii **712**
0044-460X Zhurnal Obshchei Khimii **2085**
0044-4618 Zhurnal Prikladnoi Khimii **3258**
0044-4642 Zhurnal Tekhnicheskoi Fiziki **7047**
0044-4650 Zhurnal Ushnykh, Nosovykh i Gorlovykh Boleznei **6086**
0044-4669 Zhurnal Vychislitel'noi Matematiki i Matematicheskoi Fiziki **5548**
0044-4677 Zhurnal Vysshei Nervnoi Deyatel'nosti **929**
0044-4707 Ziekenfondsgids†
0044-474X Alte und Neue Zinnfiguren†
0044-4758 Zion **7732**
0044-4766 Zionist Collegiate†
0044-4774 Zionist Literature†
0044-4782 Zionist Record and S.A. Jewish Chronicle†
0044-4812 Ziva **712**
0044-4855 Zivot i Skola **2929**
0044-4863 Zivotne Prostredie **3477**
0044-4871 Zlaty Maj†
0044-488X Znak **7697**
0044-4928 Zobozdravstveni Vestnik
0044-4952 Zodiaque† **9000**
0044-4979 Zolnierz Polski **6455**
0044-4987 Zona Franca†
0044-4995 Zona: Revista de Comercio Latino-Americana
0044-5010 Zone
0044-5037 Zoo†
0044-5088 Zoologica **969**
0044-510X Zoologica Poloniae **969**
0044-5134 Zoologicheskii Zhurnal **970**
0044-5150 Zoologische Beitraege†
0044-5169 Der Zoologische Garten **970**
0044-5231 Zoologischer Anzeiger **970**
0044-5258 Zoologisk Revy†
0044-5274 Zoon†
0044-5282 Zoonooz **971**
0044-5290 Zooprofilassi†
0044-5312 Zootechnia†
0044-5320 Zootecnia **305**
0044-5363 Divadelni Ustav. Zpravy†
0044-5398 Die Zuckerruebe **260**
0044-5401 Zuechtungskunde **305**
0044-5428 Zuid-Afrika **7198**
0044-5436 Zuivelnieuws **270**
0044-5452 Die Zukunft **5247**
0044-5460 Zukunft **7732**
0044-5479 Zulqarnain **7198**
0044-5487 Zum Nachdenken **7198**
0044-5517 Cuadernos de Historia Jeronimo Zurita *changed to* 0214-0993 **4257**
0044-5525 Zvaranie **6345**
0044-5576 Zwingli
0044-5584 Zycie i Mysl **6962**
0044-5614 A B C Decor
0044-5649 A D P Newsletter†
0044-5657 A F - Architekturforum
0044-5681 A I M Newsletter (Print) *changed to* A I M Newsletter **8554**
0044-5711 A R I S†
0044-5746 Aboriginal Quarterly†
0044-5800 Abstracts of Hungarian Economic Literature†
0044-5819 Abstracts on Health Effects of Environmental Pollutants†
0044-5827 Abundance†
0044-5835 Academy of Parish Clergy. Journal†
0044-5843 Acadia Bulletin **2271**
0044-5851 Acadiensis **4281**
0044-586X Acarologia†
0044-5878 Accident Prevention **6672**
0044-5894 Accion Empresarial **1723**
0044-5916 Accountants and Secretaries Educational Journal
0044-5924 Accountants' Washington Taxletter†
0044-5932 A C E†
0044-5940 Acoma†
0044-5967 Acta Amazonica **7831**
0044-5975 Acta Antiqua Academiae Scientiarum Hungaricae **2229**
0044-5991 Acta Histochemica et Cytochemica (Print)†
0044-6009 Acta Hospitalia **4087**
0044-6025 Acta Medica Iranica **5566**
0044-605X Acta Veterinaria Scandinavica (Print)† **8928**
0044-6068 Action
0044-6092 Action Era Vehicle **362**
0044-6106 Action Populaire **7102**
0044-6130 Actualidade Universitaria†
0044-6157 Actualite Fiduciaire†
0044-6165 Actualites Industrielles Lorraines **6303**
0044-6173 Aktuelle Traumatologie *changed to* 1864-6697 **6075**
0044-6181 Adam and Eve
0044-622X Adelaide. Stock Exchange. Official Record†
0044-6238 Adelante (Orlando)
0044-6262 Administracion, Desarrollo, Integracion†
0044-6289 A C O A†
0044-6297 Administrative Court Digest†
0044-6300 Administrative Scene†
0044-6319 Administrator†
0044-6327 Administrator†
0044-6335 Adolescent Medicine (Washington)†
0044-636X Advanced Technology Libraries **4987**
0044-6378 Advances in Urethane Science and Technology†
0044-6394 Adverse Drug Reaction Bulletin **6819**
0044-6408 Ad. Activities†
0044-6416 The Advocate (Vancouver) **4611**
0044-6432 Aero News†
0044-6467 Affirm **7744**
0044-6475 Africa (London)†
0044-6483 Africa Confidential **7102**
0044-6491 Africa Letter **7102**
0044-653X African Crescent **7708**
0044-6556 African Jewish Newspaper
0044-6564 African Journal of Pharmacy and Pharmaceutical Sciences†
0044-6610 African Studies Association of the West Indies. Bulletin
0044-6661 Afrique et Parole†
0044-667X Afriscope
0044-6696 After School
0044-670X Afterthought
0044-6726 Agora **2824**
0044-6734 Agra University. Bulletin **2966**
0044-6742 Agregation†
0044-6769 Agrichemical Age†
0044-6785 Agricultura†
0044-6793 Agricultura em Sao Paulo **191**
0044-6823 Agriculture and Farming†
0044-6831 Agrifack **86**
0044-6858 Agronomia Mocambicana **88**
0044-6874 Agronomist†
0044-6882 Agrosintesis **88**
0044-6890 Agua **3360**
0044-6904 Ahead: Australian Health Advisory Digest†
0044-6912 Aichi Gakuin Daigaku Shigakkai-shi **5833**
0044-6920 Aikamerkki†
0044-6955 Air Combat†
0044-698X Air over Arizona†
0044-7021 Airport Report **8537**
0044-703X Laisve†
0044-7048 Akron Business and Economic Review†
0044-7064 Alaluz†
0044-7080 Alberta Bowhunter and Archer
0044-7099 Alberta Builder†
0044-7129 Alberta Education Council. Newsletter†
0044-7145 Alberta Landrace Association. Newsletter
0044-7153 Alberta, Lands, Forests, Parks, Wildlife†
0044-7218 Alcheringa†
0044-7234 Alert (Wahroonga)†
0044-7250 Alexandria Journal of Agricultural Research **90**
0044-7277 Alianza Federal de Pueblos Libres. Vox de la Alianza
0044-7293 All India Institute of Medical Sciences, New Delhi. Bulletin†
0044-7331 Allergy Information
0044-7366 Allotrope
0044-7412 Amanuensis†
0044-7439 Ambassador†
0044-7447 Ambio **3402**
0044-7463 Amenagement et Nature **3402**
0044-7471 Amerasia Journal **8086**
0044-748X Latinskaya Amerika **4301**
0044-7501 American Alumni Council Commentary†
0044-751X American Antiquarian Society. Proceedings **4988**
0044-7544 American Baby **2143**
0044-7560 A L I - A B A C L E Review **4607**
0044-7587 A C S Single Article Announcement†
0044-7595 S C A L A C S **2080**
0044-7617 American Chronicle†
0044-7625 American Cinemeditor†
0044-7633 American Classical Review **2229**
0044-7676 A F T R A **2356**
0044-7684 American Film Institute Report†
0044-7722 A S†
0044-7749 American Laboratory **2097**
0044-7757 A L A Zurnals†
0044-7765 A M A Update†
0044-7773 American Notary **4615**
0044-7781 Nursing Research Report†
0044-779X American Philological Association. Directory of Members
0044-7811 The American Postal Worker **2353**
0044-7838 American Revolution†
0044-7854 A S E A Newsletter†
0044-7889 A S M News (Materials Park)†
0044-7897 A S M News (Washington) *changed to* 1558-7452 **891**
0044-7900 American Society for Neo-Hellenic Studies. Newsletter
0044-7919 A S P R Newsletter **6740**
0044-7927 A S T R Newsletter **8464**
0044-7943 American Society of Cartographers. Bulletin†
0044-8060 American Studies in Scandinavia **4283**
0044-8079 American Zionist Federation. News and Views†
0044-8133 Amis d'Andre Gide. Bulletin **5253**
0044-8141 Amministrare **7420**
0044-815X Ampute de Guerre
0044-8168 Amra†
0044-8176 Analecta Linguistica†
0044-8184 Anales de Ortopedia y Traumatologia
0044-8192 Analysen und Prognosen ueber die Welt von Morgen†
0044-8206 Anapress†
0044-8222 Ancestor **3758**
0044-8249 Angewandte Chemie **2050**
0044-8257 A C A Review **3582**
0044-8265 Anglo-Soviet Journal†
0044-8273 Anglo-Ukrainian News†
0044-832X Annals of Economic and Social Measurement†
0044-8362 Antepasados **4283**
0044-8370 Anthropological Society of Oxford. Journal **326**
0044-8389 Antioquia Medica†
0044-8419 Apero†

0044-8427 Apiculture in Western Australia†
0044-8435 Apidologie **839**
0044-8486 Aquaculture **3584**
0044-8508 Aquarium Society of New South Wales. Monthly Journal
0044-8524 Aqui **8088**
0044-8559 Arab News†
0044-8591 Archaeology in Montana **378**
0044-8613 Archipel **542**
0044-8621 De Architect **428**
0044-863X Architectura **429**
0044-8648 A A Notes†
0044-8672 Architekt
0044-8680 Architektura & Urbanizmus **432**
0044-8699 Archiv Orientalni **543**
0044-8710 Archives of Child Health
0044-8737 Archivio Storico Siracusano **4200**
0044-8745 Archivium Hibernicum **4200**
0044-8753 Archivum Mathematicum **5473**
0044-877X Arctic Frontiers†
0044-8788 Areas of Concern†
0044-8818 Argosy **2272**
0044-8877 University of Arizona Library. Bibliographic Bulletin†
0044-8885 Ark River Review
0044-8907 Arkansas Poultry Times†
0044-8915 Arkkitehtiuutiset **433**
0044-8931 Armed Citizen News†
0044-894X Armenian Observer **3519**
0044-8966 Armor **3840**
0044-8974 Armstrong Logic†
0044-8982 Arquivos Fluminenses de Odontologia†
0044-9008 Ars **467**
0044-9075 Artefact **381**
0044-9105 Artificial Rainfall Newsletter†
0044-913X Artistic Pakistan†
0044-9148 Asahi Camera **6964**
0044-9164 Asia Focus†
0044-9172 Asia Research Bulletin†
0044-9180 Asian Beacon **7732**
0044-9202 Asian Music **6546**
0044-9229 A P O News **1878**
0044-9237 Asiatic Studies
0044-9245 Asian Studies Professional Review†
0044-9261 A I T I M Boletin de Informacion Tecnica **3709**
0044-9318 Asociacion Peruana de Astronomia. Boletin
0044-9326 Asociacion Rural del Uruguay. Revista **93**
0044-9342 Assessors Review†
0044-9369 Associacao Brasileira de Educacao Agricola Superior. A B E A S Informa
0044-9423 Archives **4990**
0044-9490 A I L A Bulletin
0044-9539 Association of British Columbia Librarians. Newsletter†
0044-9547 A C D Bulletin†
0044-9598 Association of Engineers, India. Journal **3182**
0044-9660 A S L A President's Newsletter†
0044-9687 A T S S Bulletin
0044-9695 A U A Newsletter†
0044-9709 Association pour l'Histoire de Belle-Ile-en-Mer. Bulletin Trimestriel†
0044-9733 A I C Bollettino **4014**
0044-9741 A P A C Inform
0044-975X *see* 1971-5730 **8628**
0044-9768 Astarte†
0044-9784 Astrological Review
0044-9792 Astrology and Athrishta
0044-9806 The Bulletin **572**
0044-9814 Astronomical Society of Victoria. Journal†
0044-9822 Astronomy & Space†
0044-9865 Athenes-Presse Libre†
0044-9873 Athletics Administration **8159**
0044-9881 Atlantic Control States Beverage Journal *changed to* 1054-6561 **612**
0044-9911 Atlantic Review (St. Johns)
0044-992X Atlantic Salmon Journal **3586**
0044-9938 Atlantic Shepherd
0044-9989 Audience and Programme Research†
0045-0006 Auditor's Computer Update Digest†
0045-0014 Audubon Leader†
0045-0030 Auris **4072**
0045-0073 Australasian Insurance Journal†
0045-0081 Australasian Kennel Review and Dog News†
0045-0103 A S E Journal
0045-012X Industrial Information Bulletin†
0045-0138 Australia. Department of National Development. Nat/Dev†
0045-0146 Australia. Department of the Northern Territory. Northern Territory Affairs†
0045-0170 A N Z A News **3793**
0045-0197 Australia Now†
0045-0219 Australian and New Zealand Association for Medieval and Renaissance Studies. Bulletin†
0045-0243 Australian Apprenticeship Advisory Committee. Apprenticeship News†
0045-026X Australian Author **7552**
0045-0294 Australian Bee Journal **93**
0045-0308 Australian Biblical Review **7624**
0045-0316 Australian Bird Watcher *changed to* 1448-0107 **902**
0045-0324 Australian Boating Industry†
0045-0340 Australian Chemical Industry Directory†
0045-0413 Australian Current Law Review†
0045-0421 Australian Dental Journal **5835**
0045-0448 Australian Films†
0045-0472 Australian Goat World **280**
0045-0480 Australian Government News†
0045-0510 Australian Hand Weaver and Spinner
0045-0537 Australian Home Gardener†
0045-0588 Australian Jersey Journal
0045-0618 Australian Journal of Forensic Sciences **5912**
0045-0626 Australian Journal of Instrumentation and Control†
0045-0677 Australian Maps†
0045-0685 Australian Mathematics Teacher **3051**
0045-0707 A M D E L Bulletin
0045-0715 A M R A Journal **4326**
0045-0731 A N C O L D Bulletin **3258**
0045-0766 Australian Occupational Therapy Journal **6107**
0045-0782 Australian Orchid Review **3724**
0045-0839 Australian Road Transport Federation. A.R.T.F. Digest
0045-0847 Australian Roads†
0045-0898 Australia Stevedoring Industry Authority. Monthly Statistics
0045-0936 Australian Tobacco Journal†
0045-0944 Australian Trader
0045-0960 Australian Welding Research†
0045-1002 Auto-Neige†
0045-1010 Auto und Reise **8684**
0045-1061 Automobile Connoisseur
0045-1088 Automotive Messenger
0045-110X Automotive Transport Labour Relations Association. Monthly Labour Bulletin†
0045-1118 Autonomi
0045-1142 Auvergne Economique **1439**
0045-1150 L'Avant-Scene. Cinema **6490**
0045-1169 L'Avant-Scene. Theatre **8466**
0045-1177 Aviacion y Astronautica
0045-1207 Aviation Safety Digest†
0045-1223 Aware†
0045-1231 Awareness†
0045-124X Ayn Rand Letter†
0045-1290 Background to South African and World News†
0045-1304 Badger Herald **2273**
0045-1312 Badminton U.S.A.†
0045-1320 Baha'i World **7709**
0045-1339 Bakery Worker
0045-1347 Ballet-Hoo **2682**
0045-138X Bamah (Jerusalem) **8466**
0045-1401 Banco de Guatemala. Informe Economico†
0045-1444 Bank Melli Iran. Bulletin
0045-1460 Bank of Canada. Review **1313**
0045-1487 Bank Operations Report†
0045-1495 Bank Pembangunan Indonesia. Newsletter **1315**
0045-1533 Banque Canadienne Nationale. Bulletin Mensuel†
0045-1541 Bar Executive Key Handbook†
0045-155X Barnet Marksman
0045-1622 Beef & You†
0045-1649 Beer in Canada†
0045-1673 B R S Monthly Index†
0045-1681 Beitraege zur Historischen Sozialkunde†
0045-169X Beitraege zur Konfliktforschung†
0045-1703 Belgium. Institut National de Statistique. Bulletin de Statistique **1214**
0045-1711 Bella Gente†
0045-1738 Bensiiniuutiset **6763**
0045-1770 Beseda Nasi Vesnice†
0045-1797 Better Boating†
0045-1800 Better Business Bureau of Metropolitan New York. News Review†
0045-1835 Bias
0045-186X Bibliografie van de Nederlandse Taal- en Literatuur Wetenschap†
0045-1878 Bibliographic Society of Canada. Index Committee. Newsletter†
0045-1886 Bibliographie Nationale de la Tunisie†
0045-1894 Bibliographie Selective des Publications Officielles Francaise†
0045-1908 Bibliographies of Chemists†
0045-1916 Bibliographische Informationen aus der Technik und Ihren Grundlagenwissenschaften†
0045-1932 Bibliography on High Pressure Research
0045-1983 Big Book of Metalworking Machinery
0045-1991 Big Byte
0045-2033 Seibutsu Kagaku **703**
0045-205X Biologie in Unserer Zeit **659**
0045-2068 Bioorganic Chemistry **2120**
0045-2076 Bird Keeping in Australia **902**
0045-2084 Black Bag†
0045-2114 Black Books Bulletin†
0045-2157 Black Flag **7110**
0045-2165 Black Graphics International
0045-219X Black Lechwe **2604**
0045-2203 Black Lines: a Journal of Black Studies†
0045-222X Black Maria
0045-2238 Black News Digest†
0045-2270 Blackfish†
0045-2319 Bodyshop (English Edition) **8570**
0045-2351 Boian News Service†
0045-2378 Boletim de Materiais Dentarios
0045-2386 Boletim de Vulgarizacao Veterinaria†
0045-2424 Bollettino di Magistratura Democratica†
0045-2432 Bollettino Bibliografico Sardo e Archivio Tradizioni Popolari
0045-2467 Bolsa de Cereales. Revista Institucional†
0045-2483 Bonsai in Australia†
0045-2505 Book Angles†
0045-2521 Bookplates in the News *changed to* 1535-0320 **4334**
0045-2564 Books in Canada† **8937**
0045-2572 Books in English **620**
0045-2599 Bosch Kurier†
0045-2629 The Botanica **780**
0045-2696 Brannmannen **3575**
0045-270X Brasil Florestal†
0045-2742 Brazil. Superintendencia do Desenvolvimento da Amazonia. S U D A M Documenta
0045-2750 Bread Manufacturer and Pastrycook of Western Australia
0045-2769 Break Through†
0045-2777 Breakthrough†
0045-2831 Church Lads' and Church Girls' Brigade. Annual Report **7751**
0045-2866 Britain and Overseas **1553**
0045-2890 British Caribbean Philatelic Journal **6892**
0045-2998 British Columbia Mountaineer **8307**
0045-3005 British Columbia Museums Association. Museum Round Up **6521**
0045-3013 B C Outdoors *changed to* 1496-7642 **8305**
0045-3013 B C Outdoors *changed to* 1496-7634 **8305**
0045-303X British Columbia Snow Survey Bulletin **6348**
0045-3056 British Columbia Tax Reporter **1913**
0045-3064 British Columbia Thoroughbred
0045-3072 Phycological Newsletter (Print) *changed to* Phycological Newsletter (Online) **808**
0045-3080 B C Voice **8852**
0045-3102 The British Journal of Social Work **8028**
0045-3110 British Naturopathic Journal and Osteopathic Review†
0045-3129 B N A Topics **6892**
0045-3137 British Racing News†
0045-3226 Broken Spoke **8570**
0045-3234 Bromeletter
0045-3269 Brush
0045-3277 Belgium. Institut Royal Meteorologique. Bulletin Mensuel: Pollution Atmospherique. Fumee et So Deux†
0045-3285 Buckeye Review **3524**
0045-3293 Buck's Safety Management AID†
0045-3307 Buckskin Bulletin **4286**
0045-334X Buffalo **2146**
0045-3366 Milwaukee Bugle
0045-3374 Buhiti†
0045-3412 Building Ideas†
0045-3439 Building Specification
0045-3471 Bulb Horn **364**
0045-348X Bullet **4591**
0045-3501 Bulletin de l'Afrique Noire **7111**
0045-351X Bulletin Jugend und Literatur **4998**
0045-3536 Bulwark **7749**
0045-3552 Burning Spear†
0045-3587 Business and Professional Woman†
0045-3595 Business and Professional Woman†
0045-3609 Business and Society Review **1070**
0045-3633 Business Ideas and Facts†
0045-3641 Business Venezuela **1397**
0045-3676 Bust†
0045-3684 Buyers' Market
0045-3706 C I D X Messenger **2357**
0045-3714 Cable **3297**
0045-3730 Cahiers Bibliographiques des Lettres Quebecoise†
0045-3749 Cahiers de Litterature et de Linguistique Applique†
0045-3781 Cahiers du Travailleur Intellectuel†
0045-379X Cahiers Spartacus†
0045-3803 University of Cairo. Faculty of Medicine. Medical Journal **5727**
0045-3811 Caisses et Emballages en Bois†
0045-382X Calamus
0045-3838 Calcutta Gazette **7425**
0045-3846 Calcutta Review **3879**
0045-3854 Calcutta Weekly Notes **4636**
0045-3862 Calcuttan **7112**
0045-3870 Caledonian
0045-3889 Calgary Livestock Market Journal†
0045-3900 California Builder & Engineer **989**
0045-3919 C C A C Review **2275**
0045-3935 California Grocers Advocate†
0045-3951 California News Index†
0045-396X California News Reporter†
0045-3978 California Quarterly†
0045-3986 University of California at Los Angeles. Chicano Studies Research Center. Creative Series†
0045-4001 Caliper **4077**
0045-401X Call **5210**
0045-4036 Call and Post (Cleveland Edition) **3525**
0045-4044 Callboard†
0045-4052 Calquarium **6805**
0045-4087 Cameroun Litteraire†
0045-4095 CAMmunique†
0045-4109 Campaigner
0045-4176 Canada. Department of Energy, Mines, and Resources. Departmental Map Library. Acquisitions of Maps, Atlases and Gazeteers†
0045-4192 Canada Gazette: Part 1 **4638**
0045-4206 Canada Gazette: Part 2 **4638**
0045-4214 Canada Japan Trade Council. Newsletter **1398**
0045-4230 Canada Supreme Court Reports
0045-4249 Canada-Svensken†
0045-4257 Canada Today†
0045-4265 Canada Travel Digest†
0045-4273 Canada Trust Bulletin†
0045-4354 Canadian Association for Laboratory Animal Science Newsletter **5903**
0045-4362 Canadian Association of Exhibitions. Ex-Site
0045-4370 Canadian Association of Marine Equipment Industries. Newsletter
0045-4419 Canadian Association of Social Workers. Newsletter†
0045-4427 Canadian Athletic Director and Coach†
0045-4435 C. B. A. Bulletin†
0045-4486 Canadian Biographical Studies†
0045-4494 Canadian Boating
0045-4508 Canadian Building News†
0045-4524 Canadian Chamber of Commerce. Newsletter†
0045-4540 Canadian Chess Chat **8164**
0045-4559 Transit Canada†
0045-4567 Canadian Coach†
0045-4680 Canadian Earnings Estimator
0045-4710 Canadian Elk
0045-4737 Canadian Far Eastern Newsletter†
0045-4788 Canadian Field Hockey News†
0045-4796 C O S S I P†
0045-4834 Canadian Football News
0045-4842 Canadian Footwear News
0045-4869 C F A News†
0045-4877 Canadian Forwarder†
0045-4893 Canadian Government Programs and Services **7428**
0045-4915 Canadian Handgun
0045-4931 Canadian Imperial Bank of Commerce. Foreign Trade News†
0045-4958 Canadian India Times
0045-4966 Canadian Industrial Relations and Personnel Developments Guide *changed to* 1912-1806 **1669**
0045-5008 Canadian Interline News†
0045-5024 Canadian Ionospheric Data†

0045-5032 Canadian Jewish Digest Selections
0045-5040 Canadian Jewish Magazine
0045-5067 Canadian Journal of Forest Research **3685**
0045-5091 Canadian Journal of Philosophy **6909**
0045-5113 C L V Reports **1668**
0045-5121 Canadian Leathercraft **532**
0045-5156 Canadian Manager **1732**
0045-5202 Canadian Numismatic Research Society. Transactions **6649**
0045-5210 C O M D A Key **1850**
0045-5253 Canadian Philatelist **6893**
0045-527X Canadian Red Book **8571**
0045-5296 C R H A Reporter *changed to* 1706-1121
0045-5334 Canadian Scene
0045-5342 Canadian Securities Law Reporter **4640**
0045-5385 Canadian Sports Digest
0045-5393 Canadian Steam
0045-5407 Canadian Stock Market Point and Figure Summary†
0045-544X Canadian Theosophist **6909**
0045-5466 Canadian Transport
0045-5520 Canadian Vocational Journal **2834**
0045-558X Canadian Woodman
0045-5628 Canberra Survey
0045-5636 Candido
0045-5660 Capella†
0045-5695 Caps and Flints **4331**
0045-5709 Car Buyer†
0045-5717 Car Tips†
0045-5741 Cardiac Rehabilitation†
0045-575X Cardiovascular & Metabolic Diseases†
0045-5768 Care on the Road **7512**
0045-5776 Career Development†
0045-5792 Caribbean Business News
0045-5806 Caribbean Farming
0045-5830 Carleton Education Bulletin†
0045-5857 Carolina Centerscope†
0045-5865 Carolina Tips **664**
0045-5873 Carolinian
0045-5881 Cartologica†
0045-5903 Cash & Carry
0045-5946 Catalogue of Replacement Books for Children's Library Collections†
0045-5962 Catalyst for the Scottish Viewpoint
0045-5970 Catholic Agitator **7788**
0045-5989 Catholic Citizen
0045-5997 Cavalletto e Tavolozza
0045-6012 Cayuse Conserver
0045-6020 Celebrity Bulletin **641**
0045-6047 Cent Blagues†
0045-6055 C R R I Road Abstracts **3229**
0045-6098 C H I S S Cahiers†
0045-6152 Ceramurgia *changed to* 1970-0393 **2038**
0045-6209 Ceylon Trade Journal†
0045-6217 Congress News **4592**
0045-6225 Chakra†
0045-625X Challenge in Educational Administration†
0045-6268 Challenger†
0045-6276 Chambre de Commerce, d'Agriculture, d'Industrie et des Mines du Gabon. Bulletin **1399**
0045-6314 Champion†
0045-6330 Channel (Wellesley)†
0045-6349 Chaplin†
0045-6365 Chat†
0045-6381 Chelsea Spelaeological Society. Newsletter **2728**
0045-639X Chemical Industry Notes†
0045-6403 Chemical Insight **2054**
0045-6497 Chemical Take-Off **2055**
0045-6500 Chemical Weekly **2055**
0045-6519 Chemische Technik†
0045-6535 Chemosphere **3495**
0045-656X Chesapeake Bay Magazine **8274**
0045-6578 Chess Canada
0045-6594 Chess Player†
0045-6608 La Chevre **283**
0045-6624 Chicagoland Development†
0045-6713 Children's Literature in Education **2149**
0045-673X Chimie-Science **3241**
0045-6756 China Monthly†
0045-6799 Christian Communications Journal in Africa†
0045-6810 Christian Institute for Ethnic Studies in Asia. Bulletin
0045-6829 Christian Patriot†
0045-6861 Church and Clergy Finance†
0045-687X Church and School Equipment News
0045-6888 Ciencia Agronomica **101**
0045-6896 El Ciervo **3951**
0045-6926 Cinema (Year)†
0045-6942 Circulo Odontologico de Cordoba. Revista **5838**
0045-6969 C L News†
0045-6977 Citta Futura†
0045-6985 City and Suburban Travel
0045-7027 Civic Affairs
0045-7043 Civil & Military Law Journal **4971**
0045-706X Civil Rights Newsletter
0045-7108 Classiques Bretons
0045-7116 Clave†
0045-7140 Clest†
0045-7159 Climbing **8309**
0045-7167 Horumon to Rinsho **5894**
0045-7175 Clinical Trends in Anesthesiology†
0045-7183 Clio Medica **5598**
0045-7205 Club Management in Australia **1733**
0045-7213 Club Mirror **2265**
0045-7221 Co-Op Commentary
0045-723X Coastal Zone Management
0045-7256 Cocoa Growers Bulletin **225**
0045-7272 Coin Launderer and Cleaner
0045-7310 C O D I A **3261**
0045-7345 Collective Bargaining Settlements in New York State†
0045-737X College Law Digest†
0045-7388 College of Physicians and Surgeons of Ontario. Interim Report†
0045-7426 Colorado Journal of Educational Research†
0045-7434 C T R C Newsletter†
0045-7558 Commerce et Distribution†
0045-7566 Commercial Bank of Australia. Economic Review†
0045-7574 Commercial Bank of Ethiopia. Market Report **1328**
0045-7620 Commonwealth and Colonial History Newsletter†
0045-7647 Commonwealth Scientific and Industrial Research Organization. Industrial Research News†
0045-7663 Communication (London, 1967) **3038**
0045-7698 Communika†
0045-7736 Community Education Journal **2838**
0045-7779 Community Planning in British Columbia
0045-7787 Company Law Institute of India. Reports of Company Cases Including Banking & Insurance **4861**
0045-7795 Comparative Literature in Canada†
0045-7809 Compass
0045-7817 Compulsory Military Service and the Objector†
0045-7825 Computer Methods in Applied Mechanics and Engineering **3289**
0045-7833 Computer Operations†
0045-7841 Computer Price Guide **2412**
0045-785X Computer Program Abstracts†
0045-7868 Computer Programs in Science and Technology†
0045-7906 Computers & Electrical Engineering **3290**
0045-7930 Computers & Fluids **3290**
0045-7949 Computers & Structures **3290**
0045-7965 Computing Newsletter for Instructors of Data Processing
0045-7981 Comunita Mediterranea†
0045-799X Concerns **2692**
0045-8007 Concrete Abstracts†
0045-8015 Concrete Pipe News **993**
0045-8023 Confederation Nationale de la Construction. Annuaire†
0045-804X Conference Board of the Mathematical Sciences. Newsletter†
0045-8066 Conflux†
0045-8120 Connecticut Nutmegger **3763**
0045-8139 I P S Local Government Newsletter†
0045-8155 Conservation Council of Ontario. Bulletin†
0045-8163 Consolidated Report of the Condition of Banks Operating in Puerto Rico
0045-8171 Consoliere†
0045-8201 Consultants News **1735**
0045-8236 Consumer Comment†
0045-8252 Consumer Interest†
0045-8260 Consumer News†
0045-8279 Consumerism-New Developments for Business†
0045-8325 Contacts (Paris, 1949) **7635**
0045-8333 Contemporary Indian Literature†
0045-8341 Contemporary Surgery **6240**
0045-8368 Contents of Recent Economics Journals
0045-8384 Continuing Education Directory for Metropolitan Toronto†
0045-8406 Contractspeler **8167**
0045-8414 Contrasts
0045-8449 Conventions, Meetings, Incentive World†
0045-8457 Cooperateur de France†
0045-849X Cooperator†
0045-8503 Cooperator's Bulletin†
0045-8511 Copeia **939**
0045-8538 Core Teacher†
0045-8554 Cormorant News Bulletin **365**
0045-8562 Cornell University. Libraries. Bulletin†
0045-8570 Cornish Nation **4212**
0045-8597 Corporation Journal
0045-8619 Corporation of Psychologists of the Province of Quebec. News Bulletin
0045-8643 Correio Portugues **3528**
0045-8651 Correo Hispano-Americano
0045-866X Corriere Canadese **3528**
0045-8716 Cosmorama†
0045-8732 C O S P A R Information Bulletin (Committee on Space Research) *changed to* 1752-9298 **71**
0045-8740 Costa Rica. Instituto Geografico Nacional. Informe Semestral†
0045-8759 Cotton Development†
0045-8775 Council for Planning & Conservation. Newsletter†
0045-8791 C P L Newsletter†
0045-8813 Countdown (Wichita)†
0045-8848 Country Bizarre
0045-8856 Country Life **3863**
0045-8872 C F B Cold Lake Courier **6414**
0045-8880 Courrier de Politique Etrangere†
0045-8899 Courrier du Parlement **7432**
0045-8902 Courrier du Vietnam **7126**
0045-8988 Creative Teacher†
0045-8996 Creative Urge†
0045-9011 Creditalk†
0045-902X Crime and Delinquency Abstracts†
0045-9038 Criminal Justice Newsletter **2649**
0045-9046 Crisis Intervention†
0045-9054 Cristiani nel Mondo
0045-9062 Critic†
0045-9070 Critical Digest
0045-9089 Critique Socialiste†
0045-9097 Critiques de l'Economie Politique†
0045-9119 Crossroads (Indianapolis) **7734**
0045-9127 Crown **5109**
0045-9135 Crucible (Columbia)
0045-9143 Crusader: Justice for Hungary
0045-9151 Cryptogram†
0045-9186 Cuadernos de Historia Economica de Cataluna†
0045-9194 Cuadernos de Informacion Cientifica†
0045-9232 Cultura Antiqua
0045-9259 Cultured Dairy Products Journal†
0045-9291 Current Engineering Practice **3186**
0045-933X Current Physics Advance Abstracts: Solid State†
0045-9348 Current Physics Microform†
0045-9429 Cyprus To-day **2841**
0045-9445 Czas **3529**
0045-9453 Czasopismo Geograficzne **4003**
0045-947X Czechoslovak Science & Technology Digest†
0045-9488 Czechoslovak Scientific and Technical Periodicals Contents†
0045-9496 Dafni†
0045-9542 Dalka
0045-9550 Dallas. Methodist Hospital. Bulletin of the Medical Staff†
0045-9577 Dance - America†
0045-9585 Danmarks Handels Tidende†
0045-9607 Dansk Erhvervsfjerkrae **285**
0045-9615 Dansk Handelsblad **3677**
0045-9658 Darshak **485**
0045-9666 Data†
0045-9674 Data-Canada†
0045-9690 Data Processing Management Association. Magazine†
0045-9739 Davidsonia†
0045-9747 De Nos Mains†
0045-9771 The Deacon **7754**
0045-9801 Deccan College. Postgraduate & Research Institute. Bulletin **7958**
0045-981X Decennie 2†
0045-9836 Defending All Outdoors†
0045-9844 Delaware Basin Bulletin†
0045-9879 Delikt en Delinkwent **4889**
0045-9895 Delta del Parana†
0045-9909 Democratic Commitment
0045-9917 Dental Association of Thailand. Journal **5839**
0045-9941 Dental Radiography and Photography†
0045-995X Dental Student News†
0045-9968 Dentoscope†
0045-9992 Derecho Penal Contemporaneo
0046-0001 Dermatology in Practice†
0046-001X Desarrollo Economico **1883**
0046-0028 Desarrollo Rural en las Americas†
0046-0036 Descent **8311**
0046-0044 Desert Rancher
0046-0060 Designer & Builder in Asia†
0046-0079 Despatch
0046-0095 Detective†
0046-0141 Deutsche Vereinigung von Winnipeg. Mitteilungen **3530**
0046-0168 Deux-Tiers†
0046-0184 Devonport News†
0046-0192 Diabetes **5886**
0046-0206 Dialogo Social **8098**
0046-0222 Diana's Bimonthly
0046-0249 Digest of Executive Opportunities†
0046-0265 Dimension
0046-029X Dinny's Digest
0046-0303 Dio e Popolo
0046-0338 Direct from Cuba **7130**
0046-0370 Disposables International†
0046-0389 Dissonance†
0046-0400 Dividend **1092**
0046-0427 Divine Toad Sweat
0046-0443 Djassin'foue
0046-0451 Doctor **5606**
0046-0478 Documentation par l'Image **7851**
0046-0494 Doings†
0046-0508 Dokita†
0046-0567 Dominion Tax Cases **1920**
0046-0575 Dominionaire
0046-0591 La Donna di Casa
0046-0605 Donnybrook Report: Photography†
0046-063X Doshisha Literature **5285**
0046-0648 Down Under†
0046-0656 Downtown Athletic Club Journal **2265**
0046-0664 Downtown Developments†
0046-0672 Dravo Review†
0046-0702 Drilling Contractor **6767**
0046-0729 Driveway Reporter
0046-0753 Drug Forum†
0046-0796 Duesseldorf Magazin†
0046-0818 DukEngineer
0046-0826 Duodecimal Bulletin **5484**
0046-0877 E F B†
0046-0885 E I (Print) *changed to* E I (Online) **361**
0046-0915 Eagle's Eye **3531**
0046-094X East African Pharmaceutical Journal
0046-0958 East Anglian Bibliography† **8952**
0046-0966 East St. Louis Monitor **3531**
0046-0974 Eastern Film†
0046-0990 Easyriders **8258**
0046-1016 L'Eau Vive **3809**
0046-1024 Eburnea **3789**
0046-1032 Ecclaire†
0046-1040 Echo†
0046-1059 The Echo (Huntsville) **2651**
0046-1067 Echo (Skokie)
0046-1091 Echoes of History†
0046-1105 Eclectic Theosophist†
0046-1121 Ecology Law Quarterly **4663**
0046-113X Economia **1098**
0046-1148 Economia Cafetera **196**
0046-1180 Economic Research Corporation. Research Review†
0046-1237 Ecosphere **3418**
0046-1245 EdCentric†
0046-1253 Edge†
0046-127X Editor's Newsletter†
0046-1296 Edmonton Native News **6634**
0046-1318 Edmonton Stamp Club Bulletin **6894**
0046-1326 Edseletter **8578**
0046-1334 Educacao (Brasilia)†
0046-1369 Education†
0046-1377 Education and Culture†
0046-1385 Education and Psychology Review†
0046-1407 Education Commission of the States Bulletin†
0046-1415 Education Equipment Selector
0046-1423 Education in Eastern Africa
0046-1431 Education Mathematique†
0046-1482 Educational Digest **2850**
0046-1504 Educational Forum†
0046-1520 Educational Psychologist **7353**
0046-1539 Educational Reporter
0046-1547 E T S Developments **2978**
0046-158X Educator's Purchasing Guide†
0046-1598 Effective Teaching with Programmed Instruction†

ISSN

0046-7693 Hockey Digest†
0046-7715 Hoefslag **8292**
0046-7723 Hogar y Moda†
0046-7758 Home Beer and Winemaking
0046-7782 Homeo Doctor
0046-7812 Homoeopathic World†
0046-7820 Homoeopathy **5805**
0046-7839 Hon: a Book-Bin for Scholars†
0046-7855 Honneur et Fidelite **6424**
0046-7863 Honourable Artillery Company Journal **6424**
0046-7898 Horizons Africains
0046-7901 Horizons du Fantastique†
0046-791X Horizont (Berlin)†
0046-7928 The Horn Call **6573**
0046-7936 Horses **8293**
0046-8010 Hospital Medical Practice
0046-8045 Hot Bike **8259**
0046-8061 Hotuys
0046-8134 Human Behavior†
0046-8150 Human Design
0046-8169 Human Ecology (Park Ridge)†
0046-8177 Human Pathology **5631**
0046-8185 Human Rights (Chicago) **7208**
0046-8207 H R W Newsletter†
0046-8215 Human Rights in U.S.S.R†
0046-824X Humanistische Union. Mitteilungen **6924**
0046-8258 Humanitas†
0046-8274 Humbard Christian Report
0046-8282 Humour Variety
0046-8304 Hungarian Library and Information Science Abstracts **5058**
0046-8312 Hunter Natural History†
0046-8339 Husdjur **288**
0046-8398 I E T: Zeitschrift fuer Elektrische Informations- und Energietechnik†
0046-8401 I S L A **4297**
0046-841X I S M†
0046-8428 I W K **4596**
0046-8436 University of Ibadan. Library. Library Record **5053**
0046-8444 Ibero-Americana **4170**
0046-8452 Icelandic Canadian **3811**
0046-8487 Idaho Economic Indicators
0046-8517 Ide (Oslo, 1967)†
0046-8541 Idealistic Studies **6924**
0046-8568 Idiom **3064**
0046-8576 Idoles†
0046-8622 Illinois State Genealogical Society Quarterly **3771**
0046-869X Impact (Ottawa)†
0046-8703 Impact (London) **7711**
0046-872X Impianti Manutenzione Trasporti†
0046-8762 In-Short†
0046-8797 Inbavan Tanah Air
0046-8819 Inchiesta **8046**
0046-8835 Independence
0046-8843 Independent Republic Quarterly **4297**
0046-8851 Independent Weekly
0046-8908 Index to Current Urban Documents **7481**
0046-8932 India Abroad **3539**
0046-8959 India Weekly
0046-8967 Indian Affairs **6635**
0046-8983 Indian Geotechnical Journal **2709**
0046-8991 Indian Journal of Microbiology **887**
0046-9017 Indian Journal of Regional Science **7972**
0046-9025 Indian Manager **1752**
0046-9033 I P I R I Journal **3712**
0046-9068 Indian Tourist
0046-9076 Indian Trader **3539**
0046-9092 Indian Welding Journal **6343**
0046-9122 M E R P Memo†
0046-9130 Indiana University. School of Medicine. Review†
0046-9157 Exceptional Parent **3040**
0046-9165 Indonesian Current Affairs Translation Bulletin†
0046-9173 Indonesian Review of International Affairs **7241**
0046-9181 Industria Lechera **265**
0046-9203 Industrial Informika†
0046-9211 Industrial Launderer **2243**
0046-9262 Industrial Wastes†
0046-9270 Industrialist†
0046-9289 Industrie- und Handelszeitung
0046-9319 Brewers Association of Canada. Industry Notes†
0046-9327 Informateur des Chefs d'Entreprises Libres†
0046-9343 Information G†
0046-9351 L'Information Historique†
0046-936X L'Information Immobiliere **7595**
0046-9408 Informationen zur Politischen Bildung **7142**
0046-9416 Informations Aerauliques et Thermiques†
0046-9432 Informations Laitieres†
0046-9459 Informations Sociales **8046**
0046-9513 Ingenieur - Constructeur†
0046-9564 Innovation World
0046-9572 Innovator (Ann Arbor) **2288**
0046-9580 Inquiry (Rochester) **5635**
0046-9599 Inquisitor **2194**
0046-9610 Inside†
0046-9629 Inside Canberra **7142**
0046-9653 Insight (St. Paul)†
0046-9688 I F E P P Informations†
0046-9696 Institut fuer Gesellschaftspolitik. Mitteilungen†
0046-970X I P W Berichte†
0046-9718 I I E E Bulletin†
0046-9726 Belgium. Institut National d'Assurance Maladie Invalidite. I N A M I Bulletin d'Information **4494**
0046-9750 Institute of Brewing. Journal **605**
0046-9777 C F A Digest **1323**
0046-9785 Institute of Club Managers and Secretaries. Club Guide
0046-9831 I P L O Quarterly
0046-984X Institute of Southeast Asian Studies. Library. Accessions List **564**
0046-9874 Institution of Engineers Australia. South Australian Division. Bulletin†
0046-9882 Institution of Engineers, Jamaica. Journal **3199**
0046-9890 Instituto Agricola Catalan de San Isidro. Revista†
0046-9912 Instituto Brasileiro de Mercado de Capitais. Boletim de Documentacao†
0046-9920 I C A Informa†
0046-9939 Instituto de Pesca, Sao Paulo. Boletim **3598**
0046-9947 Instituto de Pesquisa Agropecuaria do l'Este. Pesquisa e Experimentos. Comunicado Tecnico†
0046-9955 Instituto de Soldadura. Boletim†
0046-9998 Pan American Institute of Geography and History. Commission on Cartography. Cartografia†
0047-0023 Institutul National de Informare si Documentare Stiintifica si Tehnica Revista de Titluri: Arhitectura. Sistematizare. Constructii†
0047-0058 Institutul National de Informare si Documentare Stiintifica si Tehnica Revista de Titluri: Constructii de Masini†
0047-0074 Institutul National de Informare si Documentare Stiintifica si Tehnica. Revista de Titluri: Coroziune. Protectia Suprafetelor†
0047-0082 Institutul National de Informare si Documentare Stiintifica si Tehnica Revista de Titluri: Conducerea si Organizarea Intreprinderilor†
0047-0104 Institutul National de Informare si Documentare Stiintifica si Tehnica Revista de Titluri: Eficienta Economica. Pret de Cost. Evidenta Contabila si Statistica†
0047-0120 Institutul National de Informare si Documentare Stiintifica si Tehnica Revista de Titluri: Frecare. Uzura. Ungere. Intretinerea si Repararea Utilajelor†
0047-0147 Institutul National de Informare si Documentare Stiintifica si Tehnica Revista de Titluri: Industria Alimentara†
0047-0163 Institutul National de Informare si Documentare Stiintifica si Tehnica Revista de Titluri: Informare Documentare†
0047-018X Institutul National de Informare si Documentare Stiintifica si Tehnica Revista de Titluri: Industria Miniera†
0047-0201 Institutul National de Informare si Documentare Stiintifica si Tehnica Revista de Titluri: Industria Usoara†
0047-021X Institutul National de Informare si Documentare Stiintifica si Tehnica Revista de Titluri: Metalurgie†
0047-0244 Institutul National de Informare si Documentare Stiintifica si Tehnica, Revista de Titluri: Mecanica. Rezistenta Materialelor. Mecanisme†
0047-0260 Institutul National de Informare si Documentare Stiintifica si Tehnica Revista de Titluri Organizarea Productiei si a Muncii†
0047-0287 Institutul National de Informare si Documentare Stiintifica si Technica. Revista de Titluri: Protectia Muncii†
0047-0325 Institutul National de Informare si Documentare Stiintifica si Tehnica Revista de Titluri: Tehnica Fotografica si Cinematografica†
0047-0333 Institutul National de Informare si Documentare Stiintifica si Technica. Revista de Titluri: Transport Intern. Ambalare. Depozitare.†
0047-0341 Institutul National de Informare si Documentare Stiintifica si Tehnica Revista de Titluri: Tehnica Masurarii. Controlul Calitatii†
0047-035X Institutul National de Informare si Documentare Stiintifica si Tehnica Revista de Titluri: Transporturi Cai de Comunicatie†
0047-0368 Institutul National de Informare si Documentare Stiintifica si Tehnica. Revista de Titluri: Scientica. Cercetare. Proiectare. Estetica Industriala†
0047-0376 Instruments India **4488**
0047-0392 Integration
0047-0406 Intelligence Survey
0047-0414 Intercom *changed to* 1942-3225 **5000**
0047-0430 Interchange†
0047-0449 Interchange†
0047-0457 Interchange (Portland) **3013**
0047-0473 Intercom (Atlanta)†
0047-0503 Intermode†
0047-0511 Intermountain Jewish News **7722**
0047-0554 I A C P Law Enforcement Legislation and Litigation Report†
0047-0562 I A C P Law Enforcement Legislative Research Digest†
0047-0570 International Bank for Reconstruction and Development. Statement of Loans†
0047-0597 International Barbed Wire Gazette†
0047-0627 International Business Digest†
0047-0651 I C M A Newsletter **7494**
0047-0694 International Export Association. Export News
0047-0724 International Journal of Government Auditing (Print Edition)†
0047-0732 International Journal of Group Tensions†
0047-0759 International Journal of Radiation Engineering†
0047-0767 International Journal of Sport Psychology **6230**
0047-0783 Co-operative Information†
0047-0791 International Labour Office. Minutes of the Governing Body†
0047-0813 International Law News **4931**
0047-083X International Monetary Fund Survey **1244**
0047-0856 I N I S Newsletter†
0047-0937 International Press Cutting Service: Electronics and Electricals Industry†
0047-0953 International Press Cutting Service: Import - Export - Licenses **1571**
0047-0961 International Press Cutting Service: Jute, Gunny, Hessian, Burlap, Coir†
0047-097X International Press Cutting Service: Labour Welfare - Industrial Legislation and Personnel Management **1689**
0047-0988 Leather, Hides, Skins, Footwear Report **4974**
0047-0996 International Press Cutting Service: Machine Tool and Iron Steel Industry†
0047-1011 International Press Cutting Service: Non-Ferrous Metals - Aluminium†
0047-1054 International Press Cutting Service: Plywood - Timber - Particle Board†
0047-1097 International Press Cutting Service: Taxation - Finance - Company Law **1930**
0047-1100 International Press Cutting Service: Tea and Coffee News†
0047-1127 International Press Cutting Service: Tender Notifications (Indian & Global) **1571**
0047-1151 International Press Cutting Service: Processed Food Products - Spices†
0047-116X International Psychologist **7366**
0047-1178 International Relations **7245**
0047-1186 International Review†
0047-1216 I T C C Review†
0047-1224 International Telecommunication Union. Operational Bulletin **2368**
0047-1240 International Understanding at School†
0047-1291 L'Interprete **5130**
0047-1321 Intervention **8048**
0047-1356 Investor's Digest of Canada **1634**
0047-1372 Invitation to Snowmobiling†
0047-1410 Iran Family Planning Bulletin†
0047-1429 Iraq News Bulletin **4322**
0047-1437 Irish Ancestor†
0047-1445 Irish Bacon News†
0047-1453 Irish Equipment News **5453**
0047-147X Irish Medical Times **5641**
0047-1488 Irish Pulse†
0047-1496 IronMan **6990**
0047-150X Ironwood†
0047-1518 Irrigation Journal†
0047-1526 Is
0047-1542 Islas **2288**
0047-1585 Israel Oil News† **8966**
0047-1607 Issue (New Brunswick) *changed to* 1548-4505
0047-1631 I A I Informa†
0047-164X It Ain't Me Babe†
0047-1658 Italian-Australian Bulletin of Commerce
0047-1666 Italix†
0047-1674 Ivoire Dimanche **3789**
0047-1704 Jackson Advocate **3541**
0047-1712 Jakemate
0047-1720 Jamaica Churchman **7762**
0047-1739 Janus†
0047-1755 Japan Chemical Week **3248**
0047-1763 Nihon Shika Ishikai Zasshi **5857**
0047-1771 Japan Foreign Trade Journal†
0047-1801 Nippon Daicho Komonbyo Gakkai Zasshi **5930**
0047-181X Japanese Business Journal†
0047-1844 Hokenfu Zasshi *changed to* 1348-8333 **5963**
0047-1852 Nippon Rinsho **5687**
0047-1860 Japanese Journal of Clinical Pathology **5643**
0047-1887 Nippon Hoigaku Zasshi **5916**
0047-1895 Kango Kyoiku **5968**
0047-1917 Japanese Journal of Veterinary Research **8800**
0047-1925 J N R Bulletin
0047-1933 Jasmin†
0047-1968 Jeremiad†
0047-1984 Jeunesse Ouvriere†
0047-200X Jewish Radical **7145**
0047-2018 Jewish Veteran **6428**
0047-2034 Jobs in Social Work†
0047-2077 Jornal Brasileiro de Medicina **5645**
0047-2085 Jornal Brasileiro de Psiquiatria **6149**
0047-2093 Jornal de Letras
0047-2107 Jornal Portugues
0047-2115 Journal Constructo **1018**
0047-2123 Journal de la Navigation†
0047-2131 Journal de la Police Nationale†
0047-214X Journal de la Publicite et des Techniques de la Promotion et Publi-Magazine†
0047-2158 Journal de Mathematiques Elementaires†
0047-2166 Journal de Pharmacie de Belgique **6852**
0047-2174 Journal de Tanger **3913**
0047-2204 Journal du Bricoleur†
0047-2212 Journal for the Study of Judaism **7725**
0047-2220 Journal of Applied Rehabilitation Counseling **8048**
0047-2255 Journal of Canadian Fiction
0047-2263 Journal of Caribbean History **4299**
0047-231X Journal of College Science Teaching **7872**
0047-2328 Journal of Comparative Family Studies **8112**
0047-2336 Journal of Contemporary Asia **4184**
0047-2352 Journal of Criminal Justice **4892**
0047-2360 Journal of Development Administration **7448**
0047-2379 Journal of Drug Education **2695**
0047-2387 Journal of Economics for Schools
0047-2395 Journal of Educational Technology Systems **2949**
0047-2425 Journal of Environmental Quality **3446**
0047-2433 Journal of Environmental Systems **3447**
0047-2441 Journal of European Studies (Chalfont Saint Giles) **4235**
0047-245X Journal of Food Distribution Research **3650**
0047-2468 Journal of Geometry **5503**
0047-2476 Journal of Geriatrics†
0047-2484 Journal of Human Evolution **874**
0047-2492 Journal of Intergroup Relations **7211**
0047-2506 Journal of International Business Studies **1137**
0047-2514 Journal of Irish Literature†
0047-2522 Journal of Korean Affairs†
0047-2530 The Journal of Legal Studies (Chicago) **4703**
0047-2549 Journal of Marketing and Economic Research
0047-2557 Journal of Mathematical and Physical Sciences **5505**
0047-2565 Journal of Medical Primatology **952**
0047-2581 Journal of Mexican American History
0047-259X Journal of Multivariate Analysis **5506**
0047-262X Huli Zazhi **5960**
0047-2638 Journal of Operational Psychiatry†
0047-2646 Journal of Organizational Communication†
0047-2662 Journal of Phenomenological Psychology **7378**
0047-2689 Journal of Physical and Chemical Reference Data **2068**
0047-2697 Journal of Political and Military Sociology **8115**
0047-2700 Journal of Political Studies **7148**
0047-2727 Journal of Public Economics **1545**
0047-2735 The Journal of Religious Studies **7656**
0047-2743 Journal of Remote Sensing†
0047-2751 Journal of Rural Development and Administration **7449**

ISSN

0047-8512	Mylord†
0047-8539	Mysore Journal of Agricultural Sciences 137
0047-8555	Mythic Society. Quarterly Journal 3620
0047-8563	N P†
0047-8598	Nachrichten zur Wirtschafts- und Sozialpolitik†
0047-8601	Naering i Nord†
0047-861X	Naftika Chronika 8654
0047-8628	Nairang Da'ijist
0047-8636	Nairobi Handbook
0047-8644	Nande†
0047-8660	Nashotah Review†
0047-8679	Nashville, Tennessee. Children's Museum. Museum Notes†
0047-8687	N C P C Newsletter†
0047-8695	Nassau Lawyer 4738
0047-8733	National Association of Conservation Districts. Tuesday Letter 2620
0047-8768	National Braille Mail†
0047-8792	National Council of Women of Australia. Quarterly Bulletin
0047-8806	National Council on Alcoholism. Friday Letter†
0047-8822	National C F News Bulletin†
0047-8830	National Democrat†
0047-8865	National Folk†
0047-8989	N O L P E School Law Journal†
0047-9012	National Parks Journal 2620
0047-9020	N.P.A. Journal 4568
0047-9039	National Police Gazette
0047-9047	National Police Journal†
0047-9055	National Research Council, Canada. Division of Mechanical Engineering and National Aeronautical Establishment. Quarterly Bulletin†
0047-9071	National Savings Newsletter†
0047-908X	N S S F N S News
0047-911X	National Times†
0047-9144	Native People†
0047-9152	Natural Health Bulletin†
0047-9160	Natural Life Styles†
0047-9209	Nebraska Law Review 4740
0047-9217	Nebraska Resources 2622
0047-925X	Needle Arts 6640
0047-9276	Neerlandica Extra Muros†
0047-9306	Negro Lawmaker Journal†
0047-9314	Neighbors - Interracial Living
0047-9330	Nepal Digest
0047-9349	Nepalese Perspective†
0047-9357	Nepriklausoma Lietuva
0047-9365	Netherlands Journal of Veterinary Science†
0047-9373	Network - Urban Coalition†
0047-9381	Neue Apotheken Illustrierte 6863
0047-9411	Neurocirugia†
0047-942X	Neuroelectric News†
0047-9446	Neutron Activation Analysis Abstracts
0047-9454	Nevada Engineer†
0047-9462	Nevada Historical Society Quarterly 4304
0047-9470	Nevada Livestock and Agriculture Journal†
0047-9489	The Nevada Rancher 294
0047-9497	R C U Report†
0047-9500	New Age 7157
0047-9519	New American Electronics Literature and Technical Data
0047-9527	New Banner†
0047-9543	New Brunswick Historical Society. Historical Review†
0047-9551	N B Naturalist 7885
0047-956X	New Chislehurst Announcer
0047-9578	New Church Herald†
0047-9624	New Electronics 3109
0047-9632	New Engineer†
0047-9640	N E A P Q News†
0047-9691	New French Books†
0047-9705	New Frontiers in Education 2996
0047-9721	New Hellas
0047-9772	New Jersey Historical Commission Newsletter 4305
0047-9810	New Mexico Transporter†
0047-9829	New Patriot
0047-9853	New Promotions and Competitions
0047-987X	The New Shetlander 3968
0047-9888	Bush Fire Bulletin†
0047-990X	Fire News 3577
0047-9934	New South Wales Police News
0047-9950	New Unity†
0047-9969	New Wave 3886
0047-9977	New Ways†
0047-9985	New Writing†
0047-9993	New York (City) Economic Development Administration. Office of Public Affairs. Economic and Other Indicators†
0048-0002	New York Denik†
0048-0037	New York Liberty Dispatch†
0048-0045	New York State Migrant Center. Newsletter†
0048-0053	New York State Environment†
0048-0061	New York (State) Office of Planning Coordination. O P C News Summary†
0048-0134	New Zealand Journal of Forestry Science 3698
0048-0150	New Zealand Surveyor 2759
0048-0169	New Zealand Veterinary Journal 8803
0048-0177	Newfoundland Amateur†
0048-0215	News and Farmer
0048-0223	News from Zambia†
0048-0231	News of the New World†
0048-0339	Niedersaechsischer Jaeger 8325
0048-0363	Nigeria Confidential
0048-0371	Nigerian Accountant
0048-038X	Nigerian Business Digest
0048-0398	Nigerian Insurance Monitor
0048-0401	Nigerian Journal of Contemporary Law 4747
0048-041X	Nile Gazette
0048-0428	Nippon Igaku Hoshasen Gakkai Zasshi 6204
0048-0452	Nippon Steel News 6327
0048-0460	Niv Hamidrashia†
0048-0479	Noir et Rouge†
0048-0495	Nordisk Jordbruksforskning 142
0048-0509	Nordisk Tidsskrift for Spesialpedagogikk†
0048-0568	Norrona†

0048-0592	Norsk Husflid 537
0048-0649	North American Scotsman
0048-0665	North Carolina Researcher†
0048-0673	N C I Catalyst†
0048-0681	North Dakota Education News 2892
0048-069X	North Dakota Society of Medical Technologists. Newsletter 5910
0048-0738	Northeast Historical Archaeology 408
0048-0746	Northeastern Regional Antipollution Conference. Proceedings†
0048-0754	Northern Air†
0048-0762	Northern Industry
0048-0770	Northern Ireland. Ministry of Education. Education Statistics
0048-0789	Northern Libraries Bulletin
0048-0797	Northern Teacher†
0048-0835	Nos Chasses†
0048-0843	Nos Maisons Familiales de Vacances†
0048-0916	Notizie dall'Albania
0048-0924	Notre Comte†
0048-0932	Notre Dame Journal 2892
0048-0967	Nouvelle Ecole 5231
0048-0975	Nouvelle Revue Internationale†
0048-0983	Nova Scotia Reports 4749
0048-1009	Novum Testamentum 7666
0048-1017	Nowi Dni†
0048-1025	Nuclear Active†
0048-1033	Nuclear Magnetic Resonance Spectrometry Abstracts
0048-105X	Nucleonics Week 3143
0048-1084	Nueva Narrativa Hispanoamericana†
0048-1092	Nuevos Aires
0048-1106	Nuggets
0048-1114	Numismatic Messenger†
0048-1122	Nuova Tradotta
0048-1149	Nuovo Impegno
0048-1165	Ha-Achot be-Yisre'el†
0048-119X	Midland News 3949
0048-1211	Nya Cyklisten 8265
0048-122X	Det Nye 8878
0048-1289	Objectif Monde Uni†
0048-1319	Observateur Africain
0048-1335	Observations from the Treadmill
0048-1394	Ochrana Fauny†
0048-1408	Odd Fellow 2268
0048-1416	Oesterreichische Bau-Wirtschaft
0048-1440	Oesterreichische Militaerische Zeitschrift 6440
0048-1459	Oesterreichische Foto-Zeitung
0048-1483	Oesterreichische Touristenzeitung 8742
0048-1505	Official Karate†
0048-1521	Pan-American Coffee Bureau. Boletin Mensual†
0048-153X	Ohio Archaeologist 409
0048-1548	Ohio Insect Information†
0048-1556	Ohio Jersey News 295
0048-1564	Ohio Researcher†
0048-1572	Ohio State Law Journal 4752
0048-1602	Oklahoma Highwayman†
0048-1629	Okyeame†
0048-1637	Old Cars 8596
0048-1645	Old Contemptible
0048-1653	Old Time Music
0048-1696	Onderwatersport 8326
0048-1734	Ontario Amateur
0048-1742	Ontario Archaeological Society. Arch Notes 409
0048-1785	Ontario Forests†
0048-1807	Ontario Journal and Tax Sale Register
0048-1815	Ontario Numismatist 6652
0048-1823	Ontario Plumbing Inspectors Association. Bulletin 4124
0048-1866	Ontario Tax Reporter 1938
0048-1882	Onward†
0048-1890	Op Safari†
0048-1904	Open Access
0048-1920	Open Home†
0048-1939	Open Letter 5346
0048-1955	Ophthalmology Digest†
0048-198X	Opinion Economica
0048-203X	Optometry Today 6050
0048-2080	Orben Comedy Letter†
0048-2099	Orben's Comedy Fillers†
0048-2110	Orbit Weekly†
0048-2129	Ordo 1784
0048-2161	Organists' Review 6603
0048-217X	Organizacija i Kadrovi†
0048-220X	Orient
0048-2234	Origins
0048-2242	Orissa Homoeopathic Bulletin†
0048-2269	Orthodox Church 7705
0048-2277	Volund 8445
0048-2331	Ottawa Law Review 4754
0048-234X	University of Ottawa. Aesculapian Society. Medical Review†
0048-2358	A P M Bulletin 362
0048-2366	Ouest Medical†
0048-2390	Our Local Sixty Six†
0048-2420	Outdoor Guide†
0048-2447	Outdoorman†
0048-2455	Outdoorsman†
0048-2471	Outlook†
0048-2498	Ouvrier Senegalais
0048-251X	Overseas Advertising 31
0048-2528	Overseas Books 7569
0048-2536	Overseas Hindustan Times†
0048-2560	Oxford Consumer
0048-2587	P D & D International†
0048-2609	P R Reporter 31
0048-2625	P A T A Indonesia
0048-2633	Pacific Marketer†
0048-2668	Package
0048-2692	Pakistan Educational Review†
0048-2706	Pakistan Heart Journal 5797
0048-2714	P L A Newsletter 5038
0048-2722	Pakistan Pediatric Journal 6099
0048-2757	Pakistan Textile Journal 8456

0048-2765	Palabra†
0048-2773	Palette†
0048-2781	Palmetto Piper†
0048-282X	Panorama (Boston) 8746
0048-2846	Panorama des Entreprises†
0048-2854	Papel Impreso†
0048-2862	Paperprintpack India 6736
0048-2889	Papetier 6736
0048-2919	Papua and New Guinea Education Gazette 2895
0048-2935	Paragraphic 6173
0048-2951	Parassitologia 5824
0048-2994	Parliamentary Journal 7164
0048-301X	Parnassos 4468
0048-3028	Parnassus: Poetry in Review 5429
0048-3044	Partisan
0048-3095	Pazifische Rundschau†
0048-3109	Pearl Gazette†
0048-3133	Pediatric Clinics of India†
0048-315X	Pedra e Cal
0048-3192	Pennant 6441
0048-3206	Pennsylvania Academy of Ophthalmology and Otolaryngology. Transactions†
0048-3214	Pennsylvania Geology 2762
0048-3249	Pennsylvania Researcher†
0048-3257	Pennsylvania Road Builder
0048-3273	Penny Wise Motoring
0048-3281	Pensioners Voice 8061
0048-329X	People 3920
0048-3303	People
0048-3311	People for Progress†
0048-332X	People United to Save Humanity. P.U.S.H.-Operation Push 5233
0048-3338	People Watching†
0048-3362	People's Voice†
0048-3370	Periodista 4581
0048-3397	Periscoop†
0048-3400	Periscope†
0048-3435	Personal Injury Researcher†
0048-3451	Personnel Guide to Canada's Travel Industry 8747
0048-3486	Personnel Review 1872
0048-3508	Perspectives (Washington, 1971)†
0048-3516	Perspectives Euro Africaines
0048-3524	Perspectives in Defense Management†
0048-3540	Royal Perth Hospital. Journal†
0048-3559	Perth. Stock Exchange. Official Record†
0048-3567	Pesquisa Medica
0048-3575	Pesticide Biochemistry and Physiology 246
0048-3591	Petroleum Gazette†
0048-3605	Petts Wood Post
0048-3613	P.G. Football Newsletter
0048-363X	Pharmacognosy Titles†
0048-3648	Pharmascope†
0048-3656	Pharmazeutische Praxis†
0048-3664	Pharmazie in Unserer Zeit 6875
0048-3710	Philatelic Journalist†
0048-3737	Philatopic Magazine†
0048-3745	Philippine Economy and Industrial Journal
0048-3753	The Philippine Entomologist 857
0048-3761	Philippine Journal of Animal Industry†
0048-377X	Philippine Journal of Fisheries 3605
0048-3796	Philippine Journal of Linguistics 5160
0048-380X	Philippine Journal of Mental Health†
0048-3818	Philippine Journal of Nursing 5978
0048-3826	Philippine Journal of Plant Industry 247
0048-3834	Philippine Journal of Soils†
0048-3842	Philippine Mining & Engineering Journal 6476
0048-3850	Philippine Planning Journal 4422
0048-3877	Philippines Quarterly†
0048-3893	Philosophia 6940
0048-3915	Philosophy and Public Affairs 7165
0048-3931	Philosophy of the Social Sciences 7992
0048-3966	Der Foto-Markt†
0048-3974	Photo-Memo
0048-3982	Photo Reporter†
0048-3990	Photographe Professionnel†
0048-4008	Photographic Journal of the Sun†
0048-4016	Photography North
0048-4024	Physical Review Abstracts†
0048-4083	Physiotherapists' Quarterly 6114
0048-4105	Piano-Tuners Quarterly 4084
0048-4113	Pick's World Currency Report†
0048-4148	Pielegniarka i Polozna
0048-4156	Pig Breeders Gazette
0048-4172	Piltdown Newsletter†
0048-4199	Pioneer 6441
0048-4202	Pioneer†
0048-4229	Pirogue†
0048-4253	Place†
0048-4261	Placedart†
0048-427X	Plaisirs de la Chasse 8329
0048-4288	Planet (Aberystwyth) 5351
0048-4318	Planning in Northeastern Illinois†
0048-4326	P I B C News 4421
0048-4342	Plant Varieties and Seeds Gazette 248
0048-4350	Plaste und Kautschuk†
0048-4385	Plastics Southern Africa 7098
0048-4415	Playboard 8476
0048-4423	Playfair Cricket Monthly†
0048-444X	Plebeian†
0048-4466	P L E R U S 4421
0048-4474	Ploughshares 5352
0048-4482	Plural Societies†
0048-4490	Plymothian
0048-4512	Poder Politico
0048-4520	Poemes Inedits
0048-4547	Poesia Hispanica†
0048-4555	Poesie
0048-4563	Poesie Presente†
0048-458X	Poetry
0048-4601	Poetry Miscellany 5431
0048-461X	Poetry of Our Times†
0048-4636	Point and Figure Digest†

9084 0048-4695 ULRICH'S PERIODICALS

0048-4695 Police Nationale†
0048-4717 Il Policlinico. Sezione Medica
0048-4741 Polish Institute of Arts and Sciences in America. Information Bulletin†
0048-475X Politieke Dokumentatie **7171**
0048-4768 Polizeiblatt fuer das Land Baden-Wuerttemberg†
0048-4784 Pollution **3490**
0048-4806 Polymer India†
0048-4830 Popular Dogs†
0048-4857 Porfeydd†
0048-4881 Portland Magazine **4084**
0048-489X Portside **8657**
0048-4903 Portugaliae Physica **7035**
0048-4911 Positif **6510**
0048-4946 Postgraduate Medicine Quarterly Abstracts†
0048-4962 Poultry Fancier
0048-5012 P M I - Powder Metallurgy International†
0048-5020 Powder Metallurgy Science & Technology†
0048-5039 Power
0048-5047 Power & Industry in Asia†
0048-508X Practical Forms & Precedents N S W **4759**
0048-511X Prairies Tax Reports†
0048-5136 Praxis der Beregnungswirtschaft†
0048-5144 Precision Shooting **8194**
0048-5160 Premisa
0048-5179 Prensa Chilena y Sus Comentarios
0048-5195 Presence Francophone†
0048-5233 Prevention†
0048-525X Preview Abstracts in Physics and Astronomy†
0048-5268 Preview Bermuda **8748**
0048-5276 Prim-Aid†
0048-5284 Primary Education†
0048-5306 Principality of Liechtenstein - A Documentary Handbook†
0048-5314 Print-Equip News **7326**
0048-5322 Printers News†
0048-5330 Printers News†
0048-5357 Prisma
0048-5365 Prison Law Reporter†
0048-5411 Problemi di Ulisse†
0048-5446 Professional Engineer in Industry Newsletter†
0048-5454 Professional Officer†
0048-5489 Progreso **5163**
0048-5497 Progress in Fire Retardancy†
0048-5500 Progress in Materials Science†
0048-5519 Progress in Physical Therapy†
0048-5535 Prometheus (Washington, DC)
0048-5543 Promise M/R†
0048-5551 The Propeller Club Quarterly **8657**
0048-5578 Prophetic Expositor **7672**
0048-5586 Proscope†
0048-5608 Prosperity **1513**
0048-5616 Protection†
0048-5632 Proud **3559**
0048-5640 Proud Black Images†
0048-5659 Proust Research Association Newsletter†
0048-5675 Przeglad Psychologiczny **7392**
0048-5691 Psicologia e Lavoro **7393**
0048-5705 Psihologija **7394**
0048-5713 Psychiatric Annals **6176**
0048-5721 Psychiatric Outpatient Services in Los Angeles County†
0048-573X Psychic Observer†
0048-5748 Psychological Issues†
0048-5756 Psychologie Medicale†
0048-5764 Psychopharmacology Bulletin **6877**
0048-5772 Psychophysiology **6179**
0048-5802 Public Affairs†
0048-5829 Public Choice **1162**
0048-5896 Public Relations Australia†
0048-5942 Publishers' Auxiliary **4582**
0048-5950 Publius **7174**
0048-5977 Puhelin **2371**
0048-6000 Pulse (London, 1959) **5700**
0048-6019 Punjab Agricultural University. Journal of Research **149**
0048-6027 Punjab Punch†
0048-6035 Purchasing Management Newsletter†
0048-6043 Pyrethrum Post **814**
0048-6086 Quaderni di Radiologia†
0048-6094 Quaderni Piacentini†
0048-6167 Quarterly Bulletin on Solar Activity **580**
0048-6183 Quarterly Market Projection†
0048-6191 Quarterly Statistical Bulletin for Africa†
0048-6205 Quarto Mondo† **8983**
0048-6213 Quasi
0048-6221 Que Pasa†
0048-6248 Quebec Aujourd' Hui†
0048-6256 Quebec-Histoire†
0048-6299 Quebec Tax Reporter **1941**
0048-6302 Queens Bar Bulletin **4764**
0048-6329 Queens Own Highlander
0048-6361 Queensland Master Builder
0048-637X Queensland Master Plumber **4125**
0048-6388 Queensland Roads†
0048-6396 Australia. Bureau of Statistics. Queensland Office. Monthly Summary of Statistics, Queensland†
0048-6418 Administrators' Bulletin†
0048-6434 Quest in Education†
0048-6442 Questo Nostro Ambiente†
0048-6477 Journal de la Quincaillerie†
0048-6493 La Quinzaine Litteraire **5357**
0048-654X Radharc†
0048-6604 Radio Science **2788**
0048-6639 Railroad Modeler†
0048-6647 Railway Digest International
0048-6663 Rakennustaito **1031**
0048-668X Rally **7813**
0048-671X Ramus **2239**
0048-6736 Rassegna Alpina†
0048-6744 Rassegna di Medicina del Traffico†
0048-6760 Rassegna di Neuropsichiatria e Scienze Affini†
0048-6779 Rassegna Internazionale di Logica†
0048-6787 La Rassegna Odontotecnica†
0048-6809 Ratcliffian **2298**
0048-6817 Rating and Valuation Reporter
0048-6833 Rautatieliikenne
0048-685X Real Estate Journal (Queensland) *changed to* 1442-9683 **7606**
0048-6868 Real Estate Law Journal **4765**
0048-6884 Realist†
0048-6906 Reason **5236**
0048-6914 Receptarius
0048-6930 Recherche Spatiale†
0048-6965 Records Management Report†
0048-6981 Recursos Hidricos
0048-7023 Red Cross Quarterly
0048-7066 Reeves Journal **4125**
0048-7090 Regione Toscana†
0048-7112 R N A O News†
0048-7120 Rehabilitacion **6115**
0048-7139 Rehabilitation Digest†
0048-7155 Reign of the Sacred Heart **7814**
0048-7163 Universite de Reims. Institut de Geographie. Travaux **4032**
0048-7171 Reinsurance **4520**
0048-7198 Relazioni Clinico Scientifiche
0048-7201 Relevo†
0048-721X Religion **7674**
0048-7260 Report on Indian Legislation†
0048-7287 Die Republik†
0048-7325 Research Journal of Philosophy and Social Sciences **6947**
0048-7333 Research Policy **7903**
0048-7368 Reserve Bank of Australia. Currency†
0048-7376 Resources (Washington) **2626**
0048-7384 Resources for American Literary Study **5360**
0048-7406 Restaurant News
0048-7422 Retail Operations News Bulletin†
0048-7449 Reumatismo **6226**
0048-7457 Reuse - Recycle† **8985**
0048-7481 Review of Law & Social Change **4769**
0048-749X Review of Regional Studies **4425**
0048-7511 Reviews in American History **4310**
0048-752X Reviews in Analytical Chemistry **2105**
0048-7554 Reviews on Environmental Health **3463**
0048-7597 Revista Agropecuaria **150**
0048-7600 Revista Argentina de Cirugia **6256**
0048-7619 Revista Argentina de Radiologia **6207**
0048-7651 Revista Chilena de Literatura **5361**
0048-766X Revista Chilena de Obstetricia y Ginecologia **6003**
0048-7678 Revista Cubana de Ciencias Veterinarias **8806**
0048-7694 Revista de Estudios Politicos **7178**
0048-7708 Revista de Geografia **4026**
0048-7716 Revista de la Sanidad Militar Argentina
0048-7732 Revista de Obstetricia y Ginecologia de Venezuela **6003**
0048-7740 Revista de Psicologia Normal e Patologica†
0048-7759 Revista de Soldadura†
0048-7767 Revista Dental
0048-7775 Revista Ecuatoriana de Higiene y Medicina Tropical **5825**
0048-7783 Revista Educativa†
0048-7813 L T R. Revista
0048-7848 Societatea de Medici si Naturalisti din Iasi. Revista Medico-Chirurgicala
0048-7856 Revista Odonto-Estomatologica
0048-7864 Revista Paulista de Hospitais
0048-7880 Revista Portuguesa de Pediatria e Puericultura
0048-7902 Revue Avicole **298**
0048-7937 Revue de Jurisprudence Commerciale
0048-7953 Revue de l'Habitat Francais *changed to* 1954-9075 **7611**
0048-8003 Revue d'Histoire Moderne et Contemporaine **4159**
0048-8011 Revue du Materiel d'Entreprise†
0048-802X Canadian Arab World Review **3525**
0048-8038 Revue Economique Franco-Allemande *changed to* 0753-5724 **1401**
0048-8046 Revue Europeenne des Sciences Sociales **7998**
0048-8097 Revue Generale de Botanique†
0048-8119 Revue Generale d'Etudes de la Police Francaise†
0048-8135 Revue Internationale de Pediatrie **6103**
0048-8143 Revue Internationale de Philosophie **6949**
0048-816X Revue Ivoirienne de Droit **4774**
0048-8178 Revue Roumaine d'Etudes Internationales **7263**
0048-8186 Revue Technique du Batiment *changed to* 0397-9296 **1033**
0048-8216 Rhode Island. University. U. R. I. Commercial Fisheries Newsletter†
0048-8224 Rhodes Report†
0048-8267 Ricardian **4258**
0048-8291 Ricerche di Automatica†
0048-8305 Right On! **3561**
0048-8348 Verniciatura Industriale **6721**
0048-8364 Rivista di Anatomia Patologica e di Oncologia†
0048-8372 Rivista di Diritto Sportivo†
0048-8399 Rivista di Idrobiologia
0048-8402 Rivista Italiana di Scienza Politica **7179**
0048-8429 Rivista Tributaria Ticinese†
0048-8445 Rock & Folk **6612**
0048-8453 Rock & Gem **4345**
0048-8461 Rocket **7180**
0048-847X Rockhound†
0048-8496 Rod & Line†
0048-8518 Roeien **8281**
0048-8526 Roerfag **4126**
0048-8534 The Rogue Digger **3781**
0048-8542 Rolling Along **8510**
0048-8577 Rumanian Journal of Chemistry†
0048-8585 Romanian Medical Review
0048-8593 Romantisme **5364**
0048-8631 Rotary Down Under **2269**
0048-864X Roughneck Magazine
0048-8658 Romania: Documents - Events **3933**
0048-8674 Rountree Report†
0048-8690 Royal Canadian Legion's Coaching Review†
0048-8771 The Running Board **8602**
0048-878X Rural Arkansas **3987**
0048-8798 Rural Education Review†
0048-881X Russian Literature Triquarterly†
0048-8828 Russian Ultrasonics†
0048-8860 Rx Bulletin†
0048-8879 The Ryde Recorder **4194**
0048-8895 S F Greats†
0048-8925 Sabam Magazine **4583**
0048-8933 Sabretache **6444**
0048-8941 Sackbut†
0048-895X Saddle and Striker **4345**
0048-8968 Safety Canada **7540**
0048-8976 Sage Professional Papers in International Studies†
0048-8992 Saint Louis Chronicle **3001**
0048-9018 Saisons d'Alsace **3842**
0048-9034 Sales and Marketing in Australia†
0048-9069 S A E **1706**
0048-9077 San Bernardino County Museum Association. Newsletter†
0048-9107 Sante Publique†
0048-9115 Santiago **5238**
0048-9182 Saskatchewan Genealogical Society. Bulletin **3782**
0048-9190 Saskatchewan Guidance and Counselling Association. Guidelines **2909**
0048-9204 Saskatchewan Indian **3562**
0048-9212 Saskatchewan Journal of Educational Research and Development†
0048-9220 Saskatchewan Medical Quarterly†
0048-9239 Saturday Evening Post **3988**
0048-9247 Savings Banks Institute. Journal
0048-9255 Scalpel and Tongs **6899**
0048-9263 Scandinavian - American Bulletin **3562**
0048-928X Scandinavian Canadian Businessman†
0048-931X Scene (Northridge)†
0048-9328 Schach **8199**
0048-9336 Scheidewege **6951**
0048-9344 Schietsport **8199**
0048-9352 Schiltrom†
0048-9387 School Bell **3031**
0048-9425 School Library Association of Queensland. Journal†
0048-9433 School Library Newsletter†
0048-9441 S M S G Newsletter†
0048-9476 School Services Curriculum Perspectives†
0048-9484 Schulverwaltungsblatt fuer Niedersachsen **3033**
0048-9492 Schuss **5172**
0048-9506 Die Schwalbe **8199**
0048-9514 Schweizer Hotel Journal
0048-9530 Schweizerische Zeitschrift fuer Nachwuchs und Ausbildung†
0048-9557 Scienca Revuo **7908**
0048-9581 Science and Government Report **7468**
0048-9603 Science Education News
0048-962X Science Fantasy†
0048-9654 Science Fiction Times†
0048-9662 Science for the People†
0048-9689 Science of Man†
0048-9697 Science of the Total Environment **3465**
0048-9727 Sciences Medicales†
0048-9751 Scots Magazine **3870**
0048-9778 Scottish Institute of Missionary Studies Bulletin **7680**
0048-9808 Scottish Transport **8510**
0048-9824 Scrap and Waste Reclamation and Disposal†
0048-9832 Screenings **416**
0048-9867 Sea Classics **8660**
0048-9883 Sealandair **6445**
0048-9891 Seaposter **6899**
0048-9905 Sear
0048-9913 Search (Nashville)†
0048-9948 Seattle Centerstage
0048-9956 Second Coming†
0048-9964 Second Order **6951**
0048-9980 Second Wave†
0049-0008 Secularist
0049-0016 Security Distributing & Marketing **1843**
0049-0024 Security Gazette **2680**
0049-0040 Seed Scoop **251**
0049-0059 Seguranca†
0049-0067 Selecciones Municipales
0049-0075 Selecoes Odontologicas
0049-0083 Select†
0049-0091 Select Bibliography on Higher Education†
0049-0105 Selected References on Environmental Quality as It Relates to Health†
0049-0164 Semina *changed to* 1796-6116 **6841**
0049-0172 Seminars in Arthritis and Rheumatism **6227**
0049-0199 Senior Citizens Today
0049-0229 Service to Business and Industry - B P L†
0049-0253 Sesame Street **2212**
0049-027X Seventeen's Make It!†
0049-0296 Severn and Wye Review†
0049-0318 Sex Problems Court Digest
0049-0326 Sexologie†
0049-0334 Shareholder and New Investor†
0049-0342 Shawensis†
0049-0385 Sh'ma **7729**
0049-0393 Shopping Center World *changed to* 1544-4236 **1841**
0049-0415 Shotgun News **8200**
0049-0423 Shuttle, Spindle & Dyepot **8457**
0049-044X Sierra Club. National News Report†
0049-0466 Sign World **35**
0049-0482 Sikh Digest
0049-0490 Silent News†
0049-0504 Sillon†
0049-0512 Simmons Review **2301**
0049-0547 Singapore Undergrad
0049-0555 Singles-Mingles
0049-0598 Sintesis
0049-0601 Sinteza
0049-061X Sioniste†
0049-0628 Sirjana
0049-0636 Sistema Nervoso†

Link to your serials resources and content with ulrichsweb.com

0049-0652 Ski Scene†
0049-0717 Slesse News
0049-0733 Slice of Pizza†
0049-0776 Smoke Signals
0049-0792 SNAP
0049-0814 Sno-Mo-Go
0049-0857 Social Change 8132
0049-0865 Social Dimension Newsletter†
0049-0881 Social Reformer
0049-089X Social Science Research 8004
0049-092X Social Sciences in Canada†
0049-0938 Socialisme Quebecois†
0049-0946 Socialist Affairs 7183
0049-0954 Socialist Press Bulletin
0049-0962 Socialni Politika changed to Prace & Socialni Politika 8062
0049-0989 Boletin S A C M†
0049-0997 Sociedad Dominicana de Geografia Boletin†
0049-1004 Sociedad Mexicana de Geografia y Estadistica. Boletin 4036
0049-1039 Sociedade de Lingua Portuguesa. Boletim 5175
0049-1055 Societe des Ecrivains Canadiens. Bulletin†
0049-1063 Societe d'Etudes. Revue d'Etudes†
0049-1098 Societe Historique Acadienne. Cahiers 4312
0049-111X Etudes Prehistoriques†
0049-1152 Society for Ancient Numismatics. S A N Journal
0049-1160 S A A D Digest 5864
0049-1209 Society of Manufacturing Engineers. Technical Digest†
0049-1217 Sociolinguistics†
0049-1225 Sociologia 8135
0049-1241 Sociological Methods & Research 8137
0049-125X Soenderjysk Maanedsskrift 4266
0049-1276 Sol
0049-1292 Solidarite Ouvriere†
0049-1306 Somerset and Dorset Notes and Queries 4266
0049-1349 Sotainvalidi 8072
0049-1357 Soufflest
0049-1381 S A Athlete†
0049-1403 South African Financial Gazette 1383
0049-1411 South African Metrication News†
0049-142X South African Studies†
0049-1454 South Australian Garden Guide†
0049-1470 South Australian State Reports 4785
0049-1489 South Carolina Dental Journal†
0049-1519 South Coast Sun 3950
0049-1527 South Eastern Latin Americanist changed to 1557-2021 4151
0049-1535 South Vietnam in Struggle†
0049-1543 S.W.A. Boer†
0049-1551 Southeast Asia†
0049-1616 Southern MotoRacing 8202
0049-1624 Southern Purchaser 1844
0049-1640 Southern Stars 582
0049-1675 Southwestern American Literature 5376
0049-1683 Southwestern Journal of Social Education†
0049-1705 Sou'wester 3609
0049-1713 Soviet Analyst 7185
0049-1756 Soviet Power Engineering†
0049-1764 Soviet Progress in Polyurethanes†
0049-1780 Space Adventures†
0049-1829 Spear†
0049-1837 Special Education Newsletter†
0049-1845 Special Interest Autos 8604
0049-187X Spoke Wheels†
0049-1888 Spokesman†
0049-1926 Sport und Mode 8205
0049-1934 Sporting Investor Method Magazine†
0049-1950 Sporting Star†
0049-2000 Spotlight (Bath)†
0049-2027 Squadron†
0049-2035 Stagione delle Arti, del Libro, e del Turismo†
0049-2051 Stampa Sud
0049-206X Standard-Bearer (New York)†
0049-2078 Standpunkte und Dokumente
0049-2086 Stanford Law School Journal†
0049-2116 The Star (Carville)
0049-2140 State of the Nation†
0049-2159 State Supplies
0049-2205 Steel Construction 1037
0049-2213 Steel Pipe News†
0049-223X Der Steuerberater 1945
0049-2248 Sti og Varde 8336
0049-2272 Stock Car†
0049-2280 Stockowners' Digest
0049-2302 Strada
0049-2337 Street Level†
0049-2345 Strobe†
0049-2353 Stromata 6953
0049-2361 Studi e Problemi di Critica Testuale 5179
0049-237X Studies in Logic and the Foundations of Mathematics 5539
0049-2388 Studies in the Linguistic Sciences 5183
0049-2396 Studii si Cercetari de Biochimie†
0049-2426 Sub-Stance 5383
0049-2442 Success (Peterborough)†
0049-2450 Sud changed to 1286-7160 5417
0049-2477 Sugar News
0049-2531 Sundet Rundt†
0049-2558 Sunstone Review (Santa Fe)†
0049-2590 Supermarket and Retailer 3681
0049-2612 Supreme Court Researcher†
0049-2620 Sur les Sentiers de l'Ecole Active†
0049-2639 Surface Wave Abstracts†
0049-2663 Svensk Idrott 8210
0049-2671 Svensk Skidsport changed to Svensk SkidsportSki & Board Magazine 8336
0049-2701 Swedish Journal of Agricultural Research†
0049-271X Swinton Journal
0049-2728 Swiss Canadian News 3567
0049-2736 Syndicats de Roumanie†
0049-2744 Syndicats Vietnamiens†
0049-2752 Synergist (Washington)†

0049-2760 B E C Synoptic
0049-2817 Taamuli 7187
0049-2825 Die Tabak Zeitung 8488
0049-2833 Tactile†
0049-2868 Take Over
0049-2884 Taliesin
0049-2906 Talk 4076
0049-2914 Tallow Light 4314
0049-2922 Tambor†
0049-2930 Tamkang Journal of Mathematics 5540
0049-2949 Tamkang Review 5385
0049-2957 Tangley Oaks Reading Guide†
0049-2981 Tanzania Police Journal
0049-3023 Tasmanian Hotel Review†
0049-304X Taxi 8512
0049-3058 Taxi Drivers Voice†
0049-3066 Tchad et Culture 3790
0049-3082 Teacher in Wales†
0049-3090 Teacher and Librarian
0049-3112 Teacher Today†
0049-3155 Technical Communication 2340
0049-3163 Technical Teachers Association of Victoria. Associate News
0049-3198 Technology Mart†
0049-3201 I I T Tecnologia†
0049-321X Teenager Monthly
0049-3228 Teen's Star†
0049-3252 Tele Presse 2395
0049-3287 Telecine†
0049-3295 Teleguide†
0049-3317 Television Sponsors Directory 2030
0049-3325 Televizier 2397
0049-3333 Temas de Orientacion Agropecuaria 161
0049-335X Tempo
0049-3368 Tempus†
0049-3376 Tenants Outlook†
0049-3422 Tennessee Vo-Tech News†
0049-3430 Tenth†
0049-3449 Teologia y Vida 7820
0049-3473 Terre Africaine
0049-3481 Teton†
0049-349X Texas Agricultural Progress†
0049-3511 Texas Farm and Ranch News†
0049-352X Texas Metro†
0049-3546 Textil†
0049-3554 Textile Asia 8459
0049-3570 Textiles Panamericanos 8461
0049-3589 Thai Journal of Agricultural Science 162
0049-3597 Theatre Enfance et Jeunesse†
0049-3619 Theatre-Quebec†
0049-3635 Theologia 7706
0049-3651 Theological Times 7777
0049-366X Theologie und Glaube 7820
0049-3686 Theoria to Theory†
0049-3708 Theosophy in New Zealand changed to 1177-8032 6957
0049-3724 Thin-Layer Chromatography Abstracts
0049-3740 Third World Reports
0049-3759 This Fortnight in Pakistan†
0049-3783 This Week†
0049-3791 This Week in Israel
0049-3848 Thrombosis Research 5800
0049-3864 Tieraerztliche Umschau 8808
0049-3899 Tijdschrift voor Gastro-Enterologie†
0049-3929 Times Higher Education Supplement changed to Times Higher Education 3005
0049-3937 Tips
0049-3945 Tobacco International 8488
0049-3953 Tobacco Review†
0049-397X Tocher 3623
0049-3988 Today in Mining†
0049-4003 Today's Girl†
0049-402X Tohoku Regional Fisheries Research Laboratory. Bulletin†
0049-4038 Toike Oike 3223
0049-4062 Museum News changed to Toledo Museum of Art Members Newsletter 6538
0049-4070 Tomorrow's Newspaper†
0049-4089 Tonnage Club Farm News†
0049-4100 Top Management Abstracts†
0049-4119 Top of the News with Fulton Lewis†
0049-4127 Topic (Washington) 4478
0049-4135 Topical Stamp Handbooks 6900
0049-4143 Torax 6220
0049-4178 Torch of Homoeopathy†
0049-4186 Toronto Jewish Press 3568
0049-4194 Toronto Life 3818
0049-4216 Toronto Stock Exchange Review 1656
0049-4240 Torontoer Zeitung
0049-4283 Touristik Aktuell 8764
0049-4291 Town and Countryside†
0049-4321 Trade and Commerce 1433
0049-433X Trade Unions International of Workers in Commerce. Bulletin
0049-4348 Trade Winds from Japan†
0049-4356 Traedgaardsnytt 3752
0049-4402 Transit News†
0049-4410 Transit - Times (Oakland)†
0049-4429 Transition 8144
0049-4461 Transport
0049-447X Transport Routier du Quebec†
0049-4488 Transportation 8515
0049-450X Transportation Law Journal 4798
0049-4518 Transportation Safety Association of Ontario. Bulletin
0049-4526 Transportation Safety Association of Ontario. Drivers' News Letter
0049-4534 Travail Theatral†
0049-4569 Travel Times
0049-4593 Treasure
0049-4615 Trefoil Trail†
0049-4623 Trend 1184
0049-4631 Tribuna Farmaceutica

0049-464X Tribuna Italiana†
0049-4658 Sackville Tribune-Post 3817
0049-4666 Tribune Psychique†
0049-4674 Tribune Socialiste†
0049-4682 Revista Tricontinental 7262
0049-4690 Trident 8664
0049-4704 Universita degli Studi di Trieste. Istituto di Matematica. Rendiconti 5543
0049-4712 Trinitarian Bible Society. Quarterly Record† 8994
0049-4720 Tripura Review†
0049-4747 Tropical Animal Health and Production 8809
0049-4755 Tropical Doctor 5827
0049-4763 Tropical Grasslands 255
0049-4801 Tundra Times
0049-481X Tungsten News†
0049-4828 Tungsten Statistics 6341
0049-4836 Tupart Monthly Reports on the Underground Press†
0049-4852 Turkiye Muhendislik Haberleri 3286
0049-4917 Two Tone
0049-4933 Tydskrif vir Volkskunde en Volkstaal 3623
0049-495X Typog†
0049-4968 New York Typographical Union Number Six. Bulletin 4599
0049-4976 U F O - Nyt 73
0049-4984 U N I C E F Information Bulletin†
0049-500X Ubique 4031
0049-5026 Uganda Schools Newsletter 2921
0049-5034 Ugens Politik†
0049-5042 Uhrenfachgeschaeft 4570
0049-5069 Uj Konyvek 637
0049-5077 Ukrainian Canadian†
0049-5107 Ulster Tatler 3872
0049-5123 Umeni 523
0049-5131 Umweltschutz 7544
0049-514X The Unabashed Librarian 5052
0049-5174 Underground Lamp Post†
0049-5204 UNESCO Centro de Documentacion Cultural, Havana. Informaciones Trimestrales 4479
0049-5220 Unidad Latina†
0049-5239 Unifier†
0049-5263 Union des Epiciers
0049-528X Union Herald 4604
0049-5298 New York Metro Area Postal Union. Union Mail 2354
0049-5301 Union Research Service†
0049-531X The Unitarian 7743
0049-5379 U N I D O Documents Checklist†
0049-5433 United Reformed Church History Society. Journal 7778
0049-5484 U.S. National Clearinghouse for Poison Control Centers. Bulletin†
0049-5506 Universe 583
0049-5530 Universitas 3007
0049-5557 Unmuzzled Ox 5437
0049-5565 Uno en Dos
0049-559X Unspeakable Visions of the Individual†
0049-5638 Urban Affairs Today†
0049-5689 Urban Rights†
0049-5700 Urethane Plastics and Products†
0049-5719 Urogallo†
0049-5727 Utah Nurse 5983
0049-5778 V E 6 2364
0049-5794 Valeurs Actuelles 3842
0049-5808 Valiseesti†
0049-5816 Vancouver Calendar Magazine
0049-5824 Vancouver Numismatic Society. News Bulletin 6653
0049-5883 Vasama 4605
0049-5891 Vasculum 7927
0049-5905 Vegetarian Courier
0049-5913 Velocidad 8610
0049-5921 Verbindungstechnik†
0049-5956 Vermont Libraries†
0049-5972 La Vernice†
0049-5980 Vers la Vie Nouvelle†
0049-5999 Der Versandhausberater 1847
0049-6014 Versicherungsvermittlung 4527
0049-6022 Vertical
0049-6057 Die Veterinaermedizin†
0049-6065 Veterinary Doctor and Veterinary Digest†
0049-6073 Vibration 3570
0049-609X Vickers News†
0049-6103 Victoria. Department of Agriculture. Dairyfarming Digest†
0049-6111 Victoria, Australia. Education Department. Curriculum and Research Bulletin†
0049-6146 Victorian Horticulture Digest†
0049-6170 Victorian Municipal Directory
0049-6200 Victorian Tobacco Grower†
0049-6286 Vie Mutualiste
0049-6294 Vie Publique†
0049-6340 Vietnam Digest
0049-6359 Vietnam Economic Report†
0049-6367 Vietnam: Yesterday and Today†
0049-6375 Vietnam Youth 2219
0049-6405 Viewpoint†
0049-643X Vigneron Champenois 257
0049-6456 Vintage†
0049-6472 Virginia Dental Journal 5869
0049-6499 Virginia Researcher†
0049-6510 Vision Index†
0049-6529 Visite†
0049-6537 Visor
0049-6545 Vista Femenina Centroamericana
0049-657X Vivre†
0049-6588 Magazine Vivre†
0049-6618 V F I Information Bulletin†
0049-6626 Voce dell'Africa†
0049-6650 Vogelwarte 916
0049-6669 Voice (Grandville) 7693
0049-6677 Voix de la Construction†
0049-6685 Voix de la Resistance†
0049-6693 Voix des Parents 2925
0049-6707 Voix du Retraite 4057
0049-6715 Volare Necesse Est
0049-6790 A Voz de Portugal 3571

0066-3417 Annuaire National des Specialistes Qualifies en Chirurgie†
0066-3425 Annuaire National des Specialistes Qualifies Exclusifs des Maladies de l'Appareil Digestif†
0066-3441 Annuaire National des Specialistes Qualifies Exclusifs en Cardiologie
0066-345X Annuaire National des Specialistes Qualifies Exclusifs en Dermatologie et Venereologie†
0066-3468 Annuaire National des Specialistes Qualifies Exclusifs en Electroradiologie†
0066-3476 Annuaire National des Specialistes Qualifies Exclusifs en Neuropsychiatrie†
0066-3492 Annuaire National des Specialistes Qualifies Exclusifs en Pneumophtisiologie
0066-3506 Annuaire National des Specialistes Qualifies Exclusifs en Ophtalmologie
0066-3514 Annuaire National des Specialistes Qualifies Exclusifs en Pediatrie†
0066-3522 Annuaire National des Specialistes Qualifies Exclusifs en Rhumatologie†
0066-3549 Annuaire National des Transports *changed to* 1965-2321 **8490**
0066-3557 Annuaire National du Verre†
0066-3573 Repertoire Officiel des Relations Internationales des Communes du Monde†
0066-3581 Annuaire Paris: Bijoux
0066-3638 Quatre Mille Imprimeries Francaises†
0066-3654 Annuaire Statistique de la France **8345**
0066-3689 Annuaire Statistique de la Tunisie **8345**
0066-3697 Annuaire Statistique de l'Industrie Francaise du Jute†
0066-376X Annual Banff Regional Conference for School Administrators. Report†
0066-3786 Annual Bibliography of English Language and Literature **5406**
0066-3816 Annual Bulletin of Electric Energy Statistics for Europe†
0066-3824 Annual Bulletin of Gas Statistics for Europe†
0066-3832 Annual Bulletin of Historical Literature **4199**
0066-3840 Annual Bulletin of Housing and Building Statistics for Europe **4432**
0066-3883 Annual Conference of Model Reporting Area for Blindness Statistics. Proceedings†
0066-3891 Annual Development Plan of Madhya Pradesh
0066-3913 Annual Directory of Booksellers in the British Isles Specialising in Antiquarian and Out-of-Print Books†
0066-3972 N U T Guide to Careers Work†
0066-3999 Annual Industry Survey of Computer and Software and Services Industry†
0066-4030 Annual Progress in Child Psychiatry and Child Development **6123**
0066-4049 Annual Register of Grant Support **2966**
0066-409X Annual Reports in Organic Synthesis **2133**
0066-4103 Annual Reports on N M R Spectroscopy **7073**
0066-412X Hawaii Visitors Bureau. Annual Research Report
0066-4146 Annual Review of Astronomy and Astrophysics **568**
0066-4154 Annual Review of Biochemistry **722**
0066-4162 Annual Review of Ecology and Systematics *changed to* 1543-592X **3403**
0066-4170 Annual Review of Entomology **838**
0066-4189 Annual Review of Fluid Mechanics **7057**
0066-4197 Annual Review of Genetics **862**
0066-4200 Annual Review of Information Science and Technology **4989**
0066-4219 Annual Review of Medicine **5576**
0066-4227 Annual Review of Microbiology **881**
0066-426X Annual Review of Physical Chemistry **2133**
0066-4278 Annual Review of Physiology **919**
0066-4286 Annual Review of Phytopathology **775**
0066-4308 Annual Review of Psychology **7335**
0066-4332 Silver Market†
0066-4340 Annual Review of United Nations Affairs **7221**
0066-4359 Annual Safety Education Review†
0066-4367 Annual Statistical Review: The Distilled Spirits Industry†
0066-4375 Annual Summary of Business Statistics, New York State†
0066-4383 Annual Summary of Information on Natural Disasters†
0066-4405 Annual Survey of African Law
0066-4413 Annual Survey of American Law *changed to* New York University Annual Survey of American Law **4746**
0066-443X Annual Survey of Psychoanalysis†
0066-4456 Annuale Mediaevale†
0066-4464 Annuario Cattolico d'Italia **7783**
0066-4472 Annuario Ceramica† **8930**
0066-4480 Annuario della Comunita Lombarda†
0066-4510 Annuario Politecnico Italiano†
0066-4545 Annuario Statistico Italiano **8345**
0066-4618 Anson G. Phelps Lectureship on Early American History†
0066-4626 Antarctic Bibliography†
0066-4642 Antemurale†
0066-4677 Anthropological Forum **325**
0066-4685 Anthropologie **326**
0066-4693 Anthropologische Gesellschaft, Vienna. Mitteilungen **326**
0066-4715 Anthropology of the North. Translations from Russian Sources†
0066-4758 Antibiotics and Chemotherapy **6821**
0066-4766 Antichita Classica e Cristiana
0066-4774 Antichthon **2230**
0066-4782 Antike Kunst. Beihefte **374**
0066-4804 Antimicrobial Agents and Chemotherapy **881**
0066-4812 Antipode **3998**
0066-4839 Antiquitas. Reihe 1. Abhandlungen zur Alten Geschichte **4130**
0066-4847 Antiquitas. Reihe 2. Abhandlungen aus dem Gebiete der Vor- und Fruehgeschichte **4130**
0066-4855 Antiquitas. Reihe 3. Abhandlungen zur Vor- und Fruehgeschichte, zur Klassischen und Provinzial-Roemischen Archaeologie und zur Geschichte des Altertums **4130**
0066-4863 Antiquitas. Reihe 4. Beitraege zur Historia-Augusta-Forschung **4130**
0066-4871 Antiquites Africaines **4173**
0066-4928 Antologia del Folklore Musical Chileno†
0066-4936 Antologias del Pensamiento Politico†
0066-4979 Kunsthistorische Musea, Antwerp. Schone Kunsten†
0066-5010 Anuario Bibliografico Costarricense **615**
0066-5053 Anuario de Cinema†
0066-5061 Anuario de Estudios Medievales **4199**
0066-507X Anuario de Filologia†
0066-5088 Anuario de Historia Economica y Social†
0066-5096 Anuario de la Mineria de Chile **6456**
0066-510X Anuario de Relojeria y Arte en Metal para Espana e Hispanoamerica†
0066-5118 Anuario del Comercio Exterior Latino-Americano†
0066-5126 Anuario de Psicologia **7335**
0066-5169 Mexico. Direccion General de Estadistica. Anuario Estadistico Compendiado†
0066-5177 Instituto Nacional de Estadistica. Anuario Estadistico de Espana: Edicion Extensa **8379**
0066-5185 Anuario Estadistico de los Andes: Venezuela†
0066-5193 Angola. Direccao dos Servicos de Estatistica. Anuario Estatistico **8345**
0066-5207 Anuario F.H.I. Argentina: Frutas y Hortalizas Industrializadas y Frescas **218**
0066-5215 Anuario Filosofico **6904**
0066-5223 Anuario Geografico del Peru **4284**
0066-5274 Yearbook for Inter-American Musical Research†
0066-5282 Anzeiger fuer Slavische Philologie **5095**
0066-5304 Aphidologists' Newsletter†
0066-5320 Apocrypha Novi Testamenti†
0066-5339 Apollonia†
0066-5347 Apotheker - Jahrbuch **6822**
0066-5363 Financial Review (Kingston)†
0066-5371 Appalachian Gas Measurement Short Course, West Virginia University. Proceedings†
0066-538X Appalachian Underground Corrosion Short Course, West Virginia University. Proceedings†
0066-5398 Appel Service; Repertoire d'Adresses Utiles pour le Commerce et l'Industrie
0066-5401 Appliance Technical Conference. Preprints†
0066-541X Applied Chemistry Series†
0066-5436 A F R I Miscellaneous Report†
0066-5444 Applied Forestry Research Institute. Research Report†
0066-5452 Applied Mathematical Sciences **5472**
0066-5479 Applied Mathematics and Mechanics **5472**
0066-5487 Applied Mineralogy - Technische Mineralogie **6456**
0066-5495 Applied Optics. Supplement†
0066-5509 Applied Physics and Engineering†
0066-5517 Applied Polymer Symposium. Papers†
0066-5533 Applied Solid State Science†
0066-5576 Approaches to Semiotics *changed to* 1612-6769 **5095**
0066-5592 Aquatica†
0066-5606 Aqui **5256**
0066-5614 Aquinas Lecture Series **6905**
0066-5630 Al-Kitab al-Arabi Fi Aam
0066-5657 Arabidopsis Information Service. Newsletter†
0066-5673 Arbeiten zur Angewandten Statistik†
0066-569X Arbeiten zur Paedagogik†
0066-5703 Arbeiten zur Rechtsvergleichung **4620**
0066-5738 Arbeitsblaetter fuer Restauratoren†
0066-5746 A R D - Jahrbuch **2356**
0066-5770 Arbeitsgemeinschaft zur Verbesserung der Agrarstruktur in Hessen. A V A-Beratungsunterlagen†
0066-5789 Arbeitsgemeinschaft zur Verbesserung der Agrarstruktur in Hessen. A V A-Hefte†
0066-5797 Arbeitsgemeinschaft zur Verbesserung der Agrarstruktur in Hessen. A V A-Materialsammlungen†
0066-5800 Arbeitsgemeinschaft zur Verbesserung der Agrarstruktur in Hessen. A V A-Sonderhefte†
0066-5819 Arbeitsgemeinschaft zur Verbesserung der Agrarstruktur in Hessen. A V A Bezugshefte†
0066-5827 Arbeitshefte zur Gemeinschaftskunde
0066-5843 Arbeitsmedizin†
0066-5851 Arbeitsmedizinische Fragen in der Ophthalmologie†
0066-5886 Archaeo-Physika **374**
0066-5894 Archaeologia Cantiana **375**
0066-5908 Archaeologia Geographica
0066-5916 Archaeologia Hungarica. Series Nova†
0066-5924 Archaeologia Polona **375**
0066-5932 Archaeologica Slovaca. Catalogi **375**
0066-5940 Archaeologica Slovaca. Fontes **375**
0066-5967 Archaeological Bibliography for Great Britain and Ireland†
0066-5975 Archaeological Exploration of Sardis. Monographs **376**
0066-5983 Archaeological Journal **376**
0066-6009 Archaeologische Funde und Denkmaeler des Rheinlandes†
0066-6017 Archaeologische Gesellschaft Koeln. Schriftenreihe†
0066-6025 Archeologische Kaarten van Belgie†
0066-6041 Archeion (Warsaw) **4199**
0066-605X Archeologia **378**
0066-6068 Archeologie et Civilisation†
0066-6084 Archeologie Mediterraneenne **379**
0066-6092 Archigram†
0066-6114 Architect and Contractors Yearbook
0066-6149 Architects, Builders and Contractors Pocket Book†
0066-6157 Architects, Contractors & Engineers Guide to Construction Costs **976**
0066-6165 Architect's Detail Library†
0066-6173 Architect's Handbook of Professional Practice **428**
0066-619X Architects' Year Book†
0066-6211 A A Papers†
0066-622X Architectural History **429**
0066-6238 Architecture at Rice University
0066-6262 Architecture in Greece **430**
0066-6270 Architectura **429**
0066-6297 Archiv fuer Diplomatik, Schriftgeschichte, Siegel- und Wappenkunde **4199**
0066-6327 Archiv fuer Geschichte des Buchwesens **7551**
0066-6335 Archiv fuer Geschichte von Oberfranken **4199**
0066-636X Archiv fuer Hessische Geschichte und Altertumskunde **4199**
0066-6386 Archiv fuer Liturgiewissenschaft **7622**
0066-6432 Archiv fuer Mittelrheinische Kirchengeschichte **7622**
0066-6440 Archiv fuer Orientforschung **4320**
0066-6459 Archiv fuer Papyrusforschung und Verwandte Gebiete **4131**
0066-6475 Archiv fuer Psychologie†
0066-6491 Archiv fuer Schlesische Kirchengeschichte **7622**
0066-6505 Archiv fuer Sozialgeschichte **4199**
0066-6513 Archiv fuer Voelkerkunde
0066-6521 Archivalia Medica†
0066-653X Archives and the User **4990**
0066-6548 Archives Bakounine†
0066-6556 Archives Claudeliennes†
0066-6564 Archives de Philosophie du Droit **4620**
0066-6572 Archives des Lettres Canadiennes **5256**
0066-6599 Archives in Trade Union History and Theory Series†
0066-6602 Archives Internationales de Finances Publiques†
0066-6610 Archives Internationales d'Histoire des Idees **6905**
0066-6629 Archives of Archaeology†
0066-6637 Archives of Asian Art **467**
0066-6645 Archives of Maryland†
0066-6661 Archivio del Teatro Italiano **8465**
0066-667X Archivio di Oceanografia e Limonologia† **8931**
0066-6688 Archivio Italiano per la Storia della Pieta **7623**
0066-670X Archivio Putti di Chirurgia degli Organi di Movimento
0066-6718 Archivio Storico Italiano. Biblioteca **4200**
0066-6734 Archivo Epistolar Colombiano **5256**
0066-6742 Archivo Espanol de Arqueologia **380**
0066-6750 Archivos Argentinos de Dermatologia **5872**
0066-6777 Archivos de Oftalmologia de Buenos Aires **6038**
0066-6785 Archivum Historiae Pontificiae **7697**
0066-6793 Archivum *changed to* 1680-1865
0066-6807 Archivum Romanicum. Biblioteca. Serie 1: Storia Letteratura Paleografia **5256**
0066-6815 Archivum Romanicum. Biblioteca. Serie 2: Linguistica **5096**
0066-6823 Archiwum Akustyki†
0066-6831 Archiwum z Dziejow Oswiaty **2827**
0066-684X Archiwum Energetyki **3182**
0066-6858 Archiwum Etnograficzne†
0066-6866 Archiwum Filologiczne† **2230**
0066-6874 Archiwum Historii Filozofii i Mysli Spolecznej **6905**
0066-6882 Archiwum Iuridicum Cracoviense **4620**
0066-6890 Archiwum Kryminologii **2644**
0066-6904 Archiwum Literackie **5256**
0066-6912 Archiwum Mineralogiczne **2725**
0066-6939 Arctic Anthropology **329**
0066-6947 Arctic Bibliography†
0066-6955 Arctic Institute of North America. Annual Report†
0066-6971 Arctic Institute of North America. Research Paper†
0066-698X Arctic Institute of North America. Technical Paper†
0066-6998 Arctos; Acta Philologica Fennica. Supplementum **2230**
0066-7005 Argentina. Consejo Federal de Inversiones. Bibliografia Sobre el Desarrollo Economico Nacional†
0066-7021 Argentina. Departamento de Estadistica Educativa. Boletin Informativo.
0066-703X Argentina. Departamento de Estudios Historicos Navales. Serie A: Cultura Nautica
0066-7048 Argentina. Departamento de Estudios Historicos Navales. Serie B: Historia Naval Argentina
0066-7056 Argentina. Departamento de Estudios Historicos Navales. Serie C: Biografias Navales Argentinas
0066-7064 Argentina. Departamento de Estudios Historicos Navales. Serie G: Cuentos, Poemas y Narraciones Marineras
0066-7072 Argentina. Departamento de Estudios Historicos Navales. Serie H: Iconografia
0066-7080 Argentina. Departamento de Estudios Historicos Navales. Serie J: Libros y Impresos Raros
0066-7099 Argentina. Direccion de Investigaciones Forestales. Miscelaneas Forestales†
0066-7102 Argentina. Direccion de Investigaciones Forestales. Notas Silvicolas†
0066-7129 Argentina. Direccion de Investigaciones Forestales. Planificacion del Desarrollo Forestal†
0066-7137 Argentina. Direccion General de Obra Social y Ministerio de Educacion. Memoria y Balance†
0066-7153 Argentina. Servicio Nacional Minero Geologico. Boletin
0066-7161 Argentina. Servicio Nacional Minero Geologico. Estadistica Minera
0066-717X Argentina. Servicio Nacional Minero Geologico. Revista
0066-7188 Argentina. Instituto Nacional de Derecho Aeronautico y Espacial†
0066-7196 Argentina. Instituto Nacional de Estadistica y Censos. Informe Serie E: Edificacion†
0066-7242 Argentina. Estacion Experimental Agropecuaria Manfredi. Serie Informacion Tecnica†
0066-7269 Argentina. Junta Nacional de Carnes. Sintesis Estadistica **175**
0066-7307 Argentina. Comando en Jefe del Ejercito. Direccion de Estudios Historicos. Boletin Informativo
0066-7331 Argentina. Servicio de Inteligencia Naval. Bibliotecas de la Armada. Boletin Bibliografico **6455**
0066-734X Argus de la Poesie Francaise†
0066-7358 Arheologia Moldovei **4200**
0066-7366 Arid Zone Research†
0066-7374 Aristotelian Society. Proceedings (Paper Back Edition) **6905**
0066-7382 Arizona. Department of Public Safety. Annual Report†
0066-7404 Arizona Forestry Notes
0066-7412 Arizona Geological Society Digest **2725**
0066-7447 Arizona Model United Nations†
0066-7455 Arizona State University. Bureau of Educational Research and Services. Educational Services Bulletin.†
0066-7463 Arizona State University. Bureau of Educational Research and Services. Research and Services Bulletin.†
0066-7501 University of Arizona. Anthropological Papers **359**
0066-751X University of Arizona. College of Education. Monograph Series†
0066-7560 E E S Series Report†
0066-7587 University of Arizona. Laboratory of Tree-Ring Research. Papers†

ISSN

9090 0066-7609 ULRICH'S PERIODICALS

0066-7609 University of Arizona. Optical Sciences Center. Newsletter†
0066-7617 University of Arizona. Optical Sciences Center. Technical Report†
0066-7641 Continuing Education in Business Administration†
0066-7668 Arkiv foer Nordisk Filologi **5096**
0066-7676 Arkkitehtuurikilpailuja **433**
0066-7684 Arlington Historical Magazine **4284**
0066-7706 University of New England. Department of Geography. Monograph Series in Geography†
0066-7714 University of New England. Department of Geography and Planning. Research Series in Applied Geography†
0066-7730 University of New England. Exploration Society. Report†
0066-7749 Armorial†
0066-7803 Arqueologicas†
0066-7811 Arquivo de Anatomia e Antropologia†
0066-782X Arquivos Brasileiros de Cardiologia **5777**
0066-7846 Arquivos de Cirurgia Clinica e Experimental†
0066-7854 Arquivos de Patologia Geral e Anatomia Patologica
0066-7862 Arquivos de Tisiologia†
0066-7870 Arquivos de Zoologia **934**
0066-7900 Ars Quatuor Coronatorum **2264**
0066-7919 Ars Suetica **467**
0066-7927 Art and Artists of the Monterey Peninsula
0066-7935 Art Bulletin of Victoria **6519**
0066-7943 Art Directors Club Milano†
0066-7951 L'Art et les Grandes Civilisations **469**
0066-796X Art Gallery of South Australia. Special Exhibitions†
0066-7978 Art in Its Context: Studies in Ethno-Aesthetics. Field Reports†
0066-7986 Art in Its Context: Studies in Ethno-Aesthetics. Museum Series†
0066-8036 Arthropods of Florida and Neighboring Land Areas **840**
0066-8044 Arthur Holmes Society. Journal **2701**
0066-8079 Universidade de Lisboa. Instituto Botanico. Artigo de Divulgacao **821**
0066-8087 Artists' Guide†
0066-8095 Arts **474**
0066-815X Arts of Mankind†
0066-8168 Arts Patronage Series†
0066-8176 Arv **3615**
0066-8184 Arvernia Biologica: Botanique **777**
0066-8192 Arznei-Telegramm **6822**
0066-8214 Handbook of Asbestos Textiles†
0066-8222 Ascidian News
0066-8230 Asia - Africa World Trade Register
0066-8249 Centro de Estudios Orientales. Anuario **4181**
0066-8265 Asia Monograph Series
0066-8281 Asian and African Studies†
0066-829X Asian and Pacific Archaeology Series†
0066-8303 Asian and Pacific Council. Cultural and Social Centre. Annual Report†
0066-8311 A S P A C Seminar on Audio-Visual Education. Proceedings†
0066-8346 Asian and Pacific Marketing Conference. Proceedings†
0066-8354 Asian Annual
0066-8362 Asian Book Trade Directory†
0066-8389 Asian Development Bank. Board of Governors. Summary of Proceedings. **1591**
0066-8397 Asian Development Bank. Occasional Papers†
0066-8419 Asian Journal of Pharmacy
0066-8435 Asian Perspectives **381**
0066-8443 Asian Philosophical Studies†
0066-8451 United Nations. Economic and Social Commission for Asia and the Pacific. Asian Population Studies Series **7294**
0066-846X A P O Annual Report **1878**
0066-8478 Asian Social Science Bibliography with Annotations and Abstracts **8019**
0066-8486 Asian Studies at Hawaii Monograph Series
0066-8524 Aslib Membership List
0066-8532 Aslib Occasional Publications†
0066-8567 Asociacion Nacional del Cafe. Departamento de Asuntos Agricolas. Informe Anual **597**
0066-8591 Asociacion Venezolana de Archiveros. Coleccion Doctrina†
0066-8613 Asociacion Venezolana de Enfermeras Profesionales. Boletin
0066-8672 Aspects of Education†
0066-8710 Associated Church Press. Directory†
0066-8729 Associated Colleges of Illinois. Report **2967**
0066-8753 Associated Public Schools Systems. Yearbook
0066-8796 Association Belge pour l'Etude, l'Essai et l'Emploi des Materiaux. Publication A.B.E.M **3341**
0066-880X Association Belge pour l'Etude, l'Essai et l'Emploi des Materiaux. Publication Groupement†
0066-8818 Association Belge pour l'Etude, l'Essai et l'Emploi des Materiaux. Proces Verbal de l'Assemblee Generale Ordinaire **3341**
0066-8842 Association Canadienne - Francaise pour l'Avancement des Sciences. Annales **7837**
0066-8893 Association des Amis d'Alfred de Vigny. Bulletin **5257**
0066-8907 Association des Amis de Pierre Teilhard de Chardin. Bulletin† **8931**
0066-8931 Association des Bibliothecaires Francais. Annuaire†
0066-894X Documents A B F†
0066-8982 I C A M Annuaire†
0066-8990 Association des Institutions d'Enseignement Secondaire. Annuaire†
0066-9016 Association des Traducteurs et Interpretes de l'Ontario. Repertoire **5097**
0066-9024 Association des Universites Partiellement ou Entierement de Langue Francaise. Cahiers†
0066-9032 Association des Universites Partiellement ou Entierement de Langue Francaise. Colloques et Congres. Comptes Rendus†
0066-9059 Association for Asian Studies. Monographs **4180**
0066-9075 Association for Childhood Education International. Yearbook†
0066-9091 Association for Computing Machinery. Proceedings of National Conference†
0066-9105 Association for Education of the Visually Handicapped. Selected Papers from A E V H Biennial Conferences†
0066-913X Association for Protection of Fur-Bearing Animals. Annual Report
0066-9172 Association for Social Anthropology in Oceania. Monograph Series **329**
0066-9210 A D B S Annuaire†
0066-9237 Association Francaise des Ingenieurs et Chefs d'Entretien. Annuaire†
0066-927X Association Francaise des Techniciens et Ingenieurs de Securite et des Medecins du Travail. Annuaire
0066-9288 Association Francaise des Experts de la Cooperation Technique Internationale. Annuaire
0066-9318 Association Nationale de la Recherche Technique. Information et Documentation†
0066-9350 Association of American Geographers. Commission on College Geography. General Series Publications†
0066-9393 Association of American Geographers. Monograph Series†
0066-9407 Association of American Law Schools. Proceedings **4622**
0066-9431 Association of American Pesticide Control Officials. Official Publication **219**
0066-944X Association of American Pesticide Control Officials. Pesticide Chemicals Official Compendium†
0066-9555 Association of Faculties of Pharmacy of Canada. Proceedings **6823**
0066-9563 Association of Graduate Schools in Association of American Universities. Journal of Proceedings and Addresses†
0066-958X Association of Japanese Geographers. Special Publication **3999**
0066-9628 Association of Pacific Coast Geographers. Yearbook **4035**
0066-9687 Association of Southeast Asian Institutions of Higher Learning. Handbook: Southeast Asian Institutions of Higher Learning **2968**
0066-9695 A S A I H L Seminar Reports **2964**
0066-9717 Association of Russian - American Scholars in the U S A. Transactions **3520**
0066-9725 Association of Universities and Colleges of Canada. Annual Meeting. Proceedings†
0066-975X Association of University Summer Sessions. Summary of Reports **2968**
0066-9776 T A Documents **5185**
0066-9784 A E T F A T Index
0066-9792 Association Scientifique de la Precontrainte. Sessions d'Etudes
0066-9806 Association Technique de l'Industrie du Gaz en France. Compte Rendu du Congres†
0066-9814 Association Technique Maritime et Aeronautique Bulletin **8639**
0066-9857 Associazione Internazionale della Stampa Medica. Bollettino Bibliografico†
0066-9865 Associazione Italiana Laringectomizzati. Atti (del) Convegno Nazionale **6078**
0066-9873 Associazione Medica Chirurgica di Tivoli e della Val d'Aniene. Atti e Memorie
0066-9903 Assyriological Studies **5097**
0066-9911 Asterisks†
0066-992X Asticou
0066-9938 Astrology and Horse Racing†
0066-9946 Astronautics Year†
0066-9970 Astronomical Ephemeris of Geocentric Places of Planets **569**
0067-0006 Astronomical Society of Victoria. Astronomical Yearbook **570**
0067-0014 Astronomische Grundlagen fuer den Kalender **570**
0067-0022 Astronomy and Astrophysics Abstracts†
0067-0030 Astrophysica Norvegica†
0067-0049 The Astrophysical Journal Supplement Series **572**
0067-0057 Astrophysics and Space Science Library **572**
0067-0065 At the Court of St. James's†
0067-0081 Scuola Archeologica di Atene e delle Missioni Italiane in Oriente. Annuario **416**
0067-0103 Centre des Sciences Sociales d'Athenes. Publications†
0067-0162 Atlantic Provinces Economic Council. Annual Report **1438**
0067-0197 Atlantic Provinces Inter-University Committee on the Sciences. Annual Report
0067-0200 Atlantic Provinces Studies†
0067-0227 Attantide Report **934**
0067-0243 Atlas Arqueologico de la Republica Mexicana†
0067-0251 Atlas de la Economia Colombiana†
0067-026X Atlas d'Attraction Urbaine.†
0067-0286 Atlas des Structures Agraires au Sud du Sahara†
0067-0294 Atlas Flory Polskiej i Ziem Osciennych **777**
0067-0308 Atlas of External Diseases of the Eye†
0067-0316 Atlas Polskich Strojow Ludowych **329**
0067-0324 Atlas Rozmieszczenia Drzew i Krzewow w Polsce†
0067-0332 Atlas Rozmieszczenia Roslin Zarodnikowych w Polsce. Seria IV. Watrobowce. Hepaticae†
0067-0340 Colorado State University. Atmospheric Science Paper†
0067-0367 A E C L Report Series **3164**
0067-0383 Atomic Energy of Canada. Annual Report
0067-0421 Auburn Forestry Forum†
0067-0480 University of Auckland Historical Society. Annual *changed to* 1176-3094 **4194**
0067-0499 University of Auckland Library. Bibliographical Bulletin†
0067-0510 Auckland University Law Review **4623**
0067-057X Augustana Library Publications **4443**
0067-0588 Augustana Historical Society, Rock Island, Illinois. Publications **4132**
0067-0618 Aus dem Schweizerischen Landesmuseum†
0067-0642 Aus Forschung und Kunst **477**
0067-0650 Ausgewaehlte Quellen zur Deutschen Geschichte des Mittelalters **4201**
0067-0669 Auslaendische Aktiengesetze **4623**
0067-0685 Ausruestung in Luft- und Raumfahrt†
0067-0707 University of Texas, Austin. Center for Neo-Hellenic Studies. Bulletin†
0067-0715 Australasian Corrosion Directory†
0067-0731 Australia. Bureau of Statistics. Banking and Currency Bulletin†
0067-074X Australia. Bureau of Statistics. Building and Construction Bulletin†
0067-0758 Australia. Bureau of Statistics. Commonwealth Finance†
0067-0774 Australia. Bureau of Statistics. Commonwealth Taxation Assessment Bulletin†
0067-0782 Australia. Bureau of Statistics. Demography (Population and Vital) Bulletin†
0067-0790 Australia. Bureau of Statistics. Insurance and Other Private Finance Bulletin†
0067-0804 Australia. Bureau of Statistics. Imports Cleared for Home Consumption, Australia†
0067-0820 Australia. Bureau of Statistics. Manufacturing Commodities Bulletin†
0067-0839 Australia. Bureau of Statistics. Manufacturing Industry Bulletin†
0067-0847 Australia. Bureau of Statistics. Non-Rural Primary Industries†
0067-0871 Australia. Bureau of Statistics. Rural Industries Bulletin†
0067-0936 Australia. Bureau of Statistics. South Australian Office. General Insurance†
0067-0979 Australia. Bureau of Statistics. South Australian Office. Projections of Population†
0067-0987 Australia. Bureau of Statistics. South Australian Office. Agriculture: General Summary-South Australia†
0067-1002 Australia. Bureau of Statistics. Transport and Communication Bulletin†
0067-1126 Australia. Bureau of Statistics. Victorian Office. Hospital Morbidity†
0067-1169 Australia. Bureau of Statistics. Value of Production Bulletin†
0067-1193 Australia. Bureau of Statistics. Victorian Office. Tertiary Education†
0067-1223 Australia. Bureau of Statistics. Victorian Office. Victorian Year Book† **8933**
0067-1282 Australia. Bureau of Statistics. Western Australian Office. Local Government Revenue and Expenditure: Budget Estimates†
0067-1290 Australia. Bureau of Statistics. Western Australian Office. Population, Dwellings and Vital Statistics†
0067-1312 Australia. Bureau of Meteorology. Bulletin†
0067-1320 Australia. Bureau of Meteorology. Meteorological Study†
0067-1339 Australia. Bureau of Mineral Resources, Geology and Geophysics. Pictorial Index of Activities†
0067-1355 Australia. Department of Education. A.C.T. Education Directory†
0067-1436 Operation of the Fishing Industry Act Annual Report†
0067-1444 Australia. Department of the Treasury. Income Tax Statistics†
0067-1495 Australia Handbook†
0067-1517 Australia. National Capital Development Commission. Annual Report†
0067-1584 Australian Academy of Science. Yearbook†
0067-1592 Australian Academy of the Humanities. Proceedings **4444**
0067-1630 Australian Association of Adult Education. Monograph†
0067-1649 Australian Association of Adult Education. Proceedings of the National Conference†
0067-172X Australian Books in Print† **8933**
0067-1738 Australian Books†
0067-1762 Australian Coal Industry Research Laboratories. Annual Report
0067-1819 Australian Computer Society. Council. Report†
0067-1835 Australian Council for Educational Research. Occasional Papers†
0067-1843 Australian Digest **4623**
0067-1878 Australian Government Publications†
0067-1894 Australian Honey Board. Annual Report†
0067-1924 Australian Journal of Botany **777**
0067-1959 Australian Market Guide† **8933**
0067-1975 Australian Museum. Records **934**
0067-2017 Australian National University, Canberra. Department of International Relations. Documents and Data Paper†
0067-2025 Australian National University, Canberra. Department of International Relations. Workpaper†
0067-2041 Australian National University, Canberra. Faculty of Asian Studies. Occasional Papers†
0067-205X Federal Law Review **4951**
0067-2165 Australian Studies in Health Service Administration† **8933**
0067-2181 Australian Telecommunication Monographs†
0067-219X Australia. Australian Water Resources Council. Hydrological Series†
0067-2238 Australian Zoologist **935**
0067-2246 Australiana Facsimile Editions†
0067-2254 Austria. Bundeskammer fuer die Gewerbliche Wirtschaft
0067-2289 Austria. Bundesministerium fuer Unterricht und Kunst. Jahresbericht†
0067-2297 Oesterreichisches Staatsarchiv. Mitteilungen **4251**
0067-2319 Beitraege zur Oesterreichischen Statistik **8357**
0067-2343 Oesterreichische Hochschulstatistik **2935**
0067-2351 Austria. Zentralanstalt fuer Meteorologie und Geodynamik. Jahrbuch **6347**
0067-236X Austrian Historical Bibliography
0067-2378 Austrian History Yearbook **4202**
0067-2394 Auto Auction
0067-2408 Auto Racing Guide†
0067-2416 Auto-Universum†
0067-2424 Autocatalogue†
0067-2432 Autocourse **8160**
0067-2483 A P I C Studies in Data Processing **2505**
0067-2521 Automobile Buyers' Guide†
0067-2548 Automobile News Annual
0067-2610 Avant-Siecle
0067-2629 Aventure des Civilisations†
0067-2637 Aves del Arca **5259**
0067-2645 Aviation Directory of Asia†
0067-2653 Aviation et Astronautique†
0067-2661 Aviation Medical Education Series
0067-270X Azania **4173**
0067-2734 B B A Library†

Link to your serials resources and content with ulrichsweb.com

0067-2742 B.G. Rudolph Lectures in Judaic Studies **7718**
0067-2793 Badania z Dziejow Spolecznych i Gospodarczych†
0067-2807 Badania Fizjograficzne nad Polska Zachodnia. Seria A. Geografia Fizyczna **4000**
0067-2815 Badania Fizjograficzne nad Polska Zachodnia. Seria B. Botanika **778**
0067-2823 Badania nad Dziejami Przemyslu i Klasy Robotniczej w Polsce†
0067-2831 Kommission fuer geschichtliche Landeskunde in Baden-Wuerttemberg. Veroeffentlichungen. Reihe A. Quellen **4238**
0067-284X Staatliche Kunstsammlungen in Baden-Wuerttemberg. Jahrbuch **6537**
0067-2858 Badischer Landesverein fuer Naturkunde und Naturschutz, Freiburg. Mitteilungen. Neue Folge **655**
0067-2866 Badlands Natural History Association. Bulletin†
0067-2874 Badman†
0067-2904 Iraqi Journal of Science
0067-2912 Bahamas Handbook and Businessman's Annual **1440**
0067-2947 Baily's Hunting Directory **1974**
0067-2955 Baja California Travels Series†
0067-2963 Baker and Bakery Management Handbook and Buyers Guide†
0067-298X Balance of Payments of Japan†
0067-3005 Balance of Payments of Trinidad and Tobago **1212**
0067-3064 Baltica **2726**
0067-3072 Baltimore College of Dental Surgery, Journal†
0067-3080 Baltimore Museum of Art. Annual†
0067-3099 Baltische Studien **4203**
0067-3102 Baltisches Recht; das Recht Estlands, Lettlands und Litauens in Vergangenheit und Gegenwart†
0067-3110 Chambre de Commerce et d'Industrie du Mali. Precis Fiscal, Commercial, des Changes et des Echanges
0067-3129 Bampton Lectures in America **7624**
0067-320X Banco Central de Costa Rica. Memoria Anual
0067-3226 Banco Central de Nicaragua. Informe Anual
0067-3250 Banco Central de Venezuela. Informe Economico **1440**
0067-3285 Banco Central del Paraguay. Memoria **1311**
0067-3315 Banco de Espana. Informe Anual **1311**
0067-3323 Banco de la Republica Cuentas Nacionales†
0067-3331 Banco de la Republica Disposiciones†
0067-334X Guia para el Inversionista.†
0067-3366 Banco de la Republica Series Estadisticas y Graficos.†
0067-3412 Bancroftiana **4993**
0067-3439 Indian Statistical Institute. Documentation Research and Training Centre. D R T C Annual Seminar **5015**
0067-3455 University of Agricultural Sciences, Bangalore. Annual Report **165**
0067-3463 University of Agricultural Sciences, Bangalore. Research Series†
0067-3471 U A S Extension Series **163**
0067-348X U A S Miscellaneous Series **163**
0067-3498 Bangkok, Thailand. College of Education. Thesis Abstract Series
0067-3501 Bank Administration Institute. Accounting Bulletins†
0067-351X Bank Administration Institute. Annual Report†
0067-3544 Bank Administration Institute. Security Bulletins†
0067-3579 Bank Leumi le-Israel. Report and Accounts
0067-3587 Bank of Canada. Governor to the Minister of Finance and Statement of Accounts. Annual Report **1313**
0067-3641 Bank of Israel. Main Points of the Annual Report†
0067-365X Bank of Israel. Annual Report **1314**
0067-3668 Bank of Jamaica. Report and Statement of Accounts **1314**
0067-3684 Bank of Japan. Business Report†
0067-3692 Bank of Japan. Special Paper†
0067-3706 Bank of Korea. Annual Report **1315**
0067-3714 Bank of Libya. Annual Report of the Board of Directors
0067-3722 Bank of Mauritius. Annual Report **1315**
0067-3749 Bank of Sudan. Report **1315**
0067-3757 Bank of Tanzania. Economic and Operations Report (Year) **1441**
0067-3803 Bankers' Who's Who
0067-3811 Banking Statistics of Pakistan **1318**
0067-3838 Bankwirtschaftliche Studien
0067-3854 Banque Centrale de Tunisie. Bulletin **1319**
0067-3862 Banque Centrale de Tunisie. Rapport d'Activite **1319**
0067-3889 Banque Centrale des Etats de l'Afrique de l'Ouest. Rapport Annuel **1319**
0067-3897 Banque Centrale des Etats de l'Afrique de l'Ouest. Rapport d'Activite. **1319**
0067-3900 Banque des Etats de l'Afrique Centrale. Rapport d'Activite **1320**
0067-3951 Banque des Mots **4994**
0067-4028 Banque Populaire Suisse. Information **1320**
0067-4060 Baptist Missionary Society, Didcot. Annual Report **7747**
0067-4079 Baptist Missionary Society. Directory and Financial Report **7747**
0067-4087 Baptist Union of Western Canada. Yearbook **7747**
0067-4095 Baptist World Alliance. Congress Reports **7748**
0067-4109 Bar-Ilan: Annual of Bar-Ilan University **7719**
0067-4125 Barbados. Statistical Service. Overseas Trade Report†
0067-4168 Patronato Municipal de la Vivienda de Barcelona. Memoria
0067-4176 Universidad de Barcelona. Facultad de Farmacia. Memoria†
0067-4184 Universidad de Barcelona. Instituto de Arqueologia y Prehistoria. Publicaciones Eventuales **421**
0067-4222 Baroque†
0067-4230 Barque's Pakistan Trade Directory and Who's Who
0067-4249 Barsoomian†
0067-4273 Baseball Guide†
0067-4303 Gewerbemuseum Basel. Schriften†
0067-4338 Basic Auto Repair Manual†
0067-4362 Basic Bodywork and Painting†
0067-4370 Basic Cams, Valves and Exhaust Systems†
0067-4389 Basic Carburetion and Fuel Systems†
0067-4397 Basic Chassis, Suspension and Brakes†
0067-4400 Basic Clutches and Transmissions†
0067-4419 Basic Facts about the United Nations **7223**
0067-4427 Basic Ignition and Electrical Systems†
0067-4443 Basic Science Symposium Series†
0067-446X Basis†
0067-4478 Basler Beitraege zur Ethnologie **330**
0067-4486 Basler Beitraege zur Geographie **4000**
0067-4494 Basler Drucke†
0067-4508 Basler Studien zur Deutschen Sprache und Literatur **5260**
0067-4532 Basler Wirtschaftswissenschaftliche Vortraege†
0067-4540 Basler Zeitschrift fuer Geschichte und Altertumskunde **4203**
0067-4575 Bau und Baustoff Handbuch†
0067-4583 Baubeschlag-Taschenbuch **1053**
0067-4591 Bauernhaeuser der Schweiz **3615**
0067-4605 Bauhinia **778**
0067-463X Bausteine zur Sprachgeschichte des Neuhochdeutschen†
0067-4648 Instituto Nacional de la Pesca de Cuba. Centro de Investigaciones Pesqueras. Boletin de Divulgacion Tecnica†
0067-4672 Bayer-Symposien†
0067-4702 Bayerisches Beamten-Jahrbuch (Year)
0067-4710 Bayerisches Forstdienst-Taschenbuch **3684**
0067-4729 Bayerisches Jahrbuch fuer Volkskunde **3615**
0067-4745 Beaufortia Bulletin Zoological Museum†
0067-4826 Bedfordshire Historical Record Society. Publications **4203**
0067-4834 Bedrijfschap voor de Lederwarenindustrie. Jaarverslag†
0067-4893 Beihefte der Bonner Jahrbuecher **383**
0067-4907 Sonderbaende zur Theologischen Zeitschrift **7682**
0067-4915 Beilsteins Handbuch der Organischen Chemie. Supplement† **8935**
0067-494X Beitraege aus der Allgemeinen Medizin
0067-4966 Beitraege zum Rundfunkrecht **2375**
0067-4974 Technische Beitraege zur Archaeologie†
0067-5008 Beitraege zur Geologie von Thueringen†
0067-5016 Beitraege zur Gerichtlichen Medizin
0067-5024 Beitraege zur Geschichte der Philosophie und Theologie des Mittelalters. Neue Folge **6907**
0067-5040 Geschichte des Buchwesens. Beitraege†
0067-5059 Beitraege zur Geschichte des Religioesen und Wissenschaftlichen Denkens†
0067-5067 Beitraege zur Harmonikalen Grundlagenforschung **6548**
0067-5075 Beitraege zur Heilpaedagogik und Heilpaedagogischen Psychologie†
0067-5083 Beitraege zur Hygiene und Epidemiologie†
0067-5091 Beitraege zur Inkunabelkunde. Dritte Folge†
0067-5105 Beitraege zur Kinderpsychotherapie **2145**
0067-5113 Krebsforschung. Beitraege†
0067-5121 Beitraege zur Kunst des Christlichen Ostens **478**
0067-5148 Beitraege zur Meereskunde†
0067-5156 Beitraege zur Neurochirurgie†
0067-5164 Beitraege zur Oberpfalzforschung†
0067-5172 Beitraege zur Oekumenischen Theologie **7785**
0067-5180 Beitraege zur Praktischen Medizin†
0067-5199 Beitraege zur Rheumatologie
0067-5202 Beitraege zur Romanischen Philologie des Mittelalters†
0067-5210 Beitraege zur Sexualforschung **7340**
0067-5229 Beitraege zur Silikose-Forschung. Pneumokoniose†
0067-5237 Beitraege zur Strafvollzugswissenschaft†
0067-5245 Beitraege zur Ur- und Fruehgeschichtlichen Archaeologie des Mittelmeerkulturraumes **383**
0067-5261 Beitraege zur Westfaelischen Familienforschung **3760**
0067-527X Brazil. Instituto de Pesquisas Agropecuarias do Norte. Boletim Tecnico†
0067-5288 Instituto de Pesquisas Agropecuarias do Norte. Circular†
0067-5296 Instituto de Pesquisas Agropecuarias do Norte. Comunicado Tecnico†
0067-5342 Belfast and Northern Ireland Directory
0067-5350 Belfast History and Philosophical Society. Proceedings and Reports
0067-5385 Belgium. Conseil National du Travail. Rapport du Secretaire sur l'Activite du Conseil†
0067-5393 Belgium. Conseil Superieur des Classes Moyennes. Rapport Annuel **1957**
0067-5407 Belgium. Fonds voor Wetenschappelijk Onderzoek - Vlaanderen. Jaarverslag (Print Edition) *changed to* Belgium. Fonds voor Wetenschappelijk Onderzoek - Vlaanderen. Jaarverslag (Online Edition) **7840**
0067-5466 Belgium. Institut National de Statistique. Statistiques Agricoles *changed to* 1379-4752 **175**
0067-5490 Belgium. Institut National de Statistique. Statistiques Demographiques *changed to* 1379-4051 **7303**
0067-5547 Belgium. Institut National de Statistique. Statistique du Tourisme et de l'Hotellerie **8778**
0067-5563 Belgium. Institut National de Statistique. Statistiques Sociales **8081**
0067-5601 Bibliotheque Africaine. Catalogue des Acquisitions. Catologus van de Aanwinsten†
0067-561X Belgium. Office Belge du Commerce Exterieur. Bijvoegsel B B H. Reeks B
0067-5628 I C E Supplement. Serie C
0067-5652 Societe National du Logement. Rapport Annuel†
0067-5660 Vojni Muzej Beograd. Vesnik **6453**
0067-5687 Universidade Federal de Minas Gerais. Instituto de Pesquisas Radioativas. Relatorios Anuais†
0067-5695 Beloit Poetry Journal. Chapbook **5417**
0067-5709 B E M A Engineering Directory **3182**
0067-5717 Benjamin F. Fairless Lectures **7109**
0067-5733 Bent†
0067-5768 Berg- und Huettenmaennische Monatshefte. Supplement†
0067-5792 Bergischer Geschichtsverein. Zeitschrift **4204**
0067-5806 Berichte des Vereins Natur und Heimat und des Naturhistorischen Museums zu Luebeck **7840**
0067-5822 Berkeley Analyses of Molecular Spectra†
0067-5830 Berkeley Journal of Sociology **8090**
0067-5849 Biologische Bundesanstalt fuer Land- und Forstwirtschaft, Berlin-Dahlem. Mitteilungen *changed to* 1867-1268 **129**
0067-5857 Historische Kommission zu Berlin. Einzelveroeffentlichungen
0067-5881 Freie Universitaet Berlin. Osteuropa-Institut. Bibliographische Mitteilungen **4170**
0067-589X Freie Universitaet Berlin. Osteuropa-Institut. Erziehungswissenschaftliche Veroeffentlichungen **7137**
0067-5903 Freie Universitaet Berlin. Osteuropa-Institut. Historische Veroeffentlichungen **4221**
0067-5911 Freie Universitaet Berlin. Osteuropa-Institut. Philosophische und Soziologische Veroeffentlichungen **6921**
0067-592X Freie Universitaet Berlin. Osteuropa-Institut. Slavistische Veroeffentlichungen **5298**
0067-5938 Freie Universitaet Berlin. Osteuropa-Institut. Wirtschaftswissenschaftliche Veroeffentlichungen **1112**
0067-5954 Hochschule fuer Oekonomie "Bruno Leuschner" Berlin. Wissenschaftliche Zeitschrift†
0067-5962 Museum fuer Voelkerkunde, Berlin. Veroeffentlichungen. Neue Folge. Abteilung: Afrika **349**
0067-5989 Museum fuer Voelkerkunde, Berlin. Veroeffentlichungen. Neue Folge. Abteilung: Suedsee **349**
0067-6004 Staatliche Museen zu Berlin. Jahrbuch. Forschungen und Berichte†
0067-6047 Berlin, Theater und Drama†
0067-6055 Berliner Byzantinistische Arbeiten
0067-6071 Historische Kommission zu Berlin. Veroeffentlichungen†
0067-6098 Berliner Tierpark-Buch **936**
0067-611X Berlinische Reminiszenzen **4204**
0067-6128 Berner Beitraege zur Nationaloekonomie **1066**
0067-6136 Berner Beitraege zur Soziologie†
0067-6144 Berner Kriminologische Untersuchungen†
0067-6152 Berner Studien zum Fremdenverkehr†
0067-6179 Bernice Pauahi Bishop Museum, Honolulu. Special Publications **7840**
0067-6195 Berytus Archeological Studies **383**
0067-6209 Besonders Wertvoll. Kurzfilme **6490**
0067-6217 Besonders Wertvoll. Langfilme **6490**
0067-6233 Best American Short Stories **5262**
0067-6276 Borestone Mountain Poetry Awards†
0067-6292 Best Sports Stories†
0067-6306 Bestands-Statistik der Kraftfahrzeuge in Oesterreich
0067-6314 Bestimmungsbuecher zur Bodenfauna Europas†
0067-6330 Bestsellers du Monde Entier†
0067-6349 Bestuurlike Informasie†
0067-6357 Beta Phi Mu Chapbook†
0067-6365 Beton- und Fertigteil-Jahrbuch **3260**
0067-6381 Schriftenreihe Betriebswirtschaftliche Beitraege zur Organisation und Automation†
0067-642X Better Building Bulletin†
0067-6454 Bharat Krishak Samaj. Year Book†
0067-6462 Basic Road Statistics of India **8522**
0067-6470 Bialostockie Towarzystwo Naukowe. Prace **4204**
0067-6489 Akademia Medyczna w Bialymstoku. Roczniki *changed to* 1896-1126 **5568**
0067-6535 Biblical Research **7627**
0067-6543 Bibliografi over Danmarks Offentlige Publikationer†
0067-6551 Bibliografia Analitica a Periodicelor Romanesti†
0067-656X Bibliografia Bibliotecologica Argentina **5057**
0067-6586 Bibliografia Brasileira de Botanica†
0067-6608 Bibliografia Brasileira de Ciencias Sociais†
0067-6616 Bibliografia Brasileira de Direito†
0067-6624 Bibliografia Brasileira de Documentacao†
0067-6632 Bibliografia Brasileira de Educacao†
0067-6640 Bibliografia Brasileira de Fisica†
0067-6659 Bibliografia Brasileira de Livros Infantis†
0067-6667 Bibliografia Brasileira de Matematica†
0067-6675 Bibliografia Brasileira de Medicina†
0067-6691 Bibliografia Brasileira de Zoologia†
0067-6705 Bibliografia Cubana **616**
0067-6721 Bibliografia Historii Polskiej **4169**
0067-6748 Bibliografia Oficial Colombiana†
0067-6764 Bibliografia Sobre a Economia Portuguesa†
0067-6772 Bibliografia Ticinese†
0067-6780 Bibliograficky Zbornik†
0067-6799 Bibliografija Medicinske Periodike Jugoslavije†
0067-6802 Bibliographia Medica Cechoslovaca (Print Edition) *changed to* 1212-3854 **5741**
0067-6829 Bibliographia Scientiae Naturalis Helvetica **7936**
0067-6837 Bibliographic Annual in Speech Communication†
0067-6853 Bibliographica Judaica **7698**
0067-687X Bibliographical Society of Canada. Facsimile Series†
0067-6888 Bibliographical Society of Canada. Monographs†
0067-6896 Bibliographical Society of Canada. Papers **618**
0067-690X Bibliographie Americaniste†
0067-6918 Bibliographie Annuelle de l'Histoire de France **4169**
0067-6926 Bibliographie Annuelle de Madagascar **618**
0067-6934 Bibliographie Cartographique Internationale†
0067-6942 Bibliographie de la Litterature Francaise du Moyen Age a Nos Jours†
0067-6950 Bibliographie der Chemisch-Archaeologischen Literatur†
0067-6969 Bibliographie der Paedagogischen Veroeffentlichungen in der Deutschen Demokratischen Republik†
0067-6977 Bibliographie der Sozialethik†
0067-6985 Bibliographie en Langue Francaise d'Histoire du Droit de 987 a 1940 **4821**
0067-7000 Bibliographie Internationale de l'Humanisme et de la Renaissance **4484**
0067-7043 Bibliographie d'Histoire Luxembourgeoise **4169**
0067-706X Bibliographie zur Symbolik, Ikonographie und Mythologie **361**
0067-7094 Bibliographies in Paint Technology†
0067-7116 Bibliographies on the Near East†
0067-7132 Bibliography and Reference Series†
0067-7159 Bibliography of Asian Studies (Print Edition)†
0067-7175 Bibliography of Canadian Bibliographies†
0067-7183 Bibliography of Developmental Medicine and Child Neurology. Books and Articles Received†
0067-7191 Bibliography of Historical Works Issued in the United Kingdom†
0067-7205 Bibliography of Interlingual Scientific and Technical Dictionaries†
0067-7213 Bibliography of Old Norse-Icelandic Studies†
0067-7256 Bibliography of South African Government Publications†
0067-7264 Bibliography of Surgery of the Hand†

ISSN

9092 0067-7272 ULRICH'S PERIODICALS

0067-7272 Bibliography of the Geology of Missouri **2719**
0067-7280 Bibliography of the History of Medicine **5741**
0067-7302 Bibliography of the Middle East
0067-7310 Bibliography of Works by Polish Scholars and Scientists Published Outside Poland in Languages Other Than Polish†
0067-7361 Bibliography on Smoking and Health†
0067-737X Bibliografichnyi Pokazhchyk Ukrains'koi Presy Poza Mezhamy Ukrainy†
0067-7388 Biblioteca de Arheologie **384**
0067-7396 Biblioteca de Cultura Vasca†
0067-740X Biblioteca de Teologia **7627**
0067-7418 Biblioteca di Bibliografia Italiana **619**
0067-7434 Biblioteca di Labeo **4445**
0067-7442 Biblioteca di Storia Toscana Moderna e Contemporanea. Studi e Documenti
0067-7450 Biblioteca di Studi Etruschi **5100**
0067-7469 Biblioteca do Educador Profissional **4445**
0067-7477 Bibliotheca Germanica **5100**
0067-7493 Biblioteca Istorica **4204**
0067-7507 Biblioteca Prehistorica Hispana†
0067-7515 Bibliotheca Romanica **5100**
0067-7531 Biblioteconomia e Bibliografia. Saggi e Studi
0067-754X Biblioteczka Ateisty†
0067-7558 Biblioteczka Kopernikanska†
0067-7566 Biblioteczka Matematyczna
0067-7582 Biblioteczka Wiedzy O Slasku. Seria Archeologiczna†
0067-7590 Biblioteczka Wiedzy O Slasku. Seria Etnograficzna†
0067-7604 Biblioteczka Wiedzy O Slasku. Seria Historyczna†
0067-7612 Biblioteczka Wiedzy O Slasku. Seria Literatura Ludowa†
0067-7620 Biblioteczka Wiedzy O Slasku. Seria Przyrodnicza†
0067-7639 Biblioteka Archeologiczna†
0067-7655 Biblioteka Etnografii Polskiej **330**
0067-7671 Biblioteka Klasykow Pedagogiki†
0067-7698 Biblioteka Krakowska **478**
0067-7701 Biblioteka Mechaniki Stosowanej **3342**
0067-7728 Biblioteka Nawigatora†
0067-7744 Biblioteka "Polonistyki"
0067-7760 Biblioteka Popularnonaukowa†
0067-7779 Biblioteka Sluchacza Koncertowego. Seria Wprowadzajaca†
0067-7787 Towarzystwo Literackie im. A. Mickiewicza. Biblioteka **5389**
0067-7809 Biblioteka Zagadnien Gospodarczych Polski†
0067-7817 Bibliotheca Aegyptiaca **384**
0067-7825 Bibliotheca Africana Droz†
0067-7841 Bibliotheca Arnamagnaeana† **8936**
0067-785X Bibliotheca Arnamagnaeana. Supplementum† **8936**
0067-7868 Bibliotheca Athena
0067-7876 Bibliotheca Australiana†
0067-7884 Bibliotheca Bibliographica Aureliana **619**
0067-7892 Bibliotheca Botanica **779**
0067-7906 Bibliotheca Cardiologica†
0067-7922 Biblioteca del Planeamiento Educativo
0067-7930 Bibliotheca Emblematica†
0067-7965 Bibliotheca Helvetica Romana **2231**
0067-7981 Bibliotheca Historica Romaniae. Studies **4205**
0067-799X Bibliotheca Historica Romaniae. Monographies **4204**
0067-8007 Bibliotheca Hungarica Antiqua **7553**
0067-8015 Bibliotheca Ibero-Americana **7199**
0067-8023 Bibliotheca Indonesica **330**
0067-8031 Bibliotheca Latina Medii et Recentioris Aevi **2231**
0067-8066 Bibliotheca Mycologica **779**
0067-8082 Bibliotheca Oeconomica **1067**
0067-8104 Bibliotheca Orientalis Hungarica **545**
0067-8112 Bibliotheca Phycologica **779**
0067-8120 Bibliotheca Phonetica†
0067-8147 Bibliotheca Psychiatrica *changed to* 1662-4874 **6157**
0067-8155 Bibliotheca Radiologica†
0067-8163 Bibliotheca Seraphico-Capuccina. Sectio Historica **7786**
0067-8201 Bibliothek der Klassischen Altertumswissenschaften. Neue Folge **4133**
0067-821X Bilder aus Deutscher Vergangenheit†
0067-8228 Bibliothek fuer das Gesamtgebiet der Lungenkrankheiten†
0067-8236 Bibliothek und Wissenschaft **4996**
0067-8244 Bibliotheque Arctique et Antarctique†
0067-8260 Bibliotheque de la Mer **8218**
0067-8279 Bibliotheque de la Revue d'Histoire Ecclesiastique **7786**
0067-8295 Bibliotheque de Sciences Religieuses†
0067-8325 Bibliotheque d'Etudes Balkaniques **5100**
0067-8333 Bibliotheque Europeenne†
0067-8341 Bibliotheque Francaise et Romane. Serie A: Manuels et Etudes Linguistiques **5100**
0067-835X Bibliotheque Francaise et Romane. Serie B: Editions Critiques de Textes **5263**
0067-8368 Bibliotheque Francaise et Romane. Serie C: Etudes Litteraires **5263**
0067-8376 Bibliotheque Francaise et Romane. Serie D: Initiation, Textes et Documents **5263**
0067-8384 Bibliotheque Francaise et Romane. Serie E: Langue et Litterature Francaises au Canada **5100**
0067-8406 Bibliotheque Historique Vaudoise
0067-8414 Bibliotheque Ideale†
0067-8422 Bibliotheque Introuvable
0067-8430 Bibliotheque Philosophique de Louvain **6907**
0067-8457 Bibliotheque Rencontre des Lettres Anciennes et Modernes†
0067-8473 Bidrag til H.C. Andersens Bibliografi†
0067-8481 Bidrag till Kaennedom av Finlands Natur och Folk **7950**
0067-8538 Bijdragen tot de Bibliotheekwetenschap†
0067-8554 Bijdragen tot de Geschiedenis van Arnhem†
0067-8562 Bilateral Studies in Private International Law†
0067-8570 Bild des Menschen in der Wissenschaft†
0067-8589 Bildungsplanung in Oesterreich†
0067-8643 Die Binnengewaesser **2793**
0067-8651 Binsted's Directory of Food Trade Marks and Brand Names **3628**
0067-866X Bio-Information
0067-8678 Biochemistry of Disease†
0067-8686 Biochemical Preparations†
0067-8694 Biochemical Society Symposia **724**
0067-8716 Nihon Seibutsu Chiri Gakkai Kaiho **694**
0067-8724 Biograficke Studie **640**
0067-8732 Biographical Encyclopedia of Pakistan†
0067-8740 Biographies de Personnalites Francaises Vivantes†
0067-8767 Biologia Pesquera **3587**
0067-8775 Biological Macromolecules Series†
0067-8783 B S C S Bulletin Series†
0067-8791 B S C S Special Publication†
0067-8821 Biomathematics†
0067-8856 Biomedical Sciences Instrumentation (Print) *changed to* 1938-1158 **5586**
0067-8864 Biomembranes†
0067-8872 Biometeorological Research Centre. Monograph Series
0067-8880 Biometeorological Research Centre. Special Monograph Series
0067-8899 Verzeichnis Lieferbarer Buecher **638**
0067-8902 Biometeorology†
0067-8929 Biophysics Series†
0067-8945 Bird Control Seminar. Proceedings†
0067-8953 University of Birmingham. Centre for Urban and Regional Studies. Occasional Papers **4429**
0067-8961 University of Birmingham. Centre for Urban and Regional Studies. Urban and Regional Studies **4429**
0067-8996 Biuletyn Fonograficzny†
0067-9003 Uniwersytet Warszawski. Wydzial Geologii. Biuletyn Geologiczny†
0067-902X Biuletyn Polonistyczny **5100**
0067-9038 Biuletyn Peryglacjalny **2778**
0067-9070 Black Experience in Children's Books **2173**
0067-9100 Black Orpheus **5264**
0067-9119 Black Review†
0067-9127 Blaetter fuer Technikgeschichte†
0067-9178 Blick hinter die Fassade
0067-9186 Association for Education and Rehabilitation of the Blind and Visually Impaired. Yearbook†
0067-9208 Nasionale Museum, Bloemfontein. Navorsinge **691**
0067-9216 University of the Orange Free State. Opsommings van Proefskrifte en Verhandelinge. Abstracts of Dissertations and Theses†
0067-9224 Bloodstock Breeders' Review **8288**
0067-9232 Bloomsbury Geographer† **8937**
0067-9240 Blue Book: Leaders of the English-Speaking World†
0067-9267 Blue Book of Europe; European Export Directory
0067-9283 Blue Book of Optometrists **6039**
0067-933X Boat World†
0067-9356 Boating Almanac, Volume 1: Massachusetts, Maine, New Hampshire **8273**
0067-9399 Boating Guide†
0067-9437 Stadt Bochum. Amt fuer Statistik und Stadtforschung. Statistisches Jahrbuch **7483**
0067-9453 Bochumer Universitaetsreden†
0067-947X Bydgoskie Towarzystwo Naukowe. Wydzial Nauk Humanistycznych. Prace. Seria D (Sztuka) **480**
0067-9488 Bodleian Library Record **4997**
0067-9496 Boersen- und Wirtschaftshandbuch†
0067-9518 Colombia. Observatorio Astronomico Nacional. Publicaciones **573**
0067-9526 Universidad Nacional de Colombia. Centro de Estudios Folkloriques. Anuario†
0067-9534 Universidad Nacional de Colombia. Centro de Estudios Folkloricos. Monografias **3623**
0067-9542 Bois-Chantiers†
0067-9585 Boletim Climatologico **6347**
0067-9593 Boletim de Ciencias do Mar†
0067-9607 Boletim de Engenharia de Producao†
0067-9615 Boletim de Industria Animal **281**
0067-9631 Boletim Oficial de Angola
0067-964X Boletim Paranaense de Geociencias†
0067-9674 Boletin de Filologia†
0067-9690 Boletin de Literatura Argentina e Iberoamericana†
0067-9720 Boletin Genetico **864**
0067-9747 Boletin Hidrologico **2793**
0067-981X Bolivia Information Handbook†
0067-9836 Bolivia. Servicio Geologico. Circular†
0067-9844 Bolivia. Servicio Geologico. Informe†
0067-9852 Bolivia. Servicio Geologico. Serie Mineralogica. Contribuciones†
0067-9860 B R A D S†
0067-9879 Bollettino dell'Atlante Linguistico Mediterraneo **5101**
0067-9887 Universita degli Studi di Bologna. Osservatorio Astronomico. Notizie e Rassegne†
0067-9895 Universita degli Studi di Bologna. Osservatorio Astronomico. Pubblicazioni†
0067-9909 Bolsilibros **5265**
0067-9917 Bombay Labour Journal†
0067-9925 Bombay Technologist **2051**
0067-995X Institut "Finanzen und Steuern." Schriftenreihe **1929**
0067-9968 Rheinisches Landesmuseum Bonn. Schriften†
0068-001X Bonner Arbeiten zur Deutschen Literatur†
0068-0028 Bonner Beitraege zur Bibliotheks- und Buecherkunde†
0068-0036 Bonner Beitraege zur Kunstwissenschaft **479**
0068-0044 Bonner Beitraege zur Soziologie†
0068-0052 Bonner Geschichtsblaetter **4206**
0068-0087 Station Biologique de Bonnevaux (Doubs). Section de Biologie et d'Ecologie Animales. Publications†
0068-0095 Book Auction Records†
0068-0117 Book of Bantams **281**
0068-0125 The Book of the States **7110**
0068-0133 Bookman's Guide to Americana **7555**
0068-0141 Bookman's Price Index **7555**
0068-0168 Books about Canada†
0068-0176 Books about Singapore **8778**
0068-0184 Books for Secondary School Libraries
0068-0192 Books for the Teen Age **5057**
0068-0206 Books from Pakistan **620**
0068-0214 Books in Print **620**
0068-0222 Books of the Theatre Series†
0068-0257 Booksellers Association of Great Britain and Ireland. Trade Reference Book†
0068-0265 Bord Iascaigh Mhara. Annual Report and Accounts **3587**
0068-0273 Universite de Bordeaux. Collection Sinologique†
0068-0338 Boston College. Bureau of Public Affairs. Community Analysis and Action Series. Monograph†
0068-0346 Boston Studies in the Philosophy of Science **7841**
0068-0354 Bostwick Paper
0068-0370 Botanica Gothoburgensia **780**
0068-0427 Botanische Studien†
0068-0443 Botschaft des Alten Testaments†
0068-0451 Botswana. Annual Statements of Accounts **1913**
0068-046X Botswana. Commissioner of the Police. Annual Report **2645**
0068-0478 Botswana. Ministry of Agriculture. Annual Report **97**
0068-0486 Botswana. Forest Department. Report
0068-0494 Bottin International†
0068-0508 Bottlers Year Book
0068-0524 Boundary Historical Society. Report
0068-0532 Boutique†
0068-0540 The Bowker Annual Library and Book Trade Almanac (Year) *changed to* Library and Book Trade Almanac (Year) **5026**
0068-0559 Bowling and Billiard Buyers Guide **8224**
0068-0567 Bowling Guide†
0068-0605 Boys' Brigade. Annual Report **2180**
0068-0613 Svenska Riksbyggen. Byggteknisk Information†
0068-0672 Brandeis University. Society of Bibliophiles. Publications
0068-0710 Brauereien und Maelzereien in Europa **600**
0068-0737 Braunschweigische Wissenschaftliche Gesellschaft. Abhandlungen **7841**
0068-0761 Technion-Israel Institute of Technology. Braverman Memorial Lecture†
0068-080X Brazil. Instituto Nacional de Estudos e Pesquisas Educacionais. Conferencia Nacional de Educacao. Anais†
0068-0850 Brazil. Servico de Piscicultura. Publicacao
0068-0877 Breifne **4206**
0068-0907 Bremer Archaeologische Blaetter **384**
0068-0915 Institut fuer Meeresforschung, Bremerhaven. Veroeffentlichungen†
0068-094X Brewing and Malting Barley Research Institute. Annual Report **601**
0068-0958 Brewing Industry Survey†
0068-1008 Brigham Young University. College of Engineering Sciences and Technology. Annual Engineering Symposium. Abstracts†
0068-1032 Bristol and Gloucestershire Archaeological Society, Bristol, England. Transactions **384**
0068-1075 Britain: An Official Handbook *changed to* U K **4274**
0068-1105 Britain in the World Today†
0068-113X Britannia **2231**
0068-1148 Britannica Atlas **4000**
0068-1156 Britannica Book of the Year **3118**
0068-1202 British Academy. Proceedings **384**
0068-1245 British and Foreign State Papers†
0068-1261 British Antarctic Survey. Scientific Reports **7842**
0068-1288 British Archaeological Association. Journal **384**
0068-130X British Astronomical Association. Handbook **572**
0068-1318 British Astronomical Association. Memoirs†
0068-1342 British Aviation Year Book†
0068-1377 B B C Annual Report and Handbook†
0068-1407 The British Catalogue of Music **6551**
0068-1431 University of British Columbia. Department of Geophysics and Astronomy. Publications†
0068-144X British Columbia. Department of Mines and Petroleum Resources. Bulletin **2727**
0068-1458 British Columbia. Department of Recreation and Conservation. Annual Report†
0068-1563 British Columbia Fruit Growers Association. Minutes of the Proceedings of the Annual Convention†
0068-1571 British Columbia Geographical Series: Occasional Papers in Geography†
0068-1598 British Columbia Insurance Directory **4496**
0068-1601 British Columbia Lumberman's Greenbook†
0068-1628 Natural History Handbook Series†
0068-1636 Royal British Columbia Museum. Occasional Papers Series†
0068-1687 University of British Columbia Library. Asian Studies Division. List of Catalogued Books. Supplement†
0068-1695 University of British Columbia. Center for Continuing Education. Occasional Papers in Continuing Education†
0068-1709 University of British Columbia. Department of Civil Engineering. Soil Mechanics Series†
0068-1725 University of British Columbia. Department of Geophysics and Astronomy. Annual Report†
0068-1768 University of British Columbia. Faculty of Education. Journal of Education†
0068-1784 University of British Columbia. Faculty of Forestry. Research Notes†
0068-1792 University of British Columbia. Faculty of Forestry. Research Papers†
0068-1806 University of British Columbia. Faculty of Forestry. Translations†
0068-1830 University of British Columbia. Institute of Oceanography. Data Report **2820**
0068-1849 University of British Columbia Law Review **4803**
0068-1857 University of British Columbia Library. Reference Publication†
0068-1938 British Cycling Federation. Handbook **8163**
0068-1954 British Ecological Society. Symposium **3407**
0068-2004 British Film Fund Agency. Annual Report
0068-2039 British Goat Society. Herd Book **281**
0068-2047 British Goat Society. Year Book **281**
0068-208X British Hospitals Contributory Schemes Association. Directory of Convalescent Homes Serving the Provinces
0068-2098 British Hospitals Contributory Schemes Association. Directory of Hospitals Contributory Scheme Benefits
0068-2101 British Hospitals Contributory Schemes Association. Report†
0068-211X British Hospitals Home and Overseas†
0068-2144 British Initials and Abbreviations†
0068-2152 British Institute in Eastern Africa. Annual Report **4173**
0068-2179 British Institute of International and Comparative Law. International Law Series
0068-2306 British Museum (Natural History) Bulletin. Historical†

Link to your serials resources and content with ulrichsweb.com

0068-2314 British Orthoptic Journal *changed to* 1743-9868 **6039**
0068-2349 British Paper and Board Industry Federation. Technical Section. Yearbook†
0068-2365 British Petroleum Equipment and Services
0068-2411 British Rabbit Council Year Book **282**
0068-2454 British School at Athens. Annual **385**
0068-2462 British School at Rome. Papers **385**
0068-2497 British Society for Parasitology. Symposia **882**
0068-2519 British Society for the History of Pharmacy. Transactions†
0068-2616 British Tourist Authority. Digest of Tourist Statistics†
0068-2624 B T H A Directory†
0068-2640 British Transport Commission. Annual Report and Accounts†
0068-2675 British Trust for Ornithology. Annual Report **904**
0068-2691 British Year Book of International Law **4919**
0068-2721 Broadman Comments; International Sunday School Lessons **7628**
0068-273X Broads Book†
0068-2748 Broadside (New York, 1940) **8467**
0068-2780 Brookfield Bandarlog **937**
0068-2799 Brookhaven Symposia in Biology **663**
0068-2853 Brookside Monographs†
0068-2861 Brown and Haley Lecture Series†
0068-290X Brown's Nautical Almanac **8273**
0068-2918 Brunei Museum Journal **6521**
0068-2926 Bibliotheque Royale Albert 1er. Catalogue Collectif des Periodiques Etrangers†
0068-2934 Discotheque Nationale de Belgique. Catalogue General†
0068-2942 Annuaire et Statistique de l'Enseignement Catholique†
0068-2985 Universite Libre de Bruxelles. Institut de Sociologie. Cahiers†
0068-2993 Universite Libre de Bruxelles. Institut d'Etudes Europeennes. Enseignement Complementaire. Nouvelle Serie†
0068-3000 Universite Libre de Bruxelles. Institut d'Etudes Europeennes. Theses et Travaux Economiques†
0068-3019 Universite Libre de Bruxelles. Institut d'Etudes Europeennes. Theses et Travaux Juridiques†
0068-3035 Bryn Mawr-Haverford Review†
0068-3043 Das Buch der Jugend†
0068-3159 Analele Universitatii Bucuresti. Estetica†
0068-3175 Analele Universitatii Bucuresti. Filozofie†
0068-3213 Analele Universitatii Bucuresti. Limbi Clasice†
0068-323X Analele Universitatii Bucuresti. Limbi Romanice†
0068-3272 Analele Universitatii Bucuresti. Matematica-Mecanica†
0068-3280 Analele Universitatii Bucuresti. Pedagogie†
0068-3299 Analele Universitatii Bucuresti. Psihologie†
0068-3302 Analele Universitatii Bucuresti. Sociologie†
0068-3310 Analele Universitatii Bucuresti. Stiinte Juridice†
0068-3337 Budapest Varostorteneti Monografiai†
0068-3345 Buddhist Publication Society. Report†
0068-3361 Buecherei des Augenarztes†
0068-337X Buecherei des Frauenarztes†
0068-3388 Buecherei des Orthopaeden
0068-3396 Ein Buechertagebuch
0068-340X Buenos Aires. Centro de Investigacion de Biologia Marina. Contribucion Cientifica†
0068-3418 Buenos Aires. Instituto de Fitotecnia. Boletin Informativo†
0068-3485 Universidad del Salvador. Anales†
0068-3493 Universidad de Buenos Aires. Instituto Bibliotecologico. Publicacion†
0068-3507 B and C J Directory†
0068-3523 Building Board Directory†
0068-3531 Building Construction Cost Data (Year) **985**
0068-3620 Bulgarska Akademiia na Naukite. Arkheologicheski Institut. Izvestiia **385**
0068-3671 Bulgarska Akademiia na Naukite. Tsentralna Biblioteka. Izvestiia†
0068-371X Bulgarska Akademiia na Naukite. Tsentralna Khelmintologichna Laboratoriia. Izvestiia†
0068-3817 Bulgarska Akademiia na Naukite. Institut po Morfologiia. Izvestiia†
0068-3841 Bulgarska Akademiia na Naukite. Institut po Obshta i Sravnitelna Patalogiia. Izvestiia†
0068-385X Bulgarska Akademiia na Naukite. Institut po Tekhnicheska Kibernetika. Izvestiia†
0068-3884 Bulgarska Akademiia na Naukite. Institut za Pravni Nauki. Izvestiia†
0068-3949 Bulgarian Academy of Sciences, Sofia. Mathematical Institute. Bulletin†
0068-3957 Bulgarska Akademiia na Naukite. Mikrobiologichni Institut. Izvestiia†
0068-3965 Bulgarska Akademiia na Naukite. Institut za Muzikoznanie. Izvestiia†
0068-3973 Bulgarska Akademiia na Naukite. Institut po Filosofiia. Izvestiia†
0068-4007 Institut de Recherches Agronomiques Tropicales et des Cultures Vivrieres. Bulletin Agronomique†
0068-4015 Bulletin d'Archeologie Marocaine **385**
0068-4023 Bulletin de Philosophie Medievale **6909**
0068-4031 Bulletin des Jeunes Romanistes†
0068-4066 Bulletin Linguistique et Ethnologique
0068-4104 Bulletin of Suicidology†
0068-4112 Bulletin of Suicidology. Supplements†
0068-4120 Bulletin of the European Communities and Supplements **1443**
0068-4171 Institut National des Industries Extractives. Bulletin Technique: Securite et Salubrite†
0068-4198 Bulletins of Marine Ecology†
0068-4201 Bullinger's Postal and Shippers Guide for the United States and Canada
0068-4287 Burt Franklin American Classics in History and Social Sciences
0068-4295 Burt Franklin Art History and Art Reference Series
0068-4309 Burt Franklin Bibliography and Reference Series
0068-4317 Burt Franklin Essays in History, Economics, and Social Sciences
0068-4325 Burt Franklin Essays in Literature and Criticism
0068-4333 Monographs in Philosophy and Religious History
0068-4341 Burt Franklin Research and Source Works Series
0068-4384 Business Almanac Series
0068-4392 West Virginia University. Business and Economic Studies†
0068-4414 Business Education Index†
0068-4430 University of New Mexico. Bureau of Business and Economic Research. Business Information Series†
0068-4449 Business Monitor: Miscellaneous Series. M2 Cinemas†
0068-4503 The Business Who's Who of Australia **1977**
0068-4562 Buying and Selling United States Coins†
0068-4570 Bydgoskie Towarzystwo Naukowe. Wydzial Nauk Humanistycznych. Prace. Seria B (Jezyk i Literatura) **5102**
0068-4589 Bydgoskie Towarzystwo Naukowe. Wydzial Nauk Humanistycznych. Prace. Seria C (Historia i Archeologia) **4207**
0068-4597 Bydgoskie Towarzystwo Naukowe. Wydzial Nauk Technicznych. Prace. Seria Z (Prace Zbiorowe) **8417**
0068-4600 Byers National Industrial Directory
0068-4635 Muzeum Gornoslaskie w Bytomiu. Rocznik. Seria Archeologia **407**
0068-4643 Muzeum Gornoslaskie w Bytomiu. Rocznik. Seria Etnografia **349**
0068-4651 Muzeum Gornoslaskie w Bytomiu. Rocznik. Seria Historia **4247**
0068-466X Muzeum Gornoslaskie w Bytomiu. Rocznik. Seria Przyroda†
0068-4678 Muzeum Gornoslaskie w Bytomiu. Rocznik. Seria Sztuka **507**
0068-4686 Byzantinobulgarica†
0068-4708 C. C. Williamson Memorial Lecture†
0068-4759 C A T V Buyer's Guide†
0068-4775 Cadastro Brasileiro de Materias-Primas Farmaceuticas, Por Produto, Por Fabricante†
0068-4791 Centre de Geomorphologie, Caen. Bulletin†
0068-4805 Universita degli Studi di Cagliari. Istituto di Storia Medioevale. Pubblicazioni†
0068-4813 Economies et Societes. Serie F. Developpement, Croissance, Progres des Pays en Voie de Developpement **1595**
0068-4821 Economies et Societes. Serie AB. Economie du Travail **1101**
0068-483X Economies et Societes. Serie G. Economie Planifiee†
0068-4848 Economies et Societes. Serie L. Economie Regionale†
0068-4856 Economies et Societes. Serie S. Etudes de Marxologie†
0068-4864 Economies et Societes. Serie AF. Histoire Quantitative de l'Economie Francaise†
0068-4872 Economies et Societies. Serie T. Information - Recherche Innovation†
0068-4880 Economies et Societes. Serie M. Philosophie - Sciences Sociales Economie†
0068-4899 Economies et Societes. Serie AG. Progres et Agriculture **196**
0068-4902 Economies et Societes. Serie P. Relations Economiques Internationales **1540**
0068-4937 Cahiers Andre Gide **5268**
0068-4945 Cahiers Archeologiques†
0068-4953 Cahiers Bretons **7952**
0068-4961 Cahiers Canadiens Claudel†
0068-502X Cahiers de Droit d'Auteur†
0068-5038 Cahiers de la Quatrieme Internationale
0068-5046 Cahiers de l'Homme **332**
0068-5054 Cahiers de Micropaleontologie†
0068-5070 Cahiers de Psychomecanique de Langage **5103**
0068-5097 Cahiers de Sciences Sociales†
0068-5119 Cahiers des Universites Francaises†
0068-5135 Cahiers d'Odonto-Stomatologie
0068-5151 Cahiers du Tourisme. Serie A: France **8690**
0068-516X Cahiers Ferdinand de Saussure **5103**
0068-5178 Cahiers Jean Cocteau **5269**
0068-5194 Cahiers Nepalais **7112**
0068-5208 Office de la Recherche Scientifique et Technique Outre-Mer. Cahiers. Serie Biologie†
0068-5224 Cahiers Rouge. Nouvelle Serie Internationale
0068-5259 Cain
0068-5267 Cairngorm Club Journal **8164**
0068-5283 Societe d'Archeologie Copte. Bibliotheque de Manuscrits
0068-5305 Societe d'Archeologie Copte. Textes et Documents
0068-5356 Calcutta Management Association. Annual Report **1732**
0068-5364 Calcutta Research Series†
0068-5372 School of Tropical Medicine, Calcutta. Bulletin†
0068-5380 University of Calcutta. Centre of Advanced Study in Ancient Indian History and Culture. Lectures
0068-5399 University of Calcutta. Centre of Advanced Study in Ancient Indian History and Culture. Proceedings of Seminars
0068-5410 Calendars of American Literary Manuscripts†
0068-5461 California Academy of Sciences. Occasional Papers†
0068-547X California Academy of Sciences. Proceedings **664**
0068-5518 Preservation, Organization and Display of State of California's Historic Documents: Report to the California State Legislature†
0068-5526 Annotated Bibliography of Research in Economically Important Species of California Fish and Game. Supplement†
0068-5542 California Design†
0068-5569 California. Department of Forestry. Range Improvement Studies†
0068-5585 California Environmental Law: A Guide†
0068-5607 California Government Notes†
0068-5615 California Handbook†
0068-5631 California Insect Survey. Bulletin **842**
0068-5682 U.S. National Aeronautics and Space Administration. Jet Propulsion Laboratory. Technical Memorandum†
0068-5720 California Macadamia Society. Yearbook **223**
0068-5739 California Manufacturers Register **1978**
0068-5755 California Natural History Guides **664**
0068-5771 California Public School Directory **2954**
0068-5798 California Slavic Studies†
0068-5801 California. State Board of Equalization. Annual Report **1914**
0068-5836 San Diego State University. Bureau of Business and Economic Research. Monographs
0068-5844 San Diego State University. Bureau of Business and Economic Research. Research Studies and Position Papers
0068-5879 California County Law Library Basic List†
0068-5909 California Studies in the History of Art **480**
0068-5917 California Studies in Urbanization and Environmental Design†
0068-5933 University of California at Berkeley. Archaeological Research Facility. Contributions **422**
0068-5968 University of California at Berkeley. Fisher Center for Real Estate and Urban Economics. Reprint Series **7614**
0068-600X University of California. Center for South and Southeast Asia Studies. Occasional Papers†
0068-6077 University of California. Institute of Business and Economic Research. Publications†
0068-6093 University of California at Berkeley. International and Area Studies. Research Series **7271**
0068-6115 University of California. Institute of Transportation Studies. Library References **8532**
0068-6123 University of California, Berkeley. Institute of Transportation Studies. Selected List of Recent Acquisitions of the Transportation Library†
0068-6166 University of California, Santa Barbara. Library. Annual Report†
0068-6182 University of California, Los Angeles. Institute of Archaeology. Archaeological Survey. Annual Report†
0068-6190 University of California, Los Angeles. African Studies Center. Occasional Paper†
0068-6212 University of California, Los Angeles. Biotechnology Laboratory. Progress Report†
0068-6220 University of California at Los Angeles. Center for Medieval and Renaissance Studies. Publications **4165**
0068-6239 University of California at Los Angeles. Center for Medieval and Renaissance Studies. Contributions **4165**
0068-6247 University of California Publications in Folklore and Mythology **3623**
0068-6263 University of California at Los Angeles. Latin American Center. Reference Series **4316**
0068-631X University of California Engineering and Physical Sciences Extension Series†
0068-6336 University of California Publications in Anthropological Records†
0068-6344 University of California Publications. Classical Studies†
0068-6352 University of California Publications. English Studies†
0068-6379 University of California Publications in Anthropology†
0068-6387 University of California Publications in Automatic Computation†
0068-6395 University of California Publications in Botany *changed to* 1559-4041 **784**
0068-6409 University of California Publications in Contemporary Music†
0068-6417 University of California Publications in Entomology **860**
0068-6433 University of California Publications in Egyptian Archaeology†
0068-6441 University of California Publications in Geography†
0068-645X University of California Publications in Geological Sciences **2718**
0068-6468 University of California Publications in History†
0068-6476 University of California Publications in Librarianship†
0068-6484 University of California Publications in Linguistics **5191**
0068-6492 University of California Publications in Modern Philology†
0068-6506 University of California Publications in Zoology **966**
0068-6514 University of California Publications. Near Eastern Studies†
0068-6522 University of California Publications. Occasional Papers†
0068-6530 Californians in Congress†
0068-6549 Calwer Hefte†
0068-659X Cambridge Air Surveys† **8939**
0068-6603 Cambridge Authors' and Printers' Guides
0068-6611 Cambridge Bibliographical Society. Transactions **5000**
0068-6638 Cambridge Classical Texts and Commentaries **2232**
0068-6654 Cambridge Geographical Studies **4001**
0068-6689 Cambridge Latin American Studies **4287**
0068-6697 Cambridge Monographs in Experimental Biology†
0068-6719 Cambridge Papers in Social Anthropology†
0068-6727 Cambridge Papers in Sociology†
0068-6743 Cambridge Philological Society. Proceedings. Supplement **2232**
0068-6751 Cambridge Studies in International and Comparative Law **4919**
0068-676X Cambridge Studies in Linguistics **5104**
0068-6808 Cambridge Studies in Sociology†
0068-6816 Cambridge Texts and Studies in the History of Education
0068-6832 Cambridge University. Department of Applied Economics. Monographs†
0068-6883 University of Cambridge. Institute of Criminology. Bibliographical Series†
0068-6891 Cambridge University. Oriental Publications **4180**
0068-693X Campground Guide for Tent and Trailer Tourists†
0068-6948 Camping Caravanning and Sports Equipment Trades Directory
0068-6964 Camping Guide†
0068-7057 Canada. Statistics Canada. Aviation Statistics Centre. Service Bulletin **8523**
0068-7111 Canada. Statistics Canada. Dairy Statistics†
0068-712X Canada. Statistics Canada. Farm Net Income†
0068-7146 Canada. Statistics Canada. Index of Farm Production†
0068-7154 Canada. Statistics Canada. Livestock and Animal Products Statistics†
0068-7189 Canada. Statistics Canada. Production of Poultry and Eggs **177**
0068-7251 Canada Commerce
0068-7278 Canada. Department of Agriculture. Analytical Chemistry Research Service. Research Report†
0068-7308 Canada. Agriculture Canada. Food Research Institute, Ottawa. Research Report†

0069-2352 Sri Lanka. Department of National Museums. Translations Series†
0069-2360 Sri Lanka Export Directory **1583**
0069-2379 Ceylon Journal of Science. Biological Sciences **665**
0069-2387 Chain Shoe Stores and Leased Shoe Department Operators†
0069-2395 Chain Store Age Supermarket Sales Manual†
0069-2417 Chalmers Tekniska Hoegskola. Handlingar†
0069-2441 Survey of Local Chambers of Commerce **1410**
0069-245X Chamber of Mines of South Africa. Research Review†
0069-2484 Chambers Trades Register. Midlands†
0069-2506 Chambers Trades Register. South Wales and South West England†
0069-2514 Chambers Trades Register. Yorkshire Northumberland and Durham†
0069-2530 Chambre de Commerce, d'Industrie et des Mines du Cameroun. Rapport Annuel **6460**
0069-2549 Chambre de Commerce et d'Industrie d'Alger. Centre d'Etudes Economiques. Publication†
0069-2565 Chambre de Commerce Japonaise en France. Annuaire *changed to* Chambre de Commerce et d'Industrie Japonaise en France. Annuaire **1400**
0069-2573 Chambre de Commerce Suedoise en France. Annuaire†
0069-259X Chambre Syndicale des Mines de Fer de France. Rapport d'Activite†
0069-2603 Union des Industries et Entreprises de l'Eau et de l'Environnement. Annuaire **3472**
0069-2611 Chambre des Ingenieurs-Conseils de France. Annuaire†
0069-2646 Champlain Society, Toronto. Report **4135**
0069-2654 Chanakya Defence Annual **6415**
0069-2727 Charles E. Merrill Monograph Series in the Humanities and Social Sciences†
0069-2751 Charles W. Hunt Lecture†
0069-276X Charles Warren Center for Studies in American History. Annual Report†
0069-2778 Chart **5955**
0069-2786 Charter **4447**
0069-2824 Checklists in the Humanities and Education†
0069-2840 Chefs-d'Oeuvre de la Science-Fiction†
0069-2859 Chefs-d'Oeuvre Interdits†
0069-2867 Chelates in Analytical Chemistry: A Collection of Monographs†
0069-2875 ChemBooks†
0069-2883 Chemical Analysis **2099**
0069-2921 Chemical Engineering Progress. Reprint Manuals†
0069-2964 Chemical Guide to Europe†
0069-2972 Chemical Guide to the United States†
0069-2999 Chemical Peddler†
0069-3030 Royal Society of Chemistry. Annual Reports on the Progress of Chemistry. Section B: Organic Chemistry **2130**
0069-3111 Chemistry and Biochemistry of Amino Acids, Peptides, and Proteins†
0069-312X Chemistry and Industry Buyers' Guide†
0069-3138 Chemistry and Physics of Carbon: A Series of Advances **2121**
0069-3146 Chemistry of Functional Groups **2057**
0069-3154 Chemistry of Heterocyclic Compounds (New York, 1951) **2121**
0069-3162 Chemistry of Natural Products†
0069-3219 Chiba University. Faculty of Horticulture. Transactions†
0069-3227 Chiba Daigaku Engeigakubu Gakujutsu Hokoku/Chiba University. Faculty of Horticulture. Technical Bulletin *changed to* 1880-8824 **3750**
0069-3235 Art Institute of Chicago. Museum Studies **6519**
0069-3251 Chicago, Cook County and Illinois Industrial Directory†
0069-326X Chicago Crime Commission. Annual Report†
0069-3278 Chicago History of American Civilization **4288**
0069-3286 Chicago Lectures in Mathematics **5478**
0069-3294 Chicago Lectures in Physics **7008**
0069-3316 University of Chicago. Center for Health Administration Studies. Research Series†
0069-3324 University of Chicago. Center for Middle Eastern Studies. Publications†
0069-3359 University of Chicago. Graduate School of Business. Selected Papers
0069-3367 University of Chicago Oriental Institute. Publications **4326**
0069-3375 University of Chicago Studies in Library Science **5053**
0069-3391 Chigiana **6555**
0069-3413 Child Health in Israel
0069-3464 Children's Books; a List of Books for Preschool through Junior High School Age
0069-3472 Children's Books: Awards and Prizes **7558**
0069-3480 Children's Books in Print **5407**
0069-3499 Children's Books of the Year†
0069-3510 Chile. Comision de Planeamiento Integral de la Educacion. Bibliografia de Investigaciones y Estudios en Educacion†
0069-3529 Chile. Comision de Planeamiento Integral de la Educacion. Publicacion†
0069-3545 Chile. Superintendencia de Educacion Publica. Cuadernos†
0069-3553 Universidad de Chile. Departamento de Astronomia. Publicaciones†
0069-357X Universidad de Chile. Departamento de Geologia. Serie Comunicaciones **2718**
0069-3588 Universidad de Chile. Departamento de Geologia. Serie Publicaciones†
0069-3596 Universidad Catolica de Chile. Facultad de Teologia. Anales **7821**
0069-3642 Chimes
0069-3677 China Glass and Tableware Red Book Directory
0069-3685 China Medical Board of New York. Annual Report†
0069-3693 China Research Monographs
0069-3715 Chiron **387**
0069-3758 Chord and Discord†
0069-3804 Lincoln College. Agricultural Economics Research Unit. Technical Paper†
0069-3820 Lincoln College. Department of Horticulture. Bulletin†
0069-3839 Lincoln College. Farmers' Conference. Proceedings†
0069-3871 Christian Periodical Index **7698**
0069-388X Christian School Directory
0069-3898 Christian Service Training Series†
0069-3936 Chromatographic Science Series **2099**
0069-3944 Chromosomes Today†
0069-3952 Chronologie des Communautes Europeennes†
0069-3960 Chronology of the United Nations†
0069-3979 Church and Society Series†
0069-3987 Church of England Yearbook **7751**
0069-3995 Church of Scotland. Yearbook **7751**
0069-4002 Church Pulpit Year Book (Year) **7633**
0069-4037 CIBA Foundation. Study Groups†
0069-4045 CIBA Zeitschriften†
0069-4053 Ciencia e Sociedade: Temas e Debates†
0069-4088 Cincinnati Classical Studies. Supplementary Monograph†
0069-410X Excavations of the University of Cincinati: Guide Book†
0069-4118 Cine Club del Uruguay. Cuadernos
0069-4134 Cineguia **6493**
0069-4177 Circe
0069-4215 Circum-Spice
0069-4231 C R F Listing of Contributions of National Level Political Committees to Incumbents and Candidates for Public Offices†
0069-424X C R F Listing of Political Contributions of Five Hundred Dollars or More†
0069-4266 University of Illinois at Urbana-Champaign. Civil Engineering Studies. Construction Research†
0069-4274 University of Illinois at Urbana-Champaign. Civil Engineering Studies. Structural Research Series
0069-4290 Civilisations et Societes **4210**
0069-4304 Civilization of the American Indian **6634**
0069-4312 Civilta Asiatiche
0069-4339 Civilta Veneziana. Dizionari Dialettali e Studi Linguistici **5106**
0069-4347 Civilta Veneziana. Fonti e Testi. Serie Terza **4211**
0069-4355 Civilta Veneziana. Fonti e Testi. Serie Prima: Fonti e Testi per la Storia dell'Arte Veneta **482**
0069-4371 Civilta Veneziana. Saggi **4211**
0069-438X Civilta Veneziana. Studi **4211**
0069-4401 Clark Guidebooks†
0069-441X Clarke Institute of Psychiatry. Monograph Series
0069-4444 Clasicos Colombianos **5274**
0069-4452 Classic European Historians†
0069-4460 Classical Association. Proceedings† **8941**
0069-4479 Classici Greci e Latini
0069-4487 Classics in Anthropology
0069-4495 Classics in Education†
0069-4509 Classics of British Historical Literature†
0069-4517 Classified Business Directory of the State of Connecticut†
0069-4533 Classiques de la Pensee Politique **7116**
0069-4541 Classiques de la Renaissance en France. Premiere Serie†
0069-4584 Clausthaler Tektonische Hefte **2729**
0069-4592 Louisiana Geological Survey. Clay Resources Bulletin **6469**
0069-4614 Clegg's International Directory of the World's Book Trade†
0069-4630 Poultry Health and Management Short Course. Proceedings†
0069-4649 Clemson University Review of Industrial Management and Textile Science†
0069-4657 Clemson University. Water Resources Center. Report **8820**
0069-469X Universite de Clermont-Ferrand II. Annales Scientifiques. Serie Biologie Vegetale†
0069-4703 Universite de Clermont-Ferrand II. Annales Scientifiques. Serie Chemie†
0069-4711 Universite de Clermont-Ferrand II. Annales Scientifiques. Serie Geologie et Mineralogie†
0069-4738 Universite de Clermont-Ferrand II. Annales Scientifiques. Serie Physique†
0069-4746 Universite de Clermont-Ferrand II. Annales Scientifiques. Serie Physiologie Animale†
0069-4754 Cles de l'Entreprise†
0069-4770 Clin-Alert **6889**
0069-4789 University of Illinois at Urbana-Champaign. Clinic on Library Applications of Data Processing. Proceedings†
0069-4797 Clinical Approaches to the Problems of Childhood: The Langley Porter Child Psychiatry Series†
0069-4800 Clinical Conference on Cancer. Papers†
0069-4819 Clinical Endocrinology†
0069-4827 Clinical Neurosurgery **6132**
0069-4835 Clinics in Developmental Medicine **6090**
0069-4843 Closed-Circuit Television and Educational Television; Bibliographical References
0069-4851 Co-Operation†
0069-4894 Coal Mines in Canada†
0069-4924 Coates's Herd Book (Beef) **284**
0069-4932 Coates's Herd Book (Dairy) **262**
0069-4967 Coffee Drinking in the United States†
0069-4991 Coke Oven Managers' Association. Year Book **6460**
0069-5017 Colecao Filosofia†
0069-5025 Coleccion Aberri ta Azkatasuna†
0069-5033 Coleccion "Aniversarios Culturales" **641**
0069-505X Coleccion Canonica **7634**
0069-5068 Coleccion Ciencia Urbanistica†
0069-5076 Coleccion Filosofica **6910**
0069-5084 Coleccion "Foros y Seminarios." Serie Foros **4289**
0069-5092 Coleccion "Foros y Seminarios." Serie Seminarios **4289**
0069-5106 Coleccion Historica **4211**
0069-5114 Coleccion "Humanismo y Ciencia" **4447**
0069-5122 Coleccion Juridica **4947**
0069-5130 Coleccion Monografica Africana†
0069-5149 Coleccion Pensamiento Argentino†
0069-5165 Collana di Cultura **5275**
0069-5181 Monografie delle Biblioteche d'Italia **5032**
0069-5203 Collana di Studi e Saggi
0069-5246 Collana "Insegnare"
0069-5254 Collana Ricciana. Fonti† **8942**
0069-5262 Collect British Stamps **6893**
0069-5270 Collectanea Historiae Musicae†
0069-5319 Collected Works on Cardio-Pulmonary Disease†
0069-5335 Collection de Sociologie Generale et de Philosophie Sociale†
0069-5343 Collection d'Histoire Contemporaine
0069-5351 Collection Dictionnaires des Idees dans les Litteratures Occidentales. Litterature Francaise†
0069-5378 Collection Etudes et Travaux de la Revue "Mediterranee"†
0069-5386 Figures de Wallonie†
0069-5416 Collection "Pilotes"†
0069-5440 Collection PSI†
0069-5459 Litteratures Anciennes†
0069-5467 Collection U. Serie Droit des Affaires et de l'Economie
0069-5475 Collection U. Serie Droit des Communautes Europeennes
0069-5483 Collection U. Serie Etudes Allemandes
0069-5491 Collection U. Serie Histoire Ancienne
0069-5505 Collection U. Serie Relations et Institutions Internationales
0069-5513 Collections: Les Idees du Jour
0069-5548 Football Guide†
0069-5580 College de France. Annuaire **2972**
0069-5602 Baccalaureate Education in Nursing: Key to a Professional Career in Nursing†
0069-5688 College Facts Chart†
0069-5696 College Music Symposium **6558**
0069-5726 College of Physicians and Surgeons of British Columbia. Medical Directory **5599**
0069-5769 Collegium Internationale Neuropsycho-Pharmacologicum
0069-5777 Collezione di Filosofia
0069-5785 Collezione di Testi e di Studi Storiografia
0069-5793 Collier's Year Book†
0069-5807 Colloque de Metallurgie†
0069-5815 Colloques Internationaux d'Histoire Maritime. Travaux
0069-5831 Colloquium on the Law of Outer Space. Proceedings **51**
0069-5882 Universitaet zu Koeln. Institut fuer Geophysik und Meteorologie. Mitteilungen **2791**
0069-5904 Banco de la Republica Estadisticas Basicas.†
0069-5939 Colombo Law Review
0069-5971 Colonial Williamsburg Archaeological Series **387**
0069-598X Coloquio de Estudos Luso Brasileiros. Anais
0069-5998 Color Photography†
0069-6005 Colorado. Cooperative Wildlife Research Unit. Special Scientific Reports. Technical Papers†
0069-6048 Colorado Rail Annual†
0069-6056 Colorado School of Mines. Professional Contributions†
0069-6099 Colorado State University. Fluid Mechanics Papers†
0069-6110 Colorado State University. Hydrology Papers†
0069-6129 Colorado State University. Sanitary Engineering Papers†
0069-6145 University of Colorado. Institute of Arctic and Alpine Research. Occasional Papers **7927**
0069-6161 University of Colorado Libraries. Report†
0069-6277 Colston Research Society, Bristol, England. Proceedings of the Symposium. Colston Research Papers†
0069-6285 Columbia Biological Series†
0069-6293 Columbia County History (Oregon)
0069-6307 Columbia Essays in International Affairs. The Dean's Papers†
0069-6315 Columbia Essays on Modern Writers†
0069-6323 Columbia Essays on the Great Economists†
0069-6331 Columbia Studies in Economics **1084**
0069-6358 Columbia University Studies in International Organization†
0069-6366 Columbia University Studies in Jewish History, Culture, and Institutions†
0069-6412 Comitatus **5276**
0069-6463 Comite International des Poids et Mesures. Comite Consultatif de Thermometrie. Rapports et Annexes† **8942**
0069-651X Comite National de l'Organisation Francaise. Annuaire†
0069-6528 Comite National Francais de Geodesie et Geophysique. Comptes-Rendus†
0069-6536 Comite National Francais de Geodesie et Geophysique. Rapport National Francais a l'U G G I†
0069-6544 Comite pour l'Independence de l'Europe. Bulletin d'Information
0069-6552 Petrole (Year)†
0069-6579 Commentationes Biologicae†
0069-6587 Commentationes Humanarum Litterarum **4448**
0069-6617 Commerce Exterieur de la Republique du Chad
0069-6625 Annuaire du Commerce Franco-Italien
0069-6722 Commission of the European Communities. Etudes: Serie Informations Internes sur l'Agriculture†
0069-6765 Commission of the European Communities. Studies: Agricultural Series†
0069-6773 Commission of the European Communities. Studies: Economic and Financial Series†
0069-679X Commission of the European Communities. Studies: Transport Series†
0069-6811 Commissione Italiana per la Geofisica. Pubblicazioni. Serie I Q S Y†
0069-682X C E D Newsletter†
0069-6838 Committee for International Cooperation in Information Retrieval Among Patent Offices. Bulletin.†
0069-6846 Committee for International Cooperation in Information Retrieval Among Patent Offices. Proceedings of Annual Meetings†
0069-6854 Committee on Institutional Cooperation. Annual Report **2973**
0069-6897 Commonwealth Agricultural Bureaux. List of Research Workers†
0069-6927 Commonwealth Bureau of Animal Health. Review Series†
0069-6986 Commonwealth Bureau of Horticulture and Plantation Crops. Horticultural Review†
0069-6994 Commonwealth Bureau of Horticulture and Plantation Crops. Research Reviews†
0069-7001 Commonwealth Bureau of Horticulture and Plantation Crops. Technical Communications†
0069-7044 Commonwealth Entomological Conference. Report
0069-7087 Commonwealth Foundation Occasional Paper (No.)†
0069-7109 Commonwealth Institute, London. Annual Report **4003**

9096 0069-7133 ULRICH'S PERIODICALS

0069-7133 Commonwealth Law Reports **4947**
0069-7141 Phytopathological Papers **809**
0069-7168 Commonwealth Press Union. Book of Quinquennial Conference†
0069-7192 C S I R O Film Catalogue†
0069-7222 Commonwealth Scientific and Industrial Research Organization. Division of Applied Geomechanics. Report†
0069-7249 Commonwealth Scientific and Industrial Research Organization. Division of Applied Geomechanics. Technical Report†
0069-7257 Commonwealth Scientific and Industrial Research Organization. Division of Geomechanics. Technical Paper†
0069-7265 Commonwealth Scientific and Industrial Research Organization. Division of Applied Geomechanics. Technical Memorandum†
0069-729X Commonwealth Scientific and Industrial Research Organization. Division of Building Research. Building Study†
0069-7338 Commonwealth Scientific and Industrial Research Organization. Division of Entomology. Technical Paper†
0069-7346 Commonwealth Scientific and Industrial Research Organization. Division of Fisheries and Oceanography. Fisheries Synopsis†
0069-7443 Commonwealth Scientific and Industrial Research Organization. Division of Irrigation Research. Report†
0069-7486 Commonwealth Scientific and Industrial Research Organization. Division of Mechanical Engineering. Circular†
0069-7508 Commonwealth Scientific and Industrial Research Organization. Division of Mechanical Engineering. Annual Report†
0069-7524 Commonwealth Scientific and Industrial Research Organization. Division of Mathematical Statistics. Technical Paper†
0069-7591 Commonwealth Scientific and Industrial Research Organization. Division of Soils. Soil Publications†
0069-7648 Commonwealth Scientific and Industrial Research Organization. Land Research Series†
0069-7680 Commonwealth Scientific and Industrial Research Organization. Wheat Research Unit. Report†
0069-7699 Commonwealth Secretariat. Commodities Division. Dairy Produce†
0069-7702 Commonwealth Secretariat. Commodities Division. Fruit†
0069-7710 Commonwealth Secretariat. Commodities Division. Meat†
0069-7729 Commonwealth Secretariat. Commodities Division. Plantation Crops†
0069-7737 Commonwealth Secretariat. Commodities Division. Vegetable Oils and Oilseeds†
0069-7745 Commonwealth Universities Yearbook **2973**
0069-777X Communications Handbook
0069-7788 Communist China Problem Research Series
0069-7796 Communist China Yearbook Series
0069-7818 Community Council of Greater New York. Budget Standard Service. Annual Price Survey and Family Budget Costs†
0069-7850 Community Mental Health Journal Monograph Series†
0069-7893 Comparative Juridical Review†
0069-794X Comparazione dei Salari e del Costo del Lavoro in Europa†
0069-7958 Compendio Statistico Italiano **8364**
0069-7966 Compendium of Pharmaceuticals and Specialties **6830**
0069-7982 Complete Chevrolet Book†
0069-7990 Complete Ford Book†
0069-8008 Complete Volkswagen Book†
0069-8016 Composers of the Americas†
0069-8032 Comprehensive Biochemistry **729**
0069-8040 Comprehensive Chemical Kinetics **2134**
0069-8067 Comprehensive Media Guide: Korea†
0069-8075 Belgium. Institut National de Statistique. Etudes Statistiques **8357**
0069-8121 Computer Index†
0069-8148 Association for Computing Machinery. Annual Computer Personnel Research Conference Proceedings†
0069-8164 Computer Service Buyers Guide†
0069-8210 Comunidad. Suplementos†
0069-8245 Concise Statistical Yearbook of Greece **8364**
0069-827X Concrete Industries Yearbook
0069-8288 The Concrete Yearbook†
0069-8296 Condon Lectures†
0069-8326 Confederation Nationale des Groupes Folkloriques Francais. Annuaire†
0069-8334 Annuario†
0069-8393 Conference in Reading. Proceedings†
0069-8407 Conference in the Study of Twentieth-Century Literature, Michigan State University. Proceedings†
0069-8415 Conference of Chief Justices. Proceedings†
0069-8458 United Nations Conference of European Statisticians. Statistical Standards and Studies **8412**
0069-8474 Conference of State Sanitary Engineers. Report of Proceedings†
0069-8512 Conference on Biological Sonar and Diving Mammals. Proceedings†
0069-8520 Perugia Quadrennial International Conferences on Cancer. Proceedings† **8980**
0069-8555 Conference on Human Relations in Industry. Proceedings†
9096-8571 Conference on Land Surveying, Purdue University. Proceedings†
0069-8598 Conference on Latin American History. Publications†
0069-8636 American Meteorological Society. Conference on Radar Meteorology. Preprint
0069-8652 Studies in Income and Wealth **1721**
0069-8679 American Meteorological Society. Conference on Severe Local Storms. Preprint
0069-8687 National Tax Association. Proceedings of the Annual Conference on Taxation and Minutes of the Annual Meeting **1936**
0069-8784 Conferencias de Bioquimica
0069-8792 Conflict Studies **7228**
0069-8806 Conflits
0069-8814 Confluence. Etats des Recherches en Sciences Sociales: Surveys of Research in the Social Sciences†
0069-8881 Congres Archeologique de France **388**
0069-889X Congres National des Peches et Industries Maritimes. Compte Rendu
0069-8911 Congres National de Speleologie. Actes **2729**
0069-892X Congressional Record Digest and Tally of Roll Call Votes†
0069-8946 Coniectanea Biblica. New Testament Series **7635**
0069-8954 Coniectanea Biblica. Old Testament Series **7635**
0069-8970 Connecticut Academy of Arts and Sciences. Memoirs **7848**
0069-8989 Connecticut Academy of Arts and Sciences. Transactions **4448**
0069-8997 Storrs Agricultural Experiment Station. Research Report **158**
0069-9012 Connecticut College Monograph†
0069-9039 Connecticut Master Transportation Plan **8494**
0069-9047 University of Connecticut. Center for Real Estate and Urban Economic Studies. General Series
0069-9055 Connecticut Urban Research Report†
0069-9063 University of Connecticut. Institute of Water Resources. Report Series **8834**
0069-908X Connolly's Suppressed Writings
0069-9101 U.S. Department of the Interior. Conservation Bulletins†
0069-911X Conservation Directory† **8943**
0069-9128 Fish and Wildlife Facts†
0069-9136 Conservation of Library Materials†
0069-9152 U.S. Department of the Interior. Conservation Yearbook.†
0069-9160 Consortium for the Study of Nigerian Rural Development†
0069-9179 Consortium for the Study of Nigerian Rural Development. C S N R D Working Paper†
0069-9187 Construction in Hawaii **996**
0069-9195 Israel. Central Bureau of Statistics. Construction in Israel **1047**
0069-9225 Consulting Engineer Who's Who and Year Book†
0069-9233 U. S. Federal Trade Commission. Consumer Bulletins†
0069-9241 Consumers' Research Magazine Handbook of Buying†
0069-9276 U.S. National Bureau of Standards. Consumer Information Series†
0069-9292 Contabilidad Nacional de Espana **1917**
0069-9306 Contact (Marburg-Lahn)†
0069-9314 Containerization: A Bibliography
0069-9322 Contamination Control Directory†
0069-9330 Contemporary African Monographs
0069-9357 Contemporary American History Series **4290**
0069-9381 Contemporary Drama Series†
0069-942X Contemporary Issues Series **8095**
0069-9446 Contemporary Neurology Series **6133**
0069-9454 Contemporary Neurology Symposia†
0069-9527 Continental Camping & Caravan Sites†
0069-9535 Continental Research Series **4181**
0069-9578 Contract Carpeting†
0069-9616 Contributii Botanice **784**
0069-9624 Contributions in Afro-American and African Studies **4174**
0069-9640 Texas A & M University. College of Geosciences. Contributions in Oceanography **2818**
0069-9659 Contributions to Indian Sociology - New Series **8096**
0069-9683 Contributions to Library Literature†
0069-9691 Contributions to Marine Science†
0069-9705 Contributions to Sensory Physiology†
0069-973X Control Magazine **483**
0069-9748 Convegno di Studi Sulla Magna Grecia. Atti **388**
0069-9764 Convegno Nazionale dei Commercianti de Mobili. Atti e Relazioni†
0069-9772 Convegno Nazionale per la Civilta del Lavoro. Atti.†
0069-9799 Cooperador Dental
0069-9810 Cooperative Education Association Membership Directory
0069-9837 Cooperative Trade Directory for Southeast Asia **1423**
0069-9845 Coordination Chemistry†
0069-9861 Danmarks Biblioteksskole. Skrifter†
0069-9896 Denmark. Kongelige Bibliotek. Fund og Forskning **5006**
0069-9918 Koebenhavns Universitet. Filosofiska Fakultet. Extracts†
0069-9942 Copperfield
0069-9950 Copyright Law Symposium **6748**
0069-9969 Copyright Laws and Treaties of the World†
0069-9977 Coral Gables Conference on Fundamental Interactions at High Energy. (Proceedings)†
0069-9993 Corn Annual **225**
0070-0002 Cornell Biennial Electrical Engineering Conference **3298**
0070-0029 Cornell International Industrial and Labor Relations Reports **1673**
0070-0053 Cornell Studies in Industrial and Labor Relations **1673**
0070-0096 Cornell University. Modern Indonesia Project. Bibliography Series†
0070-0126 Cornell University. New York State School of Industrial and Labor Relations. Annual Institute for Training Specialists. (Publication)†
0070-0134 New York State School of Industrial and Labor Relations. Bulletin **1699**
0070-0142 Industrial and Labor Relations Bibliography Series **1242**
0070-0177 I L R Paperbacks†
0070-0185 New York State School of Industrial and Labor Relations. Key Issues Series†
0070-0207 Cornell University. New York State School of Industrial and Labor Relations. Technical Monograph Series†
0070-0215 Cornell University. Southeast Asia Program. Data Papers†
0070-0223 Cornell University. Thailand Project. Interim Reports Series†
0070-024X Cornish Archaeology **388**
0070-0258 Cornwall Archaeological Society. Field Guide
0070-0282 Corporate Management Tax Conference **1918**
0070-0290 Corporate Pension Fund Seminar. Proceedings†
0070-0312 Corpus Antiquitatum Americanensium†
0070-0320 Corpus Catholicorum **7793**
0070-0339 Corpus der Romanischen Kunst im Saechsisch-Thueringischen Gebiet†
0070-0347 Corpus Medicorum Graecorum **5600**
0070-0355 Corpus Medicorum Latinorum†
0070-0363 Corpus Mensurabilis Musicae **6559**
0070-038X Corpus Palladianum†
0070-0398 Corpus Scriptorum Christianorum Orientalium: Aethiopica **7704**
0070-0401 Corpus Scriptorum Christianorum Orientalium: Arabica **7704**
0070-041X Corpus Scriptorum Christianorum Orientalium: Armeniaca **7704**
0070-0428 Corpus Scriptorum Christianorum Orientalium: Coptica **7704**
0070-0436 Corpus Scriptorum Christianorum Orientalium: Iberica **7704**
0070-0444 Corpus Scriptorum Christianorum Orientalium: Subsidia **7704**
0070-0452 Corpus Scriptorum Christianorum Orientalium: Syriaca **7704**
0070-0460 Corpus Scriptorum de Musica **6559**
0070-0495 Corpus Vasorum Antiquorum. Pologne†
0070-0509 Correctional Literature Published in Canada†
0070-0517 Correspondance d'Orient†
0070-0533 Cosmetic Formulary†
0070-0576 Costa Rica. Ministerio de Hacienda Oficina del Presupesto. Informe
0070-0584 Universidad de Costa Rica. Serie Agronomia†
0070-0592 Universidad de Costa Rica. Serie Bibliotecologia†
0070-0606 Universidad de Costa Rica. Series Ciencias Juridicas y Sociales†
0070-0614 Universidad de Costa Rica. Serie de Filosofia†
0070-0622 Universidad de Costa Rica. Serie Educacion†
0070-0630 Universidad de Costa Rica. Serie Economia y Estadistica†
0070-0649 Universidad de Costa Rica. Serie Economia y Estadistica. Estadistica Universitaria†
0070-0657 Universidad de Costa Rica. Serie Historia y Geografia†
0070-0665 Universidad de Costa Rica. Serie Textos Universitarios†
0070-0673 Cotton International **8449**
0070-072X Council for Old World Archaeology: C O W A Surveys and Bibliographies. Area 1: British Isle†
0070-0738 Council for Old World Archaeology: C O W A Surveys and Bibliographies. Area 2: Scandinavia†
0070-0746 Council for Old World Archaeology: C O W A Surveys and Bibliographies. Area 3: Western Europe: Part 1†
0070-0754 Council for Old World Archaeology: C O W A Surveys and Bibliographies. Area 3: Western Europe: Part 2†
0070-0762 Council for Old World Archaeology: C O W A Surveys and Bibliographies. Area 4: Western Mediterranean†
0070-0770 Council for Old World Archaeology: C O W A Surveys and Bibliographies. Area 5: Central Europe†
0070-0789 Council for Old World Archaeology: C O W A Surveys and Bibliographies. Area 6: Balkans†
0070-0797 Council for Old World Archaeology: C O W A Surveys and Bibliographies. Area 7: Eastern Mediterranean†
0070-0800 Council for Old World Archaeology: C O W A Surveys and Bibliographies. Area 8: European Russia†
0070-0819 Council for Old World Archaeology: C O W A Surveys and Bibliographies. Area 9: Northeast Africa†
0070-0827 Council for Old World Archaeology: C O W A Surveys and Bibliographies. Area 10. Northwest Africa†
0070-0835 Council for Old World Archaeology: C O W A Surveys and Bibliographies. Area 11. West Africa†
0070-0843 Council for Old World Archaeology: C O W A Surveys and Bibliographies. Area 12. Equatorial Africa†
0070-0851 Council for Old World Archaeology: C O W A Surveys and Bibliographies. Area 13. South Africa†
0070-086X Council for Old World Archaeology: C O W A Surveys and Bibliographies. Area 14. East Africa†
0070-0878 Council for Old World Archaeology: C O W A Surveys and Bibliographies. Area 15. Western Asia†
0070-0886 Council for Old World Archaeology: C O W A Surveys and Bibliographies. Area 16. Southern Asia†
0070-0894 Council for Old World Archaeology: C O W A Surveys and Bibliographies. Area 17. Far East†
0070-0916 Council for Old World Archaeology: C O W A Surveys and Bibliographies. Area 18. Northern Asia†
0070-0924 Council for Old World Archaeology: C O W A Surveys and Bibliographies. Area 19. Southeast Asia†
0070-0932 Council for Old World Archaeology: C O W A Surveys and Bibliographies. Area 20. Indonesia†
0070-0940 Council for Old World Archaeology: C O W A Surveys and Bibliographies. Area 21. Pacific Islands†
0070-0959 Council for Old World Archaeology: C O W A Surveys and Bibliographies. Area 22. Australia†
0070-105X Council of Europe. European Treaty Series **4922**
0070-1068 Council of Europe. Joint Meeting of the Members of the Consultative Assembly and the European Parliament. Official Report of Debates
0070-1076 Council of Graduate Schools. Proceedings of the Annual Meeting†
0070-1106 Council of Organizations Serving the Deaf. Annual Forum Proceedings†
0070-1114 Council of Organizations Serving the Deaf. Council Membership Directory†
0070-1157 Suggested State Legislation **4852**
0070-1173 Council on Legal Education for Professional Responsibility. Newsletter†
0070-119X C R I A Special Studies†
0070-1262 Country Dance and Song†
0070-1270 Country Life Annual†
0070-1327 County Louth Archaeological and Historical Society. Journal **388**
0070-1394 Courtenay Library of Reformation Classics **4212**
0070-1408 Courtenay Studies in Reformation Theology **7752**
0070-1416 Cranbrook Institute of Science, Bloomfield Hills, Michigan. Bulletin **7848**
0070-1424 Cranfield Fluidics Conference. Proceedings†
0070-1475 Cremation Society of Great Britain. Conference Report†
0070-1483 Cri du Peuple
0070-1521 Criminal Appeal Reports **2649**

Link to your serials resources and content with ulrichsweb.com

0070-153X   Critical Essays in Modern Literature†
0070-1548   Critical Review† 8947
0070-1556   Critiques de Notre Temps Et...†
0070-1572   Croissance Urbaine et Progres des Nations
0070-1580   Croner's Reference Book for Employers 1859
0070-1599   Croner's Reference Book for Exporters 1560
0070-1602   Croner's Reference Book for Importers 1560
0070-1610   Croner's Road Transport Operation 8670
0070-167X   Crystal Structures†
0070-1688   Cuadernos de Historia del Arte 484
0070-170X   Cuadernos de Orientacion†
0070-1718   Cuadernos de Pedagogia†
0070-1726   Cuadernos de Sintesis†
0070-1734   Cuadernos de Sociologia†
0070-1750   Cuadernos del Mexico Prehispanico†
0070-1769   Cuadernos del Sur 4448
0070-1785   Cuadernos para Estudiantes: Los Poetas
0070-1858   Current British Directories 1981
0070-1866   Current Caribbean Bibliography
0070-1882   Current Coins of the World†
0070-1890   Current Concepts in Clinical Nursing
0070-1904   Current Concerns in Clinical Psychology†
0070-1912   Current Diagnosis 5602
0070-1947   Index of Current Equine Research†
0070-1955   Current European Directories 1981
0070-1963   Current History Annual 4290
0070-1971   Current Issues in Higher Education†
0070-198X   Current Issues in Music Education†
0070-1998   Current Legal Problems 4654
0070-2005   Current Medical Information and Terminology†
0070-203X   Current Practice in Orthopaedic Surgery†
0070-2080   Current Psychiatric Therapies†
0070-2110   Current Therapy in Dentistry†
0070-2129   Current Topics in Bioenergetics†
0070-2137   Current Topics in Cellular Regulation 667
0070-2145   Current Topics in Clinical and Community Psychology†
0070-2153   Current Topics in Developmental Biology 667
0070-217X   Current Topics in Microbiology and Immunology 884
0070-2188   Current Topics in Pathology†
0070-2196   Current Topics in Surgical Research†
0070-2234   Cusanus-Gesellschaft. Buchreihe 7636
0070-2242   Cushman Foundation for Foraminiferal Research. Special Publication 6724
0070-2277   Cycle Buyers Guide†
0070-2315   Agricultural Research Institute. Technical Bulletin 84
0070-2323   Cyprus. Budget: Estimates of Revenue and Expenditure 1919
0070-2331   Cyprus Chamber of Commerce and Industry Directory 1981
0070-2366   Cyprus. Department of Antiquities. Monographs
0070-2374   Cyprus. Department of Antiquities. Report 389
0070-2390   Cyprus. Ministry of Labour and Social Insurance. Annual Report 1674
0070-2404   Cyprus. Department of Social Welfare Services. Annual Report†
0070-2412   Cyprus. Department of Statistics and Research. Economic Report 1223
0070-2420   Cyprus. Department of Statistics and Research. Statistics of Imports and Exports 1223
0070-2439   Cyprus. Department of Statistics and Research. Shipping Statistics†
0070-2447   Cystic Fibrosis: A Bibliography†
0070-2455   Cystic Fibrosis Club Abstracts†
0070-2471   Czasopismo Prawno-Historyczne 4213
0070-251X   Dacia: Revue d'Archeologie et d'Histoire Ancienne 389
0070-2528   Daedalus (Stockholm) 6523
0070-2587   Dairy Industries Catalog†
0070-2617   Institut Fondamental d'Afrique Noire. Catalogues et Documents 4175
0070-2625   Institut Fondamental d'Afrique Noire. Initiations et Etudes Africaines 4175
0070-2633   Institut Fondamental d'Afrique Noire. Memoires†
0070-2668   Dana-Report†
0070-2676   Dance Directory (Year)†
0070-2692   Dance World†
0070-2714   Dania Polyglotta†
0070-2749   Danish Yearbook of Philosophy 6913
0070-279X   Dans le Fantastique†
0070-2811   Danske Bogauktioner med en Oversigt over Bogpriserne†
0070-282X   Danske Forlaeggerforening. Faelleslagerkatalog†
0070-2846   Danske Magazin 4213
0070-2854   Oplagstal og Markedstal 4581
0070-2862   Dante Studies 5283
0070-2889   Data Processing in Medicine†
0070-2897   Datos y Cifras de la Ensenanza en Espana 2841
0070-2900   David Davies Memorial Institute of International Studies. Annual Memorial Lecture†
0070-2927   University of Toronto. David Dunlap Observatory. Publications†
0070-2943   Davison's Knit Goods Trade†
0070-2951   Davison's Textile Blue Book 8449
0070-2986   Davy's Devon Herd Book 285
0070-2994   Dawn in Central Asia
0070-3001   Dawn Song and All Day†
0070-3044   University of Dayton. School of Education. Abstracts of Research Projects†
0070-3052   University of Dayton. School of Education. Workshop Proceedings
0070-3060   De Proprietatibus Litterarum. Series Major†
0070-3079   De Proprietatibus Litterarum. Series Minor†
0070-3087   De Proprietatibus Litterarum. Series Practica†
0070-3095   Dead Sea Works, Beersheba, Israel. Report of the Directors
0070-3109   Dealers in Coins
0070-3141   December 5283
0070-315X   Dechema Monographien 2099
0070-3176   Decisions of the United States Courts Involving Copyrights†
0070-3192   Decorating Contractor Annual Directory†
0070-3206   Decorative Art and Modern Interiors†
0070-3214   Decouverte de l'Histoire

0070-3222   Deems Lectureship†
0070-3249   Deiches Fund Studies of Public Library Service†
0070-3257   Dein Kind†
0070-3273   Delaware Geological Survey. Bulletin 2730
0070-329X   Delaware. Department of Highways and Transportation. Traffic Summary 8630
0070-3303   Delegations to the United Nations†
0070-3311   Institute of Economic Growth. Census Studies 7285
0070-3338   Delphica†
0070-3346   Democrat
0070-3362   Demographie et Societes 7281
0070-3370   Demography 7281
0070-3389   Demokratische Existenz Heute†
0070-3419   Denken, Schauen, Sinnen†
0070-3427   Denkmaeler des Rheinlandes†
0070-3443   Denmark. Ministeriet for Foedevarer, Landbrug og Fiskeri. Skrifter fra Danmarks Fiskeri- og Havundersogelser 3590
0070-346X   Denmark. Danmarks Statistik. Arbejdsloesheden†
0070-3478   Denmark. Danmarks Statistik. Befolkningens Bevaegelser changed to 1902-049X 7306
0070-3486   Danmarks Skibe og Skibsfart†
0070-3508   Denmark. Danmarks Statistik. Ejendomssalg†
0070-3516   Denmark. Danmarks Statistik. Faerdselsuheld 7306
0070-3532   Denmark. Danmarks Statistik. Industristatistik†
0070-3567   Denmark. Danmarks Statistik. Statistisk Aarbog 8366
0070-3583   Denmark. Danmarks Statistik. Statistisk Tiaarsoversigt 8366
0070-3648   Dental Delineator
0070-3656   Dental Guide (Don Mills) 5840
0070-3664   Dental Images 5840
0070-3710   Ninth District Dental Society. Bulletin changed to Ninth District Dental Association. Bulletin 5857
0070-3737   Dentistry in Japan changed to 1882-7616 5850
0070-3745   Denver Museum of Natural History. Museum Pictorial†
0070-3753   Denver Museum of Natural History. Proceedings 940
0070-3788   Derbyshire Archaeological Journal 389
0070-3826   Description and Analysis of Contemporary Standard Russian
0070-3885   Detroit Studies in Music Bibliography 6631
0070-3893   Deutsch-Slawische Forschungen zur Namenkunde und Siedlungsgeschichte 4214
0070-3907   Deutsche Akademie der Landwirtschaftswissenschaften, Berlin. Jahrbuch†
0070-3915   Akademie fuer Aerztliche Fortbildung der DDR. Bibliographie†
0070-3923   Deutsche Akademie fuer Sprache und Dichtung. Jahrbuch 5111
0070-3931   Bibliographischer Informationsdienst der Deutschen Buecherei†
0070-394X   Deutsche Bundesbank. Geschaeftsbericht 1335
0070-3958   Deutsche Dendrologische Gesellschaft. Mitteilungen 786
0070-3974   Deutsche Forschungsgemeinschaft. Denkschriften zur Lage der Deutschen Wissenschaft 7850
0070-3982   Deutsche Forschungsgemeinschaft. Forschungsberichte 7850
0070-3990   Deutsche Forschungsgemeinschaft. Kommissionenmitteilungen 7850
0070-4016   Deutsche Gaue 4214
0070-4067   Deutsche Gesellschaft fuer Innere Medizin. Verhandlungen†
0070-4075   Deutsche Gesellschaft fuer Kreislaufforschung. Verhandlungen
0070-4083   D G L R Jahrbuecher 52
0070-4113   Deutsche Gesellschaft fuer Pathologie. Verhandlungen 5604
0070-4156   Bibliothek des Deutschen Historischen Instituts in Rom 4205
0070-4199   Deutsche Keramische Gesellschaft. Fachausschussberichte 2040
0070-4210   Deutsche Kraftfahrtforschung und Strassenverkehrstechnik†
0070-4229   Deutsches Krebsforschungszentrum. Veroeffentlichungen† 8950
0070-430X   Deutsche Physikalische Gesellschaft. D P G - Nachrichten†
0070-4318   Deutsche Schillergesellschaft. Jahrbuch 5284
0070-4334   Deutsche Texte des Mittelalters 5284
0070-4342   Deutsche Zoologische Gesellschaft. Verhandlungen 940
0070-4350   Deutsche Gesellschaft fuer Arbeitsschutz. Verhandlungen† 8949
0070-4377   Deutscher Kuesten-Almanach 8642
0070-4385   Deutscher Hochschulfuehrer† 8949
0070-4415   Deutsches Archaeologisches Institut. Jahrbuch 390
0070-4423   Deutsches Beamten-Jahrbuch; Bundesausgabe 7433
0070-4431   Deutsches Buehnen-Jahrbuch 8469
0070-444X   Deutsches Dante-Jahrbuch 5284
0070-4490   Deutsches Institut fuer Puppenspiel. Forschung und Lehre†
0070-4563   Developments in Industrial Microbiology Series†
0070-4571   Developments in Sedimentology 2731
0070-4598   Developments in Theoretical and Applied Mechanics†
0070-4601   Developpement Economique
0070-4695   Dichter und Zeichner†
0070-4709   Dictionary of African Biography†
0070-4717   Dictionary of Canadian Biography 642
0070-4725   Dictionary of Dairying. Supplement††
0070-4733   Dictionary of Latin American and Caribbean Biography†
0070-475X   Dictionnaire des Parfums de France et des Lignes pour Hommes
0070-4776   Dictionnaire des Valeurs des Meubles et Objets d'Art 486
0070-4792   Didactica Classica Gandensia 2233
0070-4806   Diderot Studies 6914
0070-4830   Diesel Locomotive Question & Answer Manual
0070-4857   Digest of Legal Activities of International Organizations and Other Institutions 4923
0070-4873   Digest of World Events 4137
0070-4903   Dine Israel 4658
0070-492X   Diplomaciai Iratok Magyarorszag Kulpolitikajahoz†
0070-4938   Diplomatarium Danicum†

0070-4946   Diplomatic Corps of Belgrade†
0070-4962   Diplomat's Annual†
0070-4997   Directories of Science Information Sources†
0070-5012   Directory for Exceptional Children 3038
0070-5039   Directory Iron and Steel Plants 6310
0070-5063   Directory of American College Theatre†
0070-5071   Directory of American Firms Operating in Foreign Countries 1561
0070-508X   Directory of American Philosophers 6914
0070-5098   Directory of American Savings and Loan Associations†
0070-5101   Directory of American Scholars†
0070-5160   Directory of British Recruitment Services
0070-5195   Directory of Buying Offices and Accounts†
0070-5217   Directory of Canadian Map Collections 4004
0070-5225   Directory of Canadian Trust Companies
0070-525X   Directory of Chemical Engineering Research in Canada†
0070-5276   Directory of College and University Libraries in New York State 5006
0070-5306   Directory of Community Services in Maryland†
0070-5322   Directory of Company Secretaries 1739
0070-5330   Directory of Computerized Information in Science and Technology†
0070-5357   Directory of Cooperative Education†
0070-5403   Directory of Current Scientific Research Projects in Pakistan†
0070-542X   Directory of Directors 642
0070-5438   Directory of Directors 1739
0070-5543   Directory of Foreign Firms Operating in the United States 1986
0070-556X   Directory of Franchising Organizations†
0070-5586   Directory of Government Agencies Safeguarding Consumer and Environment†
0070-5624   The Directory of Grant-Making Trusts†
0070-5632   Hawaii's Scientific Resources Directory†
0070-5675   Directory of Institutions of Higher Education in Missouri
0070-5691   Directory of Insurance Companies Licensed in New York State 4501
0070-5756   Directory of Lawyer Referral Services, Legal Aid and Defender Offices and Legal Assistance Offices of the Armed Forces†
0070-5780   Directory of Magazine Editorial Shopping Sections
0070-5799   Directory of Maryland Exporters-Importers†
0070-5810   Directory of Medical Libraries in New York State†
0070-5837   Directory of Mental Health Resources in Florida†
0070-5861   Directory of Mineral Producers in Oklahoma†
0070-5926   Directory of Nebraska Manufacturers 1987
0070-5942   New York Importers. Directory 2020
0070-6000   Directory of On-Going Research in Smoking and Health†
0070-6019   Directory of Opportunities for Graduates†
0070-6027   Directory of Oregon Manufacturers†
0070-6051   Directory of Overseas Summer Jobs 1988
0070-606X   Directory of Pakistani Scholars Abroad 3012
0070-6078   Directory of Pakistan's Periodicals in Social Sciences†
0070-6086   Directory of Pathology Training Programs (Year) 2978
0070-6094   Directory of Periodicals Publishing Articles on English and American Literature and Language
0070-6140   Directory of Professional Photography
0070-6213   Directory of Research Reports Relating to Produce Packaging and Marketing†
0070-6280   Directory of Scientific Research in Nigeria 7851
0070-6302   Directory of Serials in Pure and Applied Science and Economics Published in Israel†
0070-637X   Directory of Special Libraries in Israel
0070-640X   Directory of State and Federal Funds Available for Business Development†
0070-6418   Directory of State Arts Councils†
0070-6515   World Directory of Travel Agencies†
0070-6590   Directory of Worlds Chambers of Commerce and Trade Association
0070-6612   Diretorio Brasileiro da Industria Farmaceutica
0070-6663   Discourse Units in Human Communication for Librarians†
0070-668X   Discoveries in the Judaean Desert of Jordan 390
0070-6698   Discovery Reports†
0070-671X   Disquisitiones Mathematicae Hungaricae†
0070-6728   Dissertationes Botanicae 786
0070-6760   Dix-Huitieme Siecle 4215
0070-6779   Do-It-Yourself. Annual†
0070-6787   Do-It-Yourself Gardening Annual†
0070-6795   Doblingers Verlagsnachrichten†
0070-6809   Doctoral Dissertations on Transportation†
0070-6817   Documentologie†
0070-6825   Documenta Romaniae Historica. Serie A: La Moldavie 4215
0070-6833   Documenta Romaniae Historica. Serie B: La Valachie 4215
0070-6841   Documentacion Bibliotecologica†
0070-685X   Documentatio Didactica Classica
0070-6868   Documentation du Batiment†
0070-6884   Documente Istorice†
0070-6892   Documente si Manuscrise Literare†
0070-6906   Documenti sulle Arti del Libro 624
0070-6922   Documentos Latino Americanos†
0070-6930   Universidad de Navarra. Documentos Medievales 4275
0070-7007   Dod's Parliamentary Companion 7130
0070-7015   Dog World Annual 6807
0070-7031   Dokumente zur Deutschlandpolitik 7130
0070-704X   Dollars & Cents of Shopping Centers 7589
0070-7074   Donauschwaebisches Schrifttum†
0070-7112   Dorset Natural History and Archaeological Society. Proceedings 7851
0070-7120   Dorset Worthies 642
0070-7155   Dossiers du Cinema†
0070-7171   Downdraft
0070-718X   Downhill Only Journal
0070-7198   Dramascripts Series 5286
0070-7201   Landesmuseum fuer Vorgeschichte Dresden. Veroeffentlichungen 6527
0070-721X   Medizinische Akademie "Carl Gustav Carus" Dresden. Schriften†

ISSN

0070-7228 Staatliches Museum fuer Mineralogie und Geologie, Dresden. Abhandlungen†
0070-7260 Staatliches Museum fuer Tierkunde Dresden. Malakologische Abhandlungen *changed to* 1864-5127 **964**
0070-7295 Staatliches Museum fuer Voelkerkunde Dresden. Abhandlungen und Berichte *changed to* 1865-4355 **6531**
0070-7325 Droit Polonais Contemporain **4661**
0070-7333 Drosophila Information Service **866**
0070-7341 Drug Abuse Law Review†
0070-735X Drug Abuse Papers†
0070-7368 Drug Dependence†
0070-7406 Drugs of Choice
0070-7414 Dublin Institute for Advanced Studies. Communications. Series A **7010**
0070-7422 Dublin Institute for Advanced Studies. School of Cosmic Physics. Geophysical Bulletin **2780**
0070-7430 Dudley, England (West Midlands) Public Libraries. Archives Department. Transcripts†
0070-7457 Universitaet Duesseldorf. Jahrbuch†
0070-7481 Duke University. Cooperative Oceanographic Program. Progress Report†
0070-7546 Dumbarton Oaks Papers **391**
0070-7554 Dumbarton Oaks Studies **391**
0070-7562 Dumbarton Oaks Texts **4138**
0070-7589 Electronic Marketing Directory **1991**
0070-7643 Dunsink Observatory. Publications **574**
0070-7708 Duquesne Studies. Philosophical Series†
0070-7716 Duquesne Studies. Psychological Series†
0070-7732 Duquesne Studies. Theological Series†
0070-7767 Durch Stipendien Studieren
0070-7783 Dutch Studies in Russian Literature†
0070-7791 Dzieje Polskiej Granicy Zachodniej **4216**
0070-7805 E D P Conference for Retailers†
0070-7872 Early English Text Society. Original Series **5287**
0070-7910 Earth Sciences Series **2706**
0070-797X East African Law Journal **4662**
0070-7988 Maktaba **5031**
0070-8062 University of Kansas. Center for East Asian Studies. International Studies: East Asian Series. Research Series **4190**
0070-8070 University of Kansas. Center for East Asian Studies. International Studies: East Asian Series. Reference Series **4189**
0070-8089 East Carolina University Publications in History
0070-8097 East Europe in German Books†
0070-8100 East Europe Monographs†
0070-8127 East Lakes Geographer **4005**
0070-8135 Bangladesh. Education Directorate. Report on Pilot Project on Adult Education **2939**
0070-8143 Bangladesh. Directorate of Agricultural Marketing. Agricultural Marketing Series
0070-8151 Bangladesh. Directorate of Agriculture. Season and Crop Report
0070-8178 Bangladesh Research and Evaluation Centre. Report
0070-8186 Bangladesh University of Engineering and Technology, Dhaka. Technical Journal **3182**
0070-8208 East Yorkshire Local History Series **4216**
0070-8232 Eastern New Mexico University. Contributions in Anthropology **336**
0070-8259 University of Eastern Philippines. Research Center. Report **2922**
0070-8275 Eaton Electronics Research Laboratories. Technical Report†
0070-8321 Ecole Francaise des Attaches de Presse. Association des Anciens Eleves. Annuaire **4574**
0070-8348 Ecological Society of Australia. Proceedings†
0070-8356 Ecological Studies **670**
0070-8364 Ecologie Marina†
0070-8372 Ecology and Conservation Series†
0070-8437 Economic and Scientific Research Foundation. Annual Report **1099**
0070-8453 National Institute of Economic and Social Research, London. Economic and Social Studies **1152**
0070-8461 African Economic and Social Review†
0070-847X Economic Council of Canada. Annual Report†
0070-8488 Economic Council of Canada. Annual Review†
0070-8518 Economic Development Programme for the Republic of South Africa†
0070-8534 Economic Education Experiences of Enterprising Teachers
0070-8550 Economic Handbook of the Machine Tool Industry **5451**
0070-8593 Economic Picture of Japan†
0070-8615 Economic Questions for Illinois Agriculture†
0070-8623 Economic Research Studies†
0070-8631 Economic Review
0070-864X Economic Review of World Tourism†
0070-8674 Economic Studies†
0070-8712 Economic Survey of Europe **1480**
0070-8747 Economic Yearbook of Tunisia
0070-8763 Economics of Fruit Farming†
0070-8771 Economie Belge et Internationale†
0070-878X Economie de la Tunisie en Chiffres **1481**
0070-8801 Economie et Societe **1101**
0070-881X Luxembourg. Service Central de la Statistique et des Etudes Economiques. Cahiers Economiques. Serie A: Economie Luxembourgeoise†
0070-8860 Ecrits Libres **7639**
0070-8879 Ecriture **5287**
0070-8887 Ecuador. Centro de Desarrollo Industrial. Informe de Labores
0070-8895 Ecuador. Instituto Nacional de Estadistica y Censos. Anuario de Estadisticas Hospitalarias **4092**
0070-8909 Ecuador. Instituto Nacional de Estadistica y Censos. Anuario de Estadisticas Vitales **7282**
0070-8917 Ecuador. Instituto Nacional de Estadistica y Censos. Estadistica del Trabajo; Indice de Empleo y Remuneraciones **1225**
0070-8925 Ecuador Economico†
0070-8976 Edgar Brookes Academic and Human Freedom Lecture **2979**
0070-8992 University of Edinburgh. Architecture Research Unit. Report
0070-9018 University of Edinburgh. Publications. Language and Literature†
0070-9034 University of Edinburgh. Publications. Science†
0070-9069 Editiones Arnamagnaeanae. Series A **5288**
0070-9077 Editiones Arnamagnaeanae. Series B† **8953**
0070-9085 Editiones Arnamagnaeanae. Supplementum† **8953**
0070-9093 Editori Librai Cartolibrai e Biblioteche d'Italia†
0070-9107 Editorial Offices in the West†
0070-9131 Education Authorities' Directory and Annual **2847**
0070-9166 Education for Nursing: The Diploma Way†
0070-9182 Education in Europe. Section 1: Higher Education and Research†
0070-9190 Education in Europe. Section 2: General and Technical Education
0070-9212 Education in Europe. Section 4 (General)†
0070-9220 Education in Japan **2848**
0070-9239 Education in Large Cities Series†
0070-9263 Educational and Psychological Interactions **2849**
0070-9271 Educational Directory of Malaysia and Singapore
0070-931X Educational/Instructional Broadcasting Buyers Guide†
0070-9344 Educational Studies and Documents Series **2851**
0070-9352 Educational Technology Bibliography Series†
0070-9360 Educational Theatre Journal. Supplement†
0070-9379 Educational Therapy†
0070-9387 Educators Grade Guide to Free Teaching Aids†
0070-9417 Educators Guide to Free Guidance Materials **3060**
0070-9425 Educators Guide to Free Science Materials **3060**
0070-9433 Educators Guide to Free Social Studies Materials **3060**
0070-945X Edward Shann Memorial Lecture in Economics†
0070-9484 Egyptian Dental Journal **5842**
0070-9492 Egyptian Religious Texts and Representation†
0070-9506 Egyptian Society of Endocrinology and Metabolism. Journal†
0070-9514 Eidgenoessische Zukunft: Bausteine fuer Die Kommende Schweiz†
0070-9522 Einfuehrung in die Information und Dokumentation†
0070-9573 El Paso Archaeological Society. Special Reports **392**
0070-959X Eldridge Reeves Johnson Foundation for Medical Physics. Colloquium. Proceedings
0070-9603 Electeur†
0070-962X Electric Power in Canada **3157**
0070-9638 Electrical and Electronic Trader Year Book†
0070-9646 Electrical and Electronics Trades Directory†
0070-9662 Electrical Engineering Research Abstracts. Canadian Universities†
0070-9670 Electrical Engineer's Pocket Book†
0070-9689 Electrical Equipment Representatives Association. Directory **3303**
0070-9697 Electrical - Electronics Insulation Conference. Record
0070-9719 Electrical Process Heating in Industry. Technical Conference. Record†
0070-9735 Electricite de France. Rapport d'Activite **3304**
0070-976X Electricity Supply Handbook *changed to* Energy Supply Handbook (Year) **3307**
0070-9778 Electroanalytical Chemistry: A Series of Advances **2100**
0070-9816 Electron Technology (Print) *changed to* 1897-2381
0070-9840 Electronic Connection Techniques and Equipment†
0070-9913 Electronics in Japan†
0070-9972 Acta Nuntiaturae Polonae†
0070-9980 Elementary Teachers Guide to Free Curriculum Materials **3060**
0070-9999 Elements de Mathematique†
0071-0008 Elements du Bilan Economique
0071-0016 Elizabethan Bibliographies Supplements
0071-0032 Elizabethan Theatre†
0071-0067 Der Elsner **3266**
0071-0148 Employment Opportunities for Advanced Post-Graduate Scientists and Engineers
0071-0156 En Direct avec l'Histoire
0071-0164 Encore (Blacksburg)
0071-0180 Encyclopaedia Chimica Internationalis†
0071-0199 Encyclopaedic Dictionary of Physics. Supplement†
0071-0202 Encyclopedia of Associations **3119**
0071-0210 Encyclopedia of Business Information Sources **1741**
0071-0237 Encyclopedia of Social Work **8038**
0071-0326 Engineering Geology Case Histories†
0071-0342 Engineering Industries Association. Classified Directory and Buyers Guide **3190**
0071-0350 Engineering Laboratories Series†
0071-0369 Tennessee Valley Authority. Engineering Laboratory. Research in the Fields of Civil Engineering, Mechanical Engineering, Instrumentation†
0071-0490 English and American Studies in German **5114**
0071-0547 English Ceramic Circle. Transactions **2040**
0071-0571 English Guernsey Herd Book **286**
0071-058X English Historical Documents
0071-0598 English Institute. Selected Essays
0071-0601 English Language and Orientation Programs in the United States
0071-061X English Little Magazines†
0071-0628 English Monarchs Series **4217**
0071-0636 English Place-Name Society
0071-0679 Ensayo y Testimonio **5290**
0071-0687 Ente Nazionale Idrocarburi. Report and Statement of Accounts†
0071-0695 Entertainment Industry Series
0071-0709 Entomological Society of Alberta. Proceedings **845**
0071-0717 Entomological Society of America. Miscellaneous Publications†
0071-0733 Entomological Society of British Columbia. Journal **845**
0071-0741 Entomological Society of Canada. Bulletin **845**
0071-075X Entomological Society of Canada. Memoirs†
0071-0768 Entomological Society of Ontario. Proceedings *changed to* 1713-7845 **845**
0071-0776 Entomological Society of Pennsylvania. Newsletter **845**
0071-0784 Societe Entomologique du Quebec. Memoires **859**
0071-0792 Entomologicke Problemy *changed to* 1335-5899 **844**
0071-0822 Entretiens sur l'Antiquite Classique **2234**
0071-0873 Environmental Health Engineering Series†
0071-0962 Ephemeris of the Sun, Polaris and Other Selected Stars with Companion Data and Tables†
0071-0989 Epigraphische Studien **4138**
0071-1004 Epimeleia: Beitraege zur Philosophie†
0071-1039 Equal Opportunity **3532**
0071-1055 Eranos Yearbook. Papers†
0071-1063 Erasmus in English†
0071-1071 Erbivore
0071-108X Eretz-Israel. Archaeological, Historical and Geographical Studies **392**
0071-111X Ergebnisse der Inneren Medizin und Kinderheilkunde. New Series†
0071-1128 Ergebnisse der Limnologie *changed to* 1612-166X **2792**
0071-1136 Ergebnisse der Mathematik und Ihrer Grenzgebiete. Neue Folge **5486**
0071-1152 Denmark. Statens Arkiver. Erhvervsarkivet. Aarbog (year) **4214**
0071-1160 Erlanger Geologische Abhandlungen **2733**
0071-1179 Ernaehrungsforschung†
0071-1187 Ernest Bloch Lectures **6565**
0071-1233 Ertekezesek a Torteneti Tudomanyok Korebol†
0071-125X Erziehung und Unterricht†
0071-1268 Esakia **847**
0071-1284 Universidade de Sao Paulo. Escola Superior de Agricultura "Luis de Queiroz." Boletim Didactico†
0071-1292 Escola Superior de Agricultura "Luiz de Queiroz". Boletim de Divulgacao†
0071-1306 Universidade de Sao Paulo. Escola Superior de Agricultura "Luis de Queiroz." Boletim Tecnico-Cientifico†
0071-1314 Escuela Interamericana de Bibliotecologia. Estadisticas†
0071-1349 Essais Philosophiques†
0071-1357 Essays and Studies **5291**
0071-1365 Essays in Biochemistry **731**
0071-1373 Essays in Chemistry†
0071-139X Essays in French Literature *changed to* 1835-7040 **5291**
0071-1438 Essays in Physics†
0071-1446 Essays in Toxicology†
0071-1470 Essential Articles†
0071-1489 Essex Naturalist **671**
0071-1527 Estadistica del Comercio Exterior de Espana†
0071-1543 Mexico. Instituto Nacional de Estadistica, Geografia e Informatica. Estadistica Industrial Anual†
0071-1578 Estate Planning, Quick Reference Outline†
0071-1594 Mid-Year Estimates of Population of New Mexico Counties†
0071-1632 Coleccion Estructuras y Formas†
0071-1640 Estudios de Arte Moderno†
0071-1659 Estudios de Arte y Estetica **488**
0071-1675 Estudios de Cultura Nahuatl **4292**
0071-1705 Estudios de Literatura Contemporanea **5291**
0071-1713 Estudios Filologicos **5116**
0071-1721 Estudios Filologicos. Anejo†
0071-173X Estudios Oceanologicos **2804**
0071-1772 Ethiopian Publications: Books, Pamphlets, Annuals and Periodical Articles **624**
0071-1780 Ethnic Chronology Series†
0071-1845 Ethnologia†
0071-1853 Ethnomedizin†
0071-1861 Etnografia Polska **338**
0071-187X Etudes Africaines†
0071-1896 Etudes de Cas de Conflits Internationaux†
0071-190X Etudes de Linguistique Appliquee **5117**
0071-1926 Etudes de Philologie, d'Archeologie et d'Histoire Ancienne **5117**
0071-1942 Etudes de Pollution Atmospherique a Paris et dans les Departments Peripheriques
0071-1969 Etudes d'Histoire de l'Art **488**
0071-1977 Etudes d'Histoire Economique et Sociale **1541**
0071-1993 Etudes d'Histoire Africaine†
0071-2027 Etudes et Travaux d'Archeologie Marocaine **393**
0071-2035 Etudes Ethnologiques†
0071-2043 Etudes Europeennes†
0071-2051 Etudes Finno-Ougriennes **5117**
0071-206X Etudes Foreziennes
0071-2078 Etudes Gobiniennes†
0071-2086 Etudes Gregoriennes **6565**
0071-2116 Etudes Juives†
0071-2124 Etudes Linguistiques **5117**
0071-2140 Etudes Picardes†
0071-2191 Studies on Taxation and Economic Development†
0071-2205 Etudes sur l'Histoire, l'Economie et la Sociologie des Pays Slaves†
0071-223X Eugenics Society Symposia†
0071-2248 Eureka: the Archimedean's Journal **5486**
0071-2264 European Company for the Financing of Railway Rolling Stock. Annual Report **8617**
0071-2272 Europa Camping und Caravaning. Internationaler Fuehrer **8312**
0071-2299 Europa. Revue de Presse Europeenne
0071-2329 Europaeische Schriften **7233**
0071-2396 European and Mediterranean Plant Protection Organization. Publications. Series B: Plant Health Newsletter†
0071-2418 European and Mediterranean Plant Protection Organization. Publications. Series D: Miscellaneous†
0071-2426 European Art Exhibitions. Catalog†
0071-2477 European Association for Animal Production. Scientific Series **286**
0071-2485 European Association for Animal Production. Symposia on Energy Metabolism†
0071-2493 European Association for Personnel Management. Congress Reports **1861**
0071-2515 European Association for Research on Plant Breeding. Report of the Congress **3729**
0071-2558 European Civil Aviation Conference (Report of Session) **8540**
0071-2582 European Companies **1227**
0071-2647 European Congress on Electron Microscopy. Proceeding **899**
0071-2671 European Congress of Anaesthesiology. Proceedings

0072-4106 Germany. Statistisches Bundesamt. Warenverzeichnis fuer die Aussenhandelsstatistik **1234**
0072-4114 Germany. Statistisches Bundesamt. Zahlenkompass **8374**
0072-4122 Annalen der Meteorologie. Neue Folge **6346**
0072-4130 Deutscher Wetterdienst. Berichte **6352**
0072-4149 Deutscher Wetterdienst. Bibliographien†
0072-4157 Geron†
0072-4165 Gesamtverzeichnis Oesterreichischer Dissertationen†
0072-4173 Geschichte der Ethik†
0072-4203 Geschichtliche Landeskunde **4223**
0072-422X Gesellschaft fuer die Geschichte und Bibliographie des Brauwesens. Jahrbuch *changed to* 1860-8922 **604**
0072-4238 Gesellschaft fuer Niedersaechsische Kirchengeschichte. Jahrbuch **7759**
0072-4254 Gesellschaft fuer Schleswig-Holsteinische Geschichte. Zeitschrift **4224**
0072-4270 Gesellschaft Pro Vindonissa. Jahresbericht **395**
0072-4289 Gesellschaft Pro Vindonissa. Veroeffentlichungen **395**
0072-4327 Geyer's Who Makes It Directory†
0072-436X Ghana Law Reports **4680**
0072-4408 Ghana. Railway and Ports Administration. Report†
0072-4491 Universitaetsbibliothek Giessen. Kurzberichte aus den Papyrus-Sammlungen **4165**
0072-4513 Gifu Daigaku Nogakubu Kenkyu Hokoku **115**
0072-4521 Gifu Daigaku Igakubu Kiyo **5619**
0072-4548 Gioventu Passionista† **8959**
0072-4556 Girios Aidas†
0072-4580 Gladiolus Annual **3756**
0072-4610 University of Glasgow. Social and Economic Studies. Occasional Papers†
0072-4629 University of Glasgow. Social and Economic Research Studies†
0072-4661 Glaxo Volume; an Occasional Contribution to the Science and Art of Medicine†
0072-4688 Politechnika Slaska. Zeszyty Naukowe. Elektryka **3327**
0072-470X Politechnika Slaska. Zeszyty Naukowe. Matematyka - Fizyka **5525**
0072-4718 Politechnika Slaska. Zeszyty Naukowe. Nauki Spoleczne **7992**
0072-4742 Global Focus Series†
0072-4750 Glossaria Interpretum†
0072-4769 Glottodidactica **5123**
0072-4777 Glove News
0072-4793 Goeteborger Germanistische Forschungen **5123**
0072-4807 Acta Regiae Societatis Scientiarum et Litterarum Gothoburgensis. Zoologica **929**
0072-4815 Acta Regiae Societatis Scientiarum et Litterarum Gothoburgensis. Geophysica **2777**
0072-4823 Acta Regiae Societatis Scientiarum et Litterarum Gothoburgensis. Humaniora **4441**
0072-4831 Goeteborgs Tandlaekare Saellskap. Aarsbok†
0072-4866 Niedersaechsische Staats- und Universitaetsbibliothek, Goettingen. Arbeiten†
0072-4874 Goettinger Abhandlungen zur Soziologie
0072-4882 Goettinger Jahrbuch **4225**
0072-4904 Going-to-College Handbook†
0072-4920 Gold†
0072-4947 Golf Course Superintendents Association of America. Proceedings of the International Golf Course Conference and Show†
0072-4955 Golf Guide
0072-4963 Golf Rules Illustrated
0072-4998 Gondwana Newsletter†
0072-5005 The Good Food Guide **4387**
0072-5013 Gornoslaskie Studia Socjologiczne **8104**
0072-503X Gothenburg Studies in English **5123**
0072-5048 Gothenburg Studies in Philosophy†
0072-5056 Gothenburg Studies in Physics†
0072-5064 Demografiska Forskargruppen, Goeteborg. Reports†
0072-5099 Goeteborgs Universitet. Sociologiska Institutionen. Forsknings-Rapport **7967**
0072-5110 Goeteborgs Universitet. Statistiska Institutionen. Skriftserie. Publications **8374**
0072-5145 Government Contracts Guide†
0072-5153 Government Contracts Monographs **7440**
0072-5161 Government Finance Brief. New Series†
0072-517X Government in Hawaii **7440**
0072-5188 Government Reference Books†
0072-520X Governmental Research Association Directory **1997**
0072-5234 Graduate Assistantship Directory in Computer Sciences†
0072-5250 Graduate Fellowship Awards Announced by National Science Foundation†
0072-5285 Graduate Texts in Mathematics **5490**
0072-5315 Grafton Fashions for Men†
0072-534X Grain Crops†
0072-5358 Grain Trade of Canada†
0072-5366 Grammatiken und Woerterbuecher des Schweizerdeutschen
0072-5382 Universidad de Granada. Coleccion Monografica†
0072-5404 Grandes Figures de la Charite†
0072-5439 Grandes Todos **5302**
0072-5455 Grands Courants de la Pensee Mondiale Contemporaine†
0072-5471 The Grants Register (Year) **2983**
0072-548X Japan Graphic Arts **7324**
0072-5501 Graphic Directory†
0072-5536 Graphis Packaging†
0072-5544 Grass†
0072-5579 Great Black Athletes†
0072-5587 Great Britain. Admiralty Advisory Committee Reports: Structural Steel†
0072-5595 Great Britain. Aeronautical Research Council. Current Paper Series†
0072-5609 Great Britain. Aeronautical Research Council. Reports and Memoranda Series†
0072-5625 Ancient Monuments Board for England. Annual Report†
0072-5641 Great Britain. Civil Aviation Authority. Civil Aviation Publications†
0072-565X Great Britain. Department of Trade. Companies: General Annual Report†
0072-5668 Great Britain. Department of Trade. Export of Works of Art
0072-5676 Great Britain. Department of Trade. Import Duties Act 1958. Annual Report
0072-5706 Great Britain. Department of Trade. Patents, Design and Trade Marks (Annual Report) **6750**
0072-5714 Great Britain. Central Health Services Council. Report†
0072-5722 Great Britain. Central Office of Information. Overseas Publications Division. Reference Pamphlets Series†
0072-5757 Great Britain. Central Statistical Office. Research Series†
0072-5773 Great Britain. Cinematograph Films Council. Annual Report
0072-579X Great Britain. Commission on Industrial Relations. Reports†
0072-5803 Great Britain. Department of the Environment. Committee on Synthetic Detergents. Progress Report†
0072-5811 Great Britain. Committee on Tribology. Report†
0072-582X Great Britain. Department of Education and Science. Computer Board for Universities and Research Councils. Report†
0072-5838 Great Britain. Consumer Council. Report†
0072-5846 Annual Statement of the Overseas Trade of the United Kingdom†
0072-5889 Great Britain. Department of Education and Science. Education Planning Paper†
0072-5897 Great Britain. Department of Education and Science. Education Surveys†
0072-5919 Great Britain. Department of Education and Science. Science Policy Studies
0072-5935 Great Britain. Department of Employment and Productivity. Safety, Health and Welfare. New Series Booklets†
0072-5943 Great Britain. Department of Employment. Training Information Papers†
0072-5994 Great Britain. Department of Health and Social Security. Hospital Building Bulletins†
0072-6001 Great Britain. Department of Health and Social Security. Hospital Building, England and Wales: Progress Report†
0072-6036 Great Britain. Department of Health and Social Security. Hospital In-Patient Inquiry†
0072-6044 Great Britain. Department of Health and Social Security. Hospital Organization and Methods Service Reports†
0072-6052 Great Britain. Department of Health and Social Security. Health Service Design Notes†
0072-6060 Great Britain. Department of Health and Social Security. Hospital Technical Memoranda†
0072-6087 Great Britain. Department of Health. On the State of the Public Health **7519**
0072-6168 Great Britain. Foreign and Commonwealth Office. Antigua. Report†
0072-6184 Great Britain. Foreign and Commonwealth Office. Bahamas. Report†
0072-6192 Great Britain. Foreign and Commonwealth Office. Bermuda. Report†
0072-6230 Great Britain. Foreign and Commonwealth Office. Colonial Numbered Series†
0072-6249 Great Britain. Foreign and Commonwealth Office. Dominica. Report†
0072-6257 Great Britain. Foreign and Commonwealth Office. Falkland Islands. Report†
0072-629X Xianggang (Year) **7295**
0072-6303 Great Britain. Foreign and Commonwealth Office. Montserrat. Report†
0072-632X Great Britain. Foreign and Commonwealth Office. Overseas Research Publications†
0072-6338 Great Britain. Foreign and Commonwealth Office. St. Christopher-Nevis-Anguilla. Report†
0072-6354 Great Britain. Foreign and Commonwealth Office. St. Lucia. Report†
0072-6362 Great Britain. Foreign and Commonwealth Office. Seychelles. Report†
0072-6370 Great Britain. Foreign and Commonwealth Office. St. Vincent. Report†
0072-6397 Great Britain. Foreign and Commonwealth Office. Treaty Series **7238**
0072-6400 Great Britain. Studies on Medical and Population Subjects **7284**
0072-6435 Great Britain. Home Office. Research Studies **2653**
0072-6443 Great Britain. Home Office. Studies in the Causes of Delinquency and the Treatment of Offenders
0072-6478 Great Britain. Industrial Reorganization Corporation. Report and Accounts†
0072-6508 Great Britain. Iron and Steel Consumers' Council. Report†
0072-6516 Great Britain. Keeper of Public Records. Annual Report of the Keeper of Public Records on the Work of the Public Record Office and the Report of the Advisory Council on Public Records
0072-6524 Great Britain. Laboratory of the Government Chemist. Annual Report of the Government Chemist **2062**
0072-6532 Great Britain. Manpower Research Unit. Manpower Studies
0072-6575 Great Britain. Medical Research Council. Special Report Series†
0072-6583 Great Britain. Medical Research Council. Memoranda†
0072-6591 Great Britain. Mercantile Navy List
0072-6605 Great Britain. Meteorological Office. Annual Report†
0072-6613 Great Britain. Meteorological Office. Geophysical Memoirs†
0072-6621 Great Britain. Meteorological Office. Scientific Paper†
0072-6664 Great Britain. Ministry of Agriculture, Fisheries and Food. Animal Disease Surveys†
0072-6680 Great Britain. Ministry of Agriculture, Fisheries and Food. Fishery Investigations. Series II: Sea Fisheries†
0072-6729 Great Britain. Ministry of Agriculture, Fisheries and Food. Technical Bulletin†
0072-677X Great Britain. Ministry of Housing and Local Government. Handbook of Statistics†
0072-680X Great Britain. Ministry of Housing and Local Government. Report†
0072-6842 Great Britain. Department of the Environment. Archaeological Reports
0072-6850 Great Britain. Department of the Environment. Engineering Specifications
0072-6869 Great Britain. Department of the Environment. Metrication in the Construction Industry
0072-6907 Great Britain. National Advisory Council on Art Education. Report†
0072-6923 Great Britain. National Agricultural Advisory Service. Experimental Husbandry Farms and Experimental Horticulture Stations. Progress Report†
0072-694X Great Britain. National Economic Development Office. Monographs†
0072-6958 Great Britain. National Film Finance Corporation. Annual Report†
0072-6990 Great Britain. National Savings Committee. Report
0072-7008 Natural Environment Research Council. Report **3455**
0072-7016 Great Britain. Public Record Office. Handbooks
0072-7032 Great Britain. Public Works Loan Board. Annual Report **7442**
0072-7059 Great Britain. Road Research Laboratory. Technical Papers†
0072-7083 Great Britain. Royal Commission on Historical Manuscripts. Commissioners' Reports to the Crown
0072-7091 Great Britain. Royal Commission on Historical Manuscripts. Joint Publication
0072-7105 Great Britain. Royal Mint. Annual Report
0072-7113 Great Britain. Schools Council Publications. Curriculum Bulletins† **8960**
0072-7121 Great Britain. Schools Council Publications. Examinations Bulletins† **8960**
0072-713X Great Britain. Schools Council Publications. Working Papers
0072-7164 Great Britain. Soil Survey of England and Wales. Bulletin **233**
0072-7172 Great Britain. Soil Survey of England and Wales. Memoirs†
0072-7199 Great Britain. Soil Survey of England and Wales. Report†
0072-7202 Great Britain. Soil Survey of England and Wales. Special Surveys **233**
0072-7210 Great Britain. Soil Survey of England and Wales. Technical Monographs **233**
0072-7229 Great Britain Specialised Stamp Catalogue **6895**
0072-7237 Great Britain. University Grants Committee. Annual Survey†
0072-7245 Great Britain. Water Resources Board. Publication†
0072-7253 Great Britain. Water Resources Board. Report
0072-727X Great Decisions **7239**
0072-7288 Great Ideas Today†
0072-7296 Great Lakes Fishery Commission (United States and Canada) Annual Report†
0072-730X Great Lakes Fishery Commission (United States and Canada) Technical Report Series **3596**
0072-7318 Great Lakes Red Book†
0072-7326 Great Lakes Research Checklist **8824**
0072-7334 Great Ormond Street Gazette†
0072-7342 Great West and Indian Series **4294**
0072-7350 Greater London Papers **7443**
0072-7385 Greek National Committee for Astronomy. Annual Reports of the Astronomical Institutes of Greece **575**
0072-7393 Greece. National Statistical Service. Annual Industrial Survey **1235**
0072-7415 Greece. National Statistical Service. Annual Statistical Survey on Mines, Quarries and Salterns **6485**
0072-7423 Greece. National Statistical Service. Shipping Statistics **8525**
0072-7458 State of Greek Industry in (Year) **1904**
0072-7466 Greek Mathematical Society. Bulletin **5490**
0072-7474 Greek, Roman and Byzantine Monographs **2234**
0072-7482 Greek, Roman, and Byzantine Studies. Scholarly Aids **2234**
0072-7490 Greenwood's Guide to Great Lakes Shipping **8645**
0072-7520 Bibliotheque Universitaire, Grenoble. Publications†
0072-7539 Universite des Sciences Sociales de Grenoble. Centre de Recherche d'Histoire Economique, Sociale et Institutionnelle. Collection. Serie Histoire Institutionnelle†
0072-7547 Universite des Sciences Sociales de Grenoble. Centre de Recherche d'Histoire Economique, Sociale et Institutionnelle. Collection. Serie Histoire Sociale†
0072-7555 Universite des Sciences Sociales de Grenoble. Centre de Recherche Economique et Sociale. Collection. Serie Agriculture et Devenir Social†
0072-7563 Universite des Sciences Sociales de Grenoble. Centre de Recherche Economique et Sociale. Collection. Serie Economie du Financement†
0072-7571 Universite des Sciences Sociales de Grenoble. Centre de Recherche Economique et Sociale. Collection. Serie Etudes d'Economie de l'Energie†
0072-758X Universite des Sciences Sociales de Grenoble. Centre de Recherche Economique et Sociale. Collection. Serie Economie du Developpement†
0072-7598 Universite des Sciences Sociales de Grenoble. Centre de Recherche Juridique. Collection. Serie Droit de la Propriete Industrielle†
0072-7601 Universite des Sciences Sociales de Grenoble. Centre de Recherche Juridique. Collection. Serie Droit du Tourisme†
0072-761X Universite des Sciences Sociales de Grenoble. Centre de Recherche Juridique. Collection. Serie Droits Etrangers et Droit Compare†
0072-7628 Universite des Sciences Sociales de Grenoble. Collection Generale†
0072-7636 Universite des Sciences Sociales de Grenoble. Institut d'Etudes Politiques. Serie Essais et Travaux†
0072-7644 Universite des Sciences Sociales de Grenoble. Institut d'Etudes Politiques. Serie Textes et Documents†
0072-7652 Universite de Grenoble. Institut Francais de Florence. Publication. Serie 1: Collection d'Etudes d'Histoire
0072-7660 Universite de Grenoble. Institut Francais de Florence. Publication. Serie 2: Collection d'Etudes Bibliographiques

ISSN

ISSN

9104 0073-7720 ULRICH'S PERIODICALS

0073-7720 Industrie de la Manutention dans les Ports Francais **8646**
0073-7739 Industrie et Artisanat†
0073-7747 Industrie Francaise des Moteurs a Combustion Interne **8585**
0073-7755 Industrieabwaesser **3362**
0073-7763 Industries Directory, Capitals
0073-7771 Industries Directory, Delhi
0073-7798 Industries Directory, Northern India
0073-781X Industry in East Africa
0073-7828 Inedits Russes
0073-7836 Informatheque†
0073-7844 Information Display Buyers Guide†
0073-7879 Information Processing Association of Israel. National Conference on Data Processing. Proceedings† **8964**
0073-7895 Information Service of the European Communities. Newsletter on the Common Agricultural Policy **200**
0073-7917 Informations Annuelles de Caryosystematique et Cytogenetique
0073-7925 Informations et Etudes Socialistes†
0073-800X Inglis Lecture†
0073-8018 Initiation a la Linguistique. Serie A. Lectures **5127**
0073-8026 Initiation a la Linguistique. Serie B. Problemes et Methodes **5127**
0073-8034 Initiation. Serie Textes, Bibliographies
0073-8042 Inland Printer - American Lithographer Buyer's Guide†
0073-8077 Inorganic Syntheses Series **2135**
0073-8093 Canada. Insect Pathology Research Institute. Program Review†
0073-8115 Insects of Micronesia **850**
0073-8123 Insights (St. Catherines) **2867**
0073-8166 Institut Belge d'Information et de Documentation. Repertoire de l'Information
0073-8182 Institut de Droit International. Annuaire **4929**
0073-8190 Institut de France. Annuaire
0073-8212 Institut de Recherche et d'Histoire des Textes, Paris. Documents, Etudes et Repertoires **5309**
0073-8247 Institut d'Emission d'Outre Mer, Paris. Rapport d'Activite *changed to* 1635-2262 **1598**
0073-8263 Institut des Etudes Occitanes. Publications†
0073-8271 Institut des Hautes Etudes de l'Amerique Latine. Cahiers†
0073-828X Institut des Hautes Etudes de l'Amerique Latine. Centre d'Etudes Politiques, Economiques et Sociales. Publications Multigraphiees.†
0073-8301 Institut des Hautes Etudes Scientifiques, Paris. Publications Mathematiques **5493**
0073-8352 Institut Francais de Pondichery. Departement d'Indologie. Publications **551**
0073-8360 Institut Francais du Petrole. Collection Colloques et Seminaires **6773**
0073-8379 Institut Francais du Petrole. Rapport Annuel **6773**
0073-8387 Institut fuer Asienkunde. Schriften†
0073-8417 Institut fuer den Wissenschaftlichen Film. Publikationen zu Wissenschaftlichen Filmen. Sektion Biologie†
0073-8433 Publikationen zu Wissenschaftlichen Filmen. Sektion Technische Wissenschaften, Naturwissenschaften†
0073-8468 Institut fuer Gewerbeforschung, Vienna. Taetigkeitsbericht
0073-8484 Institut fuer Oesterreichische Geschichtsforschung. Mitteilungen **4232**
0073-8492 Institut fuer Ostrecht. Studien **4693**
0073-8522 Institut Historique Belge de Rome. Bibliotheque **4232**
0073-8530 Institut Historique Belge de Rome. Bulletin **4232**
0073-8557 Institut Jules Destree. Etudes et Documents **4232**
0073-8565 Institut Michel Pacha. Annales†
0073-8573 Institut Pasteur de Lille. Annales†
0073-859X Universite de Geneve. Institut Universitaire de Hautes Etudes Internationales. Etudes et Travaux†
0073-8603 Universite de Geneve. Institut Universitaire de Hautes Etudes Internationales. Publication†
0073-8611 Instituta et Monumenta. Serie I: Monumenta
0073-862X Institute for Balkan Studies. Publications **4232**
0073-8654 Institute for Defense Analyses. Papers
0073-8662 Institute for Defense Analyses. Reports
0073-8670 Institute for Defense Analyses. Studies
0073-8697 I D E A Monographs†
0073-8700 I D E A Occasional Papers†
0073-8751 Institute for Fermentation, Osaka. Research Communications†
0073-8778 Institute for Monetary Research. Monographs†
0073-8786 Institute for Palestine Studies. Anthology Series†
0073-8808 Institute for Palestine Studies. International Annual Documentary Series†
0073-8816 Institute for Palestine Studies. Monograph Series **4321**
0073-8832 Institute for Petroleum Research and Geophysics, Holon, Israel. Report†
0073-8840 I P D Economic Analyses and Surveys. Information Bulletin
0073-8859 I P D Projects. Information Bulletin
0073-8867 I P D Sociological Analyses and Surveys. Information Bulletin
0073-8921 I S M A Papers **342**
0073-893X I S M A Occasional Papers **342**
0073-8948 Institut fuer Iberoamerika-Kunde. Schriftenreihe†
0073-8999 Institute of Bankers in Pakistan. Council. Report and Accounts **1354**
0073-9006 Institute of British Geographers. Special Publication†
0073-9030 Institute of Chartered Accountants in England and Wales. Management Information Series†
0073-9057 Institute of Chartered Accountants of Scotland. Official Directory **1291**
0073-9065 C F A Monograph Series†
0073-9073 Institute of Clerk of Works of Great Britain Incorporated. Year Book
0073-909X Institute of Economic Affairs. Occasional Papers **1124**
0073-9103 Institute of Economic Affairs. Research Monographs **1125**
0073-9146 I E E E Membership Directory
0073-9154 I E E E Power Engineering Society. Winter Meeting. Preprints† **8963**
0073-9197 I E E E Region 5 Conference. Record†
0073-9200 Institution of Engineers. Technical Journal **3199**
0073-9219 Institution of Engineers. Year Book **3199**
0073-926X Institute of European Studies. Announcements
0073-9278 Institute of European Studies. Papers and Addresses of the Annual Conference and Academic Council
0073-9286 I F T World Directory and Buyers' Guide†
0073-9316 Great Britain. Natural Environment Research Council. British Geological Survey. Geomagnetic Bulletin **2783**
0073-9324 Great Britain. Institute of Geological Sciences. Geophysical Papers†
0073-9340 Institute of Geological Sciences, London. Overseas Geology and Mineral Resources. Supplement Series†
0073-9375 Great Britain. Institute of Geological Sciences. Water Supply Papers†
0073-9383 Great Britain. Institute of Geological Sciences. Water Supply Papers. Research Reports†
0073-9391 Great Britain. Institute of Geological Sciences. Water Supply Papers. Technical Communications†
0073-9413 Institute of Judicial Administration. Calendar Status Study†
0073-9421 Institute of Labor and Industrial Relations. Policy Papers in Human Resources and Industrial Relations†
0073-943X Institute of Labor and Industrial Relations. Reprint Series
0073-9456 Institute of Mennonite Studies Series†
0073-9464 Institute of Metals. Monograph and Report Series†
0073-9472 Institute of Nuclear Materials Management. Proceedings of Annual Meeting **3169**
0073-9529 Institute of Petroleum, London. Report of the Summer Meeting†
0073-9537 I P C Monographs **8106**
0073-9545 I P C Papers **8106**
0073-9561 Institute of Psychophysical Research. Proceedings
0073-957X Institute of Public Administration, Dublin. Administrative Procedure Series†
0073-9588 Institute of Public Administration, Dublin. Annual Report **7446**
0073-9596 Institute of Public Administration, Dublin. Administration Yearbook and Diary **7446**
0073-960X Institute of Public Administration, Dublin. Research Series†
0073-9618 Institute of Public Administration, Khartoum. Occasional Papers **7446**
0073-9626 Institute of Public Administration, Khartoum. Proceedings of the Annual Round Table Conference **7446**
0073-9650 Institute of Purchasing and Supply. Yearbook†
0073-9677 Institute of Refrigeration. Proceedings **4121**
0073-9693 Institute of Social Studies, The Hague. Publications. Paperback Series†
0073-9707 Institute of Social Studies, The Hague. Publications. Series Major†
0073-9731 Institute of Southeast Asian Studies. Occasional Paper **7973**
0073-9766 I E E Monograph Series†
0073-9782 Institution of Engineers (India). Directory†
0073-9790 Institution of Engineers of Ireland. Transactions **3199**
0073-9804 Institution of Municipal Engineers, London. Annual Conference. Proceedings†
0073-9812 Institution of Nuclear Engineers. Year Book†
0073-9839 Institution of Railway Signal Engineers. Proceedings **8619**
0073-9855 Instituto Adolfo Lutz. Revista **887**
0073-9871 Instituto Antartico Chileno. Contribution. Serie Cientifica **2710**
0073-988X Instituto Brasileiro do Cafe. Departamento Economico. Anuario Estatistico do Cafe
0073-9901 Instituto Butantan. Memorias **947**
0073-991X Instituto Caro y Cuervo. Serie Bibliografica **627**
0073-9928 Instituto Caro y Cuervo. Serie Minor **5309**
0073-9936 Instituto Centro Americano de Investigacion y Tecnologia Industrial. Publicaciones Geologicas†
0073-9944 Instituto Centroamericano de Administracion Publica. Serie 100. Aspectos Humanos de la Administracion†
0073-9952 Instituto Centroamericano de Administracion Publica. Serie 200. Ciencia de la Administracion†
0073-9960 Instituto Centroamericano de Administracion Publica. Serie 300: Investigacion†
0073-9979 Instituto Centroamericano de Administracion Publica. Serie 400: Economia y Finanzas†
0073-9995 Instituto Centroamericano de Administracion Publica. Serie 600: Informes de Seminarios†
0074-0004 Instituto Centroamericano de Administracion Publica. Serie 700: Materiales de Informacion†
0074-0012 Instituto Centroamericano de Administracion Publica. Serie 800: Metodologia de la Administracion†
0074-0020 Instituto Centroamericano de Administracion Publica. Serie 900: Miscelaneas†
0074-0039 Instituto Costarricense de Cultura Hispanica. Publicacion†
0074-0047 Informe de Operacion de las Principales Empresas Productoras y Distribuidoras de Energia Electrica de Costa Rica **3319**
0074-0055 Instituto de Botanica. Boletim **794**
0074-0063 Instituto de Ciencia Politica Rafael Bielsa. Anuario **7143**
0074-008X Instituto de Investigacao Cientifica de Angola. Bibliograficas Tematicas **7937**
0074-0098 Instituto de Investigacao Cientifica de Angola. Memorias e Trabalhos **7866**
0074-0144 Instituto de Tecnologia de Alimentos. Instrucoes Praticas†
0074-0152 Instituto de Tecnologia de Alimentos. Instrucoes Tecnicas
0074-0160 Anthologica Annua **4130**
0074-0195 Instituto Espanol de Oceanografia. Boletin **2807**
0074-0233 Instituto Hondureno de Seguridad Social. Departamento de Estadistica y Procesamiento de Datos. Anuario Estadistico **4506**
0074-025X Fundacion Miguel Lillo. Miscelanea **790**
0074-0276 Instituto Oswaldo Cruz, Rio de Janeiro. Memorias **678**
0074-0284 Instituto Paranaense de Botanica. Revista. Serie: Flora do Parana
0074-0292 I T A Humanidades†
0074-0306 Instituto Tecnologico y de Estudios Superiores. Publicaciones. Serie: Catalogos de Biblioteca†
0074-0330 Instituto Torcuato di Tella. Centro de Estudios Urbanos Regionales. Documentos de Trabajo†
0074-0349 Instituto Torcuato di Tella. Centro de Investigaciones Economicas. Documentos de Trabajo†
0074-0357 Instituto Torcuato di Tella. Centro de Investigaciones Sociales. Documentos de Trabajo†
0074-0446 Instituut voor Planteziektenkundig Onderzoek. Jaarverslag† **8965**
0074-0462 Koninklijk Instituut voor Taal-, Land- en Volkenkunde. Bibliographical Series **362**
0074-0470 Koninklijk Instituut voor Taal-, Land- en Volkenkunde. Translation Series **346**
0074-0543 Instrumentation in Nuclear Medicine†
0074-0551 Instrumentation in the Chemical and Petroleum Industries†
0074-0586 Instytut Gospodarki Wodnej. Prace†
0074-0616 Instytut Slaski. Kommunikaty. Seria Niemcoznawcza†
0074-0632 Instytut Slaski. Wydawnictwa†
0074-0640 Instytut Badan Jadrowych. Zaklad Radiobiologii i Ochrony Zdrowia. Prace Doswiadczalne†
0074-0667 Insulation Handbook **1015**
0074-0675 Insurance Almanac: Who, What, When and Where in Insurance **4506**
0074-0683 Insurance Casebook†
0074-0705 Israel. Central Bureau of Statistics. Insurance in Israel
0074-0756 Asociacion Interamericana de Bibliotecarios y Documentalistas Agricolas. Boletin Tecnico†
0074-0764 Inter-American Commission of Women. Special Assembly. Final Act†
0074-0780 Inter-American Commission on Human Rights. Report on the Work Accomplished During Its Special Sessions†
0074-0799 Inter-American Conference of Ministers of Labor on the Alliance for Progress. Final Act†
0074-0802 Inter-American Conference on Community Development. Final Act†
0074-0810 Congresos Indigenistas Interamericanos. Actas
0074-0829 Inter-American Council for Education, Science, and Culture. Final Report†
0074-0837 Work Accomplished by the Inter-American Juridical Committee during Its Meeting†
0074-0861 Inter-American Development Bank. Board of Governors. Proceedings of the Meeting **1355**
0074-0918 Inter-American Economic and Social Council. Final Report of the Annual Meeting at the Ministerial Level†
0074-0934 Inter-American Music Monograph Series†
0074-0942 Inter-American Nuclear Energy Commission. Final Report†
0074-0950 Inter-American Port and Harbor Conferences. Final Act†
0074-0969 Inter-American Statistical Conferences. Final Report†
0074-0985 Inter-American Travel Congresses. Final Act†
0074-0993 Inter-American Tropical Tuna Commission. Bulletin **3598**
0074-1000 Inter-American Tropical Tuna Commission. Annual Report **3598**
0074-1019 Inter-Documentation Company. Newsletter†
0074-1035 Inter - Nord **2710**
0074-106X Inter-University Case Program. Case Study **7446**
0074-1078 Inter-University Consortium for Political and Social Research. Annual Report **7143**
0074-1086 Interamerican Conference on Materials Technology. (Proceedings)†
0074-1132 Interdisciplinary Topics in Gerontology **4048**
0074-1140 Interferences, Arts, Lettres
0074-1175 Intergovernmental Oceanographic Commission. Technical Series **2808**
0074-1191 Design + Art in Greece **440**
0074-1205 Internal Revenue Guide to Your Federal Income Tax†
0074-1213 Internal Trade of Iran **1430**
0074-123X International Academy of Indian Culture. Satapitaka Series **4184**
0074-1256 International Academy of Oral Pathology. Proceedings†
0074-1264 International Actuarial Congress. Transactions†
0074-1337 International Air Transport Association. Symposium Papers from the Annual General Meeting†
0074-1353 International Anatomical Congress. Proceedings
0074-137X International Archery Federation. Bulletin Officiel
0074-1388 International Arthurian Society. Bibliographical Bulletin **5407**
0074-140X International Association for Bridge and Structural Engineering. Bulletin†
0074-1434 International Association for Bridge and Structural Engineering. Preliminary Report (of Congress)†
0074-1469 International Association for Classical Archaeology. Proceedings of Congress
0074-1507 International Association for Statistics in Physical Sciences. Proceedings (of Meetings)†
0074-1574 International Association of Applied Psychology. Proceedings of Congress
0074-1604 International Association of Democratic Lawyers. Congress Report
0074-1620 International Association of Gerontology. European Clinical Section Proceedings
0074-1639 International Association of Gerontology. Proceedings of the Congress
0074-1647 International Association of Hail Insurers. Congress Report **4509**
0074-1655 International Association of Logopedics and Phoniatrics. Reports of Congress **6146**
0074-1663 International Association of Meteorology and Atmospheric Physics. Report of Proceedings of General Assembly **6357**
0074-1671 International Association of Milk Control Agencies. Proceedings of Annual Meetings **265**
0074-1698 A.I.J.P. Yearbook
0074-1701 International Association of Philatelic Journalists. Bulletin **6896**
0074-171X International Association of Philatelic Journalists. Minutes of Annual Congresses

Link to your serials resources and content with ulrichsweb.com

DIRECTORY 2010 0074-6320 9105

0074-1728 International Association of Physical Education and Sports for Girls and Women. Proceedings of the International Congress **8180**
0074-1736 International Association of Seed Crushers. Proceedings of the Annual Congress
0074-1744 International Association of State Lotteries. (Reports of Congress) **1930**
0074-1752 International Association of Students in Economics and Management. International Compendium. Annual Report
0074-1760 International Association of Thalassotherapy. Congress Reports
0074-1809 International Astronomical Union. Proceedings of Symposia **576**
0074-1833 International Atomic Energy Agency. Bibliographical Series†
0074-1841 I A E A Laboratory Activities†
0074-185X I A E A Research Contracts†
0074-1868 International Atomic Energy Agency. Legal Series **4694**
0074-1876 International Atomic Energy Agency. Panel Proceedings Series **3169**
0074-1884 International Atomic Energy Agency. Proceedings Series **3169**
0074-1906 International Atomic Energy Agency. Technical Directories **3169**
0074-1914 International Atomic Energy Agency. Technical Report Series **3169**
0074-1922 International Auction Records
0074-1930 International Audio-Visual Technical Centre. Bibliographical References
0074-1949 International Audio-Visual Technical Centre. Studies and Reports
0074-199X World Bank Staff Occasional Papers†
0074-2007 International Beekeeping Congress. Reports **122**
0074-2015 International Bibliography of Historical Sciences **4170**
0074-2031 International Bibliography of Rice Research†
0074-204X International Bibliography of Studies on Alcohol **2701**
0074-2066 International Biennial Exhibition of Prints in Tokyo†
0074-2074 I B P Handbooks†
0074-2090 International Botanical Congress. Abstracts of Papers **716**
0074-2104 International Bureau of Fiscal Documentation. Annual Report† **8965**
0074-2139 International Businessmen's Who's Who†
0074-2147 International Catalogue of Occupational Safety and Health Films
0074-2163 International Centre for Settlement of Investment Disputes. Annual Report **1630**
0074-2171 International Centre of Fertilizers. World Congress. Acts
0074-218X International Ceramic Congress. Proceedings
0074-221X International Civil Aviation Organization. Aeronautical Agreements and Arrangements. Annual Supplement **8545**
0074-2228 International Civil Aviation Organization. (Panel On) Application of Space Techniques Relating to Aviation. Report of Meeting†
0074-2244 International Civil Aviation Organization. Airworthiness Committee. Report of Meeting†
0074-2252 International Civil Aviation Organization. Automated Data Interchange Systems Panel. Report of Meeting†
0074-2287 International Civil Aviation Organization. Air Navigation Plan. Africa - Indian Ocean Region **60**
0074-2295 International Civil Aviation Organization. Air Navigation Plan. Caribbean and South American Regions **60**
0074-2309 International Civil Aviation Organization. Air Navigation Plan. European Region†
0074-2325 International Civil Aviation Organization. Air Navigation Plan. North Atlantic, North American and Pacific Regions **60**
0074-2333 International Civil Aviation Organization. All-Weather Operations Panel. Report of Meeting†
0074-235X International Civil Aviation Organization. Assembly. Resolutions **8545**
0074-2368 International Civil Aviation Organization. Assembly. Report and Minutes of the Legal Commission **8545**
0074-2376 International Civil Aviation Organization. Assembly. Report and Minutes of the Economic Commission **8545**
0074-2384 International Civil Aviation Organization. Assembly. Report of the Technical Commission **60**
0074-2422 International Civil Aviation Organization. Digests of Statistics. Series AT. Airport Traffic **8526**
0074-2430 International Civil Aviation Organization. Digests of Statistics. Series F. Financial Data - Commercial Air Carriers **8526**
0074-2457 International Civil Aviation Organization. Digests of Statistics. Series R. Civil Aircraft on Register **8526**
0074-249X International Civil Aviation Organization. Index of I C A O Publications. Annual Cumulation **76**
0074-2503 International Civil Aviation Organization. Legal Committee. Minutes and Documents (of Sessions) **8545**
0074-252X International Civil Aviation Organization. Obstacle Clearance Panel. Report of Meeting†
0074-2546 International Civil Aviation Organization. Report of the Air Navigation Conference **8546**
0074-2570 International Civil Aviation Organization. Technical Panel on Supersonic Transport. Report of Meeting **60**
0074-2589 International Civil Aviation Organization. Visual Aids Panel. Report of Meeting†
0074-2597 International Clay Conference. Proceedings†
0074-2600 International College of Dentists. India Section. Newsletter
0074-2694 International Commission of Agricultural Engineering. Reports of Congress (proceedings)
0074-2708 International Commission of Sugar Technology. Proceedings of the General Assembly **3648**
0074-2724 International Commission on Illumination. Proceedings
0074-2732 International Commission on Irrigation and Drainage. Congress Reports **8826**
0074-2759 International Commission on Radiological Protection. Report†
0074-2783 International Committee for Historical Science. Bulletin d'Information **4147**
0074-2813 International Comparative Literature Association. Proceedings of the Congress **5309**
0074-283X International Computer Bibliography†
0074-2856 International Confederation for Agricultural Credit. Assembly and Congress Reports **200**
0074-2872 International Confederation of Free Trade Unions. World Congress Reports **4596**
0074-2880 International Confederation of Midwives. Congress Reports **5993**
0074-2899 International Confederation of Societies of Authors and Composers **6753**
0074-2902 International Conference of Agricultural Economists. Proceedings **200**
0074-2929 International Conference of Economic History. Contributions
0074-2945 International Conference of Ethiopian Studies. Proceedings **4175**
0074-2961 International Conference on Social Welfare. Conference Proceedings **8047**
0074-3011 International Conference on Cloud Physics. Proceedings **6357**
0074-302X International Conference on Congenital Malformation. Abstracts
0074-3038 International Conference on Congenital Malformations. Proceedings†
0074-3046 International Conference on Cosmic Rays. Proceedings **7067**
0074-3054 International Conference on Endodontics. Transactions†
0074-3097 International Conference on Global Impacts of Applied Microbiology. Proceedings
0074-3127 World Congresses on Information Processing. Proceedings
0074-3135 International Conference on Intra-Uterine Contraception. Proceedings
0074-3143 International Conference on Phenomena in Ionized Gases. Proceedings†
0074-3151 International Conference on Large High Voltage Electric Systems. Proceedings **3159**
0074-316X International Conference on Lead. Proceedings **6316**
0074-3178 International Conference on Low Temperature Physics. Reports
0074-3259 International Conference on Planned Parenthood. Proceedings†
0074-3305 International Conference on Social Welfare. Proceedings
0074-3356 International Commission on Trichinellosis. Proceedings
0074-3364 International Congress for Analytical Psychology. Proceedings **7363**
0074-3372 International Congress for Child Psychiatry. Proceedings
0074-3380 International Congress for Cybernetics. Proceedings **2527**
0074-3402 International Congress for Logic, Methodology and Philosophy of Science. Proceedings
0074-3410 International Congress for Microbiology. Proceedings
0074-3429 International Congress for Papyrology. Proceedings **398**
0074-3437 International Congress for Stereology. Proceedings **3346**
0074-3445 International Congress of Acarology. Proceedings
0074-347X International Congress of Angiology. Proceedings
0074-3488 International Congress of Animal Production. Proceedings†
0074-3534 International Congress of Biochemistry. Proceedings†
0074-3542 International Congress for Byzantine Studies. Acts
0074-3550 International Congress of Cell Biology. Summaries of Reports and Communications
0074-3577 International Congress of Chemotherapy. Proceedings†
0074-3615 International Congress of Cybernetic Medicine. Proceedings
0074-3631 International Congress of Electroencephalography and Clinical Neurophysiology (Proceedings) **6146**
0074-364X International Congress of Entomology **850**
0074-3666 International Congress of Food Science and Technology. Proceedings *changed to* World Congress of Food Science and Technology. Proceedings **3668**
0074-3682 International Congress of Hematology. Proceedings†
0074-3690 International Congress of Histochemistry and Cytochemistry. Proceedings **734**
0074-3704 International Congress of History of Medicine. Proceedings†
0074-3712 International Congress of Home Economics. Report
0074-3747 International Congress of Life Assurance Medicine. Proceedings
0074-3755 International Congress of Linguists. Proceedings **5129**
0074-378X International Congress of Nephrology. Proceedings†
0074-3798 International Congress of Neuro-Genetics and Neuro-Ophthalmology. Proceedings
0074-3801 International Congress of Neurological Surgery. Abstracts of Papers
0074-3828 International Congress of Occupational Therapy. Proceedings **6679**
0074-3844 International Congress of Orthoptists. Transactions
0074-3860 International Congress of Parasitology. Proceedings **948**
0074-3879 International Congress of Pharmaceutical Sciences. Proceedings **6849**
0074-3887 International Congress of Physical Medicine. Abstracts of Papers Presented
0074-3895 International Congress of Primatology. Proceedings **948**
0074-3917 International Congress of Psychotherapy. Proceedings/Verhandlungen/Comptes Rendus†
0074-3933 International Congress of Radiology. Reports **6198**
0074-3968 International Congress of Sugarcane Technologists. Proceedings **3648**
0074-3984 Transplantation Today†
0074-400X International Conference on Acoustics. Reports†
0074-4034 International Congress on Canned Foods. Report
0074-4042 International Congress on Clinical Chemistry. Abstracts†
0074-4050 International Congress on Clinical Chemistry. Proceedings†
0074-4069 International Congress on Clinical Chemistry. Papers
0074-4077 International Congress on Combustion Engines. Proceedings **3381**
0074-4107 International Congress on Hormonal Steroids. Abstracts of Papers Presented
0074-4123 International Congress on Metallic Corrosion. (Proceedings)†
0074-4131 International Congress on Occupational Health. Proceedings†
0074-414X International Congress on Phonetic Sciences. Proceedings†
0074-4158 International Congress on Project Planning by Network Analysis. Congress Book
0074-4166 International Congress on Radiation Research. Proceedings
0074-4182 International Congress on Rheology. Proceedings
0074-4190 International Congress on the History of Art. Proceedings **496**
0074-4204 International Congress on Underground Techniques and Town-Planning. Reports†
0074-4212 International Congresses on Tropical Medicine and Malaria. (Proceedings)†
0074-4220 International Convocation on Immunology. Papers†
0074-4247 International Cooperative Alliance. Congress Report†
0074-4255 International Cooperative Alliance. Cooperative Series **1423**
0074-4263 International Council for Bird Preservation. British Section. Report†
0074-4271 BirdLife International. Proceedings of Conferences†
0074-428X International Council for Building Research, Studies and Documentation. Congress Reports†
0074-4360 International Council of Homehelp Services. Reports of Congress
0074-4395 International Council of Voluntary Agencies. Documents Series†
0074-4409 International Council of Voluntary Agencies. General Conference. Record of Proceedings†
0074-4425 International Council on Social Welfare. European Symposium. Proceedings†
0074-4433 International Court of Justice. Pleadings, Oral Arguments, Documents **4930**
0074-4441 International Court of Justice: Reports of Judgments, Advisory Opinions and Orders **4953**
0074-445X International Court of Justice. Yearbook **4930**
0074-4468 Credit Union Yearbook†
0074-4565 International Directory of Arts **496**
0074-4573 International Directory of Biological Deterioration Research†
0074-4581 International Directory of Computer and Information System Services†
0074-4603 International Directory of Philosophy and Philosophers **6925**
0074-4611 International Directory of Programs in Business and Commerce†
0074-462X International Directory of 16MM Film Collectors†
0074-4646 International Economic Association. Proceedings of the Conferences and Congresses **1126**
0074-4697 International Electrotechnical Commission. Yearbook - Annuaire†
0074-5766 International Encyclopedia on Packaging Machines
0074-5774 International Engineering Directory†
0074-5782 International Eucharist Congress. Proceedings **7801**
0074-5790 International Falcon Movement. Conference Reports
0074-5804 F I D - C R Report Series†
0074-5820 F I D Annual Report†
0074-5855 International Federation for Modern Languages and Literature. Congress Reports
0074-5863 International Federation of Agricultural Producers. General Conference Proceedings
0074-588X International Federation of Asian and Western Pacific Contractors' Associations. Proceedings of the Annual Convention **6280**
0074-5898 International Federation of Associations of Textile Chemists and Colorists. Reports of Congress
0074-5901 International Federation of Automobile Engineers and Technicians Associations. Reports of Congress
0074-591X International Federation of Children's Communities. Documents
0074-5928 International Federation of Children's Communities. Etudes Pedagogiques
0074-5936 International Federation of Children's Communities. Recherches et Temoignages
0074-5952 Federation Internationale des Producteurs de Jus de Fruits. Compte-Rendu du Congres **603**
0074-5960 I F I Information†
0074-5979 International Federation of Journalists and Travel Writers. Official List **8723**
0074-5987 I F L A Annual†
0074-6002 I F L A Directory **5013**
0074-6037 International Federation of Medical Students' Associations. Minutes and Reports of the General Assembly†
0074-6045 International Federation of Prestressing. Congress Proceedings†
0074-610X International Football Book **8236**
0074-6118 International Foundry Congress. Papers and Communications **6316**
0074-6134 International Geographical Union. Papers
0074-6142 International Geophysics Series **2783**
0074-6177 International Graphical Federation. Report of Activities **4596**
0074-6185 International Grassland Congress. Proceedings **237**
0074-6193 International Green Book†
0074-6223 International Hop Growers Convention. Report of Congress
0074-6231 International Horticultural Congress. Proceedings **3739**
0074-624X International Hotel Guide†
0074-6258 International Humanist and Ethical Union. Proceedings of the Congress
0074-6274 International Hydrographic Conference. Reports of Proceedings **2808**
0074-6312 International IFIP/IFAC Prolamat Conference. Proceedings
0074-6320 International Indian Ocean Expedition. Collected Reprints†

ISSN

9106 0074-6401 ULRICH'S PERIODICALS

0074-6401 I I E P Occasional Papers **3024**
0074-641X International Institute for Labour Studies. International Educational Materials Exchange. List of Available Materials†
0074-6436 International Institute for Land Reclamation and Improvement. Bibliography† **8966**
0074-6444 International Institute for Land Reclamation and Improvement. Bulletin†
0074-6452 International Institute for Land Reclamation and Improvement. Publication **237**
0074-6479 International Institute of Administrative Sciences. Reports of the International Congress **7446**
0074-6487 International Institute of Differing Civilizations. (Session Papers)
0074-6495 International Institute of Ibero-American Literature. Congress Proceedings. Memoria **5310**
0074-6509 International Institute for Labour Studies. Publications†
0074-6525 International Institute of Philosophy. Actes **6926**
0074-6533 International Institute of Public Finance. Papers and Proceedings†
0074-6541 Institut International du Froid. Comptes Rendus de Reunions de Commissions **4121**
0074-655X International Institute of Seismology and Earthquake Engineering. Bulletin **2783**
0074-6568 International Institute of Seismology and Earthquake Engineering. Earthquake Report†
0074-6584 International Institute of Seismology and Earthquake Engineering. Lecture Note†
0074-6592 International Institute of Seismology and Earthquake Engineering. Progress Report†
0074-6614 International Institute of Seismology and Earthquake Engineering. Year Book **2784**
0074-6622 International Institute on the Prevention and Treatment of Alcoholism. Selected Papers
0074-6657 International Labor Studies†
0074-6665 International Labour and Industrial Film Triennial. Catalogue of the Participating Films
0074-6673 International Labour Conference. Record of Proceedings **1689**
0074-6681 International Labour Conference. Reports **1689**
0074-6703 Management Development Series **1775**
0074-6738 International Law Association. Reports of Conferences **4931**
0074-6770 International Lesson Annual **7651**
0074-6797 International Linguistic Association. Monograph
0074-6800 International Linguistic Association. Special Publications **5130**
0074-6819 International Literary and Artistic Association. Proceedings and Reports of Congress **4458**
0074-6827 International Literary Market Place **7563**
0074-6835 International Machine Tool Design and Research Conference. Proceedings†
0074-6878 International Maize and Wheat Improvement Center. Research Bulletin†
0074-6959 International Meeting of Animal Nutrition Experts. Proceedings **290**
0074-6983 International Metalworkers' Congress. Reports **6317**
0074-7017 International Mineralogical Association. Proceedings of Meetings **6467**
0074-7025 International Monetary Fund. Summary Proceedings of the Annual Meeting of the Board of Governors **1358**
0074-7033 International Monographs on Advanced Biology and Biophysics
0074-7041 International Monographs on Advanced Chemistry†
0074-705X International Monographs on Advanced Mathematics and Physics **5498**
0074-7068 International Monographs on Studies in Indian Economics†
0074-7084 International Motion Picture Almanac **6504**
0074-7122 International Naturist Guide
0074-7130 International Newsletter: Educational Evaluation and Research
0074-7157 International North Pacific Fisheries Commission. Bulletin†
0074-7173 International Olive Growers Federation. Congress Reports†
0074-7181 International Olympic Academy. Report of the Sessions **8181**
0074-7203 International Organization of Citrus Virologists. Proceedings of the Conference
0074-7211 International Ornithological Congress. Proceedings **908**
0074-7238 International Pacific Halibut Commission. Annual Report **3598**
0074-7262 International Pacific Salmon Fisheries Commission. Bulletin†
0074-7270 International Pacific Salmon Fisheries Commission. Progress Report†
0074-7289 I P R A Studies in Peace Research†
0074-7297 International Peace Research Association. Proceedings of the Conference†
0074-7300 International Pediatric Association. Proceedings of Congress **6093**
0074-7335 International Pharmacological Congress. Proceedings
0074-7343 International Philatelic Federation. General Assembly. Proces-Verbal **6896**
0074-7351 International Photobiological Congress. Proceedings†
0074-7386 International Planned Parenthood Federation. Proceedings of the Conference of the Europe and Near East Region†
0074-7394 International Planned Parenthood Federation. Working Papers†
0074-7408 International Association of Plant Breeders for the Protection of Plant Varieties. Congress Reports **3739**
0074-7416 I P A Conference Report†
0074-7475 International Poplar Commission. Session Reports†
0074-7483 International Poster Annual†
0074-7556 International Publishers Association. Proceedings of Congress **7563**
0074-7580 International Railway Statistics (Year) **8526**
0074-7599 International Rayon and Synthetic Fibres Committee. Statistical Yearbook **8463**
0074-7602 International Rayon and Synthetic Fibres Committee. Technical Conference. Reports†
0074-7610 International Rayon and Synthetic Fibres Committee. World Congress. Report†
0074-7637 International Real Estate Federation. Reports of Congress†
0074-7645 International Reference Annual for Building and Equipment of Sports, Tourism, Recreation Installations **8181**
0074-7696 International Review of Cytology *changed to* 1937-6448 **833**
0074-7718 International Review of Experimental Pathology†
0074-7726 International Review of Forestry Research†
0074-7734 International Review of General and Experimental Zoology†
0074-7742 International Review of Neurobiology **6148**
0074-7750 International Review of Research in Mental Retardation **6148**
0074-7777 International Review of Tropical Medicine†
0074-7785 International Reviews in Aerosol Physics and Chemistry†
0074-7815 International Road Congresses. Proceedings **8632**
0074-7823 International Rubber Study Group. Summary of Proceedings of the Group Meetings and Assemblies†
0074-784X International School of Physics "Enrico Fermi." Proceedings **7018**
0074-7866 International Science Review Series†
0074-7874 International Seaweed Symposium. Proceedings **795**
0074-7890 International Security Directory†
0074-7904 International Sedimentological Congress. Guidebook **2748**
0074-7920 International Seminar on Reproductive Physiology and Sexual Endocrinology. Proceedings†
0074-8021 International Series on Chemical Engineering†
0074-803X International Series of Monographs in Electrical Engineering†
0074-8056 International Series of Monographs in Mechanical Engineering†
0074-8064 International Series in Natural Philosophy†
0074-8080 International Series on Automation and Automatic Control†
0074-8099 International Series on Analytical Chemistry†
0074-8129 International Series on Electronics and Instrumentation†
0074-820X International Series in Library and Information Sciences†
0074-8234 International Series on Oral Biology†
0074-8242 International Series on Organic Chemistry†
0074-8315 International Series on Semiconductors†
0074-8358 International Shipping and Shipbuilding Directory†
0074-8404 International Social Science Council. Publications†
0074-8447 International Society for Cell Biology. Symposia†
0074-8455 International Society for Labour Law and Social Legislation. Proceedings of Congress **4696**
0074-8471 International Society for Research on the Moors. Report of Congress
0074-848X International Society for Rock Mechanics. Congress. Proceedings **3273**
0074-8498 International Society for Terrain-Vehicle Systems. Proceedings of International Conference **3273**
0074-8528 International Society of Blood Transfusion. Proceedings of the Congress†
0074-8536 International Society of Geographical Pathology. Proceedings of the Conference†
0074-8544 International Society of Internal Medicine. Congress Proceedings†
0074-8560 International Society of Surgery. Comptes-Rendus†
0074-8579 International Society of Urology. Reports of Congress
0074-8595 International Spectroscopy Colloquium. Proceedings†
0074-8609 International Statistical Institute. Bulletin. Proceedings of the Biennial Sessions **8379**
0074-8617 International Statistical Yearbook of Large Towns†
0074-8684 International Studies in Sociology and Social Anthropology **8110**
0074-8692 International Study Week in Traffic Engineering and International Road Safety Congress
0074-8706 International Sugar Organization. Annual Report†
0074-8722 International Symposia on Comparative Law. Proceedings†
0074-8749 International Symposium of Flavins and Flavoproteins. Proceedings
0074-8765 International Symposium on Atherosclerosis. Proceedings
0074-8897 International Symposium on Regional Development. Papers and Proceedings **4416**
0074-8927 International Symposium on the Continuous Cultivation of Microorganisms. Proceedings†
0074-8935 International Symposium on the Reactivity of Solids. Proceedings†
0074-8951 International T N O Conference. (Proceedings)†
0074-896X International Tax Agreements **1930**
0074-9001 List of Cables Forming the World Submarine Network **2369**
0074-9028 List of International Telephone Routes **2369**
0074-9044 International Telecommunication Union. List of Telegraph Offices Open for International Service **2368**
0074-9052 Table of International Telex Relations and Traffic **2371**
0074-9087 International Textile Machinery†
0074-9095 International Thyroid Conference. Proceedings†
0074-9133 International Touring Alliance. Minutes of the General Assembly
0074-9141 International Tracts in Computer Science and Technology and Their Application†
0074-915X I T C - Publications. Series A (Photogrammetry)†
0074-9192 International Union Against Cancer. Manual†
0074-9206 International Union Against Cancer. Proceedings of Congress **6023**
0074-9214 International Union Against Cancer. U I C C Monograph Series†
0074-9222 U I C C Technical Report Series†
0074-9273 I U C N Publications. New Series†
0074-9281 International Union for Conservation of Nature and Natural Resources. Proceedings and Papers of the Technical Meeting†
0074-9311 International Union for Inland Navigation. Annual Report **8500**
0074-932X International Union for Quaternary Research. Congress Proceedings **2748**
0074-9338 International Population Conference. Proceedings
0074-9346 Union Academique Internationale. Compte Rendu de la Session Annuelle du Comite **4479**
0074-9354 International Union of Biochemistry and Molecular Biology. Symposium Series **734**
0074-9400 International Union of Forestry Research Organizations. Congress Proceedings
0074-9419 International Union of Geodesy and Geophysics. Proceedings of the General Assembly **2784**
0074-9427 Commission for the Geological Map of the World. Bulletin **2729**
0074-9435 International Union of Latin Notaries. Proceedings of Congress† **8966**
0074-9443 International Union of Local Authorities. Reports of Congress†
0074-9451 International Union of Official Travel Organizations. Minutes of the IUOTO General Assemblies†
0074-946X International Union of Physiological Sciences. Proceedings of Congress†
0074-9508 International Union of Pure and Applied Chemistry. Comptes Rendus of IUPAC Conference†
0074-9524 International Union of School and University Health and Medicine. Congress Reports
0074-9540 Congres International d'Histoire des Sciences. Actes **7848**
0074-9613 International Who's Who (Year) **643**
0074-9621 International Year Book and Statesmen's Who's Who **643**
0074-9648 International Yearbook of the Underwater World†
0074-9664 International Zoo Yearbook **948**
0074-9672 Internationale Bibliographie der Fachadressbuecher†
0074-9729 Internationale Gesellschaft fuer Geschichte der Pharmazie. Veroeffentlichungen. Neue Folge *changed to* Deutsche Gesellschaft fuer Geschichte der Pharmazie. Veroeffentlichungen zur Pharmaziegeschichte **6832**
0074-9737 Internationale Volkskundliche Bibliographie **3624**
0074-9745 International Review of Biblical Studies **7698**
0074-980X Internationales Forschungszentrum fuer Grundfragen der Wissenschaften, Salzburg. Forschungsgespraeche†
0074-9818 Internationales Jahrbuch der Erwachsenenbildung **2943**
0074-9907 Internationales Zucker-Jahrbuch
0074-9931 Interscience Monographs and Texts in Physics and Astronomy†
0074-9958 Interscience Tracts on Physics and Astronomy†
0074-9974 North American Conference on Labor Statistics. Selected Papers†
0075-0018 Inventaire General des Monuments et des Richesses Artistiques de la France **446**
0075-0026 Inventari dei Manoscritti delle Biblioteche d'Italia **5058**
0075-0034 Inventaria Archaeologica Belgique†
0075-0042 Inventaria Archaeologica Ceskoslovensko†
0075-0050 Inventaria Archaeologica Denmark†
0075-0069 Inventaria Archaeologica Deutschland†
0075-0077 Inventaria Archaeologica Espana†
0075-0085 Inventaria Archaeologica France†
0075-0093 Inventaria Archaeologica Great Britain†
0075-0107 Inventaria Archaeologica Italia†
0075-0115 Inventaria Archaeologica Jugoslavija†
0075-0123 Inventaria Archaeologica Norway†
0075-0131 Inventaria Archaeologica Oesterreich†
0075-014X Inventaria Archaeologica Pologne†
0075-0158 Inventaria Archaeologica Ungarn†
0075-0166 Inventaris van Het Kunstpatrimonium van Oost-Vlaanderen
0075-0174 Inventory of Programs in Maryland's Private and Public Universities and Colleges†
0075-0255 I B A Occasional Paper†
0075-0263 Securities Industry Association. State and Local Pension Funds†
0075-0301 Invitation to Photography†
0075-0336 Ionenaustauscher in Einzeldarstellungen†
0075-0344 I A S Bulletin†
0075-0360 Iowa Development Commission. Digest†
0075-0387 Iowa Nurses' Association. Bulletin†
0075-0395 Iowa Publications in Philosophy†
0075-0425 Iowa State University. Library. Annual Report†
0075-0433 Iowa State University. Engineering Research Institute. Engineering Research Report†
0075-0468 I P E K†
0075-0476 Iran Almanac and Book of Facts **3891**
0075-0484 Iran. Geological Survey. Report
0075-0492 Foreign Trade Statistics of Iran. Yearbook
0075-0506 Iranian Industrial Statistics **1244**
0075-0514 Iranian Mineral Statistics **6485**
0075-0522 Iranian National Bibliography **628**
0075-0603 Ireland. Central Statistics Office. National Income and Expenditure **1245**
0075-0611 Ireland (Eire) Central Statistics Office. Statistics of Wages, Earnings and Hours of Work†
0075-062X Ireland. Central Statistics Office. Report on Vital Statistics - Tuarascail Ar Staidreamh Beatha **7310**
0075-0638 Ireland. Central Statistics Office. Trend of Employment and Unemployment†
0075-0654 Ireland (Eire) Department of Agriculture and Fisheries. Journal†
0075-0662 Ireland. Department of Education. List of Recognised Post-Primary Schools
0075-0670 Ireland. Department of Finance. Financial Statement of the Minister for Finance **1931**
0075-0697 Ireland (Eire) National Industrial Economic Council. Report†
0075-0700 Iris Year Book **3739**
0075-0727 Irish Baptist Historical Society. Journal **7762**
0075-0735 Irish Catholic Directory **7801**
0075-0743 Historical Studies

DIRECTORY 2010 0075-5524 9107

0075-076X Irish Drama Series†
0075-0778 Irish Geography **4016**
0075-0816 Irish Play Series†
0075-0824 Irodalom - Szocializmus†
0075-0832 Irodalomelmelet Klasszikusai†
0075-0840 Irodalomtorteneti Fuzetek **5311**
0075-0859 Irodalomtorteneti Konyvtar†
0075-0875 Iron and Steel Works of the World **6317**
0075-0883 Iron Ore
0075-0921 Islam in Paperback
0075-093X Islamic Surveys
0075-0948 Islamic World†
0075-0980 Israel. Atomic Energy Commission. I A - Reports
0075-0999 Israel. Central Bureau of Statistics. Causes of Death in Israel
0075-1006 Israel. Central Bureau of Statistics. Criminal Statistics
0075-1014 Israel. Central Bureau of Statistics. Diagnostic Statistics of Hospitalizations
0075-1022 Israel. Central Bureau of Statistics. Juvenile Delinquency†
0075-1030 Israel. Central Bureau of Statistics. Judicial Statistics **4823**
0075-1049 Israel. Central Bureau of Statistics. Labour Force Surveys **1245**
0075-1057 Israel. Central Bureau of Statistics. Motor Vehicles
0075-1065 Israel. Central Bureau of Statistics. Schools and Kindergartens
0075-109X Israel. Central Bureau of Statistics. Survey of Housing Conditions
0075-1111 Israel. Central Bureau of Statistics. Vital Statistics **7310**
0075-1138 Israel. Department of Surveys. Geodetic Papers†
0075-1146 Israel Discount Bank. Report
0075-1154 Israel Export Directory
0075-1189 Israel. Ministry of Agriculture. Department of Fisheries. Israel Fisheries in Figures†
0075-1200 Israel. Geological Survey. Bulletin
0075-1219 Israel. Hydrological Service. Hydrological Paper†
0075-1227 Israel Institute of Applied Social Research. Research Report† **8966**
0075-1235 Israel Institute of Productivity. Report of Activities†
0075-1243 Israel Journal of Entomology **851**
0075-1251 Israel Medical Bibliography†
0075-126X Israel. Meteorological Service. Series B: Observational Data. Annual Rainfall Summary†
0075-1278 Israel. Meteorological Service. Series A (Meteorological Notes)†
0075-1286 Israel. Meteorological Service. Series B: Observational Data. Annual Weather Report
0075-1308 Israel. Ministry of Communications. Statistics
0075-1367 Israel Petroleum and Energy Year Book
0075-1383 Israel Society for Rehabilitation of the Disabled. Annual
0075-1391 Israel Studies in Criminology **2656**
0075-143X Issues (New York)†
0075-1456 Istituto Agostino Gemelli. Collana di Studi Sull' Informazione Visiva
0075-1464 Istituto di Studi e Ricerche Carlo Cattaneo. Quaderni
0075-1472 Studi Etruschi **4268**
0075-1480 Istituto di Studi Pirandelliani e Sul Teatro Contemporaneo
0075-1499 Istituto e Museo di Storia della Scienza. Biblioteca **7869**
0075-1502 Istituto Ellenico di Studi Bizantini e Postbizantini di Venezia. Biblioteca **4233**
0075-1529 Istituto Mobiliare Italiano. Annual Report† **8967**
0075-1537 Istituto Nazionale per l'Assicurazione Contro le Malattie, Rome. Bilancio Consuntivo†
0075-1545 Istituto Siciliano di Studi Bizantini e Neoellenici. Quaderni **4233**
0075-1553 Istituto Siciliano di Studi Bizantini e Neoellenici. Testi e Monumenti. Testi **4233**
0075-1561 Istituto Storico della Resistenza in Modena e Provincia. Quaderni†
0075-157X Istituto Storico della Resistenza in Modena e Provincia. Rassegna Annuale†
0075-160X Istoria Limbii Romane†
0075-1626 Istorie si Civilizatie **4148**
0075-1634 Italian Studies **5311**
0075-1642 Italy: An Economic Profile†
0075-1650 Italy. Direzione Generale delle Fonti di Energia e delle Industrie di Base. Bilanci Energetici†
0075-1820 Italy. Istituto Centrale di Statistica. Bilanci delle Amministrazioni Regionali, Provinciali e Comunali†
0075-1863 Italy. Istituto Nazionale di Statistica. Popolazione e Movimento Anagrafico dei Comuni **7310**
0075-188X Italy. Istituto Nazionale di Statistica. Statistica degli Incidenti Stradali **8527**
0075-1901 Istituto di Fisica dell'Atmosfera, Rome. Bibliografia Generale
0075-191X Istituto di Fisica dell'Atmosfera, Rome. Contributi Scientifici: Pubblicazioni di Fisica dell'Atmosfera e di Meteorologia
0075-1928 Istituto di Fisica dell'Atmosfera, Rome. Pubblicazioni Didattiche
0075-1936 Istituto di Fisica dell'Atmosfera, Rome. Pubblicazioni Scientifiche **6358**
0075-1944 Istituto di Fisica dell'Atmosfera, Rome. Pubblicazioni Varie
0075-1952 Istituto di Fisica dell'Atmosfera, Rome. Rapporti Interni Provvisori a Diffusione Limitata
0075-1960 Istituto di Fisica dell'Atmosfera, Rome. Rapporti Scientifici
0075-1979 Istituto di Fisica dell'Atmosfera, Rome. Rapporti Tecnici
0075-1987 Italy. Istituto Nazionale per lo Studio della Congiuntura. Quaderni Analitici
0075-2002 Itinera Romana†
0075-2010 Itsuu Laboratory, Tokyo. Annual Report **2124**
0075-2029 Ius Romanum in Helvetia†
0075-2037 Ius Romanum Medii Aevi
0075-2045 J. Anderson Fitzgerald Lecture†
0075-2053 Miller's Sporting Annual and Athletic Record†
0075-2061 J.K. Lasser's Your Income Tax, Professional Edition **1931**
0075-207X J. L. B. Smith Institute of Ichthyology. Occasional Paper†
0075-2088 J L B Smith Institute of Ichthyology. Special Publication *changed to* 1684-4149 **963**
0075-2118 Vooraziatisch-Egyptisch Genootschap "Ex Oriente Lux". Jaarbericht **4326**
0075-2142 Jacob Blaustein Lectures in International Affairs **7246**
0075-2150 Jaeger's Intertravel†
0075-2177 Jahrbuch der Albertus Universitaet zu Koenigsberg - Pr **2988**
0075-2193 Jahrbuch der Auktionspreise fuer Buecher, Handschriften und Autographen **7564**
0075-2207 Jahrbuch der Berliner Museen **6526**
0075-2215 Jahrbuch der Bibliotheken, Archive und Informationseinrichtungen der Deutschen Demokratischen Republik†
0075-2223 Jahrbuch der Deutschen Bibliotheken **5019**
0075-224X Jahrbuch der Export- und Versandtleiter *changed to* Handbuch fuer Export und Versand **1568**
0075-2266 Graphische Unternehmungen Oesterreichs. Jahrbuch **7322**
0075-2282 Jahrbuch des Heeres†
0075-2312 Kunsthistorische Sammlungen in Wien. Jahrbuch **501**
0075-2320 Jahrbuch der Luftwaffe†
0075-2363 Jahrbuch der Psychoanalyse **7367**
0075-2371 Raabe-Gesellschaft. Jahrbuch **5357**
0075-238X Jahrbuch der Schiffart†
0075-241X Jahrbuch der Wehrmedizin†
0075-2428 Jahrbuch der Wehrtechnik†
0075-2436 Jahrbuch des Baltischen Deutschtums **4234**
0075-2517 Jahrbuch des Oeffentlichen Rechts der Gegenwart **4850**
0075-2541 Jahrbuch fuer Antike und Christentum **7652**
0075-2568 Jahrbuch fuer Berlin-Brandenburgische Kirchengeschichte **7652**
0075-2576 Jahrbuch fuer Bundesbahnbeamte
0075-2584 Jahrbuch fuer Christliche Sozialwissenschaften **8111**
0075-2592 Jahrbuch fuer das Textil-Reinigungs-Gewerbe: Waescherei und Chemischreinigung†
0075-2606 Jahrbuch fuer den Oesterreichischen Tierarzt
0075-2614 Jahrbuch fuer die Geschichte Mittel- und Ostdeutschlands
0075-2622 Erziehungs- und Schulgeschichte Jahrbuch†
0075-2649 Jahrbuch fuer Fremdenverkehr **8725**
0075-2665 Jahrbuch fuer Geschichte der Sozialistischen Laender Europas†
0075-2681 Jahrbuch fuer Liturgik und Hymnologie **7762**
0075-2703 Jahrbuch fuer Musikalische Volks- und Voelkerkunde
0075-2711 Jahrbuch fuer Numismatik und Geldgeschichte†
0075-272X Jahrbuch fuer Optik und Feinmechanik **7077**
0075-2746 Jahrbuch fuer Ostrecht **4698**
0075-2754 Jahrbuch fuer Salesianische Studien **7801**
0075-2762 Jahrbuch fuer Schlesische Kirchengeschichte
0075-2800 Jahrbuch fuer Wirtschaftsgeschichte **1543**
0075-2819 Jahrbuch Oberflaechentechnik (Year) **6318**
0075-2851 Jahresbericht ueber die Deutsche Fischwirtschaft† **8967**
0075-286X Jahresberichte fuer Deutsche Geschichte **4234**
0075-2878 Jahresberichte ueber Holzschutz†
0075-2886 Jahresfachkatalog Recht - Wirtschaft - Steuern†
0075-2924 Jahreskatalog Psychologie
0075-2932 Jahresschrift fuer Mitteldeutsche Vorgeschichte **4234**
0075-2991 Jamaican National Bibliography **628**
0075-3009 James Terry Duce Memorial Series†
0075-3017 Jane's All the World's Aircraft **62**
0075-3025 Jane's Fighting Ships **6426**
0075-3084 Jane's World Railways **8619**
0075-3092 Janua Linguarum. Series Critica†
0075-3106 Janua Linguarum. Series Didactica†
0075-3114 Janua Linguarum. Series Major†
0075-3122 Janua Linguarum. Series Minor†
0075-3130 Janua Linguarum. Series Practica†
0075-3157 Japan Annual of Law and Politics†
0075-3165 Japan Anti-Tuberculosis Association. Reports on Medical Research Problems†
0075-319X Japan Chemical Annual†
0075-3203 Japan Chemical Directory (Year) **3248**
0075-3238 Japan Center for Economic Research. Center Paper Series
0075-3246 Japan Economic Year Book†
0075-3270 Kouseiroudoushou. Jinko Dotai Tokei **8384**
0075-3289 Japan Census of Manufactures: Report by Commodities
0075-3319 Japan Road Association. Annual Report of Roads†
0075-3327 Japan Society for Cancer Therapy. Proceedings of the Congress†
0075-3343 Japanese Antarctic Research Expedition Data Reports **2711**
0075-3440 Japanese Miniature Electronic Components Data†
0075-3459 Japanese Phonograph Records of Folk Songs, Classical and Popular Music
0075-3467 Japanese Progress in Climatology **6358**
0075-3475 Japan's Iron and Steel Industry
0075-3491 Jarlibro **5131**
0075-3548 Jawaharlal Nehru University. School of International Studies Series
0075-3556 Jazz Catalogue†
0075-3572 Jazzforschung **6579**
0075-3580 Jean-Paul-Gesellschaft. Jahrbuch **5313**
0075-3599 Jefferson Memorial Lecture Series†
0075-3610 Jerome Lectures
0075-3726 Jewish Book Annual† **8967**
0075-3742 Jewish Social Service Yearbook†
0075-3750 Jewish Travel Guide **8725**
0075-3769 Jewish Year Book **7724**
0075-3807 University of the Witwatersrand, Johannesburg. Library. Annual Report of the University Librarian†
0075-3815 John Alexander Monograph Series on Various Phases of Thoracic Surgery†
0075-384X John E. Owens Memorial Foundation. Publications†
0075-3858 Johns Hopkins Oceanographic Studies
0075-3866 Johns Hopkins Series in Integration and Community Building in Eastern Europe†
0075-3874 Johns Hopkins Symposia in Comparative History **4148**
0075-3904 Johns Hopkins University Studies in Historical and Political Science **4148**
0075-3912 Johnson Photographic Year Book
0075-3920 Johnsonia†
0075-3947 Joint Center for Urban Studies. Publications **4416**
0075-3963 Joint F A O - W H O Expert Committee on Food Additives Report†
0075-3971 Joint F A O - W H O Expert Committee on Nutrition. Report†
0075-4005 Ahmedabad Textile Industry's Research Association. Joint Technological Conferences. Proceedings **8448**
0075-4013 Jordan. Department of Statistics. Annual Statistical Yearbook **8382**
0075-4021 Jordan. Department of Statistics. External Trade Statistics **1246**
0075-4056 Jouets et Jeux†
0075-4072 Journal de Biologie et de Medicine Nucleaires†
0075-4099 Journal for the Protection of All Beings†
0075-4102 Journal fuer die Reine und Angewandte Mathematik **5500**
0075-4110 Journal of Ancient Indian History
0075-4161 Journal of Byelorussian Studies†
0075-417X Journal of Child Psychotherapy **7370**
0075-4188 Journal of Civil Procedure **4833**
0075-4196 Journal of Commerce Annual Review†
0075-4218 Journal of Croatian Studies **4235**
0075-4242 Journal of English Linguistics **5133**
0075-4250 Journal of Glass Studies **536**
0075-4269 Journal of Hellenic Studies **2236**
0075-4277 The Journal of Juristic Papyrology **401**
0075-4285 Journal of Maltese Studies **4235**
0075-4293 Tokushima University. Journal of Mathematics *changed to* 1346-7387 **5545**
0075-4307 Journal of Natural Science **7872**
0075-4315 Journal of Nuclear Medicine. Supplement†
0075-4331 Journal of Periodontal Research. Supplementum†
0075-4358 Journal of Roman Studies **2236**
0075-4366 Hiroshima University. Journal of Science. Series B. Division 2. Botany†
0075-4390 Journal of the Warburg and Courtauld Institutes **4461**
0075-4404 Journal of Ultrastructure Research. Supplement†
0075-4439 Journees Annuelles de Diabetologie de l'Hotel Dieu **5896**
0075-4447 Journees Biochimiques Latines. Rapports
0075-4455 Journees de Physiologie Appliquee au Travail Humain†
0075-4463 Acquisitions Medicales Recentes.†
0075-4501 Judean Desert Studies
0075-4544 Sir Moses Montefiore Collections des Juifs Celebres†
0075-4579 Juntendo University. Medical Ultrasonics Research Center. Annual Report
0075-4595 Justice
0075-4609 Universitaet Giessen. Ergebnisse Landwirtschaftlicher Forschung **165**
0075-4625 Jyvaskyla Studies in Education, Psychology and Social Research **2879**
0075-4633 Jyvaskyla Studies in the Arts **499**
0075-4641 University of Jyvaskyla. Department of Mathematics. Report *changed to* 1457-8905 **5545**
0075-4668 Kaiser Foundation Medical Care Program. Annual Report
0075-4722 Makerere University. Department of Geography. Occasional Paper **4019**
0075-4730 Makerere University. Faculty of Agriculture. Handbook
0075-4773 Makerere University. Faculty of Agriculture. Technical Bulletin **135**
0075-4781 Makerere University. Faculty of Law. Handbook **4727**
0075-4854 Makerere University. Library. Makerere Library Publications **5031**
0075-4927 Kansas Geological Survey. Computer Contribution†
0075-4935 Kansas Geological Survey. Short Papers in Research†
0075-4951 Kansas State University. Library Bibliography Series†
0075-4986 University of Kansas. Center for Latin American Studies. Graduate Studies on Latin America†
0075-4994 University of Kansas. Department of Geology. Special Publications†
0075-5001 University of Kansas Libraries. Library Series. **5053**
0075-5060 Kappa Tau Alpha Yearbook†
0075-5079 Karachi. Chamber of Commerce and Industry. Annual Report **1406**
0075-5095 Karachi Law Journal†
0075-5109 Karachi Port Trust. Year Book of Information, Port of Karachi, Pakistan **8501**
0075-5133 Staatliche Kunsthalle Karlsruhe. Bildhefte **6537**
0075-5141 Staatliche Kunsthalle Karlsruhe. Graphik-Schriftenreihe
0075-515X Karnatak University, Dharwad, India. Journal. Humanities **4461**
0075-5168 Karnatak University, Dharwad, India. Journal. Science **7874**
0075-5176 Karnatak University, Dharwad, India. Journal. Social Sciences **7981**
0075-5192 Kasetsart Journal **130**
0075-5222 Kasmera **5656**
0075-5230 Katalog Fauny Pasozytniczej Polski **953**
0075-5257 Katalog Zabytkow Sztuki w Polsce **499**
0075-5265 Katherine Asher Engel Lectures **4461**
0075-5281 Wyzsza Szkola Pedagogiczna, Katowice. Zeszyty Naukowe. Sekcja Jezykoznawstwa†
0075-529X Kazakhskii Nauchno-Issledovatel'skii Institut Onkologii i Radiologii. Trudy†
0075-5303 Keeping Track, Current News from the Department of Agricultural Economics at Purdue†
0075-5311 Keepsake (Davis)
0075-532X Keilschrifturkunden aus Boghazkoei†
0075-5346 Keio Monographs of Business and Commerce **1139**
0075-5397 A Kemia Ujabb Eredmenyei **2069**
0075-5400 Kempe's Engineers Year-Book† **8969**
0075-5419 Kemps Directory†
0075-5443 Kemp's Jersey Holiday Guide†
0075-546X Kent Studies in Anthropology and Archaeology†
0075-5508 Kentucky Folklore Series†
0075-5524 Kentucky Nature Studies†

ISSN

9108 0075-5559 ULRICH'S PERIODICALS

0075-5559 Kentucky Geological Survey. Bulletin **2751**
0075-5567 Kentucky Geological Survey. County Report **2751**
0075-5575 Kentucky Geological Survey. Guidebook to Geological Field Trips **2751**
0075-5583 Kentucky Geological Survey. Information Circular **2751**
0075-5591 Kentucky Geological Survey. Report of Investigations **2751**
0075-5605 Kentucky Geological Survey. Reprints **2751**
0075-5613 Kentucky Geological Survey. Special Publication **2752**
0075-5621 Kentucky Geological Survey. Thesis Series **2752**
0075-5761 K I A Occasional Papers
0075-580X Kenya. Mines and Geological Department. Annual Report†
0075-5834 Kenya. Central Bureau of Statistics. Estimates of Recurrent Expenditures **1247**
0075-5842 Kenya. Central Bureau of Statistics. Economic Survey **1495**
0075-5869 Kenya. Ministry of Education. Annual Report **2880**
0075-5915 Kenya. National Irrigation Board. Reports and Accounts **240**
0075-5923 Kenya National Library Service Board. Annual and Audit Report **5022**
0075-5931 Kenya. Public Accounts Committee. Annual Report **1932**
0075-594X Kenya. Public Service Commission. Annual Report **8052**
0075-5966 Keswick Week†
0075-5974 Kew Bulletin **799**
0075-5982 Kew Bulletin. Additional Series†
0075-6008 Keys to Music Bibliography†
0075-6016 Khosla's Industrial and Commercial Directory of India, Afghanistan, Burma, Ceylon, Japan and Foreign
0075-6032 Kierkegaardiana **6930**
0075-6040 Kime's International Law Directory
0075-6067 Kinetics and Mechanisms of Polymerization†
0075-6083 Kings of Tomorrow Series **644**
0075-6091 Queen's University at Kingston. Department of Electrical Engineering. Research Report†
0075-6113 Queen's University at Kingston. Douglas Library. Occasional Papers **5059**
0075-6121 Queen's University. Engineering Society. Proceedings†
0075-613X Queen's University at Kingston. Industrial Relations Centre. Bibliography Series†
0075-6148 Queen's University at Kingston. Industrial Relations Centre. Report of Activities†
0075-6156 Queen's University at Kingston. Industrial Relations Centre. Reprint Series†
0075-6199 Kirchenmusikalisches Jahrbuch **6582**
0075-6202 Kirchenreform†
0075-6210 Kirchliches Jahrbuch fuer die Evangelische Kirche in Deutschland **7763**
0075-6245 Kirtlandia **7876**
0075-6288 Klassieken Nederlandse Letterkunde†
0075-6318 Kleine Deutsche Prosadenkmaeler des Mittelalters **5318**
0075-6326 Kleine Museumshefte†
0075-6334 Klio **2236**
0075-6342 Klucze do Oznaczania Kregowcow Polski†
0075-6350 Klucze do Oznaczania Owadow Polski **853**
0075-6369 Kniznicny Zbornik†
0075-6385 Knotty Problems of Baseball†
0075-6407 Kobe Economic and Business Review **1140**
0075-6415 Kobe Economic and Business Research Series **1140**
0075-6423 Kobe University Law Review. International Edition **4710**
0075-6431 Kobe Daigaku Igakubu Kiyo **5658**
0075-6458 Koedoe **953**
0075-6466 Koedoe. Monographs **2616**
0075-6474 Koehlers Flottenkalender **8649**
0075-6482 Koeln†
0075-6490 Koelner Ethnologische Mitteilungen **346**
0075-6520 Koelner Romanistische Arbeiten **4462**
0075-6539 Koelner Schriften zur Politischen Wissenschaft **7149**
0075-6547 Koleopterologische Rundschau **686**
0075-6555 Kolloid-Gesellschaft. Verhandlungsberichte†
0075-6563 Kolloquium ueber Spaetantike und Fruehmittelalterliche Skulptur†
0075-6628 Kompass Australia **2011**
0075-6644 Kompass Espana
0075-6660 Kompass Holland† **8969**
0075-6679 Kompass Hong Kong†
0075-6687 Kompass Italia†
0075-6695 Kompass Maroc **2011**
0075-6709 Kompass Norge **2011**
0075-6717 Kompass Schweiz - Liechtenstein **2012**
0075-6725 Kompass Sverige **2012**
0075-6741 Koninklijk Nederlands Geologisch Mijnbouwkundig Genootschap. Verhandelingen† **8970**
0075-6768 Konstruktionsbuecher†
0075-6776 Kontrollraadet foer Betongvaror. Meddelande†
0075-6784 Konyvtartudomanyi Tanulmanyok†
0075-6792 Koranyi Sandor Tarsasag. Tudomanyos Ulesek†
0075-6806 Korea Development Bank: Its Functions and Activities **1364**
0075-6857 Korea (Republic). National Bureau of Statistics. Wholesale and Retail Trade Census Report†
0075-6865 Nongsa Sihom Yon'gu Pogo *changed to* R D A Journal of Agricultural Science **8983**
0075-6873 Han'gug Tong'gye Yeon'gam **7307**
0075-6911 Korosi Csoma Kiskonyvtar **4185**
0075-6938 Korrosion†
0075-6946 Korunk Tudomanya†
0075-6954 Kosten en Financiering van de Gezondheidszorg in Nederland†
0075-6962 Koszen es Koolaj Anyagismereti Monografiak†
0075-6970 Kothari's World of Reference Works **628**
0075-6989 Kozgazdasagi Ertekezesek†
0075-7004 Akademia Gorniczo-Hutnicza im. Stanislawa Staszica. Zeszyty Naukowe. Hutnictwo†
0075-7020 Krakow Dawniej i Dzis†
0075-7039 Muzeum Archeologiczne, Krakow. Materialy Archeologiczne **407**
0075-7047 Uniwersytet Jagiellonski. Obserwatorium Krakowskie. Rocznik Astronomiczny. Dodatek Miedzynarodowy *see* Uniwersytet Jagiellonski. Obserwatorium Krakowskie. Rocznik Astronomiczny **583**
0075-7063 Jahrbuch Krankenhaus
0075-708X Krankenhaus-Probleme der Gegenwart†
0075-7101 Beitraege zur Kardiologie und Angiologie†
0075-7136 Kriminologische Gegenwartsfragen
0075-7144 Kriminologie
0075-7152 Kriminologische Abhandlungen†
0075-7160 Kryptadia: Journal of Erotic Folklore†
0075-7179 Ksiazka w Dawnej Kulturze Polskiej **4462**
0075-7217 Kumamoto University. Institute of Constitutional Medicine. Bulletin. Supplement†
0075-7225 University of Science and Technology. Journal *changed to* 0855-0395 **7873**
0075-7233 Kungliga Skogs- och Lantbruksakademiens Tidskrift, Supplement *see* 0023-5350 **131**
0075-7241 Kunst-Katalog: Auktionen **501**
0075-725X Kunst und Altertum am Rhein **403**
0075-7268 Kunstdenkmaeler des Rheinlandes. Beihefte†
0075-7276 Die Kunststoff-Industrie und Ihre Helfer **7094**
0075-7292 Kunststoffe im Lebensmittelverkehr **7094**
0075-7306 Kuratorium fuer Verkehrssicherheit. Kleine Fachbuchreihe
0075-7314 Kurtziana **799**
0075-7322 Kurzauszuege Oesterreichischer Dissertationen: Geistes- und Sozialwissenschaften†
0075-7330 Kurzauszuege Oesterreichischer Dissertationen: Naturwissenschaften und Technik†
0075-7349 Kush
0075-7357 Kyoto University. Institute for Virus Research. Annual Report **890**
0075-7365 Kyoto University. Research Activities in Civil Engineering and Related Fields **3278**
0075-7403 Universidad Nacional Agraria. Programa Cooperativo de Investigaciones en Maiz. Boletin†
0075-742X Instituto de Estudios Sociales y del Pensamiento Argentino. Cuadernos de Extension Universitaria†
0075-7446 Lab World. Labstracts. Annual Reference Guide†
0075-7489 Labor Relations Yearbook†
0075-7500 Laboratory Guide†
0075-7535 Laboratory Techniques in Biochemistry and Molecular Biology **737**
0075-756X Labour Literature: A Bibliography†
0075-7594 Lackrohstoff-Tabellen
0075-7608 Lafayette Clinic Handbooks in Psychiatry†
0075-7616 Lafayette Clinic Monographs in Psychiatry†
0075-7624 National Library of Nigeria. Annual Report **5034**
0075-7632 National Library of Nigeria. National Library Occasional Publication **5034**
0075-7640 Lagos Notes and Records†
0075-7659 University of Lagos. Inaugural Lecture Series **4480**
0075-7667 University of Lagos. Continuing Education Centre. Occasional Papers†
0075-7675 University of Lagos. Humanities Series
0075-7691 University of Lagos. Law Series†
0075-7705 University of Lagos. Library. Annual Report **5053**
0075-7713 University of Lagos. Scientific Monograph Series
0075-7721 Universidad de la Laguna. Facultad de Ciencias. Anales **7926**
0075-773X Universidad de la Laguna. Facultad de Derecho. Anales **4801**
0075-7748 Lake Carriers' Association. Annual Report **8649**
0075-7772 Lamar Lecture Series **4150**
0075-7780 Lammergeyer **2617**
0075-7799 Lancashire Dialect Society. Journal†
0075-7810 University of Lancaster. Library. Occasional Papers†
0075-7837 Land Economics Monographs†
0075-790X Landolt-Boernstein: Zahlenwerte und Funktionen aus Naturwissenschaften und Technik. Neue Serie. Group V: Geophysics†
0075-7950 Language Monographs†
0075-7969 Language Science Monographs†
0075-7993 Langues et Litteratures de l'Afrique Noire†
0075-8035 Lasers: A Series of Advances†
0075-8108 Latin American Monographs†
0075-8124 Latin American Political Guide†
0075-8167 Latin American Urban Research†
0075-8175 Latin Language Mathematicians Group. Actes et Travaux du Congres†
0075-8183 Societe de Conservation de la Region de Quebec-Maurice. Annual Report
0075-8191 Universite de Lausanne. Ecole des Sciences Sociales et Politiques. Publications†
0075-8213 World Legal Directory†
0075-823X Law in Eastern Europe **4934**
0075-8272 Lazy Man's Guide to Holidays Afloat
0075-8310 Leading Advertisers in Business Publications†
0075-8329 Leahy's Hotel-Motel Guide and Travel Atlas†
0075-8337 Learning Disorders†
0075-8345 Leather Buyers Guide and Leather Trade Marks†
0075-8353 Lebanese Industrial and Commercial Directory **2013**
0075-8361 Year-Book of the Lebanese Joint-Stock Companies **1660**
0075-837X Lebanon. Direction Centrale de la Statistique. Comptes Economiques†
0075-8388 Lebanon. Direction Centrale de la Statistique. Recueil de Statistiques Libanaises†
0075-8396 The LeBaron Russell Briggs Prize Honors Essays in English†
0075-8418 Lebensdarstellungen Deutscher Naturforscher†
0075-8426 Lectura Dantis Romana†
0075-8434 Lecture Notes in Mathematics **5508**
0075-8442 Lecture Notes in Economics and Mathematical Systems **5508**
0075-8469 Lecture Notes in Pure and Applied Mathematics **5508**
0075-8485 Lectures in Applied Mathematics **5508**
0075-8493 Lectures in Biblical Studies†
0075-8523 Lectures on Mathematics in the Life Sciences **5508**
0075-8531 Lectures on the History of Religions. New Series **7659**
0075-854X University of Leeds. Institute of Education. Papers†
0075-8558 University of Leeds. Research Institute of African Geology. Annual Report†
0075-8566 Leeds Studies in English **5320**
0075-8574 Leeds Texts and Monographs. New Series **5320**
0075-8639 Leidse Geologische Mededelingen†
0075-8655 Sportmedizinische Schriftenreihe
0075-8663 Museum fuer Voelkerkunde, Leipzig. Jahrbuch *changed to* 1865-4347 **6531**
0075-8671 Museum fuer Voelkerkunde, Leipzig. Veroeffentlichungen†
0075-8736 Lekarske Prace†
0075-8744 Leo Baeck Institute. Year Book **4151**
0075-8760 Il Leonardo†
0075-8779 Lepetit Colloquia on Biology and Medicine. Proceedings†
0075-8787 Lepidoptera **854**
0075-8795 Lepidopterists' Society. Memoirs **854**
0075-8809 Leprosy Mission. Annual Report **5822**
0075-8817 Lesotho. Treasury. Report on the Finances and Accounts **1933**
0075-8825 Lessico Intellettuale Europeo **5143**
0075-8833 Lessing Yearbook **5321**
0075-8892 Lettere Italiane. Biblioteca **5321**
0075-8906 La Lettre†
0075-8914 Levant **403**
0075-8922 Lewis Henry Morgan Lectures†
0075-8973 Librarians, Censorship and Intellectual Freedom†
0075-8981 Libraries in Nigeria: A Directory **5026**
0075-9007 Library and Documentation Journals†
0075-9031 Library Association. Library History Group. Occasional Publication†
0075-9058 Library Association. Reference, Special and Information Section. North Western Group. Occasional Papers†
0075-9066 Library Association. Yearbook *changed to* 1746-9929 **4999**
0075-9082 Library Journal Book Review†
0075-9090 Library of Christian Classics† **8971**
0075-9104 Library of Exact Philosophy **7880**
0075-9120 Library of Law and Contemporary Problems†
0075-9139 Library of Living Philosophers **6932**
0075-9201 Libros y Material de Ensenanza†
0075-921X Bank of Libya. Balance of Payments
0075-9228 Libya. Census and Statistics Department. External Trade Statistics **1249**
0075-9236 Libya. Census and Statistics Department. General Population Census **7311**
0075-9244 Libya. Census and Statistics Department. Industrial Census **1249**
0075-9252 Libya. Census and Statistics Department. Report of the Annual Survey of Large Manufacturing Establishments **1249**
0075-9260 Libya. Census and Statistics Department. Report of the Annual Survey of Petroleum Mining Industry **6800**
0075-9279 Libya. Census and Statistics Department. Report of the Survey of Licensed Construction Units **1047**
0075-9287 Libya. Census and Statistics Department. Statistical Abstract **8385**
0075-9295 Libya. Census and Statistics Department. Wholesale Prices in Tripoli Town **1249**
0075-9325 Lick Observatory. Publications†
0075-9333 Universite de Liege. Faculte des Sciences Appliquees. Collection des Publications **8444**
0075-935X Universite de Liege. Institut de Pharmacie. Travaux Publies†
0075-9368 Universite de Liege. Laboratoire d'Analyse Statistique des Langues Anciennes. Travaux Publies†
0075-9376 Lieux et les Dieux†
0075-9384 Life Around Us: A Commercial Directory†
0075-9414 Life Insurers Conference. Annual Meeting. Proceedings†
0075-9457 Lightweight Concrete Information Sheets **1020**
0075-9465 Ligue Antituberculeuse de Quebec. Rapport
0075-9473 Institut de Medecine Legale et de Medecine Sociale. Archives†
0075-9481 Lilloa **800**
0075-949X Lilies and Other Liliaceae†
0075-9511 Limnologica **2796**
0075-9554 Lindley Lecture **6932**
0075-9597 Linguistic Circle of Manitoba and North Dakota. Proceedings **5323**
0075-9600 Linguistic Society of America. Meeting Handbooks **5146**
0075-9627 Linguistic Society of India. Bulletin **5146**
0075-9635 Linguistic Structures†
0075-9651 Linguistics in Documentation; Current Abstracts†
0075-966X La Linguistique **5147**
0075-9686 Linguistische Reihe†
0075-9740 Hebrew University of Jerusalem. Lionel Cohen Lectures†
0075-9775 Lisbon. Universidade. Faculdade de Ciencias. Revista. Serie 2. Seccao B. Ciencias Fisico-Quimicas†
0075-9813 List Bio-Med†
0075-9821 L I S T†
0075-9872 Literarny Archiv **5323**
0075-9880 Literary and Library Prizes†
0075-9902 Literary Monographs†
0075-9929 Literary Prizes in Pakistan **5324**
0075-9937 Literatur und Wirklichkeit **5324**
0075-9945 Literatura Piekna. Adnotowany Rocznik Bibliograficzny†
0075-9961 Literatures of the World in English Translation: A Bibliography†
0075-997X Literaturwissenschaftliches Jahrbuch. Neue Folge **5326**
0075-9988 Litomericko†
0076-0013 Little Red Book (Year) **8502**
0076-003X University of Notre Dame. Department of Theology. Liturgical Studies **7821**
0076-0048 Liturgiewissenschaftliche Quellen und Forschungen **7660**
0076-0072 Living History of the World†
0076-0080 Living Word Commentary†
0076-0102 Livre Contemporain et les Bibliophiles Francosuisses†
0076-0129 Livre et Societes†
0076-0137 Bulletin Bibliographique Thematique
0076-0153 Livres et Auteurs Quebecois†

0076-0188 Llen Cymru **5327**
0076-020X Lloyd's Maritime Atlas **8650**
0076-0269 Locations of Industries in Gujarat State **1897**
0076-0285 Locomotive Maintenance Officers Association. Annual Proceedings
0076-0293 Locomotive Maintenance Officers Association. Preconvention Report
0076-0315 Muzeum Archeologiczne i Etnograficzne, Lodz. Prace i Materialy. Seria Etnograficzna **349**
0076-0323 Politechnika Lodzka. Zeszyty Naukowe. Budownictwo **3280**
0076-0331 Politechnika Lodzka. Zeszyty Naukowe. Wlokiennictwo **8456**
0076-034X Uniwersytet Lodzki. Prace
0076-0382 Lodzkie Studia Etnograficzne†
0076-0390 Lodzkie Towarzystwo Naukowe. Rozprawy Komisji Jezykowej **5148**
0076-0404 Lodzkie Towarzystwo Naukowe. Prace Wydzialu Jezykoznawstwa, Nauki o Literaturze i Filozofii **5327**
0076-0412 Lodzkie Towarzystwo Naukowe. Wydzial III Nauk Matematyczno-Przyrodniczych. Prace†
0076-0420 Lodzkie Towarzystwo Naukowe. Wydzial IV. Nauk Lekarskich. Prace†
0076-0439 Lodzkie Towarzystwo Naukowe. Wydzial V. Nauk Technicznych. Prace†
0076-0447 Log (Long Beach)
0076-0455 Log of the Star Class **8277**
0076-0471 Logos†
0076-0501 London and Middlesex Archaeological Society. Transactions **404**
0076-0536 London Divinity Series. New Testament†
0076-0544 London History Studies
0076-0552 London Mathematical Society. Lecture Note Series **5509**
0076-0579 London Naturalist **687**
0076-0587 University of Western Ontario. Centre for Radio Science. Annual Report†
0076-0595 University of Western Ontario. D.B. Weldon Library. Library Bulletin†
0076-0609 University of Western Ontario. Museums. Museum Bulletin†
0076-0641 London School of Economics and Political Science. Department of Geography. Geographical Papers†
0076-0668 L S E Research Monographs†
0076-0692 University of London Historical Studies†
0076-0714 University of London Legal Series†
0076-0730 University of London. Institute of Classical Studies. Bulletin **2241**
0076-0749 University of London. Institute of Classical Studies. Bulletin Supplement **2241**
0076-0765 University of London. Institute of Commonwealth Studies. Commonwealth Papers†
0076-0773 University of London. Institute of Commonwealth Studies. Collected Seminar Papers **8012**
0076-0781 University of London. Institute of Commonwealth Studies. Annual Report **8012**
0076-079X Education Libraries Bulletin Supplements†
0076-0803 University of London. Institute of Germanic Studies. Library Publications **5408**
0076-0811 University of London. Institute of Germanic Studies. Publications **5393**
0076-0846 University of London. Institute of Latin American Studies. Monographs†
0076-0854 University of London. Royal Postgraduate Medical School. Annual Report†
0076-0862 Looking for Leisure†
0076-0870 Looking Forward†
0076-0889 Looking into Leadership Series
0076-0897 Lorentzia **800**
0076-0927 Natural History Museum of Los Angeles County. Contributions in History†
0076-0943 Natural History Museum of Los Angeles County. Science Series **7888**
0076-096X Los Angeles Geographical Society. Publication
0076-0986 Southwest Museum. Frederick Webb Hodge Anniversary Publication Fund. Publications
0076-0994 Southwest Museum. Papers
0076-1001 Lost Play Series†
0076-1044 Louisiana Tech University. Division of Life Sciences Research. Research Bulletin†
0076-1109 L S U Wood Utilization Notes†
0076-1168 Instituto de Investigacao Cientifica de Mocambique. Memorias. Series A (Ciencias Biologicas)†
0076-1176 Instituto de Investigacao Cientifica de Mocambique. Memorias. Serie B (Ciencias Geograficas-Geologicas)†
0076-1184 Instituto de Investigacao Cientifica de Mocambique. Memorias. Serie C (Ciencias Humanas)†
0076-1192 Centre Belge d'Histoire Rurale. Publications **4209**
0076-1206 Universite Catholique de Louvain. Centre d'Etudes Politiques. Working Group "American Foreign Policy." Cahier†
0076-1214 Universite Catholique de Louvain. Ecole des Sciences Politiques et Sociales. Collection†
0076-1222 Universite Catholique de Louvain. Faculte de Philosophie et Lettres. Travaux **4480**
0076-1230 Universite Catholique de Louvain. Faculte de Theologie et de Droit Canonique. Travaux de Doctorat. Nouvelle Serie **7821**
0076-1249 Universite Catholique de Louvain. Institut des Langues Vivantes. Cahiers **5191**
0076-1265 Universite Catholique de Louvain. Institut Orientaliste. Publications **4189**
0076-1273 Universite Catholique de Louvain. Institut Superieur de Philosophie. Cours Publies **6959**
0076-1281 Universite Catholique de Louvain. Laboratoire de Pedagogie Experimentale. Cahiers de Recherches†
0076-129X Universite Catholique de Louvain. Section de Philologie Germanique. Serie Microfiches†
0076-1303 Universite Catholique de Louvain. Institut de Recherches Economiques, Politiques et Sociales. Publications†
0076-132X Lovejoy's College Guide†
0076-1346 Lovejoy's Career and Vocational School Guide†
0076-1354 Lovoe Geomagnetic Observatory Yearbook†
0076-1389 Lower Paleozic Rocks of the New World†
0076-1419 National Botanical Research Institute, Lucknow. Bulletin†
0076-1427 Lucknow Law Journal†
0076-1435 Lud **8119**
0076-1443 Lueneburger Blaetter†
0076-1451 Lund Studies in English **5148**
0076-1508 Lusitania Sacra **7661**
0076-1516 Lustracje Dobr Krolewskich XVI-XVIII Wieku **4241**
0076-1524 Lute Society of America. Journal **6585**
0076-1532 L E A Yearbook†
0076-1540 Lutheran World Federation. Proceedings of the Assembly†
0076-1559 Luxembourg. Ministere des Finances. Budget de l'Etat **1933**
0076-1575 Luxembourg. Service Central de la Statistique et des Etudes Economiques. Annuaire Statistique **1249**
0076-1583 Luxembourg. Service Central de la Statistique et des Etudes Economiques. Bulletin du STATEC **1249**
0076-1591 Luxembourg. Service Central de la Statistique et des Etudes Economiques. Collection D et M: Definitions et Methodes†
0076-1605 Luxembourg. Service Central de la Statistique et des Etudes Economiques. Cahiers Economiques **1249**
0076-163X Lychnos-Bibliotek†
0076-1648 Lychnos **7880**
0076-1656 Universite Claude Bernard. Departement de Mathematiques. Publications†
0076-1699 Lyrical Iowa **5426**
0076-1729 M L Seidman Memorial Town Hall Lecture Series **7152**
0076-1745 Asta-Press†
0076-1753 M T P International Review of Science. Inorganic Chemistry, Series 1
0076-1761 M T P International Review of Science. Organic Chemistry
0076-177X M T P International Review of Science. Physical Chemistry
0076-1818 Universita degli Studi di Macerata. Facolta di Lettere e Filosofia. Annali **422**
0076-1842 McGill University, Montreal. Department of Meteorology. Publication in Meteorology†
0076-1850 McGill University, Montreal. Axel Heiberg Island Research Reports†
0076-1893 McGill University, Montreal. Centre for Developing-Area Studies. Annual Report†
0076-1915 McGill University, Montreal. Centre for Developing-Area Studies. Reprint Series†
0076-1931 McGill University, Montreal. Department of Geography. Climatological Research Series†
0076-194X McGill University, Montreal. Industrial Relations Centre. Annual Conference Proceedings†
0076-1966 McGill University, Montreal. Mechanical Engineering Research Laboratories. Report **3389**
0076-1974 McGill University, Montreal. Mechanical Engineering Research Laboratories. Technical Note **3389**
0076-1982 McGill Sub-Arctic Research Papers†
0076-2016 McGraw-Hill Yearbook of Science and Technology **7882**
0076-2032 Machine Intelligence Workshop†
0076-2059 McMaster University, Hamilton, Ontario. Institute for Materials Research. Annual Report†
0076-2075 Macromolecular Chemistry†
0076-2083 Macromolecular Reviews†
0076-2091 Macromolecular Syntheses†
0076-2105 Made in Austria†
0076-213X Madison Avenue Europe†
0076-2156 Madison Avenue London†
0076-2164 Madison Avenue Paris†
0076-2180 Madison Avenue West Germany†
0076-2202 University of Madras. Archaeological Series
0076-2210 University of Madras. Endowment Lectures
0076-2229 University of Madras. Historical Series
0076-2237 University of Madras. Kannada Series
0076-2245 University of Madras. Malayalam Series
0076-2253 University of Madras. Philosophical Series
0076-2261 University of Madras. Sanskrit Series
0076-227X University of Madras. Tamil Series
0076-2288 University of Madras. Telugu Series
0076-2296 University of Madras. Urdu Series
0076-230X Les Melanges de la Casa de Velazquez **505**
0076-2318 Real Conservatorio Superior de Musica. Anuario†
0076-2326 Maerchen der Europaeischen Voelker†
0076-2342 Magazine of Albemarle County History **4302**
0076-2350 Magenta Frog†
0076-2369 Magon. Serie Scientifique
0076-2377 Magon. Serie Technique
0076-2385 Magyar Irodalomtortenetiras Forrasai†
0076-2393 Magyar Konyv†
0076-2407 Magyar Kozlony **4242**
0076-2415 Magyar Munkasmozgalmi Muzeum. Evkonyv†
0076-2431 Magyar Tudomanyos Akademia. Mikrobiologiai Kutato Intezet. Proceedings†
0076-244X Studia Biologica Academiae Scientiarum Hungarica†
0076-2458 Studia Historica Academiae Scientiarum Hungaricae†
0076-2466 Studia Philosophica Academiae Scientiarum Hungaricae†
0076-2474 Magyarorszag Allatvilaga **954**
0076-2482 Magyarorszag Kulturfloraja **800**
0076-2490 Magyarorszag Muemleki Topografiaja†
0076-2504 Magyarorszag Regeszeti Topografiaja† **8972**
0076-2512 Magyarorszag Tajfoldrajza†
0076-2520 Maharaja Sayajirao University of Baroda. Department of Archaeology and Ancient History. Archaeology Series **404**
0076-2547 Maharashtra Archives Bulletin
0076-2555 Maharashtra State Budget in Brief **1934**
0076-2563 Maharashtra State Financial Corporation. Annual Report **1366**
0076-2571 Mahratta **4185**
0076-258X Maia†
0076-2652 Maine Heritage Series
0076-2709 Maine That Was Series†
0076-2717 Maine Writers' Conference Chapbook†
0076-2725 Mainfraenkisches Jahrbuch fuer Geschichte und Kunst **4242**
0076-2733 Roemisch-Germanisches Zentralmuseum, Mainz. Ausstellungskataloge†
0076-2741 Roemisch-Germanisches Zentralmuseum, Mainz. Jahrbuch **4259**
0076-275X Roemisch-Germanisches Zentralmuseum, Mainz. Kataloge Vor- und Fruehgeschichtlicher Altertuemer **4159**
0076-2768 Mainzer Amerikanistische Beitraege
0076-2776 Mainzer Philosophische Forschungen†
0076-2784 Mainzer Reihe
0076-2792 Mainzer Zeitschrift **504**
0076-2806 Maison des Sciences de l'Homme. Collection de Reeditions†
0076-2822 Maitres-Cuisiniers de France†
0076-2849 Major League Baseball†
0076-2865 Major Problems in Clinical Pediatrics **6096**
0076-2881 Major Problems in Pathology†
0076-289X Makedonika **4242**
0076-2989 Mala Biblioteka Baletowa†
0076-2997 Malacologia **954**
0076-3004 Malacological Review **954**
0076-3020 Malawi. Accountant General. Report **1934**
0076-3055 Malawi. Department of Civil Aviation. Annual Report **8548**
0076-3063 Malawi. Department of Customs and Excise. Annual Report†
0076-3071 Malawi. Department of Forestry and Game. Report **3696**
0076-308X Malawi. Police Force. Annual Report **2660**
0076-3101 Malawi Economic Report **1497**
0076-311X Malawi. Geological Survey Department. Annual Report **2753**
0076-3128 Malawi. Geological Survey Department. Bulletin†
0076-3136 Malawi. Geological Survey Department. Memoir†
0076-3144 Malawi. Geological Survey Department. Records†
0076-3152 Malawi. Judicial Department. Annual Report†
0076-3160 Malawi. Ministry of Justice. Annual Report **4955**
0076-3179 Malawi. Lands Department. Annual Report†
0076-3195 Malawi. Ministry of Finance. Budget Statement **1934**
0076-3225 Malawi. Ministry of Local Government. Annual Report **7153**
0076-3233 Malawi. Ministry of Works and Supplies. Annual Report†
0076-3241 Malawi. National Statistical Office. Annual Survey of Economic Activities **1250**
0076-325X Malawi. National Statistical Office. Annual Statement of External Trade **1250**
0076-3284 Malawi. National Statistical Office. National Accounts Report **8387**
0076-3292 Malawi. National Statistical Office. National Sample Survey of Agriculture **183**
0076-3306 Malawi. National Statistical Office. Population Census Final Report **7312**
0076-3314 Malawi. Office of the Auditor General. Report **1934**
0076-3322 Malawi. Post Office Savings Bank. Annual Report **1366**
0076-3330 Malawi Railways. Annual Reports and Accounts **8620**
0076-3349 Malawi. Registrar of Insurance. Report **4513**
0076-3357 Malawi Treaty Series **4935**
0076-3365 Malawi. Department of Veterinary Services and Animal Industry. Annual Report†
0076-3381 National Archives of Malaysia. Annual Report **4186**
0076-342X Malignant Intrigue
0076-3470 Malta. Central Office of Statistics. Demographic Review of the Maltese Islands **7312**
0076-3489 Malta. Central Office of Statistics. Education Statistics **2934**
0076-3519 Mammalian Species (Print)† **8972**
0076-356X Management Aids Annuals†
0076-3586 Management and Labor Studies. English Series†
0076-3616 Management, Fonctions, Methodes, Experiences†
0076-3624 Management Guide to N C†
0076-3667 Management Advisory Services Technical Study†
0076-3705 Manchester Association of Engineers. Transactions†
0076-3713 Manchester Guardian Society for the Protection of Trade. Annual Report†
0076-3748 La Mandragore Qui Chante†
0076-3756 National Museum of the Philippines. Annual Report **6534**
0076-3764 National Museum of the Philippines. Museum Publications (Pamphlet Series)†
0076-3772 National Museum of the Philippines. Monograph Series†
0076-3780 Philippine Normal College. Language Study Center. Occasional Paper†
0076-3810 Manitoba Entomologist†
0076-3829 Manitoba Historical Society. Transactions†
0076-3853 Manitoba Labour - Management Review Committee. Annual Report **1696**
0076-3861 Manitoba Law Journal **4727**
0076-3896 Manitoba Record Society. Publications **4302**
0076-390X Manitoba Trade Directory†
0076-3918 University of Manitoba. Center for Settlement Studies. Publication Series†
0076-3926 University of Manitoba. Center for Settlement Studies. Series 1. Annual Reports†
0076-3934 University of Manitoba. Center for Settlement Studies. Series 2. Research Report†
0076-3942 University of Manitoba. Center for Settlement Studies. Series 3. Bibliography and Information†
0076-3950 University of Manitoba. Center for Settlement Studies. Series 4. Proceedings†
0076-3969 University of Manitoba. Center for Settlement Studies. Series 5. Occasional Papers†
0076-3993 University of Manitoba. Center for Transportation Studies. Seminar Series on Transportation. Proceedings†
0076-4000 University of Manitoba. Department of Agricultural Economics and Farm Management. Occasional Papers
0076-4035 University of Manitoba. Department of Slavic Studies. Readings in Slavic Literature†

ISSN

Link to your serials resources and content with ulrichsweb.com

9110 0076-4116 ULRICH'S PERIODICALS

0076-4116 Mankind Quarterly Monograph Series **347**
0076-4124 Manna†
0076-4140 Manpower/Automation Research Notices†
0076-4205 Manuels Pratiques d'Economie†
0076-423X Manufacturing Chemists Association. Statistical Summary†
0076-4256 Manufacturing Management Series†
0076-4264 Manx Museum, Douglas, Isle of Man. Journal†
0076-4310 Instituto de Biologia Marina. Memoria Anual†
0076-4337 Universidad Nacional del Zulia. Facultad de Humanidades y Educacion. Artes y Letras†
0076-4345 Universidad Nacional del Zulia. Facultad de Humanidades y Educacion. Conferencias y Coloquios†
0076-4353 Universidad Nacional del Zulia. Facultad de Humanidades y Educacion. Fuera de Serie†
0076-4361 Universidad Nacional del Zulia. Facultad de Humanidades y Educacion. Manuales de la Escuela de Educacion†
0076-437X Universidad Nacional del Zulia. Facultad de Humanidades y Educacion. Monografias y Ensayos†
0076-4418 Marconi's International Register†
0076-4434 Marian Library Studies. New Series **7806**
0076-4442 Marine Biology†
0076-4469 Marine Engineering Log Annual Maritime Review and Yearbook Issue **8651**
0076-4493 Marine Research†
0076-4515 Maritime Bank of Israel. Annual Report
0076-4620 Marketing Research Techniques Series†
0076-4647 Markets Year Book **1834**
0076-4671 Marquette Slavic Studies†
0076-4701 Marsyas†
0076-471X Martin Classical Lectures **2237**
0076-4728 Mary C. Richardson Lecture†
0076-4752 Maryland. Department of State Planning. Activities Report†
0076-4779 Maryland. Geological Survey. Bulletin **2754**
0076-4787 Maryland. Geological Survey. Educational Series **2754**
0076-4795 Maryland. Geological Survey. Information Circular **2754**
0076-4809 Maryland. Geological Survey. Report of Investigations **2754**
0076-4817 Maryland. Geological Survey. Water Resources Basic Data Report **8828**
0076-4833 University of Maryland. College of Library and Information Services. Conference Proceedings†
0076-4841 University of Maryland. College of Library and Information Services. Student Contribution Series†
0076-4906 Massachusetts. Department of Mental Health. Newsletter†
0076-4930 Massachusetts. Division of Employment Security. Annual Planning Report†
0076-4949 Massachusetts. Division of Employment Security. Statistical Digest†
0076-499X Massachusetts Housing Finance Agency. Annual Report **4419**
0076-5015 M I T Press Research Monographs
0076-5066 University of Massachusetts. Department of Anthropology. Research Reports†
0076-5171 Materialien zur Roemisch-Germanischen Keramik **2044**
0076-5201 Materials Science Research†
0076-521X Materialy i Prace Antropologiczne†
0076-5228 Materialy i Studia do Historii Prasy i Czasopismiennictwa Polskiego†
0076-5236 Materialy Zachodniopomorskie **6529**
0076-5244 Materialy Zrodlowe do Dziejow Kosciola W Polsce **7806**
0076-5252 Materiaux pour l'Etude de l'Extreme-Orient Moderne et Contemporain. Etudes Linguistiques†
0076-5260 Materiaux pour l'Etude de l'Extreme-Orient Moderne et Contemporain. Textes†
0076-5279 Materiaux pour l'Etude de l'Extreme-Orient Moderne et Contemporain. Travaux†
0076-5287 Materiaux pour l'Histoire du Socialisme International. Serie 2. Essais Bibliographiques†
0076-5295 Materiaux pour l'Histoire du Socialisme International. Serie 1. Textes et Documents†
0076-5317 Mathematical and Physical Society of U A R. Proceedings *changed to* 1110-0613
0076-5333 Mathematical Expositions†
0076-5341 University of Notre Dame. Department of Mathematics. Mathematical Lectures **5545**
0076-5384 Mathematical Table Series†
0076-5392 Mathematics in Science and Engineering **5515**
0076-5406 Mathematiques et Sciences de l'Homme
0076-5414 Mathematische Forschungsberichte†
0076-5422 Mathematische Lehrbuecher und Monographien. Abteilung 1: Mathematische Lehrbuecher **5516**
0076-5430 Mathematische Lehrbuecher und Monographien. Abteilung 2: Mathematische Monographien **5516**
0076-5449 Mathematische Schuelerbuecherei
0076-5465 Maudsley Monographs **6159**
0076-5481 Mauritius. Archives Department. Annual Report **5031**
0076-549X Mauritius. Customs and Excise Department. Annual Report†
0076-5503 Mauritius. Legislative Assembly. Sessional Paper†
0076-5511 Mauritius. Meteorological Services. Report†
0076-552X Mauritius. Ministry of Housing, Lands and Town and Country Planning. Annual Reports†
0076-5554 Mauritius. Ministry of Works and Internal Communications. Report†
0076-5562 Mauritius. Public Accounts Committee. Report **1934**
0076-5589 Max C. Fleischmann College of Agriculture. Publications. B (Series)†
0076-5597 Max C. Fleischmann College of Agriculture. Publications. C (Series)†
0076-5600 Max C. Fleischmann College of Agriculture. Publications. R (Series)†
0076-5619 Max C. Fleischmann College of Agriculture. Publications. T (Series)†
0076-5627 Studien und Berichte **2915**
0076-5643 Max-Planck-Institut fuer Aeronomie. Mitteilungen†
0076-566X Max-Planck-Institut fuer Silikatforschung, Wuerzburg. Veroeffentlichungen†
0076-5694 Max-Reger-Institut, Bonn. Mitteilungen†
0076-5716 Meat and Livestock Commission, Bucks, England. Index of Research†
0076-5732 Mechanical Engineering Monographs†
0076-5783 Mechanics **7061**
0076-5791 Mechanisms of Molecular Migrations†
0076-5821 Media Scandinavia **29**
0076-5856 Mediaeval Philosophical Texts in Translation **6933**
0076-5864 Mediaeval Scandinavia **4243**
0076-5872 Mediaeval Studies **4243**
0076-5880 Mediaevalia Philosophica Polonorum **6933**
0076-5899 Medical Annual†
0076-5945 Medical Library Association. Publication†
0076-5953 Medical Physics Series†
0076-5988 Kenya Medical Research Institute. Annual Report **5657**
0076-5996 Medical Research Council (Ireland). Report†
0076-6011 Medical Society of London. Transactions **5671**
0076-6038 Medical Ultrasonics†
0076-6046 Medicina **5673**
0076-6054 Medicinal Chemistry†
0076-6097 Medieval Archaeology **405**
0076-6119 Medieval India; a Miscellany
0076-6127 Medievalia et Humanistica **4243**
0076-6135 Medium Aevum Monographs†
0076-6151 Medizinische Laenderkunde†
0076-616X Medizinische Praxis†
0076-6178 Medizinische Radiographie und Photographie†
0076-6194 Meet the U. S. A†
0076-6216 Meister des Puppenspiels†
0076-6224 Melanderia†
0076-6232 Melbourne Historical Journal **4193**
0076-6259 Melbourne Monographs in Germanic Studies†
0076-6275 Melbourne Studies in Education *changed to* 1750-8487 **2840**
0076-6283 University of Melbourne. Institute of Applied Economic and Social Research. Monographs†
0076-6291 University of Melbourne. Institute of Applied Economic and Social Research. Technical Papers†
0076-6321 Melsheimer Entomological Series†
0076-6356 Membranes: a Series of Advances†
0076-6364 Memoires de Photo-Interpretation **6971**
0076-6372 Memorabilia Zoologica†
0076-6380 Junta de Estudios Historicos de Mendoza. Revista **4300**
0076-6399 Universidad Nacional de Cuyo. Biblioteca Central. Boletin Bibliografico†
0076-6402 Universidad Nacional de Cuyo. Biblioteca Central. Cuadernos de la Biblioteca†
0076-6429 Mennonite History Series†
0076-6437 Men's Wear Year Book and Diary†
0076-6461 Mental Measurements Yearbook **7385**
0076-650X Merchant Vessels of the United States
0076-6518 The Merck Index: An Encyclopedia of Chemicals and Drugs **6890**
0076-6526 The Merck Manual of Diagnosis and Therapy **5678**
0076-6542 The Merck Veterinary Manual **8803**
0076-6550 Universidad de Los Andes. Facultad de Ciencias Juridicas y Politicas. Anuario de Derecho **4802**
0076-6569 Universidad de Los Andes. Instituto de Geografia y Conservacion de Recursos Naturales. Cuadernos Geograficos **4032**
0076-6607 Mesoamerican Studies†
0076-6615 Mesopotamia **406**
0076-6623 Universita degli Studi di Messina. Istituto di Filologia Moderna. Biblioteca Letteraria
0076-6631 Universita degli Studi di Messina. Istituto di Storia Medievale e Moderna. Pubblicazioni
0076-6658 Metal Statistics†
0076-6674 Metallische Rohstoffe
0076-6682 Metall Statistik (Frankfurt Am Main)†
0076-6720 Metaphysische Rundschau
0076-6739 Meteorological Yearbook of Finland. Part 1B: Climatological Data from Jokioinen and Sodankyla Observatories†
0076-6771 Methodensammlung der Elektronenmikroskopie **899**
0076-678X Methodes de la Sociologie†
0076-6798 Methodes Mathematiques des Sciences de l'Homme
0076-681X Methods and Achievements in Experimental Pathology†
0076-6828 Methods and Models in the Social Sciences
0076-6836 Methods and Techniques in Geophysics†
0076-6852 Methods in Cancer Research†
0076-6860 Methods in Computational Physics: Advances in Research and Applications†
0076-6879 Methods in Enzymology **738**
0076-6887 Methods in Free-Radical Chemistry†
0076-6895 Methods in Geochemistry and Geophysics **2713**
0076-6917 Methods in Immunology and Immunochemistry†
0076-6925 Methods in Neurochemistry†
0076-6933 Methods in Virology†
0076-6941 Methods of Biochemical Analysis **738**
0076-6984 Metodicke Prirucky Experimentalni Botaniky†
0076-6992 Metodyki Nauczania i Wychowania
0076-700X Metro Building Industry Directory†
0076-7050 Metropolitan Library Service Agency. Annual Report†
0076-7085 Metropolitan Politics†
0076-7093 Metropolitan Toronto†
0076-7107 Metropolitan Washington Council of Governments. Annual Report†
0076-7115 Metropolitan Washington Council of Governments. Regional Directory
0076-7158 Museo Nacional de Antropologia. Cuadernos†
0076-7182 Universidad Nacional Autonoma de Mexico. Instituto de Geofisica. Anales†
0076-7204 Universidad Nacional Autonoma de Mexico. Instituto de Geofisica. Monografias **2791**
0076-7212 Universidad Nacional Autonoma de Mexico. Instituto de Investigaciones Historicas. Serie de Cultura Nahuatl. Fuentes†
0076-7247 Universidad Nacional Autonoma de Mexico. Instituto de Investigaciones Esteticas. Anales. Suplemento†
0076-7255 Universidad Nacional Autonoma de Mexico. Instituto de Investigaciones Esteticas. Publicaciones Especiales†
0076-7271 Universidad Nacional Autonoma de Mexico. Instituto de Investigaciones Historicas. Serie Documental. Cuadernos†
0076-7298 Instituto de Investigaciones Antropologicas. Serie Antropologica†
0076-7301 Universidad Nacional Autonoma de Mexico. Instituto de Investigaciones Historicas. Serie Bibliografica **4316**
0076-731X Universidad Nacional Autonoma de Mexico. Instituto de Investigaciones Historicas. Serie Documental **4316**
0076-7328 Universidad Nacional Autonoma de Mexico. Instituto de Investigaciones Historicas. Serie Culturas Mesoamericanas **4316**
0076-7344 Universidad Nacional Autonoma de Mexico. Instituto de Investigaciones Historicas. Serie de Cultura Nahuatl. Monografias†
0076-7352 Universidad Nacional Autonoma de Mexico. Instituto de Investigaciones Historicas. Serie Historia General **4316**
0076-7379 Universidad Nacional Autonoma de Mexico. Instituto de Investigaciones Historicas. Serie Historia Novohispana **4316**
0076-7387 Universidad Nacional Autonoma de Mexico. Instituto de Investigaciones Historicas. Serie Historiadores y Cronistas **4316**
0076-7468 Universidad Nacional Autonoma de Mexico. Seminario de Investigaciones Bibliotecologica. Publicaciones. Serie B. Bibliografia†
0076-7476 Instituto Nacional de Energia Nuclear. Publication†
0076-7492 Mexico. Secretaria de Programacion y Presupuesto†
0076-7506 Instituto Nacional de Antropologia e Historia. Departamento de Monumentos Coloniales. (Publicaciones)†
0076-7514 Instituto Nacional de Antropologia e Historia. Departamento de Monumentos Prehispanicos. (Publicaciones)†
0076-7530 Mexico. Direccion General de Prensa, Memorias, Bibliotecas y Publicaciones. Coleccion: Documentos Economicos de la Administracion Publica
0076-7565 Instituto Nacional de Antropologia e Historia. Coleccion Breve†
0076-7573 Instituto Nacional de Antropologia e Historia. Investigaciones†
0076-759X Instituto Nacional de Antropologia e Historia. Memorias†
0076-7611 Instituto Nacional de Antropologia e Historia. Coleccion Cientifica **343**
0076-762X Instituto Nacional de Antropologia e Historia. Serie Culturas del Mundo†
0076-7670 Meyers Grosses Jahreslexikon†
0076-7689 Meyniana **2755**
0076-7697 Miami Linguistic Series†
0076-7719 University of Miami Hispanic-American Studies†
0076-7727 Michel-Briefmarken-Kataloge **6897**
0076-7824 Michigan Beef Cattle Day Report†
0076-7832 Michigan Business Cases†
0076-7840 Michigan Business Papers†
0076-7859 Michigan Business Reports†
0076-7867 Michigan Business Studies†
0076-7905 Michigan. Department of Natural Resources. Institute for Fisheries Research. Miscellaneous Publication†
0076-7913 Michigan. Division of Vocational Education. Report†
0076-7948 Michigan Geographical Publications†
0076-7956 Michigan Governmental Studies†
0076-7964 Michigan. Department of Natural Resources. Institute for Fisheries Research. Lake Inventory Summary†
0076-7972 Michigan International Business Studies†
0076-7999 Michigan International Labor Studies†
0076-8014 Michigan Municipal League. Municipal Legal Briefs **7497**
0076-8057 Michigan Natural Resources Council. Scientific Advisory Committee. Annual Report†
0076-8073 Michigan. Plant Industry Division. Plant Pest Control Programs†
0076-8103 Michigan Slavic Contributions **5333**
0076-8111 Michigan State Plan for Construction of Community Mental Health Facilities†
0076-812X Michigan State University. Asian Studies Center. Occasional Papers: East Asia Series†
0076-8138 Michigan State University. Asian Studies Center. Occasional Papers: South Asia Series **4186**
0076-8189 Michigan State University. Latin American Studies Center. Monograph Series **4303**
0076-8197 Michigan State University. Latin American Studies Center. Occasional Papers†
0076-8200 Michigan State University. Latin American Studies Center. Research Reports **4303**
0076-8227 Michigan State University. Museum Publications. Biological Series†
0076-8235 Michigan State University. Museum Publications. Cultural Series **6529**
0076-8243 Michigan State University. Public Administration Program. Research Report†
0076-8308 Michigan Statistical Abstract†
0076-8332 University of Michigan. Graduate School of Business Administration. Leadership Award Lecture†
0076-8340 University of Michigan. Center for Japanese Studies. Bibliographical Series†
0076-8367 University of Michigan. Museum of Anthropology. Anthropological Papers **359**
0076-8375 University of Michigan. Museum of Anthropology. Memoirs **359**
0076-8405 University of Michigan. Museum of Zoology. Miscellaneous Publications **966**
0076-8413 University of Michigan. Museum of Zoology. Occasional Papers **966**
0076-8421 University of Michigan Observatories. Publications†
0076-8480 Microfiche Foundation. Newsletter†
0076-8502 Middle East and North Africa (Year) **7154**
0076-8510 Middle East Economic Papers†
0076-8529 Middle East Record† **8974**
0076-8537 Middle Eastern Monographs†
0076-857X University of Chicago. Midwest Administration Center. Monograph Series†
0076-8588 Midwest Electrical Buyers' Guide†

Link to your serials resources and content with ulrichsweb.com

0076-8596 Midwest Monographs. Series 1 (Drama)†
0076-860X Midwest Monographs. Series 2 (Poetry)†
0076-8618 Midwest Monographs. Series 3 (Graphic Works)†
0076-8626 Midwest Monographs. Series 4 (Translation)†
0076-8634 Midwest Monographs. Series 5 (Culture and Criticism)†
0076-8642 Mikrochimica Acta **2104**
0076-8650 Istituto di Ricerche Agrarie, Milan. Contributi†
0076-8669 Universita Cattolica del Sacro Cuore. Contributi. Serie Terza. Scienze Storiche†
0076-8677 Universita Cattolica del Sacro Cuore. Contributi. Serie Terza. Scienze Filosofiche†
0076-8685 Universita Cattolica del Sacro Cuore. Contributi. Serie Terza. Scienze Filologiche e Letteratura†
0076-8693 Universita Cattolica del Sacro Cuore. Contributi. Serie Terza. Scienze Psicologiche†
0076-8707 Universita Cattolica del Sacro Cuore. Istituto di Archeologia. Contributi†
0076-8715 Universita Cattolica del Sacro Cuore. Saggi e Ricerche. Serie Terza. Scienze Filologiche e Letteratura†
0076-8723 Universita Cattolica del Sacro Cuore. Saggi e Ricerche. Serie Terza. Scienze Filosofiche†
0076-8731 Universita Cattolica del Sacro Cuore. Saggi e Ricerche. Serie Terza. Scienze Geografiche†
0076-8758 Universita Cattolica del Sacro Cuore. Saggi e Ricerche. Serie Terza. Scienze Storiche†
0076-8766 Mildex Motor Book†
0076-8774 Military Research Series†
0076-8782 Military Yearbook **6436**
0076-8790 Milla Wa-Milla†
0076-8812 Millesime **1779**
0076-8820 Milton Studies **5334**
0076-8839 Milu: Wissenschaftliche und Kulturelle Mitteilungen aus dem Tierpark Berlin **955**
0076-8847 M I M S Desk Reference **6859**
0076-8855 Brazil. Tribunal Regional do Trabalho. Tercera Regiao. Revista **4631**
0076-8871 Universidade Federal de Minas Gerais. Revista†
0076-891X M W V Jahresbericht **2126**
0076-8936 M A C Newsletter *changed to* 1811-5209 **6461**
0076-8952 Minerals Yearbook **6471**
0076-8995 Mining Annual Review **6472**
0076-9029 Minkus Austria, Switzerland, Lichtenstein Stamp Catalog†
0076-9037 Minkus British Commonwealth Stamp Catalog†
0076-9045 Minkus Germany and Colonies Stamp Catalog†
0076-9053 Minkus Italy, San Marino and Vatican Stamp Catalog†
0076-907X Minkus New World Wide Stamp Catalog†
0076-9088 Minkus Russia, Poland, Hungary, Romania, Czechoslovakia Stamp Catalog†
0076-9096 Minneapolis Institute of Arts. Annual Report **6529**
0076-910X Minneapolis Institute of Arts. Bulletin†
0076-9142 Minnesota Drama Editions†
0076-9169 Minnesota Geological Survey. Bulletin **2755**
0076-9177 Minnesota Geological Survey. Report of Investigations **2755**
0076-9185 Minnesota. Geological Survey. Special Publication Series†
0076-9215 Minnesota Monographs in the Humanities†
0076-9258 Minnesota Studies in the Philosophy of Science **6934**
0076-9266 Minnesota Symposia on Child Psychology Series **7386**
0076-9274 University of Minnesota. Audio-Visual Library Service. Educational Resources Bulletin
0076-9290 University of Minnesota. Graduate School Research Center. Inventory of Faculty Research†
0076-9312 University of Minnesota Studies in Economics and Business.†
0076-9347 Miscellanea Byzantina Monacensia **4245**
0076-9355 Miscellanea Musicologica†
0076-9371 Mision Arqueologica Espanola en Nubia. Memorias†
0076-941X Missionswissenschaftliche Abhandlungen und Texte†
0076-9428 Missionswissenschaftliche Forschungen†
0076-9436 Mississippi Academy of Science. Journal **7882**
0076-9460 Mississippi Congress of Parents and Teachers. Proceedings†
0076-9479 Mississippi Congress of Parents and Teachers. Yearbook **2887**
0076-9517 Mississippi State University. Christian Student Center. Annual Lectureship
0076-9525 M V C Bulletin†
0076-9533 Mississippi Water Resources Conference. Proceedings†
0076-9541 Missouri Archaeological Society. Memoir Series†
0076-9568 Missouri Archaeological Society. Research Series†
0076-9576 Missouri Archaeologist **406**
0076-9606 Missouri. Division of Geological Survey and Water Resources. Engineering Geology Series **3278**
0076-9614 Missouri. Division of Geological Survey and Water Resources. Water Resources Report **8829**
0076-9630 Missouri Handbook Series†
0076-9649 Missouri Literary Frontiers Series†
0076-9657 University of Missouri, St. Louis. Center for International Studies. Monograph†
0076-969X University of Missouri. College of Business and Public Administration. Office of Research, Annual Report†
0076-9703 University of Missouri Studies†
0076-9711 University of Missouri at Columbia. Veterinary Medical Diagnostic Laboratory. Annual Report
0076-9754 Mittellateinische Studien und Texte **4245**
0076-9762 Mittellateinisches Jahrbuch **4245**
0076-9770 Moana: Estudios de Antropologia Oceanica **348**
0076-9894 Modern America†
0076-9908 Modern Analytic and Computational Methods in Science and Mathematics†
0076-9916 Modern Approaches to the Diagnosis and Instruction of Multi-Handicapped Children†
0076-9924 Modern Aspects of Electrochemistry **2114**
0076-9932 Modern Brewery Age Blue Book **607**
0076-9959 Modern Drug Encyclopedia and Therapeutic Index†
0076-9967 Modern Filologiai Fuzetek **5151**
0077-0000 Modern Materials. Advances in Development and Applications†
0077-0027 Modern Middle East Series **4186**
0077-0043 Modern Perspectives in Psychiatry†
0077-0094 Modern Problems of Pharmacopsychiatry *changed to* 1662-2685 **6161**
0077-0167 Modern Vocational Trends Reference Handbook†
0077-0191 Modicum
0077-0205 Die Moebel-Industrie und Ihre Helfer **4560**
0077-0221 Molecular Biology, Biochemistry and Biophysics†
0077-023X Molecular Biology; Proceedings of the International Conference†
0077-0264 University of the West Indies, Jamaica. Department of Geography. Occasional Publications Series†
0077-0272 University of the West Indies, Jamaica. Department of Geography. Research Notes Series†
0077-0280 Monarchist Book Review **4171**
0077-0299 Monarchist Press Association. Historical Series **4246**
0077-0310 Monde d'Outre-Mer, Passe et Present. 1 Serie: Etudes†
0077-0329 Monde d'Outre-Mer, Passe et Present. 2 Serie: Documents†
0077-0337 Monde d'Outre-Mer, Passe et Present. 3 Serie: Essais†
0077-0345 Monde d'Outre-Mer, Passe et Present. 4 Serie: Bibliographies et Instruments de Travail†
0077-0353 Centre pour l'Etude des Problemes de Monde Musulman Contemporain. Initiations†
0077-0361 Mondo†
0077-0396 Mongolia Society. Occasional Papers **4186**
0077-040X Monitor (Albany)†
0077-0442 Monografias de Filosofia Juridica y Social†
0077-0450 Monografias de Matematica†
0077-0469 Monografias de Psicologia, Normal y Patologica†
0077-0485 Monografie Biochemiczne **740**
0077-0493 Monografie di Archeologia Libica **406**
0077-0507 Monografie Matematyczne†
0077-0515 Monografie Psychologiczne†
0077-0523 Monografie Slaskie Ossolineum†
0077-0531 Monografie Slawistyczne **5336**
0077-054X Monografie z Dziejow Nauki i Techniki **7883**
0077-0558 Monografie z Dziejow Oswiaty **3073**
0077-0574 Monograph Series in Probability and Statistics†
0077-0582 G S I S Monograph Series in World Affairs†
0077-0620 Monograph Series on Schizophrenia **6161**
0077-0639 Monographiae Biologicae **690**
0077-0647 Monographiae Biologicae Canarienses†
0077-0655 Monographiae Botanicae **802**
0077-0663 Monographie der Flaumeichen-Buschwaelder†
0077-0671 Monographien aus dem Gesamtgebiete der Psychiatrie **6161**
0077-0701 Monographies de l'Industrie et du Commerce en France
0077-071X Monographies Francaises de Psychologie
0077-0728 Monographies Juridiques†
0077-0744 Monographs and Textbooks in Material Science†
0077-0752 Monographs and Texts in the Behavioral Sciences†
0077-0760 Monographs in Allergy† **8975**
0077-0795 Monographs in Chemistry in Non-Aqueous Ionizing Solvents
0077-0809 Monographs in Clinical Cytology **5680**
0077-0825 Monographs in Developmental Biology†
0077-0833 Monographs in Electroanalytical Chemistry and Electrochemistry Series†
0077-085X Monographs in Geology and Paleontology†
0077-0884 Monographs in Macromolecular Chemistry†
0077-0892 Monographs in Oral Science **5856**
0077-0922 Monographs in Pathology†
0077-0930 Monographs in Population Biology **690**
0077-0949 Monographs in Statistical Physics and Thermodynamics†
0077-0965 Monographs in Virology **893**
0077-099X Monographs on Atherosclerosis†
0077-1007 Monographs on Education†
0077-1015 Monographs on Endocrinology†
0077-1031 Monographs on Linguistic Analysis†
0077-104X Monographs on Oceanographic Methodology Series **2813**
0077-1074 London School of Economics Monographs on Social Anthropology **346**
0077-1090 Montana. Bureau of Mines and Geology. Bulletin **2756**
0077-1104 Montana. Bureau of Mines and Geology. Montana Mining Directory **6474**
0077-1120 Montana. Bureau of Mines and Geology. Memoir **2756**
0077-1139 Montana. Bureau of Mines and Geology. Special Publications **2756**
0077-1147 Montana Journalism Review†
0077-1163 University of Montana. Forest and Conservation Experiment Station, Missoula. Research Notes **3706**
0077-1198 Montana Vital Statistics **7312**
0077-1201 Montana. Water Resources Board. Inventory Series†
0077-1228 Instituto Tecnologico y de Estudios Superiores. Publicaciones. Serie Historia†
0077-1236 Instituto Tecnologico y de Estudios Superiores. Publicaciones. Serie Letras†
0077-1244 Museo Nacional de Historia Natural. Comunicaciones Antropologicas
0077-1252 Universidad de Uruguay. Departamento de Literatura Iberoamericana. Publicaciones
0077-1260 Universidad de la Republica. Facultad de Agronomia. Boletin **165**
0077-1279 Universidad de la Republica. Facultad de Agronomia. Publicacion Miscelanea†
0077-1287 Universidad de la Republica. Instituto de Administracion. Cuaderno **1799**
0077-1295 Universidad de Uruguay. Instituto de Mathematica y Estadistica. Publicaciones Didacticas†
0077-1317 Jardin Botanique de Montreal. Annuelles et Legumes†
0077-1325 Jardin Botanique de Montreal. Memoire†
0077-1341 Universite de Montreal. Ecole de Bibliotheconomie. Publications†
0077-1368 Montreal Women's Liberation Newsletter
0077-1376 Monumenta Aegyptiaca **406**
0077-1384 Monumenta Americana **406**
0077-1392 Monumenta Antiquitatis Extra Fines Hungariae Reperta Quae in Museo Artium Hungarico Aliisque Museis et Collectionibus Hungaricis Conservantur†
0077-1406 Monumenta Artis Romanae **406**
0077-1414 Monumenta Chartae Papyraceae Historiam Illustrantia **6735**
0077-1430 Monumenta Historica Budapestinensia†
0077-1449 Monumenta Historica Ordinis Minorum Capuccinorum **7808**
0077-1457 Monumenta Iuris Canonici. Series A, Corpus Glossatorium **7808**
0077-1465 Monumenta Musicae in Polonia. Series B: Collectanea Musicae Artis†
0077-1473 Monumenta Musicae Suecicae **6588**
0077-1481 Monumenta Paedagogica†
0077-1503 Monuments of Renaissance Music **6588**
0077-1554 Moscow Mathematical Society. Transactions **5518**
0077-1562 Gosudarstvennyi Muzei Izobrazitel'nykh Iskusstv im. Pushkina. Soobshcheniya†
0077-1570 Motocyclo Catalogue†
0077-1589 Motor Cycle Diary†
0077-1600 Motor Manual†
0077-1619 Motor Traffic in Sweden **8593**
0077-1627 Motor Transport Fact Book
0077-166X Motorboote und Yachten†
0077-1694 Motoring in Malaya
0077-1740 Mount Zion Hospital and Medical Center, San Francisco. Bulletin†
0077-1759 Mountain World†
0077-1775 Moyens de la Recherche Scientifique et Technique en Haute-Normandie.†
0077-1791 Instituto de Investigacao Agronomica de Mocambique. Centro de Documentacao Agraria. Memorias **122**
0077-1813 Muelleria **802**
0077-183X Muenchener Historische Studien. Abteilung Mittelalterliche Geschichte **4246**
0077-1856 Muenchner Universitaets-Schriften. Reihe der Philosophischen Fakultaet **6935**
0077-1872 Muenchner Germanistische Beitraege **5337**
0077-1880 Muenchener Indologische Studien†
0077-1899 Muenchener Jahrbuch der Bildenden Kunst **506**
0077-1902 Muenchener Studien zur Sozial- und Wirtschaftsgeographie†
0077-1910 Muenchener Studien zur Sprachwissenschaft **5153**
0077-1929 Universitaet Muenster. Astronomisches Institut. Mitteilungen†
0077-1937 Universitaet Muenster. Astronomisches Institut. Sonderdrucke†
0077-1945 Universitaet Muenster. Institut fuer Christliche Sozialwissenschaften. Schriften†
0077-1953 Fontes et Commentationes†
0077-197X Universitaet Muenster. Institut fuer Missionswissenschaft. Veroeffentlichungen†
0077-1996 Muenstersche Beitraege zur Deutschen Literaturwissenschaft†
0077-2011 Muensterschwarzacher Studien†
0077-202X Multihull International Catalogue Annual†
0077-2046 Multilingual Forestry Terminology Series
0077-2054 Coleccion Mundo Antiguo **4135**
0077-2089 Technische Universitaet Muenchen. Jahrbuch **8441**
0077-2119 Westfaelische Wilhelms-Universitaet Muenster. Institut fuer Kreditwesen. Schriftenreihe†
0077-2127 Universitaet Muenchen. Wirtschaftsgeographisches Institut. "W G I"-Berichte zur Regionalforschung†
0077-2143 Municipal Association of Victoria. Minutes of Proceedings of Annual Session **7498**
0077-2186 Municipal Year Book **7498**
0077-2194 Muse (Columbia) **507**
0077-2208 Museion **5033**
0077-2240 Museu Paraense Emilio Goeldi. Publicacoes Avulsas†
0077-2275 Museum Boymans-van Beuningen. Agenda **6531**
0077-2313 Museum Publications†
0077-233X Museums and Monuments Series **6532**
0077-2348 Museums Journal of Pakistan
0077-2356 Insects†
0077-2364 Mushroom Science **802**
0077-2372 Music Handbook†
0077-2380 Music and Artists Annual Directory
0077-2402 Music Educators National Conference. Selective Music Lists: Vocal Solos and Ensembles†
0077-2410 Music in Higher Education†
0077-2429 Music Indexes and Bibliographies†
0077-2437 Music Journal Anthology
0077-2453 Music World Year Book†
0077-2461 Musica Disciplina **6592**
0077-247X Musica Medii Aevi†
0077-2496 Musicological Studies and Documents **6594**
0077-2518 Musik i Sverige **6595**
0077-2526 Musikalische Denkmaeler†
0077-2542 Musk-Ox†
0077-2550 Mutual Fund Fact Book *changed to* 1938-6729 **1632**
0077-2577 Muzea Walki†
0077-2615 Mystic Seaport Manuscripts Inventory†
0077-2623 N A S A - University Conference on Manual Control (Papers)
0077-2631 N H K Technical Monograph†
0077-2666 Nairobi Airport. Annual Report
0077-2690 Names in South Carolina†
0077-2704 Namn och Bygd **5154**
0077-2712 Universite de Nancy II. Centre de Recherches et d'Applications Pedagogiques en Langues. Melanges **3086**
0077-2720 Universite de Nancy II. Centre Europeen Universitaire. Memoires†
0077-2739 Nanta Mathematica†
0077-2747 Nanyang University Journal†
0077-2801 Narradores de Arca **5338**
0077-2828 University of Rhode Island. Narragansett Marine Laboratory. Occasional Publication†
0077-2844 Narrativa Latinoamericana **4304**
0077-2879 Nassau Review **5338**
0077-2887 Nassauische Annalen **4247**
0077-2895 Natal Regional Survey. Additional Report†
0077-2909 Nathaniel Hawthorne Journal†
0077-2925 National Academy of Sciences. Annual Report†

0077-7889 Nevada. Division of Personnel. Biennial Report†
0077-7897 Nevada. State Museum, Carson City. Anthropological Papers **350**
0077-7900 Nevada. State Museum, Carson City. Natural History Publications **7891**
0077-7919 Nevada. State Museum, Carson City. Occasional Papers **6534**
0077-7927 Nevada. State Museum, Carson City. Popular Series **6534**
0077-7943 University of Nevada. Bureau of Business and Economic Research. Research Report†
0077-7994 New African Literature and the Arts†
0077-801X New Babylon: Studies in the Social Sciences **7988**
0077-8060 New Brunswick. Department of Municipal Affairs. Report†
0077-8079 New Brunswick. Department of Youth. Report†
0077-8087 New Brunswick. Liquor Control Commission. Report†
0077-8109 New Brunswick. Mineral Resources Branch. Report of Investigations
0077-8168 New Campus†
0077-8206 N D T†
0077-8230 New England Papers on Education†
0077-832X New Hampshire. Agricultural Experiment Station, Durham. Research Reports **139**
0077-8338 New Hampshire. Agricultural Experiment Station, Durham. Station Bulletins **139**
0077-8346 New Hampshire Archeologist **408**
0077-8354 New Hampshire Camping Guide
0077-8362 New Hampshire. Fish and Game Department. Biennial Report **2622**
0077-8370 New Hampshire. Fish and Game Department. Game Management and Research Division. Biological Survey Series†
0077-8389 New Hampshire. Fish and Game Department. Game Management and Research Division. Technical Circular Series†
0077-8397 New Hampshire. Fish and Game Department. Game Management and Research Division. Biological Survey Bulletin†
0077-8400 University of New Hampshire. Institute of Natural and Environmental Resources. Research Reports
0077-8427 New Hampshire Winter Holidays†
0077-8451 New Jersey Clean Air Council. Report **3489**
0077-8478 New Jersey. Economic Policy Council. Annual Report of Economic Policy Council and Office of Economic Policy†
0077-8508 New Jersey Public Employer-Employee Relations†
0077-8540 New Mexico Agricultural Statistics **184**
0077-8567 New Mexico Geological Society. Guidebook, Field Conference **2758**
0077-8575 New Mexico Statistical Abstract†
0077-8583 University of New Mexico Art Museum. Bulletin **6539**
0077-8591 New Official Guide: Japan†
0077-8605 New Orleans Academy of Ophthalmology. Transactions **6046**
0077-8613 New Perspectives in Political Science†
0077-8621 New Poetry
0077-8672 New South Wales. Department of Mines. Chemical Laboratory. Report†
0077-8680 New South Wales. Department of Mines. Coalfields Branch. Reports†
0077-8699 New South Wales. Geological Survey. Memoirs: Palaeontology **6727**
0077-8729 New South Wales. Geological Survey. Mineral Industry of New South Wales **6474**
0077-8737 New South Wales. Geological Survey. Mineral Resources Series **6474**
0077-8788 New South Wales. State Fisheries. Research Bulletin†
0077-8796 University of New South Wales. School of Civil Engineering. U N I C I V Reports. Series I
0077-880X University of New South Wales. School of Civil Engineering. U N I C I V Reports. Series R **3286**
0077-8818 University of New South Wales. Water Research Laboratory, Manly Vale. Laboratory Research Reports **8834**
0077-8826 New Teacher **2891**
0077-8842 New Testament Tools and Studies *changed to* New Testament Tools, Studies and Documents **7666**
0077-8877 New Trends in Biology Teaching Series†
0077-8885 New Trends in Chemistry Teaching Series†
0077-8893 New Trends in Mathematics Teaching†
0077-8907 New Trends in Physics Teaching Series†
0077-8915 New World Archaeological Foundation. Papers **408**
0077-8923 New York Academy of Sciences. Annals **7892**
0077-8931 New York Botanical Garden. Memoirs **805**
0077-894X City College Papers†
0077-8958 Metropolitan Museum Journal **6529**
0077-9008 New York Psychoanalytic Institute. Kris Study Group. Monographs **7388**
0077-9016 New York Public Library. Films†
0077-9059 New York State Archeological Association. Occasional Papers†
0077-9067 New York State Archeological Association. Researches and Transactions†
0077-9083 New York State Business Fact Book. Part 1: Business and Manufacturing†
0077-9091 New York State Business Fact Book. Part 2: Population and Housing†
0077-9105 New York State Business Fact Book. Supplement†
0077-9113 A F R I Research Note†
0077-9172 College and University Degrees Conferred, New York State **2972**
0077-9210 Distribution of High School Graduates and College Going Rate, New York State **2932**
0077-9229 Public School Professional Personnel Report, New York State†
0077-9253 Nonpublic School Enrollment and Staff, New York State **2892**
0077-927X New York (State) Interdepartmental Committee on Indian Affairs. Report†
0077-9296 Checklist of Official Publications of the State of New York **7480**
0077-930X New York State Library, Albany. Library Development. Excerpts from New York State Education Law, Rules of the Board of Regents, and Regulations of the Commissioner of Education Pertaining to Public and Free Association Libraries, Library Systems, Trustees and Librarians **5035**
0077-9318 New York State Library, Albany. Library Development. Institution Libraries Statistics†
0077-9326 New York State Library, Albany. Library Development. Public and Association Libraries Statistics **5059**
0077-9334 New York State Statistical Yearbook **8390**
0077-9342 Analysis of School Finances, New York State School Districts **3017**
0077-9407 New York (State) Upstate Medical Center, Syracuse. Library. Faculty Bibliography†
0077-9415 New York (State) Upstate Medical Center, Syracuse. Library. Library Guide†
0077-9423 New York State Urban Development Corporation. Annual Report
0077-9504 New York University Studies in Comparative Literature†
0077-9520 New Zealand Agricultural Engineering Institute. Annual Report†
0077-9539 Lincoln College. New Zealand Agricultural Engineering Institute. Extension Bulletin†
0077-9563 Lincoln College. New Zealand Agricultural Engineering Institute. Research Publication†
0077-9571 New Zealand Business Who's Who **2020**
0077-958X New Zealand. Central Advisory Committee on the Appointments and Promotion of Primary Teachers. Report to the Minister of Education†
0077-9601 New Zealand. Department of Scientific and Industrial Research. Annual Report†
0077-961X New Zealand. Department of Scientific and Industrial Research. Bulletin†
0077-9636 New Zealand. Department of Scientific and Industrial Research. Information Series†
0077-9644 New Zealand. Soil Bureau. Bulletin†
0077-9652 New Zealand. Department of Statistics. Annual Report of the Government Statistician†
0077-9784 New Zealand. Statistics New Zealand. Census Reports. Religious Professions **7313**
0077-9865 New Zealand. Department of Statistics. Industrial Production†
0077-9954 New Zealand Economic Papers **1153**
0077-9962 New Zealand Entomologist **856**
0078-0006 New Zealand. Forest Research Institute. Technical Paper†
0078-0022 New Zealand Geographical Society. Miscellaneous Series **4022**
0078-0030 New Zealand Geography Conference Proceedings Series† **8977**
0078-0049 New Zealand Institute of Economic Research. Discussion Paper† **8977**
0078-0057 New Zealand Institute of Economic Research. Annual Report **1153**
0078-0073 New Zealand Institute of Economic Research. Technical Memorandum†
0078-009X New Zealand Library School, Wellington. Bibliographical Series†
0078-0103 New Zealand Library School, Wellington. Occasional Papers†
0078-0111 New Zealand. Marine Department. Annual Report on Fisheries†
0078-0146 New Zealand Medical Records Officers' Association. Conference Proceedings†
0078-0170 New Zealand Official YearBook **4193**
0078-0189 New Zealand Pottery and Ceramics Research Association. Technical Report†
0078-0197 New Zealand Poultry Board. Report and New Zealand Marketing Authority Report and Statement of Accounts†
0078-0219 New Zealand Wheat Review†
0078-0243 Newcastle History Monographs **4193**
0078-0251 University of Newcastle-Upon-Tyne. Philosophical Society. Proceedings
0078-026X University of Newcastle-Upon-Tyne. Department of Geography. Research Series†
0078-0278 Newfoundland and Labrador. Department of Education. Statistical Supplement to the Annual Report†
0078-0286 Newfoundland and Labrador Who's Who†
0078-0316 Newfoundland Medical Directory **5686**
0078-0367 Newfoundland. Mines Branch. Annual Report Series†
0078-0421 Newsletters on Stratigraphy **2759**
0078-0448 Israel. Government Press Office. Newspapers and Periodicals Appearing in Israel†
0078-0502 Niagara Parks Commission. Annual Report **2622**
0078-0510 Nicaragua. Direccion General de Aduanas. Memoria **1431**
0078-0537 Niederdeutsche Beitraege zur Kunstgeschichte **508**
0078-0545 Niederdeutsches Wort **5155**
0078-057X Nigeria Annual and Trading Directory
0078-0588 Nigeria Assistance Programs of U.S. Non-Profit Organizations†
0078-0596 Nigeria Business Directory
0078-060X Nigeria Buyers Guide; A Pointer to Nigeria Market†
0078-0626 Nigeria. Federal Office of Statistics. Annual Abstract of Statistics **8391**
0078-0634 Nigeria. Federal Office of Statistics. Review of External Trade **1255**
0078-0642 Nigeria. Federal Office of Statistics. Trade Report†
0078-0650 Nigeria Trade Summary **1579**
0078-0677 University of Nigeria. Report on Research†
0078-0685 Nigeria Year Book **7255**
0078-0693 Nigerian Books in Print **632**
0078-0707 Nigerian Chamber of Mines. Annual Review
0078-0723 Nigerian Institute of International Affairs. Digest of Selected Articles on International Questions†
0078-074X Nigerian Institute of Social and Economic Research. Annual Report **7989**
0078-0758 Nigerian Institute of Social and Economic Research. Information Bulletin†
0078-0766 Nigerian Institute of Social and Economic Research. Library. List of Accessions **8021**
0078-0774 Nigerian Law Journal†
0078-0782 Nigerian Medical Directory
0078-0804 Nigerian National Advisory Council for the Blind. Annual Report
0078-0847 N I B S Bulletin of Biological Research†
0078-0855 Nityanand Universal Series **4187**
0078-0863 Nivel de la Economia Argentina
0078-0898 NMR Data Table for Organic Compounds†
0078-091X Noble Official Catalog of Canada Precancels
0078-0928 Noble Official Catalog of United States Bureau Precancels
0078-0936 Noctes Romanae†
0078-0944 Noda Institute for Scientific Research. Report **7893**
0078-0952 Nomenclator Zoologicus **958**
0078-0960 Nomenclature des Entreprises Nationales a Caractere Industriel ou Commercial et des Societies d'Economie Mixte d'Interet National **1900**
0078-0979 Nomos **7159**
0078-0987 Non-Ferrous Metal Works of the World **6327**
0078-0995 Non-Metallic Solids†
0078-1037 Nordelbingen **4248**
0078-1045 Nordfriesisches Jahrbuch **4248**
0078-1053 Collection Nordicana **333**
0078-107X Nordisk Numismatisk Aarsskrift **6652**
0078-1096 Nordisk Statistisk Skriftserie†
0078-110X Nordiska Afrikainstitutet. Skriftserie†
0078-1118 Nordic Association for American Studies. Publications†
0078-1126 N K B Skriftserie
0078-1134 Nordistica Gothoburgensia **5155**
0078-1169 Norfolk Record Society. Publications **4249**
0078-1185 Norges Bank. Report and Accounts **1372**
0078-1193 Norges Geotekniske Institutt. Publikasjon **3279**
0078-1207 Norwegian Geotechnical Institute. Technical Report†
0078-1231 Norges Teknisk-Naturvitenskapelige Forskningsraad. Aarsberetning†
0078-1266 Norsk Litteraer Aarbok **5342**
0078-1304 North American Fauna **959**
0078-1312 North American Flora **805**
0078-1320 North American Forest Soils Conference. Proceedings†
0078-1347 North American Radio-T V Guide†
0078-1355 North American Wildlife and Natural Resources Conference. Transactions **2623**
0078-1371 North Carolina Vital Statistics **7313**
0078-141X North Carolina. State Commission on Higher Education Facilities. Facilities Inventory and Utilization Study, for the State of North Carolina
0078-1444 North Carolina State University. School of Design. (Student Publication Magazine) **451**
0078-1452 University of North Carolina, Chapel Hill. Graduate School of Business Administration. Technical Papers†
0078-1460 University of North Carolina, Greensboro. Faculty Publications†
0078-1495 University of North Carolina, Chapel Hill. Institute of Statistics. Mimeo Series **8413**
0078-1525 University of North Carolina. Water Resources Research Institute. Report **8834**
0078-1576 North Dakota. Geological Survey. Miscellaneous Series **2759**
0078-1592 North-Holland Linguistic Series **5156**
0078-1622 North Pacific Fur Seal Commission. Proceedings of the Annual Meeting†
0078-1681 Northeast Folklore **3621**
0078-169X Northeastern University Studies in Rehabilitation†
0078-1703 Northeastern Weed Science Society. Proceedings **806**
0078-172X Northern History **4249**
0078-1738 Northern House Pamphlet Poets†
0078-1754 Northern Ireland. Department of Agriculture. Record of Agricultural Research†
0078-1770 Northern Virginia Planning District Commission. Annual Report†
0078-1789 Northwest Historical Series **4306**
0078-1797 Northwest Wood Products Clinic. Proceedings†
0078-1843 Norway. Fiskeridirektoratet. Skrifter. Serie Fiskeri†
0078-186X Norway. Fiskeridirektoratet. Skrifter. Serie Teknologiske Undersoekelser†
0078-1894 Norway. Statistisk Sentralbyraa. Jordbruksstatistikk **184**
0078-1908 Norway. Statistisk Sentralbyraa. Kredittmarked Statistikk†
0078-1916 Norway. Statistisk Sentralbyraa. Loennsstatistikk **1256**
0078-1959 Norway. Statistisk Sentralbyraa. Varehandelsstatistikk **1256**
0078-1967 Norwegian-American Historical Association. Newsletter **4306**
0078-1975 Norwegian-American Historical Association. Travel and Description Series **4306**
0078-1983 Norwegian-American Studies **8123**
0078-1991 Norwegian Studies in English†
0078-2009 Notas de Algebra y Analisis **5521**
0078-2017 Notas de Logica Matematica **5521**
0078-2041 Notes in Anthropology†
0078-2076 University of Notre Dame. Department of Economics. Union-Management Conference. Proceeding†
0078-2084 Geographical Field Group (Nottingham). Regional Studies†
0078-2106 University of Nottingham. School of Agriculture. Report†
0078-2122 Nottingham Medieval Studies **4249**
0078-2157 Nouveautes Techniques Maritimes **8655**
0078-2165 Nouvelle Bibliotheque Nervalienne
0078-2211 Nouvelles Economiques
0078-2238 Nova Hedwiga, Beihefte **806**
0078-2246 Nova Kepleriana. Neue Folge **578**
0078-2254 Instituto de Investigacao Agronomica de Angola. Relatorio
0078-2262 Instituto de Investigacao Agronomica de Angola. Serie Cientifica
0078-2270 Instituto de Investigacao Agronomica de Angola. Serie Tecnica
0078-2300 Nova Scotia Community Planning Conference Proceedings†
0078-2319 Nova Scotia. Department of Bacteriology. Annual Report†
0078-2351 Nova Scotia. Department of Pathology. Annual Report†

9114 0078-236X ULRICH'S PERIODICALS

0078-236X Nova Scotia. Department of Health. Nutrition Division. Annual Report†
0078-2378 Nova Scotia. Emergency Measures Organization. Report†
0078-2386 Nova Scotia Fruit Growers Association. Annual Report and Proceedings **244**
0078-2483 Nova Scotia Research Foundation. Bulletin†
0078-2521 Nova Scotian Institute of Science. Proceedings **7894**
0078-253X Novarien **7810**
0078-2564 Novos Taxa Entomologicos†
0078-2602 Nuclear Medicine Seminar†
0078-2653 Nuernberger Forschungen **4250**
0078-2696 Numismatic Chronicle **6652**
0078-270X Numismatic Literature. Supplement†
0078-2718 Numismatic Notes and Monographs **6652**
0078-2726 Numismatica Moravica†
0078-2734 Numismatiska Meddelanden **6652**
0078-2742 Nuntiaturberichte aus Deutschland nebst Ergaenzenden Aktenstuecken **4154**
0078-2769 Nuovi Saggi **4467**
0078-2777 Stadtbibliothek Nuernberg. Ausstellungskatalog **6537**
0078-2785 Beitraege zur Geschichte und Kultur der Stadt Nuernberg **4203**
0078-2807 S I N - Staedtebauinstitut. Schriftenreihe **4426**
0078-2815 S I N - Staedtebauinstitut. Studienhefte **4426**
0078-2823 S I N - Staedtebauinstitut. Werkberichte **4426**
0078-2831 Nursing Education Monographs†
0078-284X Nutrition News in Zambia **3658**
0078-2858 Nyelveszeti Tanulmanyok†
0078-2866 Nyelvtudomanyi Ertekezesek **5157**
0078-2874 O.I.G.G.†
0078-2912 Obeche
0078-2939 Oberrheinische Geologische Abhandlungen†
0078-2947 Oberrheinischer Geologischer Verein. Jahresberichte und Mitteilungen **2759**
0078-2955 Objecta
0078-2963 Obraz Literatury Polskiej†
0078-3005 Occasional Papers in Anthropology **350**
0078-303X Occasional Papers in English Local History†
0078-3048 Occasional Papers in Estate Management†
0078-3064 Occasional Papers in Industrial Relations†
0078-3080 Occasional Papers in Librarianship†
0078-3129 Occupational Safety and Health Series **6683**
0078-3137 Ocean Engineering Information Series
0078-3153 Ocean Technology†
0078-3161 Oceana Docket Classics†
0078-317X Oceana Docket Series†
0078-3188 Oceanic Linguistics. Special Publications
0078-320X Oceanographic Research Institute. Investigational Report **695**
0078-3218 Oceanography and Marine Biology **2815**
0078-3234 Oceanologia **2815**
0078-3269 Octagon Lectures†
0078-3277 Odense University Slavic Studies **5157**
0078-3285 Odense University Studies in Art History†
0078-3293 Odense University Studies in English†
0078-3315 Odense University. Studies in Linguistics *changed to* 1602-5113 **5192**
0078-3323 University of Southern Denmark Studies in Literature **5393**
0078-3358 Odontologiska Samfundet i Finland. Aarsbok **5858**
0078-3366 Odrodzenie w Polsce†
0078-3374 O'Dwyer's Directory of Public Relations Firms **2022**
0078-3390 Oekonometrie und Unternehmensforschung†
0078-3412 Oenologie Pratique†
0078-3420 Oerlikon Schweissmitteilungen **6328**
0078-3439 Oesterreichisches Ost- und Suedosteuropa Institut. Schriftenreihe **4251**
0078-3463 Oesterreichische Gesellschaft fuer Aussenpolitik und Internationale Beziehungen. Schriftenreihe†
0078-3471 Oesterreichische Gesellschaft fuer Musik. Beitraege **6600**
0078-3498 Oesterreichische Gesellschaft fuer Raumforschung und Raumplanung. Schriftenreihe†
0078-351X Oesterreichische Moorforschung†
0078-3536 Oesterreichische Schriften zur Entwicklungshilfe **1602**
0078-3544 Oesterreichische Schul-Statistik†
0078-3579 Oesterreichisches Archaeologisches Institut. Jahreshefte **409**
0078-3595 Oesterreichisches Wirtschaftsinstitut fuer Strukturforschung und Strukturpolitik. Schriftenreihe†
0078-3617 Oesterreichisches Institut fuer Raumplanung. Taetigkeitsbericht†
0078-3633 Oesterreichisches Jahrbuch fuer Exlibris und Gebrauchsgraphik
0078-3668 Oesterreichisches Ost- und Suedost-Europa Institut. Veroeffentlichungen
0078-3684 Oesterreichs Industrie
0078-3692 Offshore Europe†
0078-3714 Offa-Jahrbuch **4251**
0078-3722 Office des Communications Sociales, Montreal. Cahiers d'Etudes et de Recherches†
0078-3749 Rydge's Office Equipment Buyers Guide†
0078-3781 France. Office National d'Etudes et de Recherches Aerospatiales. Notes Techniques
0078-379X France. Office National d'Etudes et de Recherches Aerospatiales. Publications
0078-3803 Office Universitaire de Recherche Socialiste. Cahiers†
0078-382X Official American Basketball Association Guide†
0078-3846 Official Baseball Rules **8241**
0078-3854 Official Catholic Directory **7810**
0078-3862 Sporting News Books Official N B A Guide **8246**
0078-3900 Official World Series Records†
0078-3951 Ohio Agricultural Research and Development Center, Wooster. Research Bulletin **143**
0078-396X Ohio Agricultural Research and Development Center, Wooster. Research Circular **143**
0078-3978 Ohio Agricultural Research and Development Center, Wooster. Research Summary†
0078-3986 Ohio Biological Survey. Biological Notes†
0078-3994 Ohio Biological Survey. Bulletin. New Series **695**
0078-4001 Ohio. Division of State Personnel. Annual Report **1870**
0078-4052 Ohio Speech Journal **5157**
0078-4087 Ohio State University. College of Administrative Science. Monograph†
0078-4095 Ohio State University. College of Law. Law Forum Series†
0078-4184 Kent State University. Center for Business and Economic Research. Comparative Administration Research Institute Series†
0078-4192 Kent State University. Center for Business and Economic Research. Labor and Industrial Relations Series†
0078-4206 Kent State University. Center for Business and Economic Research. Printed Series†
0078-4214 Kent State University. Center for Business and Economic Research. Research Papers†
0078-4222 Kent State University. Libraries. Occasional Paper†
0078-4265 Oikos. Supplementum†
0078-429X Okayama University. Faculty of Science. Research Laboratory for Surface Science. Reports **2139**
0078-4303 Oklahoma Academy of Science. Proceedings **7895**
0078-4311 Oklahoma Academy of Science. Annals†
0078-432X Oklahoma Anthropological Society. Bulletin†
0078-4338 Oklahoma Anthropological Society. Newsletter **351**
0078-4370 Oklahoma. Fishery Research Laboratory, Norman. Bulletin†
0078-4389 Oklahoma Geological Survey. Bulletin **2760**
0078-4397 Oklahoma Geological Survey. Circular **2760**
0078-4400 Oklahoma Geological Survey. Guidebook **2760**
0078-4435 University of Oklahoma. Center for Economic and Management Research. Monograph Series†
0078-4508 Oklahoma. Grand River Dam Authority. Annual Report **3363**
0078-4516 The Old Farmer's Almanac **3121**
0078-4540 Old Salem Gleaner†
0078-4559 Old Sturbridge Village Booklet Series†
0078-4575 Olsen's Fisherman's Nautical Almanack
0078-4591 Ombres de l'Histoire
0078-463X Onoma **5157**
0078-4648 Onomastica **5158**
0078-4656 Onomastica Canadiana **5158**
0078-4672 Ontario Archaeology **409**
0078-4680 Ontario Association for Curriculum Development. Annual Conference (Report)
0078-4702 Ontario Catholic Directory
0078-4745 Ontario. Ministry of Transportation and Communications. Research and Development Division. Research Report†
0078-4826 Ontario Federation of Labour. Report of Proceedings†
0078-4834 Ontario Field Biologist†
0078-5040 Ontario Petroleum Institute. Annual Conference Proceedings **6785**
0078-5091 Champlain Society. Ontario Series **4288**
0078-5148 Ontario. Ministry of the Environment. Pollution Control Branch. Research Publication **3490**
0078-5156 Ontario. Ministry of the Environment. Ground Water Bulletin†
0078-5164 Open Door International for the Emancipation of the Woman Worker. Report of Congress **1701**
0078-5172 Open Doors
0078-5237 Opera Botanica **806**
0078-5245 Opera Lilloana **806**
0078-5261 C O R S I Bulletin
0078-5326 Ophelia *changed to* 1745-1000 **688**
0078-5415 Wyzsza Szkola Pedagogiczna, Opole. Zeszyty Naukowe. Seria A. Historia Slaska†
0078-5466 Optica Applicata (Online) **7081**
0078-5482 Optical Physics and Engineering†
0078-5504 Optics and Spectroscopy. Supplement†
0078-5512 Optik und Feinmechanik in Einzeldarstellungen†
0078-5520 Opuscula Atheniensia **2238**
0078-5539 Opuscula - aus Wissenschaft und Dichtung†
0078-5547 Orange Free State. Director of Hospital Services. Report†
0078-5555 Orbis Antiquus **2238**
0078-5563 Orbis Artium†
0078-5571 Orbis Pictus†
0078-5598 Dictionnaire National des Architectes
0078-5601 Ordre des Geometres-Experts. Annuaire **7896**
0078-5644 Oregon Research Institute. Research Bulletins†
0078-5652 Oregon Research Institute. Research Monographs†
0078-5679 Oregon School Directory **2961**
0078-5709 Oregon. Department of Geology and Mineral Industries. Bulletin **2761**
0078-5717 Oregon. State Department of Geology and Mineral Industries. G M I Short Papers†
0078-5725 Oregon. State Department of Geology and Mineral Industries. Miscellaneous Papers†
0078-5733 Oregon. State Department of Geology and Mineral Industries. Miscellaneous Publications†
0078-5741 Oregon. Department of Geology and Mineral Industries. Oil and Gas Investigations **6785**
0078-575X Oregon State Plan for the Construction and Modernization of Hospitals, Public Health Centers and Medical Facilities†
0078-5768 Oregon State Monographs. Bibliographic Series†
0078-5776 Oregon State Monographs. Studies in Botany†
0078-5784 Oregon State Monographs. Studies in Economics†
0078-5792 Oregon State Monographs. Studies in Education and Guidance†
0078-5806 Oregon State Monographs. Studies in Entomology†
0078-5814 Oregon State Monographs. Studies in Geology†
0078-5822 Oregon State Monographs. Studies in History†
0078-5830 Oregon State Monographs. Studies in Zoology†
0078-5849 Oregon State University. Water Resources Research Institute. Water Research Summary†
0078-5938 Oregon State University. School of Engineering. Graduate Research and Education†
0078-5946 Oregon State University. School of Engineering. Research Activities†
0078-5962 University of Oregon. Bureau of Business Research. Research Studies†
0078-5970 University of Oregon. Bureau of Governmental Research and Service. Information Bulletin†
0078-5989 University of Oregon. Bureau of Governmental Research and Service. Legal Bulletin†
0078-5997 University of Oregon. Bureau of Governmental Research and Service. Local Government Notes and Information: Policy and Practice Series†
0078-6020 University of Oregon. Center for Educational Policy and Management. Technical Reports†
0078-6039 University of Oregon. Library. Occasional Paper†
0078-6047 University of Oregon. Museum of Natural History. Bulletin†
0078-6063 University of Oregon. Bureau of Business Research. Business Publications†
0078-6071 University of Oregon Anthropological Papers **359**
0078-608X Orestes Brownson Series on Contemporary Thought and Affairs†
0078-611X Organic Chemistry **2127**
0078-6128 Organic Directory†
0078-6136 Organic Electronic Spectral Data **2104**
0078-6144 Organic Photochemical Syntheses†
0078-6160 Organic Reaction Mechanisms. Annual Survey **2128**
0078-6179 Organic Reactions **2128**
0078-6187 Organic Substances of Natural Origin†
0078-6209 Organic Syntheses **2128**
0078-6217 Organic Syntheses - Collective Volumes **2128**
0078-6225 Organische Chemie in Einzeldarstellungen†
0078-6233 Afro-Asian Peoples' Solidarity Organization. Council. Documents of the Session†
0078-6276 O E C D High Temperature Reactor Project Dragon†
0078-6284 O E C D Halden Reactor Project†
0078-6292 List of Research Institutes and Scientists in O E C D Member Countries†
0078-6306 O A U Review **4177**
0078-6314 Organization of American States. Department of Scientific Affairs. Serie de Biologia: Monografias†
0078-6322 Organization of American States. Department of Scientific Affairs. Serie de Fisica: Monografias†
0078-6330 Organization of American States. Department of Scientific Affairs. Serie de Matematica: Monografias†
0078-6357 Organization of American States. Department of Cultural Affairs. Cuadernos Bibliotecologicos†
0078-6373 Organization of American States. Department of Cultural Affairs. Estudios Bibliotecarios†
0078-6381 Organization of American States. Department of Cultural Affairs. Manuales del Bibliotecario†
0078-6403 O A S. General Secretariat. Annual Report **4306**
0078-642X Organization of American States. Official Records. Indice y Lista General **4307**
0078-6438 Organization of American States. Permanent Council. Decisions Taken at Meetings (Cumulated Edition)†
0078-6489 Organometallic Compounds of the Group IV Elements†
0078-6500 Organon **7896**
0078-6527 Oriens **557**
0078-6543 Oriental Notes and Studies
0078-6551 Oriental Studies **510**
0078-656X Orientalia Gothoburgensia **558**
0078-6578 Orientalia Suecana **558**
0078-6586 Original Manuscript Music for Wind and Percussion Instruments†
0078-6594 Ornithological Monographs **912**
0078-6608 L'Orthodontie Francaise **5860**
0078-6632 Center for Adult Diseases, Osaka. Annual Report†
0078-6640 Osaka City University Economic Review
0078-6659 Osaka City University. Faculty of Engineering. Memoirs
0078-6667 Osaka Medical School, Takatsuki. Bulletin. Supplement†
0078-6675 Oosaka Shiritsu-shizenshi Hakubutsukan Kenkyu Hokoku **7895**
0078-6683 Shizenshi Kenkyu **7916**
0078-6705 Osaka University. Institute for Protein Research. Memoirs **741**
0078-6721 Norges Veterinaerhoegskole. Publikasjoner†
0078-673X Norway. Statens Institutt for Alkoholforskning. Skrifter†
0078-6748 Universitetet i Oslo. Etnografiske Museum. Aarbok†
0078-6764 Universitetet i Oslo. Institutt for Bibelvitenskap. Smaarskrifter†
0078-6772 Universitetet i Oslo. Instituttet for Statsvitenskap. Skrifter†
0078-6780 Physica Mathematica Universitatis Osloensis†
0078-6802 Osservatorio di Economia Agraria per l'Europa. Studi e Ricerche
0078-6810 Ost-West Paedagogik†
0078-6845 Ostbairische Grenzmarken **4251**
0078-687X Osteuropa Institut Muenchen. Veroeffentlichungen. Reihe Geschichte **4251**
0078-6888 Osteuropastudien der Hochschulen des Landes Hessen. Reihe 1. Giessener Abhandlungen zur Agrar- und Wirtschaftsforschung des Europaeischen Ostens **204**
0078-6896 Ostpanorama
0078-690X Otago Geographer†
0078-6918 Otago Law Review **4754**
0078-6926 Other Lands, Other Peoples†
0078-6934 Ottawa. Board of Trade. Annual Report
0078-6950 Dominion Astrophysical Observatory, Victoria. Publications†
0078-6985 National Gallery of Canada. Library. Canadiana in the Library of the National Gallery of Canada: Supplement†
0078-706X Our Vanishing Heritage
0078-7094 Outline of Japanese Tax **1938**
0078-7108 Overseas Development Council. Monograph Series†
0078-7124 Overseas Directories, Who's Who, Press Guides, Year Books and Overseas Periodical Subscriptions **633**
0078-7159 Overseas Newspapers and Periodicals **7569**
0078-7175 Oxford Bibliographical Society. Occasional Publications†
0078-7183 Oxford Bibliographical Society. Publications. New Series†
0078-7191 Oxford German Studies **5347**
0078-7256 Oxford Slavonic Papers†
0078-7264 Oxford Studies of Composers **6603**
0078-7272 Oxford Theological Monographs **7668**
0078-7353 P A S Reporter†
0078-7388 P I - L T; Occasional Papers on Programmed Instruction and Language Teaching†
0078-740X Pacific Anthropological Records **351**

Link to your serials resources and content with ulrichsweb.com

0078-7418 Pacific Anthropologists†
0078-7426 Pacific Botanists†
0078-7442 Pacific Coast Obstetrical and Gynecological Society. Transactions†
0078-7469 Pacific Coast Philology **5347**
0078-7507 Pacific History Series†
0078-7515 Pacific Insects Monographs†
0078-7523 Pacific Islands Year Book **4193**
0078-7582 Pacific Marine Fisheries Commission. Bulletin†
0078-7620 Pacific Northwest Conference on Higher Education. Proceedings†
0078-7663 Pacific Trollers Association Newsletter
0078-768X Packaging Directory†
0078-7698 Packaging Machinery Manufacturers Institute. Official Packaging Machinery Directory (Print) *changed to* Packaging Machinery Manufacturers Institute. Official Packaging Machinery Directory (CD-ROM) **6713**
0078-771X Universita degli Studi di Padova. Centro per la Storia della Tradizione Artistotelica nel Veneto. Saggi e Testi
0078-7728 Universita degli Studi di Padova. Facolta di Lettere e Filosofia. Opuscoli Accademici **5392**
0078-7744 Universita degli Studi di Padova. Istituto di Storia Antica. Pubblicazioni
0078-7760 Quaderni per la Storia dell'Universita di Padova **2999**
0078-7779 Universita degli Studi di Padova. Scuola di Perfezionamento in Filosofia. Pubblicazioni†
0078-7795 Paediatrische Fortbildungskurse fuer die Praxis†
0078-7809 Paideuma **351**
0078-7817 Polymers Paint Color Year Book (Year) **6720**
0078-785X Pakistan Annual Law Digest **4755**
0078-7868 Pakistan Archaeology **410**
0078-7884 Pakistan Banking Directory
0078-7892 Pakistan Basic Facts **1938**
0078-7914 Pakistan. Central Bureau of Education. Educational Statistics Bulletin Series **2935**
0078-7930 Pakistan Central Cotton Committee. Agricultural Survey Report **245**
0078-7949 Pakistan Central Cotton Committee. Technological Bulletin. Series A **245**
0078-7957 Pakistan Central Cotton Committee. Technological Bulletin. Series B **245**
0078-7965 Pakistan. Central Statistical Office. Census of Electricity Undertakings†
0078-7973 Pakistan. Central Statistical Office. Consumer Price Index Numbers for Industrial Workers†
0078-7981 Pakistan. Statistics Division. Consumer Price Index: Scope and Limitations
0078-799X Pakistan. Statistics Division. Key to Official Statistics
0078-8007 Pakistan. Statistics Division. N S S Series
0078-8015 Pakistan. Central Statistical Office. Some Socio-Economic Trends†
0078-8031 Pakistan Conference of Linguists. Pakistani Linguistics; Selected Papers
0078-804X Pakistan Council of Scientific and Industrial Research. Annual Report **7897**
0078-8058 Pakistan Customs Tariff **1580**
0078-8082 Pakistan Economic Survey **1510**
0078-8104 Pakistan. Export Promotion Bureau. Export Guide Series†
0078-8112 Pakistan. Export Promotion Bureau. Fresh Fruits†
0078-8147 Pakistan Forest Institute, Peshawar. Annual Progress Report **3699**
0078-8155 Pakistan. Geological Survey. Memoirs; Paleontologia Pakistanica **6727**
0078-8163 Pakistan. Geological Survey. Records **2761**
0078-8171 Pakistan Historical Society. Memoir **4187**
0078-818X Pakistan Historical Society. Proceedings of the Pakistan History Conference **4187**
0078-8198 P I C I C Annual Report **1643**
0078-8201 Pakistan Industrial Development Corporation. Report **1900**
0078-821X Pakistan Institute of Development Economics. Report†
0078-8228 Pakistan Institute of Development Economics. Research Reports†
0078-8236 Pakistan Insurance Year Book
0078-8252 Pakistan Leather Year Book†
0078-8287 Pakistan. Ministry of Education. Yearbook **2895**
0078-8333 Pakistan. National Assembly. Debates. Official Report **7459**
0078-8341 Pakistan National Bibliography
0078-8376 Pakistan Nursing and Health Review†
0078-8392 Pakistan. Office of the Economic Adviser. Government Sponsored Corporations and Other Institutions **1900**
0078-8406 Pakistan Philosophical Congress. Proceedings **6938**
0078-8414 Pakistan. Planning and Development Division. Development Programme **1900**
0078-8422 Pakistan Postage Stamps
0078-8430 Pakistan Science Conference. Proceedings **7897**
0078-8449 Pakistan Sociological Association. Papers from the Conference
0078-8457 Pakistan Standards Institution. Report†
0078-8473 Pakistan Statistical Association. Proceedings **8393**
0078-8481 Pakistan. Survey of Pakistan. General Report†
0078-849X Bangladesh Tea Board. Annual Review†
0078-852X Pakistan's Balance of Payments (Annual) **1938**
0078-8546 Palaeontographica Americana **6728**
0078-8554 Palaeontologia Africana **6728**
0078-8562 Palaeontologia Polonica **6728**
0078-8570 Paleoecologia†
0078-8597 Paleontological Society. Memoir **6729**
0078-8600 Zentrales Geologisches Institut. Palaeontologische Abhandlungen†
0078-8627 Universita degli Studi di Palermo. Istituto di Filologia Greca. Quaderni **5190**
0078-866X Pamietnik Slowianski **5348**
0078-8732 Universidad de Navarra. Escuela de Arquitectura. Coleccion de Arquitectura **459**
0078-8740 Universidad de Navarra. Escuela de Bibliotecarias. Coleccion Bibliotecarias **5052**
0078-8759 Universidad de Navarra. Facultad de Derecho Canonico. Manuales: Derecho Canonico **7691**
0078-8783 Universidad de Navarra. Facultad de Ciencias de la Informacion. Manuales: Periodismo **4584**
0078-8791 Pan American Federation of Engineering Societies. Bulletin
0078-8805 Pan American Highway Congresses. Final Acts†
0078-8813 Pan American Institute of Geography and History. Commission on History. Bibliografias **4307**
0078-8821 Pan American Institute of Geography and History. Commission on History. Guias†
0078-883X Pan American Institute of Geography and History. Commission on History. Historiografias Americanas†
0078-8848 Pan American Institute of Geography and History. Commission on History. Historiadores de America†
0078-8856 Pan American Institute of Geography and History. Commission on History. Monumentos Historicos y Arqueologicos†
0078-8864 Pan American Medical Women's Alliance. Newsletter
0078-8899 Panama Canal Company. Meteorological and Hydrographic Branch. Climatological Data: Canal Zone and Panama†
0078-8996 Panama en Cifras **1257**
0078-9054 Papers in Anthropology†
0078-9062 Papers in Australian Linguistics†
0078-9151 Papers in Public Administration†
0078-916X Papers in Public Administration (Ann Arbor)†
0078-9178 Papers in Southeast Asian Linguistics **5159**
0078-9216 Papers on Modern Japan†
0078-9224 London School of Economics Papers in Soviet and East European Law, Economics and Politics†
0078-9232 Papiermusterheft†
0078-9240 Papiri Greci e Latini
0078-9283 Papua New Guinea. Bureau of Statistics. Private Overseas Investment†
0078-9356 Papua New Guinea. Bureau of Statistics. Statistics of Religious Organisations†
0078-9402 Papyrologica Bruxellensia **411**
0078-9429 Paralogue
0078-9437 Parapsychological Monographs **6743**
0078-9445 Parathyroid Conference. Proceedings
0078-947X Aeroports de Paris. Service Statistique. Statistique de Trafic **8521**
0078-9496 Paris - Bijoux Exportation
0078-950X Bureau Universitaire de Recherche Operationnelle. Cahiers†
0078-9550 Ecole Pratique des Hautes Etudes, Paris. Centre d'Etudes des Techniques Economiques Modernes. Cahiers
0078-9577 Sciences Humaines Africanistes
0078-9593 Ecole Pratique des Hautes Etudes, Paris. Centre de Psychiatrie Sociale. Publications†
0078-9615 Ecole Pratique des Hautes Etudes, Paris. Centre de Sociologie Europeenne. Cahiers†
0078-9631 Ecole Pratique des Hautes Etudes, Paris. Division des Aires Culturelles. Congres et Colloques†
0078-9666 France. Imprimerie Nationale. Annuaire. **7561**
0078-9674 Institut de Recherches Agronomiques Tropicales et des Cultures Vivrieres. Bulletin Scientifique.†
0078-9682 Institut Oceanographique. Annales†
0078-9704 Musee Guimet, Paris. Bibliotheque d'Etudes
0078-9712 Musee Guimet, Paris. Etude des Collections du Musee
0078-9720 Museum National d'Histoire Naturelle, Paris. Annuaire†
0078-978X Universite de Paris. Centre de Recherche d'Art Contemporain, Nanterre. Publications
0078-9798 Universite de Paris. Faculte de Droit et des Sciences Economiques. Travaux et Recherches. Serie Afrique
0078-9801 Universite de Paris. Faculte de Droit et des Sciences Economiques. Travaux et Recherches. Serie Droit Prive
0078-981X Universite de Paris. Faculte de Droit et des Sciences Economiques. Travaux et Recherches. Serie Droit Public
0078-9828 Universite de Paris. Faculte de Droit et des Sciences Economiques. Travaux et Recherches. Serie Europe
0078-9836 Universite de Paris. Faculte de Droit et des Sciences Economiques. Travaux et Recherches
0078-9844 Universite de Paris. Faculte de Droit et des Sciences Economiques. Trauvaux et Recherches. Series Sciences Economiques
0078-9852 Universite de Paris. Faculte de Droit et des Sciences Economiques. Travaux et Recherches. Serie Science Administrative
0078-9860 Universite de Paris. Faculte de Droit et des Sciences Economiques. Travaux et Recherches. Serie Science Politique
0078-9879 Universite de Paris. Faculte de Droit et des Sciences Economiques. Travaux et Recherches. Serie Sciences Historiques
0078-9887 Universite de Paris. Faculte des Lettres et Sciences Humaines. Publications. Serie Acta†
0078-9895 Universite de Paris. Faculte des Lettres et Sciences Humaines. Publications. Serie Recherches†
0078-9909 Universite de Paris VI (Pierre et Marie Curie). Institut Henri Poincare. Seminaire Choquet. Initiation a l'Analyse†
0078-9917 Universite de Paris. Institut de Physique du Globe. Observations Magnetiques
0078-995X Institut d'Etudes Politiques de Paris. Livret†
0078-9968 Institut d'Etudes Slaves, Paris. Annuaire†
0078-9976 Institut d'Etudes Slaves, Paris. Bibliotheque Russe **5309**
0078-9984 Institut d'Etudes Slaves, Paris. Collection de Grammaires **5128**
0078-9992 Institut d'Etudes Slaves, Paris. Collection de Manuels **5128**
0079-0001 Institut d'Etudes Slaves, Paris. Collection Historique **4231**
0079-001X Institut d'Etudes Slaves, Paris. Textes **5309**
0079-0028 Institut d'Etudes Slaves, Paris. Travaux **5309**
0079-0036 Universite de Paris VI (Pierre et Marie Curie). Institut Henri Poincare. Seminaire Lions†
0079-0052 Parkes Library Pamphlets†
0079-0060 Parkinson's Disease and Related Disorders. Cumulative Bibliography†
0079-0079 Parkinson's Disease and Related Disorders: Citations from the Literature†
0079-0095 Parliament House Book **4755**
0079-0117 Partners in Learning **7770**
0079-0141 Pastoral Psychology Series†
0079-015X Patent and Trademark Institute of Canada. Annual Proceedings **6755**
0079-0184 Pathology Annual†
0079-0206 Patterns of Literary Criticism†
0079-0214 Patterns of Religious Commitment†
0079-0230 Patterson's American Education **2961**
0079-0249 Paul Anthony Brick Lectures **6938**
0079-0257 Paul Carus Lectures **6938**
0079-0281 Pax Romana†
0079-029X Peabody Museum of Archaeology and Ethnology. Memoirs **411**
0079-0303 Peabody Museum of Archaeology and Ethnology. Papers **411**
0079-032X Peabody Museum of Natural History. Bulletin **7897**
0079-0338 Peabody Museum of Natural History. Special Publication†
0079-0354 Pearce-Sellards Series **6535**
0079-0362 Pears Cyclopaedia **3121**
0079-0370 Paedagogica Belgica Academica†
0079-0400 Pediatrics; a Medical World News Publication†
0079-0451 Penn State Studies†
0079-046X Pennsylvania. Agricultural Statistics Service. Crop and Livestock Annual Summary **246**
0079-0486 P.E.L. State Bulletin†
0079-0494 Indiana University of Pennsylvania. Annual Research Bulletin†
0079-0508 Pennsylvania School Study Council. Reports **2897**
0079-0524 Millersville State College. Contributions to Research: Faculty and Student Publications†
0079-0540 Pennsylvania State University. College of Business Administration. Center for Research. Occasional Papers†
0079-0567 Pennsylvania State University. College of Engineering. Engineering Research Bulletin†
0079-0591 Pennsylvania State University. Earth and Mineral Sciences Experiment Station. Bulletin†
0079-0613 Pennsylvania State University. Earth and Mineral Sciences Experiment Station. Circular†
0079-0621 Pennsylvania State University. Institute for Research on Land and Water Resources. Information Reports†
0079-063X Pennsylvania State University. Institute for Research on Land and Water Resources. Research Publication†
0079-0656 Pennsylvania State University. Libraries. Bibliographical Series **5039**
0079-0710 Penrose Annual†
0079-0729 People from the Past Series **645**
0079-0737 Peoples' Appalachia†
0079-0745 Peoria Academy of Science. Proceedings†
0079-0753 Peptides†
0079-0826 Pergamon Mathematical Tables Series†
0079-0834 Pergamon Series of Monographs in Laboratory Techniques†
0079-0842 Pergamon Series of Monographs on Furniture and Timber†
0079-0869 Pergamon Unified Engineering Series†
0079-0885 Periscope 2000†
0079-0893 Persica **4187**
0079-0958 Perspecta **453**
0079-0966 Perspective (Winnipeg, 1950)†
0079-0982 Perspectives de l'Economique. Serie 1. Fondateurs de l'Economie†
0079-1008 Perspectives in Criticism†
0079-1024 Perspectives in Medicine†
0079-1040 Perspectives in Social Work†
0079-1059 Perspectives in Structural Chemistry†
0079-1075 Peru Problema **8125**
0079-1083 Instituto Nacional de Enfermedades Neoplasicas. Trabajos de Investigacion Clinica y Experimental†
0079-1091 Sociedad Geologica del Peru. Boletin **2767**
0079-1148 Pesticide Review†
0079-1296 Petroleum Refineries in Canada†
0079-130X Pets Welcome **8747**
0079-1334 Pflanzenschuetzer†
0079-1342 Pflanzenschutz-Nachrichten† **8980**
0079-1350 Phaenomenologica **6939**
0079-1369 Phanerogamarum Monographiae **807**
0079-1393 Pharmaceutical Historian **6869**
0079-1423 Philippine Education Abstracts†
0079-1466 Philippine Scientist **7898**
0079-1490 Philippines Nuclear Journal **7070**
0079-1504 Philippines. Board of Investments. Annual Report **1644**
0079-1520 Philippines. Bureau of Agricultural Economics. Report†
0079-1547 Philippines. National Tax Research Center. Report
0079-1598 Philologen-Jahrbuch
0079-1628 Philological Monographs **5160**
0079-1636 Philological Society. Transactions **5161**
0079-1644 Philologische Beitraege zur Suedost- und Osteuropaforschung†
0079-1660 Philosophes Contemporains **6939**
0079-1679 Philosophes Medievaux **6939**
0079-1687 Philosophia Antiqua **6940**
0079-1695 Philosophical Society of the Sudan. Proceedings of the Annual Conference
0079-175X PHILSOM
0079-1768 Phineas L. Windsor Lecture in Librarianship†
0079-1776 Phoenix†
0079-1784 Phoenix. Supplementary Volume **2239**
0079-1806 Photochemistry†
0079-1849 Photography Annual†
0079-1881 Physical Chemistry†
0079-189X Physical Education Around the World. Monograph†
0079-1903 Physical Education Association of Great Britain and Northern Ireland. Report†
0079-1911 Physical Education Year Book†
0079-192X Physician's Handbook†
0079-1938 Physics and Chemistry in Space†
0079-1954 Physics and Chemistry of the Organic Solid State†

ISSN

0079-1989 Physik und Technik†
0079-1997 Physikalisch-Chemische Trenn- und Messmethoden
0079-2004 Physikalisch-Medizinische Sozietaet Erlangen. Sitzungsberichte
0079-2012 Physiologia Plantarum. Supplementum†
0079-2020 Physiological Society, London. Monographs†
0079-2047 Phyton. Annales Rei Botanicae **809**
0079-2055 Pianeta Fresco
0079-2071 Pilot Studies Approved for State Aid in Public School Systems in Virginia†
0079-208X Pion Applied Physics Series†
0079-211X Pisarze Slascy 19 i 20 Wieku **5351**
0079-2144 Pittsburgh Studies in Library and Information Sciences†
0079-2179 L R D C News†
0079-2225 Plant Breeding Institute, Cambridge. Annual Report†
0079-2233 Plant Monograph: Reprints†
0079-225X Plant Protection Abstracts. Supplement†
0079-2268 Plante et l'Homme
0079-2276 Planung und Kontrolle in der Unternehmung†
0079-2284 Planungsstudien **1901**
0079-2314 Playfair Cricket Annual **8242**
0079-2322 Playfair Football Annual **8242**
0079-2373 Poche-Couleurs Larousse†
0079-2381 Pocket Book of Transport Statistics of India **8528**
0079-2403 Pocket Data Book, USA†
0079-242X Pocket Library of Studies in Art
0079-2438 Pocket Poets Series **5430**
0079-2446 Australia. Bureau of Statistics. South Australian Office. Pocket Year Book of South Australia†
0079-2462 Poesia **5430**
0079-2470 Poetes et Prosateurs du Portugal†
0079-2500 Poeti e Prosatori Tedeschi† **8981**
0079-2519 Poetry Eastwest†
0079-2527 Poetyka. Zarys Encyklopedyczny **5432**
0079-2535 Points. Films† **8981**
0079-2543 Points for Emphasis; International Sunday School Lessons in Pocket Size **7670**
0079-2586 Poland. Glowny Urzad Statystyczny. Atlas Statystyczny†
0079-2594 Poland. Glowny Urzad Statystyczny. Budzet Panstwa†
0079-2608 Poland. Glowny Urzad Statystyczny. Maly Rocznik Statystyczny *changed to* 1640-3630 **8394**
0079-2632 Poland. Glowny Urzad Statystyczny. Rocznik Statystyczny Budownictwa†
0079-2667 Poland. Glowny Urzad Statystyczny. Rocznik Statystyczny Gospodarki Morskiej†
0079-2675 Poland. Glowny Urzad Statystyczny. Rocznik Statystyczny Gornictwa†
0079-2683 Poland. Glowny Urzad Statystyczny. Rocznik Statystyczny Handlu Wewnetrznego†
0079-2713 Poland. Glowny Urzad Statystyczny. Rocznik Statystyczny Kultury†
0079-2756 Poland. Glowny Urzad Statystyczny. Rocznik Statystyczny Powiatow†
0079-2802 Poland. Glowny Urzad Statystyczny. Rocznik Statystyczny Transportu†
0079-2853 Poland. Glowny Urzad Statystyczny. Ubezpieczenia Majatkowe i Osobowe†
0079-287X Poland. Glowny Urzad Statystyczny. Wypadki Drogowe†
0079-2888 Poland. Glowny Urzad Statystyczny. Wypadki przy Pracy†
0079-290X Poland. Glowny Urzad Statystyczny. Zwierzeta Gospodarskie†
0079-2918 Polar Notes†
0079-2926 Polemologische Studien†
0079-2950 Police Yearbook†
0079-2969 Polis. Evangelische Zeitbuchreihe
0079-2985 Polish Journal of Soil Science **248**
0079-2993 Polish Psychological Bulletin **7391**
0079-3027 Politica **7167**
0079-3043 Political Science Annual†
0079-3051 Maharaja Sayajirao University of Baroda. Political Science Series†
0079-3078 Politics†
0079-3094 Politics of Modernization Series†
0079-3108 Politique Belge†
0079-3124 K-W Probe†
0079-3132 Polonia Typographica Saeculi Sedecimi†
0079-3140 Polska Akademia Nauk. Biblioteka, Krakow. Rocznik *changed to* 1642-2503 **5039**
0079-3159 Academie Polonaise des Sciences. Centre Scientifique, Paris. Conferences†
0079-3183 Sredniowiecze. Studia o Kulturze†
0079-323X Polish Academy of Sciences. Institute of Fundamental Technological Research. Scientific Activities†
0079-3256 Polska Akademia Nauk. Oddzial w Krakowie. Komisja Archeologiczna. Prace **411**
0079-3264 Polska Akademia Nauk. Oddzial w Krakowie. Komisja Ceramiczna. Prace: Ceramika **2044**
0079-3272 Polska Akademia Nauk. Oddzial w Krakowie. Komisja Filologii Klasycznej. Prace **5162**
0079-3280 Polska Akademia Nauk. Oddzial w Krakowie. Komisja Gorniczo-Geodezyjna. Prace: Gornictwo **6476**
0079-3299 Polska Akademia Nauk. Oddzial w Krakowie. Komisja Geodezji i Inzynierii Srodowiska. Prace: Geodezja **4024**
0079-3310 Polska Akademia Nauk. Oddzial w Krakowie. Komisja Jezykoznawstwa. Prace **5162**
0079-3329 Polska Akademia Nauk. Komitet Jezykoznawstwa. Wydawnictwa Zrodlowe†
0079-3337 Polska Akademia Nauk. Oddzial w Krakowie. Komisja Mechaniki Stosowanej. Prace: Mechanika **7062**
0079-3345 Polska Akademia Nauk. Oddzial w Krakowie. Komisja Metalurgiczno-Odlewnicza. Prace: Metalurgia **6329**
0079-3353 Polska Akademia Nauk. Oddzial w Krakowie. Komisja Nauk Ekonomicznych. Prace **1160**
0079-3361 Polska Akademia Nauk. Oddzial w Krakowie. Komisja Nauk Geologicznych. Prace Geologiczne **2762**
0079-337X Polska Akademia Nauk. Oddzial w Krakowie. Komisja Historycznoliteracka. Rocznik **4156**
0079-3396 Polska Akademia Nauk. Oddzial w Krakowie. Komisja Nauk Mineralogicznych. Prace Mineralogiczne **2762**
0079-340X Polska Akademia Nauk. Oddzial w Krakowie. Komisja Nauk Pedagogicznych. Prace **2898**
0079-3418 Polska Akademia Nauk. Oddzial w Krakowie. Komisja Nauk Pedagogicznych. Rocznik **2898**
0079-3426 Polska Akademia Nauk. Oddzial w Krakowie. Komisja Orientalistyczna. Prace **559**
0079-3434 Polska Akademia Nauk. Oddzial w Krakowie. Komisja Slowianoznawstwa. Prace **5353**
0079-3442 Polska Akademia Nauk. Oddzial w Krakowie. Komisja Socjologiczna. Prace **8125**
0079-3450 Polska Akademia Nauk. Oddzial w Krakowie. Komisja Urbanistyki i Architektury. Teka **453**
0079-3477 Polska Akademia Nauk. Komitet Gospodarki Wodnej. Prace i Studia **8830**
0079-3485 Polska Akademia Nauk. Komitet Jezykoznawstwa. Prace Jezykoznawcze **5162**
0079-3493 Polska Akademia Nauk. Komitet Przestrzennego Zagospodarowania Kraju. Biuletyn **4424**
0079-3507 Polska Akademia Nauk. Komitet Przestrzennego Zagospodarowania Kraju. Studia **4424**
0079-3531 Polska Akademia Nauk. Oddzial w Krakowie. Rocznik **7899**
0079-354X Polska Akademia Nauk. Oddzial w Krakowie. Sprawozdania z Posiedzen Komisji Naukowych **7899**
0079-3566 Academie Polonaise des Sciences. Centre d'Archeologie Mediterraneenne. Etudes et Travaux **370**
0079-3590 Polska Bibliografia Literacka **5408**
0079-3612 Polska Piesn i Muzyka Ludowa. Zrodla i Materialy†
0079-3639 Polski Slownik Biograficzny
0079-371X Polskie Towarzystwo Naukowe na Obczyznie. Rocznik†
0079-3728 Polymer Engineering and Technology Series†
0079-3736 Polymer Reviews†
0079-3795 Pomologia Republicii Socialiste Romania†
0079-3809 University of Poona. Centre of Advanced Study in Sanskrit. Publications **5192**
0079-3833 Popes through History†
0079-3841 Popular Lectures in Mathematics Series†
0079-3868 Population Census of Papua New Guinea. Population Characteristics Bulletin Series **7290**
0079-3876 Population Council, New York. Country Profiles†
0079-3892 Population Council, New York. Reports on Population/Family Planning†
0079-3914 Population Health Survey Research Bulletin†
0079-3922 University of California, Berkeley. Institute of International Studies. Population Monograph Series†
0079-3957 University of Port Elizabeth. Publications. General Series **4480**
0079-3965 University of Port Elizabeth. Publications. Research Papers **4480**
0079-4007 Port Phillip Authority. Annual Report
0079-4066 Ports of the World†
0079-4074 Ports - Routes - Trafics† **8982**
0079-4201 Portugal. Ministerio das Financas. Relatorio do Orcamento Geral do Estado
0079-421X Portugiesische Forschungen der Goerresgesellschaft. Reihe 1: Aufsaetze zur Portugiesischen Kulturgeschichte **4254**
0079-4228 Portugiesische Forschungen der Goerresgesellschaft. Reihe 2: Monographien **4254**
0079-4236 Post-Medieval Archaeology **411**
0079-4252 Postepy Mikrobiologii **895**
0079-4260 Postepy Napedu Elektrycznego **3327**
0079-4279 Postepy Pediatrii
0079-4295 Postilla **7899**
0079-4309 Potato Marketing Board, Oxford. Annual Report and Accounts†
0079-4317 Abstracts of Theses and Dissertations Accepted for Higher Degrees in the Potchefstroom University for Christian Higher Education†
0079-4325 Union Catalogue of Theses and Dissertations of the South African Universities†
0079-4333 Potchefstroom University for Christian Higher Education. Wetenskaplike Bydraes. Reeks A: Geesteswetenskappe **4470**
0079-4341 Potchefstroom University for Christian Higher Education. Wetenskaplike Bydraes. Reeks B: Natuurwetenskappe. Series **2998**
0079-4457 Power Sources Symposium. Proceedings†
0079-4465 Powstanie Styczniowe. Materialy i Dokumenty†
0079-4481 Materialy Historyczno-Metodyczne†
0079-449X Politechnika Poznanska. Zeszyty Naukowe. Budownictwo Ladowe *changed to* 1642-9303 **3267**
0079-4503 Politechnika Poznanska. Zeszyty Naukowe. Elektryka **3327**
0079-4511 Politechnika Poznanska. Zeszyty Naukowe. Fizyka†
0079-4538 Politechnika Poznanska. Zeszyty Naukowe. Mechanika **7062**
0079-4554 Akademia Ekonomiczna, Poznan. Zeszyty Naukowe. Seria 2. Prace Habilitacyjne i Doktorskie *changed to* Akademia Ekonomiczna, Poznan. Zeszyty Naukowe. Seria 2. Prace Habilitacyjne **1058**
0079-4597 Poznanskie Towarzystwo Przyjaciol Nauk. Komisja Budownictwa i Architektury. Prace†
0079-4600 Poznanskie Towarzystwo Przyjaciol Nauk. Komisja Budowy Maszyn. Prace **5458**
0079-4619 Poznanskie Towarzystwo Przyjaciol Nauk. Komisja Biologiczna. Prace†
0079-4627 Poznanskie Towarzystwo Przyjaciol Nauk. Komisja Elektrotechniki. Prace†
0079-4635 Poznanskie Towarzystwo Przyjaciol Nauk. Komisja Filozoficzna. Prace†
0079-4651 Poznanskie Towarzystwo Przyjaciol Nauk. Komisja Historyczna. Prace **4254**
0079-466X Poznanskie Towarzystwo Przyjaciol Nauk. Komisja Historii Sztuki. Prace **512**
0079-4678 Poznanskie Towarzystwo Przyjaciol Nauk. Komisja Jezykoznawcza. Prace **5162**
0079-4708 Poznanskie Towarzystwo Przyjaciol Nauk. Komisja Nauk Rolniczych i Lesnych. Prace **147**
0079-4716 Poznanskie Towarzystwo Przyjaciol Nauk. Komisja Nauk Spolecznych. Prace†
0079-4724 Poznanskie Towarzystwo Przyjaciol Nauk. Komisja Technologii Drewna. Prace†
0079-4740 Lingua Posnaniensis **5145**
0079-4759 Prace i Materialy Etnograficzne†
0079-4767 Acta Universitatis Wratislaviensis. Prace Literackie **5249**
0079-4775 Polska Akademia Nauk. Komitet Jezykoznawstwa. Prace Onomastyczne **5162**
0079-4783 Polska Akademia Nauk. Komitet Nauk Orientalistycznych. Prace Orientalistyczne **559**
0079-4791 Lodzkie Towarzystwo Naukowe. Prace Polonistyczne **5327**
0079-4805 Towarzystwo Naukowe w Toruniu. Prace Popularnonaukowe **7924**
0079-4813 Practical Householder *changed to* 1740-5734
0079-4821 Practical Table Series†
0079-4848 Praehistorische Zeitschrift **412**
0079-4856 Prague Studies in Mathematical Linguistics†
0079-4872 Prakseologia **6944**
0079-4880 Praktische Betriebswirtschaft†
0079-4899 Praktische Chirurgie
0079-4902 Prameny Ceske a Slovenske Lingvistiky. Rada Ceska†
0079-4929 Pravnehistoricke Studie†
0079-4937 Pravoslavny Theologicky Sbornik†
0079-4945 Praxis der Klinischen Psychologie†
0079-4961 Predigtstudien **7671**
0079-497X Prehistoric Society, London. Proceedings **412**
0079-4988 Preparative Inorganic Reactions†
0079-4996 Presbyterian Church in Canada. General Assembly. Acts and Proceedings **7771**
0079-5046 Press Radio and T.V. Guide†
0079-5062 Pretoria College for Advanced Technical Education. Annual/Jaarblad†
0079-5089 Primary Socialization, Language, and Education†
0079-5100 Primates†
0079-5119 Primates in Medicine†
0079-5127 Primatologia†
0079-5186 Princeton Essays in Literature†
0079-5194 Princeton Mathematical Series **5525**
0079-5208 Princeton Monographs in Art and Archaeology **512**
0079-5240 Princeton Studies in Mathematical Economics†
0079-5259 Princeton Studies in Music†
0079-5267 Princeton University. Center of International Studies. Policy Memorandum Series†
0079-5275 Princeton University. Committee for the Excavation of Antioch. Publications†
0079-5291 Princeton University. Econometric Research Program. Research Memorandum **1161**
0079-5305 Princeton University. Industrial Relations Section. Research Report **1703**
0079-5313 Prindle, Weber and Schmidt Complementary Series in Mathematics†
0079-5321 Printing Historical Society. Journal **7326**
0079-533X Printing Magazine Purchasing Guide†
0079-5372 Printing Trades Directory† **8982**
0079-5402 Private Press Books **633**
0079-5534 Pro Football†
0079-5550 Pro Helvetia†
0079-5569 N.H.L. Pro Hockey†
0079-5577 Pro Hockey Guide†
0079-5607 Probability and Mathematical Statistics **5525**
0079-5623 Probau
0079-5631 Probe
0079-564X Probleme der Festkoerperelektronik†
0079-5666 Problemes Actuels d'Endocrinologie et de Nutrition†
0079-5682 Problemi e Ricerche di Storia Antica **2239**
0079-5690 Problemi Economici d'Oggi†
0079-5704 Problems behind the Iron Curtain Series†
0079-5739 Problems in Mathematical Analysis Report†
0079-5763 Problems of the Contemporary World
0079-5771 Problems of the North†
0079-578X Problemy Ekonomiczne†
0079-5801 Problemy Rad Narodowych. Studia i Materialy†
0079-581X Problemy Rejonow Uprzemyslawianych†
0079-5836 Prodei **2024**
0079-5852 Produccion Rural Argentina†
0079-5895 Producto Neto de la Agricultura Espanola†
0079-5925 Professional and Trade Organisations in India **2024**
0079-595X Profitability of Cotton Growing in Israel
0079-5968 Profitability of Poultry Farming in Israel
0079-5976 Profitability of Sugarbeet Growing in Israel†
0079-5984 Profits†
0079-600X Programmed Learning and Teaching Machines; Bibliographical References
0079-6042 Progress in Analytical Chemistry†
0079-6050 Progress in Astronautics and Aeronautics Series†
0079-6077 Progress in Bio-Organic Chemistry†
0079-6085 Progress in Biochemical Pharmacology†
0079-6107 Progress in Biophysics & Molecular Biology **754**
0079-6115 Progress in Boron Chemistry†
0079-6123 Progress in Brain Research **6174**
0079-614X Progress in Ceramic Science†
0079-6158 Progress in Chemical Toxicology†
0079-6166 Progress in Clinical Cancer†
0079-6174 Progress in Clinical Pathology†
0079-6182 Progress in Clinical Psychology†
0079-6190 Progress in Community Mental Health†
0079-6212 Progress in Control Engineering†
0079-6247 Progress in Elementary Particle and Cosmic Ray Physics†
0079-6263 Progress in Experimental Tumor Research **6032**
0079-6271 Progress in Gastroenterology†
0079-628X Progress in Geophysics†
0079-6298 Progress in Gynecology†
0079-6301 Progress in Hematology†
0079-631X Progress in Heat and Mass Transfer†
0079-6328 Progress in High Temperature Physics and Chemistry†
0079-6336 Progress in Histochemistry and Cytochemistry **742**
0079-6352 Progress in Industrial Microbiology **895**
0079-6379 Progress in Inorganic Chemistry **2117**
0079-6387 Progress in Learning Disabilities†
0079-6417 Progress in Low Temperature Physics **7056**
0079-6425 Progress in Materials Science **3356**
0079-645X Progress in Medical Virology†
0079-6468 Progress in Medicinal Chemistry **2077**
0079-6484 Progress in Molecular and Subcellular Biology **836**

0079-6492 Progress in Neurological Surgery **6174**
0079-6506 Progress in Neurology and Psychiatry†
0079-6565 Progress in Nuclear Magnetic Resonance Spectroscopy **2104**
0079-6573 Progress in Nuclear Medicine (Basel)†
0079-6603 Progress in Nucleic Acid Research and Molecular Biology *changed to* Progress in Molecular Biology and Translational Science **698**
0079-6611 Progress in Oceanography **2816**
0079-6638 Progress in Optics **7084**
0079-6646 Progress in Pediatric Radiology†
0079-6654 Progress in Pediatric Surgery†
0079-6662 Progress in Physical Organic Chemistry **2139**
0079-6689 Progress in Phytochemistry†
0079-6697 Progress in Polarography†
0079-6700 Progress in Polymer Science **2130**
0079-6719 Progress in Powder Metallurgy†
0079-6727 Progress in Quantum Electronics **3111**
0079-6735 Progress in Radiation Therapy†
0079-6786 Progress in Solid State Chemistry **2140**
0079-6808 Progress in Stereochemistry†
0079-6816 Progress in Surface Science **7036**
0079-6824 Progress in Surgery **6256**
0079-6840 Progress in the Science and Technology of the Rare Earths†
0079-6859 Progress in Theoretical Biology†
0079-6883 Progress Polimernoi Khimii
0079-6913 Progress Report on Clays and Shales of Montana†
0079-6956 Project Skywater. Annual Report†
0079-6972 Promotrans
0079-6980 Proof: The Yearbook of American Bibliographical and Textual Studies†
0079-6999 Proportions†
0079-7014 Prospects for America†
0079-7022 Prospezioni Archeologiche **412**
0079-7049 Protein Synthesis: a Series of Advances†
0079-7065 Protides of the Biological Fluids†
0079-7111 Pruefen und Entscheiden†
0079-7138 Przeglad Archeologiczny **412**
0079-7154 Przeglad Naukowej Literatury Rolniczej i Lesnej **249**
0079-7170 Przeglad Zagranicznej Literatury Geograficznej†
0079-7189 Przeszlosc Demograficzna Polski **7291**
0079-7197 Pseudepigrapha Veteris Testamenti Graece **7672**
0079-7227 Psychiatria Fennica **6176**
0079-726X La Psychiatrie de l'Enfant **6103**
0079-7278 Psychiatry; a Medical World News Publication†
0079-7286 Psychiatry and Art†
0079-7294 Psychoanalytic Study of Society†
0079-7308 Psychoanalytic Study of the Child **7395**
0079-7324 Psychologen Adresboek†
0079-7340 Psychologia Africana. Monograph Supplement†
0079-7391 Psychological Studies. Minor Series†
0079-7405 Psychologie und Person **7398**
0079-7413 Psychologische Praxis†
0079-7421 Psychology of Learning and Motivation: Advances in Research and Theory **7399**
0079-743X Psychopharmacology Handbook: Animal Research in Psychopharmacology†
0079-7448 Psychotheque†
0079-7456 Pszichologia a Gyakorlatban†
0079-7464 Pszichologiai Tanulmanyok **7402**
0079-7472 Pubblicita in Italia†
0079-7499 Public Administration in Israel and Abroad†
0079-7588 Public Health Conference on Records and Statistics. Proceedings **7549**
0079-7596 Public Health Monograph†
0079-7618 University of Kansas Libraries. Annual Public Lecture on Books and Bibliography†
0079-7626 Public Papers of the Presidents of the United States **7462**
0079-7634 Public Policy Issues in Resource Management **1902**
0079-7642 Public Affairs Manual for the Bench and Bar of California†
0079-7650 Public Schools Careers Guide†
0079-7677 Publications in Medieval Studies **4255**
0079-7685 Publications in Medieval Science†
0079-7707 Publications in Near and Middle East Studies. Series A†
0079-7715 Publications in Near and Middle East Studies. Series B†
0079-7731 Publications in Psychology†
0079-774X University of Helsinki. Institute of Seismology. Publications **2791**
0079-7758 McGill University Savanna Research Project - Savanna Research Series†
0079-7804 Publications on Social History†
0079-7812 Publications Romanes et Francaises **5355**
0079-7847 Publishers International Yearbook†
0079-7855 Publishers Trade List Annual†
0079-7871 Puerto Rico. Department of the Treasury. Economy & Finances
0079-7960 Pulp and Paper Research Institute of Canada. Annual Report **6738**
0079-8029 University of the Punjab. Arabic and Persian Society. Journal
0079-8037 University of the Punjab. Institute of Geology. Geological Bulletin **2773**
0079-8061 Pupila: Libros de Nuestro Tiempo **4157**
0079-807X Purdue Opinion Panel, Lafayette, Indiana. Report†
0079-8096 Purdue University. Civil Engineering Reprints†
0079-810X Purdue University. Engineering Experiment Station. Joint Highway Research Project. Research Reports†
0079-8126 Materials Research in Science and Engineering at Purdue University. Progress Report†
0079-8142 Purdue University. Road School. Proceedings of Annual Road School **8633**
0079-8150 Pure and Applied Cryogenics†
0079-8169 Pure and Applied Mathematics **5526**
0079-8177 Pure and Applied Mathematics Series **5526**
0079-8193 Pure and Applied Physics†
0079-8215 Pyrenae: Cronica Arqueologica **412**
0079-8223 Pyttersen's Nederlandse Almanak **3122**
0079-824X Quaderni dei Padri Benedettini di San Giorgio Maggiore†
0079-8258 Quaderni di Archeologia della Libia **412**
0079-8274 Quaderni di Poesia Neogreca **5432**
0079-8282 Quaderni e Guide di Archeologia **412**
0079-8304 Quality of Surface Waters of the United States†
0079-8347 Universite Laval. Centre d'Etudes Nordiques. Travaux et Documents†
0079-8355 Universite Laval. Departement d'Exploitation et Utilisation des Bois. Note de Recherches **3717**
0079-8363 Universite Laval. Departement d'Exploitation et Utilisation des Bois. Note Technique **3717**
0079-838X Universite Laval. Fonds de Recherches Forestieres. Contribution†
0079-8444 Quebec (Province) Bureau of Statistics. Agriculture Section. Statistiques Agricoles. Agricultural Statistics
0079-8789 Queen's Medical Review **5702**
0079-8797 Queen's Papers in Pure and Applied Mathematics **5527**
0079-8819 Geological Survey of Queensland. Report†
0079-8835 Queensland Museum. Memoirs **7901**
0079-8843 Queensland Naturalist **699**
0079-886X University of Queensland. Computer Centre. Papers†
0079-8878 University of Queensland. Department of Agriculture. Papers†
0079-8886 University of Queensland. Department of Architecture. Papers†
0079-8908 University of Queensland. Department of Botany. Papers†
0079-8916 University of Queensland. Department of Entomology. Papers†
0079-8924 University of Queensland. Departments of Government and History. Paper†
0079-8932 University of Queensland. Department of Geology. Papers†
0079-8940 University of Queensland. Department of Social Sciences. Papers†
0079-8959 University of Queensland. Department of Zoology. Papers†
0079-8975 University of Queensland. Faculty of Arts. Papers†
0079-8983 University of Queensland. Faculty of Education. Papers†
0079-8991 University of Queensland. Faculty of Law. Papers†
0079-9009 University of Queensland. Faculty of Medicine. Papers†
0079-9017 University of Queensland. Faculty of Veterinary Science. Papers†
0079-9033 University of Queensland Inaugural Lectures†
0079-9041 Queensland's Health†
0079-905X Quellenkataloge zur Musikgeschichte **6608**
0079-9068 Quellen und Forschungen aus Italienischen Archiven und Bibliotheken **4157**
0079-9076 Quellen und Forschungen zur Basler Geschichte **4255**
0079-9084 Quellen und Forschungen zur Wuerttembergischen Kirchengeschichte†
0079-9114 Quellen und Studien zur Geschichte Osteuropas†
0079-9149 Quellenschriften zur Westdeutschen Vor- und Fruehgeschichte **413**
0079-9157 Quellenwerke zur Alten Geschichte Amerikas **4309**
0079-919X Question†
0079-9211 Quetico-Superior Wilderness Research Center, Ely, Minnesota. Annual Report
0079-922X Quetico-Superior Wilderness Research Center, Ely, Minnesota. Technical Notes
0079-9238 University of the Philippines. Asian Center. Monograph Series **4190**
0079-9246 University of the Philippines. Community Development Research Council. Study Series
0079-9270 Qui Vend et Achete Quoi?†
0079-9300 R I C†
0079-9327 Universidade Federal de Minas Gerais. Corpo Discente. Revista Literaria. **5392**
0079-9343 R.M. Bucke Memorial Society for the Study of Religious Experience. Newsletter-Review†
0079-9351 R.M. Bucke Memorial Society for the Study of Religious Experience. Proceedings of the Conference†
0079-9386 Rabindranath Tagore Memorial Lectureship†
0079-9408 Racehorses **8297**
0079-9416 Racial Policies of American Industry. Reports†
0079-9467 Radio Handbook†
0079-9491 Radner Lectures **7176**
0079-9521 Railway Fuel and Operating Officers Association. Proceedings **8623**
0079-9548 Railway Technical Review **8624**
0079-9556 Rajasthan, India. Directorate of Economics and Statistics. Budget Study **1941**
0079-9564 Rajasthan, India. Directorate of Economics and Statistics. Basic Statistics **1259**
0079-9572 Rajasthan Year Book and Who's Who†
0079-9580 Incidenca Raka v Sloveniji **6022**
0079-9599 Rampenlicht†
0079-9602 Ranchi University Mathematical Journal **5528**
0079-9637 Rand McNally Discover Historic America†
0079-967X Ranganathan Series in Library Science†
0079-9688 Rapport Annuel sur l'Economie Arabe†
0079-9696 Rapport Annuel sur l'Economie Syrienne **1513**
0079-9726 Rassegna Internazionale del Film Scientifico - Didattico†
0079-9734 Rassegna Italiana di Sociologia. Quaderni
0079-9815 Raymond Dart Lectures†
0079-9823 Reaction Mechanisms in Organic Chemistry†
0079-9831 Reader's Digest Almanac and Yearbook†
0079-9866 Reading University Studies on Contemporary Europe†
0079-9890 Real Estate Reports
0079-9904 Reanimation et Organes Artificiels. Revue Internationale de Physiologie, Medecine, Chirurgie et des Techniques Appliquees aux Sciences Biologiques
0079-9912 Recent Advances in Food Science†
0079-9920 Recent Advances in Phytochemistry **814**
0079-9939 Recent Advances in Plasma Diagnostics†
0079-9947 Recent Developments in the Chemistry of Natural Carbon Compounds†
0079-9955 Recent Developments of Neurobiology in Hungary†
0079-998X Recent Publications in the Social and Behavioral Sciences. A B S Guide Supplement†
0080-0015 Recent Results in Cancer Research **6033**
0080-0023 Recent Sociology†
0080-0031 Recherches Africaines†
0080-004X Recherches Cooperatives†
0080-0058 Recherches de Psychologie Experimentale et Comparee†
0080-0066 Recherches de Psychopedagogie et de Pedagogie Experimentale†
0080-0074 Recherches et Documents d'Art et d'Archeologie
0080-0082 Recherches Historiques et Litteraires
0080-0090 Recherches Mediterraneennes. Bibliographies†
0080-0104 Recherches Mediterraneennes. Serie 1. Etudes†
0080-0112 Recherches Mediterraneennes. Serie 2 Documents†
0080-0120 Recherches Mediterraneennes. Serie 3: Textes et Etudes Linguistiques†
0080-0139 Vie Musicale en France sous les Rois Bourbons. Serie 2: Recherches sur la Musique Francaise Classique **6626**
0080-0155 Recht und Wettbewerb†
0080-0163 Rechts- und Staatswissenschaften†
0080-018X Rechtspflege Jahrbuch†
0080-0228 Universidade Federal de Pernambuco. Instituto de Antibioticos. Revista†
0080-0260 Reconstruction Surgery and Traumatology†
0080-0287 Records of Civilization, Sources and Studies **4158**
0080-0309 Recueil Complet des Budgets de la Syrie **1942**
0080-0341 Recurring Bibliography, Education in the Allied Health Professions†
0080-0368 Red Book; A Comprehensive Cross Reference of Hong-Kong's Manufacturers, Exporters and Products
0080-0392 New Zealand Red Cross Society. Report
0080-0414 Reducing Your Income Tax†
0080-0449 Reference Book - Argentina **1513**
0080-0457 Reference Book - Republic of South Africa **1513**
0080-0481 Reformed Church of America. Historical Series
0080-049X Refractory Materials†
0080-0511 Refrigeration Annual†
0080-0538 Regency International Directory **2025**
0080-0554 Regesta Regum Scottorum
0080-0562 Regi Magyar Dallamok Tara†
0080-0570 Regi Magyar Prozai Emlekek **5359**
0080-0589 Regional Conference on Water Resources Development in Asia and the Far East. Proceedings†
0080-0619 Regional Science Research Institute. Bibliography Series†
0080-0627 Regional Science Research Institute. Monograph Series†
0080-0643 Regions
0080-066X Registre Aeronautique International **8551**
0080-0686 Registry of Accredited Facilities and Certified Individuals in Orthotics and Prosthetics†
0080-0694 Regnum Vegetabile **815**
0080-0708 Rehabilitation der Entwicklungsgehemmten†
0080-0724 Rehabilitation Industries Corporation. Annual Report†
0080-0759 Rehovot Conference on Science in the Advancement of New States. (Proceedings)†
0080-0813 Reliability and Maintainability†
0080-0848 Religion and Reason **7674**
0080-0864 Religion et Sciences de l'Homme
0080-0880 Chetham Society Publications - Remains, Historical and Literary, Connected with the Palatine Counties of Lancaster and Chester **4210**
0080-0899 Remedia Hoechst†
0080-0937 Commission Belge de Bibliographie, Repertoire des Comptes-Rendus de Congres Scientifiques†
0080-0945 Repertoire Complementaire Alphabetique des Valeurs Mobilieres Francaises et Etrangeres non Cotees en France†
0080-0988 Annuaire des Entreprises du Mali
0080-1011 Repertoire des Principaux Textes Legislatifs et Reglementaires Promulgues en Republique du Mali
0080-102X Repertoire des Productions de l'Industrie Cotonniere Francaise†
0080-1038 France. Delegation Generale a la Recherche Scientifique et Technique. Repertoire des Scientifiques Francais. Tome 3: Biologie†
0080-1046 France. Delegation Generale a la Recherche Scientifique et Technique. Repertoire des Scientifiques Francais. Tome 4: Chimie†
0080-1062 France. Delegation Generale a la Recherche Scientifique et Technique. Repertoire des Scientifiques Francais. Tome 5: Physique†
0080-1070 Repertoire des Societes de Commerce Exterieur Francaises
0080-1097 Repertoire du Marketing et du Management
0080-1127 Repertoire General Alphabetique des Valeurs Cotees en France et des Valeurs non Cotees†
0080-1135 Repertoire General des Clubs Sportifs de France
0080-1151 Repertoire International des Medievistes **4257**
0080-116X France. Delegation Generale a la Recherche Scientifique et Technique. Repertoire National des Chercheurs: Sciences Sociales et Humaines. Tome 1: Ethnologie, Linguistique, Psychologie, Psychologie Sociale, Sociologie†
0080-1194 Repertoire Pratique de la Publicite†
0080-1216 Repertorio delle Industrie Siderurgiche Italiane†
0080-1224 Repertorium van Werken, in Vlaanderen Uitgegeven, of door Monopoliehouders Ingevoerd†
0080-1283 Fisheries of Scotland Report†
0080-1313 Israel. Ministry of Labour. Registrar of Cooperative Societies. Report on the Cooperative Movement in Israel† **8966**
0080-1321 Development of Education in Pakistan **2842**
0080-133X Reportages Fantastiques
0080-1348 Reports and Papers in the Social Sciences **7995**
0080-1356 Reports and Papers on Mass Communications Series **8128**
0080-1364 Reports of Patent, Design and Trade Mark Cases **6757**
0080-1380 Reprints in International Finance **1378**
0080-1437 Requirements for Teaching Certificates in Canada†
0080-1461 Research and Development Directory†
0080-147X Register of Research and Investigation in Adult Education†
0080-1488 Research and Publications in New York State History†

ISSN

0080-729X Schweizerische Geisteswissenschaftliche Gesellschaft. Schriften†
0080-732X Schweizerische Gesellschaft fuer Volkskunde. Schriften **3622**
0080-7338 Schweizerische Meteorologische Anstalt. Annalen
0080-7354 Schweizerische Musikforschende Gesellschaft. Publikationen. Serie 2 **6615**
0080-7389 Schweizerische Palaeontologische Abhandlungen **6730**
0080-7400 Schweizerisches Medizinisches Jahrbuch **5711**
0080-7419 Schweizerisches Sozialarchiv
0080-7540 Science Nouvelle
0080-7559 Science of Advanced Material and Process Engineering Series
0080-7591 Science Policy Studies and Documents **7910**
0080-7605 Science Record†
0080-7613 Science Surveys†
0080-7621 Science Year **3122**
0080-7648 Sciences de l'Education†
0080-7672 Sciences Secretes†
0080-7680 Scientific and Learned Societies of Great Britain†
0080-7702 Scientific and Technical Periodicals Published in South Africa†
0080-7729 Scientific Basis of Medicine Annual Reviews†
0080-7745 Scientific Research in British Universities and Colleges†
0080-7753 Israel. National Council for Research and Development. Scientific Research in Israel
0080-7788 Scotland by Road†
0080-7796 Great Britain. Department of Agriculture and Fisheries for Scotland. Advisory Bulletins†
0080-7842 Scotland-Home of Golf†
0080-7869 Scotland. Registrar General. Annual Report†
0080-7877 Great Britain. Scottish Health Services Planning Council. Annual Report†
0080-7885 Scotland. Scottish Home and Health Department. Hospital Design in Use†
0080-7915 Great Britain. Scottish Law Commission. Annual Report **4682**
0080-8024 Scottish Gaelic Studies†
0080-8032 Scottish Graduate
0080-8059 Scottish Hardware and Drysalters Association. Yearbook
0080-8075 Scottish Journal of Science
0080-8083 The Scottish Law Directory **4780**
0080-8105 Scottish Licensed Trade Association. Annual Handbook†
0080-8113 Scottish Licensed Trade Directory†
0080-8121 S.M.B.A. Collected Reprints†
0080-813X Scottish Mountaineering Club. Journal **8332**
0080-8164 Scottish Postmark Group. Handbook
0080-8202 Scottish Sea Fisheries Statistical Tables **3607**
0080-8245 Scottish Typographical Annual Report†
0080-830X Scripps Clinic and Research Foundation. Annual Report **8438**
0080-8318 Scripps Institution of Oceanography. Bulletin **2817**
0080-8350 Scripta Artis Monographia **516**
0080-8369 Scripta Hierosolymitana **4474**
0080-8377 Scripta Mongolica†
0080-8385 Scriptores Byzantini†
0080-8393 Scriptores Latini **2240**
0080-8474 Securities Law Review **1382**
0080-8504 Seed Trade Buyer's Guide **252**
0080-8512 Seeker's Guide **2027**
0080-8539 Kihara Seibutsugaku Kenkyujo. Seiken Jiho **875**
0080-8547 Seishin Igaku Kenkyujo Gyosekishu **6184**
0080-858X Selected Documents of the International Petroleum Industry†
0080-8628 Selected Studies on Indonesia†
0080-8636 Selected Topics in Solid State Physics†
0080-8660 Selective Organic Transformations†
0080-875X Selysia†
0080-8768 Semainier Beaux Pays de France
0080-8776 Semiconductors and Integrated Circuits
0080-8784 Semiconductors and Semimetals **3330**
0080-8792 Seminaire Belge de Perfectionnement aux Affaires. Exposes†
0080-8806 Seminar de Fizica Teoretica†
0080-8857 Seminar on the Acquisition of Latin American Library Materials. Microfilming Projects Newsletter **5047**
0080-8881 Semitic Texts with Translations†
0080-889X Senckenbergiana Maritima *changed to* 1867-1616 **2811**
0080-8938 Serie Afrique Noire†
0080-8946 Universidad de Costa Rica Serie Ciencias Naturales†
0080-8962 Series in Decision and Control†
0080-8997 Series on Company Approaches to Industrial Relations†
0080-9004 Series on Rock and Soil Mechanics **2716**
0080-9012 Series Paedopsychiatrica†
0080-9039 Service d'Echange d'Informations Scientifiques. Serie A: Bibliographies†
0080-9047 Service d'Echange d'Informations Scientifiques. Serie B: Guides et Repertoires†
0080-9055 Service d'Echange d'Informations Scientifiques. Serie C: Catalogues et Inventaires†
0080-9063 Service d'Echange d'Informations Scientifiques. Serie D: Methodes et Techniques†
0080-9071 Servitor di Piazza†
0080-9101 Universidad de Sevilla. Seminario de Antropologia Americana. Publicaciones
0080-9152 Shakespeare Survey **5370**
0080-9195 Fuel Society Journal†
0080-9209 University of Sheffield. Metallurgical Society. Journal†
0080-9241 Sherborn Fund Facsimiles†
0080-9292 Ships and Aircraft of the United States Fleet **6446**
0080-9330 Shoe Buyers Guide†
0080-9349 Shoe Trades Directory **7942**
0080-9365 Shooter's Bible **8200**
0080-9403 Short Play Series†
0080-9411 Short Studies in Political Science†
0080-9446 Shuttle Craft Guild. Monographs†
0080-9462 Siam Society. Natural History Bulletin **7916**
0080-9519 Sierra Club Exhibit Format Series†
0080-9527 Chamber of Commerce of Sierra Leone. Journal
0080-9535 Sierra Leone in Figures†
0080-9551 Sierra Leone. Ministry of Education. Report **2912**
0080-956X Sigma†
0080-9578 Sigma Zetan **7916**
0080-9594 Silesia Antiqua **416**
0080-9608 Sinclair Lewis Newsletter†
0080-9616 University of Sind. Research Journal. Arts Series: Humanities and Social Sciences
0080-9624 University of Sind. Research Journal. Science Series **7927**
0080-9640 Singapore Accountant
0080-9659 Singapore Book World **7573**
0080-9667 University of Singapore. Chinese Society. Journal†
0080-9675 Singapore. Economic Development Board. Report on the Census of Industrial Production **1263**
0080-9683 Singapore. Economic Development Board. Annual Report **1903**
0080-9691 Singapore Law Review **4784**
0080-973X Singapore. National Library. Board Report†
0080-9748 Sinologica†
0080-9756 Sinopsis Dun - Brazil
0080-9772 Sintesis Bibliografica **1263**
0080-9780 Sir George Earle Memorial Lecture on Industry and Government **1174**
0080-9829 Situation Economique de Cote d'Ivoire†
0080-9837 Situation Economique de l'Algerie†
0080-9845 Situation Economique du Maroc†
0080-9888 Sjoefartshistorisk Aarbok **8662**
0080-9918 Skier's Guide†
0080-9950 Skolens Aarbok†
0080-9985 S L A M: Trade Year Book of Africa†
0080-9993 Slavia Antiqua **416**
0081-0002 Slavia Occidentalis **5174**
0081-0010 Slavica Gothoburgensia **5174**
0081-0029 Slavistic Printing and Reprintings†
0081-0053 Slog-Europa†
0081-0061 Slovaci v Zahranici†
0081-007X Slovanske Historicke Studie **4264**
0081-0088 Slovenska Numizmatika **6653**
0081-0096 Small Boat Handling
0081-0118 Small Business Management Series†
0081-0126 Small Business Research Series†
0081-0142 Family Hotel and Guest House†
0081-0169 Small Marketers Aids†
0081-0177 Small Marketers Aids Annuals†
0081-0193 Smith College Studies in History **4161**
0081-0207 Smithsonian Annals of Flight†
0081-0223 Smithsonian Contributions to Anthropology **355**
0081-0231 Smithsonian Contributions to Astrophysics†
0081-024X Smithsonian Contributions to Botany **817**
0081-0258 Smithsonian Studies in History and Technology **4161**
0081-0266 Smithsonian Contributions to Paleobiology **6730**
0081-0274 Smithsonian Contributions to the Earth Sciences **2716**
0081-0282 Smithsonian Contributions to Zoology **963**
0081-0304 International Astronomical Union. Central Bureau for Astronomical Telegrams. Circular **576**
0081-0312 International Association of Geodesy. Central Bureau for Satellite Geodesy. Information Bulletin **4016**
0081-0320 Smithsonian Institution. Astrophysical Observatory. S A O Special Report†
0081-038X Soccer Year Book for Northern Ireland **8246**
0081-0398 Sociaal-Geografische Studien†
0081-0401 Sociaal-Historische Studien†
0081-041X Social and Economic Studies. New Series†
0081-0460 Social Science Studies†
0081-0487 Social Scientist **8004**
0081-0495 Social Security Handbook†
0081-0525 Social Welfare Forum. Papers
0081-055X Social Work and Social Issues **8070**
0081-0568 Social Work Practice *changed to* 0734-2004
0081-0606 Socialist Register **7183**
0081-0630 Sociedad Rural Argentina. Memoria **301**
0081-0649 Sociedad Uruguaya **8135**
0081-0657 Sociedade Broteriana. Boletim **818**
0081-0665 Sociedade Broteriana. Memorias†
0081-0681 Societa di Studi Romagnoli. Guide **4264**
0081-0703 S I S F Documenti† **8986**
0081-0711 Societatis Scientiarum Lodziensis. Acta Chimica†
0081-0738 Societe Astronomique de Bordeaux. Bulletin†
0081-0746 Societe Belge d'Ophtalmologie. Bulletin **6052**
0081-0754 Societe Chateaubriand. Bulletin. Nouvelle Serie†
0081-0770 Societe de Chimie Physique. Annuaire†
0081-0819 Societe d'Emulation Historique et Litteraire d'Abbeville. Bulletin†
0081-0835 Societe d'Ergonomie de Langue Francaise. Actes du Congres
0081-0843 Societe des Auteurs, Compositeurs, Editeurs pour la Gerance des Droits de Reproduction Mecanique. Bulletin **4784**
0081-086X Societe des Explorateurs et des Voyageurs Francais. Annuaire General **4029**
0081-0878 Societe des Francs-Bibliophiles. Annuaire **7574**
0081-0894 Societe des Oceanistes. Publications **8005**
0081-0908 Societe des Poetes Francais. Annuaire **5435**
0081-0924 Bulletin S.E.D.E.I.S†
0081-0940 Societe d'Histoire de France. Annuaire **4265**
0081-0967 Societe d'Histoire et d'Archeologie de la Goele. Bulletin d'Information **417**
0081-1033 Societe Francaise de Chirurgie Orthopedique et Traumatologique. Conferences d'Enseignement **6073**
0081-105X Societe Francaise de Metallurgie. Annuaire†
0081-1076 Societe Francaise de Physique. Annuaire **7040**
0081-1084 Societe Francaise des Ingenieurs d'Outre-Mer. Annuaire†
0081-1106 Societe Franco-Japonaise de Biologie. Bulletin **705**
0081-1114 Societe Generale de Belgique. Rapport - Report **1383**
0081-1122 Bulgarsko Istorichesko Druzhestvo. Izvestiia†
0081-1130 Societe Historique de Quebec. Textes†
0081-1149 Societe Medico-Chirurgicale des Hopitaux Libres de France. Annuaire
0081-1157 Societe Mouvements Sociaux et Ideologies. 1 Serie: Etudes†
0081-1165 Societe Mouvements Sociaux et Ideologies. 2 Serie: Documents et Temoignages†
0081-1173 Societe Mouvements Sociaux et Ideologies. 3 Serie: Bibliographies†
0081-1181 Societe Nationale des Antiquaires de France. Bulletin†
0081-119X Societe Nationale des Chemins de Fer Belges. Rapport Annuel **8625**
0081-1262 Federation Nationale des Societes d'Economie Mixte de Construction, d'Amenagement et de Renovation. Annuaire
0081-1270 Societes d'Ophtalmologie de France. Bulletin **6052**
0081-1297 Society for African Church History. Bulletin†
0081-1300 Society for American Archaeology. Memoirs†
0081-1319 Asian Music Publications. Series A: Bibliographic and Research Aids†
0081-1327 Asian Music Publications. Series B. Translations†
0081-1335 Asian Music Publications. Series C: Reprints†
0081-1343 Asian Music Publications. Series D: Monographs†
0081-136X Society for Endocrinology (Great Britain) Memoirs
0081-1386 Society for Experimental Biology. Symposia **705**
0081-1394 Society for General Microbiology. Symposium† **8989**
0081-1416 Society for International Development. World Conference Proceedings†
0081-1424 Society for Italian Historical Studies. Newsletter **4265**
0081-1432 Society for New Testament Studies. Monograph Series **7682**
0081-1440 Society for Old Testament Study. Book List **7699**
0081-1475 Society for Psychical Research. Proceedings **6744**
0081-1483 Society for the Advancement of Food Service Research. Proceedings
0081-1491 Society for the History of Technology. Monograph Series†
0081-1564 Society of Antiquaries of Scotland. Proceedings **4265**
0081-1580 Society of Cypriot Studies. Bulletin **4265**
0081-1599 Society of Exploration Geophysicists. Yearbook†
0081-1637 Society of Manufacturing Engineers. Collected Papers and Technical Papers Presented at Southeastern Engineering and Tool Exposition†
0081-1645 Society of Manufacturing Engineers. Collected Papers and Technical Papers Presented at Western Metal and Tool Exposition and Conference†
0081-1661 Society of Naval Architects and Marine Engineers. Transactions **8662**
0081-1718 Society of Professional Well Log Analysts. S P W L A Annual Logging Symposium Transactions **6793**
0081-1734 Sociologia I†
0081-1742 Sociologia II†
0081-1750 Sociological Methodology **8136**
0081-1769 Sociological Review. Monograph **8137**
0081-1777 Sociological Yearbook of Religion in Britain†
0081-1807 Sociologist
0081-1866 Sofiiski Universitet Sv. Kliment Ohridski. Yuridiheski Fakultet. Godishnik **4784**
0081-1882 Soil Conservation Society of America. Proceedings of the Annual Meeting†
0081-1912 Soils and Land Use Series†
0081-1947 Solid State Physics **7041**
0081-1955 Solid State Physics: Advances in Research and Applications. Supplement **7041**
0081-1963 Solid State Physics Literature Guides†
0081-1971 Solid State Surface Science†
0081-2048 Somerset Birds **914**
0081-2056 Somerset Archaeology and Natural History **418**
0081-2080 Soundings: A Music Journal†
0081-2110 Sources in Ancient History†
0081-2129 Sources of Supply - Buyers Guide†
0081-2145 South Africa. Department of Agriculture. Agricultural Research†
0081-220X South Africa. Department of Higher Education. Annual Report†
0081-2250 University of South Africa. Communications†
0081-2307 South Africa. Weather Bureau. Notos†
0081-2323 South Africa. Weather Bureau. Report on Meteorological Data of the Year/Verslag Oor Weerkundige Data van die Jaar†
0081-2331 South Africa. Weather Bureau. W.B. Series **6395**
0081-2390 C S I R Organisation and Activities†
0081-2455 South African Journal of Antarctic Research†
0081-2463 South African Journal of Psychology **7409**
0081-2498 South African Mining and Engineering Yearbook†
0081-2501 S.A.N.T.A. Annual Report **6219**
0081-251X South African Pollen Grains and Spores†
0081-2528 South African Reserve Bank. Annual Economic Report **1518**
0081-2544 South African Statistics **8402**
0081-2552 S A F T O Annual Report **1582**
0081-2579 South American Handbook
0081-2587 South and Southeast Asia Urban Affairs Bi-Annuals†
0081-2633 Libraries Board of South Australia. Annual Report **5026**
0081-2641 South Australia. Libraries Board. Books for Young People†
0081-2684 South Carolina Arts Commission. Annual Report†
0081-2706 University of South Carolina. Libraries. Report of the Director of Libraries
0081-2714 University of South Carolina. School of Education. Proceedings of the Reading Conference†
0081-2803 South London Field Studies Society. Journal
0081-2811 South Pacific Commission. Handbook **1605**
0081-2838 South Pacific Commission. Information Document†
0081-2862 South Pacific Commission. Technical Paper **8439**
0081-2889 South Seas Society. Journal **4188**
0081-2897 South Seas Society. Monograph **4188**
0081-2935 University of Southampton. Library. Automation Project Report†
0081-2951 S E C O L A S Annals **4311**
0081-296X Southeastern Geology. Special Publication†
0081-2986 Southern Angler's and Hunter's Guide†
0081-2994 Southern Anthropological Society. Proceedings **356**
0081-3001 Southern Baptist Convention. Annual **7775**
0081-301X Southern Baptist Convention. Historical Commission. Microfilm Catalogue†
0081-3028 Southern Baptist Periodical Index **7699**
0081-3036 Southern Historical Publications†
0081-3044 Southern Illinois Studies†

ISSN

DIRECTORY 2010 0082-2418 9121

0081-7732 Studies in Communism, Revisionism and Revolution†
0081-7767 Studies in Comparative Literature (Los Angeles)†
0081-7775 Studies in Comparative Literature† **8991**
0081-7783 Studies in Compulsory Education†
0081-7791 Studies in Consumer Installment Financing†
0081-7805 Studies in Corporate Bond Financing†
0081-7813 Studies in Development Progress†
0081-783X Finnish Meteorological Institute. Studies on Earth Magnetism†
0081-7856 Studies in Economics†
0081-7872 Studies in Economics and Business Administration†
0081-7899 Studies in English Literature†
0081-7902 Studies in Ethnomusicology†
0081-7910 Studies in European History
0081-7929 Studies in Federal Taxation† **8991**
0081-7937 Studies in French Literature†
0081-7945 Studies in General and Comparative Literature
0081-7953 Studies in General Anthropology
0081-7961 Studies in Geography in Hungary†
0081-797X Studies in German Literature†
0081-7988 Studies in Higher Education in Canada†
0081-7996 Studies in Historical and Political Science. Extra Volumes **7187**
0081-8011 Studies in Industrial Economics†
0081-802X Studies in International Affairs (Baltimore)
0081-8046 Studies in International Affairs (Boulder)
0081-8054 Studies in International Communism†
0081-8062 Studies in International Economic Relations†
0081-8070 Studies in International Finance **1385**
0081-8097 Studies in Irish History†
0081-8100 Studies in Irish History. Second Series†
0081-8119 Studies in Italian Literature
0081-8127 Studies in Japanese Culture†
0081-8135 University of Texas, Austin. Bureau of Business Research. Studies in Latin American Business†
0081-8151 Studies in Librarianship†
0081-8178 Studies in Manuscript Illumination **520**
0081-8186 University of Texas, Austin. Bureau of Business Research. Studies in Marketing†
0081-8194 Studies in Mathematical and Managerial Economics **1795**
0081-8208 Studies in Mathematics (Washington) **5539**
0081-8224 Studies in Medieval and Renaissance History **4271**
0081-8232 Studies in Mediterranean Archaeology. Monograph Series **419**
0081-8240 Studies in Money in Politics†
0081-8259 Studies in Museology
0081-8267 Studies in Music†
0081-8275 Studies in Mycenaean Inscriptions and Dialect†
0081-8291 New York University. Studies in Near Eastern Civilization **557**
0081-8305 Studies in Neuro-Anatomy†
0081-8313 Great Britain. Central Statistical Office. Studies in Official Statistics **8374**
0081-8321 Studies in Oriental Culture **561**
0081-8348 University of Texas, Austin. Bureau of Business Research. Studies in Personnel and Management†
0081-8364 Studies in Personnel Psychology†
0081-8380 Studies in Philosophy
0081-8399 Studies in Philosophy
0081-8402 Studies in Political Development†
0081-8437 University of Pennsylvania. Wharton School of Finance and Commerce. Studies in Quantitative Economics†
0081-8453 Studies in Rural Land Use†
0081-8461 Studies in Semitic Languages and Linguistics **5183**
0081-8496 Studies in Social Anthropology†
0081-850X Studies in Social History†
0081-8518 Studies in Social Life
0081-8534 Studies in Spanish Literature†
0081-8542 Studies in Statistical Mechanics† **8991**
0081-8569 Studies in the Economic Development of India†
0081-8577 Studies in the Foundations, Methodology and Philosophy of Science†
0081-8585 Mehkarim Bageografiya Shel Eretz Yisrael† **8973**
0081-8593 Studies in the Germanic Languages and Literatures† **8991**
0081-8607 Studies in the History of Christian Thought *changed to* 1573-5664 **7686**
0081-8615 Studies in the History of Discoveries†
0081-8623 Studies in the Humanities†
0081-8631 Studies in the Modern Russian Language
0081-864X Studies in the National Income and Expenditure of the United Kingdom† **8991**
0081-8674 Studies in the Social Sciences
0081-8682 State University of West Georgia. Studies in the Social Sciences **8007**
0081-8690 Studies in the Structure of Power: Decision Making in Canada†
0081-8704 Studies in the Theory of Science†
0081-8720 Studies in Tropical Oceanography†
0081-8747 Studies in Vermont Geology **2770**
0081-8771 Studies of Developing Countries†
0081-878X Studies of Negro Employment†
0081-8798 Studies of Northern Peoples†
0081-8801 Studies of Urban Society
0081-8844 Studii Clasice **2241**
0081-8852 Studii de Literatura Universala si Comparata†
0081-8860 Studii de Slavistica†
0081-8879 Studii si Cercetari de Bibliologie. Serie Noua†
0081-8887 Studii si Cercetari de Numismatica†
0081-8909 Studium Biblicum Franciscanum. Analecta
0081-8917 Studium Biblicum Franciscanum. Collectio Maior
0081-8925 Studium Biblicum Franciscanum. Collectio Minor
0081-8933 Liber Annuus **403**
0081-895X Study Abroad **3015**
0081-8992 Bibliothek fuer Zeitgeschichte, Stuttgart. Jahresbibliographie†
0081-900X Bibliothek fuer Zeitgeschichte, Stuttgart. Schriften **4133**
0081-9018 I L
0081-9077 Suedost-Forschungen **4271**
0081-9085 Suedostdeutsches Archiv *changed to* 1863-9887 **4213**
0081-9131 Suedosteuropa - Bibliographie **636**
0081-914X Suedosteuropa - Jahrbuch **4272**
0081-9158 Suedosteuropa - Schriften **4272**
0081-9166 Suedosteuropa - Studien **4272**
0081-9212 Sugar y Azucar Yearbook†
0081-9220 Suid-Afrikaanse Guernsey
0081-9255 Sulphur Institute. Technical Bulletin†
0081-9271 Sumer
0081-928X Sumitomo Sangyo Eisei†
0081-9301 Summary of Floods in the United States†
0081-931X Summary of State Laws and Regulations Relating to Distilled Spirits (Print Edition) *changed to* Summary of State Laws and Regulations Relating to Distilled Spirits (CD-ROM) **610**
0081-9387 Summer Theatre Directory†
0081-9395 Suomen Aikakauslehti-Indeksi†
0081-9417 Suomen Historiallinen Seura. Kasikirjoja **4171**
0081-9425 Suomen Historian Laehteitae **4272**
0081-9433 Suomen Naishammaslaakarit Ryhma. Julkaisu†
0081-9557 The Supreme Court Review **4965**
0081-9573 Surface and Colloid Science **2141**
0081-9581 Surface Water Supply of the United States†
0081-959X Surface Water Year Book of Great Britain
0081-9603 Surfactant Science Series **2082**
0081-9638 Surgery Annual†
0081-9646 Ackerman's Surgical Pathology
0081-9662 Surplus Dealers Directory†
0081-9670 Surrey Papers in Economics
0081-9697 Survey of Biological Progress†
0081-9743 Surveys and Development Plans of Industry in Israel† **8991**
0081-9751 Survey of London **458**
0081-976X Survey of Progress in Chemistry† **2141**
0081-9808 Svensk Geografisk Aarsbok **4030**
0081-9816 Svensk Tidskrift foer Musikforskning **6621**
0081-9824 Statens Musiksamlingar. Svenskt Visarkiv. Handlingar **6619**
0081-9832 Statens Musiksamlingar. Svenskt Visarkiv. Meddelanden **6619**
0081-9840 Statens Musiksamlingar. Svenskt Visarkiv. Skrifter **6619**
0081-9859 Svenska Bokfoerlaeggarefoereningen. Matrikel
0081-9867 Svenska Filminstitutet. Dokumentationsavdelningen. Skrifter†
0081-9905 Cement- och Betonginstitutet. Utredningar. Applied Studies†
0081-9913 Svenska Handelsbanken. Annual Report **1385**
0081-9921 Svenska Institutet i Athen. Skrifter. Serie 8 **420**
0081-993X Svenska Institutet i Rom. Skrifter. Acta Series Prima. 4:o **420**
0081-9956 Kungliga Vetenskapsakademien. Bidrag till Kungliga Vetenskapsakademiens Historia **7877**
0081-9980 Swansea Geographer **4030**
0081-9999 Swaziland. Geological Survey and Mines Department. Annual Report **2770**
0082-0008 Swaziland. Geological Survey and Mines Department. Bulletin **2770**
0082-0067 Sweden. Konjunkturinstitutet. Occasional Paper†
0082-0083 Swedish Social Security Scheme†
0082-0105 Sweden. Sjukvaardens och Socialvaardens Planerings- och Rationaliseringsinstitut. S P R I Specifikationer†
0082-0113 Sweden. Sjukvaardens och Socialvaardens Planerings- och Rationaliseringsinstitut. S P R I Raad†
0082-0180 Sweden. Statistiska Centralbyraan. Information i Prognosfragor/Forecasting Information†
0082-0199 Sweden. Statistiska Centralbyraan. Jordbruksstatistisk Aarsbok **186**
0082-0210 Sweden. Statistiska Centralbyraan. Loener†
0082-0229 Sweden. Statistiska Centralbyraan. Meddelanden i Samordningsfraagor **8408**
0082-0237 Sweden. Statistiska Centralbyraan. Statistiska Meddelanden. Serie Am, Arbetsmarknad **1269**
0082-0245 Sweden. Statistiska Centralbyraan. Statistiska Meddelanden. Serie Be, Befolkning och Levnadsfoerhaalanden **7316**
0082-030X Sweden. Statistiska Centralbyraan. Statistiska Meddelanden. Serie P, Priser och Konsumtion **1269**
0082-0318 Sweden. Statistiska Centralbyraan. Statistiska Meddelanden. Serie R, Raettsvaesen **4825**
0082-0350 Sweden. Statistiska Centralbyraan. Urval Skriftseries - Selection Series **8408**
0082-0393 Swedish Budget†
0082-0415 Swedish Nutrition Foundation. Symposia†
0082-0423 Swedish Theological Institute, Jerusalem. Annual†
0082-044X Swiatowit†
0082-0458 Rocznik Magnetyczny†
0082-0482 Swiss Society of Plastic and Reconstructive Surgeons. Proceedings (of) Annual Meeting
0082-0504 Switzerland. Bundesamt fuer Sozialversicherung. Spezialitaetenliste - Liste des Specialites - Elenco delle Specialita **6882**
0082-0512 The Sydney Law Review **4792**
0082-0520 Sydney Studies in Literature†
0082-0547 University of Sydney. Basser Department of Computer Science. Technical Report
0082-0563 University of Sydney. Department of Agricultural Economics. Research Bulletin†
0082-0571 University of Sydney. Department of Architectural Science. Reports†
0082-0598 Sydowia **819**
0082-0644 Symbolae Botanicae Upsalienses **819**
0082-0660 Symbolon†
0082-0695 Symposia Biologica Hungarica†
0082-0717 American Mathematical Society. Proceedings of Symposia in Pure Mathematics **5469**
0082-0725 Symposia Mathematica **5540**
0082-0733 Symposia on Fundamental Cancer Research. Papers
0082-0741 Symposia on Naval Structural Mechanics. Proceedings†
0082-0776 International Television Symposium and Technical Exhibition, Montreux. Symposium Record†
0082-0806 Symposium on Advanced Propulsion Concepts. Proceedings†
0082-0849 Symposium on Naval Hydrodynamics. Proceedings **7063**
0082-0873 Symposium on Ocular Therapy†
0082-089X Symposium on Particleboard - Composite Materials. Proceedings **3716**
0082-0911 Institute of Management Sciences. Symposium on Planning. Proceedings†
0082-0954 Special Ceramics†
0082-0970 Symposium on the Nondestructive Testing of Wood. Proceedings†
0082-1012 Symposium on Water Resources Research. Proceedings†
0082-1047 Syndicat General de l'Industrie Cotonniere Francaise. Annuaire
0082-1098 Syndromes de la Douleur†
0082-1101 Synopses of the British Fauna **964**
0082-1144 Synthetic Organic Chemicals, United States Production and Sales†
0082-1152 Synthetic Procedures in Nucleic Acid Chemistry†
0082-1160 Syracuse Geographical Series†
0082-1179 Syracuse University Publications in Continuing Education. Occasional Papers
0082-1195 System of Ophthalmology
0082-1209 Systemes - Decisions. Section 2. Gestion Financiere et Comptabilite†
0082-1217 Systems Engineering of Education Series **3221**
0082-1241 Szczecinskie Towarzystwo Naukowe. Sprawozdania **7922**
0082-125X Szczecinskie Towarzystwo Naukowe. Wydzial Nauk Lekarskich. Prace **5719**
0082-1268 Szczecinskie Towarzystwo Naukowe. Wydzial Nauk Matematyczno Technicznych. Prace†
0082-1276 Szczecinskie Towarzystwo Naukowe. Wydzial Nauk Przyrodniczo-Rolniczych. Prace **255**
0082-1292 Szczecinskie Towarzystwo Naukowe. Wydzial Nauk Spolecznych. Prace **8009**
0082-1306 Szilikatkemiai Monografiak†
0082-1322 Szociologiai Tanulmanyok†
0082-1330 T.B. Davie Memorial Lecture†
0082-1365 T V - Film Filebook
0082-1381 T V "Free" Film Source Book†
0082-139X T V in Psychiatry Newsletter
0082-1403 Table Ronde Francaise. Annuaire *changed to* 1953-132X **4272**
0082-1411 Tables of Constants and Numerical Data†
0082-1446 Il Taccuino dell'Azionista **1654**
0082-1454 Tagore Studies†
0082-1470 Taiwan Buyers' Guide (Print)†
0082-1497 Taiwan. Fisheries Research Institute, Keelung. Laboratory of Fishery Biology. Report†
0082-1519 Talking Books, Adult (Large Print Edition)†
0082-156X Tamagawa University. Faculty of Agriculture. Bulletin **160**
0082-1578 Tamil Nadu. Department of Statistics. Annual Statistical Abstract **8408**
0082-1586 Tamil Nadu. Department of Statistics. Season and Crop Report **187**
0082-1594 Tamil Nadu. Legislative Council. Quinquennial Review†
0082-1608 Tamworth Annual **302**
0082-1624 Universite de Madagascar. Annales. Serie Sciences de la Nature et Mathematiques†
0082-1632 Tanulmanyok a Nevelestudomany Korebol **2917**
0082-1659 Review of the Mineral Industry in Tanzania **6477**
0082-1675 National Museum of Tanzania. Annual Report **6534**
0082-1705 Tappert†
0082-1713 Tarbell's Teacher's Guide **7687**
0082-1748 Tarsadalomtudomanyi Kismonografiak†
0082-1772 Taschenbuch der Giesserei-Praxis **6334**
0082-1799 Taschenbuch der Pflanzenarztes **255**
0082-1802 Deutscher Werbekalender **24**
0082-1810 Taschenbuch der Werkzeugmaschinen und Werkzeuge
0082-1829 Taschenbuch des Oeffentlichen Lebens **7484**
0082-1845 Taschenbuch fuer Agrarjournalisten **160**
0082-1861 Taschenbuch fuer den Fernmeldedienst†
0082-1888 B A T: Taschenbuch fuer den Oeffentlichen Dienst **7422**
0082-1896 Taschenbuch fuer die Textil-Industrie **8458**
0082-1918 Taschenbuch fuer Ingenieure und Techniker im Industrie und Wirtschaft†
0082-1926 Taschenbuch fuer Ingenieure und Techniker im Oeffentlichen Dienst†
0082-1934 Taschenbuch fuer Kriminalisten†
0082-1942 Taschenbuch fuer Logistik†
0082-1950 Taschenbuch Geschichte
0082-1969 Taschenbuecher zur Musikwissenschaft **6622**
0082-1985 Information about Investment in Tasmania†
0082-2051 Tasmania. Department of Mines. Geological Survey Record†
0082-206X Tasmania. Department of Mines. Geological Survey Reports†
0082-2078 Tasmania. Department of Mines. Technical Reports†
0082-2086 Tasmania. Department of Mines. Underground Water Supply Papers†
0082-2108 University of Tasmania Law Review **4805**
0082-2116 Australia. Bureau of Statistics. Tasmanian Office. Tasmanian Year Book† **8933**
0082-2132 Tatzlil†
0082-2159 Tax Foundation. Research Publications. New Series†
0082-2167 Taxation in Western Europe†
0082-2175 Taxation Tables†
0082-2183 Taylor's Encyclopedia of Government Officials, Federal and State **7188**
0082-2205 Teacher Education†
0082-2213 Teachers' Associations. Associations d'Enseignants. Asociaciones de Personal Docente†
0082-223X Teaching
0082-2256 Teatro Clasico de Mexico. Boletin. Notas y Comentarios†
0082-2264 Technical Aids for Small Manufacturers†
0082-2272 Technical and Scientific Books in Print†
0082-2299 T A G A Proceedings **7328**
0082-2310 Technical Papers in Hydrology Series **2798**
0082-2361 Technikgeschichte in Einzeldarstellungen†
0082-2418 Techniques and Applications in Organic Synthesis Series†

ISSN

Link to your serials resources and content with ulrichsweb.com

DIRECTORY 2010 0083-2383 9123

0082-6898 Turk Etnografya Dergisi† **8994**
0082-6944 Turkey. Devlet Planama Teskilati. Yili Programi Ucuncu Bes Yil
0082-6952 Turkish Trade Directory & Telex Index
0082-6979 Turun Yliopisto. Julkaisuja. Sarja A. II. Biologica - Geographica - Geologica **708**
0082-6987 Turun Yliopisto. Julkaisuja. Sarja B. Humaniora **4478**
0082-6995 Turun Yliopisto. Julkaisuja. Sarja C. Scripta Lingua Fennica Edita **4479**
0082-7002 Turun Yliopisto. Julkaisuja. Sarja A. I. Astronomica - Chemica - Physica - Mathematica **7925**
0082-7010 Turun Yliopisto. Kirjasto. Julkaisuja **5051**
0082-7029 Turun Yliopisto. Klassillisen Filologian Laitos. Opera Ex Instituto Philologiae Classicae Universitatis Turkuensis Edita†
0082-7088 Twentieth Century Legal Philosophy Series†
0082-7118 Tyndale Bulletin **7691**
0082-7134 U C L A Forum in Medical Sciences†
0082-7150 Ub'†
0082-7169 Uganda. Geological Survey and Mines Department. Memoirs†
0082-7177 Uganda. Forestry Department. Annual Report **3706**
0082-7185 Uganda. Forestry Department. Bulletins†
0082-7193 Uganda. Forestry Department. Technical Notes **3706**
0082-724X Uganda. Ministry of Planning and Economic Development. Statistics Division. Enumeration of Employees†
0082-7282 Uhrmacher-Jahrbuch†
0082-7312 Uj Magyar Nepkoltesi Gyujtemeny† **8995**
0082-7347 Ulster Folklife **3623**
0082-7355 Ulster Journal of Archaeology **421**
0082-7363 Ulster-Scot Historical Series†
0082-7371 Ulster Year Book†
0082-7444 Underwater Acoustics†
0082-7452 Underwriting Results in Canada†
0082-7479 UNESCO Earthquake Study Missions†
0082-7487 Unesco Handbook of International Exchanges†
0082-7509 UNESCO Records of the General Conference. Proceedings **7270**
0082-7517 UNESCO Records of the General Conference. Resolutions **7270**
0082-7525 UNESCO Report of the Director - General on the Activities of the Organization **7270**
0082-7533 UNESCO Statistical Reports and Studies Series **8412**
0082-7541 UNESCO Statistical Yearbook†
0082-755X Ungarn - Jahrbuch†
0082-7568 Uniatec Congress. Records
0082-7576 Uniespana-Cine Espanol
0082-7592 Uniform Crime Reports for the United States **2670**
0082-7630 Union List of Publications in Opaque Microforms†
0082-7649 Union List of Scientific and Technical Periodicals Held in the Principal Libraries of East Africa†
0082-7711 Union Nationale de l'Enseignement Agricole Prive. Annuaire†
0082-7746 Union of British Columbia Municipalities. Minutes of Annual Convention **7473**
0082-7762 Union of Nova Scotia Municipalities. Proceedings of the Annual Convention†
0082-7770 Union Professionnelle Feminine. Annuaire
0082-7789 Index to Titles of English News Releases of Hsinhua News Agency
0082-7800 Unitarian Historical Society, London. Transactions **7743**
0082-7827 Unitarian Universalist Directory **7743**
0082-7843 United Baptist Convention of the Atlantic Provinces. Yearbook **7778**
0082-786X United Church of Canada. Committee on Archives. Bulletin. Records and Proceedings†
0082-7878 United Church of Canada. General Council. Record of Proceedings
0082-7894 United Community Funds and Councils of America. Addresses Delivered at the United Way Staff Conference†
0082-7908 United Free Church of Scotland. Handbook **7778**
0082-7940 United Kingdom Atomic Energy Authority. Annual Report†
0082-8009 United Nations and What You Should Know about It†
0082-8025 United Nations Congress on the Prevention of Crime and the Treatment of Offenders. Report† **8996**
0082-8041 United Nations. Demographic Yearbook **7294**
0082-805X United Nations. Population Studies **7295**
0082-8068 Report on the World Social Situation (Year) **8128**
0082-8084 United Nations. Economic and Social Council. Index to Proceedings **7201**
0082-8092 United Nations. Economic and Social Council. Official Records **7270**
0082-8106 United Nations Economic and Social Commission for Asia and the Pacific. Development Programming Techniques Series†
0082-8114 United Nations. Economic and Social Commission for Asia and the Pacific. Mineral Resources Development Series†
0082-8122 United Nations Economic and Social Commission for Asia and the Pacific. Regional Economic Cooperation Series†
0082-8130 United Nations. Economic and Social Commission for Asia and the Pacific. Water Resources Series **8834**
0082-8157 United Nations. General Assembly. Index to Proceedings **7201**
0082-8173 United Nations. Report of the Secretary-General on the Work of the Organization **4943**
0082-822X Report of the International Commission on the Work of Its (Year) Session, United Nations **4768**
0082-8289 United Nations. International Law Commission Yearbook†
0082-8297 United Nations Juridical Yearbook **4943**
0082-8300 United Nations Legislative Series
0082-8386 United Nations Relief and Works Agency for Palestine Refugees in the Near East. Report of the Commissioner-General **8075**
0082-8408 United Nations. Security Council. Index to Proceedings **7201**
0082-8416 United Nations. Security Council. Official Records **7271**
0082-8459 United Nations. Statistical Yearbook **8413**
0082-8491 United Nations. Trusteeship Council. Index to Proceedings **7201**
0082-8505 United Nations. Trusteeship Council. Official Records **7271**
0082-8513 United Nations. Trusteeship Council. Official Records. Supplements **7271**
0082-8521 United Nations. Yearbook **7271**
0082-8556 U S O Annual Report **8075**
0082-8599 U S A Oil Industry Directory
0082-8637 U.S. Agency for International Development. Proposed Foreign Aid Program, Summary Presentation to Congress†
0082-8661 Tables on Hatchery and Flock Participation in the National Poultry Improvement Plan
0082-8688 U.S. Air Force Academy Assembly. Proceedings
0082-8696 U.S. Air Force Academy Library. Special Bibliography Series
0082-8742 United States and Canadian Publications on Africa†
0082-8750 United States Animal Health Association. Proceedings of the Annual Meeting **8809**
0082-8823 U. S. Atomic Energy Commission. Annual Report to Congress. Supplement. Atomic Energy Research Reports†
0082-8831 U. S. Atomic Energy Commission. Division of Plans and Reports. Fundamental Nuclear Energy Research†
0082-884X U. S. Atomic Energy Commission. Safety and Fire Protection Technical Bulletins†
0082-8939 U.S. Bureau of International Commerce. Annual Reports
0082-9013 U.S. Bureau of Labor Statistics. Analysis of Work Stoppages†
0082-9021 U.S. Bureau of Labor Statistics. Bulletin **1271**
0082-903X U.S. Bureau of Labor Statistics. B L S Staff Paper†
0082-9056 Handbook of Labor Statistics†
0082-9072 Occupational Outlook Handbook **6707**
0082-9099 U.S. Bureau of Labor Statistics. Union Wages and Hours Surveys†
0082-9102 U.S. Bureau of Labor Statistics. Wage Chronologies†
0082-9110 U.S. Bureau of Land Management. Public Land Statistics **4436**
0082-9129 U.S. Bureau of Mines. Bulletin†
0082-9250 U. S. Bureau of Radiological Health. Seminar Paper Series†
0082-9307 Annual Survey of Manufactures†
0082-9331 U. S. Bureau of the Census. Census of Commercial Fisheries
0082-9358 Census of Governments (Final Reports) (Print)† **8940**
0082-9366 Census of Housing† **8940**
0082-9412 U.S. Bureau of the Census. Census Tract Manual†
0082-9439 City Government Finances† **8941**
0082-9455 County and City Data Book **8365**
0082-9536 U.S. Bureau of the Census. Technical Notes†
0082-9544 U.S. Bureau of the Census. Technical Papers
0082-9552 U.S. Bureau of the Census. Working Papers
0082-9609 U.S. Civil Aeronautics Board. Aircraft Operating Cost and Performance Report†
0082-9625 U.S. Coast Guard. Oceanographic Reports (CG-373 Series)†
0082-9641 U.S. Commission on Civil Rights. Clearinghouse Publications **7216**
0082-965X World Refugee Report†
0082-9714 U.S. Department of Agriculture. National Agricultural Statistics Service. Agricultural Statistics **187**
0082-9722 Hatcheries and Dealers Participating in the National Poultry Improvement Plan
0082-9781 U.S. Department of Agriculture, Marketing Research Report **207**
0082-979X U.S. Department of Agriculture. Production Research Reports **207**
0082-9811 U.S. Department of Agriculture. Technical Bulletin **164**
0082-9846 U.S. International Trade Administration†
0082-9862 U.S. Department of Defense. Defense Program and Defense Budget
0082-9889 U.S. Department of Health, Education, and Welfare. Catalog of H E W Assistance Providing Financial Support and Service to States, Communities, Organizations, Individuals†
0082-9897 U.S. Department of Health, Education and Welfare. Health, Education and Welfare Trends†
0082-9951 U.S. Department of Justice. Opinions of Attorney General *changed to* 0270-2134 **4800**
0083-0003 U.S. Department of State. African Series†
0083-0011 U.S. Department of State. Biographic Register
0083-002X U.S. Department of State. Commercial Policy Series
0083-0038 U.S. Department of State. Department and Foreign Service Series†
0083-0054 U.S. Department of State. East Asian and Pacific Series†
0083-0062 U.S. Department of State. Economic Cooperation Series
0083-0070 U.S. Department of State. European and British Commonwealth Series†
0083-0097 U.S. Department of State. General Foreign Policy Series†
0083-0100 U.S. Department of State. Geographic Bulletins†
0083-0119 U.S. Department of State. International Information and Cultural Series†
0083-0127 U.S. Department of State. International Organization and Conference Series†
0083-0135 U.S. Department of State. International Organization Series†
0083-0143 U.S. Department of State. Inter-American Series†
0083-0186 U.S. Department of State. Treaties and Other International Acts Series **4943**
0083-0194 U.S. Department of State. Treaties in Force **4943**
0083-0208 United States Participation in the United Nations **7271**
0083-0305 U.S. Army. Corps of Engineers. Port Series†
0083-0313 U.S. Army Corps of Engineers. Technical Reports Series†
0083-0364 U.S. Department of the Interior. Safety Conference Guides†
0083-0380 U.S. Department of Transportation. Bibliographic Lists†
0083-0445 U.S. Department of Agriculture. Agricultural Economic Reports **207**
0083-050X Sewage Facilities Construction†
0083-0518 U.S. Environmental Protection Agency. Pesticides Enforcement Division. Notices of Judgment under Federal Insecticide, Fungicide, and Rodenticide Act **256**
0083-0526 U.S. Equal Employment Opportunity Commission. Equal Opportunity Report. Job Patterns for Minorities and Women in Private Industry **6707**
0083-0534 U.S. Excise Tax Guide *changed to* U.S. Master Excise Tax Guide **1953**
0083-0607 U.S. Federal Communications Commission. I N F Bulletins **2343**
0083-0631 U. S. Federal Council for Science and Technology. Interdepartmental Committee for Atmospheric Sciences. I C A S Reports†
0083-0666 U.S. Federal Deposit Insurance Corporation. Bank Operating Statistics†
0083-0674 U.S. Federal Deposit Insurance Corporation. Changes Among Operating Banks and Branches†
0083-0682 U.S. Federal Fire Council. Federal Fire Experience for Fiscal Year†
0083-0690 U.S. Federal Fire Council. Minutes of Annual Meeting†
0083-0704 U.S. Federal Fire Council. Recommended Practices†
0083-0720 U.S. Federal Home Loan Bank Board. Report
0083-0747 U.S. Federal Home Loan Bank Board. Trends in the Savings and Loan Field
0083-0755 U.S. Federal Maritime Commission. Annual Report **8664**
0083-078X U.S. Federal Power Commission. Annual Report†
0083-0887 U.S. Federal Reserve System. Annual Report **1388**
0083-0941 U.S. Fish and Wildlife Service. Research Reports†
0083-0976 Food and Agricultural Export Directory **198**
0083-0984 Foreign Agriculture Reports†
0083-0992 U.S. Foreign Agricultural Service. Miscellaneous Reports†
0083-1018 U.S. Forest Service. Forest Products Laboratory, Madison, Wisconsin. Report of Research at the Forest Products Laboratory.†
0083-1026 U.S. Forest Service. Annual Fire Report for National Forests
0083-1077 U.S. Forest Service. Technical Equipment Reports
0083-1093 U.S. Geological Survey. Bulletin **2771**
0083-1166 U.S. Government Films for Public Educational Use†
0083-1263 United States Import Duties Annotated†
0083-1328 U.S. Industrial College of the Armed Forces. Monographs. R Series
0083-1425 U.S. Institute of Tropical Forestry. Annual Report†
0083-1476 U.S. Internal Revenue Service. Annual Report
0083-1484 U.S. Internal Revenue Service. Tax Guide for Small Business **1953**
0083-1506 U.S. Interstate Commerce Commission. Advance Bulletin of Interstate Commerce Acts Annotated†
0083-1514 U.S. Interstate Commerce Commission. Annual Report†
0083-1522 U.S. Interstate Commerce Commission. Interstate Commerce Acts Annotated†
0083-1530 U.S. Interstate Commerce Commission Reports. Decisions of the Interstate Commerce Commission of the United States†
0083-1565 U.S. Library of Congress. Annual Report of the Librarian of Congress **5052**
0083-1581 U.S. Library of Congress. Hispanic Foundation. Bibliographic Series
0083-1603 U.S. Library of Congress. Library of Congress Publications in Print†
0083-1611 U.S. Library of Congress. Manuscript Division. Registers of Papers **4165**
0083-1697 U.S. Maritime Administration. Technical Report Index, Maritime Administration Research and Development†
0083-1700 (Year) U.S. Master Tax Guide **1953**
0083-1786 U.S. National Bureau of Standards. Applied Mathematics Series *changed to* National Institute of Standards and Technology. Applied Mathematics Series
0083-1956 U.S. National Center for Health Statistics. Health Resources Statistics†
0083-1972 U.S. National Center for Health Statistics. Vital and Health Statistics. Series 10. Data from the Health Interview Survey **7549**
0083-2014 U.S. National Center for Health Statistics. Vital and Health Statistics. Series 1. Programs and Collection Procedures **7549**
0083-2022 U.S. National Center for Health Statistics. Vital and Health Statistics. Series 20. Data on Mortality **7549**
0083-2057 U.S. National Center for Health Statistics. Vital and Health Statistics. Series 2. Data Evaluation and Methods Research **7549**
0083-2073 U.S. National Center for Health Statistics. Vital and Health Statistics. Series 4. Documents and Committee Report **7550**
0083-209X N C R P Report **7532**
0083-2103 U.S. National Endowment for the Arts. Annual Report **523**
0083-2162 U.S. National Institute of Neurological Diseases and Stroke. N I N D S Research Profiles: Summary of Research†
0083-2200 U.S. National Labor Relations Board. Annual Report **1712**
0083-2219 U.S. National Labor Relations Board. Court Decisions Relating to the National Labor Relations Act **1712**
0083-2227 Decisions and Orders of the National Labor Relations Board **1674**
0083-2278 U.S. National Mediation Board. (Reports of Emergency Boards) **1712**
0083-2286 U.S. National Mediation Board. Annual Report **1712**
0083-2294 National Medical Audiovisual Center. Catalog†
0083-2316 U.S. National Park Service. Historical Handbook Series **8770**
0083-2324 U.S. National Park Service. Source Books Series†
0083-2375 U.S. National Science Foundation. N S F Factbook†
0083-2383 U.S. National Science Foundation. Research and Development in Industry **8447**

ISSN

9124 0083-2405 ULRICH'S PERIODICALS

0083-2405 U.S. National Science Foundation. Surveys of Science Resources Series
0083-2421 Astronomical Phenomena **569**
0083-2448 U.S. Naval Observatory. Publications. Second Series†
0083-2480 U.S. Forest Service. Annual Report N E **3706**
0083-2618 U.S. Office of Education. Accredited Higher Institutions†
0083-2715 U.S. Office of Education. Guide to Organized Occupational Curriculums in Higher Education†
0083-2723 U.S. Office of Education. International Teacher Development Program. Annual Report to Bureau of Education and Cultural Affairs, Department of State†
0083-2774 U.S. Office of Education. Public School Finance Program†
0083-2790 U.S. Office of Education. Residence and Migration of College Students, Analytic Report†
0083-2855 U.S. Office of Education. Studies in Comparative Education. Education in (Country)†
0083-288X U.S. Office of Education. Title VII: New Educational Media News and Reports†
0083-2898 U. S. Office of Education. Vocational and Technical Education, Annual Report†
0083-2901 U.S. Office of Saline Water. Desalting Plants Inventory Report†
0083-291X U.S. Office of Saline Water. Saline Water Conversion Report†
0083-2979 U.S. Office of the Federal Register. Guide to Record Retention Requirements
0083-2987 U.S. Forest Service. Pacific Northwest Forest and Range Experiment Station. Annual Report†
0083-2995 U.S. Forest Service. Pacific Southwest Forest and Range Experiment Station. Annual Report†
0083-3010 U.S. Patent and Trademark Office. Classification Bulletins **6759**
0083-3088 U.S. Peace Corps. Annual Report **7270**
0083-3118 United States Polo Association. Yearbook **8250**
0083-3134 U.S. Renewal Assistance Administration. Technical Guides†
0083-3142 U.S. Renewal Assistance Administration. Urban Renewal Project Characteristics†
0083-3150 U.S. Renewal Assistance Administration. Urban Renewal Service Bulletins†
0083-3169 U.S. Rocky Mountain Forest and Range Experiment Station. Annual Report of Research at the Station†
0083-3177 U.S. Rural Electrification Administration. Annual Statistical Report. Rural Electrification Borrowers†
0083-3215 U.S. Securities and Exchange Commission. Annual Report *changed to* U.S. Securities and Exchange Commission. Performance and Accountability Report **1657**
0083-3223 U.S. Securities and Exchange Commission. Decisions and Reports **1657**
0083-3231 U.S. Securities and Exchange Commission. Judicial Decisions **1657**
0083-3258 United States Ski Association. Directory
0083-3266 U.S. Small Business Administration. Administrative Management Course Program. Topics
0083-3274 U.S. Small Business Administration. Annual Report **1968**
0083-3304 U.S. Natural Resources Conservation Service. National Engineering Handbook Sections **256**
0083-3320 U.S. Natural Resources Conservation Service. Soil Survey Investigation Reports **256**
0083-3339 U.S. Natural Resources Conservation Service. Technical Publications **256**
0083-3398 United States Squash Racquets Association. Official Year Book **8250**
0083-3401 United States Statutes at Large **4801**
0083-3436 U.S. International Trade Commission. Imports of Benzenoid Chemicals and Products†
0083-3487 United States Treaties and Other International Agreements **4943**
0083-3509 Trotting and Pacing Guide **8299**
0083-3517 U S T A Year Book **8300**
0083-3533 U.S. Department of Veterans Affairs. Annual Report
0083-3541 Medical Research in the V.A.†
0083-355X U.S. Veterans Administration. Medical Research Program†
0083-3673 Univers Historique **7925**
0083-3681 Univers Politique: Relations Internationales
0083-3835 Universal Business Directories West Victoria Country Business and Trade Directory†
0083-3843 Universal Business Directories, Western Australia Country Business and Trade Directory†
0083-3851 Kongresa Libro **6281**
0083-3886 Universalist Historical Society. Journal†
0083-3908 Universidade Federal de Pernambuco. Faculdade de Odontologia. Anais†
0083-3924 Universite Autonome†
0083-3940 Universities-National Bureau Conference Series†
0083-3967 U C E A Case Series in Educational Administration†
0083-3975 University Geographer **4032**
0083-4025 University of Kansas Law Review **4804**
0083-4041 University of Queensland Law Journal **4805**
0083-405X University of Singapore Science Journal†
0083-4114 Univerzita Komenskeho. Filozoficka Fakulta. Zbornik: Graecolatina et Orientalia **2241**
0083-4122 Univerzita Komenskeho. Filozoficka Fakulta. Zbornik: Historica **4165**
0083-4130 Univerzita Komenskeho. Filozoficka Fakulta. Zbornik: Musaica **524**
0083-4165 Univerzita Komenskeho. Filozoficka Fakulta. Zbornik: Paedagogica **2923**
0083-4173 Univerzita Komenskeho. Filozoficka Fakulta. Zbornik: Philologica **5192**
0083-4181 Univerzita Komenskeho. Filozoficka Fakulta. Zbornik: Philosophica **6959**
0083-419X Univerzita Komenskeho. Filozoficka Fakulta. Zbornik: Psychologica **7414**
0083-422X Univerzita Komenskeho. Filozoficka Fakulta. Zbornik: Zurnalistika **4584**
0083-4254 Uniwersytet im. Adama Mickiewicza. Psychologia-Pedagogika **2923**
0083-4262 Uniwersytet im. Adama Mickiewicza. Prawo **4806**
0083-4289 Uniwersytet Jagiellonski. Zeszyty Naukowe. Prace Geograficzne. Prace z Geografii Ekonomicznej†
0083-4300 Uniwersytet Jagiellonski. Zeszyty Naukowe. Prace Archeologiczne **422**
0083-4327 Uniwersytet Jagiellonski. Zeszyty Naukowe. Prace Etnograficzne **360**
0083-4351 Uniwersytet Jagiellonski. Zeszyty Naukowe. Prace Historyczne **4275**
0083-436X Uniwersytet Jagiellonski. Zeszyty Naukowe. Prace Historyczno-Literackie **5394**
0083-4378 Uniwersytet Jagiellonski. Zeszyty Naukowe. Prace Jezykoznawcze **5192**
0083-4394 Uniwersytet Jagiellonski. Zeszyty Naukowe. Prace Prawnicze **4806**
0083-4416 Uniwersytet Jagiellonski. Zeszyty Naukowe. Prace Zoologiczne†
0083-453X Unternehmensforschung fuer die Wirtschaftspraxis†
0083-4548 Unternehmung und Unternehmungsfuehrung†
0083-4564 Untersuchungen zur Deutschen Literaturgeschichte **5394**
0083-4572 Untersuchungen zur Deutschen Staats- und Rechtsgeschichte. Neue Folge†
0083-4580 Untersuchungen zur Sprach- und Literaturgeschichte der Romanischen Voelker **5192**
0083-4602 Up the Tube with One I (Open)-Pomes†
0083-4661 Uppsala Universitet. Institutionen foer Nordiska Spraak. Skrifter†
0083-4688 Urban Affairs Annual Reviews†
0083-4696 Urban Environment†
0083-470X Urban Land Institute. Research Report†
0083-4718 Urban Land Institute. Technical Bulletin†
0083-4769 Uro-Nephro: Annuaire de l'Urologie et de la Nephrologie†
0083-484X Utah Geological Association. Annual Guidebook **2773**
0083-4858 Utah State University of Agriculture and Applied Science. Monograph Series†
0083-4947 University of Utah Anthropological Papers **359**
0083-4963 Utrecht Micropaleontological Bulletins **6731**
0083-4998 Disputationes Rheno-Trajectinae†
0083-5013 Uttar Pradesh, India. Scientific Research Committee Monograph Series **7927**
0083-5021 V W Z **8636**
0083-5072 Vade-Mecum
0083-5080 Vademecum Deutscher Lehr- und Forschungsstaetten. Staetten der Forschung **7927**
0083-5102 Vaikunth Mehta National Institute of Cooperative Management. Publications **1800**
0083-5137 Value Engineering Association. Proceedings†
0083-5145 Van Nostrand Mathematical Studies†
0083-5161 Vancouver Art Gallery. Annual Report **6539**
0083-517X Vancouver Board of Trade. Annual Report **1434**
0083-5196 Vancouver Neurological Centre. Annual Reports
0083-520X Vancouver Stock Exchange. Annual Report†
0083-5218 Vanderbilt Rubber Handbook **7827**
0083-5226 Vanderbilt Sociology Conference. Proceedings†
0083-5242 Varia†
0083-5269 Vascular Flora of Ohio
0083-5277 Vaskohaszati Enciklopedia†
0083-5323 Die Vegetation Ungarischer Landschaften†
0083-5358 Vejtransporten i Tal og Tekst†
0083-5366 Venezuela. Ministerio de Agricultura y Cria. Direccion de Economica y Estadistica Agropecuaria. Anuario Estadistico Agropecuario **189**
0083-5412 Universidad Central de Venezuela. Facultad de Derecho. Coleccion Tesis de Doctorado†
0083-5420 Universidad Central de Venezuela. Instituto de Estudios Politicos. Cuadernos†
0083-5439 Universidad Central de Venezuela. Consejo de Desarrollo Cientifico y Humanistico. Bibliografia de Humanidades y Ciencias Sociales y Bibliografia de Ciencia y Tecnologia del Profesorado†
0083-5455 Venture Capital†
0083-5463 Ver Sacrum†
0083-5536 Varbergs Museum. Aarsbok **6539**
0083-5544 Verdensmarkedet og Danmark†
0083-5560 V D I - Berichte **3226**
0083-5579 Verein fuer Geschichte der Stadt Nuernberg. Mitteilungen **4276**
0083-5587 Verein fuer Hamburgische Geschichte. Zeitschrift **4277**
0083-5609 Verein fuer Luebeckische Geschichte und Altertumskunde. Zeitschrift **4277**
0083-5617 Jahrbuch des Vereins fuer Niederdeutsche Sprachforschung **5131**
0083-5633 Vereinigte Evangelisch-Lutherische Kirche Deutschlands. Amtsblatt†
0083-565X Vereinigung Freunde der Universitaet Mainz. Jahrbuch†
0083-5676 Verfassung und Verfassungswirklichkeit **7192**
0083-5684 Verhandlungen des Deutschen Geographentages **4033**
0083-5706 Vermont. Agricultural Experiment Station, Burlington. Research Report M P **168**
0083-5714 Vermont. Agricultural Experiment Station, Burlington. Station Bulletin Series **168**
0083-5722 Vermont. Agricultural Experiment Station, Burlington. Station Pamphlet Series **168**
0083-5781 Vermont Year Book **2033**
0083-579X Vermont's Game Annual†
0083-5803 Verpackungs-Magazin†
0083-5811 Verpackungsfolien - Verpackungspapiere†
0083-582X Verse Speaking Anthology†
0083-5846 Verstaendliche Wissenschaft†
0083-5862 Veterinaer-Medizinische Nachrichten†
0083-5870 Veterinary Annual†
0083-5889 Vetus Testamentum. Supplements **7731**
0083-5897 Viator **4166**
0083-5919 Great Britain. Victoria and Albert Museum. Monographs†
0083-5927 Victoria and Albert Museum, South Kensington. Yearbook†
0083-5935 Victoria, Australia. Department of Agriculture. Agricultural Economics Branch. Contract Rates†
0083-5943 Victoria, Australia. Department of Agriculture. Agricultural Economics Branch. Farm Credit (Sources and Terms)†
0083-5951 Victoria, Australia. Department of Agriculture. Pig Industry Branch. Pig Farm Management Study†
0083-596X Victoria, Australia. Department of Agriculture. Poultry Branch. Poultry Farm Management Study†
0083-5978 Victoria, Australia. Forests Commission. Forestry Technical Papers†
0083-601X Victoria League for Commonwealth Friendship. Annual Report† **8997**
0083-6079 Victorian Society. Annual **460**
0083-6087 Victorian Society. Conference Reports†
0083-6095 Vie des Affaires
0083-6109 Vie Musicale en France sous les Rois Bourbons. Serie 1: Etudes **6626**
0083-6125 Informationen zu Aktuellen Fragen der Sozial- und Wirtschaftpolitik
0083-6141 Naturhistorisches Museum in Wien. Flugblatt†
0083-615X Oesterreichische Galerie. Mitteilungen†
0083-6168 Universitaet Wien. Institut fuer Statistik. Schriftenreihe. Neue Folge†
0083-6230 Viewpoints in Biology†
0083-6249 Viking Fund Publications in Anthropology†
0083-6257 Viking Society for Northern Research. Text Series **5395**
0083-6265 Vilagtortenet†
0083-6273 Villa Guide
0083-6281 Vincentian Studies†
0083-6311 Virginia Baptist Register **7779**
0083-6354 Virginia Educational Directory **2924**
0083-6389 Virginia Historical Society. Documents **4317**
0083-6397 Virginia Institute of Marine Science, Gloucester Point. Translation Series.†
0083-6419 Virginia Institute of Marine Science, Gloucester Point. Data Reports
0083-6427 Virginia Institute of Marine Science. Educational Series **710**
0083-6435 Virginia Institute of Marine Science. Marine Resources Advisory Series **710**
0083-6443 Virginia Institute of Marine Science. Special Scientific Report **710**
0083-6451 Virginia Military Institute, Lexington. Publications, Theses, and Dissertations of the Staff and Faculty†
0083-6516 Virginia Port Authority. Foreign Trade Annual Report: The Ports of Virginia†
0083-6524 Virginia. State Library. Publications†
0083-6532 Virginia Port Authority. Board of Commissioners. Annual Report†
0083-6540 Virginia Union List of Biomedical Serials
0083-6575 Virginia's Supply of Public School Instructional Personnel†
0083-6591 Virology Monographs†
0083-6613 Vishveshvaranand Indological Paper Series **4190**
0083-6621 Vishveshvaranand Indological Series **5194**
0083-6672 Visti Iz Sarseliu **8014**
0083-6680 Visual Education Yearbook†
0083-6729 Vitamins and Hormones **6885**
0083-6737 Kungliga Vitterhets Historie och Antikvitets Akademien. Antikvariskt Arkiv **501**
0083-6745 Kungliga Vitterhets Historie och Antikvitets Akademien. Filologiskt Arkiv **5137**
0083-6753 Kungliga Vitterhets Historie och Antikvitets Akademien. Historiskt Arkiv **4239**
0083-6761 Kungliga Vitterhets Historie och Antikvitets Akademien. Handlingar. Antikvariska Serien **501**
0083-677X Kungliga Vitterhets Historie och Antikvitets Akademien. Handlingar. Filologisk-Filosofiska Serien **5138**
0083-6788 Kungliga Vitterhets Historie och Antikvitets Akademien. Handlingar. Historiska Serien **4239**
0083-6796 Kungliga Vitterhets Historie och Antikvitets Akademien. Aarsbok **4239**
0083-6826 Voix dans le Monde
0083-6877 Volkstum der Schweiz† **8998**
0083-6893 Vollschlank†
0083-6915 Vom Wasser **8835**
0083-6923 Vorreformationsgeschichtliche Forschungen
0083-6982 Waermelehre und Waermewirtschaft in Einzeldarstellungen†
0083-7016 Tasmanian Almanac†
0083-7067 Walker's Old Moore's Almanac
0083-7091 Wallace Wurth Memorial Lecture†
0083-7121 Walter Lynwood Fleming Lectures in Southern History **4317**
0083-7148 Walter W.S. Cook Alumni Lecture† **8998**
0083-7172 Wanderlust†
0083-7210 Ward - Phillips Lectures in English Language and Literature **5396**
0083-7229 Ward's Automotive Yearbook **8532**
0083-7261 Biblioteka Narodowa. Rocznik **4995**
0083-7296 Akademia Rolnicza, Warsaw. Zeszyty Naukowe. Seria Historyczna†
0083-730X Szkola Glowna Planowania i Statystyki. Zeszyty Naukowe†
0083-7326 Uniwersytet Warszawski. Instytut Geograficzny. Prace i Studia.†
0083-7334 Uniwersytet Warszawski. Katedra Klimatologii. Prace i Studia†
0083-7342 Uniwersytet Warszawski. Roczniki†
0083-7350 Warwick Economic Research Papers†
0083-7393 Washington (Year) **1193**
0083-7407 The Textile Museum Journal **8460**
0083-744X Washington (State). Department of Fisheries. Fisheries Research Papers†
0083-7466 Washington (State). Department of Fisheries. Research Bulletin†
0083-7474 Washington (State) Department of Fisheries. Technical Report†
0083-7520 University of Washington. Department of Oceanography. Contribution†
0083-7539 University of Washington. Department of Oceanography. Fishery Report†
0083-7547 University of Washington. Department of Oceanography. Special Report†
0083-7555 Research in Fisheries†

Link to your serials resources and content with ulrichsweb.com

0083-7563   Washington State University, Pullman. Library Staff Association. L S A Open Stacks†
0083-7571   University of Washington Publications in Biology†
0083-758X   Washington (State) Utilities and Transportation Commission. Transportation Report†
0083-761X   Waste Management Research Abstracts **7550**
0083-7636   Water†
0083-7652   Water in Biological Systems†
0083-7660   Water Pollution Research†
0083-7679   Water Pollution Research Laboratory, Stevenage, England. Technical Papers†
0083-7709   University of Texas at Austin. Center for Research in Water Resources. Water Resources Symposium Series†
0083-7725   Waterborne Commerce of the United States **8664**
0083-7792   Webbia **822**
0083-7849   Weizmann Institute of Science, Rehovot, Israel. Scientific Activities **7928**
0083-789X   New Zealand Oceanographic Institute. Collected Reprints†
0083-7911   Welsh Bibliographical Society. Journal†
0083-7938   Welsh Soils Discussion Group. Report **259**
0083-7946   Welsh Studies in Education Series†
0083-7954   Weltstaedte der Kunst. Edition Leipzig†
0083-7962   Wendehorst, Baustoffkunde
0083-8004   Wentworth Bygones **4317**
0083-8047   Werken und Wohnen **3624**
0083-8098   Wessen Geographer
0083-8136   Wessex Geographical Year
0083-8144   West Africa Annual **4179**
0083-8187   West African Religion **7694**
0083-8195   West Canadian Research Publications of Geology and Related Sciences†
0083-8217   West Coast Reliability Symposium† **8998**
0083-8276   Pakistan Agricultural University. Research Studies
0083-8292   Pakistan. Directorate of Livestock Farms. Report **295**
0083-8306   Pakistan. Directorate of Rural Works Programme. Evaluation Report
0083-8322   Pakistan. Official Language Committee. Urdu Translation of Official Terms and Phraseology
0083-8349   Pakistan. Water and Power Development Authority. Report **3363**
0083-8403   West Virginia University. Center for Appalachian Studies and Development. Information Series†
0083-842X   West Virginia Coal Mining Institute. Proceedings†
0083-8438   West Virginia. Commission on Aging. Annual Progress Report **4057**
0083-8446   West Virginia. Commission on Mental Retardation. Annual Report†
0083-8489   West Virginia Geological Survey. Archaeological Series†
0083-8500   West Virginia Geological Survey. Bulletin†
0083-8519   West Virginia Geological Survey. Circular†
0083-8527   West Virginia Geological Survey. Geological Publications. Volumes†
0083-8586   West Virginia Government†
0083-8594   West Virginia. Human Rights Commission. Report **7218**
0083-8608   West Virginia University. Bureau for Government Research. Publications†
0083-8640   West Virginia University. Engineering Experiment Station. Bulletin†
0083-8659   West Virginia University. Engineering Experiment Station. Report†
0083-8691   Western Australia. Office of Director General of Transport. Annual Report†
0083-8705   University of Western Australia. Institute of Agriculture. Research Report: Agricultural Economics†
0083-8713   University of Western Australia. Library. Report on the Library†
0083-8721   Western Australian Museum. Annual Report (Print) *changed to* Western Australian Museum. Annual Report (Online) **6540**
0083-873X   Western Australian Museum, Perth. Special Publication†
0083-8748   Western Australian Naturalists' Club. Handbook†
0083-8772   Australia. Bureau of Statistics. Western Australian Office. Western Australian Year Book†
0083-8810   Western Canadian Society for Horticulture. Reports of Proceedings of Annual Meeting†
0083-8829   Western Canadian Studies in Modern Languages and Literature†
0083-887X   Western Frontier Library **4317**
0083-8888   Western Frontiersmen Series **4317**
0083-890X   Western Highway Institute. State Motor Carriers Handbook
0083-8918   Western Highway Institute. Research Committee. Report
0083-8934   Western Lands and Waters Series **2632**
0083-8942   Western Market Almanac†
0083-8969   Western Pharmacology Society. Proceedings **6885**
0083-8977   W P S Professional Handbook Series
0083-9000   Western Thoroughbred
0083-9019   Westernlore Ghost Town Series **4318**
0083-9027   Westfaelische Forschungen **4278**
0083-9043   Westfaelische Zeitschrift†
0083-906X   Westminster Series†
0083-9078   Weyers Flottentaschenbuch **6454**
0083-9108   What Every Veteran Should Know **6454**
0083-9116   What Research Says to the Teacher Series
0083-9132   What You Should Know about Taxes in Puerto Rico
0083-9167   Where America's Large Foundations Make Their Grants†
0083-9256   Whitaker's Almanack **3122**
0083-9337   Who Represents Whom†
0083-937X   Who's Who (Year) **646**
0083-9396   Who's Who in America **646**
0083-9450   Who's Who in Canada (Year) *changed to* Canadian Who's Who (Year) **641**
0083-9469   Who's Who in Canadian Placement
0083-9477   Who's Who in Communist China
0083-9485   Who's Who in Consulting†
0083-9493   Who's Who in East Africa†
0083-9515   Who's Who in Europe
0083-9531   Who's Who in France **647**
0083-9558   Who's Who in Indian Engineering and Industry **647**
0083-9566   Who's Who in Indian Science **647**

0083-9574   Who's Who in Insurance **4528**
0083-9582   Who's Who in International Organizations **647**
0083-9590   Who's Who in Israel
0083-9612   Who's Who in Lebanon **647**
0083-9620   Who's Who in Malaysia and Singapore
0083-9639   Who's Who in Movies†
0083-9655   Who's Who in New Zealand†
0083-9671   Who's Who in Pakistan
0083-968X   Who's Who in Science in Europe†
0083-9701   Who's Who in Soviet Science and Technology†
0083-971X   Who's Who in Soviet Social Sciences, Humanities, Art and Government†
0083-9728   Who's Who in Space†
0083-9736   Who's Who in Switzerland **647**
0083-9744   Agricultural Institute of Canada. Membership Directory
0083-9752   Who's Who in the Arab World **647**
0083-9760   Who's Who in the East **647**
0083-9787   Who's Who in the Midwest **647**
0083-9809   Who's Who in the South and Southwest **647**
0083-9825   Who's Who in the World **648**
0083-9841   Who's Who of American Women **648**
0083-985X   Who's Who of British Engineers†
0083-9892   Widener Library Shelflist†
0083-9930   Wiener Beitraege zur Theologie†
0083-9957   Wiener Geographische Schriften **4034**
0083-9965   Wiener Humanistische Blaetter
0083-9973   W I S T-Informationen
0083-9981   Wiener Jahrbuch fuer Kunstgeschichte **526**
0083-999X   Wiener Jahrbuch fuer Philosophie **6960**
0084-0009   Wiener Katholische Akademie. Studien†
0084-0017   Wiener Musikhochschule. Publikationen†
0084-0025   Wiener Rechtswissenschaftliche Studien **4814**
0084-0033   Wiener Romanistische Arbeiten **5195**
0084-0041   Wiener Slavistisches Jahrbuch **5195**
0084-005X   Wiener Studien **5195**
0084-0068   Wiener Voelkerkundliche Mitteilungen **361**
0084-0076   Wiener Zeitschrift fuer die Kunde des Morgenlandes **563**
0084-0084   Wiener Zeitschrift fuer die Kunde Suedasiens und Archiv fuer Indische Philosophie **6961**
0084-0092   Wiener Zeitschrift fuer Nervenheilkunde und deren Grenzgebiete. Supplement†
0084-0106   Wijsgerige Teksten en Studies†
0084-0114   Wilderness Report†
0084-0122   Wildlife Behavior and Ecology **711**
0084-0149   Wildlife Circular, Victoria†
0084-0173   Wildlife Monographs **968**
0084-0181   Wiley American Republic Series†
0084-019X   Wiley Series on Systems Engineering and Analysis†
0084-0203   Wiley Series on the Science and Technology of Materials†
0084-0238   William-Frederick Poets Series†
0084-0246   William K. McInally Lecture **1194**
0084-0270   William Morris Society. Annual Report **648**
0084-0297   Williamsburg in America Series
0084-0300   Williamsburg Research Studies†
0084-036X   Child Guidance Clinic of Winnipeg. Annual Report†
0084-0386   Winter Sports in Scotland†
0084-0394   Winter's Tales†
0084-0416   Winterthur Portfolio **526**
0084-0424   Wire Industry Yearbook *changed to* Equip4wire.Com **6311**
0084-0459   Wireless World Diary†
0084-0467   Wirkung der Literatur†
0084-0505   Wisconsin Academy of Sciences, Arts and Letters. Transactions **7929**
0084-0513   Wisconsin Business Monographs
0084-0521   Wisconsin Business Papers†
0084-053X   Wisconsin China Series†
0084-0556   Wisconsin. Department of Natural Resources. Research Report **3475**
0084-0564   Wisconsin. Department of Natural Resources. Technical Bulletin Series **2633**
0084-0572   Wisconsin. Department of Transportation. Division of Planning and Budget. Highway Mileage Data **8532**
0084-0580   Wisconsin. Department of Transportation. Division of Planning. Highway Traffic
0084-0599   Wisconsin Economy Studies **1195**
0084-0602   Wisconsin. Governor's Advocacy Committee on Children and Youth Annual Report†
0084-0610   Wisconsin Project Reports†
0084-067X   Wisconsin State Historical Society. Urban History Group. Newsletter†
0084-0734   University of Wisconsin, Madison. Applied Population Laboratory. Population Notes **7295**
0084-0742   University of Wisconsin, Madison. Applied Population Laboratory. Population Series **7295**
0084-0769   University of Wisconsin at Madison. Institute for Research on Poverty. Reprint Series **8013**
0084-0785   Land Tenure Center. Newsletter†
0084-0793   Land Tenure Center. Paper†
0084-0807   University of Wisconsin, Madison. Land Tenure Center. Reprint **208**
0084-0815   Land Tenure Center. Research Paper **202**
0084-0823   University of Wisconsin, Madison. Land Tenure Center. Training and Methods Series†
0084-0831   University of Wisconsin-Milwaukee. Center for Latin America. Discussion Paper Series **4316**
0084-084X   University of Wisconsin at Milwaukee. Center for Latin America. Essay Series†
0084-0890   University of Wisconsin. Mathematical Research Center Series†
0084-0904   Wisdom†
0084-0912   Wissenschaftliche Alpenvereinshefte **4034**
0084-0947   Wissenschaftliche Normung†
0084-0955   Die Wissenschaftliche Redaktion†
0084-0963   Wissenschaftliche Taschenbuecher. Reihe Biologie†
0084-0971   Wissenschaftliche Taschenbuecher. Reihe Chemie†
0084-098X   Wissenschaftliche Taschenbuecher. Reihe Mathematik - Physik†
0084-1013   Wistar Institute Symposium Monograph†

0084-1137   Woodrow Wilson National Fellowship Foundation. Newsletter **3010**
0084-1145   Woodrow Wilson National Fellowship Foundation. Annual Report **3010**
0084-117X   Woodstock Papers: Occasional Essays for Theology†
0084-1226   Woolhope Naturalists' Field Club, Herefordshire. Transactions **424**
0084-1242   Woolner Indological Series **6961**
0084-1250   Words: Wai-Te-Ata Studies in Literature†
0084-1323   Working Press of the Nation *changed to* 0000-1783 **8937**
0084-1366   World Air Transport Statistics **8532**
0084-1374   World Airline Record†
0084-1382   The World Almanac and Book of Facts **3123**
0084-1404   World Association for the Advancement of Veterinary Parasitology. Proceedings of Conference†
0084-1412   World Association of Girl Guides and Girl Scouts. Report of Conference
0084-1439   World Book Year Book
0084-1455   WorldBusiness Perspectives†
0084-1463   World Cars†
0084-1471   World Cartography† **8999**
0084-1498   World Collectors Annuary†
0084-1501   World Commerce Annual
0084-151X   World Confederation for Physical Therapy. Proceedings of the Congress
0084-1544   Trade Unions International of Chemical, Oil and Allied Workers. International Trade Conference. Documents **4603**
0084-1552   World Conference on Animal Production. Proceedings **304**
0084-1560   World Conference on Earthquake Engineering. Proceedings†
0084-1595   World Congress of Anaesthesiologists. Proceedings
0084-1609   World Congress of Psychiatry. Proceedings **6189**
0084-1641   World Congress on Fertility and Sterility. Proceedings **6006**
0084-165X   World Congress on the Prevention of Occupational Accidents and Diseases. Proceedings **6689**
0084-1668   World Council of Churches. Commission on World Mission and Evangelism. Research Pamphlets†
0084-1676   World Council of Churches. General Assembly. Assembly - Reports **7695**
0084-1684   World Council of Churches. Minutes and Reports of the Central Committee Meeting **7695**
0084-1692   World Council of Churches. World Council Studies†
0084-1706   World Crafts Council. General Assembly. Proceedings of the Biennial Meeting
0084-1722   World Energy Conference. Plenary Conferences. Transactions
0084-1730   World Energy Conference. Survey of Energy Resources
0084-1765   World Federation of Hemophilia. Proceedings of Congress **5942**
0084-1781   World Fellowship of Buddhists. Book Series **7703**
0084-179X   World Food Problems†
0084-1811   World Forestry Congress. Proceedings†
0084-182X   World Grain Trade Statistics†
0084-1854   World Jersey Cattle Bureau. Conference Reports
0084-1862   World Jute Directory
0084-1870   World List of Social Science Periodicals **8022**
0084-1897   World Medical Association. General Assembly. Proceedings†
0084-1927   World Meteorological Organization. Congress. Abridged Report with Resolutions **6399**
0084-1935   World Meteorological Congress. Proceedings *see* 0250-9237 **6393**
0084-1978   Global Atmospheric Research Programme. Publication Series†
0084-1986   Global Atmospheric Research Programme. G A R P Special Reports†
0084-1994   World Meteorological Organization. Annual Report *see* 0250-8893 **6397**
0084-2001   World Meteorological Organization. Reports on Marine Science Affairs **2821**
0084-201X   World Meteorological Organization. Technical Notes **6399**
0084-2028   World Money Guide†
0084-2036   World Motor Vehicle Production and Registration†
0084-2044   World Movement of Mothers. Reports of Meetings **8079**
0084-2052   World Muslim Conference. Proceedings **7717**
0084-2060   World Muslim Gazetteer **7717**
0084-2117   World of Learning (Year) **2963**
0084-2141   World Peace through Law Center. Pamphlet Series†
0084-2176   World Petroleum Congress. Proceedings **6797**
0084-2206   World Psychiatric Association. Bulletin†
0084-2230   World Review of Nutrition and Dietetics **6671**
0084-2257   U.S. Department of State. World Strength of the Communist Party Organizations. Annual Report.†
0084-2273   World Tobacco Directory **8489**
0084-2281   World Today Series: Africa **4179**
0084-2311   World Today Series: Middle East and South Asia **4190**
0084-2338   World Today Series: Western Europe **4279**
0084-2346   World Touring and Automobile Organization. Documentation for Traffic Engineering and Safety Study Weeks
0084-2370   World Trade Union Congress. Reports†
0084-2419   World University Service. Annual Report†
0084-2427   World University Service. Programme of Action†
0084-2435   World Veterinary Association. Catalogue of Veterinary Films and Films of Veterinary Interest
0084-2443   World Veterinary Congress. Proceedings **8815**
0084-2451   World Weather Watch Planning Reports **6400**
0084-2486   Worldwide Register of Adult Education **2947**
0084-2494   World Wildlife Series†
0084-2508   World Yearbook of Education **2926**
0084-2516   World Zionist Organization. General Council. Addresses, Debates, Resolutions
0084-2559   Worldview†
0084-2567   Worldwide Directory of National Technical Information Services†
0084-2583   Worldwide Petrochemical Directory
0084-2613   Der Wormsgau **4279**

ISSN

ISSN

0085-7653 Venezuela. Ministerio de Agricultura y Cria. Direccion de Economia y Estadistica Agropecuaria. Division de Estadistica. Plan de Trabajo
0085-7661 Verbaende, Behoerden, Organisationen der Wirtschaft **1524**
0085-770X Victoria, Australia. Department of Agriculture. Technical Bulletin†
0085-7718 Vegetable Growers Digest†
0085-7726 Victoria, Australia. Education Department. Curriculum and Research Branch. Research Reports†
0085-7769 Victoria, Australia. Geological Survey. Memoirs†
0085-7823 Vietnamese Studies **4190**
0085-784X Vocational Training in New York City: Where to Find It†
0085-7858 Wagga Wagga and District Historical Society. Journal† **8998**
0085-7866 Waigani Seminar. Papers **4194**
0085-7904 Washington Center for Metropolitan Studies. Metropolitan Bulletin†
0085-7920 University of Washington Publications in Anthropology†
0085-7939 University of Washington Publications in Fisheries†
0085-7947 University of Washington Publications on Language and Literature†
0085-798X Washington University. Institute for Urban and Regional Studies. Working Paper†
0085-8021 Water Research Foundation of Australia. Research Report†
0085-803X Weed Society of New South Wales. Proceedings†
0085-8099 West Virginia Education Directory **2926**
0085-8137 Western Australia. Geological Survey. Bulletin **2774**
0085-8161 Western Australia Law Almanac **4812**
0085-8188 Western Canadian Steam Locomotive Directory
0085-820X Whiteacre
0085-8226 Wisconsin. Department of Administration. Annual Fiscal Report **7477**
0085-8250 Witchcraft Digest†
0085-8269 Women's Rights Law Reporter **4815**
0085-8293 World Bank Atlas *changed to* The Atlas of Global Development **1591**
0085-8307 World Motor Vehicle Data†
0085-8315 World Population Data Sheet **7295**
0085-834X Yamagata Daigaku Kiyo (Kogaku) **3227**
0085-8374 York Journal of Convocation **7695**
0085-8382 Your Australian Garden
0085-8420 Eidgenoessische Sternwarte, Zurich. Astronomische Mitteilungen†
0088-7714 Materiali e Documenti Ticinesi **4242**
0090-0036 American Journal of Public Health **7507**
0090-0044 National Union Catalog of Manuscript Collections†
0090-0079 MEDI-KWOC Index†
0090-0222 The Great Lakes Entomologist **848**
0090-0427 Environmental Science Research **3429**
0090-0443 Current Concepts in Nutrition†
0090-0486 Environment Film Review†
0090-0494 Obesity & Bariatric Medicine†
0090-0508 Current Contents: Agriculture, Biology & Environmental Sciences **178**
0090-0559 Clinical Trends in Family Practice†
0090-0575 International Bibliography on Burns
0090-0591 C T F A Cosmetic Journal†
0090-0648 Fodor's Ireland **8707**
0090-0656 Fishery Bulletin **3593**
0090-0729 Institute of Environmental Sciences and Technology. Tutorial Series **3440**
0090-0737 Pennsylvania Crop Reporting Service. Pennsylvania Orchard and Vineyard Survey†
0090-0753 Index of Tissue Culture†
0090-077X New Jersey Developmental Disabilities Council. Annual Report **8058**
0090-0834 Optical Management†
0090-0842 Consensus†
0090-0893 N F A I S Newsletter†
0090-0923 Family Planning - Population Reporter†
0090-1032 Harvard Political Review **7140**
0090-1059 Oregon. Department of Education. Racial and Ethnic Survey†
0090-1091 Journal of Clinical Computing
0090-1156 U.S. Centers for Disease Control. Brucellosis Surveillance: Annual Summary†
0090-1164 Current Citations on Strabismus, Amblyopia, and Other Diseases of Ocular Motility†
0090-1237 Claudel Studies†
0090-1245 Index of Dermatology†
0090-1326 Recurring Bibliography of Hypertension†
0090-1377 Cumulated Abridged Index Medicus†
0090-1393 Annual Bibliography of Orthopaedic Surgery†
0090-1407 Cerebrovascular Bibliography†
0090-1423 Cumulated Index Medicus†
0090-1482 Journal of Alcohol and Drug Education **2695**
0090-1520 Florida. Legislature. Joint Legislative Management Committee. Summary of General Legislation†
0090-161X Bio-Medical Insight†
0090-1652 Biology of Brain Dysfunction†
0090-1830 Marine Fisheries Review **3601**
0090-1881 American Psychiatric Association. Scientific Proceedings in Summary Form†
0090-1903 Norda Briefs†
0090-1911 Vibrational Spectra and Structure **2142**
0090-192X Key Systems Guide†
0090-1938 Journal of Erie Studies **4299**
0090-1954 Symposium on Creation†
0090-1989 Directory: North Dakota City Officials **7491**
0090-1997 Florida Symposium on Automata and Semigroups†
0090-2020 Penthouse **6297**
0090-2047 Oui
0090-2071 Proteus†
0090-2233 Hawaii. Commission on Aging. Report of Achievements of Programs for the Aging
0090-239X U.S. Forest Service. Forest Service Research Accomplishments
0090-2403 U.S. National Cancer Institute. Report of the Carcinogenesis Program†
0090-2411 A E Legal Newsletter **4607**
0090-242X The Budget **7733**
0090-2462 Cotton Digest International†
0090-2500 Adit†
0090-2519 Contamination Control/Biomedical Environments†
0090-2578 Sunset Christmas Ideas and Answers†
0090-2594 Vanderbilt Journal of Transnational Law **4944**
0090-2616 Organizational Dynamics **1784**
0090-2683 Hourly Precipitation Data. Arkansas **6354**
0090-2756 Connecticut. Department of Correction. Research Report
0090-2764 University of Georgia. College of Agriculture. Cooperative Extension Service. Leaflet **166**
0090-2810 World Currency Charts
0090-2845 U.S. Copyright Office. Annual Report of the Register of Copyrights **6759**
0090-287X Annual Review of the Schizophrenic Syndrome†
0090-2926 U.S. Environmental Protection Agency. Journal Holdings Report†
0090-2934 Dialysis & Transplantation **6267**
0090-2977 Neurophysiology **6167**
0090-2985 Carnival & Circus Booking Guide†
0090-3000 Cinemagic†
0090-3019 Surgical Neurology **6260**
0090-3108 Current Citations on Communications Disorders: Language, Speech, and Voice†
0090-3132 National Library of Medicine. Current Catalog†
0090-3159 Contemporary Ob-Gyn **5988**
0090-3213 Planetarian **579**
0090-3221 State of Nebraska Uniform Crime Report **2669**
0090-3248 Illinois. Housing Development Authority. Annual Report **4415**
0090-3280 Non-G P O Imprints Received in the Library of Congress†
0090-3353 Rock Scene
0090-3361 Keyboard Arts
0090-3493 Critical Care Medicine **5601**
0090-3507 Petroleum and Chemical Industry Conference. Record of Conference Papers **3252**
0090-3558 Journal of Wildlife Diseases **8802**
0090-3612 Puerto Rico Official Industrial Directory **2024**
0090-3647 American Bar Association. Section of Administrative Law. Annual Reports of Committees†
0090-3663 Music World Magazine†
0090-3671 Year Book of Surgery **6263**
0090-3736 U.S. Library of Congress. Accessions List: Sri Lanka†
0090-3744 U.S. Library of Congress. Accessions List: Nepal†
0090-3752 Nuclear Data Sheets **3171**
0090-3779 Appalachian Journal **4284**
0090-3817 Lutheran Historical Conference. Essays and Reports **7765**
0090-3825 Management World†
0090-3833 Destination: Philadelphia†
0090-3949 Cross-Talk†
0090-3973 Journal of Testing and Evaluation **3351**
0090-3981 High Fidelity's Test Reports†
0090-399X Realty Bluebook
0090-4007 Country Music†
0090-4023 Successful Ventures in Contemporary Education in Oklahoma†
0090-4066 Directory of Corporate Urban Affairs Officers†
0090-4074 National Directory of Providers of Psychiatric Services to Religious Institutions†
0090-4082 Outstanding Elementary Teachers of America†
0090-4112 Critiques†
0090-4171 Stations†
0090-418X Who's Who in the Securities Industry†
0090-4198 Indiana Law Review **4692**
0090-4244 Journal of Adult Education **2943**
0090-4260 Literature Film Quarterly **6506**
0090-4295 Urology **6276**
0090-4309 Annual Editions: Business and Management†
0090-4325 Montana. Office of the Legislative Auditor. Department of Institutions Reimbursements Program; Report on Audit†
0090-4341 Archives of Environmental Contamination and Toxicology **3494**
0090-4368 G H S Foot-Notes *changed to* Georgia History Today **4293**
0090-4392 Journal of Community Psychology **7371**
0090-4406 Photography Year†
0090-4414 Amateur Athletic Union of the United States. Official A A U Basketball Handbook†
0090-4449 Evaluation and Change†
0090-4481 Pediatric Annals **6100**
0090-449X Clark County History **4289**
0090-452X Catskills†
0090-4546 Virginia Woolf Quarterly†
0090-4570 Rag Times **6609**
0090-4589 Job Safety and Health†
0090-4600 Tax Management International Journal **1948**
0090-4848 Human Resource Management **1864**
0090-4856 Iowa Wildlife Research Bulletin
0090-4945 Directory of Consulting Specialists†
0090-4961 Sunday Clothes†
0090-502X Memory and Cognition **7384**
0090-5070 The Groundwater Newsletter†
0090-5089 K A F P Journal **5656**
0090-516X Pollution Technology Review†
0090-5232 L C Science Tracer Bullet **7937**
0090-5259 Scene†
0090-5267 Control and Dynamic Systems: Advances in Theory and Applications†
0090-5291 Electronics Buyers' Guide†
0090-5305 Pocket Playboy†
0090-5364 Annals of Statistics **8345**
0090-5402 Modern Paint & Coatings Paint Red Book **6719**
0090-5496 Oregon. State Board of Education. ESEA Title III State Plan†
0090-5542 Basic Life Sciences **656**
0090-5550 Rehabilitation Psychology **7402**
0090-5569 Selected Abstracts on Animal Models for Biomedical Research†
0090-5631 Meat Science Institute. Proceedings **3656**
0090-5674 Paideuma **5348**
0090-5747 Sage Urban Studies Abstracts *changed to* Urban Studies Abstracts **4437**
0090-5771 Chrysanthemum **3727**
0090-5844 North Carolina Folklore Journal **3621**
0090-5917 Political Theory **7169**
0090-5968 Management of the California State Water Project†
0090-5992 Nationalities Papers **7987**
0090-6034 Cricket **2184**
0090-6077 Connecticut. Department on Aging. Report to the Governor and General Assembly†
0090-6093 Cowan Clan United. Newsletter†
0090-6360 Atomic Physics†
0090-6425 Minnesota. State Board of Health. Biennial Report†
0090-6433 Better Homes and Gardens Hundreds of Ideas†
0090-6484 Directory of Executive Recruiters *changed to* The Directory of Executive and Professional Recruiters **1986**
0090-6514 Telos **6956**
0090-6549 Infectious Disease Reviews†
0090-6557 Tennessee Pocket Data Book†
0090-6611 Popular Computing (Calabasas)†
0090-6654 Evaluations of Drug Interactions **6839**
0090-6670 M H†
0090-6700 Official Museum Directory **6535**
0090-6743 Montana. Department of Public Instruction. Descriptive Report of Program Activities for Vocational Education†
0090-6778 I E E E Transactions on Communications **2324**
0090-6808 U.S. Environmental Protection Agency. Office of Research and Development. Selected Irrigation Return Flow Quality Abstracts†
0090-6816 U S A N and the U S P Dictionary of Drug Names *changed to* 1076-4275 **6884**
0090-6883 Synthesis (Cambridge)†
0090-6905 Journal of Psycholinguistic Research **5135**
0090-693X Community-Clinical Psychology Series†
0090-6964 Annals of Biomedical Engineering **5575**
0090-709X New Mexico. Bureau of Geology and Mineral Resources. Hydrologic Report†
0090-7103 World Affairs Report **7274**
0090-7111 Census of Maine Manufactures **1882**
0090-712X Waterway Guide - Northern **8284**
0090-7286 Topical New Issues†
0090-7324 Reference Services Review **5042**
0090-7383 Conference on Data Systems Languages. Data Base Task Group. Report
0090-7421 Journal of Allied Health **7528**
0090-7790 Black Perspective in Music†
0090-7820 Bonnes Feuilles†
0090-7847 Railroad History **8623**
0090-7855 P A A B S Revista†
0090-7863 U.S. National Credit Union Administration. N C U A Quarterly†
0090-7944 Columbia Human Rights Law Review **4645**
0090-7987 Children's Book Review Service†
0090-8002 U.S. Emergency Loan Guarantee Board. Annual Report†
0090-8029 Auto Racing Digest† **8934**
0090-8142 Western Society of Weed Science. Research Progress Report **822**
0090-8177 Minnesota. Department of Natural Resources. Biennial Report
0090-8185 Dirt Bike Buyer's Guide†
0090-8258 Gynecologic Oncology **5992**
0090-8266 Graduate & Professional School Opportunities for Minority Students†
0090-8282 Insect World Digest†
0090-8290 Canadian - American Slavic Studies **4446**
0090-8304 U.S. Library of Congress. Accessions List. Bangladesh†
0090-8312 Energy Sources *changed to* 1556-7036 **3133**
0090-8312 Energy Sources *changed to* 1556-7249 **3133**
0090-8320 Ocean Development and International Law **2814**
0090-8363 Chemical Abstracts - Applied Chemistry and Chemical Engineering Sections **2093**
0090-8479 Venereal Disease Bibliography†
0090-8517 Connecticut River Valley Covered Bridge Society. Bulletin†
0090-8584 Current Topics in Comparative Pathobiology†
0090-8592 Behavior of Nonhuman Primates: Modern Research Trends†
0090-8614 A L A Sights to See Book†
0090-8622 American Review†
0090-8657 Tire Science and Technology **7827**
0090-8738 Bromeliad Society. Journal **782**
0090-8762 Practical Horseman **8296**
0090-8800 Contemporary Topics in Molecular Immunology†
0090-8843 Alabama Marine Resources Bulletin†
0090-8878 Household & Personal Products Industry **1819**
0090-8886 Infectious Diseases†
0090-8932 Render **150**
0090-8967 Illinois Institute for Environmental Quality. Annual Report†
0090-8991 New York Mercantile Exchange Statistical Yearbook†
0090-905X Iowa Genealogical Society. Surname Index†
0090-9084 Journal of Police Science and Administration†
0090-9114 Americana *changed to* 1077-8780
0090-9130 Index of American Periodical Verse† **8964**
0090-9203 H I S S News-Journal†
0090-9300 Maryland Geographer†
0090-9319 Woman's Day 101 Gardening & Outdoor Ideas†
0090-9327 Penny Stock Handbook
0090-9386 Maine. Criminal Justice Planning & Assistance Agency. Criminal Justice Internship Program. Report and Evaluation
0090-9440 Hawaii. Department of Education. Office of Business Services. Report on Federally Connected Pupils: Hawaii Public Schools†
0090-9467 Foreign Economic Trends and Their Implications for the United States†
0090-9475 Exporter's Encyclopedia-United States Marketing Guide†
0090-9521 Architecture Plus†

ISSN

0091-8873 Alaska State Chamber of Commerce. Membership Directory†
0091-8903 Rhode Island Dental Journal†
0091-8938 Student Enrollment Report; West Virginia Institutions of Higher Education†
0091-8954 Product Safety Up to Date†
0091-8962 Iowa. Department of Public Instruction. Summary of Federal Programs†
0091-9004 North Dakota. Geological Survey. Educational Series **2759**
0091-9047 Michigan Business and Economic Research Bibliography†
0091-9128 Nebraska. Commission on Law Enforcement and Criminal Justice. Criminal Justice Comprehensive Plan†
0091-9144 Centrum†
0091-9195 Nebraska. Commission on Law Enforcement and Criminal Justice. Criminal Justice Action Plan†
0091-9217 Best Science Fiction†
0091-9233 Puerto Rico. Department of Labor. Bureau of Labor Statistics. Employment Hours and Earnings in the Manufacturing Establishments Promoted by the Economic Development Administration of the Puerto Rican Industrial Development Company†
0091-925X Johns Hopkins University. Population Information Program. Population Reports. Series J. Family Planning Programs
0091-9276 Johns Hopkins University. Population Information Program. Population Reports. Series G. Prostaglandins†
0091-9284 Johns Hopkins University. Population Information Program. Population Reports. Series F. Pregnancy Termination†
0091-9322 Temperature: Its Measurement and Control in Science and Industry†
0091-9357 American Book Prices Current **7577**
0091-9403 U.S. Bureau of Labor Statistics. Employment and Wages†
0091-9446 North Dakota. Milk Stabilization Board. Annual Report of Administrative Activities **268**
0091-9500 U.S. National Oceanographic Data Center. Key to Oceanographic Records Documentation†
0091-956X Report from N J D A†
0091-9578 Plastics Engineering **7097**
0091-9586 Kansas Country Living **130**
0091-9659 Northwest Journal of African and Black American Studies†
0091-9691 Utah Bar Journal **4806**
0091-9721 Contraceptive Technology **971**
0091-9837 Environmental Defense Fund. Annual Report **3424**
0091-9845 Hawaii Observer†
0091-9942 Florida. Governor. Annual Report on State Housing Goals†
0091-9993 No-Till Farmer **140**
0092-0002 International Decade of Ocean Exploration. Progress Report†
0092-0177 Florida. Division of Motor Vehicles. Tags and Revenue **8496**
0092-0193 Ion Exchange and Solvent Extraction **2136**
0092-0258 Stanford Review†
0092-0320 U.S. Coast Guard. Polluting Incidents in and Around U.S. Waters†
0092-0371 A A M C Curriculum Directory (Print Edition) *changed to* A A M C Curriculum Directory (Online Edition) **3049**
0092-0436 Disc and That
0092-0479 Powder Coating Conference†
0092-0509 Powder Diffraction File Search Manual. Alphabetical Listing. Inorganic **2104**
0092-0517 Journal of Country Music **6580**
0092-0525 Jazz Digest
0092-0541 Solid Waste Management: Abstracts from the Literature†
0092-055X Teaching Sociology **8143**
0092-0576 Powder Diffraction File Search Manual. Organic **2129**
0092-0606 Journal of Biological Physics **753**
0092-0614 Directory of Louisiana Cities, Towns and Villages†
0092-0673 Louisiana Annual Rural Manpower Report†
0092-0703 Academy of Marketing Science. Journal **1803**
0092-0789 Devil's Box†
0092-0959 Baldwin's Ohio Legislative Service **4625**
0092-1025 Outstanding Secondary Educators of America†
0092-1068 American Hunter **8303**
0092-1084 Nevada. Commission on Crime, Delinquency and Corrections. Comprehensive Law Enforcement Plan†
0092-1270 Virgin Islands Register†
0092-1289 Camp Fire Leadership†
0092-1300 Powder Diffraction File Search Manual. Fink Method. Inorganic†
0092-1327 American Art Review **465**
0092-1335 Annual Reports in Inorganic and General Syntheses†
0092-1491 National Defense **6438**
0092-1505 Nebraska. Commission on Law Enforcement and Criminal Justice. Legislative Reporter†
0092-153X Texas Field Crop Statistics†
0092-1548 Brookhaven Highlights **3165**
0092-1599 U.S. National Credit Union Administration. Research Report†
0092-1602 New Jersey. Division of Water Resources. Special Report†
0092-1661 Symposium on Incremental Motion Control Systems and Devices. Proceedings **5460**
0092-1696 Nebraska. Fisheries Division. Annual Report **3602**
0092-1726 North Carolina. Secretary of State. North Carolina Elections†
0092-1734 New Fishing
0092-1777 Hawaii. Department of Education. Educational Directory: State & District Office **2862**
0092-1785 U.S. Agricultural Research Service. A R S - N C **164**
0092-1793 Fremontia **790**
0092-1815 International Journal of Instructional Media **3065**
0092-1858 Alaska Blue Book†
0092-1866 Intercultural Studies Information Service†
0092-1904 United States Government Manual **7190**
0092-1912 Fiction International **5296**

0092-1939 U.S. Agricultural Research Service. A R S-S†
0092-2056 National Hurricane Operations Plan **6392**
0092-2102 Interfaces (Hanover) **1754**
0092-2242 University of California, Los Angeles. Latin American Center. Latin American Activities and Resources†
0092-2307 H I S S Titles and Review†
0092-2315 American Journal of Criminal Law **2643**
0092-2323 Journal of Indo-European Studies **7979**
0092-2374 Utah Export Directory†
0092-2463 New Times (New York)†
0092-2471 Chicagoan†
0092-2501 Electrical World Directory of Electric Utilities in Latin America, Bermuda and the Caribbean Islands **3157**
0092-2528 Oklahoma Water Resources Research Institute. Annual Report **8830**
0092-2560 Weekly California Citator
0092-2633 National Peach Council. Proceedings†
0092-2684 Colorado Water Resources Circulars†
0092-2811 American Coin-Op **2242**
0092-2870 Air Freight Directory **8534**
0092-2900 Perspectives in Nephrology and Hypertension†
0092-3052 Homosexual Counseling Journal†
0092-3060 Oregon. Office of Community Health Services. Local Health Services Annual Summary†
0092-3117 U.S. Department of Transportation. Fiscal Year Budget in Brief†
0092-3168 Guide to U S Government Publications **7480**
0092-3311 New Jersey. Department of Environmental Protection. Annual Report **3456**
0092-332X U.S. Geological Survey. Water Resources Investigations **2798**
0092-3362 Massachusetts. Division of Mineral Resources. Annual Report†
0092-3419 National Indian Law Library. Catalogue†
0092-3427 Tennessee Thrusts†
0092-3435 Occupational Safety and Health Decisions†
0092-3478 American Baptist Churches in the U S A Yearbook†
0092-3486 Annual Index to Popular Music Record Reviews†
0092-3524 Iustitia (Bloomington)†
0092-3540 Texscope: U S A Textile Industry Overview **8459**
0092-3591 Overview of the F A A Engineering & Development Programs **67**
0092-3664 Fluoridation Census **5845**
0092-3761 Data on Iowa's Area Schools†
0092-380X Washington State†
0092-3818 Illinois Services Directory **2005**
0092-3826 Alcoholism Treatment Facilities Directory: United States and Canada†
0092-3877 Bar†
0092-394X Newsletter for Research in Mental Health & Behavioral Sciences†
0092-3974 International Directory of Little Magazines and Small Presses **7578**
0092-4032 Medical Challenge†
0092-4091 Present Tense†
0092-4113 W P A S Museletter **6627**
0092-4148 World Today Series: Latin America **4318**
0092-4164 Where the Trails Cross **3787**
0092-4180 Better Homes and Gardens Crafts & Sewing†
0092-4229 Speed (Beloit)†
0092-4245 Wesleyan Theological Journal **7780**
0092-427X Arctic Bulletin†
0092-4288 University of Nevada. Seismological Laboratory. Bulletin **2791**
0092-430X Pepperdine Law Review **4757**
0092-4318 Platte Valley Review **2297**
0092-4334 B I S Conference Report†
0092-4369 University of Arizona. Agricultural Experiment Station. Research Report **166**
0092-4407 Managers†
0092-4415 Primitive Baptist Yearbook
0092-4423 Resource Guide to Reading & Language Arts Programs & Materials†
0092-4458 L D A Journal **5854**
0092-4466 Hearing Instruments†
0092-4520 Equity News **4593**
0092-4563 Syntax and Semantics **5184**
0092-4571 Border States **4286**
0092-4598 Who's Who in Training and Development† **8998**
0092-4601 N A D A Recreation Vehicle Appraisal Guide **8594**
0092-4679 National Security Traders Association. Traders' Annual†
0092-4733 Michigan State University. Institute for Community Development and Services. Population Report. Community Development Series†
0092-4768 American Institute of Certified Public Accountants. Committee on Minority Recruitment and Equal Opportunity. Report†
0092-4857 M E I Marketing Economics Guide†
0092-4865 R E I T Handbook of Member Trusts†
0092-4873 A P W A Reporter **3258**
0092-489X Artes Visuales
0092-4989 International Directory of Executive Recruiters†
0092-5012 Polymer-Plastics Technology and Engineering (Hardcover Edition) *see* 0360-2559 **2129**
0092-5039 Franklin Mint Almanac†
0092-5055 Annual of Psychoanalysis **7334**
0092-5144 Vermont Facts and Figures†
0092-5268 Grants and Awards Available to American Writers **5302**
0092-5306 Best of National Lampoon†
0092-5322 Fusilier (La Puente)†
0092-5349 Michigan. State Library Services. Catalog of Books on Magnetic Tape†
0092-5438 Youth Reporter†
0092-5470 Developments in Human Services Series†
0092-5535 Panjandrum Poetry Journal **5429**
0092-5594 U.S. Centers for Disease Control. Congenital Malformations Surveillance **5828**
0092-5659 American Lung Association. Bulletin†
0092-5667 Healthnews†
0092-5675 Academy Awards Oscar Annual
0092-5691 National Education Association of the United States. Annual Summative Evaluation Report

0092-5756 Bibliography of Noise†
0092-5764 Connecticut Walk Book **8310**
0092-5810 Vermont's Fisheries Annual†
0092-5853 American Journal of Political Science **7105**
0092-590X American History and Culture†
0092-5950 N M R I Compensation in Mass Retailing, Salaries and Incentives†
0092-5969 Popular Sports Face-off†
0092-6000 Current Literature in Family Planning†
0092-6019 Immunology Series†
0092-6027 Microbiology Series†
0092-606X Degrees Conferred by West Virginia Institutions of Higher Education†
0092-6108 Title Varies†
0092-6175 Transportation and Products Legal Directory†
0092-623X Journal of Sex & Marital Therapy **7380**
0092-6256 Aurora A F X Road Racing Handbook†
0092-6280 Association for Educational Data Systems. Handbook and Directory†
0092-6302 Semiconductor Heat Sink, Socket & Associated Hardware D.A.T.A. Book†
0092-6345 Iowa State Journal of Research†
0092-6353 Horse Play†
0092-6361 Current Contents: Social & Behavioral Sciences **7417**
0092-640X Atomic Data and Nuclear Data Tables **7065**
0092-6426 Limits in the Seas **4970**
0092-6493 Annual Antitrust Law Institute **4855**
0092-6507 Auerbach Annual: Best Computer Papers†
0092-654X Illustrated Digest of Pro Football†
0092-6558 Interdenominational Theological Center. Journal **7650**
0092-6566 Journal of Research in Personality **7379**
0092-6639 Women's Organizations & Leaders Directory
0092-6736 Alaska. Department of Revenue. State Investment Portfolio **1610**
0092-6752 Pesticides (Sacramento)†
0092-6876 Automatic Taxfinder and Tax Preparer's Handbook†
0092-6884 Daily Tax Report **1919**
0092-6930 Cajal Club. Proceedings
0092-7147 Daily Bread **7734**
0092-718X Letters & Papers on the Social Sciences: an Undergraduate Review†
0092-7201 Linear Integrated Circuits and M.O.S. Devices†
0092-721X R C A Corporation. Solid State Division. R. F. Power Devices†
0092-7228 Thyristors, Rectifiers, and Diacs†
0092-735X Continuing Education for the Family Physician†
0092-7392 Index to the Contemporary Scene†
0092-7481 Urban Institute. Annual Report **1190**
0092-7643 Overseas Development Council. Annual Report **1602**
0092-7651 Archives of Podiatric Medicine and Foot Surgery†
0092-7678 Asian Affairs: An American Review **7222**
0092-7686 Booklegger†
0092-7694 Cason Quarterly
0092-7708 Conch Review of Books
0092-7724 Past and Likely Future of 58 Research Libraries, 1951-1980: a Statistical Study of Growth and Change†
0092-7732 Product Safety and Liability Reporter **7536**
0092-7767 Predicasts Source Directory†
0092-7813 Children's Hospital National Medical Center. Clinical Proceedings†
0092-7864 Commodity Journal†
0092-7872 Communications in Algebra **5479**
0092-7880 Department of the Army Historical Summary **6419**
0092-7899 Mississippi Educational Directory†
0092-7929 Annual of New Art and Artists†
0092-7937 Pennsylvania. Citizens Advisory Council to the Department of Environmental Protection. Annual Report **3459**
0092-7953 Genealogical Society of Old Tryon County. Bulletin **3768**
0092-797X Keeping Up with Orff Schulwerk in the Classroom†
0092-7996 Texas Yearbook†
0092-8089 Adsorption and Adsorbents†
0092-8119 Best Science Fiction Stories of the Year
0092-8208 Children's Literature (Baltimore) **5273**
0092-8216 Cord Sportfacts: Hunting†
0092-8240 Bulletin of Mathematical Biology **663**
0092-833X Maine Library Directory **5031**
0092-8364 District of Columbia. City Council. Annual Report†
0092-8372 The Disciple (Saint Louis)†
0092-8380 Encyclopedia of Governmental Advisory Organizations **7435**
0092-8410 N A C D S Lilly Digest†
0092-8429 U.S. Library of Congress. Processing Department. Newsletter
0092-847X University of Wisconsin, Madison. Institute for Research on Poverty. Research Report†
0092-8488 State Planning Issues (Washington)
0092-8518 Directory: Who's Who in Nuclear Energy
0092-8526 Directory Listing Curriculums Offered in the Community Colleges of Pennsylvania†
0092-8550 U.S. General Accounting Office. Office of the General Counsel. Quarterly Digest of Unpublished Decisions of the Comptroller General of the United States; Procurement Law†
0092-8577 Health Affairs†
0092-8593 A P C D Digest†
0092-8607 Biomedical Communications†
0092-8615 Drug Information Journal **6835**
0092-8631 St. Luke's Hospital. Medical Staff Journal
0092-8666 Bell Tower **4330**
0092-8674 Cell **828**
0092-8682 Current Medical Diagnosis and Treatment **5602**
0092-8712 Occupational Safety and Health Statistics of the Federal Government **6691**
0092-8828 P B X Systems Guide
0092-8887 Creative Guitar International†
0092-8933 Police and Law Enforcement† **8981**
0092-9018 Inspiration Three†
0092-9077 University of Georgia. Cooperative Extension Service. Bulletin **166**

0093-9390 Michigan. Office of Criminal Justice. Comprehensive Law Enforcement and Criminal Justice Plan†
0093-9404 Overview of Blood†
0093-9528 Dun & Bradstreet Reference Book of Transportation
0093-9552 Illinois State and Regional Economic Data Book†
0093-9579 Semiotexte
0093-9625 Hawaii Review **5304**
0093-9692 U.S. Department of Commerce. Effects of Pollution Abatement on International Trade†
0093-9714 Research Advances in Alcohol & Drug Problems†
0093-9722 Urology Times **6276**
0093-9811 Parrott Talk **3778**
0093-982X E M Bibliography for Consumers†
0093-9854 Heart of Texas Records **3769**
0093-9889 Tennessee. State Board for Vocational Education. Information Series
0093-9897 U.S. Department of Transportation. Year-End Report†
0093-9951 Roster of Black Elected Officials in the South
0093-9986 New Jersey. Legislature. Office of Fiscal Affairs. Annual Report†
0093-9994 I E E E Transactions on Industry Applications **3315**
0094-0003 Physical Review - Index **7048**
0094-002X American Indian Law Review **4614**
0094-0038 American Association of Petroleum Geologists and Society of Economic Paleontologists and Mineralogists. Annual Meetings Abstracts†
0094-0143 Urologic Clinics of North America **6276**
0094-0178 Old-House Journal **1028**
0094-0194 New York Culture Review
0094-0208 N A E P Newsletter†
0094-0232 Imprint: Oregon†
0094-0240 First Friday **1423**
0094-0259 Alfantics
0094-0283 Genealogy†
0094-0291 Hiking (Highland Park)†
0094-0305 McCall's Cooking School†
0094-033X New German Critique **4466**
0094-0364 Multitype Library Cooperative News
0094-0372 Cockshaw's Construction Labor News & Opinion **1670**
0094-0488 Arkansas Nurse†
0094-0496 American Ethnologist **324**
0094-050X S C A G Annual Report†
0094-0534 Consumers Index†
0094-0615 Law & Liberty†
0094-0623 Legal Notes for Insurance†
0094-0658 Sage International Yearbook of Foreign Policy Studies†
0094-0763 Huber Law Survey†
0094-0771 Middle School Journal **3073**
0094-0798 Oral History Review **4155**
0094-0801 University of Florida. Growth Conference. Prepared Papers†
0094-0844 The Thorny Trail **3785**
0094-0852 Explorations in Economic Research†
0094-0887 Far-Western Forum†
0094-0933 U.S. Centers for Disease Control. Abortion Surveillance **974**
0094-0968 University of Chicago. Law School. Law Alumni Journal†
0094-1034 Environmental Resources
0094-1093 Administrative Law Newsletter†
0094-1115 Basic Economic Data for Idaho **1442**
0094-114X Mechanism and Machine Theory **3389**
0094-1182 Civil War Collectors' Dealer Directory
0094-1190 Journal of Urban Economics **1138**
0094-1247 Nebraska. State Patrol. Annual Report **2674**
0094-1255 Book of Names†
0094-128X Northeast Pacific Pink and Chum Salmon Workshop. Proceedings†
0094-1298 Clinics in Plastic Surgery **6240**
0094-1344 Country Music World
0094-1352 IndustriScope†
0094-1360 Jeffersonian Review†
0094-1409 Minnesota. Office of Ombudsman for Corrections. Annual Report
0094-1417 Astrograph (Print) *changed to* Astrograph (CD-ROM)
0094-1476 Philadelphia Association for Psychoanalysis. Journal†
0094-1484 Magyar Evkonyv
0094-1492 Materials Performance **3353**
0094-1506 Michigan State Plan for Vocational Education
0094-1514 Motor Handbook†
0094-1557 Georgia. Department of Education. Statistical Report†
0094-1581 American Osteopathic Association. Directory Osteopathic Specialists†
0094-159X American College of Surgeons. Directory *changed to* 0094-1999 **6235**
0094-1611 Internationales Verzeichnis der Wirtschaftsverbaende **2009**
0094-162X Tenth Muse†
0094-1638 Sociology: Reviews of New Books†
0094-1670 Conservation in Kansas
0094-1700 Journal of Sport History **8182**
0094-1727 Minnesota Statutes. Supplement **4956**
0094-1786 Alaska. State Board of Registration for Architects, Engineers and Land Surveyors. Directory of Architects, Engineers and Land Surveyors
0094-1794 Estate Planning (New York, 1973) **4902**
0094-1832 Hydraulic Research in the United States and Canada†
0094-1859 Journal of Afro-American Issues†
0094-1875 National Traffic Law News
0094-1921 Campaign Law Reporter
0094-1956 Journal of Instructional Psychology **2876**
0094-1964 Paintbrush **5348**
0094-1972 Review of Applied Urban Research†
0094-1999 American College of Surgeons. Yearbook **6235**
0094-2006 University of Washington Medicine†
0094-2057 California School Law Digest **3018**
0094-2065 Communio **7793**
0094-209X Directories of Hawaii†
0094-2200 South Dakota. Department of Labor. Research and Statistics. Annual Report on State and Area Occupational Requirements for Vocational Education†
0094-2235 Illinois Student Lawyer†
0094-2243 Cincinnati Bar Association. Journal†
0094-226X Newsletter & Digest of Selected Opinions of State Attorneys General†
0094-2278 Railway Passenger Car Annual **8624**
0094-2294 Florida. Mental Health Program Office. Statistical Report of Hospitals†
0094-2308 Supply and Demand: Educational Personnel in Delaware
0094-2316 World of Politics **7196**
0094-2324 Community Development Digest **4407**
0094-2367 Everyman†
0094-2375 Fantasiae (Los Angeles)
0094-2383 Journal of Abstracts in International Education†
0094-2405 Medical Physics **5670**
0094-2413 Juvenile Justice Digest **2658**
0094-2421 Celebration (Kansas City) **7791**
0094-243X A I P Conference Proceedings Series **7002**
0094-2464 Small Businessman's Clinic†
0094-2472 Race Relations Reporter†
0094-2499 The Journal of Biocommunication **5646**
0094-2502 Business Regulation Law Report†
0094-2510 Marketing California Dried Fruits: Prunes, Raisins, Dried Apricots & Peaches†
0094-2553 United States Judicial Reporter†
0094-2561 Disclosure Record
0094-257X Weekly Record†
0094-2588 Communication Directory†
0094-2626 Library Statistics of Illinois Colleges and Universities: Institutional Data†
0094-2634 Index to Foreign Market Reports†
0094-2650 International Yearbooks of Drug Addiction and Society†
0094-2677 Ohio Juvenile Court Statistics†
0094-2715 Inscape (Pasadena) **5424**
0094-2766 Monthly Summary of Texas Natural Gas **6778**
0094-2871 U.S. Environmental Protection Agency. Office of Air Quality Planning and Standards. State Air Pollution Implementation Plan Progress Report†
0094-288X Russian History **4260**
0094-2898 Southeastern Symposium on System Theory. Proceedings **2525**
0094-291X Rhode Island. Department of Mental Health, Retardation and Hospitals. Mental Health, Retardation and Hospitals
0094-2987 Illinois. Department of Public Instruction. Publications Resource Manual†
0094-3002 Broker-Dealer Directory†
0094-3029 Carnegie Endowment for International Peace. Financial Report†
0094-3037 East Central Europe **4216**
0094-3061 Contemporary Sociology **8095**
0094-3134 Probe Directory of Foreign Direct Investment in the United States
0094-3142 U.S. Environmental Protection Agency. Summaries of Foreign Government Environmental Reports†
0094-3231 Environmental Information Systems Directory†
0094-3282 Empress Chinchilla Breeder **4973**
0094-3320 13th Moon **5405**
0094-3339 East-West Markets†
0094-3347 Eutrophication†
0094-3355 Horse and Horseman†
0094-3452 Places†
0094-3487 Material for Thought†
0094-3495 Journal of Social Welfare†
0094-3509 The Journal of Family Practice **5649**
0094-3568 Arts In Alaska *changed to* Alaska State Council on the Arts. Communique **464**
0094-3630 Missouri. Division of Fisheries. Abstracts of Fishery Research Reports†
0094-3681 Chem Sources - Europe†
0094-372X South Dakota Indian Recipients of Social Welfare†
0094-3770 American Bibliography of Slavic and East European Studies **4168**
0094-3800 California Plant Pathology†
0094-3819 U.S. Department of Agriculture. National Agricultural Statistics Service. Cattle (Print) *changed to* 1948-9099 **187**
0094-3851 U.S. Department of Agriculture. National Agricultural Statistics Service. Sheep and Goats (Print)† **8995**
0094-3894 Recipe Index Series†
0094-3932 Advances in Fire Retardants†
0094-3940 Department of Alcoholic Beverage Control. Annual Report **602**
0094-3983 Minnesota Pocket Data Book†
0094-3991 Narcotics and Drug Abuse A to Z **2697**
0094-4033 Union Catalog of Maps†
0094-4076 Emory Law Journal **4664**
0094-4084 International Directory of Behavior and Design Research†
0094-4114 Nantucket Review
0094-422X American Society of Pension Actuaries. Transcribings. Annual Conference†
0094-4246 Arizona Legislative Service **4621**
0094-4262 Facts About South Dakota†
0094-4270 I.C.C. Supplemental Reports†
0094-4289 Journal of Engineering Materials and Technology **3349**
0094-4335 Statistics for Water Utilities Including Water Authorities in Pennsylvania†
0094-4424 Family Planning Services: Annual Summary
0094-4459 National Collegiate Athletic Association. Proceedings of the Special Convention†
0094-4467 Southeastern Europe **4266**
0094-4491 Maryland Manual **7452**
0094-4505 Guide to American Scientific and Technical Directories†
0094-4602 Annual Report on Ground Water in Arizona†
0094-467X Securities Investor Protection Corporation. Annual Report
0094-4742 World Environmental Directory†
0094-4831 Bibliography of Society, Ethics and the Life Sciences†
0094-4920 Social Sciences Index **8021**
0094-5048 Maine. Department of Transportation. Annual Report†
0094-5056 Eastern Economic Journal **1097**
0094-5072 The InterDependent **7242**
0094-5110 Gegenwartszeit der Unicycle *see* 0566-778X **368**
0094-5129 New Human Services Review†
0094-5145 Journal of Community Health **5647**
0094-5307 Advances in Satellite Meteorology†
0094-5323 Augustinian Studies **6906**
0094-534X Ohio Northern University Law Review **4752**
0094-5366 Bilingual Review **2831**
0094-5404 Essays in Literature†
0094-5420 Judicial Education News†
0094-5439 Maine Prosecutor Bulletin†
0094-5447 Metallurgy - Materials Education Yearbook **6325**
0094-5463 Product Safety & the Law†
0094-5471 Directory of Women Physicians in the U.S.†
0094-5609 Examination of Financial Statements Inter-American Foundation **1340**
0094-5617 Hastings Constitutional Law Quarterly **4849**
0094-5633 Measuring Mormonism†
0094-5641 Minnesota Health Statistics **7548**
0094-5676 Oppositions†
0094-5714 Synthesis and Reactivity in Inorganic and Metal-Organic Chemistry *changed to* 1553-3174 **2141**
0094-5765 Acta Astronautica **41**
0094-579X Stone Soup **2215**
0094-5803 University of Wisconsin, Madison. Bureau of Business Research and Service. Research in the School of Business†
0094-582X Latin American Perspectives **7982**
0094-5846 Fundamentals of Cosmic Physics†
0094-5862 Family Album
0094-5870 Dine Bizaad Manil'iih
0094-5900 Syracuse University. Libraries. Annual Report†
0094-5943 The Reader's Adviser†
0094-6028 Computer Medicine†
0094-6109 Ohio Higher Education. Basic Data Series **2935**
0094-6168 Current Cardiovascular Topics†
0094-6176 Seminars in Thrombosis and Hemostasis **5941**
0094-6184 Serial Handbook of Modern Psychiatry†
0094-6206 Origins of Behavior Series†
0094-6249 Chemical Reference Manual
0094-6265 Maryland. State Highway Administration. Traffic Trends **8632**
0094-629X National Archives Microfilm Publications. Catalog **5034**
0094-6303 Global Directory of Gas Companies†
0094-6338 South Carolina Vital and Morbidity Statistics **7316**
0094-6354 A A N A Journal **5949**
0094-6389 American Foundation for the Blind. International Research Information Service. Index of Publications Issued by I R I S†
0094-6427 Susquehanna River Basin Commission. Annual Report **8832**
0094-6478 Music Library Association. Index and Bibliography Series **6632**
0094-6494 Illinois. Department of Public Health. Poison Control Program Report†
0094-6567 Chem Sources U S A **1979**
0094-6575 Emergency Medical Services *changed to* 1946-4967 **6058**
0094-6710 Western Livestock Journal Weekly **304**
0094-6761 Current Topics in Molecular Endocrinology†
0094-6818 International Index to Multi Media Information†
0094-6842 Systems and Management Annual†
0094-6907 Cantwell Tapestry†
0094-6915 Backtracker **3759**
0094-6923 International Telex Book. Americas Edition
0094-6958 Sage Public Administration Abstracts *changed to* Public Administration Abstracts **7483**
0094-7008 U.S. National Marine Fisheries Service. Grant-in-Aid for Fisheries: Program Activities **3610**
0094-7024 S S I E Science Newsletter†
0094-7032 Advances in Image Pickup and Display†
0094-7040 Aldine Crime and Justice Annual†
0094-7091 Geokhimiya Translations†
0094-7148 Report of Cases Determined in the Supreme Court and Court of Appeals of the State of New Mexico (Print) *changed to* New Mexico Reports and West's New Mexico Statutes (Premise CD-ROM) **4744**
0094-7156 Federal Home Loan Mortgage Corporation. Report **1341**
0094-7180 Special Management Bulletin
0094-7237 Environmental Biology
0094-7288 Engineering and Society Series†
0094-7296 Federal Aid Fact Book†
0094-730X Journal of Fluency Disorders **7374**
0094-7326 New Mexico. Veterans' Service Commission. Report **6439**
0094-7342 Journal of Mormon History **7737**
0094-7393 Highway User Quarterly†
0094-7415 Average Daily Traffic Volumes on Interstate, Arterial and Primary Routes *changed to* Average Daily Traffic Volumes with Vehicle Classification Data on Interstate, Arterial and Primary Routes **8522**
0094-7466 International Symposium on Transport and Handling of Minerals. Proceedings†
0094-7474 Summer Computer Simulation Conference. Proceedings **2518**
0094-7482 Status of the Market Nuclear Fuel Fabrication†
0094-7490 American Printmakers†
0094-7504 Annual Statistical Report of the Colorado Judiciary **4820**
0094-7512 Directory of Counseling Services†
0094-7547 New York (City). Schedules Supporting the Executive Budget **7499**
0094-7555 Banking Legislation in the Congress†
0094-7598 Land Use Law and Zoning Digest *changed to* 1548-0755 **7604**
0094-761X National Transportation Safety Board Decisions **8506**
0094-7660 Illinois Insurance **4505**
0094-7679 Journalism History **4578**
0094-7687 New Hampshire Annual Rural Manpower Report†
0094-7733 Society of General Physiologists Series†
0094-7768 International Studies Notes†
0094-7776 U.S. Occupational Safety and Health Review Commission. Administrative Law Judge and Commission Decisions†

0094-7857 U.S. National Science Foundation. Division of Environmental Systems and Resources. Summary of Awards†
0094-7865 Ripon Quarterly **7179**
0094-792X The C P A Letter (Print)† **8938**
0094-7962 University of California, Davis. Food Protection and Toxicology Center. Summary Report†
0094-7989 Bergen County History†
0094-8039 Journal of Muscle Shoals History **4299**
0094-8055 Peace Science Society (International). Papers†
0094-8063 Energy Review (Santa Barbara)†
0094-8098 Readers Advisory Service
0094-8101 Outboard Boating Handbook†
0094-8136 Yachting Yearbook of Northern California **8285**
0094-8187 Surgery Update†
0094-8233 Alloys Index **6338**
0094-8268 Summary of Expenditure Data for Michigan Public Schools†
0094-8276 Geophysical Research Letters **2782**
0094-8322 Illinois. Board of Higher Education. Directory of Higher Education **2986**
0094-8365 Program for Control of Electromagnetic Pollution of the Environment. The Assessment of Biological Hazards of Nonionizing Electromagnetic Radiation. Report **3490**
0094-8373 Paleobiology **6728**
0094-8381 Air Force Law Review **4971**
0094-8411 U.S. Export Administration Regulations **7473**
0094-8454 Official Southern California Ports Maritime Directory and Guide
0094-8462 People. Biennial Report
0094-8470 Progress in Radiation Protection†
0094-8500 Enzyme Engineering **731**
0094-8543 American Arabic Speaking Community Almanac†
0094-8551 Florida. Department of Banking & Finance. Annual Local Government Financial Report†
0094-8705 Journal of the Philosophy of Sport **8183**
0094-8764 Association of American Plant Food Control Officials. Official Publication **219**
0094-8829 Library Development in Alaska: Long Range Program
0094-8837 Selected Tables in Mathematical Statistics **5533**
0094-8845 St. Lawrence University. Conference on the Adirondack Park (Proceedings)†
0094-890X New Jersey. State Library. Union List of Serials†
0094-8934 Folk Harp Journal **6567**
0094-8950 Monographs in Lipid Research†
0094-8969 A H A Guide to the Health Care Field **4086**
0094-8977 Non Solus†
0094-9000 Theory of Probability and Mathematical Statistics **5541**
0094-9027 Young Students Encyclopedia Yearbook†
0094-9043 Ohio Geographers: Recent Research Themes†
0094-9086 Hopkins Quarterly **5423**
0094-9108 Physical Fitness Research Digest†
0094-9205 University of Georgia. Institute of Ecology. Annual Report **3472**
0094-9264 Principles and Techniques of Human Research and Therapeutics†
0094-9302 Concise Clinical Neurology Review†
0094-9329 Modern Sawmill Techniques†
0094-9426 Book Forum†
0094-9450 Nassau County Historical Society Journal
0094-9477 Previews of Heat and Mass Transfer†
0094-9531 Shepard's Federal Law Citations in Selected Law Reviews **4783**
0094-9582 U.S. National Institute of Neurological Diseases and Stroke. Research Program Reports†
0094-9620 American Optometric Association News **6038**
0094-9655 Journal of Statistical Computation and Simulation **2443**
0094-9663 National Directory of Minority Manufacturers **2018**
0094-9671 Conference on Ground Water. Proceedings **2793**
0094-9698 Three Forks of Muddy Creek **4315**
0094-9701 Ha-Metivta **4733**
0094-9744 Basenji **6804**
0094-9779 Geothermal World Directory†
0094-9787 Olympian†
0094-9914 Your Highway Department, Arkansas†
0094-9922 Transportation U S A
0094-9930 Journal of Pressure Vessel Technology **3386**
0095-0025 Job Corps Happenings†
0095-0084 Business Digest†
0095-0106 Communique (Boston)†
0095-0157 Florida Marine Research Publications†
0095-0165 Homegrown†
0095-019X Osiris (Deerfield) **5428**
0095-0203 Personal Finance Letter†
0095-036X Texas Nursing **5982**
0095-0386 Mort's Guide to Low-Cost Vacations & Lodgings on College Campuses†
0095-053X National Library Reporter†
0095-0629 L C Foreign Acquisitions Newsletter†
0095-067X The Woodenboat **8285**
0095-0688 Manhattan Directory of Commercial & Industrial Properties†
0095-0696 Journal of Environmental Economics and Management **3445**
0095-0726 Commerce Reporter†
0095-084X Electrical Installation & Repair Projects†
0095-0858 Social Psychiatry†
0095-0963 Automedica†
0095-0971 Bio-Medical Scoreboard†
0095-0998 Medical School Rounds†
0095-1005 Search and Seizure Law Report **4898**
0095-1013 Lifestyle†
0095-1021 I.F.T. Journal†
0095-1102 New Hampshire Occupational Outlook†
0095-1137 Journal of Clinical Microbiology **5647**
0095-1145 Psychology†
0095-1188 Women Law Reporter†
0095-1250 Water Resources Research in Virginia. Annual Report†
0095-1439 Central Kentucky Researcher **3761**
0095-1498 Kentucky Local Debt Report **1932**
0095-1528 Urban Planning Quarterly†
0095-1536 Women (Washington)†
0095-1587 Foster Natural Gas Report **6769**
0095-1609 Washington (State). Department of Social and Health Services. Income Maintenance, Community Social Services and Medical Assistance†
0095-1633 North Dakota. Social Service Board. Statistics†
0095-165X El Dorado†
0095-1676 Indiana. Division of Fish and Wildlife. Management Series
0095-1684 American Poetry and Poetics†
0095-1714 Imprint (Richmond)†
0095-1730 Seems **5369**
0095-1811 American Clean Car†
0095-182X American Indian Quarterly **6634**
0095-1870 Industrial Contact List for North Carolina Communities†
0095-1900 Texas. Department of Criminal Justice. Institutional Division. Research Report **2669**
0095-1978 Virginia. State Water Control Board. Annual Report†
0095-1994 Tennessee. Department of Safety. Annual Report **8635**
0095-2044 Washington D.C. Council on Environmental Quality. Environmental Quality **3474**
0095-2060 Florida. Department of Transportation. Annual Report†
0095-2109 U.S. Office of Technology Assessment. Annual Report to the Congress†
0095-2117 Comptroller General's Procurement Decisions **4648**
0095-2125 Energy: a Continuing Bibliography with Indexes†
0095-2141 U.S. Bureau of Health Resources Development. Division of Nursing. Special Project Grants and Contracts Awarded for Improvement in Nurse Training†
0095-2214 Chromatography Newsletter†
0095-2222 Consumers' Research Magazine†
0095-2273 N Y S S A Sphere **5772**
0095-2338 Journal of Chemical Information and Computer Sciences *changed to* 1549-9596 **2108**
0095-2427 Harvard Magazine **5219**
0095-2443 Journal of Elastomers and Plastics **7093**
0095-2486 University of Kentucky. Cooperative Extension Service. A G R **166**
0095-2494 University of Kentucky. Cooperative Extension Service. A S C **166**
0095-2583 Economic Inquiry **1100**
0095-2591 International Netsuke Collectors Society Journal†
0095-2605 Keeping Up with Experimental Music in the Schools†
0095-2613 The Orff Echo **6602**
0095-263X Rare Coin Review **6653**
0095-2648 Transportation Research Abstracts†
0095-2664 Tunneling Technology Newsletter†
0095-2699 Agricultural Libraries Information Notes†
0095-2702 Serials Updating Service Annual†
0095-2737 Computers & Society (Print Edition) *changed to* Computers & Society (Online Edition) **8151**
0095-2753 Taxable Sales in California. Sales and Use Tax Annual Report **1950**
0095-2788 Vogue Patterns **2263**
0095-280X Studies in American Humor **5241**
0095-2826 American Society for Personnel Administration. Personnel and Industrial Relations Colleges†
0095-2842 Handbook of Illinois Government
0095-2850 Economic and Social Progress in Latin America. Report **1479**
0095-2869 Directory of American Book Specialists†
0095-2893 Illinois. State Museum. Inventory of the Collections **6525**
0095-2907 Dickson Mounds Museum Anthropological Studies†
0095-2915 Illinois. State Museum. Research Series. Papers in Anthropology†
0095-2923 Insurance Forum **4507**
0095-2931 Outlook *changed to* 1930-0808 **1399**
0095-294X The Forecaster **1111**
0095-2958 Biology Digest **713**
0095-2966 Resources (Houston)†
0095-2974 New World Communications†
0095-2990 American Journal of Drug and Alcohol Abuse **2691**
0095-3024 Minnesota. Department of Revenue. Petroleum Division. Annual Report **6778**
0095-3059 T T O S Bulletin **4348**
0095-3075 Virginia. Employment Commission. Manpower Research Division. Economic Assumptions†
0095-3105 Nebraska Statistical Report of Abortions **973**
0095-3113 National Directory of State Agencies†
0095-3121 Family Planning Programs in Oklahoma **972**
0095-313X Epidemiologic Notes and Communicable Disease Morbidity Report†
0095-3237 Occupational Safety & Health Reporter **6683**
0095-327X Armed Forces and Society **6410**
0095-3369 Digest of the United States Practice in International Law†
0095-3415 Alaska. Violent Crimes Compensation Board. Annual Report **2643**
0095-3423 Commerce Business Daily†
0095-3431 Alabama's Vital Events **8343**
0095-344X U.S. Federal Highway Administration. Highway Statistics **8532**
0095-3539 Health Information for International Travel **7522**
0095-3628 Microbial Ecology **891**
0095-3830 Economic Outlook U.S.A.†
0095-3865 Alaska. Legislature. Budget and Audit Committee. Annual Report **7104**
0095-389X Wyoming. Employment Security Commission. Research and Analysis Section. Farm Labor Report†
0095-3911 St. Clair County Historical Society. Journal
0095-392X State University of New York at Buffalo. Law Library. Law Library Periodicals†
0095-3997 Administration & Society **7418**
0095-4004 Wisconsin. Division of Corrections. Bureau of Planning, Development, and Research. Adult Probation Admissions†
0095-4020 Massachusetts. Department of Public Welfare. State Advisory Board. Annual Report†
0095-4047 New York (State). Division of Criminal Justice Services. Annual Report **2662**
0095-4063 Communications World†
0095-4098 Library Resources Notes
0095-4101 Popular Music Periodicals Index†
0095-4144 Executive Compensation Service. Reports on International Compensation. Argentina†
0095-4209 Hawaii. State Law Enforcement and Juvenile Delinquency Planning Agency. Annual Action Program†
0095-425X Christianity Applied†
0095-4306 Wisconsin. Division of Corrections. Office of Information Management. Juvenile Probation Admissions†
0095-4314 Wisconsin Trails **3993**
0095-4322 World Mines Register†
0095-4330 Washington Agricultural Statistics **189**
0095-4365 U.S. National Climatic Center. Climatological Data; National Summary†
0095-4373 Climatological Data. Hawaii and Pacific **6350**
0095-4403 American Society for Information Science. Bulletin *changed to* 1931-6550
0095-442X Oklahoma. Conservation Commission. Biennial Report **2623**
0095-4438 Columban Mission **7793**
0095-4470 Journal of Phonetics **5135**
0095-4489 Studies in Browning and His Circle **5380**
0095-4500 Journal of Clinical Issues in Psychology
0095-4519 Innovations†
0095-4527 Cytology and Genetics **865**
0095-4543 Primary Care: Clinics in Office Practice **5699**
0095-4594 Corrections Magazine†
0095-4608 Byzantine Studies **4445**
0095-4616 Applied Mathematics and Optimization **5472**
0095-4624 Connecticut. Council on Environmental Quality. Annual Report **3412**
0095-4640 Benchmark Papers in Ecology†
0095-4659 West Virginia. Department of Natural Resources. Annual Report on the Comprehensive Water Resources Plan†
0095-4667 Alaska Medicaid Status Report†
0095-4683 Airline Handbook **8536**
0095-4721 Hawaii. State Public Library System. L S C A Annual Program†
0095-4829 Advances and Technical Standards in Neurosurgery **6119**
0095-4837 U.S. Bureau of Labor Statistics. Chartbook on Prices, Wages, and Productivity†
0095-4861 Clinical and Biochemical Analysis†
0095-4888 Directory of Minnesota's Area Mental Health, Mental Retardation, Inebriety Programs†
0095-4918 The Journal of Portfolio Management **1635**
0095-4942 North Carolina. Department of Human Resources. Annual Plan of Work†
0095-4977 Curriculum Materials Clearinghouse. Index and Curriculum Briefs†
0095-4993 Journal of African Studies†
0095-5086 Public Utilities Law Anthology†
0095-5108 Clinics in Perinatology **5988**
0095-5175 Florida. Office of the Governor. Budget in Brief
0095-5213 Kaleidoscope (Boston)†
0095-5221 Interest-Adjusted Index†
0095-5248 New Frontiers (Seattle)†
0095-5264 Nevada. Bureau of Mines and Geology. Report **2758**
0095-5310 Arizona. Department of Education. Superintendent of Public Instruction. Annual Report **3017**
0095-5329 Consolidated Report on Elementary and Secondary Education in Colorado†
0095-537X Weighing & Measurement **6407**
0095-5388 Voyages to the Inland Sea **5396**
0095-5396 American Bankers Association. National Operations & Automation Conference. Proceedings†
0095-5418 Strictly U.S.†
0095-5515 Occupational Safety and Health Cases **6683**
0095-5523 New Hampshire Vital Statistics **7312**
0095-5531 Buyers' Guide to Outdoor Advertising **22**
0095-5574 Kentucky Manpower Development. Annual Report
0095-5590 New York (State). Consumer Protection Board. Annual Report **2640**
0095-5620 G S A Supply Catalog **7438**
0095-5655 Gallaudet Almanac†
0095-5698 Access: The Supplementary Index to Periodicals **1**
0095-571X Semeia *changed to* 1567-200X **7680**
0095-5744 Viking **3009**
0095-5760 Alaska Hunting Guide†
0095-5809 Arion **2230**
0095-585X Montana Federal Grants-in-Aid Report†
0095-5876 San Diego Biomedical Symposium. Proceedings
0095-5892 Training **1798**
0095-5981 Humanities Index **4484**
0095-599X Drug Interactions†
0095-6074 Pollution Control Journal
0095-6139 Ethnicity†
0095-6317 Technical Education Reporter†
0095-6325 North Dakota. Social Service Board. Report
0095-6333 North Dakota. Social Service Board. Area Social Service Centers†
0095-635X Military Media Review†
0095-6384 Kentucky Law Enforcement Council. Annual Report†
0095-6422 Delaware. Department of Health and Social Service. Annual Report
0095-6430 State of Florida Comprehensive Manpower Plan
0095-6449 Computer Design's Data Sheet Directory of Digital Electronics†
0095-6457 Carpet Specifier's Handbook **8449**
0095-6465 California Historical Courier†
0095-6481 National Conference on Power Transmission. Proceedings†
0095-6562 Aviation, Space, and Environmental Medicine **5581**
0095-6619 Hawaii. Legislative Reference Bureau. Digest and Index of Laws Enacted†
0095-6686 Illinois. Department of Transportation. Physical Research Report
0095-6694 O S S C Bulletin†
0095-6708 Impact (Ann Arbor)†
0095-6740 Blue Cross Association. Research Series†
0095-6775 Damon Runyon - Walter Winchell Cancer Research Fund. Annual Report **6018**
0095-6783 Mississippi Marine Resources Council. Annual Report

0095-683X International Directory of the Nonwoven Fabrics Industry **8453**
0095-6848 Journal of Japanese Studies **553**
0095-6910 Homegrown†
0095-6945 Intersections†
0095-697X Juvenile Law Newsletter†
0095-702X Rendezvous of Western Art†
0095-7046 U.S. Industrial Directory **2032**
0095-7089 Mathematics Student†
0095-7119 Best Science Fiction of the Year **5440**
0095-7186 Election Index†
0095-7216 Hip†
0095-7224 Review of Allied Health Education **5703**
0095-7232 Reviews in European History†
0095-7240 World Almanac Guide to Pro Hockey†
0095-7267 California. Office of Criminal Justice Planning. Bulletin
0095-7291 Foreign Tax Law Bi-Weekly Bulletin *changed to* R I A Worldwide Tax Law Bulletin
0095-733X Michigan. Department of Management and Budget. Annual Report†
0095-7356 U.S. Department of Energy. Energy Information Administration. Monthly Energy Review (Print)†
0095-7550 Reviews of Neuroscience†
0095-7577 Journal of Space Law **4933**
0095-7607 European Parliament Digest†
0095-7755 Software Briefs†
0095-7771 Foreign Trade Reports. U.S. Airborne Exports and General Imports†
0095-7895 Cancer Therapy Abstracts†
0095-7925 Directory of Health Sciences Libraries in the United States†
0095-7984 Journal of Black Psychology **7369**
0095-8034 California Union List of Periodicals
0095-8115 Discography Series†
0095-8123 Interface Journal†
0095-8174 Virginia. Department of Labor and Industry. Division of Research and Statistics. Occupational Injuries and Illnesses by Industry†
0095-8247 Illinois. Fire Protection Personnel Standards and Education Commission. Annual Report†
0095-8301 Diabetes Forecast **5887**
0095-8387 The Del-Chem Bulletin **2059**
0095-862X Cassinia **905**
0095-8638 State Geological and Natural History Survey of Connecticut. Bulletin **2769**
0095-8778 Computers in Chemical and Biochemical Research†
0095-8808 DuPont Magazine **1093**
0095-8948 Engineering & Mining Journal **6461**
0095-8956 Journal of Combinatorial Theory. Series B **5501**
0095-8964 The Journal of Environmental Education **3445**
0095-8972 Journal of Coordination Chemistry **2068**
0095-926X U.S. Bureau of Labor Statistics. C P I Detailed Report (Print)† **8995**
0095-9286 New Silver Technology†
0095-9669 C O M S A T Technical Review†
0095-9782 Journal of Solution Chemistry **2138**
0095-9960 Ceramic Abstracts **2047**
0096-0365 American Rabbit Journal
0096-0772 Foote Prints†
0096-0985 California. Department of Fish and Game. Fish Bulletin **3588**
0096-1159 Graphic Arts Technical Foundation. Research Project Report†
0096-1191 Journal of Foraminiferal Research **6725**
0096-1221 International Pacific Halibut Commission. Report *changed to* 0304-016X **3598**
0096-1337 Journal of Undergraduate Psychological Research†
0096-1353 Ford's Deck Plan Guide†
0096-1388 Annual Report of the Arts Activities in Alabama†
0096-140X Aggressive Behavior **7332**
0096-1442 Journal of Urban History **4150**
0096-1507 A I D Research and Development Abstracts†
0096-1523 Journal of Experimental Psychology: Human Perception and Performance **7373**
0096-2279 Colorado-Wyoming Academy of Sciences. Journal **7848**
0096-2309 R S C, Railway System Controls **8622**
0096-2341 U.S. Library of Congress. Accessions List: Southeast Asia†
0096-2651 Fieldiana: Geology **2733**
0096-2708 Horizons in Biochemistry and Biophysics†
0096-2716 Contact Lens Journal†
0096-2902 Research Methods in Neurochemistry
0096-3003 Applied Mathematics and Computation **5472**
0096-3070 Florida State University Law Review **4675**
0096-3135 Politeia†
0096-3143 Orange County Bar Journal†
0096-3216 Karter News **8587**
0096-3259 Translator Referral Directory†
0096-3291 Yearbook of Science and the Future†
0096-3364 Current Aviation Statistics†
0096-3402 Bulletin of the Atomic Scientists **7224**
0096-3445 Journal of Experimental Psychology: General **7373**
0096-3496 International Plastic Modelers Society - United States Quarterly Journal†
0096-3720 Louisiana Geological Survey. Geological Bulletin **2753**
0096-3755 Denison University. Journal of the Scientific Laboratories†
0096-378X South Dakota Academy of Science. Proceedings **7919**
0096-3917 Cancer Letter **6013**
0096-3925 Moscow University Biological Sciences Bulletin **690**
0096-3941 E O S **2780**
0096-4131 Buffalo Society of Natural Sciences. Bulletin†
0096-414X South Carolina Academy of Science. Bulletin **7919**
0096-4158 Maryland Naturalist **7881**
0096-4166 Rochester Academy of Science. Proceedings **7904**
0096-4263 West Virginia Academy of Science. Proceedings **7929**
0096-4271 Geological Society of America, Inc. Proceedings Volume† **8959**
0096-428X Progress in Physiological Sciences
0096-4298 Progress in Surface and Membrane Science†
0096-4522 Soil and Crop Science Society of Florida. Annual Proceedings **253**
0096-4581 New Mexico. Bureau of Geology and Mineral Resources. Bulletin **6474**
0096-4859 Mines Magazine **6472**
0096-5804 J P L Quarterly Technical Review†
0096-5839 Entomological Society of Washington. Memoirs **845**
0096-5960 California Avocado Society. Yearbook **223**
0096-6851 American Otological Society. Transactions **6077**
0096-7343 University of Kentucky. Agricultural Experiment Station. Regulatory Bulletin **166**
0096-736X S A E Transactions *changed to* 1946-3979 **3357**
0096-736X S A E Transactions *changed to* 1946-3952 **6790**
0096-736X S A E Transactions *changed to* 1946-391X **8510**
0096-736X S A E Transactions *changed to* 1946-4614 **3329**
0096-736X S A E Transactions *changed to* 1946-3936 **8602**
0096-736X S A E Transactions *changed to* 1946-3995 **3395**
0096-736X S A E Transactions *changed to* 1946-3855 **69**
0096-7629 Welding Research **6345**
0096-7688 Michigan State Horticultural Society. Annual Report†
0096-7750 Academy of Natural Sciences of Philadelphia. Monographs **7831**
0096-7769 Northwest Geology†
0096-7866 State of Tennessee. Department of Conservation. Division of Geology. Bulletin **2769**
0096-7947 Metal Finishing. Guidebook Directory†
0096-7963 Symposium on Instrumentation for the Process Industries. Proceedings **3256**
0096-8056 Annals of Otology, Rhinology & Laryngology. Supplement *see* 0003-4894 **6077**
0096-848X Yearbook of Physical Anthropology **361**
0096-8498 University of Georgia. Agricultural Experiment Stations. Southern Cooperative Series Bulletin **257**
0096-8684 Begonian **3724**
0096-8692 Bell Telephone Magazine†
0096-8714 Tree Planters' Notes†
0096-879X Current Antarctic Literature **7936**
0096-882X Journal of Studies on Alcohol *changed to* 1937-1888 **2696**
0096-8846 Italian Americana **3541**
0096-8854 Federal Judicial Center. Annual Report **4951**
0096-8870 Gas Processors Association. Annual Convention. Proceedings **6770**
0096-8951 University of California Publications in Public Health†
0096-9109 Natural History Miscellanea†
0096-9184 Preparation and Properties of Solid State Materials†
0096-9192 Louisiana Academy of Sciences. Proceedings **7880**
0096-9214 North Dakota Academy of Science. Proceedings **7893**
0096-9311 University of California Publications in Engineering† **8996**
0096-9419 Navy Civil Engineer **6439**
0096-9842 Wyoming Mineral Yearbook **2775**
0097-0042 Railroad Research Bulletin†
0097-0204 Maine Geological Survey. Bulletin **2753**
0097-0212 U.S. Department of Agriculture. Miscellaneous Publication **164**
0097-0298 Biological Society of Washington. Bulletin **659**
0097-0395 N S R D S - N B S: National Standard Reference Data Series†
0097-0433 Proceedings of the Berkeley Symposium on Mathematical Statistics and Probability†
0097-0484 Kansas Agricultural Experiment Station. Bulletin **130**
0097-0549 Neuroscience and Behavioral Physiology **6169**
0097-059X Heat Transfer and Fluid Mechanics Institute. Proceedings **3379**
0097-0638 American Fisheries Society. Special Publications **3583**
0097-0689 University of Idaho. Agricultural Experiment Station. Research Bulletin **166**
0097-0883 Mount Desert Island Biological Laboratory. Bulletin **690**
0097-0891 University of Kentucky. Agricultural Experiment Station. Bulletin **166**
0097-0905 Connecticut. Agricultural Experiment Station, New Haven. Bulletin **843**
0097-1014 Clinical Immunobiology†
0097-109X Progress in Cardiology (Malvern)†
0097-1138 The Absolute Sound **8151**
0097-1146 Anima†
0097-1154 Indian Law Reporter **4691**
0097-1189 State O'Maine Facts†
0097-1251 Storrs Agricultural Experiment Station. Bulletin **158**
0097-1618 Contributions from the United States National Herbarium **784**
0097-191X Nevada. Bureau of Mines and Geology. Bulletin **2758**
0097-1936 Air Quality Instrumentation†
0097-2126 American Power Conference. Proceedings†
0097-2312 Loss Prevention (New York) **3250**
0097-2398 Pacific Northwest Forest and Range Experiment Station. Research Notes **3699**
0097-2533 Modern Hi-Fi & Music
0097-2584 Virginia. Water Resources Research Center. Bulletin **8835**
0097-2703 Biological Effects of Magnetic Fields†
0097-3041 Foreign Commerce Weekly†
0097-3149 Geological Survey of Alabama. Circular **2739**
0097-3157 Academy of Natural Sciences of Philadelphia. Proceedings **7831**
0097-3165 Journal of Combinatorial Theory, Series A **5501**
0097-3211 Allyn Museum. Bulletin **931**
0097-3254 Academy of Natural Sciences of Philadelphia. Special Publications **7831**
0097-3262 Geological Survey of Alabama. Bulletin **2739**
0097-3270 Society of Economic Paleontologists and Mineralogists. Special Publication *changed to* 1060-071X **2768**
0097-3416 Iowa Agriculture and Home Economics Experiment Station. Research Bulletin **123**
0097-3505 Auburn University. Agricultural Experiment Station. Circular **93**
0097-3556 University of Michigan. Museum of Paleontology. Contributions **6731**
0097-3793 New York State Museum. Map and Chart Series **2758**
0097-3939 Washington (State). Department of Fish and Wildlife. Annual Report **3611**
0097-4145 American Concrete Institute. Proceedings†
0097-4153 American Society for Testing and Materials. Proceedings†
0097-4374 Arkansas Academy of Science. Proceedings *changed to* Arkansas Academy of Science. Journal **7837**
0097-4382 Gulf Coast Research Laboratory. Publications of the Museum†
0097-4463 Carnegie Museum of Natural History. Annals **7844**
0097-4471 Kansas Geological Survey. Bulletin **2751**
0097-4536 Crossties **8616**
0097-4706 J.C.C.: Journal of Clinical Chiropractic†
0097-4749 American Paint & Coatings Journal. Convention Daily
0097-4803 Brassey's Defence Yearbook†
0097-496X Pembroke Magazine **5233**
0097-5184 Nineteenth Century (Philadelphia)†
0097-5222 Shale Country†
0097-5230 Cold Spring Harbor Conferences on Cell Proliferation†
0097-5257 Pediatric Nephrology†
0097-5311 Monthly Abstract Bulletin from the Kodak Research Laboratories *changed to* 0001-3633
0097-5338 North Dakota Farm Research†
0097-5370 Arkansas. Agricultural Experiment Station. Report Series†
0097-5397 S I A M Journal on Computing **5555**
0097-5419 Southern Medicine†
0097-5451 South Dakota State University. Agricultural Experiment Station. Bulletin **157**
0097-5478 Ohio. Division of Geological Survey. Bulletin **2760**
0097-5524 Illinois State Water Survey. Circular **8825**
0097-5605 Ohio. Division of Geological Survey. Information Circular **2760**
0097-5680 State of Ohio. Department of Natural Resources. Division of Geological Survey. Report of Investigations **2769**
0097-577X American Photography†
0097-5915 Marine Technology Society. Annual Conference Preprints **2812**
0097-5982 Pediatric Conferences†
0097-6008 Sonix†
0097-6024 Middle East Newsletter
0097-6075 Creativity (Glenbrook) **24**
0097-6156 A C S Symposium Series **2047**
0097-6199 Current Awareness in Real Estate and Planning†
0097-627X American Dance Therapy Association. Monographs†
0097-6288 Principal International Businesses **1838**
0097-6326 Federal Register **4673**
0097-6474 Chemical Abstracts. Collective Index **2093**
0097-6482 Analog Sounds†
0097-6539 Hype†
0097-6563 Sigma Phi Epsilon Journal **2301**
0097-6822 American Society of Mechanical Engineers. Transactions **3373**
0097-7004 Modern China **4186**
0097-7039 Amtrak Annual Report **8614**
0097-7136 Audubon **2603**
0097-7209 Crystal Mirror **7701**
0097-7314 International Tax Journal **1930**
0097-7330 Magnetic Resonance Review
0097-739X Wyoming Area Manpower Review†
0097-7403 Journal of Experimental Psychology: Animal Behavior Processes **7373**
0097-7519 Water Quality Monitoring Data for Georgia Streams†
0097-7721 G T E Journal of Research and Development†
0097-7799 U.S. General Services Administration. Catalog of Federal Domestic Assistance **7473**
0097-7977 U.S. Administrative Office of the United States Courts. Report on Applications for Orders Authorizing or Approving the Interception of Wire or Oral Communications **4799**
0097-7985 U.S. Library of Congress. Accessions List: Pakistan†
0097-8035 Paid My Dues†
0097-8043 Restaurant Business **4396**
0097-8051 San Jose Studies†
0097-806X Exploration†
0097-8078 Water Resources **8838**
0097-8124 Babe Ruth Baseball's Athletes of the Year†
0097-8140 Creative Computing†
0097-8159 Energy Communications†
0097-8175 Gebbie Press All-in-One Directory **1997**
0097-8221 Occasional Review†
0097-8299 Transit Journal†
0097-8329 Consumer Electronics Product News
0097-8337 Consumer Guide Magazine **8576**
0097-8345 Credit†
0097-8353 Current Concepts in Ophthalmology (St. Louis)†
0097-8434 New Jersey Municipal Bond News
0097-8442 Ancient Interface†
0097-8493 Computers & Graphics **2484**
0097-8507 Language (Washington) **5139**
0097-8515 Transportation Research Circular **8516**
0097-8620 Current Prescribing†
0097-8663 Estreno **8470**
0097-871X Interscholastic Athletic Administration **3025**
0097-8779 O A G Cruise & Shipline Guide - Worldwide Edition†
0097-8833 Times Magazine†
0097-8884 Bittersweet†
0097-8892 Journal of Developmental Disabilities†
0097-8957 Consumer Guide Magazine: Stereo & Tape Equipment Test Reports†
0097-9007 Government Reports Announcements & Index†
0097-9074 Johns Hopkins University. Population Information Program. Population Reports. Series A. Oral Contraceptives
0097-9082 Johns Hopkins University. Population Information Program. Population Reports. Series E. Law and Policy
0097-9090 Johns Hopkins University. Population Information Program. Population Reports. Series I. Periodic Abstinence
0097-9104 Johns Hopkins University. Population Information Program. Population Reports. Series K. Injectables and Implants
0097-9171 Wisconsin. Employment Relations Commission. Reporter

ISSN

Link to your serials resources and content with ulrichsweb.com

0099-0876 Index to Pravda†
0099-0973 Survey of Business†
0099-099X The Los Angeles Market **1829**
0099-1007 The New York Market **1836**
0099-1015 County Year Book†
0099-1031 Bar Leader **4627**
0099-1066 Agricultural Outlook *changed to* 1545-8741 **90**
0099-1112 Photogrammetric Engineering and Remote Sensing **4023**
0099-1147 Advances in Pathobiology†
0099-1236 B A R - B R I Bar Review. Corporations **4857**
0099-1244 B A R - B R I Bar Review. Civil Procedure **4827**
0099-1260 Oregon. Employment Division. Annual Report†
0099-1279 Wyoming. Department of Environmental Quality. Annual Report†
0099-1295 Congress and Foreign Policy **7228**
0099-1333 The Journal of Academic Librarianship **5020**
0099-1414 Sage Annual Reviews of Communication Research†
0099-1465 Southern University Law Review **4786**
0099-1546 Progress in Anesthesiology†
0099-1554 Training Directory of the Rehabilitation Research and Training Centers†
0099-1716 A-E Concepts in Wood Design†
0099-1759 Faith for the Family†
0099-1767 Journal of Emergency Nursing **5964**
0099-1791 Luptonian†
0099-183X Social Thought *changed to* 1542-6432 **8051**
0099-1848 Collier Bankruptcy Cases **1327**
0099-1864 Martin Family Quarterly†
0099-1929 Louisiana. Department of Agriculture. Analysis of Official Pesticide Samples. Annual Report†
0099-2100 State Health Benefits Program of New Jersey. Annual Report
0099-2151 National Register of Health Service Providers in Psychology **7386**
0099-2224 Management Research (Amherst)†
0099-2232 Lutheran New Yorker†
0099-2240 Applied and Environmental Microbiology **881**
0099-2267 U.S. Department of Transportation. Office of University Research. Awards to Academic Institutions by the Department of Transportation†
0099-2313 Sunset Ideas for Improving Your Home†
0099-2399 The Journal of Endodontics **5851**
0099-2410 State of Louisiana Public Documents **7470**
0099-2445 Financial Analysis of the Motor Carrier Industry†
0099-2453 Human Resources Abstracts **1240**
0099-2496 Virginia Tidewater Genealogy
0099-3468 U S D A Forest Service. Research Note I N T *changed to* U S D A Forest Service. Rocky Mountain Research Station. Research Note **3705**
0099-3778 Electro-Technology Newsletter
0099-4227 North Dakota. Geological Survey. Report of Investigations **2759**
0099-426X New England Fruit Meetings **243**
0099-4480 Illuminating Engineering Society. Journal **3318**
0099-4936 Carnegie Institution of Washington. Publication **573**
0099-5355 The Lancet (North American Edition) **5660**
0099-5444 Nematropica **958**
0099-5851 Iowa State University Veterinarian **8799**
0099-5894 Santa Barbara Museum of Natural History. Contributions in Science **962**
0099-5908 S A E Special Publications **3218**
0099-6246 Advances in Behavioral Biology **7331**
0099-6343 Water Pollution Control Federation. Abstracts of Technical Papers
0099-6416 Communications of the Lunar and Planetary Laboratory **573**
0099-6459 Colorado Geological Survey. Special Publication **2729**
0099-7676 Florida Cooperative Extension Service. Circular **113**
0099-7838 Northern Nut Growers Association. Annual Report **3745**
0099-801X Federation Series on Coatings Technology **6717**
0099-8400 McIlvainea **800**
0099-8745 Na Okika O Hawaii **803**
0099-9016 Progress in Neuropathology†
0099-9598 The Alkaloids: Chemistry and Pharmacology *changed to* 1099-4831 **2119**
0099-9660 Wall Street Journal (Eastern Edition) **1390**
0100-0039 Cientifica **224**
0100-008X Museu Botanico Municipal. Boletim **802**
0100-0187 Odontologo Moderno†
0100-0195 Revista Medica do Estado do Rio de Janeiro†
0100-0217 Revista Pernambucana de Desenvolvimento
0100-0233 Revista Baiana de Saude Publica **7538**
0100-039X Perspectiva Economica **1159**
0100-0519 Jornal Brasileiro de Urologia *see* 1677-5538 **6269**
0100-0551 Pesquisa e Planejamento Economico **1900**
0100-0683 Revista Brasileira de Ciencia do Solo **250**
0100-0691 Revista Brasileira de Biblioteconomia e Documentacao **5043**
0100-0705 Bibliografia Brasileira de Engenharia†
0100-0748 Medicina de Hoje†
0100-0756 Bibliografia Brasileira de Quimica e Quimica Tecnologica†
0100-0780 Medicina do Esporte
0100-0845 Centro de Pesquisas do Cacau. Boletim Tecnico **100**
0100-0888 Revista Letras **5361**
0100-0934 Monografias de Matematica **5518**
0100-0977 Amazonia - Bibliografia†
0100-1213 Brazil. Ministerio da Justicia. Arquivos
0100-1248 Navigator†
0100-1299 Anuario Estatistico do Brasil **8347**
0100-1302 Universidade Federal do Ceara. Centro de Ciencias da Saude. Revista de Medicina **5726**
0100-1345 Sinopse Estatistica do Brasil†
0100-1574 Cadernos de Pesquisa **2833**
0100-1582 Revista de Direito Agrario **4771**
0100-1655 Alter **7332**
0100-1671 Construcao Rio de Janeiro **994**
0100-1752 Instituto dos Advogados Brasileiros. Revista **4693**
0100-1892 Boletim Demografico C B E D *changed to* 0101-0662 **7283**
0100-1922 Biblioteca Nacional de Brasil. Anais **4995**
0100-1965 Ciencia da Informacao **5002**
0100-1981 Revista de Processo **4772**
0100-204X Pesquisa Agropecuaria Brasileira **146**
0100-2104 Eletricidade Moderna **3306**
0100-2120 Federacao dos Trabalhadores na Agricultura do Estado do Parana. Relatorio
0100-2147 Ars Curandi em Odontologia
0100-2171 Revista Brasileira de Cirurgia da Cabeca e Pescoco **6256**
0100-2228 Sistemas†
0100-2538 Estudos Juridicos **4668**
0100-2546 Instituto de Pesquisas Zootecnicas "Francisco Osorio". Anuario Tecnico†
0100-2589 Revista Brasileira de Direito Processual **4770**
0100-2635 Estudos Brasileiros†
0100-2694 Faculdade de Ciencias Agrarias do Para. Boletim **110**
0100-2767 Periodicos Brasileiros de Ciencias e Tecnologia†
0100-2775 Dens **5839**
0100-2910 Brazilian Economic Studies†
0100-2945 Revista Brasileira de Fruticultura **250**
0100-2953 Instituto Historico e Geografico de Sao Paulo. Revista **4015**
0100-3127 Acta Oncologica Brasileira **6007**
0100-3143 Educacao e Realidade **2845**
0100-3151 Instituto Florestal. Boletim Tecnico†
0100-3232 Revista Brasileira de Clinica e Terapeutica†
0100-3283 Hansenologia Internationalis **5814**
0100-3321 Sao Paulo, Brazil (State). Secretaria da Educacao. Atividades Desenvolvidas
0100-3364 Informe Agropecuario **121**
0100-3518 Revista Brasileira de Armazenamento **151**
0100-3577 Brazil. Departamento Nacional da Producao Mineral. Boletim **6458**
0100-3593 Energia Nuclear e Agricultura **107**
0100-3674 Instituto de Laticinios Candido Tostes. Revista **265**
0100-381X Anuario Estatistico do Rio Grande do Sul†
0100-3909 Correio Agricola
0100-3941 Rede Ferroviaria Federal. Lista de Artigos Selecionados†
0100-3984 Radiologia Brasileira **6206**
0100-4042 Quimica Nova **2077**
0100-4158 Fitopatologia Brasileira *changed to* 1982-5676 **821**
0100-4204 Fitossanidade **788**
0100-4271 Brasil(Year)
0100-4298 Agroanalysis **193**
0100-431X Instituto Geologico. Boletim **2747**
0100-459X Brazil Trade and Industry *see* 0101-3645
0100-4670 Ecletica Quimica **2060**
0100-4700 Natureza em Revista†
0100-4891 Jornal dos Transportes
0100-4956 Revista Economica do Nordeste **1515**
0100-4964 Instituto de Tecnologia de Alimentos. Estudos Economicos. Alimentos Processados **3647**
0100-4980 Brazil. Ministerio da Agricultura. Escritorio de Estatistica. Pecuaria, Avicultura, Apicultura, Sericicultura†
0100-512X Kriterion **6931**
0100-5138 Pesquisa Industrial **1258**
0100-5146 Universidade de Sao Paulo. Instituto Oceanografico. Publicacao Especial **2820**
0100-5162 Precos Medios do Boi Gordo e La†
0100-5197 Universidade de Sao Paulo. Instituto Oceanografico. Relatorio de Cruzeiros **2820**
0100-5219 Precos Recebidos pelos Agricultores†
0100-526X Prognostico†
0100-5316 Prognostico Regiao Centro-Sul†
0100-5405 Summa Phytopathologica **819**
0100-5502 Revista Brasileira de Educacao Medica **5704**
0100-5545 Universidade de Sao Paulo. Instituto Astronomico e Geofisico. Anuario Astronomico
0100-560X Acompanhamento da Situacao Agropecuaria do Parana **78**
0100-5790 Instituto de Resseguros do Brasil. Secretaria Geral da Presidencia. Relatorio do Exercicio†
0100-6045 Manuscrito **6933**
0100-607X Revista do Setor de Ciencias Agrarias **151**
0100-6142 Data News
0100-6266 Bibliografia Brasileira de Odontologia (Print Edition)†
0100-6304 Museu Nacional. Publicacoes Avulsas **7884**
0100-655X Literatura Economica†
0100-6657 Rio de Janeiro, Brazil (City). Arquivo Geral da Cidade do Rio de Janeiro. Boletim Informativo
0100-6711 Revista Brasileira de Tecnologia†
0100-6762 Revista Arvore **3715**
0100-6908 Mineracao Metalurgia **6470**
0100-6916 Engenharia Agricola **107**
0100-6932 Historia: Questoes e Debates **4295**
0100-6991 Colegio Brasileiro de Cirurgioes. Revista **6240**
0100-705X Revista Paulista de Odontologia **5864**
0100-7068 Universidade Federal do Rio Grande do Norte. Centro de Biociencias. Departamento de Oceanografia e Limnologia. Boletim **709**
0100-7122 Veja **3804**
0100-7157 Revista de Biblioteconomia de Brasilia†
0100-7173 Informe Demografico **7285**
0100-7203 Revista Brasileira de Ginecologia e Obstetricia **6003**
0100-722X Bibliografia de Publicacoes Oficiais Brasileiras†
0100-7238 Brazil. Fundacao Nacional do Livro Infantil e Juvenil. Boletim Informativo†
0100-7351 Arquivos de Anatomia e Antropologia **329**
0100-736X Pesquisa Veterinaria Brasileira **8804**
0100-7521 Revista do Sistema Estadual de Informacao Tecnica e Estadistica†
0100-7653 Revista Nordestina de Biologia **701**
0100-767X Balanco Financeiro **1611**
0100-7904 Centro Nacional de Pesquisa de Gado de Leite. Relatorio Tecnico **262**
0100-7912 Geografia **4008**
0100-7955 Revista Catarinense de Odontologia **5863**
0100-8013 Brazil. Centro Nacional de Pesquisa de Milho e Sorgo. Circular Tecnica†
0100-8153 Africa **4172**
0100-8226 Hanseniasis Letter†
0100-8307 Ciencia e Natura **7847**
0100-8358 Planta Daninha **813**
0100-8404 Revista Brasileira de Botanica **815**
0100-8501 Pesquisa Agropecuaria Pernambucana **146**
0100-8587 Religiao & Sociedade **7674**
0100-8633 Annuario Brasileiro de Ceramica
0100-8730 Anuario Estatistico do Estado de Sao Paulo **8347**
0100-8781 Perfil Municipal **7500**
0100-879X Brazilian Journal of Medical and Biological Research **5588**
0100-8889 Revista Paulista de Enfermagem **5980**
0100-896X Empresa de Pesquisa Agropecuaria do Estado do Rio de Janeiro. Comunicado Tecnico **107**
0100-9079 Direito & Justica **4659**
0100-9087 Revista A B R A V A **4126**
0100-9125 Suinocultura Industrial **301**
0100-929X Instituto Geologico. Revista **2747**
0100-9303 Anuario Mineral Brasileiro **6456**
0100-9397 Alimentacao **3626**
0100-9591 Forum Educacional†
0100-9605 Dados Sobre a Situacao da Agropecuaria Municipal no Estado do Parana **196**
0100-9699 Revista da Imagem (Print) *changed to* Revista da Imagem (Online) **6207**
0100-9729 Centro de Pesquisa Agropecuaria do Tropico Semi-Arido. Documentos *changed to* 1516-1633 **228**
0100-9745 Anuario das Industrias **1972**
0100-9761 Boletim de Geografia Teoretica†
0100-977X Revista Amazonense de Desenvolvimento†
0100-9974 Brazil. Ministerio de Educacao. Faculdade de Ciencias Agrarias do Para. Informe Tecnico **97**
0101-0093 Revista Telebras
0101-0352 Universidade Federal do Parana. Centro de Estudos Portugueses. Arquivos†
0101-0360 Retrospectiva da Agropecuaria†
0101-0484 Brazil. Museu do Indio. Boletim. Documentacao **331**
0101-059X Didatica†
0101-0646 Banco do Brasil. Annual Report **1312**
0101-0662 Fundacao Instituto Brasileiro de Geografia e Estatistica. Boletim Demografico **7283**
0101-0697 Banco de Bibliografias†
0101-0794 C & I
0101-1049 Laudo
0101-1057 Boletim de Pesquisa Florestal **3684**
0101-1138 Tecnicouro **4975**
0101-1251 Brazil. Centro Nacional de Pesquisa de Milho e Sorgo. Relatorio Tecnico Anual **222**
0101-1480 Rio Grande do Sul, Brazil. Procuradoria Geral do Estado. Revista **4775**
0101-1529 Spectrum
0101-1642 Carta Geologica do Brasil ao Milionesimo **2728**
0101-1723 Ensaios F E E **1540**
0101-1766 Projeto
0101-1774 Universidade Estadual Paulista. Revista de Odontologia **5868**
0101-1812 Revista Signo **4472**
0101-1944 Naturalia **692**
0101-1960 A B C Z **276**
0101-1979 Engenharia Industrial
0101-2053 Sumario Mineral **6480**
0101-2061 Ciencia e Tecnologia de Alimentos **3631**
0101-207X Filme Cultura
0101-2207 Brazil. Fundacao Instituto Brasileiro de Geografia e Estadistica. Estatisticas do Registro Civil **7304**
0101-2223 Nordeste: Analise Conjuntural†
0101-2304 Som†
0101-2320 Banco Central do Brasil. Monthly Newsletter†
0101-255X Granja Avicola
0101-2657 Comunicacao e Sociedade **2317**
0101-2800 Jornal Brasileiro de Nefrologia **6270**
0101-2886 Balanco Mineral Brasileiro†
0101-3033 Estatisticas da Saude: Assistencia Medico-Sanitaria **5744**
0101-3122 Revista Brasileira de Sementes **250**
0101-3130 Estudos Teologicos **7756**
0101-3157 Revista de Economia Politica **7178**
0101-3173 Trans - Form - Acao **6958**
0101-3262 C E D E S Cadernos **2833**
0101-3289 Revista Brasileira de Ciencias do Esporte **8196**
0101-3300 Centro Brasileiro de Analise e Planejamento. Novos Estudos **7953**
0101-3327 Meio & Mensagem
0101-3335 Letras de Hoje **5143**
0101-3424 Cadernos de Historia e Filosofia da Ciencia **7843**
0101-3459 Perspectivas **7991**
0101-3505 Revista de Letras **5361**
0101-3548 Cadernos de Linguistica e Teoria da Literatura **5103**
0101-3580 Boletim de Zoologia†
0101-3599 Brasil Comercio e Industria *see* 0101-3645
0101-3645 Brazil Comercio e Industria
0101-3653 Cultura†
0101-3742 Semina (Londrina) **2300**
0101-3769 Empresa de Pesquisa Agropecuaria do Rio de Janeiro. Informe Tecnico **107**
0101-3793 Revista de Ciencias Farmaceuticas *changed to* 1808-4532 **6879**
0101-3963 Producao Agricola Municipal **185**
0101-4064 Estudos Ibero-Americanos **3532**
0101-4161 Estudos Economicos **1106**
0101-4218 Digesto Economico **1477**
0101-4234 Producao da Pecuaria Municipal **185**
0101-4242 Boletim de Fisiologia Animal **663**
0101-4269 Problemas Brasileiros **3804**
0101-4315 Confederacao Nacional do Comercio. Conselho Tecnico Consultivo. Carta Mensal **1426**
0101-4331 Informacao Psiquiatrica **6146**
0101-4366 Instituto Historico e Geografico Brasileiro. Revista **4298**
0101-4412 Bresil Commerce et Industrie *see* 0101-3645
0101-451X Universidade Federal de Santa Catarina. Museu de Antropologia. Anais **359**
0101-4617 Mimesis†

ISSN

9138 0101-4625 ULRICH'S PERIODICALS

0101-4625 Brazil. Coordenacao de Assistencia Medica e Hospitalar. Cadastro de Estabelecimentos de Saude†
0101-465X Educacao (Porto Alegre) **2845**
0101-4668 Banco Central do Brasil. Boletim **1311**
0101-4714 Universidade de Sao Paulo. Museu Paulista. Anais **4316**
0101-4781 Revista do Medico†
0101-4838 Tempo Psicanalitico **7411**
0101-4846 Ilha do Desterro **5308**
0101-4854 Documentacao Amazonica
0101-4862 Lingua e Literatura **5145**
0101-4919 Noticia Bibliografica **4154**
0101-5001 Revista de Ensino de Engenharia **3217**
0101-5028 A N D E **2822**
0101-515X Revista Goiana de Artes **514**
0101-5303 Estudos Tecnologicos **7853**
0101-5354 Acta Biologica Leopoldensia **649**
0101-5370 Memoria e Historia
0101-5400 Universidade Federal do Rio Grande do Norte. Departamento de Geologia. Boletim **2772**
0101-546X Estudos Afro-Asiaticos **7962**
0101-5559 Pesquisa em Andamento - Milho e Sorgo†
0101-563X Revista Brasileira de Mandioca†
0101-5664 Portos e Navios
0101-5680 Brazil. Departamento Nacional de Obras Contra as Secas. Relatorio **7423**
0101-5710 Anuario de Portos e Navios
0101-5818 Cadernos de Seguro **4497**
0101-5931 Informativo Anual da Industria Carbonifera **6465**
0101-6083 Revista de Psiquiatria Clinica **6182**
0101-6253 Empresa Brasileira de Pesquisa Agropecuaria. Servico Nacional de Levantamento e Conservacao de Solos. Boletim de Pesquisa†
0101-6261 Micro Mundo
0101-630X C T A A Boletim de Pesquisa†
0101-6377 Informe Conjuntural†
0101-6547 Clube Militar. Revista **6416**
0101-658X Destaques†
0101-6628 Servico Sociale e Sociedade **8068**
0101-6636 Balanco Energetico Nacional **3151**
0101-6822 Pesquisa Nacional por Amostra de Domicilios **8394**
0101-6903 Camara Brasileira do Livro. Centro de Catalogacao na Fonte. Oficina de Livros†
0101-6954 Universidade Catolica de Goias. Gabinete de Arqueologia. Anuario de Divulgacao Cientifica†
0101-7012 Revista de Econometria *changed to* Brazilian Review of Econometrics **1536**
0101-7136 Inter-Acao **2987**
0101-7217 Revista DocPop **7292**
0101-7284 Revista do Exercito Brasileiro **6443**
0101-7330 Educacao e Sociedade **2845**
0101-7438 Pesquisa Operacional **3214**
0101-7616 Roessleria†
0101-7659 Revista Brasileira de Aplicacoes de Vacuo **3394**
0101-7683 Empresa Capixaba de Pesquisa Agropecuaria. Comunicado Tecnico **107**
0101-7748 Fundacao Universidade do Rio Grande. Departamento de Oceanografia. Documentos Tecnicos **2804**
0101-7772 G E D **5923**
0101-7934 Centro de Estudos Portugueses. Boletim **4447**
0101-7969 Tudo e Historia
0101-7993 Cadernos do Terceiro Mundo **7112**
0101-8108 Revista de Psiquiatria do Rio Grande do Sul **6182**
0101-8140 Revista Regional de Aracatuba **5864**
0101-8159 Brazil. Departamento Nacional da Producao Mineral. Serie Tecnologia Mineral **6458**
0101-8175 Revista Brasileira de Zoologia *changed to* 1984-4670 **969**
0101-8191 Revista Tecnologia **8437**
0101-8205 Computational and Applied Mathematics **5551**
0101-8248 Revista Brasileira de Lingua e Literatura†
0101-8353 Indicadores I B G E†
0101-837X Estudos Germanicos **5291**
0101-8418 Universidade Federal da Bahia. Facultade de Odontologia. Revista **5868**
0101-8426 Cadernos Brasileiros de Arquitetura
0101-8434 Revista Eclesiastica Brasileira **7677**
0101-8469 Revista Brasileira de Neurologia **6181**
0101-8515 Ciencia Hoje **7847**
0101-8531 Ars Curandi Gastro†
0101-8698 Uniletras **5392**
0101-8892 Revista do Gas†
0101-9031 Educacao (Santa Maria) **2845**
0101-9074 Historia **4142**
0101-9082 Geociencias **2708**
0101-9112 Antenna - Eletronica Popular **2375**
0101-9236 Centro Brasileiro de Pesquisas Fisicas. Monografias†
0101-9252 Jornal Brasileiro de Reabilitacao **6081**
0101-9457 Revista de Geografia†
0101-9570 Travessia **5390**
0101-9589 Revista de Ciencias Humanas (Florianopolis) **7996**
0101-9619 Pesquisas: Publicacoes de Historia **4156**
0101-9635 Leopoldianum **2992**
0101-9708 Reuniao Geral de Cultura do Arroz. Anais **275**
0101-9759 Instituto de Geociencias. Anuario **2710**
0101-9783 Centro de Biologia da Reproducao. Boletim **665**
0101-9864 Brazil. Centro Nacional de Pesquisa de Milho e Sorgo. Documentos†
0101-9872 Revista Ibero-Latino-Americana de Dermatologia†
0101-9880 Revista Brasileira de Coloproctologia **6256**
0101-9902 Enfermagem
0101-9910 Salusvita **5709**
0102-0145 Mundo Mecanico
0102-0188 Revista Brasileira de Historia **4310**
0102-0218 Mensario Estatistico Sul-Rio-Grandense†
0102-0226 Resenha Estatistica do Rio Grande do Sul†
0102-0242 Comunicarte **2317**
0102-0250 Letras **5321**
0102-0269 Reflexao **6947**
0102-0285 Dados e Ideias
0102-0323 Centro de Pesquisa e Processamento de Alimentos. Boletim **3630**
0102-0358 Estatisticas Economicas do Setor Publico†
0102-0382 Clube Naval. Revista **6416**
0102-0420 Revista de Arqueologia **413**
0102-0501 Construcao Minas Centro Oeste **994**
0102-051X Construcao Norte Nordeste **894**
0102-0528 Construcao Regiao Sul **994**
0102-0536 Horticultura Brasileira **234**
0102-0560 Diagnosticos A P E C†
0102-0617 Ensayos E C I E L
0102-065X Suplemento Literario de Minas Gerais **5383**
0102-0676 Anuario Estatistico da Bahia **8346**
0102-0692 Bahia, Brazil (State). Centro de Planejamento. Comercio Exterior da Bahia: Exportacao Segundo as Firmas e Mercadorias
0102-0803 Revista Brasileira de Reproducao Animal (Online) **961**
0102-0811 Revista de Matematica e Estatistica **5529**
0102-0897 Revista Comunicacoes e Artes **8128**
0102-0900 Revista Brasileira de Cirugia, Protese e Traumatologia Buco - Maxilo - Facial **5863**
0102-0935 Arquivo Brasileiro de Medicina Veterinaria e Zootecnia **8793**
0102-1028 Anuario Estatistico de Energia Electrica. Autoprodutores do Estado de Sao Paulo†
0102-1249 Acta Geologica Leopoldensia **7832**
0102-1397 Curso de Direito. Revista **4654**
0102-1656 Atlantica **2800**
0102-1788 Escola Superior de Guerra. Revista
0102-1915 Anuario Estatistico do Distrito Federal
0102-1931 Plastico Moderno **7096**
0102-2040 Cadernos P U C **1445**
0102-2067 Estudos de Biologia **671**
0102-2105 Revista A M R I G S **5704**
0102-2253 Congresso Brasileiro de Economia e Sociologia Rural. Anais **196**
0102-2555 Universidade de Sao Paulo. Faculdade de Educacao. Revista *changed to* 1517-9702 **2845**
0102-261X Revista Brasileira de Geofisica **2788**
0102-2636 Politica e Estrategia†
0102-2660 Revista Brasileira de Engenharia. Caderno de Engenharia Eletrica **3329**
0102-2679 Revista Brasileira de Engenharia. Caderno de Engenharia Naval **3217**
0102-2881 Exame **1107**
0102-2997 Nematologia Brasileira **957**
0102-3098 Revista Brasileira de Estudos de Populacao **7292**
0102-311X Cadernos de Saude Publica **7511**
0102-3144 Biblioteca Nacional. Bibliografia Brasileira **619**
0102-3225 Guia Panrotas **8715**
0102-3292 Sociedade Paranaense de Matematica. Monografias†
0102-3306 Acta Botanica Brasilica **772**
0102-3314 Iheringia. Serie Miscelanea†
0102-3357 Art
0102-3519 Energia: Bibliografia Seletiva†
0102-3527 Letras & Letras **5143**
0102-3586 Jornal de Pneumologia *changed to* 1806-3713 **6215**
0102-3594 Caderno Catarinense de Ensino de Fisica **7007**
0102-3608 Expedicionario
0102-3616 Revista Brasileira de Ortopedia **6072**
0102-3772 Psicologia: Teoria e Pesquisa **7393**
0102-387X Leitura: Teoria e Pratica
0102-3896 Matemarica Fisica **7881**
0102-4205 Revista de Psicanalise Integral **7403**
0102-4248 Cadernos de Estudos Sociais **7952**
0102-4256 Centro de Pesquisas do Cacau. Informe de Pesquisas **100**
0102-4264 Acta Semiotica et Linguistica **5090**
0102-4272 Museu de Historia Natural. Arquivos **7884**
0102-4302 Anuario Antropologico **328**
0102-4442 Projeto Historia **4157**
0102-4450 Documentacao de Estudos em Linguistica Teorica e Aplicada **5112**
0102-4469 Perspectiva Teologica (Belo Horizonte) **7669**
0102-4531 Rochas de Qualidade **6478**
0102-4620 Universidade Federal do Rio Grande do Sul. Faculdade de Agronomia. Boletim Tecnico†
0102-4671 Anuario Estatistico dos Transportes **8490**
0102-4698 Educacao em Revista **2845**
0102-4728 Brasil Mineral **6458**
0102-4876 Aviacao em Revista **47**
0102-4884 Revista Fundacentro
0102-4906 Estudos Anglo-Americanos **5291**
0102-4930 R F F S A Anuario Estatistico†
0102-4957 Sistema Ferroviario do Brasil†
0102-4965 Anuario Estatistico das Ferrovias do Brasil†
0102-5074 Revista Brasileira de Comercio Exterior **1581**
0102-5473 Perspectiva **2897**
0102-549X Brazil. Servico Nacional de Aprendizagem Comercial. Boletim Tecnico **2832**
0102-5678 Universitas. Cultura **4480**
0102-5694 Sintese Ferroviaria Brasileira†
0102-5716 Veterinaria e Zootecnia **8810**
0102-5767 Cadernos de Estudos Linguisticos **5103**
0102-5813 Associacao Brasileira de Cibernetica Social. Revista **7949**
0102-597X Universidade Federal do Rio Grande do Sul. Instituto de Biociencias. Boletim **709**
0102-6054 Universitas. Ciencia **7926**
0102-6089 L I L A C S - S P†
0102-6178 Globo Rural **115**
0102-6224 Neritica **2813**
0102-6275 I G - U S P. Boletim. Publicacao Especial **2709**
0102-6283 I G - U S P. Boletim. Serie Cientifica **2709**
0102-6291 I G - U S P. Boletim. Serie Didatica **2709**
0102-6348 *see* 0101-0093
0102-6380 Ars Veterinaria **8793**
0102-6445 Lua Nova **7152**
0102-6453 InterCom **2326**
0102-6496 Socialismo & Democracia
0102-6518 Cadernos Rioarte **8091**
0102-6526 Summer Institute of Linguistics. Serie Linguistica **5184**
0102-6550 Arte U N E S P **472**
0102-6631 Universidade Federal do Rio de Janeiro. Instituto de Matematica. Memorias de Matematica **5549**
0102-6712 Acta Limnologica Brasiliensia **2792**
0102-6720 Arquivos Brasileiros de Cirurgia Digestiva **5920**
0102-6798 Revista Brasileira de Linguistica **5166**
0102-6801 Educacao e Filosofia **2845**
0102-6887 Paulo-Coutiana†
0102-6895 Revista de Fisica Aplicada e Instrumentacao **7038**
0102-6909 Revista Brasileira de Ciencias Sociais **7996**
0102-6933 Revista Gaucha de Enfermagem **5980**
0102-695X Revista Brasileira de Farmacognosia **6878**
0102-6968 Centro de Letras e Ciencias Humanas **4447**
0102-6976 Pontificia Universidade Catolica do Rio Grande do Sul. Museu de Ciencias e Tecnologia. Comunicacoes. Serie Botanica **813**
0102-6984 Diogenes (Brazilian Edition) *see* 0392-1921 **7959**
0102-6992 Sociedade e Estado **8135**
0102-700X Acervo **4281**
0102-7077 The Especialist **5116**
0102-7085 Revista Analise e Conjuntura
0102-7115 Quem e Quem na Economia Brasileira **2025**
0102-7182 Psicologia & Sociedade **7993**
0102-731X Universidade Federal de Pelotas. Departamento de Pesquisa e Pos-Graduacao. Trabalhos Publicados: Resumos **2306**
0102-7336 Revista de Teatro **8477**
0102-7484 Mimesis (Bauru) **7985**
0102-7603 Pesquisa e Debate **1159**
0102-762X Disturbios de Comunicacao **2319**
0102-7638 Revista Brasileira de Cirurgia Cardiovascular **5798**
0102-7670 Revista Brasileira de Engenharia. Caderno de Engenharia Nuclear **3174**
0102-7735 Revista de Educacao em Questao **2906**
0102-7743 Ciencias Humanas **5210**
0102-7778 Artus **6982**
0102-7786 Revista Brasileira de Meteorologia **6394**
0102-7972 Psicologia: Reflexao e Critica **7393**
0102-8030 Terra Livre **4031**
0102-8049 Revista de Direito Mercantil, Industrial, Economico, e Financeiro **4771**
0102-8200 Revista de Ciencias Sociais (Porto Alegre) **7996**
0102-8227 Cadernos de Divulgacao Cultural **5590**
0102-8413 Revista Forense **4772**
0102-843X A M B *changed to* 0104-4230 **5580**
0102-8464 Revista de Educacao Fisica **3079**
0102-8529 Pontificia Universidade Catolica de Rio de Janeiro. Instituto de Relacoes Internacionais. Contexto Internacional **7172**
0102-8537 Revista Brasileira de Angiologia e Cirugia Vascular **5798**
0102-8650 Acta Cirurgica Brasileira **6234**
0102-8758 Contexto e Educacao **2839**
0102-8774 Revista de Direito do Trabalho (Sao Paulo) **4771**
0102-8782 Tempo Brasileiro **2919**
0102-8820 Academia Cearense de Letras. Revista **5248**
0102-8839 Sao Paulo em Perspectiva **7999**
0102-8901 Manchete Rural **135**
0102-8936 P & T†
0102-8979 Arquitetura e Urbanismo **434**
0102-9010 Revista Brasileira de Ciencias Morfologicas **927**
0102-9150 Guia Rural†
0102-9223 Associacao Brasileira de Engenharia Militar. Revista **6412**
0102-9304 Boletim de Geociencias da Petrobras **6764**
0102-9460 Revista Odonto Ciencia **5864**
0102-9479 Humanidades **4455**
0102-9568 Bioikos **657**
0102-9592 Acta Cirurgica Brasileira. Suplemento **6234**
0102-9711 C E A S Cadernos **8091**
0102-9789 Revista A B N T **6405**
0102-9797 Revista Brasileira de Mercado de Capitais **1167**
0102-9843 Revista Brasileira de Engenharia Quimica **3254**
0102-986X Sociedade Brasileira de Telecomunicacoes. Revista **2339**
0103-0000 Cadernos de Educacao Especial **3037**
0103-0116 Nova Escola **2892**
0103-0205 Empresa Brasileira de Pesquisa Agropecuaria. Embrapa Algodao. Documentos **229**
0103-0582 Revista Paulista de Pediatria **6103**
0103-0809 Arquivos de Saude Mental do Estado de Sao Paulo **6124**
0103-0817 Arquivos de Saude Mental do Estado de Sao Paulo. Suplemento **6124**
0103-1015 Universidade Federal do Rio de Janeiro. Instituto de Matematica. Estudos e Comunicacoes **5543**
0103-1090 Brasil. Tribunal de Contas da Uniao. Revista **1913**
0103-1104 Saude em Debate **7541**
0103-1414 Verso e Reverso **4481**
0103-1562 Face **5118**
0103-1570 Sociedade e Natureza **4029**
0103-1589 Boletim Cultural **7841**
0103-1597 Cadernos de Geociencias **2703**
0103-1643 Biotemas **662**
0103-166X Estudos de Psicologia (Campinas) **7355**
0103-1759 S B A **2463**
0103-1767 Instituto de Pesca. Boletim Tecnico (Print Edition) **3598**
0103-1813 Trabalhos em Linguistica Aplicada **5188**
0103-1821 Estudos Portugueses e Africanos **7962**
0103-183X Remate de Males **7995**
0103-1880 Filosofia Politica **7136**
0103-1899 Sociedade Brasileira de Historia da Ciencia. Boletim **7917**
0103-2003 Revista de Economia e Sociologia Rural **205**
0103-2038 Bibliografia de Politica Industrial **1214**
0103-2070 Tempo Social **8143**
0103-2100 Acta Paulista de Enfermagem **5950**
0103-2186 Estudos Historicos **4292**
0103-2259 Revista Brasileira de Alergia e Imunopatologia **5765**
0103-2283 Presenca Filosofica **6945**
0103-2380 Chronos **482**
0103-2437 Terra Indigena **3568**
0103-2550 Jardim Botanico do Rio de Janeiro. Arquivos **795**

ISSN

ISSN

ISSN

9144 0109-4599 ULRICH'S PERIODICALS

0109-4599 Muldvarpen
0109-467X Trade Directory for Denmark† **8994**
0109-4718 Ask†
0109-4777 Horse Holidays in W. Europe†
0109-4831 P S†
0109-4890 Entreprenoeren **1007**
0109-4947 Vaekst **3707**
0109-4955 Fortegnelse over Dansk Udviklingsforskning†
0109-5013 Data om Markedet†
0109-5072 NU!†
0109-5129 Fravaer ved Anmeldte Arbejdsulykker†
0109-5196 R F Avisen†
0109-5250 A 5 - Bogen†
0109-5277 Kvartalsvis Statistik for Koebenhavnsomraadet†
0109-534X Pladeanmeldelser, Rytmisk Musik†
0109-5358 Dansk-Tjekkoslovakisk Selskab. Kvartalsnyt†
0109-5366 I F L A Communications†
0109-5390 Litteratur, Aestetik, Sprog†
0109-5420 Denmark. Danmarks Statistik. Udenrigshandelen Fordelt paa Varer og Lande *changed to* 1902-8512 **8949**
0109-548X R D F Bulletin†
0109-5544 Ny Abstraktion†
0109-5579 Penge†
0109-5625 Socialisten†
0109-5641 Dental Materials **5840**
0109-565X Gerodontics†
0109-5668 Cancer Reviews†
0109-5749 Cancer Incidents in Denmark (Year) **6013**
0109-5757 Denmark. Forsvarsministeriet. Aarlige Redegoerelse† **8949**
0109-5781 Hele Fyns Erhvervsliv†
0109-579X Sydslesvig i Dag **7268**
0109-5811 Farvandvaesenets Trafikanalyse†
0109-596X Sammenslutningen af Danske Fodplejere - Fagtidsskrift **591**
0109-5978 Liber Academiae Kierkegaardiensis† **8971**
0109-6028 Siden Saxo **4263**
0109-6109 Edb Nyt†
0109-6125 Danmarks Turist Vejviser† **8948**
0109-6257 Handelshoejskolen i Koebenhavn. Center for Uddannelsesforskning. Rapport†
0109-6311 Politikens Computer Aarbog†
0109-6397 En Tern†
0109-646X Matrix **7384**
0109-6486 Dansk Faellesrejse Forening. Medlemsblad† **8948**
0109-6664 Fysiktips†
0109-6672 Denmark. Direktoratet for Toldvaesenet. Toldvaesenets Aarsberetning†
0109-6699 Lokalhistorisk Arkiv, Aalestrup. Aarsskrift **4241**
0109-6702 Feature fra Danmark†
0109-6796 Dannebrog Comics†
0109-6834 Sundhed og Samfund†
0109-6923 Tal om Landbruget **186**
0109-6966 Alt om Mad†
0109-7164 Danmarks Dyreliv† **8948**
0109-7172 Vaern om Danmark **6451**
0109-7202 Pulsen†
0109-7318 Windpower Monthly **3179**
0109-7334 Service- og Varevogne†
0109-7342 Installations Nyt. Leverandoerregister **3319**
0109-7423 Transport- og Shippingbladet†
0109-7490 Motor-Magasinet **8592**
0109-7539 Nordisk Flagkontakt **3777**
0109-758X Dansk Beton *changed to* 1903-1025 **982**
0109-7598 Managements Erhvervspolitiske Forum. Rapport†
0109-7644 Dagens Danmark† **8948**
0109-7679 Landscentralen for Undervisningsmidler. Teknisk Information†
0109-7687 Cielo dei Vichinghi†
0109-7695 Denmark. Miljoeministeriet. Miljoeministeriets Publikationsregister.†
0109-7709 Barn og Kultur i Norden†
0109-7717 Video. Vaerd at Se†
0109-7733 Vente Journalen†
0109-792X Erhvervslederen **1105**
0109-8047 Aktuell Nordisk Statistik†
0109-8071 Telex Danmark†
0109-8195 Virksomheds Nyt. Leverandoerregister†
0109-8314 Denmark. Danmarks Statistik. Vejviser i Statistikken† **8949**
0109-8365 Folk Fortaeller **4220**
0109-8519 Blindesagen **4079**
0109-8551 Lokalhistorisk Aarskrift **4241**
0109-856X Feltundersoegelser† **8956**
0109-8632 Den Frie Laererskole *changed to* 1903-5632 **2919**
0109-8640 Bibliotek og Uddannelse†
0109-8667 Hele Aarhus Amts Erhvervsliv†
0109-8853 Folkebibliotekernes Udenlanske Boernebogssamling. Katalog†
0109-890X K T†
0109-8985 Skolan i Norden (Print Edition) *changed to* 1602-8155 **2913**
0109-8993 Pohjoismaiden Kouluoloista (Finnish Edition) *changed to* 1602-8155 **2913**
0109-9019 Videofilm der er og for Boern†
0109-9035 Aarhus Universitet. Center for Latinamerikastudier. Nyhedsbrev†
0109-9043 Exportoeren†
0109-9051 Grusavisen†
0109-906X Lyrik & Prosa†
0109-9078 Fuglelivet ved Roskilde Fjord†
0109-9108 Freinet Nyt† **8958**
0109-9124 Denmark. Socialstyrelsen. Redegoerelse om Social- og Sundhedsplanlaegning†
0109-9140 Homeservice Stations Outside the Tropical Bands†
0109-9213 Datatid **2416**
0109-923X Biblioteksbistorie **4996**
0109-9264 Historisk Samfund for Soenderjylland. Skrifter **4229**
0109-9272 Avisaarbogen (year) **4132**
0109-9280 Den Jyske Historiker **4236**
0109-9299 Leder-Kursuskatalog† **8970**
0109-9310 Erhvervs-Orientering Stat Amt, Kommune **1105**
0109-9418 Jern- og Maskinindustrien **6318**
0109-9485 Om Gymnasiet, Studenterkursus og Hoejre Forberedelseseksamen†
0109-9779 Roskilde Universitetscenter. Datalogisk Afdeling. Datalogiske Skrifter **2436**
0109-9787 Sporten† **8989**
0109-9876 Fodbold, Danske Kampe **8228**
0109-9973 Aarhus Universitet. Socialmedicinsk Institut. Rapport†
0110-0041 Productivity & Technology.†
0110-0068 Miorita†
0110-0084 Outrigger†
0110-022X New Zealand Family Physician† **8977**
0110-0246 New Zealand Tax Reports†
0110-0262 New Zealand International Review **7255**
0110-0297 New Zealand Gymnast†
0110-036X Noumenon†
0110-0394 Soccer News†
0110-0483 Country Side of Music†
0110-0599 New Zealand Motorman†
0110-070X Butterworths Current Law **4634**
0110-084X Farming Statistics†
0110-0858 Islands†
0110-0947 University of Waikato. Department of Earth Sciences. Occasional Report *changed to* 1177-3871 **2718**
0110-1048 What's New in Forest Research†
0110-1080 New Zealand Alpine Journal **8324**
0110-1102 Art New Zealand **470**
0110-1145 Spiral†
0110-1277 New Zealand Administrative Reports **4746**
0110-148X New Zealand Law Reports **4746**
0110-1501 New Zealand Deer Farming Annual **294**
0110-1625 The Turnbull Library Record **4194**
0110-165X New Zealand. Soil Bureau. Bibliographic Report†
0110-1730 Commercial Fishing†
0110-1803 New Zealand Library Symbols† **8977**
0110-1900 New Zealand. Health Statistical Services. Hospital Management Data†
0110-1951 United Nations Handbook (Year) **7271**
0110-2079 New Zealand. Soil Bureau. Soil Survey Reports†
0110-2192 University of Waikato. Antarctic Research Unit. Report **2773**
0110-2656 New Zealand Export-Import Corporation. Report
0110-3245 New Zealand Bookworld†
0110-3458 New Zealand. Department of Statistics. Transport Statistics†
0110-3466 New Zealand. Statistics New Zealand. Local Authority Statistics (Print)†
0110-3474 New Zealand. Department of Statistics. Insurance Statistics†
0110-3490 New Zealand. Department of Statistics. Building Statistics†
0110-3539 Electrical Industry Directory Yearbook† **8953**
0110-3563 Engineering Management & Equipment Digest†
0110-3571 Engineering Reference Handbook† **8953**
0110-4004 Whakatane & District Historical Society. Monographs **4194**
0110-4012 New Zealand Genealogist **3776**
0110-4233 New Zealand Tax Planning Report
0110-4381 Build Magazine **984**
0110-4454 Out!† **8979**
0110-4470 New Zealand Institute of Economic Research. Quarterly Survey of Business Opinion **1153**
0110-4527 Entomological Society of New Zealand. Bulletin **845**
0110-4586 New Zealand. Department of Statistics. Vital Statistics†
0110-4640 New Zealand. Department of Statistics. Census of Building and Construction†
0110-4675 Motor Industry Year Book†
0110-4748 Delta Research Monograph **2841**
0110-4802 New Zealand. Ministry of Foreign Affairs. Development†
0110-4853 Tablet† **8992**
0110-487X Prudentia **4157**
0110-4896 Onslow Historian **4193**
0110-4926 The Stockade **4194**
0110-5027 New Zealand. Department of Statistics. Part B: Wages and Labour†
0110-5124 New Zealand Antarctic Record†
0110-5191 Public Sector **7463**
0110-5205 N Z O I Oceanographic Field Report†
0110-5221 D S I R Discussion Paper†
0110-523X Reserve Bank of New Zealand. Research Papers **1514**
0110-5248 New Zealand Runner† **8977**
0110-5264 New Zealand Health Statistics Report†
0110-5337 N Z A R T Amateur Radio Callbook†
0110-540X New Zealand Journal of Archaeology **408**
0110-5493 Aviation Historical Society of New Zealand. Journal **48**
0110-5558 Massey University. Centre for Applied Economics and Policy Studies. Agricultural Policy Paper† **8973**
0110-5566 Chemistry in New Zealand **2057**
0110-5655 The Capital Letter **7429**
0110-5892 Canterbury Botanical Society. Journal **783**
0110-5949 Consumer **2636**
0110-6015 Wool†
0110-604X Wildlife - a Review†
0110-6155 Rails† **8984**
0110-618X N Z O I Records†
0110-6287 New Zealand Environment† **8977**
0110-6325 New Zealand Beekeeper **856**
0110-6376 Set (Wellington) **2911**
0110-6384 New Zealand Journal of Sports Medicine **6231**
0110-6465 New Zealand Journal of Ecology **693**
0110-6635 New Zealand Justices' Quarterly **4746**
0110-666X Directory of Australian Associations **1985**
0110-6813 National Business Review **1500**
0110-6872 New Zealand. Ministry of Transport. Traffic Research Report†
0110-6945 Public Service Association Journal **7463**
0110-7070 Reserve Bank of New Zealand. Annual Report **1379**
0110-7321 Inter-Industry Study of the New Zealand Economy†
0110-7380 New Zealand Journal of French Studies **5341**
0110-7771 Canzona **6554**
0110-7968 New Zealand Nursing Forum†
0110-7992 The Deer Farmer **285**
0110-8085 Celluloid Strip†
0110-8247 People & Planning†
0110-8476 New Zealand Fishing News **8324**
0110-8530 Horticulture News **3737**
0110-8603 Broadsheet†
0110-9510 New Ethicals Catalogue *changed to* 1176-5844 **6859**
0110-9596 New Zealand Journal of Business†
0110-9618 New Zealand Fishing Industry Board. Report†
0110-9790 Headliner **1628**
0111-0136 University of Auckland. School of Engineering. Report **3225**
0111-0225 New Zealand. Statistics New Zealand. New Zealand Life Tables. **4530**
0111-0365 Critic **2279**
0111-0586 Chem N Z **2053**
0111-0756 New Zealand. Road Research Unit. Occasional Paper†
0111-0829 New Zealand Agricultural Engineering Institute. Current Publications†
0111-1108 Economic Review of New Zealand Agriculture†
0111-1124 New Zealand. Ministry of Transport. Traffic Research Circular†
0111-1302 N Z O I Oceanographic Summary†
0111-1485 New Zealand Society of Periodontology. Journal **5857**
0111-1736 Meteorological Society of New Zealand. Newsletter **6391**
0111-1760 University of Otago. Economics Discussion Papers **1189**
0111-1957 Alpha **7834**
0111-199X New Zealand Population Review **7288**
0111-2473 Agricultural Economist†
0111-2767 Tenders Gazette **5460**
0111-2805 Roll Back the Years†
0111-3119 Paper Clip†
0111-3232 Freshwater Catch†
0111-3364 New Zealand Pottery and Ceramics Research Association. Annual Report†
0111-378X N.Z.A.E.I. Newsletter†
0111-3895 Royal Society of New Zealand. Miscellaneous Series **7905**
0111-3933 University of Canterbury. Department of Psychology. Research Report†
0111-3976 New Zealand Society of Animal Production. Occasional Publication **294**
0111-4123 Planning Research Index†
0111-4158 Q-NewZ **1788**
0111-431X New Zealand Pharmacy Journal **6863**
0111-5162 Packaging Industry†
0111-5308 Centrepoint†
0111-5383 Fauna of New Zealand **943**
0111-5499 Weather and Climate **6398**
0111-5626 Statutes of New Zealand **4788**
0111-5642 Parliamentary Debates (Wellington) **7459**
0111-5650 New Zealand Gazette **7456**
0111-5677 Carrier
0111-5715 New Zealand Archaeological Association Monograph **408**
0111-5839 Energy Journal†
0111-6053 Report of the Administrator of Tokelau **7465**
0111-6207 N Z A S I A *changed to* 0114-0280
0111-6339 Massey University. Centre for Applied Economics and Policy Studies. Agricultural Policy Proceedings† **8973**
0111-6355 New Zealand School Journal **2205**
0111-672X New Zealand Science Abstracts†
0111-686X New Zealand. Nature Conservation Council. Newsletter†
0111-7122 Ionospheric Data, New Zealand†
0111-7289 Signature (Auckland)†
0111-7343 Russell Review **4194**
0111-7653 Auckland-Waikato Historical Journal†
0111-7696 The Weta **861**
0111-8021 New Zealand Financial Review†
0111-803X Wellington Orchid Society. Journal *changed to* 1177-0864 **3754**
0111-8587 D S I R Industrial Information Series†
0111-8676 Parallax†
0111-8781 New Zealand Bookseller & Publisher†
0111-8854 Mentalities **4153**
0111-8889 Access **2823**
0111-8994 Crescendo **6560**
0111-9044 Marketing Magazine *changed to* N Z Marketing Magazine **1835**
0111-9168 Economic News†
0111-9184 Agronomy Society of New Zealand. Special Publication. **217**
0111-9435 New Zealand Planning Institute. Planning Quarterly **4421**
0111-946X Institution of Professional Engineers New Zealand. Electrical, Mechanical and Chemical Engineering Section. Transactions† **8965**
0111-9508 Institution of Professional Engineers New Zealand. Civil Engineering Section. Transactions†
0112-0212 New Zealand Journal of Environmental Health **7533**
0112-0328 Future Times **8103**
0112-0395 N Z O I Hydrology Station Data†
0112-0433 N Z Micro *changed to* 1178-2773 **2572**
0112-0581 Canterbury Law Review **4640**
0112-0603 Massey University. Centre for Applied Economics and Policy Studies. Agricultural Policy Discussion Paper **203**
0112-109X New Zealand Journal of Psychology **7388**
0112-1138 New Zealand Scout News *changed to* 1177-8911 **2204**
0112-1227 Journal of New Zealand Literature **5315**
0112-1421 Asparagus Research Newsletter **219**
0112-1537 Merchandise Trade with Australia†
0112-1545 University of Auckland. Department of Geography. Occasional Publication *changed to* 1175-8457 **4032**
0112-1642 Sports Medicine **6233**
0112-1669 Street Rodder **8209**
0112-1758 H E R A Report **3194**
0112-2061 New Zealand Planning Council. Monitoring Reports†
0112-224X New Zealand Journal of Adult Learning *changed to* Journal of Adult Learning **2943**
0112-2320 AgLink Index and Catalogue†

0112-2339 New Zealand. Department of Scientific and Industrial Research. Social Science Series†
0112-238X Peace Office Newsletter **7740**
0112-2479 Collected Papers from the Journal of the Royal Society of New Zealand **7847**
0112-255X Hospital Therapeutics†
0112-2606 New Zealand Packaging Yearbook†
0112-2649 New Zealand Statistical Association. Newsletter **5520**
0112-2754 Wool Research Organisation of New Zealand Special Publications **8462**
0112-2789 Onfilm **6509**
0112-2851 Wool Research Organisation of New Zealand Reports† **8999**
0112-2908 Wool Research Organisation of New Zealand Communications†
0112-2932 Wool Research Organisation of New Zealand. Technical Papers†
0112-3114 New Zealand Field & Stream†
0112-3386 Real Estate Market in New Zealand. Provisional Report *changed to* 1176-9947 **7602**
0112-3475 Autofile **8562**
0112-3572 Profile New Zealand - The Electrical Industry†
0112-3629 New Zealand. Department of Statistics. Census of Transport, Storage & Communication†
0112-3718 New Zealand Census of Agricultural Contracting Services†
0112-3823 New Zealand Tax Cases
0112-3890 New Zealand Journal of Technology†
0112-3939 New Zealand. Department of Statistics. Statistics of Incomes and Income Tax of Persons†
0112-3998 New Zealand. Department of Statistics. Statistics of Incomes and Income Tax of Companies†
0112-4099 Women's Studies Journal† **8999**
0112-4226 New Zealand Hardware Journal (Auckland, 1981) **1054**
0112-4447 New Zealand. Department of Statistics. Justice Statistics: Part A†
0112-4501 New Zealand. Department of Statistics. Justice Statistics: Part B†
0112-4927 Surveillance **8808**
0112-4951 Dance News **2684**
0112-5117 New Zealand. Department of Statistics. Overseas Balance of Payments†
0112-5265 Deer Course for Veterinarians. Proceedings **8796**
0112-5443 New Zealand Stamp Collector **6897**
0112-5842 Business Keynote†
0112-6121 Technology Reviews
0112-6202 Straight Furrow **214**
0112-6393 New Zealand Trucking Magazine **8673**
0112-6598 New Zealand. Department of Statistics. Prices Statistics†
0112-6709 New Zealand. Department of Statistics. External Migration Statistics†
0112-6997 AdMedia **19**
0112-739X Meat and Wool Boards' Economic Service. Annual Review of the New Zealand Sheep & Beef Industry† **8973**
0112-7438 Nursing Praxis in New Zealand **5975**
0112-7497 Marketing Services Directory **1833**
0112-8337 University of Auckland. Calendar **3008**
0112-8876 Ad/Media's Agencies & Clients **19**
0112-8922 New Zealand Disabled†
0112-9023 North & South **3918**
0112-921X New Zealand Sociology **8123**
0112-9341 Illusions **6503**
0112-9643 Massey University. Veterinary Continuing Education. Publication *changed to* 1176-7979 **8814**
0112-9759 University of Auckland. Department of Economics. Policy Discussion Papers† **8996**
0112-9791 New Zealand Income Tax Legislation
0112-9805 Ergonomics New Zealand **3344**
0112-9910 Southland Times **3919**
0113-0374 Matangi Tonga **3962**
0113-0501 N Z Petroleum Exploration News†
0113-0641 New Zealand Harness Racing Weekly **8295**
0113-0668 Metro **3918**
0113-0838 Boating New Zealand **8273**
0113-1044 New Zealand Institute of International Affairs. Occasional Paper (No.)† **8977**
0113-115X Butterworths Conveyancing Bulletin **4634**
0113-1176 New Zealand. House of Representatives. Parliamentary Bulletin **7456**
0113-1184 Volunteers **6453**
0113-1206 Cuisine **4355**
0113-1222 New Zealand Labour Force **1700**
0113-1494 Computerworld New Zealand **2414**
0113-1680 Quarterly Predictions **1721**
0113-1850 Grocers' Review **3679**
0113-1877 New Zealand Institute of Economic Research. Research Monographs **1153**
0113-2016 Victoria University of Wellington. Decision Research Centre. Working Paper Series†
0113-2180 New Zealand Fisheries Technical Report†
0113-2202 Media Directory **29**
0113-2261 New Zealand Fisheries Research Bulletin†
0113-227X New Zealand Fisheries Occasional Publication†
0113-2288 New Zealand Fisheries. Data Report†
0113-2334 New Zealand Law Commission. Report **4746**
0113-2415 Antipodas **5094**
0113-2903 New Zealand. Department of Scientific and Industrial Research. Geophysics Division. Research Report†
0113-3055 New Zealand. Department of Scientific and Industrial Research. Geophysics Division. Technical Report†
0113-3144 New Zealand Business Bulletin†
0113-3292 Contraband **1556**
0113-3403 Tearaway Magazine **2216**
0113-3462 Interface†
0113-3667 New Zealand. Statistics New Zealand. Demographic Trends **7313**
0113-4043 New Zealand Traveltrade **8741**
0113-423X Psychiatria **6176**
0113-4566 Architecture New Zealand **431**
0113-4795 Radiation Protection News and Notes†
0113-4957 N Z Business **1151**
0113-5376 Oral History in New Zealand **4193**
0113-5597 New Zealand Chart Catalogue **8655**
0113-6224 Wood Processing Newsletter **3718**
0113-6976 Commercial Horticulture **3755**
0113-6984 Freshwater Fisheries Centre. Annual Report **3595**
0113-714X Butterworths District Court Reports **4634**
0113-7492 New Zealand Natural Sciences **693**
0113-7646 Rural News **153**
0113-7662 Social Work Review *changed to* 1178-5527 **8025**
0113-7751 Quantity Surveyor **4025**
0113-7832 Archaeology in New Zealand **378**
0113-7859 New Zealand Bloodhorse† **8977**
0113-7867 English in Aotearoa **5114**
0113-8596 New Zealand Film **6508**
0113-8642 Little Treasures **2160**
0113-8685 Paneltalk **6719**
0113-8901 Food Industry News†
0113-9371 Industrial Equipment News†
0113-9479 New Zealand Society for Music Therapy. Annual Journal *changed to* 1176-3264 **6599**
0113-9533 Safeguard (Auckland) **6685**
0113-9606 New Zealand Fisherman†
0113-9762 Press (Christchurch) **3918**
0113-9932 Environment Update *changed to* 1176-0486 **2610**
0113-9967 New Zealand Geographic **4022**
0114-0213 Customs Release **1560**
0114-023X Reserve Bank of New Zealand. Economic Forecasts†
0114-0280 N Z ASIA N†
0114-0582 Pacific Accounting Review **1373**
0114-0671 New Zealand Journal of Crop and Horticultural Science **140**
0114-0876 Rip It Up **6612**
0114-0892 Clinical Pharmacokinetics Drug Data Handbook (Year)†
0114-1090 Te Puna Matauranga†
0114-1260 Companies Registered in New Zealand - Nominal Index
0114-1279 Companies Registered in New Zealand - Address Index
0114-1406 Rugby News **8244**
0114-1473 The Dairyman **264**
0114-1481 Royal New Zealand Institute of Horticulture. Newsletter†
0114-2720 New Zealand. Commerce Commission. Decision **4877**
0114-3344 New Zealand Windsurfer† **8977**
0114-3468 New Zealand Stamp Collection *changed to* 1177-2271 **6897**
0114-3727 New Zealand Health & Hospital **4108**
0114-3999 New Zealand External Relations Review†
0114-4081 Computers in New Zealand Schools† **8942**
0114-4138 Takahe **5385**
0114-4189 New Zealand Legacy **4193**
0114-426X Otago Daily Times **3918**
0114-4618 New Zealand Real Estate *changed to* 1176-9718 **7606**
0114-4693 New Zealand. Ministry of External Relations and Trade. Moore Report†
0114-541X Consumer Voice†
0114-5436 Consumer Food and Health†
0114-5770 Poetry N Z **5431**
0114-5916 Drug Safety **6836**
0114-6017 He Muka **5153**
0114-622X Woman's Day New Zealand **8889**
0114-6602 Operational Research Society of New Zealand. Proceedings of the Annual Conference **1157**
0114-6912 New Zealand. Department of Statistics. Economy Wide Census†
0114-6971 New Zealand. Ministry of Foreign Affairs and Trade. Overseas Posts† **8977**
0114-7161 Inland Revenue Department. Tax Information Bulletin **1929**
0114-7277 National Farming News†
0114-7285 P C World New Zealand **2582**
0114-7870 New Zealand College of Midwives. Journal **5999**
0114-8052 Export Levels of New Zealand Wool Products and Their Current Markets†
0114-8206 N Z E I Rourou **2889**
0114-8745 Athletics New Zealand News *changed to* 1177-5254 **8932**
0114-8818 D S I R Plant Protection Report†
0114-8966 New Zealand Surfing **8325**
0114-9032 New Zealand Musician **6599**
0114-9083 Style†
0114-9172 New Zealand Historic Places *changed to* 1175-9615 **4192**
0114-975X Dairy Statistics **179**
0114-989X LawTalk **4717**
0114-9954 Reactions Weekly **6890**
0115-0022 Sylvatrop **3704**
0115-0235 Business Outlook in the Philippines and Asia
0115-0243 Philippine Quarterly of Culture and Society **4469**
0115-0251 Forest Products Research and Industries Development Commission. Annual Report **3712**
0115-0340 Philippine Coconut Authority. Agricultural Research Annual Report **247**
0115-0405 C L S U Scientific Journal **99**
0115-0421 Philippines. Public Information Office. Official Gazette
0115-0464 Private Development Corporation of the Philippines. Monthly Economic Letter†
0115-0553 Kalikasan
0115-0804 Philippine Phytopathology **807**
0115-0820 Araneta Research Journal
0115-0952 Plant Protection News†
0115-0960 Canopy International **3685**
0115-1169 P S S C Social Science Information **7990**
0115-1207 Philippine Astronomical Handbook **579**
0115-1266 University of the Philippines at Los Banos. College of Forestry. Conservation Circular†
0115-1312 Construction & Engineering
0115-1525 Hospital Journal **4100**
0115-1541 P C A Coconut Farmers Bulletin†
0115-155X Philippines. National Census and Statistics Office. Annual Survey of Wholesale and Retail Establishments†
0115-1746 Philippine Business Review†
0115-1843 Builder of Progress†
0115-1894 Education Quarterly **2979**
0115-205X Manila Review†
0115-2092 N S O Monthly Bulletin of Statistics **8389**
0115-2106 Philippine Biota
0115-2130 Kimika **2070**
0115-2157 Trends in Technology
0115-2173 Philippine Journal of Veterinary and Animal Sciences **8804**
0115-2181 Initiatives in Population†
0115-2297 Journal of History **4184**
0115-2300 Nucleus
0115-2351 Philippine Textile Digest†
0115-2394 Trade Post†
0115-2408 Journal of Northern Luzon **3545**
0115-2467 I R R I Reporter†
0115-2521 University of Baguio Journal†
0115-2629 Philippine Labor Review **1703**
0115-2661 Social Development News†
0115-2742 Mindanao Journal **7986**
0115-2971 Homelife **3928**
0115-3005 Philippines Yearbook of the Fookien Times **1374**
0115-3110 The Graduate School Journal **3434**
0115-3188 American Chamber of Commerce of the Philippines. Weekly Executive Update **1395**
0115-3226 American Historical Collection. Bulletin **4169**
0115-3307 Table of Sunrise, Sunset, Twilight, Moonrise and Moonset **582**
0115-3757 Atomedia†
0115-3994 Balikatanews†
0115-4141 WorldFish Center. Translations **3612**
0115-4192 Philippine Business and Industry Index **1258**
0115-4249 Philippines. Ministry of Education, Culture and Sports. National Scholarship Center. Annual Report
0115-4389 WorldFish Center. Studies and Reviews **3612**
0115-4419 Private Development Corporation of the Philippines. Industry Digest **1901**
0115-4435 WorldFish Center. Conference Proceedings **968**
0115-4729 Abstract Bibliography on Coconut†
0115-4842 World Executive's Digest *changed to* Chief Executive Asia
0115-4974 Asian Aquaculture **3586**
0115-4990 Habitat Philippines†
0115-5032 Ang Tagamasid **6346**
0115-5067 Agriculture at Los Banos†
0115-5113 National Security Review **6438**
0115-5490 P F N P Newsletter†
0115-5547 WorldFish Center. Technical Reports **3612**
0115-5555 Philippines Chinese Historical Association. Annals **4187**
0115-5814 Ang Tala†
0115-5997 WorldFish Center. Bibliographies **3614**
0115-6012 Kinaadman **554**
0115-6144 Likha **5323**
0115-6195 Malay **4464**
0115-625X Scientia Filipinas†
0115-6276 De La Salle University. Department of History and Area Studies. Anuaryo - Annales **4181**
0115-6292 Kaya Tao†
0115-6349 Religious Studies Journal **7676**
0115-6403 P B S Bulletin *changed to* P S B M B Newsletter **741**
0115-6594 D L S U Dialogue **4449**
0115-6608 Philippines Footwear Leathergoods & Accesories Journal
0115-6640 D L S U Graduate Journal†
0115-6853 Mindanao Art & Culture **3620**
0115-690X Journal of Fisheries & Aquaculture†
0115-6926 Matimyas Matematika **5517**
0115-6950 Arts & Sciences Journal†
0115-7000 Development Administration Journal†
0115-7167 Philippines. National Library. T N L News **5039**
0115-7205 Philippine Law Report **4758**
0115-7213 Philippines. National Library. T N L Research Guide Series **633**
0115-7809 Science Diliman **7909**
0115-8090 F A P E Review **2856**
0115-8341 S L U - E I S S I F Newsletter **1169**
0115-835X Likas-Yaman
0115-8473 N F E - W I D Exchange - Asia. Occasional Paper†
0115-8503 Network of Aquaculture Centres in Asia-Pacific. Newsletter **958**
0115-852X N F E - W I D Exchange - Asia. Newsletter **3014**
0115-8635 Sangwika†
0115-866X Dansalan Quarterly **7710**
0115-8686 Computer Issues **2412**
0115-8805 Philippine Yearbook of International Law **4938**
0115-9011 Philippine Review of Economics and Business *changed to* 1655-1516 **1159**
0115-9097 Development Research News **1594**
0115-9151 Danyag **4449**
0115-9194 P I D S Monograph Series†
0115-9259 Bagong Sibol†
0115-950X Fisheries Journal **3592**
0115-9577 Philippiniana Sacra **7669**
0115-9984 R & D Philippines **8447**
0116-0109 Philippine Journal of Volcanology†
0116-0257 East Asian Pastoral Review **7795**
0116-0710 Annals of Tropical Research **92**
0116-1091 The Youngster **2223**
0116-1105 Asian Development Review **1591**
0116-1164 Asian Development Bank. Annual Report **1308**
0116-1520 Philippine Yearbook **7313**
0116-1784 Forest Products Technoflow **3712**
0116-1792 Metropolitan Computer Times†
0116-1822 Foreign Trade Statistics of the Philippines **1233**
0116-1830 Boletin Eclesiastico de Filipinas **7786**
0116-2187 Kapawa News **3928**
0116-2462 Philippine Daily Inquirer **3928**
0116-2624 Philippines. National Statistics Office. Integrated Survey of Households Bulletin **8394**
0116-2640 Philippines. National Statistics Office. Special Releases **8394**
0116-2659 Philippines. National Statistics Office. Annual Survey of Establishments **1258**

ISSN

0137-2149 Akademia Rolnicza w Szczecinie. Informatory **89**
0137-2173 Monografie Fauny Polski **956**
0137-219X Eksploatacja Kolei†
0137-2270 Politechnika Warszawska. Instytut Technologii i Organizacji Produkcji Budowlanej. Prace†
0137-2297 Politechnika Warszawska. Prace Naukowe. Budownictwo **1029**
0137-2300 Politechnika Warszawska. Prace Naukowe. Chemia **2076**
0137-2319 Politechnika Warszawska. Prace Naukowe. Elektryka **3327**
0137-2327 Politechnika Warszawska. Prace Naukowe. Geodezja **4024**
0137-2335 Politechnika Warszawska. Prace Naukowe. Mechanika **3393**
0137-2343 Politechnika Warszawska. Prace Naukowe. Elektronika **3110**
0137-2351 Uniwersytet Jagiellonski. Zeszyty Naukowe. Prace z Biologii Molekularnej†
0137-236X Uniwersytet Jagiellonski. Zeszyty Naukowe. Prace z Wynalazczosci i Ochrony Wlanosci Intelektualnej **4806**
0137-2378 Uniwersytet Jagiellonski. Zeszyty Naukowe. Prace z Nauk Politycznych **7191**
0137-2386 Uniwersytet Jagiellonski. Zeszyty Naukowe. Acta Cosmologica†
0137-2408 Uniwersytet Jagiellonski. Zeszyty Naukowe. Prace Socjologiczne†
0137-2416 Uniwersytet Jagiellonski. Zeszyty Naukowe. Prace Polonijne **4275**
0137-2432 Uniwersytet Jagiellonski. Zeszyty Naukowe. Studia Religiologica **7692**
0137-2440 Polish Academy of Sciences. Institute of Geophysics. Publications. Series A: Physics of the Earth's Interior **2788**
0137-2467 Studia Germanica Posnaniensia **5379**
0137-2475 Studia Romanica Posnaniensia **5379**
0137-2548 Literatura†
0137-2599 Politechnika Lodzka. Zeszyty Naukowe. Organizacja i Zarzadzanie **7992**
0137-2645 Przemysl Fermentacyjny i Owocowo Warzywny **3661**
0137-2661 Politechnika Lodzka. Zeszyty Naukowe. Cieplne Maszyny Przeplywowe **3392**
0137-2777 Instytut Badania Prawa Sadowego. Zeszyty Naukowe†
0137-2831 Panstwowe Muzeum Archeologiczne. Materialy Starozytne i Wczesnosredniowieczne **410**
0137-284X Drogi Kolejowe†
0137-2858 Automatyka Kolejowa†
0137-2904 Reports on Mathematical Logic **5528**
0137-2939 Polska Akademia Nauk. Oddzial w Krakowie. Osrodek Dokumentacji Fizjograficznej. Studia **4024**
0137-2955 Panorama Polska (Nasza Ojczyzna)†
0137-2963 Trakcja i Wagony†
0137-2971 Materialy Budowlane **1022**
0137-298X Przeglad Rusycystyczny **5163**
0137-2998 Kwartalnik Historii Prasy Polskiej†
0137-3005 Delta **5482**
0137-303X Przeglad Polonijny **4255**
0137-3056 Uniwersytet Warszawski. Wydzial Nauk Ekonomicznych. Ekonomia†
0137-3064 Acta Mediaevalia **7782**
0137-3080 Estudios Latinoamericanos **4292**
0137-3099 Kronika Warszawy **4238**
0137-3102 Kronika Wielkopolski **4238**
0137-3218 Nasza Przeszlosc **7808**
0137-3234 Pamietnikarstwo Polskie **4252**
0137-3242 Zdanie **7197**
0137-3250 Poznanskie Towarzystwo Przyjaciol Nauk. Komisja Archeologiczna. Prace **411**
0137-3277 Uniwersytet Slaski w Katowicach. Prace Naukowe. Historia i Wspolczesnosc†
0137-3366 Rocznik Swidnicki **4259**
0137-3390 Studia Historyczne (Bydgoszcz)†
0137-3404 Studia o Ksiazce†
0137-3420 Studia Teologiczno-Historyczne Slaska Opolskiego **7684**
0137-3447 Slaskie Studia Historyczno-Teologiczne **7817**
0137-3471 Wolnosc i Lud†
0137-3501 Rocznik Kaliski
0137-3536 Polish-American Studies†
0137-3544 Polska Akademia Nauk. Instytut Krajow Socjalistycznych. Biuletyn Informacyjny†
0137-3552 Kronika Miasta Poznania **4238**
0137-3587 Studia Maritima **4163**
0137-3595 Postepy Cybernetyki†
0137-3609 Prezentacje†
0137-3617 Czlowiek i Srodowisko **4408**
0137-3668 Aura **3405**
0137-3676 Cieplownictwo, Ogrzewnictwo, Wentylacja **4117**
0137-3692 Konfrontacje†
0137-3803 Zarzadzanie†
0137-3838 Wiadomosci Zielarskie **170**
0137-3935 Paginet†
0137-3943 Paideia **2945**
0137-4001 Questiones Medii Aevi†
0137-4060 Ksiegarz†
0137-4079 Ethnologia Polona **337**
0137-4087 Czestochowskie Studia Teologiczne **7794**
0137-4141 Rocznik Ziemi Klodzkiej **4259**
0137-4176 Roczniki Nauk Spolecznych **7998**
0137-4192 Literary Studies in Poland†
0137-4354 Studia Kieleckie **4269**
0137-4389 Studia Polono-Slavica Orientalia. Acta Litteraria†
0137-4435 Transport Museums **8515**
0137-4478 Postepy Technologii Maszyn i Urzadzen **3393**
0137-463X Film **6498**
0137-4729 Polityka Spoleczna **8062**
0137-4761 Przeglad Lubuski†
0137-477X Quaestiones Geographicae **4025**
0137-4788 Sad Nowoczesny **3749**
0137-4885 Polish Archaeological Abstracts **425**
0137-4982 Problemy Szkolnictwa i Nauk Medycznych†
0137-4990 Ergonomia **7853**
0137-5040 Biblioteka Chemii **2085**
0137-5059 Biblioteka Fizyki **7006**
0137-5075 Archives of Acoustics **7086**
0137-5083 Polish Journal of Chemistry **2076**
0137-5156 Radomskie Towarzystwo Naukowe. Biuletyn Kwartalny
0137-5164 Zeszyty Gorzowskie†
0137-5172 Z Badan nad Polskimi Ksiegozbiorami Historycznymi **5055**
0137-5180 Slaskie Studia Historyczne†
0137-5210 Studia Polonijne **7294**
0137-5253 Instytut Baltycki. Komunikaty†
0137-5288 Polska Klasa Robotnicza. Studia Historyczne†
0137-530X Studia i Materialy do Dziejow Zup Solnych w Polsce **419**
0137-5326 Szkice Legnickie **7922**
0137-5350 Poznanskie Roczniki Medyczne **5698**
0137-5377 Stutthof†
0137-5393 Studia z Zakresu Inzynierii **3284**
0137-5415 Przestepczosc na Swiecie†
0137-5431 Biuletyn Slawistyczny†
0137-544X Przeglad Glottodydaktyczny **5163**
0137-5466 Organizacja i Kierowanie **1784**
0137-5474 Zagadnienia Eksploatacji Maszyn **3399**
0137-5482 Uniwersytet Slaski w Katowicach. Prace Naukowe. Kras i Speleologia **2773**
0137-5490 Przeglad Ustawodawstwa Gospodarczego **1513**
0137-5520 Bank i Kredyt **1313**
0137-5695 Muzeum Narodowe w Krakowie. Rozprawy i Sprawozdania†
0137-5733 Studia do Dziejow Dawnego Uzbrojenia i Ubioru Wojskowego **6448**
0137-5806 Oeconomica Polona†
0137-5814 Uniwersytet Gdanski. Wydzial Humanistyczny. Zeszyty Naukowe. Historia†
0137-5822 Uniwersytet Warszawski. Instytut Nauk Politycznych. Zeszyty Naukowe†
0137-5881 Acta Physiologiae Plantarum **773**
0137-589X Instytut Metali Niezelaznych. Prace†
0137-608X Nea Paphos†
0137-611X Chow Bydla **284**
0137-6217 Politechnika Wroclawska. Biblioteka Glowna i Osrodek Informacji Naukowo-Technicznej. Prace Naukowe. Konferencje†
0137-6225 Politechnika Wroclawska. Biblioteka Glowna i Osrodek Informacji Naukowo-Technicznej. Prace Naukowe. Studia i Materialy†
0137-6233 Politechnika Wroclawska. Instytut Architektury i Urbanistyki. Prace Naukowe. Konferencje†
0137-6241 Politechnika Wroclawska. Instytut Budownictwa. Prace Naukowe. Studia i Materialy†
0137-625X Politechnika Wroclawska. Instytut Fizyki. Prace Naukowe. Konferencje†
0137-6268 Politechnika Wroclawska. Instytut Matematyki. Prace Naukowe. Konferencje†
0137-6276 Politechnika Wroclawska. Instytut Podstaw Elektrotechniki i Elektrotechnologii. Prace Naukowe. Wspolpraca†
0137-6292 Politechnika Wroclawska. Instytut Ukladow Elektromaszynowych. Prace Naukowe. Przemysl†
0137-6306 Politechnika Wroclawska. Osrodek Badan Prognostycznych. Prace Naukowe. Konferencje†
0137-6314 Politechnika Wroclawska. Osrodek Badan Prognostycznych. Prace Naukowe. Monografie†
0137-6322 Politechnika Wroclawska. Osrodek Badan Prognostycznych. Prace Naukowe. Studia i Materialy†
0137-6330 Politechnika Wroclawska. Osrodek Badan Prognostycznych. Prace Naukowe. Wspolpraca.†
0137-6365 Studia Geotechnica et Mechanica **3221**
0137-6381 Z Dziejow Stosunkow Polsko-Radzieckich i Rozwoju Wspolnoty Panstw Socjalistycznych†
0137-642X Poznanskie Towarzystwo Przyjaciol Nauk. Komisja Filologiczna. Prace **5162**
0137-6446 Deir el-Bahari **389**
0137-6462 Fluid Dynamics Transactions†
0137-6543 Medycyna Dydaktyka Wychowanie **5678**
0137-6578 Akademia Wychowania Fizycznego im. Eugeniusza Piaseckiego w Poznaniu. Roczniki Naukowe **6981**
0137-6586 Problemy Agrofizyki†
0137-6608 Studia Semiotyczne **5180**
0137-6616 Acta Universitatis Nicolai Copernici. Nauki Humanistyczno-Spoleczne. Archeologia **371**
0137-6667 Acta Universitatis Nicolai Copernici. Nauki Humanistyczno-Spoleczne. Nauki Polityczne†
0137-6683 Badania Fizjograficzne nad Polska Zachodnia. Seria C. Zoologia **935**
0137-6705 Haslo Ogrodnicze **3735**
0137-673X Owoce Warzywa Kwiaty **3746**
0137-6772 Integracje†
0137-6780 Poradnik Gospodarski **147**
0137-6802 Radioelektronik **2363**
0137-6853 Annales Universitatis Mariae Curie-Sklodowska. Sectio AA. Chemia **2050**
0137-6861 Annales Universitatis Mariae Curie-Sklodowska. Sectio AAA. Physica **7005**
0137-6918 Politechnika Poznanska. Zeszyty Naukowe. Maszyny Robocze i Pojazdy *changed to* 1642-6606 **3393**
0137-6934 Banach Center Publications **5475**
0137-6969 Politechnika Czestochowska. Zeszyty Naukowe. Nauki Techniczne. Mechanika†
0137-6977 Politechnika Czestochowska. Zeszyty Naukowe. Nauki Techniczne. Elektrotechnika†
0137-6985 Collectanea Theologica **7792**
0137-7043 Bezpieczenstwo Pracy **6674**
0137-706X Chowanna **2836**
0137-7094 Ideologia i Polityka†
0137-7213 Przeglad Obrony Cywilnej **2228**
0137-7221 Przeglad Organizacji **1787**
0137-723X Przeglad Pediatryczny **6103**
0137-7256 Twoje Dziecko **8886**
0137-7299 Zycie Gospodarcze†
0137-7310 Zycie Szkoly **2930**
0137-7523 Poland. Ministerstwo Administracji, Gospodarki Terenowej i Ochrony Srodowiska. Dziennik Urzedowy *changed to* Dziennik Urzedowy Ministra Srodowiska i Glownego Inspektora Ochrony Srodowiska **7434**
0137-7566 Geografia w Szkole **4009**
0137-7612 Hotelarz
0137-7639 Jestem **8869**
0137-7671 Kultura Fizyczna **6991**
0137-771X Monitor Spoldzielczy **7453**
0137-7922 Poland. Ministerstwo Finansow. Dziennik Urzedowy *changed to* Dziennik Urzedowy Ministra Finansow **7434**
0137-8015 Poland. Urzad Patentowy. Biuletyn **6757**
0137-8031 Biologia w Szkole **657**
0137-8066 Zdrowie **7001**
0137-8082 Wychowanie w Przedszkolu **2927**
0137-8171 Szkola Zawodowa†
0137-818X Szkola Specjalna **3048**
0137-8198 Szachy†
0137-8325 Regiony **5236**
0137-8333 Razem†
0137-8384 Przewodnik Katolicki **7813**
0137-8473 Polska Bibliografia Wojskowa **6455**
0137-8562 Nowe Ksiazki **7569**
0137-8627 Poland. Ministerstwo Sprawiedliwosci. Dziennik Urzedowy *changed to* Dziennik Urzedowy Ministra Sprawiedliwosci **7434**
0137-8651 Problemy Jakosci **6405**
0137-8708 Przekazy i Opinie†
0137-8783 Przeglad Techniczny **8435**
0137-8805 A B C Technik†
0137-8848 Matematyka (Warsaw) **5511**
0137-8856 Kalejdoskop Techniki†
0137-8929 Wiedza i Zycie **3930**
0137-8996 Poznanskie Towarzystwo Przyjaciol Nauk. Komisja Matematyczno-Przyrodnicza. Prace†
0137-9011 Echo Krakowa **3929**
0137-902X Echo Dnia **3929**
0137-9038 Dziennik Zachodni **3929**
0137-9046 Dziennik Wieczorny **3928**
0137-9062 Dziennik Baltycki **3928**
0137-9089 Dziennik Polski **3928**
0137-9097 Express Ilustrowany **3929**
0137-9100 Express Poznanski **3929**
0137-9119 Express Wieczorny†
0137-9178 Glos Szczecinski **3930**
0137-9186 Glos Wielkopolski **3930**
0137-9208 Gromada - Rolnik Polski†
0137-9232 Kurier Polski†
0137-9267 Przeglad Sportowy **8194**
0137-9305 Sport **8203**
0137-933X Tempo **8211**
0137-9399 Zielony Sztandar **7198**
0137-9437 Zycie Warszawy **3931**
0137-9518 Gazeta Lubuska **3929**
0137-9550 Gazeta Targowa **1818**
0137-9585 Polska Akademia Nauk. Komitet Nauk Pedagogicznych. Rocznik Pedagogiczny **2898**
0137-9623 Acta Biologica **649**
0137-9666 Humanitas†
0137-9704 Studia Ubezpieczeniowe **4524**
0137-9712 Polonica **5162**
0137-9771 Poznanskie Towarzystwo Przyjaciol Nauk. Komisja Geograficzno-Geologiczna. Prace **2762**
0137-9798 Quaternary Studies in Poland *changed to* 1641-5558 **2770**
0137-9860 Studies on the Developing Countries†
0137-9941 Instytut Metalurgii Zelaza. Prace **6316**
0138-0109 Polish Academy of Sciences. Institute of Geophysics. Publications. Series B: Seismology **2788**
0138-0117 Polish Academy of Sciences. Institute of Geophysics. Publications. Series C: Geomagnetism **2788**
0138-0125 Polish Academy of Sciences. Institute of Geophysics. Publications. Series D: Physics of the Atmosphere **2788**
0138-0133 Polish Academy of Sciences. Institute of Geophysics. Publications. Series E: Water Resources **2788**
0138-0141 Polish Academy of Sciences. Institute of Geophysics. Publications. Series F: Planetary Geodesy **2788**
0138-015X Polish Academy of Sciences. Institute of Geophysics. Publications. Series M: Miscellanea **2788**
0138-0311 Praxiology **6944**
0138-032X Archiwum Nauki o Materialach *changed to* Archives of Materials Science and Engineering **3341**
0138-0338 Polish Polar Research **2715**
0138-0389 Geology of Poland **2742**
0138-0419 Spoldzielczy Kwartalnik Naukowy†
0138-0478 Problemy Turystyki **8748**
0138-0486 Alexandrie **372**
0138-0508 Prace Popularnonaukowe. Biblioteczka Prawnicza
0138-0516 Prace Popularnonaukowe. Zabytki Polski Polnocnej **512**
0138-0532 Science of Science†
0138-0567 Uniwersytet Warszawski. Instytut Jezyka Polskiego. Prace Filologiczne†
0138-0648 Polska Akademia Nauk. Instytut Podstaw Informatyki. Prace **2435**
0138-0680 University of Lodz. Department of Logic. Bulletin of the Section of Logic **5545**
0138-0702 Bibliografia Pomorza Zachodniego. Pismiennictwo Zagraniczne **617**
0138-0737 Wiadomosci Entomologiczne **861**
0138-0796 Instytut Techniki Budowlanej. Prace **3272**
0138-0818 Biophysics of Membrane Transport **752**
0138-0826 Elektronizacja *changed to* Elektronika - Konstrukcje, Zastosowania, Technologie **3098**
0138-0907 Panorama Leszczynska **3930**
0138-0923 Akademia Gorniczo-Hutnicza im. Stanislawa Staszica. Zeszyty Naukowe. Sozologia i Sozotechnika†
0138-094X Biblioteka Polonijna **7109**
0138-0974 Geologia **2736**
0138-0990 Akademia Gorniczo-Hutnicza im. Stanislawa Staszica. Gornictwo. Kwartalnik *changed to* 1732-6702 **6463**
0138-1008 Mikrobielle Umwelt und Antimikrobielle Massnahmen†

ISSN

DIRECTORY 2010 0141-1896 9153

0139-8865 Rustinar†
0139-8903 Pedagogicka Fakulta v Usti nad Labem. Sbornik: Rada Chemicka†
0139-8911 Ohnik **2205**
0139-8962 Zornicka **2224**
0139-9055 Pedagogicka Fakulta v Usti nad Labem. Sbornik: Rada Bohemisticka†
0139-9179 Czechoslovak Medicine†
0139-925X Opera Corcontica **2623**
0139-9268 Rossica Olomucensia **5170**
0139-9292 Czech Seismological Stations: Pruhonice, Praha, Kasperske Hory. Bulletin†
0139-9349 Slovak Seismographic Stations: Bratislava, Srobarova, Hurbanovo and Skalnate Pleso. Bulletin **2789**
0139-9446 Novinky Literatury: Marxismus-Leninismus. Spolecenske Vedy†
0139-9462 Vlastivedny Sbornik Okresu Novy Jicin *changed to* 1214-8032 **4277**
0139-9535 Conference on Coordination Chemistry Proceedings **2059**
0139-9667 Folia Musei Rerum Naturalium Bohemiae Occidentalis. Botanica† **8957**
0139-9713 Folia Musei Rerum Naturalium Bohemiae Occidentalis. Zoologica† **8957**
0139-9764 Folia Musei Rerum Naturalium Bohemiae Occidentalis. Geologica† **8957**
0139-9810 Z Dejin Hutnictvi **6337**
0139-9861 Physics and Applications **7033**
0139-9918 Mathematica Slovaca **5512**
0140-0010 Foraminifera **6724**
0140-0037 Forestry. Supplement *see* 0015-752X **3690**
0140-0053 Emergency Services News†
0140-0061 Economic and Social History Surveys†
0140-0096 The Conservator **2608**
0140-0118 Medical & Biological Engineering & Computing **826**
0140-0142 Chartered Institute of Public Finance and Accountancy. Waste Disposal Statistics. Estimates†
0140-0193 Coarse Angler†
0140-0223 Dark Horizons **5441**
0140-0266 Faith and Heritage **7642**
0140-038X Staffordshire Guide Industry and Commerce
0140-0428 Educational Administration and History Monographs **3021**
0140-0460 The Times **3872**
0140-0568 Catalysis **2133**
0140-0649 International Communist†
0140-0657 Agricultural & Veterinary Chemicals†
0140-0711 Felix **2283**
0140-072X International Advances in Nondestructive Testing†
0140-0835 Topics in Enzyme and Fermentation Biotechnology†
0140-0843 Topics in Antibiotic Chemistry†
0140-0991 The Kingsman **6430**
0140-1033 Paper Conservation News **511**
0140-1149 Coin Hoards **6650**
0140-1165 Sepia†
0140-1238 Alcuin Club Collections **7745**
0140-1270 Labour Review†
0140-1319 Traveller's Guide to the Middle East†
0140-1408 Artful Reporter†
0140-1599 Acoustics Letters†
0140-1610 European Journal of Rheumatology and Inflammation (English Edition)
0140-1696 Early Music News
0140-170X Great Britain. Department of the Environment and Department of Transport. Library. Library Bulletin†
0140-1742 Water Services Yearbook **3365**
0140-1769 International Symposium on Dredging Technology. Proceedings†
0140-1874 Arab Business Yearbook†
0140-1890 Antenna **838**
0140-1939 Clover Information Index **7578**
0140-1963 Journal of Arid Environments **4016**
0140-1971 Journal of Adolescence **2156**
0140-2145 British Pump Manufacturers Association. Technical Conference Proceedings†
0140-2161 Great Britain. Department of the Environment. Development Control Statistics
0140-2226 Yearbook of Symbolic Anthropology
0140-2285 Jazz Journal International **6578**
0140-2382 West European Politics **7273**
0140-2390 The Journal of Strategic Studies **7249**
0140-2447 New Literature on Old Age **4058**
0140-2498 Marine Stores International†
0140-2587 Great Britain. Government Statistical Service. Birth Statistics. England and Wales **7307**
0140-2625 Advances in Aquatic Microbiology†
0140-2714 Advisor†
0140-2722 British Medicine†
0140-2803 Scottish Sports Council. Information Digest **8199**
0140-2889 B A P I P Bulletin†
0140-2935 Envoy International†
0140-2986 Health & Hygiene **7520**
0140-3001 Illustrators†
0140-3028 Medical Laboratory World **5909**
0140-3117 Bucks and Berks Countryside
0140-315X Concetto **2279**
0140-3222 Natural Gas **6779**
0140-3249 Computers & Law **4844**
0140-3273 Health Education Index and Guide to Voluntary Social Welfare Organisations
0140-332X Historic Society of Lancashire and Cheshire. Transactions **4228**
0140-3397 Quinquereme† **8983**
0140-3427 Fantastic Worlds of Edgar Rice Burroughs
0140-3435 Which Computer?†
0140-3494 Browne Records
0140-3664 Computer Communications **2533**
0140-3672 Dangerous Goods Bulletin **8540**
0140-3729 Isle of Wight Natural History and Archaeological Society. Proceedings **399**
0140-3826 Zero†
0140-3990 Leicestershire Archaeological and Historical Society. Transactions **403**
0140-4016 University of Aberdeen. Undergraduate Prospectus **3008**
0140-4032 Merseyside Archaeological Society. Journal **406**
0140-4067 Nuclear Energy *changed to* 1745-2058 **3213**
0140-4113 British Library of Political and Economic Science. Quarterly List of Additions in Russian and East European Languages†
0140-4156 R A P R A Recent Literature on Hazardous Environments in Industry†
0140-4199 National Institute of Agricultural Botany. Technical Leaflets†
0140-4202 Birmingham & Warwickshire Archaeological Society. Transactions **384**
0140-4237 International Building Services Abstracts (Print)†
0140-427X Map Collector†
0140-4296 World Pharmaceutical Introductions
0140-4415 M I M S Africa **6859**
0140-4482 Welsh Local Government Financial Statistics **7485**
0140-4512 Scottish Hosteller **4398**
0140-4539 Treasure Hunting **4349**
0140-4547 Bike **8255**
0140-4563 Association of National Health Service Supplies Officers. Reference Book & Buyer's Guide†
0140-458X Climate Monitor **6349**
0140-4768 Rural Development Abstracts **4436**
0140-4776 Rural Extension, Education and Training Abstracts†
0140-4784 Forest Products Abstracts **3709**
0140-4806 World Drug Market Manual. Company **6885**
0140-4822 Agricultural Supply Industry **85**
0140-4857 Bio-Medical Applications of Polymers†
0140-489X Economic Outlook **1480**
0140-4903 Library Management News†
0140-4962 People's Dispensary for Sick Animals. Guild News†
0140-5039 Edinburgh Architecture Research **441**
0140-5098 Middle East Water & Sewage†
0140-511X Journal of Audiovisual Media in Medicine *changed to* 1745-3054 **5655**
0140-5136 Alembic†
0140-5209 F P A Newsletter **7517**
0140-525X Behavioral and Brain Sciences **7339**
0140-5357 Countryside Commission. Advisory Series **2608**
0140-5365 Toxicology Abstracts **3481**
0140-5373 Aquatic Sciences & Fisheries Abstracts. Part 1: Biological Sciences and Living Resources **2634**
0140-5381 Aquatic Sciences & Fisheries Abstracts. Part 2: Ocean Technology, Policy and Non-living Resources **8842**
0140-542X Rally Sport **8600**
0140-5497 Tennis Today **8249**
0140-5500 International Accounting and Financial Report†
0140-5624 Economist Financial Report†
0140-5683 London Transport Scrapbook **8503**
0140-5721 Country Music Round Up **6559**
0140-5772 British Exporters†
0140-5810 Scottish Women's Liberation Journal
0140-5845 New City (Sheffield)†
0140-5918 Polytechnic of Central London. Faculty of Business, Management and Social Studies. Research Working Paper **7993**
0140-5926 Commonwealth Institute. Working Party on Library Holdings of Commonwealth Literature. Annual Report **623**
0140-6000 Darts World **8168**
0140-6078 Musica Asiatica†
0140-6116 Afrique†
0140-6337 British Furniture for the World†
0140-6388 Meat and Livestock Commission. Economics Services. Meat Demand Trends **293**
0140-654X Stonehenge Viewpoint†
0140-6566 M C L C Letters†
0140-6582 Who Owns Whom. Continental Europe **1801**
0140-6647 Pension Funds & Their Advisers **4518**
0140-668X International Monograph Series on Early Child Care†
0140-6701 Fuel and Energy Abstracts **6800**
0140-6736 The Lancet **5660**
0140-6957 Recent Advances in Clinical Immunology†
0140-7007 International Journal of Refrigeration **4122**
0140-7023 British Library of Political and Economic Science. Annual Report **5057**
0140-7260 University of London. School of Slavonic and East European Studies. Library. Bibliographical Guides **638**
0140-7430 National Gallery, London. Technical Bulletin **508**
0140-7457 New City Specials **7665**
0140-7503 Essex Family Historian **3765**
0140-7562 Kevren
0140-7570 The Great Outdoors **8316**
0140-7589 Player Piano Group Bulletin **6606**
0140-7597 Iron†
0140-7619 Middle East Electronics†
0140-766X British Electrotechnical Approvals Board. Annual List of Approved Electrotechnical Equipment **8417**
0140-7686 British Journal of Obstetrics & Gynaecology. Supplement **5987**
0140-7694 Gay Christian
0140-7724 Postgraduate Doctor: Middle East **5698**
0140-7732 School Technology†
0140-7740 Animations *changed to* 1754-3053 **8465**
0140-7767 Pellison's Researcher
0140-7775 Journal of Fish Diseases **3599**
0140-7783 Journal of Veterinary Pharmacology and Therapeutics **6857**
0140-7791 Plant, Cell and Environment **697**
0140-7805 Books in the Earth Sciences†
0140-7813 British Geological Literature†
0140-7821 Zapis†
0140-7953 Middle East Living Costs†
0140-7961 Matter of Degree†
0140-8003 Private Post†
0140-8011 Arab Business
0140-8046 Reed's Special Ships†
0140-8089 Leeds Medieval Studies†
0140-8186 Coventry Chamber of Commerce & Industry Directory†
0140-8240 Studies in Public Policy **7187**
0140-8267 Light For Our Path **7765**
0140-8321 Middle East Travel **8736**
0140-8356 London Underground Rolling Stock **8620**
0140-8364 London Transport Buses **8503**
0140-8372 London Country Buses and Green Line Coaches **8503**
0140-8399 Minor Metals Survey†
0140-8402 Iron & Manganese Ores Survey†
0140-8410 Revealer Cassettes†
0140-8429 Flintshire Historical Society. Publications, Journal and Record Series **4219**
0140-8488 Building with Steel†
0140-8518 Consumer Law Today - The Fair Trading Monitor **4649**
0140-8526 Pensions Today **1644**
0140-8534 Health & Safety Monitor **6678**
0140-8623 Banyan Tree **3759**
0140-8682 Overseas Development Institute. Briefing Paper **1602**
0140-8690 Footpath Worker **2611**
0140-8798 Waterborne & High Solids Coatings Bulletin **6721**
0140-895X Irish Literary Studies **5310**
0140-9018 Welsh Social Trends†
0140-9069 Rabies Magazine†
0140-9115 Annual Reports on Fermentation Processes†
0140-9123 Recent Advances in Endocrinology and Metabolism†
0140-9131 Northamptonshire Past and Present **4249**
0140-9158 Medicine Digest **5674**
0140-9174 Management Research News *changed to* 0140-9174 **1776**
0140-9174 Management Research Review **1776**
0140-9220 Aerial Archaeology† **8928**
0140-9352 Aggie Weston's
0140-9360 Machine Tool Enterprise **3388**
0140-9387 Politics (London) **7170**
0140-9441 I T M Yearbook
0140-9468 Equal Opportunities Commission. Annual Report **7206**
0140-9506 New Equals†
0140-9565 Kent Field Club. Bulletin **2712**
0140-9573 C C E T S W Study
0140-9727 Modern Chess Theory†
0140-9743 General Review of the World Coal Industry. Progress Report†
0140-9875 University of Southampton. Department of Geography. Discussion Papers **4033**
0140-9883 Energy Economics **3130**
0140-9948 Clothing Research Journal†
0141-0008 University of Nottingham. Department of Adult Education. Bulletin of Local History, East Midlands Region†
0141-0016 Walpole Society. Volume **525**
0141-0121 Aquarian Arrow **6741**
0141-0156 School of Oriental and African Studies. Collected Papers on South Asia **560**
0141-0164 Rice Abstracts **186**
0141-0172 Soybean Abstracts (Print)†
0141-0180 Seed Abstracts **720**
0141-0229 Enzyme and Microbial Technology **763**
0141-0288 National Association of Plumbing, Heating and Mechanical Services Contractors Yearbook†
0141-0296 Engineering Structures **3266**
0141-030X Studies in Welsh History **4271**
0141-0334 Proteus (Milton Keynes)† **8983**
0141-0423 Journal of Research in Reading **2878**
0141-0490 British Machine Tools and Equipment **3374**
0141-0547 Harpers & Queen **8867**
0141-0555 Cosmopolitan (British Edition) **8856**
0141-061X Electronic Technology†
0141-0644 Medicine in Society†
0141-0660 W E A Southern District Journal†
0141-0741 Financial Times World Tax Report
0141-0768 Royal Society of Medicine. Journal **5707**
0141-0792 The Liszt Society. Journal **6585**
0141-0806 World Stainless Steel Statistics **6342**
0141-0822 Veterinary Review†
0141-0857 Practical Wireless **2387**
0141-0962 Forensic Photography
0141-1004 Studies in Operations Research
0141-1012 Library of Anthropology
0141-1020 American Business Overseas†
0141-1039 Overseas American
0141-1047 European and Middle East Tax Report†
0141-1101 Association for Korean Studies in Europe. Newsletter **4180**
0141-1128 Monographs on Astronomical Subjects†
0141-1136 Marine Environmental Research **3488**
0141-1144 Company **8856**
0141-1152 Oxford Theatre Texts **8475**
0141-1160 Educational Change and Development†
0141-1179 Dramau'r Byd†
0141-1187 Applied Ocean Research **2800**
0141-1225 Kent Field Club. Transactions **2712**
0141-1241 Global Tapestry Journal **5423**
0141-1268 National Maritime Museum. Occasional Lectures Series†
0141-1292 Dumfriesshire and Galloway Natural History and Antiquarian Society. Transactions
0141-1314 I D S Research Reports **1597**
0141-1381 Diesel Engines for the World†
0141-1403 Great Britain. Department of Health and Social Security. Health Equipment Notes **4094**
0141-1446 Food Worker **3678**
0141-1470 The British Clothing Industry Yearbook **2245**
0141-1500 Butterworths Orange Tax Handbook **1914**
0141-1594 Phase Transitions **7030**
0141-1608 Memoirs of the Geological Survey of Great Britain. Palaeontology†
0141-1667 State Research
0141-1810 Serials Monograph **5047**
0141-187X Chartered Institute of Public Finance and Accountancy. Leisure and Recreation Statistics. Estimates **8218**
0141-1896 Journal of Musicological Research **6581**

ISSN

ISSN

0143-6996 Peatain Family History Newsletter†
0143-7208 Dyes and Pigments **2060**
0143-7232 Steam Railway **8625**
0143-7275 Transducer Technology†
0143-7283 University of Strathclyde. Department of Architecture & Building Science. Research Bulletin†
0143-7380 Labour Party. Economic Review†
0143-7410 Reports Index
0143-7429 Glasgow Directory of Voluntary Organizations **8042**
0143-7453 International Bar News **4929**
0143-7488 Academus Poetry Magazine
0143-7496 International Journal of Adhesion and Adhesives **7093**
0143-7518 Christian Fellowship†
0143-7526 Sensory Perception and Information Processing†
0143-7534 Learning and Memory†
0143-7550 Mental Retardation†
0143-7585 Reactive Personal Distress†
0143-7593 Psychotherapy†
0143-7607 Metal Traders of the World **6323**
0143-764X British Journal of Audiology. Supplement†
0143-7690 Scrip **6880**
0143-7704 Community Studies Series **7955**
0143-7720 International Journal of Manpower **1689**
0143-7739 Leadership & Organization Development Journal **1772**
0143-7755 Tableware International **2046**
0143-7771 Fish Trader (Redhill) **3592**
0143-7798 Steel Times International **6334**
0143-781X History of Political Thought **7140**
0143-7836 Glass International **2042**
0143-7844 Sheet Metal Industries International†
0143-7895 Conference World **6279**
0143-7917 Family Life†
0143-7925 Focus (Grantham) **7758**
0143-7941 Tax Management International Forum **1948**
0143-7968 Hair **588**
0143-7984 Wellcome Unit for the History of Medicine. Research Publications **5730**
0143-8026 Lundy Field Society. Annual Report **2618**
0143-8042 Journal of Chinese Medicine **311**
0143-8115 Numerical Engineering
0143-8123 Comments on Molecular and Cellular Biophysics†
0143-8131 Artistes & Agents **8465**
0143-814X Journal of Public Policy **7979**
0143-8158 West Midlands Archives Newsletter†
0143-8166 Optics and Lasers in Engineering **7082**
0143-8255 Airgun World **8157**
0143-831X Economic and Industrial Democracy **7131**
0143-8328 Pay and Benefits Bulletin **1870**
0143-8387 Attendance Centre News **2644**
0143-8395 Recent Advances in Surgery **6256**
0143-8484 Plunkett Development Series†
0143-8492 Times Educational Supplement Scotland *see* 0140-0460 **3872**
0143-8492 Times Educational Supplement Scotland *see* 0307-661X **5384**
0143-8492 Times Educational Supplement Scotland *see* Times Higher Education **3005**
0143-8492 Times Educational Supplement Scotland *see* 0040-7887 **2920**
0143-8492 Times Educational Supplement Scotland *see* 0040-7887 **2920**
0143-8514 Thinking Mission **7690**
0143-8565 Yesteryear Transport†
0143-8573 Video Rights†
0143-859X N I M L A **5153**
0143-8611 Electronics Engineer†
0143-8654 School of Agriculture, Aberdeen. Annual Report†
0143-8689 Curriculum†
0143-8751 Target Gun **8211**
0143-8786 Outlook (Milton Keynes)†
0143-8859 Strays **3784**
0143-8875 Platform (Yorkshire) **8621**
0143-8883 Prospect (Belfast)†
0143-8921 Centre for the Study of Islam and Christian Muslim Relations. Newsletter *changed to* The Centre for Islamic Studies and The Centre for the Study of Interreligious Relations. Newsletter **7709**
0143-8956 British Numismatic Journal **6649**
0143-8972 Scottish Planning Appeal Decisions **4426**
0143-8980 Entertainment and Arts Management *changed to* Entertainment & Arts Manager
0143-8999 Planning Exchange Information Bulletin†
0143-9014 Pig News & Information **184**
0143-9030 N C V O Information Service†
0143-9073 Ecos **2609**
0143-909X Books for Keeps **7555**
0143-9111 British Business†
0143-912X Interim (Birmingham)
0143-9138 Waifarers†
0143-9162 Bus Fayre **8491**
0143-926X Cosmatom†
0143-9286 Geological Society of Norfolk. Bulletin **2739**
0143-9294 Clinical and Experimental Pharmacology & Physiology. Supplement *see* 0305-1870 **921**
0143-9308 War on Wants Outlook†
0143-9316 Resident Abroad
0143-9405 China Business Report†
0143-9529 Consumer Credit Bulletin
0143-9553 Keyword Index to Serial Titles **5058**
0143-9588 Employment News **1679**
0143-9596 What's New in Farming†
0143-9618 Careers Adviser
0143-9634 Nature in Devon
0143-9642 Computer Performance†
0143-9669 Re Report **4520**
0143-9677 Tax Haven & Shelter Report-North American Edition†
0143-9685 Historical Journal of Film, Radio and Television **4143**
0143-9693 Sussex Genealogist and Local Historian
0143-9715 European Muslims and Christian-Muslim Relations. Abstracts†
0143-974X Journal of Constructional Steel Research **3275**
0143-9766 World Gas Report
0143-9774 News of Muslims in Europe†
0143-9782 Journal of Time Series Analysis **8383**
0143-9863 Ramp†
0143-9871 Inklings†
0143-991X Industrial Robot **2584**
0143-9952 Jane's Armour and Artillery **6426**
0143-9995 Medisport
0144-0004 Jane's Military Communications **6427**
0144-008X Eighteen Nineties Society. Journal **5288**
0144-0160 Penny Share Guide†
0144-0179 British Archaeological Association. Conference Transactions **384**
0144-0209 I D S Focus†
0144-0322 Society of Leather Technologists and Chemists. Journal **4975**
0144-0330 Royal College of Pathologists. Symposia†
0144-0349 Association of Clinical Pathologists. Symposia†
0144-0357 Prose Studies **5354**
0144-0365 The Journal of Legal History **4149**
0144-039X Slavery and Abolition **4161**
0144-0411 Medicine International (Quarterly Edition)
0144-042X Medicine International. Irish Edition†
0144-0446 P R Bulletin
0144-0462 Scope (Belfast)† **8987**
0144-0497 Middle Thames Naturalist
0144-0519 Recent Advances in Geriatric Medicine†
0144-0535 Recent Advances in Neuropathology†
0144-0543 Franchise World **1961**
0144-0551 Mushroom Journal **802**
0144-0586 Northamptonshire Natural History Society and Field Club Journal **7893**
0144-0594 Major Companies of the Arab World (Year) **2014**
0144-0683 Nottinghamshire Link
0144-0713 Radio Modeller†
0144-0764 Stirling Technical Reports in Education†
0144-0918 Politics and Power†
0144-0969 Social Work Information Bulletin†
0144-1019 Seaways **8660**
0144-1027 Company Lawyer **4862**
0144-1078 Recent Advances in Infection†
0144-1086 Recent Advances in Clinical Psychiatry†
0144-123X Northern Bibliography†
0144-1256 Recent Advances in Community Medicine†
0144-1302 Scottish Pottery Historical Review **539**
0144-1396 A Y R S Journal **8271**
0144-1558 International Yearbook of Organization Studies†
0144-1647 Transport Reviews **8515**
0144-1671 European Digest†
0144-171X Grove Pastoral Series **7646**
0144-1728 Grove Worship Series **7759**
0144-1752 Socialist Librarians Journal†
0144-1779 Radical Bookseller†
0144-1825 Ceramic Review **2039**
0144-1957 R R L Report†
0144-1973 La Societe Guernesiaise. Report and Transactions **4265**
0144-2104 Shellfish Information Leaflet† **8988**
0144-2147 British Ceramic Research. Special Publications **2038**
0144-221X Natural History Society of Northumbria. Transactions **7888**
0144-2244 Suffolk Natural History **964**
0144-2317 U.V. Spectrometry Group. Bulletin†
0144-235X International Reviews in Physical Chemistry **2136**
0144-2376 Felt and Damaging Earthquakes†
0144-2384 Refer **5042**
0144-2406 E E C Food Legislation Manual†
0144-2457 Logos
0144-249X Stanley Gibbons Postcard Catalogue†
0144-252X Magnetic Fluids†
0144-2589 National Association of Pension Funds. Year Book **1253**
0144-2694 Walk
0144-2708 Tiddly Dyke **8626**
0144-2740 Major Companies of Nigeria†
0144-2767 Business Yearbook of Brazil, Mexico & Venezuela†
0144-2791 History Journal
0144-2821 Scottish Arts Council. Bulletin†
0144-2848 T O P S: The Old Police Station†
0144-2872 Policy Studies **7166**
0144-2902 Christian Jewish Relations†
0144-2910 Model Boats **8278**
0144-2937 Popular Crafts†
0144-2945 Journal of Laryngology and Otology. Supplement *see* 0022-2151 **6081**
0144-2988 Macromolecular Chemistry (London)†
0144-3054 E C L R: European Competition Law Review **4924**
0144-3062 Scots Philosophical Monographs† **8987**
0144-3127 Studies in Language Disability and Remediation
0144-3313 University of Edinburgh. Department of Archaeology. Occasional Papers **422**
0144-3321 Criminal Appeal Reports (Sentencing) **4886**
0144-333X International Journal of Sociology and Social Policy **8109**
0144-3356 School of Agriculture, Aberdeen. Research Investigations and Field Trials†
0144-3399 Context (Leeds)†
0144-3410 Educational Psychology **2850**
0144-3461 Caprice†
0144-347X Transport Ticket Society. Journal **8515**
0144-3488 Interchange (Glasgow) **8047**
0144-3496 Automotive & Commercial Refinisher
0144-3577 International Journal of Operations and Production Management **1760**
0144-3585 Journal of Economic Studies **1135**
0144-3593 Statute Law Review **4788**
0144-3607 Zoological Record **720**
0144-3615 Journal of Obstetrics and Gynaecology **5996**
0144-3631 British Ceramic Research Limited. Technical Notes†
0144-3674 Computer Age (London)
0144-3690 Auction Prices of American Artists†
0144-3704 Hospitality **4388**
0144-3755 Hovercraft Bulletin **58**
0144-3771 Spanish Studies **5376**
0144-378X Foundations (St. Albans) **7644**
0144-3828 Gardening World†
0144-3879 Animal Disease Occurrence†
0144-3968 Haverhill and District Archaeological Group. Journal
0144-3976 Aviation Postcard Collector
0144-4018 Kent Recusant History
0144-4034 Boat Technology International†
0144-4212 P S L G **7459**
0144-4247 Energy R & D Summary and Sources†
0144-4271 Medeconomics **5666**
0144-4360 Literary Review **5225**
0144-4379 Paper Bag
0144-4387 M E E D Arab Report†
0144-4425 Paint Titles **6722**
0144-4484 Co-Operative Fishermen's Bulletin†
0144-4492 Solar System Today†
0144-4514 Chartered Institute of Public Finance and Accountancy. Homelessness Statistics. Actuals **4435**
0144-4549 Lloyd's Shipping Index **8650**
0144-4557 Lloyd's Voyage Record **8651**
0144-4581 State Enterprise
0144-459X Doncaster Ancestor **3764**
0144-4646 Communication Research Trends **8094**
0144-4727 Works and Plant Maintenance
0144-4751 Venezuela
0144-476X E R A Technology News **1815**
0144-4816 Essex Review of Children's Literature†
0144-4948 Health Now
0144-5014 B I P Plastics Review†
0144-5049 Trades Union Press Service **1711**
0144-5081 Social Work Services Group. Statistical Bulletin **8071**
0144-5138 History of Universities **2985**
0144-5154 Assembly Automation **2457**
0144-5243 Miltronics†
0144-5251 Dairyman's Yearbook†
0144-5294 Geological Curator **6524**
0144-5340 History and Philosophy of Logic **6923**
0144-5359 Wessex Studies in Special Education **3049**
0144-5464 Hobby's Annual (Year) **4336**
0144-5596 Social Policy and Administration **8069**
0144-560X Focus (London, 1979) **5442**
0144-5685 Health and Safety Commission. Newsletter *changed to* 1751-7850 **7521**
0144-5707 Chichester Cathedral Journal **7750**
0144-5766 Over 21†
0144-5774 Sounds†
0144-5847 Other Poetry†
0144-5863 Anglo-Catalan Society. Occasional Publications **4198**
0144-5898 Lookback†
0144-5960 Wolff's Guide to the London Metal Exchange **6337**
0144-5987 Energy Exploration & Exploitation **3131**
0144-5995 Termite Abstracts†
0144-6002 Orbit (London)†
0144-6010 Video Today†
0144-6053 Harwell Information Bulletin†
0144-6096 Business Scotland **1444**
0144-610X Chartered Institute of Public Finance and Accountancy. Personal Social Services Statistics. Estimates **8082**
0144-6118 Enterprise (London, 1978)
0144-6169 Farm Animal Welfare Co-ordinating Executive. Newsletter **286**
0144-6193 Construction Management and Economics **997**
0144-624X Recreation Management Handbook†
0144-6258 Ecology & Conservation Studies **2609**
0144-6274 Grow Together†
0144-6282 Surgery Today
0144-6304 Insurance Index
0144-6339 Arthritis News **4077**
0144-6347 B S H S Newsletter **7838**
0144-6363 Heritage and Destiny†
0144-6371 Quest (Cardiff)†
0144-638X University of Aberdeen. University Library. Occasional Publications **5053**
0144-6398 A R V A C Pamphlet†
0144-6428 Slade Magazine†
0144-6436 Loot†
0144-6517 Property Law Bulletin **4762**
0144-6525 R I P A Report
0144-6533 Legion **2267**
0144-655X Dine Out **4384**
0144-6592 Recent Advances in Nursing†
0144-6630 New Age†
0144-6649 Computerworld UK†
0144-6657 British Journal of Clinical Psychology **7341**
0144-6665 British Journal of Social Psychology **7342**
0144-6673 Lloyd's Shipping Economist **8650**
0144-6681 Lloyd's Loading List **8650**
0144-672X Brentford and Chiswick Local History Society. Journal†
0144-6754 The Astrological Journal **565**
0144-6800 I C O Library Monthly Entries - Coffeeline
0144-6835 Retail Review **1840**
0144-6843 National Council for Educational Standards. Bulletin†
0144-686X Ageing and Society **4039**
0144-6878 Sussex Yesterdays†
0144-6916 Midland Bonsai Society Journal **3743**
0144-6924 Child's Play
0144-6932 Majesty **3774**
0144-7033 Consumer News†
0144-7076 P N Review **5429**
0144-7122 The Assyrian Observer **3520**
0144-7130 Textile News†
0144-7149 Chronicle (London)
0144-7181 Sport and Leisure (London)†
0144-722X Scottish Chamber Orchestra. Yearbook
0144-7238 Wood Based Panels International **3717**
0144-7262 Rock Drill **5433**
0144-7386 Shipbuilding News
0144-7394 Teaching Public Administration **7471**
0144-7416 Bailey and Litchfield's Ritz Newspaper†
0144-7424 Arrowhead **8159**
0144-7459 Directory of Arts Centres†
0144-7475 Thomas Cook Overseas Timetable **8513**
0144-7505 Printing Historical Society Bulletin **7326**

0144-7548 Republican Englishman **7177**
0144-7572 Heatline†
0144-7637 Traveller's Guide to North Africa†
0144-7645 Traveller's Guide to West Africa†
0144-7653 Traveller's Guide to East Africa and the Indian Ocean†
0144-7661 Traveller's Guide to Central and Southern Africa†
0144-7750 World Radio T V Handbook **2365**
0144-7777 Clinica **5595**
0144-7785 Noise & Vibration Bulletin **7088**
0144-7815 I A H S Proceedings and Reports **2795**
0144-7831 Res Mechanica Letters†
0144-784X Bucks Advertiser **3862**
0144-7866 London Drinker **606**
0144-8005 New Celtic Review†
0144-8021 Transport Statistics Great Britain **8531**
0144-8048 Great Britain. Department of Education and Science. Primary Mathematics Survey. Summary Report
0144-8072 Early Music Record Services. Monthly Review **6563**
0144-8099 Tourism†
0144-8129 Slimming **6669**
0144-8137 Picture Postcard Monthly **4343**
0144-8153 Evangelical Review of Theology **7641**
0144-8188 International Review of Law and Economics **4696**
0144-820X Lloyd's List **8650**
0144-8234 Africa Economic Digest† **8928**
0144-8242 British Shipbuilder†
0144-8250 Car Parts & Accessories†
0144-8285 Catholic Commission for Racial Justice. Notes & Reports†
0144-8315 Staffordshire Post
0144-8374 Baking Today†
0144-8382 County Trades Finder. Section 3: Southern
0144-8390 County Trades Finder. Section 1: Northern
0144-8412 Artery
0144-8420 Radiation Protection Dosimetry **7072**
0144-8439 Conduit **4212**
0144-8447 Science for People†
0144-8455 Postgraduate Doctor: Asia†
0144-8463 Bioscience Reports **828**
0144-8471 Insight (London, 1978)†
0144-8498 Quarterly Energy Review: Far East & Australasia†
0144-8587 Chartered Institute of Building. Construction Papers†
0144-8595 One Earth†
0144-8609 Aquacultural Engineering **3584**
0144-8617 Carbohydrate Polymers **2120**
0144-8633 Techniques of Measurement in Medicine Series†
0144-8676 Royal Society of Medicine. Annual Report **5707**
0144-8684 Current Topics in Anaesthesia
0144-8692 Management of Malignant Disease Series
0144-8722 Sobornost **7706**
0144-8765 Biological Agriculture and Horticulture **96**
0144-8773 Heterocyclic Chemistry†
0144-8781 Far East Shipping†
0144-8803 British Journal of Pharmaceutical Practice†
0144-8994 Quarterly Energy Review: Middle East†
0144-9036 B M P Monthly Statistical Bulletin **1044**
0144-9052 B M P Information **978**
0144-9060 B M P Forecasts **978**
0144-9117 O R C Notes
0144-9206 Quarterly Energy Review: North America†
0144-9214 Quarterly Energy Review: Latin America & the Caribbean†
0144-9222 Quarterly Energy Review: Western Europe†
0144-9230 Quarterly Energy Review: U.S.S.R. & Eastern Europe†
0144-9249 Quarterly Energy Review: Africa†
0144-9281 Environmental Education and Information†
0144-929X Behaviour and Information Technology **7340**
0144-9311 Transmission (Doncaster)†
0144-932X Liverpool Law Review **4724**
0144-9338 Henry Williamson Society Journal **5305**
0144-9346 Tried & Tested†
0144-946X Purvadesh
0144-9478 Butterworths International Medical Reviews: Obstetrics and Gynecology†
0144-9486 University College of Swansea. Centre for Development Studies. Monograph Series†
0144-9494 University College of Swansea. Centre for Development Studies. Occasional Papers Series†
0144-9524 Production Management and Control
0144-9613 Association Management†
0144-9621 B A S C A News†
0144-9664 Clinical Science. Supplement *see* 0143-5221 **5597**
0144-9702 Directory of Marine Technology **2803**
0144-9745 A R C News†
0144-9818 Western Buddhist **7703**
0144-9826 Conchological Society Special Publication **667**
0144-9842 Not Poetry†
0144-9850 University of London. Institute of Germanic Studies. Bithell Memorial Lectures **5393**
0144-9877 Chelmer Working Papers in Environmental Planning **3410**
0144-9931 Catalyst (London) **5001**
0144-994X New Books Quarterly on Islam & the Muslim World **7699**
0144-9966 Bibliography in Socio-Legal Studies†
0145-0050 Climatological Data. Alabama **6349**
0145-0069 Climatological Data. California **6350**
0145-0093 Kansas State University. Center for Energy Studies. Report†
0145-0239 U.S. Department of the Treasury. Financial Management Service. Daily Treasury Statement **1953**
0145-0301 U.S. Federal Reserve System. Research Library - Recent Acquisitions **636**
0145-0352 U S Export Sales Reports **1585**
0145-0360 Weekly Cotton Market Review **208**
0145-0379 Berkeley Papers in History of Science **7936**
0145-0387 Climatological Data. Arizona **6349**
0145-0409 Climatological Data. Louisiana **6350**
0145-0425 Climatological Data. Mississippi **6350**
0145-0433 Climatological Data. Kentucky **6350**
0145-0468 Climatological Data. Iowa **6350**
0145-0484 Climatological Data. Florida **6350**
0145-0492 Climatological Data. Georgia **6350**
0145-0506 Climatological Data. Colorado **6350**
0145-0514 Climatological Data. Idaho **6350**
0145-0522 Climatological Data. Illinois **6350**
0145-0530 Climatological Data. Indiana **6350**
0145-0549 Climatological Data. Maryland and Delaware **6350**
0145-062X Public Documents Highlights†
0145-0646 Daily Depository Shipping List **5005**
0145-0662 Molasses Market News **3657**
0145-0670 N S F Bulletin†
0145-0689 River Currents†
0145-0700 U.S. Central Intelligence Agency. Appearances of Soviet Leaders
0145-0786 International Poetry Review **5424**
0145-0875 World Cotton Situation†
0145-1014 Aviation Monthly **48**
0145-1022 Real Estate Investing Letter
0145-1030 Money Management Digest†
0145-1073 Surface Warfare **6448**
0145-112X Profile (Norfolk) **6442**
0145-1146 Vessel Safety Review†
0145-1189 E P A Journal†
0145-1227 Fireword†
0145-1391 Epoch (Ithaca) **5421**
0145-1464 International Journal of Radiation: Oncology - Biology - Physics. Supplement *see* 0360-3016 **6199**
0145-1472 College Student and the Courts **2973**
0145-1499 Authors in the News†
0145-1502 U.S. General Accounting Office. Office of the General Counsel. Digests of Unpublished Decisions of the Comptroller General of the United States†
0145-1677 First Monday (Washington, D.C.)†
0145-1707 Finance and Development (Print) **1343**
0145-1715 Downtown Planning & Development Annual†
0145-1901 Reserves of Crude Oil, Natural Gas Liquids and Natural Gas in the United States and Canada and United States Productive Capacity
0145-1928 Report of the Secretary of the Commonwealth to the Governor and General Assembly of Virginia **7465**
0145-1987 N A G W S Guide. Volleyball†
0145-2037 Educational Commission for Foreign Medical Graduates. Annual Report **5608**
0145-2096 Diplomatic History **4137**
0145-210X Songsmith's Journal†
0145-2118 Design Abstracts International†
0145-2126 Leukemia Research **5940**
0145-2134 Child Abuse & Neglect **2147**
0145-2258 African Economic History **1535**
0145-2290 I I M C News Digest **7494**
0145-2371 Alpine Information†
0145-2517 Music & Musicians: Instructional Disc Recordings Catalog (Large Print Edition)†
0145-2525 Music & Musicians: Instructional Cassette Recordings Catalog
0145-2681 De Colores
0145-2711 Society of Biblical Literature. Seminar Papers (Year)†
0145-2754 Septuagint and Cognate Studies *changed to* 1044-6761 **7680**
0145-2770 Society of Biblical Literature. Disseration Series *changed to* 1570-1980 **7619**
0145-2800 Water Operation and Maintenance Bulletin **8837**
0145-2843 Jazz
0145-2908 Vermont Law Review **4808**
0145-2932 People (Raleigh) **1702**
0145-3017 Corporate Buyers of Design Services/U S A
0145-3041 Social Services U.S.A.†
0145-305X Developmental & Comparative Immunology **5757**
0145-3076 State Court Journal†
0145-3084 Bibliography Newsletter
0145-3130 Music & Musicians: Braille Scores Catalog - Piano
0145-3149 Music & Musicians: Braille Scores Catalog - Organ
0145-3165 Music & Musicians: Braille Scores Catalog - Instrumental
0145-3173 Music & Musicians: Braille Scores Catalog - Choral
0145-319X N A S A Tech Briefs **66**
0145-3378 Journal of Psychohistory **7378**
0145-3408 Executive Disclosure Guide†
0145-3416 Immigration Newsletter **4928**
0145-3432 Southern Illinois University Law Journal **4786**
0145-3483 Cinegram
0145-3505 Professional Liability Reporter **4762**
0145-3513 International Trombone Association. Journal **6577**
0145-3637 South Carolina Economic Report **1519**
0145-370X International Ophthalmological Reporter
0145-3718 Advances in Modern Nutrition†
0145-3726 Progress in Cancer Research and Therapy†
0145-3890 International Organization for Septuagint and Cognate Studies. Bulletin **4458**
0145-3904 U.S. Department of Agriculture. National Agricultural Statistics Service. Egg Products **188**
0145-3963 Executive (Ithaca) *changed to* 0897-1447 **1735**
0145-3971 Review of Regional Economics and Business
0145-4064 Firehouse (Fort Atkinson) **3578**
0145-4072 Exchange (Columbia)†
0145-4145 Year Book of Cardiology **5802**
0145-417X Coal Data†
0145-4250 American Handgunner **4327**
0145-4269 Oregon Property Tax Statistics **1257**
0145-4455 Behavior Modification **7339**
0145-4471 Powder **8329**
0145-448X New York Law School Law Review **4745**
0145-4498 Current Concepts in Emergency Medicine†
0145-4560 C B Radio - S 9
0145-4773 Mountain Call
0145-479X Journal of Bioenergetics and Biomembranes **735**
0145-482X Journal of Visual Impairment & Blindness **4082**
0145-4927 Current Industrial Reports: Manufacturers' Export Sales and Orders of Durable Goods†
0145-5168 Current Industrial Reports: Fats and Oils. Oilseed Crushings†
0145-5265 A S C A P Symphonic Catalog **6541**
0145-5281 Circus Maximus†
0145-5303 Phantasm†
0145-5311 Recently Published Articles†
0145-532X Government Reports Annual Index†
0145-5338 Benchmark Papers in Analytical Chemistry†
0145-5346 Advances in Sleep Research†
0145-5397 Library Developments **5027**
0145-5400 G.P.U. News
0145-546X Mountain Review†
0145-5516 Illinois Speech and Theatre Association. Journal **2325**
0145-5532 Social Science History **8003**
0145-5559 Tradeshow **36**
0145-5575 Thorndyke File **5412**
0145-5605 Earth Resources: A Continuing Bibliography with Indexes†
0145-5613 Ear, Nose & Throat Journal **6079**
0145-5656 U.S. Department of Housing and Urban Development. F H A Monthly Report of Operations. Project Insurance Programs **4437**
0145-5664 Current Business Reports: Canned Food†
0145-5680 Cellular and Molecular Biology **665**
0145-5699 Communications in Psychopharmacology†
0145-5753 Rohmer Review†
0145-5788 Teaching Philosophy **6956**
0145-5818 Criminal Justice Periodical Index **2674**
0145-5869 Foodservice Distributor Salesman†
0145-6008 Alcoholism: Clinical and Experimental Research **2691**
0145-6016 Hobby Artist News†
0145-6024 Country Messenger†
0145-6032 Cinefantastique (Print) *changed to* Cinefantastique (Online) **5441**
0145-613X Daiwa Fishing Annual†
0145-6180 M P L A Newsletter **5030**
0145-6202 Federal Yellow Book **7437**
0145-6210 Body Forum†
0145-6237 Soundboard **6618**
0145-6261 Feed-Back (San Francisco)†
0145-627X Book Talk (Albuquerque)†
0145-6288 International Plant Protection Center. Infoletter†
0145-6296 Veterinary and Human Toxicology **3503**
0145-630X Meeting News **6281**
0145-6334 Assur **4320**
0145-644X Washington Watch†
0145-6466 Indian Opinion†
0145-6555 Museum Scope†
0145-6571 Law Officers' Bulletin **2659**
0145-6598 Government Contracts Service **1748**
0145-6628 Wisconsin Session Laws **7477**
0145-6636 Pastoral Music Notebook **6604**
0145-6644 Fund Sources in Health and Allied Fields†
0145-6776 Auto Index†
0145-6784 Soldier of Fortune **6446**
0145-6792 Glassworks†
0145-6814 Current Awareness Profile on Quantum Chemistry†
0145-6857 Alabama's Health **7506**
0145-692X Corporate Profiles for Executives & Investors†
0145-7055 McCutcheon's Emulsifiers and Detergents (North American Edition) **2072**
0145-7071 Business People in the News†
0145-7217 The Diabetes Educator **5887**
0145-7233 Concordia Journal **7634**
0145-7241 Artnewsletter **474**
0145-7284 U.S. Federal Election Commission. Annual Report **7190**
0145-7314 Summary Information on Master of Social Work Programs† **8991**
0145-7322 Criminal Law Outline **4887**
0145-7330 Geographic Profile of Employment and Unemployment **1683**
0145-7594 International School of Hydrocarbon Measurement. Proceedings **6774**
0145-7632 Heat Transfer Engineering **3245**
0145-7659 Privacy Journal **2515**
0145-7667 Liberty Bell†
0145-7675 The Other Side†
0145-7683 Significant Advances in Science†
0145-7780 Graham House Review†
0145-787X Mime Journal **8474**
0145-7888 Studies in Twentieth Century Literature *changed to* 1555-7839 **5382**
0145-7918 Blaisdell Institute. Journal.†
0145-7950 Orthodox Church in America. Yearbook and Church Directory **7705**
0145-7985 W I N News **8904**
0145-7993 American Indian Journal†
0145-8035 Guide to Graduate and Professional Study†
0145-8124 Election Administration Reports **7132**
0145-8213 Scale Cabinetmaker†
0145-8299 Feminist Press. News/Notes
0145-8302 Grantechs
0145-8310 Cathartic **5271**
0145-837X Pharmaceutical Trends†
0145-8388 New Laurel Review **5340**
0145-8396 Institute for Studies in American Music. Newsletter *changed to* 1943-9385 **6544**
0145-840X Korean Studies **554**
0145-8418 Eastern Electrical Buyers' Guide†
0145-8426 Southern Electrical Buyers' Guide†
0145-8442 Customer Service Newsletter **1737**
0145-8450 The Customer Communicator **1859**
0145-8566 Federal Election Commission. Record **7135**
0145-8582 New Directions in Legal Services†
0145-8701 Institute for Briquetting and Agglomeration. Proceedings **6465**
0145-8752 Moscow University Geology Bulletin **2756**
0145-8779 Marianne Moore Newsletter†
0145-8787 Pulp†
0145-8795 Joint Conference†
0145-8809 Astrology Now†
0145-8825 Greater Llano Estacado Southwest Heritage†
0145-8841 Stanley Foundation. Policy Paper†
0145-885X Gnostica†
0145-8868 Llewellyn's Astrological Calendar†
0145-8876 Journal of Food Process Engineering **3650**

0146-9371 U.S. Senate. Committee on Foreign Relations. Legislative Activities Report **7270**
0146-9428 Journal of Food Quality **3651**
0146-9436 M A S K C Komondor News **292**
0146-9460 Alaska. Division of Geological and Geophysical Surveys.Biennnial Report†
0146-9487 Homemaker†
0146-9568 Toledo†
0146-9576 San Francisco Theatre Magazine
0146-9584 Journal of Legislation **4703**
0146-9592 Optics Letters **7083**
0146-9673 Employment and Training Reporter **1678**
0146-9711 New Perspectives in Powder Metallurgy **6327**
0146-9738 Dental Lab Products **5840**
0146-9770 A I C P A Washington Report†
0146-9819 Auditing Research Monographs†
0146-9843 Race Relations & the Law *see* 0033-7315
0146-9924 Circuit Rider (Nashville) **7752**
0146-9959 Meteor News **577**
0146-9967 Longest Revolution†
0146-9975 N S O A Bulletin†
0146-9983 Postal History U.S.A†
0146-9991 Colorado Express **8694**
0147-0027 Railroad Station Historical Society. The Bulletin **8623**
0147-0051 Fire & Movement **8173**
0147-006X Annual Review of Neuroscience **6123**
0147-0078 Recent Researches in American Music **6609**
0147-0086 Recent Researches in the Music of the Classical Era **6609**
0147-0108 Collegium Musicum: Yale University **6558**
0147-0124 N O R C Report†
0147-0248 Applied Biochemistry and Bioengineering†
0147-0272 Current Problems in Cancer **6018**
0147-0302 Motor Skills: Theory into Practice†
0147-0310 Association of American Publishers. Exhibits Directory†
0147-037X Ming Studies **555**
0147-0396 Rebis Chapbook Series **5433**
0147-0442 Accounting Articles Digest†
0147-0469 Codification of Statements on Auditing Standards **1285**
0147-0515 N I A A A - R U C A S Alcoholism Treatment Series **2697**
0147-0590 Regulation (Washington, 1977) **7176**
0147-0604 Michigan State University. Library. Africana: Select Recent Acquisitions
0147-0612 Michigan State University. Library. Latin America: Select Recent Acquisitions†
0147-0620 Michigan State University. Library. Asia: Select Recent Acquisitions†
0147-0639 Maine Antique Digest **367**
0147-0647 I N S Reporter†
0147-0671 International Progress in Urethanes†
0147-071X Advances in Behavioral Pharmacology†
0147-0728 Gay Community News (Boston)†
0147-0779 Modern Greek Society: A Social Science Newsletter **4245**
0147-0787 Books at Brown **620**
0147-0809 Light Metals (Year) **6320**
0147-0868 Wittenberg Review of Literature and Art **5399**
0147-0965 Curwood Collector†
0147-099X Medical Subject Headings - Tree Structure (Year)†
0147-1015 Ukrainian Orthodox Word **7706**
0147-1023 Contributions in Family Studies† **8943**
0147-1031 Contributions in Intercultural and Comparative Studies† **8943**
0147-104X Contributions in Women's Studies **8895**
0147-1066 Contributions in Political Science† **8943**
0147-1074 Contributions in Legal Studies† **8943**
0147-1082 Contemporary Problems of Childhood†
0147-1104 Studies in Population and Urban Demography† **8991**
0147-1120 Association of College Unions - International. Proceedings of the Annual Conference†
0147-1139 Dignity - U S A **7795**
0147-121X Light (New York)†
0147-1228 Hoosier Journal of Ancestry†
0147-1236 A C T F L Foreign Language Education Series **3049**
0147-1260 Child Protection Report *changed to* 1554-3684
0147-1295 Arkansas Football Magazine†
0147-1309 Annual Immigration and Naturalization Institute **4827**
0147-1341 Social Change†
0147-1473 Social Development Issues **8068**
0147-1481 Offshore Rig Newsletter *changed to* Gulf of Mexico Rig Report **6772**
0147-149X Cottonwood **5279**
0147-1503 International Data Series. Selected Data on Mixtures. Series A. Thermodynamic Properties of Non-reacting Binary Systems of Organic Substances **2136**
0147-1570 CompFlash†
0147-1619 Corporation Law and Tax Report†
0147-1627 Calyx **5269**
0147-1635 Journal of Basic Writing **5314**
0147-1686 Floating Island **5297**
0147-1694 Contemporary Jewry **3528**
0147-1724 Southwestern Entomologist **859**
0147-1740 Urban League Review†
0147-1759 Women & Literature **5399**
0147-1767 International Journal of Intercultural Relations **8109**
0147-1783 Washington (State). Department of Natural Resources. Division of Geology and Earth Resources. Information Circular **2774**
0147-1821 Graduate Programs: Physics, Astronomy, and Related Fields (Year) **7014**
0147-1902 Georgia Museum of Art. Bulletin **491**
0147-1937 Real Analysis Exchange **5528**
0147-197X Current Problems in Anesthesia and Critical Care Medicine†
0147-1996 Year Book of Family Practice (Year) **5733**
0147-2003 Southwest Regional Conference for Astronomy and Astrophysics. Proceedings†
0147-2011 Society **8005**
0147-2135 A R L Statistics **5056**
0147-2186 Mississippi Agricultural & Forestry Experiment Station. Research Report **137**
0147-2208 Laventhol and Horwath Perspective†
0147-2275 Seriatim
0147-2410 Western Investor†
0147-2429 Plastics in Building Construction†
0147-2453 Curriculum Review **3057**
0147-247X Photographer's Market **6974**
0147-2488 Richardson Family Researcher and Historical News **3780**
0147-250X Bibliography of Books for Children†
0147-2526 Dance Chronicle **2683**
0147-2542 Ohio Documents **633**
0147-2550 Massachusetts Music News **6586**
0147-2569 Chess Horizons **8166**
0147-2593 The Lion and the Unicorn **5323**
0147-2615 Abstracts of Popular Culture†
0147-2631 Hollow Spring Review of Poetry
0147-264X Dental Research in the United States and Other Countries†
0147-2682 Biomedical Technology Information Service†
0147-2704 Seventh Ray
0147-2771 National Health Directory (Year) **4107**
0147-281X West Point Museum Bulletin†
0147-2828 Black Press Information Handbook†
0147-2860 Illinois. State Board of Education. Annual Report **3024**
0147-2909 Nuclear Regulatory Commission Issuances **7070**
0147-2968 Running Times **8198**
0147-3077 Periodical Guide for Computerists†
0147-3085 Celestinesca **5271**
0147-3166 Winesburg Eagle **5399**
0147-3204 I E E E Transactions on Cable Television†
0147-3247 Nuestro
0147-3301 Cablelines
0147-345X Eastman Notes **6564**
0147-3565 Porsche Panorama **8599**
0147-3654 Scienceland
0147-3689 John Marshall Law Journal **4699**
0147-3743 Safety Sadistics†
0147-3751 Americans Abroad†
0147-3786 Quest (Year)†
0147-3883 United States House of Representatives. Committee on Appropriations. Report of Committee Activities **7474**
0147-3956 U.S. Department of Health and Human Services. National Center for Health Statistics. Advance Data from Vital and Health Statistics **7549**
0147-3964 Multivariate Experimental Clinical Research *changed to* Applied Multivariate Research **7335**
0147-3972 Dental Guidance Council on the Handicapped. Journal†
0147-4006 Carcinogenesis†
0147-4030 How to Fly for Less†
0147-4049 Bright Lights (Print Edition) *changed to* Bright Lights (Online Edition) **6491**
0147-4065 Population Dynamics Quarterly†
0147-4103 United States Senate. Committee on Agriculture, Nutrition and Forestry. Legislative Calendar **7474**
0147-4316 Israel Securities Review†
0147-4367 Voice of Washington Music Educators **6627**
0147-4391 B I A Education Research Bulletin†
0147-4413 American Liszt Society. Journal **6543**
0147-443X National Nosocomial Infections Study Report†
0147-4502 West Coast Plays†
0147-4642 Communication Yearbook **5276**
0147-4650 Checklist of Official Publications of the State of Oregon†
0147-4693 On the Line Magazine (New York)
0147-4804 World Wide Printer†
0147-4847 A A S H T O Quarterly **3258**
0147-4863 Advances in Microbial Ecology **880**
0147-4871 Feedback **2381**
0147-4928 Country Gentleman
0147-4936 Invisible City **5424**
0147-507X First World
0147-5118 Toxic Substances Sourcebook†
0147-5185 American Journal of Surgical Pathology **5573**
0147-5207 Mon - Khmer Studies
0147-5231 Somatics **6997**
0147-5304 Profitable Craft Merchandising†
0147-538X The New York Times Index **4587**
0147-5401 Industrial Hygiene News **6678**
0147-5428 West Coast Writer's Conspiracy
0147-5436 Aloha†
0147-5452 Telephone†
0147-5460 Journal of Hispanic Philology **5315**
0147-5479 International Labor and Working-Class History **1689**
0147-5630 Index to Free Periodicals†
0147-5681 Children's Book Review Index **2173**
0147-5711 Medical Subject Headings - Annotated Alphabetic List†
0147-572X M R I S Abstracts†
0147-5754 Intermedia Magazine†
0147-5762 Alive & Kicking†
0147-5770 Finders International Newsletter
0147-5851 E M T Journal†
0147-5894 College and University Admissions and Enrollment, New York State **2972**
0147-5916 Cognitive Therapy and Research **7347**
0147-5924 Info Franchise Newsletter **1962**
0147-5959 Catholic Telephone Guide **7790**
0147-5967 Journal of Comparative Economics **1134**
0147-5983 Index to Record and Tape Reviews†
0147-6041 State Legislatures **7186**
0147-6149 University Journal†
0147-6165 Roaring Twenties, Gay Nineties†
0147-619X Plasmid **698**
0147-6254 Bedside Care†
0147-6262 C R C Handbook of Chemistry and Physics **2052**
0147-6335 Korean Studies Forum
0147-6491 Bibliographic Guide to North American History†
0147-6505 Bibliographic Guide to Education†
0147-6513 Ecotoxicology and Environmental Safety **3496**
0147-6521 Energy Information Abstracts†
0147-6548 New Atlantean Journal†
0147-6564 Counterpoint
0147-6572 United States Senate. Committee on Governmental Affairs. Legislative Calendar **7474**
0147-6629 Seattle Review **5369**
0147-6742 Medical Ultrasound†
0147-6874 Moscow University Soil Science Bulletin **242**
0147-6882 Scientific and Technical Information Processing **5046**
0147-6890 Fiscal Observer†
0147-698X Journal of Powder & Bulk Solids Technology†
0147-7129 Attic Press†
0147-7145 Personal Communications†
0147-7161 Georgia Courts Journal **4952**
0147-7188 Managing the Leisure Facility†
0147-720X Outdoors in Georgia†
0147-7218 Law and Behavior†
0147-7226 Hope Reports Perspective†
0147-7307 Law and Human Behavior **4713**
0147-7315 West's Military Justice Reporter **4972**
0147-7366 International Review of Biochemistry†
0147-7447 Orthopedics **6070**
0147-7463 Human Nature†
0147-7471 Adventure Travel (Seattle)†
0147-7501 Resources for Change **2905**
0147-7536 Musica Judaica **6593**
0147-7544 Dialogue in Instrumental Music Education†
0147-7625 New Realities†
0147-7668 Aerophile **4327**
0147-7684 Car Care Handbook†
0147-7706 Short Story International **5372**
0147-7714 Environmental Law Handbook **3425**
0147-779X American Phytopathological Society. Proceedings†
0147-782X International Psychic Register†
0147-7870 U.S. Department of Housing and Urban Development. Statistical Yearbook†
0147-7889 N S C Alliance Newsletter *changed to* Alliance Gazette **6518**
0147-7927 Perinatology - Neonatology†
0147-7935 Microstate Studies **7985**
0147-796X Dressage & C T
0147-7986 Florida Outlook†
0147-8044 Ganley's Catholic Schools in America **2956**
0147-8176 Fodor's Egypt **8705**
0147-8257 Harvard Environmental Law Review **4684**
0147-8265 Who's Who in Chiropractic, International Conditions†
0147-8311 Conditions†
0147-8389 Pacing and Clinical Electrophysiology **5797**
0147-8559 South Atlantic Urban Studies†
0147-8656 Fodor's Southwest†
0147-8680 Fodor's the South **8709**
0147-877X Business Officer **2969**
0147-8826 College Planning - Search Book†
0147-8834 Flyfisher **8314**
0147-8885 Journal of Histotechnology **834**
0147-8893 Diagnostic Medicine†
0147-9024 Journal of New World Archaeology†
0147-9032 Review (Binghamton) **1548**
0147-9121 Research in Labor Economics **1705**
0147-9156 Contemporary French Civilization **4212**
0147-9229 Review of Taxation of Individuals†
0147-9253 Intermedia Arts and Communication Resource Newsletter†
0147-9288 American Alpine News **8303**
0147-9296 Association for Educational Data Systems. Annual Convention Proceedings†
0147-9369 Georgia Journal of Science **7857**
0147-9512 Global Political Assessment†
0147-9563 Heart & Lung **5959**
0147-9571 Comparative Immunology, Microbiology & Infectious Diseases **883**
0147-958X Clinical and Investigative Medicine (Print)† **8941**
0147-9660 D R I - McGraw-Hill Energy Review
0147-9679 Basal Facts†
0147-9695 Vintage Triumph **8611**
0147-9725 Maryland Birdlife **910**
0147-9733 Colorado Libraries **5003**
0147-9741 Center on Evaluation, Development and Research. Quarterly†
0147-9822 Ward's Who's Who Among U.S. Motor Vehicle Manufacturers†
0147-9857 Loyola of Los Angeles Law Review **4726**
0147-9865 Georgia Labor Market Trends **1683**
0147-9911 The Aviation Consumer **48**
0147-992X McElroy Family Newsletter†
0147-9970 Litigation News (Chicago) **4724**
0147-9989 Restaurant Hospitality **4397**
0148-0006 U.S. House of Representatives. Committee on Standards of Official Conduct. Summary of Activities. Report **7473**
0148-0057 Measurements & Control†
0148-009X The Consolidated Tax Return **1917**
0148-0146 Manhattan Business†
0148-0162 Raccoon
0148-0227 Journal of Geophysical Research **2785**
0148-0243 American Go Journal **8158**
0148-0294 Princeton Journal of the Arts and Sciences
0148-0324 California Environmental Directory†
0148-0375 International Petroleum Encyclopedia **6774**
0148-0537 Fusion (New York)†
0148-0545 Drug and Chemical Toxicology **6833**
0148-0553 Law Lines **5025**
0148-0561 Kxe6s Verein Newsletter **8185**
0148-057X Kxe6s Verein Chess Society. Advisory Board Record **8185**
0148-0588 National Lawyers Guild. Guild Notes **4851**
0148-060X United States Military Posture **6451**
0148-0650 Illinois Health Sciences Libraries Serials Holdings List†
0148-0731 Journal of Biomechanical Engineering **5646**
0148-0766 Lodging Hospitality **4393**
0148-0863 Public Revenues from Alcohol Beverages†
0148-0944 Missouri Academy of Science. Occasional Paper **7882**
0148-0987 Laser Interaction and Related Plasma Phenomena **7024**
0148-1002 Rocky Mountain Bioengineering Symposium. Annual Proceedings **751**
0148-1029 Studies in Iconography **520**

ISSN

0149-4635 Hustler **6292**
0149-466X Players **3558**
0149-4732 Advances in Clinical Child Psychology†
0149-4740 National N O W Times **8877**
0149-4872 Sociological Observations **8137**
0149-4899 Plastics Machinery & Equipment†
0149-4902 M O T A
0149-4910 N A C T A Journal **138**
0149-4929 Marriage & Family Review **8119**
0149-4953 Money (New York) **1368**
0149-5046 Heard Heritage **3769**
0149-5070 Western New York Magazine†
0149-516X Southern Accents† **8989**
0149-5267 National Petroleum News **6779**
0149-5372 Checklist of Human Rights Documents†
0149-5380 W W D **2250**
0149-5437 Olson†
0149-5526 Oak Ridge National Laboratory. Technical Memorandum **3173**
0149-5534 Industry Mart†
0149-5585 International Construction Week†
0149-5682 Textile Booklist†
0149-5712 Maarav **5149**
0149-5739 Journal of Thermal Stresses **3387**
0149-5747 Advanced Lighter-Than-Air Review†
0149-5771 Electrical Marketing **1815**
0149-5801 Keystone News Bulletin†
0149-5836 European Marketscan **6768**
0149-5879 Sewage Treatment Construction Grants Manual†
0149-5887 Tiger Report†
0149-5895 Food, Drug & Cosmetic Manufacturing†
0149-5909 Convenience Store News-Executive/Store Manager Edition
0149-5917 Inspiration (Los Angeles)†
0149-5925 Vans & Pickups†
0149-5933 Comparative Strategy **7118**
0149-5992 Diabetes Care **5887**
0149-6018 Routes
0149-6026 Inner Paths **6645**
0149-6077 Washout Review†
0149-6085 Journal of Food Safety **3651**
0149-6115 Geotechnical Testing Journal **3268**
0149-6123 Cement, Concrete, and Aggregates†
0149-6166 Index to Federal Tax Articles **1241**
0149-6255 Employment Practices Decisions **1679**
0149-631X Fodor's London **8707**
0149-6352 Hospital Week†
0149-6395 Separation Science and Technology **2105**
0149-6425 Rodeo News†
0149-6433 Orthopaedic Research Society. Transactions of the Annual Meeting **6069**
0149-6441 West Branch **5438**
0149-645X I E E E - M T T S International Microwave Symposium. Digest **3312**
0149-6530 Decennial Digest: American Digest System *see* 0511-8522 **4813**
0149-6573 Environmental Comment†
0149-6581 Directory of Companies Required to File Annual Reports with the Securities and Exchange Commission Under the Securities Exchange Act of 1934†
0149-6646 Alaska. Department of Natural Resources. Annual Report†
0149-6700 Studies in History of Biology†
0149-6719 Cardiopulmonary Medicine†
0149-6727 Medical Imaging†
0149-6743 Nutrition Planning†
0149-676X American Wine Society Manual **597**
0149-6778 American Wine Society Bulletin **597**
0149-6840 Folklife Center News **3617**
0149-6859 Cross Reference†
0149-6891 Unearth†
0149-6948 Case Analysis†
0149-6956 Crain's Chicago Business **1959**
0149-6972 Far West†
0149-6980 Media & Values†
0149-7014 On Location Magazine
0149-709X R F D **4378**
0149-7162 Down's Syndrome
0149-7189 Evaluation and Program Planning **7963**
0149-7197 Retired Military Almanac **6443**
0149-7219 Yearbook of Romanian Studies
0149-7308 A S B C Newsletter **597**
0149-7324 Impresario†
0149-7332 Somos
0149-7413 Senior Tribune **4055**
0149-7421 Developments in Marketing Science **1813**
0149-7448 Regulators†
0149-7499 Floral Underawl & Gazette Times **4335**
0149-7537 Who's Who in Engineering **647**
0149-7618 Washington (State). Department of Revenue. Quarterly Business Review **1193**
0149-7634 Neuroscience & Biobehavioral Reviews **6169**
0149-7642 Red Book of Housing Manufacturers†
0149-7677 Dance Research Journal **2684**
0149-7707 Modern Silver Coinage (Year)†
0149-7820 Beehive†
0149-7847 Directory of Conservative and Libertarian Serials, Publishers, and Freelance Markets
0149-7863 Pushcart Prize: Best of the Small Presses **5355**
0149-7898 Silicon Gulch Gazette†
0149-7901 Journal of Applied Management†
0149-791X New Mexico Studies in the Fine Arts†
0149-7944 Current Surgery *changed to* 1931-7204 **6250**
0149-7952 German Studies Review **4223**
0149-7987 Arizona Bicentennial Review†
0149-8029 OpFlow **3214**
0149-8088 Index to Scientific & Technical Proceedings **7937**
0149-810X Subject Guide to Reprints†
0149-8134 World Products†
0149-8142 Dunsworld Marketing Management†
0149-8231 New York Business Change Service†
0149-824X New Jersey Business Change Service†
0149-8304 Directory of Personnel Responsible for Radiological Health Programs **3495**
0149-8347 Adult Bible Studies **7744**
0149-8398 Ecolibrium†
0149-8428 Religion Index One: Periodicals **7699**
0149-8436 Religion Index Two: Multi-Author Works†
0149-8444 Keystone Folklore†
0149-8452 New York (City). Commission on the Status of Women. Status Report†
0149-8487 Gratz College Annual of Jewish Studies†
0149-8606 Encyclopedia of Food Technology and Food Science Series†
0149-869X Work in America Institute Studies in Productivity **1274**
0149-8703 Work in America Institute: Highlights of the Literature **1274**
0149-8711 Omni†
0149-8738 International Environment Reporter **3441**
0149-8754 Phi Alpha Delta Reporter **2268**
0149-8827 Corporation Law Review†
0149-8851 River Styx **5237**
0149-886X Journal of Optometric Vision Development *changed to* 1557-4113 **6049**
0149-8886 Academy of Rehabilitative Audiology. Journal **6076**
0149-8924 Sourcebook of Equal Educational Opportunity†
0149-8932 Interview (New York) **3979**
0149-8991 Geothermal Resources Council. Special Report **2782**
0149-9009 Contemporary Diagnostic Radiology **6194**
0149-9025 Kobunshi Ronbunshu (English Edition)†
0149-9106 Architecture Minnesota **431**
0149-9114 Kansas History **4300**
0149-9246 Hastings International and Comparative Law Review **4927**
0149-9262 Access (Washington, 1975)†
0149-9270 Princeton Alumni Weekly **2297**
0149-9319 Shorthorn Country **300**
0149-9378 Compendium of Organic Synthetic Methods **2122**
0149-9386 Energy Magazine† **8953**
0149-9408 American Book Review **5205**
0149-9483 Advances in Nutritional Research **6654**
0149-953X Prana Yoga Life **6944**
0149-9726 Bonsai Journal **3725**
0149-9807 Immigration and Nationality Law Review **4928**
0149-9815 Inland Shores†
0149-9939 National Library of Medicine. Audiovisuals Catalog†
0149-9963 American Statistical Association. Statistical Computing Section. Proceedings *changed to* 1543-3218 **8344**
0149-9971 Review of International Broadcasting†
0150-0112 Dossiers de l'Elevage†
0150-1313 Rail Syndicaliste **4601**
0150-1844 Points de Vente **1837**
0150-2441 Confluent†
0150-2581 Tele Star **2396**
0150-3065 News from Prospace **67**
0150-3855 Bulletin Signaletique de Documentation Generale *changed to* 0396-4388 **8981**
0150-391X Dernieres Nouvelles d'Alsace **3840**
0150-4185 Femmes en Litterature **5295**
0150-4428 Lys Rouge **7152**
0150-4576 Touring†
0150-5467 Feuillet Rapide Fiscal Social **1924**
0150-5602 Medica Gestion†
0150-6943 Cahiers Jean Giraudoux **5269**
0150-7206 Revue Technique Carrosserie **8601**
0150-7214 Revue Moto Technique **8267**
0150-7230 Auto Expertise **8558**
0150-7516 Revue des Ingenieurs†
0150-7540 Toutes les Nouvelles de l'Hotellerie et du Tourisme† **8993**
0150-9373 Atlas de Radiologie Clinique de la Presse Medicale†
0150-9780 Revue de Chirurgie Orthopedique et Reparatrice de l'Appareil Moteur. Supplement *see* 1877-0517 **6072**
0150-9861 Journal of Neuroradiology **6201**
0151-007X Juris-Classeur Contrats-Distribution **4873**
0151-0193 Gerontologie et Societe **4046**
0151-0304 Sciences **7911**
0151-0479 Cahiers C E R T-C I R C E†
0151-0568 Syndicat General des Fondeurs de France et Industries Connexes. Annuaire†
0151-0770 France. Service d'Etude des Strategies et des Statistiques Industrielles. Bulletin Mensuel de Statistique Industrielle†
0151-0827 Documents **4169**
0151-1173 Societe Zoologique de France. Bulletin. Supplement†
0151-1475 France. Institut National de la Statistique et des Etudes Economiques. Informations Rapides **1233**
0151-1637 Science et Technique du Froid **4126**
0151-1793 Economie Champenoise†
0151-1874 Universite de Grenoble. U F R de Lettres. Recherches et Travaux **5393**
0151-1904 Vers l'Education Nouvelle **2924**
0151-1998 Sante de l'Homme **5709**
0151-2188 La Vie de l'Auto **369**
0151-2846 Naut Argus†
0151-2897 Journee des Fruits & Legumes†
0151-2943 Indicateur Bertrand **7595**
0151-3605 Visages du Vingtieme Siecle†
0151-3648 Special Bricolage†
0151-3656 Quincaillerie Moderne†
0151-4016 Renaitre 2000†
0151-4040 Chausser Magazine **7940**
0151-4105 Revue d'Histoire des Sciences **7903**
0151-4261 Or du Rhine
0151-4377 Journee Vinicole Export†
0151-4393 La Journee Vinicole **605**
0151-4695 Jardineries Vegetal **3739**
0151-5055 Economia†
0151-5713 Theatre d'Aujourd'hui **8482**
0151-5772 Royaliste **7180**
0151-5845 Psychomotricite†
0151-5861 Transports Actualites **8518**
0151-6353 Sport Auto **8203**
0151-685X Sciences et Techniques Biomedicales†
0151-6914 Journal de l'Amateur d'Art†
0151-6981 Aquarama†
0151-7163 Al Islam **7711**
0151-7341 Alsace Historique†
0151-7791 Fou Parle†
0151-8720 Societe Generale pour Favoriser de Developpement du Commerce et de l'Industrie en France. Bulletin†
0151-9093 L'Actualite Chimique **2048**
0151-9107 Annales de Chimie, Science des Materiaux **2050**
0151-9514 France. Institut National de la Statistique et des Etudes Economiques. Courrier des Statistiques **8373**
0151-9522 Cutis†
0151-9638 Annales de Dermatologie et de Venereologie **5871**
0152-0032 Po&Sie **5432**
0152-0768 Pouvoirs **7172**
0152-1454 A R P A Cahiers de Recherche Poetique†
0152-2418 Metiers d'Art†
0152-2590 La Nouvelle Republique du Centre Ouest **3841**
0152-3295 France. Ministere de l'Agriculture et de la Foret. Bulletin d'Information **114**
0152-3791 La Cote des Arts†
0152-4119 Photo Work† **8981**
0152-4305 Plastiques et Environnement Informations†
0152-4682 Grand N **5490**
0152-5778 Centre Interprofessionnel Technique d'Etudes de la Pollution Atmospherique. Etudes Documentaires **3484**
0152-6456 Sillon des Landes et des Pyrenees. Edition 64 **156**
0152-7401 Revue Francaise d'Administration Publique **7466**
0152-7886 Phreatique†
0152-7975 Unite†
0152-8521 Flash Environnement†
0152-9668 Annales des Ponts et Chaussees†
0152-9757 Directory of Demographic Research Centers† **8950**
0152-979X Show Magazine†
0152-9994 Registre Maritime **8658**
0153-0216 La Foret Privee **3691**
0153-0313 Lengas **5143**
0153-0747 Tele 7 Jours **2395**
0153-1069 L'Equipe **8171**
0153-162X France. Ministere de l'Agriculture. Informations Rapides. Situation Agricole†
0153-1662 La Medaille Militaire†
0153-1700 Etudes Canadiennes **4451**
0153-2006 Artisanat Batiment 34 **1956**
0153-226X Energie Solaire Actualites†
0153-288X Bulletin International d'Informations - Droit et Pharmacie *changed to* 1165-5372 **6833**
0153-3142 Distributeur Automobile† **8951**
0153-3231 Clefs d'Or **4591**
0153-3320 Cahiers de Linguistique Asie Orientale **5103**
0153-3401 Al Mostakbal†
0153-341X Al-Nahar al-Arabi wal-Dawli†
0153-3428 Watan al-Arabi
0153-3533 Annuaire du Diocese de Lyon **7783**
0153-3614 L'Argus International†
0153-3657 Association pour l'Etude des Problemes d'Outre Mer. Documentation-Developpement† **8931**
0153-4092 Pour la Science **7899**
0153-4157 Maghreb Selection **1577**
0153-4165 Haga†
0153-419X Le Monde. Dossiers et Documents **3841**
0153-4270 Mediatheques Publiques†
0153-4351 Histoire pour Tous†
0153-4459 Institut d'Economie Regionale Bourgogne-Franche-Comte. Cahiers†
0153-4602 Escargot Folk?†
0153-4742 Lettre Medicale†
0153-4831 Les Echos **1478**
0153-5021 Institut de Papyrologie et d'Egyptologie de Lille. Cahiers de Recherche **4175**
0153-5048 Cahiers de Philologie
0153-5196 C.T.N.E.R.H.I. Recherches†
0153-520X Nature et Mieux-Vivre
0153-5374 A l'Ecoute du Monde, Chronique Sociale†
0153-6001 Supplement au Registre Maritime **8663**
0153-6028 Bretagne Economique **1396**
0153-6052 Supplement Trimestriel au Registre Maritime **8663**
0153-6087 Cahiers Albert Schweitzer **6909**
0153-6184 Institut d'Amenagement et d'Urbanisme de la Region d'Ile de France. Cahiers **4416**
0153-6281 B T I A
0153-775X Juris-Classeur Concurrence-Consommation **4873**
0153-8438 Macadam†
0153-8519 Cine 9,5 Revue **6492**
0153-8756 Ecologia Mediterranea **669**
0153-9019 Marche de l'Innovation†
0153-9027 Nous Voulons Lire **5343**
0153-9035 Metaux Deformation† **8974**
0153-906X Etudes et Documentation de la Revue Technique Automobile **8579**
0153-9086 Fiches Techniques R T A†
0153-9094 Fiches Techniques R T D **8580**
0153-9108 Fiches Techniques R T C **8580**
0153-9124 Revue Archeologique Narbonnaise. Supplements *see* 0557-7705
0153-9167 Monde et Mineraux†
0153-9205 Tarif Pieces Detachees **8512**
0153-9213 Ciments et Chaux†
0153-9221 Etudes Vauclusiennes **4218**
0153-9299 Societe des Sciences Naturelles et d'Archeologie de Toulon et du Var. Annales **7918**
0153-9337 Archeologie Medievale **379**
0153-9345 Paleorient **6729**
0153-9361 Societe d'Etudes Scientifiques de l'Anjou. Bulletin **7918**
0153-9396 Electro-Negoce **3095**
0153-9442 Enerpresse **3134**
0153-9841 Analyse Financiere **1280**
0153-985X Courrier du C N R S†
0153-9868 Information Fiscale et Sociale
0153-9884 Interets Prives **1630**
0153-9914 Service Public et Bon Langage†

ISSN

0158-7358 Bargain Shoppers Guide to Sydney **2635**
0158-7366 Oral History Association of Australia. Journal **4193**
0158-7374 Period Building Restoration Trades & Suppliers Directory†
0158-7382 Commonwealth Scientific and Industrial Research Organization. Bureau of Scientific Services. Annual Report†
0158-7765 Zinc Today†
0158-7919 Distance Education **2940**
0158-8230 Seamen's Journal†
0158-8273 James Cook University of North Queensland. Department of Geography. Monograph Series†
0158-8346 Airflow **8301**
0158-9024 Consumers Affairs Council of Tasmania. Annual Report
0158-9032 Directory of Higher Education Courses
0158-9172 School Libraries in Australia†
0158-9245 Labor Essays† **8970**
0158-9539 Network News **2162**
0158-9776 Flinders Institute for Atmospheric and Marine Sciences. Technical Reports†
0158-9830 Research Discussion Papers†
0158-9938 Australasian Physical & Engineering Sciences in Medicine **5580**
0159-0073 Butterworths Trade Practices†
0159-0340 Guiding in Australia†
0159-0677 Tasmanian Ancestry **3784**
0159-1088 Instep†
0159-1096 Contact (Sydney, 1976)†
0159-110X Now†
0159-1290 The Australian Cottongrower **220**
0159-1428 South Australia. Department of Agriculture. Rural Marketing and Policy†
0159-1584 Australia. Bureau of Statistics. Research and Experimental Development, Business Enterprises, Australia, Preliminary† **8933**
0159-1843 Packaging Today **6714**
0159-1878 Who's Drilling **6797**
0159-2033 Lab Talk **3069**
0159-2165 Macquarie University Research Report **2993**
0159-2254 Institute of Medical and Veterinary Science. Annual Report **5636**
0159-2319 Australian Lithographer, Printer, and Packager
0159-2483 Legal Reporter†
0159-2920 Farrago **2283**
0159-2939 Australian Electronics Bulletin†
0159-2947 Australian Electronics Directory **3089**
0159-2955 Australian Engineering Directory **3182**
0159-3129 Today's Child Leaflets†
0159-3242 National Outlook†
0159-3285 Victorian Bar News **4808**
0159-3544 Labor Voice†
0159-3641 South Australia. Department of Environment and Planning. Directory of Non-Government Environmental Groups in South Australia†
0159-3803 Quest†
0159-3951 Australia. Bureau of Statistics. Government Financial Estimates, Australia†
0159-3978 Fine Print **2857**
0159-4443 A.A.U. News
0159-4702 National Reporter†
0159-4958 Australian Chess Magazine† **8933**
0159-5172 City Survival Kit
0159-5962 Photo Forum†
0159-6012 Crane Australasia†
0159-6071 Genetic Resources Communication **232**
0159-6306 Discourse (Abingdon) **3020**
0159-6330 Dance Australia **2683**
0159-656X International Camellia Journal **3739**
0159-6586 Bogong *changed to* 1446-9359
0159-6667 Australian Criminal Reports **2644**
0159-6861 Bargain Shopper's Guide to Melbourne **2635**
0159-7027 Coiffure†
0159-7132 Chalkface†
0159-7191 Morocco Bound
0159-7345 News Digest - International†
0159-7868 Curriculum Perspectives (Journal Edition) **2976**
0159-8090 Clinical Biochemist Reviews **729**
0159-8872 Challenge (Petersham North)
0159-9178 Commonwealth Scientific and Industrial Research Organization. Institute of Energy and Earth Resources. Minerals & Energy Bulletin†
0159-9321 Australia. Bureau of Statistics. New South Wales Office. Pocket Year Book of New South Wales†
0159-9364 Flinders Institute for Atmospheric and Marine Sciences. Research Reports†
0159-9372 Flinders Institute for Atmospheric and Marine Sciences. Computing Reports†
0159-950X Monash Review†
0159-9585 Photoworld Buyer's Guide. Index†
0159-9593 Photoworld Buyer's Guide. Darkrooms†
0160-001X Washington Report (Washington, 1966)†
0160-0028 Drug Abuse and Alcoholism Newsletter†
0160-0079 Institute of International Education. Annual Report **3013**
0160-0087 U.S. National Endowment for the Arts. Application Guidelines. Expansion Arts†
0160-0141 I E E E Power Engineering Society. Discussions and Closures of Abstracted Papers from the Summer Meeting **3196**
0160-0176 International Regional Science Review **7975**
0160-0184 Pediatric Alert **6099**
0160-0265 Law Studies **4717**
0160-0281 American Journal of Trial Advocacy **4614**
0160-0303 Graphic Communications Marketplace
0160-0311 Military Journal†
0160-0338 Texas Woman†
0160-0346 Logging Management†
0160-0354 Spiritual Community Guide†
0160-0362 Professional Marketing Report†
0160-0419 French-American Review†
0160-0567 U.S. National Endowment for the Arts. Application Guidelines: Dance†
0160-0583 New York Times Theatre Reviews†
0160-0621 Face the Nation†
0160-0656 Index of Legislation **7445**
0160-0680 Sulphur in Agriculture **159**
0160-0699 Umbrella† **8995**
0160-0850 Fiddle and a Bow†
0160-0885 United Methodist Church. Curriculum Plans†
0160-0893 Cornell Review†
0160-0923 Helios **5304**
0160-1040 I A **8424**
0160-1067 Society for Industrial Archeology Newsletter **8439**
0160-1075 New Directions for Women†
0160-1121 Western Birds **916**
0160-1148 Electronotes
0160-1199 Illinois Reports **4690**
0160-127X Interface (Carmel)†
0160-130X Bank Expansion Quarterly†
0160-1504 D I S C U S Facts Book†
0160-1598 Cleveland Bar Journal *changed to* 1946-9853 **4643**
0160-1644 Motor Early Model Crash Estimating Guide **8592**
0160-1652 Communicating Nursing Research†
0160-1660 Cumitechs **5602**
0160-1792 A R I S E†
0160-1830 Sports Afield Deer†
0160-1857 Left Curve **5224**
0160-1873 American Anthropological Association. Abstracts of Meetings **324**
0160-2004 Resources in Vocational Education†
0160-2071 Micropaleontology Special Papers **6726**
0160-2098 Journal of Juvenile Law *changed to* 1944-382X **4915**
0160-2144 Great River Review **5302**
0160-2179 Advances in Polyamine Research†
0160-2217 New Brooklyn
0160-2349 Science - Fantasy Correspondent
0160-2365 American Musical Instrument Society. Newsletter **6544**
0160-2373 Gleanings (Cambridge)†
0160-239X Great Basin Naturalist Memoirs *changed to* 1545-0228 **967**
0160-242X Comprehensive Endocrinology†
0160-2438 E E G Interpretation†
0160-2446 Journal of Cardiovascular Pharmacology **6852**
0160-2454 M.D. Anderson Clinical Conferences on Cancer†
0160-2462 Membrane Transport Processes†
0160-2470 Nutrition in Health and Disease†
0160-2489 Seminars in Neurological Surgery†
0160-2497 S I G C P R Newsletter†
0160-2500 Case Western Reserve University. Warner Swasey Observatory. Publications†
0160-2527 International Journal of Law and Psychiatry **4695**
0160-2543 Cynegeticus†
0160-2578 The American Bench **4614**
0160-2624 Coaching: Women's Athletics†
0160-2659 Kansas Water Resources Research Institute. Annual Report†
0160-2675 Policy Grants Directory **7166**
0160-2713 Journal of African-Afro-American Affairs†
0160-2721 Aging (Thousand Oaks)
0160-2748 Neurotoxicology†
0160-2764 Mester **5333**
0160-2802 Plains Anthropologist. Memoir **351**
0160-2829 Wyoming Geological Association. Guidebook **6798**
0160-2853 Georgetown University Papers on Languages and Linguistics†
0160-2896 Intelligence (Kidlington) **7363**
0160-2985 U.S. Department of Labor. Bureau of Labor Statistics. Major Programs **1523**
0160-3000 Woodall's Trailer & R V Travel†
0160-3051 Indiana. Geological Survey Bulletin **2747**
0160-3078 University of Oklahoma. Archaeological Research and Management Center. Project Report Series
0160-3086 University of Oklahoma. Archaeological Research and Management Center. Research Series
0160-3124 The Philological Review **5161**
0160-3183 Topics in Bioelectrochemistry and Bioenergetics†
0160-323X State and Local Government Review **7503**
0160-3302 Illinois Manufacturers Directory **2005**
0160-3310 Land and Life†
0160-3345 Alaska Economic Trends **1436**
0160-3353 Physics News **7033**
0160-337X Enhanced Oil-Recovery Field Reports†
0160-3477 Journal of Post Keynesian Economics **1545**
0160-3493 Hispano-Italic Studies†
0160-354X Michigan Papers on South and Southeast Asia **4186**
0160-3566 Black Sociologist†
0160-3582 S P E C Kit **5045**
0160-3604 Energy Research Abstracts†
0160-3612 Beltsville Symposia in Agricultural Research **95**
0160-3663 Off-Shore Technology Conference. Proceedings **6782**
0160-368X Solar Energy Utilization: a Bibliography. Vol. 3. Solar Thermal Heating and Cooling†
0160-371X Tabs†
0160-3728 Who's Who in Religion†
0160-3779 Mineral Economics Abstracts†
0160-3787 Isozymes: Current Topics in Biological and Medical Research†
0160-3817 Weaver's Journal†
0160-3825 Student Press Law Center Report **4790**
0160-3876 Musical Heritage Review Magazine **6593**
0160-3906 Fodor's Canada **8705**
0160-3922 Nutritional Perspectives **6667**
0160-3949 Rapid Readers Series **1164**
0160-3957 Delta Pi Epsilon. Service Bulletins **1091**
0160-4120 Environment International **3421**
0160-4147 Downtown Implementation Guide†
0160-4163 Conference of Insurance Legislators†
0160-4201 Voice of Youth Advocates **2171**
0160-4317 Freshwater and Marine Aquarium **6808**
0160-4341 Humboldt Journal of Social Relations **7970**
0160-4422 Perspectives in Law and Psychology **4758**
0160-4430 Self-in-Process Series
0160-4457 Platt's Oil Price Handbook & Oilmanac†
0160-449X Labor Studies Journal **1693**
0160-4570 F & O S Motor Carrier Annual Report *changed to* Motor Carrier Annual Reports **8527**
0160-4643 Virginia. Division of Mineral Resources. Publications **6483**
0160-4724 Chief Executive Magazine **1733**
0160-4740 Fish and Wildlife Reference Service Newsletter†
0160-4767 Pizzazz†
0160-4872 Weekly Insiders Poultry Report (Print)† **8998**
0160-4880 Fiction Catalog *changed to* Fiction Core Collection **5407**
0160-4929 Politics Today (Santa Barbara)†
0160-4937 Southern California Paleontological Society. Bulletin **6730**
0160-4953 Collection Building **5002**
0160-4961 Health Services Administration Education *changed to* 1930-8361 **2955**
0160-5070 Kentucky Warbler **909**
0160-5119 Florida Friends of Bluegrass Society. Newsletter **6567**
0160-5143 Forest Insect and Disease Conditions in the United States
0160-5313 Contributions in Biology and Geology **667**
0160-5429 International Education **3013**
0160-5526 Port of Detroit World Handbook **8656**
0160-5585 School Psychologist **7406**
0160-5607 Construction News **997**
0160-564X Artificial Organs **5903**
0160-5658 Annual Survey of Colorado Law (Year) **4618**
0160-5682 Operational Research Society. Journal **2433**
0160-5704 Horse, of Course!†
0160-5720 M L A Newsletter (New York) **2993**
0160-5747 Basketball Forecast (Year)†
0160-5836 Defense Foreign Affairs Handbook **6419**
0160-5895 House & Garden Decorating Guide†
0160-5976 Humanity & Society **8106**
0160-5992 In These Times **7141**
0160-6077 Directory of Library Reprographic Services†
0160-6123 Information Manager†
0160-614X Made in U S A
0160-6158 Standard (New York)
0160-6166 Club Living†
0160-6174 Diamond Report†
0160-6247 U.S. Interagency Committee on Population Research. Inventory and Analysis of Federal Population Research†
0160-628X Blake **5264**
0160-6298 Gordon's Print Price Annual (Year) **491**
0160-6336 Knitovations
0160-6360 Chemical New Product Directory†
0160-6379 Family and Community Health **7517**
0160-6395 N A E A News **507**
0160-6433 Timber Harvesting *changed to* Timber Harvesting & Wood Fiber Operations **3716**
0160-6468 Directory of Medical Schools Worldwide†
0160-6565 Guest Author†
0160-659X Common Law Lawyer
0160-6662 National Conference on Individual Onsite Wastewater Systems. Proceedings†
0160-6689 Journal of Clinical Psychiatry **6150**
0160-6778 Secondary Education Today†
0160-6786 American Maritime Cases **4969**
0160-6808 Golf Illustrated **8231**
0160-6824 Golf Industry
0160-6840 Wide Angle†
0160-6883 New Car Yearbook†
0160-6891 Research in Nursing & Health **5980**
0160-6913 Passenger Train Journal†
0160-6921 TourBook: Hawaii **8762**
0160-6972 Journal of Oral Implantology **5852**
0160-6980 Continuing Education for Health Care Providers†
0160-7006 Health Care Education†
0160-7057 Conference of Presidents of Major American Jewish Organizations. Annual Report
0160-7065 Diesel Car Digest†
0160-7081 Foundation of Thanatology. Archives†
0160-7146 Jacob Marschak Interdisciplinary Colloquium on Mathematics in the Behavioral Sciences **1762**
0160-7154 U.S. Health Care Financing Administration Forum†
0160-7219 Perinatal Press†
0160-7243 Stone in America†
0160-726X Mountain Gazette **8323**
0160-7332 Amateur Boxer†
0160-7340 Guide to Manufactured Homes†
0160-7383 Annals of Tourism Research **8683**
0160-7464 American Carbon Society. Biennial Conference on Carbon - Extended Abstracts and Program **3235**
0160-7480 Modern Healthcare **4107**
0160-7499 Irrigation Association. Technical Conference Proceedings **238**
0160-7537 Salt **6976**
0160-7545 Ellen Glasgow Newsletter **5289**
0160-7553 I D O C/International Documentation†
0160-7561 Philosophical Studies in Education **2898**
0160-757X Infusion (Westhampton Beach)†
0160-7626 Infertility
0160-7634 American Mathematical Society. Proceedings of Symposia in Applied Mathematics **5469**
0160-7642 American Mathematical Society. C B M S Regional Conference Series in Mathematics **5469**
0160-7650 The Crafts Report **533**
0160-7677 Slackwater Review†
0160-7715 Journal of Behavioral Medicine **6149**
0160-7731 Bill of Rights in Action **7203**
0160-7774 Journal of Supervision and Training in Ministry **7657**
0160-7782 Geothermal Resources Council. Bulletin **3162**
0160-7847 Fundamenta Scientiae†
0160-788X Reclamation Review†
0160-791X Technology in Society **8143**
0160-7960 Counseling and Values **7794**
0160-8029 U.S. Library of Congress. Cataloging Service Bulletin **5052**
0160-8037 Developing Country Courier†
0160-8061 Journal of Organizational Behavior Management **7377**
0160-8126 Public Education Directory
0160-8177 Practical Law Books Review†

ISSN

0161-7796	U.S. Environmental Protection Agency. Radiation Protection Activities†
0161-780X	Current Neurology†
0161-7818	Current Radiology†
0161-7842	Saddle Horse Report **8298**
0161-7885	Illinois Horizons†
0161-7893	The Woodbook†
0161-7966	National Racquetball
0161-7990	N A E B Bulletin **2994**
0161-8032	Predicasts Overview of Markets and Technology†
0161-8059	Practical Sailor **8280**
0161-8091	Energy Developments in Japan†
0161-8105	Sleep **6185**
0161-8113	Zoning and Planning Law Report **4432**
0161-813X	NeuroToxicology **6170**
0161-8202	Journal of Arachnology **950**
0161-8237	American Agriculturist **90**
0161-8261	United States Supreme Court Reports (Lawyer's Edition) **4966**
0161-827X	Journal of College and University Student Housing **2989**
0161-830X	Gilbert Law Summaries. Civil Procedure **4831**
0161-8415	Pharmaceutical Representative **6870**
0161-8423	Theodore Roosevelt Association Journal **646**
0161-8490	E P A Activities Under the Resource Conservation and Recovery Act of 1976†
0161-8555	Cosmic Search†
0161-8598	V F W Magazine **6451**
0161-8628	U.S. Department of Transportation. National Transportation Statistics. Annual **8532**
0161-8695	Vital Statistics of Iowa **7317**
0161-8741	Dallas-Fort Worth Home & Garden†
0161-8768	Officemation Product Reports†
0161-8776	Primary Prevention of Psychopathology†
0161-8784	Realites (Horsham)
0161-8792	Perspectives in Ophthalmology†
0161-8822	Papers in Slavic Philology **5159**
0161-8830	United States Oceanborne Foreign Trade Routes **8664**
0161-8938	Journal of Policy Modeling **7147**
0161-9020	Football News†
0161-9160	Treatise on Materials Science & Technology **3359**
0161-9225	Ideologies & Literature†
0161-9268	Advances in Nursing Science **5950**
0161-9284	The Magazine Antiques **367**
0161-9314	International President's Bulletin†
0161-9365	Label Letter **4597**
0161-9373	Maritime Newsletter **4598**
0161-9454	Life-Span Development and Behavior†
0161-9470	Index to the U.S. Patent Classification System **6760**
0161-9500	Executive Educator†
0161-956X	P J E, Peabody Journal of Education **2894**
0161-9721	Journal of Surgical Practice†
0161-973X	RetailWeek†
0161-9772	Commercial News U S A **1556**
0161-9780	Administration of the Toxic Substances Control Act. Annual Report *changed to* 0883-0576 **3501**
0161-987X	Notre Dame Magazine **2294**
0161-9896	Highlands Voice **2613**
0161-990X	Construction Labor News **1673**
0161-9934	Contemporary Issues in Nephrology†
0162-0029	Garcia Lorca Review†
0162-0061	Pawn Review†
0162-007X	Physical Education - Sports Index
0162-0088	World Wide Shipping Guide
0162-0134	Journal of Inorganic Biochemistry **736**
0162-0169	Red M(irage)
0162-0266	Hit Parader **6573**
0162-0290	Directory and Statistics of Oregon Libraries†
0162-0363	Catholic Sentinel (Diocese of Baker) **7790**
0162-0401	Frets Magazine†
0162-0436	Qualitative Sociology **8127**
0162-0444	Significant Decisions of the Supreme Court†
0162-0517	Swift River†
0162-0592	Work Experience of the Population **6707**
0162-0770	N P R A Question & Answer Session on Refining and Petrochemical Technology Transcripts (Print Edition) *changed to* N P R A Question & Answer Session on Refining and Petrochemical Technology Transcripts (CD-ROM Edition) **6779**
0162-0789	China Geographer†
0162-0800	Olmstead's Genealogy Recorded†
0162-0843	Health Sciences Serials†
0162-0851	L'Heritage **3770**
0162-0894	Tamarack
0162-0908	Year Book of Sports Medicine **6234**
0162-0932	Verbatim (Chicago) **5193**
0162-0975	Update: Cardiology†
0162-1017	Tamarisk
0162-1025	Fleet Owner: Small Fleet Edition†
0162-1033	Collectors News & the Antique Reporter **365**
0162-105X	Personnel Alert (Roseville)†
0162-1068	Spotlight (Bethlehem)†
0162-1084	Federal Securities Law Reports **4673**
0162-1092	Federal Tax Articles **1923**
0162-1106	Federal Carriers Reports *changed to* Federal Carriers Reporter **8496**
0162-1114	Federal Estate and Gift Tax Reports **4902**
0162-1122	Food, Drug, and Cosmetic Law Reporter (Rx Edition) **6842**
0162-1149	Gargoyle (Washington, DC) **5299**
0162-1157	Federal Banking Law Reporter **1341**
0162-1165	Cost Accounting Standards Guide **1286**
0162-1173	Corporation Law Guide†
0162-119X	Consumer Product Safety Guide **2636**
0162-1203	Congressional Index **4821**
0162-122X	Products Liability Reports *changed to* Products Liability Reporter **4762**
0162-1238	Pollution Control Guide†
0162-1246	Professional Corporations Handbook†
0162-1254	Medicare and Medicaid Guide **4514**
0162-1289	Seven Days†
0162-1297	Rugby **8244**
0162-1300	Impact Journal **2638**
0162-1327	Peninsula Magazine
0162-1343	Play Meter **8193**
0162-1378	Mode International
0162-1424	Home Health Care Services Quarterly **4098**
0162-1440	Tree Tracers **3786**
0162-1459	American Statistical Association. Journal **8344**
0162-1467	N C A A Directory **8189**
0162-153X	American Shotgunner
0162-1564	Tennessee Librarian (Print) *changed to* 1935-7052 **5050**
0162-1599	New England States Limited†
0162-1610	Payroll Management Guide **1374**
0162-1637	Pension Plan Guide **4518**
0162-1696	State Motor Carrier Guide†
0162-1718	Utilities Law Reports *changed to* Utilities Law Reporter **7475**
0162-1726	Boycott Law Bulletin **4919**
0162-1742	United States Supreme Court Bulletin†
0162-1750	State Tax Review **1945**
0162-1777	State Tax Guide **1944**
0162-1785	Automobile Law Reports - Insurance Cases†
0162-1815	Tax Court Reports **1947**
0162-1866	S T T H†
0162-1890	Evangel **7756**
0162-1904	Zone†
0162-1939	Illinois. State Museum. Guidebooklet Series†
0162-1955	Accent (Birmingham) **7744**
0162-1963	General Science Index **7937**
0162-198X	Discovery (Birmingham) **7754**
0162-2005	West's Federal Case News **4967**
0162-2102	Catholic Sentinel (Archdiocese of Portland, Oregon) **7790**
0162-2110	World of Rodeo and Western Heritage
0162-217X	Charles Redd Monographs in Western History†
0162-220X	Cancer Nursing **5954**
0162-2226	Professional Remodeling†
0162-2234	Assemblies of God Home Missions†
0162-2242	SportStyle†
0162-2250	Journal of Commerce & Industry
0162-2269	Clinical Behavior Therapy Review†
0162-2285	Medical Selfcare†
0162-2293	Update in Oral Surgery†
0162-234X	Philosopher's Annual†
0162-2382	Medical Computing Series†
0162-2404	Soviet World Outlook†
0162-2412	Iowa R E C News **3159**
0162-2439	Science, Technology & Human Values **7911**
0162-2617	F B News *changed to* 1062-8983 **161**
0162-2692	Young Spartacus†
0162-2706	Chartered Property & Casualty Underwriters Society. Journal (Print Edition) *changed to* C P C U eJournal **4497**
0162-2714	Coal Outlook **6460**
0162-2722	Charleston Magazine **3972**
0162-2730	Fuel Oil Week†
0162-2757	Detroit in Perspective†
0162-2765	Goodfellow Review of Crafts†
0162-2773	L A E Journal†
0162-2781	Milk Marketer†
0162-2811	Communication Abstracts **2347**
0162-282X	Memphis **3981**
0162-2846	P E R Report†
0162-2854	Journal of Commerce Export Bulletin†
0162-2870	October **509**
0162-2889	International Security **7245**
0162-2897	California History (San Francisco) **4287**
0162-2900	Los Angeles Lawyer **4725**
0162-2951	Chiefs of State and Cabinet Members of Foreign Governments **7226**
0162-296X	Orpheus
0162-3001	Texas Agriculture. West Texas Regional Edition† **8993**
0162-301X	Texas Agriculture. North Texas Regional Edition *see* 0162-3001 **8993**
0162-3052	L A E News *changed to* L A E Voice **2881**
0162-3060	Post Scripts (Indianapolis) **3985**
0162-3079	Jurisdocs **5022**
0162-315X	Weimaraner Magazine **6816**
0162-3176	Construction Briefings **4649**
0162-3184	Extraordinary Contractual Relief Reporter **1485**
0162-3206	National Security Record†
0162-3214	Petersen's 4 Wheel & Off-Road **8266**
0162-3257	Journal of Autism and Developmental Disorders **3042**
0162-3281	Related Patent Index†
0162-329X	Dual Dictionary to Petroleum Abstracts†
0162-3338	Professional Woman
0162-3354	Periodical Update†
0162-3362	Prep
0162-3370	Better Living
0162-3389	Actuator Systems†
0162-3397	The American Lawyer **4615**
0162-3400	Savor†
0162-3451	Moneytree
0162-3486	Taxes on Parade **1951**
0162-3532	Journal for the Education of the Gifted **3042**
0162-3559	P S B A Bulletin **3029**
0162-3567	Unity Magazine **7743**
0162-3583	Rifle **8330**
0162-3605	The Blue Sheet (Print) *changed to* 1556-4525
0162-3737	Educational Evaluation & Policy Analysis **3021**
0162-3745	Communique (Washington)†
0162-3753	Crystal Structure†
0162-3761	Contemporary Pharmacy Practice†
0162-3788	Charge, Spin and Momentum Density†
0162-3796	Woodall's Campground Management **8342**
0162-380X	Southwestern Musician **6618**
0162-3869	United Rubber Worker†
0162-3885	Business Communications Review† **8938**
0162-3893	Columbia (New York) **2278**
0162-3907	American Physical Therapy Association. Progress Report†
0162-3923	Supercycle
0162-3974	Neighbors **139**
0162-4040	Financial Review (New York)†
0162-4067	World Naturopathic Journal†
0162-4075	Concrete International **993**
0162-4083	E P O†
0162-4148	Advanced Bible Study. Commentary **7744**
0162-4172	Adult Leadership†
0162-4180	Baptist Adults **7747**
0162-4199	Baptist Youth†
0162-4245	Family Heritage†
0162-4253	Living (Nashville)†
0162-4261	Living with Teenagers **7765**
0162-427X	Mature Living **7766**
0162-4288	More (Nashville) **7768**
0162-4296	Open Windows **7769**
0162-4326	Proclaim (Nashville)†
0162-4334	Southern Baptist Convention. Sunday School Board. Quarterly Review†
0162-4342	El Interprete†
0162-4369	Look and Listen†
0162-4377	Music Makers (Nashville)†
0162-4385	On the Wing†
0162-4393	Preschool Leadership†
0162-4539	Care for Leaders†
0162-4547	Encounter!†
0162-4598	Come Alive for Leaders†
0162-461X	Children's Leadership†
0162-4660	Bible Learners. Teacher†
0162-4679	Bible Learners†
0162-4687	Bible Discoverers. Teacher†
0162-4695	Bible Discoverers†
0162-4717	Bible Reader's Guide†
0162-4741	Bible Study. Pocket Commentary†
0162-475X	Bible Study. Leaflet†
0162-4768	Youth in Discovery. Teacher†
0162-4776	Youth in Discovery†
0162-4784	Youth in Action†
0162-4792	Youth in Action. Teacher†
0162-4857	Bible Lesson Digest†
0162-489X	Sunday School Youth B†
0162-4903	Sunday School Young Adults†
0162-492X	C L A S S Forum†
0162-4962	Biography (Honolulu) **640**
0162-4989	Impact (Washington, 1975) **8585**
0162-5047	Livestock Weekly **292**
0162-5098	Crops and Soils Magazine **227**
0162-5144	Eagle (Champaign)†
0162-5160	Pennsylvania Township News **7500**
0162-5179	Oregon Farm Bureau News **144**
0162-5241	Profile (Omaha) **1409**
0162-5276	Kiwanis **2267**
0162-5284	New Hampshire Audubon **2622**
0162-5306	Action Line (Memphis)†
0162-5403	Alaska Review of Social and Economic Conditions **1436**
0162-5411	Official Baseball Dope Book†
0162-5519	Hadronic Journal **7014**
0162-5594	Intercontinental Press Combined with Imprecor†
0162-5667	Hearing & Speech Action†
0162-5691	Corporate Practice Series **4865**
0162-573X	Daisy†
0162-5748	The Review of Higher Education **3000**
0162-5764	Licensing Law and Business Report†
0162-5772	Jesuit†
0162-5780	Current Interests of the Ford Foundation **8036**
0162-5799	University of South Carolina. Institute of Archeology and Anthropology. Annual Report **422**
0162-5810	Alembic†
0162-5837	Who
0162-5861	Dining In & Out†
0162-587X	Canadian Automobile Agreement **4920**
0162-5888	The Joint Economic Report **7448**
0162-5918	Alpha
0162-5934	S W L†
0162-5942	Emergency (Print Edition)†
0162-5950	On-Your-Own Guide to Asia†
0162-5977	C S P Directory of Suppliers of Educational Foreign Language Materials†
0162-5993	D I S C U S Newsletter†
0162-6051	U.S. National Marine Fisheries Service. Imports and Exports of Fishery Products. Annual Summary **3610**
0162-6108	Frozen Fishery Products. Annual Summary **3613**
0162-6140	Canned Fishery Products. Annual Summary†
0162-6191	Constructor **999**
0162-6248	Measure
0162-6256	Sanitary Services in Tennessee†
0162-6280	Folklore and Mythology Studies†
0162-6337	Defenders **2608**
0162-6345	Footwear Focus†
0162-6353	Carolinas Companies†
0162-637X	Chemical Worker **4591**
0162-6426	Library of Congress†
0162-6434	Journal of Special Education Technology **3043**
0162-6442	Customs Bulletin and Decisions **1919**
0162-6469	Archaeological Institute of America. Annual Meeting Abstracts **425**
0162-6477	Correspondence Society of Surgeons. Collected Letters†
0162-6493	Infectious Disease Practice **5817**
0162-6574	Journal of Experiential Learning and Simulation†
0162-6604	Aftermarket Executive†
0162-6620	Action in Teacher Education **2824**
0162-6639	Index of N L M Serial Titles†
0162-6655	Mpls. - Saint Paul Magazine **3982**
0162-6671	Primroses **3748**
0162-6728	American Fisheries Directory and Reference Book†
0162-6760	Spirituality Today†
0162-6795	Journal of Asian Culture **553**
0162-6809	Regional Official Guides: Tractors and Farm Equipment **214**
0162-6817	Market Logic†
0162-6833	Aware **7746**
0162-6841	Start (Birmingham) **7776**

ISSN

ISSN

0165-7267 Amsterdam Studies in the Theory and History of Linguistic Science. Series 5: Library and Information Sources in Linguistics **5200**
0165-7305 Amsterdamer Beitraege zur Aelteren Germanistik **5253**
0165-7380 Veterinary Research Communications **8814**
0165-7445 V N Informatie†
0165-7518 Skript **4161**
0165-7569 Lingvisticae Investigationes: Supplementa **5147**
0165-7607 Recht en Kritiek†
0165-7615 Vicus Cuadernos: Arqueologia, Antropologia Cultural, Etnologia†
0165-7666 Vicus Cuadernos: Linguistica†
0165-7763 Studies in Language Companion Series **5182**
0165-7798 Bres **5209**
0165-7828 Onze Taal **5158**
0165-7836 Fisheries Research **3592**
0165-7895 De Gemeentestem **7438**
0165-7909 Het Verzekeringsblad **4527**
0165-8042 Lover **8900**
0165-8107 Neuro-Ophthalmology **6163**
0165-8131 S W Journaal **1706**
0165-8158 Hermeneus **4141**
0165-8174 N A V A S *changed to* 1569-0520 **1025**
0165-8204 Lampas **5320**
0165-8220 Nu
0165-8425 De Werkgever†
0165-8433 Mi Doro
0165-8476 W P N R **4810**
0165-8484 Nieuwspoort Nieuws *changed to* 1873-8990 **4581**
0165-8573 Zuivelzicht **270**
0165-859X Marine Biology Letters†
0165-8603 Advent **7744**
0165-8638 Redoc†
0165-8646 Photobiochemistry and Photobiophysics†
0165-8654 Beeldenaar **6649**
0165-8719 Core Journals in Gastroenterology **5743**
0165-8735 Sociaal Den Haag†
0165-8743 Purdue University Monographs in Romance Language†
0165-8786 Speelgoed & Hobby **4061**
0165-8794 Science of Religion **7699**
0165-8859 Moto 73 **8261**
0165-8867 Pen en Toets†
0165-8905 Onze Eigen Krant *changed to* 1574-7638 **8978**
0165-9030 Van Taal tot Taal†
0165-9111 Annual Egyptological Bibliography **4169**
0165-9162 Netherlands Institute for Sea Research. Annual Report **2813**
0165-9200 Tabu **5185**
0165-9227 Grazer Philosophische Studien **6922**
0165-9278 Amstelodamum **4198**
0165-9294 Beeldpraat†
0165-9308 ZOA Nieuws *changed to* 1871-0727 **8079**
0165-9367 Bulletin Antieke Beschaving **385**
0165-9375 C S M Informatie† **8938**
0165-9405 Core Journals in Cardiology **5742**
0165-9421 London Studies in Classical Philology **5148**
0165-9510 Rijksmuseum. Bulletin **515**
0165-9545 Milieudefensie *changed to* 1569-3368 **2619**
0165-9618 Costerus **5108**
0165-9677 Finish†
0165-9839 Toorts **2946**
0165-9863 Internationale Licht Rundschau *see* 1871-3661 **1016**
0165-988X Wereld en Zending **7694**
0165-9936 Trends in Analytical Chemistry **2107**
0165-9952 Het Nederlands Zangersblad
0166-0004 De Nederlandse Jager **8324**
0166-0101 Het Orgel **6603**
0166-0268 Netherlands. Centraal Bureau voor de Statistiek. Maandschrift†
0166-0276 Vogelvrije Fietser **8520**
0166-0381 Kroniek van Het Rembrandthuis **500**
0166-0438 Brieven van Paulus **4206**
0166-0462 Regional Science and Urban Economics **4425**
0166-0470 Koninklijke Nederlandse Oudheidkundige Bond. Bulletin **403**
0166-0586 Het Nederlandse Boek† **8976**
0166-0616 Studies in Mycology **819**
0166-0624 Horeca Info **4388**
0166-0667 Volkskundig Bulletin†
0166-0829 Linguistik Aktuell **5147**
0166-0861 Developments in Bioenergetics and Biomembranes†
0166-0918 Developments in Soil Science **228**
0166-0934 Journal of Virological Methods **890**
0166-0993 Homologie†
0166-1116 Studies in Environmental Science **3468**
0166-1256 Management Team **1777**
0166-1280 Journal of Molecular Structure: THEOCHEM **2068**
0166-1302 Columbia Studies in the Classical Tradition **2233**
0166-1345 De Poezenkrant **6813**
0166-137X Betoniek **982**
0166-1426 Boogie Woogie and Blues Collector
0166-1558 Amro Relais†
0166-1590 Zeggenschap (Leiderdorp) *changed to* 1569-6561 **1717**
0166-1736 Skoop†
0166-1760 Grafisch Orgaan†
0166-1787 Skrien **6513**
0166-1809 Ons Amsterdam **4251**
0166-1868 De Tweede Ronde **5391**
0166-1957 Transport Policy and Decision Making†
0166-1965 Machinist **3388**
0166-2007 Opzij **8879**
0166-2015 Spectator Waterstaatswerken
0166-2058 Over Multatuli **5347**
0166-2074 Museumvisie **6533**
0166-2082 Topics in Environmental Health†
0166-2112 Hydro Delft† **8962**
0166-218X Discrete Applied Mathematics **5483**
0166-2236 Trends in Neurosciences **6189**
0166-2287 Developments in Agricultural and Managed Forest Ecology **3687**
0166-2309 Doctor Jazz Magazine **6562**
0166-2333 Current Topics in Veterinary Medicine and Animal Science **8796**
0166-2392 Ouderlingenblad **7668**
0166-2406 Felikat Magazine **6808**
0166-2430 Jonxis Lectures
0166-2481 Developments in Psychiatry†
0166-2511 Holland **4230**
0166-252X Logopedie en Foniatrie **4075**
0166-2538 Developments in Plant Biology†
0166-2570 Natuur en Milieu *changed to* 1574-9711 **2629**
0166-2627 Natuurbehoud **2714**
0166-2635 Developments in Precambrian Geology **2731**
0166-2678 Op Weg *changed to* 1872-079X **1009**
0166-2740 Exchange **7642**
0166-2767 Niet Zo Benauwd
0166-2791 Heilsfontein†
0166-2813 Nieuw Zicht†
0166-2880 De Geheel-Onthouder **2694**
0166-3119 Komby **2198**
0166-3178 Molecular Physiology†
0166-3437 Filatelie **6898**
0166-3461 Toerusting *changed to* 1568-8763 **8993**
0166-3534 Groen **3734**
0166-3542 Antiviral Research **881**
0166-3607 In de Strengen **8293**
0166-3615 Computers in Industry **1415**
0166-3704 De Kleine Aarde **3741**
0166-3801 Nederlandse Historien **4247**
0166-3828 Officiele Bekendmakingen†
0166-3844 De Poelier *changed to* 1574-1710 **294**
0166-3860 Kwik†
0166-3992 Contrastma *changed to* 1574-1893 **6216**
0166-4069 Ruimzicht†
0166-4115 Advances in Psychology **7331**
0166-4166 Uitdaging **7691**
0166-4204 Vastgoed **7615**
0166-4298 Raakpunt **6180**
0166-4301 Westerheem **423**
0166-4328 Behavioural Brain Research **6126**
0166-4360 In Search
0166-445X Aquatic Toxicology **3493**
0166-4492 Tableau **521**
0166-4662 Landelijke Contactraad voor de Gemeentelijke Bemoelingen met de Lichamelijke Opvoeding en de Sport. Landelijk Contact *changed to* 1872-2210 **8204**
0166-4751 Nederlands Tijdschrift voor Ergotherapie **6113**
0166-4824 Waddenbulletin *changed to* 1572-3453 **2631**
0166-4948 Noorderbreedte **4248**
0166-4972 Technovation **8443**
0166-4980 De Dagbladpers†
0166-5030 Philosophia Patrum† **8980**
0166-5057 Economic Titles - Abstracts†
0166-5111 Schippersweekblad†
0166-5146 Oost-Europa Verkenningen†
0166-5154 Zeeuws Tijdschrift **4280**
0166-5162 International Journal of Coal Geology **2748**
0166-526X Comprehensive Analytical Chemistry **2099**
0166-5294 Tijdschrift voor Milieu Aansprakelijkheid *changed to* 1574-9851 **3470**
0166-5316 Performance Evaluation **2435**
0166-5324 Journal of Pipelines†
0166-5405 Buxbaumiella **782**
0166-5677 Van Horen Zeggen **4076**
0166-5766 Ports and Dredging **3363**
0166-5782 Klik **8053**
0166-5790 Glot†
0166-5839 De Landeigenaar **7598**
0166-5936 Nederlands Tijdschrift voor Chiropodie *changed to* 0922-4742 **2260**
0166-5952 Varkens **303**
0166-5960 Developments in Neurology **6136**
0166-6002 Verbum *changed to* 1569-3015 **2889**
0166-6010 Materials Science Monographs **3209**
0166-6029 Lyts Frisia
0166-6061 Studies in Modern Thermodynamics†
0166-6096 Media†
0166-6150 Achtergrond†
0166-6223 OMOlogie **2893**
0166-6363 Bouwen met Staal **983**
0166-641X Bouwmarkt (Doetinchem) **983**
0166-6495 Gewasbescherming **233**
0166-6584 Notulae Odonatologicae **694**
0166-6614 De Vrije Gedachte *changed to* 1872-1478 **6960**
0166-6762 Milieu Actief **3452**
0166-6789 Registratie†
0166-6851 Molecular and Biochemical Parasitology **738**
0166-6894 Rij - Instructie **2945**
0166-6967 Sigma **1793**
0166-6983 Structure Reports. Section A: Metals and Inorganic Compounds†
0166-6991 Synthese Library **6956**
0166-7025 Jazz Nu *changed to* 1568-2714 **6578**
0166-7033 Structure Reports. Section B: Organic Compounds†
0166-7068 Specifiek *changed to* 0169-9261 **1720**
0166-7149 Fobie-Vizier *changed to* 1872-4396 **6185**
0166-7203 Nederlands Tijdschrift voor Dietisten **6664**
0166-7297 Kunstschrift **502**
0166-7416 Compres **7319**
0166-7629 Diabc **5886**
0166-7688 Analyse **5902**
0166-7831 Contour **2939**
0166-784X Bomennieuws **3725**
0166-7890 Bouwbedrijf†
0166-8072 Landbouw-Economisch Instituut. Maandblad Prijsstatistiek†
0166-8129 Landbouw-Economisch Instituut. Mededelingen **183**
0166-8250 Pluimveehouderij **296**
0166-8358 Trias
0166-8439 H2O **8824**
0166-8471 Wetenschapsbeleid†
0166-8498 Vrijheid en Democratie *changed to* 1872-0862 **7151**
0166-8528 B & G **1911**
0166-8544 Reviews in Cancer Epidemiology†
0166-8595 Photosynthesis Research **742**
0166-8641 Topology and Its Applications **5542**
0166-8706 Het Zee-Aquarium **968**
0166-9079 Publikatieblad Sociale Verzekering
0166-915X Nederlandsche Bank N.V. Kwartaalbericht *see* 0922-6184 **1370**
0166-9176 Sociale Verzekering *changed to* 1568-8992 **4501**
0166-9222 Beleidsanalyse†
0166-929X Voetbal Totaal **8250**
0166-932X Berichten aan Zeevarenden
0166-9478 Netherlands. Centraal Planbureau. Centraal Economisch Plan **1899**
0166-9524 Jurisprudentie Onderwijswetten *changed to* 1570-0011 **3031**
0166-9648 Rugby Nieuws **8244**
0166-9656 Woningraad Extra†
0166-9680 Netherlands. Centraal Bureau voor de Statistiek. Statistisch Bulletin **1254**
0166-9842 Developments in Cardiovascular Medicine **5785**
0166-9966 Bibliografie van Nederlandse Proefschriften†
0167-0018 T V B **4056**
0167-0034 Democraat **7128**
0167-0115 Regulatory Peptides **744**
0167-0247 Volleybal†
0167-028X Ons Burgerschap *changed to* 1571-4365 **7140**
0167-0441 Doopsgezinde Bijdragen **7735**
0167-0468 H B O Journaal† **8960**
0167-0581 Tijdschrift Financieel Management *changed to* 1567-553X **1342**
0167-0689 Bestuursforum **7423**
0167-0840 Organist en Eredienst *changed to* 1569-416X **6597**
0167-0883 Liberaal Reveil **5224**
0167-0980 Lokaal Bestuur **7497**
0167-1006 Strijdkreet **7776**
0167-1057 Tijding **7742**
0167-1146 Binnenlands Bestuur **7423**
0167-1200 Concilium†
0167-1227 De Wekker **7780**
0167-1251 Nederlandse Vliegtuigencyclopedie
0167-1359 Tijdschrift voor Arbitrage
0167-1685 Tandartspraktijk **5867**
0167-1715 Algemeen Doopsgezind Weekblad *changed to* 1872-2229 **7754**
0167-1723 Rechte Sporen *changed to* 1574-7697 **7690**
0167-1782 World Crops: Production, Utilization and Description†
0167-1839 French-Language Psychology†
0167-1847 Atlantisch Perspectief **7222**
0167-1871 Wapenveld **7693**
0167-191X Science Policy in the Netherlands†
0167-1987 Soil & Tillage Research **157**
0167-2134 Semasia†
0167-2185 Deutsche Buecher **7199**
0167-2258 Bijbel en Wetenschap *changed to* 1570-2057 **7640**
0167-2274 Muziekbode **6597**
0167-2304 Credo **7753**
0167-2320 Sociology of the Sciences. Yearbook **7918**
0167-2355 De Christen *changed to* 1872-5678 **7748**
0167-2363 Vandaar **7779**
0167-238X Dth **7353**
0167-2436 Kind en Adolescent **6096**
0167-2444 Filosofie & Praktijk **6920**
0167-2495 Wiskundig Genootschap. Mededelingen†
0167-2533 Human Systems Management **1750**
0167-2622 Scheut Hier en Elders
0167-2657 Calvijn
0167-2681 Journal of Economic Behavior & Organization **1134**
0167-2738 Solid State Ionics **7041**
0167-2770 Vrede over Israel **7693**
0167-2789 Physica D: Nonlinear Phenomena **7031**
0167-2843 Applied Methods in Oncology†
0167-2878 Dutch Birding **906**
0167-2894 Developments in Petrology **2731**
0167-2924 Woord en Daad *changed to* 1871-9570 **8078**
0167-2932 Grasduinen **791**
0167-2940 Trends in Analytical Chemistry (Library Edition) **2107**
0167-2967 Nederlandse Jezuieten *changed to* 1871-1944 **7802**
0167-2991 Studies in Surface Science and Catalysis **7063**
0167-3114 Schrift **7816**
0167-319X Sponsorbulletin†
0167-3211 F M (Utrecht) **7797**
0167-3467 Gereformeerd Kerkhistorisch Tijdschrift†
0167-3491 B K-Informatie **477**
0167-3572 Planning†
0167-3599 Annual Review of the Social Sciences of Religion†
0167-3602 Nieuw Leven **7769**
0167-3696 Ins and Outs† **8964**
0167-3785 Handbook of Powder Technology **3268**
0167-3831 Grotiana **4683**
0167-3882 Assurantie Magazine **4493**
0167-3890 Durability of Building Materials†
0167-403X Studies in Electrical and Electronic Engineering **3331**
0167-4048 Computers & Security **2512**
0167-4064 U T C *changed to* 1569-352X **1920**
0167-4080 Clinically Important Adverse Drug Interactions†
0167-4099 Oso **351**
0167-4102 Studien zur Oesterreichischen Philosophie **6954**
0167-4110 Natural Resources Forum Library†
0167-4129 Studies in Automation and Control†
0167-4137 Developments in Agricultural Engineering **228**
0167-4161 Studies of Classical India **6956**
0167-4188 Chemical Engineering Monographs **3239**
0167-4242 Agrarisch Recht *changed to* 1874-9674 **162**
0167-4293 Belastingblad **1912**
0167-4323 Telecontact
0167-4331 Studies in Generative Grammar **5182**
0167-4366 Agroforestry Systems **87**
0167-4412 Plant Molecular Biology **697**
0167-4447 Culture, Illness and Healing **335**
0167-4471 Aspects of Homogeneous Catalysis: a Series of Advances†
0167-4501 Developments in Food Science **2122**

ISSN

0170-5652 I F O Studien zur Verkehrswirtschaft **8498**
0170-5660 I F O Studien zur Industriewirtschaft **1888**
0170-5695 I F O Studien zu Handels- und Dienstleistungsfragen **1120**
0170-5709 I F O Studien zur Entwicklungsforschung **1597**
0170-5725 Ur- und Fruehzeit†
0170-5768 Schrifttums fuer den Bereich Haushalt und Verbauch. Bibliographie†
0170-5776 Archaeologische Mitteilungen aus Nordwestdeutschland *changed to* 1862-9083 **407**
0170-5784 Beitraege zur Quantitativen Wirtschaftsforschung **1066**
0170-5792 Motorik **6993**
0170-589X Materialkundlich-Technische Reihe†
0170-5903 Hormone and Metabolic Research. Supplement **5893**
0170-592X Schriften zur Mittelstandsforschung **8131**
0170-5946 Sprache und Geschichte in Afrika **5177**
0170-5989 N M R†
0170-6004 Orthopaedic Practitioner†
0170-6012 Informatik-Spektrum **3291**
0170-608X Daten und Dokumente Zum Umweltschutz†
0170-6128 Schoenberger Hefte
0170-6195 Kultur und Leben
0170-6233 Berichte zur Wissenschaftsgeschichte **7840**
0170-6241 Zeitschrift fuer Semiotik **6962**
0170-6306 Bergbau in der Bundesrepublik Deutschland†
0170-656X Systematische Politikwissenschaft†
0170-6632 Chip **2570**
0170-6659 Bankfachklasse **1065**
0170-6748 M I Z - Materialien und Informationen zur Zeit **5225**
0170-6799 Ostalb-Einhorn **3854**
0170-6802 An Rems und Murr **3843**
0170-6845 Steuer Training
0170-6977 Wissenschaft und Umwelt†
0170-6993 Instandhaltung **5453**
0170-7213 Who's Who at the Frankfurt Book Fair **7576**
0170-7256 Datenschutz-Berater **2513**
0170-7302 Katholisches Leben und Kirchenreform im Zeitalter der Glaubensspaltung **7803**
0170-7434 Physics Briefs - Physikalische Berichte†
0170-7558 Quickborn **5164**
0170-7620 Steuer Telex **1945**
0170-7671 Agrarsoziale Gesellschaft. Kleine Reihe **8086**
0170-7779 I F O Studien zur Energiewirtschaft **3137**
0170-7787 South Asian Digest of Regional Writing†
0170-7817 Jahrbuch der Deutschen Bundespost†
0170-7922 Schulleiter Handbuch *changed to* 1618-5978 **3032**
0170-8007 Balkan-Archiv Neue Folge†
0170-8058 Tribuna Alema†
0170-8082 Nepal Research Centre Publications **557**
0170-8163 Anglo-American Forum† **8930**
0170-8171 Forum Linguisticum **5120**
0170-821X Bonner Romanistische Arbeiten **5101**
0170-8252 Finanzwissenschaftliche Schriften **1541**
0170-8406 Organization Studies **7990**
0170-8422 Z M P Bilanz Kartoffeln *changed to* Z M P Marktbilanz Kartoffeln **260**
0170-8473 Brille und Mode **586**
0170-8570 Hispanistische Studien **5125**
0170-8643 Lecture Notes in Control and Information Sciences **5025**
0170-8805 Kasseler Arbeiten zur Sprache und Literatur†
0170-883X Berliner Hochschulschriften zum Gewerblichen Rechtsschutz und Urheberrecht **4857**
0170-8848 Neue Studien zur Anglistik und Amerikanistik **5339**
0170-8864 Monographien zur Indischen Archaeologie, Kunst und Philologie **556**
0170-8872 Regensburger Beitraege zur Deutschen Sprach- und Literaturwissenschaft. Reihe B: Untersuchungen **5359**
0170-8929 Muenchner Zeitschrift fuer Balkankunde **4246**
0170-902X Das Band **3037**
0170-9089 Lateinische Sprache und Literatur des Mittelalters **5142**
0170-9097 Bauwirtschaft im Zahlenbild **981**
0170-9127 Moderne Geschichte und Politik **4245**
0170-9135 Mainzer Studien zur Amerikanistik **5329**
0170-9143 Mikrokosmos (Frankfurt) **5334**
0170-9240 Studies in the Intercultural History of Christianity **7742**
0170-9267 Bautenschutz und Bausanierung **981**
0170-9291 Europaeisches Patentamt. Amtsblatt **6749**
0170-9305 Europaeisches Patentblatt (Print)† **8954**
0170-9321 Methoden und Verfahren der Mathemathischen Physik†
0170-9348 International Books in Print†
0170-9364 Die Alte Stadt **4403**
0170-9518 Beitraege zur Allgemeinen und Vergleichenden Archaeologie **383**
0170-9526 V D I Informationsdienst. Blechbearbeitung *changed to* Informationsdienst F I Z Technik. Blechbearbeitung **6315**
0170-9550 Informationsdienst Kaltmassivumformung *changed to* 1437-451X **6339**
0170-9569 Informationsdienst Verein Deutscher Ingenieure. Elektrisch Abtragende Fertigungsverfahren *changed to* Informationsdienst F I Z Technik. Elektrisch Abtragende Fertigungsverfahren **6315**
0170-9577 T Z fuer Metallbearbeitung†
0170-9690 V G A Nachrichten **4526**
0170-9704 The Study of Time **582**
0170-9771 Consulting. Ausgabe A†
0170-9828 Allgemeine Fleischer Zeitung **3626**
0170-9909 Unterrichtswissenschaft. Beiheft†
0171-0079 Atalanta **840**
0171-0087 Basler Afrika Bibliographien. Nachrichten†
0171-0125 Bibliographien zur Romanistik **5406**
0171-0133 Neue Musikzeitung **6599**
0171-015X Lagertechnik **1829**
0171-0591 Das Bad (Luebeck)
0171-0621 Muensterische Beitraege zur Ur- und Fruehgeschichte†
0171-0796 Rheinisch-Westfaelischer Jaeger **8330**
0171-0826 Lexikon des Steuer- und Wirtschaftsrechts **4723**
0171-0834 Kodikas - Code - Ars Semeiotica **8117**
0171-0850 Universitaet Dortmund. Forschungsbericht **8012**
0171-0869 Universitaet Dortmund. Schriftenreihe **8012**
0171-0958 E L C O M P Magazine†
0171-1113 Gesellschaft fuer Oekologie. Verhandlungen **675**
0171-1288 Perspektiven der Philosophie. Neues Jahrbuch **6939**
0171-1334 Paedagogik Heute†
0171-1407 Beitraege zur Strukturforschung **1066**
0171-1423 Hessische Bibliographie†
0171-1474 Roemisch-Germanisches Zentralmuseum, Mainz. Monographien **4259**
0171-1490 Forum Sozialstation **8041**
0171-1547 Forschung Stadtverkehr: Sonderreihe†
0171-1644 Bromberg **3845**
0171-1660 Beitraege zur Afrikakunde†
0171-1687 Geomethodica†
0171-1695 Hard Times **5219**
0171-175X Abfallwirtschaft in Forschung und Praxis **3503**
0171-1814 Anaesthesiologie und Intensivmedizin†
0171-1873 Springer Series in Solid State Sciences **7041**
0171-1911 Umweltbundesamt. Berichte **3472**
0171-1938 Kontakt und Studium **7877**
0171-1970 Briefmarkenwelt†
0171-2004 Handbook of Experimental Pharmacology **6845**
0171-2012 Nordrhein Verkehr **8621**
0171-2160 Topics in Infectious Diseases†
0171-2217 Seminars in Infectious Disease†
0171-2276 Informations Bayer pour l'Industrie du Caoutchouc†
0171-2284 Informaciones Bayer para la Industria del Caucho†
0171-2365 Handbuch der Steuerveranlagungen: Einkommensteuer, Koerperschaftsteuer, Gewerbesteuer, Umsatzsteuer **1928**
0171-2594 Lebensmittelrecht **4719**
0171-2713 Kommentar Fertigpackungsrecht **6711**
0171-2721 Polizeiliche Kriminalstatistik Niedersachsen mit Informationen aus dem Landeskriminalamt **2675**
0171-2802 Polizeiliche Kriminalstatistik Nordrhein-Westfalen **2675**
0171-290X Portugiesische Forschungen der Goerresgesellschaft. Reihe 3: Vieira-Texte und Vieira-Studien†
0171-2977 Analysen†
0171-2985 Immunobiology **5759**
0171-3183 Perspektiven†
0171-3302 Berliner Wissenschaftliche Gesellschaft. Jahrbuch **7840**
0171-3426 Pulheimer Beitraege zur Geschichte und Heimatkunde **4255**
0171-3434 Psychosozial **7400**
0171-3469 Reformationsgeschichtliche Studien und Texte **7772**
0171-3523 Privates Eigentum **7604**
0171-3558 Taeckkolmia† **8992**
0171-3604 Prisma (Kassel) **7899**
0171-3647 Informationsdienst Verein Deutscher Ingenieure. Schmieden und Pressen *changed to* Informationsdienst F I Z Technik. Schmieden und Pressen **6339**
0171-3655 Projektbereich Auslaendische Arbeiter. Materialien†
0171-3760 Soester Beitraege **4266**
0171-3825 Technik Heute†
0171-3841 Meditation **7662**
0171-385X Studien zur Europaeischen Geschichte
0171-3876 Medikament & Meinung† **8973**
0171-3973 Meisterwerke der Kunst **505**
0171-399X Digest **2040**
0171-4058 Archivpflege in Westfalen und Lippe **4200**
0171-4090 Articulata **840**
0171-4104 Archiv fuer Musikorganologie†
0171-4147 Audio **7086**
0171-4163 Test-Index
0171-4171 Lebendige Katechese **7804**
0171-4198 Elektronik Heute†
0171-4260 Uhren - Juwelen - Schmuck. Jahrbuch *see* 0720-6607 **4570**
0171-4317 Verband der Automobilindustrie. Auto **8610**
0171-4457 Wer und Was in der Deutschen Getraenke - Industrie *changed to* 1610-2150 **612**
0171-4481 Auslaendisches Lebensmittelrecht. Codex Alimentarius **4918**
0171-449X Auslaendisches Lebensmittelrecht. E G - Vorschriften **4918**
0171-4538 Sozialpsychiatrische Informationen **7409**
0171-4546 G S I Report **7066**
0171-466X Mannheimer Vortraege zur Versicherungswissenschaft **4514**
0171-4694 Verein zum Schutz der Bergwelt. Jahrbuch **2630**
0171-4880 Unispiegel (Heidelberg) **3006**
0171-4902 Taschenbuch des Textil- und Lederwareneinzelhandels *changed to* 1864-7189 **8458**
0171-4910 Goettinger Orientforschungen. Reihe: Grundlagen und Ergebnisse
0171-4953 Sportpaedagogik **3082**
0171-4961 Germany. Statistisches Bundesamt. Fachserie 6: Handel, Gastgewerbe, Reiseverkehr; Reihe 5: Warenverkehr mit Berlin (West)†
0171-4996 Italienisch **5131**
0171-5038 W E M A Bezugsquellenverzeichnis†
0171-5054 Jahrbuch fuer Vulkanisation und Reifentechnik† **8967**
0171-5062 Fertigung und Betrieb†
0171-5089 Der Weihenstephaner **612**
0171-5178 Praxis Geographie **4025**
0171-5208 Kulleraugen **6506**
0171-5216 Journal of Cancer Research and Clinical Oncology **6024**
0171-5275 Reiter-Spiegel†
0171-533X Pelz International†
0171-5364 Welt der Grossen und Kleinen Eisenbahn†
0171-5410 Arbeiten aus Anglistik und Amerikanistik **5256**
0171-5445 Bauphysik **980**
0171-5461 Muenchener Statistik. Monatsbericht **7482**
0171-5496 Licht **3323**
0171-564X H L K - Heizung - Lueftung - Klimatechnik **4119**
0171-5658 Hoppenstedt Boersenfuehrer **1351**
0171-5666 Brennpunkt Seelsorge **7628**
0171-5720 Der Mineralbrunnen **607**
0171-5860 Analyse & Kritik **7947**
0171-5895 Liboriusblatt **7804**
0171-5976 Menschenrechte **7212**
0171-6018 Geld-Profi **1349**
0171-6026 Homosexuelle Emanzipation†
0171-6042 Made in Europe. Furniture and Interiors†
0171-614X SelberMachen **4346**
0171-6204 Erneuerung in Kirche und Gesellschaft **7756**
0171-628X Elektro-Blitz **3305**
0171-6298 Spiridon Laufmagazin **6997**
0171-6425 The Thoracic and Cardiovascular Surgeon **6261**
0171-6433 Wissenschaftliche Vereinigung fuer Augenoptik und Optometrie. Fachvortraege des W V A O Jahreskongresses **6053**
0171-6441 Zeitschrift fuer die Neutestamentliche Wissenschaft und die Kunde der Aelteren Kirche. Beihefte **7696**
0171-645X Beitraege zur Hochschulforschung **2968**
0171-6530 Aurora-Buchreihe **5258**
0171-6662 Britische und Irische Studien zur Deutschen Sprache und Literatur **5101**
0171-6786 Beitraege zur Kommunikationswissenschaft und Medienforschung **8090**
0171-6794 Studies in Descriptive Linguistics†
0171-6859 Canadian Studies in German Language and Literature **5270**
0171-6867 Australian and New Zealand Studies in German Language and Literature **5258**
0171-6913 Information†
0171-693X Polizei Journal†
0171-6964 Keramik-Boutique†
0171-7073 Hamburger Gartenfreund **3735**
0171-7081 Schriften zur Umwelt- und Ressourcenoekonomie **1516**
0171-709X Polymers - Properties and Applications†
0171-7111 Haematology and Blood Transfusion **5937**
0171-7170 Regensburger Beitraege zur Deutschen Sprach- und Literaturwissenschaft. Reihe A: Quellen **5359**
0171-7197 Deutscher Ausschuss fuer Stahlbeton. Schriftenreihe **1002**
0171-7200 Schweizerische Versicherungszeitschrift **4522**
0171-7219 Stanford German Studies **5377**
0171-7227 Anwaltsblatt **4619**
0171-7235 Tuebinger Studien zur Deutschen Literatur **5390**
0171-726X Utah Studies in Literature and Linguistics **5394**
0171-7278 Studien zur Philosophie des 18. Jahrhunderts **6955**
0171-7316 Slavica Helvetica **5174**
0171-7391 Schweizer Asiatische Studien. Studienhefte **560**
0171-7502 Der Baeckermeister **3671**
0171-7510 KommunalPraxis. Ausgabe Bayern **7495**
0171-7537 Bielefelder Studien zur Entwicklungssoziologie **8090**
0171-7596 Studienbuecher Deutsch als Fremdsprache **5182**
0171-7634 Extracta Otorhinolaryngologica†
0171-7669 Forum Jugendhilfe **8041**
0171-7928 Architektur und Wohnen **432**
0171-7936 Offenbacher Verein fuer Naturkunde. Abhandlungen
0171-7952 Bauen fuer die Landwirtschaft **979**
0171-8096 Technisches Messen - T M **4490**
0171-8118 Aristo - Mitteilungen fuer Ingenieur- und Hochschulen†
0171-8126 Aussenhandelsblaetter† **8932**
0171-8177 Entomologia Generalis **844**
0171-8185 N W B - Dokumentation Steuerrecht **1935**
0171-8312 Printing & Packaging†
0171-8320 Jahrbuch fuer Internationale Germanistik. Reihe A: Kongressberichte **5131**
0171-838X B T E Marketing-Berater **1806**
0171-8452 Auto Zeitung **8561**
0171-8495 B L L V Bayerische Schule **2829**
0171-8533 Haus- und Grundbesitz in Recht und Praxis **1011**
0171-8630 Marine Ecology - Progress Series **688**
0171-8649 Geographie und Schule **4012**
0171-8789 B F G: Aussenhandelsdienst†
0171-8819 Arbeit und Soziales†
0171-8908 B D - Baumaschinendienst **977**
0171-8932 Zeitschriften - Datenbank (Z D B)†
0171-9033 Militaerpolitik Dokumentation **6434**
0171-9157 Barmer **4494**
0171-9173 Barmer Bruecke†
0171-922X Bernard und Graefe Aktuell†
0171-9238 Herzmedizin **5789**
0171-9254 Germany (Federal Republic, 1949-). Statistisches Bundesamt. Fachserie 4, Produzierendes Gewerbe. Reihe 4.1.2: Betriebe, Beschaeftigte und Umsatz im Bergbau und im Verarbeitenden Gewerbe nach Beschaeftigtengroessenklassen
0171-9289 Freibeuter†
0171-9319 Begegnen und Helfen **8027**
0171-9335 European Journal of Cell Biology **832**
0171-9378 Studien zu Nichteuropaeischen Rechtstheorien†
0171-9386 Junges Forum **4236**
0171-9408 Balatros Berichtet†
0171-9416 Bayerisch-Schwaebische Wirtschaft **1396**
0171-9505 Bielefelder Katalog - Jazz **6549**
0171-9513 Der Bayerische Steuerzahler
0171-9572 Bayernsport **8161**
0171-9610 Hessische Staedte- und Gemeinde-Zeitung **4412**
0171-9661 Hessisches Aerzteblatt **5628**
0171-967X Calcified Tissue International **5884**
0171-9718 Behindertenhilfe Durch Erziehung, Unterricht und Therapie **3037**
0171-9750 Archives of Toxicology. Supplement†
0171-9904 Jahrbuch fuer Volkskunde *changed to* 1868-131X **3619**
0172-0023 Nationalpark Berchtesgaden. Forschungsberichte **2620**
0172-0147 Bildung Konkret†
0172-0171 Bildung und Wissenschaft (Bonn) **2831**
0172-018X Blaetter fuer Vorgesetzte **1880**
0172-0236 Berliner Bank. Boersenbrief† **8935**
0172-0457 Literarisches Arbeitsjournal†
0172-049X Wettbewerb in Recht und Praxis **4814**
0172-0538 Bremer-Universitaets-Zeitung†
0172-0570 Agrarmeteorologischer Wochenhinweis fuer das Gebiet Bundesrepublik Deutschland†
0172-0589 Brauerei Journal† **8937**
0172-0597 International Music Education†
0172-0643 Pediatric Cardiology **5797**
0172-0805 Bleib Gesund *changed to* Bleibgesund Life **6983**
0172-0872 Blaetter fuer Oberdeutsche Namenforschung
0172-0899 Micro Extra†
0172-0929 Priesterjahrheft **7813**

ISSN

0173-9921 Theoretische und Experimentelle Methoden der Regelungstechnik†
0173-9980 Bulk Solids Handling **3236**
0174-0008 Ernaehrungs Umschau **6658**
0174-0091 Regulae Benedicti Studia. Annuarium Internationale† **8985**
0174-0105 Regulae Benedicti Studia. Supplementa *changed to* Regulae Benedicti Studia. Traditio et Receptio **7673**
0174-0156 Rechtspfleger - Studienhefte **4766**
0174-0164 D D Z - Deutsche Drogisten Zeitung *changed to* D W Z - D D Z **6832**
0174-0199 Earth Evolution Sciences†
0174-0202 Zeitschrift fuer Rechtssoziologie **8148**
0174-0350 Der Sonntagsbrief *changed to* 1619-2001 **7633**
0174-0423 Frau Aktuell **8864**
0174-0474 Texte zur Forschung **6957**
0174-0512 Bayerns Pferde Zucht und Sport **8288**
0174-0652 Ural-Altaische Jahrbuecher. Neue Folge **5192**
0174-0660 Actualites de Rohde et Schwarz *see* 0548-3093 **2335**
0174-0679 Grundriss der Literaturgeschichten nach Gattungen† **8960**
0174-0695 Ertraege der Forschung **6916**
0174-0814 G S I Scientific Report (Print) *changed to* G S I Scientific Report (Online) **7066**
0174-0830 Zeitschrift fuer Berufs- und Wirtschaftspaedagogik. Beihefte **3088**
0174-1004 Charadrius **905**
0174-1039 Beitraege zur Avifauna des Rheinlandes **902**
0174-108X Krankenpflege Journal (Print) *changed to* Krankenpflege Journal (Online) **5968**
0174-1098 Zeitschrift fuer Laermbekaempfung *changed to* 1863-4672 **7088**
0174-1136 Zeitschrift fuer Kommunalfinanzen **1425**
0174-1144 Sporthandbuch Nordrhein-Westfalen
0174-1152 Sporthandbuch Niedersachsen†
0174-1225 Arbeitsrecht im Betrieb **4620**
0174-1357 Markscheidewesen **6469**
0174-1446 Recycling†
0174-1551 Cardiovascular and Interventional Radiology **6193**
0174-1578 Journal of Comparative Physiology B **924**
0174-1756 L W F Documentation **7764**
0174-1772 Spielmittel **4061**
0174-1845 Das Geltende Seevoelkerrecht in Einzeldarstellungen **4926**
0174-1942 Die Information ueber Steuer und Wirtschaft *changed to* I N F - Die Information fuer Steuerberater und Wirtschaftspruefer **1928**
0174-2086 Hephaistos (Hamburg) **396**
0174-2108 Informationsbrief Auslaenderrecht **4928**
0174-2132 Schreibheft **5367**
0174-2175 Bayerische Landjugend **2145**
0174-2345 Schuetz-Jahrbuch **6615**
0174-2442 Colo-Proctology **5921**
0174-2450 ColoProctology (International Edition)†
0174-2469 Klinische Ernaehrung *changed to* Stoffwechselmanagement **6669**
0174-2477 Berliner Islamstudien **7709**
0174-254X Apparent Places of Fundamental Stars **569**
0174-2582 Kulleraugen - Materialsammlung **6506**
0174-2612 Die Gemeindekasse Baden-Wuerttemberg **7492**
0174-268X Arbeiten zur Geschichte der Medizin in Giessen **5577**
0174-2701 Container Contacts **8494**
0174-2744 Aktuelle Onkologie **6007**
0174-2752 Klinische und Experimentelle Urologie **6271**
0174-2795 Zentralinstitut fuer Versuchstierzucht. Jahresbericht†
0174-2876 Rheinland-Pfalz Heute **7483**
0174-2914 Rheinland-Pfalz. Statistisches Landesamt Rheinland-Pfalz. Statistische Monatshefte **7483**
0174-304X Neuropediatrics **6097**
0174-3120 W Z B - Mitteilungen **8014**
0174-3147 Der Kieselstein **3043**
0174-3163 F L F **1923**
0174-318X Kantinen Anzeiger†
0174-3376 Evangelisches Sonntagsblatt aus Bayern **7641**
0174-3384 Braunschweiger Naturkundliche Schriften **936**
0174-3465 Die Eule†
0174-3538 V T F - Post **6744**
0174-3589 Berliner Gartenfreund **3724**
0174-3600 Siedlung und Eigenheim **4427**
0174-3635 Standort **4030**
0174-3740 Kapitalanlagen Steuer-Dienst
0174-3775 Taxi Heute **8606**
0174-4038 Bongo **936**
0174-4224 Early Man News†
0174-4399 Medien in Forschung und Unterricht. Serie A **8120**
0174-4410 Studien und Texte zur Sozialgeschichte der Literatur **5380**
0174-4429 Texte und Textgeschichte **5387**
0174-4445 Esslinger Studien - Jahrbuch **4218**
0174-4534 N C Fertigung **6326**
0174-4631 Landkreises Birkenfeld. Heimatkalender **4239**
0174-4704 Human Rights Law Journal **4849**
0174-4747 Analysis **5469**
0174-478X Gesetzblatt fuer Baden-Wuerttemberg **4680**
0174-4860 Pathogenese und Klinik der Harnsteine **6273**
0174-4909 Frankfurter Allgemeine **3848**
0174-4917 Sueddeutsche Zeitung **3857**
0174-4984 Das Rathaus **7501**
0174-5336 D S B **1001**
0174-5395 Betriebspruefung **1913**
0174-5506 Diakrisis **7754**
0174-5522 elektronik industrie **3098**
0174-559X Transportrecht **8518**
0174-5735 Magazin fuer Heimwerker†
0174-5832 Stafette **2214**
0174-5875 Freiburger Theologische Studien **7644**
0174-6065 Ueben & Musizieren **6625**
0174-6073 Mikrocomputer-Jahrbuch† **8974**
0174-6081 Erlanger Forschungen. Reihe B: Naturwissenschaften und Medizin **5610**
0174-6146 Industrie-Service **1889**
0174-6170 Wirtschaft und Erziehung **1550**
0174-6200 Basistexte Personalwesen
0174-6227 Fussballtraining **8229**
0174-6324 Lateinamerika Nachrichten **1601**
0174-6545 Epigraphica Anatolica **4218**
0174-6626 Mainzer Naturwissenschaftliches Archiv. Beiheft **687**
0174-6863 Autokaufmann **8562**
0174-6944 Instant
0174-6979 Felsbau *changed to* 1865-7362 **2743**
0174-6979 Felsbau *changed to* 1866-0134 **2733**
0174-6995 Lazarus **7738**
0174-7363 Financial Times (Frankfurt Edition) **1346**
0174-738X Verdauungskrankheiten **5728**
0174-786X Deutsche Waldenser *changed to* 1867-0644 **7693**
0174-8246 Die Antike† **8930**
0174-8386 Bayerisches Jahrbuch **7488**
0174-870X Abhandlungen zur Geschichte der Medizin und der Naturwissenschaften **5564**
0175-0135 Dilthey-Jahrbuch **6914**
0175-0143 Pilot und Flugzeug **8550**
0175-0496 P C Welt **2581**
0175-0992 Forschung Frankfurt **7855**
0175-1336 L D V - Forum **5203**
0175-1344 Segelsport†
0175-162X Traber-Rundschau **8299**
0175-2073 Plant Gene Research **877**
0175-2081 Die Bar
0175-2200 Fachdienst Germanistik **5295**
0175-2235 Mathematik Lehren **3072**
0175-2413 Demokratie- und Arbeitergeschichte†
0175-2464 Sozialoekonomische Schriften zur Ruralen Entwicklung **207**
0175-2502 European Economics Editor†
0175-2723 Beispiele
0175-274X Sicherheit und Frieden **7265**
0175-2936 Pet **6813**
0175-2944 I F O Studien zur Arbeitsmarktforschung **1686**
0175-2960 Pro Familia Magazin **7391**
0175-2987 Mannheimer Beitraege zur Slavischen Philologie **5150**
0175-3053 Medizinische Kongresse **6281**
0175-3061 Werkverkehr und Verlader† **8998**
0175-3096 Zeitschrift fuer Empirische Paedagogik und Paedagogische Psychologie
0175-3169 Mannheimer Beitraege zur Sprach- und Literaturwissenschaft **5150**
0175-3347 Exilforschung **8101**
0175-3479 Hessische Blaetter fuer Volks- und Kulturforschung **3537**
0175-3495 Westfaelischen Museum fuer Naturkunde. Abhandlungen **7929**
0175-3622 Beitraege zur Altertumswissenschaft **2231**
0175-3754 Beitraege zur Augsburger Bistumsgeschichte **7785**
0175-3851 Intensivmedizin und Notfallmedizin **5636**
0175-3886 Frankfurter Althistorische Studien†
0175-4211 WaBoLu Hefte **3474**
0175-4262 VetMed Hefte
0175-4467 Streit **7216**
0175-4548 F & W - Fuehren und Wirtschaften im Krankenhaus **4093**
0175-4564 Hoerspiele in der A R D†
0175-4645 Beitraege zur Geschichte der Carolo-Wilhelmina **4203**
0175-4793 Beitraege zur Geschichte der Stadt Moenchengladbach **4203**
0175-4815 Deutsches Polizeiblatt **2650**
0175-5021 Fossilien **6724**
0175-503X Goettinger Quellenhefte†
0175-5080 Beitraege zur Geschichte und Quellenkunde des Mittelalters†
0175-5137 Beitraege zur Gesellschaftspolitik **8090**
0175-5293 Dokumentation Deutsche Finanzrechtsprechung†
0175-5307 Informationen fuer Steuerberatende Berufe†
0175-5315 Verfahrenstechnik **3257**
0175-5323 Beitraege zur Geschichte und Lehre der Reformierten Kirche **7624**
0175-5366 Bundessteuerblatt. Ausgabe A **1913**
0175-5382 Westfaelische Wilhelms-Universitaet Muenster. Institut fuer Allgemeine Sprachwissenschaft. Arbeitshefte **5195**
0175-5447 Beitraege zur Iranistik **544**
0175-551X Neue Muenchner Beitraege zur Kunstgeschichte†
0175-5617 Beitraege zur Mittelstandsforschung†
0175-5676 Beitraege zur Oekonomischen Forschung†
0175-5811 Aerzte Zeitung **5569**
0175-5838 Oekumene am Ort†
0175-5889 Theaterpaedagogik†
0175-5943 Beitraege zur Psychopathologie†
0175-5994 Beitraege zur Sozialpolitik und zum Sozialrecht **8027**
0175-6087 Beitraege zur Sozialforschung **7223**
0175-6168 Beitraege zur Stadt- und Regionalforschung **4404**
0175-6206 Lexicographica **5144**
0175-6281 European Truck & Trailer†
0175-6303 Beitraege zur Sozialgeschichte Bremen **4204**
0175-6486 Wissenschaft und Gegenwart. Geisteswissenschaftliche Reihe†
0175-6494 Wissenschaft und Gegenwart. Juristische Reihe†
0175-6508 Philosophische Abhandlungen **6942**
0175-6524 Lansky: Bibliotheksrechtliche Vorschriften **5024**
0175-6532 Max-Planck-Institut fuer Europaeische Rechtsgeschichte. Veroeffentlichungen. Ius Commune. Sonderhefte **4935**
0175-6559 Sozialwissenschaftliche Literaturrundschau **8007**
0175-6753 Kunststoffverarbeitung Deutschland **7094**
0175-6796 Bibliotheken der Bundesrepublik Deutschland. Datierte Handschriften **4996**
0175-6877 DX Magazine **2358**
0175-6893 D B I - Pressespiegel†
0175-7016 Hebraeische Beitraege zur Wissenschaft des Judentums **5304**
0175-7024 Israel und Palaestina **7246**
0175-7261 Universitaet Hamburg. Seminar fuer Allgemeine Betriebswirtschaftslehre. Schriftenreihe **1187**
0175-7490 Bastel-Boutique
0175-7571 European Biophysics Journal **753**
0175-7598 Applied Microbiology and Biotechnology **756**
0175-7601 Das Logbuch **4338**
0175-761X Siebenbuergische Familienforschung **3782**
0175-7695 E M W - Informationen **7639**
0175-7717 Schriftenreihe Unternehmensfuehrung und Marketing†
0175-7776 Giessener Beitraege zur Fremdsprachendidaktik **5122**
0175-7989 Horizont (Frankfurt) **26**
0175-8055 Studien zu Bildung und Wissenschaft
0175-8128 Weiss - Blaetter†
0175-8136 Dokumentation Sprachwissenschaftliche Lehrveranstaltungen†
0175-8152 Laurentius†
0175-825X Badminton - Report†
0175-8314 Alles ueber Wein **3626**
0175-8330 I F O Studien zur Umweltoekonomie **1120**
0175-8411 Altertumswissenschaftliche Texte und Studien **5251**
0175-842X Auslandsdeutsche Literatur der Gegenwart **5258**
0175-8446 Berlin in Geschichte und Gegenwart **4204**
0175-8586 Alpha-Omega. Reihe A, Lexika, Indizes, Konkordanzen zur Klassischen Philologie **5092**
0175-8659 Journal of Applied Ichthyology **950**
0175-873X Documenta Linguistica. Studienreihe **5112**
0175-8985 Schriften zur Unternehmensplanung **1171**
0175-9035 Deutsche Volksbuecher in Faksimiledrucken. Reihe A **624**
0175-9191 Allensbacher Jahrbuch der Demoskopie **8086**
0175-9264 Lexicographica. Series Maior **5144**
0175-9299 Der Personalrat **1871**
0175-9388 Germanistische Texte und Studien **5122**
0175-9434 Roemische Forschungen der Bibliotheca Hertziana **515**
0175-9469 Das Geld A B C
0175-9485 Wir Selbst†
0175-9515 Judaistische Texte und Studien **7725**
0175-9558 Studien zur Kunstgeschichte **519**
0175-9574 Philosophische Texte und Studien **6942**
0175-9590 Studien zur Filmgeschichte **6514**
0175-9809 Mensch Guten Willens†
0176-036X Uni Ulm Intern **2305**
0176-0513 Wohnung & Gesundheit **461**
0176-053X Management und Krankenhaus **4106**
0176-0599 Deutsche Tennis Zeitung **8226**
0176-067X Gemeinschaftskatalog (Year)†
0176-0785 Photo-Technik International *changed to* 1863-1509 **6973**
0176-0874 I F O Studien zur Strukturforschung **1120**
0176-0882 Mein Tennis Aktuell†
0176-0920 Ex Magazine **6677**
0176-0947 Sozialistische Praxis†
0176-0955 Agrar-Praxis†
0176-1110 Filmfaust†
0176-1188 Die Schaubuehne†
0176-1196 Volkskunde in Niedersachsen **3624**
0176-1218 D G S P Schriftenreihe **6135**
0176-1285 Mineralien-Magazin Lapis **2755**
0176-148X Geologie und Palaeontologie in Westfalen **2741**
0176-1536 T K Aktuell **4524**
0176-1617 Journal of Plant Physiology **798**
0176-1625 Gummi, Fasern, Kunststoffe **7824**
0176-1633 Fernerkundung in Raumordnung und Stadtebau†
0176-1714 Social Choice and Welfare **8068**
0176-1749 Lung and Respiration†
0176-1765 Klinische und Experimentelle Notfallmedizin **5658**
0176-1900 Goldmann-Nachrichten
0176-1919 Computer Business†
0176-1927 Run†
0176-1943 Mainzer Afrika-Studien **4176**
0176-2044 E P D Film **6496**
0176-2087 Der Fliegenfischer **8314**
0176-2206 Vortraege zum Thema Mensch und Tier
0176-2257 Der Schachwoche **8199**
0176-232X Forum Buerowirtschaft
0176-2354 Damaszener Mitteilungen *changed to* 1868-9078 **424**
0176-2397 Bibliothek fuer Alle
0176-2400 Computer-Schach und -Spiele **2475**
0176-246X Kontakt **1691**
0176-2494 Bio Garten†
0176-2532 Lanius **909**
0176-2591 Hessischer Kleingaertner **3736**
0176-2621 Heldia **945**
0176-263X Forschung Aktuell **7855**
0176-2656 Sekundaer-Rohstoffe **5459**
0176-2680 European Journal of Political Economy **7134**
0176-2753 Fundevogel
0176-277X Spektrum (Muenster) **8141**
0176-2834 Wolkenkratzer Art Journal†
0176-2923 Chips und Kabel† **8941**
0176-2931 Contacts. Serie 1: Theatrica **8468**
0176-2966 Friedrich Jahresheft **2858**
0176-2982 Paten **8061**
0176-3008 Spiegel der Forschung **7919**
0176-3083 Stahlbau - Nachrichten **1037**
0176-3148 Gypsy **5303**
0176-3156 Videofilmen **2404**
0176-3245 Fachbereich Versicherungswesen der Fachhochschule Koeln **4502**
0176-3261 P K V Publik **4518**
0176-3288 Datacom† **8948**
0176-3318 Heinrich-Mann-Jahrbuch **5304**
0176-3369 Research in Khoisan Studies **5166**
0176-3385 Niedersachsen†
0176-3466 Neue Woche **8877**
0176-3539 Der Maueranker **449**
0176-3547 Entscheidungen zum Mitbestimmungsgesetz **1680**
0176-358X TransportMarkt **8518**
0176-3679 Pharmacopsychiatry **6173**
0176-3687 Das Forum (Munich, 1961)† **8957**
0176-3695 Deutsches Aerzteblatt. Ausgabe C *see* 0012-1207 **5604**
0176-3733 Inklings **5443**
0176-375X Motor und Reisen. Ausgabe A†
0176-3792 Motor und Reisen **8593**
0176-3822 Extrablatt†
0176-3849 Medien-Kritik†
0176-3911 Umform Produkte†
0176-3946 Soester Zeitschrift **4266**

ISSN

Link to your serials resources and content with ulrichsweb.com

0177-9141 Sozialwissenschaftliches Institut der Bundeswehr. Vortraege **8007**
0177-9184 Kommunalpolitische Blaetter **7149**
0177-9214 Acta Biologica Benrodis **649**
0177-9222 Archaeologie der Literarischen Kommunikation **5256**
0177-9249 Kabel & Satellit†
0177-9265 Agora (Eichstaett) **2271**
0177-9303 Entscheidungen zum Wirtschaftsrecht - E W I R **1483**
0177-932X Centrifuga†
0177-9338 Collectanea Artis Historiae†
0177-9354 Ars Grammatica†
0177-9362 Altdeutsche Texte in Kritischen Ausgaben†
0177-9370 Forschungen zur Geschichte der Aelteren Deutschen Literatur **5297**
0177-9389 Die Geistesgeschichte und Ihre Methoden **5443**
0177-9397 Grundfragen der Literaturwissenschaft. Neue Folge†
0177-9419 Zeitungs - Dokumentation Bildungswesen **2937**
0177-9451 Kritische Stichwoerter†
0177-946X Houston German Studies **4230**
0177-9478 Humanistische Bibliothek. Reihe I: Abhandlungen **626**
0177-9486 Humanistische Bibliothek. Reihe II: Texte **626**
0177-9494 Humanistische Bibliothek. Reihe III: Skripten **626**
0177-9524 M N - Magazin fuer Naturheilkunde
0177-9540 Contrapunct†
0177-9591 Apotheke und Krankenhaus† **8930**
0177-9656 Steuer Seminar **1945**
0177-9672 Steuer-Lexicon. Teil III. B F H Rechtsprechung **1945**
0177-9761 V K G - Nachrichten†
0177-9796 Guss Produkte†
0177-980X Steuer-Lexikon. Teil I-G. Gesetze, Verordnungen **1945**
0177-9818 Steuer Lexicon. Teil I-R. Richtlinien **1945**
0177-9990 Chirurgische Gastroenterologie *changed to* 1662-6664 **5932**
0178-000X Bateria†
0178-0018 Ikarus†
0178-0034 Bayreuth African Studies Series **3522**
0178-0069 Springers Angewandte Informatik **2538**
0178-0085 Literatur im Dialog
0178-0107 Literaturgeschichte und Literaturkritik **5326**
0178-0115 Literatur-Kabinett. Deutsche Literatur in Reprints†
0178-0123 Motive. Freiburger Folkloristische Forschungen
0178-0166 Kraut und Rueben **3741**
0178-0301 Buchkalender Erzgebirge, Saazerland **3524**
0178-0328 Clinical Perspectives in Obstetrics and Gynecology **5988**
0178-0352 Muskelreport **6067**
0178-0409 Fliegenfischen **8314**
0178-0417 Deutsch - Betrifft Uns **5110**
0178-0425 Muenstersche Mittelalter-Schriften **5337**
0178-045X Archaeologische Nachrichten aus Baden **377**
0178-0492 Muenchner Archaeologische Studien **406**
0178-0506 Muenchner Romanistische Arbeiten
0178-0522 Myosotis†
0178-0530 Personal- und Vorlesungsverzeichnis der Universitaet zu Wuerzburg
0178-0778 Zuercher Germanistische Studien **5405**
0178-0867 Archiv der D L G **92**
0178-0875 Harvard Series in Ukrainian Studies **4226**
0178-0905 Eselsohr **2188**
0178-0913 Poetik und Hermeneutik **5430**
0178-093X Hypnose und Kognition *changed to* 1862-4731 **5943**
0178-1073 Ariadne **8851**
0178-1154 Archaeologische Gesellschaft zu Berlin. Winckelmannsprogramm **377**
0178-1197 Offset-Technik†
0178-126X Studien zur Theoretischen Linguistik **5181**
0178-1278 Musil-Studien **5337**
0178-1294 Romanica Monacensia **5364**
0178-1308 Mein Schoener Garten **3743**
0178-1367 Sozialphilosophische Studien
0178-1375 Spaetmittelalterliche Texte
0178-1383 Texte und Untersuchungen zur Englischen Philologie **4477**
0178-1391 Reihe Rhetorik
0178-1405 Uebergaenge
0178-1421 Gruenstift (Berlin) **2613**
0178-1448 Betriebsecho†
0178-160X Statistisches Jahrbuch der Stadt Koeln **7484**
0178-1626 Forum Katholische Theologie **7798**
0178-1634 Kritische Information **4462**
0178-1677 Wandermagazin **8340**
0178-1715 O P Journal **6254**
0178-1723 Beitraege zur Phonetik und Linguistik **5099**
0178-1731 Geschiebekunde Aktuell **6725**
0178-1758 Augsburger Jahrbuch fuer Musikwissenschaft†
0178-1804 Marburger Gelehrten Gesellschaft. Abhandlungen **2885**
0178-1812 iBau Planungsinformationen. Regionalausgabe Stuttgart **4415**
0178-1820 iBau Planungsinformationen. Regionalausgabe Freiburg **4415**
0178-1839 iBau Planungsinformationen. Regionalausgabe Hamburg **4415**
0178-1847 iBau Planungsinformationen. Regionalausgabe Koblenz - Trier **4415**
0178-1855 iBau Planungsinformationen. Regionalausgabe Tuebingen **4415**
0178-1863 iBau Planungsinformationen. Regionalausgabe Schleswig-Holstein **4415**
0178-188X iBau Planungsinformationen. Regionalausgabe Schwaben **4415**
0178-1936 iBau Planungsinformationen. Regionalausgabe Berlin **4414**
0178-1944 Praxis Sonderschule†
0178-1987 American Studies **5253**
0178-2010 R F L **3661**
0178-2096 Die Steuer-Warte **7470**
0178-2134 Advances in Immunity and Cancer Therapy†
0178-2142 Internationale Hoelderlin Bibliographie **4232**
0178-2177 Schottische Terrier Gazette†
0178-2312 Automatisierungstechnik **2458**
0178-2320 Automatisierungstechnische Praxis **4486**
0178-2479 Akademische Reden und Kolloquien **2966**
0178-2495 German Maritime Industry Journal†
0178-2509 Wohnbaden **4563**
0178-2525 Rettungsdienst **5703**
0178-2568 Bibliographica Romanica *changed to* Bibliographica et Fundamenta Romanica **5099**
0178-269X C Q - D L **2357**
0178-2762 Biology and Fertility of Soils **221**
0178-2770 Distributed Computing **2417**
0178-2789 The Visual Computer **2490**
0178-2835 Der Siebdruck **7328**
0178-2916 Obstbauversuchsring des Altes Landes. Mitteilungen **244**
0178-2967 Biblische Notizen **7628**
0178-2983 Handball Magazin **8234**
0178-2991 *see* 0172-0171 **2831**
0178-3009 *see* 0172-0171 **2831**
0178-322X T Ue V Journal *changed to* 1863-8198 **8440**
0178-3262 Forschungen und Berichte der Archaeologie des Mittelalters in Baden-Wuerttemberg **394**
0178-3343 D N I *changed to* 1861-9894 **1024**
0178-3521 W W T - Weiterbildung in Wirtschaft und Technik†
0178-3556 Manipulator
0178-3564 Informatik - Forschung und Entwicklung *changed to* 1865-2034 **2526**
0178-3629 Jahrbuch der Religionspaedagogik **7652**
0178-367X Der Waldbesitzer **3707**
0178-3696 Advances in Neurotraumatology†
0178-384X Winckelmann Pelzmarket
0178-4099 Transfer (Wuerzburg)†
0178-4161 Bayerische Blasmusik **6548**
0178-4250 Auszuege aus den Patentschriften **6746**
0178-434X Construction Annual†
0178-4390 Germanisch-Romanische Monatsschrift. Beiheft **5300**
0178-4412 Brossapress **6716**
0178-4528 Bahn-Report **8615**
0178-4617 Algorithmica **2406**
0178-4625 Deutsche Gesellschaft fuer Urologie. Mitteilungen **6267**
0178-4641 Keyboards **6582**
0178-4692 Bodensee Magazin **8688**
0178-4757 Johannes Gutenberg Universitaet Mainz. Forschungsmagazin **7871**
0178-4765 Bio Nachrichten **221**
0178-4781 Cell and Developmental Biology of the Eye†
0178-4811 Auto and Service†
0178-4862 Apotheker-Zeitung **6822**
0178-4978 L R E - Sammlung Lebensmittelrechtlicher Entscheidungen **4711**
0178-5001 Betriebs- und Wirtschaftsinformatik **1413**
0178-5044 Woodworking Review
0178-5052 In Leder†
0178-5109 Grauer Panther **4047**
0178-5125 Cash **1616**
0178-5176 Volkstanz **2688**
0178-5192 Comprehensive Manuals in Pediatrics†
0178-5214 Der Feuerwehrmann **3576**
0178-5354 Communications and Control Engineering Series **3185**
0178-5621 Casebooks in Earth Sciences†
0178-5737 Contraste **1086**
0178-5893 Verkaufsleiter Service **1800**
0178-594X K M I Buerowirtschaft - Lehre und Praxis **1852**
0178-6083 Wir Frauen **8889**
0178-6156 HiFi Vision†
0178-6199 Allgaeuer Geschichtsfreund
0178-6202 Nord-Handwerk. Ausgabe Luebeck **1408**
0178-6210 Nord-Handwerk. Ausgabe Flensburg **1408**
0178-6326 D G L R Bericht **52**
0178-644X Sprachreport **5177**
0178-6563 Forum Wissenschaft **7855**
0178-6571 Stahlmarkt **6332**
0178-658X Agenturen und Marken Adress **20**
0178-6660 Technische Universitaet Muenchen. Vorlesungsverzeichnis **3034**
0178-6717 Deutsche Angestellten Zeitung **1675**
0178-6768 Wissenschaften in der D.D.R.†
0178-6806 D J V - Journal **4574**
0178-6830 Spex **3857**
0178-6849 Sheet Metal Tubes Sections†
0178-6857 Literatur in Bayern **5324**
0178-692X Schmerzdiagnostik und Therapie†
0178-7039 Universitaet Stuttgart. Vorlesungsverzeichnis **2962**
0178-7128 Aufklaerung **4201**
0178-7179 Flora (Hamburg) *changed to* 1610-3157 **3729**
0178-7209 Wirtschafts Kompass
0178-7225 Laser **7079**
0178-7241 Buchjournal **5266**
0178-725X Afrikanistische Arbeitspapiere *changed to* 1613-3730 **5094**
0178-7284 Journal fuer die Frau†
0178-7349 Funkgeschichte **2381**
0178-7373 Wellensittich Magazin **916**
0178-7438 China-Handel†
0178-7489 Mimesis **5334**
0178-7578 Bulldok - Bauphysik, Waerme†
0178-7586 Hard and Soft
0178-7624 Orthomolekular†
0178-7640 Muenchener Studien zur Literarischen Kultur in Deutschland **5337**
0178-7667 Forum der Psychoanalyse **7357**
0178-7675 Computational Mechanics **5551**
0178-7748 Anubis†
0178-7764 Internationales Sauna - Archiv†
0178-787X Neue Aerztliche†
0178-7888 Mycotoxin Research **3500**
0178-7896 Berliner Gesellschaft fuer Anthropologie, Ethnologie und Urgeschichte. Mitteilungen **330**
0178-8051 Probability Theory and Related Fields **5526**
0178-8116 Angewandte Versicherungsmathematik **4492**
0178-8183 Marktorientierte Unternehmensfuehrung **1147**
0178-8310 Studien zur Modernen Geschichte **4163**
0178-8345 Diagnose und Labor†
0178-837X Der Staudengarten **3751**
0178-8515 Abhandlungen zur Sprache und Literatur **5248**
0178-8558 MediumMagazin **4580**
0178-8612 Nepal Information **557**
0178-8744 Publikationen des Faust-Archivs und der Faust-Gesellschaft†
0178-8876 Aussenwirtschaftsbrief† **8932**
0178-8884 MusikTexte **6597**
0178-8906 Kirchlicher Dienst in der Arbeitswelt *changed to* 1614-4589 **7768**
0178-8930 Recht der Datenverarbeitung **2515**
0178-8965 Deutscher Forschungsdienst Magazin†
0178-9058 Banatica
0178-9090 Infektionen und Klinikhygiene†
0178-9120 Nord-Handwerk. Ausgabe Hamburg **1408**
0178-9163 Rinderproduktion *changed to* 1867-2809 **293**
0178-918X Materialien zur Bevoelkerungswissenschaft **7287**
0178-9279 Basketball News† **8935**
0178-9287 International Listening Guide
0178-9406 Fortschritt-Berichte V D I. Reihe 2: Fertigungstechnik **3367**
0178-9414 Fortschritt-Berichte V D I. Reihe 6: Energieerzeugung **3135**
0178-9422 Fortschritt-Berichte V D I. Reihe 9: Elektronik **3308**
0178-9449 Fortschritt-Berichte V D I. Reihe 12: Verkehrstechnik - Fahrzeugtechnik **8581**
0178-9457 Fortschritt-Berichte V D I. Reihe 18: Mechanik - Bruchmechanik **3378**
0178-9465 Fortschritt-Berichte V D I. Reihe 19: Waermetechnik - Kaeltetechnik **4119**
0178-9473 Fortschritt-Berichte V D I. Reihe 20: Rechnerunterstuetzte Verfahren **3291**
0178-9481 Fortschritt-Berichte V D I. Reihe 21: Elektrotechnik **3308**
0178-949X Fortschritt-Berichte V D I. Reihe 1: Konstruktionstechnik - Maschinenelemente **3267**
0178-9503 Fortschritt-Berichte V D I. Reihe 3: Verfahrenstechnik **3193**
0178-9511 Fortschritt-Berichte V D I. Reihe 4: Bauingenieurwesen **3267**
0178-952X Fortschritt-Berichte V D I. Reihe 5: Grund- und Werkstoffe **3345**
0178-9538 Fortschritt-Berichte V D I. Reihe 7: Stroemungstechnik **3308**
0178-9546 Fortschritt-Berichte V D I. Reihe 8: Mess-, Steuerungs- und Regelungstechnik **3367**
0178-9554 Fortschritt-Berichte V D I. Reihe 11: Schwingungstechnik **3345**
0178-9562 Fortschritt-Berichte V D I. Reihe 13: Foerdertechnik **3378**
0178-9570 Fortschritt-Berichte V D I. Reihe 14: Landtechnik - Lebensmitteltechnik **3643**
0178-9589 Fortschritt-Berichte V D I. Reihe 15: Umwelttechnik **3432**
0178-9597 Fortschritt-Berichte V D I. Reihe 16: Technik und Wirtschaft **3192**
0178-9627 Fortschritt-Berichte V D I. Reihe 10: Informatik - Kommunikationstechnik **2470**
0178-9643 Auto Motor und Sport Testjahrbuch **8559**
0178-9813 Versicherungs Betriebswirt **4527**
0178-983X Der Tankstellenberater **8606**
0178-9945 Swingtrend **1654**
0178-9953 Der Punkt†
0178-9988 Buskursbuch†
0179-0048 Kiels Feine Adressen†
0179-0102 Missionsblaetter **7807**
0179-0145 Giessener Schriften zur Agrar- und Ernaehrungswirtschaft **115**
0179-0153 T U S Info **8211**
0179-0161 Steuer Aktuell **1945**
0179-017X D N R - Kurier†
0179-0269 Informationsdienst F I Z Technik. Alternative Energien **3153**
0179-0307 Computational Microelectronics **3091**
0179-0315 Beto†
0179-0358 Pediatric Surgery International **6255**
0179-0374 Applied Agricultural Research†
0179-0382 MiniMicro Magazin†
0179-0404 Medizin Heute† **8973**
0179-0498 B F H - N V **7422**
0179-051X Dysphagia **6079**
0179-0579 Strick und Schick†
0179-0595 P T B-Bericht. Mechanik und Akustik **7062**
0179-0668 Frankfurter Beitraege zur Geschichte, Theorie und Ethik der Medizin **5616**
0179-0676 Konzepte **5318**
0179-0749 Forschungsberichte zur Oekonomie im Gartenbau **1111**
0179-0765 F H - Report†
0179-079X R W T H - Themen **7901**
0179-0811 Informationsdienst F I Z Technik. Regelungstechnik† **8964**
0179-0900 Ausgaben Deutscher Literatur des XV. bis XVIII. Jahrhunderts **5258**
0179-0986 De Gruyter Studies in Mathematics **5482**
0179-1109 Universitaet Passau. Vorlesungsverzeichnis **2306**
0179-1281 Vivarium, Darmstadts Tiergarten†
0179-1389 Anglistische Forschungen **5254**
0179-1419 Berg (Year) **8305**
0179-146X Deutsche Gesellschaft fuer Volkstanz. Schriftenreihe **2685**
0179-1583 Erweckliche Stimme **7756**
0179-1591 Schloss & Beschlag-Markt **1055**
0179-1605 Gesellschaft, Recht, Wirtschaft†
0179-1613 Ethology **942**
0179-1621 Mediterranean Language and Culture Monograph Series **555**
0179-163X Erinnyen **6916**
0179-1826 Medical Corps International **5667**
0179-1834 Goeppinger Arbeiten zur Germanistik **5301**
0179-1842 Ludwigsburger Geschichtsblaetter **4241**
0179-1869 Hoeruebersicht International† **8962**
0179-1958 International Journal of Colorectal Disease **6246**
0179-1990 Computer und Recht **2492**
0179-2075 Strahlenschutzkommission. Veroeffentlichungen **3174**

ISSN

DIRECTORY 2010 0187-4233 9179

0184-0266 Memoires de Biospeologie *changed to* Subterranean Biology **706**
0184-041X Annuaire de l'Education Permanente *changed to* 0245-0712
0184-0584 Journal du Travail Temporaire et des Services†
0184-1025 Cahiers Charles V **5103**
0184-1068 Documents d'Archeologie Meridionale **390**
0184-1238 Le Cycle **8256**
0184-2595 Montagnes Magazine **8322**
0184-3400 Annuaire des Hypermarches†
0184-4067 Technica **1182**
0184-5691 Guide International de l'Energie Nucleaire†
0184-6469 France. Caisse Nationale des Allocations Familiales. Statistiques Prestations de Logement†
0184-6655 Bleu et Rouge†
0184-6949 L'Annee Philologique **2242**
0184-7155 Collection des Universites de France **2233**
0184-7414 Progres de la Gendarmerie†
0184-7457 Universite de Grenoble III. Institut de Phonetique. Bulletin†
0184-7473 Combat Nature†
0184-7503 Connaissance des Ceramiques†
0184-7570 Les Langues Neo-latines **5142**
0184-7589 Geographie et Recherche†
0184-7678 Cahiers Elisabethains†
0184-7732 Le Francais Aujourd'hui **5120**
0184-7783 Population et Societes **7290**
0184-7899 Universite de Poitiers. Centre d'Etudes Superieures de Civilisation Medievale. Publications **4165**
0184-8100 Jalons **5424**
0184-8127 Bridgerama **8163**
0184-8550 Paysan du Haut-Rhin **146**
0184-8895 Banc-Titre - Animation Stand†
0184-9336 Le Figaro Magazine **3840**
0184-9646 S F E N. Bulletin de Liaison *changed to* 1620-9583 **3174**
0184-9662 Agri-Afrique†
0184-9697 Equip-Afric†
0184-9719 Banque Afrique **1553**
0184-9832 Nous **2640**
0185-0008 Ciencia y Desarrollo **7847**
0185-0059 Instituto de Investigaciones Electricas. Boletin **3319**
0185-0067 Universidad Nacional Autonoma de Mexico. Instituto de Investigaciones Bibliografica. Instrumenta Bibliographica **5052**
0185-0083 Bibliotecas y Archivos†
0185-0105 C B†
0185-0113 Dialogos†
0185-0121 Nueva Revista de Filologia Hispanica **5156**
0185-013X Foro Internacional **7236**
0185-0164 Estudios de Asia y Africa **549**
0185-0172 Historia Mexicana **4295**
0185-027X Cuadernos Politicos†
0185-0326 Biotica†
0185-0334 Ciencia Pesquera **3589**
0185-0350 Estados Unidos: Perspectiva Latinoamericana. Cuadernos Semestrales†
0185-0377 Asociacion de Bibliotecarios de Instituciones de Ensenanza Superior e Investigacion. Boletin **4991**
0185-0458 Economia Mexicana **1098**
0185-0504 Economia de America Latina†
0185-0539 El Colegio Nacional. Memoria **7955**
0185-0547 Educacion **2845**
0185-058X Mexico Indigena†
0185-0601 Comercio Exterior **1556**
0185-0636 Nueva Antropologia **350**
0185-0644 Universidad Nacional Autonoma de Mexico. Instituto de Matematicas. Anales **5543**
0185-0695 Semana Medica de Mexico†
0185-075X Ciencia. Academia Mexicana de Ciencias *changed to* 1405-6550 **7846**
0185-0784 Siempre! **5239**
0185-0814 Relaciones Internacionales **7262**
0185-0830 Texto Critico **5387**
0185-0849 Economia Informa **1098**
0185-092X Ingenieria Sismica **2710**
0185-0946 Instituto Politecnico Nacional. Escuela Nacional de Ciencias Biologicas. Anales **678**
0185-0970 Enfermera al Dia†
0185-0989 Tlalocan **358**
0185-0997 Instituto Politecnico Nacional. Escuela Nacional de Ciencias Biologicas. Boletin Bibliografico†
0185-1004 Periodica. Indice de Revistas Latinoamericanas en Ciencias **7938**
0185-1063 Revista Medica del Hospital General de Mexico S.S.A. **5706**
0185-1098 Banco de Mexico. Informe Anual **1312**
0185-1101 Revista Mexicana de Astronomia y Astrofisica **580**
0185-1136 Monetaria **1367**
0185-1160 J A M A en Mexico†
0185-1179 America Indigena **323**
0185-1217 J A M A en Centroamerica†
0185-1225 Anales de Antropologia **324**
0185-125X K I N A M†
0185-1268 Mercado de Valores **1638**
0185-1276 Instituto de Investigaciones Esteticas. Anales **496**
0185-1284 Revista Latinoamericana de Estudios Educativos **2907**
0185-1314 Geomimet **6463**
0185-1322 Universidad Nacional Autonoma de Mexico. Anuario de Geografia **4032**
0185-1330 Universidad de Mexico **2922**
0185-1357 Naturaleza†
0185-1373 Anuario de Letras **5255**
0185-1411 Avance y Perspectiva **7838**
0185-1535 Nexos **7989**
0185-1586 Vuelta†
0185-1594 Ensenanza e Investigacion en Psicologia **7354**
0185-1616 Estudios Politicos **7133**
0185-1632 Proceso **3910**
0185-1659 Cuicuilco **334**
0185-1667 Investigacion Economica **1543**
0185-1675 Mexico. Comision Nacional Bancaria. Boletin Estadistico **1367**
0185-1691 Cuadernos de Historia del Arte **484**
0185-1780 Construccion Mexicana
0185-1799 Universidad Nacional Autonoma de Mexico. Instituto de Investigaciones Esteticas. Monografias de Arte **523**
0185-1810 Universidad Nacional Autonoma de Mexico. Facultad de Derecho de Mexico. Revista **4802**
0185-1845 Estudios y Fuentes del Arte en Mexico **488**
0185-1861 Revista Interamericana de Planificacion
0185-1896 Cuadernos de Musica **6560**
0185-1918 Revista Mexicana de Ciencias Politicas y Sociales **7179**
0185-1926 Mexico. Archivo General de la Nacion. Boletin **4303**
0185-1934 Compendium de Investigaciones Clinicas Latinoamericanas†
0185-1969 Vision (New York)
0185-1985 Decision **1401**
0185-2000 Biologia†
0185-2027 Boletin Bibliografico Mexicano **7577**
0185-2108 Investigacion Medica Internacional **5641**
0185-2140 Hombre y Trabajo†
0185-2175 Controversia
0185-2248 Nuestra America†
0185-2302 Mundo Medico
0185-2353 Condiciones de Trabajo
0185-2426 Caribe Contemporaneo†
0185-2450 Dianoia **6914**
0185-2477 El Cuento **3908**
0185-2493 C N I D A Informa **7557**
0185-2523 Estudios de Historia Novohispana **4292**
0185-2558 Universidad Nacional Autonoma de Mexico. Instituto de Investigaciones Filosoficas. Cuadernos†
0185-2574 Estudios de Cultura Maya **4292**
0185-2604 Cuadernos de Critica†
0185-2620 Estudios de Historia Moderna y Contemporanea de Mexico **4292**
0185-2647 Estudios de Linguistica Applicada **5116**
0185-2698 Perfiles Educativos **2897**
0185-2728 Expansion **1885**
0185-2752 Universidad de Guadalajara. Instituto de Astronomia y Meteorologia. Boletin Informativo Mensual **583**
0185-2760 Revista de la Educacion Superior **3000**
0185-2779 Union de Universidades de America Latina. Gaceta **3006**
0185-2876 Historia Obrera†
0185-2884 Bibliografia Latinoamericana **617**
0185-2930 Bibliografia Latinoamericana: Part II†
0185-3058 Nova Tellus **4467**
0185-3082 Acta Poetica **5415**
0185-3198 Asociacion Latinoamericana de Psicologia Social. Revista†
0185-3252 Anales Medicos **5574**
0185-3279 U N A M. Instituto de Ciencias del Mar y Limnologia. Publicaciones Especiales *see* 0185-3287 **2819**
0185-3287 U N A M. Instituto de Ciencias del Mar y Limnologia. Anales **2819**
0185-3295 Anuario Juridico **4619**
0185-3309 Revista Mexicana de Fitopatologia **250**
0185-3325 Salud Mental **6183**
0185-3481 Revista de Filosofia **6948**
0185-3597 Docencia Postsecundaria **2978**
0185-3872 Didac **2977**
0185-3880 Ciencias Marinas **2802**
0185-3899 Ingenieria Petrolera **6773**
0185-3929 Relaciones (Zamora) **4310**
0185-3937 Analisis Economico **1436**
0185-4003 Sociedad Mexicana de Mecanica de Suelos. Boletin **3283**
0185-4011 Nabor Carrillo Lecture Series. Proceedings **3279**
0185-402X Mexican Society for Soil Mechanics Meeting. Proceedings **3278**
0185-4038 Dermatologia **5874**
0185-4143 Los Universitarios **3007**
0185-4186 Estudios Sociologicos **8100**
0185-4259 Iztapalapa **7976**
0185-4305 Patologia **697**
0185-4399 Informe†
0185-4534 Revista Mexicana de Analisis de la Conducta **7404**
0185-464X Obras **1028**
0185-4658 Energeticos†
0185-4666 Fem **8862**
0185-4925 Plural **5352**
0185-4968 Nacional Financiera. Annual Report **1369**
0185-5093 Quipu†
0185-5107 Sociedad Latinoamericana de Historia de la Ciencia y la Tecnologia. Boletin Informativo **7917**
0185-5131 Cuadernos de Arquitectura Mesoamericana **439**
0185-5271 Estudios de Caso. Serie Estados Unidos **1484**
0185-5530 Universidad Nacional Autonoma de Mexico. Instituto de Geologia. Boletin **2772**
0185-5727 La Palabra y el Hombre **4468**
0185-5751 Bioquimia **2051**
0185-5905 Practica Odontologica†
0185-6014 Revista Mexicana de Patologia Clinica **5706**
0185-6022 Revista Mexicana de Politica Exterior **7262**
0185-6073 Revista Mexicana de Psicologia **7405**
0185-6200 Mathesis **5517**
0185-6235 Atencion Medica **5580**
0185-6278 Indian News from the Americas†
0185-6286 T R A C E **357**
0185-6391 Estrategia†
0185-6480 Voz Informativa **6744**
0185-6588 Perfumeria Moderna **596**
0185-6596 Jueves de Excelsior **3909**
0185-6944 Analisis de la Agricultura Sinaloense **193**
0185-7126 Anuario Estadistico de los Estados Unidos Mexicanos **8345**
0185-7282 Panorama Medico
0185-7444 Universidad Nacional Autonoma de Mexico. Instituto de Geografia. Serie Varia **4032**
0185-7770 Dialectica **7959**
0185-8114 Comunidad Informatica **2443**
0185-822X Cuadernos de Comunicacion†
0185-8572 Cuadernos de Arquitectura Virreinal **439**
0185-8599 Gaceta Mexicana de Administracion Publica Estatal y Municipal **7438**
0185-9099 Directorio M P M - Medios Audio-visuales **38**
0185-9439 Textual **8143**
0185-9641 Contactos Extraterrestres†
0186-0186 Clinicas Odontologicas de Norteamerica
0186-0194 Clinicas Medicas de Norteamerica
0186-0216 Clinicas Quirurgicas de Norteamerica
0186-0224 Clinicas Cardiologicas de Norteamerica
0186-0348 Secuencia **4312**
0186-0437 Instituto Nacional de Estadistica, Geografia e Informatica. Catalogo de Publicaciones **8379**
0186-0445 Cuaderno de Informacion Oportuna **1476**
0186-0453 Agenda Estadistica **8343**
0186-0461 Boletin de Politica Informatica **7110**
0186-047X Cuaderno de Informacion Oportuna Regional **1476**
0186-0488 Mexico. Instituto Nacional de Estadistica, Geografia e Informatica. Encuesta Industrial Mensual **1252**
0186-0496 Comercio Exterior de Mexico. Informacion Preliminar **1221**
0186-050X Sector Electrico en Mexico **3161**
0186-0526 Anuario de Letras Modernas **5255**
0186-1042 Contaduria y Administracion **1285**
0186-1077 Higiene y Seguridad **5815**
0186-1166 Muebletecnic†
0186-1336 Chilango **3908**
0186-1395 Memoria **7154**
0186-159X Clinicas Pediatricas de Norteamerica **6090**
0186-176X E N P Gaceta **2978**
0186-1840 El Cotidiano **3908**
0186-2146 Opcion **4468**
0186-2243 Libros de Mexico **7566**
0186-2391 Acta Pediatrica de Mexico **6087**
0186-2707 Mexico. Instituto Nacional de Estadistica, Geografia e Informatica. Revista de Estadistica **8388**
0186-2766 Panorama (La Paz) **2997**
0186-2774 Panorama. Suplemento *see* 0186-2766 **2997**
0186-2863 U N A M Gaceta **3006**
0186-2901 Momento Economico **1149**
0186-2979 Universidad y Ciencia **7926**
0186-2987 Universidad Nacional Autonoma de Mexico. Facultad de Medicina. Gaceta **5726**
0186-3266 Instituto Mexicano del Petroleo. Boletin Informativo†
0186-3274 Cuadernos de Nutricion **6657**
0186-3401 Pemex. Boletin Bibliografico **6801**
0186-3924 Colegio de Mexico. Boletin Editorial **5275**
0186-4076 Ingenieria Hidraulica en Mexico **3362**
0186-422X Buenhogar **4353**
0186-4262 Contaduria Publica
0186-4386 Pesca Marina y el Barco Pesquero **3604**
0186-4394 Revista de Geografia Agricola **151**
0186-4742 Omnia **2996**
0186-484X Matematicas y Ensenanza†
0186-4866 Medicina Interna de Mexico **5947**
0186-4963 Renglones **7995**
0186-5609 Management Today **1777**
0186-5730 Tiempos de Ciencia **7923**
0186-5757 El Correo Fronterizo†
0186-5897 Geotermia **3162**
0186-6028 Acta Sociologica **8085**
0186-6036 Tecnologia, Ciencia, Educacion **7922**
0186-6486 Empresa Publica†
0186-7067 Infame Turba†
0186-7180 Universidad Autonoma de Yucatan. Revista **4479**
0186-7210 Estudios Demograficos y Urbanos **7283**
0186-7229 Centro de Estudios Monetarios Latinoamericanos. Boletin Bimensual **1326**
0186-7377 Prometeo (Guadalajara)†
0186-7687 Funcion **5121**
0186-7792 Directorio M P M - Medios Impresos **38**
0186-8470 Economia Nacional **1098**
0186-8543 Ferrocarriles Mexicanos **8617**
0186-8985 Instituto de Seguridad y Servicios Sociales de los Trabajadores al Servicio del Estado. Revista Medica **5636**
0186-9027 Boletin de Informacion Oportuna del Sector Alimentario **3669**
0186-9035 Encuesta Trimestral sobre la Industria de la Construccion **1046**
0186-9345 Cuadernos de Psicoanalisis **7350**
0186-9418 Voices of Mexico **4033**
0186-9787 Antropologia y Tecnica **328**
0187-0173 Sociologica **8136**
0187-0203 Universidad Nacional Autonoma de Mexico. Instituto de Investigaciones Juridicas. Cuadernos†
0187-022X Sociedad Mexicana de Lepidopterologia. Revista **859**
0187-0785 Tecnologia y Comunicacion Educativas **8443**
0187-1447 Instituto de Seguridad y Servicios Sociales de los Trabajadores al Servicio del Estado. Boletin Medico **5636**
0187-1455 Business Mexico†
0187-1552 Militancia: Temas del Socialismo
0187-1560 Mexico Desconocido **8733**
0187-1811 Estudios Latinoamericanos **4451**
0187-182X Historicas **4296**
0187-2818 Asociacion de Bibliotecarios de Instituciones de Ensenanza Superior e Investigacion. Cuadernos†
0187-3148 Salud Problema **5708**
0187-3180 Revista Mexicana de Micologia **815**
0187-3229 Mexico. Centro de Informacion Tecnica y Documentacion. Indice de Revistas. Seccion de Humanidades y Ciencias Sociales†
0187-3407 Review of the Economic Situation of Mexico *see* 0014-3960 **1485**
0187-3474 Industri-Noticias
0187-358X Investigacion Bibliotecologica **5019**
0187-3601 Banmar **1065**
0187-3962 Sonido†
0187-4160 Tramoya **8483**
0187-4233 Natura†

ISSN

DIRECTORY 2010 0191-3034 9181

0189-336X Nigeria. National Integrated Survey of Households. Report on National Consumer Survey **1255**
0189-3556 Times International **3921**
0189-3963 Headlines **3920**
0189-4242 Lagos State Today
0189-4412 Nigerian Library and Information Science Review **5036**
0189-5001 Nigerian Journal of International Studies†
0189-5036 Nigerian Business Journal **1407**
0189-5117 Tropical Journal of Obstetrics and Gynaecology **6005**
0189-6016 African Journal of Traditional, Complementary and Alternative Medicines **5570**
0189-6067 Social Statistics in Nigeria **8021**
0189-6652 Journal of English Studies **5133**
0189-6709 African Journal of Academic Librarianship **4987**
0189-6725 African Journal of Paediatric Surgery **6087**
0189-8000 Food Security **3642**
0189-8442 Journal of Pharmacy and Bioresources **6856**
0189-8671 Nigerian Journal of Social Science Research Abstracts **8021**
0189-8892 Newswatch **3920**
0189-8965 Nigerian Mathematical Society. Journal **5520**
0189-9007 Nigerian Society of Engineers. Special Publications - Conference Proceedings **3212**
0189-9171 Nigerian Journal of Ophthalmology **6046**
0189-9228 Fun Times **3920**
0189-9686 Nigerian Journal of Genetics **876**
0190-0005 City Hall Digest†
0190-0013 Philosophy and Literature **6942**
0190-0218 Advances in Inorganic Biochemistry†
0190-0226 Boarding Kennel Proprietor†
0190-0234 Inklings†
0190-0242 Children's Rights Report†
0190-0277 8th District Dental Society. Bulletin **5842**
0190-0331 Allied Health and Behavioral Sciences†
0190-051X Medicine (New York)
0190-0528 Rangelands **297**
0190-0536 Philosophical Investigations **6940**
0190-0692 International Journal of Public Administration **7447**
0190-0943 I T E M *changed to* Interference Technology **3319**
0190-0951 Biomedical Engineering and Health Systems†
0190-096X Chemistry of Organometallic Compounds†
0190-0978 Clinical Monographs in Obstetrics and Gynecology†
0190-1052 American Society for Engineering Education. Annual Conference Proceedings **3181**
0190-1079 Comparative Studies in Behavioral Science: A Wiley Series†
0190-1087 Real Estate for Professional Practitioners†
0190-1133 Survey of Retirement, Thrift and Profit Sharing Plans Covering Salaried Employees of the 50 Largest U. S. Industrial Companies
0190-1141 U.S. Department of Energy. Fossil Energy Research and Development Program†
0190-1168 New Spirit†
0190-1176 Paideia (Buffalo)†
0190-1192 Community Association Law Reporter **4407**
0190-1222 Society of General Physiologists. Distinguished Lecture Series†
0190-1249 Sports Afield Outdoor Almanac†
0190-1281 Research in Economic Anthropology **353**
0190-1370 Electrical Apparatus **3302**
0190-1397 Forge
0190-1400 Photoletter **6975**
0190-1486 Current Topics in Hematology†
0190-1559 Banjo Newsletter **6547**
0190-1567 Free Stock Photography Directory†
0190-1648 New York (State). Department of Health. Monograph†
0190-1737 Street Magazine†
0190-1788 Poetry in Motion†
0190-1796 Professional Women and Minorities **6702**
0190-1818 Journal of Homeopathic Practice
0190-1850 Denver Museum of Natural History. Annual Report **7850**
0190-1974 Learning Resources (Washington)†
0190-1982 C B S News Review
0190-1990 The New York Times Current Events Edition **4154**
0190-2008 Journal of Caribbean Studies **3544**
0190-2075 Speech Communication Association. Directory†
0190-2083 World Financial Markets **1391**
0190-2148 Experimental Lung Research **6214**
0190-2156 Annual Review of Birth Defects†
0190-2180 Humanities Report†
0190-2210 State Consumer Action†
0190-2253 Gusto†
0190-227X John Simon Guggenheim Memorial Foundation. Reports of the President and the Treasurer **2988**
0190-2342 Chutzpah
0190-2350 Legal Aspects of Medical Practice†
0190-2369 Modern Chinese Literature **5335**
0190-2377 Tennessee Out-of-Doors†
0190-2407 Studies in the Age of Chaucer **5382**
0190-2458 In Business (Emmaus)† **8963**
0190-2563 Corrections Today **2648**
0190-2571 On the Line (Laurel) **2662**
0190-2709 Special Astrophysical Observatory - North Caucasus. Bulletin†
0190-2717 Crimean Astrophysical Observatory. Bulletin **573**
0190-2725 Social Psychology Quarterly **8134**
0190-2733 The Examiner (Raleigh) **1287**
0190-2741 Co-Op (Ann Arbor)†
0190-2814 Federal Reserve Bank of San Francisco. Annual Report **1342**
0190-2903 Plate Collector
0190-2911 MidAmerica **5333**
0190-292X Policy Studies Journal **7167**
0190-2946 Academe **2965**
0190-2962 U.S. Office of Consumer Affairs. Directory: Federal, State, and Local Government Consumer Offices†
0190-2970 Current Topics in Eye Research†
0190-3012 Northern New England Review **5343**
0190-3039 Alexandria History†
0190-3047 Directory of Manufacturers, State of Hawaii†
0190-3055 Rhode Island Genealogical Register **3780**
0190-3063 Contract Management **1735**
0190-3187 International Family Planning Perspectives *changed to* 1944-0391 **5994**
0190-3195 Perspectivas Internacionales en Planificacion Familiar **6001**
0190-3225 Management Aids for Small Business Annual†
0190-3233 Review (Charlottesville) **5360**
0190-3241 Future Survey *changed to* 1946-7567 **7930**
0190-3268 West Virginia A F L - C I O Observer **4605**
0190-3276 Copley Mail Order Advisor
0190-3284 Zero
0190-3306 Faceplate†
0190-3314 Green Feather
0190-3322 Appalachian Voice **4284**
0190-3330 Thinking **6957**
0190-3349 Food Marketing Industry Speaks *changed to* 1936-3923 **3678**
0190-3357 Foundation Center. Annual Report **8082**
0190-3365 E D I S†
0190-3373 Anthropological Literature **361**
0190-3454 Handbook of Antimicrobial Therapy **5814**
0190-3586 Bostonian Society. Proceedings†
0190-3608 Conser Tables†
0190-3632 The A R R L Repeater Directory **2356**
0190-3640 Sez
0190-3659 Boundary 2 **5265**
0190-3667 Mongolian Studies **556**
0190-3683 Technology Transfer **3469**
0190-373X U.S. Community Services Administration. Annual Report†
0190-3802 High Adventure *changed to* Rangers Now **7740**
0190-3845 Live (Springfield) **7738**
0190-3896 U.S. Administration on Aging. Elderly Population: Estimates by County†
0190-3918 International Conference on Parallel Processing. Proceedings **2467**
0190-406X Museums New York **6532**
0190-4132 International Conference on Lasers. Proceedings (Year) **7077**
0190-4167 Journal of Plant Nutrition **798**
0190-4175 Electric Vehicle Progress *changed to* 1548-7997 **8584**
0190-4183 Practical Parenting†
0190-4205 St. Louis Home - Garden
0190-4280 At Ease **7623**
0190-4507 Boating Product News†
0190-4531 Technical Conference on Artificial Insemination and Reproduction. Proceedings **269**
0190-4566 Youth Leader†
0190-4620 Woman's Touch†
0190-4639 Paraclete†
0190-4655 Cooperative Education Quarterly
0190-4671 Geolinguistics **5121**
0190-4701 Furman Studies **4453**
0190-4744 1262 Banner **4606**
0190-4752 Paragraph†
0190-4817 Advances in Cancer Chemotherapy†
0190-485X Counter Pentagon†
0190-4876 Energy Research Reports†
0190-4906 Black Review
0190-4914 The Business Owner **1958**
0190-4922 Contributions to Music Education **6559**
0190-4930 Plans for the Implementation of the Post-Vietnam Era Veterans' Educational Assistance Act of 1977
0190-4965 Utility Reporter **4604**
0190-4981 Combined Cumulative Index to Pediatrics
0190-5066 Same-Day Surgery **6257**
0190-5074 International Psoriasis Bulletin†
0190-5104 Sage Annual Reviews of Drug and Alcohol Abuse†
0190-5147 American Cancer Society. Annual Report (Online) **6007**
0190-521X Political Science Discussion Papers†
0190-5252 United States Law Week Summary and Analysis **4801**
0190-5279 American Druggist†
0190-535X Oncology Nursing Forum **5976**
0190-5368 Toxicon. Supplement *see* 0041-0101 **6883**
0190-5457 Daily Guideposts **7636**
0190-552X Air Transport **8535**
0190-5554 Toll Reporter
0190-5570 Telescope Making†
0190-5724 Carnivore†
0190-5740 Government Procurement Newsletter†
0190-5805 United States House of Representatives. Committee on Rules. Legislative Calendar **7474**
0190-5821 I L A Newsletter **4928**
0190-5848 Frontiers in Education Conference. Proceedings **3308**
0190-5872 Meeting Site Selector
0190-597X SciQuest†
0190-6011 Journal of Orthopaedic and Sports Physical Therapy **6230**
0190-602X China Facts and Figures Annual **7305**
0190-6097 Wesleyan Christian Advocate **7780**
0190-6135 Hampden-Sydney Poetry Review **5423**
0190-6313 Federal Reserve System. Board of Governors. Annual Report **1486**
0190-6526 Flying Yearbook†
0190-6569 Light' n' Heavy†
0190-6577 Folk Music Magazine
0190-6585 DataWorld
0190-6593 Western New England Law Review **4812**
0190-6615 National Association of Schools of Music. Proceedings of the Annual Meeting **6598**
0190-6623 State Government Research Checklist†
0190-6631 A C H Newsletter **4485**
0190-6682 Poet (Mishawaka)
0190-6690 Official Intermodal Equipment Register **8507**
0190-6739 R V Aftermarket†
0190-678X Format
0190-6798 The Speedy Bee **158**
0190-7034 Boston College Environmental Affairs Law Review **3407**
0190-7077 Bibliography of Agricultural Bibliographies
0190-7107 John O'Hara Journal†
0190-7166 Ad $ Summary **19**
0190-731X The Scriblerian and the Kit-Cats **5368**
0190-7409 Children and Youth Services Review **2148**
0190-745X Bulletin of Bibliography†
0190-7492 Marketing California Ornamental Crops **203**
0190-7522 Tax Guide for College Teachers and Other College Personnel **1947**
0190-7573 Los Angeles Firefighter **4598**
0190-7808 National Waste News†
0190-7891 French 20 Bibliography. Provencal Supplement *see* 0085-0888 **5201**
0190-8049 National Arts Guide†
0190-8189 Folk and Kinfolk of Harris County†
0190-8227 Applewood Journal†
0190-8235 Colorado Labor Advocate **4592**
0190-826X South Carolina Magazine of Ancestral Research **3783**
0190-8375 Reactive Intermediates in Organic Chemistry†
0190-8553 Commercial Kitchen & Institutional Dining Room†
0190-860X U.S. National Geophysical Data Center. Key to Geophysical Records Documentation **2791**
0190-8715 Reports on Research Assisted by the Petroleum Research Fund†
0190-8723 California Native Plant Society. Special Publication **783**
0190-8766 ProFile (Atlanta) **454**
0190-9185 Monitoring the Future **2887**
0190-9215 Carnivorous Plant Newsletter **783**
0190-9320 Political Behavior **7168**
0190-9363 N A G W S Guide. Flag Football, Speedball, Speed-a-Way†
0190-941X C A Selects. Proton Magnetic Resonance **2092**
0190-9428 C A Selects. Infrared Spectroscopy (Organic Aspects) **2087**
0190-9436 C A Selects. Infrared Spectroscopy (Physicochemical Aspects) **7047**
0190-9444 C A Selects. Colloids (Macromolecular Aspects) **2086**
0190-9614 New Jersey Mosquito Control Association. Proceedings. Supplement **243**
0190-9622 American Academy of Dermatology. Journal **5871**
0190-9630 United Way of America. Annual Report **8075**
0190-9703 Advances in the Study of Communication and Affect†
0190-9789 The Green Scene **3734**
0190-9797 U.S. Civil Service Commission. Annual Report†
0190-9819 National Preservation Report†
0190-9835 White Walls **526**
0190-9851 Private Label **1901**
0190-986X Lens' on Campus†
0190-9940 Archaeoastronomy **374**
0191-0051 O'Dwyer's Directory of Public Relations Executives† **8978**
0191-0132 The Asian Wall Street Journal Weekly†
0191-0167 Restoration Witness **7741**
0191-0310 Statistical Abstract of Oklahoma **1267**
0191-0329 Fielding's Favorites: Hotels & Inns, Europe†
0191-0531 U.S. Department of Agriculture. National Agricultural Statistics Service. Farm Production Expenditures **188**
0191-0574 Index to Social Sciences & Humanities Proceedings **8020**
0191-0760 Gravida
0191-0825 National Academy of Design. Annual Exhibition Catalogue **508**
0191-0841 Society of Manufacturing Engineers. Technical Paper EE **3358**
0191-085X Society of Manufacturing Engineers. Technical Paper MF **3358**
0191-0914 Reading Research. Advances in Theory and Practice†
0191-0930 Texas Journal of Political Studies **7188**
0191-0965 Yoga Journal **6648**
0191-1031 Kentucky Review **4461**
0191-104X Illinois Blue Book **7445**
0191-1058 Illinois. State Library, Springfield. Publications of the State of Illinois. **7199**
0191-118X U.S. Chamber of Commerce. Analysis of Workers' Compensation Laws (Year) **1711**
0191-1422 Congressional Yellow Book **7431**
0191-1430 A S A Annual Meeting Papers **3515**
0191-1473 Congressional Roll Call (Year) **7119**
0191-152X O A G Cargo Guide Worldwide **8549**
0191-1554 Performing Woman
0191-1562 Minnesota Statutes **4956**
0191-1600 Developmental Disabilities Abstracts†
0191-1708 Fundamentals of Pure and Applied Economics Series
0191-1716 South Dakota State University. Agricultural Experiment Station. T B **157**
0191-1759 National Health†
0191-183X Florida Business Publications Index
0191-1872 Update in Clinical Dentistry†
0191-1937 Research in Corporate Social Performance and Policy†
0191-1953 Full Blast†
0191-1961 The Missouri Review **5335**
0191-1988 Memory and Learning - Research in the Nervous System†
0191-2208 Expense Analysis: Condominiums, Cooperatives and Planned Unit Developments **7590**
0191-2259 Black Box†
0191-2283 High - Low Report†
0191-2291 Nurses' Drug Alert **5972**
0191-2453 Current Topics in Nutrition and Disease†
0191-247X Contemporary Anesthesia Practice†
0191-250X Current Perspectives in Oncologic Nursing†
0191-2518 Perception and Perceptual Development†
0191-2542 Dental Dimensions **5840**
0191-2615 Transportation Research. Part B: Methodological **8517**
0191-2690 Ballet News†
0191-2704 Fannie Mae Annual Report **7590**
0191-2763 Loss Prevention and Control†
0191-2798 Library and Reference Facilities in the Area of the District of Columbia†
0191-2836 Arthritis Foundation. Annual Report **6222**
0191-2887 Advances in Heterocyclic Chemistry. Supplement†
0191-2917 Plant Disease **247**
0191-2925 Stamp Show News & Philatelic Review†
0191-2933 Plants, Sites & Parks†
0191-2941 Nature and System†
0191-3026 Research in Marketing **1840**
0191-3034 Jewish Civilization: Essays and Studies†

ISSN

0194-8733 Convenience Store News **3677**
0194-8784 N L R B Advice Memorandum Reporter **4737**
0194-8814 Horse & Chariot†
0194-8849 A E A Advocate **2822**
0194-8903 Construction Dimensions Magazine **995**
0194-9039 Flight Reports **8703**
0194-9047 Eagle Leader **2265**
0194-9063 Scientific American Medicine†
0194-9098 Tennis Week **8249**
0194-9101 Mercer Business Magazine **1407**
0194-911X Hypertension **5789**
0194-9144 Fashionews†
0194-9225 News Front Business Trends†
0194-9268 N A H R O Monitor **4420**
0194-9276 Ohio Engineer **3213**
0194-9314 Surfing **8336**
0194-9349 Yesteryear **369**
0194-939X National Bus Trader **8505**
0194-9535 Esquire **6289**
0194-9543 Angus Journal **278**
0194-9756 Dog (Marshall) **6807**
0194-9772 Cotton Grower **225**
0194-9799 The Leaven (Kansas City) **7804**
0194-9802 T P A Messenger *changed to* 1521-7523 **4584**
0194-9888 Choppers & Big Bike Magazine†
0194-9977 Space Gamer†
0194-9993 Atlantic City Magazine **3970**
0195-0002 Mississippi Business Journal **1964**
0195-0061 Urban Concerns
0195-0118 Textile Rental **2250**
0195-0150 N S D C A Times **2687**
0195-0193 Interactions (Dayton) **3013**
0195-0223 Eastern Basketball Magazine†
0195-0290 Law Enforcement Legal Reporter **4714**
0195-0320 B M X Plus **8254**
0195-0347 Aviators Hot Line **49**
0195-0509 Sport Trucking†
0195-0525 Ukrains'ke Pravoslavne Slovo *see* 0147-1015 **7706**
0195-0541 Blind Justice†
0195-0576 Oil Express **6784**
0195-0614 Filtration Engineering Catalog
0195-0673 Washington Agricultural Record **169**
0195-072X Gallery **6291**
0195-0738 Journal of Energy Resources Technology **3140**
0195-0746 Executive Wealth Advisory **1622**
0195-0819 Chicago Apparel News†
0195-0851 Astrology: Your Daily Horoscope
0195-0894 Springfield! Magazine (Springfield, 1979)† **8990**
0195-0908 B A S Speaker **8152**
0195-0924 Organic Consumer Report†
0195-0932 Abrasive Technology *changed to* Abrasive Engineering Society Magazine
0195-0983 New Jersey Lawyer Magazine (New Brunswick) **4743**
0195-1009 Communique (Dallas)†
0195-105X Members Calendar **6529**
0195-1165 Iron Horse†
0195-1238 Estate Planning & Taxation Coordinator **4902**
0195-1246 Business Farmer **98**
0195-1297 Gospel Advocate **7645**
0195-1335 Pura Verdad†
0195-1351 Biblical Illustrator **7748**
0195-136X Baptist Young Adults†
0195-1467 Military Modeler†
0195-1513 N F I B **1964**
0195-1521 New York Teacher **4599**
0195-153X S N E A Impact: The Student Voice of the United Teaching Profession†
0195-1548 Pulpit Resource **7672**
0195-1564 N A D A's Automotive Executive **8594**
0195-1599 New Gun Week **8190**
0195-1653 North Shore **3983**
0195-1661 Corvette Fever **8576**
0195-1688 Women's Political Times
0195-1696 Obscenity Law Bulletin **4896**
0195-1785 Solar Law Reporter†
0195-1793 Minnesota (St. Paul)†
0195-1858 Insurance Litigation Reporter **4693**
0195-1874 Home Energy Digest & Wood Burning Quarterly†
0195-1920 Phalanx **6441**
0195-2056 AsianWeek **3520**
0195-2099 Illinois Pharmacist **6847**
0195-2137 Teens' and Boys' Magazine†
0195-2250 Global Communications†
0195-2293 E P V A Monthly Report **4065**
0195-2358 Informer (Washington)†
0195-2366 Material Handling Product News **2462**
0195-2390 Equal Employment News
0195-2420 Visit U S A Guide
0195-2552 Yankee Food Service **4400**
0195-2617 Federal Grants Management Handbook **1745**
0195-2633 British Heritage **4206**
0195-265X Christian Crusade **7631**
0195-2692 Lost Treasure **4338**
0195-282X Carolina Lifestyle†
0195-2986 A A P G Explorer **6761**
0195-3036 Cosmetic Technology†
0195-3052 San Francisco Business Journal†
0195-3095 Economic Week†
0195-3117 True Story **5412**
0195-315X Internal Medicine Alert **5945**
0195-3184 Home Textiles Today **8451**
0195-3192 New Jersey Reporter **3983**
0195-3303 American Book Trade Directory. Updating Service *see* 0065-759X **7551**
0195-3346 F C X Carolina Cooperator†
0195-3354 Nursing Abstracts†
0195-3370 Technology Tomorrow†
0195-3389 Education Tomorrow†
0195-3397 Business Tomorrow†
0195-3443 Maryland Documents **7481**
0195-3451 Leavenworth Papers **6431**
0195-346X B U C New Boat Price Guide†
0195-3478 Inside Sports†
0195-3508 Channel (Los Angeles)†
0195-3516 Exit **5294**
0195-3524 Oil Spill Intelligence Report **3490**
0195-3567 Computer Law Bibliography†
0195-3591 C F T C Databook†
0195-3613 Journal of Labor Research **1691**
0195-363X A L L-O-Grams
0195-3664 Civil Engineering Series **3263**
0195-3729 Giustizia†
0195-377X L A C U S Forum **5138**
0195-3842 Current Clinical Topics in Infectious Diseases **5812**
0195-3869 H R A F Newsletter†
0195-3966 M M I Press Symposium Series
0195-3974 World Trade & Business Digest†
0195-3982 Griffith Observer **575**
0195-3990 College and University Administrators Directory†
0195-4016 Finger Lakes Library System. Newsletter **5009**
0195-4040 Joel Whitburn's Top Pop Singles **6580**
0195-4091 High Technology
0195-4121 County Lines **5069**
0195-4148 Art Criticism **469**
0195-4156 Careers (Saratoga)
0195-4202 Oxbridge Directory of Ethnic Periodicals†
0195-4288 Society of Plastics Engineers. Monographs **7100**
0195-4482 Disability Newsletter **4501**
0195-4490 Daily Traffic World
0195-4555 Marine Fish Management
0195-4563 Lundberg Letter **6800**
0195-4636 The Workbook†
0195-4644 West Virginia Business Index **1193**
0195-4695 Urban Transport News *changed to* 0275-3758 **8627**
0195-4741 Arms Control Impact Statements **7221**
0195-475X Journal of Mayan Linguistics **5134**
0195-4784 Annual Editions: Readings in Management *changed to* 1092-4876 **1725**
0195-4857 Technical Services Law Librarian **5050**
0195-4903 Center for Southern Folklore Magazine†
0195-4911 C A Selects. Atomic Spectroscopy **7047**
0195-4938 C A Selects. Chemical Instrumentation **4490**
0195-4946 C A Selects. Chemical Processing Apparatus **3237**
0195-4970 C A Selects. Emulsion Polymerization **2087**
0195-4989 C A Selects. Fluidized Solids Technology **2087**
0195-4997 C A Selects. Fuel & Lubricant Additives **2087**
0195-5012 C A Selects. Inorganic & Organometallic Reaction Mechanisms **2088**
0195-5020 C A Selects. Ion-Containing Polymers **2088**
0195-5039 C A Selects. Laser Applications **2088**
0195-5063 C A Selects. Optical and Photosensitive Materials **7048**
0195-5071 C A Selects. Optimization of Organic Reactions **2089**
0195-508X C A Selects. Organic Stereochemistry **2089**
0195-5101 C A Selects. Organotin Chemistry **2089**
0195-511X C A Selects. Plastic Films **7100**
0195-5128 C A Selects. Polymer Morphology **2091**
0195-5136 C A Selects. Porphyrins **2091**
0195-5152 C A Selects. Surface Analysis **2092**
0195-5160 C A Selects. Synfuels **2092**
0195-5179 C A Selects. Synthetic Macrocyclic Compounds **2092**
0195-5187 C A Selects. Thermal Analysis **2092**
0195-5209 C A Selects. Ultraviolet & Visible Spectroscopy†
0195-5233 Washington Action Reporter†
0195-5314 Pennmarva†
0195-5330 Federal Election Campaign Financing Guide **1341**
0195-5349 Enlisted Times
0195-5365 Science Fiction Chronicle *changed to* 1552-9983 **5440**
0195-5373 Atomic Spectroscopy **2098**
0195-539X Who's Who in California Business and Finance†
0195-5594 Genesis of Behavior†
0195-5616 Veterinary Clinics of North America: Small Animal Practice **8812**
0195-5632 Army Motors **4327**
0195-5705 Focus (Madison) **8040**
0195-5756 Annual Institute on Securities Regulation **1308**
0195-5764 Landscape Architecture Technical Information Series†
0195-5780 Plate World†
0195-5799 Piegan Storyteller†
0195-5802 Music Psychology Index†
0195-5810 Massachusetts Directory of Manufacturers **2015**
0195-5861 Forestry Research West†
0195-5888 Constitution, Jefferson's Manual, and Rules of the House of Representatives of the United States **4847**
0195-590X Canadian Oil Industry Directory†
0195-5926 Pediatric Social Work†
0195-5934 Prime Times Magazine (Madison)†
0195-5977 Journal of Holistic Medicine†
0195-6000 Journal of Public and International Affairs†
0195-6051 Journal of Popular Film and Television **6505**
0195-6086 Symbolic Interaction **8008**
0195-6108 American Journal of Neuroradiology **6192**
0195-6124 Outdoor Writers Association of America. Directory **4581**
0195-6159 Missouri Economic Indicators **1499**
0195-6167 Music Theory Spectrum **6592**
0195-6175 California Political Week **7112**
0195-6183 Woman Poet **5438**
0195-6191 Mean Mountain Music†
0195-623X International Symposium on Multiple-Valued Logic **2472**
0195-6310 Comparative Social Research **8095**
0195-6337 Archaeological Society of New Jersey. Newsletter **376**
0195-6442 Index to the Chicago Sun-Times†
0195-6450 Defense Monitor **6419**
0195-6515 Pacific Fishing **3604**
0195-6574 The Energy Journal **3132**
0195-6612 Communications and Information Handling Equipment & Services: Semi-Annual Directory/Index†
0195-6620 Stanger Report **1653**
0195-6655 Inter-American Music Review **6576**
0195-6663 Appetite **6655**
0195-6671 Cretaceous Research **2705**
0195-668X European Heart Journal **5786**
0195-6698 European Journal of Combinatorics **5487**
0195-6701 Journal of Hospital Infection **5820**
0195-6728 Discotheque Magazine
0195-6744 American Journal of Education **2826**
0195-6752 Journal of Historical Review **4149**
0195-6760 Swim Swim†
0195-6779 Media History Digest†
0195-6876 Engineering Times *changed to* 1930-5745 **3214**
0195-6884 Eton Journal of Real Estate Investment†
0195-6981 Association of Executive Recruiting Consultants. Directory†
0195-7031 C I S Highlights†
0195-7074 Louisiana Contractor *changed to* 1550-2821 **1036**
0195-7163 Arcadia Bibliographica Virorum Eruditorum **615**
0195-7171 Multiple Linear Regression Viewpoints **2888**
0195-7198 Naukove Tovarystvo Imeni Shevchenka. Proceedings of the Section of Chemistry, Biology and Medicine **2074**
0195-7252 International Prisoners Aid Association. Newsletter
0195-7260 Papers in Romance†
0195-7279 Pleasures of Cooking†
0195-7287 E F T Report *changed to* 1558-7398 **1393**
0195-7384 Je Me Souviens **3772**
0195-7449 Research in Race and Ethnic Relations **3561**
0195-749X Federal Regulatory Directory **7135**
0195-7554 International Journal for the Study of Animal Problems†
0195-7597 Journal for Vocational Special Needs Education (Print Edition)†
0195-7627 New Jersey Bell
0195-7643 Whittier Law Review **4814**
0195-7651 Small Business Reporter†
0195-7678 The Comparatist **5276**
0195-7716 Volumes: The Jewish Book Report†
0195-7732 Women & Politics *changed to* 1554-477X **7148**
0195-7740 N C R P Proceedings of the Annual Meeting **7532**
0195-7759 Myra Waldo's Travel Guide to the Orient and Asia
0195-7783 Illinois Government Research†
0195-7791 Social Science Monitor†
0195-7805 Indiana Underwriter†
0195-7813 The Manuscript Society News **5031**
0195-7848 Cumberland Journal†
0195-7910 American Journal of Forensic Medicine and Pathology **5912**
0195-7961 Watch†
0195-7988 Social Planning - Policy & Development Abstracts†
0195-7996 United States Pharmacopeia. National Formulary **6884**
0195-8011 A M S Studies in the Renaissance **5247**
0195-802X Hofstra University Cultural and Intercultural Studies†
0195-8054 Silver and Gold Report†
0195-8100 Sports Literature Index
0195-8127 Journal of Psychiatric Treatment and Evaluation†
0195-8186 Interloop†
0195-8194 Mobility (Washington) **7600**
0195-8208 Art & Antiques **364**
0195-8224 Little Big Horn Associates. Research Review **6635**
0195-8259 Comparative Climatic Data for the United States **6351**
0195-8267 American Classic Screen **6489**
0195-8437 Farm, Ranch & Country Vacations **8703**
0195-8461 Blue Book of Major Home Builders†
0195-847X Gold Book of MultiHousing
0195-8496 Plumbers Ink†
0195-8550 Economic Forum (Salt Lake City)†
0195-8569 Electric Vehicle Council Newsletter†
0195-8631 Health Care Financing Review **5624**
0195-8682 Metas
0195-8690 National Cancer Institute. Annual Report†
0195-8720 S T D Fact Sheet†
0195-8763 Myra Waldo's Travel Guide to Northern Europe
0195-878X Advances in Shock Research†
0195-8895 World Press Review†
0195-8933 Human Sexuality Update†
0195-8941 Hudson Home Products Directory†
0195-895X Best Newspaper Writing **4572**
0195-9034 Yearbook of American and Canadian Churches **7695**
0195-9050 C S A Journal **3524**
0195-9069 Federal Energy Regulatory Commission. Annual Report **3135**
0195-9085 Horizons in Biblical Theology **7648**
0195-9093 U.S. Library of Congress. Name Authorities Cumulative Microform Edition†
0195-9107 Hazardous Materials Management Journal†
0195-9131 Medicine and Science in Sports and Exercise **6231**
0195-9204 Leadership (Washington, 1980) **1772**
0195-9212 Baha'i News†
0195-9255 Environmental Impact Assessment Review **3425**
0195-9271 International Journal of Infrared and Millimeter Waves *changed to* 1866-6892 **7078**
0195-928X International Journal of Thermophysics **7055**
0195-9298 Journal of Nondestructive Evaluation **3350**
0195-9301 International Journal of Policy Analysis and Information Systems†
0195-931X Western Wood Products Association. Statistical Yearbook **3709**
0195-9336 Destination of Shipments of Western Wood Species by State†
0195-9344 Western Wood Products Association. Quarterly Injury & Illness Incidence Report **6691**
0195-9352 New Jersey Directory of Manufacturers **2020**
0195-9425 Journal of Security Administration **2678**
0195-945X American Theatre Annual†
0195-9468 Spenser Studies **5435**
0195-9476 Popular Sports. Soccer Illustrated
0195-9530 Progress in Cardiac Rehabilitation†
0195-962X The Gallup Poll Annual Series **7966**
0195-9646 The Packet **5038**
0195-9700 Education's Federal Funding Alert†
0195-9735 Contest Hotline
0195-9743 Woman in History **8889**
0195-9867 Advances in Parapsychological Research†
0195-9921 New York Arts Journal
0195-9964 Poetry Texas†
0196-0016 F T C Watch **1565**
0196-0024 Myra Waldo's Travel Guide to South America
0196-0075 Library & Archival Security **5026**
0196-0091 E P A Publications Bibliography Quarterly Abstracts Bulletin **3478**

ISSN

0198-084X	Local Climatological Data. Santa Maria, California. Monthly Summary **6384**	
0198-0858	Local Climatological Data. Stockton, California. Monthly Summary **6386**	
0198-0866	Local Climatological Data. Bishop, California. Annual Summary with Comparative Data **6363**	
0198-0874	Local Climatological Data. Blue Canyon, California. Annual Summary with Comparative Data **6364**	
0198-0882	Local Climatological Data. Eureka, California. Annual Summary with Comparative Data **6369**	
0198-0890	Local Climatological Data. Fresno, California. Annual Summary with Comparative Data **6370**	
0198-0904	Local Climatological Data. Long Beach, California. Annual Summary with Comparative Data **6375**	
0198-0912	Local Climatological Data. Los Angeles, California. International Airport. Annual Summary with Comparative Data **6376**	
0198-0920	Local Climatological Data. Los Angeles, California. Civic Center. Annual Summary with Comparative Data **6376**	
0198-0939	Local Climatological Data. Mount Shasta, California. Annual Summary with Comparative Data **6378**	
0198-0947	Local Climatological Data. Oakland, California. Annual Summary with Comparative Data†	
0198-0955	Local Climatological Data. Red Bluff, California. Annual Summary with Comparative Data **6382**	
0198-0963	Local Climatological Data. Sacramento, California. Annual Summary with Comparative Data **6383**	
0198-0971	Local Climatological Data. San Diego, California. Annual Summary with Comparative Data **6384**	
0198-098X	Local Climatological Data. San Francisco, California. International Airport. Annual Summary with Comparative Data. **6384**	
0198-0998	Local Climatological Data. San Francisco, California. Federal Office Building. Annual Summary with Comparative Data. **6384**	
0198-1005	Local Climatological Data. Santa Maria, California. Annual Summary with Comparative Data **6384**	
0198-1013	Local Climatological Data. Stockton, California. Annual Summary with Comparative Data **6386**	
0198-1021	Carta Abierta†	
0198-103X	Advances in the Management of Cardiovascular Disease†	
0198-1056	Cinefex **6493**	
0198-1064	Cinemacabre†	
0198-1080	Purser's Magazine†	
0198-1129	Local Climatological Data. Bridgeport, Connecticut. Annual Summary with Comparative Data **6364**	
0198-1137	Local Climatological Data. Hartford, Connecticut. Annual Summary with Comparative Data **6371**	
0198-1145	Local Climatological Data. Wilmington, Delaware. Annual Summary with Comparative Data **6389**	
0198-1153	Local Climatological Data. Bridgeport, Connecticut. Monthly Summary **6364**	
0198-1161	Local Climatological Data. Hartford, Connecticut. Monthly Summary **6371**	
0198-117X	Local Climatological Data. Wilmington, Delaware. Monthly Summary **6389**	
0198-1188	Local Climatological Data. Washington D.C. National Airport. Monthly Summary **6388**	
0198-1196	Local Climatological Data. Washington, D.C. National Airport. Annual Summary with Comparative Data **6388**	
0198-120X	Local Climatological Data. Washington, D.C. Dulles International Airport. Annual Summary with Comparative Data **6388**	
0198-1218	Local Climatological Data. Apalachicola, Florida. Annual Summary with Comparative Data **6361**	
0198-1226	Local Climatological Data. Daytona Beach, Florida. Annual Summary with Comparative Data **6367**	
0198-1234	Local Climatological Data. Fort Myers, Florida. Annual Summary with Comparative Data **6369**	
0198-1242	Local Climatological Data. Jacksonville, Florida. Annual Summary with Comparative Data **6373**	
0198-1250	Local Climatological Data. Key West, Florida. Annual Summary with Comparative Data **6374**	
0198-1269	Local Climatological Data. Miami, Florida. Annual Summary with Comparative Data **6377**	
0198-1277	Local Climatological Data. Orlando, Florida. Annual Summary with Comparative Data **6380**	
0198-1285	Local Climatological Data. Pensacola, Florida. Annual Summary with Comparative Data **6380**	
0198-1293	Local Climatological Data. Tallahassee, Florida. Annual Summary with Comparative Data **6386**	
0198-1307	Local Climatological Data. Tampa, Florida. Annual Summary with Comparative Data **6386**	
0198-1315	Local Climatological Data. West Palm Beach, Florida. Annual Summary with Comparative Data **6388**	
0198-1323	Local Climatological Data. Washington D.C. Dulles International Airport. Monthly Summary **6388**	
0198-134X	Local Climatological Data. Daytona Beach, Florida. Monthly Summary **6367**	
0198-1358	Local Climatological Data. Fort Myers, Florida. Monthly Summary **6369**	
0198-1366	Local Climatological Data. Jacksonville, Florida. Monthly Summary **6373**	
0198-1374	Local Climatological Data. Key West, Florida. Monthly Summary **6374**	
0198-1382	Local Climatological Data. Miami, Florida. Monthly Summary **6377**	
0198-1390	Local Climatological Data. Orlando, Florida. Monthly Summary	
0198-1404	Local Climatological Data. Pensacola, Florida. Monthly Summary **6380**	
0198-1412	Local Climatological Data. Tallahassee, Florida. Monthly Summary **6386**	
0198-1420	Local Climatological Data. Tampa, Florida. Monthly Summary **6386**	
0198-1439	Local Climatological Data. West Palm Beach, Florida. Monthly Summary **6388**	
0198-1501	Safe Boating†	
0198-1544	Local Climatological Data. Athens, Georgia. Annual Summary with Comparative Data **6361**	

0198-1552	Local Climatological Data. Athens, Georgia. Monthly Summary **6361**
0198-1560	Local Climatological Data. Atlanta, Georgia. Annual Summary with Comparative Data **6361**
0198-1579	Local Climatological Data. Atlanta, Georgia. Monthly Summary **6361**
0198-1587	Local Climatological Data. Augusta, Georgia. Annual Summary with Comparative Data **6362**
0198-1595	Local Climatological Data. Augusta, Georgia. Monthly Summary **6362**
0198-1609	Local Climatological Data. Columbus, Georgia. Annual Summary with Comparative Data **6366**
0198-1617	Local Climatological Data. Columbus, Georgia. Monthly Summary **6366**
0198-1625	Local Climatological Data. Macon, Georgia. Annual Summary with Comparative Data **6376**
0198-1633	Local Climatological Data. Macon, Georgia. Monthly Summary **6376**
0198-1641	Local Climatological Data. Rome, Georgia. Annual Summary with Comparative Data **6383**
0198-1668	Local Climatological Data. Savannah, Georgia. Annual Summary with Comparative Data **6384**
0198-1676	Local Climatological Data. Savannah, Georgia. Monthly Summary **6384**
0198-1684	Local Climatological Data. Hilo, Hawaii. Annual Summary with Comparative Data **6372**
0198-1692	Local Climatological Data. Hilo, Hawaii. Monthly Summary **6372**
0198-1706	Local Climatological Data. Honolulu, Hawaii. Annual Summary with Comparative Data **6372**
0198-1714	Local Climatological Data. Honolulu, Hawaii. Monthly Summary **6372**
0198-1722	Local Climatological Data. Kahului, Hawaii. Annual Summary with Comparative Data **6373**
0198-1730	Local Climatological Data. Kahului, Hawaii. Monthly Summary **6373**
0198-1749	Local Climatological Data. Lihue, Hawaii. Annual Summary with Comparative Data **6375**
0198-1757	Local Climatological Data. Lihue, Hawaii. Monthly Summary **6375**
0198-1765	Local Climatological Data. Boise, Idaho. Annual Summary with Comparative Data **6364**
0198-1773	Local Climatological Data. Boise, Idaho. Monthly Summary **6364**
0198-1781	Local Climatological Data. Lewiston, Idaho. Annual Summary with Comparative Data **6375**
0198-179X	Local Climatological Data. Lewiston, Idaho. Monthly Summary **6375**
0198-1803	Local Climatological Data. Pocatello, Idaho. Annual Summary with Comparative Data **6381**
0198-1811	Local Climatological Data. Pocatello, Idaho. Monthly Summary **6381**
0198-182X	Local Climatological Data. Cairo, Illinois. Annual Summary with Comparative Data **6365**
0198-1846	Local Climatological Data. Chicago, Illinois. O'Hare International Airport. Annual Summary with Comparative Data **6365**
0198-1854	Local Climatological Data. Chicago Illinois O'Hare International Airport. Monthly Summary **6366**
0198-1862	Local Climatological Data. Moline, Illinois. Annual Summary with Comparative Data **6378**
0198-1870	Local Climatological Data. Moline, Illinois. Monthly Summary **6378**
0198-1889	Local Climatological Data. Peoria, Illinois. Annual Summary with Comparative Data **6380**
0198-1897	Local Climatological Data. Peoria, Illinois. Monthly Summary **6380**
0198-1900	Local Climatological Data. Rockford, Illinois. Annual Summary with Comparative Data **6383**
0198-1919	Local Climatological Data. Rockford, Illinois. Monthly Summary **6383**
0198-1927	Local Climatological Data. Springfield, Illinois. Annual Summary with Comparative Data **6385**
0198-1935	Local Climatological Data. Springfield, Illinois. Monthly Summary **6385**
0198-1943	Local Climatological Data. Evansville, Indiana. Annual Summary with Comparative Data **6369**
0198-1951	Local Climatological Data. Evansville, Indiana. Monthly Summary **6369**
0198-196X	Local Climatological Data. Fort Wayne, Indiana. Annual Summary with Comparative Data **6370**
0198-1978	Local Climatological Data. Fort Wayne, Indiana. Monthly Summary **6370**
0198-1986	Local Climatological Data. Indianapolis, Indiana. Annual Summary with Comparative Data **6372**
0198-2001	Local Climatological Data. Indianapolis, Indiana. Monthly Summary **6373**
0198-201X	Local Climatological Data. South Bend, Indiana. Annual Summary with Comparative Data **6385**
0198-2028	Local Climatological Data. South Bend, Indiana. Monthly Summary **6385**
0198-2036	Local Climatological Data. Burlington, Iowa. Annual Summary with Comparative Data **6364**
0198-2052	Local Climatological Data. Des Moines, Iowa. Annual Summary with Comparative Data **6367**
0198-2060	Local Climatological Data. Des Moines, Iowa. Monthly Summary **6368**
0198-2079	Local Climatological Data. Dubuque, Iowa. Annual Summary with Comparative Data **6368**
0198-2087	Local Climatological Data. Dubuque, Iowa. Monthly Summary **6368**
0198-2095	Local Climatological Data. Sioux City, Iowa. Annual Summary with Comparative Data **6385**
0198-2109	Local Climatological Data. Sioux City, Iowa. Monthly Summary **6385**
0198-2117	Local Climatological Data. Waterloo, Iowa. Annual Summary with Comparative Data **6388**
0198-2125	Local Climatological Data. Waterloo, Iowa. Monthly Summary **6388**
0198-2133	Local Climatological Data. Concordia, Kansas. Annual Summary with Comparative Data **6367**

0198-2141	Local Climatological Data. Concordia, Kansas. Monthly Summary
0198-215X	Local Climatological Data. Dodge City, Kansas. Annual Summary with Comparative Data **6368**
0198-2168	Local Climatological Data. Dodge City, Kansas. Monthly Summary **6368**
0198-2176	Local Climatological Data. Goodland, Kansas. Annual Summary with Comparative Data **6370**
0198-2184	Local Climatological Data. Goodland, Kansas. Monthly Summary **6370**
0198-2192	Local Climatological Data. Topeka, Kansas. Annual Summary with Comparative Data **6387**
0198-2206	Local Climatological Data. Topeka, Kansas. Monthly Summary **6387**
0198-2214	Local Climatological Data. Wichita, Kansas. Annual Summary with Comparative Data **6389**
0198-2222	Local Climatological Data. Wichita, Kansas. Monthly Summary **6389**
0198-2230	Local Climatological Data. Lexington, Kentucky. Annual Summary with Comparative Data **6375**
0198-2249	Local Climatological Data. Lexington, Kentucky. Monthly Summary **6375**
0198-2257	Local Climatological Data. Louisville, Kentucky. Annual Summary with Comparative Data **6376**
0198-2265	Local Climatological Data. Louisville, Kentucky. Monthly Summary **6376**
0198-2273	Local Climatological Data. Baton Rouge, Louisiana. Annual Summary with Comparative Data **6362**
0198-2281	Local Climatological Data. Baton Rouge, Louisiana. Monthly Summary **6363**
0198-229X	Local Climatological Data. Lake Charles, Louisiana. Annual Summary with Comparative Data **6374**
0198-2303	Local Climatological Data. Lake Charles, Louisiana. Monthly Summary **6375**
0198-2311	Local Climatological Data. New Orleans, Louisiana. Annual Summary with Comparative Data **6378**
0198-232X	Local Climatological Data. New Orleans, Louisiana. Monthly Summary **6378**
0198-2338	Local Climatological Data. Shreveport, Louisiana. Annual Summary with Comparative Data **6385**
0198-2346	Local Climatological Data. Shreveport, Louisiana. Monthly Summary **6385**
0198-2354	Local Climatological Data. Caribou, Maine. Annual Summary with Comparative Data **6365**
0198-2362	Local Climatological Data. Caribou, Maine. Monthly Summary **6365**
0198-2370	Local Climatological Data. Portland, Maine. Annual Summary with Comparative Data **6381**
0198-2389	Local Climatological Data. Portland, Maine. Monthly Summary **6381**
0198-2397	Local Climatological Data. Baltimore, Maryland. Annual Summary with Comparative Data **6362**
0198-2400	Local Climatological Data. Baltimore, Maryland. Monthly Summary **6362**
0198-2419	Local Climatological Data. Boston, Massachusetts. Annual Summary with Comparative Data **6364**
0198-2427	Local Climatological Data. Boston, Massachusetts. Monthly Summary **6364**
0198-2435	Local Climatological Data. Blue Hill Observatory. Milton, Massachusetts. Annual Summary with Comparative Data **6364**
0198-2443	Local Climatological Data. Blue Hill Observatory, Milton, Massachusetts. Monthly Summary **6364**
0198-2451	Local Climatological Data. Worcester, Massachusetts. Annual Summary with Comparative Data **6389**
0198-246X	Local Climatological Data. Worcester, Massachusetts. Monthly Summary **6390**
0198-2486	Local Climatological Data. Clayton, New Mexico. Monthly Summary **6366**
0198-2494	Local Climatological Data. Alpena, Michigan. Annual Summary with Comparative Data **6361**
0198-2508	Local Climatological Data. Alpena, Michigan. Monthly Summary **6361**
0198-2516	Local Climatological Data. Detroit, Michigan. City Airport. Annual Summary with Comparative Data **6368**
0198-2532	Local Climatological Data. Detroit, Michigan. Metropolitan Airport. Annual Summary with Comparative Data **6368**
0198-2540	Local Climatological Data. Detroit, Michigan. Metropolitan Airport. Monthly Summary **6368**
0198-2559	Local Climatological Data. Flint, Michigan. Annual Summary with Comparative Data **6369**
0198-2567	Local Climatological Data. Flint, Michigan. Monthly Summary **6369**
0198-2575	Local Climatological Data. Grand Rapids, Michigan. Annual Summary with Comparative Data **6371**
0198-2583	Local Climatological Data. Grand Rapids, Michigan. Monthly Summary **6371**
0198-2591	Local Climatological Data. Houghton, Lake, Michigan. Annual Summary with Comparative Data **6372**
0198-2605	Local Climatological Data. Houghton Lake, Michigan. Monthly Summary **6372**
0198-2613	Local Climatological Data. Lansing, Michigan. Annual Summary with Comparative Data **6375**
0198-2621	Local Climatological Data. Lansing, Michigan. Monthly Summary **6375**
0198-2648	Local Climatological Data. Marquette, Michigan. Monthly Summary **6377**
0198-2656	Local Climatological Data. Muskegon, Michigan. Annual Summary with Comparative Data **6378**
0198-2664	Local Climatological Data. Muskegon, Michigan. Monthly Summary **6378**
0198-2672	Local Climatological Data. Sault Ste. Marie, Michigan. Annual Summary with Comparative Data **6384**
0198-2680	Local Climatological Data. Sault Ste. Marie, Michigan. Monthly Summary **6384**
0198-2699	Local Climatological Data. Duluth, Minnesota. Annual Summary with Comparative Data **6368**
0198-2702	Local Climatological Data. Duluth, Minnesota. Monthly Summary **6368**

0198-2710 Local Climatological Data. International Falls, Minnesota. Annual Summary with Comparative Data **6373**

0198-2729 Local Climatological Data. International Falls, Minnesota. Monthly Summary **6373**

0198-2737 Local Climatological Data. Minneapolis-St. Paul, Minnesota. Annual Summary with Comparative Data

0198-2745 Local Climatological Data. Minneapolis-St. Paul, Minnesota. Monthly Summary **6378**

0198-2753 Local Climatological Data. Rochester, Minnesota. Annual Summary with Comparative Data **6382**

0198-2761 Local Climatological Data. Rochester, Minnesota. Monthly Summary **6382**

0198-277X Local Climatological Data. Saint Cloud, Minnesota. Annual Summary with Comparative Data **6383**

0198-2788 Local Climatological Data. Saint Cloud, Minnesota. Monthly Summary **6383**

0198-2796 Local Climatological Data. Jackson, Mississippi. Annual Summary with Comparative Data **6373**

0198-280X Local Climatological Data. Jackson, Mississippi. Monthly Summary **6373**

0198-2818 Local Climatological Data. Meridian, Mississippi. Annual Summary with Comparative Data **6377**

0198-2826 Local Climatological Data. Meridian, Mississippi. Monthly Summary **6377**

0198-2834 Local Climatological Data. Columbia, Missouri. Annual Summary with Comparative Data **6366**

0198-2842 Local Climatological Data. Columbia, Missouri. Monthly Summary **6366**

0198-2850 Local Climatological Data. Kansas City, Missouri. International Airport. Annual Summary with Comparative Data **6374**

0198-2877 Local Climatological Data. Kansas City Missouri International Airport. Monthly Summary **6374**

0198-2885 Local Climatological Data. Saint Joseph, Missouri. Annual Summary with Comparative Data† **8971**

0198-2907 Local Climatological Data. St. Louis, Missouri. Annual Summary with Comparative Data **6386**

0198-2915 Local Climatological Data. St. Louis, Missouri. Monthly Summary **6386**

0198-2923 Local Climatological Data. Springfield, Missouri. Annual Summary with Comparative Data **6386**

0198-2931 Local Climatological Data. Springfield, Missouri. Monthly Summary **6386**

0198-294X Local Climatological Data. Billings, Montana. Annual Summary with Comparative Data **6363**

0198-2958 Local Climatological Data. Billings, Montana. Monthly Summary **6363**

0198-2966 Local Climatological Data. Glasgow, Montana. Annual Summary with Comparative Data **6370**

0198-2974 Local Climatological Data. Glasgow, Montana. Monthly Summary **6370**

0198-2982 Local Climatological Data. Great Falls, Montana. Annual Summary with Comparative Data **6371**

0198-2990 Local Climatological Data. Great Falls, Michigan. Monthly Summary **6371**

0198-3008 Local Climatological Data. Havre, Montana. Annual Summary with Comparative Data **6371**

0198-3024 Local Climatological Data. Helena, Montana. Annual Summary with Comparative Data **6372**

0198-3032 Local Climatological Data. Helena, Montana. Monthly Summary **6372**

0198-3040 Local Climatological Data. Kalispell, Montana. Annual Summary with Comparative Data **6373**

0198-3059 Local Climatological Data. Kalispell, Montana. Monthly Summary **6373**

0198-3067 Local Climatological Data. Miles City, Montana. Annual Summary with Comparative Data **6377**

0198-3083 Local Climatological Data. Missoula, Montana. Annual Summary with Comparative Data **6378**

0198-3091 Local Climatological Data. Missoula, Montana. Monthly Summary **6378**

0198-3105 Local Climatological Data. Grand Island, Nebraska. Annual Summary with Comparative Data **6370**

0198-3113 Local Climatological Data. Lincoln, Nebraska. Annual Summary with Comparative Data **6375**

0198-3121 Local Climatological Data. Lincoln, Nebraska. Monthly Summary **6375**

0198-313X Local Climatological Data. Norfolk, Nebraska. Annual Summary with Comparative Data **6379**

0198-3148 Local Climatological Data. Norfolk, Nebraska. Monthly Summary **6379**

0198-3156 Local Climatological Data. North Platte, Nebraska. Annual Summary with Comparative Data **6379**

0198-3164 Local Climatological Data. North Platte, Nebraska. Monthly Summary **6379**

0198-3172 Local Climatological Data. Omaha, Nebraska. Annual Summary with Comparative Data **6380**

0198-3180 Local Climatological Data. Omaha, Nebraska. Monthly Summary **6380**

0198-3199 Local Climatological Data. Omaha (North), Nebraska. Annual Summary with Comparative Data **6380**

0198-3202 Local Climatological Data. Omaha (North), Nebraska. Monthly Summary **6380**

0198-3210 Local Climatological Data. Scottsbluff, Nebraska. Annual Summary with Comparative Data **6384**

0198-3229 Local Climatological Data. Scottsbluff, Nebraska. Monthly Summary **6385**

0198-3237 Local Climatological Data. Valentine, Nebraska. Annual Summary with Comparative Data **6387**

0198-3245 Local Climatological Data. Valentine, Nebraska. Monthly Summary **6387**

0198-3253 Local Climatological Data. Grand Island, Nebraska. Monthly Summary **6370**

0198-3261 Local Climatological Data. Elko, Nevada. Annual Summary with Comparative Data **6368**

0198-327X Local Climatological Data. Elko, Nevada. Monthly Summary **6368**

0198-3288 Local Climatological Data. Ely, Nevada. Annual Summary with Comparative Data **6368**

0198-3296 Local Climatological Data. Ely, Nevada. Monthly Summary **6368**

0198-330X Local Climatological Data. Las Vegas, Nevada. Annual Summary with Comparative Data **6375**

0198-3318 Local Climatological Data. Las Vegas, Nevada. Monthly Summary **6375**

0198-3326 Local Climatological Data. Reno, Nevada. Annual Summary with Comparative Data **6382**

0198-3334 Local Climatological Data. Reno, Nevada. Monthly Summary **6382**

0198-3342 Local Climatological Data. Winnemucca, Nevada. Annual Summary with Comparative Data **6389**

0198-3350 Local Climatological Data. Winnemucca, Nevada. Monthly Summary **6389**

0198-3369 Local Climatological Data. Concord, New Hampshire. Annual Summary with Comparative Data **6367**

0198-3377 Local Climatological Data. Concord, New Hampshire. Monthly Summary **6367**

0198-3385 Local Climatological Data. Mount Washington Observatory. Gorham, New Hampshire. Annual Summary with Comparative Data

0198-3393 Local Climatological Data. Mount Washington Observatory, Gorham, New Hampshire. Monthly Summary **6378**

0198-3415 Local Climatological Data. Atlantic City, New Jersey. National Weather Service Office. Aviation Facilities Expertise Center. Monthly Summary **6362**

0198-3423 Local Climatological Data. Atlantic City, New Jersey. National Weather Service Urban Site. Atlantic City State Marina. Monthly Summary **6362**

0198-3431 Local Climatological Data. Newark, New Jersey. Annual Summary with Comparative Data **6379**

0198-344X Local Climatological Data. Newark, New Jersey. Monthly Summary **6379**

0198-3458 Local Climatological Data. Trenton, New Jersey. Annual Summary with Comparative Data†

0198-3474 Local Climatological Data. Albuquerque, New Mexico. Annual Summary with Comparative Data **6360**

0198-3482 Local Climatological Data. Albuquerque, New Mexico. Monthly Summary **6360**

0198-3490 Local Climatological Data. Clayton, New Mexico. Annual Summary with Comparative Data **6366**

0198-3512 Local Climatological Data. Roswell, New Mexico. Annual Summary with Comparative Data **6383**

0198-3520 Local Climatological Data. Roswell, New Mexico. Monthly Summary

0198-3539 Local Climatological Data. Albany, New York. Annual Summary with Comparative Data **6360**

0198-3547 Local Climatological Data. Albany, New York. Monthly Summary **6360**

0198-3555 Local Climatological Data. Binghamton, New York. Annual Summary with Comparative Data **6363**

0198-3563 Local Climatological Data. Binghamton, New York. Monthly Summary **6363**

0198-3571 Local Climatological Data. Buffalo, New York. Annual Summary with Comparative Data **6364**

0198-358X Local Climatological Data. Buffalo, New York. Monthly Summary **6364**

0198-3598 Local Climatological Data. New York, New York Central Park. Annual Summary with Comparative Data **6378**

0198-3601 Local Climatological Data. New York, New York Central Park Observatory. Monthly Summary **6379**

0198-3628 Local Climatological Data. New York, New York John F Kennedy International Airport. Monthly Summary **6379**

0198-3644 Local Climatological Data. New York, New York La Guardia Airport. Monthly Summary **6379**

0198-3652 Local Climatological Data. Rochester, New York. Annual Summary with Comparative Data **6383**

0198-3660 Local Climatological Data. Rochester, New York. Monthly Summary **6383**

0198-3679 Local Climatological Data. Syracuse, New York. Annual Summary with Comparative Data **6386**

0198-3687 Local Climatological Data. Syracuse, New York. Monthly Summary **6386**

0198-3695 Local Climatological Data. Asheville, North Carolina. Annual Summary with Comparative Data **6361**

0198-3709 Local Climatological Data. Asheville, North Carolina. Monthly Summary **6361**

0198-3717 Local Climatological Data. Cape Hatteras, North Carolina. Annual Summary with Comparative Data **6365**

0198-3725 Local Climatological Data. Cape Hatteras, North Carolina. Monthly Summary **6365**

0198-3733 Local Climatological Data. Charlotte, North Carolina. Annual Summary with Comparative Data **6365**

0198-3741 Local Climatological Data. Charlotte, North Carolina. Monthly Summary **6365**

0198-375X Local Climatological Data. Greensboro, North Carolina. Annual Summary with Comparative Data **6371**

0198-3768 Local Climatological Data. Greensboro, High Point, Winston-Salem AP, North Carolina. Monthly Summary

0198-3776 Local Climatological Data. Raleigh, North Carolina. Annual Summary with Comparative Data **6382**

0198-3784 Local Climatological Data. Raleigh, North Carolina. Monthly Summary **6382**

0198-3792 Local Climatological Data. Wilmington, North Carolina. Annual Summary with Comparative Data **6389**

0198-3806 Local Climatological Data. Wilmington, North Carolina. Monthly Summary **6389**

0198-3814 Local Climatological Data. Bismarck, North Dakota. Annual Summary with Comparative Data **6363**

0198-3822 Local Climatological Data. Bismarck, North Dakota. Monthly Summary **6363**

0198-3830 Local Climatological Data. Fargo, North Dakota. Annual Summary with Comparative Data **6369**

0198-3849 Local Climatological Data. Fargo, North Dakota. Monthly Summary **6369**

0198-3857 Local Climatological Data. Williston, North Dakota. Annual Summary with Comparative Data **6389**

0198-3865 Local Climatological Data. Williston, North Dakota. Monthly Summary **6389**

0198-3873 Local Climatological Data. Akron, Ohio. Annual Summary with Comparative Data **6360**

0198-3881 Local Climatological Data. Akron, Ohio. Monthly Summary **6360**

0198-389X Local Climatological Data. Cincinnati, Ohio. Abbe Observatory. Annual Summary with Comparative Data†

0198-3911 Local Climatological Data. Cincinnati, Ohio. Greater Cincinnati Airport. Annual Summary with Comparative Data **6366**

0198-392X Local Climatological Data. Cincinnati, Ohio. Greater Cincinnati Airport, Boone County, Kentucky. Monthly Summary **6366**

0198-3938 Local Climatological Data. Cleveland, Ohio. Annual Summary with Comparative Data **6366**

0198-3946 Local Climatological Data. Cleveland, Ohio. Monthly Summary **6366**

0198-3954 Local Climatological Data. Columbus, Ohio. Annual Summary with Comparative Data **6367**

0198-3962 Local Climatological Data. Columbus, Ohio. Monthly Summary **6367**

0198-3970 Local Climatological Data. Dayton, Ohio. Annual Summary with Comparative Data **6367**

0198-3989 Local Climatological Data. Dayton, Ohio. Monthly Summary **6367**

0198-3997 Local Climatological Data. Mansfield, Ohio. Annual Summary with Comparative Data **6376**

0198-4004 Local Climatological Data. Mansfield, Ohio. Monthly Summary **6376**

0198-4012 Local Climatological Data. Toledo, Ohio. Annual Summary with Comparative Data **6387**

0198-4020 Local Climatological Data. Toledo, Ohio. Monthly Summary **6387**

0198-4039 Local Climatological Data. Youngstown, Ohio. Annual Summary with Comparative Data **6390**

0198-4047 Local Climatological Data. Youngstown, Ohio. Monthly Summary **6390**

0198-4055 Local Climatological Data. Oklahoma City, Oklahoma. Annual Summary with Comparative Data **6379**

0198-4063 Local Climatological Data. Oklahoma City, Oklahoma. Monthly Summary **6380**

0198-4071 Local Climatological Data. Tulsa, Oklahoma. Annual Summary with Comparative Data **6387**

0198-408X Local Climatological Data. Tulsa, Oklahoma. Monthly Summary **6387**

0198-4098 Local Climatological Data. Astoria, Oregon. Annual Summary with Comparative Data **6361**

0198-4101 Local Climatological Data. Astoria, Oregon. Monthly Summary **6361**

0198-411X Local Climatological Data. Burns, Oregon. Annual Summary with Comparative Data **6365**

0198-4128 Local Climatological Data. Burns, Oregon. Monthly Summary **6365**

0198-4136 Local Climatological Data. Eugene, Oregon. Annual Summary with Comparative Data **6369**

0198-4144 Local Climatological Data. Eugene, Oregon. Monthly Summary **6369**

0198-4152 Local Climatological Data. Medford, Oregon. Annual Summary with Comparative Data **6377**

0198-4160 Local Climatological Data. Medford, Oregon. Monthly Summary **6377**

0198-4179 Local Climatological Data. Pendleton, Oregon. Annual Summary with Comparative Data **6380**

0198-4187 Local Climatological Data. Pendleton, Oregon. Monthly Summary **6380**

0198-4195 Local Climatological Data. Portland, Oregon. Annual Summary with Comparative Data **6381**

0198-4209 Local Climatological Data. Portland, Oregon. Monthly Summary **6381**

0198-4217 Local Climatological Data. Salem, Oregon. Annual Summary with Comparative Data **6383**

0198-4225 Local Climatological Data. Salem, Oregon. Monthly Summary **6383**

0198-425X Local Climatological Data. Guam, Pacific. Annual Summary with Comparative Data **6371**

0198-4268 Local Climatological Data. Guam, Pacific. Monthly Summary **6371**

0198-4276 Local Climatological Data. Johnston Island, Pacific. Annual Summary with Comparative Data **6373**

0198-4292 Local Climatological Data. Koror Island, Pacific. Annual Summary with Comparative Data **6374**

0198-4306 Local Climatological Data. Koror Island, Pacific. Monthly Summary **6374**

0198-4314 Local Climatological Data. Kwajalein, Marshall Islands, Pacific. Annual Summary with Comparative Data **6374**

0198-4322 Local Climatological Data. Kwajalein, Pacific. Monthly Summary **6374**

0198-4330 Local Climatological Data. Majuro, Marshall Islands, Pacific. Annual Summary with Comparative Data **6376**

0198-4349 Local Climatological Data. Majuro, Marshall Island, Pacific. Monthly Summary **6376**

0198-4357 Local Climatological Data. Pago Pago, American Samoa. Annual Summary with Comparative Data **6380**

0198-4365 Local Climatological Data. Pago Pago, American Samoa, Monthly Summary

0198-4373 Local Climatological Data. Ponape Island, Pacific. Annual Summary with Comparative Data **6381**

0198-4381 Local Climatological Data. Ponape Island, Pacific. Monthly Summary **6381**

0198-439X Local Climatological Data. Truk, Eastern Caroline Island, Pacific. Annual Summary with Comparative Data **6387**

0198-4403 Local Climatological Data. Truk Caroline Island Pacific. Monthly Summary **6387**

0198-4411 Local Climatological Data. Wake Island, Pacific. Annual Summary with Comparative Data **6388**

0198-442X Local Climatological Data. Wake Island, Pacific. Monthly Summary **6388**

0198-4438 Local Climatological Data. Yap Island, Pacific. Annual Summary with Comparative Data **6390**

0198-4446 Local Climatological Data. Yap Island, Pacific. Monthly Summary **6390**

0198-4454 Local Climatological Data. Allentown, Pennsylvania. Annual Summary with Comparative Data **6360**

0198-4462 Local Climatological Data. Allentown, Pennsylvania. Monthly Summary **6360**

0198-4470 Local Climatological Data. Avoca, Pennsylvania. Annual Summary with Comparative Data **6362**

DIRECTORY 2010 0202-7127 9191

0198-9634 Contact Quarterly **2683**
0198-9669 Country Reports on Human Rights Practices for (Year) **7205**
0198-9693 Capital University Law Review **2646**
0198-9715 Computers, Environment and Urban Systems **3481**
0198-9731 Annual Review of Family Therapy†
0198-9839 Journal of Information Management†
0198-9855 Sing Heavenly Muse!
0198-9863 American Society of Animal Science. Abstracts **8791**
0198-9871 Contributions to the Study of Popular Culture **333**
0198-9901 Blueline (Potsdam) **5264**
0198-9936 Powell Alert†
0198-9960 Manhattan Book Hound†
0199-0012 True Experience **5415**
0199-0020 True Romance **5412**
0199-0039 Population and Environment **7391**
0199-0101 Engineer's Digest†
0199-0128 Baseball Bulletin†
0199-0144 Pythian International **2269**
0199-0187 Journal of Veterinary Orthopedics†
0199-0217 Christmas Trees Magazine **101**
0199-0233 Olde Time Needlework, Patterns and Design†
0199-025X Travel Holiday†
0199-0330 City Limits (Print) *changed to* City Limits (Online) **7955**
0199-0349 Hispanic Business Magazine **1118**
0199-0357 Gourmet Retailer **3645**
0199-0365 Maine Sportsman **8321**
0199-0373 Modern Truckstop News
0199-0411 Keystone Builder **1019**
0199-0454 Wichita Business *changed to* 1048-8782
0199-0462 Glos Polek **3535**
0199-0705 The Predicament **8194**
0199-0721 Heritage Florida Jewish News **7721**
0199-0802 Civil Litigation Reporter **4829**
0199-0837 Nautical Quarterly†
0199-0918 Ohio P T A News **2893**
0199-1248 Nevada **8741**
0199-1280 The Shield of Phi Kappa Psi Fraternity
0199-1310 Alaskan Malamute Club of America. Newsletter **6802**
0199-1337 Sea Power **6445**
0199-1345 Virginia's Health **7544**
0199-137X University of Hawaii. Sea Grant College Program. Sea Grant Quarterly†
0199-1388 Aquaculture Magazine **3585**
0199-1574 Atlanta Skier **8304**
0199-1604 Pattern World†
0199-1671 Agribusiness Worldwide†
0199-1728 Greater Portland Magazine
0199-1752 Volcano Review†
0199-1779 Cotton Economic Review **225**
0199-1833 Medical Liability Reporter†
0199-1876 Advocate (Los Angeles, 1973) **4611**
0199-1892 Woodworker's Journal **4439**
0199-1914 Model Railroading **4341**
0199-1973 State and Local Taxes: Property Taxes
0199-2066 Chicago Nurse
0199-2155 Northeast Optician
0199-2260 Execu-Time†
0199-2317 Milk and Liquid Food Transporter **8672**
0199-2333 Kind†
0199-2414 C A L Underwriter
0199-2422 News Photographer **6971**
0199-252X Wentzville Union and St. Charles County Record *changed to* 1523-6358 **1179**
0199-2538 Y Drych **3530**
0199-2783 Viewpoint (Willow Grove)†
0199-2805 Southeast Food Service News **3664**
0199-2864 Adweek: Eastern Edition *changed to* 1549-9553 **20**
0199-2899 Long Island Jewish World **3548**
0199-2988 Taxidermy Review
0199-3003 Soap Opera Stars **2390**
0199-3046 Yakama Nation Review **3573**
0199-3070 Stovall Journal **3784**
0199-3100 Benefits News Analysis **1856**
0199-3186 The Director (Brookfield) **3719**
0199-3291 Bassmaster Magazine **8305**
0199-3313 Keyboard World
0199-3356 West Coast Peddler **369**
0199-3429 God's Word Today **7799**
0199-350X The People (Mountain View) **7164**
0199-3518 New Horizons (Willow Grove) **7768**
0199-3607 Kansas Business News†
0199-3658 Utmost†
0199-3720 Entree (New York)†
0199-378X Music World†
0199-3887 Master Salesmanship **1834**
0199-3933 House & Garden Building & Remodeling Guide†
0199-3941 Nit & Wit
0199-3992 Texas Homes†
0199-4050 The Short Line†
0199-4239 Holstein World **265**
0199-4336 Grain Storage and Handling†
0199-4395 T W N†
0199-4433 Mission Journal†
0199-4441 The Jewish World **7724**
0199-4468 Import Automotive Parts & Accesories **8585**
0199-4514 Tole World†
0199-4530 News & Views (Pendleton) **2162**
0199-4557 New Jersey Interact†
0199-4646 Fordham Urban Law Journal **4676**
0199-4654 The Sensible Sound† **8988**
0199-4662 Public Employee Bargaining†
0199-4697 Current Concepts in Oncology
0199-4735 Garden Glories **3731**
0199-4751 Flowers& **3756**
0199-4786 Occupational Outlook Quarterly **6707**
0199-4883 Federal Labor Relations Reporter **1681**
0199-4905 Medical Sciences Bulletin†
0199-4913 Petersen's Photographic† **8980**
0199-5014 Indian River Life
0199-5030 Supreme Court Bulletin **4965**
0199-5073 Inland Empire Magazine **3978**
0199-5103 Group Practice Journal **5621**
0199-5111 Cruise Travel **8696**
0199-5162 O A G Pocket Travel Planner **8742**
0199-5197 Cobblestone **2183**
0199-5235 Massachusetts Discrimination Law Reporter **4729**
0199-5243 M A P A LOG Magazine **65**
0199-5278 Sportswear Graphics†
0199-5316 Safari Magazine **8331**
0199-5405 Hustler Humor **6292**
0199-5421 Mainline Modeler **4339**
0199-543X The A F A Watchbird **900**
0199-5553 Museum Magazine†
0199-5650 Energy Management†
0199-5685 I U P I W Views **6773**
0199-5782 West's Bankruptcy Reporter **1390**
0199-5839 Florida Realtor **7591**
0199-5855 Whitchappel's Herbal†
0199-6037 Academy Reporter†
0199-6045 The Mailbox **3071**
0199-6096 Bus Tours Magazine **8492**
0199-6231 Journal of Solar Energy Engineering **3176**
0199-6258 Wrestling U S A (Missoula) **8216**
0199-6290 Back Home in Kentucky **3970**
0199-6304 Employee Health and Fitness†
0199-6401 Rural Montana **3987**
0199-6487 Chinmaya Mission West News **7631**
0199-6495 Terrier Type **6816**
0199-6509 Management Digest (Chicago)†
0199-6517 Georgia Sportsman **8315**
0199-6649 InfoWorld†
0199-6657 Kicks **6582**
0199-669X California Business Law Reporter **4860**
0199-6738 Setter Quarterly†
0199-6762 N R H A Reiner **8295**
0199-6819 Slovak v Amerike **3564**
0199-6827 Risk Management Reports (Print) *changed to* Risk Management Reports (Online) **4522**
0199-6835 Alarm Signal†
0199-686X C B I A News **1445**
0199-7025 California Peace Officer†
0199-7068 Model Ship Builder
0199-7092 Spirit of Aloha **8786**
0199-7114 Program Manager *changed to* 1547-5476 **2520**
0199-7149 Sexology Today†
0199-7238 Cape Cod Life **3971**
0199-7297 American Brittany **6803**
0199-7319 Output†
0199-7327 Scale R - C Modeler† **8987**
0199-7335 Pet Gazette†
0199-7343 Colorado Medicine **5599**
0199-736X Dental Practice†
0199-7424 Israel Scene†
0199-7505 Prime of Life†
0199-7602 Inside (Philadelphia) **3539**
0199-7610 Specialist (Radnor)†
0199-7653 C P M Aspects†
0199-7661 Leadership (Carol Stream) **7659**
0199-7696 Foodservice Product News†
0199-7777 Reach (Oklahoma City)†
0199-7890 Vette **8610**
0199-7912 Drug Metabolism Newsletter†
0199-7947 Senior Citizen Sentinel†
0199-7955 Microsystems†
0199-8013 Plant Services **3392**
0199-8153 Sequoia (San Francisco)
0199-817X Nematology Newsletter **958**
0199-820X Current Health 1 **3055**
0199-8293 World Around You **3049**
0199-8307 Marketing Times
0199-8315 Bichon Frise Reporter **6804**
0199-834X Going Places (Schaumburg)†
0199-8366 Groom & Board†
0199-8374 Chicago Lawyer **4642**
0199-8404 Bartender **598**
0199-8498 Sugar Producer **159**
0199-8501 Inside Kung Fu **8179**
0199-8536 Powerlifting U S A **8194**
0199-8552 Healthwire **5959**
0199-8595 Energy Engineering **3131**
0199-865X V F W Auxiliary *changed to* Ladies Auxiliary V F W **2267**
0199-8668 Southern Struggle†
0199-8714 Unfinished Furniture Industry†
0199-8730 Biz†
0199-8803 Today's Missal **7820**
0199-8838 M I S Week†
0199-8951 Systems User **2525**
0199-8986 Human Resource Planning *changed to* 1946-4606 **1871**
0199-9028 Communique (Chicago) **7587**
0199-9060 Soil and Water Conservation News†
0199-9095 Wisconsin Law Reporter **4815**
0199-9184 Miniature Collector **4340**
0199-9206 Arizona Realtor Digest **7582**
0199-9214 Dayton Magazine
0199-9230 Crossroads (Evanston)†
0199-9257 Prevue **6510**
0199-9273 Media Review†
0199-9303 Los Angeles Home and Garden Magazine†
0199-9346 Communities **1422**
0199-9362 Lowrider **8589**
0199-9419 Asia Record†
0199-9451 Halifax Magazine **3977**
0199-946X Baseball Hobby News
0199-9486 Classic Images Review†
0199-9559 Orchid Digest **3746**
0199-9583 Huguenot Historian
0199-9591 Acadian Genealogy Exchange **3757**
0199-9613 U.S. Department of Energy. Strategic Petroleum Reserve Office. Annual Report†
0199-9664 Nebraska State Historical Society. Historical Newsletter **4304**
0199-9753 Diamond Registry. Bulletin **4565**
0199-9788 Games **8174**
0199-9885 Annual Review of Nutrition **6655**
0199-9915 Retail Automation Report†
0199-9931 The Dartmouth **2281**
0199-994X Geographical Perspectives†
0200-5344 Zalai Tukor†
0200-5352 Magyar Nepmuveszet Evszazadai†
0201-419X Kul'tura Slova **5319**
0201-4211 Sel'skoe Stroitel'stvo **1035**
0201-4335 Byulleten' Registratsii N I R i O K R. Seriya 13. Lesnaya i Derevoobrabatyvayushchaya Promyshlennost' **3118**
0201-4432 Perestroika†
0201-4521 Byulleten' Registratsii N I R i O K R. Seriya 11. Naukovedenie. Informatika. Patentnoe Delo. Izobretatel'stvo. Ratsionalizatorstvo **3118**
0201-453X Byulleten' Registratsii N I R i O K R. Seriya 12. Pishchevaya Promyshlennost' **3118**
0201-4564 Elektricheskie Stantsii (Moscow, 1930) **3188**
0201-4610 Byulleten' Registratsii N I R i O K R. Seriya 10. Geodeziya. Kartografiya. Geofizika. Geologiya. Geografiya. **3118**
0201-4785 Olimp **8191**
0201-4793 Primiritel' **7671**
0201-5137 Geodeziya, Aeros'emka, Kartografiya: Sostoyanie i Perspektivy Razvitiya Tsifrovogo Kartografii **2781**
0201-5218 Referativnyi Zhurnal. Biologiya. Obshchie Problemy Biologii. Razdel-Tom **718**
0201-5226 Referativnyi Zhurnal. Virusologiya. Mikrobiologiya **719**
0201-5307 Signal'naya Informatsiya. Kvantovaya Radiotekhnika - Kriogennaya Radioehlektronika†
0201-5315 Signal'naya Informatsiya. Antenny - Volnovody - Ob'emnye Rezonatory - Rasprostranenie Radiovoln†
0201-5323 Signal'naya Informatsiya. Ehlektrosvyaz†
0201-5331 Signal'naya Informatsiya. Radiolokatsiya. Radionavigatsiya - Televidenie - Impul'snaya Tekhnika†
0201-6265 Letopis' Periodicheskikh i Prodolzhayushchikhsya Izdanii **629**
0201-6354 Knigi Rossiskoi Federatsii **628**
0201-7032 Kontrol' Diagnostika **3387**
0201-7288 Kommercheskii Vestnik†
0201-7318 Moscow Patriarchate. Journal *see* 0132-862X **7706**
0201-7369 Akademiya Meditsinskikh Nauk S.S.S.R. Vsesoyuznyi Kardiologicheskii Nauchnyi Tsentr. Byulleten'†
0201-7385 Moskovskii Gosudarstvennyi Universitet. Vestnik. Seriya 7: Filosofiya **6935**
0201-7474 Khimiya Drevesiny†
0201-7539 Arkheologicheskie Raboty v Tadzhikistane†
0201-7563 Anesteziologiya i Reanimatologiya **5769**
0201-7628 Vsemirnoe Profsoyuznoe Dvizhenie†
0201-7636 Bibliotechka Profsoyuznogo Aktivista *changed to* Bibliotechka Profsoyuznogo Aktiva i Predprinimatelei **7950**
0201-7776 Za Bezopasnost' Dvizheniya **2228**
0201-7806 Efemeridy Malykh Planet **574**
0201-8039 Latviesu Valodas Kulturas Jautajumi†
0201-8373 Soviet Film†
0201-890X Geodeziya, Topografiya, Kartografiya. Seriya: Distantsionnoe Zondirovanie Zemli dlya Ekologii i Prirodopol'zovaniya **2781**
0201-9280 Ezhegodnik Vsesouznogo Paleonlologiceskogo Obshchestva **6724**
0202-0718 Itogi Nauki i Tekhniki. Bionika†
0202-0726 Itogi Nauki i Tekhniki. Geodeziya i Aeros'emka†
0202-0734 Itogi Nauki i Tekhniki. Issledovanie Kosmicheskogo Prostranstva†
0202-0742 Itogi Nauki i Tekhniki. Astronomiya†
0202-0769 Itogi Nauki i Tekhniki. Radiotekhnika†
0202-1250 Sbornik Opisanii Izobretenii, Rekomendovannykh dlya Vnedreniya na Zheleznodorozhnom Transporte **8624**
0202-1382 Kompleksnoe Ispol'zovanie Mineral'nogo Syr'ya **6468**
0202-1811 Eesti Geograafia Seltsi. Aastaraamat **4005**
0202-2001 Lituanistika v S.S.S.R. Filosofiya i Psikhologiya†
0202-201X Lituanistika v S.S.S.R. Yazykoznanie†
0202-2028 Lituanistika v S.S.S.R. Pravo†
0202-2036 Obshchestvennye Nauki v S.S.S.R. Seriya 1: Problemy Nauchnogo Kommunizma†
0202-2125 Obshchestvennye Nauki za Rubezhom. Problemy Nauchnogo Kommunizma†
0202-2257 Paramagnitnyi Rezonans **7029**
0202-2354 Problemy Difraktsii i Rasprostraneniya Voln **7089**
0202-2745 Aviatsionnaya i Raketnaya Tekhnika **49**
0202-2893 Gravitation & Cosmology **7014**
0202-3342 Lietuvos Istorijos Metrastis **4240**
0202-3350 Sborka v Mashinostroenii, Priborostroenii **3395**
0202-3776 Obogashchenie Rud **6475**
0202-4101 Referativnyi Zhurnal. Avtomatika i Telemekhanika **2444**
0202-4241 Referativnyi Zhurnal. Fiziologiya i Biokhimiya Rastenii **719**
0202-4977 Trenie i Iznos **3397**
0202-5132 Referativnyi Zhurnal. Farmakologiya Effektornykh Sistem. Khimioterapevticheskie Sredstva *changed to* Referativnyi Zhurnal. Farmakologiia Obshchaia. Khimioterapevtitcheskie Sredstva **6890**
0202-5442 Byulleten' Mezhdunarodnykh Nauchnykh S'ezdov, Konferentsii, Kongressov, Vystavok **6283**
0202-6120 Deponirovannye Nauchnye Raboty. Bibliograficheskii Ukazatel' **7936**
0202-6309 Mestnyi Proizvodstvennyi Opyt v Promyshlennosti†
0202-6317 Mestnyi Proizvodstvennyi Opyt v Stroitel'stve†
0202-6325 Mestnyi Proizvodstvennyi Opyt v Sel'skom Khozyaistve†
0202-6619 Geodeziya, Topografiya, Kartografiya. Seriya: Kartografiya i Geograficheskie Informatsionnye Sistemy **2781**
0202-7011 Itogi Nauki i Tekhniki. Zoologiya Bespozvonochnykh†
0202-702X Itogi Nauki i Tekhniki. Zoologiya Pozvonochnykh†
0202-7046 Itogi Nauki i Tekhniki. Immunologiya†
0202-7070 Itogi Nauki i Tekhniki. Molekulyarnaya Biologiya†
0202-7089 Itogi Nauki i Tekhniki. Seriya Morfologiya Cheloveka i Zhivotnykh. Antropologiya†
0202-7097 Itogi Nauki i Tekhniki. Obshchaya Genetika†
0202-7127 Itogi Nauki i Tekhniki. Onkologiya†

ISSN

0202-7135 Itogi Nauki i Tekhniki. Patologicheskaya Anatomiya†

0202-7143 Itogi Nauki i Tekhniki. Pochvovedenie i Agrokhimiya†

0202-7151 Itogi Nauki i Tekhniki. Radyatsionnaya Biologiya†

0202-716X Itogi Nauki i Tekhniki. Rastenievodstvo†

0202-7186 Itogi Nauki i Tekhniki. Fiziologiya Rastenii†

0202-7208 Itogi Nauki i Tekhniki. Geografiya Zarubezhnykh Stran†

0202-7216 Itogi Nauki i Tekhniki. Geografiya SSSR†

0202-7232 Itogi Nauki i Tekhniki. Seriya Gidrologiya Sushi†

0202-7240 Itogi Nauki i Tekhniki. Kartografiya†

0202-7259 Itogi Nauki i Tekhniki. Meditsinskaya Geografiya†

0202-7267 Itogi Nauki i Tekhniki. Teoreticheskie i Obshchie Voprosy Geografii†

0202-7275 Itogi Nauki i Tekhniki. Geomagnetizm i Vysokie Sloi Atmosfery†

0202-7283 Itogi Nauki i Tekhniki. Glyatsiologiya†

0202-7291 Itogi Nauki i Tekhniki. Meteorologiya i Klimatologiya†

0202-7305 Itogi Nauki i Tekhniki. Okeanologiya†

0202-7313 Itogi Nauki i Tekhniki. Fizika Zemli†

0202-7321 Itogi Nauki i Tekhniki. Okhrana Prirody i Vosproizvodstvo Prirodnykh Resursov†

0202-733X Itogi Nauki i Tekhniki. Geologicheskie i Geokhimicheskie Metody Poiskov†

0202-7348 Itogi Nauki i Tekhniki. Geokhimiya - Mineralogiya - Petrografiya†

0202-7356 Itogi Nauki i Tekhniki. Gidrogeologiya. Inzhenernaya Geologiya†

0202-7372 Itogi Nauki i Tekhniki. Obshchaya Geologiya†

0202-7380 Itogi Nauki i Tekhniki. Rudnye Mestorozhdeniya†

0202-7399 Itogi Nauki i Tekhniki. Stratigrafiya, Paleontologiya†

0202-7402 Itogi Nauki i Tekhniki. Tekhnika Geologorazvedochnykh Rabot†

0202-7410 Itogi Nauki i Tekhniki. Razrabotka Mestorozhdenii Tverdykh Poleznykh Iskopaemykh†

0202-7429 Itogi Nauki i Tekhniki. Razrabotka Neftyanykh i Gazovykh Mestorozhdenii†

0202-7437 Itogi Nauki i Tekhniki. Obogashchenie Poleznykh Iskopaemykh†

0202-7445 Itogi Nauki i Tekhniki. Algebra - Topologiya - Geometriya†

0202-7453 Itogi Nauki i Tekhniki. Matematicheskii Analiz†

0202-7461 Itogi Nauki i Tekhniki. Problemy Geometrii†

0202-7488 Itogi Nauki i Tekhniki. Teoriya Veroyatnostei - Matematicheskaya Statistika-Teoreticheskaya Kibernetika†

0202-7496 Itogi Nauki i Tekhniki. Aviastroenie†

0202-750X Itogi Nauki i Tekhniki. Aviatsionnye i Raketnye Dvigateli†

0202-7518 Itogi Nauki i Tekhniki. Avtomobilestroenie†

0202-7542 Itogi Nauki i Tekhniki. Dvigateli Vnutrennego Sgoraniya†

0202-7569 Itogi Nauki i Tekhniki. Mashiny i Oborudovanie dlya Tekstil'noi Promyshlennosti†

0202-7585 Itogi Nauki i Tekhniki. Metrologiya i Izmeritel'naya Tekhnika†

0202-7615 Itogi Nauki i Tekhniki. Raketostroenie i Kosmicheskaya Tekhnika†

0202-7623 Itogi Nauki i Tekhniki. Rezanie Materialov. Stanki i Instrumenty†

0202-7658 Itogi Nauki i Tekhniki. Sudostroenie†

0202-7704 Itogi Nauki i Tekhniki. Turbostroenie†

0202-7739 Itogi Nauki i Tekhniki. Metallovedenie i Termicheskaya Obrabotka†

0202-7747 Itogi Nauki i Tekhniki. Metallurgiya Tsvetnykh Metallov†

0202-7755 Itogi Nauki i Tekhniki. Metallurgicheskaya Teplotekhnika†

0202-7763 Itogi Nauki i Tekhniki. Proizvodstvo i Stali†

0202-7771 Itogi Nauki i Tekhniki. Prokatnoe i Volochilnoe Proizvodstvo†

0202-778X Itogi Nauki i Tekhniki. Svarka†

0202-7798 Itogi Nauki i Tekhniki. Teoriya Metallurgicheskikh Protsessov†

0202-7801 Itogi Nauki i Tekhniki. Seriya Tekhnicheskii Analiz v Metallurgii†

0202-781X Itogi Nauki i Tekhniki. Mekhanika Zhidkosti i Gaza†

0202-7828 Itogi Nauki i Tekhniki. Mekhanika Deformiruemogo Tverdogo Tela†

0202-7836 Itogi Nauki i Tekhniki. Obshchaya Mekhanika†

0202-7844 Itogi Nauki i Tekhniki. Avtomobil'nyi i Gorodskoi Transport†

0202-7860 Itogi Nauki i Tekhniki. Vzaimodeistvie Raznykh Vidov Transporta i Konteinernye Perevozki†

0202-7879 Itogi Nauki i Tekhniki. Vodnyi Transport†

0202-7887 Itogi Nauki i Tekhniki. Vozdushnyi Transport†

0202-7895 Itogi Nauki i Tekhniki. Zheleznodorozhnyi Transport†

0202-7909 Itogi Nauki i Tekhniki. Promyshlennyi Transport†

0202-7917 Itogi Nauki i Tekhniki. Truboprovodnyi Transport†

0202-7933 Itogi Nauki i Tekhniki. Fizika Plazmy†

0202-7941 Itogi Nauki i Tekhniki. Analiticheskaya Khimiya†

0202-795X Itogi Nauki i Tekhniki. Biologicheskaya Khimiya†

0202-7968 Itogi Nauki i Tekhniki. Kinetika. Kataliz†

0202-7976 Itogi Nauki i Tekhniki. Korroziya i Zashchita ot Korrozii†

0202-7984 Itogi Nauki i Tekhniki. Kristallokhimiya†

0202-8018 Itogi Nauki i Tekhniki. Protsessy i Apparaty Khimicheskoi Tekhnologii†

0202-8050 Itogi Nauki i Tekhniki. Khimicheskaya Termodinamika i Ravnovesiya†

0202-8069 Itogi Nauki i Tekhniki. Khimiya i Tekhnologiya Vysokomolekulyarnykh Soedinenii†

0202-8077 Itogi Nauki i Tekhniki. Seriya Khimiya Tverdogo Tela†

0202-8093 Itogi Nauki i Tekhniki. Elektrokhimiya†

0202-8123 Itogi Nauki i Tekhniki. Obshcheotraslevye Voprosy Ekonomiki i Organizatsii Proizvodstva†

0202-814X Itogi Nauki i Tekhniki. Seriya Informatika†

0202-8166 Referativnyi Zhurnal. Atomnaya Energetika **3174**

0202-8190 Itogi Nauki i Tekhniki. Kotel'nye Ustanovki i Vodopodgotovka†

0202-8247 Itogi Nauki i Tekhniki. Teplo- i Massoobmen†

0202-8255 Itogi Nauki i Tekhniki. Teplovye Elektrostantsii. Teplosnabzhenie†

0202-8298 Itogi Nauki i Tekhniki. Elektrooborudovanie Transporta†

0202-8301 Itogi Nauki i Tekhniki. Elektricheskie Apparaty†

0202-831X Itogi Nauki i Tekhniki. Elektricheskie Mashiny i Transformatory†

0202-8344 Itogi Nauki i Tekhniki. Elektroprivod i Avtomatizatsiya Promyshlennykh Ustanovok†

0202-8387 Signal'naya Informatsiya. Genetika Cheloveka†

0202-8395 Signal'naya Informatsiya. Ikhtiologiya†

0202-8425 Signal'naya Informatsiya. Obmen Veshchestv, Pitanie i Pishchevarenie†

0202-8433 Signal'naya Informatsiya. Obshchaya Genetika†

0202-8441 Signal'naya Informatsiya. Obshchaya Mikrobiologiya†

0202-845X Signal'naya Informatsiya. Obshchie Problemy Biologii†

0202-8468 Signal'naya Informatsiya. Obshchie Problemy Fiziologii Cheloveka i Zhivotnykh. Prikladnaya Fiziologiya†

0202-8476 Signal'naya Informatsiya. Onkologiya: Opukholi u Cheloveka†

0202-8484 Signal'naya Informatsiya. Onkologiya: Terapiya Opukholei†

0202-8492 Signal'naya Informatsiya. Onkologiya: Eksperimental'naya†

0202-8506 Signal'naya Informatsiya. Prikladnaya Mikrobiologiya†

0202-8522 Signal'naya Informatsiya. Farmakologiya: Khimioterapevticheskie Sredstva†

0202-8530 Signal'naya Informatsiya. Fiziologiya Krovoobrashcheniya i Dykhaniya: Pochki†

0202-8549 Signal'naya Informatsiya. Tsitologiya - Tsitogenetika†

0202-8638 Signal'naya Informatsiya. Vysokomolekulyarnye Soedineniya†

0202-8646 Signal'naya Informatsiya. Zhiry, Masla, Moyushchie Sredstva i Dushistye Veshchestva†

0202-8662 Signal'naya Informatsiya. Kinetika - Kataliz - Fotokhimiya - Radiatsionnaya Khimiya†

0202-8670 Signal'naya Informatsiya. Korroziya i Zashchita ot Korrozii†

0202-8689 Signal'naya Informatsiya. Kristallokhimiya i Kristallografiya†

0202-8697 Signal'naya Informatsiya. Laki - Kraski - Organicheskie Pokrytiya†

0202-8727 Signal'naya Informatsiya. Natural'nyi Kauchuk-Rezina†

0202-8735 Signal'naya Informatsiya. Neorganicheskaya Khimiya-Kompleksnye Soedineniya-Radiokhimiya†

0202-8743 Signal'naya Informatsiya. Obshchie Voprosy Khimii†

0202-8751 Signal'naya Informatsiya. Obshchie i Teoreticheskie Voprosy Organicheskoi Khimii†

0202-876X Signal'naya Informatsiya. Osnovy Khimicheskoi Tekhnologii†

0202-8778 Signal'naya Informatsiya. Pererabotka Tverdykh Goryuchikh Iskopaemykh, Nefti, Gazov, Drevesiny†

0202-8786 Signal'naya Informatsiya. Pestitsidy†

0202-8794 Signal'naya Informatsiya. Pishchevaya, Brodil'naya i Sakharnaya Promyshlennost'†

0202-8808 Signal'naya Informatsiya. Plastmassy i Ionoobmennye Materialy†

0202-8816 Signal'naya Informatsiya. Poverkhnostnye Yavleniya - Khimiya Kolloidov†

0202-8824 Signal'naya Informatsiya. Prirodnye Soedineniya i Ikh Sinteticheskie Analogi†

0202-8832 Signal'naya Informatsiya. Promyshlennyi Organicheskii Sintez i Sintez Krasitelei†

0202-8840 Signal'naya Informatsiya. Silikatnye Materialy†

0202-8859 Signal'naya Informatsiya. Sinteticheskaya Organicheskaya Khimiya†

0202-8867 Signal'naya Informatsiya. Sinteticheskie i Prirodnye Lekarstvennye Veshchestva†

0202-8875 Signal'naya Informatsiya. Stroenie Molekul i Khimicheskaya Svyaz'†

0202-8883 Signal'naya Informatsiya. Struktura i Svoistva Vysokomolekulyarnykh Soedinenii†

0202-8891 Signal'naya Informatsiya. Termodinamika - Termokhimiya - Ravnovesiya - Rastvory†

0202-8905 Signal'naya Informatsiya. Tekhnika Bezopasnosti. Sanitarnaya Tekhnika†

0202-8921 Signal'naya Informatsiya. Tekhnologiya Neorganicheskikh Veshchestv†

0202-893X Signal'naya Informatsiya. Khimicheskie Volokna - Tekstil - Kozha - Mekh†

0202-8948 Signal'naya Informatsiya. Khimiya Vody **2096**

0202-8956 Signal'naya Informatsiya. Khimiya Tverdogo Tela - Gazy - Zhidkosti - Amorfnye Tela†

0202-8980 Signal'naya Informatsiya. Enzimologiya†

0202-8999 Signal'naya Informatsiya. Razrabotka Neftyanykh i Gazovykh Mestorozhdenii†

0202-9103 Referativnyi Zhurnal. Tsitologiya **719**

0202-9111 Referativnyi Zhurnal. Entomologiya **718**

0202-912X Referativnyi Zhurnal. Bionika. Biokibernetika. Bioinzheneriya **718**

0202-9138 Referativnyi Zhurnal. Genetika i Selektsiya Vozdelyvaemykh Rastenii **719**

0202-9146 Referativnyi Zhurnal. Genetika Cheloveka **719**

0202-9154 Referativnyi Zhurnal. Immunologiya. Allergologiya **5750**

0202-9162 Referativnyi Zhurnal. Klinicheskaya Farmakologiya **6890**

0202-9197 Referativnyi Zhurnal. Onkologiya **5750**

0202-9200 Referativnyi Zhurnal. Rastenievodstvo (Biologicheskie Osnovy) **719**

0202-9219 Referativnyi Zhurnal. Toksikologiya **6890**

0202-9227 Referativnyi Zhurnal. Farmakologiya. Khimioterapevticheskie Sredstva. Toksikologiya†

0202-9235 Referativnyi Zhurnal. Fitopatologiya **718**

0202-9243 Referativnyi Zhurnal. Biogeografiya. Geografiya Pochv **718**

0202-9251 Referativnyi Zhurnal. Geografiya Ameriki, Avstralii, Okeanii i Antarktiki **4036**

0202-926X Referativnyi Zhurnal. Geografiya Zarubezhnoi Azii i Afriki **4036**

0202-9278 Referativnyi Zhurnal. Geografiya Zarubezhnoi Evropy **4036**

0202-9286 Referativnyi Zhurnal. Geografiya Stran na Territorii Byvshego S S S R *changed to* Referativnyi Zhurnal. Geografiya Rossiiskoi Federatsii **4036**

0202-9294 Referativnyi Zhurnal. Kartografiya **4036**

0202-9308 Referativnyi Zhurnal. Meteorologiya i Klimatologiya **6400**

0202-9316 Referativnyi Zhurnal. Okeanologiya. Gidrologiya Sushi. Glyatsiologiya **2721**

0202-9324 Referativnyi Zhurnal. Teoreticheskie i Obshchie Voprosy Geografii **4036**

0202-9332 Referativnyi Zhurnal. Okhrana Prirody i Vosproizvodstvo Prirodnykh Resursov **3480**

0202-9340 Referativnyi Zhurnal. Antropogenovyi Period. Geomorfologiya Sushi i Morskogo Dna **2720**

0202-9359 Referativnyi Zhurnal. Geologicheskie i Geokhimicheskie Metody Poiskov Poleznykh Iskopaemykh. Metody Razvedki i Otsenki Mestorozhdenii. Razvedotchnaya i Promyslovaya Geofizika **2721**

0202-9367 Referativnyi Zhurnal. Geokhimiya, Mineralogiya, Petrografiya **2721**

0202-9375 Referativnyi Zhurnal. Gidrogeologiya, Inzhenernaya Geologiya, Merzlotovedenie **2721**

0202-9383 Referativnyi Zhurnal. Mestorozhdeniya Goryuchikh Poleznykh Iskopaemykh **6486**

0202-9391 Referativnyi Zhurnal. Nemetallicheskie Poleznye Iskopaemye **2721**

0202-9405 Referativnyi Zhurnal. Obshchaya Geologiya **2721**

0202-9413 Referativnyi Zhurnal. Rudnye Mestorozhdeniya **6477**

0202-9421 Referativnyi Zhurnal. Stratigrafiya. Paleontologiya **6731**

0202-943X Referativnyi Zhurnal. Tekhnika Geologo-Razvedochnykh Rabot **2721**

0202-9448 Referativnyi Zhurnal. Geomagnetizm i Vysokie Sloi Atmosfery **2721**

0202-9456 Referativnyi Zhurnal. Fizika Zemli **2720**

0202-9464 Referativnyi Zhurnal. Obogashchenie Poleznykh Iskopaemykh **6486**

0202-9472 Referativnyi Zhurnal. Razrabotka Mestorozhdenii Tverdykh Poleznykh Iskopaemykh. Vspomogatelnye Protsessy **6486**

0202-9480 Referativnyi Zhurnal. Razrabotka Mestorozhdenii Tverdykh Poleznykh Iskopaemykh. Obshchie Problemy, Promyshlennost, Ekonomika, Stroitelstvo **6486**

0202-9499 Referativnyi Zhurnal. Razrabotka Mestorozhdenii Tverdykh Poleznykh Iskopaemykh. Osnovnye Protsessy **6486**

0202-9502 Referativnyi Zhurnal. Razrabotka Neftyanykh i Gazovykh Mestorozhdenii **6801**

0202-9510 Referativnyi Zhurnal. Mashiny i Oborudovanie dlya Tekstil'noi Promyshlennosti. Vypusk Svodnogo Toma *changed to* 0034-2432 **1260**

0202-9529 Referativnyi Zhurnal. Tekhnologiya i Organizatsiya Proizvodstva Tekstil'noi Promyshlennosti. Vypusk Svodnogo Toma *changed to* 0034-2432 **1260**

0202-9537 Referativnyi Zhurnal. Trikotazhnaya, Shveinaya i Kozhevenno-Obuvnaya Promyshlennosti. Vypusk Svodnogo Toma *changed to* 0034-2432 **1260**

0202-9545 Referativnyi Zhurnal. Matematicheskii Analiz **5548**

0202-9553 Referativnyi Zhurnal. Obshchie Voprosy Matematiki. Matematicheskaya Logika. Teoriya Chisel. Algebra. Topologiya. Geometriya **5549**

0202-9561 Referativnyi Zhurnal. Teoriya Veroyatnostei i Matematicheskaya Statistika **5549**

0202-957X Referativnyi Zhurnal. Rezanie Materyalov. Stanki i Instrumenty **5462**

0202-9596 Referativnyi Zhurnal. Tekhnologiya i Oborudovanie Kuznechno-Shtampovochnogo Proizvodstva **6341**

0202-960X Referativnyi Zhurnal. Tekhnologiya i Oborudovanie Liteinogo Proizvodstva **6341**

0202-9618 Referativnyi Zhurnal. Tekhnologiya i Oborudovanie Mekhanosborochnogo Proizvodstva **5462**

0202-9626 Referativnyi Zhurnal. Metallovedenie i Termicheskaya Obrabotka **6341**

0202-9634 Referativnyi Zhurnal. Metallurgicheskaya Teplotekhnika. Oborudovanie, Izmereniya, Kontrol i Avtomatizatsiya v Metallurgicheskom Proizvodstve **6341**

0202-9650 Referativnyi Zhurnal. Proizvodstvo Chuguna i Stali **6341**

0202-9669 Referativnyi Zhurnal. Prokatnoye i Volochil'noye Proizvodstvo **6341**

0202-9677 Referativnyi Zhurnal. Teoriya Metallurgicheskikh Protsessov **6341**

0202-9685 Referativnyi Zhurnal. Tekhnicheskii Analiz v Metalurgii† **8984**

0202-9693 Referativnyi Zhurnal. Mekhanika Deformiruemogo Tverdogo Tela **7049**

0202-9707 Referativnyi Zhurnal. Mekhanika Zhidkosti i Gaza **7049**

0202-9715 Referativnyi Zhurnal. Obshchie Voprosy Mekhaniki. Obshchaya Mekhanika **7049**

0202-9723 Referativnyi Zhurnal. Iskusstvennye Sooruzheniya na Avtomobil'nykh Dorogakh. Vypusk Svodnogo Toma *changed to* 0486-2252 **8528**

0202-9731 Referativnyi Zhurnal. Stroitel'stvo i Ekspluatatsiya Avtomobilnykh Dorog. Vypusk Svodnogo Toma *changed to* 0486-2252 **8528**

0202-974X Referativnyi Zhurnal. Avtomobilestroenie **8528**

0202-9758 Referativnyi Zhurnal. Avtomobil'nyi Transport **8528**

0202-9766 Referativnyi Zhurnal. Gorodskoi Transport **8529**

0202-9790 Referativnyi Zhurnal. Aviastroenie **8528**

0202-9847 Referativnyi Zhurnal. Avtomatika, Telemekhanika i Sviaz' na Zheleznykh Dorogakh **8528**

0202-9855 Referativnyi Zhurnal. Lokomotivostroenie i Vagonostroenie **8529**

0202-9863 Referativnyi Zhurnal. Stroitelstvo Zheleznykh Dorog. Put' i Putevoe Khozyaistvo **8529**

0202-9871 Referativnyi Zhurnal. Tekhnicheskaya Ekspluatatsiya Podvizhnogo Sostava i Tyaga Poezdov **8529**

0202-988X Referativnyi Zhurnal. Upravlenie Perevozochnym Protsessom na Zheleznykh Dorogakh **8529**

0202-9898 Referativnyi Zhurnal. Pozharnaya Okhrana. Otdel'nyi Vypusk **3582**

0202-9901 Referativnyi Zhurnal. Pozharnaia Bezopasnost. Vypusk Svodnogo Toma *changed to* 0202-9898 **3582**

0202-991X Referativnyi Zhurnal. Pozharnaia Okhrana. Vypusk Svodnogo Toma *changed to* 0202-9898 **3582**

0202-9936 Referativnyi Zhurnal. Pod'emno-Transportnoe Mashinostroenie **3233**

0202-9944 Referativnyi Zhurnal. Transportnoe Khozyaistvo Promyshlennykh Predpriyatii†

0202-9952 Referativnyi Zhurnal. Organizatsiya i Bezopasnost' Dorozhnogo Dvizheniya **8529**

0202-9979 Referativnyi Zhurnal. Radiofizika i Fizicheskie Osnovy Elektroniki **7049**
0203-0454 Pogranichnik **4024**
0203-1272 Mekhanika Kompozitnykh Materialov **7061**
0203-137X Itogi Nauki i Tekhniki. Klassicheskaya Teoriya Polei i Teoriya Gravitatsii†
0203-1841 Zheleznodorozhnyi Transport. Seriya. Gruzovaya i Kommercheskaya Rabota. Konteinernye Perevozki **8628**
0203-1876 Zheleznodorozhnyi Transport. Seriya. Organizatsiya Dvizheniya i Passazhirskie Perevozki **8628**
0203-1884 Zheleznodorozhnyi Transport. Seriya. Bezopasnost' Truda **8628**
0203-1914 Zheleznodorozhnyi Transport. Seriya. Podvizhnoi Sostav. Lokomotivnoe i Vagonnoe Khozyaistvo **8628**
0203-2406 Avtomatizirovannye Sistemy Upravleniya
0203-3054 Informatics Abstracts *see* 0486-235X **5059**
0203-3100 Geofizicheskii Zhurnal **2781**
0203-3119 Sverkhtverdye Materialy **2118**
0203-3275 Kompositsionnye Polimernye Materialy†
0203-347X Spravochnik. Inzhenernyi Zhurnal **3220**
0203-3488 Al'fa i Omega **7620**
0203-3569 Sel'skaya Molodezh **2212**
0203-4646 Ekologiya Morya **2803**
0203-4654 Fizika i Tekhnika Vysokikh Davlenii **7058**
0203-493X Neirokhimiya **2074**
0203-5146 Referativnyi Zhurnal. Kompleksnye i Spetsyal'nye Razdely Mekhaniki **7049**
0203-5154 Referativnyi Zhurnal. Prochnost' Konstruktsii i Materyalov **1048**
0203-5170 Referativnyi Zhurnal. Metallurgiya Tsvetnykh Metallov **6341**
0203-5197 Referativnyi Zhurnal. Obshchie Voprosy i Teoreticheskie Osnovy Elektrotekhniki. Elektrobezopasnost' **3329**
0203-5200 Referativnyi Zhurnal. Svetotekhnika i Infrakrasnaya Tekhnika **3233**
0203-5219 Referativnyi Zhurnal. Silovaya Preobrazovatel'naya Tekhnika **3117**
0203-5227 Referativnyi Zhurnal. Elektrifikatsiya Byta†
0203-5243 Referativnyi Zhurnal. Elektricheskie Apparaty **3233**
0203-5251 Referativnyi Zhurnal. Elektricheskie Mashiny i Transformatory **3233**
0203-526X Referativnyi Zhurnal. Elektrooborudovanie Transporta **3233**
0203-5278 Referativnyi Zhurnal. Elektroprivod i Avtomatizatsiya Promyshlennykh Ustanovok **3233**
0203-5286 Referativnyi Zhurnal. Elektrotekhnicheskie Materialy, Elektricheskie Kondensatory, Provoda i Kabeli **3233**
0203-5294 Referativnyi Zhurnal. Elektrotekhnologiya **3233**
0203-5308 Referativnyi Zhurnal. Energetika **3154**
0203-5324 Referativnyi Zhurnal. Generatory Pryamogo Preobrazovaniya Teplovoi i Khimicheskoi Energii v Elektricheskuyu **3154**
0203-5332 Referativnyi Zhurnal. Gidroenergetika **3154**
0203-5340 Referativnyi Zhurnal. Kotelnye Ustanovki i Vodopodgotovka **3154**
0203-5375 Referativnyi Zhurnal. Teplovye Elektrostantsii. Teplosnabzhenie **3154**
0203-5383 Referativnyi Zhurnal. Elektricheskie Stantsii i Seti **3154**
0203-5391 Referativnyi Zhurnal. Energeticheskie Sistemy i ikh Avtomatizatsiya **3154**
0203-5405 Itogi Nauki i Tekhniki. Obshchie Problemy Biologii†
0203-5413 Signal'naya Informatsiya. Metallurgiya Blagorodnykh, Redkikh, Redkozemel'nykh i Radioaktivnykh Metallov i Splavov. Proizvodstvo Tsvetnykh Metallov i Splavov iz Vtorichnogo Syr'ya†
0203-5421 Signal'naya Informatsiya. Metallurgiya Legkikh i Tyazhelykh Metallov i Splavov†
0203-543X Signal'naya Informatsiya. Metallurgicheskaya Teplotekhnika†
0203-5448 Signal'naya Informatsiya. Metodika Issledovanii Metallov i Splavov i Laboratornoe Oborudovanie. Termicheskaya i Khimiko-Termicheskaya Obrabotka Metallov i Splavov†
0203-5456 Signal'naya Informatsiya. Obshchie Voprosy Metallovedenya i Termicheskoi Obrabotki. Fazovye Ravnovesiya Metallov i Splavov. Fazovye i Strukturnye Prevrashcheniya v Metallakh i Splavakh†
0203-5464 Signal'naya Informatsiya. Obshchie Voprosy Prokatnogo Proizvodstva. Teoriya Prokatki Metallov. Proizvodstvo Blyumov, Slyabov, Zagotovok i Profilei Prokata Chernykh Metallov†
0203-5472 Signal'naya Informatsiya. Obshchie Voprosy Tsvetnoi Metallurgii. Obogashchenie Rud Tsvetnykh Metallov†
0203-5480 Signal'naya Informatsiya. Obshchie Voprosy Chernoi Metallurgii. Obshchezavodskoe Khozyaistvo Chernoi Metallurgii†
0203-5499 Signal'naya Informatsiya. Podgotovka Syr'evykh Materialov Chernoi Metallurgii. Proizvodstvo Chuguna i Ferrosplavov. Pryamoe Poluchenie Zheleza i Stali†
0203-5502 Signal'naya Informatsiya. Proizvodstvo Listov Chernykh Metallov†
0203-5510 Signal'naya Informatsiya. Proizvodstvo Zagotovok, Profilei, Katanki, Listov i Fol'gi iz Tsvetnykh Metallov i Splavov. Volochil'noe i Metiznoe Proizvodstvo. Proizvodstvo Trub†
0203-5529 Signal'naya Informatsiya. Proizvodstvo Stali†
0203-5537 Signal'naya Informatsiya. Struktura i Svoistva Tsvetnykh Metallov i Splavov i Kompozitsionnykh Materialov na Ikh Osnove. Metally i Splavy v Atomnoi i Termoyadernoi Ehnergetike†
0203-5545 Signal'naya Informatsiya. Atomnoe Yadro†
0203-5553 Signal'naya Informatsiya. Nelineinaya Optika i Kvantovaya Elektronika†
0203-5561 Signal'naya Informatsiya. Struktura i Dinamika Reshetki Tverdykh Tel†
0203-5847 Literaturnaya Ucheba **2200**
0203-6002 Referativnyi Zhurnal. Fizika Gazov i Zhidkostei: Termodinamika i Statisticheskaya Fizika **7049**
0203-6010 Referativnyi Zhurnal. Fizika Plazmy **7049**
0203-6037 Referativnyi Zhurnal. Yadernaya Fizika i Fizika Yadernykh Reaktorov **7049**
0203-6045 Referativnyi Zhurnal. Analiticheskaya Khimiya. Oborudovanie Laboratorii **2095**
0203-607X Referativnyi Zhurnal. Obshchie Voprosy Khimicheskoi Tekhnologii **2095**
0203-6088 Referativnyi Zhurnal. Organicheskaya Khimiya **2095**
0203-6126 Referativnyi Zhurnal. Tekhnologiya Organicheskikh Veshchestv **2096**
0203-6134 Referativnyi Zhurnal. Tekhnologiya Organicheskikh Lekarstvennykh Veshchestv, Veterinarnykh Preparatov i Pestitsidov **2095**
0203-6150 Referativnyi Zhurnal. Khimiya Vysokomolekuliarnykh Soedinenii **2095**
0203-6169 Referativnyi Zhurnal. Khimiya i Pererabotka Goryuchikh Iskopaemykh i Prirodnykh Gazov **2095**
0203-6223 Referativnyi Zhurnal. Ekonomika Promyshlennosti **1260**
0203-6436 Referativnyi Zhurnal. Teplomassobmen **3154**
0203-6460 Mezhdunarodnyi Forum po Informatsii **5032**
0203-6495 F I D - R I Series on Problems of Information Science†
0203-7483 Protection of Atmosphere Against Pollution†
0203-7807 Ekonomika i Upravlenie v Ugol'noj Promyshlennosti†
0203-8889 Ekspress Informatsiya. Informatika†
0203-9494 Problemy Slov'yanoznavstva†
0203-9699 Polutehniline Instituut Tallinn. Narodonaselenie i Rabochaya Sila†
0203-9710 Polutehniline Instituut Tallinn. Teoriya i Tekhnologiya Poluchenie Stroitel'nykh Materialov iz Zol Tverdykh Topliv†
0203-9745 Polutehniline Instituut Tallinn. Optimal'nye Sistemy i Algoritmy†
0203-9788 Polutehniline Instituut Tallinn. Voprosy Povysheniya Kachestva Pishchevykh Produktov†
0204-0476 Argumenty i Fakty **3934**
0204-0956 Meditsinski Pregled. Akusherstvo i Ginekologiia **5998**
0204-2061 Knygotyra **5023**
0204-2177 Olimpiiskaya Panorama **8191**
0204-241X Panorama Olimpico *see* 0204-2177 **8191**
0204-2592 Olympic Panorama *see* 0204-2177 **8191**
0204-2606 Panorama Olympique *see* 0204-2177 **8191**
0204-2614 Olympisches Panorama *see* 0204-2177 **8191**
0204-3327 Izvestiya Vysshikh Uchebnykh Zavedenii. Yadernaya Energetika **7067**
0204-3386 Bibliografiya Rossiiskoi Bibliografii **618**
0204-3432 Zhivaya Starina **541**
0204-3467 Physics of Low-Dimensional Structures **7071**
0204-3483 Inzhenernaya Ekologiya **3203**
0204-3513 Poligrafist i Izdatel' **7325**
0204-3548 Mineralogicheskii Zhurnal **6471**
0204-3556 Khimiya i Tekhnolohiya Vody **2070**
0204-3564 Eksperimental'naya Onkologiya *changed to* 1812-9269 **6019**
0204-3572 Elektronnoe Modelirovanie **2517**
0204-3602 Promyshlennaya Teplotekhnika **3394**
0204-3726 Byulleten' Registratsii N I R i O K R. Seriya 9. Metallurgiya **3119**
0204-3734 Byulleten' Registratsii N I R i O K R. Seriya 8. Meditsina i Zdravookhranenie. Okhrana Truda **3119**
0204-3777 Referativnyi Zhurnal. Ekonomika Otraslei Pishchevoi i Legkoi Promyshlennosti *changed to* 0135-9800 **1260**
0204-3777 Referativnyi Zhurnal. Ekonomika Otraslei Pishchevoi i Legkoi Promyshlennosti *changed to* Referativnyi Zhurnal. Ekonomika Otraslei Pishchevoi Promyshlennosti **3670**
0204-3777 Referativnyi Zhurnal. Ekonomika Otraslei Pishchevoi Promyshlennosti *changed to* Referativnyi Zhurnal. Ekonomika Otraslei Pishchevoi i Legkoi Promyshlennosti **8984**
0204-3785 Referativnyi Zhurnal. Ekonomika Otraslei Toplivno-Energeticheskogo Kompleksa **1260**
0204-3793 Referativnyi Zhurnal. Ekonomika Otraslei Metallurgicheskogo i Mashinostroitelnogo Kompleksov **1260**
0204-3807 Referativnyi Zhurnal. Mirovaya Ekonomika. Sotsyal'no-Ekonomicheskoe Razvitie Stran Mira **1260**
0204-3815 Referativnyi Zhurnal. Biokhimiya. Biokhimiya Ksenobiotikov *changed to* Referativnyi Zhurnal. Biokhimiya **718**
0204-4005 Sofiiski Universitet Sv. Kliment Ohridski. Istoricheski Fakultet. Godishnik **4162**
0204-4013 Izvestiya na Muzeite v Severozapadna Bulgariya†
0204-4021 Palaeobulgarica **4252**
0204-403X Izvestiya na Muzeite ot Iugoiztochna Bulgariya **399**
0204-4048 Godishnik na Muzeite ot Severna Bulgariia **4224**
0204-4072 Izvestiya na Muzeite ot Iuzhna Bulgariya **399**
0204-4080 Voennoistoricheski Sbornik **4278**
0204-4099 Natsionalen Muzei na Revoliutsionnogo Dvizhenie v Bulgariya. Godishnik†
0204-4110 Serdika Matematichesko Spisanie **5534**
0204-4218 Shumen. Pedagogicheski Institut. Godishnik **3805**
0204-4684 Statisticeski Danni za Bibliotekite v Bulgaria†
0204-5079 Ribno Stopanstvo†
0204-5109 Neftena i Vuglishtna Geologiia†
0204-5117 Rodna Rech **2210**
0204-5311 Rudoobrazuvatelni Protsesi i Mineralni Nakhodishta **2765**
0204-5389 Meditsinski Pregled. Khirurgichni Zaboliavaniia **6252**
0204-563X Statisticheski Izvestiia **8405**
0204-577X Abstracts of Bulgarian Scientific Literature. Industry, Building and Transport†
0204-5958 Fiziko-Khimicheska Mekhanika **2135**
0204-6083 Abstracts of Bulgarian Scientific Literature. Economics and Law†
0204-6091 Narodna Biblioteka Sv.sv. Kiril i Metodii. Izvestiya†
0204-6105 Nefrologiia, Hemodializa i Transplantatsiia **6272**
0204-6253 Teatur **8481**
0204-6415 Stomatologichen Pregled†
0204-6865 Meditsinski Pregled. Sardechno-Sadovi Zaboliavaniia **5795**
0204-6962 Suvremennik **5383**
0204-6989 Yaderna Energiya **3176**
0204-7004 Preduchilishtno Vuzpitanie **2899**
0204-711X Ikonomika **1352**
0204-7209 Problemi na Geografijata **4025**
0204-7217 Paleontologiia, Stratigrafiia i Litologiia **6729**
0204-7373 Bibliografia na Bulgarskata Bibliografiia†
0204-7535 Materialozanie i Tekhnologiia **3352**
0204-7594 Biomekhanika
0204-7934 Inzenerna Geologiia i Khidrogeologiia **2710**
0204-8043 Folia Medica **5614**
0204-8124 Armeiski Pregled†
0204-8132 Arkhiven Pregled **4991**
0204-8205 *see* 0204-8884
0204-8213 Bulgaro-Suvetska Druzhba†
0204-823X Bulgarsko Muzikoznanie **6552**
0204-8248 Vodni Problemi **8835**
0204-8329 Estrada **8470**
0204-8418 Discover Bulgaria†
0204-868X Starobulgarska Literatura **5377**
0204-8701 Sapostavitelno Ezikoznanie **5171**
0204-8728 Tantsovo Izkustvo†
0204-8752 Filatelen Pregled **6894**
0204-8809 Acta Microbiologica Bulgarica†
0204-8884 Bulgarian Films
0204-8973 *see* 0204-8884
0204-9155 Problems of Infectious and Parasitic Diseases **5825**
0204-9260 Istoriya i Obshtestvoznanie†
0204-9406 Abstracts of Bulgarian Scientific Literature. Geosciences†
0204-9449 Abstracts of Bulgarian Scientific Literature. Mathematical and Physical Sciences†
0204-9600 Sofiiski Universitet Sv. Kliment Ohridski. Fakultet po Klasicheski i Novi Filologii. Godishnik **5176**
0204-9716 Meditsinski Pregled. Klinichna Laboratoriia **738**
0204-9724 Meditsinski Pregled. Alergologiia i Klinichna Imunologiia **5764**
0204-9783 Fakel **5295**
0204-9805 Pliska Bulgarski Matematicheski Studii **5524**
0204-9848 Problemi na Tekhnicheskata Kibernetika i Robotika **2528**
0204-9880 Studia Praehistorica **419**
0205-0013 Panorama **5348**
0205-0617 Naselenie **7288**
0205-0625 Uspehi na Moleculiarnata Biologia†
0205-0900 Durzhaven Vestnik **3804**
0205-0919 Erevan **3532**
0205-0994 Ikonomicheski Zhivot **1121**
0205-1273 Starshel **5240**
0205-1281 Televiziia i Radio **2397**
0205-1338 Trud **3805**
0205-1362 Tsurkoven Vestnik **7706**
0205-1656 Savremenna Zhurnalistika **4583**
0205-1834 Chuzhdoyezikovo Obuchenie **5106**
0205-2253 Kirilo-Metodievski Studii **4237**
0205-2679 Sbornik za Narodni Umotvoreniya **3622**
0205-3217 Mathematica Balkanica **5512**
0205-3292 Ikonomicheski Izsledvania **1121**
0205-3640 Historia Naturalis Bulgarica **7861**
0205-3772 Abstracts of Bulgarian Scientific Literature. History, Archaeology and Ethnography†
0205-3845 Ikonomika i Upravlenie na Selskoto Stopanstvo **200**
0205-4027 Morskoi Transport. Seriya: Tekhnicheskaya Ekspluatatsiya Flota **8653**
0205-406X Morskoi Transport. Seriya: Tekhnologiya Morskikh Perevozok i Morskie Porty **8653**
0205-4108 Morskoi Transport. Seriya: Sudoremont **8653**
0205-5767 Yunyi Naturalist **2223**
0205-5791 Yunyi Khudozhnik **2223**
0205-8316 64 - Shakhmatnoe Obozrenie **8217**
0205-9592 Psikhologicheskii Zhurnal **7394**
0205-9606 Voprosy Istorii Estestvoznaniya i Tekhniki **7928**
0205-9614 Issledovanie Zemli iz Kosmosa *see* 1024-5251
0205-9975 Garagum **4453**
0206-0388 Vedomosti Medzhlisa Turkmenistana **7191**
0206-0477 Rossiiskaya Akademiya Nauk. Zoologicheskii Institut. Trudy **962**
0206-0582 Shpion **5415**
0206-1325 Byulleten' Registratsii N I R i O K R. Seriya 4. Yazykoznanie. Literatura. Literaturovedenie. Narodnoe Poeticheskoe Tvorchestvo **3119**
0206-1333 Byulleten' Registratsii N I R i O K R. Seriya 5. Biologiya. Biotekhnologiya **3119**
0206-1473 New Times *see* 0137-0723 **3938**
0206-149X Far Eastern Affairs **5215**
0206-1619 Geografiya i Prirodnye Resursy **4009**
0206-3131 Nadezhnost' i Dolgovechnost' Mashin i Sooruzhennii†
0206-3638 Fizika Mnogochastichnykh Sistem†
0206-3735 Emakeele Seltsi Aastaraamat **5114**
0206-3743 Byulleten' Registratsii N I R i O K R. Seriya 3. Kul'tura. Narodnoe Obrazovanie. Pedagogika. Fizicheskaya Kul'tura i Sport **3119**
0206-3859 Byulleten' Registratsii N I R i O K R. Seriya 7b. Tekhnologiya Mashinostroeniya **3119**
0206-3875 Byulleten' Registratsii N I R i O K R. Seriya 7a. Otraslevoe Mashinostroenie **3119**
0206-4189 Kazan Utlary **4461**
0206-4952 Immunologiya **5760**
0206-5231 Kul'tura v Sovremennom Mire: Opyt, Problemy, Resheniya **7981**
0206-5398 Signal'naya Informatsiya. Tekhnologiya Proizvodstva Radioapparatury†
0206-5401 Signal'naya Informatsiya. Ehlektrovakuumnye Pribory i Ustroistva†
0206-541X Signal'naya Informatsiya. Materialy Elektronnoi Tekhniki†
0206-5428 Signal'naya Informatsiya. Optoehlektronnye Pribory†
0206-5452 Referativnyi Zhurnal. Elektronika **3117**
0206-5487 Referativnyi Zhurnal. Optoelektronnye Pribory†
0206-5517 Referativnyi Zhurnal. Mikrobiologiya Sanitarnaya i Meditsinskaya **719**
0206-5525 Referativnyi Zhurnal. Veterinariya†
0206-572X Mekhanizatsiya i Elektrifikatsiya Sel'skogo Khozyaistva **212**
0206-6130 Referativnyi Zhurnal. Tekhnologicheskie Aspekty Okhrany Okruzhayushchei Sredy **3480**
0206-6149 Referativnyi Zhurnal. Sistemy, Pribory i Metody Kontrolya Kachestva Okruzhayushchei Sredy **3480**

ISSN

ISSN

9196 0210-7007 ULRICH'S PERIODICALS

0210-7007 Alerta Informativa. Serie D: el Mundo Rural†
0210-7023 Alerta Informativa. Serie E: Economia de la Empresa†
0210-7074 Estudios Josefinos **7796**
0210-7112 Revista Espanola de Teologia **7677**
0210-7120 Instituto Nacional de Estadistica. Anuario Estadistico de Espana: Edicion Manual†
0210-7171 Avances en Obstetricia y Ginecologia†
0210-7228 Instituto Gemologico Espanol. Boletin **4566**
0210-7260 Estudios Segovianos **4451**
0210-7279 Informaciones Psiquiatricas **6146**
0210-7295 Tribuna Cooperativa
0210-7309 O.R.L. Dips **6083**
0210-7317 Institucion Tello Tellez de Meneses. Publicaciones **4457**
0210-735X Almanaque Nautico **568**
0210-7465 Anales de Medicina†
0210-7481 Real Academia de Buenas Letras de Barcelona. Boletin **5165**
0210-749X Catedra Miguel de Unamuno. Cuadernos **6910**
0210-7546 Studia Paedagogica†
0210-7597 Acta Botanica Barcinonensia **772**
0210-7694 Revista Habis **2239**
0210-7708 Lagascalia **799**
0210-7716 Historia, Instituciones, Documentos **7140**
0210-7732 Anuario de Esuko-Folklore **328**
0210-7775 Medios Audiovisuales
0210-7791 Museo de Pontevedra **6530**
0210-7821 Stochastica†
0210-7872 Universidad Complutense de Madrid. Revista†
0210-7945 Clinica Rural
0210-7953 Estudios de Filologia Inglesa†
0210-7988 Revista de Ferreteria†
0210-8046 Almanaque Nautico Reducido para Uso con Maquinas de Calcular†
0210-8062 Institut Botanic de Barcelona. Treballs *changed to* 1695-8950 **956**
0210-8127 Fenomenos Astronomicos **574**
0210-8135 M T A Pediatria **6096**
0210-8143 Museo del Prado. Boletin **6530**
0210-8178 Universidad de Extremadura. Facultad de Filosofia y Letras. Anuario de Estudios Filologicos **5190**
0210-8194 Asociacion Espanola de Neuropsiquiatria. Boletin **6124**
0210-8224 Cuadernos de Estudios Borjanos **4213**
0210-8259 Mientras Tanto **8121**
0210-8275 Nueva Enfermeria†
0210-8283 Pathos†
0210-8291 Quaderns de Treball†
0210-8348 Psiquis†
0210-8364 Sociologia del Trabajo **8135**
0210-8380 Geographicalia **4011**
0210-8437 Instituto de Estudios Maritimos Juan de la Cosa. Anales†
0210-8445 Boletin Auriense **6521**
0210-8453 Civitas. Revista Espanola de Derecho Financiero **4860**
0210-8461 Revista Espanola de Derecho Administrativo **4772**
0210-847X Cuadernos de Estudios Gallegos **7957**
0210-8496 Jabega **3952**
0210-8518 Revista General de Legislacion y Jurisprudencia **4772**
0210-8550 Berceo **4444**
0210-8577 Real Sociedad Geografica. Boletin **4026**
0210-8615 Llull **7880**
0210-8623 Centro de Edafologia y Biologia Aplicada. Anuario†
0210-8674 Industria Conservera†
0210-8704 Estudis d'Historia Contemporania del Pais Valencia **4218**
0210-8720 Studium Ophthalmologicum **6052**
0210-8739 Studia Silensia **7684**
0210-8747 Seguritecnia **2680**
0210-8801 Nueva Lente **6972**
0210-8836 Spain. Instituto de Estudios Laborales y de la Seguridad Social. Jurisprudencial Laboral y de Seguridad Social.†
0210-8852 F A C: Revista Practica de Medicina†
0210-8917 Anuarios de Geomagnetismo (Year)†
0210-895X Biologia & Clinica Hematologica†
0210-8984 Asociacion Espanola de Entomologia. Boletin **840**
0210-900X Harvard - Deusto Business Review **1117**
0210-9093 Estudis **4218**
0210-9107 Papeles de Economia Espanola **1510**
0210-9123 Air Sonic
0210-9174 Revista de Filologia Espanola **5167**
0210-9352 Oecologia Aquatica **2816**
0210-9395 Estudios de Psicologia **7355**
0210-9425 Investigaciones Historicas **4232**
0210-9433 Medicina Integral **5673**
0210-9441 Narria **6533**
0210-945X Vieraea **710**
0210-9476 Asociacion Espanola de A T S en Urologia. Revista **6265**
0210-9492 Centro de Informacion Documental de Archivos. Boletin de Informacion **5001**
0210-9506 Acta Botanica Malacitana **772**
0210-9522 Miscelanea Comillas **7663**
0210-9565 Instituto de Estudios Economicos. Revista **1491**
0210-9573 Seminario de Estudios de Arte y Arqueologia. Boletin **517**
0210-9581 Revista de Ciencias de la Educacion **2905**
0210-959X Antropologia y Paleoecologia Humana **328**
0210-9611 Chronica Nova **4210**
0210-962X Universidad de Granada. Cuadernos de Arte **523**
0210-9689 Revista "Es" **5167**
0210-9700 Eguzkilore **4663**
0210-9727 Cuadernos Universitarios de Planificacion Empresarial†
0210-9743 Universidad Complutense de Madrid. Centro de Calculo. Boletin†
0210-976X Studia Archaeologica **419**
0210-9778 Lazaroa **799**
0210-9794 Revista de Estudios Internacionales†
0210-9832 Acta Obstetrica y Ginecologica Hispano-Lusitana†
0210-9859 Alcantara
0210-9891 Escuela de Optica Cuantica. Cursos† **8954**
0210-9913 J A M A en Colombia†
0210-9921 J A M A en Venezuela†
0210-9956 Playamar† **8981**
0210-9980 Saitabi **4261**
0210-9999 Tiempos Medicos **5722**
0211-0040 Revista de Historia de la Psicologia **7403**
0211-0075 Cuadernos Valencianos de Historia de la Medicina y de la Ciencia. Serie A. Monografias
0211-0083 Cuadernos Valencianos de Historia de la Medicina y de la Ciencia. Serie B. Textos Clasicos
0211-0091 Cuadernos Valencianos de Historia de la Medicina y de la Ciencia. Serie C. Repertorios Biobibliograficos
0211-0105 Boletin Oficial de la Propiedad Industrial. 2: Patentes y Modelos de Utilidad **6746**
0211-0121 Boletin Oficial de la Propiedad Industrial. 1: Marcas y Otros Signos Distintivos **6746**
0211-013X Boletin Oficial de la Propiedad Industrial. 3: Modelos y Dibujos Industriales y Artisticos **6746**
0211-030X Agrishell **86**
0211-0326 Boletin de Ciencias de la Naturaleza **663**
0211-0334 Boletin de Estudios y Documentacion de Servicios Sociales†
0211-0407 Consejo General de Colegios Veterinarios de Espana. Circular Informativa **8795**
0211-0547 Cuadernos de Investigacion Filologica **5109**
0211-0555 Cuadernos del Norte†
0211-0563 Eria **4005**
0211-058X Gastrum **5925**
0211-0652 Quaderns d'Ecologia Aplicada **3461**
0211-0741 Studium Ovetense **7686**
0211-0768 D'Art *changed to* 1579-2641 **504**
0211-0822 Revista de Psicoterapia y Psicosomatica **7404**
0211-0830 Resistor **3112**
0211-0865 Cuadernos Aragoneses de Economia **1476**
0211-0873 Sant Pau **4111**
0211-0903 Revista del Foro Canario **4772**
0211-0938 Espana Hostelera **8701**
0211-0946 Eina **107**
0211-0954 Economia Vascongada†
0211-1071 Bouquet **600**
0211-111X Real Sociedad Bascongada de los Amigos del Pais. Boletin **7995**
0211-1136 Fluidos **3361**
0211-1179 Geographicalia. Serie Monographica **4011**
0211-1187 Huelva Arqueologica **396**
0211-1217 Revista Juridica de Asturias **4772**
0211-1241 Anuario Iberoamericano de Seguros†
0211-125X Anuario Espanol de Seguros **4492**
0211-1268 Boletin de Coyuntura y Estadistica del Pais Vasco† **8937**
0211-1284 Coyuntura Industrial y Utilizacion de la Capacidad Productiva de Alava†
0211-1314 Spain. Instituto Nacional de Investigaciones Agrarias. Comunicaciones. Serie: Higiene y Sanidad†
0211-1322 Jardin Botanico de Madrid. Anales **796**
0211-139X Revista Espanola de Geriatria y Gerontologia **4054**
0211-142X Quaderns d'Historia Tarraconense **412**
0211-1535 Circulo de Empresarios. Boletin† **8941**
0211-1608 Cuadernos de Prehistoria y Arqueologia **388**
0211-1721 Real Academia de Ciencias Exactas, Fisicas y Naturales. Memoria. Serie de Ciencias Exactas **5528**
0211-1748 Noticiario Arqueologico Hispanico†
0211-1799 Recien Nacido **2166**
0211-1810 Revista de Folklore **3622**
0211-1993 Revistas Espanolas con I S S N†
0211-2000 Nueva Publicidad **31**
0211-2027 Arcano
0211-2035 Archivo Agustiniano **7784**
0211-2086 Spain. Ministerio de Agricultura, Pesca y Alimentacion. Cuentas del Sector Agrario†
0211-2124 Novatica **2433**
0211-2140 Boletin Millares Carlo† **8937**
0211-2159 Psicologica **7393**
0211-2175 Analisi **7947**
0211-2256 Seminarios de Estratigrafia. Serie Monografias **2766**
0211-2264 Servicio de Investigacion Prehistorica. Serie de Trabajos Varios **416**
0211-2337 Anales del Seminario de Historia de la Filosofia **6904**
0211-2361 Aviacion y Turismo **8685**
0211-2388 Fundacion Universidad - Empresa. Boletin† **8958**
0211-2426 Boletin Informativo de Legislacion Fiscal *changed to* 1699-2318 **4858**
0211-2477 Instituto de Estudios Gerundenses. Serie Monografica **3540**
0211-2558 Folia Neuropsiquiatrica del Sur de Espana†
0211-2574 Lino: Revista de Arte **503**
0211-2612 Naturalia Hispanica†
0211-2663 Revista de Girona **3953**
0211-2698 Sociedad Canaria de Oftalmologia. Archivos **6051**
0211-2728 Agricola Vergel **216**
0211-2744 La Ley (Bimonthly Edition) *see* 1138-9907 **4723**
0211-285X Cambio 16 **5210**
0211-2876 Imprempres **6734**
0211-2892 Rotacion **8659**
0211-2914 Artepiel†
0211-2930 Cambus†
0211-2957 Dismoda†
0211-2965 Envaspres **6709**
0211-2973 Eurofach Electronica **3099**
0211-299X Mecanipel **4974**
0211-304X Sernaval **8660**
0211-3058 Mundo Cientifico†
0211-3171 Museo e Instituto Camon Aznar. Boletin **6530**
0211-318X Brigantium **6521**
0211-3228 Cuadernos de Prehistoria† **8947**
0211-3295 One†
0211-3325 Quimera **5357**
0211-3333 Revista Internacional de Comunicacion y Relaciones Publicas **34**
0211-3341 Tecnicas de Transporte y Almacenaje
0211-3465 Pediatrika†
0211-3473 Medievalia **4153**
0211-3481 Cuadernos de Psicologia **7350**
0211-3538 Anuario Musical **6545**
0211-3546 Radiorama **2388**
0211-3589 Al-Qantara **5164**
0211-3708 Confeccion Industrial **2246**
0211-3732 Defensa **6418**
0211-3767 Frisona Espanola **287**
0211-3945 Revista de Libreria Antiquaria **4257**
0211-3961 Tecnica del Calzado **7942**
0211-397X Elektor **3305**
0211-4003 Altamira **7487**
0211-4011 Liceo Franciscano **7660**
0211-402X Enrahonar **6915**
0211-4046 Boletin de Traducciones†
0211-4143 Actualidad Bibliografica de Filosofia y Teologia **7697**
0211-4267 Spain. Ministerio de Justicia. Boletin de Informacion **4786**
0211-4356 Cuadernos de Ciencias Economicas y Empresariales **1089**
0211-4364 Revista de Estudios de Juventud **8065**
0211-4399 Guia de Centros de Ensenanza Media de la Iglesia *changed to* 0211-4410 **2956**
0211-4410 Guia de Centros Educativos Catolicos **2956**
0211-4488 Memorial de Ingenieria de Armamento† **8974**
0211-450X Museo Canario
0211-4526 Persona y Derecho **4757**
0211-4534 Observatorio del Ebro. Publicaciones. Miscelanea **2787**
0211-4550 Revista de Menorca **5236**
0211-4623 Studia Oecologica† **8991**
0211-4704 Campo y Mecanica **99**
0211-4763 Economia Guipuzcoana† **8952**
0211-4844 Urania **583**
0211-4917 Guia del Comercio y de la Industria de Madrid **1404**
0211-495X Jakin **6927**
0211-5166 Observatorio del Ebro. Boletin, Ionsofera **2787**
0211-5174 Trabajos de Arqueologia Navarra **421**
0211-5239 Alxebra **5468**
0211-5247 Centro de Albacete. Anales† **8940**
0211-5255 Archivo Dominicano **7784**
0211-5379 Coyuntura Comercial. Alava†
0211-5425 Estudis Historics i Documents dels Arxius de Protocols **4668**
0211-5441 Imagenes de la Fe **7649**
0211-5468 Informe Economico de Aragon **1405**
0211-5514 El Olivo **7667**
0211-5530 Pontevedra **7500**
0211-5549 Psicopatologia **6175**
0211-5557 Institut Catala d'Antropologia. Quaderns **342**
0211-5581 Revista Politica Comparada **7179**
0211-5603 Actualidad Juridica
0211-5638 Fisioterapia **5959**
0211-5700 Cuadernos de Investigacion Biologica **667**
0211-5727 Estudios Internacionales†
0211-5735 Asociacion Espanola de Neuropsiquiatria. Revista **6124**
0211-5743 Revista Espanola de Derecho Constitucional **4852**
0211-5786 Anuario de Energia†
0211-5808 Archivo de Arte Valenciano **467**
0211-5840 Kalathos **402**
0211-5891 Lurralde **4019**
0211-5913 Revista Canaria de Estudios Ingleses **5167**
0211-5921 Boletin de Jurisprudencia Constitucional **4846**
0211-593X Affar **5091**
0211-6030 Universitat de Girona. Facultat de Lletres. Estudi General **5191**
0211-6057 Nutricion Clinica†
0211-6065 Obradoiro **451**
0211-6073 Obradoiro. Suplemento *see* 0211-6065 **451**
0211-609X Paleontologia i Evolucio **6729**
0211-612X Revista Agustiniana **7814**
0211-6138 Revista de Derecho Bancario y Bursatil **1380**
0211-6200 La Bici
0211-6391 Recerca Musicologica **6609**
0211-6561 Mensajero **7662**
0211-657X Guia del Comprador de Coches **8583**
0211-6642 Agora (Santiago de Compostela) **6902**
0211-6707 Areas **7948**
0211-6820 Cuadernos de Investigacion Geografica **4003**
0211-6944 Jurisprudencia Aragonesa **4706**
0211-6995 Nefrologia **6271**
0211-7029 PhotoVision **6975**
0211-7045 Stereofonia† **8990**
0211-707X Institucio Catalana d'Historia Natural. Treballs **794**
0211-7142 Banco Central. Boletin Informativo†
0211-7150 Botanica Macaronesica **780**
0211-7207 Turiaso **7821**
0211-7274 Rheuma **6226**
0211-7290 Tecnica Ceramica **2046**
0211-7339 Analisis y Modificacion de Conducta **7334**
0211-7649 Cuadernos de Estudios Caspolinos **4213**
0211-772X Ethnografia Espanola **336**
0211-7754 Justicia **4708**
0211-7827 Modapiel **7941**
0211-7916 Tarraco **4030**
0211-7932 Tecnica del Punto **2250**
0211-7959 Arte Regalo **4059**
0211-7967 Azulejo **2037**
0211-7975 Textiles para el Hogar **8461**
0211-8173 Tecnologia del Agua **8832**
0211-8181 Equivalencias **5421**
0211-819X Educar **2846**
0211-8319 A T E M C O P **3258**
0211-8327 Studia Geologica Salmanticensia **2770**
0211-8335 International Bulletin of Bibliography on Education **2934**
0211-8343 Instituto Cajal. Trabajos†
0211-836X Resultados Expediciones Cientificas†
0211-8378 La Madera **3713**
0211-8386 Acta Numismatica **6648**
0211-8408 Alcalde†
0211-8432 Anuario de Derecho Maritimo **4969**
0211-8483 Boletin de Arte **479**
0211-8513 Colegios de Abogados de Aragon. Boletin **4644**
0211-853X Cuadernos de Estadistica Matematica **8365**
0211-8556 Documentacion Laboral **1676**
0211-8572 Estudis Romanics **5116**
0211-8629 Foro de las Ciencias y de las Letras† **8957**

ISSN

DIRECTORY 2010 0226-840X 9201

0221-0347 Ecole Nationale Superieure de Biologie Appliquee a la Nutrition et a l'Alimentation. Cahiers†
0221-0363 Journal de Radiologie 6200
0221-0436 Mondes et Cultures 7883
0221-1777 Genealogie Lorraine 3768
0221-2102 Expertises des Systemes d'Information 4670
0221-2536 France. Bureau de Recherches Geologiques et Minieres. Documents 2734
0221-2781 Politique Internationale 7260
0221-2870 Inter Auto Ecoles de Conduite†
0221-301X Vinetec† 8997
0221-4245 Argent†
0221-4784 Absous†
0221-4792 Archeologie en Languedoc 379
0221-5004 Studia Iranica 561
0221-508X Aurore Paysanne 93
0221-5225 Bigre†
0221-5780 Cote-d'Ivoire Selection 1556
0221-5896 Ktema 4322
0221-5918 Annuaire Europeen d'Administration Publique 7420
0221-6280 Histoire de l'Education 2863
0221-7090 Bulletin des Elus Locaux 7111
0221-7279 Toulouse Magazine†
0221-7821 Franchise Magazine 1112
0221-7945 Societe Theophile Gautier. Bulletin 5374
0221-7996 Biba 2251
0221-8127 Tennis Info 8248
0221-833X Speakeasy 5240
0221-8836 Club Maison†
0221-8852 Amerindia 5093
0222-0334 La France Latine 5120
0222-0377 Charcuterie et Gastronomie 3676
0222-061X Tourhebdo†
0222-1543 Russkoe Vozrozhdenie 7706
0222-2094 Spicae†
0222-3074 Tutti†
0222-3856 Audition et Parole†
0222-3996 Auto Verte 8561
0222-4194 Le Droit Ouvrier 1676
0222-4259 Religieuses en Mission Educative
0222-447X Minis Autos†
0222-4828 Jeux d'Afrique
0222-5123 Met Mar 2755
0222-559X Securite Civile et Industrielle 2228
0222-5751 Actualites Digestives†
0222-593X Bamerkhav†
0222-5956 Cahiers Confrontation† 8939
0222-6650 Energ'hic†
0222-674X A F A E 3016
0222-6782 La Revue Francaise de Genealogie
0222-7762 Institut des Recherches Marxistes. Issues† 8965
0222-7797 Velo Magazine†
0222-8394 France. Laboratoire Central des Ponts et Chausees. Rapport de Recherche†
0222-9307 Soins - Pathologie Tropicale†
0222-9420 France des Points Chauds†
0222-9536 Aguiaine 323
0222-9617 Neuropsychiatrie de l'Enfance et de l'Adolescence 6097
0222-9706 Documents Autour de la Bible†
0222-9714 Cahiers Evangile 7629
0222-979X Jura Agricole et Rural 129
0222-9838 L'Information Grammaticale 5127
0223-0011 Batiment Artisanal 979
0223-0038 Air Fan 6409
0223-0127 Videoglyphes†
0223-0135 Revue Technique Machinisme Agricole 214
0223-0143 La Revue du Financier 1380
0223-0976 Ovni-Presence†
0223-1077 La Revue des Fabricants *changed to* 0990-1914
0223-1603 Galerie des Arts†
0223-3002 Sillages†
0223-3045 30 Jours d'Europe†
0223-3398 B O P I Dessins & Modeles 3365
0223-3401 B O P I Marques de Fabrique, de Commerce ou de Service 6746
0223-3533 Nouveau Commerce de la Lecture†
0223-3592 Dialogue (Ivry) 3057
0223-3711 Revue des Langues Romanes 5168
0223-3843 Le Medieviste et l'Ordinateur (Online) 4172
0223-4211 Officiel de la Sage-Femme†
0223-4270 Connaissance de la Region†
0223-4289 Livres Jeunes Aujourd'hui 5327
0223-4300 Tresors Monetaires 6653
0223-4637 Semaine Sociale Lamy 4782
0223-4718 La Revue Fiduciaire 1648
0223-4726 Legi - Social†
0223-4742 Fiction†
0223-4785 Galaxie - Bis
0223-4866 Enjeux 6402
0223-5099 Ecole Francaise de Rome. Collection 391
0223-5102 Ecole Francaise de Rome. Melanges: Antiquite 391
0223-5137 Neuroptera International†
0223-5234 European Journal of Medicinal Chemistry 731
0223-534X Instructions Nautiques 8646
0223-5358 Feux et Signaux de Brume
0223-5404 Revue Internationale de Droit Penal 4940
0223-5420 Accueillir†
0223-5439 Administration 7418
0223-5536 Justice 4708
0223-5633 Metropolis†
0223-565X Nouvelle Revue de Psychanalyse†
0223-5692 Personnel 1872
0223-5714 Proletariat†
0223-5749 Reforme 7772
0223-5803 Communisme†
0223-582X Cahiers de Defense Sociale 2645
0223-5838 Questions de Securite Sociale†
0223-5846 Hommes et Commerce†
0223-5862 Europe Outremer†
0223-5927 L'Assurance Mutuelle
0223-5986 Enseignement Public 2853
0223-7105 Memoire des Femmes
0223-7237 Genealogies Bourbonnaises et du Centre
0223-758X Batiment Parisien 979
0223-7741 La Bievre 902
0223-8756 Magazine de la Discotheque et des Disc-Jockeys
0223-9027 Message aux Adherents†
0223-9159 Bibliographie Internationale des Industries Agro-Alimentaires *changed to* 0245-985X
0223-9272 Centre de Geographie Humaine et Sociale. Travaux
0223-9353 Masques†
0223-9434 Lettre du Psychiatre†
0223-9469 Universite de Saint Etienne. Centre Jean Palerne. Memoires 4480
0224-0041 Recherches sur le Francais Parle 5165
0224-0424 Strategique 6448
0224-098X Stateco 1267
0224-1404 Fondation pour la Recherche et le Developpement dans l'Ocean Indien. Documents et Recherches
0224-2222 Repertoire du Notariat Defrenois. Supplement Rapide 4768
0224-2249 Repertoire du Notariat Defrenois 4768
0224-2265 Semaine de l'Energie†
0224-3911 Diagrammes 5482
0224-4365 Travail et Emploi 1711
0224-4772 Geopolitique du Petrole†
0224-5469 Nice Matin Magazine 3841
0224-5477 Nice Matin 3841
0224-7283 Sport-Auto. Hors-Serie
0224-747X Collection Psychologie et Pedagogie de la Musique
0224-7534 Racing
0224-7836 Collection Le Monde Indien. A: Textes 5275
0224-7844 Collection Le Monde Indien. B: Etudes 5275
0224-8042 C.T.N.E.R.H.I. Documents†
0224-8700 Ce Temps de Lire†
0224-8999 Gazette des Mathematiciens 5489
0224-960X Azur et Or†
0224-9928 J Magazine†
0225-0004 *see* 1910-2089 4316
0225-0233 Bonne Nouvelle 7786
0225-0500 Canadian Journal of Netherlandic Studies 5270
0225-0608 The Canadian Taxpayer 1916
0225-0934 Canada. Inland Waters Directorate. Historical Water Levels Summary. Quebec 2793
0225-1140 Italcommerce 1405
0225-1205 Minjoong Shinmoon
0225-1507 Canada. Statistics Canada. Coastwise Shipping Statistics†
0225-1574 Canadiana Authorities 5000
0225-1582 Moebius
0225-1604 Innisfil Scope 3811
0225-1760 U T L A S Newsletter†
0225-1965 Au Fil des Evenements 2828
0225-1981 Terminologie 5186
0225-2112 Feuillet Biblique 7797
0225-2279 Canadian Native Law Reporter 4640
0225-2287 Legal Information Service Reports†
0225-2384 Social Sciences and Humanities Research Council of Canada. Annual Report 8004
0225-2392 Canadian Bookseller 7557
0225-2783 Real Estate News 7609
0225-2910 Banque Nationale du Canada. Revue Economique†
0225-3151 Cinema au Quebec, Repertoire
0225-316X Quebec Film Industry Handbook *see* 0225-3151
0225-3194 Terminogramme 5186
0225-3216 Canadiana on Microfiche 622
0225-3488 Western Hog Journal 304
0225-3550 S P E A Q Journal
0225-3569 Entremetteur 2283
0225-3895 Medicine North America†
0225-4050 Foodservice & Hospitality News†
0225-4115 Justice - Directory of Services 8052
0225-4190 Handbook of Canadian Consumer Markets†
0225-4212 Plasmapheresis and Plasma Exchange†
0225-4239 Assessment Report Index 3150
0225-4271 Gerontophile *changed to* 1707-0104 4057
0225-4530 Quebec (Province) Pension Board. Supplemental Pension Plans-Characteristics and Membership Statistics†
0225-4700 Ma Caisse 1323
0225-476X Atlantic Year Book and Almanac†
0225-4913 Horses All 8293
0225-509X British Columbia. Housing Management Commission. Annual Report 4405
0225-5170 A S T I S Occasional Publications 2718
0225-5189 Canadian Journal of Development Studies 7952
0225-5316 Ontario Geological Survey. Geoscience Research Grant Program. Summary of Research†
0225-5456 Ports Annual 8657
0225-5693 B C Counsellor 3052
0225-5804 Resilog 3511
0225-5847 Canadian Legislative Report†
0225-6096 Forum *changed to* 1719-010X 2965
0225-610X Writer's Lifeline 7576
0225-6134 Sanitation Canada 3512
0225-6282 Air Transportation Annual†
0225-6363 Coatings 6716
0225-6398 Landscape Trades 3741
0225-6533 Adventuring in Conservation 3683
0225-6843 Broadside
0225-686X Musicworks 6595
0225-6932 Canadian Federation for the Humanities. Annual Report†
0225-7068 Mandate 7661
0225-7211 Simmental Country 156
0225-7629 Atlantic Life Business
0225-7874 Devil's Artisan 7319
0225-8285 Meetings & Incentive Travel 6281
0225-8315 Scope Camping News 8332
0225-9036 Index to Commonwealth Legal Periodicals†
0225-9044 Spirale 4476
0225-9206 Bath & Kitchen Marketer†
0225-9435 Canadian Music Trade 6554
0225-9443 Directory of Retail Chains in Canada 1988
0225-9451 Canadian Medical Education Statistics 5742
0225-9494 Statutes of the Province of British Columbia 4789
0225-9591 Medecin Veterinaire du Quebec 8803
0225-9885 Revue Quebecoise de Psychologie 7405
0225-9907 Northwest Territories. Bureau of Statistics. Statistics Quarterly 1255
0225-9923 Canada. Labour Canada. Annual Review - Revue Annuelle†
0225-9958 Canadian Review of Physical Anthropology†
0226-0174 Le Moyen Francais 5153
0226-0336 Canada Mortgage and Housing Corporation. Annual Report 4406
0226-0344 Cottager Magazine†
0226-0360 Public Service Commission of Canada. Appeal Board Decisions 4851
0226-0409 Canadian Book of Charities 8030
0226-0786 Forintek Canada Corp., Western Laboratory. Review Reports†
0226-0840 The Pottersfield Portfolio 5353
0226-093X Canadian Homeowner
0226-1413 Annual Aid Review†
0226-1456 Contact (Vancouver)
0226-1480 M I M I
0226-1502 Furniture Retailer†
0226-1510 Healthsharing†
0226-1537 Index of Industrial Relations Literature†
0226-1561 Ontario Wrestler Magazine
0226-157X Canadian Railway Club. Newsletter 8615
0226-1685 A S T I S Bibliography†
0226-1758 Today's Bride 5561
0226-1766 Connections (Alhambra) 7956
0226-1804 Repertoire Theatral du Quebec (Year)†
0226-1928 Ethnocultural Directory of Ontario†
0226-210X Quebecensia
0226-2169 Le Sagamien 4028
0226-2177 Canadian Human Rights Reporter 7203
0226-224X Au Courant†
0226-2320 Canada. Statistics Canada. Restaurant, Caterer and Tavern Statistics 4401
0226-2347 Candid Facts 5592
0226-2576 Marche du Travail†
0226-2630 Track & Field Journal†
0226-2916 Interuniversity Centre for European Studies. Research Report†
0226-3068 Zapad†
0226-3114 Repertoire des Cooperatives du Quebec†
0226-3300 University of Guelph Library. Collection Update 5053
0226-3440 University College Review†
0226-3467 Caducee 2276
0226-3491 Studies in Aboriginal Rights†
0226-3505 Contact (Laval) 3807
0226-353X Skylark (Saskatoon) 5174
0226-3882 Negotiated Working Conditions from Collective Agreements in Nova Scotia†
0226-3947 Economics of Milk Production in Alberta 264
0226-420X Newfoundland. Department of Social Services. Annual Report 8058
0226-4323 Quebec (Province). Conseil des Affaires Sociales et de la Famille. Rapport Annuel†
0226-4595 Canada. Statistics Canada. Metal Mines (Print Edition) *changed to* 1708-6299 6485
0226-4617 Canada. Statistics Canada. Quarries and Sand Pits 6459
0226-4781 Ici Radio Canada Television†
0226-479X Remote Sensing in Canada 2715
0226-501X Today Magazine†
0226-5044 Manitoba History 4302
0226-5117 Eastern News 3531
0226-5125 Canadian Theatre Checklist†
0226-5346 Quebec (Province). Regie de l'Assurance-Maladie. Statistiques Annuelles 4530
0226-5389 Carleton University Magazine 2971
0226-5419 Directory of Long-Term Care Centres in Canada†
0226-5664 Canadian Collector†
0226-5702 The Ontario Water Skier 8326
0226-577X Canadian Amateur Softball Association. Facts & Figures†
0226-5788 Health Care†
0226-5893 Policy Options 7166
0226-5923 Catholic Health Association of Canada Review†
0226-6083 Croc
0226-6091 Data Product News
0226-6105 Generations (Winnipeg) 3768
0226-6121 Age d'Or - Vie Nouvelle
0226-6245 Entraide Genealogique 3765
0226-627X Atlantic Post Calls 8287
0226-6326 Guelph This Week
0226-6377 Telegraph (Battleford) 3818
0226-6628 Thyroid Disorders†
0226-6776 Moving to Houston†
0226-6822 Financial Accounting Problems with Detailed Solutions
0226-6881 Dialogues et Cultures 5112
0226-7004 Summer Breezes†
0226-7063 Cahiers d'Histoire de Deux-Montagnes
0226-7101 Kingston Business Review†
0226-7144 Langues et Linguistique 5142
0226-7365 Quality of Working Life†
0226-7446 Canadian Gemmologist 4564
0226-7454 Universites 3007
0226-7462 Whiskey Jack†
0226-7527 Carleton University. Library. Serials List†
0226-7551 Shopping Centre Canada†
0226-7586 McGill University. Register 4152
0226-7616 Centre for Resources Studies. Working Papers†
0226-7691 B.C. Archer 8160
0226-773X Federation of Canadian Archers. Rules Book 8173
0226-7748 E I C†
0226-7934 Laurentian University. Gazette†
0226-8043 Quaderni d'Italianistica 5356
0226-8264 Canadian Real Estate Journal†
0226-8361 Marine Affairs Bibliography†
0226-840X Samisdat†

ISSN

0226-8418	Scripta Mediterranea **4325**
0226-8531	Co-opservations†
0226-854X	I P Sharp Newsletter†
0226-8620	Musick **6594**
0226-8760	Canadian Network Papers†
0226-8841	Health Law in Canada **5913**
0226-8922	Conventions & Meetings Canada **6279**
0226-8965	Coaching Science Update†
0226-9252	Quebec Chronicle - Telegraph **3816**
0226-9325	O S C Bulletin†
0226-9368	British Columbia. Ministry of Forests. Research Notes **3685**
0226-9422	At the Centre†
0226-9430	British Columbia. Ministry of Energy, Mines and Petroleum Resources. Paper Series†
0226-9554	Urgences changed to 1189-4563 **5385**
0226-9597	Practical Homes **1029**
0226-9686	Suburban **3818**
0226-9864	Canadian Retailer (Toronto) **1809**
0226-9902	Femmes d'Action
0227-0072	University of Manitoba Anthropology Papers **359**
0227-0129	Canadian Nuclear Society. Annual Conference Summaries **3166**
0227-017X	Canada. Statistics Canada. Retail Chain and Department Stores **1218**
0227-0315	Filles d'Aujourd'hui changed to 1714-9134 **2255**
0227-034X	Service **8068**
0227-0390	Federal Court of Appeal Decisions†
0227-0455	The New Quarterly **5340**
0227-0579	Alberta Wild Rose Quarter Horse Journal†
0227-0722	Veux-tu Savoir? changed to 1712-7637 **2142**
0227-0773	Island (Lantzville)
0227-0994	Family Genealogies†
0227-1230	Juice & Cookie
0227-1265	Tax Principles to Remember†
0227-1338	I A S C - S C A D Bulletin **5012**
0227-1362	Trends in Collective Agreement Settlement Wage Rate Changes in Nova Scotia†
0227-1370	Gaspesie†
0227-1397	Ontario Business†
0227-1400	Annual Bibliography of Victorian Studies **5406**
0227-1532	Newfoundland T V Topics†
0227-1559	U F O Update
0227-1699	Lyman's Standard Catalogue of Canada-B N A Postage Stamps†
0227-1761	Canada. Statistics Canada. Production of Selected Biscuits†
0227-1834	Soccer Canada†
0227-1907	Canadian Nuclear Society. Annual Conference Proceedings **3166**
0227-2091	Circle†
0227-2199	University of Waterloo Courier **2307**
0227-227X	Liaison (Vanier) **503**
0227-2393	F A M L I†
0227-2636	L M G Report on Data and Word Processing
0227-2806	Graphic Monthly **7322**
0227-2865	National Bank of Canada. Economic Review†
0227-3020	Transport - Action **8514**
0227-3160	Helicopters **8544**
0227-3268	Ontario. Federal Cabinet. Orders-in-Council†
0227-3411	Who's Who in Canadian Business (Year)†
0227-3713	Geolog **2736**
0227-3780	School Libraries in Canada†
0227-3802	British Columbia. Ministry of Agriculture and Food. Agricultural Aid to Developing Countries†
0227-3853	Mid-North Monitor **3813**
0227-4272	Style Buyers' Guide see 0039-4246 **2261**
0227-4302	Directory of Restaurant & Fast Food Chains in Canada **3634**
0227-4310	Amateur Musician **6543**
0227-4337	Canadian Council of Churches. Triennial Assembly Proceedings†
0227-4752	Nova Scotia Historical Review†
0227-4779	Feuillet Meteorologique†
0227-4787	Canada Water Act. Annual Report†
0227-5090	Scrivener Creative Review **5368**
0227-5872	Saskatchewan Archaeology **415**
0227-5910	Crisis (Kirkland) **7350**
0227-6178	Court Cases of Interest to the Ombudsman Institution†
0227-6313	Ressources see 0709-0439
0227-6658	Orienteering Canada **8326**
0227-7514	Saskatchewan Archaeological Society Newsletter **415**
0227-793X	Seasons changed to 1711-9138 **2623**
0227-7980	Canadian Pest Management Society Proceedings†
0227-8073	Chief Electoral Officer. Annual Report **7430**
0227-809X	Canadian Business Management Developments†
0227-8731	Micro-Scope†
0227-9207	Statement of Votes - General Election and By-Election **7186**
0227-986X	Ontario Fisheries. Technical Report Series **3604**
0227-9916	Ontario Hydro Research Review
0228-0108	Supreme Court Law Review **4791**
0228-0116	T V Plus†
0228-0132	Conference Board of Canada. The Provincial Economies
0228-0140	Conference Board of Canada. The Canadian Economy
0228-0531	Northumberland News **3814**
0228-0620	J A M
0228-0671	For the Learning of Mathematics **5488**
0228-0736	Canada. Petawawa National Forestry Institute. Information Reports†
0228-0906	Victorian Order of Nurses for Canada. National Office. Newsletter†
0228-0914	Canadian School Executive†
0228-1023	Niagara Farmers' Monthly **295**
0228-1201	Stress Journal†
0228-1244	Ennui
0228-1546	Growing up Whole†
0228-1554	Media West
0228-1635	Journal of Ukrainian Studies **5316**
0228-1686	Producteur de Lait Quebecois **268**
0228-1821	C R S Perspectives†

0228-2127	C P A Review†
0228-2194	Nicola Indian†
0228-2356	Aspen†
0228-250X	Tricolorul
0228-2518	In Summary†
0228-2828	Messenger **3549**
0228-2984	Westminster Institute Review†
0228-3344	Potboiler Magazine
0228-3530	La Plongee†
0228-3980	Canada. Service de l'Environnement Atmospherique. Memoires Techniques see 0708-2878
0228-4642	Ontario Science Centre. Newscience†
0228-4723	Cape Breton Development Corporation. Annual Report changed to 0848-5267 **7435**
0228-5134	Canada. Statistics Canada. Listing of Supplementary Documents†
0228-5452	La Barrique **598**
0228-5479	La Vie en Rose
0228-5584	Agriweek **86**
0228-5622	Saskatchewan Energy & Mines. Monthly Oil and Gas Production Report **6791**
0228-5630	Drilling Activity Report **6767**
0228-5657	Saskatchewan Geological Survey. Summary of Investigations (Print Edition) changed to 1912-4996 **2765**
0228-5789	Quebec. Ministere de l'Education. Rapport Annuel changed to 1715-8818 **2902**
0228-5843	Noticias do Canada†
0228-5851	Regina Geographical Studies **4026**
0228-586X	Alive **6981**
0228-6157	Wine Tidings **613**
0228-6203	International Journal of Modelling & Simulation **3347**
0228-6246	Science Council of Canada. Annual Review†
0228-6351	Quebec Soccer **8243**
0228-6637	Arpenteur-Geometre
0228-6726	Video Guide **2403**
0228-698X	Voila Quebec **8786**
0228-7099	Le Polyscope **2297**
0228-734X	Le Collectif (Sherbrooke) **2278**
0228-7404	Moosehead Anthology **5427**
0228-7498	The Craft Factor **533**
0228-7587	Drillsite†
0228-7749	Made in Canada **503**
0228-7781	Sound Heritage Series†
0228-7951	Ecriture Francaise dans le Monde†
0228-8117	British Columbia. Ministry of Agriculture Fisheries and Food. Field Crop Production Guide to Weed, Disease, Insect, Bird and Rodent Control **98**
0228-8311	Manitoba Industry, Trade and Mines. Economic Geology Report Series **2753**
0228-8397	Canadian Association of African Studies. Newsletter **2971**
0228-8605	Papers in Mediaeval Studies **4253**
0228-863X	Directory of Alcohol and Drug Treatment Resources in Ontario
0228-8648	Substance Abuse Book Review Index†
0228-8699	Chronic Diseases in Canada **5944**
0228-8702	Maladies Chroniques au Canada **5947**
0228-877X	Ontario Medical Technologist†
0228-8788	Construction Canada **995**
0228-8842	B.C. Naturalist changed to 1912-3280 **7838**
0228-8877	Memorial University of Newfoundland. Gazette **2291**
0228-894X	National Loss Prevention
0228-9091	Signal **6687**
0228-9636	Les Diplomes **2282**
0228-9652	Reading Manitoba **2903**
0228-9806	Science Express
0228-9989	Canada. Environment Canada. Forestry Service Research Notes†
0229-012X	Mal-I-Mic News **6635**
0229-0235	B C A T M L Newsletter **3052**
0229-0391	Northern Pen **3814**
0229-0685	Proletarian Revolution
0229-0693	Revolution Proletarienne see 0229-0685
0229-0812	Digest on Gay Rights **4658**
0229-1134	Coptologia **7704**
0229-1150	British Columbia. Ministry of Environment, Lands and Parks. Fisheries Branch. Fisheries Technical Circular **3587**
0229-1320	Ontario Craft **538**
0229-1622	British Columbia. Ministry of Forests. Land Management Handbooks **3685**
0229-1886	British Columbia. Ministry of Forests. Five-Year Forest and Range Resources Program **2604**
0229-1916	Quaker Concern **7740**
0229-1932	New Canadian Fandom **5445**
0229-2068	L'Infomane **2287**
0229-2181	International Ombudsman Institute. Newsletter **4696**
0229-2408	Transport Montreal
0229-2548	Canadian Parliamentary Review **7113**
0229-2556	see 0229-2548 **7113**
0229-2653	Action for Canada's Children†
0229-2807	Arc **7622**
0229-2947	Projection (Toronto)
0229-3099	Alberta Science Teacher
0229-3196	Toronto Clarion
0229-3404	Les Affaires **1306**
0229-3455	Champion†
0229-365X	British Columbia Federation of Labour. Annual Convention. Summary of Proceedings
0229-379X	Careers
0229-382X	In Tune†
0229-4141	Trustee†
0229-4362	Transporteur **7777**
0229-4435	Artisan†
0229-4958	Collective Agreement Expiration in Nova Scotia†
0229-4966	Athletics **8159**
0229-5024	Birdfinding in Canada†
0229-5032	Moving to Washington, D.C.†
0229-5040	Moving to Dallas - Fort Worth†
0229-5113	Refuge **7291**
0229-5121	see 0229-5113 **7291**

0229-527X	British Columbia Genealogical Society. Newsletter†
0229-5385	Hysteria†
0229-5415	Spartacist Canada **7185**
0229-5466	Touring **8763**
0229-5628	C-CORE Publication **3183**
0229-5679	R I A Digest†
0229-5792	Conference Board of Canada. Consumer Markets Update
0229-6098	Canada. Statistics Canada. Mineral Wool Including Fibrous Glass Insulation **1045**
0229-6276	Alberta Law Reform Institute. Annual Report **4613**
0229-6357	Vancouver Board of Trade Roster and Purchasers' Guide **1411**
0229-6373	Clan Suibhne Association. Newsletter†
0229-6829	Questions de Culture†
0229-7051	Canadian Journal of Philosophy. Supplementary Volume Series **6909**
0229-7094	Fifth Column **442**
0229-7175	His Dominion†
0229-7205	Saamis Seeker **3781**
0229-7248	Thornhill Month
0229-7256	Canadian Research Institute for the Advancement of Women. Newsletter **8854**
0229-737X	Sugar World†
0229-7493	Iota **2288**
0229-7876	Producteur de Porc Quebecois†
0229-8090	Grainews **272**
0229-8139	Commission Municipale du Quebec. Rapport Annuel changed to 1709-6235 **7490**
0229-8325	Canada. Mineral Policy Sector. Mineral Survey†
0229-8422	Toy Report **4062**
0229-8473	Northern Pipeline Agency. Annual Report **3143**
0229-8546	Alberta's Reserve of Gas: Complete Listing **6761**
0229-8651	R S - S I†
0229-8961	Canadian Art Sales Index **480**
0229-9119	Varsity Student Handbook **2308**
0229-9429	L'Actualite Medicale **5567**
0229-9666	Saskatchewan Trucking **8675**
0230-0508	Pszichologia **7402**
0230-0648	Malakologiai Tajekoztato **954**
0230-1806	Egyutt†
0230-1814	Allattenyesztes es Takarmanyozas **277**
0230-1911	Adam†
0230-2780	Acta Universitatis Szegediensis. Papers in English and American Studies **5090**
0230-3558	Acta Universitatis Szegediensis de Attila Jozsef Nominatae. Sectio Scientiae Socialismi†
0230-4139	Hungarian Panorama†
0230-4414	Hungary. Kozponti Statisztikai Hivatal. Idegenforgalmi Evkonyv **8779**
0230-4430	Rovid Uton†
0230-4619	Informatika es Tudomanyelemzes†
0230-5151	Levelezesi Sakkhirado **8185**
0230-5348	Anyagmozgatasi es Csomagolasi Szakirodalmi Tajekoztato **8521**
0230-5755	Hungary see 0230-5828 **8386**
0230-581X	Magyar Korhazak es Klinikak Evkonyve
0230-5828	Magyarorszag **8386**
0230-5909	Ungarn see 0230-5828 **8386**
0230-5925	Vengria v Godu see 0230-5828 **8386**
0230-6476	Acta Paedagogica Debrecina **2823**
0230-6972	Uj Technika
0230-7065	Geologiai es Geofizikai Szakirodalmi Tajekoztato **2719**
0230-8223	Musicalia Danubiana **6594**
0230-8452	Monumenta Linguae Mongolicae Collecta†
0230-9017	Miscellanea Zoologica Hungarica†
0230-9718	Public Finance in Hungary†
0231-0007	Symposium on Reliability in Electronics **3114**
0231-0643	Automatizalasi, Szamitastechnikai es Merestechnikai Szakirodalmi Tajekoztato **7047**
0231-0651	Banyaszati Szakirodalmi Tajekoztato **6485**
0231-066X	Elektronikai es Hiradastechnikai Szakirodalmi **2347**
0231-0678	Energiaipari es Energiagazdalkodasi Tajekoztato **3152**
0231-0686	Gepeszeti Szakirodalmi Tajekoztato **3230**
0231-0694	Gepgyartastechnologiai es Szerszamgepipari Szakirodalmi Tajekoztato **3230**
0231-0708	Kohaszati es Onteszeti Szakirodalmi Tajekoztato **6340**
0231-0716	Kornyezetvedelmi Szakirodalmi Tajekoztato **3480**
0231-0724	Kozuti Kozlekedesi Szakirodalmi Tajekoztato **8527**
0231-0732	Melyepitesi es Vizepitesi Szakirodalmi Tajekoztato **3232**
0231-0740	Papiripari es Nyomdaipari Szakirodalmi Tajekoztato **6740**
0231-0759	Vallalatszervezesi es Ipargazdasagi Szakirodalmi Tajekoztato **1273**
0231-0767	Vasuti Kozlekedesi Szakirodalmi Tajekoztato **8532**
0231-0775	Vegyipari Szakirodalmi Tajekoztato **2096**
0231-0783	Elektrotechnikai Szakirodalmi Tajekoztato **3229**
0231-1941	Hajozasi Szakirodalmi Tajekoztato **8525**
0231-195X	Ipari Formatervezesi Szakirodalmi Tajekoztato **3232**
0231-2522	Tarsadalomkutatas **8143**
0231-2670	Acta Universitatis Szegediensis de Attila Jozsef Nominatae. Sectio Philosophica†
0231-3316	Szamitogepes Muszaki Tervezes **3234**
0231-3596	ATOMKI Annual Report **7065**
0231-3928	Repulesi Szakirodalmi Tajekoztato **8529**
0231-424X	Acta Physiologica Hungarica **918**
0231-4398	O G Y I Kozlemenyek changed to 1787-1204 **6845**
0231-441X	Acta Paediatrica Hungarica†
0231-4592	Magyar Nemzeti Bibliografia. Idoszaki Kiadvanyok Bibliografiaja **630**
0231-4614	Acta Chirurgica Hungarica†
0231-5335	Acta Dendrobiologica **3682**
0231-5513	Populacni Zpravy†
0231-5548	Travaux Geophysiques†
0231-5629	Pionyrska Stafeta†
0231-5653	Acta Museorum Agriculturae†
0231-5718	Partelet†
0231-5742	Agricultura Tropica et Subtropica **83**
0231-5785	Acta Facultatis Forestalis, Zvolen **3682**
0231-5823	Archaeologia Historica **375**
0231-5882	General Physiology and Biophysics **922**
0231-5904	Pamatnik Narodniho Pisemnictvi. Sbornik **5348**

0235-2109 Referativnyi Zhurnal. Proektirovanie, Konstruirovanie, Tekhnologiya i Oborudovanie dlya Radiotekhnicheskogo Proizvodstva **3117**
0235-2117 Referativnyi Zhurnal. Radiolokatsiya, Radionavigatsiya, Radioupravlenie, Televizionnaya Tekhnika **3117**
0235-2133 Referativnyi Zhurnal. Teoreticheskaya Radiotekhnika. Antenny. Volnovody. Ob'emnye Rezonatory. Rasprostranenie Radiovoln **3117**
0235-215X Referativnyi Zhurnal. Kvantovaya Elektronika. Krioelektronika. Golografiya **7049**
0235-2168 Referativnyi Zhurnal. Materialy dlya Elektroniki **3117**
0235-2184 Referativnyi Zhurnal. Vychislitel'naya Matematika. Matematicheskaya Kibernetika **5549**
0235-2206 Referativnyi Zhurnal. Tekhnologiya Silikatnykh i Tugoplavkikh Nemetallicheskikh Materialov **3234**
0235-2222 Referativnyi Zhurnal. Izdatel'skoe Delo i Poligrafiya **7329**
0235-2257 Itogi Nauki i Tekhniki. Promyshlennye Roboty i Manipulyatory†
0235-2265 Itogi Nauki i Tekhniki. Svyaz'†
0235-2281 Itogi Nauki i Tekhniki. Khimiya i Tekhnologiya Pishchevykh Produktov†
0235-2443 A P K: Ekonomika, Upravlenie **190**
0235-2451 Dostizheniya Nauki i Tekhniki A P K **106**
0235-2478 Zootekhniya **305**
0235-2486 Pishchevaya Promyshlennost' **3660**
0235-2494 Ekonomika Sel'skokhozyaistvennykh i Pererabatyvayushchikh Predpriyatii **1103**
0235-2508 Khleboproducty **274**
0235-2524 Melioratsiya i Vodnoe Khozyaistvo **8829**
0235-2532 Zernovye Kul'tury **260**
0235-2559 Tekhnicheskie Kul'tury†
0235-2591 Sadovodstvo i Vinogradarstvo **3749**
0235-2605 Kombikormovaya Promyshlennost' **274**
0235-2990 Antibiotiki i Khimioterapiya **6821**
0235-3105 Referativnyi Zhurnal. Biologiya Sel's'kokhozyaistvennykh Zhivotnykh **718**
0235-3148 Referativnyi Zhurnal. Prirodnye Organicheskie Soedineniya i ikh Sinteticheskie Analogi **2095**
0235-3156 Referativnyi Zhurnal. Khimiya i Tekhnologiya Pishchevykh Produktov **2095**
0235-3164 Referativnyi Zhurnal. Tekhnologiya Proizvodstva Produktov Bytovoi Khimii. Parfumeriya i Kosmetika **2096**
0235-3199 Itogi Nauki i Tekhniki. Izdatel'skoe Delo i Poligrafiya†
0235-3202 Itogi Nauki i Tekhniki. Ekonomiya Topliva Teplovoi i Elektricheskoi Energii†
0235-3474 Tekhnicheskaya Diagnostika i Nerazrushayushchii Kontrol' **7043**
0235-3490 Arkheolohiya **381**
0235-3520 Mir P K **2432**
0235-4160 Oftal'mokhirurgiya **6047**
0235-4241 Rasskaz **5357**
0235-5000 Obzornaya Informatsiya. Problemy Bezopasnosti Poletov **76**
0235-5019 Obzornaya Informatsiya. Problemy Okruzhayushchei Sredy i Prirodnykh Resursov **3480**
0235-5043 Klub **4597**
0235-5051 Narodnoe Tvorchestvo **537**
0235-5116 Pod'emno-Transportnaya Tekhnika i Sklady†
0235-5531 Obzornaya Informatsiya. Geologiya, Metody Poiskov, Razvedki i Otsenki Mestorozhdenii Tverdykh Poleznykh Iskopaemykh **2760**
0235-554X Obzornaya Informatsiya. Geologiya, Metody Poiskov, Razvedki i Otsenki Mestorozhdenii Toplivnoenergeticheskogo Syr'ia **2760**
0235-5620 Aktual'nye Problemy Evropy **7220**
0235-5884 Protsessy Lit'ya **6330**
0235-635X Sil's'ki Obrii **156**
0235-6368 Dom, Sad, Gorod **196**
0235-6384 Krantai†
0235-6821 Sotsial'nye i Gumanitarnye Nauki. Zarubezhnaya Literatura. Kitaevedenie†
0235-6848 Nork **5342**
0235-6856 Referativnyi Zhurnal. Sverkhprovodimost' **7049**
0235-6899 Maakodu **135**
0235-7089 Rodina **4259**
0235-7119 Problemy Mashinostroeniya i Nadezhnosti Mashin **5458**
0235-716X Lituanistica **5148**
0235-7186 Filosofija, Sociologija **6920**
0235-7208 Lietuvos Mokslu Akademija. Energetika **3141**
0235-7216 Lietuvos Mokslu Akademija. Chemija **2071**
0235-7224 Ekologija **671**
0235-7259 Arkhitektura i Stroitel'stvo Rossii **433**
0235-7607 Delovye Svyazi
0235-764X Business Contact *see* 0235-7607
0235-7771 Akadeemia **4441**
0235-7801 Mezhdunarodnyi Agropromyshlennyi Zhurnal **136**
0235-7941 Filosofska Dumka **6920**
0235-8026 Eesti Arst **7515**
0235-8050 Kataliku Pasaulis **7802**
0235-8573 Traktory i Sel'skokhozyaistvennye Mashiny **214**
0235-8824 Referativnyi Zhurnal. Nauchno-Tekhnicheskii Progress. Integratsiya Nauki s Proizvodstvom. Organizatsiya i Finansirovanie **8447**
0235-8832 Referativnyi Zhurnal. Kadry, Ekonomika Obrazovaniya **1260**
0235-8859 Referativnyi Zhurnal. Fizika Tverdykh Tel: Magnitnye Svoistva **7049**
0235-8867 Referativnyi Zhurnal. Fizika Tverdykh Tel: Elektricheskie Svoistva **7049**
0235-8875 Referativnyi Zhurnal. Optika i Yadernaya Fizika **7049**
0235-8883 Referativnyi Zhurnal. Ekonomicheskie Aspekty Organizatsii i Tekhniki Sistem Upravleniya **1259**
0235-8891 Referativnyi Zhurnal. Metody Upravleniya Ekonomikoi **1260**
0235-8913 Referativnyi Zhurnal. Genetika i Selektsiya Mikroorganizmov **719**
0235-8921 Referativnyi Zhurnal. Genetika i Selektsiya Sel'skokhozyaistvennykh Zhivotnykh **719**
0235-8964 Superconductivity: Physics, Chemistry, Technology†
0235-9146 Haridus **2862**
0235-974X Idel **5308**
0236-0551 Liaudies Kultura **346**
0236-0942 Dialog **7130**
0236-1019 Spadcyna **4266**
0236-1205 Morskoi Transport. Seriya: Ekonomika i Kommercheskaya Rabota na Morskom Transporte **8653**
0236-1426 Vneshneekonomicheskie Svyazi Rossii **1524**
0236-1639 Proizvodstvo i Ispol'zovanie Elastomerov **3254**
0236-1914 Obzornaya Informatsiya. Transport: Nauka, Tekhnika, Upravlenie **8528**
0236-2007 Chelovek **4447**
0236-2058 Voennaya Mysl' **6452**
0236-235X Programmnye Produkty i Sistemy *see* 0257-9928 **1786**
0236-2414 Opyt Morskikh Uchebnykh Zavedenii **8507**
0236-2619 Sport v S S S R i v Mire†
0236-2716 Caritas **7787**
0236-2791 Grudnaya i Serdechno-Sosudistaya Khirurgiya **6244**
0236-3054 Vrach **5729**
0236-3100 Revista de Istorie a Moldovei **4257**
0236-3127 Itogi Nauki i Tekhniki. Seriya Vychislitelnye Nauki†
0236-3135 Itogi Nauki i Tekhniki. Seriya Koordinatsionnaya Khimiya Metallorganicheskaya†
0236-3143 Itogi Nauki i Tekhniki. Nauchno-Tekhnicheskii Progress. Integratsiya Nauki s Proizvodstvom†
0236-3194 Itogi Nauki i Tekhniki. Fizicheskie i Matematicheskie Modeli Neironnykh Setei†
0236-3208 Itogi Nauki i Tekhniki. Yadernye Reaktory†
0236-3496 Shchit i Mech **8200**
0236-3593 Zheleznodorozhnyi Transport. Seriya. Elektrosnabzhenie Zheleznykh Dorog **8628**
0236-3607 Zheleznodorozhnyi Transport. Seriya. Signalizatsiya i Svyaz' **8628**
0236-3615 Zheleznodorozhnyi Transport. Seriya. Vychislitel'naya Tekhnika i Avtomatizirovannye Sistemy Upravleniya **8628**
0236-3674 Ekspress-Informatsiya. Geologiya, Metody Poiskov, Razvedki i Otsenki Mestorozhdenii Tverdykh Poleznykh Iskopaemykh **2733**
0236-3879 Kur'ier Yunesko **7250**
0236-3933 Moskovskii Gosudarstvennyi Tekhnicheskii Universitet. Vestnik. Priborostroenie **4489**
0236-3941 Moskovskii Gosudarstvennyi Tekhnicheskii Universitet. Vestnik. Mashinostroenie **3390**
0236-4719 Magazyn Wilenski **3549**
0236-4964 Radiolyubitel' **2363**
0236-4999 Psikhologiya Zrelosti i Stareniya **4053**
0236-5200 Konyvtari es Informatikai Kozponti Gyarapodasi Jegyzek†
0236-5278 Acta Geologica Hungarica *changed to* 1788-2281 **2728**
0236-5286 Acta Medica Hungarica†
0236-5294 Acta Mathematica Hungarica **5464**
0236-5383 Acta Biologica Hungarica **649**
0236-5391 Acta Morphologica Hungarica†
0236-5731 Journal of Radioanalytical and Nuclear Chemistry **2102**
0236-607X Munkavedelem Munka- es Uzemegeszsegugy†
0236-6134 Magyar Elektronika **3108**
0236-6290 Acta Veterinaria Hungarica **8790**
0236-6495 Acta Botanica Hungarica **772**
0236-6568 Hungarian Studies **4456**
0236-705X Elelmiszertudomanyi es Elelmiszeripari Szakirodalmi Tajekoztato†
0236-7408 Muszaki Konyv-Magazin†
0236-8676 Elektronikai Technologia, Mikrotechnika†
0236-8722 International Agrophysics **237**
0236-9168 Agria **4197**
0236-9591 Studies in Modern Philology **5183**
0236-9702 Scientific Films and Videocassettes†
0236-9842 Hungary. Kozponti Statisztikai Hivatal. Szamitastechnikai Statisztikai Zsebkonyv **2443**
0237-0115 Biotechnology Information†
0237-028X Acta I M E K O **6400**
0237-0298 Hungary. Kozponti Statisztikai Hivatal. Epitoipari Arak Alakulasa†
0237-0301 Etudes Historiques Hongroises **4139**
0237-0719 Baranyai Konyvtaros†
0237-0808 Hungarian R and D Abstracts. Science and Technology **7937**
0237-0840 Kulfoldi Kozgazdasagi Irodalmi Szemle. Series A†
0237-0859 Kulfoldi Kozgazdasagi Irodalmi Szemle. Series B†
0237-1545 Ungarische Wirtschaftshefte *changed to* 1416-3586 **1847**
0237-1553 Hungarian Business Herald **1819**
0237-2169 Scientific Society of the Silicate Industry. Conference on Silicate Industry and Silicate Science **2045**
0237-2215 International Symposium of the Technical Committee on Photon-Detectors†
0237-2525 Sakkelet **8198**
0237-2738 Universitatis Scientiarum Budapestinensis de Rolando Eotvos Nominatae. Annales. Sectio Geophysica et Meteorologica **2791**
0237-322X Tudomany **7925**
0237-3785 Nepszava (National Edition) *see* 0133-1701 **3876**
0237-3831 Business Partner Hungary **1074**
0237-384X Vasarnapi Hirek **3877**
0237-4021 Medipress
0237-4323 A Falu **198**
0237-5249 Turizmus **8770**
0237-5419 Universitas Budapestinensis. Institutum Zoosystematicum et Oecologicum. Opuscula Zoologica **966**
0237-5478 Geschaeftspartner Ungarn **1113**
0237-5516 Kepes 7†
0237-7837 Computerworld Szamotastechnika **2414**
0237-7896 Psychiatria Hungarica **6176**
0237-7934 Aetas **4129**
0237-8280 Hungary. Kozponti Statisztikai Hivatal. Kozlekedesi Evkonyv **8526**
0237-9554 Acta Universitatis Szegediensis. Dissertationes Slavicae. Sectio Linguistica **5090**
0237-9562 Acta Universitatis Szegediensis de Attila Jozsef Nominatae. Dissertationes Slavicae. Sectio Historiae Litterarum†
0237-9996 Studies in Central and Eastern European Music†
0238-0161 Acta Agronomica Hungarica **78**
0238-0196 Hungarika Informacio†
0238-0218 Antaeus **374**
0238-0668 Comparative History of Literatures in European Languages **5277**
0238-1249 Acta Phytopathologica et Entomologica Hungarica **773**
0238-132X Danubian Historical Studies†
0238-1486 European Review of Native American Studies **6634**
0238-1613 Review of Historical Demography†
0238-2423 Eotvos University. Astronomy Department. Publications **574**
0238-2571 Medicina Thoracalis **6216**
0238-2865 Ezredveg **5294**
0238-4000 Foci†
0238-4043 Notarius†
0238-5562 Eotvos Lorand Tudomanyegyetem. Tudomanyos Tajekoztato†
0238-5759 Popcorn **2208**
0238-602X Hungarian Trade Journal†
0238-7891 Hungary. Kozponti Statisztikai Hivatal. Mezogazdasagi Elelmiszeripari Statisztikai Zsebkonyv **181**
0238-8197 Agrarvilag†
0238-8308 Mediterran Tanulmanyok **4323**
0238-9037 Reform **3877**
0238-9401 Hungarian Music Quarterly†
0238-9878 Muszaki-Gazdasagi Magazin **1252**
0238-9932 Hungarian Observer†
0239-0345 Soon to Appear...†
0239-0426 Autopiac **8566**
0239-152X Heti Budapest†
0239-1589 Hungary. Kozponti Statisztikai Hivatal. Gazdasag es Statisztika **1240**
0239-1619 The Arabist **5095**
0239-2275 Acta Academiae Scientiarum Poloniae†
0239-2356 Wyzsza Szkola Pedagogiczna im. Komisji Edukacji Narodowej w Krakowie. Rocznik Naukowo-Dydaktyczny. Prace Pedagogiczne†
0239-2666 Zielony Sztandar. Dodatek Ilustrowany *see* 0137-9399 **7198**
0239-3174 Projektowanie i Systemy **8435**
0239-3182 Politechnika Wroclawska. Instytut Konstrukcji i Eksploatacji Maszyn. Prace Naukowe. Wspolpraca†
0239-3204 Politechnika Wroclawska. Instytut Nauk Ekonomiczno-Spolecznych. Prace Naukowe. Monografie†
0239-3212 Politechnika Wroclawska. Instytut Nauk Ekonomiczno-Spolecznych. Prace Naukowe. Studia i Materialy†
0239-3271 Czlowiek i Spoleczenstwo **7958**
0239-3433 Politechnika Wroclawska. Instytut Sterowania i Techniki Systemow. Prace Naukowe. Konferencje†
0239-3506 Studia Rossica **5379**
0239-3646 Maszyny Elektryczne **3325**
0239-3670 Chrzescijanskie Stowarzyszenie Spoleczne. Materialy Problemowe†
0239-4170 Psychoterapia **6179**
0239-4243 Annales Universitatis Mariae Curie-Sklodowska. Sectio EE. Zootechnika **8792**
0239-4251 Annales Universitatis Mariae Curie-Sklodowska. Sectio F. Historia **4130**
0239-426X Annales Universitatis Mariae Curie-Sklodowska. Sectio FF. Philologiae **5094**
0239-4421 Bibliografia Wydawnictw Ciaglych **617**
0239-4472 Tarnowskie Studia Teologiczne **7819**
0239-4499 Wiadomosci Polskiego Autokefalicznego Kosciola Prawoslawnego **7707**
0239-4596 Wroclawska Stomatologia *changed to* 1644-387X **5839**
0239-4855 Instytut Transportu Samochodowego. Zeszyty Naukowe **8499**
0239-488X Politechnika Poznanska. Zeszyty Naukowe. Geometria **5525**
0239-5096 Stan Hodowli i Wyniki Oceny Swin **301**
0239-5231 I.B. Informacja Biezaca†
0239-5282 Akademia Gorniczo-Hutnicza im. Stanislawa Staszica. Mechanika. Kwartalnik *changed to* 1734-8927 **3389**
0239-5312 Akademia Gorniczo-Hutnicza im. Stanislawa Staszica. Zeszyty Naukowe. Elektrotechnika†
0239-5320 Akademia Gorniczo-Hutnicza im. Stanislawa Staszica. Zeszyty Naukowe. Mechanika†
0239-541X Przeglad Dokumentacyjny z Zakresu Handlu Wewnetrznego i Uslug
0239-5428 Uniwersytet Jagiellonski. Zeszyty Naukowe. Prace Psychologiczne **7414**
0239-5436 Uniwersytet Jagiellonski. Zeszyty Naukowe. Prace Pedagogiczne **2923**
0239-5452 Archaeologia Interregionalis†
0239-5460 Svitanok **3567**
0239-5495 Politechnika Wroclawska. Instytut Technologii Organicznej i Tworzyw Sztucznych. Prace Naukowe. Monografie†
0239-5606 Bibliografia Wydawnictw Ciaglych Nowych, Zawieszonych i Zmieniajacych Tytul **617**
0239-5622 Akademia Gorniczo-Hutnicza im. Stanislawa Staszica. Zeszyty Naukowe. Zagadnienia Spoleczno-Filozoficzne†
0239-5894 Uniwersytet Gdanski. Zeszyty Naukowe. Rozprawy i Monografie†
0239-622X Bibliografia Gospodarki i Inzynierii Wodnej
0239-6238 Instytut Meteorologii i Gospodarki Wodnej. Materialy Badawcze. Seria: Gospodarka Wodna i Ochrona Wod **8826**
0239-6246 Bibliografia Hydrologii i Oceanologii
0239-6254 Instytut Meteorologii i Gospodarki Wodnej. Materialy Badawcze. Seria: Inzynieria Wodna **3362**
0239-6262 Instytut Meteorologii i Gospodarki Wodnej. Materialy Badawcze. Seria: Meteorologia **6357**
0239-6270 Bibliografia Meteorologii
0239-6297 Instytut Meteorologii i Gospodarki Wodnej. Materialy Badawcze. Seria: Hydrologia i Oceanologia **2795**
0239-6319 Przedsiebiorstwo i Rynek
0239-6327 Biuletyn Informacyjny Cointe
0239-6440 Auto-Technika Motoryzacyjna

0239-6467 Akademia Rolnicza w Szczecinie. Rozprawy 89
0239-6483 Instytut Obrobki Skrawaniem. Prace. Materialy Instruktazowe 3346
0239-6661 Acta Universitatis Wratislaviensis. Niemcoznawstwo 4196
0239-667X Teatr Lalek 8481
0239-6769 Wyzsza Szkola Pedagogiczna im. Komisji Edukacji Narodowej w Krakowie. Problemy Studiow Nauczycielskich†
0239-6815 Colloquia Communia 6911
0239-6858 Edukacja 2852
0239-6866 Murator 450
0239-6904 Magazyn Muzyczny†
0239-7013 Narodowy Bank Polski. Dziennik Urzedowy 1369
0239-7080 Akademia Muzyczna. Prace Specjalne 6542
0239-7269 Polish Academy of Sciences. Bulletin. Mathematics 5524
0239-7277 Polish Academy of Sciences. Bulletin. Earth Sciences†
0239-7285 Polish Academy of Sciences. Bulletin. Chemistry†
0239-7404 Problemy Projektowe†
0239-7528 Polish Academy of Sciences. Bulletin. Technical Sciences 8434
0239-7560 Uniwersytet im. Adama Mickiewicza. Geologia 2773
0239-7730 Machine Dynamics Problems 3388
0239-7757 Pedagogika Pracy 2945
0239-7846 Instytut Zachodni. Studium Niemcoznawcze 4232
0239-7854 Osrodek Badan Naukowych im. Wojciecha Ketrzynskiego. Biblioteka Olsztynska 4251
0239-7927 Polska Akademia Nauk. Oddzial w Krakowie. Komisja Historyczna. Materialy 4156
0239-7986 Wyzsza Szkola Pedagogiczna im. Komisji Edukacji Narodowej w Krakowie. Rocznik Naukowo-Dydaktyczny. Prace Rusycystyczne†
0239-801X Studia Teologiczne 7819
0239-8044 Techniki Komputerowe 2528
0239-8508 Folia Histochemica et Cytobiologica 832
0239-8524 Folia Praehistorica Posnaniensia 393
0239-8532 Akademia Ekonomiczna im. Oskara Langego we Wroclawiu. Prace Naukowe. Seria: Monografie i Opracowania *changed to* Uniwersytet Ekonomiczny we Wroclawiu. Prace Naukowe. Seria: Monografie i Opracowania 1190
0239-8567 Chopin Studies 6555
0239-8605 Accademia Polacca delle Scienze. Conferenze†
0239-8613 Szkola Glowna Gospodarstwa Wiejskiego. Rozprawy Naukowe i Monografie 160
0239-8710 Zamojski Kwartalnik Kulturalny 5246
0239-8818 Hemispheres†
0239-8834 Monumenta Musicae in Polonia. Series C: Tractatus de Musica†
0239-8931 Centralny Katalog Zagranicznych Wydawnictw Ciaglych w Bibliotekach Polskich 622
0239-9067 Uniwersytet Gdanski. Wydzial Ekonomiki Produkcji. Zeszyty Naukowe. Ekonomika i Organizacja Turystyki i Uslug†
0239-9148 Szkice o Kulturze Muzycznej XIX Wieku. Studia i Materialy†
0239-9253 Informator dla Kandydaton na Studia Podyplomowe i Doktoranckie
0239-927X Akademia Rolnicza im. Hugona Kollataja w Krakowie. Zeszyty Naukowe. Seria: Ekonomika†
0239-9288 Akademia Rolnicza im. Hugona Kollataja w Krakowie. Zeszyty Naukowe. Seria: Geodezja 2777
0239-9296 Akademia Rolnicza im. Hugona Kollataja w Krakowie. Zeszyty Naukowe. Seria: Historia Rolnictwa†
0239-930X Akademia Rolnicza im. Hugona Kollataja w Krakowie. Zeszyty Naukowe. Seria: Lesnictwo†
0239-9326 Akademia Rolnicza im. Hugona Kollataja w Krakowie. Zeszyty Naukowe. Seria: Ogrodnictwo†
0239-9334 Akademia Rolnicza im. Hugona Kollataja w Krakowie. Zeszyty Naukowe. Seria: Rolnictwo†
0239-9415 Politechnika Poznanska. Zeszyty Naukowe. Organizacja i Zarzadzanie 1901
0239-958X Bibliografia Agrometeorologii†
0239-9679 Budownictwo Weglowe. Projekty - Problemy†
0239-9709 Hodowca Golebi Pocztowych 908
0239-9776 Akademia Wychowania Fizycznego im. Eugeniusza Piaseckiego w Poznaniu. Kronika 6981
0239-989X Polish Trade Magazine†
0239-9954 Monumenta Musicae in Polonia. Series D: Bibliotheca Antiqua†
0239-9962 Monumenta Musicae in Polonia. Series A: Works by Polish Composers†
0239-9989 Uniwersytet Jagiellonski. Zeszyty Naukowe. Opuscula Musealia 6539
0239-9997 Studies in the Theory and Philosophy of Law†
0240-172X Gyn Obs - La Medecine et la Femme† 8960
0240-2041 Langues et Civilisations a Tradition Orale 5142
0240-2963 Universite Paul Sabatier. Faculte des Sciences. Annales 5544
0240-396X Echange - Travail†
0240-4656 Celebrer 7791
0240-4729 France. Ministere de l'Interieur. Repertoire Mensuel 7438
0240-4869 Experiences et Gestions Municipales†
0240-4958 L'Est Republicain 3840
0240-5024 Jardin Familial de France†
0240-5164 Federation Protestante de France. Annuaire 7758
0240-5172 Les Hotels de France 4390
0240-5709 A P M E P. Bulletin 5463
0240-6411 Avenir et Sante†
0240-642X Acta Endoscopica 5919
0240-6608 Livres Disponibles 630
0240-7418 Chroniques d'Histoire Maconnique 2265
0240-7426 Commerce et Industrie†
0240-7914 Journal Francais d'Orthoptique 6044
0240-8236 Actualites Reglementaires 1551
0240-8368 Epimenides
0240-8376 Epidecides Lunaires†
0240-8430 Perspectives Mediterraneennes†
0240-8678 Cahiers de Civilisation Medievale. Bibliographie 4133
0240-8759 Vie et Milieu 710
0240-8783 Revue d'Hydrobiologie Tropicale†
0240-8813 Sciences des Aliments 3663
0240-8864 Centre Aixois de Recherches Anglaises. Actes du Colloque 5271
0240-8910 Abstracta Iranica 4168
0240-902X Alta Nizza† 8929
0240-9399 Teleobjectif†
0240-9925 Inter Regions 1889
0241-0109 Journal International de Medecine†
0241-0257 Cameroun Selection 1554
0241-0311 Revue Pyreneenne 8330
0241-0389 Viandes et Produits Carnes 303
0241-0702 Tricot Prestige 6642
0241-130X La Revue du Secretariat et de la Comptabilite. Edition Professeurs†
0241-1393 Wind Magazine 8342
0241-2438 Opera International†
0241-2640 Infotecture†
0241-2799 Cahiers Philosophiques 6909
0241-2926 Greenpeace Magazine 3435
0241-3663 Musique Bretonne 6597
0241-5224 Toques Blanches†
0241-6794 Cahiers Techniques du Batiment 989
0241-6972 Soins Psychiatrie 5982
0241-7286 Planete Survie 3841
0241-7413 Revue de Pau et du Bearn 4473
0241-8185 A - Ya†
0241-8231 Parc National de Port Cros. Travaux Scientifiques 2624
0241-9092 Le Paysan Vosgien
0241-9890 Cahiers Tristan l'Hermite
0242-035X International Association of Literary Critics. Revue 7563
0242-0805 Journal de l'Automobile 8587
0242-0821 Dialogue (Montpellier)†
0242-1275 Profils Poetiques des Pays Latins†
0242-1283 Commutation et Transmission†
0242-1593 Cahiers de Grammaire 5103
0242-1623 Revue Internationale de la Propriete Industrielle et Artistique 6758
0242-1771 Spelunca 2769
0242-259X Centre I N F F O. Guides Techniques 1858
0242-2794 Villes en Parallele 4033
0242-2999 Inter - C D I 2957
0242-312X Vae Victis 8214
0242-3332 La Forge
0242-3456 France Industrie†
0242-3502 Hudson Letter†
0242-3960 Inter Bloc 5961
0242-4002 Association Nationale d'Etude et de Lutte contre les Fleaux Atmospheriques. Rapport de Campagne 6346
0242-4878 L'Annee du Tennis 8220
0242-4959 Les Quatre Saisons du Jardinage *changed to* 1962-5790 3748
0242-5157 Prevue 5432
0242-5424 Revue des Societes, Journal des Societes 4774
0242-5599 Fiscalite Europeenne 1925
0242-5602 Economie et Comptabilite 1287
0242-5629 Revue des Loyers, des Fermages et de la Copropriete *changed to* 1779-6903 4425
0242-5637 Archives de Politique Criminelle 4884
0242-5645 Cour de Cassation. Bulletin des Arrets. Chambres Civiles 4830
0242-5769 Le Monde Informatique (Print) *changed to* Le Monde Informatique (Online) 2432
0242-5777 La Semaine Juridique. Edition Generale 4782
0242-5785 La Semaine Juridique. Notariale et Immobiliere 4782
0242-5815 Banque de France. Enquete Mensuelle de Conjoncture (Print) *changed to* 1762-5912 1441
0242-5866 Banque de France. La Monnaie en...† 8935
0242-5874 Bulletin Social 1668
0242-5912 Bulletin Fiscal 1913
0242-598X France. Ministere de l'Economie et des Finances. Statistiques et Etudes Financieres. Finance Publique. Serie Bleue†
0242-6005 Le Point 3841
0242-6056 La Croix 7794
0242-6110 Annales des Falsifications de l'Expertise Chimique et Toxicologique 3493
0242-6218 Revue d'Etude de Relations Internationales†
0242-6331 Gazette du Palais 4679
0242-6366 Announces Judiciaires et Legales 4618
0242-6382 Legislation 4722
0242-6390 Gazette du Palais. Recueil Bimestriel 4679
0242-648X Journal de Readaptation Medicale 6110
0242-6498 Annales de Pathologie 653
0242-6595 Revue de l'Alimentation Animale 275
0242-6706 Union Girondine des Vins de Bordeaux 256
0242-6765 Journal Officiel de la Republique Francaise. Debats Parlamentaires. Assemblee Nationale. Compte Rendu Integral 7449
0242-6781 Le Bulletin des Annonces Legales Obligatoires† 8938
0242-6838 Revue Historique de Bordeaux et du Departement de la Gironde 4258
0242-7052 Cahiers Tarnais†
0242-7206 Textes et Manuscrits 5387
0242-7540 Chroniques de l'Annuaire de l'Afrique du Nord 7954
0242-7702 Les Nouvelles de l'Archeologie 409
0242-830X Monuments Historiques†
0242-8962 Dialogue 8098
0242-9063 Entraid'oc 108
0242-9217 Mickey Parade *changed to* 1631-5227 2202
0242-9225 Journal de Mickey 2195
0242-9284 Auto-Loisirs†
0242-9322 Equipement des Commerces, Enseignes, Eclairage†
0242-9616 Psychoanalistes†
0242-9705 Gavroche 4222
0242-9772 Practiciens et Troisieme Age 4053
0242-9780 Revue Francaise de Gestion Industrielle 1791
0243-0150 Rassemblement pour la Republique†
0243-0738 Echo de l'Union 4043
0243-1203 Journal Europeen de Radiotherapie†
0243-1327 Casus Belli 4331
0243-1335 Ca M'Interesse 3840
0243-1947 C E P I I Lettre 1445
0243-2331 Perspectives Internationales 7259
0243-2412 Recherches Institutionnelles. Institutions et Histoire 7673
0243-2633 Dunkerque Expansion 1401
0243-3397 Medicographia 5795
0243-3559 Association Nationale Hector Berlioz. Bulletin de Liaison 6546
0243-3567 P L M 295
0243-3672 Anna 6636
0243-3699 Mode Europe (Ed. Francaise)
0243-4504 CinemAction 6494
0243-4911 Electronique Pratique 3097
0243-4938 Sono Magazine 8154
0243-5624 Collection Sciences et Techniques Agro-Alimentaires 102
0243-6019 L'Armement†
0243-6345 France. Ministere de l'Agriculture. Situation Agricole en France. Note de Conjoncture Production Animale†
0243-6450 M O T S 7152
0243-6795 Les Routiers 8675
0243-6825 Annuaire de Statistique Agricole 174
0243-7473 Travaux Scientifiques des Chercheurs du Service de Sante des Armees 4112
0243-7589 La Mucoviscidose *changed to* 1961-3210 6221
0243-8461 France. Direction des Affaires Economiques et Internationales. Etudes sur la Construction et l'Equipement *changed to* 1274-865X 4435
0243-8518 Enquete Permanente sur l'Utilisation des Vehicules de Transport en Commun de Personnes en (Year)†
0243-8585 France. Ministere de l'Agriculture. Series "S". Methodes et Applications Scientifiques†
0243-881X Reunion. Institut National de la Statistique et des Etudes Economiques. Collection: Documents†
0243-9808 Le Progres 3842
0244-0008 Amina 8851
0244-0342 African Defence Journal†
0244-1136 Maison et Travaux 1022
0244-1462 Temoignage Chretien 5241
0244-2019 Isolation†
0244-2906 Les Amis de George Sand 5253
0244-4771 Havre Port†
0244-4860 Viti Vinicole 257
0244-5603 Universite de Rouen. Publications†
0244-6014 Societe Francaise de Photogrammetrie et de Teledetection. Bulletin *changed to* 1768-9791 4027
0244-6316 Caisse Nationale des Autoroutes. Rapport Annuel 8630
0244-6936 Recherches Institutionnelles. Recherche Documentaire 7673
0244-7118 France. Service d'Etude des Strategies et des Statistiques Industrielles. Collections: Traits Fondamentaux du Systeme Industriel Francais†
0244-7428 Continent†
0244-7827 Politique Africaine 7171
0244-7878 Le Nouvel Humanisme 7160
0244-8327 Abbay†
0244-8459 L'Union Agricole 164
0244-9358 Revue Trimestrielle de Droit Commercial et de Droit Economique 4775
0244-9404 Centre d'Histoire Contemporaine du Languedoc-Roussillon. Bulletin†
0244-9412 Societe Archeologique et Historique de la Charente. Bulletins et Memoires 4264
0244-9870 Traitement de Texte
0245-0011 Annuaire National Automobile†
0245-0429 La France Cycliste 8259
0245-0712 Annuaire National de l'Education Permanente†
0245-1875 Les Editeurs et Diffuseurs de Langue Francaise† 8952
0245-2030 Annuaire des Communautes d'Enfants 2826
0245-2057 Ben's Book†
0245-3169 Courrier A N V A R Magazine†
0245-3185 36000 Communes 7505
0245-3312 L'Equipe Magazine 8171
0245-3355 Reproduire 6976
0245-3614 Cheval Magazine 8289
0245-4505 Industries des Cereales 3647
0245-484X Foret Mediterraneenne 3691
0245-5552 Journal d'Echographie et de Medicine Ultrasonore *changed to* 0221-0363 6200
0245-5668 Association Nationale des Communautes Educatives. Bulletin Mensuel d'Informations† 8931
0245-5676 Art Press 471
0245-5781 Confection 2000 Nouveles Techniques de l'Habillement†
0245-5811 Journal de Traumatologie†
0245-5919 Motricite Cerebrale 6161
0245-663X L'Alsace 3997
0245-7318 Cheminot de France 4591
0245-7466 Bulletin Epidemiologique Hebdomadaire 7510
0245-761X Banque de l'Union Europeenne. Chiffres et Commentaires†
0245-8160 Afrique Litteraire†
0245-8659 Actualites d'Angeiologie†
0245-8756 Statistiques de Trafic 8530
0245-8829 Confluents Psychanalytiques 7348
0245-8969 Revue E P S 3079
0245-8977 Education Physique et Sportive au 1er Degre 8171
0245-9310 Guide Offshore†
0245-9329 L'Etendard de la Bible et Heraut du Royaume de Christ 7641
0245-9337 International Pediatric Association. Bulletin†
0245-9345 France. Bureau de Recherches Geologiques et Minieres. Manuels et Methodes 2734
0245-940X Chimie Magazine *changed to* 1286-0921 2065
0245-9418 Oceanographie Tropicale†
0245-9442 Groupe de Recherche pour l'Education et la Prospective. Pour 2861
0245-9450 Officiel du Batiment et des Travaux Publics de Toulouse et de Midi-Pyrenees†
0245-9469 Revue de Droit Sanitaire et Social 7466
0245-9590 Techniques de l'Ingenieur. Construction 3285
0245-9604 Techniques de l'Ingenieur. Constantes Physico-Chimiques 3256

ISSN

0250-5266 Indian Veterinary Medical Journal **8799**
0250-5339 Journal of Science and Technology **7873**
0250-5347 Shivaji University. Journal (Science) **7916**
0250-5363 Karachi Journal of Science **7874**
0250-5371 Legume Research **241**
0250-538X Maadini **2753**
0250-541X National Academy of Sciences, India. Science Letters **7886**
0250-5509 Universite du Burundi. Revue **3805**
0250-5517 Revue Roumaine de Biologie. Serie Biologie Vegetale **815**
0250-5525 Schweizerische Medizinische Wochenschrift (Supplementum) **5711**
0250-5584 U N D O C: Current Index†
0250-5649 Ciencias Veterinarias **8795**
0250-5657 Zambian Geographical Journal
0250-5665 Bibliographie der Berner Geschichte **4169**
0250-5673 Historischer Verein des Kantons Bern. Archiv **4229**
0250-5681 Auszuege der Revue Internationale de la Croix-Rouge *see* 1816-3831 **4932**
0250-5738 Europees Parlement **4925**
0250-5754 E P News **4924**
0250-5940 Rechtsbibliographie
0250-5959 I I C A in the Americas†
0250-5991 Journal of Biosciences **682**
0250-6017 Indian Institute of Tropical Meteorology. Annual Report **6357**
0250-6025 Boletin de la O M M *see* 0042-9767 **6397**
0250-6041 Documentacion de la Seguridad Social Americana **4501**
0250-605X Revista Internacional de Seguridad Social **4521**
0250-6068 Pharmanual†
0250-6076 Byulleten' V M O *see* 0042-9767 **6397**
0250-6092 Organizacion de los Estados Americanos. Boletin Estadistico†
0250-6114 Chiefs of State and Cabinet Ministers of the American Republics†
0250-6149 Development Newsletter
0250-6173 Juventud†
0250-6262 Inter-American Review of Bibliography†
0250-6300 Sintesis de las Decisiones Tomadas en las Sesiones y Textos de las Resoluciones Aprobadas *see* 0250-6319 **7476**
0250-6319 Washington. General Secretariat Organization of American States. Summary of the Decisions Taken at the Meetings and Texts of the Resolutions Approved **7476**
0250-6335 Journal of Astrophysics and Astronomy **576**
0250-636X Tropical Gastroenterology **5932**
0250-6386 Arnoldia Zimbabwe **654**
0250-6394 N A F O Statistical Bulletin **3613**
0250-6408 Journal of Northwest Atlantic Fishery Science **3600**
0250-6416 N A F O Scientific Council Reports **3602**
0250-6424 I C N A F Sampling Yearbook (International Commission for the Northwest Atlantic Fisheries)†
0250-6432 N A F O Scientific Council Studies **3602**
0250-6440 Der Gesellschafter **4868**
0250-6459 Zeitschrift fuer Neuere Rechtsgeschichte **4819**
0250-6467 Zeitschrift fuer Hochschuldidaktik **2928**
0250-6505 Regional Development Dialogue **1604**
0250-6521 Universidad de la Republica. Facultad de Humanidades y Ciencias. Revista. Serie Ciencias de la Tierra **2718**
0250-653X Universidad de la Republica. Facultad de Humanidades y Ciencias. Revista. Serie Ciencias Biologicas **709**
0250-6548 Universidad de la Republica. Facultad de Humanidades y Ciencias. Revista. Serie Linguistica **5190**
0250-6556 Universidad de la Republica. Facultad de Humanidades y Ciencias. Revista. Serie Letras **5392**
0250-6564 Universidad de la Republica. Facultad de Humanidades y Ciencias. Revista. Serie Ciencias Antropologicas **359**
0250-6807 Annals of Nutrition and Metabolism **6655**
0250-6831 Belizean Studies **4285**
0250-6882 Emirates Medical Journal **5609**
0250-6963 Biocenosis **2604**
0250-6971 Revue de Theologie et de Philosophie. Cahiers **7677**
0250-698X Africa Link **971**
0250-6998 Cinema Vision India **6494**
0250-7005 Anticancer Research **6008**
0250-7072 *see* 1998-1430 **2612**
0250-7080 *see* 1998-1430 **2612**
0250-7099 *see* 1998-1430 **2612**
0250-7102 Naturopa *changed to* 1998-1430 **2612**
0250-7161 Revista Latinoamericana de Estudios Urbano Regionales **4425**
0250-7188 Hamdard Medicus **5623**
0250-7196 Hamdard Islamicus **7710**
0250-7234 Fiji. Mineral Resources Department. Report **2734**
0250-7277 Fiji. Mineral Resources Department. Geothermal Report **2734**
0250-7307 International Monetary Fund. By-Laws Rules and Regulations **1358**
0250-7366 International Monetary Fund. Annual Report on Exchange Arrangements and Exchange Restrictions **1358**
0250-7374 International Monetary Fund. Government Finance Statistics Yearbook **1244**
0250-7412 Bulletin du F M I *see* 0047-083X **1244**
0250-7420 Boletin del F M I *see* 0047-083X **1244**
0250-7439 Finanzierung und Entwicklung *see* 0145-1707 **1343**
0250-7439 Finanzierung und Entwicklung *see* 0430-473X **1343**
0250-7447 Finanzas y Desarrollo (Print Edition) *see* 0430-473X **1343**
0250-7447 Finanzas y Desarrollo (Print Edition) *see* 0145-1707 **1343**
0250-7455 Tamwil wa-al-tanmiyat *see* 0145-1707 **1343**
0250-7455 Tamwil wa-al-tanmiyat *see* 0430-473X **1343**
0250-7463 International Financial Statistics Yearbook **1243**
0250-7498 International Monetary Fund. Annual Report of the Executive Board **1358**
0250-7501 Fonds Monetaire International. Rapport Annuel du Conseil d'Administration *see* 0250-7498 **1358**
0250-751X Fondo Monetario Internacional. Informe Anual del Directorio Ejectivo *see* 0250-7498 **1358**
0250-7528 Internationaler Waehrungsfonds. Jahresbericht der Exekutivdirektoren *see* 0250-7498 **1358**
0250-7595 Index Indiana **8**
0250-7609 Geosur **7237**
0250-7617 Carindex: Social Sciences and Humanities **8020**
0250-7625 I I A S A Reports **3482**
0250-7633 I D O C Monthly Bulletin†
0250-7641 I D O C Internazionale† **8963**
0250-7676 Swiss Gay **4379**
0250-7684 Groene Band *changed to* 1378-5990 **3685**
0250-7730 International Designs Bulletin **6753**
0250-7765 Petroleum News†
0250-7773 The Weekly Gleaner **3995**
0250-7781 European Parliament's Official Handbook **7134**
0250-7803 Aardkundige Mededelingen **3996**
0250-7811 N A F O List of Fishing Vessels†
0250-7935 Industry and Development†
0250-7994 Guide to Training Opportunities for Industrial Development†
0250-801X United Nations Industrial Development Organization. Development and Transfer of Technology Series†
0250-8052 E P P O Bulletin **228**
0250-8060 Water International **8837**
0250-8087 Pseudo-Allergic Reactions†
0250-8095 American Journal of Nephrology **6265**
0250-8109 Z G A Occasional Studies
0250-8117 Z G A School Supplement
0250-8125 Z G A Bibliographic Series
0250-8133 Zambia Geographical Association. Regional Handbook
0250-815X Episeme Efemerida ton Europaikon Koinoteton. C. Anakoinoseis Kai Plerofories *see* 1725-2423 **7256**
0250-815X Episeme Efemerida ton Europaikon Koinoteton. C. Anakoinoseis Kai Plerofories *see* 0257-7763 **4923**
0250-8168 Episeme Efemerida ton Europaikon Koinoteton. L: Nomothesia *see* Official Journal of the European Union. L Series: Legislation **7256**
0250-8281 Tourism Recreation Research **8763**
0250-829X Indian Journal of Botany **793**
0250-832X Dentomaxillofacial Radiology **6195**
0250-8346 Journal of Himalayan Studies and Regional Development **3447**
0250-8443 A F R O Technical Report Series
0250-846X Criteres d'Hygiene de l'Environnement *see* 0250-863X **3425**
0250-8478 Criterios de Salud Ambiental *see* 0250-863X **3425**
0250-8524 E M R O Technical Publication *changed to* 1020-0428 **7514**
0250-8567 Serie de Rapports Techniques A F R O *see* 0250-8443
0250-8575 Organisation Mondiale de la Sante. Publications Regionales. Serie Europeenne *see* 0378-2255 **7545**
0250-8613 I A R C Biennial Report **6021**
0250-8621 A F R O Technical Papers†
0250-863X Environmental Health Criteria **3425**
0250-8648 Kriterii Sanitarno-Gigienicheskogo Sostoyaniya Okruzhayushchei Sredy *see* 0250-863X **3425**
0250-8664 Ezhegodnik Mirovoi Sanitarnoi Statistiki†
0250-8699 Vsemirnaya Organizatsiya Zdravookhraneniya. Byulleten' *see* 0042-9686 **5731**
0250-8710 Euro Reports and Studies†
0250-8737 Vsemirnaya Organizatsiya Zdravookhraneniya. Seriya Tekhnicheskikh Dokladov **5729**
0250-8893 Vsemirnaya Meteorologicheskaya Organizatsiya. Godovoi Otchet **6397**
0250-8931 *see* 0031-0336 **8061**
0250-8958 *see* 0082-8386 **8075**
0250-8966 *see* 0082-8386 **8075**
0250-8974 *see* 0082-8386 **8075**
0250-9032 Organisation Meteorologique Mondiale. Association Regionale V (Pacifique Sud-Ouest). Rapport Final Abrege de la (No.) Session *see* 0250-9040 **6399**
0250-9040 World Meteorological Organization. Regional Association V (South West Pacific). Abridged Final Report of the (No.) Session **6399**
0250-9059 Organisation Meteorolgique Mondiale. Association Regionale I (Afrique). Rapport Final Abrege de la Session *see* 0510-9124 **6399**
0250-9105 Vsemirnaya Meteorologicheskaya Organizatsiya. Regional'naya Assotsiatsiya II (Aziya). Okonchatel'nyi Sokrashchennyi Otchet (No.) Sessii *see* 0509-3007 **6399**
0250-9113 Organisation Meteorologique Mondiale. Association Regionale II (Asie). Rapport Final Abrege de la (No.) Session *see* 0509-3007 **6399**
0250-9121 World Meteorological Organization. Regional Association IV (North America and Central America). Abridged Final Report of the (No.) Session **6399**
0250-913X Organizacion Meteorologica Mundial. Asociacion Regional IV (America del Norte y America Central). Informe Final Abreviado de la (No.) Reunion *see* 0250-9121 **6399**
0250-9148 Organizacion Meteorologica Mundial. Asociacion Regional III (America del Sur). Informe Final Abreviado de la (No.) Reunion *see* 0510-9132 **6399**
0250-9156 Organisation Meteorologique Mondiale. Commission des Sciences de l'Atmosphere. Rapport Final Abrege de la (No) Session *see* 0250-9172 **6398**
0250-9164 Vsemirnaya Meteorologicheskaya Organizatsiya. Komissiya po Atmosfernym Naukam. Okonchatel'nyi Sokrashchennyi Otchet (No) Sessii *see* 0250-9172 **6398**
0250-9172 World Meteorological Organization. Commission for Atmospheric Sciences. Abridged Final Report of the (No.) Session **6398**
0250-9180 Organizacion Meteorologico Mundial. Comision de Ciencias Atmosfericas. Informe Final Abrevido de la (No) Reunion *see* 0250-9172 **6398**
0250-9237 Organisation Meteorologique Mondiale. Congres. Proces - Verbaux **6393**
0250-9245 Vsemirnaya Meteorologicheskaya Organizatsiya. Kongress. Sokrashechennyi Otchet s Rezolyutsiyami *see* 0084-1927 **6399**
0250-9253 Organizacion Meteorologica Mundial. Congreso. Informe Abrevido y Resoluciones *see* 0084-1927 **6399**
0250-9261 Organisation Meteorologique Mondiale. Congres. Rapport Abrege et Resolutions *see* 0084-1927 **6399**
0250-9288 Composition of the W M O **6351**
0250-9393 World Meteorological Organization. Weather Reporting. Volume A: Observing Stations **6399**
0250-9407 World Meteorological Organization. Weather Reporting. Volume B: Data Processing **6399**
0250-9415 World Meteorological Organization. Weather Reporting. Volume C2: Transmissions **6399**
0250-9423 World Meteorological Organization. Weather Reporting. Volume D: Information for Shipping **6399**
0250-961X Inside China Mainland†
0250-9628 Journal of Combinatorics, Information & System Sciences
0250-9636 Indian Society of Statistics and Operations Research. Journal **2422**
0250-9644 Annales Nestle (French Edition) **5575**
0250-9652 Annales Nestle (German Edition) **5575**
0250-9660 I C S S R Journal of Abstracts and Reviews: Political Science **7199**
0250-9687 I C S S R Journal of Abstracts and Reviews: Geography **4036**
0250-9695 I C S S R Journal of Abstracts and Reviews: Economics **1241**
0250-9709 Indian Dissertation Abstracts†
0250-9725 Bibliotheek voor Hedendaagse Dokumentatie. Bulletin **5060**
0250-975X Bhashavimarsa†
0250-9768 Journal of Economic and Taxonomic Botany **796**
0250-9792 Resumen Semanal **7177**
0250-9806 QueHacer **7175**
0250-9814 Serie Praxis†
0250-9881 Arab Mining Journal **6456**
0250-9903 Annual Bulletin of Steel Statistics for Europe†
0250-9938 Mezdunarodnoe Agentstvo po Atomnoj Energii Bulleten' *see* 0020-6067 **3168**
0250-9989 Ecoforum **3416**
0251-0030 United Nations. Population and Vital Statistics Report **7317**
0251-0073 Statistical Indicators of Short Term Economic Changes in E.C.E. Countries† **8990**
0251-0081 Annual Bulletin of Trade in Chemical Products†
0251-009X Forum de Comercio Internacional *see* 0020-8957 **1571**
0251-0111 Munazzamat al-Sihhah al-'Alamiyyah. Silsilat al-Taqarir al-Fanniyyah **5681**
0251-012X Indian Musicological Society. Journal **6575**
0251-0170 Experimental Hematology Today†
0251-0189 Nations Unies. Commission Economique pour l'Europe. Rapport Annuel *see* 0251-0197 **1099**
0251-0197 Economic Commission for Europe. Annual Report **1099**
0251-0200 Organizatsiya Ob'edinennykh Natsii. Evropeiskaya Ekonomicheskaya Komissiya. Godovoi Doklad *see* 0251-0197 **1099**
0251-0332 Executive **1485**
0251-0340 Msafiri **8739**
0251-0391 Transafrican Journal of History **4164**
0251-0405 Journal of Eastern African Research & Development **7978**
0251-0421 Language Association of Eastern Africa. Journal†
0251-0480 Pakistan Journal of Agricultural Research **145**
0251-0499 Aquarius **3586**
0251-0669 Cour Internationale de Justice. Annuaire *see* 0074-445X **4930**
0251-0677 Europaike Trapeza Ependuseon. Plerofories *see* 0250-3891 **1622**
0251-0774 E S I S. Newsletter
0251-0790 Gaodeng Xuexiao Huaxue Xuebao **2062**
0251-0952 Seed Science and Technology **816**
0251-1029 Vasa. Supplementum *see* 0301-1526 **5801**
0251-1045 The Zimbabwe Journal of Agricultural Research **173**
0251-1053 *see* 0041-6436 **3706**
0251-107X International Astronomical Union. Transactions **576**
0251-1088 The Environmentalist **3429**
0251-1096 Institution of Engineers (India). Electronics and Telecommunication Engineering Division. Journal **3104**
0251-110X Institution of Engineers (India). Environmental Engineering Division. Journal **3440**
0251-1126 Chemie Kunststoffe Aktuell
0251-1134 Dumortiera **786**
0251-1150 Electronique†
0251-1223 Geobios **675**
0251-1231 Heizung und Lueftung **4120**
0251-1258 J L B Smith Institute of Ichthyology. Ichthyological Bulletin **949**
0251-1290 Nouvelles Africaines de Securite Sociale **4517**
0251-1339 International Social Security Association. Reports of the General Assemblies of the I S S A **4509**
0251-1371 Estado Mundial de la Agricultura y la Alimentacion *see* 0081-4539 **158**
0251-1460 Situation Mondiale de l'Alimentation et de l'Agriculture *see* 0081-4539 **158**
0251-1525 F A O Fertilizer Yearbook *changed to* 1014-7675 **230**
0251-1584 *see* 0041-6436 **3706**
0251-1630 Indian Institute of World Culture. Bulletin **4456**
0251-1649 International Journal of Clinical Pharmacology Research **6849**
0251-1657 Swiss Dent **5867**
0251-1673 Swiss Pharma **6882**
0251-169X Swiss Plastics†
0251-1703 Swiss Chem†
0251-172X Odonto-Stomatologie Tropicale **5858**
0251-1738 P N G L A Nius†
0251-1746 Shree Hari Katha **7708**
0251-1754 Basler Adressbuch **1974**
0251-1770 Journal of Engineering Production†
0251-1789 Invasion and Metastasis†
0251-1819 Reserve Bank of Zimbabwe. Quarterly Economic and Statistical Review **1379**
0251-1835 O C D E. Nouvelles *see* 0258-6347

ISSN

0251-1878 Reforme Agraire, Colonisation et Cooperatives *see* 0251-1894 **202**
0251-1886 Reforma Agraria, Colonizacion y Cooperativas *see* 0251-1894 **202**
0251-1894 Land Reform, Land Settlement and Cooperatives **202**
0251-1924 Nyala **959**
0251-1940 Handbok Baenda **117**
0251-1959 Food Outlook **198**
0251-1967 Cour Internationale de Justice. Actes et Documents **4922**
0251-2068 Concepts in Pediatric Neurosurgery†
0251-2394 Local Finance†
0251-2408 De Franse Nederlanden **5216**
0251-2416 Revue de Coree†
0251-2440 Agricultural Abstracts for Tanzania **173**
0251-2467 Child Health and Development†
0251-2483 Estudios Paraguayos **7962**
0251-2491 Andean Report **1436**
0251-2521 A S E A N Briefing **1435**
0251-2653 Nepal - Antiquary **557**
0251-2661 Bunadarrit†
0251-267X International Civil Aviation Organization. Digests of Statistics. Series OFOD. On-Flight Origin and Destination **8526**
0251-2750 Annuaire International de l'Education *see* 0252-5496
0251-2912 Benelux Dossier†
0251-2920 C E P A L Review **1445**
0251-2955 Turkish Public Administration Annual **7472**
0251-2998 Documentation Europeene **8366**
0251-3013 Banque Marocaine du Commerce Exterieur. Revue d'Informations **1320**
0251-3056 Journal of Government and Political Studies **7147**
0251-3072 Mediterranean Studies†
0251-3110 Asian and Pacific Quarterly†
0251-3137 Beijing Information **3822**
0251-3153 Comunicacion **8095**
0251-317X Development Policy and Administrative Review **7433**
0251-3218 Conference Internationale du Travail. Compte Rendu des Travaux *see* 0074-6681 **1689**
0251-3226 Conferencia Internacional del Trabajo. Actas *see* 0074-6681 **1689**
0251-3412 Derecho **4656**
0251-348X Social Sciences Research Journal **8004**
0251-3498 Revue Olympique *see* 0377-192X **8191**
0251-351X Politische Rundschau **7171**
0251-3528 Revue Roumaine *see* 0035-8088 **5237**
0251-3552 Nueva Sociedad **7160**
0251-3587 Lamalif **5223**
0251-3609 Francia†
0251-3617 Informations Constitutionnelles et Parlementaires **7142**
0251-3625 D I S P **4409**
0251-3706 Bulletin des Stupefiant *see* 0007-523X **2700**
0251-379X B I T Commission des Employes et des Travailleurs Intellectuels. Rapport *see* 0251-3803 **1686**
0251-3803 I L O Committee on Salaried Employees and Professional Workers. Report **1686**
0251-3994 Anquan lishihui huiyi biaoti suoyin, Lianheguo *see* 0082-8408 **7201**
0251-401X Commodity Trade and Price Trends†
0251-4044 Agence Internationale de l'Energie Atomique Bulletin *see* 0020-6067 **3168**
0251-4095 I A O Internationale Arbeitskonferenz. Bericht *see* 0074-6681 **1689**
0251-4125 Documentation, Libraries and Archives: Bibliographies and Reference Works†
0251-415X Oil and Arab Cooperation **6783**
0251-4184 Acta Mathematica Vietnamica **5465**
0251-4214 Universite d'Abidjan. Annales. Serie C. Sciences **7926**
0251-4257 Commission des Nations Unies pour le Droit Commercial International. Annuaire **4921**
0251-4265 United Nations Commission on International Trade Law. Yearbook **4943**
0251-4273 Comision de las Naciones Unidas para el Derecho Mercantil Internacional. Anuario **4921**
0251-4281 Komissiya Organizatsii Ob'edinennykh Natsii po Pravu Mezhdunarodnoi Torgovli. Ezegodnik **4934**
0251-432X Documentation, Bibliotheques et Archives: Bibliographies et Ouvrages de Reference†
0251-4389 Annuaire des Droits de l'Homme *see* 0251-6519 **8999**
0251-4451 Bulletin International des Sciences de la Mer *see* 0020-7918 **2806**
0251-4559 Informes y Documentos de Ciencias Sociales *see* 0080-1348 **7995**
0251-463X Educational Building Digest†
0251-4710 E P I Newsletter *changed to* 1814-6244 **5759**
0251-4761 La Revue Juridique, Politique et Economique du Maroc **4959**
0251-4788 Taiwan Shenxue Lukan **7687**
0251-4931 Principes de la Planification de l'Education *see* 0071-9862 **3023**
0251-5040 Musees et Monuments *see* 0077-233X **6532**
0251-5105 Etudes et Documents d'Information *see* 0080-1356 **8128**
0251-5253 TermNet News **5186**
0251-5342 Frontiers in Diabetes **5893**
0251-5350 Neuroepidemiology **6164**
0251-5369 Corporacion Financiera Internacional. Informe Anual *see* 0251-5385 **1356**
0251-5377 Societe Financiere Internationale. Rapport Annuel *see* 0251-5385 **1356**
0251-5385 International Finance Corporation. Annual Report **1356**
0251-544X Rapports et Documents de Sciences Sociales *see* 0080-1348 **7995**
0251-5539 Educational Research and Practice†
0251-5601 Progres en Neonatologie†
0251-5695 Etudes et Documents de Politique Scientifique *see* 0080-7591 **7910**
0251-5768 Coleccion Unesco, Programas y Metodos de Ensenanza†
0251-5776 Collection Unesco, Programmes et Methodes d'Enseignement†
0251-5865 Studies and Surveys in Comparative Education **2915**
0251-5989 U I E Case Studies†
0251-6020 Intergovernmental Oceanographic Commission. Manuals and Guides **2807**
0251-6047 Commission Oceanographique Intergouvernementale. Manuels et Guides **2802**
0251-6365 International Monetary Fund. Occasional Papers **1358**
0251-6438 Monthly Commodity Price Bulletin **1252**
0251-6519 Yearbook on Human Rights† **8999**
0251-6535 Helliniki Epitheorissis Evropaikou Dikaiou **4927**
0251-6594 Informe Sobre la Situacion Social en el Mundo *see* 0082-8068 **8128**
0251-6608 Rapport sur la Situation Sociale dans le Monde *see* 0082-8068 **8128**
0251-6632 Development Forum **1594**
0251-6640 Forum du Developpement *see* 0251-6632 **1594**
0251-6659 Forum *see* 0251-6632 **1594**
0251-6667 Foro del Desarrollo *see* 0251-6632 **1594**
0251-6683 United Nations Commission on Narcotic Drugs. Summary of Annual Reports of Governments Relating to Narcotic Drugs and Psychotropic Substances
0251-6691 Resume de Rapports Annuels des Gouvernements Relatifs aux Stupefiants et aux Substances Psychotropes *see* 0251-6683
0251-6705 Resumen de los Informes Anuales de los Gobiernos, Relativos a los Estupefacientes y las Sustancias Sicotropicas *see* 0251-6683
0251-6748 United Nations Commission on Narcotic Drugs. Laws and Regulations
0251-6756 *see* 0251-6748
0251-6764 Trafic Illicite *see* 0251-6772
0251-6772 United Nations Commission on Narcotic Drugs. Illicit Traffic
0251-6780 Trafico Illicito *see* 0251-6772
0251-6802 Bulletin on Ageing *changed to* Bulletin on Social Integration Policies **4042**
0251-6810 International Colloquium on Prospective Biology (Proceedings)†
0251-6845 Social Development Newsletter **8133**
0251-6861 Populi†
0251-6896 Ce Qu'il Faut Savoir des Nations Unies *see* 0251-690X **8955**
0251-690X Everyone's United Nations† **8955**
0251-6918 Naciones Unidas. Origenes, Organizacion, Actividades *see* 0251-690X **8955**
0251-7019 Human Rights Bulletin†
0251-7086 Boletin de Estupefacientes *see* 0007-523X **2700**
0251-7094 Byulleten' po Narkoticheskim Sredstvam *see* 0007-523X **2700**
0251-7329 U N Chronicle **7269**
0251-737X Psychotherapies **7401**
0251-7388 France. Ministere de la Culture et des Affaires Sociales. Lectures **5010**
0251-7418 Sawasdee **8785**
0251-7469 International Conference on Data Processing in the Field of Social Security. Reports **4509**
0251-7493 Oesterreichische Geologische Gesellschaft. Mitteilungen **2760**
0251-7558 Nations Unies Annuaire Juridique *see* 0082-8297 **4943**
0251-7566 Naciones Unidas Anuario Juridico *see* 0082-8297 **4943**
0251-7574 Organizatsiya Ob'edinennykh Natsii. Yuridicheskiy Ezhegodnik *see* 0082-8297 **4943**
0251-7582 United Nations. Statement of Treaties and International Agreements **7271**
0251-7590 Boletin de Poblacion de las Naciones Unidas *see* 0251-7604 **7289**
0251-7604 Population Bulletin of the United Nations **7289**
0251-7612 Bulletin Demographique des Nations Unies *see* 0251-7604 **7289**
0251-7647 Biaoti suoyin dahui huiyi jilu, Lianheguo *see* 0082-8157 **7201**
0251-7655 Fihris a'mal al-gam'iyyat al-'ammatt - al-Umam al-Muttahidat *see* 0082-8157 **7201**
0251-7833 United Nations. Reports of International Arbitral Awards **4801**
0251-7965 *see* 0082-8386 **8075**
0251-7973 *see* 0082-8386 **8075**
0251-8694 Mazuipin Gongbao *see* 0007-523X **2700**
0251-8740 Organisation Meteorologique Mondiale. Commission de'Hydrologie. Rapport Final Abege de la (No) Session *see* 0251-8775 **6399**
0251-8759 Organizacion Meteorologica Mundial. Comision de Hidrologia. Informe Final Abrevido de la (No) Reunion *see* 0251-8775 **6399**
0251-8767 Vsemirnaya Meteorologicheskaya Organizatsiya. Komissiya po Gidrologii. Okonchatel'nyi Sokrashchennyi Otchet (No) Sessii *see* 0251-8775 **6399**
0251-8775 World Meteorological Organization. Commission for Hydrology. Abridged Final Report of the (No.) Session **6399**
0251-8783 World Meteorological Organization. Commission for Instruments and Methods of Observation. Abridged Final Report of the (No.) Session **6399**
0251-8791 Organisation Meteorologique Mondiale. Commission des Instruments et des Methodes d'Observation. Rapport Final Abrege de la (No) Session *see* 0251-8783 **6399**
0251-8813 Vsemirnaya Meteorologicheskaya Organizatsiya. Komissiya po Priboram i Metodam Nablyudenii. Okonchatel'nyi Sokrashchennyi Otchet (No) Sessii *see* 0251-8783 **6399**
0251-8821 Organizacion Meteorologica Mundial. Comision de Meteorologia Agricola. Informe Final Abrevido de la (No) Reunion *see* 0510-9078 **6398**
0251-883X Organisation Meteorologique Mondiale. Commission de Meteorologie Agricole. Rapport Final Abrege de la (No) Session *see* 0510-9078 **6398**
0251-8848 Vsemirnaya Meteorologicheskaya Organizatsiya Komissiya po Sel'skokhozyaistvennoi Meteorologii. Okonchatel'nyi Sokrashchennyi Otchet (No) Sessii *see* 0510-9078 **6398**
0251-8856 Vsemirnaya Meteorologicheskaya Organizatsiya. Komissiya po Morskoi Meteorologii. Okonchatel'nyi Sokrashchennyi Otchet (No) Sessii *see* 1011-3207 **6399**
0251-8864 Organizacion Meteorologica Mundial. Comision de Meteorologia Marina. Informe Final Abrevido de la (No) Reunion *see* 1011-3207 **6399**
0251-8872 Organisation Meteorologique Mondiale. Commission de Meteorologie Maritime. Rapport Final Abrege de la (No) Session *see* 1011-3207 **6399**
0251-8880 Vsemirnaya Meteorologicheskaya Organizatsiya. Komissiya po Aviatsionnoi Meteorologii. Okonchatel'nyi Sokrashchennyi Otchet (No) Sessii *see* 0510-906X **6398**
0251-8899 Organisation Meteorologique Mondiale. Commission de Meteorologie Aeronautique. Rapport Final Abrege de la (No) Session *see* 0510-906X **6398**
0251-8902 Organizacion Meteorologica Mundial. Comision de Meteorologia Aeronautica. Informe Final Abrevido de la (No) Reunion *see* 0510-906X **6398**
0251-8945 World Meteorological Organization. Commission for Special Applications of Meteorology and Climatology. Abridged Final Report of the (No.) Session†
0251-8953 World Meteorological Organization. Commission for Basic Systems. Abridged Final Report of the (No.) Session **6398**
0251-8961 Vsemirnaya Meteologicheskaya Organizatsiya. Komissiya po Osnovnym Sistemam. Okonchatel'nyi Sokrashchennyi Otchet (No) Sessii *see* 0251-8953 **6398**
0251-897X Organizacion Meteorologica Mundial. Comision de Sistemas Basicos. Informe Final Abrevido de la (No) Reunion *see* 0251-8953 **6398**
0251-8988 Organisation Meteorologique Mondiale. Commission des Systems de Base. Rapport Final Abrege de la (No) Session *see* 0251-8953 **6398**
0251-8996 Population†
0251-9089 Caribbean Documentation Centre. Current Awareness Bulletin **622**
0251-9100 State of the World's Children **8073**
0251-9119 Estado Mundial de la Infancia **8039**
0251-9127 United Nations Commission on International Trade Law. Report on the Work of Its Session **4943**
0251-9135 Doklad Komissii Organizatsii Ob'edinennykh Natsii po Pravu Mezhdunarodnoi Torgovli o Rabote ee Sessii **4923**
0251-9143 Comision de las Naciones Unidas para el Derecho Mercantil Internacional. Informe sobre la Labor Realizada en su Periodo de Sesiones **4921**
0251-9151 Commission des Nations Unies pour le Droit Commercial International. Rapport des Travaux de sa Session **4921**
0251-916X Lianhegui Guoji Maoyifa Weiyuanhui Huiyi Gongzuo Baogao **4935**
0251-9178 Al-Umam al-Muttahidah. Lajnah lil-Qanun at-Tijari ad-Duwali. Tarrir 'an 'Amal Dawratiha **4916**
0251-9380 *see* 0251-9410 **1186**
0251-9399 *see* 0251-9410 **1186**
0251-9402 *see* 0251-9410 **1186**
0251-9410 United Nations Economic and Social Council. Resolutions and Decisions **1186**
0251-9429 *see* 0251-9410 **1186**
0251-9437 Cuadernos Estadisticos de la C E P A L **8365**
0251-9461 Handbook of International Trade and Development Statistics - United Nations†
0251-9518 Disarmament†
0251-9569 Intergovernmental Oceanographic Commission. Workshop Report **2808**
0251-9593 Mezpravitel'stvennaja Okeanograficeskaja Komissija. Mehaniceskaja Serija *see* 0074-1175 **2808**
0251-9607 Commission Oceanographique Intergouvernementale. Serie Technique *see* 0074-1175 **2808**
0251-9674 U I E Monographs†
0251-9682 Monographie de l'I U E†
0252-0001 *see* 0082-8173 **4943**
0252-001X *see* 0082-8173 **4943**
0252-0028 *see* 0082-8173 **4943**
0252-0036 *see* 0082-8173 **4943**
0252-0044 *see* 0082-8173 **4943**
0252-0052 *see* 0082-8173 **4943**
0252-0060 Missions Permanentes aupres de l'Organisation des Nations Unies *see* 0252-0079 **7259**
0252-0079 Permanent Missions to the United Nations **7259**
0252-0206 M A B Report Series **3451**
0252-0214 Serie de informes del M A B *see* 0252-0206 **3451**
0252-0222 Serie des Rapports du M A B *see* 0252-0206 **3451**
0252-0230 Seriya Dokladov M A B *see* 0252-0206 **3451**
0252-0249 Al Taqrir al-Niha'i-Barnamag al-Insan Wa-al-Muhit al-Hayawi (al-Mab) *see* 0252-0206 **3451**
0252-0257 Revista de la C E P A L **1515**
0252-029X Statistiques Financieres Internationales Annuaire *see* 0250-7463 **1243**
0252-0346 I C J Newsletter **4928**
0252-0354 C I J L Yearbook
0252-0389 S N V Bulletin **6406**
0252-0397 Journal of Higher Education **2990**
0252-0567 Collection Sauvegarde de la Nature *see* 0252-0575 **2621**
0252-0575 Nature and Environment Series **2621**
0252-0583 Council of Europe. Information Bulletin on Social Policy†
0252-0591 Council of Europe. Documentation Centre for Education in Europe. Newsletter†
0252-063X International Exchange of Information on Current Criminological Research Projects in Member States†
0252-0648 Exchange of Information on Research in European Law†
0252-0656 Council of Europe. Parliamentary Assembly. Documents: Working Papers **4922**
0252-0664 Council of Europe. Parliamentary Assembly. Official Report of Debates **4922**
0252-0699 Council of Europe. Study Series: Local and Regional Authorities in Europe **7490**

DIRECTORY 2010 0253-2484 9209

0252-0869 Cultural Policy **7229**
0252-0877 Council of Europe. Directorate of Legal Affairs. Information Bulletin on Legislative Activities†
0252-0958 Council of Europe Forum†
0252-0982 Amenagement du Territoire Europeen. Serie Etudes *see* 0252-0990 **7492**
0252-0990 European Regional Planning Study Series **7492**
0252-1032 Acta de Odontologia Pediatrica **5833**
0252-1040 Revista Peruana de Lenguas Indoamericanas **5168**
0252-1075 Indian Institute of Tropical Meteorology. Contributions **6357**
0252-1105 Information Resources Annual†
0252-1121 Le Bulletin Celinien **5266**
0252-1164 Clinical Physiology and Biochemistry†
0252-1172 Applied Pathology†
0252-1679 Union Internationale des Telecommunications. Rapport des Activites *see* 0085-2201 **2368**
0252-1687 Union Internacional de Telecomunicaciones. Informe sobre las Actividades *see* 0085-2201 **2368**
0252-1725 International Frequency List. Preface **2383**
0252-1792 Nomenclature des Voies de Telecommunication Utilisees pour la Transmission des Telegrammes **2370**
0252-1814 Nomenclature des Stations de Radiocommunications Spatiales et des Stations de Radioastronomie **2361**
0252-1865 Apuntes **7948**
0252-1881 Schweizerische Gesellschaft fuer Ur- und Fruehgeschichte. Jahrbuch *changed to* 1661-8394 **399**
0252-189X Centre National de Recherches Oceanographiques. Document **2801**
0252-1911 Zoologisch-Botanische Gesellschaft in Oesterreich. Verhandlungen **970**
0252-192X Stapfia **706**
0252-1938 Studia Universitatis "Babes-Bolyai". Mathematica **5538**
0252-1962 Revista de Investigaciones Marinas **701**
0252-1970 Geoscience Journal **2743**
0252-2012 Foreign Trade Statistics of Africa. Series C: Summary Tables **1233**
0252-2128 United Nations Economic Commission for Africa. Biennial Report of the Executive Secretary **1606**
0252-2195 C E P A L Cuadernos **1422**
0252-2209 Naciones Unidas. Comision Economica para America Latina y el Caribe. Boletin de Planificacion **1547**
0252-2276 Nations Unies. Commission Economique et Sociale pour l'Asie et le Pacifique. Rapport Annuel *see* 0252-2284 **1595**
0252-2284 Economic and Social Commission for Asia and the Pacific. Annual Report **1595**
0252-2462 Fiji. Mineral Resources Department. Annual Report **6462**
0252-2497 Fiji. Mineral Resources Department. Memoir **2734**
0252-2519 Aide a l'Eglise en Detresse. Bulletin *see* 0252-2535 **7807**
0252-2519 Aide a l'Eglise en Detresse. Bulletin *see* 0252-2527 **7796**
0252-2527 Echo der Liebe **7796**
0252-2535 Mirror **7807**
0252-2543 Echo der Liefde *see* 0252-2527 **7796**
0252-2543 Echo der Liefde *see* 0252-2535 **7807**
0252-2551 L'Eco dell'Amore *see* 0252-2527 **7796**
0252-2551 L'Eco dell'Amore *see* 0252-2535 **7807**
0252-256X Ayuda a la Iglesia Necesitada. Boletin *see* 0252-2527 **7796**
0252-256X Ayuda a la Iglesia Necesitada. Boletin *see* 0252-2535 **7807**
0252-2578 Chretiens de l'Est **7791**
0252-2659 Weekly Analysis of Ecuadorian Issues **1524**
0252-2667 Journal of Information & Optimization Sciences **2429**
0252-2683 Informations Recentes sur les Comptes Nationaux des Pays en Developpement†
0252-2691 Latest Information on National Accounts of Developing Countries *changed to* 0252-2683
0252-2942 World Bank. Annual Report **1607**
0252-2977 Statistiques Financieres Internationales *see* 0020-6725 **1243**
0252-2985 Fonds Monetaire International. Serie des Brochures **1348**
0252-2993 Fondo Monetario Internacional. Serie de Folletos **1348**
0252-3019 International Monetary Fund. Direction of Trade Statistics. Yearbook *see* 0252-306X **1243**
0252-3027 International Financial Statistics. Supplement†
0252-3035 International Monetary Fund. Balance of Payments Statistics Yearbook **1243**
0252-3043 Estadisticas Financieras Internacionales Anuario *see* 0250-7463 **1243**
0252-306X International Monetary Fund. Direction of Trade Statistics **1243**
0252-3078 Estadisticas Financieras Internacionales *see* 0020-6725 **1243**
0252-3108 Per Jacobsson Foundation. Lectures **1374**
0252-3116 Tushuguan Qingbao Gongzuo **5051**
0252-3213 International Directory of Sources. Infoterra **3441**
0252-3221 Repertoire International des Sources. Infoterra *see* 0252-3213 **3441**
0252-323X Directorio Internacional de Fuentes. Infoterra *see* 0252-3213 **3441**
0252-3248 Mezhdunarodnyi Spravochnyi Registr Istochnikov Informatsii. Infoterra *see* 0252-3213 **3441**
0252-3310 United Nations Environment Programme. The State of the Environment; Report of the Executive Director *changed to* 1014-5990 **3472**
0252-3353 Date Palm Journal†
0252-337X Academia de Geografia e Historia de Guatemala. Anales **3997**
0252-3426 Small Industry Bulletin for Asia and the Pacific†
0252-354X Regional Information Support Service†
0252-3639 Population Headliners **7290**
0252-3647 United Nations Economic and Social Commission for Asia and the Pacific. Statistical Newsletter **1273**
0252-3655 Statistical Yearbook for Asia and the Pacific **1267**
0252-3752 Union Postale Universelle. Statistique des Services Postaux **2355**
0252-3973 Union Postale Universelle. Actes **2355**
0252-3981 Universal Postal Union. Acts *see* 0252-3973 **2355**
0252-4368 United Nations. Economic Commission for Asia and the Pacific. Energy Resources Development Series **3149**
0252-4392 Transport & Communications Bulletin for Asia & the Pacific **8514**
0252-4406 Electric Power in Asia and the Pacific **3302**
0252-4457 Statistical Indicators for Asia and the Pacific **1267**
0252-4473 C C O P Newsletter **2703**
0252-452X United Nations Economic and Social Commission for Asia and the Pacific. Social Development Division. Social Work Education and Development†
0252-4848 African Trade†
0252-5038 Rural Progress†
0252-5224 Guide to U N C T A D Publications. Supplement†
0252-5321 United Nations. Treaty Series. Cumulative Index **4825**
0252-5348 Mekong Bulletin†
0252-5356 Bihdasht-i Jahan†
0252-5364 Documentation, Bibliotecas y Archivos: Bibliografias y Obras de Referencia†
0252-5410 El Transporte Maritimo en... *see* 0566-7682 **8658**
0252-5429 Etude sur les Transports Maritimes *see* 0566-7682 **8658**
0252-5437 Isti'rau al-Naql al-Bauri 'am *see* 0566-7682 **8658**
0252-5445 Nian Haiyun Gailan *see* 0566-7682 **8658**
0252-5453 Obzor Morskogo Transporta *see* 0566-7682 **8658**
0252-5461 Nations Unies. Recueil des Traites. Index Cumulatif *see* 0252-5321 **4825**
0252-547X *see* 0082-8084 **7201**
0252-5488 African Statistical Yearbook†
0252-5496 International Yearbook of Education Series†
0252-5577 Guanyu junhei guanzhi he caijun duobian xieding de xiankuang - Lianheguo *see* 0252-5607 **7270**
0252-5585 Sostoanie mnogostoronnih soglasenij o regulirovanii vooruzenij i razoruzenii - Organizacia Obedinennyh Nacij *see* 0252-5607 **7270**
0252-5593 Naciones Unidas. Anuario sobre Desarme *see* 0252-5607 **7270**
0252-5607 United Nations Disarmament Yearbook **7270**
0252-5615 Nations Unies Annuaire de Desarmement *see* 0252-5607 **7270**
0252-5704 Economic and Social Survey of Asia and the Pacific **1479**
0252-5712 Survey of Economic and Social Conditions in Africa **1605**
0252-5720 Coordinating Committee for Geoscience Programmes in East and Southeast Asia. Technical Publication **2705**
0252-6964 *see* 0252-7014 **4943**
0252-6972 *see* 0252-7014 **4943**
0252-6980 *see* 0252-7014 **4943**
0252-6999 *see* 0252-7014 **4943**
0252-7006 *see* 0252-7014 **4943**
0252-7014 United Nations. Resolutions and Decisions Adopted by the General Assembly During Its Session **4943**
0252-7235 International Frequency List **2383**
0252-791X Refugees **7261**
0252-7960 Societe de Physique et d'Histoire Naturelle de Geneve. Memoires **7918**
0252-7979 Guide to Current Literature in Environmental Health Engineering and Science **626**
0252-7987 Repindex **3480**
0252-8150 Zygos (Bi-monthly Edition)†
0252-8169 Journal of Comparative Literature and Aesthetics **5314**
0252-8177 N S C Symposium Series†
0252-8185 Annales Nestle (Spanish Edition) *see* 0250-9644 **5575**
0252-8185 Annales Nestle (Spanish Edition) *see* 0517-8606 **5574**
0252-8185 Annales Nestle (Spanish Edition) *see* 0250-9652 **5575**
0252-8266 Eurostatistik. Daten zuer Konjunkturanalyse **8368**
0252-8274 Ernstia **787**
0252-8282 Bibliotheque Franco Simone **4205**
0252-8290 Revue d'Etudes Palestiniennes **3561**
0252-8347 Papua New Guinea National Bibliography **633**
0252-8398 Bibliography of the Geology of Fiji **2719**
0252-841X Boletin de Antropologia Americana **331**
0252-8444 Agencia de Noticias Fides. Notas **7103**
0252-8460 Revista Minera Bamin **6477**
0252-8479 Repertorio Americano **5359**
0252-8576 International Journal of Educational Sciences **2870**
0252-8584 Economia y Desarrollo **1098**
0252-8606 Signos **3622**
0252-8614 Museo del Hombre Dominicano. Boletin **348**
0252-8622 Archivo Historico del Guayas. Revista†
0252-8630 Sarance **355**
0252-8649 Anuario Bibliografico Ecuatoriano **615**
0252-8657 Cultura (Quito) **1334**
0252-8673 Cuestiones Economicas **1334**
0252-8681 Revista Ciencias Sociales **7996**
0252-8711 Alero **5251**
0252-872X Tradicion Popular **3623**
0252-8754 Inforpress Centroamericana **7142**
0252-8762 Revista de la Integracion y el Desarrollo de Centroamerica **1604**
0252-8770 Universidad Nacional Autonoma de Honduras. Instituto de Investigaciones Economicas y Sociales. Boletin **8012**
0252-8789 Boletin Nicaraguense de Bibliografia y Documentacion
0252-8800 Nicarauac **4466**
0252-8819 Tarea **2917**
0252-8827 Socialismo y Participacion **7183**
0252-8835 Allpanchis **7946**
0252-8843 Revista de Critica Literaria Latinoamericana **5361**
0252-8851 Analisis **7105**
0252-886X Amazonia Peruana **323**
0252-8878 Actualidad Economica del Peru
0252-8894 Historica **4296**
0252-8908 Homines **7969**
0252-8924 Paraguay Economico
0252-8932 Anuario Estadistico del Paraguay **8346**
0252-8983 Revista Historica†
0252-8991 Banco Central de Venezuela. Boletin Mensual **1212**
0252-9017 Revista de Literatura Hispanoamericana **5361**
0252-905X Actualidades
0252-9076 Montalban **4465**
0252-9084 Cultura Universitaria **4449**
0252-9114 European Commission of Human Rights. Annual Review†
0252-9157 The Weekly Review **3902**
0252-9173 Uranium: Ressources, Production et Demande *see* 1996-3459 **6483**
0252-9181 Universitaet Zuerich. Soziologisches Institut. Bulletin†
0252-9203 Social Sciences in China **8004**
0252-9246 C I E - Journal†
0252-9254 Indian Journal of Physics. Part B *changed to* 0973-1458 **7016**
0252-9262 Indian Journal of Physics. Part A *changed to* 0973-1458 **7016**
0252-9289 Archives des Sciences et Compte Rendu des Seances de la Societe de Physique et d'Histoire Naturelle de Geneve *changed to* 1661-464X **7836**
0252-9319 Progres Economique et Social en Amerique Latine. Rapport *see* 0095-2850 **1479**
0252-9335 Eidgenoessische Technische Hochschule Zuerich. Institut fuer Geodaesie und Photogrammetrie. Mitteilungen **2780**
0252-936X E S A Rapport Annuel *see* 0258-025X **53**
0252-9378 Northwest Atlantic Fisheries Organization. Provisional Index and List of Titles of Scientific Council Meeting Documents **3603**
0252-9416 Mausam **6390**
0252-9505 Transnational Perspectives **7269**
0252-9521 Ciencias Economicas **1537**
0252-9572 Options **3482**
0252-9599 Chinese Annals of Mathematics. Series B **5478**
0252-9602 Acta Mathematica Scientia **5464**
0252-9610 Cargonews Asia†
0252-9629 Travel News Asia†
0252-967X Saudi Economic Survey **1171**
0252-9688 Turk Folklor Arastirmalari
0252-9696 Acta Reproductiva Turcica†
0252-9718 Ege Universitesi. Fen Fakultesi Dergisi. Seri B
0252-9742 European Association for Theoretical Computer Science. Bulletin **2600**
0252-9750 Tropical Diseases Research Series†
0252-9769 Revista Geofisica **2788**
0252-9793 Armada International **47**
0252-9920 Unemployment Monthly Bulletin†
0252-9939 Caribbean Geography **4001**
0252-9947 N S C Special Publication†
0252-9963 Mesoamerica **7985**
0252-998X Educacion Especial
0253-0015 Boletin de Lima **7841**
0253-0090 United Nations. Economic Commission for Europe. Information **1186**
0253-0112 UNESCO Reports in Marine Science†
0253-018X Compstat **8364**
0253-0198 Neues vom Bau **1026**
0253-035X Schweizerische Gesellschaft fuer Klinische Chemie. Bulletin†
0253-0368 Archives de Psychologie. Monographies **7336**
0253-0465 Krankenpflege†
0253-0503 Zimbabwe Geological Survey. Bulletin **2776**
0253-052X African Journal of Clinical and Experimental Immunology†
0253-0538 Carib-Latin Energy Consultant **3126**
0253-0597 Garcia de Orta: Serie de Zoologia **944**
0253-066X Caribbean Journal of Religious Studies **7630**
0253-0678 Ingenieria Hidraulica *changed to* 1680-0338 **3362**
0253-0716 Iranian Journal of Medical Sciences **5641**
0253-0724 Ahari Children's Hospital. Medical Center. Proceedings
0253-0910 Oikogeneia kai Skoleio **2163**
0253-0937 Laographike Kypros
0253-0961 Medicom **5675**
0253-097X Archiv fuer Lagerstaettenforschung **2725**
0253-1062 Geotermia†
0253-1097 Journal of the Social Sciences **7980**
0253-1151 Revista Cubana de Higiene y Epidemiologia **7539**
0253-116X Linzer Biologische Beitraege **687**
0253-1194 Contributions to Current Research in Geophysics†
0253-1321 F I O D S Revue†
0253-1453 Botanica Helvetica **780**
0253-1496 Agricultural Reviews **84**
0253-150X Agricultural Science Digest **84**
0253-1593 Analecta Cartusiana **7621**
0253-1607 Monumentet
0253-1623 Bulletin d'Etudes Orientales **545**
0253-1631 Bibliographie Luxembourgeoise **618**
0253-164X Universite Saint Joseph. Melanges **4480**
0253-1674 Didaskalia **7794**
0253-1879 Ocrotirea Naturii si a Mediului Inconjurator **7894**
0253-1933 O I E Revue Scientifique et Technique **8803**
0253-1941 Pakistan and Gulf Economist **1158**
0253-195X Unir Cinema **6516**
0253-1968 Regional and Local Affairs News†
0253-200X Theilheimer's Synthetic Methods of Organic Chemistry **2132**
0253-2050 F A O Soils Bulletin **230**
0253-2069 Biology International: I U B S Newsmagazine†
0253-2093 Advances in Pharmacotherapy†
0253-2123 World Bank Country Study **1608**
0253-2131 World Bank. Reprint Series **1391**
0253-2166 Comite International des Poids et Mesures. Comite Consultatif de Photometrie et Radiometrie. (Rapport et Annexes)† **8942**
0253-2239 Guangxue Xuebao **7076**
0253-2301 Fujian Nongye Keji **114**
0253-231X Gongcheng Rewuli Xuebao **7054**
0253-2328 Ningxia Daxue Xuebao. (Ziran Kexue Ban) **7893**
0253-2336 Meitan Kexue Jishu **3250**
0253-2352 Zhonghua Guke Zazhi **6076**
0253-2395 Shanxi Daxue Xuebao (Ziran Kexue Ban) **7914**
0253-2409 Ranliao Huaxue Xuebao **3254**
0253-2417 Linchan Huaxue yu Gongye **2071**
0253-2468 Huanjing Kexue Xuebao **3437**
0253-2484 Entomologica Basiliensia **844**

ISSN

9210 0253-2492 ULRICH'S PERIODICALS

0253-2492 Consejo Nacional para Investigaciones Cientificas y Tecnologicas, Costa Rica. Informe Anual 8419
0253-2506 N E A Data Bank. Newsletter
0253-2549 Collection F A O, Alimentation et Nutrition see 1014-3181 6658
0253-2654 Weishengwuxue Tongbao 898
0253-2670 Zhongcaoyao 5735
0253-2697 Shiyou Xuebao 6792
0253-2700 Yunnan Zhiwu Yanjiu 823
0253-2727 Zhonghua Xueyexue Zazhi 5942
0253-2743 Jiguang Zazhi 7077
0253-2778 Zhongguo Kexue Jishu Daxue Xuebao 7934
0253-2786 Youji Huaxue 2132
0253-2808 Scientific Committee on Oceanic Research. Proceedings 2817
0253-2875 Newsletter for Research in Chinese Studies 557
0253-2913 Point Series 559
0253-293X New Muses
0253-2948 Revista Costarricense de Ciencias Medicas 5704
0253-2964 Korean Chemical Society. Bulletin 2071
0253-3006 Zhonghua Xiaoer Waike Zazhi 6105
0253-3073 Sengyakhak-Hoeji 6880
0253-3200 Peolpeu Jong'i Gi'sul 6737
0253-3219 Hejishu 3168
0253-3243 Institut Scientifique. Bulletin 7866
0253-3294 Ratio Humana 6946
0253-3340 Geobios New Reports 675
0253-3413 Boletim de Bibliografia Portuguesa. Monografias 5057
0253-3421 Boletim de Bibliografia Portuguesa. Publicacoes em Serie 5057
0253-343X Boletim de Bibliografia Portuguesa. Documentos nao Textuais 5057
0253-357X Shengzhi yu Biyun 973
0253-3596 Yuanzineng Nongye Yingyong 3176
0253-360X Hanjie Xuebao 6342
0253-3618 Hangzhou Daxue Xuebao (Lixue Ban)/Hangzhou University. Journal (Natural Science Edition) changed to 1008-9497 7933
0253-3626 Chongqing Yike Daxue Xuebao 5594
0253-3685 Jiangsu Yiyao 5643
0253-3707 Baiqiuen Yike Daxue Xuebao/Bethune Medical University. Journal changed to 1671-587X 5644
0253-3758 Zhonghua Xin-Xueguanbing Zazhi 5802
0253-3766 Zhonghua Zhongliu Zazhi 6037
0253-3782 Dizhen Xuebao 2780
0253-3790 Yuanzihe Wuli†
0253-3804 Journal of Civil and Hydraulic Engineering 3274
0253-3820 Fenxi Huaxue 2100
0253-3839 Zhongguo Gongcheng Xuekan 3228
0253-3847 Daehan Geumsog Haghoeji 6310
0253-3863 Report on Geoscience and Mineral Resources†
0253-3952 Social Dynamics 8002
0253-3960 Punjab Journal of Politics 7261
0253-3987 La Vie Economique see 1011-386X 1192
0253-4002 Statistical Information Bulletin for Africa†
0253-4010 I U S S P Papers
0253-4142 Indian Academy of Sciences. Proceedings. Mathematical Sciences 5493
0253-4177 Bandaoti Xuebao 3089
0253-4193 Haiyang Xuebao 2805
0253-4231 Bangsa'seon Bang'eo Haghoeji 7065
0253-4304 Guangxi Yixue 5621
0253-4312 Tuliao Gongye 6721
0253-4320 Modern Chemical Industry 3251
0253-4355 Indian Journal of Plant Protection 235
0253-4401 Naturhistorisches Museum Bern. Jahrbuch 7889
0253-441X Universite d'Abidjan. Annales. Serie B. Medecine 5727
0253-4436 Indian Review of Life Sciences†
0253-4517 L S M S Working Paper 1601
0253-4533 Sprache & Kognition†
0253-4703 F A O Bulletin d'Irrigation et de Drainage 8823
0253-4754 International Journal of Structures 3273
0253-4800 National Central University. Bulletin of Geophysics†
0253-4827 Applied Mathematics and Mechanics 5472
0253-4843 Survey of Drug Research in Immunologic Disease†
0253-4851 Tropical Veterinarian†
0253-4886 Digestive Surgery 6241
0253-4894 I C M E News†
0253-4924 Food Technology Abstracts 3669
0253-4959 Dicengxue Zazhi 2731
0253-4967 Dizhen Dizhi 2779
0253-4975 Guoji Dizhen Dongtai 2783
0253-5025 Indian Food Industry 3647
0253-5033 Sistema Nacional de Informacion Cientifica y Tecnologia. Boletin 7917
0253-505X Acta Oceanologica Sinica 2799
0253-5068 Blood Purification 5934
0253-5092 Anthropologika 374
0253-5106 Chemical Society of Pakistan. Journal 2055
0253-519X Discourse 7735
0253-5211 Schweizerische Laboratoriums Zeitschrift 5911
0253-5416 Bangladesh Journal of Botany 778
0253-5424 Bangladesh Journal of Jute & Fibre Research 8448
0253-5432 Bangladesh Journal of Scientific Research 724
0253-5440 Bangladesh Journal of Soil Science 220
0253-5483 Tea Journal of Bangladesh
0253-5629 Botswana. Ministry of Health. Report†
0253-5637 Ciencias de la Tierra y el Espacio 2704
0253-5645 Ingenieria Energetica 3138
0253-5688 Revista C E N I C. Ciencias Biologicas 700
0253-5696 Jardin Botanico Nacional. Revista 796
0253-570X Revista de Salud Animal 8806
0253-5742 Boletin de Psicologia†
0253-5750 Ciencia y Tecnica en la Agricultura. Serie: Veterinaria
0253-5777 Cuba. Ministerio de Educacion Superior. Centro Azucar 227
0253-5785 Cuba. Ministerio de Educacion Superior. Centro Agricola 103
0253-584X Unir: Echo de Saint Louis 5392
0253-5858 Unir Cine Media 8145
0253-5955 African Journal of Agricultural Sciences
0253-5963 Post 7899
0253-6005 A R P E L Boletin Tecnico†
0253-6013 Progreso Economico y Social en America Latina. Informe see 0095-2850 1479
0253-6021 Progresso Socio-Economico na America Latina. Relatorio see 0095-2850 1479
0253-6099 Kuangye Gongcheng 6468
0253-6102 Communications in Theoretical Physics 7008
0253-6188 Italienische Studien 5312
0253-6226 Advances in Bryology 773
0253-6250 Junnan Nuidaiji 5656
0253-6269 Archives of Pharmacal Research 6822
0253-6374 Sri Lanka Association for the Advancement of Science. Proceedings of the Annual Session changed to 1391-0248 7920
0253-6374 Sri Lanka Association for the Advancement of Science. Proceedings of the Annual Session changed to 1391-023X 7920
0253-6455 A B C Teaching Human Rights
0253-6463 A B C Enseignement des Droits de l'Homme see 0253-6455
0253-6498 Han'gug Weon'ye Haghoeji/Korean Society for Horticultural Science. Journal changed to Horticulture, Environment and Biotechnology 3737
0253-651X Hangug Gynnhaghoi Ji 792
0253-6544 Supreme Court Cases (Criminal) 4898
0253-6552 Supreme Court Cases (Labour and Services) 4965
0253-6560 Supreme Court Cases (Taxation)†
0253-6579 Current Central Legislation 4653
0253-6587 Uttar Pradesh Services Cases†
0253-6730 Revue de Paleobiologie 2764
0253-6749 Agricultural Research Institute. Miscellaneous Reports 84
0253-6757 N I H F W Technical Reports 8056
0253-6803 Health and Population: Perspectives and Issues 972
0253-682X Arogya 6982
0253-6889 Bulletin of Medico-Ethno-Botanical Research 307
0253-6951 Demographic Statistics (Year) 7281
0253-7141 Indian Journal of Environmental Protection 3439
0253-7176 Indian Journal of Psychological Medicine 6145
0253-7184 Indian Journal of Sexually Transmitted Diseases 5945
0253-7206 International Bio-Sciences Monographs†
0253-7214 Journal of Advanced Zoology 949
0253-7222 Journal of Dharma 7654
0253-7230 Journal of Scientific Research 952
0253-7249 Journal of Scientific Research in Plants & Medicines 6856
0253-7257 Acoustical Society of India. Journal 7003
0253-7273 Journal of Zoological Research 952
0253-732X Acta Ciencia Indica. Physics 7003
0253-7338 Acta Ciencia Indica. Chemistry 2048
0253-7370 West Indian Law Journal 4812
0253-7397 Ciencias Tecnicas Fisicas y Matematicas 8418
0253-7400 Archiv der Geschichte der Naturwissenschaften†
0253-7419 Medequip†
0253-7427 Eurosocial Newsletter†
0253-7508 Glimpse 7519
0253-7516 Amax News
0253-7567 Nutrition Society of India. Proceedings 6667
0253-7583 Physics News 7033
0253-7605 The Journal of Cytology and Genetics 873
0253-7613 Indian Journal of Pharmacology 6848
0253-7621 Handbook of Medical Education (Year)
0253-7818 O I T Comision Paritaria del Servicio Publico. Informe see 0253-7834 1686
0253-7826 B I T Commission Paritaire de la Fonction Publique. Rapport see 0253-7834 1686
0253-7834 I L O Joint Committee on the Public Service. Report 1686
0253-8040 Indian Journal of Weed Science 235
0253-8199 I M O News 8646
0253-8229 Sri Lanka National Bibliography 7579
0253-8253 Qatar Medical Journal 5701
0253-8261 Nepal Pharmaceutical Association. Journal 6863
0253-8296 Speleological Abstracts 2721
0253-8318 Pakistan Veterinary Journal 8804
0253-8482 Sierra Leone Medical and Dental Association. Journal
0253-8512 The Medical Letter on Drugs and Therapeutics (French Edition) 6860
0253-8539 IndustrieArchaeologie 4146
0253-8555 Cyprus. Department of Statistics and Research. Monthly Economic Indicators 1476
0253-8563 Tourism, Migration and Travel Statistics†
0253-858X Cyprus. Department of Statistics and Research. Imports and Exports Statistics 1223
0253-8598 Cyprus. Department of Statistics and Research. Services Survey†
0253-8601 Health Statistics†
0253-8628 Hospital Statistics†
0253-8636 Sales of Vine Products Manufactured in Cyprus†
0253-8660 Cyprus. Department of Statistics and Research. Wages, Salaries and Hours of Work†
0253-8687 Cyprus. Department of Statistics and Research. Analysis of Wholesale and Retail Trade†
0253-8695 Cyprus. Department of Statistics and Research. Criminal Statistics 2674
0253-8709 Cyprus. Department of Statistics and Research. Tourism, Migration and Travel Statistics 8778
0253-8741 Cypriot Students Abroad†
0253-875X Cyprus. Department of Statistics and Research. Statistical Abstract 8020
0253-8776 J I S T A 5131
0253-9071 Language Forum 5140
0253-9187 Zhongguo Xumu Xuehui Huizhi 969
0253-9268 Revista Cubana de Fisica 7037
0253-9276 Tecnologia Quimica 2082
0253-9306 Research Journal: Science 7902
0253-9365 Bangalore Theological Forum 7624
0253-939X South African Journal for Enology and Viticulture 610
0253-9411 Wiener Tieraerztliche Monatsschrift 8815
0253-9454 Greece. National Statistical Service. Social Welfare and Health Statistics 8083
0253-9543 China Daily 3823
0253-9578 Yingyong Jiemian Huaxue/Applied Surface Chemistry changed to 1026-325X 3248
0253-9608 Ziran Zazhi 7935
0253-9616 F F T C Book Series 230
0253-9624 Zhonghua Yufang Yixue Zazhi 5738
0253-9667 Egyptian Association of Physical Medicine and Rehabilitation. Journal changed to 1110-161X 6223
0253-9713 Beijing Yixue 5584
0253-9721 Fangzhi Xuebao 8450
0253-973X Zhonghua Yixue Jianyan Zazhi/Chinese Journal of Medical Laboratory Technology changed to 1009-9158 5912
0253-9748 Zhenkong Kexue yu Jishu 3400
0253-9772 Yichuan 879
0253-9780 Zhonghua Heyixue Zazhi 6211
0253-9802 Xinyixue 5732
0253-9810 Recht 4766
0253-9829 Turang 2717
0253-9837 Cuihua Xuebao 2115
0253-987X Xi'an Jiaotong Daxue Xuebao 7931
0253-9888 Wuhan Daxue Xuebao (Ziran Kexue Ban) changed to 1671-8836 7930
0253-9896 Tianjin Yiyao 6883
0253-990X Shiping yu Fayiao Gongye 3663
0253-9926 Shanxi Yiyao Zazhi 6880
0253-9934 Shanghai Yixue 5713
0253-9950 Hehuaxue yu Fangshe Huaxue 2063
0253-9977 Xibao Shengwuxue Zazhi 837
0253-9985 Shiyou yu Tianranqi Dizhi 2767
0253-9993 Meitan Xuebao 6470
0254-0010 Huanjing Baohu 3437
0254-0037 Beijing Gongye Daxue Xuebao 7839
0254-0053 Shanghai Lixue 7062
0254-0096 Taiyang Neng Xuebao 3178
0254-010X Turangxue Jinzhan 2717
0254-0126 International Journal of Tropical Plant Diseases 795
0254-0150 Runhua yu Mifeng 3395
0254-0185 Studies in Education and Teaching Techniques†
0254-0193 Series in English Language and Literature†
0254-0207 Language Forum Monograph Series†
0254-0215 Series in Sikh History and Culture†
0254-0355 Universite d'Abidjan. Annales. Serie A. Droit 4802
0254-0533 Textile Industries Dyegest Southern Africa 8460
0254-0576 Social Security Documentation. Caribbean Series 4523
0254-0584 Materials Chemistry and Physics 3352
0254-0592 I W S A Year Book
0254-0649 Statistical Office of the European Communities. Industrial Production†
0254-0657 Melanesian Law Journal 4732
0254-0665 Research in Melanesia†
0254-0681 Yagl-Ambu 8017
0254-0703 International Commission on Large Dams. Transactions 3272
0254-072X Actas Procesales del Derecho Vivo
0254-0770 Universidad del Zulia. Facultad de Ingenieria. Revista Tecnica 3225
0254-0789 Sudan Journal of Food Science and Technology 3664
0254-0819 Acute Care†
0254-0878 Bustard Studies 2605
0254-0886 N I M H A N S Journal 6162
0254-105X Progress in Reproductive Biology and Medicine†
0254-1092 Current Agriculture 104
0254-1106 Revista Critica de Ciencias Sociais 7996
0254-1114 Asian Sources Electronics changed to 1751-9284 3100
0254-1173 Asian Sources Timepieces changed to Global Sources Fashion Accessories 2256
0254-1173 Asian Sources Timepieces changed to Global Sources Gifts & Home Products 4060
0254-119X Mustaqbaliyyat see 0304-3045 2897
0254-119X Mustaqbaliyyat see 0033-1538 2900
0254-1262 Revue Suisse de la Securite et de l'Environnement 3463
0254-1270 Karger Continuing Education Series†
0254-1300 Review of Tropical Plant Pathology 815
0254-1319 Mazuixue Zazhi/Anaesthesiologica Sinica changed to Acta Anaesthesiologica Taiwanica 5768
0254-1335 Iceland. Landsbokasafn Islands. Arbok†
0254-1378 Islensk Bokaskra 5058
0254-1394 Laeknabladid. Fylgirit 5659
0254-1416 Zhonghua Mazuixue Zazhi 5775
0254-1432 Zhonghua Xiaohua Zazhi 5933
0254-1459 Kommissionen for de Europaeiske Faelleskaber. Dokumenter see 0254-1475 7227
0254-1467 Kommision der Europaischen Gemeinschaften. Dokumente see 0254-1475 7227
0254-1475 Commission of the European Communities. Documents 7227
0254-1483 Epitrope ton Europaikon Koinoteton. Eggrafa see 0254-1475 7227
0254-1491 Commission des Communautes Europeennes. Documents see 0254-1475 7227
0254-1505 Commissione delle Comunita Europee. Documenti see 0254-1475 7227
0254-1513 Commissie van de Europese Gemeenschappen. Dokumenten see 0254-1475 7227
0254-1521 Samisdat
0254-1629 Anthropos 327
0254-1637 Argos 7948
0254-1645 Sic 7817
0254-167X Actividad Economica†
0254-1688 Amanecer 7782
0254-1696 Estudios Sociales 7133
0254-170X Mesoamerica 3830
0254-1718 Nouvelles de l'UNITAR see 1014-7853
0254-1769 Zhonghua Huli Zazhi 5984
0254-1785 Zhonghua Qiguan Yizhi Zazhi 6264
0254-1793 Yaowu Fenxi Zazhi 6886
0254-1807 Scriptura 7774
0254-184X University of Cape Town. Department of Obstetrics and Gynaecology. Annual Report 6006
0254-1971 International Centre for Mechanical Sciences. Courses and Lectures 3381

Link to your serials resources and content with ulrichsweb.com

0254-2005 International Association for the Physical Sciences of the Oceans. Proces Verbaux **2808**
0254-2013 Sur†
0254-2021 Shupihui **7681**
0254-203X Latinamerica Press **7982**
0254-2129 Chasqui **8093**
0254-2153 Notas de Desarrollo **1900**
0254-217X Asian Computer Monthly†
0254-2188 Computerweek **2413**
0254-2196 Computing S A **2415**
0254-2226 Sysdata **2439**
0254-2234 Polyscope **2435**
0254-2242 Electrotehnica, Electronica si Automatica. Automatica si Electronica **2460**
0254-2307 Romanian Journal of Gerontology and Geriatrics **4055**
0254-2404 Caribbean Information System for Economic and Social Planning. Carispan Abstracts
0254-2412 Development Information Abstracts†
0254-2420 Directory of On-Going Research in Cancer Epidemiology†
0254-2447 United Nations Children's Fund. Annual Report **8075**
0254-2471 Central America Report **7114**
0254-2528 Interamerican Society for Tropical Horticulture. Proceedings **3739**
0254-2617 Organization of American States. Executive Secretariat for Education, Science and Culture. Newsletter†
0254-2765 Zimbabwe Scientific Association. Transactions **7935**
0254-282X Annales Islamologiques. Supplement
0254-2897 International Union of Geological Sciences. Publication **2748**
0254-2935 Cell and Chromosome Research Journal **828**
0254-2951 University of Zimbabwe. Institute of Mining Research. Report **6483**
0254-3028 Ariel **5256**
0254-3036 I F D A Dossier†
0254-3052 Gaoneng Wuli yu Hewuli *changed to* 1674-1137 **7065**
0254-3079 Yingyong Shuxue Xuebao **5547**
0254-3087 Yiqi Yibiao Xuebao **4490**
0254-3109 International Federation of Automatic Control. Newsletter†
0254-3133 A C C I S Newsletter **2519**
0254-3184 Kypriakos Logos **4239**
0254-3206 Eso - Etimos **3832**
0254-3478 Journal of Research in Ayurveda and Siddha **312**
0254-3486 Suid Afrikaanse Tydskrif vir Natuurwetenskap en Tegnologie **7921**
0254-3494 Paper Southern Africa **6736**
0254-3567 Fuel Science and Technology **3135**
0254-3710 Turicum **3959**
0254-3729 Asian Business†
0254-380X Central Marine Fisheries Research Institute. Technical and Extension Series **938**
0254-3834 Statistical Office of the European Communities. Agricultural Prices **186**
0254-3869 Freshwater and Aquaculture Contents Tables†
0254-3885 O E C D Steel Market in (Year) and Outlook for (Year)†
0254-3893 W W F News **2631**
0254-3923 Animals International **318**
0254-3966 Risk Book Series **7678**
0254-4059 Chinese Journal of Oceanology and Limnology **2801**
0254-4067 Islensk Hljodritaskra **8156**
0254-4091 Indian Botanical Reporter **793**
0254-4105 Indian Journal of Veterinary Surgery **8799**
0254-4113 Cerrahpasa Medical Review†
0254-413X King Abdul Aziz Medical Journal **5657**
0254-4156 Zidonghua Xuebao **2464**
0254-4164 Jisuanji Xuebao **2468**
0254-4210 Revista Centroamericana de Economia **1515**
0254-4261 Assuntos Europeus
0254-4288 Journal of the Gulf and Arabian Peninsula Studies **4322**
0254-4296 Annales Aequatoria **324**
0254-4318 Elektronikschau *changed to* 0013-5674 **3098**
0254-4326 O E G A I Journal **2455**
0254-4342 Business Information Digest **1073**
0254-4377 Glaube in der 2. Welt **7645**
0254-4407 Zwingliana **7781**
0254-4415 Economia **1098**
0254-4466 Hanxue Yanjiu **4182**
0254-4474 Language Research **5141**
0254-4571 Nizam Pezeshki Jomhuriye Islamiye Iran. Majalleh†
0254-461X Muenzen-Revue **6651**
0254-4660 World Directory of Social Science Institutions†
0254-4725 F A O Food and Nutrition Paper **3635**
0254-4733 Hagskyrslur Islands **8375**
0254-4784 Library Association of China. Newsletter **5027**
0254-4903 Chinese Science Abstracts. Part B **7936**
0254-4962 Psychopathology **6179**
0254-5020 Medicine and Sport Science **6231**
0254-5047 P R O S I **3659**
0254-508X Zhongguo Zaozhi **6740**
0254-5098 Zhonghua Fangshe Yixue yu Fanghu Zazhi **6211**
0254-5101 Zhonghua Weishengwuxue he Mianyixue Zazhi **5767**
0254-5179 Chinese Science Abstracts. Part A **7936**
0254-5209 2 Plus 2†
0254-5217 Congres International de la Population. Proceedings *see* 0074-9338
0254-5241 J B I Journal **6467**
0254-5268 Business India **1426**
0254-5276 Buletini i Shkencave Gjeologjike **2727**
0254-5284 F A O Irrigation and Drainage Papers **8823**
0254-5314 Verkehr **8637**
0254-5330 Annals of Operations Research **2406**
0254-5357 Yankuang Ceshi **2775**
0254-5373 Karger Biobehavioral Medicine Series†
0254-5381 Entomologia Hellenica **844**
0254-5446 Turkish Journal of Nuclear Sciences **3175**
0254-5527 Ege Universitesi. Fen Fakultesi Dergisi. Seri A
0254-556X Mauritius Chamber of Commerce and Industry. Newsletter†
0254-5578 Aracnologia **933**
0254-5705 Revista Medica de Mocambique **7539**
0254-5853 Dongwuxue Yanjiu **940**
0254-5861 Jiegou Huaxue **2066**
0254-587X Jinshu Rechuli Xuebao/Transactions of Metal Heat Treatment *changed to* 1009-6264 **6307**
0254-5888 Jishu yu Xunlian **6318**
0254-5934 Korean Journal of Genetics/Han'gug Yujeon Haghoeji *changed to* 1976-9571 **867**
0254-6019 F A O Animal Production and Health Papers **286**
0254-6051 Jinshu Rechuli **3348**
0254-6086 Hejubian yu Denglizitiwuli **7066**
0254-6094 Huagong Jixie **3245**
0254-6108 Huanjing Huaxue **2063**
0254-6124 Kongjian Kexue Xuebao **64**
0254-6175 Chronicle of Current Events†
0254-6183 Asian Literary Market Review **7552**
0254-6205 Knanayamithram **2198**
0254-6213 S E A S Anniversary Meeting. Proceedings **2550**
0254-6221 Daseinsanalyse†
0254-623X Progress in Critical Care Medicine†
0254-6299 South African Journal of Botany **818**
0254-6302 Structural Engineering Documents **3284**
0254-6337 Swiss Vet†
0254-6426 Evergreen **3688**
0254-6434 Jardin Botanico Nacional "Dr. Rafael M. Moscoso." Boletin **796**
0254-6442 Moscosoa **802**
0254-6450 Zhonghua Liuxingbingxue Zazhi **5738**
0254-6493 Aquiculture†
0254-6523 Linchan Gongye **3696**
0254-7066 Taiwan Tudi Jinrong Jikan†
0254-7147 Consulting Medical Laboratories. Bulletin **5600**
0254-7317 Venezuela. Oficina Central de Estadistica e Informatica. Anuario Estadistico
0254-7325 Academia Nacional de la Historia. Boletin **4281**
0254-7376 Revista Musical de Venezuela **6611**
0254-7457 El Diario **3802**
0254-7511 Prisma Latinoamericano **3831**
0254-7597 Aula
0254-7627 Yaxkin **361**
0254-7678 Miscelanea Antropologica Ecuatoriana **348**
0254-7694 Short Book Reviews *changed to* 0306-7734 **8379**
0254-7783 Banco Mundial Noticias†
0254-7791 Jisuan Shuxue **5499**
0254-7805 Guti Lixue Xuebao **7059**
0254-7813 Computer Science and Informatics **2412**
0254-7821 Mehran University Research Journal of Engineering and Technology **3210**
0254-783X S I N Newsletter†
0254-7856 Al-Mushir **7664**
0254-7902 Texte **6187**
0254-7937 Janus *changed to* 1680-1865
0254-797X Garabato **5299**
0254-7988 Regional Studies **7176**
0254-802X Barricada Internacional
0254-8054 Amazonia Indigena†
0254-8062 Arqueologia y Sociedad **381**
0254-8119 Debate **5213**
0254-8151 San Marcos **516**
0254-816X Semana Economica **1172**
0254-8178 Nemity **4466**
0254-8186 Revue Internationale d'Histoire Militaire **6444**
0254-8240 Gaceta Arqueologica Andina **395**
0254-8275 Beitraege zur Intensiv- und Notfallmedizin†
0254-8313 International Center for Agricultural Research in the Dry Areas. Annual Report **122**
0254-833X Arab News **3912**
0254-8356 Neotestamentica **7665**
0254-8372 Journal of Economic Development **1600**
0254-8399 India Today **3883**
0254-8410 Cronica de las Naciones Unidas *see* 1025-8523 **7227**
0254-8410 Cronica de las Naciones Unidas *see* 0251-7329 **7269**
0254-8445 Revista Energetica **3147**
0254-8453 Flora del Paraguay **788**
0254-8631 I B A Review
0254-8682 Jiaoyu Zhanwang† **8968**
0254-8704 Journal of Environmental Biology **3445**
0254-8712 Nova Acta Paracelsica **5688**
0254-8739 Concepts in Toxicology†
0254-8747 Advances in Audiology†
0254-8755 International Journal of Tropical Agriculture **123**
0254-8763 Kexue Dui Shehui de Yingxiang **7981**
0254-8798 Environmental Awareness **3423**
0254-8801 Agrindex†
0254-8844 International Organization of Plant Biosystematists. Newsletter **795**
0254-8852 Discussions in Neuroscience†
0254-8860 Indian Journal of Gastroenterology **5926**
0254-8895 Analele Universitatii Bucuresti. Fizica **7005**
0254-8992 Der Steuerentscheid **4789**
0254-9026 Zhonghua Laonian Yixue Zazhi **4058**
0254-9042 Zhongguo Yixue Wenzhai (Zhongyi) **5752**
0254-9077 J A M A: The Journal of the American Medical Association (Swiss Edition)†
0254-9204 Pakistan Journal of Applied Economics **1510**
0254-9212 Anthropologica **325**
0254-9220 Debates en Sociologia **8098**
0254-9239 Lexis **5144**
0254-9247 Revista de Psicologia **7404**
0254-9263 Health for All Series **4096**
0254-928X Internationale Zeitschrift fuer Sozialpsychologie und Gruppendynamik **7366**
0254-9298 Lebensmittel- und Biotechnologie **3654**
0254-9352 I J B - Bulletin†
0254-9379 Proche-Orient Etudes Economiques†
0254-9395 Indian Journal of Leprosy **5816**
0254-9409 Journal of Computational Mathematics **5502**
0254-9433 Geobotanisches Institut E T H, Stiftung Ruebel, Zurich. Veroeffentlichungen **791**
0254-945X Zeitschrift fuer Schweizerisches Recht **4819**
0254-9492 Arab Medical Bulletin **5577**
0254-9549 The New Voices **5341**
0254-9565 Nova Giulianiad
0254-9611 Majallah-i Fizik **7025**
0254-962X Caribbean Community Perspective **1446**
0254-9662 Youth of the 21†
0254-9670 Experimental and Clinical Immunogenetics†
0254-9697 Thexis *changed to* 1865-6544 **1833**
0254-9727 F A O Plant Protection Bulletin (Multilingual Edition) **787**
0254-9743 Earthscan Bulletin†
0254-9794 Calcutta Historical Journal **4180**
0254-9808 Tibetan Bulletin **7702**
0254-9824 U I S Bulletin (Print) *changed to* U I S Bulletin (Online) **2771**
0254-9921 Aux Ecoutes **4072**
0254-9948 Monumenta Serica **556**
0255-0024 I L C A Newsletter **288**
0255-0032 *see* 0255-0024 **288**
0255-0059 International Directory of New and Renewable Energy Information Sources and Research Centres† **8965**
0255-0067 Bermuda National Bibliography **616**
0255-0083 Meiguo Yanjiu *changed to* 1021-3058 **4307**
0255-0091 Naturhistorisches Museum in Wien. Annalen. Serie A, Mineralogie und Petrographie, Geologie und Palaeontologie, Anthropologie und Praehistorie **7889**
0255-0105 Naturhistorisches Museum in Wien. Annalen. Serie B: Botanik und Zoologie **957**
0255-0113 Naturhistorisches Museum in Wien. Annalen. Serie C: Jahresbericht†
0255-013X I N A Newsletter **2806**
0255-0148 Journal of Water Resources
0255-0156 Operator Theory **5523**
0255-0172 Transvaal Museum. Monographs **965**
0255-0180 South Africa. Department of Agriculture. Entomology Memoir **859**
0255-027X Ecuador. Direccion General de Geologia y Minas. Revista†
0255-0326 I F H O H Journal **4074**
0255-0385 Omaly sy Anio **4177**
0255-0539 Transilvania **7691**
0255-058X South African Tunnelling **3283**
0255-0695 Zambia Educational Review
0255-0776 Social Europe†
0255-0822 O E C D Economic Studies *changed to* 1995-2805 **1155**
0255-0830 Revue Economique de l'O C D E†
0255-0849 International Bibliography of Historical Demography†
0255-0857 Indian Journal of Medical Microbiology **5760**
0255-0903 Groupe International d'Etude de la Ceramique Egyptienne. Bulletin de Liaison **396**
0255-0911 Containers†
0255-0962 Institut Francais d'Archeologie Orientale du Caire. Bulletin **397**
0255-2701 Chemical Engineering and Processing **3238**
0255-2779 Literary Endeavour **5324**
0255-2809 Litterae Numismaticae Vindobonenses†
0255-2922 Journal of Traditional Chinese Medicine *see* 1130-4405
0255-2922 Journal of Traditional Chinese Medicine *see* 1001-1668 **316**
0255-2930 Zhongguo Zhenjiu **316**
0255-3066 Machinery and Steel **5455**
0255-3104 Bauen in Stahl **435**
0255-3139 International Council on Archives. Committee on Conservation and Restoration. Committee on Archival Reprography. Bulletin†
0255-3430 Entscheidungen der Beschwerdekammern des Europaeischen Patentamts† **8954**
0255-3465 Statistical Sources and Methods **1267**
0255-3570 Treffpunkt Bibliothek **7575**
0255-3627 Quarterly Labour Force Statistics† **8983**
0255-3635 Revista Internacional de Ciencias Administrativas *see* 0020-8523 **7447**
0255-3635 Revista Internacional de Ciencias Administrativas *see* 0303-965X **7466**
0255-3678 Kriminalsoziologische Bibliographie†
0255-3686 Progress in Veterinary Microbiology and Immunology†
0255-3813 N A T O Review (Print)†
0255-3910 Pain and Headache **6172**
0255-4003 Commission of the European Communities. Operation of Nuclear Power Stations **3166**
0255-4054 Sudan Science Abstracts **7939**
0255-4062 Eye Care **6042**
0255-4070 Ahfad Journal **8893**
0255-4100 Cocos **101**
0255-4119 Coconut Bulletin **101**
0255-4321 Revista Internacional de Policia Criminal†
0255-4402 Sociedad Zoologica del Uruguay. Boletin **963**
0255-4429 World Badminton **8216**
0255-4437 International Badminton Federation. Annual Statute Book **8180**
0255-4445 Zygos (Annual Edition)† **1837**
0255-4607 Trade and Development Report **1584**
0255-4720 Institouton Okeanografikon kai Alieutikon Ereunon. Eidike Ekdose **2807**
0255-4887 Apacheta†
0255-4925 Pacifico Sur **696**
0255-4992 Revue Internationale de Droit Contemporain *see* International Review of Contemporary Law
0255-5018 Disaster Management
0255-5131 Market Trends & Prospects for Chemical Products†
0255-5182 List of E C A Documents Issued **1601**
0255-5190 New Acquisitions in the U N E C A Library **632**
0255-5263 Census of Motor Traffic on Main International Traffic Arteries **8630**
0255-5336 Antenne Francaise de Sinologie a Hong Kong. Bulletin Mensuel *changed to* 1021-9013 **7259**
0255-5352 O C E A C Bulletin de Liaison et de Documentation
0255-5425 Turkologischer Anzeiger **564**
0255-5476 Materials Science Forum **7026**
0255-5484 Documentation Indian National Affairs†
0255-5506 Travail dans le Monde *see* 0255-5514 **1716**
0255-5514 World Labour Report **1716**
0255-5522 Trabajo en el Mundo *see* 0255-5514 **1716**
0255-5581 Taiwan Sugar Research Institute. Annual Report **255**
0255-5697 Taiwan Economy **1521**
0255-5905 Taizhong-qu Nongye Gailiang Chang Yanjiu Huibao **160**

ISSN

0256-7423 University of Durban-Westville. Bulletin for Academic Staff
0256-7458 Bulletin of the Industrial Development Decade for Africa
0256-7512 Bulletin of Agricultural Research in Botswana **98**
0256-7563 The Engineering industries in O E C D Member Countries†
0256-7571 National Accounts of O E C D Countries. Volume 2 Detailed Tables **1252**
0256-758X National Accounts of O E C D Countries. Volume 1 Main Aggregates **1252**
0256-7601 National Accounts E S A - Aggregates (Years) **1152**
0256-7679 Chinese Journal of Polymer Science **2121**
0256-7687 World Data (Year)†
0256-7709 National Bibliography of Barbados **631**
0256-7857 Statistical Yearbook of the Republic of China **1268**
0256-7873 Terminologie et Traduction **5186**
0256-7911 Journal of Solar Energy Research
0256-7970 Greece. National Statistical Service. Building Activity Statistics **1046**
0256-8047 Malta. Central Office of Statistics. Annual Abstract of Statistics **8387**
0256-8063 Fiji. Bureau of Statistics. Shipping Statistics **8524**
0256-8071 Fiji. Bureau of Statistics. Aircraft Statistics **76**
0256-808X Sri Lanka Yearbook **1266**
0256-8144 Boletin del Instituto Nacional de Salud *changed to* 1606-6979 **5636**
0256-8187 Tin Statistics†
0256-8209 Avgerinos†
0256-8314 Cyprus. Ministry of Labour and Social Insurance. Labour Review†
0256-8411 Saga **4160**
0256-842X Islenskt Maal og Almenn Maalfraedi **5130**
0256-8446 Skirnir **5373**
0256-8462 Hid Islenzka Fornleifafelag. Arbok **4233**
0256-8470 Ferdafelag Islands. Arbok **8703**
0256-8500 Cyprus Bulletin†
0256-8543 Journal of Research in Childhood Education **2878**
0256-8551 Journal of Microbial Biotechnology
0256-856X Melanesian Journal of Theology **7662**
0256-8578 Salzburger Romanistische Schriften **5366**
0256-8829 Educare *changed to* 1814-6627 **2966**
0256-8837 Musicus **6595**
0256-8845 Politeia **7167**
0256-8853 Progressio **3078**
0256-8861 South African Journal of Library and Information Science **5048**
0256-8896 U N I S A Psychologia *changed to* 1812-6731 **7388**
0256-8934 Dataweek **8419**
0256-8993 Freidenker **5216**
0256-9000 Nashrat al-Mukhaddirat *see* 0007-523X **2700**
0256-9043 Sinorama **3960**
0256-9051 *see* 0256-9043 **3960**
0256-906X *see* 0256-9043 **3960**
0256-9175 Bontebok†
0256-9280 Experimental Hematology. Supplement **5936**
0256-940X Energy Balances of O E C D Countries **3130**
0256-9426 Analele Banatului. Etnografie **324**
0256-9493 Swamy Botanical Club. Journal **819**
0256-9507 Missionalia **7699**
0256-954X Papua New Guinea Journal of Agriculture, Forestry and Fisheries **145**
0256-9574 S A M J South African Medical Journal **5708**
0256-9590 Society
0256-9604 Versants **5394**
0256-9655 Current Contents of Foreign Periodicals in Chinese Studies **5004**
0256-9671 Tushuguan Xuekan **5051**
0256-9701 Soilless Culture†
0256-971X Uttar Pradesh Journal of Zoology **966**
0256-9795 Estudios e Informes de la C E P A L **1595**
0256-9868 L'Industrie Siderurgique en (Year) **6315**
0256-9957 Asia Pacific Tech Monitor **8416**
0257-0017 Dialogue **3789**
0257-005X Spectrum **3082**
0257-0076 Actes des Colloques Insectes Sociaux **837**
0257-0114 Paginas de Contenido: Ciencias de la Informacion†
0257-0130 Queueing Systems **3328**
0257-0149 Baogao Wenxue **4572**
0257-0165 Dangdai **5282**
0257-0173 Dianying Chuangzuo **6496**
0257-0181 Dianying Yishu **6496**
0257-0203 Fangyan **5118**
0257-0211 Fujian Xiju/Fujian Theater *changed to* 1004-2075 **8471**
0257-022X Guangzhou Wenyi **5302**
0257-0238 Gushihui **5303**
0257-0246 Shehui Kexue Zhanxian **8001**
0257-0254 Wenyi Lilun Yanjiu **5398**
0257-0262 Beijing Wenxue **5261**
0257-0270 Dushu **5286**
0257-0289 Fudan Xuebao (Shehui Kexue Ban) **7965**
0257-0297 Fujian Wenxue†
0257-0300 Huanjing **3437**
0257-0335 Ekonomicheskaya i Social'naya Komissiya Dlya Azii i Tikhogo Okeana. Godovoi Doklad *see* 0252-2284 **1595**
0257-0343 Yazhou ji Taipingyang Jingji Shehui Weiyuanhui. Niandu Baogao *see* 0252-2284 **1595**
0257-0521 E A R Se L Newsletter **2705**
0257-053X E A R Se L Directory†
0257-067X United Nations. Security Council. Official Records. Supplement **7271**
0257-0769 Nations Unies. Conseil de Securite. Documents Officials. Supplement *see* 0257-067X **7271**
0257-0971 Naciones Unidas. Consejo de Seguridad. Documentos Oficiales. Suplemento *see* 0257-067X **7271**
0257-1072 Patient Care†
0257-1145 *see* 0251-9410 **1186**
0257-1250 Organizatsiya Ob'edinennykh Natsii. Sovet Bezopasnosti. Ofitsial'nye Otchety. Dopolnenie *see* 0257-067X **7271**
0257-1412 Association of Exploration Geophysicists. Journal **2778**
0257-1420 International Angler **8319**
0257-1447 Institute for Strategic Studies. Bulletin **7242**
0257-1617 O P E C Annual Report **6782**
0257-1625 Artesanias de America†
0257-1668 Domodomo **335**
0257-1749 Tecnologica **8443**
0257-1846 Notes et Documents Burkinabe†
0257-1862 South African Journal of Plant and Soil **254**
0257-1897 Disarmament Newsletter†
0257-196X Engineering Week **3190**
0257-1978 Institution of Municipal Engineers of Southern Africa. Journal
0257-1994 Meson†
0257-2001 Rossing Magazine **2626**
0257-201X South African Poultry Bulletin **301**
0257-2036 Ensovoort **5421**
0257-2044 Golden Fleece†
0257-2095 South African Citrus and Sub-Tropical Fruit Journal†
0257-2109 N A C News†
0257-2117 South African Journal of African Languages **5176**
0257-2141 Defence Journal **6418**
0257-2168 Notas sobre la Economia y el Desarrollo†
0257-2176 Estudio Economico de America Latina y el Caribe **1484**
0257-2184 Economic Survey of Latin America and the Caribbean **1480**
0257-2354 Hellenic Veterinary Medical Society. Bulletin **8798**
0257-2389 San'eob Misaengmul Haghoeji/Korean Journal of Applied Microbiology and Biotechnology *changed to* 1598-642X **886**
0257-2419 Statistical Office of the European Communities. Transport, Communications, Tourisme - Annuaire Statistique **8530**
0257-2605 Ethiopian Journal of Agricultural Sciences **108**
0257-2753 Digestive Diseases **5922**
0257-277X Immunologic Research **5759**
0257-2796 International College of Dentists. European Section. Newsletter **5848**
0257-2826 Jiaoxue yu Yanjiu **3066**
0257-2834 Jilin Daxue Shehui Kexue Xuebao **7977**
0257-2850 Minzu Wenxue **5334**
0257-2885 Nanfeng **5338**
0257-2915 Jinyang Wenyi†
0257-3032 World Bank Research Observer **1391**
0257-3105 B F B Bericht **655**
0257-3113 Oesterreichische Akademie der Wissenschaft. Institut fuer Limnologie. Biologische Station Lunz. Jahresbericht **695**
0257-3180 Fernfahrer **8670**
0257-3199 Allgemeinmedizin†
0257-3229 International Association of School Librarianship. Annual Conference **5018**
0257-3245 Research and Development Reporter **249**
0257-3377 De Kat **3949**
0257-3423 Institution of Engineers (India). Aerospace Engineering Division. Journal **60**
0257-3431 Institution of Engineers (India). Agricultural Engineering Division. Journal **122**
0257-344X Institution of Engineers (India). Architectural Engineering **3272**
0257-3512 Conditions of Work Digest†
0257-3555 Libros Paraguayos **5322**
0257-3563 The Island Sun **3995**
0257-358X Shandong Zhongyi Zazhi **5713**
0257-3598 Umriss†
0257-3601 Werkblatt **7414**
0257-3636 Hong Kong Countdown: Perspectives on Change†
0257-3695 Columbus Logbook†
0257-3717 International Narcotics Control Board. Report for (Year) **6850**
0257-3725 L'Organe International de Controle des Stupefiants pour (Year). Rapport *see* 0257-3717 **6850**
0257-3741 Guoji Mazuipin Guanzhiju (Year) Baogao *see* 0257-3717 **6850**
0257-375X Al Hay'a al-Duwaliyyatt li-Muraqaba al-Muhaddirat li'Am (Year). Taqrir *see* 0257-3717 **6850**
0257-3768 Mezdunarodnyi Komitet po Kontrolu nad Narkotikami. Doklad za (God) *see* 0257-3717 **6850**
0257-3822 Medien und Recht International **4732**
0257-3830 Neue Helvetische Gesellschaft. Mitteilungen **2268**
0257-3849 Interface **3065**
0257-3881 Nauchnaya Apparatura†
0257-389X *see* 0251-9410 **1186**
0257-3962 Environment Newsletter **3422**
0257-4063 Textes Litteraires Francais **5387**
0257-4098 Voyageurs Occidentaux en Egypte **563**
0257-411X Institut Francais d'Archeologie Orientale du Caire. Memoires **398**
0257-4136 Textes Arabes et Etudes Islamiques **7716**
0257-4152 Tarih Incelemeleri Dergisi **4325**
0257-4284 Tidal Gravity Corrections†
0257-4292 Tipografia
0257-4306 Investigacion Operacional **5498**
0257-4314 Revista Cubana de Educacion Superior **3000**
0257-4322 Revista Cubana de Psicologia **7403**
0257-4349 Banque de la Republique d'Haiti. Bulletin **1320**
0257-4357 Banque de la Republique d'Haiti. Rapport Annuel **1320**
0257-439X Fihrist **624**
0257-4403 World Population Projections†
0257-442X Institution of Engineers (India). Mining Engineering Division. Journal **6466**
0257-4438 Institution of Engineers (India). Textile Engineering Division. Journal **8453**
0257-4667 Biserica Ortodoxa Romana **7703**
0257-4985 Pakistan Journal of Otolaryngology **6084**
0257-4993 Journal of Potassium Research **6319**
0257-5035 Agro-Chemicals News in Brief **217**
0257-5256 Directory of Community Legislation in Force **4658**
0257-5310 Hindu International Edition **3882**
0257-5418 Transkei Government Gazette Index†
0257-5426 Wiel **8520**
0257-5434 South Pacific Journal of Psychology (Print) *changed to* 1834-4909 **7377**
0257-5604 Xiaoshuo Xuankan **5402**
0257-5639 Xinju Zuo *changed to* Shanghai Yishujia **8478**
0257-5647 Xin Wenxue Shiliao **5402**
0257-5663 Taiwan, Republic of China. Executive Yuan. Directorate-General of Budget, Accounting & Statistics. Quarterly National Economic Trends, Taiwan Area **1521**
0257-5671 Taiwan, Republic of China. Executive Yuan. Directorate-General of Budget, Accounting & Statistics. National Income in Taiwan Area, R.O.C. **1269**
0257-5698 Commodity Price Monthly†
0257-5728 Commodity Price Statistics Monthly in Taiwan Area **1221**
0257-5736 Taiwan, Republic of China. Executive Yuan. Directorate-General of Budget, Accounting & Statistics. Social Indicators in Taiwan Area (Year) **8408**
0257-5779 Minzu Yuwen **5151**
0257-5809 Sanwen **5367**
0257-5817 Shandong Wenxue **5371**
0257-5833 Shehui Kexue (Shanghai) **8001**
0257-5841 Shi Yue **5371**
0257-585X Shuofang **5372**
0257-5876 Wenyi Yanjiu **5398**
0257-5892 Nanjing Daxue Xuebao (Zhexue Shehui Kexue Ban) *changed to* 1007-7278 **7885**
0257-5906 Shanxi Wenxue **5371**
0257-5914 Wenxue Yichan **5398**
0257-5930 Xinwen Zhanxian **4586**
0257-5973 A T A S Bulletin **8415**
0257-599X Munazzamat al-Sihhiyyah al-'Alamiyyah. Nashrah *see* 0042-9686 **5731**
0257-6015 Sante pour Tous. Serie *see* 0254-9263 **4096**
0257-6023 Salud para Todos. Serie *see* 0254-9263 **4096**
0257-6074 Culture Populaire Albanaise **3616**
0257-6082 Kultura Popullore **3619**
0257-6090 C D B News **1323**
0257-6120 Caribbean Development Bank. Annual Report **1325**
0257-6236 International Rivers and Lakes **2796**
0257-6309 F P Revista C I N T E R F O R **5009**
0257-6376 Nuclear Data Newsletter **3171**
0257-6430 Studies in History (New Delhi) **4189**
0257-6449 Winak **3010**
0257-6457 Cuadernos de Poetica†
0257-6503 A I L A Bulletin *changed to* 1461-0213 **5088**
0257-6562 Ertong Wenxue **2188**
0257-6651 International Union of Anthropological and Ethnological Sciences. Newsletter **343**
0257-6686 Terra Plana **8760**
0257-6708 Institution of Engineers (India). Production Engineering Division. Journal **3199**
0257-6775 Bokasafnid **4997**
0257-702X E I S Newsletter
0257-7038 Fauna Europaea Evertebrata **942**
0257-7046 Paiperlek†
0257-7062 Tydskrif vir Islamkunde **7716**
0257-7070 Paraguay **633**
0257-7216 United Nations Centre for Human Settlements. Bibliographic Notes **4437**
0257-7240 Greek Economy in Figures (Year) **1236**
0257-7291 I O J Newsletter†
0257-7305 Manushi **8900**
0257-7313 N G O News on Human Settlements†
0257-7321 Nouvelles de l'O I J†
0257-7348 South Asian Anthropologist **356**
0257-7364 South East Asian Review **4188**
0257-7488 Universitatea din Timisoara. Analele. Stiinte Fizice *changed to* Universitatea de Vest din Timisoara. Analele. Seria Stiinte Fizice **7044**
0257-750X Boletin Antropologico **331**
0257-7534 Muzeul de Istorie al Republicii Socialiste Romania. Cercetari de Conservare si Restaurare a Patrimoniului Muzeal†
0257-7550 Least Developed Countries Report **1575**
0257-7615 South African Journal of Marine Science *changed to* 1814-232X **3583**
0257-7631 South Africa. Sea Fisheries Research Institute. Special Report **3608**
0257-7712 Huaxi Yike Daxue Xuebao/West China University of Medical Sciences. Journal *changed to* 1672-173X **5714**
0257-7739 Message of the Library **5032**
0257-7747 Tydskrif vir die Suid-Afrikaanse Reg **4799**
0257-7755 Banque Europeenne d'Investissement. Cahiers **1320**
0257-7763 Diario Oficial de las Comunidades Europeas. C: Comunicaciones e Informaciones **4923**
0257-7771 Jornal Oficial das Comunidades Europeias. C: Comunicacoes e Informacoes *see* 0257-7763 **4923**
0257-7771 Jornal Oficial das Comunidades Europeias. C: Comunicacoes e Informacoes *see* 1725-2423 **7256**
0257-7801 Quarterly National Accounts **1941**
0257-7828 International Journal of Science & Engineering **7867**
0257-7852 Filmbulletin **6500**
0257-7860 Carn **7225**
0257-7941 Ancient Science of Life **306**
0257-8018 Export Times†
0257-8034 Fertiliser Marketing News **230**
0257-8050 Pollution Research **3460**
0257-8069 A S C I Journal of Management **1722**
0257-8093 Informe Sobre el Comercio y el Desarrollo *see* 0255-4607 **1584**
0257-8158 Taiwan International Trade **1583**
0257-8166 Taiwan Electronics Industry **3114**
0257-8174 Target Electronics Industry Components†
0257-8301 Kenya Past and Present **4176**
0257-8409 I L C A Research Report **288**
0257-8573 Aeronautica Meridiana **42**
0257-859X Rubber Reporter
0257-8611 Boletin de Geociencias†
0257-8646 Engineering News **3190**
0257-8697 Upbeat
0257-8700 Water Sewage and Effluent **8840**
0257-8719 South African Pharmaceutical Journal **6881**
0257-8727 Pact **410**
0257-8921 Woord & Daad **7780**
0257-8972 Surface and Coatings Technology **2106**
0257-9022 Plasticulture **7098**

ISSN

0259-0883 Demographische Informationen *changed to* 1728-4414 **7295**
0259-0948 Geographical Journal of Nepal†
0259-0956 Journal of Development and Administrative Studies **1544**
0259-0964 Tribhuvan University. Natural History Museum. Journal **820**
0259-0972 Institute of Medicine. Journal **5636**
0259-1049 Revista Estudios Dominicanos **7178**
0259-1081 Thraco-Dacica **4273**
0259-1111 Voice of History **4190**
0259-1146 Directory of Chinese External Economic Organizations & Industrial - Commercial Enterprises **1986**
0259-1162 Anaesthesia Essays and Researches **5768**
0259-1235 Electronic News for China **3096**
0259-126X Personality **3949**
0259-1340 Models in Dermatology†
0259-1405 Himalayan Economist **1118**
0259-1413 Himalayan Review **4014**
0259-1499 Kuensel (English Edition) **3802**
0259-1618 Ramjham†
0259-1642 The Rising Nepal **3914**
0259-1839 N I P R News†
0259-1855 South African Exporters **1582**
0259-1871 University of Pretoria. Annual Report **2307**
0259-188X Indicator South Africa† **8964**
0259-1901 Journal of Dendrology **796**
0259-191X Orion **2434**
0259-1944 Studies in the History of Cape Town†
0259-1952 Suid-Afrikaanse Oorsig†
0259-2010 Namibiana **4176**
0259-2029 Education & Culture†
0259-207X Education Journal†
0259-2185 Desarmement. Serie D'etudes *see* 1014-2177 **7270**
0259-2193 Nepala Kanuna Paricarca **4740**
0259-2215 Etudes F A O: Developpement Economique et Social *see* 0259-2460 **1108**
0259-2282 Hacettepe Medical Journal
0259-2312 Per Linguam **5160**
0259-2347 Journal of Korean Pharmaceutical Sciences **6854**
0259-2371 Archivo General de la Nacion. Revista†
0259-238X Asia - Pacific Population Journal **7277**
0259-2460 F A O Economic and Social Development Paper **1108**
0259-2495 F A O Fertilizer and Plant Nutrition Bulletin **197**
0259-2509 F A O Fisheries Series **3591**
0259-2517 F A O Plant Production and Protection Papers **229**
0259-2533 F A O Training Series† **8955**
0259-2568 F A O Land and Water Development Series **109**
0259-2673 Farming for Development††
0259-2770 F A O Better Farming Series **109**
0259-2789 C O P E S C A L. Documento Tecnico **3588**
0259-2916 Codex Alimentarius (English Edition) **3631**
0259-2940 United Nations Environment Programme. Evaluation Report (Year)†
0259-3009 United Nations. National Accounts Statistics. Government Accounts and Tables† **8996**
0259-3017 United Nations. National Accounts Statistics. Analysis of Main Aggregates **1273**
0259-3025 United Nations. National Accounts Statistics. Main Aggregates and Detailed Tables **1273**
0259-3041 Pulp and Paper Industry in O E C D Member Countries†
0259-3076 Swazi Life **3954**
0259-3157 European Commission. Report on Competition Policy *changed to* 1609-5111 **1885**
0259-3165 Schweizer Jahrbuch fuer Musikwissenschaft **6615**
0259-3238 Commercial Agriculture in Zimbabwe†
0259-3300 B I T Commission des Industries Mecaniques. Rapport *see* 1010-2388 **1686**
0259-3491 Turkey. Turkiye Istatistik Kurumu. Turkiye Istatistik Yilligi (Year) **8410**
0259-353X Beitraege zur Lehrerbildung **3052**
0259-3556 Eleuthere Kythrea
0259-3580 Touristika Chronika **8764**
0259-3599 Schaffhauser Beitraege zur Geschichte **4261**
0259-3629 Disarmament Times **7231**
0259-3696 International Children's Rights Monitor **7210**
0259-370X Tribune Internationale des Droits de l'Enfant **7216**
0259-3726 Catalogue des Publications du B I T *see* 1011-0569 **1220**
0259-3734 Hamdard Naunehal **6659**
0259-3742 Soochow University Journal of Chinese Art History†
0259-3750 Soochow Law Review **4784**
0259-3769 Soochow Journal of Economics and Business **1176**
0259-3777 Soochow Journal of Foreign Languages and Literatures **5176**
0259-3793 Index to Chinese Legal Periodicals **4822**
0259-3823 Institut Francais d'Archeologie Orientale du Caire. Bibliotheque d'Etude **397**
0259-3882 Cooperation South **8096**
0259-3904 Educational Innovation and Information **2850**
0259-3963 General Report on the Activities of the European Communities **1488**
0259-4021 Kompass Taiwan **2012**
0259-4072 Hunde Haltung Zucht Sport **6809**
0259-4137 Liechtenstein Politische Schriften **7152**
0259-4153 Mitteilungen des Oesterreichischen Staatsarchivs **4245**
0259-4285 United Nations University. Work in Progress **1606**
0259-4323 Timber Bulletin **3716**
0259-4331 N A T O Handbook **7253**
0259-4366 L'Intermediaire des Casanovistes **5309**
0259-4374 Envio **3920**
0259-4412 Kontekst
0259-4463 Sobesednik **3941**
0259-4676 Statistisches Jahrbuch Fuerstentum Liechtenstein **8407**
0259-4692 Braby's Highway Directory **1976**
0259-4730 Emplo Review - Tydskrift
0259-4773 Freight World
0259-4862 University of Stellenbosch. Bureau for Economic Research. Economic Prospects **1523**
0259-4943 Klagenfurter Beitraege zur Philosophie. Reihe: Diplomarbeiten & Dissertationen **6931**

0259-4951 Klagenfurter Beitraege zur Philosophie. Reihe: Gruppendynamik & Organisationsentwicklung **6931**
0259-496X Klagenfurter Beitraege zur Philosophie. Reihe: Lehrmaterialen **6931**
0259-4978 Klagenfurter Beitraege zur Philosophie. Reihe: Referate **6931**
0259-5036 Turkey. Turkiye Istatistik Kurumu. Hanehalki Isgucu Istatistikleri (Year) **1271**
0259-5141 Turkey. Turkiye Istatistik Kurumu. Yillik Imalat Sanayi Istatistikleri† **8995**
0259-515X Encuesta Industrial: Resultados Nacionales **1226**
0259-5192 Strassenverkehrsunfaelle in der Schweiz **8605**
0259-5222 Meat Balances in O E C D Countries†
0259-5257 Milk and Milk Products Balances in O E C D Countries *changed to* 1028-8031
0259-5281 Iraq. Central Statistical Organization. Annual Abstract of Statistics
0259-532X Kuwait. Central Statistical Office. Annual Statistical Abstract **8384**
0259-5338 Turkey. Turkiye Istatistik Kurumu. Dis Ticaret Istatistikleri Yilligi **1270**
0259-5400 Revista de Tecnologia Educativa **2906**
0259-5443 Collection Theologique Hockma **7634**
0259-5591 Die Unie **2922**
0259-5605 Applied Plant Science **776**
0259-563X Denteksa†
0259-5729 Braby's Chatsworth Directory†
0259-5796 Africa Press Clips
0259-5893 Development Business (New York, 1978) **1593**
0259-5915 Jahrbuecher fuer Kunstwissenschaft†
0259-6016 Fiji. Bureau of Statistics. Census of Building and Construction **1046**
0259-6024 Fiji. Bureau of Statistics. Census of Distribution and Services **1230**
0259-6083 Statistisches Jahrbuch der Stadt Wien **8407**
0259-6148 Korea (Republic). Ministry of Agriculture and Foresty, Rural Development Administration. Annual Report **131**
0259-6180 Bulletin F A O d'Engrais et Nutrition Vegetale *see* 0259-2495 **197**
0259-6199 Cahiers de Linguistique Francaise **5103**
0259-627X F A O Document Technique du Centre d'Investissement *see* 1011-5366 **8955**
0259-6334 Nufusbilim Dergisi† **8978**
0259-6415 Simpliciana **5372**
0259-6512 V W A **5394**
0259-6563 Annales Jean-Jacques Rousseau **5255**
0259-6768 Foerdertechnik *changed to* 1661-674X **1897**
0259-6776 Balance of Payments of Jamaica **1553**
0259-6911 Newspot **3962**
0259-7349 Photographia **6974**
0259-7381 Cahiers de la Ceramique Egyptienne **386**
0259-7454 Papier und Druck
0259-7527 Rapport Mensuel sur l'Europe *see* 1021-4224 **7253**
0259-7764 Bern Universitaet. Seminar fuer Klassische Archaeologie. Hefte **383**
0259-7985 Statistisches Taschenbuch der Stadt Wien **8407**
0259-8086 Statistical Abstract of the Democratic Socialist Republic of Sri Lanka **8403**
0259-8108 Luxembourg. Inspection Generale de la Securite Sociale. Rapport General sur la Securite Sociale au Grand-Duche de Luxembourg **4513**
0259-8124 Revista Asea Brown Boveri *see* 1013-3119 **3293**
0259-8183 International Markets for Meat **290**
0259-8191 Marches Internationaux de la Viande *see* 0259-8183 **290**
0259-8205 Mercados Internacionales de la Carne *see* 0259-8183 **290**
0259-8213 World Market for Dairy Products **170**
0259-8264 World Translations Index†
0259-8280 Camera International†
0259-8299 Revista Estadistica **1515**
0259-8361 Tribute†
0259-8388 International Quarterly of Analytical Chemistry†
0259-8396 International Quarterly of Antibiotic Research
0259-840X International Quarterly of Cancer Research
0259-8418 International Quarterly of Materials Science
0259-8426 International Quarterly of Virology
0259-8434 International Dairy Federation. Bulletin **265**
0259-8582 Revue Internationale des Services de Sante des Forces Armees†
0259-8590 Solar Energy Research and Development in the European Community. Series H. Solar Energy in Agriculture and Industry†
0259-868X Empangeni - Richards Bay Directory **1991**
0259-8957 Das Waldviertel **4278**
0259-9023 Sophia Perennis†
0259-904X Luqman **7713**
0259-9082 Majalle-ye Zabanshenasi **5149**
0259-9090 Nashr-i Danish **4466**
0259-9139 Pashtu Quarterly
0259-9198 South African Panorama (French Edition)†
0259-9201 South African Panorama (Portuguese Edition)†
0259-921X South African Panorama (Spanish Edition)†
0259-9228 Realta Sudafricana†
0259-9236 South African Panorama (German Edition)†
0259-9287 Yaghma†
0259-9333 Modern Medicine of South Africa **5680**
0259-9341 Ons Eie **144**
0259-9422 Hervormde Teologiese Studies **7647**
0259-949X Die Hervormer **7760**
0259-9570 Tydskrif vir Taalonderrig **5189**
0259-9600 Revista Andina **7996**
0259-9627 Middle East Times†
0259-9635 Caribbean Contact†
0259-9651 Africana Research Bulletin
0259-9678 Societe Internationale de Conchyliologie. Bulletin **963**
0259-9686 Korea & World Affairs **7250**
0259-9775 Economic Review **1100**
0259-9791 Journal of Mathematical Chemistry **5505**
0259-9864 Proceso **7173**
0259-9872 Revista Latinoamericana de Teologia **7677**
0259-9880 Trade Winds Monthly **1585**

0259-9945 Rumbo **3821**
0259-9953 Al-Raida **8902**
0259-997X Greece. National Statistical Service. Provisional National Accounts of Greece **1235**
0259-9996 Namah-yi Anjuman-i Hasharahshinasan-i Iran **855**
0260-0005 Serials in the British Library **5059**
0260-0064 Butterworths International Medical Reviews: Cardiology†
0260-0072 Butterworths International Medical Reviews: Clinical Endocrinology†
0260-0099 Butterworths International Medical Reviews: Clinical Pharmacology and Therapeutics†
0260-0102 Butterworths International Medical Reviews: Otolaryngology†
0260-0110 Butterworths International Medical Reviews: Gastroenterology†
0260-0129 Butterworths International Medical Reviews: Hematology† **8938**
0260-0137 Butterworths International Medical Reviews: Neurology†
0260-0145 Butterworths International Medical Reviews: Ophthalmology†
0260-0153 Butterworths International Medical Reviews: Orthopaedics†
0260-0161 Butterworths International Medical Reviews: Pediatrics†
0260-017X Butterworths International Medical Reviews: Rheumatology†
0260-0188 Butterworths International Medical Reviews: Surgery†
0260-0218 Scottish Council of Social Service. News Bulletin†
0260-0226 Multiracial Education†
0260-0234 Printers Pie†
0260-0250 Clwyd Historian **4211**
0260-0315 Bookmark **5265**
0260-0374 Lincolnshire Dragon
0260-0382 The Shepherd **7706**
0260-0439 English Horizon†
0260-0447 Current Transnational Corporations Bibliography†
0260-0463 Geologist's Directory **2742**
0260-0471 Great Britain. Department of Education and Science. Architects and Building Branch. Broadsheets†
0260-0498 Eurovet Bulletin†
0260-0544 Castle Lodge News and Views†
0260-0552 Alternative Alternative **8148**
0260-0595 Paperback Inferno *changed to* 0505-0448 **5448**
0260-0617 Scottish Episcopal Church Yearbook **7774**
0260-0668 Times Index **4588**
0260-0684 University of Liverpool. Research Report†
0260-0765 I B I D†
0260-0781 Qarch **5527**
0260-079X County Trades Finder. Section 2: Central
0260-0803 B A A F Practice Series **8027**
0260-0811 B A A F Research Series **8027**
0260-082X B A A F Discussion Series **8027**
0260-0854 Oxford Reviews of Reproductive Biology†
0260-0935 Bible Translator. Technical Papers **5099**
0260-0943 Bible Translator. Practical Papers **5099**
0260-0986 Popular D I Y†
0260-1001 The Estate Agent **7589**
0260-101X Retail Security & Fire Prevention†
0260-1036 Leeds Naturalists' Club and Scientific Association. Newsletter **7879**
0260-1044 Herefordshire Family History Society. Journal **3770**
0260-1060 Nutrition and Health **6665**
0260-1079 Journal of Interdisciplinary Economics **1137**
0260-1087 International Bulk Journal **8646**
0260-1117 A C T H and Related Peptides†
0260-1141 Purines†
0260-115X Energy Review†
0260-1176 Finance Director's Review **1343**
0260-1230 Journal of Molluscan Studies **952**
0260-1265 Yearbook and Philatelic Societies' Directory **6901**
0260-1370 International Journal of Lifelong Education **2942**
0260-146X Barclays U.K. Financial Survey†
0260-1508 Exhibitor's Handbook†
0260-1559 Focus on Tourism†
0260-1664 Current Topics in Infection
0260-1729 Trent Papers in Education†
0260-1745 Kitchens†
0260-1753 Hel Achau **3770**
0260-180X Bus News†
0260-1818 Royal Society of Chemistry. Annual Reports on the Progress of Chemistry. Section A: Inorganic Chemistry **2118**
0260-1826 Royal Society of Chemistry. Annual Reports on the Progress of Chemistry. Section C: Physical Chemistry **2140**
0260-1842 Phototrain Express
0260-1869 Manpower: Glass Industry
0260-1974 Food World News **3643**
0260-2016 Wool Statistics **8464**
0260-2067 Irish Slavonic Studies **4232**
0260-2091 Essex Education†
0260-2105 Review of International Studies **7262**
0260-2113 Ecuatorial†
0260-2199 The Conference Green Book *changed to* 1756-1159 **6278**
0260-2202 Cubit†
0260-2245 The Sorby Record **7919**
0260-2288 Sensor Review **5459**
0260-2334 Medicine International (Southern African Edition)†
0260-2342 Medicine in Practice†
0260-2350 Palestine Report†
0260-2377 Brazilian Agriculture & Commodities
0260-2385 Insurance Brokers' Monthly and Insurance Adviser *changed to* 1472-2275 **4506**
0260-2393 Fur Review†
0260-2415 North of Scotland Visitor†
0260-2423 Radio Advertisers' Guide†
0260-2431 The Conference Blue Book *changed to* 1756-1140 **6278**
0260-2474 Aspis **1973**
0260-2504 Grampian English Views†
0260-2539 Horwath - E T B English Hotel Occupancy Survey (Year)†
0260-261X Barclays Commodities Survey†

0260-2695 N B A Technical Note†
0260-2733 Leeds and Harrogate Graphic
0260-2776 Writer (Penzance) **5401**
0260-2784 Marine Biological Association of the United Kingdom. Occasional Publications **688**
0260-2792 New Life (London, 1971) **7665**
0260-2938 Assessment & Evaluation in Higher Education **2967**
0260-2946 Physiological Principles in Medicine
0260-2954 Avon Past†
0260-2970 Locomotives Large & Small
0260-3004 Smash Hits†
0260-3020 Atomic Energy News†
0260-3055 Annals of Glaciology **2724**
0260-3063 Muslim World Book Review **7715**
0260-311X Educational Drama Association. Newsletter
0260-3225 John Buchan Journal **5313**
0260-3241 North Herts Medical Journal
0260-3306 Great Britain. Advisory Council for Adult and Continuing Education. Annual Report
0260-3322 Rutland Record **4261**
0260-3330 New Gandy Dancer **6599**
0260-342X Sing Tao Daily **3564**
0260-3594 Comments on Inorganic Chemistry **2115**
0260-3667 American Trust for the British Library. Newsletter **4989**
0260-3675 Transit Packaging†
0260-3683 Fuel Poverty News
0260-3691 W E F Communications Report†
0260-3705 W E A Theological News **7693**
0260-3772 Research Papers: Muslims in Europe†
0260-3780 Beatrix Potter Society. Newsletter **5261**
0260-3799 Wader Study Group. Bulletin **916**
0260-3810 Labour Party. Campaign Briefing†
0260-3853 Conspectus For...Of Further Education in the Inner and Outer London Region†
0260-390X Clarinet and Saxophone **6556**
0260-3926 Whillans's Tax Tables **1955**
0260-3934 Edinburgh Medicine†
0260-3985 British-Israel Trade
0260-3993 Vive la Difference **3571**
0260-4019 Intercede (Manchester)
0260-4027 World Futures **6961**
0260-4043 Ultrasound Patents & Papers
0260-406X Chartered Institute of Public Finance and Accountancy. Housing Rents Statistics. Actuals **4435**
0260-4094 Housing Corporation. Quarterly Review†
0260-4108 Disability Rights Bulletin† **8950**
0260-4116 Traditional Kent Buildings†
0260-4256 Textile Digest†
0260-4272 Arabia: The Islamic World Review
0260-4280 Perspective of Physics†
0260-4299 International Coal Report **6466**
0260-4345 Developments in Food Carbohydrate† **8950**
0260-4353 Fluid Mechanics of Astrophysics and Geophysics
0260-437X Journal of Applied Toxicology **3498**
0260-4388 Manchester Training Handbooks **7452**
0260-440X Carnivorous Plant Society Journal
0260-4426 West of Scotland Visitor†
0260-4450 Adhesion†
0260-4515 Stock Car Reporter
0260-4523 I A P S Newsletter†
0260-4531 Spindrift†
0260-454X Afrosport
0260-4671 Axbridge Archaeological and Local History Society. Journal **4202**
0260-4698 Expired British Patents & Licences of Right
0260-471X Short Stories Magazine
0260-4736 Sandgrouse **914**
0260-4752 Practical English Teaching†
0260-4809 British Compressed Gases Association. Code of Practice **3366**
0260-4833 I E S Proceedings†
0260-4868 European Human Rights Reports **7206**
0260-4876 I. P. Reports from Socialist Countries†
0260-4884 The Dozenal Journal **5484**
0260-4906 Top Fruit Times†
0260-4914 London and Middlesex Genealogical Directory†
0260-4930 Graphics World. Services and Supplies Directory†
0260-4957 Heritage (Loughborough) **4226**
0260-4965 Fighters **8173**
0260-5007 Directory of Land and Hydrographic Survey Services in the United Kingdom†
0260-504X Wind and Water Mills
0260-5058 F E R N Journal **2980**
0260-5090 Movie News†
0260-5112 Free Life **7137**
0260-5139 Gloucestershire Local History Newsletter **4224**
0260-5171 Business History Newsletter **1536**
0260-5244 Community View†
0260-5295 Home Care Services, Day Care Establishments, Day Services - Scotland†
0260-5325 School Nurse†
0260-535X British National Formulary **6826**
0260-5414 Extro
0260-5457 Staff of Scottish Social Work Departments **8073**
0260-5473 Children in Care or Under Supervision (Year) **8033**
0260-5511 Abstracts on Hygiene and Communicable Diseases **5739**
0260-5546 Chartered Institute of Public Finance and Accountancy. Revenue Collection Statistics. Actuals **1221**
0260-5554 Problem - Solving News **3077**
0260-5570 Handbooks in Maritime Archaeology†
0260-5619 Catalogue of British Official Publications Not Published by H.M.S.O. **622**
0260-5627 Labrador Retriever Club of Wales. Yearbook **6810**
0260-5643 Nottingham Lingusitic Circular **5156**
0260-5716 Light and Design International
0260-5724 Business Computing
0260-5732 Shetland Life **3870**
0260-5759 Market Assessment
0260-5821 C T O†
0260-583X Kington History Society. Papers
0260-5848 Royal College of Midwives. Current Awareness Service†
0260-5864 Holdsworth Law Review **4687**
0260-5872 Clinical Cytogenetics
0260-5880 Haemic and Lymphatic Cell Culture†
0260-5902 Plant Biotechnology
0260-5910 Development of Social Skills†
0260-5929 University of London. Institute of Germanic Studies. Research in Germanic Studies†
0260-597X Turner Studies†
0260-5988 Timecraft†
0260-5996 British Acupuncture Association. Newsletter†
0260-6003 Bicycle Trade Times
0260-6054 Kelly's Directory of British Industry & Services in Eastern England†
0260-6097 Bicycle Times
0260-6127 Workers Education Association. Women's Studies Newsletter†
0260-6151 Kelly's Directory of British Industry & Services in Northern England†
0260-6186 Guide to Banks & Other Financial Institutions in Asia (Including Iran & the Arab Region)
0260-6194 Kelly's Directory of British Industry & Services in The Midlands†
0260-6208 Bulletin of Scottish Politics
0260-6216 B C I S Quarterly Review of Building Prices **977**
0260-6267 International Journal of Pharmaceutical Technology & Product Manufacture
0260-6275 Journal of Separation Process Technology
0260-6291 Royal Society of Chemistry. Special Publications **2079**
0260-6313 Crosscurrent†
0260-6321 Glass and Glazing News **2041**
0260-633X Kelly's Directory of British Industry & Services in Scotland and Northern Ireland†
0260-6348 Lyle Official Books Review†
0260-6356 Homeopathic Alternative†
0260-6399 Steel Industry Monitor†
0260-6402 Outsider **7213**
0260-6410 C P A G Newsletter
0260-6429 C O A D Words†
0260-6445 P.S. (London)
0260-6488 A - Z of U.K. Marketing Data†
0260-6496 Institute of Chartered Accountants in England and Wales. Tax Digest **1929**
0260-6526 Grocery Stores Directories†
0260-6550 Bulletin of Northern Ireland Law **4633**
0260-6585 Koleinu **7726**
0260-664X Austin Healey Year Book†
0260-6674 Sheffield Studies in Japanese†
0260-6704 People's Power†
0260-6739 Philatelist and Philatelic Journal of Great Britain
0260-6755 Parliaments, Estates & Representation **4155**
0260-6801 Arts London Review†
0260-681X Cephalopod Newsletter **938**
0260-6844 Terminus
0260-6917 Nurse Education Today **5971**
0260-6925 Great Britain. Institute of Terrestrial Ecology. Bangor Occasional Paper
0260-6941 Scientific & Technical Books†
0260-695X Newth-Nuth Family History Society. Newsletter **3776**
0260-6976 South (London, 1980)†
0260-7042 Wiltshire Monographs
0260-7050 Computer Price Guide for Large Computers†
0260-7093 County Guide to Marine Companies† **8946**
0260-7123 Combat (Cleckheaton)
0260-714X Black Country Geologist **2726**
0260-7174 Wiltshire Family History Society. Journal **3788**
0260-7212 Marxist Humanism
0260-728X Sea Angling Monthly†
0260-7352 Canadean World New Products
0260-7409 International Packaging Abstracts *changed to* 1475-598X **6715**
0260-7425 Tonic **6623**
0260-745X Cranes Today Handbook **1000**
0260-7468 European Racehorse
0260-7476 Journal of Education for Teaching **2875**
0260-7492 Wild Cat **2632**
0260-7514 Parents **2164**
0260-7522 I C S A Bulletin
0260-7549 Twirling Times
0260-7565 Oxfordshire Local History **4252**
0260-7573 Coaches & Parties Welcome **8693**
0260-759X Liverpool Family Historian **3773**
0260-7638 Liverpool Software Gazette
0260-7654 Zip
0260-7735 National Council on Inland Transportation. Newsletter **8632**
0260-7743 London Federation of Museum and Art Galleries. Newsletter
0260-7751 P.P.A. North West Region Newsletter†
0260-776X Conferences Meetings & Exhibitions Welcome†
0260-7786 Hong Kong Handbook
0260-7794 Darlington Astronomical Society. Newsletter **574**
0260-7808 Early Childhood†
0260-7824 Cipher
0260-7840 Modern Power Systems **3142**
0260-7891 Union Fact Sheet
0260-7921 Fellowship in Prayer†
0260-7964 Irish Drama Selections **8472**
0260-7972 Scottish Pottery Studies **2045**
0260-8081 Fairfield Experimental Horticulture Station. Summary Annual Review
0260-809X Energy Matters†
0260-8103 Equi†
0260-8111 Equestrian Year†
0260-812X Strider
0260-8189 Probe Report† **8982**
0260-8243 Which? Wine Monthly†
0260-8251 Fantasy Macabre
0260-8278 Creative Mind
0260-8294 Nottingham Licensed Taxi Owners & Drivers Association. Newsletter **1964**
0260-8308 Everything Has a Value†
0260-8324 Illustrators Despatch†
0260-8367 Clinical Research Reviews†
0260-8383 Tuition, Entertainment, News, Views **523**
0260-8391 Caraher Family History Society. Journal
0260-8405 Lincolnshire Population†
0260-8456 Faba Bean Abstracts†
0260-8480 Irish Studies†
0260-8499 Reflections **3870**
0260-8553 Knitting Industry Technical Review†
0260-860X Overseas Development Institute. Annual Report **1602**
0260-8634 Business News†
0260-8642 Chartered Institute of Public Finance and Accountancy. Planning and Development Statistics. Actuals†
0260-8677 Epoxy Resins & Plastics†
0260-8685 Head and Hand
0260-8693 Handgunner: Britain's Foremost Firearms Journal **8176**
0260-8707 Historic House **444**
0260-8723 Arts Report†
0260-8774 Journal of Food Engineering **3650**
0260-8790 Correlation **565**
0260-8812 Forecast of Shop Rents†
0260-8839 London Port Handbook (Year) **8651**
0260-8847 Journal of Synthetic Methods **2069**
0260-8855 Knitstats **8464**
0260-8944 ComLon†
0260-8952 Bradford Center Occasional Papers
0260-8979 Euroednews†
0260-9061 Weekender
0260-9088 Soil Survey and Land Evaluation†
0260-910X Visit California with Fyfe Robertson†
0260-9126 Journal of Education in Museums **6526**
0260-9150 New Computer Careers
0260-9177 Pelham Golf Year†
0260-924X Ireland Ports & Shipping Handbook
0260-9282 Falmouth Port and Industry Handbook 1984
0260-9290 City Handbook†
0260-9339 Poetry and Little Press Information†
0260-9355 Edmonton Hundred Historical Society. Chronicle
0260-9363 Instant Record
0260-9398 Stereotype
0260-9436 Polymicros†
0260-9452 Boating Business **8273**
0260-9460 Biblical Creation
0260-9517 Great Yarmouth Port and Industry Handbook **8644**
0260-9533 Asklepios
0260-9541 Archives of Natural History **7836**
0260-955X Annual Register of Pharmaceutical Chemists **6821**
0260-9576 Loss Prevention Bulletin **3250**
0260-9584 Quaker Peace & Service. Annual Report†
0260-9592 London Review of Books **5225**
0260-9746 British Catalogue of Audio-Visual Materials†
0260-9762 Chartered Institute of Public Finance and Accountancy. Local Government Comparative Statistics. Estimates **7480**
0260-9770 Multicultural Education Abstracts (Print) **2934**
0260-9819 Communist Affairs†
0260-9835 T.E. Lawrence Studies Newsletter
0260-986X Irish Hare **2615**
0260-9886 Chartered Institute of Public Finance and Accountancy. Highways and Transportation. Actuals & Estimates **8523**
0260-9924 Canterbury Diocesan News Service†
0260-9975 Chartered Institute of Public Finance and Accountancy. Airport Financial Statistics. Estimates†
0260-9983 U K I R T Report†
0261-0035 *see* British Shopping Centre Development Master List
0261-0078 Bedford Way Papers **2830**
0261-0094 Anbar Management Publications Joint Index†
0261-0124 Aireings **5416**
0261-0140 Progress in Obstetrics and Gynaecology **6002**
0261-0159 Equal Opportunities International *changed to* 2040-7149 **8895**
0261-0183 Critical Social Policy **8036**
0261-023X Bulletin of Inventions and Summary of Patent Specifications **6747**
0261-0272 Reviewing Sociology **8128**
0261-0280 Housing†
0261-0299 A T L A S **4986**
0261-0310 International Who's Who in the Arab World
0261-0329 Glazed Expressions **2042**
0261-0337 Training Action†
0261-0388 Afghan Voice
0261-0558 Curious Woman
0261-0582 Alternatives to "A" Level†
0261-0604 Nucleus (Cambridge)†
0261-0620 Property Guide: Homes in Essex & Hertfordshire†
0261-0647 Property Guide: Homes in Sussex & Kent†
0261-0655 Property Guide: Homes in Beds/Bucks/Berks & Oxon†
0261-0663 Estuaries and Coastal Waters of the British Isles **3479**
0261-0752 Lincolnshire, Housing†
0261-0760 Resources†
0261-0795 Poetry into Print†
0261-0868 Magpie
0261-0876 Al-Majalla **3912**
0261-0884 Insist
0261-0892 Popular Astronomy **580**
0261-099X Strathclyde Modern Language Studies†
0261-1023 Okikiolu Scientific and Industrial Organization. Bulletin of Mathematics†
0261-1066 Literary Drivel Society. Transactions
0261-1104 Cronicl Powys **3763**
0261-1139 Greentrees **3769**
0261-1171 Crimp Journal
0261-1279 Early Music History **6563**
0261-1325 I S Annual†
0261-1341 Moz-Art†
0261-135X Shropshire Family History Journal **3782**
0261-1376 Explorations in Knowledge†
0261-1392 Leisure, Recreation and Tourism Abstracts **8779**
0261-1430 Popular Music **6607**
0261-152X I F L A Art Libraries Section. Newsletter **5013**
0261-1538 Liverpool Monographs in Hispanic Studies†
0261-1589 Fire Research News **3577**
0261-1600 Beatles Book Monthly **6548**

0263-3698 British Distilling Industry†
0263-3701 C O M E C O N Data†
0263-3809 Sponsorship News **8202**
0263-3957 Politics (Oxford) **7170**
0263-4023 Christian Aid News **7750**
0263-4066 Golf Guide - Where to Play and Where to Stay **8231**
0263-4104 European Conference on Mixing. Papers†
0263-4112 International Conference on Fluid Sealing. Papers Presented **3381**
0263-4163 Pneumotransport†
0263-4171 Hydrotransport **3362**
0263-4228 Large Mixed Retailing†
0263-4260 Panama Handbook
0263-4317 International Symposium on the Aerodynamics and Ventilation of Vehicle Tunnels. Papers Presented **3273**
0263-4376 Developments in Food Preservation† **8950**
0263-4422 Clinical Surgery International
0263-4430 Busy Solicitors' Digest†
0263-4457 Journal of Applied Language Study†
0263-4503 Marketing Intelligence & Planning **1832**
0263-4600 U F A W Annual Report and Accounts **322**
0263-4678 Management in Government **1775**
0263-4708 Developments in Food Proteins† **8950**
0263-4872 Photography Report†
0263-4929 Journal of Metamorphic Geology **2750**
0263-4937 Central Asian Survey **7115**
0263-5046 First Break **2780**
0263-5054 Aberdeen Petroleum Report **6761**
0263-5143 Research in Science & Technological Education **2904**
0263-5232 Hegel Society of Great Britain. Bulletin **6922**
0263-5275 Classified List of Fodder Crop Varieties. England & Wales **225**
0263-5372 Informe Latinoamericano **1491**
0263-5380 Nine to Five
0263-5402 Institute of Development Studies. Commissioned Studies†
0263-5429 New Generation **5999**
0263-5488 International Tax-Free Trade Buyers Guide & Directory†
0263-5534 Aqualine Abstracts **8842**
0263-5577 Industrial Management + Data Systems **1418**
0263-5666 Journal of Molluscan Studies. Supplement *see* 0260-1230 **952**
0263-5747 Robotica **2586**
0263-5798 Papers in Slavonic Linguistics†
0263-5852 I E E Telecommunications Series *changed to* I E T Telecommunications Series **2324**
0263-5860 I E E Electromagnetic Waves Series *changed to* The I E T Electromagnetic Waves Series **3317**
0263-5879 International Textile Calendar **8453**
0263-5909 Journal of Community Education†
0263-5917 Critical Reports on Applied Chemistry†
0263-5933 Royal Society of Edinburgh. Transactions. Earth Sciences *changed to* 1755-6910 **2716**
0263-5968 University of Aberdeen. Staff Lists **2962**
0263-6050 World Cement **1043**
0263-6107 Teaching Science **7922**
0263-6123 Bank of England. Technical Series Discussion Papers† **8934**
0263-6131 Wool Record *changed to* 1759-0418 **8461**
0263-6174 Adsorption Science and Technology **3235**
0263-6190 C A D - C A M Digest
0263-6212 Keyboards and Music Player
0263-6263 Truck and Bus Builder
0263-6271 Science in Parliament **7910**
0263-6336 Robotics in Japan†
0263-6344 Theatre Ireland†
0263-6352 Journal of Hypertension **5793**
0263-6395 International Media Law†
0263-6409 B A C M I Review†
0263-6484 Cell Biochemistry & Function **728**
0263-6506 North West Kent Family History **3777**
0263-6522 Integrated Circuits International†
0263-6565 Fiction Magazine
0263-6697 Compass Sport - Orienteer **8167**
0263-6700 Policy Market
0263-6727 Atlantic Quarterly†
0263-6735 Information Technology Training†
0263-6743 Clarity
0263-6751 Anglo-Saxon England **4198**
0263-676X Themes in Drama†
0263-6786 Vox Evangelica†
0263-6794 Tube International **6336**
0263-6921 Young Farmer†
0263-6980 D I G Around†
0263-7030 Jane's Merchant Ships **8648**
0263-7057 Golfing Handbook†
0263-7073 Canary Islands Shipping Handbook (Year)
0263-7081 Wheels & Tracks **8612**
0263-709X Art Book Review
0263-7162 Tatler **3872**
0263-7170 News of Liturgy **7666**
0263-7189 Libyan Studies **403**
0263-7227 Bacterial Cell Surface†
0263-7235 Beta Lactams†
0263-7243 Cardiovascular Pharmacology
0263-7251 Cell Cycle†
0263-726X Cell Differentiation†
0263-7286 Complement (Sheffield)†
0263-7294 Diabetes Mellitus†
0263-7324 Hearing†
0263-7340 Motor Activity†
0263-7359 Neonatal Physiology†
0263-7367 Polyamines†
0263-7383 Annales Benjamin Constant **4443**
0263-7472 Property Management **7605**
0263-7499 Rent Review and Lease Renewal **7611**
0263-7529 Vintage Tractor **215**
0263-7537 Housing Law Reports **4688**
0263-7553 Picture House **6509**
0263-7561 Beebug†
0263-7669 Money Observer **1640**
0263-7685 Executive Travel†
0263-7693 Floors **4540**
0263-7707 The Medal **6651**
0263-7715 Christian Action Journal†
0263-774X Environment and Planning C: Government & Policy **7435**
0263-7758 Environment and Planning D: Society and Space **4410**
0263-7790 Office Systems†
0263-7839 The Russell Society. Journal **6478**
0263-7863 International Journal of Project Management **1419**
0263-7952 Industrial Research in United Kingdom†
0263-7960 Built Environment **436**
0263-8029 Biotech News†
0263-8126 Wastes Management *changed to* 1751-5602 **3504**
0263-8169 The Voice **3571**
0263-8223 Composite Structures **3263**
0263-8231 Thin-Walled Structures **3397**
0263-8266 Standards in Defence News **6406**
0263-8371 Changes *changed to* 1471-7646 **8049**
0263-841X In Practice (London) **8798**
0263-8460 Jane's Urban Transport Systems **8500**
0263-8525 What Mortgage **1193**
0263-8614 Great Britain. Institute of Terrestrial Ecology. Symposia
0263-8665 Petcare†
0263-8746 Sports Teacher **8208**
0263-8762 Chemical Engineering Research & Design **3239**
0263-8878 The Mail on Sunday **3868**
0263-8894 Orbit†
0263-9041 The Wisden Cricket Monthly *changed to* The Wisden Cricketer **8251**
0263-9076 Tax Insight **1948**
0263-9106 Which Camera? **6978**
0263-9114 European Journal of Chiropractic†
0263-9157 Sick Pay Bulletin†
0263-9181 Public Library Expenditure in Scotland†
0263-9203 Middle East Computing†
0263-9319 Surgery **6259**
0263-9351 Construction Law Digest†
0263-936X Pickup in Progress†
0263-9378 Community Transport Magazine **8494**
0263-9424 Cambridge Studies in Mathematical Biology **664**
0263-9432 Whitaker's Classified Monthly Book List†
0263-9459 Cruciferae Newsletter† **8947**
0263-9475 Circa Art Magazine **482**
0263-953X What Investment **1659**
0263-9629 Welsh House Condition Survey **4437**
0263-9653 Road Accidents: Wales **8529**
0263-967X British Society of Animal Science. Occasional Publication **282**
0263-9696 Inspection and Advice† **8965**
0263-9831 Stockmarket Confidential†
0263-9904 Romance Studies **5364**
0263-9947 V A T Intelligence†
0263-9971 Energy-Saving Marketguide **1992**
0264-0155 Euro-Asia Business Review†
0264-0198 Scottish Language **5172**
0264-0260 Food Production
0264-0384 Biotechnology Reports *see* 0261-6904
0264-0406 British Naturism **6983**
0264-0414 Journal of Sports Sciences **8183**
0264-0422 Glasgow Magazine†
0264-0449 Sinclair Projects†
0264-0473 The Electronic Library **5061**
0264-0562 Catering†
0264-0619 Which Bike†
0264-0643 A D I U Report†
0264-0732 World Leasing Yearbook (Year) **1525**
0264-0783 World Ports and Harbours News†
0264-083X The World of Interiors **4553**
0264-0856 Cencrastus†
0264-0910 U K Offshore Oil & Gas Directory†
0264-0929 Magazine for London Living
0264-0937 The Treasurer **1387**
0264-0996 Sound Scrutiny
0264-1011 Templar†
0264-1062 Model Flyer†
0264-1097 Law Reports: Chancery Division **4912**
0264-1100 *see* 0967-6686 **2122**
0264-1119 Law Reports. Family Division **4912**
0264-1127 Law Reports: Queen's Bench Division **4716**
0264-1135 Law Reports: House of Lords **4716**
0264-1143 Scottish Development Department. Statistical Bulletin **1432**
0264-1259 Antwerp Handbook 1984†
0264-1275 Materials & Design **3352**
0264-1283 British Micro Software News **2588**
0264-1291 Horticultural Trades Association Members' Reference Book†
0264-1380 Bank of England. Occasional Paper **1314**
0264-1453 Amar Deep **3518**
0264-1461 Prison Service News **2666**
0264-1496 Strathclyde Papers on Government and Politics **7470**
0264-1607 Communicable Disease Report. Supplement **5811**
0264-1615 Interlending & Document Supply **5018**
0264-1704 Museum Ethnographers Group. Occasional Paper **349**
0264-1763 Triangle **8769**
0264-1801 Psychological Medicine. Monograph Supplement† **8983**
0264-1828 Arts & the Islamic World
0264-1887 Technology
0264-1933 A F T Occasional Papers **6117**
0264-2069 The Service Industries Journal **1172**
0264-2190 Society for Italian Studies. Bulletin†
0264-2220 Model Shipwright **4341**
0264-2247 International Pharmaceutical Technology & Product Manufacture Abstracts†
0264-2336 Who's Who in the Commonwealth†
0264-2441 U A P Newsletter **5051**
0264-2506 Finishing **6717**
0264-2557 Amateur Radio **2356**
0264-259X Aquanaut **6762**
0264-2611 Data Business†
0264-2689 British Association for Psychopharmacology. Monograph†
0264-2719 Community Service by Offenders†
0264-2751 Cities **7489**
0264-2786 Medieval English Theatre Modern Spelling Texts **8474**
0264-2824 Parliamentary History **4155**
0264-2867 Latin American Special Reports **1637**
0264-2875 Dance Research **2684**
0264-3022 Developments in Oriented Polymers† **8950**
0264-3049 Crop Research†
0264-3081 Recent Advances in Renal Medicine†
0264-312X Shaw's Directory of Courts in the United Kingdom **4960**
0264-3138 C A S T M E Journal **7842**
0264-3219 Book Marketing News†
0264-3278 Amnesty **7202**
0264-3294 Cognitive Neuropsychology **6133**
0264-3340 Asian Electricity
0264-3405 British Cactus & Succulent Journal *changed to* 1751-1429 **782**
0264-3596 Interzone **5443**
0264-3669 Classified List of Herbage Varieties. England & Wales **225**
0264-3693 Bookplate Journal **7555**
0264-3707 Journal of Geodynamics **2785**
0264-3723 Weekly Law Digest **4826**
0264-3731 Justice of the Peace Reports **4708**
0264-3758 Journal of Applied Philosophy **6928**
0264-3774 British Journal of Clinical Pharmacology. Supplement **6826**
0264-3871 Benson and Hedges Cricket Year **8223**
0264-3944 Pastoral Care in Education **2896**
0264-4002 Rural Viewpoint†
0264-4061 Stationary Engine **3220**
0264-4088 Community Currents **8082**
0264-410X Vaccine **5766**
0264-4126 Bibliography of Economic Geology **2719**
0264-4150 Showcall **8478**
0264-4177 Greenwich Time Report **575**
0264-4185 British Astronomical Association. Circular **572**
0264-4401 Engineering Computations **3291**
0264-4479 Computer Answers†
0264-4509 Communicate **2367**
0264-4525 Journal of Practical Civil Defence†
0264-4568 Telecommunications News **2372**
0264-4576 Communications Management **1734**
0264-4606 B O C A A D†
0264-4622 Art Magazine†
0264-4703 Precision Toolmaker **6329**
0264-4738 I F L A Section on Serial Publications. Newsletter *changed to* I F L A Serials and Other Continuing Resources Section. Newsletter **5014**
0264-4746 The Organbuilder†
0264-4770 Texas Personal Injury Law Reporter
0264-4835 Dredging & Port Construction **8642**
0264-486X Country Profile. Denmark† **8945**
0264-4886 Country Profile. Netherlands† **8946**
0264-4932 Industry Northwest **1889**
0264-4940 Ideas and Productions†
0264-4975 Directory of British Caving Clubs (Year)
0264-4991 Home Computing Weekly†
0264-5033 Primary Health Care **8063**
0264-5041 European Tableware Buyers Guide **535**
0264-5092 Hypotenuse **7863**
0264-5122 Action Research†
0264-5130 Fisheries Research Data Report **3593**
0264-5157 Tiles & Architectural Ceramics Society Journal **2046**
0264-519X Research, Policy and Planning **8065**
0264-5211 Communique **6911**
0264-522X The Regionalist **7176**
0264-5254 Anglo-Saxon Studies in Archaeology and History **373**
0264-5262 Social Affairs Unit. Research Reports **8002**
0264-5300 Mozambique Information Office News Review†
0264-5319 Foundry Yearbook and Castings Buyers' Directory (Year) **1996**
0264-5351 Business Librarian
0264-5378 Coffee International Directory **3631**
0264-5440 Glamorgan Family History Society. Journal **3768**
0264-5467 Research and Development in Agriculture†
0264-5505 Probation Journal **2666**
0264-553X Microprocessor Software Quarterly†
0264-5564 Vinaver Studies in French†
0264-5572 Scottish Church History Society. Records **7680**
0264-5661 Vancouver Port Handbook†
0264-5688 Scottish Health Education Group Bulletin†
0264-5769 French Railway Review†
0264-5793 Suffolk Birds **915**
0264-5807 Society for Environmental Therapy. Newsletter†
0264-5890 Formaos
0264-598X Christian Arena†
0264-6013 Colchester Archaeological Report **387**
0264-6021 Biochemical Journal **724**
0264-6099 Country Profile. Belgium† **8944**
0264-6102 Country Profile. Iceland† **8945**
0264-6129 Country Profile. Luxembourg† **8945**
0264-6137 Bare Nibs **8466**
0264-6196 British Journal of Visual Impairment **4080**
0264-6358 Videodisc Newsletter†
0264-6412 Rad Magazine **6205**
0264-6420 Maritime Guide†
0264-6447 Tanker Casualty Bulletin
0264-6501 Uncensored Poland News Bulletin†
0264-6579 Irish Christian Study Centre. Journal†
0264-6684 Clinical Courier **5596**
0264-6706 Euromoney Trade Finance Report **1338**
0264-6781 Imprint (York)
0264-679X Collect Birds on Stamps **6893**
0264-6811 Journal of Energy and Natural Resources Law **4701**
0264-6838 Journal of Reproductive and Infant Psychology **7379**
0264-6854 Construction Computing **3290**
0264-6900 Cerebral Circulation and Metabolism†
0264-6943 Graduate Management Research†
0264-7028 Main Line **8620**

ISSN

0265-9484 World Banking Abstracts 1391
0265-9581 Health and Safety Executive. Research Paper 6678
0265-962X B R E News of Fire Research 978
0265-9646 Space Policy 71
0265-9654 Glass Cone 2042
0265-9670 Great Britain. Office for National Statistics. Mortality Statistics. Cause changed to 2040-252X 7307
0265-9786 Landscape Issues 448
0265-9808 Sightline 8478
0265-9816 Ansible 5439
0265-9883 British Journal of Psychotherapy 6128
0266-0016 Folio Poetry Magazine
0266-0032 Soil Use and Management 253
0266-0091 Statistics of Agricultural Co-Operatives in the United Kingdom†
0266-0172 Strathclyde Regional Council. Annual Report & Financial Statement 7470
0266-0180 Index to Business Reports†
0266-0377 Conflict Bulletin†
0266-0466 Home Furnishings Survey†
0266-0512 Risk in Society
0266-0520 First Time 5422
0266-0539 Hardware and Garden Review 1054
0266-0563 Marcom
0266-0598 Leibniz Newsletter 6931
0266-0601 Contemporary Issues in Computed Tomography†
0266-0628 Building Law Monthly 4633
0266-0644 Los Angeles Port and Shipping Handbook
0266-0784 English Today 5115
0266-0806 Texas Health Law Reporter
0266-0814 Texas Evidence Reporter
0266-0822 Serica 8457
0266-0830 Studies in the Education of Adults 2946
0266-0865 Banking Technology 1318
0266-0962 British Isles Airlines Schedule†
0266-0970 Care of the Critically Ill 6057
0266-0997 Peace Research Reports†
0266-1004 British Tax Cases 1913
0266-1020 British Value Added Tax Cases 1913
0266-1144 Geotextiles and Geomembranes 8451
0266-1241 Social Action and the Media
0266-1322 Perspectives in American History New Series†
0266-139X Civil Engineering Surveyor 3263
0266-1500 Linen Hall Review†
0266-1616 INSPEC Matters 7939
0266-1640 Pteridologist 814
0266-1667 Escape†
0266-1713 Control changed to 1755-1501 1783
0266-1721 History of Technology Series 8424
0266-1772 Warburg Institute. Surveys and Texts 4482
0266-1799 University of Edinburgh. Department of Archaeology. Project Papers 422
0266-2043 Great Britain. Economic and Social Research Council. Annual Report 7967
0266-2078 Medical Textiles 5672
0266-2108 Laser and Optics International†
0266-2132 Airfinance Annual 1306
0266-2140 International Labour Reports†
0266-2159 Great Britain. Economic and Social Research Council. Research Supported by the Economic and Social Research Council†
0266-2183 Muhyiddin Ibn Arabi Society. Journal 7714
0266-2205 Subsea Engineering News 6793
0266-2256 Professional Video International Yearbook†
0266-2426 International Small Business Journal 1962
0266-2442 Anglo-Israel Archaeological Society. Bulletin 373
0266-2450 Electrotechnical News†
0266-2485 The Road 5446
0266-254X Expedition Planners' Guidebook and Directory 4006
0266-2639 E S R C Newsletter†
0266-2671 Economics and Philosophy 1481
0266-2698 Local History Magazine 4240
0266-2701 Afkar Inquiry†
0266-2736 Gulf Construction & Saudi Arabia Review Directory 1010
0266-2914 Latin American Informes Especiales 1637
0266-2922 Iota 5310
0266-2930 International Process Technology Abstracts
0266-2949 Chartered Institute of Public Finance and Accountancy. School Meals Statistics†
0266-2957 Ghana Studies Bulletin†
0266-3031 Chemist & Druggist Generics see 0957-7831 6865
0266-3031 Chemist & Druggist Generics see 1369-3980 6828
0266-3031 Chemist & Druggist Generics see 0009-3033 6828
0266-304X Binary: Computing in Microbiology†
0266-3120 Destiny†
0266-3147 International Banking & Financial Law Bulletin†
0266-318X Security Retailer†
0266-321X P C Review†
0266-3228 Miniature Wargames 6437
0266-3236 Cambridge Computer Science Texts† 8939
0266-3295 Trophy & Engraving News 1855
0266-3368 Educational Technology Abstracts 2932
0266-3392 Selly Oak Journal†
0266-3414 The Dentist
0266-352X Computers and Geotechnics 3290
0266-3538 Composites Science and Technology 8419
0266-3554 German History 4223
0266-366X Peter Warlock Society Newsletter 6605
0266-3775 Recent Advances in Tropical Medicine†
0266-3821 Business Information Review 1730
0266-3856 Port Kelang Shipping Handbook†
0266-3880 Biology and Society†
0266-3910 Home Plus†
0266-3953 Legal Action 4719
0266-4003 Manna 7726
0266-402X Hobsons Finance Casebook 1351
0266-4070 International Industry†
0266-4097 Hobsons Engineering Casebook 3195
0266-4119 Your Horse 8300
0266-4127 ChaCom 1398
0266-4151 European Rubber Journal 7824

0266-4208 Booknews†
0266-4224 Air Gunner 8157
0266-4283 Computing Equipment††
0266-4356 British Journal of Oral and Maxillofacial Surgery 6238
0266-4410 Staple 5435
0266-4429 Holiday Parks†
0266-4437 Camping and Caravan Site Selector†
0266-4615 Water Science Reviews†
0266-4623 International Journal of Technology Assessment in Health Care 5906
0266-464X N T Q. New Theatre Quarterly 8474
0266-4658 Economic Policy 1100
0266-4666 Econometric Theory 1539
0266-4674 Journal of Tropical Ecology 3448
0266-4720 Expert Systems 2448
0266-4763 Journal of Applied Statistics 8382
0266-4771 Harvest 7360
0266-481X Football Monthly 8228
0266-4860 Indexers Available 7563
0266-4879 MicroIndexer†
0266-4909 Journal of Computer Assisted Learning 2469
0266-4992 Staffordshire Archaeological Studies 418
0266-5212 Fitness
0266-5263 Third World Book News see 0265-1432
0266-5328 No. 1†
0266-5433 Planning Perspectives 4156
0266-5441 Scotlink
0266-5611 Inverse Problems 5553
0266-562X Chef†
0266-5697 Middle East Expatriate 3912
0266-5719 Battle Action Force
0266-5883 Frontier 1112
0266-5905 Middle East Agribusiness†
0266-6014 P A X 7811
0266-6022 Potato Statistics in Great Britain 185
0266-6030 South Asian Studies 4188
0266-6065 Campaigner (London, 1989)†
0266-6073 Dental Annual†
0266-6138 Midwifery 5998
0266-6154 Physiotherapy Practice†
0266-6170 The Annual Register (Year) 7106
0266-6197 Lloyd's Ports of the World (Year) changed to 1478-4696 8650
0266-6200 Across Architecture†
0266-6227 World List of Forensic Science Laboratories and Practices 5917
0266-6251 Genoa Port and Shipping Handbook
0266-6278 A C E Bulletin changed to 1754-7202 3017
0266-6286 Word & Image 5246
0266-6294 Blood Coagulation Factors†
0266-6308 D N A Probes
0266-6316 Biocompatible Materials†
0266-6340 Immunodeficiency†
0266-6375 Mammary Gland†
0266-6413 Shell Commercial Vehicle & P S V Buyer's Guide
0266-6421 Issues in the Islamic Movement†
0266-6448 Collective Bargaining†
0266-6480 Urban Design Quarterly 4430
0266-660X Reproductive Immunology†
0266-6618 Thymus†
0266-6650 Postgraduate Doctor: Pakistan†
0266-6669 Information Development 5016
0266-6731 Africa Bibliography 4168
0266-6871 Air Conditioning & Refrigeration News 4116
0266-688X Ethics & Medicine 5610
0266-6898 Scottish Museum News†
0266-6936 British Occupational Hygiene Society. Technical Guide Series 6674
0266-6979 Geology Today 2742
0266-7037 Intensive Care World 5636
0266-7045 Contractor Report - Transport and Road Research Laboratory†
0266-7053 Institute of Chartered Accountants in England and Wales. Update 1291
0266-707X Who's Who in Arts Management†
0266-7088 Congregational Year Book 7752
0266-7142 Optical & Electron Microscopy†
0266-7169 Laboratory News 5908
0266-7177 Modern Theology 7664
0266-7207 Future Computing Systems†
0266-7215 European Sociological Review 8101
0266-7274 Virginia Ports and Shipping Handbook
0266-7339 City University Business School. Economic Review†
0266-7347 World Wrought Copper Statistics 6342
0266-7355 World Metal Statistics. Yearbook 6337
0266-7363 Educational Psychology in Practice 2850
0266-7401 Cricketer Quarterly Facts and Figures† 8947
0266-7428 Scottish Industrial History 8438
0266-7452 Trolleybus Magazine 8518
0266-7525 Third World Women's News
0266-7533 Newcomen Bulletin changed to 1478-484X 8431
0266-7665 Science Education Newsletter 7909
0266-7681 Journal of Hand Surgery (British Volume) changed to 1753-1934 6248
0266-7703 Profitable Greetings†
0266-7738 R E Today 2902
0266-7762 Industrial Heritage Magazine†
0266-7800 European Paint and Resin News 6717
0266-7835 New Ground 7158
0266-7908 International Management Development Review†
0266-7924 Royal Agricultural Society of England. Reference Book and Buyers' Guide†
0266-7932 University of London. Institute of Germanic Studies. Bithell Series of Dissertations 5393
0266-7975 Dogs Monthly 6807
0266-7991 Promotions and Incentives 1838
0266-8017 African Farming and Food Processing 79
0266-8025 Far Eastern Agriculture 110
0266-8033 Memory Lane
0266-8068 The National Trust 2620
0266-8106 Classic Racer 8256
0266-8130 Professional Nurse changed to 0954-7762 5975

0266-8254 Letters in Applied Microbiology 890
0266-8262 Briefings for Surveyors 4000
0266-8297 Business Informer 1957
0266-8343 Sessional Information Digest 7468
0266-8351 The Amateur Entomologist 838
0266-836X Amateur Entomologists' Society. Bulletin 838
0266-8394 Knitting International 8454
0266-8459 Directory of Post-Graduate and Post-Experience Courses†
0266-8491 Townswoman
0266-8505 Machine Knitting News†
0266-8521 Altrive Chapbooks†
0266-8548 Quarterly Journal of Social Affairs†
0266-8610 Air Force List 6409
0266-8629 Animal Health 278
0266-8653 Reinsurance Market Report†
0266-867X World Marxist Review
0266-8688 Media International 29
0266-8734 Psychoanalytic Psychotherapy 7395
0266-8750 Liverpool Link 8054
0266-8831 Label
0266-8920 Probabilistic Engineering Mechanics 3393
0266-8947 Vintage Roadscene 8637
0266-8963 Sport & Fitness
0266-8971 100A1†
0266-9013 Chartered Institute of Public Finance and Accountancy. Block Grant Statistics†
0266-903X Oxford Review of Economic Policy 1158
0266-9056 T H S Health Summary† 8992
0266-9072 Journal of Complementary Medicine 5648
0266-9080 Irish Philosophical Journal†
0266-9102 Leisure Management 4979
0266-9137 Road Accident Statistics English Regions 8634
0266-9145 Education for Tomorrow
0266-9153 Sikh Messenger 7741
0266-9374 International Ceramic Directory 2043
0266-9382 International Gas Report 6774
0266-9390 Optical Receptionist†
0266-9412 U S Business Briefing†
0266-9455 Landscape Industry International†
0266-9536 Anti-Cancer Drug Design changed to 0965-0407 6031
0266-9552 Chartered Institute of Public Finance and Accountancy. Environmental Health Statistics. Actuals 7547
0266-9560 Chartered Institute of Public Finance and Accountancy. Leisure Usage. Actuals†
0266-9870 River and Flood Control Abstracts†
0266-9897 Who's Who in Local Government
0266-9927 Current Problems in Tumour Pathology†
0266-9994 Foundry Practice 6312
0267-0003 Lectures in Anaesthesiology†
0267-0054 Housing Information Digest†
0267-0224 End Journal†
0267-0240 Nemcon 5035
0267-0267 Athletics Coach†
0267-0275 Postgraduate Doctor: Caribbean 5698
0267-033X Sesame 2300
0267-0348 Selected Bibliographies on Ageing 4058
0267-0372 C E G B Abstracts†
0267-0380 International Perspectives in Physical Therapy†
0267-050X Road Engineering Intelligence and Research†
0267-0836 Materials Science and Technology 3353
0267-0844 Surface Engineering 6334
0267-0887 Free Associations† 8958
0267-0925 Which Compact Disc & Hi-Fi for Pleasure†
0267-095X Great Britain. H M Treasury. Civil Service Statistics 7480
0267-1131 Family Tree Magazine 3766
0267-1166 Golf Club Management 8230
0267-1174 Chartered Institute of Public Finance and Accountancy. Teaching Hospital Statistics. Actuals†
0267-1182 Chartered Institute of Public Finance and Accountancy. Non-Teaching Hospital Costs. Statistics†
0267-1190 Royal Bank of Scotland Review†
0267-1255 Mobile Telecommunications News
0267-1263 London Energy News†
0267-1344 Delawarr Laboratories Information Service Newsletter†
0267-1360 Writers' Own Magazine†
0267-1379 Current Opinion in Gastroenterology 5922
0267-1395 Communications Systems Worldwide†
0267-1409 Mineral Planning 2755
0267-1425 Scottish Library and Information Resources 5046
0267-145X Butterworths Company Law Cases 4859
0267-1468 Britain's Best Holidays - A Quick Reference Guide 8688
0267-1476 Industrial Maintenance†
0267-1492 Home Computer Advanced Course
0267-1522 Research Papers in Education 2905
0267-1557 Codex: Journal of the Centre for the Study of Christianity in Islamic Lands†
0267-1611 Educational & Child Psychology 7353
0267-1719 Management Digest†
0267-1727 Great Britain. H.M.S.O. Books in Print 625
0267-1891 Pelargonium News 3747
0267-1905 Annual Review of Applied Linguistics 5094
0267-1948 Current Research in Britain. Physical Sciences
0267-1956 Current Research in Britain. Biological Sciences
0267-1964 Current Research in Britain. Social Sciences 8020
0267-1972 Current Research in Britain. Humanities
0267-2006 Institute of Chartered Shipbrokers. Reference Book and List of Members (Year)
0267-2022 Local Government Administrators' Official Source Book†
0267-2030 Institute of Maintenance and Building Management. Reference Book and List of Members
0267-2049 Plant Manager's Directory†
0267-2243 Boston Sea and Air Port Handbook
0267-2286 Darts Player 8168
0267-2294 Everywoman
0267-2316 Sharjah Ports Handbook
0267-2359 Construction Law Journal 996
0267-2391 You and Your Wedding 5562
0267-2472 Index of Middle English Prose 5407
0267-2499 Third World Affairs†
0267-2510 Manuscript Studies 5330

ISSN

DIRECTORY 2010 **0269-5340** **9223**

0268-3393 B C I R A Abstracts of International Literature on Metal Castings Production†
0268-3407 Cole's Register of British Antiquarian & Secondhand Bookdealers†
0268-3555 Phlebology **5797**
0268-3601 Wool Trade Directory of the World **2035**
0268-3644 Planning Appeal Decisions **4758**
0268-3660 Scope†
0268-3679 Teaching Mathematics and Its Applications **5541**
0268-3687 Software Alert
0268-3695 Medical Electronics Japan
0268-3709 Interights Bulletin **7210**
0268-375X Directory of Management Consultants in the U K **1739**
0268-3768 International Journal of Advanced Manufacturing Technology **3381**
0268-3784 Counsel **4651**
0268-3792 Current Reviews in Paediatrics†
0268-3830 Verse **5394**
0268-3946 Journal of Managerial Psychology **1768**
0268-3954 Information Technology Intelligence (Luton)†
0268-3962 Journal of Information Technology **5021**
0268-3989 Business in Kent†
0268-4012 International Journal of Information Management **2547**
0268-4020 Papers in the Administration of Development **1603**
0268-4047 This Caring Business **8074**
0268-4055 Complementary Medical Research†
0268-4160 Continuity and Change **7280**
0268-4179 A I S B Quarterly **2445**
0268-4225 H & V Engineer†
0268-4306 F R A M E News **319**
0268-4314 Retail Banker's Yearbook†
0268-4349 Cross Post **6893**
0268-4373 British Ceramic Proceedings† **8937**
0268-4519 Elektor Electronics *changed to* 1757-0875 **3097**
0268-4527 Intelligence and National Security **7242**
0268-4543 Voluntary Voice
0268-4578 Kitcars & Specials
0268-4705 Current Opinion in Cardiology **5784**
0268-4713 Spaceflight News†
0268-4721 Tolley's Personal Finance Letter†
0268-4764 Textile Outlook International **8460**
0268-4780 The Beekeeper's Quarterly **840**
0268-4861 Arab Medicare
0268-487X Phoenix (Somersham) **697**
0268-490X Science and Public Affairs *changed to* 2040-3968 **7897**
0268-4926 Blueprint (Chelmsford) **435**
0268-4934 Computing Age **2415**
0268-4942 Performance Bikes **8266**
0268-4993 Abstracts: Cellular Pathology
0268-5000 Jennings Magazine†
0268-5027 Dartmoor Magazine **3864**
0268-5116 Geneva Theological College. The Forum
0268-5167 Health at School
0268-5248 Radio Control Boat Modeller†
0268-5256 Directory of International Film and Video Festivals (Year) **6496**
0268-537X Journal of Irish Archaeology **401**
0268-540X Anthropology Today **327**
0268-5418 Thomas Hardy Journal **5388**
0268-5450 C I O L A Directory **6694**
0268-5485 Optometry Today **6050**
0268-5531 Netlink†
0268-5620 Patchwork & Quilting **6641**
0268-5639 The Ergonomist **3191**
0268-5671 International Meeting Place
0268-5809 International Sociology **8110**
0268-5892 Business Ratio Report: Educational Equipment Industry†
0268-5914 Anti-Piracy News
0268-5930 Modern German Studies† **8975**
0268-5949 Electricity for China†
0268-5965 Linguist **5145**
0268-5973 Health Information Service†
0268-5981 The Rialto **5433**
0268-6112 Irish Biblical Studies **7651**
0268-6120 Motor Caravan **8323**
0268-6171 I E E Management of Technology Series *changed to* The I E T Management of Technology Series **8424**
0268-6287 Chromatography Abstracts **2093**
0268-6309 Marine Money†
0268-6317 Navigation News **8654**
0268-6376 Radical Statistics **8395**
0268-6384 Business†
0268-6392 Business Success
0268-6414 Key Note Market Report: Insurance Companies **1894**
0268-6457 Business Ratio Report: Insurance Companies†
0268-6481 Oakland Port and Shipping Handbook
0268-649X Cherbourg Port Handbook
0268-6503 Darwin Port Handbook†
0268-6511 Southampton Port Handbook
0268-6538 Books at Boston Spa†
0268-6708 The Software Users Year Book *changed to* Computing M I I T Software Directory (Year) **2588**
0268-6716 Historical Research for Higher Degrees in the United Kingdom. Part 1: Theses Completed **4143**
0268-6724 Historical Research for Higher Degrees in the United Kingdom. Part 2: Theses in Progress **4143**
0268-6821 Computer Users' Year Book **2413**
0268-6864 Latin American Economic Report **1496**
0268-6872 Exe†
0268-6902 Managerial Auditing Journal **1778**
0268-6910 Expatriate
0268-6929 Andover Business
0268-702X Rouen Port and Shipping Handbook
0268-7038 Aphasiology **6123**
0268-7135 Knitting and Sewing Machine Times†
0268-7143 Equal Opportunities Review **1680**
0268-716X Computergram International **2413**
0268-7194 Scootering Magazine **8268**
0268-7232 Fund Management International†
0268-7291 Biotechnology Insight†
0268-7305 Platinum (Year) **6329**
0268-733X Workboat International†
0268-7364 Progress in the Psychology of Language **7392**
0268-7402 U K Centre for Economic and Environmental Development Bulletin **3471**
0268-7410 Family Policy†
0268-7429 Lighting & Sound International **8473**
0268-7518 Church Monuments
0268-7526 Research Notes in Artificial Intelligence **2456**
0268-7542 Editors Media Directories. Vol. 1: National Newspapers, Radio, TV **1991**
0268-7569 Editors Media Directories. Vol. 3: Provincial Newspapers & Town Guide **1991**
0268-7615 Airline Business **8536**
0268-764X Benefits & Compensation International **4495**
0268-7666 Marine Conservation **688**
0268-7682 Venture U K **1800**
0268-7712 Airport
0268-7801 Expression†
0268-7844 Weekly Petroleum Argus **6797**
0268-7852 Mid-Week Petroleum Argus **6778**
0268-7860 Industrial Computing **2422**
0268-8050 Condition Monitor **3185**
0268-8212 Impact International **605**
0268-8328 Military Illustrated **6435**
0268-8336 Law Library Information Reports **4715**
0268-8352 Link International: Educational Newsletter **7713**
0268-8360 AIDS Newsletter†
0268-8387 Career Secretary
0268-8395 The Franchise Magazine **1817**
0268-8417 G P **5617**
0268-8425 Satellite T V Europe
0268-8476 Northern Earth **408**
0268-8581 Finance Director International†
0268-8638 Mediaeval and Renaissance Studies† **8973**
0268-8654 Proprietary Articles Trade Association. Publication†
0268-8697 British Journal of Neurosurgery **6238**
0268-876X Agriculture in Scotland **86**
0268-8786 One to One (London, 1985) **8154**
0268-8921 Lasers in Medical Science **5660**
0268-893X Public Library Journal **5040**
0268-8948 Government Contracting Review†
0268-8999 Horse International
0268-9111 The Consort **6558**
0268-9146 Animal Genetics **862**
0268-9154 *see* 0268-9146 **862**
0268-9219 Liquids Handling†
0268-9502 Dog & Country†
0268-9561 Who's Who in Publishing
0268-957X The Tennis Times
0268-960X Blood Reviews **5934**
0268-9650 B M T Abstracts **8522**
0268-9669 Professional Liability Today†
0268-9685 I E E Power Engineering Series†
0268-9766 Surface Coating & Raw Material Directory†
0268-9847 Advanced Ceramics Report **2037**
0268-9863 Farm Tax Brief **1923**
0268-991X You & Your Vet **6817**
0268-9960 International Telecommunications Intelligence **2328**
0269-0012 Current British Journals†
0269-0020 Steam Days **8625**
0269-0039 Construction Industry Law Letter **4649**
0269-0055 Wasafiri: Caribbean, African, Asian and Associated Literatures in English **5396**
0269-0071 Advances in Pineal Research†
0269-011X National Association of Pension Funds. Annual Survey of Occupational Pension Schemes *changed to* National Association of Pension Funds. Annual Survey **1253**
0269-0179 Serie d'Ecriture **5369**
0269-0217 Travel Trade London **8768**
0269-0225 Diagnostic Engineering **3376**
0269-0292 Music Business
0269-0357 International Public Relations Review **7244**
0269-0365 United Kingdom. Ministry of Defence. Contracts Bulletin **6451**
0269-0403 Royal Musical Association. Journal **6613**
0269-0489 D E C Today **2573**
0269-0543 Agricultural Zoology Reviews†
0269-056X C L W Contents Monthly†
0269-0608 Railways Restored (Year) **8624**
0269-0640 P C Management **1420**
0269-0659 Glass & Glazing Products **2041**
0269-0713 Developments in Applied Biology **668**
0269-0756 Snooker Scene **8201**
0269-0780 N A G Newsletter†
0269-0802 European Patent Office Reports **6749**
0269-0829 Royal Institute of British Architects. Members **456**
0269-0837 International Architects **446**
0269-0942 Local Economy **1145**
0269-1035 Business Ratio Report: Confectioners, Tobacconists and Newsagents†
0269-1191 French History **4222**
0269-1205 Literature and Theology **5325**
0269-1213 Renaissance Studies **4158**
0269-123X Evergreen **3865**
0269-1302 Athletics Today†
0269-1310 What House? (London, 1978)
0269-1329 Hotel Specification International *changed to* 1753-3813 **4390**
0269-1361 Llyfrgell Genedlaethol Cymru. Adroddiad Blynyddol **5030**
0269-1396 Pratique **2355**
0269-1434 Bird Watching **903**
0269-1469 Sheppard's Bookdealers in North America **7573**
0269-1574 Rhodesian Study Circle Journal **6899**
0269-1701 Industrial Minerals Directory - World Guide to Producers and Processors **6465**
0269-1728 Social Epistemology **6952**
0269-1736 Who's Who in Scotland **647**
0269-1744 Journalist's Handbook
0269-1752 Press Briefing†
0269-1760 Centre for South-East Asian Studies. Bibliography and Literature Series **546**
0269-1779 Centre for South-East Asian Studies. Occasional Papers **4181**
0269-1825 Van User **8610**
0269-1876 Convention and Exhibition London†
0269-1922 Denning Law Journal **4656**
0269-1973 Forbes Handbook of Home Economics & Consumer Education†
0269-2023 B A P L A Directory **6964**
0269-2058 What's New in Marketing (Print) *changed to* What's New in Marketing (Online) **1848**
0269-2147 Oxbow Book News **7569**
0269-2155 Clinical Rehabilitation **6107**
0269-2163 Palliative Medicine **5693**
0269-2171 International Review of Applied Economics **1129**
0269-2244 Royal Historical Society Studies in History **4260**
0269-2309 Electronics Showcase†
0269-2317 Local Studies Index†
0269-2368 Steam Heritage Museums & Rally Guide (Year) *changed to* Steam Heritage Guide (Year) **8511**
0269-2422 Construction Products (Sevenoaks)†
0269-2465 Primary Science Review **2899**
0269-2473 B M X Bi-Weekly
0269-249X Diatom Research **786**
0269-2511 Constitutional Reform†
0269-2554 E S R C Studentship Handbook **7960**
0269-2597 Elle (U K Edition) **8860**
0269-2600 World Cinema **6517**
0269-2619 Princess Grace Irish Library **5354**
0269-2694 Butterworths Journal of International Banking and Financial Law **4634**
0269-2805 Butterworths Trading Law Cases†
0269-2813 Alimentary Pharmacology and Therapeutics **5920**
0269-2821 Artificial Intelligence Review **2446**
0269-283X Medical & Veterinary Entomology **5667**
0269-297X Quality Assurance Abstracts†
0269-2996 Warehouse Computing **1855**
0269-3011 P C Week **2581**
0269-3046 Office Magazine†
0269-3062 I E E Software Engineering Series†
0269-3208 On the Move†
0269-3259 Anthroposophy Today†
0269-3275 MacUser **2577**
0269-3445 Palaeontographical Society. Monographs (London) **2761**
0269-3518 Journal of Cell Science. Supplement *see* 0021-9533 **833**
0269-3534 Euromoney Annual Financing Report†
0269-3615 Interspace *changed to* 0161-3448
0269-3658 Paterson's Licensing Acts **4756**
0269-3682 Stone's Justices' Manual **4789**
0269-3720 Tax Practitioner's Diary **1949**
0269-3755 Travel & Tourism Analyst **8766**
0269-3828 Used Motorcycle Guide **8270**
0269-3836 Keyboard Player **6582**
0269-3844 Africa Review **1435**
0269-3852 Europe Review (Saffron Walden) **1484**
0269-3879 Biomedical Chromatography **2098**
0269-3933 Institute of European Finance. School of Accounting, Banking and Economics. Research Papers in Banking and Finance **1355**
0269-400X Royal Economic Society. Conference Papers *see* 0013-0133 **1100**
0269-4018 Propliner **68**
0269-4042 Environmental Geochemistry and Health **3424**
0269-4166 Country Report. Canada **1451**
0269-4174 Country Report. Sri Lanka **1461**
0269-4182 Country Report. Norway **1459**
0269-4204 Country Report. Nigeria **1459**
0269-4212 Country Report. Argentina **1449**
0269-4239 Country Report. Kenya **1456**
0269-4263 Country Report. Spain **1461**
0269-428X Country Report. Philippines **1460**
0269-4301 Country Report. Hungary **1455**
0269-431X Country Report. Bangladesh **1450**
0269-4328 Country Report. Libya **1457**
0269-4360 Country Profile. Zimbabwe† **8946**
0269-4379 Country Profile. Canada† **8944**
0269-4395 Country Profile. Iraq† **8945**
0269-4433 Agricultural Research Institute of Northern Ireland. Annual Report **84**
0269-4468 Country Profile. Argentina† **8944**
0269-4476 Country Profile. Australia† **8944**
0269-4484 Country Profile. Austria† **8944**
0269-4492 Country Profile. Brazil† **8944**
0269-4522 Country Profile. Malawi† **8945**
0269-4530 Country Profile. Kenya† **8945**
0269-4549 Country Profile. Ghana† **8945**
0269-4573 Banking Fintac Report†
0269-4670 Underground†
0269-4727 Journal of Clinical Pharmacy and Therapeutics **6852**
0269-4735 Pro Sound News Europe **8154**
0269-4824 Tuba **5437**
0269-4921 Expatriates Tax & Investment Intelligence†
0269-493X Broadcast Hardware International **2357**
0269-5006 France & Colonies Philatelic Society of Great Britain. Journal **6895**
0269-5022 Paediatric and Perinatal Epidemiology (Print) **6098**
0269-5073 Country Profile. Sri Lanka† **8946**
0269-5081 Country Profile. Chile† **8945**
0269-5103 Country Profile. Colombia† **8945**
0269-5111 Country Profile. Cuba† **8945**
0269-5162 Country Report. United Arab Emirates **1463**
0269-5170 Country Report. Austria **1450**
0269-5197 Country Report. Chile **1452**
0269-5219 Country Profile. Poland† **8946**
0269-5227 Country Profile. Egypt† **8945**
0269-526X Country Report. Egypt **1453**
0269-5278 Country Report. Ireland **1456**
0269-5286 Country Report. France **1454**
0269-5316 S C R E Publications†
0269-5324 Country Profile. Ireland† **8945**
0269-5332 Country Profile. Finland† **8945**
0269-5340 Country Profile. France† **8945**

ISSN

0271-6925 Ripley P. Bullen Monographs in Anthropology and History **414**
0271-7069 Alaska Sea Grant Report **652**
0271-7085 Enhanced Energy Recovery News†
0271-7093 Battery & E V Technology News **3296**
0271-7182 Law Officer's Pocket Manual **2659**
0271-7190 C A R D Report (Ames, 1971)†
0271-728X Parish Visitor **7812**
0271-7395 Progress in Resource Management and Environmental Planning
0271-7409 Rhode Island Review
0271-7417 T M S A Aerospace Market Outlook†
0271-7514 N A G W S Guide. Bowling-Fencing *changed to* 0736-4458
0271-7565 Police and Security Bulletin†
0271-7662 Directory of Foodservice Distributors (Year) **1986**
0271-7735 Little Balkans Review **503**
0271-776X National Technical Association. Journal
0271-7794 Masters of Science Fiction†
0271-7808 Fantasy Voices†
0271-7832 Florida Geological Survey. Bulletin **2734**
0271-7956 Year Book of Clinical Pharmacy†
0271-7964 Year Book of Emergency Medicine **6075**
0271-8014 Entertainment Industry Directory
0271-8022 Indiana Theory Review **6575**
0271-8189 Best of Micro†
0271-8197 New Pages **7568**
0271-8227 Iowa Woman†
0271-8235 Seminars in Neurology **6184**
0271-8294 Topics in Language Disorders **3048**
0271-8472 News on Tests†
0271-8480 A A V S O Solar Bulletin **567**
0271-8502 Wisconsin Geological and Natural History Survey. Field Trip Guide Books **2775**
0271-8510 A A P G Studies in Geology Series **6761**
0271-8529 A A P G Memoir **2722**
0271-8685 Midwest Historical and Genealogical Register. Quarterly **3775**
0271-8774 Paleo Data Banks†
0271-8812 South Carolina Geological Survey. Bulletin **2768**
0271-8979 Geothermal World Journal
0271-8987 Alaska Shippers Guide†
0271-8995 Crop Dust†
0271-9002 Micro†
0271-9029 Alternate Energy Transportation Newsletter†
0271-9053 A A V S O Journal **567**
0271-9061 I.O. Evans Studies in the Philosophy & Criticism of Literature†
0271-9126 Landscaping, Lawns and Gardens
0271-9142 Journal of Clinical Immunology **5762**
0271-9150 National Consultor
0271-9177 Cross-Cultural Research and Methodology Series†
0271-9274 Studies in American Jewish Literature **3566**
0271-9347 Wistar Symposium Series†
0271-9355 Biological Regulation & Development†
0271-9460 Journal of Applied Polymer Science. Applied Polymer Symposium **3248**
0271-9487 American Man†
0271-9509 The Greenwood Encyclopedia of American Institutions **2860**
0271-9517 N A C A D A Journal **2994**
0271-955X Frontiers in Aging Series†
0271-9606 Michigan State University. Institute of Water Research. Annual Report **8829**
0271-9657 Private School Quarterly†
0271-972X S C O P E Report **3464**
0271-9738 Advances in Analysis of Behavior
0271-9746 Trustee Quarterly **2920**
0271-9797 U.S. Merit Systems Protection Board. Annual Report **7473**
0271-9800 Annual of Armenian Linguistics **5094**
0271-9835 University of Hawaii Law Review **4804**
0271-9940 Dance Book Forum
0271-9967 National Mastitis Council. Annual Meeting Proceedings **267**
0272-0086 China Exchange News†
0272-0108 Nuclear Medicine Annual **6204**
0272-0116 The Construction Lawyer **996**
0272-0167 Directory of Home Center Operators & Hardware Chains (Year) **1987**
0272-0264 Greenwood Encyclopedia of Black Music **6570**
0272-0272 Ellis Horwood Series in Engineering Science **3188**
0272-0280 Niepodleglosc **4248**
0272-0345 Update (Smithsonian Institution Traveling Exhibition Service) **6539**
0272-037X D L A Bulletin†
0272-0426 Ancestoring **3758**
0272-0434 Advances in the Mechanics and Physics of Surfaces Series
0272-0469 Washington Consumers' Checkbook **2642**
0272-0485 Metals Daily†
0272-0493 Wise Giving Bulletin†
0272-0515 Women & Health Roundtable Reports
0272-0558 Enterprise (Cincinnati)†
0272-0574 Primer of Labor Relations†
0272-0582 P C R **7417**
0272-0671 Policy Publishers and Associations Directory **7166**
0272-068X Advances in Human Psychopharmacology†
0272-0701 Free Inquiry **6921**
0272-0787 Advances in Neurogerontology†
0272-0795 Geological Society of America. Map and Chart Series **2738**
0272-0809 Evolutionary Monographs **672**
0272-0817 Rental House & Condo Investor†
0272-0825 National Fund Raiser†
0272-0868 Mark Skousen's Forecasts & Strategies on Inflation, Taxes and Government Controls *changed to* 1556-4037 **1478**
0272-0884 Technicalities **5050**
0272-0906 American Institute of Architects. International Directory†
0272-0965 Pneuma **7770**
0272-1007 U.S. Forest Service. Report **3706**
0272-1015 Irish-American Genealogist†
0272-1082 Century
0272-1090 International Pipe Line Industry† **8966**
0272-1120 EnviroSouth
0272-1155 Heritage Lectures **7444**
0272-1163 American Export Register (Year)†
0272-1171 I C P Directory†
0272-1236 Video Programs Index†
0272-1279 St. Louis **3987**
0272-1384 Landmarks Observer **4301**
0272-1406 Tampa Bay History†
0272-1465 Current Histopathology **5944**
0272-1473 Springer Series on the Teaching of Nursing **5982**
0272-1570 Northwest Discovery
0272-1589 East Asian Executive Reports **1478**
0272-1635 Anales de la Literatura Espanola Contemporanea **5254**
0272-166X Comparative Political Economy and Public Policy Series†
0272-1678 Crosscurrents in Contemporary Psychology **7350**
0272-1686 Artificial Intelligence†
0272-1716 I E E E Computer Graphics and Applications **2486**
0272-1732 I E E E Micro **2571**
0272-1740 Advances in Substance Abuse: Behavioral and Biological Research†
0272-1783 M L A Abstracts of Articles in Scholarly Journals†
0272-1902 New Hearer
0272-1937 Afro-American Historical and Genealogical Society. Journal **3758**
0272-1953 American Subsidiaries of German Firms **1395**
0272-1961 Legal Assistants Update†
0272-1988 Reference Book Review **634**
0272-1996 W L W Journal†
0272-2011 American Review of Canadian Studies **7947**
0272-202X Springer Series: Focus on Women† **8990**
0272-2062 International Banjo†
0272-2089 Family Journal
0272-2135 Directory of College Recruiting Personnel†
0272-2151 Leading Constitutional Cases on Criminal Justice **4850**
0272-2275 Moped and Economy Motorcycle Buyer's Guide†
0272-2348 Journal of Refugee Resettlement†
0272-2410 Pace Law Review **4755**
0272-2461 Accent on Living Buyer's Guide†
0272-247X National Directory of Landscape Architecture Firms†
0272-2488 Contemporary Concepts in Physics Series
0272-2631 Studies in Second Language Acquisition **5183**
0272-2658 University of Kansas. Museum of Natural History. Public Education Series
0272-2666 Perfumer & Flavorist **595**
0272-2690 Language Problems and Language Planning **5141**
0272-2712 Clinics in Laboratory Medicine **5904**
0272-2747 Ram's Horn **5165**
0272-2771 Tobacco Market Review. Fire-Cured and Dark Air-Cured **8488**
0272-3328 N R D C Newsletter†
0272-3336 Datapro Reports on Word Processing†
0272-3417 Farming Uncle **112**
0272-3433 The Public Historian **4157**
0272-3484 Service Corporation Directory†
0272-3506 A S M E Boiler and Pressure Vessel Code. Section 7: Recommended Guidelines for the Care of Power Boilers **3372**
0272-3530 Drug-Nutrient Interactions†
0272-3565 Benzene Magazine†
0272-3581 Today's Education: Social Studies Edition†
0272-359X Today's Education: Elementary Edition†
0272-3638 Urban Geography **4430**
0272-3646 Physical Geography **2714**
0272-3700 I F P R I Report (Print) *changed to* 1933-5202 **200**
0272-3751 Pets and People of the World
0272-3778 Laboratory Regulation Manual†
0272-3794 Annual Editions: Psychology **7334**
0272-3808 Annual Editions: Aging **4040**
0272-3816 Annual Editions: Criminal Justice **2644**
0272-3840 Advances in Biomaterials†
0272-3913 T S F Bulletin†
0272-4065 Directory of Corporate Counsel†
0272-4103 Today's Education: Vocational-Career Education Edition†
0272-4111 Today's Education: Mathematics-Science Edition†
0272-4146 Alaska Housing Finance Corporation. Annual Report **4403**
0272-4154 Better Homes and Gardens Brides Book†
0272-4294 Seafood America
0272-4308 International Journal of Partial Hospitalization†
0272-4316 Journal of Early Adolescence **2156**
0272-4324 Plasma Chemistry & Plasma Processing **3252**
0272-4332 Risk Analysis **5530**
0272-4340 Cellular & Molecular Neurobiology **6130**
0272-4359 Another Chicago Magazine **5255**
0272-4367 Freedom Socialist **8864**
0272-4391 Drug Development Research **6834**
0272-4456 Annual Editions: Early Childhood Education **2826**
0272-4464 Annual Editions: Social Problems **8025**
0272-4499 McCall's Country Decorating†
0272-4537 Faxon Librarians' Guide to Continuations†
0272-4561 Construction Claims Monthly **995**
0272-4626 European Applied Research Reports: Environmental and Natural Resources Section†
0272-4634 Journal of Vertebrate Paleontology **6726**
0272-4669 Veterinary Pharmaceuticals and Biologicals†
0272-4685 I E E E Conference of Electrical Engineering Problems in the Rubber and Plastics Industries. Conference Record†
0272-4693 Antennas and Propagation **3295**
0272-4790 Advances in Drying†
0272-4804 Series in Computational Methods in Mechanics and Thermal Sciences
0272-4855 Office Automation Conference Digest†
0272-4936 Annals of Tropical Paediatrics **6087**
0272-4944 Journal of Environmental Psychology **7373**
0272-4952 Power Industry Research†
0272-4960 I M A Journal of Applied Mathematics **5492**
0272-4979 I M A Journal of Numerical Analysis **5492**
0272-4987 Quarterly Journal of Experimental Psychology. Section A: Human Experimental Psychology *changed to* 1747-0218 **7402**
0272-4995 Quarterly Journal of Experimental Psychology. Section B: Comparative and Physiological Psychology *changed to* 1747-0218 **7402**
0272-5010 Annual Editions: Education **2826**
0272-5037 American Society of International Law. Proceedings of the Annual Meeting **4916**
0272-507X Reviews of Hematology†
0272-5088 Accelerators and Storage Rings Series *changed to* Physics and Technology of Particle and Photon Beams **7070**
0272-5231 Clinics in Chest Medicine **6213**
0272-5282 Association for Supervision and Curriculum Development. Annual Conference† **8931**
0272-5371 Western Bank Directory
0272-5452 California Anthropologist **332**
0272-5495 OncoLogic†
0272-5541 Masson Today†
0272-5657 Me **504**
0272-5665 Journal of Therapeutic Humor†
0272-5673 American Society of Mechanical Engineers. Heat Transfer Division. Publication HTD **3336**
0272-572X JazzTimes **6579**
0272-5800 Compendium of Research Reports **4408**
0272-5827 Search (Brattleboro)†
0272-5835 Springer Series on Adulthood and Aging *changed to* Springer Series on Life Styles & Issues on Aging **8990**
0272-5959 Libertarian Digest†
0272-5967 Maize†
0272-5991 West's Bankruptcy Digest **4813**
0272-6017 Changing Public Attitudes on Governments and Taxes **1916**
0272-6076 Texas A & M University. Department of Oceanography. Technical Report **2818**
0272-6122 International Bulletin of Missionary Research **7762**
0272-6211 Financial Disclosure Reports of Members of the U.S. House of Representatives **7437**
0272-6319 Childbirth Alternatives Quarterly†
0272-6327 Perspectives in Biomechanics†
0272-6343 Electromagnetics **3304**
0272-6351 Particulate Science and Technology **3251**
0272-6378 Mark Twain Society Bulletin†
0272-6386 American Journal of Kidney Diseases **6265**
0272-6408 Experimental and Clinical Psychiatry†
0272-6505 Current Population Reports. Population Characteristics. Fertility of American Women **7281**
0272-6513 Connections (New York)†
0272-6521 Pyrotechnica **3254**
0272-6742 Woodrose†
0272-6750 Democracy†
0272-6793 U.S. Department of Agriculture. National Agricultural Statistics Service. Floriculture Crops **188**
0272-684X International Quarterly of Community Health Education **7527**
0272-6904 Colorado Homes & Lifestyles **4535**
0272-6939 Tentmaker's Journal†
0272-6963 Journal of Operations Management **3369**
0272-7145 Children's Digest† **8941**
0272-717X Mid-Hudson Language Studies†
0272-7250 Albanian Catholic Bulletin†
0272-7323 Rep Talk
0272-7358 Clinical Psychology Review **7345**
0272-7404 Comedy
0272-7560 Southeastern Law Librarian **5048**
0272-7595 Journal of Contemporary Studies†
0272-7617 Death Penalty Reporter†
0272-765X Social Action and the Law†
0272-7714 Estuarine, Coastal and Shelf Science **2804**
0272-7757 Economics of Education Review **3020**
0272-7765 John M. MacEachran Memorial Lectures†
0272-782X National Fluid Power Association. Reporter **3390**
0272-7846 S E C Monthly Statistical Review†
0272-7870 Chemical Briefs Report
0272-7897 Annual Editions: Marriage and Family *changed to* Annual Editions: The Family **5556**
0272-7900 Pulmonary Disease Reviews†
0272-7919 International Journal of Turkish Studies **4321**
0272-8060 Houston Monthly Magazine
0272-8087 Seminars in Liver Disease **5931**
0272-8117 Delaware Directory of Commerce and Industry **1983**
0272-8141 I S A Directory of Instrumentation *changed to* I S A Directory of Automation **4487**
0272-8230 First Tuesday†
0272-8362 Setting Municipal Priorities†
0272-8370 American Association of Petroleum Landmen. Membership Directory
0272-8397 Polymer Composites **7098**
0272-8419 Asantesem†
0272-8443 Health Facilities Energy Report†
0272-8486 Bulletin on Training†
0272-8494 Folklore Bibliography for (Year)†
0272-8532 Base Line **4000**
0272-8540 Chicago History **4288**
0272-8583 Minnesota Industrial Minerals Directory
0272-863X N A G W S Guide. Tennis†
0272-8710 P M R Conference. Proceedings **4252**
0272-8761 Life Insurance Index†
0272-880X International Centre for Heat and Mass Transfer. Proceedings **3200**
0272-8842 Ceramics International **2039**
0272-8850 Periodicals Digest in Dentistry
0272-8869 Bibliography of Fossil Vertebrates† **8936**
0272-8885 Math Notebook **5512**
0272-8893 Focus on Learning Problems in Mathematics *changed to* 1947-7503 **5498**
0272-8923 Cycle Street and Touring Guide†
0272-8931 Capstone Journal of Education†
0272-8966 Sanctuary

0272-8974 U.S. Urban Initiatives Anti-Crime Program. Annual Report to Congress **2670**
0272-9008 Annual Editions: Environment **3403**
0272-9016 University of Southern California. School of Social Work. Social Work Papers†
0272-9032 Genetic Technology News **869**
0272-9067 Articulator†
0272-9164 California State Health Plan†
0272-9172 Materials Research Society Symposium Proceedings **7025**
0272-9199 Pedalpoint **6604**
0272-930X Merrill - Palmer Quarterly **7385**
0272-9334 West's Military Justice Digest **4972**
0272-9377 Colorado Heritage **4289**
0272-9490 American Journal of Occupational Therapy **6672**
0272-9520 Tarakan Music Letter†
0272-9539 Deep Drilling and Production Symposium. Proceedings **6766**
0272-9598 RiverSedge
0272-9601 Prooftexts **5354**
0272-961X Woman's World **8890**
0272-9660 Telematics†
0272-9709 Promoting Health†
0272-9741 American Board of Medical Specialties. Annual Report & Reference Handbook **5571**
0272-9784 Evaluation Notes†
0272-9814 Alcohol (Boca Raton)†
0272-9822 Corrections†
0272-9830 Communication (Boca Raton)†
0272-9849 Crime†
0272-9857 Energy (Boca Raton)†
0272-9865 Ethnic Groups (Boca Raton)†
0272-9873 South Carolina Geology†
0272-9881 Clinical Biochemistry Reviews (Tarrytown)†
0272-989X Medical Decision Making **5667**
0272-9911 August Derleth Society. Newsletter **5258**
0272-992X Family (Boca Raton)†
0272-9938 Food†
0272-9946 Habitat†
0272-9954 Health (Boca Raton)†
0272-9962 Mental Health†
0272-9970 Money (Boca Raton)†
0272-9989 Privacy†
0272-9997 School†
0273-0014 Women (Boca Raton)†
0273-0022 Work (Boca Raton)†
0273-009X Focus (Moscow)†
0273-0189 Association for Research in Vision and Ophthalmology. Spring Meeting†
0273-0197 Needle and Bobbin Club Bulletin
0273-0200 Harris Postage Stamp Price Index†
0273-0227 Linda Hall Library. Miscellany†
0273-0278 Postgraduate Radiology†
0273-0324 Source (Jamaica)†
0273-0340 The Henry James Review **5305**
0273-0413 Perspectives on Medicaid and Medicare Management†
0273-0561 Medical Directory of New York State **5668**
0273-057X Urban League News†
0273-0685 Securities and Federal Corporate Law Report **4880**
0273-0693 Scotia **4262**
0273-0758 International Conference of Building Officials. (Year) Accumulative Supplement to the Uniform Codes and Related Publications†
0273-0979 American Mathematical Society. Bulletin. New Series **5469**
0273-0995 The Brief (Chicago) **4631**
0273-1061 Federal Librarian *changed to* Federal and Armed Forces Libraries **5009**
0273-1177 Advances in Space Research **41**
0273-1223 Water Science and Technology **8840**
0273-1231 Studies in Freedom† **8991**
0273-124X Contributions to the Study of Childhood and Youth†
0273-1312 Income Taxes Worldwide†
0273-1371 Geopolitics of Energy **7237**
0273-138X Federal Tobacco Firearms Explosives Reports†
0273-1428 Country Music Sourcebook†
0273-1576 Sesame Street Parents' Newsletter†
0273-1606 Metamorfosis†
0273-1665 Plum Magazine†
0273-1673 E E R Energy Price Forecast†
0273-1770 Iowa A F L - C I O News **4596**
0273-1800 Gulf Solidarity
0273-1886 Committee for Economic Development. Annual Report **1448**
0273-1916 Alaska. Oil and Gas Conservation Commission. Statistical Report†
0273-2017 Survival Tomorrow
0273-2033 One Show **31**
0273-2041 B H M Support†
0273-2122 National Center for Professional Responsibility Advance Sheets†
0273-2157 Directory of Special Opportunities for Women†
0273-2173 Sociological Spectrum **8137**
0273-2238 Water Engineering and Management†
0273-2246 Shooting Commercials (Melville)†
0273-2254 Dermatology & Allergy†
0273-2289 Applied Biochemistry and Biotechnology **723**
0273-2297 Developmental Review **7352**
0273-2300 Regulatory Toxicology and Pharmacology **3500**
0273-2335 Los Chihuahuas **6806**
0273-2343 S H A R E†
0273-2351 Research Libraries in O C L C: A Quarterly†
0273-236X Employee Benefit Cases **1677**
0273-2378 Energy Purchasing Report†
0273-2467 Aging (Boca Raton)†
0273-2475 Consumerism†
0273-2483 Death and Dying†
0273-2491 Defense (Boca Raton)†
0273-2505 Drugs†
0273-2513 Ethics (Boca Raton)†
0273-2521 Human Rights (Boca Raton)†
0273-253X Pollution†
0273-2548 Population (Boca Raton)†
0273-2556 Religion†
0273-2564 Sexuality†
0273-2572 Sports†
0273-2580 Technology (Boca Raton)†
0273-2599 Third World†
0273-2602 Transportation (Boca Raton)†
0273-2610 Youth (Boca Raton)†
0273-267X Revue de Louisiane†
0273-2696 Syntax†
0273-270X New Jersey Monthly **3983**
0273-2858 Metropolitan Home **4546**
0273-2920 Song of Zion **6617**
0273-298X Current Energy Patents†
0273-2998 European Applied Research Reports Special Topics Series
0273-3013 Benchmark Soils News†
0273-303X Home Planet News **5423**
0273-3056 RadioNews†
0273-3072 The Cato Journal **7114**
0273-3080 Scan Newsletter†
0273-3102 Energy Clearinghouse†
0273-3145 Action (Winona Lake)†
0273-3196 Initiative News Report†
0273-320X Nursing (Year) Drug Handbook **5972**
0273-3218 A W W A Mainstream† **8927**
0273-3226 Biotechnology News **761**
0273-3234 Work Related Abstracts†
0273-3250 C T I Journal **6765**
0273-3269 Coptic Church Review **7635**
0273-3285 The Journal of Plastic and Reconstructive Surgical Nursing *changed to* 0741-5206 **5978**
0273-3323 Central Park†
0273-3366 Fanon Center Journal
0273-3382 Journal of International Student Personnel†
0273-3552 Accomplishments in Cancer Research†
0273-3579 Psychology Information Guide Series†
0273-3684 Business Index†
0273-3722 Yearbook of Substance Use and Abuse†
0273-382X Occupational Projections and Training Data *see* 0082-9072 **6707**
0273-3978 U S D A Forest Service. Rocky Mountain Research Station. Annual Western International Forest Disease Work Conference. Proceedings **3705**
0273-4079 Dial†
0273-4117 Nevada R N Formation **5971**
0273-4125 Findex (Year)†
0273-4230 Corrections Yearbook†
0273-4257 Professional Practice Management†
0273-429X Chinese Physics†
0273-4311 Berita **4180**
0273-4370 Air Force Report **6409**
0273-4397 Current Industrial Reports. M311K, Fats and Oils: Production, Consumption, and Stocks (Print)†
0273-4419 Whalewatcher **2632**
0273-4443 Education Funding News†
0273-446X Rural Educator **2908**
0273-4516 U.S. Coast Guard. Office of Research and Development. Report *changed to* U.S. Coast Guard. Research and Development Center. Report **8664**
0273-4613 Consulting Opportunities Journal **1735**
0273-4621 Perspectives in Computing (Armonk)†
0273-4699 West Coast Sailors **8665**
0273-4737 American Society of Safety Engineers. Society Update **3181**
0273-4753 Journal of Marketing Education **1825**
0273-480X World's Fair†
0273-4931 Armstrong Oil Directories: Louisiana, Texas Gulf Coast, East Texas, Arkansas and Mississippi Edition **6763**
0273-4974 National Report on Computers and Health†
0273-4982 Smithsonian Year **7468**
0273-5024 Journal of Teaching in Physical Education **3068**
0273-5032 U.S. Bureau of Alcohol, Tobacco and Firearms. Explosives Incidents **2670**
0273-5229 Armstrong Oil Directories: Rocky Mountain - Central United States Edition **6763**
0273-5253 Annual Institute on Mineral Law **4618**
0273-5261 German American Journal **3535**
0273-5415 Precancel Forum **6899**
0273-5520 Restaurants & Institutions **4397**
0273-5598 Philatelic Observer†
0273-5601 Goal†
0273-5636 On Cable†
0273-5652 Art Business News **4870**
0273-5687 Western H V A C R News *changed to* H V A C R Business **4120**
0273-5768 Brewing Industry News†
0273-5822 Mini-Storage Messenger **1431**
0273-5865 Discipleship Journal **7754**
0273-5954 Contractors Guide†
0273-5970 National Comment†
0273-6004 San Francisco Wholesale Ornamental Crops Report **154**
0273-608X Ninety-Nine News **67**
0273-6101 Fireplug **3578**
0273-6160 Better Living
0273-6187 Intermountain Catholic **7801**
0273-6225 Builder Developer West
0273-6241 S Gaugian **4345**
0273-6268 Petroleum Marketing Management†
0273-6314 Executive Intelligence Review **7135**
0273-642X Skier's World†
0273-6462 Sheet Music Magazine. Standard Piano - Guitar Edition **6616**
0273-6497 Adoptalk **8023**
0273-6519 Appaloosa World **8287**
0273-6527 This People†
0273-6551 Broker World **4496**
0273-6586 Leisure Time Electronics†
0273-6691 Gray's Sporting Journal **8316**
0273-6705 Quote†
0273-6713 Commercial Fisheries News **3589**
0273-6837 The Wall Paper *changed to* Wall Fashions
0273-6896 C A H P E R D Journal/Times **8164**
0273-6918 Playgirl†
0273-6950 Arizona Business Gazette **1061**
0273-6977 M S U Alumni Magazine **2290**
0273-7000 Annual Energy Litigation Institute. Effective Strategies and Techniques
0273-7027 Estate Planning and California Probate Reporter **4902**
0273-7078 Stamp Auction News *changed to* 1095-0443 **6897**
0273-7086 Housewares Retailing†
0273-7116 Los Alamos Science†
0273-7124 Nursing Careers
0273-7159 Railroad Evangelist **7740**
0273-7302 C C H Financial and Estate Planning **1322**
0273-7310 Aviation Law Reports *changed to* Aviation Law Reporter **8538**
0273-7345 West Texas Angelus **7823**
0273-7353 E S A Newsletter **843**
0273-7434 Bowhunter **8306**
0273-7485 Interservice†
0273-7590 Humpty Dumpty's Magazine **2193**
0273-7612 Executive Compensation & Taxation Coordinator **1922**
0273-7620 Common Faith†
0273-7655 Surgical Practice News†
0273-768X Employee Benefits Compliance Coordinator **1860**
0273-7752 Low Priced Stock Survey **1638**
0273-7884 B G R Newsletter†
0273-7957 Crafts Fair Guide **533**
0273-7973 Winning Negotiator†
0273-8023 Alliance Update *changed to* UPDATE (Reston) **6999**
0273-804X California Optometry **6039**
0273-8066 Big E
0273-8120 Sew News **2260**
0273-8139 Pharmaceutical Engineering **3215**
0273-8163 Alternative Energy Retailer† **8929**
0273-8198 Northern California Electronics News†
0273-821X Employee Benefits Alert†
0273-8279 L'Italo Americano Newspaper **3541**
0273-8295 Way of St. Francis **7822**
0273-8333 The Lhasa Apso Reporter **6811**
0273-8392 View (New York)†
0273-8481 Journal of Burn Care & Rehabilitation *changed to* 1559-047X **5646**
0273-8562 Taegliche Andachten†
0273-8570 Journal of Field Ornithology **909**
0273-8589 Diver **8170**
0273-8597 Quarter Horse News **8296**
0273-8724 Book and Magazine Production†
0273-8910 E A P Digest **2693**
0273-8945 Wolfpacker **8215**
0273-9240 Creative Products News†
0273-9267 Credit Union Management **1333**
0273-9313 Industrial Chemical News†
0273-9348 The Ukrainian Weekly **3569**
0273-9380 Leading Edge†
0273-9402 Truck Blue Book **8677**
0273-9453 Rough Rider **8602**
0273-9550 Print & Graphics†
0273-9569 Compliance Management Report†
0273-9615 Children's Health Care **8033**
0273-964X Office Guide†
0273-9658 Official Railway Guide. North American Travel Edition†
0273-9712 West Plains Gazette†
0273-9747 Florida Funeral Director **3719**
0273-978X Stamp Dealer†
0273-9895 Kansas City Aviation†
0273-9917 Education in Photojournalism. Journal†
0273-9933 Indiana Musicator **6575**
0273-9992 Urner Barry's Price-Current **303**
0274-4805 Bottom Line, Personal **2635**
0274-4872 Keepers' Voice†
0274-4929 Indianapolis Business Journal **1429**
0274-4961 Las Vegas Israelite **7726**
0274-4996 Packaging Technology†
0274-5003 V-8 Times **369**
0274-502X Audubon Society of Rhode Island. Report **2603**
0274-5097 Prints (Alton)†
0274-5143 Penthouse Variations **6297**
0274-5186 Foundation Drilling **1008**
0274-5348 Northern Automotive News†
0274-547X Indiana Beverage Journal **605**
0274-5496 Greater Washington Board of Trade News **1428**
0274-5526 Plexus
0274-5569 Increase†
0274-564X Ornithological Newsletter **912**
0274-5720 Muzzleloader **8323**
0274-5771 Feed International **272**
0274-5828 Today's Art and Graphics
0274-5852 William Winter Comments†
0274-5976 Graphic Arts Product News (Chicago)†
0274-600X Prayers for Worship **7671**
0274-6034 Bow & Swing **2683**
0274-6050 Big Farmer Entrepreneur†
0274-6085 Antiques & Collectibles Magazine **363**
0274-6093 California Inntouch†
0274-6115 Marblehead Magazine **3981**
0274-6190 Dell Word Search Puzzles
0274-6212 Profitunities - Better Buys†
0274-6239 Official Crossword Puzzles *changed to* 1556-4177
0274-6298 Federal Tax Forms **1924**
0274-6301 Dell Crossword Puzzles
0274-6336 Pennsylvania Sportsman†
0274-6425 Dell Pocket Crossword Puzzles
0274-6441 Second Boat†
0274-645X Supervisory Sense†
0274-6484 New England Engineering Journal **3212**
0274-6530 I R T Communication Quarterly†
0274-6565 American Farriers Journal **8286**
0274-6638 I E E E Geoscience and Remote Sensing Society Newsletter **3311**
0274-6662 Volleyball Magazine **8251**
0274-6743 Total Health **6670**

ISSN

0275-8873 Apparel Plant Wages Survey **8448**
0275-889X Annual of American Architecture†
0275-8911 Georgia Journal of Accounting†
0275-9098 Current Topics of Contemporary Thought†
0275-9101 Body Bulletin Newsletter†
0275-9128 Geophysical Journal†
0275-9160 A S I S News†
0275-9179 Wythe County Historical Review **4319**
0275-9187 Rock Yearbook
0275-9314 Swedish American Genealogist **3784**
0275-9357 N R C S A Directory of Educational Programs **2888**
0275-939X Applied Research Summary of Awards
0275-9470 A I G A Graphic Design U S A†
0275-9527 South Asian Review **5375**
0275-9586 Methods in Microanalysis
0275-9594 Demographic Monographs
0275-9608 Ferroelectricity and Related Phenomena
0275-9616 U.S. Library of Congress. Manuscript Division. Acquisitions **5052**
0275-9624 Journal of Somatic Experience†
0275-9640 Handmade†
0275-9667 Ages 3-4 Church and Home Leaflets†
0275-9942 Journal of Linguistic Research†
0275-9977 Slit Wrist Magazine
0275-9993 Hebrew Union College Annual Supplements **7721**
0276-0045 The Review of Contemporary Fiction **5360**
0276-0061 International Petroleum Industry Data Service: North America†
0276-0142 Journal of Freshwater†
0276-0185 U.S. Department of Agriculture. Program Aid **207**
0276-0193 Utah Agricultural Statistics **189**
0276-0231 Colorado. Division of Wildlife. Division Report **3411**
0276-0290 Nous Letter†
0276-0347 Cosmetic Surgery†
0276-0355 Chronicle Career Index†
0276-0363 Chronicle Guide for Transfers†
0276-0371 Chronicle Vocational School Manual **2954**
0276-0401 Research and Invention†
0276-0428 C A I News†
0276-0436 Pulpsmith (Year)†
0276-0444 Mananam Publication Series **7707**
0276-0460 Geo-Marine Letters **2735**
0276-055X Recent Ethics Opinions **4766**
0276-0592 Focus (Princeton) **2981**
0276-0606 Kastlemusick Monthly Bulletin†
0276-0681 E P R I-EL **3301**
0276-0746 Workers Vanguard **7194**
0276-0843 Public Affairs Review†
0276-086X Psi News†
0276-0959 Modern's Market Guide†
0276-0983 Larson's Workers' Compensation Law **4512**
0276-1025 Alaska Bar Rag **4612**
0276-1076 Interferon **887**
0276-1092 Year Book of Orthopedics **5752**
0276-1106 University of Texas Publications in Astronomy†
0276-1114 Modern Judaism **3551**
0276-119X N B E R Reporter **1546**
0276-1289 Water Resources Data for Connecticut **8839**
0276-1319 Water Resources Data for Virginia **8839**
0276-1378 Statement of Financial Accounting Concepts **1302**
0276-1416 Byelorussian Times
0276-1432 Jewish Jurisprudence Series
0276-1440 Computer Graphics News†
0276-1467 Journal of Macromarketing **1825**
0276-1483 Society of Prospective Medicine. Proceedings of the Annual Meeting **5716**
0276-1505 Bench & Bar of Minnesota **4628**
0276-1521 Schnauzer Shorts **6815**
0276-1564 Bloomsbury Review **5264**
0276-1610 Psychic Studies
0276-1653 Research in Domestic and International Agribusiness Management†
0276-1661 Court Management Journal†
0276-170X Farm and Ranch Living **110**
0276-1769 University of Illinois at Urbana-Champaign. Graduate School of Library and Information Science. Occasional Papers **5053**
0276-1858 Energy Newsletter Index
0276-1890 Coal Statistics International†
0276-1904 Am-Pol Eagle **3517**
0276-1947 Griffin **2285**
0276-203X Center for Law and Education. Newsnotes†
0276-2048 Rural Libraries **5044**
0276-2056 I S T F News **3692**
0276-2072 Fat Tuesday **5295**
0276-2080 Philosophical Topics **6941**
0276-2226 A R C Bulletin†
0276-2234 Oncology Times **6031**
0276-2277 World Pharmaceutical Directory†
0276-2285 Journal of Rural Community Psychology (Print) changed to Journal of Rural Community Psychology (Online) **8115**
0276-2293 National Reye's Syndrome Foundation†
0276-2307 The Sporting News Pro Football Yearbook **8247**
0276-2315 International Perspectives in Urology
0276-2323 Hospital Safety Information Service†
0276-2358 Accent on Worship†
0276-2366 Imagination, Cognition and Personality **7362**
0276-2374 Empirical Study of the Arts **487**
0276-2412 Advances in Hydrogen Energy **3164**
0276-2560 Fodor's Rome **8708**
0276-2684 Data Processing Magazine†
0276-2714 Kahane†
0276-2730 Princeton History†
0276-2846 Coal Daily **6460**
0276-2854 Erasmus of Rotterdam Society Yearbook **6916**
0276-2897 Nuclear Waste News **3509**
0276-2919 Fusion Power Report†
0276-2994 American Meteorological Society. Conference on Hydrometeorology. Preprint
0276-3052 Interval

0276-3109 BIOSIS CAS Selects: Biochemistry of Fermented Foods†
0276-3117 BIOSIS CAS Selects: Biological Clocks†
0276-3125 BIOSIS CAS Selects: Cancer Immunology†
0276-3133 BIOSIS CAS Selects: Endorphins†
0276-3141 BIOSIS CAS Selects: Geriatric Pharmacology†
0276-315X BIOSIS CAS Selects: Histochemistry and Cytochemistry†
0276-3176 BIOSIS CAS Selects: Interferon†
0276-3184 BIOSIS CAS Selects: Mammalian Birth Defects†
0276-3192 BIOSIS CAS Selects: Pediatric Pharmacology†
0276-3206 BIOSIS CAS Selects: Plant Genetics†
0276-3214 BIOSIS CAS Selects: Schizophrenia†
0276-3222 BIOSIS CAS Selects: Transplantation†
0276-3303 Zoo View **969**
0276-3338 Old Mill News **4307**
0276-3362 The Hemingway Review **5305**
0276-3397 The Tamarind Papers
0276-3478 International Journal of Eating Disorders **6660**
0276-3494 Moving Image†
0276-3508 Advances in Ophthalmic Plastic & Reconstructive Surgery†
0276-3559 Tennis Directory
0276-3583 Boston College Third World Law Journal **4918**
0276-3605 Black Music Research Journal **6549**
0276-3613 The Alcoholism Report†
0276-3621 Proletarian Internationalism†
0276-363X Workers' Advocate†
0276-3737 The Poe Messenger **5430**
0276-377X Mixed Voices†
0276-3788 Montana Lawyer **4736**
0276-3826 U.S. Environmental Protection Agency. Monthly Awards for Construction Grants for Wastewater Treatment Works†
0276-3869 Medical Reference Services Quarterly **5031**
0276-3877 The Reference Librarian **5042**
0276-3885 Women & History†
0276-3893 Journal of Housing for the Elderly **4049**
0276-3915 Community & Junior College Libraries **5003**
0276-4040 International Gas Technology Highlights†
0276-4148 Himalayan International Institute. Eleanor N. Dana Laboratory. Research Bulletin†
0276-4156 Wisconsin Preservation **4318**
0276-4164 Palmetto **3747**
0276-4245 Broadcast Databook†
0276-4296 Cardiologist's Compendium of Drug Therapy†
0276-4318 Family Physician's Compendium of Drug Therapy†
0276-4342 Internist's Compendium of Drug Therapy†
0276-4415 Housing Finance Review†
0276-4512 Marriage & Family changed to 1054-0202
0276-4563 Dialogue on Liberty
0276-461X N A P E H E Proceedings†
0276-4644 Costa Rica Report
0276-4679 Fulness†
0276-4695 Cold Spring Harbor Reports in the Neurosciences†
0276-4733 D H H S Publication **4092**
0276-4741 Mountain Research and Development **2713**
0276-4768 Saxophone Journal **6615**
0276-4792 Real Estate Investment Digest†
0276-4806 B I S G Bulletin†
0276-4830 Pro Rege **2297**
0276-4849 U.S. Hydrographic Conference. Biennial Meeting. Proceedings **2799**
0276-4857 Knox County, Kentucky Kinfolk
0276-4865 Worldwide Hunting Annual†
0276-4873 Trailer Life's Recreational Vehicle Buyers Guide†
0276-4881 Firehouse Magazine Buyers Guide†
0276-489X Municipal Year Book Directories†
0276-492X U.S. Coastal Engineering Research Center. Special Report **3364**
0276-4954 Estandarte Obrero
0276-5055 BioCycle **3504**
0276-5063 Advances in Modern Environmental Toxicology†
0276-5098 Microcomputer Systems D.A.T.A. Book†
0276-5128 P L†
0276-5241 Newport Review†
0276-5322 Small Business Tax Review **1943**
0276-5330 Critical Perspectives on Contemporary Psychology†
0276-5349 Association of American Publishers. Annual Report **7552**
0276-5357 Trends in the Hotel Industry. U S A Edition **4399**
0276-539X O P D Chemical Buyers Directory **2022**
0276-5411 Upper Atmospheric Programs. Bulletin†
0276-5519 American Register of Printing and Graphic Arts Services
0276-5543 South Dakota Archaeology **418**
0276-556X Export Documentation Handbook†
0276-5594 Group and Family Therapy†
0276-5608 Chemical Dependencies: Behavioral & Biomedical Issues†
0276-5624 Research in Social Stratification and Mobility **8128**
0276-5632 Middle East Policy Survey **7253**
0276-5675 D E S Litigation Reporter† **8948**
0276-5683 Thomas Wolfe Review **5388**
0276-5756 Computing Resources for the Professional†
0276-5853 E E O Report†
0276-590X La Opinion **3556**
0276-5918 L N G Digest **6776**
0276-5934 Daily Munger Oilogram **6766**
0276-5985 Oil in the Rockies†
0276-5993 Herold's Comparative Appraisal Reports - Sector 1
0276-606X Health of Kansas Chart Book†
0276-6256 Journal of Children in Contemporary Society†
0276-6280 Insurance Theft Report Passenger Cars, Cargo Vans, Pickups and Utility Vehicles **4508**
0276-6345 Syracuse Scholar†
0276-6353 Operating Room Research Institute. Journal†
0276-6361 Insurance Service Quarterly Review
0276-640X Illinois Aviation **8544**
0276-6469 U.S. Agency for International Development. Congressional Presentation, Fiscal Year **1606**
0276-6493 Georgia Genealogical Survey†
0276-6515 Richmond Quarterly **4311**

0276-6523 Washington Tribune changed to Washington Afro-American Newspaper **3572**
0276-6531 C D F Reports†
0276-6558 Studies in Visual Communications†
0276-6566 State and Metropolitan Area Data Book **7316**
0276-6574 Computers in Cardiology **5830**
0276-6582 Surfboard
0276-6612 Adweek: Midwest Edition changed to 1549-9553 **20**
0276-6701 S.O.S. Directory†
0276-6744 Yearbook of Podiatric Medicine and Surgery†
0276-6795 Ex Tempore†
0276-6949 Bibliography of the English-Speaking Caribbean†
0276-6957 Annual Estate Planning Institute **4900**
0276-6965 Probation and Parole Law Reports **4959**
0276-6973 California State Library Newsletter **5000**
0276-7031 New on the Charts **6599**
0276-7066 Network (Washington, 1981)
0276-7074 Driving Digest Magazine
0276-7090 Tournament Chess
0276-7120 Q C: The Magazine of Queens County
0276-7139 United States House of Representatives. Committee on the Budget. Activities and Summary Report **7474**
0276-7155 Southwestern Review **5376**
0276-718X Education Law Bulletin†
0276-7244 United States Postal Card Catalog
0276-7317 Industry International†
0276-7333 Organometallics **2128**
0276-7449 Journal of the Alleghenies **4300**
0276-7473 Recycling News†
0276-7546 National Law Review Reporter
0276-7554 Motions in Proteins, Peptides & Amino Acids†
0276-7562 Phase-Transfer Reactions†
0276-7570 U C M P Quarterly†
0276-7589 Effective Speech Writer's Newsletter†
0276-7597 Airbrush Digest
0276-7600 Wood Pulp and Fiber Statistics†
0276-7643 Sacred Heart University Review **4473**
0276-7651 State Laws and Published Ordinances, Firearms **4788**
0276-7783 M I S Quarterly **2523**
0276-7805 Directory of Faculty Contracts and Bargaining Agents in Institutions of Higher Education **4593**
0276-783X Directory of Consumer Finance Companies†
0276-7856 Chimeres: A Journal of French and Italian Literature†
0276-7872 Burrelle's Pennsylvania Media Directory (Year)†
0276-7910 Gavea - Brown **5299**
0276-7929 Southeastern Association of Fish and Wildlife Agencies. Proceedings **3609**
0276-7953 Journal of Industrial Fabrics†
0276-7961 Microwave World **3656**
0276-8135 Short-Timer's Journal†
0276-8151 Peter W. Rodino Institute of Criminal Justice. Annual Journal†
0276-816X Something About the Author **5375**
0276-8178 Twentieth-Century Literary Criticism **5391**
0276-8186 National Parks **4981**
0276-8259 Technology (Boulder)†
0276-8267 Computer State of the Art Reports†
0276-8275 Washington Tariff & Trade Letter **4944**
0276-8291 Abbey Newsletter†
0276-8313 Historical Journal of Massachusetts **4296**
0276-8356 Nevada Official Publications†
0276-8445 Code of Federal Regulations. Title 30, Mineral Resources **6460**
0276-8577 Comments on Geochemistry and Cosmochemistry†
0276-8585 Journal of Ecological and Life Chemistry†
0276-8593 Multichannel News **2385**
0276-8607 Occasional Publications in Northeastern Anthropology†
0276-8631 Specialized Transportation Planning and Practice†
0276-8704 Protein Semisynthesis†
0276-8712 Current Awareness Profile on Chemical Information†
0276-8739 Journal of Policy Analysis and Management **7448**
0276-8747 Opt
0276-8798 New York Agricultural Statistics **184**
0276-8852 Transportation Safety Information Report **8517**
0276-8860 Journal of Clinical Laboratory Automation†
0276-8879 Journal of Clinical Surgery†
0276-8887 Milieu Therapy†
0276-8895 Sports Afield Hunting†
0276-8917 Yachtsman's Pocket Almanac†
0276-8925 Physics: A Series of Monographs & Tracts
0276-8976 Applications of Management Science **1725**
0276-8992 Colorado Wildlife Research Review†
0276-9018 Fodor's Colorado†
0276-9042 Knife World **4338**
0276-9212 F A A Aviation Forecasts **54**
0276-9220 Borderlands Journal†
0276-9239 Modern Recording & Music's Buyer's Guide†
0276-928X Journal of Staff Development **1868**
0276-9387 Modern Technics in Surgery. Plastic Surgery†
0276-9433 Grower Talks Magazine **3735**
0276-9573 Indo-China Philatelist†
0276-9581 Reports of Cases Decided in the Appellate Division of the Supreme Court, State of New York **4959**
0276-959X Directory of Government Document Collections and Librarians **5006**
0276-9603 Juvenile Law Reports†
0276-9751 Advertising Age Yearbook†
0276-9883 Crime Digest†
0276-9905 In-Fisherman **8318**
0276-9913 Advances in Descriptive Psychology†
0276-993X Tennessee Williams Review†
0276-9948 University of Illinois Law Review **4804**
0276-9956 Enfo
0276-9964 Sunspeak†
0276-9972 Computer Publicity News†
0276-9980 The Almanac of Virginia Politics **7104**
0276-9999 The Almanac of Virginia Politics. Supplement see 0276-9980 **7104**
0277-0008 Pharmacotherapy **6872**
0277-0059 Micro Moonlighter†
0277-0121 Research in Urban Economics **7501**
0277-013X Lymphokines†

0278-1425 Professional Surveyor **4025**
0278-1433 Outside (Santa Fe) **8327**
0278-1468 Group of Thirty. Occasional Paper **1488**
0278-1557 Knowledge and Society **8116**
0278-1565 American Bus Association. Report†
0278-1581 Energy Information Directory (Year)†
0278-1603 Wildrows†
0278-1700 Contemporary Nephrology **6266**
0278-1743 Research Services Directory†
0278-176X Drug Law Reporter†
0278-1808 Focal Points†
0278-1816 Criminal Law Monthly†
0278-1832 Chemical Abstracts - Physical, Inorganic and Analytical Chemistry Sections **2093**
0278-1867 National Baseball Hall of Fame & Museum Yearbook **8239**
0278-1891 Pynchon Notes **5355**
0278-193X Working Mother **8892**
0278-1980 B Y U Studies†
0278-2200 American Enterprise Institute for Public Policy Research. Memorandum†
0278-2219 A S A News (Print) *changed to* 1942-4949 **3515**
0278-2251 Sephardic Scholar **7729**
0278-226X Platt's Energy Litigation Report†
0278-2308 International Social Science Review **7975**
0278-2324 Conjunctions **5277**
0278-2340 B I H E P†
0278-2359 Advances in the Psychology of Human Intelligence†
0278-2367 Advances in Personality Assessment†
0278-2375 Developments in Business Simulation & Experiential Exercises **2517**
0278-2383 Information and Referral **8046**
0278-2391 Journal of Oral and Maxillofacial Surgery **5852**
0278-2421 Ecos†
0278-2448 International Construction Week: Asia Construction Business Report†
0278-2456 International Construction Week: Latin America Construction Business Report†
0278-2464 International Construction Week: Mideast Construction Business Report†
0278-2618 Washington Letter on Latin America†
0278-2626 Brain and Cognition **7341**
0278-2693 Sports Collectors Digest **4347**
0278-2715 Health Affairs **7520**
0278-2731 International Research Centers Directory **2871**
0278-2774 Computer Graphics Marketplace†
0278-2790 Photographer's Market Newsletter†
0278-2820 Abstracts Strengthening Research Library Resources Program
0278-2839 Home† **8962**
0278-2863 Community Animal Control†
0278-2871 Rock Art†
0278-288X Nuevo Amanecer†
0278-2901 Journal of Photoacoustics†
0278-291X Rocky Mountain Symposium on Microcomputers: Systems, Software, Architecture. Proceedings†
0278-3126 School Age NOTES **2167**
0278-3134 Smith Papers†
0278-3177 New Hampshire Media Directory†
0278-3193 Roeper Review **3079**
0278-3231 International Series of Monographs in Pure and Applied Mathematics†
0278-324X Coral Reef Newsletter **784**
0278-3274 Novitates Arthropodae†
0278-3282 Spring (Emmaus)†
0278-3355 New York State Museum. Bulletin **7892**
0278-3398 Georgia Geological Survey. Information Circular **2743**
0278-3452 Health Devices Sourcebook **5625**
0278-3487 U.S. Nuclear Regulatory Commission. Licensed Operating Reactors. Status Summary Report†
0278-3509 Mergent International Manual and News Reports **1639**
0278-3517 Moody's International News Reports **1640**
0278-355X Property & Liability Insurance Index†
0278-3630 Ebsconet Newsletter†
0278-3649 International Journal of Robotics Research **2585**
0278-3703 Oregon. Department of Geology and Mineral Industries. Special Papers **2761**
0278-372X How to Find Information About Companies **1119**
0278-3738 Neuroscience Newsletter *changed to* Neuroscience Quarterly **6169**
0278-3819 Transportation Studies
0278-3916 *see* Law - Technology **4845**
0278-4017 Science and Technology Series **70**
0278-4092 Connecticut Nursing News **5956**
0278-4114 Loose Change†
0278-4149 Legal Systems Letter†
0278-4165 Journal of Anthropological Archaeology **344**
0278-4173 Hot Water Review **5424**
0278-4203 Famous Monsters **6497**
0278-4238 Translations Index *changed to* 1352-7940
0278-4246 Ruralamerica†
0278-4254 Journal of Accounting and Public Policy **1293**
0278-4262 Astrology for the 80's†
0278-4289 Annals of Public Administration†
0278-4297 Journal of Ultrasound in Medicine **6201**
0278-4300 Ecology of Disease†
0278-4319 International Journal of Hospitality Management **4391**
0278-4343 Continental Shelf Research **2802**
0278-436X J A P O S Bulletin†
0278-4378 Source I
0278-4386 Source II
0278-4408 Northern Sun News
0278-4424 Manufacturing Technology Horizons†
0278-4432 Mendy and the Golem
0278-4440 Organizing Notes†
0278-4491 Environmental Progress (New York) *changed to* 1944-7442 **3427**
0278-4521 Energy Progress†
0278-4602 Psychiatry Digest†
0278-4645 Selected Papers From the Annual Meeting *changed to* 1540-7942 **7682**
0278-4653 Annual Editions: Health **6982**
0278-4661 Annual Editions: Human Development **919**
0278-467X Tours and Visits Directory†
0278-4750 Problems of Desert Development†
0278-4777 Louisiana Geological Survey. Resources Information Series **2753**
0278-4807 Rehabilitation Nursing **5979**
0278-4858 Washington State Library News†
0278-4882 Occasional Papers in Middle Eastern Librarianship†
0278-4912 U.S. National Center for Health Statistics. Catalog of Publications **7575**
0278-4947 What's Cooking in Congress?
0278-4998 Pediatric Mental Health†
0278-5013 Video Age International **2398**
0278-503X Cable T V Programming†
0278-5048 Sales Rep's Advisor† **8986**
0278-5099 Energy & Minerals Resources†
0278-5226 Journal of Arboriculture *changed to* 1935-5297 **3723**
0278-5234 U.S. National Center for Health Statistics. Vital and Health Statistics. Series 23. Data from the National Survey of Family Growth **7550**
0278-5277 Criminal Justice Career Digest†
0278-5293 Electronic Education†
0278-5307 Libertas Mathematica **5509**
0278-5439 International Business Report **1570**
0278-551X Axios **7703**
0278-5641 O'Casey Annual†
0278-565X Pockets **7771**
0278-5676 Microwave Discontinued Devices D.A.T.A. Book†
0278-5692 U.S. Federal Deposit Insurance Corporation. Trust Assets of Banks and Trust Companies **1388**
0278-5706 Job Catalog
0278-5749 Training and Development Organizations Directory†
0278-5846 Progress in Neuro-Psychopharmacology & Biological Psychiatry **6876**
0278-5919 Clinics in Sports Medicine **6229**
0278-5927 Journal of American Ethnic History **3544**
0278-5943 American Classical Studies **2229**
0278-5994 Diesel & Gas Turbine Worldwide **3376**
0278-6079 Nightsun **5341**
0278-6087 Journal of Business Forecasting Methods and Systems *changed to* 1930-126X **1134**
0278-6125 Journal of Manufacturing Systems **3386**
0278-6133 Health Psychology **7360**
0278-6168 National Council on Family Relations. Report **8122**
0278-6265 Chemical Industry Institute of Toxicology Series†
0278-6273 Laser Chemistry **7079**
0278-6281 Life Chemistry Reports†
0278-632X Kidstuff†
0278-6397 Reruns
0278-6419 Moscow University Computational Mathematics and Cybernetics **2527**
0278-6516 Who's Who in the Motion Picture Industry **6517**
0278-6524 Market Guide Continental Europe†
0278-6567 Financial Statements and Operating Ratios for the Mortgage Banking Industry†
0278-6591 Universal Black Writer†
0278-6613 Maverick Guide to Hawaii†
0278-663X Terrorism†
0278-6648 I E E E Potentials **3313**
0278-6656 Classical Antiquity **2232**
0278-6680 International Country Risk Guide **1492**
0278-6729 Springer Series on Behavior Therapy and Behavioral Medicine† **8990**
0278-6745 Legal Notes and Viewpoints Quarterly†
0278-6826 Aerosol Science and Technology **2049**
0278-6850 PharmAlert
0278-6915 Food and Chemical Toxicology **3497**
0278-6990 The American Freshman: National Norms (Year) **2966**
0278-7016 Raise the Stakes **3462**
0278-7024 Cleveland Electrical/Electronics Conference and Exposition. Conference Record†
0278-7067 Welding and Fabricating Data Book†
0278-7091 Geoscience Texts† **8959**
0278-7121 Publishing Abstracts†
0278-713X Special Report to the U S Congress on Alcohol and Health from the Secretary of Health and Human Services **2699**
0278-7210 Children's Legal Rights Journal **4908**
0278-7261 Critica Hispanica **5280**
0278-7334 Parks & Recreation Resources†
0278-7393 Journal of Experimental Psychology: Learning, Memory, and Cognition **7373**
0278-7407 Tectonics **2791**
0278-7431 Western Pennsylvania Genealogical Society Quarterly
0278-7490 Better Homes and Gardens Holiday Crafts **531**
0278-7601 Growth Capital
0278-761X Minnesota Family Law Journal **4913**
0278-7628 Minnesota Real Estate Law Journal† **8974**
0278-7660 Vistas†
0278-7695 Decisions of the Federal Labor Relations Authority **1674**
0278-7784 Religious Socialism **7177**
0278-7946 O M S Annual Report†
0278-8004 West's Washington Legislative Service **7505**
0278-8047 World Technology†
0278-8071 Blue Grass Roots **3760**
0278-808X Medical Device Register **5668**
0278-8128 American Showcase Illustration *changed to* 1554-6268 **517**
0278-8209 Patient Education Newsletter†
0278-8225 Mainstream (San Diego)†
0278-825X Electronic & Electrical Engineering Research Studies. Pattern Recognition and Image Processing Series **3304**
0278-8292 Chemometrics Series†
0278-8381 Economic Indicators (Charleston) **1480**
0278-839X Journal of Social, Political and Economic Studies **7148**
0278-8403 The Behavior Therapist **7339**
0278-842X Who's Who in Special Libraries† **8998**
0278-8799 Dun's Industrial Guide - The Metalworking Directory **1989**
0278-8888 Annual Insider Index to Public Policy Studies†
0278-8950 Light Plane Maintenance **65**
0278-8969 Afro-Hispanic Review **3517**
0278-8985 American Association of Engineering Societies. Engineering Workforce Commission. Engineering and Technology Enrollments (Year) **3181**
0278-9000 American Academy of Dermatology. Directory **5871**
0278-906X Handbook of Food Preparation†
0278-9078 Ethnic Forum†
0278-9132 Global Atmospheric Background Monitoring for Selected Environmental Parameters. B A P Mo N Data
0278-9140 Local Climatological Data. Jackson, Kentucky. Annual Summary with Comparative Data **6373**
0278-9159 Local Climatological Data. Jackson, Kentucky. Monthly Summary **6373**
0278-9213 Cross Country Skier **8310**
0278-937X Washington Papers **7272**
0278-940X Critical Reviews in Biomedical Engineering **748**
0278-9426 Glass Art Society Journal **491**
0278-9434 Transportation Quarterly **8516**
0278-9442 Yet Another Small Magazine **5246**
0278-9469 PALINET News **5063**
0278-9485 Livability Digest†
0278-9507 American Ceramics
0278-9566 Bi-Annual Review of Allergy†
0278-9612 Wrestling's Main Event†
0278-9620 Science and Engineering Personnel **1707**
0278-9647 Computer Technology Review **2412**
0278-9671 Literature and Medicine **5325**
0278-9728 Biotechnology Press Digest†
0278-9736 Agricultural Genetics Report†
0278-9752 Borgo Political Scenarios†
0278-9779 Medico Interamericano **5675**
0278-9795 Rug News **8456**
0278-9884 Official Pencil Puzzles and Word Games†
0278-9892 The Washington Blade **4380**
0278-9922 Electronic Servicing & Technology†
0278-999X Management (Los Angeles)†
0279-0033 Pennsylvania Journal of Health, Physical Education, Recreation and Dance **3076**
0279-0106 Arbor Age **3683**
0279-0203 Chihuahua News†
0279-0211 Tax News **1949**
0279-022X T S T A Advocate **2917**
0279-0238 The Giants Newsweekly†
0279-0246 The California Eye **7112**
0279-0254 Open Wheel **8597**
0279-0327 Typographer†
0279-0459 Religious Life **7814**
0279-0467 Labor and Investments†
0279-0483 Orange Coast Magazine **3984**
0279-0491 Illinois Vocational Education Journal†
0279-0521 Professional Geologist **2762**
0279-053X Screenprinting & Graphic Imaging Association International Tabloid *changed to* 1544-0060 **7327**
0279-0548 Services **1035**
0279-0556 Poetry Magazine
0279-0645 Catholic Voice (Oakland) **7790**
0279-0653 Purple Heart Magazine **6442**
0279-067X Essex Genealogist **3765**
0279-0688 Education and Psychological Research†
0279-0696 Info (Nordman)†
0279-070X Computers and Programming†
0279-0718 Black Family
0279-0734 Media General Financial Weekly†
0279-0750 Pacific Philosophical Quarterly **6938**
0279-0785 The Chamber Today **1399**
0279-0815 Uncle Sam
0279-0858 Clavier's Piano Explorer **6557**
0279-0882 Rhode Island Lawyers Weekly **4775**
0279-0939 Commodex System **1617**
0279-0947 Commodity Futures Forecast Service **1617**
0279-0998 Sporting Classics **8335**
0279-1021 C P A Marketing Report **1809**
0279-103X Objector†
0279-1072 Journal of Psychoactive Drugs **2696**
0279-1102 Construction Litigation Reporter **996**
0279-1153 College and Junior Tennis **8225**
0279-1161 California English **3053**
0279-1188 Hawaii Coastal Zone News†
0279-1196 Communicare†
0279-1226 Avenue **3970**
0279-1242 Hard Hat News **1011**
0279-1250 Letters Magazine (Teaneck) **6294**
0279-1293 Serbian Struggle†
0279-1323 Orlando Magazine *changed to* 1059-3624 **8745**
0279-1382 Executive Report†
0279-1420 Buying for the Farm†
0279-1447 Robb Report **3987**
0279-1501 N L B A News†
0279-151X Radio World. International Edition†
0279-1552 Buildings Journal†
0279-1579 Unisphere†
0279-1633 The Land **132**
0279-1692 A H C A Notes **8022**
0279-1749 Sportsman Pilot **72**
0279-1773 Michigan Runner **8322**
0279-1889 The Bottomline **1281**
0279-2028 Skill† **8988**
0279-2109 Tax Ideas **1948**
0279-2125 New Health
0279-2133 Stateways **610**
0279-2176 Truck & Equipment Salesman†
0279-2230 Federal Career Opportunities **6697**
0279-2257 Juvenile and Family Law Digest **4912**
0279-2338 Saving Energy†
0279-2346 Missouri. Department of Agriculture. Weekly Market Summary **137**
0279-2419 Northern Line **3457**
0279-2427 Exempt Organizations Reports *changed to* Exempt Organizations Reports Library **1923**
0279-246X Epic Illustrated†
0279-2656 California. Agricultural Statistics Service. Crop Weather Report **176**
0279-2664 Interact **2574**

ISSN

0281-5893 Stoppa Rasismen **3566**
0281-5923 Maanadens Standard†
0281-627X I L G A Bulletin **4375**
0281-6296 Stockholms Universitet. Pedagogiska Institutionen. Seminariet om Miljoepedagofik och Kunskapsbildning. Rapport **2915**
0281-658X Bygg & Teknik **987**
0281-6768 Umeaa Universitet. Pedagogiska Institutionen. Akademiska Avhandlingar **2921**
0281-6814 Working Papers in African Studies **8015**
0281-6873 D I K - Forum **5004**
0281-6881 Sweden. Sjukvaardens och Socialvaardens Planerings- och Rationaliseringsinstitut. S P R I Tryck†
0281-6903 Faaglar i Norrbotten **906**
0281-6989 Svenskt Naeringsliv *changed to* 1651-9264 **1879**
0281-7020 Klinik och Terapi foer Tandlaekare†
0281-7241 Nordisk Papperskalender *changed to* 1652-7259 **6735**
0281-7276 Nya Byggregler **1048**
0281-7403 M C - Folket **8260**
0281-7411 Gurklisten **8618**
0281-7446 Arbetarhistoria **4590**
0281-7489 Socialistiskt Perspektiv†
0281-7519 S V A Vet **8807**
0281-7578 Information **2783**
0281-7632 Nyheter Fraan Nicaragua **4306**
0281-7691 TS-Boken **7579**
0281-7888 Oehman Guide†
0281-790X Faaglar i Blekinge **906**
0281-7993 Bistaandsantropologen†
0281-806X Lantbruksekonomen†
0281-8205 Noetkoett **141**
0281-8515 Energy, Environment and Development in Africa†
0281-871X Sportskytten **8208**
0281-9198 Tekniska Museet. Rapportserie **3223**
0281-9341 Illustrerad Vetenskap **7864**
0281-9422 Nordisk Tidskrift foer Folkbildning och Vuxenundervisning†
0281-966X Linkoeping Universitet. Department of Water and Environmental Studies. Tema V Report **8828**
0281-9902 Saharabulletinen *changed to* 1652-2052 **4179**
0282-0005 Gustaf **2191**
0282-0080 Glycoconjugate Journal **733**
0282-0099 Kommunal Ekonomi **7495**
0282-020X Presshistorisk Aarsbok **4582**
0282-0226 Dialekt-, Ortnamns- och Folkminnesarkivet i Umeaa. Skrifter. Serie D, Meddelanden **5111**
0282-0234 Kateketnytt **7803**
0282-0390 Restauranger & Storkoek **3662**
0282-0463 Sydasien **4189**
0282-0536 Bilismen i Sverige **8569**
0282-0595 Kyrkogaarden **3720**
0282-0668 E F S Missionstidning Budbaeraren **7755**
0282-082X Windahlia *changed to* 1653-0357 **819**
0282-0889 Gnosis†
0282-0900 Race and Cruising Segling *changed to* Segling **8282**
0282-0919 Svensk Reklamtaxa **636**
0282-1168 Rent **2244**
0282-1184 Naalsoegat†
0282-1192 Motstaand†
0282-1354 Aelvraeddaren **3401**
0282-1524 Foereningen Svenska Atheninstitutets Vaenner. Skriftserie **4219**
0282-1540 Acidification Research in Sweden†
0282-1575 Axplock **5259**
0282-2024 Sweden. Statens Jaernvaegars Huvudkontor. Geoteknik och Ingenjoergeologi. Meddelanden†
0282-2113 Miljoetidningen **3453**
0282-227X Groblad **5302**
0282-258X Fjaerde Vaerlden **3534**
0282-2628 Aluminium Scandinavia **6304**
0282-2768 Affaersideer†
0282-3454 Aarets Skisport†
0282-3489 Sweden. Statistiska Centralbyraan. Statistiska Meddelanden. Serie N, Nationalraekenskaperna **1269**
0282-3497 Sweden. Statistiska Centralbyraan. Statistiska Meddelanden. Serie O, Offentliga Finanser **1269**
0282-3500 Sweden. Statistiska Centralbyraan. Statistiska Meddelanden. Serie Na, Naturresurser och Miljoe **3481**
0282-3519 Sweden. Statistiska Centralbyraan. Statistiska Meddelanden. Serie Ku, Kultur **362**
0282-390X Naturhistoriska Riksmuseet. Ringmaerkningscentralen. Report of Swedish Bird Ringing **910**
0282-3926 Bladmagen **8794**
0282-3934 Baatliv **8272**
0282-4108 Svensk Tull **1946**
0282-4132 Lantbrukspraktika **134**
0282-4175 Guldsmedstidningen†
0282-423X Journal of Official Statistics **8383**
0282-440X Klinisk Kemi **5658**
0282-4434 Statens Straalskyddsinstitut. S S I-Rapport **7470**
0282-4485 Landstingsvaerlden *changed to* 1652-6511 **7491**
0282-454X Barnen Framfoer Allt **8027**
0282-4582 Bergslagspoeten†
0282-4655 Initiativ†
0282-4760 Faaglar i Jaemtland - Haerjedalen **906**
0282-4809 Svensk Bridge **8210**
0282-4906 Exlibriscirkulaeret **5009**
0282-4922 Skrifter Utgivna av Stiftelsen Hallands Laensmuseer, Halmstad och Varberg **4264**
0282-4949 Restaurang & Storhushaall - Nytt *changed to* 1654-6350 **4396**
0282-4973 Universitetslaeraren **2922**
0282-5066 Studia Baltica Stockholmiensia **5179**
0282-5090 Hypnos **5943**
0282-5449 Hasselblad Forum (English Edition) **6969**
0282-5554 Faaglar i Medelpad **906**
0282-5678 Sportscar **8208**
0282-5783 Drug Effects in Clinical Chemistry†
0282-5813 Sveriges Stoersta Foeretag **2029**
0282-5856 Vaermlaendsk Kultur **4276**
0282-5902 Kulturens Vaerld **501**
0282-6062 Res Publica **5236**
0282-6135 Studie-Cirkeln *changed to* 1652-1595 **2837**
0282-6283 C B I Informerar **988**
0282-6364 Audio, Video†
0282-6372 Nytt fraan Industrifoerbundet†
0282-6534 Statens Musiksamlingar. Musikmuseet. Rapporter **6619**
0282-6607 Journal of Social and Administrative Pharmacy. Supplement†
0282-6623 Studia Multiethnica Upsaliensia **3566**
0282-6747 Arkitekttavlingar†
0282-6860 Gotarc. Serie B, Gothenburg Archaeological Theses **395**
0282-7271 Allmaenna Raad *changed to* 1650-2361 **3455**
0282-7298 Sweden. Naturvaardsverket. Rapport **3469**
0282-7301 Fynd **6524**
0282-7336 Aktuell Saekerhet **1725**
0282-7344 Calidris Supplement *see* 0346-9395 **905**
0282-7476 Comprehensive Summaries of Uppsala Dissertations from the Faculty of Medicine **5599**
0282-7484 Comprehensive Summaries of Uppsala Dissertations from the Faculty of Pharmacy **6830**
0282-7492 Comprehensive Summaries of Uppsala Dissertations from the Faculty of Social Sciences (Print Edition) *changed to* 1652-9030 **7959**
0282-7581 Scandinavian Journal of Forest Research **3701**
0282-7662 Varghunden **6816**
0282-8006 Strindbergiana **5378**
0282-8057 Nationellt Pistolskytte *changed to* 1404-8647 **8189**
0282-8154 Stadsarkivets Skriftserie *changed to* 1653-5464 **4276**
0282-8200 Antik & Auktion **362**
0282-8278 Studier i Arbetarroerelsens Historia
0282-860X Aarets Ishockey **8156**
0282-8677 Studies in Plant Ecology†
0282-8731 N I A Informerar†
0282-8839 Baltic Marine Biologists. Publication **656**
0282-888X Benelux Rail **8615**
0282-8928 Uppsala Dissertations from the Faculty of Medicine **5727**
0282-8952 Statens Musiksamlingar. Musikmuseet. Skrifter **6619**
0282-910X Arbetarskyddsregler Byggarbete *changed to* 1654-4277 **6673**
0282-9134 M C M **8260**
0282-9479 Gotarc. Serie C, Arkeologiska Skrifter **395**
0282-9525 Nytt Juridiskt Arkiv. Avd. 1 - Raettsfall fraan Hoegsta Domstolen **4750**
0282-955X Miljoe och Haelsa **3453**
0282-9800 Linkoeping Studies in Arts and Science **4463**
0282-9967 Konjunkturen **1496**
0283-0175 S G I - Nu **2789**
0283-0302 Svensk Religionshistorisk Aarsskrift **7686**
0283-0345 Akademix **2966**
0283-0418 Kartbladet *changed to* 1651-8705 **4018**
0283-0558 BoRaett **4405**
0283-0647 Fib-Aktuellt **6290**
0283-071X Svensk Numismatisk Tidskrift **6653**
0283-0779 Norra Sveriges Affaerer & Foeretag†
0283-0892 Vaestra Sveriges Affaerer & Foeretag†
0283-0973 Sweden. Riksfoersaekringsverket. Anser *changed to* 1653-2937 **4969**
0283-1007 Small Scale Forestry†
0283-1015 Marathonloeparen **8186**
0283-104X Musikbiblioteksnytt **5033**
0283-1104 S M H I Reports. Hydrology **2798**
0283-1112 S M H I Reports. Oceanography **2817**
0283-1155 Brand & Raeddning **3575**
0283-1244 Studia Byzantina Upsaliensia **4269**
0283-1333 Antikvariatet **4989**
0283-149X Psychologia et Sociologia Religionum **7672**
0283-1503 Slitz **3956**
0283-1511 I V L Referat **3487**
0283-166X Drogfri Arbetsmiljoe†
0283-1724 Sveriges Lantbruksuniversitet. Skogsvetenskapliga Fakulteten. Rapport *changed to* 1653-008X **3704**
0283-1910 S S R - Tidningen *changed to* 1652-9898 **8024**
0283-1929 Socionomen **8072**
0283-1961 Nordiska Hoegskolan foer Folkhaelsovetenskap. N H V-Rapport **7534**
0283-202X Social Forskning **8002**
0283-2208 Svensk Innebandy **8210**
0283-2224 Sy & Sticka†
0283-2267 Massoeren
0283-2348 Faglar i Norrbotten. Supplement **907**
0283-2372 Internationell Revolution **7144**
0283-2380 Acta Philosophica Gothoburgensia **6902**
0283-2526 Svensk Musik (Print) *changed to* Svensk Musik (Online) **6621**
0283-2577 Economic Perspective on Scandinavia†
0283-2631 Nordic Pulp & Paper Research Journal **3714**
0283-2852 Faaglar i Kvismaren **906**
0283-2887 Konstnaeren **500**
0283-2925 Comunidad **7118**
0283-3190 S T I M - Nytt **6614**
0283-3298 Svenska Forskningsinstitutet i Istanbul. Skrifter
0283-3301 Forntida Teknik†
0283-3352 Brottsfoerebyggande Raadets Tidskrift Apropaa **2645**
0283-3387 Aperitif **4382**
0283-3395 Elevforum **2853**
0283-3484 Jabbok **7652**
0283-3492 Islandspostur **3877**
0283-3654 Qvartilen **8395**
0283-3883 Studentidrott **8210**
0283-4081 K K S - Meddelanden†
0283-4138 Beagle (Tyresoe) **6804**
0283-4146 Kammarmusik-Nytt *changed to* Musikant och Kammarmusik-Nytt **6596**
0283-4197 Handelspolitik†
0283-4251 Fakta om Folkvalda **7436**
0283-4391 Aktuellt foer Kontor†
0283-4529 Goeteborgs Stad. Stadskansliet. Boersmeddelanden†
0283-4537 Teknik och Kultur†
0283-4545 Ortodox Tidning **7705**
0283-4669 Verko **3399**
0283-474X Gitarr och Luta **6569**
0283-4995 Uppsala Women's Studies. B, Women in the Humanities **8904**
0283-5088 R S V -Nytt *changed to* 1653-8447 **1943**
0283-5193 Bokfoermedlaren†
0283-5207 Dialoger **8469**
0283-5215 Biogen†
0283-5363 V - Byggaren **3287**
0283-5371 Ankkuri†
0283-541X Sjukskoetersketidningen†
0283-5452 Skydd & Saekerhet **2681**
0283-5533 Vasaloeparen **8339**
0283-5576 Taxi Idag **8512**
0283-572X Habit Butik†
0283-5762 Dekanalen **7637**
0283-5835 Country News†
0283-5843 God News from Sweden†
0283-586X International Society of Arctic Char Fanatics. Information Series **948**
0283-5983 Filmjournalen†
0283-6025 Vest **7928**
0283-6335 Kometen†
0283-636X Droemmen om Elin **1093**
0283-6408 Kaervent†
0283-653X Opsis Kalopsis **2163**
0283-6580 Marknadspolitik†
0283-6726 Agora†
0283-6750 Droemskrinet **5286**
0283-684X Salaam **7716**
0283-6874 Lund Studies in Medieval Archaeology *changed to* 1653-1183 **404**
0283-6890 Babian†
0283-6971 Afghaner **6802**
0283-7129 Haent Extra **3955**
0283-7234 Nordtest. N T Techn Report **3213**
0283-751X Valoer **524**
0283-7560 Fria Tider **4977**
0283-7587 Revansch! **6181**
0283-7692 Studies of Higher Education and Research†
0283-7714 S M H I Oceanografi **2817**
0283-7722 S M H I Hydrologi **2798**
0283-7730 S M H I Meteorologi **6394**
0283-7803 Svensk Leverantoerstidning **1845**
0283-7846 Kyrkfack **7764**
0283-7862 Carlshamniana **4134**
0283-7986 Tidningen Trafikmagasinet **8635**
0283-7994 Fraan Ransberg och Kirkefalla **4221**
0283-8117 Drug Abuse *changed to* Nordrug 2000 (Print)
0283-8273 Wycliffe Rapport *changed to* 1651-8365 **7643**
0283-8389 Svenska Institutet i Rom. Skrifter. Series Altera in 8o **4272**
0283-8400 Militaerhistorisk Tidskrift **4245**
0283-8486 Journal of Prehistoric Religion **401**
0283-8494 Studies in Mediterranean Archaeology and Literature. Pocket-Book Series **419**
0283-8567 Arena (Stockholm, 1986)†
0283-8605 Sweden. Statistiska Centralbyraan. Statistiska Meddelanden. Serie S, Socialtjaenst och Socialfoersaekring **8084**
0283-8664 Bokboden **5265**
0283-877X I V L Rapport. B **3487**
0283-880X Konjunkturen Verkstadsindustrin†
0283-8958 Lapphunden **6810**
0283-8974 Research Institute of Industrial Economics. Yearbook *changed to* 1654-0824 **1889**
0283-8982 Valda Avhandlingar **822**
0283-913X Foeretagsskoeterskan **5959**
0283-9318 Scandinavian Journal of Caring Sciences **5710**
0283-944X Uppsala Women's Studies. A, Women in Religion **8904**
0283-9571 Friluftsliv, i Alla Vaeder **8315**
0283-9830 Distriktlaekaren **5606**
0283-9865 Sirenen **3581**
0283-989X Sydfoerfattaren **5384**
0284-0049 Tidningen Fotboll†
0284-0103 R A Rapporter†
0284-0162 Boersinsikt **1613**
0284-0235 Nordisk Sattelit- och Kabel-TV-Nytt†
0284-0413 Reklambyraaer i Sverige *changed to* 1650-7924 **22**
0284-0448 Bergsmannen med Jernkontorets Annaler **6458**
0284-0618 S P O V†
0284-0693 Bulletin foer Socialistisk Politik†
0284-0707 Reflexen **8634**
0284-0758 Scan Ref **4126**
0284-088X Nya Budkavle†
0284-0901 Mjoelkspegeln
0284-1215 Flygbranschen **56**
0284-1428 Arte et Marte **3759**
0284-1541 University of Stockholm. Center for Pacific Asia Studies. Occasional Paper **4190**
0284-155X University of Stockholm. Center for Pacific Asia Studies. Working Papers **4190**
0284-169X Swedish Institute of Space Physics. Annual Report **2790**
0284-1703 Swedish Institute of Space Physics. I R F Scientific Report **2790**
0284-1711 Swedish Institute of Space Physics. Preprint†
0284-172X Swedish Institute of Space Physics. Software Report†
0284-1738 Swedish Institute of Space Physics. I R F Technical Report **2790**
0284-1827 R V F-Nytt *changed to* 1654-5087 **3504**
0284-1843 Svensk Skogsteknik *changed to* 1650-8092 **3704**
0284-1851 Acta Radiologica **6192**
0284-186X Acta Oncologica **6007**
0284-2270 Skrot och Miljoeteknik†
0284-2319 Fotbollmagasinet *changed to* 1651-4459 **8238**
0284-2785 Bygg-magasinet†
0284-2807 Foeretagsmagasinet†
0284-284X Skolhaelsan **5981**
0284-2955 Q.S.
0284-3005 Macworld Sweden **2577**
0284-3242 Argus (Dalaroe) **6519**
0284-3366 Ovako Steel A B. Technical Report **6328**
0284-3765 Bataljonsbladet **6413**

ISSN

0286-4266 Seiji Keizai Shigaku **4160**
0286-4339 Iwate University Forests. Bulletin **3694**
0286-4444 Aomoriken Seibutsu Gakkaishi **653**
0286-4487 Rigaku Senkoka Zasshi†
0286-4568 Kyoto Daigaku. Reichorui Kenkyujo Nenpo **346**
0286-4622 Kenchiku Kenkyujo Nenpo **1019**
0286-4630 Kenchiku Kenkyu Shiryo **1019**
0286-4673 Computerworld Japan†
0286-4754 Eiyo Seiri Kenkyukaiho **286**
0286-4827 Tokai Monthly Economic Letter†
0286-4835 Kino Zairyo **3351**
0286-486X Login **2431**
0286-5092 Tezukayama Tanki Daigaku Kiyo. Shizen Kagaku Hen **7923**
0286-5122 New Electronic Products Japan **3326**
0286-522X Bulletin of Informatics and Cybernetics **5476**
0286-5300 Omni Japan†
0286-5394 Kansetsu Geka **6066**
0286-5408 Environmental Research Center Papers **3428**
0286-5491 Hakodate Technical College. Research Reports **8423**
0286-5548 Koshien Daigaku Kiyo/Koshien University. Bulletin *changed to* 0913-5537 **6662**
0286-5629 Denkai Chikudenki Hyoron†
0286-5769 Kumamoto Daigaku Kyoyobu Kiyo. Shizen Kagaku Hen **7877**
0286-5858 Shika Zairyo, Kikai **5865**
0286-5904 Tohoku Gakuin Daigaku Kogakubu Kenkyu Hokoku **3223**
0286-598X Solid State Technology (Japanese Edition)†
0286-6013 Zairyo Shisutemu **3228**
0286-6064 Shi Pawa†
0286-6102 Shokuchu Shokubutsu Kenkyukai Kaishi **817**
0286-6153 Iyakuhin Fukusayo Joho **6851**
0286-617X Kyoto Furitsu Kaiyo Senta Kenkyu Ronbun **2811**
0286-6226 Kyoiku Jissen†
0286-6293 Utsunomiya Daigaku Kyoyobu Kenkyu Hokoku. Dai-2-bu†
0286-6366 Seitoku Eiyo Tanki Daigaku Kiyo†
0286-6722 Hoshasen Kagaku (Tokyo) **2063**
0286-6773 Jimbun Ronkyu **4458**
0286-6943 Kogyo Toso **6718**
0286-7052 Nihon Rinsho Seiri Gakkai Zasshi **5687**
0286-7125 Niigata Rikagaku **7028**
0286-715X Recent Progress of Natural Sciences in Japan†
0286-7184 Seimitsu Chosa Hokokusho **6479**
0286-7303 Shizuoka Daigaku Kyoikugakubu Kenkyu Hokoku. Jinbun, Shakai Kagaku Hen **4475**
0286-7311 Shizuoka Daigaku Kyoikugakubu Kenkyu Hokoku. Shizen Kagaku Hen **7916**
0286-732X Shizuoka Daigaku Kyoikugakubu Kenkyu Hokoku. Kyoka Kyoikugaku Hen **2912**
0286-7400 Kokuritsu Rekishi Minzoku Hakubutsukan Kenkyu Hokoku **4185**
0286-7427 Marine Technology Research Abstracts & Index (MATRAX)†
0286-7486 Hikaku Ganka Kenkyu **6043**
0286-7656 Akitaken Ishikai Zasshi **5570**
0286-7737 Oyo Chishitsu **2761**
0286-7745 Kozui
0286-7761 Seibutsu Fukuoka **703**
0286-780X Kyushu Sangyo Daigaku Kyoyobu Kiyo/Kyushu Sangyo University. College of Liberal Arts. Bulletin *changed to* 1340-9425 **7250**
0286-7877 Will **1801**
0286-7966 Kankeigaku Kenkyu **4461**
0286-8016 Daiichi Yakka Daigaku Kenkyu Nenpo†
0286-8172 Rikusui Seibutsugakuho **701**
0286-8180 Kyushu Tokai Daigaku Nogakubu Kiyo **132**
0286-8202 Nihon Rinsho Eiyo Gakkai Zasshi **6664**
0286-8210 Japan Semiconductor Technology News†
0286-8385 Sabo Gakkaishi **3282**
0286-8474 Ryokakusen **8659**
0286-8660 Ishikawa-ken Hakusan Shizen Hogo Senta Kenkyu Hokoku **2615**
0286-8768 Tokyo-to Takao Shizen Kagaku Hakubutsukan Kenkyu Hokoku **7924**
0286-8873 Hoshasen to Sangyo **7066**
0286-8970 Kagoshima Joshi Tanki Daigaku Kiyo **4461**
0286-9152 Kaiji Sangyo Kenkyujoho **8649**
0286-9179 Kotsuzai Shigen **3277**
0286-9187 Aichi Ika Daigaku Kiso Kagakuka Kiyo **5570**
0286-9306 Bifidobacteria and Microflora *changed to* 1342-1441 **661**
0286-9314 Kokyu **6215**
0286-9500 Kuoku†
0286-9543 Iwate Iho **5642**
0286-9640 University of the Ryukyus. College of Science. Bulletin **5545**
0286-9659 Oputoronikusu **7083**
0286-9667 African Study Monographs. Supplementary Issue **323**
0286-9713 Soshiki Kagaku **1794**
0286-9810 Konchugaku Hyoron **853**
0286-9837 Mikkyo Bunka **7702**
0286-9853 Studies in British & American Literature **5380**
0287-0002 Fukuoka Daigaku Sogo Kenkyujoho. Shizen Kagaku Hen **5488**
0287-0029 Japan. Ministry of Agriculture, Forestry and Fisheries. National Research Institute of Agricultural Engineering. Technical Report **212**
0287-0142 Societe Franco-Japonaise de Geographie. Bulletin
0287-0185 Arerugia
0287-024X Asahikawa Shiritsu Byoin Ishi **5579**
0287-0266 Yasukawa Denki **3334**
0287-041X Japan Foundrymen's Society. Transactions†
0287-0517 Environmental Medicine **5609**
0287-0606 Hozon Kagaku **2613**
0287-0894 Iyakuhin Kenkyu **5642**
0287-0916 Oita Daigaku Keizai Kenkyusho Kenkyujcho **1156**
0287-0932 Kaigai Jijo Kenkyu **7249**
0287-0940 Daito Hogaku **4654**
0287-1092 Nishinihon Sekitsui Kenkyukaishi **6068**
0287-1122 Kyoka Kyoiku Kenkyu†
0287-1173 Tohoku no Nogyo Kisho **6396**
0287-119X Seibutsu Kyoiku **703**
0287-122X Nichinairen Joho **3391**
0287-1238 Japanese Cosmetic Science Society. Journal **594**
0287-1319 Nagasaki Daigaku Kyoyobu Kiyo. Shizen Kagaku Hen **7885**
0287-1394 Oosaka Sangyo Daigaku Ronshu. Shizen Kagaku Hen **7895**
0287-1467 Tokai Daigaku Kaiyo Kenkyujo Nenpo **2819**
0287-1513 Institute for the Comprehensive Study of Lotus Sutra. Journal **7701**
0287-1521 Iryo to Fukushi **5642**
0287-1564 Nihon Musen Giho **2361**
0287-1629 Poetica **5161**
0287-1645 Bessatsu Seikei Geka **6056**
0287-1688 Tottori-kenritsu Hakubutsukan Kenkyu Hokoku **7924**
0287-170X Kyoryo to Kiso **3278**
0287-1777 Ishikawa Kenritsu Chuo Byoin Igakushi **5642**
0287-1785 I C M R Annals†
0287-203X Marine Engineer **8651**
0287-2064 Josai Jinbun Kenkyu **4459**
0287-2099 Tokai Daigaku Kaiyo Kagaku Hakubutsukan Nenpo **2818**
0287-2137 Kikanshigaku **6215**
0287-2153 Doai Igaku Zasshi†
0287-2218 Bijutsu Techo **478**
0287-2285 Kossetsu **6066**
0287-2293 Kaiyo Kansoku Deta†
0287-2358 Kapuseru **6857**
0287-2404 L T C B Research **1897**
0287-2420 J A L T Journal **5131**
0287-2609 J O D C News **2808**
0287-2633 Kaijo Hoancho. Suirobu Kansoku Hokoku. Tenmon Sokuchi Hen **2785**
0287-2706 Eigo Seinen **5114**
0287-2846 Denchi Kigu†
0287-2900 Utan **7927**
0287-3052 Needs **7891**
0287-3125 Kogyo Shoyukenho Kenkyu **6754**
0287-3214 Nihon Ryumachi Kansetsu Geka Gakkai Zasshi **6225**
0287-3257 Nippon Shida no Kai Kaiho **805**
0287-3427 Toyoda Gosei Giho **8608**
0287-3494 Fuji Takerui Shokubutsuen Hokoku **790**
0287-3516 Nippon Eiyo Shokuryo Gakkaishi **6664**
0287-3532 Iwatani Naoji Kinen Zaidan Kenkyu Hokokusho **7869**
0287-3672 Toa Nyusu†
0287-3796 Saibo Kogaku **770**
0287-4075 Atypus†
0287-4466 Setsunan University. Scientific Review. Series A, Natural Sciences†
0287-4474 Setsunan University. Scientific Review. Series B, Human Studies and Social Sciences†
0287-4547 Dental Materials Journal **5840**
0287-4660 Kikan Suiro
0287-4733 Kowan **3277**
0287-4741 Iyaku Journal **6851**
0287-475X Oosaka-fu Suisan Shikenjo. Kenkyu Hokoku **3604**
0287-4970 Kishu Seibutsu **686**
0287-5063 Ishikawa Koshi Gijutsu Nyusu **3203**
0287-5098 R N O D C Newsletter for WestPac **2816**
0287-5128 Japan Shipbuilding Information Notes†
0287-5187 Hakuyo Kogyo
0287-5195 Hakuyo Kogyo Sokuho
0287-5276 Umi no Kisho **6397**
0287-5306 Kinyu Kenkyu **1364**
0287-5330 Nihon Kango Kagakkaishi **5971**
0287-5349 Kuroshio (Wakayamaken) **686**
0287-5357 Sophia Linguistica **5176**
0287-5594 Mediya Sakuru†
0287-5632 Tottori Seibutsu **708**
0287-5802 J M A Janaru **1762**
0287-590X Sagyosen **8659**
0287-5950 Igaku to Kikai†
0287-6000 Ryukoku Daigaku Ronshu **3000**
0287-6108 Mie University. Fisheries Research Laboratory. Report **955**
0287-6132 Shokaki Shudan Kenshin *changed to* 1345-4110 **5929**
0287-623X Nihonkaiiki Kenkyujo Hokoku **2814**
0287-6256 Chiikigaku Kenkyu **4002**
0287-6280 Funtai to Kogyo **3193**
0287-637X Shishunkigaku **2168**
0287-6450 Denpa Koho **8642**
0287-6477 Kakocho **853**
0287-6485 Kusuri no Chishiki
0287-6507 Kobe University. Graduate School of Science and Technology. Memoirs. Series A **8430**
0287-6515 Kobe Daigaku Daigakuin Shizen Kagaku Kenkyuka Kiyo B **7877**
0287-6531 Kagawa Seibutsu **685**
0287-6760 Ido no Nippon **310**
0287-6779 Galaxea†
0287-7007 Waseda Seiji Keizaigaku Zasshi **7193**
0287-7023 Shogaku Shushi **1174**
0287-7082 Kanagawa University. Institute for Humanities Research. Bulletin **4461**
0287-7112 Japan Press Weekly: News & Comments **3900**
0287-718X Rikagakkaishi **7904**
0287-7406 Sumitomo Bank Economic Survey†
0287-7651 Kiso Shinrigaku Kenkyu **7382**
0287-7775 Seicho **703**
0287-7805 Tsudajuku Daigaku Kiyo **7925**
0287-7902 Kyoto Sangyo Daigaku Ronshu. Shizen Kagaku Keiretsu **7878**
0287-802X Chosen Shogakkai Gakujutsu Ronbunshu **5478**
0287-8119 Chuki Keizai Yosoku **1447**
0287-816X Shimane Daigaku Chishitsugaku Kenkyu Hokoku **2767**
0287-8305 Un'yu to Keizai **8519**
0287-8313 Nihon Neji Kenkyu Kyokaishi **3391**
0287-8321 Jidosha Gijutsukai Ronbunshu **8587**
0287-8445 Karento Terapi **5656**
0287-8585 Trigger **8444**
0287-864X Nihon Rikagaku Kyokai. Kenkyu Kiyo **7028**
0287-8828 Energi Keizai **3134**
0287-900X Number **8191**
0287-9085 Mejikaru Nyusu†
0287-9247 Kisho Eisei Senta Nyusu **6359**
0287-9263 Kyushu Denryoku K.K. Sogo Kenkyujo Kenkyu Kiho **3323**
0287-9506 Nikkei Personal Computing **2578**
0287-9530 Japan Directory of Professional Associations **7564**
0287-9549 Nara Joshi Daigaku Hoken Kanri Senta Nenpo **7532**
0287-9794 Botany **781**
0287-9808 Kyoto University. Research Reactor Institute. Technical Report **3170**
0287-9824 Nogyo Kisho Kenkyu Shuroku **6392**
0287-9859 Kasen **8828**
0287-9980 Kyushu Daigaku Kyoyobu Sugaku Zasshi†
0288-0059 Sangyo Keiei Kenkyujoho **1792**
0288-0180 Ritsumeikan Keizaigaku **1168**
0288-030X Yamagata Medical Journal **5733**
0288-0490 Netsu Shori **6327**
0288-0822 Nihongogaku **5155**
0288-089X Kaihatsu Ronshu **1495**
0288-1012 Shika Yakubutsu Ryoho **6880**
0288-111X Kyotofu Yakuzaishikai Shiken Kenkyu Senta Nenpo†
0288-1233 Senpaku Hyojunka Giho†
0288-1330 Shigaken Biwako Kenkyujo Shoho†
0288-139X Mizukusa Kenkyukai Kaiho **801**
0288-1500 Review on Liberal Arts **4472**
0288-1527 Institute of Malacology of Tokyo. Bulletin **947**
0288-1578 Seimei Kagaku Kenkyujo Kiyo **704**
0288-1829 Donan Igakkaishi†
0288-1977 Tenmon Gaido **582**
0288-2027 Nihon Biyo Geka Gakkai Kaiho **6253**
0288-2043 Radiation Medicine *changed to* 1867-1071 **6199**
0288-2051 Journal of Kokugakuin University **6526**
0288-2124 Sabo to Chisui **3282**
0288-2302 Haikan to Sochi **3378**
0288-2329 Tokyo-to no Shizen **7924**
0288-2485 Kanpo Igaku **312**
0288-2701 Toshiba Gijutsu Kokaishu **3115**
0288-2876 Eigo Eibungaku Kenkyu **5288**
0288-2906 Iyaku Anzensei Kenkyukai Kaiho†
0288-3015 Nihon Joshi Daigaku Ei-Bei Bungaku Kenkyu **5341**
0288-3031 Nihon Joshi Daigaku Kiyo. Bungakubu **4466**
0288-3112 Mizu Shigen Kaihatsu Kodan. Shikenjo Hokoku **8829**
0288-3139 Mogura†
0288-3155 Urban Kubota **2718**
0288-3422 Niigata Daigaku Kyoikugakubu Kiyo. Shizen Kagaku Hen **7893**
0288-3473 Raifu Saiensu
0288-349X Gakujutsu Zasshi†
0288-3503 Acta Slavica Iaponica **3515**
0288-3538 Bukkyo Daigaku Shinrigaku Kenkyujo Kiyo†
0288-3570 Japanese Journal of American Studies **4298**
0288-3635 New Generation Computing **2572**
0288-366X Shobo Kenshu **3581**
0288-3740 Forest Pests **3689**
0288-3821 Kanagawa Chuho **853**
0288-3864 Packaging Japan **6713**
0288-3872 Nanzan Review of American Studies **4304**
0288-3929 Lotus **6933**
0288-4216 Gekkan Tenmon **575**
0288-4232 Yamaguchi Kenritsu Yamaguchi Hakubutsukan Kenkyu Hokoku **7932**
0288-4240 Yamaguchiken no Shizen **7932**
0288-433X Institute of Space and Astronautical Science. Report. Special Publication **576**
0288-4348 Sosei **5716**
0288-4402 Amica **838**
0288-450X Medical Imaging Technology **6203**
0288-4712 Aichi Kyoiku Daigaku Taiiku Kyoshitsu Kenkyu Kiyo **2825**
0288-4771 Yosetsu Gakkai Ronbunshu **6345**
0288-4887 Dobutsu to Dobutsuen **940**
0288-500X Akademia. Shizen Kagaku, Hoken Taiiku Hen **5467**
0288-5026 Nikkei New Media
0288-5301 Suirobu Giho **2798**
0288-5441 Fujita Gakuen Igakkaishi **5616**
0288-5492 Kunitachi Ongaku Daigaku Kenkyu Kiyo
0288-5514 Jikken Igaku **5906**
0288-5530 Tokyo Denki University. Faculty of Engineering. General Education. Research Reports **8010**
0288-5581 Monken **3278**
0288-559X Diteruman *changed to* 1341-3864 **5618**
0288-5603 Ea Warudo
0288-5611 Saitama-kenritsu Shizenshi Hakubutsukan Kenkyu Hokoku **7906**
0288-562X Zeisei†
0288-5654 Goyo Kensetsu Gijutsu Kenkyujo Nenpo
0288-5751 Nihon Sanka Fujinka Gakkai Tokyo Chiho Bukai Kaishi **6000**
0288-5867 Kinoshi Kenkyukaishi **6735**
0288-5980 Geological Survey of Japan. Cruise Report **2740**
0288-6022 Current Science and Technology Research in Japan **7936**
0288-6030 Musashino Art University. Bulletin **507**
0288-609X Nihon Shoni Geka Gakkai Zasshi **6097**
0288-6103 Dempa Digest†
0288-6138 Kirisutokyo Ronso **7658**
0288-6146 Seikatsu Kagaku Ronso **704**
0288-6154 Shoin Literary Review **5371**
0288-6170 Bunrin **5267**
0288-6200 Nippon Laser Igakkaishi **5687**
0288-6243 Calanus **664**
0288-6340 Kokugakuin University Economic Review **1141**
0288-6472 Bukkyo Shigaku Kenkyu **7700**
0288-6502 Tochi Zosei Kogaku Kenkyu Shisetsu Hokoku†
0288-6537 Ginseng Review†
0288-7118 Jumin Katsudo†
0288-7126 Shakaigaku Nenshi **8132**
0288-7142 People and National Land Policy
0288-7223 Chugaikai Nyuzu†
0288-724X Fukuyama Daigaku Yakugakubu Kenkyu Nenpo **6843**

ISSN

0293-9525	Societe d'Agriculture, Commerce, Sciences et Arts du Departement de la Marne. Memoires *changed to* 1768-6814 **4451**
0293-9614	Bulletin Signaletique d'Information Administrative†
0293-9789	Actualite des Arts Plastiques **464**
0293-9908	Comptes Rendus de Therapeutique et de Pharmacologie Clinique†
0293-9932	Voix d'Afrique (Paris) **7693**
0294-0000	Livres Hebdo **7578**
0294-0019	Livres de France **7566**
0294-0027	Les Livres du Mois **7566**
0294-0035	Trois Mois de Nouveautes†
0294-0043	Six Mois de Nouveautes†
0294-0051	Perspectives (Paris)†
0294-0264	Sciences et Techniques en Perspective **4160**
0294-0337	Sciences Sociales et Sante **7541**
0294-0442	Journal of the Short Story in English **5316**
0294-0671	Mises au Point de Biochimie Pharmacologique† **8974**
0294-0736	Journal d'Economie Medicale **5645**
0294-0752	Office des Prix du Batiment - Edition Maconnerie Peinture
0294-0809	Dossiers de l'Education†
0294-0817	Medecine Aeronautique et Spatiale **5666**
0294-0833	Revue Francaise de Finances Publiques **1942**
0294-0868	Education et Formations **2847**
0294-0949	Choisir†
0294-0957	Filmo†
0294-1090	Un An de Nouveaute†
0294-1228	Annales Francaises de Microtechniques et de Chronometrie **3374**
0294-1260	Annales de Chirurgie Plastique Esthetique **6236**
0294-1341	Israel & Palestine Political Report†
0294-1414	La Nouvelle Revue du Seizieme Siecle *changed to* 1774-4466 **5369**
0294-1449	l'Institut Henri Poincare. Annales (C). Analyse Non Lineaire **5493**
0294-1465	Juris-Classeur Commercial **4873**
0294-1546	Code General des Impots **1917**
0294-1643	Juris-Classeur de Procedure Civile **4706**
0294-1759	Vingtieme Siecle **4277**
0294-1805	Philosophie (Paris) **6941**
0294-1945	Ordres Sociaux
0294-2623	Revue de Parapsychologie
0294-2925	International Viewpoint **7246**
0294-3069	Recherches Internationales **7176**
0294-3107	Artension **472**
0294-3506	Biofutur†
0294-4030	Nouvelle Tour de Feu†
0294-4081	Cahiers de la Photographie† **8939**
0294-4480	O R A C L†
0294-474X	Revue Internationale de Rhumatologie†
0294-5495	Societe Speleologique et Prehistorique de Bordeaux. Memoire†
0294-6068	Pom's†
0294-6467	Lettre de l'Ocean Indien *see* 0294-6475 **7241**
0294-6475	Indian Ocean Newsletter **7241**
0294-653X	L'A N E†
0294-6831	Cahiers du Tourisme. Serie D: Statistiques **8778**
0294-6904	L'Epoque Conradienne **5290**
0294-6939	Les Cahiers de la Guitare **6553**
0294-7080	Systemes de Pensee en Afrique Noire **357**
0294-7382	Revue Genealogique Normande **3780**
0294-7579	Youthlink **2223**
0294-7749	Albatros
0294-8052	International Herald Tribune **3841**
0294-8095	Journal des Maires **7494**
0294-8117	Le Mois en Afrique†
0294-8141	Intersocial†
0294-8168	Liaisons Sociales. Bref Social *changed to* 1955-5024 **1695**
0294-8281	Dirigeant **7130**
0294-8303	Cooperation-Distribution-Consommation†
0294-8346	Communes Modernes†
0294-8362	Paris Projet (Revue) *changed to* 1773-7974 **4422**
0294-8451	France. Ministere de la Culture et Communication. Developpement Culturel **5010**
0294-8567	Architecture Interieure, C R E E **430**
0295-0251	Sociolinguistique **5175**
0295-0448	Aqua Revue **92**
0295-060X	Centre International de Documentation Arachnologique. Liste des Travaux Arachnologiques†
0295-0847	Materiaux Arabes et Sudarabiques **4464**
0295-1347	Association Francaise pour l'Etude du Sol. Lettre **219**
0295-1371	L'Avant-Scene. Opera **6546**
0295-1630	Pleine Marge **5352**
0295-1843	T L E **5384**
0295-1967	Spectra Biologie **706**
0295-2211	Unilactualites†
0295-2319	Politix **7172**
0295-317X	La Pisciculture Francaise d'Eau Vive et d'Etang Saumatre et Marine†
0295-3420	A G E C O P Liaison†
0295-3722	Analyse Musicale†
0295-3730	Etudes Retiviennes **5292**
0295-3803	Compagnie des Ecrivains Mediterraneens et des Amis des Lettres. Bulletin *changed to* 0985-7427
0295-3943	Midi Media **1835**
0295-4192	Logistiques Magazine **3352**
0295-4397	Gerer et Comprendre **6463**
0295-4591	Les Cahiers Hospitaliers **4089**
0295-5024	Roman 20 - 50 **5363**
0295-5075	Europhysics Letters **7012**
0295-5245	Etudes et Documents Berberes **3532**
0295-5261	Rhumatologie Pratique **6227**
0295-5385	Lutte de Classe **7251**
0295-5652	Pardes†
0295-5830	Revue de Droit des Affaires Internationales **4939**
0295-5873	Systemes Solaires **3178**
0295-5989	La Peche en Mer **3604**
0295-6047	Spectacles Infos† **8989**
0295-6292	Tout Prevoir - Revue de l'A G M F
0295-6977	Fondements des Sciences **7855**
0295-7108	Manuscrits Medievaux en Caracteres Hebraiques **5330**
0295-7736	Logiques Sociales **8118**
0295-7787	Kompass Regional Economique et Industriel. Midi-Pyrenees **1141**
0295-7795	Kompass Regional Economique et Industriel. Languedoc - Roussillon **1141**
0295-7841	Maraicher Nantais **136**
0295-7868	Annuaire de la Meunerie Francaise **270**
0295-7906	Kompass Regional Economique et Industriel. Pays de la Loire *changed to* 1767-6509 **1142**
0295-7914	Kompass Regional Economique et Industriel. Lorraine **1141**
0295-7922	Kompass Regional Economique et Industriel. Bourgogne **1141**
0295-7930	Kompass Regional Economique et Industriel. Champagne - Ardennes **1141**
0295-7949	Kompass Regional Economique et Industriel. Franche-Comte **1141**
0295-7957	Kompass Regional Economique et Industriel. Auvergne **1141**
0295-7965	Kompass Regional Economique et Industriel. Alsace **1141**
0295-7973	Kompass Regional Economique et Industriel. Nord, Pas-de-Calais **1142**
0295-7981	Kompass Regional Economique et Industriel. Aquitaine **1141**
0295-8899	Encyclopedie Periodique Economique, Politique et Administrative. L'Assemblee Nationale *changed to* 1954-4251 **640**
0295-9151	Ethnies **3532**
0295-9909	Groupe Interdisciplinaire du Theatre Antique. Cahiers **8471**
0296-0877	Multicoques Magazine **8278**
0296-1288	Connaissance des Religions† **8943**
0296-1830	Paris. Bulletin Municipal Officiel - Bulletin Departemental Officiel **7459**
0296-2292	Arts du Spectacle **8465**
0296-3086	Association des Naturalistes de la Vallee du Loing et du Massif de Fontainebleau. Bulletin **777**
0296-3140	Be Star Newsletter **572**
0296-3361	France Tabac **8486**
0296-3981	Neuro-psy *changed to* 1633-5767 **6167**
0296-399X	Lettre du Continent **7251**
0296-4333	Solidarite Atlantique†
0296-4449	Ecoflash **1097**
0296-4961	Sport Eco
0296-533X	B G V. Bulletin Grande Vitesse *see* 0240-5709 **5463**
0296-6131	Cosmopolitiques†
0296-6395	Jukebox Magazine **6581**
0296-6700	Animalerie **6803**
0296-6867	Societe des Poetes Francais. Bulletin Trimestriel **5435**
0296-8274	Toupie **2218**
0296-8576	Winnie **2221**
0296-8622	Arts et Livres de Provence†
0296-8673	Eglise du Mans *changed to* 1777-3245 **7796**
0296-8746	Ami du Professionnel en Alimentation†
0296-8770	Psychologie et Psychometrie†
0296-8789	Nouvelles Economiques†
0296-9009	La Lettre de l'Infectiologue **5822**
0296-9017	Conseils Sols Murs et Papiers Peints†
0296-9076	Porc Magazine **296**
0296-9386	Le Pneumatique **7826**
0296-9904	Hard Force†
0297-0376	Revue Francaise de Service Social **8065**
0297-0651	Securiscope†
0297-1062	Technologies et Formations
0297-1194	Revue de Psychotherapie Psychanalytique de Groupe **7405**
0297-2301	Expression d'Entreprise **2320**
0297-2964	Recherche en Soins Infirmiers†
0297-4592	Revue Francaise de Logistique
0297-4932	Ostreiculteur Francais *changed to* 1779-0220 **3589**
0297-5785	L'Oiseau Magazine **321**
0297-6005	Kinesitherapeute Praticien†
0297-8253	Presence du Cinema Francais†
0297-8350	I D - L'Information Dentaire **5846**
0297-8644	ArMen **3999**
0297-8695	Tele Loisirs **2395**
0297-9101	Securite Informatique† **8987**
0297-9373	Aster **2828**
0297-9977	Centre d'Etudes et de Recherches Amazigh. Publications **5271**
0298-055X	Pratiques de Formation **2898**
0298-2196	Dits et Vecus Populaires **2842**
0298-2250	Dossiers de Documentation Archeologique **391**
0298-2285	Zero - Un Informatique (Hebdomadaire) **2551**
0298-248X	Cahiers de Paleontologie Est-Africaine
0298-2919	Atout Chien **6804**
0298-3141	Escrime Magazine **8171**
0298-3540	Le Technicien d'Agriculture Tropicale **161**
0298-3788	Les Inrockuptibles **3841**
0298-3834	E R Q
0298-461X	Linguistique Generale **5147**
0298-511X	Le Bulletin Officiel de la Concurrence, de la Consommation et de la Repression des Fraudes† **8938**
0298-5268	Actions Sante **5567**
0298-5632	Histoire Biographique de l'Enseignement **3064**
0298-6191	Limonadier - Restaurateur Hotelier†
0298-6248	Clefs C E A **7847**
0298-6477	Glossa **5122**
0298-7104	Bulletin Difrap
0298-7139	Filigrane†
0298-7201	Universite Sportive d'Ete. Cahiers **8214**
0298-7449	Le Bouilleur de France
0298-7538	Cour de Cassation. Bulletin des Arrets. Chambre Criminelle **4886**
0298-7783	Revue Generale Nucleaire: International Edition
0298-7899	Cahiers d'Etude et de Recherche†
0298-7902	Notebooks for Study and Research†
0298-7996	Histoire et Defense†
0298-8550	Pharmascope
0298-8682	Medexpres†
0298-9204	Maroc Repression†
0298-9239	Lettre du Sponsoring et du Mecenat†
0299-0628	C R L H. Cahiers Annuels **331**
0299-0733	Institut National de Recherche en Informatique et en Automatique. Collection Didactique **2537**
0299-0865	Matulu†
0299-1098	Ethnosciences **337**
0299-1705	B T P Magazine **978**
0299-2213	Annales de Chirurgie Vasculaire **6236**
0299-2388	Collection Astraea **5275**
0299-3007	Afrique Medecine et Sante†
0299-3147	Popi **2208**
0299-3201	Ethnomusicologie **6565**
0299-3511	Les Cahiers d'Action Familiale **8091**
0299-3570	Le Journal de l'Atelier *changed to* 1631-1132 **1432**
0299-3600	Archaeozoologia† **8931**
0299-3635	Notre Terroir† **8978**
0299-3678	Profession Textile
0299-3856	Officiel des Bainistes†
0299-3953	J A M I F **5643**
0299-4208	V T T Magazine **8270**
0299-6065	Qui Represente Quit†
0299-6081	Kompass Professionnel. Precision†
0299-609X	Kompass Professionnel. Services, Industries Graphiques **2011**
0299-6103	Kompass Professionnel. Machines - Outils, Robotique, Mecanique Generale†
0299-6111	Kompass Professionnel. Chimie, Plastiques, Caoutchouc, Produits Mineraux **2011**
0299-612X	Kompass Professionnel. Electricite, Electronique, Informatique **2011**
0299-6138	Kompass Professionnel. Produits du Metal **2011**
0299-6146	Kompass Professionnel. Textile, Habillement, Cuirs et Peaux **2012**
0299-6154	Kompass Professionnel. Agriculture, Alimentation **2011**
0299-6162	Kompass Professionnel. Batiment et Genie Civil, Manutention - Levage, Bois - Meubles **2011**
0299-6170	Kompass Professionnel. Siderurgie, Metallurgie, Fonderie **2012**
0299-6197	Kompass Professionnel. Techniques Hydrauliques et Pneumatiques, Climatisation **2012**
0299-6898	Panorama **7668**
0299-7061	Nous Deux **3841**
0299-7258	Techniques Sciences Methodes, Genie Urbain Genie Rural **3469**
0299-7827	Griffon
0299-8459	Info D G A† **8964**
0299-8572	Afrique Elite†
0299-8661	Bulletin Technique du Machinisme et de l'Equipement Agricoles†
0299-9781	Papercast **6736**
0300-0087	Annali di Ostetricia, Ginecologia e Medicina Perinatale† **8930**
0300-0109	Archivio e Rassegna Italiana di Ottalmologia†
0300-0265	Canada. Statistics Canada. Wool Production and Supply†
0300-0273	Canadian Statistical Review. Weekly Supplement†
0300-029X	Chiken Ishiyaku Joho **6828**
0300-032X	Rinsho Seishin Igaku **6183**
0300-0338	Chokaku Gengo Shogai†
0300-0443	Psychological Reader's Guide†
0300-0486	Society of Biological Chemists. Proceedings **745**
0300-0508	Physiotherapy Canada **6114**
0300-0540	Karl-Marx-Universitaet Leipzig. Mathematisch-Naturwissenschaftliche Reihe. Wissenschaftliche Zeitschrift† **8969**
0300-0559	Revue de Medecine du Travail†
0300-0583	Caraibe Medical†
0300-0605	Journal of International Medical Research **5650**
0300-0664	Clinical Endocrinology **5885**
0300-0702	Mises a Jour Cardiologiques†
0300-0729	Rhinology **6085**
0300-0753	Canada. Statistics Canada. Dairy Review **177**
0300-0818	Jinko Zoki **5644**
0300-0923	W H O Food Additives Series **3667**
0300-0958	Flora of New South Wales.†
0300-1016	Versuchstierkunde
0300-1067	Studia Phonologica **5180**
0300-1202	Canada. Statistics Canada. Wool Yarn and Cloth Mills†
0300-1245	Pediatrician†
0300-1342	New Zealand Journal of Dairy Science and Technology†
0300-1407	Carbohydrate Chemistry and Metabolism Abstracts†
0300-1555	South Africa. Prisons Department. Report of the Commissioner of Prisons†
0300-1628	International Tax Report **1930**
0300-1644	Berlin-Magazin†
0300-1652	Nigerian Medical Journal **5686**
0300-1695	Pilot (Clapham) **68**
0300-1725	Current Problems in Clinical Biochemistry†
0300-1881	Nigeria. Federal Ministry of Trade. Quarterly Information Bulletin†
0300-1903	Universita Cattolica del Sacro Cuore. Saggi e Ricerche. Serie Terza. Scienze Psicologiche†
0300-1989	Karl-May-Gesellschaft. Jahrbuch **5317**
0300-1997	Tiroler Verkehrswirtschaftliche Zahlen
0300-2004	Journalismus **4578**
0300-2012	Wolfenbuetteler Beitraege **5055**
0300-2039	Bruecke-Archiv **480**
0300-2047	Germany. Bundesministerium fuer Bildung, Wissenschaft, Forschung und Technologie. Bundesbericht Forschung *changed to* Bundesministerium fuer Bildung und Forschung. Bundesbericht Forschung und Innovation **7425**
0300-2055	Foerteckning Oever Advokater och Advokatbyraaer **4676**
0300-208X	Who's Notable in Mexico
0300-211X	Radical Philosophy **6946**
0300-2144	Management Journal **1776**
0300-2241	Liberia. Department of State. Newsletter
0300-225X	World Peace

ISSN

9238 0300-2373 ULRICH'S PERIODICALS

0300-2373 Kenya. Central Bureau of Statistics. Agricultural Census (Large Farm Areas) **183**
0300-2403 Nigeria. Federal Department of Forest Research. Research Paper **3698**
0300-242X List of Approved Hospitals and Recognised House Officer Posts†
0300-2497 Neki Pokazatelji Tehnickog Razvoja Privrede Jugoslavije†
0300-2527 Drustveni Proizvod i Narodni Dohodak **1225**
0300-2535 Licni Dohoci **1249**
0300-2551 Australia. Department of the Treasury. Taxation Branch. Taxation Statistics†
0300-2594 Institut d'Etudes Slaves, Paris. Documents Pedagogiques **5128**
0300-2659 Prevent†
0300-2667 Management Information Service **1776**
0300-2713 Oriental Insects Supplements Series†
0300-2721 Insaat Muhendisleri Odasi. Teknik Bulten†
0300-2802 Planen und Streuen: Fachwerbung
0300-2853 Planen und Streuen: Publikumswerbung
0300-287X Bibliothekspraxis **4996**
0300-2896 Archivos de Bronconeumologia **6211**
0300-2942 Avenir Agricole et Viticole Aquitain **220**
0300-2977 Netherlands Journal of Medicine **5947**
0300-3035 Nihon Hozon Shikagaku Zasshi *changed to* 0387-2343 **5857**
0300-306X Nippon Steel Technical Report **6327**
0300-3094 Nordisk Statutsamling†
0300-3132 Tavola Rotonda†
0300-3159 Tekawennake **3568**
0300-3167 Umformtechnik **6336**
0300-3175 Valori Umani†
0300-3183 Vida Hospitalar†
0300-3205 Voice of Malta
0300-3213 Voxair **6453**
0300-3256 Zoologica Scripta **969**
0300-3264 Young Soldier *changed to* Kid Zone **7763**
0300-3272 Talyllyn News **8625**
0300-3302 Sun Yat-sen Cultural Foundation Bulletin **8008**
0300-3310 Skip†
0300-3329 Sicherheitsingenieur **1707**
0300-3337 Sicherheitsbeauftragter **1707**
0300-3345 Angus Herd Book of New Zealand **278**
0300-3361 Science Chelsea† **8987**
0300-337X The Scottish Genealogist **3782**
0300-3388 Salamandra **5238**
0300-340X Rivista Storica dell'Antichita **4159**
0300-3418 Revista de Quimica Textil **8456**
0300-3434 Renal Physiology
0300-3442 Hospital Career†
0300-3450 Rechentechnik - Datenverarbeitung
0300-3469 The Reader **7772**
0300-3477 Razza Bovina Piemontese
0300-3485 Rassegna di Diritto, Legislazione e Medicina Legale Veterinaria†
0300-3493 Foreign Compound Metabolism in Mammals†
0300-3515 Rally†
0300-3523 Protee **4470**
0300-3558 Prison Service Journal **2666**
0300-3574 Pollustop
0300-3604 Photosynthetica **807**
0300-3612 University of the Philippines. Institute of Library Science. Newsletter **5053**
0300-3620 Civil Service Reporter **7430**
0300-3639 Phenix†
0300-3647 Itogi Nauki i Tekhniki. Seriya Entomologiya†
0300-3655 Personalhistorisk Tidsskrift **3779**
0300-368X Nigerian Agricultural Journal **140**
0300-3701 Orquidea (Mex) **806**
0300-3752 New Linguist†
0300-3779 Muchachas†
0300-3787 Mundo Electronico **3109**
0300-3809 Natun Thikana **5229**
0300-3817 Magyar Tortenelmi Szemle **4242**
0300-3825 Medico†
0300-3876 Ministikok
0300-3884 El Mundo Financiero **1369**
0300-3906 Mindanao Mail **3928**
0300-3922 Multinational Business†
0300-3930 Local Government Studies **7497**
0300-3957 Kerala Homoeo Journal†
0300-3973 Informazione Radio TV† **8964**
0300-4007 Indranil **5221**
0300-4023 Indochina
0300-4031 In Terris **5424**
0300-4058 International Law Reporter **4931**
0300-4074 Kanara Chamber of Commerce & Industry Journal **1406**
0300-4090 H K I M S
0300-4112 Forstarchiv **3691**
0300-4139 Germinal
0300-4147 I I M S
0300-4155 Impact **7971**
0300-4171 I D E **6710**
0300-418X Hong Kong Monthly Digest of Statistics **7308**
0300-4198 D I M S
0300-4228 Fleet Street Letter **1624**
0300-4252 European Federation of Finance House Associations. Newsletter **1339**
0300-4279 Education 3-13 **2846**
0300-4309 Dhandha **5482**
0300-4317 Desarrollo del Tropico Americano†
0300-4333 University of Calgary Gazette *changed to* OnCampus **2295**
0300-435X Canadian Guider **2146**
0300-4368 Charadista **3931**
0300-4376 Current Titles in Electrochemistry **2094**
0300-4384 Concord
0300-4406 Common Market News†
0300-4414 Dejiny Ved a Techniky **7850**
0300-4422 Deputazione di Storia Patria per l'Umbria. Bollettino **4214**
0300-4430 Early Child Development and Care **2151**
0300-4465 Cooperator†
0300-4473 Cidade†
0300-4481 Cerveza y Malta **601**
0300-449X Transport and Tourism Journal
0300-4511 Canada Rides
0300-452X Camouflage Air Journal†
0300-4538 Cahiers de la Presse Francaise†
0300-4546 Society and Commerce **1433**
0300-4554 B I P **6763**
0300-4562 British Lichen Society Bulletin **782**
0300-4589 Bollettino di Collegamento
0300-4597 Epidemiological Surveillance of Rabies for the Americas
0300-4600 Athletic Echo **8159**
0300-4627 Blatt fuer Sortenwesen **176**
0300-4651 Odini **7810**
0300-4686 Acrida†
0300-4740 Cayman Islands. Legislative Assembly. Minutes **7114**
0300-483X Toxicology **3502**
0300-4864 Journal of Neurocytology *changed to* 1559-7105
0300-4872 Beitraege zur Kryomedizin† **8935**
0300-4880 Public Health in Europe†
0300-4937 Medecine et Armees **5666**
0300-4953 Artes de Mexico **472**
0300-5038 I A R C Scientific Publications **6021**
0300-5127 Biochemical Society Transactions **725**
0300-5143 Clean Air **3484**
0300-5178 Wiener Klinische Wochenschrift. Supplementum **5730**
0300-5194 Excerpta Medica. Section 46: Environmental Health and Pollution Control **3479**
0300-5224 Nieren- und Hochdruckkrankheiten **5796**
0300-5232 Society of Chemical Industry. Bulletin†
0300-5267 S H I L A P **858**
0300-5275 Ontario Dentist **5858**
0300-5283 Medical Journal of Malaysia **5669**
0300-533X Institute of Child Health, Calcutta, Annals†
0300-5356 Arhitectura **432**
0300-5402 Acta Universitatis Carolinae. Geographica **3997**
0300-5429 Environmental Physiology & Biochemistry†
0300-5453 Al Huda al-Jadida
0300-5461 Hospital and Health Service Purchasing†
0300-5526 Intervirology **888**
0300-5550 Revista Espanola de Lecheria†
0300-5577 Journal of Perinatal Medicine **5996**
0300-5585 Norges Offisielle Statistikk **1255**
0300-5607 Courses et Elevage **8289**
0300-5623 Urological Research **6276**
0300-5658 Eperon†
0300-5712 Journal of Dentistry **5851**
0300-5720 Hospital Development **4100**
0300-5747 South Africa. Maize Board. Report on Grain Sorghum and Buckwheat for the Financial Year†
0300-5755 Alimentaria **3626**
0300-5771 International Journal of Epidemiology **5638**
0300-5860 Zeitschrift fuer Kardiologie *changed to* 1861-0684 **5783**
0300-600X Venture Management†
0300-6026 Trends in Housing†
0300-6034 Pratt's Consumer Credit and Truth in Lending Compliance Report **4760**
0300-6050 Texas State and Region Newsletter†
0300-6069 New Jersey Register
0300-6077 Under Twenty-Five Newsletter
0300-6093 Royalton Review†
0300-6107 California Teachers Association. Chapter News Service†
0300-6123 Rubber & Plastics News **7826**
0300-6158 Miesiecznik Franciszkanski†
0300-6182 South Dakota Municipalities **7502**
0300-6190 Tube Topics
0300-6204 Business & Government Insider Newsletter†
0300-6212 Svithiod Journal **3567**
0300-6239 Southern Tobacco Journal†
0300-6247 Talking Leaf
0300-6301 Motor North
0300-6328 The Rawhide Press **3560**
0300-6336 Union W.A.G.E.†
0300-6379 Rainbow (Jersey City)†
0300-6387 Sports Car **8604**
0300-6425 Recovering Literature **5358**
0300-6433 T E P S A Journal **3034**
0300-645X Virginia Genealogist† **8997**
0300-6484 Palestine Digest†
0300-6506 Transportation Business Report†
0300-6514 Pan-American Trader†
0300-6530 West Virginia Record and West Virginia Merchant
0300-6549 Walker's Manual Supplements
0300-6557 Trailer Boats **8283**
0300-6565 Whispering Wind **3572**
0300-6573 Whitmore Investment Letter†
0300-6603 Twin Cities Courier†
0300-6611 Women's Advocate†
0300-662X Western Mining News†
0300-6646 National On-Campus Report **2293**
0300-6654 R H G H Vital Signs†
0300-6689 N A T E News **7727**
0300-6727 North Carolina Agribusiness†
0300-6743 Noticiero Obrero Norteamericano†
0300-676X Oshkosh Advance - Titan *changed to* Advance - Titan **2271**
0300-6786 Post Eagle **3558**
0300-6794 Nostalgia Newsletter†
0300-6808 Ute Bulletin **3570**
0300-6816 P A A Affairs **7288**
0300-6832 North Dakota Publisher†
0300-6859 Urban Affairs Abstracts†
0300-6867 W E A L Washington Report
0300-6883 I A L News **6080**
0300-6905 Highway Safety Literature†
0300-6921 Chicago Reporter **8093**
0300-693X Daphnis **5283**
0300-6964 Augsburg College Now **2273**
0300-7006 World Education Reports **8147**
0300-7014 Feminist Art Journal†
0300-7022 A D R I S Newsletter **7619**
0300-7030 Concerned Business Students' Report†
0300-7049 Inside Industry
0300-7073 Family Practice News **5613**
0300-7081 Chicago. Municipal Reference Library. Recent Additions†
0300-7103 Essecondsex†
0300-7111 Fashion Newsletter **2255**
0300-712X Chicago. Municipal Reference Library. Checklist of Publications Issued by the City of Chicago†
0300-7138 Du Pont Context†
0300-7162 Diacritics **5284**
0300-7170 Environmental Pollution Control Journal†
0300-7200 Medic Alert Newsletter†
0300-7219 American Challenge
0300-7227 Bibliography and Index of Micropaleontology (Print)†
0300-7235 Bay View†
0300-7243 Clyde LaMotte's Washington Energy Memo
0300-7278 American Indian News†
0300-7316 Discovery (Richmond)†
0300-7324 Dow Theory Forecasts **1621**
0300-7359 Media Ecology Review†
0300-7367 Commodity Exchange Bulletin
0300-7405 Intermountain Logging News†
0300-743X C O R E Magazine **7203**
0300-7464 Brazilian American Chamber of Commerce News Bulletin **1396**
0300-7472 Afterimage **6963**
0300-7480 Beer Marketer's Insights **598**
0300-7499 Buffalo Spree **3971**
0300-7510 Bnai Yiddish†
0300-7553 Margins†
0300-7561 The Crab **5004**
0300-757X Inside R & D **8426**
0300-7618 Poblacion†
0300-7626 American Whitewater **8271**
0300-7634 Correio Operario Norteamericano†
0300-7693 Performance Guide Publications. Mutual Funds and Timing†
0300-7723 Photo Industry Newsletter
0300-7731 Plus-Profit Publicity†
0300-7766 Popular Music & Society **6607**
0300-7812 Goddard Journal†
0300-7820 Suomi-Opiston Viesti†
0300-7839 Human Ecology (New York) **341**
0300-7898 New York (State) University. Division of Continuing Education. Newsletter†
0300-7901 Know News Service†
0300-7960 Shmuessen mit Kinder un Yugent
0300-7995 Current Medical Research and Opinion **5602**
0300-8002 Junior High-Middle School Bulletin†
0300-8029 Inforasia†
0300-8045 United Kingdom. Department of Health and Social Security. Reports on Health and Social Subjects **7544**
0300-8096 D T I†
0300-810X Italian Heritage Newsletter†
0300-8126 Infection **5634**
0300-8134 Journal of Human Ergology **5650**
0300-8142 Libri Oncologici **6026**
0300-8169 Medicina e Historia†
0300-8177 Molecular and Cellular Biochemistry **738**
0300-8207 Connective Tissue Research **831**
0300-8223 M I M S Ireland **5663**
0300-824X Environmental Quality and Safety: Chemistry, Toxicology and Technology†
0300-8258 Connecticut Fireside **3973**
0300-8274 Actualites Psychiatriques†
0300-8371 Neue Muenchner Beitraege zur Geschichte der Medizin und Naturwissenschaften. Medizinhistorische Serie†
0300-838X Microbiology Abstracts: Section A. Industrial & Applied Microbiology **717**
0300-8398 Microbiology Abstracts: Section B. Bacteriology **717**
0300-8428 Basic Research in Cardiology **5778**
0300-8436 Jahresverzeichnis der Verlagsschriften und einer Auswahl der Ausserhalb des Buchhandels Erschienenen Veroeffentlichungen der D.D.R., der B.R.D. und Westberlins Sowie der Deutschsprachigen Werke Anderer Laender†
0300-8495 Australian Family Physician **5581**
0300-8509 Fore **8229**
0300-8533 Oyo Yakuri **6865**
0300-8584 Medical Microbiology and Immunology **5763**
0300-8622 Leber Magen Darm†
0300-8630 Klinische Paediatrie **6096**
0300-8665 Verein fuer Wasser-, Boden- und Lufthygiene. Schriftenreihe **2630**
0300-8703 Studebaker Story†
0300-8797 Sotilaslaaketieteellinen Aikakauslehti **5716**
0300-8819 Neurobiology†
0300-8827 Acta Orthopaedica Scandinavica. Supplementum (Print Edition) *changed to* 1745-3690 **6054**
0300-8835 Acta Obstetrica et Gynecologica Scandinavica. Supplement†
0300-8851 Herold der Wahrheit **7736**
0300-8878 Scandinavian Journal of Infectious Diseases. Supplementum **5826**
0300-8886 Scandinavian Journal of Urology and Nephrology. Supplement **6274**
0300-8908 Nevada Planner†
0300-8916 Tumori **6035**
0300-8924 Acta Vitaminologica et Enzymologica†
0300-8932 Revista Espanola de Cardiologia (Print) **5799**
0300-8967 Acta Psychiatrica Belgica
0300-9009 Acta Neurologica Belgica **6118**
0300-9033 Acta Gastroenterologica Latinoamericana **5919**
0300-9041 Ginecologia y Obstetricia de Mexico **5991**
0300-9068 Revista Latinoamericana de Patologia **5705**
0300-9084 Biochimie **726**
0300-9092 Akusherstvo i Ginekologiya **5985**
0300-9149 Kokubyo Gakkai Zasshi **5928**
0300-9157 Ryumachi†
0300-9165 Nihon Sanka Fujinka Gakkai Zasshi **6000**
0300-9173 Nihon Ronen Igakkai Zasshi **4052**

0300-9181 Nihon Byori Gakkai Kaishi **5686**
0300-919X Kumamoto Igakkai Zasshi†
0300-9440 Progress in Organic Coatings **6720**
0300-9475 Scandinavian Journal of Immunology **5765**
0300-9483 Boreas **2726**
0300-9491 Fossils and Strata†
0300-9505 Revue d'Histoire de l'Eglise de France **7677**
0300-953X Societe des Oceanistes. Journal **8005**
0300-9556 Paediatrie und Paedologie. Supplement†
0300-9572 Resuscitation **6219**
0300-9645 *see* 0021-9320 **8112**
0300-9726 Upsala Journal of Medical Sciences. Supplement **5727**
0300-9734 Upsala Journal of Medical Sciences **5727**
0300-9742 Scandinavian Journal of Rheumatology **6227**
0300-9815 Revue d'Odontostomatologie **5864**
0300-9831 International Journal for Vitamin and Nutrition Research **6849**
0300-984X Archiv fuer Genetik†
0300-9858 Veterinary Pathology **8813**
0300-9947 Nursing Bibliography†
0300-9963 Selected Annual Reviews of the Analytical Sciences†
0300-9998 International Journal of Chronobiology†
0301-0066 Perception **7390**
0301-0074 Organometallic Chemistry **2128**
0301-0082 Progress in Neurobiology **927**
0301-0104 Chemical Physics **2133**
0301-0139 Pigment Cell†
0301-0155 Frontiers of Matrix Biology†
0301-0163 Hormone Research *changed to* 1663-2818 **5894**
0301-018X Australasian Nurses Journal†
0301-0287 Psychiatries†
0301-0325 Ambio Special Report **652**
0301-0333 Kenya Nursing Journal **5968**
0301-035X Bangladesh Medical Journal **5583**
0301-0368 Asian Archives of Anaesthesiology and Resuscitation†
0301-0384 Health of the People†
0301-0392 Clinica; Portavoz del Internado **5595**
0301-0406 Revista de Patologia Tropical **815**
0301-0422 Public Health Reviews† **8983**
0301-0430 Clinical Nephrology **6266**
0301-0449 Pediatric Radiology **6205**
0301-0457 Behring Institute Mitteilungen†
0301-0481 Zeitschrift fuer Hautkrankheiten H & G *changed to* 1610-0379 **5878**
0301-049X Food Irradiation Information†
0301-0511 Biological Psychology **7340**
0301-0546 Allergologia et Immunopathologia **5753**
0301-0635 Sciences Pharmaceutiques et Biologique de Lorraine†
0301-0643 Epoch (Croydon)
0301-0716 Radiochemistry†
0301-0724 Folia Veterinaria Latina†
0301-0740 World Health Organization. Handbook of Resolutions and Decisions of the World Health Assembly and the Executive Board. **7545**
0301-0767 Hospital Infantil de Mexico. Boletin Medico. Suplemento *see* 0539-6115 **4100**
0301-0791 Cahiers de Chirurgie†
0301-0864 Anaesthesia, Resuscitation and Intensive Therapy†
0301-0902 Aichi Ika Daigaku Igakkai Zasshi **5570**
0301-0996 Goeteborg Psychological Reports **7358**
0301-102X John Rylands University Library of Manchester. Bulletin **4459**
0301-1089 Fiji Medical Journal **5614**
0301-1178 Cahiers de Biotherapie **5590**
0301-1208 Indian Journal of Biochemistry and Biophysics **733**
0301-1216 Indian Journal of Preventive and Social Medicine **5634**
0301-1348 Pharma International **6867**
0301-150X Electromyography and Clinical Neurophysiology **6137**
0301-1526 Vasa **5801**
0301-1569 O R L **6083**
0301-1577 Inhaled Particles **4102**
0301-1623 International Urology and Nephrology **6269**
0301-1798 Uspekhi Fiziologicheskikh Nauk **7045**
0301-1941 Bibliografia Publikacji Naukowych Pracownikow Akademii Medycznej w Bialymstoku†
0301-2115 European Journal of Obstetrics & Gynecology and Reproductive Biology **5990**
0301-2123 Acta Biologica Paranaense **649**
0301-2212 Social Behavior and Personality **7408**
0301-2328 Microbiology Abstracts: Section C. Algology, Mycology and Protozoology **717**
0301-2425 Biofizika Zhivoi Kletki†
0301-2514 Acta Universitatis Palackianae Olomucensis. Facultatis Medicae†
0301-2581 Nissei Byoin Igaku Zasshi **4108**
0301-2603 Neurological Surgery **6252**
0301-2611 Kensa to Gijutsu **5907**
0301-262X Nihon Hoken Igakkai Shi **5686**
0301-2689 Berichte ueber Landwirtschaft. Sonderhefte **95**
0301-2719 Gaertnerische Berufspraxis
0301-2735 Advances in Agronomy and Crop Science†
0301-276X Monumenta Venatoria†
0301-2778 Mammalia Depicta†
0301-2867 Daehan Bangsaseon Yihag Hoeji/Korean Radiological Society. Journal *changed to* 1738-2637 **6195**
0301-2883 Daehan Sohwa'gi'byeong Haghoe Jabji *changed to* 1598-9992 **5928**
0301-2972 International Business Report†
0301-3006 Analytische Psychologie **7334**
0301-3057 Monographs on Drugs†
0301-3073 Frontiers of Hormone Research **5893**
0301-309X International Symposium on Brain-Endocrine Interaction. Proceedings†
0301-3138 Equine Infectious Diseases†
0301-3146 Canadian Society for Immunology. International Symposium. Proceedings†
0301-326X European Ophthalmological Society. Congress **6041**
0301-3294 Zeitschrift fuer Germanistische Linguistik **5199**
0301-3529 Monday Morning **3905**
0301-374X New Techniques in Biophysics and Cell Biology†
0301-3782 Basel Institute for Immunology. Annual Report†
0301-3847 Scandinavian Journal of Rheumatology. Supplement **6227**
0301-3898 Abstracts of World Medicine†
0301-3901 Institut d'Hygiene des Mines. Revue†
0301-391X Itogi Nauki i Tekhniki. Genetika Cheloveka†
0301-3952 Journal de Biologie Buccale†
0301-4029 Taehan Pangsason Uihakhoe Chapchi **6209**
0301-4126 Societe de l'Histoire de l'Art Francais. Bulletin **518**
0301-4134 Archives de l'Art Francais **467**
0301-4185 Digital Processes†
0301-4193 Contributions to Human Development†
0301-4207 Resources Policy **3146**
0301-4215 Energy Policy **3132**
0301-4223 New Zealand Journal of Zoology **958**
0301-4231 Contributions to Primatology†
0301-4347 Zimbabwe. National Archives. Annual Report **4179**
0301-438X Inter-American Centre for Agricultural Documentation and Information. Documentacion e Informacion Agricola†
0301-441X Excelsa **787**
0301-4428 Theoretical Linguistics **5187**
0301-4436 R & D Projects in Documentation and Librarianship†
0301-4444 Annales de Medecine de Reims Champagne-Ardennes†
0301-4460 Annals of Human Biology **653**
0301-4495 Annee Therapeutique et Clinique en Ophtalmologie†
0301-4576 Revista Peruana de Medicina Tropical **5706**
0301-4606 Bangladesh Pharmaceutical Journal **6824**
0301-4614 Bibliographie der Bibliographien†
0301-4622 Biophysical Chemistry **752**
0301-4657 Current Research and Development Projects in Israel: Natural Sciences and Technology†
0301-4681 Differentiation **669**
0301-469X Eastern Archives of Ophthalmology†
0301-4703 Essays in Fundamental Immunology†
0301-472X Experimental Hematology **5936**
0301-4738 Indian Journal of Ophthalmology **6043**
0301-4746 Industrial Safety Chronicle†
0301-4770 Journal of Chromatography Library **2101**
0301-4797 Journal of Environmental Management **3446**
0301-4800 Journal of Nutritional Science and Vitaminology **6662**
0301-4827 Kerala Medical Journal **5657**
0301-4835 Die Krankenversicherung **4512**
0301-4843 Kupat-Holim Yearbook†
0301-4851 Molecular Biology Reports **739**
0301-486X Mycopathologia **803**
0301-4894 Nippon Geka Gakkai Zasshi **6253**
0301-5068 Egyptian Journal of Pharmaceutical Sciences **6837**
0301-5106 Who's Who in India (Calcutta) **647**
0301-5165 Zhonghua Minguo Chuban Tushu Mulu†
0301-5262 Universidad de Sevilla. Revista Medica†
0301-5335 Settimana del Sordo†
0301-5386 Nekotorye Filosofskie Voprosy Sovremennogo Estestvoznaniya
0301-5467 Universitas Comeniana. Acta Facultatis Pharmaceuticae **6884**
0301-5491 Lekar a Technika†
0301-5556 Advances in Anatomy, Embryology and Cell Biology **650**
0301-5572 British Journal of Sexual Medicine†
0301-5599 Major Problems in Anaesthesia†
0301-5602 Major Problems in Neurology†
0301-5629 Ultrasound in Medicine & Biology **709**
0301-5645 People†
0301-5661 Community Dentistry and Oral Epidemiology **5838**
0301-567X Beitraege zur Tropischen Landwirtschaft und Veterinaermedizin *changed to* 1612-9830 **126**
0301-5688 Jahrbuch der Psychoanalyse. Beiheft *see* 0075-2363 **7367**
0301-5718 Update. Journal of Postgraduate General Practice *changed to* 1753-9773 **5619**
0301-5742 Indian Orthodontic Society. Journal **5847**
0301-5769 Schmuck†
0301-5785 Australian Outlook **3793**
0301-603X South African Journal of Agricultural Extension **157**
0301-6056 Cinema & T V†
0301-6129 Acta Diurna Historica†
0301-6137 Your Family **8892**
0301-6145 C S I R Publications†
0301-620X Journal of Bone and Joint Surgery: British Volume **6063**
0301-6226 Livestock Production Science *changed to* 1871-1413 **292**
0301-6242 Petroleum International
0301-6307 Quaderni Storici **4157**
0301-6323 Scandinavian Journal of Immunology. Supplement **5766**
0301-6331 University of Otago Medical School. Proceedings†
0301-634X Radiation and Environmental Biophysics **754**
0301-6374 N G M†
0301-6404 North-Eastern Affairs **7159**
0301-6412 Neurolinguistics†
0301-6420 Studia Historica Slavo-Germanica **4269**
0301-6455 Studi e Documenti di Architettura† **8991**
0301-6528 Rockville International†
0301-6587 Anthropologica **325**
0301-6625 Central Bank of Yemen. Annual Report **1326**
0301-6722 Universidade Federal do Para. Revista†
0301-679X Tribology International **3398**
0301-6900 Lingvisticheskie Issledovaniya
0301-6919 Voprosy Fiziki Tverdogo Tela†
0301-6943 Veterinary History **8812**
0301-696X Revista de Sanidad Militar **6443**
0301-6994 Sociedade Brasileira
0301-7001 Studia Botanica Hungarica **818**
0301-701X Teoria y Praxis†
0301-7028 Water Services *changed to* 1364-4513 **8836**
0301-7036 Problemas del Desarrollo **1603**
0301-7095 Malaysia in Brief **4185**
0301-7168 Guyana. Auditor General. Report on the Public Accounts **1236**
0301-7176 Danmarks Tekniske Universitet. Institute of Hydrodynamics and Water Resources. Progress Report†
0301-7222 Fisheries Statistics of Indonesia **3613**
0301-7230 Revista de Financas Publicas
0301-7257 Byron Journal **5418**
0301-7265 Community Medicine†
0301-732X Archivos de Medicina Veterinaria **8793**
0301-7443 Anuario Financiero y de Sociedades Anonimas de Espana†
0301-7478 Survey of Construction Activities of the Private Sector in Urban Areas of Iran **1038**
0301-7516 International Journal of Mineral Processing **6466**
0301-7524 Greater London Council. Housing Facts and Figures†
0301-7559 Financial Statistics of Education in Cyprus†
0301-7567 Guia de Reuniones Cientificas y Tecnicas en la Argentina **6280**
0301-7575 Electron Spin Resonance Spectroscopy Abstracts
0301-7605 Critique **7127**
0301-7621 Almanak Jakarta
0301-7656 Probleme der Ernaehrungs- und Lebensmittelwissenschaft **6668**
0301-7729 Universidade Federal de Minas Gerais. Faculdade de Medicina. Anais†
0301-7737 Annales Universitatis Mariae Curie-Sklodowska. Sectio DD. Medicina Veterinaria **8792**
0301-7753 Cameroon Year Book **4001**
0301-7761 Daily Mail Year Book†
0301-7788 Iter†
0301-7796 Facts and Figures
0301-7818 Argentina. Congreso de la Nacion. Biblioteca. Boletin Legislativo†
0301-7826 Wiener Medizinische Wochenschrift. Supplement *see* 0043-5341 **5730**
0301-7826 Wiener Medizinische Wochenschrift. Supplement *see* W M W Skriptum **5729**
0301-7877 Finish Digest†
0301-7966 Acta Universitatis Wratislaviensis. Anglica Wratislaviensia **5090**
0301-8059 Sociedade Entomologica do Brasil. Anais *changed to* 1519-566X **855**
0301-8113 Institut d'Anesthesiologie. Acta† **8965**
0301-8121 Journal of Chinese Philosophy **6928**
0301-8156 Rio Grande do Sul, Brazil. Fundacao de Economia e Estatistica. Indicadores Sociais†
0301-8202 Hart Bulletin **5787**
0301-8210 Baroda Journal of Nutrition **6655**
0301-8407 National Dairy Research Institute. Annual Report **267**
0301-8423 Gambia. Produce Marketing Board. Annual Report **199**
0301-8636 Archives Belges de Dermatologie†
0301-8660 Egyptian Journal of Physiological Science **921**
0301-8695 Animal Behavior Abstracts **712**
0301-8776 Cahiers des Amis de Valery Larbaud **5268**
0301-8881 Let's Square Dance **2686**
0301-889X Asturiensia Medievalia **4131**
0301-8911 Universidad de Buenos Aires. Catedra de Patologia y Clinica de la Tuberculosis. Anales†
0301-8938 Fluorocarbon and Related Chemistry†
0301-9004 In†
0301-9020 Botswana Handbook **3803**
0301-9047 Democratic World **7129**
0301-9055 Democratic Forum
0301-9063 Derecho
0301-9187 Institut de Speologie Emil Racovitza. Travaux **2783**
0301-9195 British Pteridological Society. Bulletin **782**
0301-9209 Etudes Zairoises **7134**
0301-9225 Handbuch der Oeffentlichen Bibliotheken†
0301-9233 Ironmaking & Steelmaking **3348**
0301-9268 Precambrian Research **2762**
0301-9322 International Journal of Multiphase Flow **3382**
0301-9349 Confederacion General de la Industria. Memoria y Balance General
0301-9578 Sichuan Wenyi *changed to* 1003-9678 **5438**
0301-9780 Shokuhin Sogo Kenkyujo Kenkyu Hokoku **3663**
0301-9837 Catalogue of Statistical Materials of Developing Countries **1220**
0302-0029 Hanzaigaku Zasshi **2654**
0302-0479 Kanazawa Daigaku Kyoyobu Ronshu. Shizen Kagaku Hen **7874**
0302-0622 Euro Cooperation†
0302-0665 Frontiers of Gastrointestinal Research **5923**
0302-069X Geological Correlation **2738**
0302-0703 Correlation Geologique *see* 0302-069X **2738**
0302-0762 Hot Buttered Soul†
0302-0797 The Chemical Engineer **3238**
0302-0851 National Institute for Research in Dairying. Report†
0302-0924 Universite d'Abidjan. Annales. Serie G: Geographie **4032**
0302-0967 Schriften zur Weingeschichte **610**
0302-1033 Annales Musei Goulandris **6519**
0302-1068 Kodix Nomikou Vematos **4710**
0302-1114 Greece. National Statistical Service. Statistics on the Declared Income of Physical Persons and Its Taxation **1235**
0302-1122 Anthropines Scheseis
0302-1173 Koinonike Epitheoresis†
0302-1181 Vivliographika **5054**
0302-119X Liechtenstein. Botanisch-Zoologische Gesellschaft Liechtenstein Sargans-Werdenberg. Bericht **686**
0302-1254 Big Beat†
0302-1319 Journal of Indian Writing in English **5315**
0302-1416 Greece. National Statistical Service. Statistics of the Declared Income of Legal Entities and Its Taxation **1235**
0302-1432 Colegio Notarial de Granada. Boletin de Informacion **4644**
0302-1475 Sign Language Studies **5174**
0302-1599 Himalangue
0302-1610 Indian Journal of Psychiatric Social Work
0302-1629 Anuario do Estado de Mocambique
0302-167X P T A Heute **6866**
0302-1750 Rivista di Farmacologia e Terapia†
0302-1998 National Children's Bureau. Annual Review **2162**
0302-2013 Bank Indonesia. Data Kredit Perbankan†

ISSN

0303-7002 Kerrygold International†
0303-7169 Singapore Bulletin†
0303-7193 New Zealand Journal of Physiotherapy **6113**
0303-7207 Molecular and Cellular Endocrinology **5897**
0303-7312 Rechtspraak Sociale Verzekering **4520**
0303-7339 Tijdschrift voor Psychiatrie **6188**
0303-7495 Institut Francais d'Etudes Andines. Bulletin **7973**
0303-7657 Revista Brasileira de Saude Ocupacional **6685**
0303-7762 Instituto de Higiene e Medicina Tropical. Anais **7525**
0303-7800 Periodica Polytechnica. Transport Engineering **3280**
0303-7819 Encyclopaedia Judaica Year Book† **8953**
0303-7827 Biblioteka Pediatry **6089**
0303-7878 W H O Offset Publications†
0303-7908 Socijalna Psihijatrija **6186**
0303-7932 Majalah Kedokteran Surabaya†
0303-7940 Archifacts **4990**
0303-7967 Prakriti Vani
0303-805X I S O Bulletin (English Edition) *changed to* 1729-8709 **6402**
0303-8106 Audiology Japan
0303-8157 Poznan Studies in the Philosophy of the Sciences and the Humanities **6944**
0303-8173 Acta Medica Austriaca *changed to* 0043-5325 **5730**
0303-8300 Social Indicators Research **8150**
0303-8408 Sozial- und Praeventivmedizin *changed to* 1661-8556 **5639**
0303-8459 Excerpta Medica. Section 49: Forensic Science Abstracts **5746**
0303-8467 Clinical Neurology and Neurosurgery **6132**
0303-853X Economic Survey of Liberia
0303-8564 Archipelago†
0303-8777 Cayman Islands. Education Department. Report of the Chief Education Officer **2835**
0303-8874 Anales Otorrinolaringologicos Ibero-Americanos†
0303-8939 Revista Internacional de Auditoria Gubernamental *see* 0047-0724
0303-8947 Revue Internationale de la Verification des Comptes Publics *see* 0047-0724
0303-8971 Institut Economique Agricole. Cahiers†
0303-9021 Vlaams Diergeneeskundig Tijdschrift **8815**
0303-903X Belgium. Rijksstation voor Sierplantenteelt. Mededelingen†
0303-9056 Belgium. Rijksstation voor Landbouwtechniek. Mededelingen
0303-9099 Annales de Gembloux†
0303-9102 Rijksuniversiteit te Gent. Mededelingen van de Fakulteit Diergeneeskunde†
0303-9145 Institut Royal Belge pour l'Amelioration de la Betterave. Publication Trimestrielle†
0303-9234 Jammu and Kashmir. Directorate of Economics and Statistics. Digest of Statistics **1246**
0303-9277 External Trade Statistics of Gambia **1228**
0303-9293 Journal of Commerce, Industry & Transportation
0303-9315 Sierra Leone Trade Fairs and Exhibitions
0303-9382 M E R A D O News†
0303-965X Revue Internationale des Sciences Administratives **7466**
0303-9676 Estudios Sociales Centroamericanos†
0303-9692 Schweizerische Zeitschrift fuer Volkswirtschaft und Statistik **1171**
0303-9714 Studi Parlamentari e di Politica Costituzionale **4790**
0303-9722 L'Amministrazione Italiana **7420**
0303-9757 Politeia **7167**
0303-9773 Universidade de Coimbra. Faculdade de Direito. Boletim **4944**
0303-9803 Cahiers Zairois de la Recherche et du Developpement
0303-9838 Universidade de Sao Paulo. Faculdade de Direito. Revista **4802**
0303-9862 Revista de Ciencias Sociais (Fortaleza) **7996**
0303-9889 Revista de Estudios Sociales†
0303-9897 De Economia†
0303-9900 Boletin Informativo de Ciencia Politica†
0303-9919 Anales de Economia†
0303-9935 Tijdschrift voor Social Geschiedenis *changed to* 1572-1701 **8144**
0303-9951 Indian Journal of Politics **7142**
0303-9986 Revista de Derecho U de C **4771**
0304-0003 L I A S: Sources and Documents Relating to the Early Modern History of Ideas **4150**
0304-002X Cultures (French Edition)†
0304-0100 I I C A en America†
0304-0119 Indice Agricola de America Latina y el Caribe†
0304-016X International Pacific Halibut Commission. Scientific Report **3598**
0304-0208 North-Holland Mathematics Studies **5521**
0304-0313 Patologia e Clinica Ostetrica e Ginecologica†
0304-0356 Rassegna Medica. English Edition†
0304-0550 Istituto Sperimentale per la Floricoltura. Annali†
0304-0593 Rivista di Ingegneria Agraria **251**
0304-0607 Rivista di Zootecnia e Veterinaria
0304-0615 Istituto Sperimentale Agronomico. Annali
0304-064X Giornale di Agricoltura†
0304-0658 Laboratorio di Entomologia Agraria Filippo Silvestri. Bollettino
0304-0666 Annuario dell'Agricoltura Italiana **92**
0304-0712 Amsterdam Studies in the Theory and History of Linguistic Science. Series 1: Amsterdam Classics in Linguistics, 1800-1925†
0304-0720 Amsterdam Studies in the Theory and History of Linguistic Science. Series 3: Studies in the History of the Language Sciences **5093**
0304-0763 Amsterdam Studies in the Theory and History of Linguistic Science. Series 4: Current Issues in Linguistic Theory **5093**
0304-078X Cultures†
0304-0941 Decision **1738**
0304-095X Bangladesh Development Studies **1440**
0304-0992 Statistical Yearbook of Jamaica **8405**
0304-100X Services Law Cases **4782**
0304-1042 Japanese Journal of Religious Studies **7737**
0304-1158 Indian School of Mines. Annual Report **2866**
0304-1166 Chemical India Annual
0304-1190 Ghana†
0304-1204 Free China Today†
0304-1239 K L O E Impulse†
0304-1409 Atheist†
0304-1476 Dens **5839**
0304-162X Times of India. Index†
0304-1662 Association of Medical Women in India. Journal
0304-1735 New Zealand. Soil Bureau. Scientific Report†
0304-1743 Norwegian Maritime Research†
0304-176X Planning and Administration† **8981**
0304-1786 Prospect†
0304-1840 Remedia
0304-1913 Sociedad y Derecho
0304-1972 Trinity College Journal **3005**
0304-2065 Energie†
0304-2081 Hokkaido Rihabiriteshon Gakkai Zasshi **6110**
0304-2138 Fundacao Servicos de Saude Publica. Revista
0304-2146 Nihon Nettai Igakkai Zasshi/Japanese Journal of Tropical Medicine and Hygiene *changed to* 1348-8945 **5827**
0304-2154 Akademie der Wissenschaften der D.D.R. Jahrbuch†
0304-2162 Le Mois Economique et Financier†
0304-2170 Indonesian Quarterly **7142**
0304-2189 Irian: Bulletin of Irian Jaya **343**
0304-2197 Jahrbuch Internationale Politik und Wirtschaft†
0304-2227 Burma Research Society. Journal†
0304-2243 Journal of Ethiopian Studies **4176**
0304-226X Siam Society. Journal **8001**
0304-2286 University of Bombay. Journal **8012**
0304-2294 Linguistica Antverpiensia *changed to* Linguistica Antverpiensia. New Series **5146**
0304-2324 Al Qanun Wa-al Iqtisad **1162**
0304-2340 Universidade Federal de Minas Gerais. Faculdade de Direito. Revista **4802**
0304-2367 Museo Nacional. Revista†
0304-2383 Revue Zairoise de Droit†
0304-2405 Social Praxis†
0304-2421 Theory and Society **8143**
0304-243X Trabalhos de Antropologia e Etnologia **358**
0304-2448 Toho Gakuho **562**
0304-2499 Tecnica Pesquera†
0304-2502 Pastizales **295**
0304-2529 Actividades en Turrialba†
0304-2561 Buhuth **7951**
0304-2588 Pontificio Museo Missionario Etnologico. Annali†
0304-2596 Anuario Indigenista **328**
0304-260X Asian Economies
0304-2618 Berichte und Informationen†
0304-2669 Cadernos de Estudos Rurais e Urbanos†
0304-2685 Ciencia & Tropico **7955**
0304-2707 Cahiers Zairois d'Etudes Politiques et Sociales **7112**
0304-2731 Drejtesia Popullore
0304-274X National Bank of Egypt. Economic Bulletin **1500**
0304-2758 Estudios de Economia **1106**
0304-2774 Etudes Senegalaises
0304-2782 Europaeische Rundschau **7233**
0304-2820 Revista de Derecho y Reforma Agraria **4771**
0304-2839 Documentacion e Informacion para el Desarrollo Agricola†
0304-2847 Facultad Nacional de Agronomia Medellin. Revista **110**
0304-2863 Colloquium Internationale†
0304-2871 European Organization for Nuclear Research. List of Scientific Publications **7048**
0304-288X C E R N Courier **7065**
0304-2898 C E R N School of Computing. Proceedings **7939**
0304-2901 C E R N Annual Report
0304-291X C E R N Rapport Annuel *see* 0304-2901
0304-3037 Revue Internationale des Sciences Sociales **7998**
0304-3045 Perspectives (Paris, 1971) **2897**
0304-3053 Perspectivas *see* 0304-3045 **2897**
0304-3053 Perspectivas *see* 0033-1538 **2900**
0304-310X El Correo de la Unesco†
0304-3118 Le Courrier de l'Unesco†
0304-3126 O Correio da Unesco†
0304-3134 Il Corriere Unesco†
0304-324X Gerontology **4046**
0304-3274 Perspectives Economiques de l'O E C D **1159**
0304-3282 O E C D Guide to Legislation on Restrictive Business Practices Supplements†
0304-3320 Recherche en Matiere d'Economie des Transports **8509**
0304-3363 O C D E. Etudes Economiques **1502**
0304-3398 Observateur de l'O C D E *see* 0029-7054 **1504**
0304-341X Nuclear Law Bulletin **3172**
0304-3460 Goodwin Series. Occasional Papers **395**
0304-3479 Russian Literature **5365**
0304-3487 Russian Linguistics **5170**
0304-3495 Rumanian Studies†
0304-3509 Revista Pedagogjike **2907**
0304-3517 Romania Libera **3933**
0304-3525 Romanian Orthodox Church News†
0304-355X China Forum **4181**
0304-3584 Actualidades Biologicas **650**
0304-3606 Irrinews†
0304-3665 Bulletin Legislatif Belge **4633**
0304-3681 Extern†
0304-3703 Vinculos **360**
0304-3711 Brenesia **7841**
0304-3754 Alternatives **7220**
0304-3770 Aquatic Botany **776**
0304-3797 European Journal of Engineering Education **3192**
0304-3800 Ecological Modelling **3481**
0304-3835 Cancer Letters **6013**
0304-3843 Hyperfine Interactions **7015**
0304-3851 Journal of Applied Science and Engineering Section A. Electrical Power and Information Systems†
0304-386X Hydrometallurgy **6315**
0304-3878 Journal of Development Economics **1600**
0304-3886 Journal of Electrostatics **3322**
0304-3894 Journal of Hazardous Materials **3508**
0304-3932 Journal of Monetary Economics **1362**
0304-3940 Neuroscience Letters **6169**
0304-3959 Pain **6172**
0304-3975 Theoretical Computer Science **2601**
0304-3991 Ultramicroscopy **7044**
0304-4017 Veterinary Parasitology **8813**
0304-4025 Wave Electronics†
0304-4033 Revista Centroamericana de Nutricion y Ciencias de Alimentos†
0304-405X Journal of Financial Economics **1136**
0304-4068 Journal of Mathematical Economics **1545**
0304-4076 Journal of Econometrics **1544**
0304-4092 Dialectical Anthropology **335**
0304-4114 Mass Emergencies†
0304-4130 European Journal of Political Research **7134**
0304-4149 Stochastic Processes and Their Applications **5538**
0304-4165 B B A - General Subjects **723**
0304-4173 B B A - Reviews on Bioenergetics†
0304-4181 Journal of Medieval History **4236**
0304-419X B B A - Reviews on Cancer **6009**
0304-4203 Marine Chemistry **2712**
0304-422X Poetics **5352**
0304-4238 Scientia Horticulturae **3750**
0304-4246 Contributions to Gynecology and Obstetrics **5988**
0304-4254 Pediatric and Adolescent Endocrinology†
0304-4270 INSEAD Alumni Association Address Book **2288**
0304-4289 Pramana **7035**
0304-4300 Analecta Sacra Tarraconensia **7621**
0304-4319 Anuario de Historia del Derecho Espanol **4619**
0304-4408 Rejuvenation†
0304-4475 Barcelona Quirurgica†
0304-4521 Madras Institute of Neurology. Proceedings
0304-4556 Iranian Journal of Public Health **7527**
0304-4602 Academy of Medicine, Singapore. Annals **5565**
0304-4629 Geneesmiddelenbulletin **6844**
0304-4645 Handbook of Electroencephalography and Clinical Neurophysiology
0304-4793 Turk Otolarengoloji Arsivi **6086**
0304-4831 The Egyptian Journal of Gastroenterology **5922**
0304-4858 Gaceta Medica de Bilbao **5617**
0304-4866 Galicia Clinica†
0304-4920 Chinese Journal of Physiology **921**
0304-5013 Progresos de Obstetricia y Ginecologia **6002**
0304-5048 Siemens-Albis. Berichte†
0304-5056 Revista Espanola de Cirugia Osteoarticular†
0304-5218 Islamabad Journal of Sciences **7869**
0304-5242 Journal of Plantation Crops **239**
0304-5250 Indian Journal of Ecology **3439**
0304-5277 Chemical Education **2054**
0304-5293 Academia Sinica. Institute of Physics. Annual Report **7003**
0304-5323 Museum Memoir†
0304-5331 Administration for Development†
0304-534X I N S D O C Russian Scientific and Technical Publications. Accessions List†
0304-5358 Contents List of Soviet Scientific Periodicals†
0304-5374 Comparative Animal Nutrition†
0304-5412 Medicine **5674**
0304-5439 C I M M Y T Report on Wheat Improvement†
0304-5447 C I M M Y T Today†
0304-5463 C I M M Y T Review†
0304-548X C I M M Y T Report on Maize Improvement†
0304-551X C I M M Y T Information Bulletin†
0304-5544 C I I D Informa *see* 0315-9981 **1597**
0304-5609 Ciencia e Investigacion Agraria **101**
0304-5617 Investigacion Agricola†
0304-5692 Zaire. Institut National de la Statistique. Annuaire des Statistiques du Commerce Exterieur†
0304-5714 Institut Oceanographique. Memoires **2807**
0304-5722 Institut Oceanographique. Bulletin **2807**
0304-5757 Conjonction **3874**
0304-5765 Tropical Grain Legume Bulletin†
0304-582X F A O Documentation - Current Bibliography†
0304-5897 Cerberus Electronic†
0304-5935 Abstracts of Geochronology and Isotope Geology†
0304-5978 G E R V Activiteitsverslag†
0304-6117 Administrator **3016**
0304-6125 Afghanistan Journal†
0304-615X Africanus **7103**
0304-6184 Madhya Pradesh. Directorate of Agriculture. Agricultural Statistics **183**
0304-6214 A I I S Quarterly Newsletter **541**
0304-6257 Amsterdamer Beitraege zur Neueren Germanistik **5253**
0304-6451 Association of Urban Authorities. Annual Bulletin **7488**
0304-6478 Pakistan. Finance Division. Annual Budget Statement (Final) **1938**
0304-6729 Arab Fund for Economic and Social Development. Annual Report **1590**
0304-6796 Central Bank of Barbados. Annual Report **1446**
0304-6818 Central Sericultural Research and Training Institute. Annual Report **100**
0304-6907 Cotton Corporation of India. Annual Report **196**
0304-6915 Creditanstalt-Bankverein. Annual Report **1333**
0304-6931 Zambia. Department of Legal Aid. Annual Report **4818**
0304-6966 Deposit Insurance Corporation. Annual Report: Directors' Report, Balance Sheet and Accounts **4501**
0304-7032 Indian Council of Historical Research. Annual Report **4183**
0304-7067 Indian Veterinary Research Institute. Annual Report **8799**
0304-7083 Institute of Secretariat Training and Management. Annual Report **1866**
0304-7121 I I A S A Annual Report **3482**
0304-7164 Jammu & Kashmir Minerals Limited. Annual Report **6467**
0304-7202 Kenya National Trading Corporation. Annual Report **1430**
0304-7237 Kuwait National Petroleum Company. Annual Report **6776**
0304-7245 Madhya Pradesh State Agro-Industries Development Corporation Ltd. Annual Report **203**
0304-727X Liberia. Ministry of Finance. Annual Report
0304-730X Liberia. Ministry of Local Government, Rural Development & Urban Reconstruction. Annual Report
0304-7326 Liberia. Ministry of Public Works. Annual Report

ISSN

9242 0304-7350 ULRICH'S PERIODICALS

0304-7350 Singapore. National Statistical Commission. Annual Report†
0304-7652 International Civil Aviation Organization. Air Navigation Plan. European Region **60**
0304-7709 Marga Institute. Annual Report **7984**
0304-7725 Lusaka. Medical Officer of Health. Annual Report†
0304-7849 Fiji. Office of the Ombudsman. Annual Report of the Ombudsman **4674**
0304-8101 Punjab National Bank. Annual Report **1377**
0304-811X Republic Forge Company. Annual Report **1903**
0304-8152 Salar Jung Museum. Annual Report **6536**
0304-8179 Shellac Export Promotion Council. Annual Report **6721**
0304-8233 University of Rajasthan. South Asian Studies Centre. Annual Report **563**
0304-8349 United Planting Association of Malaysia. Annual Report **208**
0304-8365 University of Malawi. Centre for Extension Studies. Annual Report†
0304-8373 Jamaica. Urban Development Corporation. Annual Report **4416**
0304-8551 Arab Oil & Gas Directory **6762**
0304-8608 Archives of Virology **881**
0304-8616 Archivos de Farmacologia y Toxicologia†
0304-8624 Armenian Studies
0304-8667 Asian Press
0304-8675 Asian Profile **543**
0304-8683 Asiryada
0304-8705 Astronautical Research†
0304-8713 Austria Today **3797**
0304-8721 Automobil **8563**
0304-8764 Medio Ambiente **3452**
0304-8799 Bosque **3685**
0304-8802 Agro Sur **86**
0304-8845 P T L†
0304-8853 Journal of Magnetism and Magnetic Materials **7020**
0304-8861 Anuario Bibliografico Uruguayo **615**
0304-9027 Bangladesh Journal of Zoology **935**
0304-9078 Behaviorometric **7949**
0304-9124 Bhopal University Research Journal
0304-9272 Brahmana-Gaurava
0304-9345 Bangladesh Bank. Bulletin **1440**
0304-9515 Haffkine Institute. Bulletin†
0304-9523 Astronomical Society of India. Bulletin **569**
0304-9558 Indian Institute of History of Medicine. Bulletin **5633**
0304-9620 Societe des Naturalistes Luxembourgeois. Bulletin **705**
0304-968X Buy from India **1977**
0304-971X Revista de Biologia del Uruguay
0304-9787 Aligarh Bulletin of Mathematics **5468**
0304-9795 Annals of Systems Research†
0304-9809 Bangladesh Journal of Scientific and Industrial Research **7839**
0304-9825 Academia Sinica. Institute of Mathematics. Bulletin *changed to* Academia Sinica. Institute of Mathematics. Bulletin. New Series **5464**
0304-985X Delft Progress Report†
0304-9876 Electronics Information and Planning
0304-9884 Indian Journal of Engineering Mathematics **5493**
0304-9914 Korean Mathematical Society. Journal **5508**
0304-9957 Instituto de Optica "Daza de Valdes". Publicacion **7077**
0305-0009 Journal of Child Language **2156**
0305-0041 Cambridge Philosophical Society. Mathematical Proceedings **5477**
0305-0068 Comparative Education **2838**
0305-0122 The Bulk Carrier Register **8640**
0305-0130 Local Government Companion **7496**
0305-0173 Northern Architect
0305-0270 Journal of Biogeography **4017**
0305-0319 Cosmetic World News† **8944**
0305-0351 C I P Descriptions of Plant-Parasitic Nematodes†
0305-0394 Geological Society of London. Miscellaneous Paper **2739**
0305-0440 Historical Breechloading Smallarms Association. Journal **6424**
0305-0467 Freezer Foods†
0305-0475 Computer Applications in Archaeology **425**
0305-0483 Omega **1782**
0305-0548 Computers & Operations Research **2413**
0305-0629 International Interactions **7243**
0305-0637 Classified World
0305-0688 Rock Carling Fellowship **5707**
0305-0718 Commonwealth Law Bulletin **4646**
0305-0734 The Middle East **5227**
0305-0742 A A Members Handbook. Ireland **8553**
0305-0920 Appropriate Technology **194**
0305-0998 Norwegian Chamber of Commerce. Year Book and Directory of Members
0305-103X Urban Abstracts **4437**
0305-1048 Nucleic Acids Research **741**
0305-1064 The Collegian **2278**
0305-1218 Ratel **961**
0305-1293 Laboratory Reports†
0305-1366 Environmental Directory†
0305-1420 British Railways Board. Annual Report and Accounts†
0305-1439 N E L Report **3211**
0305-1471 N M M News†
0305-1498 Oxford Literary Review **5347**
0305-1536 Home and School†
0305-1706 Film Dope **6498**
0305-1765 Loughton Review **28**
0305-1781 C I R I A Technical Note **3261**
0305-179X The Tanker Register **8663**
0305-1803 The Liquid Gas Carrier Register *changed to* 1478-4610 **8644**
0305-182X Journal of Oral Rehabilitation **5852**
0305-1838 Mammal Review **954**
0305-1846 Neuropathology and Applied Neurobiology **6167**
0305-1862 Child: Care, Health and Development **6089**
0305-1870 Clinical and Experimental Pharmacology & Physiology **921**
0305-196X Ecological Abstracts **715**
0305-1978 Biochemical Systematics and Ecology **725**
0305-1986 Concrete Society Technical Report **993**
0305-2001 Royal Observatory, Edinburgh. Publications†
0305-2109 Communications International†
0305-215X Engineering Optimization **3190**
0305-2257 National Electronics Review†
0305-2680 Descriptions of Plant Viruses†
0305-2729 C I P Keys to the Nematode Parasites of Vertebrates†
0305-3067 Grove Booklet on Ministry & Worship **7759**
0305-3121 Machinery Buyers' Guide **5455**
0305-3326 University of East Anglia. Calendar **2962**
0305-3342 The Medical Directory
0305-3555 Fabian Research Series†
0305-3601 Communication & Broadcasting†
0305-3679 Essex Union List of Serials†
0305-3717 Zambezi Press International
0305-3849 Par Golf
0305-3903 University of Durham Calendar
0305-3954 Who Owns What in World Banking
0305-4047 C I R I A Annual Report **3261**
0305-408X C I R I A Report **3261**
0305-411X Council of Legal Education. Calendar
0305-4136 Hospital Update†
0305-4179 Burns **6057**
0305-4284 Offshore Drilling Register†
0305-439X Processing†
0305-4403 Journal of Archaeological Science **400**
0305-442X Kennel Club Yearbook **6810**
0305-4438 Music and Liturgy **6589**
0305-4470 Journal of Physics A: Mathematical and General (Print) *changed to* 1751-8113 **7022**
0305-4543 Spon's Mechanical & Electrical Services Price Book **1037**
0305-4659 Northamptonshire Archaeology **408**
0305-4756 Camden History Review **4209**
0305-4780 News of the World Football Annual **8240**
0305-4829 Heat Treatment of Metals†
0305-4934 Ornamental Horticulture **3755**
0305-4985 Oxford Review of Education **2894**
0305-5000 Dental Update **5841**
0305-5132 Year Book of Chess **8217**
0305-5167 The British Library Journal†
0305-5426 Programming Index†
0305-5477 Vernacular Architecture **460**
0305-5493 Locomotion Papers **8502**
0305-5582 Urban and Regional Planning Series†
0305-5604 Health Education News†
0305-5663 Wireless World Annual†
0305-5698 Educational Studies **2851**
0305-5728 V I N E **5064**
0305-5736 Policy and Politics **7166**
0305-5752 Property Studies in the U K and Overseas†
0305-5795 Devon Archaeological Society. Proceedings **390**
0305-5892 Register of Thoroughbred Stallions†
0305-5906 Municipal Year Book **7498**
0305-5914 University of Reading. Department of Geography. Geographical Papers Series **4033**
0305-5973 B S R I A Application Guides **4116**
0305-5981 Omnibus (Bracknell)†
0305-6104 Independent Broadcasting†
0305-6120 Circuit World **8418**
0305-6147 Radical Education
0305-6198 Saturated Heterocyclic Chemistry†
0305-6244 Review of African Political Economy **7262**
0305-6325 World of Tennis **8252**
0305-6481 I R C S Journal of Medical Science†
0305-649X I R C S Medical Science: Classified List†
0305-652X Pick
0305-6848 I R C S Medical Science: Neurobiology and Neurophysiology†
0305-6856 I R C S Medical Science: Neurology and Neurosurgery†
0305-6864 I R C S Medical Science: Pediatrics†
0305-6899 I R C S Medical Science: Psychiatry and Clinical Psychology†
0305-6902 I R C S Medical Science: Psychology†
0305-6961 I R C S Medical Science: Veterinary Science†
0305-697X Inorganic Chemistry of the Main Group Elements†
0305-7046 Clothing Machinery Times†
0305-7070 Journal of Southern African Studies **7980**
0305-7194 C E G B Research†
0305-7232 Cancer Biochemistry Biophysics
0305-7240 Journal of Moral Education **2877**
0305-7259 Mathematics in School **5515**
0305-7267 Studies in Science Education **3083**
0305-733X Blinds and Shutters **4554**
0305-7348 Ideas†
0305-7356 Psychology of Music **6608**
0305-7364 Annals of Botany **775**
0305-7372 Cancer Treatment Reviews **6014**
0305-7402 Containerisation International Yearbook **8641**
0305-7410 China Quarterly **546**
0305-7429 Modern China Studies. International Bulletin†
0305-7453 Journal of Antimicrobial Chemotherapy **5819**
0305-7488 Journal of Historical Geography **4017**
0305-750X World Development **1608**
0305-7518 Leprosy Review **5822**
0305-7593 Modern Languages in Scotland†
0305-764X Cambridge Journal of Education **2970**
0305-7674 Cambridge Anthropology **332**
0305-7712 Environmental Chemistry†
0305-7755 Teaching English†
0305-781X Association of British Theological and Philosophical Libraries. Bulletin **4992**
0305-7828 Aether
0305-7844 Fire Prevention Science and Technology†
0305-7887 British Library. Annual Report (Year) **4998**
0305-7925 Compare **2838**
0305-7984 University of Manchester. School of Education. Gazette†
0305-7992 Proof†
0305-8018 Teaching Geography **4030**
0305-8034 London Journal **4241**
0305-8069 C B I Overseas Reports
0305-8131 B C R A Review†
0305-814X Reading in Political Economy **1164**
0305-8174 Offshore Fishing†
0305-8190 University of Oxford. School of Geography. Research Papers **4032**
0305-8204 Current Topics in Immunology
0305-8298 Millennium **7253**
0305-8344 New Review (London, 1974)†
0305-8417 Primate Eye **352**
0305-8506 Borthwick Texts and Calendars *changed to* 1748-9474 **4206**
0305-8549 Devon Historian **4214**
0305-8611 The Association for Scottish Literary Studies. Occasional Paper **5257**
0305-862X African Research and Documentation **3516**
0305-8646 University of Glasgow. Institute of Latin American Studies. Occasional Papers†
0305-8689 Background Data on the Common Market†
0305-8719 Geological Society Special Publication **2739**
0305-8727 Bristol Record Society. Publications **7488**
0305-876X Offshore Engineer **6782**
0305-8824 University of Aberdeen. Annual Report **2306**
0305-8832 Aberdeen University Awards **2271**
0305-8921 Tolley's Corporation Tax **1952**
0305-893X Tolley's Income Tax **1952**
0305-9006 Progress in Planning **4424**
0305-9049 Oxford Bulletin of Economics and Statistics **1157**
0305-9111 Classroom Geographer†
0305-9154 Plant Growth Regulator Abstracts **185**
0305-9189 State Librarian *changed to* 1750-6883
0305-9219 Viking Society for Northern Research. Saga-Book **4277**
0305-9227 University of Liverpool Calendar **3008**
0305-9243 Omnibus Magazine **8507**
0305-926X Housman Society Journal **5306**
0305-9308 Writer (Zennor)†
0305-9324 Fellowship for Freedom in Medicine. Newsletter
0305-9332 Industrial Law Journal **1687**
0305-9340 Health and Welfare Libraries Quarterly†
0305-9367 Insurance†
0305-9464 Teaching Geography. Occasional Paper **4030**
0305-9499 Applecon†
0305-9529 New Internationalist **7255**
0305-9545 Carbonization Research Report†
0305-9553 Standard Chartered Review†
0305-9596 I E E Medical Electronics Monographs†
0305-960X Religious Books in Print†
0305-9642 Hospital Life†
0305-9669 Family Practitioner Services†
0305-9677 Open University Gazette **2295**
0305-9715 Aromatic and Heteroaromatic Chemistry†
0305-9723 Colloid Science†
0305-9731 Chemical Thermodynamics†
0305-974X Dielectric and Related Molecular Processes†
0305-9766 Electronic Structure & Magnetism of Inorganic Compounds†
0305-9774 Inorganic Chemistry of the Transition Elements†
0305-9782 Molecular Spectroscopy†
0305-9790 Molecular Structure by Diffraction Methods†
0305-9804 Nuclear Magnetic Resonance **2139**
0305-9812 Organic Compounds of Sulphur, Selenium and Tellurium†
0305-9839 Hard Cheese
0305-9863 Buying Antiques
0305-988X Modern Purchasing†
0305-9898 Borthwick Institute Bulletin†
0305-9928 Henley Centre for Forecasting. Costs & Prices†
0305-9936 Framework Forecast for the E E C Economies†
0305-9960 Statistical Mechanics†
0305-9979 Electrochemistry†
0305-9987 Mass Spectrometry†
0305-9995 Theoretical Chemistry†
0306-0012 Chemical Society Reviews **2055**
0306-0020 Mantatoforos†
0306-0128 Dance Gazette **2684**
0306-0152 Great Britain. Property Services Agency. Construction References†
0306-0160 Leicestershire, Northamptonshire & Rutland Farmer **134**
0306-0179 Engineering Capacity **3189**
0306-0195 Poetry Post **5431**
0306-0209 The Naval Architect **8654**
0306-0284 Bibliography of Insecticide Materials of Vegetable Origin†
0306-0314 C I P A **6747**
0306-0322 The African Book Publishing Record **7577**
0306-0349 Airtrade†
0306-0357 Organ Club Journal **6603**
0306-0373 Delius Society Journal **6561**
0306-0403 Swimming Teacher
0306-0470 Public Authorities Directory *changed to* Local Government Directory (Year) **7496**
0306-0497 Self & Society **7407**
0306-0519 Furniture Manufacturer **4557**
0306-056X Street Research Bulletin
0306-0586 High-Speed Ground Transportation and Urban Rapid Transit Systems Bibliography Service†
0306-0594 Air-Cushion and Hydrofoil Systems Bibliography Service†
0306-0608 Grove Liturgical Studies **7759**
0306-0624 University of York. Institute of Advanced Architectural Studies. Research Papers **460**
0306-0659 Stable Management
0306-0675 North Riding and Durham Farmer. Whole Edition **142**
0306-0713 Organophosphorus Chemistry **2128**
0306-0837 Llafur **1696**
0306-0861 Scottish Small Presses
0306-0888 Walker Art Gallery. Annual Report and Bulletin **6540**
0306-0896 Pacifica **6897**
0306-0926 The Oriental Ceramic Society. Transactions **2044**
0306-0942 Service Point **5047**
0306-1051 Antiques Trade Gazette **363**
0306-1078 Early Music **6563**
0306-1108 University of Sussex. Centre for Continuing Education. Occasional Paper **2947**
0306-1124 Commonwealth Bibliographies†

9244 0307-2444 ULRICH'S PERIODICALS

0307-2444 Studies for Trade Unionists†
0307-2460 East Anglian Archaeology. Report **391**
0307-2517 Knitting World & Textile Manufacturer†
0307-2606 Locke Newsletter *changed to* 1476-0290 **6932**
0307-2614 S E E Journal
0307-2657 B S B I Abstracts **713**
0307-2681 Sun (London) **3871**
0307-269X Sunday Telegraph **3871**
0307-2711 Evening Echo, Bournemouth† **8955**
0307-2738 Western Daily Press **3873**
0307-2770 New German Studies†
0307-2835 Kew Record of Taxonomic Literature Relating to Vascular Plants **717**
0307-2851 Midland Ancestor
0307-2916 Fireweed†
0307-2991 What Car? **8612**
0307-3017 Dinghy Sailing
0307-3025 Corporate Planner's Yearbook
0307-3041 The Management Specialist **1777**
0307-3149 Jane's Ocean Technology†
0307-3238 York Papers in Linguistics **5197**
0307-3262 Iberian Studies† **8963**
0307-3319 Great North Review **8618**
0307-3335 Matrix **5444**
0307-3378 Bulletin of Economic Research **1070**
0307-3394 Cardiff Medical Society. Scientific Proceedings†
0307-3408 Bard† **8935**
0307-3459 Warlord†
0307-353X Insight: Soviet Jews†
0307-3572 Tennyson Society (England). Occasional Papers **5386**
0307-3610 Telegraph & Argus **3872**
0307-4293 New Fiction†
0307-4331 Austria
0307-434X British Directory of Little Magazines and Small Presses†
0307-4358 Managerial Finance **1778**
0307-4366 Lady Golfer's Handbook **8237**
0307-4382 Club **5106**
0307-4463 Population Trends **7291**
0307-4552 Barclays Country Reports†
0307-4617 Screen International **6512**
0307-4625 Centerpiece†
0307-4676 Security and Fire Equipment Selector†
0307-4706 International Fireball **8276**
0307-4722 Art Libraries Journal **4991**
0307-4730 British Journal of Clinical Equipment†
0307-4803 New Library World **5035**
0307-4811 The Vegan **6670**
0307-4870 Journal of Planning and Environment Law **4704**
0307-4951 International Financial Bulletin
0307-5036 Royal Scottish Museum Information Series: Natural History†
0307-5044 Royal Scottish Museum Information Series: Technology†
0307-5052 Royal Scottish Museum Information Series: Geology†
0307-5079 Studies in Higher Education **3003**
0307-5087 Contrebis **388**
0307-5095 Journal of Electrophysiological Technology *changed to* 1757-8973 **920**
0307-5133 Journal of Egyptian Archaeology **400**
0307-5265 Y Faner **5215**
0307-5281 Watford and District Industrial History Society. Journal **4278**
0307-529X The Kist **4237**
0307-532X Countryside Commission. Research Register **2608**
0307-5354 S P E L†
0307-5362 The Surtees Society. Publications **4272**
0307-5397 Tabard†
0307-5400 European Law Review **4669**
0307-5451 History of Technology **8424**
0307-546X Tangent
0307-5508 Community Care (Sutton) **8034**
0307-5532 The Way. Supplement†
0307-5583 Cromwelliana **4212**
0307-5591 Industrial Relations Law Reports **1688**
0307-5664 Belfast Telegraph **3861**
0307-5753 The Sunday Post **3871**
0307-5761 Evening News (Edinburgh) **3865**
0307-577X Electric Vehicles
0307-580X Jeweller†
0307-5850 The Scotsman **3870**
0307-5869 The Courier & Advertiser **3863**
0307-5877 Sunday Mail **3871**
0307-5923 The Belfast News Letter **3892**
0307-5958 Mount Carmel **7808**
0307-5966 Journal of Meteorology *changed to* 1748-2992 **6358**
0307-6032 Who's Who in Finance†
0307-6040 Who's Who in Corrugated **6739**
0307-6067 Community Work†
0307-6113 International Directory of Current Research in the History of Cartography and in Carto-Bibliography†
0307-6164 British Plastics and Rubber Magazine **7091**
0307-6172 Derry Journal **3864**
0307-6202 Sheffield University Calendar **3002**
0307-6334 Church Music Quarterly **6556**
0307-6490 Automotive Engineer **8564**
0307-6539 Commonwealth Magistrates' Conference. Report
0307-6547 Great Britain. Department of Energy. Report on Research and Development†
0307-6571 Coin Yearbook **6650**
0307-6598 Topics in Gastroenterology **5932**
0307-6601 Exhibitions & Conferences†
0307-661X T L S **5384**
0307-6628 Cheshire Archaeological Bulletin†
0307-6652 Notes on Water Research†
0307-6679 Stamp Magazine **6900**
0307-6687 Tolley's Tax Tables (Year) **1952**
0307-6695 New Aspects of Breast Cancer†
0307-6717 Criminal Statistics, Scotland
0307-6741 Toy Retailing News†
0307-6768 Management Services **1777**
0307-6822 Road Accidents in Great Britain **8634**
0307-6903 S C O C L I S News†
0307-6911 Roof **4426**
0307-6938 Clinical and Experimental Dermatology **5873**
0307-6946 Ecological Entomology **843**
0307-6962 Physiological Entomology **857**
0307-6970 Systematic Entomology **860**
0307-7039 Politics Today†
0307-7055 Agent's Hotel Gazetteer: Resorts of Europe **4381**
0307-7144 Lore and Language **5148**
0307-7195 Printing Industries†
0307-7225 Church of England. General Synod. Report of Proceedings **7751**
0307-7233 German Political Studies†
0307-7276 Weyfarers **5438**
0307-7349 Soviet Non-Ferrous Metals Research†
0307-7403 Recent Advances in Clinical Neurology†
0307-7411 Air Extra†
0307-7497 Occasional Papers in German Studies (Coventry) **5345**
0307-7543 Trade Union Register†
0307-7578 Daily Mail **3863**
0307-7608 International Steel Statistics - United Kingdom **6340**
0307-7667 Quarterly Review of Marketing†
0307-7683 New Civil Engineer **3279**
0307-7691 National Coal Board Statistical Tables†
0307-7748 Lyles Official Arms & Armour Review†
0307-7861 Accountants Weekly†
0307-7942 Energy World **3134**
0307-7950 Heating and Air Conditioning Journal **4120**
0307-8051 Courtauld Institute Illustration Archives. Archive 1†
0307-806X Courtauld Institute Illustration Archives. Archive 2†
0307-8078 Courtauld Institute Illustration Archives. Archive 3†
0307-8086 Courtauld Institute Illustration Archives. Archive 4†
0307-8140 Northumberland & Durham Family History Society. Journal **3777**
0307-8175 Bank of England. Statistical Abstract†
0307-823X Sussex Anthropology†
0307-8388 Themelios **7688**
0307-8477 Newscheck **6701**
0307-8531 Rare Earth Bulletin† **8984**
0307-8590 Maritime Monographs and Reports†
0307-8647 Bar Quarterly†
0307-8698 Ringing and Migration **913**
0307-8833 Theatre Research International **8483**
0307-8884 Seed
0307-904X Applied Mathematical Modelling **5550**
0307-9058 Great Britain. Centre for Overseas Pest Research. Miscellaneous Report†
0307-9074 Stream **8832**
0307-9082 Great Britain. Centre for Overseas Pest Research. Report†
0307-9112 London Mystery Selection†
0307-9163 Association of Art Historians. Bulletin **476**
0307-9201 Sage Race Relations Abstracts *changed to* Race Relations Abstracts **8150**
0307-9244 Le Nurb **2294**
0307-9252 Communicator†
0307-9325 Brick Bulletin **983**
0307-9384 NRCd Publication **6972**
0307-9457 Avian Pathology **8794**
0307-9481 British Library News†
0307-9562 Thames Poetry†
0307-9570 Moonshine†
0307-9589 Great Britain. Civil Service Department. Report†
0307-9708 School and Community†
0307-9767 New Library Buildings†
0307-9813 Gay Left†
0307-9821 Halsbury's Laws of England Monthly Review **4952**
0307-9872 Greenwood Tree **3769**
0307-9929 Under 5†
0307-9961 ARTbibliographies Current Titles (Print Edition) *changed to* ARTbibliographies Current Titles (Email Edition)
0308-003X Tape and Hi-Fi Test†
0308-0110 Medical Education **5668**
0308-0129 English Philological Studies†
0308-0161 International Journal of Pressure Vessels and Piping **3383**
0308-017X Thomas Hardy Society. Newsletter†
0308-0188 Interdisciplinary Science Reviews **7867**
0308-0226 British Journal of Occupational Therapy **5589**
0308-034X Chile Fights†
0308-0382 Epworth Review **7756**
0308-0404 Enthusiasm **6497**
0308-0463 Harvard Business School Club of London Address Book **2286**
0308-048X Cranfield School of Management Address Book **2279**
0308-0501 Fire and Materials **3344**
0308-051X Pharmatherapeutica†
0308-0528 Middle East Construction†
0308-0544 Briefing† **8937**
0308-0587 Modern English Teacher **3073**
0308-0617 Catholic Life†
0308-0641 Truck **8676**
0308-065X Interfish
0308-0676 Warfare **6453**
0308-0757 I'Anson Times†
0308-0765 Human Rights Review†
0308-082X Town and Country Planning Association. Annual Report **4428**
0308-0838 Fern Gazette **787**
0308-0889 Four Decades†
0308-0900 London Facts and Figures†
0308-0943 Skinner's British Textile Register†
0308-0951 Charles Lamb Bulletin **5272**
0308-0978 Manx Life **3968**
0308-1060 Transportation Planning and Technology **8516**
0308-1079 International Journal of General Systems **2522**
0308-1087 Linear and Multilinear Algebra **5509**
0308-1222 Energy Trends **3133**
0308-1230 On Target **7161**
0308-1265 Brewing & Distilling International *changed to* 1753-2086 **600**
0308-1273 Netherlands-British Trade Directory **2019**
0308-129X Royal Society of Edinburgh. Communications, Physical Sciences†
0308-1656 Akhbar-E-Watan
0308-1745 Great Britain. Department of the Environment. Local Government Financial Statistics: England and Wales **7480**
0308-180X Natural History Book Reviews†
0308-1907 N A T F H E Journal†
0308-1958 Impact of Tax Changes on Income Distribution†
0308-1990 Footnote†
0308-2075 Occasional Papers in Linguistics and Language Learning
0308-2105 Royal Society of Edinburgh. Proceedings. Section A (Mathematics) **5530**
0308-213X International Planned Parenthood Federation. Report to Donors, Programme Development & Financial Statements
0308-2172 Management and Marketing Abstracts **1251**
0308-2199 British Mining **6459**
0308-2253 The Sea **8660**
0308-2261 Clinics in Hematology *see* Ematologia Clinica
0308-2318 Span (Stowmarket)†
0308-2342 Journal of Chemical Research. Synopses (Print Edition) *changed to* 1747-5198 **2067**
0308-2350 Journal of Chemical Research. Miniprint (Print Edition) *changed to* 1747-5198 **2067**
0308-2369 B C Engineering†
0308-2482 British Institute of International and Comparative Law. Newsletter **4919**
0308-2644 Trevithick Society. Journal **8444**
0308-2695 Chapman **5272**
0308-2717 International African Institute. Bulletin **4175**
0308-2725 African Languages **5091**
0308-275X Critique of Anthropology **334**
0308-2776 Prospice†
0308-2857 Survival International Review†
0308-2881 Christian Educator†
0308-2938 International Marketing Data and Statistics (Year) **1243**
0308-2997 Feeding-Weight and Obesity Abstracts†
0308-3039 Lace **8454**
0308-3047 Market Research G B **1830**
0308-3217 International†
0308-3233 Issues in Race and Education†
0308-3241 Advancement of Science† **8928**
0308-3306 Farming Industry†
0308-3322 Great Britain. Royal Greenwich Observatory. Annual Report†
0308-3330 Vintage Aircraft Magazine
0308-3381 Bananas
0308-342X Surrey Archaeological Society. Research Volumes **419**
0308-3446 Market Research Europe **1830**
0308-3462 Essex Archaeology and History **392**
0308-3497 City of London Recorder
0308-3594 Local Council Review **7496**
0308-3624 Lifeline **7660**
0308-3675 Great Britain. Institute of Terrestrial Ecology. Merlewood Research and Development Paper†
0308-3683 University of Oxford. Department of Engineering Science. Report **3225**
0308-3705 Consuming Interest†
0308-3748 Countryside Recreation Research Advisory Group. Abstracts **8778**
0308-3764 Court†
0308-3772 Belgian Patents Abstracts†
0308-390X United States Patents Abstracts. Part 3: Electrical†
0308-3918 United States Patents Abstracts. Part 2: General - Mechanical†
0308-3926 United States Patents Abstracts. Part 1: Chemical†
0308-3950 German Patents Gazette. Part 2. Mechanical & General†
0308-3969 German Patents Gazette. Part 3: Electrical†
0308-4183 Bristol and Avon Family History Society. Journal **3760**
0308-4205 Professional Printer† **8982**
0308-4221 Computer Applications†
0308-423X I B A Technical Review
0308-4272 Radiological Protection Bulletin *changed to* eBulletin
0308-4337 Ricardian Bulletin **4258**
0308-437X Acoustics Bulletin **7086**
0308-4450 West African Journal of Sociology and Political Science **8146**
0308-4469 Quarterly Bulletin of Cocoa Statistics **3661**
0308-4485 Offset Data Index†
0308-4531 Stella Polaris **6647**
0308-454X Television (London, 1927) **2396**
0308-4574 Bracton Law Journal **4631**
0308-4698 British Country Music Association. Yearbook
0308-4752 Omens **5428**
0308-4809 Northumbriana **4467**
0308-4914 Recent Advances in Orthopaedics†
0308-4949 Royal British Legion. Journal.†
0308-4957 Vida Hispanica **5193**
0308-499X Great Britain. Department of Trade. Insurance Business: Annual Report **4504**
0308-5074 Great Britain. Royal Greenwich Observatory. Bulletins†
0308-5104 Commonwealth Judicial Journal **4921**
0308-5147 Economy and Society **7961**
0308-518X Environment and Planning A **4410**
0308-5198 Defence Materiel†
0308-521X Agricultural Systems **85**
0308-5244 Manchester Business School Review **1147**
0308-5252 C W I Herald **7733**
0308-5368 Well Inventory Series. Metric Units **2774**
0308-5384 Biological Structure and Function†
0308-5392 Techniques of Physics **7043**
0308-5422 Proceedings of the International Cryogenic Engineering Conference *see* 0011-2275 **7053**
0308-5430 National Radiological Protection Board. Report **7069**
0308-5457 The Garden **3730**
0308-5538 Documents on International Affairs†
0308-5562 Oxoniensia **410**
0308-566X Industrial Specification†
0308-5694 Imago Mundi **4146**
0308-5759 Adoption and Fostering **8023**
0308-5791 British Flower

0308-5821 Africa Woman†
0308-5864 I D S Discussion Paper **1597**
0308-5899 Fortean Times **6741**
0308-5961 Telecommunications Policy **2341**
0308-597X Marine Policy **2812**
0308-602X Chest, Heart and Stroke Journal†
0308-6089 Theological Renewal **7777**
0308-6100 Craft & Hobby Dealer
0308-6119 University of London. Contemporary China Institute. Research Notes and Studies **563**
0308-6135 Portsmouth Magazine
0308-616X Housing Outlook†
0308-6194 Christian Parapsychologist
0308-6224 B S R I A Statistics Bulletin **4128**
0308-6259 Commercial Food Information
0308-6275 Dyslexia Review **3038**
0308-6283 New Poetry†
0308-6305 Ushaw Magazine†
0308-633X Transport Bibliography **8531**
0308-6348 Nottinghamshire Historian **4249**
0308-6380 Marfleet Society Newsletter **3774**
0308-6402 Fact Paper on Southern Africa†
0308-6461 Canadian Daily Record
0308-6534 The Journal of Imperial and Commonwealth History **4149**
0308-6623 Recent Advances in Respiratory Medicine†
0308-6631 Mining Magazine **6473**
0308-6666 Monthly Digest of Statistics **8389**
0308-6674 Mallorn **5444**
0308-6739 Freshwater Biological Association. Occasional Publications **673**
0308-6747 Architecture West Midlands†
0308-6763 University of East Anglia. Prospectus **2962**
0308-6771 University of East Anglia. Accounts **3034**
0308-6798 Survey of International Affairs†
0308-6852 Red Letters†
0308-6909 C O R E†
0308-695X Monthly Art Sales Index†
0308-6992 Geographers **4010**
0308-7026 Gas Marketing
0308-7085 I D S Handbook Series **1686**
0308-7123 Directory of Summer Jobs Abroad **1988**
0308-7166 Scottish Current Law Year Book†
0308-7212 In Touch (London) **1569**
0308-7298 History of Photography **6969**
0308-731X Cherwell **2277**
0308-7344 Potato Abstracts **185**
0308-7379 Scottish Diver **8199**
0308-7441 Lifeboat International **8649**
0308-745X Partners **5824**
0308-7484 Registered Accountant†
0308-7506 Tertiary Research Special Papers†
0308-7565 Canoeing†
0308-762X International Newsletter†
0308-7638 Forestry and British Timber *changed to* 1756-3275 **3712**
0308-7662 D H Lawrence Society. Journal **5282**
0308-7794 Metallurgical Plantmakers of the World **6324**
0308-7980 Oncology Abstracts†
0308-7999 Gazelle Review of Literature on the Middle East†
0308-8006 Steel Traders of the World **6334**
0308-8022 Scottish Fisheries Research Reports **3607**
0308-8030 Simon's Tax Cases **1943**
0308-809X ARLIS News-sheet **4991**
0308-812X Ley Hunter
0308-8146 Food Chemistry **2061**
0308-8197 Dairy Industries International **3633**
0308-8219 Bar List of the United Kingdom†
0308-8367 Laboratory Equipment Index†
0308-8405 Manchester United Football Book†
0308-8421 Seminar for Arabian Studies. Proceedings **416**
0308-8448 Design Engineering *changed to* 0013-7758 **3188**
0308-8456 Archaeology in Britain (Year)†
0308-8464 World Hotel Directory†
0308-8480 C A B News†
0308-8537 Bectis Bulletin **4994**
0308-8650 Wiring - Installations - Supplies†
0308-8669 Labour Weekly†
0308-8677 L A N S A **6651**
0308-8766 Society of Osteopaths. Journal†
0308-8774 Latest Literature in Family Planning†
0308-8790 Open University. B A Degree Handbook **2961**
0308-8839 Maritime Policy and Management **8652**
0308-8863 Agricultural Engineering Abstracts **174**
0308-888X Essays in Poetics†
0308-8928 Sweet and Maxwell's Students' Law Reporter† **8992**
0308-9002 Interest Rate Service **1355**
0308-9037 Kent Family History Society. Record Publication
0308-9088 City Directory (Year)
0308-9134 Security & Protection Equipment†
0308-9142 Iron and Steel International Directory (Year) **6317**
0308-924X D O E and C I R I A Piling Development Group. Report P G **1001**
0308-9274 A G M Service†
0308-9290 Research Fields in Physics at United Kingdom Universities and Polytechnics†
0308-9304 A B C Freight Guide **8666**
0308-9312 I D S Brief *changed to* 1748-2828 **1685**
0308-9339 I D S Studies *changed to* I D S H R Studies **1686**
0308-9347 Music Master
0308-9398 Footwear Industry Statistical Review **7942**
0308-9460 Car Buyer **8572**
0308-955X Food Industry Statistics Digest†
0308-9568 L A C News†
0308-9584 Agent's Hotel Gazetteer: Tourist Cities of Europe **4381**
0308-9614 Domestic Heating and Air Conditioning
0308-969X Registered Names of Horses†
0308-9770 Iron and Steel Industry: Monthly Statistics†
0308-9827 Spotlight Actresses **8479**
0308-9886 Body Lines
0309-0108 Royal Observatory, Edinburgh. Annual Report†
0309-0132 Great Britain. Medical Research Council. Handbook (Year)†
0309-0140 Recent Advances in Paediatrics **6103**
0309-0167 Histopathology **6021**
0309-0183 Spotlight Actors **8479**
0309-0248 B S R I A Technical Notes **4116**
0309-0256 Media Reporter **4579**
0309-0329 Canada - U.K. Year Book **1398**
0309-040X The Offshore Service Vessel Register *changed to* 1477-5395 **8656**
0309-0426 House Magazine **7444**
0309-0450 International Gas Bearing Symposium. Proceedings†
0309-0485 Degree Course Guides (Year) **2955**
0309-0531 Nutrition Information Centre. Bulletin†
0309-0558 Managerial Law *changed to* 1754-243X **1689**
0309-0566 European Journal of Marketing **1816**
0309-0574 Recommended Recordings†
0309-0590 Journal of European Industrial Training **1765**
0309-0671 International Law Reports **4931**
0309-068X Amnesty International Report **7221**
0309-0698 Monographs on Physical Biochemistry
0309-0701 Oxford Editions of Cuneiform Texts **410**
0309-0728 Industrial Archaeology Review **397**
0309-0787 Journal for the Study of the Old Testament. Supplement Series **7653**
0309-0809 Milk Bulletin **267**
0309-0817 Automobile Abstracts (Print Edition) *changed to* 1743-260X **8522**
0309-0825 The International Law List
0309-0892 Journal for the Study of the Old Testament **7653**
0309-099X Royal Observatory. Occasional Reports†
0309-1031 Dog News and Family Pets
0309-118X InterMedia **2383**
0309-1252 Bristow's Book of Yachts†
0309-1287 Protozoological Abstracts **718**
0309-1295 Nutrition Abstracts and Reviews. Series A: Human and Experimental **6671**
0309-1309 Mervyn Peake Review **5444**
0309-1317 International Journal of Urban and Regional Research **4416**
0309-1325 Progress in Human Geography **4025**
0309-1333 Progress in Physical Geography **4025**
0309-135X Nutrition Abstracts and Reviews. Series B: Livestock Feeds and Feeding **184**
0309-1414 Jane's Police Review **2656**
0309-1422 Waterways World **8284**
0309-1430 Institute of Automotive Engineer Assessors. Journal **8585**
0309-1619 Powys Review **5353**
0309-1627 Faith & Worship **7642**
0309-1643 Land Resource Bibliography†
0309-166X Cambridge Journal of Economics **1079**
0309-1708 Advances in Water Resources **8817**
0309-1740 Meat Science **3656**
0309-1783 Hobart Paperbacks†
0309-1813 Atomic Absorption & Emission Spectrometry Abstracts
0309-1821 Guinea-Pig News Letter†
0309-1848 Rat News Letter†
0309-1880 Institute of Petroleum **6773**
0309-1902 Journal of Medical Engineering & Technology **5651**
0309-1929 Geophysical and Astrophysical Fluid Dynamics **2781**
0309-1945 Greater London Arts Association. Annual Report†
0309-2143 Converter Directory **6733**
0309-2178 University of London King's College. Department of Geography. Occasional Paper†
0309-2216 International Copper Information Bulletin†
0309-2224 Conservation News **2607**
0309-2275 The Oxfordshire Family Historian **3778**
0309-2283 Recent Advances in Rheumatology†
0309-233X Vision†
0309-2356 U K Chemical Industry Statistics Handbook†
0309-2402 Journal of Advanced Nursing **5964**
0309-2437 Recent Advances in Ophthalmology†
0309-2445 Publishing History **7571**
0309-2526 Hands off Ireland
0309-2534 Advances in Raman Spectroscopy†
0309-2569 Family Planning Association. Medical Newsletter†
0309-2666 Medical Technologist and Scientist†
0309-2674 Recent Advances in Plastic Surgery†
0309-2747 Recent Advances in Dermatology†
0309-2771 The College of Law. Crash Course Lecture **4644**
0309-2968 Sutton Bridge Annual Review **207**
0309-3069 N P L Report M O M **6404**
0309-3077 L P Gas Review†
0309-3093 Berkshire Archaeological Journal **383**
0309-3166 The College of Law. Lectures **4644**
0309-3247 Journal of Strain Analysis for Engineering Design **3351**
0309-3263 Reading Geographer†
0309-3298 In the Making **1423**
0309-3328 Counterpoint†
0309-3344 Dorchester Magazine†
0309-345X African Environment Special Reports†
0309-3484 Junior Education *changed to* 1755-8905 **2879**
0309-3492 Third Way (Harrow) **7690**
0309-3557 Recycling and Waste Disposal†
0309-359X Chester Archaeological Society. Journal **387**
0309-3603 Cambridge Antiquarian Society. Proceedings **4208**
0309-3646 Prosthetics and Orthotics International **6071**
0309-3654 Messenger (Grantham) **7767**
0309-3689 Labour Student **7150**
0309-3700 Liverpool Classical Monthly **2237**
0309-3786 G L A D Journal†
0309-393X Royal Scottish Museum Information Series: Art & Archaeology†
0309-4073 Leveller†
0309-409X Chelsea Speleological Society. Records **2728**
0309-4170 Christian Librarian **5002**
0309-4189 Offshore Research Focus (Print)†
0309-4227 Paper Conservator **6535**
0309-4251 Rescue Publication **413**
0309-4294 Great Britain. Sea Fish Industry Authority. Fisheries Economics Newsletter **3596**
0309-4308 Liturgy†
0309-4413 Directory for Disabled People
0309-4529 South American Handbook (Year) **8757**
0309-4545 Fertility and Contraception†
0309-457X The Maghreb Review **4176**
0309-4642 Motocourse **8262**
0309-4693 Social Service Abstracts†
0309-4707 Middle East Electricity *changed to* 0032-5929 **3393**
0309-474X European Bulletin and Press **7134**
0309-4758 Walter Skinner's North Sea and Europe Offshore Yearbook and Buyers' Guide† **8998**
0309-4766 Big Farm Weekly†
0309-4812 Apparel News†
0309-4960 Worldwide Marketing Opportunities Digest **1849**
0309-507X Goff's Guide to Cater Yourself Holidays
0309-5118 Hatcher Review†
0309-5150 Optics Abstracts†
0309-5177 Systems International
0309-5207 The Journal of Beckett Studies **5314**
0309-524X Wind Engineering **3178**
0309-5304 L G O R U Transportation News†
0309-5312 X-Ray Diffraction Abstracts
0309-5320 Laser Raman & Infrared Spectroscopy Abstracts
0309-5371 Statistics - Asia & Australasia: Sources for Market Research†
0309-5452 Statistics - America†
0309-5460 Current African Directories
0309-5487 Directory of British Associations & Associations in Ireland **1985**
0309-5495 Newsrelease
0309-5541 Arca **2230**
0309-5584 On Two Wheels† **8978**
0309-5614 Chartered Institute of Public Finance and Accountancy. Education Statistics. Actuals **2931**
0309-5630 Chambers Trades Register of Scotland and North East England†
0309-5649 Chambers Trades Register of the Wirral to the Wash†
0309-5657 Journal of Informatics **5021**
0309-5703 Tenders and Contracts Journal
0309-5770 Catalysts in Chemistry
0309-5789 T S B Gazette
0309-5991 Semiconductors and Insulators†
0309-6149 Croydon Natural History & Scientific Society. Bulletin **7849**
0309-6270 Logophile†
0309-6297 Successful Slimming†
0309-653X Chartered Institute of Public Finance and Accountancy. Personal Social Services Statistics. Actuals **8082**
0309-6564 Dutch Crossing **5214**
0309-6629 Chartered Institute of Public Finance and Accountancy. Public Libraries Statistics. Actuals **5057**
0309-6653 M D A Information†
0309-667X Great Britain. Civil Aviation Authority. General Aviation Safety Information Leaflets **8542**
0309-6688 Finite Element News **3291**
0309-6831 Society for Experimental Biology. Seminar Series†
0309-6890 Gas Kinetics and Energy Transfer†
0309-6904 I P P F Co-operative Information Service†
0309-6998 Textes Litteraires *changed to* Exeter Textes Litteraires **5294**
0309-7013 Aristotelian Society. Proceedings. Supplementary Volume **6906**
0309-703X Company Secretary's Review **4862**
0309-7234 European Industrial Relations Review *changed to* 1754-0143 **1680**
0309-7285 Cienfuegos Press Anarchist Review
0309-7323 Scottish Opera News†
0309-7374 North West Industrial Development Association. Newsletter†
0309-7382 Laboratory Animals. Buyers Guide **5908**
0309-7463 Institute of Oceanographic Sciences. Collected Reprints†
0309-7471 Material Matters†
0309-7544 Social Science Teacher **3082**
0309-7552 Science Bulletin†
0309-7560 Forth Naturalist and Historian Series **7855**
0309-7625 Brewers Guild Directory **601**
0309-7676 International Business Lawyer†
0309-7684 International Legal Practitioner **4932**
0309-7714 Journal of Environmental Planning and Pollution Control†
0309-7773 British Psychological Society. Annual Report **7342**
0309-7803 Surrey Archaeological Collections **419**
0309-7846 Hydrographic Journal **2709**
0309-7854 Economic Bulletin (London)†
0309-7889 International Flyfisher
0309-7900 Tax Planning International **1949**
0309-7935 Bookplate Society Newsletter **7555**
0309-7986 Cumberland and Westmorland Antiquarian and Archaeological Society. Transactions **389**
0309-7994 Devonshire Association for the Advancement of Science, Literature and the Arts. Report and Transactions **4449**
0309-8036 Theatre Papers†
0309-8079 Handicapped Children
0309-8095 Weight Watchers Magazine **7000**
0309-8117 Institute of Acoustics. Proceedings **7087**
0309-8168 Capital and Class **1536**
0309-8184 Offshore Technology Papers **6783**
0309-8249 Journal of Philosophy of Education **6929**
0309-8265 Journal of Geography in Higher Education **4017**
0309-8281 Coarse Fisherman **8309**
0309-829X Motorcycle Racing
0309-8303 Hydrographic Society. International Headquarters. Special Publications **8825**
0309-8338 Cumbria Guide Industry and Commerce
0309-8389 Kirklees Chamber of Commerce. Member's Directory
0309-8397 Bradford and Halifax Chambers of Commerce Members Directory
0309-8435 B S R I A Annual Report **4116**
0309-8451 Environmental Education **3424**
0309-8486 Northamptoniana† **8977**

ISSN

0311-8347 Thoroughbred Breeders' Handbook
0311-8479 Womanspeak
0311-872X I B M Quarterly
0311-8754 Right to Choose†
0311-8924 Historical Journal†
0311-8983 National Acoustic Laboratories, Sydney. Annual Report†
0311-8991 Commonwealth Teaching Service. Annual Report†
0311-905X Current Therapeutics†
0311-9300 University of New England. Management Forum†
0311-9319 Overseas Map Acquisitions†
0311-9491 Queensland. Department of Local Government. Conference of Local Authority Engineers. Proceedings†
0311-9629 Australian Directory of Services for Alcoholism and Drug Dependence†
0312-004X Stereo Buyer's Guide. Directory†
0312-0074 Stereo Buyer's Guide. Speakers†
0312-0104 Stereo Buyer's Guide. Cassettes†
0312-0112 Australasian Small Press Review†
0312-0325 Australian Women's Wear†
0312-0627 International Research and Information Association. Survey
0312-1356 Australia. Bureau of Statistics. Tasmanian Office. Public Justice†
0312-1372 Chain Reaction **3410**
0312-1437 Australia. Bureau of Statistics. Trade Union Statistics, Australia†
0312-1585 Australia. Bureau of Statistics. Foreign Ownership and Control of the Mining Industry, Australia† **8932**
0312-1658 Queensland Lawyer **4764**
0312-1674 New South Wales Law Reports **4957**
0312-200X C H O M I - Das†
0312-2115 Australian Road Index†
0312-2417 Australian Archaeology **382**
0312-2530 Australian History Teacher†
0312-259X Australia. National Library. Acquisitions Newsletter†
0312-2654 Metro **6507**
0312-3162 Western Australian Museum. Records **6540**
0312-3480 Working Kelpie Council. National Stud Book **304**
0312-3502 Caring *changed to* Inspire (Adelaide) **8047**
0312-3685 The Mathematical Scientist **5514**
0312-407X Australian Social Work **8027**
0312-4134 A F C O Quarterly†
0312-4371 Cataloguing Australia†
0312-4711 The Australian Geologist **2726**
0312-4738 Endocrine Society of Australia. Proceedings **5891**
0312-4991 Australian Society of Archivists. Bulletin **4993**
0312-5033 Australian Journal of Early Childhood **2144**
0312-5203 Scout Association of Australia. Annual Report *changed to* Scouts Australia. Annual Report **2270**
0312-5211 C S I R O Textile News†
0312-5327 Australian Giftguide **4059**
0312-5467 Working Papers in Language & Linguistics†
0312-5807 Australian Naval Institute. Journal *changed to* 1833-6531 **6423**
0312-5831 Brief **4631**
0312-5963 Clinical Pharmacokinetics **6829**
0312-5998 Open House **4395**
0312-6072 Australia. Bureau of Statistics. Western Australian Office. Local Government, Western Australia†
0312-6145 Early Days **4191**
0312-6307 The Age **3793**
0312-6315 Sydney Morning Herald **3796**
0312-6757 Cover Note **4500**
0312-6994 Australia. Law Reform Commission. Annual Report†
0312-7044 The Summit **7819**
0312-7273 Australia. Bureau of Statistics. New South Wales Office. Mining, New South Wales†
0312-7397 Australia. Bureau of Statistics. Queensland Office. List of Publications†
0312-7559 Nepean Review†
0312-7915 Working Papers in Sex, Science and Culture†
0312-8008 Australian Prescriber **6823**
0312-8059 A N Z A A S Congress Papers† **8927**
0312-8121 Astronautical Society of Western Australia. News Bulletin†
0312-8741 University of New England. Department of Geography and Planning. Monograph Series (No.)†
0312-889X Professional Farm Management Guidebook† **8982**
0312-8962 Australian Journal of Management **1727**
0312-8989 Quandong **249**
0312-9195 Golf Victoria **8233**
0312-9640 Historical Society of South Australia. Journal **4192**
0312-973X Factory Management
0312-9764 Telopea **820**
0312-9837 Petroleum Newsletter†
0312-9888 Luna
0313-0096 University of New South Wales Law Journal **4804**
0313-0134 Cordell's Quarterly Review of Construction in N.S.W. and the A.C.T.†
0313-0525 Australia. Bureau of Statistics. Victorian Office.. Survey of Tourist Accommodation Establishments *changed to* Australia. Bureau of Statistics. Victorian Office. Tourist Accommodation, Small Area Data, Victoria **4401**
0313-0568 Thomson's Liquor Guide **2641**
0313-0843 Management Diary *changed to* 1440-5636 **1777**
0313-122X Western Australian Museum. Records. Supplement **6540**
0313-1459 Span **5376**
0313-153X Reform **4767**
0313-1823 Caravan Test†
0313-1912 Australia. Bureau of Statistics. Queensland Office. Labour Force, Queensland†
0313-1971 National Library of Australia. Annual Report **5034**
0313-2080 Theatre Australia
0313-2153 New Doctor **5685**
0313-220X Art Almanac **468**
0313-251X The Ancestral Searcher **3758**
0313-2560 Build
0313-2846 Australian Speleo Abstracts†
0313-2919 Health Action†
0313-3192 Australian Plant Introduction Review†
0313-3249 Instead
0313-3311 Australian Computer Society. Conference Proceedings†
0313-3761 Campaign Australia†
0313-377X Agricultural Economics Bulletin (No.)†
0313-3834 Hrvatski List
0313-4075 Ports of New South Wales Journal†
0313-4083 Adelaide Botanic Garden. Journal **773**
0313-427X University of New South Wales. Library. Annual Report **5053**
0313-4288 L I P
0313-4423 Scarlet Woman†
0313-4474 University of Sydney. Annual Report **3009**
0313-5055 McCabe-McMiles Letter
0313-5276 Custom Vans & Trucks†
0313-5373 Australian Journal of Teacher Education **2968**
0313-5780 University of Tasmania. Centre for Environmental Studies. Working Papers† **8996**
0313-5888 Bird Observer **903**
0313-5926 Economic Analysis and Policy **1098**
0313-5934 J A S S A **1634**
0313-5977 Canberra Historical Journal **4191**
0313-6221 Parergon **4468**
0313-6647 Australian Journal of Public Administration **7421**
0313-6701 Heritage News†
0313-6728 Queensland. Department of Education. Division of Special Education. Special Education Bulletin
0313-6744 Tableaus
0313-6825 Function† **8958**
0313-685X S C O P P
0313-6906 University of Wollongong. Annual Report†
0313-6922 Institution of Engineers, Australia. National Conference Publications **3199**
0313-7112 Australian Graduate School of Management. Handbook†
0313-7155 Issues in Educational Research **2872**
0313-7546 Pioneer Books Monographs Literary Series† **8981**
0313-766X Australian Powerboat **8271**
0313-7767 Teaching Mathematics **5541**
0313-7813 Queensland Government Publications†
0313-7864 Enterprise: Western Australia†
0313-7872 Beach Conservation†
0313-8143 Queensland Education Digest†
0313-8682 Teachers Guild of New South Wales. Proceedings
0313-8704 University of Sydney. Department of Agricultural Economics. Agricultural Extension Bulletin†
0313-8747 Explore **2856**
0313-8860 Western Geographer **4034**
0313-895X Australian Road Research Board. Technical Manuals†
0313-9581 University of Western Australia. Centre for East Asian Studies. Occasional Papers†
0313-9603 Australian Commonwealth Specialists' Catalogue†
0313-9611 Australian Banknote Catalogue†
0313-9921 University of Wollongong. Research Bulletin†
0313-9948 Australia. National Capital Development Commission. Technical Papers†
0314-0164 Complan Handbook† **8942**
0314-0326 Movie† **8975**
0314-0377 Australasian Shipping Record **8639**
0314-0679 Graduate Outlook
0314-1160 Criminal Law Journal **4887**
0314-1306 Wool Outlook†
0314-1357 Research Laboratories Review of Activities†
0314-1608 Salssah on Com†
0314-1705 Australia. Bureau of Statistics. Tasmanian Office. Education†
0314-1888 Australia. Bureau of Statistics. Tasmanian Office. Mining, Tasmania†
0314-1950 Australia. Bureau of Statistics. Tasmanian Office. Motor Vehicle Registrations, Tasmania†
0314-2019 Australia. Bureau of Statistics. Tasmanian Office. Foreign Trade, Tasmania†
0314-2051 Australia. Bureau of Statistics. Tasmanian Office. Value of Agricultural Commodities Produced, Tasmania†
0314-2205 A R R B Regional Symposium†
0314-2531 Panorama (Hobart)†
0314-2779 Australia. Bureau of Statistics. Labour Statistics, Australia†
0314-285X Inprint†
0314-2868 A C T U Bulletin†
0314-2981 Helen Vale Foundation. Journal†
0314-3058 Trust News. Victoria *changed to* Front Row
0314-3155 Simply Living† **8988**
0314-3171 Australian Institute of Petroleum. Annual Report **6763**
0314-3287 Australia. Bureau of Statistics. Queensland Office. Sawmill Statistics, Queensland†
0314-3457 Queensland Geographer
0314-3767 Australian Society of Indexers. Newsletter *changed to* 1832-3855 **1**
0314-3775 Fremantle Gazette **3794**
0314-3937 Applied Linguistics Association of Australia. Occasional Papers† **8930**
0314-4216 Institution of Engineers, Australia. Queensland Division. Technical Papers†
0314-4224 The Earthmover and Civil Contractor **3266**
0314-4240 Chemistry in Australia **2057**
0314-4607 Mining Review†
0314-4623 O H T A News **6600**
0314-464X Australian Musician
0314-5468 Sports Coach **8207**
0314-5514 Life: Be in It /Y S R News†
0314-5913 Mattoid **5331**
0314-6138 Australian Family Law Cases
0314-6154 Australasian Institute of Mining and Metallurgy Symposia Series *changed to* 1324-6240 **6457**
0314-6316 Pharmacy Review **6874**
0314-6510 Reeflections (Townsville)†
0314-6677 Science Fiction **5447**
0314-6782 M A R G I N **5328**
0314-6804 Monash University. Centre of Southeast Asian Studies. Working Papers **4186**
0314-6820 Statistical Society of Australia. Newsletter **8405**
0314-7177 The Instrumentality **5443**
0314-724X V I S E News†
0314-7312 Fleece and Flock **287**
0314-7320 Currency†
0314-7487 Energy†
0314-7495 New Literature Review **5340**
0314-7525 Studies in Western Australian History **4194**
0314-7592 Journal of Industry and Commerce†
0314-7894 Candy Family History Newsletter†
0314-8009 Compass†
0314-8696 Tasmanian Manufacturers Directory **2030**
0314-8742 Environmental Newsletter†
0314-8769 Aboriginal History **4191**
0314-9099 Canberra Anthropology *changed to* 1444-2213 **329**
0315-0062 Canadian Frontier†
0315-0143 Urban Focus†
0315-0208 Spear
0315-0224 A.N. & A.F. Journal
0315-033X Around the North
0315-0380 Eco-Log Week *changed to* 1910-2240 **3478**
0315-0399 Barrique
0315-047X Decormag **4537**
0315-0496 Stuffed Crocodile†
0315-0542 Outdoor Canada **8327**
0315-0550 Cuttings and Comments†
0315-0607 Articles et Commentaires†
0315-0623 Lodgistiks†
0315-0631 Directory of Community Services in Metropolitan Toronto
0315-0682 Canadian Road Knight
0315-0771 Ottawa Ethnic Groups Directory†
0315-0836 Canadian Theatre Review **8467**
0315-0860 Historia Mathematica **5491**
0315-0879 Canadian Key Business Directory **1978**
0315-0887 Volleyball Technical Journal†
0315-0909 Canadian Amateur Boxing News†
0315-0941 Geoscience Canada **2743**
0315-1042 On Continuing Practice†
0315-1131 M S Canada **6159**
0315-1190 Canadian Review†
0315-1204 Cooperateur Agricole **102**
0315-1301 Cosmetics
0315-1409 Canadian and International Education **3012**
0315-1417 C O R S Bulletin **2409**
0315-1433 Canadian Annual Review of Politics and Public Affairs **4287**
0315-1468 Canadian Journal of Civil Engineering **3261**
0315-162X Journal of Rheumatology **6224**
0315-1654 Energy Analects **3130**
0315-1700 World Directory of Historians of Mathematics **5546**
0315-1727 Teeoff†
0315-1808 T A S A
0315-1840 L S M News†
0315-1859 The Charlatan **2277**
0315-1867 Le Consommateur Canadien†
0315-1999 Canadian Books in Print - Subject Index†
0315-2146 Entomological Society of Manitoba. Proceedings **845**
0315-2154 Country Estate Magazine
0315-2235 Venture Forth **2924**
0315-2286 National (Ottawa, 1974) **4738**
0315-2340 Documentation et Bibliotheques **5007**
0315-2359 Beaux-Arts
0315-2685 Jewish Dialogue
0315-2804 Raincoast Chronicles†
0315-3010 Westwater†
0315-3037 Ego†
0315-307X Focus on Beef
0315-3088 Where to Eat in Canada **4400**
0315-310X Hellenic View
0315-3118 Skimania†
0315-3290 Creative Canada†
0315-3339 Accelerator (Ottawa)†
0315-3355 B. C. Affairs Quarterly
0315-3371 History Collection: Canadian Catholic Church†
0315-3452 Canadian Layman
0315-3495 Canadian Defence Quarterly†
0315-3525 Canadian Rehabilitation Council for the Disabled. Employment Bulletin†
0315-355X Alberta-Westmorland-Kent Regional Library. Extension Department. News†
0315-3584 Pathfinder Travel Parks Directory
0315-3606 Body Politic†
0315-3630 Northern Journey†
0315-3673 Strategie
0315-3681 Utilitas Mathematica **5546**
0315-369X Reporting Classroom Research†
0315-3754 Capilano Review **5270**
0315-3770 Event **5293**
0315-3835 British Columbia Genealogist **3760**
0315-3932 Waves†
0315-3959 Canadian Dancers News†
0315-3967 Cahiers Linguistiques d'Ottawa **5103**
0315-3975 Video-Presse†
0315-4114 Concern International
0315-4149 International Fiction Review **5309**
0315-4254 C B Newsletter†
0315-4297 The Journal of Canadian Art History **498**
0315-4351 Comment on Education†
0315-4459 Forgotten People
0315-4661 Computernews
0315-467X Chien d'Or **5273**
0315-4793 Better Vending & Catering†
0315-484X Actrascope News†
0315-4874 Landscape Canada†
0315-4920 C P A C Review†
0315-5021 Waterloo Historical Society **4317**
0315-5064 Manitoba Nature†
0315-5153 Vie Medicale au Canada Francais†
0315-5226 Vanguard (Vancouver)†
0315-5412 Journal of Automatic Writing
0315-5757 Insight (Toronto)
0315-5943 Repertoire de l'Edition au Quebec†
0315-5986 I N F O R Journal **2536**
0315-6087 Independencer
0315-6168 Canadian Parliamentary Guide (Year) **7113**
0315-6389 Lookout **6431**

ISSN

0317-7173 Cartographica **4002**
0317-7203 Guidelines for Pastoral Liturgy *changed to* 1912-0680 **7810**
0317-7254 Carleton Germanic Papers†
0317-7262 Manitoba. Horse Racing Commission. Annual Report **8294**
0317-7319 Saskatchewan. Office of the Ombudsman. Annual Report **7467**
0317-7327 Commission Consultative de l'Enseignement Prive. Rapport Annuel **2837**
0317-7335 Saskatchewan Labour Report†
0317-7483 Canada's Trade in Agricultural Products **195**
0317-7785 Canadian Rodeo News **8288**
0317-7815 Automobile Insurance Experience
0317-7831 Model Aviation Canada **4340**
0317-7882 Canada. Statistics Canada. Aggregate Productivity Measures *changed to* 1492-8612 **1218**
0317-7904 Canadian Review of Studies in Nationalism†
0317-7920 Canadian Art Auction Record†
0317-8161 Ontario. Ministry of Consumer and Commercial Relations. Statistical Review†
0317-8196 Canada. Road and Motor Vehicle Traffic Safety Branch. Road Safety Annual Report. Rapport Annuel, Securite Routiere
0317-8382 Papers on European and Mediterranean Societies†
0317-8498 Michael **7807**
0317-851X En Eglise **7796**
0317-8536 Directory of Libraries in Manitoba†
0317-8722 Youth Science News†
0317-9044 Canadian Drama†
0317-9060 Canadian Income Tax Act with Regulations **1915**
0317-9087 Canadian Council on International Law. Proceedings of the Annual Conference **4920**
0317-9095 Kinesis **8870**
0317-9311 U F O - Quebec†
0317-9508 Mining - What Mining Means to Canada†
0317-9575 Long Point Bird Observatory Newsletter **910**
0317-9656 Universite de Sherbrooke. Revue de Droit **4802**
0317-9737 Dance in Canada†
0317-9893 University of Toronto. Department of Geography. Discussion Paper Series†
0318-000X Indian Education Newsletter†
0318-0069 Cable Communications Magazine†
0318-0077 Learning Resources
0318-0107 Gargoyle **2284**
0318-0123 Donum Dei†
0318-0131 *see* 0318-0123
0318-0220 The Courier (Edmonton)†
0318-0344 Fraser's Construction & Building Directory†
0318-0352 Canadian Insurance Claims Directory **4498**
0318-0417 Shipping Register†
0318-0522 Canadian Structural Engineering Conference. Proceedings†
0318-0646 Professional Institute of the Public Service of Canada. Communications **7460**
0318-0859 Canadian Process Equipment & Control News **1080**
0318-0883 I M P I Newsletter **3318**
0318-1235 University of Toronto-York University Joint Program in Transportation. Newsletter†
0318-1251 University of Toronto - York University. Joint Program in Transportation. Annual Report†
0318-1340 Liaison (Montreal)†
0318-1693 Quebec Construction†
0318-1944 Canadian Information Processing Society. Canadian Salary Survey†
0318-2037 Current Soviet Leaders†
0318-2118 Manitoba Spectra *changed to* 1910-782X **3058**
0318-2126 Association of New Brunswick Land Surveyors. Annual Report
0318-2266 Canada. Inland Waters Directorate. Surface Water Data. Yukon and Northwest Territories **8819**
0318-2452 Femme
0318-2460 Windsor This Month†
0318-2789 Canadian Conservation Directory†
0318-2967 Dairy Policy **263**
0318-3122 University of Waterloo. Solid Mechanics Division. Studies Series **3359**
0318-3319 Erasmus Studies **4451**
0318-3556 Ontario Annual Practice **4753**
0318-3610 Matrix **504**
0318-3661 British Columbia. Ministry of Agriculture Fisheries and Food. Vegetable Production Guide **223**
0318-3726 British Columbia Hunter's Annual
0318-3912 Manitoba. Water Services Board. Annual Report **8828**
0318-3971 Alberta Opportunity Company. Annual Report
0318-4099 Canada Manpower and Immigration Review
0318-4137 Recherches Amerindiennes au Quebec **352**
0318-4277 Canadian Forest Industries **3710**
0318-434X St. Anne de Beaupre. The Annals **7816**
0318-4366 Sainte Anne de Beaupre *see* 0318-434X **7816**
0318-4412 Phi Zero: Revue d'Etudes Philosophiques
0318-4501 Nutrition Forum **6665**
0318-4560 Commerce Montreal†
0318-4714 Official Rules of Baseball **8241**
0318-479X Revue des Sciences de l'Education **2907**
0318-4900 Uniform Law Conference of Canada. Proceedings of the Annual Meeting **4843**
0318-4935 Canadian Bar Association. Annual Report of Proceedings **4638**
0318-4943 Alberta Fishing Guide **8302**
0318-5133 Canadian Society of Environmental Biologists Newsletter **3409**
0318-5176 Alberta Modern Language Journal†
0318-5184 Canada. Statistics Canada. Survey of Canadian Nursery Trades Industry†
0318-5273 Canada. Statistics Canada. Household Facilities and Equipment **4370**
0318-5311 Issues in Canadian Science Policy†
0318-532X Aspects de la Politique Scientifique du Canada†
0318-5427 Manual of Social Services in Manitoba
0318-5540 Alberta Naturalist *changed to* 1713-8639 **2621**
0318-5729 Amigo
0318-5737 Amisol
0318-5753 Amber
0318-5796 Canada. Inland Waters Directorate. Surface Water Data. Reference Index. Canada **8843**
0318-5877 Canada. Inland Waters Directorate. Historical Streamflow Summary, Alberta **2793**
0318-5885 Canada. Inland Waters Directorate. Historical Streamflow Summary, Atlantic Provinces **2793**
0318-5893 Canada. Inland Waters Directorate. Historical Streamflow Summary, British Columbia **2793**
0318-5907 Canada. Inland Waters Directorate. Historical Streamflow Summary, Manitoba **2793**
0318-5915 Canada. Inland Waters Directorate. Historical Streamflow Summary, Ontario **2793**
0318-6075 Cross Country†
0318-6210 Training Aids Action Service†
0318-6229 Careers for Graduates†
0318-6237 Short Courses and Seminars
0318-6385 Metric Message†
0318-6431 Canadian Journal of Sociology (Print)†
0318-6725 Fabreries **847**
0318-675X Canadian Government Publications: Catalogue†
0318-6938 Revue d'Ethnologie du Quebec†
0318-6954 Archivaria **4284**
0318-7020 Parachute **511**
0318-7063 Forest Engineering Research Institute of Canada. Technical Report **3711**
0318-7160 Canada. Statistics Canada. Statistical Information on Schools of Social Work in Canada†
0318-7276 Directory of Canadian Urban Information Sources
0318-7306 Action Canada - France **1394**
0318-742X C G A Magazine **1282**
0318-7489 Fine
0318-7527 Ontario Municipal Board Reports **4753**
0318-7551 Eskimo **6634**
0318-756X Eskimo. Edition Francaise **6634**
0318-7721 Hospitality Canada
0318-7888 Canada. Statistics Canada. Report on Fur Farms†
0318-8116 L U A C Monitor†
0318-8140 Urban Forum†
0318-8329 Inventory of Research into Higher Education in Canada†
0318-8442 Canadian Issues **4446**
0318-8612 Maritime Provinces Higher Education Commission. Annual Report **2993**
0318-8655 Black Moss†
0318-8701 Fashion Textiles Mode
0318-871X Fem Ego†
0318-8752 Franchise Annual **1996**
0318-8787 Canada. Statistics Canada. Selected Financial Statistics of Charitable Organizations†
0318-8809 Canada. Statistics Canada. Building Permits **1045**
0318-8841 Canada. Statistics Canada. Contract Drilling for Petroleum and Other Contract Drilling†
0318-8914 Canada. Statistics Canada. Shipping Report. Part 1: International Seaborne Shipping (by Country)†
0318-8930 Canada. Statistics Canada. Shipping Report. Part 3: Coastwise Shipping†
0318-8949 Canada. Statistics Canada. Shipping Report. Part 5: Origin and Destination for Selected Commodities†
0318-8957 Cooperatives Canada
0318-9007 Canada. Statistics Canada. Estimates of Labour Income†
0318-9090 Canadian Journal of University Continuing Education†
0318-9171 University of British Columbia. Faculty of Forestry. Bulletin†
0318-9201 Voix et Images **5395**
0318-9236 Poumons†
0318-9392 Vie Oblate **7822**
0318-9422 Sanford Evans Gold Book of Snowmobile Data and Used Prices **8219**
0318-9651 Apartment & Building
0318-9872 Echo Missionaire†
0318-9937 American Society for Information Science. Western Canada Chapter. Annual Meeting Proceedings†
0319-003X Atlantic Canada Economics Association. Annual Conference Proceedings **1063**
0319-0080 C C L **7557**
0319-0110 Structural Engineering Report **3284**
0319-0161 Computing Canada *changed to* 1484-9089 **2511**
0319-0188 Sphinx **5376**
0319-0323 Inside Oxfam **8047**
0319-0439 Tourist Guide Book of Ontario†
0319-051X Canadian Review of Comparative Literature†
0319-0528 Metalworking Management†
0319-0552 York Dance Review†
0319-0595 Harlequin†
0319-0714 The Globe and Mail **3810**
0319-0722 Le Devoir **3808**
0319-0781 Toronto Star **3818**
0319-1001 Pedestal
0319-1095 Interuniversity Centre for European Studies. Bulletin†
0319-1214 Pangnirtung†
0319-1249 Chateauguay Valley Historical Society Annual Journal **4288**
0319-1362 Bull & Bear Financial Newspaper **1614**
0319-1443 Family Involvement
0319-1648 Kabalarian Courier†
0319-2148 Canadian Office†
0319-2156 Connection†
0319-2385 Constructive Citizen Participation†
0319-2431 Canadian Tax News†
0319-2547 Canadian Appaloosa Journal†
0319-258X Directory of Community Services of Greater Montreal **8037**
0319-2644 Canadian Public Health Association. Proceedings of the Annual Meeting†
0319-2725 Queen's Gazette **2999**
0319-2776 Gulf Wings†
0319-2822 Cycle Canada **8256**
0319-2865 Moto Journal **8261**
0319-3225 Canadian Funeral Director **3719**
0319-3322 Canadian Business Law Journal **4860**
0319-3403 Canadian Energy News **3125**
0319-3438 Yardsticks for Costing **461**
0319-3780 Routes et Transports **8634**
0319-3896 CanPara **8308**
0319-4019 Monarchy Canada **7155**
0319-4183 Municipal Statistics. Annual Report **7454**
0319-4264 Alberta Economic Accounts†
0319-4345 Nouveau Cosmos-Express
0319-4620 Centre for Urban and Community Studies. Major Report Series **4406**
0319-4639 Cape Breton's Magazine **4287**
0319-4728 Centre Stage†
0319-485X Religious Studies Review **7699**
0319-4930 Canada. Statistics Canada. Labour Costs in Canada: Finance, Insurance and Real Estate†
0319-4957 Canada. Statistics Canada. Feldspar and Quartz Mines†
0319-4973 Prince Edward Island. Legislative Assembly. Journal **7501**
0319-5066 Zwiazkowiec *changed to* 1494-6610
0319-5082 Summer in Canada†
0319-5147 Polish Canadian Courier **3558**
0319-5228 Canoma **4001**
0319-5465 Sanavik Cooperative. Baker Lake Prints
0319-5724 Canadian Journal of Statistics **8362**
0319-5759 Energy Processing Canada **3133**
0319-583X Canada North Almanac
0319-5864 Canada. National Museums of Canada. Journal†
0319-5902 Canadian Industrial Equipment News **5450**
0319-6038 Huron Soil and Crop News **234**
0319-6461 Canadian Political Science Association. Bulletin
0319-6771 Environmental Health Review **7516**
0319-681X Cegepropos
0319-6860 Rikka
0319-6887 Bharati
0319-6984 Alerte au Quebec
0319-7085 Cannons of Construction **4640**
0319-7107 Canadian Travel News†
0319-7247 Canada Pension Plan Contributors **1615**
0319-7336 Hume Studies **6924**
0319-7468 Communique (Ottawa)†
0319-7492 Truck & Trailer **8677**
0319-7549 Common Sense Economics†
0319-7697 Manitoba Moods†
0319-7751 Ontario Statistics†
0319-7980 Alberta Decisions. Civil and Criminal Cases **4612**
0319-7999 Saskatchewan Decisions, Civil and Criminal Cases **4779**
0319-8049 Canada. Statistics Canada. Federal Government Activities in the Human Sciences†
0319-8103 Communitronics
0319-8332 Coupler **8616**
0319-8367 Delta-K
0319-8413 Design Product News **3187**
0319-8480 Discovery **7851**
0319-8561 Cross Trail News **2683**
0319-8650 Envers du Decor **8470**
0319-8715 Canadian India Star
0319-891X Canada. Statistics Canada. Textile Products Industries **8463**
0319-9118 Ontario. Ministry of Natural Resources. Forest Research Information Paper **3699**
0319-9223 L'Assemblee Legislative du Nouveau-Brunswick. Journeaux *see* 0706-0629 **7424**
0319-9649 Statement of the Assets and Liabilities of the Chartered Banks of Canada†
0320-006X Dinamika Izluchayuschego Gaza
0320-0108 Pis'ma v Astronomicheskii Zhurnal **579**
0320-0116 Pis'ma v Zhurnal Tekhnicheskoi Fiziki **7035**
0320-0213 Bogoslovskie Trudy **7703**
0320-0914 Asimptoticheskie Metody v Teorii Sistem **5474**
0320-1031 Druzhba **2187**
0320-1058 Ekspress Informatsiya. Peredacha Informatsii†
0320-216X Morskaya Geologiya i Geofizika†
0320-2372 Inozemna Filolohija†
0320-3123 Signal'naya Informatsiya. Akustika†
0320-314X Signal'naya Informatsiya. Fizika Yadernykh Reaktorov†
0320-3166 Signal'naya Informatsiya. Elektricheskie Svoistva Tverdykh Tel†
0320-3182 Signal'naya Informatsiya. Chastitsy i Polya†
0320-331X Tekhnika Molodezhi **8443**
0320-3352 Polutehniline Instituut Tallinn. Issledovanie Dvumernogo Vozmushchennogo Polya Napryazheniya†
0320-3379 Polutehniline Instituut Tallinn. Neorganicheskaya Khimiya i Tekhnologiya†
0320-4421 Istoriya Narodnoho Hospodarstva ta Ekonomichnoi Dumky Ukrainy **1543**
0320-4529 Byulleten' Inostrannoi Kommercheskoi Informatsii **1554**
0320-5452 Filosofskie Nauki (Alma-Ata)†
0320-6475 Teploprovodnost' i Diffuziya†
0320-6777 Voprosy Istorii Dal'nego Vostoka
0320-6858 Avrora **5259**
0320-7102 Avtometriya **7074**
0320-7218 Absorbtsiya i Absorbenty†
0320-734X Aktual'nye Problemy Leksikologii i Slovoobrazovaniya†
0320-7390 Literaturnyi Kyrgyzstan **5326**
0320-7420 G P N T B Rossii. Algoritmy i Programmy **2590**
0320-7455 Baigal **3934**
0320-7544 Belarus' **3800**
0320-7552 Belaruskaya Lingvistyka **5099**
0320-7579 Biarozka **4444**
0320-7633 Referativnyi Zhurnal. Biokhimiya. Assimiliyatsiya i Metabolizm Azota. Belki. Biosintez i Metabolizm *changed to* Referativnyi Zhurnal. Biokhimiya **718**
0320-765X Ekspress Informatsiya. Pravovye Voprosy Okhrany Okruzhayushchei Sredy **4822**
0320-7838 Bibliotekovedenie i Bibliografiya za Rubezhom **4995**
0320-7919 Akusticheskii Zhurnal **7086**
0320-7978 Vidomosti Verkhovnoi Rady Ukrainy **7476**
0320-7986 Twentieth Century and Peace
0320-7994 Siglo 20 y la Paz *see* 0320-7986
0320-8001 Vek 20 i Mir *see* 0320-7986

ISSN

0324-7627	Honismeret **4230**
0324-7775	Kritika
0324-802X	Politechnika Slaska. Zeszyty Naukowe. Hutnictwo **6329**
0324-8038	Politechnika Slaska. Zeszyty Naukowe. Jezyki Obce†
0324-8046	Politechnika Slaska. Zeszyty Naukowe. Organizacja†
0324-8194	Zagadnienia Informacji Naukowej **5055**
0324-8232	Sztuka **520**
0324-8240	Szpitalnictwo Polskie†
0324-8267	Archiwum Medycyny Sadowej i Kriminologii **5912**
0324-8291	Studies in Physical Anthropology†
0324-8305	Literatura na Swiecie **5325**
0324-8313	Journal of Technical Physics **7088**
0324-8321	Polski Przeglad Kartograficzny **4024**
0324-833X	Postepy Biologii Komorki **835**
0324-8380	Politechnika Warszawska. Instytut Fizyki. Prace **7035**
0324-8445	Akademia Ekonomiczna im. Oskara Langego we Wroclawiu. Prace Naukowe *changed to* 1899-3192 **1190**
0324-8453	Foto **6967**
0324-8461	Archiwum Ochrony Srodowiska **3404**
0324-8526	Zagadnienia Wychowawcze a Zdrowie Psychiczne **6190**
0324-8569	Control and Cybernetics **2526**
0324-8585	Roczniki Historyczne **4259**
0324-8666	Studies in Human Ecology†
0324-8712	Reports on Philosophy **6947**
0324-8739	Przemyslowy Instytut Maszyn Rolniczych. Prace†
0324-8763	Polish Ecological Studies†
0324-8801	Jazz Forum **6578**
0324-8828	Environment Protection Engineering **3422**
0324-8925	Muzeum Literatury im. Adama Mickiewicza. Blok-Notes **5337**
0324-8968	Wyzsza Szkola Pedagogiczna, Opole. Zeszyty Naukowe. Seria A. Dydaktyka†
0324-8976	Uniwersytet Slaski w Katowicach. Prace Fizyczne†
0324-9328	Politechnika Wroclawska. Instytut Telekomunikacji i Akustyki. Prace Naukowe. Monografie†
0324-9336	Politechnika Wroclawska. Instytut Telekomunikacji i Akustyki. Prace Naukowe. Studia i Materialy†
0324-9344	Politechnika Wroclawska. Instytut Telekomunikacji i Akustyki. Prace Naukowe. Konferencje†
0324-9387	Politechnika Wroclawska. Instytut Techniki Cieplnej i Mechaniki Plynow. Prace Naukowe. Monografie†
0324-9395	Politechnika Wroclawska. Instytut Techniki Cieplnej i Mechaniki Plynow. Prace Naukowe. Konferencje†
0324-9409	Politechnika Wroclawska. Instytut Techniki Cieplnej i Mechaniki Plynow. Prace Naukowe. Studia i Materialy†
0324-9441	Politechnika Wroclawska. Instytut Podstaw Elektrotechniki i Elektrotechnologii. Prace Naukowe. Konferencje†
0324-945X	Politechnika Wroclawska. Instytut Podstaw Elektrotechniki i Elektrotechnologii. Prace Naukowe. Monografie†
0324-9468	Politechnika Wroclawska. Instytut Organizacji i Zarzadzania. Prace Naukowe. Studia i Materialy†
0324-9484	Politechnika Wroclawska. Instytut Organizacji i Zarzadzania. Prace Naukowe. Konferencje†
0324-9492	Politechnika Wroclawska. Instytut Organizacji i Zarzadzania. Prace Naukowe. Monografie†
0324-9530	Politechnika Wroclawska. Instytut Metrologii Elektrycznej. Prace Naukowe. Przemysl†
0324-9549	Politechnika Wroclawska. Instytut Metrologii Elektrycznej. Prace Naukowe. Monografie†
0324-9557	Politechnika Wroclawska. Instytut Metrologii Elektrycznej. Prace Naukowe. Konferencje†
0324-9565	Politechnika Wroclawska. Instytut Materialoznawstwa i Mechaniki Technicznej. Prace Naukowe. Monografie†
0324-9573	Politechnika Wroclawska. Instytut Materialoznawstwa i Mechaniki Technicznej. Prace Naukowe. Konferencje†
0324-9603	Politechnika Wroclawska. Instytut Matematyki. Prace Naukowe. Monografie†
0324-9611	Politechnika Wroclawska. Instytut Matematyki. Prace Naukowe. Studia i Materialy†
0324-962X	Politechnika Wroclawska. Instytut Konstrukcji i Eksploatacji Maszyn. Prace Naukowe. Monografie†
0324-9638	Politechnika Wroclawska. Instytut Konstrukcji i Eksploatacji Maszyn. Prace Naukowe. Studia i Materialy†
0324-9646	Politechnika Wroclawska. Instytut Konstrukcji i Eksploatacji Maszyn. Prace Naukowe. Konferencje†
0324-9654	Politechnika Wroclawska. Instytut Historii Architektury, Sztuki i Techniki. Prace Naukowe. Studia i Materialy†
0324-9662	Politechnika Wroclawska. Instytut Historii Architektury, Sztuki i Techniki. Prace Naukowe. Monografie†
0324-9670	Politechnika Wroclawska. Instytut Gornictwa. Prace Naukowe. Konferencje†
0324-9689	Politechnika Wroclawska. Instytut Gornictwa. Prace Naukowe. Monografie†
0324-9697	Politechnika Wroclawska. Instytut Fizyki. Prace Naukowe. Studia i Materialy†
0324-9719	Politechnika Wroclawska. Instytut Inzynierii Ochrony Srodowiska. Prace Naukowe. Konferencje†
0324-9727	Politechnika Wroclawska. Instytut Inzynierii Ladowej. Prace Naukowe. Monografie†
0324-9735	Politechnika Wroclawska. Instytut Inzynierii Ladowej. Prace Naukowe. Konferencje†
0324-9743	Politechnika Wroclawska. Instytut Inzynierii Chemicznej i Urzadzen Cieplnych. Prace Naukowe. Konferencje†
0324-9751	Politechnika Wroclawska. Instytut Inzynierii Chemicznej i Urzadzen Cieplnych. Prace Naukowe. Studia i Materialy†
0324-976X	Politechnika Wroclawska. Instytut Energoelektryki. Prace Naukowe. Monografie†
0324-9778	Politechnika Wroclawska. Instytut Energoelektryki. Prace Naukowe. Konferencje†
0324-9786	Politechnika Wroclawska. Instytut Cybernetyki Technicznej. Prace Naukowe. Monografie†
0324-9794	Politechnika Wroclawska. Instytut Cybernetyki Technicznej. Prace Naukowe. Konferencje†
0324-9808	Politechnika Wroclawska. Instytut Cybernetyki Technicznej. Prace Naukowe. Studia i Materialy†
0324-9816	Politechnika Wroclawska. Instytut Chemii Organicznej i Fizycznej. Prace Naukowe. Monografie†
0324-9824	Politechnika Wroclawska. Instytut Chemii Organicznej i Fizycznej. Prace Naukowe. Konferencje†
0324-9832	Politechnika Wroclawska. Instytut Chemii Nieorganicznej i Metalurgii Pierwiastkow Rzadkich. Prace Naukowe. Konferencje†
0324-9840	Politechnika Wroclawska. Instytut Chemii Nieorganicznej i Metalurgii Pierwiastkow Rzadkich. Prace Naukowe. Monografie†
0324-9859	Politechnika Wroclawska. Instytut Chemii i Technologii Nafty i Wegla. Prace Naukowe. Monografie†
0324-9867	Politechnika Wroclawska. Instytut Chemii i Technologii Nafty i Wegla. Prace Naukowe. Konferencje†
0324-9875	Politechnika Wroclawska. Instytut Budownictwa. Prace Naukowe. Monografie†
0324-9883	Politechnika Wroclawska. Instytut Budownictwa. Prace Naukowe. Konferencje†
0324-9891	Politechnika Wroclawska. Instytut Architektury i Urbanistyki. Prace Naukowe. Studia i Materialy†
0324-9905	Politechnika Wroclawska. Instytut Architektury i Urbanistyki. Prace Naukowe. Monografie†
0325-0075	Archivos Argentinos de Pediatria **6088**
0325-0202	Metalurgia Moderna
0325-0229	Ceramica y Cristal **2039**
0325-0245	Tesis Presentadas a la Universidad de Buenos Aires†
0325-0253	Asociacion Argentina de Mineralogia, Petrologia y Sedimentologia. Revista **2702**
0325-0288	Anales de Arqueologia y Etnologia **373**
0325-0326	Industria Azucarera **3647**
0325-0407	Noticiero del Plastico **7095**
0325-0415	Envasamiento **6709**
0325-0482	Academia Nacional de la Historia. Boletin **4128**
0325-058X	Revista de la Union Industrial†
0325-0598	Liberacion y Derecho†
0325-0601	Revista de Ciencias Juridicas Sociales **4770**
0325-0679	Indice de la Literatura Dental en Castellano†
0325-0687	Mercado **1498**
0325-0695	Psicologia Medica†
0325-0725	Revista Latinoamericana de Filosofia **6949**
0325-0741	Salud Bucal **5864**
0325-0792	Argentina. Escuela de Defensa Nacional. Revista **7221**
0325-0814	Administracion **1723**
0325-0830	Economia **1098**
0325-0938	Revista Neurologica Argentina **6182**
0325-0946	La Nacion **3791**
0325-1071	Universidad Nacional de Cordoba. Facultad de Odontologia. Revista†
0325-108X	Ecosur
0325-1195	Cuadernos de Historia de Espana **4213**
0325-1209	Universidad de Buenos Aires. Instituto de Historia Antigua Oriental. Revista **4326**
0325-1217	Runa **354**
0325-125X	Facultad de Odontologia. Revista **5844**
0325-1306	Centro de Investigacion y Accion Social. Revista **7953**
0325-173X	Trabajos y Comunicaciones†
0325-1772	Instituto Nacional de Tecnologia Agropecuaria. Estacion Experimental Regional Agropecuaria. Boletin de Divulgacion Tecnica **122**
0325-1799	Estacion Experimental Region Agropecuaria Pergamino. Informe Tecnico **108**
0325-187X	Meteorologica **6390**
0325-1888	Revista Argentina de Relaciones Internacionales
0325-1918	Revista de Historia de Derecho **4771**
0325-1926	Realidad Economica **1513**
0325-1942	Redaccion **7572**
0325-1969	Argentina. Instituto Nacional de Estadistica y Censos. Boletin Estadistico Trimestral†
0325-2051	Academia Nacional de Ciencias. Boletin **7829**
0325-2221	Relaciones **352**
0325-2256	Museo de la Plata. Notas. Paleontologia **6727**
0325-2280	Patristica et Mediaevalia **4155**
0325-2345	Quiron **5702**
0325-237X	Informacion Economica de la Argentina
0325-2388	Economic Information of Argentina *see* 0325-237X
0325-2426	Conector†
0325-2434	Revista Argentina de Psiquiatria y Psicologia de la Infancia y de la Adolescencia **6181**
0325-2582	Ambito Financiero **1910**
0325-2620	Congreso Geologico Argentino. Actas **2730**
0325-2698	Sociedad Argentina de Estudios Geograficos. Boletin **4028**
0325-2701	La Ingenieria **3197**
0325-2736	Revista de Educacion y Cultura
0325-2787	Revista Argentina de Dermatologia **5881**
0325-2868	Archivo General de la Nacion. Revista **4990**
0325-2957	Acta Bioquimica Clinica Latinoamericana **721**
0325-3147	Argentina. Congreso de la Nacion. Biblioteca. Serie Bibliografica†
0325-3228	Rassegna. Revista de Informacion Medica y Cultural
0325-3384	La Alimentacion Latinoamericana **3626**
0325-3406	Academia Nacional de Ciencias. Miscelanea **7830**
0325-352X	Megavatios **3325**
0325-3627	Derecho del Trabajo **1675**
0325-3635	Impuestos **1929**
0325-3732	Hickenia†
0325-3767	Pediatria†
0325-383X	Argentina. Ministerio de Economia, Hacienda y Finanzas. Boletin Semanal de Economia **1437**
0325-3856	Argentina. Museo Provincial de Ciencias Naturales. Comunicaciones **654**
0325-3937	Ensayos Economicos **1105**
0325-3961	Toxicomanias
0325-402X	Argentina Forestal **3710**
0325-4097	Geografica **4009**
0325-4186	Centro de Investigacion y Desarrollo en Tecnologia de Pinturas. Anales **6716**
0325-4194	Argos **2230**
0325-4216	F A C E N A **672**
0325-4291	Cuadernos de Planeamiento†
0325-4453	Nudos en la Cultura Argentina
0325-4569	Imago
0325-4755	Revista Argentina de Micologia **815**
0325-4798	Guia de Refrigeracion y Aire Acondicionado **4119**
0325-4933	Estudios de Filosofia **6917**
0325-4984	Bolsa **1396**
0325-4992	Bolsa. Suplemento **1396**
0325-500X	Bolsa. Suplemento Semanal **1396**
0325-5069	Pensamiento Economico **1408**
0325-5182	Acta Oceanographica Argentina†
0325-5212	El Cronista Comercial **3791**
0325-5247	Sociedad Argentina de Diabetes. Revista **5900**
0325-5387	Ethos **6918**
0325-5395	Ingenieria Quimica **3246**
0325-5425	Academia Nacional de Derecho y Ciencias Sociales de Cordoba. Anales **4608**
0325-5476	F I D E Coyuntura y Desarrollo†
0325-5956	Accion (Buenos Aires) **5204**
0325-6030	Revista Argentina de Transfusion **5941**
0325-6081	Archivo General de la Provincia de Santa Fe. Boletin **4990**
0325-6146	S C A R Boletin **7906**
0325-6251	Bibliotecologia y Documentacion Argentina†
0325-6278	Argentina. Instituto Nacional de Tecnologia Industria. Boletin Tecnico†
0325-6375	Revista de Investigacion y Desarrollo Pesquero **3606**
0325-6391	Revista de Medicina Veterinaria **8806**
0325-6448	Summarios
0325-6502	Psychologica†
0325-6669	Scripta Ethnologica **355**
0325-6790	Instituto Nacional de Investigacion y Desarrollo Pesquero. Serie Contribuciones†
0325-6987	Instituto Nacional de Investigacion y Desarrollo Pesquero. Memoria†
0325-7150	Fotomundo **6968**
0325-724X	Actualidad Administrativa **7418**
0325-7282	Homeopatia **5805**
0325-7479	Circulo Argentino de Odontologia. Revista
0325-7525	C A I Informa **3183**
0325-7541	Revista Argentina de Microbiologia **895**
0325-7592	Limnobios†
0325-7622	Instituto de Numismatica e Historia de San Nicolas de los Arroyos. Boletin
0325-7657	Cuadernos de Numismatica y Ciencias Historicas
0325-7665	Revista Historica†
0325-772X	Res Gesta **4158**
0325-7886	Informacion Economique sur l'Argentine *see* 0325-237X
0325-7894	Wirtschaftsinfomation ueber Argentinien *see* 0325-237X
0325-7932	Chacra y Campo Moderno **100**
0325-805X	Filosofar Cristiano **6919**
0325-819X	Psicoanalisis **7392**
0325-8203	Interdisciplinaria **7363**
0325-8238	Folia Historica del Nordeste **4293**
0325-8246	Cuadernos de Geohistoria Regional **4003**
0325-8637	Lectura y Vida **5143**
0325-8718	R I A. Revista de Investigaciones Agropecuarias **149**
0325-8807	El Protesista Dental **5862**
0325-8815	Boletin de Educacion y Cultura†
0325-8955	Colegio de Abogados de Buenos Aires. Revista **4644**
0325-8963	Notas de Geometria y Topologia†
0325-9072	Instituto para el Desarrollo de Ejecutivos en la Argentina. Revista **1754**
0325-9153	Encuesta de Expectativas Agropecuarias†
0325-9161	Situacion Coyuntural del Sector Agropecuario†
0325-9250	Universidad de Buenos Aires. Facultad de Agronomia. Revista **165**
0325-9293	Aeronavegacion Comercial Argentina†
0325-9331	C A I C H A **3629**
0325-934X	I N T I†
0325-9501	Revista Argentina de Ciencias Penales **2667**
0325-951X	Medicina. Suplemento **5673**
0325-9552	Medicina y Sociedad **7531**
0325-9609	Patria
0325-9625	Serie Conservacion de la Naturaleza **2627**
0325-9676	Critica y Utopia
0325-9684	Parodiana **807**
0325-9781	Argentina. Direccion de Investigaciones Forestales. Folleto Tecnico Forestal†
0325-9986	Boletin Bibliotecologico de la Plata†
0326-0003	Cuadernos de Administracion Publica **7432**
0326-0011	El Rey **8196**
0326-0089	Energia Nuclear
0326-0380	Autotecnica
0326-0429	Semanario **3792**
0326-0550	Revista Argentina de Produccion Animal **298**
0326-0658	Revista Patagonica
0326-0666	Mutantia **6646**
0326-0690	Instituto de Matematica Beppo Levi. Cuadernos **5494**
0326-0704	Asociacion Escuela Argentina de Psicoterapia para Graduados. Revista **6124**
0326-0941	Incipit **5308**
0326-0992	Gaceta Agronomica†
0326-1050	Guia Argentina de Trafico Aereo **8543**
0326-1166	Revista Universitaria de Letras **5168**
0326-1182	Jurisprudencia Argentina (Buenos Aires, 1918) **4706**
0326-1190	Jurisprudencia Argentina (Buenos Aires, 1954) **4706**
0326-1301	Analisis Filosofico **6904**
0326-1336	Notas de Matematica Discreta†
0326-1352	Historia **4295**
0326-1417	Centro de Estudios Urbanos y Regionales. Cuadernos **8093**
0326-1441	Physis **960**
0326-145X	Anthropos **327**
0326-1638	Biologia Acuatica **657**
0326-1778	Historia Natural **7861**
0326-1913	Interdisciplinaria Monographs†
0326-1956	Comunicaciones Biologicas†
0326-1980	Bimestre
0326-2219	Revista Argentina de Mastologia **6256**
0326-226X	L E A†
0326-2383	Acta Farmaceutica Bonaerense *changed to* Latin American Journal of Pharmacy **6858**
0326-2766	Cuadernos Docentes **4003**
0326-2774	Prudentia Iuris **4763**
0326-2898	Nueva Radio Tecnica
0326-2928	Letras de Buenos Aires **5321**

ISSN

DIRECTORY 2010 0332-5784 9253

0328-7335 P C Magazine **2434**
0328-7769 Maquinas y Equipos, Herramientas e Insumos Industriales **5456**
0328-7823 Noticias de la Semana Extra *see* 0328-4298 **3791**
0328-7947 Sociedad Argentina de Ginecologia Infanto Juvenil. Revista **6005**
0328-7998 Coleccion **7117**
0328-8064 Alternativas. Serie: Espacio Pedagogico **2825**
0328-8188 Orbis Tertius **5346**
0328-8242 Cosmopolitan Argentina **8857**
0328-8269 Parabrisas Libro de Los Tests *see* 0328-4387 **8597**
0328-8277 Crucigrama Clasicos *see* 0328-4328 **8168**
0328-8285 Parabrisas Libro Guia Todos Los 4 x 4 *see* 0328-4387 **8597**
0328-8323 60 x 60 - Noticias de Medios y Comunicacion **2346**
0328-8331 Condorito **2183**
0328-8390 Cuadernos de Bioetica **5601**
0328-8501 Para Ti **8879**
0328-8560 Gente **3791**
0328-8579 Negocios **1152**
0328-865X Ingenieria Alimentaria **3647**
0328-8773 Mora **8121**
0328-8854 Revista Forestal Yvyrareta **3701**
0328-8951 Cuentas Nacionales Oferta y Demanda Globales **1476**
0328-9036 Weekend Guia de Camping *see* 0328-4271 **8340**
0328-9184 Cuadernos de Literatura Inglesa y Norteamericana **5281**
0328-9206 Revista Argentina de Residentes de Cirugia **6256**
0328-9230 Teatro XXI **8481**
0328-929X Estudios del Habitat **442**
0328-932X Energias Renovables y Medio Ambiente **3128**
0328-9621 Crucigrama Extra *see* 0328-4328 **8168**
0328-9702 Praxis Educativa **2898**
0328-9885 Luna **8872**
0329-0069 Lecturas Educacion Fisica y Deportes **8185**
0329-0573 Huellas **4014**
0329-0638 Manual Farmaceutico
0329-0883 Diseases of the Colon Rectum (Spanish Edition) **6241**
0329-093X Documentos e Investigaciones sobre la Historia del Tango **2685**
0329-1006 Mastozoologia Neotropical. Publicaciones Especiales **955**
0329-1367 Fundacion Argentina de Psicoterapia Simbolica. Revista **6142**
0329-1421 Salud Vital **6996**
0329-2045 Aportes y Transferencias. Tiempo Libre: Turismo y Recreacion **8683**
0329-2142 Apuntes de Investigacion del CECYP **7106**
0329-2177 Natura Neotropicalis **7888**
0329-224X Musica e Investigacion **6593**
0329-2665 Quinto Sol **4157**
0329-2967 Internet World **2562**
0329-3009 Electro Gremio **3188**
0329-3068 Los Archivos de Internet World **2552**
0329-3076 Argentine Foreign Trade Statistics†
0329-3092 Revista Argentina de Ciencia Politica **7178**
0329-322X El Jardin **3739**
0329-3319 Autos de Epoca **8566**
0329-3327 Auto Test Libro de Pruebas **8560**
0329-3335 Autocatalogo **8561**
0329-3343 Los Mejores Automoviles del Mundo **8590**
0329-3416 Intramuros **643**
0329-3475 Invenio **7975**
0329-3602 R C A. Revista Cientifica Agropecuaria **149**
0329-3807 Anclajes **5093**
0329-4633 Lugares **8731**
0329-4897 Arquitectura Digital **433**
0329-5192 Revista de Educacion en Biologia **701**
0329-5257 Revista Argentina de Bioingenieria **3217**
0329-5265 Revista Argentina de Bibliotecologia† **5043**
0329-5559 F A B I C I B **732**
0329-5583 S A E. Revista **8397**
0329-5591 AeDP. Actualidad en el Derecho Publico **4611**
0329-5656 Rolling Stone **6613**
0329-5796 Comercio Exterior Argentino y Entrerriano **1556**
0329-5885 Universidad de Buenos Aires. Facultad de Psicologia. Anuario de Investigaciones **7413**
0329-5893 Investigaciones en Psicologia **7366**
0329-6288 Block **435**
0329-6415 Flash **3791**
0329-6598 Jockey Club Biblioteca. Boletin **8294**
0329-7322 Universidad Nacional del Sur. Escuela de Perfeccionamiento en Investigacion Operativa. Revista **1799**
0329-7462 Desidamos **8845**
0329-7489 Fundamentos (Rio Cuarto) **1487**
0329-7888 Informe Anual sobre la Situacion de los Derechos Humanos en la Argentina **7209**
0329-8159 E N A. Encuesta Nacional Agropecuaria Provincia de Entre Rios **106**
0329-8221 Ateneo Psicoanalitico. Revista **7337**
0329-8434 Derecho y Cambio **105**
0329-8485 Alternativas. Serie: Historia y Practicas Pedagogicas **2825**
0329-8728 Escenarios Alternativos **7133**
0329-8922 Revista de Ciencia y Tecnologia **7903**
0329-9112 Como Estar Bien **8856**
0329-9147 Acheronta **7330**
0329-9368 Cuadernos Para la Otra Historia **4137**
0330-1516 Courrier de l'Industrie **1088**
0330-163X Statistiques du Commerce Exterieur **1268**
0330-258X Maghreb Medical **5664**
0330-5961 Tunisie Chirurgicale **6262**
0330-7530 Revue Tunisienne de l'Energie **3147**
0330-7549 Magallat Dirasat Andalusiyyat **4241**
0330-7611 Revue Maghrebine de Pediatrie **6104**
0330-7719 Tunisia News **3962**
0330-7956 Revue des Regions Arides **4027**
0330-8030 Microbiologie Hygiene Alimentaire **891**
0330-8081 Arab Historical Review for Ottoman Studies **4319**
0330-8480 Revue Tunisienne de Communication **2337**
0330-8987 Revue d'Histoire Maghrebine **4177**
0330-9290 Guide Economique de la Tunisie **1998**
0330-9436 Dialogue **3789**
0330-9584 Chambre de Commerce et d'Industrie du Sud. Bulletin **1400**
0330-9924 Revue Tunisienne de Geographie **4027**
0330-9932 R T A P **7464**
0330-9983 Le Temps **3962**
0331-0019 National Bibliography of Nigeria **631**
0331-0086 Barrister **4627**
0331-0094 Nigerian Journal of Entomology **856**
0331-0124 Journal of Medical and Pharmaceutical Marketing **1826**
0331-0191 I F E African Studies **4175**
0331-0205 Ikenga **3538**
0331-0213 Benin Review **5208**
0331-0337 Kwara News
0331-0361 Nigerian Economic Society. Proceedings of the Annual Conference **1153**
0331-0388 Association for Teacher Education in Africa. Western Council. Report of the Annual Conference
0331-0515 West African Journal of Educational and Vocational Measurement **2925**
0331-0523 Savanna†
0331-0531 West African Journal of Modern Languages **5195**
0331-0566 Okike **5345**
0331-0604 Journal of Pharmaceutical and Medical Sciences†
0331-0612 Nigerian Journal of Business Management **1781**
0331-0809 University of Ibadan. Student Affairs Office. Student Handbook of Information on University Policies and Practices **3008**
0331-0817 University of Ibadan. Institute of Education. Annual Report **2922**
0331-085X Civil Servant
0331-0965 Agriculture **85**
0331-0973 Nigerian Yellow Pages **1852**
0331-1376 Teachers' Forum
0331-1414 Newbreed
0331-1422 Oduma†
0331-1457 Happy Home **8867**
0331-1481 Nsukka Library Notes **5037**
0331-1570 Nigeria. National Integrated Survey of Households. Industrial Survey **1255**
0331-1686 University of Nigeria. Annual Report **3009**
0331-1805 *see* Kano State of Nigeria Gazette **7449**
0331-2062 Nigerian Journal of Animal Production **295**
0331-2151 Nigeria Bulletin on Foreign Affairs **7255**
0331-2569 Sunday Tribune **3921**
0331-2585 Business Times **1076**
0331-2658 Sunday Times **3921**
0331-2712 Nigerian Tribune **3920**
0331-2739 Daily Times†
0331-2747 Gboungboun†
0331-2755 New Nigerian **3920**
0331-3026 Nigeria Veterinary Journal **8803**
0331-3131 Annals of Nigerian Medicine **5575**
0331-3158 West African Journal of Archaeology **423**
0331-3468 Muse **5337**
0331-3646 Nigerian Journal of International Affairs **7255**
0331-3735 Nigeria Society of Physiotherapy. Journal **6113**
0331-3778 Home Studies **3920**
0331-4162 Woman's World **8890**
0331-4219 Museum Africum†
0331-426X Aworerin **2829**
0331-4367 Ibadan Review†
0331-443X Nigerian Tobacco Company. Annual Report and Accounts **8486**
0331-4448 Nigerian Nurse **5971**
0331-4464 Ntieyong Business Review **1155**
0331-4472 Nitel Journal
0331-4502 Teen and Twenty **2216**
0331-4774 Nigerian Radio - T V Times **2361**
0331-4782 Medipharm **6861**
0331-5126 Northern States Review
0331-5134 Tarikh **4178**
0331-5177 Centre of Arabic Documentation. Research Bulletin **5105**
0331-5193 The Leader **7804**
0331-5967 Nigeria Engineer **3212**
0331-5975 The Truth **7716**
0331-6173 B P News†
0331-6254 Nigerian Institute of International Affairs. Monograph Series **7255**
0331-6262 Nigerian Institute of International Affairs. Lecture Series **7255**
0331-6289 Apollo **2176**
0331-6351 Ife Journal of Agriculture **120**
0331-6742 Noma **141**
0331-7080 New Culture **508**
0331-7110 The Independent **7800**
0331-7285 Samaru Journal of Agricultural Research **154**
0331-7714 The Publisher **7570**
0331-8109 School Libraries Bulletin **5045**
0331-8400 Marketing in Nigeria **1832**
0331-8494 Healthy Living†
0331-8524 Nigerian Journal of Political Science **7255**
0331-9237 Lagos Education Review **2881**
0331-9296 Kainji Lake Research Institute. Annual Report **2796**
0331-9911 Positive Review†
0332-0006 National Library of Ireland. Council of Trustees. Annual Report *changed to* 2009-020X **5034**
0332-0111 Irish Birds **909**
0332-0162 Community Report
0332-0189 Progressive Farmer†
0332-0197 Irish Computer **2427**
0332-0235 Glasra **791**
0332-0294 Teangeolas **5186**
0332-0502 Social Studies†
0332-0510 Irish Journal of Psychiatric Nursing†
0332-0561 Irish Rod & Gun
0332-0588 Irish Grassland and Animal Protection Association. Journal *changed to* Irish Grassland Association. Journal **266**
0332-0618 Search **7774**
0332-0650 Development†
0332-0707 Irish Pharmacy Journal **6851**
0332-0758 Eriu **5290**
0332-0782 County Kildare Archaeological Society. Journal **388**
0332-0847 Hot Press **3893**
0332-0863 University College Cork Calendar **3008**
0332-1045 Irish Bystander
0332-1118 Irish Business and Administrative Research *changed to* 1649-248X **1130**
0332-1150 Scripture in Church **7817**
0332-1169 Saothar **4261**
0332-1185 Irish Biogeographical Society. Bulletin **4016**
0332-1266 Co-Op Ireland **3485**
0332-1274 Gaelic World **8174**
0332-1428 Milltown Studies **7807**
0332-1452 Irish Boats and Yachting†
0332-1460 Irish Studies in International Affairs **7246**
0332-1541 Soundpost†
0332-1568 Aontas Review†
0332-1592 Peritia **4253**
0332-1649 Compel **5551**
0332-1665 Irish Journal of Environmental Science†
0332-1673 Gaelic Games Monthly
0332-1711 Engineers Journal **3191**
0332-1754 Magill **3894**
0332-1789 Fishery Leaflet **3593**
0332-1800 Royal Dublin Society. Journal of Life Sciences†
0332-1940 Sunday Tribune **3895**
0332-2033 Workers Life†
0332-205X Teanga **5186**
0332-2130 I P U Review **6847**
0332-2262 Farm Machinery†
0332-2300 Ireland, a Directory and Yearbook *changed to* 0790-1070 **7447**
0332-2386 School and College
0332-2408 Irish Farmers Monthly **124**
0332-2483 Inside Ireland **8721**
0332-253X Blazes
0332-2580 Cork Review **483**
0332-2629 Sherkin Island. Journal†
0332-2637 Chemistry in Action **2057**
0332-267X Marketing Opinion **29**
0332-2696 Central Bank of Ireland. Irish Economic Statistics **1220**
0332-270X Bealoideas **3615**
0332-2947 Irish Runner **8181**
0332-298X Irish Folk Music Studies **6578**
0332-2998 Poetry Ireland Review **5431**
0332-3102 Irish Medical Journal **5641**
0332-317X Irish Stamp News†
0332-3188 Beau†
0332-320X Allied Irish Bank Review **1306**
0332-3250 Dublin University Law Journal **4661**
0332-3293 Irish Law Reports Monthly **4833**
0332-3315 Irish Educational Studies **2871**
0332-3536 Irish Greyhound Review **8181**
0332-3625 Church & State **7116**
0332-3633 Irish History Workshop
0332-3641 Institute of Guidance Counsellors. Journal **6699**
0332-3889 Trinity College. Centre for Language and Communication Studies. Occasional Paper **5189**
0332-3951 Economic Trends **1101**
0332-4036 Identity (Dublin)†
0332-4095 International Civil Engineering Abstracts **3232**
0332-4117 Cathair na Mart **4209**
0332-4214 Scriptores Latini Hiberniae **5368**
0332-4222 Mediaeval and Modern Breton Series **5150**
0332-4230 Mediaeval and Modern Welsh Series **5331**
0332-4249 Scribhinni Gaeilgena na Brathar Mionur **5368**
0332-4265 Mediaeval and Modern Irish Series **5331**
0332-4273 Moorea **3744**
0332-4281 Dawn Train†
0332-4338 Fisheries Bulletin **943**
0332-4346 Religious Life Review **7814**
0332-4354 Irish Business
0332-4400 Hotel and Catering Review **4389**
0332-4427 Irish Biblical Association. Proceedings **7651**
0332-4443 Gralton
0332-446X Women's Clubs Magazine **8891**
0332-4567 Aspect **1610**
0332-463X Garda News **2653**
0332-4680 Practical Farmer
0332-4788 Evening Echo **3892**
0332-4834 Cork Weekly Examiner†
0332-4869 Maynooth Review
0332-4877 Geographical Viewpoint **4011**
0332-4893 Irish Economic and Social History **4232**
0332-5024 Studia Musicologica Norvegica **6620**
0332-5083 Norway. Fiskeridirektoratet. Skrifter. Serie Ernaering†
0332-5105 Sirene†
0332-5121 Gyldendals Aktuelle Magasin†
0332-513X Foreldre og Barn **2153**
0332-5210 European Offshore Petroleum Newsletter **6768**
0332-5229 Jord og Myr†
0332-5334 Scandinavian Oil - Gas Magazine **6791**
0332-5407 University of Bergen. Department of Pure Mathematics. Report **5545**
0332-5415 Fokus paa Familien **6141**
0332-5423 Kapital **1770**
0332-5474 Norsk Landbruk **142**
0332-5482 Norsk Musikktidsskrift†
0332-5490 Norsk Oljerevy†
0332-5512 Tidsskrift om Edruskapsspoersmaal†
0332-5555 Oekonomisk Rapport **1900**
0332-5598 Penger og Kreditt **1374**
0332-5601 Vaar Fuglefauna **915**
0332-561X Symbolae Osloenses. Fasciculi Suppletorii *see* 0039-7679 **2241**
0332-5652 N I P H Annals†
0332-5733 Mur *changed to* 1504-7903 **450**
0332-5741 Norsk Veterinaer-Tidsskrift **8803**
0332-5768 Norges Geologiske Undersoekelse. Bulletin†
0332-5784 Dugnad (Oslo) *changed to* 1502-7473 **358**

ISSN

0332-5792 Dyade **6915**
0332-5806 Ergo†
0332-5814 Videregaaende Opplaering†
0332-5822 Basar†
0332-5865 Nordic Journal of Linguistics **5155**
0332-5881 Taxi **8512**
0332-5903 Geophysica Norvegica†
0332-5938 Teknikk og Miljoe†
0332-5997 Tradisjon *changed to* 1502-7473 **358**
0332-6004 Nordnorsk Magasin **5342**
0332-608X Viking **423**
0332-611X IngenioerNytt **3198**
0332-6144 North Sea Observer *changed to* 0803-3773 **6782**
0332-6152 Byggherren **988**
0332-6195 Tromura. Naturvitenskap **7925**
0332-6306 A m S - Varia **370**
0332-6330 Sosiologi i Dag **8139**
0332-6411 A m S - Smaatrykk **370**
0332-6470 Norsk Psykologforening. Tidsskrift **7388**
0332-6500 Universitetet i Bergen. Arkeologisk Institutt. Arkeologiske Skrifter†
0332-6535 Legemiddelforbruket i Norge **6890**
0332-6543 Tromura. Museologi **6538**
0332-656X Synopsis†
0332-6578 Norske Arkitektkonkurranser **451**
0332-6756 Bergen Banks Kvartalsskrift†
0332-6772 Hytteliv **4542**
0332-6802 Personal-Opplaering†
0332-6926 Musikk og Skole *changed to* 0809-0807 **6545**
0332-6934 FlyNytt **56**
0332-6942 Doeves Tidsskrift **4073**
0332-6950 Apotekteknikeren **4589**
0332-7078 Kjoettbransjen **3680**
0332-7086 Byggeindustrien **988**
0332-7108 Journalisten **4578**
0332-7116 Me'a *changed to* 1504-7466 **3601**
0332-7124 Arbeidervern **6672**
0332-7132 Norsk Fiskeoppdrett **3603**
0332-7159 Offisersbladet **6440**
0332-7221 Byggmesteren **988**
0332-723X Billedkunstneren **478**
0332-7264 Norsklaereren **5156**
0332-7280 Vaare Nyttevekster *changed to* 1504-4165 **818**
0332-7299 Norsk Utenrikspolitisk Aarbok†
0332-7353 Modeling, Identification and Control (Print) *changed to* 1890-1328 **2463**
0332-7426 Aktuelt Perspektiv **7104**
0332-7434 Sunnhetsbladet **6998**
0332-7442 Villmarksliv **8339**
0332-7469 Natur og Samfunn **3455**
0332-7531 Nordlyd **5156**
0332-7574 Tre og Moebler *changed to* 1504-2510 **4545**
0332-7582 Bo **4404**
0332-7590 Juristkontakt **4707**
0332-7647 Tromura. Fellesserie **6538**
0332-7779 Diedut **4214**
0332-7795 Revisjon og Regnskap **1300**
0332-7868 Marius **4935**
0332-7892 Roede Fane *changed to* 1504-4777 **7180**
0332-7906 Norway. Statistisk Sentralbyraa. Helsestatistikk **7548**
0332-7957 Norway. Statistisk Sentralbyraa. Familie Statistikk†
0332-7965 Norway. Statistisk Sentralbyraa. Alkohol og Andre Rusmidler†
0332-8015 Norway. Statistisk Sentralbyraa. Framskriving av Folkemengden **7313**
0332-8023 Norway. Statistisk Sentralbyraa. Kommunestyrevalget **7482**
0332-8066 Handelsbestyreren **1749**
0332-8074 Norges Kjoebmannsblad **3680**
0332-8295 Allergologen **5753**
0332-8317 Arkitektur- og Designhoegskolen i Oslo. AHO-Skrift **433**
0332-8414 Bondebladet **97**
0332-8457 Spesialpedagogikk **3047**
0332-8554 Gunneria **7859**
0332-8597 Norsk Fotografisk Tidsskrift **6972**
0332-8643 Fiskerioekonomiske Smaaskrifter **3594**
0332-8775 Fjell og Vidde **8313**
0332-8813 Hundesport **6809**
0332-883X Politiembetsmennenes Blad **2664**
0332-8848 Norsk Filatelistisk Tidsskrift **6897**
0332-8856 Jogging†
0332-8864 Motorbransjen **8593**
0332-8929 Papirhandleren **6737**
0332-8937 Nicolay **408**
0332-8988 Samferdsel **8634**
0332-9046 Kjoekkenskriveren **6662**
0332-9062 Forsvarets Forum *changed to* 1503-8505 **6421**
0332-9097 Befalsbladet **6413**
0332-9119 Polarflokken **813**
0332-9410 Hold Pusten **6197**
0332-9453 Teknisk Tegning†
0332-9526 Sygeforsikringsbladet *changed to* 0809-5302 **8146**
0332-9666 Friidrett **8174**
0332-9690 Vestlandsk Landbruk **168**
0332-9771 Norsk Sjakkblad **8191**
0332-9798 Cockpit Forum **4592**
0333-0044 Homoeopatisk Tidsskrift **5805**
0333-0079 Bankoekonoment†
0333-0141 Kroppsoeving **2881**
0333-0176 Norsk Kirkemusikk **6600**
0333-0273 Forskningspolitikk **4453**
0333-0370 Spelemannsbladet for Folkemusikk og Bygdedans **6619**
0333-0389 Skolepsykologi **2913**
0333-0451 Avis- og Bladlista†
0333-0656 Stavanger Museum. Aarbok **519**
0333-0664 Stavanger Museum. Skrifter **6537**
0333-0753 Norsk Lovtidend. Avd. I Lover og Sentrale Forskrifter m.v. **4851**
0333-0761 Norsk Lovtidend. Avd. II Regionale og Lokale Forskrifter m.v. **4851**
0333-080X Frimerke Forum **6895**
0333-0869 Gamalt fraa Voss **8713**
0333-0915 Gauldalsminne†
0333-0974 Maihaugen **4242**
0333-1024 Cephalalgia **6130**
0333-1059 Kunsthaandverk **536**
0333-1172 Parapsykologiske Notiser **6743**
0333-1342 Nordisk Sosialt Arbeid **8059**
0333-1393 Verden og Vi†
0333-1423 Norsk Skattelovsamling *changed to* 1504-6001 **1931**
0333-1504 Norway. Statistisk Sentralbyraa. Bank- og Kredittstatistikk. Aktuelle Tall†
0333-1512 Acta ad Archaeologiam et Artium Historiam Pertinentia. Series Altera **370**
0333-1865 University of Bergen. Department of Mathematics. Statistical Report **5545**
0333-1911 Yrkesbil **8679**
0333-1997 Bygdeungdommen **2181**
0333-2020 Norsk Treteknisk Institutt. Rapport **3714**
0333-2055 Norway. Statistisk Sentralbyraa. Sosialstatistikk *changed to* 1504-2316 **8150**
0333-208X Norway. Statistisk Sentralbyraa. Reiselivsstatistikk *changed to* 1503-4119 **8780**
0333-2241 I C L A S Bulletin†
0333-2306 Norges Offentlige Utredninger **3924**
0333-2314 Universitetet i Trondheim. Norges Tekniske Hoegskole. Biblioteket. Meldinger og Boklister†
0333-2411 Supplement till Norsk Skattelovsamling *changed to* 0809-6600 **1942**
0333-2500 Driftsgranskinger i Jord- og Skogbruk **196**
0333-2551 Riksantikvaren. Rapporter **4426**
0333-256X Rangifer **298**
0333-2578 S I N T E F Rapport†
0333-2624 Spillerom†
0333-273X European Political Data Newsletter†
0333-2802 Tromura. Kulturhistorie **4274**
0333-2810 Skatterett **4784**
0333-2861 Helsenytt for Alle **7524**
0333-2969 Flair Business **8863**
0333-3205 Sosiolog-Nytt **8139**
0333-3310 Ledelse†
0333-3329 Huseierens Magasin†
0333-3469 Jernvarehandleren†
0333-3477 Byggenytt **988**
0333-3507 Fiskerinytt
0333-3531 Maleren **6719**
0333-354X Moebelhandleren *changed to* 1504-4858 **4560**
0333-3566 Wiwar **4279**
0333-3620 I A S P Newsletter **7563**
0333-3639 Sport **8203**
0333-3671 Institutt for Samfunnsforskning. Rapport **8107**
0333-3701 Norway. Statistisk Sentralbyraa. Helseinstitusjoner†
0333-3728 Norway. Statistisk Sentralbyraa. Fiskeristatistikk **3614**
0333-3760 Norges Musikhoegskole. N M H Publikasjoner **6600**
0333-3779 Norway. Statistisk Sentralbyraa. Elektrisitesstatistikk **3153**
0333-3825 Spraaknytt **5177**
0333-3868 Skattebetaleren **4905**
0333-3973 SkiSport **8333**
0333-3981 Forsvarsstudier *changed to* 1504-6532 **2226**
0333-4031 Reindriftsnytt **298**
0333-4325 University of Bergen. Institute of Psychology. Psychological Report Series†
0333-4384 European Rig- and Supplyship Owners. Yearbook†
0333-452X Norsk Svoemming **8191**
0333-4538 Norsk Skyttertidende **8191**
0333-4589 Diakonos **7637**
0333-4872 Porselensmaling *changed to* 1890-2928 **534**
0333-5100 Ba'avoda Kehilatit
0333-5151 Dapim Leheker Tekufat Hashoa **4137**
0333-5194 I O L R Collected Reprints†
0333-5259 Physical Education and Sport† **8981**
0333-5321 Union List of Serials in Israel Libraries **638**
0333-533X English Teachers' Journal (Israel)† **8953**
0333-5372 Poetics Today **5234**
0333-5380 Diamond World Review **4565**
0333-5461 Ma'ariv Lano'ar **2200**
0333-5526 United States-Israel Binational Science Foundation. Project-Report Abstracts†
0333-5623 Survey of Israel. Cartographic Papers† **8991**
0333-5658 Nihul **1781**
0333-5666 Yeda Lemeda **1955**
0333-5720 Survey of Israel. Photogrammetric Papers† **8991**
0333-5739 Israel Institute of Animal Science. Scientific Activities
0333-5771 Israel. Atomic Energy Commission. Annual Report
0333-578X Agricultural Research Organization. Scientific Activities†
0333-5836 Israel Institute of Horticulture. Scientific Activities
0333-5844 Qedem **412**
0333-5879 Technion - Israel Institute of Technology. Faculty of Agricultural Engineering. Publications†
0333-5895 Isra - Counter-Source†
0333-5925 Israel Yearbook on Human Rights **7211**
0333-5933 Israel C P A†
0333-600X Israel. Central Bureau of Statistics. Staff in Universities†
0333-6018 Israel Book Trade Directory **7564**
0333-6050 Israel. Central Bureau of Statistics. Road Accidents with Casualties. Part 1 **8527**
0333-6107 Israel. Central Bureau of Statistics. Road Accidents with Casualties. Part 2 **8527**
0333-6131 Calendar of Scientific and Technological Meetings in Israel
0333-6166 Books from Israel†
0333-6174 Seridim† **8988**
0333-6190 Israel Academy of Sciences and Humanities. Section of Sciences. Proceedings† **8966**
0333-6204 Israel. Central Bureau of Statistics. Tourism **8779**
0333-6212 Tierra Santa *see* 0040-3784
0333-6255 Family Expenditure Survey
0333-6271 Out of Jerusalem†
0333-6298 B'Or Ha-Torah **7719**
0333-6379 Kibbutz Studien†
0333-6387 Noga† **8977**
0333-6425 Israel. Geological Survey. Current Research **2748**
0333-6476 Assaph. Section B: Studies in Art History **476**
0333-6514 Israel Public Council for Soviet Jewry. Scientists' Committee. News Bulletin†
0333-6603 Israel. Central Bureau of Statistics. Survey of Travelling Habits **8779**
0333-6611 Tel Aviv University. David Horowitz Institute for the Research of Developing Countries. Annual Report† **8992**
0333-6697 Sevivot
0333-6735 Environmental Planning† **8954**
0333-676X Voices Israel **5437**
0333-6875 Holy Land Postal History **6895**
0333-6883 Techumin **7730**
0333-6948 Pi Ha'atom† **8981**
0333-6964 Hebrew University of Jerusalem. Authority for Research and Development. Research† **8961**
0333-7073 Bank of Israel. Recent Economic Developments **1441**
0333-7081 Mehq're Yerushalayim B'Mahshevet Yisra'el **7726**
0333-712X Hello Israel
0333-7189 Holy Land Review **7721**
0333-7219 Z'manim **4168**
0333-7235 Ammudim **1422**
0333-7286 A.B. - The Samaritan News **3514**
0333-7308 Israel Journal of Psychiatry and Related Sciences **6148**
0333-7383 Torgos **915**
0333-7413 Machshevim P C† **8972**
0333-7499 Israel Museum Journal **6526**
0333-7502 Mivnim **1024**
0333-7553 Tikshoret
0333-7588 Hadarim
0333-7596 Yad L'achim Wall Calendar† **8999**
0333-7618 Jerusalem Cathedra†
0333-7634 Israel. Central Bureau of Statistics. Victimization Survey **2674**
0333-7685 Meda'on **2431**
0333-7839 Maurice Falk Institute for Economic Research in Israel. Report and Discussion Paper Series **1147**
0333-7936 Israel. Meteorological Service. Monthly Agroclimatological Report†
0333-8037 Madrich Legrote Chove†
0333-8169 Israel. Central Bureau of Statistics. Suicides and Attempted Suicides
0333-8266 Israel. Central Bureau of Statistics. Survey of Trucks **8527**
0333-8428 I D F Journal†
0333-8436 Israel. Central Bureau of Statistics. Foreign Trade Statistics (Annual) - Exports **1245**
0333-8479 Etzb'oni **2188**
0333-8487 Israel. Central Bureau of Statistics. Foreign Trade Statistics (Annual) - Imports **1245**
0333-8584 Kolot
0333-8649 National Insurance Institute, Jerusalem. Annual Survey **4516**
0333-8835 Mayim ve-Hashkaya **8829**
0333-886X Israel. Central Bureau of Statistics. Local Authorities in Israel: Financial Data
0333-8886 Alon Hanotea **218**
0333-9025 Ikkare Yisra'el **120**
0333-9041 Families in Israel
0333-9068 World Union of Jewish Studies. Proceedings† **8999**
0333-9076 Hed ha-Ulpan† **8961**
0333-9270 Oraita
0333-9378 Spiegel Lectures in European Jewish History†
0333-9440 Israel. Central Bureau of Statistics. National Accounts of Judea, Samaria, and the Gaza Area
0333-9491 Israel. Central Bureau of Statistics. Energy in Israel **3153**
0333-9505 Israel. Central Bureau of Statistics. Students in Universities
0333-9521 Technologies **8441**
0333-953X Israel Book News
0333-9637 Rimmonim **515**
0333-9661 Studies in Jewish Education **7730**
0333-9688 Lammed Leshon'kha **5138**
0333-9718 World of Art† **8999**
0333-9726 Mesilot **7726**
0333-9793 Israel. Central Bureau of Statistics. Survey on Research and Development in Industry
0333-9815 Alon Lemoreh Habiologia†
0333-9874 Integrated Rural Development. Publications
0333-9882 Israel Film Industry Directory
0333-9904 Rotem† **8986**
0333-9971 Tnuah Vetachbura†
0334-0082 International Journal of Turbo and Jet Engines **61**
0334-0139 International Journal of Adolescent Medicine and Health **6093**
0334-018X Journal of Pediatric Endocrinology & Metabolism **5896**
0334-0236 Journal of Orthopedic Surgical Techniques
0334-0309 Israel. Knesset. Divrei ha-Knesset **7144**
0334-0430 Bisdeh Habniya† **8936**
0334-049X Israel. Central Bureau of Statistics. Inputs in Research and Development in Universities
0334-0570 Hardun†
0334-0600 Yedi'on† **8999**
0334-0686 Dappim L'Mehqar B'sifrut **5283**
0334-0694 Israel Geological Society. Annual Meeting Proceedings
0334-0716 Mehq're Mishpat **4732**
0334-0740 Mittuv T'veria
0334-0899 Apiryon
0334-0902 Ma K'dai† **8972**
0334-0953 Jews of the Soviet Union†
0334-0996 D E C U S Israel News†
0334-1003 Yalkut Lemachshava Sotzialistit†
0334-1100 Interface **7867**
0334-1151 Weizmann Institute of Science. Research†
0334-1186 Perspectives in Drug Abuse **2698**
0334-1208 Shappirit†
0334-1380 Barkai† **8935**
0334-1461 Re'em† **8984**
0334-1488 Mazon Umitbach
0334-1674 Massorot **7726**
0334-1763 Reviews in the Neurosciences **6181**
0334-1798 Yisrael-Am ve-Eretz†

0334-1860 Journal of Intelligent Systems 2527
0334-200X Yad Laqore changed to 1565-544X 5031
0334-2026 Israel Studies in Musicology†
0334-2050 Environment in Israel. Selected Papers†
0334-2093 Bank of Israel. Israel's Banking System 1314
0334-2123 Phytoparasitica 247
0334-2182 Kibbutz (Tel Aviv)
0334-2212 Kidma†
0334-2220 Israel. Central Bureau of Statistics. Transport Statistics Quarterly 8527
0334-2255 Beer-Sheva 7719
0334-2263 Hed HaGan 2863
0334-231X Social Security 4523
0334-2336 Da'at 7720
0334-2360 Gerontology 4046
0334-2425 Trade Marks Journal
0334-2476 Israel. Central Bureau of Statistics. Tourism and Hotel Services Statistics Quarterly 8779
0334-2484 Agricultural Research Organization. Special Publications†
0334-2492 Financial Statements for the Year 1345
0334-2506 Forum†
0334-2514 State, Government and International Relations†
0334-2565 Iyyunim B'-Hinnukh 2988
0334-2573 Israel. Central Bureau of Statistics. Agricultural Statistics Quarterly
0334-2603 Israel Pharmaceutical Journal†
0334-2611 Shefa Quarterly†
0334-2751 Sapanut†
0334-276X Sifrut Yeladim Vanoar 2213
0334-2786 Jerusalem Papers on Peace Problems†
0334-2816 Divre ha-Akademia ha-Le'umit ha-Yisr'elit Le-Madda'im 4450
0334-2824 Directory of Scientific and Technical Associations in Israel
0334-2867 Ma'agale Keri'a
0334-2921 Mapfte'ah L'khit've 'Et B'ivrit 10
0334-2948 Journalism Yearbook†
0334-2956 Shma Yisrael
0334-2972 Israel. Central Bureau of Statistics. Foreign Trade Statistics Quarterly
0334-3022 Pashosh† 8980
0334-3049 International Journal of Medicine and Law†
0334-3057 Israel Electronics
0334-3065 Ha-Riv'on ha-Yisre'eli I'Missim 1927
0334-309X Bibliography of Modern Hebrew Literature in Translation† 8936
0334-3170 B'eretz Yisra'el
0334-3197 Directory of Research Institutes and Industrial Laboratories in Israel†
0334-3251 Siach†
0334-326X Argamon†
0334-3278 Israel. Central Bureau of Statistics. New Statistical Projects and Publications in Israel 8381
0334-3332 Patents and Design Journal (Print) changed to Patents and Design Journal (Online) 6756
0334-3405 Slavica Hierosolymitana†
0334-3553 Folklore Research Center Studies†
0334-357X Ha-Lohem 6423
0334-360X Italia 3541
0334-3626 Leshonenu 5143
0334-3650 Tarbiz 7730
0334-3715 Levantina†
0334-3758 Yuval Monograph Series† 8999
0334-3774 Ofaqim B'geografiya 4023
0334-3804 Israel Environment Bulletin 3444
0334-3847 Innovation†
0334-3871 Assia 5579
0334-3898 Israel Business†
0334-3928 Etanim changed to Derekh Hayyim 7514
0334-4002 Shvut 3564
0334-4029 Society and Welfare 8072
0334-4053 Yeda-Am†
0334-4088 Pe'amim 7728
0334-4118 Jerusalem Studies in Arabic and Islam
0334-4150 Michael 3550
0334-4169 Maeda Lerofei†
0334-4258 Gal-ed 3534
0334-4266 Modern Hebrew Literature 5335
0334-4304 Sinai 7729
0334-4355 Tel Aviv 420
0334-438X Jews and the Jewish People - Jewish Samizdat†
0334-4401 Israel Oriental Studies 552
0334-4436 Jews and the Jewish People. Excerpts from the Soviet Press†
0334-4479 Salit†
0334-4487 Jews and the Jewish People - Petitions, Letters and Appeals from Soviet Jews† 8967
0334-4509 Scripta Classica Israelica
0334-4525 Avareyanut Usetiya Chevrati†
0334-4576 Tel Aviv University. Law Review 4793
0334-4622 Arachim†
0334-4657 Cathedra 4320
0334-4754 Ale Sefer 5056
0334-4762 Social Research Review†
0334-4770 Iyyunim B'minhal Uv'Irgun Ha-hinnukh 3025
0334-4800 Jerusalem Quarterly
0334-4827 Ale Siah
0334-4843 Historia 4142
0334-4878 Itton 77 Lesifrut Uletarbut 5424
0334-4975 Proza† 8983
0334-5076 Alon Lamorah Lesifrut
0334-5084 Alim† 8929
0334-5114 Symbiosis
0334-5262 Sifre Ya'ats Hadashim 635
0334-5572 Igra 5308
0334-5831 Adam Hofshi
0334-5963 Assaph. Section C: Studies in the Theatre 8466
0334-5971 S S D A Yedi'on - Newsletter† 8986
0334-6005 Corrosion Reviews 6309
0334-6056 I C A Information†
0334-6137 Seven Gates†

0334-6234 Neto Plus 1870
0334-6307 Israel High-Tech & Investment Report 8428
0334-6447 Journal of Polymer Engineering 3249
0334-6455 High Temperature Materials and Processes 3345
0334-648X Kulanu† 8970
0334-6579 Tel Aviv University. Wiener Library. Bibliography of New Acquisitions†
0334-6595 Financial Data of T A - 100 Companies - Quarterly† 8956
0334-6943 Seratim
0334-6986 Sidra 7729
0334-6994 Kabbalah
0334-701X Jewish History 7723
0334-715X Hadshot Sappanut Uteufah - Yidion 8645
0334-7311 Michmanim 406
0334-7397 Inyan Hadash†
0334-7524 Preventive Pediatrics
0334-7532 Mehkar Hakla'i Be-Yisrael†
0334-7591 Scopus 2300
0334-7680 Elektronika Umachshevim
0334-7826 Tsillum Miktso'i† 8994
0334-7869 Keshev
0334-794X Adrichalut
0334-8113 Hinnukh Meyuhad Weshiqum
0334-8121 Haroshet† 8961
0334-8466 Romah†
0334-8547 Al-Karmil 5317
0334-8814 Megadim 7662
0334-8865 see 0932-8408 4273
0334-889X Semana
0334-8903 Dispersion y Unidad†
0334-8938 Journal of the Mechanical Behavior of Materials 6319
0334-8954 Aurora 3895
0334-8970 Secular Humanistic Judaism
0334-9101 J D C - Brookdale Institute of Gerontology and Human Development. International Forum†
0334-9144 Aging in the Jewish World†
0334-9152 Israel Journal of Veterinary Medicine 8800
0334-9160 Leumi Review 1497
0334-9330 Sihot
0334-9470 Lo Nishkach† 8971
0334-9527 Taglit
0334-9578 Eretz Magazine 2610
0334-9594 Yerusholaimer Almanakh† 8999
0334-9659 Al Hapereq† 8929
0334-9810 Mishkafayim† 8974
0334-9853 Missim 1935
0344-9942 Halikhot Sadeh 117
0334-9977 Journal of Social Work and Policy in Israel 8051
0335-0088 Ardenne Economique (Carleville-Mezieres) 1395
0335-0274 I N R S Bulletin de Documentation
0335-038X Centre d'Etudes et de Recherches Litteraires et Scientifiques de Mende. Bulletin 4209
0335-0479 C X P Informations†
0335-136X Action Sociale et Sante 1661
0335-1793 Liberation 3841
0335-1947 Cite Nouvelle†
0335-1971 Numismatique & Change 6652
0335-2013 Relations Internationales 7262
0335-2021 Construction Neuve et Ancienne†
0335-2927 Theatre Public 8483
0335-315X Digraphe†
0335-3265 Interaction† 8965
0335-3559 Repertoire de Materiaux et Elements Controles du Batiment†
0335-3710 Bulletin Technique Apicole 98
0335-377X Pulp and Paper†
0335-394X Guide de l'Acheteur NF†
0335-3958 Quercy Recherche 4256
0335-4105 Conseil de l'Europe. Bulletin d'Information sur la Politique Sociale†
0335-4377 Monde Rural†
0335-4997 Point Veterinaire 8804
0335-5004 Revue Generale Nucleaire 3174
0335-5012 Assemblee Nouvelle†
0335-5047 Droit et Pratique du Commerce International†
0335-508X Bulletin des Etudes Valeryennes†
0335-5160 Annales du Museum du Havre 6519
0335-5233 Archeologie en Bretagne†
0335-5306 Coeur et Sante† 8941
0335-5322 Actes de la Recherche en Sciences Sociales 7945
0335-5721 Ciconia 905
0335-5950 Dossiers Noirs 7231
0335-5985 Archives de Sciences Sociales des Religions 7623
0335-6035 Nouvelles Feministes†
0335-6124 Cogito†
0335-6280 Cinema Politique†
0335-6469 Calao†
0335-6566 Mineraux et Fossiles 6726
0335-6809 Figures 4452
0335-7163 Centre de Promotion de la Presse Industrielle et Scientifique Francaise. Revue des Sommaires†
0335-7457 Revue Francaise d'Allergologie et d'Immunologie Clinique changed to 1877-0320 5765
0335-752X Nouvelles du Livre Ancien 7569
0335-7619 Tribune Medicale†
0335-7791 Bulletin Climatologique des Deux-Sevres changed to 1774-9298 6348
0335-7856 Vaucluse Agricole 168
0335-7899 Le Coq Heron 6133
0335-8178 Institut de Montpellier. Memoires et Travaux 2747
0335-8402 Centre Interdisciplinaire d'Etude et de Recherche sur l'Expression Contemporaine. Travaux 4446
0335-878X Grues et Chariots†
0335-9190 L.S.I.
0335-9255 Sciences de la Terre: Serie Informatique Geologique 2766
0335-9956 Officiel†
0336-0296 Hellequin†
0336-030X Heimdal† 8961
0336-142X Vie et Sciences Economiques 1191
0336-1438 L'Ethnographie 336

0336-1446 Espaces 8312
0336-1454 France. Institut National de la Statistique et des Etudes Economiques. Economie et Statistique 1233
0336-1462 Echanges Internationaux et Developpement 7960
0336-1470 Centre d'Etude des Revenus et des Couts. Documents†
0336-1489 Defense Nationale changed to 1950-3253 6419
0336-1500 Communication et Langages 5107
0336-1519 Ecole Francaise d'Extreme-Orient. Bulletin 549
0336-156X Revue des Etudes Islamiques 559
0336-1578 Revue des Sciences Sociales de la France de l'Est changed to 1623-6572 7998
0336-1640 Regard sur la Biochimie 744
0336-1721 Pluriel 7992
0336-2698 Archontes†
0336-321X Presence des Lettres et des Arts†
0336-3449 Diagnostics†
0336-3686 International Copyright Information Centre. Information Bulletin†
0336-4895 Recherche, Pedagogie et Culture†
0336-4917 Annales du Museum d'Histoire Naturelle de Nice
0336-4933 Lithoclastia†
0336-5689 Enseignements Professionnels†
0336-5913 Cahiers de Sexologie Clinique 5591
0336-626X Aeroports Magazine changed to 1954-5231 8785
0336-6596 Moto Flash 8591
0336-7266 Creations Lingerie
0336-7525 Revue de Chirurgie Esthetique de Langue Francaise 6257
0336-8424 Bouliste†
0336-9331 Fiches du Cinema 6497
0336-9420 Combat Socialiste†
0336-9455 Connaissance du Pays d'Oc† 8943
0336-9609 Revue Sexpol†
0336-9722 Urbapress Informations 4431
0336-9730 Traverses† 8994
0337-0216 Informations sur les Maladies Veneriennes†
0337-0402 Voyages Contact 8773
0337-1573 France. Laboratoire Central des Ponts et Chaussees. Rapport General d'Activite 3267
0337-1603 Arts d'Afrique Noire† 8931
0337-1883 Le Haut-Parleur†
0337-2014 Paradoxes†
0337-2154 La Hulotte 2193
0337-274X Ingeniere-Edition Regionale, Sud-Ouest de la France
0337-307X Futuribles 8103
0337-3126 Connexions 7348
0337-3371 Cahiers Turcica
0337-4092 Actualite, Combustibles, Energie†
0337-4149 Qui Fabrique et Fournit Quoi†
0337-5781 Guide du Feu 3579
0337-579X Societe Archeologique et Historique de l'Orleanais. Bulletin 417
0337-5935 Annuaire National des Masseurs Kinesitherapeutes
0337-5978 Mots en Liberte, Bulletin d'Etudes Lexicales†
0337-5986 Lexique Dernier†
0337-6176 Universite de la Reunion. Cahier†
0337-6818 Revue des Ingenieurs et Techniciens Europeens
0337-6877 Revue Francaise d'Acupuncture 314
0337-7091 Regards sur l'Actualite 7465
0337-7148 Bulletin de Saint-Sulpice 7787
0337-730X Revue Francaise du Dommage Corporel 5916
0337-7393 Revue de Jurisprudence Fiscale 4774
0337-792X College de France. Institut des Hautes Etudes Chinoises. Memoirs 547
0337-839X Universite de Droit, Economie et de Sciences Sociales de Paris. Travaux du Seminaire de Recherches sur les Faits Electoraux de Monsieur le Professeur Robert Villers 4802
0337-8500 Journal des Electriciens 3322
0337-8659 Eclats de Rire†
0337-8810 Cuisine et Vins de France 3632
0337-8888 Nostra†
0337-9515 Afrique Agriculture
0337-9736 Revue d'Orthopedie Dento-Faciale 5864
0338-0181 Khamsin†
0338-0548 Bulletin d'Informations Proustiennes 5267
0338-0599 Revue d'Etudes Comparatives Est-Ouest 1548
0338-0610 Diagonal 4409
0338-1439 Cahiers Medicaux†
0338-1552 Nouveau Pouvoir Judiciaire 4958
0338-1595 L'Essor de la Gendarmerie Nationale 2651
0338-1757 Solidaires (Paris) 8072
0338-1811 Tempe Informations† 8993
0338-182X Action Agricole de Tarn et Garonne 79
0338-1889 V R S†
0338-1900 Oeuvres et Critiques 5345
0338-1927 Port of le Havre Flashes 8657
0338-1978 La Revue Lorraine Populaire† 8985
0338-2052 Signes d'Aujourd'hui 6616
0338-2060 Revue Francaise d'Etudes Politiques Mediterraneennes†
0338-2079 Revue du Magnetisme-Etude du Psychisme Experimental†
0338-2338 Perspectives Medievales 5160
0338-2389 Pratiques 5163
0338-2397 Psychanalyse a l'Universite†
0338-263X Collection de Biologie Evolutive 666
0338-3520 Armees d'Aujourd'hui 6411
0338-361X Etudes Corses 338
0338-3849 La S O F C O T. Cahiers d'Enseignement 6257
0338-4241 France. Direction de la Prevision. Rationalisation des Choix Budgetaires†
0338-4330 Esclavage†
0338-4454 France. Ministere des Affaires Etrangeres. Documents d'Actualite Internationale 4926
0338-4551 Revue Francaise de Gestion 1791
0338-487X Herodote 4014
0338-5019 Lire 5323
0338-5353 Rustica Hebdo changed to Rustica 153
0338-5469 S U Syndicalisme universitaire changed to 1143-2705 2900

ISSN

0340-6350 Goettinger Orientforschungen. Reihe VI: Hellenistica
0340-6369 Giorgio Levi della Vida Conferences. Reports of the Conference† **8959**
0340-6377 Bonner Orientalistische Studien†
0340-6385 Neuindische Studien **5155**
0340-6393 Codices Arabici Antiqui **547**
0340-6407 Oriens Christianus **7668**
0340-6423 Societas Uralo-Altaica. Veroeffentlichungen **5175**
0340-644X Saarlaendisches Aerzteblatt **5708**
0340-6490 Schriften zur Geistesgeschichte des Oestlichen Europa **4262**
0340-6628 Materialien zur Psychoanalyse und Analytisch Orientierten Psychotherapie†
0340-6644 Fotowirtschaft **6968**
0340-6660 FotoMagazin **6968**
0340-6687 Ruhr-Universitaet Bochum. Ostasien Institut. Veroeffentlichungen **4188**
0340-6717 Human Genetics **871**
0340-6792 Studies in Oriental Religions **7742**
0340-6849 Hoelderlin-Jahrbuch **5306**
0340-6857 Contubernium **7848**
0340-6881 Die Deutsche Rechtsprechung auf dem Gebiete des Internationalen Privatrechts **4923**
0340-6970 Kieler Vortraege† **8969**
0340-6989 Kieler Studien **1574**
0340-7004 Cancer Immunology, Immunotherapy **6012**
0340-7063 Die Schaltung†
0340-7071 Strassenbahn Magazin **8625**
0340-7195 Studien zur Fuggergeschichte **4270**
0340-7217 Soziale Forschung und Praxis†
0340-7225 U T B **7691**
0340-7349 Public International Law **4824**
0340-7403 Kritische Berichte **500**
0340-742X Geoexploration Monographs. Series 1†
0340-7489 Baurecht **980**
0340-7497 Zeitschrift fuer Miet- und Raumrecht **7616**
0340-7519 Strompraxis **3331**
0340-7578 Contact†
0340-7586 Bayerische Akademie der Wissenschaften. Mathematisch-Naturwissenschaftliche Klasse. Sitzungsberichte **7839**
0340-7594 Journal of Comparative Physiology A **924**
0340-7691 Bayerische Kommission fuer die Internationale Erdmessung. Veroeffentlichungen **2778**
0340-7705 Forum Ware **1111**
0340-7829 Die Pirsch **8329**
0340-7853 Bibliothek der Griechischen Literatur **2231**
0340-787X D L Z Agrarmagazin **104**
0340-7888 Literarischer Verein in Stuttgart. Bibliothek **5323**
0340-7896 Glueckauf **6463**
0340-7918 Betriebs-Berater **4629**
0340-7926 Recht der Internationalen Wirtschaft **4938**
0340-7969 Allgemeine Zeitschrift fuer Philosophie **6903**
0340-7993 Paepste und Papsttum **7811**
0340-8035 Monumenta Germaniae Historica. Staatsschriften des Spaeteren Mittelalters†
0340-8051 Bibliothek des Buchwesens (B B) **4996**
0340-8078 Der Deutsche Dermatologe **5875**
0340-8094 Indices Naturwissenschaftlich-Medizinischer Periodica bis 1850†
0340-8132 Dahlem Workshop Reports. Life Sciences Research Report†
0340-8140 Mendelssohn Studien **4153**
0340-8159 Zeitschrift fuer Pflanzenkrankheiten und Pflanzenschutz *changed to* 1861-3829 **798**
0340-8183 M M G†
0340-823X Kriminalitaet und ihre Verwalter
0340-8248 Sozialforschung und Gesellschaftspolitik
0340-8256 Kunst und Gesellschaft
0340-8280 Renovatio **7814**
0340-8329 Zeitschrift fuer Luft- und Weltraumrecht **4945**
0340-8388 Dokumentation Rheologie†
0340-8396 Deutsches Mittelalter, Kritische Studientexte der Monumenta Germaniae Historica†
0340-840X Agrarrecht *changed to* Agrar- und Umweltrecht **80**
0340-8434 Arbeit und Sozialpolitik *changed to* 1611-5821 **1683**
0340-8450 Records of the Ancient Near East†
0340-8469 Sozialmagazin **8072**
0340-8515 Physik und Didaktik†
0340-8574 Blaetter der Wohlfahrtspflege **8028**
0340-8590 Demokratie und Recht†
0340-8604 Deutsche Notar-Zeitschrift **7433**
0340-8612 Deutsche Richterzeitung **4657**
0340-8671 Biologische Medizin
0340-871X I B Z - Internationaler Betriebswirtschaftlicher Zeitschriften-Report **4870**
0340-8728 V S W G - Vierteljahrschrift fuer Sozial- und Wirtschaftsgeschichte **8013**
0340-8744 Empirica **1483**
0340-8779 Entscheidungen der Oberverwaltungsgerichte fuer das Land Nordrhein-Westfalen in Muenster sowie fuer die Laender Niedersachsen und Schleswig-Holstein in Lueneburg **4666**
0340-8833 Ernst-Mach-Institut, Freiburg. Bericht **7853**
0340-8973 Forschungsdokumentation zur Arbeitsmarkt- und Berufsforschung† **8957**
0340-9023 Studien zur Literatur der Moderne† **8991**
0340-9031 WPg - Die Wirtschaftspruefung **1304**
0340-9066 Fisch und Umwelt†
0340-9090 N A B D - Mitteilungen†
0340-918X Soziologie **8141**
0340-9198 S O P O - Sozialistische Politik†
0340-9201 Sozialisation und Kommunikation†
0340-9244 Politikwissenschaftliche Forschung†
0340-9260 Neues Steuerrecht von A bis Z†
0340-9341 Deutsche Sprache **5111**
0340-9384 Deutsches Institut fuer Bautechnik. Schriften. Reihe A **3264**
0340-9392 Grundlagen und Praxis des Bank- und Boersenwesens **1350**
0340-9406 Recht der Wirtschaft (Berlin) **4879**
0340-949X Beitraege zur Umweltgestaltung. Reihe B.
0340-9503 Die Steuerliche Betriebspruefung **1945**
0340-9716 Beitraege zur Umweltgestaltung. Reihe A **3406**
0340-9767 Kritikon Litterarum **5318**
0340-9783 Hohenheimer Arbeiten **118**
0340-9821 Veroeffentlichungen der Astronomischen Institut der Universitaet Bonn† **8997**
0340-983X Materialiensammlung Staedtebau†
0340-9880 Der Landkreis (Bavarian State Edition) *see* 0342-2259 **7451**
0340-9937 Herz **5789**
0340-9961 Chemie Technik **3240**
0340-997X Hospital-Hygiene†
0341-0005 R U **7813**
0341-003X F F H - Funk Fachhaendler†
0341-0056 Historia. Einzelschriften **2235**
0341-0064 Hermes - Einzelschriften **2235**
0341-0102 Universitas (Spanish Edition)†
0341-0110 Apotheker und Kunst†
0341-0129 Universitas (English Edition)†
0341-0137 Deutsche Morgenlaendische Gesellschaft. Zeitschrift **547**
0341-0145 Stuttgarter Beitraege zur Naturkunde. Serie A. Biologie **706**
0341-0153 Stuttgarter Beitraege zur Naturkunde. Serie B. Geologie und Palaeontologie *changed to* 1867-6294 **2761**
0341-0161 Stuttgarter Beitraege zur Naturkunde. Serie C. Allgemeinverstaendliche Aufsaetze **7920**
0341-017X Angestellten Magazin†
0341-0218 Max-Planck-Gesellschaft. Jahrbuch **7881**
0341-0293 W K S B **4127**
0341-034X Zeitschrift fuer Praeklinische und Klinische Geriatrie†
0341-0390 N V - Neue Verpackung **6712**
0341-0412 D L G - Mitteilungen **104**
0341-0455 Altenpflege **5951**
0341-0463 Archiv fuer Eisenbahntechnik†
0341-0501 Aktuelle Ernaehrungsmedizin **6654**
0341-051X Aktuelle Rheumatologie **6221**
0341-0552 Z I International **2047**
0341-0595 Informationsdienst Krankenhauswesen **4102**
0341-0609 Kopfklinik†
0341-0676 Sprechsaal
0341-0730 Medizin in Unserer Zeit†
0341-0757 Internationales Jahrbuch fuer Wissens- und Religionssoziologie†
0341-0765 Studia Leibnitiana. Sonderhefte **6954**
0341-0773 Sudhoffs Archiv. Beihefte **7921**
0341-0781 Melliand Textilberichte **8455**
0341-079X Archiv fuer Rechts- und Sozialphilosophie. Beihefte **6905**
0341-0803 Deutsche Morgenlandischen Gesellschaft. Zeitschrift. Supplement *see* 0341-0137 **547**
0341-0811 Zeitschrift fuer Franzoesische Sprache und Literatur. Beihefte. Neue Folge **5199**
0341-0838 Zeitschrift fuer Dialektologie und Linguistik. Beihefte **5198**
0341-0846 Vierteljahrschrift fuer Sozial- und Wirtschaftsgeschichte. Beihefte **8014**
0341-0900 Angewandte Arbeitswissenschaft **1663**
0341-0935 Betriebsverpflegung†
0341-0943 Jahrbuch Kritische Medizin **5643**
0341-0951 Forschung Stadtverkehr†
0341-0986 Internationales Jahrbuch fuer Kartographie†
0341-101X H T M - Haerterie-Technische Mitteilungen *changed to* 1867-2493 **6314**
0341-1044 Betrieb und Personal **1067**
0341-1095 Bundesgesetzblatt. Teil 1 **4827**
0341-1109 Bundesgesetzblatt. Teil 2 **4828**
0341-1117 Sozialpolitische Informationen **7185**
0341-1184 Acta Praehistorica et Archaeologica **371**
0341-1230 Aurora **5258**
0341-1281 Aerokurier **42**
0341-1508 Fortschritte der Sozialpaediatrie **7965**
0341-1869 I K O - Innere Kolonisation - Land und Gemeinde†
0341-1893 Mineraloeltechnik **6778**
0341-1915 Neue Juristische Wochenschrift **4740**
0341-1966 Kriminologisches Journal **2659**
0341-1982 Niedersaechsische Wirtschaft **1501**
0341-1990 Sichere Chemiearbeit **3255**
0341-2024 T B Report† **8992**
0341-2032 T A B **4127**
0341-2040 Lung **6216**
0341-2059 Communications **2316**
0341-2067 Kleinbrennerei **767**
0341-2105 Gartenpraxis **3733**
0341-2148 Verkehrs Rundschau. Ausgabe A **8519**
0341-2172 Schriftenreihe Literatur **5368**
0341-2245 Die Gemeindekasse Bayern **7492**
0341-2253 Wolfenbuetteler Notizen zur Buchgeschichte **7576**
0341-230X V F I - Der Versuchs- und Forschungsingenieur
0341-2318 V I K - Mitteilungen **3149**
0341-2350 Klinikarzt **5658**
0341-2377 Reactivity and Structure: Concepts of Organic Chemistry†
0341-2431 Dokumentation zur Raumentwicklung†
0341-244X Forschungen zur Raumentwicklung†
0341-2458 Aerztin **5569**
0341-2474 Denkmaeler der Buchkunst **485**
0341-2482 Die Allgemeine Sonntagszeitung
0341-2490 Allgemeine Baecker-Zeitung **3670**
0341-2512 Referateblatt zur Raumentwicklung† **8984**
0341-2563 Altoettinger Liebfrauenbote **7620**
0341-2601 C C B†
0341-2636 F & H - Foerdern und Heben **3377**
0341-2660 O & P - Oelhydraulik und Pneumatik **3392**
0341-2687 Z F B F **1802**
0341-2695 International Orthopaedics **6062**
0341-2709 Aquarium†
0341-275X Vereinigung von Afrikanisten in Deutschland. Schriften†
0341-2776 Bayrischer Bauernkalender **95**
0341-2792 Personal-Buero in Recht und Praxis **4757**
0341-2865 Heidelberger Akademie der Wissenschaften. Jahrbuch **7860**
0341-2873 Archaeologische Informationen **377**
0341-289X Historischen Vereins fuer den Niederrhein. Annalen **4228**
0341-2954 Steuer und Wirtschaft **1945**
0341-3055 Atemwegs- und Lungenkrankheiten **6212**
0341-311X Fenno-Ugrica†
0341-3136 Universitaet Bonn. Institut fuer Kommunikationsforschung und Phonetik. Forschungsberichte†
0341-3144 Forum Phoneticum†
0341-3152 Hamburger Beitraege zur Archaeologie **396**
0341-3179 Hamburger Juristische Studien
0341-3195 Papiere zur Textlinguistik **5160**
0341-3217 Bibliotheca Russica†
0341-3225 Linguarum Minorum Documenta Historiographica†
0341-3233 Universitaet Hamburg. Institut fuer Internationale Angelegenheiten. Veroeffentlichungen **7271**
0341-3241 Universitaet Hamburg. Institut fuer Internationale Angelegenheiten. Werkhefte **4944**
0341-3276 Dokumente zur Deutschlandpolitik. Beihefte **7130**
0341-3322 Regnum **7814**
0341-339X Wirtschaft und Berufserziehung **6705**
0341-3403 Atem und Mensch†
0341-3489 Industrie der Steine und Erden **6465**
0341-3497 Niedersaechsisches Gesetz- und Verordnungsblatt **7457**
0341-3500 Niedersaechsisches Ministerialblatt **7457**
0341-356X Fliesen und Platten **3267**
0341-3608 Baukeramik **2037**
0341-3616 Die Bahnhofsgaststaette†
0341-3624 Baum-Zeitung **778**
0341-3659 B M **4554**
0341-3675 Deutsch Lernen *changed to* 1619-8433 **2940**
0341-3721 Lift-Report **5454**
0341-3756 Die Industriefeuerung†
0341-3772 Scripta Geobotanica **816**
0341-3780 Goettinger Geographische Abhandlungen **4013**
0341-3888 Behindertenrecht **4064**
0341-3896 B I **977**
0341-3918 Bayerische Vorgeschichtsblaetter **4203**
0341-3934 E T G - Fachberichte **3301**
0341-3977 Das Standesamt **4787**
0341-3993 Bayerische Staatszeitung und Bayerischer Staatsanzeiger **3844**
0341-4019 Zeitschrift fuer das Gesamte Kreditwesen **1391**
0341-4027 Geologisches Jahrbuch Hessen **2741**
0341-4043 Geologische Abhandlungen Hessen **2741**
0341-406X Drosera†
0341-4086 Kleine Senckenberg Reihe **7877**
0341-4094 Senckenbergische Naturforschende Gesellschaft. Aufsaetze und Reden†
0341-4108 Senckenberg Buecher **7913**
0341-4116 C F S† **8938**
0341-4159 Kunst & Antiquitaeten†
0341-4175 E L O†
0341-4183 Bibliothek Forschung und Praxis **4996**
0341-4191 Studien zur Indologie und Iranistik **4189**
0341-4213 A T W News†
0341-4248 Svetsaren **6344**
0341-4388 Verkehrsdienst **8637**
0341-440X R A K - Riechstoffe, Aromen, Kosmetica†
0341-4418 Manager Magazin **1777**
0341-4434 Arzt und Auto **5578**
0341-4477 Betrieb und Meister **1880**
0341-4485 Die Besinnung†
0341-4507 Beschaffung Aktuell **1807**
0341-4515 Berufsbildung in Wissenschaft und Praxis **6693**
0341-468X Kraftfahrt-Bundesamt. Statistische Mitteilungen **8588**
0341-4698 Personalwirtschaft (Neuwied) **1872**
0341-471X Schulbibliothek Aktuell†
0341-4728 Schnellstatistik Allgemeiner Oeffentlicher Bibliotheken†
0341-4906 Bild am Sonntag **3845**
0341-4922 Bildung Aktuell **3018**
0341-5023 Klinische Anaesthesiologie und Intensivtherapie **5772**
0341-5066 Moebel Wirtschaft†
0341-5104 Modell Fan **4341**
0341-5112 Mobil **6225**
0341-5155 Mais **242**
0341-521X Butonia **2245**
0341-5228 Bus und Bahn **8492**
0341-5244 Bus-Fahrt **8689**
0341-5260 Unterricht Biologie **710**
0341-5279 Praxis Deutsch **5163**
0341-5295 Rationelle Hauswirtschaft **4366**
0341-5376 Monographs on Theoretical and Applied Genetics†
0341-5406 Computer Zeitung **2413**
0341-5414 Chinchilla Post **938**
0341-5449 D S W R†
0341-5457 D D R Report†
0341-5589 Elektronikpraxis **3098**
0341-5759 Du und das Tier **6807**
0341-5775 M M - Maschinenmarkt **5455**
0341-5783 Europa Industrie Revue†
0341-5864 Zielsprache Deutsch **5200**
0341-5872 Forschungsarbeiten aus dem Strassenwesen. Schriftenreihe **3267**
0341-5910 Publikationen zu Wissenschaftlichen Filmen. Sektion Ethnologie†
0341-5929 Publikationen zu Wissenschaftlichen Filmen. Sektion Medizin†
0341-5937 Publikationen zu Wissenschaftlichen Filmen. Sektion Geschichte, Publizistik†
0341-6151 Law and State†
0341-616X Institute for Scientific Co-operation with Developing Countries. Economics†
0341-6178 Education†
0341-6186 Educacion†
0341-6208 Bankhistorisches Archiv **1317**
0341-633X Lecture Notes in Biomathematics†
0341-6356 Monograph Series on Mineral Deposits†

ISSN

ISSN	Title
0342-507X	Halbjaehrliches Verzeichniss Taschenbuecher†
0342-5096	Die Glocke (Sachsenheim)†
0342-5118	Heim und Garten
0342-5142	Glas und Rahmen **2041**
0342-5169	Hoch- und Tiefbau **1011**
0342-5177	H I S Brief†
0342-5231	Gymnasium **2235**
0342-5258	Unsere Jugend **2170**
0342-5282	International Journal of Rehabilitation Research **6110**
0342-5452	Beitraege zur Naturkunde in Osthessen **656**
0342-5517	Katechetische Blaetter **7803**
0342-5525	R A B S **7772**
0342-5576	Bibliographie Moderner Fremdsprachenunterricht **5100**
0342-5592	Verwaltungsrundschau **4808**
0342-5622	Oil Gas European Magazine **6784**
0342-5630	D V G W - Schriftenreihe Wasser **8820**
0342-5673	Der Niederrhein **3854**
0342-5681	Bergbau **6458**
0342-5703	Fischer und Teichwirt **3591**
0342-5746	Politik - Aktuell fuer den Unterricht **7171**
0342-5789	Antimilitarismus Information†
0342-5800	Confructa†
0342-5827	Heimatjahrbuch Kreis Ahrweiler **5304**
0342-5835	Jahrbuch des Kreises Dueren **3850**
0342-5851	Zeitlupe **7218**
0342-5886	Z D F Jahrbuch **2399**
0342-5932	Wuerzburger Jahrbuecher fuer die Altertumswissenschaft†
0342-5940	Wolfenbuetteler Studien zur Aufklaerung. Schriftenreihe **4167**
0342-5967	Wohnmedizin **7545**
0342-5991	Bayerische Akademie der Wissenschaften. Philosophisch-Historische Klasse. Sitzungsberichte **4444**
0342-6068	Gewaesserschutz - Wasser - Abwasser **8824**
0342-6106	Staedte- und Gemeinderat **7469**
0342-6165	B D V I - Forum **3260**
0342-6173	Zielsprache Englisch **5200**
0342-619X	Zielsprache Spanisch†
0342-6203	Zielsprache Franzoesisch **5200**
0342-622X	Tankstelle **8606**
0342-6254	T U - Zeitschrift fuer Technik im Unterricht **8440**
0342-6270	Archiv und Wirtschaft **1060**
0342-6297	Jugend in Schule und Beruf†
0342-6300	Jahrbuch Deutsch als Fremdsprache **5131**
0342-6319	I W - Report†
0342-6335	Weltkonjunkturdienst†
0342-6378	Wort und Antwort **7695**
0342-6386	Jetzt†
0342-6416	Das Zeichen **7823**
0342-6505	Ja **7652**
0342-6513	Ja, das Wort fuer Alle **7652**
0342-6521	Der Zimmermann **1053**
0342-6602	Westfaelischer Jaegerbote†
0342-6610	Uebersee-Museum Bremen. Veroeffentlichungen. Reihe G: Bremer Suedpazifik-Archiv†
0342-6661	Altdeutsche Textbibliothek **5251**
0342-6734	Verkehrsrechtliche Mitteilungen **8519**
0342-6769	Das Vertriebene Landvolk† **8997**
0342-6777	Politische Didaktik†
0342-6785	Alexander von Humboldt-Stiftung. Jahresbericht **4442**
0342-6793	Topics in Current Physics†
0342-6831	Integrative Therapie **7363**
0342-6874	W M Allgemeine Verlosungstabelle **1389**
0342-6882	W M: Wertpapierberatung
0342-6904	Zur Zeit†
0342-6939	W M Teil II: Nachrichten ueber Deutsche Festverzinsliche Werte **1389**
0342-6955	W M Teil III: Nachrichten ueber Deutsche Aktien, Anteile, Genussscheine, Kuxe *changed to* 0944-3568 **1389**
0342-6971	W M Teil IV: Zeitschrift fuer Wirtschafts- und Bankrecht **4810**
0342-6998	W M Teil Va: Nachrichten ueber Auslaendische Aktien und Aktienaehnliche Werte *changed to* 0944-1026 **1389**
0342-7005	W M Teil Vb: Nachrichten ueber Auslaendische Festverzinsliche Wertpapiere **1389**
0342-7064	Die Betriebswirtschaft **1728**
0342-7072	Der Landbote *changed to* 1439-6432 **241**
0342-7145	Theorie und Praxis der Sozialpaedagogik **2169**
0342-7161	Teddy†
0342-7188	Irrigation Science **124**
0342-7331	Unser Pferd **8300**
0342-734X	Archaeologisches Korrespondenzblatt **377**
0342-7366	Sonderpaedagogik **3046**
0342-7439	Arnes Journal fuer Guten Geschmack†
0342-751X	Schule Heute **2945**
0342-7528	Segeln **8282**
0342-7536	Nota Lepidopterologica **856**
0342-7595	Schwaebische Heimat **3856**
0342-7609	Koelner Aerztliche Nachrichten†
0342-7617	Beton-Kalender **982**
0342-7625	Kuechenforum†
0342-7633	Adult Education and Development **2937**
0342-7641	Leder- und Haeutemarkt **4974**
0342-765X	Landwirtschaftliches Wochenblatt Westfalen-Lippe: Ausgabe A **133**
0342-7684	Sammler Journal†
0342-7722	Schwartzsche Vakanzen-Zeitung **7468**
0342-7749	Der Spediteur†
0342-7757	Unsere Katze†
0342-782X	Ludwig-Maximilians-Universitaet. Institut fuer Phonetik und Sprachliche Kommunikation. Forschungsberichte **5148**
0342-7862	Unser Milchvieh†
0342-7951	T W **6283**
0342-801X	D I N - Taschenbuecher **6401**
0342-8036	Bargfelder Bote **5098**
0342-8044	Arbeiten zur Theologie†
0342-8052	Calwer Theologische Monographien. Reihe A: Bibelwissenschaft†
0342-8060	Calwer Theologische Monographien. Reihe B: Systematische Theologie und Kirchengeschichte†
0342-8079	Calwer Theologische Monographien. Reihe C: Praktische Theologie und Missionswissenschaft†
0342-8095	Bimbo **2604**
0342-8117	Phaenomenologische Forschungen **6939**
0342-8176	Prokla **8126**
0342-8206	S B Z - Monteur **4126**
0342-8281	Rudersport **8281**
0342-8303	Hamburger Jahrbuch fuer Musikwissenschaft **6572**
0342-8311	Geo **3433**
0342-8397	P T A - Repetitorium **6866**
0342-8419	Der Uebungsleiter **8214**
0342-8427	Skandinavistik **5373**
0342-8494	Altes Haus Modern†
0342-8613	Photoblaetter†
0342-8699	Altfraenkische Bilder und Wappenkalender *changed to* 1862-7404 **4197**
0342-8702	P R - Magazin **31**
0342-8761	R T F†
0342-880X	Biotechnische Umschau†
0342-8869	Das Recht der Wirtschaft **4766**
0342-8893	Cancer Campaign†
0342-8915	Bayern Tennis **8223**
0342-8923	Cinclus **905**
0342-8974	Wochenschau fuer Politische Erziehung, Sozial- und Gemeinschaftskunde. Ausgabe fuer Sekundarstufe II **8015**
0342-8982	Studium Linguistik†
0342-8990	Wochenschau fuer Politische Erziehung, Sozial- und Gemeinschaftskunde. Ausgabe fuer Sekundarstufe I **8015**
0342-9148	Nachrichtentechnik†
0342-9423	Zeitschrift fuer Mission **7696**
0342-9512	Lebensmittel Zeitung **3654**
0342-9547	Neue Beitraege zur George-Forschung **5427**
0342-9571	Staatliche Zentralstelle fuer Fernunterricht. Amtliches Mitteilungsblatt **2946**
0342-958X	Microscopica Acta. Supplementa†
0342-9601	Medizinische Monatsschrift fuer Pharmazeuten **5677**
0342-9776	Neue Fleischer-Zeitung
0342-9806	Nationalpark **2620**
0342-9830	Neues Rheinland **5339**
0342-9849	Nahverkehrs-Praxis **8505**
0342-9857	Neue Praxis **8057**
0342-9873	Oberpfalz **4250**
0342-9911	Baecker-Zeitung **3671**
0342-9954	Der Motorjournalist **4580**
0342-9962	Die Mitarbeiterin **8875**
0342-9989	Magazin der Tierfreunde†
0343-0103	Loyal **6431**
0343-0162	Mitteilungsblatt Berliner Zahnaerzte **5856**
0343-0170	Lernzielorientierter Unterricht†
0343-0200	Die Milchpraxis und Rindermast *changed to* Milchpraxis **267**
0343-0235	Olympische Jugend (Print)†
0343-0359	Modell Magazin **4341**
0343-043X	Maschinen Anlagen Verfahren **1779**
0343-0456	Kunst Magazin†
0343-0553	Der Ueberblick **7270**
0343-0642	M D **4545**
0343-0758	Papers on French Seventeenth Century Literature **5348**
0343-0936	Kuerschners Deutscher Literatur-Kalender **628**
0343-0987	Beitraege zur Hydrologie†
0343-1002	Medizin Bibliothek Dokumentation†
0343-1088	Kleine Aegyptische Texte **554**
0343-1096	Goettinger Orientforschungen. Reihe V: Biblica et Patristica
0343-1258	Gratia **4225**
0343-1312	Umweltbrief (Berlin)† **8995**
0343-1401	Publik-Forum **7672**
0343-1444	Baufachblatt **979**
0343-1452	Ruhrwirtschaft **1409**
0343-1460	Umwelt **3471**
0343-1495	Structur†
0343-1525	Das Warnkreuz **6688**
0343-1614	B D H Kurier **5582**
0343-1630	*see* 1437-8175 **6825**
0343-1657	Literatur fuer Leser **5324**
0343-1711	Bergische Handwerk **478**
0343-186X	Aus dem Antiquariat **7552**
0343-1886	Arbeit und Beruf **1664**
0343-1983	Landes-Bausparkasse†
0343-2009	Saecula Spiritalia **4160**
0343-2092	Gas **6769**
0343-2157	Monumenta Germaniae Historica. Scriptores **4246**
0343-2181	Minerals and Rocks **2755**
0343-2246	K K - die Kaelte und Klimatechnik **4122**
0343-2521	GeoJournal **4012**
0343-2564	Computer Address†
0343-2785	Beitraege zur Heimatkunde der Stadt Schwelm und ihrer Umgebung **4203**
0343-2793	Offenbacher Verein fuer Naturkunde. Bericht
0343-2807	Betriebsstatistik Wissenschaftlicher Bibliotheken†
0343-2963	Yorkshire Terrier Journal†
0343-3048	Zentralblatt Haut- und Geschlechtskrankheiten†
0343-3102	Color Foto **6965**
0343-3153	W L B Report **3474**
0343-3277	Duisburger Journal **4216**
0343-3366	Lady International
0343-3420	Dokumentation Neusprachlicher Unterricht†
0343-3463	Elektroboerse *changed to* 1613-9984 **3305**
0343-3463	Elektroboerse *changed to* 1613-9992 **3305**
0343-3471	Maschine und Werkzeug **5456**
0343-348X	Chefbuero†
0343-3498	Behavioural Analysis and Modification†
0343-3528	Primate Report **960**
0343-3560	Schadenprisma **3581**
0343-3587	Progress in Orthopaedic Surgery†
0343-3668	Deutsches Schiffahrtsarchiv **8642**
0343-3722	Deutsches Taschenbuch fuer Maler und Lackierer *changed to* 1866-4067 **6717**
0343-3722	Deutsches Taschenbuch fuer Maler und Lackierer (Year) *changed to* 1866-4059 **6717**
0343-3749	W M Teil IIa: Neuemissionen - Schnelldienst
0343-3757	Hessische Polizeirundschau **2654**
0343-379X	Romanistische Zeitschrift fuer Literaturgeschichte **5364**
0343-382X	Der Dachdeckermeister *changed to* 1618-9612 **1001**
0343-3838	Der Deutsche Badebetrieb†
0343-3846	Deutsche Bauern-Korrespondenz **105**
0343-3854	Creditreform **1334**
0343-3889	Der Einzelhaendler†
0343-4060	Accessories†
0343-4109	Soziologische Revue **8141**
0343-4117	Bibliographie zur Geschichte der Deutschen Arbeiterbewegung **1215**
0343-4133	P z L - Papiere zur Linguistik†
0343-415X	Position **1432**
0343-4184	Paderborner Almanach†
0343-4192	Links und Rechts der Autobahn **4393**
0343-4206	HiFi und TV†
0343-4583	Bildung Real **3018**
0343-4591	Lebendige Seelsorge **7764**
0343-4605	Katholische Bildung **7803**
0343-4648	Geschichte, Politik und ihre Didaktik **4223**
0343-4842	Drug Development and Evolution†
0343-4958	Schwimmbad und Sauna **1035**
0343-5113	Unser Oberschlesien **4275**
0343-5121	Express (Offenbach) **7135**
0343-5202	Sprache und Datenverarbeitung **2538**
0343-5210	Kataloge der Praehistorischen Staatssammlung **4237**
0343-5245	Vol'noe Slovo†
0343-527X	Theater *see* 0040-5507 **8481**
0343-5318	Deutsches Turnen **8169**
0343-5334	Didaktik der Mathematik†
0343-5369	Leichtathletik **8321**
0343-5377	Zeitschrift fuer Energiewirtschaft **3150**
0343-5474	Deutsche Wachtelhund-Zeitung **6806**
0343-5520	Forschungsberichte aus Technik und Naturwissenschaften†
0343-5571	Film und T V Kameramann **6500**
0343-558X	Dokument und Analyse†
0343-5598	D N V **7559**
0343-5733	Arztrecht **5579**
0343-5857	Deutsche Annalen **4214**
0343-5903	Baustoff Umschau†
0343-5970	Schriften zum Marketing **1842**
0343-642X	Fachbuchverzeichnis Elektrotechnik - Elektronik (Year)
0343-6462	Entwicklung und Laendlicher Raum *changed to* Rural 21 **152**
0343-6489	Notes from Europe†
0343-6500	Erdstall **392**
0343-6519	Entwurf **7756**
0343-6640	Documenta Homoeopathica **5606**
0343-6675	Elektronik Informationen **3098**
0343-6683	Esquire†
0343-6853	Haustex **4558**
0343-6861	Reiter und Pferde in Westfalen **8297**
0343-6950	Japan **7145**
0343-6993	The Mathematical Intelligencer **5513**
0343-7035	Archiv fuer Begriffsgeschichte. Supplementheft *see* 0003-8946 **6905**
0343-7051	Abhandlungen aus dem Gebiet der Auslandskunde. Series B & C†
0343-7078	Edit†
0343-7205	Feierabend **7797**
0343-7256	Geographie und Ihre Didaktik **4012**
0343-7388	Entscheidungen des Bundesoberseeamtes und der Seeamter der Bundesrepublik Deutschland†
0343-7477	Germany. Bundesministerium fuer Ernaehrung, Landwirtschaft und Forsten. Jahresbericht. Forschung im Geschaeftsbereich des Bundesministeriums fuer Ernaerung, Land, Wirtschaft und Forsten†
0343-7493	Universitaet Muenchen. Geophysikalisches Observatorium, Fuerstenfeldbruck. Veroeffentlichungen. Serie A **2791**
0343-754X	Economic Bulletin† **8952**
0343-7604	Muenchener Beitraege zur Theaterwissenschaft†
0343-7620	Philippia **6535**
0343-7647	A Z - Nachrichten **900**
0343-768X	Heilbad und Kurort **309**
0343-7701	Atom-Informationen†
0343-7728	Boersen Zeitung **1068**
0343-7736	Frauen und Film **6501**
0343-7744	Forum Religion **7644**
0343-7752	Freiheit der Wissenschaft **7856**
0343-7833	Forschungsdokumentation Stadt- und Regionalforschung†
0343-785X	Ozean und Technik†
0343-7868	Informationen - Bildung, Wissenschaft†
0343-7906	Stuttgarter Geographische Studien **4030**
0343-7965	Probleme der Kuestenforschung im Suedlichen Nordseegebiet **7899**
0343-8090	Institut fuer Wasserwirtschaft, Hydrologie und Landwirtschaftlichen Wasserbau. Mitteilungen **8825**
0343-8198	Unser Betrieb† **8996**
0343-8228	Schriften zur Oeffentlichen Verwaltung und Oeffentlichen Wirtschaft **7467**
0343-835X	Freie Universitaet Berlin. Osteuropa-Institut. Rechtswissenschaftliche Veroeffentlichungen **4678**
0343-8392	Fernmelde Impulse†
0343-8449	Fakten
0343-8554	Zeitschrift fuer Lymphologie†
0343-8651	Current Microbiology **883**
0343-8694	Arbeitspapiere zur Linguistik **5096**
0343-8732	Gottesdienst **7799**
0343-8740	Geldinstitute **1349**
0343-8759	Handling **2460**
0343-9003	Junge Radio-, Fernseh- und Industrie-Elektroniker
0343-9011	K F Z Zeitschrift fuer den Nachwuchs des Kraftfahrzeughandwerks
0343-9062	Federal Republic of Germany - Partner of the World **1485**
0343-9429	Klinische Psychologie und Psychopathologie

ISSN

0345-486X Haesten **8291**
0345-5068 Ica-Kuriren **4361**
0345-5106 Idrottsbladet **8178**
0345-5114 Idrottsbladet. Special **8178**
0345-5165 I M *changed to* 1653-932X **1601**
0345-5246 Impuls **2942**
0345-5300 Information†
0345-5467 Internationalen **7144**
0345-5505 Invandrarrapport†
0345-5564 Journal of Traffic Medicine
0345-5580 Judisk Kroenika **3545**
0345-5599 Jules Verne - Magasinet **5444**
0345-5637 Jaktjournalen **8320**
0345-5653 Jefferson **6580**
0345-5718 Jordbruksaktuellt **125**
0345-5734 Jury **5414**
0345-5807 Kinarapport **3826**
0345-5998 Kvinnobulletinen†
0345-6005 Kvaekartidskrift **7738**
0345-6048 Kalle Anka & Co **2196**
0345-6056 Kalle Ankas Pocket **2196**
0345-6188 Klasskampen **7149**
0345-620X Knasen **2198**
0345-6293 Kolonitraedgaarden **3741**
0345-6307 Kommunalarbetaren **1691**
0345-6358 Lantarbetaren†
0345-6471 Kontakten **2369**
0345-6498 Kontaktstencil **403**
0345-6579 Kristendom och Skola†
0345-6609 Kryssdax **8184**
0345-6617 Krysset **8184**
0345-6633 K T H-Nytt *changed to* 1653-2872 **2991**
0345-6706 Kustbon **3546**
0345-6757 Kyrka och Folk **7764**
0345-682X Kyrklig Samling Kring Bibeln och Bekaennelsen **7764**
0345-696X Laboratoriet **5908**
0345-7001 Lantbruksnytt†
0345-7060 Ledartips **8053**
0345-7109 Lektyr **6293**
0345-7133 Leveranstidningen Entreprenad **1020**
0345-7338 Lundagaard **2267**
0345-7354 Lunds Universitet Meddelar *changed to* 1653-2295 **2992**
0345-746X Laekarsekreteraren **1852**
0345-7478 Laenk-nytt **2696**
0345-7524 Linkoeping Studies in Science and Technology **7880**
0345-7621 Miljoe i Sverige†
0345-763X Miljoeaktuellt *changed to* 1654-6946 **3453**
0345-7699 Musiktidningen†
0345-7702 Maal & Medel **3654**
0345-7710 Maalarnas Facktidning **6718**
0345-7737 Moebler & Miljoe **4561**
0345-7788 MaskinKontakt **5456**
0345-7850 Foerbundet foer Art, Bild, Copy och Design. Meddelandet **25**
0345-7907 Menorah **3956**
0345-7958 Miljoe och Framtid†
0345-7966 Miljoejournalen†
0345-7982 Bygd och Natur (Tidskrift) **2605**
0345-7990 Min Haest **8294**
0345-8083 Mitt Livs Novell†
0345-8105 Mixturen†
0345-813X Modellflygnytt **8187**
0345-8202 Munskaenken med Vinjournalen **607**
0345-8210 Musikant *changed to* Musikant och Kammarmusik-Nytt **6596**
0345-8210 Musikant *changed to* 1650-089X **6614**
0345-8296 Naturvetaren **7890**
0345-8326 Nord Refo†
0345-8350 Ny Solidaritet **3956**
0345-8377 Nya Kraftsport *changed to* 1404-594X **8213**
0345-8512 Nordisk Kamp **7159**
0345-8539 Nordisk Posttidsskrift†
0345-8571 Nordisk Oestmission **7769**
0345-858X Nordiska Rikspartiet **7159**
0345-8601 Nord-Sverige **3956**
0345-8628 Norrbottningen†
0345-8792 Nytt Juridiskt Arkiv. Avd. 2 - Tidskrift foer Lagstiftning m.m. **4750**
0345-8865 Ossa†
0345-8997 Orientaliska Studier **558**
0345-9071 Praktiskt Butiksarbete **3681**
0345-9225 Pensionaeren /PRO **8061**
0345-9314 Petroleumhandeln **6788**
0345-9454 Polistidningen **2664**
0345-9578 Proletaeren **7174**
0345-9616 P S O - Aktuellt *changed to* 1404-4056 **5881**
0345-9667 Paa Kryss Till Rors *changed to* 1404-9597 **8279**
0345-973X Ridsport **8298**
0345-9896 Regeringsraettens Aarsbok **7465**
0346-0320 Samefolket **4261**
0346-0509 Sloejdforum **539**
0346-0576 Hifi & Musik **8153**
0346-0657 Svenska Frisoertidningen **591**
0346-0762 S C C News†
0346-0770 Schacknytt **8199**
0346-0789 Schweden Heute†
0346-1033 S I A **3715**
0346-1238 Scandinavian Actuarial Journal **4522**
0346-1254 Skattenytt **1943**
0346-1289 Skogsmannen†
0346-1297 Skogssport **8333**
0346-1300 Skohandlaren *changed to* 1653-7793 **7942**
0346-1351 Skorstensfejaremaestaren **3581**
0346-1386 Skraedderi **2249**
0346-1467 Socialfoersaekring *changed to* 1652-9472 **8036**
0346-1491 Socialistisk Debatt **7184**
0346-1505 Socialistiskt Forum†
0346-1750 Starlet **2214**
0346-1815 Statstjaenstemannen *changed to* 1652-3075 **1706**
0346-1823 Status **7542**
0346-1866 Sten **1037**
0346-1890 Stridsropet **7683**
0346-2048 Svensk Curling **8336**
0346-2072 Svensk Fiskhandel **3609**
0346-2080 Svensk Fotboll†
0346-2099 Svensk Froetidning **255**
0346-2102 Svensk Golf **8248**
0346-2129 Svensk Handikapptidskrift **8074**
0346-2137 Svensk Hotellrevy **4399**
0346-2145 Svensk Industritidning†
0346-2161 Svensk Linje **7187**
0346-217X Svensk Missionstidskrift **7776**
0346-2196 Svensk Patenttidning **6758**
0346-2218 Svensk Skattetidning **1946**
0346-2250 Svensk Veterinaertidning **8808**
0346-2315 Svenska Journalen **3957**
0346-2323 Svenska Jaernvaegstidningen **8625**
0346-2366 Svenska Nyheter **7187**
0346-2420 Svenskt Skytte **8248**
0346-2439 Sverigekontakt **3957**
0346-2463 Svezia Oggi†
0346-251X System **3083**
0346-2560 Saeljaren **1432**
0346-2595 Soermlandslaaten **6617**
0346-2617 Tandskoetersketidningen **5867**
0346-2641 Teknik foer Alla†
0346-2692 Tidningen Byggkontakt **1040**
0346-2765 Tobakshandlaren†
0346-2773 T H - Transport & Hantering†
0346-2854 Tullinformation **1953**
0346-2935 T C O - Tidningen **1710**
0346-3001 Teratology Lookout†
0346-3222 Tidsspegel *changed to* 1652-9464 **2886**
0346-329X Tonfallet†
0346-332X Trav- och Galoppronden **8299**
0346-3427 TS-Tidningen **7579**
0346-3605 Undervisningsteknologi†
0346-363X Ung Vaerld†
0346-377X Utrikespolitiska Institutet. Kalendarium†
0346-3788 Utsikt **7191**
0346-3869 Verdandisten **2700**
0346-3893 Vi Maenskor **8887**
0346-4008 Vaegmaestaren **8519**
0346-4105 Vecko-Revyn **2219**
0346-4164 Vertex **2308**
0346-4180 Vi **3957**
0346-4210 Vi Bilaegare **8610**
0346-4245 Vi Foeraeldrar **2170**
0346-427X Vi Laenkar **2700**
0346-430X Vi och Vaar Landsbygd
0346-444X Villaegaren **7615**
0346-4601 World Pollen and Spore Flora†
0346-4644 V V S - Forum **4127**
0346-4679 Vaar Loesen†
0346-4687 Vaar Ponny†
0346-4873 Vaerld och Vetande **7927**
0346-4881 Vaerlden och Vi **7191**
0346-4938 Vaesterbotten **4276**
0346-4954 Vaestgoetabygden **4276**
0346-4997 Vaextskyddskuriren **257**
0346-5004 Pedagogisk-Psykologiska Problem **7389**
0346-5039 Pedagogisk Dokumentation†
0346-5047 Pedagogiska Hjaelpmedel†
0346-5233 91: an **5247**
0346-5365 Sveriges Socialfoerbunds Tidskrift†
0346-5373 Teknikens Vaerld **8606**
0346-5438 Bibliotheca Historico-Ecclesiastica Lundensis **7748**
0346-5446 Studia Philosophiae Religionis **6954**
0346-5462 Acta Universitatis Upsaliensis **7832**
0346-5470 Sveriges Riksdag. Aarsbok **7471**
0346-5764 Sweden. Statens Lantmaeteriverk. L M V Information†
0346-5845 Svensk Foerfattningssamling **4791**
0346-5926 Studia Psychologica et Paedagogica. Series Altera **2915**
0346-5942 Goeteborg Studies in Politics **7138**
0346-6000 Sweden. Socialstyrelsen. Foerfattningssamling: Medical **5719**
0346-6019 Sweden. Socialstyrelsen. Foerfattningssamling: Social **8074**
0346-606X Sweden. Statistiska Centralbyraan. Statistiska Meddelanden. Subgroup F (Entreprises) **1269**
0346-6086 Fraan Riksdag & Departement **7438**
0346-6272 Stockholm Studies in English **5178**
0346-6280 Maa Bra **6992**
0346-6329 Socialmedicinsk Tidskrift Skriftserie *see* 0037-833X **5715**
0346-640X Dagens Industri **1089**
0346-6418 Acta Universitatis Stockholmiensis **4441**
0346-6434 Verkstadstidningen **3399**
0346-6442 Boreas (Uppsala) **4320**
0346-6469 Studia Indoeuropaea Upsaliensia **5180**
0346-6477 Studia Turcica Upsaliensia **5181**
0346-6493 Uppsala Studies in Economic History **1550**
0346-6507 Uppsala Studies in Social Ethics **6959**
0346-6523 Nova Acta Regiae Societatis Scientiarum Upsaliensis. A, Astronomy and Mathematical Sciences **7894**
0346-6566 Invandrare och Minoriteter *changed to* 1404-6857 **7284**
0346-6590 Sweden. Statens Raad foer Byggnadsforskning. Aarsbok†
0346-6612 Umeaa Universitet. Medical Dissertations **5725**
0346-6620 Stockholm Studies in Politics **7186**
0346-6728 Norna - Rapporter **5156**
0346-6787 Meddelanden fraan Lunds Universitets Geografiska Institute. Avhandlingar **4019**
0346-6868 Ecological Bulletins **3416**
0346-6892 University of Stockholm. Institute for International Economic Studies. Monograph Series **1189**
0346-7090 Svenska Traeskyddsinstitutet. Meddelanden **3716**
0346-718X Chalmers Tekniska Hoegskola. Doktorsavhandlingar. Ny Serie **3184**
0346-7341 Vaar Foeda. Supplement†
0346-7392 Stockholm Studies in Finnish Language and Literature **5178**
0346-7449 Foereningen foer Orientaliska Studier. Skrifter **549**
0346-7465 Acta Bibliothecae R. Universitatis Upsaliensis **4987**
0346-7538 Statsvetenskapliga Foereningen i Uppsala. Skrifter **7186**
0346-7724 Svenska Spraaknamnden. Skrifter **5184**
0346-7740 Acta Universitatis Gothoburgensis **4441**
0346-7775 Scanorama **8785**
0346-7805 Arbetarskydd **6673**
0346-7821 Arbete och Haelsa **4590**
0346-7856 Uppsala Universitet. Litteraturvetenskapliga Institutionen. Skrifter **5394**
0346-8100 Scandinavian Journal of Behavior Therapy. Supplement *see* 1650-6073 **7346**
0346-8186 Eastern Business Magazine†
0346-8208 Balans **1281**
0346-8240 C B I Rapporter - Reports **988**
0346-8305 Stockholm Studies in Economic History **1179**
0346-8313 Nobel Symposium **4467**
0346-8445 S P R I Informerar†
0346-8453 Sjukhusfarmaci
0346-847X Svensk Kirurgi **6260**
0346-8496 Stockholm Studies in Russian Literature **5377**
0346-8577 Svetsaren (English Edition) *see* 0341-4248 **6344**
0346-8666 Sweden. Fishery Board. Institute of Marine Research. Report†
0346-8712 Slavica Lundensia **5174**
0346-8755 Scandinavian Journal of History **4160**
0346-895X L O-Tidningen **4597**
0346-8968 Svenska Foereningen Foer Psykisk Haelsa. Monografserie **7411**
0346-8992 Sweden. Statistiska Centralbyraan. Statistiska Meddelanden. Subgroup HS (Public Health and Medical Care)†
0346-900X Studia Ethnologica Upsaliensia **357**
0346-9018 Hembygden **2686**
0346-9182 Aktuellt Maaleri **6715**
0346-9190 Allt om Husvagn & Camping **8302**
0346-9344 Bostonterriern **6804**
0346-9352 Boxning†
0346-9387 Baatologen **8522**
0346-9395 Calidris **905**
0346-9468 Current Business in Sweden†
0346-9662 Faaglar i X-Laen **906**
0346-9727 GrafikNytt **7321**
0346-9735 Historiska Institutionens Tidskrift†
0346-9751 Haessle Information†
0347-0024 Metamorfos **5333**
0347-030X Railway Scene†
0347-0377 Schackkorrespondenten **8199**
0347-0423 Signum **7817**
0347-0482 Solhjulet **7184**
0347-0520 Scandinavian Journal of Economics **1171**
0347-058X Arkitekten **433**
0347-0652 Traebiten **8283**
0347-0717 Utbildningskontakt†
0347-0822 Etudes Romanes de Lund **5117**
0347-0911 Vaardfacket **5983**
0347-0970 Transportforskningkommissionen. Rapport **8518**
0347-0989 Motpol†
0347-1136 F A S S Vet **6840**
0347-1314 Uppsala Studies in Education **2923**
0347-1322 Pockettidningen R **2698**
0347-1438 V A V - Nytt *changed to* 1651-0674 **8832**
0347-1772 Vetenskapssocieteten i Lund. Skrifter **4481**
0347-1837 Svenska Landsmaal och Svenskt Folkliv **3623**
0347-1845 Jernvaegsnytt **8619**
0347-2035 Bilsport **8569**
0347-2078 Contract†
0347-2116 S M H I Rapporter. Meteorologi och Klimatologi **6394**
0347-2159 Religion & Livsfraagor (RoL) **2904**
0347-237X Golf i Sverige
0347-2558 Lunds Universitet, Department of Linguistics and Phonetics. Travaux **5148**
0347-2612 Kriminalvaardsverkets Foerfattningssamling *changed to* 1653-6665 **2659**
0347-2647 Baatvaerlden (Stockholm) **8272**
0347-2663 Hockeyboken **8178**
0347-2744 Idrottsboken **8235**
0347-2752 Fotboll (Stockholm) **8229**
0347-2787 Bible Researcher **7625**
0347-2922 Myntboken **6651**
0347-2965 Arbetarroerelsen. Aarsbok†
0347-299X Bocken **6413**
0347-3023 Riksskatteverkets Foerfattningssamling *changed to* 1652-1420 **1943**
0347-3198 Sveriges Riksbank. Foervaltningsberaettelse†
0347-3236 Vaextskyddsrapporter†
0347-3414 Bland Tomatar och Troll **5264**
0347-3546 Brev **5266**
0347-3597 Liekki **5322**
0347-3783 Sveriges Rikes Lag **4791**
0347-4178 Svensk Kyrkomusik (Edition B for Choir Members)†
0347-4232 Lasernytt **8277**
0347-4240 A I C A R C Bulletin†
0347-4275 Yrkesfiskaren **3612**
0347-4283 Jernkontorets Bergshistoriska Skriftserie **6318**
0347-4364 Halland **4225**
0347-4372 Halland i Litteraturen†
0347-4402 Vaestergoetlands Fornminnesfoerenings Tidskrift **423**
0347-4453 Konstperspektiv **500**
0347-4585 R A - Nytt†
0347-4836 Narkotikafraagan **2697**
0347-4917 Acta Regiae Societatis Scientiarum et Litterarum Gothoburgensis. Botanica **773**
0347-4925 Acta Regiae Societatis Scientiarum et Litterarum Gothoburgensis. Interdisciplinaria **4441**
0347-500X Patent- och Registreringsverkets Foerfattningssamling **6756**
0347-5042 Sveriges Riksbank. Annual Report **1385**
0347-5123 Acta Regiae Societatis Humaniorum Litterarum Lundensis **371**
0347-5158 Kungliga Musikaliska Akademien. Skriftserie **6583**

0354-8724   International Scientific Journal Geographica Pannonica 4016
0354-8759   Beogradska Defektoloska Skola 3037
0354-8996   Tribology in Industry see 0351-1642 3398
0354-9283   Blic 3944
0354-9313   Muzicki Talas 6597
0354-9410   Acta Entomologica Serbica 929
0354-9461   Srpska Akademija Nauka i Umetnosti. Zbornik za Istoriju Bosne i Hercegovine 4267
0354-950X   Acta Chirurgica Iugoslavica 6234
0354-964X   Kodovi Slovenskih Kultura 3619
0354-9682   Trece Oko 7924
0354-9720   Jezik Danas 5132
0354-9798   Analiza Rada Visokoskolskih Biblioteka u Vojvodini 4989
0354-9836   Thermal Science 3148
0355-001X   Suomen Kirjallisuus†
0355-0036   Signum 5048
0355-0044   Kansallis-Osake-Pankki. Taloudellinen Katsaus†
0355-0133   Union Bank of Finland. Annual Report 1388
0355-0141   Castrenianumin Toimitteita changed to 1797-3945 360
0355-0192   Societe Neophilologique de Helsinki. Memoires 5175
0355-0206   N I F Newsletter†
0355-0214   Suomalais-Ugrilaisen Seuran Aikakauskirja 357
0355-0230   Suomalais-Ugrilaisen Seuran Toimituksia 357
0355-0303   Kanava 5222
0355-0311   Kalevalaseuran Vuosikirja 3619
0355-0346   Business Contacts in Finland 1977
0355-0451   Maamies†
0355-0567   Teho A 161
0355-0575   Turkistalous 4975
0355-0656   Suomen Riista 3609
0355-0680   L o A 132
0355-0729   Koneviesti 5454
0355-1059   Musiikki 6595
0355-1067   Psykologia 7401
0355-1075   Kaytannon Laakari 6857
0355-113X   Annales Academiae Scientiarum Fennicae. Dissertationes Humanarum Litterarum†
0355-1253   Finnisch-Ugrische Forschungen 5119
0355-1350   Helsingin Yliopiston Kirjaston. Julkaisuja 5012
0355-1393   Keski-Suomi 4237
0355-144X   Research Institute of the Lutheran Church in Finland. Publications 7676
0355-1555   Koti 4362
0355-1571   Finland. Kuluttaja-Asiain Osaston. Julkaisu. Sarja B changed to 0788-544X 2638
0355-1628   Kemia - Kemi 2069
0355-1644   Aarni 4195
0355-1717   Finland. Ilmatieteen Laitos. Tutkimusseloste†
0355-1725   Ajatus 6902
0355-1733   Finnish Meteorological Institute. Technical Report†
0355-1768   Suomalaisen Kirjallisuuden Seura. Toimituksia 5383
0355-1776   Ethnologia Fennica 337
0355-1784   Ylioppilasaineita 2963
0355-1792   Acta Philosophica Fennica 6902
0355-1814   Finskt Museum 393
0355-1822   Suomen Muinaismuistoyhdistyksen Aikakauskirja 419
0355-1830   Kansatieteellinen Arkisto 345
0355-1849   Paasikivi - Seruan. Monistesarja†
0355-1865   Pientalo-Omakoti†
0355-1873   Tee Itse†
0355-1911   Non Stop†
0355-1938   Taidehistoriallisia Tutkimuksia 521
0355-1962   Suomen Geodeettinen Laitos. Tiedonantoja 2790
0355-2004   Finnish Meteorological Institute. Observations of Satellites. Visual Observations of Artificial Earth Satellites in Finland†
0355-2047   Helsingin Sanomat 3838
0355-2055   Ilta - Sanomat 3838
0355-2063   Finland. Tilastokeskus. Kasikirjoja 8370
0355-2071   Finland. Tilastokeskus. Tutkimuksia 8372
0355-208X   Finland. Tilastokeskus. Tilastollisia Tiedonantoja 8372
0355-2101   Aku Ankka 2175
0355-2179   Finland. Tilastokeskus. Rikollisuus. Tuomioistuinten Tutkimat Rikokset†
0355-2187   Finland. Tilastokeskus. Tuomioistuinten Toiminta†
0355-2195   Finland. Tilastokeskus. Valtiolliset Vaalit. Tasavallan Presidentin Vaalit Valisijamiesten†
0355-2225   Finland. Tilastokeskus. Korkeakoulut†
0355-2446   Finland. Tilastokeskus. Yleissivistaevaet Oppilaitokset†
0355-2527   Teho B 4368
0355-256X   Commentationes Scientiarum Socialium 7955
0355-2659   Kinolehti†
0355-2667   Acta Wasaensia 1535
0355-2675   Kielikello 5317
0355-2683   Jaegaren see 0047-6986 2618
0355-2691   Suomen Autolehti 8605
0355-2705   Acta Polytechnica Scandinavica. C I. Civil Engineering and Building Construction Series†
0355-2721   Acta Polytechnica Scandinavica. P H. Applied Physics Series 7003
0355-2772   Seksi†
0355-2896   Autolla Ulkomaille changed to 1796-7031 8685
0355-2918   Ketju 8052
0355-2950   Avotakka 4553
0355-2969   Katso 2384
0355-2993   Nakke
0355-3000   Ravi ja Ratsastus†
0355-3027   Eevaneule†
0355-3035   Anna 8851
0355-3043   U M: Uusi Maailma†
0355-3051   Apu 3838
0355-3108   Iskos 399
0355-3140   Scandinavian Journal of Work, Environment & Health 6687
0355-3175   Suomen Sukututkimusseura. Julkaisuja 4272
0355-3183   Suomen Sukututkimusseura. Vuosikirja 3784
0355-3191   Acta Universitatis Ouluensis. Series A. Scientiae Rerum Naturalium 7832
0355-3205   Acta Universitatis Ouluensis. Series B. Humaniora 4441
0355-3213   Acta Universitatis Ouluensis. Series C. Technica 8415

0355-3221   Acta Universitatis Ouluensis. Series D. Medica 5567
0355-323X   Acta Universitatis Ouluensis. Series E. Scientiae Rerum Socialium 7102
0355-3256   Myyntineuvoja changed to 1457-0637 1904
0355-3280   Nykyaika 7769
0355-3299   see 0355-3280 7769
0355-337X   Technical Research Centre of Finland. Publication. Building Technology and Community Development†
0355-3388   Technical Research Centre of Finland. Publication. Materials and Processing Technology†
0355-3396   Technical Research Centre of Finland. Publication. Electrical and Nuclear Technology†
0355-3434   Valtion Teknillinen Tutkimuskeskus. Kojetekniikan Laboratorio. Tiedonanto†
0355-3450   Valtion Teknillinen Tutkimuskeskus. Geotekniikan Laboratorio. Tiedonanto†
0355-3477   Valtion Teknillinen Tutkimuskeskus. Maankayton Laboratorio. Tiedonanto†
0355-3485   Valtion Teknillinen Tutkimuskeskus. Palotekniikan Laboratorio. Tiedonanto†
0355-354X   Valtion Teknillinen Tutkimuskeskus. Biotekniikan Labboratorio. Tiedonanto†
0355-3558   Valtion Teknillinen Tutkimuskeskus. Elintarvikelabboratorio. Tiedonanto†
0355-3566   Valtion Teknillinen Tutkimuskeskus. Graafinen Labboratorio. Tiedonanto†
0355-3574   Valtion Teknillinen Tutkimuskeskus. Kemian Laboratorio. Tiedonanto†
0355-3590   Valtion Teknillinen Tutkimuskeskus. Polttl- ja Voiteluainelaboratorio. Tiedonanto†
0355-3639   Valtion Teknillinen Tutkimuskeskus. Tekstiililaboratorio. Tiedonanto†
0355-3663   Valtion Teknillinen Tutkimuskeskus. Reaktorilaboratorio. Tiedonanto†
0355-3671   Valtion Teknillinen Tutkimuskeskus. Sahkotekniikan Laboratorio. Tiedonanto†
0355-368X   Valtion Teknillinen Tutkimuskeskus. Teletekniikan Laboratorio. Tiedonanto†
0355-3698   Valtion Teknillinen Tutkimuskeskus. Ydinvoimatekniikan Laboratorio. Tiedonanto†
0355-3701   Valtion Teknillinen Tutkimuskeskus. Teknillinen Informaatiopalvelulaitos. Tiedonanto†
0355-3728   Lounais-Hameen Luonto 7880
0355-3752   Tuottavuus
0355-3779   Siirtolaisuus 7292
0355-3787   Maaseudun Tulevaisuus 135
0355-3930   Suomen Antropologi 357
0355-3949   Help!†
0355-3965   Opettaja 2894
0355-4074   Suomen Sanomalehtien Mikrofilmit 4588
0355-4090   Suomen Hammaslaakarilehti 5866
0355-4236   Jaana†
0355-4252   Kaks'plus 3838
0355-4260   Suosikki 2215
0355-4287   T M. Tekniikan Maailma 2641
0355-4295   V M 8609
0355-4317   Hymy 3838
0355-4481   Finland. Patentti- ja Rekisterihallitus. Mallioikeuslehti 6750
0355-4511   Kaltio 5222
0355-4651   Finnish Dental Society. Proceedings. Supplement†
0355-4767   Finland. Sosiaalihallitus. Kodinhoitoapu.
0355-4791   Baptria 840
0355-4848   Finland. Kansanelakelaitos. Julkaisuja. Sarja E†
0355-4856   Finland. Kansanelakelaitos. Julkaisuja. Sarja EL†
0355-5003   Finland. Kansanelakelaitos. Toimintakertomus†
0355-5054   Rondo 6613
0355-5097   Sosiaalilaaketieteellinen Aikakauslehti 5716
0355-550X   Rakentajain Kalenteri 1031
0355-5615   Numismaatikko 6652
0355-578X   Acta Academiae Aboensis. Series A: Humaniora†
0355-5895   4H -Tiedotuksia
0355-6050   Suomen Pankki. Julkaisuja. Kasvututkimuksia†
0355-6085   Urheilulehti 8214
0355-614X   Sparkassen see 0036-2123
0355-6395   Valtion Teknillinen Tutkimuskeskus. Metallilaboratorio. Tiedonanto†
0355-6654   Liikenneturva. Reports 7530
0355-6832   Joensuun Korkeakoulu. Julkaisuja. Sarja B2†
0355-6913   Aamulehti 3838
0355-6980   Purjehtija 8281
0355-7073   Liikuntakasvatus†
0355-7235   Koiramme 6810
0355-7294   Vakuutussanomat 4526
0355-7308   Foersaekringstidning 4503
0355-7375   Finland. Posti-ja Lennatinlaitos. Ulkomaisten Sanoma- ja Aikakauslehtien Hinnasto
0355-7448   Hallinto 7443
0355-7596   Metsanhoitaja 3697
0355-7650   Abophil 6891
0355-7820   Suomen Tukkukauppa 1583
0355-7839   Muoviuutiset†
0355-7847   Kansantaloudellisia Tutkimuksia 1139
0355-7855   Tie ja Liikenne 3285
0355-7871   Navigator 8654
0355-7936   Suomen Tukkukauppiaiden Liitto. Yearbook†
0355-7995   Kotimaisten Kielten Tutkimuskeskus. Skrifter 5137
0355-8045   Teosofi 6957
0355-8096   Suomen Shakki 8210
0355-8215   Oikeustiede-Jurisprudentia 4752
0355-841X   Regina 8882
0355-8614   Rakentaja 1031
0355-8746   Satakunnan Kansa 3839
0355-8924   N I F Publications†
0355-8991   Tekstiiliopettaja 8458
0355-9076   Valtion Teknillinen Tutkimuskeskus. Sairaalatekniikan Laboratorio. Tiedonanto†
0355-9106   Narinkka 4247
0355-9149   Tidningen Aaland 3839
0355-9378   Y V†
0355-9459   Tahdet (Year) 582
0355-9467   Tahdet ja Avaruus 582

0355-9483   Turun Yliopisto. Julkaisuja. Sarja D. Medica - Odontologica 5725
0355-953X   Puumies 1051
0355-9610   Aja 8555
0355-9637   Nykyposti 3839
0355-984X   Finnish Institute of Occupational Health. Current Research Projects 4093
0355-9874   Annales Chirurgiae et Gynaecologiae. Supplementum 6236
0355-9912   Uudistuva Konttori changed to 1459-6636 1854
0355-9963   Folkkulturdarkivet. Meddelanden 3617
0356-004X   Valtion Teknillinen Tutkimuskeskus. A T K-Palvelutoimisto. Tiedonanto†
0356-021X   Avaruusluotain 47
0356-0376   Studier i Nordisk Filologi 5182
0356-0473   A T S Ydintekniikka 3164
0356-0481   Suomen Antropologisen Seura. Toimituksia 357
0356-0635   Urkki†
0356-0724   Hufvudstadsbladet 3838
0356-0759   Suomen Kiorjallisen Seura. Toimituksia 7686
0356-0767   Suomen Kirkkohistoriallinen Seura. Vuosikirja 7686
0356-0783   Rakennusteollisuus†
0356-0910   Nordenskiold-Samfundets Tidskrift 694
0356-1003   Aalaendsk Odling 4195
0356-1070   Studies in Sport, Physical Education and Health 6997
0356-1089   S F S - Tiedotus 6406
0356-1135   Kotimaa 3839
0356-1283   Ilkka 3838
0356-133X   Turun Sanomat 3839
0356-1356   Kaleva 3838
0356-1364   University of Helsinki. Institute for Co-operative Studies. Publications 1425
0356-1380   Kansan Tahto 3838
0356-1402   Keskisuomalainen 3838
0356-1496   Skrifter Utgivna af Historiska Samfundet i Aabo 4263
0356-1534   Kotiristikko changed to 1796-590X 8184
0356-1577   Taskuristikko 8211
0356-1585   Kalastaja 3600
0356-1623   Lansi - Savo 3839
0356-1631   Tiedonantaja 3839
0356-1674   Hyvinkaan Sanomat changed to 1459-8663 3838
0356-1682   Etela - Pohjanmaa 3838
0356-1704   Vapaa-Aika-Eurosport†
0356-1755   Svenskbygden 2946
0356-178X   Finuc-S†
0356-1844   Vasabladet 3839
0356-2298   Iisalmen Sanomat 3838
0356-2395   Latu ja Polku 8321
0356-2751   Hameen Sanomat 3838
0356-276X   Savon Luonto†
0356-3014   Mallas ja Olut 607
0356-3081   Syopa 6035
0356-3189   Savonia†
0356-3464   Era 8311
0356-3472   P.S.†
0356-3502   Kainuun Sanomat 3838
0356-3510   Savon Sanomat 3839
0356-3545   Kristityn Vastuu 3839
0356-3553   Oesterbottningen changed to 1797-5492 3839
0356-3588   Suomenmaa (Helsinki) 3839
0356-3677   Tiede & Edistys 3839
0356-3693   Sibelius-Akatemia. Vuosikertomus changed to 1797-4763 3002
0356-3987   Tikkurilan Viesti 1040
0356-3995   Dickursby Meddelanden see 0356-3987 1040
0356-4096   Projektio†
0356-4444   Ita - Savo 3838
0356-4509   Finlands Natur 788
0356-4541   Lalli 3839
0356-472X   Tampereen Teknillinen Korkeakoulu. Opintomoniste changed to 1795-2824 3221
0356-4843   Tampereen Teknillinen Korkeakoulu. Arkkitehtuurin Osasto. Raportti changed to 1459-8868 458
0356-4940   Tampereen Teknillinen Korkeakoulu. Julkaisuja changed to 1459-2045 3221
0356-5092   Hinnat ja Kilpailu†
0356-5106   Talouselama 1181
0356-5122   Kemira changed to 1797-7738 3249
0356-5629   Faravid 4219
0356-5769   Lexica Societatis Fenno-Ugricae 5144
0356-5785   Apuneuvoja Suomalais-Ugrilaisten Kielten Opintoja Varten 5095
0356-6528   Scandinavian Journal of Work, Environment and Health. Supplement see 0355-3140 6687
0356-6927   Suomalainen Tiedeakatemia. Vuosikirja 7921
0356-7249   I T - Invalidityoe 8046
0356-746X   Liikuntatieteellisen Seura. Julkaisuja 8185
0356-7753   Finnish Boatbuilding Industry 8275
0356-780X   Migration Studies, C see 0356-9659 7293
0356-7818   Kemistin Kalenteri 2069
0356-7826   Suomen Vakuutusvuosikirja 4524
0356-7834   Foersaekringsaarsbok foer Finland 4503
0356-7842   Laeraren 2881
0356-7893   Current Research on Peace and Violence†
0356-7923   Muusikko 6597
0356-7931   Osto†
0356-794X   Pistis†
0356-8067   Tahti†
0356-8075   Valokuvauksen Vuosikirja 6978
0356-8083   Vaatturi 2250
0356-8091   Valtionyhtiot 1908
0356-813X   Lammin Notes 686
0356-8164   Helsingin Kauppakorkeakoulu. Julkaisusarja D. 1236
0356-8172   Svenska Tekniska Vetenskapsakademien i Finland. Meddelande 3221
0356-8199   Studia Historica Septentrionalia 4269
0356-8202   Makasiini†
0356-827X   Finland†
0356-861X   Kevo Notes 685
0356-8741   Turun Yliopisto. Psykologian Tutkimuksia 7413
0356-875X   Helsingfors i Forna Tider 3838

9266 0356-889X ULRICH'S PERIODICALS

0356-889X Helsingin Kauppakorkeakoulu. Julkaisusarja B. Tutkimuksia **1117**
0356-892X Helsingin Kauppakorkeakoulu. Julkaisusarja C. Oppikirjoja. **1117**
0356-9276 Energiakatsaus **3128**
0356-9349 Suomalainen Teologinen Kirjallisuusseura. Julkaiau **7686**
0356-9624 Nordinfo-Nytt†
0356-9659 Siirtolaisuustutkimuksia, A **7293**
0356-9691 Synkooppi **6622**
0356-9993 Insurance in Finland†
0357-0010 Tampereen Yliopisto. Musiikintutkimuksen Laitos. Julkaisu **3623**
0357-0126 Oikeuspoliittisen Tutkimuslaitos. Julkaisu *changed to* 1797-562X **4752**
0357-0363 Finland. Tilastokeskus. Taskutilasto *changed to* 1795-732X **8371**
0357-0371 Finland. Tilastokeskus. Finland in Figures **8370**
0357-0614 Finland. Tilastokeskus. Valtion Tilastojulkaisut†
0357-0738 Hifi-Lehti *changed to* 0781-2078 **2578**
0357-0797 Juridiska Foereningen i Finland. Publiktionsserie **4705**
0357-0975 Etela-Saimaa **3838**
0357-1068 Svenska Folkskolans Vaenners Kalender **4272**
0357-1084 Ohoi **7458**
0357-1432 Liehuvan Varit **3773**
0357-1440 Oulun Yliopiston Kirjaston Julkaisuja **5038**
0357-1521 Kansan Uutiset **3838**
0357-1823 Westermarck-Seura. Transactions **8146**
0357-1831 Valtion Teknillinen Tutkimuskeskus. Metallurgian ja Mineraalitekniikan Laboratorio. Tiedonanto†
0357-1858 Uusimaa **3839**
0357-1947 Tammerkoski **4272**
0357-1955 N O S P - Mikro†
0357-2021 Keski - Uusimaa **3838**
0357-2129 Turub Yliopisto. Historian Laitos. Julkaisu **4274**
0357-2234 Riista- ja Kalatalouden Tutkimuslaitos. Toimintakertomus **3606**
0357-2366 Suuri Ristikko **8210**
0357-2463 Yla - Vuoksi **3839**
0357-2498 Liikunnan ja Kansanterveyden Edistamissaatio. Julkaisuja **6231**
0357-2714 Koululainen **2881**
0357-2854 Kuluttajansuoja *changed to* 1796-5497 **2634**
0357-2862 Mark†
0357-2994 Baltic Sea Environment Proceedings **3405**
0357-3583 Jatuli **4235**
0357-3672 I F - Rapport **3618**
0357-3737 Valtion Teknillinen Tutkimuskeskus. Betoni- ja Silikaattitekniikan Laboratorio. Tiedonanto†
0357-4083 Tutkijaliito. Julkaisusarja **3839**
0357-4121 Prosessori **2463**
0357-4296 Tyoterveyslaitos. Katsauksia **6688**
0357-4377 Me Miehet†
0357-4725 Vaestoliitto. Vaestontutkimuslaitoksen. Julkaisusarja. D **7295**
0357-4962 Finland. Tilastokeskus. Finland i Siffror **8370**
0357-511X Ethnos-Toimite **3616**
0357-542X Alibi **4883**
0357-5535 Jyvaskylan Yliopisto. Biologian Laitos. Tiedonantoja *changed to* 1795-6900 **685**
0357-6493 Tom & Jerry **2217**
0357-6574 Bygdeserien **436**
0357-7031 Valtion Teknillinen Tutkimuskeskus. Rakennetekniikan Laboratorio. Tiedonanto†
0357-7163 Liikearkistoyhdistys. Julkaisuja†
0357-749X Vitriini **4400**
0357-7937 Tahtitieteellinen Yhdistys Ursa. Ursan Julkaisuja **582**
0357-8070 Tampereen Yliopisto. Tiedotusopillinen Yhdistys. Tiedotustutkimus **4584**
0357-816X Sotahistoriallinen Aikakauskirja **6447**
0357-8755 Roope-Seta **2211**
0357-9387 Valtion Teknillinen Tutkimuskeskus. V T T Symposium **8444**
0357-9484 Puu **1051**
0357-9492 Sukuviesti **4272**
0357-9921 Jyvaskyla Studies in Computer Science, Economics and Statistics **2430**
0357-9956 Oesterbotten **4250**
0358-0083 Migrationsstudier, B *see* 0356-9659 **7293**
0358-0474 Valtakunnallisen Tutkimus- ja Kokeiluyksikon. Julkaisuja *changed to* 1797-0466 **8052**
0358-0520 Scanp†
0358-0628 Kehittyva Yritys†
0358-1071 Kirjeshakki **8184**
0358-1489 Finland. Ulkoasiainministerio. Julkaisuja **7234**
0358-1705 Karjalainen **3838**
0358-1861 V T T Toimintakertomus **3226**
0358-190X Historian ja Yhteiskuntaopin Opettajien Liitto H Y O L Ry. Vuosikirja **4228**
0358-2671 Finland. Ilmatieteen Laitos. Ilmasahkohavaintoja†
0358-2973 Helsingin Kauppakorkeakoulu. F, Tyopapereita†
0358-3279 Kilpisjarvi Notes **686**
0358-3406 Tvarminne Studies **720**
0358-3414 Arx Tavastica **4201**
0358-3511 Muoto *changed to* 1796-9751
0358-4038 Tehy **5982**
0358-4208 Yritystalous **1802**
0358-4283 Metsantutkimuslaitos. Tiedonanto **3697**
0358-4313 Vi i Norden†
0358-5522 Scandinavian Economic History Review **1549**
0358-5581 Opusculum†
0358-5654 Aabo Akademi. Ekonomisk-statsvetenskapliga Fakulteten. Meddelanden **7944**
0358-5697 *see* 0079-7227 **6176**
0358-6197 Aikuiskasvatus **2938**
0358-626X Fakta **1745**
0358-6294 Borgaabladet **3838**
0358-6464 Jyvaskyla Cross - Language Studies **5136**
0358-6758 Walter and Andree de Nottbeck Foundation. Scientific Reports **898**
0358-7010 Liikunta & Tiede **8185**
0358-7045 Nordinfo Publikation†
0358-7061 Arkiv foer Svenska Oesterbotten **4201**
0358-7088 S S I D Liaison Bulletin†
0358-710X Scripta Historica **4263**
0358-7517 Terminfo **5186**
0358-7673 Teollisuusviikko†
0358-7703 Blue Wings **8782**
0358-7711 V R - Express
0358-8017 Seura **3839**
0358-8351 Eeva **8859**
0358-8424 Uppsatser **4276**
0358-870X University of Vaasa. Proceedings. Discussion Papers **1550**
0358-8815 Tanssi **2688**
0358-8882 Tiede ja Ase **6449**
0358-8904 Form Function Finland *changed to* 1458-7904 **452**
0358-8998 Finland. Tilastokeskus. Finlyandiya v Tsifrakh *see* 0357-4962 **8370**
0358-8998 Finland. Tilastokeskus. Finlyandiya v Tsifrakh *see* 0357-0371 **8370**
0358-8998 Finland. Tilastokeskus. Finlyandiya v Tsifrakh *see* 0781-657X **8370**
0358-8998 Finland. Tilastokeskus. Finlyandiya v Tsifrakh *see* 1795-732X **8371**
0358-8998 Finland. Tilastokeskus. Finlyandiya v Tsifrakh *see* 0782-7326 **8372**
0358-9153 Suomen Akatemia. Julkaisuja **7921**
0358-9293 Spraakbruk **5177**
0359-0216 University of Turku. Psychological Research Reports **7414**
0359-0267 Sina, Mina **8884**
0359-0569 Skimbaaja **8333**
0359-095X Suomen Logopedis-Foniatrinen Aikakauslehti *changed to* 1458-3410 **5163**
0359-1034 Psychiatria Fennica. Monographs **6176**
0359-1174 Nalle Puh **2204**
0359-1255 Tyoeterveiset **6688**
0359-1301 Forma Uutiset *changed to* 1795-3715 **4540**
0359-1832 Lounais-Haemeen Kotiseutu- ja Museoyhdistys. Vuosikirja **4241**
0359-2189 Perfis **5861**
0359-3207 Psychiatria Fennica. Reports **6176**
0359-3223 Historiallinen Kirjasto **4142**
0359-3568 Sorbifolia **818**
0359-4203 Helsingin Yliopisto. Opettajankoulutuslaitos. Tutkimuksia *changed to* 1795-2158 **2863**
0359-4378 Futari **8229**
0359-4947 Tietokone **2583**
0359-5056 Etela-Suomen Sanomat **3838**
0359-5749 University of Helsinki. Department of Education. Research Bulletin **2922**
0359-6079 Prima†
0359-629X Jyvaskylan Yliopisto. Musiikin Laitos. Julkaisusarja. A, Tutkielmia ja Raportteja **6581**
0359-6648 Frisk Bris **8275**
0359-6729 Finland. Oikeusministerio. Tietojarjestelmayksikko. B **7437**
0359-6753 Lapin Kansa **3839**
0359-6788 Documenta Septentrionalia **4215**
0359-7008 Technik aus Finnland†
0359-7016 Finlande Industrielle†
0359-7024 N A D - Publikation **2697**
0359-7105 D A T U T O P **439**
0359-7601 N T K F - Publikation†
0359-7636 Moottori **8591**
0359-7679 Suomalais-Ugrilaisen Seuran Kansatieteellisia Julkaisuja **357**
0359-811X Tampereen Teknillinen Korkeakoulu. Sahkotekniikan Osasto. Fysiikka. Raportti *changed to* 1459-3742 **3332**
0359-8543 Tietoviikko **2439**
0359-9108 Tulosuunta†
0359-9124 Metsatilastotiedote (Print) *changed to* 1797-3074 **3709**
0359-968X Metsatilastollinen Vuosikirja **3709**
0360-0017 Multiple Sclerosis Indicative Abstracts†
0360-0025 Sex Roles **7407**
0360-005X Maine Fish and Wildlife **2618**
0360-0114 Florida Bar News **4675**
0360-0157 Young Socialist
0360-0181 New Conversations **7665**
0360-0270 Illinois. State Museum. Reports of Investigations **7864**
0360-0289 Illinois. State Museum. Story of Illinois Series†
0360-0297 Illinois. State Museum. Popular Science Series **7864**
0360-0300 A C M Computing Surveys **2405**
0360-0467 Areito†
0360-0564 Advances in Catalysis **2132**
0360-0572 Annual Review of Sociology **8088**
0360-0637 Ebsco Bulletin of Serials Changes **5008**
0360-0661 Index to Scientific Reviews **7937**
0360-0688 CLENExchange **5002**
0360-0696 Behavior Change†
0360-0726 Rehabilitation - World†
0360-0734 Washington. Utilities and Transportation Commission. Railroad-Highway Grade Crossing Accidents. Summary and Analysis†
0360-0815 National Panorama of American Youth
0360-1005 Mandate† **8972**
0360-1013 The Ohio Review†
0360-1021 Archaeology of Eastern North America **378**
0360-1056 North Carolina Genealogical Society Journal **3777**
0360-1102 Needlework Guild of America. Annual Report†
0360-1234 Journal of Environmental Science and Health. Part B: Pesticides, Food Contaminants, and Agricultural Wastes **3447**
0360-1250 Current Book Review Citations†
0360-1277 Educational Gerontology **4044**
0360-1285 Progress in Energy and Combustion Science **3145**
0360-1293 Acupuncture and Electro-Therapeutics Research **306**
0360-1315 Computers & Education **2974**
0360-1323 Building and Environment **984**
0360-1404 Abraxas†
0360-1420 Journal of Christian Reconstruction **7654**
0360-1455 New River Review†
0360-151X Brigham Young University Law Review **4632**
0360-1757 E I A Electronics Multimedia Handbook†
0360-1765 Leviathan (Colorado Springs) **5224**
0360-1773 Market Chronicle†
0360-1862 TeleSystems Journal†
0360-1897 Pacific Theological Review†
0360-1927 Journal of Latin American Lore **3619**
0360-1935 Main Title†
0360-196X Corrections Court Digest
0360-1978 Richmond Historian†
0360-1986 Women's Work (Washington)
0360-2109 Paul's Record Magazine **6604**
0360-215X Dictionary of Contemporary Quotations **5285**
0360-2192 Masks†
0360-2206 Balkanistica **4202**
0360-2273 Popular Mechanics Do-It-Yourself Yearbook†
0360-2370 Studies in Eighteenth Century Culture **4476**
0360-2397 Harper's Weekly†
0360-2400 Management Contents†
0360-2486 Advances in Liquid Crystals†
0360-2508 Current Governments Reports: Chart Book on Government Data. Organization, Finances and Employment†
0360-2516 Billboard Index†
0360-2532 Drug Metabolism Reviews **5607**
0360-2559 Polymer-Plastics Technology and Engineering **2129**
0360-2583 Drugs and the Pharmaceutical Sciences **6836**
0360-2672 Scree **5238**
0360-2702 Bibliographic Guide to Business and Economics†
0360-2745 Bibliographic Guide to Law†
0360-2753 Bibliographic Guide to Music†
0360-2761 Bibliographic Guide to Technology†
0360-277X Bibliographic Guide to Psychology†
0360-2788 Bibliographic Guide to Theatre Arts†
0360-2796 Bibliographic Guide to Government Publications - U S†
0360-2834 Maryland Register **7452**
0360-2877 Concrete Pipe Industry Statistics **3229**
0360-3016 International Journal of Radiation: Oncology - Biology - Physics **6199**
0360-3024 Family Motor Coaching **8496**
0360-3032 Trinity Journal **7691**
0360-3059 Vermont. Agency of Environmental Conservation. Biennial Report†
0360-3083 Wood Industry Abstracts†
0360-3164 Plating and Surface Finishing **6328**
0360-3199 International Journal of Hydrogen Energy **3139**
0360-3318 Viewpoint (Atlanta)†
0360-3334 Calendar of Folk Festivals and Related Events†
0360-3342 Liberty, Then and Now†
0360-3350 L A D O C†
0360-3385 Tristania **5390**
0360-3407 Guide to National Endowment for the Arts **492**
0360-3431 Sourcebook of Criminal Justice Statistics **2675**
0360-3482 Microorganisms and Infectious Diseases†
0360-3512 The Federal Directory **7436**
0360-3520 Body Fashions - Intimate Apparel†
0360-3601 Genesis III†
0360-3636 Arithmoi†
0360-3679 Institutes of Religion and Health. Institutes Reporter†
0360-3695 Film & History **6498**
0360-3709 American Poetry Review **5416**
0360-3725 A M E Church Review **7743**
0360-3733 Theological Currents†
0360-3741 Black Church†
0360-3768 Candler Review†
0360-3814 Performing Arts Resources **8476**
0360-3881 Alaska. Division of Geological and Geophysical Surveys. Special Report **2724**
0360-389X Adventist Heritage **7744**
0360-392X U.S. National Transportation Safety Board. Briefs of Accidents Involving Midair Collisions, U.S. General Aviation†
0360-3938 Business Outlook†
0360-3954 U.S. National Transportation Safety Board. Listing of Aircraft Accidents-Incidents by Make and Model, U.S. Civil Aviation†
0360-3989 Human Communication Research **7360**
0360-3997 Inflammation **5635**
0360-4012 Journal of Neuroscience Research **6155**
0360-4020 Association of Military Dermatologists. Journal
0360-4039 Nursing (Year) **5972**
0360-4055 C S Journal
0360-4071 Quality Rock Reader
0360-4217 National Journal **7156**
0360-4225 Visual Dialog†
0360-4365 In Theory Only **6575**
0360-4381 River City
0360-4411 Who's Where in Music
0360-4438 Appalachian Notes
0360-4543 U.S. Department of the Interior. Oil Shale Environmental Advisory Panel. Annual Report†
0360-4594 U.S. Food and Nutrition Service. Food and Nutrition Programs†
0360-4608 Record (Nashville) **8064**
0360-4756 Honolulu Academy of Arts. Journal **493**
0360-487X U.S. Social and Rehabilitation Service. Annual Report of Welfare Programs†
0360-4918 Presidential Studies Quarterly **7173**
0360-4993 Budget Decorating & Remodeling†
0360-5108 Looking Back to Those Wonderful Days Gone by†
0360-5132 U.S. Patent and Trademark Office. Official Gazette. Trademarks **6759**
0360-5167 American Hospital Association. House of Delegates. Proceedings†
0360-5272 Rail Transit Directory†
0360-5302 Communications in Partial Differential Equations **5480**
0360-5310 The Journal of Medicine and Philosophy **5652**
0360-5434 Occupational Education†
0360-5442 Energy **3130**
0360-5450 Vertica†
0360-5485 Affiliate **4611**
0360-5531 Old Northwest†
0360-5590 Texas Tech Journal of Education†

Link to your serials resources and content with ulrichsweb.com

ISSN

9270 0363-8480 ULRICH'S PERIODICALS

0363-8480 Recent Advances in Tobacco Science
0363-8499 U.S. Internal Revenue Service. Bulletin Index - Digest System: Service 4. Excise Taxes†
0363-8502 U.S. Internal Revenue Service. Bulletin Index - Digest System: Part 3. Employment Taxes
0363-8545 U.S. Department of Agriculture. National Agricultural Statistics Service. Farm Labor (Print)† **8995**
0363-8553 Current Business Reports: Monthly Wholesale Trade, Sales and Inventories (Print)† **8947**
0363-8561 U.S. Department of Agriculture. National Agricultural Statistics Service. Crop Production **188**
0363-860X Reserve Forces Almanac **6443**
0363-8618 National Guard Almanac **6438**
0363-8642 Cements Research Progress†
0363-8715 Journal of Computer Assisted Tomography **6200**
0363-8782 Texas Speech Communication Journal **5187**
0363-8812 Federal Design Matters†
0363-8820 Energy Reporter
0363-8855 Journal of Clinical Engineering **750**
0363-891X Psychohistory Review†
0363-8952 Psychiatry and the Humanities
0363-8960 Old Time Songs and Poems (Seabrook)†
0363-8979 North American Bird Bander **911**
0363-8987 Financial Studies of the Small Business **1345**
0363-9010 Tamarind Institute Report†
0363-9029 Cassette Books **4071**
0363-9037 Maledicta Press Publications **5150**
0363-9045 Drug Development and Industrial Pharmacy **6834**
0363-9061 International Journal for Numerical and Analytical Methods in Geomechanics **3272**
0363-907X International Journal of Energy Research **3139**
0363-910X B A I Index of Bank Performance†
0363-9185 Help (Washington)
0363-9282 N A G W S Guide. Gymnastics†
0363-9290 Republican Almanac **7177**
0363-9347 International League for Human Rights. Annual Report†
0363-9401 S.C.A., State & County Administrator†
0363-941X U.S. House of Representatives. Committee on Science and Technology. Legislative Calendar **7473**
0363-9452 Grand Jury Report†
0363-9460 Confrontation - Change Review **1085**
0363-9487 T V Season†
0363-9509 Community College Frontiers†
0363-9525 37 Design & Environment Projects†
0363-9568 Nursing Administration Quarterly **5973**
0363-9614 National Pro-Life Journal
0363-972X Directory of Dance Companies
0363-9762 Clinical Nuclear Medicine **6194**
0363-9819 U.S. Environmental Protection Agency. Radiological Quality of the Environment in the United States†
0363-9991 Interstate
0364-0000 Cutting Edge†
0364-0078 Country Style
0364-0086 TourBook: Mid-Atlantic **8762**
0364-0094 A J S Review **7717**
0364-0132 Finance Companies **1343**
0364-0213 Cognitive Science **7347**
0364-0256 Annual Evaluation Report on Programs Administered by the U.S. Office of Education **8025**
0364-0302 Libertarian Review†
0364-0418 International Flight Information Manual **61**
0364-0426 Advisor, Navy Civilian Manpower Management†
0364-0531 N I A A A Information and Feature Service†
0364-0558 Calendars of the United States House of Representatives and History of Legislation **6278**
0364-0620 Internal Revenue Cumulative Bulletin **1930**
0364-0655 Flow of Funds Account **1487**
0364-071X Colt American Handgunning Annual†
0364-0728 Arkansas Vital Statistics **7296**
0364-0760 Charities U S A **8031**
0364-0779 Institute for Socioeconomic Studies. Journal **7143**
0364-0841 International Series in Experimental Psychology
0364-0868 Biweekly Cryogenics Current Awareness Service†
0364-0876 U.S. Bureau of Mines. Mineral Industry Surveys - Commodities: Cement†
0364-0930 U.S. Department of Housing and Urban Development. Office of International Affairs. Foreign Publications Accessions List†
0364-0973 Official Reports of the Supreme Court **4958**
0364-0981 U.S. Coast Guard Marine Safety Council. Proceedings *changed to* 1547-9676 **6432**
0364-1007 U.S. Department of the Treasury. Financial Management Service. Monthly Treasury Statement of Receipts and Outlays of the United States Government **1388**
0364-1015 U.S. Department of the Treasury. Bureau of Public Debt. Monthly Statement of the Public Debt of the United States **1388**
0364-1074 E I S **3478**
0364-118X E L C†
0364-1236 Library Resources for the Blind and Physically Handicapped **5029**
0364-1252 Production, Prices, Employment and Trade in Northwest Forest Industries **3700**
0364-1260 Government Paper Specification Standards **6733**
0364-1287 The Army Lawyer **4971**
0364-1325 Federal Trainer†
0364-1333 *see* 0364-1341 **1348**
0364-1341 Foreign Exchange Rates **1348**
0364-1368 U.S. Food Safety and Quality Service. Issuances of the Meat and Poultry Inspection Program†
0364-1376 New Publications of the Bureau of Mines†
0364-1449 Handbook on International Study for U.S. Nationals. Vol. 1: Study in Europe†
0364-152X Environmental Management (New York) **3426**
0364-1538 Stereopus
0364-1546 Dirt Bike **8258**
0364-1678 Federal Government†
0364-1708 Glyph
0364-1724 Law Enforcement News†
0364-1805 Copper-Base Mill and Foundry Products
0364-1880 Current Industrial Reports. M3-1, Manufacturers' Shipments, Inventories, and Orders (Print)†
0364-1910 Chemical Information Bulletin **2054**
0364-2011 E T A Interchange†
0364-202X U.S. Department of Agriculture. National Agricultural Statistics Service. Cattle on Feed **187**
0364-2089 Input†
0364-2151 Environment Midwest†
0364-216X Aesthetic Plastic Surgery **6235**
0364-2194 Barbeque Planet†
0364-2216 Journal of the Graduate Music Students at the Ohio State University **6581**
0364-2232 Voice for the Defense **4809**
0364-2267 U.S. Securities and Exchange Commission. Official Summary of Security Transactions and Holdings **1657**
0364-2313 World Journal of Surgery **6262**
0364-2348 Skeletal Radiology **6208**
0364-2410 M E L A Notes **5030**
0364-2429 Money Digest†
0364-2437 Afro-Americans in New York Life and History **3517**
0364-2453 U.S. Patent and Trademark Office. Manual of Patent Examining Procedure **6759**
0364-2461 U.S.Geological Survey. New Publications†
0364-2569 Monographs in Pharmacology and Physiology†
0364-2577 Guidelines to Metabolic Therapy†
0364-2615 Tennessee Valley Perspective†
0364-2666 U.S. Department of Housing and Urban Development. F H A Trends of Home Mortgage Characteristics **4437**
0364-2682 U.S. Department of Agriculture. National Agricultural Statistics Service. Poultry Slaughter (Print) *changed to* 1949-1581 **189**
0364-2690 U.S. Department of Agriculture. Agricultural Statistics Board Reports: Celery†
0364-2887 Writings on American History†
0364-2895 California Economic Indicators **1445**
0364-2976 Journal of the Hellenic Diaspora **3545**
0364-2984 Geological Survey of Alabama. Oil and Gas Report **6771**
0364-3026 Urban Life in New and Renewing Communities†
0364-3107 Administration in Social Work **8023**
0364-3115 Grantsmanship Center News†
0364-3190 Neurochemical Research **6164**
0364-3344 Box 749
0364-3417 Annual Review of Population Law†
0364-345X Passenger Transport **8508**
0364-3468 U.S. Federal Highway Administration. Highway and Urban Mass Transportation†
0364-3484 Mass Transit **8503**
0364-3557 Water Resources Data for Washington **8839**
0364-3565 Water Resources Data for Wyoming **8839**
0364-3581 Federal Rules of Evidence News **4673**
0364-359X Dragonfly (Talent)†
0364-3603 The Claims Forum†
0364-362X North Carolina Attorney General Reports **4747**
0364-3670 International CODEN Directory†
0364-3719 National Locksmith **2679**
0364-3824 Taste
0364-4014 The Spirit That Moves Us **5376**
0364-4022 Poesie - U.S.A.
0364-4065 Water Resources Data for New Mexico **8839**
0364-4073 Water Resources Data for Montana **8839**
0364-4081 Water Resources Data for Kentucky **8839**
0364-4103 J S A C Grapevine†
0364-4146 United States Senate. House Armed Services Committee. Legislative Calendar **4853**
0364-4154 United States Senate. Committee on Rules and Administration. Legislative Calendar **7474**
0364-4162 United States Senate. Committee on Finance. Legislative Calendar **1389**
0364-4197 United States Senate. Committee on Banking, Housing, and Urban Affairs. Legislative Calendar **7474**
0364-4200 United States House of Representatives. Committee on Veterans' Affairs. Legislative Calendar **6451**
0364-4243 United States Senate. Committee on Foreign Policy. Legislative Calendar **7474**
0364-4294 United States House of Representatives. Committee on the Judiciary. Legislative Calendar **7474**
0364-4308 Yiddish **7732**
0364-4324 Water Resources Data for Idaho **8839**
0364-4332 Water Resources Data for Illinois **8839**
0364-4340 Water Resources Data for Indiana **8839**
0364-4359 Water Resources Data for Iowa **8839**
0364-4367 Water Resources Data for Maryland and Delaware **8839**
0364-4375 Water Resources Data for Michigan **8839**
0364-4383 Water Resources Data for Minnesota **8839**
0364-4405 Water Resources Data for North Dakota **8839**
0364-4421 Water Resources Data for West Virginia **8839**
0364-457X Studio One **5436**
0364-474X Electric Perspectives **3302**
0364-4782 Journal of Human Services Abstracts†
0364-5010 Climatological Data. Tennessee **6351**
0364-507X Wisconsin Public Documents **7485**
0364-5134 Annals of Neurology **6123**
0364-5193 Bioethics Digest†
0364-5274 The Energy Daily **3130**
0364-5282 Location Identifiers **65**
0364-5312 Climatological Data. Nevada **6350**
0364-5339 Climatological Data. New England **6351**
0364-5371 Climatological Data. West Virginia **6351**
0364-538X Hourly Precipitation Data. Maryland & Delaware **6355**
0364-5398 Hourly Precipitation Data. Louisiana **6355**
0364-5401 Hourly Precipitation Data. Kentucky **6355**
0364-5479 Informer (Los Angeles)
0364-5487 Peters Notes†
0364-5541 Journal of Mental Imagery **7376**
0364-555X Russian-English Translators Exchange†
0364-5568 Professional Translator†
0364-5584 Climatological Data. Ohio **6351**
0364-5592 Climatological Data. Utah **6351**
0364-5606 Climatological Data. New York **6351**
0364-5614 Climatological Data. New Jersey **6351**
0364-5630 Climatological Data. Virginia **6351**
0364-5711 Standard & Poor's International Stock Report†
0364-5754 N C J R S Document Retrieval Index†
0364-5843 Climatological Data. Pennsylvania **6351**
0364-5851 Climatological Data. Oregon **2704**
0364-586X Downtown Mall Annual & Urban Design Report†
0364-5886 U.S. Senate. Calendar of Business **7473**
0364-5916 CALPHAD **2107**
0364-5924 Hayes Historical Journal†
0364-6068 Climatological Data. Missouri **6350**
0364-6076 Hourly Precipitation Data. Alabama **6354**
0364-6084 Hourly Precipitation Data. Arizona **6354**
0364-6092 Hourly Precipitation Data. California **6354**
0364-6106 Hourly Precipitation Data. Colorado **6354**
0364-6114 Hourly Precipitation Data. Florida **6354**
0364-6122 Hourly Precipitation Data. Georgia **6354**
0364-6149 Hourly Precipitation Data. Idaho **6354**
0364-6157 Hourly Precipitation Data. Illinois **6354**
0364-6165 Hourly Precipitation Data. Indiana **6355**
0364-6173 Hourly Precipitation Data. Iowa **6355**
0364-6181 Hourly Precipitation Data. Kansas **6355**
0364-619X Hourly Precipitation Data. Pennsylvania **6356**
0364-6203 Hourly Precipitation Data. Michigan **6355**
0364-6211 Hourly Precipitation Data. Minnesota **6355**
0364-622X Hourly Precipitation Data. Mississippi **6355**
0364-6238 Hourly Precipitation Data. Missouri **6355**
0364-6246 Hourly Precipitation Data. Montana **6355**
0364-6254 Hourly Precipitation Data. Nebraska **6355**
0364-6262 Hourly Precipitation Data. Nevada **6355**
0364-6270 Hourly Precipitation Data. New England **6355**
0364-6289 Hourly Precipitation Data. New Jersey **6355**
0364-6297 Hourly Precipitation Data. New Mexico **6355**
0364-6300 Hourly Precipitation Data. New York **6355**
0364-6319 Hourly Precipitation Data. North Carolina **6355**
0364-6327 Hourly Precipitation Data. North Dakota **6355**
0364-6335 Hourly Precipitation Data. Ohio **6355**
0364-6343 Hourly Precipitation Data. Oklahoma **6356**
0364-6351 Hourly Precipitation Data. Oregon **6356**
0364-636X Hourly Precipitation Data. South Carolina **6356**
0364-6378 Hourly Precipitation Data. South Dakota **6356**
0364-6386 Hourly Precipitation Data. Tennessee **6356**
0364-6645 Harvard Business School. Baker Library. Working Papers in Baker Library†
0364-6661 Report from the Capital **7773**
0364-6696 U.S. Office of the Secretary of the Treasury. Treasury Papers†
0364-6718 S E C News Digest **1648**
0364-6742 International Notices to Airmen **61**
0364-6858 Federal Motor Vehicle Safety Standards and Regulations **8580**
0364-6866 Nuclear Reactors Built, Being Built, or Planned in the United States†
0364-6874 Hourly Precipitation Data. Virginia **6356**
0364-6882 Hourly Precipitation Data. Texas **6356**
0364-6890 Hourly Precipitation Data. Wyoming **6356**
0364-6904 Hourly Precipitation Data. West Virginia **6356**
0364-6912 Hourly Precipitation Data. Washington **6356**
0364-6920 Hourly Precipitation Data. Utah **6356**
0364-6939 Hourly Precipitation Data. Wisconsin **6356**
0364-6947 United States Senate. Committee on the Judiciary. Legislative and Executive Calendar **4966**
0364-698X American Wine Society Journal **597**
0364-6998 Solar Energy Update†
0364-7072 U.S. Geological Survey. National Earthquake Information Service. Preliminary Determination of Epicenters, Monthly Listing **2791**
0364-7145 Maintenance†
0364-720X Lake Superior Review†
0364-7218 Entrepreneur†
0364-7234 World Economic Conditions in Relation to Agricultural Trade†
0364-7374 American Merchant Marine Conference. Proceedings **8638**
0364-7390 Evaluation Studies Review Annual†
0364-7501 Musical Mainstream (Large Print Edition) **6593**
0364-7544 Congressional Record Index **7431**
0364-7609 Primavera (Chicago) **8881**
0364-7625 Access Reports **7201**
0364-765X Mathematics of Operations Research **2431**
0364-7668 Rising Tide
0364-7692 Harvard University Gazette **2286**
0364-7714 Water Supply and Management†
0364-7927 U.S. Bureau of Mines. Mineral Industry Surveys - Commodities: Molybdenum†
0364-7943 Titanium (Year): A Statistical Review **6335**
0364-8028 Indian Leader **2287**
0364-8044 Panama Canal Spillway
0364-8079 President's Council of Physical Fitness & Sports. Newsletter†
0364-8087 Rice Market News **275**
0364-8109 U.S. National Labor Relations Board. Weekly Summary of the National Labor Relations Board Cases **1712**
0364-815X Marquee (Anaheim)
0364-8176 United States Senate. Committee on Veterans' Affairs. Legislative Calendar **6451**
0364-8184 New Horizon - Polish American Cultural Review† **8976**
0364-8265 U.S. General Accounting Office. Monthly List of G A O Reports *changed to* 1936-6620 **7485**
0364-8273 Football Forecast (Year)†
0364-8303 International and Comparative Public Policy†
0364-8370 U.S. Federal Reserve System. Selected Interest and Exchange Rates. Weekly Series of Charts† **8995**
0364-8575 World This Year†
0364-8583 The World Tomorrow *changed to* 0009-5281 **7631**
0364-8591 Old Testament Abstracts **7699**
0364-863X The Postal Bulletin **2355**
0364-8753 U.S. Coast Guard. Register of Officers **6450**
0364-8796 American Candlemaker†
0364-8877 Financial Aids for Higher Education
0364-9024 Journal of Graph Theory **5504**
0364-9040 Iowa Agricultural Statistics†
0364-9059 I E E E Journal of Oceanic Engineering **3312**
0364-9156 Directors & Boards **1739**
0364-9210 Ethnodisc Journal of Recorded Sound†

ISSN

9272 0368-0827 ULRICH'S PERIODICALS

0368-0827 Inzynieria i Aparatura Chemiczna **3247**
0368-1025 Izmeritel'naya Tekhnika **4488**
0368-1084 Journal of Applied Chemistry & Biotechnology. Abstracts *see* 0268-2575 **767**
0368-1157 Journal of Agricultural Research **126**
0368-1254 Nassauischer Verein fuer Naturkunde. Jahrbuecher **7886**
0368-1327 Agricultural Society of Trinidad & Tobago. Journal **128**
0368-1416 Jornal Brasileiro de Ginecologia†
0368-1521 Jahresbericht der Pharmazie† **8967**
0368-1653 Chinese Institute of Chemical Engineers. Journal *changed to* 1876-1070 **3256**
0368-2048 Journal of Electron Spectroscopy and Related Phenomena **7078**
0368-2145 Hokkaido University. Faculty of Science. Journal. Series 5: Botany†
0368-2188 Hokkaido University. Faculty of Science. Journal. Series 6: Zoology†
0368-2196 University of Tokyo. Faculty of Science. Journal. Section 3: Botany†
0368-220X University of Tokyo. Faculty of Science. Journal. Section 4: Zoology†
0368-2307 Gesellschaft fuer Naturkunde in Wuerttemberg. Jahreshefte **675**
0368-2315 Journal de Gynecologie Obstetrique et Biologie de la Reproduction **5994**
0368-2323 Geochemical Society of India. Journal **2735**
0368-2331 Geological Society of the Philippines. Journal
0368-2625 Journal of the Indian Medical Profession†
0368-2781 Japanese Journal of Antibiotics **5643**
0368-2811 Japanese Journal of Clinical Oncology **6023**
0368-2897 Hanguk Nonghwahakhoechi/Agricultural Chemistry and Biotechnology *changed to* 1738-2203 **234**
0368-3141 Japan Congress on Materials Research. Proceedings **3348**
0368-3206 Mine Ventilation Society of South Africa. Journal **6470**
0368-3303 Asiatic Society. Journal **544**
0368-4040 Journal Suisse d'Apiculture **129**
0368-4113 Hiroshima University. Journal of Science. Series B. Division 1: Zoology†
0368-4199 Shivaji University. Journal (Humanities) **4475**
0368-444X Japan Steel Works Technical News **6318**
0368-4571 Shinshu University. Faculty of Textile Science and Technology. Journal. Series F: Physics and Mathematics†
0368-458X Shinshu University. Faculty of Textile Science and Technology. Journal. Series D: Arts†
0368-4598 Shinshu University. Faculty of Textile Science and Technology. Journal. Series A: Biology†
0368-4601 Shinshu University. Faculty of Textile Science and Technology. Journal. Series C: Chemistry†
0368-461X Shinshu University. Faculty of Textile Science and Technology. Journal. Series E: Agriculture and Sericulture†
0368-4628 Shinshu University. Faculty of Textile Science and Technology. Journal. Series B: Textile Engineering†
0368-4636 Textile Association (India). Journal **8459**
0368-4741 Kagaku Asahi **7874**
0368-4814 Kazanskii Meditsinskii Zhurnal **5657**
0368-489X Musee Royal de l'Afrique Centrale. Annales - Sciences Geologiques. Serie in 8 **2756**
0368-492X Kybernetes **2527**
0368-4954 Kurashiki Chuo Byoin Nempo **5659**
0368-5039 Kyoto Daigaku Genshi Enerugi Kenkyujo Iho **3170**
0368-5063 Kagoshima Daigaku Igaku Zasshi **5656**
0368-5098 Kogakuin Daigaku. Kenkyu Hokoku **7877**
0368-511X Kyoto Daigaku Nogakubu Enshurin Hokoku/Kyoto University Forests. Bulletin *changed to* 1344-4174 **3702**
0368-5128 Kagawa Daigaku Nogakubu Gakujutsu Hokoku **129**
0368-5179 Keio Igaku/Keio Medical Society. Journal *changed to* 0022-9717 **5657**
0368-5187 Koshu Eisei **7530**
0368-5306 Keikinzoku Yosetsu **6320**
0368-5365 Kogyo Gijutsuin. Biseibutsu Kogyo Gijutsu Kenkyujo. Kenkyu Hokoku
0368-5470 Kagaku. Zokan **2069**
0368-5632 Khimiya v Shkole **2070**
0368-5713 Kikai no Kenkyu **5454**
0368-5780 Keiso **4488**
0368-5810 Kurume Igakkai Zasshi **5659**
0368-5829 Kyorin Igakkai Zasshi **5659**
0368-5918 Kagaku to Kogyo (Osaka) **8430**
0368-5942 Journal of Meteorological Research **6358**
0368-5969 Kobe Kaiyo Kishodai. Iho **2810**
0368-6000 Kagawa Kenritsu Noka Daigaku Kiyo/Kagawa Agricultural College. Memoirs *changed to* 0453-0764 **129**
0368-6051 Keiryo Kenkyusho Hokoku/National Research Laboratory of Metrology. Reports *changed to* 1347-1473 **6406**
0368-6132 Klinische Medizin† **8969**
0368-6213 Kosmos **7024**
0368-623X Kita Nihon Byogaichu Kenkyukaiho **240**
0368-6302 Kongelige Norske Videnskabers Selskab. Forhandlinger *changed to* 0803-1983 **7877**
0368-6310 Kongelige Norske Videnskabers Selskab. Skrifter **7877**
0368-6337 Kinzoku **6320**
0368-6396 Kexue (Shanghai) **7875**
0368-6558 Koryo **595**
0368-6795 Kumamoto Journal of Science, Biology†
0368-6833 Kyushu Shika Gakkai Zasshi **5854**
0368-7147 Kvantovaya Elektronika (Moscow) **7079**
0368-7155 Kvantovaya Elektronika (Kyiv) **3323**
0368-7163 Kimya ve Sanayi†
0368-7171 Kongelige Veterinaer- og Landbohoejskole. Aarskrift†
0368-7201 Kongelige Danske Videnskabernes Selskab. Oversigt over Selskabets Virksomhed **7877**
0368-7279 Kyushu Yakugakkai Kaiho **6858**
0368-7295 Kozharska i Obuvna Promishlenost†
0368-7368 Lab Instrumenten *changed to* 1567-1828 **5908**
0368-7481 Libyan Journal of Sciences **7880**
0368-7619 Lesnaya Promyshlennost' **3713**
0368-8275 Muenchener Beitraege zur Abwasser-, Fischerei- und Flussbiologie
0368-8283 Real Academia de Ciencias y Artes de Barcelona. Memorias **7902**
0368-8666 Matematicheskii Sbornik **5511**
0368-8798 Bundesforschungsanstalt fuer Forst- und Holzwirtschaft. Mitteilungen **3710**
0368-9123 Il Mondo del Latte, il Latte nel Mondo **267**
0368-9379 Hokkaido University. Faculty of Engineering. Memoirs **3195**
0368-9395 Minzoku Eisei **689**
0368-9530 Technische Hochschule Aachen. Eisenhuettenmaennische Institut. Mitteilungen† **8992**
0368-9638 Kobe University. Faculty of Engineering. Memoirs **3207**
0368-9654 Muenstersche Forschungen zur Geologie und Palaeontologie **2756**
0368-9689 Kyoto University. Faculty of Science. Memoirs. Series of Physics, Astrophysics, Geophysics and Chemistry **7878**
0368-9751 A Magyar Allami Foldtani Intezet evi jelentese **2722**
0368-9913 Mitteilungen zur Geschichte der Medizin der Naturwissenschaften und Technik† **8974**
0369-0369 Osaka University. Institute of Scientific and Industrial Research. Memoirs **8434**
0369-061X Metallurgical Engineer†
0369-1136 Naturwissenschaftlicher Verein fuer Steiermark. Mitteilungen **7890**
0369-1179 Laboratorio Nacional de Engenharia Civil. Memoria **3278**
0369-1276 Morskoi Flot **8653**
0369-1527 Medicinski Podmladak†
0369-1799 Societe Royale des Sciences de Liege. Memoires. Collection in 8†
0369-1829 Royal Astronomical Society, England. Memoirs†
0369-1896 Academie des Sciences, Inscriptions, et Belles Lettres de Toulouse. Memoires **4440**
0369-1950 Waseda University. School of Science and Engineering. Memoirs
0369-2035 Mauritius Sugar Industry Research Institute. Occasional Paper **3655**
0369-2043 Mauritius Sugar Industry Research Institute. Annual Report **3655**
0369-2086 Mineralia Slovaca **6470**
0369-223X Maden Tetkik ve Arama Enstitusu Mecmuasi *see* 0026-4563
0369-2302 Mitsubishi Denki Giho **3325**
0369-2345 Metallgesellschaft Aktiengesellschaft. Review of the Activities† **8974**
0369-3228 Nagasaki Igakkai Zasshi **5682**
0369-3562 Nihon Daigaku Bunrigakubu Shizen Kagaku Kenkyujo Kenkyu Kiyo **7892**
0369-3570 Nagoya Daigaku Kankyo Igaku Kenkyujo Nenpo **5682**
0369-3902 New Zealand Grassland Association. Proceedings **140**
0369-3961 Nippon Genshiryoku Kenkyusho. Kokai J A E R I-Memo†
0369-4232 Nihon Onkyo Gakkaishi **7088**
0369-4275 Nippon Genshiryoku Kenkyusho Kenkyu Hokoku/J A E R I Research Report *changed to* J A E A - Research **3169**
0369-4305 Nippon Hoshasen Gijutsu Gakkai Zasshi **7069**
0369-4313 Nihon Daigaku Rikogaku Kenkyujo Shoho **8433**
0369-4356 Niigata University. Faculty of Science. Science Reports. Series C: Chemistry **2075**
0369-4550 Nihon Kaisui Gakkaishi **2814**
0369-4577 Nippon Kagaku Kaishi†
0369-4585 Nihon Kessho Gakkaishi **2111**
0369-4658 Noyaku Kensasho Hokoku **244**
0369-4771 Nova Acta Leopoldina. Supplementum **7894**
0369-478X N L R Report **66**
0369-5034 Nova Acta Leopoldina **7894**
0369-5123 Nogyo Doboku Gakkai-Shi/Japanese Society of Irrigation, Drainage and Reclamation Engineering. Journal *changed to* 1882-2770 **159**
0369-5247 Nogyo Oyobi Engei **141**
0369-5255 Norsk Pelsdyrblad **4974**
0369-5271 Nova Thalassia† **8978**
0369-5638 Niigata University. Faculty of Science. Science Reports. Series E: Geology and Mineralogy **2759**
0369-5662 Nihon Shashin Gakkaishi **6972**
0369-5867 New South Wales. Department of Agriculture. Science Bulletin **140**
0369-6243 Natura **7887**
0369-6464 Nutrition News (Rosemont)†
0369-674X Nippon Yakuzaishikai Zasshi **6864**
0369-707X Oceanographical Magazine **2815**
0369-710X Osaka Daigaku Igaku Zasshi *changed to* 0030-6169
0369-7649 Onkologia†
0369-7665 Onsen Kogakkaishi **2760**
0369-7762 Organorama†
0369-7827 Osiris (Chicago) **7896**
0369-7843 L'Ospedale Maggiore†
0369-8009 Oyo Buturi **7029**
0369-8106 Akademia Athenon. Praktika **4197**
0369-8114 Pathologie et Biologie **5693**
0369-8173 Progres Agricole et Viticole **249**
0369-8203 National Academy of Sciences, India. Proceedings. Section A. Physical Sciences **7886**
0369-8211 National Academy of Sciences, India. Proceedings. Section B. Biological Sciences **691**
0369-8629 Pchelovodstvo **146**
0369-8963 Periodico di Mineralogia **6475**
0369-9382 Bureau d'Etudes Geologiques et Minieres Coloniales. Publications† **8938**
0369-9420 Pigment & Resin Technology **6720**
0369-9560 Le Photographe **6974**
0369-979X Pharmazie Heute **6875**
0369-9986 Leeds Philosophical and Literary Society. Scientific Section. Proceedings†
0370-0046 Indian National Science Academy. Proceedings. Part A: Physical Sciences *changed to* Indian National Science Academy. Proceedings **7865**
0370-047X Linnean Society of New South Wales. Proceedings **953**
0370-0593 Postgraduate Medical Journal. Supplement **5698**
0370-0747 Polimery w Medycynie **2129**
0370-0755 Politechnika Wroclawska. Instytut Chemii Nieorganicznej i Metalurgii Pierwiastkow Rzadkich. Prace Naukowe. Studia i Materialy†
0370-0798 Politechnika Wroclawska. Instytut Gornictwa. Prace Naukowe. Studia i Materialy†
0370-081X Politechnika Wroclawska. Instytut Chemii Organicznej i Fizycznej. Prace Naukowe. Studia i Materialy†
0370-0828 Politechnika Wroclawska. Instytut Fizyki. Prace Naukowe. Monografie†
0370-0844 Politechnika Wroclawska. Instytut Inzynierii Ladowej. Prace Naukowe. Studia i Materialy†
0370-0852 Politechnika Wroclawska. Instytut Podstaw Elektrotechniki i Elektrotechnologii. Prace Naukowe. Studia i Materialy†
0370-0879 Politechnika Wroclawska. Instytut Technologii Organicznej i Tworzyw Sztucznych. Prace Naukowe. Studia i Materialy†
0370-0887 Politechnika Wroclawska. Instytut Technologii Elektronowej. Prace Naukowe. Konferencje†
0370-0917 Politechnika Wroclawska. Instytut Materialoznawstwa i Mechaniki Technicznej. Prace Naukowe. Studia i Materialy†
0370-1093 Oregon Academy of Science. Proceedings†
0370-1514 Il Progresso Medico†
0370-1573 Physics Reports **7034**
0370-1743 Przeglad Skorzany†
0370-1859 Process Engineering **3253**
0370-1972 Physica Status Solidi. B: Basic Research **7031**
0370-2138 Pontificia Academia Scientiarum. Acta **7899**
0370-2529 Problems of Control and Information Theory†
0370-2596 Comite International des Poids et Mesures. Proces-Verbaux des Seances **6401**
0370-2693 Physics Letters. Section B: Nuclear, Elementary Particle and High-Energy Physics **7071**
0370-2731 New Zealand Society of Animal Production. Proceedings **294**
0370-274X Pis'ma v Zhurnal Eksperimental'noi i Teoreticheskoi Fiziki **7035**
0370-3207 Academia de Ciencias Exactas, Fisico-Quimicas y Naturales. Revista **7829**
0370-3568 Accademia delle Scienze Fisiche e Matematiche. Rendiconto **7831**
0370-3576 Revue Agricole et Sucriere de Maurice **250**
0370-369X Revista Brasileira de Analises Clinicas **5910**
0370-372X Revista Brasileira de Farmacia **6878**
0370-3878 Canterbury Museum. Records **2606**
0370-3908 Academia Colombiana de Ciencias Exactas, Fisicas y Naturales. Revista **7829**
0370-4009 Revista Chilena de Ingenieria **3217**
0370-4106 Revista Chilena de Pediatria **6103**
0370-4165 Rassegna Clinico - Scientifica
0370-4246 University of the Ryukyus. College of Agriculture. Science Bulletin **167**
0370-4254 Ritsumeikan Daigaku Rikogaku Kenkyujo Kiyo **3218**
0370-4327 Redia **298**
0370-4467 Revista da Escola de Minas **3281**
0370-4661 Universidad Nacional de Cuyo. Facultad de Ciencias Agrarias. Revista **165**
0370-5404 Revista Industrial y Agricola de Tucuman **151**
0370-5579 Rinsho Ganka **6051**
0370-5633 Rinsho Kagaku **5707**
0370-5943 Revista Latinoamericana de Quimica **2078**
0370-629X Revue Medicale de Liege **5706**
0370-6486 Revista Mexicana de Radiologia **6207**
0370-6583 Rodriguesia **815**
0370-663X Rostlinna Vyroba *changed to* 1214-1178 **147**
0370-7024 Nihon University. Research Institute of Science and Technology. Report **7892**
0370-7164 Revue Scientifique du Bourbonnais et du Centre de la France **7904**
0370-727X Universita degli Studi di Cagliari. Facolta di Scienze. Seminario. Rendiconti **7926**
0370-7342 Ricerche Spettroscopiche†
0370-7415 Sociedad Mexicana de Historia Natural. Revista **2716**
0370-7466 Research on Steroids **6232**
0370-7687 Universidad Nacional de Cordoba. Revista **2922**
0370-7792 Revista Argentina de Anestesiologia **5773**
0370-7830 Revista de Cirugia *changed to* Hospital Juarez de Mexico. Revista **6245**
0370-7857 Revista Electrotecnica **3329**
0370-7865 Rivista di Viticoltura e di Enologia† **8986**
0370-8047 Ryusan To Kogyo **2079**
0370-8063 Referativnyi Zhurnal. Fotokinotekhnika†
0370-808X Rezanie i Instrument **7062**
0370-8098 Referativnyi Zhurnal. Khimicheskoe, Neftepererabatyvayuschchee i Polimernoe Mashinostroenie **3233**
0370-8179 Srpski Arhiv za Celokupno Lekarstvo **5717**
0370-8241 Saishin Igaku **5708**
0370-8314 South African Museums Association. Bulletin **6537**
0370-8446 Sanfujinka no Shinpo
0370-8462 South African Association for the Advancement of Science. Special Publication *see* 0038-2353 **7919**
0370-8799 Sibirskii Vestnik Sel'skokhozyaistvennoi Nauki **156**
0370-8918 Scottish Beekeeper **155**
0370-9108 Schweizerische Milchzeitung *changed to* Alimenta **261**
0370-9213 Schweizer Strahler **6479**
0370-923X Studia Chemica† **8991**
0370-9361 Suisan Daigakko Kenkyu Hokoku **3609**
0370-9531 Seitai no Kagaku **704**
0370-9574 Senshoku Kogyo **8457**
0370-9590 La Semana Medica **5712**
0370-9736 Siemens Forschungs- und Entwicklungsberichte†
0370-9868 Sekiyu Gijutsu Kyokaishi **6791**
0370-999X Shindan To Chiryo **5714**
0371-0025 Shengxue Xuebao **7089**
0371-005X Shimazu Hyoron **3395**
0371-0424 Societa Italiana per il Progresso delle Scienze. Atti della Riunione **7917**
0371-0459 Scandinavian Journal of Metallurgy *changed to* 1611-3683 **6333**

0371-0548 Ecological Review 670
0371-0580 Sen'i Kikai Gakkaishi 8457
0371-0688 Suhak Kwa Mulli 7042
0371-0785 Suido Kyokai Zasshi 8832
0371-0874 Shengli Xuebao 928
0371-1447 Saneamiento
0371-1838 Soryushiron Kenkyu 7072
0371-1900 Sogo Rinsho 5716
0371-2672 Niigata University. Faculty of Science. Science Reports. Series D: Biology†
0371-2699 Niigata University. Faculty of Science. Science Reports. Series B: Physics 7028
0371-2761 Tohoku University. Science Reports of the Research Institutes. Series C: Medicine†
0371-3067 Sogo Shikenjo Nenpo 3220
0371-3172 Studi Sassaresi
0371-327X Saechsische Akademie der Wissenschaften, Leipzig. Mathematisch-Naturwissenschaftliche Klasse. Sitzungsberichte 7906
0371-3385 Shiga-kenritsu Tanki Daigaku Gakujutsu Zasshi 214
0371-3520 Santo Tomas Journal of Medicine 5709
0371-375X Towarzystwo Naukowe w Toruniu. Sprawozdania
0371-3903 Tohoku University. Science Reports. Series 3: Mineralogy, Petrology and Economic Geology 6480
0371-3970 Prikladnaya Geofizika 2788
0371-4039 Srpska Akademija Nauka i Umetnosti. Odeljenje Medicinskih Nauka. Glas 5717
0371-411X Sumitomo Kinzoku 6334
0371-4217 Suisanzoshoku 3609
0371-4756 Wroclawskie Towarzystwo Naukowe. Sprawozdania. Seria A 7930
0371-5264 Osram-Gesellschaft. Technisch-Wissenschaftliche Abhandlungen†
0371-5345 Tanso 2082
0371-5728 Tecnicas de Laboratorio 5911
0371-5736 Dizhi Lun-Ping 2732
0371-6023 Office de la Recherche Scientifique et Technique Outre-Mer. Travaux et Documents 4023
0371-6147 Technique de l'Eau et de l'Assainissement††
0371-6813 Tokyo Gakugei Daigaku Kiyo†
0371-683X Tijdschrift voor Geneeskunde 5722
0371-6910 Gesellschaft fuer Innere Medizin der Deutschen Demokratischen Republik. Tagungsbericht†† 8959
0371-7453 Institute of Materials, Minerals and Mining. Transactions. Section B: Applied Earth Science 6465
0371-750X Indian Ceramic Society. Transactions 2043
0371-7690 Indian Institute of Chemical Engineers. Transactions 3246
0371-8271 Taiwan Gongcheng Jie changed to 1015-0773 3194
0371-9553 Institute of Materials, Minerals and Mining. Transactions. Section C: Mineral Processing & Extractive Metallurgy 6465
0371-9588 The Mining, Geological and Metallurgical Institute of India. Transactions 6472
0371-9685 Matematicheskii Institut im. V.A. Steklova. Trudy 5511
0372-0187 Newcomen Society for the Study of the History of Engineering and Technology. Transactions changed to 1758-1206 3200
0372-0330 Toyo Daigaku Kiyo. Kyoyo Katei Hen. Shizen Kagaku 7924
0372-0349 Tottori Daigaku Nogakubu Kenkyu Hokoku 163
0372-0365 Toso Gijutsu 6721
0372-039X Toyoda Kenkyu Hokoku 7044
0372-0462 Toshiba Rebyu 3115
0372-1043 Kyoto University. Institute of Atomic Energy. Technical Reports†
0372-1426 Royal Society of South Australia. Transactions 7905
0372-2112 Dianzi Xuebao 3092
0372-2929 Tsvetnye Metally 6336
0372-3283 Vsesoyuznyi Nauchno-Issledovatel'skii Institut Zernovogo Khozyaistva. Trudy
0372-333X Taiwania 707
0372-400X Ukrains'kyi Fizychnyi Zhurnal 7044
0372-4123 Ukrain'skyi Botanichnyi Zhurnal 821
0372-4204 Ukrains'kyi Khimichnyi Zhurnal see 0041-6045 2083
0372-4530 Museo de la Plata. Notas. Geologia 2756
0372-4549 Museo de la Plata. Notas. Zoologia 956
0372-4557 Museo de la Plata. Notas. Botanica 802
0372-4611 Museo de La Plata. Revista. Seccion Botanica 802
0372-462X Museo de La Plata. Revista. Seccion Geologia 2756
0372-4638 Museo de La Plata. Revista. Seccion Zoologia 956
0372-5480 Veterinarski Arhiv 8811
0372-5510 Verniciature e Decorazioni
0372-5715 V G B Kraftwerkstechnik 3333
0372-5758 Voprosy Geografii 4033
0372-588X Voprosy Inzhenernoi Geologii i Gruntovedeniya
0372-5898 Victoria, Australia. Geological Survey. Bulletin†
0372-6053 Kievskii Politekhnicheskii Institut. Vestnik. Mashinostroenie changed to Natsional'nyi Tekhnichnyi Universytet Ukrainy "Kyiv's'kyi Politekhnichnyi Instytut". Visnyk. Mashynobuduvannya 5457
0372-6827 Veterinaria†
0372-7025 Vojenske Zdravotnicke Listy 5728
0372-7114 Waerme
0372-7181 Waseda Daigaku Rikogaku Kenkyujo Hokoku†
0372-7327 Korean Nuclear Society. Journal changed to 1738-5733 7069
0372-7629 Yakuzaigaku 6886
0372-7661 Yamaguchi Daigaku Kogakubu Kenkyu Hokoku (Print) changed to 1345-5583 3227
0372-7726 Yokohama Medical Journal 5734
0372-7785 Tsuruoka: Yamagata Norin Gakkai 163
0372-7858 Yonsei Journal of Medical Science†
0372-798X Zasso Kenkyu 823
0372-8854 Zeitschrift fuer Geomorphologie 2776
0372-9311 Zhurnal Mikrobiologii, Epidemiologii i Immunobiologii 898
0372-9400 Akademia Gorniczo-Hutnicza im. Stanislawa Staszica. Zeszyty Naukowe. Gornictwo†
0372-9427 Akademia Gorniczo-Hutnicza im. Stanislawa Staszica. Zeszyty Naukowe. Geologia†

0372-9443 Akademia Gorniczo-Hutnicza im. Stanislawa Staszica. Zeszyty Naukowe. Metalurgia i Odlewnictwo†
0372-9486 Politechnika Krakowska. Zeszyty Naukowe. Mechanika 7062
0372-9494 Politechnika Slaska. Zeszyty Naukowe. Chemia 2076
0372-9508 Politechnika Slaska. Zeszyty Naukowe. Gornictwo 6476
0372-9524 Politechnika Czestochowska. Zeszyty Naukowe. Nauki Techniczne. Hutnictwo†
0372-9796 Politechnika Slaska. Zeszyty Naukowe. Energetyka 3144
0373-0425 Journal Officiel de la Republique Francaise. Lois et Decrets 4704
0373-045X South African Sugar Technologists' Association. Proceedings 254
0373-0468 Bonner Geographische Abhandlungen 4000
0373-0697 Observatoire Royal de Belgique. Bulletin Astronomique 579
0373-0719 Techniques et Architecture†
0373-0778 Academie Royale des Sciences, des Lettres et des Beaux-Arts de Belgique. Annuaire 4440
0373-0786 Indian Science Congress Association. Proceedings 7865
0373-0840 Livres de l'Annee, Bibliot
0373-0875 Societe Linneenne de Provence. Bulletin†
0373-0883 International Journal for Vitamin and Nutrition Research. Supplement see 0300-9831 6849
0373-0891 Annales des Travaux Publics de Belgique 3259
0373-0956 Institut Fourier. Annales 5493
0373-0972 Palaeontographia Italica 6727
0373-1006 Seppyo 2716
0373-1022 Journal of Pharmacy and Pharmacology. Supplement see 0022-3573 6856
0373-1170 Facultad de Veterinaria de Leon. Anales 8797
0373-1243 Universita e Politecnico di Torino. Seminario Matematico. Rendiconti 5544
0373-1332 Sumarski List 3703
0373-174X Glowna Biblioteka Lekarska. Biuletyn 5620
0373-1928 Etudes Celtiques 5117
0373-1944 Travail et Securite 6688
0373-1987 Bibliografia Geologiczna Polski 2719
0373-1995 Institution of Engineers (India). Civil Engineering Division. Journal 3272
0373-2002 Revista de Psicologia General y Aplicada 7404
0373-2010 Officiel des Textiles†
0373-2029 Archives of Mechanics 7057
0373-2061 Bulletin Scientifique de Bourgogne 7842
0373-2134 Prirodnjacki Muzej u Beogradu. Glasnik. Serija B: Bioloske Nauke changed to Natural History Museum in Belgrade. Bulletin 2757
0373-2266 Ardea 901
0373-241X Glasgow Naturalist 675
0373-2428 Zarubezhnaya Radioelektronika changed to Zarubezhnaya Radioelektronika. Uspekhi Sovremennoi Elektroniki 3116
0373-2444 Rossiiskaya Akademiya Nauk. Izvestiya. Seriya Geograficheskaya 4027
0373-2517 Revue de Pathologie Comparee et de Medecine Experimentale†
0373-2525 Saussurea 816
0373-2541 Istituto Veneto di Scienze, Lettere ed Arti. Atti. Classe Scienze Morali, Fisiche e Parte Generale e Atti Ufficiali 7869
0373-2568 Pirineos 697
0373-2630 Revue d'Economie Politique 1167
0373-2681 Gazeta de Matematica 5489
0373-2746 Maanedsskrift for Praktisk Laegegerning 5663
0373-2851 Revue des Sciences Naturelles d'Auvergne 701
0373-286X Office International des Epizooties. Statistiques
0373-2916 Le Strade 3283
0373-2959 Schweizerische Zeitschrift fuer Pilzkunde 816
0373-2967 Candollea 783
0373-2975 Boissiera 780
0373-3009 Archivio per l'Antropologia e la Etnologia† 8931
0373-3076 Societe Neuchateloise de Geographie. Bulletin 356
0373-3092 Naturforschende Gesellschaft Schaffhausen. Mitteilungen 7889
0373-3114 Annali di Matematica Pura ed Applicata 5470
0373-3149 International Series of Numerical Mathematics 5498
0373-3165 Buecherei des Paediaters
0373-3181 Comite International des Poids et Mesures. Comite Consultatif des Unites (Rapport et Annexes)† 8942
0373-3297 Societe Languedocienne de Geographie. Bulletin changed to 1637-6978
0373-3343 Astronomicheskii Ezhegodnik 570
0373-3491 Societa Entomologica Italiana. Bollettino 859
0373-3505 Le Matematiche 5510
0373-3602 Japan. Maritime Safety Agency. Hydrographic Department. Report of Hydrographic Research 2711
0373-3629 Annales Hydrographiques 8638
0373-3823 Museo de La Plata. Revista. Seccion Paleontologia 6727
0373-384X Naturforschende Gesellschaft Graubuenden. Jahresbericht 7889
0373-3874 Dansk Naturhistorisk Forening. Videnskabelige Meddelelser†
0373-3998 Organisation Mondiale de la Sante. Serie de Rapports Techniques 5690
0373-403X Chmelarstvi
0373-4064 Metal Bulletin Monthly 6323
0373-4102 Rivista Italiana del Petrolio e delle Altre Fonti di Energia†
0373-4110 Universita degli Studi di Genova. Musei e Istituti Biologici. Bollettino 709
0373-4153 Osservatorio Astrofisico di Arcetri. Osservazioni e Memorie 579
0373-4242 Entomological Society of Southern Africa. Memoirs 845
0373-4250 Associated Scientific and Technical Societies of South Africa. Annual Proceedings 7837
0373-4285 Recherche et Architecture†
0373-4293 Blumea. Supplement 780
0373-4331 Betonwerk und Fertigteil-Technik 982

0373-434X Commission Internationale pour l'Exploitation Scientifique de la Mer Mediterranee. Rapport du Congres 666
0373-4447 Library and Information Science 5026
0373-4463 Meteorologiske Annaler 6391
0373-4544 Societe Entomologique de Mulhouse. Bulletin 859
0373-4625 Abeille de France et l'Apiculteur 78
0373-4633 Journal of Navigation 8648
0373-4641 Sociedade Broteriana. Anuario 818
0373-465X Koninklijke Nederlandse Akademie van Wetenschappen. Afdeling Natuurkunde. Verhandelingen. Tweede Reeks
0373-4722 University of Tokyo. Faculty of Science. Journal. Section 5: Anthropology†
0373-4838 Canada Department of Energy, Mines and Resources. Publications of the Earth Physics Branch 3125
0373-4854 Auroral Observatory. Magnetic Observations 572
0373-5125 Observatorio Astronomico de Madrid. Anuario 579
0373-5133 Revue du Bois et de ses Applications†
0373-5346 Railway Gazette International 8623
0373-5354 Tudomanyos Tajekoztatas Elmelete es Gyakorlata†
0373-5478 Archives d'Histoire Doctrinale et Litteraire du Moyen Age 6905
0373-5656 Anthropologische Gesellschaft in Wien. Mitteilungen 326
0373-5680 Sociedad Entomologica Argentina. Revista 859
0373-5737 Revue des Etudes Latines 2239
0373-580X Sociedad Argentina de Botanica. Boletin 817
0373-5834 Cahiers d'Outre-Mer†
0373-5842 Koso Kishodai Iho 6360
0373-5850 Station Biologique de Besse en Chandesse. Annales†
0373-5885 Welt des Kindes 7823
0373-5893 Zoological Society, Calcutta. Proceedings 970
0373-5907 Universita di Ferrara. Annali. Sezione 3: Biologia Animale 709
0373-5915 Universita di Ferrara. Annali. Sezione 13: Anatomia e Fisiologia Comparata 928
0373-5923 Universita di Ferrara. Annali. Sezione 6: Fisiologia e Chimica Biologica 928
0373-5931 Universita di Ferrara. Annali. Sezione 4: Botanica 821
0373-5982 Postepy Astronautyki 68
0373-6067 Universite de Grenoble. Laboratoire d'Hydrologie et de Pisciculture. Travaux†
0373-6075 Revue d'Histoire des Textes 5362
0373-6156 Revue Generale de Droit International Public 4939
0373-6172 Paris et Ile de France 4253
0373-6237 Bibliotheque de l'Ecole des Chartes 4133
0373-6245 South African Geographical Journal 4029
0373-6296 Etudes Nigeriennes 338
0373-630X Semitica 4474
0373-6407 Referativnyi Zhurnal. Aviatsionnye i Raketnye Dvigateli 76
0373-6415 Referativnyi Zhurnal. Gornoe i Neftepromyslovoe Mashinostroenie 6486
0373-6474 Universidade de Coimbra. Museu e Laboratorio Mineralogico e Geologico. Publicacoes. Memorias e Noticas 2772
0373-6512 Excerpta Medica. Section 7: Pediatrics and Pediatric Surgery 5746
0373-6547 Polska Akademia Nauk. Instytut Geografii i Przestrzennego Zagospodarowania. Prace Geograficzne 4024
0373-658X Voprosy Yazykoznaniya 5194
0373-6601 R F M Revue Francaise de Mecanique changed to 1296-2139 3389
0373-6687 Journal of Bryology 796
0373-675X Rybarstvi 3606
0373-6776 Mechanizace Zemedelstvi 212
0373-6873 Societas pro Fauna et Flora Fennica. Memoranda 705
0373-689X Zeitschrift fuer die Binnenfischerei der DDR†
0373-7063 Academie Royale des Sciences d'Outre-Mer. Classe des Sciences Techniques. Collection in 4 7830
0373-7101 Spain. Observatorio Astronomico Nacional. Boletin Astronomico†
0373-7160 Geographical Survey Institute, Tokyo. Bulletin 4011
0373-7187 Arbeiten zur Rheinischen Landeskunde 3999
0373-7500 Grotte d'Italia† 8960
0373-7586 Naturkundemuseums Goerlitz. Abhandlungen und Berichte 804
0373-7640 Bayerische Botanische Gesellschaft. Berichte 778
0373-7837 Instytut Hodowli i Aklimatyzacji Roslin. Biuletyn 181
0373-7934 Acta Cardiologica. Supplementum 5775
0373-8221 Mathematischen Seminar Giessen. Mitteilungen
0373-8256 Electronique Nouvelle
0373-8299 Annales Societatis Mathematicae Polonae. Series 1: Commentationes Mathematicae - Prace Matematyczne 5470
0373-8302 Polskie Towarzystwo Matematyczne. Roczniki. Seria 2: Wiadomosci Matematyczne 5525
0373-8361 Nippon Veterinary and Zootechnical College. Bulletin changed to Nippon Veterinary and Life Science University. Bulletin 8803
0373-840X Pesquisas: Publicacoes de Botanica 807
0373-8418 Pesquisas: Publicacoes de Zoologia 960
0373-8442 Societe d'Histoire Naturelle des Ardennes. Bulletin 705
0373-8531 Filmoteca Ultramarina Portuguesa. Boletim 4139
0373-8558 Akademia Gorniczo-Hutnicza im. Stanislawa Staszica. Zeszyty Naukowe†
0373-8647 Politechnika Gdanska. Zeszyty Naukowe. Elektryka 3327
0373-8663 Politechnika Gdanska. Zeszyty Naukowe. Budownictwo Wodne 3363
0373-8671 Politechnika Gdanska. Zeszyty Naukowe. Budownictwo Ladowe 3280
0373-868X Politechnika Gdanska. Zeszyty Naukowe. Budownictwo Okretowe 8656
0373-8698 Politechnika Gdanska. Zeszyty Naukowe. Elektronika 2463
0373-8701 Societe d'Horticulture et d'Histoire Naturelle de l'Herault. Annales 7918
0373-8868 R & D Kobe Seiko Giho 6330
0373-8884 Elektro Radio Handel†
0373-8957 Societe des Etudes Oceaniennes. Bulletin 356

9274 0373-8981 ULRICH'S PERIODICALS

0373-8981 Staatliches Museum fuer Tierkunde Dresden. Entomologische Abhandlungen *changed to* 1863-7221 **839**
0373-9066 Museo Argentino de Ciencias Naturales "Bernardino Rivadavia." Instituto Nacional de Investigacion de las Ciencias Naturales. Revista. Zoologia†
0373-9090 Association Internationale de Signalisation Maritime. Bulletin **8639**
0373-9139 Ciel et Espace **573**
0373-9252 Algebra i Logika **5468**
0373-9260 Anais Hidrograficos **8817**
0373-9465 Folia Entomologica Hungarica **848**
0373-9570 Terra **7923**
0373-9767 Akademie der Wissenschaften zu Goettingen. Jahrbuch **7833**
0373-9856 Przemysl Drzewny **3715**
0373-9864 Poligrafika **7325**
0373-9929 Societe des Sciences Naturelles de la Charente-Maritime. Annales **914**
0374-0056 Eidgenoessische Technische Hochschule Zuerich. Versuchsanstalt fuer Wasserbau, Hydrologie und Glaziologie. Mitteilungen **2794**
0374-0315 Slovenska Akademija Znanosti in Umetnosti. Letopis **518**
0374-0323 Sociedad Argentina de Estudios Geograficos. Anales **4028**
0374-0390 Greek Speleological Society. Deltion **2745**
0374-0463 Acta Linguistica Hafniensia **5089**
0374-048X Deutsche Gesellschaft fuer Gerontologie. Veroeffentlichungen† **8949**
0374-0501 Universo **583**
0374-0641 Differentsial'nye Uravneniya **5483**
0374-0676 Information Bulletin on Variable Stars **575**
0374-0706 Societe d'Histoire Naturelle de Colmar. Bulletin **818**
0374-0730 Univerzitet u Novom Sadu. Filozofski Fakultet. Godisnjak **6959**
0374-0781 Academie Serbe des Sciences et des Arts. Classe des Sciences Techniques.Bulletin **8415**
0374-082X Srpska Akademija Nauka i Umetnosti. Glasnik†
0374-0854 Techniques Industrielles du Japon
0374-1036 Musei Nationalis Pragae. Acta Entomologica **855**
0374-1222 Schiffbautechnischen Gesellschaft. Jahrbuch **8660**
0374-1257 Max-Planck-Institut fuer Stroemungsforschung. Mitteilungen†
0374-1338 Reumatizam **6226**
0374-1346 Association des Geologues du Bassin de Paris. Bulletin d'Information **2725**
0374-1583 Abhandlungen aus der Hamburger Sternwarte **568**
0374-1834 Bulletin Analytique de la Litterature Scientifique et Technique Roumaine†
0374-1893 Geologica Hungarica. Series Palaeontologica **6725**
0374-1958 Astronomische Gesellschaft. Mitteilungen **570**
0374-1990 Funktsional'nyi Analiz i Ego Prilozheniya **5489**
0374-2105 Oftalmologia†
0374-2113 Conferenze del Seminario di Matematica dell'Universita di Bari *changed to* 1660-5446 **5517**
0374-2261 Le Trefile
0374-2288 Courrier C E R N *see* 0304-288X **7065**
0374-2466 Tenmon Geppo **582**
0374-258X A E C L Research and Development in Engineering†
0374-2687 Israel Physical Society. Bulletin **7018**
0374-2725 Mechanical Engineering Laboratory. Bulletin **3389**
0374-2822 C A M A C Bulletin **2459**
0374-3063 Electronics Today (Bombay) **3097**
0374-3098 Das Elektron International
0374-3101 Electro-Revue **3304**
0374-3136 E R A Journal†
0374-3268 Geos†
0374-339X Ingenieria Mecanica y Electrica **3379**
0374-3535 Journal of Elasticity **3349**
0374-3632 Kodaikanal Observatory Bulletin. Series A **577**
0374-3667 Kodaikanal Observatory Bulletin. Series B **577**
0374-3721 London Gazette **4725**
0374-3799 Materials Research in A E C L†
0374-387X Universita degli Studi di Roma. Istituto di Automatica. Notiziario†
0374-3896 Naukovedenie i Informatika†
0374-406X Perkin-Elmer N M R Quarterly† **8980**
0374-4256 La Revue Polytechnique **8437**
0374-4272 Revista Astronomica **580**
0374-4329 Nagoya University. Faculty of Engineering. Automatic Control Laboratory. Research Reports†
0374-4345 Niigata Daigaku Kogakubu Kenkyu Hokoku **3212**
0374-4353 Research Disclosure **6757**
0374-4361 Radio & Electronics Constructor†
0374-4493 Systemes Logiques†
0374-4663 Takenaka Gijutsu Kenkyu Hokoku **1039**
0374-4779 Vrashchenie i Prilivnye Deformatsii Zemli†
0374-4795 Works Management **1801**
0374-4809 X-Ray Focus†
0374-4817 Politechnika Lodzka. Zeszyty Naukowe. Elektryka **3327**
0374-4884 Korean Physical Society. Journal **7024**
0374-4914 Sae Mulli **7039**
0374-4981 Universita degli Studi di Perugia. Facolta di Agraria. Annali† **8996**
0374-504X Denmark. Ministeriet for Foedevarer, Landbrug og Fiskeri. Aarsberetning **227**
0374-5066 Acta Botanica Islandica **772**
0374-5147 Australian Entomological Society. Miscellaneous Publications **840**
0374-5317 Instituto Nacional de Antropologia e Historia. Anales†
0374-535X Istituto Sperimentale per la Cerealicoltura. Annali†
0374-549X Universite de Madagascar. Etablissement d'Enseignement Superieur des Sciences. Annales: Serie Sciences de la Nature et Mathematiques **7926**
0374-5686 Arquivos de Ciencias do Mar **2800**
0374-5708 Aquila†
0374-5791 Istituto Sperimentale per l'Enologia Asti. Annali **605**
0374-5929 Nova Acta Regiae Societatis Scientiarum Upsaliensis. C, Botany, General Geology, Physical Geography, Palaeontology and Zoology **7894**
0374-5961 Aberdeen University Studies
0374-6003 Ecole Nationale Superieure d'Agronomie et des Industries Alimentaires. Bulletin†
0374-6054 Naturhistorische Gesellschaft Hannover. Beihefte zu den Berichten **693**
0374-6070 Hospitais Civis de Lisboa. Boletim Clinico **5629**
0374-6097 Instituto Nacional de Pesca del Ecuador. Boletin Cientifico y Tecnico **3598**
0374-6232 Institut Royal des Sciences Naturelles de Belgique. Bulletin. Serie Entomologie **850**
0374-6240 Florida Genealogical Society Journal **3766**
0374-6291 Institut Royal des Sciences Naturelles de Belgique. Bulletin. Serie Sciences de la Terre **2747**
0374-6402 Bulletin de la Murithienne **2703**
0374-6429 Institut Royal des Sciences Naturelles de Belgique. Bulletin. Serie Biologie **678**
0374-647X Academia Nacional de Medicina. Boletin **5564**
0374-6569 Bionika†
0374-6658 Brazil. Departamento Nacional de Obras Contra as Secas. Boletim Tecnico **3587**
0374-6771 Carinthia II **4209**
0374-7042 Caribbean Medical Journal†
0374-7115 Central Plantation Crops Research Institute. Annual Report **100**
0374-7123 Museo de Historia Natural de Montevideo. Comunicaciones Paleontologicas **6727**
0374-7387 E A N H S Bulletin **669**
0374-7417 Epistemonike Epeteris Kteniatrikes Scholes
0374-7506 Ergebnisse der Experimentellen Medizin†
0374-7530 Etnologiska Studier **338**
0374-7638 Folia Anatomica Universitatis Conimbricensis
0374-776X Rofeh ha-Mishpacha†
0374-7859 Gardens' Bulletin, Singapore **791**
0374-7867 Dep. Plantengenetica en-Veredeling. Activiteitenverslag **3728**
0374-7913 Giornale Italiano delle Malattie del Torace. Supplemento *see* 1127-0810 **6214**
0374-7921 Goeteborgs Naturhistoriska Museum. Aarstryck **6524**
0374-7956 Srpska Akademija Nauka i Umetnosti. Odeljenje Prirodno-Matematickih Nauka. Glas **7920**
0374-8014 Health Bulletin
0374-8111 Hangug Susan Haghoi Ji **3596**
0374-8189 Instituto de Economia y Producciones Ganaderas del Ebro. Comunicaciones **122**
0374-826X Indian Journal of Heredity **872**
0374-8278 Inmersion y Ciencia†
0374-8405 Irish Colleges of Physicians and Surgeons. Journal *changed to* 1479-666X **6259**
0374-8545 College of Radiologists of Australasia. Journal *changed to* 1754-9477 **6200**
0374-860X Kerala Academy of Biology. Journal†
0374-8669 Journal of Phytopathology of the United Arab Republic *changed to* 1110-0230 **786**
0374-8715 Kinki Daigaku Genshiryoku Kenkyujo Nenpo **3170**
0374-874X Kyoto-Furitsu Daigaku Nogakubu Enshurin Hokoku **3695**
0374-8804 Kagawa Prefecture Agricultural Experiment Station. Bulletin **129**
0374-9002 Academie Malgache. Memoires **7830**
0374-9037 Forstliche Bundesversuchsanstalt. Mitteilungen **3691**
0374-9045 Medicina Fisica y Rehabilitacion **6112**
0374-9061 Geographische Gesellschaft in Hamburg. Mitteilungen **4012**
0374-9096 Mikrobiyoloji Bulteni **892**
0374-9169 Mikrobiyoloji Bulteni Supplement†
0374-9231 Societe Nationale des Sciences Naturelles et Mathematiques de Cherbourg. Memoires **7918**
0374-955X Natuurhistorisch Genootschap in Limburg. Publicaties **693**
0374-9584 Nigerian Journal of Forestry **3698**
0374-9797 Nouvelle Revue d'Entomologie **856**
0374-9800 National Centre for Occupational Health. Annual Report **6681**
0374-9851 Nihon Contact Lens Gakkaishi **6046**
0374-9894 Nature Canada **2621**
0375-0183 Odonatologica **695**
0375-0191 Oosaka Kogyo Daigaku Kiyo. Riko Hen **8434**
0375-0299 Palaeontographica. Abt. B: Palaeophytologie **6728**
0375-0442 Palaeontographica. Abt. A: Palaeozoologie - Stratigraphie **6727**
0375-0752 Universidad Nacional de Rosario. Facultad de Ciencias Medicas. Revista **5726**
0375-0760 Revista Cubana de Medicina Tropical **5825**
0375-0884 Universidad de San Carlos de Guatemala. Facultad de Medicina Veterinaria y Zootecnia Revista **8809**
0375-0906 Revista de Gastroenterologia de Mexico **5930**
0375-0922 Rehabilitacia **6115**
0375-1155 Museo Municipal de Historia Natural de San Rafael. Revista **7883**
0375-1325 Revue Suisse d'Agriculture **152**
0375-1430 Revue Suisse de Viticulture, Arboriculture et Horticulture **251**
0375-1465 Revue Vervietoise d'Histoire Naturelle **701**
0375-1511 India. Zoological Survey. Records **947**
0375-1589 South African Journal of Animal Science **301**
0375-1651 Sellowia **816**
0375-1821 Saito Ho-on Kai Museum of Natural History. Research Bulletin **7906**
0375-2038 Svenska Linne-Saellskapet. Aarsskrift **819**
0375-2135 Staatliches Museum fuer Tierkunde Dresden. Faunistische Abhandlungen **964**
0375-250X Statens Offentliga Utredningar **7470**
0375-2682 South African Sugar Association Experiment Station. Annual Report **254**
0375-2909 Steenstrupia **964**
0375-2984 Sudan Notes and Records **4325**
0375-3050 Sarawak Museum Journal **355**
0375-3077 Tea Research Association. Advisory Bulletin **611**
0375-3220 Colleges of Medicine of South Africa. Transactions **5599**
0375-3417 Instituto de Economia y Producciones Ganaderas del Ebro. Trabajos **122**
0375-4065 Zimbabwe. Tobacco Research Board. Annual Report and Accounts **8489**
0375-4588 University of New England. Annual Report **3009**
0375-4634 Museo de la Plata. Notas. Antropologia **348**
0375-4855 Zemedelske Muzeum. Vedecke Prace†
0375-4928 Vyskumny Ustav Luk a Pasienkov v Banskej Bystrici. Vedecke Prace†
0375-5207 Yonsei Reports on Tropical Medicine† **8999**
0375-5231 Staatliches Museum fuer Tierkunde Dresden. Zoologische Abhandlungen *changed to* 1864-5755 **966**
0375-5290 Zeitschrift des Koelner Zoos **968**
0375-5363 Victoria University of Wellington Zoology Publications†
0375-538X Universidad del Zulia. Centro de Investigaciones Biologicas. Boletin **709**
0375-5444 Dili Xuebao **4004**
0375-5452 Acta Humboldtiana. Series Geologica, Palaeontologica et Biologica†
0375-605X Canadian Rock Mechanics Symposium. Proceedings†
0375-6068 Carinthia II. Sonderheft *see* 0374-6771 **4209**
0375-6084 Catalogus Fossilium Austria†
0375-6157 Colorado Geological Survey. Bulletin **2729**
0375-6343 Forschungen zur Deutschen Landeskunde **4006**
0375-6386 Geographical Review of India **4011**
0375-6505 Geothermics **2708**
0375-6718 Johns Hopkins University Studies in Geology
0375-6742 Journal of Geochemical Exploration **2711**
0375-7145 New Mexico State University. Water Resources Research Institute. Report **8830**
0375-7226 Norfolk and Norwich Naturalists' Society. Transactions **2622**
0375-7315 Oak Ridge National Laboratory. Report **3173**
0375-7331 University of Ottawa. Department of Geography. Research Notes†
0375-7471 Quartaer **412**
0375-7536 Revista Brasileira de Geociencias **2715**
0375-7587 Scripta Geologica **2766**
0375-7633 Societa Paleontologica Italiana. Bollettino **6730**
0375-7765 Tecnia **3222**
0375-7773 Tektonika i Stratigrafiya†
0375-7854 Tohoku University. Science Reports. Series 7: Geography **4031**
0375-8265 Wisconsin Geological and Natural History Survey. Bulletin **2774**
0375-8370 Acta Cientifica Venezolana. Suplemento *see* 0001-5504 **7832**
0375-8419 Rossiiskaya Akademiya Nauk. Institut Okeanologii im. P.P. Shirshova. Trudy
0375-8427 Veterinarni Medicina **8811**
0375-8621 Bayerisches Landwirtschaftliches Jahrbuch†
0375-880X Current Topics in Radiation Research Quarterly†
0375-8842 Energetika **3158**
0375-8990 Gidrobiologicheskii Zhurnal **675**
0375-9172 Tokyo Jikeikai Ika Daigaku Zasshi *see* 0021-6968 **5644**
0375-9202 Tokyo Nogyo Daigaku Nogaku Shuho **162**
0375-9237 Egyptian Journal of Botany
0375-9253 Kagaku Kogaku **3249**
0375-9318 Material und Organismen. Beihefte†
0375-9342 Medicinski Glasnik†
0375-9393 Minerva Anestesiologica **5772**
0375-9415 Molekulyarnaya Biologiya (Kiev)†
0375-9474 Nuclear Physics, Section A **7069**
0375-9504 Banyaszati es Kohaszati Lapok - Ontode†
0375-9598 Physical Society of Japan. Journal. Supplement **7032**
0375-9601 Physics Letters. Section A: General, Atomic and Solid State Physics **7070**
0375-9636 Pollen et Spores†
0375-9660 Problemy Endokrinologii **5899**
0375-9687 Progress of Theoretical Physics. Supplement **7036**
0375-9717 Referativnyi Zhurnal. Geodeziya i Aeros'emka **2720**
0375-9857 Societa Geologica Italiana. Memorie **2767**
0376-0030 Universidad Central de Venezuela. Facultad de Agronomia. Revista Alcance **165**
0376-0421 Progress in Aerospace Sciences **68**
0376-0456 Universidad Nacional del Litoral. Facultad de Ingenieria Quimica. Revista†
0376-0537 Iwate Daigaku Kogakubu Kenkyu Hokoku **3204**
0376-2025 Societe Royale Belge d'Entomologie. Memoires **859**
0376-2041 Museo Nacional de Historia Natural. Noticiario Mensual **7884**
0376-2149 Museo de La Plata. Revista. Seccion Antropologia **348**
0376-2173 Roczniki Nauk Rolniczych. Seria H. Rybactwo†
0376-2491 Zhonghua Yixue Zazhi **5738**
0376-2599 Visindafelag Islendinga. Rit **7928**
0376-2726 Societa Italiana di Scienze Naturali e del Museo Civico di Storia Naturale. Memorie **7917**
0376-2793 Museo Argentino de Ciencias Naturales "Bernardino Rivadavia." Instituto Nacional de Investigacion de las Ciencias Naturales. Revista. Botanica†
0376-4001 Utrechtse Geografische Studies†
0376-401X Die Sprache **5177**
0376-4087 S C I M A
0376-4109 Indian Philosophical Annual **6925**
0376-415X Indian Philosophical Quarterly **6925**
0376-4206 I C S S R Research Abstracts Quarterly†
0376-4230 Contributions to Vertebrate Evolution†
0376-4249 Current Topics in Critical Care Medicine†
0376-4265 E S A Bulletin **53**
0376-429X American Journal of Arabic Studies†
0376-4354 Black Review†
0376-4370 Revista de Investigaciones Pecuarias *changed to* 1682-3419 **8806**
0376-4435 A G A R D Manual
0376-4605 Annual Survey of South African Law **4618**
0376-4672 Daehan Ci'gwa Yisa Hyeob'hoeji **5839**
0376-4699 Indian Journal of Chemistry. Section B: Organic and Medicinal Chemistry **2064**
0376-4710 Indian Journal of Chemistry. Section A: Inorganic, Physical, Theoretical and Analytical Chemistry **2064**
0376-4745 Electrotehnica, Electronica si Automatica. Electrotehnica **3305**
0376-4753 E S A R B I C A Journal **5007**

0376-477X Zhonghua Nongye Yanjiu/Journal of Agricultural Research of China *changed to* 0022-4847 160
0376-4788 Indian Roads Congress. Highway Research Bulltein 8631
0376-480X Advances in Pollen Spore Research 774
0376-4826 Steirische Beitraege zur Hydrogeologie 2798
0376-4842 Current Awareness in Particle Technology†
0376-4974 Agroconocimiento 87
0376-5016 O P T I M A Newsletter 806
0376-5024 Asociacion de Escribanos del Uruguay. Revista 4622
0376-5032 Print Letter†
0376-5040 Core Journals in Pediatrics 5743
0376-5059 Core Journals in Obstetrics / Gynecology 5743
0376-5067 Trends in Biochemical Sciences (Reference Edition)†
0376-5083 I R R I C A B: Current Annotated Bibliography of Irrigation†
0376-5091 Excerpta Medica. Section 37: Drug Literature Index†
0376-5156 Geophytology 6725
0376-5202 Guyanese National Bibliography 626
0376-5229 Guide to Electronics Industry in India 3100
0376-5253 Graezer Beitraege 396
0376-5423 Meghalaya Industrial Development Corporation. Annual Report 1148
0376-5466 India. Department of Space. Annual Report 59
0376-5482 European Commission. Joint Research Center. Annual Report 7134
0376-5512 Andhra Pradesh State Trading Corporation Limited. Annual Report 1805
0376-5695 Foreign Trade Statistics of Yemen Arab Republic 1233
0376-5725 Reserve Bank of Malawi. Financial and Economic Review 1514
0376-5776 Congress Marches Ahead 7118
0376-6039 Books Ireland 7555
0376-6357 Behavioural Processes 6126
0376-6411 Terra et Aqua 8663
0376-6438 O E C D Economic Surveys 1502
0376-6608 Masihi Avaza 7662
0376-6616 Banker's World Directory
0376-6764 Moniteur Belge 4736
0376-6802 N I V A G Contour
0376-6829 Neue Zuercher Zeitung 3958
0376-6853 Schweizer Bauwirtschaft 1035
0376-6861 Rivista Tecnica 3218
0376-6918 Auto + Motor Techniek 8557
0376-6926 Cantieri 990
0376-7124 Instituto de Ciencias de la Construccion Eduardo Torroja. Monografias†
0376-7191 Quarterly Economic Commentary 1163
0376-7213 Construction and Property News 994
0376-723X I M M E Boletin Tecnico 3269
0376-7256 Indian Highways 3269
0376-7272 Vaare Veger 3287
0376-7299 Revista Latinoamericana de Geotecnia 3282
0376-7302 Plan 453
0376-7329 Advances in Research and Technology of Seeds†
0376-7361 Developments in Petroleum Science 6767
0376-737X Journal of Chromatography. Supplementary Volume *see* 0021-9673 2101
0376-737X Journal of Chromatography. Supplementary Volume *see* 0301-4770 2101
0376-7388 Journal of Membrane Science 2137
0376-7396 Meyler's Side Effects of Drugs 6861
0376-7418 Philosophy and Medicine 6942
0376-7442 Tijdschrift voor Kindergeneeskunde 6104
0376-7450 Cobalt and Cobalt Abstracts†
0376-7558 Fiji. Bureau of Statistics. Consumer Price Index†
0376-7574 Contributions to Nepalese Studies 4181
0376-7582 Corps Medical 5600
0376-7604 Current Management Literature 1223
0376-7639 Cahiers de Medecine du Travail
0376-7655 Cajanus 6656
0376-7701 Caribbean Journal of Education†
0376-771X Carte d'Identite du Senegal†
0376-7787 C C A I Monthly News Letter 6459
0376-7868 Chartered Secretary
0376-7892 Cirugia Plastica Ibero Latinoamericana 6239
0376-7965 Conservation of Cultural Property in India 388
0376-804X Andhra Pradesh Small Scale Industrial Development Corporation. Annual Report 1956
0376-8090 Damilica
0376-8163 Degres 5110
0376-818X Dengue Newsletter for the Americas
0376-8201 Depthnews Indonesia 3891
0376-835X Development Southern Africa 1594
0376-8430 International Association of Law Libraries. Directory 5018
0376-8465 Kenya. Ministry of Foreign Affairs. Directory of Diplomatic Corps & International Organizations 7249
0376-8481 Kenya. Central Bureau of Statistics. Directory of Industries 2010
0376-8546 Directory of Public Enterprises in India
0376-8554 Directory of Scientific Research in Indian Universities†
0376-8678 International Labour Conference. Draft Programme and Budget and Other Financial Questions 1689
0376-8686 Dutch Studies†
0376-8716 Drug and Alcohol Dependence 2693
0376-8791 Economic Survey of Singapore 1481
0376-8864 Kenya. Central Bureau of Statistics. Employment and Earnings in the Modern Sector 1247
0376-8902 English in Africa 5215
0376-8929 Environmental Conservation 3423
0376-9011 Pakistan. Finance Division. Estimates of Foreign Assistance 1938
0376-9100 Everest Review
0376-9208 Pakistan. Finance Division. Economic Analysis of the Budget 1938
0376-933X Fiji Library Directory 5009
0376-9410 I Z A 6678
0376-9429 International Journal of Fracture 3347
0376-9453 Amtsblatt der Europaeischen Gemeinschaften. L: Rechtsvorschriften *see* Official Journal of the European Union. L Series: Legislation 7256

0376-9461 Amtsblatt der Europaischen Gemeinschaften. C: Mitteilungen und Bekanntmachungen *see* 1725-2423 7256
0376-9461 Amtsblatt der Europaischen Gemeinschaften. C: Mitteilungen und Bekanntmachungen *see* 0257-7763 4923
0376-9496 Connexion *see* 0250-4499 3412
0376-9569 Highlander 4014
0376-9631 History in Malawi 4175
0376-9682 I C H R Newsletter 4183
0376-9771 India International Centre Quarterly 7241
0376-9836 Indian Historical Review 4183
0376-9844 Indian Journal of Criminology 2654
0376-9852 Indian Journal of Engineers†
0376-9879 Indian Journal of Social Sciences 7972
0376-9887 Indian Miller
0376-9909 Indian Railways Yearbook 8526
0376-9941 Indice Industrial - Anuario de la Industria Uruguaya 1888
0376-9968 Indo-Burma Petroleum Company. Annual Report 6773
0376-9976 Indonesian Shipping Directory
0376-9984 Indonesia Statistics†
0377-0001 Indonesian Commercial Newsletter 1429
0377-0036 Industrial Herald 1888
0377-0087 Inkworld 4596
0377-0125 Sudan. Department of Statistics. Internal Trade and Other Statistics 1268
0377-0141 International Journal of Critical Sociology 8109
0377-015X International Journal of Ecology and Environmental Sciences 3441
0377-0168 International Journal of Zoonoses†
0377-0192 Commission of the European Communities. Directorate of Taxation. Inventory of Taxes 1917
0377-0214 Iran Banking Almanac
0377-0257 Journal of Non-Newtonian Fluid Mechanics 7059
0377-0265 Dynamics of Atmospheres and Oceans 6352
0377-0273 Journal of Volcanology and Geothermal Research 2785
0377-0400 Journal of Applied Medicine†
0377-0427 Journal of Computational and Applied Mathematics 5502
0377-0435 Journal of Indian Education 2876
0377-0443 Journal of Kerala Studies 4184
0377-0451 Korean Journal of International Studies† 8970
0377-046X Journal of Molecular Medicine†
0377-0486 Journal of Raman Spectroscopy 2103
0377-0494 Journal of Shipping, Customs, and Transport Law
0377-0508 Journal of Social and Economic Studies 7980
0377-0524 All India Institute of Speech and Hearing. Journal
0377-0648 Jawaharlal Nehru University. School of Languages. Journal†
0377-0699 Kerala Journal of Psychiatry
0377-0729 Korean Journal of International Law *changed to* Korean Journal of International and Comparative Law 4934
0377-0745 Wiener Gesellschaft fuer Theaterforschung. Jahrbuch†
0377-077X Labour in the Public Sector Undertakings: Basic Information
0377-0850 Law and Progress
0377-0885 Law Reports of Tanzania 4955
0377-0907 Legal History 4720
0377-1083 Lore 5328
0377-1121 Majalah Kedokteran Indonesia 5664
0377-1237 Medical Journal Armed Forces India 5669
0377-1253 Medicina y Cirugia
0377-1261 Meghalaya Chronicle†
0377-1385 Kenya. Central Bureau of Statistics. Migration and Tourism Statistics 8779
0377-144X Barbados. Legislature. House of Assembly. Minutes of Proceedings 7109
0377-1458 Barbados. Legislature. Senate. Minutes of Proceedings 7109
0377-1482 M M T C News 6469
0377-1490 Modern Fibres†
0377-1504 Modern Medicine of Asia†
0377-1555 Monthly Statistical Bulletin of Bangladesh 8389
0377-1636 National Bibliography of Zambia 631
0377-1652 Sudan. Department of Statistics. National Income Accounts and Supporting Tables 1721
0377-1717 N E O N†
0377-1725 Technik Report 3397
0377-1741 New Botanist 804
0377-1806 Norwegian Offshore Index 6800
0377-192X Olympic Review (Year) 8191
0377-1962 Council of Europe. Parliamentary Assembly. Orders of the Day, Minutes of Proceedings 4922
0377-2012 Molecular Structures and Dimensions. Bibliography 2111
0377-2039 South Pacific Commission. Statistical Bulletin 8402
0377-208X Nederlands Tijdschrift voor Fysioterapie *changed to* Dutch Journal of Physical Therapy 6108
0377-2152 Portugal. Instituto Nacional de Estatistica. Boletim Mensal das Estatisticas da Agricultura e da Pesca. Continente, Acores e Madeira†
0377-2179 Portugal. Instituto Nacional de Estatistica. Boletim Mensal das Estatisticas Industrias. Continente, Acores e Madeira†
0377-2187 Portugal. Instituto Nacional de Estatistica. Boletim Trimestral das Estatisticas Monetarias e Financeiras. Continente, Acores e Madeira†
0377-2217 European Journal of Operational Research 1742
0377-2233 Portugal. Estatisticas da Energia: Continente, Acores e Madeira†
0377-225X Estatisticas da Pesca - Statistiques de la Peche 3613
0377-2268 Portugal. Instituto Nacional de Estatistica. Estatisticas da Saude 5697
0377-2284 Estatisticas Demograficas 7306
0377-2306 Estatisticas do Turismo 8779
0377-2314 Estatisticas Industrais. Suplemento 1227
0377-2322 Estatisticas Monetarias e Financieras 1338
0377-2365 Portugal. Instituto Nacional de Estatistica. Inquerito as Receitas e Despesas Familiares 8062
0377-2454 Portugal. Instituto Nacional de Estatistica. Recenseamento da Populacao e Habitacao 4365

0377-2497 Turk Tip Dernegi Dergisi
0377-256X Pakistan Digest 3926
0377-2586 Pakistan Pictorial 3926
0377-2667 Party Life 7164
0377-2713 People's Power 7165
0377-2748 Council of Europe. Standing Committee on the European Convention on Establishment (Individuals). Periodical Report 7204
0377-2772 Philosophy & Social Action 7992
0377-2780 Planning *changed to* 1811-9107 436
0377-2969 Pakistan Academy of Sciences. Proceedings 7897
0377-3086 Proletarian Path 7174
0377-3132 Psycho-Lingua 5163
0377-3213 Central Bank of Syria. Quarterly Bulletin 1446
0377-3302 Rajasthan Forest Statistics 3709
0377-3310 Rajasthan Journal of English Studies†
0377-3418 Institut Pasteur de Dakar. Rapport sur le Fonctionnement Technique 887
0377-3426 Reading Journal
0377-3450 R E C S A M Annual Report 2902
0377-3515 Renditions 559
0377-3574 Contributions to Epidemiology and Biostatistics†
0377-368X International Commission for the Conservation of Atlantic Tunas. Report 948
0377-3744 National Institute of Nutrition. Annual Report 6664
0377-4422 Fiji. Printing Department Report 4575
0377-449X Singapore International Chamber of Commerce. Report 1409
0377-4503 Malta. Department of Information. Reports on the Working of Government Departments 7481
0377-452X South Pacific Commission. Report of Meetings 1519
0377-4554 University of Nairobi. Institute for Development Studies. Research and Publications†
0377-466X Council of the European Communities. Review of the Council's Work 1448
0377-4686 Revista Servico de Administracao Militar 6443
0377-4708 Revista de Farmacia y Bioquimica 6879
0377-4724 Revista de Chirurgie, Oncologie, Radiologie, O.R.L., Oftalmologie, Stomatologie. Oncologie†
0377-4732 Revista Espanola de Medicina Legal 5916
0377-4740 Revista Mexicana de Angiologia 5799
0377-4902 Homeopathic Herald
0377-4910 I C M R Bulletin 5631
0377-4929 Indian Journal of Pathology & Microbiology 887
0377-497X Revista de Medicina Interna, Neurologie, Psihiatrie, Neuro-Chirurgie, Dermato-Venerologie. Series Neurologie, Psihiatrie, Neurochirugie†
0377-5070 Schweizer Landtechnik 154
0377-5119 Pan American Health 7534
0377-5135 Sciences, Techniques, Informations C R I A C 1903
0377-5240 Seoul National University. Faculty Papers. A & B, Humanities and Social Science Series†
0377-5291 Singapore Dental Journal 5865
0377-5305 Singapore Family Physician 5715
0377-5321 Sino-American Relations 7265
0377-5380 Social and Labour Bulletin†
0377-5429 South African Labour Bulletin 1708
0377-5437 Southeast Asian Affairs 7184
0377-547X Spices Newsletter†
0377-5690 Iraq. Central Statistical Organization. Statistical Pocket Book
0377-5704 Statistical Review of Tourism in Hong Kong 8780
0377-5712 Statistical Survey of the East African Community Institutions 1267
0377-5828 Sudan Journal of Economic and Social Studies 8008
0377-6093 Council of Europe. Parliamentary Assembly. Texts Adopted by the Assembly 4922
0377-628X Revista de Filologia y Linguistica 5167
0377-6336 Universities Handbook (Year) 2962
0377-6352 Uplift 8076
0377-6360 Vedic Light 7708
0377-6433 Viva
0377-6611 The Working Class 4605
0377-6719 Yearly All India Criminal Digest†
0377-6832 Data India 3881
0377-6921 Ethiopian Chamber of Commerce. Directory of Agriculture†
0377-7081 Documentation in Public Administration 7480
0377-7103 Eastern Africa Journal of Rural Development 196
0377-7154 Egyptian Computer Journal 2417
0377-7316 Anuario de Estudios Centroamericanos 7947
0377-7332 Empirical Economics 1104
0377-7359 Indian Films 6503
0377-7367 Indian Library Movement 5015
0377-7391 Industrial Welder 6343
0377-743X Jijnasa 4184
0377-7464 I E S Journal *changed to* 1937-3260 3269
0377-7464 The I E S Journal *changed to* The I E S Journal. Part C: Power Engineering
0377-7464 The I E S Journal *changed to* The I E S Journal. Part B: Intelligent Devices and Systems
0377-7480 Journal of Rural Cooperation 1424
0377-7499 Kailash 4185
0377-7537 Man-Made Textiles in India 8454
0377-7553 Bank of Jamaica. Monthly Review†
0377-757X Municipalities and Corporation Cases 4737
0377-7596 Oh Calcutta 3886
0377-7669 North Atlantic Treaty Organization. Expert Panel on Air Pollution Modeling. Proceedings 3490
0377-7774 Family Planning Association of India. Report 972
0377-791X Malta. Central Office of Statistics. Shipping and Aviation Statistics 8527
0377-7928 Singapore Periodicals Index 16
0377-8002 Tamil Nadu Journal of Co-operation 1424
0377-8053 Water Resources Journal 8840
0377-8096 Youth News
0377-8118 Zambia Mining Yearbook 6484
0377-8142 Revue Roumaine de Biologie. Serie Biologie Animale 962
0377-8231 Academie Royale de Medecine de Belgique. Bulletin et Memoires 5565
0377-8282 Drugs of the Future 6837

9276 0377-8312 ULRICH'S PERIODICALS

0377-8312 Von Karman Institute for Fluid Dynamics. Lecture Series **74**
0377-8320 Psicodeia†
0377-8347 Schweizerische Zeitschrift fuer Militaer- und Katastrophenmedizin†
0377-8398 Marine Micropaleontology **6726**
0377-8401 Animal Feed Science and Technology **270**
0377-8444 Journal of Chemical Sciences (Amritsar) **2067**
0377-8487 Vignana Bharathi
0377-8495 Verkeerskunde **8637**
0377-8533 University of Durban-Westville. Institute for Social and Economic Research. Annual Report **8012**
0377-8541 University of Durban-Westville Journal†
0377-8576 Paidonomia **6232**
0377-8592 Safety Management **6686**
0377-8657 Purchasing South Africa†
0377-8665 Snarl†
0377-8711 Corrosion and Coatings **6717**
0377-8908 Norway. Statistisk Sentralbyraa. Statistisk Aarbok **8392**
0377-8959 Revue des Revues Demographiques *see* Review of Population Reviews (Online) **7292**
0377-9017 Letters in Mathematical Physics **7025**
0377-9025 Methods and Phenomena† **8974**
0377-905X Wasser, Energie, Luft **8836**
0377-9084 Fabrimetal Magazine†
0377-9165 Annual Bulletin of General Energy Statistics for Europe†
0377-919X Journal of Palestine Studies **4322**
0377-9211 Arabian Journal for Science and Engineering **3181**
0377-9238 Bangladesh Medical Research Council Bulletin **5583**
0377-9335 Entomon **846**
0377-9343 The Indian Journal of Chest Diseases and Allied Sciences **5945**
0377-936X Timber Development Association of India. Journal **3716**
0377-9378 Karnataka Medical Journal **5656**
0377-9408 Tool and Alloy Steels **6335**
0377-9424 Agronomia Costarricense **88**
0377-9556 Yakhak Hoeji **6886**
0377-9696 The Leech
0377-9920 The Asian Wall Street Journal **1309**
0377-9955 Commission de Pacifique Sud. Manuel *see* 0081-2811 **1605**
0377-9963 Medical Progress (Hong Kong Edition) **5670**
0377-9971 Pontificia Academia Scientiarum. Scripta Varia **7899**
0378-0392 Mineral and Electrolyte Metabolism†
0378-0449 Plant Protection Bulletin **812**
0378-0473 Kanina **5317**
0378-052X Ciencia y Tecnologia **7847**
0378-0546 I N S E R M Symposia **5632**
0378-0597 African Studies
0378-0600 Hong Kong Law Journal **4688**
0378-0643 Poesie
0378-0651 Muziek en Onderwijs *changed to* 1570-7989 **6583**
0378-066X Entretiens d'Actualite†
0378-0716 Academie Royale des Sciences, des Lettres et des Beaux-Arts de Belgique. Classe des Beaux-Arts. Bulletin **4440**
0378-0732 History in Zambia
0378-0759 Indian Linguistics **5127**
0378-0783 Documentation Legislative Africaine **4660**
0378-0813 Ethiopian Journal of Development Research **1885**
0378-0856 Indo-Iranica **5308**
0378-0864 Geologische Bundesanstalt. Abhandlungen **2741**
0378-0880 Communication & Cognition **8094**
0378-0902 Belgium. Geological Survey of Belgium. Professional Papers **2726**
0378-0953 Musee Royal de l'Afrique Centrale. Departement de Geologie et de Mineralogie. Rapport Annuel **2756**
0378-0961 Sociedad Nacional de Mineria. Boletin Minero **6479**
0378-097X Cuadernos de Psicologia†
0378-1003 Indian Journal of Psychometry and Education **7362**
0378-1046 Journal of the Earth and Space Physics **7023**
0378-1097 F E M S Microbiology Letters **885**
0378-1119 Gene **764**
0378-1127 Forest Ecology and Management **3688**
0378-1135 Veterinary Microbiology **897**
0378-1143 Bhandarkar Oriental Research Institute. Annals **545**
0378-116X Academia das Ciencias de Lisboa. Classe de Letras. Memorias **4439**
0378-1240 Garcia de Orta: Serie de Geologia **2735**
0378-1593 Central Bank of Swaziland. Quarterly Review
0378-178X Central Bank of Barbados. Economic and Financial Statistics **1325**
0378-181X Pedofauna†
0378-1844 Interciencia **7867**
0378-1879 Investigacion Pediatrica
0378-1909 Environmental Biology of Fishes **941**
0378-1925 Tijdschrift voor Verloskundigen **6005**
0378-1933 Macaskill Letter
0378-195X Metro: A Bibliography†
0378-1968 International Statistical Handbook of Urban Public Transport **8526**
0378-1984 Bharatya Vidya **7733**
0378-200X Revista Castilla **5361**
0378-2034 Etudes Maliennes **4174**
0378-2166 Journal of Pragmatics **5203**
0378-2255 World Health Organization Regional Publications. European Series **7545**
0378-2271 Europhysics Conference Abstracts **7048**
0378-2352 Istanbul Universitesi. Veteriner Fakultesi Dergisi **8800**
0378-2387 C M F R I Bulletin **3588**
0378-2395 Journal of Maharashtra Agricultural Universities **127**
0378-2409 Journal of Root Crops **239**
0378-2484 I J D L **5126**
0378-2506 Byzantion **545**
0378-2514 Ceylon Geographer **4002**
0378-2522 Estadistica Panamena. Situacion Economica. Seccion 351. Indice de Precios al por Mayor y al Consumidor **1226**
0378-2530 Estadistica Panamena. Situacion Economica. Seccion 351. Precios Pagados por el Productor Agropecuario **179**
0378-2549 Estadistica Panamena. Situacion Economica. Seccion 351. Precios Recibidos por el Productor Agropecuario. Compendio **179**
0378-2557 Estadistica Panamena. Situacion Economica. Seccion 314, 323, 324, 325, 353. Industria **1226**
0378-2565 Estadistica Panamena. Situacion Economica. Seccion 312. Superficie Sembrada y Cosecha de Arroz, Maiz y Frijol de Bejuco **179**
0378-2581 Estadistica Panamena. Situacion Economica. Seccion 312. Produccion Pecuaria **179**
0378-259X Estadistica Panamena. Situacion Politica, Administrativa y Justicia. Seccion 631. Justicia **4822**
0378-2603 Estadistica Panamena. Situacion Economica. Seccion 342. Cuentas Nacionales **1226**
0378-2611 Estadistica Panamena. Situacion Economica. Seccion 351. Precios Recibidos por el Productor Agropecuario **179**
0378-2654 Industrial Development Abstracts†
0378-2689 University of Hong Kong. Centre of Asian Studies. Occasional Papers and Monographs **563**
0378-2697 Plant Systematics and Evolution **813**
0378-2700 Egyptian Journal of Dairy Science **264**
0378-2778 Tijdschrift voor Alcohol, Drugs en Andere Psychotrope Stoffen
0378-2808 Archivum Ottomanicum **4320**
0378-2832 Government Oriental Manuscripts Library. Bulletin†
0378-2883 Armaghan†
0378-2905 Ankara Universitesi. Dil ve Tarih-Cografya Fakultesi Dergisi **4319**
0378-2921 Ankara Universitesi. Siyasal Bilgiler Fakultesi Dergisi **7106**
0378-2964 Indian Horizons **4183**
0378-3146 Belgium. Rijksdienst voor Arbeidsvoorziening. Jaarverslag *see* Belgium. Office National de l'Emploi. Etudes Economiques et Sociales **1667**
0378-3227 Portugal. Instituto Nacional de Estatistica. Serie Estatisticas Regionais **8395**
0378-3235 Portugal. Instituto Nacional de Estatistica. Serie Estimativas Provisorias **8395**
0378-3286 United Nations Commission on Narcotic Drugs. Summary of Reports on Illicit Transactions and Seizures of Narcotic Drugs and Psychotropic Substances
0378-3316 Rocas y Minerales **6478**
0378-3758 Journal of Statistical Planning and Inference **8383**
0378-3766 T I M S Studies in the Management Sciences†
0378-3774 Agricultural Water Management **217**
0378-3782 Early Human Development **5989**
0378-3790 Inorganic Perspectives in Biology and Medicine†
0378-3812 Fluid Phase Equilibria **2135**
0378-3820 Fuel Processing Technology **6769**
0378-3839 Coastal Engineering **3263**
0378-3928 Hindustani Zaban†
0378-4010 Al-Hilal
0378-4029 Geological Survey of India. News **2740**
0378-4045 Progress in Clinical Neurophysiology†
0378-407X Gereformeerde Vrouweblad **7759**
0378-4088 Imbongi Yenkosi **7761**
0378-410X Molaetsa-Molaetsa **7768**
0378-4126 Murumiwa **7768**
0378-4134 Umthombo Wamandla **7778**
0378-4150 German Language and Literature Monographs†
0378-4169 Lingvisticae Investigationes **5147**
0378-4177 Studies in Language **5182**
0378-4215 Acta Iranica **541**
0378-424X Documentation Cistercienne
0378-4266 Journal of Banking & Finance **1360**
0378-4274 Toxicology Letters **3502**
0378-4282 Animal Regulation Studies†
0378-4290 Field Crops Research **231**
0378-4320 Animal Reproduction Science **278**
0378-4371 Physica A: Statistical Mechanics and its Applications **7030**
0378-4479 Results of the Business Survey Carried Out Among Managements in the Community **1903**
0378-4509 Avances en Produccion Animal **280**
0378-4525 Zambian Ornithological Society. Bulletin†
0378-4533 Zambian Ornithological Society. Newsletter **917**
0378-4568 Anvesak **1060**
0378-4584 Bibliographie der Schweizergeschichte **618**
0378-4592 Linguistic Bibliography **5201**
0378-4606 Universite de Bruxelles. Revue **4480**
0378-4657 De Gids op Maatschappelijk Gebied **4595**
0378-469X Balafon†
0378-4703 Moyo **3906**
0378-4738 Water S A (Print) *changed to* 1816-7950 **8840**
0378-4754 Mathematics and Computers in Simulation **2517**
0378-4770 W E P Studies†
0378-4789 Independent Journal of Philosophy **6925**
0378-4835 Oncologia†
0378-4843 F C T L†
0378-4851 Afya **5570**
0378-486X The Sri Lanka Journal of the Humanities **4476**
0378-4878 Letras **4463**
0378-4908 University of Cape Town. Studies in English†
0378-4916 Collectanea Cisterciensia **7792**
0378-4967 Estadistica Panamena. Situacion Cultural. Seccion 511. Educacion **2933**
0378-4983 Estadistica Panamena. Situacion Economica. Seccion 331. Comercio. Anuario de Comercio Exterior **1226**
0378-4991 Estadistica Panamena. Situacion Economica. Seccion 352. Hoja de Balance de Alimentos **179**
0378-5092 Revue Europeenne Formation Professionnelle *see* European Journal Vocational Training **2855**
0378-5106 Europaeische Zeitschrift Berufsbildung *see* European Journal Vocational Training **2855**
0378-5122 Maturitas **5998**
0378-5130 Wirtschaft und Gesellschaft **1194**
0378-5165 International Journal of Political Education†
0378-5173 International Journal of Pharmaceutics **6850**
0378-519X Developments in Crop Science **228**
0378-5203 Journal of Organometallic Chemistry Library†
0378-522X Auto Data Digest **8557**
0378-5335 University of the North. Communique†
0378-5378 D O C P A L Resumenes sobre Poblacion en America Latina **7305**
0378-5386 Centro Latinoamericano de Demografia. Boletin Demografico **7279**
0378-5408 Labour and Society†
0378-5424 Travail et Societe†
0378-5432 Bureau International du Travail. Bulletin Officiel. Serie A *see* 0378-5882 **1689**
0378-5467 Labour Education **1694**
0378-5505 Supplement du Bulletin des Statistiques du Travail **1269**
0378-5513 Oficina Internacional del Trabajo. Boletin Oficial. Serie A *see* 0378-5882 **1689**
0378-5521 Oficina Internacional del Trabajo. Boletin Oficial. Serie B *see* 0378-5890 **1689**
0378-5548 Revista Internacional del Trabajo **1705**
0378-5564 Educacion Obrera *see* 0378-5467 **1694**
0378-5572 Education Ouvriere *see* 0378-5467 **1694**
0378-5599 Revue Internationale du Travail **1705**
0378-5726 Etudes Mesoamericaines **338**
0378-584X Onkologie **6031**
0378-5866 Developmental Neuroscience **6136**
0378-5882 International Labour Office. Official Bulletin. Series A **1689**
0378-5890 International Labour Office. Official Bulletin. Series B **1689**
0378-5904 I L O Publications†
0378-5912 Trends in Neurosciences (Reference Edition)†
0378-5920 The World Economy **1196**
0378-5955 Hearing Research **6080**
0378-603X The Egyptian Journal of Radiology and Nuclear Medicine
0378-6080 Side Effects of Drugs Annual **6881**
0378-6099 Topics in Photosynthesis†
0378-6110 Cell Surface Reviews†
0378-6129 Research Monographs in Cell and Tissue Physiology†
0378-6161 Epidemiological Bulletin†
0378-620X Integral Equations and Operator Theory **5494**
0378-6242 Indian National Science Academy. Bulletin **7865**
0378-6285 Enfermeria **5958**
0378-6307 Geophysical Research Bulletin†
0378-6323 Indian Journal of Dermatology, Venereology and Leprology **5877**
0378-6358 Istanbul Medical Faculty. Medical Bulletin **5642**
0378-6366 Minerals & Metals Review **6326**
0378-6420 Revista Venezolana de Cirugia **6257**
0378-6471 Daehan An'gwa Hag'hoeji **6041**
0378-6501 Drugs under Experimental and Clinical Research **6837**
0378-651X Financial Market Trends *changed to* 1995-2805 **1155**
0378-6749 Estadistica Panamena. Situacion Demografica. Seccion 221. Estadisticas Vitales - Cifras Preliminares†
0378-6765 Estadistica Panamena. Situacion Social. Seccion 451. Accidentes de Transito **8524**
0378-6862 Landesmuseum Joanneum Graz. Jahresbericht **7878**
0378-6870 Geologisch-Palaeontologische Mitteilungen Innsbruck *changed to* 1824-7741 **6725**
0378-6900 Advances in Cardiovascular Physics†
0378-6919 Schweizer Foerster†
0378-6927 Plusminus 20†
0378-6935 Theater-Zytig **8482**
0378-6978 Official Journal of the European Communities. L Series: Legislation *changed to* Official Journal of the European Union. L Series: Legislation **7256**
0378-6986 European Communities. Official Journal. C: Information and Notices *changed to* 1725-2423 **7256**
0378-6994 Europaeiske Faellesskabers Tidende. L: Retsforskrifter *see* Official Journal of the European Union. L Series: Legislation **7256**
0378-7001 De Europaiske Fallesskabers Tidende. C: Meddelelser og Oplysninger *see* 1725-2423 **7256**
0378-7001 De Europaiske Fallesskabers Tidende. C: Meddelelser og Oplysninger *see* 0257-7763 **4923**
0378-701X Gazzetta Ufficiale delle Comunita Europee. C: Comunicazioni ed Informazioni *see* 0257-7763 **4923**
0378-701X Gazzetta Ufficiale delle Comunita Europee. C: Comunicazioni ed Informazioni *see* 1725-2423 **7256**
0378-7028 Gazzetta Ufficiale delle Comunita Europee. L: Legislazione *see* Official Journal of the European Union. L Series: Legislation **7256**
0378-7052 Journal Officiel des Communautes Europeennes. C: Communications et Informations *see* 1725-2423 **7256**
0378-7052 Journal Officiel des Communautes Europeennes. C: Communications et Informations *see* 0257-7763 **4923**
0378-7060 Journal Officiel des Communautes Europeennes. L: Legislation *see* Official Journal of the European Union. L Series: Legislation **7256**
0378-7079 Publikatieblad van de Europese Gemeenschappen. C: Mededelingen en Bekendmakingen *see* 1725-2423 **7256**
0378-7079 Publikatieblad van de Europese Gemeenschappen. C: Mededelingen en Bekendmakingen *see* 0257-7763 **4923**
0378-7087 Publikatieblad van de Europese Gemeenschappen. L Serie: Wetgeving *see* Official Journal of the European Union. L Series: Legislation **7256**
0378-7184 Arab Oil & Gas Magazine (Monthly) **6762**
0378-7206 Information & Management **2521**
0378-7273 Official Journal of the European Union. S Series: Tendering Procedures for Public Contracts **4937**
0378-7346 Gynecologic and Obstetric Investigation **5992**
0378-7354 Advances in Biological Psychiatry **6120**
0378-7362 I L O Judgements of the Administrative Tribunal **4689**
0378-7397 Estadistica Panamena. Situacion Economica. Seccion 341. Balanza de Pagos **1226**
0378-7400 Magallat al-batrul wa-al-gaz al-'arabi *see* 0378-7184 **6762**
0378-746X I R E B I†
0378-7478 Research in Tourism **8752**
0378-7494 Creative Book Selection Index **7578**
0378-7508 Library History Review **5027**
0378-7516 Asian Journal of European Studies **4201**
0378-7524 History of Agriculture **118**

DIRECTORY 2010 0379-7074 9277

0378-7532 Management Development
0378-7540 Current Trends in Life Sciences **667**
0378-7559 Statistical Office of the European Communities. Monthly Statistics Iron and Steel†
0378-7656 International Federation for Documentation. P-Notes†
0378-7680 Ciencia y Sociedad **7847**
0378-7699 Instituto del Mar del Peru. Boletin **3598**
0378-7702 Instituto del Mar del Peru. Informe **3598**
0378-7710 Swaziland National Bibliography **7579**
0378-7753 Journal of Power Sources **3322**
0378-777X Environmental Policy and Law **3427**
0378-7788 Energy and Buildings **3130**
0378-7796 Electric Power Systems Research **3302**
0378-7818 Universidad del Zulia. Facultad de Agronomia. Revista **165**
0378-7826 Namibia Today†
0378-7923 Academie Royale des Sciences, des Lettres et des Beaux-Arts de Belgique. Classe des Beaux-Arts. Memoires **463**
0378-7931 Deviance et Societe **8098**
0378-7958 Pharma-Flash **6867**
0378-7966 European Journal of Drug Metabolism and Pharmacokinetics **6838**
0378-7974 Revista de Estudios Hispanicos **4472**
0378-8024 Journal of Turkish Phytopathology
0378-8032 Garcia de Orta: Serie de Estudos Agronomicos **115**
0378-8059 Sudanow **4325**
0378-8113 Bangladesh Veterinary Journal **8794**
0378-8121 Bangladesh Academy of Sciences. Journal **7839**
0378-813X P K V Research Journal **145**
0378-8156 Indian Journal of Physical Anthropology and Human Genetics **872**
0378-8172 Nouvelles Universitaires Europeennes **2892**
0378-8180 Journal of Oman Studies†
0378-8202 Naturhistorisches Museum in Wien. Veroeffentlichungen. Neue Folge **7890**
0378-8253 An-Nahar **3905**
0378-8350 Langues et Terminologies†
0378-8407 Tempo Medical†
0378-8482 Revista Geografica de Chile Terra Australis **4027**
0378-8490 Karger Highlights: Nephrology†
0378-8504 Aktuelle Probleme in Chirurgie und Orthopadie†
0378-8628 Dirim Aylik Tip Gazetesi **5605**
0378-8644 Oesterreichische Akademie der Wissenschaften. Almanach **7895**
0378-8652 Oesterreichische Akademie der Wissenschaften. Philosophisch-Historische Klasse. Anzeiger **4250**
0378-8660 Jahrbuch der Oesterreichischen Byzantinistik **4234**
0378-8717 Science Teacher
0378-8733 Social Networks **8003**
0378-8741 Journal of Ethnopharmacology **6853**
0378-875X Ciencia Biologica: Biologia Molecular e Celular **728**
0378-8865 Harvest **234**
0378-8873 Barbados. Statistical Service. Monthly Digest of Statistics **8357**
0378-8938 Kenya. Ministry of Cooperatives and Social Services. Sessional Papers **7450**
0378-8970 Arabian Year Book†
0378-8989 Analele Universitatii Bucuresti. Biologie **7835**
0378-9004 International Institute for Applied Systems Analysis. Research Reports **3482**
0378-9012 European Illustration **488**
0378-9020 Building Industries Federation. Annual Report **985**
0378-9098 South African Journal of Business Management **1794**
0378-9128 Bike S.A. **8255**
0378-9144 Boardroom **1850**
0378-9160 Bowls†
0378-9217 Braby's East London Directory **1976**
0378-9225 Braby's East Rand Directory†
0378-9241 Braby's Greytown Directory **1976**
0378-925X Braby's Howick Directory **1976**
0378-9268 Ladysmith Directory **2012**
0378-9306 Braby's Pietermaritzburg Directory **1976**
0378-9314 Braby's Pretoria Directory **1976**
0378-9365 Business Digest†
0378-9411 South African Optometrist **6052**
0378-9454 Vistas in Plant Sciences†
0378-9497 Acta Rhumatologica Belgica **6221**
0378-9519 Journal of Entomological Research **852**
0378-9535 Urja
0378-9551 Revista Seguridad†
0378-956X Instituto Tecnologico de Santo Domingo. Documentos **7866**
0378-9608 Universidade de Coimbra. Faculdade de Farmacia. Boletim†
0378-9721 Bulletin of Animal Health and Production in Africa **282**
0378-9748 W H O Pesticide Residue Series†
0378-9845 Health Communications and Informatics†
0378-9853 Karger Highlights: Cardiology†
0378-9888 Nederduitse Gereformeerde Teologiese Tydskrif **7768**
0378-9896 Universidad Catolica Nuestra Senora de la Asuncion. Centro de Estudios Antropologicos. Suplemento Antropologico **359**
0378-990X Iranian Review of International Relations **7246**
0378-9918 Universidad de la Republica. Facultad de Ciencias Economicas y de Administracion. Revista **1187**
0378-9926 Reseaux - Ciephum **6947**
0378-9942 Bibliographie du Senegal **618**
0378-9977 International Background†
0378-9993 Industry and Environment† **8964**
0379-0002 Reviews on Powder Metallurgy & Physical Ceramics†
0379-0037 Indian Journal of Applied Linguistics **5127**
0379-0045 Vigilancia Epidemiologica de la Rabia en las Americas
0379-0053 Vigilancia Epidemiologica de las Encefalitis en las Americas†
0379-0207 Oesterreichische Akademie der Wissenschaften, Vienna. Mathematisch - Naturwissenschaftliche Klasse. Denkschriften **5522**
0379-0231 Tiroler Landesmuseum Ferdinandeum, Innsbruck. Veroeffentlichungen **6538**
0379-0258 Automatic Data Processing Information Bulletin†
0379-0282 Internationale Revue fuer Soziale Sicherheit **7975**
0379-0290 Current Research in Social Security†
0379-0304 Seguridad Social **8067**
0379-0312 Revue Internationale de Securite Sociale **8065**
0379-0347 U N C R D Newsletter **1606**
0379-0355 Methods and Findings in Experimental and Clinical Pharmacology **6861**
0379-038X National Academy of Medical Sciences. Annals **5683**
0379-0401 Bismuth Institute. Bulletin **6306**
0379-0436 Comparative Physiology and Ecology†
0379-0479 Indian Journal of Cryogenics **7054**
0379-0495 I P I Research Topics **235**
0379-0533 Revista de Ciencias Farmaceuticas†
0379-055X Tobacco Research **8488**
0379-0584 Index to South African Periodicals **8**
0379-0622 Zambezia **8018**
0379-0649 Penpals **4343**
0379-0703 Journal of Oman Studies Special Report†
0379-0738 Forensic Science International **5913**
0379-0762 Revista Internacional de Ciencias Sociales†
0379-0827 Agricultural Research Institute. Agricultural Economics Report **192**
0379-0851 Cyprus. Tmimatos Georgias. Etisia Ekthesi (Year)†
0379-086X Cyprus. Department of Fisheries. Annual Report on the Department of Fisheries and the Cyprus Fisheries **3589**
0379-0916 Cyprus. Meteorological Service. Summary of the Weather in Cyprus†
0379-0924 Cyprus. Department of Statistics and Research. Agricultural Statistics **178**
0379-0932 Cyprus. Agricultural Research Institute. Technical Paper†
0379-0940 Americas (English Edition) **4442**
0379-0975 Americas (Spanish Edition) *see* 0379-0940 **4442**
0379-0991 European Economy **1484**
0379-1068 Karger Highlights: Gerontology†
0379-1130 Rubber Research Institute of Sri Lanka. Journal **7827**
0379-119X Botswana. Geological Survey Department. District Memoirs **2726**
0379-1203 Instituto de Investigacao Agronomica de Angola. Divisao de Meteorologia Agricola. Anuario
0379-122X Unesco Journal of Information Science, Librarianship and Archives Administration†
0379-1254 Societa Ticinese di Scienze Naturali. Bollettino **7917**
0379-1335 Operational Hydrology Report **2797**
0379-1416 Naturwissenschaftlich - Medizinischen Vereins in Innsbruck. Berichte **693**
0379-1424 Universitaet Wien. Dissertationen
0379-153X Porrime **3252**
0379-1564 Bibliographical Series on Coconut†
0379-1580 Fiji. Mineral Resources Department. Bulletin **2734**
0379-1653 Jaslok Hospital & Research Centre. Bulletin **5643**
0379-1726 Diqiu Huaxue **2731**
0379-1785 Musee Royal de l'Afrique Centrale. Annales - Sciences Zoologiques. Serie in 8 **956**
0379-1815 Belgian Environmental Research Index†
0379-1890 Flore Illustree des Champignons d'Afrique Centrale **789**
0379-1920 Academie Royale des Sciences d'Outre-Mer. Classe des Sciences Naturelles et Medicales. Collection in 4 **7830**
0379-1998 Karger Highlights: Oncology†
0379-2005 Karger Highlights: Oral Science†
0379-220X O H O L O Biological Conferences. Proceedings
0379-2218 General Information Program - U N I S I S T Newsletter **5010**
0379-2226 Programme General d'Information - Bulletin de l'U N I S I S T **5040**
0379-2234 Obshchaya Programa po Informatsii - Byulleten' J U N I S I S T **5037**
0379-2242 Programa General de Informacion - Boletin del U N I S I S T **5040**
0379-2269 Children in the Tropics†
0379-2285 E S A Journal†
0379-2366 Studien zur Theologischen Ethik **7684**
0379-2447 Ozone Layer Bulletin†
0379-2463 Siren†
0379-2501 Output†
0379-2617 Mother and Child†
0379-2722 Aargauische Naturforschende Gesellschaft. Mitteilungen **7829**
0379-2854 U N I C E F News†
0379-2862 China Letter **1447**
0379-2870 Philippine Letter **1511**
0379-2889 Japan Letter **1494**
0379-2897 Sinet **7916**
0379-2927 Journal for the History of Arabic Science **7871**
0379-296X Fiji. Mineral Resources Department. Economic Investigation **6462**
0379-3109 Dossier de l'Europe *see* 0379-3133 **1563**
0379-3117 Notities over Europa *see* 0379-3133 **1563**
0379-3125 Schede Europee *see* 0379-3133 **1563**
0379-3133 European File **1563**
0379-3141 Stichwort Europa *see* 0379-3133 **1563**
0379-315X Europa Noter *see* 0379-3133 **1563**
0379-3168 Pure and Applied Mathematika Sciences **5526**
0379-3338 World Union for the Safeguard of Youth. Bulletin†
0379-3400 Teacher Education **2917**
0379-3435 Inland Fisheries Society of India. Journal **3598**
0379-3486 European Communities Trade with ACP States and the South Mediterranean States†
0379-3532 Q R Journal
0379-3540 Zoological Survey of India. Memoirs **970**
0379-3575 Egyptian Journal of Agronomy **106**
0379-3621 Codices Manuscripti **5002**
0379-363X Paracelsus†
0379-3664 Schweizerische Zeitschrift fuer Soziologie **8131**
0379-3680 F I D Directory†
0379-3710 Era Socialista†
0379-3729 Problemes Sociaux Zairois **8126**
0379-3737 Sri Lanka Labour Gazette **1708**
0379-3753 Wallonie **1524**
0379-3877 Jaffna Medical Journal†
0379-3885 Journal of Indian Psychology **7375**
0379-3893 Revista Chilena de Cirugia **6256**
0379-3923 Ciencias Forestales **3686**
0379-3974 Comunicacion **2838**
0379-3982 Tecnologia en Marcha **8443**
0379-3990 Thesis Abstracts **187**
0379-4008 Haryana Agricultural University. Journal of Research **117**
0379-4024 Journal of Operator Theory **5506**
0379-4032 Islam and the Modern World
0379-4059 European Space Agency. Procedures, Standards and Specifications Series
0379-4067 European Space Agency. Scientific and Technical Reports **53**
0379-4075 European Space Agency. Scientific and Technical Memoranda **53**
0379-4105 Cahiers Philosophiques Africains **6909**
0379-4148 Wuli **7046**
0379-4156 Kexue Shiyan†
0379-4180 Taiwan Shuichan Xuehui Kan **3609**
0379-4229 European Applied Research Reports: Nuclear Science and Technology Section
0379-4237 Estadistica Panamena. Situacion Demografica. Seccion 221. Estadisticas Vitales **7306**
0379-4261 Estadistica Panamena. Situacion Economica. Seccion 331. Comercio Exterior. Preliminar†
0379-4288 Bangladesh Horticulture **3724**
0379-4296 Bangladesh Journal of Agricultural Sciences **94**
0379-430X Bangladesh Journal of Animal Science **280**
0379-4318 Institution of Engineers, Bangladesh. Journal **3199**
0379-4342 S I N A S B I. Revista†
0379-4350 South African Journal of Chemistry **2081**
0379-4369 South African Journal of Wildlife Research **2627**
0379-4377 South African Journal of Physics†
0379-4407 Oesterreichische Zeitschrift fuer Wirtschaftsrecht **1937**
0379-4415 Recht der Schule†
0379-4423 Rundfunkrecht **4841**
0379-4474 Karger Highlights: Medical Imaging†
0379-4482 Periodicals in Southern African Libraries†
0379-4504 Current Literature on Science of Science **7936**
0379-4520 Chamber of Mines of South Africa. Annual Report **6460**
0379-458X Call of St. John†
0379-4636 Caravan and Outdoor Life **8692**
0379-4652 Catholic Directory of Southern Africa **7788**
0379-4695 Christiaan de Wet Annale **4174**
0379-4792 Transport and Road Digest†
0379-4830 Cabo **4174**
0379-4857 Acta Medica Dominicana **5566**
0379-4997 Destin International†
0379-508X Acta Botanica Indica **772**
0379-5098 Indian Geologists' Association. Bulletin **2747**
0379-511X Indian Geological Index†
0379-5128 Indian Journal of Earth Sciences **2709**
0379-5136 Indian Journal of Marine Sciences **2806**
0379-5144 M A C T. Journal *changed to* M A N I T. Journal **3208**
0379-5160 Indian Academy of Geoscience. Journal **2709**
0379-5179 Kavaka
0379-5187 Mineral Research
0379-525X Pacific Perspective **7990**
0379-5268 Mana **5329**
0379-5276 Boletin Internacional de Ciencias del Mar *see* 0020-7918 **2806**
0379-5284 Saudi Medical Journal **5709**
0379-5314 Oesterreichische Chemie Zeitschrift **2075**
0379-5349 Wiener Mitteilungen: Wasser, Abwasser, Gewaesser **8842**
0379-5373 Forschungsinstitut der Eidgenoessischen Turn- und Sportschule Magglingen. Wissenschaftliche Schriftenreihe†
0379-542X Cheiron *changed to* 0973-2942 **8808**
0379-5446 Indian Foundry Journal **6315**
0379-5462 I P P T A **6734**
0379-5489 Journal of Nuclear Agriculture and Biology **239**
0379-5527 Mechanical Engineering Bulletin **3389**
0379-556X Pharmstudent **6875**
0379-5594 Seed Research **251**
0379-5608 Soaps, Detergents & Toiletries Review **596**
0379-5616 C I F A Technical Papers **3588**
0379-5721 Food and Nutrition Bulletin **6659**
0379-573X Asset†
0379-5845 Chile Agricola **101**
0379-5853 HongKongiana†
0379-587X Bogazici University Journal: Engineering†
0379-5888 Bogazici University Journal: Sciences†
0379-5896 Chimica Acta Turcica **2058**
0379-5918 Hacettepe Bulletin of Natural Sciences and Engineering†
0379-6175 South African Journal of Physiotherapy **6116**
0379-6191 University of Stellenbosch. Bureau for Economic Research. Trends **1434**
0379-6205 Journal for Studies in Economics and Econometrics **1544**
0379-6256 Sonnenenergie **3177**
0379-6272 Noticias S I N A S B I†
0379-6302 African Freedom Annual†
0379-6310 African Soccer Mirror†
0379-6485 Ars Nova *changed to* 1812-5980 **6597**
0379-6507 Audio South Africa†
0379-6531 Adler Museum Bulletin **5567**
0379-654X Animal Anti-Cruelty League. Chairman's Report **317**
0379-6566 E S A - S P **574**
0379-6574 Africana Society. Yearbook **4173**
0379-6590 Uruguay Economico†
0379-6604 Agricultural Engineering in South Africa **209**
0379-6736 South Africa. Weather Bureau. Technical Paper **6395**
0379-6779 Synthetic Metals **3358**
0379-6906 Cailiao Kexue **6307**
0379-6922 Mundo Nuevo **3950**
0379-6930 African Journal of Plant Protection **216**
0379-7007 Portugal. Instituto Nacional de Estatistica. Centro de Estudos Demograficos. Cadernos **7314**
0379-7031 Weleda Korrespondenzblaetter fuer Aerzte **5729**
0379-704X Social Security Documentation: African Series **4523**
0379-7074 African News Sheet *see* 0251-1290 **4517**

ISSN

0381-6907 Quebec (Province) Centrale des Bibliotheques. Bulletin de Bibliographie†
0381-694X Motoneigiste Canadien†
0381-7008 Canadian Gregg News
0381-7024 Dalhousie University. Institute of Public Affairs. Occasional Papers†
0381-7032 Ars Combinatoria 5473
0381-7059 Canadian Amateur Photographer†
0381-7245 Blue Book of Canadian Business (Year) 1442
0381-7482 Rassembler 7813
0381-7547 Philatelie Quebec 6898
0381-7695 Harness World
0381-7717 Native Perspective†
0381-7733 Forest Engineering Research Institute of Canada. Special Report 3688
0381-7741 Forest Engineering Research Institute of Canada. Technical Note 3688
0381-7857 Interest
0381-7946 Maria†
0381-8004 Ontario Industrial Arts Association. Bulletin
0381-8047 Crucible 7849
0381-8063 Gens du Quebec
0381-811X Saskatchewan Association of Teachers of French. Bulletin de Service 5171
0381-8179 Sanford Evans Gold Book of Used Car Prices 8603
0381-8187 Scope†
0381-8349 Evasion
0381-8365 Smiths Falls Star
0381-8535 Fur Trade Journal of Canada
0381-856X Caledonian†
0381-8632 O C S Nouvelles 2335
0381-8896 Dominion Report Service†
0381-890X Prelude (Calgary) 6607
0381-8950 Deutsche Katholik in Kanada†
0381-9027 Silahis
0381-9035 Speaking of Mime
0381-9132 Olifant 5428
0381-9140 New Review of East-European History†
0381-9167 Toronto Tree 3785
0381-9191 Herstory†
0381-9345 Atlantic Provinces Transportation Commission. Tips & Topics 8490
0381-9361 Teiresias 2241
0381-9388 Societe Historique Nicolas Denys. Revue d'Histoire 4313
0381-9418 Status of Women News†
0381-9485 Tricot Journal
0381-9507 Canadian L P & Tape Catalogue
0381-9515 Artviews†
0381-9582 Tema 5186
0381-9612 The Trust 3048
0381-9663 Alberta Construction and Resource Industries Directory. Purchasing Guide†
0381-9868 Motive Power International†
0381-9884 Jewish Public Library Bulletin†
0381-9930 Toys & Games
0381-9965 Association des Traducteurs et Interpretes de l'Ontario. Translatio†
0382-0068 Voice of United Senior Citizens of Ontario
0382-0122 Vietnam Report
0382-0149 Ishtar News
0382-0157 Western Ontario Historical Notes†
0382-0203 Village Squire
0382-0262 Vie Francaise†
0382-0289 Vista (Saskatoon) 4369
0382-0327 Voice of Radom
0382-0335 Jeu 8472
0382-0416 Western Voice
0382-0424 Vision
0382-0467 Arctic in Colour†
0382-0610 Undzer Veg 3569
0382-0661 U B C Library News†
0382-0718 Vector†
0382-0734 Hollinger Mines Limited. Annual Report
0382-0750 Transition†
0382-0769 I D E E S†
0382-0831 Westmorland Historical Society. Newsletter
0382-084X Lettres Quebecoises 5322
0382-0912 Town and Country Librarian†
0382-0939 Canada. Statistics Canada. For-Hire Trucking Survey†
0382-0998 Canada. Statistics Canada. Principal Taxes in Canada†
0382-1005 Computers†
0382-1048 Novia Scotia. Department of Labour and Manpower. Monthly Summary of Activities-Industrial Relations Division†
0382-1072 Canadian Coast Guard. List of Lights, Buoys and Fog Signals: Newfoundland 8640
0382-1080 List of Lights, Buoys and Fog Signals. Pacific Coast 6431
0382-1102 Current Labour Force Statistics for Nova Scotia†
0382-1110 Education Nova Scotia†
0382-1145 Fire Losses in Canada. Annual Report†
0382-1161 Canada. Commissioner of Official Languages. Annual Report 7426
0382-1242 Wage Rates, Salaries and Hours of Labour in Nova Scotia†
0382-1420 New Brunswick. Office of the Auditor General. Report of the Auditor General to the Legislative Assembly 7455
0382-1455 National Arts Centre. Annual Report 508
0382-1463 Canada. Law Reform Commission. Annual Report†
0382-1498 Canada Deposit Insurance Corporation. Annual Report 4497
0382-151X National Film Board of Canada. Annual Report 2386
0382-1587 Canada. Pension Review Board. Reports†
0382-1838 Saskatchewan Universities Commission. Annual Report
0382-1889 Labour Research Bulletin†
0382-2028 Manitoba Grassland Projects†
0382-2281 Canadian Commercial Corporation. Annual Report 7428
0382-2486 Annual Northern Expenditure Plan 7488
0382-2788 Environment Ontario Legacy†
0382-2834 Ontario Hydro. Statistical Yearbook

0382-2850 New Brunswick. Department of Education. Annual Report 2890
0382-2915 Selected Streamflow Data for Ontario
0382-3083 Public Accounts of the Province of Prince Edward Island 1940
0382-3229 Canadian Dairy Commission. Annual Report 262
0382-3601 Varieties of Grain Crops for Saskatchewan 275
0382-3814 Education Quebec†
0382-392X Canada. Anti-Inflation Board. Consumer Information†
0382-4012 Canada. Statistics Canada. Manufacturing Industries of Canada: Sub-Provincial Areas†
0382-4020 Canada. Statistics Canada. Manufacturing Industries Division. Potash Mines†
0382-408X Teacher (Halifax) 3034
0382-411X Canada. Statistics Canada. Educational Staff in Community Colleges†
0382-4144 Canada. Statistics Canada. Manufacturing Industries of Canada. National and Provincial Areas 1079
0382-4276 Airport News
0382-4314 Crusader (Toronto) 7753
0382-4365 Avec "Lui"
0382-4373 Aim 8157
0382-442X Animal News
0382-4438 Athletica†
0382-4497 Courrier S P C A 6806
0382-4500 Arrow†
0382-456X Advocate (Toronto) 4611
0382-4624 Canadian Living 5067
0382-4756 Banque de Commerce Canadienne Imperiale. Lettre Commerciale†
0382-4772 C S A S Newsletter
0382-4926 Vie Montante. Edition Canadienne
0382-4942 Auctioneer
0382-5078 Criteria†
0382-5124 Ateliers†
0382-5167 Alberta Counsellor
0382-5175 Alberta English Notes†
0382-5191 Alberta English
0382-5205 Urban Reader†
0382-5264 Branching Out
0382-5272 British Columbia Monthly 5418
0382-5345 Alberta Liberal†
0382-5485 B. C. Rehabilitation News
0382-5493 Teaching Mathematics†
0382-5590 Book Commentator
0382-5604 Bouscueil†
0382-5655 Blue Bill 904
0382-5671 British Columbia Primary Teachers' Association. Newsletter 3053
0382-5728 Miners' Voice†
0382-5795 Canadian Hackney Stud Book 8288
0382-5809 Canadian Gem and Family Visitor
0382-5825 Auto Revue (Montreal)
0382-5868 Long Time Coming†
0382-5876 Canadian Funeral News 3719
0382-5884 Outdoor Echo
0382-5906 Ontario Real Estate Law Guide 4753
0382-5914 Repertoire des Cours d'Ete†
0382-6031 Canadian Manhood†
0382-6147 Canadian Nationalist
0382-6171 Canadian Negro
0382-6295 Amnesty International (Toronto Group) Newsletter
0382-6376 Canadian Century and Canadian Life & Resources
0382-6384 Beacon 7785
0382-6406 Canadian Jersey Herd Record 283
0382-6627 Owl 2206
0382-6651 Clansman (Dorval)†
0382-6880 Canadian Homes†
0382-6996 Heating, Plumbing, Air Conditioning Buyers' Guide 4120
0382-7003 Canadian Guild of Organists. Journal
0382-7038 Comment 4499
0382-7046 Commentaires 4499
0382-7453 Canadian Practitioner and Review†
0382-7518 Powell River Progress
0382-7577 Big Country Voice
0382-7658 Canadian Friend 7733
0382-7712 Canadian Mining and Financial News
0382-7879 School Calendar 3031
0382-8115 Canada Crafts†
0382-8255 C O F Newsletter
0382-8352 Backgrounder
0382-8409 Challenge (Winnipeg)
0382-845X Chamber Pot
0382-8476 Nurscene 5971
0382-8557 Ciao 3527
0382-8565 Brick 5209
0382-8603 Canadian Professional Film Directory
0382-8727 Christian Bus Driver
0382-876X Iconomatrix†
0382-8824 Laomedon Review
0382-8832 Cultural Horizons of the Deaf in Canada†
0382-8883 Le Nord 3814
0382-8980 Deaf Herald†
0382-909X Descant 5283
0382-912X Council of Ontario Universities. Application Statistics 2931
0382-9251 Abaka 3515
0382-9391 Diocesan Times 7754
0383-0047 Au Fil du Bois†
0383-008X Canada. Statistics Canada. Fruit and Vegetable Production 177
0383-0381 Canadian Science Digest
0383-0640 Stationery & Office Products†
0383-0713 Canadian Music and Radio Trades
0383-0721 Ecouri Rumanesti†
0383-073X Canadian Transceiver
0383-0837 Tetes de Pioche
0383-087X Arab Dawn
0383-090X Metalworking Production & Purchasing 6326
0383-1027 Canadian Musical News
0383-1213 Goldstream Gazette 3810
0383-1264 International Nickel Company of Canada. Annual Report

0383-1329 Nieuwe Weg (Montreal)
0383-137X Canadian Wheelman
0383-1418 Eastern Light
0383-1590 Canadian Writer and Editor
0383-1620 Catholic Register 7789
0383-1825 Microscopical Society of Canada. Bulletin 899
0383-199X P E I T F Newsletter 2894
0383-2031 Waters†
0383-2066 Digeste Francais
0383-2244 Farm Trends†
0383-2406 Canadian Campus Career Directory†
0383-2538 Evanhel'skyi Holos
0383-2554 Aujourd'hui Credo 3806
0383-2635 Jesus Marie Notre Temps 7802
0383-2651 Ievanhelyst
0383-2694 Mountain Breeze
0383-2708 Focus on Vancouver†
0383-2813 Canada-Mongolia Review†
0383-283X Squatchberry Journal†
0383-2848 Norman Paterson School of International Affairs. Bibliography Series 7200
0383-2929 Metropolitan Toronto Library Board. Theatre Section. Selected List of Acquisitions for Reference Use
0383-3003 Living Places†
0383-3356 Forage Crop Recommendations 272
0383-3372 Labour Legislation in Nova Scotia 1694
0383-3402 Electricity Today†
0383-3437 Labour Organizations in Nova Scotia 4598
0383-3623 Alberta Hansard 4613
0383-3712 Alberta. Legislature Library. Annual Report†
0383-3925 Manitoba. Health Services Commission. Annual Report†
0383-4301 Oecumenisme see 0383-431X 7639
0383-431X Ecumenism 7639
0383-4352 Saskatchewan Trading Corporation. Annual Report
0383-4379 Canada. Correctional Investigator. Annual Report 2646
0383-4417 Grain Matters 272
0383-4514 Documents in the History of Canadian Art†
0383-4638 Canada. Department of National Defence. Defence (Year) 6414
0383-4654 Cooperation Canada†
0383-4840 Annual Report of Municipal Statistics 7478
0383-4948 Province of New Brunswick. Department of Supply and Services. Annual Report 7461
0383-5030 Home†
0383-5154 Canada. Department of Industry, Trade and Commerce. Annual Report.†
0383-5359 Alberta Research Council. Bulletin 2701
0383-5391 Masterpieces in the National Gallery of Canada 504
0383-5405 Canadian Artists Series 481
0383-5588 Manitoba. Human Rights Commission. Annual Report 7212
0383-5766 Canada. Statistics Canada. Passenger Bus and Urban Transit Statistics 8523
0383-6037 Manisquare
0383-6061 Intercom (Guelph) 7761
0383-610X Maritime Professional
0383-6207 Dairy Contact
0383-6215 Record Week†
0383-624X Christian Nationalist Party News
0383-6266 Artswest
0383-6312 Smallholder 157
0383-6320 Sante Mentale au Quebec 7406
0383-6363 Hello Ottawa
0383-641X Comeback†
0383-6436 Countdown
0383-6479 Ontario Conservation News†
0383-6509 Caledonia Diocesan Times 7749
0383-6576 Canadian Oral History Association. Bulletin†
0383-669X Revue du Barreau 4774
0383-6711 Global Village Voice 1596
0383-7009 Ontario Snowmobiler 8326
0383-7300 Gift Magazine†
0383-7521 Derives†
0383-7653 Prairie Harvester 2297
0383-770X Canadian Book Review Annual 7557
0383-7769 Main Deck†
0383-7920 Canadian Rental Service 1080
0383-8277 Prions en Eglise - Edition Dominicale 7813
0383-8285 Prions en Eglise - Edition Complete 7813
0383-8307 Pretre et Pasteur 7813
0383-8358 Directory of Law Teachers 4658
0383-8420 Nova Scotia Historical Society. Collections
0383-8455 Universite de Montreal. Faculte de Medecine Veterinaire. Annuaire 8810
0383-8528 Dialect 8037
0383-8536 Nuclear Canada. Yearbook 3171
0383-8714 L'Actualite 3805
0383-9133 Lillooet District Historical Society. Bulletin†
0383-9184 Metric Fact Sheets 6404
0383-9230 Ontario Credit Union News†
0383-9249 Bruce Trail News 8307
0383-9257 Landscape Ontario†
0383-9370 Speak Up! 7185
0383-9486 Brotherhood of Railway Running Trades. Communique
0383-9494 Criminal Reports (Fifth Series) 4888
0383-9516 A M L F C Bulletin 5564
0383-9575 dANDelion 5420
0383-9648 Commercial Monthly
0383-9672 Color Spotlight
0383-9737 Commerce Journal†
0383-9745 Southam Business†
0383-9753 Society for the Study of Egyptian Antiquities. Journal 417
0383-9818 Jewellery World†
0383-9893 Canadian Business Conditions 1079
0383-9982 Connexion
0384-0158 Societe Historique de Saint-Boniface. Bulletin 4312
0384-0174 Critere†
0384-0298 Le Colombien 2265
0384-0425 Simgames†
0384-0433 Contemporary Poetry of British Columbia†
0384-062X Egale: a Journal on Women and the Law†

ISSN

0386-0779 International Latitude Observatory of Mizusawa. Publications†
0386-0795 Petroleum Industry in Japan
0386-0809 Kyoto University. Geophysical Institute. Contributions†
0386-0817 Sendai Astronomiaj Reportoj **581**
0386-0884 N G K Rebyu **7052**
0386-1058 Shinrigaku Hyoron **7408**
0386-1104 I A T S S Review **8631**
0386-1112 I A T S S Research **8584**
0386-118X Fukuoka Daigaku Rigaku Shuho **5488**
0386-1198 Institute for Sea Training. Journal **8646**
0386-1430 Atomu Fukushima **3165**
0386-1449 Way†
0386-1465 Furusato Tenbo†
0386-1511 Iwatsu Giho†
0386-1538 Reito to Kucho **4126**
0386-1570 Meiden Jiho
0386-183X Kagaku Saron†
0386-1856 Baiofidobakku Kenkyu **7338**
0386-2003 Shuppan Nyusu
0386-2054 Kensetsu Gyokai *changed to* 1349-2799 **3261**
0386-2062 Yakugaku Toshokan **5055**
0386-2097 Journal of Humanities (Chiba) **4460**
0386-2143 Kagaku Shoho **2094**
0386-2151 Kagaku Kyoiku *changed to* Kagaku to Kyoiku **2069**
0386-216X Kagaku Kogaku Ronbunshu **3249**
0386-2178 Bunseki **2098**
0386-2186 Kobunshi Ronbunshu **2126**
0386-2194 Japan Academy. Proceedings. Series A: Mathematical Sciences **5499**
0386-2208 Japan Academy. Proceedings. Series B: Physical and Biological Sciences **7870**
0386-2224 Hokkaido Nogyo Shikenjo Kenkyu Shiryo **118**
0386-2240 Suri Kagaku **5540**
0386-2321 Gendai Ringyo **3691**
0386-233X Speleological Society of Japan. Journal **2717**
0386-2372 Japan Meat Processing Journal **3649**
0386-2380 Okinawa Kannai Kisho Kenkyukaishi **6392**
0386-250X Vegetable and Ornamental Crops Research Station. Bulletin. Series B†
0386-2550 Seidenki Gakkaishi **7039**
0386-2615 Netsu Sokutei **7056**
0386-2682 Domyaku Koka†
0386-2704 Hiroshima Daigaku Keizai Ronso **1118**
0386-2755 Shiso (Tokyo) **4475**
0386-2763 Petorotekku **6786**
0386-2828 Purometeusu†
0386-2895 Denryoku Doboku
0386-300X Acta Medica Okayama **5566**
0386-3034 Hiroshima University. Journal of Science. Series A. Physics and Chemistry **7015**
0386-3042 J C A Journal **1573**
0386-3158 Hiroshima Forum for Psychology†
0386-3166 Hiroshima University. Laboratory for Amphibian Biology. Scientific Report†
0386-3271 Tokyo Gakugei Daigaku Tokushu Kyoiku Kenkyu Shisetsu Hokoku **3048**
0386-3425 Snake†
0386-3433 Yamaguchi University. Faculty of Engineering. Technology Reports **8445**
0386-3506 Sogo Toshi Kenkyu **8139**
0386-3530 Hokuriku Koshu Eisei Gakkaishi **7524**
0386-3565 Hiroshima Heiwa Kagaku **7140**
0386-3603 Yakuri to Chiryo **6886**
0386-3638 Nikkei Mechanical **3391**
0386-3980 Nihon Raigakkai Zasshi/Japanese Journal of Leprosy *changed to* 1342-3681 **5823**
0386-4006 Tokyo Joshi Daigaku Kiyo. Ronshu. Kagaku Bumon Hokoku **7923**
0386-4049 Kisho Kenkyujo Gijutsu Hokoku **6359**
0386-4073 Chikyu Kagaku **2704**
0386-4081 Kuki Chowa Eisei Kogaku **7530**
0386-4103 Oosaka-shi Igakkai Zasshi **5690**
0386-412X Kyoto Daigaku Bosai Kenkyujo Nenpo **7530**
0386-4138 Shizen Hogo **2627**
0386-4197 Umi no Hakubutsukan **2819**
0386-4200 Nihon Jakushi Shashi Gakkaiho **6046**
0386-4243 Sendai Denpa Kogyo Koto Senmon Gakko Kenkyu Kiyo **7999**
0386-4251 Young East†
0386-426X Tohokai†
0386-4286 Yokosuka-shi Hakubutsukan Shiryoshu **7933**
0386-4294 Gunma University. Faculty of Education. Annual Report: Cultural Science Series **4454**
0386-4383 Senshu Keizaigaku Ronshu **1172**
0386-4464 Hokkaido Kyoiku Daigaku Taisetsuzan Shizen Kyoiku Kenkyu Shisetsu Kenkyu Hokoku **7862**
0386-4502 Aimikku
0386-4553 Kagaku Kyoiku Kenkyu **2879**
0386-4766 Gekkan Saibo **832**
0386-4812 Nihon Keikei Kogakkaishi **1781**
0386-4928 Kinki Daigaku Rikogakubu Kenkyu Hokoku **7876**
0386-4944 Meiji Daigaku Kagaku Gijutsu Kenkyujo Kiyo **8431**
0386-4952 Meijo Daigaku Rikogakubu Kenkyu Hokoku **8432**
0386-4960 Sugaku Semina **5539**
0386-4987 Oosaka Denki Tsushin Daigaku Kenkyu Ronshu. Shizen Kagaku Hen **2335**
0386-4995 Doboku Kenkyujo Hokoku **3265**
0386-5037 Enshu no Shizen **7853**
0386-5096 Mitsubishi Electric Advance **3325**
0386-5126 Japan. Ministry of Agriculture, Forestry and Fisheries. National Research Institute of Agricultural Engineering. Abstracts from Research Reports **212**
0386-5290 Kyoto Furitsu Kaiyo Senta Kenkyu Hokoku **2811**
0386-5304 Hiroshimashi Shokubutsu Koen Kiyo **792**
0386-5428 A S C I I **2406**
0386-5444 Solar Terrestrial Environmental Research in Japan†
0386-5479 Denki to Koji **3299**
0386-5487 Shin Denki **3331**
0386-5525 National Institute of Polar Research. Memoirs. Series B: Meteorology **6392**
0386-5533 National Institute of Polar Research. Memoirs. Series C: Earth Sciences **2713**
0386-5541 National Institute of Polar Research. Memoirs. Series E: Biology and Medical Science **691**
0386-555X National Institute of Polar Research. Memoirs. Series F: Logistics **7887**
0386-5576 Ohm **3326**
0386-5819 Senshu Syogaku Ronshu **1172**
0386-5827 Senshu Shizen Kagaku Kiyo **7913**
0386-5835 Nihon Shika Masui Gakkai Zasshi **5772**
0386-5843 N G K Review. Overseas Edition **7052**
0386-586X Doboku Kenkyujo Iho **3265**
0386-5878 Doboku Kenkyujo Shiryo **3265**
0386-5886 Doboku Gijutsu Shiryo **3265**
0386-5924 Kawasaki Igakkai Shi **5657**
0386-5959 Shimane Journal of Medical Science **5714**
0386-5991 Kodai Mathematical Journal **5507**
0386-6092 Acta Medica Kinki University **5566**
0386-6106 Akita Igaku **5570**
0386-6157 Society of Powder Technology, Japan. Journal **3220**
0386-6262 Fukui-kenritsu Tanki Daigaku Kenkyu Kiyo
0386-6289 Shoni Kango **5981**
0386-6297 Price Indexes Monthly **1259**
0386-6319 Basic Sugaku **5475**
0386-6572 Nihon Denshi News **3109**
0386-6688 Pollen Science†
0386-6890 Takayama Tanki Daigaku Kenkyu Kiyo **7922**
0386-7080 Nara Shokubutsu Kenkyu **803**
0386-7196 Cell Structure and Function **830**
0386-720X Nanzan Institute for Religion and Culture. Bulletin **7664**
0386-7293 Current Contents of Academic Journals in Japan **623**
0386-7471 Chosetsu Koho Niigata **3360**
0386-7498 Dobutsuen Suizokukan Zasshi **940**
0386-7617 Seicho Kagaku Kyokai Kenkyu Nenpo **703**
0386-7668 Ibaraki Daigaku Kyoikugakubu Kiyo. Shizen Kagaku **7864**
0386-7722 Rinsho Kango **5980**
0386-7889 Nihon Deta Tsushin
0386-8109 Chiryogaku **748**
0386-8133 Boei Ika Daigakko Shingaku Katei Kenkyu Kiyo **4445**
0386-8141 Seitai Kagaku†
0386-8176 Ogasawara Kenkyu **7895**
0386-8192 Kosaku Kikai Nyusu **5454**
0386-8230 Hinshitsu **1750**
0386-8311 Jinkogaku Kenkyu **7286**
0386-8362 Sekai no Chikusan†
0386-8419 Nikuyogyu Kenkyukaiho
0386-8435 Research and Clinical Center for Child Development. Annual Report **2167**
0386-8559 Nagasakiken Chigakkaishi **2713**
0386-8605 Okinawa Toshokan Kyokai Shi **5038**
0386-8710 Tokyo Metropolitan University. Department of Geography. Geographical Reports **4031**
0386-8729 Jimbun Gakuho **4458**
0386-8761 Institute of Noise Control Engineering. Journal **7087**
0386-8796 Tobishima Giho, Doboku **3285**
0386-8850 Nihonshi Kenkyu **4187**
0386-8907 Rekishi Hyoron **4187**
0386-8931 Shiso (Kyoto) **4161**
0386-9059 Toyoshi-Kenkyu **4189**
0386-9113 Keiei Shigaku **1139**
0386-9164 Nihon Rekishi **4187**
0386-9237 Journal of Historical Studies **4170**
0386-9253 Seiyoshigaku **4263**
0386-9369 Shirin **4188**
0386-9512 Kagakushu Kenkyu (Tokyo, 1974) **2069**
0386-9539 Seibutsugakushi Kenkyu **703**
0386-9555 Sugakushi Kenkyu **5539**
0386-9571 Byoin Kanri **4089**
0386-9598 Gakkou Hoken Kenkyuu **7518**
0386-9601 Ganka Rinsho Iho **6042**
0386-961X Gendai Kagaku **2062**
0386-9628 Haigan **6020**
0386-9644 Igaku Kyoiku **5632**
0386-9687 Jibi Inkoka Tembo **6081**
0386-9695 Rinsho Men'eki/Clinical Immunology *changed to* 1881-1930 **5765**
0386-9709 Shinkei Naika **6185**
0386-9733 Recent Advances in Reticulo Endothelial System Research†
0386-9768 Nihon Shokaki Geka Gakkai Zasshi **5929**
0386-9784 Nishinihon Hifuka **5880**
0386-9792 Sanka to Fujinka
0386-9806 Shonika Shinryo **6104**
0386-9822 Sogo Rihabiriteshon **6116**
0386-9830 Kangogaku Zasshi **5968**
0386-9849 Rigaku Ryoho to Sagyo Ryoho/Japanese Journal of Physical Therapy and Occupational Therapy *changed to* 0915-1354 **6686**
0386-9857 Rinsho Geka **6257**
0386-9865 Rinsho Fujinka Sanka **6003**
0386-9873 Sanfujinka no Sekai **6004**
0386-9881 Shusanki Igaku **6004**
0386-9903 Nihon Bungaku **5341**
0387-0006 Igaku Chuo Zasshi **5632**
0387-0014 Shizen **8438**
0387-0022 Iden **872**
0387-0057 Chubu Denryoku K.K. Kenkyu Shiryo **3297**
0387-0138 Aomori Kenritsu Chuo Byoin Ishi **4088**
0387-0154 Atsuryoku Gijutsu **3182**
0387-0162 Boira Kenkyu **5449**
0387-0197 Yosetu Gijutsu **6345**
0387-0200 Reza Kenkyu **7084**
0387-0235 Nippon Shingo Giho **2335**
0387-0324 Kanagawa Daigaku Kogaku Kenkyujo Shoho **3206**
0387-0502 Chutanzo, Netsushori **6308**
0387-0707 Shokubutsu Boekijo Chosa Kenkyu Hokoku **252**
0387-0723 Uchu Koku Kankyo Igaku **5725**
0387-074X Hokuriku Daigaku Kiyo **2864**
0387-0758 Denki Kyokai Zasshi **3299**
0387-0766 Micro Computer & Electronics†
0387-0774 Denshi Zairyo **3092**
0387-0790 Doboku Seko **3265**
0387-0804 Aichi Kogyo Daigaku Kenkyu Hokoku. A Kyoyo Kankei Ronbunshu **3180**
0387-0812 Aichi Kogyo Daigaku Kenkyu Hokoku. B Senmon Kankei Ronbunshu **3180**
0387-0855 Fukushima Daigaku Kyoiku Gakubu Ronshu Rika Hokoku/Fukushima University. Faculty of Education. Science Reports *changed to* 1880-3903 **340**
0387-0863 Fune no Kagaku†
0387-088X Genshiryoku Chosa Jiho†
0387-0928 Genshiryoku Shiryo **3167**
0387-0936 Gosei Jushi **7092**
0387-0960 Kajima Kensetsu Gijutsu Kenkyujo Nenpo *changed to* 0918-015X **3277**
0387-0995 Kanazawa Daigaku Kyoikugakubu Kiyo. Shizen Kagaku Hen **7874**
0387-1002 Kansai Byochugai Kenkyukaiho **240**
0387-1010 Kansen, Ensho, Men'eki **5821**
0387-1029 Karyoku Genshiryoku Hatsuden **3176**
0387-1045 Machine Design **3388**
0387-1053 Kikai to Kogu **3387**
0387-1061 Konkurito Kogaku **1019**
0387-1088 Geriatric Medicine
0387-1096 Koon Gakkaishi **7055**
0387-1126 Myakkangaku **5796**
0387-1142 Nainen Kikan **3390**
0387-1150 Nara Kogyo Koto Senmon Gakko Kenkyu Kiyo **8433**
0387-1193 Nippon Rinsho Saibo Gakkai Zasshi **5687**
0387-1207 Gastroenterological Endoscopy **5924**
0387-1231 Rinsho Seijimbyo *changed to* 1347-0418 **5711**
0387-1304 Sumitomo Jukikai Giho
0387-1312 Sumitomo Kagaku Tokushugo **2081**
0387-1339 Toyama Daigaku Kogakubu Kiyo **3223**
0387-1452 Norinsho Koho **142**
0387-1533 Nihon Reoroji Gakkaishi **7061**
0387-1541 Clinician **5598**
0387-1592 Nanzan Law Review **4738**
0387-1711 Asia Pacific Community†
0387-172X Tohoku Nogyo Shikenjo Kenkyu Shiryo†
0387-1819 Sho Energi **3220**
0387-1851 Nihon Kafun Gakkai Kaishi **6727**
0387-1924 Kaseki Kenkyukai Kaishi **6726**
0387-1940 Robotto **2586**
0387-1975 Shokuhin Shosha **3663**
0387-1983 Puresutoresuto Konkurito **1030**
0387-2203 Zosen Gijutsu **8666**
0387-2254 Taisei Kensetsu Gijutsu Kenkyujoho **1039**
0387-2319 Sangyo to Denki **3330**
0387-2335 Nogyo Doboku Gakkai Rombunshu **141**
0387-2343 Nihon Shika Hozongaku Zasshi **5857**
0387-2351 Nova Angiologicae
0387-2432 Mitsubishi Juko Giho **8432**
0387-2440 Gakujutsu Geppo **7857**
0387-2483 Shakai Jinruigaku Nenpo **355**
0387-2645 Shokaki Geka **5931**
0387-2653 Bunben to Masui **5987**
0387-2688 Bijutsushigaku **478**
0387-2718 Hiryo Kagaku **234**
0387-2785 Asahi Ajia Rebyu†
0387-2793 Jinko Mondai Kenkyu **7286**
0387-2807 Ajia, Afurika Gengo Bunka Kenkyu **4179**
0387-2815 American Review **4282**
0387-2831 Doitsu Bungaku **5285**
0387-2882 Journal of Law and Politics **4702**
0387-2939 Journal of Insurance Science **4510**
0387-2955 K S U Economic and Business Review **1139**
0387-3005 Katorikku Kenkyu **7803**
0387-3021 Doshisha University Economic Review **1093**
0387-3064 Kikan Shakai Hosho Kenkyu **7286**
0387-3099 Koeki Jigyo Kenkyu **3141**
0387-3102 Public Law Review **4763**
0387-3110 Kokugo to Kokubungaku **5137**
0387-3129 Kokumin Keizai Zasshi **1141**
0387-3145 Kyoiku Shakaigaku Kenkyu **2881**
0387-3161 Kyoikugaku Kenkyu **2881**
0387-3196 Nippon Chugoku Gakkaiho **4187**
0387-3234 Nogyo Keizai Kenkyu **204**
0387-3242 Nogyo Sogo Kenkyu **204**
0387-3307 Shakai Kagaku Kenkyu **8000**
0387-3374 Tokushu Kyokugaku Kenkyu **3048**
0387-3382 Toshi Mondai **7504**
0387-3404 Waseda Shogaku **1434**
0387-3439 *see* 0039-3649 **5288**
0387-3447 Kokubungaku Kenkyu Shiryokan Kiyo *changed to* 1880-2230 **5318**
0387-3498 Gekkan Chikyu **2707**
0387-351X Nasu Suteshon†
0387-3528 National Institute of Special Education. Bulletin **3044**
0387-3544 Press Working **5458**
0387-365X Oosaka Furitsu Kogyo Koto Senmon Gakko Kenkyu Kiyo **8434**
0387-3668 Rinsho Masui **5774**
0387-3730 Nanzan Journal of Theological Studies **7665**
0387-3773 Kokusai Noringyo Kyoryoku **131**
0387-3803 Jidosha Kenkyu **8587**
0387-382X Kaiyo Kagaku Gijutsu Senta Shiken Kenkyu Hokoku **2810**
0387-3870 Tokyo Journal of Mathematics **5542**
0387-3927 J P G Letter **7564**
0387-4001 Kagaku Gijutsu Bunken Sokuho. Energi-hen†
0387-4028 Meteorological Satellite Center. Monthly Report **6391**
0387-4087 Yamaguchi Daigaku Kyoyobu Kiyo. Shizen Kagaku Hen **7932**
0387-4095 Sekei Saigai Geka **6072**
0387-4133 Dokkyo Ika Daigaku Kyoyo Igakka Kiyo/Dokkyo University School of Medicine. Bulletin of General Education *changed to* 1348-9917 **4467**
0387-4141 Hissu Aminosan Kenkyu **733**
0387-4168 Nihon Gasu Tabin Gakkaishi **3391**
0387-4249 Nagasakiken Seibutsu Gakkaishi **691**
0387-4338 Sekai no Norinsuisan **155**
0387-4419 Oosaka Daigaku Teion Senta Dayori **7056**

ISSN

9282 0387-446X ULRICH'S PERIODICALS

0387-446X Oosaka Daigaku Iryo Gijutsu Tanki Daigakubu Kenkyu Kiyo. Shizen Kagaku Iryo Kagaku Hen†
0387-4508 Osaka University. Joining & Welding Research Institute. Transactions **6343**
0387-4532 Nagoya Daigaku Kyoyobu Kiyo B. Shizen Kagaku, Shinrigaku†
0387-4605 Oyo Shinrigaku Kenkyu **7389**
0387-4745 Pacific Society. Journal **351**
0387-4753 Seijo University Economic Papers **1172**
0387-494X Oosaka Shika Daigaku Seirigaku Kyoshitsu Ronbunshu
0387-4982 Tsukuba Journal of Mathematics **5542**
0387-4990 Tokyo Daigaku Chokoatsu Denshi Kenbikyoshitsu Nenpo **7052**
0387-5008 Nihon Kikai Gakkai Ronbunshu. A Hen **3391**
0387-5016 Nihon Kikai Gakkai Ronbunshu. B Hen **3391**
0387-5024 Nihon Kikai Gakkai Ronbunshu. C Hen **3391**
0387-5040 Foreign Press Center Japan. Press Guide†
0387-5113 Tobishima Giho, Kenchiku **3285**
0387-5172 Nihon Shino Kunrenshi Kyokaishi **6046**
0387-5245 Office Equipment and Products†
0387-5253 Society of Cosmetic Chemists of Japan. Journal **596**
0387-5350 Dobutsutachi
0387-5369 Kishou Kenkyu Noto **6359**
0387-5385 Meiden Review
0387-5504 Journal of Naval Architecture and Ocean Engineering **2809**
0387-5512 Zugaku Kenkyu **529**
0387-5547 Teikyo Igaku Zasshi **5720**
0387-5695 Yugato **861**
0387-5733 Elytra **843**
0387-5784 Yamaguchi Keibingu Kurabu Kaiho **6731**
0387-5857 Standard Frequency and Time Service Bulletin†
0387-5911 Kansenshogaku Zasshi **5821**
0387-5970 Dharma World **7701**
0387-6004 Senri Ethnological Studies **355**
0387-6055 Tokyo Kogei Daigaku Kogakubu Kiyo **3223**
0387-6101 Journal of Information Processing†
0387-6144 Research Laboratory for Nuclear Reactors. Bulletin **3174**
0387-6195 Kondensa Hyoron†
0387-6454 Hiroshima Kenritsu Byoin Ishi **5628**
0387-6837 Rikkyo Daigaku Kenkyu Hokoku. Shizen Kagaku†
0387-7000 Zasshi Shinbun Sokatarogu **639**
0387-7019 Gekkan Media Deeta **1997**
0387-7035 Kitami Kogyo Daigaku Kenkyu Hokoku **8430**
0387-7310 Keizai Kagaku Ronshu **1139**
0387-7337 Erekutoroniku Seramikkusu†
0387-7361 Kitakyushu Shokubutsu Tomo no Kai Kaiho **799**
0387-7434 Educational Technology Research **8421**
0387-7515 Bungei Gengo Kenkyu. Gengo-hen **5102**
0387-7523 Bungei Gengo Kenkyu. Bungei-hen **5267**
0387-754X Denki Kako Gakkaishi **3299**
0387-7590 Shiron **5371**
0387-7604 Brain & Development **6127**
0387-7833 Kyoto Kyoiku Daigaku Kiyo. A: Jimbun, Shakai/Kyoto University of Education. Bulletin. Series A. Education, Social Sciences, Literature and Arts *changed to* Kyouto Kyouiku Daigaku Kiyou **7878**
0387-7868 Oita Daigaku Kogakubu Kenkyu Hokoku **3213**
0387-7906 Kawasaki Juko Giho **3369**
0387-7973 Jikken Shakai Shinrigaku Kenkyu **7367**
0387-8007 Karento Aweanesu **5022**
0387-8023 Shoni no Noshinkei **6185**
0387-8082 Acta Sumerologica **5090**
0387-821X Sangyo Ika Daigaku Zasshi **6686**
0387-8236 Niigata Daigaku Rigakubu Fuzoku Sado Rinkai Jikkenjo Tokubetsu Hokoku†
0387-8341 Okinawa Gijutsu Noto **6392**
0387-8406 Winds†
0387-8503 Japanese Periodicals Index. Medical Sciences and Pharmacology†
0387-8511 National Science Museum. Bulletin. Series E: Physical Sciences and Engineering **3212**
0387-8538 Saga University. Faculty of Science and Engineering. Department of Mathematics. Reports. Mathematics **5532**
0387-8597 Hiroshimashi Shokubutsu Koen Saibai Kiroku **792**
0387-8716 Shiretoko Hakubutsukan Kenkyu Hokoku **7915**
0387-8805 Journal of Light & Visual Environment **7078**
0387-8929 Tokyo Gakugei Daigaku Kiyo. Dai 2-bumon, Jimbun Kagaku/Tokyo Gakugei University. Bulletin. Series 2, Humanities *changed to* 1880-4314 **4478**
0387-8937 Tokyo Gakugei Daigaku Kiyo. Dai 3-bumon, Shakai Kagaku/Tokyo Gakugei University. Bulletin. Series 3, Social Sciences *changed to* 1880-4322 **4478**
0387-8961 Nihon Purankuton Gakkaiho **694**
0387-9003 Nihon Oyo Dobutsu Konchu Gakkai Chugoku Shibu Kaiho **856**
0387-9089 Toyama-shi Kagaku Bunka Senta Kenkyu Hokoku **7924**
0387-9097 Shimane Ika Daigaku Kiyo **5713**
0387-9119 Rinboku no Ikushu **3701**
0387-9194 Nippon Biyo Geka Gakkaishi **6253**
0387-9259 Toyoda Machine Works Technical Review **5460**
0387-9283 Toba Shosen Koto Senmon Gakko Kiyo **8663**
0387-9313 Saitama Daigaku Kiyo. Kyoikugakubu. Sugaku, Shizen Kagaku†
0387-9348 Heron†
0387-9364 Saitama Daigaku Kogakubu Kensetsukei Kenkyu Hokoku **3282**
0387-9569 Interface **2423**
0387-964X Kitakyushu Shiritsu Shizenshi Hakubutsukan Kenkyu Hokoku/Kitakyushu Museum of Natural History. Bulletin *changed to* 1348-2653 **7876**
0387-964X Kitakyushu Shiritsu Shizenshi Hakubutsukan Kenkyu Hokoku/Kitakyushu Museum of Natural History. Bulletin *changed to* 1349-323X **345**
0387-9666 Byotai Seiri (Tokyo) **920**
0387-9674 Genshiryoku Anzen Iinkai Geppo **7066**
0387-9690 Gekkan Oroshi Yakugyo
0387-981X My Passport†
0387-9844 Ogasawara Kenkyu Nenpo **7895**
0388-0001 Language Sciences **5141**
0388-001X Rakuno Gakuen Daigaku Kiyo. Shizen Kagaku Hen **269**
0388-0028 Rakuno Gakuen Daigaku Kiyo. Jinbun Shakai Kagaku Hen **149**
0388-0036 Nippon Gakushiin Kiyo **7989**
0388-0079 Marine Engineering Society in Japan. Bulletin **3209**
0388-0125 Niigata Airglow Observatory. Bulletin **7028**
0388-0168 Tokyo Metropolitan Rehabilitation Center for the Physically and Mentally Handicapped. Bulletin†
0388-0176 Chu-Shikoku Studies in American Literature **5273**
0388-0192 Cancer Research Institute Report **6014**
0388-0206 Climatological Notes **6351**
0388-0214 Contemporary Japan†
0388-0230 Kyoto University. Department of Astronomy. Contributions **577**
0388-0303 Farming Japan **112**
0388-0311 Focus Japan†
0388-032X Now in Japan
0388-0435 Japan Echo **4184**
0388-0508 Journal of Intercultural Studies **345**
0388-0532 Kyoto Review†
0388-0605 Monthly Finance Review **1368**
0388-0648 National Theatre of Japan **8474**
0388-0664 Nippon Tungsten Review **2117**
0388-0702 Rajio Nippon Nyusu *see* 0033-7927 **2362**
0388-0761 Pacific Friend *changed to* 1348-4419
0388-0788 Tokai University. Faculty of Engineering. Proceedings **3223**
0388-0796 Renaissance Bulletin **5359**
0388-080X Agency of Industrial Science and Technology. Electrotechnical Laboratory. Summaries of Reports **3294**
0388-0834 Electric Power Survey
0388-0966 Tokyo University of Fisheries. Transactions†
0388-1008 Waseda Business and Economic Studies **1193**
0388-1032 Wing Newsletter
0388-113X Cahiers du Japon *see* 0388-0435 **4184**
0388-1237 Iberoamericana **7971**
0388-127X J J P E N: Japanese Journal of Parenteral and Enteral Nutrition†
0388-130X Meisei Daigaku Kenkyu Kiyo. Rikogakubu **3210**
0388-1350 Journal of Toxicological Sciences **3499**
0388-1423 A M J Newsletter†
0388-1512 Bosei Eisei **8844**
0388-158X J A S Journal **8153**
0388-1601 Rinsho Yakuri **6879**
0388-1717 Kyushu Daigaku Daigakuin Sogo Rikogaku Kenkyuka Hokoku **3208**
0388-1865 World Traders†
0388-1911 Junkankika **5794**
0388-1989 Tokyo Denki University. Faculty of Science and Engineering. Research Activities **3223**
0388-208X Kindai Judo **8184**
0388-211X Kokusai Iyakuhin Joho **6858**
0388-2128 Jitchuken Zenrinsho Igaku Kenkyujo Nenpo†
0388-2217 Mitsubachi Kagaku **855**
0388-225X Fujikura Technical Review **3309**
0388-2314 Kosei Nenkin Byoin Nenpo **4105**
0388-2330 Kyoto University. College of Agriculture. Memoirs **131**
0388-2349 Kyoto University. Kwasan and Hida Observatories. Contributions **577**
0388-2403 Norin Suisansho Kachiku Eisei Shikenjo Kenkyu Hokoku/Japan. National Institute of Animal Health. Bulletin *changed to* 1347-2542 **8796**
0388-2616 Hiroshimaken Byoin Yakuzaishikai Gakujutsu Nenpo **6846**
0388-2845 Hana no Wa **792**
0388-2926 Takuma Denpa Kogyo Koto Senmon Gakko. Kenkyu Kiyo **3332**
0388-3051 Nihon Hakuyo Kikan Gakkaishi/Marine Engineering Society in Japan. Journal *changed to* 1346-1427 **3209**
0388-3345 Zenitakagumi Giho **3287**
0388-3396 Mitsubishi Genshiryoku Giho
0388-3515 Seikei Kisho Kansokujo Hokoku **6400**
0388-3647 Kyoritsu Joshi Tanki Daigaku. Bunka. Kiyo **5319**
0388-3698 Peptide Chemistry **741**
0388-3752 Gensei Dobutsugaku Zasshi **944**
0388-3841 Jidosha Kogaku **8587**
0388-3906 Waseda Journal of Asian Studies **4190**
0388-3930 Zairyo Kagaku *changed to* 1347-4774 **3360**
0388-4015 Kaigai Denryoku **3323**
0388-4066 Kensetsu Kikaika Kenkyujo Nenpo **1019**
0388-4112 National Defense Academy. Memoirs. Mathematics, Physics, Chemistry and Engineering **7886**
0388-418X Mushi **855**
0388-4252 Kikai Gijutsu Kenkyujo Shoho†
0388-4449 Iwate Horticulture Experiment Station. Bulletin **238**
0388-449X Yokohama Port News **8665**
0388-4627 Chiba Kogyo Daigaku Kenkyu Hokoku *changed to* 0385-7026 **8418**
0388-4732 Hakusan **2613**
0388-4783 Minophagen Medical Review **6861**
0388-4953 Sprout (Tokyo, 1980)†
0388-5070 Shizuoka Daigaku Daigakuin Denshi Kagaku Kenkyuka Kenkyu Hokoku **3113**
0388-5119 Diamond Box (Year) **3900**
0388-5186 J A I C I Forum **2066**
0388-5208 Chigaku Dantai Kenkyukai. Sokuho **2728**
0388-5216 Research for Religion & Parapsychology†
0388-5267 Energy Forum **3131**
0388-5321 Hyomen Kagaku **7015**
0388-5461 Uo **966**
0388-550X Gifu-ken Hakubutsukan Chosa Kenkyu Hokoku **7858**
0388-5585 Kurinikaru Sutadi **5968**
0388-5607 Tohoku University. Science Reports. Series 8: Physics and Astronomy **7043**
0388-5704 Nenpo Keizaigaku **1152**
0388-5712 Nittsuko Giho **3326**
0388-5852 Tenmon Kaiho **582**
0388-5976 Norin Suisan Tosho Shiryo Geppo **184**
0388-600X N K K News **3390**
0388-6107 Biomedical Research **5586**
0388-6115 Japan Pictorial†
0388-6174 University of Tsukuba. Institute of Geoscience. Science Reports. Section A: Geographical Sciences **4033**
0388-6182 University of Tsukuba. Institute of Geoscience. Science Reports. Section B: Geological Sciences **2773**
0388-6212 Shokubutsu Chiri Bunrui Kenkyu **817**
0388-6298 Shizuoka Daigaku Chikyu Kagaku Kenkyu Hokoku **2716**
0388-631X Okayama Prefectural Dairy Experiment Station. Bulletin†
0388-6417 Jochi Eigo Bungaku Kenkyu **5132**
0388-645X Taisho Daigaku Sogo Bukkyo Kenkyujo Nenpo **7702**
0388-6492 Celastrina **842**
0388-659X Ionics
0388-6719 Gendai Toyo Igaku†
0388-6735 Nihon Chinetsu Gakkaishi **2787**
0388-6859 Shimane Daigaku Hobungakubu Kiyo. Bungakuka Hen **8001**
0388-6999 Gijutsu Kenkyujoho **3268**
0388-7081 Patents and Licensing **6756**
0388-709X Nikko Foramu **1900**
0388-7154 Niigataken Seibutsu Kyoiku Kenkyukaishi **694**
0388-7219 Kodai Oriento Hakubutsukan Kiyo **402**
0388-7359 Kishocho Jishin Kansokujo Gijutsu Hokoku **2786**
0388-7367 Aichi Kyoiku Daigaku Kenkyu Hokoku. Geijutsu, Hoken Taiiku, Kasei, Gijutsu Kagaku **7833**
0388-7405 Nihon Kokai Gakkai Ronbunshu **8655**
0388-7421 Dobutsu Iyakuhin Kensajo Nenpo **8796**
0388-743X Gifuken Koseiren Igaku Zasshi†
0388-7480 Kyoiku Ongaku, Shogaku-ban **6583**
0388-7502 Kyoiku Ongaku, Chugaku Koko-ban **6583**
0388-7529 Meintenansu†
0388-7561 Hyogoken Ishikaiho **5631**
0388-7596 Keio Communications Review **7981**
0388-788X Gyobyo Kenkyu **945**
0388-8231 Kanagawa-ken Nogyo Sogo Kenkyujo Kenkyu Hokoku **130**
0388-8266 Kinjin Kenkyujo Kenkyu Hokoku **799**
0388-8401 Nagasaki-ken Suisan Shikenjo. Kenkyu Hokoku **3602**
0388-8738 Yoshida Kagaku Gijutsu Zaidan Nyusu **8445**
0388-886X Kansai University Review of Law and Politics **4709**
0388-9009 Kanagawa Shizenshi Shiryo **7874**
0388-9327 Yamaguchi-ken Nogyo Shikenjo KenkyuHhokoku **171**
0388-9408 Tan to Sui **5900**
0388-9459 Kankyo Gijutsu **3449**
0388-9475 Kawasaki Steel Technical Report *changed to* 1348-0677 **6318**
0388-9491 Shiroari **858**
0388-9653 Kisho Eisei Senta Gijutsu Hokoku **6359**
0388-9718 Suisan Kogaku Kenkyujo Kenkyu Hokoku **3609**
0388-9734 Shojinkai Igakushi **5714**
0389-0023 Musashi Kogyo Daigaku Genshiroto Kyodo Riyo Kenkyu Seika Hokokusho†
0389-0066 G A Document **443**
0389-0244 Kochi Daigaku Gakujutsu Kenkyu Hokoku. Shizen Kagaku **7877**
0389-0260 Kochi University. Faculty of Science. Memoirs. Series B, Physics **7024**
0389-0279 Kochi University. Faculty of Science. Memoirs. Series C, Chemistry **2070**
0389-0287 Kochi University. Faculty of Science. Memoirs. Series D, Biology **686**
0389-0295 Kochi University. Faculty of Science. Memoirs. Series E, Geology **2752**
0389-0341 Hoshi no Tomo **575**
0389-0449 Kochi Daigaku Kyoikugakubu Kenkyu Hokoku. Dai-3-Bu **2881**
0389-0457 Kochi Daigaku Gakujutsu Kenkyu Hokoku. Jinbun Kagaku **4462**
0389-0473 Kochi Daigaku Gakujutsu Kenkyu Hokoku. Nogaku **131**
0389-0503 Economic Eye†
0389-0538 Hogaku Kenkyu **4687**
0389-0988 Gurin Pawa **3692**
0389-102X Ryukyu Daigaku Kogakubu Kiyo **3218**
0389-1046 Denpa Kenkyujo Nyusu *changed to* N I C T News **2334**
0389-116X Keio Law Review **4709**
0389-1186 Japanese Slavic & East European Studies **7247**
0389-1194 I C U to C C U†
0389-1313 Nihon Seikisho Gakkai Zasshi **6392**
0389-1445 Edaphologia **941**
0389-1550 Denki Kako Gijutsu **3299**
0389-1631 Kumatoto Chigakkaishi **4018**
0389-1658 Kobe Jogakuin Daigaku Ronshu **2992**
0389-1755 Chikei **2729**
0389-1771 Kazi **8277**
0389-1836 Azabu Daigaku Juigakubu Kenkyu Hokoku *changed to* 1346-5880 **935**
0389-1844 Junkan Seigyo **5821**
0389-1879 Seko **1035**
0389-1887 Medical Technology **5672**
0389-1895 Shika Giko **5865**
0389-2050 Toukai Daigaku Kaiyogakubu Gyosekishu†
0389-2131 Hoshi no Techo **575**
0389-214X Eizo Joho Medikaru *changed to* 1346-1354 **6195**
0389-2166 Shinrin Bunka Kenkyu **3702**
0389-2441 Teion Kogaku **7056**
0389-2514 Nippon Kogyo Daigaku Knkyu Hokoku **7893**
0389-2751 Akitu **838**
0389-3030 Kagawa Daigaku Keizai Ronso **1495**
0389-3057 Kagawa Daigaku Kyoikugakubu Kenkyu Hokoku. Dai-2-Bu **2879**
0389-3081 Tokai Daigaku Kiyo. Gaikokugo Kyoiku Senta **5188**
0389-312X Doshisha Shinri **7352**
0389-3502 Japan: An International Comparison **8382**
0389-3510 Speaking of Japan†
0389-3626 Shoka to Kyushu **5931**
0389-3634 Hip Joint **6061**
0389-3723 Rinsho Seishin Byori **7405**
0389-3847 Kaseki no Tomo **6726**
0389-3898 Igaku to Yakugaku **6847**
0389-3928 Hokuriku Ishi **5629**
0389-4002 Nihon Zenkoku Shoshi **632**
0389-4010 Koku Uchu Gijutsu Kenkyujo Hokoku **64**
0389-4029 Bungaku **5267**
0389-4037 Nihongo Kyoiku **5155**

0389-4045 Gaku Ganmen Hotetsu **6244**
0389-4061 Hiroshimaken Hospital Pharmacists Association. Drug Information News **6846**
0389-4088 Kochi Gakuen College. Bulletin
0389-4118 Arukoru Kenkyu to Yakubutsu Izon/Japanese Journal of Alcohol Studies and Drug Dependence (Kyoto, 1981) *changed to* 1341-8963 **2697**
0389-4150 Japan. Ministry of Construction. Public Works Research Institute. Newsletter†
0389-4215 Industrial Design
0389-4304 J S A E Review *changed to* 1349-4724 **8601**
0389-4703 Nihon Keisei Geka Gakkai Kaishi **6253**
0389-4843 Chui Rinsho **308**
0389-4894 Chusei Sogo Byoin Zasshi/Chusei General Hospital. Journal *changed to* 1340-7015
0389-4983 Hokuden Gijutsu Kaihatsu Nyusu **3310**
0389-4991 Kan, Tan, Sui, Japan **5896**
0389-5025 Suzugamine Joshi Tandai Kenkyu Shuho. Shizen Kagaku **7921**
0389-5068 Fujita Kogyo Gijutsu Kenkyujoho **3267**
0389-5122 Hachinohe Shiritsu Shimin Byoin Ishi†
0389-5246 Nihon Shokubutsuen Kyokaishi **805**
0389-5386 Nihon Hotetsu Shika Gakkai Zasshi *changed to* 1883-1958 **5853**
0389-5491 Hiba Kagaku **7861**
0389-5505 Koyoju Kenkyu **3695**
0389-5564 Geka to Taisha Eiyo **6244**
0389-5602 Nihon Tokei Gakkaishi (Tokyo, 1971) **1255**
0389-5610 Shinkei Gaisho **6185**
0389-5793 Chizu Nyusu†
0389-5858 National Research Institute of Aquaculture. Bulletin **3602**
0389-617X Tokyo Denki University. Faculty of Engineering. Research Reports **3223**
0389-6390 Hokuriku Denryoku K.K. Gijutsu Kenkyujo Gijutsu Kenkyu Hokoku **3310**
0389-6609 Seto Marine Biological Laboratory. Special Publication Series **704**
0389-6625 Kogaku **7079**
0389-6633 Kankyo Joho Kagaku **3449**
0389-6692 Kagoshima Daigaku Kyoikugakubu Kenkyu Kiyo. Shizen Kagaku Hen **7874**
0389-6838 Suzukuri **964**
0389-6897 Kurume Kogyo Daigaku Kenkyu Hokoku **8430**
0389-6951 Watashitachi no Shizenshi **7928**
0389-696X Hosupitaru
0389-7087 Kanto Seikei Saigai Geka Gakkai Zasshi **6066**
0389-729X Bunkazai no Chu-kin-gai **223**
0389-7303 Dokuta Saron **5606**
0389-7389 Abstracts of the Current Literature on Respiratory Diseases and T B†
0389-7451 Kurinikku Magajin **5659**
0389-746X Drug Magazine **6835**
0389-7540 Gunma Daigaku Iryo Gijutsu Tanki Daigakubu Kiyo/Gunma University. College of Medical Care and Technology. Annual Reports *changed to* 1343-4179 **5621**
0389-7605 Hokkyokusei Hoikakuhyo **575**
0389-7834 Kagoshima Daigaku Shigakubu Kiyo **5854**
0389-7842 Nanki Seibutsu **691**
0389-7850 Nanki Seibutsukaiho/Nanki Biological Society. News *changed to* 0287-5349 **686**
0389-8067 Hoso Kenkyu†
0389-8105 Oosaka-shiritsu Shizenshi Hakubutsukan Kanpo **6535**
0389-8148 Higuma **946**
0389-8237 Ionospheric Data at Showa Station (Antarctica) **6358**
0389-827X Hiroshima Mushi no Kai Kaiho **848**
0389-8326 Gekkan Nashingu **5959**
0389-8431 Academia. Bungaku, Gogaku Hen **5248**
0389-8458 Academia. Jinbun, Shakai Kagaku Hen **4439**
0389-8865 Shumi no San'yaso **817**
0389-8970 National Institute of Hygienic Sciences. Monthly Report†
0389-9004 Japan. Statistics Bureau. Management and Coordination Agency. Japan Statistical Yearbook **8382**
0389-9047 Oosaka-shiritsu Shizenshi Hakubutsukan Shuzo Shiryo Mokuroku **695**
0389-9071 Tairyoku Kenkyu **6998**
0389-9098 Byoin Yakugaku/Japanese Journal of Hospital Pharmacy *changed to* 1346-342X **6851**
0389-911X Seibu Zosenkai Kaiho/West-Japan Society of Naval Architects. Transactions *changed to* 1880-3717 **8655**
0389-9128 Shiga Shizen Kyoiku Kenkyu Shisetsu Kenkyu Gyoseki **2716**
0389-9160 A + U **425**
0389-9225 Mie Daigaku Kyoiku Gakubu Kenkyu Kiyo. Shizen Kagaku/Mie University. Faculty of Education. Bulletin. Natural Science *changed to* 1880-2419 **2886**
0389-9233 Mie Daigaku Kyoiku Gakubu Kenkyu Kiyo. Jimbun Kagaku/Mie University. Faculty of Education. Bulletin. Humanities *changed to* 1880-2419 **2886**
0389-925X Mie Daigaku Kyoiku Gakubu Kenkyu Kiyo. Kyoiku Kagaku/Mie University. Faculty of Education. Bulletin. Educational Science *changed to* 1880-2419 **2886**
0389-9306 Asahikawa Kogyo Koto Senmon Gakko kenkyu Hobun/Asahikawa Technical College. Journal *changed to* Asahikawa National College of Technology. Journal **2967**
0389-9357 Nihon Shikisai Gakkaishi **7081**
0389-9500 Kikai Shinko **5454**
0389-9551 Kogakkan Daigaku Kiyo *changed to* 1344-4468 **5318**
0389-9578 Kobe Tokiwa Tanki Daigaku Kiyo **7877**
0389-9705 Shika Hoshasen **5865**
0389-9713 Kazan Funka Yochi Renrakukai Kaiho **2786**
0389-9780 Cosmica **5108**
0389-9861 Komazawa Daigaku Keizai Gakubu Kenkyu Kiyo **1141**
0390-0010 Istituto Sperimentale per la Selvicoltura. Annali **3694**
0390-0037 Chronobiologia
0390-0088 Clinica Neuropsichiatrica†
0390-0096 Rassegna di Studi Etiopici **4177**
0390-010X Rassegna Economica **1513**
0390-0134 Giornale Italiano di Ortopedia e Traumatologia **6061**
0390-0142 Critica Letteraria **5280**
0390-0150 Altri Termini†
0390-0304 La Moto† **8975**
0390-0320 Quadrangolo
0390-0347 Medico e Paziente **5675**
0390-0355 Terzo Occhio **522**
0390-038X Unita Proletaria† **8996**
0390-0398 Musica Popolare
0390-0444 Colture Protette **3727**
0390-0460 Micologia Italiana **801**
0390-0479 VigneVini **257**
0390-0495 Rassegna Italiana di Chirurgia Pediatrica† **8984**
0390-0517 Oncologia Clinica†
0390-0541 Industrie delle Bevande **605**
0390-0584 Antichita Pisane†
0390-0592 Archeologia Medievale **379**
0390-0606 Archivio Amministrativo ed Urbanistico Subalpino
0390-0614 Universita degli Studi di Lecce. Bollettino di Storia della Filosofia† **8996**
0390-0657 Critica del Diritto† **8947**
0390-0711 Medioevo Romanzo **5150**
0390-0738 Nuovo Diritto Agrario *changed to* 1826-0373 **106**
0390-0746 Gli Ospedali della Vita† **8979**
0390-0851 Sociologia del Diritto **4784**
0390-0886 Anarchismo† **8930**
0390-0975 Informatica e Diritto **5016**
0390-0991 Lavoro e Sindacato (Print) *changed to* 1826-2422 **1695**
0390-1009 Archivio Storico Civico e Biblioteca Trivulziana. Libri & Documenti **615**
0390-1025 Modulo **1025**
0390-105X Quaderni di Economia del Lavoro **1704**
0390-1076 La Repubblica **3898**
0390-1106 Giornale di Astronomia **575**
0390-1173 Aerei **4326**
0390-1181 Affari Sociali Internazionali **8085**
0390-1289 Anthropos **327**
0390-1297 Archivio Sardo del Movimento Operaio Contadino e Antonomistico
0390-1319 Arte Naive† **8931**
0390-1378 Banche e Banchieri **1311**
0390-1513 Casa Stile **4535**
0390-1521 Casaviva **4555**
0390-1572 Civilta del Bere† **8941**
0390-1750 Costarossa
0390-1807 Cronorama†
0390-1882 Il Diritto di Famiglia e delle Persone **4908**
0390-2048 Enohobby† **8953**
0390-2102 Europa Domani
0390-2153 Forme del Significato†
0390-2196 Geo - Archeologia **395**
0390-2269 Giurisprudenza Commerciale **4869**
0390-2285 Gong
0390-2358 I C P **3246**
0390-2412 Incontri Linguistici **5126**
0390-2420 Infanzia
0390-2439 Informatica & Documentazione
0390-2447 Informazioni Aziendali e Professionali†
0390-2455 Informazione Elettronica† **8964**
0390-2498 Iterarte
0390-251X Lavoro e Previdenza Oggi **4713**
0390-2528 Lavoro Sicuro† **8970**
0390-2617 Libri delle Biblioteche Trentine **5029**
0390-2692 M C Meeting e Congress **6281**
0390-2811 Mondo Cinese† **8975**
0390-2897 Naifs e l'Arte Popolare
0390-2927 Navigazione Interna† **8976**
0390-2935 Nicolaus **7809**
0390-3036 Nuova Stoa **6937**
0390-3044 Nuovi Orientamenti†
0390-3079 Oggi e Domani
0390-3087 Onda Quadra† **8978**
0390-3141 Pan **5159**
0390-3230 Piscine Oggi **8193**
0390-329X Presenza Tecnica **3216**
0390-3311 Prima Comunicazione **2336**
0390-3338 Primo Maggio
0390-346X Psicologia Contemporanea **7392**
0390-3605 Quaderni Siciliani†
0390-3656 Quinta Generazione
0390-3877 Rivista di Studi Fenici **415**
0390-4148 Settimanale
0390-4229 Sociologia dell'Organizzazione **8136**
0390-4253 Storia Architettura
0390-4296 Strumenti (Rome) **458**
0390-4393 Studia Historica et Philologica: Sectio Slavica† **8991**
0390-4415 Il Subacqueo **8336**
0390-4520 Trasporti†
0390-4539 30 Giorni **7824**
0390-4555 Tuscia†
0390-4601 Uomo Mare†
0390-4628 La Voce della Campania *changed to* La Voce delle Voci **7192**
0390-4717 Manifesto. Quaderno *see* 0025-2158 **3897**
0390-492X Memorie di Biologia Marina e di Oceanografia **2813**
0390-5128 Nuovo Corriere Filatelico
0390-5187 Tribuna Postale e delle Telecomunicazioni†
0390-5195 Problemi dell'Informazione **8126**
0390-5276 Lo Scalpello **6072**
0390-5349 Giornale Italiano di Psicologia **7358**
0390-5403 Cardiostimolazione†
0390-5454 Ospedale Maria Vittoria di Torino. Annali†
0390-5462 Giornale di Batteriologia, Virologia ed Immunologia†
0390-5527 Attualita in Chirurgia†
0390-5543 Archimede **5473**
0390-5616 Journal of Neurosurgical Sciences **6249**
0390-5764 Aggiornamenti di Terapia Oftalmologica **6037**
0390-5780 Istituto Italiano degli Attuari. Giornale **4510**
0390-5845 Gaslini **6092**
0390-590X Statistica
0390-6019 Rivista di Tossicologia Sperimentale e Clinica†
0390-6078 Haematologica **5936**
0390-6140 Economia Pubblica **1884**
0390-6167 Seminario Matematico di Messina. Rendiconti **5534**
0390-6272 I R I Gruppo Yearbook†
0390-6329 Istituto di Ricerca sulle Acque. Quaderni **8826**
0390-6353 Universita di Ferrara. Annali. Sezione 18: Ecologia **3472**
0390-6361 Scienza e Tecnica Lattiero-Casearia **269**
0390-6434 Italy. Istituto Centrale di Statistica. Bollettino Mensile di Statistica. Supplementi†
0390-6523 Italy. Istituto Nazionale di Statistica. Annuario di Contabilita Nazionale†
0390-6558 Italy. Istituto Nazionale di Statistica. Statistica Annuale del Commercio con l'Estero. Tomo 1. Dati Generali e Riassuntivi **1246**
0390-6566 Italy. Istituto Nazionale di Statistica. Statistica Annuale del Commercio con l'Estero. Tomo 2: Merci per Paesi **1246**
0390-6574 Conti degli Italiani **1222**
0390-6582 Annuario Statistico dell'Istruzione - Tomo 1†
0390-6590 Annuario Statistico dell'Istruzione - Tomo 2†
0390-6620 Italy. Istituto Nazionale di Statistica. Indicatori Mensili† **8967**
0390-6639 Monografie di Natura Bresciana **690**
0390-6647 Il Giappone **4182**
0390-6663 Clinical and Experimental Obstetrics and Gynecology **5988**
0390-6671 Atleticastudi **8159**
0390-6701 International Review of Sociology **8110**
0390-6779 Cooperation in Education†
0390-6809 Studi Italiani di Linguistica Teorica ed Applicata **5179**
0390-6841 Quintessenza†
0390-7139 Quaderni di Anatomia Pratica†
0390-7252 Annuario Pontificio **639**
0390-7368 Archivio di Ortopedia e Reumatologia **6056**
0390-7740 Rays†
0390-7783 Accademia delle Scienze di Siena Detta de Fisiocritici. Atti **5565**
0390-8127 Ricerca Operativa *changed to* 1619-4500 **2441**
0390-8240 Archivio per la Storia del Movimento Sociale Cattolico in Italia. Bollettino **7784**
0390-8283 Societa Medico Chirurgica di Pavia. Bollettino
0390-8542 Diritto e Societa (Naples)†
0390-8712 La Clinica Termale **6107**
0390-8739 Collegamento *changed to* Nuovo Collegamento **6864**
0390-8798 Corriere Medico **5601**
0390-8844 Critica Penale **4653**
0390-9166 Fronte Sanitario
0390-9379 L'Informatore Legislativo† **8964**
0390-9522 Banca Borsa e Titoli di Credito **1310**
0391-0121 E N A S A R C O. Notiziario **1096**
0391-0377 Patologo Clinico **5694**
0391-0946 Rivista di Teologia Morale **7815**
0391-108X Rocca **7815**
0391-1470 Vita Ospedaliera **4112**
0391-1535 Cronache Ercolanesi **5109**
0391-1551 Rivista di Biologia Normale e Patologica†
0391-156X Natura Bresciana **7888**
0391-1586 L'Industria Mineraria **6465**
0391-1594 Ercole Marelli
0391-1624 Minerva Ecologica Idroclimatologica Fisicosanitaria†
0391-1632 Monitore Zoologico Italiano. Monografie†
0391-1640 Studi Linguistici Salentini
0391-1675 Rivista dei Cuscinetti *see* 1104-8158 **3377**
0391-1683 Tecnologie Meccaniche **6334**
0391-173X Scuola Normale Superiore di Pisa. Annali. Classe di Scienze **5533**
0391-1764 Commissione Grotte Eugenio Boegan. Atti e Memorie **8309**
0391-1772 Minerva Psichiatrica **6161**
0391-1780 Bollettino Storico Pisano **4205**
0391-1810 Istituto di Diritto Romano. Bullettino **4697**
0391-1845 Rivista Giuridica della Scuola†
0391-1853 Giurisprudenza delle Imposte (Print)†
0391-187X Responsabilita Civile e Previdenza **4520**
0391-1888 Rivista del Notariato **4841**
0391-1896 Rivista Trimestrale di Diritto e Procedura Civile **4841**
0391-190X Rivista Trimestrale di Scienza dell'Amministrazione **7467**
0391-1926 Contributi di Sociologia†
0391-1934 Capitalismo e Socialismo†
0391-1942 Strumenti Linguistici†
0391-1950 Romanica Neapolitana **5169**
0391-1969 Istituzione Italiana di Cardio-Chirurgia. Giornale†
0391-1977 Minerva Endocrinologica **5897**
0391-2000 Mondo Ortodontico **5856**
0391-2035 Clinica e Laboratorio†
0391-2043 Medicina Illustrata†
0391-2051 Fondazione Giorgio Ronchi. Atti **7075**
0391-2078 Economia e Politica Industriale **1098**
0391-2108 Rivista di Letterature Moderne e Comparate **5363**
0391-2124 Tecniche dell'Imballaggio†
0391-2159 Tribuna Stampa
0391-2221 Rivista Italiana di Chirurgia Plastica
0391-2248 Storia Urbana **4428**
0391-2264 Politica ed Economia† **8981**
0391-2302 Antiqua
0391-2337 Archivio Storico Sardo† **8931**
0391-2353 Blue Guitar†
0391-2396 Confronto **7118**
0391-2418 Il Contributo†
0391-2426 Critica Giudiziaria
0391-2434 Diritto e Pratica dell'Aviazione Civile **8540**
0391-2485 Filologia Moderna†
0391-2493 Filologia e Critica (Rome) **5118**
0391-2515 Giornale Storico di Psicologia Dinamica *changed to* 1828-4353 **7344**
0391-2566 Medioevo (Padua) **6934**
0391-2604 Nuova Rivista Europea
0391-2612 Ofioliti **2714**
0391-2639 Otto-Novecento†
0391-2647 Policordo
0391-2655 Problemi di Amministrazione Pubblica†
0391-2698 Prometheus (Florence)
0391-271X Prospettive nel Mondo†

9284 0391-2787 ULRICH'S PERIODICALS

0391-2787 Rassegna della Giustizia Militare 4972
0391-2817 Rivista Italiana di Drammaturgia†
0391-2825 Rivista di Medicina del Lavoro ed Igiene Industriale†
0391-285X Romanobarbarica 2240
0391-2868 Terapia Familiare 4914
0391-2965 Dimensione Psi
0391-2973 L'Immagine Riflessa 5308
0391-3023 Mondo Archeologico†
0391-3066 Occasioni Giudiziarie
0391-3074 Per Un Analisi Storica e Critica della Psicologia†
0391-3082 Punto† 8983
0391-3090 Quaderni Portoghesi 5164
0391-3155 Vuoto, Scienza e Tecnologia 7192
0391-3171 Contributi di Sociologia. Readings†
0391-321X Istituzioni Culturali†
0391-3228 Le Lingue e le Civilta Straniere Moderne†
0391-3236 Quaderni di Analisi Matematica†
0391-3244 Scienze della Materia†
0391-3252 Serie di Matematica e Fisica 5534
0391-3260 Societa e Diritto di Roma†
0391-3295 Teorie Economiche†
0391-3317 Abruzzo Notizie† 8927
0391-3368 Italianistica 5311
0391-3457 Dossier Europa - Emigrazione†
0391-349X Fai da Te Motoverde
0391-3619 La Medicina Estetica 5673
0391-3635 Modo
0391-3716 Notiziario Vinciano
0391-3724 Nuova Rassegna di Studi Musicali† 8978
0391-3740 Le Nuove Leggi Civili Commentate 4839
0391-3813 Istituto di Storia dell'Arte Medioevale e Moderna. Quaderni 497
0391-383X Radio Kit Elettronica 3112
0391-3872 Rivista Italiana di Elettroencefalografia e Neurofisiologia†
0391-3929 Storia della Citta†
0391-3988 The International Journal of Artificial Organs 5637
0391-4097 Journal of Endocrinological Investigation 5896
0391-4100 Panorama Farmaceutico†
0391-4119 La Difesa delle Piante†
0391-4127 Ricerche Slavistiche 5169
0391-4143 Studia Historica et Philologica: Sectio Romanica† 8991
0391-4151 Studi di Grammatica Italiana 5178
0391-416X Studia Historica et Philologica: Sectio Slavo-Romanica† 8991
0391-4186 Verifiche 6960
0391-4216 Spicilegio Moderno 5177
0391-4224 Scrittura (Urbino) 7407
0391-4240 Rivista di Storia Contemporanea†
0391-4259 Stazione Sperimentale del Vetro. Rivista 2045
0391-4275 Restauro†
0391-4291 Radioindustria-Elettronica-Televisione†
0391-4356 Nuovi Studi Politici†
0391-4364 Notizie da Palazzo Albani 509
0391-4380 Musica Domani 6592
0391-4550 Bollettino Storico della Citta di Foligno 4205
0391-4631 Rivista di Meccanica International Edition†
0391-464X Carte d'Acquisto†
0391-4712 Banca d'Italia. Assemblea Generale Ordinaria dei Partecipanti 1310
0391-4739 Ferrovie dello Stato. Ufficio Statistiche. Direzione Generale. Bollettino Statistico Mensile
0391-481X Bulletin of Molecular Biology and Medicine† 8938
0391-4844 Medicina Geriatrica
0391-500X Universita degli Studi di Firenze. Facolta di Architettura. Biblioteca. Bollettino di Segnalazioni e Notizie Bibliografiche†
0391-5018 Doc Italia 2978
0391-5026 Economic Notes 1100
0391-5107 Italian Yearbook of International Law 4933
0391-5115 Journal of European Economic History†
0391-5182 Bibliografia Geografica della Regione Italiana†
0391-5190 Societa Geografica Italiana. Memorie 4029
0391-5239 Il Diritto Fallimentare e delle Societa Commerciali 4659
0391-5360 Energie Alternative: Habitat, Territorio, Energia†
0391-5379 C S E L T Infotel†
0391-5417 Maglieria†
0391-5425 Armonia di Voci 6546
0391-5433 Catechesi 7787
0391-545X Diagroup 7794
0391-5468 Dimensioni Nuove 2185
0391-5476 Espressione Giovani†
0391-5484 Mondo Erre 2203
0391-5492 Migranti-Press 7287
0391-5506 Presenza Nuova degli Anziani†
0391-5514 Progetto (Turin)†
0391-5522 Apitalia 933
0391-5573 Universita di Ferrara. Annali. Sezione 17: Scienze Mineralogiche e Petrografiche 6482
0391-5581 Italian Communists†
0391-5603 Urologia 6275
0391-5611 Rivista Italiana degli Odontotecnici - Dental Press†
0391-5638 Statistiche per la Prevenzione. Serie Dati Globali *see* 1592-6818 6690
0391-5646 Archivio Giuridico Filippo Serafini 4620
0391-5654 Cultura Neolatina 5281
0391-5662 Ufficio Moderno
0391-5670 Giornale di Anestesia Stomatologica†
0391-5816 Andar per Ceramiche nel Mondo
0391-5832 Orpheus
0391-5840 Vetrina
0391-5859 Gortania 7858
0391-5867 Il Bollettino Salesiano 7786
0391-5891 Lamiera 6320
0391-5905 Giornale di Fisica. Quaderni†
0391-5972 Istituto Centrale per la Patologia del Libro. Bollettino
0391-6030 Forme Materiali ed Ideologie del Mondo Antico†
0391-6049 Nuovo Medioevo 4250
0391-6065 Dossier di Le Monde Diplomatique†
0391-6073 Journal of Italian History†
0391-6081 Ricerche di Psicologia 7405
0391-609X Societa e la Scienza†
0391-6103 Studi d'Economia†
0391-6111 Diritto Comunitario e degli Scambi Internazionali 1561
0391-6146 Quale Impresa 1902
0391-6162 Rivista Aeronautica 69
0391-6170 Rivista di Politica Economica. Selected Papers† 8986
0391-6219 Approvvigionamenti
0391-6227 Antifurto 2644
0391-6243 Chimica e Petrolchimica
0391-6251 Il Coltivatore†
0391-6278 Coop Italia
0391-6286 Corriere dei Costruttori
0391-6308 Criminologia†
0391-6324 Docete 2843
0391-6332 Economia Brindisina
0391-6359 Economia Pesarese
0391-6375 L'Educatore 2852
0391-6391 Elettronica Oggi 3099
0391-6405 Fiorino† 8956
0391-6456 Motor Italia. Euromotor† 8975
0391-6537 Ingegneri Architetti Costruttori 3270
0391-6545 Italy's Contribution to the Promotion of World Wide Prosperity†
0391-6553 Linea Estetica
0391-6561 Lipe
0391-6588 Management e Informatica†
0391-660X Micromegas†
0391-6618 Meccanica Italiana†
0391-6626 Modena Economica 1407
0391-6677 Argomenti Radicali†
0391-6715 Bollettino Storico-Bibliografico Subalpino 4205
0391-6723 Bozze†
0391-6731 Clio 4135
0391-674X Cooperazione†
0391-6774 Il Corriere di Roma† 8944
0391-6782 Fiera di Milano†
0391-6812 L'Informazione Bibliografica *changed to* 1824-0771 632
0391-6855 Il Mondo 1150
0391-6863 La Nazione 3898
0391-688X L'Osservatore Romano (Daily) 7811
0391-6901 Popolo
0391-6936 Quaderni di Storia 2239
0391-6952 Societa Romana di Storia Patria. Archivio 6617
0391-6960 Riforma Amministrativa 1791
0391-6987 Societa e Storia 4161
0391-7002 L'Unita 7190
0391-7010 Istituto Storico Italiano per l'Eta Moderna e Contemporanea. Annuario 4233
0391-7029 Archivio di Chirurgia Toracica e Cardiovascolare†
0391-7045 Sviluppo e Organizzazione 1796
0391-707X Artigianato Oggi† 8931
0391-7096 Castelli Romani†
0391-7150 L'Italia Cooperativa 1423
0391-7169 Madonna† 8972
0391-7231 Medicina Ospedaliera Romana
0391-7274 Gli Argonauti 6124
0391-7290 V G Vendogiocattoli†
0391-7304 Aquileia Nostra
0391-7312 Quaderni Terzo Mondo
0391-7320 Archivum Fratrum Praedicatorum 4200
0391-7339 A E S†
0391-7347 E D I†
0391-7371 Italian Toys†
0391-738X Italian Technology 8428
0391-7398 Market Espresso†
0391-7401 Plast 7096
0391-741X Progetto (Milan)†
0391-7428 Diritto e Societa 4659
0391-7452 Isto Cito Patologia†
0391-7487 Ottagono 4548
0391-7495 Italia Medievale e Umanistica 4233
0391-7509 Italia Francescana 6927
0391-7517 Felix Ravenna† 8956
0391-7576 Le Regioni 4767
0391-7622 Parma nell'Arte
0391-7681 Citta Nuova (Rome) 3896
0391-769X Fiuggi
0391-7711 La Lettera Finanziaria 1365
0391-772X Il Massimo
0391-7738 Aviazione†
0391-7746 Animalia 932
0391-7754 Giornale del Maiscoltore†
0391-7762 Studi Etruschi 4268
0391-7770 Archivio Storico Italiano 4200
0391-7789 Studi Musicali 6620
0391-7797 Prospettiva Sindacale†
0391-7819 Il Santo 7816
0391-7835 Studi Danteschi 5378
0391-786X Il Sole 24 Ore 3898
0391-7894 Potere Locale†
0391-7924 Stadium 8209
0391-7940 Tendenze della Occupazione†
0391-7959 Tribunali Amministrativi Regionali *changed to* 1828-4418 4681
0391-7967 Tuttoscuola 2921
0391-7983 La Spezia Oggi 1410
0391-805X Accademia Nazionale dei Lincei. Atti dei Convegni Lincei 4440
0391-8068 Igea Medica
0391-8130 Accademia Nazionale dei Lincei. Fondazione Leone Caetani 7708
0391-8157 Accademia Nazionale dei Lincei. Atti. Notizie degli Scavi di Antichita 4440
0391-8165 Archeologia Classica 379
0391-8181 Accademia Nazionale dei Lincei. Atti. Scienze Morali, Storiche e Filologiche. Rendiconti 4129
0391-8211 Istituto Storico Artistico Orvietano. Bollettino 4233
0391-8246 Guida delle Regioni d'Italia†
0391-8319 Pavia Economica 1408
0391-8351 La Programmazione in Sardegna 1902
0391-836X Prospettive Settanta†
0391-8424 Ricerche per la Storia Religiosa di Roma 7678
0391-8459 Studi Gregoriani
0391-8467 Studi Medievali 4268
0391-8505 La Cultura (Rome) 4448
0391-8513 Informazioni Librarie
0391-8521 Qualita della Vita 8127
0391-853X Religione e Societa (Rome) 7814
0391-8548 Nuova Universale Studium 5344
0391-8564 Verba Seniorum 7692
0391-8572 S I P E-Famiglia† 8986
0391-8580 I C U Papers†
0391-8599 S I P E† 8986
0391-8602 Memorie di Scienze Geologiche 2755
0391-8637 In Tema di Medicina e Cultura†
0391-8645 Oleodinamica Pneumatica Lubrificazione 3392
0391-8653 Poliedro
0391-8661 Rassegna Tecnica di Problemi dell'Energia Elettrica†
0391-867X Realta Nuova 3898
0391-8688 Risicoltore 152
0391-8696 Rivista di Diritto Agrario 152
0391-8718 Samnium
0391-8726 Sardegna Agricoltura† 8987
0391-8734 Sorpasso C.B.
0391-8750 Studi Economici e Sociali
0391-8769 Studi Organizzativi 1795
0391-8785 Trentino 3471
0391-8866 Il Giornale dei Congressi Medici†
0391-8904 Cuore e Vasi 5602
0391-8912 Il Dermatologo 5875
0391-8920 Ginecorama 5991
0391-8939 Il Gastroenterologo 5924
0391-8963 Il Reumatologo 6226
0391-898X Pediatria Oggi Medica e Chirurgica 6099
0391-8998 Clinica Oculistica e Patologia Oculare
0391-9005 Il Giornale di Chirurgia 6244
0391-9013 Giornale Italiano di Ostetricia e Ginecologia 5991
0391-9048 Giornale di Neuropsicofarmacologia 6143
0391-9056 Giornale Italiano di Senologia†
0391-9064 Artibus et Historiae 473
0391-9099 La Ricerca Folklorica 3622
0391-9110 Arte e Archeologia 472
0391-9293 Museo Archeologico di Tarquinia. Materiali 6530
0391-948X Antichita, Archeologia, Storia dell'Arte†
0391-9641 Rivista Mineralogica Italiana 6478
0391-9714 History and Philosophy of the Life Sciences 676
0391-9730 Facolta di Magistero di Firenze. Istituto di Storia. Annali†
0391-9749 Nematologia Mediterranea 242
0391-9838 Geografia Fisica e Dinamica Quaternaria 2736
0391-9919 Petrolieri International
0391-9994 Actum Luce 4196
0392-0003 Fondazione Basso. Annali 4139
0392-0011 Istituto Storico Italo-Germanico in Trento. Annali 4233
0392-0038 Archeografo Triestino 378
0392-0062 Museo Civico di Storia Naturale di Verona. Bollettino *changed to* 1590-8399 802
0392-0062 Museo Civico di Storia Naturale di Verona. Bollettino *changed to* 1590-8402 2756
0392-0070 Museo Civico di Storia Naturale di Verona. Memorie. Serie 2, Sezione C: Scienze dell'Uomo 7883
0392-0089 Museo Civico di Storia Naturale di Verona. Memorie. Serie 2, Sezione B: Scienze della Terra 2713
0392-0097 Museo Civico di Storia Naturale di Verona. Memorie. Serie 2, Sezione A: Scienze della Vita 691
0392-0100 Nuova Polizia e Riforma dello Stato
0392-0143 Centro di Riferimento Italiano Diane. Notiziario†
0392-016X Rivista di Storia e Letteratura Religiosa. Biblioteca. Testi e Documenti 7678
0392-0224 Interpres 4458
0392-0232 Archivio Storico Lombardo 4200
0392-0283 Archivio Storico per le Province Parmensi† 8931
0392-0321 Societa Istriana di Archeologia e Storia Patria. Atti e Memorie 416
0392-033X Societa Savonese di Storia Patria. Atti e Memorie 4264
0392-0356 Benedictina
0392-0402 Societa per gli Studi Storici, Archeologici ed Artistici della Provincia di Cuneo. Bollettino 416
0392-0437 Studi Veneziani 4268
0392-0445 Rivista Italiana E P P O S† 8986
0392-047X Folia Oncologica†
0392-0488 Giornale Italiano di Dermatologia e Venereologia 5877
0392-0534 Studi Trentini di Scienze Naturali. Acta Geologica 2770
0392-0542 Studi Trentini di Scienze Naturali. Acta Biologica 706
0392-0550 Biblioteca Statale e Libreria Civica di Cremona. Annali 4204
0392-0615 Notiziario Pediatrico
0392-0658 Eta Evolutiva 7355
0392-0771 Chirurgia del Piede 6239
0392-0836 Accademia Toscana di Scienze e Lettere La Colombaria. Atti e Memorie 7831
0392-0879 Collezioni e Musei Archeologici del Veneto 387
0392-0887 Kokalos 403
0392-0895 Rivista di Archeologia 414
0392-0909 Sikelika. Serie Archeologica 416
0392-0917 Sikelika. Serie Storica 4161
0392-0925 Novita Bibliografiche: Antichita Greca e Romana
0392-095X Scuola Normale Superiore di Pisa. Annali. Classe di Lettere e Filosofia 4474
0392-100X Acta Otorhinolaryngologica Italica 6077
0392-1026 L'Assistenza Sociale† 8931
0392-1050 Archivio per l'Alto Adige 5096
0392-1107 Bollettino Storico per la Provincia di Novara 4205
0392-1115 MondOperaio 7155
0392-1131 Ricerca Sociale†
0392-1212 Economia del Lavoro (Rome)†
0392-128X Giornale Italiano di Oncologia 6020
0392-1328 Testimonia Siciliae Antiqua 420
0392-1336 Istituto Veneto di Scienze, Lettere ed Arti. Atti. Classe di Scienze Morali, Lettere ed Arti 5311
0392-1344 Clinica & Terapia Cardiovascolare
0392-1352 Campania Sacra 4209
0392-1360 Rivista Italiana di Otorinolaringologia, Audiologia e Foniatria 6085
0392-1387 Giornale Italiano di Angiologia†

0392-1395 Dermatologia Clinica **5874**
0392-1409 Cenacolo (Taranto)† **8940**
0392-1433 La Nuova Clinica Otorinolaringoiatrica†
0392-1492 Pio IX†
0392-1530 Quadrivium **4471**
0392-1581 Ricerche di Storia Sociale e Religiosa **8130**
0392-162X Ricerche Storiche **4159**
0392-1670 Rivista di Sessuologia **5707**
0392-1689 Picenum Seraphicum
0392-1697 Scrittura e Civilta *changed to* 1825-9189 **2237**
0392-1700 Thesaurus Ecclesiarum Italiae
0392-1719 Studia Picena **4269**
0392-1727 Studi Bitontini **4268**
0392-1735 Studi Goriziani **8007**
0392-1794 Proposte e Ricerche **4255**
0392-1816 Regesta Chartarum **4256**
0392-1832 Fonti per la Storia d'Italia†
0392-1867 Quaderni Fiorentini per la Storia del Pensiero Giuridico Moderno **4764**
0392-1875 Quaderni Medievali† **8983**
0392-1883 Quaderni Culturali Bolognesi
0392-1913 Obiettivi e Documenti Veterinari **8804**
0392-1921 Diogenes (English Edition) **7959**
0392-1948 Studi di Storia dell'Educazione†
0392-2065 Archivio Storico di Belluno Feltre e Cadore **4200**
0392-209X Psichiatria e Cultura†
0392-2111 Cultura e Mass Media†
0392-2146 Studi sull'Educazione **2915**
0392-2227 Giornale Italiano di Chimica Clinica†
0392-226X Astra **565**
0392-2278 Autonomie Locali e Servizi Sociali **8027**
0392-2308 Astronomia (Naples)
0392-2316 L'Audio Giornale
0392-2324 Azeta† **8934**
0392-2332 Nouvelles de la Republique des Lettres **6937**
0392-2359 Apollinaris **7784**
0392-2367 Atti dello Psicodramma
0392-2375 L'Appennino **8304**
0392-2391 Index. Quaderni Camerti di Studi Romanistici **4691**
0392-2413 Museo Bodoniano di Parma. Bollettino **6530**
0392-2510 Biologi Italiani **657**
0392-2529 Biopsyche
0392-2561 Best Boomerang† **8935**
0392-2642 Bergamo 15 **3896**
0392-2669 Beauty Line **585**
0392-2707 bargiornale **4382**
0392-2715 Il Bagno Oggi e Domani **4532**
0392-2723 Bagno e Accessori **978**
0392-2758 Automondo
0392-2774 La Famiglia **7964**
0392-2790 Professionalita **2998**
0392-2804 Tempo Sereno†
0392-2812 Direzione Scuola *see* 0036-9888 **2911**
0392-2820 Scuola Materna **2911**
0392-2855 Analecta Augustiniana **7783**
0392-2863 Aquarium
0392-2898 Universita degli Studi di Roma. Facolta di Architettura. Bolletino della Biblioteca **459**
0392-2936 European Journal of Gynecological Oncology **6019**
0392-2952 Psicobiettivo **7392**
0392-2987 Annuario della Specola Cidnea **568**
0392-3002 Aggiornamento Medico **5570**
0392-3010 L'Informatore Farmaceutico **6848**
0392-3029 E S A R D A Bulletin **7514**
0392-3037 Societa Geologica Italiana. Rendiconti†
0392-3061 Acquasport† **8928**
0392-3088 Acta Phoniatrica Latina **6235**
0392-3126 Bollettino per le Farmacodipendenze e l'Alcoolismo **2692**
0392-3134 Bollettino Informativo Fiscale†
0392-3320 Capital **1080**
0392-3347 Il Carrobbio† **8940**
0392-3355 Castellum **437**
0392-3398 Centro Ricerche Biopsichiche
0392-3460 Tecnologie Elettriche International†
0392-3479 Commercio Elettrico **3297**
0392-3487 Tecnologie Meccaniche International†
0392-3495 Esperienze Letterarie **5215**
0392-3525 Italian Journal of Surgical Sciences†
0392-3568 Italia Contemporanea **4233**
0392-3584 Notiziario Chirurgico
0392-3614 Il Giornale degli Apparecchi Domestici
0392-3622 Il Giornale della Subfornitura **6314**
0392-3630 Il Giornale dell'Installatore Elettrico **3309**
0392-3665 Il Mese di Caccia **8322**
0392-3673 Monthly Review†
0392-3681 Motitalia **8261**
0392-369X Nautica **8279**
0392-3789 Bollettino di Legislazione Tecnica **983**
0392-3827 Rivista del Latte **269**
0392-3886 Il Bolscevico **7110**
0392-3894 Brutium† **8937**
0392-3940 Cammello
0392-3983 Meccanizzazione Agricola†
0392-4033 Unione Matematica Italiana. Bollettino. Sezione A: La Matematica nella Societa e nella Cultura *changed to* 1972-7356 **5510**
0392-4041 Unione Matematica Italiana. Bollettino. Sezione B: Articoli di Ricerca Matematica *changed to* 1972-6724 **5543**
0392-4130 Rendiconti Accademia Nazionale delle Scienze detta dei XL. Memorie di Scienze Fisiche e Naturali **7037**
0392-4149 Natura Alpina **2713**
0392-4173 Naturismo† **8976**
0392-419X Ateneo Parmense. Acta Naturalia
0392-4203 Ateneo Parmense. Acta BioMedica **5580**
0392-4432 Bollettino di Storia delle Scienze Matematiche **5476**
0392-4440 Castoro Cinema†
0392-4475 Energia e Materie Prime†
0392-4483 Giornale di Neuropsichiatria dell'Eta Evolutiva **6143**
0392-4505 Salute e Territorio **8067**
0392-4513 Storia dell'Arte **519**
0392-4548 Medicina Oggi† **8973**
0392-4556 Teresianum **7820**
0392-4564 Memoria†
0392-4629 N U A International Journal of Nephrology, Urology, Andrology
0392-4645 Opus
0392-4653 Bank of Italy. Economic Papers†
0392-470X L'Antenna† **8930**
0392-4718 Pasticceria Internazionale **3675**
0392-4777 Rassegna Iberistica
0392-4823 Il Progettista Industriale **5458**
0392-4831 Tecnica Ospedaliera **4112**
0392-4858 La Rivista del Medico Pratico **5707**
0392-4866 Rivista degli Studi Orientali **560**
0392-4912 Responsabilita del Sapere
0392-4939 Sociologia Urbana e Rurale **8136**
0392-4947 Spazio e Societa†
0392-4955 Storia e Critica della Psicologia†
0392-498X Il Torchio Artistico e Letterario
0392-5005 Urbanistica Informazioni **4431**
0392-5013 Volonta†
0392-5021 Studi Marittimi† **8991**
0392-5048 Sociologia del Lavoro **8005**
0392-5056 Il Picentino† **8981**
0392-5080 Riscontri
0392-5099 Sandalion† **8987**
0392-5110 Studi di Filologia Italiana **5178**
0392-5145 Archivio di Medicina Legale e delle Assicurazioni **5912**
0392-5153 L'Operatore Sanitario† **8979**
0392-5218 Studi di Lessicografia Italiana **5179**
0392-5234 Arte Veneta **472**
0392-5285 Istituto Nazionale d' Archeologia e Storia dell'Arte. Rivista **399**
0392-5404 Schede Medievali **4261**
0392-5439 Medaglia†
0392-5463 Mezzalira
0392-5498 Il Millimetro† **8974**
0392-5528 Museologia (Florence)†
0392-5536 Music
0392-5544 Musica **6592**
0392-5617 Agricoop†
0392-5692 Altrimedia
0392-5730 L'Ambiente Cucina **4531**
0392-5765 Amici dei Musei
0392-5773 Amici della Pipa
0392-5803 Cronache Castellane **439**
0392-5854 L'Anestesista *changed to* Il Nuovo Anestesista Rianimatore **5772**
0392-5862 Animali Natura Habitat
0392-5870 Animazione Sociale **8087**
0392-6044 Energia Solare e Fonti Alternative†
0392-6052 Export†
0392-6060 Il Latte **266**
0392-6079 Mondo dei Gioielli
0392-6095 Inventario†
0392-615X Archivio delle Locazioni e del Condominio **4620**
0392-6176 L'Arengo
0392-6206 Ars-Uomo
0392-629X Instituta et Monumenta. Serie II: Instituta
0392-6303 Marmomacchine **6469**
0392-6338 Materiali e Discussioni per l'Analisi dei Testi Classici **2237**
0392-6346 Il Messaggero Avventista **7767**
0392-6397 Misure Critiche **5335**
0392-6443 Mondo Legno **3714**
0392-6508 Musica e Assemblea **6592**
0392-6516 Medicina†
0392-6567 Utensil
0392-6613 OEbalia† **8978**
0392-6621 Otorinolaringologia **6084**
0392-6664 Quaderni Costituzionali **4851**
0392-6672 International Journal of Speleology **2748**
0392-6680 Istituto Veneto di Scienze, Lettere ed Arti. Atti. Classe di Scienze Fisiche, Matematiche e Naturali **7869**
0392-6699 Eos **5757**
0392-6710 Societa Sarda di Scienze Naturali. Bollettino **7917**
0392-6788 Studi per l'Ecologia del Quaternario **356**
0392-6796 Le Grandi Automobili
0392-680X Psicologia e Scuola **2901**
0392-6834 Cer Annuario **2038**
0392-6850 Cer Fornitori **2038**
0392-6877 L'Avvenire Medico† **8934**
0392-6885 Egitto e Vicino Oriente **4174**
0392-6907 Linguistica Computazionale† **8971**
0392-6915 Linguistica e Letteratura **5146**
0392-6931 Museum Criticum† **8975**
0392-7032 Istituto Nazionale per la Storia del Movimento di Liberazione in Italia. Notizie e Documenti†
0392-7059 Nuova Rassegna di Legislazione, Dottrina e Giurisprudenza **4750**
0392-7113 Rassegna di Diritto e Tecnica dell'Alimentazione†
0392-713X Saggi e Memorie di Storia dell'Arte **516**
0392-7148 Rassegna di Meccanica†
0392-7156 Rassegna Penitenziaria e Criminologica **2667**
0392-7199 Medical Tribune
0392-7202 Ricerche di Storia dell'Arte **515**
0392-7229 Rivista Giuridica del Lavoro e della Previdenza Sociale **4601**
0392-7253 Settimana Giuridica† **8988**
0392-7261 Studi Piemontesi **4476**
0392-7288 Islamochristiana **7651**
0392-7296 Giornale Italiano di Entomologia
0392-7318 La Clinica Dietologica†
0392-7326 Studi Settecenteschi **4162**
0392-7334 Centro di Studi Vichiani. Bollettino **6910**
0392-7342 Elenchos **6915**
0392-7393 Il Biologo†
0392-7504 Comunicazioni Scientifiche di Psicologia Generale†
0392-7512 Alimentazione Nutrizione Metabolismo†
0392-7571 Istituto per la Documentazione Giuridica. Bibliografia. Diritto Civile **4823**
0392-758X Museo Regionale di Scienze Naturali. Bollettino **691**
0392-7601 Italica
0392-7636 Commissione Archeologica Comunale di Roma. Bullettino **388**
0392-7652 Istituto dei Tumori di Napoli. Bollettino†
0392-7660 Balcanica
0392-7733 Fisiopatologia della Riproduzione†
0392-7792 Rassegna della Stampa Estera†
0392-7903 Conservazione degli Alimenti†
0392-7911 Energia† **8953**
0392-792X Imbottigliamento **6710**
0392-7938 Panis†
0392-7946 Scienzasocieta
0392-8020 Tuttoturismo **8770**
0392-8055 Macchine del Legno†
0392-8063 Serramenti & Falegnameria **1051**
0392-8098 Ceramica Informacion **2039**
0392-8136 Tecnica della Confezione e della Maglieria
0392-8217 Pixel†
0392-8233 Elettronica Viva
0392-825X Rivista di Letteratura Italiana **5363**
0392-8268 Rivista Teletra Review (English Edition)
0392-8276 Rivista Teletra Review (Italian Edition)
0392-8306 Agora (Rome)†
0392-8322 Impegno Ospedaliero. Sezione Scientifica **5633**
0392-839X Chimica Oggi **2058**
0392-8411 Universita degli Studi in Italia. Annuario **2962**
0392-842X Bollettino dei Classici **2231**
0392-8470 Universita di Ferrara. Annali. Sezione 1: Anatomia Umana **928**
0392-8497 Zerouno **2441**
0392-8543 Journal of Applied Cosmetology† **8968**
0392-856X Clinical and Experimental Rheumatology **6223**
0392-8586 Biblioteche Oggi **4995**
0392-8608 Rassegna di Architettura e Urbanistica **455**
0392-8667 Comunicazioni Sociali **8095**
0392-8675 Il Contesto
0392-8713 Annali di Ricerche e Studi di Geografia† **8930**
0392-8748 Rivista di Diritto Valutario e di Economia Internazionale
0392-8764 International Journal of Heat and Technology **7055**
0392-8772 Impegno Ottanta
0392-8810 Le Scienze, la Matematica e il Loro Insegnamento
0392-8829 Automazione Oggi **2459**
0392-8837 Bit†
0392-8845 Computerworld Italia **2414**
0392-8926 Storia della Storiografia **4268**
0392-8942 C n S. La Chimica nella Scuola **2052**
0392-8950 Difesa Ambientale†
0392-9027 Linea E D P **2538**
0392-9035 Antropologia Contemporanea† **8930**
0392-9043 Il Solidale
0392-9078 Journal of Experimental and Clinical Cancer Research (Print) *changed to* 1756-9966 **6024**
0392-9094 Seminario di Scienze Antropologiche
0392-9116 Algologia
0392-9140 Rivista Oto-Neuro-Oftalmologica†
0392-9221 Club Alpino Italiano. La Rivista *changed to* 1825-8743 **8330**
0392-9264 Il Polso†
0392-9345 Universita degli Studi di Siena. Facolta di Lettere e Filosofia. Annali **5392**
0392-9418 Annali di Medicina Navale†
0392-9442 Aggiornamenti di Medicina e Chirurgia
0392-9450 Societa Veneziana di Scienze Naturali. Lavori **7917**
0392-9485 Archeologia Viva **379**
0392-9507 Journal of Foetal Medicine†
0392-9515 Acta Mediterranea di Patologia Infettiva e Tropicale **5808**
0392-9523 Istituto Lombardo. Accademia di Scienze e Lettere. Rendiconti. A: Scienze Matematiche e Applicazioni **7869**
0392-9531 Istituto Lombardo. Accademia di Scienze e Lettere. Rendiconti. B: Scienze Chimiche e Fisiche, Geologiche, Biologiche e Mediche. **7869**
0392-954X Rivista di Frutticoltura e di Ortofloricoltura **251**
0392-9574 Associazione Genetica Italiana. Atti
0392-9590 International Angiology **5790**
0392-9639 Scienza Veterinaria e Biologia Animale†
0392-9647 Sport & Medicina **6233**
0392-9663 Geriatrics†
0392-9698 Acta Cardiologica Mediterranea **5775**
0392-9701 Stato e Mercato **7186**
0392-971X Bollettino di Numismatica **6649**
0392-9744 Filosofia Oggi
0392-9752 L'Esopo† **8954**
0392-9760 Epistemologia **6916**
0392-9779 Filosofia e Societa
0392-9787 Rivista di Psicologia Analitica **7405**
0392-9884 Circolo Culturale B.G. Duns Scoto di Roccarainola. Atti **3896**
0392-9965 Bollettino di Notizie e Ricerche da Archivi e Biblioteche†
0392-9981 Cinema d'Oggi **6493**
0393-0033 F M R (Italian Edition) **489**
0393-0076 Industria Orafa Italiana
0393-0092 Medioevo Latino
0393-0149 Padusa **410**
0393-0157 Preistoria Alpina **412**
0393-0203 Rassegna **4366**
0393-022X Rivista Storica Calabrese **4259**
0393-0238 Romagna Arte e Storia **4473**
0393-0246 Studi Eblaiti† **8991**
0393-0300 Vicino Oriente **423**
0393-0327 Communicationes **7793**
0393-0343 Dimensione Energia†
0393-0394 Impegno Ospedaliero **5633**
0393-0416 Sinistra Europea†
0393-0440 Journal of Geometry and Physics **5503**
0393-0483 A M U† **8927**
0393-0505 Junior Dental e Bocca Nuda†
0393-0521 Ambiente Risorse Salute **3402**
0393-0564 Biochimica Clinica **726**
0393-0572 Informatica 70† **8964**
0393-0599 Media Duemila **2538**

ISSN

0393-0637	The Lancet (Edizione Italiana)†
0393-0645	Quaderni Italiani di Psichiatria 6180
0393-0653	La Presse Medicale (Italian Edition) 5699
0393-067X	Giornale dell'Odontoiatra 5845
0393-0726	Antologia Medica Italiana†
0393-0742	Bollettino Geofisico
0393-0750	Museo Civico di Padova. Bollettino 4465
0393-0785	La Gazzetta della Fotografia† 8958
0393-0807	Labyrinthos 502
0393-0890	Tennis Italiano 8248
0393-0904	Istituto Siciliano di Studi Bizantini e Neoellenici. Monumenti 497
0393-098X	E D A V 3058
0393-0998	Unione Matematica Italiana. Notiziario 5543
0393-1005	Nova Astronautica 67
0393-1056	Congresso Internazionale di Studi sull'Alto Medioevo. Atti 4212
0393-1064	Psicologia Italiana 7393
0393-1072	Pulizia Industriale e Sanificazione 7538
0393-1110	Rivista Italiana di Acustica 7089
0393-1129	Rivista Italiana di Agopuntura 5707
0393-1137	Rivista Italiana di Biologia e Medicina†
0393-1218	Gli Uccelli d'Italia 915
0393-1226	Quaderni di Semantica 5164
0393-1307	Cronaca Filatelica 6893
0393-1315	Diritto Processuale Amministrativo 4659
0393-1331	L'Industria Meccanica 3379
0393-134X	La Legislazione Penale 4722
0393-1358	The Federalist† 8956
0393-1382	Societa Italiana di Buiatria. Atti changed to 1828-4078 8794
0393-1412	Universita Cattolica. Istituto di Storia Antica. Ricerche†
0393-1420	Ingegneria Sismica 3197
0393-1455	Rassegna della Protezione Civile†
0393-1471	Chirurgia Epatobiliare†
0393-1560	La Cultura 4448
0393-1641	Gallerie e Grandi Opere Sotterranee 3193
0393-182X	Rassegna di Diritto Civile 4765
0393-1838	Anterem 5255
0393-2028	Rivista di Cardiologia Preventiva e Riabilitativa†
0393-2087	Informatica & Documentazione. Supplemento
0393-2095	Kos 5659
0393-2214	Firenze Chirurgica†
0393-2230	Koinonia 4462
0393-2249	Minerva Urologica e Nefrologica 6271
0393-2346	Voce di Fiume
0393-2362	Zeta 5438
0393-2397	Accademia Petrarca di Lettere, Arti e Scienza. Atti e Memorie 4440
0393-2400	Banca d'Italia. Bollettino Economico 1440
0393-2427	Carte Scoperte
0393-2451	Intersezioni 4458
0393-246X	Islam†
0393-2494	Rivista Italiana di Diritto del Lavoro 4776
0393-2516	Rivista di Storia della Filosofia 6950
0393-2532	Studi Verdiani 6620
0393-2648	C S E L T Technical Reports
0393-2664	Anteprima Libri†
0393-2680	Istruzione Tecnica e Professionale†
0393-2702	Universitas†
0393-2729	The International Spectator 7245
0393-2834	Teorie & Modelli 5541
0393-2842	Match-Ball†
0393-2850	Super Football†
0393-2893	Culture Musicali
0393-2907	Literatura Foiro 5148
0393-2915	Informazioni e Studi Vivaldiani changed to 1594-0012 646
0393-2931	Accademia di Archeologia Lettere e Belle Arti. Rendiconti 4129
0393-2990	European Journal of Epidemiology 5611
0393-3024	see 0032-3101 7260
0393-3180	Istituto Universitario Orientale. Annali 4458
0393-3202	Calendario Atlante De Agostini 4001
0393-330X	Datalignum† 8948
0393-3318	Ferrarissima
0393-3377	Museo di Storia Naturale di Livorno. Quaderni 7883
0393-3385	Storia Nordamericana†
0393-3393	Audiologia Italiana†
0393-3415	Rivista di Storia Economica 1549
0393-3547	Dossier Catechista 7795
0393-3555	Famiglia Domani 7797
0393-3571	Istituto Ricerche Pesca Marittima. Quaderni† 8967
0393-3598	Cristianesimo nella Storia 7636
0393-361X	Psichiatria dell'Infanzia e dell'Adolescenza 6175
0393-3660	Gazzetta Medica Italiana Archivio per le Scienze Mediche 5618
0393-3687	Studi Ecumenici 7684
0393-3725	Italy Italy 8724
0393-3733	N C F. Notiziario Chimico e Farmaceutico 6862
0393-3741	Il Calendario del Popolo 7952
0393-3830	Ricerche Storiche Salesiane 7815
0393-3849	Rivista di Scienze dell'Educazione 3000
0393-3857	Griffithiana 6502
0393-3865	SegnoCinema 6512
0393-3903	L'Indice dei Libri del Mese 7563
0393-3911	Automazione Integrata 2459
0393-3938	A N C I Rivista 7487
0393-3954	Fondazione Giangiacomo Feltrinelli. Annali 7964
0393-3970	Il Labirinto
0393-4012	Gli Oratori del Giorno† 8979
0393-4039	Rassegna di Diritto Farmaceutico†
0393-4047	Statistiche per la Prevenzione. Serie Monografica see 1592-6818 6690
0393-408X	Trimestre 5243
0393-4098	Rassegna Mensile della Imposte Dirette† 8984
0393-4101	Sanita Pubblica changed to 1722-7194 7541
0393-4195	La Favilla
0393-4209	Bambini 2145
0393-4217	Rivista della Montagna 8330
0393-4330	Zoom 6979
0393-4365	Lavaggio Industriale 2243

0393-4373	Verniciatura del Legno 1052
0393-4411	Riabita 1033
0393-4470	Interfaccia†
0393-4489	Casa Classica†
0393-4500	Il Giornale dell'Arredamento 4540
0393-4551	Savings and Development 1381
0393-4578	Il Nuovo Saggiatore 7029
0393-4594	Societa Chimica Italiana. Bollettino† 8989
0393-4608	Giornale dell'Industria† 8959
0393-4624	Rivista Dalmatica 4259
0393-4675	Societa per la Preistoria e Protostoria della Regione Friuli-Venezia Giulia. Atti
0393-4713	Unione Matematica Italiana. Bollettino. Sezione D: Algebra e Geometria†
0393-4748	Reflex Foto Market
0393-4780	Amici di Brugg. Rivista di Odontoiatria 5834
0393-4802	Universita degli Studi di Parma. Facolta di Medicina Veterinaria. Annali 8809
0393-4810	Rivista di Politica Agraria†
0393-4853	Bollettino di Psichiatria Biologica†
0393-487X	Clot and Hematologic Malignancies†
0393-4888	Confezione 2246
0393-4969	Frames Architettura dei Serramenti 1008
0393-4977	La Cittanova
0393-506X	Lengua†
0393-5108	Sinergie
0393-5132	Arredostile Middle East†
0393-5140	Casarredo Middle East†
0393-5167	Forwood International†
0393-5183	A A R P Environment Design
0393-5221	Rivista Italiana di Ortopedia e Traumatologia Pediatrica
0393-523X	Previsioni a Breve Termine†
0393-5264	Functional Neurology 6142
0393-5302	New Trends in Arrhythmias†
0393-5310	New Trends in Experimental and Clinical Psychiatry†
0393-5337	Ginecologia dell'Infanzia e dell'Adolescenza 5991
0393-5345	New Trends in Clinical Neuropharmacology†
0393-5418	Fogli di Informazione 7357
0393-5442	Centauro†
0393-5469	Itinerario
0393-5493	Sistemi Urbani†
0393-554X	J A M A (Italian Edition)†
0393-5582	Rivista Italiana di Nutrizione Parenterale ed Enterale changed to 1828-6232 6667
0393-5590	Giornale Italiano di Nefrologia 6268
0393-5620	Istituto Superiore di Sanita. Congressi 7527
0393-5671	Frate Indovino 3120
0393-5744	Political Economy†
0393-5825	Autobus Oggi
0393-585X	Gardenia 3732
0393-5884	Lancillotto e Nausica†
0393-5930	Quaderni di Medicina e Chirurgia
0393-5949	I Tatti Studies 4272
0393-5957	Giornale Italiano di Ricerche Cliniche e Terapeutiche†
0393-5965	Aerobiologia 651
0393-5981	Brevetti & Invenzioni
0393-599X	Industria Mercato 3379
0393-6074	Metallurgical Science & Technology 6325
0393-6082	Qualestoria 4255
0393-6139	Primary Cardiology (Italian Edition)
0393-6147	Il Vesuvio† 8997
0393-6155	The International Journal of Biological Markers 678
0393-6163	Studi di Psicologia dell'Educazione 2915
0393-6317	E N E A (Rapporti Tecnici) R T - STUDI 3166
0393-635X	Acta Toxicologica et Therapeutica†
0393-6368	Annuario D E A delle Universita e Istituti di Studio e Ricerca in Italia† 8930
0393-6376	Acta Chirurgica Mediterranea 6234
0393-6384	Acta Medica Mediterranea 5808
0393-6392	Acta Pediatrica Mediterranea 6087
0393-6414	San Martino
0393-6449	La Citta Nuova (Naples)† 8941
0393-6457	Lettera dall'Italia†
0393-6503	Institut International J. Maritain. Notes et Documents 7143
0393-652X	Selezione Chimica Tintoria†
0393-6732	Cemento†
0393-6740	Comunismo 7118
0393-6805	Henoch 7721
0393-6813	Latium 4239
0393-697X	Societa Italiana di Fisica. Rivista del Nuovo Cimento 7040
0393-7046	Bibliografia Agricola†
0393-7054	Ambiente e Sicurezza sul Lavoro 6672
0393-7062	Bancamatica 1310
0393-7089	Antincendio 3575
0393-7186	Universita Cattolica del Sacro Cuore. Annuario 2922
0393-7267	Arte Medievale 472
0393-7445	Il Lanternino 5660
0393-7496	Quaderni di Retorica e Poetica†
0393-7518	Riabilitazione e Apprendimento
0393-7526	Ruotaspring† 8986
0393-7534	La Tribuna del Collezionista
0393-7542	Acta Oncologica†
0393-7550	Assistenza Infermieristica del Nord America†
0393-7577	Clinica Chirurgica del Nord America†
0393-7585	Clinica Medica del Nord America†
0393-7593	Clinica Odontoiatrica del Nord America†
0393-7607	Clinica Ostetrica e Ginecologica†
0393-7615	Clinica Pediatrica del Nord America†
0393-7623	La Medicina di Laboratorio†
0393-764X	Progressi Clinici: Chirurgia†
0393-7658	Progressi Clinici: Medicina†
0393-7666	Motori† 8975
0393-7704	Banca d'Italia. Economic Bulletin see 0393-2400 1440
0393-7720	Mediabook Italia
0393-7798	Tutela 8075
0393-7801	Ultrasonica†
0393-781X	Radioamatore
0393-7844	Politica Meridionalista 1511
0393-7852	SuperBasket 8248
0393-7860	Gente Motori 8582

0393-7879	Tuttomoto 8269
0393-7895	Gente Viaggi 8713
0393-7909	Il Piacere†
0393-7925	Gente Money† 8959
0393-7941	Gente Mese† 8959
0393-795X	Donna† 8951
0393-7976	Acta Otorhinolaryngologica Italica. Supplement 6077
0393-7984	Comunita Sportiva
0393-800X	J D† 8967
0393-8026	Prometheus (Milan)†
0393-8034	Reggio Storia 4256
0393-8050	Le Fiere† 8956
0393-8069	Italian Building and Construction 1017
0393-8077	Vie e Trasporti 8520
0393-8085	Mondo Uomo†
0393-8115	Gioielli (Milan, 1974)†
0393-8131	Phytophaga 247
0393-814X	Onda Tivu 2387
0393-8166	Italian Journal of Medicine 5642
0393-8190	Manualita Creativita Maestria 537
0393-8204	Tecno Show†
0393-8212	Il Nuovo Governo Locale†
0393-8255	Vs†
0393-8263	Arsenale† 8931
0393-8379	Quaderni di Cinema
0393-8387	Auto & Design 8557
0393-8417	Studi e Materiali di Storia delle Religioni 7683
0393-8476	Il Giornale del Farmacista 6844
0393-8492	Giornale del Medico 5619
0393-8506	Medicina Toracica† 8973
0393-8522	Aesthetica Preprint 6902
0393-859X	Accademia Nazionale di San Luca. Annuario 427
0393-8638	L'Impegno 4231
0393-8700	Museo Civico di Scienze Naturali "E.Caffi". Rivista 7883
0393-876X	Marmor 6469
0393-8875	Natura e Societa 3455
0393-9014	D W F 8858
0393-9170	Electronic Mass Media Age† 8953
0393-9200	Giornale della Soia† 8959
0393-9243	Economia e Banca†
0393-9332	Nuova Scienza
0393-9340	Annali Italiani di Medicina Interna changed to 1828-0447 5945
0393-9367	Hyria† 8962
0393-9375	Human Evolution 341
0393-9383	International Journal of Anthropology 343
0393-9391	The Medical Letter on Drugs and Therapeutics (Italian Edition) 6860
0393-9413	Pubblico Esercizio†
0393-9448	Piazza Mercato† 8981
0393-9464	Il Segnale† 8987
0393-9480	Steve 5435
0393-9499	Adverse Drug Reaction Bulletin (Italian Edition) 6819
0393-9510	Prospettive Sociali e Sanitarie 8063
0393-9529	Quaderni di Sanita Pubblica 7538
0393-9561	Vision†
0393-9626	Aerei Modellismo 4326
0393-9693	Farmaci & Terapia† 8955
0393-9715	Rivista Internazionale di Chirurgia Vertebrale e dei Nervi Periferici†
0393-9723	Il Corriere Termo Idro Sanitario 4118
0393-974X	Journal of Biological Regulators and Homeostatic Agents
0393-9758	Almanacco di Fotografare 6963
0393-9774	Psichiatria e Psicoterapia Analitica changed to 1724-4919 6175
0393-9871	Almanacco dello Specchio 5416
0393-9898	Rivista di Psicologia dell'Arte
0393-9901	Il Cenacolo 7791
0393-9936	Filosofia Oggi. Collana
0393-9944	Studi Sciacchiani
0393-9960	Prevenzione & Assistenza Dentale 5861
0394-0055	Area (Milan, 1990) 4403
0394-0063	Il Naturalista Siciliano 7888
0394-008X	Bianco & Nero 6490
0394-0128	Automobilismo 8564
0394-0136	Antologia di Belle Arti 466
0394-0152	La Conchiglia† 8943
0394-0179	Art e Dossier 469
0394-0187	Musica e Dossier†
0394-0195	Scienza e Dossier†
0394-0209	Storia e Dossier
0394-0225	Giornale Italiano di Endoscopia Digestiva 5925
0394-0276	Eta Verde
0394-0284	Il Cristiano 7753
0394-0314	L'Oroptero
0394-0403	Istituto Universitario Orientale di Napoli. Seminario di Studi dell'Europa Orientale. Sezione Linguistico - Filologica. Annali 5131
0394-0411	Istituto Universitario Orientale di Napoli. Seminario di Studi dell'Europa Orientale. Arte e Letteratura. 497
0394-0438	Agricoltura Mediterranea 82
0394-0454	F M R (French Edition) see 0393-0033 489
0394-0462	F M R (English Edition) see 0393-0033 489
0394-0519	Catalogo dell'Arte Italiana dell'Ottocento
0394-0543	Il Giornale dell'Arte 491
0394-0594	Rivista di Ascetica e Mistica 7815
0394-0616	Studi e Ricerche sull'Oriente Cristiano†
0394-0691	Atti Ticinensi di Scienze della Terra 2702
0394-0705	Centro Linceo Interdisciplinare Beniamino Segre. Contributi 7844
0394-073X	Cardiomyology†
0394-0748	Connective Tissue Diseases
0394-0756	Orizzonti di Chirurgia†
0394-0764	Rassegna di Medicina d'Urgenza†
0394-0772	Rivista di Patologia dell'Apparato Locomotore†
0394-0802	Prospettiva 513
0394-0810	L'Indicizzazione†
0394-0853	Giardini 3733
0394-0888	Minerva Psicogeriatrica†
0394-0896	Monitor - Radio T V 2385
0394-090X	Pesca in Fiumi, Laghi e Torrenti 8328

0394-0918 Pesca in Mare **8328**
0394-0942 Rivista Giuridica Sarda†
0394-0969 Umus†
0394-1051 Eupalino†
0394-1132 Harper's Gran Bazaar† **8961**
0394-1248 Teoria Politica **7188**
0394-1310 Ecologia della Mente† **8952**
0394-1361 Microelettronica e Imprese† **8974**
0394-1418 Trasgressioni **7189**
0394-1434 C I R V I Bollettino
0394-1442 Spazio Abitato†
0394-1493 Flash Art International **489**
0394-1574 Italian Current Radiology†
0394-1582 Impiantistica Italiana **3367**
0394-1590 Costruire in Laterizio†
0394-1612 Obiettivo Marca†
0394-1620 Minerva Medicopratica†
0394-1639 Prometeo **4470**
0394-1647 Pratica Odontoiatrica†
0394-1655 Rassegna sulla Sperimentazione Organizzativa e Didattica nelle Universita†
0394-1663 Societa Tiburtina di Storia e d'Arte. Atti e Memorie **416**
0394-1671 Rivista di Musicoterapia
0394-168X Minerva Ortognatodontica **5856**
0394-1736 Annali Accademici Canadesi
0394-1809 Annuario Filosofico (Year) **6904**
0394-1841 Bollettino Storico della Basilicata **7786**
0394-1914 Hystrix **946**
0394-2120 Annali di Sociologia (Trent) **8087**
0394-2147 L'Arca **428**
0394-2155 Azienditalia **1727**
0394-2287 Rivista Giuridica dell'Ambiente **3464**
0394-2309 Universita degli Studi di Pavia. Scientifica Acta. Quaderni del Dottorato **7926**
0394-2341 Teatro Festival†
0394-2368 Unioncamere†
0394-2384 V R† **8996**
0394-2473 Diorama Letterario **5213**
0394-249X Gene Geography†
0394-252X Minerva Ospedaliera. La Settimana degli Ospedali. II Medico Ospedaliero†
0394-2538 Risparmio Energetico
0394-2597 Micologia e Vegetazione Mediterranea **801**
0394-2627 Medicina Moderna Oggi
0394-266X Orientalia Venetiana
0394-2678 Oris Medicina† **8979**
0394-2694 Quaderni Veneti **4471**
0394-2732 Coscienza e Liberta **7635**
0394-2740 Il Fallimento e le Altre Procedure Concorsuali **4867**
0394-2759 Fenomenologia e Societa **6919**
0394-2775 Harvard Espansione
0394-2783 Hinterland†
0394-2791 Lacio Drom†
0394-283X Organizzazione Sanitaria **4108**
0394-2856 Psicologia e Societa **7393**
0394-2864 Psicoterapia e Scienze Umane **6175**
0394-2902 Euro Annuario Carne **3634**
0394-2910 Eurocarni **3634**
0394-2929 Il Pesce **3605**
0394-2937 Picus **913**
0394-2953 Archivio di Scienze del Lavoro† **8931**
0394-3054 Idee **6924**
0394-3119 Shop & Decoration
0394-3143 Yacht Digest **8285**
0394-3151 Veterinaria **8810**
0394-3216 Nuova Finestra **1055**
0394-3240 Laboratorio di Scienze dell'Uomo†
0394-3283 Terra†
0394-3291 Caleidoscopio **5591**
0394-3356 Quaternario **2715**
0394-3372 Prevenzione e Salute
0394-3399 Argonauta **934**
0394-3402 Diabetes, Nutrition & Metabolism, Clinical and Experimental†
0394-3410 Minerva Ortopedica e Traumatologica **6067**
0394-3429 Panorama Difesa **6441**
0394-3437 J P 4 Mensile di Aeronautica **62**
0394-3445 Giornale Italiano di Medicina Tropicale **5814**
0394-3453 Macplas **7095**
0394-347X Made in Italy
0394-3518 Taverna di Auerbach
0394-3569 Studi Linguistici Italiani **5179**
0394-3623 Notiziario del Lavoro e Previdenza **4877**
0394-3631 Societa Bilancio e Contabilita†
0394-364X Segni dei Tempi **7680**
0394-3682 Spobabella
0394-3704 Linea Verde **3742**
0394-3747 Attualita Grafologica **7337**
0394-3755 New Trends in Ophthalmology†
0394-3801 Quetzal
0394-3933 Journal of Regional Policy†
0394-395X Il Golfo
0394-4115 Meridiana **4153**
0394-4131 Per la Filosofia **6938**
0394-414X Attraverso il Mondo† **8932**
0394-4166 Minerva Mesoterapeutica†
0394-4204 I Quaderni di Ventotene **7261**
0394-4247 Popoli **3898**
0394-4298 Venezia Arti **524**
0394-4344 Carteggi Umanistici **4209**
0394-4360 Corpus Philosophorum Medii Aevi. Serie I. Subsidia
0394-4379 Corpus Philosophorum Medii Aevi. Serie II. Testi e Studi
0394-4387 Rinascimento. Quaderni **4473**
0394-4395 Rivista Italiana di Musicologia. Quaderni **6612**
0394-4409 Istituto Nazionale di Studi sul Rinascimento. Studi e Testi **4233**
0394-4417 Studi di Musica Veneta **6620**
0394-4549 Rivista di Patologia e Sperimentazione Clinica†
0394-4573 Bollettino d'Arte **479**
0394-459X Giornale Italiano di Patologia Clinica†
0394-4611 Bollettino d'Arte, Supplemento **479**
0394-4808 Museo degli Strumenti Musicali. Rassegna di Studi e Notizie **6589**
0394-4883 Pluteus **4254**
0394-4921 Quaderni di Letterature Iberiche e Iberoamericane **5356**
0394-5057 Speleo† **8989**
0394-5065 Biblioteca di Storia della Scienza **7840**
0394-5073 Universita degli Sudi di Firenze. Dipartimento di Filosofia. Annali **6958**
0394-509X Museum Patavinum†
0394-5103 European Earthquake Engineering† **8954**
0394-512X T P - Il Giornale della Trasmissione di Potenza†
0394-5138 Associazione Internazionale "Amici di Pompei". Bollettino†
0394-5359 Padania†
0394-5367 Previsioni dell'Economia Italiana† **8982**
0394-5391 R S. Rifiuti Solidi **3510**
0394-5413 Tecnologie Tessili **8458**
0394-5596 Annales Tectonicae†
0394-560X Lega Italiana contro l'Epilessia. Bollettino **6158**
0394-5618 Erba d'Arno **5290**
0394-5634 L'Impianto Elettrico **3318**
0394-5669 Uomo Citta Territorio **3899**
0394-5723 Rivista Italiana di Ipnosi Clinica e Sperimentale†
0394-5758 Rassegna di Psicoterapie - Ipnosi†
0394-5782 Museo Civico di Storia Naturale di Ferrara. Stazione di Ecologia. Quaderni **855**
0394-5847 Quaderni di Palazzo Te **513**
0394-5871 Ingegneria Ambientale **7525**
0394-5898 Quattro Zampe **6814**
0394-591X Progressio (French Edition) **7672**
0394-5928 Progressio (Spanish Edition) **7672**
0394-5936 Progressio (English Edition) **7672**
0394-5944 Arredo Urbano† **8931**
0394-5952 Arredo Urbano Bis† **8931**
0394-5987 Amici Miei† **8929**
0394-6029 Abruzzo nel Mondo **3896**
0394-6088 Crocevia **7490**
0394-6169 Advances in Horticultural Science **3721**
0394-6282 Rivista Internazionale di Musica Sacra **6612**
0394-6320 International Journal of Immunopathology and Pharmacology **5761**
0394-6428 Next† **8977**
0394-6444 The European Journal of International Affairs **7233**
0394-6479 A S P E†
0394-6495 Rivista Internazionale dei Diritti dell'Uomo†
0394-6568 Aqua† **8930**
0394-6584 Beni Culturali e Ambiente
0394-6592 Bollettino del Lavoro e dei Tributi **4631**
0394-6657 Controluce†
0394-6681 E O News **3094**
0394-6835 Metamorfosi **450**
0394-6916 Rivista del Consulente Tecnico **1033**
0394-6924 Quale Sviluppo **4309**
0394-6932 Teatro e Storia†
0394-6940 Vita Italiana. Cultura e Scienza† **8997**
0394-6975 Tropical Zoology **965**
0394-7122 Lamborghini Review
0394-7149 Societa Italiana di Malacologia. Bollettino Malacologico **963**
0394-7157 Accademia Clementina. Atti e Memorie **4195**
0394-7181 A Tavola **3625**
0394-719X Avventura
0394-7203 Bell'Italia **8686**
0394-7211 Progetto Legno†
0394-7270 La Fenice **4139**
0394-7297 Filosofia Politica **7136**
0394-7335 Lavorosocieta†
0394-7394 Nuncius **7894**
0394-7440 Pace, Diritti dell'Uomo, Diritti dei Popoli **7213**
0394-7580 Sale e Pepe **4366**
0394-7688 Viaggiando in Autostrada
0394-7726 Analecta Ordinis Carmelitarum **7783**
0394-7734 Archivium Historicum Carmelitanum **7784**
0394-7742 Carmel in the World **7787**
0394-7750 Carmel in the World Paperbacks **7787**
0394-7769 Collationes Mariales Instituti Carmelitani **7792**
0394-7777 Collectanea Bibliographica Carmelitana **7698**
0394-7785 Presenza del Carmelo†
0394-7793 Textus et Studia Historica Carmelitana **7820**
0394-7807 Vacare Deo **7821**
0394-7858 Medioevo e Rinascimento **4243**
0394-7866 Miscellanea Marciana
0394-7874 Mondo Cucina
0394-7947 Piccola Impresa† **8981**
0394-7963 Storia, Antropologia e Scienze del Linguaggio
0394-8048 Linea Intima **2248**
0394-8064 R M 1 Maglieria in Italia†
0394-8080 Attualita Cinematografiche†
0394-8137 Danzare
0394-8153 Voce dell'Emigrante **8077**
0394-820X Aeronautica e Difesa **42**
0394-8218 Jura Medica
0394-8226 Annales Theologici **7783**
0394-8234 G E C Il Giornale del Cartolaio **2321**
0394-8250 Vanita†
0394-8277 Comuni d'Italia **7490**
0394-8285 Il Vigile Urbano **2671**
0394-8293 L'Ufficio Tecnico **1041**
0394-8307 La Finanza Locale **1925**
0394-8323 I Servizi Demografici **7292**
0394-8331 Informatica ed Enti Locali†
0394-8358 Politica del Turismo†
0394-8366 Diritto ed Economia† **8950**
0394-8374 Rivista Trimestrale degli Appalti **4880**
0394-8382 Gea *changed to* 1971-5455 **3402**
0394-8390 L'Unione dei Segretari **4604**
0394-8420 Rivista Giuridica di Urbanistica **4426**
0394-8439 Rivista del Personale dell'Ente Locale *changed to* 1723-9877 **7501**
0394-8447 Rivista dell'Istruzione **2908**
0394-8471 Sistemi di Trasporto **8511**
0394-848X Reporter
0394-8501 Accademia Leonardo da Vinci: Journal of Leonardo Studies and Bibliography of Vinciana
0394-8528 Spazio Tessile
0394-8536 Tourispress Italia
0394-8609 Il Cobold **4447**
0394-8625 Essecome **2677**
0394-8684 Sardinia When & Where†
0394-8706 C I B Edifici Intelligenti†
0394-8811 Accademia della Scienze Mediche. Atti
0394-882X Casa Tessil Reporter
0394-8862 Columbus 92
0394-8889 Nuovi Argomenti di Medicina
0394-8900 Informatore Giuridico dell'Operatore Turistico† **8964**
0394-9001 Medicina nei Secoli **5673**
0394-901X Il Diabete **5886**
0394-9028 Rivista delle Cancelliere **4776**
0394-9036 La Difesa Penale†
0394-9044 Archivi per la Storia *changed to* 1970-4070 **4990**
0394-9060 Biologia Oggi†
0394-9079 Chirurgia della Testa e del Collo
0394-9109 Rivista Italiana di Colon-Proctologia†
0394-9214 Matecon
0394-9230 Zodiac
0394-9249 Zodiac (English Edition)†
0394-9257 Journal of Genetics & Breeding **874**
0394-929X Sistemi e Impresa **2525**
0394-9303 Istituto Superiore di Sanita. Notiziario **7527**
0394-9338 Irrigazione e Drenaggio†
0394-9362 Giornale di Tecniche Nefrologiche e Dialitiche **6268**
0394-9370 Ethology Ecology & Evolution **942**
0394-9389 Il Castello di Elsinore **8467**
0394-9397 Religioni e Societa **7675**
0394-9427 Alba Pompeia **372**
0394-9486 Rivista di Micologia **815**
0394-9508 Chirurgia **6239**
0394-9559 La Lettera della Ipertensione
0394-9575 Mediaforum† **8973**
0394-9583 Nuovo†
0394-9591 Target†
0394-9605 Unificazione & Certificazione **1550**
0394-977X Rivista di Ostetricia e Ginecologia† **8986**
0394-9796 Tecnica Calzaturiera **7942**
0394-980X Ricerche Storico Bibliche **7815**
0394-9826 Alcologia **2691**
0394-9834 Italy Export
0394-9850 Euntes Docete **7797**
0394-9869 Bibliografia Missionaria **7697**
0394-9893 Glass Machinery Plants & Accessories **2042**
0394-9915 Gioielli e Orologi†
0394-994X Il Confronto Letterario **5107**
0394-9982 Riza Psicosomatica **5707**
0395-000X Ordinaire du Psychanalyste†
0395-0018 Action Poetique. Supplement *see* 0001-7477 **5415**
0395-0026 Cle des Mots†
0395-0328 Reunion Agricole†
0395-0395 Riviera Scientifique **7904**
0395-0530 Afro Music†
0395-0840 Animation et Education **2826**
0395-0913 Batiment-Actualite **978**
0395-1081 Kyrn†
0395-1200 Cahiers Debussy **6553**
0395-1294 France Transports†
0395-1804 Argus du Bateau et de Tout le Materiel Nautique† **8931**
0395-2037 Le Monde **3841**
0395-2096 Forum Chirurgical
0395-2126 Hetero†
0395-2649 Annales (Paris) **8087**
0395-2673 Conseils Sols et Murs *changed to* 0296-9017
0395-269X Ex Libris Francais **7560**
0395-2894 Specialement Votre†
0395-2916 Paysage Actualites
0395-3491 Sports Equestres†
0395-3599 Courses Hippiques†
0395-3661 SIONA Information
0395-367X Technic Hebdo
0395-3750 Bulletin Technique du Genie Militaire†
0395-3998 Boreales **4206**
0395-403X Societe Francaise de Cardiologie. Bulletin d'Informations†
0395-4269 Le Bolchevik **7110**
0395-4366 Autohebdo†
0395-4382 Karate Cinema†
0395-451X Bulletin Rapide de Droit des Affaires **1729**
0395-5621 C F D T Magazine **7951**
0395-5958 Syndicalisme - Fonction Publique **7503**
0395-6458 Le Nouvel Economiste†
0395-6601 Centre National de Documentation Pedagogique. Textes et Documents pour la Classe. **2835**
0395-6725 Quinzaine Universitaire **2999**
0395-6989 Commonwealth **5211**
0395-6997 Crochet d'Art **6638**
0395-7152 Agriculture de Groupe **85**
0395-7306 Societe Entomologique du Nord de la France. Bulletin **859**
0395-7349 Medecine, Sciences et Documents
0395-7527 Societe Mycologique de France. Bulletin Trimestriel **818**
0395-7632 Etudes Philosophiques (Aix-en-Provence) **6918**
0395-7691 Education Rurale **2849**
0395-773X Traduire **5188**
0395-7837 Chantiers de Pedagogie Mathematique **3054**
0395-7845 Chants des Peuples **5272**
0395-8086 Universite d'Aix-Marseille 3. Centre des Hautes Etudes Touristiques. Essais **8781**
0395-8108 Etudes de Paleographie Hebraique **5117**
0395-8175 Cahiers du Credit Mutuel†
0395-8183 Charolais **283**
0395-837X Espace 90†
0395-8396 Euroviande†
0395-8507 Foret - Loisirs et Equipements de Plein Air†
0395-8531 Horticulture Francaise†
0395-8582 L'Antenne **8638**

ISSN

ISSN

ISSN

Link to your serials resources and content with ulrichsweb.com

0451-0712 Gong Lu **8631**
0451-0887 Kunsterziehung†
0451-1476 Kyoto Daigaku Shokuryo Kagaku Kenkyusho Hokoku **131**
0451-1611 Kyushu Hematological Society. Journal†
0451-1646 K Mitteilungen **7094**
0451-1964 Kagaku (Kyoto) **2069**
0451-1999 Kagaku Keisatsu Kenkyujo Hokoku Bohan Shonen Hen *changed to* 1881-347X **2658**
0451-2006 Kagaku Keisatsu Kenkyujo Hokoku Kotsu Ken *changed to* 1881-347X **2658**
0451-2030 Kagaku Kojo **3249**
0451-2065 Kagami **5222**
0451-2081 Kagawa Daigaku Keizai Gakubu Kenkyu Nenpo **1139**
0451-212X Kagoshima Daigaku Kogakubu Kenkyu Hokoku **3206**
0451-2219 Kaigan **3276**
0451-243X K V Convertible Fact Finder Service†
0451-2715 Kalmar Laen **4236**
0451-307X Kanpo no Rinsho **312**
0451-3118 Gansu Huabao **3824**
0451-3371 Kansa Taisteli - Miehet Kertovat†
0451-3991 Kansas City Genealogist†
0451-4084 Kansas Kin **3772**
0451-4203 Kanzo **5928**
0451-4475 Karger Gazette **5656**
0451-4874 Kasseler Statistik **7481**
0451-5560 Kauppalehti **1139**
0451-5994 Keikinzoku **6319**
0451-6001 Keikinzoku Kogyo Tokei Nenpo **6340**
0451-6109 National Research Laboratory of Metrology. Bulletin **6405**
0451-6222 Keizai Riron **1770**
0451-6265 Keizaigaku Kenkyu (Sapporo) **1140**
0451-6338 Kelsey Review **5317**
0451-6486 Kenchiku Kenkyu Hokoku
0451-7490 Kepes Ujsag
0451-937X Kiho Kyosanken Mondai/Communist Bloc Problems *changed to* 0918-7030 **7263**
0451-9396 Kikai Gijutsu **3387**
0451-9930 Kirkia **799**
0452-2486 Kochi Joshi Daigaku Kiyo. Shizen Kagaku Hen **7877**
0452-2516 Kodai **402**
0452-2591 Kodak Tech Bits†
0452-2834 Kogyo Zairyo **3351**
0452-2907 Kokalos. Supplementi *see* 0392-0887 **403**
0452-3016 Kokubungaku, Kaishaku to Kyozai no Kenkyu **5318**
0452-3318 Kyoiku Kenkyu **2881**
0452-3377 Kokusai Mondai **7250**
0452-3385 Japan Commercial Arbitration Association. Quarterly **1573**
0452-3458 Kokyu to Junkan **6215**
0452-361X Komazawa Daigaku Kenkyu Kiyo *changed to* 0389-9861 **1141**
0452-361X Komazawa Daigaku Kenkyu Kiyo/Komazawa University. Journal *changed to* 0452-3628 **7701**
0452-3628 Komazawa Daigaku Bukkyo Gakubu Kenkyu Kiyo **7701**
0452-3636 Komazawa Daigaku Bungakubu Kenkyu Kiyo **5318**
0452-389X Kommunalteknikk **3207**
0452-4160 Konan Daigaku Kiyo. Rigaku Hen **7877**
0452-4780 Konjunkturpolitik. Beihefte†
0452-4918 Konstanzer Blaetter fuer Hochschulfragen†
0452-5914 Korean Stamps
0452-599X Koroze a Ochrana Materialu **3250**
0452-621X Kosmos Bibliothek†
0452-7208 Kristofer Lehmkuhl Forelesning **1142**
0452-7402 Gugong Bowuyuan Yuankan **4454**
0452-7739 Die Kueste **2811**
0452-8255 Kunchong Zhishi **854**
0452-8514 Kunst in Hessen und am Mittelrhein†
0452-8778 Guoji Zhanwang **7239**
0452-8832 Guoji Wenti Yanjiu **7239**
0452-9081 Kurtrierisches Jahrbuch **4239**
0452-9456 Kwansei Gakuin Daigaku Shakai Gakubu Kiyo **7982**
0452-9502 Kwartalnik Filmowy **6506**
0452-9650 Kyoiku Shinrigaku Nenpo **2881**
0452-9731 Kyoritsu Yakka Daigaku Kenkyu Nenpo†
0452-9987 Kyoto University. Biological Laboratory. Contributions **686**
0452-9995 Kyoto University. Research Institute for Food Science. Memoirs†
0453-0276 Kyushu Daigaku Kyoyobu Chigaku Kenkyu Hokoku **2712**
0453-0314 Kyushu Daigaku Nogakubu Suisangakka Gyosekishu **3600**
0453-0349 Kyushu Institute of Technology. Bulletin: Humanities, Social Sciences **4462**
0453-0357 Kyushu Institute of Technology. Bulletin: Science and Technology **8430**
0453-0535 Japan. Norin-sho Kachiku Eisei Shikenjo Nenpo†
0453-0578 Kacic **4236**
0453-0586 Kadmos. Supplement **402**
0453-0616 Kaerntner Bibliographie **4236**
0453-0667 Kagaku Keisatsu Kenkyujo Nenpo **2658**
0453-0675 Kagaku Keisatsu Kenkyujo Shiryo†
0453-0691 Japan Association for Philosophy of Science. Annals **7870**
0453-073X Kagaku to Seibutsu **737**
0453-0764 Kagawa Daigaku Nogakubu Kiyo **129**
0453-0845 Kagoshima Daigaku Nogakubu Gakujutsu Hokoku **129**
0453-0853 Kagoshima University. Faculty of Agriculture. Memoirs **129**
0453-087X Kagoshima Daigaku. Suisan Gakubu Kiyo **3600**
0453-0950 Journal of World Affairs **7249**
0453-1116 Kaj
0453-1388 Kalmia†
0453-1507 Kami Parupu Gijutsu Taimusu **6734**
0453-1515 Kami Parupu Tokei Nenpo **6734**
0453-185X Kanagawa Hogaku **4708**
0453-1906 Kanagawa-kenritsu Hakubutsukan Kenkyu Hokoku. Shizen Kagaku **7874**
0453-1981 Kanazawa University. Faculty of Law and Literature. Studies and Essays **5317**
0453-2198 Kansai University Technology Reports **8430**
0453-2201 Kansanelaman Kuvauksia **3619**
0453-2600 Kansas Statistical Abstract (Print) *changed to* 1934-9319 **8384**
0453-2805 Kansas Sportsman
0453-2899 Kaogu **402**
0453-2902 Kaogu Xuebao **402**
0453-3283 Karlsruher Juristische Bibliographie **4823**
0453-3402 Karstenia **799**
0453-3429 Karthago **402**
0453-3585 Kataliz i Katalizatory†
0453-3623 Katalog Fauny Polski **953**
0453-3992 Katunob†
0453-4360 Volcanological Society of Japan. Bulletin **2791**
0453-4387 Keats - Shelley Journal **5425**
0453-4441 Keeping Track **8619**
0453-4514 Operations Research Society of Japan. Journal **1783**
0453-4557 Keio Business Review **1139**
0453-4654 Keisoku Jido Seigyo Gakkai Ronbunshu **3207**
0453-4662 Keisoku to Seigyo **6403**
0453-4778 Keizaigaku Ronsan **1140**
0453-4786 Keizaigakushi Gakkai Nenpo **1546**
0453-4972 B R I Research Papers **978**
0453-512X Kennedy Quarterly†
0453-5723 Kentucky Genealogist
0453-5812 Kentucky Travel Guide **8727**
0453-5944 Kenya. Dairy Board. Annual Report
0453-6002 Kenya Statistical Digest **8384**
0453-6460 Kenya Export News†
0453-7440 Kerala **1495**
0453-7580 Keramos **2044**
0453-767X Kernkraft Zentrale, Gundremmingen. Jahresberichte†
0453-7831 Kevo Subarctic Research Institute. Reports **685**
0453-7998 Elektroenergetika i Avtomatizatsiya Energoustanovok **3188**
0453-8048 Kahrkivs'kyi Natsional'nyi Universytet. Visnyk **2991**
0453-8129 Sudan Research Information Bulletin **4477**
0453-8463 Kieler Beitraege zur Anglistik und Amerikanistik **5317**
0453-8811 Kinetika i Kataliz **2138**
0453-8854 Kingston Law Review†
0453-8889 Kinki Daigaku. Nogakubu Kiyo **131**
0453-9249 Kiplinger California Letter **1636**
0453-9273 Kirche im Osten **7763**
0453-929X Kirche und Konfession **7658**
0453-9346 Alt-Katholiken in Deutschland. Kirchliches Jahrbuch†
0453-9478 Kiruna Geophysical Data **2786**
0453-9834 Klassische Texte des Romanischen Mittelalterszweisprachigen Ausgaben **628**
0453-9842 Klaus Groth Gesellschaft. Jahresgaben **5137**
0454-0689 Knjizevnost i Jezik
0454-0816 Gequ **6569**
0454-1111 Kobe University Economic Review **1140**
0454-1138 Kobunshi **2125**
0454-1197 Kodak Photonews†
0454-1286 Koelner Beitraege zur Sozialen Forschung und Angewandten Soziologie†
0454-1308 Koelner Germanistische Studien **5137**
0454-1383 Koepfe des 20. Jahrhunderts
0454-1405 Kogaku to Gijutsu **3207**
0454-1634 Gekkan Kokogaku Journal **395**
0454-1723 Kokugakuin University. Faculty of Law and Politics. Journal **7149**
0454-191X Foreign Aero-Space Literature†
0454-1960 Toshokan Kenkyu Sirizu **5050**
0454-2134 Journal of Social Science **7980**
0454-2150 Asian Cultural Studies **4180**
0454-255X Kommunale Dienstleistungen
0454-3491 Konyvtari es Dokumentacios Szakirodalom†
0454-4072 Korea Today **7149**
0454-4102 Korean Business Directory **2012**
0454-4196 Korean Trade Unions†
0454-420X Korean Youth and Students **2159**
0454-4439 Vychodoslovenske Muzeum v Kosiciach. Sbornik. Seria A. Prirodne Vedy *changed to* 1335-3535 **2713**
0454-448X Kosmosophie **6931**
0454-4544 Kotai Butsuri **7060**
0454-4617 Za Casopis: Kovcezic
0454-4641 Kowan Gijutsu Kenkyujo Hokoku **3277**
0454-4668 Kowan Giken Shiryo **3277**
0454-4811 Akademia Gorniczo-Hutnicza im. Stanislawa Staszica. Zeszyty Naukowe. Zagadnienia Techniczno-Ekonomiczne†
0454-482X Muzeum Etnograficzne im. Seweryna Udzieli w Krakowie. Rocznik **349**
0454-5230 Krigshistorisk Tidsskrift **6430**
0454-5265 Kriminalwissenschaftliche Abhandlungen†
0454-5354 Kritik **5318**
0454-5478 Krs Jugoslavije†
0454-5508 Krugozor†
0454-5524 Krystalinikum† **8970**
0454-5648 Guisuanyan Xuebao **2116**
0454-6059 Cultuurpatronen†
0454-6148 Kumamoto Daigaku Kyoikugakubu Kiyo. Shizen Kagaku **7877**
0454-6245 Kuml **403**
0454-6296 Kunchong Xuebao **853**
0454-6520 Kunst og Museum†
0454-6601 Kunstjahrbuch der Stadt Linz **501**
0454-7063 Kuwait. Central Statistical Office. Monthly Bulletin of Foreign Trade Statistics **1248**
0454-7217 Meddelande fraan Kvismare Faagelstation **910**
0454-7586 Kyosai Iho **5659**
0454-7659 Kyoto University. Abuyama Seismological Observatory. Seismological Bulletin **2786**
0454-7675 Kyoto University. Disaster Prevention Research Institute. Bulletin†
0454-7802 Kyoto University. Faculty of Science. Memoirs. Series of Biology **686**
0454-7810 Kyoto University. Faculty of Science. Memoirs. Series of Geology and Mineralogy **2752**
0454-8086 Kytoesavut†
0454-8132 Kyushu American Literature **5319**
0454-8302 Kanagawa Shigaku **5854**
0454-8833 Khimiya i Termodinamika Rastvorov†
0454-8973 Knight Letter **3773**
0454-9244 Kyoto University. Research Reactor Institute. Annual Reports†
0454-949X Kenya Newsletter **3902**
0454-9910 Kibernetika i Vychislitel'naya Tekhnika **2527**
0455-0250 Katastrophenmedizin† **8969**
0455-0374 Kernenergie Forschungsschiff "Otto Hahn". Jahresbericht†
0455-0420 Kieler Diskussionsbeitraege **1495**
0455-0463 Knjizevna Smotra **5318**
0455-0595 Kratkie Soobshcheniya po Fizike *see* 1068-3356 **7024**
0455-0609 Krcki Zbornik **4238**
0455-2059 Lanzhou Daxue Xuebao (Ziran Kexue Ban) **7878**
0455-2342 Landarbeit und Technik†
0455-8154 De Letzeburger Bauer **134**
0456-2666 Literaturspiegel
0456-3867 Canadian Hardware, Electrical & Building Supply Directory **1978**
0456-4804 Ramsay Society of Chemical Engineers. Journal†
0456-5339 Look Japan *changed to* Japan Journal (English Edition) **1599**
0456-5959 Louisiana Agricultural Experiment Station. Report of Projects **134**
0456-7463 Louisiana English Journal **5328**
0456-829X L'udove Noviny
0457-088X Landman **6777**
0457-1320 Langues et Styles
0457-1673 Universidad Nacional de la Plata. Instituto de la Produccion. Serie Contribuciones
0457-2483 Law Library Lights **5025**
0457-3633 Legislative Trends†
0457-3897 Neujahrsgabe der Deutschen Buecherei†
0457-3900 Sonderbibliographien der Deutschen Bucherei
0457-4184 Lejeunia **800**
0457-4206 Univerzita Karlova. Lekarska Fakulta Hradec Kralove. Lekarske Zpravy† **8996**
0457-4214 Lekarsky Obzor **5661**
0457-5792 Letecky Obzor†
0457-6039 Levante Agricola **241**
0457-6047 Leveltari Szemle **4240**
0457-6241 Lishi Jiaoxue **4151**
0457-6306 Liaoning Huabao† **8971**
0457-7019 County Newsletter†
0457-8074 United Nations Association of the Republic of China Newsletter **7270**
0457-8090 Lianhuan Huabao **3826**
0457-8910 Lilly Endowment. Report†
0457-9976 Liste des Societes Savantes et Litteraires†
0458-0036 Listy Biometryczne **687**
0458-063X Liturgy **7660**
0458-1520 Muzeum Archeologiczne i Etnograficzne, Lodz. Prace i Materialy. Seria Archeologiczna **407**
0458-1547 Politechnika Lodzka. Zeszyty Naukowe. Zeszyt Specjalny†
0458-1555 Politechnika Lodzka. Zeszyty Naukowe. Chemia **2076**
0458-1822 Lok Magazin **8620**
0458-3329 Louisiana Geological Survey. Folio Series **2753**
0458-4244 Lozarstvo i Vinarstvo **607**
0458-4317 Annales Universitatis Mariae Curie-Sklodowska. Sectio G. Ius **4617**
0458-497X Lutheran Digest **7765**
0458-5674 L P V-Listos para Vencer†
0458-5682 L S U Forestry Notes **3695**
0458-5933 Laboratory Animal Handbooks **5908**
0458-6026 Labour Law Cases†
0458-6506 Lalit Kala **502**
0458-6859 Landbauforschung Voelkenrode *changed to* Landbauforschung **241**
0458-6905 Landeskundliche Vierteljahrsblaetter **4239**
0458-6972 Landmark (Waukesha) **4301**
0458-7251 Le Langage et l'Homme **5138**
0458-726X Langages **5139**
0458-7367 Language Research in Progress†
0458-7871 Laser and Unconventional Optics Journal†
0458-7944 Lateinamerika (Rostock)†
0458-8460 Law and Legislation in the German Democratic Republic†
0458-8584 Law in Japan **4715**
0458-8592 Law in Society **4715**
0458-8665 Law Quadrangle Notes **2290**
0458-8711 Law Society of Scotland. Journal (Year) **4717**
0458-9564 Legal Bulletin **4719**
0458-998X Leidse Historische Reeks†
0459-0007 Leidse Wijsgerige Reeks†
0459-004X Deutsche Buecherei. Jahrbuch†
0459-021X Leitfaeden der Angewandten Mathematik und Mechanik **5509**
0459-0236 Deutscher Wetterdienst. Leitfaeden fuer die Ausbildung **6352**
0459-0953 Lens and Speaker†
0459-1283 Letras (Caracas) **5143**
0459-1356 Letras Nacionales
0459-1623 Letture Classensi **5322**
0459-1801 Nationaal Natuurhistorisch Museum. Zoologische Bijdragen **957**
0459-1879 Lixue Xuebao **7060**
0459-1909 Lishi Yanjiu **4151**
0459-1992 Liberal **7151**
0459-2034 Safety Education **7540**
0459-2476 Y L G News†
0459-2603 Library of Theoria **6932**
0459-2980 Libya Antiqua **4323**
0459-3030 Libyca†
0459-3650 American Council of Life Insurance. Economic and Investment Report†
0459-3774 Life Sciences†
0459-3871 Ligue Internationale Contre la Concurrence Deloyale. Annuaire
0459-388X Ligue Internationale Contre la Concurrence Deloyale. Communication

ISSN

0475-0209 One World
0475-025X Ontario Bird Banding
0475-0608 O P E C Annual Statistical Bulletin **6782**
0475-0756 Otemon Economic Studies **1157**
0475-0926 Oklahoma. Attorney General's Office. Opinions of the Attorney General **4958**
0475-0942 Ontario. Ministry of the Environment. Water Resources Branch. Water Resources Report†
0475-1388 Old Athlone Society Journal†
0475-1450 Ontogenez **695**
0475-1671 Oyez **4754**
0475-171X Oceans†
0475-1906 Optimum†
0475-2058 Osaka Dental University. Journal **5860**
0475-2953 P S **5458**
0475-302X P T T Syndicaliste **2335**
0475-4816 La Palabra Diaria **7668**
0475-6347 Panorama **3930**
0475-9141 Patre *changed to* 1638-4830 **298**
0476-0069 Pediatria Internazionale†
0476-0301 Beijing Shifan Daxue Xuebao (Ziran Kexue Ban) **7840**
0476-031X Beifang Wenxue **5261**
0476-0441 Pellicce Moda **4974**
0476-1103 Pennsylvania Statistical Abstract†
0476-3475 Die Personalvertretung **1871**
0476-4854 Le Phare†
0476-5532 Philippine Government Rulings
0476-8612 Pionierleiter†
0476-9465 Plana†
0476-9546 Planned Parenthood **973**
0477-0250 Universitet po Khranitelni Tekhnologii. Nauchni Trudove **3666**
0477-1664 Poland. Ministerstwo Oswiaty. Dziennik Urzedowy *changed to* 1644-292X **2843**
0477-2008 Police & Constabulary Almanac **2663**
0477-244X Politica dei Trasporti
0477-5449 Poodle Review **6813**
0477-7255 Portugal Illustrado†
0477-8685 Pozemni Stavby†
0478-1376 Presenza† **8982**
0478-1392 Preservation Progress (Charleston) **454**
0478-1546 Presse†
0478-1805 Previdenza Sociale nell'Agricoltura†
0478-3166 Pro Austria Romana **412**
0478-4049 Asbestos Producer
0478-4251 Products Finishing Directory **6720**
0478-5118 Progressiste
0478-6378 Proyeccion **7672**
0478-6599 Przeglad Mleczarski **268**
0478-6866 Psychobiologie†
0479-1290 Padova†
0479-1320 Universita di Padova. Facolta di Scienze Politiche. Pubblicazioni **7575**
0479-1363 Beihefte Paedagogik†
0479-4346 Panorama Economico **1510**
0479-4419 Panorami **1785**
0479-480X Magyar Grafika **7324**
0479-4826 Papua New Guinea. National Statistical Office. Building Statistics **1048**
0479-5997 Pariser Historische Studien **4253**
0479-611X Aus Politik und Zeitgeschichte **7108**
0479-7876 Pediatria **6099**
0479-8023 Beijing Daxue Xuebao (Ziran Kexue Ban) **7839**
0479-8244 Pembrokeshire Historian†
0479-9054 Pennsylvania State University. Agricultural Extension Service. Leaflet **146**
0479-947X P H S News **3746**
0479-9534 Pennsylvania Osteopathic Medical Association. Journal **5695**
0480-0257 Performing Arts Magazine (San Francisco Edition)†
0480-2160 Petroleum Intelligence Weekly **6787**
0480-2624 Der Pharmazeutische Betrieb **6874**
0480-2853 Philanthropic Digest
0480-3981 Series of Philippine Scientific Bibliographies†
0480-7480 Quellen und Abhandlungen zur Mittelrheinischen Kirchengeschichte **7672**
0480-9106 Quartaer-Bibliothek **412**
0481-0023 Quellen zur Geschichte des Islamischen Aegyptens
0481-1089 Quaderni di Studi Senesi *see* 0039-3010 **4790**
0481-1224 Quaestiones Oeconomicae **1163**
0481-1275 Quantum Physics and Its Applications†
0481-2158 Quarterly Medical Review **5702**
0481-2735 Quebec (Province) Service de l'Hydrometrie. Annuaire Hydrologique
0481-3375 Queensland. Registrar of Co-Operative and Other Societies. Report
0481-3510 Quellen und Beitraege zur Geschichte der Universitaet Wuerzburg **2999**
0481-3537 Quellen und Darstellungen zur Schlesischen Geschichte **4255**
0481-3650 Quellen zur Geschichte des Parlamentarismus und der Politischen Parteien. Erste Reihe: Von der Konstitutionellen Monarchie zur Parlamentarischen Republik **7175**
0481-4118 Quimica e Derivados **2077**
0481-4142 Die Quintessenz des Steuerrechts **1941**
0481-5084 R F D News **149**
0481-5475 Rachunkowosc **1299**
0481-6048 Radio es Televizioujsag†
0481-6684 Revista de Chirurgie, Oncologie, Radiologie, O.R.L., Oftalmologie, Stomatologie. Radiologie†
0481-780X Rassegna di Medicina Omeopatica† **8984**
0481-9004 Realty†
0481-9357 Recht und Organisation der Parlamente **7465**
0482-0819 Reform Judaism **7728**
0482-086X Reformatusok Lapja **7772**
0482-2803 Report on Credit Unions†
0482-458X Otaru Shoka Daigaku Jimbun Kenkyu **4468**
0482-5004 Revista Brasileira de Reumatologia **6226**
0482-5209 Revista de Administracion Publica **7466**
0482-5276 Revista de Ciencias Sociales **7996**
0482-5527 Revista de Educacao e Cultura†
0482-5748 Revista de Historia Militar **6443**
0482-5772 Revista de Ingenieria **3217**
0482-5985 Revista de Ortopedia y Traumatologia (Print) *changed to* 1888-4415 **6072**
0482-6019 Revista de Psiquiatria y Psicologia Medica de Europa y America Latinas
0482-640X Revista Nacional de Oncologia†
0482-6760 Revista Medica†
0482-6876 Revista Mexicana de Seguridad Social†
0482-7171 Revista Portuguesa de Medicina Militar†
0482-8062 Revue du Travail **1705**
0483-0466 Riesgo†
0483-1330 Ritsumeikan Hogaku **4940**
0483-142X Rivista del Lavoro
0483-2027 Robotnik **7180**
0483-5654 Rund um die Boerse†
0483-5689 Rundbrief der Dobrudscha-Deutschen†
0483-7495 R C A Technical Notes **2337**
0483-786X Revue Technique Veterinaire de l'Alimentation†
0483-8009 Annales de la Recherche Forestiere au Maroc **3683**
0483-8785 Radnor Historical Society. Bulletin **4309**
0483-9080 Rajamme Vartijat **6442**
0483-9218 Rajshahi University Studies
0483-9420 Random Lengths **3715**
0483-9722 Rassegna di Diritto e Tecnica Doganale e delle Imposte di Fabbricazione† **8984**
0483-9811 Rassegna Italiana di Gastroenterologia†
0484-0305 Readaptation **3045**
0484-0828 Recent Researches in the Music of the Baroque Era **6609**
0484-0887 Recherches Augustiniennes **7673**
0484-1689 Redbook of Used Gun Values†
0484-2286 Referativnyi Zhurnal. Kommunal'noe, Bytovoe i Torgovoe Oborudovanie **5462**
0484-2480 Referativnyi Zhurnal. Stroitel'nye i Dorozhnye Mashiny **3233**
0484-2502 Referativnyi Zhurnal. Teploenergetika†
0484-2545 Referativnyi Zhurnal. Vodnyi Transport **8529**
0484-2561 Referativnyi Zhurnal. Vozdushnyi Transport **8529**
0484-2596 Referativnyi Zhurnal. Zheleznodorozhnyi Transport **8529**
0484-2650 Reflection **5358**
0484-5412 Reserve Bank of Australia. Annual Report **1378**
0484-6125 Revealer **6899**
0484-6710 Taiikugaku Kenkyu **2917**
0484-6885 Revista de Derecho Financiero y de Hacienda Publica† **8985**
0484-6923 Revista de Derecho Social Ecuatoriano **4771**
0484-7784 Revista Juridica del Peru **4773**
0484-7903 Revista Mexicana de Anestesiologia **5774**
0484-8039 Revista Oftalmologica Venezolana **6051**
0484-811X Revista Portuguesa de Farmacia **6879**
0484-8268 Revista Uruguaya de Psicoanalisis **7405**
0484-8284 Revista Veterinaria Venezolana **8806**
0484-8365 Revolution et Travail **7179**
0484-8616 Revue des Etudes Juives **7729**
0484-8764 Revue Francaise de Comptabilite **1300**
0484-8934 Revue Metapsychique **6743**
0484-8942 Revue Numismatique **6653**
0484-9019 Rit Fiskideildar **3606**
0485-1412 Rinsho Eiyo **6669**
0485-1420 Rinsho Kensa **5910**
0485-1439 Rinsho Ketsueki **5941**
0485-1447 Rinsho Noha **6183**
0485-1854 Universidade Federal do Rio de Janeiro. Departamento de Microbiologia Geral. Anais de Microbiologia **746**
0485-2281 Rivista dei Dottori Commercialisti **1168**
0485-2435 Rivista Giuridica dell'Edilizia **1033**
0485-2877 Rocket News **69**
0485-3504 Rodzina i Szkola†
0485-4098 Istituto di Diritto Processuale Civile. Pubblicazioni **4833**
0485-4152 Universita di Roma. Istituto di Storia dell'Architettura. Quaderni **460**
0485-5175 Roving Commissions **8281**
0485-6724 Old Sturbridge Visitor **4307**
0485-8255 Regional Science Research Institute. Discussion Paper Series†
0485-8972 Radiotekhnika†
0485-9561 Rajasthan Medical Journal
0485-9642 Rajio no Seisaku†
0485-9960 Random Lengths Yearbook **3709**
0486-0306 Rassegna Geriatrica
0486-0349 Rassegna Italiana di Sociologia **8127**
0486-0373 Rassegna Parlamentare **4851**
0486-0845 University of Reading. Department of Agricultural Economics & Management. Miscellaneous Studies†
0486-0993 Reales Sitios **455**
0486-1019 Realidade†
0486-106X Realites Gabonaises **7176**
0486-123X Recent Researches in the Music of the Renaissance **6609**
0486-1426 Recherches Voltaiques†
0486-1469 Recht der Landwirtschaft **150**
0486-1493 Recht und Geschichte†
0486-2236 Referativnyi Zhurnal. Astronomiya **584**
0486-2252 Referativnyi Zhurnal. Avtomobil'nye Dorogi. Otdel'nyi Vypusk **8528**
0486-2279 Referativnyi Zhurnal. Dvigateli Vnutrennego Sgoraniya **3233**
0486-2309 Referativnyi Zhurnal. Geologiya **2721**
0486-2325 Referativnyi Zhurnal. Khimiya **2095**
0486-235X Referativnyi Zhurnal. Informatika **5059**
0486-350X Relacion Criminologica
0486-3518 Relaciones Financieras **1647**
0486-3739 Renaissance Drama **8477**
0486-3887 Renewal of Town and Village†
0486-400X Rentgenologia i Radiologia **6207**
0486-4271 Repertorium Plantarum Succulentarum **815**
0486-4433 Reporter†
0486-4476 Reports on Progress in Polymer Physics in Japan†
0486-4689 Res Facta†
0486-4700 Res Publica **7177**
0486-5111 Research Progress in Organic, Biological and Medicinal Chemistry†
0486-5383 Reserve Bank of Malawi. Report and Accounts **1379**
0486-5561 Resources for the Future. Annual Report **2626**
0486-5588 Responsa Meridiana **4769**
0486-5642 Restoration Quarterly **7676**
0486-6096 Review of International Affairs *see* 0543-3657 **7252**
0486-6134 Review of Radical Political Economics **1548**
0486-6347 Revista Brasileira de Bebidas e Alimentos†
0486-641X Revista Brasileira de Psicanalise **7403**
0486-6460 Revista Camoniana†
0486-6525 Revista Colombiana de Antropologia **353**
0486-8161 Sacramento Newsletter†
0486-8234 Saechsische Heimatblaetter **4261**
0486-8927 Schweizerisches Institut fuer Gewerbliche Wirtschaft an der Universitaet St. Gallen. Schriftenreihe **1171**
0487-1596 I C A P Lista de Nuevas Adquisiciones†
0487-2088 St. Hedwigsblatt†
0487-3491 Seminario de Arte Aragones **517**
0487-3750 Guida Sardegna d'Oggi
0487-5648 Sbornik Vlastivednych Praci z Podblanicka
0487-577X Scanner (Croydon) **2338**
0487-6423 Statistisches Jahrbuch Schleswig-Holstein **8407**
0487-6598 Schoenhengster Jahrbuch **3856**
0487-6830 School Sister of Notre Dame†
0487-8965 Scientific Meetings **6282**
0488-1281 Seishin Igaku **6184**
0488-2024 Semaine Africaine **7817**
0488-3721 Servex **1582**
0488-3896 Service Station Management†
0488-4965 The Settler **4312**
0488-5406 Shanghai Jiaoyu (Chengren Jiaoyu Ban) **2945**
0488-6097 Shepard's Alaska Citations **4960**
0488-6119 Shepard's Mississippi Citations **4962**
0488-6364 Shijie Jingji Wenhui **1173**
0488-6720 Shipmate **2301**
0488-728X Free Albanian
0488-7387 Shuxue Jiaoxue **3082**
0488-7395 Shuxue Tongxun **5535**
0488-7476 Shukan Josei **8883**
0488-7484 Shukan Shincho **3901**
0488-7557 Svetlosc **5241**
0488-8812 Simplicity School Catalog†
0489-0280 Sites et Monuments **416**
0489-0760 Skolhistoriskt Arkiv **4263**
0489-1090 Slaekt och Haevd **3783**
0489-1376 Literarny Almanach Slovaka V Amerike†
0489-2089 Norsk Etnologisk Gransking. Smaaskrifter†
0489-2313 Smithsonian Institution. Annual Symposia Publications†
0489-3824 Sociedad Valenciana de Pediatria. Boletin **6104**
0489-4006 Societa Emiliana Romagnola Triveneta di Ortopedia e Traumatologia. Atti†
0489-4138 Societa Italiana per il Progresso delle Scienze. Rassegna d'Informazioni†
0489-5606 Engineering Know-How in Engine Design†
0489-6432 Sophia (Tokyo, 1952)†
0489-7293 Sondages **8139**
0489-7617 Kiho Soren Mondai/Soviet Problems *changed to* 0918-7030 **7263**
0489-8567 South African Licensee's Guardian **4398**
0489-9563 South of the Mountains **4313**
0489-958X Commission de Pacifique Sud. Document Technique *see* 0081-2862 **8439**
0489-9598 Commission de Pacifique Sud. Rapport Annuel *see* 1017-1983 **7266**
0490-1606 Soziale Arbeit **8072**
0490-1630 Soziale Sicherheit **8072**
0490-2270 Instituto de Aclimatacion. Archives†
0490-2602 Instituto Nacional del Carbon. Memoria **2123**
0490-3323 Spain. Ministerio de la Vivienda. Boletin Oficial **4427**
0490-4176 Spex Speaker **7085**
0490-4788 Spoletium
0490-5113 Sport Universitario **8205**
0490-5326 Sports Afield Gun Annual†
0490-6381 Sri Lanka
0490-6659 Srpska Akademija Nauka i Umetnosti. Odeljenje Likovne i Muzicke Umetnosti. Muzicka Izdanja **6619**
0490-6756 Sichuan Daxue Xuebao (Ziran Kexue Ban) **7916**
0490-8287 State Agencies Cooperating with the U.S. Department of Agriculture Forest Service in Administration of Various Forestry Programs
0490-9348 Steirischer Burgenverein. Mitteilungen
0490-9631 Steuer- und Zollblatt fuer Berlin†
0490-9658 Die Steuerberatung **1945**
0490-9690 Der Steuerzahler **1946**
0491-0850 Stockholm Studies in History of Art **519**
0491-0869 Stockholm Studies in History of Literature **5377**
0491-0877 Stockholm Studies in Philosophy **6953**
0491-0885 Stockholm Studies in Sociology **8141**
0491-0893 Stockholmer Germanistische Forschungen **5178**
0491-0982 Stomatologia†
0491-2705 Studia Ethnographica Upsaliensia **357**
0491-2764 Studia Latina Stockholmiensia **5180**
0491-2853 Studia Theologica Lundensia **7684**
0491-3310 Studies in Public Opinion†
0491-3337 Kokugogaku **5137**
0491-3418 Studii de Muzicologie†
0491-3949 Subastas y Concursos
0491-4481 Sudan Medical Journal†
0491-4783 South African Panorama (Afrikaans Edition)†
0491-6204 Surmach **6448**
0491-6263 Survey of Compounds Which Have Been Tested for Carcinogenic Activity **6035**
0491-6441 Svarochnoe Proizvodstvo **6344**
0491-6522 Svensk Annonstaxa **636**
0491-6786 Svenska Kyrkohistoriska Foereningen. Skrifter II, Ny Foeljd **7687**
0491-807X Utrikesfraagor **7272**
0491-9424 Szabad Foldmuves†
0492-004X Transportarbetaren **8515**
0492-0716 T V Star Annual†
0492-0929 Dazhong Dianying **6495**

ISSN

0507-0252 Viola da Gamba Society of America. Journal **6626**
0507-1259 Virginia Polytechnic Institute and State University. Department of Geological Sciences. Geological Guidebooks **2773**
0507-1305 Virginia Social Science Journal **8014**
0507-1410 Vishveshvaranand Indological Journal **4482**
0507-1658 Visual Communications Journal **525**
0507-1690 Vita Evangelica†
0507-1712 Vita Italiana. Documenti e Informazioni† **8997**
0507-1747 Vital **6999**
0507-1925 Vjesnik Bibliotekara Hrvatske **5054**
0507-1992 Muzeum Vysociny. Oddeleni Ved Spolecenskych. Vlastivedny Sbornik Vysociny **6533**
0507-2379 Voice of the Pharmacist **6885**
0507-2921 Voprosy Antropologii **360**
0507-3758 Voprosy Onkologii **6036**
0507-3952 Voprosy Teatra **8484**
0507-4088 Voprosy Virusologii **898**
0507-4150 Vorgaenge **7192**
0507-5386 Vychislitel'nye Metody i Programirovaniye **2510**
0507-570X Universidad Central de Venezuela. Instituto de Ciencias Penales y Criminologicas. Anuario **2670**
0507-6544 Valley Leaves **3786**
0507-6714 Verein Deutscher Zementwerke. Forschungsinstitut der Zementindustrie. Taetigkeitsbericht **1042**
0507-6773 Vertebrate Pest Conference. Proceedings **257**
0507-6986 Vajra Bodhi Sea **7702**
0507-7184 Vida Pastoral **7692**
0507-7230 Vierteljahrsschrift fuer Wissenschaftliche Paedagogik **2924**
0507-9683 Waseda Daigaku Daigakuin Rikogaku Kenkyu Iho **3234**
0508-1254 Wasserrecht und Wasserwirtschaft **8836**
0508-2404 Weinberg und Keller†
0508-2757 Welt der Arbeit
0508-3133 Werden **1714**
0508-4741 Western Australia. Geological Survey. Report **2774**
0508-5942 Westfalenspiegel **4278**
0508-6191 Westwind (Los Angeles) **526**
0508-6213 Wetterauer Geschichtsblaetter **4278**
0508-6795 Who's Where†
0508-8445 Wir vom Konsum
0508-850X Guide to Broadcasting Stations
0509-0652 Wochenpost†
0509-089X Women's Circle†
0509-1632 World and Press **4585**
0509-2507 Organizacion Mundial de la Salud. Serie de Informes Tecnicos **5690**
0509-3007 World Meteorological Organization. Regional Association II (Asia). Abridged Final Report of the (No.) Session **6399**
0509-3015 World Meteorological Organization. Regional Association VI (Europe). Abridged Final Report of the (No.) Session†
0509-4038 Wuli Tongbao **7046**
0509-5166 W.C.J. Meredith Memorial Lectures **4810**
0509-5409 Vaart Blad†
0509-5832 Waksman Foundation of Japan. Report **6885**
0509-6057 Walter E. Edge Lectures†
0509-6510 Centralny Instytut Ochrony Pracy. Prace†
0509-6936 Muzeum Narodowe w Warszawie. Rocznik†
0509-7053 Przemyslowy Instytut Elektroniki. Prace **3111**
0509-769X Environmental Radiation Surveillance in Washington State. Annual Report **3428**
0509-7967 Washington State Traffic Accident Facts†
0509-8262 Manufacturers and Distributors Directory of the Washington, D.C. Area†
0509-8858 Wassertriebwerk **3164**
0509-917X Waterway Guide - Mid-Atlantic **8284**
0509-9528 The Weekly of Business Aviation **8552**
0510-0054 N Z O I Miscellaneous Publications†
0510-0380 Wenyi Xuexi **526**
0510-2014 Western Australia. Geological Survey. Mineral Resources Bulletin†
0510-2332 Western Express
0510-243X Western Material Handling - Packaging - Shipping
0510-3746 Belaruski Instytut Navukii Mastatstva. Zapisy
0510-4262 Wiadomosci Melioracyjne i Lakarskie **3365**
0510-4270 Wiadomosci Naftowe†
0510-4882 William Nelson Cromwell Foundation. Legal Studies†
0510-5285 Wir Bauen†
0510-5315 Die Wirbelsaeule in Forschung und Praxis
0510-5587 Wirtschaftswissenschaftliche Abhandlungen **1195**
0510-5595 Wirtschaftswissenschaftliche Schriften†
0510-5609 Wirtschaftszahl†
0510-7148 Women Ai Kexue **2222**
0510-7350 Women's Comfort†
0510-7385 Women's Household†
0510-8055 World Branches Conference of the English Speaking Unions. Principal Addresses and Summary of the Proceedings†
0510-8284 World Congress of Sodalities of Our Lady. Proceedings†
0510-8292 World Congress of the W F D. Proceedings **4077**
0510-8837 World Health Organization. Regional Office for Africa. Report of the Regional Director†
0510-8845 World Health Organization. Regional Office for the Western Pacific. Report on the Regional Seminar on the Role of the Hospital in the Public Health Programme
0510-9019 Bulletin de l'O M M *see* 0042-9767 **6397**
0510-906X World Meteorological Organization. Commission for Aeronautical Meteorology. Abridged Final Report of the (No.) Session **6398**
0510-9078 World Meteorological Organization. Commission for Agricultural Meteorology. Abridged Final Report of the (No.) Session **6398**
0510-9124 World Meteorological Organization. Regional Association I (Africa). Abridged Final Report of the (No.) Session **6399**
0510-9132 World Meteorological Organization. Regional Association III (South America). Abridged Final Report of the (No.) Session **6399**
0510-9175 World O R T Union. Congress Report
0510-9337 World Press Photo **6978**
0510-9833 Wuerzburger Geographische Arbeiten **4034**
0510-9884 Wychowanie Techniczne w Szkole **3227**
0511-0440 Wyoming Trucker **8637**
0511-0726 A A G Bijdragen **4195**
0511-084X Wakayama Medical Reports **5729**
0511-1110 Regional Engineering College Warangal. Research Bulletin **3217**
0511-1145 Warehouse Distributor News†
0511-1196 Ruch Wydawniczy w Liczbach **7579**
0511-1625 Panstwowe Muzeum Etnograficzne w Warszawie. Zeszyty **351**
0511-1633 Opady Atmosferyczne†
0511-1765 Studia Nauk Politycznych†
0511-196X Waseda Political Studies **7193**
0511-1978 Waseda Seibutsu **711**
0511-2141 Washington (State) Department of Fisheries. Information Booklet†
0511-2400 Washington Economic Indicators†
0511-2834 University of Washington. College of Business Administration. Occasional Paper†
0511-3202 Washington Library Letter†
0511-3520 Wasser - Kalender† **8998**
0511-3806 Waterway Guide - Southern **8284**
0511-4063 Wedgwood Society. Proceedings
0511-4187 Weekly Compilation of Presidential Documents *changed to* 1946-6986 **7128**
0511-4268 Weiqi†
0511-4381 Welding Research News **6345**
0511-4683 Wenxue Pinglun **5397**
0511-4721 Wen Shi Zhe **4482**
0511-4772 Wenwu **423**
0511-4934 Wesleyan Poetry Program **5437**
0511-5493 West Bengal. Bureau of Applied Economics and Statistics. Statistical Handbook **1274**
0511-568X West-European Symposia on Clinical Chemistry†
0511-6775 West Virginia Statistical Handbook†
0511-6848 Western Association of Graduate Schools. Proceedings of the Annual Meeting **3010**
0511-6872 Western Australia. Agriculture Protection Board. Annual Report (Years) **170**
0511-6910 Western Australia. Major Investment Projects, Public and Private, Current and Proposed†
0511-6996 Western Australia. Geological Survey. Annual Report†
0511-7542 Western Foundation of Vertebrate Zoology. Occasional Papers **967**
0511-7550 Western Foundation of Vertebrate Zoology. Proceedings **967**
0511-7666 W I C H E Reports†
0511-8255 Barometer (Portland) **3708**
0511-8484 Westpreussen - Jahrbuch **4278**
0511-8522 West's General Digest **4813**
0511-8719 Where to Retire on a Small Income†
0511-8794 Whitmark Directory†
0511-8824 Whitney Review
0511-8832 Whittier Newsletter **5438**
0511-8891 Who's Who Among Students in American Junior Colleges **3010**
0511-8905 Who's Who in Advertising
0511-8948 Who's Who in California **647**
0511-8964 Who's Who in Floriculture†
0511-9022 Who's Who in Public Relations (International) **647**
0511-9030 Who's Who in Spain†
0511-9138 Who's Who in World Jewry†
0511-9162 Wiadomosci Historyczne **4167**
0511-9405 Wiez **7823**
0511-9510 Wildlife Review†
0511-9618 Willdenowia **823**
0511-9715 William L. Bryant Foundation American Studies. Report†
0511-9723 William L. Hutcheson Memorial Forest. Bulletin **3707**
0512-0640 Wisconsin Geological and Natural History Survey. Information Circulars **2775**
0512-0659 Wisconsin. Geological and Natural History Survey. Special Report **2775**
0512-1175 Wisconsin Academy Review *changed to* 1558-9633 **5245**
0512-1213 Wisconsin English Journal **3088**
0512-1507 Johann Wolfgang Goethe Universitaet Frankfurt am Main. Wissenschaftliche Gesellschaft. Schriften **7977**
0512-1523 Universitaet Frankfurt. Wissenschaftliche Gesellschaft. Sitzungsberichte **7926**
0512-1582 Wissenschaftliche Monographien zum Alten und Neuen Testament **7694**
0512-1604 Wissenschaftliche Untersuchungen zum Neuen Testament **7694**
0512-2511 World Confederation of Organizations of the Teaching Profession. Occasional Papers†
0512-252X W C O T P Theme Study†
0512-2589 Faith and Order Papers **7642**
0512-2724 World Directory of Crystallographers and of Other Scientists Employing Crystallographic Methods **2112**
0512-2740 World Directory of Mathematicians **5546**
0512-2759 World Directory of Medical Schools **5731**
0512-2783 World Directory of Schools of Public Health†
0512-2953 World Fertilizer Plant List and Atlas **259**
0512-3003 World Health Organization. Basic Documents **4945**
0512-3038 World Health Organization. Monograph Series†
0512-3054 W H O Technical Report Series **5729**
0512-3186 World Land Use Survey. Occasional Papers†
0512-3194 World Land Use Survey. Regional Monograph†
0512-3453 World Peace Through Law Center. Report of the Director-General†
0512-350X Estatistica Brasileira de Energia **3152**
0512-3739 World Trade Annual **1274**
0512-3747 World Trade Annual Supplement **1275**
0512-4077 Wrangler **4318**
0512-4174 Wuxiandian **2365**
0512-4204 Wudao **2688**
0512-4255 Wychowanie Muzyczne w Szkole **6629**
0512-4395 Wyoming Statistical Review†
0512-4409 Wyoming Labor Force Trends **1716**
0512-4638 W.A. Cargill Memorial Lectures in Fine Art†
0512-4743 West Virginia Union List of Serials **639**
0512-4921 World Health Organization. Regional Office for the Western Pacific. Annual Report of the Regional Director to the Regional Committee for the Western Pacific†
0512-493X Wyoming State Geological Survey. Memoir **2775**
0512-5030 Wasser und Abwasser in Forschung und Praxis **8836**
0512-5235 Western Catholic Reporter **7823**
0512-5278 What's Happening on the Chinese Mainland†
0512-5456 Wisconsin Studies in Vocational Rehabilitation. Monographs†
0512-5472 Works in Progress†
0512-5804 What They Said
0512-5901 Woman's Day Christmas Ideas for Children†
0512-610X Washington Notes on Africa **7272**
0512-6355 Occupational Opportunities Information for Wisconsin†
0512-7920 Yinyue Shenghuo **6629**
0512-7939 Yinyue Yanjiu **6630**
0512-7955 Yingyang Xuebao **6671**
0513-0832 Yugoslavia. Savezni Zavod za Statistiku. Ucenici u Privredi†
0513-0883 Yugoslavia. Savezni Zavod za Statistiku. Zaposleno Osoblje†
0513-0891 Yugoslavia. Savezni Zavod za Statistiku. Zaposlenost *changed to* Srbija i Crna Gora Zavod za Statistiku. Zaposlenost **1266**
0513-1405 Yale Law School Studies
0513-1545 Western Historical Series†
0513-1693 Yamaguchi Daigaku Kyoikugakubu Kenkyu Ronso. Dai-2-bu. Shizen Kagaku **7932**
0513-1715 Yamaguchi University. Faculty of Agriculture. Bulletin **171**
0513-1812 Yamaguchi University. School of Medicine. Bulletin **5733**
0513-1871 Yamanashi Daigaku Kogakubu Kenkyu Hokoku **3227**
0513-2088 Yearly Digest of Criminal Cases†
0513-2436 Yinyue Chuangzuo **6629**
0513-2541 Hokkaido-ku Suisan Kenkyujo. Kenkyu Hokoku†
0513-2592 Yokohama National University. Faculty of Engineering. Bulletin **3227**
0513-2622 Yokosuka-shi Hakubutsukan Kenkyu Hokoku. Shizen Kagaku **7933**
0513-2711 York Pioneer **4319**
0513-2762 Yorkshire Dialect Society. Summer Bulletin **5197**
0513-353X Yuanyi Xuebao **3754**
0513-417X Yadoriga **861**
0513-4501 Yale Southeast Asia Studies. Monograph Series **563**
0513-4617 Yalkut Moreshet **4279**
0513-4668 Yamagata Daigaku Kiyo (Kyoiku Kagaku) **2927**
0513-4676 Yamagata Daigaku Kiyo (Nogaku) **171**
0513-4684 Yamagata Daigaku Kiyo (Shakai Kagaku) **8017**
0513-4692 Yamagata Daigaku Kiyo (Shizen Kagaku) **711**
0513-4870 Yaoxue Xuebao **6886**
0513-5117 Year Book of Neurology and Neurosurgery **6190**
0513-5303 Yeni Yayinlar
0513-5419 Dos Yiddishe Vort **7732**
0513-5532 Yokogawa Giho **3334**
0513-5621 Yokohama Kokuritsu Daigaku Jinbun Kiyo Dai-1-rui, Tetsugaku, Shakai Kagaku **8017**
0513-563X Yokohama Kouritsu Daigaku Jinbun Kiyo. Dai-2-rui. Gogaku, Bungaku **5197**
0513-5656 Yokohama National University. Educational Sciences **2927**
0513-5710 Yonago Acta Medica **6190**
0513-5796 Yonsei Medical Journal **5734**
0513-5982 Young Fabian Pamphlet **7197**
0513-6032 World Alliance of Y M C A's Directory **2271**
0513-6261 Yrke och Framtid **6706**
0513-6342 Yuasa Jiho†
0513-6547 Yugoslavia. Savezni Zavod za Statistiku. Metodoloski Materijali *changed to* Srbija i Crna Gora Zavod za Statistiku. Metodoloski Materijali **8402**
0513-6555 Yugoslavia. Savezni Zavod za Statistiku. Studije, Analize i Prikazi *changed to* Srbija i Crna Gora Zavod za Statistiku. Studije, Analize i Prikazi **8403**
0513-6776 Yakima Valley Genealogical Society Bulletin **3788**
0513-7926 Zahntechnik†
0513-8809 Zdrowie i Trzezwosc†
0513-9066 Zeitschrift fuer Heilpaedagogik **3049**
0513-9147 Zeitschrift fuer Theologie und Kirche. Beiheft **7781**
0513-9198 Z f K - Zeitung fuer Kommunale Wirtschaft **4431**
0513-9465 Zen Notes **7703**
0513-9473 Zena **8892**
0513-9856 Zhinochyi Svit **8892**
0514-017X Zivljenje in Tehnika **8446**
0514-2482 Zeal **7823**
0514-2571 Zeitschrift fuer Beamtenrecht **4818**
0514-2717 Zeitschrift fuer Paedagogik. Beiheft **3035**
0514-2776 Zeitschrift fuer Sozialreform **7197**
0514-2784 Zeitschrift fuer Versicherungswesen **4529**
0514-2938 Zement - Taschenbuch†
0514-2946 Zement und Beton **1044**
0514-3292 Genealogisches Jahrbuch **3768**
0514-342X Zeszyty "Argumentow"†
0514-3446 Zeszyty Gliwickie **4280**
0514-4264 Zuercher Medizingeschichtliche Abhandlungen **5739**
0514-5090 Zavod za Slavensku Filologiju. Radovi†
0514-5163 Zairyo **3360**
0514-5171 Japanese Congress for Testing Materials. Proceedings *changed to* 0368-3141 **3348**
0514-5392 Zambia. Central Statistical Office. Transport Statistics **8533**
0514-5457 Zambia. Educational and Occupational Assessment Service. Annual Report **6706**
0514-5724 Zane Grey Collector†
0514-5899 Zastita Prirode **3476**
0514-616X Zbornik Zastite Spomenika Kulture†
0514-6321 Zeitschrift fuer Allgemeine und Textile Marktwirtschaft†
0514-6364 Zeitschrift fuer Bibliothekswesen und Bibliographie. Sonderhefte **5056**
0514-6488 Zeitschrift fuer Philosophische Forschung. Beihefte†
0514-6496 Zeitschrift fuer Rechtspolitik **4819**

ISSN

0537-6246 Information Processing in Japan†
0537-6297 Documentation Europeenne - Serie Agricole†
0537-6300 Documentazione Europea - Serie Agricola†
0537-6327 Europaeische Dokumentation - Schriftenreihe Landwirtschaft†
0537-6645 Informator **1123**
0537-667X Informator Nauki Polskiej **7865**
0537-6858 Informazione Scientifica
0537-6998 In'gu Munje Nonjip
0537-779X Institut Francais d'Archeologie d'Istanbul. Bibliotheque Archeologique et Historique†
0537-7900 Institut fuer Deutsche Sprache. Jahrbuch **5128**
0537-9024 Studies in Biology
0537-9032 Institute of Biology. Symposia **678**
0537-9202 I D E Occasional Papers Series **1120**
0537-9423 Gesamtausgaben **6569**
0537-9679 Institute of Town Planners, India. Journal **4416**
0537-9989 I E E Conference Publication Series *changed to* The I E T Conference Publication Series **3316**
0538-0391 Instituto Colombiano Agropecuario. Boletin Tecnico **122**
0538-0898 Instituto de Investigacion de Recursos Naturales. Publicacion
0538-1347 Instituto Latinoamericano de Mercadeo Agricola. I L M A - RR†
0538-1355 Instituto Latinoamericano de Mercadeo Agricola. Information Bulletin†
0538-1428 Instituto Mexicano del Petroleo. Revista†
0538-1983 Anales Toledanos **4198**
0538-2270 Institutum Romanum Finlandiae. Acta **398**
0538-2351 Instrument Maintenance Management†
0538-2378 Instrument Society of America. Monographs†
0538-2629 Insurance Marketplace **4508**
0538-2769 Organization of African Unity. Inter-African Bureau for Soils. Bibliographie
0538-2785 Inter-African Conference on Food and Nutrition. Report†
0538-2807 Inter-African Labour Conference Reports, Recommendations and Conclusions
0538-2912 Inter-American Commission of Women. News Bulletin†
0538-2920 Inter-American Commission of Women. Noticiero†
0538-3048 Inter-American Council of Commerce and Production. Uruguayan Section. Publicaciones **1598**
0538-3110 Inter-American Development Bank. Institute for Latin American Integration. Annual Report†
0538-3579 Inter-American Statistical Institute. Committee on Improvement of National Statistics. Report
0538-3609 Inter-American Tropical Tuna Commission. Data Report **3598**
0538-3641 Interbank
0538-3900 Comision Oceanografica Intergubernamental. Coleccion Tecnica *see* 0074-1175 **2808**
0538-4141 I A A World Directory of Marketing Communications Periodicals†
0538-4168 International Advertising Association. United Kingdom Chapter. Concise Guide to International Markets†
0538-4427 International Association for the Exchange of Students for Technical Experience. Annual Report **3013**
0538-4680 International Association of Theoretical and Applied Limnology. Communications† **8965**
0538-4753 International Astronomical Union. Information Bulletin **576**
0538-4893 International Atomic Energy Agency. Law Library. Books and Articles in the I A E A Law Library. List†
0538-5105 International Bibliography of the History of Religions†
0538-5342 International Centre for African Social and Economic Documentation. (Bibliographical Index Cards)†
0538-5482 International Children's Center. Courrier†
0538-5490 International Children's Centre. Paris. Report of the Director-General to the Executive Board
0538-5504 International China Painting Teachers Organizations. News
0538-5644 International Colloquium on Rapid Mixing and Sampling Techniques Applicable to the Study of Biochemical Reactions. Proceedings†
0538-5687 Commission Internationale pour l'Exploitation Scientifique de la Mer Mediterranee. Bulletin de Liaison des Laboratoires†
0538-5768 International Commission on Irrigation and Drainage. Report **8826**
0538-5946 International Confederation of Free Trade Unions. Features†
0538-6128 International Conference on Lighthouses and Other Aids to Navigation. Reports **8646**
0538-6349 International Congress Calendar **6280**
0538-6381 International Congress for the Study of Pre-Columbian Cultures of the Lesser Antilles. Proceedings **343**
0538-6462 International Congress of Endocrinology. Proceedings
0538-6527 International Congress of Libraries and Museums of the Performing Arts. Acts
0538-6586 International Congress of Radiation Research. Proceedings†
0538-6640 International Congress on Catalysis. Proceedings†
0538-6675 Association Internationale de Cybernetique. Congres International de Cybernetique. Actes *see* 0074-3380 **2527**
0538-6772 International Congress Science Series **6280**
0538-6829 International Cotton Industry Statistics **8463**
0538-6918 C O D A T A Newsletter **7843**
0538-7051 International Cryogenics Monograph Series†
0538-7078 International Dairy Federation. Annual Memento
0538-7086 International Dairy Federation. Catalogue of I D F Publications **182**
0538-7094 International Dairy Federation. International Standard **265**
0538-7159 International Directory of Antiquarian Booksellers **7563**
0538-7191 International Directory of Prisoners Aid Agencies
0538-7302 F I D Publications Catalogue†
0538-7353 I A G Communications†
0538-740X International Federation of Film Archives. Annuaire. Yearbook†
0538-7434 International Federation of Municipal Engineers. Questionaires and General Reports on Themes of the Congress
0538-7442 International Federation of Operational Research Societies. Airline Group. Proceedings **8546**
0538-7477 International Federation of Plantation, Agricultural and Allied Workers. Report of the Secretariat to the I F P A A W World Congress†
0538-7736 International Histological Classification of Tumours†
0538-7965 Worldwide Bibliography of Space Law and Related Matters†
0538-8066 International Journal of Chemical Kinetics **2136**
0538-8228 International Journal of Slavic Linguistics and Poetics **5129**
0538-8295 The Cost of Social Security **8035**
0538-8325 Labour-Management Relations Series **1694**
0538-8333 International Labour Office. Special Report of the Director-General on the Application of the Declaration Concerning the Policy of Apartheid of the Republic of South Africa†
0538-8759 International Monetary Fund. Pamphlet Series **1358**
0538-8880 International Oceanographic Tables†
0538-8988 International Organization of Consumers Unions. Proceedings
0538-9089 Family Planning in Five Continents†
0538-9127 Victor-Bostrom Fund. Report
0538-9143 International Plant Propagators' Society. Combined Proceedings of Annual Meetings **3739**
0538-933X International Reading Association. Annual Report†
0538-9461 International Rescue Committee. Annual Report **8048**
0538-9550 International Rice Commission. Newsletter†
0538-9755 International Secretariat of Entertainment Trade Unions. Newsletter
0538-978X International Seismological Centre. P-Nodal Solutions for Earthquakes†
0538-9887 International Series on Civil Engineering†
0538-9895 International Series on Heating, Ventilation and Refrigeration†
0538-9968 International Series on Cerebrovisceral and Behavioral Psychology and Conditioned Reflexes†
0538-9984 International Series on Earth Sciences†
0538-9992 International Series on Electromagnetic Waves†
0539-0133 International Series in Solid State Physics†
0539-0184 Social Science Information **8003**
0539-0230 I E S A Information
0539-032X International Society of Criminology. Bulletin **2656**
0539-0338 International Society of Food Service Consultants. Directory†
0539-0346 International Society of Plant Morphologists. Yearbook **795**
0539-0559 International Symposium on Comparative Endocrinology. Proceedings†
0539-0613 International Symposium on Rarefied Gas Dynamics. Proceedings
0539-080X International Textile Bulletin Weaving Edition†
0539-0893 I T C Publications. Series B. Photo-Interpretation†
0539-0915 International Transport Workers' Federation Report on Activities **4596**
0539-0990 Commission on Crystallographic Apparatus†
0539-1016 International Union of Geodesy and Geophysics. Monograph†
0539-1326 International Wheat Council. Secretariat Papers†
0539-1512 Internationale Gesellschaft fuer Urheberrecht. Yearbook†
0539-2063 Legal Report of Oil and Gas Conservation Activities†
0539-2306 Inventaria Archaeologica Roumanie†
0539-242X Academia Nacional de la Historia. Investigaciones y Ensayos **4281**
0539-2896 Memminger Geschichtsblaetter **4244**
0539-3027 Museo Municipal de Historia Natural de San Rafael. Instituto de Ciencias Naturales. Notas
0539-323X Meng Ya **5332**
0539-3728 Mercado Mundial **1577**
0539-385X Mercer County Law Journal **4732**
0539-3973 Mereni a Regulace†
0539-421X Meshek Ha-ofot
0539-4511 Metal Center News **6323**
0539-6115 Hospital Infantil de Mexico. Boletin Medico **4100**
0539-7413 Michigan Health Statistics†
0539-8452 University of Michigan. Mental Health Research Institute. Annual Report†
0539-8703 Michigan Aviation **65**
0539-8908 Michigan Sportsman **8322**
0539-9149 Micro-Bibliotheca Anthropos†
0540-049X Universita Cattolica del Sacro Cuore. Facolta di Agraria. Annali **165**
0540-0694 Milford Historical Society Newsletter†
0540-0910 Milliyet **3962**
0540-0961 Milton Society of America. Proceedings
0540-1151 Minjian Wenxue **3620**
0540-1224 Minzu Huabao **3550**
0540-1259 Minami Oosaka Byoin Igaku Zasshi **5679**
0540-3995 Mississippi Genealogical Exchange
0540-410X Mississippi's Health†
0540-4193 Missouri's New and Expanding Industry **1899**
0540-4428 Missouri Business **1407**
0540-4568 Misuljaryo **506**
0540-469X Mitsubishi Technical Bulletin†
0540-4746 Mitteilungen fuer die Archivpflege in Bayern†
0540-4924 Miyazaki University. Faculty of Engineering. Memoirs **3210**
0540-4932 Miyazaki Daigaku Kogakubu Kenkyu Hokoku *changed to* 0540-4924 **3210**
0540-5203 Modell **4341**
0540-5556 Modern Surgical Monographs†
0540-6226 Monatshefte fuer Evangelische Kirchengeschichte des Rheinlandes **7768**
0540-6722 Monografie Parazytologiczne **893**
0540-830X Monumenta Germaniae Historica. Quellen zur Geistesgeschichte des Mittelalters **4246**
0540-8962 Mortgage Market†
0541-2331 Internationale Stiftung Mozarteum. Mitteilungen **6577**
0541-2404 Muehlviertler Heimatblaetter†
0541-2439 Muemlekvedelem
0541-2447 Muenchener Historische Studien. Abteilung Geschichtliche Hilfswissenschaften **4246**
0541-3370 Deutsches Wirtschaftswissenschaftliches Institut fuer Fremdenverkehr. Schriftenreihe **8698**
0541-377X Museoscienza **6531**
0541-3869 Mushroom News **242**
0541-4040 Musica **6592**
0541-4393 Muskeg Research Conference. Proceedings†
0541-4466 Muster und Farbe†
0541-4873 Mwana Shaba **6474**
0541-5357 M B I's Indian Industries Annual **1897**
0541-5462 M.I.I. Series
0541-5489 M L A News (Chicago) **5663**
0541-5632 Mitzion Tetzeh Torah. M.T.T.
0541-5829 Mabua
0541-623X Keith Callard Lecture Series†
0541-6256 Canadian Meteorological and Oceanographic Society. Climatological Bulletin†
0541-6388 Machine Building Industry **5455**
0541-6434 Machine Tool Engineer†
0541-6507 Mackinac History†
0541-7406 Majalah Perusahaan Gula **8431**
0541-7562 Institute of Traditional Cultures, Madras. Bulletin **343**
0541-881X Magazin Istoric **4241**
0541-8836 Magazin Polovnika†
0541-8968 Magdeburger Telemann Studien **6586**
0541-9093 Magyar Bibliografiak Bibliografiaja†
0541-9220 Magyar Kulpolitikai Evkonyv **7251**
0541-9298 Magyar Nyelvjarasok **5149**
0541-9344 Magyar Szo Naptara **3121**
0541-9492 Magyar Tudomanyos Akademia Konyvtara Kezirattaranak Katalogusai **630**
0541-9522 Nepi Kultura - Nepi Tarsadalom *changed to* 1787-9396 **8100**
0542-0938 Mahasagar (Goa) **2811**
0542-0997 The Mail Coach **6896**
0542-1136 Maine Geological Survey. Special Economic Studies Series†
0542-1292 Maine Archeological Society Bulletin **404**
0542-1462 Mainstream **3885**
0542-1470 Maintenant†
0542-1497 Universitaet Mainz. Forschungsinstitut fuer Wirtschaftspolitik. Veroeffentlichungen **1187**
0542-1535 Mainzer Naturwissenschaftliches Archiv **687**
0542-1551 Mainzer Romanistische Arbeiten†
0542-1748 The Egyptian Statistical Journal **8367**
0542-2108 Makedonski Folklor **3620**
0542-3007 Guide to Agricultural Production in Malawi **117**
0542-397X Malaysian Chinese Association. Annual Report **4185**
0542-4550 Malta Yearbook **7153**
0542-5395 Manitoba Crop Insurance Corporation. Annual Report **4513**
0542-5492 Legislative Assembly of Manitoba. Debates and Proceedings **7451**
0542-5808 Manpower Journal **1696**
0542-6243 Map Collectors Circle†
0542-626X Maps†
0542-6375 Universidad del Zulia. Facultad de Medicina. Revista†
0542-6480 Marburger Abhandlungen zur Politischen Wissenschaft†
0542-6537 Marburger Ostforschungen†
0542-657X Marburger Theologische Studien **7661**
0542-6669 Marche Romane **5150**
0542-6685 Marches Publics†
0542-6758 Mare Balticum **7251**
0542-6766 Association Internationale de Geodesie. Commission des Marees Terrestres. Marees Terrestres Bulletin d'Information **2778**
0542-6987 Marine Invertebrates of Scandinavia†
0542-7029 Marine Resources of the Atlantic Coast†
0542-7398 Marketing Science Institute. Review **1833**
0542-7770 Marxistische Blaetter **7153**
0542-8343 Maryland English Journal
0542-8351 Maryland Genealogical Society Bulletin *changed to* 1948-0962 **3774**
0542-836X Maryland Lawyer's Manual **4728**
0542-8386 Maryland Nutrition Conference for Feed Manufacturers. Proceedings *changed to* Maryland and Mid-Atlantic Nutrition Conference for Feed Manufacturers. Proceedings **274**
0542-9943 Massu'a **3549**
0542-9951 Informatyka†
0543-0313 Materials Management Journal of India **1834**
0543-0941 Mathematics and Its Applications†
0543-100X Mathematik fuer Naturwissenschaft und Technik
0543-1042 Mathematische Monographien
0543-1220 Zbornik Matice Srpske za Knjizevnost i Jezik **5198**
0543-1433 Mauritania. Direction de la Statistique et des Etudes Economiques. Bulletin Mensuel Statistique **8388**
0543-1565 Mauritius. Director of Audit. Report **1934**
0543-1719 Max Freiherr von Oppenheim-Stiftung. Schriften **555**
0543-1735 Veroeffentlichungen des Max-Reger-Institutes **6626**
0543-1786 Ma'yanot† **8973**
0543-1972 Measurement Techniques **6404**
0543-2073 Mechanical Translation and Computational Linguistics† **8973**
0543-2146 Med-Events†
0543-2243 Medecine de l'Homme†
0543-2464 *see* 0268-8638 **8973**
0543-2618 Medical Digest **5668**
0543-2936 Medical Tribune **5672**
0543-3533 Medium Aevum†
0543-3657 Medjunarodna Politika **7252**
0543-3754 Meet the Press **4580**
0543-3770 Meeting on Soil Correlation for North America. (Report)†
0543-3789 Meeting on Soil Survey Correlation and Interpretation for Latin America. Report†
0543-3916 Meiji Daigaku Kagaku Gijutsu Kenkyujo Nenpo **8432**
0543-3975 Meiji Yakka Daigaku Kenkyu Kiyo **6861**
0543-4033 Meisterwerke der Musik
0543-4726 Der Mensch als Soziales und Personales Wesen **8121**
0543-5056 Merchant Explorer **4244**
0543-5099 Mercurius†

ISSN

DIRECTORY 2010 0557-8507 9303

0552-007X The President†
0552-1645 Probleme de Lingvistica Generala **5163**
0552-1734 Problemes de l'Europe
0552-2005 Problems of the Baltic†
0552-2056 Problemy Fiziki Atmosfery†
0552-2188 Problemy Opiekunczo-Wychowawcze **2900**
0552-2234 Problemy Rodziny **8126**
0552-2323 La Procellaria† **8982**
0552-3702 Il Protagora **6945**
0552-4245 Przeglad Zachodniopomorski **4470**
0552-4466 Psychologische Achtergronden†
0552-5276 Census of Manufacturing Industries of Puerto Rico **1882**
0552-5934 Pulsen†
0552-6426 Persatuan Pure Life. Annual Report **8061**
0552-6450 Push Pin Graphic†
0552-6981 Publizistikwissenschaftlicher Referatedienst†
0552-7252 Pacific Coast Archaeological Society Quarterly **410**
0552-7333 Pacific Geology†
0552-8100 World Peace Through Law Center. Bulletin†
0552-8259 Pakistan's Key Economic Indicators
0552-9034 Pakistan Journal of Agricultural Sciences **145**
0552-9050 Pakistan Journal of Scientific Research **7897**
0552-9115 Pakistan Petroleum Limited. Annual Report **6786**
0552-914X Pakistan Philosophical Journal **6938**
0552-9263 Pakistan Year Book **3926**
0552-9344 Palaeohistoria **410**
0552-9352 Palaeontologia Jugoslavica†
0552-9360 Palaeontological Society of India. Journal **6728**
0552-9395 Palante **5233**
0552-9506 Osservatorio Regionale per le Malattie della Vite. Osservazioni di Meteorologia, Fenologia e Patologia della Vite
0552-9638 Palingenesia **2238**
0552-9832 Instituto de Lengua y Cultura Espanola para Extranjeros. Coleccion **5128**
0552-9913 Pan American Development Foundation. Annual Report **1603**
0553-0067 Pan American Highway Congress. Boletin Informativo†
0553-013X Pan American Institute of Geography and History. Commission on History. Bulletin†
0553-0237 Studies in Export Promotion†
0553-0326 Pan American Associations in the United States; A Directory with Supplementary Lists of Other Associations. Inter-American and General†
0553-0377 Organization of American States. Department of Scientific Affairs. Serie de Quimica: Monografias†
0553-0385 Estudio Social de America Latina†
0553-0407 Pan American Union. Department of Social Affairs. Studies and Monographs†
0553-058X Inter-American Briefs†
0553-0601 Pan Am World Guide†
0553-0644 Pan T'ai Hsueh Pao
0553-1098 Panorama **3898**
0553-1454 Grocers Bags and Grocers Sacks
0553-1594 Papua New Guinea. National Statistical Office. Taxation Statistics. Preliminary Bulletin†
0553-1721 Instituto do Desenvolvimento Economico-Social do Para. Para Desenvolvimento **1492**
0553-206X International Journal of Parasychology **6742**
0553-2159 Parents **2164**
0553-2361 Materiaux pour le Manuel de l'Histoire des Song†
0553-2507 Musee de l'Homme, Paris. Catalogues. Serie B: Afrique Blanche et Levant†
0553-2515 Musee de l'Homme, Paris. Catalogues. Serie G: Arctiques†
0553-2930 Universite de Paris VI. Institut de Statistique. Publications *changed to* 1626-1607 **5548**
0553-3163 Parlamentsspiegel **7459**
0553-3864 Southwestern Legal Foundation. Patent Law Annual†
0553-4003 Patristische Texte und Studien **7669**
0553-4054 Patterson's Schools Classified **2961**
0553-4283 Peace Research Reviews **7259**
0553-4429 Janus Pannonius Muzeum. Evkonyve **6526**
0553-4917 Penguin Modern Poets†
0553-4992 Penn ar Bed **697**
0553-5700 Educational Series - Pennsylvania Geologic Survey **2732**
0553-5816 University of Pennsylvania. Population Studies Center. Analytical and Technical Report†
0553-5980 Pennsylvania Geographer **4023**
0553-6448 Peraba **7812**
0553-6502 Percussive Notes **6604**
0553-6626 Periodica Polytechnica. Civil Engineering **3280**
0553-6707 Peristil **453**
0553-6812 Permanent International Committee of Linguists. Committee on Linguistic Statistics. Publication†
0553-6863 Convenios Centroamericanos de Integration Economica **1593**
0553-6898 General Treaty for Central American Economic Integration. Permanent Secretariat. Newsletter **1596**
0553-6901 Permian Historical Annual **4308**
0553-6979 Peparimi
0553-7371 Perspective (Cincinnati)†
0553-738X Perspective†
0553-8467 Pesquisas: Publicacoes de Antropologia **351**
0553-8483 Pesquisas: Publicacoes de Communications **2336**
0553-8521 Pesticide Handbook (Entoma)†
0553-8882 Petroleum Geology
0553-8890 Petroleum Geology of Taiwan **6787**
0553-9382 Pharmacopoea Internationalis *see* 0042-9686 **5731**
0553-9536 Phi Theta Papers†
0553-9587 Philadelphia Herpetological Society. Bulletin **960**
0554-0674 Philologische Studien und Quellen **5351**
0554-0828 Philosophische Rundschau. Beiheft **6942**
0554-1069 Photogrammetric Journal of Finland **6974**
0554-1182 Phykos **808**
0554-2308 Pivarstvo
0554-2324 Pivot **5430**
0554-2375 Plains Talk **4308**
0554-2537 Planiranje i Analiza Poslovanja
0554-2626 Planning News†
0554-2731 Plant Location†
0554-2901 Plasticheskie Massy **7096**
0554-291X Plasticos†
0554-2952 Plastics Focus **7097**
0554-3037 Play Index **5408**
0554-3045 Plays. A Classified Guide to Play Selection **8476**
0554-3363 Pneumatiki Kypros **5234**
0554-3762 Poesie und Wissenschaft
0554-436X Central Statistical Office. Concise Statistical Year Book of Poland **8362**
0554-4386 Poland. Glowny Urzad Statystyczny. Rocznik Statystyczny Gospodarski Mieszkaniowej i Komunalnej†
0554-4629 Poland. Ministerstwo Oswiaty i Szkolnictwa Wyzszego. B, Dzial Oswiaty. Dziennik Urzedowy *changed to* 1644-292X **2843**
0554-498X Polish Yearbook of International Law **4938**
0554-5196 Political Science Review **7169**
0554-534X Politik und Waehler†
0554-5455 Politische Bildung **3077**
0554-5579 Poljoprivreda i Sumarstvo **3700**
0554-5625 Polonica Zagraniczne. Bibliografia **633**
0554-579X Polska Akademia Nauk. Oddzial w Krakowie. Komisja Historycznoliteracka. Prace **5352**
0554-5927 Academie Polonaise des Sciences. Centre d'Archeologie Mediterraneenne. Travaux **370**
0554-6648 Pontificia Academia Scientiarum. Commentarii **7899**
0554-6877 Popular†
0554-7040 Poreditsa Balkani†
0554-7342 Porta Linguarum Orientalium **5162**
0554-7555 Ports and Harbors **3281**
0554-7598 Portsmouth Papers **4254**
0554-8039 Uniwersytet im. Adama Mickiewicza. Akustyka **7090**
0554-811X Uniwersytet im. Adama Mickiewicza. Biologia **710**
0554-8128 Uniwersytet im. Adama Mickiewicza. Geografia **4033**
0554-8136 Uniwersytet im. Adama Mickiewicza. Zoologia **966**
0554-8144 Uniwersytet im. Adama Mickiewicza. Filologia Angielska **5192**
0554-8160 Uniwersytet im. Adama Mickiewicza. Filologia Klasyczna **5192**
0554-8179 Filologia Polska **5118**
0554-8195 Uniwersytet im. Adama Mickiewicza. Archeologia **422**
0554-8233 Uniwersytet im. Adama Mickiewicza. Astronomia **583**
0554-8241 Uniwersytet im. Adama Mickiewicza. Chemia **2083**
0554-825X Uniwersytet im. Adama Mickiewicza. Fizyka **7045**
0554-8373 Postal Stationery **2355**
0554-873X Pount
0554-9043 Prace Instytutow i Laboratoriow Badawczych Przemyslu Spozywczego **3660**
0554-9051 Acta Universitatis Wratislaviensis. Prace Zoologiczne **930**
0554-9221 Rocenka Povetrnostnich Pozorovani Observatore Karlov†
0554-9884 Prajna **2998**
0554-9906 Prakit Jain Institute Research Publication Series **7740**
0554-9965 Der Praktiker **6343**
0555-0025 Uniwersytet Jagiellonski. Osrodek Badan Prasoznawczych. Zeszyty Prasoznawcze **4584**
0555-0114 Pravoslavlje **7705**
0555-0122 Pravoslavni Misionar
0555-0238 Prazsky Sbornik Historicky†
0555-0572 Presbyterian Layman†
0555-1099 Prikladnaya Biokhimiya i Mikrobiologiya **742**
0555-1137 Prilozi Proucavanju Jezika **5163**
0555-1501 Princeton University. Center of International Studies. Research Monograph Series†
0555-2222 Probleme de Automatizare†
0555-2257 Probleme der Dichtung **5354**
0555-2354 Problemes Actuels de Biochimie Appliquee† **8982**
0555-2648 Problemy Arktiki i Antarktiki **6393**
0555-2656 Problemy Bioniki†
0555-2788 Problemy Kosmicheskoi Biologii **698**
0555-2923 Problemy Peredachi Informatsii **2534**
0555-2966 Problemy Rozwoju Budownictwa **1030**
0555-2982 Problemy Severa **633**
0555-3385 Professional Liability Newsletter†
0555-3830 Progress in Applied Materials Research†
0555-4276 Progress in Solid Mechanics†
0555-4349 Progress of Medical Parasitology in Japan†
0555-4810 Prospettive dell'Industria Italiana†
0555-5027 Protokolle†
0555-5299 Psichiatria Generale e dell'Eta Evolutiva **6175**
0555-5574 Psychologia a Patopsychologia Dietata **7396**
0555-5582 Psychologia Universalis
0555-5620 Psychological Research Bulletin†
0555-5795 Psychopathology and Pictorial Expression†
0555-5914 Public Affairs **7174**
0555-5973 Public Education in Virginia†
0555-6015 Public Health Papers†
0555-6023 Public Library Abstracts†
0555-6031 Public Library Reporters†
0555-621X Public Works in Canada†
0555-6392 Publishing, Entertainment and Advertising and Allied Fields Law Quarterly†
0555-6562 Puerto Rico. Planning Board. Statistics Coordination Section. Programas Estadisticos†
0555-6635 Empleo y Desempleo en Puerto Rico **1677**
0555-6945 Pulse†
0555-6953 Pulse (Cypress) **8805**
0555-7631 Panjab University Research Bulletin (Sciences) **7897**
0555-7674 Journal of Scientific Research *changed to* 1812-1128 **4481**
0555-7747 Bulletin of Education and Research **2833**
0555-781X Punsok Hwahak **7900**
0555-7860 Puranam. Bulletin
0555-8026 Purdue University. Water Resources Research Center. Technical Report **8831**
0555-8158 Pushto **5163**
0555-8581 Pacific Southwest Directory **2023**
0555-9308 Pastoraltheologische Informationen **7812**
0555-9456 Farm Economics **198**
0555-974X Perspective (Indiana) **4023**
0555-9952 Peuples du Monde
0556-0071 Philippine Journal of Internal Medicine **5948**
0556-0152 Phyllis Schlafly Report **7992**
0556-056X Police Research Bulletin†
0556-0691 Pomorania Antiqua†
0556-1019 Uniwersytet im. Adama Mickiewicza. Historia Sztuki **524**
0556-1183 Universita Karlova. Pedagogicky Fakulta. Sbornik. Historie†
0556-137X Preparons l'Avenir†
0556-1442 Pressure Research Notes†
0556-171X Problemy Prochnosti **3356**
0556-1906 Progress of Science in India†
0556-2813 Physical Review C (Nuclear Physics) **7070**
0556-3100 Problems in Education and Nation Building†
0556-3321 Pakistan Journal of Botany **807**
0556-3488 Partio **2206**
0556-350X Pasquim
0556-3585 Exports by Pennsylvania Manufacturers†
0556-3593 Pennsylvania. Department of Commerce. Bureau of Statistics. Statistics by Industry and Size of Establishment†
0556-3615 Pennsylvania. Department of Commerce. Bureau of Statistics, Research and Planning. Statistics for Manufacturing Industries†
0556-3860 Photochemistry **2076**
0556-4409 Paintindia **6719**
0556-4417 Pakha Sanjam **5159**
0556-5693 Revista de Derecho
0556-5782 Revista de Economia **1167**
0556-5960 Revista de Historia Americana y Argentina **4310**
0556-5987 Revista de Historia de las Ideas†
0556-5995 Revista de Historia de Rosario **4310**
0556-6134 Revista de Literaturas Modernas **5361**
0556-6177 Revista de Medicina **5705**
0556-6274 Revista de Psicologia (La Plata)†
0556-6436 Revista del Folklore Ecuatoriano†
0556-6533 Revista Espanola de Antropologia Americana **353**
0556-655X Revista Espanola de Micropaleontologia **6730**
0556-6606 Revista Forestal Venezolana **3701**
0556-6703 Revista Interamericana de Ciencias Sociales†
0556-6835 Revista Mexicana de Fianzas **1380**
0556-6908 Revista Paraguaya de Microbiologia
0556-6916 Revista Paranaense de Desenvolvimento†
0556-7238 Revue Bibliographique des Ouvrages de Droit, de Jurisprudence, d'Economie Politique, de Science Financiere, de Sociologie, d'Histoire et de Philosophie†
0556-7297 Revue d'Economie et de Droit Immobilier†
0556-7300 Revue d'Histoire de l'Art Dentaire **5864**
0556-7335 Revue Annuelle d'Histoire du Quatorzieme Arrondissement de Paris **4258**
0556-7343 Revue d'Histoire et de Civilisation du Maghreb **4177**
0556-7378 Revue de Droit Canonique **4774**
0556-7432 Revue de Geomorphologie Dynamique†
0556-7440 Revue de l'Arbitrage **4939**
0556-7459 Revue de l'Atherosclerose et des Arteriopathies Peripheriques†
0556-7734 Acta Technica Belgica. Revue E P E: Energie Primaire
0556-7793 Revue Francaise de Dietetique†
0556-7807 Revue Francaise de Pedagogie **2907**
0556-7963 Revue Juridique Themis **4775**
0556-8072 Revue Roumaine d'Histoire **4258**
0556-8080 Revue Roumaine d'Histoire de l'Art. Serie Beaux-Arts **515**
0556-8218 Rheinisch-Westfaelische Zeitschrift fuer Volkskunde **4258**
0556-8609 Rhode Island Jewish Historical Notes **7729**
0556-8641 Philosophical Papers **6941**
0556-8692 Zimbabwe. Registrar of Insurance. Report **4530**
0556-9001 Zambia. Teaching Service Commission. Annual Report **2928**
0556-9664 La Ricerca Scientifica. Quaderni†
0557-0220 Rikagaku Kenkyujo Kenkyu Nenpo **7050**
0557-0395 Japan. Government Forest Experiment Station. Kyushu Branch. Annual Report **3694**
0557-0433 Rinsho Seikei Geka **6072**
0557-0506 Bolsa de Valores do Rio de Janeiro. Resumo Anual **1613**
0557-0689 Museu Nacional. Relatorio Anual **7884**
0557-1359 Rivista di Storia dell'Agricoltura **152**
0557-1367 Rivista di Studi Bizantini e Neoellenici **4259**
0557-1391 Rivista Italiana di Diritto e Procedura Penale **4897**
0557-1405 Rivista Italiana di Geotecnica **2764**
0557-1464 Rivista Trimestrale di Diritto Pubblico **4776**
0557-1588 The Welch Foundation. Conferences on Chemical Research. Proceedings†
0557-1693 Rocenka Odborara **4601**
0557-2088 Rocznik Nadnotecki†
0557-2282 Rodna Gruda **3561**
0557-2614 Romanfuehrer **5364**
0557-2657 Romanica Stockholmiensia **5169**
0557-2665 Acta Universitatis Wratislaviensis. Romanica Wratislaviensia **5091**
0557-272X Romanoslavica **5170**
0557-2738 The Romantic Movement *see* 0013-8282 **5290**
0557-3254 University of Roorkee Research Journal†
0557-3467 Ross Conference on Pediatric Research. Report **6669**
0557-4161 Royal Society of New Zealand. Proceedings†
0557-4250 Rozhlad **3561**
0557-6466 Revista Argentina de Psicologia **7403**
0557-6644 Rural Reconstruction
0557-6857 Rassegna di Letteratura Tomistica†
0557-6873 Rassegna Forense
0557-6911 University of Reading. Department of Agricultural and Food Economics. Farm Business Data **208**
0557-6989 Recherches Anglaises et Americaines†
0557-7330 Research into Disease†
0557-739X R M A Ontario Bulletin
0557-7527 Review of Plant Protection Research†
0557-7705 Revue Archeologique Narbonnaise
0557-7853 Rheinische Ausgrabungen **414**
0557-8019 Rivista di Studi Salernitani†
0557-8213 Bulletin Agricole du Rwanda **98**
0557-8507 Revista de Antropologia **353**

ISSN

9304 0557-8582 ULRICH'S PERIODICALS

0557-8582 Revue de Medecine Fonctionelle† **8985**
0557-8590 Revue Medicale Rwandaise
0557-8620 Law of the Sea Institute. Proceedings of the Annual Conference **4970**
0557-8639 University of Rhode Island. Law of the Sea Institute. Special Publications†
0557-9147 Record Exchanger **6610**
0557-9295 Res Gestae **4769**
0557-9325 Review of Progress in Coloration and Related Topics **8436**
0557-9414 Revue Libanaise des Sciences Politiques†
0557-9430 La Riabilitazione† **8985**
0557-9465 Rijeci **4258**
0558-0293 S I A M Series in Applied Mathematics†
0558-0439 Norsk Senter for Informatikk. Artikkel Indeks†
0558-0846 Statistisches Amt des Saarlandes. Kurzbericht *changed to* 1864-2594 **7483**
0558-1257 Safn til Soegu Islands og Islenskra Bokmennta **5366**
0558-1931 St. Lawrence County Historical Association. Quarterly **4311**
0558-194X U.S. Saint Lawrence Seaway Development Corporation. Annual Report **8664**
0558-244X Saitama University. Science Reports. Series B: Biology and Earth Sciences†
0558-3624 Sammelblatt fuer Rechtsvorschriften des Bundes und der Laender **4778**
0558-3667 Sammlung Metzler **5366**
0558-4639 Sananjalka (Turku) **5171**
0558-471X Sanfujinka Chiryo **6004**
0558-4728 Sanfujinka no Jissai **6004**
0558-4779 Industry and Commerce†
0558-4809 Sangyo Kikai **5459**
0558-5201 Camara Oficial de Comercio, Industria y Navegacion de Santa Cruz de Tenerife. Boletin Informativo **1398**
0558-6208 Saobracaj **8634**
0558-6291 Universidad de Zaragoza. Facultad de Medicina. Archivos **5726**
0558-6976 Saskatchewan Economic Review **1516**
0558-7220 Saudi Arabian Monetary Agency. Annual Report **1942**
0558-9118 Schriften zum Deutschen und Europaeischen Zivil-, Handels- und Prozessrecht **4780**
0558-9126 Schriften zum Strafrecht **2668**
0558-9274 Schriften zur Phonetik, Sprachwissenschaft und Kommunikationsforschung†
0558-9746 Schriftenreihe fuer Raumforschung und Raumplanung.†
0559-1414 Scientia et Praxis
0559-1422 Scientia Juridica **4780**
0559-1791 Scottish Fisheries Bulletin†
0559-1996 Scottish Society of the History of Medicine. Report of Proceedings **5711**
0559-2526 Seattle Genealogical Society. Bulletin **3782**
0559-2674 Sedar†
0559-3840 Semaine Internationale d'Etudes Superieures des Methodes Physiques d'Analyse. (Papers)
0559-4065 Seminar of African Christian Students in Europe. Report
0559-6645 Universidad de Sevilla. Serie: Ciencias **7926**
0559-698X Social Development Research Institute. Organization and Activities
0559-717X Shanxi Huabao **3827**
0559-7218 Shanhua **5371**
0559-7234 Shandong Daxue Xuebao (Ziran Kexue Ban) *changed to* 1671-9352 **7914**
0559-7269 Shanghai Zhongyiyao Zazhi **315**
0559-7277 Shanghai Xiju **8478**
0559-7331 Shangying Huabao **6513**
0559-7692 Sheltie Special
0559-7765 Shengli Kexue Jinzhan **928**
0559-7781 Shepard's California Reporter Citations **4960**
0559-8095 Shixue Jikan **4161**
0559-8516 Shinku **7040**
0559-8958 Shokubai **2141**
0559-8974 Shokuhin Eisei Kenkyu **3663**
0559-8990 Shokuhin Kogyo **3663**
0559-9091 Shopping Center Newsletter†
0559-9202 Shosetsu Gendai **5372**
0559-9342 Shuili Fadian **8831**
0559-9350 Shuili Xuebao **3364**
0559-9385 *see* 1000-3207 **704**
0559-9822 Sieboldia Acta Biologica†
0560-0391 Silence†
0560-0871 Sind University Journal of Education†
0560-1878 Skaansk Senmedeltid och Renaessans **4263**
0560-1894 Skalk **4263**
0560-2416 Kungliga Skytteanska Samfundet. Handlingar **4239**
0560-2793 Slovenska Akademia Vied. Archeologicky Ustav. Studijne Zvesti **416**
0560-2920 Slovenska Akademija Znanosti in Umetnosti. Razred za Filoloske in Literarne Vede. Razprave **5175**
0560-3617 Soccer Journal **8245**
0560-3870 Social Welfare History Group. Newsletter **8070**
0560-4168 Boletin de la Sociedad Cientifica del Paraguay y del Museo Etnografico†
0560-4567 Sociedad Venezolana de Historia de la Medicina. Revista **5716**
0560-4613 Revista Brasileira de Cartografia **4026**
0560-5296 Societe des Etudes Juives. Memoires†
0560-6152 Society of Archer-Antiquaries. Journal **8202**
0560-642X S P E **3395**
0560-6675 Socijalizam†
0560-8325 Songwriter's Annual Directory†
0560-8996 Sources in Western Political Thought
0561-0095 A E - South Carolina Crop and Livestock Reporting Service **77**
0561-015X Checklist of South Carolina State Publications†
0561-2454 Soviet Metal Technology **6332**
0561-2551 Sovietica†
0561-3590 Instituto de Estudios Giennenses. Boletin **4232**
0561-3663 Anejos de Archivo Espanol de Arqueologia **373**
0561-4619 Spain. Ministerio de Educacion y Ciencia. Junta Nacional Contra el Analfabetismo. Boletin†
0561-4902 Spain. Ministerio de la Vivienda. Estadistica de la Industria de la Construccion **1048**
0561-5062 Evolucion de la Economia Espanola†
0561-5402 Sparkassenfachbuch (Year) **1384**
0561-6271 Hochschule Speyer. Schriftenreihe **7444**
0561-6360 Institut za Oceanografiju i Ribarstvo Split. Biljeske **2807**
0561-7332 Academie Serbe des Sciences et des Arts. Classe des Sciences Mathematiques et Naturelles. Bulletin Sciences Mathematiques **5464**
0561-7383 Srpska Akademija Nauka i Umetnosti. Predavanja†
0561-7626 Sichuan Wenxue *changed to* 1003-9678 **5438**
0561-7855 Stahlbau - Rundschau†
0561-8738 State Bank of Pakistan. State Bank News **1384**
0561-922X National Federation of Statistical Associations of Japan. Statistical Notes of Japan **8389**
0561-9726 Steam Automobile **8605**
0562-0031 Stepping Stones **4314**
0562-1062 Stockholm Studies in Classical Archaeology **2240**
0562-1070 Stockholm Studies in Comparative Religion **7683**
0562-1089 Stockholm Studies in Educational Psychology **7410**
0562-1666 Strazak **3581**
0562-1690 Stream of History **4314**
0562-1852 Stroitel'stvo **1038**
0562-1887 Strojarstvo **3396**
0562-2646 Studi Parmensi **4790**
0562-2719 Studia Anglistica Upsalienses **5179**
0562-2743 Studia Graeca Upsaliensia **2240**
0562-2751 Studia Historico-Ecclesiastica Upsaliensia **7684**
0562-2786 Studia i Materialy do Historii Wojskowosci **6448**
0562-2840 Studia Juridica Stockholmiensia **4790**
0562-2859 Studia Latina Upsaliensia **5180**
0562-2867 Studia Litteraria **5379**
0562-3022 Studia Romanica Upsaliensia **5180**
0562-3030 Studia Slavica Upsaliensia **5181**
0562-3359 Studien zur Koelner Kirchengeschichte **4270**
0562-3871 Studies in North-European Archeology **419**
0562-4096 Studies of Color **7085**
0562-4649 Subsidia Scientifica Franciscalia **7819**
0562-5033 Sudan Cotton Bulletin **8457**
0562-5068 Sudan Cotton Review **255**
0562-5122 Sudan Silva **3703**
0562-5130 Sudan Society **357**
0562-5297 Suedostdeutsche Vierteljahresblaetter **4271**
0562-5351 Suelos Ecuatoriales **2717**
0562-5548 Suimon Tekkan **3364**
0562-6048 Sunrise **6956**
0562-6579 Slavic Studies **3564**
0562-6927 Survey of German Federal Statistics **8408**
0562-7192 Suvremenna Medicina **5719**
0562-7370 Svensk Polis **2669**
0562-9020 Nouvelles Economiques de Suisse†
0563-0355 Systemation Letter†
0563-0592 Acta Universitatis de Attila Jozsef Nominatae. Acta Biologica *changed to* 1588-385X **649**
0563-0606 Acta Universitatis Szegediensis. Acta Iuridica et Politica **4609**
0563-0614 Acta Climatologica **6345**
0563-0819 Berzsenyi Daniel Megyei Konyvtar. Evkonyve **4994**
0563-0991 Supesu Dezain†
0563-1475 Annales Universitatis Saraviensis. Rechts- und Wirtschaftswissenschaftliche Abteilung. Schriftenreihe **4617**
0563-1483 Annales Universitatis Saraviensis. Reihe Philosophische Fakultaet **6904**
0563-1637 Terre Malgache **255**
0563-2595 University of Texas. Humanities Research Center. Tower Bibliographical Series†
0563-2897 The Texas Gulf Historical & Biographical Record **4314**
0563-3079 Texte des Spaeten Mittelalters und der Fruehen Neuzeit **5387**
0563-3737 Thailand Year Book†
0563-3745 Thalassia Salentina **820**
0563-4040 Theatre News (Washington)†
0563-4245 Au Coeur de l'Afrique **7623**
0563-4288 Theologische Bibliothek Toepelmann **7689**
0563-4407 Theorie des Systemes†
0563-4415 Theorie und Geschichte der Literatur und der Schoenen Kuenste **5388**
0563-4458 Theorie und Praxis der Koerperkultur†
0563-4784 This Is Malawi **1522**
0563-4806 This Week in Public Health†
0563-4822 Thomas Mann Studien **5388**
0563-4970 Thurn und Taxis Studien **4273**
0563-5020 Dizhi Kexue **2731**
0563-5446 Timber Tax Journal†
0563-5489 Timeless Fellowship **5050**
0563-573X Buletini i Shkencave Bujqesore **98**
0563-5780 Studime Filologjike **5184**
0563-5799 Studime Historike **4163**
0563-587X Tiscia **708**
0563-6140 Tobacco Bibliography†
0563-6191 Tax Burden on Tobacco
0563-6493 Tohoku Chiho Kisho Kenkyukaishi **6396**
0563-6531 Tohoku University. Research Institute of Electrical Communication. Reports†
0563-6590 Tohoku University. Research Institute for Strength and Fracture of Materials. Reports **3359**
0563-6760 Tokai Daigaku Kiyo. Bungakubu **4478**
0563-6841 *see* 0020-3157 **5494**
0563-6981 Tokushima Daigaku Kyoyobu Kiyo. Shizen Kagaku†
0563-7848 University of Tokyo. Institute for Nuclear Study. INS-PT†
0563-7856 University of Tokyo. Institute for Nuclear Study. INS-TCA†
0563-7864 University of Tokyo. Institute for Nuclear Study. INS-TCB†
0563-7872 University of Tokyo. Institute for Nuclear Study. INS-TH†
0563-7880 University of Tokyo. Institute for Nuclear Study. INS-TL†
0563-7902 Strong-Motion Earthquake Records in Japan **2790**
0563-7929 Tokyo Daigaku Kogakubu. Denki Kogaku Denshi Kogaku Iho **3333**
0563-8038 University of Tokyo. Department of Astronomy. Contributions **583**
0563-8151 Tokyo Geijutsu Daigaku Bijutsu Gakubu Kiyo **522**
0563-8186 Institute for Comparative Studies of Culture. Annals **7973**
0563-8313 Tokyo University of Agriculture and Technology. Annual Report **255**
0563-8372 Tokyo University of Fisheries. Report **3610**
0563-8488 Tokyo Toritsu Aisotopu Sogo Kenkyujo Nenpo **3175**
0563-8682 South East Asian Studies **8006**
0563-8887 Tools and Tillage†
0563-8895 Top Companies **1905**
0563-9093 Tops **3704**
0563-9239 Archaeological Newsletter **376**
0563-9425 Torreia†
0563-9727 Universite des Sciences Sociales de Toulouse. Annales *changed to* 1634-8664 **8012**
0563-9743 Homo† **8962**
0563-9751 Litteratures (Toulouse)
0563-9786 Via Domitia†
0563-9794 Universite de Toulouse II (le Mirail). Institut d'Art Prehistorique. Travaux†
0564-0334 Trabajo **1711**
0564-0342 Trabalho **1711**
0564-0482 Trade Directories of the World **2031**
0564-0571 Tradiciones de Guatemala **358**
0564-1373 Transports **8518**
0564-1470 Trauma† **8994**
0564-1497 Travail et Maitrise (Edition Industrie Chimique)†
0564-1500 Travail et Profession d'Outre- Mer†
0564-2159 Tribal Research and Development Institute. Bulletin
0564-2280 Tributi **1952**
0564-2612 Trinidad and Tobago. Central Statistical Office. Continuous Sample Survey of Population **7316**
0564-3295 Tropical Ecology **821**
0564-3392 Truck Data Book **8677**
0564-3619 Trziste, Novac, Kapital **1846**
0564-3783 Tsitologiya i Genetika **879**
0564-3929 Turang Xuebao **2717**
0564-4070 Cuadernos de Humanitas *see* 0441-4217 **4455**
0564-4232 Tuebinger Geographische Studien **4031**
0564-4402 Tulane Tax Institute **1953**
0564-4437 Tulsa Annals **3786**
0564-5042 Turk Arkeoloji Dergisi† **8994**
0564-5050 Turk Dili Arastirmalari Yilligi Belleten **5391**
0564-5093 Turk Kulturu Arastirmalari **562**
0564-559X Twayne's English Authors Series **5391**
0564-5603 Twayne's World Authors Series **5391**
0564-5654 Twentieth Century Series†
0564-6103 Tavkozlesi Kutato Intezet Evkonyve†
0564-6162 Teoreticheskaya i Matematicheskaya Fizika **7043**
0564-6197 Texas Tech Law Review **4795**
0564-6278 Tilburg Studies in Econometrics†
0564-6294 Topics in Astrophysics and Space Physics†
0564-6723 Tea Research Association. Tocklai Experimental Station. Scientific Annual Report **611**
0564-6758 Tecnologia de Alimentos **3666**
0564-6855 University of Texas. Humanities Research Center. Bibliographical Monograph Series†
0564-6898 University of Tokyo. Ocean Research Institute. Bulletin **2820**
0564-7150 T.M.†
0564-7169 T A I U S†
0564-7207 Tall Timbers Conference on Ecological Animal Control by Habitat Management. Proceedings†
0564-724X Tanzania Directory of Trades
0564-7568 Dagspressens Detaljspridning **7578**
0564-7630 University of Tokyo. Research Institute of Logopedics and Phoniatrics. Annual Bulletin†
0564-7959 Tuebinger Beitraege zur Linguistik **5189**
0564-7975 C E R E S Cahiers. Serie Linguistique
0564-836X Report on Tourism Statistics in Tanzania **8780**
0564-8602 University of Memphis. Anthropological Research Center. Occasional Papers **359**
0564-8742 University of Tokyo. Computer Center. Report†
0564-9021 Tutzinger Studien **7190**
0564-9048 25 Weekend Build-It Projects†
0565-0704 U.S. Fish and Wildlife Service. Investigations in Fish Control†
0565-0828 U.S. Bureau of the Census. Census Bureau Methodological Research†
0565-0933 Guide to Foreign Trade Statistics (Print) *changed to* Guide to Foreign Trade Statistics (Online) **1236**
0565-1034 Current Business Reports: Monthly Department Store Sales for Selected Areas†
0565-1557 Light List **8649**
0565-1603 U.S. Coastal Engineering Research Center. Bulletin and Progress Reports†
0565-1611 U.S. Coastal Engineering Research Center. Miscellaneous Papers *changed to* 0193-5992 **2802**
0565-1980 Poultry Market Statistics **185**
0565-2189 U.S. Department of Agriculture. National Agricultural Statistics Service. Hogs and Pigs **188**
0565-2820 U.S. Department of Housing and Urban Development. Annual Report **4429**
0565-4408 U.S. Economic Development Administration. Annual Report **1906**
0565-4688 U.S. Equal Employment Opportunity Commission. Annual Report **1712**
0565-4866 Flight Standards Information Manual†
0565-596X U.S. Geological Survey. Techniques of Water-Resources Investigations **8833**
0565-6567 U.S. Law Enforcement Assistance Administration. Annual Report†
0565-7024 National Advisory Council on the Education of Disadvantaged Children. Annual Report to the President and the Congress
0565-7059 N A S A. Contractor Report **7884**
0565-7199 Management (Baltimore)†
0565-7717 Motor Vehicle Safety Defect Recall Campaigns **8593**
0565-811X Medical Subject Headings **5672**
0565-873X U.S. Forest Service. Resource Bulletin N C **3706**
0565-9248 Federal Plan for Meteorological Services and Supporting Research (Year) **6352**

0565-9310 U.S. Department of Labor. Register of Reporting Labor Organizations†
0566-0327 U.S. Social Security Administration. O R S I P Notes†
0566-0335 U.S. Social Security Administration. Research Report
0566-0351 Social Security Programs Throughout the World†
0566-0637 Report of the Visa Office†
0566-0785 United States Attorney's Bulletin **4801**
0566-0963 United Steelworkers of America. Information **4604**
0566-1854 Faculdade de Odontologia de Porto Alegre. Revista **5844**
0566-201X Universite de Yaounde. Faculte des Sciences. Annales **7926**
0566-2257 University News **3008**
0566-2389 University of Richmond Law Review **4805**
0566-2540 Unnatkrishi **167**
0566-2575 Unser Bocholt **3859**
0566-2621 Unsere Jagd **8339**
0566-2672 Unservile State Papers†
0566-2680 Untei†
0566-2710 Die Unternehmung im Markt **1550**
0566-2753 Untersuchungen ueber Gruppen und Verbaende **1425**
0566-2796 Untersuchungen zur Oesterreichischen Literatur des 20. Jahrhunderts *changed to* 1814-5698 **5405**
0566-2818 Untersuchungen zur Romanischen Philologie†
0566-3091 Skrifter Roerande Uppsala Universitet. B, Inbjudningar **2301**
0566-3628 Monthly Price Review **3657**
0566-3911 Uspekhi Fotoniki†
0566-4128 Utah Geological and Mineralogical Survey. Special Studies *changed to* 1063-4916 **2773**
0566-4152 Utah. Juvenile Courts. Annual Report **4966**
0566-4543 Utopie
0566-4640 Utrecht Publications in General and Comparative Literature†
0566-4691 Utsunomiya Daigaku Nogakubu Gakujutsu Hokoku **167**
0566-5302 Demographic Handbook for Africa†
0566-6201 UNESCO Asian Fiction Series†
0566-666X *see* 0566-778X **368**
0566-7038 U.S. National Institute of Mental Health. Report Series on Mental Health Statistics. Series C: Methodology Reports†
0566-7186 Aeronautics and Space Report of the President *changed to* 0277-6499 **7833**
0566-7682 Review of Maritime Transport **8658**
0566-778X Re-Unicycling the Past **368**
0566-8301 N I H Public Advisory Groups†
0566-8549 Selected United States Government Publications†
0566-8654 Univers des Sciences et Techniques†
0566-8700 U F A W News-Sheet **322**
0566-8794 Uomo & Cultura
0566-8808 Uppsala University. Department of Peace and Conflict Research. Report **8146**
0566-9618 F A A Statistical Handbook of Aviation **8524**
0566-9901 U.S. Centers for Disease Control. Diphtheria Surveillance Report†
0567-1795 Auto Ja Tie **8522**
0567-2392 Autopista **8566**
0567-2848 Avicultura Tecnica
0567-2899 Avionics News Magazine **49**
0567-428X A U C A†
0567-4565 Aarets Fotboll *changed to* 0347-2752 **8229**
0567-4840 Kano Studies
0567-4980 Abhandlungen fuer die Kunde des Morgenlandes **541**
0567-4999 Abhandlungen zur Kunst-, Musik- und Literaturwissenschaft† **8927**
0567-560X Academia (Madrid, 1881) **463**
0567-5782 Academia de Ciencias de Cuba. Instituto de Oceanologia. Serie Oceanologica†
0567-5871 Academia Dominicana de la Historia. Publicaciones **4281**
0567-6029 Academia Provincial de la Historia. Boletin
0567-6037 Academia Puertorriquena de la Historia. Boletin
0567-6223 Nyelv- es Irodalomtudomanyi Kozlemenyek **5157**
0567-6304 Studii si Materiale de Istorie Medie†
0567-6320 Studii si Materiale de Istorie Moderna **4271**
0567-6584 Academie Royale de Langue et de Litterature Francaises. Annuaires **5089**
0567-6592 Academie Royale des Sciences d'Outre Mer. Revue Bibliographique†
0567-6630 Academy of American Franciscan History. Bibliographical Series†
0567-672X Acarologie
0567-7246 Acta Universitatis Szegediensis. Acta Antiqua et Archaeologica **2229**
0567-7254 Acta Asiatica **541**
0567-7289 Acta Baltica†
0567-7327 Acta Biologica Debrecina†
0567-7351 Huaxue Xuebao **2063**
0567-7386 Acta Clinica Belgica. Supplementum *see* 1784-3286 **5565**
0567-7505 Acta Geologica Hispanica *changed to* 1695-6133 **2737**
0567-7513 Acta Geologica Lilloana **2722**
0567-753X Acta Herediana **3927**
0567-7572 Acta Horticulturae **3721**
0567-7599 Acta Humboldtiana. Series Historica†
0567-7661 Acta Litteraria Academiae Scientiarum Hungarica†
0567-7718 Acta Mechanica Sinica **7057**
0567-7734 Acta Medica et Biologica **5566**
0567-7785 Acta Mexicana de Ciencia y Tecnologia **7832**
0567-784X Acta Neophilologica **5090**
0567-7874 Acta Organologica **6542**
0567-7920 Acta Palaeontologica Polonica **6722**
0567-7947 Acta Physica et Chimica Debrecina **7003**
0567-8099 Acta Universitatis Szegediensis. Acta Romanica **5090**
0567-8250 Acta Universitatis Carolinae. Medica. Monographia **5567**
0567-8293 Acta Universitatis Carolinae. Philosophica et Historica **4196**
0567-8315 Acta Veterinaria **8790**
0567-8560 Actualidad Antropologia
0567-8587 Organization of American States. Department of Educational Affairs. Actualidades†
0567-882X Actualites Neurophysiologiques **6119**
0567-932X The Adelphi Papers *changed to* 1944-5571 **7219**
0567-977X *see* 0749-7075 **1792**
0567-9931 Advances in Fluorine Chemistry†
0568-000X Advances in Mass Spectrometry **2097**
0568-0018 Advances in Materials Research†
0568-0301 World Advertising Expenditures†
0568-0352 Advertising Research Foundation. Conference Proceedings†
0568-0425 The Advocate (Boston) **4610**
0568-0476 Aegyptologische Abhandlungen **541**
0568-0530 Aero West†
0568-0581 University of Illinois at Urbana-Champaign. Department of Electrical Engineering. Aeronomy Laboratory. Aeronomy Report†
0568-062X Aerosol Review†
0568-1278 African Christian Student Seminar in Europe. Papers
0568-1308 African Development Bank. Report by the Board of Directors **1590**
0568-1499 African Student Christian Seminar (Report)†
0568-2517 Agricultura Tecnica en Mexico **83**
0568-2800 Index of Current Research on Pigs **181**
0568-2894 Ontario. Ministry of Agriculture, Food and Rural Affairs. Agricultural Statistics for Ontario (Year)†
0568-3114 Agrotecnia de Cuba **88**
0568-3343 Ailleurs
0568-3653 Air Quality Monograph Series†
0568-3866 Airplane, Missile and Spacecraft Structure Series†
0568-3939 Aisthesis **464**
0568-4307 Akademie der Wissenschaften in Goettingen. Sonderheft *see* 0341-9843 **5467**
0568-434X Schwaebische Forschungsgemeinschaft. Reihe 1: Studien zur Geschichte des Bayerischen Schwaben **4262**
0568-4447 Akademie der Wissenschaften und der Literatur, Mainz. Orientalische Kommission. Veroeffentlichungen **542**
0568-465X Rastenievudni Nauki **249**
0568-5281 Rossiiskaya Akademiya Nauk. Izvestiya. Mekhanika Zhidkosti i Gaza **7062**
0568-6245 Rezul'taty Issledovanii po Mezhdunarodnym Geofizicheskim Proektam. Glyatsiologicheskie Issledovaniya†
0568-6776 Akademiya Nauk S.S.S.R. Sibirskoe Otdelenie. Ural'skii Nauchnyi Tsentr. Institut Elektrokhimii. Trudy†
0568-7276 Der Akademiker in Wirtschaft und Verwaltung†
0568-7306 Akhshav
0568-7594 Aktuelle Fragen des Landbaues†
0568-806X Alabama Genealogical Society Magazine **3758**
0568-8442 Alaska. State Library, Juneau. State and Local Publications Received-Alaska
0568-8604 University of Alaska. Biological Papers **709**
0568-8760 University of Alaska. Mineral Industry Research Laboratory. Annual Report of Research Progress **6482**
0568-8876 Economia Alavesa **1401**
0568-8957 Albanische Forschungen **4197**
0568-9589 Alexandria University. Faculty of Engineering. Bulletin *changed to* 1110-0168 **3180**
0568-9619 University of Alexandria. Faculty of Science. Bulletin **7927**
0568-9848 Revue Algerienne du Travail
0569-0609 Allgemeiner Caecilien-Verband. Schriftenreihe **6543**
0569-0838 Almanac for Geodetic Engineers **568**
0569-0870 Almanach Africain†
0569-1338 Altalanos Nyelveszeti Tanulmanyok **5092**
0569-1346 Altamura **6519**
0569-1451 Altnuernberger Landschaft. Mitteilungen†
0569-163X Am Ve-admato†
0569-1796 Amateur Wrestling News **8157**
0569-1966 America by Car†
0569-2032 American Academy of Actuaries. Yearbook **4492**
0569-2245 American Assembly. Report **7104**
0569-230X School Nursing Monographs†
0569-2393 American Association for the Advancement of Science. Committee on Desert and Arid Zone Research. Contributions†
0569-2423 A A B G A Newsletter (American Association of Botanical Gardens and Arboretums) *changed to* American Public Gardens Association. Newsletter **3722**
0569-2628 A A F M Proceedings of Annual Meeting†
0569-2954 C U S I P Master Directory†
0569-3667 American Chamber of Commerce in Italy. Yearbook **1394**
0569-3799 American Chemical Society. Petroleum Chemistry Division. Preprints **2119**
0569-3845 American Christmas Tree Journal **3722**
0569-3993 A C T Research Report **2964**
0569-4043 Industrial Ventilation **4121**
0569-4221 American Crystallographic Association. Program & Abstracts **2085**
0569-4345 American Economist **1436**
0569-4353 American Educational Research Association. Directory of Members†
0569-4450 American Entomological Institute. Contributions **838**
0569-4515 A F L - C I O. Constitutional Convention. Proceedings **4589**
0569-4833 American Foundation for the Study of Man. Publications†
0569-5341 A I A Emerging Techniques†
0569-5376 Research Problems in Biology†
0569-5457 A I Ch E Workshop Series†
0569-5473 A I Ch E Equipment Testing Procedures Series **3234**
0569-5686 American Institute of Physics. Annual Report **7004**
0569-5716 Physics Manpower - Education and Employment Statistics†
0569-5961 American Italian Historical Association. Newsletter **3518**
0569-6461 American Mathematical Society, Mathematical Association of America, and the Society for Industrial and Applied Mathematics. Combined Membership List **5469**
0569-6666 American Musicological Society. Greater New York Chapter. Publications†
0569-6720 American Numismatic Society. Annual Report **6648**
0569-6941 American Philological Association. Newsletter **5252**
0569-7344 American Review of Art and Science†
0569-7425 Excavations at the Athenian Agora. Picture Book **393**
0569-7840 A S A Monograph (Washington)†
0569-7859 American Society of Appraisers. Appraisal and Valuation Manual†
0569-8057 Reinforced Concrete Research Council. Bulletins†
0569-8219 American Society of Mammalogists. Special Publications **932**
0569-8243 Reports on Diesel and Gas Engines Power Costs†
0569-9053 American Wedgwoodian†
0569-9460 Amministrazione della Difesa†
0569-9479 Amministrazione Tributi e Finanze†
0569-9789 Analecta Calasanctiana
0569-9827 Analecta Musicologica **6545**
0569-986X Analecta Romanica **5093**
0569-9878 Anales Cervantinos **5093**
0569-9924 Anales Galdosianos **5254**
0570-0027 Analytical Advances†
0570-0035 Analytical Methods for Pesticides, Plant Growth Regulators, and Food Additives *changed to* 0091-7486
0570-023X Ancient Peoples and Places†
0570-0655 Andhra Pradesh **4179**
0570-0930 Anglistische Studien **5254**
0570-1600 Annales de Normandie. Cahiers *see* 0003-4134 **4198**
0570-1716 Annales Islamologiques **7709**
0570-1783 Annals of Agricultural Science **91**
0570-1791 Annals of Arid Zone **218**
0570-183X Annals of Internal Medicine. Supplement *see* 0003-4819 **5943**
0570-1864 The Annals of Regional Science **1060**
0570-1937 Annee Africaine†
0570-1953 L'Annee Canonique **4855**
0570-202X Annotationes Zoologicae et Botanicae **933**
0570-2070 Union of European Football Associations. Handbook of U E F A **8250**
0570-2194 Geneva International Year Book†
0570-2259 Annuaire Roumain d'Anthropologie **324**
0570-2658 Annual Survey of Commonwealth Law†
0570-2666 Annual Survey of Indian Law **4618**
0570-2674 Annual Survey of Massachusetts Law†
0570-2976 Anthropological Studies†
0570-3085 Studia Instituti Anthropos **357**
0570-3697 Antropologia Social†
0570-393X Anuario Bibliografico Colombiano **615**
0570-3956 Anuario Brasileiro de Propaganda
0570-3980 Anuario Comercial Iberoamericano
0570-4006 Anuario Cultural del Peru
0570-4200 Anuario del Desarrollo de la Educacion, la Ciencia y la Cultura en America Latina†
0570-4251 Anuario Ecuatoriano de Derecho Internacional **4917**
0570-426X Anuario Estadistico Centroamericano de Comercio Exterior **1200**
0570-4324 Anuario Iberoamericano **7947**
0570-4359 Anuario Latinoamericano
0570-4480 Anzen Kogaku **3181**
0570-4561 Gyomu Nenpo - Aomori-ken Ringo Shikenjo **117**
0570-4839 Applied Economic Papers **1060**
0570-488X Applied Physics Quarterly†
0570-4928 Applied Spectroscopy Reviews **7074**
0570-5029 Approdo Letterario†
0570-507X Aqlam Journal
0570-5169 Aquilo. Serie Botanica **776**
0570-5177 Aquilo. Serie Zoologica **933**
0570-5258 Arab Observer†
0570-5398 Arabica **542**
0570-5479 Arbeiten zur Fruehmittelalterforschung **4199**
0570-5487 Arbeiten zur Geschichte des Kirchenkampfes†
0570-5509 Arbeiten zur Neutestamentlichen Textforschung **7622**
0570-5517 Arbeiten zur Pastoraltheologie **7622**
0570-5886 Arbeitsmethoden der Medizinischen und Naturwissenschaftlichen Kriminalistik **5912**
0570-6068 Archaeologia Zambiana **375**
0570-6084 Archaeological Reports (London) **376**
0570-6211 Archaiologike Hetaireia. To Ergon Kata to (Year) **378**
0570-622X Archaiologikon Deltion **378**
0570-6262 Archenhold-Sternwarte. Vortraege und Schriften **569**
0570-6270 Archeologia **379**
0570-6300 Archeological Society of Virginia. Newsletter **379**
0570-6483 Architectural Index **462**
0570-6602 Architektur Aktuell **431**
0570-6742 Beihefte zum Archiv fuer Kulturgeschichte **4132**
0570-6769 Archiv fuer Musikwissenschaft. Beihefte **6545**
0570-6793 Archiv fuer Vergleichende Kulturwissenschaft†
0570-6815 Archiv Orientalni. Supplementa **543**
0570-6955 Archives Medicales de l'Ouest†
0570-7196 Archivos Venezolanos de Folklore†
0570-720X Archivs†
0570-7218 Archivum (Oviedo) **5096**
0570-7293 Arco
0570-734X Arctos; Acta Philologica Fennica **2230**
0570-7358 Ardeola **901**
0570-7439 Arena†
0570-751X Areopag†
0570-8834 Argentina. Instituto Forestal Nacional. Anuario de Estadistica Forestal†
0570-8869 Argo **4200**
0570-8915 L'Argus de la Legislation Libanaise **4620**
0570-8958 Arheoloski Radovi i Rasprave **380**
0570-8966 Arheoloski Vestnik **380**
0570-9008 Arhivski Vjesnik **4200**
0570-9520 Arizona Geological Survey. Oil, Gas & Helium Production **6762**
0570-9601 Arizona State University. Faculty of Industrial Engineering. Industrial Engineering Research Bulletin†
0571-0111 Arizona Political Almanac†
0571-0189 Arkansas. Agricultural Experiment Station. Special Reports†
0571-0278 Arkansas. Geological Commission. Water Resources Circulars **8818**
0571-0456 Arkansas Almanac
0571-0472 Arkansas Family Historian **3759**

ISSN

ISSN

0587-2421 Acta Europaea Fertilitatis†
0587-2448 Acta Musicologica Fennica **6542**
0587-2634 Airline Management and Marketing Including American Aviation†
0587-2871 American Animal Hospital Association. Journal (Print Edition) *changed to* 1547-3317 **8791**
0587-2936 American Bar Association. Section of Local Government Law. Committee Reports†
0587-3428 Aquila†
0587-3452 Archplus **432**
0587-3460 Archaeographie†
0587-3533 Arkansas Archeological Survey. Publications on Archeology. Popular Series **380**
0587-3584 Art - Language†
0587-3746 Assure Social **8089**
0587-3835 Aussenpolitik (English Edition)†
0587-3908 Australian Orthodontic Journal **5835**
0587-4076 Aarbok for Telemark **4195**
0587-4114 Universite d'Abidjan. Annales. Serie D. Lettres, Litterature **5393**
0587-4122 Universite d'Abidjan. Annales. Serie E. Ecologie **3472**
0587-4246 Acta Physica Polonica. Series A: General Physics, Physics of Condensed Matter, Optics and Quantum Electronics, Atomic and Molecular Physics, Applied Physics **7003**
0587-4254 Acta Physica Polonica. Series B: Elementary Particle Physics, Nuclear Physics, Statistical Physics, Theory of Relativity, Field Theory **7003**
0587-4300 Actualidad Pastoral **7732**
0587-4416 Advances in Primatology **930**
0587-484X Universitaet Innsbruck. Alpin-Biologische Studien
0587-5064 American Studies Association of Texas. Journal **4283**
0587-5161 Anthropos **7335**
0587-5196 Anuario del Cuento Costarricense†
0587-5234 Angewandte Sozialforschung **8087**
0587-5277 Archiv der Deutschen Jugendbewegung. Jahrbuch *changed to* 1863-1185 **4228**
0587-5447 Arte y Arqueologia†
0587-5455 Arti Musices **6546**
0587-5471 Asian Pacific Congress of Cardiology. Symposia **5778**
0587-5560 Bulletin de l'A N E C L A†
0587-565X Astronomie und Raumfahrt†
0587-5846 Australian Conservation Foundation. Annual Report **2603**
0587-5919 Automobile Electronic Equipment
0587-5943 Pesticide Residues in Food **7535**
0587-6435 Coleccao de Estudos Filologicos†
0588-0912 Collana di Testi e di Critica†
0588-2583 Le Collectionneur Francais **4332**
0588-2699 College Chemistry Faculties **2972**
0588-2990 Colleges Classified†
0588-3237 Colloquium **7634**
0588-3253 Colloquium Geographicum **4003**
0588-4462 Colorado Fisheries Research Review†
0588-4543 Colorado. State Department of Public Health. Annual Progress Report. State Migrant Plan for Public Health Services†
0588-4934 Colorado College Studies **2973**
0588-5094 Colour Society. Journal **6716**
0588-5108 Colourage Annual **2243**
0588-6228 Comite International des Poids et Mesures. Comite Consultatif pour la Definition de la Seconde. (Rapport et Annexes)†
0588-6414 Commentationes Balticae†
0588-649X Euromarket News†
0588-6562 Canadian Insurance Law Reporter **4639**
0588-6694 Commercial Bank of Ethiopia. Annual Report **1328**
0588-6783 Commission for Technical Co-Operation in Africa. Joint Project†
0588-6953 Commission of the European Communities. Expose Annuel sur les Activities d'Orientation Professionnelle dans la Communaute†
0588-702X Mines Safety and Health Commission. Report
0588-7445 Common Market Law Reports **4646**
0588-7720 Commonwealth Geological Liaison Office. Liaison Report†
0588-7755 Commonwealth Geological Liaison Office. Report (on) Resources of the British Commonwealth†
0588-7763 Commonwealth Geological Liaison Office. Special Publication
0588-7933 Commonwealth Trade†
0588-8018 Communications **8094**
0588-8093 Communicator†
0588-8360 Community
0588-8611 Easter Commemoration Digest†
0588-9049 Comparative Education Society in Europe. Proceedings of the General Meeting **2838**
0588-912X Compendio Estadistico Centroamericano†
0588-9138 Compendio Estadistico de America†
0588-9278 Comprehensive Education
0588-9405 Computer Programs for Chemistry†
0588-9545 Comunicaciones - Revista Tecnica†
0588-9804 Concilium **7634**
0589-0365 Conseil International des Archives. Table Ronde Internationale des Archives. Actes *changed to* 1680-1865
0589-1019 Alliance for Engineering in Medicine and Biology. Proceedings of the Annual Conference†
0589-1485 Conference on Precision Electromagnetic Measurements. Digest†
0589-1663 Caribbean Conference Series†
0589-2546 Association Internationale pour l'Histoire du Verre. Annales des Congres **2037**
0589-2813 Congreso Latinoamericano de Siderurgia. Memoria Tecnica
0589-3151 Congressional Pictorial Directory **7431**
0589-3178 Congressional Staff Directory **7119**
0589-3267 Congresso Europeo di Storia Ospitaliera. Atti
0589-3305 Congresso Latinoamericano de Hidraulica (Papers)
0589-381X University of Connecticut. Center for Real Estate and Urban Economic Studies. Annual Report **7614**
0589-400X Connecticut Water Resources Bulletins†
0589-4069 Conscientia **6911**
0589-4301 Consejo Superior Universitario Centroamericano. Actas de la Reunion Ordinaria **2974**
0589-4360 Consejo Superior Universitario Centroamericano. Publicaciones†
0589-4468 Conservation Court Digest
0589-4522 Conservative Journal
0589-4735 Construction-Amenagement†
0589-5081 Contacto†
0589-5227 Contemporary China†
0589-5286 Contemporary Music Newsletter†
0589-5820 Contributions a l'Etude des Sciences de l'Homme
0589-6185 Convivium
0589-6355 Cooperative Housing Journal **4408**
0589-6525 Danmarks Biblioteksskole. Studier†
0589-6665 Denmark. Statens Byggeforskningsinstitut. Landbrugsbyggeri†
0589-686X Corax **905**
0589-7483 Corning Research **7075**
0589-7742 Corporacion Nacional de Fertilizantes. Memoria Anual
0589-7920 Corporate Report Fact Book **1981**
0589-7963 Corpus Christianorum. Continuatio Mediaevalis **7793**
0589-7998 Corpus Consuetudinum Monasticarum **7793**
0589-8056 Corpus Hispanorum de Pace†
0589-8366 Corriere Africano
0589-8447 Cosmetic World **586**
0589-8544 Costa Rica. Direccion General de Estadistica y Censos. Inventario de las Estadisticas Nacionales **8365**
0589-8765 Costruttori Italiani nel Mondo
0589-9028 C B A Annual Report **385**
0589-9036 C B A Research Reports **385**
0589-9362 Council of Europe. Exchange of Information Between the Member States on Their Legislative Activity and Regulations (New Series)†
0589-9478 Council of Europe. Council for Cultural Cooperation. Annual Report†
0589-9508 Council of Europe. Concise Handbook†
0589-9575 European Co-Operation **4925**
0589-9591 Council of Europe Film Weeks†
0589-9788 State Headlines†
0590-0174 Courier (Nashville)
0590-0239 Courrier des Pays de l'Est† **8946**
0590-0581 Cranwells Building Supplies Catalogue†
0590-0727 Creditanstalt-Bankverein. Wirtschaftsberichte†
0590-0832 Crime and Delinquency in California *changed to* Crime in California **2673**
0590-0980 Criterion **7636**
0590-1111 Cronache Meridionali†
0590-1545 Cuadernos Bibliograficos†
0590-160X Cuadernos de Antropologia **334**
0590-1626 Cuadernos de Aragon **4213**
0590-1731 Cuadernos de Cristianismo y Sociedad **7636**
0590-1871 Cuadernos de Etnologia y Etnografia de Navarra **334**
0590-1901 Cuadernos de Filosofia†
0590-1928 Cuadernos de Historia *see* 0018-2141 **4227**
0590-1987 Cuadernos de Alhambra **484**
0590-2525 Cuadernos Republicanos
0590-2568 Cuadernos Uruguayos de Filosofia†
0590-2916 Cuba Azucar **227**
0590-3343 Universidad de Oriente. Instituto Oceanografico Biblioteca. Boletin Bibliografico **2721**
0590-3351 Universidad de Oriente. Instituto Oceanografico. Cuadernos Oceanograficos†
0590-3890 Current Soviet Policies†
0590-4102 Current Primate References **715**
0590-417X Current Research in British Studies by American and Canadian Scholars†
0590-4501 Cusanus-Gesellschaft. Kleine Schriften **7794**
0590-451X Cusanus-Gesellschaft. Mitteilungen und Forschungsbeitraege **7794**
0590-4846 Cyprus. Department of Statistics and Research. Demographic Report **7305**
0590-501X C T K Dokumentacni Prehled†
0590-5702 Canada. Statistics Canada. Direct Selling in Canada **1217**
0590-5966 Casopis za Zgodovino in Narodopisje **4209**
0590-6008 Catholic International Education Office. Etudes et Documents†
0590-6105 Informes Latinoamericanos de Fisica†
0590-6334 Cicindela
0590-6563 Commission of the European Communities. Community Law **4921**
0590-6776 Cord Sportfacts Guns Guide†
0590-711X C P D A News†
0590-7225 Cours et Documents de Biologie†
0590-7233 Bibliographie de Jurisprudence Europeenne Concernant les Decisions Judiciaires Relatives aux Traites Institutant les Communautes Europeennes†
0590-8434 Cleveland and Teesside Local History Society. Bulletin
0590-8450 Coating **7319**
0590-8876 Costume **2253**
0590-9325 Canada. Statistics Canada. Market Research Handbook **1218**
0590-9384 Canadian Coast Guard. List of Lights, Buoys and Fog Signals: Atlantic Coast **8640**
0590-9449 Canada. Public Service Staff Relations Board. Annual Report **7427**
0590-9597 Casopis za Suvremenu Povijest **4209**
0590-966X Centro Calouste Gulbenkian. Archivos **5407**
0590-9775 British Shipping Statistics†
0590-9783 Charities Digest (Year) **8031**
0590-9945 Coin Bulletin
0591-0110 Commission of the European Communities. Expose Annuel sur les Activities des Services de Main-d'Ouvre des Etats Membres de la Communaute†
0591-0129 Committee for Economic Development of Australia. C E D A Occasional Papers†
0591-0188 Comentarios Economicos†
0591-0358 Universite de Copenhague. Institut du Moyen-Age Grec et Latin. Cahiers **4275**
0591-0447 Country Corner†
0591-0471 Courrier de l'Extreme-Orient
0591-0633 Cahiers Marxistes **7112**
0591-0986 Catalogue of Little Press Books in Print Published in the UK†
0591-1036 Centrale Nucleare Garigliano. Relazione Annuale†
0591-1044 Centrale Elettronucleare Latina. Relazione Annuale†
0591-1133 Geschied- en Oudheidkundige Kring van Ronse en het Tenement van Inde. Annalen **4223**
0591-1281 Chips and Ships†
0591-1710 Commerce Yearbook of Public Sector†
0591-2237 Country Music People **6559**
0591-2296 Crux of the News **7636**
0591-2334 Custom Car **8576**
0591-2369 Zycie Literackie†
0591-2377 Zycie Szkoly Wyzszej†
0591-2385 Zygon **7697**
0591-2512 Forum du Commerce International *see* 0020-8957 **1571**
0591-2539 Wenti yu Yanjiu **7273**
0591-2628 Panorama
0591-2776 Acta Universitatis Wratislaviensis. Studia Geograficzne **3997**
0591-2806 Cartographie Mondiale *see* 0084-1471 **8999**
0700-0278 Canada. Statistics Canada. Canvas Products and Cotton and Jute Bag Industries†
0700-0731 Canada. Statistics Canada. Felt and Fibre Processing Mills†
0700-1207 National Building Code of Canada **4738**
0700-124X National Fire Code of Canada (Year) **3580**
0700-141X Canada. Statistics Canada. Continuing Education: Universities†
0700-1444 Canada. Statistics Canada. Continuing Education: Elementary-Secondary†
0700-1517 Capacity Utilization Rates in Canadian Manufacturing†
0700-1568 Canada. Chief Electoral Officer. Report **7113**
0700-1576 Fisheries Improvement Loans Act. Annual Report **1926**
0700-1584 T E S L Talk **3083**
0700-1681 Quebec (Province) Ministere du Travail et de la Main d'Oeuvre. Jurisprudence en Droit du Travail: Tribunal du Travail†
0700-1754 National Research Council, Canada. Institute for Research in Construction. Research Program†
0700-1770 ForesTalk†
0700-2033 Industry Price Indexes **1242**
0700-205X Canada. Statistics Canada. Quarterly Estimates of Trusteed Pension Funds **1218**
0700-2092 Public Sector†
0700-2114 Canada. Department of Industry, Trade and Commerce. Trade News: Food and Agriculture *changed to* 0823-3330 **1554**
0700-2181 Canada. Statistics Canada. University Financial Statistics†
0700-2467 New Brunswick. Department of Finance. Main Estimates **7454**
0700-2866 Canada Grains Council. Annual Report†
0700-2971 Manitoba Statistical Review **8387**
0700-3021 Photo Life **6973**
0700-3048 Dialogue (Ottawa)†
0700-3102 Worklife (Kingston) **1716**
0700-3226 Korean Journal†
0700-3528 Monday Report on Retailers **1835**
0700-3617 Overview **1505**
0700-365X Estuaire **5421**
0700-3684 Manitoba Library Association. Newsline **5031**
0700-3722 Information-Status of Women†
0700-3838 Music Research News
0700-3862 Labour **1693**
0700-4192 Missions des Franciscains **7807**
0700-432X Equipement et Methodes
0700-4400 International View†
0700-4532 Metropolitan Toronto Library Board. Annual Report†
0700-463X Intralogue†
0700-4745 Musicanada†
0700-480X Sources **2028**
0700-4982 London Community Services Directory
0700-5008 Marquee **8473**
0700-5040 Habitabec Montreal *changed to* 1203-3103
0700-5105 Laurier Campus **2289**
0700-5121 Collective Bargaining
0700-5199 Szamadas
0700-5202 Slavna Nadeje **7775**
0700-5237 Canadian Council on Animal Care. Resource *see* 0700-5245
0700-5245 Conseil Canadien de Protection des Animaux. Ressource
0700-527X Northern Life (Sudbury) **3814**
0700-5318 Opus
0700-5369 Literacy
0700-5385 Rural Voice **153**
0700-5423 Canadian Traveller
0700-5539 Investment Reporter **1633**
0700-5989 Association of Ontario Land Surveyors. Annual Report **3259**
0700-6004 Reseau†
0700-6500 Revue Notre Dame du Cap **7678**
0700-6802 Scarboro Missions **7679**
0700-723X Voice of the Kent Farmer **169**
0700-7388 Boating News†
0700-7396 Action Sports
0700-8066 Mennonite Historian **7738**
0700-8104 Early Canadian Life
0700-8392 Animals' Voice **318**
0700-8406 Acta Victoriana **5249**
0700-9003 Peace Arch News **3815**
0700-9070 Federation of Catholic Parent-Teacher Associations of Ontario. Newsletter **2856**
0700-9178 Construction Alberta News **994**
0700-9224 Applied Mathematics Notes†
0700-933X Up the Gatineau! **3786**
0700-9380 Gifts & Tablewares **4060**
0700-9445 Name Gleaner
0700-9712 Community Information Service. Newsletter
0700-9771 A R C Arabic Journal **3515**
0700-9801 Journal of Psychology and Judaism†

ISSN

0704-206X Canadian Ethnology Service. Annual Review *see* 1709-5875 **332**
0704-2086 Canada Mortgage and Housing Corporation. Monthly Housing Statistics **4434**
0704-2493 British Columbia. Alcohol and Drug Commission. Annual Report†
0704-2582 Ontario Geological Survey. Report **6475**
0704-2590 Ontario Geological Survey. Study **6475**
0704-2663 Ontario Advisory Council on Senior Citizens. Annual Report **7458**
0704-2671 Education Manitoba†
0704-2701 Ocean Dumping Report†
0704-2752 Ontario Geological Survey. Miscellaneous Paper **6475**
0704-2833 The Economy **1481**
0704-2884 Canada. Geological Survey. Current Research **2727**
0704-2965 Horizons (Montreal) **3811**
0704-2973 *see* 0704-2965 **3811**
0704-3481 Conseil des Sciences du Canada. Rapport *see* 0840-1950
0704-3694 Canadian Industry Report of Fisheries and Aquatic Sciences **3588**
0704-3708 Rapport Canadien a l'Industrie sur les Sciences Halieutiques et Aquatiques *see* 0704-3694 **3588**
0704-3716 Canadian Translation of Fisheries and Aquatic Sciences **664**
0704-3724 Canadian Occupational Safety & Health Law†
0704-3899 Medical Research Council of Canada. Reference List of Health Science Research in Canada†
0704-4550 Gazette des Femmes **8865**
0704-4585 Manitoba. Social Services Advisory Committee. Annual Report†
0704-464X Acts of New Brunswick **4609**
0704-4658 Acts of the Legislature of New Brunswick *changed to* 0704-464X **4609**
0704-4747 Eye†
0704-4771 N A F O Meeting Proceedings†
0704-4798 N A F O Annual Report **3602**
0704-4860 Hearsay **2286**
0704-514X Barreau du Quebec. Rapport Annuel **4627**
0704-5263 Perception **8061**
0704-5352 Voix Sepharade **3571**
0704-5387 Canada. Statistics Canada. Public Warehousing†
0704-5522 Concerned Canadian
0704-5565 *see* 1910-944X **7433**
0704-5603 Canada. Parliament. House of Commons Debates **7427**
0704-5638 Canada. Parliament. Chambre des Communes. Debats **7427**
0704-5646 Canadian Poetry **5419**
0704-5697 Y E R Monograph Series†
0704-5700 Yeats Eliot Review **5438**
0704-5824 Occasional
0704-5883 New Religions Newsletter
0704-5905 Targumic and Cognate Studies. Newsletter **7730**
0704-6022 British Columbia. Ministry of the Attorney-General. Annual Report *changed to* 1499-0210 **7424**
0704-6278 British Columbia Manufacturer's Directory **1425**
0704-6286 Germination **5423**
0704-6359 L'Hospitalite†
0704-6588 Crosscurrents **6560**
0704-6596 Canada. Statistics Canada. Elementary - Secondary School Enrolment†
0704-6618 Alberta Genealogical Society. Ancestor Index†
0704-6715 Synthesis†
0704-6766 Construction Safety Journal
0704-6804 Airforce **6409**
0704-6839 Northern Titles: K W I C Index†
0704-6936 Issues, Events & Ideas **2872**
0704-7002 Polyphony†
0704-7177 Forum F C M *see* 0381-1352
0704-7223 Taxipresse
0704-7231 The Recorder **6610**
0704-7290 Intrinsic
0704-7339 Toronto International Auto Show Program **8607**
0704-7428 Image de la Mauricie **2638**
0704-7509 B C Journal of Special Education†
0704-7576 Grande Replique
0704-7584 International Development Research Centre. Annual Report **1126**
0704-7630 Recueil des Sentences de l'Education **3030**
0704-7673 Canadian Forestry Service. Northern Forest Research Centre. Information Report *changed to* 0831-8247 **3685**
0704-7916 Arts Atlantic **474**
0704-7975 Gardenland†
0704-8017 Edmonton Chamber of Commerce. Commerce News **1402**
0704-8025 Reports on Separatism†
0704-8394 Nova Scotia Barristers' Society. Annual Report **4749**
0704-8475 Virus Montreal
0704-8726 Prairie Provinces Water Board Annual Report **8831**
0704-8874 Labour Topics
0704-9153 Ovo Magazine
0704-9161 Magazine OVO *see* 0704-9153
0704-9226 Halton Farm News
0704-9420 Poultry in Canada†
0704-9463 This Is Entertainment
0704-9471 Hamilton-Burlington Month
0704-9528 Administrateur Hospitalier†
0704-9536 Freeze Frame **6501**
0704-9641 Ontario. Advisory Committee on Confederation. Report†
0704-982X Quebec (Province) Conseil Superieur de l'Education. Conseil-Education
0705-0453 Theatre **8482**
0705-0534 Australia. Bureau of Statistics. Australian Exports, Country by Commodity†
0705-0542 Australia. Bureau of Statistics. Australian Imports, Country by Commodity†
0705-0585 Decor a Coeur†
0705-064X Development Directions†
0705-0992 Adsum **6408**
0705-1026 Federation des Associations de Parents et Instituteurs Langues Francaise de l'Ontario. Liaison
0705-1085 Dionysius
0705-1093 Decoration Chez-Soi **4537**
0705-1123 Echo (Ottawa)†
0705-1166 I N D E C Communicator
0705-1328 Journal of Canadian Poetry **5424**
0705-1360 All Canada Weekly Summaries - National **4613**
0705-1379 Freelance **5298**
0705-1433 Canadian Footwear Journal **7940**
0705-1549 Activities Digest†
0705-1840 Sanford Evans Gold Book of Motorcycle Data & Used Prices **8268**
0705-1867 Vani
0705-1883 Books in Finnish†
0705-1913 Review of Architecture and Landscape Architecture†
0705-2006 Canadian Journal of Archaeology **386**
0705-212X Lawn & Garden Trade **1829**
0705-2146 Australia. Bureau of Statistics. Western Australian Office. Fisheries, Western Australia†
0705-2162 Canadian Federation of Film Societies. Newsletter†
0705-2170 Toronto Stock Exchange Daily Record **1656**
0705-2294 Books in Dutch†
0705-2332 Books in Danish†
0705-2367 Coal Miner†
0705-2731 Caribbean Year Book
0705-2855 Archivist†
0705-3045 Eastern Ontario Construction Industry Directory and Purchasing Guide†
0705-3061 Jurisprudence Express **4706**
0705-3150 Wilderness Arts and Recreation
0705-3207 University of British Columbia. Department of Geological Sciences. Report **2772**
0705-3215 C'Est pour Quand **2147**
0705-3436 Loisir et Societe **4980**
0705-3657 Canadian Journal of Communication **8092**
0705-369X Injured Athlete
0705-372X Directory of Social Services in the A.C.T.†
0705-3754 Crescent International **7710**
0705-3797 Episodes **2733**
0705-3851 Femmes d'Ici **8863**
0705-386X Canadian Council of Teachers of English. Newsletter **3053**
0705-3894 Free Throw†
0705-3983 University of Alberta. Agriculture and Forestry Bulletin†
0705-4041 Mennonitische Post **3549**
0705-405X Edmonton Sun **3809**
0705-4157 Alumi-News†
0705-4165 Incidences†
0705-4319 Canada. Statistics Canada. Control and Sale of Alcoholic Beverages in Canada†
0705-4343 Canada. Statistics Canada. Air Passenger Origin and Destination. Canada - United States Report **8523**
0705-4572 Chinook†
0705-4580 Canadian Journal of Regional Science **1536**
0705-470X British Columbia. Ministry of Agriculture Fisheries and Food. Tree Fruit Production Guide for Interior Districts **223**
0705-4831 Nova Scotia Trappers Newsletter **4974**
0705-4890 Library Association of Alberta. Letter **5027**
0705-5137 Canadian Report
0705-5196 C A N M E T Reports†
0705-5242 Canada. Statistics Canada. Report on Livestock Surveys: Cattle, Sheep†
0705-5269 Canada. Statistics Canada. International Travel, Advance Information **8778**
0705-5390 British Columbia. Ministry of Environment, Lands and Parks. Fisheries Branch. Fisheries Management Report **3587**
0705-548X Canadian Film Series **6492**
0705-5587 Canada Addictions Foundation. Directory
0705-5595 Canada. Statistics Canada. New Motor Vehicle Sales **8523**
0705-5617 Coaching Review†
0705-5765 Canada. Statistics Canada. Canadian Statistical Review. Annual Supplement to Section 1†
0705-5811 Alberta. Environment Council of Alberta. Annual Report†
0705-5900 Atmosphere - Ocean **6347**
0705-6028 Canadian Advisory Council on the Status of Women. Annual Report - Rapport Annuel *changed to* 1187-6654
0705-6087 Alberta Library News†
0705-6109 Misleading Advertising Bulletin†
0705-6311 Physician's Management Manuals **5696**
0705-6346 Lumiere et Paix
0705-6397 Arc *changed to* 1910-3239 **5416**
0705-6435 Conseil du Statut de la Femme. Rapport Annuel Quebec *changed to* 1706-9750 **7204**
0705-6494 Books in Hungarian†
0705-6605 Televiews†
0705-663X Canadian Union of Public Employees. The Public Employee†
0705-6656 Continuo **6559**
0705-6672 Court Judgement Report
0705-6680 Canadian Perspective†
0705-6702 Newfoundland Medical Association Journal†
0705-6710 Canadian Paper Analyst†
0705-6761 Embouteilleur Quebecois
0705-6907 Inprint
0705-6923 Quebec Vert **3748**
0705-6931 Leadline†
0705-7040 L'Echo du Transport **8670**
0705-7113 A J A S **4281**
0705-7156 Books in Spanish†
0705-7172 Books in Arabic†
0705-7199 Geographie Physique et Quaternaire **4011**
0705-7423 University of Wollongong. Handbook for Undergraduates†
0705-7504 Canadian Soccer Association. Technical Manual†
0705-7520 Gite **4387**
0705-7814 Wise Owl News (Toronto)†
0705-7822 Nayer Dor†
0705-7830 Alberta Teachers' Association. Journal of Home Economics Education
0705-7857 Sunday Star *see* 0319-0781 **3818**
0705-7970 Liban au Canada
0705-8160 Directory of Courses: Tourism, Hospitality, Recreation†
0705-8209 Books in Armenian†
0705-825X Books in Urdu†
0705-8292 Conseil de la Jeunesse Scientifique. Bottin
0705-8314 Guide du Camping
0705-8330 Canadian Business Economics **1079**
0705-8365 Cuvantul Romanesc
0705-8373 Books in Hindi†
0705-8454 A S T I S Current Awareness Bulletin†
0705-856X Facts†
0705-8594 Middle East Focus
0705-8748 Farm Gate **110**
0705-8799 Trade News North
0705-8810 Canadian Police College. Journal†
0705-8861 Asianadian†
0705-8993 Marine Trades
0705-9019 B.C. Music Educator **6547**
0705-906X Western Grocer Magazine **3682**
0705-9175 Movie Works Weekly
0705-9205 Trufax
0705-9388 Occupational Health in Ontario†
0705-9485 Canada Gazette: Part 3 **7426**
0705-9981 Canada Livestock Meat Trade Report **282**
0706-0092 Ontario Education Relations Commission. Annual Report†
0706-0114 Datafacts
0706-0300 Bicycling News Canada†
0706-0424 Charlton's Standard Catalogue of Canadian Coins *changed to* 1716-0782 **6649**
0706-0459 Charlton Coin Guide **6649**
0706-0556 Esplumoir
0706-0629 British Columbia. Legislative Assembly. Journals **7424**
0706-0661 Canadian Journal of Plant Pathology **783**
0706-067X Canada. Statistics Canada. Road Motor Vehicles, Registrations **8523**
0706-0793 Science Statistics (Print Edition) *changed to* 1209-1278 **7938**
0706-0823 Canadian Forces Personnel Newsletter **6415**
0706-0955 Northward Journal **5343**
0706-098X Musees **6530**
0706-1005 Concordia University Magazine
0706-1021 Annuaire Franco-Ontarien†
0706-1382 C A F C Dialogue
0706-1420 Alberta Electric Industry, Annual Statistics **3155**
0706-151X Input†
0706-1706 Labour, Capital and Society **1601**
0706-1889 Writing
0706-1994 Academie des Sciences. Comptes Rendus Mathematiques **5464**
0706-2141 New Breed†
0706-215X Bulletin Voyages **8689**
0706-2168 Canadian Geographic **4001**
0706-2265 Quebec (Province). Services Documentation Multimedia. Choix Jeunesse: Documentation Imprimee *changed to* 1719-5284 **634**
0706-2338 The Directory of Canadian Universities (Year) **2955**
0706-2346 Canada. Hydrographic Service. Water Levels. Vol. 2: Tidal Highs and Lows†
0706-2354 Canada. Hydrographic Service. Water Levels. Vol. 1: Daily Means†
0706-2419 Parlure†
0706-246X Institute of Man and Resources Reports†
0706-2613 Conseil des Sciences du Canada. Agenda
0706-280X Canadian Jewish Herald†
0706-2869 Gouvernement du Quebec. Ministere des Finances. Comptes Publics **7439**
0706-2893 British Columbia Police Journal†
0706-2915 School Library Newsletter†
0706-2966 Canada. Statistics Canada. Annual Review of Science Statistics†
0706-3105 Canada. Statistics Canada. Road and Street Length and Financing†
0706-3180 Livret des Reglements de la Federation Canadienne des Archers *see* 0226-773X **8173**
0706-3253 Action (Hull, Que.)†
0706-3350 Manitoba Gazette **4727**
0706-3369 Alberta. Horticultural Research Center. Annual Report†
0706-3393 Canada. Inland Waters Directorate. Historical Water Levels Summary. Atlantic Provinces **2793**
0706-3423 Canada. Inland Waters Directorate. Historical Water Levels Summary. Saskatchewan **2793**
0706-3431 La Chronique **5002**
0706-3466 Canada. Inland Waters Directorate. Historical Water Levels Summary. Yukon and Northwest Territories **2793**
0706-3474 Canada. Inland Waters Directorate. Historical Water Levels Summary. British Columbia **2793**
0706-3598 Gazette Officielle du Quebec: Laws and Regulations *see* 0703-5721 **4679**
0706-3601 B.C. Economic Development†
0706-3679 Canada. Statistics Canada. Education in Canada **2931**
0706-3717 Canada. Statistics Canada. Minority and Second Language Education, Elementary and Secondary Levels **5201**
0706-3792 Manitoba. Municipal Employees Benefits Board. Annual Report **1696**
0706-3857 Fireweed†
0706-3954 Transpo†
0706-4152 C C I Technical Bulletins **6521**
0706-425X Agricultural Research Institute of Ontario. Annual Report **84**
0706-4284 Physio-Quebec **5696**
0706-4292 British Columbia. Ministry of Agriculture Fisheries and Food. Mushroom Production Guide **3725**
0706-4403 Prince Edward Island. Department of Municipal Affairs. Annual Report†
0706-4454 Canada. Department of Agriculture. Union list of Serials in Canada Department of Agriculture Library†
0706-4551 Ontario Geological Survey. Mineral Deposits Circular **6475**
0706-4713 U - Choose: A Guide to Canadian Universities†
0706-4845 Canadian Journal of Anthropology†

ISSN

DIRECTORY 2010 0713-7095 9313

0709-1443 Export Credits Insurance Corporation. Annual Report and Financial Statements changed to 1707-4533 1564
0709-1532 Western Sportsman 8341
0709-1605 Export Development Corporation. Annual Report (Print Edition) changed to 1707-4533 1564
0709-1915 Voice of the Middlesex Farmer 169
0709-2016 Le Temps (Ottawa)†
0709-2334 Dimensions (Montreal)
0709-2377 Canada Grains Council. Proceedings of Annual Meeting 270
0709-2423 Manitoba Business Magazine 1498
0709-2563 Pulp & Paper Canada Annual Directory 6737
0709-2652 Arctic Seas†
0709-2679 Coup d'Oeil sur le Saguenay-Lac-Saint-Jean†
0709-292X Production of Canada's Leading Minerals 6486
0709-3403 Canadian Security 2676
0709-3632 Journal des Debats 7448
0709-3748 Weekly Well Activity Report 6797
0709-3756 Bibliographical Society of Canada. Bulletin 618
0709-3845 Le Communiste†
0709-4035 Wot†
0709-4515 Survey of Wage Rates from Collective Agreement Settlements in Nova Scotia†
0709-4531 British Columbia Liquor Distribution Branch. Financial Statements 7424
0709-4604 A C A Bulletin 4985
0709-4647 Share 3563
0709-4671 Ontario Geological Survey. Northern Ontario Engineering Geology Terrain Study
0709-4698 Victorian Periodicals Review 5395
0709-4744 Sailing Canada†
0709-5112 Eclipse†
0709-5139 Provincial Judges Journal 4762
0709-5201 Florilegium 4219
0709-5236 Canadian Secretary†
0709-5252 Canadian Occupational Health & Safety News 6675
0709-5333 Alberta Chamber of Commerce. Legislative Report†
0709-5341 Motor Vehicle Reports (4th Series) 8504
0709-5368 Transpotech†
0709-549X Ultimate Reality and Meaning 6958
0709-5562 Historic Guelph 4296
0709-5600 Supreme Court of Canada Decisions 4965
0709-5724 Loto - Quebec. Rapport Annuel 1933
0709-5740 Loto - Quebec. Annual Report see 0709-5724 1933
0709-602X Canadian Pulp and Paper Association. Monthly Newsprint Statistics 6732
0709-6607 Public School Programs (Year) 2901
0709-681X Nickle's Daily Oil Bulletin 6780
0709-6941 Participation 7164
0709-6968 Cases to be Heard by the Supreme Court of Canada†
0709-7093 Leisure Wheels 8589
0709-7727 Creative Source†
0709-7751 Language and Society†
0709-776X B.C. Sea Angling Guide†
0709-7778 B.C. Fresh Water Fishing Guide†
0709-8103 Aviation Safety Letter (Print Edition) 48
0709-812X Securite Aerienne, Nouvelles (Print Edition) see 0709-8103 48
0709-8146 The Saskatchewan Educational Administrator 3031
0709-8219 Composers West†
0709-8227 Kino - Nouvelles†
0709-8502 Annales de Biochimie Clinique du Quebec changed to 1705-6322 5902
0709-874X Collection Choix†
0709-8847 Environnement†
0709-8855 Imagine†
0709-8863 Solaris
0709-8936 Canadian Dental Association. Journal 5837
0709-8987 University of Toronto. Library Automation Systems. New Publications Awareness List†
0709-9010 Indian Book Review Digest†
0709-9177 Hibou†
0709-9487 Rencontre 3561
0709-9495 Rencontre (English Edition) see 0709-9487 3561
0709-955X Museums in Manitoba (Year) 6532
0709-9762 Canada: Travel Information†
0709-9959 Canada. Northern Forestry Centre. Forestry Report†
0710-0140 Phys 13 News 7030
0710-0167 Revue Quebecoise de Linguistique 5168
0710-0353 Canadian University Music Review changed to 1911-0146 6577
0710-0469 Pappus 3747
0710-0574 Butterflies of Ontario & Summaries of Lepidoptera Encountered in Ontario changed to 1713-9481 856
0710-068X Cross-Cultural Psychology Bulletin 7350
0710-0744 B C A T A Journal for Art Teachers 3052
0710-0825 Canadian Society for Computational Studies of Intelligence. Proceedings of the Biennial Conference†
0710-0841 Windsor Yearbook of Access to Justice 4815
0710-0868 Geographie et Teledetection. Bulletin de Recherche 4011
0710-1023 Canada. Statistics Canada. Provincial Government Finance: Assets, Liabilities, Source and Application of Funds†
0710-1244 Hands Magazine
0710-1309 Holstein Journal 265
0710-1422 Delta Optimist 3808
0710-1457 Phoenix Rising†
0710-1481 Canadian Journal of Native Education 2834
0710-1511 Personal Financial Planning Letter†
0710-1678 Time Out†
0710-1759 Loi de l'Impot sur le Revenu du Canada et Reglement 1933
0710-1805 Martin's Related Criminal Statutes 4893
0710-2038 Audible†
0710-2054 Vie et Camping†
0710-2224 Canadian Imperial Bank of Commerce. Spectrum†
0710-2305 C R S S S de Quebec. Rapport Annuel changed to 1719-8593 8024
0710-2720 Equipment Journal 1007
0710-2747 Gryphon Theatre News†
0710-2755 Northern Ontario Business 1155
0710-2801 Ontario Golf News changed to 1709-2922 8241
0710-3034 Pig Paper 5233
0710-3360 Northwest Travel Guide - Northwest Territories†
0710-3417 M A L T Newsletter 5030
0710-362X P E M: Plant Engineering and Maintenance 1785
0710-3883 Beverly Page
0710-3891 Pass Herald Ltd. 3815
0710-3948 40-Mile County Commentator 3821
0710-4103 Camrose Booster 3807
0710-4278 Initiales 5127
0710-4340 Canadian Journal of Educational Communication changed to 1499-6677 3054
0710-4421 Canadian Equestrian News†
0710-4537 The Strand 2302
0710-4693 Cahiers de Recherche Ethique 7629
0710-4847 The Osprey 7896
0710-510X Fraternity for Canadian Astrologers. Fraternity News†
0710-5118 Communiqu'elles†
0710-5185 Le Pasquin†
0710-5371 Western Medical News†
0710-5568 Centrale de l'Enseignement du Quebec. Nouvelles 2835
0710-622X Canadian Oil & Gas Handbook†
0710-6629 Who's Who in Canadian Law
0710-6637 Conference Board of Canada. Fiscal Position of the Provinces
0710-6858 Saskatchewan Industry and Commerce. Annual Report†
0710-6874 Alberta Energy Resource Industries. Monthly Statistics 3150
0710-7269 see 0711-852X 8375
0710-7412 British Columbia Board of Parole. Annual Report 7423
0710-7544 Statistiques sur les Incendies de Foret au Canada changed to 0708-5788 3708
0710-7935 Pest Management Report 3700
0710-8648 Liquor Distribution Branch. Annual Report 7451
0710-8982 Bon Vivant
0710-9628 Key to Kingston 8727
0710-9911 Equinox†
0711-0014 British Columbia Summer Games. General Rules 8307
0711-0081 The Upper Canadian 369
0711-0316 Profits 1965
0711-0383 Ombudsman and Other Complaint-Handling Systems Survey
0711-0529 Societe Historique du Marigot, Longueuil. Cahier 4313
0711-0677 Choices 7115
0711-0685 Choix 7115
0711-0707 Great Lakes Pilotage Authority. Annual Report (Print Edition) 8644
0711-0782 Canada. Department of Fisheries and Oceans. Annual Report†
0711-0901 Rig Locator 6790
0711-0995 McGill-Queen's Studies in the History of Ideas 6933
0711-1215 Yukon Water Studies†
0711-124X Badminton Canada 8221
0711-1320 Canada. Environment Canada. Annual Report†
0711-1703 Directory of Labour Organizations in Canada 4593
0711-2157 Information Proche-Orient†
0711-2173 Canadian C.S. Lewis Journal 5270
0711-222X Journal of Leisurability†
0711-2270 Red Menace
0711-2416 Canadian Association of College and University Student Services. Bulletin†
0711-2521 Alberta Teachers' Association. Math Monograph
0711-2718 P A C Newsletter 3557
0711-2866 Canada. National Museums of Canada. Annual Bulletin†
0711-2998 Pool & Spa Marketing 1837
0711-3048 Choosing Life†
0711-3226 Score 8245
0711-3242 Canadian Energy Trends changed to 0848-9114 3125
0711-3277 Mining Review changed to 1911-0138 6470
0711-3374 Diesel Magazine
0711-3765 Dismantler†
0711-3773 Winnipeg Sun 3820
0711-382X Algonquian and Iroquoian Linguistics 5092
0711-4044 Red Cross Today†
0711-4222 Pakeeza International 3557
0711-4370 Cannon†
0711-4818 Cahiers des Arts Visuels au Quebec
0711-5210 Moving to Los Angeles & Orange Counties†
0711-5229 Moving to Greater San Diego†
0711-5342 Nexus (Hamilton)†
0711-5377 The Leader 2159
0711-5598 Quebec en Revue
0711-5601 Corpus Agribusiness Report†
0711-561X Corpus Plastics Report†
0711-5784 Energy Pricing News†
0711-589X Edmonton†
0711-6039 Centre for Resource Studies. Proceedings†
0711-6225 Chile Business Update
0711-6381 Energy changed to 0008-3100 1079
0711-6454 Snow Goer 8334
0711-6659 Canadian Acoustics 7087
0711-6683 S I M Now 7679
0711-6705 Capital Chinese News 3525
0711-6721 Canadian Data Report of Hydrography and Ocean Sciences 2801
0711-6748 Canadian Contractor Report of Hydrography and Ocean Sciences 2801
0711-6764 Canadian Technical Report of Hydrography and Ocean Sciences 2801
0711-6780 Environments 3429
0711-6829 L'Alliance (Montreal)†
0711-6896 Ontario Universities Benefits Survey 2997
0711-7108 Globehopper Magazine
0711-7140 Hazardous Waste Management Handbook†
0711-7388 Human: Life Issues for Canadians†
0711-7450 Langley Times 3812
0711-7485 Herizons 8867
0711-7590 Broadwater Market Letter†
0711-7884 D P Market Facts
0711-7914 Videomania
0711-7957 Sentier Chasse - Peche 8332
0711-7965 Polymetric Report. N Y S E Edition 1645
0711-818X Canada. Livestock Feed Board of Canada. Annual Report†
0711-8244 British Columbia Export-Import Opportunities†
0711-8422 Manitoba. Environmental Council. Topics†
0711-849X Ontario. Labour Relations Board. Annual Report 1701
0711-852X Gross Domestic Product by Industry 8375
0711-8635 Canadian Directory of Awards for Graduate Study (Year)†
0711-8813 Dalhousie French Studies 5110
0711-9828 C B C Classical Record Reference Book 6552
0712-0508 British Columbia. Office of the Ombudsman. Public Report Series 7424
0712-0761 Canada. Department of External Affairs. Statements and Speeches†
0712-1180 L'Etat du Monde (Year) 1563
0712-1318 Pundit 5355
0712-1326 Now 3815
0712-1539 Strike!†
0712-1571 see 0828-797X 8108
0712-2012 Econoscope 1481
0712-2470 Canadian Technical Asphalt Association. Proceedings of the Annual Conference†
0712-2519 C U E†
0712-2632 Jim Rennie's Sports Letter 8182
0712-2683 Truck News 8677
0712-2705 Petite Caisse
0712-3280 Canada Rugby News†
0712-337X Globule Rouge 2285
0712-3426 Atlantic Business†
0712-3620 Information for Collectors 6465
0712-3906 Montreal Office Space Directory
0712-435X Science Express X
0712-4384 Literary Markets†
0712-4422 Statutes of Quebec 4789
0712-4597 Province of British Columbia. Estimates 1259
0712-4627 Technostyle 5385
0712-4635 E D U Q†
0712-4724 Coulee Continue†
0712-4767 Renaissance Universal Journal
0712-4791 Monthly Economic Review 1720
0712-4813 Spectroscopy 745
0712-4996 Greenhouse Canada 3734
0712-5046 Health Management Forum†
0712-5143 Alberta Women†
0712-5348 North Shore News 3814
0712-5704 Shama 3563
0712-5747 Leisureways changed to 1910-0140 8690
0712-5828 Population Studies Centre. Highlights 7291
0712-5895 Toronto Construction News†
0712-6115 LibSat 5030
0712-6417 Windmill Herald: U.S. Edition 3572
0712-6662 Canada Tax Letter†
0712-6689 Ontario Medicine†
0712-6778 Canadian Operating Room Nursing Journal 5954
0712-6875 Canadian Clinical Laboratory
0712-7243 Resource-Mag†
0712-7456 Training Resources Tourism, Hospitality, Recreation†
0712-7561 Etudes Strategiques et Militaires (Collection) 5201
0712-774X Industrial Accident Prevention Association. Annual Review 6678
0712-8177 John Kettle's Futureletter†
0712-8231 Quebec (Province). Regie des Rentes du Quebec. Statistical Outlook†
0712-8290 The Record
0712-8304 Black Express†
0712-841X Legal Alert 4719
0712-8657 Teoros 8760
0712-8762 Canada. Statistics Canada. System of National Accounts, Provincial Gross Domestic Product by Industry†
0712-8991 White Wall Review 5398
0712-9068 Kingston This Week 3812
0712-9092 Steel Design 458
0712-9343 Alberta Insurance Directory 4492
0712-936X Human Factors Association of Canada. Communique changed to 1491-7971 6673
0712-9467 Technology Today†
0712-9939 Technical University of Nova Scotia. Newsletter†
0713-0082 Legislative Assembly of the Northwest Territories. Hansard 4835
0713-0341 Export News†
0713-0651 Legal Services Society of British Columbia. Annual Report changed to 1708-3605 4720
0713-0910 Supplementary Information to the Public Accounts. Details of Expenditure by Payee
0713-1348 Canadian Fisheries. Landings 1882
0713-214X Neologie en Marche†
0713-2158 Canadian Fisheries Annual Statistical Review 3588
0713-2840 Canada. Statistics Canada. Travel-log 8778
0713-3111 Connaissons Nos Voisins†
0713-3235 Canadian Woman Studies 8894
0713-3286 Canadian MoneySaver 1615
0713-3383 Pastoral Sciences changed to 1910-703X 6644
0713-3391 Worldview†
0713-3421 C S S E Contact†
0713-3545 Gamut
0713-357X Canadian Institute of Chartered Accountants. Uniform Final Examination Report 1284
0713-3901 Tales of the Twelve 6537
0713-3936 Canadian Journal of Community Mental Health (Print) changed to Canadian Journal of Community Mental Health (Online) 7343
0713-4118 Jeux et Jouets†
0713-4789 New Maritimes†
0713-4800 Municipalite 7454
0713-4819 Moving to Denver†
0713-5424 Graphics Interface. Proceedings 2486
0713-5815 Nyame Akuma 409
0713-6315 Antique Showcase changed to 1708-6469 8930
0713-6919 Information Construction
0713-7095 Saskatchewan Reports 4779

ISSN

0716-6117 Instituto de Chile. Anales **4457**
0716-6184 Terapia Psicologica **7412**
0716-6222 Revista Medica del Sur **5706**
0716-6311 Innovacion **8426**
0716-6346 Nueva Revista del Pacifico **5156**
0716-6427 Judaica Iberoamericana **3545**
0716-6478 Instituto de la Patagonia. Anales. Serie Ciencias Sociales **7973**
0716-6486 Instituto de la Patagonia. Anales. Serie Ciencias Naturales **678**
0716-677X Visiones Cientificas **7928**
0716-6869 Actas de Lengua y Literatura Mapuche **5091**
0716-6931 Revista Chilena de Obesidad **6668**
0716-7040 Cuadernos de Cirugia **6241**
0716-7105 Revista Chilena de Cardiologia **5798**
0716-730X Persona y Sociedad **7991**
0716-7334 Pontificia Universidad Catolica de Chile. Instituto de Economia. Documentos de Trabajo **1160**
0716-7555 Carta Hidrogeologica de Chile *changed to* 0717-7267 **2728**
0716-7628 Administracion y Economia UC **1723**
0716-775X Mercado de Suelo **449**
0716-7776 Cubo **5481**
0716-7784 Sociedad Chilena de Ciencia de Computacion. Boletin **2438**
0716-792X Revista de Ciencias Penales
0716-7989 Revista de Derecho Procesal†
0716-8039 Revista de Psicologia **7404**
0716-8098 Actas Colombinas **4281**
0716-8101 Ediciones de la Mujeres **8895**
0716-8136 Siglo XXI Ciencia and Tecnologia **7916**
0716-842X Chile. Instituto Nacional de Estadisticas. Industrias Manufactureras **1221**
0716-8446 Scientia. Series A: Mathematical Sciences **5533**
0716-8462 Estadisticas del Cobre y Otros Minerales Anuario **6485**
0716-8500 Universidad de Chile. Facultad de Odontologia. Revista **5868**
0716-8535 Revista Educarte **514**
0716-8594 Gastroenterologia Latinoamericana **5924**
0716-8756 Informacion Tecnologica **7865**
0716-8764 Agroeconomico **193**
0716-8810 La Bicicleta
0716-8861 Horizonte de Enfermeria **5960**
0716-8942 Nutram†
0716-8950 Veintiuno
0716-9108 Revista de Historia **4310**
0716-9132 Revista de Derecho (Valdivia) **4770**
0716-9140 Ladeco America
0716-9213 Universidad y Sociedad *changed to* 0717-991X **8135**
0716-9337 Revista Chilena de Ciencias Medico - Biologicas **5704**
0716-9396 Contribucion Arqueologica **388**
0716-9663 Actualidad Farmaceutica **6818**
0716-9671 Revista Tiempo y Espacio **4158**
0716-9698 Vas **6715**
0716-9760 Biological Research **658**
0716-9868 Revista Chilena de Anatomia *changed to* 0717-9367 **5639**
0717-0033 Economia y Trabajo en Chile **1098**
0717-005X Export Directory Chile **1992**
0717-0165 L I D E R **7286**
0717-0173 De Familias y Terapias **7351**
0717-0211 Revista Chilena de Investigacion Educacional **2905**
0717-0297 Psikhe **7394**
0717-036X Notas Historicas y Geograficas **4154**
0717-0572 Ingeniero Andino **6465**
0717-0580 Latinomineria **6468**
0717-0610 Investigacion y Desarrollo **7868**
0717-0653 Estudios de Administracion **1106**
0717-070X Revista Chilena de Administracion Publica **7466**
0717-0785 Revista Eidisis **5043**
0717-0815 Revista Chilena de Obstetricia y Ginecologia Infantil y de la Adolescencia **6003**
0717-0882 Revista del Profesor de Matematicas **5529**
0717-1013 Pensamiento Educativo **2897**
0717-1056 Mundo Precolombino **507**
0717-1072 Universidad de Tarapaca. Facultad de Ingenieria. Revista *changed to* 0718-3291 **3379**
0717-1099 Pentukun **351**
0717-1137 Revista Chilena de Docencia e Investigacion en Salud **2905**
0717-1285 Onomazein **5158**
0717-1404 Universidad de Santiago de Chile. Facultad de Humanidades. Revista **4479**
0717-1420 Educacion y Humanidades **4450**
0717-1463 Chile. Instituto Nacional de Estadisticas. Ciudades, Pueblos y Aldeas **8363**
0717-1498 Revista Fuerzas Armadas y Sociedad **7997**
0717-1587 Revista De Historia Indigena **4310**
0717-1609 Tierra Adentro **162**
0717-1641 Electricidad Interamericana **3157**
0717-182X Bionoticias **661**
0717-1846 Universidad Academia Humanismo Cristiano. Revista **4479**
0717-1862 Chile. Instituto Nacional de Estadisticas. Consumo Regional de Energia en la Industria Manufacturera **3151**
0717-1897 Boletin Chileno de Ornitologia **904**
0717-1900 Mujeres y Hombres en Chile. Cifras y Realidades **8389**
0717-1927 Boletin de Anestesiologia **5770**
0717-196X Theoria **3005**
0717-1978 Chile. Instituto Nacional de Estadisticas. Division Politico - Administrativa **8363**
0717-201X Revista Chilena de Radiologia **6207**
0717-2028 Plan Nacional de Recopilacion Estadistica **8394**
0717-2079 Ciencia y Enfermeria **5955**
0717-2087 Revista Chilena de Temas Sociologicos **8128**
0717-2117 Revista de Derecho de Aguas **8831**
0717-2125 Revista de Derecho de Minas **6477**
0717-2168 Humanitas **342**
0717-2257 Revista de Ciencias Sociales **7996**
0717-2273 Revista Chilena de Dermatologia **5881**
0717-229X Tercer Millenio **4584**
0717-2311 Agenda Salud **8843**
0717-2354 Pares cum Paribus **5349**
0717-2443 Instituto de Estudios del Pacifico. Boletin **1491**
0717-2478 Instituto de la Patagonia. Anales. Serie Ciencias Humanas *changed to* 0718-0209 **7984**
0717-2494 Boletin de Investigacion Educacional **2832**
0717-2532 Mapas Geologicos **2754**
0717-2567 Perspectivas†
0717-2621 Revista de Ciencias de la Salud **701**
0717-2664 Revista C & T **7903**
0717-2680 Consumidores y Desarrollo **1448**
0717-2761 Nomadias **7989**
0717-277X Chile. Servicio Nacional de Geologia y Mineria. Documentos de Trabajo **2729**
0717-2796 Carta Gravimetrica de Chile *changed to* 0717-7275 **7007**
0717-2869 Cyber Humanitatis **4449**
0717-2877 Ius et Praxis **4697**
0717-2885 Universidad de Valparaiso. Facultad de Arquitectura. Revista *changed to* 0718-4034 **449**
0717-2931 I S P R S Highlights **4014**
0717-2958 Ethno **2854**
0717-2966 Guia Silber. Directorio de Instituciones Chilenas **1998**
0717-3024 Correo de la Innovacion **7848**
0717-3075 Revista Chilena de Semiotica **5167**
0717-3105 Universidad Metropolitana de Ciencias de la Educacion. Revista **2922**
0717-313X Revista Chilena Cooperacion **7466**
0717-3172 Telemedia Internacional†
0717-3202 Revista Austral de Ciencias Sociales **7996**
0717-3210 Revista Chilena de Cancerologia y Hematologia **6033**
0717-327X Oikos **1782**
0717-3326 Revista de Biologia Marina y Oceanografia **701**
0717-3407 Chile. Servicio Nacional de Geologia y Mineria. Miscelanea **2729**
0717-344X Abante **1722**
0717-3458 Electronic Journal of Biotechnology **763**
0717-3504 Aerea **5415**
0717-3539 Conserva **4289**
0717-3644 Maderas **3713**
0717-3652 Revista Chilena de Salud Publica **7539**
0717-3660 Anuario de Cuentas Nacionales **1308**
0717-3695 Revista Chilena de Ultrasonografia **6207**
0717-3768 Perspectivas en Politica, Economia y Gestion **7165**
0717-3830 Economia Chilena **1098**
0717-3849 Ciencia al Dia Internacional **7846**
0717-3911 E P I Vision **5608**
0717-392X El Vigia **5828**
0717-3997 Urbano **460**
0717-4004 Calidad en la Educacion **2834**
0717-4055 A L A S B I M N Journal **6191**
0717-4063 Ius Publicum **4849**
0717-4101 Agronomia y Forestal UC **88**
0717-4195 Ingenieria Informatica **2423**
0717-4276 Sociedad Chilena de Ciencia de Computacion. Revista **2438**
0717-4292 Diadokhe **6914**
0717-4586 Asociacion Chilena de Seguridad. Boletin Cientifico *changed to* 0718-0306 **6675**
0717-4632 Chloris Chilensis **783**
0717-4659 Revista Chilena de Fonoaudiologia **6084**
0717-4667 Et Cetera **6917**
0717-4691 Ultima Decada **8145**
0717-4918 Gestion Ambiental **3433**
0717-4985 Castalia **7344**
0717-5000 C L E I Electronic Journal **4999**
0717-5051 Revista de Urbanismo **4425**
0717-5256 Revista de Estudios Trasandinos **4158**
0717-5302 Bioplanet **758**
0717-5337 Revista Chilena de Epilepsia **6181**
0717-5345 Revista de Derecho (Coquimbo) **4770**
0717-554X Cinta de Moebio **6910**
0717-5639 Werken **423**
0717-5698 Revista Chilena de Enfermedades Respiratorias **6219**
0717-5701 Doxa **6915**
0717-5744 Revista de Estudios Criminologicos y Penitenciarios **4897**
0717-5833 Revista Chilena de Medicina Intensiva **6072**
0717-5906 Acta Bioethica **5565**
0717-5965 Revista Chilena de Medicina Familiar **5704**
0717-6007 Akikai Chile (Print) *changed to* 0718-5669 **8156**
0717-6147 Revista Investigaciones en Educacion **2907**
0717-6163 *see* 0034-9887 **5706**
0717-6171 *see* 0071-1713 **5116**
0717-6201 *see* 0301-732X **8793**
0717-621X *see* 0716-5811 **5148**
0717-6228 *see* 0370-4106 **6103**
0717-6236 *see* 0250-7161 **4425**
0717-6252 *see* 0716-2790 **6611**
0717-6260 *see* 0716-5455 **4959**
0717-6279 *see* 0716-0917 **5526**
0717-6287 *see* 0716-9760 **658**
0717-6295 *see* 0049-3449 **7820**
0717-6317 *see* 0716-078X **700**
0717-6341 *see* 0716-1018 **5825**
0717-635X Revista de la Ciencia del Suelo y Nutricion Vegetal **250**
0717-6392 Estudios Politicos Militares **7133**
0717-6481 Voluntarios **8077**
0717-652X Gayana **944**
0717-6538 *see* 0717-652X **944**
0717-6554 Polis **7992**
0717-6643 *see* 0016-5301 **716**
0717-6732 Avance Agricola **93**
0717-6759 Estado, Gobierno, Gestion Publica **7435**
0717-6767 Revista Chilena de Terapia Ocupacional **6115**
0717-6821 *see* 0716-0046 **1089**
0717-6848 *see* 0716-0909 **5249**
0717-6945 R E X E **2902**
0717-6996 *see* 0716-0852 **426**
0717-7178 *see* 0716-1069 **701**
0717-7186 M E C E S U P. Boletin **2884**
0717-7194 *see* 0073-2435 **4295**
0717-7224 Pensamiento Critico
0717-7267 Carta Geologica de Chile. Serie Hidrogeologia **2728**
0717-7275 Carta Geologica de Chile. Serie Geofisica **7007**
0717-7283 Carta Geologica de Chile. Serie Geologica Basica **2728**
0717-7348 *see* 0717-5698 **6219**
0717-7356 Chungara (Arica) **387**
0717-7364 En Concreto **1006**
0717-7488 Revista Praxis†
0717-7518 *see* 0716-1549 **6668**
0717-7526 *see* 0048-766X **6003**
0717-7593 *see* 0716-7334 **1160**
0717-7704 Parasitologia Latinoamericana **894**
0717-7712 *see* 0717-7704 **894**
0717-7747 Bicentenario: Revista de Historia de Chile y America **4285**
0717-7798 Psicoperspectivas (Print) *changed to* 0718-6924 **7393**
0717-7887 Delegation Regionale de Cooperation dans le Cone Sud et le Bresil. Bulletin Eletronique **7850**
0717-7917 Boletin Latinoamericano y del Caribe de Plantas Medicinales y Aromaticas **780**
0717-7925 Revista de la Construccion **3282**
0717-8085 *see* 0716-3576 **3822**
0717-8506 *see* 0718-1655 **484**
0717-8573 *see* 0717-5302 **758**
0717-8697 *see* 0716-162X **2318**
0717-876X Revista Chilena de Antropologia Visual **353**
0717-8816 Aldea Periodismo **4571**
0717-8883 *see* 0365-7779 **5243**
0717-8891 Universidad de Chile. Facultad de Ciencias Fisicas y Matematicas. Boletin Informativo **5543**
0717-8905 Universidad de Chile. Facultad de Medicina. Boletin Informativo **5726**
0717-8913 Boletin Climatico **6347**
0717-8948 Ciencia Abierta **7846**
0717-8956 Circular de Extension. Publicacion Tecnico Ganadera **101**
0717-8972 *see* 0378-4509 **280**
0717-8980 *see* 0717-6759 **7435**
0717-9154 Jurimetria **4706**
0717-9162 Revista Chilena de Derecho Informatico **4770**
0717-9200 *see* 0304-8799 **3685**
0717-9227 *see* 0034-7388 **6181**
0717-9235 Fosil **6724**
0717-9308 *see* 0717-201X **6207**
0717-9324 The Chilean Chemical Society. Journal **2058**
0717-9367 International Journal of Morphology **5639**
0717-9502 *see* 0717-9367 **5639**
0717-9553 *see* 0717-2079 **5955**
0717-9618 Revista Chilena de Educacion Cientifica **7903**
0717-9707 *see* 0717-9324 **2058**
0717-9758 Diseno Urbano y Paisaje **4409**
0717-9812 Innova **446**
0717-9863 Clinic@s de Medicina Critica **5598**
0717-9898 E-rural **2844**
0717-991X Sociedad & Conocimiento **8135**
0718-0012 *see* 0717-2877 **4697**
0718-0039 Pez de Plata **5039**
0718-0179 Actuel Marx Intervenciones **7102**
0718-0195 Estudios Constitucionales **4848**
0718-0209 Magallania **7984**
0718-0233 Revista Chilena de Derecho Privado **4841**
0718-0241 Revista Enfoques **7466**
0718-0306 Ciencia & Trabajo **6675**
0718-0330 Boletin Olivicola **281**
0718-0349 Boletin de Flores **97**
0718-0357 Boletin de Plantas Medicinales y Aromaticas **780**
0718-0365 Boletin de Hortalizas **3725**
0718-0373 Boletin de Frutales de Nuez **222**
0718-039X Boletin de Caprinos **281**
0718-0403 Boletin de Ovinos **281**
0718-0411 Boletin de Camelidos **281**
0718-042X Boletin de Bovinos **281**
0718-0438 Boletin de Frutales **97**
0718-0446 Suma Psicologia UST **7411**
0718-0454 Ecoengen **3416**
0718-0462 *see* 0716-1840 **4443**
0718-0527 Revista M A D **354**
0718-0543 Chile. Ministerio Publico. Boletin **4642**
0718-0551 Revista Chilena de Neuropsicologia **6181**
0718-056X Parthenon **3280**
0718-0586 Cuadernos Interculturales **8096**
0718-0705 *see* 0716-050X **2980**
0718-073X Ingenieria al Dia **7866**
0718-0764 *see* 0716-8756 **7865**
0718-0888 Visiones de la Educacion **2925**
0718-090X *see* 0716-1417 **7262**
0718-0918 Revista Pediatria Electronica **6103**
0718-0934 *see* 0035-0451 **5361**
0718-0950 *see* 0716-9132 **4770**
0718-0969 *see* 0716-2006 **2802**
0718-1043 *see* 0716-0925 **392**
0718-1094 Revista para la Gestion del Trabajo **4601**
0718-1124 Centros de Documentacion. Boletin **100**
0718-1132 Bifurcaciones **8090**
0718-1140 Revista Chilena de Periodoncia y Oseointegracion **5863**
0718-1213 Revista Chilena de Educacion Matematica **5529**
0718-1221 Ciudadano de Dos Mundos **5274**
0718-123X Agenda Publica **7419**
0718-1299 Instituto Nacional de la Vivienda. Revista **446**
0718-1302 Revista de Derecho de la Empresa **4880**
0718-1329 Iter **5131**
0718-1361 Limite **6932**
0718-1442 Ingenerare **3197**
0718-1515 Complexus **7513**
0718-1566 *see* 0716-1921 **1158**
0718-1655 Culturart **484**
0718-1671 Ciencias Sociales Online **7955**
0718-1698 Sociedad de Psiquiatria y Neurologia de la Infancia y Adolescencia. Revista *changed to* Revista Chilena de Psiquiatria y Neurologia de la Infiancia y la Adolescencia **6181**
0718-1795 *see* 1871-0204 **1289**

ISSN

ISSN

0723-7871 Jahrbuch des Museums fur Kunst und Gewerbe Hamburg **6526**
0723-791X Oesterreichische Akademie der Wissenschaften. Abteilung 1: Biologische Wissenschaften und Erdwissenschaften. Sitzungsberichte und Anzeiger **695**
0723-7928 Lehrer im Berufsfeld Koerperpflege†
0723-8010 Aerztliches Mitteilungsblatt Schwaben†
0723-8029 Deutsche Gesellschaft fuer Gynaekologie und Geburtshilfe. Mitteilungen **5989**
0723-8037 V W D - Vieh und Fleisch **1657**
0723-8061 WerWasWo? im Taschenbuch†
0723-8088 Kulturrevolution **7150**
0723-8177 Turmschreiber Kalender **5391**
0723-8274 Der Gemeinderat **7492**
0723-8398 East Asia†
0723-8428 Documenta Naturae **2732**
0723-8630 Funde und Ausgrabungen im Bezirk Trier **395**
0723-8649 Forschungen und Berichte zur Volkskunde in Baden-Wuerttemberg **4220**
0723-8673 Hermetika†
0723-8886 Medizinrecht **5915**
0723-8975 I F O Studien zur Entwicklungsforschung. Sonderreihe Information und Dokumentation **1597**
0723-9289 Mad **5226**
0723-9297 Budo und Transkulturelle Bewegungsforschung†
0723-9408 Praxis der Werbung **32**
0723-9416 Zeitschrift fuer Wirtschaftsrecht - Z I P **4819**
0723-9505 Zeitschrift fuer Systemische Therapie *changed to* Zeitschrift fuer Systemische Therapie und Beratung **7416**
0723-9580 Frau in Unserer Zeit†
0723-9629 Betriebswirtschaftliche Blaetter **1728**
0723-9653 Ostsprachige Fachliteratur: Ausgabe Osteuropa Bauwesen†
0723-9688 Ostsprachige Fachliteratur: Ausgabe Osteuropa, Chemie, Chemische Technik, Kunststoffe†
0723-970X Ostsprachige Fachliteratur: Ausgabe Osteuropa Elektrotechnik, Energietechnik†
0723-9726 Ostsprachige Fachliteratur: Ausgabe Osteuropa Geowissenschaften, Bergbau†
0723-9734 Ostsprachige Fachliteratur: Ausgabe Osteuropa Huettenwesen, Werkstoffkunde†
0723-9750 Ostsprachige Fachliteratur: Ausgabe Osteuropa Maschinenbau, Apparatebau, Fertigungstechnik, Technik der Verkehrsmittel†
0723-9769 International Joseph Martin Kraus-Gesellschaft. Mitteilungen **6576**
0723-9793 Ostsprachige Fachliteratur: Ausgabe Osteuropa Mathematik, Physik†
0723-9807 Ostsprachige Fachliteratur: Ausgabe Osteuropa Regelungstechnik, Automation, Kybernetik†
0723-9815 Ostsprachige Fachliteratur: Ausgabe Osteuropa Umweltprobleme†
0723-9874 Kieler Geographische Schriften **4018**
0723-9912 Entomologischer Verein Apollo. Nachrichten **846**
0723-9920 Nachrichten des Entomologischen Vereins Apollo. Supplementum *see* 0723-9912 **846**
0724-0090 Sprichwoerterforschung **5178**
0724-0155 Die Bromelie **782**
0724-0252 Der Dialysepatient **6267**
0724-0279 Horizont (Cologne)
0724-0376 Zahnaerzte Wirtschaftsdienst **5869**
0724-0686 Ausschuss Volkswirtschaft des G D V **4493**
0724-0708 Passauer Pegasus
0724-0775 Fachhochschule fuer Bibliotheks- und Dokumentationswesen in Koeln. Amtliche Mitteilungen†
0724-0856 B M F T Journal†
0724-1054 Chemical Plants & Processing **3239**
0724-1062 Tanzen **2688**
0724-1119 Baby Post **2144**
0724-1194 Flugasche†
0724-1208 Rheinische Friedrich-Wilhelms-Universitaet. Institut fuer Tierzuchtwissenschaft. Arbeiten **298**
0724-1348 Heterocera Sumatrana **848**
0724-1445 American University Studies. Series 3. Comparative Literature **5253**
0724-1569 Teppe und Gelaender†
0724-1593 Technische Revue **8441**
0724-1631 Bagatelle†
0724-1720 Process Engineering Magazine†
0724-1747 Randspringer†
0724-1976 Verein Deutscher Ingenieure. Informationsdienst. Instandhaltung *changed to* Informationsdienst F I Z Technik. Instandhaltung **3230**
0724-2034 Arcus†
0724-2050 Verkehrsunfall und Fahrzeugtechnik **8610**
0724-2174 African Biographies†
0724-2247 Recht & Psychiatrie **7402**
0724-2263 Islamic Book Review Index†
0724-2298 International Annual Bibliography of Festschriften **627**
0724-2344 V D L - Journal **167**
0724-2514 Bunte Blaetter†
0724-2522 Marburger Germanistische Studien†
0724-2557 Schriften des Werksarchivs
0724-2565 Bau-Trends†
0724-2573 Diabetes Mellitus†
0724-2603 Horvath Blaetter†
0724-2654 Deutsche Jagd-Zeitung **8311**
0724-2689 Delfin
0724-2778 Una Voce Korrespondenz **7822**
0724-3103 Sprachwissenschaft - Computerlinguistik **5204**
0724-3227 Norddeutscher Molkerei- und Kaeserei-Adresskalender
0724-3235 Sueddeutscher Molkerei- und Kaeserei-Adresskalender **269**
0724-3324 Wechselwirkungen **3010**
0724-3332 Gruppe und Spiel **3063**
0724-3375 Seibt Pharma-Technik†
0724-343X Kultur-Chronik (German Edition) *changed to* 1614-595X
0724-3464 Sozialwissenschaften und Berufspraxis **8007**
0724-3472 Tribologie und Schmierungstechnik **3257**
0724-3529 Militaria **6435**
0724-360X Das Personal A B C **4757**
0724-3618 Kindergesundheit†
0724-3707 Speisen und Reisen†
0724-3766 Zwischenschritte **7416**
0724-3790 Baden-Wuerttemberg. Statistisches Landesamt. Statistisch-Prognostischer Bericht **7478**
0724-3820 Leben und Weg **8053**
0724-3847 Punto Tecnica y Moda
0724-3901 S S I P - Bulletin **8130**
0724-3944 Handel†
0724-4096 Beitraege zur Volkskultur in Nordwestdeutschland **4204**
0724-4142 Wirtschaft im Revier **1412**
0724-4177 Agrargeographie†
0724-4215 Camp **8307**
0724-4223 Bombus **841**
0724-4266 Deutsche Getraenke Wirtschaft **602**
0724-4290 Bau-Intern **8818**
0724-4304 Marburger Studien zur Vor- und Fruehgeschichte **4242**
0724-4339 G M D - Spiegel† **8958**
0724-4347 Forschungen und Berichte zur Vor- und Fruehgeschichte in Baden-Wuerttemberg **394**
0724-4401 Dokumentationsdienst Bildung und Kultur†
0724-441X Fortschritte der Medizinischen Mikrobiologie†
0724-4479 Philosophie und Geschichte der Wissenschaften **6942**
0724-4495 Revier und Werk **6477**
0724-4509 Export-Markt, Euro-Revue†
0724-4606 Raps **249**
0724-4681 I C-Wissen Buerokommunikation
0724-4703 Freiburger Fernoestliche Forschungen **549**
0724-472X Wolfenbuetteler Arbeiten zur Barockforschung **4279**
0724-4770 Schwebstaubmessungen in Hessen. Bericht im Messjahr **3491**
0724-486X Aspekte der Englischen Geistes- und Kulturgeschichte **5097**
0724-4908 Eberbacher Geschichtsblatt **4216**
0724-4967 W B K Forschungsberichte **3226**
0724-4983 World Journal of Urology **6277**
0724-5130 European Journal of Cell Biology. Supplement *see* 0171-9335 **832**
0724-5165 Die Kerbe **8052**
0724-5246 Orientierungen zur Gesellschafts- und Wirtschaftspolitik **7990**
0724-5262 Das Schullandheim **2962**
0724-5343 Der Deutsche Lehrer im Ausland **5111**
0724-5572 Selbsthilfe **8067**
0724-5580 L Z Rheinland **132**
0724-5637 Deutsche Steuer-Zeitung **1920**
0724-567X Neue Arzneimittel **6863**
0724-5688 Karlsruher Paedagogische Beitraege **3069**
0724-6110 OrganisationsEntwicklung **1157**
0724-6137 Berliner Theologische Zeitschrift **7748**
0724-6145 Advances in Biochemical Engineering. Biotechnology **755**
0724-6153 Getraenkefachgrosshandel **604**
0724-6226 Contactologia-Bucherei
0724-6234 Trialog **4428**
0724-6285 Muenchner Studien zur Neueren und Neuesten Geschichte **4246**
0724-6307 Trichogramma News†
0724-6331 Palaeo Ichthyologica **960**
0724-6358 Gemeinsame Koerperschaftsdatei†
0724-6404 Patientenpost†
0724-6412 Dichtungsring **5284**
0724-6471 Holz Aktuell†
0724-6528 Haeuser **4411**
0724-6579 Universitaetsbibliothek Eichstaett. Schriften **5052**
0724-6609 Bad Homburger Aktuell†
0724-6617 Deutsche Wohnungswirtschaft **7588**
0724-6633 Deutsches Bundes-Adressbuch: Industrie, Gross- und Aussenhandel, Dienstleistungen, Organisationen†
0724-6706 Einstein Quarterly Journal of Biology and Medicine *changed to* 1559-5501 **670**
0724-6722 Abacus (New York)†
0724-6803 J M C I: Journal of Molecular and Cellular Immunology†
0724-6811 M.D. Computing (New York)†
0724-696X Brauwelt **600**
0724-6978 Discret **6562**
0724-6994 Arbeitsgestaltung fuer Behinderte†
0724-7001 Buchwissenschaftliche Beitraege aus dem Deutschen Bucharchiv Muenchen **7556**
0724-715X Arbeitskreis Deutsche England-Forschung. Veroeffentlichung **4199**
0724-7192 Bahnsport Aktuell **8254**
0724-7265 Thyssen Edelstahl Technische Berichte†
0724-7281 GaFa - Gartenfachhandel Saatgutwirtschaft
0724-7389 Horus **4081**
0724-7435 D C G Informationen **939**
0724-7508 Journal Film **6504**
0724-7567 Mediterranean Language Review **555**
0724-7613 Kaufmaennische Schule **2880**
0724-7656 Zelluloid†
0724-7664 Omnibusspiegel **8507**
0724-7699 Architekten- und Ingenieurhandbuch **431**
0724-7729 European Patent Office. Annual Report **6749**
0724-7885 Staatsanzeiger fuer das Land Hessen **4787**
0724-7923 System ubw **7411**
0724-8016 Ilco-Praxis **6021**
0724-8156 Jahrbuch fuer Opernforschung†
0724-8164 Besprechungen Annotationen **4994**
0724-8199 Speedway International†
0724-8342 Fahren in Europa **8703**
0724-8415 Bibliography of Chinese Studies†
0724-8482 Jahrbuch Stahl **6318**
0724-8490 Packung und Transport†
0724-8679 C'T **2415**
0724-8717 World Guide to Special Libraries **5055**
0724-8741 Pharmaceutical Research **6870**
0724-8784 Schriftenreihe Lebensmittelchemie, Lebensmittelqualitaet **3662**
0724-8822 Archivum Eurasiae Medii Aevi **543**
0724-8857 Bayerisches Bienen-Blatt **95**
0724-8954 Archaeologische Ausgrabungen in Baden-Wuerttemberg **377**
0724-9012 Piscium Catalogus **6729**
0724-9144 Theorie und Vermittlung der Sprache **5187**
0724-9152 Mannheimer Beitraege zum Arbeitsrecht†
0724-9519 Z Das Neue Zeitalter†
0724-956X Wolfenbuetteler Abhandlungen zur Renaissanceforschung **4279**
0724-9578 Repertorien zur Erforschung der Freuhen Neuzeit **4257**
0724-9586 Wolfenbuetteler Schriften zur Geschichte des Buchwesens **7329**
0724-9594 Wolfenbuetteler Forschungen **4279**
0724-9616 Informationen Deutsch als Fremdsprache **2986**
0724-9624 Das Abendland **4439**
0724-9632 Planung & Analyse **1837**
0724-9756 Abhandlungen zu den Wirtschaftlichen Staatswissenschaften **1535**
0724-9764 German Chapter of the A C M. Berichte **2419**
0724-9780 Forum Loccum **7758**
0724-9950 Apotheken-Magazin **6822**
0725-0096 Scripsi†
0725-0207 S L A N T News†
0725-0290 Labour Resourcer
0725-0320 Reserve Bank of Australia. Bulletin **1260**
0725-0355 Tasmanian Conservationist **2628**
0725-0371 Commonwealth Taxation Board of Review Decisions†
0725-0509 Copyright Reporter **6748**
0725-0568 Victorian Gemmology Newsletter
0725-0665 Australian Credit Unions Magazine
0725-1122 Health in Schools†
0725-1181 Australia. Bureau of Statistics. Victorian Office. Victoria at a Glance†
0725-1394 Australian Sound & Broadcast
0725-1424 Herpetofauna **946**
0725-1831 Spanish Herald **3565**
0725-184X Emek†
0725-2110 Interlocking Concrete Paving Review†
0725-2293 Australia. Australian Water Resources Council. Occasional Papers Series†
0725-2323 Philas News **6898**
0725-2390 A P S A Newsletter†
0725-2455 Diary of Social Legislation and Policy†
0725-2803 Social Sciences Bibliography Series†
0725-2919 Technical Aid to the Disabled Journal **4070**
0725-3079 Byzantina Australiensia **4208**
0725-3141 Communicable Diseases Intelligence *changed to* 1447-4514 **5812**
0725-3915 Historic Australia
0725-3931 Your Computer†
0725-4415 Australian Personal Computer **2574**
0725-4644 Insurance Record of Australia & New Zealand† **8965**
0725-4695 Australia. Australian Water Resources Council. Conference Series†
0725-4709 M I M S Annual **6859**
0725-4857 Australia. Bureau of Statistics. Queensland Office. Hospital Morbidity, Queensland†
0725-4946 This Australia†
0725-4989 Arbovirus Research in Australia **5810**
0725-5136 Thesis Eleven **7188**
0725-5454 Agricultural Trends†
0725-5489 Infocab† **8964**
0725-5543 Brave New Word
0725-5810 Australian Transport Literature Information System. Bulletin†
0725-6108 Hearsay† **8961**
0725-6361 New South Wales. Agriculture and Fisheries. Plant Disease Survey†
0725-6590 Ghalib **3535**
0725-6639 Tension
0725-6701 Horticultural Trends†
0725-6868 Journal of Intercultural Studies **3544**
0725-7066 Sterilization in Australia **7542**
0725-7333 Pig Industry News†
0725-8526 Commonwealth Scientific and Industrial Research Organization. Division of Soils. Divisional Report†
0725-8968 Hostelling†
0725-9107 Guide to Collections of Manuscripts Relating to Australia†
0725-914X Progenitor **3780**
0725-9158 Register of Australian Mining **6477**
0725-9417 Diving Down Under
0726-0458 Nelen Yubu† **8976**
0726-0784 Queensland Law Reporter **4764**
0726-0822 Australian Society of Sugar Cane Technologists. Proceedings **3627**
0726-0865 Steel Profile† **8990**
0726-1152 Friends of the Australian Ballet. Bulletin
0726-125X Traverse
0726-1268 Between the Leaves **3684**
0726-1276 A B N Authorities†
0726-1292 Australian Songs. Series†
0726-1306 Songs of New South Wales. Series†
0726-1314 Songs of Victoria. Series†
0726-1322 Songs of South Australia. Series†
0726-1330 Songs of Queensland. Series†
0726-1349 Songs of Western Australia. Series†
0726-1357 Songs of Tasmania. Series†
0726-1365 Songs of Northern Territory. Series†
0726-1527 South Australia. Department of Mines and Energy. Special Publications†
0726-1772 Commonwealth Scientific and Industrial Research Organization. Institute of Energy and Earth Resources. Technical Communication†
0726-1780 Commonwealth Scientific and Industrial Research Organization. Institute of Energy and Earth Resources. Investigation Report†
0726-1799 National Buckskin Society. Newsletter **8295**
0726-1810 Mad Magazine Australia **2200**
0726-1888 The Stilt **915**
0726-2256 Australian Horticulture **3723**
0726-2418 4 x 4 Australia **8613**
0726-2469 Western Australian Nature Reserve Management Plan†
0726-2566 Australian Beauty Counter†
0726-2612 New Times **7768**

ISSN

0726-2639	Ed Notes: Australian Union of Students Research Briefs	
0726-2655	Education and Society **2847**	
0726-3252	Australian Communication Review†	
0726-3449	Flora of Australia **789**	
0726-3554	Royal Australian Historical Society. Annual Report and Statement of Accounts *see* 0035-8762 **4194**	
0726-3554	Royal Australian Historical Society. Annual Report and Statement of Accounts *see* 1031-9476 **4194**	
0726-3589	Creative Source Australia	
0726-3759	Queensland Reports **4959**	
0726-3872	South Australian Pamphlets of Verse **5435**	
0726-3929	University of Western Australia. School of Music. Music Monograph **6625**	
0726-4097	Victorian Baptist Witness **7779**	
0726-4127	Scan (Ryde) **5045**	
0726-4143	Editor's Clip Sheets **7755**	
0726-416X	Curriculum and Teaching **3056**	
0726-4275	Commonwealth Scientific and Industrial Research Organization. Marine Laboratories. Circular†	
0726-4283	Commonwealth Scientific and Industrial Research Organization. Marine Laboratories. Microfiche Report†	
0726-4305	Lutheran Church of Australia. Yearbook **7765**	
0726-4399	Primitiae†	
0726-4607	Austra-Link **2692**	
0726-4623	Plantline†	
0726-4844	University of Wollongong. Legislation†	
0726-4860	Die Woche in Australien **3572**	
0726-4941	Australian Folk Directory	
0726-4976	Australia. Bureau of Statistics. Selected Agricultural Commodities, Australia, Preliminary†	
0726-5018	Australian Optometry **6039**	
0726-5093	Sunshine Express **8625**	
0726-5247	Periodontology **5861**	
0726-5646	Australian Sailing **8271**	
0726-5816	Administrative Law Decisions **4610**	
0726-5824	Family Law Reports **4910**	
0726-5883	Australian Industrial Law Review†	
0726-5956	Australian Consumer Sales and Credit Law Reporter	
0726-6065	Australian Company Law & Practice†	
0726-626X	Leaping **7738**	
0726-6472	Maritime Studies **8653**	
0726-6510	Commonwealth Scientific and Industrial Research Organization. Division of Geomechanics. Geomechanics of Coal Mining Report	
0726-657X	C S I R O Net News†	
0726-6715	Historic Environment	
0726-6987	Australian Waste Disposal Catalogue†	
0726-7002	Victoria, Australia. Department of Education. Education Nationally and Internationally†	
0726-7215	Flinders Journal of History and Politics **4191**	
0726-7304	News Weekly **3795**	
0726-7819	Australian Coal Miner	
0726-8416	University of New England. Animal Genetics and Breeding Unit. Occasional Report†	
0726-8602	Australian Journal of Linguistics **5097**	
0726-9072	Mask **3072**	
0726-934X	Western Australia. Department of Agriculture. Farmnote **170**	
0726-9498	Wine Industry Newsletter **259**	
0726-9501	Western Australia. Department of Industrial Development. Building Investment†	
0726-951X	Western Australia Products Directory†	
0726-9587	Joint Serials Catalogue of Western Australian Academic Libraries†	
0726-9609	The Western Australian Naturalist **7929**	
0726-9897	The Skeptic **6743**	
0727-0003	Asphalt Review **3259**	
0727-0046	Altro Polo† **8929**	
0727-0097	Advances in the Study of the Sydney Basin. Symposium Proceedings **2723**	
0727-0119	Green Pages: Directory of Non-Government Environmental Groups in Australia **2613**	
0727-078X	Australian Retail Tobacconist **8485**	
0727-1239	Artlink **473**	
0727-1255	Classroom **3054**	
0727-1301	Communitas **2317**	
0727-1409	1:100 000 Geological Map Commentary **2776**	
0727-145X	Australia. Bureau of Statistics. Pocket Year Book, Australia†	
0727-2170	Australia. Bureau of Statistics. Western Australian Office. Value of Agricultural Commodities Produced, Western Australia†	
0727-2200	Australia. Bureau of Statistics. Western Australian Office. Census of Manufacturing Establishments. Summary of Operations by Group, Western Australia†	
0727-2308	Australia. Bureau of Statistics. Western Australian Office. Motor Vehicle Registrations, Western Australia (Annual)†	
0727-2456	Facts on Women at Work in Australia†	
0727-2596	Australian Energy Statistics†	
0727-2731	Australia. Air Transport Statistics. Airline Aircraft Utilisation†	
0727-2758	Australia. Air Transport Statistics. Aerial Agriculture Operations†	
0727-2774	Australia. Air Transport Statistics. Flight Crew Licences†	
0727-2790	Australia. Air Transport Statistics. Monthly Provisional Statistics of International Scheduled Air Transport (print) *changed to* Australia. Air Transport Statistics. Monthly Provisional Statistics of International Scheduled Air Transport (Online) **8521**	
0727-2979	Business Indicators†	
0727-2987	Australia. Australia - China Council Annual Report†	
0727-3061	Historical Records of Australian Science **7861**	
0727-307X	Biology in Action	
0727-3126	Australian Rowing†	
0727-3215	Australasian Catholic Record **7785**	
0727-338X	Australian Air Pilot **8538**	
0727-3541	The Australian Gas Industry Directory **6763**	
0727-3851	Australian Medliner†	
0727-386X	A N U Reporter **2271**	
0727-3975	Cameras & Lenses†	
0727-3983	Photoworld Buyer's Guide. Photoguide†	

0727-4076	Annual Survey of Australian Law†	
0727-4092	Australian Arabian Horse News **8287**	
0727-4181	Commonwealth of Australia. Parliament. Parliamentary Paper **7431**	
0727-419X	Australian Journal of Coal Mining Technology and Research†	
0727-4211	Collection of Australian Stamps **6893**	
0727-517X	Australia. Bureau of Statistics. Western Australian Office. Agriculture, Western Australia†	
0727-5366	Environment Victoria	
0727-5757	New South Wales Mineral Industry Review†	
0727-5803	Victorian Consultative Committee on Social Development. Annual Review†	
0727-6125	Australia. Sea Transport Statistics. Stevedoring Industrial Disputes. Nature of Issue and Extent†	
0727-615X	Freesail†	
0727-6281	Queensland. Department of Primary Industries. Project Report **149**	
0727-6311	Acts of the Parliament of the Commonwealth of Australia **7418**	
0727-6346	Property Law & Practice in Queensland **4762**	
0727-6672	Australia. Air Transport Statistics. Australian Air Distances **8521**	
0727-6680	Monash University. Centre of Southeast Asian Studies. Monash Papers on Southeast Asia **4186**	
0727-6753	Directory of C S I R O Research Programs†	
0727-6982	Review of Australia's Demographic Trends†	
0727-758X	B R W **1064**	
0727-7830	Local Government Law & Practice New South Wales **7496**	
0727-792X	Planning & Development Service New South Wales **4758**	
0727-7946	Jacobs' County Court Practice†	
0727-7954	Jackson and Byron Local Courts (Civil Claims) Practice *changed to* N S W Civil Practice & Procedure **4838**	
0727-7989	Local Government Index New South Wales **7481**	
0727-8047	Baalman & Wells Land Titles Office Practice N S W **4625**	
0727-8101	Light Railways **8620**	
0727-8225	Study at Macquarie **3003**	
0727-8926	A P A I S: Australian Public Affairs Information Service (Print)†	
0727-9078	New South Wales. Department of Agriculture. Soil Survey Bulletin	
0727-9264	New South Wales. Department of Mineral Resources. Annual Report. Statistical Supplement†	
0727-9620	Cunninghamia **785**	
0728-0351	Christophany† **8941**	
0728-0394	Totline **2170**	
0728-0408	Plumbers News *changed to* Plumbing Union News **4125**	
0728-0556	Traveltalk *changed to* 1832-4134 **8768**	
0728-067X	Queensland. Department of Primary Industries. Conference and Workshop Series **1902**	
0728-0696	Queensland Department of Primary Industries. Study Tour Report **149**	
0728-0734	Trends in Animal Industries†	
0728-0858	Queensland Potters Association. Annual Report of the Directors **2044**	
0728-0874	Government Equipment News *changed to* 1447-0500	
0728-0904	Ragtrader **2249**	
0728-0912	Vox Reformata **7779**	
0728-1897	Melbourne Citymission. Annual Report **8055**	
0728-2249	Australia. Bureau of Statistics. New South Wales Office. Deaths, New South Wales†	
0728-2311	Western Australia. Geological Survey. Records **2774**	
0728-2400	Australian Uranium Association. Newsletter **6457**	
0728-294X	Australia. Bureau of Statistics. Queensland Office. Health and Welfare Establishments, Queensland†	
0728-3008	Consuming Interest†	
0728-3873	What's New in Electronics **3116**	
0728-4152	High Court of Australia. Annual Report **4952**	
0728-4217	Australia. Bureau of Statistics. Tasmanian Office. Principal Agricultural Commodities, Tasmania, Preliminary†	
0728-4527	Australia. Bureau of Statistics. Shearing and Wool Production Forecast, Australia, Preliminary†	
0728-4543	Australia. Bureau of Statistics. Child Care Arrangements, Australia, Preliminary†	
0728-4632	Australian Pharmacist **6823**	
0728-4764	The South Sea Digest†	
0728-4845	Newsmonth **4599**	
0728-5132	Australia. Bureau of Statistics. Queensland Office. Census of Mining Establishments: Details of Operations by Industry Sub-division, Queensland†	
0728-5167	Australian Footballer	
0728-5582	Council and Community† **8944**	
0728-5620	Australian Chess Lore†	
0728-5701	Image **6969**	
0728-5884	Monash University. Centre of Policy Studies. Discussion Paper Series†	
0728-5914	Meridian **5333**	
0728-5965	Animal Production in Australia (Print)†	
0728-5981	Motor Vehicle Law. Queensland **4736**	
0728-6309	Australian Planning Appeal Decisions†	
0728-635X	Employers' Review†	
0728-6414	A N A R E News†	
0728-6422	Heritage Australia†	
0728-6481	Dixson Library Report†	
0728-6503	In Unity (Online) **8046**	
0728-6910	Australia. National Health and Medical Research Council. Department of Health. Report of the (No.) Session†	
0728-6929	Australia. Department of Primary Industry. Poultry Industry Assistance. Annual Report†	
0728-7143	Australian Tourist Commission. Annual Report *changed to* Tourism Australia. Annual Report **8763**	
0728-7216	Remuneration Tribunal. Annual Report **7465**	
0728-7275	Owner Builder Magazine **1028**	
0728-7372	Scarp†	
0728-7399	Australien Kurier† **8934**	
0728-7445	Martin Place Papers†	

0728-7550	Peace Dossier†	
0728-7569	Contact (Goodna)	
0728-7704	Government of South Australia. Department for Environment and Heritage. Board of the Botanic Gardens and State Herbarium. Annual Report **791**	
0728-7933	South Australian Housing Trust. Annual Report **4427**	
0728-8409	Pacific Economic Papers *changed to* 1834-8971 **1552**	
0728-8417	Industrial Arbitration Service. Industrial Reports **4870**	
0728-859X	A I A S Occasional Publication **77**	
0728-8727	National Dog **6811**	
0728-9006	Secondary Journal (Sydney)†	
0728-909X	Sunshine Bulletin **2270**	
0728-912X	Working Together Nationally†	
0728-9359	Majalah Ikawiria	
0728-9405	Australia. Department of the Treasury. Annual Report **1438**	
0728-9413	F E N **8422**	
0728-9502	Australia. Australian Water Resources Council. Water Management Series†	
0729-011X	Geological Society of Australia. Abstracts Series **2719**	
0729-0403	Ebb and Flow†	
0729-0446	Social Accounting Monitor†	
0729-056X	Commonwealth Scientific and Industrial Research Organization. Institute of Energy and Earth Resources. Annual Report†	
0729-1485	Journal of Law and Information Science **4702**	
0729-154X	The History Teacher *changed to* 1834-5131 **2901**	
0729-1957	Videoworld†	
0729-1965	Videoworld Buyer's Guide Annual†	
0729-199X	Public Libraries in Western Australia. Statistical Bulletin† **8983**	
0729-2236	Nation (Melbourne)†	
0729-2368	New Zealand and Dependencies Stamp Catalogue†	
0729-2384	Auditopics	
0729-2430	Queensland Manufacturers Directory†	
0729-2449	Hermit Press Pamphlets† **8962**	
0729-2473	War & Society **4166**	
0729-2570	Supreme and District Courts Practice N S W *changed to* N S W Civil Practice & Procedure **4838**	
0729-2716	Human Rights: Newsletter of the Human Rights Commission	
0729-2759	Breastfeeding Review **6656**	
0729-2775	Company and Securities Law Journal **4861**	
0729-2910	Promissory Note Survey	
0729-3356	Australian Journal of Law and Society†	
0729-3445	Golden Egg Farms Newsletter **287**	
0729-3542	Presbyterian Banner **7771**	
0729-3623	Monash University. Centre of Southeast Asian Studies. Annual Indonesian Lecture Series **4186**	
0729-3682	Australian Planner **4404**	
0729-3720	Western Australia. Geological Survey. 1: 250,000 Geological Series. Explanatory Notes **2774**	
0729-3828	Superfunds **4524**	
0729-3836	Money Matters **1640**	
0729-4026	North West Express **5036**	
0729-4069	P E S A Journal **6786**	
0729-4115	Creve Salope	
0729-4271	Directory of Australian Public Libraries **5006**	
0729-4352	Australian Aboriginal Studies **330**	
0729-4360	Higher Education Research and Development **2985**	
0729-5030	Hunter Valley Research Foundation. Working Papers **8377**	
0729-5081	Mode Brides†	
0729-512X	Australia. Bureau of Statistics. Western Australian Office. Principal Agricultural Commodities, Western Australia, Preliminary†	
0729-5154	Southern Courier†	
0729-5472	State Library of New South Wales. Library Deposit List†	
0729-5545	Prime Time	
0729-560X	Herbology Magazine **310**	
0729-5685	Army **6411**	
0729-5936	Domestic Travel in Queensland†	
0729-5944	International Travel in Queensland†	
0729-5987	New South Wales Statutes Annotation and References **4744**	
0729-6096	Australia. Air Transport Statistics. Airport Traffic Data **8521**	
0729-6339	V A T - C H A T†	
0729-6436	Solar Progress **3177**	
0729-6509	State Trends†	
0729-6533	A N A R E Research Notes† **8927**	
0729-6568	Directory of Company Histories of the Book Industries†	
0729-6762	Australia. Bureau of Statistics. Interstate Freight Movement, Australia†	
0729-7823	Epilepsy Victoria **6138**	
0729-8242	Review (Melbourne)†	
0729-8463	A C R O D Newsletter†	
0729-8595	Australian Society†	
0729-8684	Australia. Bureau of Statistics. South Australian Office. Principal Agricultural Commodities, South Australia, Preliminary†	
0729-8757	Rural Quarterly†	
0729-8773	Ringing Towers	
0729-9389	Sonics Yearbook†	
0729-9486	Sonics†	
0729-9745	Medical Practice†	
0730-0018	Maverick Guide to Australia†	
0730-0050	Journal of Acoustic Emission	
0730-0069	Center Journal (Notre Dame)†	
0730-0158	Keyboard **6582**	
0730-0212	Mortgage Banking **1369**	
0730-0220	Literatura Chilena†	
0730-028X	Swedish-American Historical Quarterly **3784**	
0730-0301	A C M Transactions on Graphics **2483**	
0730-031X	Biotechnology Law Report **761**	
0730-0743	U.S. Internal Revenue Service. Statistics of Income Bulletin **1272**	
0730-0794	Edmund's Prescription Drug Prices†	
0730-0808	Mirror (Washington)†	
0730-0832	Neonatal Network **5970**	
0730-093X	C A M L S News	
0730-1049	T'ai Chi **562**	

0731-1222 Telltale Compass†
0731-1230 Photonics Spectra **7083**
0731-1265 International Journal of Legal Information **5019**
0731-129X Criminal Justice Ethics **6912**
0731-1370 Best of A C L D†
0731-1400 Advances in Perinatal Medicine **5985**
0731-1524 University of California Publications. Folklore & Mythology Studies†
0731-1613 Journal of Korean Studies **4184**
0731-1680 Science and Practice of Surgery Series†
0731-1745 Educational Measurement: Issues and Practice **2850**
0731-1788 Laughing Matters **7383**
0731-1850 Educational Computer Magazine†
0731-1869 Carbon-Graphite Composite Material Study **2115**
0731-1907 Wisconsin Court Rules and Procedure *changed to* Court Rules Pamphlet(s). Wisconsin Court Rules and Procedure, State and Federal **4949**
0731-1966 State of Michigan's Annual Highway Safety Plan.
0731-1974 Creditweek **1620**
0731-2024 Alaska Woman
0731-2040 Focus (Washington, D.C. 1981) **5488**
0731-2148 Journal of Religion & Psychical Research *changed to* 1932-5770 **6742**
0731-2164 Country Decorating Ideas *changed to* 1946-0651 **4549**
0731-2180 Sextant†
0731-2199 Advances in Health Economics and Health Services Research†
0731-227X The Poetry Exchange†
0731-2326 Problem Behavior Management†
0731-2334 Innovation (Dulles) **3368**
0731-2342 A M S Studies in the Seventeenth Century **5248**
0731-2350 Ask! **1726**
0731-2369 Worldwide Synthetic Fuels and Alternate Energy Directory†
0731-2377 C M P Bulletin†
0731-2385 Notes (New York)†
0731-2547 Orthodox Observer **7705**
0731-2652 International Life
0731-2768 El Promotor de Educacion Cristiana
0731-2784 Kentucky Geological Survey. Annual Report†
0731-2849 Progress in Mutation Research†
0731-2911 Inter-Society Color Council News **7077**
0731-2946 Missouri Folklore Society. Journal **3620**
0731-2970 Solar Engineering & Contracting†
0731-3012 The Messenger of the Chesterfield Historical Society of Virginia **4303**
0731-311X Kansas Geological Survey. Subsurface Geology Series†
0731-3144 Army Trainer†
0731-3284 Ohio Arts Council. Biennial Report **510**
0731-3292 Geographical Bulletin **4010**
0731-3403 Medieval and Renaissance Drama in England **8473**
0731-3411 C A B Air Carrier Traffic Statistics **8523**
0731-342X Ski Coach†
0731-3470 Motorcycle Industry Business Journal†
0731-3500 Linguistics of the Tibeto-Burman Area **5147**
0731-3527 News from the Library of Congress **5036**
0731-3616 Desktop Computing†
0731-3675 Media Spectrum **3072**
0731-3764 Journal of Undergraduate Research in Physics **7023**
0731-3772 Limerence Forum†
0731-3799 Food & Beverage Marketing†
0731-3802 Apparel Sales - Marketing Compensation Survey†
0731-3810 Journal of Toxicology. Clinical Toxicology *changed to* 1556-3650 **6829**
0731-3829 Journal of Toxicology. Cutaneous and Ocular Toxicology *changed to* 1556-9527 **6832**
0731-3837 Journal of Toxicology. Toxin Reviews *changed to* 1556-9543 **6883**
0731-3896 Delaware Genealogical Society. Journal **3764**
0731-4019 Virrasztó†
0731-4035 Texas Builders and Contractors Resource Guide†
0731-4043 Classification Literature Automated Search Service **5478**
0731-4108 American Ethnological Society. Proceedings†
0731-4116 Index: Foreign Broadcast Information Service Daily Reports: Eastern Europe†
0731-4191 Wire Association International. Annual Convention Proceedings **3334**
0731-4213 Collegiate Microcomputer†
0731-4345 Annual Planning Information: Sacramento Metropolitan Statistical Area†
0731-4361 Journal of Obesity and Weight Regulation†
0731-437X Aviation Accident Investigator†
0731-4388 The Book Report *changed to* 1542-4715 **5028**
0731-4450 United States Merit Systems Protection Board. Decisions **4853**
0731-4515 Accessions List, Brazil **4987**
0731-4523 New Plays U S A†
0731-4531 International Society of Certified Employee Benefit Specialists. Newsbriefs **1867**
0731-454X Business and Technology Videolog†
0731-4582 Journal of Urban Psychiatry†
0731-4612 Labor Relations Forms and Agreements†
0731-4647 Human Resource Management Newsletter†
0731-4655 Mideast Press Report
0731-4663 Passaic Review **5233**
0731-4698 Tractor Digest†
0731-4728 World Affairs Journal†
0731-4817 Rackham Journal of the Arts and Humanities†
0731-4833 Dispute Resolution Program Directory (Year)†
0731-5082 Stanford Journal of International Law **4941**
0731-5090 Journal of Guidance, Control, and Dynamics **63**
0731-5112 CampBook: Southeastern **8691**
0731-5171 Ferroelectrics Letters Section **3308**
0731-518X I D Handbook of Foodservice Distribution (Year)†
0731-5236 Poetics Journal **5234**
0731-5244 Contemporary Education Review (Washington)†
0731-5341 International Energy Annual (Year) (Print)†
0731-535X CampBook: South Central **8691**
0731-5376 Better Homes and Gardens Country Crafts†
0731-5384 Cornell Journal of Architecture **438**
0731-5481 Lucky Start†
0731-549X Freelance Writer's Report **4575**
0731-5589 Trends Update†
0731-5600 Better Homes and Gardens Kitchen & Bath Ideas **4533**
0731-5627 Weather Almanac† **8998**
0731-566X People with Special Needs - Down Syndrome Report **3045**
0731-5724 American College of Nutrition. Journal **6654**
0731-5732 Environmental Forum (Washington, DC) **3424**
0731-5775 Bulletins on Science and Technology for the Handicapped†
0731-5783 Licensing Law Handbook **4723**
0731-5791 Zoning and Planning Law Handbook **4432**
0731-5805 Securities Handbook Series. Securities Law Handbook **1650**
0731-5813 Trademark Law Handbook **4797**
0731-583X Going Public Handbook **1927**
0731-5848 Creditors' Rights in Bankruptcy **4865**
0731-5902 Pediatric Habilitation Series†
0731-5910 Current Trends in Urology†
0731-5945 Health Sciences Videolog†
0731-6011 Institute for Contemporary Studies. Letter†
0731-602X American Association of Colleges for Teacher Education. Briefs **2966**
0731-6100 Directory of Accredited Allied Medical Educational Programs *changed to* Health Care Careers Directory **5624**
0731-616X Kansas Geological Survey. Educational Series **2751**
0731-6291 Energygrams†
0731-6305 Middle East Business Intelligence **1577**
0731-6313 Energy and Housing Report
0731-6321 University of California at Berkeley. International and Area Studies. Policy Papers in International Affairs **7271**
0731-633X Directory of Special Libraries and Information Centers **5006**
0731-6445 Hydro-Abstracts
0731-650X Corporate Capital Transactions Coordinator†
0731-6518 Sunstone Review (Salt Lake City)†
0731-6526 Woodall's Retirement Directory†
0731-6844 Journal of Reinforced Plastics & Composites **3351**
0731-6933 Slick
0731-6941 Economic Development and Law Center Report†
0731-7085 Journal of Pharmaceutical and Biomedical Analysis **6855**
0731-7107 Child & Family Behavior Therapy **7344**
0731-7115 Clinical Gerontologist **4043**
0731-7131 Technical Services Quarterly **5050**
0731-7174 Texas Vision†
0731-7220 International Health News†
0731-7557 W R R I Report **8835**
0731-759X S E P M Reprint Series **6730**
0731-762X U.S. Bureau of Mines. Special Publications†
0731-7662 Illinois. State Geological Survey. Cooperative Groundwater Report **8825**
0731-7824 Herbarium News†
0731-7840 Encyclopedia of Occultism and Parapsychology
0731-7867 Dictionary of Literary Biography Yearbook†
0731-7883 S U N Y L A Newsletter **5045**
0731-7891 Worldwide Videotex Update **2569**
0731-7948 Abundant Life Magazine†
0731-7964 Colorado Courts **4947**
0731-7980 Cumberland Poetry Review†
0731-7999 Research in Real Estate†
0731-8014 Heisey News **366**
0731-8081 Directory of Unpublished Experimental Mental Measures†
0731-8103 Campbook: Southwestern **8691**
0731-8111 Boletin Anglohispano†
0731-812X Batter Performance Handbook
0731-8138 Pitcher Performance Handbook
0731-8146 Insiders Baseball Fact-Book Extra†
0731-8162 Insiders Baseball Fact-Book
0731-8189 Current Treaty Index **4822**
0731-8359 American Academy of Otolaryngology - Head and Neck Surgery. Bulletin **6077**
0731-8367 On-Line (Durham) **2502**
0731-8375 Cornsilk from DeKalb County, Il. **3763**
0731-8413 Special Aspects of Education
0731-843X Disc Collector **6562**
0731-8510 Directory of Multihospital Systems†
0731-8529 Dallas Opera Magazine†
0731-8545 Chicago Architectural Journal
0731-8561 International Union of Crystallography. Collected Abstracts of the Triennial Congress **2110**
0731-8618 Advances in Solar Energy: An Annual Review of Research and Development **3176**
0731-8634 Cook's Index (Print Edition)†
0731-8650 Occupational Programs in California Public Community Colleges **2961**
0731-8693 National Real Estate Investor. Directory Issue†
0731-8758 C B C Quarterly†
0731-8774 Chemical Business†
0731-8812 Chatham House Annual Review **7226**
0731-8820 California Criminal Defense Practice Reporter **4885**
0731-8863 Statistics of Paper, Paperboard and Wood Pulp **6740**
0731-8898 Journal of Environmental Pathology, Toxicology and Oncology **3499**
0731-8979 Johnson Reporter **3772**
0731-8987 Atavist†
0731-9029 The Atlanta Journal - The Atlanta Constitution Index *see* The Atlanta Constitution and Journal Index **4586**
0731-9045 The Chicago Tribune Index†
0731-9053 Advances in Econometrics **1435**
0731-9096 Oregon International Trade Directory†
0731-9150 Runzheimer Reports on Relocation **1874**
0731-9177 Financial Planning Strategist†
0731-9185 National Five Digit Zip Code and Post Office Directory†
0731-924X U S Crude Oil, Natural Gas and Natural Gas Liquids Reserves. Annual Report (Year) (Print)†
0731-9258 Journal of Computers in Mathematics and Science Teaching **5553**
0731-9274 Sharing (Yuma)
0731-9290 Wordwatching†
0731-9371 Middle East Insight†
0731-938X Veridian
0731-9444 Jenks Southeastern Business Letter†
0731-9487 Learning Disability Quarterly **3043**
0731-9533 Football Rules - Simplified and Illustrated **8229**
0731-9649 Virginia Tech Research **3009**
0731-9711 L R E Report†
0731-9770 Sports Medicine Digest†
0731-9916 Lady's Circle Patchwork Quilts
0731-9991 Teen Bag†
0732-0051 Public Press Newsletter†
0732-006X Collectibles Illustrated†
0732-0124 Billboard International Talent and Touring Directory (Year) **6549**
0732-0132 Directory of Jewish Resident Summer Camps
0732-0167 Nutrition & the M.D. *changed to* 1938-8640 **6656**
0732-0175 International Symposium on Computer-Aided Seismic Analysis and Discrimination. Proceedings†
0732-0183 Medical Update (Chicago) **5672**
0732-0205 McCarville - Hill Report
0732-0280 Lupus News **6224**
0732-0418 Foreign Direct Investment in the United States† **8957**
0732-0469 The Bond Buyer **1613**
0732-0485 Everybody's Money Complaint Directory for Consumers†
0732-054X Woman's Day Crosswords†
0732-0566 Advances in Host Defense Mechanisms†
0732-0582 Annual Review of Immunology **5754**
0732-0590 Canadian County Connections†
0732-0639 Tennessee Williams Newsletter†
0732-0671 Advances in Library Administration and Organization **4987**
0732-071X Colorado City Retail Sales by Standard Industrial Classification **1426**
0732-0736 Cincinnati Bar Association. Report **4642**
0732-0825 Massachusetts Appellate Tax Board Reporter **1934**
0732-085X Contributions to the Study of Aging† **8943**
0732-0868 Psychiatric Medicine†
0732-0914 Heritage (Waltham) **7721**
0732-0965 Probation and Parole Directory **2666**
0732-0981 Origin to Destination†
0732-099X Salaries (Year)†
0732-1015 Colorado State and County Retail Sales by Standard Industrial Classification **1084**
0732-1031 American Judicature Society. Annual Report†
0732-1139 Topics in Geriatrics†
0732-118X New Ideas in Psychology **7387**
0732-1295 Cognitive Science Series (Cambridge)
0732-1317 Research in Public Policy Analysis and Management **7177**
0732-1325 Dentist's Desk Reference†
0732-1503 Nebraska Music Educator†
0732-1511 Picture†
0732-1562 Women's Studies Quarterly **8905**
0732-1686 Towards†
0732-1805 Atlanta Regional Commission. Annual Report **4404**
0732-1813 Federal Reserve Bank of Atlanta. Economic Review **1485**
0732-183X Journal of Clinical Oncology **6024**
0732-1856 National Cooperative Transit Research and Development Program Synthesis of Transit Practice†
0732-1864 Nineteenth-Century Literature Criticism **5342**
0732-1872 Homily Service **7648**
0732-1880 Entertainment and Sports Lawyer **4666**
0732-1902 The Sporting News Pro Football Guide **8246**
0732-1929 Literature and Belief **7660**
0732-1988 P E R B News **7459**
0732-2038 The Chronicle (Chicago) **1285**
0732-2224 Beckett Circle **5261**
0732-2283 Kagan Census of Cable and Pay T V†
0732-2305 Electric Power Monthly (Print Edition)†
0732-233X Facts about Store Development **3677**
0732-2364 Workers Under Communism†
0732-2399 Marketing Science **1833**
0732-2402 Impulse (Fresno) **5015**
0732-2569 Country Living (New York) **4536**
0732-2577 CampBook: Northwestern **8691**
0732-2585 CampBook: North Central **8690**
0732-2631 Supply and Demand for Scientists and Engineers *changed to* Supply & Demand Indicators for New Science and Engineering Doctorates **6704**
0732-2666 Risk Management for Executive Women†
0732-2674 Working Papers in Irish Studies **3572**
0732-2755 Directory of Graduate Programs in the Communication Arts and Sciences†
0732-281X North Carolina Rules of Court with Amendments Received *changed to* Court Rules Pamphlet(s). North Carolina Rules of Court, State & Federal **4949**
0732-2852 Art Com **469**
0732-2860 Upstate New York Directory of Manufacturers **2032**
0732-2917 I R A Compliance Manual†
0732-2933 Response (Fairfax)†
0732-2941 Co-Op Development Report†
0732-2992 Muqarnas **507**
0732-300X Theatre Times†
0732-3034 Guide to the Evaluation of Educational Experiences in the Armed Services (Year) **2861**
0732-3042 Language Quarterly†
0732-3093 Official New Mexico Blue Book **4306**
0732-3115 Upper Midwest Report†
0732-3123 The Journal of Mathematical Behavior **5505**
0732-3336 Pyramid Guide†
0732-3395 Meyer's Directory of Genealogical Societies in the U S A & Canada
0732-3581 Your Public Lands†
0732-393X Victorian†
0732-4030 Town Hall *changed to* 1545-9071 **8075**
0732-4243 Journal of Forms Management†
0732-4308 Essays in Contemporary Economic Problems†
0732-4375 Photovoltaics
0732-4383 Current Topics in Chinese Science. Section A: Physics

0734-9890	Emotions and Behavior. Monograph **6137**
0734-9920	The National Hispanic Journal **3552**
0734-9963	CutBank **5420**
0734-9998	Mutual Aid†
0735-0015	Journal of Business and Economic Statistics **1247**
0735-0023	Streamlined Seminar†
0735-0031	Here's How†
0735-004X	Advances in Learning and Behavioral Disabilities **3036**
0735-0082	Superintendent's Digest†
0735-0104	Advances in Viral Oncology†
0735-0120	The International Journal of Orofacial Myology **5849**
0735-0171	Advances in Reading - Language Research **2824**
0735-018X	Timber Trails **3785**
0735-0198	Rhetoric Review **5362**
0735-0287	Genealogical Computer Pioneer†
0735-0295	Bookmark (Moscow) **4998**
0735-0317	Photron†
0735-0341	Classics in Psychoanalysis†
0735-0384	Antioch Law Journal†
0735-0392	Annual Editions: Western Civilization **4130**
0735-0414	Alcohol and Alcoholism **2690**
0735-0503	Geothermal Hotline **3162**
0735-066X	Lumber Price Index. P N W Coast Index **3709**
0735-0724	College Sports
0735-0783	Tennessee Philological Bulletin **5186**
0735-0821	National Association of Administrative Law Judges. Journal *changed to* National Association of Administrative Law Judiciary. Journal **4738**
0735-0864	Anselm Studies†
0735-1097	American College of Cardiology. Journal **5776**
0735-1100	North Carolina Foreign Language Review†
0735-1135	Tennessee's Business **1968**
0735-1240	Mark **5226**
0735-1259	Journal of Teaching Writing **4577**
0735-1267	Arena Review†
0735-1283	American Review of Diagnostics
0735-1291	Learning and Media **5025**
0735-1313	Molecular Biology and Medicine†
0735-1321	Satsang **154**
0735-1348	Ancient T L **373**
0735-1364	Tibet Society Journal† **8993**
0735-1437	The State of Small Business: A Report of the President Transmitted to the Congress *changed to* 1932-3573 **1967**
0735-1534	Reference Report
0735-1550	Saul Bellow Journal **5367**
0735-1607	Space Commerce News
0735-1631	American Journal of Perinatology **5985**
0735-164X	Applied Developmental Psychology **7335**
0735-1690	Psychoanalytic Inquiry **7395**
0735-1755	Horizons (Washington, 1981)†
0735-1771	Costs and Indexes for Domestic Oil and Gas Field Equipment and Production Operations *changed to* Oil and Gas Lease Equipment and Operating Costs **1900**
0735-1828	United States Foreign Trade. Bunker Fuels†
0735-1844	Integrated Service Digital Network†
0735-1887	All Area
0735-1895	Theaterwork
0735-1909	Vitae Scholasticae **646**
0735-1925	Microcomputer Market Place†
0735-1933	International Communications in Heat and Mass Transfer **3381**
0735-2026	Art Directors Annual **469**
0735-2034	Group of Thirty. Annual Report **1488**
0735-2166	Journal of Urban Affairs **4417**
0735-2336	Harvard Business School. Baker Library. Recent Additions to Baker Library†
0735-2387	Hillsdale Review†
0735-2409	New York Sea Grant Law and Policy Journal†
0735-2417	Indiana Manufacturers Directory **2005**
0735-2425	Annual Editions: Urban Society **8088**
0735-2484	Direct Energy Conversion (Oak Ridge, 1982)†
0735-2492	Nuclear Reactor Safety†
0735-2506	Nuclear Fuel Cycle†
0735-2530	Clinical Infant Reports. Monograph **6089**
0735-2689	Critical Reviews in Plant Sciences **226**
0735-2727	Radioelectronics and Communications Systems **3112**
0735-2751	Sociological Theory **8137**
0735-2794	Terrebonne Life Lines **3784**
0735-3073	Deep Sky†
0735-3081	Resource Recovery Report **3511**
0735-309X	Pioneer Wagon **3779**
0735-3278	Freestone Frontiers **3767**
0735-3324	Federal Staff Directory **7437**
0735-3413	Arizona Literary Magazine
0735-3480	Advances in Applied Biology†
0735-3618	A S R C Membership Directory
0735-3723	E T C†
0735-3766	Journal of Business Logistics **1764**
0735-3847	Integrative Psychiatry†
0735-3863	Data Processing Auditing Report†
0735-388X	Telecommunications Counselor†
0735-3928	Crime and Justice†
0735-3936	Behavioral Sciences & the Law **7339**
0735-3944	Insurance and Employee Benefits Literature†
0735-3995	World S F Newsletter **5449**
0735-4037	Perspectives in Psychotherapy
0735-4134	Peace Newsletter **7258**
0735-4355	Dirt Rider Magazine **8258**
0735-4398	Celibate Woman†
0735-4401	New York State Museum. Educational Leaflet Series **7892**
0735-4444	Nationwide Directory of Corporate Meeting Planners **6282**
0735-455X	The People Take the Lead† **8980**
0735-4576	Hyst'ry Myst'ry Magazine†
0735-4665	Sagetrieb **5434**
0735-469X	Home Video and Cable Yearbook†
0735-4703	Public Administrator and the Courts†
0735-4711	Tri-State Bluegrass Association Band and Festival Guide **6624**
0735-4738	Employee Relations Report†
0735-4754	Mason Memories†
0735-4762	Nutrition Update **6667**
0735-4789	Steppingstones†
0735-4843	Law Office Management & Administration Report **4715**
0735-5424	Western Water **8842**
0735-5467	Missouri Archaeological Society. Special Publications†
0735-5572	Archive (Tucson) **6964**
0735-5653	Arctic Policy Review†
0735-5688	Sightsaving†
0735-5696	Caring (Chicago)†
0735-570X	The Rodale Report†
0735-5920	Quarterly Review of Doublespeak†
0735-6161	Wood and Fiber Science **3717**
0735-6196	CrossRoad Trails **3763**
0735-6250	International Journal of Entomology†
0735-6323	National Centurion
0735-6331	Journal of Educational Computing Research **2949**
0735-6358	Choices: A Core Collection for Young Reluctant Readers **2182**
0735-6471	Ethnic Racial Review
0735-648X	Journal of Crime & Justice **2656**
0735-6498	Reference Book of Corporate Managements *changed to* 1098-7266 **1737**
0735-6501	Critique (West Vancouver)
0735-6536	Quarto (New York) **5235**
0735-6544	Street Pharmacologist†
0735-6552	Language Planning Newsletter†
0735-6595	Delaware Lawyer **4655**
0735-665X	Publishers' Catalogs Annual†
0735-6676	Outdoor Power Equipment Official Guide **213**
0735-6722	Journal of Health Administration Education **4103**
0735-6757	American Journal of Emergency Medicine **6055**
0735-6765	American Association of Housing Educators. Proceedings **4403**
0735-6773	Modeling and Simulation on Microcomputers†
0735-682X	Family Backtracking **3765**
0735-6838	Court Rules Pamphlet(s). Florida Rules of Court, State and Federal **4652**
0735-6870	Southern Echoes **3783**
0735-6889	Spring (New York) **5240**
0735-6897	Theory and Research in Behavioral Pediatrics†
0735-696X	Georgia Farm Bureau News **115**
0735-6986	Teen Times **2216**
0735-7028	Professional Psychology: Research and Practice **7392**
0735-7036	Journal of Comparative Psychology **7371**
0735-7044	Behavioral Neuroscience **7339**
0735-7133	Sundog (Tallahassee) **5436**
0735-7362	Consumer Comments **2636**
0735-7540	V L A Shipping List (Print) *changed to* V L A Shipping List (Online) **5054**
0735-7672	Johnson's Investment Company Charts **1634**
0735-7788	Musical America International Directory of the Performing Arts *changed to* 1933-3250 **6593**
0735-7850	American Association of Engineering Societies. Engineering Workforce Commission. Professional Income of Engineers (Year) **3181**
0735-7885	Kalliope **5425**
0735-7893	Puerto Rico Taxes **1941**
0735-7907	Cancer Investigation **6013**
0735-7923	Journal of Industrial Irradiation Technology†
0735-7958	Aber Bulletin **3757**
0735-8016	Shiawassee County Genealogical Society. Journal **3782**
0735-8032	Allertonia **774**
0735-8202	Another Season†
0735-8210	Alkaloids: Chemical and Biological Perspectives **722**
0735-8237	China Spring **7204**
0735-8253	Steam Coal Watch†
0735-8296	S C O P E†
0735-8318	U S Catholic Historian **7821**
0735-8342	Southern Studies **8006**
0735-8407	L I N K Line†
0735-8423	Electronic Office
0735-8458	Datapro Reports on Telecommunications†
0735-8490	Editors Only **4574**
0735-8571	The New Library Scene *changed to* 1935-5246 **5047**
0735-8652	Agave†
0735-8660	Keraulophon **6582**
0735-8733	State Legislative Report (Denver) **7185**
0735-8741	Popular Culture Association. Newsletter and Popular Culture Methods **8126**
0735-8776	Daily Guide to Richer Living†
0735-8881	Energy Directory†
0735-8938	Rutgers Computer & Technology Law Journal **4845**
0735-9004	Virginia Tax Review **1954**
0735-9055	Swallow's Tale Magazine†
0735-9098	Institutional Investor Directory **1630**
0735-9144	Taylor Quarterly (Alexandria)
0735-9152	The Family Therapy Collections **7357**
0735-9209	Polish Heritage **3558**
0735-9225	Investing & Trading with Spanish Speaking Countries†
0735-9276	Simulation Series **2518**
0735-9314	Commercial Space Report†
0735-9322	Curran's Ginseng Farmer
0735-9330	Code News *changed to* 1932-099X **1028**
0735-9381	Processed World†
0735-9411	Woodrow Wilson School of Public and International Affairs. Discussion Papers in Economics **1195**
0735-9462	Park Science **3459**
0735-9543	U C L A Symposium Series on Molecular and Cellular Biology†
0735-9551	Ob-Gyn Litigation Reporter†
0735-9640	Plant Molecular Biology Reporter **742**
0735-9683	Health Marketing Quarterly **7522**
0735-9713	Painting and Wallcovering Contractor **6719**
0735-973X	B U C Used Boat Price Guide **8271**
0735-9780	Heart
0735-9810	Kansas Geological Survey. Geology Series†
0735-9861	O R N L **3143**
0735-9985	Auerbach Systems Development Management† **8932**
0736-0010	Foodlines†
0736-0037	Nutrition Research Newsletter **6666**
0736-0053	The Opera Quarterly **6602**
0736-007X	Al Hanson's Economic Newsletter **1609**
0736-0096	Nutrition Week **6667**
0736-0126	The Insurance and Financial Review†
0736-0142	C L S Quarterly†
0736-0150	Inside (Albany) **4870**
0736-0258	Journal of Clinical Neurophysiology **6150**
0736-0266	Journal of Orthopaedic Research **6064**
0736-0274	Catalyst Media Review†
0736-0282	World Federation of Health Agencies for the Advancement of Voluntary Surgical Contraception. Communique
0736-0339	Crittenden Report Real Estate Financing **7588**
0736-0401	Security Letter Source Book **2680**
0736-0460	Indo-Pacific Fishes **947**
0736-0509	Contributions from the New York Botanical Garden **784**
0736-0517	Commercial Lease Law Insider **7586**
0736-0525	New York Co-op & Condo Insider†
0736-0673	Notes on Linguistics†
0736-0681	Parenteral Drug Association. Technical Information Bulletin†
0736-0703	Cost of Doing Business for Retail Sporting Goods Stores **1427**
0736-0711	Plays in Process†
0736-0770	Visual Arts Research **525**
0736-0797	Higher Education Directory (Year) **2984**
0736-0800	Appleland Bulletin **3758**
0736-0886	Kershner Kinfolk†
0736-0932	Forum for Social Economics **1541**
0736-0975	Fiduciary Tax Return Guide
0736-0983	Planning for Higher Education **2998**
0736-0991	Solar Utilization News (Estes Park)†
0736-1084	Linden Lane Magazine†
0736-1122	Barnhart Dictionary Companion **5098**
0736-1149	Threshold (Chicago)†
0736-1157	Alaska Statutes. Advance Legislative Service **4612**
0736-1238	Reproduction Bulletin **7327**
0736-167X	Telemarketing Update **1845**
0736-1688	Refunding Update **2641**
0736-1696	Continuing Education Alternatives Update **2939**
0736-170X	Almost Free Cookbooks & Recipes Update **4351**
0736-1750	Media Law Notes **4579**
0736-1793	Chilton's Automotive Service Manual **8574**
0736-1823	International C A D/C A M Industry Directory
0736-1858	Family Records Today **3766**
0736-1882	Self Publishing Update **2338**
0736-1890	Recycling Update **3511**
0736-1904	Barter Update **1957**
0736-1912	Self-Employment Update **1966**
0736-1920	Career Planning and Adult Development Journal **2939**
0736-1963	Fundamentalist Journal†
0736-198X	W W I Aero **74**
0736-2048	E L T Documents†
0736-2056	Avicultura Profesional **280**
0736-2099	Community (Alexandria)†
0736-2129	Operating Small Business Investment Companies. Directory **1964**
0736-217X	Reporting from the Russell Sage Foundation†
0736-2196	Family Practice Survey†
0736-220X	Beverage Alcohol Market Report (Print Edition) *changed to* Beverage Alcohol Market Report (Email Edition) **599**
0736-2277	Wisconsin Natural Resources **2633**
0736-2358	Fielding's Caribbean†
0736-2374	Ocular Inflammation and Therapeutics
0736-2390	Chambers Helping Chambers **3762**
0736-2412	Dohner Family Newsletter†
0736-248X	Journal of Insurance Regulation **4510**
0736-2498	Mar-Marr-Marrs-Mars Exchange†
0736-2501	Noise Control Engineering Journal **3391**
0736-251X	Virginia Woolf Miscellany **5395**
0736-2536	Aerospace Engineering Magazine *changed to* 1937-5212 **43**
0736-2609	National Water Conditions†
0736-2625	Byelorussian Youth
0736-2633	Davenport Newsletter†
0736-265X	Indian - Artifact Magazine **397**
0736-2676	Wildlife Publications Review†
0736-2684	Answer Man Newsletter†
0736-2692	Book of Apple Software†
0736-2706	Book of Atari Software†
0736-2714	Contributions in Psychology **7349**
0736-2722	Software Catalog: Microcomputers†
0736-2730	Software Catalog: Minicomputers **2574**
0736-2803	Clinical Rheumatology in Practice†
0736-2854	Dodd Diggings†
0736-2870	Michigan Purchasing Directory†
0736-2889	Michigan Manufacturers Directory **2017**
0736-2900	Coastal Plains Farmer†
0736-2919	Investment Horizons
0736-2935	Noise-Con Proceedings **3489**
0736-2951	Bits'n Bytes Gazette†
0736-2986	T V Executive **2392**
0736-2994	Stochastic Analysis and Applications **5538**
0736-3044	Center for Self-Sufficiency Update **2939**
0736-3435	Court Rules Pamphlet(s). Texas Rules of Court, State and Federal **4949**
0736-3443	Health Lawyer **4686**
0736-3559	Almanac of Seapower **6410**
0736-3583	Bulletin of Clinical Neurosciences†
0736-3605	Focus on Critical Care†
0736-3621	Computer Programming Management†
0736-3680	Planetary Report **579**
0736-3737	Automation News†
0736-3745	Facets Features **6497**
0736-3761	Journal of Consumer Marketing **1823**
0736-3796	Autoharpoholic†
0736-3885	ComputerTalk for the Physician†
0736-3907	Mosasaur **6727**
0736-3974	Text **5386**
0736-3982	C U N Y English Forum†
0736-3990	Frugal Consumers Dollar-Stretching Possibility Newsletter **4359**
0736-4024	Area Footprints **3759**

0737-5158	Paedonoson
0737-5166	Acta Paedologica†
0737-5174	Trisomy 21
0737-5182	Chiaroscuro†
0737-5190	Impromptu†
0737-5204	National Federation Handbook **8189**
0737-5212	Basketball - Simplified & Illustrated Rules **8222**
0737-5239	Ill-la-Mo Searcher†
0737-5255	Government Programs and Projects Directory†
0737-5298	Luna Tack†
0737-5328	Teacher Education Quarterly **3084**
0737-5344	Design Book Review†
0737-5379	New York Spectator†
0737-5387	New Observations **508**
0737-5409	American Academy of Podiatry Administration News-Letter†
0737-5425	Program on Environment and Behavior Monograph Series **8126**
0737-545X	Surveys, Polls, Censuses and Forecasts Directory†
0737-5468	Journal Record (Oklahoma City) **1138**
0737-5506	Salthouse†
0737-5522	Black Messiah†
0737-5549	Palestine Human Rights Campaign Newsletter†
0737-5581	United Methodist Reporter **7778**
0737-5670	U.S. National Endowment for the Arts. Application Guidelines: Media Arts - Film, Radio, Television†
0737-5689	Education Update (Washington)†
0737-5700	Robotics Update†
0737-5778	Social Work and Christianity **7681**
0737-5883	Creative **23**
0737-5905	American Prometheus†
0737-5921	Society of Vacuum Coaters. Annual Technical Conference Proceedings **6721**
0737-5980	Biotechnology Education Report†
0737-6022	Alaska. Division of Geological and Geophysical Surveys. Professional Reports **2724**
0737-612X	Science, Medicine and Technology in East Asia†
0737-6146	Advances in Anesthesia **5768**
0737-6154	Sun Sign Book **567**
0737-6278	The Bridge (Washington) **3183**
0737-6308	Wealthbuilding†
0737-6340	Bronte Newsletter†
0737-6413	Banking World†
0737-6421	The Astronomical Almanac **569**
0737-6553	Electronic Imaging†
0737-6642	American Illustration†
0737-6650	American Asian Review
0737-6707	Notes on Literacy†
0737-6731	Farmers' Almanac **3120**
0737-6766	Occultation Newsletter **579**
0737-6782	Journal of Product Innovation Management **1890**
0737-6839	Personal Property Section News **4519**
0737-6855	Muppet Magazine†
0737-6871	Social Process in Hawaii **8134**
0737-688X	Engel-Poh Family History Newsletter†
0737-7002	Slavic and East European Arts†
0737-7029	Hispanic Focus **3574**
0737-7037	Journal of Folklore Research **3619**
0737-7169	Hemlocks and Balsams†
0737-7282	Report of the Ross Roundtable on Critical Approaches to Common Pediatric Problems in Collaboration with the Ambulatory Pediatric Association **6103**
0737-7320	Medical Digest†
0737-7363	Journal of Continuing Higher Education **2943**
0737-738X	Patristic and Byzantine Review **4253**
0737-7436	Journal of the Print World, Inc. **7564**
0737-7452	Advances in Developmental and Behavioral Pediatrics†
0737-7495	Ohio Manufacturers Directory **2022**
0737-7576	Light Impressions Review†
0737-7592	O A - F A Update†
0737-7622	Communications Lawyer **4647**
0737-7665	U.S. National Endowment for the Arts. Application Guidelines: Museums†
0737-769X	Journal of Chinese Religions **7737**
0737-772X	Recent Transportation Literature for Planning and Engineering Librarians†
0737-7754	Writing Teacher (Orono)†
0737-7762	Social Concept†
0737-7797	Resource Sharing & Information Networks **5043**
0737-7843	Periodical Title Abbreviations† **8980**
0737-7908	Robotics World†
0737-7932	Itawamba Settlers **3772**
0737-7940	Iowa Manufacturers Register **2009**
0737-8017	Annual A C M Symposium on the Theory of Computing. Proceedings **2600**
0737-8025	Chemical Industries Series **3239**
0737-8033	Chemistry and Pharmacology of Drugs†
0737-8076	Hot Off the Computer†
0737-8092	Center for Holocaust Studies Newsletter†
0737-8130	L D R C Bulletin **4834**
0737-8173	Lighted Pathway†
0737-8181	International Dredging Review **3362**
0737-8211	Systematic Botany Monographs **819**
0737-8246	Quaker Yeomen **7740**
0737-8335	Kahawai†
0737-8483	Membrane and Separation Technology News **768**
0737-8505	Personal Robotics News†
0737-8548	World Spaceflight News **75**
0737-8610	N C I W Newsletter†
0737-8726	The Expert and the Law **4670**
0737-8823	Euphorbia Journal **3729**
0737-8831	Library Hi Tech **5062**
0737-8939	P C World **2581**
0737-8947	Boston University International Law Journal **4918**
0737-9005	Zoobooks **969**
0737-9021	The E M I E Bulletin **3531**
0737-9080	Film Review Annual†
0737-920X	Connecticut Family Law Journal
0737-9218	White House Weekly **7477**
0737-9242	Roots and Branches **3781**
0737-9269	Blind Alleys **5418**
0737-9285	National Center for the Study of Collective Bargaining in Higher Education and the Professions. Newsletter†
0737-9412	Carte Italiane **5271**
0737-948X	Agricultural Credit Conditions Survey†
0737-9498	Best Editorial Cartoons of the Year **5208**
0737-9501	Software Publishing Report†
0737-9544	Contemporary Psychotherapy Review **7349**
0737-9633	Employment Outlook Survey **1679**
0738-0070	Wisconsin Manufacturers Register **2035**
0738-0143	Winning Sweepstakes Newsletter
0738-0151	Child and Adolescent Social Work Journal **8093**
0738-0194	P C Tech Journal†
0738-0208	Jobless Newsletter†
0738-0232	Hazardous Waste Consultant **3507**
0738-0372	U.S. National Cancer Institute. Division of Extramural Activities. Annual Report **7544**
0738-0429	Modern Master Series **506**
0738-0461	Aerospace Defense Markets & Technology†
0738-050X	Southeast Asia Chronicle†
0738-0518	Consumer Sourcebook **2637**
0738-0534	Homiletic (Print)† **8962**
0738-0550	Federation News (Los Angeles)
0738-0569	Computers in the Schools **2948**
0738-0577	Occupational Therapy in Health Care **5689**
0738-0593	International Journal of Educational Development **2869**
0738-0615	Consumer Pharmacist **6830**
0738-0623	Police Misconduct and Civil Rights Law Report **2664**
0738-064X	A M S Studies in Anthropology **322**
0738-0658	Puerto Rico Health Sciences Journal **5700**
0738-0674	New Relationships†
0738-0690	Preview (Northbrook)†
0738-0739	Holocaust Studies Annual†
0738-0755	Studies in Black American Literature†
0738-0763	Essays in Graham Greene†
0738-0771	Smart Machines†
0738-0798	Wake Forest University School of Law. Continuing Legal Education. Annual Review, North Carolina **4810**
0738-081X	Clinics in Dermatology **5873**
0738-0895	Journal of Architectural and Planning Research **447**
0738-0917	Pulp & Paper Week **6738**
0738-0925	Recent Publications in Natural History†
0738-0941	5 Great Romances†
0738-095X	World's Greatest Love Stories†
0738-0968	Space Age Times **70**
0738-0976	P A Outlook **5691**
0738-0984	Hospital Law Newsletter†
0738-100X	A C M / I E E E Design Automation Conference. Proceedings **2457**
0738-1018	Anesthesiology Malpractice Reporter†
0738-1026	Malpractice Reporter†
0738-1034	Compensation & Benefits Report (Washington) **1671**
0738-1085	Microsurgery **6252**
0738-1093	Overland Journal (Indepedence) **4307**
0738-1131	Architecture California **430**
0738-114X	Planning & Zoning News **4423**
0738-1220	Portable Computer†
0738-1247	Parascope **4755**
0738-1360	Marine Resource Economics **2812**
0738-1387	Robot - X News
0738-1425	International Development Resource Books† **8965**
0738-1433	The Women's Review of Books **5245**
0738-1441	Lens Research†
0738-145X	Agricell Report **774**
0738-1514	Minnesota Manufacturers Register **2017**
0738-1522	Information America†
0738-159X	Flower of the Forest Black Genealogical Journal **3766**
0738-1611	N C A A Football Records **8239**
0738-1719	Ethnic Information Sources of the U S†
0738-1727	Journal of Modern Greek Studies **4236**
0738-1743	Polymer Yearbook Series **2077**
0738-1859	Small Farm Advocate†
0738-1891	Oregon Genealogical Society Quarterly **3778**
0738-1913	Collective Bargaining in Higher Education and the Professions. Annual Bibliography†
0738-1948	Malpractice Reporter. Ob-Gyn†
0738-1956	Malpractice Reporter. Hospitals Edition†
0738-1964	Malpractice Reporter. Surgeon's†
0738-2022	Journal of Forth Application and Research†
0738-2030	Journal of Intermountain Archeology
0738-2049	Laws Quarterly **4717**
0738-2146	U.S. Office of the Comptroller of the Currency. Quarterly Journal (Print)†
0738-2170	B O M A Experience Exchange Report **7583**
0738-2227	New Products Marketplace†
0738-2278	Advances in Orthopaedic Surgery†
0738-2294	Gesar†
0738-2324	Guide to the High Technology and Industries†
0738-2332	Clearing Up: Northwest Energy Markets **3126**
0738-2340	Where to Write for Vital Records **7295**
0738-2391	Roots & Shoots Quarterly **3781**
0738-2405	Kovel's Antiques and Collectibles Price List **367**
0738-2421	Holly Society Journal **3736**
0738-2448	S Corporations (New York, 1983) **1942**
0738-2464	Texas Paleontology Series **6731**
0738-2472	Coastal Ocean Pollution Assessment News†
0738-2480	Law and History Review **4713**
0738-2502	Precious Metals Performance Digest†
0738-2669	The Juggler **499**
0738-2758	National Directory of College Athletics (Men's Edition) **8189**
0738-2766	Consumer Health Reporter†
0738-2812	New Haven Studies in International Law and World Public Order **4936**
0738-2839	Society of Petroleum Engineers. California Regional Meeting. Proceedings
0738-2898	Journal of Environmental Horticulture **3740**
0738-291X	Contacts **23**
0738-2944	The Journal of Christian Healing **7370**
0738-3053	Magnolia Society. Journal **3742**
0738-3088	Monthly Truck Tonnage Report **8673**
0738-3096	Government Tender Report†
0738-310X	Government Traffic Bulletin†
0738-3185	C W A S Newsletter
0738-3266	Federal Software Exchange Catalog
0738-3290	American Carnival Glass News **2037**
0738-3312	Government Union Critique†
0738-3355	Technical Analysis of Stocks & Commodities **1655**
0738-3371	New-Radio Cable Audio & Pay Radio Report†
0738-3398	I B C D: International Business Conditions Digest
0738-3401	Administration and Policy Journal†
0738-3576	Digit Magazine
0738-3614	Computers in Psychiatry - Psychology†
0738-3770	Genealogical Goldmine **3767**
0738-386X	Indiana Review **5308**
0738-3932	Recipes for Sale **3661**
0738-3967	M S Quarterly Report **6159**
0738-3991	Patient Education and Counseling **7535**
0738-4203	For Your Eyes Only†
0738-4211	Selling Direct†
0738-422X	Recent Developments in Alcoholism **2698**
0738-4262	Computer Security, Auditing and Controls **2512**
0738-4270	Computer Audit News and Developments **1285**
0738-4300	G C N **7486**
0738-4319	Cognotes **5002**
0738-4351	Securities Traders' Monthly†
0738-4394	Perspectives in Ethology **960**
0738-4440	Futures Conditional†
0738-4467	Sampan **3562**
0738-453X	Current Population Reports: Series P-25, Population Estimates and Projections **7305**
0738-4548	Indochina Issues†
0738-4556	M D S News **5855**
0738-4580	Vascular Medicine†
0738-4602	A I Magazine **2445**
0738-467X	Caring (Washington) **5954**
0738-4726	Child Nurturance†
0738-4750	Translation Services Directory **5188**
0738-4793	United States House of Representatives. Committee on Veterans' Affairs. Activities Report **6451**
0738-484X	Freeland and Allied Families **3767**
0738-4866	Gunn Salute **3769**
0738-4912	T A I C H Directory†
0738-5102	Southern Historian **4313**
0738-5161	Boycott Report†
0738-517X	Puerto del Sol **5355**
0738-5226	Genealogical Aids Bulletin†
0738-5285	Tax Management Primary Sources **1948**
0738-5382	Rockpile **6612**
0738-5560	Chismearte
0738-5579	Bond Fund Survey
0738-5587	Fortune International **1111**
0738-5625	Hispanic American Arts†
0738-565X	Wheels of Time **8679**
0738-5676	Power Line†
0738-5765	Busby Papers†
0738-5919	Antitrust Law Handbook **4856**
0738-5927	Public Citizen **2640**
0738-596X	The Nut Kernel **3745**
0738-5978	AgriComp
0738-5994	Fulton County Historical & Genealogical Society Newsletter **4293**
0738-6060	Medical School Admission Requirements. United States and Canada†
0738-6087	Teaching and Computers†
0738-6176	The Psychotherapy Patient *changed to* 1540-1383 **7372**
0738-6206	Pace Environmental Law Review **4755**
0738-6222	*see* 0001-0634 **2093**
0738-6230	A A C O M Annual Statistical Report *changed to* Osteopathic Medical Education. Annual Report **5749**
0738-6249	Current Drug Handbook†
0738-6354	Micro Software Marketing†
0738-6362	Salesman's Insider
0738-6419	The Good News Letter **7799**
0738-6435	C S I Congressional Record Abstracts: Energy Edition
0738-6443	C S I Congressional Record Abstracts: Master Edition
0738-6451	C S I Congressional Record Abstracts: Foreign Affairs Edition
0738-646X	C S I Federal Register Abstracts: Master Edition
0738-6486	C S I Congressional Record Abstracts: National Defense Edition
0738-6494	Just Compensation
0738-6508	International Policy Report **7244**
0738-6516	Sizzle Sheet
0738-6532	Renewable Resources Journal **3462**
0738-6583	Executive Housekeeping Today **4385**
0738-6648	Jacksoniana†
0738-6656	Ranger Rick **2210**
0738-6729	The Behavior Analyst **7338**
0738-6745	Urner Barry's Meat & Poultry Directory **303**
0738-6761	Midwest Labor & Employment Law Journal†
0738-677X	Illinois Journal of Family Law†
0738-6788	Texas Memorial Museum. Conservation Notes†
0738-6826	T R News **8512**
0738-6869	Business News (San Diego)
0738-6931	D.C. Real Estate Reporter **7588**
0738-694X	California in Print†
0738-6974	Administrative Radiology Journal†
0738-6982	Executive Compensation Reports†
0738-7008	Crab Creek Review **5279**
0738-7024	Business Ideas†
0738-7075	Career Center Bulletin†
0738-7105	Institute of Modern Russian Culture Newsletter **8107**
0738-7113	Latin America in Books†
0738-7148	Boy Meets Girl†
0738-7164	Studies in Medievalism **4271**
0738-7172	Book of IBM Software†
0738-7202	Overseas Press Club Bulletin **4581**
0738-7237	Mirror (Lancaster) **4303**
0738-7245	Nautical Research Journal **8654**
0738-7253	Business & Acquisition Newsletter **1322**
0738-7261	Jewelry Newsletter International **4567**
0738-7288	Bowser Report **1613**
0738-7318	Religious Herald **7773**
0738-7326	Investor's Guide to High Technology Corporations†

ISSN

9328 0738-7342 ULRICH'S PERIODICALS

0738-7342 High Technology Outlook†
0738-7393 High Technology Overviews†
0738-7415 How to Be Your Own Publisher Update **7562**
0738-7431 Kids Rhyme Newsletter **2197**
0738-7458 Smorgasboard - Plenty to Eat **4367**
0738-7490 Home Business Idea Possibility Newsletter **1750**
0738-7512 High Technology Growth Trends†
0738-7571 Marshall County Historical Quarterly **4303**
0738-761X Folding Carton†
0738-7644 Texas Optometry **6052**
0738-7687 Living Off the Land
0738-7717 Rockin' 50s **6612**
0738-7741 The Alabama Baptist **7744**
0738-775X Mississippi Archaeology **406**
0738-7776 ChemEcology
0738-7792 A I M Report **4570**
0738-7806 Generations (San Francisco) **4045**
0738-7857 Personal Fitness **6994**
0738-7911 Talkin' Union†
0738-7946 Hospital Gift Shop Management†
0738-7954 Augsburg Media Messenger†
0738-7962 Parish Teacher†
0738-7989 Journal of Materials Education **3206**
0738-8004 The Written Word†
0738-8012 Word from Washington (Washington, D.C.) **4070**
0738-8020 Pottery Southwest **411**
0738-8039 Western Photographer
0738-8063 W A S Newsletter **423**
0738-811X HealthFacts **5627**
0738-8128 Documentation Newsletter†
0738-8144 Corrections Compendium **2647**
0738-8209 Central Georgia Genealogical Society. Quarterly **3761**
0738-825X Reynolds Family Newsletter†
0738-8268 Goodlet Family Newsletter†
0738-8330 Teamster Convoy Dispatch **4603**
0738-8357 Folk Art Finder†
0738-8365 New York Antique Almanac†
0738-8381 Rocky Mountain Quarter Horse Magazine **8298**
0738-8446 Exchange (Washington)†
0738-8489 Evangelist (Albany) **7735**
0738-8497 Roundup (Washington)†
0738-8543 List†
0738-8551 Critical Reviews in Biotechnology **762**
0738-8578 Single Source Newsletter **7943**
0738-8586 Victor Valley Magazine†
0738-8608 Western Boatman†
0738-8632 Federal Tax Coordinator 2d **1923**
0738-8640 Knowledge†
0738-8667 Prismal-Cabral†
0738-8675 American Radio **2346**
0738-8705 The Panhandler *changed to* 1935-1305 **5260**
0738-8713 Hearing Research Developments
0738-8748 C I R R†
0738-8756 Penny Stock Performance Digest†
0738-8772 Laboratory Computer Letter
0738-8845 C M C News†
0738-8861 Progressive Platter Music Review†
0738-8888 International Currency Report†
0738-890X Furniture World **4557**
0738-8942 Conflict Management and Peace Science **7227**
0738-8950 Journal of Agribusiness **201**
0738-8977 Business Worcester
0738-9000 Creative Black Book†
0738-9035 Pacific Rim Intelligence Report†
0738-9094 Travelwriter Marketletter **4584**
0738-9116 Impartial Citizen
0738-9124 Land Mobile Product News†
0738-9159 National Council News **6162**
0738-9183 La Prensa San Diego **3559**
0738-9191 International Terrorism Newsletter†
0738-9213 Computer Buyer's Guide and Handbook†
0738-9264 Futurific *changed to* Futurific Leading Indicators **1112**
0738-9299 Frank
0738-9302 Ligature
0738-9310 Science of Food and Agriculture†
0738-9337 International Patent Litigation
0738-9345 Contributions to the Study of World Literature **5279**
0738-9361 Arts & Sciences (Evanston)†
0738-9388 Festivus **3591**
0738-9396 Mid-Atlantic Archivist **5032**
0738-9450 Iowa Legislative News Service Bulletin **7447**
0738-9477 N E C N P Newsletter **3142**
0738-9515 Travel Industry World Yearbook **8781**
0738-9604 Carefree Enterprise†
0738-9620 Textile Flammability Digest†
0738-9639 The Older American **4052**
0738-9655 John Donne Journal **5313**
0738-9663 Illinois Issues **7141**
0738-9671 New Mexico Humanities Review†
0738-968X I P M Practitioner **235**
0738-9728 International Lawyers' Newsletter†
0738-9736 Kanhistique **366**
0738-9744 Dental Computer Newsletter **5830**
0738-9752 Q J I **7175**
0738-9779 The Tribune (New York) **8886**
0738-9833 Ocean Realm **2623**
0738-985X Natchez Trace Traveler **3776**
0738-9906 Predicasts Basebook†
0738-9949 The U S Archer **8214**
0738-9981 Collectrix
0738-999X Florida Field Naturalist **907**
0739-0025 Luren†
0739-0033 Fillers for Publications
0739-0041 Florida Geographer **4006**
0739-0068 The Near East Archaeological Society. Bulletin **407**
0739-0084 Teachers & Writers **3084**
0739-0092 Today's Farmer **162**
0739-0130 Ohio United Way. Legislative Bulletin
0739-0157 Kansas English **3069**
0739-022X Spudletter **254**
0739-0270 A A M I News **4486**
0739-0289 Morticians of the Southwest **3720**
0739-0319 Miami Times **3550**
0739-0327 Waterfowler's World†
0739-0351 A N A R C Newsletter†
0739-036X Closed Loop†
0739-0378 CinemaTexas Program Notes
0739-0386 L O E X News *changed to* 1547-0172 **5024**
0739-0394 Campus Law Enforcement Journal **2646**
0739-0408 Tennessee Education **3034**
0739-0424 Mississippi Mud†
0739-0432 Sycamore Leaves†
0739-0440 Wesleyan World **7694**
0739-0483 California Pharmacist **6827**
0739-0491 Textile Business Outlook
0739-0505 Muslim World Pulse†
0739-0548 Asia Pulse†
0739-0572 Journal of Atmospheric and Oceanic Technology **6358**
0739-0602 Outdoor Press†
0739-0653 Peek 65†
0739-0718 Hue Points†
0739-0734 Urner Barry's National Weekly Hatch Report **189**
0739-0750 Fielding's Economy Caribbean
0739-0769 Fielding's Bermuda and the Bahamas†
0739-0793 Fielding's Mexico†
0739-0874 Computer Economics Report **2535**
0739-0904 Cornerstone Clues **3763**
0739-0939 Airpost Journal **6891**
0739-098X International Journal of Applied Philosophy **6926**
0739-0998 Jail and Prisoner Law Bulletin **4892**
0739-1048 Star Tech Journal **1904**
0739-1056 College Media Review **4573**
0739-1072 Baylor Business Review **1065**
0739-1102 Journal of Biomolecular Structure & Dynamics **735**
0739-1110 The Industrial-Organizational Psychologist **7362**
0739-1137 I A S S I S T Quarterly **5012**
0739-1153 O L A C Newsletter **5037**
0739-117X Motor Coach Age **8504**
0739-1218 Philosophy and the Arts†
0739-1226 National Directory of College Athletics (Women's Edition) **8189**
0739-1242 Noninvasive Medical Imaging†
0739-1250 Communal Societies **4136**
0739-1277 Willow Springs **5399**
0739-134X Landers Landing†
0739-1382 U.S. National Advisory Council on Continuing Education. Annual Report
0739-1390 International Council for Traditional Music. Bulletin **6576**
0739-1404 U.S. Office of Personnel Management. Personnel Systems and Oversight Group. Federal Civilian Workforce Statistics. Occupations of Federal White-Collar and Blue-Collar Workers **1272**
0739-1439 Restaurant Industry Operations Report **4397**
0739-1471 National Online Meeting. Proceedings†
0739-148X Illinois Teacher of Home Economics†
0739-1544 N C E C A Journal **537**
0739-1587 Corporate & Incentive Travel **8695**
0739-1617 National Educator
0739-1684 Federal Jobs Digest **6697**
0739-1692 Cancer Update†
0739-1706 Lawyer Hiring & Training Report† **8970**
0739-1714 Southern Partisan **3989**
0739-1722 Car Prices†
0739-1730 The Carolina Indian Voice **3525**
0739-1749 Daughters of Sarah†
0739-1781 Journal of Weather Modification **6359**
0739-1803 Lesbian News **4376**
0739-1811 Natural Gas Intelligence **6779**
0739-182X Society for Spanish and Portuguese Historical Studies. Bulletin **4265**
0739-1838 Red River Valley Heritage Press **4309**
0739-1854 Harvard International Review **7239**
0739-1862 Predicasts Company Thesaurus†
0739-1889 Limited Offering Exemptions: Regulation D **4875**
0739-1897 Entertainment, Publishing and the Arts Handbook **2380**
0739-1935 Satellite Audio Report†
0739-1943 Journal of Southwest Georgia History **4300**
0739-196X Real Life Magazine
0739-2001 Gray Panther Network†
0739-2044 Medicine & Computer†
0739-2117 Family Treebune **3766**
0739-2141 Magill's Cinema Annual **6506**
0739-2168 The I R A Reporter **1629**
0739-2257 Boats & Harbors **8273**
0739-2281 Searching Together **7774**
0739-229X Sonus **6617**
0739-2303 Teilhard Studies **7687**
0739-2311 Utah Holiday†
0739-232X Wind River Rendezvous **4318**
0739-2354 Crosscurrents†
0739-2494 Barrister (Philadelphia) **4627**
0739-2532 Catalyst for Change **3019**
0739-2559 Spectrum (Minneapolis) **7293**
0739-2958 All About Mail Order†
0739-2974 Northern Lights Studies in Creativity **509**
0739-2982 Fitness Business†
0739-2990 Managing International Development†
0739-3024 Association of American University Presses Directory **7552**
0739-3067 The Sporting News Official N B A Register **8246**
0739-3075 Energy Statistics†
0739-3121 Reporter - Your Editorial Assistant
0739-3148 New Political Science **7158**
0739-3156 The Office Professional **1853**
0739-3164 University R & D
0739-3172 Issues in Accounting Education **1293**
0739-3199 Higdon Family Newsletter **3770**
0739-3202 Texas Books in Review **636**
0739-3210 National Institute for Trial Advocacy. Docket†
0739-3253 High-Tech New Issues Advisory†
0739-3261 Islamic Art† **8966**
0739-327X National Auction Bulletin **1835**
0739-3369 Journal of Vocational Education Research *changed to* 1554-754X **2834**
0739-3393 Cataloging Service Bulletin Index **5001**
0739-344X Tradeswomen†
0739-3474 Carrier Pidgin **5104**
0739-3482 Virginia Appalachian Notes **3786**
0739-3490 National Association of Railroad Passengers News **8621**
0739-3520 Commodity Trading Digest†
0739-3547 Gulf Coast Oil Directory **1998**
0739-3555 Houston - Texas Oil Directory **6772**
0739-3571 Line of March†
0739-358X Research Alert (New York) **1839**
0739-3601 Paralegal **4755**
0739-3679 Energy Information Abstracts Annual†
0739-3695 Counterman **8576**
0739-3709 American Fire Journal†
0739-3733 Atterbury Letter - Wine, Dining & Travel†
0739-3784 Road Race Management Newsletter **8330**
0739-3830 North Carolina Plumbing, Heating & Cooling Forum **4124**
0739-3865 Point of Beginning **3280**
0739-3873 Business Mailers Review **2353**
0739-3881 Affaire de Coeur **5408**
0739-392X N A C A A News **2640**
0739-3938 Southern Political Report **7184**
0739-4144 Textile Pricing Outlook
0739-4233 e - lab *changed to* 1942-4671 **3131**
0739-4241 Provenance **4309**
0739-425X Children's Advocate **2148**
0739-4330 County Agents Directory **103**
0739-4381 Wisconsin Business Journal
0739-439X University of California at Los Angeles. Institute of Industrial Relations. Monograph and Research Series **1713**
0739-4403 Gun Digest Hunting Annual†
0739-4462 Archives of Insect Biochemistry and Physiology **839**
0739-456X Journal of Planning Education and Research **4417**
0739-4586 V A H P E R D Journal **6999**
0739-4640 Global Risk Assessments **1567**
0739-4667 Book on Starting Pitchers
0739-4691 Texas Blue Book of Life Insurance Statistics†
0739-4772 Heritage of the Great Plains **4295**
0739-4810 Current Hematology and Oncology†
0739-4829 P V News **3177**
0739-4837 La Prensa De Los Angeles†
0739-4853 Against the Current **7103**
0739-4896 Community Spirit Magazine (Carmel)
0739-4934 History of Science Society Newsletter **7862**
0739-4942 Warren Family Historian†
0739-4969 Outerbridge **5346**
0739-4977 International Water Conference. Official Proceedings **8826**
0739-4993 Small Animal Practice (Monrovia)
0739-5043 Career Opportunities News **6694**
0739-506X Library and Information Science Education Statistical Report **5059**
0739-5086 Judaica Librarianship **5022**
0739-5124 Chicago Theological Seminary Register **7630**
0739-5132 L.O.G.I.C.†
0739-5159 Electrical Overstress-Electrostatic Discharge Symposium Proceedings **3303**
0739-5175 I E E E Engineering in Medicine and Biology Magazine **748**
0739-5183 Organization of American States. Legal Newsletter†
0739-5272 Motheroot Journal†
0739-5329 Newspaper Research Journal **4581**
0739-5388 Advanced Vehicle News†
0739-5396 International Olympic Lifter†
0739-540X Current References in Fish Research†
0739-5418 A Friendly Letter†
0739-5442 One to One (Fresno) **2361**
0739-5523 Selected Readings in Plastic Surgery **6258**
0739-5531 Television Index **2397**
0739-5558 Children's Folklore Review **2148**
0739-5566 Economic News from Italy†
0739-5612 Archaeological Society of Connecticut. Bulletin **376**
0739-568X Scuba Times **8200**
0739-5698 Travel Weekly's World Travel Directory†
0739-5728 Helicopter Annual **8544**
0739-5736 Museum of Fine Arts, Boston. Bulletin†
0739-5914 Mind: The Meetings Index (Print)†
0739-5949 The Year Book of Hand Surgery *changed to* 1551-7977 **6263**
0739-5957 West Texas Geological Society. Bulletin **2774**
0739-6023 Catholic Northwest Progress **7789**
0739-6074 Nationwide Directory of Sporting Goods Buyers **8190**
0739-6155 Pioneer Times†
0739-6163 Federal Taxation of Insurance Companies†
0739-618X Business Publications Index and Abstracts†
0739-6198 Philateli-Graphics **6898**
0739-6201 ComputerTalk Directory of Medical Computer Systems†
0739-6236 Service Dealer's Newsletter **1793**
0739-6244 Asia - Pacific Currency Report†
0739-6279 Baseline Data Report†
0739-6376 Land Development Law Reporter **7597**
0739-6392 American University Studies. Series 5. Philosophy **6903**
0739-6406 American University Studies. Series 6. Foreign Language Instruction **5093**
0739-6422 Christian Life Communities Harvest **7792**
0739-6449 Investment Column Quarterly **1632**
0739-6538 Washington Remote Sensing Letter **74**
0739-6546 American Clay Exchange†
0739-6554 Medical Documentation Update†
0739-6562 Drug Abuse Update†
0739-6643 Trail Seekers **3785**
0739-6651 Savage Family Depository Newsletter
0739-6686 Annual Review of Nursing Research **5951**
0739-6694 Beginning (Iowa City)†
0739-6767 N C T V News
0739-6791 The Food and Fiber Letter **198**
0739-6821 Exhibitor Magazine **1816**
0739-6961 Almanac for Farmers and City Folk **3117**
0739-697X Newsletter of Engineering Analysis Software

0739-7003 Tinta **5389**
0739-7011 F I U Hospitality Review **4385**
0739-7046 Faith and Philosophy **6919**
0739-7062 New York State Pharmacist - Century II **6863**
0739-7097 Special Libraries Association. Washington D.C. Chapter. Chapter Notes **5048**
0739-7100 U M T R I Research Review **8518**
0739-7151 Facts about Blacks†
0739-7194 Bus Industry Magazine **8492**
0739-7240 Domestic Animal Endocrinology **8796**
0739-7259 Local Climatological Data. Tupelo, Missouri. Monthly Summary **6387**
0739-7313 Advances in Child Behavioral Analysis and Therapy **7331**
0739-7348 Infectious Disease Alert **5817**
0739-7437 Collision **8575**
0739-7453 G L A D News
0739-747X Nor'westing **8279**
0739-7569 American Journal of Tax Policy **1910**
0739-7666 Academy News (Colorado Springs) **5912**
0739-7712 School Library Media Annual†
0739-7747 Aviso **6520**
0739-7771 Computer Law Reporter **4648**
0739-7801 Hemingway Newsletter **5304**
0739-7828 Currents (Des Moines)
0739-7852 John Whitmer Historical Association. Journal **4148**
0739-7860 California Regulatory Law Reporter†
0739-7895 Book Arts Review†
0739-7917 Central Issues in Anthropology†
0739-7933 Shoreline/Coastal Zone Management†
0739-8042 California Today **3408**
0739-8050 Texas Energy Reporter **3148**
0739-8069 Middle States Council for the Social Studies. Journal **7985**
0739-8077 Practical Winery & Vineyard **609**
0739-8093 Fayette Connection†
0739-8123 Personal Electronics†
0739-8158 Fram
0739-8166 Cable Video Briefs
0739-8182 Impact: Office Automation†
0739-8239 Franchise Legal Digest†
0739-8328 Problems in General Surgery† **8982**
0739-8352 Advances in Petroleum Geochemistry **6761**
0739-8360 Pacific Review (San Diego) **4468**
0739-8395 Business Week. Industrial Edition *see* 0007-7135 **1077**
0739-8409 Business Week International **1076**
0739-8417 Cybernetics and Computing Technology†
0739-8433 Soviet Immunology†
0739-8468 MacRae's North Dakota - South Dakota State Industrial Directory†
0739-8476 MacRae's Arizona - New Mexico State Industrial Directory†
0739-8484 MacRae's Texas State Industrial Directory†
0739-8506 Catalyst (Seattle) **481**
0739-8549 Old English Newsletter. Subsidia **5345**
0739-8565 Dutchess County Historical Society. Yearbook **4291**
0739-8573 Current Emergency Therapy†
0739-862X N A R F Legal Review **6635**
0739-8646 Artpaper
0739-8662 Arts Journal†
0739-8689 Securities & Syndication Review **1650**
0739-8700 Minnesota Monthly **3981**
0739-8743 Automated Office Systems
0739-8859 Research in Transportation Economics **8510**
0739-8905 National Cancer Advisory Board. United States. Annual Report†
0739-8913 Christian Education Journal **7631**
0739-8921 Candy Industry Buyer's Guide **3672**
0739-8956 Economic Growth in Tennessee, Annual Report **1884**
0739-8972 Occasional Papers in Slavic Languages and Literature **5345**
0739-9022 Automated Materials Handling and Storage†
0739-909X L D A Newsbriefs **3043**
0739-9111 N L A D A Cornerstone **4968**
0739-9138 Investment Guide **1632**
0739-9170 American Dane†
0739-9189 C A L C Report
0739-9235 Farmer-Stockman of the Midwest **111**
0739-9243 The Frat **4074**
0739-9308 South Carolina Statistical Abstract **8402**
0739-9324 Voice of the Turtle **967**
0739-9332 Health Care for Women International **8846**
0739-9405 Programmer's Market†
0739-9413 Business and Health (Print Edition)†
0739-9480 Detroit Legal News **4657**
0739-9502 Gallup Monthly Report on Eating Out†
0739-9529 Seminars in Interventional Radiology **6208**
0739-9561 Hospital Pharmacy Service Instant Up-Date **6846**
0739-957X Hospital Pharmacy Director's Monthly Management Series **6846**
0739-9588 Vital Signs Pharmacy Services Newsletter **6885**
0739-9596 Pharmacy Health-Line **6873**
0739-9723 Merchant Magazine **3714**
0739-9731 Stetson Law Review **4789**
0739-9766 P A H A Newsletter†
0739-9774 Inside M S *changed to* 1940-3410 **6161**
0739-9847 Medical Month†
0739-9863 Hispanic Journal of Behavioral Sciences **7360**
0739-991X Current (Washington, 1980) **2379**
0739-9928 Computer Negotiations Report
0739-9936 Bank Acquisition Report†
0739-9987 President's Cancer Panel. Report of the Chairman **6032**
0739-9995 United States Congress. House Committee on Agriculture. Report on Activities **208**
0740-0004 Central America and the Caribbean: Development Assistance Abroad†
0740-0020 Food Microbiology **886**
0740-008X The Journal of Equipment Lease Financing **1136**
0740-011X Virginia Forests **3707**
0740-0179 T A C D A Alert **2228**
0740-0187 Construction Bargaineer†
0740-0195 Focus (Washington, D.C. 1986) **7206**
0740-0217 Spencer's Research Reports on Employee Benefits **1875**
0740-0225 Our Life **3556**
0740-0276 Fraser Opinion Letter†
0740-0357 EdCal **2845**
0740-0365 Accent West Amarillo **8680**
0740-0403 Museum Year **6532**
0740-0411 Supervisor's Newsletter†
0740-042X A L A Yearbook of Library and Information Services†
0740-0446 American University Studies. Series 7. Theology and Religion **7621**
0740-0454 American University Studies. Series 8. Psychology **7333**
0740-0462 American University Studies. Series 9. History **4129**
0740-0470 American University Studies. Series 10. Political Science **4615**
0740-0489 American University Studies. Series 11. Anthropology and Sociology **7947**
0740-0497 American University Studies. Series 12. Slavic Languages and Literature **5093**
0740-0535 Washington Federal Science Newsletter **7928**
0740-0586 Canadian Veterinary Pharmaceuticals & Biologicals **6828**
0740-0608 Ye Olde Newes
0740-0624 Perspectives on Local Public Finance and Public Policy†
0740-0632 A L D E E U. Cuadernos **2264**
0740-0640 Radiation Protection Management **6684**
0740-0659 Faith and Mission **7757**
0740-0667 American Chemical Society. Division of Environmental Chemistry. Preprints of Extended Abstracts†
0740-0675 History of Philosophy Quarterly **6923**
0740-0683 C A Selects. Automated Chemical Analysis†
0740-0691 C A Selects. Natural Product Synthesis **2088**
0740-0713 C A Selects. Fermentation Chemicals **2087**
0740-0721 C A Selects. Crosslinking Reactions **2086**
0740-0780 Carrousel Art
0740-0802 Spotlight on Youth Sports **8209**
0740-0845 Monographs in Epidemiology and Biostatistics **7532**
0740-0853 Saybrook Review†
0740-090X Law and Legal Information Directory **4713**
0740-0942 Lawyer's P C **4845**
0740-1035 Alcohol Clinical Update†
0740-1108 Shijie Ribao (Monterey Park) **3564**
0740-1116 Hunger Notes (Print Edition) *changed to* Hunger Notes (Online Edition) **8045**
0740-1183 Council Spotlight Booknotes†
0740-1205 Mr. Cogito†
0740-1248 Quarterly Review of Wines **609**
0740-1361 Ohio Beverage Journal **608**
0740-137X Protection of Assets Bulletin **2679**
0740-1418 O S H A News **6682**
0740-1434 Ag-Pilot International **44**
0740-1477 Ellis Cousins Newsletter **3764**
0740-154X Saga of Southern Illinois **3781**
0740-1558 Yearbook for Traditional Music **6629**
0740-1663 Study of Financial Results and Reporting Trends in the Gaming Industry†
0740-1744 D.C. Code Updater **7491**
0740-1809 Wire Rope News and Sling Technology **6715**
0740-1817 Petroleum Frontiers **6787**
0740-185X School Tech News†
0740-1892 Media Profiles: Health Sciences Edition†
0740-1906 Media Profiles: Career Development Edition
0740-1914 Anesthesia File Notebook†
0740-1922 The Electron **3095**
0740-1949 Daily Court Review **4865**
0740-1957 Madness Network News†
0740-1965 Schatzkammer **5172**
0740-1973 Florida Specifier **3431**
0740-2007 Ancient Philosophy **6904**
0740-2074 Draft Review and Preview†
0740-2155 Software Supermarket†
0740-218X On the Beam **5689**
0740-2201 Equal Play†
0740-2252 Acid Precipitation Digest†
0740-235X A L P S Monthly†
0740-2368 Mole†
0740-2384 New York Sports†
0740-2392 Agada **5250**
0740-2430 Quarterly Index: Information Access for the Small Animal Practitioner†
0740-252X Technology Network†
0740-2562 Peanut Industry Guide **205**
0740-2570 Seminars in Diagnostic Pathology **5712**
0740-2619 Synapse (San Francisco) **2303**
0740-2678 U S Association Executive **1799**
0740-2708 Journal of Correctional Education **2656**
0740-2716 Advertising Specialty Register: Product Research and Source Data
0740-2740 Sellers Letters†
0740-2775 World Policy Journal **7274**
0740-2783 American Malacological Bulletin **931**
0740-2791 Seminars, Workshops & Classes **2945**
0740-283X Creative Black Book. Portfolio Edition
0740-2856 Boca Raton Magazine **3971**
0740-2872 Film Directors: A Complete Guide **1993**
0740-2880 Literature Criticism from 1400 to 1800 **5325**
0740-2899 Business Journal Serving Greater Milwaukee **1073**
0740-2902 MacRae's Virginia State Industrial Directory†
0740-2910 MacRae's State Industrial Directory: Georgia†
0740-2929 MacRae's State Industrial Directory: Maryland - District of Columbia - Delaware†
0740-2945 MacRae's State Industrial Directory: Maine - New Hampshire - Vermont†
0740-2961 A S T M Standards Infobriefs†
0740-2996 Pennsylvania. Department of Agriculture. Seed Report **274**
0740-3046 Cousins et Cousines **3763**
0740-3119 Catalog Age *changed to* 1554-8961 **30**
0740-3127 S I R S Social Issues†
0740-3151 Iowa Legislative News Service Bulletin (Interim Report Edition) *see* 0738-9450 **7447**
0740-3194 Magnetic Resonance in Medicine **6202**
0740-3224 Optical Society of America. Journal B: Optical Physics **7082**
0740-3291 Cultural Survival Quarterly **3529**
0740-3313 DNotes†
0740-3437 L A Parent **2159**
0740-3550 New from Japan†
0740-3569 New from Europe†
0740-3577 New from U S†
0740-3585 World Electronic Developments†
0740-3593 Sex over Forty†
0740-3690 Federal Parks & Recreation (Print) *changed to* Federal Parks & Recreation (Online) **2611**
0740-3704 Capital Press **100**
0740-3739 Fine Chemicals Directory†
0740-3755 Music Industry Products†
0740-3801 Product Alert **3661**
0740-3852 Lookout - Nonfoods **595**
0740-3860 Lookout - Foods **3654**
0740-3909 U.S. Department of Energy. Energy Information Administration. Annual Energy Review (Year) **3148**
0740-395X College By Mail Newsletter - Etc. Newsletter **2972**
0740-3968 Computer User (Cerritos)†
0740-3984 D.C. Directory†
0740-4018 America's Corporate Families and International Affiliates **1972**
0740-4050 A B A / B N A Lawyers' Manual on Professional Conduct Current Reports **4606**
0740-4077 Work America **1525**
0740-4085 Computer Publishers & Publications†
0740-4093 Quilt Digest†
0740-4131 Camping Magazine **2146**
0740-4174 U S P - D I. Vol. 1. Drug Information for the Health Care Professional† **8995**
0740-4182 Credences: A Journal of Twentieth Century Poets and Poetics†
0740-4190 U.S. Department of Energy. Energy Information Administration. Annual Energy Outlook (Year) **3154**
0740-4212 Springer Series in Psychiatry† **8990**
0740-4247 Video Marketing Surveys and Forecasts†
0740-4271 Secondary Mortgage Markets†
0740-428X MacRae's Iowa - Nebraska State Industrial Directory†
0740-4298 MacRae's State Industrial Directory: Pennsylvania†
0740-4328 MacRae's Kentucky - West Virginia State Industrial Directory†
0740-4336 MacRae's Illinois State Industrial Directory†
0740-4409 Under Construction
0740-4417 San Diego Leaves & Saplings **3781**
0740-4549 Source Book: Social and Health Services in the Greater New York Area **8072**
0740-4557 American University Studies. Series 13. Linguistics **5093**
0740-4565 American University Studies. Series 14. Education **3017**
0740-4603 Unity (Oakland)†
0740-4638 MacRae's State Industrial Directory: California†
0740-4646 MacRae's State Industrial Directory: Tennessee†
0740-4654 MacRae's Mississippi State Industrial Directory†
0740-4662 MacRae's Oklahoma State Industrial Directory†
0740-4670 MacRae's Arkansas State Industrial Directory†
0740-4697 MacRae's Florida State Industrial Directory†
0740-4727 Valley Journal
0740-476X Music Industry Directory†
0740-4816 Supermicro†
0740-4824 Brooklyn Journal of International Law **4919**
0740-4832 Grassroots Fundraising Journal **8042**
0740-4840 Publishing Northwest Newsletter†
0740-4859 Hyatt's P C News Report†
0740-4921 Details **6288**
0740-4956 Focus: Library Service to Older Adults, People with Disabilities†
0740-4964 Consumer Alert Comments **2636**
0740-4980 F T Systems **2520**
0740-4999 Northwest Trail Tracer **3777**
0740-5006 Iredell County Tracks (NC) **3772**
0740-5022 Software Publishers' Catalogs Annual†
0740-5065 Military Living **6435**
0740-5073 Military Living's R & R Report **6436**
0740-5103 Investment Decisions†
0740-5111 American University Studies. Series 15. Communications **2312**
0740-5138 International Journal of Reviews in Library and Information Science†
0740-5154 Keepsake (Scottsdale)†
0740-5162 International Coal Testing Conference†
0740-5197 B A S H Magazine†
0740-5251 Tips & Techniques†
0740-5278 Gas Processors Report **6770**
0740-5294 Rehabfilm Newsletter†
0740-5324 Perspective on A T & T and Boc Products and Marketing†
0740-5367 Timbertown Log **3785**
0740-5375 International Journal of Islamic and Arabic Studies†
0740-5383 Grant Advisor **2983**
0740-5391 Columbia Review (Columbia)†
0740-5405 Cyrano's Journal **2318**
0740-543X Society of Exploration Geophysicists. International Meeting. Abstracts *changed to* 0737-0164 **2789**
0740-5472 Journal of Substance Abuse Treatment **2696**
0740-5502 Information and Behavior **7362**
0740-5529 Pelican Guide to the Bahamas **8747**
0740-5537 Journal of Civil Defense **2227**
0740-557X United Mutual Fund Selector†
0740-5596 Insights into Open Education†
0740-560X Gifted Unlimited
0740-5618 Friendly Woman
0740-5669 Better Business†
0740-5685 Programming Trends in Therapeutic Recreation†
0740-5723 Art & Artists†
0740-5804 Ampersand **7551**
0740-5812 MadAminA! **6586**

ISSN

9330 0740-5820 ULRICH'S PERIODICALS

0740-5820 Latham Letter 8053
0740-588X American Canals 8638
0740-5901 Jews for Jesus Newsletter 7737
0740-591X Irish Herald 3541
0740-5928 Jersey Jazz 6580
0740-5944 Gwiazda Polarna 3536
0740-5960 Academic Journal
0740-5979 Herbarist 3736
0740-6045 MacRae's Indiana State Industrial Directory†
0740-6053 MacRae's Wisconsin State Industrial Directory†
0740-6061 MacRae's Minnesota State Industrial Directory†
0740-607X MacRae's Missouri State Industrial Directory†
0740-6088 MacRae's Idaho - Montana - Wyoming State Industrial Directory†
0740-610X MacRae's Oregon State Industrial Directory†
0740-6118 MacRae's Kansas State Industrial Directory†
0740-6126 MacRae's Colorado - Utah - Nevada State Industrial Directory†
0740-6134 MacRae's Washington State Industrial Directory†
0740-6231 Computer Publishing & Advertising Report†
0740-624X Government Information Quarterly 7440
0740-6258 Business of Fur†
0740-6452 Correspondent (Appleton)† 8944
0740-6460 M A R C Newsletter 7661
0740-6673 Carpenter and Related Family Historical Journal†
0740-669X International Report (Irvine)†
0740-672X Mutual Magazine 8620
0740-6746 International Old Lacers, Inc. Bulletin 6639
0740-6754 The Word (Rochester, NY) 6648
0740-6797 Society for Modeling and Simulation International. Transactions 2518
0740-6800 Data Base Product Reports†
0740-6819 Automated Law Office Consultant†
0740-6835 Conscience 7793
0740-6916 U S P - D I. Vol. 2. Advice for the Patient 6883
0740-6959 Profession 3077
0740-6967 Cataract; International Journal of Cataract Surgery†
0740-719X Contemporary German Philosophy†
0740-7211 Homes International†
0740-722X Aerospace America 42
0740-736X Library Hotline 5027
0740-7378 Biotechnology Series 761
0740-7394 Linscott's Directory of Immunological and Biological Reagents 737
0740-7416 Frontiers of Entrepreneurship Research 1112
0740-7459 I E E E Software 2590
0740-7475 I E E E Design & Test of Computers 2471
0740-7564 Toth-Maatian Review†
0740-7580 Computers in Medical Practice 5830
0740-7688 California Library Directory 5000
0740-770X Women & Performance 8484
0740-7750 Somatic Cell and Molecular Genetics†
0740-7785 Exhibit Reporter†
0740-784X Cell Membranes: Methods and Reviews†
0740-7874 E R S Spectrum 2844
0740-7890 Permafrost 5350
0740-7998 The Biblical Evangelist 7748
0740-8005 China Briefing†
0740-8013 Oak Leaves 3777
0740-8048 Yale Law & Policy Review 4817
0740-8056 Save Energy†
0740-8064 Envoy (New York)†
0740-8102 Guide to Graduate Degree Programs in Architectural History†
0740-8161 Mushroom 3744
0740-817X I I E Transactions 3367
0740-8188 Library & Information Science Research 5027
0740-8218 Indiana Medical History Quarterly†
0740-8226 Medical and Pediatric Oncology. Supplement 6027
0740-8250 Directory of Psychiatry Residency Training Programs 6136
0740-8269 House Committee on Rules. Survey of Activities 7444
0740-8285 Casual Living 4555
0740-8293 Buried Treasure from Aceto Genealogical Files†
0740-8307 E I D O S 8859
0740-8358 American Archeology 372
0740-8366 Minnesota Insurance 4515
0740-8404 A M A T Y C Review 5463
0740-8439 The Book 7554
0740-8498 The Wellness Newsletter†
0740-8501 Washington Counseletter 6705
0740-851X U C L A Business Forecast for California†
0740-8528 American Council for Judaism. Special Interest Report 7717
0740-8625 Studies in Contemporary Jewry 3566
0740-8684 Nutrition Report†
0740-8706 Conference on Electron Beam Melting and Refining. Proceedings†
0740-8765 P M T
0740-8803 Water Resources Data for Wisconsin 8839
0740-8900 Mechanisms of Inorganic and Organometallic Reactions†
0740-8935 Poetry Review
0740-8943 Communications from the International Brecht Society 5276
0740-8951 Olde Mecklenburg Genealogical Society Quarterly 3778
0740-896X Tri-State Packet 3786
0740-8978 American Public Opinion Index
0740-8994 New England Journal on Criminal and Civil Confinement 4741
0740-9133 Northeast African Studies 3555
0740-9141 Tar River Poetry 5436
0740-9214 Arts Quarterly 475
0740-9222 Milk Facts 267
0740-9257 American University Studies. Series 2. Romance Languages and Literature 5253
0740-9303 Ophthalmic Plastic and Reconstructive Surgery 6048
0740-9311 Clockwatch Review†
0740-9354 Teleconnect† 8992
0740-9451 Microcirculation, Endothelium and Lymphatics
0740-946X Siglo XX†
0740-9478 Mississippi Philological Association. Publications 5334
0740-9524 Stamp Journals Index
0740-9540 U.S. Court of International Trade. Reports 1585
0740-9567 Africa Research and Publications Project. Working Papers Series†
0740-9583 Genetic Epistemologist 7358
0740-9613 Let's Pray Together†
0740-9648 Escape Magazine 3975
0740-9664 Indiana Daily Student 2287
0740-9680 Times of Restoration 7690
0740-9699 The Mohawk 3775
0740-9702 The Saratoga 3781
0740-9710 Food and Foodways 6659
0740-9729 Monographs in Primatology 956
0740-9737 Genewatch 870
0740-9745 Benchmark Sites News†
0740-9834 Senate Election Law Guidebook 4782
0740-9893 Excellence in Teaching†
0740-9982 Hospital Manager†
0741-0034 El Tecolote 3568
0741-0042 C A D - C A M: Management Strategies†
0741-0050 Executive Computing†
0741-0077 Online Database Search Services Directory†
0741-0085 Caribe Magazine 481
0741-0107 The Licensing Book 6754
0741-0115 N B A Magazine 4737
0741-0123 Reviews in Economic Geology 2764
0741-0131 International Review of Mental Imagery†
0741-0182 Georgia Descriptions in Data†
0741-0204 Global Perspectives†
0741-0212 The Year's Best Mystery and Suspense Stories†
0741-0263 Dynamic 7131
0741-0271 Sunrust†
0741-0298 Brasilians Journal
0741-031X California Library Statistics 5057
0741-0344 California State Library Foundation Bulletin 5000
0741-0352 Issues (San Francisco) 7737
0741-0360 The Pied Cow 3779
0741-0379 M A C Newsletter 5030
0741-0395 Genetic Epidemiology 869
0741-0506 The New Brewer 608
0741-059X American Quaternary Association. Conference. Program and Abstracts 2719
0741-0611 Geographic Distribution of V A Expenditures 6422
0741-0689 Water Resources Data for Alaska 8839
0741-0697 Water Resources Data for Colorado 8839
0741-0700 American University Studies. Series 4. English Language and Literature 5253
0741-0727 N A I C News 4515
0741-076X A L A Worldwide Directory and Fact Book 6408
0741-0794 Ceilidh†
0741-0808 High-Tech Materials Alert 3345
0741-0816 Scentouri News 3988
0741-0840 Utah Geological and Mineral Survey. Open-File Report *changed to* Utah Geological Survey. Open-File Reports 2773
0741-0883 Written Communication 2345
0741-0921 N A S D A Q Fact Book 1642
0741-1111 American Politics
0741-1162 Pre Law Journal 4760
0741-1170 Law School Administrator's Journal 4716
0741-1189 Legal Bibliography Journal 4823
0741-1197 Law Teacher's Journal 4717
0741-1200 Bridge (Ames) 3523
0741-1219 Patent, Trademark and Copyright Laws (Year) 6756
0741-1235 Sociology of Sport Journal 8139
0741-1243 Milwaukee Magazine 3981
0741-126X International Daily News 3540
0741-1278 Mutual Fund Specialist
0741-1286 Hermes Americanus 2235
0741-1294 The Masonry Society Journal 1022
0741-1308 Urban Resources†
0741-1316 Nebo 5338
0741-1340 Military Manpower Statistics 6455
0741-1359 U.S. Nuclear Regulatory Commission. Power Reactor Events†
0741-1391 California Linguistic Newsletter *changed to* California Linguistic Notes 5104
0741-1413 International Electrochemical Progress†
0741-1448 Florida Foliage†
0741-1537 Folio *changed to* 1945-2381 7779
0741-160X Radiology and Imaging Letter†
0741-1626 Current Advances in Cell & Developmental Biology 714
0741-1634 Current Advances in Endocrinology†
0741-1642 Current Advances in Genetics & Molecular Biology 714
0741-1677 Current Advances in Neuroscience 5743
0741-1707 Gold Skills†
0741-1715 Sound & Video Contractor 8155
0741-1723 National Accident Sampling System *changed to* National Automotive Sampling System 8527
0741-1731 Space Calendar 70
0741-1758 Evangelical Journal 7641
0741-1790 Avalon to Camelot†
0741-191X Chronicle of the O A S *changed to* 1945-4708
0741-1952 Hideaways Guide *changed to* 1930-2622 8718
0741-1995 Concerned Investors Guide
0741-2037 Crossroads 4181
0741-2045 Kates Kin 3772
0741-2088 Belli Law Journal†
0741-2150 American University Studies. Series 16. Economics 1535
0741-2207 Blue & Gray Magazine 4285
0741-2223 Journal of Robotic Systems *changed to* 1556-4959 2585
0741-2290 Women's Health†
0741-2312 Child and Family Policy†
0741-2320 Today's Therapeutic Trends 5722
0741-2347 Apple Index
0741-2355 I B M - P C Index
0741-2363 Business Computer Index
0741-238X Advances in Therapy 5568
0741-2460 Wavelength (New Orleans)
0741-2576 Texas Linguistic Forum 5187
0741-2592 Afrique Histoire
0741-2673 Mystic Light of the Aladdin Knights 367
0741-2827 Yearbook of German - American Studies 5403
0741-286X Open Systems Data Transfer
0741-2878 C I S Federal Register Index†
0741-2894 Senior Voice 4055
0741-2940 I S C A Quarterly 494
0741-3017 Health Letter (New York)†
0741-3106 I E E E Electron Device Letters 3101
0741-3149 Midway Review†
0741-3157 Party Mail†
0741-3173 Local/State Funding Report 1933
0741-3335 Plasma Physics and Controlled Fusion 7035
0741-3343 Oil Industry Outlook for the U S A†
0741-3351 The Artist's Magazine 473
0741-336X Standard for Auditing Computer Applications†
0741-3432 San Antonio Living
0741-3467 From the State Capitals. Consumer Protection†
0741-3599 Minnesota Genealogical Journal 3775
0741-3610 C P A Digest†
0741-3629 Energy Design Update 1006
0741-367X Annual Report on Industrial Robots†
0741-3696 Sports - Nutrition News
0741-3742 Voice of Local 880 4605
0741-3750 Opportunity Magazine†
0741-4110 West's Social Security Reporting Service 4528
0741-4129 Paperboard Packaging's International Container Directory *changed to* International Container Directory 8965
0741-4188 Library Currents 5027
0741-4218 Clinical Cardiology Alert 5783
0741-4234 Neurology Alert 6166
0741-4242 The Long Story 5327
0741-4250 Teilhard Perspectives 7687
0741-4285 Run†
0741-4307 Advent Christian Witness 7744
0741-434X Louisiana. Department of Public Safety. Summary of Motor Vehicle Traffic Accidents. Rural 8385
0741-4358 Louisiana. Department of Public Safety. Summary of Motor Vehicle Traffic Accidents. Statewide 8386
0741-4382 Louisiana. Department of Public Safety. Summary of Motor Vehicle Traffic Accidents. Shreveport 8385
0741-4439 Louisiana. Department of Public Safety. Summary of Motor Vehicle Traffic Accidents. Kenner 8385
0741-4498 Growing Edge†
0741-451X Water Resources Data for South Dakota 8839
0741-4579 Arts Review†
0741-4587 U S S E A Update 74
0741-4617 Contractor Profit News†
0741-4641 Business Computing†
0741-465X American Council for Judaism. Issues 7717
0741-4773 Hidden Valley Journal 3770
0741-4803 Water Resources Data for Kansas 8839
0741-482X Security and Special Police Legal Update†
0741-4862 U S Economy Lodging Industry†
0741-4927 Paper Collector's Marketplace 368
0741-496X Art-Talk 471
0741-501X Assessor's Data Exchange†
0741-5028 Bluefish
0741-5141 Mental Health Law Reporter *changed to* Joint Commission Advisor for Behavioral Health 4833
0741-5168 Alaska. Division of Geological and Geophysical Surveys. Alaska's Mineral Industry 2723
0741-5184 West's Federal Taxation. Comprehensive Volume 1954
0741-5192 K Power†
0741-5206 Plastic Surgical Nursing 5978
0741-5214 Journal of Vascular Surgery 6250
0741-5222 Laser Research†
0741-5230 Acid Precipitation†
0741-5249 Solar Thermal Energy Technology†
0741-5257 Coal Preparation and Pollution Control†
0741-5273 Dunrobin Piper 3530
0741-5346 West's Education Law Digest
0741-5362 The I S C Newsletter†
0741-5400 Journal of Leukocyte Biology 683
0741-5435 Tomahawk (Indianapolis) 2304
0741-5516 Living (Phoenix Edition)†
0741-5702 Formations†
0741-5737 American Salon 585
0741-5745 Human Intelligence International Newsletter†
0741-5753 Society for German - American Studies. Newsletter 5374
0741-5788 Bulwark 4827
0741-5796 W O H R C News†
0741-580X Modem Notes 2564
0741-5818 Travel Smart for Business†
0741-5826 Travel Smart 8767
0741-5834 Lightwave 2331
0741-5842 Shaw 5371
0741-5877 International Series in Heat and Mass Transfer†
0741-5885 Jazziz 6579
0741-5893 Computers - R - Digital†
0741-5958 Third Rail 5242
0741-6016 Microcomputer Industry Update†
0741-6024 Fiction Network Magazine†
0741-6075 Journal of Christian Jurisprudence†
0741-6091 Kovels on Antiques and Collectibles 367
0741-6156 Theory and Practice 6623
0741-6164 The Phonetician 5161
0741-6210 Croton Review†
0741-6229 Zetetic Scholar 6744
0741-6245 Mayo Clinic Health Letter 5665
0741-6253 Diabetes Self-Management 5888
0741-6261 RAND Journal of Economics 1164
0741-6296 Water Resources Data. Missouri 8839
0741-6423 American Productivity & Quality Center. Case Study†
0741-6512 D R G Monitor†
0741-6547 Dunn Report†
0741-6555 Feminist Bookstore News 7561
0741-6563 The Primary Source 5040
0741-6571 Survey of Jewish Affairs 7730
0741-6601 Sales & Marketing Digest (Boca Raton)†

Link to your serials resources and content with ulrichsweb.com

0741-6881 Woodson Watcher Plus Allied Lines
0741-6903 Directory of General Merchandise, Variety & Specialty Stores (Year)†
0741-692X Federal Court Management Statistics **4951**
0741-6989 C G S M Enterprise *changed to* 0897-1447 **1735**
0741-6997 H R Reporter†
0741-7004 Foundation Giving Watch†
0741-7136 Adult Education Quarterly **2938**
0741-7233 Annual Editions: Comparative Politics **7106**
0741-7284 Knox County Illinois Genealogical Society. Quarterly **3773**
0741-739X C S C Reports†
0741-7403 Familia Latina†
0741-7497 Northern California Review of Business and Economics†
0741-7527 Annali d'Italianistica **5255**
0741-756X Poetry North Review†
0741-7586 Pacific Maritime Magazine **8656**
0741-7594 Young Authors Magazine **2223**
0741-7632 Bateman Datum
0741-7659 The Double Reed **6562**
0741-7713 Coal-Based Synfuels†
0741-7721 Unconventional Petroleum†
0741-7748 Consuming Passions†
0741-7780 Sheet Music Exchange
0741-7802 Harford Historical Bulletin **4294**
0741-8124 Railroad Notes†
0741-8132 Business Book Review **1071**
0741-8264 Circuit Rider (Springfield) **3762**
0741-8280 Advances in Economic Botany **773**
0741-8329 Alcohol (New York) **2690**
0741-8345 Blue Chip Financial Forecasts **1612**
0741-837X School Finance News†
0741-8388 State Telephone Regulation Report **2371**
0741-8450 Simon Wiesenthal Center Annual†
0741-8477 Boston University Journal of Tax Law†
0741-8485 Urban Institute. Policy and Research Report†
0741-8507 I G W M C Ground Water Modeling Newsletter **2795**
0741-8531 Wrap Up on Latin American Agriculture, Food, Fishing & Livestock†
0741-854X Wrap Up on Latin American Banking & Finance†
0741-8558 Wrap Up on Latin American Chemicals, Cosmetics, Pharmaceuticals & Medical Equipment†
0741-8566 Wrap Up on Latin American Construction, Housing & Real Estate†
0741-8574 Wrap Up on Latin American Mining & Forestry†
0741-8582 Wrap Up on Latin American Textile & Leather, Rubber & Plastic Industries†
0741-8590 Wrap Up on Latin American Machinery, Electronics & Communications†
0741-8604 Wrap Up on Latin American Energy†
0741-8620 Journal of Dental Practice Administration†
0741-8639 Sage: A Scholarly Journal on Black Women†
0741-8647 MacWorld **2577**
0741-8655 Author Biographies Master Index†
0741-8760 Locomotive **5455**
0741-8779 Aerospace Material Specifications **43**
0741-8795 Esoteric Review
0741-8809 Computer Law Monitor†
0741-8825 Justice Quarterly **2658**
0741-8841 Packaging Patents Newsletter†
0741-885X Plastics Processing Patents Newsletter†
0741-8868 Plastics Materials Patents Newsletter†
0741-9015 Food & Wine **3637**
0741-9023 Preservation Tech Notes **1029**
0741-9031 Kentucky Manufacturers Register **2010**
0741-9058 Library Hi Tech News **5062**
0741-9147 National Women's Health Report **8847**
0741-9155 The Chattahoochee Review **5272**
0741-9163 Sacred Art Journal†
0741-9228 American Institute of Indian Studies. Biennial Report†
0741-9279 N C A A Men's and Women's Skiing Rules **8323**
0741-9309 American University Studies. Series 17. Classical Language and Literature **2230**
0741-9325 Remedial and Special Education **3046**
0741-9333 Cogitations on Law and Government **4644**
0741-9341 Advances in Computing Research†
0741-9368 Healthcare Marketing Report **6988**
0741-9384 Hora
0741-9414 Washington Informer **3572**
0741-9430 Electric Utility Instrumentation†
0741-9449 Minnesota Journal†
0741-9457 The Yale Journal on Regulation **4817**
0741-9481 Journal of Child and Youth Care Work **2156**
0741-9643 U.S. Department of Energy. Energy Information Administration. Petroleum Marketing Monthly (Print)†
0741-9767 Metropolitan Life Insurance Company. Statistical Bulletin S B†
0741-9791 SoftNews†
0741-9805 Pennsylvania English **5350**
0741-9821 Writers West†
0741-9848 American Vegetable Grower **218**
0741-9872 Concord (Chicago) **7752**
0741-9899 Annotated Guide to Women's Periodicals in the United States and Canada†
0741-9910 North American Lily Society. Yearbook **3745**
0741-9937 Algebras, Groups and Geometries **5468**
0741-9945 Polish Music History Series **6606**
0741-9953 International Book Collectors Almanac. Newsletter†
0741-997X Absolute Reference **2570**
0742-0013 Prism (Fort Lauderdale)†
0742-0021 Real Estate Finance Today†
0742-0226 Arizona State University Law Forum **4621**
0742-0242 Sponsored Research in the History of Art†
0742-0277 Black Issues in Higher Education *changed to* 1557-5411 **2978**
0742-0293 Word Processing News (Burbank)†
0742-0315 Chilton's Truck and Van Repair Manual *changed to* Chilton's Truck and Van Service Manual **8574**
0742-034X Arizona Trends **5065**
0742-0412 Public Works Manual†
0742-0420 Antique Toy World **4327**
0742-0463 Volcanology & Seismology **2791**
0742-0498 State Budget and Tax News†
0742-0501 Publisher's Directory **7570**
0742-051X Teaching and Teacher Education **3084**
0742-0528 Chronobiology International **666**
0742-0552 Blueprints **435**
0742-0587 Sports Afield Fishing†
0742-0595 Sports Afield Fishing Secrets†
0742-0633 Computer Security Alert **2512**
0742-065X Daily Bible Study **7753**
0742-0757 Tennessee Tax Guide **1951**
0742-0889 Construction Claims Citator **995**
0742-0897 Chiron **7344**
0742-0919 Dow Jones-Irwin Mutal Fund Yearbook†
0742-0935 Mature Outlook†
0742-096X Allegheny Review **5251**
0742-1036 Professional Computing†
0742-1044 Aletheia
0742-1087 U.S. District Court Federal Filings Alert **4966**
0742-1095 Want's Federal-State Court Directory *changed to* 1938-565X **4951**
0742-1109 Aids and Research Tools in Middle Eastern Studies **4319**
0742-1117 Bibliotheca Afroasiatica **5100**
0742-1125 Islamic Art and Architecture **497**
0742-1133 Invited Lectures on the Middle East at the University of Texas at Austin†
0742-1141 Byzantina Kai Metabyzantina†
0742-115X Humana Civilitas†
0742-1168 Studies in Near Eastern Culture and Society **4325**
0742-1176 Interplay (Malibu) **5310**
0742-1184 Other Realities **351**
0742-1206 U-News†
0742-1222 Journal of Management Information Systems **2548**
0742-1419 Family History Capers **3765**
0742-1427 Data Sets: Cuneiform Texts†
0742-1478 Health Care Strategic Management†
0742-1494 Vintage '45†
0742-1508 Cockpit **51**
0742-1516 Connecticut Greenhouse Newsletter *changed to* Yankee Grower **259**
0742-1575 Water Resources Data for Texas **8839**
0742-1621 Software in Healthcare†
0742-1656 Art Therapy **6106**
0742-1753 A S C E Annual Combined Index†
0742-1796 Biomedical Ethics Reviews **5586**
0742-1850 Railroad Facts
0742-1915 Journal of Clinical Psychiatry Monograph Series **6150**
0742-1923 American University Studies. Series 18. African Literature **5253**
0742-1931 International Journal of Adult Orthodontics and Orthognathic Surgery†
0742-194X The Year Book of Podiatric Medicine and Surgery†
0742-1974 The Engineering Index Monthly **3229**
0742-2032 Ultrasport†
0742-2075 Hudson Valley Regional Review **2287**
0742-2091 Cell Biology and Toxicology **3495**
0742-2113 Stories†
0742-2334 Computer Aided Research in Near Eastern Studies **4171**
0742-2393 Trinity University Monograph Series in Religion†
0742-2466 Florida Review **5297**
0742-2474 Indiana Directory of Music Teachers **6575**
0742-2520 Directory of International Music Education Dissertations in Progress†
0742-2644 Real Estate Quarterly†
0742-2652 N R C Regulatory Agenda **8432**
0742-2733 Philosophy in Context†
0742-2741 Telecommunications Patents Newsletter†
0742-2768 Rag Mag **5236**
0742-2822 Echocardiography **5785**
0742-2962 Affirmative Action Information. Yakima County *see* Washington (State). Employment Security Department. Affirmative Action Information **1274**
0742-2970 Affirmative Action Information. Pasco and Franklin Counties *see* Washington (State). Employment Security Department. Affirmative Action Information **1274**
0742-3071 Diabetic Medicine **5889**
0742-3098 Journal of Pineal Research **6156**
0742-3101 Engineering Geology Abstracts†
0742-3152 Abstracts of the Midwinter Research Meeting **6076**
0742-3187 American Group Psychotherapy Monograph Series **7332**
0742-3217 Dermatology (New York, 1982)†
0742-3225 Family Medicine **5613**
0742-3233 Computers in Life Science Education†
0742-3322 Advances in Strategic Management **1724**
0742-3330 Serbian Studies **4475**
0742-339X Evaluating Your Firm's Injury & Illness Record. Services Industries†
0742-3403 Evaluating Your Firm's Injury & Illness Record. Transportation & Public Utilities Industries†
0742-3411 Evaluating Your Firm's Injury & Illness Record. Wholesale & Retail Trade Industries†
0742-3438 Aging Network News†
0742-3446 Merritt Risk Management News **4515**
0742-3470 Afro-American Journal of Philosophy
0742-3497 Nonprofit Counsel *changed to* 1542-8419 **4632**
0742-3519 Columbus Computer Xchange
0742-3551 Channel 9000†
0742-3578 Techniques†
0742-3640 International Journal on World Peace **7244**
0742-3667 National Center for the Study of Collective Bargaining in Higher Education and the Professions. Annual Conference Proceedings **2994**
0742-3675 United States Trade Fair
0742-3705 Society of Experimental Test Pilots. Symposium Proceedings **70**
0742-3713 Economic Development Review **1884**
0742-3780 Michie's Texas Tort Reporter†
0742-3802 U.S. Small Business Administration. Office of the Inspector General. Semi-Annual Report **1968**
0742-3837 Progressive Forensics†
0742-3896 L E R S Monograph Series **5659**
0742-390X Current Ornithology **906**
0742-3934 Copper in the United States†
0742-3985 International Periodicals and Reference Works†
0742-4043 National Winter Storms Operations Plan **2227**
0742-406X Gates Researcher†
0742-4078 United States Senate. Committee on the Judiciary. Report on the Activities during the Congress **4966**
0742-4108 Receptors and Ligands in Intercellular Communication Series†
0742-4248 Clues **5275**
0742-4256 Soviet Scientific Reviews Supplement Series. Physicochemical Biology†
0742-4299 U S F L Guide and Register†
0742-4329 Tennessee Attorneys Directory and Buyers Guide **4793**
0742-4337 Energy Meetings & Trade Shows Directory†
0742-4434 Raw†
0742-4469 Compute's P C & P C jr.†
0742-4477 Agribusiness (New York) **191**
0742-4485 Golf Digest Almanac (Year)†
0742-4507 Netback **1642**
0742-4515 Good Money **1627**
0742-4531 Termino **5386**
0742-454X Red Fox Review at Mohegan Community College†
0742-4574 Boxes and Arrows†
0742-4612 The Mississippi Rag **6588**
0742-4639 The Word Among Us **7823**
0742-4647 Mealey's Litigation Report: Asbestos **4836**
0742-4655 Mealey's Litigation Report: Iranian Claims†
0742-4671 Journal of Film and Video **6505**
0742-4779 Heir Lines **3770**
0742-4787 Journal of Tribology **6776**
0742-4795 Journal of Engineering for Gas Turbines and Power **3385**
0742-4817 The Los Angeles Times Index **4587**
0742-4876 Interpreter (Sacramento)†
0742-4906 Opera Digest
0742-4914 Bibliography on Cable Television **2346**
0742-5031 Kol ha-T'nuah **7726**
0742-504X I B R O Handbook Series†
0742-5066 Chesapeake Bay Foundation. Annual Report **3410**
0742-5252 Elliott Wave Theorist **1621**
0742-5279 Election Politics†
0742-5287 Hispanic Linguistics **5125**
0742-5317 Federal Bar Association. Section of Taxation. Report **1923**
0742-5341 The Report on I B M **2541**
0742-535X World Right-to-Die Newsletter†
0742-5368 Pantheist Vision **7740**
0742-5414 Central America Monitor†
0742-5457 Asian Theatre Journal **8466**
0742-5473 Dickens Quarterly **5284**
0742-5503 Mystics Quarterly **7664**
0742-5511 Grounds Management Forum **3735**
0742-552X Detention Reporter **2650**
0742-5538 Historical Guides to the World's Periodicals and Newspapers **4576**
0742-5562 Midwest Modern Language Association. Journal **5334**
0742-5600 Real Estate Computer Review
0742-5619 Disability Income and Health Insurance†
0742-5627 Innovative Higher Education **2987**
0742-5635 Wild and Free†
0742-5678 Carolina Real Estate Journal†
0742-5686 Comput-A-Cal†
0742-5694 Building Products Digest **986**
0742-5708 Hospital Capital Finance†
0742-5783 Radio P C Report†
0742-5813 Trademark Alert†
0742-5821 International Directory of Nuclear Utilities **3169**
0742-5929 American Journal of Chinese Studies **542**
0742-597X Journal of Management in Engineering **3205**
0742-5996 Ring Systems Handbook **2130**
0742-602X Merger and Acquisition Sourcebook (Year) **1148**
0742-6046 Psychology & Marketing **7398**
0742-6089 Used Computer Guide
0742-6119 Visionary Company: A Magazine of the Twenties†
0742-6151 G T E Network Systems World-Wide Communications Journal **2350**
0742-6186 Advances in Industrial and Labor Relations **1662**
0742-6208 R V Buyers Guide **8509**
0742-6216 Uniform C P A Examination. Questions and Unofficial Answers†
0742-6224 Yeats **5403**
0742-6313 Advances in Mental Retardation and Developmental Disabilities†
0742-6348 Northern Journal of Applied Forestry **3698**
0742-6380 Organizational Ethics Newsletter†
0742-6445 Telecom Insider†
0742-6453 Office Automation Reporting Service†
0742-6496 Computers in Banking†
0742-6534 Catalyst (Montpelier)†
0742-6542 Administrator's Update†
0742-6550 Business Journal (Portland) **1444**
0742-6569 News Basket†
0742-6615 Dziennik Zwiazkowy **3530**
0742-6631 Germantown Crier **4293**
0742-6712 Studies in the Humanities (New York) **4477**
0742-6747 Hi-Res†
0742-678X Directions (Austin)
0742-6801 Bibliographies and Indexes in World Literature† **8936**
0742-681X Bibliographies and Indexes in Psychology **7416**
0742-6828 Bibliographies and Indexes in American History **4169**
0742-6836 Bibliographies and Indexes in Religious Studies **7698**
0742-6844 Bibliographies and Indexes in Anthropology† **8936**
0742-6852 Bibliographies and Indexes in World History **4169**
0742-6860 Bibliographies and Indexes in American Literature† **8936**
0742-6879 Bibliographies and Indexes in Library and Information Science† **8936**
0742-6887 Bibliographies and Indexes in Philosophy† **8936**
0742-6895 Bibliographies and Indexes in Sociology† **8936**

ISSN

0743-7927 National Insurance Law Review **4739**
0743-7935 BiblioFile **4994**
0743-7951 Wisconsin International Law Journal **4944**
0743-7978 Lake Line **3600**
0743-8044 Views (Boston)†
0743-8079 Medical Benefits **4514**
0743-8095 Magazine of Virginia Genealogy **3774**
0743-815X C P A Examination Review *changed to* Wiley C P A Examination Review **1303**
0743-8176 Primary Care & Cancer
0743-8346 Journal of Perinatology **5996**
0743-8354 Ob/Gyn Clinical Alert **6000**
0743-8389 Cinema Blue **6287**
0743-8397 Daily Territorial **1090**
0743-8400 Agrichemical Briefing
0743-846X S A F E Symposium Proceedings **69**
0743-8494 C S P A Statesider†
0743-8508 Gold Mining Stock Report **1627**
0743-8591 Edwards Journal **3764**
0743-8753 E P R I Guide†
0743-880X Praxis†
0743-8826 Hazard Prevention *changed to* Journal of System Safety **3206**
0743-8834 A C O A Action News **7219**
0743-8915 University of Kentucky Libraries. Occasional Papers **5053**
0743-894X Better Homes and Gardens Wood **4437**
0743-8958 Bridge Builder (Print) *changed to* Bridges **3260**
0743-8982 Space R & D Alert
0743-9016 A C M Symposium on Principles of Programming Languages. Conference Record *changed to* 0730-8566 **2457**
0743-913X Light Year†
0743-9156 Journal of Public Policy & Marketing **1826**
0743-9180 United Nations Issues Conference. Report **7271**
0743-9199 Classics of Soviet Mathematics **5478**
0743-9229 Medical Heritage†
0743-9237 New Concepts in Cardiac Imaging†
0743-9261 Year Book of Infectious Diseases†
0743-927X Vox Mediaevalis†
0743-9288 Videosat News†
0743-9296 Journal of Management Case Studies†
0743-930X Current Oncology Series†
0743-9326 Fodor's Chicago **8705**
0743-9342 Texas Family Law Reporter **4914**
0743-9385 Fodor's New Orleans **8707**
0743-9407 Master Brewers Association of the Americas. Technical Quarterly *changed to* 1558-0628 **611**
0743-9466 I B M Compatibles Plus†
0743-9563 The Sport Americana Team Baseball Card Checklist **4347**
0743-9628 Borgo Bioviews†
0743-9709 TradeShow & Convention Guide†
0743-9725 Directory of Voluntary Agencies†
0743-9741 Fodor's Washington, D.C. **8710**
0743-9814 North Dakota Court Rules *changed to* Court Rules Pamphlet(s). North Dakota Court Rules, State and Federal **4949**
0743-9822 Studies in the History of Music **6621**
0743-9873 Children's Magazine Guide **2174**
0743-989X Caveat Emptor Consumers Bulletin **2635**
0743-9962 Rural Living (Lansing) *changed to* Benefits Advisor **95**
0743-9989 Small Farmer's Journal **156**
0743-9997 Arizona Business Reports
0744-0006 Yankees Magazine **8252**
0744-0081 Computer Industry Update†
0744-0103 U S C T A News **8299**
0744-0154 N E A Now†
0744-0200 The S A B Choir **6614**
0744-0219 Daylily Journal **3728**
0744-0251 Respuesta†
0744-0359 American Sunbeam†
0744-0405 Fast Service/Family Restaurants†
0744-0456 The City Pages **3972**
0744-057X Ecphorizer†
0744-0596 Genesis (Washington)†
0744-060X New York Native†
0744-0626 Daily Construction Report *changed to* 1553-3816 **1024**
0744-0669 Windhound†
0744-0731 Collie Review†
0744-074X MotorHome **8323**
0744-0863 Clinch River Breeder Reactor Plant. Technical Review
0744-0901 Doll Reader **4333**
0744-0987 Texas Gardener **3751**
0744-1002 Career World **6695**
0744-1010 National Clearinghouse for Census Data Services. Address List† **8976**
0744-1088 Associations Report†
0744-1177 Focus Quarterly†
0744-1193 Builder (Washington) **984**
0744-1231 Arizona Today's Business
0744-1266 Walleye
0744-1274 Cavalcade of Auto Racing†
0744-1282 Dairy Market News **263**
0744-1320 Texas Water Resources **8832**
0744-1355 Speech Technology (New York)†
0744-1363 American Skating World
0744-138X Upholstering Today†
0744-1444 Herzl Institute Bulletin
0744-1495 Orthodox Herald **7705**
0744-155X The Star (Lakewood) **8605**
0744-1576 Home & Away *changed to* 1932-1767 **8679**
0744-1606 TravelAge Mid-America†
0744-1657 Test & Measurement World **3332**
0744-1673 Data Sources† **8948**
0744-1681 Units **4429**
0744-172X Business Times **1444**
0744-1738 Hobby Merchandiser **4336**
0744-1754 Pacific Magazine **1580**
0744-1770 New Generating Plants *see* 0032-5961 **3328**
0744-1916 Foodservice Technology Int'l. (Kitchen Planning)†
0744-2009 Conservogram (Print) *changed to* Conservogram (Online) **2608**
0744-2106 Southern Loggin' Times **3716**
0744-2149 Construction Times
0744-2386 Commline **3289**
0744-2416 National Masters News **8323**
0744-2467 Winning! (Tulsa)†
0744-2475 Peelings II†
0744-2483 Carolina Food Dealer†
0744-2513 Modern Jeweler **4568**
0744-253X Beef Business Bulletin **280**
0744-2548 Rural Telecommunications **2371**
0744-2572 Mustang Times **8594**
0744-2629 A O P A General Aviation National Report†
0744-2653 California Ornamental Crops Report **99**
0744-267X Catholic Sun (Syracuse) **7790**
0744-2777 Coal-Energy News **3126**
0744-2785 Predicasts F & S Index of Corporate Change†
0744-2807 Sertoman **8131**
0744-2823 Drugs & Drug Abuse Education. Newsletter†
0744-2866 Basketball Times **8223**
0744-2947 Internal Auditing Alert
0744-2955 Detective (Falls Church)†
0744-3056 Side-Saddle News *changed to* Aside World **8287**
0744-3064 Shreveport†
0744-3102 Magazine & Bookseller†
0744-3129 The Ensign **8643**
0744-3226 Dolphin Digest **8170**
0744-3234 Diario Las Americas **3530**
0744-3315 Focus (Washington, D.C. 1977) **2611**
0744-3439 Southern Runner **8202**
0744-348X Good Ideas†
0744-3528 Podiatry Management **6071**
0744-3587 Philadelphia Business Journal **1511**
0744-3609 UltraRunning **8339**
0744-3625 Supervisor's Bulletin: Office Edition†
0744-3676 Employee Services Management **1741**
0744-3692 Louisiana Game & Fish **8321**
0744-3749 Antique Angler **8304**
0744-3765 Making It! Careers Newsmagazine†
0744-3773 Shotgun Sports **8332**
0744-379X Huttlinger's Pipeline Report **6772**
0744-3927 Mortgage Marketplace†
0744-3943 Jonquil **2267**
0744-396X Kentucky Dental Journal
0744-4044 Tennessee Professional Engineer
0744-4052 Christian Missions in Many Lands **7632**
0744-4060 Christian Index (Memphis)
0744-415X Victorian Homes **4552**
0744-4184 Arkansas Sportsman **8304**
0744-4192 Mississippi Game & Fish **8322**
0744-4230 Pennsylvania Magazine **3985**
0744-4249 ByLine **4572**
0744-432X Rays from the Rose Cross **6743**
0744-4370 Christian Advertising Forum **23**
0744-4443 Manufacturing Midwest
0744-4451 Georgia Cattleman **287**
0744-4516 The Real Estate Professional **7609**
0744-4540 Barr's Post Card News **4328**
0744-4567 Microcomputing†
0744-4575 Community Education Today **2838**
0744-4583 Voice of North Carolina School Boards Association **3035**
0744-4680 Northwest Arts†
0744-4702 U S A C News **8213**
0744-4710 Resource Recycling *changed to* 1536-3856 **3505**
0744-4761 Texas Hereford **302**
0744-4796 Quiet Miracle **7673**
0744-4885 Playboy Fashion **6298**
0744-4958 Beverage Retailer Weekly†
0744-5059 Model Aviation **4340**
0744-5105 Muscle & Fitness **6993**
0744-5121 Shape **8848**
0744-513X Virginia Crops and Livestock **257**
0744-5199 Santa Barbara Magazine **3987**
0744-5253 Labor Arbitration Information System **4873**
0744-5288 Mackinac **2618**
0744-5296 PlasticsBrief: Reinforced Plastic Edition **7098**
0744-5466 North Carolina. Department of Agriculture. Agricultural Review **142**
0744-5474 Arizona Land and People **93**
0744-5555 The Round Up **2299**
0744-5598 Agri-News (Des Moines) **82**
0744-561X Long Island Life†
0744-5660 International Trade Alert **1570**
0744-5709 National Leader†
0744-5784 American Society of Media Photographers. Bulletin **6963**
0744-5881 Oil and Gas Investor **6783**
0744-5962 Kart Sport **8587**
0744-5989 Collectors' Showcase **365**
0744-6020 Orthopaedic Nursing Journal **5977**
0744-6233 Travel Printout†
0744-625X Alimentos Procesados†
0744-6306 National Clothesline **2243**
0744-6314 Nursing Management **5974**
0744-6349 FirstHand Magazine **4373**
0744-6357 Pest Management†
0744-6373 Washington Living **3572**
0744-6381 Pacific Union Recorder **7739**
0744-6403 Apparel News South†
0744-642X Real Estate Business **7608**
0744-6470 Hospital Employee Health **4100**
0744-6489 J E I Report†
0744-6586 Denni Hlasatel **3529**
0744-6594 Nasinec **3552**
0744-6608 Sheltie Pacesetter **6815**
0744-6616 American Printer **7318**
0744-6640 Home Shop Machinist **5452**
0744-6691 Federal Rules of Evidence Service **4673**
0744-6713 Journal of State Taxation **1932**
0744-6756 California Tort Reporter **4637**
0744-6829 The Racking Review **8297**
0744-6918 Flute Talk **6567**
0744-6985 Baptist Courier **7747**
0744-7132 Journal of Ophthalmic Nursing & Technology†
0744-7140 National Ad Search†
0744-7167 Construction Supervision & Safety Letter†
0744-723X Big Reel† **8936**
0744-7418 River Cities†
0744-7434 First Teacher **2857**
0744-7477 Arizona Capitol Times **7420**
0744-7523 Nebraska Agri-facts **183**
0744-7612 Communication World **1734**
0744-7671 Bankruptcy Law Letter **1318**
0744-7701 Fur Rancher **4973**
0744-771X Steubenville Register **7818**
0744-7809 A T V News†
0744-7841 Satellite T V Week†
0744-7868 80 Micro†
0744-7876 Farmer's Report **230**
0744-7884 Voice of Universarius†
0744-7981 Texas Public Utility News†
0744-8120 Woodall's Campgrounds **8775**
0744-8155 Pacific Automotive News†
0744-8163 Diversity
0744-818X Massachusetts Decisions Report in North Eastern Reporter. Second Series
0744-8201 Wisconsin Fire Journal **3582**
0744-8295 Breakout
0744-8317 Oregon Coast **3984**
0744-8333 Source (Seattle) **7682**
0744-8341 In Touch for Men **4375**
0744-8376 Ohio State Bar Association Report **4752**
0744-8481 The Journal of American College Health **6990**
0744-8546 Pomeranian Review **6813**
0744-8570 Cable Connection **2377**
0744-8600 Californiai Magyarsag **3525**
0744-8635 Interiorscape **4543**
0744-8686 California Tomorrow†
0744-8716 West's Education Law Reporter **4813**
0744-8724 Commodore Magazine†
0744-8767 Bank Wage-Hour & Personnel Report **4857**
0744-8783 Evangelical Newsletter†
0744-8821 University of Washington. Academic Computing Services. Newsletter†
0744-8864 Warehousing Supervisor's Bulletin†
0744-8961 Jacksonville Monthly†
0744-8996 Technical Soaring **72**
0744-9100 Daily Devotions for the Deaf **4073**
0744-9143 Apartment Management Newsletter **7582**
0744-9194 Lakeland Boating **8277**
0744-933X Pilot†
0744-9348 San Francisco Attorney **4778**
0744-9372 3rd Coast†
0744-9488 The Champion **4886**
0744-9518 Baptist Messenger **7747**
0744-9569 R V Business **8219**
0744-9585 Catholic Voice (Omaha) **7791**
0744-9631 A C F A Bulletin **6802**
0744-9666 The Sun (Chapel Hill) **5241**
0744-9798 County News (Washington) **7490**
0744-9852 Farm and Ranch Guide **110**
0744-9860 Sproutletter **6669**
0744-9917 A.N.A.L.O.G. Computing†
0744-9941 I A W C M Bulletin†
0745-0079 Gulfshore Life **5072**
0745-0095 Sokol Times **2270**
0745-0109 Iowa Crop Report†
0745-0257 Southern Cross (San Diego) **7818**
0745-0346 Exploring 1 for Leaders†
0745-0389 R V Trade Digest **8674**
0745-0397 Manufactured Housing Trade Digest
0745-0427 The Witness (Diocesan) Newspaper **7823**
0745-0478 Vanderbilt Register *changed to* Vanderbilt View **2308**
0745-0575 Women's Household Crochet†
0745-0621 Human Resources Management - Personnel Practices & Communications **1865**
0745-063X Human Resources Management - Compensation **1865**
0745-0656 Iowa Livestock Report†
0745-0745 Business Computer Systems†
0745-0753 Multi Level Marketing News
0745-0850 Systems & Software†
0745-0877 C P A Personnel Report **1857**
0745-0885 Physician & Patient†
0745-0915 Illinois Snowmobiler **8318**
0745-0958 Delta Epsilon Sigma Journal **2281**
0745-1032 Candy Industry **3672**
0745-113X Electronics West†
0745-1148 Hospital Security and Safety Management†
0745-1172 Between Times†
0745-1202 Geriatric Consultant†
0745-1237 Missouri Schools†
0745-1245 Sharing the Victory **7681**
0745-1253 Brookings Review†
0745-1261 Pacific Business
0745-1296 Akita World **6802**
0745-1342 C P A Computer Report†
0745-1458 Computers & Electronics†
0745-1474 Tennessee Business
0745-1490 Stamp Review†
0745-1512 Water Quality Association Membership Directory **8838**
0745-1520 Wassaja†
0745-1539 Illinois Advance **4074**
0745-161X Wisconsin Snowmobile News **8342**
0745-1636 Corporate Meetings & Incentives **6279**
0745-1679 The Record of Sigma Alpha Epsilon **2298**
0745-1687 Builder (Scottdale) **7628**
0745-1709 Geriatric Medicine Today†
0745-1784 The Grower **233**
0745-1849 German Shepherd Quarterly **6808**
0745-1911 Carnegie Mellon Magazine†
0745-1962 Circle K **2277**
0745-2012 Sheltie International **6815**

ISSN

DIRECTORY 2010 0748-5107 9335

0747-2218 Clearwater Navigator 3411
0747-2293 Trailblazer 8765
0747-2536 Prepared Foods 3660
0747-2544 Fleet Equipment 8670
0747-2560 Fine Dining
0747-2757 France - Amerique 3534
0747-3028 University of Hartford Observer 2306
0747-3060 A M O A Location
0747-3087 Modern Dentalab†
0747-3109 A O S Awards Quarterly 3721
0747-315X Athletic Business 8159
0747-3168 Advertising & Graphic Arts Techniques
0747-3176 Homeowner†
0747-3206 Spirits, Wine & Beer Marketing in Minnesota, North & South Dakota†
0747-3265 National Billiard News 8239
0747-3397 The Fish Sniffer 8313
0747-3508 Wisconsin Appellate Reporter†
0747-3575 Comic Reader†
0747-3605 Rock Products 1033
0747-3613 Public Power Weekly 3161
0747-3648 MidWest Outdoors 8322
0747-3680 Law Enforcement Technology 2659
0747-3699 Capital District Business Review *changed to* 1537-4254 1075
0747-3753 Fur World 4973
0747-380X Intimacy 5410
0747-3818 Contact (Berkeley)†
0747-3869 Den Danske Pioneer 3529
0747-3885 Housewares Merchandising†
0747-4059 OnSat 2387
0747-4172 American Iris Society. Bulletin 3722
0747-4261 Glass Magazine 2042
0747-4288 Brethren Evangelist 7749
0747-4296 National Job Market
0747-4504 Columbia University Record 2279
0747-4563 California (Beverly Hills)†
0747-4636 Vizsla News 6816
0747-4652 The Greater Baton Rouge Business Report 1488
0747-4679 Anesthesiology News 5770
0747-4695 Teen Machine†
0747-475X Travelware†
0747-4768 Creative Ideas for Living†
0747-4784 Rural Electric News Letter†
0747-4857 Data Book of Social Studies Materials and Resources†
0747-489X Imagine (Boston)
0747-4911 Illinois Runner†
0747-4938 Econometric Reviews 1478
0747-4946 Sequential Analysis 8399
0747-4962 Harbor Review†
0747-5020 Transition (Cincinnati)†
0747-5071 Shijie Ribao (San Francisco) 3564
0747-5160 Papers and Proceedings of Applied Geography Conferences 4023
0747-5179 Architectural Designs 429
0747-5187 An Analysis of the President's Budgetary Proposals for Fiscal Year 7420
0747-5241 Annals of Theoretical Psychology†
0747-525X Looking Ahead (Washington)†
0747-5276 Reinsurance Directory†
0747-5284 Sculpture Review 517
0747-5306 Oil and Gas 6783
0747-5314 Annual Report on Tobacco Statistics 8489
0747-5322 Folklife Annual†
0747-5403 Speedway Scene 8202
0747-5411 Serials Perspective
0747-5438 B N A Online†
0747-5500 A W E A Wind Energy Weekly 3178
0747-5527 National Stampagraphic†
0747-5535 Quarterly Journal of Business and Economics *changed to* 1939-8123 1163
0747-5551 P A†
0747-5608 Letter to Libraries†
0747-5616 Federal R & D Funding by Budget Function 1230
0747-5624 Relatively Seeking 3780
0747-5632 Computers in Human Behavior 8151
0747-5667 Missouri State Genealogical Association Journal 3775
0747-5675 Hughes Family Letter†
0747-5705 The Official Price Guide to Pottery & Porcelain 538
0747-573X Recruiter Journal†
0747-5810 Eswau Huppeday 3765
0747-5853 American Swimming Coaches Association World Clinic Yearbook 8158
0747-5861 Programmer's Journal†
0747-587X Micro Cornucopia†
0747-5993 Journal of Swimming Research 8183
0747-6000 A S C A Newsletter 8156
0747-606X American Homeopathy
0747-6086 Community Service Business†
0747-6108 African Urban Quarterly 4402
0747-6140 Working Parents†
0747-6159 Tennessee School Boards Journal 3034
0747-6175 A J L Newsletter 4985
0747-6213 Inside Drug Law†
0747-6221 I F M A News 1751
0747-623X S O L Etter†
0747-6337 I R M Multinational Reports†
0747-6353 Advances in Forensic Psychology and Psychiatry†
0747-640X Expanding Horizons†
0747-6558 Die Pommerschen Leute 3558
0747-6566 Leonard's Annual Price Index of Art Auctions 502
0747-6612 Advanced Annotation Service to the Code of Alabama (Year)
0747-6663 Latah County Genealogical Society. Quarterly†
0747-668X I E E E International Conference on Consumer Electronics. Digest of Technical Papers 3101
0747-6752 Sports & Lifestyle Marketing†
0747-6817 Center for Sports Sponsorship's Sponsor Quest
0747-6914 Advance Annotation Service to Colorado Revised Statutes (Year)
0747-6949 District of Columbia Court Rules Annotated 4660
0747-6965 Official Code of Georgia Annotated. Advance Information Service 4751
0747-6973 Georgia Rules of Court Annotated 4952
0747-7007 Burns Indiana Statutes Annotated. Advance Annotation Service
0747-7023 Advance Annotation Service to Annotated Code of Maryland 4610
0747-7074 Tennessee Code Annotated Advance Annotation Service 4793
0747-7082 General Laws of Rhode Island Advance Annotation Service
0747-7090 Virginia Rules Annotated 4967
0747-7171 Journal of Symbolic Computation 5553
0747-7201 A L A Survey of Librarian Salaries 4985
0747-7236 The Cheap Investor 1616
0747-7287 Streletz
0747-7333 Report on Ohio Mineral Industries 6477
0747-735X Michigan Environmental Report 3452
0747-7368 Journal of Gastronomy†
0747-7406 Modern Chlor-Alkali Technology 2073
0747-7430 Houston Building and Construction Directory†
0747-7449 Air and Space Lawyer 4612
0747-7465 Unique Homes 7614
0747-749X Computer Media Directory 2412
0747-7511 Growth Stock Report†
0747-7538 Who's Who in Indian Relics
0747-7600 Pulp Voices or Science Fiction Voices†
0747-7716 National Culinary Review 3657
0747-7759 Advances in Human Fertility & Reproductive Endocrinology†
0747-7805 Western Maryland Genealogy 3787
0747-7872 McKinney's New York Rules of Court *changed to* Court Rules Pamphlet(s). McKinney's New York Rules of Court, State & Federal 4949
0747-7902 Annals of Child Development†
0747-7961 Law Enforcement Officers Killed and Assaulted 2659
0747-7988 Gas Turbine World 3136
0747-8003 Corporate Giving Watch†
0747-8011 Ulula 5190
0747-8070 American Society of Missiology Series
0747-8127 Washington Weekly
0747-8194 North Carolina Agricultural Research Service. Technical Bulletin 142
0747-8216 Microcosm - Lyrical Ways 5227
0747-8283 Club Industry *changed to* 1552-5503 6984
0747-8291 Ultrapure Water 8833
0747-8445 Huxford Genealogical Society. Magazine 3771
0747-8453 Southern Indiana Genealogical Society Quarterly 3783
0747-847X BookNotes: Resource Information for the Small and Self-Publisher†
0747-8607 Tax Management Compensation Planning Journal 1797
0747-8615 Toy Soldier Review 4349
0747-8712 Sacramento Magazine 3987
0747-8739 News from the Northwest 3776
0747-8763 Outside Plant Magazine 2370
0747-8836 College Transfer Guide 2954
0747-8887 Hot Wire†
0747-8895 Mid-American Review 5227
0747-8909 A E J M C News 4570
0747-8917 Bankruptcy Strategist 1318
0747-8925 Medical Malpractice Law & Strategy 4837
0747-8968 Welcome to Planet Earth 567
0747-9026 Knitter's Magazine 6639
0747-9107 Almanac of Business and Industrial Financial Ratios 1307
0747-9115 Journal of Taxation of Investments 1932
0747-9131 Benefits Today†
0747-9182 Minerals and Metallurgical Processing 6471
0747-9239 Seismic Instruments 2789
0747-9255 Colorado Monthly Magazine
0747-9298 Legal Information Management Index 4823
0747-9301 Society for Armenian Studies. Journal 3565
0747-931X Unveiling
0747-9360 Design Issues 486
0747-9395 Fordham International Law Journal 4926
0747-9409 Sites†
0747-9417 A C S M Bulletin 3996
0747-9549 Data Entry Awareness Report†
0747-9573 Packaged Software Reports†
0747-9581 The Yearbook of Landscape Architecture†
0747-962X Identification Journal†
0747-9662 Journal of Economic and Social Measurement 8382
0747-9670 Computer Graphics Today†
0747-9697 Prickly Pear Tucson†
0747-9700 Federal Contract Disputes 4867
0747-9727 Thirteen†
0747-9751 National Airspace System Plan: Facilities, Equipment and Associated Development†
0747-9794 Illinois Magazine†
0747-9840 Champ Channels 938
0747-9964 Journal of Engineering Technology 3205
0747-9980 Unicycling Galore *see* 0566-778X 368
0748-0016 Personal Engineering & Instrumentation News†
0748-0059 Image Understanding†
0748-0067 Advances in Teacher Education 3050
0748-0113 Florida Armchair Researcher
0748-0164 Cross Currents (New Haven)†
0748-027X Case Studies in Emergency Medicine†
0748-0318 U.S. Department of Agriculture. National Agricultural Statistics Service. Meat Animals: Production, Disposition and Income 188
0748-0334 Springer Series on Health Care and Society† 8990
0748-0458 Sorkins Directory of Business & Government (St. Louis Edition) *see* 1055-906X 1904
0748-0466 Carolina ChemTips†
0748-0474 Computer-Integrated Manufacturing Review†
0748-0512 Journal of Veterinary Oncology†
0748-0539 American Society of Ichthyologists and Herpetologists. Special Publication 931
0748-0571 Report of a Vantage Conference 7262
0748-0628 Salon Talk†
0748-0709 International Trade Reporter Decisions 1572
0748-0725 Peacework 7164
0748-075X Journal of Health Care Technology†
0748-0792 Cable Advertising, Merchandising & Programming Report†
0748-0806 Educational Change 2849
0748-0814 Journal of Law and Religion 4702
0748-0881 The Video Source Book 2403
0748-0903 Turbomachinery International Handbook 3398
0748-0970 Foothills Inquirer 3766
0748-1012 Licking Lantern 3773
0748-1071 Lancaster County Connections 3773
0748-111X Official Price Guide to Music Collectibles
0748-1179 District Council Journal†
0748-1187 Death Studies 7351
0748-1195 December Rose†
0748-1225 Research Paper S O *changed to* U S D A Forest Service. Southern Research Station. Research Paper 3705
0748-125X Washington State University. Cooperative Extension. Extension Bulletin 169
0748-1276 Dividends from Wood Research 3708
0748-1284 U.S. Forest Service. Resource Bulletin P N W 3706
0748-1314 U.S. Forest Service. General Technical Report N E 3706
0748-1357 U.S. Forest Service. Resource Bulletin N E 3706
0748-1438 U S D A Forest Service. Rocky Mountain Research Station. New Publications 3705
0748-1489 Oceanic Abstracts 2720
0748-1578 Futures (East Lansing) 115
0748-1691 Lawson Letters
0748-1756 Measurement and Evaluation in Counseling and Development 2886
0748-1780 Image Magazine†
0748-1845 Financial Advertising Review 25
0748-2043 Small Computers in the Arts News
0748-2051 Micropsych Network†
0748-2116 Logos (Argonne) 3208
0748-2272 I S K C O N Report†
0748-2302 Minorities in America. Annual Bibliography†
0748-2337 Toxicology and Industrial Health 3502
0748-237X Clipper Studies in the Theatre†
0748-2388 Michigan Energy Journal
0748-2469 Official Directory of New Jersey Libraries and Media Centers 5037
0748-2485 Roots & Leaves 3781
0748-2493 Rutland Historical Society Quarterly 4311
0748-2507 Whatcom Genealogical Society. Bulletin 3787
0748-2515 Western Montana Genealogical Society Bulletin 3787
0748-2558 Shakespeare Bulletin 8478
0748-2590 Texas Kin†
0748-2604 American Arts Project
0748-2663 Employee Benefits in Medium and Large Firms†
0748-2671 U.S. Industrial Outlook (Year)†
0748-2760 Contemporary Geriatric Medicine
0748-2841 Foreign Policy (San Diego)†
0748-285X Death and Dying†
0748-2868 Criminal Justice (San Diego)†
0748-2876 Nuclear Arms†
0748-2906 Bet-Nahrain 4320
0748-2922 Economic Trends (Cleveland) 1481
0748-2930 Romanian Philatelic Studies†
0748-3007 Cladistics 666
0748-3015 Hibiscus†
0748-304X Ceramic World†
0748-3058 Esto America
0748-3082 List of Proprietary Substances and Nonfood Compounds Authorized for Use under U S D A Inspection and Grading Programs†
0748-3090 Laugh Factory 5224
0748-3104 Comunicaciones 2317
0748-3155 Exercise Physiology: Current Selected Research 6985
0748-318X Real Estate Finance 7608
0748-321X Journal of Veterinary Medical Education 8801
0748-3228 A F F†
0748-3406 Venture Inward 6744
0748-4011 Review of New Energy Technology†
0748-4054 Preschool Perspectives†
0748-4062 Poet Magazine
0748-4089 Asia - Pacific - Africa - Middle East Petroleum†
0748-4135 Workers' Compensation Laws of California 4816
0748-4151 U.S. Nuclear Regulatory Commission. Report to Congress on Abnormal Occurrences 3175
0748-4321 Legacy (Lincoln) 5320
0748-433X United Nations of the Next Decade Conference. Report 7271
0748-4356 Africa Insider 7219
0748-4364 Higher Education Abstracts 2933
0748-4372 North Dakota Research Report 142
0748-4410 Advances in Clinical Neuropsychology 6120
0748-4461 Computer Games†
0748-4518 Journal of Quantitative Criminology 2658
0748-4526 Negotiation Journal 7254
0748-4585 Lange's Handbook of Chemistry 2071
0748-4593 La Tribune *see* 0738-9779 8886
0748-4607 La Tribuna *see* 0738-9779 8886
0748-4631 Interflo 1570
0748-4658 Journal of Propulsion and Power 63
0748-4666 The Dental Advisor 5839
0748-4674 New Connections
0748-4682 Doxology 7638
0748-4720 Iowa Agri-News†
0748-4739 Runzheimer International Letter†
0748-4755 Pricing Advisor 2640
0748-478X Currents (Washington) 2976
0748-4895 Strategic Planning Management†
0748-4925 Vermont Bar Journal and Law Digest *changed to* Vermont Bar Journal 4807
0748-4976 V I Newspapers - Substantive Index†
0748-5050 Journal of Regional Cultures†
0748-5093 Catalog of University Presentations 7547
0748-5107 American Society for Conservation Archaeology Report 372

ISSN

Link to your serials resources and content with ulrichsweb.com

DIRECTORY 2010 0755-4338 9337

0749-8667 Insurance Review (New York)†
0749-8683 U.S. Department of Agriculture. National Agricultural Statistics Service. Mink **188**
0749-8799 C U B Communicator **8091**
0749-890X Industrial Fire World **3579**
0749-8969 Cave Geology **2728**
0749-9043 King's International Coal Trade **6468**
0749-9051 New York Image
0749-9078 Lex Collegii **4723**
0749-9132 Foreign Intelligence Literary Scene
0749-9213 Carpatho-Rusyn American†
0749-9310 Texas Lone Star **3034**
0749-9345 N O A Newsletter **6598**
0749-9361 Showboat Centennials Newsletter†
0749-937X N B M G. Open-File Report **2757**
0749-9418 Business First (Buffalo) **1072**
0749-9531 U R I S A News **2551**
0749-9566 Nelson-Atkins Museum of Art. Bulletin†
0749-9736 National Directory of Corporate Public Affairs **2018**
0749-9779 Stockowners' News†
0749-9809 Lone Star Review†
0749-9841 Play Source†
0749-9884 National Report for Training and Development†
0749-9930 Tennessee. Labor Market Information Directory **1710**
0749-9957 Wool & Wattles **304**
0749-9973 Medical and Health Information Directory **6992**
0750-0416 Le Bulletin Officiel du Ministere de la Justice† **8938**
0750-0750 Reunion. Institut National de la Statistique et des Etudes Economiques. Indicateurs Conjoncturels†
0750-0769 L'Economie de la Reunion **1481**
0750-1080 Informatique Professionnelle†
0750-1099 Travaux d'Archeologie Limousine **4164**
0750-1269 Assemblages† **8931**
0750-1552 C.F.P. Chaud - Froid - Plomberie **4117**
0750-1900 Collections (Paris)
0750-1919 Lectio Divina **7659**
0750-1978 Sources Chretiennes **7682**
0750-2036 Langues et Cultures du Pacifique **5142**
0750-2079 Musique et Culture†
0750-2389 Moselle Agricole **137**
0750-3288 Le Journal de la Maison **4544**
0750-3334 Le Chasseur Francais **8309**
0750-3407 Images du Mois **7800**
0750-3490 Officiel de la Coiffure et de la Beaute†
0750-3520 Lui *changed to* 1266-8672
0750-3547 Etudes Indo - Europeennes **338**
0750-3628 Vogue (France) **2263**
0750-3695 Lettre de Taize **7804**
0750-3717 L'Hotellerie **4390**
0750-3725 Vogue Homme†
0750-3806 Jeannette **2195**
0750-3849 Vogue Espana **8888**
0750-4039 Les Veillees des Chaumieres **3842**
0750-4047 Woodcraft *changed to* 1955-8864 **2271**
0750-4152 Guide de France **2191**
0750-4160 Cap Levant†
0750-4497 Vie Agricole et Cooperative
0750-4586 Info-Nature†
0750-5299 Societe Francaise Shakespeare. Actes du Congres **5374**
0750-6066 Ecole Pratique des Hautes Etudes. Laboratoire de Geomorphologie. Memoires **2706**
0750-6244 Archives of Otolaryngology†
0750-6473 Societe d'Etudes Scientifiques de l'Anjou. Memoires **7918**
0750-6635 Laboratoires de Geologie Lyon. Documents **2752**
0750-6651 Observatoire de Haute Provence. Rapport d'Activite **579**
0750-6848 Societe Linneenne de Bordeaux. Bulletin **963**
0750-7046 Catalogue Afnor (Normes Francaises) **6401**
0750-7151 Laboratoire de Glaciologie et Geophysique de l'Environnement. Rapport d'Activite **3449**
0750-7321 Biologia Gallo-Hellenica
0750-747X Societe Zoologique de France. Memoires **964**
0750-7569 S N E C M A Informations **69**
0750-7658 Annales Francaises d'Anesthesie et de Reanimation **5770**
0750-7682 Sciences Veterinaires - Medecine Comparee **8807**
0750-7933 Societe des Sciences Naturelles. Miscellanea Entomologia†
0750-8042 Informations Rapides de la Copropriete **7595**
0750-8069 Histoire Epistemologie Langage **5125**
0750-8093 Terres d'Ariege **161**
0750-8123 Casse-Tete de Poche
0750-8131 Carrosserie **8573**
0750-8158 Les Enfants S' Amusent **2187**
0750-8247 Juris-Classeur de Droit Compare **4706**
0750-8271 Juris-Classeur Construction Urbanisme **4873**
0750-8298 Juris-Classeur Civil. Annexes *see* 0448-0732 **4833**
0750-8301 Juris-Classeur de la Responsabilite Civile et des Assurances **4706**
0750-831X Juris-Classeur Rural **4706**
0750-8328 Juris-Classeur des Loyers et de la Propriete Commerciale **4706**
0750-8336 Juris-Classeur des Baux. Baux Ruraux **4873**
0750-845X Juris-Classeur Propriete Litteraire et Artistique **4706**
0750-8468 Codes et Lois. Traites de l'Europe Occidentale et Textes d'Application **4643**
0750-8565 Juris-Classeur Travail Traite **4706**
0750-8573 Juris-Classeur Copropriete **4873**
0750-862X Action Agricole Picarde **79**
0750-8638 Juris-Classeur Encyclopedie des Huissiers de Justice **4706**
0750-8743 I S T P M Rapports Techniques†
0750-8794 Travail et Maitrise (Edition Mines)†
0750-8999 Travail et Maitrise (Edition Textiles)†
0750-9170 Lalies **5138**
0750-9189 Planedenn†
0750-9219 L'Etoile Absinthe **5292**
0750-9278 Revue des Deux Mondes **5237**
0751-0357 Zeszyty Literackie **5404**
0751-1000 Europe Afrique Service†
0751-1418 Institut d'Allemand d'Asnieres. Publications **2987**
0751-1787 Le Monde Arabe Economique et les Affaires Internationales†
0751-1809 Revue des Caisses d'Epargne†
0751-266X Cahiers Henri Pourrat *changed to* Correspondance Henri Pourrat - Suzanne Renaud **5279**
0751-2708 Medievales **4153**
0751-2856 Recherches sur les Societes Mediterraneennes
0751-2902 Universite de Franche-Comte. Centre de Documentation et de Bibliographie Philosophiques. Travaux **6959**
0751-3496 Communisme **7117**
0751-3860 Centre de Genealogie et d'Histoire des Iles d'Amerique. Cahiers† **8940**
0751-3879 813: Les Amis de la Litterature Policiere **5415**
0751-4239 Universite de Provence. Centre d'Aix. Cahiers d'Etudes Germaniques **4480**
0751-428X Depeche de Tahiti **3842**
0751-4417 Challenges **1082**
0751-4794 Job Pratique Magazine *changed to* 1955-9631 **1964**
0751-4875 L A C I T O Documents Asie - Austronesie **5138**
0751-4883 L A C I T O Documents Eurasie **5138**
0751-5022 Corps Ecrit†
0751-5405 Voiles et Voiliers **8284**
0751-5464 Publi 10†
0751-5537 Parfums Beaute International **595**
0751-5545 L'Argus de l'Automobile et des Locomotions **8556**
0751-5553 Crapouillot†
0751-557X Automobiliste†
0751-5596 France Aviation†
0751-5685 Louveteau† **8972**
0751-5731 Scouts† **8987**
0751-5766 Hospitalisation Nouvelle **4101**
0751-5804 Revue des Sciences Morales et Politiques†
0751-5812 Demain† **8949**
0751-5839 Universite Syndicaliste **3007**
0751-5871 Activite Economique *changed to* 1778-8315 **1057**
0751-588X Entreprises Rhone - Alpes **1885**
0751-591X Moto Journal **8261**
0751-5936 Journal du Batiment et des Travaux Publics†
0751-5944 Travaux Publics et Batiment du Midi†
0751-5960 Coiffure de Paris
0751-5987 Pour la Verite **7771**
0751-6002 Okapi **2205**
0751-6010 Points de Repere **7670**
0751-6037 Circuits Culture **225**
0751-6169 Familles de France **8102**
0751-6231 Agriculteur Normand. Calvados **82**
0751-624X Agriculteur Normand. Orne **82**
0751-6266 Agriculteur Normand. Manche **82**
0751-6460 Ange Gardien **7621**
0751-6657 Tourisme†
0751-7033 Iris (Paris)†
0751-7599 Institut National de la Statistique et des Etudes Economiques. Service Departemental de la Guyane. Bulletin Trimestriel de Statistiques†
0751-7688 Karstologia **2751**
0751-7696 Adolescence **6119**
0751-7718 Consultation†
0751-7963 Le Cormoran **905**
0751-7971 Reseaux **8128**
0751-8145 F E N - Hebdo *changed to* 1628-1306
0751-8447 Ekaina†
0751-9044 Debout Guyane **7128**
0751-9478 Legipresse **2331**
0752-0360 Journees Equations aux Derivees Partielles **5507**
0752-1537 France, Belgique, Luxembourg†
0752-1693 Geopolitique **7237**
0752-1855 Courrier Economique **1475**
0752-2452 A R I E S *changed to* 1567-9896 **6643**
0752-2525 Voix des Sports **8215**
0752-272X Poesie† **8981**
0752-2878 Novecento *changed to* 1770-9571 **5268**
0752-4072 T S I. Technique et Sciences Informatiques **2528**
0752-4250 L'Officiel Jardin-Motoculture†
0752-4676 I C A Executive Search Newsletter
0752-4749 Modelisme C L A P†
0752-5192 Action Commerciale **1056**
0752-5222 L'Ecrit-Voir†
0752-5346 Connaissance des Peres de l'Eglise **7635**
0752-5370 Nouvelles Dermatologiques **5880**
0752-5443 Mandenkan **5150**
0752-5508 Mediagaz†
0752-5656 Revue Archeologique de Picardie **414**
0752-5702 Histoire, Economie et Societe **1542**
0752-5729 Recherche en Danse†
0752-5974 Foret - Entreprise **3690**
0752-6180 Finance **1342**
0752-6903 Les Cahiers de Philosophie† **8939**
0752-7055 Annuaire International des Collectionneurs†
0752-7535 Annuaire de l'Alimentation Animale†
0752-921X Kompass Regional Economique et Industriel. Rhone - Alpes **1142**
0752-9236 Union des Associations Francaises de Relations Publiques. Annuaire†
0752-9309 Kompass Regional Economique et Industriel. Normandie **1142**
0752-9864 Institut Catholique de Paris. Annuaire
0753-0056 Volonte de l'Industrie, du Commerce et des Prestataires de Services *changed to* 1630-3792 **1434**
0753-1419 Logement et Famille **8118**
0753-1605 Revue des Tabacs **8487**
0753-1877 Militaria Magazine **6435**
0753-2415 Negoce Agriculture **204**
0753-2830 Journal de Toxicologie Clinique et Experimentale†
0753-2989 Presse Environnement†
0753-3098 Revue de Presse et de Documentation Allemande† **8985**
0753-311X France. Direction du Tourisme. Economie du Tourisme†
0753-3322 Biomedicine & Pharmacotherapy **5587**
0753-3454 Relais†
0753-3918 Actualites Biologiques†
0753-3969 Annales de Paleontologie **6723**
0753-4000 Nouveau Detective†
0753-4159 Bois du Sud† **8937**
0753-4183 Centre Genealogique de l'Ouest. Revue Trimestrielle *changed to* Centre Genealogique de Loire-Atlantique. Revue **3761**
0753-4418 Les Cahiers de la Fonction Publique et de l' Administration **7489**
0753-4590 Cahiers Henri Bosco **5406**
0753-4639 Centre de Genealogie Protestante. Cahiers **7750**
0753-4655 Societe d'Histoire Naturelle du Doubs. Bulletin **7918**
0753-4973 Alytes **931**
0753-5015 Gazette du Livre Medieval **4222**
0753-521X Handisport Magazine **8176**
0753-5724 Contact - Chambre Officielle Franco-Allemande de Commerce et d'Industrie **1401**
0753-5732 Feuillet Rapide Social **1682**
0753-650X Bicross Magazine†
0753-6712 Cahiers d'Histoire et de Philosophie des Sciences **7843**
0753-6852 Loisirs Sante **3071**
0753-7409 L E D. Loisirs Electroniques d'Aujourd'hui *changed to* 0243-4911 **3097**
0753-7417 Societe Francaise de Cancerologie Privee. Bulletin†
0753-759X Communiquer† **8942**
0753-874X Actualite Legislative Dalloz†
0753-986X Gaultmillau Magazine†
0754-023X L'Infini **5221**
0754-054X Ouvertures†
0754-0590 Emballages Magazine **6709**
0754-068X Jeux & Jouets Magazine (Paris) **4060**
0754-121X Tracteurs et Machines Agricoles†
0754-1384 Lire au College **3070**
0754-1678 Take It Easy **5241**
0754-1996 Industrie de l'Information†
0754-2275 Roman†
0754-2348 Fait Main (Paris, 1982) **2254**
0754-2445 L A C I T O Documents Afrique **5138**
0754-2623 Ondes Courtes Informations†
0754-2712 Maxi Basket†
0754-281X Travailleurs†
0754-331X Recherches sur la Philosophie et le Langage **6947**
0754-3786 Nouvelles du Vietnam **7256**
0754-4200 Change† **8940**
0754-4219 Change des Monnaies Etrangeres *changed to* 0754-4200 **8940**
0754-4766 M'Bolo† **8973**
0754-5215 La Lettre Afrique Energies *changed to* 1635-9003 **6761**
0754-7188 La Lettre d'Oto-rhino-laryngologie **6082**
0754-7234 Lire pour Comprendre **5323**
0754-7560 Plainpied†
0754-7625 A.F.P. Cahiers de l'Afrique Occidentale et de l'Afrique Equatoriale†
0754-8826 Naturellement **3455**
0754-9172 Revue Professionnelle des Metiers de l'Ameublement et de la Decoration† **8985**
0754-927X Luvah **5328**
0754-944X Lesbia Magazine **4376**
0754-9725 Ge Magazine†
0754-9962 Societe Herpetologique de France. Bulletin **963**
0755-0006 Juris Associations **1770**
0755-0251 Gai Pied Hebdo†
0755-0960 Fabula†
0755-1088 Chronique du Transporteur†
0755-110X L'Expert Automobile **8580**
0755-1150 Thesindex Pharmaceutique†
0755-138X Mission de l'Eglise **7807**
0755-1460 Officiel des Congres et du Tourisme d'Affaires†
0755-1533 Manuel General de la Peinture et de la Decoration **6719**
0755-1541 Bulletin des Metiers et de l'Artisanat† **8938**
0755-1673 Cinema et Sciences Humaines
0755-1924 Societe d'Etude des Sciences Naturelles de Nimes et du Gard. Bulletin **7918**
0755-1940 Agence Economique et Financiere *changed to* 1776-3193 **1305**
0755-1959 Classiques Francais du Moyen Age **5274**
0755-2068 Revue d'Histoire de la Spiritualite†
0755-2130 Provence Medicale†
0755-219X Mesures **2463**
0755-2238 Bilans Hebdomadaires **1067**
0755-2270 France. Ministere des Armees. Bulletin Officiel des Armees. Edition Chronologique. Partie Principale† **8958**
0755-2289 France. Ministere des Armees. Bulletin Officiel des Armees. Edition Chronologique† **8958**
0755-2378 Ordre National des Chirurgiens- Dentistes. Conseil National. Bulletin Officiel†
0755-2386 Securite et Medecine du Travail **6687**
0755-2459 Informateur Social†
0755-2483 Societe des Etudes Litteraires, Scientifiques et Artistiques du Lot. Bulletin **4265**
0755-2491 Societe d'Histoire Naturelle du Pays de Montbeliard. Bulletin **818**
0755-2513 Unichamp **5392**
0755-2629 Patriote Guadeloupeen†
0755-2742 Revolution Socialiste Antilles **1705**
0755-2793 France. Parlement. Assemblee Nationale. Bulletin *changed to* 1952-448X **7136**
0755-284X Exploitant Familial **109**
0755-2947 Etincelle **7133**
0755-3110 Annuaire Sucrier **3670**
0755-3374 France. Ministere de l'Emploi et de la Solidarite. Annuaire des Statistiques Sanitaires et Sociales **7518**
0755-3390 Institut de Recherche Mathematique Avancee de Strasbourg. Publication **5493**
0755-3617 Academie des Sciences, Arts et Belles Lettres de Dijon. Memoires **4440**
0755-379X Nord Matin†
0755-3854 Notre Librairie *changed to* 1956-984X **5281**
0755-4168 Institut National de la Sante et de la Recherche Medicale. Actualites **7525**
0755-4249 Ordi 5
0755-4338 Inter-Parents **4078**

ISSN

0764-8499 Les Cahiers de la Cinematheque **6491**
0764-8510 Cahiers de la Cinematheque. Collection *see* 0764-8499 **6491**
0764-8804 Traversieres Magazine **6624**
0764-8928 Gradhiva **340**
0764-9169 Collection Amphi 7 **2972**
0764-9185 Docavia **53**
0764-9614 C D S. Publication Speciale
0764-9878 Cahiers d'Etudes sur la Mediterranee Orientale et le Monde Turco-Iranien **7112**
0765-0019 Traitement du Signal **7044**
0765-006X Entrainements & Systemes† **8954**
0765-0078 Repertoire de l'Administration Francaise **7465**
0765-0094 La Lettre Europeenne du Progres Technique *changed to* 1770-9547 **8416**
0765-0116 Guide du Cheval Arabe en France†
0765-0213 Cultures et Societes de l'Est **8097**
0765-0302 Laboratoire d'Informatique pour la Mecanique et les Sciences de l'Ingenieur. Rapport d'Activite **3208**
0765-040X Bareme des Coefficients
0765-0574 European Space Directory **53**
0765-0639 Bibliotheque du C N A M **3374**
0765-0698 France Auto **8581**
0765-0752 Revue Europeenne des Migrations Internationales **7292**
0765-0779 Recherche Technologie†
0765-0817 Atlas Historique des Villes de France **4201**
0765-104X Delegation Archeologique Francaise en Iran. Cahiers **389**
0765-1104 Tableaux de l'Economie Polynesienne **1269**
0765-1120 Dossiers de Teledetection
0765-1155 Recherches sur l'Imaginaire **5358**
0765-1325 Bases **5060**
0765-1333 Problemes d'Amerique Latine **4309**
0765-1376 Kouakou†
0765-1457 L'Echappement **8578**
0765-1597 Science & Sports **6232**
0765-1635 Travaux de Didactique du Francais Langue Etrangere **5189**
0765-1899 Institut National des Langues et Civilisations Orientales. Livret de l'Etudiant **4184**
0765-1937 C R E D I F Bulletin Bibliographique†
0765-2046 European Biotechnology Newsletter†
0765-2399 Annuaire de l'Enseignement Assiste par Ordinateur†
0765-2887 Micro P C† **8974**
0765-3069 Technologies Bancaires† **8992**
0765-3522 Circuler *changed to* 1956-9629 **8493**
0765-3697 Societes **8135**
0765-4405 Laser (Paris)†
0765-4413 Autre Journal†
0765-4448 Mercure 10 **1431**
0765-4812 L'Etudiant. Guide Pratique **2283**
0765-4871 Angiologie *changed to* 1622-3810
0765-4944 Cahiers de Praxematique **5103**
0765-5010 Notes Pediatriques
0765-5290 Reanimation, Soins Intensifs, Medecine d'Urgence†
0765-5762 Entreprises Formation *changed to* 1952-3637 **1877**
0765-5991 Culture et Recherche **5004**
0765-6017 Ecoles des Lettres. Second Cycle† **8952**
0765-6386 Practic Export **8508**
0765-703X Sante Gestion†
0765-9849 Camera International†
0766-0278 Societe d'Etudes Historiques de la Nouvelle-Caledonie. Bulletin **4194**
0766-0502 Cahiers de Paleontologie. Section Vertebres
0766-057X Magwa†
0766-0707 Ragazzi **5165**
0766-0715 Kinder **5137**
0766-0723 Freunde **5121**
0766-0731 Teen **5186**
0766-0758 A Tot of English **5188**
0766-0766 Muchachos **5153**
0766-0774 Adulescens **5091**
0766-0782 Iuvenis **5131**
0766-0847 Moto Crampons **8261**
0766-1177 Cahiers d'Extreme - Asie **7733**
0766-1398 Philosophies **6942**
0766-169X Auto 8† **8934**
0766-1827 Histoire et ses Representations **4227**
0766-1924 Polyphonies†
0766-2130 P & A: Paysage et Amenagement *changed to* 1296-0101
0766-2262 Kine Actualite **6112**
0766-2610 Association Francis Jammes. Bulletin **5257**
0766-2750 I T A Press (French Edition) **59**
0766-2823 Froid et Climatisation Cuisines Professionnelles†
0766-3366 I T A Press (English Edition) **59**
0766-3633 Cardiologie Pratique **5779**
0766-3706 Polio-France†
0766-3838 Droits **4661**
0766-3889 Vos Chiens **6816**
0766-4125 France Catholique **7798**
0766-4133 S O S Amitie **8066**
0766-4451 Textuel 34 - 44 **5050**
0766-446X Cahiers Textuel 34 - 44 *see* 0766-4451 **5050**
0766-4516 Bulletin d'Histoire de la Revolution Francaise† **8938**
0766-4877 Vol Libre **8340**
0766-5024 F M T Medical *changed to* 1778-915X **6109**
0766-5075 Etudes Mongoles et Siberiennes *changed to* Etudes Mongoles et Siberiennes, Centrasiatiques et Tibetaines **338**
0766-5105 Geodynamique†
0766-5229 Bureau et Informatique†
0766-5350 Dires†
0766-5466 Lyon Mediterranee Medical - Medecine du Sud Est *changed to* 1628-0741
0766-5520 C N P F la Revue des Entreprises *changed to* 1282-5247 **8985**
0766-5598 Revue des Etudes Byzantines **4324**
0766-5601 L'Acces aux Documents Administratifs *changed to* 1952-9759 **7430**
0766-5644 Remedes†
0766-5725 Technique et Biologie†
0766-5784 Maquettes Plastique Magazine†
0766-5830 Echanges (Paris, 1971)†
0766-5849 Bulletin Quotidien **7111**
0766-608X Vie Foraine **1191**
0766-6101 Eaux - Vives **7795**
0766-6241 Informations M M M **1123**
0766-6268 France. Institut National de la Statistique et des Etudes Economiques. Note de Conjoncture **1111**
0766-6314 Revue Periodique de la Physiophile **7903**
0766-6330 L'Etudiant **2283**
0766-6349 L'Etudiant Plus **2283**
0766-639X P A S C A L Lexique Francaise - Anglaise - Allemand. Metallurgie†
0766-6500 Remisis† **8985**
0766-6934 Le Bijoutier **4564**
0766-7078 Directions† **8950**
0766-7159 Charbonnages de France. Publications Techniques†
0766-7175 France. Bureau de Recherches Geologiques et Minieres. Principaux Resultats Scientifiques†
0766-7302 Le Syndicat Agricole (Pas-de-Calais Edition) **160**
0766-740X Agriculteur de la Dordogne, le Paysan du Prigord†
0766-7531 Revue 9 et 2†
0766-916X La Lettre du Musicien **6584**
0766-9402 Information Economique†
0766-9755 Gestion Sociale **1747**
0767-0192 F I A B C I Press **7590**
0767-0303 Lieux de l'Enfance†
0767-0311 Lettres et Cultures de Langue Francaise **5322**
0767-0672 Conquerir **1811**
0767-0869 Bibliotheque de l'Information Grammaticale **5100**
0767-094X Revue de la Navigation Fluviale Europeenne, Ports et Industries *changed to* 1769-8588 **8654**
0767-0974 Medecine Sciences **5666**
0767-0982 Revue de Medecine et d'Internat†
0767-1075 Etudes Traditionnelles†
0767-1237 France. Direction Generale des Impots. Precis de Fiscalite **1926**
0767-1555 Dictionnaire Permanent: Difficultes des Entreprises **1738**
0767-2004 Revue Medicale de l'Assurance Maladie *changed to* 1952-9201 **4519**
0767-2187 Dictionnaire Permanent: Securite et Conditions de Travail **1675**
0767-2640 Documentation Touristique: Bibliographie Analytique Internationale†
0767-2659 Touristic Analysis Review†
0767-2667 Cahiers du Tourisme. Serie E: Legislation **8690**
0767-2888 Institut Francais de Recherche Scientifique pour le Developpement en Cooperation. Etudes et Theses **7866**
0767-2896 Institut Francais de Recherche Scientifique pour le Developpement en Cooperation. Colloques et Seminaires **7866**
0767-3558 Le Parisien **3841**
0767-3701 Recherche et Applications en Marketing **1839**
0767-3795 Moniteur du Tourisme Africain **8737**
0767-3841 Annuaire de la Maree et de l'Aquaculture†
0767-3981 Fundamental and Clinical Pharmacology **6843**
0767-4007 La Montagne **3841**
0767-4775 Dossiers de l'Audiovisuel *changed to* 1769-101X **8978**
0767-4910 Lettre de l'Intelligence Artificielle† **8971**
0767-6379 La Lettre de la Pierre **7598**
0767-6468 Cahiers de l'Orient†
0767-6794 L'Observateur de l'Immobilier **4421**
0767-6891 Sciences Orgonomiques†
0767-709X Revue Archeologique de l'Ouest **414**
0767-7367 Societe Geologique du Nord. Annales **2768**
0767-7480 Monnaie, Prix, Conjoncture† **8975**
0767-7529 Institut d'Etudes Germaniques. Cahiers **5309**
0767-7987 Surf Session **8210**
0767-807X Picsou **2207**
0767-8150 Artstudio†
0767-8177 Guide Cuisine **4359**
0767-8193 Les Dossiers de l'Obstetrique **5989**
0767-869X Gazette des Armes **4335**
0767-8711 Action Agricole de Touraine **79**
0767-8959 Ophtalmologiste Praticien†
0767-9432 Qualitique **1163**
0767-9491 Marches Asiatiques†
0767-9505 Banque de France. Comptes Annuels des Etablissements de Credit† **8935**
0767-9513 Hermes **7969**
0767-9556 Barbacane **5260**
0767-9742 Musique en Jeu†
0767-9793 Encyclopedie Periodique Economique Politique et Administrative. Conseil Economique et Social *changed to* 1954-4340 **640**
0767-9807 Encyclopedie Periodique Economique Politique et Administrative. Conseil de Paris *changed to* 1954-4316 **640**
0767-9815 Encyclopedie Periodique Economique Politique et Administrative. Documentation Electorale *changed to* 1957-6587 **7423**
0767-9831 Encyclopedie Periodique Economique Politique et Administrative. Presidents des Conseils generaux *changed to* 1954-4308 **640**
0767-9866 Bareme Social Periodique **1065**
0767-9874 Journees de la Recherche Porcine en France **291**
0767-9920 Batirama *changed to* 1266-2089 **979**
0767-9939 Administrer **7581**
0768-0279 Cahiers du Tourisme. Serie C: Recherche Fondamentale et Appliquee - Methodologie **8690**
0768-0627 J'ai Lu. Roman Policier **5414**
0768-0635 J'ai Lu. Science Fiction **5444**
0768-0805 Philosophie d'Aujourd'hui **6941**
0768-0856 Tribune Libre (Paris) **5242**
0768-1305 Centre Interuniversitaire de Recherche sur la Renaissance Italienne **5271**
0768-1380 Institut d'Ethnologie (Musee de l'Homme). Memoires
0768-1593 Revue Musicale†
0768-1674 Bibliotheque du XVe Siecle **5263**
0768-1852 Perspectives de l'Economique. Serie 3. Critique†
0768-1887 Ecole et la Famille†
0768-1968 I R E D U. Cahier **2865**
0768-2034 Guide du Routard **8716**
0768-231X Ce Que Je Crois **5271**
0768-2352 Etudes d'Antiquites Africaines **4174**
0768-2557 Documents Relatifs a l'Histoire des Croisades **4215**
0768-2662 Education 2000 **3059**
0768-2964 Institut Francais d'Archeologie Orientale du Caire. Documents de Fouilles **397**
0768-3154 Institut National de la Sante et de la Recherche Medicale. Colloques **5635**
0768-3162 Cahiers du Tourisme. Serie B: Etranger **8690**
0768-3537 Archives Royales de Mari **380**
0768-3685 Laboratoire d'Anthropologie, Prehistoire, Protohistoire et Quaternaire Armoricains. Travaux **346**
0768-3847 Bibliotheque de l'Ecole des Hautes Etudes. Quatrieme Section, Sciences Historiques et Philologiques **4133**
0768-3979 Trois Pommes **2218**
0768-4053 Documents d'Histoire Maghrebine **548**
0768-424X Institut Francais d'Etudes Andines. Travaux **7973**
0768-4258 Univers de la France et des Pays Francophones **4275**
0768-4479 Universite de Besancon. Annales Litteraires. Serie Linguistique et Semiotique **5191**
0768-4703 Institut Francais d'Archeologie Orientale du Caire. Fouilles **398**
0768-5475 Universite de Liege. Faculte de Philosophie et Lettres. Bibliotheque **4480**
0768-5785 Archiscopie **428**
0768-598X Toxicologie Analytique. Annales **2106**
0768-6374 Gazet Sifon Ble **7966**
0768-7028 Flash Alternative†
0768-7516 Gammes Jardin†
0768-8008 Atakpame *changed to* 1957-5130 **8096**
0768-827X Video Broadcast†
0768-9047 Lamy Fiscal **4712**
0768-9098 Informations Canadiennes†
0768-9136 Lettre Informatique et Collectivites Locales **7486**
0768-9179 Le Pharmacien Hospitalier **6871**
0768-9209 France. Statistiques du Commerce Exterieur de la France. Annuaire Abrege†
0768-9403 Muntu†
0768-9454 Technologie **3085**
0768-956X Sonovision **2339**
0768-9756 Rapport **8509**
0768-9942 Medecin du Midi
0769-0088 Hor Yezh **5219**
0769-010X Documents d'Archeologie Francaise **390**
0769-0126 Quadrant **5356**
0769-0142 Cle Pour
0769-0266 Actes **8489**
0769-0274 Synthese **8512**
0769-0398 France. Office National d'Immigration. Annuaire des Migrations
0769-0479 Revue Francaise d'Economie **1548**
0769-0509 Scribecot†
0769-0541 Centre International pour la Formation et les Echanges Geologiques. Publication Occasionnelle **2728**
0769-055X Social Pratique **1176**
0769-0584 Transports Routiers de Marchandises Effectues par des Transporteurs Etrangers sur le Territoire Francais†
0769-0681 Iris **5443**
0769-0770 Universite de Perpignan. Les Cahiers
0769-0819 Le Cardiologue **5779**
0769-0878 Observations et Travaux† **8978**
0769-0886 Recherches sur Diderot et sur l'Encyclopedie **5358**
0769-0940 Nouvelle Bibliotheque du Moyen Age **5343**
0769-0959 1895 **6517**
0769-0975 Archimag **4990**
0769-1025 Satellites de Saturne I to VIII†
0769-1033 Satellites Galileens de Jupiter†
0769-1041 Ephemerides of the Faint Satellites of Jupiter and Saturn†
0769-1343 G A N I L. Nouvelles **7014**
0769-184X Fortuna **7357**
0769-1920 L'Ecran Fantastique **6496**
0769-3206 Materiaux pour l'Histoire de Notre Temps **4242**
0769-3249 Camping-Car Magazine **8492**
0769-3362 Revue Droit et Societe **4774**
0769-3397 Lithiques†
0769-3478 Dossiers de l'Outre-Mer†
0769-3508 Gazette des Communes, des Departements, des Regions **1747**
0769-3656 Etudes Danubiennes **4218**
0769-3710 Intramuros **446**
0769-4113 Intellectica **7363**
0769-4377 Les Jeux de Notre Temps **8182**
0769-4407 Depeche Mode†
0769-4679 Pas Tant†
0769-4814 Raids **6442**
0769-4830 Sports Loisirs Tourisme†
0769-489X France. Institut National de la Statistique et des Etudes Economiques. Annales d'Economie et de Statistique **1233**
0769-5918 Dossiers du Marketing Direct† **8951**
0769-6027 Atout Chat **6804**
0769-6094 Savoirs et Formation **2909**
0769-6361 Aquarium Magazine† **8930**
0769-7120 Informatique Magazine
0769-7635 Dix-Neuvieme Siecle **5285**
0769-7864 Emblemes et Pavillons **3765**
0769-8372 Amateur de Bordeaux **597**
0770-0148 Industrial Relations Europe **1688**
0770-0164 Institut Royal Meteorologique de Belgique. Bulletin Trimestriel: Observations d'Ozone **6357**
0770-0261 Institut Royal Meteorologique de Belgique. Miscellanea. Serie A **6357**
0770-0369 Belgium. Institut National de Statistique. Annuaire de Statistiques Regionales **1214**
0770-0415 Annuaire Statistique de la Belgique†
0770-0512 Belgian Journal of Operations Research, Statistics and Computer Science†
0770-0520 Physicalia Magazine **7032**

ISSN

0773-476X Fast Food Magazine (Nederlandse Editie) **4386**
0773-4778 Vraag en Aanbod **1908**
0773-4980 Enquete du Musee de la Vie Wallonne **336**
0773-5006 Musee Royal de l'Afrique Centrale. Annales - Sciences Historiques. Serie in 8 **4176**
0773-557X Home Digest (French Edition)†
0773-5812 Universite Libre de Bruxelles. Institut de Philologie et d'Histoire Orientales et Slaves. Annuaire†
0773-5901 Het Spoor **8625**
0773-591X Grafisch Nieuws *see* 0029-4926 **7325**
0773-5995 Radio Revue
0773-6347 E C E T O C Monograph **3496**
0773-6509 Europe-Magazine
0773-6959 Rechtsdocumentatie **4824**
0773-6991 Saisons
0773-7378 Mathematique et Pedagogie **5516**
0773-7386 *see* 0417-5271
0773-7467 Bulletin Usuel des Lois et Arretes **4633**
0773-7661 Vooruitgang *see* 0033-0434
0773-7688 Dialectes de Wallonie **5111**
0773-7777 Reseau Automatique Belge de la Pollution Atmospherique†
0773-7912 Etudes Phenomenologiques **6741**
0773-8072 E C E T O C Technical Report **3496**
0773-8560 Musee Royal de l'Afrique Centrale. Catalogue des Editions **631**
0773-8625 Samsom Audit & Revisoraat **1301**
0773-9273 Gemeentekrediet van Belgie. Driemaandelijks Tijdschrift *see* 0011-099X **1333**
0773-9400 L'Erable **671**
0773-9532 La Part de l'Oeil **511**
0773-9559 Stad Antwerpen. Cultureel Jaarboek **6537**
0773-9664 Belgium. Ministere des Affaires Economiques. Administration de l'Information Economique. Apercu Trimestriel de l'Economie†
0773-9826 Centre d'Etudes et de Documentation Africaines. Bulletin Bibliographique†
0774-0115 Revue Belge du Cinema†
0774-0484 Bulletin Jean Ray†
0774-0557 Talkabout **5185**
0774-0670 Yachting Sud sur l'Eau **8285**
0774-0689 European Aquaculture Society. Special Publications **3590**
0774-112X Recherches Universitaires sur l'Integration Europeenne **7261**
0774-1200 *see* 0014-9640
0774-1324 Uit **8770**
0774-1383 Auto†
0774-1391 Promotor
0774-1413 Dobbit Professional (Dutch Edition) *see* 0774-1421 **1003**
0774-1421 Dobbit Professional (French Edition) **1003**
0774-1847 Tijdschrift voor de Studie van de Verlichting en van het Vrije Denken†
0774-2398 Taalbeheersing in de Praktijk *changed to* 1373-5470 **5158**
0774-2606 Cahiers Nivellois **5418**
0774-2711 Le Vif - L'Express **3802**
0774-2754 Laicite. La Pensee et les Hommes **6931**
0774-2797 De Boekarbeider *see* 0041-1876
0774-2819 Lambillionea **854**
0774-2827 Ons Geestelijk Erf **7667**
0774-2908 Humanistica Lovaniensia **2235**
0774-3106 Albums de Croy **4197**
0774-3114 *see* 0774-3106 **4197**
0774-3289 Fiscolex B T W **1925**
0774-3548 Sambre et Heure **4160**
0774-3696 Mars Magazine (Edition Francaise)
0774-370X Mars Magazine (Nederlandse Edition) *see* 0774-3696
0774-3998 Tractebel. Annual Report
0774-4110 Chaleur et Climats (Edition Bilingue) *changed to* 1376-8816
0774-4137 Le Journal des Poetes **5424**
0774-4706 Cactussen en Vetplanten **783**
0774-5141 Belgian Journal of Linguistics **5099**
0774-5435 Geschied- en Oudheidkundige Kring voor Leuven en Omgeving. Jaarboek **4223**
0774-5486 Vlaamse Stam **3787**
0774-5524 Questions Liturgiques **7673**
0774-5729 Zoo Antwerpen *see* 1373-6906 **969**
0774-5885 Revue Belge de Numismatique et de Sigillographie **6653**
0774-613X Ad Rem **8489**
0774-6326 Industrial Engineering News - Europe **3368**
0774-6415 Hobbytuin Magazine **3736**
0774-658X De Fiscale Koerier **1925**
0774-6830 Go Skiing (Edition Francaise) *see* 0774-6849 **8315**
0774-6849 Go Skiing (Nederlandse Editie) **8315**
0774-7160 De Lelie **3742**
0774-7209 Samsom Concertation Sociale *see* 0774-7217 **1874**
0774-7217 Samsom Sociaal Overleg **1874**
0774-7241 Clairlieu: Tijdschrift Gewijd aan de Geschiedenis der Kruisheren **7633**
0774-7365 Havens Zeebrugge en Oostende. Jaarboek **8645**
0774-7446 Milieuzakboekje **3453**
0774-7640 Wetboek Fiscaal Recht - Inkomstenbelasting **1955**
0774-7950 Place de la Sante
0774-8108 Revue de Jurisprudence de Liege, Mons et Bruxelles **4774**
0774-8353 Bibliotheque Africaine. Liste des Acquisitions **619**
0774-8396 Commission Royale de Toponymie et Dialectologie. Bulletin **5107**
0774-8523 De Witte Raaf **526**
0774-8698 Interface (Brussels) **5128**
0774-9015 Steps **3801**
0774-935X F N I B - Info *changed to* 1379-7476 **5959**
0774-9457 Tijdschrift voor Boek- en Bibliotheekwezen *changed to* 0014-9527 **7571**
0774-9465 Het Boek (Antwerpen) *changed to* 0014-9527 **7571**
0774-9732 De Gerechtsdeurwaarder - Digest **4952**
0774-9740 Chouette **5106**
0774-9775 Courrier Fiscal *see* 0774-658X **1925**
0774-9929 Samsom Personal Computer (Dutch Edition) *changed to* 1371-3817 **2576**
0774-9945 Flair (French Edition) **8863**
0775-0021 Flair (Flemish Edition) **8863**
0775-0234 De Belgisch Tijdschrift voor Sociale Zekerheid **7422**
0775-0285 Belgisch Tijdschrift voor Tandheelkunde *see* 0775-0293 **5864**
0775-0293 Revue Belge de Medecine Dentaire **5864**
0775-0501 Huisarts Nu **5630**
0775-051X Advances in Protein Phosphatases†
0775-0544 Transport Echo (French Edition) *see* 0775-0552 **8514**
0775-0552 Transport Echo (Dutch Edition) **8514**
0775-0560 Catering (Dutch Edition) **4383**
0775-0587 Catering (French Edition) **4383**
0775-0722 Archives et Bibliotheques de Belgique **4990**
0775-0781 Fiscaal Jaarboek **1925**
0775-0927 A V Production Book†
0775-1400 Cyperaceae Newsletter **785**
0775-1443 Belgium Economic and Commercial Information
0775-2024 Bulletin d'Acoustique **7087**
0775-2075 Equipment Construction **1007**
0775-2202 Les Cahiers de la Fonderie **4208**
0775-2784 Bulletin des Assurances **4496**
0775-2814 Tijdschrift voor Belgisch Burgerlijk Recht **4843**
0775-2857 *see* 1021-4232 **2352**
0775-2962 Ingenieur et Industrie **3198**
0775-3039 Koninklijk Museum voor Midden-Afrika. Annalen. Nieuwe Reeks in 4. Zoologische Wetenschappen *changed to* 1780-1311 **964**
0775-311X Belgium. Institut National de Statistique. Statistiques Judiciaires†
0775-3128 Volkskunde **3624**
0775-3209 Revue Europeenne de Droit de la Consommation†
0775-3217 Tijdschrift voor Gemeenterecht **7504**
0775-3314 Archaeologia Transatlantica **375**
0775-3322 Collectanea Maritima **4211**
0775-3381 Typologie des Sources du Moyen Age Occidental **4274**
0775-3411 Thorikos **420**
0775-3446 Centre de Recherche et de Promotion Forestieres. Documents†
0775-3691 Samsom Milieu & Bedrijf **3464**
0775-4205 Elga
0775-4221 Attitude **5065**
0775-4663 Revue de Droit International et de Droit Compare **4939**
0775-4671 Cercle Royal d'Histoire et d'Archeologie d'Ath et de la Region et Musees Athois. Bulletin **387**
0775-4779 Eigen Aard **8859**
0775-4795 Le Cri du Citoyen **3801**
0775-597X European Trade Union Institute. Documentation Centre. Bulletin†
0775-6178 A B C Belge pour le Commerce et l'Industrie **1970**
0775-6348 Beslagzakboekje **4946**
0775-6771 L'Echo de Nos Vergers **3728**
0775-7034 Haven Gent. Jaarboek **8645**
0775-7379 Etudes Nervaliennes et Romantiques **5292**
0775-7883 Samsom Sportsecretaris **8199**
0775-7905 Samsom Artsenpraktijk
0775-8073 Le Courrier du Passant *changed to* 1783-8509 **6522**
0775-8413 Industrie Cimentiere Belge **1014**
0775-8545 Kampeertoerist **8320**
0775-8553 Varen **8284**
0775-8596 Knipoog†
0775-8758 Recueil Annuel de Jurisprudence Belge **4767**
0775-8944 Coiffeur et Coiffures *see* 0775-8952 **589**
0775-8952 Kapper en Kapsels **589**
0775-9002 Via Secura **8637**
0775-9010 *see* 0775-9002 **8637**
0775-9053 Acta Medica Catholica **6902**
0775-9401 Notre Temps *changed to* 1377-2384 **4053**
0775-9479 Cahiers du Scenario†
0775-9592 Opera Botanica Belgica **806**
0775-9878 Play Golf (Nederlandse Editie) **8242**
0776-0116 Textyles **5187**
0776-023X Play Golf (Edition Francaise) *see* 0775-9878 **8242**
0776-0590 Samsom Actualite Comptable **1301**
0776-0604 Fast Food Magazine (Edition Francaise) **4385**
0776-0698 Stars†
0776-1023 De Leiegouw **4239**
0776-1155 Tribune de l'Eau **8833**
0776-1244 Institut Archeologique du Luxembourg. Annales **397**
0776-1260 Institut Archeologique Liegeois. Bulletin **397**
0776-1295 Societe d'Art et d'Histoire du Diocese de Liege. Bulletin **518**
0776-1309 Societe Royale Le Vieux-Liege. Bulletin **4265**
0776-1317 Mariemont. Cahiers **6528**
0776-1414 Musees Royaux d'Art et d'Histoire. Bulletin **4247**
0776-1465 Samsom Fiscale Wenken **1942**
0776-1473 Samsom Signaux Fiscaux *see* 0776-1465 **1942**
0776-1511 Samsom Cooperatieve Vennootschappen **1170**
0776-152X Samsom Societe Cooperative *see* 0776-1511 **1170**
0776-1562 Samsom Societe Privee a Responsabilite Limitee *see* 0778-127X **1170**
0776-202X Appeltjes van het Meetjesland **4199**
0776-2143 Landbouwtijdschrift. Tweetalige Editie†
0776-2461 Avimo Info **2829**
0776-2488 Inter-Presse **7650**
0776-2666 Hethitica **551**
0776-2933 Academie Royale des Sciences d'Outre-Mer. Classe des Sciences Morales et Politiques. Memoires in 8 **4440**
0776-2976 Koninklijke Kring voor Oudheidkunde Letteren en Kunst van Mechelen. Handelingen **4238**
0776-2984 Acta Archaeologica Lovaniensia - Monographiae **370**
0776-3190 Gael **8865**
0776-3387 Trends **5085**
0776-3395 Trends - Tendances **5085**
0776-3468 Academie Royale de Marine de Belgique. Communications **8638**
0776-3646 G R Infos Sentiers **8315**
0776-376X Kadath
0776-3794 *see* 0038-7770 **8202**
0776-3824 Kernos **2236**
0776-3859 Antwerp Papers in Linguistics **5094**
0776-3948 Nouvelle Biographie Nationale **644**
0776-409X L'Echo (Brussels) **1097**
0776-4111 Gezelliana, Kroniek van de Gezellestudie†
0776-4383 Samsom Vrije Beroepen **1170**
0776-4480 Mesures Art International†
0776-4642 Echos-Flash **3188**
0776-4707 Redactuel **4583**
0776-5436 Revue Internationale P M E **1966**
0776-5533 Koninklijke Geschied- en Oudheidkundige Kring van Kortrijk. Handelingen
0776-5738 Media Plan **29**
0776-5827 De Stem van de Ouders **4069**
0776-5835 La Voix des Parents **4070**
0776-7153 Silva Belgica **3702**
0776-7323 Africana Gandensia **323**
0776-7412 Militaria Belgica **6435**
0776-7943 Journal of African Zoology **949**
0776-8354 Collationes. Vlaams Tijdschrift voor Theologie en Pastoraal **7634**
0776-8605 Tijdschrift voor Vreemdelingenrecht **4942**
0776-8656 Coup de Foudre **5108**
0776-8982 Samsom Environnement et Gestion *see* 0775-3691 **3464**
0776-9121 Lettre d'Information Hebdomadaire pour la Gestion d'un Cercle Sportif *see* 0775-7883 **8199**
0776-9458 Weekberichten *see* 0577-148X **7126**
0776-9628 Verkeersveiligheid **8532**
0776-9636 Securite Routiere **8529**
0776-9954 A B C Luxembourgeois pour le Commerce et l'Industrie **1970**
0776-9989 Linguiste **5145**
0777-0006 Donnees Statistiques sur le Livre Belge de Langue Francaise **7578**
0777-0030 De Reiskrant **8751**
0777-0111 Koninklijk Belgisch Instituut voor Natuurwetenschappen. Studiedocumenten **686**
0777-0707 Cahiers Internationaux de Psychologie Sociale **7343**
0777-074X Fils d'Abraham **7643**
0777-0812 Media & Marketing **29**
0777-1266 Voir **4086**
0777-1525 Academie Royale des Sciences d'Outre-Mer. Classe des Sciences Techniques. Collection in 8 **7830**
0777-1673 Corpus Christianorum. Lingua Patrum **5108**
0777-2009 Samsom Professions Liberales *see* 0776-4383 **1170**
0777-2173 Etudes et Recherches Archeologiques de l'Universite de Liege **393**
0777-2491 Colloques d'Histoire des Connaissances Zoologiques **938**
0777-2572 Bulletin C R R **3260**
0777-3331 Bulletin d'Histoire Cistercienne **7698**
0777-3374 Photographie Ouverte **6974**
0777-3439 Feeling **8862**
0777-3579 Revue Trimestrielle des Droits de l'Homme **7214**
0777-3625 Foto Video Audio News (Dutch Edition) **6967**
0777-3641 Photo Video Audio News (French Edition) **6973**
0777-3781 International Far-Eastern Numismatics News
0777-4761 A B P Contact **4063**
0777-4931 Nationale Maatschappij van Belgische Spoorwegen. Informatie en Aanwinsten **8528**
0777-5067 De Gulden Passer **7562**
0777-5091 Varkensbedrijf **303**
0777-5288 World Directory of Cement & Concrete Associations†
0777-5814 The European Public Affairs Directory (Year) **1564**
0777-5954 Klasse **3026**
0777-611X European Cement Association. World Statistical Review **1046**
0777-6187 Anthropologie et Prehistoire *changed to* 1377-5723 **325**
0777-6276 Belgian Journal of Zoology **935**
0777-6306 V R B - Informatie **5054**
0777-6349 De Onderneming *see* 0777-6357 **4118**
0777-6357 L'Entreprise **4118**
0777-639X La Gazette Diplomatique **7237**
0777-642X Karaat **5074**
0777-7094 Medialex **2333**
0777-7302 L'Instant
0777-7418 De Huisarts *see* 0777-7426 **5619**
0777-7426 Le Generaliste **5619**
0777-7787 Sociaal Praktijkboek **4842**
0777-785X Collection de la Revue des Etudes Juives **7720**
0777-8112 Subsidia Hagiographica **7819**
0777-8473 Chrom und Flammen **8574**
0777-8600 Institut de Linguistique de Louvain. Serie Pedagogique **5127**
0777-8805 Louvain Brewing Letters†
0777-883X Tijdschrift voor Sociologie **8144**
0777-8988 De Weekkrant **3802**
0777-9100 Auschwitz - Stichting. Driemaandelijks Tijdschrift *see* La Memoire d'Auschwitz. Bulletin Trimestriel **4244**
0777-916X Infor Marechalerie-Der Huf **8293**
0777-9321 Op de Baan - T S P *see* 0777-933X **8617**
0777-933X En Lignes - P F T **8617**
0777-9364 U Z Magazine **4112**
0777-978X Orientalia Lovaniensia Analecta **558**
0777-9844 Proeftuin Nieuws **249**
0777-9909 Presse-Inter **6647**
0778-0265 Dopido (French Edition) **2186**
0778-0273 Dopido (Dutch Edition) **2186**
0778-0303 A V Industrie **2311**
0778-0443 Tijdschrift voor Onderwijsrecht en Onderwijsbeleid **4796**
0778-0583 Samsom Societe Anonyme *see* 0778-1261 **1170**
0778-0680 Codex Publiek Recht **7430**
0778-1032 C V News **22**
0778-1199 Groen Magazine **3734**
0778-1261 Samsom Naamloze Vennootschappen **1170**
0778-127X Samsom Besloten Vennootschappen met Beperkte Aansprakelijkheid **1170**
0778-1288 Samsom Geld en Onderneming **1381**
0778-1318 Tijdingen *changed to* 1377-8714 **7553**
0778-1350 Musea Nostra **6529**
0778-1695 Actualites du Droit **4609**
0778-1806 Kantieke Schoolmeester **5317**

0783-7828 Islanninhevoskuulumisia *changed to* 1797-3538 **8293**
0783-8069 Lappeenranta University of Technology. Department of Information Technology. Research Report **2473**
0783-8670 Lappeenranta University of Technology. Department of Information Technology. Lecture Notes **2473**
0783-8921 C - Lehti†
0784-0039 Gerontologia **4046**
0784-0322 Suomen Musiikkikirjastoyhdistys. Julkaisusarja **6621**
0784-1418 Vartiotorni (Tavallinen) *see* 0043-1087 **7743**
0784-1736 Meijeriteollisuus†
0784-2546 Leppis **2199**
0784-2821 Finland. Posti-ja Telelaitos. Postin Lehtiluettelo (Year)†
0784-3496 Finnish Association for Aerosol Research. Report Series in Aerosol Science **2100**
0784-3844 Naistutkimus **8901**
0784-5197 Finnish Economic Papers **1110**
0784-5502 Suomen Golflehti **8247**
0784-6010 Maritime Research News **8653**
0784-6037 Oulun Sukututkija **4252**
0784-6509 Bank of Finland. Bulletin **1314**
0784-6789 Tasa-Arvo **8885**
0784-7610 Pienoismalli **4343**
0784-7696 Lappeenranta University of Technology. Department of Industrial Engineering and Management. Report **3370**
0784-7726 Blues News **6550**
0784-7998 Finland. Tilastokeskus. Tyovoimatilasto **1232**
0784-8161 Finland. Tilastokeskus. Tilastokirjaston Uutuudet†
0784-817X Finland. Tilastokeskus. Tuottajahintaindeksit **1232**
0784-8196 Finland. Tilastokeskus. Rakennuskustannusindeksi (Kuukausitilasto) **1046**
0784-820X Finland. Tilastokeskus. Kuluttajahintaindeksi **1231**
0784-8218 Finland. Tilastokeskus. Ansiotasoindeksi **1231**
0784-8226 Finland. Tilastokeskus. Teollisuustilasto†
0784-8307 Finland. Tilastokeskus. Asuminen†
0784-8323 Finland. Tilastokeskus. Julkinen Talous†
0784-8331 Finland. Tilastokeskus. Kansantalous†
0784-834X Finland. Tilastokeskus. Kauppa **1231**
0784-8366 Finland. Tilastokeskus. Oikeus†
0784-8374 Finland. Tilastokeskus. Palkat†
0784-8382 Finland. Tilastokeskus. Rahoitus†
0784-8390 Finland. Tilastokeskus. Rakentaminen†
0784-8412 Finland. Tilastokeskus. Terveys†
0784-8420 Finland. Tilastokeskus. Tulot ja Kulutus†
0784-8439 Finland. Tilastokeskus. Vaalit†
0784-8447 Finland. Tilastokeskus. Vaestoe†
0784-8463 Finland. Tilastokeskus. Yritykset†
0784-8641 Lukufiilis **5328**
0784-8757 Finland. Tilastokeskus. Elinolot†
0784-8765 Finland. Tilastokeskus. Kulttuuri ja Viestinta†
0784-882X Finland. Tilastokeskus. Poliisin Tietoon Tullut Rikollisuus **2674**
0784-9257 University of Turku. Publications of the Institute of History. General History **4165**
0784-9346 Finland. Tilastokeskus. Vuokratilasto **4435**
0784-9354 Finland. Tilastokeskus. Energia†
0784-9370 Finland. Tilastokeskus. Kuntasektorin Kuukausipalkat *changed to* 1459-6369 **1231**
0784-9583 Finland. Tilastokeskus. Kansantalouden Tilinpito: Vuositilasto (Print) *changed to* 1795-8881 **1231**
0784-9613 Finland. Tilastokeskus. Kansantalouden Tilinpito. Taulukot **1231**
0784-9672 Finland. Tilastokeskus. Rahoitustilinpito **1232**
0784-9737 Finland. Tilastokeskus. Kuntien Talousarviot **7480**
0784-9761 Finland. Tilastokeskus. Alueellinen Luottokanta *changed to* 1459-5451 **1231**
0784-9788 Finland. Tilastokeskus. Joukkovelkakirjat†
0784-9842 Finland. Tilastokeskus. Pankit: Vuositilasto *changed to* 1795-2050 **1231**
0784-994X Finland. Tilastokeskus. Sijoitusrahastot **1232**
0784-9966 Finland. Tilastokeskus. Maatilatalouden Tulo- ja Verotustiedot *changed to* 1797-304X **180**
0784-9974 Finland. Tilastokeskus. Maatilatalouden Yritys- ja Tulotilasto (Print) *changed to* 1797-304X **180**
0785-0026 Yleisradio. Annual Report **2399**
0785-0050 Finland. Tilastokeskus. Tyovoimatilasto **1232**
0785-0107 Finland. Tilastokeskus. Tyoemarkkinat†
0785-0204 Finland. Tilastokeskus. Tyotaistelut (Neljannesvuositilasto) **1232**
0785-0387 Finland. Tilastokeskus. Ymparistotilasto **3479**
0785-0638 Finland. Tilastokeskus. Korkeakouluihin Hakeneet ja Hyvaksytyt†
0785-0719 Finland. Tilastokeskus. Tiede ja Teknologia **7854**
0785-0743 Finland. Tilastokeskus. Vaeston Koulutusrakenne Kunnittain **2933**
0785-0891 Soundi **6618**
0785-0913 E T - Lehti **4043**
0785-1324 Markkinointiviestinta†
0785-1928 Finnish Political Science Association. Books **7136**
0785-2517 Kosmoskyna **5444**
0785-2843 Intervalli (Print) *changed to* 1796-7392 **6578**
0785-3165 Finland. Tilastokeskus. Energiatilastot **3152**
0785-3416 Me Kaksit
0785-3572 Bank of Finland. Discussions Papers *changed to* Bank of Finland Research Discussions Papers **1314**
0785-3793 Sisuviesti **8603**
0785-3890 Annals of Medicine **5902**
0785-398X Aabo Underrettelser **3838**
0785-4420 Pedersoeret†
0785-4587 Steel News *changed to* 1795-357X **1054**
0785-4625 Sosiaaliturva **8084**
0785-4633 Tyolakemenotilasto Alueittain **8084**
0785-479X Finland. Tilastokeskus. Vaestonmuutokset Kunnittain *changed to* 1795-1887 **7306**
0785-5494 Futura **3838**
0785-5540 Business Finland **1977**
0785-6016 Finland. Tilastokeskus. Tulo- ja Varallisuustilasto **1232**
0785-6105 Tampereen Yliopisto. Sosiologian ja Sosiaalipsykologian Laitos. A, Tutkimuksia **8142**
0785-613X Finland. Tilastokeskus. Moottoriajoneuvot **8524**
0785-6172 Finland. Tilastokeskus. Liikennetilastollinen Vuosikirja **8524**
0785-6245 Finland. Tilastokeskus. Tieliikenneonnettomuudet **8524**
0785-6288 Finland. Tilastokeskus. Tukku- ja Vahittaiskauppa **1232**
0785-6318 Talomestari **1039**
0785-6482 Tampereen Teknillinen Korkeakoulu. Sahkotekniikan Osasto. Elektroniikan Laitos. Raportti *changed to* 1459-3270 **3332**
0785-6695 Sportti†
0785-6776 Nuori Voima **5344**
0785-6822 Aabo Akademi. Institutet foer Finlandssvensk Samhaellsforskning. Forskningsrapporter **7944**
0785-7373 Ystavien Kesken *changed to* 1797-0369 **2698**
0785-7527 Sairaanhoitaja **5980**
0785-7934 Finland. Tilastokeskus. Luottokortit **1231**
0785-8205 Finland. Tilastokeskus. Perheet **7306**
0785-8221 Finland. Tilastokeskus. Tyossakayntitilasto (Print) *changed to* Finland. Tilastokeskus. Tyossakaynti **1232**
0785-823X Lappeenrannan Teknillinen Yliopisto. Energia- ja Ymparistotekniikan Osasto. Tutkimusraportti A **3208**
0785-8256 Lappeenrannan Teknillinen Korkeakoulu. Energiatekniikan Osasto. D. Julkaisu *changed to* 1459-2657 **3208**
0785-8736 Helsingin Kaupungin Tilastollinen Vuosikirja **8376**
0785-8760 Entomologica Fennica **844**
0785-885X Finland. Tilastokeskus. Science and Technology in Finland **7854**
0785-8884 Finland. Tilastokeskus. Valtion Kuukausipalkat **1232**
0785-9880 Finland. Tilastokeskus. Tulonjakotilasto **1232**
0785-997X Tekniikka & Talous **3222**
0785-9988 Mikro P C **2578**
0786-0021 Finland. Tilastokeskus. Energian Tiotanto ja Vesihuolto **3152**
0786-0102 Tampere University of Technology. Software Systems Laboratory. Report *changed to* 1459-417X **2599**
0786-0188 Lapsen Maailma **8053**
0786-0218 Film from Finland *changed to* 1796-0738 **6501**
0786-0218 Films from Finland *changed to* 1796-072X **6501**
0786-0366 Finland. Tilastokeskus. Kuorma-Autoliikenteen Kustannusindeksi **8524**
0786-0994 Finland. Tilastokeskus. Rakennuskustannusindeksi. (Vuositilasto)†
0786-1346 Mutta-Julkaisu
0786-1877 Finland. Tilastokeskus. Tieliikenteen Tavarankuljetustilasto **8779**
0786-2016 T M. Tekniikan Maailma. Automaailma **8606**
0786-2113 Sampovisio **1792**
0786-2571 Skeptikko **6952**
0786-2857 Finland. Ministry of Agriculture and Forestry. Information Centre. Statistics. Maatilatilastollinen Vuosikirja **180**
0786-3012 Science Studies **7911**
0786-4256 Pientalo
0786-4558 Technical Research Centre of Finland. Annual Report *changed to* V T T Annual Report **3226**
0786-4612 Viikko - Eteenpain **3839**
0786-4809 Kaukolampotilasto **3153**
0786-5066 Studia Archaeologica Septentrionalia **419**
0786-5546 Suomen...Suurinta Yritysta†
0786-5686 Hoitotiede **5960**
0786-5767 Tietosuoja **4853**
0786-6135 Starlight†
0786-6453 The Finnish Yearbook of International Law **4926**
0786-7883 Kompass Finland **1574**
0786-8170 Tropical Forestry Reports **3705**
0786-8413 University of Oulu. Department of Information Processing Science. Series A, Research Papers **2538**
0786-8456 Kellon - Haukiputaan Kotiseutujulkaisu **4237**
0786-9282 Trendi **8886**
0786-9363 Filatelisti **6895**
0787-0132 Finland. Tilastokeskus. Kuolemansyyt **7306**
0787-0221 Acta Societatis Fennicae Iuris Gentium. B **4916**
0787-0604 Lappeenrannan Teknillinen Korkeakoulu. Asiantuntijaluettelo *changed to* 1459-3203 **2992**
0787-197X Tornionlaakson Vuosikirja **4273**
0787-2348 Varsinais Suomen Maakuntakirja†
0787-2399 Totto **4274**
0787-295X Arttu **475**
0787-3840 Suomen Arkkitehtiliitto. Vuosikirja **458**
0787-4421 Rakennusinsinoori **3281**
0787-5266 F P A - Bladet **4502**
0787-572X Finland. Tilastokeskus. Rakentaminen ja Asuminen: Vuosikirja **4435**
0787-6424 Lemmikki **6811**
0787-7153 Finland. Tilastokeskus. Kunnallisvaalit **7480**
0787-7439 Tennismaailma†
0787-8052 Uusi Elektroniikka†
0787-8478 Kalatutkimuksia **3600**
0787-8516 Finland. Tilastokeskus. Maailma Numeroina. Suomen Tilastollinen Vuosikirjan...Kansainvalinen Osa **8371**
0787-9156 Poiju *changed to* 1796-329X **3838**
0787-9385 Kotilaakari **6991**
0788-0308 Finland. Tilastokeskus. Asuntojen Hinnat. Vuositilasto **4435**
0788-0332 Motion **8187**
0788-1010 Yhteiskuntasuunnittelu *changed to* 1459-6806 **4431**
0788-1347 Finland. Tilastokeskus. Finnish Mass Media **8149**
0788-1576 Helsingin Kaupungin Tietokeskuksen Neljannesvuosijulkaisu. Kvartti **7444**
0788-1673 Sukutieto **3784**
0788-1738 Finland. Tilastokeskus. Suomen Yritykset **1232**
0788-2211 L E I F - Life and Education in Finland†
0788-365X Acta Futura Fennica **3838**
0788-3749 M K-Lehti **8321**
0788-3757 Studia Musica **6620**
0788-4141 Hyvinvointikatsaus **8083**
0788-4397 Acta Societatis Fennicae Iuris Gentium. A **4916**
0788-4877 African Newsletter on Occupational Health and Safety **6672**
0788-4990 Valtion Taloudellinen Tutkimuskeskus. V A T T - Julkaisuja **1191**
0788-5008 Valtion Taloudellinen Tutkimuskeskus. V A T T - Tutkimuksia **1191**
0788-5016 Valtion Taloudellinen Tutkimuskeskus. V A T T - Keskustelualoitteita **1191**
0788-5237 Finland Tilastokeskus. Vaestorakenne *changed to* 1795-1887 **7306**
0788-5245 Finland. Tilastokeskus. Vaestonmuutokset **7306**
0788-544X Finland. Kuluttajaviraston. Julkaisu **2638**
0788-5717 Commentationes Physico-Mathematicae et Chemico-Medicae **7008**
0788-5822 Asu Hyvin
0788-6012 Current Research in Physical Sciences in Finland **8168**
0788-6098 Finland. Sosiaali- ja Terveyshallitus. Kotipalvelu **8040**
0788-6101 Lastensuojelu **8053**
0788-639X Jyvaskylan Yliopiston. Perhetutkimusyksikon. Julkaisuja *changed to* 1796-105X **8116**
0788-6632 T V - Veckan och Radio†
0788-6667 Vaasan Yliopisto. Julkaisuja. Tutkimuksia **1550**
0788-6675 Vaasan Yliopisto. Julkaisuja. Tutkimuksia. Hallintotiede **7475**
0788-6683 Vaasan Yliopisto. Julkaisuja. Tutkimuksia. Kansantaloustiede **1191**
0788-6691 Vaasan Yliopisto. Julkaisuja. Tutkimuksia. Kielitiede **5193**
0788-6705 Vaasan Yliopisto. Julkaisuja. Tutkimuksia. Liiketaloustiede **1800**
0788-6713 Vaasan Yliopisto. Julkaisuja. Tutkimuksia. Maantiede *changed to* 1459-6318 **3473**
0788-6721 Vaasan Yliopisto. Julkaisuja. Tutkimuksia. Matematiikka **5546**
0788-673X Vaasan Yliopisto. Julkaisuja. Tutkimuksia. Oikeustiede **4806**
0788-6748 Vaasan Yliopisto. Julkaisuja. Tutkimuksia. Sosiologia **8146**
0788-723X Finland. Tilastokeskus. L Y - Tunnuskirja **1231**
0788-7604 Lapin Yliopisto. Acta Universitatis Lapponiensis **7879**
0788-7906 Turun Yliopisto. Taydennyskoulutuskeskus. Julkaisu. A **3005**
0788-804X Savellys ja Musiikinteoria **6615**
0788-8325 Keskipohjanmaa **3838**
0788-8430 Muovi - Plast **7095**
0788-8554 Paallystolehti **6441**
0788-9135 Taloustaito **1946**
0788-9178 Finland. Tilastokeskus. Kansanedustajain Vaalit, Ennakkotilasto **7199**
0788-9917 Bodaus **6983**
0789-0168 Finland. Tilastokeskus. Kesamokit **4435**
0789-0249 F F Network **3617**
0789-0265 Kansan Lehti†
0789-0346 Dialogi **8037**
0789-0710 Jyvaskylan Yliopisto. Chydenius-Instituutti. Tutkimuksia **1139**
0789-0737 Pohjalainen **3839**
0789-0893 Finland. Oikeusministerio. Tietohallintotoimisto. A **7437**
0789-1180 Finland. Tilastokeskus. Tyotapaturmat **1232**
0789-1393 Matkailu **8733**
0789-1776 E A N Info *changed to* 1795-8083 **6402**
0789-2462 Finland. Tilastokeskus. Hinta- ja Palkkatiedote **1231**
0789-2616 Betfaeltet *see* 0789-2667 **129**
0789-2667 Juurikassarka **129**
0789-2918 Finland. Oikeusministerio. Tietojarjestelmayksikko. D **4674**
0789-4767 Kaupparekisterilehti **6753**
0789-516X Urheiluampuja
0789-5232 Fysioterapia **6109**
0789-5437 Sahkoala **3330**
0789-578X Tampereen Teknillinen Korkeakoulu. Arkkitehtuurin Osasto. Rakennussuunnittelun Laitos. Julkaisu *changed to* 1459-5397 **458**
0789-6093 Terassi†
0789-6263 Akava-Uutiset *changed to* 1795-8822 **4589**
0789-6549 Folk och Musik **3617**
0789-6638 Suomen Kalapaikkaopas **8336**
0789-676X Sahko - Tele **3330**
0789-7286 Finnish Journal of Dairy Science **264**
0789-7332 Finnboat News **8275**
0789-743X Finland. Tullihallitus. Ulkomaankauppa *changed to* 1796-9344 **1232**
0789-7804 Tampere English Studies **5185**
0789-8525 Lapsen Elatus ja Huolto **8053**
0789-8789 Terve Elama **7543**
0789-886X Ymparisto & Tekniikka *see* 0355-0729 **5454**
0789-9238 Vauva **2170**
0789-9343 Ateneum **476**
0789-9726 Rahapuu†
0789-9920 Kodinrakentaja†
0790-004X Treoir **6624**
0790-0147 Weekend Start
0790-0260 Geological Survey of Ireland. Guide Series **2740**
0790-0279 Geological Survey of Ireland. Report Series **2740**
0790-0317 Irish Motor Industry *changed to* 1649-976X **8586**
0790-0422 National Botanic Gardens. Occasional Papers **803**
0790-0430 Food Ireland **3639**
0790-0562 The Phoenix **5233**
0790-0600 Irish Cycling Review **8260**
0790-0627 International Journal of Water Resources Development **8826**
0790-066X Irish Bank Officials Association Newsheet **1359**
0790-0724 Construction Information Services Report **996**
0790-0929 Aquaculture Ireland **3585**
0790-1070 Ireland, a Directory **7447**
0790-1186 Irish Journal of Psychiatry
0790-1216 Salesian Bulletin **7816**
0790-1232 Public Sector Times **7463**
0790-1372 Chamber Link
0790-150X Software Abstracts for Engineers†
0790-1593 Arts Council. Annual Report **474**
0790-1631 The Salmon†
0790-1658 The Property Valuer **7605**
0790-1712 Labour Comment (Cork) **7150**
0790-1763 Irish Journal of Earth Sciences **2710**
0790-2026 Irish Printer **7324**
0790-2050 Fast Food Review *see* 0332-4400 **4389**
0790-2239 Bakery World **3671**
0790-228X Irish Rugby Review **8236**
0790-2441 Irish Vexillology Newsletter†

ISSN

0792-822X The Jerusalem Post (English Edition) **3895**
0792-8262 Shalom **2945**
0792-8424 Atiqot **382**
0792-8467 Jewish Studies† **8967**
0792-8610 Israel Film Centre Information Bulletin† **8966**
0792-9080 Mikkun Ve-handasa Be-hakla'ut
0792-9145 Frick 2000†
0792-9285 P C Magazine (Israeli Edition) **2573**
0792-9307 Zav-Zav† **8999**
0792-9358 Electronics **3096**
0792-9749 Inside Israel
0792-9765 Link† **8971**
0792-9803 J T D
0792-9935 Refu'at Happe Vehashinnayim **5863**
0792-9951 Vehicles & Transportation **8519**
0792-9978 Israel Journal of Plant Sciences **795**
0793-0070 ProAnimal
0793-0089 Mifneh **8121**
0793-0232 Ma'arakhot Tekhnologiya
0793-0275 Israel. Central Bureau of Statistics. National Expenditure on Culture, Recreation and Sports **7481**
0793-0283 Heterocyclic Communications **2063**
0793-0291 Metal-Based Drugs **2103**
0793-0453 Galileo (Tel Aviv) **7857**
0793-047X Mazon *changed to* Mazon Plus **3655**
0793-0593 Aqadem **5095**
0793-0607 Basifriyot **4994**
0793-0879 Asakim & Kalkala† **8931**
0793-1050 Mideast Security and Policy Studies **7253**
0793-1069 Sociological Papers **8137**
0793-1166 Aki Yerushalayim **3517**
0793-1344 'ale Hinnukh† **8929**
0793-1395 Palestine - Israel Journal of Politics, Economics and Culture **7163**
0793-1514 Eretz Va-Teva *see* 0334-9578 **2610**
0793-176X Justice **4850**
0793-1786 Functional Differential Equations **5488**
0793-1840 Anti-Semitism Worldwide **7202**
0793-1891 Einayim **2187**
0793-2065 Yalqut L'Teqstil† **8999**
0793-2081 Bank of Israel. Annual Information on the Banking Corporations **1213**
0793-2235 Israel. Central Bureau of Statistics. National Accounts of Israel **1245**
0793-2472 Foerder Institute for Economic Research. Working Papers **1541**
0793-2839 Perspectives **6939**
0793-3606 Israel. Central Bureau of Statistics. Immigrant Population from Former U S S R - Demographic Trends **7310**
0793-3894 Bekhol Derakhekha Da'ehu **7719**
0793-4041 Jews in Eastern Europe *changed to* 1565-4907 **7211**
0793-4114 Gitelson Peace Papers **7966**
0793-4602 Tmurot†
0793-4912 Surveys & Reviews in Gerontology†
0793-4947 Israel Conventions, Trade Shows, Festivals & Special Events† **8966**
0793-4955 Israeli Forum
0793-4963 I S O 9000 Certification in Israel
0793-5439 Tat-Tarbut† **8992**
0793-6362 Orachot **7727**
0793-646X Kol N'khe Milhama **8053**
0793-6648 International Journal for Manufacturing Science and Production **3368**
0793-6664 Azure **5208**
0793-694X International Journal of Generic Drugs **6849**
0793-7121 Hayyim Aherim **309**
0793-7385 The Jerusalem Review **5313**
0793-7407 Handbook of Pharmaceutical Generic Development **6845**
0793-7466 Sichat Hashavua **7729**
0793-7474 Hitkashrous **7721**
0793-8233 The Jerusalem Times
0793-8241 Palestine Business Report
0793-8918 International Medical Journal
0793-8934 Nashim **8901**
0794-0890 Nigerian Fisheries and Aquatic Sciences Abstracts **3603**
0794-1005 Global Approaches to Extension Practice: A Journal of Agricultural Extension **115**
0794-1749 Lagos Life **3920**
0794-2877 Nigeria Business Guide Annual **1153**
0794-3008 N P A Bulletin **8654**
0794-3415 Heritage **3537**
0794-3733 Medipharm Medical Journal **5676**
0794-3865 Nigeria Periodicals Review **5036**
0794-4055 Nigeria. National Integrated Survey of Households. Report on General Household Survey **4436**
0794-439X New Horizon **7158**
0794-4713 International Journal of Natural and Applied Sciences **7867**
0794-4721 Animal Production Research Advances **278**
0794-4810 ThisWeek
0794-4845 Tropical Veterinarian **8809**
0794-4896 Ife Journal of Science **7864**
0794-5086 Zariya Veterinarian **8815**
0794-5655 Editors' Forum **7560**
0794-6406 Nigerian Periodicals Index **11**
0794-6414 Nigerian Stored Products Research Institute. Annual Report **213**
0794-6430 Nigeria Banking, Finance & Commerce **1371**
0794-6961 Nsukka Journal of Linguistics and African Languages **5156**
0794-7046 T C N N Research Bulletin **7687**
0794-7054 Nigerian Packaging News
0794-7410 Journal of Community Medicine and Primary Health Care **5648**
0794-7763 Coop News **1423**
0794-7860 Samaru Journal of Agricultural Education
0794-7968 Insight Magazine **6645**
0794-8468 Quality **3921**
0794-859X Nigerian Journal of Physiological Sciences **5948**
0794-8603 Books **7555**
0794-9804 Ife Studies in English Language **5126**
0795-0101 Tropical Freshwater Biology **3610**
0795-0152 Josy Ajoboye on Sunday
0795-0691 The Analyst
0795-2031 Abokiyar Hira **3920**
0795-2864 Saiwa **5366**
0795-3038 Port Harcourt Medical Journal **5697**
0795-4506 Journal of African Children's and Youth Literature **2156**
0795-4778 African Journal of Library, Archives and Information Science **4987**
0795-5146 Daily Champion **3920**
0795-6495 Water Resouces **8838**
0795-6762 African Journal of Genetics **861**
0795-6770 Global Science Journal **7858**
0795-7475 The Sun **3921**
0795-7602 African Journal of Biblical Studies **7782**
0795-8080 Biokemistri **726**
0795-8692 Nigerian Journal of Palms and Oil Seeds **805**
0795-896X Weekly Probes **7193**
0795-8994 Search the Scriptures **7680**
0795-9001 Building the Body **7628**
0795-932X Banking & Finance Digest **1317**
0795-9931 Nigeria. National Universities Commission. University System News **2996**
0796-000X The Nation **3843**
0796-0018 Gambia Outlook†
0796-0034 The Gambia Onward†
0796-0158 The Worker **3843**
0796-0174 The Gambia Family Planning Association Newsletter **972**
0796-0220 Central Bank of the Gambia. Quarterly Bulletin **1446**
0796-0255 The Gambian Times **3842**
0796-0573 Foroyaa **3842**
0796-0832 The Daily Observer **3842**
0796-1049 Central Bank of the Gambia. Annual Report **1326**
0796-5036 Le Pays **3805**
0797-0005 Reflexiones del Batallismo **7995**
0797-0048 Revista Uruguaya de Cardiologia **5799**
0797-0056 Revista de Administration Publica Uruguaya **7466**
0797-0064 Suma **1520**
0797-0072 C I D A E **50**
0797-0129 Archivos de la Biblioteca Nacional **4990**
0797-0137 Paz y Justicia: Sumario de Derechos Humanos†
0797-0269 Revista Juridica Estudiantil **4773**
0797-0307 Revista Uruguaya de Patologia Clinica **5706**
0797-0366 Odontologia Uruguaya **5858**
0797-0374 Odontoestomatologia **5858**
0797-0463 Anuario de Derecho Administrativo **7420**
0797-0471 Revista Uruguaya de Derecho Procesal **4773**
0797-048X Revista Uruguaya de Derecho de Familia **4914**
0797-0501 Revista de Derecho Comercial y de la Empresa†
0797-0560 Revista de Ingenieria **3218**
0797-0684 Banco Central del Uruguay. Boletin Estadistico **1212**
0797-0773 Anuario de Derecho Civil Uruguayo **4619**
0797-0803 Archivos de Ginecologia y Obstetricia **5986**
0797-1176 Guia Financiera **1350**
0797-1443 Publicaciones Matematicas del Uruguay **5526**
0797-1478 Instituto de Investigaciones Pesqueras. Boletin **3598**
0797-163X Uruguay. Poder Legislativo. Biblioteca. Anales Parlamentarios†
0797-194X Boletin Estadistico Pesquero **3587**
0797-2008 Busqueda **1445**
0797-2059 Cinemateca Revista **6494**
0797-2067 Resumenes de Formacion Profesional C I N T E R F O R†
0797-2350 Cuadernos de Marcha†
0797-258X Uruguay. Direccion General de Estadistica y Censos. Indice Medio de Salarios **1273**
0797-2695 Justicia Uruguaya **4708**
0797-2733 Mercado **1407**
0797-292X Revista de Derecho Agrario - Uruguay **151**
0797-2954 Revista de Transporte y Seguros **4521**
0797-2989 Camara Nacional de Comercio. Revista **1398**
0797-2997 Sociedad Uruguaya de Geologia. Revista **2767**
0797-3101 Informativo A L A M A R **8646**
0797-3209 Encuesta Industrial Trimestral **1226**
0797-3217 Uruguay. Direccion General de Estadistica y Censos. Estadisticas Vitales **7317**
0797-3233 Imagen **4456**
0797-3268 Uruguay. Direccion General de Estadistica y Censos. Indice del Costo de la Construccion†
0797-3306 Instituto Nacional de Pesca. Informe Tecnico **3598**
0797-3357 Uruguay. Ministerio de Agricultura y Pesca. Precios de Productos e Insumos Agropecuarios **208**
0797-3411 Revista de Derecho Penal **4771**
0797-3500 Revista Uruguaya de Derecho Internacional†
0797-3527 Seguros **4522**
0797-3594 Uruguay en Cifras **8413**
0797-3713 O Dos†
0797-3918 Gaceta Universitaria **2982**
0797-4116 Comision Administradora del Rio Uruguay. Publicacion **8820**
0797-4175 Zeta†
0797-4248 Punto 21 **2901**
0797-4264 Uruguay. Unidad Asesora de Promocion Industrial. Memoria de Actividades **3149**
0797-4302 Revista de Derecho Publico **4852**
0797-471X La Cacerola
0797-4876 Revista Uruguaya de Psicologia **7405**
0797-4884 Cirugia Plastica Uruguaya **6239**
0797-4892 Revista del Sur **7997**
0797-4930 Ingenieria Quimica **3246**
0797-5198 Bolsa de Valores de Montevideo. Boletin Mensual **1613**
0797-5333 Brecha **3993**
0797-5457 Registro Nacional de Leyes, Decretos y Otros Documentos **4767**
0797-552X Instituto de la Mujer. Revista **8899**
0797-5538 Revista de Ciencias Sociales **7997**
0797-5546 Revista de Economia **1167**
0797-5686 Camara Nacional de Comercio. Informe Anual **1398**
0797-5716 Anuario Estadistico de Existencias, Faena y Exportacion **3669**
0797-6011 Centro Estudiantes de Derecho. Revista Juridica **4641**
0797-6062 Centro Latinoamericano de Economia Humana. Cuadernos **7953**
0797-6119 Teorema†
0797-6194 Revista Uruguaya de Enfermeria **5980**
0797-6275 Uruguay. Direccion de Educacion. Revista **2924**
0797-6291 Encuesta de Hogares: Ocupacion y Desocupacion **1718**
0797-6305 Hoy es Historia
0797-6313 Garibaldi **5217**
0797-633X Encuesta Continua de Hogares **4435**
0797-6461 Uruguay. Direccion de Educacion. Serie los Departamentos **2924**
0797-6488 Temas de Comunicacion
0797-650X Serie: Educacion y Mercosur **2911**
0797-6763 Guia del Mundo **3120**
0797-6828 Museo Nacional de Historia Natural de Montevideo. Anales **6727**
0797-6852 Acta Genetica et Teratologica
0797-7050 Anuario de Derecho Tributario **4917**
0797-7522 Foro Literatio†
0797-7565 Comision de Integracion Electrica Regional. Revista **3156**
0797-7581 Ambito Empresarial†
0797-7611 Revista A L A M A R†
0797-7883 Actas de Fisiologia **918**
0797-8057 Prisma **4470**
0797-8235 Lolapress **8900**
0797-8243 Anuario de Importacion - Exportacion del Uruguay **1200**
0797-8316 Universidad de la Republica. Facultad de Derecho. Revista **4801**
0797-8375 Infancia†
0797-8855 Revista Uruguaya de Instrumentadores Quirurgicos **4489**
0797-8871 Tierra Amiga **3470**
0797-888X Biodiversidad **2604**
0797-8960 Cuadernos de Negocios Internacionales e Integracion **1560**
0797-9061 Biblioteca Nacional de Uruguay. Revista **4995**
0797-9150 Asociacion de Quimica y Farmacia del Uruguay. Revista **6823**
0797-9495 Diplomacia en Accion
0797-9517 Revista Encuentros **7997**
0797-9533 Galileo **2859**
0797-9754 Relaciones **7402**
0797-9789 Revista Uruguaya de Ciencia Politica **7179**
0798-0000 Revista de Hacienda
0798-0035 Fitopatologia Venezolana **788**
0798-0086 Bibliografia Venezolana **4994**
0798-0256 Presencia Ecumenica **7671**
0798-0264 Archivos Venezolanos de Farmacologia y Terapeutica **2692**
0798-0329 Revista de Investigacion **2906**
0798-037X Boletin de Salud Publica†
0798-0469 Universidad Central de Venezuela. Facultad de Medicina. Revista **5726**
0798-0477 Instituto Nacional de Higiene Rafael Rangel. Revista **7526**
0798-0523 Urbana **460**
0798-0582 Revista Venezolana de Oncologia **6033**
0798-0639 Instituto Oceanografico de Venezuela. Boletin **2807**
0798-0728 Tribuna Medica (Venezuela Edition) *see* Tribuna Medica (Equador Edition)
0798-0728 Tribuna Medica (Venezuela Edition) *see* 0120-2529 **5724**
0798-0728 Tribuna Medica (Venezuela Edition) *see* Tribuna Medica (Mexico Edition)
0798-0728 Tribuna Medica (Venezuela Edition) *see* Tribuna Medica (Peru Edition)
0798-0752 Anales Venezolanos de Nutricion **6655**
0798-0841 Cuadernos de Actualidad Internacional **8036**
0798-1015 Espacios **7853**
0798-1120 Scientia Guaianae **7912**
0798-1147 Politica International
0798-1171 Revista de Filosofia **6948**
0798-118X Acta Terramaris **930**
0798-1228 Educacion Superior y Sociedad **2979**
0798-1236 I T E R Revista de Teologia **7648**
0798-1406 Cuestiones Politicas **7127**
0798-1457 Academia de Ciencias Politicas y Sociales. Boletin **7101**
0798-1546 Venezuela. Oficina Central de Estadistica e Informatica. Coyuntura Economica **1273**
0798-1570 Cifra Nueva **4447**
0798-1619 Parapara Seleccion de Libros para Ninos y Jovenes **7570**
0798-1635 Petroguia **6786**
0798-1759 International Journal of Sociology of Agriculture and Food **8109**
0798-1872 Parapara Revista de Literatura Infantil†
0798-1937 Bibliografia Seleccionada de Especies y Topicos Forestales **3708**
0798-1961 Magen-Escudo **3549**
0798-197X Revista Sobre Relaciones Industriales y Laborales **1705**
0798-2003 Numero
0798-2100 Maderas Comerciales de Venezuela **3696**
0798-2259 Universidad del Zulia. Facultad de Ciencias Veterinarias. Revista Cientifica **8809**
0798-2364 Zumaque
0798-2437 Revista Forestal Latinoamericana **3700**
0798-278X Paramillo **4468**
0798-2879 Informe Annual sobre la Situacion de los Derechos Humanos en Venezuela **7209**
0798-295X Banco Central de Venezuela. Anuario de Balanza de Pagos **1212**
0798-2968 Tierra Firme **8010**
0798-2992 Anuario Ininco **8088**
0798-3069 Fermentum **8102**
0798-3166 MedULA **5677**
0798-3220 Notas de Matematica **5521**
0798-3522 Dinero **1739**
0798-3530 Producto **1161**

0803-3668 Hjerteforum. Supplement *see* 0802-1465 **5789**
0803-3722 Natur og Mijoe Bulletin *changed to* 1504-4114 **3453**
0803-3773 Offshore og Energi **6782**
0803-379X Ordet **5158**
0803-3900 S N F Bulletin **8130**
0803-3927 Ringmerkaren **913**
0803-4028 Stiftelsen for Samfunns- og Naeringslivsforskning. Arbeidsnotat **1968**
0803-4036 S N F - Rapport **1169**
0803-4222 Theoretical Physics Seminar in Trondheim **7043**
0803-4494 P C World Norge Ekspress *changed to* 1503-8408 **2493**
0803-4508 Skogeiernytt *changed to* 0809-9006 **3683**
0803-4729 Ropet fra Oest **7773**
0803-4907 Scandinavian Society for Parasitology. Bulletin *changed to* 0809-6619 **703**
0803-5172 Norsk Motorveteran **8595**
0803-5253 Acta Paediatrica **6086**
0803-5326 Acta Paediatrica. Supplement *see* 0803-5253 **6086**
0803-544X Norway. Utenriksdepartementet. Evaluation Report *changed to* 1504-2723 **7255**
0803-5903 A m S - Tilvekst **370**
0803-5946 Eutrophia *changed to* 1503-5034 **6664**
0803-5954 Aarbok for Norsk Folkemusikk **6541**
0803-5962 Norway. Royal Norwegian Ministry of Finance. The National Budget (Year)†
0803-6160 Norsk Kunstaarbok†
0803-625X N I V A-Rapport **3489**
0803-6640 Transportforum **8518**
0803-6799 Oekonomisk Fiskeriforskning **3604**
0803-6926 Apollon **7836**
0803-6969 Norsk Patenttidende†
0803-7051 Blood Pressure **5778**
0803-706X International Forum of Psychoanalysis **7363**
0803-7108 D N V Forum **8642**
0803-7132 S M R Rapport **2626**
0803-723X 3. Verden Magasinet X *changed to* 1503-4879 **7192**
0803-7345 Eiendomsmegleren **7589**
0803-7485 Bo Bygg og Bolig **4533**
0803-8023 Blood Pressure. Supplement **5778**
0803-8201 Norge-Amerika Foreningen. Yearbook **3014**
0803-8236 Visuelt **7329**
0803-8309 Paa Sekundet **4568**
0803-8562 Kjoekkesjefen **4392**
0803-8589 Kvinner Sammen **8870**
0803-8740 Nora **8901**
0803-8821 Standpunkt **4941**
0803-883X Larus Marinus *changed to* 1503-6170 **907**
0803-902X Medmenneske *changed to* 1503-9862 **8052**
0803-9364 TradeWinds **8664**
0803-9372 Dagens Naeringsliv **3922**
0803-9410 Forum for Development Studies **1596**
0803-9488 Nordic Journal of Psychiatry **6171**
0803-9496 Nordic Journal of Psychiatry. Supplement **6171**
0803-9518 Finansavisen **1110**
0803-9763 Norges Teknisk-Naturvitenskapelige Universitet. Institutt for Bygg, Anlegg og Transport. Concept Rapport **1154**
0804-0036 Paa Flukt, Bakgrunn†
0804-0079 Norges Teknisk-Naturvitenskapelige Universitet. Vitenskapsmuseet. Seksjon for Naturhistorie. Botanisk Notat **805**
0804-0281 Audiovisuelle Medier *changed to* 1504-579X **2334**
0804-0389 Norwegian Literature†
0804-0486 Sosiologisk Tidsskrift **8139**
0804-0508 Cicerone *changed to* 1504-8136 **6359**
0804-0524 Norway. Statistisk Sentralbyraa. Ukens Statistikk†
0804-0575 Norges Handelshoeyskole. Senter for Fiskerioekonomi. Monografiserie **1154**
0804-0605 Nordic Linguistic Bulletin†
0804-0729 Oslo School of Architecture and Design. Research Magazine **452**
0804-1083 Automatisering *changed to* 1504-6184 **2458**
0804-1105 Norges Handelshoeyskole. Senter for Fiskerioekonomi. Saertrykkserie†
0804-1202 Norsk Fiskaralmanakk **3603**
0804-1253 Organet **8060**
0804-1326 Birkebeiner'n **8306**
0804-1334 Bygginfo†
0804-1415 Medarbeideren *changed to* 1504-6494 **7140**
0804-1563 Rengjoering og Vedlikehold *changed to* 1501-987X **1854**
0804-1687 N B F - Nytt *changed to* 1503-5360 **6099**
0804-1830 I F I M - Notat†
0804-1997 Ny Dag **2205**
0804-2233 Posisjon **4024**
0804-2462 Det Norske Veritas. Annual Report **8655**
0804-2489 Sveiseaktuelt **6344**
0804-2543 Flux **6920**
0804-2608 Ragtime (Oslo) **5236**
0804-2926 Norway. Statistisk Sentralbyraa. Regionalstatistikk. Rogaland **8392**
0804-3086 Listen to Norway†
0804-3116 Aftenposten **3921**
0804-3159 Folkeuniversitetet†
0804-3183 Tobakk- og Kiosk†
0804-3221 Norway. Statistisk Sentralbyraa. Statistiske Analyser **8392**
0804-3272 Det Norske Videnskaps-Akademi. Senter for Hoejere Studier. Informasjonsblad *changed to* 1503-4224 **4467**
0804-3639 Chr. Michelsen Institute. Working Paper **7954**
0804-3698 Skolefokus *changed to* 1502-9778 **2924**
0804-421X N I N A Temahefte **3454**
0804-4511 C I C E R O. Policy Note **6348**
0804-452X C I C E R O. Working Paper **6348**
0804-4562 C I C E R O. Report **6348**
0804-4635 European Journal of Endocrinology. Supplement **5892**
0804-4643 European Journal of Endocrinology **5892**
0804-4910 Straalevernrapport **7543**
0804-5070 Hamsun-Nytt **5303**
0804-5372 Nordica Bergensia **5155**
0804-5488 Sjoemat **3608**
0804-5496 Havforskningsnytt **3596**
0804-5585 *see* 0803-9763 **1154**
0804-5887 Alt om Fiske **8302**
0804-5984 Det Norske Videnskaps-Akademi. Senter for Hoejere Studier. Newsletter *changed to* 1503-4232 **4467**
0804-6069 Norut Samfunn. Rapport *changed to* 1890-5226 **8123**
0804-6093 Universitetet i Tromsoe. Senter for Samiske Studier. Skrifter **5243**
0804-6166 Paa Flukt - Tema†
0804-631X Ajour **4589**
0804-676X Norges Landbrukshoegskole. Institutt for Tekniske Fag. Meldinger†
0804-6824 Norges Handelshoeyskole. Institutt for Samfunnsoekonomi. Discussion Paper **1154**
0804-6832 Institutt for Samfunnsforskning. I S F Sammendrag **8149**
0804-7235 N U P I Rapport **7254**
0804-7294 Bladboken Vi Fornyer Oss†
0804-7375 Kritisk Juss **4710**
0804-7464 Henne **2256**
0804-7529 Credo **7753**
0804-7545 Forskning **7855**
0804-7758 Appell **8025**
0804-8096 Vi over 60 **3925**
0804-8142 Filmmagasinet **6500**
0804-8150 Barbie **2178**
0804-8177 Betongindustrien *changed to* 0332-7086 **988**
0804-8185 S T E P Rapport†
0804-8266 Statoil Magasin **6793**
0804-8452 Norsk Medietidsskrift **8123**
0804-855X Goal **8230**
0804-8568 *see* 0802-085X **3193**
0804-8592 Prosopopeia **5355**
0804-8665 Gress-Forum **8316**
0804-8754 Norwegian Refugee Council. Reports†
0804-8894 Norway. Statistisk Sentralbyraa. Arbeidsmarkedstatistikk. Hefte I: Hovedtall *changed to* 1503-4712 **1256**
0804-8916 Tidens Tale **7777**
0804-8983 Bergens Tidende **3921**
0804-8991 Stavanger Aftenblad **3925**
0804-9092 Norway. Statistisk Sentralbyraa. Arbeidsmarkedstatistikk. Hefte II: Regionale Tall†
0804-9297 Broen **7786**
0804-9432 Vagabond (Oslo) **8771**
0804-9505 Norsk Polarinstitutt. Aarsmelding **2759**
0804-9807 Tankekors **8074**
0805-0260 Agent X9 **2175**
0805-0562 Jordmorbladet†
0805-0686 Telemark Handikap Info *changed to* 0809-6457 **8059**
0805-0759 Samler og Antikkboersen **368**
0805-083X Plan **1511**
0805-1224 Petrius **4938**
0805-1232 Euroreft **4926**
0805-1615 Wendy **2221**
0805-2727 Miljoerettslige Studier **3453**
0805-357X MiRA **7212**
0805-3596 Med Bil i Europa *changed to* 1503-9250 **8739**
0805-3669 Norges Handelhoegskole. Senter for Fiskerioekonomi. Rapport **3603**
0805-3766 Dagbladet **3922**
0805-3782 Nationen **3924**
0805-3804 Adresseavisen **3921**
0805-3839 Klassekampen **3923**
0805-3855 Finnmark Dagblad **3922**
0805-3901 Hockeyavisa†
0805-3944 Class Struggle†
0805-4355 Tidsskrift for Forretningsjus **4882**
0805-4460 N F - Rapport **7986**
0805-469X N I N A. Fagrapport **2619**
0805-4932 Norsk Ornitologisk Forening. N O F Rapportserie **911**
0805-5033 Nordisk Kriminologi **2662**
0805-505X Chr. Michelsen Institute. Report **7954**
0805-5130 Universitetet i Oslo. ARENA - Senter for Europaforskning. Working Papers **8012**
0805-5203 V G **3925**
0805-5238 Ramazzini **6685**
0805-5289 Fiskeribladet **3594**
0805-5300 Folkets Framtid **7136**
0805-5327 Bergensavisen **3921**
0805-5424 Vaart Land **3925**
0805-598X Norsk Maskin Tidende *changed to* 1890-6095 **8652**
0805-6048 Landslaget for Norskundervisning. Skriftserie **5138**
0805-6129 Akuttjournalen (Print) *changed to* 1757-7241 **6072**
0805-6285 *see* 0802-085X **3193**
0805-6293 *see* 0802-085X **3193**
0805-6315 Online World Monitor Newsletter **2565**
0805-6676 Acem-Nytt *changed to* 1504-4343 **6643**
0805-7028 N I L F - Rapport **138**
0805-7095 Corpus, Psyche et Societas **6984**
0805-7214 Norges Landbrukshoegskole. Institutt for Jord- og Vannfag. Rapport *changed to* 1504-3584 **256**
0805-7257 Norges Landbrukshoegskole. Institutt for Tekniske Fag. I T F Rapport *changed to* Universitetet for Miljoe- og BioVitenskap. Institutt for Matematiske Realfag og Teknologi. I M T- Rapport **7926**
0805-7508 Nordic Journal of Political Economy **1154**
0805-7575 N O S P Adresseliste til Nordiske Bibliothek **631**
0805-7656 Sjoeoffiseren *changed to* 1890-6095 **8652**
0805-7958 Vennehefte *changed to* 1504-5544 **2980**
0805-8024 Frisoer **587**
0805-8210 *see* 0333-0273 **4453**
0805-8253 *see* 0801-1818 **8652**
0805-8725 Ut i All Verden†
0805-9101 Alta Museum. Pamphlets *see* 0805-9128 **4197**
0805-911X Altta Museuma. Smavvacallosat *see* 0805-9128 **4197**
0805-9128 Alta Museum. Smaaskrifter **4197**
0805-9136 Alta Museum. Schriftreihe *see* 0805-9128 **4197**
0805-9144 Form **535**
0805-9268 Vakttarnet (Ytre Enebakk) *see* 0043-1087 **7743**
0805-9411 Norway. Statistisk Sentralbyraa. Documents **8391**
0805-9527 *see* 1504-4114 **3453**
0805-9535 *see* 0804-8452 **8123**
0805-9691 Norsk Institutt for Landbruksoekonomisk Forskning. Notat **142**
0805-9713 Allers **3921**
0805-9721 B L F - Nytt *changed to* 1651-0534 **8027**
0805-9837 Naeringseiendom **7601**
0805-9918 Det Norske Meteorologiske Institutt. D N M I- Rapport, Klima *changed to* 1504-1549 **6391**
0806-0029 Hotell Restaurant og Reiseliv **8720**
0806-0711 Norway. Statistisk Sentralbyraa. Pasientstatistikk **4114**
0806-1041 Amnestynytt (Print Edition) *changed to* 1504-6923 **7221**
0806-1173 Kvinner i Bevegelse **8870**
0806-1319 Forum *changed to* 1504-1980 **3157**
0806-1866 Bedre Gardsdrift **95**
0806-1912 Complex **4647**
0806-198X Journal of Arabic and Islamic Studies (Online Edition) **5132**
0806-2633 *see* 0333-2306 **3924**
0806-2870 *see* 0333-3825 **5177**
0806-3044 Norway. Statistisk Sentralbyraa. Ukens Statistikk Online†
0806-3222 Acta Humaniora **4441**
0806-3648 Arbeid og Helse **6672**
0806-3702 *see* 0803-6926 **7836**
0806-3710 *see* 1504-8136 **6359**
0806-4075 T U - Transport Revyen†
0806-4105 Polyteknisk Tidsskrift *changed to* 0040-2354 **8443**
0806-4555 Norges Geologiske Undersoekelse. Kartkatalog (Year)†
0806-4792 *see* 0332-5555 **1900**
0806-5063 Riss (Trondheim) **5363**
0806-5314 Hestesport **8291**
0806-5446 Basis *changed to* 1503-6944 **7492**
0806-5462 Allergi i Praksis **5753**
0806-6205 Nordic Journal of Philosophical Logic†
0806-6221 Fiskeriforskning. Rapport *changed to* 1890-579X **3603**
0806-6256 Kvinneforskning *changed to* 0809-6341 **8903**
0806-7066 Peak **3110**
0806-7120 *see* 0803-0685 **4178**
0806-7511 Sykepleien **5982**
0806-7732 Fotografi **6968**
0806-7813 Norsk Zoologisk Forening. Rapport **959**
0806-8089 Batmagasinet Online **8272**
0806-8224 Nei til E U. Skriftserie *changed to* 1504-5374 **4944**
0806-8593 Replikk **7995**
0806-8623 Boeygen **5264**
0806-8917 Datamagasinet†
0806-895X Straaleverninfo **7542**
0806-9034 K K **8870**
0806-9115 Nytt i Strafferetten *changed to* 1502-685X **4899**
0806-9123 Nytt i Ekspropriasjonsretten *changed to* 1504-3495 **4905**
0806-9271 Sanitasjon†
0806-9425 Fantomet **2188**
0806-9689 *see* 0806-8593 **7995**
0806-9859 Norges Handikapforbund. Buskerud. Medlemsnytt *changed to* 0809-6457 **8059**
0807-0164 Mann **6294**
0807-0628 Embla **8038**
0807-0946 Norges Naturvernforbund. Rapport **2623**
0807-111X V F T-aktuelt **6336**
0807-1268 Miljoestrategi **3489**
0807-1292 D B E Informerer om Farlig Gods *changed to* 1503-4682 **2226**
0807-1551 Norsk Sjoemat **3603**
0807-1721 Politihoegskolen. P H S Forskning **2665**
0807-1918 Oslo.Online *see* 0802-3786 **7214**
0807-1950 Norden Nytt *changed to* 1890-2103 **3944**
0807-2027 *see* 0804-3116 **3921**
0807-2035 *see* 0805-5327 **3921**
0807-2043 *see* 0805-3766 **3922**
0807-2051 *see* 0805-5203 **3925**
0807-2086 *see* 0803-9372 **3922**
0807-2132 Kraft Journalen **3141**
0807-2191 Genealogen **3767**
0807-2302 Flyktning *changed to* 1504-0216 **7283**
0807-271X *see* 0800-1464 **6517**
0807-2728 *see* 0801-5236 **2493**
0807-2736 *see* 0332-5792 **6915**
0807-2779 Oesten og Vi *changed to* 0809-9782 **7623**
0807-3082 Stiftelsen for Naturforskning og Kulturminneforskning. Project Report **3468**
0807-3139 Universitetet i Oslo. ARENA - Senter for Europaforskning. Report **8012**
0807-3201 Fartoeyvern **8643**
0807-3287 Bamse **2177**
0807-3619 *see* 0803-8821 **4941**
0807-3635 Norsk Institutt for Studier av Forskning og Utdanning. Rapport *changed to* 1504-1824 **4465**
0807-4763 Norway. Statistisk Sentralbyraa. Industristatistikk. Naeringstall **1256**
0807-4801 Graasteinen **2745**
0807-5069 Buskap **282**
0807-5077 Aktiv Livsstil (Print Edition) *changed to* Aktiv Livsstil (Online Edition) **8157**
0807-5239 News from N I K K *see* 1502-1521 **8901**
0807-5557 Veiledende Liste *changed to* 1503-2337 **2178**
0807-6316 3 T **8485**
0807-6375 Budbaereren **7749**
0807-6472 Upstream (Oslo) **6796**
0807-6685 Norsk Kirkesang **6600**
0807-6839 Informasjon†
0807-6855 Ernie **2187**
0807-6944 Norsk Bokfortegnelse. Aarskatalog. I S B N - Liste†
0807-6960 Norsk Bokfortegnelse. Aarskatalog. Verker utgitt i Norge†
0807-7096 *see* 0029-2001 **5688**
0807-7258 Norsk Baatindustri†
0807-741X Porcelain Painting *see* 1890-2928 **534**
0807-7428 Porzellanmalerei *see* 1890-2928 **534**
0807-7487 *see* 0332-5415 **6141**
0807-7517 K I F O Rapport **7657**
0807-7525 K I F O Perspektiv **7657**
0807-8238 Mikke Mus *changed to* 1890-0623 **2202**

ISSN

0807-8246 Donald Duck & Co. **2186**
0807-8297 Norges Geologiske Undersoekelse. Aarsrapport†
0807-8319 Hjemme P C **2576**
0807-8416 *see* 0048-122X **8878**
0807-8521 Norges Bank. Inflasjonsrapport **1501**
0807-9048 Trepleie *changed to* 1504-6028 **3752**
0807-9234 Natur og Miljoe **3455**
0807-9323 O B O S - Bladet **4421**
0807-9439 Where to Build & Where to Repair **8665**
0807-9811 *see* 0332-5423 **1770**
0807-9862 Norsk Filminstitutt. Skriftsserie **6509**
0807-9897 Arena *changed to* 1503-6944 **7492**
0808-0127 Saerpublikasjon - Norsk Skogbruksmuseum *changed to* 1504-3606 **3701**
0808-0291 Med Evangeliet til Asiens Millioner *changed to* 1504-5560 **7746**
0808-0402 Bergen Museum. Aarbok **6521**
0808-0496 Blekka *changed to* 1504-7415 **2202**
0808-1514 Parabel **6938**
0808-1522 *see* 0804-5496 **3596**
0808-1565 N I J O S-Ressursoversikt *changed to* 1504-6966 **3700**
0808-1840 Musikkorpsavisa **6596**
0808-2154 Norway. Statistisk Sentralbyraa. Statistikk over Eiendomsdrift, Forretningsmessig Tjenesteyting og Utleiervirksomhet **7618**
0808-2200 Norway. Statistisk Sentralbyraa. Saertryk **3924**
0808-2359 Rangifer. Report **298**
0808-2790 *see* 0332-7108 **4578**
0808-288X Sosiologisk Aarbok. Ny Serie **8139**
0808-3096 Fiskeriteknologisk Forskningsinstitutt. Rapport†
0808-4688 Praktisk Baatliv *changed to* 1504-3908 **8272**
0808-5005 Musikk - Kultur **6596**
0808-5013 N O V A. Rapport **8056**
0808-5293 Norway. Statistisk Sentralbyraa. Aktuelle Befolkningstall†
0808-5366 Elle (Oslo) **8860**
0808-5498 Fotballrevyen†
0808-551X Utenrikspolitiske Skrifter†
0808-6559 Fisk **3594**
0808-6567 Aktuell Sikkerhet **2676**
0808-7180 Utsyn over Norsk Landbruk **167**
0808-7857 Universitetet i Oslo. Senter for Helseadministrasjon. Rapport *changed to* 1504-1751 **4112**
0808-9183 N O V A. Skriftserie **8056**
0808-9655 Agder Naturmuseum. Aarbok **7833**
0809-0505 Tid og Tanke **4273**
0809-0521 N K-Info *changed to* 1890-4556 **6146**
0809-0742 Norway. Statistisk Sentralbyraa. Kriminalstatistikk **2675**
0809-0807 Arabesk **6545**
0809-0890 Kunnskap om Idrett *changed to* 1503-6065 **6993**
0809-0947 Fantonald **2188**
0809-1102 *see* 0804-8592 **5355**
0809-1293 Voksne for Boern. Bulletin *changed to* 0801-1346 **7383**
0809-1412 Fakta - N I N A N I K U *changed to* 1503-5158 **2619**
0809-1471 Arbok for Norsk Samtidsmusikk *changed to* 1502-8860 **6585**
0809-1498 Nordisk Rettsmedisin *changed to* 1503-9552 **5916**
0809-1668 Nordlit **5342**
0809-1846 Fastfood *changed to* 1502-5985 **3632**
0809-1919 *see* 0377-8908 **8392**
0809-2001 Norway. Statistisk Sentralbyraa. Nasjonalregnskapsstatistikk. Produksjon, Anvendelse og Sysselsetting **7482**
0809-201X Norway. Statistisk Sentralbyraa. Nasjonalregnskapsstatistikk. Institusjonelt Sektorregnskap **1256**
0809-2028 *see* 0809-201X **1256**
0809-2044 Norsk Litteraturvitenskapelig Tidsskrift **5342**
0809-2052 Tidsskrift for Velferdsforskning **8074**
0809-2109 Motmaele **5153**
0809-2168 The Bassoe Offshore Monthly **6763**
0809-2222 Parfymeriet
0809-2230 Tekstilforum **8458**
0809-2397 Sudanic Africa. Texts and Sources **4178**
0809-280X Falken Magasinet **8580**
0809-2834 Rus og Avhengighet *changed to* 1500-8614 **2698**
0809-2907 Selgeren *changed to* 1890-1360 **1843**
0809-3016 Diabetes for Helsepersonell *changed to* 1503-9609 **5889**
0809-3083 Veteran og Sportsbil *changed to* 1890-257X **369**
0809-3180 Norway. Reindriftsforvaltningen. Ressursregnskap **268**
0809-3334 A G I Norsk Grafisk Tidsskrift **7318**
0809-3369 Nordlands-dokter'n *changed to* 1503-5654 **4593**
0809-3539 Jeger, Hund og Vapen **8320**
0809-3601 Krompen *changed to* 1890-0682 **907**
0809-389X Kraft *changed to* 1502-7848 **3162**
0809-4187 Skattenytt **1943**
0809-4519 Se og Hoer **3924**
0809-4527 Fiskeopdrett **3613**
0809-4551 Norges Landbrukshoegskole. Institutt for Landskapsplanlegging. Melding **204**
0809-4713 *see* 0801-7603 **8150**
0809-5213 Arboretet og Botanisk Hage, Milde. Aarringen **776**
0809-5302 Velferd **8146**
0809-540X Natur & Vitenskap†
0809-5469 Plastforum **7096**
0809-5779 Samenes Venn **7773**
0809-6023 Norway. Statistisk Sentralbyraa. Kvartalsvis Investeringsstatistikk **1256**
0809-6058 U B A S, Nordisk **421**
0809-6066 U B A S, International **421**
0809-6082 Slektsveven **3783**
0809-6090 Sami Instituhtta. Utredning **8131**
0809-6104 Politihoegskolen. P H S -Skriftserie **2665**
0809-6120 *see* 1503-4801 **2922**
0809-6139 Store Satsinger **4476**
0809-6163 Vann & Konflikter **8835**
0809-618X AmS-nett **4129**
0809-6198 Fjoel Bibelen **8313**
0809-6201 Jakt & Fiske, Friluftsliv **8319**
0809-621X Kvinnerettslig Skriftserie **8870**
0809-6228 *see* 1504-1174 **6397**
0809-6244 Utdanningsspeilet (Year) **3035**
0809-6252 Utdanningssektoren. Tilstandsrapport (Year) *changed to* 0809-6244 **3035**
0809-6260 Oslo School of Architecture and Design. A H O **452**
0809-6287 Skvaerriggerne **8662**
0809-6333 *see* 0332-8295 **5753**
0809-6341 Tidsskrift for Kjoennsforskning **8903**
0809-635X Apotek og Legemidler **6821**
0809-6376 Digitale Impulser **2416**
0809-6414 Klepp Historielag. Aarsskrift **4237**
0809-6430 Utlendingsnemmda. Aarbok **4853**
0809-6457 Norges Handikapforbund. Oslofjord Vest. Regionsnytt **8059**
0809-6465 Boligetc.no **982**
0809-649X *see* 1501-973X **4066**
0809-6503 Byens Naeringsliv **1958**
0809-6511 Byavisa **3921**
0809-652X *see* 1503-0741 **1372**
0809-6562 Bolig i Utlandet **8688**
0809-6600 Rett til Kildene **1942**
0809-6619 Scandinavian-Baltic Society for Parasitology. Bulletin **703**
0809-666X Norway. Directorate of Immigration. Facts and Figures **7288**
0809-6678 Kamille **8870**
0809-6724 Digital Kompetanse **3058**
0809-6732 C M I Brief **7224**
0809-6740 *see* 0809-6732 **7224**
0809-6775 Universitetet i Stavanger. Doktor Ingenioer-Avhandling *changed to* 1890-1387 **3225**
0809-6813 Diakonissehjemmets Hoegskole. Arbeidsnotat **5957**
0809-6929 N I B R-Notat (Online) **4420**
0809-7062 *see* 1502-4946 **5959**
0809-7070 *see* 0809-6813 **5957**
0809-7097 *see* 0804-9297 **7786**
0809-7143 *see* 0809-6724 **3058**
0809-7275 Geronius (Online Edition) **4046**
0809-7291 Nordic Journal of Religion and Society **7666**
0809-7399 *see* 1501-6803 **269**
0809-7445 N U P I Notat (Online) **7254**
0809-7488 Universitetet i Oslo. Institutt for Kriminologi og Rettssosiologi. Bokserien **2670**
0809-750X *see* 0803-0103 **7470**
0809-7682 Hoegskolen i Agder. Doktoravhandlingar *changed to* 1504-9272 **8012**
0809-800X Arena† **8931**
0809-8026 Eureka Forskningsserie **2855**
0809-8034 Eureka Laeremiddelserie **2855**
0809-8042 Matindustrien **3655**
0809-8131 Nordic Journal of Music Therapy **6113**
0809-8158 Statens Pensjonsfond - Utland *changed to* 1890-3517 **1502**
0809-8166 Government Pension Fund - Global *changed to* 1890-3541 **1372**
0809-8212 Kuiper **5318**
0809-8271 Star School **2214**
0809-8298 Rehabilitering **4110**
0809-8352 Psykisk **7401**
0809-8409 Norsk Luftfartshistorisk Magasin **8549**
0809-8530 *see* 0809-8654 **96**
0809-8565 Visjon **315**
0809-8603 Norsk Skogmuseum. Skrifter **3698**
0809-8638 Vaapenbrevet **3786**
0809-8646 Moeteplass Middelalder **4246**
0809-8654 Bioforsk Tema **96**
0809-8662 Bioforsk Fokus **96**
0809-8670 Drift og Vedlikehold *changed to* 1504-6931 **1746**
0809-8697 Norsk Araberhest **8295**
0809-8700 G S 1 Fokus **6402**
0809-8719 *see* 0809-8700 **6402**
0809-8735 Interdisciplinary Communications **4457**
0809-8743 *see* 0809-8735 **4457**
0809-8751 E U R O H A R P Report **8823**
0809-876X *see* 0809-8751 **8823**
0809-8778 E U R O H A R P Newsletter **8823**
0809-8786 Universitetet i Oslo. Oekonomisk Institut. Memorandum **1187**
0809-8832 *see* 0809-8786 **1187**
0809-8867 *see* 0332-7582 **4404**
0809-8891 *see* 1503-4364 **8528**
0809-8921 Naturviteren **4599**
0809-8948 *see* 1504-4092 **6785**
0809-8956 *see* 1503-8386 **7191**
0809-8999 Misjonshoegskolen. Dissertation Series **7663**
0809-9006 Allskog **3683**
0809-9014 Intervet Agenda Magasin **3599**
0809-9022 Pokemon **2208**
0809-9030 Dagens I T **2318**
0809-909X G E C H S News **3432**
0809-9111 Aviso **3405**
0809-912X Arran Julevsame Guovdasj. Tjalarajddo **4201**
0809-9146 Fairies *changed to* 1891-0955 **2185**
0809-9197 Veterinaerinstituttet. Rapportserie **8810**
0809-9227 Nordand **5155**
0809-9316 *see* 0805-3804 **3921**
0809-9324 *see* 0801-3020 **4611**
0809-9375 God Bedring *changed to* 0809-8298 **4110**
0809-9456 *see* 0908-3731 **1663**
0809-9499 *see* 1503-9676 **8426**
0809-9510 *see* 0805-4355 **4882**
0809-9529 *see* 1504-3495 **4905**
0809-9537 *see* 1502-685X **4899**
0809-9545 *see* 1503-6782 **4881**
0809-9553 *see* 1503-2965 **4914**
0809-974X Appell, Medlem *see* 0804-7758 **8025**
0809-9774 Droemmefanger'n **4215**
0809-9782 Areopagos **7623**
0810-0055 Australia - New Zealand Foundation. Annual Report (Year)†
0810-0187 Street Machine **8511**
0810-0500 Par Oneri **6441**
0810-0640 Australia. Bureau of Statistics. Victorian Office. Principal Agricultural Commodities, Victoria, Preliminary†
0810-0713 Australian Journal of Clinical Hypnotherapy and Hypnosis **5942**
0810-0918 Australia. Bureau of Statistics. South Australian Office. Local Government Finance, South Australia†
0810-1906 Australian-Canadian Studies *changed to* 1832-5408 **329**
0810-2317 Education Guidelines†
0810-2333 Marc N U C O M†
0810-249X T V Week **2395**
0810-2686 Australian Journalism Review **4572**
0810-2740 Matilda Magazine: Literary and Art Magazine† **8973**
0810-3240 Bureau of Sugar Experiment Stations. Bulletin **223**
0810-4123 Australasian Drama Studies **8466**
0810-4468 Australian Short Stories†
0810-459X Australia. Bureau of Statistics. Agricultural Industries, Financial Statistics, Australia†
0810-5073 Australian Timberman
0810-5200 Sinatra International **6616**
0810-5391 Accounting and Finance **1277**
0810-5480 Australian Income Tax Legislation
0810-5596 Australian Master Tax Guide
0810-5677 Australia. Department of the Treasury. Budget **1438**
0810-6029 Design World†
0810-6142 Mathematics Students' Gazette†
0810-6150 MathMag†
0810-6355 Australia. Bureau of Statistics. South Australian Office. Crops and Pastures, South Australia†
0810-6398 Hyper Activities **3041**
0810-6681 West Australian Nut and Tree Crop Association. Yearbook **259**
0810-6983 Great Barrier Reef Marine Park Authority. Special Publication Series† **8960**
0810-7025 Contact (Scoresby) **7793**
0810-722X Australian Commonwealth Collectors Club of New South Wales. Bulletin
0810-7440 Australian Dental Association. News Bulletin **5835**
0810-7742 Australia. Bureau of Statistics. Queensland Office. Value of Agricultural Commodities Produced, Queensland†
0810-7947 Common Sense† **8942**
0810-8064 Rawlinsons Australian Construction Handbook (Year) **1031**
0810-820X On the Beach
0810-8226 Who's Who in Australia **646**
0810-8285 Road Patrol *changed to* Horizons (Perth) **8584**
0810-8315 Australian Centre for International Agricultural Research. Annual Report **93**
0810-8633 Australia. Bureau of Statistics. Year Book Australia **8356**
0810-8889 Association of Australasian Palaeontologists. Memoirs **6723**
0810-9028 Prometheus (Abingdon) **2336**
0810-9303 Australia. Bureau of Statistics. New South Wales Office. Tertiary Education, New South Wales†
0810-9435 Knox Historian **4150**
0810-9729 Journal of Professional Legal Education† **8968**
0810-9796 Zadok Perspectives **7696**
0810-9958 Australian Motoring Year†
0811-0026 Papers in Pidgin and Creole Linguistics **5159**
0811-0069 Materials in Languages of Indonesia†
0811-0174 Bibliography of Education Theses in Australia (Print)†
0811-0433 Quarternary Australasia **4025**
0811-0859 Photofile **6974**
0811-112X Australasian College Libraries (South Australia)†
0811-1146 Urban Policy and Research **4430**
0811-1197 Maffra & District Historical Society. Bulletin† **8972**
0811-1235 Film and Video Acquisitions†
0811-1863 Australia. Department of Employment and Industrial Relations. Employee Participation News†
0811-191X Storylines†
0811-2169 Outrage†
0811-2304 Trinity Occasional Papers†
0811-2762 What's New in Computing†
0811-3165 Australian Education Directory *changed to* 1834-3775 **2828**
0811-3394 Queensland Family Historian **3780**
0811-3475 Australian Macadamia Society. News Bulletin **220**
0811-3653 Beagle **6521**
0811-3661 The Australian Family **2144**
0811-3688 Australian Transport Information Directory†
0811-3696 Australasian Arachnology
0811-3742 Talking Electronics **3114**
0811-3963 Brandywine Bibliography **7329**
0811-3971 Brandywine Documents on the History of Books & Printing **7318**
0811-4293 M L A A N Z Journal† **8972**
0811-4684 Tactual Mapping Newsletter†
0811-4692 A C F O A News†
0811-5141 Australia. Bureau of Statistics. Queensland Office. Selected Agricultural Commodities, Queensland, Preliminary†
0811-5397 Australian Water Resources Council. Water Resources Series **8818**
0811-5680 Small Business Review†
0811-5796 Law in Context **4715**
0811-580X University of Tasmania. Centre for Environmental Studies. Environmental Studies Project Report **2630**
0811-594X Quorum†
0811-5982 New England Monographs in Continuing Education (No.)†
0811-6199 Australia. National Health and Medical Research Council. Department of Health. Medical Research†
0811-6202 Australian Journal of Communication **2313**
0811-6296 1:100 000 Geological Map Series. Explanatory Notes **2776**
0811-6318 Canberra Bulletin of Public Administration *changed to* 1832-0066 **7461**
0811-6407 Defender **2226**
0811-6504 South Australian Geographical Papers **4029**
0811-6652 Persons in Juvenile Corrections Institutions†
0811-6997 A V A News
0811-7098 Armidale College of Advanced Education. Annual Report†
0811-7179 Dolly **2186**

ISSN

9350 0815-8479 ULRICH'S PERIODICALS

0815-8479 Australia. Bureau of Statistics. Value of Selected Agricultural Commodities Produced, Australia, Preliminary†
0815-8495 Kalgoorlie College. Annual Report†
0815-9076 Australia Investment Quarterly†
0815-9319 Journal of Gastroenterology and Hepatology **5928**
0815-936X Queensland Nurse **5979**
0815-9424 Development Dossier†
0815-953X Meanjin **5227**
0815-9572 Sunday Territorian **3796**
0815-9769 Dairy Goat Society of Australia. Victorian Branch Newsletter **284**
0815-9777 British Alpine Breeders Group of Australia. Newsletter **262**
0815-998X Journal of Numismatic Association of Australia **6651**
0816-0031 Salt **7679**
0816-0201 The Walker†
0816-0260 What's on in Victoria
0816-0368 Hummer **4146**
0816-0430 National Liquor News **608**
0816-0465 Australia. Bureau of Statistics. Queensland Office. Deaths, Queensland†
0816-0627 Australia. Bureau of Statistics. Digest of Current Economic Statistics†
0816-0805 Australian Wine Research Institute. Technical Review **598**
0816-1070 Renewable Energy Index†
0816-1089 Australian Journal of Experimental Agriculture *changed to* 1836-0939 **218**
0816-1623 Agricultural and Veterinary Product Index
0816-1631 Enterprise (Brisbane)
0816-1658 Australian Geographic **4000**
0816-1860 Australian Society for the History of Medicine. Occasional Papers
0816-200X Informaa Quarterly **1851**
0816-2107 Workers Compensation Report **1715**
0816-2220 Abilities **4071**
0816-2239 Lantern Light†
0816-2271 Western Australian Resource Development Services. Directory **2034**
0816-2484 Management Report on the Australian Economy
0816-2735 Sir Robert Madgwick Lecture Series (No.)
0816-2905 Truck & Bus Road Tests†
0816-3030 Australian Administrative Law **7421**
0816-3057 AdArt†
0816-3065 Prints†
0816-3316 Australia. Bureau of Statistics. Queensland Office. The Labour Force: Regional Estimates†
0816-3456 Economic Advice to Business†
0816-3480 Archive of Australian Judaica. Monograph **7718**
0816-3596 Australasian Paint & Panel **6716**
0816-360X Crafts Competitions and Prizes†
0816-3642 Lucky†
0816-3650 Ad News Handbook **19**
0816-3677 Australian Photography Camera Test Reports†
0816-3685 Professional and Industrial Photographic Equipment†
0816-4347 Ashes to Dust†
0816-4436 National Emergency Response **2227**
0816-4509 Australian Trotting Register†
0816-4525 New South Wales Law Reform Commission. Annual Report **4744**
0816-455X Gold Gazette **6463**
0816-4622 Clinical and Experimental Optometry **6040**
0816-4649 Australian Feminist Studies **8894**
0816-4746 Audit Guide†
0816-5041 University of New England. Faculty of Economic Studies. Occasional Papers in Economic Development (No.)†
0816-5122 Australian Educational and Developmental Psychologist **7338**
0816-5157 Third Degree
0816-5173 Rural Development Working Papers†
0816-5181 Working Papers in Trade and Development **1587**
0816-5416 T N C Workers Research Brief†
0816-5432 Spunti e Ricerche **3566**
0816-5521 Company Director **1734**
0816-6013 Commonwealth Scientific and Industrial Research Organization. Division of Geomechanics. Geomechanics Computer Programs
0816-603X Pioneer Books Magazine†
0816-6048 Australia. Bureau of Statistics. Personal Finance, Australia†
0816-6196 Drovers Journal†
0816-651X Australian Cricket Journal
0816-6668 Organic Growing (Ulverstone)† **8979**
0816-6773 Education Department of Victoria. Textbooks†
0816-6838 Econometrics Discussion Papers† **8952**
0816-6897 Financial Monitor **1623**
0816-7141 Australian Jewish Historical Society. Newsletter **7718**
0816-7656 D O G S Newsletter
0816-7885 Fishing News†
0816-7923 A C I A R Technical Reports Series **77**
0816-8091 Indonesian Studies Newsletter†
0816-8474 Commonwealth Scientific and Industrial Research Organization. Division of Tropical Crops and Pastures. Annual Report†
0816-9020 Australian Educational Computing **2948**
0816-9330 AudioVision & Prosound†
0816-9349 Prime Number **5525**
0816-939X Studio Bambini **2261**
0816-956X Online Currents **2531**
0816-9713 Western Australia Wildlife Management Program **967**
0816-9799 Victorian Statutes Annotations **4826**
0816-990X Renal Educator†
0817-0088 Magpies **2160**
0817-024X New South Wales & Australian Capital Territory Retail Directory **2020**
0817-0444 Australian National University. National Centre for Development Studies. Pacific Policy Papers†
0817-0886 Victorian Update†
0817-1351 Access (Toorak) **5565**
0817-1416 Cars in Australia†
0817-1831 Peace Research Centre Working Papers†
0817-1904 Communications World
0817-1939 The Weekly Times **169**
0817-2285 The Sydney Organ Journal **6622**
0817-2455 Your Pharmacy†
0817-2773 Sailboard Extra
0817-2811 Ski Extra
0817-2935 Travel Australia†
0817-3052 Drugs: Australia†
0817-3176 Australian Sugar Year Book **3627**
0817-3192 Australia's Top 500 Companies† **8934**
0817-3524 Social Security Reporter† **8988**
0817-3532 Freedom of Information Review† **8958**
0817-3834 Australian Private Doctor **5581**
0817-394X Australia. Bureau of Statistics. Tertiary Education, Australia†
0817-4075 Tasmanian Numismatist **6653**
0817-4148 Gippsland Writer
0817-4296 Homes & Living **1012**
0817-4334 Peopling of the British Peripheries in the Eighteenth Century. Series: Esso Lecture: No.2
0817-4466 Journey **7763**
0817-458X L i N Q **5319**
0817-4628 Xpress
0817-4792 Excel†
0817-4830 A C C - Westpac Economic Discussion Papers†
0817-489X Queensland Geographical Journal†
0817-5586 Youth Issues Forum
0817-5802 The Western Flyer **5413**
0817-5829 Interest Rates Service
0817-5837 Comcise
0817-587X Directory of Women in Business, Professions & Management†
0817-6043 Power Equipment Australasia **213**
0817-6094 Great Barrier Reef Marine Park Authority Technical Memorandum **675**
0817-6124 This Week in Melbourne **8760**
0817-6132 This Week in Tasmania **8761**
0817-6140 This Week in Canberra **8760**
0817-6159 This Week in Brisbane **8760**
0817-6167 This Week in Adelaide†
0817-6175 This Week in Sydney **8760**
0817-623X Australian Journal of Family Law **4907**
0817-6337 Australian Plumbing Industry **4116**
0817-6345 Australian Institute of Family Studies. Working Paper†
0817-6353 Who's Pegging†
0817-6469 Encore Directory **6497**
0817-6493 Royal Australian Historical Society. Technical Information Service†
0817-6531 Australian Family Lawyer **4907**
0817-654X Australian Gold, Gem and Treasure Magazine **6457**
0817-6795 Custom Rodder†
0817-7724 Australian Oyster†
0817-7988 What's on Video and Cinema†
0817-8038 Pacific Economic Bulletin **1510**
0817-8143 Australia. Bureau of Statistics. Queensland Office. Manufacturing Establishments: Summary of Operations†
0817-8240 Australian Caver *changed to* 1449-2601 **2728**
0817-8445 Look Magazine **6528**
0817-8526 Australia. Bureau of Statistics. Queensland Office. Summary of Social Statistics, Queensland†
0817-8542 Trends and Issues in Crime and Criminal Justice **2670**
0817-8550 Australian Stock Horse Journal **8287**
0817-8585 Club Marine **5068**
0817-8771 University of Sydney. Department of Agricultural Economics. Research Report.† **8996**
0817-895X Peace Magazine Australia†
0817-9344 Australia. Bureau of Statistics. Information Paper: National Nutrition Survey, Confidentialised Unit Record File (Print) *changed to* Australia. Bureau of Statistics. Information Paper: National Nutrition Survey, Confidentialised Unit Record File (Online) **6671**
0817-9514 Australian Review of Applied Linguistics. Series 5 *see* 0155-0640 **5097**
0817-9638 Gippsland Heritage Journal **4192**
0817-9751 United Nations Review†
0818-0261 Australian Woodworker **1049**
0818-0423 Restaurant Hotel Club & Caterer
0818-0571 Australian Institute of Building Papers†
0818-0628 Time Australia *changed to* Time South Pacific **3796**
0818-0660 Land Link†
0818-0954 Hrvatska Sloboda
0818-1233 R A I A Memo†
0818-1578 TopKids†
0818-1713 Rural Update
0818-2019 A.C.T. Science Teacher†
0818-2132 Australia. Bureau of Statistics. Queensland Office. Schools, Queensland, Preliminary†
0818-2493 Good Government **1542**
0818-2515 Records of North Queensland History **4194**
0818-304X Notes on Pure Mathematics†
0818-3422 Australia. Bureau of Statistics. Price Indexes of Copper Materials, Australia†
0818-3511 Dwelling Unit Commencements, Australia, Preliminary (Online) **1045**
0818-3589 Australian Hot Talk **6286**
0818-3856 Australia. Bureau of Statistics. Register of Commonwealth Statistical Collections† **8933**
0818-4127 National Trotguide
0818-4658 Western Australia. Department of Conservation and Land Management. Annual Report *changed to* 1835-1131 **2631**
0818-4984 World Goodwill Newsletter **8079**
0818-4992 Fleet
0818-5077 Golf Australia **8230**
0818-5166 Occasional Papers in Commerce†
0818-5204 Transit Australia **8627**
0818-5352 Australian Institute of Family Studies. Policy Background Paper (No.)†
0818-5549 Motor News **8592**
0818-5646 Australasian Sound Archive
0818-5670 Environmental Health Review, Australia†
0818-6022 Australian Ballet News **2682**
0818-6065 O G: Oriental Guys **4377**
0818-6286 Interaction (Canberra)
0818-6308 Textile Fibre Forum **8459**
0818-6510 Australian Orienteer **8304**
0818-6561 Pastrycooks & Bakers News Monthly†
0818-7169 South Australian Dairyfarmer's Journal
0818-772X Australia. Bureau of Statistics. Finance Companies, Australia†
0818-7762 Senior Topics†
0818-7894 Australian Meat Livestock Research and Development Corporation. Annual Report†
0818-8068 Australian Universities' Review **2968**
0818-8122 Auditing Discussion Paper
0818-8149 Australian Slavonic and East European Studies **4444**
0818-8173 Melbourne Bride **5560**
0818-8238 Curtin University of Technology. Mulga Research Centre Journal
0818-8343 Car Australia†
0818-8491 Electric Vehicle News
0818-8734 Eyeline **489**
0818-9005 The Priest **7813**
0818-9021 Australian Communications
0818-9110 Australian Geomechanics Journal **6457**
0818-917X Yearbook of South Australian Crafts (Year)†
0818-9412 Accounting Theory Monograph **1279**
0818-9595 Blitz **8162**
0818-9641 Immunology and Cell Biology **5760**
0818-979X Australia. Bureau of Statistics. Queensland Office. Manufacturing Establishments: Small Area Statistics, Queensland†
0818-9846 Entertainment Worker
0818-9935 Asian - Pacific Economic Literature **1200**
0818-9951 Australia. Bureau of Statistics. Queensland Office. Selected Accommodation Establishments, Queensland†
0819-0194 Stereo Buyer's Guide. Loudspeakers, Amplifiers and Tuners **8155**
0819-0208 Stereo Buyer's Guide. C D Players, Turntables and Cassettes Decks† **8990**
0819-0216 Stereo Buyer's Guide. Audio Yearbook **8155**
0819-0615 Australian Jewish Historical Society. Journal **3521**
0819-0739 Blast **5264**
0819-0852 Australian Folklore **3615**
0819-0879 Lab Lines **3069**
0819-0887 Australian Prosthodontic Journal†
0819-1158 Australia. Bureau of Statistics. Australian Capital Territory Courts† **8932**
0819-1247 Kingia†
0819-1530 Creation **7635**
0819-1565 Press Press Magazine
0819-1794 Australian Official Journal of Patents (Print) *changed to* 1832-9950 **6745**
0819-1808 Australian Official Journal of Trade Marks (Print) *changed to* 1832-9969 **6745**
0819-1824 N S W Master Plumber **4123**
0819-2251 National Star Observer†
0819-2316 Australian Film, Television and Radio School. Annual Report **2356**
0819-2421 Australian and New Zealand Wine Industry Journal **598**
0819-243X All about Town†
0819-2588 Australian Institute of Family Studies. Annual Report **7277**
0819-2626 Australian Chemistry Resource Book†
0819-2642 *see* 1832-2417 **1188**
0819-2898 A F M Information Systems Series (No.)
0819-2928 Australia. Bureau of Statistics. Queensland Office. Economic Indicators, Queensland†
0819-2936 S.A. Crafts† **8986**
0819-2952 Legal Aid Commission of New South Wales. Annual Report **4968**
0819-2995 Australian Rural Science Annual **93**
0819-3053 Australian Study Opportunities
0819-3363 Australasian Cycling & Triathlon News†
0819-3592 Monthly Rainfall Review: Australia†
0819-3606 Phoenix Review† **8981**
0819-405X Australia. Bureau of Statistics. Western Australian Office. Building Approvals - Private Sector, Perth Statistical Division†
0819-4130 Qld. & N.T. Judgements Bulletin†
0819-4262 Commercial Law Quarterly **4861**
0819-4289 Australian Non-Government Railways Operating Statistics (Years)†
0819-4327 Western Australia. Fisheries Department. Fisheries Management Paper **3611**
0819-4424 A F C News *changed to* Screen Australia News **6512**
0819-4564 Australian Senior Mathematics Journal **3052**
0819-4599 Victorian Farmer **168**
0819-4610 World Council of Enterostomal Therapists Journal **5932**
0819-470X Local Government Focus (Green Edition) **7496**
0819-4734 Australian Model Engineering Magazine **4328**
0819-4823 Recent Advances in Animal Nutrition in Australia (Year)
0819-484X HERA Update **4170**
0819-4882 Tasmanian Transport Statistics†
0819-5129 Sydney Star Observer **4379**
0819-5358 Fiction Focus **5296**
0819-5447 What's New in Process Engineering *changed to* 1832-2271 **3226**
0819-5471 Victoria Government Gazette. General **7475**
0819-548X Victoria Government Gazette. Special **7475**
0819-5498 Victoria Government Gazette. Periodical **7475**
0819-5633 Record **7772**
0819-5781 Health Issues **5625**
0819-5943 Australian Technology Review†
0819-6028 New South Wales. Department of Housing. Annual Report **4420**
0819-6303 Real 2 Reel **2389**
0819-6508 Australian Mineralogist
0819-6648 Adbrief Register: Agencies & Marketers **19**
0819-677X Contemporary Art Centre of South Australia. Broadsheet **483**
0819-6826 Tasmanian Naturalist **707**
0819-6990 Scanfile **1792**

Link to your serials resources and content with ulrichsweb.com

0828-3176 Canada. Statistics Canada. Unemployment Insurance Statistics. Annual Supplement **4529**
0828-3192 Archivy†
0828-3664 Arms Control Verification Studies **7221**
0828-3737 Specialty Crop Report **254**
0828-3877 Ontario Economic Accounts **7458**
0828-3893 Canadian Journal of Counselling **7343**
0828-3907 Saskatchewan Indian Federated College Journal†
0828-4083 Grail: An Ecumenical Journal†
0828-4105 Twenty-Four†
0828-4253 Up Here **4983**
0828-4466 Hilborn's Family Newsletter Directory†
0828-4539 Table Tennis Technical†
0828-4547 Report on the Administration of the Labour Adjustment Benefits Act **1705**
0828-4679 Horse Industry Directory of Canada†
0828-4849 Viking Tourist Guide†
0828-4989 Monde Juridique†
0828-5225 Agora **2271**
0828-525X Info Outlook (Year)
0828-542X O O H N A Journal **5976**
0828-5594 Energy Equipment News†
0828-5608 X Y Z **5402**
0828-5624 WatCom News **2599**
0828-5721 Invest Canada
0828-5748 Catholic Health Association of Canada. Directory†
0828-5802 Rites
0828-6116 Aftermarket Canada **8555**
0828-6396 Perspectives in Cardiology **5797**
0828-6647 National Hockey League. Official Guide & Record Book **8219**
0828-6868 I S E R Research and Policy Papers **8106**
0828-6914 C P J - Canadian Pharmaceutical Journal *changed to* 1715-1635 **6827**
0828-6949 A T A C C Newsletter
0828-699X Tri-Fit†
0828-7023 Vista (Regina) **6539**
0828-7198 Indicator†
0828-7252 Canadian Human Rights Advocate†
0828-7341 Angler and Hunter†
0828-7600 Charolais Connection **283**
0828-7619 Canadian Garden News†
0828-7899 Big Fish Country Fishing Guide†
0828-797X Interculture **8108**
0828-7996 Guelph Dairy Research Report†
0828-802X Coming Attractions **5276**
0828-8178 Monthly Stock Charts - Canadian Companies **1640**
0828-8208 Canada. Statistics Canada. Air Charter Statistics **8523**
0828-8259 Canadian Horticultural History†
0828-833X Eagle Valley News **3809**
0828-8496 Next Exit†
0828-864X Equinews **8291**
0828-8666 Humanomics **1543**
0828-8755 Calgary STAMPede†
0828-8984 Human Resource†
0828-9239 Project Magazine
0828-9522 Resource: The Canadian Journal of Real Estate†
0828-9557 Halfyard Heritage **3769**
0828-9581 Sport Plus **8205**
0828-9638 Graphic Monthly Estimators' & Buyers Guide (Ontario Edition) **7322**
0828-9824 Canada. Statistics Canada. Communications and Other Electronic Industries†
0828-9999 Revue Quebecoise de Droit International **4940**
0829-0032 Humus
0829-0067 Rumors†
0829-0369 Travail et Sante **6688**
0829-044X Conrad Grebel Review **2279**
0829-0474 Official Directory of Canadian Museums and Related Institutions **6535**
0829-0504 British Columbia Mountaineering Club Newsletter **8307**
0829-0547 Western Canadian Anthropologist†
0829-075X Canadian Co-operative Wool Growers Magazine **282**
0829-0814 Canada Journal **3807**
0829-0857 Periodical Writers Association of Canada. Directory of Members **4581**
0829-0873 Canadian Standards Association. Catalogue **6401**
0829-0954 Liberation **7764**
0829-1098 Unemployment Insurance Statistics **1712**
0829-1349 Canadian Business Life **1079**
0829-1373 Hamilton This Month **3810**
0829-1411 Le Producteur Laitier†
0829-1667 L'Acadie Nouvelle **3812**
0829-1675 Elan
0829-1713 Voice of the Oxford Farmer†
0829-1756 Canada. Statistics Canada. Passenger Bus and Urban Transit Statistics. Monthly Edition†
0829-1764 Quarterly Hospital Information System. Hospital Indicators†
0829-1772 Canada. Agriculture Canada. Prairie Farm Rehabilitation Administration. Annual Report†
0829-1802 Bulletin de Droit Immobilier **4633**
0829-1888 Canadian Media Directors' Council. Media Digest **8092**
0829-2019 National Creditor-Debtor Review **1370**
0829-2132 Canadian Aviation News
0829-2175 Credit Union Way **1333**
0829-2507 Scientia Canadensis **7912**
0829-2531 Office Product News†
0829-254X C A A T Tracks†
0829-2809 Pharmacy Practice **6873**
0829-2922 Religious Studies and Theology **7676**
0829-2930 Corinthian Horse Sport **8289**
0829-3023 Canadian Trackside Guide **8615**
0829-3139 Weekly Stock Charts - Canadian Resource Companies **1659**
0829-318X Tree Physiology **820**
0829-3201 Canadian Journal of Law and Society **4639**
0829-321X International Insights **7243**
0829-3279 Sea Kayaker **8282**
0829-3295 Decorating Centre
0829-3309 Campus Canada **2276**
0829-3384 Xtra! **4380**
0829-352X Wastewater Technology Centre Newsletter†
0829-3627 CanPlay **8467**
0829-3678 Sound & Vision†
0829-3767 Canadian Wrestler Newsletter **8164**
0829-3929 Journal of Law and Social Policy **4968**
0829-4003 Canadian Treasury Management Review **1324**
0829-4011 Revue Canadienne de Gestion de Tresorerie **1380**
0829-4135 Alberta Native News **3517**
0829-4216 Unity **3570**
0829-4321 Alberta Association of College Librarians. Newsletter **4988**
0829-4380 Canada Reports†
0829-4399 Reportage Canada†
0829-4666 Gospel Herald **7645**
0829-4674 Construction Comment **995**
0829-4747 Face to Face With Talent **2381**
0829-4801 Agenda **464**
0829-481X B C Business **1064**
0829-4836 Canadian Journal of Marketing Research **1809**
0829-4844 Camping in Ontario **8308**
0829-4887 Canadian Programmable Control Conference and Exhibition. Conference Proceedings†
0829-4909 University of Toronto. Institute for Policy Analysis. Working Paper Series **1190**
0829-4976 From My Bookshelf†
0829-5026 Canadian West†
0829-5085 Willowdale Month†
0829-5239 Brunswick Business Journal
0829-5247 A Fleur de Pot†
0829-5344 Canadian Folk Music Bulletin (Print Edition) *changed to* Canadian Folk Music Bulletin (Online Edition) **6553**
0829-5425 University Computing and Information Services Newsletter **2440**
0829-5476 Juriste **4707**
0829-5557 Bulletin d'Information Toxicologique† **8938**
0829-5700 Hiring & Firing†
0829-5735 Canadian Journal of School Psychology **2834**
0829-576X Worker Co-ops
0829-609X Contributions to Natural Science†
0829-6359 Publiquip **1030**
0829-7010 Tyro Magazine†
0829-7142 Council of Nova Scotia Archives Newsletter **5004**
0829-7177 University Finance Trend Analysis†
0829-7460 Standing Senate Committee on Banking, Trade and Commerce. Proceedings **1384**
0829-7681 E L S Monograph Series **5287**
0829-772X Civic Public Works **7430**
0829-7983 Cap-aux-Diamants **4287**
0829-8157 Trade Asia Magazine
0829-8203 Ontario Geological Survey. Summary of Field Work **6475**
0829-8211 Biochemistry and Cell Biology **725**
0829-8297 Gerontion†
0829-8319 British Columbia Collective Bargaining Review and Outlook **4591**
0829-8351 Nickel
0829-8416 Canadian Outlook, Economic Forecast **1445**
0829-8564 The Compleat Mother **5988**
0829-8726 Bead Forum **383**
0829-8815 Entourage **3039**
0829-8947 Trucking in Canada **8678**
0829-9137 Alberta Teachers' Association. Multicultural Education Council Newsletter†
0829-9153 Edmonton Metropolitan Regional Planning Commission. Metro Planning Review
0829-917X Teachers' Money Matters **3034**
0829-948X University of Waterloo Bibliography Series **5060**
0829-9528 Canada. Law Reform Commission. Protection of Life Series. Study Papers†
0829-9676 Habitat 2000
0829-982X Azure Magazine **4532**
0829-9838 Ontario Insurance Directory **4517**
0829-9889 Housewares Canada **4559**
0830-0011 Aviso **3017**
0830-0089 National Library of Canada. Annual Report†
0830-0151 The Lawyers Weekly **4718**
0830-0305 Family Health **6985**
0830-0348 World Review of Doulton†
0830-0380 Jurisprudence Logement **4706**
0830-0445 Journal of Distance Education **2943**
0830-0453 Pacific Forestry Centre. Information Report **3699**
0830-0593 Canadian Thoroughbred **8288**
0830-0739 Okanagan History **4307**
0830-0763 Non-Wage Provisions in Saskatchewan Collective Agreements†
0830-1085 New Brunswick Government Publications Quarterly List†
0830-1417 Network **3720**
0830-1611 N W T Labour Force Survey (Year) **1698**
0830-1654 Pro-Farm **249**
0830-1743 Veterinarius **8811**
0830-176X Canada's Original Bridal Buyers' Guide†
0830-1808 Atlantic Trucking **8668**
0830-1921 Sports Business†
0830-3630 Guelph Alumnus **2286**
0830-4009 Cree-Naskapi Commission. Report
0830-5250 Business Connexions†
0830-5315 Vox Me D A L **2308**
0830-839X Canadian Specialty Foods Retailer†
0830-8535 Greater Winnipeg Business Magazine
0830-856X Elements (Dresden) **3060**
0830-8705 Port Hole **8280**
0830-8713 Victoria's Business Report **1969**
0830-8721 Guitar Canada
0830-8772 Eye Opener **4575**
0830-8810 Industrial Maintenance Repair and Overhaul News
0830-8845 C M B E S - S C G B Newsletter **5590**
0830-8888 Arabusiness International **1060**
0830-890X Universite de Montreal. Groupe de Recherche Interdisciplinaire en Sante. Rapport **7544**
0830-9000 Canadian Journal of Veterinary Research **8795**
0830-9086 Socialist Studies Bulletin **8005**
0830-9272 Scott's Directories - Ontario Manufacturers **2027**
0830-9396 Northern Miner Magazine†
0830-9434 Epson Today†
0830-9442 Ontario Advisory Council on Women's Issues. Annual Report **8879**
0830-9493 Canadian Autoparts Marketing†
0830-9507 Aviation Trade's Corporate & Commercial Aviation *see* 1180-9663
0830-9574 La Riverego **5169**
0831-0114 Quebec ce Mois-ci
0831-0122 Journal Industriel du Quebec **3369**
0831-019X Alberta Oil & Gas Directory **1971**
0831-0203 Canadian Band Journal†
0831-0254 Network (Toronto)†
0831-0319 Revue Stop
0831-0386 Canadian Donor's Guide to Fund Raising Organizations in Canada *see* 0849-0104 **8043**
0831-0661 Del Condominium Life **4537**
0831-067X En Voyage†
0831-0785 Son Hi-Fi Video†
0831-0866 Une Veritable Amie *see* 0824-1961 **8864**
0831-1048 Cahiers de Recherche Sociologique **8091**
0831-1161 Parcs Industriels Municipaux†
0831-1552 Westworld Saskatchewan **8612**
0831-1579 Westworld Alberta Magazine **8611**
0831-1625 Fugues **4373**
0831-1692 Memo (Toronto)†
0831-1846 Peace & Security
0831-1919 Breakthrough!†
0831-2133 Art Impressions†
0831-2338 Prairie Farmers Catalogue **213**
0831-2516 Dismissal and Employment Law Digest **1675**
0831-2559 Border Crossings **479**
0831-2621 Pets Magazine **6813**
0831-2796 Genome **870**
0831-2958 Le Monde de l'Auto **8591**
0831-3008 Canadian Guernsey Journal **283**
0831-3016 Saskatchewan Library Association. Forum **5045**
0831-3067 Vacances pour Tous†
0831-3083 Recueil de Jurisprudence du Quebec **4959**
0831-3202 C F L Facts, Figures and Records†
0831-3245 Manitoba Journal of Counselling **2885**
0831-3318 E A F Journal **3020**
0831-3377 Feminist Action
0831-3482 Securities and Corporate Regulation Review†
0831-3520 Atlantic Provinces Linguistic Association. Annual Meeting. Papers **5097**
0831-4020 Canadian Environmental Mediation Newsletter **3409**
0831-4039 Ven'd'Est **3819**
0831-411X Inter-Mecanique du Batiment **4121**
0831-4160 Toronto Business Magazine **1968**
0831-4268 International Conservative Insight†
0831-4306 Environmental Notes from the National Capital†
0831-4330 British Columbia Ministry of Water, Land and Air Protection. Biodiversity Branch. Wildlife Working Report **2605**
0831-4365 Seniors' Advocate **4056**
0831-4411 J A S M U
0831-4446 The Eastern Synod Lutheran **7755**
0831-4497 Canadian Archival Inventory Series, Literary Papers **5000**
0831-4527 Canadian Free Trader **1554**
0831-4535 Focus on Canadian Employment and Equality Rights **1861**
0831-4799 Oil & Gas Report†
0831-4853 OptionProfits†
0831-4888 Focus (Toronto, 1970) **6402**
0831-4985 Collection Forum **6522**
0831-5000 Geotechnical Science Laboratories. Publications, Reports, and Theses **2720**
0831-5027 Current Therapy in Allergy, Immunology, and Rheumatology **5757**
0831-5175 Film Canada Yearbook **6498**
0831-5213 Montreal Magazine
0831-5388 Reel West Magazine **6511**
0831-5477 The Bottom Line **1069**
0831-5493 Guidance & Counselling†
0831-5604 Liaison (Hamilton) **6680**
0831-5671 Algonquian Conference. Papers **323**
0831-5698 Canada. Statistics Canada. Canadian Social Trends **7304**
0831-5701 Tendances Sociales Canadiennes **7316**
0831-5825 Echange
0831-585X Native Studies Review **6636**
0831-5930 Roots, Branches and Twigs **3781**
0831-6279 C M T Newsletter†
0831-6309 Who's Who in Canadian Film and Television (Year) **647**
0831-6317 Sport Thesaurus **8219**
0831-6503 Blue Chart Report **4496**
0831-652X Current Therapy in Endocrinology and Metabolism†
0831-6708 Inuit Art Quarterly **497**
0831-7348 Canadian Labour Arbitration Summaries **4591**
0831-7445 Perspectives (Toronto, 1977)) **4053**
0831-7496 City of Ottawa. Corporate Financial and Statistical Information†
0831-7674 Gazette S C P *see* 1205-5298 **6089**
0831-7925 S A C E Bulletin **2951**
0831-795X Access (Don Mills)†
0831-8093 Atlantic Region Geographical Studies†
0831-8107 Saint Mary's University. Occasional Papers in Geography†
0831-8247 Canadian Forestry Service. Northern Forestry Centre. Information Report **3685**
0831-859X Esse **488**
0831-8603 Machinery & Equipment M R O **5455**
0831-8670 Current Therapy in Sports Medicine
0831-9111 Association of Educators of Gifted, Talented and Creative Children in B.C. Journal
0831-9227 Amnesty International. Canadian Section (English Speaking). Bulletin†
0831-9383 Bank of Canada. Summary of Government of Canada Direct and Guaranteed Securities and Loans *changed to* 1490-7291 **1912**

ISSN

0835-2445 Kola
0835-2526 Designs
0835-2623 Canada. Statistics Canada. Small Business Profiles **1219**
0835-264X Canada. Statistics Canada. Small Business Profiles, Newfoundland **1219**
0835-2666 Canada. Statistics Canada. Small Business Profiles, Prince Edward Island **1219**
0835-2682 Canada. Statistics Canada. Small Business Profiles, Nova Scotia **1219**
0835-2704 Canada. Statistics Canada. Small Business Profiles, New Brunswick **1219**
0835-2720 Canada. Statistics Canada. Small Business Profiles, Quebec **1219**
0835-2747 Canada. Statistics Canada. Small Business Profiles, Ontario **1219**
0835-2763 Canada. Statistics Canada. Small Business Profiles, Manitoba **1219**
0835-278X Canada. Statistics Canada. Small Business Profiles, Saskatchewan **1219**
0835-2801 Canada. Statistics Canada. Small Business Profiles, Alberta **1219**
0835-2828 Canada. Statistics Canada. Small Business Profiles, British Columbia **1219**
0835-2844 Canada. Statistics Canada. Small Business Profiles, Yukon **1219**
0835-2860 Canada. Statistics Canada. Small Business Profiles, Northwest Territories **1219**
0835-2933 Stone and Cox Life Insurance Tables **4524**
0835-2976 Canadian Cancer Statistics **5742**
0835-2984 Statistiques Canadiennes sur le Cancer *see* 0835-2976 **5742**
0835-3026 J C M C C **5499**
0835-3042 Lake Erie Fisheries Report **3600**
0835-3069 Medical Psychotherapy†
0835-3255 Canadian Potato Production **224**
0835-3336 Asia Horizon Azie†
0835-3433 Northern Review **4467**
0835-3530 Open File. British Columbia, Geological Survey Branch **2761**
0835-3565 Clik
0835-3573 Charlton Standard Catalogue of Canadian Government Paper Money *changed to* Canadian Bank Notes **6649**
0835-359X Cosmetics Beauty Guide
0835-3638 Ancient History Bulletin **4130**
0835-3689 Current Surgical Therapy **6241**
0835-3743 Les Expos†
0835-3778 Environmental & Waste Management World
0835-3808 Immigration Law Reporter (3rd Series) **7285**
0835-3913 Career Options **6694**
0835-3980 Climate Change Digest **6349**
0835-4057 Canada. Statistics Canada. Quarterly Demographic Statistics **7304**
0835-409X Statistiques Financieres des Institutions de Depot
0835-412X ChristianWeek **7751**
0835-4162 Passion Magazine
0835-4170 Hotel Amenities in Canada
0835-4251 Small Business World Magazine **1967**
0835-426X Atlantic Chamber Journal
0835-4545 Contemporary Radiology†
0835-4596 Rhythmology: Cardiac Arrhythmia Research and Therapy Update†
0835-4634 Canada. Statistics Canada. Trusteed Pension Funds - Financial Statistics **1219**
0835-4944 Canadian Journal for the Study of Adult Education **2939**
0835-5134 Industrial Specialties News **6465**
0835-5452 Science and Technology Dimensions†
0835-5533 Canada. Statistics Canada. Shipping in Canada **8523**
0835-5592 Market & Waterfront
0835-5819 Canadian Child Day Care Federation. Interaction **8030**
0835-5851 Alces **931**
0835-5932 Catalyst: Research at the University of Calgary†
0835-6017 Fresh Perspective†
0835-605X Environmental Science & Engineering **3428**
0835-6122 Wednesday Report†
0835-6246 Farming Facts **180**
0835-636X Ontario Family Law Reporter **4913**
0835-6378 U - Choose: A Guide to Homes for Seniors in Canada (Ontario Edition)†
0835-6386 U - Choose: A Guide to Homes for Seniors in Canada (Eastern - Atlantic Province Edition)†
0835-6394 U - Choose: A Guide to Homes for Seniors in Canada (Western Edition)†
0835-6602 Electronics & Technology Today†
0835-6661 Atout Micro **2407**
0835-6742 Canadian Journal of Administrative Law and Practice **4639**
0835-6963 Canadian Maritime Bibliography†
0835-7005 Canada. Department of Fisheries and Oceans. General Education Series **3588**
0835-7315 British Columbia. Ministry of Finance and Corporate Relations. Annual Report *changed to* 1708-0266 **7424**
0835-7447 Bowbender Magazine's Hunting Annual (Year)†
0835-748X The Charlton Standard Catalogue of Canadian Colonial Tokens **6649**
0835-7560 American & World Intellectual Property Report
0835-7625 Scat!
0835-7641 Etc. Montreal **488**
0835-7692 Montreal Business Magazine **1150**
0835-7714 J'aime Lire **2194**
0835-7900 Canadian Journal of Gastroenterology **5921**
0835-7919 Safarir **3817**
0835-8044 Hockey Coaching Journal
0835-8087 National Labour Review†
0835-8095 Pixel - The Computer Animation Newsletter†
0835-8346 The Flag & Banner **3766**
0835-8443 T T R. Traduction Terminologie Redaction **5185**
0835-8583 Pension Plan Coverage in Canada†
0835-8672 A Rayons Ouverts **4986**
0835-8702 Le Bel Age **4041**
0835-9148 Canadian Economic Observer **1220**
0835-9245 Canadian Corporate Law Reporter†
0835-9423 New Weekly Magazine **3813**
0835-9563 Protoculture Addicts **513**
0835-9628 Persuasions, Occasional Papers†
0835-9741 Venture Link†
0835-9806 Inside Hockey†
0835-9946 Canadian Fisheries. Products and Inventories **1882**
0836-0014 Le Quebec a Votre Portee **3122**
0836-0111 Status of Women Canada. Perspectives **8884**
0836-0278 Canadian Water and Wastewater Association. Bulletin **8819**
0836-0391 British Columbia Annual Practice **4632**
0836-0421 Grammateion **5218**
0836-0456 Canadian Insurance Law Review†
0836-0472 New Times
0836-0618 Leslie L. Schaffer Lectureship in Forest Science **3695**
0836-0820 Trade Monitor†
0836-0839 Intersections (Montreal, 1987)†
0836-0928 Les Naturalistes†
0836-0960 Canadian Shareowner *changed to* 1704-1082 **1651**
0836-1002 Film - Video Canadiana†
0836-1134 Aurora (Athabasca)†
0836-1142 Business Examiner (South Island Edition) **1072**
0836-1355 Equine Employment and Education Guide†
0836-1398 Physics Essays **7033**
0836-1444 The Chiropractic Report **5804**
0836-1525 Ontario. Ministry of Labour. Library. Infolink
0836-1630 Autopinion **8566**
0836-1657 Quality of Western Canadian Canola **275**
0836-2041 Directory of Archival Collections in Newfoundland and Labrador **5006**
0836-205X Tourisme Plus, le Journal des Voyages†
0836-2114 Playback **2387**
0836-2149 Scandinavian Forum†
0836-2378 In-Site†
0836-2688 New Brunswick Medical Society. Newsletter **5685**
0836-2696 Canadian Society for Horticultural Science. Newsletter **3726**
0836-2971 Saint-Jerome Vous Informe *changed to* 1719-6086 **3817**
0836-3005 Tusaayaksat **3569**
0836-303X Canadian Review of Social Policy **8030**
0836-3102 Au Pays de Matane **4285**
0836-3196 Canadian (Toronto)†
0836-320X Alpine Garden Club of British Columbia. Bulletin **3721**
0836-3463 A C M C Forum **5563**
0836-3587 Micro-Gazette†
0836-3862 Luggage, Leathergoods & Accessories
0836-4001 Canadian Life and Health Insurance Facts **4498**
0836-4176 Independent Petroleum Association of Canada. Activity update
0836-4249 Goodlife's Tastes of Toronto†
0836-4796 B.C. Woman to Woman Magazine
0836-4818 B C A M T Newsletter **3052**
0836-4966 L'Informateur Agricole†
0836-5024 Publication Profiles **33**
0836-5156 Truck World
0836-5261 Bottin Bleu†
0836-5318 Yesterday's Footprints **3788**
0836-5482 Microview **2572**
0836-5504 Manitoba Law Foundation. Annual Report *changed to* The Law Society of Manitoba (Year) Annual Report **4717**
0836-5768 Dominion Law Reports. Fourth Series: Index, Annotations, Table of Cases **4660**
0836-5911 Blakes Report on Intellectual Property **4630**
0836-6055 Video Marketing
0836-6179 Construction Economist **995**
0836-6217 Canadian Antiquer and Collector†
0836-6314 Drug Protocol
0836-6527 Canada Computes!†
0836-6594 Audrey Gostlin's Inside Fashion
0836-6632 U N B Law Journal **4799**
0836-6853 Logibase **2594**
0836-6926 Fetes et Festivals **1817**
0836-6993 Magyar Naplo **3549**
0836-7094 Socialist Worker **7184**
0836-7132 Didsbury Review **3808**
0836-7140 Congresso
0836-7353 Travel a la Carte **8765**
0836-737X Industrial Process Products and Technology **1889**
0836-7515 Match News **8874**
0836-7590 Reggae†
0836-7973 C S S H E Professional File **2970**
0836-8066 Sault Ste. Marie This Week **3817**
0836-8600 Westcoast Fisherman **3611**
0836-8635 Echo de Frontenac **3809**
0836-8880 Courtenay Comox Valley Record **3808**
0836-9925 L'Eco d'Italia **3531**
0837-0028 Maidstone Mirror **3813**
0837-0125 Richmond Hill Month
0837-015X Canadian Masonry Contractor†
0837-0443 Queen's University. Industrial Relations Centre. School of Industrial Relations Research Essay Series†
0837-0524 Canada. Law Reform Commission. Administrative Law Series. Study Papers†
0837-0648 Bielaruski Holas **3522**
0837-0672 Vaba Eestlane **3570**
0837-0680 Canada Darpan International†
0837-1059 Atlantic Salmon Federation. Annual Report **3586**
0837-1083 Greek Canadian Action - Drassis **3535**
0837-1091 Insieme **3540**
0837-1105 Popular **3558**
0837-1342 Hollandse Krant
0837-1512 Today's Trucking **8676**
0837-1571 V - The Style of the City†
0837-1652 Environmental Studies Research Funds Report **3429**
0837-1989 Packet & Times **3815**
0837-2071 Glasnik Hrvatske Seljacke Stranke **3535**
0837-2136 Agricultural Credit Corporation of Saskatchewan. Annual Report **192**
0837-2179 Yiddish Press†
0837-2446 Telefilm Canada. Annual Report **6515**
0837-2462 Nova Scotia. Department of Health. Vital Statistics. Annual Report **7288**
0837-2861 Menora
0837-3175 Toronto Sun **3818**
0837-3183 Saturday Sun *see* 0837-3175 **3818**
0837-3191 Sunday Sun *see* 0837-3175 **3818**
0837-3280 Chinese - Canadian Magazine **3527**
0837-3299 Windmill Herald: Central-Eastern Canada Edition **3572**
0837-3337 The Journal Pioneer **3811**
0837-3434 The Standard (St. Catharines) **3817**
0837-3744 Expositor **3809**
0837-3760 Journal - Saint Mary's University **2288**
0837-3809 Chinese Times†
0837-4171 Canada. Department of Tourism. Annual Report **8691**
0837-4503 Peches et Oceans. Serie de l'Education Generale **3604**
0837-4589 Royal Canadian Mounted Police. External Review Committee. Annual Report **7467**
0837-4899 British Columbia Tidal Waters Sport Fishing Guide **8307**
0837-5771 Emergency Preparedness Digest **2226**
0837-5828 Canada. Department of Finance. Quarterly Economic Review†
0837-6239 Welcome to the Best of Toronto & Ontario Guide
0837-6549 Pacific Forestry Centre. Pest Report **3699**
0837-6859 British Columbia Lottery Corporation. Annual Report **7424**
0837-7006 La Tarification en Assurance Automobile. Rapport *changed to* 1712-9389 **4524**
0837-7065 Canada. Civil Aviation Tribunal. Annual Report **4971**
0837-7251 Health Personnel in Canada **5625**
0837-7839 Art Gallery of Nova Scotia. Annual Report (Print Edition) *changed to* 1711-733X **6519**
0837-8649 Saskatchewan. Bureau of Statistics. Monthly Statistical Review **1262**
0838-0015 Guide de la Route: La Floride **8716**
0838-0163 Transactor for the Amiga
0838-0236 Canada. Statistics Canada. Canadian Economic Observer. Historical Statistical Supplement *see* 0835-9148 **1220**
0838-0341 New Freeman **7809**
0838-0368 Synergy
0838-0430 Journal of Baha'i Studies **7654**
0838-049X Newfoundland Ancestor **3776**
0838-0511 Issues Paper **4697**
0838-0651 Ryerson Review of Journalism **4583**
0838-0872 Power Boating Canada **8280**
0838-0937 Beekeeping Notes **95**
0838-0953 Teleromans†
0838-0961 Canadian Petroleum Tax Journal **6765**
0838-1313 Dance Connection†
0838-1321 A L F A†
0838-1550 Pagans for Peace **7740**
0838-164X Journal of Prisoners on Prisons **2657**
0838-1658 Gallerie: Women Artists Monographs
0838-1674 Option Serre **3746**
0838-1895 Beautiful British Columbia Magazine's Guidebook†
0838-200X Poetry Halifax Dartmouth
0838-2026 Fontanus **4453**
0838-2182 Canada. Statistics Canada. Business Services **1217**
0838-228X Canadian H R Reporter **1857**
0838-2395 Cottage Life **5068**
0838-2433 Medecines Nouvelles et Alimentation Naturelle
0838-2638 Nova Scotia Medical Journal†
0838-2875 Education & Law Journal **4663**
0838-2964 Library Editions†
0838-3502 Air Transport Management†
0838-3596 Windsor Review of Legal and Social Issues **4815**
0838-360X Library Footnotes†
0838-3677 Ontario Geological Survey. Report of Activities, Resident Geologists **6475**
0838-3693 New Brunswick. Department of Health and Community Services. Annual Report *changed to* 1499-4704 **7533**
0838-3715 Family Expenditure in Canada **1230**
0838-3871 Nuclear Sector Focus†
0838-3898 Family Food Expenditure in Canada **1230**
0838-3936 Vista
0838-4061 Sport & Leisure†
0838-4096 Winter Cities
0838-4185 Woodworking **1053**
0838-4207 F I I Q en Action *changed to* 1914-2609 **5958**
0838-4207 F I I Q en Action *changed to* 1914-2595 **5958**
0838-4223 Statistics Canada Catalogue **8406**
0838-4312 What's in a N A M E? **6628**
0838-438X Business ComputerNews†
0838-4401 Sommets *changed to* 1913-8164 **2304**
0838-4479 Recherches Feministes **8902**
0838-4525 Scrutiny†
0838-4711 Journal of Indigenous Studies **345**
0838-4789 Other Voices **5428**
0838-4843 Charter of Rights Newsletter **4847**
0838-519X Report on the Industrial Direct Discharges in Ontario **3462**
0838-522X Biennale Nationale de Ceramique *changed to* 1716-284X **478**
0838-5319 Focus Newsletter **7964**
0838-5467 Canada West Travel News
0838-5505 Island Parent Magazine **2639**
0838-553X *see* 0831-5604 **6680**
0838-5610 Vehicule des Conducteurs Proprietaires†
0838-5769 Timely Disclosure **1386**
0838-5971 Natural History Occasional Paper **7888**
0838-6021 Canadian Literature Index†
0838-603X Fuse Magazine **490**
0838-6048 Business Examiner (North Island Edition) **1072**
0838-6455 New Home Magazine†
0838-6471 Vancouver Venture Magazine
0838-6536 Y Triangle†
0838-6609 Queen's University. Industrial Relations Centre. Queen's Papers in Industrial Relations Series **1704**
0838-6749 Underpass
0838-6781 B C Farmer†
0838-679X Atlantic Firefighter **3575**
0838-6803 C C C C Bulletin **8029**

ISSN

DIRECTORY 2010 0860-4037 9359

0851-0024 Revue de l'INSEA **7292**
0851-0202 Banque Marocaine du Commerce Exterieur. Information Review **1320**
0851-0210 Construire **999**
0851-0229 M A P Actualite **7152**
0851-0431 Revue de Droit et d'Economie **1167**
0851-0458 Economie et Socialisme
0851-0474 Al-Iqtisaed Wa-al-Mugtama' *see* 0851-0458
0851-0857 Maroc Magazine **1498**
0851-0865 Morocco. Direction de la Statistique. Etudes Economiques et Statistiques†
0851-0881 Langues et Litteratures **5142**
0851-089X Annuaire Statistique du Maroc **8345**
0851-0903 Nasrat al-Ihsa'iyyat al-Sanawiyyat li-i-Magrib **8389**
0851-0946 Le Maroc en Chiffres **8387**
0851-0954 Morocco. Direction de la Statistique. Indice des Prix a la Production Industrielle, Energetique et Miniere **1252**
0851-0970 Morocco. Direction de la Statistique. Indice des Prix de Gros **1252**
0851-1128 Islam Today **7712**
0851-1470 Les Echos Africains **1336**
0851-1519 *see* 0851-0946 **8387**
0851-1667 Maroc Fruits **242**
0851-1934 Banque Nationale pour le Developpement Economique. Rapport Annuel **1880**
0851-2167 Banques et Entreprises au Maroc **1321**
0851-2914 Identity, Culture and Politics **8106**
0851-3058 Revue Marocaine de Finances Publiques et d'Economie **1380**
0851-4909 Signes du Present **1174**
0851-5115 Maroc Business **1147**
0851-5743 Economap **1097**
0851-6804 Morocco. Direction de la Statistique. Population Active Urbaine: Resultats Detailles†
0851-7762 Journal of Higher Education in Africa **2990**
0852-0321 Berita - Pusat Penelitian Perkebunan Gula Indonesia **221**
0852-0747 Edisi Chusus Bulletin Koperasi **1482**
0852-5900 Dunia Wanita **8859**
0852-596X Foto Media **6967**
0852-6729 Bola **8162**
0852-713X Journal of Population **7286**
0852-8217 Mangle **3891**
0852-8225 HumOr **5220**
0852-9736 Warta K O W A N I *see* 0852-9744 **8870**
0852-9744 K O W A N I News **8870**
0853-0300 Nova **8878**
0853-375X ArchipelaGo **3891**
0853-8360 Jurnal Bioteknologi Pertanian **129**
0853-9952 Index Medicus Indonesia **5747**
0854-0306 Daftar Terbitan Berkala Indonesia Yang Telah Mempunyai ISSN **6**
0854-1388 Majalah Ilmiah Himpunan Matematika Indonesia **5510**
0854-1566 Tropical Biodiversity **708**
0854-235X Coconut Statistical Yearbook **225**
0854-2414 Al-Hikmah **7711**
0854-5006 Cocoinfo International **101**
0854-543X A S E A N Economic Info View **1589**
0854-6711 Katalog Induk Majalart **10**
0854-6886 Statistical Report on Visitor Arrivals to Indonesia **8780**
0854-9176 Stulos **7686**
0855-000X Asemka **5257**
0855-0018 African Demography **7276**
0855-0042 Ghana Journal of Agricultural Science **115**
0855-0050 Legon Journal of the Humanities **4463**
0855-0093 Ghana National Bibliography **625**
0855-0115 Ghana Science Abstracts **7937**
0855-0174 A A U Newsletter **2963**
0855-0247 Ghana. Statistical Service. Economic Survey **1235**
0855-0352 Journal of Management Studies **1768**
0855-0395 Journal of Science and Technology **7873**
0855-0417 Ghana Commercial Bank. Quarterly Economic Review **1488**
0855-0484 Ghana Journal of Chemistry **2062**
0855-0506 Cocoa Research Institute. Annual Report **3631**
0855-0514 Oguaa Social Science Journal†
0855-0662 Ghana. Statistical Service. Quarterly Digest of Statistics **8374**
0855-076X L E C I A Bulletin **7250**
0855-0875 Ghana Journal of Literacy and Adult Education **2860**
0855-0883 University of Cape Coast. Institute of Education. Journal **2922**
0855-0913 The Oguaa Educator **2996**
0855-0948 G R M A News **5959**
0855-0964 Bank of Ghana. Quarterly Economic Bulletin **1441**
0855-1049 External Trade Statistics of Ghana (Quarterly) **1228**
0855-1073 Ghana in Figures†
0855-1308 Ghana Population Studies **7283**
0855-1537 Mirror **3861**
0855-1677 Ghanaian Chronicle **3861**
0855-1707 Ghana Journal of Forestry **3692**
0855-191X Historical Society of Ghana. Transactions **4143**
0855-2010 Ideal Woman **8868**
0855-2215 Journal of Applied Science and Technology **8429**
0855-2606 Journal of Performing Arts **8472**
0855-2983 Akwaaba†
0855-3262 Journal of African Christian Thought **7653**
0855-3823 Ghana Science Association. Journal **7858**
0855-4412 Institute of African Studies Research Review **7973**
0855-4706 Mathematics Connection **5515**
0855-6059 National Drug Information Journal **6862**
0855-6261 Legon Journal of Sociology **8118**
0855-6660 Journal of Philosophy and Culture **6929**
0855-6768 Ghana Journal of Development Studies **7857**
0856-0005 Educational Abstracts for Tanzania **2932**
0856-003X Tanzania National Bibliography **636**
0856-0048 Africa Theological Journal **7744**
0856-0056 African Review **7103**
0856-0080 T P R I Bulletin
0856-0099 Dar es Salaam Medical Journal *changed to* 0856-7212
0856-0110 Jenga **1890**
0856-0129 Mulika **5153**
0856-0161 Tanzania. Ministry of Trade. Foreign Trade News Bulletin†
0856-017X Tanzania News Review **3961**
0856-0188 Nchi Yetu **3961**
0856-0250 Studies in Curriculum Development†
0856-0323 Tanzania Official Gazette **7471**
0856-0366 Home Builders Journal†
0856-0374 Tanzania. Bureau of Standards. Announcer **6407**
0856-0382 Rasilimali **1647**
0856-0404 Industrial Abstracts for Tanzania **8446**
0856-0455 East Africana Accessions Bulletin **4169**
0856-048X Kiswahili **5137**
0856-0560 Studies in Adult Education **2946**
0856-0595 Torch **4584**
0856-065X Tanzanian Mathematical Bulletin **5540**
0856-0722 Mwenge **3552**
0856-0838 Ukulima wa Kisasa **164**
0856-0854 Umma **5391**
0856-096X Utafiti **5394**
0856-101X Bank of Tanzania. Economic Bulletin **1441**
0856-1087 Habari za Washirika **3961**
0856-1109 Journal of Adult Education **2943**
0856-1222 Ngao **4517**
0856-1265 Muislamu **3961**
0856-1435 Uongozi: Journal of Management Development **1799**
0856-1621 Tanzania Library Service. Occasional Paper **5050**
0856-1761 Tanzania Journal of Science **7922**
0856-1818 University of Dar es Salaam Library Journal **5053**
0856-1850 E A C R O T A N A L Information **5113**
0856-1931 Ija Webonere **7761**
0856-1982 Kipepeo†
0856-2105 Tanzania Trade Currents **1583**
0856-2172 Tanzania Industrial Studies and Consulting Organisation. Annual Report and Accounts **1181**
0856-227X Maji Review **3141**
0856-2423 Tanzania Investment Bank. Annual Report **1386**
0856-2539 Tanzania. Bureau of Standards. Director's Annual Report **6407**
0856-2563 Kiongozi **7803**
0856-2687 Tanzania Housing Bank. Annual Report and Statement of Accounts **1386**
0856-2806 Miombo **2619**
0856-311X Tanzania Journal of Paediatrics **6104**
0856-3152 Uhandisi **3224**
0856-3349 Azania News **3789**
0856-3373 Tanzania Economic Trends
0856-3810 Daily News **3961**
0856-3861 An-Nuur **7709**
0856-390X Mfanyakazi **3961**
0856-4043 C R H C S News **7511**
0856-4531 Tanzania Journal of Economics
0856-6259 Hoja **3961**
0856-6372 African Journal of Finance and Management **1057**
0856-6739 Huria **2864**
0856-7212 Dar es Salaam Medical Students Journal†
0856-8960 East Africa Journal of Public Health **7515**
0856-9355 AMANET Annual Report **5809**
0856-938X Habari Njema **7646**
0856-9495 Ardhi Ni Uhai **7582**
0856-9517 Jarida la Afya Morogoro **7528**
0856-9525 Morogoro Health Newsletter **7532**
0856-9673 U C C Newsletter **2440**
0856-9797 Tujielimishe **3148**
0856-9916 Mshauri Wako **3961**
0856-9940 The East African Lawyer **4663**
0856-9975 Bang Magazine **3522**
0857-0140 Microcomputer **2572**
0857-0361 S E A M E O Quarterly†
0857-0744 Journal of Infectious Diseases and Antimicrobial Agents **5820**
0857-0760 Peace Progress†
0857-1139 LookEast **8731**
0857-1155 Thai Industrial Directory **2030**
0857-1163 Secretaries Year Book **1707**
0857-1554 Buffalo Journal **282**
0857-2143 Journal of Demography **7286**
0857-233X S E A F D E C Newsletter **3606**
0857-2410 Agrometeorological Report **6346**
0857-2933 Journal of Research Methodology **7979**
0857-2968 T D R I Quarterly Review **1181**
0857-2984 Thailand Industrial Buyer's Guide **2030**
0857-6149 Warasan Loha, Watsadu lae Lae **6336**
0857-6173 R E R I C International Energy Journal **3145**
0857-6181 A I T Reports and Publications on Energy. Abstracts†
0857-6548 Thailand Eximport Review **1584**
0857-7277 Thailand Company Information (Year) **1433**
0857-748X Fishery Statistical Bulletin for South China Sea Area **3613**
0857-8702 Thailand's Investment Promotion Journal **1655**
0857-9067 Statistical Yearbook of Thailand **8405**
0857-9164 Thailand. National Statistical Office. Annotated Statistical Bibliography **8409**
0857-9253 Asian Institute of Technology. Abstracts on Management of Technology and International Business **8446**
0857-9466 Statistical Handbook of Thailand†
0857-9482 Thailand. National Statistical Office. Quarterly Bulletin of Statistics **8409**
0858-0200 Thailand. National Statistical Office. Report of the Labor Force Survey, Whole Kingdom (Year) **1270**
0858-0391 Survey of Migration into the Bangkok Metropolis†
0858-1088 Phuket Marine Biological Center. Research Bulletin **697**
0858-1630 Directory of Scientific and Technical Libraries in Thailand **5006**
0858-1886 Statistical Budget and Activities in Thailand†
0858-2114 Agricultural Engineering Journal **83**
0858-2696 Thailand. National Statistical Office. Annual Report **8409**
0858-3633 Phuket Marine Biological Center. Special Publications **697**
0858-4028 Decor International Magazine **4536**
0858-4419 Asian Energy News **3124**
0858-4869 Geotechnical Engineering Bulletin **2708**
0858-6721 S E A M E O Update†
0858-673X S E A M E O Canada Chronicler†
0858-6934 Up - Date **7927**
0858-7884 Computer Professional Information **2412**
0858-8406 Thailand Tatler **3962**
0858-9976 Hobby Electronics **3117**
0859-0095 Industrial Technology Review **8425**
0859-2527 F H M (Thailand) **6290**
0859-290X Mekong Fish Catch and Culture **3601**
0859-4074 Thammasat International Journal of Science and Technology **7923**
0859-449X Journal of Euro - Asian Management **1765**
0859-600X Aquaculture Asia **92**
0859-709X S E T Journal **1648**
0859-7685 Thai Journal of Nursing Research **5983**
0859-9920 Manusaya: Journal of Humanities **4464**
0860-0007 Fasciculi Archaeologiae Historicae **393**
0860-0023 Poznan Fair Magazine **1580**
0860-0031 Poznan Messemagazin *see* 0860-0023 **1580**
0860-0066 Lituano-Slavica Posnaniensia **4240**
0860-0074 Politechnika Slaska. Zeszyty Naukowe. Architektura **453**
0860-0120 Uniwersytet Jagiellonski. Zeszyty Naukowe. Acta Mathematica **5545**
0860-0171 Uniwersytet Gdanski. Wydzial Ekonomiki Produkcji. Zeszyty Naukowe. Finanse i Rachunek Ekonomiczny (No.)†
0860-021X Biology of Sport **6229**
0860-0260 Akademia Gorniczo-Hutnicza im. Stanislawa Staszica. Zeszyty Naukowe. Fizyka†
0860-0376 Fenix†
0860-0627 Akademia Rolnicza im. Hugona Kollataja w Krakowie. Zeszyty Naukowe. Seria: Technologia Zywnosci†
0860-0716 Acta Universitatis Wratislaviensis. Neerlandica Wratislaviensia **5090**
0860-0732 Polska Akademia Nauk. Oddzial w Krakowie. Komisja Historyczna. Prace **4171**
0860-0775 Studia Franciszkanskie **7818**
0860-0953 Gospodarka Surowcami Mineralnymi **6464**
0860-097X Politechnika Krakowska. Monografie **7898**
0860-0988 Kultura (Warsaw, 1985)†
0860-1046 Wyzsza Szkola Pedagogiczna im. Komisji Edukacji Narodowej w Krakowie. Rocznik Naukowo-Dydaktyczny. Prace z Historii Oswiaty i Wychowania *changed to* 1895-751X **2826**
0860-1100 Akademia Gorniczo-Hutnicza im. Stanislawa Staszica. Zeszyty Naukowe. Chemia†
0860-1119 Acta Universitatis Lodziensis: Turyzm **8680**
0860-1194 Politechnika Wroclawska. Instytut Historii Architektury, Sztuki i Techniki. Prace Naukowe. Konferencje†
0860-147X Towarzystwo Naukowe w Toruniu. Prace Archeologiczne
0860-1615 Politechnika Wroclawska. Centrum Obliczeniowe. Prace Naukowe. Konferencje†
0860-1623 Politechnika Wroclawska. Centrum Obliczeniowe. Prace Naukowe. Studia i Materialy†
0860-1844 Archiwum Historii i Filozofii Medycyny **5577**
0860-1917 Kociewski Magazyn Regionalny **5222**
0860-2085 Studia Phonetica Posnaniensia **5180**
0860-2107 Uniwersytet Slaski w Katowicach. Prace Naukowe. Annales Mathematicae Silesianae **5545**
0860-2212 Szczecinskie Roczniki Naukowe, Nauki Spoleczne **8009**
0860-2220 Kraje Socjalistyczne†
0860-2441 Uniwersytet Slaski w Katowicach. Prace Naukowe. Acta Biologica Silesiana **710**
0860-2492 Gdanski Rocznik Kulturalny **4222**
0860-2506 Politechnika Warszawska. Prace Naukowe. Organizacja i Zarzadzanie Przemyslem **1786**
0860-2603 Acta Academiae Agriculturae ac Technicae Olstenensis. Zootechnica†
0860-2611 Acta Academiae Agriculturae ac Technicae Olstenensis. Protectio Aquarum et Piscatoria†
0860-262X Acta Academiae Agriculturae ac Technicae Olstenensis. Geodaesia et Ruris Regulatio†
0860-2646 Polskie Towarzystwo Botaniczne. Sekcja Dendrologiczna. Rocznik Dendrologiczny **813**
0860-2670 Zagle **8286**
0860-2786 Biblioteka Chopinowska†
0860-2832 Acta Academiae Agriculturae ac Technicae Olstenensis. Agricultura†
0860-2840 Acta Academiae Agriculturae ac Technicae Olstenensis. Veterinaria†
0860-2859 Acta Academiae Agriculturae ac Technicae Olstenensis. Technologia Alimentorum†
0860-2883 Studia Austro-Polonica **4163**
0860-2948 Acta Academiae Agriculturae ac Technicae Olstenensis. Oeconomica†
0860-2956 Acta Academiae Agriculturae ac Technicae Olstenensis. Aedificatio et Mechanica†
0860-3022 Ptaki Slaska **913**
0860-309X Rada Narodowa†
0860-3111 Acta Universitatis Lodziensis: Folia Physiologica Cytologica et Genetica **773**
0860-3200 Politechnika Wroclawska. Instytut Nauk Ekonomiczno-Spolecznych. Prace Naukowe. Konferencje†
0860-3294 Szczecinskie Roczniki Naukowe, Nauki Przyrodnicze i Rolnicze **819**
0860-3324 Maszyny Przeplywowe **3209**
0860-3359 Studies in the Developing Countries†
0860-3375 Polska Akademia Nauk. Komitet Przestrzennego Zagospodarowania Kraju. Studia Regionalia **4424**
0860-3391 Materialy do Polskiej Muzyki Ludowej†
0860-3405 Problemy Medycyny Nuklearnej **6205**
0860-3421 I.B. - 1. Informacja Biezaca†
0860-3456 Gdanskie Studia Jezykoznawcze **5121**
0860-3502 I.B. - 2. Informacja Biezaca†
0860-3693 Zeszyty Tarnogorskie **4280**
0860-3723 EuroCriminology **2651**
0860-3731 Uniwersytet Gdanski. Wydzial Prawa i Administracji. Zeszyty Naukowe. Studia Prawno-Ustrojowe†
0860-3847 Novosti Veterinarnoi Farmatsii i Meditsiny†
0860-3944 Documenta Chopiniana†
0860-4037 Animal Science Papers and Reports **278**

ISSN

0864-0262 Su Voz **7776**
0864-0270 Heraldo Cristiano **7760**
0864-0289 Revista Cubana de Hematologia, Inmunologia y Hematerapia **5941**
0864-0300 Revista Cubana de Investigaciones Biomedicas **700**
0864-0319 Revista Cubana de Enfermeria **5980**
0864-0327 Muchacha **2203**
0864-0394 Pastos y Forrajes **268**
0864-0408 Cuban Journal of Agricultural Science **103**
0864-0432 Trabajadores **1711**
0864-0467 Cinco de Septiembre **7116**
0864-0505 Pionero **2207**
0864-0513 El Caiman Barbudo **5210**
0864-0521 Zunzun **2224**
0864-0564 Somos Jovenes **2168**
0864-0572 Alma Mater **7104**
0864-0769 Archivo Nacional de Cuba. Boletin **4284**
0864-0777 Bohemia **3831**
0864-084X Nucleus **3172**
0864-098X Vanguardia **7191**
0864-1110 Invasor **7144**
0864-1269 La Demajagua **7128**
0864-1277 Escambray **7133**
0864-1307 Cuba en el Ballet **2683**
0864-1315 Revolucion y Cultura
0864-1331 Del Caribe **3831**
0864-134X Temas **3831**
0864-1358 Centro de Estudios Martianos. Anuario **4288**
0864-1374 Cuba. Ministerio de Cultura. Tablas **3831**
0864-1382 Indice General de Publicaciones Periodicas Cubanas **9**
0864-1404 Clave **7116**
0864-1412 Juventud Rebelde **2157**
0864-1420 Cuba: Economia Planificada **1718**
0864-1439 Actualidades de la Economia Socialista†
0864-151X Revista Cubana de Meteorologia **2715**
0864-1587 Revue Tricontinental *see* 0049-4682 **7262**
0864-1595 Tricontinental Magazine *see* 0049-4682 **7262**
0864-1609 Tribuna de la Habana **7189**
0864-1641 Ahora **7103**
0864-165X Revista Cubana de Derecho **4770**
0864-1706 Nueva Gaceta de Cuba **5344**
0864-1870 Academia de Ciencias de Cuba. Instituto de Geologia. Serie Geologica
0864-1889 Enigma **5215**
0864-1897 Revista Tecnologica **8437**
0864-2052 Paz y Soberania **7258**
0864-2125 Revista Cubana de Medicina General Integral **5704**
0864-2133 Revista Cubana de Nutricion y Alimentacion *changed to* 0864-3466 **7539**
0864-2141 Revista Cubana de Educacion Medica Superior **5704**
0864-215X Revista Cubana de Ortopedia y Traumatologia **6072**
0864-2176 Revista Cubana de Oftalmologia **6051**
0864-2184 Resumed *changed to* 0864-2125 **5704**
0864-2362 Militante Comunista
0864-2478 C I A C Sintesis Informativa **7111**
0864-3210 Acta Medica **5566**
0864-3466 Revista Cubana de Salud Publica **7539**
0864-3490 Revista Biologia **700**
0864-3598 Publicaciones Seriadas Cubanas **7570**
0864-3784 Revista Cubana de Ortodoncia **5863**
0864-3857 Cuba Foreign Trade **1401**
0864-3873 Ciencia y Tecnologia Pesquera
0864-4462 Revista Cubana de Endocrinologia **5900**
0864-4497 Ciencia y Tecnologia de los Alimentos **3631**
0864-4551 Biotecnologia Aplicada **761**
0864-4616 Granma Internacional (Spanish Edition) **7139**
0864-4624 Granma International (English Edition) **7139**
0864-4632 Granma Internacional (Portuguese Edition) **7139**
0864-4640 Granma International (French Edition) **7139**
0864-4659 Ciencias de la Informacion **5002**
0864-4675 Cuba Economica **1089**
0864-7003 Nover **5971**
0864-7410 Hungarian Agricultural Engineering **119**
0864-7828 Poenvadaszat **4343**
0864-8166 Fakanal **3635**
0864-8492 auto Magazin **8559**
0864-8557 Igen **7800**
0864-8581 168 Ora **3877**
0864-8646 Mult es Jovo
0864-8786 Uj Periodikumok†
0864-8921 Magyar Urologia **6271**
0864-9219 Auto Extra†
0864-9227 Denise
0864-9235 Julia **5410**
0864-9243 Romana **5412**
0864-9251 Tvr-het **2398**
0864-9421 Chip **2410**
0864-960X Multunk **4154**
0864-991X Health Information and Libraries†
0865-0047 Csaladi Haz **4355**
0865-0497 Izotoptechnika, Diagnosztika†
0865-0810 Esely **7133**
0865-1035 Kismama **8870**
0865-1167 Magyar Cserkesz
0865-1329 Konyvtari Levelezo†
0865-1396 Magyar Dohanyujsag
0865-1906 Magyar Neprajzi Bibliografia **3620**
0865-2007 Otthon **4548**
0865-2090 Mathematica Pannonica **5512**
0865-350X Playboy (Budapest) **6297**
0865-3518 Auto Katalogus **8558**
0865-3682 Research Review on Hungarian Social Sciences Granted by the Government†
0865-3844 Szombat **3567**
0865-4093 Beszelo **3876**
0865-4131 Motor Revue **8262**
0865-4158 Tiffany **5412**
0865-4824 Symmetry **7921**
0865-5227 Magyar Egyhaztorteneti Vazlatok **4241**
0865-5243 Computer Panorama **2412**
0865-5251 Klasszikus Magyar Irok Keziratainak es Levelezesenek Katalogusa **5318**
0865-557X Regio (Budapest, 1990) **7261**
0865-6347 Rubicon **3877**
0865-6355 Tozsde Kurir
0865-6681 Burda **2251**
0865-6746 Investors' Guide to Hungary **1634**
0865-7165 Motor Katalogus **8262**
0865-736X Magyar Kozigazgatas†
0865-8986 Business Week (Hungarian Edition)†
0865-9028 Tolnai Nepujsag **3877**
0865-9109 Heves Megyei Hirlap **3876**
0865-9125 Somogyi Hirlap **3877**
0865-9133 Uj Dunantuli Naplo **3877**
0865-915X Uj Neplap **3877**
0865-9303 Akademiai Ertesito **3016**
0866-0042 Voila **8888**
0866-0174 Acta Academiae Paedagogicae Nyiregyhaziensis. Matematikai-informatikai Kozlemenyek†
0866-0182 Academia Paedagogica Nyiregyhaziensis. Acta Mathematica **5464**
0866-0484 Afeosz Tajekoztato†
0866-076X Gazdasagi Forum†
0866-0867 Bianca **5409**
0866-1146 Hungary. Kozponti Statisztikai Hivatal. Belkereskedelm **1240**
0866-1510 Termeszetbuvar **707**
0866-241X Hungarian University of Physical Education. Review†
0866-2452 Buci Maci **2181**
0866-2517 Nemzeti Sport **8190**
0866-2789 Gulliver Tinimagazin†
0866-4811 Lege Artis Medicine *changed to* 1217-6052 **5664**
0866-482X Feherje es Biotermek†
0866-5192 Kutatasszervezesi Tajekoztato†
0866-6024 Magyar Installateur **4123**
0866-6032 Publicationes Universitatis Miskolciensis. Series Juridica et Politica **4763**
0866-6083 Magyar Szolo- es Borgazdasag **241**
0866-7179 Vietnam Journal of Mathematics†
0866-7500 Thuongmai **1584**
0866-7837 Vietnamese Trade Unions **4605**
0866-7942 Khoa Hoc va Doi Song **7876**
0866-7950 Lao Dong **1695**
0866-806X Vietnam Pictorial **3995**
0866-8140 Vietnam Courier **3994**
0866-8345 Giao Thong-Van Tai **8497**
0866-9198 Tygodnik Gdanski†
0866-9279 Acta Universitatis Wratislaviensis. Studia i Materialy z Dziejow Universytetu Wroclawskiego **2965**
0866-9287 Business Promotion **1075**
0866-9449 Comparative Law Review **4647**
0866-9465 Panstwowy Instytut Geologiczny. Prace **2761**
0866-9546 Archives of Transport **8490**
0866-9597 Polska Akademia Nauk. Komitet Nauk Etnologicznych. Prace **352**
0866-9708 Polish Academy of Sciences. Institute of Geography and Spatial Organization. Conference Papers†
0866-9791 Mloda Polska†
0866-9961 Przeglad Uniwersytecki **4470**
0867-0005 Gospodarka Narodowa **1488**
0867-0102 Uniwersytet Gdanski. Wydzial Biologii, Geografii i Oceanologii. Zeszyty Naukowe. Geografia†
0867-0153 P C Kurier†
0867-020X Hispanica Posnaniensia **5306**
0867-0323 Forum Oswiatowe **2941**
0867-0412 Spoleczenstwo Otwarte **8007**
0867-0420 Przysposobienie Obronne w Szkole†
0867-0501 Fonorama **6568**
0867-0536 Trybuna **3930**
0867-0544 Metafora **5333**
0867-0579 Po Prostu†
0867-0609 Annales Universitatis Mariae Curie-Sklodowska. Sectio DDD. Pharmacia **6820**
0867-0625 Exit **6523**
0867-0633 Teksty Drugie **5385**
0867-0730 Polish Botanical Studies **813**
0867-0838 Poland. Glowny Urzad Statystyczny. Studia i Analizy Statystyczne†
0867-0846 Poland. Glowny Urzad Statystyczny. Materialy i Opracowania Statystyczne†
0867-0854 Poland. Glowny Urzad Statystyczny. Zeszyty Metodyczne i Klasyfikacje†
0867-0935 Wspolnota **7505**
0867-1079 Studies in Physical Culture and Tourism **6997**
0867-1095 Uniwersytet Jagiellonski. Zeszyty Naukowe. Acta Chimica **2083**
0867-1125 Kresy **5318**
0867-132X Nowa Fantastyka **5445**
0867-1370 Studia Podlaskie **4270**
0867-1389 Businessman
0867-1400 Wojsko i Wychowanie†
0867-1656 Polish Academy of Sciences. Bulletin. Biological Sciences†
0867-1710 Genus **791**
0867-1729 Polityka Polska†
0867-1761 Folia Horticulturae **3730**
0867-1788 Politechnika Krakowska. Zeszyty Naukowe. Inzynieria Ladowa **3280**
0867-1818 Magazyn Medyczny†
0867-1826 Twoj Styl **2262**
0867-1850 Orzecznictwo Sadow Polskich **4958**
0867-1915 Tygodnik Budowlany **1041**
0867-1958 Ex Libris **5293**
0867-1966 Muzeum Gornoslaskie w Bytomiu. Rocznik. Seria Entomologia **855**
0867-2008 Ordines Militares **4155**
0867-2040 Annales Universitatis Mariae Curie-Sklodowska. Sectio J. Paedagogia - Psychologia **2826**
0867-2075 Przeglad Wojsk Lotniczych i Obrony Powietrznej **6442**
0867-2105 Dom & Wnetrze **4538**
0867-2121 Archiwum Informatyki Teoretycznej i Stosowanej **2407**
0867-2148 Czas Kultury **5213**
0867-2164 Gazeta Lekarska **5618**
0867-2202 Nowosci Ksiegarskie
0867-2229 Poradnik Domowy **4365**
0867-2237 Nie **5230**
0867-2253 Media Reporter†
0867-2334 Computer World **2413**
0867-2393 Akademia Rolnicza we Wroclawiu. Zeszyty Naukowe. Monografie *changed to* Uniwersytet Przyrodniczy we Wroclawiu. Zeszyty Naukowe. Monografie **167**
0867-2512 Orzecznictwo Sadu Najwyzszego. Izba Cywilna oraz Izba Administracyjna, Pracy i Ubezpieczen Spolecznych *changed to* Orzecznictwo Sadu Najwyzszego. Izba Administracyjna, Pracy i Ubezpieczen Spolecznych **4839**
0867-2512 Orzecznictwo Sadu Najwyzszego. Izba Cywilna oraz Izba Administracyjna, Pracy i Ubezpieczen Spolecznych *changed to* Orzecznictwo Sadu Najwyzszego. Izba Cywilna **4839**
0867-2555 Format **490**
0867-2598 Notatnik Teatralny **8475**
0867-2628 Obrobka Plastyczna Metali **6328**
0867-2717 Brulion†
0867-2822 Moj Pies **6811**
0867-3055 Medyk **5678**
0867-311X Pracownia **5432**
0867-3152 Nie z tej Ziemi†
0867-3179 Reports on Geodesy **4026**
0867-3217 Poland. Glowny Urzad Statystyczny. Raport o Stanie, Zagrozeniu i Ochronie Srodowiska (Year) **3480**
0867-339X Postepy Osteoartrologii **5806**
0867-3403 Spotkania (Warsaw)†
0867-3411 Dziennik Ustaw Rzeczypospolitej Polskiej **4662**
0867-356X Politechnika Wroclawska. Studium Nauki Jezykow Obcych. Prace Naukowe. Studia i Materialy†
0867-3594 Wyzsza Szkola Pedagogiczna im. Komisji Edukacji Narodowej w Krakowie. Rocznik Naukowo-Dydaktyczny. Prace Fizyczne†
0867-3608 Dzis **7231**
0867-3675 Tygodnik Wspolczesny†
0867-3748 Fiscus **1288**
0867-3756 Akademia Rolnicza we Wroclawiu. Zeszyty Naukowe. Mechanizacja Rolnictwa† **8929**
0867-3764 Karta **4237**
0867-387X Burda **2252**
0867-3888 Folia Turistica **8710**
0867-4140 Acta Endoscopica Polona†
0867-4159 Theoria et Historia Scientiarum **7923**
0867-4175 A S - Sekretarka
0867-4264 Barbakan **8685**
0867-4299 Inzynieria Morska i Geotechnika **8647**
0867-4361 Alkoholizm i Narkomania **2691**
0867-4469 Siodma Prowincja **5239**
0867-4485 Budownictwo i Gospodarka Miejska†
0867-4507 Trybuna Slaska **3930**
0867-4523 Polska Zbrojna **6441**
0867-4566 Enter **2418**
0867-4752 Bezpieczenstwo Jadrowe i Ochrona Radiologiczna **7509**
0867-4779 Medicus **5675**
0867-4809 Rrom P-O Drom **3561**
0867-4817 Poland. Glowny Urzad Statystyczny. Przemysl†
0867-4841 Poland. Glowny Urzad Statystyczny. Demografia†
0867-4922 Wilenskie Rozmaitosci **4279**
0867-499X Medycyna Praktyczna **5678**
0867-5007 Metody Komputerowe w Inzynierii Ladowej†
0867-518X Plastyka i Wychowanie w Szkole†
0867-5325 Politechnika Wroclawska. Instytut Technologii Maszyn i Automatyzacji. Prace Naukowe. Monografie†
0867-5376 Tytul **5243**
0867-5392 Principia **6945**
0867-5600 Biblioteka w Szkole **4995**
0867-5708 Przeglad Policyjny **2666**
0867-583X Instytut Spawalnictwa. Biuletyn **6316**
0867-5872 Rota **3079**
0867-5910 Journal of Physiology and Pharmacology **925**
0867-5945 Centrum Naukowo-Techniczne Kolejnictwa. Prace†
0867-6038 Politechnika Slaska. Zeszyty Naukowe. Inzynieria Srodowiska **3460**
0867-6070 Slask Opolski **3930**
0867-6143 Panstwowy Instytut Geologiczny. Biuletyn **2761**
0867-6151 Foto Kurier **6967**
0867-6313 Poland. Glowny Urzad Statystyczny. Praca†
0867-6348 Problemy Terapii Monitorowanej **6115**
0867-6356 Foundation of Computing and Decision Sciences **3291**
0867-6380 Swiat Nauki **7921**
0867-6402 Borussia **4206**
0867-6445 Lithuania **5225**
0867-647X Nowa Krytyka **5231**
0867-6569 Uniwersytet Gdanski. Wydzial Ekonomiki Produkcji. Zeszyty Naukowe. Organizacja i Zarzadzanie†
0867-6585 Sport dla Kazdego
0867-6631 Akademia Gorniczo-Hutnicza. Rozprawy Monografie **6304**
0867-6720 Aero-technika Lotnicza **42**
0867-6747 Kwartalnik Elektroniki i Telekomunikacji **3107**
0867-6798 Poland **1160**
0867-6836 Polska Akademia Nauk. Instytut Geografii i Przestrzennego Zagospodarowania. Zeszyty†
0867-6860 Donosy **3928**
0867-6976 Polish Libraries Today **5039**
0867-7018 Sekrety Mlodosci i Urody†
0867-7026 Business Forum†
0867-7077 Pneumonologia i Alergologia Polska **6217**
0867-7093 Poland. Glowny Urzad Statystyczny. Ochrona Zdrowia†
0867-7255 Przeglad Sadowy **4763**
0867-7298 Cztery Katy **4536**
0867-7352 Auto i Zycie **8558**
0867-7387 Serce i Troska†
0867-7409 Acta Universitatis Wratislaviensis. Politologia **7102**
0867-7433 Orzecznictwo Sadow Apelacyjnych **4958**
0867-7441 Acta Universitatis Wratislaviensis. Literatura i Kultura Popularna **5249**
0867-7468 Przeglad Lesniczy **3700**
0867-7514 Przeglad Podatkowy **1940**

ISSN

0870-0060 Banco de Portugal. Report of the Directors and Economic and Financial Survey **1312**
0870-0133 Evphrosyne **2234**
0870-0141 Classica **2232**
0870-0168 Garcia de Orta: Serie de Antropobiologia†
0870-0206 Revista Lusitana **353**
0870-0214 Associacao de Empresas de Construcao e Obras Publicas do Sul. Industria da Construcao **977**
0870-0230 Farmacia Portuguesa **6841**
0870-0451 Estatisticas dos Transportes e Comunicacoes **8524**
0870-0680 Noticia B A D **5036**
0870-080X Humanistica e Teologia **7648**
0870-0923 Boletim de Estudios Operarios†
0870-094X O Arqueologo Portugues **381**
0870-0974 Bibliotecas, Arquivos e Museus
0870-0990 Antropologia Portuguesa **328**
0870-1059 Instituto dos Produtos Florestais - Cortica. Boletim†
0870-1067 Laboratorio Nacional de Investigacao Veterinaria. Repositorio de Trabalhos **8802**
0870-1121 Medicina Veterinaria **8803**
0870-1164 Corrosao e Proteccao de Materiais **6309**
0870-1199 Efemerides Astronomicas **574**
0870-1253 Ariane **5256**
0870-1326 Universidade Tecnica de Lisboa. Instituto Superior de Economia e Gestao. Estudos de Economia **1187**
0870-1407 Elektor **3097**
0870-1415 Electricista†
0870-1504 Jornal Arquitectos **447**
0870-161X P C World Portugal **2434**
0870-1695 Ciencia Biologica: Ecologia e Sistematica **938**
0870-1717 Pesca e Navegacao†
0870-1741 Recursos Hidricos **2797**
0870-1776 A Bola **8162**
0870-1857 AutoSport **8567**
0870-1865 Avante **7108**
0870-1970 Expresso **1108**
0870-1989 Gazeta dos Desportos **8174**
0870-2004 Fichero Epigrafico **393**
0870-2047 Noticias do Comercio **1431**
0870-2055 Noticias Medicas
0870-2144 Povo Livre **7172**
0870-2179 Record **8196**
0870-2306 Arqueologia **381**
0870-2551 Revista Portuguesa de Cardiologia **5799**
0870-2594 Estado das Culturas e Previsao de Colheitas **108**
0870-2608 Indices da Producao Industrial **6464**
0870-2616 Indice de Precos no Consumidor **1429**
0870-2659 Portugal. Instituto Nacional de Estatistica. Contas Nacionais **1721**
0870-273X Revista A C P **8601**
0870-287X A I P Informacao **1878**
0870-2950 Anuario Climatologico **6346**
0870-3116 Universidade de Lisboa. Faculdade de Direito. Revista
0870-3124 S O D I Livros. Analise **7572**
0870-337X Portugal. Ministerio da Justicia. Boletim **4759**
0870-340X Ciencia e Tecnica Fiscal **1917**
0870-3531 Economia (Lisbon, 1977) **1098**
0870-3701 Cruz Vermelha Portugesa. Boletim de Informacao†
0870-3841 Coloquio: Artes†
0870-3876 Museu Municipal do Funchal. Boletim **956**
0870-3884 Instituto Hidrografico. Anais **8826**
0870-399X Acta Medica Portuguesa **5566**
0870-4104 Clio **4211**
0870-4112 Biblos **5263**
0870-4139 Revista Portuguesa de Filologia **5168**
0870-4147 Revista Portuguesa de Historia **4158**
0870-418X Revista Portuguesa de Pedagogia **2907**
0870-4236 Economista **1102**
0870-4252 Universidade de Coimbra. Faculdade de Direito. Boletim de Ciencias Economicas **1187**
0870-4287 Stoma **5866**
0870-4295 O Medico Veterinario **8803**
0870-4376 Inquerito de Conjuntura ao Investimento **1630**
0870-4406 Estatisticas de Proteccao Social. Associacoes Sindicais e Patronais **8148**
0870-4422 Balancos de Aprovisionamento **8356**
0870-4449 Comunicacoes **2317**
0870-4457 Estudos de Antropologia Cultural e Social **336**
0870-452X Jornal de Letras **5221**
0870-4546 Cultura, Historia e Filosofia **4213**
0870-4600 Boletim de Filologia **5101**
0870-4635 Economia E C **1479**
0870-4643 Economia e Gestao†
0870-4686 Boletim Meteorologico **6347**
0870-4694 Boletim Meteorologico para a Agricultura **6347**
0870-4716 Centro de Fisica da Atmosfera de Lisboa. Boletim **2779**
0870-4724 Projecto I2 do P I D D A C. Boletim **6393**
0870-4732 Resumos Meteorologicos para a Aeronautica†
0870-4740 Boletim Actinometrico de Portugal†
0870-4759 Portugal. Instituto Nacional de Meteorologia e Geofisica. Revista†
0870-4783 Jornal de Psicologia
0870-4805 Investimento e Tecnologia **1631**
0870-4821 Boletim do Trabalho e Emprego 1a Serie **1667**
0870-516X Boletim do Trabalho e Emprego. 2a Serie **1667**
0870-5232 Academia das Ciencias de Lisboa. Boletim†
0870-5259 Livros de Portugal **7566**
0870-5283 Revista Portuguesa de Filosofia **6949**
0870-5291 Nova Seara Nova
0870-533X Portugal. Instituto Nacional de Estatistica. Estatisticas Agricolas **185**
0870-5364 Electricidade **3304**
0870-5429 Vida Rural
0870-5577 Macao. Direccao dos Servicos de Estatistica e Censos. Indice de Precos no Consumidor **1249**
0870-5615 Governo da Regiao Administrativa Especial de Macau. Direccao dos Servicos de Estatistica e Censos. Anuario Estatistico **8374**
0870-5631 Macao. Direccao dos Servicos de Estatistica e Censos. Indice de Precos no Consumidor (Relatorio Anual) **1250**
0870-5658 Macao. Direccao dos Servicos de Estatistica e Censos. Inquerito ao Ensino **2934**
0870-5879 Instituto de Investigacao Cientifica Tropical. Estudos de Historia e Cartografia Antiga - Memorias **4147**
0870-5968 Ingenium **3198**
0870-6018 Economia e Socialismo†
0870-6026 Economia e Sociologia **1479**
0870-6077 Revista de Historia Economica e Social **4158**
0870-6093 Livros Disponiveis (Year) **630**
0870-6182 Ler Historia **4240**
0870-6204 Garcia de Orta: Serie de Antropologia†
0870-6263 Pastagens e Forragens **145**
0870-6336 Universidade de Lisboa. Faculdade de Letras. Revista **5392**
0870-6352 Silva Lusitana **3702**
0870-6425 Cadernos de Arqueologia **385**
0870-6565 Infancia e Juventude **4911**
0870-6581 Arquipelago. Serie Ciencias da Natureza **7837**
0870-6735 Instituto de Investigacao Cientifica Tropical. Centro de Estudos de Historia e Cartografia Antiga. Serie Separatas **4147**
0870-6778 Macau em Numeros **8386**
0870-6794 Africa Hoje **3789**
0870-7081 Revista de Comunicacao e Linguagems **8129**
0870-709X Factos e Ideias
0870-7227 Sociedade Portuguesa de Entomologia. Boletim **859**
0870-7235 Broteria Genetica **864**
0870-7308 Sociedade Portuguesa de Malacologia. Publicacoes Ocasionais **963**
0870-7375 Geonovas **2743**
0870-7618 Broteria **4445**
0870-8002 Documentacao e Direito Comparado **4830**
0870-8118 Ordem dos Advogados. Revista **4753**
0870-8231 Analise Psicologica **7334**
0870-8339 Brigantia **4445**
0870-8355 Arqueologia Industrial **381**
0870-841X Professor **2900**
0870-8436 I C A L P Revista **4456**
0870-8444 Tecnometal **6334**
0870-8487 Revista de Legislacao e de Jurisprudencia **4771**
0870-8584 Estudos Italianos em Portugal **488**
0870-8789 Jornal de Contabilidade **1293**
0870-8924 Atlantis **8782**
0870-8932 Eles & Elas **3931**
0870-8967 Diacritica **5284**
0870-9025 Revista Portuguesa de Saude Publica **7466**
0870-9041 Estudos Italianos em Portugal. Quaderno *see* 0870-8584 **488**
0870-9149 Laboratorio Nacional de Engenharia Civil. Boletim de Informacao Tecnica†
0870-9173 Exportar **1565**
0870-9343 Revista da Armada **6443**
0870-9467 Vida Sovietica **8772**
0870-970X Critica **6912**
0870-9726 Arquivo de Bibliografia Portuguesa†
0870-984X Revista Portuguesa de Engenharia de Estructuras **2789**
0870-9874 Cadernos do Noroeste **7952**
0870-9912 Risco
0870-9939 Cadernos do Povo **5268**
0870-9955 Nos **5343**
0870-9963 Diario da Republica. 1a Serie **3931**
0870-9971 Diario da Republica. 2a Serie **3931**
0870-998X Diario da Republica. 3a Serie **3931**
0871-018X Revista de Ciencias Agrarias **151**
0871-0260 Revista de Etnografia†
0871-0376 Direito e Justica **4659**
0871-0430 Prelo†
0871-0554 Sociedade Portuguesa de Entomologia. Boletim. Suplemento **859**
0871-066X Al Madan **404**
0871-0759 Revista de Guimaraes **4257**
0871-0945 Cadernos de Ciencias Sociais **7952**
0871-102X Accao Socialista **7101**
0871-164X Universidade do Porto. Faculdade de Letras. Historia **4165**
0871-1666 Universidade do Porto. Faculdade de Letras. Geografia **4032**
0871-1682 Universidade do Porto. Faculdade de Letras. Linguas e Literaturas **5190**
0871-1720 Recursos da Pesca. Serie Divulgacao **3605**
0871-1739 Recursos da Pesca. Serie Estatistica **3605**
0871-1747 Instituto de Investigacao Cientifica Tropical. Comunicacoes. Serie de Ciencias da Engenharia Geografica **4015**
0871-1755 Instituto de Investigacao Cientifica Tropical. Comunicacoes. Serie de Ciencias Biologicas **678**
0871-1763 Instituto de Investigacao Cientifica Tropical. Comunicacoes. Serie de Ciencias Agrarias **122**
0871-178X Instituto de Investigacao Cientifica Tropical. Comunicacoes. Serie de Ciencias Etnologicas e Etnomuseologicas **3540**
0871-1798 Instituto de Investigacao Cientifica Tropical. Comunicacoes. Serie de Ciencias da Terra **2710**
0871-2336 Africana **7945**
0871-2344 Revista Internacional de Estudos Africanos **4177**
0871-2549 Skin Cancer **6034**
0871-2743 Nummus **6652**
0871-2778 Universidade Nova de Lisboa. Faculdade de Ciencias Sociais e Humanas. Revista **8012**
0871-326X Portugaliae Zoologica **960**
0871-3316 Portugal. Comissao para a Igualdade e Direitos das Mulheres. Noticias **8880**
0871-3413 Arquivos de Medicina **5578**
0871-3529 Geociencias **2736**
0871-3715 Claro. Escuro **482**
0871-4304 Arquivos de Reumatologia e Doencas Osted Articulares†
0871-4320 Vida Economica **1191**
0871-4657 Psychologica **7396**
0871-4673 Acata Medica Portugesa. Supplement *see* 0870-399X **5566**
0871-4835 Organizacoes e Trabalho **8124**
0871-4843 Museu Bocage. Arquivos **956**
0871-4932 Marketing e Publicidade **29**
0871-5157 Informacao Industrial
0871-5386 Geriatria **4045**
0871-5424 Gaia **2707**
0871-5742 Tecnologia Qualidade **6334**
0871-5955 Recursos da Pesca. Serie Estudos **3605**
0871-6153 Automotor **8566**
0871-6161 Personal Computer World *changed to* PC Guia **2582**
0871-6188 Hi-Fi **8153**
0871-6196 Nursing **5972**
0871-620X Update **5727**
0871-6218 Semana Informatica **2538**
0871-6412 Educacao **2845**
0871-6595 Airo **901**
0871-6625 P C Magazine (Portuguese Edition) **2580**
0871-7338 Informacao Economica **1491**
0871-7362 T V Guia **2392**
0871-7478 Guimaraes. Arquivo Municipal "Alfredo Pimenta." Boletim de Trabalhos Historicos **4225**
0871-7486 Penelope **4253**
0871-7494 Argumento
0871-7516 Cadernos de Consulta Psicologica **7343**
0871-780X Keramica **1019**
0871-7958 Educacao Medica **5608**
0871-8032 Portugal. Instituto Nacional de Estatistica. Inquerito ao Ganho dos Trabalhadores Agricolas **185**
0871-8563 Revista Portuguesa de Ciencia Criminal **4897**
0871-858X Infeccao Hospitalar **5816**
0871-8598 Jornal do Exercito **6429**
0871-8679 Selecoes do Reader's Digest (Portuguese Edition) **3931**
0871-8709 Caracterizacao das Empresas Portuguesas†
0871-8717 Portugal Social **7291**
0871-8725 Portugal em Numeros **8394**
0871-8733 Portugal in Figures *see* 0871-8725 **8394**
0871-8741 Anuario Estatistico de Portugal **8346**
0871-875X Estudos Demograficos **7306**
0871-8822 Jornal das Ciencias Medicas†
0871-8997 Indicadores da Producao Animal **181**
0871-9004 Indicadores da Producao Vegetal **181**
0871-9101 Portugal. Instituto Nacional de Estatistica. Inquerito as Ferias dos Portugueses **3621**
0871-9144 Indice do Comercio Externo **1569**
0871-9152 Precos e Rendimentos na Agricultura **185**
0871-9187 Revista Portuguesa de Educacao **2907**
0871-9292 Portugal. Instituto Nacional de Estatistica. Indicador Trimestral da Pesca†
0871-9365 Relatorio Mensal de Economia **1514**
0871-9519 Dedalus **5283**
0871-9535 Portugal. Instituto Nacional de Estatistica. Contas Economicas da Silvicultura **3709**
0871-9799 Portugal. Comissao para a Igualdade e Direitos das Mulheres. Informacao Bibliografica†
0871-9969 Estatisticas da Construcao de Edificios **1046**
0872-0223 Kompass Portugal **2011**
0872-0738 Discursos **4450**
0872-0754 Nascer e Crescer **6097**
0872-0835 Forum Canonicum **4677**
0872-1521 Inquerito Mensal de Conjuntura a Construcao e Obras Publicas **7481**
0872-1602 Contas Nacionais Trimestrais **1718**
0872-1653 Vipasca **423**
0872-1688 Semanario Economico **1172**
0872-1696 Diario Economico **1092**
0872-1769 Queirosiana **5356**
0872-1866 Exame **1885**
0872-1904 Portugaliae Electrochimica Acta **2114**
0872-1912 Ceramicas **2039**
0872-1920 Videosom†
0872-1998 Associacao dos Municipios do Distrito de Setubal. Revista **2827**
0872-2226 Arquivos Portugueses de Cirurgia **6237**
0872-2250 Arqueologia Medieval **381**
0872-2293 Producao Profissional **2388**
0872-2331 Medicamento, Historia e Sociedade **6860**
0872-2560 Museu Municipal do Funchal. Boletim. Suplemento *see* 0870-3876 **956**
0872-2692 Video Guia†
0872-279X Sete†
0872-315X Instituto de Investigacao Cientifica Tropical. Index Seminum Quae Hortus et Musaeum Agricolum Tropicum **3755**
0872-3168 Instituto de Investigacao Cientifica Tropical. Anuario de Actividades†
0872-3303 Manchete **5226**
0872-3400 AutoMais **8685**
0872-3419 Universidade do Porto. Faculdade de Letras. Sociologia **8145**
0872-3540 Visao **3931**
0872-3559 T V Mais **2393**
0872-3664 Eborensia **7639**
0872-3672 Sociedade Portuguesa de Matematica. Boletim **5537**
0872-3893 Intercompreensao **5128**
0872-3915 Quadrante **5527**
0872-4059 Facultade de Medicina. Revista **5613**
0872-4237 Macao. Direccao dos Servicos de Estatistica e Censos. Relatorio de Actividades **8386**
0872-4296 Instituto Camoes. Boletim. **5128**
0872-4482 Macao. Direccao dos Servicos de Estatistica e Censos. Estatisticas Demograficas **7311**
0872-458X Espaco **6985**
0872-4733 Notas Economicas **1502**
0872-5284 Estudos de Gestao **1742**
0872-5292 Acta Parasitologica Portuguesa **880**
0872-5632 Universidade de Coimbra. Boletim do Arquivo **5052**
0872-5675 Romanica **5364**
0872-5969 Estatisticas dos Transportes Rodoviarios de Passageiros e de Mercadorias **8524**
0872-6515 Ragazza (Lisbon) **2210**
0872-6620 Vaquiero - Saberes e Sabores **3666**
0872-671X Medicina Interna **5947**
0872-7023 Sexualidade e Planeamento Familiar **8132**
0872-7554 Ordem dos Farmaceuticos. Revista **6865**
0872-7570 Estatisticas do Emprego **1960**

ISSN

Link to your serials resources and content with ulrichsweb.com

9364 0872-7643 ULRICH'S PERIODICALS

0872-7643 Educacao, Sociedade & Culturas **2845**
0872-8178 Jornal Portugues de Gastrenterologia **5927**
0872-8224 Associacao dos Antigos Alunos do Colegio Militar. Revista **6412**
0872-8402 Sabado **3931**
0872-8429 Arqueologia & Industria **381**
0872-8496 Euro Asia Journal of Management **1106**
0872-8844 Sinais Vitais **5715**
0872-8852 Journal of Blood Rheology†
0872-8879 Estatisticas das Empresas. Industria **1227**
0872-9123 Instituto Portugues de Investigacao Maritima. Relatorios Cientificos e Tecnicos **7866**
0872-9131 Instituto Portugues de Investigacao Maritima. Boletim†
0872-914X Instituto Portugues de Investigacao Maritima. Publicacoes Avulsas†
0872-9298 Estatisticas da Producao Industrial **1227**
0872-9301 Indicadores de Conforto das Familias **4436**
0872-962X Offarm **6865**
0872-9662 Comportamento Organizacional e Gestao **7348**
0872-9786 Bank of Portugal. Economic Bulletin *see* 0872-9794 **1440**
0872-9794 Banco de Portugal. Boletim Economico **1440**
0873-0423 B M J (Portuguese Edition) *see* 0959-535X **5582**
0873-0687 Estatisticas do Comercio Internacional **1227**
0873-092X Comercio Extracomunitario **1221**
0873-1152 Engenharia Civil UM **3266**
0873-1233 Via Spiritus **7822**
0873-1632 Comunicacao Empresarial **1734**
0873-1861 Populacao e Sociedade **7289**
0873-2159 Revista Portuguesa de Pneumologia **6219**
0873-237X Relatorio do Estado do Ordenamento do Territorio†
0873-2949 Revista Portuguesa de Marketing **1841**
0873-2981 O Apicultor **92**
0873-3317 Ajuda a Igreja Que Sofre. Boletim *see* 0252-2527 **7796**
0873-3317 Ajuda a Igreja Que Sofre. Boletim *see* 0252-2535 **7807**
0873-3570 Elle (Lisbon) **8860**
0873-366X Intercambio **5128**
0873-3996 Ego **6288**
0873-4410 Prospectiva e Planeamento **1513**
0873-4569 Revista Portuguesa de Ortodoncia **5864**
0873-464X Revista de Educacao Especial e Reabilitacao **3046**
0873-4704 Arquipelago - Life and Marine Sciences **654**
0873-4798 Exame Informatica **1416**
0873-4801 100 por Cento Jovem **2224**
0873-4976 Psicologia (Braga) **7392**
0873-5301 Farmacia Distribuicao **6841**
0873-5379 DrugNet Europe **2693**
0873-5387 *see* 0873-5379 **2693**
0873-5395 *see* 0873-5379 **2693**
0873-5409 *see* 0873-5379 **2693**
0873-5522 Universidade Tecnica de Lisboa. Faculdade de Medicina Veterinaria. Anais **8809**
0873-5921 Povos e Culturas **7291**
0873-612X Revista de Psiquiatria Consiliar e de Ligacao **6182**
0873-6243 Liga **6158**
0873-626X Disputatio **6914**
0873-6308 Sociedade e Territorio **8135**
0873-6316 A Grande Ilusao
0873-6324 Estatisticas das Receitas Fiscais **1227**
0873-6529 Sociologia **8135**
0873-6561 Etnografica **338**
0873-6650 Politica Internacional **7260**
0873-7037 Kiss me!
0873-7045 Leituras **5025**
0873-7339 Casa e Campo
0873-7444 Economia Global e Gestao **1740**
0873-7630 Revista Militar†
0873-7886 Mundo Motorizado
0873-7894 Mundo Nautico†
0873-8025 Vert **8339**
0873-819X Antropologicas **328**
0873-8904 Pensar Enfermagem **5977**
0873-9129 Revista Portuguesa de Psicanalise **7405**
0873-948X Portugal. Instituto Geologico e Mineiro. Comunicacoes *changed to* Portugal. Instituto Geologico e Mineiro. Comunicacoes Geologicas **2762**
0873-9498 Instituto Geologico e Mineiro. Memorias **2710**
0873-9749 Acta Ethologica **929**
0873-9781 Acta Pediatrica Portuguesa **6087**
0873-9811 Portugal em Numeros. Situacao Socio-Economica **8395**
0873-982X Portugal. Economic and Social Indicators *see* 0873-9811 **8395**
0874-0070 A Pessoa como Centro **7391**
0874-0283 Referencia **5979**
0874-0321 Revista Portuguesa de Humanidades **4472**
0874-0437 Episteme **6916**
0874-0453 Activa **8850**
0874-047X Caras **3931**
0874-0488 Caras Decoracao **4534**
0874-050X Casa Claudia **4534**
0874-0526 Executive Digest†
0874-0534 Turbo **8608**
0874-0542 Auto Guia **8558**
0874-0569 Barbie **2178**
0874-0593 Disney Especial **2185**
0874-0607 Tio Patinhas **2217**
0874-0623 Pato Donald **2206**
0874-0801 Estudos do Quaternario **2707**
0874-1123 Arquivos da Memoria **3519**
0874-2049 Psicologia (Lisbon) **7392**
0874-2375 Africana Studia **7946**
0874-2391 Psicologia, Educacao e Cultura **7393**
0874-2677 Journal of Iberian Archaeology **401**
0874-2731 A B O **5933**
0874-3479 Enologia **603**
0874-372X Revista de Vinhos **609**
0874-4416 Museu Bocage. Publicacoes Avulsas **7884**
0874-4696 Revista Portuguesa de Psicossomatica **7405**
0874-4769 E A N Portugal **6401**
0874-4955 Mensageiro do Coracao de Jesus **7662**
0874-4963 O Clarim **2182**
0874-4971 Vida em Testemunho **7692**
0874-498X Oracao e Vida **2206**
0874-4998 Magnificant **7661**
0874-5161 Investigacao Operacional **2427**
0874-5498 Agora **5250**
0874-5560 Ex Aequo **8896**
0874-5846 Mar (Lisboa) **8651**
0874-6230 Erzats **6966**
0874-6540 GeoInova **4012**
0874-6885 Revista Faces de Eva. Estudos Sobre a Mulher **8902**
0874-7016 Radioproteccao **7072**
0874-7695 Revista Investigacao em Enfermagem **5980**
0874-8438 Bulletin of Portuguese-Japanese Studies **4180**
0874-8799 Politecnica **2998**
0874-8810 Observatorio **2335**
0874-9019 Robotica. Automacao, Controlo e Instrumentacao **3394**
0874-9035 Portugalia Acta Biologica, Sistematica, Ecologia, Biogeografia Paleontologia, Morfologia, Fisiologia, Genetica e Biologia Geral **698**
0874-9329 *see* Liberpolis **5025**
0882-0074 Fodor's Boston **8704**
0882-0104 Data General Micro World†
0882-0139 Immunological Investigations **5759**
0882-0147 Fertilizer Technology†
0882-0171 The Ardell Wellness Report†
0882-018X Rundy's Journal and Confederation Courier **8244**
0882-0228 Selections (Los Angeles)†
0882-0236 D O S S U Journal **6894**
0882-0325 Pravda†
0882-0368 Jazz Festivals International Directory†
0882-0384 Texas League Savings Account†
0882-0422 Genealogical Clearinghouse Quarterly†
0882-0430 Life Rates & Data†
0882-0465 Grayson Gateway†
0882-0481 Fitness Management **6986**
0882-049X Signature (Priairie Village)†
0882-052X Seminars in Orthopaedics†
0882-0538 Seminars in Ophthalmology **6051**
0882-0546 Seminars in Respiratory Infections†
0882-0554 New England Sampler
0882-0589 Martin Brower's Orange County Report **1431**
0882-0635 Tennessee Ancestors **3784**
0882-0643 Black Resource Guide **3523**
0882-066X Widener Review†
0882-0732 Notable Books†
0882-0783 Journal of Police and Criminal Psychology **2657**
0882-0880 Advances in Dermatology **5871**
0882-0910 Women and Work (Newbury Park) **1715**
0882-0929 California Chamber of Commerce Alert **1397**
0882-0937 V I T A News†
0882-0945 Buddhist - Christian Studies **7700**
0882-1046 The Journal of Contemporary Health Law and Policy **5648**
0882-1100 S P E Monograph Series **2908**
0882-1127 American Journalism **4571**
0882-1135 Women's Quarterly Review†
0882-116X L F L Reports **973**
0882-1178 Treasure Chest News **3785**
0882-1232 Journal of Curriculum and Supervision†
0882-1240 Dimensions: A Journal of Holocaust Studies **4137**
0882-1275 National Spiritualist **7665**
0882-133X Physician's Legal Alert†
0882-1372 Volleyball Rules Book **8251**
0882-1410 Artificial Intelligence Abstracts (US)†
0882-1429 Telecommunications Abstracts†
0882-1437 C A D - C A M Abstracts†
0882-1445 Public Technology†
0882-1453 Computer Security Digest
0882-1461 Telephone Selling Report **1845**
0882-147X Morning Coffee Chapbook Series†
0882-1496 Market Moves
0882-1526 Design Horizons†
0882-1577 Health Progress **4096**
0882-1623 Genealogical Gems **3767**
0882-1658 Zone (Waverly)†
0882-1666 Systems and Computers in Japan **2439**
0882-1674 Trident - Visnyk **6900**
0882-1720 Tele
0882-178X Option Magazine†
0882-1852 Biological Therapies in Dentistry **5836**
0882-1860 Directory of Dental Educators†
0882-1879 Island Properties Report
0882-1925 Flash (Chicago)†
0882-1933 Olschwanger Journal†
0882-1968 North American Culture†
0882-1984 Marine Equipment Catalog **8651**
0882-1992 Crain's Detroit Business **1088**
0882-200X Computer & Electronics Graduate†
0882-2042 Chicora Foundation Research Series **4288**
0882-2050 Merlyn's Pen†
0882-2085 Annual Organ Handbook **6545**
0882-2123 Ambassador Report†
0882-214X The Pitch Pipe **6606**
0882-2158 Traces (Glasgow) **3785**
0882-2190 Schabacker Investment Management. Weekly Advisory Bulletin†
0882-228X Magazine of History **4152**
0882-2301 The Child's Doctor (Print) *changed to* The Child's Doctor (Online) **6089**
0882-2360 Current Contents Address Directory - Science & Technology†
0882-2379 Current Contents Address Directory - Social Sciences, Arts & Humanities†
0882-2425 A Lot of Bunkum Yearbook **3757**
0882-245X National Foundation for Advancement in the Arts. Annual Report **508**
0882-2506 American Psychiatric Association. Biographical Directory†
0882-2514 Frost on the Vine
0882-2522 American Native Press†
0882-2549 The Duplex Planet **3616**
0882-2573 Kane's Beverage Week *changed to* 1556-6250
0882-2611 Technology Reimbursement Reports: The Beige Sheet†
0882-2689 Journal of Psychopathology and Behavioral Assessment **7379**
0882-2719 California Veckoblad **3524**
0882-2743 Contents of Periodicals on Latin America†
0882-2751 I A S News†
0882-276X D A R Systems International's White Paper Series in Computer Programming†
0882-2786 International Journal of Oral & Maxillofacial Implants **5849**
0882-2816 Poodle Variety **6814**
0882-2840 The A L A N Review **3049**
0882-2859 Buffalo Business Journal **1069**
0882-2921 Faces Rocks **6566**
0882-3006 Oesterreich in Amerikanischer Sicht **7990**
0882-3014 Systems Research and Information Science†
0882-3030 Folio (Brockport) **4452**
0882-3049 Cultura Ludens†
0882-3073 Corporate Finance Letter†
0882-3103 Peterson's Guide to Colleges in the Southwest (Year)†
0882-3111 MediaSource†
0882-312X Rangel's Reports **7261**
0882-3138 Research in Finance. Supplement **1378**
0882-3154 Western Reserve Historical Society News **4318**
0882-3189 Pitts Choice†
0882-3197 Savings Institutions Sourcebook†
0882-3219 Virginia Industrial Directory **2033**
0882-3294 Micrographics and Optical Storage Equipment Review†
0882-3316 Emerging Patterns of Work and Communications in an Information Age† **8953**
0882-3332 Pipe & Quill
0882-3340 Atari Explorer†
0882-3383 Santa Clara Computer and High Technology Law Journal **4779**
0882-3405 Index to Periodical Literature on Aging
0882-3421 California Pediatrician†
0882-3472 Attitude: The Dancers' Magazine **2682**
0882-3499 Soft - Letter **2597**
0882-3510 Social Marketing Update **8069**
0882-3588 Arc†
0882-3634 Marker **6159**
0882-3685 Pennsylvania Genealogical Magazine **3779**
0882-3693 Central Texas Archeologist†
0882-3715 Finest Hour **4139**
0882-3723 Fourth World Journal **7206**
0882-3731 The Right of Aesthetic Realism to Be Known **4473**
0882-374X Snake River Echoes **4312**
0882-3758 Thermology†
0882-3766 Government Research Directory **8423**
0882-3804 The Letter Exchange
0882-3812 Natural Resources & Environment **3455**
0882-3820 Clean Yield†
0882-3944 Monitor (Arlington)†
0882-3995 Business Computer Digest & Software Review†
0882-4010 Microbial Pathogenesis **5823**
0882-4037 Inactive or Discontinued Items from the 1950 Revision of the Classified List†
0882-4045 List of Classes of United States Government Publications Available for Selection by Depository Libraries **5059**
0882-4096 Communication Research Reports **8094**
0882-4126 Higher Education **2984**
0882-4142 Ivy Journal **3739**
0882-4150 Hamersky & Allied Families Newsletter†
0882-4266 Mountain Empire Genealogical Quarterly **3775**
0882-4274 American Conference of Governmental Industrial Hygienists. Transactions of the Annual Meeting†
0882-4347 Applied Orgonometry **7836**
0882-4371 Cultural Critique **334**
0882-438X A M S Studies in Education **2822**
0882-4401 Nautical Brass†
0882-4428 Bean Home Newsletter **5260**
0882-4460 Chocolate Singles†
0882-4606 Kosmon Voice **7738**
0882-4630 N A S F A A Newsletter **2994**
0882-4657 Exercise for Men Only **6985**
0882-4681 Corporate Times†
0882-4711 Export Today *changed to* 1530-8472 **1564**
0882-472X What's Line **5055**
0882-4738 Utah. Division of Administrative Rules. Utah State Bulletin **7475**
0882-4746 Good Stuff (Grand Forks) **5011**
0882-4843 Feminist Teacher **3062**
0882-4894 High Plains Applied Anthropologist **340**
0882-4959 I E E E Translation Journal on Magnetics in Japan†
0882-5017 C E A Voice *changed to* The Voice (Columbus) **2925**
0882-5181 Caquelin Chronicle†
0882-5289 Business News (Westford)
0882-5297 Afro-American Culture and Society Monograph Series **3517**
0882-5300 C A A S Special Publication Series **3524**
0882-5394 Hadronic Journal. Supplement **7014**
0882-5424 Tapori **2216**
0882-5440 Emerging & Special Situations†
0882-5491 Arkansas Archeological Survey. Publications on Archeology. Research Series **380**
0882-5505 The Franchise Handbook **1961**
0882-5521 Taft Nonprofit Executive†
0882-553X SportSearch†
0882-5572 Arizona Wildlife Views **2603**
0882-5637 Federal Career Insights†
0882-5645 Topics in Pain Management **5723**
0882-5726 Data Broadcasting Report
0882-5734 Flavour and Fragrance Journal **2123**
0882-5793 Federation Review†
0882-5807 Economic Trends (Chicago)†
0882-5823 Restaurant Review **4397**
0882-584X Urban Wildlife Manager's Notebook†
0882-5858 Urban Wildlife News†
0882-5866 Academic Talent†
0882-5874 Durch die Fensterscheibe **3764**
0882-5882 Heller Helper **3770**
0882-5890 Schartzer - Schertzer Connection†

Link to your serials resources and content with ulrichsweb.com

0882-5904 Schneider Connections **3782**
0882-5939 Sloane Report†
0882-5955 Constitution (Washington)†
0882-5963 Journal of Pediatric Nursing **5966**
0882-5971 Georgia Trend **1349**
0882-598X Health Letter (Washington) **5625**
0882-5998 The Year Book of Hematology†
0882-6072 Hypnosis Reports
0882-6099 Luna City Press†
0882-6110 Advances in Accounting **1279**
0882-6129 Advances in Geophysical Data Processing†
0882-6145 Advances in Group Processes **8085**
0882-6188 Ground Water Monitor†
0882-6196 Reading Plus **6946**
0882-6218 Barnard's Retail Marketing Report **1806**
0882-6250 Employment Alert†
0882-6323 Ober Income Letter†
0882-6366 Workers' Advocate Supplement†
0882-6382 New & Emerging Technology†
0882-6447 Caduceus†
0882-648X Bogg **5418**
0882-6501 Avotaynu **7718**
0882-651X Bugeye Times **6521**
0882-6528 St. Clair County Genealogical Society Quarterly **3781**
0882-6595 Blacfax **3522**
0882-6617 Mayo Clinical Update **5665**
0882-6633 Heliport Development Guide **8544**
0882-6706 Prairie Scout
0882-6714 American Academy of Matrimonial Lawyers. Journal **4906**
0882-6757 Reaper†
0882-6773 Newkirk Notes†
0882-6803 Latin Travel Review
0882-6838 Art to Zoo **6520**
0882-6846 C R I A R L Newsletter **4999**
0882-6951 Cutting Edge Quarterly (Ann Arbor)†
0882-696X Guthrie Journal **5622**
0882-7036 Preaching **7671**
0882-7044 Bio-Bibliographies in Afro-American and African Studies† **8936**
0882-7052 Bio-Bibliographies in Law and Political Science† **8936**
0882-7095 D D R Studien **4137**
0882-7133 Annual DeGarmo Lectures **2966**
0882-7141 Society of Professors of Education. Occasional Papers **2913**
0882-715X Preservation Law Reporter **454**
0882-7214 United Church News **7778**
0882-7249 Facilities Manager **3022**
0882-7311 Stalker **3784**
0882-7370 Threads **6642**
0882-7400 Published†
0882-7419 Powertechnics Magazine
0882-7427 Virginia Institute of Marine Science, Gloucester Point. Special Report in Applied Marine Science and Ocean Engineering **2820**
0882-7451 Bridal Guide **5556**
0882-7508 Mineral Processing and Extractive Metallurgy Review **6326**
0882-7516 Active and Passive Electronic Components **3294**
0882-7524 Topics in Geriatric Rehabilitation **4057**
0882-7672 Rowe Historical Society. Bulletin **4311**
0882-7753 Rehabilitation R & D Progress Reports **6443**
0882-7826 Drug Abuse and Drug Abuse Research **2693**
0882-7842 California Family Law Monthly **4907**
0882-7850 Magill's Literary Annual: History and Biography†
0882-7893 Journal of Interpretation (Rockville) **4075**
0882-7907 Hurricane Alice **8868**
0882-7958 Advanced Materials & Processes **3335**
0882-7974 Psychology and Aging **4053**
0882-7982 Yarn Market News†
0882-8016 Ward's Business Directory of Major International Companies†
0882-8024 A S H S Newsletter **3721**
0882-8040 Online International Command Chart **2433**
0882-8059 Intermodal Reporter†
0882-8067 New Accountant **1297**
0882-8075 Node†
0882-8121 Mathematical Geology *changed to* 1874-8961 **2754**
0882-8156 Weather and Forecasting **6398**
0882-8180 Kick
0882-8202 Barron Family Newsletter **3759**
0882-8245 Viral Immunology **5766**
0882-8253 Advertising Career Directory†
0882-8261 Book Publishing Career Directory†
0882-8288 Public Relations Career Directory†
0882-8377 G A S Lites†
0882-8415 Software Developer's Monthly
0882-8431 A R P E News†
0882-8458 Women's Travel Connections†
0882-8466 Lacan Study Notes†
0882-8512 Freethought Today **6921**
0882-8520 Youth Law News **4817**
0882-8539 Shofar (Ashland) **7729**
0882-8571 Arts Calendar Quarterly
0882-8598 Get - Two - Gether **7943**
0882-861X Engineering Literature Guides **3190**
0882-8644 Philippine Report†
0882-8652 Hypnotherapy Today **5943**
0882-8679 Quarterly Report†
0882-8768 Play It Safe†
0882-8849 Texas A & M Business Forum†
0882-8857 Civilian Manpower Statistics **1221**
0882-889X Metabolic, Pediatric and Systemic Ophthalmology **6046**
0882-8938 Overseas Living
0882-9004 M A R A D (Year) **8651**
0882-9020 Osprey's Seafood Newsletter†
0882-908X F L I C C Newsletter **5009**
0882-9098 Patent and Trademark Office Society. Journal **6755**
0882-9136 Compilation of State and Federal Privacy Laws **4647**
0882-9144 Real Estate Analysis and Planning Service **7608**
0882-9187 Miniatures Dealer†
0882-9225 Pediatric Reviews and Communications†
0882-9233 Surgical Research Communications†
0882-9268 College Marketing Alert†
0882-9284 Agricultural Computing†
0882-9292 Agri-Naturalist **82**
0882-9314 Performance†
0882-9365 A A H S Journal **40**
0882-9438 Florida Manufacturers Register **1995**
0882-9454 Industrial Development in the Tennessee Valley Region†
0882-956X Accounting Education News **1277**
0882-9624 P O A **8295**
0882-9640 Silent Sports **8201**
0882-9659 New Ways (Evanston)†
0882-9667 N S I Advisory **2679**
0882-9691 Wheat Grower†
0882-9802 Kinship Kronicle **3773**
0882-987X Chamberlain Association News
0883-0029 Aegis: Magazine on Ending Violence against Women†
0883-0053 Ex Auditu **7642**
0883-0061 Keeper's Log **4150**
0883-0126 Red Bass
0883-0142 Amaranth Today†
0883-0185 International Reviews of Immunology **5761**
0883-0215 New Menorah
0883-0231 Europe for Travelers!†
0883-024X Anthropology of Work Review **327**
0883-0266 Monthly Prescribing Reference **6862**
0883-0355 International Journal of Educational Research **2869**
0883-0371 Pharmacist's Letter **6871**
0883-038X Airlines†
0883-0398 Alaska Seas and Coasts†
0883-0452 HealthSpan†
0883-0487 Letter of Credit Update *changed to* 1520-0221 **1092**
0883-0568 Alaska Law Review **4612**
0883-0576 Toxic Substances Control Act: Report to Congress for Fiscal Year **3501**
0883-072X American Intelligence Journal **6410**
0883-0738 Journal of Child Neurology **6150**
0883-0754 Experimental Musical Instruments†
0883-0762 Health Care Instrumentation†
0883-0797 Just Cross Stitch **6639**
0883-0908 Stress and Coping†
0883-0940 Cloud Family Journal **3762**
0883-0975 Directory of American Fulbright Scholars†
0883-1033 Baseball Illustrated (Year) **8222**
0883-105X American Studies International†
0883-1084 Professional Insurance Agents of New Jersey **4519**
0883-1092 Professional Insurance Agents of Connecticut **4519**
0883-1157 Romance Quarterly **5364**
0883-1173 About Alfords†
0883-1181 Chapman Chatter†
0883-119X The Wise Woman **8889**
0883-1270 Soviet-American Debate†
0883-1289 Human Sexuality†
0883-1297 Legal Information Alert **5025**
0883-1300 S C P Journal **7679**
0883-1319 S C P Newsletter **7679**
0883-1327 Edutech Report **3022**
0883-1351 Palaios **6728**
0883-1378 Journal of Inferential and Deductive Biology†
0883-1424 Computer Aided Publishing Report†
0883-1475 Sida: Botanical Miscellany **817**
0883-1513 Heritage: The Yorker Scene *see* 8755-9064 **4294**
0883-153X Polymer Contents **3233**
0883-1548 New York State Museum. Biennial Report **6534**
0883-1580 Sports Periodicals Index†
0883-1599 Temblor
0883-1661 Investment Portfolio Guide **1633**
0883-1718 Character II (Chicago)†
0883-1858 Annual Systems and Processing Salaries Report†
0883-1874 Pediatric Asthma, Allergy & Immunology **6100**
0883-1890 Entertainment Magazine (Print)†
0883-1947 U.S. Congressional Record (Permanent Edition) *see* 0363-7239 **7118**
0883-1963 Consumer Health and Nutrition Index†
0883-2102 A P I Account **1275**
0883-2285 Hemochromatosis Awareness†
0883-2293 Person-Centered Review†
0883-2323 Journal of Education for Business **1136**
0883-2331 Old Westbury Review†
0883-2390 AmigaWorld†
0883-2404 American Academy of Advertising. Proceedings of the Conference **20**
0883-2455 Entertainment Law & Finance **4666**
0883-2463 Birnbaum's South America **8687**
0883-2471 Hawaii (Year) **8717**
0883-2498 Europe (Year) **8702**
0883-2501 United States (Year) **8770**
0883-251X U S A for Business Travelers **8770**
0883-2560 Spec - Com Journal
0883-265X Stanford Business School Magazine *changed to* 1094-5423 **2301**
0883-2668 Shoe Tree†
0883-2676 Organic Coatings Science and Technology†
0883-2692 Clark Clarion **3762**
0883-2714 Working Age Newsletter†
0883-2773 Venture Capital Journal **1658**
0883-2781 Collage (New Cumberland)†
0883-282X Spectrum (Olathe) **5048**
0883-2838 Collective Bargaining Contract Clauses†
0883-2870 U.S. Department of Agriculture. National Agricultural Statistics Service. Citrus Fruits **187**
0883-2919 World Englishes **5196**
0883-2927 Applied Geochemistry **2724**
0883-2935 Journal of Applied Cardiology†
0883-296X M B M (New York)
0883-3087 G D G Report
0883-3141 Steelabor *changed to* 1931-6658 **4604**
0883-315X Information Center†
0883-3311 N R C T L D Direct Radiation Monitoring Network **7069**
0883-3370 Federal Benefits for Veterans and Dependents **6421**
0883-3389 Renota Rosaldo Lecture Series Monograph **4310**
0883-3397 Small Business Sourcebook **1967**
0883-3419 Future Reflections **4081**
0883-3451 American Institute of Certified Public Accountants. Tax Division Newsletter **1910**
0883-3532 Editing History **4291**
0883-3605 Morgan Migrations **3775**
0883-3648 Notre Dame Journal of Law, Ethics & Public Policy **7457**
0883-3656 Advances in Applied Social Psychology†
0883-3664 Odysseus **8742**
0883-3680 Material Culture
0883-3753 Governments of Alabama **7440**
0883-3761 Governments of Arkansas **7440**
0883-377X Governments of California **7440**
0883-3788 Governments of Colorado **7441**
0883-3796 Governments of Connecticut **7441**
0883-380X Governments of Florida **7441**
0883-3818 Governments of Georgia **7441**
0883-3826 Governments of Illinois **7441**
0883-3834 Governments of Indiana **7441**
0883-3842 Governments of Iowa **7441**
0883-3850 Governments of Kansas **7441**
0883-3869 Governments of Kentucky **7441**
0883-3877 Governments of Louisiana **7441**
0883-3885 Governments of Maine **7441**
0883-3893 Governments of Massachusetts **7441**
0883-3907 Governments of Michigan **7441**
0883-3915 Governments of Minnesota **7441**
0883-3923 Governments of Mississippi **7441**
0883-3931 Governments of Missouri **7441**
0883-394X Governments of Nebraska **7441**
0883-3958 Governments of New Jersey **7441**
0883-3966 Governments of New York **7441**
0883-3974 Governments of North Dakota **7441**
0883-3982 Governments of Ohio **7441**
0883-3990 Governments of Oklahoma **7441**
0883-4008 Governments of Pennsylvania **7441**
0883-4016 Governments of South Dakota **7441**
0883-4024 Governments of Tennessee **7442**
0883-4032 Governments of Texas **7442**
0883-4040 Governments of Vermont **7442**
0883-4059 Governments of Virginia **7442**
0883-4067 Governments of Washington **7442**
0883-4075 Governments of West Virginia **7442**
0883-4083 Governments of Wisconsin **7442**
0883-4091 Governments of the Carolinas **7442**
0883-4105 Governments of the Northwest **7442**
0883-4113 Governments of the West **7442**
0883-4121 Governments of the Northeast **7442**
0883-4202 Cybernetic†
0883-4237 Statistical Science **8404**
0883-430X WalkWays†
0883-4334 Bay Windows **4371**
0883-4350 Computing for Business†
0883-4423 California Wine Winners **601**
0883-4431 Gun Traders Guide **8176**
0883-4539 American Association of Textile Chemists and Colorists. Technical Manual (Year) **8448**
0883-4555 Consumer Finance Law Quarterly Report **4649**
0883-458X Gas Turbine World Handbook **3136**
0883-4660 Traditional Home **4551**
0883-4687 Foreign Trade Fairs New Products Newsletter **1566**
0883-4725 Current Titles in Ocean, Coastal, Lake & Waterway Sciences†
0883-475X Scholastic Choices **3080**
0883-4881 Computer (Scottsdale) **2411**
0883-489X Camera (Year) **6965**
0883-4938 Urologist's Sportslife†
0883-4970 Forum (Santa Rosa) **7644**
0883-5330 Directory of Biomedical and Health Care Grants **3020**
0883-5365 Oral Tradition (Print)†
0883-5381 Healthcare Executive **4097**
0883-5403 Journal of Arthroplasty **6063**
0883-5462 Green Magazine (Bee) **3734**
0883-5470 Poet's Market **5432**
0883-5500 North East Linguistic Society. Proceedings **5156**
0883-5519 Combustion Science and Technology Book Series **2134**
0883-5527 World Biolicensing Report†
0883-556X Madden Family Newsletter **3774**
0883-5608 Personal Identification News
0883-5640 Phi Sigma Iota Forum **5160**
0883-5667 Church **7792**
0883-5675 Approved Crossword Puzzles. Special Issue
0883-5683 Computer Pictures†
0883-5691 Topics in Clinical Nutrition **6670**
0883-5772 Software Industry Bulletin
0883-5799 Washington Trooper **2671**
0883-5810 A T H A Newsletter†
0883-5845 News About Library Services for the Blind and Physically Handicapped **4068**
0883-5926 Allees All Around **3758**
0883-5977 Computer Industry Digest†
0883-5993 Journal of Thoracic Imaging **6201**
0883-6000 Emory Vico Studies **6915**
0883-6027 Journal of Urban Analysis and Public Management†
0883-6043 Fodor's Amsterdam†
0883-6078 A I P L A Quarterly Journal **4607**
0883-6086 Perspectives (Norwood)†
0883-6159 California Broker **1958**
0883-6183 In Fashion†
0883-6248 New School Observer **2293**
0883-6264 California Facts **3119**
0883-6337 Notebook†
0883-6353 Geoarchaeology **395**
0883-6361 Cracked **5212**
0883-6590 Pulteney St. Survey **2297**
0883-6612 Annals of Behavioral Medicine **5575**
0883-6639 Russkaya Zhizn' **3562**
0883-6671 Health Insurance Medical Records Risk Management Report†
0883-6728 Colorado Episcopalian **7752**
0883-6736 N A M B L A Topics **4377**
0883-6752 Pages (Marion) **4581**

9366 0883-6779 ULRICH'S PERIODICALS

0883-6779 Financial Reporting for American Cities and Counties†
0883-6795 A A T F National Bulletin **5088**
0883-6833 Buckeye Sports Bulletin **8163**
0883-6841 U S A Outdoors
0883-6884 Contributions in Military Studies **6417**
0883-6922 Children's Video Report
0883-6949 Mannlicher Collector **367**
0883-6973 In House Graphics **7323**
0883-7066 System Dynamics Review **1796**
0883-7090 Adult Video News **2399**
0883-7147 Topics in Hospital Law **4797**
0883-7155 International Design Yearbook **4544**
0883-7198 Clinical Pediatrics Series†
0883-721X India - West **3539**
0883-7252 Journal of Applied Econometrics **1544**
0883-7279 Pratt Journal of Architecture **454**
0883-735X Rotkin Review†
0883-7368 Ukrainian National Association. Alamanac **3966**
0883-7384 Asset **1280**
0883-7554 I E E E Electrical Insulation Magazine **3311**
0883-7597 Journal of Pharmaceutical Marketing and Management† **8968**
0883-7635 Orim: A Jewish Journal at Yale†
0883-7694 M R S Bulletin **3352**
0883-7708 Lamb's Pastures **3773**
0883-7724 Darnall, Darnell - Dawn to Dusk†
0883-7732 Tibet Society Bulletin†
0883-7767 Allergy Relief Newsletter†
0883-7783 North Carolina Law Monitor†
0883-7805 Manley Family Newsletter **3774**
0883-7813 WaterSki **8340**
0883-7856 Government Finance Review **1927**
0883-7880 C A M Magazine **988**
0883-7899 Montana Catholic **7808**
0883-7902 Mental and Physical Disability Law Reporter *changed to* Joint Commission Advisor for Behavioral Health **4833**
0883-7937 Ultralight Flying! **74**
0883-7945 Northwest Runner **8191**
0883-7953 America's Fastest Growing Companies
0883-7961 Krefeld Immigrants and Their Descendants **3773**
0883-7996 Ba Shiru†
0883-8038 Thoroughbred Business
0883-8046 Rocky Mountain High Technology Directory **2026**
0883-8062 P.A. Update†
0883-8089 Computer Entertainment†
0883-8100 World Resources Institute. Journal†
0883-8135 World Today Series: Canada **4318**
0883-8151 Journal of Broadcasting and Electronic Media **2383**
0883-816X Muslim Journal **7714**
0883-8194 Focus (Austin, 1985)†
0883-8208 Colorado High Technology Directory **8418**
0883-8216 Health Science **6660**
0883-8240 Professional Insurance Agents of New York **4519**
0883-8283 Ferroelectrics and Polar Materials†
0883-8305 Paleoceanography **2816**
0883-833X Antique Review†
0883-8348 Gastroenterology and Endoscopy News **5924**
0883-8380 Beehive History **4285**
0883-8402 Utility Supervision†
0883-8429 Racquet (New York)
0883-8437 Audio (Year) (Scottsdale) **8152**
0883-8526 Alaska Native Language Center Research Papers **5092**
0883-8534 Journal of Multicultural Counseling and Development **7376**
0883-8542 Applied Engineering in Agriculture **92**
0883-8550 Daugherty Family Newsletter†
0883-8569 Editor's Workshop Newsletter **4574**
0883-8577 Palestine Focus†
0883-8690 Government Assistance Almanac **7493**
0883-8763 Current Housing Reports. Series H-121, Homeownership Trends† **8947**
0883-8798 Penthouse Letters **6297**
0883-8828 Techletter **7543**
0883-8941 Secrets of Winners
0883-8984 Arkansas Journal†
0883-9026 Journal of Business Venturing **1134**
0883-9050 The Stockton Family Newsletter **3784**
0883-9115 Journal of Bioactive and Compatible Polymers **734**
0883-9123 Shakespearean Criticism **5371**
0883-9131 Beloit Fiction Journal **5261**
0883-9166 Fessenden Review†
0883-9174 Celebration (Baltimore) **5419**
0883-9190 Hard Rock Video†
0883-9212 Journal of Cardiopulmonary Rehabilitation *changed to* 1932-7501 **5792**
0883-9395 Social Responsibility: Business, Journalism, Law, Medicine†
0883-9409 Denver University Law Review **4656**
0883-9417 Archives of Psychiatric Nursing **5952**
0883-9425 Informatics in Pathology†
0883-9441 Journal of Critical Care **6063**
0883-9468 Guns & Ammo Action Series **8316**
0883-9484 Museum of Life Sciences. Bulletin **691**
0883-9492 Molecular Toxicology†
0883-9506 Vibration Engineering†
0883-9514 Applied Artificial Intelligence **2445**
0883-9530 Journal for Research in Mathematics Education. Monograph **3067**
0883-9611 Broomstick†
0883-9670 Wells Fargo Bank Business Review†
0883-9697 Journal of Middle Atlantic Archaeology **401**
0883-9719 Environ **3420**
0883-9727 Directions (New York) **1814**
0883-9778 Burrelle's New Jersey Media Directory (Year)†
0883-9786 Burrelle's New York State Media Directory (Year)†
0883-9816 Cincinnati Romance Review **5274**
0883-9824 Argonaut (Austin)†
0883-9832 Israeli Foreign Affairs†
0883-9859 Inventors' Digest **6753**
0883-9875 Nuclear Resister **7160**
0883-9891 Willett House Quarterly†
0883-9905 Potomac Children†
0883-9921 Modern Postal History Journal†
0883-9956 In Dance
0883-9980 C S L Bulletin **5268**
0883-9999 Burrelle's New England Media Directory (Year)† **8938**
0884-0016 Advanced Studies in Contemporary Mathematics†
0884-0032 Civil R I C O Report **4829**
0884-0040 A S H E - E R I C Higher Education Report Series *changed to* 1551-6970 **2964**
0884-0075 The California Prisoner
0884-0083 Cardiovascular Medicine
0884-0091 Academia Norteamericana de la Lengua Espanola. Boletin **5248**
0884-0180 Armenian Numismatic Journal **6649**
0884-0210 Fodor's Houston & Galveston†
0884-030X Inside Alabama Politics **7446**
0884-0326 New Horizons (Mount Prospect) **5685**
0884-0385 Hydro Review **3162**
0884-0431 Journal of Bone and Mineral Research **6063**
0884-0482 Illinois Appellate Reports **4690**
0884-0490 A S H R A E Technical Data Bulletin **3372**
0884-0601 C E A Chap Book†
0884-0628 Houston City†
0884-0695 Restaurant Briefing†
0884-0741 Research in Governmental and Non-Profit Accounting **1299**
0884-075X Littell's Living Age **3773**
0884-0768 U C L A Pacific Basin Law Journal **4799**
0884-0806 Food Protection Report **7518**
0884-0822 Forth Dimensions
0884-0946 Journal of Natural Hygiene
0884-0989 Choices†
0884-1012 Robot Experimenter. Supplement†
0884-1020 She-Ra Princess of Power Magazine†
0884-1039 Canada (Year) **8691**
0884-1055 Early Cello Series. Modern Edition
0884-1063 U.S. Department of the Treasury. Financial Management Service. United States Government Annual Report and Appendix **1953**
0884-1098 T V Dimensions **2392**
0884-1136 Ensign **7735**
0884-1144 Selected Bibliography of Recent Economic Development Publications†
0884-1179 Georgia Economic Outlook **1113**
0884-1187 U.S. Federal Deposit Insurance Corporation. Merger Decisions **1388**
0884-1209 Mexico (Year) **8733**
0884-1217 Georgia Law Letter†
0884-1233 Journal of Teaching in Social Work **3068**
0884-1241 Journal of Marketing for Higher Education **2991**
0884-1357 V M E Bus Systems *changed to* 1941-3807 **2525**
0884-1373 Southern Business Review
0884-139X Defense News **6419**
0884-1667 M S B A in Brief†
0884-173X Ohio Register of Manufacturers **2022**
0884-1756 Inter-American Law Review **4929**
0884-1799 Applications of Management Science. Supplement **1725**
0884-1829 Minority Engineer **3210**
0884-1918 Museum & Arts Washington†
0884-1926 Civil Engineering Education **3262**
0884-1934 Square One **5447**
0884-1969 Checklist of Kentucky State Publications†
0884-2019 Cahiers Cesairiens†
0884-2035 Colorado Research in Linguistics (Print Edition) *changed to* 1937-7029 **5107**
0884-2043 Clio (Ft. Wayne) **4135**
0884-2086 Genealogical Society of Okaloosa County. Journal **3767**
0884-2108 Terrell Trails **3785**
0884-2140 Phelps County Genealogical Society Quarterly **3779**
0884-2159 Petroleum Market Shares: Report on Retail Sales of Gasoline†
0884-2175 Journal of Obstetric, Gynecologic, and Neonatal Nursing **5966**
0884-2205 Mo Info **5032**
0884-2213 Appearances **5256**
0884-2272 Communications Technology **2379**
0884-2299 Peterson's College Selection Service. Two-Year Colleges†
0884-2329 U.S. Department of Agriculture. National Agricultural Statistics Service. Crop Values **188**
0884-2426 The Review of Securities & Commodities Regulation **1648**
0884-2485 Christian Review†
0884-2604 Data Training†
0884-2795 Reimbursement Advisor **4110**
0884-2817 Connecticut C P A Quarterly†
0884-2914 Journal of Materials Research **3350**
0884-2930 Wyoming
0884-2949 The Faulkner Journal **5295**
0884-2957 Belles Lettres (North Potomac)†
0884-2981 Euthanasia Review†
0884-3031 Richard C. Young's Intelligence Report **1648**
0884-3090 Publisher's Report **7571**
0884-3171 U.S. Foreign Trade Highlights (Print) *changed to* 1932-376X **1585**
0884-318X New York University. Salomon Center. Occasional Papers in Business and Finance **1371**
0884-3198 U C L A Journal of Dance Ethnology†
0884-3201 New Lebanese American Journal **4154**
0884-3228 Fourth Circuit Review†
0884-3236 Late Imperial China **4185**
0884-3244 Immigration Journal†
0884-3279 Western New York Index†
0884-3309 Pioneer America Society. Transactions **4308**
0884-3406 Washington State University. Cooperative Extension. Circular **169**
0884-3457 Cream City Review **5279**
0884-352X Leaders *see* 0277-9277 **607**
0884-3554 Refugee Reports **7291**
0884-3635 Brilliant Star **2181**
0884-3643 National Association for Gifted Children. Communique *changed to* Compass Points (Washington) **3038**
0884-3716 Research News
0884-3740 R A L Report†
0884-3848 Paint & Coatings Industry **6719**
0884-3910 News for You **2944**
0884-4011 Decorative Arts Society Newsletter **485**
0884-4054 Defense and Foreign Affairs Weekly†
0884-4194 Current Concepts of Cerebrovascular Disease: Stroke†
0884-4240 Irish America Magazine **3540**
0884-4275 C U N Y Forum†
0884-4291 Creative Child and Adult Quarterly†
0884-4313 Best's Insurance Reports - International *changed to* Best's Insurance Reports - Life & Non-Life - Non-U.S. **4495**
0884-4348 Hustler Fantasies **6292**
0884-4356 The American Voice†
0884-4437 Copyright Law Journal **6748**
0884-4461 The Dolciani Mathematical Expositions **5484**
0884-4488 Chile Economic Report†
0884-4526 Recoup's Materials Recycling Markets **3510**
0884-4550 Petroleum Management†
0884-4615 Your Computer Career†
0884-4674 Competitive Edge (Tempe)†
0884-4712 Emergency Medical Care Digest†
0884-4720 Electronic Musician **6564**
0884-4739 Bassin' **3587**
0884-4747 Artilleryman **4284**
0884-4755 Aviation Digest†
0884-4798 4-H Leader†
0884-4828 Electronic Warfare Digest **6420**
0884-4836 Emergency Medical Technician Legal Bulletin **5609**
0884-4925 Insight (Chatsworth)†
0884-495X World Trade Report†
0884-4984 Catering Today†
0884-4992 T V Game Show Magazine†
0884-5123 International Telemetering Conference†
0884-514X Addendum (Indianapolis) **4609**
0884-5166 New England Living Magazine†
0884-5336 Nutrition in Clinical Practice **6666**
0884-5352 Journal of Career Planning & Employment *changed to* 1542-2046 **1698**
0884-5379 Fides et Historia **4139**
0884-5409 Carnahan Conference on Security Technology. Proceedings†
0884-5433 Exxon Air World†
0884-5506 Christian Education Today†
0884-5514 Shining Star Magazine†
0884-5735 Palatine Immigrant **3778**
0884-5808 Hakomi Forum **7359**
0884-5816 Age of Johnson **5250**
0884-5840 Summer Theatre Directory (Year) **8480**
0884-5859 Directory of Undergraduate Political Science Faculty (Year) *changed to* A P S A Directory of Political Science Faculty (Year) **7101**
0884-5891 Ocean Drilling Program. Scientific Results. Proceedings. Scientific Results **2814**
0884-5905 Administrative Management (New York)†
0884-5913 Kinematics and Physics of Celestial Bodies **577**
0884-593X Wired Librarian's Newsletter **5064**
0884-5956 The Ohio Lepidopterist **959**
0884-6006 Directory of Literary Magazines *changed to* The Literary Press and Magazine Directory **5407**
0884-6057 Tax Management Weekly Report **1948**
0884-6154 Socialist **7183**
0884-6162 Agweek **89**
0884-6227 Update U S S R†
0884-626X Motorcycle Industry Magazine **8263**
0884-6316 A I M International **7619**
0884-6332 Educational Directions in Dental Hygiene†
0884-6421 Utah State Digest **7504**
0884-6510 Bennett Exchange†
0884-6537 Common Cause Magazine†
0884-660X Leather Today (New York)†
0884-6669 Alabama Genealogical Exchange Quarterly†
0884-6677 Y E S Quarterly†
0884-6782 Financial Times (North American Edition) **1346**
0884-6790 Progress in Leukocyte Biology†
0884-6804 Journal of Composites Technology and Research†
0884-6812 Analytical and Quantitative Cytology and Histology *changed to* 1570-5870 **830**
0884-6863 Acute Coronary Care **5775**
0884-688X The New Good Apple Newspaper†
0884-6901 Graphic Communications World **7322**
0884-6944 Malcolm Hulke Studies in Cinema & Television†
0884-6952 Studies in Judaica & the Holocaust†
0884-7010 Consecrated Life **7793**
0884-7177 Connecticut History **4289**
0884-7185 Food Broker Quarterly **1817**
0884-7282 C S C P A Newsletter *changed to* 1934-3906 **1285**
0884-7347 Guide to Graduate Education in Speech - Language Pathology and Audiology†
0884-7355 Women's Health **8849**
0884-738X Totally Gospel
0884-7398 Admissions Marketing Report *changed to* 1946-8369 **3024**
0884-741X Home Healthcare Nurse **5629**
0884-7452 C A S BioTech Updates. Environmental Biotechnology†
0884-7460 C A S BioTech Updates. Genetic Engineering†
0884-7479 C A S BioTech Updates. Biosensors†
0884-7487 C A S BioTech Updates. Pharmaceutical Applications†
0884-7533 Extension **7797**
0884-7622 Andrew Harper's Hideaway Report **8683**
0884-7657 The 401 (k) Reporter†
0884-7827 Texas Real Estate†
0884-7975 A M U S Log
0884-8076 Child Support Report **8032**
0884-8092 Combined Cumulative Index to Obstetrics and Gynecology
0884-8114 Chamber Executive **1398**
0884-8173 International Journal of Intelligent Systems **2451**
0884-8254 Informer **6896**
0884-8297 International Journal of Psychosomatics†
0884-8319 Scientific Serials Review: Biomedicine†
0884-8351 Campaign Finance Law **7113**

Link to your serials resources and content with ulrichsweb.com

0884-8394 Interstate Information Report†
0884-8416 Peterson's College Selection Service. Four-Year Colleges†
0884-8424 Association of Children's Prosthetic-Orthotic Clinics. Journal†
0884-8432 Modern Greek Studies Yearbook†
0884-8440 Index to Scientific Book Contents† **8964**
0884-8475 S R C Green Book of 5-Trend 35-Year Charts **1649**
0884-8513 Beyond Relief **1067**
0884-8610 Speaking Relatively **3783**
0884-8696 Georgia State Literary Studies **5300**
0884-870X Stress in Modern Society **8141**
0884-8726 Information Marketing Newsletter
0884-8734 Journal of General Internal Medicine **5946**
0884-8742 Update in Critical Care Medicine†
0884-8769 Art Gallery International†
0884-8815 Brookgreen Journal **3726**
0884-8823 Popular Woodworking **1051**
0884-8858 Sinsemilla Tips†
0884-8920 Man (Los Angeles)
0884-8947 Trucks†
0884-8971 Sociological Forum **8136**
0884-8998 Hospital Home Health **4100**
0884-9064 Washington's Almanac
0884-9072 Golden State Report†
0884-9129 H R - P C†
0884-9145 Arkansas Outdoors **2603**
0884-9153 Journal of Student Financial Aid **2878**
0884-9196 Peace Corps Times **7258**
0884-9331 Maryland Journal of International Law and Trade†
0884-934X Commitment - Plus Newsletter
0884-9382 The National Interest **7254**
0884-9390 American Visions†
0884-9404 Advances in Pediatric Infectious Diseases†
0884-9420 Work Dynamics
0884-948X Chemically Modified Surfaces
0884-9501 Baseball History†
0884-9528 Photo-Lab Index
0884-9536 National Directory of Bulletin Board Systems†
0884-9641 Free Venice Beachhead
0884-9757 Electronic Chemicals & Materials News†
0884-9854 Iowa Oil Spout†
0884-9889 Friends (Warren)†
0884-9919 Michigan Librarian **5032**
0885-0003 Waste Treatment Technology News†
0885-0046 Issues (Chicago) **5963**
0885-0089 American Association of State Colleges and Universities. Proceedings of the Annual Meeting†
0885-0097 C A Selects. Acid Rain & Acid Air†
0885-0100 C A Selects. Ceramic Materials (Patents) **2047**
0885-0119 C A Selects. Chemical Vapor Deposition **2086**
0885-0127 C A Selects. Color Science **2086**
0885-0135 C A Selects. Conductive Polymers **2086**
0885-0143 C A Selects. Electrically Conductive Organics **2086**
0885-0151 C A Selects. Electronic Chemicals & Materials **2087**
0885-0178 C A Selects. Laser - Induced Chemical Reactions **2088**
0885-0186 C A Selects. Organic Optical Materials **2089**
0885-0194 C A Selects. Phase Transfer Catalysis **2089**
0885-0208 C A Selects. Photochemical Organic Synthesis **2090**
0885-0216 C A Selects. Photoresists **2090**
0885-0224 C A Selects. Polymerization Kinetics & Process Control **2091**
0885-0232 C A Selects. Spectrochemical Analysis **2092**
0885-0275 Hotel - Bar - Restaurant Review **4595**
0885-0283 Counselor (Wheaton) **2184**
0885-0372 Religious Studies News **7676**
0885-0399 Art for Humanity†
0885-0429 Children's Literature Association Quarterly **5001**
0885-0437 Internal Revenue Acts **1929**
0885-050X Chain Store Age General Merchandise Trends†
0885-0577 California Lodging Industry†
0885-0607 International Journal of Intelligence and Counterintelligence **7243**
0885-0615 Human Research Report **5906**
0885-0631 Quick and Easy Crochet **6641**
0885-064X Journal of Complexity **5553**
0885-0658 Starmont Pulp & Paper Dime Novel Studies†
0885-0666 Journal of Intensive Care Medicine **5650**
0885-0690 Good Food†
0885-0704 Food & Justice†
0885-0739 Member Net†
0885-0925 Medicare Review **4515**
0885-1034 Business Accounting for Lawyers Newsletter† **8938**
0885-1123 Rehabilitation Report†
0885-114X Occupational Medicine *changed to* 1526-0046 **5598**
0885-1158 Medical Problems of Performing Artists **5670**
0885-1174 Human Stress: Current Selected Research **7361**
0885-1204 Cabbage Patch Kids†
0885-1247 Born Young Newsletter
0885-1263 Texas Conchologist **965**
0885-1271 Dallas Weekly **3529**
0885-1328 Hudson's State Capitals†
0885-1336 Domestic Uranium and Milling Industry. Viability Assessment (Year)†
0885-1352 Delaware District Digest **4830**
0885-1379 I C P Data Processing Management†
0885-1468 The Socialist Worker **7184**
0885-1476 Pinhole Journal **6975**
0885-1522 Tanning Trends **1968**
0885-1530 S I R S Science†
0885-1549 Applied Science†
0885-1557 Medical Science†
0885-1565 Earth Science†
0885-1573 Life Science†
0885-1581 Physical Science†
0885-1603 Private Schools of the United States†
0885-1751 Hazardous Substances†
0885-176X U S - Mexico Report†
0885-1808 Professional Stained Glass†
0885-1980 Current Advances in Clinical Chemistry **2094**
0885-1999 Fairfax†
0885-2006 Early Childhood Research Quarterly **2844**
0885-2014 Cognitive Development **7347**
0885-2030 Outlaw Biker **8265**
0885-2049 Boston College Magazine **2275**
0885-209X Shopping Center Digest **7612**
0885-2111 Research in Consumer Behavior **1840**
0885-212X Research in Politics and Society **7177**
0885-2200 Third World in Perspective **7188**
0885-2308 Computer Speech and Language **2506**
0885-2316 Annual Third World Conference Proceedings **4130**
0885-2332 Maat†
0885-2340 T V Program Investor† **8992**
0885-2367 Hinman Heritage **3770**
0885-2405 Advances in Meat Research Series† **8928**
0885-2448 National Air Quality and Emissions Trends Report **3489**
0885-2499 North Dakota R E C Magazine **3983**
0885-2545 Journal of Cultural Economics **1544**
0885-2650 Midwest Law Review **4734**
0885-2685 Texas Review **5386**
0885-3010 I E E E Transactions on Ultrasonics, Ferroelectrics and Frequency Control **7087**
0885-3061 The Federal Labor - Management and Employee Relations Consultant **1681**
0885-3134 Journal of Personal Selling and Sales Management **1826**
0885-3177 Pancreas **5898**
0885-3185 Movement Disorders **6162**
0885-3215 Allen Family Circle **3758**
0885-3258 The Oregon Stater **2295**
0885-3282 Journal of Biomaterials Applications **6247**
0885-3290 Washington Book Review (Washington, 1985)†
0885-3304 Environmental Compliance Update
0885-3312 Marketing Research Review
0885-3339 Advances in the Economic Analysis of Participatory and Labor-Managed Firms **1662**
0885-3347 Overture (Baltimore) **6603**
0885-3371 Poultry Times **297**
0885-3436 Southern Rural Sociology **8140**
0885-3479 Academy of Natural Sciences of Philadelphia. Journal†
0885-3517 Charles H. Tweed International Foundation. Journal **5837**
0885-3886 Phenomenological Inquiry **6939**
0885-3894 Public Garden **3748**
0885-3908 The International Trade Journal **1572**
0885-3916 Society of Logistics Engineers. Annals†
0885-3924 Journal of Pain and Symptom Management **6155**
0885-3940 Theatre Historical Society. Annual **459**
0885-3959 S I S A C News†
0885-3991 Toy Book **4061**
0885-4009 Coastal Journal
0885-4025 East Tennessee Roots **3764**
0885-4092 Katolicky Kalendar Jednota†
0885-4122 Journal of Planning Literature **4417**
0885-4149 Manufacturers Hanover Trust Company. Economic Report†
0885-4238 Labor Research Review†
0885-4262 Photomarket†
0885-4270 Photobulletin **6973**
0885-4289 Virginia Circuit Court Opinions **4809**
0885-4300 Socialism and Democracy **7183**
0885-4319 Committee on South Asian Women Bulletin†
0885-4327 Mineral News **4340**
0885-4343 Torch Romances†
0885-4378 Lucha - Struggle†
0885-4394 Livable City **4464**
0885-4416 On the Risk **4517**
0885-4513 Biotechnology and Applied Biochemistry **760**
0885-453X Jacksonville Business Journal *changed to* 1527-8611 **1073**
0885-4580 Heidegger Studies **6922**
0885-4610 MediaFile **2333**
0885-4629 California Academy of Sciences. Memoirs **664**
0885-4653 Mathematical Surveys & Monographs **5515**
0885-467X McNeese Review **5331**
0885-4718 The Capital (Rhinebeck) **3761**
0885-4726 Journal of Health Care Chaplaincy **6991**
0885-4734 Journal of Chemical Dependency Treatment *changed to* 1550-4263 **2696**
0885-4742 Midwestern Miscellany **5334**
0885-4750 Fabulous Mustangs and Exotic Fords†
0885-4777 100 Highest Yields†
0885-4807 Parkinson's Disease Update
0885-4823 Haynes Family Association. Chronicle
0885-4831 The Connecticut Historical Society Bulletin†
0885-4858 Optimal Health†
0885-4890 Brilliant Ideas for Publishers†
0885-4939 Miju Munhak
0885-4947 Pilgrim Journal†
0885-5013 Saguaro†
0885-5021 Movietone News†
0885-503X Music Forum **6590**
0885-5099 National Railway Bulletin *changed to* 1940-3615 **8621**
0885-5110 North-Holland Series in System Science and Engineering†
0885-5684 Advanced Manufacturing Technology **2584**
0885-5706 Nicaraguan Perspectives†
0885-5722 Rock & Ice **8330**
0885-5749 Patterson Post **3779**
0885-5765 Physiological and Molecular Plant Pathology **808**
0885-5773 Occasional Papers on Linguistics†
0885-5781 Metal Architecture **449**
0885-579X Journal of Personality Disorders **7378**
0885-5811 King's Gulf Grain Guide **274**
0885-5870 Northwest Energy News **3143**
0885-5889 Interchange (Rockville) **4596**
0885-5927 Oculus **452**
0885-5935 Gas Daily **6770**
0885-5943 Florida State Collection of Arthropods. Occasional Papers **847**
0885-5951 Soviet Biological Research Abstracts†
0885-6001 North Carolina Studies in the Romance Languages and Literatures **5343**
0885-6028 National Black Nurses' Association. Journal **5970**
0885-6060 Michigan Dry Bean Digest†
0885-6079 Atenea **5207**
0885-6087 Hydrological Processes **2794**
0885-6095 Western Journal of Applied Forestry **3707**
0885-6117 Hot Shots
0885-6125 Machine Learning **2454**
0885-6133 Common Ground (Alexandria) **7587**
0885-615X Bear News **935**
0885-6168 Executive AIDS Watch†
0885-6192 Dimensions in Oncology Nursing **6018**
0885-6214 Publishing and New Media Technology Newsletter†
0885-6222 Human Psychopharmacology: Clinical and Experimental **6145**
0885-6230 International Journal of Geriatric Psychiatry **4048**
0885-6257 European Journal of Special Needs Education **3039**
0885-6265 International Pediatrics **6246**
0885-6273 Current Maryland Archeology
0885-6362 Geobyte†
0885-6370 Publication Design Annual†
0885-6400 D A V Magazine **6417**
0885-6540 The New American (Appleton) **7157**
0885-6583 Ohio Chess Bulletin **8191**
0885-6648 The Single Scene (Gahanna)†
0885-6664 Inkblot
0885-6680 Plaza†
0885-6699 Pragmatist **1547**
0885-6710 Personal Communications Technology†
0885-6729 S I N E T **8150**
0885-6745 S T V Guide†
0885-6788 I C A's Newsletter†
0885-6834 Statistical Reference Index **8404**
0885-6869 St. Louis - Southern Illinois Labor Tribune **4602**
0885-6877 Foodservice East **3643**
0885-6893 American Public Opinion Data
0885-6907 Texas Banking **1386**
0885-6931 The Practicing C P A **1299**
0885-6966 The Newsletter Newsletter **7769**
0885-7024 Civil Engineering (Reston) **3262**
0885-7113 Balungan **6547**
0885-7156 Powder Diffraction **3215**
0885-7172 Fair Employment Compliance†
0885-7202 Employee Communication (New York)
0885-7229 In Depth (New York)†
0885-7237 Econews **3418**
0885-7288 Career Development for Exceptional Individuals **3037**
0885-7326 Preservation Notes **454**
0885-7342 Association of College and Research Libraries. Law and Political Science Section News **4622**
0885-7369 Glagol **5300**
0885-7377 L A Architect *changed to* 1931-5643 **442**
0885-7385 La Posta **2355**
0885-7423 Psychology and Sociology of Sport: Current Selected Research **7399**
0885-7431 Clinical Neurochemistry† **8941**
0885-7458 International Journal of Parallel Programming **2507**
0885-7466 Social Justice Research **8133**
0885-7474 Journal of Scientific Computing **7940**
0885-7482 Journal of Family Violence **2657**
0885-7490 Metabolic Brain Disease **5678**
0885-7512 Monographic Review **5336**
0885-7520 Modern British Literature†
0885-7555 Reference Guides to Archives and Manuscript Collections on Immigrant Culture† **8984**
0885-7601 The Daily Princetonian **2281**
0885-761X University of Tulsa. Monograph Series†
0885-7636 Vegetarian Journal **6670**
0885-7679 National Cattlemen **294**
0885-7687 Cornell Nutrition Conference for Feed Manufacturers. Proceedings **284**
0885-7717 Psychiatric Hospital†
0885-7741 The Recorder (New York) **3560**
0885-7792 Nutrition Action Health Letter **6665**
0885-7822 Heavy Metal **5443**
0885-7857 Virchow-Piquet Medical Society. Proceedings†
0885-7954 Augustan Reprint Society. Publication **5258**
0885-7962 C Ö D A Newsletter **4072**
0885-8039 Remodeling **1032**
0885-8055 Business Software Review†
0885-8160 Kayhan International **3891**
0885-8179 Kayhan **3891**
0885-8187 Kayhan al-Arabi **3912**
0885-8195 Journal of Cancer Education **6023**
0885-8276 American Journal of Physiologic Imaging†
0885-8284 Emergency Nursing Reports†
0885-8330 Transportation Energy Research **3154**
0885-8365 Corporate Philanthropy Report **8035**
0885-842X New Jersey Medicine†
0885-8462 Contemporary Graphic Artists†
0885-8500 Common Boundary **7348**
0885-8543 Triads†
0885-8551 Wrestling All Stars Heroes and Villains† **8999**
0885-8608 Natural Areas Journal **3455**
0885-8624 Journal of Business & Industrial Marketing **1823**
0885-8659 Shmate†
0885-8748 South Shore Business
0885-8950 I E E E Transactions on Power Systems **3159**
0885-8969 I E E E Transactions on Energy Conversion **3159**
0885-8977 I E E E Transactions on Power Delivery **3315**
0885-8985 I E E E Aerospace and Electronic Systems Magazine **3101**
0885-8993 I E E E Transactions on Power Electronics **3103**
0885-9027 Washington Crossing Card Collectors Club Newsletter **4350**
0885-906X Timber Processing **3716**
0885-9116 Exposure Draft **1288**
0885-9124 Faxnet†
0885-9159 Contributions to the Study of World History **4136**
0885-9175 Contact Lens Spectrum **6040**
0885-9183 The Complete Baseball Record Book **8225**
0885-9191 T M J Update: A Current Review of Temporomandibular Joint Developments **5719**
0885-9205 Manhattan Poetry Review **5426**

ISSN

Link to your serials resources and content with ulrichsweb.com

9368 0885-9256 ULRICH'S PERIODICALS

0885-9256 P S (Wynantskill)†
0885-9264 Contact Lens Update **5742**
0885-9302 Sixteenth Century Bibliography **4171**
0885-9337 Boulevard **5265**
0885-9361 ArtToday†
0885-9418 Mathematical Concepts and Methods in Science and Engineering **5513**
0885-9442 Quodlibet **6608**
0885-9574 West Virginia Shakespeare and Renaissance Association. Selected Papers **5398**
0885-9612 Shelterforce **4427**
0885-9647 Black Elegance†
0885-9671 Directory of Hospital Personnel **1987**
0885-968X Emblematica **4217**
0885-9698 Techniques in Orthopaedics **6073**
0885-9701 Journal of Head Trauma Rehabilitation **6064**
0885-971X Topics in Acute Care and Trauma Rehabilitation†
0885-9779 China Clipper **6893**
0885-9787 Arete **8026**
0885-9795 Again **7703**
0885-9809 R E T S Digest†
0885-9841 Shopping Centers Today **7612**
0885-985X Journal of Social Studies Research **7980**
0885-9884 Association of Teachers of Japanese. Journal *changed to* 1536-7827 **5131**
0885-9906 Ceiba **5271**
0885-9914 Indian Health Trends and Services†
0885-9922 Lutheran Partners **7766**
0885-9973 Maine Bar Journal **4727**
0886-0009 Biotech Update†
0886-0025 Photogrammetric Coyote **4023**
0886-005X Champs-Elysees **8692**
0886-0076 Directory of American Research and Technology†
0886-0092 Readers' Guide Abstracts (Microfiche Edition)†
0886-0122 Mealey's Litigation Report: Tobacco **4837**
0886-0149 Ocean Navigator **8279**
0886-0165 Non-Credit Learning News **2944**
0886-0203 Writer's Info†
0886-022X Renal Failure **6273**
0886-0246 Reading Research and Instruction *changed to* 1938-8071 **3070**
0886-0254 Boatbuilder **8272**
0886-0270 Monographs on Infancy†
0886-036X Reality Change†
0886-0408 Law Books in Review†
0886-0416 Studies in Regional Science and Urban Economics **1520**
0886-0432 Studia Linguistica et Philologica†
0886-0440 Journal of Cardiac Surgery **5792**
0886-0459 Letters of Credit Report†
0886-0467 Lasers in the Life Sciences†
0886-0475 B N A's Corporate Counsel Weekly **1727**
0886-0483 How **26**
0886-0556 Computer Shopper **2491**
0886-0564 U.S. Bureau of Mines. Mineral Industry Surveys (Print Edition)†
0886-0629 New Studies on the Left **5230**
0886-0637 Wildfowl **8341**
0886-0653 Medical Ethics Advisor **5668**
0886-0661 T E S L Reporter **3083**
0886-067X Southeastern Front **518**
0886-0750 Stanford French & Italian Studies†
0886-0807 Washington Summary **7201**
0886-0882 National Council of the Paper Industry for Air and Stream Improvement. Technical Bulletin **3489**
0886-0890 Technology Forecasts & Technology Surveys **8442**
0886-0963 Shoe Retailing Today **7942**
0886-1013 Art Law & Accounting Reporter **4621**
0886-103X Technology Management Action **1583**
0886-1064 American Academy of Gnathologic Orthopedics. Journal **5834**
0886-1080 Orienteering North America **8326**
0886-1099 Affilia **8024**
0886-1102 P S L S†
0886-117X World History Bulletin **4167**
0886-1196 America's Spirit **8025**
0886-120X Court of Appeals of Georgia. Reports of Cases **4948**
0886-1234 The American Legion **2264**
0886-1242 The Timber Producer **3704**
0886-1269 Tennessee Wildlife **965**
0886-1277 Four Worlds Journal†
0886-1293 Company **7793**
0886-1307 Washington Heritage†
0886-1315 Infant Screening†
0886-1390 Eco-Logos†
0886-1420 T E N C O N (I E E E Region 10 Conference). Proceedings **2439**
0886-1463 N C S Integrated Manufacturing†
0886-1501 Sharing Ideas News Magazine **5371**
0886-1528 International Review of Industrial and Organizational Psychology **7366**
0886-1544 Cell Motility and the Cytoskeleton **829**
0886-1609 Radio Control Car Action **4345**
0886-1641 Journal of Social Behavior and Personality
0886-165X Las Vegas Magazine
0886-1676 Homoeopathy Today **310**
0886-1684 Unmask†
0886-1730 Moravian Historical Society. Transactions *changed to* 1933-6632 **4299**
0886-1811 Catholic War Veteran **8031**
0886-1862 Hogaku†
0886-1897 The Podium†
0886-1935 Closing the Gap **3038**
0886-1986 HealthAction†
0886-1994 The Competitive Advantage **1811**
0886-2044 Community Murals†
0886-2060 Works and Days **5400**
0886-2087 VoiceNews†
0886-2117 Historic New Orleans Collection. Manuscripts Division Update†
0886-2133 Dog News **6807**
0886-2141 Religion Watch **7675**
0886-2168 The Upstart Crow **5394**
0886-2176 University of Arkansas. Lecture Notes in the Mathematical Sciences†
0886-2214 Meeting Planners Guidebook. California & Nevada Edition
0886-2230 NetManager
0886-2249 Rolling Stock **5237**
0886-2257 Air & Space - Smithsonian **44**
0886-2362 Token Perspectives Newsletter†
0886-2397 LocalNetter Newsletter†
0886-2400 Datacom Reader†
0886-2435 Change Exchange **4641**
0886-2443 Mechanics of Rigid Bodies **7061**
0886-2451 New Pathways
0886-2478 France Magazine **5216**
0886-2508 School Law Bulletin (Chapel Hill) **4779**
0886-2516 Universidad de Puerto Rico. Revista Juridica **4802**
0886-2540 New England Jury Verdict Review & Analysis **4741**
0886-2605 Journal of Interpersonal Violence **2657**
0886-2664 Upwellings **8834**
0886-2680 South Dakota Magazine **4313**
0886-2796 Dorot **3764**
0886-280X Social Science (Chapel Hill)†
0886-2818 Wind Energy News **3178**
0886-2915 Governmental Accounting Standards Board. Technical Bulletin **1927**
0886-294X Rhyme Time Poetry Newsletter **5433**
0886-2958 Mystery Time **5414**
0886-2982 Governmental Accounting Standards Board. Action Report **1289**
0886-3032 Spin **6619**
0886-3059 Investigate†
0886-3075 Montana Farm Bureau Spokesman **137**
0886-3148 Ash at Work†
0886-3210 California Western International Law Journal **4919**
0886-327X Corporate Counsel Review **4863**
0886-3288 Samoan Pacific Law Journal†
0886-330X Indiana Factbook† **8964**
0886-3350 Journal of Cataract & Refractive Surgery **6044**
0886-3369 Scene (Tacoma) **2300**
0886-3431 Private Island Inventory
0886-344X Amphibious Warfare Review **6410**
0886-3458 Wildlife Harvest **8341**
0886-3490 The Arms Control Reporter **7221**
0886-3520 Copyright Society of the U.S.A. Journal **6748**
0886-3547 Tax Management Estates, Gifts and Trusts Journal **1655**
0886-3601 Hooks Family Chronicles†
0886-361X State College **3989**
0886-3679 New York University. Annual Institute on Federal Taxation. Proceedings **1937**
0886-3687 Compensation and Benefits Review **1671**
0886-3717 U S - Arab Commerce†
0886-3741 Candy Marketer†
0886-3768 Western Investor Newsletter†
0886-3784 Readings†
0886-3806 Cypris **6724**
0886-3849 Journal of Tumor Marker Oncology **6025**
0886-3865 Victorians Institute Journal **5244**
0886-3881 National Directory of Minority - Owned Business Firms **2018**
0886-389X National Directory of Woman - Owned Business Firms **2018**
0886-3946 Regional Directory of Minority- and Women-Owned Business Firms: Western Edition **2025**
0886-3954 Dance Research Annual†
0886-3970 C A R D Report (Ames, 1986)†
0886-3997 Setters, Incorporated **6815**
0886-4047 A.Bacus (Elmwood) **5415**
0886-4071 Advanced Animal Breeder†
0886-4144 Loadstar **2594**
0886-4152 Softdisk†
0886-4187 Blue Pitcher†
0886-4217 U S Aviation Reports†
0886-4225 Computerwhat?†
0886-4268 Precious Fibers
0886-4276 World Chronology Series†
0886-4357 American Red Angus **278**
0886-4365 Almond Facts **3721**
0886-4411 Power and Motoryacht **8280**
0886-442X Popular Music†
0886-4446 Cooking Light **4354**
0886-4470 Archives of Otolaryngology - Head & Neck Surgery **6077**
0886-4535 F A S B Technical Bulletin **1288**
0886-4543 Viewpoint (New York)†
0886-4586 U.S. Merit Systems Protection Board. Reporter **4853**
0886-4594 Calendar for New Music **6553**
0886-4616 New Frontier **6646**
0886-4659 Ops: The Data Center Newsletter†
0886-4667 Guardian Index **4587**
0886-4691 U.S. National Center for Health Statistics. Vital and Health Statistics. Series 3. Analytical and Epidemiological Studies **7550**
0886-4772 K C M S Bulletin **5656**
0886-4780 Potato Country **248**
0886-4802 Young Viewers†
0886-4845 University of Florida. Food and Resource Economics Department. Economic Information Report **208**
0886-4969 Heard Journal†
0886-5051 Cotton Boll
0886-5108 Clemson University. Cooperative Extension Service. Circular **101**
0886-5132 Colorado State University. Cooperative Extension Service. Bulletin **102**
0886-5140 Comments on Toxicology†
0886-5175 Ward's Automotive Reports **8611**
0886-5213 Washington State Bar News **4811**
0886-5272 Historical Footnotes (Stonington) **4296**
0886-5280 Accounting News (New York, 1981)†
0886-5299 Your Big Backyard **3476**
0886-5302 Petite (Los Angeles)
0886-537X Telephone Bypass News†
0886-5388 Shared Tenant Service News†
0886-5396 Pay Phone News†
0886-5558 Choices (Ames) **195**
0886-5582 Private Label International **1901**
0886-5612 Copycat Magazine†
0886-5620 A S E T Newsletter **6118**
0886-5647 Nationwide Overnight Stabling Directory & Equestrian Vacation Guide **8295**
0886-5655 Journal of Borderlands Studies **7247**
0886-5663 Produce Business **3681**
0886-5698 Current Population Reports. Series P-70, Household Economic Studies **7305**
0886-5701 Journal of Reading Education **2877**
0886-571X Residential Treatment for Children & Youth **2167**
0886-5760 The Georgia Veterinarian **8797**
0886-5779 Horticultural News **3737**
0886-5868 Florida Food and Resource Economics **3636**
0886-5884 Feed and Feeding Digest **271**
0886-5906 Farm Economics: Facts and Opinions **198**
0886-5949 Exteriors†
0886-5957 Manna
0886-6104 Pro Motion **8126**
0886-6139 Toy Trade News†
0886-6155 West Texas Historical Association Yearbook **4317**
0886-6198 Global Affairs†
0886-621X Federal Litigator **4673**
0886-6236 Global Biogeochemical Cycles **7858**
0886-6287 Chesapeake and Ohio Historical Magazine **8616**
0886-6309 Mosquito Control Research. Annual Report **855**
0886-6368 Marketing Bulletin **1831**
0886-6376 Maple Syrup Digest **3655**
0886-6473 Linc: Linking Issue Networks for Cooperation
0886-6481 Thoughts for All Seasons **5242**
0886-649X New Hampshire Supreme Court Reporter
0886-6503 Sierra Heritage **3988**
0886-6511 News About the A - V Scene†
0886-6554 Vim & Vigor **6999**
0886-6570 Cinematograph **6494**
0886-6597 Valley Business Perspectives†
0886-6619 N J Audubon **2619**
0886-6643 Electronic House **3095**
0886-666X Stanford Literature Review†
0886-6678 Legal Plan Letter†
0886-6686 United Nations Resolutions. Series 1. Resolutions Adopted by the General Assembly†
0886-6694 Preventing Sexual Abuse†
0886-6708 Violence and Victims **8146**
0886-6716 Chemical Design Automation News†
0886-6724 Collection of Bibliographic and Research Resources†
0886-6791 The Gate **6741**
0886-6848 Human Nutrition†
0886-6880 Claremont Reading Conference. Yearbook†
0886-6899 American Forage and Grassland Council. Proceedings of the Annual Conference†
0886-6910 Iskcon Review **7737**
0886-6961 International Amateur - Professional Photoelectric Photometry. Communication **576**
0886-697X Hydrowire (Kansas City) **3163**
0886-7062 Connexions (Oakland)†
0886-7089 N B C C News Notes *changed to* National Certified Counselor **8056**
0886-7097 Studies in American Drama, 1945 - Present†
0886-7143 Emphasis, Nursing†
0886-7151 Noticias del Puerto de Monterey **4306**
0886-7186 Clinical Oncology Alert **6016**
0886-7194 Computer Marketing Newsletter†
0886-7208 Antiques & Fine Arts (Laguna Hills)†
0886-7267 Spirit (Princeton)†
0886-7283 Florida State Horticultural Society. Proceedings of the Annual Meeting **3730**
0886-7348 Western Writers Series **5245**
0886-7356 Cultural Anthropology **334**
0886-7372 I F P R I Research Report **200**
0886-7437 Jet Lag†
0886-7526 Geological Survey of Alabama. Monograph **2739**
0886-7623 New York State Agricultural Experiment Station. Special Report **140**
0886-764X Great Activities **2860**
0886-7666 Keystoner **6045**
0886-7690 U.S. Department of Agriculture. The Yearbook of Agriculture†
0886-7747 Inter-American Legal Materials†
0886-7771 Radius (San Francisco)
0886-778X Advance (Washington) **7219**
0886-7798 Tunnelling and Underground Space Technology **3224**
0886-7836 Federal Technology Catalog **8422**
0886-7879 Clinical Pharmacokinetic Newsletter†
0886-7909 Intrapreneurial Excellence†
0886-7976 Midland Review **5333**
0886-8018 Key Neurology and Neurosurgery†
0886-8026 Key Ophthalmology†
0886-8034 Soma: Engineering for the Human Body†
0886-8093 Q E X **2361**
0886-8115 New Art Examiner†
0886-814X News C A S T **140**
0886-8166 Business Age†
0886-8174 Puget Sound ComputerUser **2582**
0886-8204 Commercial Lending Review **1328**
0886-8220 Contributions in Medical Studies **5600**
0886-8239 Contributions in Labor Studies **1673**
0886-8255 Senior Lawyer *changed to* 1936-587X **4809**
0886-828X Alternative Energy†
0886-8298 C B E Environmental Review **2605**
0886-8409 Moravian (Bethlehem, 1912) **2293**
0886-8441 Corrie Herring Hooks Series **2608**
0886-845X Entry
0886-8476 A Delaware Sea Grant Technical Report **2608**
0886-8484 Working Classics
0886-8506 Electronic Market Trends **3095**
0886-8573 Candle (Naselle)†
0886-8611 Rural Development News **206**

0886-862X Transitions (Minneapolis) 6303
0886-8654 The Meadow 5331
0886-8662 Herold's Comparative Appraisal Reports - Sector 2
0886-8697 Oz Collector
0886-8719 Midnight Marquee 6507
0886-8743 2 A M Magazine 5449
0886-876X Minute-a-Day Health Newsletter†
0886-8778 Motor Freight Controller 8673
0886-8832 Military Club & Hospitality 3656
0886-8913 Bioethics Literature Review 5741
0886-8948 Nursing Pulse of New England
0886-9006 Pediatric Nurse Practitioner 5977
0886-9022 Plastics Industry News†
0886-9030 Overthrow 5232
0886-9049 Our Right to Know†
0886-9103 Howard Historian 3771
0886-9154 Rocky Mountain Council on Latin American Studies. Proceedings†
0886-9162 Workers' Compensation Journal of Ohio 7477
0886-9189 MacRae's Blue Book 2013
0886-9200 Airman's Information Manual/Federal Aviation Regulations†
0886-9286 Social Studies Journal 3082
0886-9308 U.S. Geological Survey. Water Supply Paper 2798
0886-9359 Donor Briefing†
0886-9383 Journal of Chemometrics 2101
0886-9634 Cranio: Journal of Craniomandibular Practice 5601
0886-9669 Window Fashions 4563
0886-9685 Civil Engineering Practice 3262
0886-9693 Empire State Farmer 107
0886-9723 Journal of Ambulatory Care Marketing†
0886-9790 Forgiveness News
0886-9812 Excellence (Microsoft Excel)†
0886-9820 International Combat Arms†
0886-9863 Resort & Hotel Management†
0886-988X Pharmacy Practice News 6873
0886-9901 Cleaning & Restoration 2242
0886-9960 International Typographical Union. Review
0886-9979 National Education Association Rhode Island. Newsline 2889
0886-9995 New Jersey Success†
0887-0004 N D Banner 4075
0887-011X Wellsprings 7731
0887-0144 Convenience Care Update†
0887-0152 Peterson's Competitive Colleges (Year) 2961
0887-0160 Journal of Law and Technology†
0887-0187 A B A Bank Compliance 1304
0887-0217 Teaching Thinking & Problem Solving Newsletter†
0887-0241 Population Reports (English Edition) 7290
0887-025X Population Reports (French Edition) 7290
0887-0268 Population Reports (Spanish Edition) 7290
0887-0276 Population Reports (Portuguese Edition) 7290
0887-0284 Hydrocarbon Processing 6772
0887-0292 AIDS Alert 5808
0887-0306 Orphan Disease Update 5691
0887-0314 Consulting Intelligence *changed to* Consulting Tips Newsletter 1086
0887-0330 Ely Heritage
0887-0365 Parent and Preschooler Newsletter 2164
0887-0373 Public Affairs Quarterly 6945
0887-0403 World Resources (Year) 2633
0887-0411 Zone (New York)†
0887-042X Creative Classroom†
0887-0446 Psychology & Health 7398
0887-0500 Soviet - East European Survey†
0887-0519 Almanac of the 50 States 8086
0887-0527 American Cities Chronologies Series†
0887-0535 Food & Nutrition Quarterly Index†
0887-0551 Directory of Grants in the Humanities 2978
0887-056X Accomplishments in Oncology†
0887-0586 Journal of Wave - Material Interaction†
0887-0594 Central America NewsPak 1398
0887-0624 Energy & Fuels 3130
0887-0764 American Jewish Congress. Congress Monthly 7718
0887-0799 Medical Laboratory Products†
0887-0896 For Poets Only†
0887-1027 Gym Dandies†
0887-1035 Superstar Wrestlers† 8991
0887-1043 I R F Newsletter†
0887-1086 Industry and Health Care†
0887-1116 Centennial State Libraries 5001
0887-1132 Charter Connections
0887-1175 Computing Information Directory†
0887-1183 Legal Handbook for Architects, Engineers and Contractors 4720
0887-1191 Civil Rights Litigation and Attorney Fees Annual Handbook *changed to* Civil Rights Litigation and Attorney Fees Handbook 4829
0887-1205 Immigration Procedures Handbook 4691
0887-123X Carmelite Digest 7787
0887-1264 Cole Chronicle
0887-1280 Pate Pioneers
0887-1299 Elkins Eagle
0887-1337 Analysis of Key S E C No-Action Letters 1610
0887-137X E B R I Issue Brief 1859
0887-1418 Hand Papermaking 6734
0887-1493 AIDS Policy and Law 4612
0887-1507 Playwright's Companion†
0887-1574 Index to Book Reviews in Religion 7698
0887-1612 Conditioned Response†
0887-1639 C M J S Centerpieces 7719
0887-1655 Van Wert County Genealogical Quarterly†
0887-1701 T V Technology 2394
0887-171X Polling Report 7200
0887-1736 Complications in Orthopedics 6058
0887-1752 L O M A Resource 4512
0887-1760 Mid-America Journal of Theology 7663
0887-1892 Founder's Sounder 6568
0887-1914 Congressional Report: Science, Energy & Environment 7431
0887-1922 John T. Reed's Real Estate Investor's Monthly 7596
0887-1973 Metro Handbook and Directory of Members (Year)†
0887-2007 High - Scope Resource 3063
0887-2023 Vedic Globe†
0887-2058 Journal of Business Strategies 1764
0887-2074 South Coast Poetry Journal†
0887-2120 Woman Engineer 3227
0887-2139 Frederick Forerunners 3767
0887-2147 Au Courant Newsmagazine
0887-2155 Duckburg Times 4334
0887-2171 Seminars in Ultrasound, C T and M R I 6208
0887-218X Debates in Medicine†
0887-2201 Private Funding Advisor†
0887-2236 Biological and Cultural Tests for Control of Plant Diseases 779
0887-2244 Thoroughbred Times 8299
0887-2279 Alaska Business Newsletter†
0887-2333 Toxicology in Vitro 3502
0887-235X Combat Studies Institute. U.S. Army Command and General Staff College. Research Survey 6416
0887-2376 Science Scope 7910
0887-2384 Creative Needle 6638
0887-2392 Soviet Medical Reviews. Section B: Physicochemical Aspects of Medicine Reviews†
0887-2406 Curly Cues 8290
0887-252X Journal of Theoretical Psychology
0887-2546 Combat Weapons†
0887-2597 Heartland Journal (Madison)†
0887-2783 Social History of Alcohol Review *changed to* 1930-8418 2699
0887-2856 Lest We Forget 3773
0887-2899 National Jury Verdict Review and Analysis 4739
0887-2910 Agri-Times Northwest 82
0887-2937 Clothing and Textile Arts Index 2250
0887-2953 Consultants' and Contractors' Newsletter
0887-3003 R T W Review† 8984
0887-302X Clothing & Textiles Research Journal 2246
0887-3046 Zingsheim Times 3788
0887-3135 Holston Pastfinder 3771
0887-3186 Citizens Informer 7116
0887-3208 Florida Real Estate and Development Update 7591
0887-3224 Biology of Extracellular Matrix 828
0887-3267 The Humanistic Psychologist 7361
0887-347X Railroad Station Historical Society. Railroad Station Monograph 8623
0887-3488 Soviet Medical Reviews. Section D: Immunology Reviews†
0887-3496 Soviet Medical Reviews. Section E: Virology Reviews†
0887-3518 Chinese Physics - Lasers†
0887-3534 Drug Therapy for the Elderly†
0887-3550 C L S Newsletter 4999
0887-3569 Contemporary Social Issues: A Bibliographic Series 8148
0887-3577 Social Theory: A Bibliographic Series 8150
0887-3593 North American Benthological Society. Journal 694
0887-3615 I C L A Bulletin 5307
0887-3631 Journal of Cultural Geography 4017
0887-364X State of the World 3467
0887-3658 Frontiers of Clinical Neuroscience 6142
0887-3682 Pennsylvania Manufacturers Register 2023
0887-3690 Creative Quilting
0887-3712 H L B Newsletter†
0887-3763 Reference and Research Book News 634
0887-3771 Utah Centennial Series 4316
0887-378X The Milbank Quarterly 7154
0887-3801 Journal of Computing in Civil Engineering 3292
0887-381X Journal of Cold Regions Engineering 3274
0887-3828 Journal of Performance of Constructed Facilities 3276
0887-3836 Video Register and Teleconferencing Resources Directory†
0887-3844 New Directions in Information Management 5035
0887-3852 AIDS & Public Policy Journal 5808
0887-3860 Wandering Wolfs 3787
0887-4034 Criminal Justice Policy Review 4886
0887-4042 Directory of Primes 1988
0887-4050 Small Business Preferential Subcontracts Opportunities Monthly 2028
0887-4085 Government Primecontracts Monthly 1886
0887-4115 Bellowing Ark 5261
0887-4131 Privileged Traveler†
0887-414X Beauty Age
0887-4174 Texas Fish & Game 8337
0887-4190 Builder News 984
0887-4220 Sea Grant Abstracts†
0887-4239 Albatross
0887-4247 Harris West Virginia Manufacturing Directory (Year) 2003
0887-428X Washington Spectator 7193
0887-4301 Northrop University Law Journal of Aerospace, Business and Taxation
0887-4328 Lighthouse (Auburn)
0887-4336 Electronic Representatives Directory (Year)†
0887-4387 University of Michigan. School of Dentistry. Alumni Bulletin 5868
0887-4409 West Virginia Association of College English Teachers. Bulletin 5398
0887-4417 Journal of Computer Information Systems 2523
0887-4468 Public Innovation Abroad 4424
0887-4476 Synapse (New York) 6187
0887-4484 H M O - P P O Directory 1999
0887-4492 Lake Effect (New York)†
0887-4514 A D L A†
0887-4557 The Communique (Milwaukee) 5956
0887-4808 Financial Managers' Statement†
0887-4824 Whitmark Magazine
0887-4840 U.S. Forest Service. General Technical Report P N W 3706
0887-4905 Attorney's Directory of Forensic Psychologists†
0887-493X Alabama Heritage 4282
0887-4980 U.S. Bureau of Reclamation. Annual Report 2630
0887-4999 The Almanac of the Canning, Freezing, Preserving Industries 3626
0887-5006 Florida Nursing Review†
0887-5049 Prism (New Brighton) 7671
0887-5057 Erotic Fiction Quarterly 5290
0887-5073 Valve News†
0887-5081 Pump News†
0887-5170 Hayden's Ferry Review 5219
0887-5200 Today's Executive†
0887-5219 M G F
0887-5227 Virginia's Press 4585
0887-5286 Motorola Technical Developments 2370
0887-5294 Resource Recovery Update
0887-5308 CrazyQuilt†
0887-5367 Hypatia 8898
0887-5413 Gloucester County Historical Society. Bulletin 4294
0887-543X Lycoming County Historical Society Journal 4302
0887-5448 Harlow's Wooden Man 4294
0887-5480 Relationship & Family Communications
0887-557X Video Buyer's Guide†
0887-5588 Charlotte Business Journal 1082
0887-5596 North Carolina English Teacher 5156
0887-5669 Dentist (Waco)†
0887-5693 Emerick Family Newsletter 3765
0887-5707 Magnets in Your Future†
0887-5715 Redneck Review
0887-5723 Black Film Review†
0887-5731 Chronicles 5210
0887-5847 T V Collector†
0887-5855 Nueva Luz 6972
0887-5863 New York Mets Inside Pitch 8240
0887-5901 Who's Who in Technology†
0887-591X Chocolatier *changed to* Dessert Professional 3673
0887-6045 Journal of Services Marketing 1827
0887-6061 Balloon Life 8161
0887-6142 Progress in Pesticide Biochemistry and Toxicology† 8983
0887-6177 Archives of Clinical Neuropsychology 6123
0887-6185 Journal of Anxiety Disorders 7368
0887-6207 BioScan 758
0887-6223 Great Lakes Travel & Living
0887-624X Journal of Polymer Science. Part A, Polymer Chemistry 2125
0887-6266 Journal of Polymer Science. Part B, Polymer Physics 2125
0887-6274 Clinical Nurse Specialist 5955
0887-6282 Coas: New Mexico Archaeology and History†
0887-6290 Georgist Journal 1542
0887-6304 InterFace (Chicago, 1984) 5848
0887-6312 Frary Family Newsletter 3767
0887-6320 Frary Family Journal 3767
0887-6371 Oakley's Insiders Money Report†
0887-6495 Biochemistry of the Elements 726
0887-6509 Journal of Compliance in Health Care†
0887-6541 Cosmetic Science and Technology Series 5601
0887-6584 N S S L H A Clinical Series 6083
0887-6665 Masterkey†
0887-6681 Xavier Review 5402
0887-6703 Spectroscopy 2105
0887-6746 Laurence Reid Gas Conditioning Conference. Proceedings 6777
0887-6827 Offshore Service Vessels†
0887-6835 Offshore Tugs†
0887-6851 Video Librarian 5054
0887-686X Hydrological Science and Technology 8825
0887-6878 Exhibit Builder 1816
0887-6916 Advances in Otolaryngology - Head and Neck Surgery†
0887-6924 Leukemia 5939
0887-6959 Whitman County Genealogical Society. Newsletter 3788
0887-6991 Latest Jokes
0887-7068 Restaurant Exchange News
0887-7084 49ers Report 8252
0887-7106 Alert!: Focus on Central America†
0887-7165 Eastern Great Lakes Biblical Society. Proceedings 7639
0887-7254 P N W 145
0887-7297 Social Sciences in Forestry†
0887-736X For Formulation Chemists Only 2100
0887-7386 Apis†
0887-7394 Toxics Law Reporter 3513
0887-7491 Capacitor and Resistor Technology Symposium. Proceedings 3090
0887-7505 Bed & Breakfast Update†
0887-7556 Printout 7329
0887-7580 Black Masks 8467
0887-7629 Political Risk Letter 1580
0887-7653 American Journal of Islamic Social Sciences 7709
0887-7661 Network World 2502
0887-7688 Jackpotunities†
0887-7696 Studies in the Age of Chaucer. Proceedings *see* 0190-2407 5382
0887-7777 Lawyer Referral Network 4718
0887-7785 Criminal Justice (Chicago, 1986) 4886
0887-7815 Pharmaceutical Litigation Reporter *changed to* 1553-6696 4826
0887-7823 General Aviation Accident Report†
0887-7858 Insurance Industry Litigation Reporter 4507
0887-7866 Andrews School Asbestos Alert†
0887-7904 Business (Little Rock) 1397
0887-7920 Rochester A F L - C I O Labor News
0887-7963 Transfusion Medicine Reviews 5942
0887-7971 American Journal of Cardiac Imaging†
0887-8005 American Journal of Cardiovascular Pathology†
0887-8013 Journal of Clinical Laboratory Analysis 5907
0887-803X Hair International News 588
0887-8048 New Jersey Folklife†
0887-8056 New York, New Jersey, Connecticut Real Estate†
0887-8064 Washington Information Directory (Year) 7193
0887-8099 Chinese Literature, Essays, Articles, Reviews 5273
0887-817X Fitness in Business†
0887-8218 Forum for Applied Research and Public Policy†
0887-8226 Providence Business News 1162
0887-8250 Journal of Sensory Studies 6157
0887-8277 Industrial Negligence Law Bulletin†
0887-8420 Private Clubs 2269
0887-8439 Consumer Reports Travel Letter† 8943
0887-8463 Wine Advocate 612

0888-8051 National Toxicology Program Technical Report Series **3455**
0888-8086 Radiological Health Bulletin†
0888-8108 M.D. Anderson Symposia in Fundamental Cancer Research†
0888-8132 National Forum of Education Administration and Supervision Journal **2995**
0888-8183 The Energy Report
0888-8191 Circulation Management *changed to* 1946-0392 **7552**
0888-8205 The Agency Automation Report *changed to* 1940-9176 **4530**
0888-8299 S C I Nursing **5708**
0888-8310 Foundation of Thanatology Series†
0888-8337 Drug and Chemical Toxicology Series†
0888-8361 Defense Systems Review and Military Communications†
0888-840X Arizona Hunter and Angler **8304**
0888-8469 Innovator (University Park) **2288**
0888-8507 P C Magazine (Print)† **8979**
0888-8574 Harmonic Research†
0888-8604 Indiana Folklore and Oral History†
0888-8612 Winds of Change **6636**
0888-8671 Callahan's Credit Union Directory **1079**
0888-868X Metropolitan Education†
0888-8698 NewsNet Action Letter†
0888-8701 American Handel Society. Newsletter **6543**
0888-8752 Middlebury Studies in Russian Language and Literature **5151**
0888-8787 University of Texas Studies in Contemporary Spanish-American Fiction†
0888-8809 Molecular Endocrinology **5897**
0888-8817 Forensic Engineering†
0888-8833 Open Hands **7769**
0888-8884 Alaska Wilderness Milepost
0888-8892 Conservation Biology **2607**
0888-9007 Jusur†
0888-9015 Cue Sheet **6560**
0888-904X Japan Electronics (Gardena)†
0888-9058 Perceptions
0888-9074 Baptist Trumpet **7747**
0888-9104 Hardwood Market Report **1050**
0888-9139 Crittenden Real Estate Buyers **7588**
0888-9201 Issues: A Critical Examination of Contemporary Ethical Issues in Health Care†
0888-9287 Advances in Motor Development Research† **8928**
0888-9376 Classmate†
0888-9384 Chrysalis (West Chester)†
0888-9406 In-Stat Electronics Report† **8963**
0888-9465 Health Professions Report†
0888-949X The N B E R Digest (Print) **1151**
0888-9546 Illinois. Natural History Survey. Special Publication **677**
0888-9570 S O P A Newsletter†
0888-9589 Sport Place International **8205**
0888-9619 Lyonia†
0888-9643 Toledo Museum of Art. Annual Report *changed to* Toledo Museum of Art Members Newsletter **6538**
0888-9678 Research Paper S E *changed to* U S D A Forest Service. Southern Research Station. Research Paper **3705**
0888-9686 U.S. Department of Agriculture. North Central Forest Experiment Station. Research Paper N C **3706**
0888-9708 U S D A Forest Service. Rocky Mountain Research Station. Resource Bulletin **3705**
0888-9732 Perspective (Madison) *changed to* 1932-5800 **2993**
0888-9740 Personality, Psychopathology and Psychotherapy†
0888-9775 New York Woman†
0888-9988 Local Climatological Data. Paducah, Kentucky. Annual Summary with Comparative Data **6380**
0889-0064 Mutual Fund Trends **1641**
0889-0072 Waste Recovery Report **3514**
0889-0102 California Forestry Note **3685**
0889-0145 New German Review **5340**
0889-0153 Drew **2282**
0889-017X Mental Health Law News **6160**
0889-0196 Electronics Purchasing†
0889-020X Soviet Spaceflight Report†
0889-0234 D W I Journal: Law & Science **4654**
0889-0242 Pressure (Bethesda) **5699**
0889-0277 Shaw Historical Library. Journal **4312**
0889-0293 International Journal of Social Education **7974**
0889-0358 Houston Medicine†
0889-0390 George D. Hall's Directory of Central Atlantic States Manufacturers†
0889-0404 Defense Daily **52**
0889-0447 Pacific Northwest Feed Market News **295**
0889-0463 Hops Market News **234**
0889-048X Agriculture and Human Values **85**
0889-0498 Land Opportunity Review†
0889-0501 Origins (Grand Rapids) **7770**
0889-0595 Vatican Voices and Notable Papal Quotes **7821**
0889-0609 American Labor†
0889-0625 Security Law Newsletter **2680**
0889-0633 Chemical Waste Litigation Reporter **3505**
0889-0641 R I C O Law Reporter **4765**
0889-0668 Journal of Explosives Engineering **3248**
0889-0692 Thrasher **8212**
0889-0722 Third Woman†
0889-0749 National School Bus Report†
0889-0765 Center Focus **8093**
0889-0781 Wherever†
0889-0803 Notus New Writing†
0889-0811 Communications Industry Report†
0889-0838 Maddux Report *changed to* Maddux Business Report **1146**
0889-0846 T A H P E R D Journal **6998**
0889-0889 Transportation in America **8516**
0889-0897 Professional Investor
0889-0935 The Valley Forge **2307**
0889-0951 Media Sports Business† **8973**
0889-1036 Better Health & Living†
0889-1575 Journal of Food Composition and Analysis **3650**
0889-1583 Journal of the Japanese and International Economies **1574**

0889-1591 Brain, Behavior, and Immunity **5755**
0889-163X Eleven Meter Times & Journal
0889-1664 Rambunctious Review **5357**
0889-1680 Anson Newsletter†
0889-1699 Turnarounds & Workouts **4799**
0889-1753 International Business Regulations Report†
0889-1761 Brazil Service
0889-177X The Anvil's Ring **531**
0889-1834 South Carolina Farmer **157**
0889-1893 American Journal of Alternative Agriculture (Print Edition) *changed to* 1742-1705 **150**
0889-1915 Temple International and Comparative Law Journal **4942**
0889-2016 Maroon Tiger **2291**
0889-2113 Reference Point: Food Industry Abstracts **3670**
0889-2121 American Fitness Quarterly†
0889-2148 Afghanistan Forum†
0889-2156 Mennonite Weekly Review **7738**
0889-2164 Different Worlds†
0889-2202 Progressive Review (Washington D.C.) **5235**
0889-2229 AIDS Research and Human Retroviruses **5809**
0889-2237 Birmingham Business Journal **1067**
0889-2288 Carlsonreport for Shopping Center Management **1732**
0889-2296 Miami Today **3981**
0889-2326 Riverside Quarterly†
0889-2377 North Texas Golfer **8240**
0889-2407 Ohio Fisherman
0889-2415 S O C M Sentinel **3464**
0889-2423 The Independent Florida Alligator **2287**
0889-2431 Daily Commercial Record **1090**
0889-2504 Cavallino Magazine **8573**
0889-258X Lindleyana **3742**
0889-2709 Kansas Libraries **5022**
0889-2741 Cities of the World **4002**
0889-2776 Metro California Media **30**
0889-2784 National Radio Publicity Outlets
0889-2857 Ketch Pen **291**
0889-2865 Voices of Youth
0889-2873 Nashville Business Journal **1152**
0889-2938 Guam and Micronesia Glimpses†
0889-2962 North Shore Life†
0889-2970 Rural Heritage **299**
0889-2989 Do-It-Yourself Retailing *changed to* 1934-8819 **4438**
0889-2997 Sabermetric Review†
0889-3012 Assemblage†
0889-3047 The Review of Austrian Economics **1548**
0889-3055 Highlights & Documents†
0889-3098 StarDate **582**
0889-311X Crystallography Reviews **2110**
0889-3128 Studies in Gender and Culture
0889-3136 The Best of Long Range Planning **1728**
0889-3144 R A P R A Review Reports **7101**
0889-3179 Elected and Appointed Black Judges in the United States **4950**
0889-3209 Sales Upbeat
0889-3217 Seafood Business **3607**
0889-3225 Roundel **8602**
0889-3241 A C I Structural Journal **974**
0889-325X A C I Materials Journal **974**
0889-3268 Journal of Business & Psychology **7369**
0889-3322 Florida Game & Fish **8314**
0889-3357 The Richmond Business Journal **1168**
0889-3365 Macroeconomics Annual **1720**
0889-3381 The Microbiological Update **891**
0889-3403 Business Journal of New Jersey†
0889-3411 Nuclear Monitor *changed to* Nuclear Monitor (North American Edition) **3172**
0889-342X N A O S†
0889-3454 Hazardous Materials Newsletter **7520**
0889-3470 Farmers Independent **112**
0889-3497 Sun Magazine†
0889-3500 National Association of State Boards of Accountancy. State Board Report **1297**
0889-3519 Alcoholic Beverage Executives' Newsletter **597**
0889-356X Sixth Circuit Review (Louisville) **4965**
0889-3578 Fourth Circuit Review (Louisville) **4952**
0889-3586 Restaurant Reporter†
0889-3594 North Dakota. Geological Survey. Newsletter **2759**
0889-3608 Meat Sheet **293**
0889-3616 Codes & Standards **4407**
0889-3640 Miami Meanderings **3775**
0889-3667 International Journal of Comparative Psychology **7364**
0889-3675 Journal of Poetry Therapy **7378**
0889-3764 Apicultural Information and Issues†
0889-3799 Missouri Game & Fish **8322**
0889-3802 Kentucky Game & Fish **8320**
0889-3888 Truck Identification Book **8677**
0889-3918 Automotive Week **8566**
0889-3934 Motion **7061**
0889-3950 Official Industrial Equipment Guide†
0889-3977 Advances in Sports Medicine and Fitness†
0889-3985 More Light Update **4377**
0889-4000 I B F A N News
0889-4019 The Career Development Quarterly **6694**
0889-4078 Home & Away (Ohio Edition) **8719**
0889-4086 Northeast Update for Insurance Women†
0889-4094 Sailing World **8281**
0889-4108 Guide to Computer Living **2419**
0889-4159 Message of the Open Bible **7663**
0889-4175 Talent Education Journal†
0889-4191 Bioelectromagnetics Society Newsletter *changed to* Bioelectromagnetics Newsletter **752**
0889-423X Dealer Communicator **7319**
0889-4256 Wine Investor: Executive Edition
0889-4299 America's Economy†
0889-4302 Apple Assembly Line†
0889-4329 Your Health (Boca Raton)†
0889-4337 Today's C P A **1302**
0889-4469 Liability & Insurance Bulletin†
0889-4477 Esthetic Dentistry Update†
0889-4493 Manager's Legal Bulletin **1778**
0889-4507 Verbum†

0889-4523 Corporate Television†
0889-454X Walker's Estimating & Construction Journal†
0889-4558 Child Care Center†
0889-4639 American Libraries (Year)†
0889-4655 The Journal of Cardiovascular Nursing **5792**
0889-468X Continuing the Conversation†
0889-4701 Problems in Critical Care†
0889-471X Problems in Urology†
0889-4744 Monthly Mini-Lessons in Care of the Aging **4051**
0889-4752 Popular Lures†
0889-4760 Mrs. Eagle **2268**
0889-4787 Valley Potato Grower **257**
0889-4795 Let's Play Hockey **8185**
0889-4825 Gulf Coast Golfer **8234**
0889-4841 Capitol Update **7429**
0889-485X Jonesreport *changed to* 1555-8347 **1823**
0889-4876 Security Affairs **7265**
0889-4884 Mailbox News **3674**
0889-4906 English for Specific Purposes **5114**
0889-4922 International Recording Equipment and Studio Directory†
0889-4965 The Printer **7326**
0889-4973 Videomaker **2404**
0889-5015 Off Main Street **5345**
0889-504X Journal of Turbomachinery **3387**
0889-5058 Youthworker Update†
0889-5074 Advances in Cardiac Surgery†
0889-5104 Brevard Business News **1069**
0889-518X Greene County Democrat **3536**
0889-5201 Bebop and Beyond
0889-5244 Pilipinas **4187**
0889-5252 Heartsong Review†
0889-5333 Target Marketing **1845**
0889-5341 Monitoring Times **2360**
0889-5392 Consortium **5481**
0889-5406 American Journal of Orthodontics and Dentofacial Orthopedics **5834**
0889-5414 Hospitality Law **4388**
0889-5422 Employee Testing & the Law†
0889-5481 Arizona Trend†
0889-5503 Wabash County Historical Society Newsletter **4317**
0889-5546 Current **2803**
0889-5589 Animator†
0889-5597 Credit Union Newswatch **1333**
0889-5619 Farmers and Consumers Market Bulletin **111**
0889-5635 Blitz†
0889-5643 Montessori Observer **3073**
0889-5678 New Horizons (Milwaukee) **2891**
0889-5740 Fire Control Digest **3577**
0889-5791 Rip
0889-5899 Ostomy - Wound Management **6070**
0889-5902 Frozen Food Digest **3644**
0889-5929 Penn State Agriculture **146**
0889-5937 New Mexico Business, Current Economic Report **1153**
0889-5988 Bigger, Faster, Stronger **8223**
0889-5996 Circus Report **8468**
0889-6003 Jury Trials & Tribulations **4707**
0889-6038 U S Fire Sprinkler Reporter†
0889-6054 Space Today **71**
0889-6089 Amateur Satellite Report **2375**
0889-6143 The Writing Center Journal **2926**
0889-6216 Start (San Francisco)†
0889-6259 The Master Teacher **2885**
0889-6267 Avanti Magazine **8567**
0889-6283 Urology Annual†
0889-6291 Iran Today **3891**
0889-6321 Maeventec Software Review†
0889-6348 Proteus (Shippensburg) **3986**
0889-6402 Organization Development Journal **1784**
0889-6410 Lake Street Review†
0889-6445 Bugle (Missoula) **2605**
0889-6461 Tech Street Journal†
0889-647X Kentucky Poetry Review†
0889-6488 A T E A Journal **2823**
0889-6518 Magazines in Special Media **4071**
0889-6607 R I D I M - R C M I Inventory of Music Iconography **6608**
0889-6712 Animals' Voice Magazine†
0889-6720 Montessori News **3073**
0889-6836 Infocus (Philadelphia) **2521**
0889-6984 Del-Gen-Data Bank†
0889-7018 Rehabilitation Education **3046**
0889-7042 Michaels on Etiquette†
0889-7077 Substance Abuse **2699**
0889-7085 Specialty Travel Index **8757**
0889-7158 Calliope (Bristol)†
0889-7174 Changing Men†
0889-7204 Progress in Cardiovascular Nursing **5798**
0889-7247 Morrell, Morrill Families Association Newsletter†
0889-728X Sculpture **516**
0889-7298 Oregon State University. Forest Research Laboratory. Biennial Report **3699**
0889-7328 Military History **4303**
0889-7352 Alaska Oil and Industry News†
0889-7395 C R A Review **1881**
0889-7425 Symbols **420**
0889-7433 Aura Literary Arts Review **5207**
0889-745X Oklahoma Baptist Chronicle **7769**
0889-7468 Alabama Development News†
0889-7549 Business Digest of Pioneer Valley
0889-7581 Pan Pipes **6604**
0889-759X Jean Rhys Review **5313**
0889-7670 Connecticut Magazine **3973**
0889-7727 Great Dane Reporter **6808**
0889-7743 Yale Journal of International Law **4945**
0889-7751 Forum (Sacramento) **4677**
0889-7794 Narc Officer **4738**
0889-7816 Handbook of Non-Prescription Drugs **6845**
0889-7840 Market Vane's Bullish Consensus **1638**
0889-7875 New Family Life **4364**
0889-7891 South American Explorer **8757**
0889-7956 W K Kellogg Foundation Annual Report **1192**

9372 0889-7972 ULRICH'S PERIODICALS

0889-7972 Fanatic Reader
0889-8022 E R I C - C U E Trends and Issues†
0889-8030 E R I C - C U E Urban Diversity Series†
0889-8049 E R I C Clearinghouse on Urban Education. Digest†
0889-8065 West Virginia University. Agricultural and Forestry Experiment Station. Circular **170**
0889-8138 Midwest Living **3981**
0889-8162 Washington Reports. 2d Series **4967**
0889-8189 China Painter **481**
0889-8227 Applied Management Newsletter
0889-8235 Guilfoyle Report **6969**
0889-8243 The C T N S Bulletin **7629**
0889-8391 Journal of Cognitive Psychotherapy **7371**
0889-8421 Everything Natural†
0889-8448 Perspectives in Mexican American Studies **3557**
0889-8464 N T I S Tech Notes†
0889-8472 Upscale†
0889-8480 Mathematical Population Studies **7287**
0889-8499 Newspapers Career Directory†
0889-8502 Magazines Career Directory†
0889-8510 Marketing and Sales Career Directory†
0889-8529 Endocrinology & Metabolism Clinics of North America **5892**
0889-8537 Anesthesiology Clinics of North America *changed to* 1932-2275 **5770**
0889-8545 Obstetrics and Gynecology Clinics of North America **6001**
0889-8553 Gastroenterology Clinics of North America **5924**
0889-8561 Immunology and Allergy Clinics of North America **5760**
0889-857X Rheumatic Diseases Clinics of North America **6226**
0889-8588 Hematology / Oncology Clinics of North America **6021**
0889-8650 South Asia in Review†
0889-8731 Al-Arabiyya **5200**
0889-8790 Remember That Song **6610**
0889-8804 Double Talk (Amelia)†
0889-8839 Overseas Academic Opportunities **3014**
0889-8847 Attitudes and Arabesques **2688**
0889-8863 Parents' Press **2165**
0889-8901 Christ for the Nations **7631**
0889-8928 Media Arts†
0889-8936 P R R C: Emerging Trends **7668**
0889-8952 Voices in the Wilderness†
0889-8979 A T & T Technology†
0889-9002 China Daily News†
0889-9010 Safe & Vault Technology **2679**
0889-9096 Monte's Mail
0889-9142 Imaging Update†
0889-9185 Latter - Day Woman†
0889-9207 Chief of Police **2646**
0889-9223 The Fed Tracker **1109**
0889-9304 Southern Magazine†
0889-9363 N A F S A Government Affairs Bulletin†
0889-9371 School Library Media Activities Monthly **5046**
0889-938X Review of Industrial Organization **1548**
0889-9398 Opera Companion
0889-9401 The Analysis of Verbal Behavior **7334**
0889-941X Corporate Monthly†
0889-9428 North American Society of Adlerian Psychology. Newsletter **7388**
0889-9436 Mission Frontiers **7664**
0889-9444 Management Strategy†
0889-9452 Financial Independence **1344**
0889-9460 Amplitude
0889-9479 Blois Voice†
0889-9495 Radiance†
0889-9509 Eye Research Seminar **6042**
0889-9517 Odontia (Print) *changed to* Odontia (Online) **5858**
0889-9525 Technical Trends **1655**
0889-9568 Proof Rock **5235**
0889-9576 Air Alaska
0889-9584 Southland High Tech†
0889-9614 Skywatchers Almanac (Year) **581**
0889-9622 Local Planet Visibility Report (Year) **577**
0889-9630 Comparative Ephemeris (Year) **573**
0889-9657 Education and Self Management of the Psychiatric Patient†
0889-9673 California Beverage Hotline
0889-9681 Wine Investor: Buyers' Guide
0889-9746 Journal of Fluids and Structures **3205**
0889-9789 The Public Employment Reporter†
0889-9797 Casino Chronicle **8164**
0889-9924 Professional Floral Designer†
0889-9967 Profit-Building Strategies for Business Owners **1162**
0889-9983 Securities Handbook Series. Mortgage-Backed Securities **1382**
0889-9991 UPstate Magazine
0890-0019 Raised Dot Computing Newsletter†
0890-0035 The GreekAmerican **3535**
0890-0108 Journal of Animal Science. Supplement. Biennial Symposium on Animal Reproduction **923**
0890-0132 Journal of Interdisciplinary Studies (Pasadena) **4460**
0890-0159 Advances in Behavioral Economics **7331**
0890-023X Market Month **1638**
0890-0256 Thundercats Magazine†
0890-0264 Spectrum (Roseville) **7775**
0890-0299 Wine & Spirits **613**
0890-0302 The California Psychologist **7343**
0890-0337 San Francisco Business Times **1432**
0890-0353 Families of Wyoming County, W V **3765**
0890-0361 Families of Yancey County, N C **3765**
0890-037X Weed Technology **258**
0890-0388 Science Weekly. Level Pre-A **2212**
0890-0426 C A R A Seminary Forum†
0890-0434 The Massachusetts Daily Collegian **2291**
0890-0450 Old Hickory Review
0890-0477 Louisiana Literature **5328**
0890-0485 Ninnau **3554**
0890-0515 Income Investor Perspectives
0890-0523 Journal of Mass Media Ethics **8114**
0890-0566 Minnesota Literature **5334**
0890-0574 Austin Magazine†
0890-0582 A I Ch E M I Modular Instruction. Series G: Design of Equipment†
0890-0590 El Lider Bautista†
0890-0604 Artificial Intelligence for Engineering Design, Analysis and Manufacturing **2446**
0890-0612 Hilliard History†
0890-0639 Connections (Kittery) **3763**
0890-0795 C M J New Music Report **6553**
0890-0841 Books and Religion†
0890-0876 Western & Eastern Treasures†
0890-0884 Adhesives & Sealants Newsletter†
0890-0914 George Odiorne Letter†
0890-0930 Sun Reporter **3567**
0890-0957 Dick Davis Digest **1620**
0890-0973 N C L C Reports: Deceptive Acts & Warranties **4737**
0890-099X Orthodox America **7705**
0890-1007 The Oklahoma Constitution **7458**
0890-104X New York Forest Owner **3698**
0890-1090 Volunteering Virginia **8077**
0890-1112 Journal of Ritual Studies **345**
0890-1120 Arthritis Today **6222**
0890-1139 Italy (Year) **8724**
0890-1155 Home Shopping Investor†
0890-1171 American Journal of Health Promotion **6982**
0890-118X Across Frontiers
0890-1201 Earthwatch Oregon **3415**
0890-121X Private Education Law Report **4761**
0890-1252 Satellite Retailer†
0890-1260 Satellite Times†
0890-1287 The S L V G S News **3781**
0890-1341 Arab Book World
0890-1392 Minergia†
0890-1406 Japan Computer Technology and Applications Abstracts†
0890-1422 Keeping Up†
0890-1449 Current Topics in Pulmonary Pharmacology and Toxicology†
0890-1465 Pennsylvania Portfolio†
0890-1473 California Staats-Zeitung **3524**
0890-1538 Interp Central Clearinghouse Newsletter†
0890-1554 Alabama Literary Review **5205**
0890-1619 New Options†
0890-1627 Council of Professional Association on Federal Statistics. News **8365**
0890-1651 Directory of Minnesota City Officials **7491**
0890-1686 Michigan Historical Review (Mt. Pleasant) **4303**
0890-1732 Plastictrends†
0890-1759 Spy†
0890-1813 C A Selects. Artificial Sweeteners **3669**
0890-1821 C A Selects. Memory & Recording Devices & Materials **2088**
0890-1856 C A Selects. Carbon & Graphite Fibers†
0890-1864 C A Selects. Catalytic & Kinetic Analysis†
0890-1872 C A Selects. Fiber Optics and Optical Communication†
0890-1880 C A Selects. Formulation Chemistry **2087**
0890-1899 C A Selects. Ion Chromatography **2088**
0890-1910 C A Selects. Pharmaceutical Chemistry (Journals) **6889**
0890-1929 C A Selects. Pharmaceutical Chemistry (Patents) **6889**
0890-1937 C A Selects. Platinum and Palladium Chemistry **2090**
0890-1945 C A Selects. Polyacrylates (Journals) **2091**
0890-1953 C A Selects. Quaternary Ammonium Compounds **2092**
0890-1961 C A Selects. Silicas & Silicates **2092**
0890-1988 Employment Health Law & Benefits†
0890-2070 European Journal of Personality **7355**
0890-2127 Colorado Springs Business†
0890-2135 C K C Report **4353**
0890-2143 Computer Entertainer
0890-2151 Mitchell Report†
0890-2194 Recreation Executive Report **4982**
0890-2208 Nolo News†
0890-2216 Confederate Veteran **4289**
0890-2224 On Our Backs†
0890-2240 Yale Daily News **2310**
0890-2267 Clinical Report on Aging†
0890-2305 International Employment Opportunities Digest†
0890-233X Horse Industry Directory **8292**
0890-2372 Gilbert Gallery
0890-2402 Cellular Marketing *changed to* 1086-7716 **2366**
0890-2461 Philosophy & Theology **6943**
0890-247X Parenting *changed to* 1947-9883 **4365**
0890-247X Parenting *changed to* 1947-1149 **4365**
0890-2518 A P V A Newsletter
0890-2593 Groce Family Newsletter†
0890-2607 N C L C Reports: Debt Collection & Repossessions **4737**
0890-2615 N C L C Reports: Consumer Credit & Usury **4737**
0890-2631 Oswald Outlines
0890-2747 Soviet Journal of Applied Physics†
0890-2755 Advances in Sensor Technology
0890-2763 Advances in R & D†
0890-2771 Advances in High-Tech Materials
0890-278X A G H E Exchange **4037**
0890-2887 Expressions (Greenville)
0890-2909 G.I. Joe Magazine†
0890-2917 The Yearbook of Langland Studies **5438**
0890-2925 The Air Charter Guide **8534**
0890-2933 Broom, Brush & Mop **1069**
0890-2941 New Law Books Reviewer
0890-2968 Redwood Researcher **3780**
0890-300X Innovator's Digest†
0890-3018 Industrial Health & Hazards Update **6678**
0890-3034 Confidential Report for Attorneys **4648**
0890-3050 Lake Superior Magazine **4300**
0890-3077 Twins **2170**
0890-3085 Peterson's Applying to Colleges and Universities in the United States: A Handbook for International Students†
0890-3093 Exploradores†
0890-3107 The Tartan **3004**
0890-3115 Estudios Biblicos para Ninos. Alumnos†
0890-3123 Estudios Biblicos para Ninos. Maestros†
0890-3158 Historias Biblicas para Preescolares. Maestros†
0890-3174 Weekly Reader. Pre-K Edition **2221**
0890-3190 Weekly Reader. Grade 4 Edition *changed to* W R News. Senior Edition **2220**
0890-3239 Weekly Reader. Senior Edition *changed to* W R News. Senior Edition **2220**
0890-3247 Historias Biblicas para Preescolares. Alumnos†
0890-3255 The Birth Gazette **5987**
0890-3271 Reports of Interest to Lawyers†
0890-3344 Journal of Human Lactation **5995**
0890-3352 Tenso **5386**
0890-3360 Gossage Regan Manager's Memo†
0890-3387 Christian Film & Video†
0890-3417 N C A H F Newsletter **7532**
0890-3433 Puckerbrush Review **5235**
0890-3476 Direction. Student Book **7638**
0890-3514 Golfweek **8234**
0890-3522 Metro Reporter **3550**
0890-3530 Network (Salt Lake City) **8877**
0890-3557 Lollipops†
0890-3565 A R R L Handbook for Radio Amateurs **2356**
0890-3573 Surprises†
0890-362X DuPont Registry: A Buyer's Gallery of Fine Automobiles **8578**
0890-3670 The Scientist **7913**
0890-3689 I D Strategies†
0890-3735 Nature Society News **7889**
0890-3891 Southwestern Discoveries
0890-3956 Campaign California Report†
0890-3972 Podiatric Products *changed to* OrthoKinetic Review **6069**
0890-4006 TeenQuest†
0890-4014 Arnold Ancestry **3759**
0890-4022 Gillet Gillette Gillett Pride 'n' Joy **3768**
0890-4049 Michigan Distributors Directory†
0890-4065 Journal of Aging Studies **4048**
0890-4073 Advances in Health Education: Current Research†
0890-4081 International Christian Digest†
0890-409X Clinical Connection†
0890-4111 A T A Scholarly Monograph Series **5088**
0890-412X American University Studies. Series 20. Fine Arts **466**
0890-4154 Changing Homes
0890-4162 Teddy Bear Review **4348**
0890-4189 Looking Fit **6992**
0890-4197 Nathaniel Hawthorne Review **5338**
0890-4227 Current Packaging Abstracts†
0890-4251 International Trade and Investment Letter **1571**
0890-426X Eximbank Letter **1108**
0890-4278 Corporate Report Wisconsin **1087**
0890-4294 Differentia
0890-4340 Los Angeles Sentinel **3548**
0890-4359 Paper Air†
0890-4413 Current Diet Review
0890-4448 The Cherokee One Feather **3526**
0890-4456 Dewitt County Genealogical Society. Quarterly **3764**
0890-4464 Asia Institute. Bulletin **543**
0890-4480 World Book Health and Medical Annual†
0890-4537 Access (New York)†
0890-4596 Scream Magazine
0890-460X Rockbill
0890-4618 Campus Report **2971**
0890-4707 Restaurant Information Abstracts†
0890-4723 Southern California New Homes†
0890-4758 Translation Perspectives **5188**
0890-4766 Worldwide Travel Planner†
0890-4847 Studies in African and African-American Culture **4178**
0890-4863 P C Life
0890-4871 California Insurance Law Report†
0890-4898 The Practical Tax Lawyer **1939**
0890-4960 International Preservation News **5019**
0890-5010 Sub Rosa (Seattle)†
0890-5037 Law and Mental Health†
0890-5053 Cope†
0890-507X G I G Newsletter **6659**
0890-5096 Annals of Vascular Surgery **6237**
0890-510X World and United States Aviation and Space Records **75**
0890-5169 Corporate Philanthropy†
0890-5185 Cherokee Voice **8032**
0890-5193 Cherokee Boys Club Newsletter **3526**
0890-5215 O N S News *changed to* 1935-1623 **6029**
0890-5223 Retirement Money†
0890-5231 Release Print **6511**
0890-524X WordStar Scroll **2601**
0890-5258 Arkansas Episcopalian **7746**
0890-5304 Outdoor Photographer **6972**
0890-5339 Journal of Orthopaedic Trauma **6065**
0890-5355 Tennessee Family Law Letter **4914**
0890-5363 Geothermal Science and Technology
0890-538X Emerging **6644**
0890-5401 Information and Computation **2422**
0890-541X Directory of Grants in the Physical Sciences†
0890-5428 Human Service Education **8045**
0890-5436 Food Biotechnology **764**
0890-5444 Membrane Separation Engineering†
0890-5460 Ocean Physics and Engineering†
0890-5487 China Ocean Engineering **3184**
0890-5495 Nineteenth-Century Contexts **5341**
0890-5509 Waste Minimization & Recycling Report†
0890-5517 Quick Frozen Foods Annual Processors' Directory and Buyers' Guide **3661**
0890-5525 Directory of Directories: Publishers Volume†
0890-5541 Avaloka†
0890-5568 Living Prayer†
0890-5584 Restaurants U S A (Online) **4397**
0890-5592 Catastrophism and Ancient History. Proceedings†
0890-5649 A P B A Journal†
0890-5673 Natural Resources Computer Newsletter
0890-5762 Review (New York, 1968) **5360**
0890-5924 Texas Weekly **7472**
0890-5959 U.S. Employment Opportunities
0890-6068 Journal of Patient Account Management **4104**
0890-6076 Ski Patrol Magazine **8201**
0890-6092 Nebraska Development News **1500**

Link to your serials resources and content with ulrichsweb.com

0890-6130 Nature, Society, and Thought **7157**
0890-6149 Alaska History **4282**
0890-6157 Miners News **6471**
0890-6165 A F L - C I O Department of International Affairs. Bulletin†
0890-622X Peregrine **5429**
0890-6238 Reproductive Toxicology **927**
0890-6246 P I C O Laptops & Portables Magazine†
0890-6270 Starmont Popular Culture Studies†
0890-6327 International Journal of Adaptive Control and Signal Processing **3320**
0890-6343 Clock Radio†
0890-6386 Leisure Arts **4338**
0890-6408 Apalachee Quarterly *changed to* Apalachee Review **5256**
0890-6440 Jazzletter **6579**
0890-6459 Teacher Education and Practice **3084**
0890-6467 Oncogene Research†
0890-6491 Weavings **7780**
0890-653X Fiberoptic Product News *changed to* 1552-5511
0890-6548 Imagen **3931**
0890-6564 Lyceum of Natural History of New York. Annals *changed to* 0077-8923 **7892**
0890-6599 Journal of Neurological and Orthopaedic Medicine & Surgery†
0890-6610 The N D A Pipeline† **8975**
0890-6645 America's Corporate Families **1879**
0890-6718 FMedia!†
0890-6785 Payphone Exchange†
0890-6793 Christian Challenge **7750**
0890-6823 Factsheet 5†
0890-684X Caribbean Action†
0890-6858 Western New York Genealogical Society Journal **3787**
0890-6866 The Universe in the Classroom **3086**
0890-6882 Natural History Inventory of Colorado **957**
0890-6890 Magazine†
0890-6904 Local Climatological Data. Redding, California. Monthly Summary **6382**
0890-6912 Sales and Marketing Training
0890-6955 International Journal of Machine Tools and Manufacture **3369**
0890-6998 Revue C E L F A N - C E L F A N Review *changed to* 1547-1942 **5268**
0890-7005 Le Mercenaire Intelligence Newsletter†
0890-703X Evangelical Studies Bulletin **7756**
0890-7048 Progress in Endocrine Research and Therapy†
0890-7064 Journal of Psychology & Human Sexuality *changed to* 1931-7611 **7366**
0890-7129 Towpaths **4315**
0890-7137 Canal Society of Ohio. Newsletter **4287**
0890-7161 Media and Society Series **8119**
0890-720X Food Industry Newsletter **3639**
0890-7218 L A S A Forum **7982**
0890-7234 Printers Buyer's Guide and Handbook†
0890-7269 Caliban†
0890-7315 Inside Litigation†
0890-7358 Soviet Journal of Contemporary Engineering Mechanics†
0890-7471 A A A Today (Greenfield)
0890-7528 C A S BioTech Updates. Agriculture†
0890-7595 Medallion **4152**
0890-7609 Corporate Annual Report Newsletter **483**
0890-7625 Land Letter **2617**
0890-7641 Directory of Manufacturers' Sales Agencies
0890-765X The Journal of Rural Health **5654**
0890-7714 Winslow Homer: An Annual†
0890-7722 Magill Book Reviews†
0890-782X Official Video Directory & Buyer's Guide **2022**
0890-7862 Emory Bankruptcy Developments Journal **4830**
0890-7889 Technology and Learning†
0890-7900 S M T Trends **3112**
0890-7935 Rasmuson Library Historical Translation Series **4309**
0890-7951 G L C Voice†
0890-796X Caribbean Treasures†
0890-8028 Whole Gay Catalog†
0890-8044 I E E E Network **2498**
0890-815X Privatization Report†
0890-8184 Chimera Connections†
0890-8192 Man from Mainz and His Descendants **3774**
0890-8206 Scouter's Digest†
0890-8214 China Spring Digest†
0890-8265 Access to Energy **3123**
0890-8281 Scrapbook Pages†
0890-8311 Rare Fruit Council International. Yearbook†
0890-8362 Kentucky Explorer **4300**
0890-8389 The British Accounting Review **1282**
0890-8400 California District Attorneys Association. Case Digest **2646**
0890-8478 First D I B S
0890-8508 Molecular and Cellular Probes **5909**
0890-8567 American Academy of Child and Adolescent Psychiatry. Journal **6121**
0890-8575 Natural Resource Modeling **5520**
0890-8583 Reformed Worship **7772**
0890-8621 Laboratory Decisions Online†
0890-8648 U S A **4429**
0890-8710 Yomiuri Shimbun (Satellite Edition) **3901**
0890-8753 Photo Business†
0890-8761 Washington Lawyer **4811**
0890-877X Biology Bulletin Monthly†
0890-8796 Bible Story Time. Younger Pupil†
0890-8826 Security **2680**
0890-8885 Cross Timbers Review
0890-8923 Bloodlines **6804**
0890-9016 Clinical Transplants **6240**
0890-9024 West Hills Review†
0890-9032 The Church Pianist **6556**
0890-9091 Oncology **6030**
0890-9113 Jewish Folklore and Ethnology Review†
0890-913X Journal of Private Enterprise **1138**
0890-9148 S A E UPdate (International Edition) *see* 0742-972X **3395**
0890-9156 Korea Automotive Review
0890-9164 The Insurance Tax Review **1929**
0890-9199 Consumer Companion: The Quarterly Digest of Consumer Product Reviews†
0890-9202 Boatracing†
0890-9229 Sting **8209**
0890-9237 Vogue Knitting International **6643**
0890-9245 Health Employment Law Update **1685**
0890-9253 Employment Law Update (Evansville) **4665**
0890-9369 Genes & Development **867**
0890-9377 Contributions to the Study of Anthropology† **8943**
0890-9423 Virginia, West Virginia Queries†
0890-9431 Stratton Notes†
0890-944X Bush Branches **3761**
0890-9458 Fisher Families†
0890-9466 Butcher Block **3761**
0890-9474 Baldwin By-lines†
0890-9482 Alexander Agenda†
0890-9490 German Queries†
0890-9520 Journal of Rural and Small Schools†
0890-9547 Yacht Vacations
0890-958X Habitat World **4411**
0890-9598 Harper's Bazaar en Espanol†
0890-961X The Journeyman Roofer & Waterproofer **1018**
0890-9695 WomenWise†
0890-9792 Perspectives (Columbus)
0890-989X Pencil Press Quarterly†
0890-9903 Chinese Journal of Infrared and Millimeter Waves†
0890-9911 Exchange Book **8702**
0890-9997 Historical Studies in the Physical and Biological Sciences *changed to* 1939-1811 **7862**
0891-0006 Current Separations *changed to* Current Separations and Drug Development **2099**
0891-0030 Johns Hopkins University. Population Information Program. Population Reports. Series C. Female Sterilization†
0891-0049 Johns Hopkins University. Population Information Program. Population Reports. Series D. Male Sterilization†
0891-0073 New Connections: Studies in Interdisciplinarity **5339**
0891-012X Recruitment and Retention in Higher Education **2999**
0891-0138 International S A M P E Symposium and Exhibition **3348**
0891-0162 American Association of Occupational Health Nurses Journal **5951**
0891-0278 Exercise Standards and Malpractice Reporter **4670**
0891-0537 Inside Bluegrass **6575**
0891-0545 Raft **5433**
0891-060X Microbial Ecology in Health & Disease **5822**
0891-0618 Journal of Chemical Neuroanatomy **6150**
0891-0634 B N A's Banking Report (Print) **1310**
0891-0685 PsycSCAN: Applied Experimental and Engineering Psychology†
0891-0707 The Wrestling News **8216**
0891-0758 Carto-Philatelist *changed to* 1930-2053 **6897**
0891-0766 Cancer Victors Journal
0891-0812 Ambulance Industry Journal
0891-0847 A P L I C Communicator **4986**
0891-0901 Society of Petroleum Engineers. Reprint Series **6793**
0891-0960 Downeast Ancestry
0891-1002 Music News†
0891-1150 Cleveland Clinic Journal of Medicine **5595**
0891-1177 Order of Buddhist Contemplatives. Journal **7702**
0891-1207 Professional Communicator†
0891-1231 Ridge Review†
0891-1258 Worry-Free Investing
0891-1371 Witness **5245**
0891-141X Equipment Today **1007**
0891-1436 United Journal†
0891-1460 Library Orientation Series **5028**
0891-1509 Cheese Market News **262**
0891-1525 C A P Today **5590**
0891-1533 Today's Catholic (Fort Wayne) **7820**
0891-1614 School of International Studies. Publications on Russia and Eastern Europe **7181**
0891-1622 Sales Promotion Monitor†
0891-1681 Promotion Digest†
0891-1703 National Air and Space Museum. Research Report†
0891-1762 Journal of Global Marketing **1824**
0891-1797 Safety and Health **6685**
0891-1800 Surgical Rounds for Orthopaedics†
0891-1835 Finding the Source† **8956**
0891-1851 Kitplanes **64**
0891-1886 C P I Digest **6722**
0891-1908 Conference on Editorial Problems: University of Toronto† **8943**
0891-1916 International Journal of Political Economy **7144**
0891-1924 Health Technology†
0891-1932 Securities Law Series **4880**
0891-1940 American Laryngological Association. Transactions of the Annual Meeting **6077**
0891-2017 Computational Linguistics† **8942**
0891-2033 Basic and Clinical Pharmacology **6824**
0891-2068 Basic & Clinical Endocrinology†
0891-2084 General Ophthalmology *changed to* 1550-0004 **6052**
0891-2092 Clinical Cardiology (Print) *changed to* Clinical Cardiology (Online) **5783**
0891-2106 Basic Histology **827**
0891-2114 Length of Stay by Diagnosis, Canada†
0891-2181 Length of Stay by Operation, Canada†
0891-2351 Gold Stocks Advisory **1627**
0891-2378 S P S M & H **5434**
0891-2386 Cicada (Bakersfield) **5419**
0891-2416 Journal of Contemporary Ethnography **8112**
0891-2424 Economic Development Quarterly **1539**
0891-2432 Gender & Society **8104**
0891-2459 Your Patient & Fitness in Internal Medicine **5949**
0891-2467 Your Patient & Fitness in Cardiology **5802**
0891-2513 Complex Systems **5551**
0891-2548 Crystal Gazing†
0891-2556 Carbonates and Evaporites **2727**
0891-2572 Kennedy's Career Strategist†
0891-2599 Professional Apartment Management *changed to* 1935-6137 **7582**
0891-2602 Ogden Newsletter†
0891-2610 Public History News **4157**
0891-2653 For the Record (Springfield)†
0891-2661 Quarterdeck **6536**
0891-270X Hollowell Heritage **3771**
0891-2718 California Cities, Towns and Counties **8148**
0891-2726 Soviet Journal of Psychology†
0891-2742 Library Personnel News **5028**
0891-2769 Fed in Print (Print) *changed to* Fed in Print (Online) **1230**
0891-2785 Academic Collective Bargaining Information Service. Fact Sheet. Newsletter
0891-2823 Asian and Pacific Population Forum†
0891-2831 Ten Million Flies Can't Be Wrong†
0891-2874 C D E Working Paper **7278**
0891-2890 Norwegian Trade Bulletin **1408**
0891-2920 Archeomaterials†
0891-2947 Secondary Marketing Executive **1382**
0891-2955 Bits & Bytes Review†
0891-2963 Historical Biology **6725**
0891-2971 Crystal Rainbow†
0891-298X Sink
0891-303X Technical Computing†
0891-3102 Geologic Index†
0891-3153 A A A Road Atlas **8553**
0891-3161 Biotech Investor
0891-3188 CD-ROM Review†
0891-3234 Dental Statistics Handbook†
0891-3242 Hayes Directory of Medical Supply Houses†
0891-3250 Health Management Quarterly†
0891-3331 American Deli-Bakery News
0891-334X Soviet Forging and Sheet Metal Stamping Technology†
0891-3358 Current Contents: Clinical Medicine **5743**
0891-3374 Hope Health Letter **6989**
0891-3390 Annual Editions: American Government **7106**
0891-351X China Report: Political, Sociological, and Military Affairs
0891-3633 Southern Surgical Association. Transactions **6259**
0891-3668 The Pediatric Infectious Disease Journal **6101**
0891-3676 Modern Concepts in Immunology†
0891-3706 Twigs Magazine†
0891-3730 Buildings Energy Technology†
0891-3749 Bibliographic Guide to Microform Publications†
0891-3757 Opera Fanatic **6602**
0891-3811 Critical Review (Columbus) **5212**
0891-382X California Planning and Development Report **7425**
0891-3846 Evangelizing Today's Child *changed to* 1554-7779 **7776**
0891-3862 Chinese Journal of Atmospheric Sciences **6349**
0891-3870 Directions in Psychiatry **6136**
0891-3978 Idea Factory†
0891-3994 Medical Subject Headings - Supplementary Chemical Records (Year)†
0891-4001 City Sports Magazine (Los Angeles Edition) *see* 0191-8400 **8166**
0891-401X City Sports Magazine (Metro Edition) *see* 0191-8400 **8166**
0891-4036 Metalworking News†
0891-4044 C I O Letter†
0891-4087 Lang Classical Studies **2236**
0891-4095 North American Studies in Nineteenth-Century German Literature **5343**
0891-4117 Reviews in Aquatic Sciences†
0891-4125 World Economic Data†
0891-4141 Labor Relations Week **1693**
0891-4168 Molecular Genetics, Microbiology and Virology **893**
0891-4176 Earthquake Research in China†
0891-4214 Read, America! **3078**
0891-4222 Research in Developmental Disabilities **6180**
0891-4249 A S H R A E Insights **4115**
0891-4265 A C M Distinguished Dissertations **2405**
0891-4303 European Chromatography News†
0891-4370 Georgetown Immigration Law Journal **4679**
0891-4397 Fiber Optics Technical Directory†
0891-4435 World Nuclear Performance†
0891-4443 Planned Gifts Counselor†
0891-4451 Systems Research in Physiology
0891-446X American Purpose†
0891-4478 International Journal of Technology & Aging†
0891-4486 International Journal of Politics, Culture, and Society **7243**
0891-4494 Journal of Near-Death Studies **6929**
0891-4516 Prentice-Hall Software Series **2596**
0891-4524 Physics of Atoms and Molecules **7033**
0891-4540 Modern Inorganic Chemistry **2117**
0891-4559 Prentice-Hall Information and System Sciences Series **2549**
0891-4591 Current Estimates from the National Health Interview Survey, United States *changed to* 1938-9892 **8407**
0891-4621 Robotics and Expert Systems†
0891-4648 Official N A S C A R Preview and Press Guide **8596**
0891-4680 Readings from Physics Today **7036**
0891-4699 McGraw-Hill Series in Management Information Systems **2531**
0891-4702 M I T Press Series in Information Systems **2431**
0891-4710 M I T Press Series in Computer Systems *changed to* Computer Systems Series **2519**
0891-4737 The Official Proceedings of Speech Tech
0891-4796 Muscle Car Review **8594**
0891-4990 Artquest Newsletter & Artquest Update
0891-5083 International Journal of Science and Technology†
0891-5121 1-2-3 User's Journal†
0891-5148 Aviation Ground Equipment Market†
0891-5199 ComeUnity†
0891-5229 P A S Newsletter **7569**
0891-5237 Professional Quilter **1965**
0891-5245 Journal of Pediatric Health Care **6095**
0891-5326 Re: View†
0891-5385 Water and Wastewater International **8837**
0891-5393 James White Review **4375**
0891-5415 Contemporary Music Studies
0891-5466 Texas Journal of Agriculture and Natural Resources **162**

ISSN

DIRECTORY 2010 0893-4452 9375

0892-4996 Visitor Behavior†
0892-5003 Novascope **3984**
0892-5038 Running Journal **8331**
0892-5046 Consulting - Specifying Engineer **3185**
0892-5070 Journal of Clinical Electrophysiology† **8968**
0892-5089 Splice
0892-5100 Slowo i Liturgia **7817**
0892-5135 High - Scope Extensions **3063**
0892-516X Limited Partnership Investment Review **1933**
0892-5178 Portu-Info **6898**
0892-5194 Fayette County (Ky.) Genealogical Society Quarterly **3766**
0892-5208 Oregon Postal History Journal
0892-5232 Corporate Jobs Outlook†
0892-5267 Mildred†
0892-5275 Marginella Marginalia **955**
0892-5380 Tennessee Public Works **7503**
0892-5410 Great Lakes Sailor†
0892-5429 Mutable Dilemma **566**
0892-5437 Violexchange†
0892-5461 Energy Books Quarterly†
0892-547X Immigration Policy & Law†
0892-5488 Work in America†
0892-550X Bratstvo†
0892-5534 Wildbird **917**
0892-5550 Bio-Bibliographies in the Performing Arts **8485**
0892-5569 Comparative Urban and Community Research **4408**
0892-5593 University of Chicago Legal Forum **4803**
0892-5658 Finger Lakes Magazine
0892-5712 Criswell Theological Review **7753**
0892-578X Onion World **244**
0892-5798 Current Comments
0892-581X Righting Words
0892-5836 Normal
0892-5895 Yell County Historical & Genealogical Society. Bulletin **3788**
0892-5909 Security and Intelligence Foundation. Nightwatch†
0892-5984 Of a Like Mind **7739**
0892-6018 I R A - Individual Retirement Account Stocks†
0892-6034 Business Information from Your Public Library†
0892-6077 Meat & Poultry **3655**
0892-6107 Orange County Business First
0892-6174 Quality Care Advocate **4109**
0892-6271 Lone Star Horse Report **8294**
0892-628X H E R S Newsletter **5992**
0892-6298 International Society for Respiratory Protection. Journal **6215**
0892-6336 Historic Schaefferstown Record **4296**
0892-6387 American Pheasant and Waterfowl Society Magazine **901**
0892-6395 California Job Journal **6694**
0892-6433 Vanguard (Milwaukee, 1970) **8076**
0892-6468 Preview (Richardson) **6510**
0892-6484 Association for the Advancement of Automotive Medicine. Proceedings *changed to* 1943-2461 **5575**
0892-6514 Cat Fancy **6805**
0892-6522 Dog Fancy **6807**
0892-6603 The Shorthorn **3002**
0892-662X Wine East **613**
0892-6638 The F A S E B Journal **672**
0892-6719 Interfaith Women's News & Network†
0892-6735 Five Owls **2152**
0892-6794 Ethics & International Affairs **7232**
0892-6808 Soviet Technology Reviews. Section B: Thermal Physics Reviews†
0892-6824 The European (Oxford)†
0892-6875 Minerals Engineering **6471**
0892-6891 Transportation Research Board. State-of-the-Art Report **8516**
0892-6905 Visions: An Art Quarterly
0892-6921 Later Years†
0892-6956 Rohwedder†
0892-6964 California Reader **3053**
0892-6999 Soviet Agricultural Biology. Part 1: Plant Biology†
0892-7006 Soviet Agricultural Biology. Part 2: Animal Biology†
0892-7014 Biofouling **3494**
0892-7022 Molecular Simulation **2073**
0892-7057 Journal of Thermoplastic Composite Materials **7094**
0892-7081 Clinical Decisions in Obstetrics & Gynecology†
0892-7103 Focus on Geriatric Care and Rehabilitation†
0892-7138 Stanford Environmental Law Journal **4787**
0892-7146 Techpak **6715**
0892-7162 Antique Comb Collector **362**
0892-7189 San Francisco Opera
0892-7219 Journal of Offshore Mechanics and Arctic Engineering **3386**
0892-726X Advances in Epileptology†
0892-7278 T W I C E **3114**
0892-7286 European Monographs in Social Psychology **7356**
0892-7308 11th Circuit Law Letter†
0892-7332 Technology for Laboratory Medicine†
0892-7340 Technology for Imaging & Radiology†
0892-7367 Finding†
0892-7375 Visibilities†
0892-7421 Voice of the Hawkeyes **8250**
0892-743X L D B Interior Textiles **4560**
0892-7537 Journal of World Prehistory **401**
0892-7545 Employee Responsibilities and Rights Journal **1677**
0892-7553 Journal of Insect Behavior **852**
0892-757X Food Service Forum†
0892-7588 Khang Chien†
0892-7626 Journal of Applied Business Research **1133**
0892-7642 American Wine & Food
0892-7669 Nursing Assistant
0892-7731 Health Industry Buyers' Guide **5625**
0892-7758 Jottings **4082**
0892-7782 Lunar Entrepreneurs Directory†
0892-7790 Journal of Endourology **6270**
0892-7812 Financial Sourcebooks' Source†
0892-7839 Alumnews†
0892-7855 C U P A News *changed to* C U P A - H R eNews **3018**
0892-7901 Advances in Psychophysiology†
0892-791X Junk Journal†
0892-7936 Anthrozoos **933**
0892-7979 Tennessee Anthropologist†
0892-807X Maryland Poetry Review **5426**
0892-810X Supreme Court Record **4791**
0892-8150 Developmental Clinical Psychology and Psychiatry **6136**
0892-8185 Medicenter Management†
0892-8193 Sales Motivation†
0892-8231 Michigan Restaurateur **4394**
0892-8282 George D. Hall's Directory of North Carolina Manufacturers†
0892-8312 Farm Industry News **111**
0892-8320 Hot Boat **8276**
0892-8339 Museum Anthropology **349**
0892-8509 University of Illinois at Urbana-Champaign. Graduate School of Library and Information Science. Monograph Series†
0892-8525 Country Woman **8857**
0892-8649 Tax Policy and the Economy **1949**
0892-8665 J A S N A News **5312**
0892-869X Austin Business Journal **1063**
0892-8762 Aging: Immunology & Infectious Disease†
0892-8789 Southern Vermont Magazine
0892-8797 Chromatography†
0892-8819 Animals' Agenda†
0892-8878 Advances in Clinical Rehabilitation†
0892-8886 University of Washington. Working Papers in Linguistics **5192**
0892-8908 U.S. National Oceanic and Atmospheric Administration. National Marine Fisheries Service. Technical Report *changed to* 1931-4590 **3610**
0892-8916 A T S News **6211**
0892-8959 U.S. National Center for Health Statistics. Vital and Health Statistics. Series 5. Comparative International Vital and Health Statistics Reports **7550**
0892-8967 International Contact Lens Clinic *changed to* 1367-0484 **6040**
0892-9084 Alabama County Data Book **7419**
0892-9092 Youth Theatre Journal **8485**
0892-922X Ellis Island Series: Immigration and the Pluralist Society
0892-9238 Bradford Compact Newsletter **3760**
0892-9270 Space Technology (Kilington)†
0892-9300 Christian Conquest **7631**
0892-9319 Corporate Fitness†
0892-9327 Cardiology Management†
0892-9343 P R Activity Report†
0892-9351 Health and Safety Science Abstracts (Print)†
0892-9386 Audio-Digest Gastroenterology **5920**
0892-9440 Let's Play Softball **8237**
0892-9459 Spectrum Magazine (Bloomsburg) **3989**
0892-953X Scanning Microscopy Supplement
0892-9548 Sensus Water Journal **8831**
0892-9556 Advances in Nonprofit Marketing†
0892-9599 Creative Kids **2184**
0892-9696 Z Miscellaneous†
0892-970X MidCoaster **5333**
0892-9742 Boston Quarterly **6804**
0892-9769 Carousel News & Trader **365**
0892-9793 Interleaf **6896**
0892-9807 WittyWorld **527**
0892-984X Low Priced Stocks†
0892-9882 Science and Global Security **7908**
0892-9912 Journal of Technology Transfer **8429**
0892-9947 Lasers & Optronics†
0892-9955 Write Age†
0892-9963 Snowshoe (Corinth) **8335**
0893-0031 Jaycees Magazine **2267**
0893-0058 University of North Carolina Sea Grant College Program. Sea Grant Publication **2820**
0893-0120 EthnoArts Index **362**
0893-0139 Index to Reproductions in Art Periodicals **530**
0893-0147 Current Neuro-Ophthalmology†
0893-0228 World Peacemakers Quarterly **7274**
0893-0252 Drood Review of Mystery **5413**
0893-0260 Lurzer's International Archive **28**
0893-0279 M O M A **6528**
0893-0309 World Productivity Forum & International Industrial Engineering Conference†
0893-0341 Alzheimer Disease and Associated Disorders **6121**
0893-0376 Connecticut English Journal **5107**
0893-0384 Continuing Higher Education Review **2974**
0893-0392 Coalition on Government Information Newsletter
0893-0414 Splash Magazine
0893-0465 City & Society **333**
0893-0473 Civil Rights Update†
0893-049X Teaching Abroad†
0893-0511 Study in the United Kingdom and Ireland†
0893-052X Federal Computer Week **7486**
0893-0538 Activities of Daily Living Update
0893-0570 Ada Strategies
0893-0597 Applications of Communications Theory **2349**
0893-0619 Defense Media Review **6419**
0893-0627 Hippocrates News
0893-0694 California Connections
0893-0708 Report from the Hill†
0893-0732 Bank of Hawaii Business Trends **1441**
0893-0775 Metro Chicago Real Estate **7599**
0893-0805 Richmond Afro-American Newspaper†
0893-0864 Montana Review†
0893-0872 Messenger (Worcester) **7705**
0893-1054 Radiology Today (Thorofare)†
0893-1089 New England Getaways†
0893-1097 Decorative Artist's Workbook† **8949**
0893-1151 La Jolla Magazine
0893-1224 O N†
0893-1240 Cruise Industry News (Newsletter) **8696**
0893-1259 T M S - Letter†
0893-1305 Abstracts of Papers Read at the Annual Meeting of the American Musicological Society **6631**
0893-1321 Journal of Aerospace Engineering **3274**
0893-133X Neuropsychopharmacology **6168**
0893-1348 Bishop Museum Occasional Papers **7841**
0893-1356 Nursing Educators MicroWorld†
0893-1550 The Caribbean Writer **5270**
0893-1593 Ohio Genealogical Society. Wood County Chapter. Newsletter **3777**
0893-1607 Jubilee **7763**
0893-1623 Llewellyn's Moon Sign Book & Gardening Guide†
0893-164X Psychology of Addictive Behaviors **2698**
0893-1674 M S U - D O E Plant Research Laboratory. Annual Report **3141**
0893-1704 B N A's Alternative Dispute Resolution Report†
0893-181X Rhode Island Queries†
0893-1828 Resource Management **6443**
0893-1909 Computers in Science†
0893-1925 Imaging on Campus†
0893-195X Chevy Outdoors†
0893-2034 Journal of Current Podiatric Medicine†
0893-2069 Tree Shaker **3785**
0893-2107 U K & U S A **1411**
0893-2115 Libertarian E-Mail Directory†
0893-214X Wildlife Society. Western Section. Transactions **2632**
0893-2174 International Journal of Prosthodontics **5849**
0893-2182 Jazziminds Magazine
0893-2190 Journal of Perinatal and Neonatal Nursing **5967**
0893-2255 Minnesota Real Estate Journal **7600**
0893-2271 Idaho Archaeologist **397**
0893-228X Chemical Research in Toxicology **3495**
0893-2298 Indiana Facts **3120**
0893-2301 Central and Inner Asian Studies **4181**
0893-2336 Neuromethods **926**
0893-2395 Hispanic Issues **5305**
0893-2409 U S A Today Index **4588**
0893-2417 St. Louis Post - Dispatch Index†
0893-2425 San Francisco Chronicle Index **4588**
0893-2433 Detroit News Index **4587**
0893-2441 Denver Post Index **4586**
0893-245X Christian Science Monitor Index **4586**
0893-2468 American Banker Index **1199**
0893-2476 Houston Post Index **4587**
0893-2484 New Orleans Times - Picayune Index **4587**
0893-2492 Barclays United States Ninth Circuit Service **4627**
0893-2522 DealerNews **8257**
0893-2565 E S D: The Electronic System Design Magazine†
0893-2573 Public and Local Acts of the Legislature of the State of Michigan **7501**
0893-2581 Alternative Fiction & Poetry†
0893-2654 Risk & Benefits Management†
0893-2662 Tradeshow and Exhibit Manager†
0893-2670 The Texas Philatelist **6900**
0893-2697 San Antonio Homes & Gardens†
0893-2700 Kagan Media Index†
0893-2719 Midwest Real Estate News **7599**
0893-2727 The Boston Globe Index **4586**
0893-276X Columbiana **2606**
0893-2816 Missouri Manufacturers Register **2017**
0893-2824 West Virginia Manufacturers Register **2034**
0893-2905 Psychiatric Times **6176**
0893-2913 Indiana University. Research Institute for Inner Asian Studies. Uralic and Altaic Series **5127**
0893-2921 Jewish Genealogical Society of Philadelphia. Chronicles **3772**
0893-293X A L F News. Newsletter **7101**
0893-2956 New Mexico Library Association Newsletter **5035**
0893-2980 Casualty Actuarial Society. Proceedings **4498**
0893-2999 S I G C U E Outlook†
0893-3014 Cwy Ye: Cherokee Blood Newsletter
0893-3022 Creative Living **5069**
0893-3030 Traffic Law Reports†
0893-3057 The Saline **3781**
0893-3065 Directory of Traditional Music† **8950**
0893-3073 Business Flyer†
0893-309X Tate Trails **3784**
0893-3103 The Quarterly (New York)†
0893-3111 Bishop Museum Bulletins in Anthropology **331**
0893-312X Bishop Museum Bulletins in Zoology **936**
0893-3138 Bishop Museum Bulletins in Botany **779**
0893-3146 Bishop Museum Bulletins in Entomology **841**
0893-3162 Gathering Gibsons **3767**
0893-3170 N Y Gold **6971**
0893-3189 Management Communication Quarterly **1775**
0893-3200 Journal of Family Psychology **7374**
0893-3340 The Local Historian **4302**
0893-3359 Stanly County Genealogical Society. Journal **3784**
0893-3375 Windfall†
0893-3383 Lowfat Lifeline†
0893-3405 Kluwer International Series in Engineering and Computer Science *changed to* 1872-082X **2406**
0893-3472 N†
0893-3499 S O L E - International Society of Logistics. Proceedings **8437**
0893-3502 El Chicano **3526**
0893-3561 Consumer Markets Abroad†
0893-357X Journal of Pesticide Reform **3488**
0893-3685 Korea Herald **3903**
0893-3758 Dempsey Canadian Letter†
0893-3855 Manufacturing Week†
0893-3871 Journal of Osteopathic Sports Medicine†
0893-388X Physical Acoustics **7089**
0893-3901 Art Calendar **469**
0893-3936 I A F C On Scene **3579**
0893-3952 Modern Pathology **5680**
0893-3960 International Journal of Engineering Fluid Mechanics†
0893-4118 AppleWorks Forum†
0893-4150 Roots & Branches **3781**
0893-4177 Night Club & Bar Magazine **4394**
0893-4215 Communication Reports **5107**
0893-4231 Protecting Children **8063**
0893-4274 InvesText Advisor†
0893-4290 African-American Family History Association Newsletter†
0893-4347 Research Recommendations **1965**
0893-438X Science Impact Letter
0893-4428 Adventures of Superman
0893-4452 Environmental Nutrition **6658**

ISSN

0895-3503 Latin American Report†
0895-3562 American Reading Forum. Yearbook (Print Edition) *changed to* American Reading Forum. Yearbook (Online Edition) **2826**
0895-3570 Planner **1298**
0895-3619 F E W's News and Views **7436**
0895-3635 Money Manager Previews†
0895-3643 American Journal of Gynecologic Health†
0895-3651 France Today **5216**
0895-366X Anchor Point Magazine **7334**
0895-3678 Workamper News **6705**
0895-3708 Electronic Manufacturing†
0895-3791 Business Digest
0895-3805 Managing Automation **2462**
0895-3856 Truck Parts & Service **8677**
0895-3880 National Forum of Applied Educational Research Journal **2890**
0895-3899 Used Car Book (Year) **8609**
0895-3961 The Daze Inc. **2040**
0895-3988 Biomedical and Environmental Sciences **5585**
0895-3996 Journal of X-Ray Science and Technology **7023**
0895-4062 Cox Heritage **3763**
0895-4070 Oklahoma Queries†
0895-4097 Annual North American Power Symposium. Proceedings *changed to* N A P S (Year) Proceedings **3326**
0895-4143 The Perfect Vision **2387**
0895-4186 Financial Executive **1745**
0895-4208 Military Police **6436**
0895-4259 Jewish Press of Pinellas County **7723**
0895-4283 India Worldwide†
0895-4313 Medical Office Report **5670**
0895-4321 National Directory of Magazines **631**
0895-4356 Journal of Clinical Epidemiology **5647**
0895-4372 The Workshop (Microsoft Works)†
0895-4488 Perkins Family Newsletter†
0895-4496 Mason Family Newsletter†
0895-450X Fenestration† **8956**
0895-4534 Irish Voice **3541**
0895-4550 Media Mergers & Acquisitions†
0895-4615 Business Starts Record **1444**
0895-4666 Industry Report (New York)
0895-4682 Places: A Directory of Public Places for Private Events and Private Places for Public Functions **2023**
0895-4690 Chinese American Forum **3527**
0895-4712 Political Pix
0895-4798 S I A M Journal on Matrix Analysis and Applications **5531**
0895-4801 S I A M Journal on Discrete Mathematics **5531**
0895-481X Buckmasters Whitetail **8307**
0895-4844 Lawrence-Leiter Digest†
0895-4852 Academic Questions **2965**
0895-4860 Arizona-Nevada Academy of Science. Journal. Proceedings Supplement **7837**
0895-4895 Fastener Age†
0895-4909 Duke University Libraries **5007**
0895-4933 American Freestyler†
0895-495X Birder's World **903**
0895-4968 Praying†
0895-500X Lewis County Historical Society. Journal **4301**
0895-5018 Third World Legal Studies (Year) **4942**
0895-5026 Ethikos **6918**
0895-5034 Orthodontic Review†
0895-5050 Peak to Peak†
0895-5093 New Research Reports†
0895-5166 Solidarity Bulletin†
0895-5182 The Claflin Review **5106**
0895-5220 L R A's Economic Notes **1691**
0895-5239 Ninth Street Center Journal **4377**
0895-5271 Foghorn†
0895-531X Library Computer Systems & Equipment Review†
0895-5409 University of North Dakota. Alumni Review **2307**
0895-5433 A P U Life **2271**
0895-5441 L C G C International (European Edition)†
0895-5549 New Yorkin Uutiset†
0895-5573 The Southern Register **4313**
0895-5581 Dogs U S A **6807**
0895-559X Albany Review†
0895-562X Journal of Productivity Analysis **1769**
0895-5638 Journal of Real Estate Finance and Economics **7597**
0895-5646 Journal of Risk and Uncertainty **1546**
0895-5662 New England Economic Indicators Monthly Update†
0895-5689 United & Babson Investment Report†
0895-5719 Messages **505**
0895-5743 How(ever)†
0895-576X Private Placement Advisory†
0895-5786 Blueprint for Social Justice **7203**
0895-5808 C A Selects. Enzyme Assays†
0895-5816 C A Selects. Structure - Activity Relationships **2092**
0895-5824 C A Selects. Solid State N M R **2092**
0895-5832 C A Selects. Siloxanes & Silicones **2092**
0895-5840 C A Selects. Polyimides **2091**
0895-5859 C A Selects. Organometallics in Organic Synthesis **2089**
0895-5867 C A Selects. Nonlinear Optical Materials **7047**
0895-5875 C A Selects. New Antibiotics **6889**
0895-5883 C A Selects. Isomerization & Catalysts†
0895-5891 C A Selects. Hot-Melt Adhesives **2087**
0895-5905 C A Selects. Free Radicals (Biochemical Aspects) **714**
0895-5913 C A Selects. Food & Feed Analysis **3669**
0895-5921 C A Selects. Fluoropolymers **2087**
0895-5948 C A Selects. Ceramic Materials (Journals) **2047**
0895-5956 C A Selects. Carbon Fiber Composites†
0895-5964 C A Selects. Alkylation & Catalysts **2085**
0895-5972 C A Selects. Free Radicals (Organic Aspects) **2087**
0895-5980 C A Selects. Air Pollution (Books & Reviews)†
0895-5999 Report on Science and Human Rights *changed to* Science and Human Rights Newsletter **7215**
0895-6014 On the Issues†
0895-6022 Casualty Actuarial Society. Yearbook **4498**
0895-6049 Southwest Profile
0895-6065 Taos Magazine **8781**
0895-609X Fall Industrial Engineering Conference. Proceedings *changed to* 1069-367X **8965**
0895-6103 Santa Clara County Connections **3781**
0895-6111 Computerized Medical Imaging and Graphics **5829**
0895-6200 The Art of Eating **3627**
0895-6219 Journal of Paralegal Education and Practice†
0895-6308 Research Technology Management **1790**
0895-6316 Neural Technology Update
0895-6324 Soviet Engineering Geology†
0895-6332 Site San Diego
0895-6340 Computing Systems†
0895-6359 Financial Services Yearbook†
0895-6405 Connection (Boston) *changed to* 1938-5978 **2995**
0895-643X Channels†
0895-6464 Vista de Mexico
0895-6472 Roots-Key **3781**
0895-6499 C A S BioTech Updates. Antibody Conjugates†
0895-6502 Yesterday's Magazette **5403**
0895-6510 New Writer's Magazine **5341**
0895-6537 R I T Industry Education Programs Update **2950**
0895-6545 Journalism and Mass Communication Directory **4577**
0895-657X Medicine - Health Information Review†
0895-660X Physics - Mathematics Information Review†
0895-6618 C A S BioTech Updates. D N A Formation & Repair†
0895-6626 C A S BioTech Updates. Biochemical Immobilization & Biocatalytic Reactors†
0895-6685 Japan Manufacturing†
0895-6693 Japan Transportation†
0895-6707 Japan Materials†
0895-6715 Japan Computers†
0895-6723 Japan Electronics (Washington)†
0895-6731 Japan Business†
0895-674X Japan Chemistry†
0895-6758 Japan Bioscience
0895-6766 Japan Telecommunications†
0895-6774 Japan Energy†
0895-6782 Guide to Muscle Cars†
0895-6820 21st Century Science & Technology (Print) *changed to* 21st Century Science & Technology (Online) **7935**
0895-6855 Rethinking Schools **2905**
0895-688X State of New York City's Municipal Hospital System **4111**
0895-6936 Cymbiosis **6560**
0895-6995 Soldier Support Advocate†
0895-7061 American Journal of Hypertension **5776**
0895-7088 Early China. Supplement *see* 1048-2520
0895-7088 Early China. Supplement *see* 0362-5028 **4181**
0895-7126 Swenson Center News **3567**
0895-7134 Labyrinth **8871**
0895-7150 Advertising Research Foundation. Annual Report
0895-7177 Mathematical and Computer Modelling **5512**
0895-7185 International Economic Review (Washington D.C.) **1493**
0895-724X Journal of Social, Political and Economic Studies Monograph Series **7148**
0895-7258 Journal of Indo-European Studies Monograph Series **7979**
0895-7304 Millwork Manufacturing **1024**
0895-7347 Applied Measurement in Education **2827**
0895-738X Epicurean Revue
0895-7428 The Children's Choir†
0895-7452 World Outlook **7274**
0895-7460 The New Mercersburg Review **7665**
0895-7517 Spectrum Review†
0895-7533 Laboratory Robotics and Automation†
0895-755X Spotlight on AIDS†
0895-7576 Nancy's Magazine **4466**
0895-7606 Native Peoples **6635**
0895-7622 Henceforth **7647**
0895-7657 Body, Mind & Spirit Magazine†
0895-7673 Journal of Training & Practice in Professional Psychology†
0895-769X A N Q: A Quarterly Journal of Short Articles, Notes and Reviews **5248**
0895-7703 Veterinary Medicine Report†
0895-7711 Obstetrics - Gynecology Report†
0895-772X Green Markets Dealer Report **116**
0895-7738 Melts†
0895-7754 N P U G News†
0895-7762 Ironic Blood **5895**
0895-786X Peelings†
0895-7916 Chaplaincy Today (Schaumburg, 1986)†
0895-7959 High Pressure Research **7059**
0895-7967 Seminars in Vascular Surgery **6258**
0895-7975 Payroll Manager's Letter **1938**
0895-7983 Harris Poll (Print) *changed to* 1946-4525 **8149**
0895-7991 Claims **4499**
0895-8009 American Association on Mental Retardation. Monographs **7332**
0895-8017 American Journal on Mental Retardation (Print) *changed to* 1944-7515 **6122**
0895-8033 American Association on Mental Retardation. News and Notes† **8929**
0895-805X CineVue **6494**
0895-8076 Urban Design Update **460**
0895-8084 Florida Facts **3120**
0895-8092 Iowa Facts **3120**
0895-8106 North Carolina Facts **3121**
0895-8114 New Hampshire Facts **3121**
0895-8211 Navy Medicine **5684**
0895-8254 Longevity†
0895-8270 Spectrum (Paxton)†
0895-8289 C I O Monthly†
0895-8335 Baseball (Year)†
0895-8378 Inhalation Toxicology **3498**
0895-8432 High Technology Business†
0895-8440 Financial Services Week (New York, 1985) **1345**
0895-8467 Mountain Bike Action **8265**
0895-8483 Stilwell - Stillwell What the 'L'
0895-8491 Western Sahara Campaign News
0895-8505 New West Notes **7158**
0895-853X Journal of Bank Accounting & Auditing†
0895-8556 Hawaii Realtor Journal **7592**
0895-8696 Journal of Molecular Neuroscience **6153**
0895-8726 Infonetics **2571**
0895-8750 Journal of Psychological Type **7378**
0895-8777 Monitor (Stamford)†
0895-8815 International Journal of Value-Based Management *changed to* 0167-4544 **1134**
0895-8831 The Journal of Clinical Dentistry **5850**
0895-8939 Calvert County Genealogy Newsletter **3761**
0895-898X Writer's N W **7576**
0895-9005 American Woodturner **1049**
0895-9013 National Electronic Packaging and Production Conference (East). Proceedings of the Technical Program **2432**
0895-9021 National Electronic Packaging and Production Conference (West). Proceedings of the Technical Program **2432**
0895-9048 Educational Policy **3022**
0895-9080 Holography News **7076**
0895-9285 Human Performance **7361**
0895-9307 Green Mountains Review **5302**
0895-9331 AIDS Bibliography (Troy)†
0895-934X Sun Belt Floor Covering
0895-9374 Advances in Dental Research **5833**
0895-9390 Maui Update **8733**
0895-9420 Journal of Aging & Social Policy **4048**
0895-9439 Short Story Criticism **5372**
0895-9471 U S Kids†
0895-9544 A C C A Docket *changed to* 1546-4776 **4854**
0895-9595 Compute's Apple Applications†
0895-9609 Maui, a Paradise Family Guide *changed to* 1544-1377 **8746**
0895-965X Who's Who of Emerging Leaders in America†
0895-9668 Mushing **8323**
0895-9706 Pinter Review: Annual Essays **8476**
0895-9722 National Dipper **3657**
0895-9773 Long Shot†
0895-9781 Agricultural Policy and Economics Issues†
0895-9803 Current Advances in Cancer Research **5743**
0895-9811 Journal of South American Earth Sciences **2711**
0895-9897 International Museum of Cultures. Publications in Ethnography **343**
0895-9919 International Yearbook for Studies of Leaders and Leadership†
0895-9927 Information Broker
0895-9935 Research in Political Sociology **8128**
0895-9943 Radiation Oncology
0895-9978 Crop Science Society of America. Special Publication **226**
0895-9986 Health Consciousness **309**
0896-0011 Classical and Medieval Literature Criticism **5274**
0896-002X The Last Days Magazine†
0896-0038 Co-Laborer Magazine **7634**
0896-0054 The Great Plains Sociologist **8104**
0896-0194 The National Black Law Journal **4738**
0896-0240 Situation & Outlook Report. Sugar & Sweetener **206**
0896-0267 Brain Topography **6128**
0896-0348 Military Robotics Newsletter **2586**
0896-0399 New American Land†
0896-0437 Super Automotive Service†
0896-0453 Texas Economic Indicators†
0896-0461 What C D?†
0896-0518 G E D Items **2941**
0896-0569 Thrombosis Research. Supplement **5800**
0896-0585 United States Telephone Association. Statistics of the Local Exchange Carriers **2349**
0896-0607 Nuclear Medicine†
0896-0615 World Watch **3475**
0896-0623 Regional Immunology†
0896-0631 Athena†
0896-064X Tampa Review **5436**
0896-0674 Government Productivity News†
0896-0720 V L A Newsletter (Print) *changed to* V L A Newsletter (Online) **5054**
0896-0747 Delaware Valley Regional Planning Commission. Annual Report **8494**
0896-0763 Executive Guide to Specialists in Industrial and Office Real Estate **7590**
0896-0798 Excellence (Novato) **8580**
0896-0801 Hinduism Today **7707**
0896-0925 Mongolia Society. Special Papers **4186**
0896-0941 Employee Assistance Program Management Letter **1677**
0896-095X India Currents **3539**
0896-0968 International Choral Bulletin **6576**
0896-0976 Electronic Photography News **6966**
0896-0984 Elementary Mathematician†
0896-100X Imaging Abstracts **6979**
0896-1018 American Romanian Academy of Arts and Sciences. Journal **465**
0896-1107 Journal of Superconductivity *changed to* 1557-1939 **7023**
0896-1220 Concepts in Neurosurgery
0896-1255 Advances in Health Education and Promotion†
0896-1263 Nephrology News & Issues **6272**
0896-1301 Iris: A Journal about Women **8869**
0896-131X Handicap News
0896-1352 Music Performance Resources†
0896-1379 Historical Roller Skating Overview **8177**
0896-1409 Argonaut (Moscow) **2272**
0896-1425 I E E E Standards Bearer *changed to* I E E E StandardsWire **6402**
0896-1441 Ideas **26**
0896-145X H P Professional†
0896-1468 Parentguide News **2164**
0896-1476 Perspectives in Clinical Pharmacy†
0896-1506 New England Entertainment Digest **4981**
0896-1530 Journal of International Consumer Marketing **1825**
0896-1549 Ophthalmology Clinics of North America **6048**
0896-1611 Manufacturing Review†
0896-1638 Sewanee Mediaeval Studies **4263**
0896-1646 Sea History Gazette **8660**

0896-1654 American Association for Crystal Growth Newsletter **2109**
0896-1670 Snack World†
0896-1689 Bibliographies in Technology and Social Change **8148**
0896-1727 La Palabra entre Nosotros **7811**
0896-1794 Florida Water Resources Journal **8823**
0896-1875 Weld County Genealogical Society. Quarterly **3787**
0896-1883 Farm Chronicle **110**
0896-1905 Studies in Technology and Social Change Series **8439**
0896-193X Nails **590**
0896-1956 Theater Week†
0896-1964 Agincourt Irregular†
0896-1972 Indian Awareness Center Newsletter **3539**
0896-1980 Fulton County Folk Finder **3767**
0896-2022 Turtle Quarterly Magazine†
0896-209X Lutheran Woman Today **7766**
0896-2103 Preanesthetic Assessment **5773**
0896-2111 Wang in the News†
0896-2138 Digest of the Arab Press†
0896-2146 Arab Press Bulletin†
0896-2154 Living World **8054**
0896-2162 Directory of Single Unit Supermarket Operators (Year) **1988**
0896-2170 Sunset Recipe Annual (Year) **4368**
0896-2189 Western Legal History **4812**
0896-2251 Gulf Coast (Houston) **5303**
0896-226X Essays in Economic and Business History **1540**
0896-2294 International Journal on the Unity of the Sciences†
0896-2308 RiskWatch **1791**
0896-2324 Parking Professional **8597**
0896-2332 Fast Forward†
0896-2367 N O B C Ch E. Proceedings **2074**
0896-2383 B Y U Journal of Public Law **4625**
0896-2413 God's Special People†
0896-243X Harmony (San Francisco) **7207**
0896-2472 Ohio State University. Byrd Polar Research Center. Report Series **7895**
0896-2510 Conference Board. Utility Investment Report†
0896-2529 Manufacturing Investment Outlook†
0896-2545 World Economic Monitor†
0896-2553 Conference Board's Management Briefing: Business Finance†
0896-2618 Mulberry Tree Papers†
0896-2642 Buena Salud *changed to* 1081-9703 **5067**
0896-2685 Sprinkler Age **3581**
0896-2693 Now & Then (Johnson City) **5344**
0896-2707 Forward (Oakland)†
0896-2715 Catholic Spirit (Austin) **7790**
0896-2774 Bit Dropper
0896-2804 Egg Industry **285**
0896-2863 Dissociation†
0896-2871 Video Choice **2403**
0896-2898 Pan-Erotic Review†
0896-2960 Critical Reviews in Physical & Rehabilitation Medicine **6108**
0896-3002 The National Report on Work & Family *changed to* 1544-9165
0896-3010 International Securities Regulation Report†
0896-3045 Browning Newsletter **6348**
0896-3053 O-blek†
0896-3126 New Jersey Journal of School Psychology†
0896-3134 A D A Today **7417**
0896-3142 TeleSpan's Business T V†
0896-3150 New Heaven - New Earth†
0896-3169 E C A Magazine **1005**
0896-3185 Tobacco Products Litigation Reporter **4796**
0896-3207 TUGboat **7328**
0896-3215 Techline **2395**
0896-3223 Nielsen's International Investment Letter†
0896-3274 Rochester Business Journal **1515**
0896-3290 The Message (Northborough) **8322**
0896-3371 Garsas†
0896-341X Thymus Update Series†
0896-3452 Employment Guide Newsletter†
0896-3517 Black Mountain Review **5208**
0896-3533 Codex Filatelica **6893**
0896-3568 Journal of Business & Finance Librarianship **5020**
0896-3576 The Acquisitions Librarian *changed to* 1941-126X **5020**
0896-3584 Budget and the Region **7424**
0896-3630 Talladega County Historical Association. Newsletter†
0896-3649 National Gay and Lesbian Task Force. Task Force Reports **4377**
0896-3703 Business Perspectives **1075**
0896-372X Close Up Magazine **6557**
0896-3746 Infants and Young Children **6093**
0896-3827 Environmental Engineering Selection Guide **3424**
0896-3835 Occupational Health & Safety News **6683**
0896-386X Tempo (New York, 1969)†
0896-3878 Timbuktu†
0896-3908 M L S: Marketing Library Services **5030**
0896-3975 Atlanta History **4284**
0896-4009 Georgia Manufacturers Register **1997**
0896-4017 Chicago & Cook County Marketing Directory†
0896-4025 Kane County Marketing Directory†
0896-4033 Lake County Marketing Directory†
0896-4041 DuPage County Marketing Directory†
0896-4068 SilverPlatter Exchange† **8988**
0896-4106 Sylvia Porter's Personal Finance†
0896-4114 A S T A Agency Management†
0896-4122 New York Education Law Report **4744**
0896-4130 Lincoln Laboratory Journal **3108**
0896-4157 InvesTech Market Analyst **1631**
0896-4165 InvesTech Mutual Fund Advisor **1631**
0896-4173 Philatelic Communicator **6898**
0896-4181 Global Finance **1349**
0896-419X Tri-County Genealogy **3786**
0896-422X Advanced Coatings & Surface Technology **2097**
0896-4254 Brittany World†
0896-4289 Behavioral Medicine **7339**
0896-4297 New Theology Review **7809**
0896-4300 Gardener Share
0896-4327 Journal of Interventional Cardiology **5793**
0896-4343 Ettore Majorana International Science Series. Life Sciences
0896-436X Neural Network Review†
0896-4394 Assemblies of God Heritage **7733**
0896-4408 S S G H S Newsletter **3781**
0896-4416 United States Population Data Sheet†
0896-4424 Train Rider Magazine **8626**
0896-4440 Rail Travel News **8623**
0896-4467 Key Obstetrics and Gynecology†
0896-4505 The Foodservice Distributor†
0896-4556 Incentive Taxation **4415**
0896-4572 Breastfeeding Abstracts **5741**
0896-4602 Luther Family Newsletter **3774**
0896-4610 Cross-Bias†
0896-4688 Long Island **1145**
0896-4696 Women's Health & Fitness News†
0896-470X Advances in Discourse Processes **5091**
0896-4742 Marketing Advents **1831**
0896-4750 M C S†
0896-4785 Milton Caniff's Steve Canyon
0896-4858 Wildflower (Austin, 1988)†
0896-4882 Breathline **5770**
0896-4904 Blue Chip Stocks **1612**
0896-4912 Newsletter for Information Executives†
0896-4920 Being Single **5066**
0896-4955 Old Abe's News **213**
0896-4998 B N A Administrative Practice Manual†
0896-5005 Soma **5239**
0896-5048 Nonprofit Times **1781**
0896-5102 Wind Energy Technology†
0896-5110 Solar Buildings Technology **3154**
0896-5137 Ocean Wave and Tidal Energy Systems†
0896-5145 Energy Storage Systems†
0896-5153 Nuclear Reactors and Technology†
0896-5161 Industrial Energy Conservation†
0896-517X Clean Coal Technologies†
0896-5188 Advanced Oil and Gas Recovery Technologies†
0896-5196 Electric Energy Systems†
0896-520X Advanced Fossil Energy Technologies†
0896-548X The Journal of Trace Elements in Experimental Medicine†
0896-5552 Professional Roofing **1030**
0896-5595 The Journal of Contemporary Legal Issues **4700**
0896-5617 Prairie Gold Rush **213**
0896-5633 American Academy of Psychiatry and the Law. Newsletter†
0896-565X International Workcamp Directory **3013**
0896-5684 Off Off Off Off Off Broadway
0896-5722 Import Service
0896-5730 Ohio Writer *changed to* 1942-275X **5337**
0896-5749 Fundamental News Service **7758**
0896-5803 Journal of Real Estate Research **7597**
0896-5811 Journal of Legal Studies Education **4703**
0896-582X Phoenix Conference on Computers and Communications. Conference Proceedings†
0896-5900 Solid State and Superconductivity Abstracts **7050**
0896-5919 Virology and AIDS Abstracts **720**
0896-5951 Turnstile†
0896-601X Soviet Medical Reviews Supplement Series. Section B: Immunology†
0896-6079 Repertoire International de la Presse Musicale **6632**
0896-6095 StarLight (Wilson)†
0896-6206 Louisiana Almanac **8731**
0896-6230 Bank Asset - Liability Management *changed to* Pratt's Bank Asset/Liability Management **1376**
0896-6257 Geothermal Energy **3152**
0896-6265 Energy from Biomass and Municipal Waste†
0896-6273 Neuron **6167**
0896-629X National Political Science Review **7156**
0896-6338 California State Poetry Quarterly
0896-6346 New Perspectives on Turkey **4186**
0896-6354 What Is to Be Read **5398**
0896-6389 Film Threat†
0896-6427 Crump Family Newsletter†
0896-6443 N C C L S Document *changed to* 1558-6502 **5596**
0896-6478 New Mexico Progress **4075**
0896-6508 International Association of Book Trade Consultants Report†
0896-6567 Managed Care Outlook **4513**
0896-6575 Airliners **8536**
0896-6591 Bibliographies and Indexes in Medical Studies† **8936**
0896-6605 Voice for Education **2925**
0896-6737 Current Construction Reports. C21, New Residential Construction in Selected Metropolitan Areas†
0896-6745 Current Construction Reports: C30, Value of New Construction Put in Place†
0896-6834 Yard and Garden **3754**
0896-6923 National Health Care Expenditures Study. Data Preview†
0896-6966 Journal of Pharmacoepidemiology *changed to* 1936-1130
0896-6982 Augsburg Adult Bible Studies. Participant Book **7746**
0896-6990 Augsburg Adult Bible Studies. Leader Guide **7746**
0896-7032 Looking Forward **4051**
0896-7075 Lawyers' Liability Review **4718**
0896-7121 Gmac Quest†
0896-7148 American Literary History **5252**
0896-7156 Marketing Higher Education Newsletter **2993**
0896-7199 New York Family **2162**
0896-7202 Political Woman†
0896-7210 Journal Watch *changed to* Journal Watch General Medicine **5748**
0896-7229 Procomm Enterprises Magazine
0896-7245 Apple Blossom Connection†
0896-7253 Pesticides and You **247**
0896-7261 Roller Coaster! **4982**
0896-7288 Miniatures Showcase†
0896-7296 Hudspeth Report **4391**
0896-7369 Sport Fishing **8335**
0896-7423 Catalyst (Atlanta)†
0896-7431 Generator **5422**
0896-7520 F D D I Report†
0896-7601 Means Light Commercial Cost Data (Year) **1023**
0896-7636 Cycles (Sharon)†
0896-7660 Chinese Theological Review **7631**
0896-7695 Referee (Gaithersburg)†
0896-7709 Who's Who in the West **647**
0896-7725 The Expert (Louisville)†
0896-7733 Out - Look†
0896-775X Corporate Restructuring†
0896-7792 Financial Aid for Veterans, Military Personnel, and Their Dependents **3022**
0896-7946 Writer's Northwest Handbook **7576**
0896-7962 Home Fashions Magazine *changed to* 1087-2124
0896-7970 Diehard **8226**
0896-8012 Daily Journal of Commerce (Portland) **1427**
0896-8039 Anglican and Episcopal History **7745**
0896-8063 Tattoo Advocate†
0896-8071 Clarion Call
0896-808X Augsburg Home Bible Studies†
0896-8098 Bibliographic Guide to Computer Science†
0896-8101 Bibliographic Guide to Anthropology and Archaeology†
0896-8152 Jewish Storytelling Newsletter **3619**
0896-8160 New England Gardener†
0896-8217 A A A A News **7201**
0896-8276 St. Paul's Family Magazine†
0896-8284 Newspaper Marketing **1836**
0896-8292 Kansas City Magazine & the Town Squire
0896-8306 Soviet Medical Reviews. Section G: Neuropharmacology Reviews†
0896-8322 DISCoveries *changed to* 1055-2685 **6570**
0896-8373 Garden Club of America. Newsletter
0896-8381 Iowa Academy of Science. Journal **7868**
0896-8411 Journal of Autoimmunity **5762**
0896-8446 The Journal of Supercritical Fluids **2103**
0896-8454 V-gram **74**
0896-8470 Yourdon Press Computing Series **2441**
0896-8497 Open Systems†
0896-8500 Investment Management Weekly **1632**
0896-8608 Peritoneal Dialysis International **5695**
0896-8659 Processing **3253**
0896-8667 Military Forum (Englewood)†
0896-8683 Great Britain (Year) **8714**
0896-8691 Ireland (Year) (New York) **8724**
0896-8705 Lactuca **5425**
0896-8713 Briefly†
0896-8756 The Learning Edge **3070**
0896-8772 Store Planning & Design Review **4551**
0896-8802 Gorezone†
0896-887X U S - Japan Economic Relations Yearbook†
0896-890X Political Behavior Annual†
0896-8926 P A M A News **67**
0896-8934 Vox Pop Newsletter†
0896-8942 Mountain Record **7702**
0896-8993 American Songwriter **6544**
0896-9035 Cancer in Puerto Rico **6013**
0896-9051 Safe Worker **6685**
0896-906X Bowne Digest for Corporate & Securities Lawyers **4821**
0896-9108 Sports Inc.†
0896-9132 Pain Management†
0896-9140 Social and Behavioral Sciences Documents†
0896-9159 Community Change **1448**
0896-9205 Critical Sociology **5212**
0896-9256 Current Construction Reports: New One-Family Houses Sold and for Sale†
0896-9345 Always Jukin' **4327**
0896-9426 Cooperative Partners†
0896-9442 Home Energy **3137**
0896-9469 Vital Statistics on Congress **7485**
0896-9531 Bad Attitude **4371**
0896-9574 Educating Able Learners: Discovering and Nurturing Talent†
0896-9590 Colton Clarion **3762**
0896-9604 Harvest (Salem)
0896-9647 Infections in Urology *changed to* 1559-4637 **6269**
0896-9671 International Conference of Building Officials. Uniform Mechanical Code† **8965**
0896-971X International Conference of Building Officials. Uniform Code for the Abatement of Dangerous Buildings†
0896-9728 International Conference of Building Officials. Dwelling Construction under the Uniform Building Code† **8965**
0896-9752 International Conference of Building Officials. Analysis of Revisions to the (Year) Uniform Codes† **8965**
0896-9779 Texas High Technology Directory **2030**
0896-9795 Quartermaster Professional Bulletin **6442**
0896-9868 I F R Refresher **59**
0896-9892 S O L *changed to* 1525-0741 **5037**
0896-9922 C J the Americas†
0896-9949 O S H A Compliance Advisor **3457**
0896-9965 Horns of Plenty
0897-0092 B O C A National Mechanical Code†
0897-0106 Ethics: Easier Said than Done
0897-0122 Mineral Law Series **4734**
0897-0149 Lear's†
0897-0157 Passport to World Band Radio **2361**
0897-0181 Business Credit **1322**
0897-0211 Indianapolis Woman **8868**
0897-022X Hardwood Floors **1050**
0897-0238 Dreams and Nightmares **5421**
0897-0262 Real Estate Accounting and Taxation†
0897-0270 Multiple Sclerosis Research Report†
0897-0289 I B M Directions **2543**
0897-0297 The E M S Leader†
0897-0378 Internal Auditing **1291**
0897-0386 Best Recipes†
0897-0394 Journal of Borderland Research **7872**
0897-0459 Christian Social Action†
0897-0475 Journal of Confederate History **6429**
0897-0483 George Sand Studies
0897-0491 Marine Log **8651**
0897-0521 Journal of the Fantastic in the Arts **5444**
0897-0556 Toward the 21st Century **7294**
0897-0602 Rhode Island Jewish Historical Association. Newsletter **4311**

ISSN

0898-1353 Career Planning and Adult Development Network Newsletter **2939**
0898-1418 Kauai Update **8727**
0898-1434 Today's Image†
0898-1485 Soap Opera Update†
0898-1507 Lasers in Engineering **7080**
0898-1515 R T F I: The Real-Time Financial Information Index†
0898-1558 Darius Milhaud Society Newsletter **6561**
0898-1574 Perkins Press†
0898-1582 Film & Video Finder **2347**
0898-1620 Insurance Law Briefings†
0898-1639 United States Congressional Serial Set Catalog *see* 0362-6830 **7482**
0898-1698 Real Property Law Reporter **4765**
0898-1728 Health Journal
0898-1744 Eastern Review (New York)†
0898-1795 Insights (Washington, 1988)
0898-1809 Inc. Office Guide **1962**
0898-1825 Computer Decisions†
0898-1930 Khosana **8116**
0898-2007 Advances in Social Cognition†
0898-2015 Online Access†
0898-2104 Journal of Liposome Research **6854**
0898-2112 Quality Engineering **3216**
0898-2139 Employers Negotiating Service†
0898-2155 Automotive Investor†
0898-2198 C R S Publications' Career Opportunity Update†
0898-2317 Directory of Postsecondary Institutions†
0898-2392 Muse (Burlington)†
0898-2457 Communications Law **2316**
0898-2481 M T A Today **2884**
0898-2503 PhillySport
0898-2511 FairTest Examiner **2856**
0898-252X The A A S A Professor *changed to* 1931-6569 **3016**
0898-2643 Journal of Aging and Health **4048**
0898-2651 Classic Cross-Stitch†
0898-2686 Directory of Public Vocational Technical Schools, Colleges and Institutes
0898-2759 Physician Executive **4109**
0898-2805 Humboldt Society Newsletter **4375**
0898-2813 Biotech Patent News **759**
0898-2848 Biotechnology Therapeutics†
0898-2864 Mountain
0898-2929 United Nations Resolutions. Series 2. Resolutions and Decisions of the Security Council†
0898-2937 National Bureau of Economic Research. Working Paper Series **1152**
0898-2961 New York Apartment Law Insider **7602**
0898-3003 Environmental and Molecular Mutagenesis. Supplement **866**
0898-3011 Satori†
0898-302X P R C News **2402**
0898-3038 Hemisphere **7240**
0898-3089 The Catalyst Review Newsletter **2053**
0898-3097 Hispanic **3537**
0898-3127 Mind-Body-Health Digest†
0898-3283 Australian & New Zealand Journal of Serials Librarianship†
0898-3364 Laboratory Animal Welfare **320**
0898-3410 Triathlete **8213**
0898-3437 Phytochemical Bulletin† **8981**
0898-3534 Facts, Figures and Bright Ideas *changed to* 1559-1611 **4405**
0898-3569 Health & You **6988**
0898-3577 Compliance Engineering†
0898-3585 Local Climatological Data. Redding, California. Annual Summary with Comparative Data **6382**
0898-3615 Parent's Guide to Children's Video†
0898-3623 California Criminal Law Reporter **4885**
0898-3690 J P R S Report. Science and Technology. U S S R Life Sciences†
0898-3720 Car Audio & Electronics **8152**
0898-3798 Flying Saucer Digest **56**
0898-3879 Statistical Abstract of Utah†
0898-3887 National Trade Estimate, Report on Foreign Trade Barriers **1578**
0898-3917 Bonneville Power Administration. Annual Report **3125**
0898-3933 Reliability Assessment **3161**
0898-3968 Rhythm
0898-4077 Science Fiction, Fantasy, & Horror†
0898-4093 Columbia University-Presbyterian Hospital. School of Nursing Alumni Association. Alumni Magazine **5955**
0898-4131 Association of Food and Drug Officials. Journal (Print Edition) *changed to* Association of Food and Drug Officials. Journal (Online Edition) **3627**
0898-4174 Hispanic Market News **3679**
0898-4204 World War II (Leesburg) **4318**
0898-4212 Abraham Lincoln Association. Journal **4128**
0898-4271 Political Resource Directory **7169**
0898-4298 N C S L Federal Update†
0898-431X Critical Care Report†
0898-4328 C E P Research Report **2635**
0898-4336 International Economy **1570**
0898-4387 Florida Leader†
0898-4417 Thomistic Papers **7820**
0898-4425 Aerospace Facts & Figures **76**
0898-4557 The Gettysburg Review **5217**
0898-4581 Uptown San Diego Examiner **4806**
0898-4646 A J N Guide†
0898-4654 American Statistical Association. Biopharmaceutical Section. Proceedings *changed to* 1543-3218 **8344**
0898-4719 Golf for Women† **8960**
0898-4735 Directory of Dance Faculties in Colleges and Universities, U S & Canada†
0898-4786 M A Training **8186**
0898-4859 Pet Health News†
0898-4867 Cruise and Vacation Views **8695**
0898-4875 Saludos Hispanos **3562**
0898-4891 Community Nursing **5956**
0898-4921 Journal of Neurosurgical Anesthesiology **5772**
0898-4948 S A R A Scope **456**
0898-4972 Small Business U S A **1967**
0898-4980 Model†
0898-5006 Means Repair and Remodeling Cost Data (Year) **1023**
0898-5030 HIV/AIDS Treatment Directory **5815**
0898-5049 Urban Design and Preservation Quarterly†
0898-509X A I A Update **40**
0898-5111 Chinese Journal of Contemporary Mathematics **5478**
0898-512X Chinese Journal of Biochemistry and Biophysics†
0898-5138 Chinese Journal of Genetics†
0898-5146 Chinese Journal of Arid Land Research†
0898-5162 Running & FitNews **6996**
0898-5197 Plum Creek Almanac **4308**
0898-5227 BioBusiness Search Guide†
0898-5316 Review of Research in Nursing Education†
0898-5367 Newman Report†
0898-5405 New Jersey Facts **3121**
0898-5413 Georgia Queries†
0898-5421 Wade World **3787**
0898-543X Hastings Herald
0898-5448 Robertson Report
0898-5456 Parker Papers
0898-5464 English Enquiries†
0898-5510 Journal of Forensic Economics **1545**
0898-5529 Tetrahedron Computer Methodology†
0898-5561 Today's Distributor†
0898-557X Long Island Monthly†
0898-560X Country Inns, Bed & Breakfast†
0898-5626 Entrepreneurship & Regional Development **1105**
0898-5634 Commercial Leasing Law and Strategy **7587**
0898-5650 Toy Shop† **8993**
0898-5669 Pediatric Physical Therapy **6101**
0898-5731 Air Taxi Commuter Safety Bulletin†
0898-5782 F S F Pilots Safety Exchange Bulletin†
0898-5839 Within and Beyond†
0898-588X Studies in American Political Development **7186**
0898-5898 Linguistics and Education **5147**
0898-5901 Laser Therapy **5660**
0898-5952 Performance Improvement Quarterly **3076**
0898-5987 American Viola Society. Journal **6544**
0898-5995 Seminars in Nutrition **6669**
0898-6002 State Resources and Services for Alcohol and Drug Abuse Problems
0898-6029 Holistic Medicine†
0898-6126 Woman's Enterprise†
0898-6169 Survey of Early Childhood Software†
0898-6193 The Voice of Walden
0898-6207 Primate Conservation†
0898-6231 The Discerning Traveler **8698**
0898-6339 Cleveland Foundation. Annual Report **8034**
0898-6355 Country Journal†
0898-6398 Clinical Pharmacology†
0898-6401 New York Doctor†
0898-6428 Advantage Point†
0898-6525 Skin Inc. **5882**
0898-6533 Teaching for Learning†
0898-6568 Cellular Signalling **830**
0898-6606 Waterwheel **8904**
0898-6614 Council of Logistics Management Annual Conference Proceedings **1812**
0898-6622 American Association for the History of Nursing. Bulletin **5951**
0898-6630 Growth, Genetics & Hormones **5893**
0898-6665 Skin Cancer Foundation Journal **6034**
0898-672X American Society of Hypertension. Symposium Series *changed to* American Society of Hypertension. Symposia Highlights **5776**
0898-6770 Perspectives in Hypertension Series **5797**
0898-6886 Pulp & Paper Forecaster†
0898-6894 H P V News **8176**
0898-6908 Human Power **8178**
0898-6916 Capital Source **7114**
0898-6924 International Journal of Cancer. Supplement **6023**
0898-6959 Horn Speaker **366**
0898-6975 Kansas Wildlife & Parks **2616**
0898-7084 Long Island Historical Journal **4302**
0898-7092 The Monocacy Valley Review†
0898-7149 Electronics Distribution Today†
0898-719X Deaf Life **4073**
0898-7270 Hospimedica†
0898-7289 Heckerling Institute on Estate Planning. Annual **4903**
0898-7297 State Legislative Sourcebook **7470**
0898-7300 Annual Bibliography of Modern Art†
0898-7378 Parkinson Report **6173**
0898-7386 Journal of Clinical Practice in Sexuality†
0898-7467 Drug Evaluations†
0898-7521 Hot Tips†
0898-753X Priscilla Papers **7671**
0898-7564 Journal of Veterinary Dentistry **8801**
0898-7629 Harvard University. Graduate School of Business. Working Papers **1749**
0898-7653 Housing Matters
0898-7661 U R I S A Membership Directory
0898-7742 Maine Environment **2618**
0898-7750 Methods in Molecular and Cellular Biology†
0898-7815 Library & Archives News **4151**
0898-784X Independent Publishers Trade Report†
0898-7955 Handel's National Directory for the Performing Arts†
0898-7963 Jewish Science Interpreter **7724**
0898-7971 Defense & Disarmament Alternatives†
0898-798X Corporate Taxation†
0898-7998 Banking Law Review†
0898-8048 Rivers†
0898-8056 Locus (Denton)†
0898-8161 Radioactive Waste Management Handbook
0898-820X Dodge Assemblies Cost Data†
0898-8277 Great American Orators **4170**
0898-8323 The Brown University S T D Update **5589**
0898-8358 Yivo News **4483**
0898-8374 State Municipal League Directory **7503**
0898-8404 Saint Louis University. Public Law Review **4778**
0898-8439 Retail Systems Alert†
0898-8463 Bulletin of the Cantigueiros **7629**
0898-8471 Texas Papers in Foreign Language Education†
0898-8498 C B T Directions†
0898-8501 Pennsylvania Birds **913**
0898-8536 Black Music Research Bulletin†
0898-8625 Locomotive Engineer Newsletter *changed to* 1549-6422 **8620**
0898-8684 Talisman **5436**
0898-8722 Pergolesi Studies **6605**
0898-8749 Safe Driver **8510**
0898-8757 Music for the Love of It **6590**
0898-8765 New Jersey Farmer **139**
0898-879X Arkansas Court Rules Annotated **4621**
0898-8838 Advances in Inorganic Chemistry **2115**
0898-8900 Nichibei Josei Journal **8901**
0898-8943 Knives Illustrated **4338**
0898-8951 Splash (Costa Mesa) **8283**
0898-8978 Handgun Illustrated
0898-8986 All Chevy†
0898-8994 Mustang Illustrated†
0898-9001 All About Beer **597**
0898-901X Digital Technical Journal†
0898-9052 Luso - Americano **3548**
0898-9060 Atlantic States Insurance
0898-9087 Telecom Resources **2372**
0898-9095 Masters Abstracts International **2934**
0898-915X Audubon Activist†
0898-9184 Memories†
0898-9222 Financial Aid for the Disabled and their Families **4065**
0898-9265 Freedom Monitor **7207**
0898-929X Journal of Cognitive Neuroscience **6151**
0898-9346 Eastern Challenge *changed to* Light Among the Least Reached **7764**
0898-9419 Survey of Research for Sexually Transmitted Diseases†
0898-9427 Legal Video Review†
0898-9451 Current Index to Legal Periodicals **4653**
0898-9508 N A S C A R News†
0898-9575 Auto/Biography Studies **640**
0898-9583 Sugaku Expositions **5539**
0898-9591 Chinese Journal of Geophysics (Print Edition)†
0898-9621 Accountability in Research **7831**
0898-9745 The Real Calvin Coolidge **645**
0898-9753 The Executive Report on Managed Care **4502**
0898-9761 Japanese Investment in U S Real Estate Review
0898-977X Florida Motor Sports†
0898-9818 Fairfield County Business Journal **1485**
0898-9842 Encyclopedia of Physical Science & Technology Yearbook†
0898-9907 Corporate Counsel's International Adviser **1556**
0898-9923 Corporate Counsel's Monitor **4864**
0898-9931 Executive Legal Summary **4867**
0898-994X Purchaser's Legal Adviser†
0898-9966 Lawyer's Brief†
0899-0042 Chirality **728**
0899-0131 National Contest Journal **2360**
0899-014X Recreational & Educational Computing†
0899-0158 The North American New Product Report
0899-0166 Research Guides in Military Studies† **8985**
0899-0174 Corporate Controller (New York, 1988)†
0899-0182 Chief Information Officer Journal†
0899-0220 Somatosensory and Motor Research **928**
0899-0247 East-West Education **2844**
0899-0255 Medico-Legal Advisor†
0899-0328 Indianapolis Monthly **3978**
0899-0417 Newsmakers **644**
0899-0425 Newsletters in Print† **8977**
0899-045X Aquarium Fish Magazine *changed to* 1942-5678 **6803**
0899-0506 East Coast Angler†
0899-0514 Original Logic Problems **4343**
0899-0530 Wall Street Digest **1390**
0899-0581 Quiltmakers Time
0899-0913 U.S. Foreign Broadcast Information Service. Daily Reports: Latin America†
0899-0956 The Journal of Applied Manufacturing Systems†
0899-1022 Swimming Pool - Spa Age†
0899-1057 Stockman - Grass Farmer **301**
0899-1111 Ranch Dog Trainer
0899-1138 Images of Excellence **643**
0899-1146 Agora†
0899-1154 Emerge *changed to* 1532-3692
0899-1227 Advances in Library Information Technology†
0899-126X Computer Protocols **2496**
0899-1308 Composite Materials: Testing and Design **3342**
0899-1332 Quaker Queries†
0899-1340 New Jersey Queries†
0899-1359 Kentucky Queries†
0899-1367 Barrett Branches†
0899-1375 Cain Connections†
0899-1391 The Moneychanger **1640**
0899-1405 Wary Canary
0899-1413 Out West **8746**
0899-1502 Journal of Sugar Beet Research **3652**
0899-1510 R E: view† **8983**
0899-1529 The Family (Boston)†
0899-1537 A T O Alive! *changed to* A T O Palm **2271**
0899-1561 Journal of Materials in Civil Engineering **3276**
0899-1596 Stafford Data†
0899-160X Talbott Tree†
0899-1618 Simonson Miscellaneous Research Data†
0899-1626 Freeman Footnotes†
0899-1634 Wiley World†
0899-1650 Invention News
0899-1782 U S Art†
0899-1804 P - P M Technology†
0899-1855 Journal of Physical Therapy Education **6111**
0899-188X Focus on Basics **5119**
0899-191X Allen's Trademark Digest **4613**
0899-1928 Aviation Tradescan **76**
0899-1944 State Child Care Fact Book (Year)†
0899-1952 HeartCorps†
0899-1987 Molecular Carcinogenesis **6028**
0899-1995 Adult Residential Care Journal†
0899-2002 Schools Abroad of Interest to Americans **3015**
0899-2150 A J C Journal† **8927**

0900-2758 Lovinformation fra Miljoestyrelsen†
0900-2812 Danish Meat Research Institute. Annual Report *changed to* 1604-7842 **3664**
0900-2839 Slagteriernes Forskningsinstitut. Aarsberetning *changed to* 1604-7842 **3664**
0900-2847 Fiske-Jul†
0900-288X Faellesudvalget til Kaninavlens Fremme. Beretning† **8955**
0900-291X Arbejdsmiljoe **6673**
0900-2944 Optikeren **6049**
0900-2995 Frankrig Information† **8958**
0900-3002 Tidsskrift for Sygeplejeforskning **5983**
0900-3037 Folkesagn i Tekst og Billed fra Noerreherred†
0900-3045 Dansk Ingenioerforening. Medlemsfortegnelse
0900-3053 Faglig Solidaritet†
0900-3126 Lokalhistorisk Arkiv for Fredericia og Omegn. Aarsskrift†
0900-3134 Bag Kulisserne†
0900-3177 Export **1564**
0900-3339 Retorik†
0900-3347 Tools†
0900-338X Argos†
0900-3401 Tidsskrift for Kaninavl **302**
0900-3452 Musikbladet†
0900-3460 Skalmejen†
0900-3606 Travel Manager C P H **8552**
0900-3665 D S B Bladet† **8948**
0900-372X Dansk Curling†
0900-3738 Denmark. Miljoe- og Energiministeriet. Miljoestyrelsen. Betaenkning **3413**
0900-3746 Miljoepolitik **7155**
0900-3762 Technical Product Update† **8992**
0900-4041 Dansk Kirurgisk Selskab. Nyhedsbrev†
0900-419X Energylab Newsletter†
0900-422X Artisten **4590**
0900-4262 Astma-Allergi Bladet **5754**
0900-4319 Dansk Landbrugs Grovvareselskab. Annual Report *see* 1604-1984 **104**
0900-4505 Handelsskolen **1117**
0900-4556 Anders And & Co.
0900-4645 Danmarks Tekniske Bibliotek med Dansk Central for Dokumentation. Periodiske Bibliografier i D T B. Katalog†
0900-470X Sidesporet†
0900-4726 Alliancebladet *changed to* 1901-533X **7757**
0900-484X Nordisk Herpetologisk Forening **958**
0900-4858 Medicintakst†
0900-5099 M S Biblioteksnyt†
0900-5226 Opdraettervejviseren **6812**
0900-5250 Danish Offshore Guide and Yearbook†
0900-5269 Mikro-Bladet†
0900-5285 Plantebeskyttelse i Land- og Skovbrug†
0900-5293 Oversigt over Landsforsoegene **245**
0900-5579 Dantec Information†
0900-5625 Psykologisk Forskningsrapport†
0900-5749 Dansk Biavl **104**
0900-5781 Danmarks Laererhoejskole. Institut for Informatik. Arbejdspapir†
0900-579X Tidsskrift for Miljoeteknik†
0900-5846 Stambog over Shetland Ponyer† **8990**
0900-615X Rummeteren *changed to* 1902-1496 **3734**
0900-6257 Danmarks Geologiske Undersoegelse. Serie D†
0900-6354 Operabladet Ascolta **6602**
0900-6362 Danmarks Geologiske Undersoegelse. Serie C†
0900-6559 Dats†
0900-6788 Denmark. Miljoe- og Energiministeriet. Miljoestyrelsen. Redegoerelse **3413**
0900-6995 Bibel og Historie **7625**
0900-7008 Idraettens Forskningsraad. Forskningsoversigt†
0900-7350 Dramapaedagogik i Nordisk Perspektiv†
0900-7679 Emigranten†
0900-7962 Helsestatistik for de Nordiske Lande **5747**
0900-7989 Kabel- og Liniemesteren **3323**
0900-7997 Karrosseribladet†
0900-8012 Haandbog for Kvaeghold **288**
0900-8047 Laegaest: Arkeologi i Nordslesvig†
0900-8063 Energi og Planlaegning **3128**
0900-8098 Environmental Radioactivity in the North Atlantic Region Including the Faroe Islands and Greenland†
0900-8160 Den Blaa Port **5263**
0900-8268 Elektrikeren **4593**
0900-8322 Oekonomistyring og Informatik **1782**
0900-8365 Cuba Bladet **4290**
0900-8632 Idraetshistorisk Aarbog **8178**
0900-8659 Bil Testen†
0900-8675 N O W E L E. Supplement **5153**
0900-8691 Guide Nyt†
0900-8764 Molsbibliotekets Lokalhistoriske Arkiv.†
0900-8772 Nordisk Psykologisk Litteratur†
0900-8799 Kniplebrevet **6639**
0900-8977 Haandbog for Svinehold **288**
0900-9132 Skipperen **8662**
0900-9558 Traelast-Tidende **3716**
0900-9582 Skolebiblioteksaarbog **5048**
0900-9671 MedieKultur **2333**
0900-9787 Fiskeriaarbogen **3594**
0900-9922 Koebenhavns Universitet. Sociologisk Institut. Afhandling **8117**
0901-0025 Micro Publications. Social Science Series†
0901-0335 Acta Jutlandica. Medicinsk Serie†
0901-0408 Fodterapeuten **6060**
0901-0505 Sportsdykkeren **8208**
0901-0556 Acta Jutlandica. Humanistisk Serie **4441**
0901-0602 Haandbog i Sociallovgivning†
0901-067X C A S - Nyt **4089**
0901-0815 Arkaeologiske Udgravninger i Danmark† **8931**
0901-0963 Statens Vejlaboratorium. Nye Publikationer†
0901-1056 Ulricks Strikkeideer†
0901-1218 Skibs og Baadebygning†
0901-1595 Fodbold Poster Bladet†
0901-1668 Dansk Fotografisk Tidsskrift† **8948**
0901-1803 Maanedsbladet Press†
0901-1811 Spotlight†
0901-1919 Koebenhavns Nyt†
0901-1943 Goedskingrapport†
0901-1986 Frit Erhverv†
0901-201X Para-nyt†
0901-2281 Kollegie Nyt†
0901-2508 Pilbladet†
0901-2567 OZ **2361**
0901-2583 Platonselskabets Skriftserie **6944**
0901-2869 Ogsaa en Avis†
0901-2982 Auditor **7733**
0901-3067 Hobby Bladet†
0901-313X Bartenderen **6692**
0901-3156 Bibliografi over Dansk Kunst†
0901-3334 K F U M Idraet **8183**
0901-3393 Scandinavian Journal of Laboratory Animal Science **5911**
0901-3601 Danmarks Sko Tidende†
0901-3652 Diabetes **5886**
0901-3768 Energy in Denmark†
0901-3814 Brandteknisk Vejledning **3575**
0901-3873 Dansk Kirketidende **7637**
0901-3946 Chauffoeren **4591**
0901-4209 Dansk Fotografi **6966**
0901-4233 Info-Text†
0901-4306 Blindes Jul **3833**
0901-4497 Aarhus Universitet. Teologiske Fakultet. Bibliografi†
0901-4500 Cystisk Fibrose **5603**
0901-4578 Fremmedsprog† **8958**
0901-4632 D O P S - Nyt **7075**
0901-4691 Oekonomaen **4108**
0901-4780 Hvem Forsker Hvad **3771**
0901-4950 Nord Nu **3944**
0901-5027 International Journal of Oral and Maxillofacial Surgery **5849**
0901-5132 Dansk Amatoermusik†
0901-5205 Nordisk Tidsskrift for Optikere†
0901-5213 Aarhus Universitet. Institut for Statskundskab. Arbejdspapir†
0901-5469 Punkt 95†
0901-5507 Dansk Historisk Bibliografi†
0901-5701 Fynsk Natur (Print) *changed to* Fynsk Natur (Online) **674**
0901-5736 Denmark. Statens Mejeriforsoeg. Report†
0901-5795 Hrymfaxe *changed to* 1901-418X **501**
0901-6120 Bilismen i Danmark†
0901-6171 I F U. Annual Report **1597**
0901-618X I F U. Rapport Annuel *see* 0901-6171 **1597**
0901-6198 I F U. Informe Anual *see* 0901-6171 **1597**
0901-6201 Greens **1998**
0901-6309 Chef Nyt†
0901-6635 A F A Skandinavien Frimaerkekatalog **6891**
0901-6643 A F A Oesteuropa Frimaerkekatalog **6891**
0901-6783 Denmark. Miljoeministeriet. Landsplansredegoerelse fra Miljoeministeren†
0901-6813 Frit Norden **7137**
0901-6945 D V Bogen† **8948**
0901-6996 A F A Danmark Fireblokke **6891**
0901-7003 A F A Danmark, Faeroeerne, Groenland, Dansk Vestindien Frimaerkekatalog **6891**
0901-702X A F A Vesteuropa Frimaerkekatalog **6891**
0901-7089 Psykolog Nyt **7401**
0901-7348 Mejeri- og Dagligvarehandel†
0901-7364 Gartnerinfo†
0901-7488 Fremtidsorientering **8103**
0901-7623 Plys **5352**
0901-7658 Hugin†
0901-7798 P T U Nyt **6172**
0901-7801 Den Roede Transportliste (Year) **8659**
0901-781X Den Blaa Besejlingsliste (Year) **8639**
0901-7917 T L - Teknikeren **8440**
0901-800X Setting Up in Denmark†
0901-8050 Nordisk Pedagogik **2892**
0901-8077 Kolding Bogen **4238**
0901-814X B I M C O Bulletin **8639**
0901-8328 Scandinavian Journal of the Old Testament **7679**
0901-8468 Architecture from Scandinavia†
0901-8484 A S F - Dansk Folkehjaelp†
0901-8735 Firmengruendung in Daenemark†
0901-8816 Nordisk Medie Nyt *changed to* 1399-3658
0901-8883 Passage **5349**
0901-9235 P E O **5347**
0901-9294 Ungdoms- og Voksenundervisning† **8996**
0901-9308 Gymnasiet og HF† **8960**
0901-9316 Erhvervsuddannelserne† **8954**
0901-9545 Se og Hoer **3834**
0901-9731 Koebenhavnerstudier i Tosprogethed **3069**
0901-9758 Nordisk List-Tech†
0901-9847 Dansk Svoemmebadsteknisk Forening. Publikation **8168**
0901-9898 Tandlaegernes Nye Tidsskrift **2169**
0902-0055 Oral Microbiology and Immunology **894**
0902-0063 Clinical Transplantation **6240**
0902-0152 Erhvervlivets Forskning og Udviklingsarbejde **8421**
0902-0179 Islam i Nutiden†
0902-0608 Det Sikkerheds- og Nedrustningspolitiske Udvalg. Aarsberetning†
0902-1523 Romansk Filmklub **6511**
0902-1612 S F Status† **8986**
0902-1620 I Form **6989**
0902-1787 Laegemagasinet **5659**
0902-2074 Denmark. Undervisningsministeriet. Nyhedsbrev†
0902-2163 Dansk Kunsthandvaerk *changed to* 1603-9092 **536**
0902-2228 E K R - Aarsberetning†
0902-2236 E F R - Aarsberetning† **8952**
0902-2341 U F O Vision **73**
0902-2597 Boernebibliotekskatalog. Billed- og Lydmedier†
0902-2767 Klinisk Sygepleje **5968**
0902-2899 Hjemmesygepleje og Forebyggende Foranstaltninger for Boern og Unge **5747**
0902-2961 Denmark. Nationalmuseet. Publications: Archaeological Historical Series **389**
0902-297X Katolsk Orientering **7803**
0902-3488 C S Bladet **6414**
0902-3518 Fortvivl-ikke† **8957**
0902-3542 Vejlaegen *changed to* Syddanske Laeger **8992**
0902-3690 Museumsforeningen for Laesoe. Laesoe Museum *changed to* 1903-8372 **6527**
0902-3704 Ledelse & Erhvervsoekonomi **1144**
0902-3879 Dyrene & Os†
0902-4034 A B Weekend†
0902-4042 Dansk Dragesport† **8948**
0902-4182 Kemi, Pharmaci, Medicin†
0902-4344 Vindue mod Oest **8014**
0902-4441 European Journal of Haematology **5936**
0902-4506 European Journal of Haematology. Supplementum†
0902-4581 P O E T **5159**
0902-4638 Vardin **3837**
0902-4905 Leverandoerhaandbogen† **8971**
0902-5057 Plus Proces **3660**
0902-5456 Dansk V V S **4118**
0902-5499 Carsten Niebuhr Institut Publications **4320**
0902-560X Data†
0902-5618 Handicapidraet **4066**
0902-5626 K C Publikation†
0902-5685 Vaerkstedsteknikeren†
0902-6061 Skoven Nyt **3703**
0902-6452 University of Copenhagen. Institute of Economics. Discussion Papers **1188**
0902-6533 Vejviser over Folkebiblioteker i Storkoebenhavn† **8997**
0902-6592 Thorslunde Ishoej Lokalhistoriske Forening **4273**
0902-6681 Danmarks Nationalbank. Statens Laantagning og Gaeld **7433**
0902-6711 Modus **6588**
0902-705X Thyras Vold **3835**
0902-7076 Navigatoer *changed to* 1901-4899 **8662**
0902-7300 Landbrugets Driftsresultater **202**
0902-7351 Nordic Journal of International Law **4936**
0902-7440 B K F - Billedkunstnernes Forbund *changed to* 1902-3618 **478**
0902-7521 Culture & History **334**
0902-753X Danida Nyt *changed to* 1601-1864 **8036**
0902-7890 Nordisk Uddannelsescenter for Doevblindepersonale. Nyhedsbrev **8059**
0902-798X Udvalg af Litteratur om Ringkoebing Amt†
0902-8161 Erhvervs - Avisen†
0902-8218 Adressefortegnelse, Voksen Kurser†
0902-8234 Teaterraadets Indstillinger, Forslag og Konklusioner†
0902-8242 Nielsen Marketing Research. News† **8977**
0902-9001 Filosofi og Videnskabsteori paa Roskilde Universitetscenter, 2. Raekke, Samlinger **6919**
0902-901X Filosofi og Videnskabsteori paa Roskilde Universitetscenter, 3. Raekke, Preprints og Reprints **6919**
0902-9028 Filosofi og Videnskabsteori paa Roskilde Universitetscenter, 1. Raekke, Enkeltpublikationer **6919**
0902-9117 Fjernsyn†
0902-9125 Den Gule Serie **2861**
0902-9206 Notat C U F†
0902-9273 Fred og Frihed **7236**
0902-9303 Formandsbladet **1008**
0902-9427 Aarbogen for Skjern **4195**
0902-9508 Hjemstavsliv *changed to* 1901-3639 **2688**
0902-9532 Indre Missions Tidende **7761**
0902-9737 Erhvervs-jordbruget†
0902-9818 Koerelaereren **4597**
0902-9907 Renaessancestudier **4257**
0902-9931 K B L Nyt *changed to* 1901-9254 **4595**
0903-0077 Kommunen **7495**
0903-0107 Koebenhavns Kronik
0903-0123 Kvindernes Fagblad *changed to* 1604-6781 **4594**
0903-0425 Haand & Vaerk **1010**
0903-062X Denmark. Statens Uddannelsesstoette. Haandbog **2977**
0903-0719 Groen Viden, Havebrug **3734**
0903-0905 Fortidsminder og Kulturhistorie†
0903-1383 Columbus†
0903-1391 Tid og Syn **4569**
0903-1588 Kommunalbladet *changed to* 1901-2209 **4595**
0903-1723 Angles on the English-Speaking World **5093**
0903-1731 Fugle og Dyr i Nordjylland **907**
0903-188X Musik og Forskning **6595**
0903-1936 The European Respiratory Journal **6214**
0903-2037 Regnskabsstatistik-Landbrug†
0903-2231 Dragonavisen *changed to* 1604-9136 **6419**
0903-2401 Humaniora **4455**
0903-2444 Dansk Filatelistisk Tidsskrift **6894**
0903-2533 Deep-Sea Newsletter† **8949**
0903-2606 I C E S Techniques in Marine Environmental Sciences **677**
0903-2738 Historisk-Topografisk Selskab for Gladsaxe Kommune. Aarbog *changed to* 1903-0916 **4224**
0903-2932 Panorama in Interlingua **5159**
0903-3033 Interieur **4543**
0903-3424 Skanderborg Museum. Aarbog **4263**
0903-3440 Nordisk Filatelistisk Tidsskrift **6897**
0903-3459 A V Haandbogen **18**
0903-3483 Current Titles in Dentistry†
0903-3521 Mit Livs Novelle†
0903-3947 Auto og Bolig Montering
0903-4404 Danish Labour News **4592**
0903-4641 Acta Pathologica Microbiologica et Immunologica Scandinavica **650**
0903-465X A P M I S Supplementum **648**
0903-4668 Tegl **1040**
0903-4714 Papyrus **4177**
0903-5079 Odense University. Department of Commercial Law and Political Science. Publications†
0903-5427 Cronicas de Dinamarca†
0903-5524 Brydning† **8937**
0903-5583 Tieteen Kuvalehti *see* 0281-9341 **7864**
0903-5583 Tieteen Kuvalehti *see* 0109-2456 **7865**
0903-5583 Tieteen Kuvalehti *see* 0800-3955 **7865**
0903-5648 WindStats Newsletter **3179**
0903-5664 Det Danske Hedeselskab. Forsoegsvirksomheden. Beretning†

ISSN

0903-5907	MiljoeDanmark **3453**
0903-6237	K C Nyt **7494**
0903-6326	Fagbladet *changed to* 1604-6781 **4594**
0903-6342	Nyt fra Nyhavn *changed to* 1903-0819 **5037**
0903-6466	Danske Musikoptagelser†
0903-6628	Denmark. Miljoeministeriet. Skov- og Naturstyrelsen. Rapport B†
0903-6814	Denmark. Socialforskningsinstituttet. Rapport *changed to* 1396-1810 **8098**
0903-6857	Aalisartunut Quppersagaq *changed to* 1603-3485 **3597**
0903-6865	Ung **2219**
0903-6946	Denmark. Folketinget. Praesidiet. Folketingstidende. Aarbog og Registre **7433**
0903-6962	Danish Illustration (Year)†
0903-7004	Nord **7159**
0903-7101	Denmark. Risoe National Laboratory. Systems Analysis Department. Annual Progress Report†
0903-7195	Bogmarkedet **7553**
0903-7349	Magisterbladet **4598**
0903-7403	Denmark. Energistyrelsen. Energiforsyning. Energiforbrug†
0903-7497	Laegesekretaer Nyt *changed to* 1903-3125 **4592**
0903-7535	Social Forskning **8069**
0903-7543	Samfundsforskning†
0903-7659	D A O Bladet *changed to* 1902-5742 **6596**
0903-806X	Metal Soefart *changed to* 1901-4570 **4591**
0903-8086	Virksomheden ved Sygehuse *changed to* 1604-8229 **4114**
0903-8108	Sport/Handel†
0903-854X	Forum for Bibelsk Eksegese **7644**
0903-868X	Supermarkedshaandbogen (Year) **1968**
0903-8809	Dansk Varemaerketidende **6748**
0903-8825	Dansk Moenstertidende *changed to* 1601-7366 **6748**
0903-8868	Oekonomiske Tendenser **1156**
0903-8876	A M I - Rapport **1661**
0903-8892	Aalborg Universitet. Institut for Sprog og Internationale Kulturstudier. Publikationer **8085**
0903-9198	Farmaci **6841**
0903-921X	Tennis Aarbogen†
0903-9295	Henry - D R U Nytt†
0903-9961	International Studies. Nordic Seminar on Human Rights. Proceedings† **8966**
0904-0234	Denmark. Danmarks Statistik. Noegletal paa Postnumre **7306**
0904-0919	L O - Ungdoms Blad†
0904-1346	Fugle i Aarhus Amt **907**
0904-1559	Mester Tidende **1023**
0904-1567	Niviarsiaq **7159**
0904-1699	Hermes **2322**
0904-1737	D S I-Rapport **4092**
0904-1796	Dansk Turisme *changed to* 1604-5807 **8772**
0904-1850	European Respiratory Journal. Supplement **6214**
0904-1893	Katalog for Skolebiblioteker. Eleverne† **8969**
0904-1907	Katalog for Skolebiblioteker. Skolebibliotekaren† **8969**
0904-1990	Denmark. Direktoratet for Kriminalforsorgen. Aarsberetning *changed to* 1901-7677 **2650**
0904-2067	Acta Hyperborea **371**
0904-2105	Provinsens Distriktsblade
0904-2180	L L - Nyt **3069**
0904-2253	Denmark. Statens Byggeforskningsinstitut. Projektresumeer†
0904-2334	Katalog **6970**
0904-2369	Dit Laegemagasin **6984**
0904-2393	Dansk Paedagogisk Tidsskrift **2841**
0904-2431	Studies in Central and East Asian Religions†
0904-2458	A G **3874**
0904-2512	Journal of Oral Pathology & Medicine **5852**
0904-2598	S U F O I News **69**
0904-2644	Att.:†
0904-275X	Patentdirektoratet Orienterer†
0904-2903	Danskeren **7281**
0904-3063	Journal of World Education **2879**
0904-3179	Nyt fra Kriminalforsorgen **4896**
0904-3241	Byggeplads Danmark **436**
0904-3535	Social Kritik **8003**
0904-3594	Anlaeg Netto **976**
0904-3616	Anlaeg Brutto **976**
0904-3624	Husbygning Netto **1013**
0904-3632	Husbygning Brutto **1013**
0904-3640	Landsudvalget for Svin. Aarsberetning **292**
0904-3683	Stavn **4267**
0904-3748	B (Copenhagen) **4404**
0904-3764	Kost og Allergi Nyt†
0904-3853	Over Broen† **8979**
0904-4310	Danish Dairy & Food Industry - Worldwide **264**
0904-4337	N I A S Nytt **556**
0904-4698	C D R Project Paper†
0904-4701	C D R Working Paper†
0904-4760	Aarhus Universitet. Center for Kulturforskning. Arbejdspapirer, Groen Series **8085**
0904-4787	Kloaktuelt **4123**
0904-4868	Tekst og Tolkning **7687**
0904-504X	Voeka **5983**
0904-5139	S R - Skat **1942**
0904-5341	Ungdomsuddannelser **2922**
0904-5589	Denmark. Nationalmuseet. Publications: Ethnographical Series†
0904-5813	Danceletter
0904-6054	Kristeligt Dagblad **3834**
0904-6216	Aeldre Sagen *changed to* 1903-2161 **4038**
0904-6216	Aeldre Sagen *changed to* 1903-2153 **4038**
0904-6267	Historisk Aarbog for Thy og Vester Hanherred **4229**
0904-6380	Nordic Theatre Studies **8474**
0904-6399	Maelk & Ost†
0904-6453	A A U Reports†
0904-6534	Trans-Inform **8513**
0904-6542	Farmaceuten *changed to* 1902-7966 **6867**
0904-6860	Greenland. Groenlands Statistik. Befolkning **7307**
0904-6895	Fynske Laeger *changed to* Syddanske Laeger **8992**
0904-6917	Turist- og Rutebilbladet†
0904-7034	Denmark. Dantest. Aarsberetning†
0904-728X	Romance†
0904-7824	Lys **3324**
0904-8022	Driftsresultater for Sommerregnskaber†
0904-8081	Handicap - Nyt **4066**
0904-8545	Menighedsraadenes Blad **7662**
0904-860X	Dansk Fjernvarmevaerkers Forening. Statistik *changed to* 1902-4258 **4128**
0904-8626	Copenhagen Discussion Papers†
0904-8987	Tordenskjold†
0904-9002	Aalborg-Bogen **4195**
0904-9339	Manteia†
0904-9363	Dansk Landbrug *changed to* 1901-9300 **133**
0904-9444	Det Ny Infodont†
0904-9681	News from D B D H *changed to* 1902-9500 **4120**
0904-9754	IN **8868**
0904-9789	Mellemoestinformation **4323**
0904-986X	Denmark. Forbrugerstyrelsen. Tekniske Meddelelser†
0905-0035	Status og Visioner **7542**
0905-006X	Boerne- og Ungdomstandplejen i Danmark†
0905-0167	Scandinavian Journal of Information Systems **2437**
0905-0515	MacWorld Danmark†
0905-0620	Rigsombudsmanden paa Faeroerne. Beretning **4258**
0905-071X	Kirkelig Forening for den Indre Mission i Danmark. Aarbog **7763**
0905-1236	Denmark. Danmarks Statistik. Forskning og Udviklingsarbejde i den Offentlige Sektor (Print) *changed to* Denmark. Danmarks Statistik. Forskning og Udviklingsarbejde i den Offentlige Sektor (Online) **8366**
0905-1503	Ung og Fri **5243**
0905-1600	Dansk Tidsskrift for Museumsformidling **6523**
0905-1678	Julegaven†
0905-1740	High Fidelity (Swedish Edition) **8153**
0905-197X	Loke†
0905-2143	Ingenioer - Hvorfor, Hvordan **3198**
0905-2151	Maskin - Aktuelt **6321**
0905-247X	Miljoetema **3489**
0905-295X	D S T **3687**
0905-3026	Teater 1 **8480**
0905-3174	Vejen Frem†
0905-3204	I T Standardnyt†
0905-3263	Denmark. Danish Meteorological Institute. Scientific Report **6351**
0905-3336	Denmark. Udenrigsministeriet. Denmark's Development Assistance. Country Memorandum†
0905-3492	Danmarks Biblioteksskole. Biblioteket. D B I Accession†
0905-3549	D M I News **8642**
0905-3883	Atletik'en†
0905-4006	Fodbold, Internationale Kampe **8228**
0905-4170	Spildevandsforskning fra Miljoestyrelsen†
0905-4332	Mandag Morgen **4242**
0905-4367	F S Rs Skattelove med Noter **1923**
0905-4383	Photodermatology, Photoimmunology & Photomedicine **5880**
0905-443X	Skat Udland **1943**
0905-4472	Kursliste for Danske Aktieselskaber og Anpartsselskaber samt Groenlandske Selskaber **1143**
0905-4545	Almen Semiotik **6903**
0905-4766	Styret **8268**
0905-4774	Soendag **3834**
0905-5029	Danske Moebler *changed to* Moebel + Interioer Brancheblade **4561**
0905-5142	Agriculture in Denmark: Statistics on Danish Agriculture **174**
0905-5193	Groenlands Fiskeriundersoegelser. Aarsberetning
0905-5215	Kalaallit Nunaani Aalisakkanik Misissuinerit. Ukiumoortumik Nalunaarusiaq
0905-5282	Erhvervs- og Boligstyrelsen - Aarsberetning **8421**
0905-5320	Kridtstregen **8237**
0905-5371	Dansk Kommentar til det Nye Testamente **7637**
0905-5487	L V U Fagbladet *changed to* 1903-7139 **2921**
0905-5525	D S U'eren **7128**
0905-5533	Det Kongelige Bibliotek. Magasin **5023**
0905-5681	Teknologidebat **8443**
0905-5878	Guldnummeret† **8960**
0905-5908	Dansk Sociologi **8098**
0905-5991	Miljoenyt **3453**
0905-6157	Pediatric Allergy and Immunology **6099**
0905-6300	Dansk Musik Aarbog **6561**
0905-6343	Teletema *changed to* 1602-799X **2319**
0905-6351	Vestkyst Fiskeren *changed to* 1396-4194 **3594**
0905-6416	Energinyt **3129**
0905-6432	Apoteksassistenten
0905-6440	Danske Malermestre **6717**
0905-6866	International Journal for the Joining of Materials† **8966**
0905-6947	Indoor Air **7525**
0905-6998	K & K **8116**
0905-7080	Avls- og Aarbog for Langhaaret Hoensehund† **8934**
0905-7161	Clinical Oral Implants Research **5838**
0905-717X	Iatrogenics†
0905-7188	Scandinavian Journal of Medicine & Science in Sports **6232**
0905-7196	Arabian Archaeology and Epigraphy **374**
0905-7218	C A S A Nyt **8091**
0905-7269	Copenhagen Studies in Language **5108**
0905-7293	Folkeskolens Nyhedskatalog†
0905-7498	Dansk Politi **2650**
0905-7501	Denmark. Statens Paedagogiske Forsoegscenter. Projektbeskrivelser **2841**
0905-7633	Emil†
0905-7676	Aarbog for Kvindeforskning (Aarhus)†
0905-7692	Statistik om Virksomheden i Hjemmesygeplejen...og Skolesundhedstjenesten†
0905-7749	Aslan (Print) *changed to* 1901-6646 **7623**
0905-7765	C E U - Bladet†
0905-815X	Danmarks Miljoeundersoegelser. Faglig Rapport **3413**
0905-8478	Kongelige Veterinaer- og Landbohoejskole. Institut for Jordbrugsvidenskab. Forskningsrapport†
0905-8567	Nordschleswiger **3834**
0905-8834	Ledoeje-Smoerum Historisk Forening og Arkiv - Aarsskrift **4239**
0905-8869	Konnichi Wa - Dansk Japansk Venskabsforenings Blad†
0905-8893	Kvant **7024**
0905-8915	Danish Polar Center. Newsletter†
0905-8958	Aktuel Astronomi **568**
0905-8966	Ledelse i Dag† **8970**
0905-9180	European Respiratory Review **6214**
0905-9415	Finans og Samfund *changed to* 1603-9947 **8969**
0905-9466	Jul i Familien†
0905-9539	Arbejdsmiljoet - Netop Nu†
0905-9717	Semiramis†
0905-9741	Fritid til Soes† **8958**
0905-975X	Specialisten **4602**
0905-9954	Over Soe og Land *changed to* 1604-5076 **8984**
0905-9962	Musikeren **6596**
0906-0081	Agrologisk **87**
0906-009X	Bovilogisk **261**
0906-0146	Blaavand Fuglestation†
0906-0294	Koebenhavns Universitet. Geologisk Centralinstitut. Aarsberetning **2752**
0906-0308	European Studies **4219**
0906-0413	Kompass Select Export. Textiles, Clothing, Footwear and Leather Goods†
0906-0499	Uddannelse og Erhver. Materialer **6518**
0906-0510	Papers in Organization† **8980**
0906-0596	I C E S Annual Report *changed to* 2070-7185 **2808**
0906-060X	I C E S Marine Science Symposia **3597**
0906-0669	Koebenhavns Universitet. Oekonomisk Institut. Cykelafdelingen. Memo **1141**
0906-0820	Alt om Mad†
0906-0928	Koebenhavns Universitet. Institut for Statskundskab. Forskningsrapport†
0906-0995	Hyologisk **288**
0906-1037	Byggeriet **988**
0906-1061	Strings and Squares **2688**
0906-1134	Odensebogen (Year) **4250**
0906-1371	U S A Trade Opportunities†
0906-1436	I S W A Times† **8963**
0906-1452	National Committee for Pig Breeding and Production. Annual Report *see* 0904-3640 **292**
0906-1614	Journalen **4236**
0906-1746	Tidsskrift for Dansk Faareavl *changed to* 1902-7168 **286**
0906-1797	Denmark. Risoe National Laboratory. Optics and Fluid Dynamics Department. Annual Progress Report† **8949**
0906-1851	Golfhaandbogen† **8960**
0906-1894	Denmark. Landbrugsministeriet. Forskningssekretariatet. Rammeplaner†
0906-219X	Psykologisk Paedagogisk Raadgivning *changed to* 1903-0002 **7389**
0906-2211	Statistisk Aarbog for Hovedstadsregionen† **8990**
0906-2254	Neriusaaq **508**
0906-2408	Zigzag *changed to* 1901-9211 **7241**
0906-2475	Fund af Storsommerfugle i Danmark **848**
0906-2483	Psykologisk Set **7401**
0906-270X	Rent i Danmark **1789**
0906-2807	Fagbladet Artur†
0906-3021	Antropologi **328**
0906-3315	Greenland. Groenlands Statistik. Konjunkturstatistik **1236**
0906-3323	Arbok fyri Foeroyar **8347**
0906-3420	Danmarks Stoerste Virksomheder†
0906-3447	Scandinavian Journal of Design History **516**
0906-3560	I OE. Annual Report **1597**
0906-3773	Havforskning fra Miljoestyrelsen†
0906-3927	Computerworld **2414**
0906-4052	Nyhedsmagasinet Elektronik & Data **3110**
0906-4060	Mad & Bolig Magasinet **4545**
0906-415X	Jaeger **8319**
0906-4184	Amnesty **7220**
0906-4397	Restauratoeren, Danmark†
0906-4664	Reflex **6947**
0906-4702	Acta Agriculturae Scandinavica. Section A. Animal Science **277**
0906-4710	Acta Agriculturae Scandinavica. Section B. Soil and Plant Science **216**
0906-4893	Folketinget efter Valget **7438**
0906-4907	Vildtinformation **8339**
0906-5202	Ildfisken **5308**
0906-5369	Danish Literary Magazine† **8948**
0906-5407	Bibliotek for Laeger **5584**
0906-5474	Bil Magasinet **8569**
0906-5504	Inuit Tusaataat†
0906-5563	Denmark. Finanstilsynet. Tilsynet med Realkreditinstitutter. Beretning† **8949**
0906-5784	Pediatric Allergy and Immunology. Supplementum **6099**
0906-5792	H K Handel *changed to* 1901-9254 **4595**
0906-5822	Denmark. Forskningsafdelingen. Forskning†
0906-6225	Kognition & Paedagogik **7382**
0906-6292	Latinamerikabladet Manana†
0906-6349	Det Bedste† **8935**
0906-642X	DataSikkerhedsBladet **2513**
0906-6489	Banana Split **5260**
0906-6632	Satellit Information (Print) *changed to* 1901-8134 **2338**
0906-6659	Aarhus Universitet. Psykologisk Skriftserie†
0906-6691	Ecology of Freshwater Fish **941**
0906-6705	Experimental Dermatology **5876**
0906-6713	Periodontology 2000 **5861**
0906-6896	Film **6498**
0906-690X	Psykologisk Paedagogisk Raadgivning. Monografi† **8983**
0906-6977	Familie Journalen **3833**
0906-7043	Jord og Viden **125**
0906-7590	Ecography **3416**
0906-7612	Odense Working Papers in Language and Communication **5157**
0906-7639	Copenhagen Working Papers in Linguistics†
0906-8147	Lederforum **4598**
0906-8317	Boersen Informatik†
0906-8643	Opgavesamling i Skatteret 1† **8979**
0906-8880	Rangfoelgen, de 3 Foerste Rangklasser†
0906-897X	Denmark. Danish Meteorological Institute. Technical Report **6351**
0906-9178	D A O **5110**
0906-9194	Design DK *changed to* 1603-1059 **8420**

DIRECTORY 2010 0910-2485 9385

0906-9305 Pigment Cell Research. Supplement *see* 1755-1471 **835**
0906-9488 Dansk Avls Nyt **285**
0906-9550 Kongelige Veterinaer- og Landbohoejskole. Jordbrugsteknisk Institut. Rapport† **8970**
0906-9666 Program of Plenary Sessions and Advance Abstracts of Short Communications
0906-9690 Euroman **6289**
0906-9976 Spring (Gentofte) **5377**
0907-0079 Risoe International Symposium on Materials Science. Proceedings **6331**
0907-0192 Finans **1346**
0907-0362 Forest & Landscape Research†
0907-0478 Skriftserie for Terapiforskning†
0907-0559 Baadmagasinet *changed to* Baadmagasinet Sejl **8271**
0907-0559 Baadmagasinet *changed to* Baadmagasinet Motor **8271**
0907-0567 Avls-Information **280**
0907-0648 Autoriserede Laeger i Danmark†
0907-0753 Nyt om Arbejdermuseet **350**
0907-0877 Cybernetics & Human Knowing **2526**
0907-0974 Salt† **8986**
0907-1016 Koebenhavns Fondsboers. Aarsrapport
0907-1040 Groenland **1010**
0907-1075 En Verden af Romantik†
0907-1156 Kulturkontakten† **8970**
0907-1296 FoQus† **8957**
0907-1423 Glasmagasinet *changed to* 1604-8016 **2041**
0907-1695 Denmark. Danmarks Meteorologiske Institut. Data Report†
0907-1814 Politiken **3834**
0907-2160 Rambam **3560**
0907-2225 Greenland. Groenlands Statistik. Uddannelse **8375**
0907-2284 Benzin-tanken†
0907-2322 Polarfronten **2715**
0907-2357 Handelshoejskolen i Koebenhavn. Aarsberetning **1749**
0907-2535 Exit†
0907-2675 Danmarks Olie og Gasproduktion **6766**
0907-2829 Roskilde Universitscenter. International Development Studies. Occasional Paper **1604**
0907-3272 Menighedsfakultetet. Videnskabelige Serie **7662**
0907-3388 Koebenhavns Universitet. Institut for Almen og Anvendt Sprogvidenskab. Arbejdspapirer **5137**
0907-3574 Konstruktoeren **1020**
0907-3612 Magasinet Kunst **503**
0907-3728 Lovregister for Faeroerne **4725**
0907-3841 Djembe *changed to* 1903-4911 **4449**
0907-404X Denmark. Danmarks Miljoeundersoegelser. Beretning og Aktiviteter **3413**
0907-4066 Vejledning i Plantevaern **257**
0907-418X Danmarks Journalisthoejskole. Beretning **4574**
0907-4449 Acta Crystallographica. Section D: Biological Crystallography **2109**
0907-4597 Dansk Brugsmodeltidende (Print edition) *changed to* 1602-6691 **6748**
0907-4732 Hendes Verden **4360**
0907-4791 Landsbynyt **8118**
0907-4821 Denmark. Statens Filmcentral. S F C Film Kataloget
0907-4856 Camping & Fritid **8308**
0907-5437 Dansk Security† **8948**
0907-5682 Childhood **2148**
0907-6069 Specialundervisning† **8989**
0907-6182 Kvinder, Koen & Forskning **8870**
0907-6581 Tidsskrift for Boerne- og Ungdomskultur **2169**
0907-676X Perspectives - Studies in Translatology **5160**
0907-6824 Viborg Stiftsmuseums Raekke† **8997**
0907-7154 Noerre-Alslev Kommune. Lokalhistorisk Forening. Aarsskrift **4248**
0907-7243 Blik & Roer **4590**
0907-7375 D A N A K's Register over Akkrediterede Proevningslaboratorier og Godkendte GLP-Laboratorier
0907-743X Tidevandstabeller. Danmark **2818**
0907-7448 Break 19†
0907-7502 Tidevandstabeller. Faeroeerne **2818**
0907-7510 Tidevandstabeller. Groenland **2818**
0907-7626 Kvinder i Musik **6583**
0907-7723 F S Rs Afgiftslove **1923**
0907-7901 Copenhagen Studies in Translation†
0907-7960 Inguirer *changed to* 1602-5334 **6509**
0907-8002 Dansk Forening for Information og Dokumentation. Skriftserie†
0907-8118 The Carlsberg Papyi **5270**
0907-8274 Beretning om den Oekonomiske Udvikling paa Faeroerne **1066**
0907-8541 Kirkegaardskultur **3720**
0907-8770 Haandbogen Dag- og Doegninstitutioner *changed to* 1602-8074 **8937**
0907-8789 Byhistorisk Samling og Arkiv i Hoje-Taastrup Kommune. Aarskrift **4207**
0907-8916 Danish Medical Bulletin (Print)†
0907-9033 Venstrebladet **3835**
0907-905X Faroe Islands. Foeroya Landsstyri. Kunngerdabladid, A **4671**
0907-9068 Faroe Islands. Foeroya Landsstyri. Kunngerdabladid, B **4671**
0907-9076 Familieplanlaegning†
0907-9300 Nyt fra Ankestyrelsen **8059**
0907-9386 Uddannelses- og Erhvervsvalget **3006**
0907-9432 Greenland. Groenlands Statistik. Greenland (Year) - Statistical Yearbook **8375**
0907-9440 Kvinder & Karriere†
0907-9556 Holstebro Museum. Skriftraekke **4230**
0907-9718 Det Danske Fjerkraeraad. Beretning **285**
0907-984X Dansk Mission†
0908-0031 Social Forskning. Tema-Nummer **8133**
0908-0260 Dansk Bioenergi *changed to* 1902-7907 **3236**
0908-0317 Danmarks Moenter og Pengesedler **6650**
0908-0465 Billedkunst **478**
0908-049X Nordisk Litteratur **5342**
0908-0570 Transport-Magasinet **8515**
0908-0627 Koebenhavns Universitet. Oesteuropainstitut. Rapporter† **8969**
0908-066X En Hel Verden†
0908-0686 Zapp Jorden Rundt **7275**
0908-0740 Omkring Gudstjenesten†
0908-0791 Markforsoeg i de Landoekonomiske Foreninger†
0908-0813 Tabelbilag til Landsforsoegene **255**
0908-0945 Raastofproduktion i Danmark. Landomraade†
0908-1208 Aalborg Universitetscenter. Institut for Elektroniske Systemer. Afdeling for Proceskontrol - Rapport **3294**
0908-1224 Aalborg Universitetscenter. Institut for Elektroniske Systemer. Afdeling for Kommunikationsteknologi. Rapport **3294**
0908-1410 Ny Poetik†
0908-164X Murernes Fagblad†
0908-1682 Boerns Hverdag **2831**
0908-1704 Oil and Gas Production in Denmark *changed to* Denmark's Oil and Gas Production **6766**
0908-1755 Danish Centre for Technical Aids for Rehabilitation and Education. Newsletter†
0908-1771 Nyt - Ho-Re-Fa†
0908-1992 Boernefilm & Video†
0908-200X The Copenhagen Diplomatic List **7228**
0908-2492 Gaia **7236**
0908-3316 Alt om Foto & Video **6963**
0908-3472 Rapport om den Kommunale Beskaeftigelsesindsats i...†
0908-3537 Skrift for Historisk Forening for Sundeved **4263**
0908-3731 Arbeidsliv i Norden **1663**
0908-3839 *see* 1901-8444 **8415**
0908-3855 Miljoe **1024**
0908-3987 Ren Viden **3511**
0908-4037 Akseltrykmaalinger **8629**
0908-4185 F S Rs Skatte- og Afgiftslove. Supplement **1923**
0908-4282 Applied Neuropsychology **6123**
0908-4398 The Nordic Countries in Figures **8391**
0908-4738 Dansk Standard. Elsektoren. Aarbog†
0908-5025 Danish Children's Literature† **8948**
0908-5165 Konditor Nyt *changed to* 1901-6069 **3674**
0908-5262 L I S **5319**
0908-5351 Passepartout **511**
0908-5491 Roskilde Universitetscenter. Datalogisk Afdeling. Datalogiske Noter **2436**
0908-5580 Instruktoermagasinet Krumspring *changed to* 1604-0988 **8214**
0908-5610 Erhvervsfremme†
0908-5890 Akademiet for de Tekniske Videnskaber. Nyhedsbrev *changed to* 1602-0081
0908-5904 F O A Bladet *changed to* 1901-5712 **4594**
0908-5904 F O A Bladet *changed to* 1901-0214 **4594**
0908-5904 F O A Bladet *changed to* 1901-0222 **4594**
0908-5904 F O A Bladet *changed to* 1901-0230 **4594**
0908-5920 Indoor Air. Supplement **7525**
0908-617X University of Copenhagen. Niels Bohr Institute, Oersted Laboratory. Report **7044**
0908-6226 Haandbog for Social- og Sundhedssektor *changed to* 1600-0293 **8069**
0908-6293 Billedpaedagogisk Tidsskrift **478**
0908-6404 Produktionsoekonomi, Planteavl **205**
0908-6625 Geographica Hafniensia. Skrifter A **4010**
0908-6633 Geographica Hafniensia. Skrifter C **4010**
0908-665X Xenotransplantation **6262**
0908-6692 TemaNord **7188**
0908-6722 Almennyttige Boligafdelingers Regnskaber **4432**
0908-6781 Rotunden **3834**
0908-7133 Isenkrambranchen *changed to* 1903-0894 **2040**
0908-715X Ord & Tekst† **8979**
0908-729X Denmark. Risoe National Laboratory. Annual Report **3166**
0908-7648 Autosport **8160**
0908-7656 Dansk Told & Skat **4592**
0908-7702 Historisk Aarbog for Roedding-Egnen **4229**
0908-7737 Brudstykker fra Blicheregnen **4207**
0908-7761 Vand & Jord **2630**
0908-777X Sprog og Kulturmoede **5178**
0908-7796 Breve Indland **2353**
0908-7885 Maritime Archaeology Newsletter from Roskilde *changed to* 1902-0708 **405**
0908-7923 RetorikMagasinet **5360**
0908-8237 Opgavesamling i Skatteret 2† **8979**
0908-8245 Naturforvaltning **2621**
0908-8431 Tidsskrift for Skatter og Afgifter **1951**
0908-8504 Denmark. Statens Arkiver. Landsarkivet for Fyn. Gemt er ikke Glemt **4214**
0908-858X Havrevimpen **676**
0908-8687 Koebenhavns Universitet. Sociologisk Institut. Rapportserie **8117**
0908-8695 Koebenhavns Universitet. Institut for Historie. Skrifter†
0908-8725 Bangsbo Museum og Arkiv. Aarbog **6521**
0908-8814 Boernebiblioteksaktalog. Baand, CD'er og Plader†
0908-8857 Journal of Avian Biology **909**
0908-8865 Teori og Aestetik **5386**
0908-8962 Centre for Labour Market and Social Research. Working Papers† **8940**
0908-9195 Denmark. Miljoe- og Energiministeriet. Miljoestyrelsen. Arbejdsrapport†
0908-9454 Doevebladet **4073**
0908-9489 Dybfrost Danmark†
0908-9594 Beredskab **2225**
0908-9659 Export Denmark **1992**
0908-973X Haandvaerksraadet. Haandbog *changed to* 1901-3795 **1961**
0908-9926 De Farver **6717**
0909-0002 Film & Video† **8956**
0909-0029 Marinehistoriske Skrifter **6432**
0909-0282 Dansk Squash† **8948**
0909-0347 D A Loenstatistik (Print) *changed to* D A Loenstatistik (Online) **1223**
0909-0452 Beskrivelsestekster **981**
0909-0495 Journal of Synchrotron Radiation **7068**
0909-0509 Boern i Tiden† **8937**
0909-0630 G H E X I S Newsletter† **8958**
0909-0703 Kongelige Veterinaer- og Landbohoejskole. Institut for Oekonomi, Skov og Landskab. Samfundsvidenskabelig Memo-Serie† **8970**
0909-0797 Musical Denmark Yearbook: Including Music in Denmark Key Directory†
0909-0878 B R I C S Report Series **2408**
0909-0886 Diwan†
0909-1025 Finansfokus†
0909-1076 Europaeisk Politik **4924**
0909-1092 Elforsyningen, Ti-aars Statistik
0909-1165 Oekonomisk Ugebrev **1505**
0909-119X Syddansk Universitet. Institut for Sundhedstjeneste Forskning. Monographs on Population Aging **4056**
0909-1351 E U-Orientering *changed to* 1904-0350 **264**
0909-1378 Denmark. Ministeriet for Foedevarer, Landbrug og Fiskeri. Plantedirektoratet. Beretning **227**
0909-1386 Denmark. Transport- og Energiministeriet. Vejteknisk Institut. Rapport **3264**
0909-1408 Installations Nyt, Special **3319**
0909-1424 Denmark. Finansministeriet. Budgetredegoerelse **1919**
0909-1459 Aviserat *changed to* 1901-8088 **4583**
0909-1904 Racefjerkrae **297**
0909-1912 Global Oekologi **3434**
0909-2757 Psoriasis Nyt **5881**
0909-3044 Vejledning og Vejledere, Adresser **2963**
0909-3206 B R I C S Notes Series **2407**
0909-3486 Aarhus Geoscience†
0909-3818 Scandinavian Food & Drink **3662**
0909-3826 Sko - Shoes & More **7942**
0909-4156 Sundhedsstatistikken (Year) **4114**
0909-4261 Nordisk Miljoeforskningsprogram†
0909-4288 Denmark. Transport- og Energiministeriet. Vejdirektoratet. Rapport **3264**
0909-5837 Bistandsloven og alle dens Regler *changed to* 1398-4403 **8135**
0909-5926 D B 3 Billedkunst **3057**
0909-6043 B R I C S Newsletter†
0909-6388 Tidsskrift for Dansk Sundhedsvaesen **4112**
0909-6396 Wildlife Biology **967**
0909-6418 Lederne **1695**
0909-6477 Folkeskolen. Katalog† **8957**
0909-7325 Fiskeri Tidende **3594**
0909-7503 Afspaendingspaedagogen *changed to* 1902-3375 **6981**
0909-752X Skin Research and Technology **5882**
0909-783X Dayanisma Gazetesi **7230**
0909-7872 Dansk Uddannelses & Erhvervs Leksikon **2955**
0909-8143 Levnedsmiddelavisen *changed to* 1902-4754 **3654**
0909-816X Politiken Weekly **3834**
0909-8208 Goal **8230**
0909-8348 *see* 0905-3549 **8642**
0909-8410 Denmark. Transport- og Energiministeriet. Vejdirektoratet. Notat **8630**
0909-8615 Sermitsiaq **3874**
0909-8801 Oerestadsselskabet. Aarsberetning *changed to* 1902-1127 **3279**
0909-8836 European Journal of Oral Sciences **5844**
0909-8976 Rask **5165**
0909-9034 Schultz Lovbibliotek **4780**
0909-9050 Espansiva **6565**
0909-9077 Arbejdsmarkedspolitisk Agenda *changed to* 1902-7915 **1662**
0909-9093 Det Kongelige Bibliotek. Aarsberetning **5023**
0909-914X Nordicom†
0909-9328 Sprogforum **5178**
0909-945X Den Gamle By **6524**
0909-9557 Dansk Landbrugsraadgivning. Dansk Kvaeg. Aarsstatistik, Avl **285**
0909-9832 Nordisk Program for Arktisk Humanistisk Forskning†
0909-9883 Musikvejviser
0909-9891 Facts & Faenomener†
0909-9905 Specialitetstakst *changed to* 1602-8910 **6861**
0910-0059 Rigaku Ryoho **6116**
0910-0067 Nihon Kotsu Taisha Gakkai Zasshi†
0910-0156 Kokusai Kenkyu **7250**
0910-0172 Wota Jetto
0910-0237 N E C Update **3326**
0910-0350 Denki Setsubi Gakkaishi **3299**
0910-0377 Hirosaki Daigaku Igakubu Eiseigaku Kyoshitsu Gyosekishu†
0910-0458 Chosekihyo 1. Nihon Oyobi Fukin **2801**
0910-0466 Chosekihyo 2. Taiheiyo Oyobi Indoyo **2802**
0910-0474 Mebio **5795**
0910-0709 Tokyo Daigaku Daigakuin Rigakukeikenkyuka Rigakubu Butsurigaku Kyoshitsu Nenji Kenkyu **7043**
0910-0717 Meidai Uchusan Kenkyushitsu Kiji **7026**
0910-0725 Hakodate Igakushi **5623**
0910-0792 Kokusai Denki Giho **3323**
0910-0822 Nagoya Daigaku Kogakubu Jinko Kessho Kenkyu Shisetsu Ronbun Yoshishu†
0910-0865 Environmental Mutagen Research/Kankyo Hen'igen Kenkyu *changed to* Genes and Environment **867**
0910-0903 Mukin Seibutsu **690**
0910-0911 Animaruzu Nyusu
0910-0938 Kasen Rebyu **8828**
0910-1004 Japan Hospitals **4103**
0910-1020 Dongjing Dumin Tongxun *see* 0916-7951 **7504**
0910-111X Pawa Dezain†
0910-1225 Sogo Seikotsu†
0910-1381 Keio University Bulletin **2991**
0910-1403 Sumitomo Bank. Annual Report **1385**
0910-1543 Iyo Gazo Joho Gakkai Zasshi (Print)†
0910-1551 Medical Practice **5670**
0910-1810 Atarashii Ganka **6038**
0910-1896 Urakawa Seismological Observatory, and Sapporo Seismological Observatory. Bulletin†
0910-2027 Japanese Yearbook on Business History *changed to* 1349-807X **1131**
0910-2159 Kikai no Songai†
0910-2205 Kidorui **6320**
0910-2213 Kaku Igaku Shorei Kentokai Shoreishu **6202**
0910-223X Kanisetsukyo **6066**
0910-2388 Yamaguchi Yacho **917**
0910-2396 Yacho Dayori **917**
0910-2485 Nihon Sanka Fujinka Gakkai Kanagawa Chiho Bukai Kaishi **5999**

ISSN

0912-1692 Shokubutsu Shunju
0912-1722 Toshi Kaihatsu Chiiki Kaihatsu Kankyo Kogai Kankei Indekkusu **3491**
0912-1838 Shizuoka Genshiryoku Dayori **3174**
0912-1862 Seishinka Chiryogaku **6184**
0912-1870 Practica Otologica Kyoto. Supplement **6084**
0912-1897 Kushiro-shiritsu Hakubutsukan Kiyo **7878**
0912-1900 Hitachiobi **946**
0912-1935 J W E. Journal of Wind Engineering **3273**
0912-1986 J A M D A†
0912-2001 Newsweek Nihon Ban **3900**
0912-2087 Hikaku Bunmei **8105**
0912-2125 Ibaraki-ken Kyukyu Igakkai Zasshi **6061**
0912-2184 Tsuchi to Biseibutsu **897**
0912-2192 Kai Nakama **953**
0912-2214 J S P P Newsletter **795**
0912-2249 Current Concepts in Magnesium Metabolism
0912-2311 Abstracts of Science and Technology in Japan: Energy Technology†
0912-2346 Daito Bunka Daigaku Kiyo. Shizen Kagaku **7849**
0912-2354 Yamada Kagaku Shinko Zaidan Nyusu **7932**
0912-2370 Research Reports on Information Sciences. Series A, Mathematical Science **2550**
0912-2419 Meiji Shinkyu Igaku **313**
0912-2451 Yaso **823**
0912-2508 Journal of Hydroscience and Hydraulic Engineering **3363**
0912-2524 Fujitsu General **3309**
0912-2664 Taigai Junkan Gijutsu **5720**
0912-2761 Fujikura Giho **3309**
0912-2826 Yokohama City Institute of Health. Annual Report **7546**
0912-2966 Saitama-ken Sanfujinka Ikaiho **6004**
0912-3016 Shiga Ika Daigaku Zasshi **5713**
0912-3075 Dream International Quarterly
0912-3156 Gyogyo to Kisho
0912-3164 Fune to Kisho
0912-3318 Chikuho Hakubutsu
0912-3474 Japan Update†
0912-3490 Miyagi-ken Genshiryoku Senta Nenpo **3171**
0912-3512 Senkyo Kenkyu **7182**
0912-3628 Saibo Kogaku, Bessatsu **770**
0912-3636 Soshiki Baiyo Kenkyu **836**
0912-3741 J J N Supesharu **5963**
0912-3814 Ecological Research **670**
0912-3881 Nikkei Regional Economic Report **1154**
0912-3938 Kokyo **3277**
0912-4047 Reichorui Kenkyu **961**
0912-4063 Genshi Shototsu Sakyura **7066**
0912-4071 Okayama no Shizen **2623**
0912-4195 Kaku Igaku Gazo Shindan **6202**
0912-4322 Ritsumeikan Law Review (International Edition) **4940**
0912-4446 Butsurigakushi **7007**
0912-4462 Tokyo-to Shika Ishikai Zasshi **5868**
0912-4764 Shigen Shori Gijutsu *changed to* 1348-6012 **6467**
0912-4772 Japanese High-Technology Monitor†
0912-4829 Kaiyo Kagaku Kenkyu **2810**
0912-4837 Jakunensha Shinshikkan Taisaku Kyogikaishi
0912-490X Pairotto **67**
0912-5019 Shigyo Taimusu **6738**
0912-5027 Kosei Busshitsu Ryoho†
0912-5094 Eisei Tsushin Kenkyu/Satellite Communications Study *changed to* 1348-4869 **2329**
0912-5108 Oosaka Daigaku Sangyo Kagaku Kenkyujo Fuzoku Hoshasen Jikkenjo Nenpo **3173**
0912-5116 Hoshasen Jikkenjo Dayori **7066**
0912-5361 Nihongo Journal **5155**
0912-5434 Optoelectronics†
0912-5566 Oki Technical Review†
0912-5639 Fukui Daigaku Sekisetsu Kenkyushitsu Kenkyu Hokoku **6352**
0912-5760 Chidanken Senpo **2728**
0912-5779 Jishin Janaru
0912-5833 DataNet **2530**
0912-5930 Hirosakishi Ishikaiho **5628**
0912-5949 Aizu Seibutsu Dokokaishi **651**
0912-5957 Kumamoto Konchu Dokokaiho **853**
0912-6015 Gengo to Kyoiku no Kenkyu **3062**
0912-6112 Tokei Suri **5549**
0912-6139 Nanzan Keizai Kenkyu **1152**
0912-6147 Nanzan Keiei Kenkyu **1780**
0912-6155 Okera **856**
0912-6317 Japan Free Press
0912-6325 Oyo Chishitsu Nenpo **2761**
0912-6449 Kyodo to Kagaku **7878**
0912-6597 Ijigaku Kenkyu†
0912-6627 Nihon Chishitsu Gakkai Kansai Shibu Kaiho **2759**
0912-6651 Nihon no Ebine
0912-6686 I C Biotech. Annual Reports†
0912-6937 Oosaka Toseki Kenkyukai Kaishi **6273**
0912-6953 Honshi Giho **3269**
0912-7089 Hirata Shiritsu Byoin Nenpo/Hirata Municipal Hospital. Journal *changed to* 1881-1566 **4103**
0912-7097 Impotence/Inpotensu Kenkyukaishi *changed to* 1345-8361 **6273**
0912-7186 Suisan no Kenkyu†
0912-7208 Chiba Daigaku Hogaku Ronshu **1082**
0912-7216 Chiba Daigaku Keizai Kenkyu **1082**
0912-7283 Ongaku Onkyo Kenkyukai Shiryo **7089**
0912-7291 Doryokuro Kaku Nenryo Kaihatsu Jigyodan. Hokoku to Koen no Kai Yokoshu†
0912-7348 Kaiyo Kaihatsu Ronbunshu **3277**
0912-7402 Kokusai Kosho Kankyo Iinkai. Nyusureta **2796**
0912-7410 International Lake Environment Committee Foundation. Newsletter **4696**
0912-7437 Umi to Anzen **2819**
0912-7518 Shimizu Technical Research Bulletin **1035**
0912-7550 Okayamaken Baiotekunoroji Kenkyujo Kenkyu Nenpo **769**
0912-7712 Sumitomo Quarterly **3901**
0912-778X Hobetsu Choritsu Hakubutsukanpo **6525**
0912-7798 Hobetsu-choritsu Hakubutsukan Kenkyu Hokoku **6725**
0912-7968 Barubu Giho **5449**
0912-7984 Butsuri Tansa **2778**
0912-8085 Jinko Chino Gakkaishi **2452**
0912-8107 The Contemporary Middle East **7119**
0912-8123 Kaiyo Sangyo Kenkyu Shiryo **1139**
0912-8204 Chono Gengogaku Kenkyu *changed to* 1347-8451 **6082**
0912-8395 Dereke Kenkyu
0912-8549 Kaiyo Kaihatsu Nyusu†
0912-8638 Japan Philately†
0912-8670 Gakkai Shinpo
0912-8921 Kiso Roka Kenkyu **737**
0912-8948 Kiso Roka Gakkai Sakyura **4050**
0912-9111 Jissen Kyoiku **2873**
0912-9200 Ceramic Society of Japan. Journal (International Edition)†
0912-9243 Japanese Biblical Institute. Annual **7652**
0912-9405 Nihon Jomyaku Keicho Eiyo Kenkyukaishi *changed to* 1344-4980 **6661**
0912-9502 Mitsubishi Research Institute. Research Review
0912-9626 Kikai Gijutsu Kyokai Nyusu **3387**
0912-9731 Noson Keikaku Gakkaishi **4421**
0912-974X Kaoku Gaichu **240**
0912-9952 Ibaraki Kenritsu Byoin Igaku Zasshi **5632**
0913-0071 Suizo **5949**
0913-0101 Mitsubishi Densen Kogyo Jiho **3325**
0913-0187 Waseda Daigaku Kyoikugakubu Gakujutsu Kenkyu. Seibutsugaku, Chigaku Hen **711**
0913-0195 Waseda Daigaku Kyoikugakubu Gakujutsu Kenkyu. Sugaku Hen **5546**
0913-0217 Hokkaido Iho **5628**
0913-0241 Hiro to Kyuyo no Kagaku†
0913-025X Materials on Asia - Accession List and Review†
0913-0322 Seirigaku Kenkyujo Gijutsuka Hokoku†
0913-039X Engeki Kenkyu **8470**
0913-0683 Yakkyoku no Tomo (Tokyo, 1975)†
0913-0748 UNIX Magazine **2599**
0913-0756 Seinan Gakuin Daigaku Kokusai Bunka Ronshu **4474**
0913-106X Denki Gijutsusha **3091**
0913-1078 Mitsubishi Genshiryoku Nyusu†
0913-1140 Robotics & Electronics Japan†
0913-1175 Vitamin Information Center. Newsletter
0913-1302 Kuroshio **2811**
0913-1361 Reza Kyokai Uinta Semina **7084**
0913-137X Pariti. Bessatsu Shirizu **7029**
0913-1442 Riron to Hoho **8130**
0913-1507 Studies in Medieval English Language and Literature **5381**
0913-1558 Kurashiki-shiritsu Shizenshi Hakubutsukanpo **6527**
0913-1566 Kurashiki-shiritsu Shizenshi Hakubutsukan Kenkyu Hokoku **7878**
0913-1620 Sophia University. Institute of Comparative Culture. Business Series†
0913-1639 G A **443**
0913-1655 Setchaku Shigaku **5865**
0913-1736 Fukuoka Daigaku Yakugaku Kiyo **6843**
0913-1760 Hokkaido Genshiryoku Kankyo Dayori **3168**
0913-1841 Quarterly Forecast of Japanese Economy **1902**
0913-199X Electronics News from Fujitsu†
0913-2082 N T T Business
0913-2147 Miyagi-ken Yakuji Joho **6861**
0913-221X Tohoku - Hokuriku Sugaku Kyoiku Kisoteki Kenkyu Hokoku **5541**
0913-2244 Kujira **953**
0913-2368 Nihon Sanka Fujinka Gakkai Kyushu Rengo Chiho Bukai Zasshi **6000**
0913-2384 Kagaku Ryoho no Ryoiki **5947**
0913-2430 Koshunai Kiho **3695**
0913-2546 Fukuoka no Shokubutsu **790**
0913-2708 Gekkan I M **6969**
0913-2864 Fukushima Kenritsu Byoin Igaku Kenkyushi **5617**
0913-2899 Manipyureshon
0913-302X Rigaku Denki Janaru **2079**
0913-3216 Kokusai Energi Doko Bunseki **3141**
0913-3348 Nihon Oyo Koso Kyokaishi **740**
0913-3410 Nikkei Real Estate - Tokyo†
0913-3429 Nikkei Design **1781**
0913-3437 Nikkei Events†
0913-3526 Nihon Yuki Kogakkaishi **3212**
0913-3615 International Christian University. Language Research Bulletin **5128**
0913-3747 C I C S J Bulletin **2052**
0913-3763 Seibutsu Shiryo Bunseki **703**
0913-3801 Information Science and Technology Association. Journal **5017**
0913-3887 Erekutoronikusu no Rinsho **5610**
0913-3941 Okayama Shigakkai Zasshi **5858**
0913-3976 Nihon Jibi Inkoka Kansensho Kenkyukai Kaishi **6083**
0913-4026 Doboku Keikakugaku Kenkyu Koenshu **3265**
0913-4034 Doboku Keikakugaku Kenkyu Ronbunshu **3265**
0913-4050 Doboku Keikakugaku Shinpojumu **3265**
0913-4077 Ganban Rikigaku ni Kansuru Shinpojumu Ronbunshu **3267**
0913-4093 Kankyo Mondai Shinpojumu Koen Ronbunshu **3277**
0913-4182 Chikasui Gakkaishi **2793**
0913-4271 Asiatic Society of Japan. Transactions. 4th Series **544**
0913-4352 R & D News Kansai **3328**
0913-4417 Asahikawa Sekijuji Byoin Igaku Zasshi **5579**
0913-4581 Aomoriken Jichitai Igakkaishi **5576**
0913-4603 Asahigawaso Kenkyu Nenpo **5579**
0913-4689 Kokagaku **2138**
0913-4751 Osaka University. Research Institute for Microbial Diseases. Annual Reports†
0913-476X Tohkai Sekitsui Geka **6074**
0913-4778 Nihon Baioreoroji Gakkaishi *changed to* 1867-0466 **754**
0913-4859 Nihon Rikusui Gakkai Koshin'etsu Shibukai Kaiho **2797**
0913-4867 Maguneshumu **5897**
0913-4913 Concrete Library International (Print) *changed to* Concrete Library International (CD-ROM) **3263**
0913-4921 Doboku Gakkai Hokkaido Shibu Ronbun Hokokushu **3264**
0913-4964 Jiritsu Kunren Kenkyu **7367**
0913-5006 Drug Delivery System **6834**
0913-5014 O P E Nursing **5976**
0913-5022 Gakujutsu Joho Senta Kiyo/National Center for Science Information System. Research Bulletin *changed to* 1349-8614 **2435**
0913-5073 Kagoshima Kyukyu Igakkaishi†
0913-5146 Amagasaki Shiritsu Eisei Kenkyujoho **7507**
0913-5200 Kyoto Journal **554**
0913-5219 Birder **662**
0913-5227 Nihon Kasei Gakkaishi **4365**
0913-5308 Bellmedico
0913-5316 Companion Animal Practice **8795**
0913-5421 Kinokuni **853**
0913-543X Rigaku Journal **7038**
0913-5480 J A M R I Report†
0913-5510 Myu **7081**
0913-5537 Koshien Daigaku Kiyo. A, Eiyogakubu Hen **6662**
0913-5545 Koshien University. College of Business Administration and Information Science. Bulletin **1420**
0913-5561 Shu Seibutsugaku Kenkyu **817**
0913-557X Plant Species Biology **812**
0913-5685 Denshi Jouhou Tsuushin Gakkai Gijutsu Kenkyuu Houkoku **3299**
0913-5693 Denshi Jouhou Tsuushin Gakkaishi **3092**
0913-5707 Denshi Jouhou Tsuushin Gakkai Rombunshi. A **3186**
0913-5847 Tohoku Konchu **860**
0913-6002 Seto Marine Biological Laboratory. Annual Report **704**
0913-6037 Iryo Keiei Joho **4102**
0913-6134 Journal of Communication between Rural Communities and Towns **202**
0913-6150 Fain Kemikaru **3243**
0913-6339 Denki Gakkai Ronbunshi. D, Sangyo Oyo Bumonshi **3299**
0913-6355 Reza Gakkai Gakujutsu Koenkai Nenji Taikai Koen Yokoshu **7049**
0913-6452 Kinsei Kagaku†
0913-6584 Sogo Gakujutsu Kenkyu Shukai **7918**
0913-6746 Nihon Doketsugaku Kenkyujo Hokoku **6727**
0913-6800 Tsukuba Daigaku Sugadaira Kogen Jikken Senta Kenkyu Hokoku **2717**
0913-7025 Kankyo Eisei Kogaku Kenkyu **3449**
0913-7262 Hyogo Kenritsu Kodomo Byoin Nenpo **4102**
0913-7335 Donaciist **843**
0913-7343 Arumeida Iho **5578**
0913-7505 Rinsho to Yakubutsu Chiryo/Clinics & Drug Therapy *changed to* 1349-4252 **5659**
0913-7556 Bio Medical Engineering†
0913-7602 Aichi Ika Daigaku Karei Ikagaku Kenkyujo Kiyo **4039**
0913-7629 Hokuriku Geka Gakkai Zasshi **6245**
0913-7718 Tokyo Financial Letter
0913-7785 Jinrui Dotai Gakkai Kaiho **7019**
0913-7815 Earth **106**
0913-7823 Ie-no-Hikari **120**
0913-7912 Niigata Kogyo Tanki Daigaku Kenkyu Kiyo **8433**
0913-7955 Nippon Kin Gakkai Nyusu **805**
0913-8005 Toshokan Kyoryoku Tsushin **5050**
0913-8013 Kodo Bunsekigaku Kenkyu **7382**
0913-8102 Living in Japan **3900**
0913-8188 Oyo Saibo Seibutsugaku Kenkyu
0913-8242 Kajitsu Nihon **240**
0913-8277 Mizu Shigen Kankyo Kenkyu **8829**
0913-8293 J A T E Tsushin **2328**
0913-8307 Aomoriken Rinsho Sanfujinka Ikaishi **5986**
0913-8323 Choken Field **842**
0913-8420 Hosei Daigaku Keisan Senta Kenkyu Hokoku **2419**
0913-8471 Iryoshoku
0913-8609 Genshiryoku Seisaku. Joho Fairu Circular **3167**
0913-865X Sanfujinka Kanpo Kenkyu no Ayumi **6004**
0913-8668 Journal of Anesthesia **5772**
0913-8684 Chubu Byoin Igaku Zasshi/Okinawa Chubu Hospital. Bulletin *changed to* 1344-1256 **5689**
0913-8706 Nihon Shoni Ketsueki Gakkai Zasshi **5940**
0913-8773 Japan Review of International Affairs **7247**
0913-882X Nihon Yoton Gakkaishi **295**
0913-8897 Tokyo Toritsu Kagaku Gijutsu Daigaku Kenkyu Hokoku **8443**
0913-8919 Innervision **6198**
0913-8927 Hyogo Kenritsu Seijinbyo Senta Kiyo **6021**
0913-9036 Japan Society for Comparative Endocrinology. Proceedings **5895**
0913-9044 Nihon Hihaku Naibunpi Gakkai Nyusu **5898**
0913-9079 Kensetsu Giho
0913-9214 Chiba Daigaku Eizo Kakusoku Kenkyu Senta. Senta Nenpo **2779**
0913-932X Hikari Shin Jidai
0913-9443 Gekkan Iryo Joho **5618**
0913-946X Netsu Bussei **7056**
0913-9532 Kessei Hanno no Ayumi†
0913-9613 Keichitsu **853**
0913-9664 Yokohama-shiritsu Daigaku Kiyo. Shizen Kagaku Hen **7932**
0913-9834 Oncology & Chemotherapy†
0914-0026 Business Tokyo†
0914-0077 Tando **5900**
0914-0085 Yamanashi Seibutsu **711**
0914-0212 Nikkei Datapro: Workstations†
0914-0255 Japan Medical Review
0914-028X Naturalists **7888**
0914-0379 Nikkei Watcher on I B M†
0914-0654 Kasen Dento Koho **8828**
0914-0727 Shinko Denki Giho†
0914-0956 Nippon Sekijujisha. Ketsueki Jigyobu. Kenkyu Hokoku†
0914-1065 Coastal Development **3263**
0914-1103 Design Scene **486**
0914-112X Kenkyu Happyokai Koen Ronbunshu - Energi, Shigen Kenkyukai **3141**
0914-126X Tokyo Erekutoron Nyusu. Handotai Seizo Sochi Hen
0914-1340 Nissan Kagaku Shinko Zaidan Jigyo Hokokusho **7893**
0914-1367 Ayuruveda Tsushin **307**
0914-1405 Gan Yakuri **6042**
0914-1413 Hitachi Maikon Giho **3100**
0914-157X Telecommunication Advancement Corporation. Report
0914-1677 Shakespeare Worldwide† **8988**
0914-1707 Naito Kinen Kagaku Shinko Zaidan Kenkyu Hokokushu†

ISSN

0914-2045 Legis-Mate
0914-2223 Biotherapy **762**
0914-2401 Sapporo-shi Seishonen Kagakukan Kiyo **7907**
0914-2487 Nakatani Denshi Keisoku Gijutsu Shinko Zaidan Nenpo
0914-2541 Harmonia **6572**
0914-2703 Toryu Kako Gakkaishi **3397**
0914-2819 Heart Nursing **5960**
0914-2843 Konsoryu
0914-2908 Report of the Research Center of Ion Beam Technology, Hosei University. Supplement **3329**
0914-3068 Shiga Daigaku Kyoikugakubu Kosho Jisshu Shisetsu Ronbunshu **2798**
0914-3106 Tosoh Kenkyu Hokoku/Journal of Tosoh Research *changed to* 1346-3039 **3256**
0914-322X Sumitomo Corporation News **3901**
0914-3378 Jochi Daigaku Sugaku Kokyuroku **5499**
0914-3467 Gan Men'eki Eiyo†
0914-3491 Jibi Inkoka, Tokeibu Geka **6081**
0914-3505 Congenital Anomalies **5600**
0914-353X Electronics Update **3097**
0914-3777 Chudoku Kenkyu **3495**
0914-3823 Kinki Shokubutsu Dokokai Kaiho **799**
0914-3890 Dainippon Koboku K.K. Gijutsu Shiryo **1001**
0914-3904 Orientaru Konsarutantsu Gijutsuho **3280**
0914-4218 Suiriho **159**
0914-4250 Kochi Iryo Gakuin Dosokaishi **5658**
0914-4277 Gekkan Chiiki Igaku **5618**
0914-4285 Tokyo Jikeikai Ika Daigaku Tairyoku Igaku Kenkyushitsu Nenpo†
0914-4307 Nihon Chorui Hyoshiki Kyokaishi **911**
0914-4412 Sekitsui Sekizui Janaru **6072**
0914-4463 Kotsu to Iryo
0914-4501 Ibarakiken Ishikaiho **5632**
0914-4528 J A C I C Report **1017**
0914-4579 Kikanshi J E T O C **3500**
0914-4587 J E T O C Newsletter†
0914-4897 Abstracts of Scientific and Technological Publications **8446**
0914-4935 Sensors and Materials **7039**
0914-496X Kanreichi Gijutsu Kenkyu Kaihatsu Senta Hokoku **6776**
0914-4994 Bane **3374**
0914-5001 Q C Circle **1788**
0914-5036 Yamanashi Shokubutsu Kenkyu **823**
0914-5079 Kitasato Daigaku Daigakuin Yakugaku Kenkyuka Rinsho Yakugaku Tokuron Kiyo **6857**
0914-5087 Journal of Cardiology **5792**
0914-5117 Ikagaku Oyo Kenkyu Zaidan Kenkyu Hokoku **7524**
0914-5249 New Machine Tools **5457**
0914-5265 Jin to Kotsu Taisha **6270**
0914-5400 Nippon Seramikkusu Kyokai Gakujutsu Ronbunshi *changed to* 1882-0743 **2039**
0914-5427 Japan International Cooperation Agency. Annual Report **1599**
0914-5478 Fakutori Otomeshon **3378**
0914-5508 No Sotchu no Geka **6254**
0914-5559 H V E M Reports **3309**
0914-5605 Nikkei Chodendo†
0914-5753 Kaijo Hoancho. Suirobu Kansoku Hokoku. Eisei Sokuchi Hen **2785**
0914-580X Oita Daigaku Kyoikugakubu Kenkyu Kiyo/Oita University. Faculty of Education. Research Bulletin *changed to* 1345-0875 **7895**
0914-5818 Nihon Hosenkin Gakkaishi **894**
0914-594X Nihon Togai Gaku Ganmen Geka Gakkaishi **6253**
0914-5958 Miyaji Giho **6326**
0914-6024 Sekizui Geka **6072**
0914-6083 Hokkaido Seikei Geka Gaisho Kenkyukai Kaishi **6061**
0914-6091 Shikoku Shigakkai Zasshi **5865**
0914-6113 Baieru Bukkuretto Shirizu
0914-6121 Gekkan Toraiboroji **3378**
0914-6172 N I R A Seisaku Kenkyu†
0914-6180 Hinyoki Geka **6268**
0914-6229 Konoikegumi Gijutsu Kenkyu Hokoku **1020**
0914-6253 Yukuatsu Gijutsu **3365**
0914-627X Mito Kagaku Gijutsu **8432**
0914-6385 Shizen Kagaku Kenkyu (Tokushima) **7916**
0914-6407 Kanpo to Men'Eki Arerugi†
0914-6415 Japanese Symposium on Plasma Chemistry. News **2066**
0914-6458 Fujitsu Ten Technical Journal **3309**
0914-6466 Osaka City University Business Review **1157**
0914-6482 Nichibunken Newsletter **557**
0914-6504 Joho Tsushin Janaru **2328**
0914-6601 C D N L A O Newsletter (Print Edition)†
0914-6628 Zairyo to Purosesu **6337**
0914-6636 Niigata Seikei Geka Kenkyukai Kaishi **6068**
0914-6660 Hyogo Rikusui Seibutsu **677**
0914-6725 Denki Kanetsu Gijutsu Joho *changed to* 0919-9721 **3307**
0914-6741 Ohkura Denki Giho
0914-675X Kumamoto Journal of Mathematics **5508**
0914-6776 Nihon Jusei Chakusho Gakkai Zasshi **5999**
0914-6806 Kikan Ganka Shujutsu **6045**
0914-6822 Nihon Parapurejia Igakkai Zasshi *changed to* 1348-3242 **6068**
0914-6830 Hokkaidoritsu Suisan Shikenjo Kenkyu Hokoku **3596**
0914-6849 Hokusuishi Dayori **3597**
0914-6873 Aomori-ken Ishikaiho **5576**
0914-7020 Kenkyu Gijutsu Keikaku **1770**
0914-7047 The Bone **6056**
0914-708X Kokusai Genshiryoku Kikan Kiho. Nihongoban†
0914-7136 Nihon Toseki Ikai Zasshi **6273**
0914-7187 Annals of Nuclear Medicine **6192**
0914-7195 Anritsu Technical Review **3295**
0914-7225 Kuroshio. Tokubetsugo **2811**
0914-7268 Atarashii Yakugaku o Mezashite†
0914-7306 Nihon Kyoryo Giho†
0914-7314 Nippon Jozo Kyokaishi **608**
0914-7357 Mie Seibutsu **689**
0914-7470 Human Cell **871**
0914-7489 National Museum of Modern Art, Tokyo. Bulletin **508**
0914-7500 Aomori Shimin Byoin Ishi **5576**
0914-7535 N H K Giken R & D **2386**
0914-7578 Doyakushi
0914-7586 Nihon Genshiryoku Bunka Shinko Zaidan Geppo
0914-7594 Apparel Production News **2245**
0914-7683 Zensoku **6221**
0914-7691 Ronenkichiho†
0914-7721 Yuseisho Tsushin Sogo Kenkyujo Nyusu *changed to* N I C T News **2334**
0914-7829 Nikkei Art†
0914-7837 Nikkei Entertainment†
0914-7845 Nikkei Restaurants **4394**
0914-7861 Kasen Joho Kenkyujo Hokoku **8828**
0914-7896 Denchuken Review **3298**
0914-790X Facial Nerve Research **6197**
0914-8019 Himeji Sekijuji Byoinshi **4098**
0914-8035 Journal of American and Canadian Studies **4459**
0914-8051 Nihongo Magazine†
0914-8108 Noshuyo Byori
0914-8124 Monthly Book Orthopaedics **6067**
0914-8159 Kaihatsu Doboku Kenkyujo Geppo *changed to* 1346-6747 **3269**
0914-8167 Kaihatsu Doboku Kenkyujo Hokoku **3277**
0914-8175 Kaihatsu Doboku Kenkyujo Nenpo†
0914-8183 Kaihatsu Doboku Kenkyujo Koenkai Tokushu-go *changed to* 1346-6747 **3269**
0914-8248 Ayuruveda Kenkyu **307**
0914-8272 Kaijo Hoancho. Suirobu Kansoku Hokoku. Choryu Hen **2796**
0914-8337 Kaunseringu Kenkyu **7382**
0914-840X Tohoku Shokubutsu Kenkyu
0914-8426 Puraimari - Kea **5701**
0914-8574 Nishinomiya Shiritsu Chuo Byoin Kiyo **4108**
0914-8620 Himarayagakushi†
0914-8663 Danso Eizo Kenkyukai Zasshi **6195**
0914-8698 Sentan Kako Gijutsu **3395**
0914-8744 Kanagawa-kenritsu Shizen Hogo Senta Hokoku **2616**
0914-8760 Rinshou Ryuumachi **6227**
0914-8779 Journal of Bone and Mineral Metabolism **5895**
0914-8833 Aera **3899**
0914-8922 Japanese Journal of Interventional Cardiology **5791**
0914-8930 Keisanki Tokeigaku **8384**
0914-8973 Hyuman Saiensu/Journal of Human Sciences *changed to* 1880-0270 **350**
0914-8981 Baiosaiensu to Indasutori **757**
0914-899X Hitachi Cable Review (Print)†
0914-9090 J J A P Series **7019**
0914-918X Technology and Development **1606**
0914-9198 Journal of Toxicologic Pathology **3499**
0914-9201 Uchu Seibutsu Kagaku **708**
0914-9244 Journal of Photopolymer Science and Technology **2125**
0914-9260 Communications Research Laboratory. Journal *changed to* 1349-3205 **2386**
0914-9279 Tsushin Sogo Kenkyujo Kiho/Communications Research Laboratory. Review *changed to* 1349-3191 **2383**
0914-9287 Hoshako
0914-9317 Nikkei Datapro: E D P†
0914-9325 Nikkei Datapro: O A†
0914-9341 Nikkei Datapro: Minicomputers†
0914-9368 Nikkei Datapro: Personal Computers†
0914-9457 Nihon Jiki Kyomei Igakkai Zasshi **6204**
0914-9465 Archives of Histology and Cytology **827**
0914-9481 Yamaguchi Ganban Kenkyu **3227**
0914-9538 Gifuken Ishikai Igaku Zasshi **5619**
0914-9554 Yokohama Gaku Ganmen Koku Geka Gakkaishi†
0914-9589 Gijutsu Kenkyujo Dayori **3309**
0914-9775 Josai Daigaku Kenkyu Nenpo. Shizen Kagaku Hen **4459**
0914-9805 Reza Kurosu **7084**
0914-9864 Hattatsu Yakuri Yakubutsu Chiryo Kenkyukai Zasshi *changed to* 1342-6753 **6864**
0914-9902 Shin Busshitsu Kenkyu Kondankai Kenkyu Happyokai Yokoshu
0914-9953 Naibunpi Geka **5898**
0915-0021 National Astronomical Observatory. Reprint **578**
0915-003X Shokuseishi Kenkyu **817**
0915-0048 Kankyo Kagakkaishi **3449**
0915-0188 Jikoketsu Yuketsu **5791**
0915-0226 Cuadernos de Japon *see* 0388-0435 **4184**
0915-0323 Fukui Chuho **848**
0915-0374 Nihon Seitai Jiki Gakkaishi **754**
0915-0447 Japanese Symposium on Plasma Chemistry. Abstract Papers **2094**
0915-0471 Mie Daigaku Seibutsu Shigen Gakubu Kiyo **3697**
0915-051X Unisys News **2494**
0915-0528 N T N Technical Review **3211**
0915-0544 N K K Technical Review *changed to* 1348-0677 **6318**
0915-0552 Rigaku Ryoho Janaru **6116**
0915-0609 I S T E C Journal **3104**
0915-0625 Kazoku Shinrigaku Kenkyu **7382**
0915-065X Seishin Hoken Kenkyu **6184**
0915-0692 Sekai no Genshiryoku Hatsuden Kaihatsu no Doko **3174**
0915-0781 Nikkei Resort†
0915-079X Nikkei Gifts†
0915-0803 Gekkan Blood
0915-0862 University of Tokyo. Earthquake Research Institute. Special Bulletin **2791**
0915-0889 Nichibunken **557**
0915-0900 Nihon Kenkyu (Kyoto) **4186**
0915-0919 Kita Nihon Kaku Igaku Danwakai
0915-0935 Denki Tsushin Daigaku Kiyo **2318**
0915-0986 Nichibunken Japan Review **557**
0915-1060 Gekkan Bakodo/Monthly Bar Code *changed to* Gekkan Jidou Ninshiki **2460**
0915-1079 Sentan Gijutsu Koenkai **7084**
0915-1125 Kotsu Kansetsu Jintai **6224**
0915-1168 Toraiborojisuto **3397**
0915-1265 Setsunan University. Law Review **4782**
0915-1281 Gaiko Foramu **7236**
0915-129X Bessatsu Medikaru Hyumaniti†
0915-1354 Sagyo Ryoho Janaru **6686**
0915-1389 Suimon Mizu Shigen Gakkaishi **2798**
0915-1400 Roka to Shikkan†
0915-1427 Nikkei High Tech Report†
0915-1451 Kanagawa Seikei Saigai Geka Ikai Zasshi *changed to* 1348-043X **6066**
0915-1478 Fuji Film Research & Development **6969**
0915-1559 I S I J International **6315**
0915-1605 Toba Suizokukan Nenpo **3610**
0915-1621 Nihon Iyaku Bunken Shorokushu **6890**
0915-1656 Kokunai Iyakuhin Tenpu Bunsho Joho†
0915-1664 Hospital Dentistry & Oral-Maxillofacial Surgery **5846**
0915-1672 Pesutoroji Gakkaishi/Pest Control Research *changed to* 1880-3415
0915-1699 Proceedings of Japanese Symposium of Plasma Chemistry
0915-1702 Car Graphic **8572**
0915-1753 Rinsho Biseibutsu Jinsoku Shindan Kenkyukaishi **896**
0915-1869 Hyomen Gijutsu **2114**
0915-1915 Denshi Joho Tsushin Gakkai Ronbunshi. D-1/I E I C E Transactions on Information and Systems, Pt.1 (Japanese Edition) *changed to* 1880-4535 **2542**
0915-1923 Denshi Joho Tsushin Gakkai Ronbunshi. D-2 *changed to* 1880-4535 **2542**
0915-194X Hiroshima Kenritsu Seibu Kogyo Gijutsu Senta Kenkyu Hokoku **1887**
0915-1982 Ibarakiken Noson Igakkai Zasshi **5632**
0915-2059 Puranta **814**
0915-2067 Nihon Semi no Kai Kaiho **856**
0915-2083 Hokkaido Daigaku Iryo Gijutsu Tanki Daigakubu Kiyo†
0915-2210 Passenger & In-Flight Service†
0915-2253 Tohkai Seikei Geka Gaisho Kenkyu Kaishi **6074**
0915-2261 Nagoya Joshi Daigaku Kiyo. Jinbun, Shakai-hen **4465**
0915-227X Ryumachika **6227**
0915-2296 Linkage†
0915-2318 N T T Gijutsu Janaru **2370**
0915-2326 N T T R & D **2370**
0915-2350 Japanese Society of Computational Statistics. Journal **8382**
0915-2490 Nikkei Datapro: Microprocessors†
0915-2563 A T R Journal **2311**
0915-2652 Sanshi Konchu Nogyo Gijutsu Kenkyusho Hokoku†
0915-2679 Sanshi. Konchu Nogyo Gijutsu Kenkyusho Shiryo **858**
0915-2687 Ezai Kenkyujo Nenpo†
0915-2695 Chugoku Shikoku Seikei Geka Gakkai Zasshi **6057**
0915-2733 Biseibutsu Iden Shigen Haifu Mokuroku **882**
0915-2830 Biseibutsu Iden Shigen Tansaku Shushu Chosa Hokokusho **882**
0915-2938 Hokkaido Denryoku K.K. Sogo Kenkyujo Kenkyu Nenpo **3310**
0915-2997 Kaiyo Chosa Gijutsu **2810**
0915-3004 T M J Nihon Gaku Kansetsu Gakkai Zasshi **6073**
0915-3012 Ehime Kenritsu Iryo Gijutsu Tanki Daigaku Kiyo **5609**
0915-3020 Lamellicornia†
0915-308X Ibaraki Kaku Igaku **6198**
0915-3098 Nagoya Joshi Daigaku Kiyo. Kasei, Shizen-hen **4364**
0915-3160 New Breeze **2335**
0915-3217 Shokaki Naishikyo **5931**
0915-3306 Nogyo Kogaku Kenkyujo Hokoku *changed to* N I R E. Bulletin **213**
0915-3411 Hyogo Baiotekunoroji Konwakai Kaiho **765**
0915-3470 Nikkei Construction **3279**
0915-3535 Skin Cancer **6034**
0915-3616 J A S M A: Journal of the Japan Society of Microgravity Application **7018**
0915-3640 National Astronomical Observatory. Publications **578**
0915-3667 Anitekkusu **5902**
0915-3691 Clinical Information†
0915-3780 National Astronomical Observatory. Mizusawa Astrogeodynamics Observatory. Mizusawa Kansoku Center. Technical Report **578**
0915-3845 Sakai no Shokubutsu
0915-3896 Shinkei Soshiki no Seicho Saisei Ishoku†
0915-3942 Journal of Robotics and Mechatronics **2585**
0915-4027 Seikei Kakou **7099**
0915-4116 Super C G†
0915-4191 Nikkei Healthcare **4108**
0915-4213 Emergency Nursing/Emajenshi Nashingu *changed to* 1349-6557 **6059**
0915-423X Fukui Ika Daigaku Kenkyu Katsudo Ichiran†
0915-4302 Nihon Hakunaishu Gakkaishi **6046**
0915-4353 C E L S S Journal **663**
0915-4418 Genshiro Jikkenjo Dayori **7066**
0915-4523 Chikyuken Nyusu Reta
0915-4531 Baiotorendo **656**
0915-4566 Shibaura Institute of Technology. Research Laboratory of Engineering. Report **3219**
0915-4620 Jerontoroji **4048**
0915-4639 Gan Chiryo to Shukushu **6020**
0915-4698 Kandokon **853**
0915-4728 Okayama-ken Sogo Chikusan Senta Kenkyu Hohkoku **295**
0915-4841 Access Nippon (Year)†
0915-4914 Newsletter of Himalayan Botany **805**
0915-4965 Gifu Shishunki Kenkyu†
0915-4981 Japan-Netherlands Institute. Journal **7247**
0915-499X Kyushu University. Institute of Tropical Agriculture. Bulletin **132**
0915-5007 Kiseichu Bunrui Keitai Danwakai Kaiho **5821**
0915-5015 Kutsu no Igaku **5659**
0915-5031 Shinko Tekuno Giho
0915-5066 Ganka Shujutsu Konnichi no Kangaekata†
0915-5074 Kamishihoro-cho Higashi Taisetsu Hakubutsukan Kenkyu Hokoku **7874**
0915-5082 Institute of International Relations. Research Papers. Series A†
0915-5090 Institute of International Relations. Research Papers. Series B†
0915-5228 Tohoku Daigaku Iden Seitai Kenkyu Senta Nenpou†
0915-5244 Nihon Hoshako Gakkai Nenkai Yokoshu
0915-5287 Journal of Physical Therapy Science **6111**
0915-5317 Tsukuba Daigaku Butsurigakukei Nenji Kenkyu Hokoku **7044**
0915-5333 Doboku Joho Shisutemu Shinpojumu Koenshu **3265**

0915-5392	Annual Report of the Kiso Observatory **568**
0915-5422	Eiju Sogo Byoin Kiyo **5905**
0915-5457	Food and Agricultural Policy Research Center. Study Group on International Issues. Report **113**
0915-5511	Hokkaido Kaitaku Kinenkan Chosa Hokoku **6525**
0915-5635	Digestive Endoscopy **5922**
0915-5651	Journal of Advanced Science **7871**
0915-5732	Idemitsu Giho **1121**
0915-5759	Brain Medical **5588**
0915-5813	Byogen Biseibutsu Kenshutsu Joho Geppo **5811**
0915-5821	Hokkaido no Shizen Seibutsu†
0915-5961	Shichokaku Joho Kenkyukai Kaiho†
0915-5988	Nihon Koku Shuyo Gakkaishi **6029**
0915-6003	Atsugi Byoin Ishi†
0915-6054	Asanumagumi Gijutsu Kenkyujoho **3259**
0915-6062	Hokkaido no Nogyo Kisho **6354**
0915-6089	Katachi no Kagakkaiho **7874**
0915-6151	Reviews on Heteroatom Chemistry **2078**
0915-6305	Ronen Seishin Igaku Zasshi **4055**
0915-6321	Kokuritsu Tenmondaiho **577**
0915-633X	N I F S Series. Research Report **7069**
0915-6348	National Institute for Fusion Science. Research Report. P R O C Series **7027**
0915-6356	National Institute for Fusion Science. Research Report. Tech Series **7027**
0915-6364	National Institute for Fusion Science. Research Report. Data Series **7069**
0915-6372	National Institute for Fusion Science. Research Report. Memo Series **7069**
0915-6445	Nature and Culture†
0915-6550	Tameike no Shizen **255**
0915-6593	Diabetes Frontier **5887**
0915-6607	The Lipid **5662**
0915-6631	I N C C Newsletter†
0915-6690	Speaking Out **3467**
0915-6704	Kaku Yuugou Kagaku Kenkyusho Nyusu **7068**
0915-6739	Kyoto Rigaku Ryohoshikai Kaishi *changed to* 1346-1710 **6116**
0915-6755	Gazo Rabo **6969**
0915-6836	Nogyo Seibutsu Shigen Kenkyujo Kenkyu Shiryo **694**
0915-6852	Female Patient†
0915-6976	Rinsho Monita†
0915-6992	Asian Journal of Oral and Maxillofacial Surgery **5835**
0915-7093	Dainippon Doboku Gijutsu Kenkyujoho **3264**
0915-7107	Nihon Seikei Geka Choonpa Kenkyukai Kaishi **6067**
0915-7204	Tokai Sanka Fujinka Gakkai Zasshi **6005**
0915-731X	Hattatsu no Shinrigaku to Igaku
0915-7344	Hoshi Sogo Byoin Nenpo **4099**
0915-7352	Trends in Glycoscience and Glycotechnology **2132**
0915-7441	Nihon Kessen Shiketsu Gakkaishi **5940**
0915-7522	Nagoya University. Plasma Science Center†
0915-7557	Gifu-ken Bosei Eisei Gakkai Zasshi†
0915-759X	Eiyou Hyoka to Chiryo **6658**
0915-7786	Kansai Kansetsukyo Hiza Kenkyukaishi†
0915-7875	Shukan S T **5173**
0915-7883	Suruga no Konchu **860**
0915-8014	Chuo Suisan Kenkyujo Kenkyu Hokoku
0915-8162	Joetsu Kyoiku Daigaku Kenkyu Kiyo **7871**
0915-8170	Hokkaido University. Catalysis Research Center. Annual Report (Year) **2135**
0915-826X	Nikkei Office†
0915-8375	Sanfujinka Shujutsu **6004**
0915-8383	Toukai Kotsu Nanbu Shuyou **6035**
0915-8472	Eiyo Kanri no Kenkyu†
0915-8502	Frontiers Science Series **7856**
0915-8529	Ketsueki Shuyoka **5939**
0915-860X	Nihon Ion Kokan Gakkaishi **2075**
0915-8634	Bobasu Janaru **8028**
0915-8693	Edogawa Igakkaishi†
0915-874X	Cardiac Practice **5779**
0915-8847	Kassei Sanso Furi Rajikaru†
0915-8863	Kokuritsu Tenmondai Nyusu **577**
0915-8944	Bungaku Kenkyu Ronshu **5267**
0915-9029	Hattatsu Shinrigaku Kenkyu **7360**
0915-9061	Edogawa†
0915-907X	Cell Science†
0915-9088	Sekai CD-ROM Soran **635**
0915-9096	Symposium on Ion Sources and Ion-Assisted Technology. Proceedings
0915-9118	Jin Ishoku Kekkan Geka **6247**
0915-9126	Natural History Museum and Institute, Chiba. Bulletin. Humanities **4186**
0915-9231	Tetsudo to Denki Gijutsu
0915-924X	Nihon Kyukyu Igakkai Zasshi **5948**
0915-9274	Biomedical Fuzzy Systems Bulletin
0915-9444	Natural History Research **7888**
0915-9452	Natural History Museum and Institute, Chiba. Journal **7888**
0915-955X	Environmental Sciences **3429**
0915-9606	Japanese Journal of Forensic Toxicology *changed to* 1860-8965 **5913**
0915-9622	Yotonkai **305**
0915-9681	Comparative Primatology Monographs†
0915-9754	Kishidaia **853**
0915-9789	Nara Sangyo Daigaku Sangyo to Keizai **1152**
0915-9851	R N O D C Activity Report **2816**
0915-9975	Hiragana Times **3900**
0916-0043	Purinto Kairo Gakkai Gakujutsu Koen Taikai Koen Ronbunshu
0916-0094	Konnichi no Ishoku **6251**
0916-0191	Rim **1168**
0916-0302	Asahi Pasokon **2574**
0916-0337	Equilibrium Research. Supplement **922**
0916-0345	N I News **3109**
0916-0396	Waseda Daigaku Ningen Kagaku Kenkyu/Waseda Studies in Human Sciences *changed to* 1880-0270 **350**
0916-0426	Tekko Gijutsu
0916-0450	Aomori-ken Noson Igakkai Zasshi **5576**
0916-0574	Nihongo **5155**
0916-0604	Photon Factory News **7070**
0916-068X	Aichi Cancer Center Research Institute. Scientific Report **6007**

0916-0701	Meikai Daigaku Shigaku Zasshi **5855**
0916-0752	Minami Taiheiyo Kenkyu **7882**
0916-0892	Kyushu Daigaku Chuo Bunseki Senta Hokoku **4488**
0916-0981	Ran/Kansai Society of Naval Architects, Japan. Bulletin *changed to* 1880-3725 **8649**
0916-1058	Japan Hymenopterists Association. Special Publications **851**
0916-1104	Nihon Daekisen Gakkaishi **926**
0916-1112	Futao **848**
0916-1139	Yakubutsu Dotai *changed to* 1347-4367 **5607**
0916-1147	Densho to Igaku†
0916-1163	Oosaka Shiritsu Shinshin Shogaisha Rihabiriteshon Senta Kenkyu Kiyo
0916-1198	Nihon Kagaku Gijutsu Kankei Chikuji Kankobutsu Soran (Print)†
0916-1287	Saikaku†
0916-1295	Symposium on Atmosphere **6396**
0916-1465	Toshiba's Selected Papers on Science & Technology **3115**
0916-1503	Shakai Shinrigaku Kenkyu **7408**
0916-152X	Tokyo Daigaku Genshiryoku Kenkyu Sogo Senta Nyusu **3175**
0916-1546	Nagare no Keisoku **6404**
0916-1562	Suisan Kaiyo Kenkyu **3609**
0916-1589	Yoyuen Oyobi Koon Kagaku **2119**
0916-1600	Shisutemu Seigyo Joho **2464**
0916-1643	Nihon Seikei Geka Supotsu Igakkaishi **6067**
0916-166X	Kikogaku Kishogaku Kenkyu Hokoku **6359**
0916-1740	Shigen Sozai **6479**
0916-1775	T A C News
0916-1783	Haseko Giho **3268**
0916-1813	*see* 0916-0191 **1168**
0916-1856	Prism: The Magazine of Japanese Industry and Lifestyles†
0916-1899	Kanagawa Koka Daigaku Kenkyu Hokoku. A, Jinbun Shakai Kagaku-hen **4461**
0916-1902	Kanagawa Koka Daigaku Kenkyu Hokoku. B Rikogaku Hen **8430**
0916-1929	Gekkan Asahi **3900**
0916-1937	Fuji Economic Review†
0916-2011	Gekkan Kaiyo **2804**
0916-2038	Hirosaki Daigaku Rigakubu Kanchi Kisho Jikkenshitsu Hokoku **6353**
0916-2062	Aichi Gakuin Dental Science **5833**
0916-2135	Handai Nihongo Kenkyu **5124**
0916-2259	Kyushu Daigaku Rigakubu Shimabara Jishin Kazan Kansokujo Kenkyu Hokoku **2786**
0916-2275	Denji Kankyo Kogaku Joho E M C **3298**
0916-2313	Ohu Daigaku Shigakushi **5858**
0916-2410	Choonpa Techno **7087**
0916-2623	Japan Petroleum and Energy Trends **6775**
0916-2682	Chiryo Kyoiku Kenkyu Kiyo†
0916-2690	Kokusaigaku Rebyu **7250**
0916-2747	Kagaku Ryoho Kenkyujo Kiyo **5997**
0916-2771	Tele Media†
0916-2844	Osaka Medical College. Bulletin **5691**
0916-2860	Tohoku Daigaku Ryutai Kagaku Kenkyujo Hokoku **7043**
0916-2879	Tohoku University. Institute of Fluid Science. Reports **7043**
0916-295X	N S K News Bulletin **4580**
0916-3085	Tokyo Kokusai Kenkyu Kurabu Ronbunshu **7268**
0916-3158	Ryugin Keizai Report **1516**
0916-3182	Semento, Konkurito Ronbunshu **1035**
0916-3255	Shinshu Daigaku Rigakubu Fuzoku Suwa Rinko Jikkenjo Hokoku **2798**
0916-328X	Kazoku Shakaigaku Kenkyu **7981**
0916-3328	Tokyo Daigaku Aisotopu Sogo Senta Nyusu **3175**
0916-3387	Iwaki Kyoritsu Byoin Iho **4103**
0916-3409	Enerugi Riyo to Chokusetsu Hatsuden Shinpojumu **3307**
0916-3441	Shokubutsu Saibo Kogaku†
0916-3492	J A S C O Report **7077**
0916-3522	Kokunai Kaiyo Chosa Hokoku Ichiran **2810**
0916-3611	Gakujutsu Koenkai Ronbunshu **4007**
0916-3662	Hakoniwa Ryohogaku Kenkyu **6143**
0916-3743	Aisotopu Senta Nyusu **3164**
0916-3751	C Y R I C News **3166**
0916-3786	Hikaku Seiri Seikagaku **922**
0916-3808	Nihon Rodo Kenkyu Zasshi **1700**
0916-3816	J I L Risachi†
0916-3999	Kami Ryutsu Tokei Geppo†
0916-4014	Kikai Tokei Geppo **5462**
0916-4065	Shinri Rinsho†
0916-4146	Osaka Prefectural Radiation Research Institute. Technical Report†
0916-4316	Purazuma Kagaku Senta Nyusu†
0916-4367	Kiso Kagaku Kenkyujo Koenkai Koenshu **2070**
0916-4405	Shinrin Sogo Kenkyujo Kenkyu Hokoku **3702**
0916-443X	Shokubutsu Kenkyu Shuroku
0916-4553	Japan Fine Ceramics Center Review **2043**
0916-460X	Clinical Engineering **5596**
0916-4650	Hokkaido University. Economic Journal **1118**
0916-4731	Kashika Joho Gakkaishi *changed to* 1346-5252 **7874**
0916-474X	Kiko Eikyo Riyo Kenkyukai Kaiho **6359**
0916-4804	Nippon Ishinkin Gakkai Zasshi **894**
0916-4812	Nihon Setchaku Gakkaishi **7095**
0916-4820	Tokyoko Haro Kansoku Nenpo **2819**
0916-4936	Nihon Maikuro Sajari Gakkai Kaishi **6253**
0916-4944	Meiji Daigaku Riko Gakubu Kenkyu Hokoku **7882**
0916-5002	Shizuokaken Kisho Geppo **6395**
0916-5010	Tochigiken Kisho Geppo **6396**
0916-5037	Hyogoken Kisho Geppo **6356**
0916-5045	Okayamaken Kisho Geppo **6392**
0916-5053	Aichiken Kisho Geppo **6346**
0916-5061	Ehimeken Kisho Geppo **6352**
0916-507X	Gifuken Kisho Geppo **6353**
0916-5088	Gunmaken Kisho Geppo **6353**
0916-5096	Hokkaido Kisho Geppo **6354**
0916-5126	Kagawaken Kisho Geppo **6359**
0916-5169	Kyotofu Kisho Geppo **6360**
0916-5185	Naganoken Kisho Geppo **6391**
0916-5231	Tokushima-ken Kisho Geppo **6396**

0916-524X	Tokyoto Kisho Geppo **6396**
0916-5258	Tottoriken Kisho Geppo **6397**
0916-5266	Toyamaken Kisho Geppo **6397**
0916-5274	Yamaguchiken Kisho Geppo **6400**
0916-5282	Yamanashiken Kisho Geppo **6400**
0916-5290	Miyazakiken Kisho Geppo **6391**
0916-5304	Ibarakiken Kisho Geppo **6356**
0916-5312	Nagasakiken Kisho Geppo **6392**
0916-5320	Oitaken Kisho Geppo **6392**
0916-5339	Okinawaken Kisho Geppo **6393**
0916-5355	Iwateken Kisho Geppo **6358**
0916-5371	Fukushimaken Kisho Geppo **6353**
0916-538X	Shimaneken Kisho Geppo **6395**
0916-5398	Miyagiken Kisho Geppo **6391**
0916-5614	Tottoriken Kisho Nenpo **6397**
0916-5630	Toyamaken Kisho Nenpo **6397**
0916-572X	Connective Tissue **5600**
0916-5746	S U T Journal of Mathematics **5532**
0916-5754	Tsushin Sogo Kenkyujo Nenpo†
0916-5800	Kokuritsu Kenko, Eiyo Kenkyujo Kenkyu Hokoku **6662**
0916-5835	Kaiyo Onkyo Gakkaishi
0916-5908	Jui Masui Gekagaku Zasshi **8802**
0916-6009	Toyama University. Mathematics Journal *changed to* 1880-6015 **5542**
0916-6033	Chubu Ryumachi **6223**
0916-6076	Yosha **6721**
0916-6165	Shinrin Sogo Kenkyujo Hokkaido Shisho Nenpo **3702**
0916-619X	Riken Nyusu **7050**
0916-6211	Kawasaki Steel Bulletin†
0916-6343	Mizusawa Astrogeodynamics Observatory. Annual Report **578**
0916-6386	The Lancet (Nihongo-ban)†
0916-6394	Saitama Daigaku Kiyo. Kogakubu **7906**
0916-6408	Thanks
0916-6424	Zekuseru Tekku Rebyu **3399**
0916-6440	Nihon Sutoma Rihabiriteshon Gakkaishi *changed to* 1882-0115 **5929**
0916-6491	Technical Report of Kirin **611**
0916-653X	Kensetsu Tokei Geppo **1047**
0916-6564	Bosai Kagaku Gijutsu Kenkyujo Kenkyu Hokoku **2702**
0916-6688	Nippon Geijutsu Ryoho Gakkaishi **509**
0916-6718	Showa Densen Rebyu **3331**
0916-6750	Nihon Yuki Kogakkai Taikai Ronbun Hokokushu **3212**
0916-6858	National Research Institute of Vegetables, Ornamental Plants and Tea. Bulletin. Series B†
0916-6890	Junkatsu Keizai **3387**
0916-6920	Cytometry Research **831**
0916-6971	Shin Netsu Sokutei no Shinpo
0916-698X	Advances in Neurotrauma Research†
0916-7005	Japan Journal of Industrial and Applied Mathematics **5499**
0916-7013	Gekkan Sogo Kea **5618**
0916-7048	Nihon Gaku Henkeisho Gakkai Zasshi **5857**
0916-7099	Tsunami Kogaku Kenkyu Hokoku **3286**
0916-7145	Itami to Kanpo
0916-7153	Sony Technical Reports **3114**
0916-717X	Biomedical Research on Trace Elements **727**
0916-7226	Sendai-shi Eisei Kenkyujoho **7541**
0916-7250	Journal of Veterinary Medical Science **8801**
0916-7269	Pawa Erekutoronikusu Kenkyukai Ronbunshi **3110**
0916-7277	Reza Kyokaishi **7084**
0916-7293	Dobokushi Kenkyu **3265**
0916-7315	Kyushu Daigaku. Rigakubu Kenkyu Hokoku, Chikyu-Wakusei-Kagaku *changed to* 1348-0545 **2752**
0916-7374	Suikogaku Ronbunshu **3364**
0916-7390	Kyushu University. Faculty of Sciences. Memoirs. Series D: Earth and Planetary Sciences **2752**
0916-7439	Nihon Ryokka Kogakkaishi **140**
0916-7471	Tohoku Daigaku. Hanno Kagaku Kenkyusho Hokoku
0916-7501	Toyota Gijutsu **8608**
0916-7544	I T U Jyanaru **2325**
0916-7587	Hyogoken Yakuzaishikaishi **6846**
0916-7617	Suisan Kogaku **3609**
0916-765X	Nihon Shakai Jigyo Daigaku Kenkyu Kiyo **8059**
0916-7668	Sagami Joshi Daigaku Kiyo. A, Jinbun, Shakai-kei **4474**
0916-7676	Sagami Joshi Daigaku Kiyo. B, Shizen-kei **7906**
0916-782X	Japan Society for Precision Engineering. International Journal†
0916-7838	Asian - Pacific Book Development **7552**
0916-7846	W W F **2631**
0916-7897	Kaigan Kogaku Ronbunshu **3277**
0916-7900	Nihon Sekigaisen Gakkaishi **7056**
0916-7927	Nihon Ashi no Geka Gakkai Zasshi **6253**
0916-7943	Nikkei Datapro Communications Newsletter†
0916-7951	Tokyo Metropolitan News **7504**
0916-796X	Komatsu Technical Report **3387**
0916-7978	New Technology Japan†
0916-8001	Tokushima Kenritsu Hakubutsukan Kenkyu Hokoku **6538**
0916-801X	Explosion **3243**
0916-8192	Senryaku Konpyuta†
0916-8265	Shinrin Yasei Dobutsu Kenkyukaishi
0916-8273	Shikaku no Kagaku **6051**
0916-8362	Umi no Kenkyu **2819**
0916-8370	Journal of Oceanography **2809**
0916-8419	Dobutsu Shinrigaku Kenkyu **940**
0916-8451	Bioscience, Biotechnology, and Biochemistry **758**
0916-8486	Toyama Daigaku Suiso Doitai Kino Kenkyu Senta Kenkyu Hokoku **2141**
0916-8508	I E I C E Transactions on Fundamentals of Electronics, Communications and Computer Sciences **3103**
0916-8516	I E I C E Transactions on Communications **2324**
0916-8524	I E I C E Transactions on Electronics **3103**
0916-8532	I E I C E Transactions on Information and Systems **2544**
0916-8621	Tokyo Nogyo Daigaku Aisotopu Senta Kenkyu Hokoku **7072**
0916-8656	Hokkaido Institute of Environmental Sciences. Report **3486**
0916-8672	Senpaku Kaihatsu Giho **8660**
0916-8699	Techno Marine/Nihon Zosen Gakkaishi *changed to* 1880-3725 **8649**

ISSN

Link to your serials resources and content with ulrichsweb.com

9394 0924-9834 ULRICH'S PERIODICALS

0924-9834 Personeel en Organisatie - Vakmatig *changed to* 1566-0613 **1856**
0924-9877 Biotechnology and Development Monitor†
0924-9907 Journal of Mathematical Imaging and Vision **5553**
0925-0018 Helen Dowling Institute for Biopsychosocial Medicine. Publication†
0925-0042 Solid Mechanics and Its Applications **7063**
0925-0069 Politiestudies
0925-0085 C A D D E T Analysis Series† **8938**
0925-0123 Language Acquisition and Language Disorders **5139**
0925-0166 Fichte - Studien **6919**
0925-0239 Boekmancahier *changed to* 1571-5949 **479**
0925-0530 Sancties **2668**
0925-062X VakWerk *changed to* 1574-3438 **4360**
0925-0689 Inzage **7564**
0925-0700 Flyer†
0925-0824 Maatgevend *changed to* 1571-1331 **4070**
0925-0832 International V A T Monitor **1930**
0925-0913 Business Magazine†
0925-0972 Helsinki Monitor *changed to* 1874-7337 **7215**
0925-0980 Politie Magazine
0925-1006 Zoogdier **969**
0925-1022 Designs, Codes and Cryptography **5482**
0925-1030 Analog Integrated Circuits and Signal Processing **2465**
0925-1413 Scan†
0925-1421 Studies in Ancient Medicine **5718**
0925-160X Horen **4074**
0925-1650 Bodem **3406**
0925-1669 Economic and Social History in the Netherlands†
0925-1820 Indikator *changed to* 1872-1869 **7875**
0925-1944 Nederlandse Cystic Fibrosis Stichting. C F Nieuws **6216**
0925-1987 Elsevier's Almanak voor Schenken en Erven **4901**
0925-2177 Circumpolar Journal *changed to* 1574-0374 **4002**
0925-2312 Neurocomputing **2455**
0925-2428 Primeur **205**
0925-2657 Schriftenreihe zur Philosophie Karl L Poppers und des Kritischen Rationalismus **6951**
0925-2665 Oorlogsdocumentatie '40-'45 *changed to* 1569-3724 **6439**
0925-2711 Nieuwsbrief Politie **2662**
0925-2738 Journal of Biomolecular N M R **735**
0925-2762 Agriloper†
0925-2789 Netherlands. Centraal Bureau voor de Statistiek. Volwasseneneducatie: Beroepsbegeleidend Onderwijs en Vormingswerk, Cursorische Ondernemersonderwijs†
0925-2819 Tijdschrift voor Geneeskunde en Ethiek *changed to* 1572-0179 **5722**
0925-2878 Symbolon **567**
0925-2916 Brill's Indological Library **545**
0925-3084 C N W S Publications **331**
0925-3122 Italie **5074**
0925-3467 Optical Materials **7082**
0925-3572 Oald Hengel *changed to* 1876-4606 **4226**
0925-3793 Drents Ondernemers Kontakt *changed to* 1871-2568 **1782**
0925-3874 Print Buyer **7326**
0925-4005 Sensors and Actuators B: Chemical **2114**
0925-4110 Forfaitair **1926**
0925-4129 Money† **8975**
0925-4153 International Series in the Psychology of Religion **7651**
0925-4161 Early Studies in Germanic Philology†
0925-4269 Kiosk *changed to* 1874-8015 **2943**
0925-4374 Medische Antropologie **5676**
0925-4390 Demo **7128**
0925-4439 B B A - Molecular Basis of Disease **863**
0925-4455 Agro Informatica **215**
0925-4471 Focus on Parkinson's Disease (German Edition) *see* 0924-2015 **6141**
0925-4544 Beloning en Belasting **1912**
0925-4552 Fiscaal Up to Date **1110**
0925-4560 Journal for General Philosophy of Science **7871**
0925-4609 Comma *changed to* 1872-0056 **8969**
0925-4617 De Grote Lijsters **5302**
0925-4668 Dynamics and Control *changed to* 1079-2724 **3369**
0925-4676 Journal of Systems Integration†
0925-4692 Inflammopharmacology **6848**
0925-4757 Reinardus **5359**
0925-4773 Mechanisms of Development **834**
0925-482X Vrouwenbelangen **8888**
0925-4927 Psychiatry Research: Neuroimaging **6178**
0925-496X Pensioen Advies **1644**
0925-4994 Crime, Law and Social Change **2648**
0925-5001 Journal of Global Optimization **7940**
0925-5125 Molecular Engineering†
0925-5133 Jaarboek voor de Belastingdienst en de Belastingadviespraktijk†
0925-5214 Postharvest Biology and Technology **769**
0925-5222 Nieuwsbrief Telematica *changed to* 1876-4584 **2341**
0925-5273 International Journal of Production Economics **3369**
0925-5338 Nederlands Tijdschrift voor Fotonica *changed to* 1871-7802 **6968**
0925-5397 Elektro Magazine - Detailhandel†
0925-5400 Elektro Magazine - Installatie†
0925-5443 Ars Aequi Katern **4621**
0925-5478 Change **3410**
0925-5532 Nieuwsbrief Milieurecht†
0925-5621 Nederlandse Organisatie voor Toegepast Natuurwetenschappelijk Onderzoek. Jaarverslag **7891**
0925-5710 International Journal of Hematology **5938**
0925-5745 P C - Active **2578**
0925-5796 Developments in Earth and Planetary Sciences†
0925-5818 North-Holland Personal Library **7029**
0925-5850 Random Materials and Processes **7036**
0925-5893 Kan Anders **7249**
0925-5923 Baksteen **978**
0925-5958 Excerpta Medica. Section 40: Drug Dependence, Alcohol Abuse and Alcoholism **2701**
0925-5982 Cardiovascular Cases†
0925-6040 Nederlands Tijdschrift voor E H B O en Reddingwezen **7533**
0925-6237 Trivizier **6449**
0925-6261 Nederlands Omroep Handboek **2386**
0925-630X R C C Koude & Luchtbehandeling **4125**
0925-6466 Bouwmanagement en Technisch Beheer **983**
0925-6482 International Law in Asian Perspective **4931**
0925-6512 Brill's Japanese Studies Library **545**
0925-6660 Nonlinear Topics in the Mathematical Sciences **5521**
0925-6679 Euro Courses. Chemical and Environmental Science **3430**
0925-6733 Issues in Business Ethics **6927**
0925-6741 Aspecten van de Verzameling Beeldhouwkunst en Kunstnijverheid†
0925-6806 Studia Copernicana - Brill Series **582**
0925-6814 Juridische Berichten voor het Notariaat **4705**
0925-6822 Fiscale Berichten voor het Notariaat **4674**
0925-6881 Tijdschrift Gezondheidsbevordering†
0925-6911 Database Magazine **2530**
0925-711X Infectieziekten Bulletin **5816**
0925-7128 Civiele Techniek **3262**
0925-7195 C P S-Krant *changed to* C P S Nieuwsbrief **2833**
0925-725X Muziek en Wetenschap†
0925-7322 Openbaar Bestuur **7458**
0925-7535 Safety Science **6686**
0925-7586 Zeven Provincien Reeks **4280**
0925-7594 Pompe Reeks **4896**
0925-7640 Developments in Biotherapy **763**
0925-7683 Medieval and Renaissance Authors and Texts **4243**
0925-7721 Computational Geometry **5551**
0925-7748 Cargovision **8539**
0925-7802 Flying Dutchman **8783**
0925-7845 Jaarboek Monumentenzorg **446**
0925-7950 I A M C R Newsletter
0925-7977 C A Techniek *changed to* 1572-4980 **2462**
0925-8175 Mixture†
0925-8191 Lier en Boog **503**
0925-8264 Informatie Management†
0925-8310 Netherlands. Centraal Bureau voor de Statistiek. Niet-Nederlanders in Nederland op 1 Januari (Year)
0925-837X Agrarisch Onderwijs *changed to* 1568-8704 **168**
0925-8388 Journal of Alloys and Compounds **6319**
0925-8396 I R V Series in Rehabilitation Research†
0925-8426 Hollandische Mission - I G V C
0925-8434 Lasers in Medicine†
0925-8507 Caribbean Abstracts†
0925-8531 Journal of Logic, Language and Information **5134**
0925-854X Natural Language Semantics **5154**
0925-8558 Journal of East Asian Linguistics **5133**
0925-8574 Ecological Engineering **3417**
0925-8582 Studies in Mathematical Physics **7041**
0925-8604 Nederlands Tijdschrift voor Dermatologie en Venereologie **5880**
0925-8612 C E R M E I L†
0925-8620 Foro Hispanico **5297**
0925-8639 Rodopi Philosophical Studies **6950**
0925-8760 F M - International *changed to* 1568-8925 **8955**
0925-8787 C N V - Opinie†
0925-9244 Computers in Psychology†
0925-9384 Velon *changed to* 1876-4622 **3005**
0925-9392 Studies in East European Thought **7187**
0925-9406 Geluid **3433**
0925-9449 Filosofie **6920**
0925-9635 Diamond and Related Materials **2110**
0925-9643 Vennootschap & Onderneming **4882**
0925-9708 Groenten & Fruit. Algemeen **3735**
0925-9724 Computer Supported Cooperative Work **2412**
0925-9759 European Tax Handbook (Year) **1922**
0925-9848 Advances in M R I - Contrast†
0925-9856 Formal Methods in System Design **2520**
0925-9864 Genetic Resources and Crop Evolution **869**
0925-9872 Information Technology and the Law†
0925-9880 Review of Central and East European Law **4769**
0925-9899 Journal of Algebraic Combinatorics **5500**
0925-9902 Journal of Intelligent Information Systems **2453**
0925-9929 Cahier V G I†
0926-0005 Project Analyse†
0926-0048 Loonbelasting en Sociale Verzekering *changed to* 1874-9682
0926-0315 P & I Magazine
0926-0455 VTM *changed to* 1381-9763 **1052**
0926-0498 Ambacht & Industrie†
0926-0684 Odeon **6600**
0926-0692 N N O Magazine **6598**
0926-0838 Kinderopvang **2159**
0926-129X Philips Telecommunication Review†
0926-1753 Financieel Management Select *changed to* 1567-553X **1342**
0926-2040 Solid State Nuclear Magnetic Resonance **2105**
0926-2067 The Immunoassay Kit Directory. Series A: Clinical Chemistry **5759**
0926-2113 Seceur†
0926-213X Food Management Milieu *see* 0168-325X **8957**
0926-2172 Factor D **1109**
0926-2245 Differential Geometry and Its Applications **5482**
0926-2261 Brill's Series in Jewish Studies **7719**
0926-227X Journal of Computer Security **2515**
0926-2326 Studies in Interreligious Dialogue **7685**
0926-2342 De Jonge Lijsters **5314**
0926-2350 Blackbirds **5264**
0926-2490 A V S Nieuwsbrief *changed to* 1872-664X **8286**
0926-2520 Nestor **4052**
0926-2571 D D A Magazine *changed to* 1871-6717 **52**
0926-2601 Potential Analysis **5525**
0926-261X Bioethics Yearbook†
0926-2644 Group Decision and Negotiation **1748**
0926-2695 Spoor en Trein *changed to* 1871-7004 **8625**
0926-2830 Plafond en Wand Info *changed to* 1872-4957 **1029**
0926-2970 Nexus **5341**
0926-2989 Wotanin Wowapi†
0926-3004 Controllers Journaal **1286**
0926-3195 Atlantis (Amsterdam)†
0926-3209 C I C I A M S Nouvelles (Multilingual Edition)†
0926-3241 V I P **2538**
0926-3292 Pantaleon Reeks **5693**
0926-3314 Rendement **1789**
0926-3357 Bijen *changed to* Bijenhouden **96**
0926-3373 Applied Catalysis B: Environmental **3236**
0926-3411 N F M - Themareeks
0926-3497 Zeepaard **7933**
0926-3527 Litteratura Serpentium (English Edition) *changed to* 1571-9006 **954**
0926-3543 Amoeba **652**
0926-3551 Societas Internationalis Odonatologica. Rapid Communications **705**
0926-3586 Litteratura Serpentium (Nederlandse Edition) *changed to* 1571-9006 **954**
0926-3691 Barbie **2178**
0926-3810 Pasarkrant **4187**
0926-3837 Geografie **4009**
0926-3853 K N A G Nieuws†
0926-3977 Sociale Interventie **8134**
0926-3985 Boekie Boekie **2180**
0926-4078 Fact *changed to* 1568-5802 **1744**
0926-4183 Selectief†
0926-4205 Voorkomen†
0926-4213 Schip en Werf de Zee **8660**
0926-4264 Nederlands Tijdschrift voor Natuurkunde **7891**
0926-4345 Analytical Spectroscopy Library **2098**
0926-440X Voorraadbeheer en Woningmarktonderzoek **4431**
0926-4639 McGill University Monographs in Classical Archaeology and History **405**
0926-4744 Interieur & Etalage **2256**
0926-485X Stichting Praktijkonderzoek Pluimveehouderij. Jaarverslag **301**
0926-4981 E R C I M News **2350**
0926-5007 N V K Publikatiereeks **4020**
0926-5074 Geotechnika **2744**
0926-5112 Fluid Mechanics and Its Applications **7058**
0926-5147 Functional Grammar Series†
0926-5155 Studies of Argumentation in Pragmatics and Discourse Analysis **5183**
0926-5201 Amsterdam Paedological Center. Publications†
0926-5279 Loon *changed to* 1874-5105 **1933**
0926-5287 Reproduction, Nutrition, Development *changed to* 1751-7311 **932**
0926-5309 Reproduction, Nutrition, Development. Supplement†
0926-5341 Applications of Fibonacci Numbers **5471**
0926-5430 Cross Cultural Psychology Monographs†
0926-5473 I F I P Transactions A: Computer Science & Technology†
0926-5481 I F I P Transactions B: Computer Applications in Technology†
0926-549X I F I P Transactions C: Communications Systems†
0926-5589 Developments in Agricultural Economics **196**
0926-5600 Amsterdam Monographs in American Studies **4442**
0926-5783 S A I Reeks **4177**
0926-5805 Automation in Construction **2458**
0926-5856 Leiden Studies in Indo-European **5143**
0926-6003 Computational Optimization and Applications **5551**
0926-602X Groninger Ondernemers Kontakt *changed to* 1871-2614 **1782**
0926-6070 Education and Society in the Middle Ages and Renaissance **2847**
0926-6097 Contributions to Biblical Exegesis and Theology **7635**
0926-6224 Algemeen Burgerlijk Pensioenfonds. Jaarverslag **1662**
0926-6240 Housing and Urban Policy Studies **4412**
0926-6267 Vandalisme, Criminaliteit en Volkshuisvesting **4431**
0926-6275 Technisch-Bestuurskundige Verkenningen **3469**
0926-6291 Volkshuisvesting in Theorie en Praktijk† **8998**
0926-6364 Random Operators and Stochastic Equations **5528**
0926-6410 Cognitive Brain Research *changed to* 0006-8993 **6128**
0926-6437 Journal of Income Distribution **1545**
0926-6445 Ontladingen
0926-6453 Studies in Spirituality **7685**
0926-6461 European Studies on Multilingualism†
0926-6534 Biochimica et Biophysica Acta. Mucoproteins and Mucopolysaccharides†
0926-6690 Industrial Crops and Products **236**
0926-6801 Journal of High Speed Networks **2500**
0926-7026 Incentive Magazine *changed to* 1871-3149 **1804**
0926-7050 Acht Mei Post†
0926-7069 ArtSchool Magazine†
0926-7093 Studies in Astronautics **72**
0926-7158 Controllers Magazine **1286**
0926-7182 Denkbeeld **7351**
0926-7212 Delft Outlook **8419**
0926-7220 Science & Education **7908**
0926-7263 Chime **6555**
0926-7417 AIDS-Bestrijding *changed to* 1573-6369 **5765**
0926-7522 Nederlands Tijdschrift voor Heelkunde **5684**
0926-759X Knip Mode **2257**
0926-7638 R S G *changed to* 1571-8654 **8205**
0926-7670 Adfomedianieuws **1804**
0926-7859 Beveiliging **2676**
0926-8197 Pantaleon Cahiers **5693**
0926-8235 Centraal Economisch Plan **1882**
0926-8456 Land + Water **3278**
0926-8537 Reflector (Doetinchem) **8601**
0926-860X Applied Catalysis A: General **3236**
0926-874X Tilburg Foreign Law Review *changed to* Tilburg Law Review **4942**
0926-8782 Distributed and Parallel Databases **2530**
0926-8812 Bruid & Bruidegom **5557**
0926-8855 Acht Mei Krant†
0926-8898 Marie Claire (Dutch Edition) **8874**
0926-8901 Esquire **6289**
0926-8952 Marie Claire. Wonen **8874**
0926-9045 International Geneva Yearbook†
0926-9061 I F L A Round Table of National Centres for Library Services. Newsletter†
0926-907X Studies in Visual Information Processing **6187**
0926-910X AvantGarde **3914**
0926-9118 Polymer Science Library **2076**
0926-9142 Ekoland **107**
0926-9282 Mechanics and Physics of Discrete Systems **3389**
0926-9312 Babesch. Supplementa *see* 0165-9367 **385**

Link to your serials resources and content with ulrichsweb.com

0926-9398 Elle (Netherlands) **8860**
0926-941X Elle Wonen **4556**
0926-9568 Institut Historique Archeologique Neerlandais de Stamboul. Publications **4321**
0926-9592 Residence **4549**
0926-9606 Physics and Evolution of the Earth's Interior†
0926-9614 Industrial Chemistry Library **2065**
0926-9622 Advances in Design and Manufacturing **2483**
0926-9630 Studies in Health Technology and Informatics **5718**
0926-9649 Interventional Cardiology **5790**
0926-9657 European Monographs **4925**
0926-9681 Semiotisch Perspectief†
0926-969X Clinical Medical Ethics **5597**
0926-9711 Environment & Management **3421**
0926-972X Studies in Risk and Uncertainty **1550**
0926-9738 Studies in Human Biology **928**
0926-9754 Ecology, Economy & Environment **3418**
0926-9762 Euro Courses. Computer and Information Science **2418**
0926-9770 Euro Courses. Health Physics and Radiation Protection **3167**
0926-9789 Euro Courses. Reliability and Risk Analysis **8421**
0926-9797 Euro Courses. Remote Sensing **8421**
0926-9800 Information Law Series **4692**
0926-9827 Primary Health Care Publications†
0926-9851 Journal of Applied Geophysics **2784**
0926-9894 Aannemer **974**
0926-9959 European Academy of Dermatology and Venereology. Journal **5876**
0927-0043 Egyptologische Uitgaven **4321**
0927-0094 Chemicals in Agriculture **224**
0927-0108 Composite Materials Series **3342**
0927-0116 Neuropsychology and Cognition **6168**
0927-0124 Computer Law Series **4648**
0927-0132 Vrije Universiteit. Faculteit der Economische Wetenschappen en Econometrie. Research Memorandum **1550**
0927-0140 GebouwBeheer **1747**
0927-0213 Stichting Praktijkonderzoek Pluimveehouderij. Onderzoekverslag
0927-0248 Solar Energy Materials & Solar Cells **3177**
0927-0256 Computational Materials Science **3343**
0927-0353 Centrum voor Onderzoek en Voorlichting voor de Pluimveehouderij "Het Spelderholt". Jaarverslag†
0927-0507 Handbooks in Operations Research and Management Science *changed to* 1876-7354 **2438**
0927-0523 Italian Studies in Law†
0927-0574 Nieuwe Drogist **6863**
0927-0760 Woonconsument *changed to* 1569-3503 **1006**
0927-0817 Topics in Molecular Organization and Engineering **3256**
0927-0833 Netherlands. Sociaal en Cultureel Planbureau. Cahiers **8122**
0927-0841 Chemical Safety Sheets†
0927-1007 Euro Courses. Technological Innovation **8421**
0927-1023 Automated Reasoning Series **2446**
0927-1198 Kennis Systemen†
0927-1279 Zeeland **4280**
0927-1392 Wie Werkt Waar in de Reclame **37**
0927-1449 Kwaliteit in Beeld **4105**
0927-1759 Mavors. Roman Army Researches **4152**
0927-1791 Alledaagse Dingen *changed to* 1872-5090 **3624**
0927-1813 Studies in Speech Pathology and Clinical Linguistics†
0927-1864 Institut Pierre Bayle. Studies **4232**
0927-1910 German Monitor **5217**
0927-202X Lokaal & Mondiaal - Vakmatig†
0927-2216 Modus *changed to* 1871-4307 **4630**
0927-2518 Idee **7141**
0927-2569 Biblical Interpretation **7627**
0927-2615 Nederlandse Jurisprudentie Kort *changed to* 1567-2298 **4740**
0927-2658 Passage *changed to* 1570-6303 **6180**
0927-2739 Computer! Totaal **2575**
0927-2747 Nederlands Tijdschrift voor Burgerlijk Recht **4838**
0927-2771 Excerpta Medica. Section 4: Microbiology: Bacteriology, Mycology, Parasitology and Virology **715**
0927-278X Excerpta Medica. Section 29: Clinical and Experimental Biochemistry **715**
0927-2798 Excerpta Medica. Section 30: Clinical and Experimental Pharmacology **6889**
0927-2852 Applied Categorical Structures **5550**
0927-2933 Blotto *changed to* 1871-6970 **6508**
0927-2941 Vagant *changed to* 1871-1332 **3003**
0927-3026 Erfgoed van Industrie en Techniek **8421**
0927-3034 Languages of Design†
0927-3042 Cancer Treatment and Research **6014**
0927-3131 Samuel Beckett Today - Aujourd'hui **5366**
0927-3204 T V Krant **2393**
0927-3255 Gramma - T T T†
0927-328X E C C Newsletter†
0927-3301 Delft Studies in Integrated Water Management **8820**
0927-3336 Tijdschrift voor Waterstaatsgeschiedenis **4273**
0927-3360 InterActions†
0927-3379 Air & Space Law **8534**
0927-3387 Bestuurskunde **7423**
0927-3417 Scramble **70**
0927-3433 Vee Dee Amok **6451**
0927-3506 Kunst en Wetenschap **7877**
0927-3514 E A I E Occasional Paper **3012**
0927-3522 The International Journal of Marine and Coastal Law **4969**
0927-3557 Letterlik *changed to* 1570-4580 **5346**
0927-3816 Fichte-Studien. Supplementa **6919**
0927-3824 Globaal *changed to* 1569-0393 **7202**
0927-3840 Frontaal†
0927-3948 Ocular Immunology and Inflammation **6047**
0927-3972 Strabismus (London) **6052**
0927-4014 Rijksmuseumkunstkrant *changed to* 1876-3561 **6535**
0927-4057 Euro Courses. Advanced Scientific Techniques **8421**
0927-4065 Studia Imagologica **5379**
0927-409X Delfia Batavorum Jaarboek
0927-4103 Aristoteles Semitico-Latinus **6905**
0927-4316 Centrum voor Plantenveredelingsonderzoek. Jaarverslag
0927-4340 Kerngetallen Nederlandse Beursfondsen†
0927-4367 Jeanswear†
0927-4375 Holland Management Review **1118**
0927-4405 Philosophie & Repraesentation **6942**
0927-4472 Glass Science and Technology (Amsterdam)
0927-4510 Isotopes in the Physical and Biomedical Sciences†
0927-4529 Kluwer Texts in the Mathematical Sciences **5507**
0927-4545 Info-bulletin Varkenshouderij†
0927-4588 Bioinformatics†
0927-460X Merkourios **4935**
0927-4626 Jaarboek Numaga **4234**
0927-4634 Jaar in Cijfers (Year) **8382**
0927-4642 Nijmeegs Katern **4248**
0927-4936 Nieuwsbrief Volkshuisvesting **4421**
0927-4987 Developments in Health Economics and Public Policy **7514**
0927-5002 European Materials Research Society. Symposia Proceedings **3344**
0927-5010 European Materials Research Society. Monographs†
0927-5029 North-Holland Delta Series **7028**
0927-5088 Studies in the History of Ideas in the Low Countries **6955**
0927-5193 Membrane Science and Technology Series **834**
0927-5207 Developments in Environmental Economics **3413**
0927-5215 Trace Metals in the Environment *changed to* 1875-1121 **3503**
0927-5290 Golf Nieuws†
0927-5304 Golfjournaal **8233**
0927-5371 Labour Economics **1694**
0927-538X Pacific-Basin Finance Journal **1373**
0927-5398 Journal of Empirical Finance **1361**
0927-5401 Clinical Trials and Meta-Analysis†
0927-5428 Highlife **5219**
0927-5436 Health Policy Monographs†
0927-5444 Studies in Computer and Communications Systems **2352**
0927-5452 Advances in Parallel Computing **2466**
0927-5460 Studies in Comparative Economic Policies **1549**
0927-5479 Optical Wave Sciences and Technology†
0927-5487 Clinical Aspects of Biomedicine†
0927-5568 The International Journal of Children's Rights **7210**
0927-5622 Circus-Gids Nederland†
0927-5746 Fiscaal Ondernemingsrecht **1925**
0927-5754 Textxet **5387**
0927-5819 Topics in Discrete Mathematics **5542**
0927-5827 X L *changed to* 1569-4461 **4371**
0927-586X Texts on Computational Mechanics **3397**
0927-5878 Chemical Thermodynamics **7053**
0927-5886 European Communities Environmental Policy Series **3430**
0927-5916 Polymer Recovery†
0927-5940 International Tax and Public Finance **1930**
0927-6076 Nieuwsbrief Administratie *changed to* 1388-2635 **1798**
0927-6203 L T Journaal *changed to* K L V Update **129**
0927-6254 Transmissie **7742**
0927-6424 N F T O Bulletin (Venlo) *changed to* 1872-0552 **3006**
0927-6440 Composite Interfaces (Print)† **8942**
0927-6467 Russian Journal of Numerical Analysis and Mathematical Modelling **5530**
0927-6505 Astroparticle Physics **571**
0927-6629 Energietechniek **3307**
0927-6769 C M Actueel
0927-6947 Set-Valued Analysis *changed to* 1877-0533 **5535**
0927-6998 Landbouwkundig Tijdschrift. Vacaturegids†
0927-7021 Weekblad Cricket **8251**
0927-703X N C H Tradeletter
0927-7048 Kwiklink *changed to* 1871-5710 **4341**
0927-7056 Interface Science *changed to* 0022-2461 **3350**
0927-7099 Computational Economics **1415**
0927-720X Scandinavian Conference on Artificial Intelligence **2456**
0927-7218 Bedrijfsuitkomsten en Financiele Positie†
0927-7293 De Trainer-Coach **8249**
0927-748X Vormen uit Vuur **541**
0927-7501 Dutch Studies in Armenian Language and Literature†
0927-751X Lincoln Smitweld Reportage **6343**
0927-7544 Journal of Real Estate Literature **7597**
0927-7633 Religions in the Graeco-Roman World **7675**
0927-7641 Stadswerk **3283**
0927-7706 Utrecht Studies in Language and Communication **5193**
0927-7749 Gelders Erfgoed **4223**
0927-7757 Colloids and Surfaces A: Physicochemical and Engineering Aspects **2134**
0927-7765 Colloids and Surfaces B: Biointerfaces **2134**
0927-7838 Het Landbouwblad†
0927-7889 De RozeLinks†
0927-7943 Horeca Nederland Visie *changed to* 1388-0411 **4388**
0927-7951 Computational Mechanics Advances†
0927-796X Materials Science and Engineering R: Reports **3353**
0927-8311 Nieuwsbrief Nederlands Fotoarchief **6971**
0927-8370 Business Supporter†
0927-894X K I W A Nieuws *changed to* 1574-7948 **8828**
0927-8982 T I N F O N **2917**
0927-9113 Intercambio†
0927-9296 Europees Belasting Toegevoegde Waarde-Nieuws *changed to* 1383-7613 **1912**
0927-9369 A I M Magazine *changed to* 1871-4250 **4486**
0927-9628 R A M†
0927-9768 Max Euwe-Centrum. Nieuwsbrief **8187**
0927-9849 Tuincomfort†
0927-9938 Ambtelijk Contact **7745**
0928-0065 Tijdschrift voor Integrale Geneeskunde *changed to* 1874-0251 **311**
0928-0189 Orientations†
0928-0200 East-West Journal of Numerical Mathematics *changed to* 1570-2820 **5553**
0928-0219 Journal of Inverse and Ill-Posed Problems **5504**
0928-0480 Genealogysk Jierboek **3768**
0928-0529 European Video Journal of Cardiology†
0928-0553 Stichting Kom Over en Help. Informatiebulletin *changed to* 1875-3027 **7683**
0928-0634 Spanish Yearbook of International Law **4941**
0928-0677 Ondernemersbrief
0928-0707 Journal of Sol-Gel Science and Technology **3351**
0928-0723 Nieuwsbrief Gemeenteraadsleden **7500**
0928-0731 Biblical Interpretation Series **7627**
0928-0979 Nederland's Patriciaat **3776**
0928-0987 European Journal of Pharmaceutical Sciences **6838**
0928-1010 Tjabe Rawit†
0928-1045 Journal of Computer-Aided Materials Design *changed to* 1874-8562
0928-1231 Pharmacy World and Science **6874**
0928-124X Feed Mix **272**
0928-1258 Medecine Nucleaire **6202**
0928-1282 Transparant **7777**
0928-1290 Arbo en Milieu *changed to* 1571-4152 **6673**
0928-1371 European Journal on Criminal Policy and Research **2651**
0928-141X Studien zur Interkulturellen Philosophie **6954**
0928-1444 Archeologische Routes in Nederland *changed to* 1871-6385 **389**
0928-1460 Indigenous Knowledge and Development Monitor *changed to* 1570-0291 **1598**
0928-1479 Advances in Image Communication **2483**
0928-1495 Kano-Sport **8277**
0928-1509 Advances in X-Ray Contrast **6192**
0928-1525 E R M **1815**
0928-1533 Studies in Bilingualism **5182**
0928-1541 I A W A Journal **793**
0928-1568 Balans Belang *changed to* 1872-0560 **3037**
0928-1576 Topics in Transportation **8513**
0928-1584 New Concepts in Polymer Science **3251**
0928-1606 Hyperthermia and Oncology†
0928-1614 New Trends in Probability and Statistics **5520**
0928-1789 Filosofie Magazine **6920**
0928-1886 Jurisprudentie Arbeidsrecht **4707**
0928-1894 Alliance Environmental Law Newsletter† **8929**
0928-2009 Developments in Marine Technology **3376**
0928-2017 Studies in the History and Philosophy of Mathematics **5539**
0928-2025 Developments in Earth Surface Processes **2730**
0928-2041 Samenwerkingsverband Jeugdhulpverlening Utrecht. Nieuwsbrief†
0928-2076 Praktijkonderzoek
0928-2122 L G R - Series **2786**
0928-2130 Amsterdam Classical Monographs **2230**
0928-2149 Process Simulation & Modeling **2518**
0928-2211 O T B Working Paper **7894**
0928-222X E I M in de Markt **1959**
0928-2440 Guides to the Identification of the Microinvertebrates of the Continental Waters of the World **945**
0928-270X De Weduwe Ida *changed to* 1872-4590 **6524**
0928-2726 Headhunters
0928-2734 Coastline **2802**
0928-2742 Morality and the Meaning of Life **7664**
0928-2750 E C Tax Review **1921**
0928-2858 Groenwerk†
0928-2998 Tijdschrift voor Hygiene en Infektiepreventie **5827**
0928-3021 Service Management (Alphen aan den Rijn) **1793**
0928-303X Gewina *changed to* 1876-9055 **3003**
0928-3196 Stichting Vrienden MS Research. Nieuwsbrief *changed to* 1574-9215 **6183**
0928-320X De Geestelijke Genezer *changed to* 1871-7241 **6113**
0928-3420 Studies in Plant Science **819**
0928-3552 Landelijke Studenten Vakbond. Nieuwsbrief *changed to* 1872-0307 **2985**
0928-3935 Topics in Secondary Metabolism†
0928-3986 Studies in Probability, Optimization and Statistics **5555**
0928-4060 Tip Culinair *changed to* 1574-809X
0928-4087 Saldi van Akkerbouwgewassen†
0928-4109 Exkies **5844**
0928-4230 Boekenpost **7553**
0928-4249 Veterinary Research **8814**
0928-4257 Journal of Physiology (Paris) **6156**
0928-432X Asian Yearbook of International Law **4917**
0928-4575 Netherlands. Centraal Bureau voor de Statistiek. Overlevingstafels naar Burgerlijke Staat†
0928-463X Netherlands. Centraal Bureau voor de Statistiek. Overlevingstafels naar Geslacht en Leeftijd†
0928-4672 Tijdschrift voor Huisartsgeneeskunde **5722**
0928-4680 Pathophysiology **926**
0928-4702 Woonboot Magazine **8285**
0928-477X Netherlands. Centraal Bureau voor de Statistiek. Leeftijdsopbouw per Gemeente, Kerncijfers (Year)
0928-4788 Netherlands. Centraal Bureau voor de Statistiek. Bevolking der Gemeenten van Nederland op 1 Januari (Year) (Diskette) *see* 1569-8033 **7312**
0928-4923 N V V K Info **6681**
0928-4931 Materials Science and Engineering C: Biomimetic Materials, Sensors and Systems *changed to* Materials Science and Engineering C: Materials for Biological Applications **3353**
0928-5008 R B Elektronica†
0928-5083 Sociaal Wetenschappelijke Studies
0928-5121 Bibliografie Nederlandse Sociale Wetenschappen (Print Edition) *changed to* Bibliografie Nederlandse Sociale Wetenschappen (Online Edition) **8148**
0928-5318 Overheid en Overleg *changed to* 1874-4052 **8978**
0928-5350 Facta *changed to* 1877-8216 **8138**
0928-5520 The Medieval Mediterranean **4152**
0928-5644 Gezondheid†
0928-5687 Horeca Journal *changed to* 1574-342X **4394**
0928-5687 Horeca Journal *changed to* 1574-3411 **4394**
0928-5687 Horeca Journal *changed to* 1574-3403 **4394**
0928-5806 Distrifood **3634**
0928-6020 Stichting Kinderboerderijen Nederland. Infobulletin *changed to* 1872-0617 **168**
0928-611X Arts Assistent **5578**
0928-6268 Groomers Europe†
0928-6527 Itch† **8967**
0928-6586 Ophthalmic Epidemiology **6047**
0928-6594 P L N International†
0928-6624 Politie, Dier en Milieu *changed to* 1574-8405 **3414**
0928-673X Klokken-Koerier *changed to* 1871-7845 **4569**
0928-6799 Dopido (Kampen) **2186**
0928-6802 Electronic Journal of Oriental Studies

ISSN

9396 0928-6853 ULRICH'S PERIODICALS

0928-6853 Financiele Gegevens van de Bedrijfspensioenfondsen, de Ondernemingspensioen- en Ondernemingsspaarfondsen en de Beroepspensioenfondsen *changed to* 1570-3894 **8956**
0928-7051 P C Koop†
0928-7132 Moniteur de la Biotechnologie et du Developpement†
0928-7167 Nieuwe Wiskrant **5520**
0928-7329 Technology and Health Care **5720**
0928-7353 Stedelijke en Regionale Verkenningen **4427**
0928-7655 Resource and Energy Economics **3146**
0928-7868 Pediatric Clinics Amsterdam **6100**
0928-7930 Wie Levert Merken **2035**
0928-7949 Wie Levert Produkten en Diensten **2035**
0928-8066 Vrije Universiteit Amsterdam. Center for the Study of Religion and Politics. Studies†
0928-8090 Nieuwsbrief Sociale Vernieuwing **8058**
0928-8120 Nederlands Jazz Archief Bulletin *changed to* 1871-9201 **6578**
0928-8201 De Boomkwekerij (The Hague)†
0928-8228 Gorteria. Supplement **791**
0928-8244 F E M S Immunology and Medical Microbiology **885**
0928-8368 Savante†
0928-8414 Cultus *changed to* 1873-6092 **358**
0928-8430 Time (Atlantic Edition) **3837**
0928-8457 Fisc *changed to* 1568-5802 **1744**
0928-8503 Overheidsmanagement **1373**
0928-8562 A V Journaal
0928-8627 Tijdschrift voor Bedrijfsadministratie *changed to* 1570-4688 **8928**
0928-8635 Eur Nieuws **7232**
0928-8759 Criminology, Penology & Police Science Abstracts†
0928-8775 Lijn†
0928-8783 Theology and Medicine **7689**
0928-883X Netherlands. Centraal Bureau voor de Statistiek. Leeftijdsopbouw per Gemeente op 1 Januari (Year)
0928-8910 Automated Software Engineering **2446**
0928-8929 Studies in Discourse and Grammar **5182**
0928-8937 Norwegian Petroleum Society. Special Publication **6781**
0928-8945 Cancer Biology and Medicine **6011**
0928-9038 Informatization Developments and the Public Sector **7486**
0928-9119 Medical Artificial Intelligence **2454**
0928-9178 Sporen in de Tijd
0928-9313 Global Journal on Crime and Criminal Law **4890**
0928-9321 Global Law Review **4681**
0928-933X Global Environmental Law Annual **4681**
0928-9372 Tennis & Coach **8248**
0928-9380 Islamic Law and Society **7712**
0928-9518 Philosophical Studies in Contemporary Culture **6941**
0928-9526 Systems Approaches for Sustainable Agricultural Development **160**
0928-9534 Euro Courses. Environmental Impact Assessment **3430**
0928-9542 European Geophysical Society Series on Hydrological Sciences† **8954**
0928-9550 Medical Science Symposia Series **5671**
0928-9569 European Journal of Crime, Criminal Law and Criminal Justice **4889**
0928-964X Journal of Constitutional Law in Eastern and Central Europe **4850**
0928-9658 Eastern and Central European Journal on Environmental Law **4663**
0928-9801 European Review of Private Law **4925**
0928-9933 A B N Amro Economic Review†
0929-0001 Kritisch Consumeren *changed to* Goede Waar **8960**
0929-0036 Landbouw, Milieu en Economie *changed to* 1571-3067 **183**
0929-0052 Cuneiform Monographs **389**
0929-0079 Arbomagazine **1664**
0929-015X Interpretatie **7651**
0929-0168 European Academy of Dermatology and Venereology. Journal. Supplement **5876**
0929-0176 Nederlands Tijdschrift voor Medische Microbiologie **5684**
0929-0184 Nederlands Tijdschrift voor Urologie **6271**
0929-0214 Tot & Met†
0929-0273 European Journal of Health Law **5611**
0929-0281 Ecology & Environment **3417**
0929-0354 Euro Courses. Mechanical and Materials Science **3344**
0929-0400 Ons Erfgoed *changed to* Ons Genealogisch Erfgoed **3778**
0929-0435 Studies in Austrian Economics
0929-046X Consumenten Geldgids *changed to* 1569-3333 **1329**
0929-0508 Transport en Logistiek **8514**
0929-0567 Technische Universiteit te Delft. Bibliotheek. Lijst van Lopende Seriele Publikaties **636**
0929-0591 Stimulus **6116**
0929-0605 Vademecum Permanente Nascholing Huisartsen **5727**
0929-0680 Kanonistische Studien und Texte **7658**
0929-0753 Sophoshare **3331**
0929-0761 Dead Sea Discoveries **7720**
0929-077X Ancient Civilizations from Scythia to Siberia **4179**
0929-0788 Environment & Assessment **3420**
0929-0826 T I Newsletter†
0929-0850 World Disasters Report **7545**
0929-0907 Pragmatics & Cognition **5204**
0929-1016 Biological Rhythm Research **658**
0929-1032 Origine **368**
0929-1083 Automobiel Management **8562**
0929-1199 Journal of Corporate Finance **1360**
0929-1261 European Journal of Law and Economics **1107**
0929-127X Natural Resource Management and Policy **3455**
0929-1296 Frontiers in Electronic Testing **3099**
0929-130X Advances in Computational Economics **1413**
0929-1318 Developments in Plant Pathology **786**
0929-1326 Alliance European Community Law News†
0929-1393 Applied Soil Ecology **218**
0929-144X De Veluwenaar **8771**
0929-1512 Bloemen & Planten **3725**
0929-1555 C J P Magazine *changed to* 1871-6652 **4976**
0929-161X Klank en Show *changed to* 1571-6791 **6590**
0929-1636 Seasons **3750**
0929-1679 Soera *changed to* 1574-6577 **4280**
0929-1776 Scripta Phlebologica†
0929-1792 Tijdschrift Management en Informatie *changed to* 1571-862X **1775**
0929-1873 European Journal of Plant Pathology **787**
0929-189X Applied Composite Materials **3341**
0929-1903 Cancer Gene Therapy **6012**
0929-1954 Nieuwsbrief Bodem **3456**
0929-2012 Textiel Beheer **2244**
0929-2039 Tijdschrift Volwassenen Educatie†
0929-208X Zending Zonder Grenzen *changed to* 1574-7824 **7758**
0929-2160 Licht **3323**
0929-2187 MO/Samenlevingsopbouw **8055**
0929-2195 Stichting Ideele Import. Info
0929-2217 Dialogos Hispanicos†
0929-2268 EUROSIM - Simulation News Europe **2517**
0929-2403 Islamic History and Civilization **7712**
0929-2411 Feit & Fictie† **8956**
0929-2470 Nag Hammadi and Manichaean Studies **7705**
0929-2640 Nederlands Theaterjaarboek **8474**
0929-2934 Tandtechnisch Magazine **5867**
0929-2950 De Aan- en Afvoer van Goederen over Zee in de Nederlandse Zeehavens†
0929-2985 Normalisatie-Nieuws **6405**
0929-3116 Kijk op Oost Nederland **1140**
0929-3256 Liftinstituut. Mededeling *changed to* 1873-9105 **3388**
0929-3302 EMBASE List of Journals Indexed **5744**
0929-3515 Missets Horeca **4394**
0929-3787 Akkoord **6543**
0929-3949 Focus on Depression and Anxiety†
0929-4082 Waarvan Akte **4810**
0929-4449 Zorg en Verzekering *changed to* 1569-948X **4529**
0929-4562 De Actuaris **4491**
0929-4589 International Humanist News **6925**
0929-4627 Kreavak **536**
0929-4678 F W Z Maritiem Magazine *changed to* 1873-9067 **8654**
0929-4716 Het Vaggeschip
0929-4821 Nederlands Tijdschrift voor Kinderrevalidatie†
0929-483X The Dutch Annual of Psychoanalysis†
0929-4848 Transfer **3005**
0929-4856 Geomechanics Research Series **2742**
0929-5054 Electromagnetic Waves **7010**
0929-5100 Clinch *changed to* 1389-1847 **7150**
0929-5216 Kijk op Noord-Holland *changed to* 1574-6100 **1720**
0929-5224 Kijk op Zuid-Holland *changed to* 1574-6100 **1720**
0929-5305 Journal of Thrombosis and Thrombolysis **5794**
0929-5313 Journal of Computational Neuroscience **6151**
0929-5380 PodoSophia **6875**
0929-5518 KvK-Magazine *changed to* 1873-9288 **1720**
0929-5577 Amerika *changed to* 1571-0351 **8682**
0929-5585 Design Automation for Embedded Systems **2460**
0929-5593 Autonomous Robots **2584**
0929-5607 Adsorption **3235**
0929-5631 Conclusies Rechtspraak van de Week†
0929-5666 Letters in Peptide Science *changed to* 1381-1991 **7068**
0929-5666 Letters in Peptide Science *changed to* 1573-3149 **734**
0929-5674 Gereedschap†
0929-5887 Argumenten†
0929-5968 Lava Literair Tijdschrift **5224**
0929-600X Tijdschrift voor Bedrijfs- en Verzekeringsgeneeskunde **5722**
0929-6042 VKVisie *changed to* 1574-2776 **7814**
0929-6050 Muziek en Beeld *changed to* 1875-2888 **6565**
0929-6174 Journal of Quantitative Linguistics **5203**
0929-6212 Wireless Personal Communications **2365**
0929-6247 AdFundum **597**
0929-6298 Library of Rhetorics **6932**
0929-6301 The Judges **4934**
0929-631X American Dialect Society. Centennial Series **5092**
0929-6328 Vienna Circle Institute Yearbook **6960**
0929-6352 Rentabiliteit en Financiering van de Glastunibouw en de Champignonteelt in Nederland†
0929-6395 Fructus **232**
0929-6425 Australasian Studies in History and Philosophy of Science *changed to* 1871-7381 **7920**
0929-6441 Journal of Medical Ultrasound **6201**
0929-6484 Manuscripta Indonesica **4185**
0929-6573 Asser Actueel† **8931**
0929-6646 Formosan Medical Association. Journal **5615**
0929-6727 European Newsletter of Southeast Asian Studies† **8955**
0929-6743 Biomedical and Health Research Series **5585**
0929-6778 Papagaio *changed to* 1872-356X **3563**
0929-6824 Geschiedenis der Geneeskunde **5619**
0929-693X Archives de Pediatrie **6088**
0929-6980 Scrinium **416**
0929-6999 Internationale Forschungen zur Allgemeinen und Vergleichenden Literaturwissenschaft **5310**
0929-7006 Current Issues in Production Ecology **8419**
0929-7049 Neuropsychology, Development, and Cognition. Section C: Child Neuropsychology **7387**
0929-7111 International Law in Japanese Perspective **4931**
0929-712X Contemporary Issues in Genetics and Evolution **865**
0929-7138 International Society on Optics within Life Sciences. Series (Proceedings)†
0929-7154 Herademing **7647**
0929-7235 Volksdans **3624**
0929-7316 Benjamins Translation Library **5099**
0929-7324 Studies in Written Language and Literacy **5183**
0929-7332 Linguistics in the Netherlands **5147**
0929-7529 Dox **6496**
0929-7537 Kenmerken *changed to* 1872-5589 **7543**
0929-760X Power Unlimited **2481**
0929-7758 A V R O-Bode **2374**
0929-7774 Nieuwsbrief Absent! **1781**
0929-7790 Actuele Ontwikkeling van Bedrijfsresultaten en Inkomens **173**
0929-7820 Gouden Hoorn
0929-7839 Coolia **784**
0929-7871 Kantoor Business Magazine **1852**
0929-7928 Milieu Forum **3452**
0929-7936 Geregeld†
0929-8215 Journal of New Music Research **2495**
0929-824X La France et les Pays-Bas†
0929-8266 European Journal of Ultrasound **6196**
0929-8274 Literatuur Zonder Leeftijd **5326**
0929-8290 Westweek *see* 1566-2616 **144**
0929-8312 Nieuwe Damspel†
0929-8436 Value Inquiry Book Series **6959**
0929-8444 Marketing Results **6860**
0929-8479 Eindhoven University of Technology. Department of Technology Management. Research Report† **8953**
0929-8525 Technische Universiteit Eindhoven. Faculteit der Wiskunde en Informatica. E U T Reports - W S K **5541**
0929-8584 Eigen Perk **4217**
0929-8592 Queeste **5356**
0929-8622 Nederlands Tijdschrift voor Traumatologie **6067**
0929-8649 Tijdschrift voor Civiele Rechtspleging **4843**
0929-8665 Protein and Peptide Letters **742**
0929-8673 Current Medicinal Chemistry **2059**
0929-8681 Pensioenbrief **1702**
0929-8703 Oncologica **6030**
0929-872X Rentabiliteit en Financiering van de Tuinbouw in de Open Grond in Nederland†
0929-8738 I I A S Newsletter **4183**
0929-8908 Jaarboek Minderheden *changed to* 1875-8916 **7286**
0929-9017 Progress in Pure and Applied Discrete Mathematics **5526**
0929-9254 Mobiel **8055**
0929-9289 ArbeidsRecht **1663**
0929-9394 Filter **5119**
0929-9408 Historia en Informatica *changed to* 1872-0374 **2536**
0929-9459 Telewerken *changed to* 0022-8893 **1852**
0929-9610 Information and Systems Engineering†
0929-9629 Monte Carlo Methods and Applications **5555**
0929-9645 Transport Logistics†
0929-967X Policy Management Brief **1603**
0929-970X Historische Reeks Breukelen **4228**
0929-9718 Hollandse Studien **4230**
0929-9726 Middeleeuwse Studies en Bronnen **4244**
0929-9734 Middelnederlandse Tekstedities **5333**
0929-9742 N W Posthumus Reeks **4247**
0929-9750 Alkmaarse Historische Reeks **4197**
0929-9769 Amsterdamse Historische Reeks. Grote Serie **4198**
0929-9777 Archiefpublikaties†
0929-9785 Centrum voor Bedrijfsgeschiedenis. Cahiers† **8940**
0929-9793 Egmondse Studien **4216**
0929-9807 Egodocumenten **642**
0929-9815 De Geschiedenis van Hilversum **4224**
0929-9823 Erasmus Universiteit. Faculteit der Historsiche en Kunstwetenschappen. Publikaties **4139**
0929-9831 Studies over Holland in de Middeleeuwen†
0929-984X Utrechtse Bijdragen tot de Medievistiek† **8996**
0929-9858 Vereeniging tot Beofening van Geldersche Geschiedenis, Oudheidkunde en Recht. Werken **4276**
0929-9866 Middeleeuwse Verzamelhandschriften uit de Nederlanden **5333**
0929-9890 De Achttiende Eeuw **4195**
0929-9904 Scope on Phlebology and Lymphology†
0929-9971 Terminology **5186**
0929-998X Functions of Language **5121**
0929-9998 Keuken Studio **4559**
0930-0007 ZauberZeit†
0930-0171 Fachblatt Musik Magazin†
0930-0198 Beitraege zur Geschichte der Medizin und Ihrer Nebengebiete **5584**
0930-021X Plattdeutsche Bibliographie†
0930-0279 Walthari **5396**
0930-0309 Caravan **8308**
0930-0317 Lecture Notes in Earth Sciences **2712**
0930-0325 Lecture Notes in Statistics **8385**
0930-0341 Theologie der Dritten Welt **7689**
0930-0392 Themen - Texte - Interpretation **3086**
0930-0503 Ketzerbriefe **5222**
0930-0597 Bilanz- und Buchhaltung **1281**
0930-0635 Biona-Report **661**
0930-0708 Mineralogy and Petrology **6471**
0930-0716 Rosa Flieder†
0930-0724 Tranvia†
0930-0791 Deutscher Tischtennis Sport *changed to* Tischtennis **8249**
0930-1038 Surgical and Radiologic Anatomy **5718**
0930-1054 Die Datenschleuder **2506**
0930-1100 Productronic **3111**
0930-1127 Muenchener Beitraege zur Mediaevistik und Renaissance-Forschung†
0930-1143 Neue Gespraeche **7809**
0930-1178 Aertztliche Monatshefte†
0930-1186 Pony†
0930-1194 Skilaeufer† **8988**
0930-1208 Heidelberger Althistorische Beitraege und Epigraphische Studien **2235**
0930-1224 Maxi **8874**
0930-1313 Unterwegs (Munich) **7692**
0930-1364 Akademie fuer Oeffentliches Gesundheitswesen. Berichte und Materialien **7506**
0930-1437 Albanische Hefte **3517**
0930-1461 Forensic Science Progress†
0930-1844 Deutsche Gesellschaft fuer Auswaertige Politik. Forschungsinstitut. Reihe Ruestungsbeschraenkung und Sicherheit†
0930-1852 Yejin Shebei he Jishu *see* 0935-7254 **6321**
0930-1852 Yejin Shebei he Jishu *see* 0934-8077 **6321**
0930-1895 Baupraxis-Zeitung **980**
0930-195X Biologische Arbeitsstoff Toleranz Werte und Expositionsaequivalente fuer Krebserzeugende Arbeitsstoffe **6674**
0930-1992 Wissenschaft und Logos†
0930-2034 Stadt Remscheid Statistisches Jahrbuch **8403**
0930-2093 Deutscher Bildungsdienst†
0930-2115 Die Offizin†
0930-2166 Studien zur Deutschen Literatur des 19 und 20 Jahrhunderts *changed to* 0946-9168 **5380**
0930-2239 B E F A - Mitteilungen

Link to your serials resources and content with ulrichsweb.com

ISSN

DIRECTORY 2010 0934-9057 9399

0933-3657 Artificial Intelligence in Medicine **2446**
0933-372X Bibliographien zur Rechts- und Sozialwissenschaft **7950**
0933-3738 Caliber **8164**
0933-3746 F Z - Der Fachanzeiger **4565**
0933-3754 Entsorga-Magazin **3191**
0933-3835 Jahrbuch fuer Evangelikale Theologie **7762**
0933-3851 Praktische Psychiatrie **6174**
0933-3894 Taschenbuch fuer Hauseigentuemer **4428**
0933-3924 Bauaufsichtliche Zulassungen† **8935**
0933-4017 Restauro **514**
0933-4033 Bundesdatenschutzgesetz **2511**
0933-4106 Celan-Jahrbuch **5271**
0933-4165 Packaging Production International†
0933-4173 Journal of Planar Chromatography - Modern TLC **2102**
0933-422X Paedagogik (Weinheim) **2895**
0933-4289 Berufskrankheitenverordnung **6674**
0933-4343 Berlinfoerderungsgesetz **7488**
0933-4351 Nyankpala Agricultural Research Report†
0933-4440 Touren-Fahrer **8269**
0933-4483 Probleme der Semiotik **6945**
0933-4491 Visier **8340**
0933-4505 Berufsbildung im Oeffentlichen Dienst **6693**
0933-4548 Versicherungsmedizin **5728**
0933-4629 B I A Handbuch *changed to* B G I A Handbuch **6674**
0933-4688 Photomed†
0933-4718 A V A - Arbeitsmaterialien zur Verwaltungs- und Hochschulausbildung†
0933-4769 Text und Kontext **5386**
0933-4807 Pteridines
0933-4947 Spots Planungsdaten Hoerfunk - Fernsehen **2029**
0933-498X Papyrologische Texte und Abhandlungen **4155**
0933-5013 Osteuropaforschung **4251**
0933-5080 Supplementa Byzantina **2241**
0933-5102 Rheinisches Archiv **4258**
0933-5137 Materialwissenschaft und Werkstofftechnik **6322**
0933-5145 Deutsche Literatur von den Anfaengen bis 1700 **5284**
0933-5293 Z I Jahrbuch **3287**
0933-5315 Bios **641**
0933-5323 Heidelberger Akademie der Wissenschaften. Philosophisch-Historische Klasse. Supplemente zu den Schriften **4141**
0933-5358 Heimat Ostbayern†
0933-5366 Grenzfragen **7858**
0933-5374 Praxis Geschichte **3077**
0933-5390 Premiere†
0933-5420 Historische Bibliographie **4170**
0933-5501 Goettinger Dissertationen **2982**
0933-5722 Politische Oekologie **3460**
0933-5846 Archive for Mathematical Logic **5473**
0933-5927 F & S **2061**
0933-596X Electronic Actuell Magazin **3095**
0933-6087 Contacts. Serie 2: Gallo-Germanica **4212**
0933-6095 Contacts. Serie 3: Etudes et Documents **4212**
0933-6222 Studies in Anthropological Linguistics†
0933-6230 Gutenberg-Gesellschaft. Kleine Drucke **7323**
0933-632X Koelner Statistische Nachrichten. Sonderhefte **7481**
0933-6346 Heimatpflege in Westfalen **3436**
0933-6354 Zur Lage der Welt *see* 0887-364X **3467**
0933-6354 Zur Lage der Welt *see* 1576-1266 **1517**
0933-6389 Paedagogische Korrespondenz
0933-646X Stint **5377**
0933-6494 Umwelt- und Technikrecht **3471**
0933-663X Druckbehaelterverordnung† **8951**
0933-6648 Sicherheitstechnik **2668**
0933-6680 Feinschmecker fuer Aerzte†
0933-6788 Update in Intensive Care and Emergency Medicine†
0933-6850 Suedosteuropaeische Arbeiten **4272**
0933-6885 Musik-, Tanz- und Kunsttherapie **5681**
0933-6907 Infosat **2383**
0933-694X Denkmalrecht der Laender und des Bundes **439**
0933-6990 Forum fuer Interdisziplinaere Forschung **6920**
0933-7024 Schwaedds **5172**
0933-7075 Club Magazin† **8941**
0933-7105 Marktforschung und Management
0933-7164 Spektrum des Geistes **5376**
0933-7253 Passagen†
0933-7334 Elbinger Nachrichten **4217**
0933-7342 Marienburger Zeitung
0933-7385 Hautfreund **5877**
0933-7407 Mycoses **5681**
0933-7431 Literatur und Geschichte
0933-7547 Blitz-Terminal†
0933-7563 Wuerzburger Medizinhistorische Forschungen. Beiheft **5731**
0933-7571 Explosionsschutz Elektrischer Anlagen **3308**
0933-758X Mitteilungen zur Altenhilfe†
0933-761X Empirical Approaches to Language Typology **5114**
0933-7636 Mouton Grammar Library **5153**
0933-7660 Prakla Seismos Report†
0933-7741 Forum Mathematicum **5488**
0933-7776 Kultus und Unterricht. Ausgabe A **3026**
0933-7792 Cross Magazin **8256**
0933-7946 Arthroskopie **5578**
0933-7954 Social Psychiatry and Psychiatric Epidemiology **6186**
0933-8012 Forschungen zur Kriminalpolitik **2653**
0933-8047 Seibt Oberflaechentechnik **7062**
0933-8055 Energiedepesche **3129**
0933-808X Schuhtechnik International†
0933-811X Endoskopie Heute **5923**
0933-8128 Techtex Forum **8458**
0933-8217 Kreisarchiv Soest. Schriften **4238**
0933-8241 Mensch und Buero **1852**
0933-8268 Annales Universitatis Saraviensis. Series Mathematicae **5470**
0933-8276 Formularbuch der Steuer- und Wirtschaftspraxis **1926**
0933-8306 E D V - Recht **4662**
0933-8314 Europaeische Gesetze gegen Wettbewerbsbeschraenkungen† **8954**
0933-8330 Schmiede Journal **6331**
0933-8349 Strips Sheets Tubes†
0933-8357 Aussendienst Informationen **4493**
0933-8381 Chinesisch - Unterricht **5106**
0933-842X Praxis der Klinischen Verhaltensmedizin und Rehabilitation **6115**
0933-8470 Golf Journal **8232**
0933-8497 Formeln fuer die Steuer- und Wirtschaftspraxis **1926**
0933-8527 Deutsches Muenzen Magazin **6650**
0933-8535 R K W Handbuch Forschung, Entwicklung, Konstruktion **7901**
0933-8586 Orthodoxes Forum **7705**
0933-8640 Deckblatt†
0933-8667 Design & Elektronik **2539**
0933-8721 Hefte fuer Ostasiatische Literatur **5304**
0933-8799 Spuren Suchen **4267**
0933-8810 M - Moderne Metalltechnik *changed to* 1864-3515 **6326**
0933-8926 Jazzthetik **6579**
0933-8934 Literaturschau "Stahl und Eisen" **6321**
0933-8993 Verordnung ueber Allgemeine Bedingungen fuer die Gasversorgung von Tarifkunden *changed to* Niederdruckanschlussverordnung - Gasgrundversorgungsverordnung **6781**
0933-9000 Sprengstoffgesetz **3255**
0933-9051 Medizinische Forschung **5677**
0933-9094 Rueckert zu Ehren **5365**
0933-9221 Winklers Illustrierte **1194**
0933-9264 Brillen Special
0933-9280 HighTech†
0933-9299 Hamburger Zahnaerzteblatt **5846**
0933-9345 Western Horse **8300**
0933-9477 Genossenschafts-Handbuch **1423**
0933-9663 Abstracts and Reviews from Zentralblatt fuer Mathematik†
0933-968X Briefmarken Magazin† **8937**
0933-9698 Kochen und Geniessen **3653**
0933-9701 Business Travel Intern†
0933-9728 Media-Daten Annuals†
0933-9736 Geo Wissen **4008**
0933-9884 Internationale Direktinvestionen **7144**
0933-9906 Zweiwochendienst Frauen und Politik **8893**
0933-9949 Bibelreport **7625**
0934-0300 Muensteraner Monographien zur Englischen Literatur **5337**
0934-0378 Film und Fakten†
0934-0394 Automobil Produktion **8563**
0934-0696 Zeitschrift fuer Tuerkeistudien **564**
0934-0734 Biomedical Progress **5934**
0934-0858 Komparatistische Bibliothek **7981**
0934-0866 Particle & Particle Systems Characterization **7029**
0934-0874 Transplant International **5724**
0934-0882 Sexual Plant Reproduction **817**
0934-0912 Werkzeug & Formenbau **5461**
0934-0939 Forum Politische Bildung†
0934-1129 AIDS†
0934-1188 Paediatrics in Europe†
0934-1234 Forschungen zur Brandenburgischen und Preussischen Geschichte **4220**
0934-1307 Neue Zeitschrift fuer Verkehrsrecht **8506**
0934-1420 Key Topics in Brain Research **6157**
0934-1455 Magira†
0934-1463 Fantasia (Print) *changed to* Fantasia (Online) **5442**
0934-1668 Interdisziplinaere Europa Studien **7242**
0934-1684 Kultur-Chronik (Spanish Edition) *changed to* 1614-595X
0934-1692 Kultur-Chronik (French Edition) *changed to* 1614-595X
0934-1706 Kultur-Chronik (English Edition) *changed to* 1614-595X
0934-1722 Informationsbrief fuer Fuehrungskraefte *changed to* 1860-9228 **3246**
0934-1730 Kuenstler - Kritisches Lexikon der Gegenwartskunst **500**
0934-1749 AutoCAD Magazin **2588**
0934-1854 Classical Homoeopathy Quarterly†
0934-1897 Z D†
0934-1951 Motorrad, Reisen und Sport†
0934-196X Quer Durch Hamburg. Spedition und Transport *changed to* 1614-4554 **8509**
0934-2028 Forum. Berichte aus der Arbeit†
0934-2192 Religionswissenschaftliche Reihe **7675**
0934-2230 Drehscheibe (Cologne) **8616**
0934-2575 Zeitschrift fuer die Alttestamentliche Wissenschaft. Beihefte **7696**
0934-2583 Lehrbogen Technik†
0934-2621 Grundgesetz der Bundesrepublik Deutschland **4848**
0934-3008 Psychiatrische Praxis. Supplement **6177**
0934-3032 Taschenlexikon Haftpflichtrechtlicher Entscheidungen **4898**
0934-3040 Deutsche Stimme **7129**
0934-3059 Taschenlexikon Sozialversicherungsrechtlicher Entscheidungen **8074**
0934-3148 Med-Report **5665**
0934-3180 T V I†
0934-3229 Taschenlexikon Steuerrechtlicher Entscheidungen **1946**
0934-3253 Centaurus-Skript **4641**
0934-3261 Produzentenhaftung **4879**
0934-327X Papageien **6812**
0934-3342 Textilkunst International **8461**
0934-3350 Deutsche Squash Zeitung†
0934-3369 Sport Bild **8203**
0934-3431 Psychologie-Almanach†
0934-3482 Muellmagazin **3509**
0934-3504 Umweltwissenschaften und Schadstoff-Forschung **3492**
0934-3571 Gefahrgut - Dangerous Goods CD-ROM **8541**
0934-361X Dachau Review†
0934-3652 Beamtenrecht **7422**
0934-3725 Studien zur Allgemeinen und Romanischen Sprachwissenschaft **5181**
0934-375X Handbuch der Steuerlichen Betriebspruefung **1116**
0934-3768 Phantastische Zeiten†
0934-3792 D E C H E M A Biotechnology Conferences **763**
0934-3814 Bausteine Grundschule **2939**
0934-3822 Media Daten: Verbreitungsatlas - Anzeigenblaetter†
0934-3865 Sticks **6620**
0934-3962 Instrumentbau-Zeitschrift - Musik International **6576**
0934-411X Rolladen & Sonnenschutz **539**
0934-4136 Sozialgesetzbuch: Allgemeiner Teil **4842**
0934-4144 Sozialgesetzbuch: Gemeinsame Vorschriften **4842**
0934-4152 Sozialgesetzbuch: Verwaltungsverfahren und Schutz der Sozialdaten **4842**
0934-4160 Sozialgesetzbuch: Zusammenarbeit der Leistungstraeger und ihre Beziehungen zu Dritten **4842**
0934-4179 Strategie- und Informationsmanagement **1795**
0934-4187 Dialyse Intern **6267**
0934-4217 Media Selection **1577**
0934-4225 Fischoekologie **3591**
0934-4241 Gitarre Aktuell **6569**
0934-4284 Das Rechts A B C **4766**
0934-4292 M D Kurier
0934-4365 Scientific Drilling†
0934-4403 Turkologie und Tuerkeikunde **562**
0934-4411 Wirtschaft und Gesellschaft im Beruf†
0934-4470 Bericht der Bayerischen Bodendenkmalpflege **4132**
0934-4500 Instituts zur Erforschung der Europaeischen Arbeiterbewegung. Mitteilungsblatt **4596**
0934-4535 Allgemeine Zeitschrift fuer Paranormologie†
0934-456X Floristische Rundbriefe **789**
0934-4586 Fussball-Jahrbuch† **8958**
0934-4632 Unabhaengige Bauernstimme **164**
0934-4640 Deutsche Gesellschaft fuer Pharmakologie und Toxikologie. Mitteilungen
0934-4713 Neue Kronstaedter Zeitung **3853**
0934-4721 Informatik Betrifft Uns† **8964**
0934-5043 Formal Aspects of Computing **2418**
0934-506X Disziplinarrecht des Bundes und der Laender **7434**
0934-5086 Geriatrie und Rehabilitation† **8959**
0934-5094 Besoldungsrecht **1667**
0934-5140 Check-in†
0934-5175 Indienrundbrief†
0934-5213 Fauna und Flora in Rheinland-Pfalz **2611**
0934-5256 Praxis Spiel und Gruppe **2899**
0934-5272 Themenzentrierte Interaktion **7412**
0934-5337 Recherches Valeryennes **5166**
0934-5531 Fruehe Neuzeit **5298**
0934-554X Aktuelle Frauenforschung **8893**
0934-5620 Mannheimer Beitraege zur Oekonomischen Oekologie **2618**
0934-5639 Immobilien-Berater **7595**
0934-5744 Personalvertretungsrecht des Bundes und der Laender **1703**
0934-5841 Software Kurier†
0934-585X Woerkshop **37**
0934-5868 Stadtforschung und Statistik **7483**
0934-5914 Element und Bau **1006**
0934-5930 Eisenbahn Ingenieur Kalender (Year) **8616**
0934-5949 Verfahrensberichte zur Abwasserbehandlung **3492**
0934-6082 C G†
0934-6112 Advances in Disease Vector Research†
0934-6155 Zwischen Orient und Okzident **564**
0934-6198 Recht der Arbeiter und Angestellten im Oeffentlichen Dienst *changed to* 1862-0655 **1705**
0934-6252 Theatron **8483**
0934-6260 Stowage and Segregation Guide to I M D G Code **8663**
0934-6317 Kontinent **5222**
0934-6465 Bayerisches Staatsministerium des Innern. Allgemeines Ministerialblatt **7422**
0934-6570 Kinderzeit **2880**
0934-6643 Mertensiella **955**
0934-6694 Operative Orthopaedie und Traumatologie **6068**
0934-6740 Euro Transport Journal†
0934-6767 Statistische Rundschau Nordrhein-Westfalen†
0934-6805 Elektro- und Solarmobilbrief **8579**
0934-683X Baustoff, Recycling und Deponietechnik **3342**
0934-7054 F B M - Fertigungs-Technologie†
0934-7062 Geschmacksmusterblatt **6750**
0934-7100 Arbeitsrecht-Blaettei (A R) **4620**
0934-7135 Informationsdienst Naturschutz Niedersachsen **2614**
0934-716X Praxis Kultur- und Sozialgeographie **4025**
0934-7186 P C fuer Einsteiger **2579**
0934-7275 Monographs to Applied Entomology†
0934-7348 Powder Handling & Processing **8435**
0934-7445 Beitraege zum Recht der Sozialen Dienste und Einrichtungen **4628**
0934-7453 Mediaevistik **4243**
0934-764X Brussels Museum of Musical Instruments. Bulletin†
0934-7658 Konstanzer Schriften zur Rechtswissenschaft **4710**
0934-7879 Studien zur Altaegyptischen Kultur. Beihefte **2240**
0934-7909 Natur- und Ganzheitsmedizin†
0934-800X Land und Leute
0934-8026 Hausbau **1011**
0934-8069 S P + T. Liteinoe Proizvodstvo i Tekhnologiya Liteinogo Dela **6343**
0934-8077 M P T. Metallurgicheskoe Proizvodstvo i Tekhnologiya Metallurgicheskih Protsessov **6321**
0934-8387 Pneumologie **6217**
0934-8395 Thermo Med†
0934-8417 A F E T - Mitglieder - Rundbrief *changed to* 1862-0329 **3038**
0934-8441 Boerse Online **1612**
0934-845X Macintosh Magazin†
0934-8522 Materialdienst des Konfessionskundlichen Instituts **7806**
0934-8549 Abgesaegt†
0934-8557 B T H - Fussboden Forum†
0934-8603 N Vw Z Rechtsprechungs Report Verwaltungsrecht **4737**
0934-8611 Jakobus-Studien **7802**
0934-8654 Pocket & Laptop Computer
0934-8662 Elternforum **2853**
0934-8719 Inventaria Archaeologica The Netherlands†
0934-8727 Protoplasma Supplementum *see* 0033-183X **836**
0934-8786 Vanessas Zeitgeist
0934-8875 Waelzlagertechnik - Industrietechnik†
0934-8883 Naturschutz Heute **2621**
0934-8913 Nikephoros **4154**
0934-8964 Amtsblatt der Stadt Moenchengladbach **7420**
0934-9014 Parkett Magazin **4561**
0934-9022 Verbands-Handbuch **2270**
0934-9049 Deutsche Forschungsgemeinschaft. Jahresbericht. Programme und Projekte **7850**
0934-9057 Deutscher Vertriebs- und Verkaufs-Anzeiger **24**

ISSN

0936-174X Journal of Perinatal Medicine. Supplement *see* 0300-5577 **5996**
0936-1928 Euro-Focus†
0936-2045 Frankfurter Vortraege zum Versicherungswesen **4503**
0936-2398 Beitraege zur Rundfunkoekonomie **2357**
0936-2479 Bluegrass - Buehne **6550**
0936-2517 Ophthalmo Chirurgie **6048**
0936-2568 Soil Technology Series
0936-2711 Koelner Kriminalwissenschaftliche Schriften **4892**
0936-2762 Muenchener Aegyptologische Untersuchungen **4176**
0936-2770 Computer Graphik Topics
0936-2800 Zeitschrift fuer Bankrecht und Bankwirtschaft **1391**
0936-2835 Exceptionality **3040**
0936-2878 *see* 0343-9445 **2045**
0936-2940 Hochschule fuer Musik Koeln. Journal **6573**
0936-2959 Schriften zur Malakozoologie aus dem Haus der Natur Cismar **962**
0936-2967 Archiv fuer Geschiebekunde **6723**
0936-2975 Advances in Feed Technology†
0936-3033 Eurocargo *changed to* 1862-7250 **8503**
0936-3084 Handlungsbedingungen und Handlungsspielraeume fuer Entwicklungspolitik **7968**
0936-3475 Dumjahn's Jahrbuch fuer Eisenbahnliteratur **8616**
0936-3483 Stadtarchiv Sankt Augustin. Beitraege zur Stadtgeschichte **4267**
0936-3572 Asien-Pazifik *changed to* Asien-Pazifik. Wirtschaftshandbuch **1438**
0936-3580 Techno Digest†
0936-3599 Oldenburgische Wirtschaft **1408**
0936-367X Software A B C
0936-3777 Kinematograph **6505**
0936-3815 Berliner Tierfreund **318**
0936-3858 Beitraege zur Geschichte des Alten Moenchtums und des Benediktinertums **7785**
0936-3890 Germanistische Symposien **5300**
0936-3904 Symbiose **6882**
0936-3912 International Contributions to Hydrogeology **2795**
0936-3971 Blaue Jungs†
0936-4005 Kieler Werkstuecke. Reihe A: Beitraege zur Schleswig-Holsteinischen und Skandinavischen Geschichte **4237**
0936-4013 Der Mittler-Brief **6437**
0936-403X Praedica Verbum **7670**
0936-4048 Schriften zur Rechts- und Sozialwissenschaften **7999**
0936-4056 Gesundheit Heute **7518**
0936-4072 I L S I Human Nutrition Reviews†
0936-4129 Getraenkeherstellung Deutschland **604**
0936-4161 Kieler Werkstuecke. Reihe D: Beitraege zur Europaeischen Geschichte des Spaeten Mittelalters **4237**
0936-4242 Lichtenberg-Jahrbuch **644**
0936-4366 Kulturanalysen **7981**
0936-4471 Das Deutsche Autojahrbuch†
0936-4544 Messung von Gefahrstoffen **3500**
0936-4579 I H K Journal Koblenz **1404**
0936-4609 Museums - Eisenbahn **8620**
0936-465X Jahrbuch fuer Soziologiegeschichte **7976**
0936-4730 Stadtarchiv Bamberg. Ausstellungen **4267**
0936-4749 Darstellungen und Quellen zur Stadtgeschichte Bambergs **4213**
0936-4757 Stadtarchiv Bamberg. Veroeffentlichungen **4267**
0936-4773 Sozialgesetzbuch: Gesetzliche Krankenversicherung **4842**
0936-4838 Badische Bauern Zeitung **94**
0936-4935 Kieler Werkstuecke. Reihe C: Beitraege zur Europaeischen Geschichte des Fruehen und Hohen Mittelalters **4237**
0936-5036 Der Knuepfteppich **4544**
0936-5117 Wirtschaftsprueferkammer. Mitteilungen *changed to* W P K Magazin **1303**
0936-5141 Religion Betrifft Uns **7674**
0936-5184 Internationale Beziehungen **7246**
0936-5206 Muell-Handbuch **3509**
0936-5214 Synlett **2131**
0936-5249 Taschenlexikon Miet- und Wohnungsrechtlicher Entscheidungen **4792**
0936-5257 Taschenlexikon Versicherungsrechtlicher Entscheidungen **4525**
0936-5281 Lernhilfen fuer den Textilunterricht *changed to* 1619-8840 **8459**
0936-5362 Series in Microelectronics **3113**
0936-5370 Florian Hessen **3578**
0936-5400 AussenWirtschaft **1552**
0936-5656 Leitsatzkartei des Deutschen Rechts **4722**
0936-5745 Kartographisches Taschenbuch **4018**
0936-5761 Nachbarsprache Niederlaendisch **5154**
0936-577X Climate Research **6349**
0936-5796 Historische Mitteilungen der Ranke-Gesellschaft **4144**
0936-5818 Wetterkarte†
0936-5869 Historischer Verein Eichstaett. Sammelblatt **4229**
0936-5877 Palstek **8280**
0936-5885 Wirtschaft im Suedwesten **1194**
0936-5907 Cognitive Linguistics **5106**
0936-5931 Medizinische Genetik **875**
0936-5982 KiTa KinderTageseinrichtungen Aktuell. Ausgabe Bayern **2159**
0936-6075 Acta Paedopsychiatrica†
0936-6148 Geotechnical Abstracts†
0936-627X Reisen und Leben†
0936-6318 European Dairy Magazine **264**
0936-6547 Kiel **3851**
0936-6555 Clinical Oncology **6016**
0936-658X P Z Schriftenreihe **6866**
0936-6644 Standbein Spielbein **6537**
0936-6709 Sales Guide Cologne **2026**
0936-6768 Reproduction in Domestic Animals **8805**
0936-6784 Historical Social Research. Supplement *see* 0172-6404 **4228**
0936-6903 Biologie Heute†
0936-6911 Elektronenmikroskopie **899**
0936-692X M S R Magazin **3324**
0936-6954 Naturschutz, Landschaftspflege, Jagd- und Forstrecht **2621**
0936-6962 Scope **1903**
0936-6970 Praxis Schule 5-10 **3077**
0936-7098 Fachhochschule Muenchen. Studienfuehrer **2981**
0936-7152 Geriatrie Praxis†
0936-7160 Perinatal-Medizin†
0936-7195 G A M M Mitteilungen **5489**
0936-7233 Abhandlungen zum Studenten- und Hochschulwesen **2823**
0936-725X Anders Leben†
0936-7292 Z A P **4817**
0936-7446 Applaus **8465**
0936-7527 E I R Strategic Alert. Deutsche Ausgabe **5214**
0936-7543 EIR Strategic Alert *see* 0936-7527 **5214**
0936-7578 Spuren und Motive†
0936-7586 Die Philosophin† **8981**
0936-7624 Bike **8255**
0936-7748 Revocatio Historiae **4159**
0936-7772 Ethik und Unterricht **6918**
0936-7802 Stripspiegel
0936-7829 Rapport d'Exercice - D G-Bank *see* 1611-4396 **1335**
0936-8043 Familien und Jugend - Gottesdienste **7642**
0936-8051 Archives of Orthopaedic and Trauma Surgery **6056**
0936-806X Grafische Palette **7321**
0936-8159 G W A **25**
0936-8205 Pretosia Cassellana **4254**
0936-8272 Sigma Series in Pure Mathematics **5536**
0936-8299 Urspring Nachrichten **2307**
0936-8302 Top Agrar: Ausgabe B **162**
0936-8310 Top Agrar: Ausgabe R **162**
0936-8329 Top Agrar: Ausgabe S **162**
0936-8345 Northeimer Jahrbuch **4249**
0936-837X Muenchner Beitraege zur Voelkerkunde **348**
0936-8507 Intensivmedizinisches Seminar **5945**
0936-8515 Haeckel Buecherei
0936-8590 Detmold-Paderborner Beitraege zur Musikwissenschaft **6561**
0936-8671 Bundesamt fuer Sera und Impfstoffe. Paul-Ehrlich-Institut. Arbeiten **5589**
0936-871X Rasant†
0936-8760 Fertigung **6312**
0936-8787 Zeitschrift fuer Planung *changed to* 1613-8392 **1197**
0936-8833 Desktop Dialog **2570**
0936-8868 Konstanzer Schriften zur Sozialwissenschaft **7981**
0936-8930 Artist **473**
0936-8957 Meteor - Berichte **2813**
0936-8965 Reihe der Villa Vigoni **7262**
0936-9066 Caliber Club†
0936-9090 Magnus†
0936-9171 Dokumentationsdienst Asien und Suedpazifik. Ausgewaehlte Neuere Literatur† **8951**
0936-9198 Sozialversicherungs-Berater **1794**
0936-9228 Ergebnisse der Diagnostik, Therapie und Nachsorge **5610**
0936-9236 Krebsnachsorge und Rehabilitation **6026**
0936-9244 Skeptiker **6647**
0936-9589 Pharmacopsychiatry. Supplement **6174**
0936-9627 Kirchenzeitung fuer das Bistum Aachen **7803**
0936-9643 Sport-Inform. Ausgabe A†
0936-966X Sport-Inform. Ausgabe C†
0936-9678 Sport-Inform. Ausgabe D†
0936-9686 Vorhang Auf (Spplingen) **2220**
0936-9724 Muenstersche Beitraege zur Romanischen Philologie **5337**
0936-9732 Urologie Poster†
0936-9856 H V - Journal **1428**
0936-9872 Jahrbuch Frieden (Year)†
0936-9902 Ichthyological Exploration of Freshwaters **947**
0936-9937 Journal of Evolutionary Economics **1545**
0937-0048 Nationalpark Bayerischer Wald **2620**
0937-0242 Beringeria **6723**
0937-0277 Pflegen Ambulant *changed to* 1866-9611 **7541**
0937-0420 D L R - Nachrichten **52**
0937-0773 Interdisziplinaere Beitraege zur Kriminologischen Forschung **2655**
0937-0862 List Forum fuer Wirtschafts- und Finanzpolitik **1144**
0937-0927 Prisma (Hamburg)†
0937-0951 Taschenlexikon Arbeitsrechtlicher Entscheidungen **1710**
0937-096X Paediatrie Aktuell **6098**
0937-0994 Informationen und Berichte **4231**
0937-101X Image-Scene **6980**
0937-1060 Max-Planck-Institut fuer Meteorologie. Report **6390**
0937-1095 Jahrbuch Alte Musik **6578**
0937-1478 Lebensmittelchemie **3654**
0937-1532 Parodontologie **5860**
0937-1540 Dialog der Kirchen **7637**
0937-1583 Profi **148**
0937-1680 Steuer-Eildienst **1945**
0937-1761 Aktuelle Beitraege zur Sozialwissenschaftlichen Forschung **7946**
0937-1826 Bauidee **980**
0937-1877 Edition Orpheus **5288**
0937-2008 Izumi **552**
0937-2032 P P M P **6172**
0937-2105 Khoj **554**
0937-2148 Chemistry of Plant Protection Series†
0937-2172 Grundlagen der Weiterbildung *changed to* 1861-0501 **2925**
0937-2180 Familie und Recht **4909**
0937-2199 Das Buero (Planegg)
0937-2253 Informationsdienst V D I. Logistik Aktuell *changed to* Informationsdienst F I Z Technik. Logistik Aktuell **1242**
0937-230X GourmeTip International†
0937-2326 Garten und Handel†
0937-2369 E G Wirtschaftsrecht Aussenwirtschaft† **8952**
0937-2385 B D I Handbuch der Forschungs- und Innovationsfoerderung **1064**
0937-2415 Wirtschaftsverkehr mit dem Ausland†
0937-2423 Anschriften fuer die Aussenwirtschaft **1552**
0937-2474 Top Hotel **4399**
0937-2539 Erziehung und Wissenschaft im Saarland **2854**
0937-2555 Schutz Aktuell†
0937-261X Boersenverein des Deutschen Buchhandels. Jahrbuch†
0937-2628 Soziale Psychiatrie **6186**
0937-2644 Schleswig-Holstein. Jahrbuch - Heimatkalender
0937-2695 Oekologie der Voegel. Beihefte **911**
0937-2725 BioTec **759**
0937-2733 Fabrik 2000†
0937-2857 Top Magazin Essen **3858**
0937-2865 Top Magazin Hamburg **3858**
0937-2873 Forschung an der Universitaet Bielefeld *changed to* 1863-8775 **7840**
0937-2881 Limnologie Aktuell **2797**
0937-289X Krankenhauspsychiatrie **7382**
0937-292X Sporthandbuch Bremen†
0937-3012 Das Personal **1871**
0937-3039 Frankfurter Afrikanistische Blaetter **5120**
0937-3055 Lecture Notes in Bio-Organic Chemistry†
0937-3071 Auslaender in der Bundesrepublik Deutschland† **8932**
0937-3128 Diplomatische Missionen, Konsularische Vertretungen **7231**
0937-3136 Archiv der Aussenwirtschaft
0937-3160 Fremdsprache Deutsch **5120**
0937-3225 Philosophy and Artificial Intelligence
0937-3365 Schriften zur Europaeischen Rechts- und Verfassungsgeschichte **4940**
0937-3381 Autokosten und Steuern Aktuell **8562**
0937-339X Jahrbuch fuer Fuehrungs Kraefte des Rechnungswesens†
0937-3438 Aussenwirtschaftsrecht (Year)† **8932**
0937-3462 International Urogynecology Journal **5994**
0937-3527 Anna **8851**
0937-3535 *see* 0937-3527 **8851**
0937-3624 Jahrbuch zur Liberalismus Forschung **4148**
0937-3632 Steuern und Recht **1946**
0937-3691 Ilex **677**
0937-3721 Paderborner Historische Forschungen **4252**
0937-373X Tuebinger Mikropalaeontologische Mitteilungen **6731**
0937-3780 Duesseldorfer Uni-Zeitung **2282**
0937-3810 Arbeit und Oekologie Briefe *changed to* Gute Arbeit **3436**
0937-3853 Sozialgesetzbuch: Gesetzliche Rentenversicherung **4842**
0937-387X Umsatzsteuer-Kartei *changed to* Umsatzsteuer B M F - B F H **1953**
0937-3888 Deutscher Staedtetag. Reihe K: Beitraege zur Staedtischen Europaarbeit **7491**
0937-3918 Meininger Magazin **607**
0937-3934 AIDS - Brief†
0937-3969 Leica-Fotografie International **6970**
0937-3977 *see* 0937-3969 **6970**
0937-4019 I D W Fachnachrichten **1290**
0937-4043 Sinolinguistica **5174**
0937-406X Forum Angewandte Linguistik **5120**
0937-4108 W M Teil VI: Nachrichten ueber Optionen und Futures **1390**
0937-4167 Konstruktionspraxis **3351**
0937-4183 Materialwirtschaft und Logistik im Unternehmen **1779**
0937-4213 Gitarre und Bass **6569**
0937-4299 Informationsdienst F I Z Technik. Fluidtechnik, Oelhydraulik, Pneumatik **3230**
0937-4302 Informationsdienst F I Z Technik. Steuern, Regeln und Automatisieren von Maschinen und Anlagen **3231**
0937-4310 Informationsdienst F I Z Technik. Spanende Fertigungsverfahren, Drehen, Fraesen, Hobeln, Bohren, Schleifen, Abtragen *changed to* Informationsdienst F I Z Technik. Spanende Fertigungsverfahren und Werkzeugmaschinen, Drehen, Fraesen, Hobeln, Bohren, Abtragen **3231**
0937-4329 Informationsdienst F I Z Technik. Klima-, Reinraum-, Entstaubungs- und Trocknungstechnik, Kaelte- und Waermepumpentechnik **3479**
0937-437X Kieler Werkstuecke. Reihe F: Beitraege zur Osteuropaeischen Geschichte **4237**
0937-4426 B f S - Berichte **3165**
0937-4469 B f S - Schriften **3165**
0937-4477 European Archives of Oto-Rhino-Laryngology **6079**
0937-4523 Ethnopsychoanalyse **7355**
0937-4574 Der Verein **2270**
0937-4639 Office Design
0937-4760 Konstanzer Schriften aus Geld- und Aussenwirtschaft **1142**
0937-4787 Goettinger Beitraege zur Internationalen Uebersetzungsforschung **5301**
0937-4906 Macwelt **2577**
0937-4922 Sporthandbuch Hessen†
0937-4973 Aktuelle Beitraege zur Angewandten Psychologie **7332**
0937-518X Muensteraner Reihe **4515**
0937-5198 Entomologischer Verein Stuttgart. Mitteilungen **846**
0937-5325 Fandom Newsletter†
0937-5406 D I Y in Europe *changed to* 1868-0038 **4437**
0937-5414 Humanitaeres Voelkerrecht **4928**
0937-5449 Top Magazin Koeln **3858**
0937-5457 Gambit Revue† **8958**
0937-5511 Algorithms and Combinatorics **5468**
0937-552X Praevention und Rehabilitation **5698**
0937-566X Sporthandbuch Hamburg†
0937-5724 Wolfenbuetteler Mittelalter Studien **4279**
0937-583X Musik in Bayern **6595**
0937-5848 Frauen in der Einen Welt **8897**
0937-5864 Clarino **6556**
0937-5929 Dokumentationsdienst Asien und Suedpazifik. Reihe A† **8951**
0937-5937 Dokumentationsdienst Vorderer Orient. Ausgewaehlte Neuere Literatur† **8951**
0937-5945 Dokumentationsdienst Vorderer Orient. Reihe A† **8951**
0937-597X Karten **1363**
0937-5996 Informationsdienst F I Z Technik. Umformtechnik, Pressen, Schmieden, Waelzen, Biegen, Sintern *changed to* Informationsdienst F I Z Technik. Umformtechnik und Werkzeugmaschinen - Pressen, Schmieden, Waelzen, Ziehen, Biegen, Sintern **3231**
0937-6178 Das Kloecknerhaus†

ISSN

DIRECTORY 2010 0940-2993 9403

0939-0634 Deutsche Nationalbibliographie. Reihe N: Vorankuendigungen, Monographien und Periodika *changed to* 1611-0145 **631**
0939-0642 Deutsche Nationalbibliographie. Reihe T: Musiktontraeger *changed to* 1613-8945 **8156**
0939-0650 Argumente (Berlin) **92**
0939-0804 Rheingutebericht N R W **8831**
0939-0839 Bus Aktuell *changed to* 1865-4657 **8597**
0939-0863 Mining & Energy†
0939-0952 Selbstorganisation. Jahrbuch fuer Komplexitaet in den Natur-, Sozial- und Geisteswissenschaften† **8987**
0939-1037 Paedagogische Fuehrung. Ausgabe Rheinland-Pfalz/Saarland **3029**
0939-1045 Paedagogische Fuehrung. Ausgabe Bayern **3029**
0939-1053 Paedagogische Fuehrung. Ausgabe Berlin, Brandenburg, Mecklenburg-Vorpommern, Sachsen, Sachsen-Anhalt, Thueringen **3029**
0939-1096 Journal of Cellular Pharmacology†
0939-1134 Elektronik Revue
0939-1169 Springer Series in Soviet Mathematics **5537**
0939-138X Lydia **8872**
0939-1517 Journal of Neurology. Supplement **6154**
0939-1533 Archive of Applied Mechanics **3182**
0939-1592 Philipps-Universitaet Marburg. Vorgeschichtliches Seminar. Veroeffentlichungen **411**
0939-1614 Finanztest **2638**
0939-1916 Binnenschiffahrt **8491**
0939-1959 Handbook of International Documentation and Information **5011**
0939-1975 Publishers' International I S B N Directory (Year) **7570**
0939-1983 Archives of Virology. Supplementum **882**
0939-2033 Cerebro†
0939-2041 Kreis Wesel. Jahrbuch **7450**
0939-205X Engineering und Automation†
0939-2106 European Music Catalog of Scores†
0939-2165 Zollrecht **1956**
0939-2335 R W I - Konjunkturbrief†
0939-2416 C A D S
0939-2505 Fernsehwoche **3847**
0939-2548 Made in Europe Buyers' Guide†
0939-2564 Trigon **8075**
0939-2580 Religionsgeschichtliche Versuche und Vorarbeiten **7675**
0939-2629 Werkstoffe - in der Fertigung **8445**
0939-2645 Sachsen-Info **3330**
0939-2661 A I N S - Anaesthesiologie, Intensivmedizin, Notfallmedizin, Schmerztherapie **5767**
0939-2688 Training Aktuell **1798**
0939-2734 Euro Brief† **8954**
0939-2807 Darmstaedter Echo **3846**
0939-2815 Beitraege zur Geschichte der Sprachwissenschaft **5099**
0939-2904 Neue Beitraege zur Juelicher Geschichte **4248**
0939-2947 Roter Morgen **7180**
0939-298X D L R - Mitteilungen **52**
0939-3013 Perspektiven D S **7165**
0939-3021 Vera's Gluecks Ratgeber **8214**
0939-3099 Aktuelle Ostinformationen **7103**
0939-3188 Lexikon Strassenverkehrsrechtlicher Entscheidungen **8632**
0939-3250 Frankfurt von Hinten†
0939-3323 Aerzteblatt Mecklenburg-Vorpommern **5569**
0939-334X Geschichte der Pharmazie **6844**
0939-3382 America **8682**
0939-3390 Astro†
0939-3439 SchulVerwaltung. Ausgabe Brandenburg, Mecklenburg-Vorpommern, Sachsen, Sachsen-Anhalt, Thueringen und Berlin
0939-3471 Brandenburgisches Aerzteblatt **5588**
0939-3498 Brief Berater **4572**
0939-3501 Deutscher Jugendbund fuer Naturbeobachtung. Naturkundliche Beitraege **2608**
0939-351X Medizin, Gesellschaft und Geschichte **5676**
0939-3684 Material und Markt†
0939-3706 Sport Sciences International **8205**
0939-3722 Kreditwesengesetz **1365**
0939-3781 Halbasien†
0939-3846 Layout†
0939-3889 Zeitschrift fuer Medizinische Physik **6117**
0939-3897 Europaeische Gesellschaft fuer Katholische Theologie. Bulletin **7797**
0939-396X Meereswissenschaftliche Berichte **2812**
0939-3986 Brandenburgischen Landeshochschule Potsdam. Wissenschaftliche Zeitschrift†
0939-401X Sozialrecht & Praxis **8072**
0939-4044 Siehste!†
0939-415X Betrieb und Wirtschaft **1442**
0939-4192 Fussbodentechnik **1050**
0939-4273 Gruppenanalyse **7359**
0939-4354 Kind - Jugend - Gesellschaft *changed to* 1865-9330 **2158**
0939-4362 Coyote **6634**
0939-4435 Fruit Processing **603**
0939-4443 Berlin - Brandenburgische Handwerk **1396**
0939-4451 Amino Acids **722**
0939-4494 Euromecum **2980**
0939-4532 Bonner Studien zur Frauengeschichte **8894**
0939-463X Stadt Bochum. Wahlbuero. Wahlen in Bochum **7483**
0939-4648 Bielefelder Universitaetszeitung *changed to* H1 **2286**
0939-4656 Im Dienst der Kirche **7800**
0939-4664 Fermate **6566**
0939-4702 Deutsche Behindertenzeitschrift **3038**
0939-4729 Gemeinsames Ministerialblatt des Auswaertigen Amtes, des Bundesministers des Innern, des Bundesministers fuer Ernaehrung, Landwirtschaft und Forsten, des Bundesministers fuer Innerdeutsche Beziehungen, des Bundesministers fuer Jugend, Familie, Frauen und Gesundheit, des Bundesministers fuer Umwelt, Naturschutz und Reaktorsicherheit, des Bundesministers fuer Raumordnung, Bauwesen und Staedtebau **7438**
0939-4753 Nutrition, Metabolism & Cardiovascular Diseases **6666**
0939-4761 Kirchenmusikalische Nachrichten **6582**
0939-477X Gesundheitsblatt A O K Aktuell†
0939-4788 Super Electronics Jahrbuch
0939-4796 Westricher Heimatblaetter
0939-4826 Unicum **2305**
0939-4966 Geldanlage Berater **1626**
0939-4982 Marketing der Agrar- und Ernaehrungswirtschaft **203**
0939-5024 Phonai **5161**
0939-5032 Adressbuch Deutscher Bibliotheken†
0939-5075 Zeitschrift fuer Naturforschung. Section C: A Journal of Biosciences **712**
0939-5113 Studien zu Finanzen, Geld und Kapital **1384**
0939-5121 Theologie fuer die Praxis **7777**
0939-5164 Klinische Pharmakologie **6857**
0939-5199 T A N Z **7687**
0939-5296 Aufwind **4327**
0939-5326 Automobil-Elektronik **8563**
0939-5342 Werkzeuge **5461**
0939-5385 Historische Mitteilungen. Beihefte **4144**
0939-544X Bibliotheca Germanica. Series Nova **5263**
0939-5458 B L Journal†
0939-5474 Unterschiede†
0939-5482 Connotations (New York) **5278**
0939-5512 Dialektik *changed to* Zeitschrift fuer Kulturphilosophie **6962**
0939-5539 Dialog der Religionen†
0939-5547 Die GmbH **1927**
0939-5555 Annals of Hematology **5933**
0939-5563 Menora **4244**
0939-5571 Baeko Magazin **3671**
0939-561X Internationale Archaeologie **398**
0939-5687 Thueringer Zahnaerzteblatt **5868**
0939-5784 Berliner Aerzte **5584**
0939-5806 Jahrbuch fuer Transkulturelle Medizin und Psychotherapie **7367**
0939-5849 Gesamtverband Autoteile-Handel. Mitgliederverzeichnis **8582**
0939-5881 Neue Steuer-Informationen
0939-589X Polizei-Trendletter†
0939-5911 Sucht **2699**
0939-592X I F F - Ferienkurses. Vorlesungsmanuskripte **7015**
0939-5946 Beihefte zu Editio **5261**
0939-5970 Metis† **8974**
0939-6039 F V W International *changed to* 1864-340X **8702**
0939-6071 Politics and the Individual†
0939-6209 Rundschau fuer den Lebensmittelhandel **3681**
0939-6241 I R I S **5307**
0939-625X Die Wohnungswirtschaft **7616**
0939-6292 Medizin ohne Nebenwirkungen **6861**
0939-6314 Vegetation History and Archaeobotany **822**
0939-6322 Journal of Maternal - Fetal Investigation†
0939-6330 Zeitschrift fuer Fischkunde **969**
0939-6365 European Journal of Pain†
0939-6381 H N O - Mitteilungen **6080**
0939-6411 European Journal of Pharmaceutics and Biopharmaceutics **6838**
0939-6462 Rhetorik-Forschungen **5362**
0939-6586 Gestalten und Verkaufen **3733**
0939-6632 Forum der Geooekologie **3432**
0939-6640 Mineralien-Welt **4568**
0939-6667 Nuovo Oltreconfine†
0939-6721 Xiangqi Kurier
0939-6764 European Journal of Pediatric Surgery. Supplement **6243**
0939-6780 European Journal of Cardiac Pacing and Electrophysiology†
0939-6802 Top Tan **591**
0939-6977 Uebergaenge†
0939-7027 Socialmanagement *changed to* 1613-0707 **8072**
0939-7086 Beitraege zur Mathematischen Geologie und Geoinformatik†
0939-7116 Klinische Neuroradiologie *changed to* Clinical Neuroradiology **6194**
0939-7140 Zoology in the Middle East **970**
0939-7167 Studies of the Environmental Law Network International†
0939-723X Ferrari World **8580**
0939-7248 European Journal of Pediatric Surgery **6243**
0939-7256 Forum (Munich, 1962)†
0939-7280 R W I - Untersuchungen†
0939-7299 Z F F - Zeitschrift fuer Fremdsprachenforschung **5198**
0939-7329 Auto Zubehoer Markt: Die Sonderseiten **8561**
0939-7418 Machine Vibration†
0939-7434 Annual Report on Reactor Safety Research Projects **3164**
0939-7507 Erzieherbrief **7232**
0939-7531 Probleme des Friedens†
0939-7620 B B E Chef-Telegramm. Apotheken Spezial **1727**
0939-7639 B B E Chef-Telegramm. Textil Spezial **1727**
0939-7647 B B E Steuerpraxis **1727**
0939-7655 Design and Light
0939-7663 Drive und Control† **8951**
0939-7736 Naturhistorischer Verein der Rheinlande und Westfalens. Arbeitsgemeinschaft Rheinischer Koleopterologen. Mitteilungen **957**
0939-7817 Kinderleicht **3069**
0939-7825 Finanzierungs Berater
0939-7868 Zeitschrift fuer Ganzheitliche Tiermedizin **8815**
0939-7906 Acta Mechanica. Supplementum†
0939-7965 Fracht-Dienst **8644**
0939-7973 Tuebinger Beitraege zur Linguistik. Series A. Language Development **5189**
0939-799X Tuebinger Beitraege zur Anglistik **5390**
0939-8007 Drive und Control† **8951**
0939-8015 Design und Licht **4555**
0939-804X D G U Nachrichten **3413**
0939-8074 A K M - Studien **8084**
0939-8104 Krankenversicherung und Unfallversicherung in Rechtsprechung und Schrifttum† **8970**
0939-8147 Cor Europaeum†
0939-8171 Schuldrucker **2945**
0939-818X Studies in Arabic Language and Literature **5182**
0939-8317 B L M Schriftenreihe **2313**
0939-8333 Acta Romanica **5090**
0939-8368 E P E Journal **3094**
0939-8392 Leichtathletiktraining **8321**
0939-8414 First Class **4386**
0939-8430 Back Journal. Spezial
0939-8457 Die Heimstatt†
0939-8481 Arbeiten aus Anglistik und Amerikanistik. Buchreihe **5256**
0939-8503 Auf Einen Blick **3844**
0939-8511 Bravo Girl! **2180**
0939-852X Das Neue **3853**
0939-8538 Das Neue Blatt **3853**
0939-8546 Playboy (Munich) **6298**
0939-8562 Tina **4368**
0939-8570 Argumente und Fakten der Medizin **5577**
0939-8600 Journal of Experimental Animal Science **5907**
0939-8619 International Contact **6970**
0939-8627 Tobacco Journal International **8488**
0939-8635 Jugendpolitik **5222**
0939-8791 Deutsches Baublatt **1002**
0939-883X Jugend Musiziert **2157**
0939-8848 Straf- und Ordnungswidrigkeitenrecht in der Sozialversicherung†
0939-8856 D V Management†
0939-8872 Arbeitsplaetze in Umschlag- und Lageranlagen von Speditionsunternehmen† **8930**
0939-8937 *see* 0171-4317 **8610**
0939-8945 Forum fuer Fachsprachen-Forschung **5120**
0939-9186 Mitteilungen fuer Anthropologie und Religionsgeschichte **7664**
0939-9259 Informationsdienst Kunst **496**
0939-9275 K L A G E **5136**
0939-9399 Language in Performance **5140**
0939-9410 Film und Medien in der Diskussion **6500**
0939-9437 European Journal of Hospital Pharmacy†
0939-9445 Wildhaltung† **8998**
0939-9488 Pharmaceutical and Pharmacological Letters†
0939-9496 Kommunikation und Institution **5137**
0939-9577 Wirtschafts- und Rechtspraxis Neue Bundeslaender
0939-9585 International Association of Geodesy Symposia **2783**
0939-9712 Medien-Skripten **2333**
0939-9763 A S B Magazin **8022**
0939-9771 Deutsches Pfarrerblatt **7754**
0939-978X Phlebologie **5695**
0939-9909 I K **1429**
0940-0060 Praxis Aktuell. Ausgabe Brandenburg, Mecklenburg-Vorpommern, Ost-Berlin, Sachsen-Anhalt, Sachsen und Thueringen **8063**
0940-0079 Bioforum **657**
0940-0109 Mellitus Lauf **8187**
0940-0117 Interferenzen† **8965**
0940-0125 Weitergehen†
0940-0141 Muenchner Uni Magazin **2293**
0940-0184 Verkehrs Rundschau. Ausgabe B **8519**
0940-0265 Santag **560**
0940-0303 ScriptOralia **5172**
0940-0311 Taschenbuch der Telekom Praxis *changed to* Jahrbuch der Telekom Praxis **2328**
0940-032X G I T Spezial Separation **2100**
0940-0354 A D A C Handbuch: Unfall Ratgeber **4607**
0940-0362 Backjournal **3671**
0940-0389 Kieler Arbeitspapiere zur Landeskunde und Raumordnung **4018**
0940-0478 S P E L L **5171**
0940-0486 A V Invest *changed to* 1863-2963 **2311**
0940-0494 Merkblaetter fuer die Wasser-, Abwasser- und Schlammuntersuchung **3489**
0940-0516 Meissner Tageblatt **3853**
0940-0524 Riesaer Tageblatt **3856**
0940-0583 Neue Post **8877**
0940-063X Bochumer Fruehneuzeitstudien **4133**
0940-0648 Zeitschrift Marxistische Erneuerung **8018**
0940-0656 T V Hoeren und Sehen **2393**
0940-0745 Current Cancer Research **6017**
0940-0788 Languages of the World **5142**
0940-0990 Stadt und Gemeinde **7469**
0940-1008 Tanzforschung **2688**
0940-1059 H N O Highlights†
0940-1091 Der Lebensmittelbrief **3680**
0940-1334 European Archives of Psychiatry and Clinical Neuroscience **6139**
0940-1369 SchulVerwaltung. Ausgabe Niedersachsen *changed to* 1618-9167 **3032**
0940-1431 Laetare Schriftenreihe†
0940-1490 Stadtstreicher **3857**
0940-1571 Studies in English and Comparative Literature **5381**
0940-1598 Frankfurter Beitraege zur Lateinamerikanistik **5298**
0940-1644 Forschungen zur Brandenburgischen und Preussischen Geschichte. Beiheft **4220**
0940-1776 Lufthygienisches Ueberwachungssystem Niedersachsen **3488**
0940-1849 Metro Man†
0940-1954 Leipziger Jahrbuch zur Buchgeschichte **7566**
0940-1997 Rolf Kaukas Bussi Baer **2908**
0940-208X Kaese-Theke **266**
0940-2098 Adipositas†
0940-2136 Bibliotheca Weidmanniana **5263**
0940-2233 Akademie Gemeinnuetziger Wissenschaften zu Erfurt. Geisteswissenschaftlichen Klasse. Sitzungsberichte **7946**
0940-2241 Adademie Gemeinnutziger Wissenschaften zu Erfurt. Mathematisch-Naturwissenschaftlichen Klasse. Sitzungsberichte **7832**
0940-2306 Chelsea Hotel **5419**
0940-2322 Filmwaerts†
0940-2330 InterCamara
0940-2454 Deutsche Gaertnerpost **3728**
0940-2470 E P E **3376**
0940-2500 Medizin Dental Magazin **5855**
0940-2691 Draht und Kabel Panorama†
0940-2721 Deutsche Nationalbibliographie. Reihe D, Monographien und Periodika. Halbjahres-Verzeichnis **623**
0940-2810 Sozialgesetzbuch: Kinder- und Jugendhilfe **4842**
0940-2993 Experimental and Toxicologic Pathology **5612**

ISSN

0943-8793 Deutsche Bundesbank. Devisenkursstatistik **1224**
0943-884X Transplant International. Supplement *see* 0934-0874 **5724**
0943-898X Ophthalmologische Nachrichten **6048**
0943-9021 Edition Discours **7961**
0943-9064 Amtsblatt fuer Berlin **7487**
0943-9080 Fabrik†
0943-9099 Studies in the Western **5412**
0943-9129 Die Deutsche Volkshochschule
0943-9145 World Court Digest **4816**
0943-917X International Journal of Sports Medicine. Supplement **6230**
0943-9188 Fritz-Hueser-Institut fuer Deutsche und Auslaendische Arbeiterliteratur. Informationen **5407**
0943-9196 Selbstverwaltungsrecht der Sozialversicherung **8067**
0943-9242 Beitraege zur Popularmusikforschung **6548**
0943-9250 Symposium Medical **5719**
0943-9323 Germany. Bundesanstalt fuer Strassenwesen. Berichte: Strassenbau **3268**
0943-934X Industriearmaturen **3368**
0943-9358 Aachener Berichte Fuegetechnik **6342**
0943-9366 Transporting
0943-9382 Journal of Cancer Research and Clinical Oncology. Supplement **6024**
0943-9404 Cancer Chemotherapy and Pharmacology. Supplement **6011**
0943-9447 Mach Mal Pause **3852**
0943-9463 Polizeispiegel **2665**
0943-9471 Philologia Fenno-Ugrica **5160**
0943-9552 Schutzgemeinschaft Deutsche Nordseekueste. Schriftenreihe **2626**
0943-9609 Berliner Reihe **4495**
0943-9676 European Journal of Pediatrics. Supplement **6091**
0943-9692 Implantologie **5847**
0943-9773 Jagen Weltweit **8319**
0943-9846 Verein fuer Thueringische Geschichte. Zeitschrift **4277**
0943-9862 Geschichte der Meteorologie in Deutschland **6353**
0943-9919 Technische Vorschriften fuer Kraftfahrzeuge **8606**
0944-0097 JUSletter†
0944-0143 Z M T Contributions **711**
0944-0178 Sendtnera† **8988**
0944-0216 Recht der Gemeinnuetzigen Organisationen und Einrichtungen **8064**
0944-0291 Rohrblatt **6613**
0944-0321 Globulus **7858**
0944-0356 I F O Studien zur Innovationsforschung **1120**
0944-0364 Beauty Forum **585**
0944-0372 Design & Design **4537**
0944-0380 Apply† **8930**
0944-0577 Gesellschaft fuer Anlagen- und Reaktorsicherheit. Jahresbericht **3193**
0944-0585 F U: Nachrichten **2283**
0944-0658 Western Mail **6628**
0944-0690 TeleTalk **1845**
0944-0704 Grundwasserbericht **8824**
0944-0828 Monographien zur Bildenden Kunst **506**
0944-0844 TenDenZen (Year)†
0944-0852 Fremdsprachen, Eurokommunikation, Management
0944-0895 iBau Planungsinformationen. Regionalausgabe Brandenburg **4414**
0944-0917 Park **5233**
0944-0968 Finanzen *changed to* Euro mit Finanzen **1338**
0944-0984 Gast und Kueche†
0944-100X Juedische Quellen†
0944-1026 W M Teil Va: Nachrichten ueber Auslaendische Aktien, Anteile, Optionsscheine und Aktienaehnliche Werte **1389**
0944-1123 Medizinland
0944-1131 Gemeindeordnung fuer den Freistaat Sachsen **7438**
0944-1166 Journal of Hepato - Biliary - Pancreatic Surgery *changed to* Journal of Hepato - Biliary - Pancreatic Sciences **6248**
0944-1174 Journal of Gastroenterology **5927**
0944-1204 Steuer-Lexikon. Teil II. Aufsaetze, Verfuegungen, Erlasse, Einzelfragen, FG-Rechtsprechung *changed to* Steuer-Lexikon. Teil II. BMF-Schreiben, Erlasse, Verfuegungen, FG-Urteile, Aufsaetze **1945**
0944-1220 Rentenversicherung der Arbeiter und Angestellten†
0944-1271 Iranica **552**
0944-128X R d E - Recht der Energiewirtschaft **3145**
0944-1344 Environmental Science and Pollution Research **3486**
0944-1352 Juedische Familienforschung
0944-1395 Plastics Information Europe **7097**
0944-1492 Statistische Nachrichten der Stadt Nuernberg **7483**
0944-1506 Nuernberger Statistik Aktuell **7482**
0944-1514 Statistisches Jahrbuch der Stadt Nuernberg **7484**
0944-1530 Z E W Wirtschaftsanalysen **1534**
0944-1557 That Was Yugoslavia†
0944-1611 Schriften zur Politischen Ethik† **8987**
0944-1646 Mjaso i Moloko **3656**
0944-1670 Z U M A - Nachrichten **8151**
0944-1735 Das Naechste Spielemagazin
0944-1743 Computer-Spiele per Post **2475**
0944-1824 Tarif Aktuell **7471**
0944-1867 Informationsmittel fuer Bibliotheken†
0944-1921 Archive of Fishery and Marine Research *changed to* 0175-8659 **950**
0944-193X Windows†
0944-1948 Archives of Dermatological Research. Supplement **5872**
0944-1972 Spotlight **3857**
0944-1999 Mitteilungen zur Astronomiegeschichte† **8974**
0944-2006 Zoology **970**
0944-2065 Pro Fertighaus **1030**
0944-2111 Feine Adressen Stuttgart - Schwaben *changed to* 1861-9193 **3847**
0944-212X Anwalt- und Notarverzeichnis **1972**
0944-2162 Kult - Ali Agenda **5223**
0944-2219 Haus- und Grund in Deutschland (Ausgabe fuer Westfalen) **7592**
0944-226X Laparo-Endoskopische Chirurgie†
0944-2294 Euroclio. Etudes et Documents **7962**
0944-2316 Oberbayerisches Amtsblatt **7500**
0944-2367 Softwarefuehrer UNIX
0944-2405 Miroir et Image **6935**
0944-2499 Praxishandbuch Buchfuehrung und Steuern fuer Freiberufler und Kleinunternehmer **1161**
0944-2502 Zentralblatt fuer Arbeitsmedizin, Arbeitsschutz und Ergonomie **6689**
0944-2626 Panu Derech **7770**
0944-2669 Calculus of Variations and Partial Differential Equations **5477**
0944-2693 Gesetzliche Unfallversicherung **4504**
0944-2758 Der Fachberater **3729**
0944-2766 Stimme und Weg **6447**
0944-2774 I T & T I *changed to* 1611-2776 **2421**
0944-2901 Paedagogische Fuehrung. Hessen **3029**
0944-291X Fuer Sie Privat
0944-2936 Globus (Radolfzell-Moeggingen)†
0944-2952 Berichte des Forschungszentrums Juelich **7065**
0944-2979 Bildungsarbeit in der Zweitsprache Deutsch *changed to* 1619-8433 **2940**
0944-2995 Quellen und Darstellungen zur Geschichte von Stadt und Kreis Uelzen **4255**
0944-3045 Hildesheimer Jahrbuch fuer Stadt und Stift Hildesheim **4227**
0944-307X S u S - Schweinezucht und Schweinemast **299**
0944-310X Comtel†
0944-3169 Energieanwendung, Energie- und Umwelttechnik†
0944-3177 Der Deutsche Weinbau **602**
0944-3207 B L Z **3017**
0944-3215 Institut fuer den Wissenschaftlichen Film. Beitraege zu Zeitgeschichtlichen Filmquellen **6504**
0944-3223 Bank Magazin **1313**
0944-324X Deutschland-Journal **3846**
0944-3266 Jahrbuch fuer Geschichte und Theorie der Biologie **680**
0944-3509 Waerland **6999**
0944-3568 W M Teil III: Nachrichten ueber Deutsche Aktien, Anteile, Genussscheine, Kuxe und Optionsscheine **1389**
0944-3606 Blickpunkt Wirtschaft (Trier) **1396**
0944-3649 Deutsch-Franzoesische Kulturbibliothek **7958**
0944-3746 Elan†
0944-3754 Verlagsvertretungen **638**
0944-3932 H W Handwerkswirtschaft **1684**
0944-4017 Aktive Fotografie†
0944-4025 Profi Kosmetik **596**
0944-4033 Point of Sale **2352**
0944-405X L.O.G.O.S. Interdisziplinaer **6158**
0944-4165 Agrarsoziale Gesellschaft. Arbeitsbericht **8086**
0944-4173 KiTa KinderTageseinrichtungen Aktuell. Ausgabe Niedersachsen, Schleswig-Holstein, Hamburg, Bremen **2159**
0944-4181 Ruprecht Karls Universitaet Heidelberg. Personalverzeichnis **2299**
0944-419X ConChem Journal
0944-4211 Versicherungs - Dienst, P K V Informationsdienst
0944-4327 Nikephoros-Beihefte **4154**
0944-4351 KulturKommerz **1771**
0944-4459 Occupational Toxicants *changed to* 1860-496X **6680**
0944-4505 Der Schwarzwald **4262**
0944-453X Live Magazin Saar **5225**
0944-4564 Natuerlich Gaertnern **3744**
0944-4580 Ad Fontes **4196**
0944-4610 Jahrbuch fuer Recht und Ethik **4698**
0944-4645 D D W - Die Weinwissenschaft† **8947**
0944-467X Blue Print **7223**
0944-4718 Architecture and Detail† **8931**
0944-4734 Brennpunkt Gemeinde **7749**
0944-4769 Feine Adressen Muenchen **3847**
0944-5005 Auto Welt **8561**
0944-5013 Microbiological Research **891**
0944-5021 G R S - F **3193**
0944-5218 Kurstabellen
0944-5277 E-T-A-Hoffmann Jahrbuch **5287**
0944-5307 Telefonkarten Journal **4349**
0944-534X Total!†
0944-5579 Rechtsdienst der Lebenshilfe **8064**
0944-5587 Public Health Forum **7537**
0944-5633 Postdienst **2355**
0944-5641 A B C Europ Production **1551**
0944-5668 Arbeitsmappe Sozial- und Wirtschaftskunde **3118**
0944-5706 Jewish Studies Quarterly **7724**
0944-5730 Berichte zum Vogelschutz **902**
0944-5749 Mikado **1024**
0944-5765 Steuer-Brief fuer das Personalbuero *changed to* Mandanten-Information fuer das Personalbuero **1869**
0944-582X Akademie **6692**
0944-5846 ChemKon - Chemie Konkret **2057**
0944-5854 Reiten und Fahren St. Georg **8297**
0944-5897 Truck Modell **4349**
0944-5943 Ambulant Operieren **6235**
0944-5951 RadioLit†
0944-6028 B L Z **3052**
0944-6052 Arbeitsmedizin, Sozialmedizin, Umweltmedizin **7508**
0944-6117 Gefahr-Gut **8496**
0944-6125 ProMed *changed to* 1866-5756 **5700**
0944-6141 Connect **2349**
0944-6192 Our Cats **6812**
0944-6222 D V S Informationen†
0944-6273 Wahre Geschichten **5413**
0944-629X Jahrbuch fuer Historische Kommunismusforschung **4234**
0944-6303 W M Teil IIb: Sammelliste Gekuendigter und Verloster Wertpapiere **1389**
0944-6311 Konstanzer Schriften zur Entwicklungspolitik **7250**
0944-632X Burda Mode fuer Maedchen und Jungen
0944-6419 Arbeitsmedizin, Sozialmedizin, Umweltmedizin. Supplement **7508**
0944-6427 Burda Unser Baby
0944-6486 Chemotherapie Journal. Supplement *see* 0940-6735 **6015**
0944-6524 Production Engineering **3371**
0944-6532 Journal of Convex Analysis **5502**
0944-6575 Krisis **7149**
0944-6672 Wirtschaft Regional (Ausgabe Stuttgart)†
0944-6699 I N E M Bulletin†
0944-6729 Analog und Digital **7485**
0944-680X Fortschritte in der Neurotraumatologie und Klinischen Neuropsychologie **6141**
0944-6826 Luftwaffen-Forum†
0944-6850 Food P P P† **8957**
0944-6869 Ostthueringer Wirtschaft **1408**
0944-6877 Psychopharmakotherapie **6877**
0944-6885 Medizinprodukte Journal **5677**
0944-6982 Family (Witten) **2152**
0944-7008 Zeitschrift fuer Kanada-Studien **4319**
0944-7059 Aerzte-Brief Kassenabrechnung Aktuell *changed to* 1438-7166 **5564**
0944-7075 P C Aktiv†
0944-7105 Sexuologie **5712**
0944-7113 Phytomedicine **5696**
0944-713X Blick **2274**
0944-730X Deutsche Bank Research. Bulletin† **8949**
0944-7350 Bergische Wirtschaft **1396**
0944-7369 Hartmannbund Magazin **5623**
0944-7482 Print und Produktion **7326**
0944-7490 ReiseRecht aktuell **8751**
0944-7512 Interdisziplinaere Studien zur Entwicklung in Laendlichen Raeumen **200**
0944-7520 Sicherheits Markt *changed to* 1615-455X **2671**
0944-7598 Aktien-Analyze **1609**
0944-7652 Zeitschrift fuer Medizinische Ethik **5734**
0944-7687 Duesseldorfer Beitraege aus Anglistik und Amerikanistik *changed to* 1615-326X **5261**
0944-7725 Papilio Curiosus†
0944-7741 Aktuelle Fragen der Vermoegensanlagepraxis **4492**
0944-7776 Der Sicherheitsschirm *changed to* Bruecke **8448**
0944-7881 Verband Deutscher Fischereiverwaltungsbeamter und Fischereiwissenschaftler. Schriftenreihe **3611**
0944-7970 Medien und Theater **8473**
0944-8039 Libertas Optima Rerum **7251**
0944-8101 WeltTrends **7273**
0944-8136 Neue Musikzeitung. Allgemeine Ausgabe J M D *see* 0171-0133 **6599**
0944-8152 Textbooks for Knowledge Organization **5050**
0944-8160 Journal of Brain Research†
0944-8195 Neues Archiv fuer Saechsische Geschichte **4248**
0944-825X Fachdienst der Lebenshilfe† **8955**
0944-8365 Paderborner Beitraege zur Geschichte **4252**
0944-8373 Korea Forum **554**
0944-8438 Ausbildung Pruefung Fortbildung (Brandenburg Edition) **7421**
0944-8446 Nordrhein-Westfaelische Akademie der Wissenschaften. Jahrbuch **2294**
0944-8594 Grenzgaenge **5302**
0944-8608 Musikwissenschaftliche Publikationen **6597**
0944-8764 Magazin fuer die Polizei **2660**
0944-8780 Tiefbau **1040**
0944-8799 Nordrhein-Westfaelische Akademie der Wissenschaften. Vortraege Natur-, Ingenieur- und Wirtschaftswissenschaften **7893**
0944-8810 Nordrhein-Westfaelische Akademie der Wissenschaften. Geisteswissenschaften Vortraege **6937**
0944-8837 Nordrhein-Westfaelische Akademie der Wissenschaften. Abhandlungen. Sonderreihe Papyrologica Coloniensia **4249**
0944-8845 Bankhistorisches Archiv. Beiheft **1317**
0944-8918 Pflege Aktuell *changed to* 0340-5303 **5981**
0944-8942 Euro Cosmetics **594**
0944-8977 Forschungsbeitraege zu Handwerk und Technik **8422**
0944-9094 Journal for the Study of British Cultures **4459**
0944-9124 Echt **7755**
0944-9248 Garten Zeitung **3732**
0944-9337 Ausbilder Handbuch **1063**
0944-937X Bildung und Wissenschaft (Ludwigsburg) **2831**
0944-9442 Aletheia
0944-954X Studien zur Geschichte des Alltags **4270**
0944-9604 Sportwissenschaftliche Dissertationen und Habilitationen **8209**
0944-9841 Politische Zeitung, Wir in Europa *changed to* 1611-1567 **2189**
0945-0041 Campus **7843**
0945-0084 Kunststoffe - Plast Europe *changed to* 1862-4243 **7094**
0945-0173 Forum Medienethik†
0945-0270 Deutscher Bauernverband. Geschaeftsbericht **196**
0945-0327 Rundbrief Fotografie **6976**
0945-0416 D B B Magazin - Ausgabe Komba Bayern **4592**
0945-0424 D B B Magazin - Ausgabe Hamburg† **8947**
0945-0459 K I - Luft- und Kaeltetechnik *changed to* K I - Kaelte Luft Klimatechnik **4122**
0945-0491 OBJEKTspektrum **2502**
0945-053X Matrix Biology **5665**
0945-0556 Tinnitus-Forum **4076**
0945-0645 HobbyArt **4336**
0945-0653 Berichte aus der Agrarwissenschaft **95**
0945-0661 Berichte aus der Architektur **435**
0945-067X Berichte aus dem Bauwesen **981**
0945-0688 Berichte aus der Biologie **656**
0945-0696 Berichte aus der Betriebswirtschaft **1728**
0945-070X Berichte aus der Chemie **2051**
0945-0742 Berichte aus der Fahrzeugtechnik **8569**
0945-0777 Berichte aus der Geowissenschaft **2702**
0945-0793 Berichte aus der Hochfrequenztechnik **7006**
0945-0807 Berichte aus der Informatik **5550**
0945-0823 Berichte aus der Kommunikationstechnik **2313**
0945-084X Berichte aus der Lasertechnik **7074**
0945-0858 Berichte aus der Literaturwissenschaft **5262**
0945-0890 Berichte aus der Medizin **5584**
0945-0904 Berichte aus der Metallurgie **6306**
0945-098X Berichte aus der Rechtswissenschaft **4629**
0945-0998 Berichte aus der Sozialwissenschaft **7950**
0945-1021 Berichte aus der Verfahrenstechnik **3236**
0945-1056 Berichte aus der Werkstofftechnik **3342**
0945-1064 Schriftenreihe Zentralblatt fuer Arbeitsmedizin† **8987**

ISSN

0947-756X Forum Wirtschaftsethik 1111
0947-7616 Flug- und Reisemedizin *changed to* 1864-4538 5614
0947-7713 KiZ fuer Kids†
0947-7748 Spektrum Hoeren 4076
0947-7756 Berichte aus der Astronomie 572
0947-7772 Bootsmarkt 8273
0947-7780 GynLit†
0947-7799 PsychNeuro Disk-Archiv†
0947-7802 Chirurgie Plus Disk-Archiv†
0947-787X Markenblatt 6754
0947-7969 Online I S D N†
0947-7993 Koelner Arbeiten zur Internationalen Politik 7250
0947-8094 Kirche und Recht 4709
0947-8116 Muenzen und Papiergeld 6651
0947-8175 Highlight 4558
0947-823X General and Diagnostic Pathology†
0947-8302 Musik in Baden-Wuerttemberg 6595
0947-8337 B J V Report 4572
0947-8353 Afrika Sued 1590
0947-8388 P C - Spiel†
0947-8396 Applied Physics A 7005
0947-8485 Tabula Rasa
0947-8493 Edi-Change†
0947-8507 P E T A's Animal Times (German Edition) 321
0947-8515 Surfers 8268
0947-854X Byzantinische Zeitschrift. Supplementum Bibliographicum *see* 0007-7704 545
0947-8582 Emslaendische Geschichte 4217
0947-8620 Forschungszentrum Karlsruhe. Wissenschaftliche Berichte 3432
0947-8655 Leipziger Beitraege zur Bach-Forschung 6584
0947-8701 Belser Kunst Quartal *changed to* 1860-0530 6527
0947-871X C D Sicherheits-Management 2676
0947-8736 Klinik & Forschung 5658
0947-8914 Renova
0947-8922 Image Hifi 3104
0947-8949 Handballwoche 8235
0947-8957 Forum Erziehungshilfen 8041
0947-8965 Der Onkologe 6031
0947-899X Designers Digest 486
0947-904X Euros†
0947-9104 Wirtschaftsreport Estland, Lettland, Litauen
0947-9155 Unterwasser 8214
0947-9163 Melliand International 8455
0947-9198 Marly - Rechtsprechung zum Computerrecht†
0947-9252 StraFo - Strafverteidiger Forum 4898
0947-9287 Klassik Uhren 4488
0947-9333 Konstruktion und Engineering 1020
0947-9368 Focus Afrika 7136
0947-9430 Metallbau und Aluminium - Kurier 1023
0947-9449 Miniboerse 7807
0947-9481 D H F *changed to* D H F Intralogistik 5451
0947-949X D H F Actuell *see* D H F Intralogistik 5451
0947-9511 Journal of European Integration History 7248
0947-9538 Volucella 861
0947-9546 Wissenschaftsmanagement 7929
0947-9597 Das Ostpreussenblatt 3854
0947-9732 Tertium Comparationis 3015
0947-9767 Bauernblatt 94
0947-9805 MessTec Jahrbuch 3370
0947-9856 Verwaltung und Management 4808
0947-9953 Funky Handy 2321
0948-003X Caritas und Pflege 5954
0948-0048 Facility Management 1851
0948-0161 Bravo Sport 8163
0948-0188 B D K J Journal 7785
0948-0218 Wissenschaftsrecht 4815
0948-0285 Bremer Jahrbuch fuer Musikkultur 6551
0948-0293 Hamburg Port Tariffs with Brunsbuettel and Cuxhaven
0948-0331 Neue Palaeontologische Abhandlungen 6727
0948-0382 Electronic Journal of Pathology and Histology†
0948-0390 Berliner Dialog 7625
0948-0463 Markant HandelsMagazin 29
0948-0528 Visier Special 8340
0948-0552 Paedagogische Fuehrung. Nordrhein-Westfalen 3029
0948-0587 Zeitschrift fuer Altorientalische und Biblische Rechtsgeschichte 563
0948-0625 W I S O SteuerBrief 1954
0948-0633 Abrechnung Aktuell 1276
0948-065X Medizin und Ethik 5676
0948-0684 Kloeckner Werke Heute 6320
0948-079X Landesumweltamt Nordrhein-Westfalen. Jahresbericht 3450
0948-0919 Forschungszentrum Karlsruhe. Nachrichten 3432
0948-0935 Arbeit und Gesundheit. Sonderausgabe Verkehr 7508
0948-1052 Wild und Hund Exklusiv 8341
0948-1125 Ugaritsch-Biblische Literatur 7691
0948-1168 Polster-Fashion 4562
0948-1214 Fassadentechnik 1008
0948-1222 Arbeitsgemeinschaft fuer Rheinische Musikgeschichte. Mitteilungen 6545
0948-1257 Leipziger Geowissenschaften 2786
0948-1354 Sprache im Kontext 5377
0948-1427 Wissenschaftliche Berichte F Z K A - P F T 3475
0948-146X Experimental and Clinical Endocrinology and Diabetes. Supplement 5892
0948-1494 Studien zur Translation 5182
0948-1605 Zeitpunkt-Kulturmagazin 3860
0948-163X Mobilcom†
0948-1680 Ost-West-Contact 1579
0948-1702 Dialog 3846
0948-1737 Altertumskunde des Vorderen Orients 542
0948-177X Bamberger Theologische Studien 7624
0948-1842 PflegePartner 6113
0948-1850 Aktuelles Steuerrecht 1910
0948-1885 Literatur zur Interkulturellen Paedagogik 8118
0948-1893 Center for International Research on Economic Tendency Surveys. Studien 1081
0948-1907 Chemical Vapor Deposition 2109
0948-1923 Indian Philology and South Asian Studies 5127
0948-1931 Publishing Praxis 7580
0948-194X Osnabruecker Jahrbuch Frieden und Wissenschaft 7896
0948-1966 Unterrichten mit Geographie Aktuell 4033
0948-2105 DEMO 7491
0948-2148 Experimental Technique of Physics†
0948-2210 Zeitschrift fuer Verkehrserziehung 8637
0948-2393 Zeitschrift fuer Geburtshilfe und Neonatologie 6006
0948-2407 Disput 7130
0948-2520 Boxsport 8163
0948-2547 Kino *changed to* German Films Quarterly 6502
0948-2598 Baby und die Ersten Lebensjahre *changed to* 1861-0552 8852
0948-2628 Deutsche Hockey Zeitung 8169
0948-2644 Oeko-Test 2640
0948-2652 TrendInfo 7485
0948-2717 T V Today 2394
0948-2725 Plexus 5773
0948-2784 Mannheimer Geschichtsblaetter. Neue Folge 4242
0948-2806 Beitraege zur Kenntnis Suedasiatischer Sprachen und Literaturen 544
0948-2822 Haut & Allergie Aktuell 5758
0948-2873 P C Go! 2595
0948-2881 Enduro 8258
0948-289X Deutsches Handwerks-Journal†
0948-2962 Niedersachsen-Tennis 8191
0948-2970 Graue Literatur zur Stadt-, Regional- und Landesplanung 4411
0948-3055 Aquatic Microbial Ecology 881
0948-311X Archaeologie in Berlin und Brandenburg 377
0948-3128 M S T News 2473
0948-3144 Abhandlungen zur Literatur Alt-Syrien-Palaestinas und Mesopotamiens 5089
0948-3209 R P G†
0948-325X Benni und Teddy 2179
0948-3276 K G K. Kautschuk, Gummi, Kunststoffe 7825
0948-3314 Kita 554
0948-3349 International Journal of Life Cycle Assessment 3443
0948-3357 Stauffenburg Discussion 3015
0948-3365 Stauffenburg Einfuehrungen 5178
0948-3403 Acta Universitatis Scodvensis 5090
0948-3411 Kuechenprofi 4560
0948-3470 B I S S 3844
0948-3535 Huddle 8235
0948-3578 Tipp Mit 8212
0948-3756 Jahrbuch der Landesmedienanstalten 2359
0948-3853 Preussischer Kulturbesitz. Staatsbibliothek zu Berlin. Beitraege 5040
0948-387X Medien und Bildung†
0948-3950 Selected Readings in Computer Graphics 2489
0948-4124 Der Budoka 8163
0948-4167 Beschreibende Sortenliste Getreide, Mais, Oelfruechte, Leguminosen und Hackfruechte 270
0948-4221 D G S Intern 284
0948-423X Soziale Systeme 8140
0948-4248 Steuer-Brief fuer Personengesellschaften† 8990
0948-4264 Altmuehlseeberichte 901
0948-4280 Journal of Marine Science and Technology 2809
0948-4310 Forschungszentrum Karlsruhe. Ergebnisbericht ueber Forschung und Entwicklung 3167
0948-4396 Zeitschrift fuer Oeffentliches Recht 4819
0948-4523 Comixene 482
0948-4531 Gala 8865
0948-4647 Lebendige Tierwelt 320
0948-4787 FEhS - Institut fuer Baustoff-Forschung. Schriftenreihe 3506
0948-4825 Netrunner†
0948-4914 Genau 7092
0948-4949 Olli und Molli 2206
0948-5007 Gesellschaft fuer das Buch 5011
0948-5023 *see* 1610-2940 2137
0948-5074 Statistisches Landesamt Rheinland-Pfalz. Statistisches Taschenbuch 7484
0948-5139 Jahrbuch fuer Wirtschaftswissenschaften 1246
0948-5155 Ersatz- und Ergaenzungsmethoden zu Tierversuchen 5905
0948-5163 Kapitalmarktrecht 1636
0948-5201 Backen Leichtgemacht 3671
0948-5228 Kontenrahmen fuer die Traeger der Gesetzlichen Krankenversicherung, Kontenrahmen fuer die Traeger der Sozialen Pflegeversicherung und den Ausgleichsfonds 7530
0948-5279 Herder Jahrbuch 4226
0948-535X F Z K A - Projekt Europaeisches Forschungszentrum fuer Massnahmen zur Luftreinhaltung†
0948-5430 A B I T International
0948-5511 F Z K A - Projekt Umwelt und Gesundheit. Berichte†
0948-5538 Beitraege zur Zuechtungsforschung† 8935
0948-5627 Implant
0948-5643 Blues News 6550
0948-5678 Music Publishers' International I S M N Directory†
0948-5945 Handbuch der Leitungs- und Wegerechte 7443
0948-5953 Umweltbrief 2630
0948-6003 Wirtschaftsreport Tschechische Republik - Slowakische Republik
0948-6011 Wirtschaftsreport - Economic Report Romania, Bulgaria
0948-602X Wirtschaftsreport Russland - Ukraine†
0948-6038 Nova Supplementa Entomologica 856
0948-6070 Hallesche Beitraege zur Europaeischen Aufklaerung 4225
0948-6097 Weltraum-Philatelie 6901
0948-6119 Equitrends 8291
0948-6135 Studium Integrale Journal 706
0948-6143 Histochemistry and Cell Biology 833
0948-6216 Klerusblatt 7804
0948-6224 Pfarramtsblatt
0948-6259 Neuropsychiatrie 6167
0948-6283 Mitteilungsblatt - Gesellschaft Deutscher Chemiker, Fachgruppe Umweltchemie und Okotoxikologie *changed to* 1617-5301 2073
0948-6402 Norddeutsches Handwerk. Ausgabe Braunschweig *see* Norddeutsches Handwerk 1900
0948-6410 Norddeutsches Handwerk. Ausgabe Hildesheim *see* Norddeutsches Handwerk 1900
0948-6429 Norddeutsches Handwerk. Ausgabe Lueneburg-Stade *see* Norddeutsches Handwerk 1900
0948-6445 Norddeutsches Handwerk. Ausgabe Oldenburg *see* Norddeutsches Handwerk 1900
0948-6453 Norddeutsches Handwerk. Ausgabe Ostfriesland *see* Norddeutsches Handwerk 1900
0948-6461 O P Druckmagazin
0948-6488 Allegra† 8929
0948-6496 Freizeit und Raetselmagazin 8174
0948-650X Frau mit Herz 8864
0948-6526 Abhandlungen der Delattinia 648
0948-6534 Schriftenreihe Aus Natur und Landschaft im Saarland. Sonderband *see* 0948-6526 648
0948-6550 Laurentius Flugschriften 5024
0948-6631 Heimatbuch des Kreises Viersen 4141
0948-6682 Autoflotte 8562
0948-6704 Zeitschrift fuer Gerontologie und Geriatrie 4057
0948-6879 Monitoring Greifvoegel und Eulen Europas. Jahresbericht 910
0948-695X Journal of Universal Computer Science 2430
0948-6976 Materialhefte zur Archaeologie des Mittelalters und der Neuzeit 405
0948-7018 Universitaet Dortmund. Lehrstuhl fuer Anlagensteuerungstechnik. Schriftenreihe 3257
0948-7026 Management, Rechnungslegung und Unternehmensbesteuerung 1934
0948-7034 Gefaesschirurgie 6244
0948-7050 Dokumente der Luft- und Raumfahrtindustrie† 8951
0948-7131 Hexenforschung 4227
0948-7247 Rinderzucht Fleckvieh 299
0948-7255 European Studies in the History of Science and Ideas 7963
0948-7263 Deine Bahn 8616
0948-728X N T Z 2334
0948-7387 E T Z 3301
0948-7395 Gemmologie 4566
0948-7417 Sprachkontakt in Afrika† 8990
0948-7441 Wohnungslos 8078
0948-7557 Matices 7252
0948-762X Kurier Bayer 241
0948-7697 Verlage - Vertretungen - Auslieferungen (Year) 638
0948-7727 Al Rafidayn - Jahrbuch zu Geschichte und Kultur des Modernen Iraq 4324
0948-7794 Der Aktuar 4491
0948-7905 Burda Fasching 2252
0948-7913 Notfallvorsorge 2227
0948-7921 Electrical Engineering 3303
0948-7964 Kicker - Sportmagazin. Sonderheft Bundesliga *see* 0023-1290 8184
0948-7980 Rundschau - Fachzeitschrift fuer Internationale Damenmode und Schnitt-Technik 2260
0948-7999 Gegenbilder 8103
0948-8030 Bausteine 981
0948-8251 Expressdienst Umweltrecht† 8955
0948-8294 Zeitschrift fuer Ostmitteleuropa-Forschung 4280
0948-8340 Markt und Mittelstand 1147
0948-8359 Archaeologisches Nachrichtenblatt 377
0948-8405 Kleine Uelzener Kunstfuehrer 4237
0948-843X Mobil und Sicher 8737
0948-8448 Rundschau - Fachzeitschrift fuer Internationale Herrenmode und Schnitt-Technik 2249
0948-8456 Rarissima Litterarum 5357
0948-8464 Verbraucherschutz, Produktsicherheit, Umweltschutz 2642
0948-8588 Apotheken-Depesche 6821
0948-8596 Praxis-Depesche 5699
0948-8634 Betrieb und Management†
0948-8642 Laura 8871
0948-8650 Handschriften des Altaegyptischen Totenbuches 550
0948-8677 Kleine Bibliothek fuer das 21. Jahrhundert†
0948-8685 Portraits Oesterreichischer Architekten 453
0948-8731 Ecos de Espana y Latinoamerica 3951
0948-8758 A G P Mitteilungen 1661
0948-8782 Zeitschrift fuer Berufliche Umweltbildung 3476
0948-8790 Praxis der Freiwilligen Gerichtsbarkeit 4840
0948-8855 Convenience Shop 3677
0948-891X Moebelfertigung 4561
0948-8928 Junges Wohnen 4559
0948-8936 Spot Markt 4562
0948-8944 Arcade 4553
0948-9002 Deutsche Seeschiffahrt 8642
0948-9053 Handbuch Milch 264
0948-9061 Anna Hardanger 6636
0948-9096 Wissenschaft Ohne Grenzen 7929
0948-9118 Rinderzucht Braunvieh 299
0948-9185 Ton - Video Report 8155
0948-9363 Sport-Kurier
0948-941X Berliner Beitraege zur Amerikanistik 4285
0948-9428 Freie Universitaet Berlin. John F. Kennedy-Institut fuer Nordamerika Studien. Materialien 4293
0948-9479 Catering Management 3630
0948-9487 G I T Spezial Sicherheit und Management 6677
0948-9533 D N W E Schriftenreihe 1674
0948-9592 Osteuropa Institut Muenchen. Veroeffentlichungen. Reihe Forschungen zum Ostseeraum 4251
0948-9770 Stadt und Gruen 3751
0948-9878 Zeitschrift des Forschungsverbundes S E D - Staat 7197
0948-9908 Der Sachverstaendige 1424
0948-9959 Umwelt- und Energie-Report
0949-0078 Bonner Illustrierte† 8937
0949-0086 Hallesche Forschungen 4225
0949-0124 Bibliographie der Deutschsprachigen Frauenliteratur 618
0949-0140 Hochzeit 5558
0949-0175 Auktionen und Investment
0949-0205 Zement - Kalk - Gips International 3287
0949-0213 Jahrbuch der Psychoonkologie 6023
0949-023X Schriften ueber Sprachen und Texte 5172
0949-0248 Nova Hotel†

DIRECTORY 2010 0950-2645 9411

0949-0345 Das Mittelalter 4245
0949-0396 Auslandskurier† 8932
0949-040X Diplomatisches Magazin 7433
0949-0426 Magazin - A E G†
0949-0434 Eurasia Antiqua 393
0949-0450 Iguana-Rundschreiben *changed to* Iguana 947
0949-0469 Puppenmachen 4061
0949-0663 G S F Mensch und Umwelt Spezial 3432
0949-0671 Mensch und Umwelt 3452
0949-0698 Die Kommunalverwaltung Sachsen-Anhalt 7495
0949-0701 Die Kommunalverwaltung Mecklenburg-Vorpommern 7495
0949-0795 Okamatsu Bunko 557
0949-0833 Markt- und Planungsdaten fuer die Bauwirtschaft†
0949-0884 Auto-Katalog 8558
0949-0892 Motorrad Katalog 8264
0949-1031 Business Law Europe†
0949-1147 Zeitschrift fuer Didaktik der Naturwissenschaften 2928
0949-1295 Facetten 5487
0949-149X International Journal of Engineering Education 3201
0949-152X Arbeitshefte Baugrund†
0949-1538 Arbeitshefte Boden†
0949-1546 Arbeitshefte Deponien† 8930
0949-1554 Arbeitshefte Geologie† 8930
0949-1589 Rechtsprechung zum Umweltschutz 3462
0949-1597 Saechsische Landesanstalt fuer Landwirtschaft. Schriftenreihe 154
0949-1619 Psych. Pflege Heute 6175
0949-1635 Forum D (Deutsche Ausgabe)†
0949-1740 Berufskraftfahrer Zeitung 8669
0949-1775 Accreditation and Quality Assurance 2096
0949-1791 Phonus 5161
0949-1821 Koelner Beitraege zur Ethnopsychologie und Transkulturellen Psychologie 7382
0949-183X Molecular Modeling Annual *see* 1610-2940 2137
0949-1872 Direkte Aktion 1477
0949-1953 Recht und Wahrheit 7176
0949-2100 A f P 4607
0949-216X EineWelt 7755
0949-2186 N St Z Volltext CD-ROM *see* 0720-1753 4894
0949-2194 Bundesliga (Year) 8224
0949-2216 B f S - E T 3165
0949-2275 Stavebni Materialy 1037
0949-2283 G M D Geschaeftsbericht 2419
0949-2321 European Journal of Medical Research 5611
0949-2356 Intelligente Architektur 446
0949-2364 Jahrbuch Leopoldina (Reihe 3) 7870
0949-2380 Shape Up 6996
0949-2402 CO'MED 308
0949-2410 Archaeologie in Eurasien 377
0949-2461 P C Intern† 8979
0949-2488 Via Medici 5728
0949-2496 Volante
0949-2526 O L G Report Bremen, Hamburg, Schleswig *changed to* 1860-5435 4750
0949-2569 Yoyo†
0949-2577 Bremer Kirchenzeitung 7749
0949-2585 Amtsblatt des Hessischen Kultusministeriums 7420
0949-2615 Hyperboreus 2235
0949-2658 Journal of Orthopaedic Science 6065
0949-2720 Glas 443
0949-2852 Schueler 2910
0949-2860 Steuer-Brief fuer Architekten und Ingenieure† 8990
0949-2917 Industrie- und Handelskammer zu Dortmund. Statistisches Jahrbuch 1242
0949-2933 Live Music Artist†
0949-2984 Finance and Stochastics 1343
0949-2992 Gemeinnuetzigkeit und Management *changed to* 1439-4057 1794
0949-3026 Ecotropica 786
0949-3131 Diners Club Magazine 8698
0949-3182 N H Z 5228
0949-3204 B f S - K T 3165
0949-3212 B f S - S T 3165
0949-3220 Dokumentation Public Health, Oeffentliches Gesundheitswesen, Gesundheitswissenschaften†
0949-3247 Jedermensch 7145
0949-328X Sport-Orthopadie - Sport-Traumatologie 6233
0949-3328 O S - 2 Softwarefuehrer
0949-3409 Jahrbuch fuer Deutsche und Osteuropaeische Volkskunde 3619
0949-3417 Adam 4370
0949-3441 Onkologie-Service Aktuell 6031
0949-3476 Lindenmaier - Moehring Nachschlagewerk des Bundesgerichtshofs 4835
0949-3506 Denkmalpflege in Sachsen-Anhalt 485
0949-3565 Schuh-Werk
0949-3581 Food, Nonfood und Getraenke 3640
0949-3867 GeschaeftsWelt *changed to* 1612-7110 1162
0949-3972 Sielmanns Abenteuer Natur†
0949-4065 Boots Boerse 8273
0949-4073 Sprint†
0949-4499 Bildwoche 3845
0949-4502 T V Neu 2393
0949-4529 Esperiana 847
0949-4596 Mainzer Vortraege 4242
0949-4618 Hamburger Abendblatt 3849
0949-4642 Bio Magazin 6983
0949-4669 D F V - Familie 2150
0949-4723 I M I S - Beitraege 7284
0949-4766 N J W Cassetten *see* 0341-1915 4740
0949-4774 DStR - Cassetten *see* 0949-7676 1920
0949-4790 Funk Uhr (Ausgabe Ost) *see* 0932-6901 2381
0949-4855 Balagan 8466
0949-5045 B Z 3844
0949-5053 B Z am Sonntag 3844
0949-5096 Bild 3845
0949-5126 Berliner Morgenpost 3844
0949-5231 Bibliographie zur Europaeischen Dimension des Bildungswesen†
0949-5304 Magdeburger Wissenschaftsjournal 7880
0949-541X Topicos 8010
0949-5428 My Lady 5411
0949-5436 MyLady Weihnachtsband 5411
0949-5479 Dortmunder Bekanntmachungen 3846
0949-5487 Lufthanseat 8548
0949-5495 Der Nord-Berliner 3854
0949-5525 Tiffany† 8993
0949-5533 Tiffany Duo† 8993
0949-5541 Wirtschaft im Suedoestlichen Westfalen 1412
0949-5568 Historical 5410
0949-5576 Historical Gold 5410
0949-5584 Historical Gold Extra 5410
0949-5614 Das Andere Deutsche Nachrichtenmagazin†
0949-5681 Berichte der Forschungsstelle Kueste 2604
0949-569X Romana 5412
0949-5703 Romana Exklusiv 5412
0949-5770 Microform and Imaging Review 5032
0949-5835 Bianca 5409
0949-5843 Bianca Hochzeitsband *changed to* 1862-9555 5410
0949-5851 Bianca Exklusiv 5409
0949-5886 Baccara 5409
0949-5894 Collection Baccara 5409
0949-5908 Evangelische Arbeitsgemeinschaft fuer Kirchliche Zeitgeschichte. Mitteilungen 7641
0949-5916 Julia 5410
0949-5924 Julia Extra 5410
0949-5932 Journal of Lie Theory 5504
0949-6025 Die Probe 3371
0949-605X Schriftenreihe zur Politischen Kultur der Weimarer Republik 4262
0949-6092 Z T 5869
0949-6130 Julia Prestige 5410
0949-6181 Journal for East European Management Studies 1763
0949-622X Aktiv (Hannover) 6120
0949-6351 Jaeger und Fischer 8319
0949-636X Schriftenschau fuer den Feldherpetologen 962
0949-6394 Parfums 595
0949-6432 Romana Valentinsband *changed to* 1862-4421 5411
0949-6459 European Aggregates†
0949-6483 Julia Exklusiv 5410
0949-6521 Moebelmarkt 4561
0949-6629 Nowoczesne Laboratorium†
0949-6637 Family O.K.
0949-6750 Amiga Plus CD-ROM†
0949-6785 Sache - Wort - Zahl 3079
0949-6807 Diskurse der Arabistik 548
0949-6815 Jenaer Beitraege zum Vorderen Orient 553
0949-6874 Bild der Frau 8853
0949-6890 Julia zum Muttertag 5411
0949-7013 Das Gesundheitswesen. Sonderheft *see* 0941-3790 7519
0949-703X Institut der Deutschen Wirtschaft. Gewerkschaftsreport† 8965
0949-7129 Neue Zeitschrift fuer Strafrecht Rechtsprechungs Report Strafrecht 4894
0949-7137 N Z A Rechtsprechungs Report Arbeitsrecht 1698
0949-7145 Geliebtes Haustier
0949-7188 Welt am Sonntag 3859
0949-720X Niedersachsenturner *changed to* N T B Magazin 8189
0949-7226 D S B Presse *changed to* D O S B Presse 8168
0949-7234 A S Vorort†
0949-7277 Kontakte (Tuebingen) 7659
0949-7323 ProCare 5978
0949-7374 MediaSeller 3108
0949-7412 Ornithologischer Verein zu Hildesheim. Naturkundliche Mitteilungen 912
0949-7420 Taipan 1654
0949-7501 Dortmunder Messebrief 6279
0949-7536 German Research Service. Special Press Reports
0949-7544 Der Bauherr 979
0949-7633 Derm 5874
0949-7641 Paed 6098
0949-7676 DStR - Deutsches Steuerrecht 1920
0949-7684 Jahrbuch fuer Regionalgeschichte und Landeskunde *changed to* 1860-8248 4234
0949-7714 Journal of Geodesy 2785
0949-7722 Associations†
0949-7811 German Research Service. Special Science Reports† 8959
0949-7900 D V W Landesvereine Hessen und Thueringen. Mitteilungen 3264
0949-7919 Euro-Atlantic Security Studies†
0949-7927 Opera Sinologica 557
0949-7943 Deutscher Forschungsdienst. D F - Digest fuer Jugend und Bildungseinrichtungen
0949-8036 Gefahrstoffe - Reinhaltung der Luft 3486
0949-8052 Public Relations Forum 33
0949-8109 Technica Didactica 8440
0949-8133 Colloquia Academica. Naturwissenschaften 7847
0949-8257 Journal of Biological Inorganic Chemistry 2117
0949-8265 Nachhaltiges Niedersachsen 2619
0949-8273 Space View 5447
0949-8400 Fachbuch - Gesamtverzeichnis Technik
0949-8508 Deutsche Baecker Zeitung 3673
0949-8567 Europaeischer Informationsbrief Bildung und Beschaeftigung 1106
0949-8621 R A S 4125
0949-863X Zeitschriften - Loseblattwerke - Jahrbuecher (Year) 639
0949-8656 Neue Energie 3178
0949-8672 Die Kirche 7763
0949-8702 Rudolstaedter Naturhistorische Schriften. Supplement *see* 0863-0844 702
0949-877X *see* 1066-8888 2532
0949-8788 Colloquia Academica. Geisteswissenschaften 7847
0949-880X Lutherische Beitraege 7766
0949-8818 Genossenschaftliches Mitteilungsblatt Weser-Ems *changed to* 1610-630X 1349
0949-8869 Alt und Jung Metten 7782
0949-8877 Brewing and Beverage Industry International 601
0949-8931 Off Kinomagazin 6509
0949-8958 Corel Draw
0949-8990 Nationaltheater Mannheim Magazin†
0949-9040 Business U S A†
0949-9199 Deutsche Muenzenzeitung†
0949-9210 Amica 8851
0949-9229 Show 6616
0949-9253 Qualitaetsmanagement in Klinik und Praxis 5701
0949-9261 Formdiskurs 442
0949-9288 Hallo Taxi 8583
0949-930X InVo - Insolvenz und Vollstreckung *changed to* 1866-0584 1348
0949-9334 Fachbuchverzeichnis Maschinenbau - Produktionstechnik
0949-9342 Fachbuchverzeichnis Mathematik - Physik - Chemie
0949-9350 Fachbuchverzeichnis Bauwesen - Architektur (Year)
0949-944X Development, Genes and Evolution 668
0949-9504 Event Partner 6566
0949-9512 Naumann - Museum. Beitraege zur Gefiederkunde und Morphologie der Voegel 911
0949-9563 Jagd in Bayern 8319
0949-9571 Zeitschrift fuer Antikes Christentum 7696
0949-9598 Samsolidam†
0949-9636 Germany. Kraftfahrt-Bundesamt. Grenzueberschreitender Strassenverkehr 8524
0949-9695 Etiketten-Labels 7320
0949-9709 Flexo und Gravure International 7320
0949-9717 Flexo- und Tief-Druck 7320
0949-9725 Erfolgreiche Computer-Praxis
0949-975X Feine Adressen Berlin *changed to* 1861-0870 3847
0949-9768 Feine Adressen Dortmund 3847
0949-9776 Feine Adressen Duisburg - Essen - Muelheim 3847
0949-9784 Feine Adressen Hof - Oberfranken - Plauen 3847
0949-9792 Feine Adressen International 3847
0949-9806 Feine Adressen Karlsruhe - Baden-Baden†
0949-9814 Feine Adressen Sylt 3847
0949-9946 Biologische Anstalt Helgoland. Zweijahresbericht 2800
0949-9989 Neue Solidaritaet 5229
0950-0006 Ceram Research News†
0950-0170 Work, Employment & Society 8147
0950-0189 Scottish Libraries *changed to* 1479-8441 5017
0950-0332 Q X†
0950-0340 Journal of Modern Optics 7078
0950-0464 University of Essex. Department of Economics. Discussion Paper Series 1188
0950-0472 Historical Diffusionism†
0950-0510 Heat Shock Proteins†
0950-0529 Luminescence†
0950-0537 Methyl Transferases†
0950-0553 Neuroimmunoendocrinology†
0950-0561 Oncogenes†
0950-057X Oxygen Radicals
0950-0588 Proteases and Inhibitors†
0950-0596 Protein Secretion†
0950-0618 Construction and Building Materials 994
0950-0642 Wind Directions 3178
0950-0650 Africa and the World†
0950-0685 Penthouse 6297
0950-0693 International Journal of Science Education 2871
0950-0707 Science, Technology & Development†
0950-0715 Sheppard's Book Dealers in British Isles 7573
0950-0731 Arab Affairs†
0950-0782 Language and Education 5139
0950-0790 Evaluation and Research in Education 2855
0950-0804 Journal of Economic Surveys 1135
0950-0839 Philosophical Magazine Letters 7030
0950-0871 Business Ratio Report: Clothing Wholesalers†
0950-091X Basin Research 2702
0950-1029 World Oil Trade 6797
0950-1037 North Sea Letter 6781
0950-1045 Oil and Energy Trends 3143
0950-1096 The Linnean 687
0950-1304 International Directory of Exhibiting Artists†
0950-138X The Astronomer 569
0950-1398 Electronic Materials Information Service Datareviews 3095
0950-1401 Handbook of Geophysical Exploration 2783
0950-141X Cambridge Astrophysics Series 572
0950-1428 Macmillan Computer Science Series 2431
0950-1436 Monographs in Electrical and Electronic Engineering 3325
0950-1487 Power International† 8982
0950-1533 Artificial Intelligence Abstracts (UK)†
0950-1568 Restoration†
0950-1576 Cadscan
0950-1584 Leadscan†
0950-1592 Zincscan
0950-1630 Staffordshire Studies 4267
0950-1657 Hortus 3738
0950-1711 Natural Product Updates 2095
0950-1746 Forktail 907
0950-1789 Science & Technology Abstracts *changed to* 1478-7946 7937
0950-1800 The Wharton Report
0950-1991 Development (Cambridge) 668
0950-2009 Photography†
0950-2092 Micronutrient Analysis†
0950-2114 Image Technology† 8963
0950-2149 Steppin Out†
0950-222X Eye (London, 1880) 6042
0950-2254 Scottish Office. Central Research Unit Papers 2668
0950-2262 World Copper Databook 6483
0950-2270 Bristol Illustrated
0950-2289 Masonry International 449
0950-2343 Tolley's Tax Computations 1952
0950-236X Textual Practice 5387
0950-2378 New Formations 5229
0950-2386 Cultural Studies 8097
0950-2394 Business Ratio Report: Airfreight Agencies†
0950-2408 Business Ratio Report: Brick & Tile Manufacturers†
0950-2416 Communist Review 7117
0950-2440 One, Two Testing & Zig Zag†
0950-2505 Copyright World 6748
0950-2513 Patent World 6756
0950-2564 Trademark World 6759
0950-2645 Insolvency Intelligence 4692

ISSN

DIRECTORY 2010 0952-701X 9413

0951-547X New Mexico Real Estate Law Reporter
0951-5631 Profile of the Worldwide Semiconductor Industry
0951-5666 A I & Society **2444**
0951-5674 Aberdeen Letters in Ecology **648**
0951-5690 E D A **3093**
0951-5852 Cycling Weekly **8257**
0951-5879 Containerisation International World Directory of Liner Shipping Agents *changed to* World Directory of Liner Shipping Agents (Year) **2035**
0951-6026 New Paradigms Newsletter **7891**
0951-6042 Health Economics Research Group. Discussion Paper **4096**
0951-6050 CAB International Database News†
0951-614X Hotlines†
0951-6158 Hakluyt Society. Extra Series†
0951-6204 British Review of New Zealand Studies **4191**
0951-6220 Incorporated Society of Musicians Yearbook **6575**
0951-6239 Register of Professional Private Music Teachers **6610**
0951-6263 R C I **1031**
0951-6298 Journal of Theoretical Politics **7148**
0951-631X Social History of Medicine **5715**
0951-6328 Journal of Refugee Studies **7249**
0951-6379 Caribbean Times **3525**
0951-6417 Practical Handbooks in Archaeology **411**
0951-6433 BioFactors **726**
0951-6530 Hospital Caterer†
0951-6549 Journal of Roman Studies Monograph Series **2236**
0951-6646 Great Britain. Natural Environment Research Council. British Geological Survey. Overseas Memoirs **2745**
0951-6654 Research Studies in Botany and Related Applied Fields **815**
0951-6816 Sound on Sound **6618**
0951-6824 Office Secretary **1870**
0951-6840 Model Collector **4340**
0951-6859 Benchmark (Glasgow) **3183**
0951-6875 Special Children **3047**
0951-6883 Prism **2962**
0951-6921 World Community Journal
0951-693X Children First!†
0951-7154 Electronic and Optical Publishing Review†
0951-7162 Automated Manufacturing Strategy†
0951-7197 Advances in Cement Research **975**
0951-7200 The Gaskell Society Journal **5299**
0951-726X Yes **7695**
0951-7308 Business Ratio Report: Painting and Decorating Contractors and Merchants **4534**
0951-7367 Current Opinion in Psychiatry **6135**
0951-7375 Current Opinion in Infectious Diseases **5812**
0951-7391 Latin and Greek Texts **2236**
0951-7405 Collected Classical Papers **2233**
0951-7472 Fertilizer Week **231**
0951-7499 Fast Car **8580**
0951-7502 Kew Index for...†
0951-7561 Forces Postal History Society. Newsletter **6895**
0951-7588 Countertrade & Barter†
0951-7626 The Teacher Trainer **3084**
0951-7677 Frontier (Oxford) **7207**
0951-7715 Nonlinearity **5521**
0951-7723 The Drink Forecast† **8951**
0951-7731 The Food Forecast†
0951-774X Advertising Statistics Yearbook (Year) **38**
0951-7758 European Advertising & Media Forecast **25**
0951-7766 Quarterly Survey of Advertising Expenditure **33**
0951-7812 D I Y Superstore *changed to* 1476-0614 **4438**
0951-7855 N U T Education Review *changed to* 1462-7272 **2979**
0951-7871 Engineering Services Management†
0951-7898 Freelance News
0951-7928 World Property†
0951-7936 Jersey Law Reports **4698**
0951-8045 Huna London†
0951-8053 United Kingdom. Ministry of Defence. News **1186**
0951-8134 Discover North America Travel Trade Directory **8698**
0951-8207 Journal for the Study of the Pseudepigrapha **7653**
0951-8215 Journal for the Study of the Pseudepigrapha. Supplement Series *changed to* Library of Second Temple Studies **7660**
0951-8231 Moores & Rowland's Yellow Tax Guide **1935**
0951-824X Groupwork **8043**
0951-8258 Medical Horizons†
0951-8266 Africa Health Marketletter†
0951-8320 Reliability Engineering & System Safety **3217**
0951-8339 Marine Structures **3388**
0951-8347 Living Stones†
0951-8363 Starting Point **7613**
0951-838X Books & Periodicals Online *changed to* 1554-2157 **7936**
0951-838X Books and Periodicals Online *changed to* 1554-2173 **5744**
0951-838X Books and Periodicals Online *changed to* 1554-2165 **4484**
0951-838X Books and Periodicals Online *changed to* Books and Periodicals ONLINE: Law, Business and News **620**
0951-8398 International Journal of Qualitative Studies in Education **2870**
0951-841X Carbohydrate Chemistry. Part 2: Macromolecules†
0951-8487 Diabetes Contents†
0951-855X Great Britain. Department of Energy. Publications†
0951-8592 Gas Consumers Council. Annual Report **6769**
0951-8622 Prima **8881**
0951-8649 The Catering Business†
0951-8673 World Airline Fleets News **8553**
0951-8681 U S Executive Report†
0951-872X Boarding Schools & Colleges **2954**
0951-8797 Overseas Road Note **8633**
0951-8819 Panoscope (London)† **8980**
0951-8843 Great Britain. H.M.S.O. Daily List **625**
0951-886X Railway Philately **6899**
0951-8878 Journal of Chinese Philately **6896**
0951-8894 Business Ratio Report: Building Insulation Contractors†
0951-8916 Monographs in Regional and Local History†
0951-8932 In Cornwall Magazine **3866**
0951-8959 Bedfordshire Naturalist **656**
0951-8967 Mediterranean Historical Review **4323**
0951-8975 L I S U - U S A Academic Book Prices Report **5024**
0951-9084 Yorkshire Artscene **528**
0951-9092 Great Britain. Central Statistical Office. Key Data **8374**
0951-9203 C H S Newsletter **988**
0951-9262 Liverpool Investment Letter **1637**
0951-9289 Estates Gazette Law Reports **7590**
0951-9297 Contemporary France†
0951-9467 The Independent **3867**
0951-9521 National Genealogical Directory **3776**
0951-953X Advanced Composites Bulletin **7090**
0951-9556 Commercial Leases **4861**
0951-9564 Design Education Yearbook†
0951-9580 Journal of Orthopaedic Rheumatology†
0951-9602 Current Medical Literature. Infectious Diseases†
0951-9610 Current Medical Literature. Paediatrics **6090**
0951-9645 Railway Technology International†
0951-9688 Defence Systems International **6418**
0951-9718 Office at Home†
0951-9726 Astronomy Now **571**
0951-9785 Exchange **5876**
0951-9815 Community Living **8035**
0951-9882 Salmon Farming **3614**
0951-9955 Baton **6892**
0951-9971 Business Library Management†
0952-0279 Sparks†
0952-0287 Welding Abstracts†
0952-0309 Carbohydrate Antigens†
0952-0317 Drug Targeting
0952-0325 Human Genome†
0952-0333 Leishmaniasis†
0952-0341 Malaria†
0952-035X Multi Drug Resistance†
0952-0368 Photochemotherapy†
0952-0376 Transcription Regulation†
0952-0384 Bio-electronics and Biosensors
0952-0406 Proteins: Post-Translational Processing
0952-0414 Ribosomes and Translation†
0952-0422 Membrane Lipids†
0952-0430 Employment Initiatives†
0952-0562 Annual of Cardiac Surgery†
0952-0570 Hispanic Bilingual Texts†
0952-0627 Current Practice in Surgery†
0952-0686 The Wire **6628**
0952-0708 International Colour Authority **2256**
0952-0724 Quarterly Economic Bulletin **1513**
0952-0759 The Lute **6585**
0952-0767 Public Policy and Administration **7462**
0952-0791 Tolley's Inheritance Tax **1952**
0952-083X Which School? **2963**
0952-0899 Travel Management International†
0952-0953 Financial Regulation Report *changed to* 1473-3323 **1345**
0952-1038 Law Reports of the Commonwealth. Criminal Law Reports **4893**
0952-1046 Law Reports of the Commonwealth. Commercial Law Reports **4874**
0952-1054 Great Britain. Department of Health and Social Security. Health Building Notes **4094**
0952-1089 Recent Advances in Critical Care Medicine†
0952-1119 Cambridge Medicine **5591**
0952-1127 Innovation in Microbiology Series **887**
0952-1178 Journal of Hypertension. Supplement **5793**
0952-1194 Keele Cognition Seminars†
0952-1216 Contax†
0952-1453 Agroforestry Abstracts (Print)†
0952-1488 Scottish Business Insider *changed to* 2040-2201 **1354**
0952-1518 Guide to European Community Grants and Loans **1596**
0952-1542 Contamination Control Abstracts†
0952-1631 Personal Financial Planning Manual **1939**
0952-1666 Booksellers Association. Directory of Members (Year) **7555**
0952-1798 Advances in Underwater Technology, Ocean Science and Offshore Engineering **2799**
0952-1895 Governance **7138**
0952-1909 Journal of Historical Sociology **8113**
0952-1917 Ratio Juris **4765**
0952-1941 European Journal of Anaesthesiology. Supplement **5771**
0952-1976 Engineering Applications of Artificial Intelligence **2448**
0952-1984 Risk Update (London, 1987)
0952-2018 Journal of Stained Glass
0952-2050 Japan Society. Proceedings **7247**
0952-2204 I U B S Monograph Series **677**
0952-2220 Scrip's Pharmaceutical Company League Tables (Year) **6880**
0952-2255 Scientific Basis of Psychiatry† **8987**
0952-2271 The Health Service Journal **4096**
0952-231X Occupational Pensions **4517**
0952-2352 Environment Now *see* 1471-9568
0952-2360 Playback **8154**
0952-2409 U K Journal of Mines and Minerals **6480**
0952-2468 Agricultural Research and Extension Network. Papers **1590**
0952-2565 P C Plus **2580**
0952-2581 Marketsearch† **8972**
0952-2603 Centre for Housing Research. Discussion Paper **4406**
0952-2654 H T F S Digest†
0952-2697 Music & Musicians International†
0952-2700 Geotitles **2720**
0952-2727 Fire & Flammability Bulletin†
0952-2743 Hydrogeological Report **2746**
0952-2751 C P E - Chemical and Process Engineering†
0952-2867 Motive Power Monthly
0952-2875 Cat World **6805**
0952-2956 Consumer and Marketing Law†
0952-3006 Atari ST User†
0952-3170 W W F News†
0952-3227 Company Information†
0952-326X Gnomon **575**
0952-3278 Prostaglandins, Leukotrienes & Essential Fatty Acids **5899**
0952-3332 Archaeological Computing Newsletter† **8930**
0952-3359 Unigram.X **2599**
0952-3367 The International Journal of the History of Sport **4147**
0952-3383 British Journal of Special Education **3037**
0952-3472 Nucleotide Sequences *see* 0261-3166 **741**
0952-3472 Nucleotide Sequences *see* 0305-1048 **741**
0952-3480 N M R in Biomedicine **6203**
0952-3499 Journal of Molecular Recognition **2124**
0952-3561 A S E A S U K. News **3515**
0952-3618 Acquisitions Monthly **1609**
0952-3626 Directory of European Industrial & Trade Associations **1986**
0952-3677 L F C S Report Series **2430**
0952-3804 Aerospace Design and Components†
0952-3839 International Who's Who in Medicine†
0952-3847 International Yearbook of Rural Planning† **8966**
0952-3855 Plants Today†
0952-3871 Journal of Human Nutrition and Dietetics **6661**
0952-3960 Explosives Engineering **3243**
0952-3979 Foolscap†
0952-3987 Educational Media International **3059**
0952-4061 U K Christian Handbook (Year) **7691**
0952-4096 The Bilingual Family Newsletter **5100**
0952-4118 Graphic Repro **7322**
0952-4126 Recent Advances in Aquaculture†
0952-4134 British Army Review **6414**
0952-4142 Keats - Shelley Review **5317**
0952-4320 Manchester Region History Review **4242**
0952-4363 Business Ratio Report: Pet Food Manufacturers & Distributors†
0952-4444 Viewfinder **3087**
0952-4452 Progress in Marketing†
0952-4495 Packaging Scotland **6713**
0952-4517 Sow's Ear
0952-4541 Squills International Racing Pigeon Year Book **8209**
0952-4622 Bioacoustics **936**
0952-4630 Sports Medicine Bulletin **6233**
0952-4649 Journal of Design History **498**
0952-4665 Jane's Airports and Handling Agents. Middle East and Africa **8546**
0952-4673 Jane's Airports and Handling Agents. Europe **8546**
0952-469X Jane's Airports and Handling Agents. Far East, Asia and Australasia **8546**
0952-4711 M & Q Environment†
0952-4746 Journal of Radiological Protection **3170**
0952-4762 Solid Mechanics Archives†
0952-4843 Court's Charge Reporter *changed to* Texas Court's Charge Reporter **4965**
0952-4894 Di C T A Journal
0952-4975 Studies in Ancient Chronology **419**
0952-5041 Journal of Molecular Endocrinology **5896**
0952-522X Wiccan Workshop News†
0952-5238 Visual Neuroscience **6189**
0952-5246 Great Britain. Department of Trade and Industry. Radiocommunications Division. Report for the Financial Year on the Radiocommunications Division of the Department of Trade and Industry†
0952-5300 Topics in Engineering **3223**
0952-5335 N W R National Newsletter
0952-5394 Lloyd's Nautical Year Book†
0952-5424 Progress in Tourism, Recreation and Hospitality Management **8749**
0952-5505 U K Iron and Steel Industry. Annual Statistics **6341**
0952-5661 Bus & Coach Management†
0952-5793 Surveying Technician†
0952-584X International Steel Statistics - Austria **6339**
0952-5858 International Steel Statistics - Belgium, Luxembourg **6339**
0952-5866 International Steel Statistics - Brazil **6339**
0952-5874 International Steel Statistics - Canada **6339**
0952-5890 International Steel Statistics - Finland **6339**
0952-5904 International Steel Statistics - France **6339**
0952-5920 International Steel Statistics - Irish Republic **6339**
0952-5939 International Steel Statistics - Italy **6339**
0952-5947 International Steel Statistics - Japan **6339**
0952-5955 Surface Topography†
0952-598X Raw Materials for the Glass and Ceramics Industries†
0952-6005 International Steel Statistics - Netherlands **6340**
0952-6013 International Steel Statistics - Norway **6340**
0952-6021 International Steel Statistics - South Africa, Rep.†
0952-603X International Steel Statistics - Korea (South) **6339**
0952-6048 International Steel Statistics - Sweden **6340**
0952-6056 International Steel Statistics - Eastern European Countries, Turkey and Yugoslavia†
0952-6064 Bedsit Briefing **7583**
0952-6080 Meat Trader†
0952-6099 International Steel Statistics - Switzerland **6340**
0952-6102 International Steel Statistics - Selected Central and South American Countries†
0952-6145 Al-Hilal Al-Dawli†
0952-617X The International Journal of Comparative Labour Law and Industrial Relations **4695**
0952-6196 New Materials - Korea†
0952-6293 Annual of Gastrointestinal Endoscopy†
0952-6315 International Journal of Computers in Adult Education and Training†
0952-6390 Priests and People *changed to* The Pastoral Review **7812**
0952-6498 Scottish Economic Bulletin **1516**
0952-6609 Rubberneck **6613**
0952-6706 Escort **6289**
0952-6757 Phonology **5161**
0952-6803 International Steel Statistics - Summary Tables **6340**
0952-6811 International Steel Statistics - U S A **6340**
0952-6846 Multiphase Update†
0952-6862 International Journal of Health Care Quality Assurance **5639**
0952-6889 Association of Christians in Higher Education. Forum **2967**
0952-6897 Interface (Glasgow)
0952-6951 History of the Human Sciences **7969**
0952-7001 What's New in Business Information **2344**
0952-701X Fashion Forecast International **2247**

ISSN

DIRECTORY 2010 0955-1115 9415

ISSN

0954-0091 Connection Science **2447**
0954-0105 Food and Agricultural Immunology **673**
0954-0121 A I D S Care **5807**
0954-0156 Traditional Woodworking *changed to* 1755-0157 **1049**
0954-0164 Volksworld **8611**
0954-0172 Yearbook of World Electronics Data Vol. 2: America, Japan, & Asia - Pacific **1908**
0954-0180 Yearbook of World Electronics Data Vol. 1: West Europe **1908**
0954-0253 Gender and Education **2859**
0954-0261 International Review of Psychiatry **6148**
0954-027X Journal of Hard Materials†
0954-0334 Books for Men†
0954-0342 Lavender Lesbian List†
0954-0350 British Association of Psychotherapists. Journal **7341**
0954-0369 Getting About Britain†
0954-0377 Music File†
0954-0393 Electronic Payments International **1392**
0954-0431 Food & Drink from Britain Buyers' Guide†
0954-0504 Geographical Abstracts: Physical Geography **4036**
0954-0512 Geological Abstracts **2719**
0954-0547 Cambridge Studies in Population, Economy and Society in Past Time† **8939**
0954-0555 N D T News **3355**
0954-0628 Offshore Investment **1373**
0954-0652 Building Today
0954-0709 Communications News **2316**
0954-075X United Kingdom Freedom Bulletin†
0954-0822 Special Educational Needs Abstracts **2936**
0954-0881 Vigil **5437**
0954-0911 Soldering & Surface Mount Technology **6344**
0954-0954 Australian Studies **4191**
0954-0962 Public Money and Management **7462**
0954-0970 Bunyan Studies **5267**
0954-1020 Antarctic Science **653**
0954-1071 Home Furnishings **4558**
0954-1136 Middle East Strategic Studies Quarterly†
0954-1179 Bulletin of Judaeo-Greek Studies **7719**
0954-1225 National Statistical Offices of the World†
0954-1306 Oxford Today **2295**
0954-1314 Journal of International Financial Management and Accounting **1362**
0954-1381 Lithium†
0954-139X Reviews in Medical Microbiology **5703**
0954-1411 Libas International **8871**
0954-1438 Interior *changed to* 1740-4053 **8453**
0954-1446 European Journal of Cognitive Psychology **7355**
0954-1470 Open Market
0954-1500 World Cruise Industry Review **8665**
0954-1543 Marketing Business *changed to* 1743-5528 **1831**
0954-1594 Business Ratio Report: Commercial and Video Equipment†
0954-1683 Institute of Grocery Distribution. Economic Commentary. Bulletin†
0954-1748 Journal of International Development **1600**
0954-1802 British Music Worldwide†
0954-1829 Library and Information Briefings **5026**
0954-190X O D I Index to Development Literature†
0954-1918 Auguries **5440**
0954-1977 Estates Gazette Planning Law Reports†
0954-1985 Economics & Politics **1540**
0954-2027 Health Psychology Update **6144**
0954-206X Social Inventions **8133**
0954-2078 Country Times
0954-2094 Distribution **8494**
0954-2116 New Welsh Review **5230**
0954-2167 Business Ratio Report: Investment Trusts†
0954-2191 Theological Book Review **7688**
0954-2205 Bartlett Review†
0954-2264 Optical Computing and Processing†
0954-2299 Chemical Speciation and Bioavailability **3410**
0954-237X R A D A R Bulletin *changed to* 1748-1414 **4068**
0954-2396 Reflections on Higher Education
0954-2485 Investment Fund Index - Investment Trusts **1632**
0954-2612 I T Link†
0954-2620 Broadcasting Press Digest
0954-2647 Transport of Goods by Road in Great Britain **8676**
0954-2760 Expat Investor **1340**
0954-2787 HairFlair **588**
0954-2809 Law for Business **4874**
0954-285X Director Drive†
0954-2868 M & S Magazine *changed to* Your M & S **3873**
0954-2892 International Journal of Public Opinion Research **7144**
0954-2906 Bonsai *changed to* 1876-6137 **3725**
0954-2965 Kerouac Connection†
0954-3007 European Journal of Clinical Nutrition **6658**
0954-3066 Liverpool Historical Studies **4151**
0954-3074 World in (Year) **1196**
0954-3139 Surface Coatings†
0954-3163 Clerical and Operative Rewards **1670**
0954-3317 Interventional Radiology†
0954-3333 Pulmonary Pharmacology (Sheffield)†
0954-3392 Ulster Editions and Monographs **5391**
0954-3406 Relate News **8065**
0954-3414 Free House *changed to* 1748-5886 **4396**
0954-3473 Mediafile†
0954-349X Structural Change and Economic Dynamics **1549**
0954-3503 Japanese New Materials Yearbook† **8967**
0954-3538 New Materials International **1899**
0954-3589 Current Military and Political Literature†
0954-3597 National Preservation Office Seminar Papers†
0954-3635 Socialist Lawyer **4784**
0954-3643 Water Fittings and Materials Directory†
0954-3694 P S I Discussion Papers **7990**
0954-3708 British Journal of Educational Psychology. Monograph Series†
0954-3716 Higher Education Policy Series†
0954-3732 National Association of Career & Guidance Teachers. Journal **2944**
0954-3759 Industrial Handling & Storage *changed to* 1751-1631 **5453**
0954-3848 Jane's Air-Launched Weapons **6426**
0954-3872 Poetry Durham†
0954-3880 Parks, Golf Courses and Sports Grounds
0954-3899 Journal of Physics G: Nuclear and Particle Physics **7067**
0954-3902 Works **5449**
0954-3945 Language Variation and Change **5142**
0954-3988 Fast Ferry International **8643**
0954-4011 EuroBrief†
0954-4054 Institution of Mechanical Engineers. Proceedings. Part B: Journal of Engineering Manufacture **3380**
0954-4062 Institution of Mechanical Engineers. Proceedings. Part C: Journal of Mechanical Engineering Science **3380**
0954-4070 Institution of Mechanical Engineers. Proceedings. Part D: Journal of Automobile Engineering **8585**
0954-4089 Institution of Mechanical Engineers. Proceedings. Part E: Journal of Process Mechanical Engineering **3380**
0954-4097 Institution of Mechanical Engineers. Proceedings. Part F: Journal of Rail and Rapid Transit **8619**
0954-4100 Institution of Mechanical Engineers. Proceedings. Part G: Journal of Aerospace Engineering **60**
0954-4119 Institution of Mechanical Engineers. Proceedings. Part H: Journal of Engineering in Medicine **749**
0954-4178 Artscribe International†
0954-4194 Science and Christian Belief **7680**
0954-4208 Great Britain. Agricultural Science Service. Research and Development Report. Agricultural Service **116**
0954-4224 Nutrition Research Reviews **6666**
0954-4232 Applied Community Studies†
0954-4240 Decanter **602**
0954-4518 Key Note Report: Printing Inks†
0954-4607 Key Note Report: Breweries†
0954-4755 Orthopaedic Product News **6069**
0954-4763 London Guildhall University. Department of Economics. Working Paper **1145**
0954-478X The T Q M Magazine *changed to* 1754-2731 **1797**
0954-4828 Journal of Engineering Design **3205**
0954-4879 Terra Nova **2717**
0954-4887 Terra Abstracts† **8993**
0954-4917 Process Industry International†
0954-4925 Grocery Wholesaling (Year) **3679**
0954-4933 The Quilter **6641**
0954-5093 Key Note Report: New Trends in Retailing†
0954-5271 ReSources Pharmaceutical and Healthcare Information News†
0954-5395 Human Resource Management Journal **1864**
0954-5492 Independent Power News **3159**
0954-5514 Insurance Systems International
0954-5581 Diamond Insight
0954-5611 Look! Hear!† **8971**
0954-562X Good News (Exeter)†
0954-5638 Water Research Centre. Annual Review **8838**
0954-5735 Liberal Democrat News **7151**
0954-5751 Pensions & Employee Benefits Magazine†
0954-576X Journal of Health and Safety†
0954-5794 Development and Psychopathology **7351**
0954-5824 Environmental Engineering (London) **3191**
0954-5832 Aerospace Composites & Materials†
0954-5867 Cambridge Opera Journal **6553**
0954-5913 Retail Marketing & Management†
0954-5964 International Cargo Handling†
0954-5972 Health and Safety Officer's Handbook
0954-6006 Dark Lily **6741**
0954-6014 Technic *changed to* Journal of Operating Department Practice **6249**
0954-6030 Politics and Society in Germany, Austria and Switzerland†
0954-6111 Respiratory Medicine **6218**
0954-612X 3-D Education†
0954-6138 Pims U S A Trade & Technical Directory **633**
0954-6146 Clay Technology **2040**
0954-6235 Vending International **1847**
0954-6316 Yorkshire Dialect Society. Transactions† **8999**
0954-6324 Wildfowl **917**
0954-6499 Samizdat†
0954-6510 WorldAIDS† **8999**
0954-6545 Revolutionary Russia **4257**
0954-6553 Terrorism and Political Violence **7268**
0954-6561 Multi-User Computing†
0954-6634 Journal of Dermatological Treatment **5879**
0954-6642 Applied and Theoretical Electrophoresis†
0954-6650 Journal of the History of Collections **6526**
0954-6677 Women's Health Newsletter **8849**
0954-6685 London Society. Journal **4241**
0954-6774 Purchasing and Supply Rewards **1704**
0954-6782 African Review of Business and Technology **8415**
0954-6820 Journal of Internal Medicine **5946**
0954-6839 Slovo (London) **8002**
0954-6898 M 8 **6294**
0954-691X European Journal of Gastroenterology and Hepatology **5923**
0954-6928 Coronary Artery Disease **5783**
0954-7037 Trout News *changed to* 1749-0669 **3591**
0954-710X European Community Cases **4669**
0954-7118 International Journal of Global Energy Issues **3139**
0954-7134 Delegates†
0954-7169 Journal of Museum Ethnography **345**
0954-7207 Chartered Building Societies Institute. Journal†
0954-7274 The Tax Journal **1948**
0954-7428 Rugby News & Monthly *changed to* 1742-7908 **8236**
0954-7495 Clinical Cancer Monographs†
0954-7525 Asia Pacific International Journal of Business Research†
0954-7533 Asia Pacific International Journal of Management Development†
0954-7541 The International Journal of Wine Marketing *changed to* 1751-1062 **605**
0954-755X Professional Practice Development†
0954-7568 Who's Who in the Meat Industry (Year) **3667**
0954-7614 European Fabrication News†
0954-7649 Jane's Airport Review **8546**
0954-7711 Waterline **8841**
0954-7762 Nursing Times **5975**
0954-7800 Society for the Study of Human Biology. Symposium Series **928**
0954-7894 Clinical and Experimental Allergy **5756**
0954-7940 I T Training **1866**
0954-7983 Restaurant Magazine **4397**
0954-8017 Fear†
0954-8076 A C E†
0954-8084 Gibbons Stamp Monthly **6895**
0954-8165 Directors Rewards **1675**
0954-8319 Key Note Report: Insurance Brokers *changed to* Key Note Market Assessment: Independent Financial Advisers **4511**
0954-8505 Model & Hobby International†
0954-8521 Phillips' International Paper Directory† **8980**
0954-853X Gas Industry Directory (Year)† **8958**
0954-8564 Card World **1324**
0954-8602 Reviews in Contemporary Pharmacotherapy **6878**
0954-8653 First Magazine **1746**
0954-8696 Mountain Biking U K **8265**
0954-8742 World Sports Cars
0954-8750 G Q (British Edition) **6291**
0954-8769 Scottish Book Collector **7573**
0954-8815 Variant **524**
0954-8823 D I Y Week **4438**
0954-8866 Auto Express **8558**
0954-8874 Dean Archaeology **389**
0954-8890 African Journal of International and Comparative Law **4916**
0954-8939 L I S U British Academic Book Prices Report **5024**
0954-8947 Surgical Nurse†
0954-8955 Best **8853**
0954-8963 Cultural Trends **484**
0954-898X Network (London, 1990) **6163**
0954-9021 Headlines (London) **4576**
0954-903X Health Matters **7522**
0954-9056 Insider **496**
0954-9072 Knowledge-Based Systems Management Review†
0954-9145 Networks†
0954-9153 Key Abstracts - Business Automation **2443**
0954-917X Information Technology for Local Government†
0954-9196 C A B L I S†
0954-9226 Baseline (East Malling) **7318**
0954-9501 Junior Holiday Fun **2196**
0954-9552 Track a Word **4349**
0954-9587 Horoscope **566**
0954-9609 Berks, Bucks and Oxon Farmer **95**
0954-9617 Cambridgeshire Farmers **99**
0954-9641 Cheshire Farmer **101**
0954-9668 Cornish Farmer and Grower **102**
0954-9684 Derbyshire Farmer **105**
0954-9692 East Riding Farmer **106**
0954-9714 Gloucestershire and North Avon Farmer **116**
0954-9749 Essex Farmer†
0954-9765 Ski Special **8333**
0954-9803 The Big Paper†
0954-982X Biochemist **725**
0954-9846 Practical Parenting *changed to* 1758-9045 **2166**
0954-9889 International Journal of Neural Networks†
0954-9897 AgBiotech News and Information **712**
0954-9900 Palaeontology Newsletter **6728**
0954-9927 Anglo-Norman Studies **4198**
0955-0011 Lancashire Farmer **132**
0955-0046 Arena (London) **6286**
0955-0119 Mizz **8875**
0955-0178 Marie Claire **8873**
0955-0208 Norfolk Farmer **142**
0955-0216 Northumberland Farmer **142**
0955-0224 Nottinghamshire Farmer **142**
0955-0240 Shropshire Farmer
0955-0267 Staffordshire Farmer **158**
0955-0275 Suffolk Farmer **159**
0955-0283 Warwickshire Farmer **169**
0955-0291 West Riding Farmer **169**
0955-0305 Worcestershire Farmer & Record **170**
0955-0313 York County Farmer **171**
0955-0321 Postman Pat Picture Paper
0955-0348 More! (London, 1988) **8876**
0955-0356 The Collector *changed to* 1756-1671 **8949**
0955-0372 Your Hair (London) **592**
0955-0445 100 Winners for (Year) **8300**
0955-047X Greyhound Star **6809**
0955-0488 Sun Guide to the Flat **8299**
0955-0496 Sun Guide to the Jumps **8299**
0955-0526 Performance Ford **8598**
0955-0534 Sun Soccer Annual†
0955-0569 Institute of Development Studies. Development Bibliography Series **1243**
0955-0631 Learning Resources News **2992**
0955-0658 Energy World Yearbook **3134**
0955-0666 Durham Medieval Texts **5286**
0955-0674 Current Opinion in Cell Biology **831**
0955-0690 Staffordshire Polytechnic. Department of Sociology. Occasional Papers†
0955-0704 Advertising Works (no.) **20**
0955-0712 Petroleum Engineering and Development Studies **6787**
0955-0747 Crockford's Clerical Directory **7753**
0955-0771 Private Villas **8748**
0955-078X What Video Book of Tests
0955-0798 Daily Law Reports Index† **8948**
0955-0801 Social Care Education†
0955-081X Salmon, Trout & Sea Trout **8331**
0955-0828 The Trader **1846**
0955-0836 Precision Marketing **1838**
0955-0852 Process Industry Journal **3253**
0955-0933 The Gate†
0955-095X New Horizon **1371**
0955-0968 Christian News World†
0955-0984 Rehabilitation Index†
0955-1034 Chartered Institute of Public Finance and Accountancy. Archives Statistics. Estimates **1221**
0955-1085 Triathlete (London) **8213**
0955-1115 Hi-Fi Choice **8153**

Link to your serials resources and content with ulrichsweb.com

DIRECTORY 2010 0960-5371 9419

0959-2431 Journal of Smoking-Related Disorders†
0959-2482 Market South East **1577**
0959-2598 Reviews in Clinical Gerontology **4054**
0959-2644 Grocery Market Bulletin†
0959-2695 Journal of French Language Studies **5133**
0959-2709 Bird Conservation International **902**
0959-2822 Progress in Underwater Science†
0959-2830 N S C A Pollution Handbook *changed to* Pollution Control Handbook (Year) **3490**
0959-2857 Black Housing *changed to* 1752-5632 **4404**
0959-289X International Journal of Obstetric Anesthesia **5994**
0959-2946 Public Health News†
0959-2989 Bio-Medical Materials and Engineering **747**
0959-3020 Isokinetics and Exercise Science **6230**
0959-3071 Geophysics Abstracts†
0959-308X Superconductivity Abstracts†
0959-311X For a Change **7964**
0959-3217 Big **6549**
0959-3330 Environmental Technology **3429**
0959-3519 Oncology Today†
0959-3535 Feminism & Psychology **7357**
0959-3543 Theory & Psychology **7412**
0959-3632 Trafodion Anrhydeddus Gymdeithas y Cymmrodorion **4478**
0959-3640 York Georgian Society. Annual Report **461**
0959-3683 English Goethe Society. Publications **5289**
0959-373X Essential Book of Kitchens, Bedrooms & Bathrooms *changed to* 0966-4114 **4560**
0959-3748 The Irish Post **5221**
0959-3780 Global Environmental Change **3434**
0959-3799 Entertainment Law Review **4666**
0959-3845 Information Technology and People **5062**
0959-3861 European Plastics Directory *changed to* 1749-5571 **7092**
0959-3896 Print Buyers Directory†
0959-3926 Co-op Commonweal **7116**
0959-3969 The International Review of Retail, Distribution and Consumer Research **1822**
0959-3977 Essays in Developmental Psychology **7355**
0959-3985 Physiotherapy Theory and Practice **6114**
0959-3993 World Journal of Microbiology and Biotechnology **771**
0959-4116 Information Technology Review **2534**
0959-4213 ARAM Periodical **4319**
0959-4361 Plant User **3747**
0959-437X Current Opinion in Genetics & Development **865**
0959-4388 Current Opinion in Neurobiology **6134**
0959-440X Current Opinion in Structural Biology **730**
0959-4450 PetDogs Magazine
0959-4493 Veterinary Dermatology **8812**
0959-4558 Exuberance **5442**
0959-4655 Morgannwg **4246**
0959-4752 Learning and Instruction **2882**
0959-4779 Essays in Cognitive Psychology **7355**
0959-4906 British Library. Document Supply Centre. Index of Conference Proceedings **6283**
0959-4914 British Library. Document Supply Centre. Current Serials Received (Year) **621**
0959-4957 Immunology and Infectious Diseases†
0959-4965 NeuroReport **6169**
0959-4973 Anti-Cancer Drugs **6008**
0959-4981 Echoes (London) **6564**
0959-5031 Third Way (London) **7188**
0959-504X The Intelligent Home†
0959-5066 Care Home Proprietor†
0959-5112 Consumer Japan (Year)†
0959-5147 European Advertising, Marketing, and Media Data†
0959-5236 Drug and Alcohol Review **2693**
0959-5244 Molecular Neuropharmacology†
0959-5287 Medico-Chirurgical Transactions *changed to* 0141-0768 **5707**
0959-535X B M J **5582**
0959-5589 Cambrensis **5269**
0959-566X Libertarian Heritage **7151**
0959-5678 Libertarian Heritage Reprints **7151**
0959-5740 Aktuell **5092**
0959-5759 Jane's Radar and Electronic Warfare Systems **6428**
0959-5767 Cambridge Studies in Medieval Literature **5269**
0959-5805 Planning History **4423**
0959-5813 Broadcast Systems International†
0959-5821 Jane's Land-Based Air Defence **6427**
0959-5848 Personnel Today **1872**
0959-5864 Mechanics of Creep Brittle Materials† **8973**
0959-5872 N A P O News **2660**
0959-5937 Fingerprint News†
0959-597X Great Britain. Home Office. Police Research Group. Crime Prevention Unit. Papers **2653**
0959-5996 Traffic Advisory Leaflet **8635**
0959-6038 International Cement Review **1015**
0959-6046 Light Rail Review†
0959-6054 Anti-Corrosion Handbook & Directory
0959-6119 International Journal of Contemporary Hospitality Management **4391**
0959-6127 World Ceramics & Refractories **2047**
0959-6186 Travel Industry Monitor†
0959-6208 Cambridge Studies in Modern Optics **7074**
0959-6259 C A D User **3289**
0959-6283 Jane's Underwater Warfare Systems **6428**
0959-6380 Progress in Heterocyclic Chemistry **2077**
0959-6410 Islam and Christian - Muslim Relations **7711**
0959-6429 DataComms Book (Year) **2533**
0959-6496 Selling Long-Haul **8755**
0959-6518 Institution of Mechanical Engineers. Proceedings. Part I: Journal of Systems and Control Engineering **3380**
0959-6526 Journal of Cleaner Production **3369**
0959-6550 Blues & Soul **6550**
0959-6623 Frontiers in Diabetes Research **5893**
0959-6631 Intelligent Highway **8631**
0959-6658 Glycobiology **733**
0959-6666 Postgraduate Dentist: Middle East
0959-6674 Postgraduate Surgery: Middle East
0959-6682 Prescriber **6876**
0959-6739 Ornithological Society of the Middle East Bulletin†
0959-6798 Quarterly Account **1163**
0959-6801 European Journal of Industrial Relations **1681**
0959-681X Tolley's Tax Investigations **1952**
0959-6828 Positive Teaching†
0959-6836 The Holocene **3437**
0959-6844 Cambridge Studies in International Relations **7225**
0959-6879 British Journal of Phytotherapy **307**
0959-6909 Model Engineers' Workshop **4340**
0959-6933 HotShoe International **6969**
0959-6941 European Business Law Review **4668**
0959-6992 Moving Pictures International **6508**
0959-7123 Classic Bike Guide **8256**
0959-7204 Classic C D†
0959-7336 European Fact File†
0959-7344 Pause **5429**
0959-7638 Francophone Business Bulletin†
0959-7646 Majority Minority Review **7984**
0959-7689 The Journal of Law & Practice†
0959-7697 Audiophile†
0959-7719 World Shipping Statistics (Year) **8533**
0959-7727 Oxford Energy Forum **3144**
0959-7743 Cambridge Archaeological Journal **386**
0959-7808 Tees Valley Writer **4584**
0959-8006 Skeleton Crew†
0959-8014 I D S Pensions Law Reports **1686**
0959-8049 European Journal of Cancer **6019**
0959-8103 Polymer International **7099**
0959-8138 B M J (Clinical Research Edition) **5582**
0959-8146 B M J (International Edition) *see* 0959-535X **5582**
0959-8154 B M J - General Practice Edition **5583**
0959-8278 European Journal of Cancer Prevention **6019**
0959-8286 Instrumentation and Control Engineering†
0959-8324 Microelectronics Journal **3109**
0959-8367 Select **6616**
0959-8375 First Voice **1960**
0959-8383 Fly Fishing and Fly Tying **8314**
0959-8391 News in Headache†
0959-8421 Licensing Review **4723**
0959-843X D-I-Y Radio†
0959-8464 Chemistry Review **2057**
0959-8472 Physics Review **7034**
0959-8480 Politics Review **7171**
0959-8499 Sociology Review **8139**
0959-860X A C B National Meeting Handbook†
0959-8642 R E M
0959-8731 London Association for Celtic Education. Directory **2884**
0959-8758 Pharmafile **6874**
0959-8782 911 and Porsche World **8614**
0959-8812 Northern Ireland Bibliography†
0959-8820 Past Sixteen Science Issues Forum†
0959-8871 N E E D I S Initiative†
0959-888X F I B A Basketball **8227**
0959-891X Dogs Today **6807**
0959-8928 Information Research News†
0959-8952 Caliologists' Series **905**
0959-9010 East Europe Business Focus†
0959-9029 A C B National Meeting Proceedings
0959-9053 Body Beautiful *see* 0309-8095 **7000**
0959-9061 The European†
0959-9096 Cheshire and Wirral Bird Report **905**
0959-9118 Prentice-Hall International Series in Optoelectronics **7084**
0959-9185 Technical Textile Markets **8458**
0959-9363 International Hatchery Practice **289**
0959-9371 Edinburgh P I C T Working Paper **2319**
0959-938X Edinburgh P I C T Student Paper Series†
0959-9428 Journal of Materials Chemistry **2068**
0959-9436 Mendeleev Communications **2072**
0959-9517 Surface Mount International†
0959-955X International Bank Accountant†
0959-9568 Investment Trusts **1633**
0959-9576 Focus on Africa **7235**
0959-9592 Seed Pathology and Microbiology†
0959-9606 Improve Your Coarse Fishing **8318**
0959-9630 Amiga Computing†
0959-9673 International Journal of Experimental Pathology **5638**
0959-969X 90 Minutes†
0959-9738 Classic Car Weekly **365**
0959-9851 Clinical Autonomic Research **5596**
0959-986X Architectural Ironmongery Journal **1053**
0959-9916 Journal of Property Research **4417**
0959-9940 Practical Law for Companies **4879**
0959-9959 Ground Engineering Yearbook† **8960**
0960-0035 International Journal of Physical Distribution & Logistics Management **8671**
0960-0124 P C Today **2581**
0960-0175 Moscow Physical Society. Journal†
0960-0191 European Retail
0960-0213 Horse Review†
0960-0272 Playdays **2207**
0960-0450 Fragmente **5422**
0960-0477 Scottish Poetry Library. Newsletter **5046**
0960-0590 Retail Design International†
0960-0647 Legal Abacus **4719**
0960-0655 Journal of Current Business Research†
0960-071X E P R U Papers **7131**
0960-0760 The Journal of Steroid Biochemistry and Molecular Biology **737**
0960-0779 Chaos, Solitons & Fractals **5478**
0960-0833 Software Testing, Verification and Reliability **2598**
0960-085X European Journal of Information Systems **2543**
0960-0884 Soviet Lightwave Communications†
0960-0906 Software Management†
0960-0949 World Arbitration & Mediation Report† **8999**
0960-0949 World Arbitration & Mediation Report *changed to* 1934-3310 **4816**
0960-0981 European Insurance Market **4502**
0960-099X Liability Risk & Insurance **4512**
0960-1163 Camden Fifth Series **4209**
0960-1252 Hannah Research Institute. Yearbook **264**
0960-1260 Green Politics†
0960-1287 Personnel Management Plus
0960-1295 Mathematical Structures in Computer Science **5554**
0960-1317 Journal of Micromechanics and Microengineering **3386**
0960-1325 Games Master International†
0960-135X European Journal of Clinical Investigation. Supplement **5611**
0960-1406 International Journal of Sustainable Development **3443**
0960-1422 Chess Post **8166**
0960-1449 Medium Companies of Europe. Volume 1. Medium Companies of the Continental European Economic Community†
0960-1473 Japan Digest†
0960-1481 Renewable Energy **3146**
0960-1503 The International (London, 1990) **7242**
0960-1511 International Current Awareness Services. Anthropology†
0960-152X International Current Awareness Services. Economics†
0960-1538 International Current Awareness Services. Political Science†
0960-1546 International Current Awareness Services. Sociology†
0960-1570 Select: National Bibliographic Service Newsletter†
0960-1619 Personnel Training and Education† **8980**
0960-1627 Mathematical Finance **1367**
0960-1635 Gas World International†
0960-1643 British Journal of General Practice **5588**
0960-1813 Judge Dredd - The Megazine **2195**
0960-2011 Neuropsychological Rehabilitation **6168**
0960-202X Biotechnology in Agriculture Series **761**
0960-2054 Military Science Index **6455**
0960-2178 Clinical and Experimental Allergy. Supplement **5756**
0960-2208 Time Out Eating & Drinking in London Guide **4399**
0960-233X Parks **2624**
0960-2356 Utilities Law Review **4806**
0960-2372 International Steel Statistics - Denmark **6339**
0960-2380 International Steel Statistics - Greece **6339**
0960-2399 Plans and Construction Guide *changed to* 1741-7791 **4344**
0960-2437 Frontier Tanzania **3432**
0960-247X Great Hospitality†
0960-2526 Institute of Mathematics and Its Applications. Conference Series† **8965**
0960-2585 Seed Science Research **251**
0960-2593 Computer Audit Update†
0960-264X Moneywise **1150**
0960-2704 Moneyfacts **1368**
0960-2720 European Journal of Theology **7756**
0960-2739 Asia Pacific Chemicals†
0960-2828 Practical Motorist **8599**
0960-2860 What Caravan? **8612**
0960-2879 Equine Welfare†
0960-2887 History of the University of Cambridge Texts and Studies **2985**
0960-2941 International Journal of Orthopaedic Trauma†
0960-2976 Phosphorus in Agriculture†
0960-2992 Chemical Industry Europe† **8941**
0960-300X Vox†
0960-3069 Turkey Briefing†
0960-3085 Food and Bioproducts Processing **764**
0960-3107 Applied Financial Economics **1437**
0960-3115 Biodiversity and Conservation **2604**
0960-3123 International Journal of Environmental Health Research **3442**
0960-3131 Journal of Electronics Manufacturing†
0960-314X Pharmacogenetics *changed to* 1744-6872 **877**
0960-3158 Processing of Advanced Materials†
0960-3166 Reviews in Fish Biology and Fisheries **961**
0960-3174 Statistics and Computing **2444**
0960-3182 Geotechnical and Geological Engineering **6463**
0960-3271 Human & Experimental Toxicology **3497**
0960-3301 Pricecheck†
0960-3328 Landscape Showcase†
0960-3360 N I R News **2104**
0960-3409 Materials at High Temperatures **3352**
0960-3581 Best of Mayfair **6286**
0960-3662 Venue Magazine **4983**
0960-3697 Passport **5233**
0960-3751 Beauty Counter
0960-376X Community Pharmacy *changed to* 1751-0902 **8980**
0960-3778 Screen & Display **7327**
0960-3786 Node **2524**
0960-3794 Electricity U K†
0960-3859 The Arts Business†
0960-3964 Clinical and Laboratory Haematology. Supplement† **8941**
0960-3999 Broadcasting Standards Council. Annual Review†
0960-4286 Edinburgh Journal of Botany **786**
0960-4308 Office Environment†
0960-4405 No - Dig International *changed to* 1756-4093 **3285**
0960-4421 Wildfowl and Wetlands *changed to* 1752-7392 **916**
0960-443X University of Aberdeen. Department of Economics. Discussion Paper **1188**
0960-4448 Jane's Naval Weapon Systems **6427**
0960-4472 Export Finance
0960-4529 Managing Service Quality **1778**
0960-4545 European English Messenger **5117**
0960-460X Mirabella†
0960-4626 Export Sales and Marketing†
0960-4669 Contract Lighting
0960-4855 Memes†
0960-5002 Managing Intellectual Property **6754**
0960-5037 Current Biotechnology† **8947**
0960-5045 Process and Chemical Engineering **3233**
0960-5053 Theoretical Chemical Engineering **3234**
0960-5061 Which European Database?†
0960-5088 Opportunities Briefing†
0960-5142 Blue Book of British Broadcasting **1976**
0960-5150 Esquire **6289**
0960-5193 Sandhurst Journal of Military Studies†
0960-5207 Butterworths International Law Directory†
0960-5231 New Review (London, 1989) **8058**
0960-5290 Contemporary Hypnosis **5942**
0960-5371 British Journal of Psychiatry. Supplement *see* 0007-1250 **6128**

ISSN

9420 0960-5398 ULRICH'S PERIODICALS

0960-5398 E L F†
0960-5436 Europe's Automotive Components Business 8579
0960-5444 Living France 8731
0960-5460 International Financial Law Practice Files 4930
0960-5533 S F E P Directory 7572
0960-5592 Transfusion Medicine. Supplement *see* 0958-7578 5942
0960-572X Focus on Political Repression in South Africa†
0960-5754 Scene Out†
0960-5762 Issue One - The Bridge†
0960-5843 M D A Evaluation Report†
0960-5886 Lancashire Magazine 3867
0960-5894 Mediation *changed to* 1476-699X 8055
0960-6025 Studies in Hogg and His World 5381
0960-6068 Ukrainian Journal of Physics 7044
0960-6076 Technical University of Kosice. Transactions 8441
0960-6106 Total Theatre 8483
0960-6130 European Research in Regional Science† 8955
0960-6157 Daily Mail Ski 8310
0960-6254 Applause 6545
0960-6289 Conspectus Gastroenterology 5921
0960-6319 Central Banking 1326
0960-6416 Access All Areas 6277
0960-6491 Industrial and Corporate Change 1543
0960-6505 Business Monitor: Catering and Allied Trades 4401
0960-6513 Perspectives in Information Management†
0960-653X World Publishing Monitor *changed to* 1475-0910 7329
0960-6556 The Art Newspaper (International Edition) 470
0960-6572 Key Abstracts - Factory Automation 2443
0960-6580 Adult and Youth Training 1855
0960-6629 Papers in Leisure and Tourism Studies† 8980
0960-6645 In Hand 2540
0960-6653 The Dark Side 5441
0960-6661 Technical Ceramics International†
0960-6785 Tax Statutes and Statutory Instruments 1950
0960-6793 Video Maker†
0960-6807 Birds of Nottinghamshire 904
0960-6823 Laxton's Building Price Book (Year) 1020
0960-720X Junior Friends†
0960-7250 Great Britain. Department of Trade and Industry. Assessment Paper 1748
0960-7323 Taxes 1951
0960-7404 Surgical Oncology 6035
0960-7412 The Plant Journal 811
0960-7439 International Journal of Paediatric Dentistry (Print) 5849
0960-7471 Audio Media 8152
0960-7560 Homeostasis *changed to* 1802-9698 6119
0960-7595 Monitor (London, 1991)†
0960-7609 General Studies Review†
0960-7692 Ultrasound in Obstetrics and Gynecology 6005
0960-7722 Cell Proliferation 830
0960-7730 Business Strategy International†
0960-7773 Contemporary European History 4212
0960-779X Eye (London, 1990) 488
0960-7870 British Brick Society. Information 983
0960-7889 Regulatory Affairs Journal *changed to* 1740-1240 6878
0960-7919 Engineering Management Journal *changed to* 1750-9637 3189
0960-7935 O I O C Newsletter 557
0960-7943 Eurofood Monitor 3635
0960-796X British Journal of Curriculum & Assessment†
0960-8230 T V Zone Special 2395
0960-8338 Dudley Chamber of Industry & Commerce Directory†
0960-8524 Bioresource Technology 758
0960-863X The Vegetable Farmer 168
0960-8648 Issues in Architecture, Art and Design†
0960-8664 Fossils Illustrated 6724
0960-8699 Children and Parliament†
0960-8702 Latin American Economy and Business 1575
0960-8710 Negocios al Dia 1578
0960-8761 Ideological Commentary†
0960-877X Watchwords G C S E English Review†
0960-8788 British Journal for the History of Philosophy 6908
0960-8796 Green Engineering†
0960-8885 Trade-It 8608
0960-8923 Obesity Surgery 6254
0960-8931 Melanoma Research 6027
0960-894X Bioorganic & Medicinal Chemistry Letters 2120
0960-8966 Neuromuscular Disorders 6167
0960-8974 Progress in Crystal Growth and Characterization of Materials 2112
0960-8982 Practice Manager *changed to* 1479-2818 5698
0960-9024 Civil Aviation Training 8539
0960-9059 Middle East Focus†
0960-9253 Printmaking Today 513
0960-9261 Aircraft Proximity Hazards Reports 8535
0960-9512 Northamptonshire Image 3869
0960-9555 Lincolnshire Past and Present 4240
0960-9644 Education Bulletin 2847
0960-9768 Journal of Cancer Care†
0960-9776 The Breast 5987
0960-9784 International Food Safety News *changed to* 0963-4894 3668
0960-9822 Current Biology 667
0960-9830 Human Systems 7361
0960-9881 Electronics Technology International
0960-989X Global Investment Management†
0960-9911 Open Systems†
0960-9938 P T R C Perspectives 8633
0961-0006 Journal of Librarianship and Information Science 5021
0961-0340 Current Issues in Economics 1089
0961-0391 Student Law Review 4790
0961-0405 European Environment *changed to* 1756-932X 3427
0961-0421 Bailliere's Clinical Neurology†
0961-0464 Fruit and Vegetable Markets 232
0961-0472 Global Trends†
0961-0804 Practitioners' Child Law Bulletin†
0961-0863 Buying Cameras† 8938
0961-088X Biomedical Letters†
0961-0898 Dendron† 8949
0961-0901 Chromatin† 8941
0961-091X P A Brief 7569
0961-0928 Dolls House World 4334
0961-0944 Teddy Bear Times 4349
0961-1002 Wales on Sunday 3872
0961-1037 Working Out
0961-1096 Racecar Engineering 8600
0961-1134 Consumer Policy Review† 8943
0961-1142 Africa Forum†
0961-1215 Leonardo Music Journal 6584
0961-124X AudIT†
0961-1258 Opportunities for Theatre Staff & Other Specialists 5977
0961-1266 He Lines 2247
0961-1290 III - Vs Review 3116
0961-1339 Street
0961-1347 Perspectives in Energy 3144
0961-1371 Plainsong & Medieval Music 6606
0961-1398 Cambridge Middle East Library† 8939
0961-1479 Midwifery Matters 5970
0961-1657 Key Note Report: Furniture†
0961-1703 Key Note Market Review: Personal Finance & Savings in the U.K. *changed to* 1741-1742 1364
0961-2025 Women's History Review 8905
0961-2033 Lupus 6224
0961-205X Social Development 8133
0961-2076 Meat Focus International†
0961-2092 The Treasurer's Handbook *changed to* The International Treasurer's Handbook 1359
0961-2114 Broker
0961-2149 Oxford Studies in Comparative Education 2894
0961-2173 Baconiana 5208
0961-2203 Books in the Media 7555
0961-2246 Current Medical Literature. Thrombosis†
0961-2513 The Avmark Aviation Economist† 8934
0961-253X Clinical Dentistry in Health and Disease 5838
0961-2548 Goat Veterinary Society Journal 8797
0961-2556 Financial Director 1344
0961-2564 Civil Protection 2225
0961-2580 Recreation 8196
0961-2653 B J R Supplement 6193
0961-2688 U K Plastics News†
0961-2696 Classical Music 6557
0961-270X Directory of Chemical Products & Buyers Guide 2060
0961-2815 Property Research Summaries†
0961-2831 International Food Hygiene 3648
0961-2904 International Steel Statistics - Australia 6339
0961-2920 Medium Companies of Europe. Volume 2. Medium Companies of the United Kingdom†
0961-2939 Medium Companies of Europe. Volume 3. Medium Companies of Western Europe Outside the European Economic Community†
0961-298X Benson and Hedges Golf Year†
0961-2998 European Regional Incentives
0961-3005 Wedding Dresses Magazine 2263
0961-3072 Realm (North American Edition) *see* 0950-5245 3866
0961-3099 Cambridge Series on Human-Computer Interaction 2409
0961-3153 Institute for Fiscal Studies. Commentary 1929
0961-3218 Building Research and Information 986
0961-3226 Major Companies of the Far East and Australasia (Year) *changed to* Major Companies of Asia and Australasia (Year) 2014
0961-3323 Hampstead & Highgate Express 3866
0961-3331 Ilford Recorder 3866
0961-3374 Newham Recorder 3869
0961-3382 Romford Recorder 3870
0961-3439 Zit 6302
0961-351X Tropical Oil Seeds†
0961-3528 Cotton and Tropical Fibres†
0961-3544 The Recorder Magazine 6610
0961-3617 Scottish Society of Anaesthetists. Annals 5774
0961-3684 Journal of Roman Military Equipment Studies 6429
0961-3730 International Fire & Security Product News† 8966
0961-4001 Global Management†
0961-4036 Managing†
0961-4060 Gazette and Herald 3865
0961-4141 Kew 799
0961-4206 Privatisation International†
0961-4249 Archbold News 4884
0961-432X Llanelli Star 3868
0961-4370 Wellington Weekly News 3873
0961-4400 Peeping Tom 5446
0961-4419 Herald Express 3866
0961-4524 Development in Practice 1594
0961-4540 Needlecraft 6640
0961-4575 The Libraries Directory 5026
0961-4591 Palliative Care Index†
0961-4613 Carmarthen Journal 3862
0961-463X Time & Society 8144
0961-4664 Freshwater Forum 674
0961-4672 Agrochemical Patent Fast-Alert 217
0961-4737 Clinical Nutrition Update
0961-477X Disney and Me 2185
0961-4834 South London Press (Tuesday) 3871
0961-4842 South London Press (Friday) 3871
0961-5202 Retail Newsagent 1965
0961-5237 The Classical Catalogue 6557
0961-5261 Treasury Today†
0961-5342 Financial Technology Insight†
0961-5415 Advances in the Synthesis and Reactivity of Solids†
0961-5423 European Journal of Cancer Care 6019
0961-5431 Developments in Politics 7129
0961-544X English Heritage. Occasional Paper 4217
0961-5490 R N I D Research Report
0961-5520 Vanity Fair 5244
0961-5539 International Journal of Numerical Methods for Heat and Fluid Flow 3272
0961-5555 M I D I R S Midwifery Digest 5997
0961-5563 Mallal's Monthly Digest 4727
0961-5628 Geoscientist 2744
0961-5652 Labour History Review 1694
0961-5679 Professional Fundraising 8063
0961-5725 London School of Economics and Political Science. Centre for Economic Performance. Discussion Paper 1145
0961-575X British Business Rankings
0961-5768 King's College Law Journal *changed to* King's Law Journal 4709
0961-5784 Journal of Co-operative Studies 1424
0961-5822 Sports & Leisure News†
0961-5865 The Finance Director†
0961-5873 Herbs 3736
0961-589X Television Producer
0961-5970 Philosophy Now 6943
0961-6004 Essex Wildlife Magazine 2610
0961-6012 Commonwealth Law Librarian†
0961-6039 Checkout Fresh 3676
0961-6047 Aircraft Maintenance International Yearbook 8535
0961-6063 Review of English Language Teaching†
0961-6152 Science Teacher Education 3081
0961-6209 Law Technology Journal†
0961-6306 Wound Management
0961-6373 Brass Band World 6551
0961-6438 European Journal of Cancer Care (French Edition) *see* 0961-5423 6019
0961-6446 European Journal of Cancer Care (Dutch Edition) *see* 0961-5423 6019
0961-6454 European Journal of Cancer Care (Italian Edition) *see* 0961-5423 6019
0961-6462 European Journal of Cancer Care (Spanish Edition)†
0961-6497 Art Business Today 468
0961-6608 Scotland's What's On
0961-6926 Recent Advances in Manufacturing Bulletin†
0961-6934 Management Week
0961-7035 Burry Post Star *see* 0961-432X 3868
0961-706X Scunthorpe Evening Telegraph 4583
0961-7132 Asian Trader 1973
0961-7140 Garavi Gujarat 3534
0961-7167 Essex Chronicle 3864
0961-7256 Banking Law Reports 1317
0961-7280 Statewatch 7215
0961-7299 Books on the Environment and Related Topics†
0961-7345 E A A N nouncements†
0961-740X Information Technology Solutions Europe†
0961-7418 Communications Technology International†
0961-7442 Planahome Guide
0961-7477 B B C Gardeners' World Magazine 3724
0961-7507 European Converting Industry Directory 6733
0961-754X Common Knowledge 6911
0961-7590 Communications Middle East - Africa 2316
0961-7612 Information Management Report 2545
0961-7647 Language Export Lexel Abroad†
0961-7655 Potato Review 147
0961-7663 Hi-Fi World 8153
0961-7671 International Journal of Pharmacy Practice 6850
0961-7698 Occasional Papers in Industrial Strategy
0961-7736 Correspondence Chess 8167
0961-7752 Marketing Success 1833
0961-7906 European Defence and Strategic Studies Annual (Year)†
0961-7922 Connecting Drinks Yearbook 602
0961-7930 British Journal of Intensive Care
0961-7981 Fast Bikes 8258
0961-8074 Building Europe†
0961-8139 Meat & Poultry News 3655
0961-8171 The Bondholder 1613
0961-8244 British Railways Illustrated 8615
0961-8309 The Systemist 8009
0961-8333 Practice Marketing International†
0961-8341 Star Trek†
0961-8368 Protein Science 743
0961-8384 British Mosquito Bulletin *changed to* 1460-6127 229
0961-8422 London Defence Studies†
0961-8481 Ahora 5091
0961-8538 What's on T V 2398
0961-8945 Tea-Break Quickie
0961-9275 Clinical M R I 6194
0961-9313 Arts Management Weekly†
0961-933X New Studies in Athletics 8190
0961-9364 Somerset Magazine *changed to* 1476-1238 3871
0961-9372 Car Design & Technology† 8939
0961-9437 British Hospital Management (Year)†
0961-9453 Streetfighters 8268
0961-9518 Animals' Defender *changed to* 1748-5452 317
0961-9534 Biomass & Bioenergy 3124
0961-9577 T V Quick (Central Edition) *changed to* 1758-4132 2394
0961-9593 T V Quick (HTV Edition) *see* 1758-4132 2394
0961-9607 T V Quick (Scottish & Grampian Edition) *see* 1758-4132 2394
0961-9658 T V Quick (Ulster Edition) *see* 1758-4132 2394
0961-9704 Dazed & Confused 6288
0961-9712 EuroProperty 7590
0961-978X Feeds and Feeding†
0961-981X Grown Ups Magazine
0961-9828 Schizophrenia Monitor†
0961-9852 Best of Electric Blue 6286
0961-9879 Visability 3049
0962-0044 Tolley's V A T Cases (Year) 1952
0962-0087 Middle East Cultures Series 4323
0962-0095 Exeter Studies in American & Commonwealth Arts 5294
0962-0184 Peak Performance
0962-0206 The Politician
0962-0214 International Studies in Sociology of Education 3066
0962-032X British Glass Manufacturers Confederation. Digest of Information and Patent Review 2038
0962-0427 Cambridge Studies in African and Caribbean Literature 5269
0962-0435 Comparative Law Yearbook of International Business 4921
0962-0443 Gissing Journal 5300
0962-0478 Great Britain. Home Office. Research and Statistics Department. Research Bulletin 7442
0962-0524 Copeland Bird Observatory Report 905
0962-0575 National Museums & Galleries of Wales. Geological Series 2757
0962-0648 Early Modern History Review†
0962-0672 Frieze 490
0962-0737 U K O P†

Link to your serials resources and content with ulrichsweb.com

0965-2914 Care Home Briefing **8030**
0965-2930 Caterer's Briefing **8493**
0965-2957 Payroll Briefing **1871**
0965-3147 Waste Planning **3514**
0965-3244 R A D A R Contact†
0965-3341 Logistics Technology International†
0965-335X Metalworking Technology Europe†
0965-3422 Anglo-American Sports
0965-3554 I N T A M E L Metro† **8963**
0965-3562 Disaster Prevention and Management **7514**
0965-3597 In Competition† **8963**
0965-3643 Expert Evidence†
0965-366X Home Cooking
0965-3732 Going U S A *changed to* 1749-9593 **8700**
0965-3740 Australian News *changed to* 1749-9550 **8700**
0965-3775 International Who's Who of Women (Year) **8899**
0965-3783 World Directory of Diplomatic Representation **7274**
0965-3805 Fishkeeping Answers **3594**
0965-3813 Environment Risk†
0965-3945 Scotland
0965-4003 Aquila **2176**
0965-4038 What's on T V (Anglia Edition) **2399**
0965-4232 The Greatest Game **8234**
0965-4283 Health Education **6988**
0965-4313 European Planning Studies **4410**
0965-433X Oxfam GB **1603**
0965-4356 London Stock Exchange. Member Firms **1637**
0965-4364 D J Magazine **6560**
0965-4380 Association for Global Strategic Information. Journal†
0965-4496 Waste & Environment Today. Bibliographic Journal†
0965-4542 Waltham International Focus (Greek Edition) *see* 1355-5413 **6816**
0965-4542 Waltham International Focus (Greek Edition) *see* Veterinary Focus **6816**
0965-4569 Waltham International Focus (Italian Edition) *see* Veterinary Focus **6816**
0965-4569 Waltham International Focus (Italian Edition) *see* 1355-5413 **6816**
0965-4577 Waltham International Focus (Spanish Edition) *see* 1355-5413 **6816**
0965-4577 Waltham International Focus (Spanish Edition) *see* Veterinary Focus **6816**
0965-4585 Waltham International Focus (French Edition) *see* 1355-5413 **6816**
0965-4585 Waltham International Focus (French Edition) *see* Veterinary Focus **6816**
0965-4593 Waltham International Focus (German Edition) *see* Veterinary Focus **6816**
0965-4593 Waltham International Focus (German Edition) *see* 1355-5413 **6816**
0965-464X Eastern Eye **3531**
0965-4682 Food Industry Bulletin *changed to* 1478-7911 **3639**
0965-4704 Freight Management International **8496**
0965-4720 Independent Caterer **4391**
0965-4739 Premises and Facilities Management **1854**
0965-4747 Design Products and Application **3187**
0965-4941 Long Eaton Herald and Post†
0965-5298 Institute for Computer Based Learning. Reports **2987**
0965-531X Bible Puzzler†
0965-5328 The Marketing Handbook **1832**
0965-5344 Scotland's Top 2000 Companies (Year)
0965-5360 Drink Pocket Book (Year)† **8951**
0965-5395 Fetal and Maternal Medicine Review **5990**
0965-5409 Pensions Pocket Book **1702**
0965-5425 Computational Mathematics and Mathematical Physics **5480**
0965-5441 Petroleum Chemistry **6787**
0965-5492 Mexico and Central America Handbook (Year) **8733**
0965-5506 O M N I
0965-5654 Advertising Standards Authority. Monthly Report **20**
0965-5662 British Psychological Society. Psychotherapy Section. Newsletter *changed to* 1747-1761 **7401**
0965-5670 FunMath **5489**
0965-5751 Clinician in Management *changed to* 1757-207X **5638**
0965-5794 The Coleopterist **842**
0965-5883 International Banking and Financial Law†
0965-6030 Directory of European Dyers, Printers and Finishers **1986**
0965-6057 T V Stars†
0965-6111 Diecasting World **6310**
0965-6138 British Health & Fitness Club Guide†
0965-6146 Foodinfo **3669**
0965-6200 Cambridge Monographs on Particle Physics, Nuclear Physics and Cosmology **7065**
0965-6545 Software Futures **2597**
0965-6626 Green's Civil Court Statutes†
0965-6707 Transport Retort **8515**
0965-674X International Banking Systems **1355**
0965-6758 V G Monographs in Mass Spectrometry **2107**
0965-6804 University and Polytechnic Libraries Book and Journal Spending **7575**
0965-6812 Imaging **6198**
0965-6928 B B C Vegetarian Good Food **4352**
0965-7029 Mining & Quarrying Technology International (Year)†
0965-7053 Arbitration and Dispute Resolution Law Journal†
0965-7061 Street Rod & Sport Truck **8605**
0965-7126 Current Medical Literature. Clinical Nutrition†
0965-7134 Current Medical Literature. Virology†
0965-7320 Drug Abstracts Monthly†
0965-7355 East European Business Law
0965-7452 European Journal of Prosthodontics and Restorative Dentistry **5844**
0965-7517 People in Power **7164**
0965-7525 Wiltshire & Wessex Life
0965-7533 Somerset & Avon & Wessex Life
0965-7576 Review of International Economics **1166**
0965-7592 International Wool Textile Overview†
0965-7711 Roskill's Lithium Digest **6331**
0965-7738 Mela
0965-7746 Dan Haul
0965-7843 Safety and E M C **3330**
0965-7959 Windows Magazine†
0965-7991 Personal Injuries and Quantum Reports **4757**
0965-8203 Port Engineering Management **8656**
0965-8211 Memory **7384**
0965-8238 Shivers **6513**
0965-8289 Active Life **4975**
0965-8297 B M Magazine **6521**
0965-8408 Musculoskeletal Medicine†
0965-8416 Language Awareness **5140**
0965-8521 Quality of Working Life News & Abstracts†
0965-8564 Transportation Research. Part A: Policy & Practice **8516**
0965-8602 Cross Stitch Collection **6638**
0965-8629 Motor Insurance Market
0965-867X Institution of Agricultural Engineers. Members' Handbook & Buyers' Guide†
0965-8726 Taxline **1951**
0965-9250 Exchange & Mart (Southern Edition) *changed to* Auto Exchange & Mart (South & West Edition) **8558**
0965-9269 Exchange and Mart (North/Midland Edition) *changed to* Auto Exchange & Mart (North and Midlands Edition) **1957**
0965-9315 University College London. Institute of Archaeology. Papers **422**
0965-9331 Financial Times Credit Ratings International *changed to* 1753-7444 **1355**
0965-934X Human Rights Case Digest† **8962**
0965-9390 Brand Strategy **22**
0965-9455 BusinessMatters **1731**
0965-9463 Woodcarving **1052**
0965-948X Psychology Teaching Review **7400**
0965-9544 Army List **6412**
0965-9552 Army List. Supplement **6412**
0965-9579 Coal U.K. **3126**
0965-9587 Screen Finance **6512**
0965-9676 East European Insurance Report **4501**
0965-9706 Principles of Psychology†
0965-9978 Advances in Engineering Software **3288**
0965-9994 Geological Conservation Review Series **2738**
0966-0011 Phasmid Studies **857**
0966-002X European Machining†
0966-0062 For Men Ultimate Collection **6290**
0966-0100 Plant Genetic Resources Abstracts **718**
0966-0224 Current Medical Literature. General Surgery†
0966-0259 Euroslot **1816**
0966-0313 BusinessAge **1077**
0966-0348 Aircraft Value Journal† **8929**
0966-0356 Scottish Affairs **7182**
0966-0380 F X **4539**
0966-0402 University of Wales. Cardiff Business School. Discussion Papers in Accounting and Finance (Print) *changed to* 1750-6638 **1284**
0966-0410 Health and Social Care in the Community (Print) **7521**
0966-0429 Journal of Nursing Management **5966**
0966-0453 Asia Pacific Handbook
0966-0461 British Journal of Nursing **5953**
0966-0550 Commerce Business Directories. Northampton **1980**
0966-0763 A C D. The Journal of the Arthur Conan Doyle Society
0966-0844 BioMetals **727**
0966-0879 Journal of Contingencies and Crisis Management **1765**
0966-0933 F H M (United Kingdom) **6290**
0966-0941 Spectroscopy Europe **2106**
0966-1018 Bulletin of Francophone Africa **3789**
0966-1026 Scroope **456**
0966-1050 C A R F **7111**
0966-1107 U F O Magazine **5448**
0966-1115 Pictish Arts Society Journal **4253**
0966-114X S C I C A T **7938**
0966-1158 The Gallipolian **6422**
0966-1166 English Nature **2610**
0966-162X Technical Education & Training Abstracts *changed to* 1943-0272 **2937**
0966-1646 European Environmental Law Review *changed to* European Energy and Environmental Law Review **4669**
0966-1689 Croner's Employment Law **4653**
0966-1867 Asian Plastics News **7090**
0966-1913 R I S C User **2573**
0966-193X Entertainment & Media Law Reports **4830**
0966-2022 Environmental Law Reports **4667**
0966-2030 Environmental Liability **4667**
0966-2065 Airline Maintenance World
0966-2081 Landscape Architecture Europe†
0966-2138 Business Information from Government† **8938**
0966-2146 Dictionary of Natural Products on CD-ROM **6833**
0966-2154 F I L Newsletter **5009**
0966-2200 Ecology & Environmental Magagment in Practice *changed to* 1754-4882 **2614**
0966-2219 What House? (London, 1992) **7616**
0966-2227 Pharmaceutical Manufacturing Review Directory
0966-2235 Latissimus **854**
0966-2278 Essex Homes & Living†
0966-2294 Colchester Express **3863**
0966-2359 Harwich and Manningtree Standard **3866**
0966-2413 A A B's Register of Wanted Publications
0966-2766 Stillwater Trout Angler†
0966-2774 Information Networking News†
0966-2790 For Women **8863**
0966-2839 European Security **7234**
0966-2855 Youthwork **7781**
0966-3061 Celtic View **8224**
0966-3142 The Whitehaven News **3873**
0966-3274 Transplant Immunology **5766**
0966-3347 Strange Attractor **5448**
0966-3363 ArtByte: Computers in Art & Art History **530**
0966-3371 The Knowledge **2384**
0966-3452 Central Asia Brief (English Edition)†
0966-3487 Clinical and Experimental Dermatology. Supplement **5873**
0966-3533 Truck & Driver Magazine **8676**
0966-3541 Business Europa†
0966-3592 Pig World **296**
0966-3622 Feminist Legal Studies **4673**
0966-369X Gender, Place and Culture **8898**
0966-3711 The Retail Pocket Book **1840**
0966-3924 Fun to Learn - Rosie & Jim†
0966-4033 Playing Card World **4343**
0966-4041 Charity Law & Practice Review **4641**
0966-4068 Portland Press Proceedings **5910**
0966-4076 The E N D S Report **3415**
0966-4114 Kitchens, Bedrooms & Bathrooms Magazine **4560**
0966-4246 University of Southampton. Department of Economics. Discussion Papers in Economics and Econometrics **1189**
0966-4270 Focus (London, 1992) **3865**
0966-4327 Daily Mail Motor Review†
0966-4343 London Stock Exchange. Quality of Markets Quarterly Review†
0966-4351 Skin Deep **518**
0966-4378 Marconi Instruments Measure Test†
0966-4394 The Moscow Letter
0966-4505 Oil and Gas†
0966-4734 European Packaging **6709**
0966-4769 I A T U L Proceedings (Print Edition) *changed to* I A T U L Proceedings (CD-ROM Edition) **5012**
0966-4793 Trends in Polymer Science†
0966-4831 Special **3046**
0966-4858 European Handbook
0966-4874 The Guide to European Business Media
0966-4882 Communications Networks **2496**
0966-4920 Prison Writing **5354**
0966-5196 Mathematics Resource Guide **5516**
0966-5250 Monocle (Goldalming) **4980**
0966-5269 Company Digest **1084**
0966-5358 Yorkshire Journal **3873**
0966-5374 Mayfair Specials **6295**
0966-5390 Women on Top **8891**
0966-5471 Soul C D
0966-5609 Purple Patch **5432**
0966-5625 Shiny Magazine **5371**
0966-5773 I A S C Update *changed to* 1474-2675 **1290**
0966-6273 R & D Efficiency†
0966-6303 Royal College of Veterinary Surgeons. Directory of Veterinary Practices (Year) **8807**
0966-6346 Dance Now† **8948**
0966-6362 Gait & Posture **5617**
0966-6370 Consumer Credit **1329**
0966-6427 Harvest Moon **6741**
0966-6443 Perfect Home **4561**
0966-6486 Nursing Home Yearbook†
0966-6494 Student B M J **5718**
0966-6532 Ambulatory Surgery†
0966-6656 Cardiff Business School. Discussion Paper Series in Financial and Banking Economics **1324**
0966-6680 In the Sticks† **8963**
0966-6729 Needlework **6640**
0966-6745 Taking Stock (Leeds) **5050**
0966-677X Logo!†
0966-6788 Top†
0966-6796 Microbial Clean-Up†
0966-6826 Journal of Sleep Research. Supplement **5654**
0966-6907 College Management Today
0966-6923 Journal of Transport Geography **4017**
0966-6931 Save the Children Overseas Department Working Paper **2167**
0966-694X Oracle World†
0966-6982 Save the Children Development Manuals **2167**
0966-7008 Price Waterhouse European Companies Handbook **2024**
0966-7040 Socialism of the Future†
0966-7067 Retail Trade International (Year) **1841**
0966-7113 Junior Focus **3069**
0966-7164 A Q **305**
0966-7180 B B C Music Magazine **6547**
0966-730X Financial Press Facts **1993**
0966-7334 Fraud Watch **1348**
0966-7350 Feminist Theology **8896**
0966-7369 Journal of Pentecostal Theology **7762**
0966-7458 The European Journal of Teleworking† **8954**
0966-7466 Footwear Business International **7940**
0966-761X Lloyd's Casualty Week **4513**
0966-7660 Overseas Jobs Express **1870**
0966-7687 World Pharmaceuticals Report†
0966-7717 European Marketing Pocket Book (Year) **1816**
0966-7733 The International Broker **4509**
0966-7806 Caribbean Focus
0966-7822 Polymer Gels and Networks†
0966-7849 Computer Finance **1329**
0966-7857 Aircraft Economics **8535**
0966-789X Voice†
0966-7903 Occupational Therapy International **6683**
0966-7911 Reptilian **961**
0966-7954 Anaesthetic Pharmacology Review†
0966-7970 East European Business Information†
0966-8012 The In-House Lawyer **4691**
0966-8071 Insight Japan† **8965**
0966-811X Cross-Stitcher **6638**
0966-8136 Europe - Asia Studies **1106**
0966-8217 Annual Country Forecast Report. Thailand *changed to* 1744-8808 **1522**
0966-8225 Property Review†
0966-8268 European Adhesives & Sealants Yearbook and Directory **6717**
0966-8306 Horse Exchange†
0966-8365 Health & Safety at Work Act Newsletter **6678**
0966-8373 European Journal of Philosophy **6918**
0966-842X Trends in Microbiology **896**
0966-8438 Classic Bus **8493**
0966-8454 Journal of Medical and Veterinary Mycology. Supplement†
0966-8497 Inside Soap **2383**
0966-8519 The Journal of Heart Valve Disease **5793**
0966-8705 Global Forecasting Service. Yugoslavia†
0966-8748 Country Forecast. Hong Kong **7121**
0966-8764 A S S I A Plus†
0966-8772 B H I Plus†

ISSN

0968-3038	The Online Manual†
0968-3062	Teaching Today **2918**
0968-3097	B N B on CD-ROM **616**
0968-3100	Microlight Flying **65**
0968-3194	Current Law Monthly Digest **4653**
0968-3224	World Coal†
0968-3240	National Renderers Association. Bulletin **3657**
0968-3291	Radio Control Jet International **4345**
0968-3305	MacFormat **2577**
0968-3364	Racing Post **8297**
0968-3372	Bridge Plus† **8937**
0968-3402	I A W Q Yearbook **8825**
0968-3445	War in History **6453**
0968-347X	Isotech Journal of Thermometry†
0968-3860	Ealing & Acton Gazette **3864**
0968-4107	T R L Reports **8635**
0968-4131	The Graduate Series in Astronomy
0968-4239	M & A Japan
0968-4328	Micron **899**
0968-4344	Middle East Broadcast and Satellite **2385**
0968-4387	Reed's Nautical Companion **8658**
0968-4468	Business Africa **1443**
0968-4476	Occasional Papers in Politics and International Relations **7160**
0968-4506	Craftworker's Year Book **533**
0968-4557	Benn's Media: World **4572**
0968-4565	Benn's Media: Europe **4572**
0968-4638	Machine Knit Today (UK edition) **1963**
0968-476X	Bunker News **1553**
0968-4794	Environmental Law Monthly **4667**
0968-4883	Quality Assurance in Education **2901**
0968-4972	Latin American Consensus Forecasts **1496**
0968-4999	Inspector
0968-5081	Psychopoetica†
0968-5227	Information Management & Computer Security **1752**
0968-5243	Magnetic Resonance Materials in Physics, Biology and Medicine **7068**
0968-5332	Medical Law International **4731**
0968-5340	Hygiene and Nutrition in Food Service and Catering†
0968-5367	The S A L T Programme for 3 to 4 **7773**
0968-5375	The S A L T Programme for 5 to 7 **7678**
0968-5383	The S A L T Programme for 8 to 10 **7678**
0968-5391	The S A L T Programme for 11 to 13 (Sharing and Learning Together) *changed to* 1743-2308 **7646**
0968-5405	The S A L T Programme for All Ages **7773**
0968-5480	AIDS Abstracts†
0968-5553	Local Authority Waste & Environment *changed to* 1750-9769 **3508**
0968-5588	Statistics of Education and Training in Wales: Schools **2936**
0968-5596	Further and Higher Education and Training Statistics for Wales **2933**
0968-5626	Current Medical Literature. Allergy†
0968-5650	Financial History Review **1344**
0968-5669	The Motor Trade Guide to Used Car Prices
0968-5685	Biological Products†
0968-5693	Eco Directory of Environmental Databases in the United Kingdom† **8952**
0968-5707	Royalty Collector's Edition **3781**
0968-5758	Gravesend Reporter **3865**
0968-5766	Dartford Times **3864**
0968-5774	Bromley & Beckenham Times **3862**
0968-5782	Orpington & Petts Wood Times **3869**
0968-5790	Chislehurst Times **3862**
0968-5804	Erith & Crayford Times **3864**
0968-5812	Eltham & Greenwich Times **3864**
0968-5820	Bexleyheath & Welling Times **3861**
0968-5863	Fun to Learn - Mr. Men†
0968-5936	Royal Institution of Cornwall. Journal **4260**
0968-6045	A C T **7619**
0968-6053	Current Diagnostic Pathology *changed to* 1756-2317 **5944**
0968-607X	P C Mart **2434**
0968-6169	Strange Adventures†
0968-6177	Fax 21†
0968-6185	Premonitions **5446**
0968-6312	Minilab Developments†
0968-6339	Conference Fast-Track. New Chemical Entities **6830**
0968-6347	Utility Finance†
0968-6355	East European Privatisation News **7131**
0968-6452	Nefte Compass **6780**
0968-6630	Management of Voluntary Organisations **8055**
0968-6673	Gender, Work and Organization **1747**
0968-669X	Generation in the 1990s†
0968-6703	Acquisitions and Diversification†
0968-672X	Asia F A B **219**
0968-6886	Port of Hamburg Handbook **8657**
0968-6940	Toybox **2218**
0968-7017	Briefing Notes in Economics **1069**
0968-7092	Pub Food†
0968-7130	Japan Management Review†
0968-7149	C O M E T **6716**
0968-7165	With Marriage in Mind **5562**
0968-7262	Choir & Organ **6555**
0968-7300	Journal of Bone and Joint Surgery: British Volume on CD-ROM *see* 0301-620X **6063**
0968-7300	Journal of Bone and Joint Surgery: British Volume on CD-ROM *see* 0301-620X **6063**
0968-7300	Journal of Bone and Joint Surgery: British Volume on CD-ROM *see* 1094-5903 **6063**
0968-7459	North African Handbook
0968-7467	Particle Characterization Abstracts†
0968-7475	Borderlines: Studies in American Culture†
0968-7599	Disability & Society **4077**
0968-7610	Addiction Abstracts **2689**
0968-7637	Drugs **2693**
0968-7645	European Urology Update Series *changed to* 1569-9056 **6268**
0968-7653	Disability, Pregnancy & Parenthood International **4065**
0968-7661	Potato Business World *changed to* 1745-2937 **3660**
0968-7688	Molecular Membrane Biology **739**
0968-7726	The Royal Life Saving Society U.K. Lifeguard **7540**
0968-7769	A L T - J **2964**
0968-7785	Fiction Furnace **5216**
0968-7807	Chart and Compass International **8032**
0968-784X	Offshore Technology **6783**
0968-7858	Country Profile. Germany† **8945**
0968-7866	Chartist **7115**
0968-7874	Scottish Memories **3870**
0968-7904	Vertigo **6516**
0968-7912	Down Syndrome Research and Practice **6137**
0968-8005	Journal of Nietzsche Studies **6929**
0968-8080	Reproductive Health Matters **8848**
0968-8153	Bale Catalogue of Israel Postage Stamps
0968-8234	Retail Monitor International†
0968-8250	First Source†
0968-8277	Take a Break's Take a Crossword **4348**
0968-8374	Noddy **2205**
0968-8382	Shout (Dundee) **2213**
0968-851X	T V & Satellite Week. North West - Anglia *see* T V & Satellite Week **2392**
0968-8528	T V & Satellite Week. North West - Border *see* T V & Satellite Week **2392**
0968-8544	T V & Satellite Week. Midlands - Wales and West *see* T V & Satellite Week **2392**
0968-8560	T V & Satellite Week. Yorkshire - Tyne - Tees *see* T V & Satellite Week **2392**
0968-8684	Kent Business **3867**
0968-8714	Max Power **8590**
0968-8773	Cellular & Molecular Biology Research†
0968-879X	Current Law Week (Print) *changed to* 2040-8730 **4653**
0968-8803	Executive Systems International
0968-8838	Carers World
0968-8846	Family Law Today†
0968-8927	Gardens Illustrated **3732**
0968-896X	Progress in Pathology **5700**
0968-9001	Logistics Europe **8502**
0968-9028	Audit in General Practice†
0968-9079	Barbour Index Building Product Compendium *changed to* 1750-323X **4532**
0968-9346	Parentwise†
0968-9400	New Leisure Markets **1836**
0968-9419	Consumer Spending
0968-9486	E D I Yearbook (Year)†
0968-9745	N. London, Herts & Beds Auto Trader *changed to* 1747-6860 **8589**
0968-9974	Bygone Birmingham
0969-0018	Optical Practitioner **6049**
0969-0069	Education U S A
0969-0131	Gastroenterology Today **5925**
0969-0158	Meat Manufacturing & Marketing International†
0969-0166	Today's Anaesthetist **5774**
0969-0174	Ship Repair and Conversion Technology **8661**
0969-0212	Quality of Service Regulation†
0969-0239	Cellulose **2121**
0969-0301	Mariani Foundation Paediatric Neurology **6096**
0969-0352	Contract Flooring Journal **4535**
0969-0409	The Resource **3462**
0969-0468	Royal National Institute for the Blind. Update **8066**
0969-059X	European Quality **8422**
0969-0603	Performing Arts Yearbook for Europe *changed to* Performing Arts Yearbook **8476**
0969-0654	Waterways **8284**
0969-0689	First Empire **4219**
0969-0700	Journal of Wound Care **6066**
0969-0719	Health Informatics Europe (Online Edition) **5830**
0969-0727	Sportsboat and Waterski International **8283**
0969-0735	Feed Legislation **272**
0969-0840	European Legal Journals Index†
0969-1022	Transport News **8515**
0969-1049	Outlook (Colchester) **7739**
0969-109X	Green's Conveyancing Statutes **4832**
0969-1103	Green's Statutes. Family Law, Succession, Trusts and Judicial Factors **4911**
0969-1111	Bibliography of European Palaeobotany & Palynology **6731**
0969-1154	Marx Memorial Library. Bulletin **7153**
0969-1162	Q E D **1965**
0969-1227	Catastrophe Reinsurance Newsletter **4498**
0969-1243	Jane's Airports and Handling Agents. Central Latin America Including the Caribbean **8546**
0969-1251	Cattle Practice **283**
0969-1332	Your Garden†
0969-1340	Enact *changed to* 1479-9499 **2607**
0969-1375	Occult Observer
0969-1413	Journal of Medical Screening **5820**
0969-1464	Passenger Rail Management†
0969-1537	Current Medical Literature. Surgical Infection†
0969-1545	Financial Reporting & Auditing Newsletter†
0969-1669	Butterworths Employment Law Bulletin **4859**
0969-1693	Russian Business International†
0969-1731	S C O R E Quarterly Report **4426**
0969-1812	C E S M M 3 Price Database
0969-1839	P C Marketplace **2573**
0969-1847	Professional Marketing **1838**
0969-1855	Developments in Chemical Engineering and Mineral Processing *changed to* 1932-2135 **3236**
0969-1901	Hardy Plant Journal **3735**
0969-1936	Context (Canterbury) **7349**
0969-1952	Optical World **6049**
0969-2037	Fish & Chips and Fast Food **3636**
0969-2061	Rainforest Action Report **2625**
0969-2126	Structure **706**
0969-2150	Kingpin **8184**
0969-2215	Nature's Place **2621**
0969-2258	Shemot **3782**
0969-2290	Review of International Political Economy **1514**
0969-2304	Care in Place: The International Journal of Networks and Community†
0969-2436	Inside Eye **1630**
0969-2568	Croner's Coach and Bus Operations **8494**
0969-2576	Cycle Sport **8168**
0969-2622	International Congress, Symposium and Seminar Series **6280**
0969-2630	Fast Ferry Operators Directory† **8956**
0969-3041	Sonic the Comic **5447**
0969-3297	I T Law Today **4689**
0969-336X	Healthlines†
0969-3386	Monographs on the Physics and Chemistry of Materials **7026**
0969-3521	Local History News **4240**
0969-3548	Aldeburgh Studies in Music **6543**
0969-3572	Modern Poetry in Translation **5427**
0969-3637	Industrial Relations Law Bulletin *changed to* 1754-1247 **1679**
0969-3645	Occasional Papers in Education and Interdisciplinary Studies†
0969-3718	Occasional Papers in Irish Studies†
0969-3726	American Car World **8490**
0969-3769	Geodrilling International **3267**
0969-3823	Quekett Journal of Microscopy **900**
0969-3831	Company Law Monitor†
0969-3858	Paso a Paso *see* 0962-2861 **8040**
0969-3963	Pharmaceutical Marketing **6869**
0969-3971	Pharmaceutical Marketing. Practical Guide Series **6869**
0969-4005	Poetry Now (Woodston) **5431**
0969-4080	Review of Employment Topics **1705**
0969-4129	Regulatory Affairs Journal. Devices **6878**
0969-4145	Machinery Update **6711**
0969-4161	The Scottish Episcopalian **7774**
0969-4218	Mining Environmental Management **6472**
0969-4234	Jane's Islamic Affairs Analyst **7145**
0969-4331	Socialist History **4161**
0969-434X	Professional Update†
0969-4501	Human Development Report **7970**
0969-4587	Directory of Continuous Market Research (Year)†
0969-4595	European Regional Prospects (Abridged Edition) **1485**
0969-4609	History Notes **4230**
0969-4625	A C L A I I R Newsletter **4985**
0969-4684	Hotel & Restaurant Magazine†
0969-4706	AIDS Treatment Update *changed to* 1756-7890 **5816**
0969-4765	Biometric Technology Today **3090**
0969-4846	Writing Ulster **5401**
0969-4862	Bookselling *changed to* 1745-3798 **7555**
0969-4900	British Journal of Midwifery **5987**
0969-5095	Occupational Therapy News **6113**
0969-5141	Team (London, 1959) **5186**
0969-5214	Fable Bulletin. Violin Improvisation Studies.†
0969-5575	British Horse Society. Register of Instructors **8288**
0969-5656	Shetland Times **3870**
0969-5893	Clinical Psychology **7345**
0969-5907	Telecoms Heritage News
0969-5915	European Utilities Yearbook (Year)†
0969-5931	International Business Review **1126**
0969-594X	Assessment in Education: Principles, Policy and Practice **2827**
0969-5958	International Journal of the Legal Profession **4695**
0969-5966	Latin America Monitor. Brazil **1496**
0969-5974	Latin America Monitor. Mexico **1496**
0969-6016	International Transactions in Operational Research **2427**
0969-6024	Birding World **903**
0969-6032	Bailrigg Papers on International Security **7223**
0969-6040	Bailrigg Memoranda **7223**
0969-6105	Used Bike Guide **8270**
0969-6113	The British Journal of Cardiology **5778**
0969-6121	E C Inform Energy *changed to* 1753-2825 **3148**
0969-613X	Interchange (Edinburgh) **2942**
0969-6202	Focus on Electronics Chemicals†
0969-6210	Focus on Pigments **6722**
0969-6229	Focus on Diagnostics†
0969-6237	Focus on Water Quality†
0969-627X	Country Profile. Russia† **8946**
0969-6288	Soho Square **5374**
0969-630X	Cross Stitch **6638**
0969-6369	Life Assurance Market†
0969-6393	Managed Derivatives
0969-6431	Careers Guidance Today **6695**
0969-6474	The Learning Organization **1869**
0969-6539	Engineering - South Wales **3190**
0969-6547	Mineral Planning Appeals in Great Britain **2755**
0969-6652	Stage Screen & Radio **4602**
0969-6695	The Professional Manager **1787**
0969-6709	Research **1839**
0969-6725	Air Traffic Management **8534**
0969-6733	ResearchPlus†
0969-675X	Building & Construction Index† **8937**
0969-6806	Medicine International (Middle Eastern Edition)
0969-6849	Journal of Advanced Materials (Commack) **3348**
0969-6881	Direct Marketing International **1813**
0969-692X	Current Clinical Cancer†
0969-6946	Popular Patchwork **538**
0969-6970	Angiogenesis **6008**
0969-6989	Journal of Retailing and Consumer Services **1826**
0969-6997	Journal of Air Transport Management **1763**
0969-7039	Arthritis Today **6222**
0969-7063	Current Medical Literature. Leukaemia and Lymphoma **6017**
0969-708X	Occupational Health Bulletin
0969-7128	Gene Therapy (Basingstoke) **5618**
0969-7136	Team Leader's Briefing†
0969-7144	Croner's Executive Companion **1736**
0969-7179	Kluwer Insurance Briefing
0969-7217	Tire Technology International (Annual Edition) *see* 1462-4729 **7827**
0969-725X	Angelaki **4443**
0969-7330	Nursing Ethics **5973**
0969-7373	Anvil **7746**
0969-7462	Iran Bulletin **7711**
0969-7500	Global Telecoms Business **2322**
0969-7527	Toy Trader Bulletin†
0969-7667	Herpes **5815**
0969-7721	Hybrid
0969-7748	Islamica Magazine **7713**
0969-7764	European Urban and Regional Studies **7963**
0969-7802	A I M Reports **1589**

ISSN

0970-6119 Indian Cement Review 1888
0970-6135 National Bureau of Fish Genetic Resources. Annual Report 876
0970-616X Central Inland Capture Fisheries Research Institute. Bulletin 3589
0970-6186 Export Gazette†
0970-6194 Beverage and Food World 599
0970-6240 Bharatiya Sugar 221
0970-6267 Central Inland Capture Fisheries Research Institute. Annual Report 3588
0970-6305 Asian Economic and Social Review 7948
0970-6380 Indian Journal of Pulses Research changed to Journal of Food Legumes 239
0970-6399 Indian Journal of Agricultural Biochemistry 733
0970-6402 Indian Journal of Asian Affairs 7241
0970-6453 Economic Trends 1402
0970-647X C S I Communications 2409
0970-6496 Maharashtra Sugar changed to 0970-6240 221
0970-6569 Bulletin of Pure & Applied Sciences. Section D: Physics 7007
0970-6577 Bulletin of Pure & Applied Sciences. Section E: Mathematics 5476
0970-6607 Awishkara 7838
0970-6666 Indian Journal of Aerospace Medicine 5633
0970-6674 Indian Airman and Spaceman 59
0970-6739 Sasmira's Bulletin†
0970-6755 Seminar Reporteur 7913
0970-6763 Pesticide Research Journal 246
0970-6852 Architects India 428
0970-6879 Indian Fisheries Abstracts 3613
0970-6887 Textile India Progress 8460
0970-6895 Industrial Products Finder 2005
0970-6925 Gram Shilp 7858
0970-695X Mycorrhiza News 803
0970-6984 Indian Water Resources Society. Journal 2795
0970-7018 see 0447-2500 1962
0970-7034 Metalworking Abstracts 5462
0970-7050 Journal of Hill Research 2711
0970-7077 Asian Journal of Chemistry 2051
0970-7131 R I L I S A R Bulletin 5041
0970-714X Journal of Library and Information Science 5022
0970-7158 Ayurveda Education Series 307
0970-7182 Poetry 5430
0970-7190 C.T.A. Journal
0970-7204 Minetech 6472
0970-7212 Endontology 5843
0970-7328 International Journal of Management and Systems 1759
0970-7387 Cottage Industries 1959
0970-7417 Sri Aurobindo International Centre of Education. Bulletin 3015
0970-7425 Sriarvimda Amtarastriya Siksha Kemdra Patrika 2914
0970-7441 Electronic Products Finder 1884
0970-7522 Hispanic Horizon 5305
0970-7530 Assam Economic Journal 1535
0970-7654 Arthik Prasanga 1061
0970-7689 Panchbati Sandesh 7740
0970-7719 Environmental Resources Abstracts 3479
0970-7727 Diamond World 4565
0970-7794 Indian Council of Philosophical Research. Journal 6925
0970-7816 Sruti 6619
0970-7867 Indian Journal of Rural Technology 8425
0970-7891 C R I Current Contents changed to 0972-3439 1048
0970-7913 North-East India Council for Social Science Research. Journal 7159
0970-7972 Indian Socio-Legal Journal 4691
0970-8111 Personality Study and Group Behaviour 7390
0970-812X Itihas
0970-8138 Wheel Fare 8612
0970-8162 Artha Suchi 1200
0970-8197 Business World 1076
0970-8235 Indian Potato Association. Journal 236
0970-8324 Sevartham 3889
0970-8332 Journal of English and Foreign Languages 5133
0970-8340 C I E F L Bulletin 5102
0970-8367 Samakalina Bharatiya Sahitya 5366
0970-8405 Personnel Today 1872
0970-8413 Indian and World Arts & Crafts
0970-8448 Prajnan (Pune) 1376
0970-8456 Vinimaya 1389
0970-8464 S E D M E 1966
0970-8472 Land Bank Journal 1365
0970-8480 Indian Association for Environmental Management. Journal
0970-8502 Skyways 70
0970-860X Third World Science & Environment Perspectives
0970-8618 Vivek 2456
0970-8626 Association of Scientific Workers of India. Bulletin
0970-8650 Krishak Jagat 131
0970-8685 Health for the Millions 6660
0970-8782 Cinemaya changed to 0973-2144 6509
0970-8863 Socialist Perspective 7183
0970-8898 Tyre Samachar 8609
0970-9037 Journal of Ecobiology 682
0970-9045 Urban India
0970-9053 Vivekananda Kendra Patrika 4482
0970-9061 I A S S I Quarterly 8020
0970-9088 Indian Journal of Geochemistry 2747
0970-9134 Indian Journal of Thoracic and Cardiovascular Surgery 5790
0970-9142 Chess Mate 8166
0970-9150 Ultra Scientist of Physical Sciences 7925
0970-9185 Journal of Anaesthesiology - Clinical Pharmacology 5771
0970-9223 Popular Electronics India 3111
0970-9231 Exploration and Research for Atomic Minerals 3167
0970-9258 River Behaviour and Control 8831
0970-9266 Directory of Periodicals Published in India 7560
0970-9274 Journal of Human Ecology 3447
0970-9290 Indian Journal of Dental Research 5847
0970-9304 Journal of Applied Zoological Researches 950
0970-9320 Indian Journal of Comparative Microbiology, Immunology and Infectious Diseases 887
0970-9371 Journal of Cytology 833
0970-938X Biomedical Research 5586
0970-9444 Biojournal 657
0970-9452 Academy of Hospital Administration. Journal 1722
0970-9517 Journal of Freshwater Biology
0970-9525 Chemical Digest 2054
0970-9606 Recent Researches in Geology 2764
0970-9649 Mendel 875
0970-9657 University of Calcutta. Business Studies 1188
0970-969X Indian Odonatology 849
0970-9738 Indian Poultry Industry Yearbook 289
0970-9754 Buddhist Studies 7700
0970-9797 India. Textiles Committee. Consumer Purchases of Textiles (Year) 8452
0970-9800 Consumer Purchases and Price Trends of Textiles 8449
0970-9819 International Journal of Translation 5130
0970-9835 Bionature 661
0970-9843 Institution of Engineers (India). Interdisciplinary Panels Journal 3199
0970-9851 Institute of Indian Geographers. Transactions 4015
0970-9894 Journal of Indian Museums 6526
0970-9908 Journal of Gandhian Studies 7147
0970-9916 Vagartha
0970-9932 Dairy India Yearbook 263
0970-9940 Indian Journal of Linguistics 5127
0970-9967 Journal of Marine and Atmospheric Research 2809
0970-9991 Journal of Energy, Heat and Mass Transfer 3140
0971-0043 Current Tax Reporter 1919
0971-0078 Popular Plastics & Packaging 7099
0971-0108 Bioved 662
0971-0116 Current Nematology 939
0971-0167 Fish Technology Newsletter 3592
0971-0191 Gasoil 6771
0971-0221 Granthana: Indian Journal of Library Studies 5011
0971-0272 Sudhanidhi
0971-0388 Aligarh Journal of Statistics 8344
0971-0396 Indian School of Political Economy. Journal 1122
0971-0426 Indian Journal of Fibre & Textile Research 8452
0971-0450 Institution of Engineers (India). Marine Engineering Division. Journal 3199
0971-0469 Institution of Engineers (India). Computer Engineering Division. Journal 2471
0971-0485 South Asian Language Review 5176
0971-0493 Allahabad Mathematical Society. Bulletin 5468
0971-0507 Advances in Horticulture & Forestry 3721
0971-0523 Asian Journal of Chemistry Reviews†
0971-0566 Indian Journal of Finance and Research 1353
0971-0612 Samskriti 7708
0971-0639 Alive 5205
0971-0647 New Agriculturist 139
0971-0663 University of Calcutta. Department of Sociology. Journal 8145
0971-0701 Journal of Veterinary and Animal Sciences 8801
0971-071X Journal International Medical Sciences Academy 5645
0971-0728 Powder Metallurgy Science & Technology 6329
0971-0817 Indian Journal of Social Science†
0971-0833 A C T 8447
0971-085X T I D E changed to 0972-6721 3148
0971-0949 Hearing Aid Journal 4074
0971-0957 P I L C Journal of Dravidic Studies 5159
0971-0965 Journal of Ecotoxicology & Environmental Monitoring 3498
0971-0973 Indian Academy of Forensic Medicine. Journal 5914
0971-1031 Journal of Veterinary Parasitology 8801
0971-104X Indian Journal of Zoological Spectrum 947
0971-1066 Hindustan Chamber Review 1404
0971-1198 Trends in Biomaterials & Artificial Organs 4078
0971-1228 Journal of Australian Literature 5314
0971-1244 Indian Construction 1014
0971-1252 Ethnobotany 787
0971-1260 Think India 3223
0971-1317 Indian Auto 8585
0971-1333 News Review on South East Asia, Australasia and Indo-China†
0971-1341 News Review on Africa†
0971-135X The Annals of Medical Entomology 5575
0971-1376 Mine and Metal Worker 6470
0971-1422 Indian Fisheries Association. Journal 3597
0971-1449 Papeles de la India 4468
0971-1481 Current Trends in Geology†
0971-149X Suman Saurabh 2215
0971-1503 Woman's Era 8889
0971-152X Grih Shobha 8866
0971-1538 Sarita 5367
0971-1554 Journal of Quantitative Economics 1138
0971-1562 Perspectives in Psychological Researches†
0971-1589 Indian Books in Print 627
0971-1600 Journal of Spacecraft Technology 64
0971-1619 People's Manifesto 7165
0971-1627 Indian Journal of Heterocyclic Chemistry 2064
0971-1643 Journal of Bombay Veterinary College 8800
0971-1651 see 0009-1332 2182
0971-166X Documentation on Women's Concerns 8858
0971-1678 Aspect of Plant Sciences 777
0971-1708 Recent Researches in Ecology, Environment and Pollution†
0971-1716 International Bioscience Series†
0971-1724 Birsa Agricultural University. Journal of Research 96
0971-1848 Media and Technology for Human Resource Development†
0971-1864 Institute of Public Enterprise. Journal 1754
0971-1899 Journal of Mining Research 6467
0971-1929 Journal of Forensic Medicine and Toxicology 5914
0971-1937 Indian Journal of Veterinary Anatomy 8799
0971-1996 Population Research Abstract 7290
0971-2038 Urja Oil and Gas International
0971-2062 Indian Journal of Dryland Agricultural Research and Development 121
0971-2097 Political Economy Journal of India 1547
0971-2119 Journal of Applied Animal Research 949
0971-2127 Indian Journal of Environment and Toxicology 3497
0971-2151 Chemical & Environmental Research 2053
0971-216X P C Quest 2580
0971-2240 Indian Historical Quarterly†
0971-2291 Election Archives and International Politics 7132
0971-2305 Screen World 6512
0971-2313 Rheedea 815
0971-233X Information Technology 5061
0971-2356 Indian Journal of Agricultural Engineering 120
0971-2372 Journal of Environmental Research 3446
0971-2402 Asian Journal of Plant Science 777
0971-2453 Junior Scientist 3069
0971-2542 Indian Journal of Petroleum Geology 6773
0971-2615 International Journal of Toxicology, Occupational and Environmental Health†
0971-2631 Energy & Fuel Users' Journal 3130
0971-2658 A A R R O Newsletter changed to A A R D O Newsletter 1589
0971-2666 W W F India Quarterly 3474
0971-2690 Indian Journal of Open Learning 2949
0971-2704 Advances in Forestry Research in India 3683
0971-2720 N F I Bulletin 6663
0971-2755 Ramakrishna Mission Institute of Culture. Bulletin 4471
0971-2828 Communications in Theoretical Physics 7008
0971-2844 Palaeontologia Indica 6728
0971-2909 Asian Journal of Psychology and Education 2827
0971-2941 Granthalaya Vijnana 5011
0971-2976 National Botanical Society. Journal 804
0971-3034 Indian Journal of Technical Education 8425
0971-3077 Bay of Bengal News 3587
0971-3085 Institut Francais de Pondichery. Departement de Sciences Sociales. Publications 7973
0971-3093 Asian Journal of Physics 7006
0971-3107 Institut Francais de Pondichery. Departement d'Ecologie. Publications 7866
0971-314X Indian Medicine 310
0971-3182 Movie 6507
0971-3190 International Journal of Behavioural Sciences 7364
0971-3204 Statistics of Marine Products Exports 1268
0971-3212 Religion and Law Review 4768
0971-3220 Journal of Objective Studies 7713
0971-3239 P R I M E 1580
0971-3263 Journal of Atomic Mineral Science 3170
0971-3328 Journal of Spices and Aromatic Crops 684
0971-3336 Psychology and Developing Societies 7398
0971-3344 Institution of Engineers (India). Technorama 3199
0971-3352 E I News 3196
0971-3425 Asian Textile Journal 8448
0971-3441 Agricultural Economics Research Review 192
0971-3492 Samiksa 7406
0971-3514 Differential Equations and Dynamical Systems 5482
0971-3549 India. Ministry of Home Affairs. Vital Statistics Division. Sample Registration Bulletin 7309
0971-3557 Journal of Entrepreneurship 1765
0971-3573 Annals of Plant Protection Sciences 775
0971-359X Sportstar 8208
0971-3611 Journal of Analysis 5500
0971-3654 Sportsworld 8208
0971-3689 Plastics News 7097
0971-3719 Journal of Mycopathological Research 890
0971-3727 Indiya Tode see 0254-8399 3883
0971-3751 Kanch 2043
0971-376X Sri Aurobindo. Archives and Research†
0971-3786 Parsiana 7740
0971-3794 Voyage 8773
0971-3808 Stock Exchange Official Directory 2029
0971-3859 Journal of Educational Planning and Administration 3026
0971-3964 Tapovan Prasad 7708
0971-4022 Annals of Forestry 3683
0971-4065 Indian Journal of Nephrology 6268
0971-4111 Hispanistica 5306
0971-4170 Indian Journal of Landscape Systems and Ecological Studies 3439
0971-4189 Indian Journal of Gerontology 4047
0971-4197 Defence Today 6418
0971-4219 Medical and Nutritional Research Communications 6663
0971-4227 Poets International 5432
0971-4251 The Indian Journal of Veterinary Research 8799
0971-426X Indian Mountaineer 8318
0971-4324 Journal of Applied Biology 680
0971-4367 Muslim & Arab Perspectives 3552
0971-4383 D E S I D O C Bulletin of Information Technology changed to 0974-0643 5004
0971-4391 D R D O Newsletter 6417
0971-4413 Technology Focus 6448
0971-443X Current Indian Forestry, Environment & Wildlife Abstracts 3708
0971-4448 D K Newsletter 623
0971-4456 Journal of Dairying, Foods & Home Sciences 266
0971-4472 Psychology in Progress
0971-4502 Indian Journal of Hematology and Blood Transfusion 6022
0971-4529 Fishing Chimes 3593
0971-4537 India Today International see 0254-8399 3883
0971-457X Indian Journal of Chemical Technology 2064
0971-4588 Indian Journal of Engineering and Materials Sciences 3197
0971-4669 Major Indian Works Annual 630
0971-4693 Allelopathy Journal 774
0971-4839 Homoeopathic Update 5805
0971-4871 Journal of Environment and Pollution changed to 0972-6268 3489
0971-4936 Delhi Law Review 4656
0971-4944 Spatio - Economic Development Record 4427
0971-4960 Loyola Journal of Social Sciences 7984
0971-5053 Life Science Advances: Experimental & Clinical Endocrinology†
0971-5134 Life Science Advances: Oncology†
0971-5150 Vikram Mathematical Journal 5546
0971-5215 Indian Journal of Gender Studies 8899
0971-5223 International Journal of Punjab Studies changed to Journal of Punjab Studies 7979

ISSN

DIRECTORY 2010 0973-7847 9429

0972-8074 Anil Aggrawal's Internet Journal of Forensic Medicine and Toxicology **5912**
0972-8201 Asian Journal of Management Cases **1726**
0972-821X Current Topics in Biotechnology **763**
0972-8279 Journal of Maxillofacial and Oral Surgery **6249**
0972-8341 B T R A Scan **8448**
0972-8589 Farm Science Journal **111**
0972-8600 A K C E International Journal of Graphs and Combinatorics **5463**
0972-8864 International Relations in a Globalising World
0972-9038 International Journal of Computer Science & Applications **2425**
0972-9062 Journal of Vector Borne Diseases **5821**
0972-9070 The I C F A I Journal of Audit Practice **1290**
0972-9089 The I C F A I Journal of Behavioral Finance **1750**
0972-9097 The I C F A I Journal of Brand Management **1819**
0972-9119 The I C F A I Journal of Derivatives Markets **1629**
0972-9151 The I C F A I Journal of Financial Economics **1352**
0972-916X The I C F A I Journal of Financial Risk Management **1750**
0972-9194 The I C F A I Journal of Infrastructure **1750**
0972-9208 The I C F A I Journal of Industrial Economics **1120**
0972-9216 The I C F A I Journal of Knowledge Management **1751**
0972-9224 The I C F A I Journal of Services Marketing **1819**
0972-9232 The I C F A I Journal of Mergers and Acquisitions **1120**
0972-9259 The I C F A I Journal of Business Strategy **1750**
0972-9267 The I C F A I Journal of Supply Chain Management **1819**
0972-9291 The I C F A I Journal of Monetary Economics **1719**
0972-9305 The I C F A I Journal of Managerial Economics **1751**
0972-9313 The I C F A I Journal of Environmental Economics **3438**
0972-933X The I C F A I Journal of Risk and Insurance **4505**
0972-9348 Indian Media Studies Journal **2325**
0972-9356 The I C F A I Journal of Public Finance **1928**
0972-9364 India Surface Finishing **6315**
0972-9380 International Journal of Economic Research **1128**
0972-9437 Indian Development Review **1598**
0972-950X Journal of Aerospace Sciences and Technologies **63**
0972-9518 Calicut Medical Journal **5591**
0972-9585 The Indian Cow **265**
0972-9607 Indian Journal of Practical Pediatrics **6093**
0972-9658 D I A S Technology Review **1089**
0972-9712 Annual Review of Plant Pathology **775**
0972-9739 Images Yearbook **2256**
0972-9747 Hepatitis B Annual **5814**
0972-9755 India Policy Forum **1719**
0972-978X Journal of Orthopaedics **6065**
0972-9828 International Journal of Pure and Applied Mathematical Sciences **5497**
0972-9836 Global Journal of Mathematics and Mathematical Sciences **5490**
0972-9852 Mathematical Forum **5513**
0972-9860 Asian Journal of Water, Environment and Pollution **3404**
0972-9917 Advances in Plant Physiology **773**
0972-9941 Journal of Minimal Access Surgery **6249**
0972-9976 International Journal of Tomography & Statistics **6199**
0972-9992 Gyan **2861**
0973-0044 Central Research Institute for Jute and Allied Fibres. Annual Report **8449**
0973-0052 International Journal of Rural Management **4016**
0973-0060 Indian Environment Online **3439**
0973-0095 Dialogue **4657**
0973-0109 Advanced Bio Tech **755**
0973-015X M I C A Communications Review **1829**
0973-0176 International Journal of Applied Mathematical Sciences **5495**
0973-0184 International Journal of Applied Mathematics and Mechanics **5495**
0973-0206 Science & Society **7908**
0973-0273 Liberal Digest **7151**
0973-029X Journal of Oral and Maxillofacial Pathology **5852**
0973-0311 The Indian Anaesthetists' Forum **5771**
0973-0338 The Journal of C P R I **3159**
0973-0419 Labour and Development **1693**
0973-0427 Awards Digest **1666**
0973-0435 Shram Vidhana **1707**
0973-0486 Kindler **1770**
0973-0508 The Indian Journal of Neurotrauma **6145**
0973-0516 Resources, Energy and Development **3146**
0973-0524 Literary Explorer **5324**
0973-0559 I-Manager's Journal of Education Technology **2865**
0973-0591 New Building Materials & Construction World **1026**
0973-0818 Indian Journal of Human Rights and the Law **7209**
0973-0826 Energy for Sustainable Development **3131**
0973-0850 Alliance Journal of Business Research **1725**
0973-0907 Journal of Arid Legumes **239**
0973-0915 North Eastern Geographer **4022**
0973-1040 Trends in Cancer Research **6035**
0973-1075 Indian Journal of Palliative Care **4102**
0973-1180 North East India Studies **7989**
0973-1229 Mens Sana Monographs **6160**
0973-1245 Biosciences Biotechnology Research Asia **758**
0973-127X Global Review of Business and Economic Research **1114**
0973-1288 A P T I Bulletin **6818**
0973-1296 Pharmacognosy Magazine **6871**
0973-1318 International Journal of Performability Engineering **3202**
0973-1326 Transfusion Bulletin *changed to* 0973-6247 **5933**
0973-1342 Indian Association for Child and Adolescent Mental Health. Journal **7362**
0973-1350 International Review of Pure and Applied Mathematics **5498**
0973-1377 International Journal of Applied Mathematics & Statistics **5495**
0973-1385 International Journal of Ecological Economics & Statistics **679**
0973-1407 Indian Birds **908**
0973-1423 Journal of Ship Technology **8649**
0973-1458 Indian Journal of Physics **7016**
0973-1482 Journal of Cancer Research and Therapeutics **6024**
0973-1598 S M A R T Journal of Business Management Studies **1792**
0973-161X egov **2536**
0973-1636 Indian Venture Capital Journal **1629**
0973-1695 Indian Ocean Turtle Newsletter **947**
0973-1725 Updates@nrsa **2718**
0973-1733 *see* 0973-1741 **1600**
0973-1741 Journal of South Asian Development **1600**
0973-175X Amity Journal of Behavioural and Forensic Sciences **7333**
0973-1768 Global Journal of Pure and Applied Mathematics **5490**
0973-1776 International Journal of Pure and Applied Physics **7017**
0973-1784 International Journal of Dynamics of Fluids **3382**
0973-1792 International Journal of Applied Chemistry **2065**
0973-1806 Delhi Journal of Orthopaedics **6058**
0973-1814 Journal of Health and Development **7529**
0973-1822 Indian Journal of Fertilisers **235**
0973-1857 Industrial Products Source **3197**
0973-1873 International Journal of Computational Intelligence Research **2425**
0973-1881 International Journal of Mechanics and Solids **3347**
0973-1938 I C S Newsletter **6651**
0973-1954 Vilakshan **1800**
0973-1970 Indian Internet Journal of Forensic Medicine & Toxicology **5914**
0973-1997 Shrimata **7708**
0973-2020 Journal of Exercise Science and Physiotherapy **924**
0973-2063 Bioinformation **657**
0973-208X International Journal of Lateral Computing **2426**
0973-2101 International Journal of Management Sciences **1759**
0973-211X Business Analyst **1070**
0973-2144 Osian's Cinemaya **6509**
0973-2152 International Journal of Fitness **6990**
0973-2179 Journal of Neonatology **6094**
0973-2187 *see* 0973-2179 **6094**
0973-2195 Trendz **5724**
0973-2209 Indian Journal of Physical Medicine and Rehabilitation **6110**
0973-2241 International Journal of Cow Science **289**
0973-225X The I C F A I Journal of Public Administration **7445**
0973-2268 The I C F A I Journal of Science and Technology **7864**
0973-2284 Indian Journal of Occupational and Environmental Medicine **5634**
0973-2314 International Gallerie **4457**
0973-2322 Ophthalmology Times India **6049**
0973-2349 Indian Dairy Industry **265**
0973-2365 Indian Ocean Survey **2806**
0973-2411 Indian Journal of Geomorphology **2709**
0973-2446 Trends in Heat and Mass Transfer **7057**
0973-2470 Asian-Pacific Business Review **1726**
0973-2497 Journal of Rehabilitation Council of India **8051**
0973-2527 Fast Forward Newsletter **1341**
0973-2586 Journal of Creative Communications **2329**
0973-2594 *see* 0973-2586 **2329**
0973-2640 The I C F A I Journal of Corporate and Securities Law **4870**
0973-2659 The I C F A I Journal of Entrepreneurship Development **1750**
0973-2667 International Journal of Oceans and Oceanography **2808**
0973-2675 International Journal of Statistics and Systems **8379**
0973-2683 Indian Journal of Applied Agricultural Research **121**
0973-2691 International Journal of Biotechnology and Biochemistry **766**
0973-2721 Kerala Mathematics Association. Bulletin **5507**
0973-273X Puzha Magazine **3887**
0973-2764 Heritage Amruth **310**
0973-2772 Rays of the Harmonist **7708**
0973-2802 Islam and Muslim Societies **7711**
0973-2861 Journal of Analysis and Computation **5500**
0973-287X Journal of Approximation Theory and Applications **5501**
0973-2896 The I C F A I Journal of Information Technology **2420**
0973-290X India Macroeconomics Annual **1719**
0973-2926 Journal of Computer Science **2428**
0973-2942 Tamilnadu Journal of Veterinary and Animal Sciences **8808**
0973-2977 Strategy **1180**
0973-3043 Genesis ... a Caravan **1747**
0973-306X Atlantic Journal of World Affairs **7222**
0973-3086 Rajagiri Journal of Social Development **8127**
0973-3094 Journal of S A T Agricultural Research **128**
0973-3159 Maritime Affairs **8652**
0973-3167 S C M S Journal of Indian Management **1792**
0973-3205 Amaltas **218**
0973-340X Indian Journal of Sleep Medicine **6229**
0973-3426 Journal of Social and Economic Policy **7148**
0973-3442 Karnataka State Dental Journal **5854**
0973-3469 Materials Science Research India **3354**
0973-3477 Acharya Nagarjuna Journal of Mathematics and Information Technology **5464**
0973-3515 V S I Vision **2474**
0973-3558 Indian Society of Toxicology. Journal **3498**
0973-3566 *see* 0973-3558 **3498**
0973-3574 International Journal of Environment and Development **3441**
0973-3582 Journal of Social Anthropology **345**
0973-3604 International Journal of Mathematics and Analysis **5497**
0973-3698 Indian Journal of Rheumatology **6224**
0973-3787 Ninad **6599**
0973-3809 Pulmon **6217**
0973-3825 Vidhigya. The Journal of Legal Awareness **4808**
0973-3841 Communications in Mathematical Analysis **5479**
0973-385X Journal of Computational Intelligence in Bioinformatics **2453**
0973-3922 *see* 0378-6323 **5877**
0973-3930 International Journal of Diabetes in Developing Countries **5894**
0973-3965 Biomed **779**
0973-4007 S A T I Journal of Science and Technology **7906**
0973-4058 P C T E Journal of Computer Sciences **2434**
0973-4066 P C T E Journal of Business Management **1784**
0973-4082 Journal of Education for Sustainable Development **3444**
0973-4139 Digital Learning **2842**
0973-4163 Trends in Information Management **5051**
0973-4198 NetPEM Newsletter **3456**
0973-421X Advances in Fuzzy Sets and Systems **5466**
0973-4228 J P Journal of Fixed Point Theory and Applications **5499**
0973-4317 Indian Journal of Industrial and Applied Mathematics **5493**
0973-4333 Business & Economy **1070**
0973-4341 4Ps Business and Marketing **1849**
0973-449X NICE Journal of Business **1781**
0973-4511 Small Change **1383**
0973-452X Pharma Times **6868**
0973-4538 J O H A R **4391**
0973-4554 Advances in Theoretical and Applied Mathematics **5467**
0973-4562 International Journal of Applied Engineering Research **3200**
0973-4570 International Journal of Lakes and Rivers **8826**
0973-4589 International Journal of Materials Science **3347**
0973-4600 Journal of Statistics and Applications **8383**
0973-4651 Current Medical Issues **5602**
0973-4678 Doon Theological Journal **7638**
0973-4686 Advances and Applications in Fluid Mechanics **3360**
0973-4708 Wave Front **7046**
0973-483X Biopesticides International **221**
0973-4864 I J S C I **2527**
0973-4872 Voyager **2441**
0973-4880 The Indian Journal of Crop Science **235**
0973-4945 E-Journal of Chemistry **2060**
0973-502X Context **438**
0973-5070 Studies on Ethno - Medicine **5718**
0973-5089 International Journal of Criminal Justice Sciences **2655**
0973-5143 J P Journal of Biostatistics **8381**
0973-5216 Socio-Legal Review **8135**
0973-5259 International Economic and Finance Journal **1356**
0973-5275 International Journal of Applied Mathematics and Engineering Sciences **5495**
0973-5313 Advances in Applied Mathematical Analysis **5466**
0973-5321 Advances in Dynamical Systems and Applications **5466**
0973-533X Advances in Fuzzy Mathematics **5466**
0973-5348 Mathematical Modelling of Natural Phenomena **5513**
0973-5399 *see* 0971-636X **128**
0973-5550 Management Today **1777**
0973-5593 Far East Journal of Ocean Research **2804**
0973-5607 Current Development in Theory and Applications of Wavelets **5481**
0973-5615 J P Journal of Solids and Structures **3273**
0973-5631 Far East Journal of Mathematical Education **5487**
0973-5666 Indian Journal of Physiotherapy and Occupational Therapy **6110**
0973-5674 *see* 0973-5666 **6110**
0973-5747 Bulletin of Political Economy **1592**
0973-5763 J P Journal of Heat and Mass Transfer **3140**
0973-5887 G G U Journal of Business **1112**
0973-5909 *see* 0970-8235 **236**
0973-5933 Bulletin of Pure and Applied Mathematics **5476**
0973-5984 Jadavpur Journal of International Relations **7246**
0973-6042 International Journal of Shoulder Surgery **6246**
0973-6069 International Journal of Applied Environmental Sciences **3441**
0973-6085 International Journal of Theoretical and Applied Mechanics **3383**
0973-6093 Mathematical Modelling and Applied Computing **5513**
0973-6107 Advances in Computational Sciences and Technology **5466**
0973-6115 A P C R I Newsletter **5564**
0973-6131 International Journal of Yoga **6990**
0973-614X Donald School Journal of Ultrasound in Obstetrics and Gynecology **6195**
0973-6247 Asian Journal of Transfusion Science **5933**
0973-6263 Research Journal of BioTechnology **770**
0973-631X International Journal of Nanotechnology and Applications **3347**
0973-6328 International Journal of Petroleum Science and Technology **6774**
0973-6336 Journal of Wavelet Theory and Applications **2351**
0973-6344 Mathematics Applied in Science and Technology **5515**
0973-6379 Journal of Lipid Science and Technology **2124**
0973-6425 Knowledge Hub **1771**
0973-6549 Physiotherapy **6114**
0973-6565 Akshara **5251**
0973-6581 Bioinformatics Trends **747**
0973-6638 Digital Library Communication **5061**
0973-6751 International Journal of General Topology **5496**
0973-693X Advances in Applied Mathematical Biosciences **5466**
0973-6964 Advances in Algebra **5465**
0973-6972 Advances in Wireless and Mobile Communications **2311**
0973-6980 Vet Scan **8810**
0973-6999 Advances in Computer Science and Engineering **2470**
0973-7006 Far East Journal of Electronics and Communications **3308**
0973-709X Journal of Clinical and Diagnostic Research **5647**
0973-7103 *see* 0974-3626 **2067**
0973-7111 *see* 0304-4289 **7035**
0973-712X *see* 0971-8044 **7903**
0973-7138 *see* 0250-5991 **682**
0973-7189 Studies on Home and Community Science **8142**
0973-7294 *see* 0972-9976 **6199**
0973-7510 Journal of Pure and Applied Microbiology **890**
0973-7669 *see* 0250-4707 **3342**
0973-7677 *see* 0256-2499 **7906**
0973-7685 *see* 0253-4142 **5493**
0973-7693 *see* 0019-5456 **6092**
0973-7707 *see* Indian Journal of Otolaryngology and Head and Neck Surgery **6080**
0973-7715 *see* 0046-8991 **887**
0973-7723 *see* 0970-9134 **5790**
0973-7731 *see* 0022-1333 **873**
0973-774X *see* Journal of Earth System Science **2711**
0973-7758 *see* 0250-6335 **576**
0973-7847 Pharmacognosy Reviews **6872**

ISSN

Link to your serials resources and content with ulrichsweb.com

0983-4796 Bibliotheque de la Psychanalyse
0983-5733 Tableaux Economiques de l'Ile-de-France. Edition (Year) *changed to* 1635-0529 **1521**
0983-6233 Exploitant Agricole de Saone et Loire **109**
0983-656X Lamy Droit Commercial **4873**
0983-6799 Lamy Societes Commerciales **4874**
0983-6829 Lamy Droit Economique **4712**
0983-8201 O P A Pratique **6083**
0983-8430 La Recherche Photographique†
0983-8651 Military Powers' Encyclopedia†
0984-0028 Association pour la Recherche Cognitive. Bulletin†
0984-1466 Tutti Insieme **5189**
0984-1695 N E I D†
0984-1725 R C E: Revue des Comites d'Entreprise et Equivalents *changed to* 1633-3284 **1698**
0984-2292 Guerres Mondiales et Conflits Contemporains **4141**
0984-2314 Wapiti **2221**
0984-2438 C T B A Info† **8939**
0984-2586 Science & Motricite (France) *changed to* 1378-1863 **6233**
0984-2594 New Caledonia. Institut de la Statistique et des Etudes Economiques. Indice et Index du B T P **1048**
0984-2616 Horizons Maghrebins **341**
0984-2632 Germanica **5300**
0984-3086 Infos - Route A 36†
0984-3779 Les Cahiers du C T N E R H I *changed to* 1295-2362 **8961**
0984-421X Tennis de Table Magazine **8248**
0984-4295 Ongle Magazine†
0984-452X La Lettre du Pharmacologue **6858**
0984-4554 Lettre de l'Environnement **3450**
0984-4554 La Lettre de l'Environnement *changed to* 1969-9468 **3430**
0984-4708 30 Millions d'Amis **6817**
0984-4899 Bato Loc International† **8935**
0984-5585 Banque de France. Commission Bancaire. Rapport (Year) **1319**
0984-6700 Statistique Annuelle de la Navigation Interieure†
0984-760X Jeune et Jolie **2195**
0984-7685 Islam et Societe au Sud du Sahara†
0984-774X Etat de l'Opinion **1816**
0984-7987 Revue Juridique et Economique du Sport **4774**
0984-8207 Cahiers Jungiens de Psychanalyse **7343**
0984-8479 Coulicou†
0984-8541 Documentation - Refugies†
0984-8983 Albatroz† **8929**
0984-9068 Top's Cars **8607**
0984-9114 Bulletin Officiel de la Comptabilite Publique **1282**
0984-9521 Marches Africains **1577**
0984-9602 Arts Graphiques Magazine† **8931**
0985-0074 Face *changed to* 1967-0176 **1402**
0985-049X Praticien du Sud Ouest†
0985-0503 France Composites†
0985-0562 Nutrition Clinique et Metabolisme **5898**
0985-0791 Centre d'Information des Utilisateurs de Progiciels. Catalogue **1415**
0985-116X Mesogee†
0985-1402 Vertigo **6516**
0985-1461 Grandes Cuisines **4387**
0985-150X Bovins Limousins **281**
0985-1534 La Toque et le Verre
0985-1542 Satellite TV Europe (Paris) *changed to* 1248-3222
0985-1739 Compagnie Nationale des Commissaires aux Comptes. Conseil National. Bulletin **4647**
0985-1798 Unir **3842**
0985-1909 Cahiers d'Etudes Arabes†
0985-1976 Propriete Agricole†
0985-200X G P L Actualite **6769**
0985-2204 Energie†
0985-2220 F T S†
0985-2395 Institut Jean Vigo. Archives **6504**
0985-2433 Mutations† **8975**
0985-2654 Flash Japon†
0985-2662 Flash Etats-Unis†
0985-3057 Oceanorama **2815**
0985-3111 Geodinamica Acta **2736**
0985-3286 Marsyas†
0985-3642 L'Orgue Francophone **6603**
0985-3685 En Mains Propres **3505**
0985-5106 Memoires et Documents d'Histoire Medievale et de Philologie **4244**
0985-5637 Tolerie **6335**
0985-5645 Quotidien du Maire†
0985-5734 Seve Eglise Aujourd'hui *changed to* 1625-5437
0985-5939 Sociocriticism†
0985-7303 Cuisine Collective Magazine **4384**
0985-7427 Souffles†
0985-7443 Compatibles P C Magazine **2575**
0985-7826 Travaux et Recherches des Universites Rhenanes **5390**
0985-8784 Infos de l'Expression d'Entreprise **1753**
0985-9195 Faiences Patriotiques
0985-9837 Universite de Bordeaux II. Cahiers Ethnologiques. Memoires† **8996**
0986-0754 La Vie Claire†
0986-1289 Courrier des Marches et d'Outre Mer†
0986-1351 A S - Actualite de la Scenographie **8464**
0986-1491 Aujourd'hui Dimanche **7746**
0986-1653 L'Enseignement Philosophique **6915**
0986-1793 P C M le Pont *changed to* Ponts & Chaussees Magazine **3280**
0986-2013 Chambre de Commerce et d'Industrie de Rouen. Bulletin Economique **1399**
0986-2226 La Societe Jules Verne. Bulletin **4265**
0986-2684 Societe des Amis du Vieux Strasbourg. Annuaire **4427**
0986-2773 Etudes Jean-Jacques Rousseau
0986-2889 Camera Video *changed to* 1289-527X **2400**
0986-2943 Environnement et Technique **3430**
0986-3354 Animaux Magazine **318**
0986-492X Etudes Montaignistes **5292**
0986-5152 L'Imaginaire du Texte
0986-5675 Plaisance Mer et Peche† **8981**
0986-6019 Modernites
0986-6124 Recherches Linguistiques de Vincennes **5165**
0986-6426 Revue Languedocienne de Sociologie Ethnologie†
0986-6884 Haute Finance†
0986-7449 Paris Passion†
0986-7481 Voici **8888**
0986-8518 Journal des Architectes
0986-9050 Le Journal des Enfants **2195**
0987-0717 Science & Nature†
0987-0806 Tangente **5540**
0987-1438 Business Bourse
0987-2205 Association pour la Promotion de la Recherche Archeologique en Alsace. Cahiers **382**
0987-2930 Lettre du Routard†
0987-3090 Memoire de Trame **2348**
0987-3201 L'Officiel des Terrains de Camping et de Caravaning†
0987-3260 Plein Droit **4851**
0987-3368 Revue d'Economie Financiere **1380**
0987-3813 Revue de l'Economie Meridionale
0987-3872 Lettre d'Orion (Magazine) **4568**
0987-4135 Bulletin d'Histore Contemporaine de l'Espagne **4207**
0987-4216 Antiane Eco†
0987-5212 Cantal Eco **1398**
0987-6014 Netcom
0987-6030 Repertoire†
0987-6278 Zusammen **5200**
0987-6421 Chambre de Commerce et d'Industrie. La Lettre† **8940**
0987-6936 Mathematiques et Sciences Humaines **5516**
0987-7053 Neurophysiologie Clinique **6167**
0987-710X Tertiaire *changed to* 1771-8414 **1540**
0987-7282 Batiprix **979**
0987-7401 Repertoire des Banques de Donnees Teletel pour l'Entreprise†
0987-741X Golf en France†
0987-7444 Magazine de la Construction†
0987-7606 Produits et Communication
0987-7622 Standpoints *changed to* 1292-8976 **3074**
0987-7738 Langues Orientales Anciennes Philologie et Linguistique†
0987-7878 Revue Internationale d'Histoire de la Psychanalyse†
0987-7924 Allo Comptoir
0987-7940 Societe Internationale d'Etudes Yourcenariennes. Bulletin **5374**
0987-7983 Journal de Pediatrie et de Puericulture **5645**
0987-8238 CD-ROM International†
0987-8254 Clinic International
0987-8270 Liquides Magazine **3208**
0987-8467 Al-Handasah†
0987-8505 Passages
0988-0895 J'ai Lu. Thriller **5414**
0988-1433 Confederation Service†
0988-1476 Elle Decoration **4556**
0988-1808 Le Vieux Marly **4277**
0988-1824 Recherche et Formation **2999**
0988-1921 Who's Working Where†
0988-1956 Aviron **8271**
0988-3215 New Caledonia. Institut Territorial de la Statistique et des Etudes Economiques. Indices des Prix a la Consommation **1254**
0988-324X Les Marches **136**
0988-3266 I N R A Sciences Sociales **200**
0988-3452 Computer Data Storage Newsletter **2539**
0988-3525 Opto†
0988-3754 R A I R O - Theoretical Informatics and Applications **2528**
0988-3789 Science et Technologie de la Conservation et de la Restoration des Oeuvres d'Art et du Patrimoine† **8987**
0988-3800 Societe des Etudes Bloyennes. Bulletin†
0988-4068 Nervure **6163**
0988-4386 France. Ministere de la Mer. Bulletin Officiel **8644**
0988-5188 Le Batisseur Europeen *changed to* 1266-2089 **979**
0988-5226 Lignes **3841**
0988-5234 Mythes, Croyances et Religions dans le Monde Anglo-Saxon *changed to* 1631-4271
0988-5560 Le Trimestre Psychanalytique *changed to* 1775-6871 **7337**
0988-5730 Systemes Experts†
0988-5838 L'Interconsulaire France Regions **1405**
0988-629X R F M†
0988-6729 Revue Francaise d'Esperanto **5168**
0988-6990 Gynecologie - Obstetrique Pratique **5992**
0988-7679 Photographies Magazine†
0988-8160 Amstrad Cent pour Cent
0988-8233 Tout en Cartes†
0988-8705 Transversales† **8994**
0988-9256 Auvergne Agricole **93**
0988-9590 Boulogne Informations† **8937**
0988-9760 Police Mutualite†
0988-9914 Trimestre du Monde†
0989-0009 Vie de la Moto **369**
0989-0025 Mutualite Sociale Agricole. Annuaire Statistique† **8975**
0989-1080 Voyages et Strategie **8773**
0989-1706 Confortique Magazine **3091**
0989-1889 Profession Nouveau Papetier **6737**
0989-1900 Option Finance **1373**
0989-2257 Centre d'Etude des Revenus et des Couts. Notes et Graphiques†
0989-2583 Sycodes Informations *changed to* 1763-7716 **1031**
0989-263X Gastroenterologie *changed to* 1622-4191 **5919**
0989-2648 Agro Performances† **8928**
0989-2737 La Revue du Praticien - Medecine Generale **5706**
0989-3091 Cuisine Actuelle **4355**
0989-3105 Ophtalmologie†
0989-3334 Savoirs Actuels **7907**
0989-4322 Litterales
0989-4454 Arctique **5096**
0989-5671 N A B U. Nouvelles Assyriologiques Breves et Utilitaires **407**
0989-5973 Le Catalogue des Cartes Marines et des Ouvrages Nautiques **8641**
0989-5981 Repertoire des Radiosignaux **2363**
0989-6023 Ligeia **503**
0989-6139 Valentiana **423**
0989-621X Journees de Strasbourg†
0989-6236 Astronomie et Sciences Humaines
0989-635X Bibliotheque Nationale de France. Autorites Collectivites **620**
0989-6686 Tribune Video des Anglicistes†
0989-697X Atout Cambresis†
0989-6988 Academie d'Agriculture de France. Comptes Rendus **78**
0989-733X Youpi **2223**
0989-7577 Mineurs de France: Edition Centre-Midi **6472**
0989-7828 Centre de Recherche et d'Information sur la Litterature pour la Jeunesse **5271**
0989-7925 Facultes de Droit et de la Science Juridique. Revue d'Histoire† **8955**
0989-8131 Marches Latino-Americains **1577**
0989-8379 Ingenieurs sans Frontieres *changed to* 1764-2558 **3180**
0989-8735 Information du Technicien Biologiste†
0989-8778 Forum Enseignements†
0989-8921 Academie Internationale de Pathologie. Division Francaise. Bulletin **4565**
0989-8972 Biological Structures and Morphogenesis†
0989-9200 Societe des Sciences Historiques et Naturelles de Semur en Auxois et des Fouilles d'Alesia. Bulletin **4265**
0990-0063 Annuaire des Arachnologistes Mondiaux†
0990-0632 Productions Animales **8805**
0990-0845 Subaqua **8336**
0990-1027 Revue Juridique de l'Ouest **4774**
0990-1159 Locaguide **1021**
0990-1310 Oxymag **5773**
0990-1760 L'Annee du Rugby **8220**
0990-1876 Maison de la Chasse et de la Nature. Revue†
0990-1914 A B C D†
0990-1930 Top Echecs†
0990-1957 Jour J†
0990-2295 Annee Gerontologique (French Edition)†
0990-2392 Gazette des Assureurs Conseils **4503**
0990-3089 Decoration†
0990-3925 Association des Sedimentologistes Francais **2725**
0990-5200 Liberte de l'Est **3841**
0990-5413 Education Economie†
0990-5669 Gerontologie Pratique **4046**
0990-6479 Glamour (Paris)†
0990-6827 Les Amis de Jean-Giraudoux. Bulletin *changed to* 1962-5952 **5267**
0990-6908 Cahiers d'Histoire de l'Aluminium **6307**
0990-7068 Ulysse **8770**
0990-7440 Aquatic Living Resources **3586**
0990-7866 Revue Carbet†
0990-820X Mineurs de France†
0990-834X Bourse de Paris. Decisions & Avis†
0990-8420 Symptomes†
0990-8498 Guide de la Securite des Entreprises et des Collectivites **3579**
0990-8536 Kompass Professionnel. Distribution, Commerce de Gros **2011**
0990-8544 Kompass Professionnel. Industries en Matieres Multiples†
0990-8552 Kompass Professionnel. Transports, Moyens de Transports **2012**
0990-9141 Centre de Recherches Historiques. Cahiers†
0990-9435 France. Institut National de la Statistique et des Etudes Economiques. Note de Conjoncture Internationale **1111**
0990-9699 France. Ministere de l'Economie et des Finances. Les Notes Bleues. Statistiques & Etudes Financieres†
0990-977X A D **426**
0991-0298 Journal du Controle Technique **8587**
0991-1944 Chambre de Commerce Franco-Asiatique. Annuaire Officiel†
0991-2118 Les Nouvelles du Patchwork *changed to* 1956-7480 **6640**
0991-2428 Territoires **7503**
0991-3009 Micro Impression†
0991-3769 Pilota **8242**
0991-4781 Guides de Charme Rivages **8717**
0991-5028 Centre de Recherche sur la Lecture Litteraire de Reims. Publication
0991-5281 Aquitania. Supplement *see* 0758-9670 **4199**
0991-532X La Boulite **3615**
0991-5877 Sciences du Langage **5172**
0991-6229 Marges **5330**
0991-6342 C N R S plus **621**
0991-6709 Agur **3517**
0991-7128 Argus des Pharmaciens *changed to* 0991-7136
0991-7136 Argus de la Sante†
0991-7357 L'Arc Boutant **8025**
0991-7799 Annuaire du Cinema Television Video *changed to* 1969-1750 **6489**
0991-8000 Assemblees de Dieu de France. Annuaire **7623**
0991-8086 Revue des Etudes Georgiennes et Caucasiennes **4258**
0991-8787 Les Belles Histoires de Pomme d'Api *changed to* 1770-4758 **2178**
0991-9236 Union Sociale des Oeuvres Privees *changed to* 0041-7041 **8075**
0991-949X Acteurs†
0991-966X Nouveaux Dirigeants
0991-9708 Le Nouvel Educateur **2892**
0991-9953 Langouste†
0992-0285 Anka† **8930**
0992-0730 Femmes au Village†
0992-0757 Levant†
0992-1060 Pixel†
0992-1893 Cycnos **5282**
0992-2059 Histoire de l'Art **493**
0992-2164 Meilleures Adresses des Traitements Thermiques†
0992-2660 Serpent a Plumes†
0992-387X Encyclopedie Periodique Economique Politique et Administrative. La Cour de Cassation *changed to* 1954-4367 **640**
0992-4302 C E M A G R E F. Groupement de Bordeaux. Etude **210**
0992-4426 Polish Agriculture†
0992-4647 Guide Professionel du Minitel†
0992-499X Revue d'Intelligence Artificielle **2456**

DIRECTORY 2010 1000-4424 9433

0999-9981 Lamy Environnement Installations Classees 3450
1000-0003 Xizang Yanjiu 563
1000-0038 Ziran Ziyuan 2634
1000-0054 Qinghua Daxue Xuebao (Ziran Kexue Ban) 7900
1000-0062 Qinghua Daxue Xuebao (Zhexue Shehui Kexue Ban) 6946
1000-0070 Zhonghua Renmin Gongheguo Quanguo Renmin Daibiao Dahui Changwu Weiyuanhui Gongbao 7478
1000-0089 Zhongguo Funu 8892
1000-0097 Shijie Tushu† 8988
1000-0100 Waiyu Xuekan 5194
1000-0119 Hangkong Zhishi 58
1000-0127 Yesheng Dongwu†
1000-0135 Qingbao Xuebao 5041
1000-0151 Dianshi Dianying Wenxue *changed to* Dian Jiang Ying Shi 8950
1000-0186 Kecheng - Jiaocai - Jiaofa 3069
1000-0194 Wenwu Tiandi 423
1000-0208 Zhengfa Luntan 4819
1000-0216 Zhexue Yanjiu 6962
1000-0224 Ziran Kexueshi Yanjiu 7935
1000-0232 Nanfang Jianzhu 450
1000-0240 Bingchuan Dongtu 2778
1000-0267 Nongye Huanjing Baohu *changed to* 1672-2043 3457
1000-0283 Yuanlin 3754
1000-0313 Fangshexue Shijian 6197
1000-033X Zhulu Jixie yu Shigong Jixiehua 5462
1000-0348 Meiguo Yixuehui Yanke Zazhi (Zhongwen Ban)† 8973
1000-0356 Hang Hai 8645
1000-0364 Yuanzi yu Fenzi Wuli Xuebao 7073
1000-0372 Tiedao Zhishi 8626
1000-0380 Zidonghua Yibiao 4490
1000-0399 Anhui Yixue 5574
1000-0429 Waiyu Jiaoxue yu Yanjiu 5194
1000-0437 Wenxian 639
1000-0461 Baxiaoshi Yiwai 3822
1000-0496 Shandong Yike Daxue Xuebao/Shandong University of Medical Sciences. Journal *changed to* 1671-7554 5712
1000-050X Wuhan Cehui Keji Daxue Xuebao (Xinwen Kexue Ban) *changed to* 1671-8860 4034
1000-0518 Yingyong Huaxue 2084
1000-0526 Qixiang 6393
1000-0534 Gaoyuan Qixiang 6353
1000-0550 Chenji Xuebao 2728
1000-0569 Yanshi Xuebao 2775
1000-0577 Xitong Kexue yu Shuxue 2525
1000-0585 Dili Yanjiu 4004
1000-0593 Guangpuxue yu Guangpu Fenxi 7075
1000-0607 Zhenci Yanjiu 316
1000-0615 Shuichan Xuebao 3608
1000-0623 Zhongguo Linye 3708
1000-064X Gang Ao Jingji 1113
1000-0658 Youkuang Dizhi 2775
1000-0666 Dizhen Yanjiu 2731
1000-0674 Weiti Gushengwu Xuebao 898
1000-0690 Dili Kexue 4004
1000-0704 Hubei Zhongyi Zazhi 5630
1000-0712 Daxue Wuli 7010
1000-0720 Fenxi Shiyanshi 7012
1000-0739 Dongwu Fenlei Xuebao 940
1000-0747 Shiyou Kantan yu Kaifa 6792
1000-0755 Dianzi Jishu 3092
1000-0763 Ziran Bianzhengfa Tongxun 8019
1000-0771 Jiliang Jishu 6403
1000-078X Geography Teaching 3063
1000-0801 Dianxin Kexue 2319
1000-081X Gaodeng Xuexiao Jisuan Shuxue Xuebao 5489
1000-0852 Shuiwen 2798
1000-0860 Shuili Shuidian Jishu 3364
1000-0879 Lixue yu Shijian 3388
1000-0887 Yingyong Shuxue he Lixue 5547
1000-0895 Qigong yu Kexue 6995
1000-0909 Neiranji Xuebao 3391
1000-0917 Shuxue Jinzhan 5535
1000-0925 Neiranji Gongcheng 3355
1000-0933 Shengtai Xuebao 3466
1000-0941 Zhongguo Shuitu Baochi 260
1000-0968 Shijie Kexue 7915
1000-0976 Tianranqi Gongye 6795
1000-0984 Shuxue de Shijian yu Renshi 5535
1000-0992 Lixue Jinzhan 7060
1000-100X Dianli Dianzi Jishu 3092
1000-1026 Dianli Xitong Zidonghua 3156
1000-1050 Shoulei Xuebao 963
1000-1069 He'nan Yike Daxue Xuebao *changed to* 1671-6825 5735
1000-1077 Dianzi yu Diannao 2416
1000-1085 Zhongguo Shipin 4369
1000-1093 Binggong Xuebao 6413
1000-1107 Zhongguo Xiaofang 3582
1000-1115 Zhongguo Pengren 4369
1000-114X Guangdong Shehui Kexue 7967
1000-1158 Jiliang Xuebao 6403
1000-1174 Zhongguo Gangchangbing Zazhi 5932
1000-1182 Huaxi Kouqiang Yixue Zazhi 5846
1000-1190 Huazhong Shifan Daxue Xuebao (Ziran Kexue Ban) 7863
1000-1212 Gongcheng Jixie 1009
1000-1220 Xiaoxing Weixing Jisuanji Xitong 2574
1000-1239 Jisuanji Yanjiu yu Fazhan 2473
1000-1247 Dianxin Jishu 2367
1000-1255 Hecheng Xiangjiao Gongye†
1000-1298 Nongye Jixie Xuebao 213
1000-1301 Dizhen Gongcheng yu Gongcheng Zhendong 2779
1000-131X Tumu Gongcheng Xuebao 3286
1000-1328 Yuhang Xuebao 76
1000-1336 Shengming de Huaxue 745
1000-1344 Dian Shijie 3299
1000-1379 Renmin Huang He 4026
1000-1395 Dianzi Kexue Jishu†
1000-1417 Wuxiandian yu Dianshi 2399
1000-1441 Shiyou Wutan 6792
1000-1476 Zhongguo Fangzhi Daxue Xuebao 8463
1000-1484 China Textile University. Journal 8449
1000-1492 Anhui Yike Daxue Xuebao 5574
1000-1506 Beifang Jiaotong Daxue Xuebao/North Communications University. Journal *changed to* 1673-0291 7839
1000-1522 Beijing Linye Daxue Xuebao 7840
1000-1549 Zhongyang Caizheng Jinrong Xueyuan Xuebao 1198
1000-1565 Hebei Daxue Xuebao (Ziran Kexue Ban) 7860
1000-1573 Hebei Nongye Daxue Xuebao 118
1000-159X Taiyuan Zhongxing Jixie Xueyuan Xuebao/Taiyuan Heavy-Machinery Institute. Journal *changed to* 1673-2057 7922
1000-1638 Nei Menggu Daxue Xuebao (Ziran Kexue Ban) 7891
1000-1646 Shenyang Gongye Daxue Xuebao 7915
1000-1670 Dalian Tiedao Xueyuan Xuebao/Dalian Institute of Railway Technology. Journal *changed to* 1673-9590 7849
1000-1700 Shenyang Nongye Daxue Xuebao 155
1000-1719 Liaoning Zhongyi Zazhi 312
1000-1735 Liaoning Shifan Daxue Xuebao (Ziran Kexue Ban) 7879
1000-1743 Zhejiang Yike Daxue Xuebao/Zhejiang Medical University. Journal *changed to* 1008-9292 5735
1000-1751 Liaoning Shifan Daxue Xuebao (Shehui Kexue Ban) 7983
1000-176X Caijing Wenti Yanjiu 1323
1000-1786 Dongwuxue Jikan 940
1000-1794 Changchun Youdian Xueyuan Xuebao/Changchun Institute of Posts and Telecommunications. Journal *changed to* 1671-5896 2548
1000-1824 Yanbian Daxue Yixue Xuebao 5733
1000-1832 Dongbei Shi-Daxuebao (Ziran Kexue Ban) 7851
1000-1840 Songliao Xuekan (Ziran Kexue Ban) 7918
1000-1891 Daqing Shiyou Xueyuan Xuebao 6766
1000-1905 Ha'erbin Yike Daxue Xuebao 5622
1000-1948 Journal of Medical Colleges of P L A 5651
1000-1964 Zhongguo Kuangye Daxue Xuebao 6484
1000-1980 Hehai Daxue Xuebao (Ziran Kexue Ban) 2794
1000-2006 Nanjing Linye Daxue Xuebao *changed to* Nanjing Linye Daxue Xuebao (Ziran Kexue Ban) 3697
1000-2022 Nanjing Qixiang Xueyuan Xuebao/Nanjing Institute of Meteorology. Journal *changed to* Nanjing Xinxi Gongcheng Daxue Xuebao 6392
1000-2030 Nanjing Nongye Daxue Xuebao 138
1000-2065 Xuzhou Yixueyuan Xuebao 5732
1000-2073 Suzhou Daxue Xuebao (Ziran Kexue Ban) 7921
1000-2081 Hangzhou Daxue Xuebao (Zhexue Shehui Kexue Ban) *changed to* 1008-942X 8018
1000-2138 Wenzhou Yixueyuan Xuebao 5730
1000-2146 Hangzhou Shifan Xueyuan Xuebao (Shehui Kexue Ban) 7968
1000-2154 Shangye Jingji yu Guanli 1793
1000-2162 Anhui Daxue Xuebao (Ziran Kexue Ban) 7835
1000-2189 Anhui Gongxueyuan Xuebao†
1000-2197 Anhui Nongxueyuan Xuebao 91
1000-2200 Bangbu Yixueyuan Xuebao 5583
1000-2219 Anhui Zhongyi Xueyuan Xuebao 5574
1000-2243 Fuzhou Daxue Xuebao (Ziran Kexue Ban) 7856
1000-2278 Jingdezhen Taoci Xueyuan Xuebao 2043
1000-2286 Jiangxi Nongye Daxue Xuebao 7870
1000-2294 Jiangxi Yixueyuan Xuebao 5644
1000-2340 Henan Nongye Daxue Xuebao 118
1000-2359 Henan Shifan Daxue Xuebao (Shehui Kexue Ban) 7969
1000-2367 Henan Shifan Daxue Xuebao (Ziran Kexue Ban) 7861
1000-2375 Hubei Daxue Xuebao (Ziran Kexue Ban) 7863
1000-2383 Diqiu Kexue 2705
1000-2405 Wuhan Gongye Daxue Xuebao *changed to* 1671-4431 7930
1000-2413 Wuhan University of Technology. Journal (Material Science Edition) 8445
1000-2421 Huazhong Nongye Daxue Xuebao 119
1000-2472 Hunan Daxue Xuebao (Shehui Kexue Ban) 7970
1000-2499 Changsha Tiedao Xueyuan Xuebao 8616
1000-2502 Zhongnan Linxueyuan Xuebao 3708
1000-2529 Hunan Shifan Daxue. Shehui Kexue Xuebao 7971
1000-2537 Hunan Shifan Daxue Xuebao (Ziran Kexue Ban) *changed to* Hunan Shifan Daxue. Ziran Kexue Xuebao 7863
1000-2561 Redai Zuowu Xuebao 814
1000-257X Zhongshan Yike Daxue Xuebao/Sun Yat-Sen University of Medical Sciences. Academic Journal *changed to* 1672-3554 5739
1000-2588 Di Yi Junyi Daxue Xuebao 5604
1000-260X Shenzhen Daxue Xuebao (Renwen Sheke Ban) 2912
1000-2618 Shenzhen Daxue Xuebao (Ligong Ban) 7915
1000-2634 Xinan Shiyou Xueyuan Xuebao 6798
1000-2642 Xinan Nongye Daxue Xuebao *changed to* Xinan Nongye Daxue Xuebao (Ziran Kexue Ban) 7931
1000-2650 Sichuan Nongye Daxue Xuebao 156
1000-2669 Luzhou Yixueyuan Xuebao 5662
1000-2677 Xinan Shifan Daxue Xuebao (Zhexue Shehui Kexue Ban)/Southwest Normal University. Journal (Philosophy and Social Science Edition) *changed to* 1673-9841 8016
1000-2707 Guiyang Yixueyuan Xuebao 5621
1000-2715 Zunyi Yixueyuan Xuebao 5739
1000-2723 Yunnan Zhongyi Xueyuan Xuebao 5734
1000-2731 Xibei Daxue Xuebao (Shehui Kexue Ban) 8015
1000-274X Xibei Daxue Xuebao (Ziran Kexue Ban) 7931
1000-2758 Xibei Gongye Daxue Xuebao 8445
1000-2790 Di Si Junyi Daxue Xuebao 5604
1000-2804 Lanzhou Daxue Xuebao (Shehui Kexue Ban) 7982
1000-2812 Lanzhou Yixueyuan Xuebao 5660
1000-2820 Xinjiang Daxue Xuebao (Zhexue Shehui Kexue Ban) *changed to* Xinjiang Daxue Xuebao (Zhexue - Renwen Shehui Kexue Ban) 8016
1000-2839 Xinjiang Daxue Xuebao (Ziran Kexue Ban) 7931
1000-2871 Boli yu Tangci 2038
1000-288X Shuitu Baochi Tongbao 252
1000-2928 Wenhua Yule 4984
1000-2952 Zhongguo Shehui Kexueyuan Yanjiu Shengyuan Xuebao 8019
1000-2979 Yuwen Yanjiu 5197
1000-2987 Jinyang Xuekan 7977
1000-2995 Keyan Guanli 7876
1000-3002 Zhongguo Yaolixue yu Dulixue Zazhi 3503
1000-3037 Ziran Ziyuan Xuebao 2718
1000-3045 Zhongguo Kexueyuan Yuankan 7934
1000-3053 Redai Haiyang *changed to* 1009-5470 2816
1000-3061 Shengwu Gongcheng Xuebao 770
1000-3088 Kexue Bolan†
1000-3096 Haiyang Kexue 2805
1000-310X Yingyong Shengxue 7090
1000-3118 Gujizhui Dongwu Xuebao 945
1000-3126 Zhongguo Kexue. A Ji (Shuxue, Wulixue, Tianwenxue, Jishu kexue) *changed to* 1672-1780 7047
1000-3126 Zhongguo Kexue. A Ji: Shuxue, Wulixue, Tianwenxue, Jishu Kexue *changed to* 1006-9232 5547
1000-3134 Zhongguo Kexue. B Ji: Huaxue, Shengwuxue, Nongxue, Yixue, Dixue *changed to* 1006-9240 7934
1000-3142 Guangxi Zhiwu 791
1000-3150 Zhongguo Chaye 3668
1000-3177 Yaogan Xinxi 4034
1000-3185 Huashi 6725
1000-3193 Renleixue Xuebao 352
1000-3207 Shuisheng Shengwu Xuebao 704
1000-3231 Ganguang Kexue yu Guanghuaxue/Photographic Science and Photochemistry *changed to* 1674-0475 6978
1000-324X Wuji Cailiao Xuebao 2119
1000-3258 Diwen Wuli Xuebao 7054
1000-3266 Shuzhi Jisuan yu Jisuanji Yingyong 7940
1000-3274 Dizhen 2779
1000-3282 Shengwu Huaxue yu Shengwu Wuli Jinzhan 745
1000-3290 Wuli Xuebao 7046
1000-3304 Gaofenzi Xuebao 2135
1000-3312 Huanjing Yaogan/Remote Sensing of Environment *changed to* 1007-4619 4034
1000-3355 Zhengzhixue Yanjiu 7197
1000-3363 Chengshi Guihua Huikan 3262
1000-338X Fujian Zhongyi Yao 309
1000-3398 Kexue yu Wenhua 7876
1000-3401 Jisuan Jiegou Lixue Jiqi Yingyong 3384
1000-341X Shuxue Yanjiu yu Pinglun 5536
1000-3428 Jisuanji Gongcheng 2473
1000-3436 Fushe Yanjiu yu Fushe Gongyi Xuebao 3167
1000-3444 Ticao†
1000-3452 Pingpang Shijie 8242
1000-3460 Lanqiu 8237
1000-3479 Qiaopai†
1000-3487 Zhongguo Diaoyu 8343
1000-3495 Youyong 8217
1000-3509 Tianjing 8337
1000-3517 Zuqiu Shijie 8252
1000-3525 Zhonghua Wushu 8217
1000-3541 Beifang Luncong 4444
1000-355X Xiandai Riben Jingji 1196
1000-3584 Xiuci Xuexi 5196
1000-3592 Fujian Huabao 3824
1000-3606 Linchuang Erke Zazhi 6096
1000-3630 Shengxue Jishu 7089
1000-3649 Sichuan Zhongyi 315
1000-3657 Zhongguo Dizhi 2776
1000-3665 Shuiwen Dizhi Gongcheng Dizhi 2798
1000-3673 Dianwang Jishu 3300
1000-3681 Zijinshan Tianwentai Taikan 584
1000-369X Journal of Tea Science 3652
1000-3703 Qiche Jishu 8600
1000-3711 Difangbing Tongbao 5812
1000-372X Yingyong Jiguang 7085
1000-3738 Jixie Gongcheng Cailiao 3384
1000-3819 Guti Dianzixue Yanjiu yu Jinzhan 3100
1000-3835 Zhendong yu Chongji 7064
1000-3851 Fuhe Cailiao Xuebao 3345
1000-386X Jisuanji Yingyong yu Ruanjian 2428
1000-3878 Zaochuan Jishu 8665
1000-3886 Dianqi Zidonghua 2460
1000-3894 Shuliang Jingji Jishu Jingji Yanjiu 1174
1000-3916 Fangzhi Wenzhai 8463
1000-3924 Shanghai Nongye Xuebao 155
1000-3932 Huagong Zidonghua ji Yibiao 4487
1000-3940 Duanya Jishu 6310
1000-3967 Zhongguo Quyu Dizhi/Regional Geology of China *changed to* Dizhi Tongbao 2732
1000-3975 Shanghai Huanjing Kexue 3466
1000-3983 Da Dianji Jishu 3376
1000-4009 Guoji Hangkong 57
1000-4017 Yin Ran 8462
1000-4025 Xibei Zhiwu Xuebao 823
1000-4033 Zhenzhi Gongye 8463
1000-4041 Daziran Tansuo 7849
1000-405X Diqiu 2705
1000-4076 Xibei Shi-Di/Historical and Geographical Review of Northwest China *changed to* Xibei Mingzu 4190
1000-4092 Youtian Huaxue 6798
1000-4106 Dunhuang Yanjiu 391
1000-4130 Xueqian Jiaoyu 2927
1000-4149 Renkou yu Jingji 7291
1000-4157 Zhiyin 8892
1000-4173 Bolan Qunshu 5265
1000-4181 Zhongguo Jingji Wenti 1722
1000-4211 Shanghai Jingji 1173
1000-422X Zhongguo Shehui Jingjishi Yanjiu 4191
1000-4238 Faxue (Shanghai) 4671
1000-4270 Yinyue Yishu 6630
1000-4289 Shijie Zongjiao Yanjiu 7681
1000-4300 Xiandai Jiating 4369
1000-4319 Weile Haizi 2171
1000-4343 Zhongguo Xitu Xuebao *see* 1002-0721 6319
1000-4351 Guowai Yixue (Liuxingbingxue Chuanranbingxue Fence) 5814
1000-436X Tongxin Xuebao 2342
1000-4378 Banhua Yishu 477
1000-4416 Meiqi yu Reli 3325
1000-4424 Gaoxiao Yingyong Shuxue Xuebao 5489

ISSN

1000-9035 Journal of Molecular Science **2068**
1000-9086 China Medical Abstracts (Internal Medicine) **5742**
1000-9094 Zhongguo Jingji Xinwen **1535**
1000-9116 Acta Seismologica Sinica **2777**
1000-9132 Litterature Chinoise† **8971**
1000-9140 Beijing Review **3822**
1000-9159 Beijing Informa *see* 1000-9140 **3822**
1000-9167 Beijing Rundschau *see* 1000-9140 **3822**
1000-9221 Approximation Theory and Its Applications *changed to* 1672-4070 **5470**
1000-9264 China im Bild **3823**
1000-9272 La Chine **3823**
1000-9280 China Revista Ilustrada **3823**
1000-9299 China†
1000-9302 China Gazeta la Picha†
1000-9310 La Cina **3823**
1000-9329 Kina†
1000-9337 Chugoku Gaho **3823**
1000-9345 Chinese Journal of Mechanical Engineering **3375**
1000-9353 Peking Syuho *see* 1000-9140 **3822**
1000-9361 Chinese Journal of Aeronautics **51**
1000-937X Nexus†
1000-9388 Women of China **8904**
1000-9396 People's Republic of China Year Book **3121**
1000-940X Journal of Partial Differential Equations **5506**
1000-9426 Chinese Journal of Geochemistry **2729**
1000-9515 Acta Geologica Sinica **2723**
1000-954X Zhongguo Duiwai Maoyi **1588**
1000-9582 Voice of Friendship **7272**
1000-9604 Chinese Journal of Cancer Research **6015**
1000-9620 Marine Science Bulletin **2812**
1000-9639 Zhongshan Daxue Xuebao (Shehui Kexue Ban) **8019**
1000-9647 Zhongguo Nianjian **3123**
1000-9671 Xiandai Qiye **1196**
1000-968X Qiye Jishu Jinbu **1162**
1000-9701 Jiefangjun Jiankang **6990**
1000-971X Shandong Jingji **1173**
1000-9736 Renmin Junyi **6256**
1000-9752 Jianghan Shiyou Xueyuan Xuebao/Jianghan Petroleum Institute. Journal *changed to* Shiyou Tianranqi Xuebao **6792**
1000-9760 Jining Yixueyuan Xuebao **5644**
1000-9817 Zhongguo Xuexiao Weisheng **7001**
1000-9825 Ruanjian Xuebao **2596**
1000-9833 Heilongjiang Shuizhuan Xuebao **3361**
1000-9841 Dadou Kexue **227**
1000-985X Rengong Jingti Xuebao **2045**
1000-9868 Nongye Jixie (Shang Chanpin Liutong, Xia Chanpin Jishu) **213**
1000-9876 Roupin Weisheng **7540**
1000-9892 Taoci Yanjiu **2046**
1000-9906 Heilongjiang Zhongyiyao **5627**
1000-9930 Xiangtan Kuangye Xueyuan Xuebao/Xiangtan Mining Institute. Journal *changed to* 1672-9102 **6464**
1000-9957 Dalian Shuichan Xueyuan Xuebao **3589**
1000-9965 Jinan Daxue Xuebao (Ziran Kexue yu Yixue Ban) **7871**
1000-9973 Zhongguo Tiaoweipin **3668**
1000-999X Zhongguo Zixingche **8270**
1001-0009 Beifang Yuanyi **3724**
1001-0017 Huaxue yu Nianhe **3245**
1001-0025 Zhongri Youhao Yiyuan Xuebao **5738**
1001-005X Senlin Caiyun Kexue *changed to* Senlin Gongcheng **3715**
1001-0076 Kuangchan Baohu yu Liyong **2616**
1001-0084 Siliao Bolan **275**
1001-0092 Malingshu Zazhi/Journal of Potatoes *changed to* Zhongguo Malingshu **260**
1001-0114 Guoji Rencai Jiaoliu **3012**
1001-0157 Haiyang Wenzhai **2805**
1001-0165 Sihai **5372**
1001-019X Jianzhu Guanli Xiandaihua **1017**
1001-0203 Jiating Yixue **5644**
1001-0211 Youse Jinshu **6337**
1001-022X Qilu Xuekan **7993**
1001-0238 Yindu Xuekan **4190**
1001-0254 Xiandaihua Nongye **171**
1001-0262 Tianjin Shangxueyuan Xuebao *changed to* 1674-2362 **1183**
1001-0270 Yingxiang Jishu **6978**
1001-0297 Xinxi Shijie **5055**
1001-0327 Jianghan Kaogu **400**
1001-0335 Zhongguo Jingkuangyan **6484**
1001-0408 Zhongguo Yaofang **6887**
1001-0432 Heilongjiang Jingrong **1351**
1001-0440 Shaanxi Huabao **3827**
1001-0459 Jingtan Fengyun **5414**
1001-0483 Beifang Wenwu **383**
1001-0505 Dongnan Daxue Xuebao (Ziran Kexue Ban) **7851**
1001-0521 Rare Metals **6330**
1001-053X Beijing Keji Daxue Xuebao **6458**
1001-0548 Dianzi Keji Daxue Xuebao **8420**
1001-0564 Beijing Fuzhuang Xueyuan Xuebao (Ziran Kexue Ban) **7839**
1001-0572 Zhongguo Gonggong Weisheng Xuebao/Chinese Journal of Public Health *changed to* 1001-9561 **7546**
1001-0580 Zhongguo Gonggong Weisheng **7546**
1001-0602 Cell Research **665**
1001-0610 Xiandai Wuli Zhishi **7047**
1001-0637 Zhongguo Haiguan **1588**
1001-0645 Beijing Ligong Daxue Xuebao **7840**
1001-0661 Hanzi Wenhua **4454**
1001-067X Zhonghua Renmin Gongheguo. Zuigao Renmin Jianchayuan Gongbao **7478**
1001-0688 Zhonghua Yingcai **3830**
1001-070X Guotu Ziyuan Yaogan **2709**
1001-0726 Zhongguo Shaoshang Chuangshang Zazhi **6076**
1001-0742 Journal of Environmental Sciences **3447**
1001-0785 Qizhong Yunshu Jixie **5459**
1001-0890 Shiyou Zuantan Jishu **6793**
1001-0912 Tiedao Yixue/Railway Medical Journal *changed to* 1671-7562 **5732**
1001-0920 Kongzhi yu Juece **3207**
1001-0939 Zhonghua Jiehe he Huxi Zazhi **6221**
1001-0963 Gangtie Yanjiu Xuebao **6313**
1001-0971 Guowai Yixue (Yaoxue Fence)/Foreign Medical Sciences (Pharmacy) *changed to* 1674-0440 **6845**
1001-098X Guowai Yixue (Fangshe Yixue Heyixue Fence) **6197**
1001-0998 Guowai Yixue (Xinxueguan Jibing Fence) **5787**
1001-1005 Guowai Yixue (Mazuixue yu Fusu Fence) **5771**
1001-1013 Guowai Yixue (Shuxue yu Xueyexue Fence) **5936**
1001-1021 Guowai Yixue (Linchuang Fangshexue Fence)/Foreign Medical Sciences (Clinical Radiology) *changed to* 1674-1897 **6197**
1001-103X Guowai Yixue (Mianyixue Fence) **5758**
1001-1048 Guowai Yixue (Yichuanxue Fence) **871**
1001-1056 Guowai Yixue (Shenjingbingxue Shenjing Waikexue Fence) **6143**
1001-1064 Guowai Yixue (Huxi Xitong Fence) **6214**
1001-1072 Guowai Yixue (Jishengbing Fence) **886**
1001-1080 Guowai Yixue (Fenzi Shengwuxue Fence) *changed to* 1672-8009 **898**
1001-1099 Guowai Yixue (Hulixue Fence) **5959**
1001-1102 Guowai Yixue (Er Bi Yanhou Kexue Fence) **6080**
1001-1110 Guowai Yixue (Shengwu Yixue Gongcheng Fence) **748**
1001-1129 Guowai Yixue (Weishengwuxue Fence) **886**
1001-1137 Guowai Yixue (Weisheng Jingji Fence) **7520**
1001-1153 Guowai Yixue (Xiaohuaxi Jibing Fence) **5925**
1001-1161 Guowai Yixue (Chuangshang yu Waike Jiben Wenti Fence) *changed to* 1009-9255 **6061**
1001-117X Guowai Yixue (Wuli Yixue yu Kangfuxue Fence) **6109**
1001-1188 Guowai Yixue (Kouqiang Yixue Fence) **5925**
1001-1196 Guowai Yixue (Yankexue Fence) **6043**
1001-120X Guowai Yixue (Jingshenbingxue Fence) **6143**
1001-1226 Guowai Yixue (Weishengxue Fence) **6987**
1001-1234 Guowai Yixue (Shehui Yixue Fence) **5622**
1001-1242 Zhongguo Kangfu Yixue Zazhi **5736**
1001-1250 Jinshu Kuangshan **6467**
1001-1269 Yejin Shebei **6337**
1001-1285 Baiyi Keji **220**
1001-1307 Zhongguo Yixue Wenzhai (Er-bi-yanhou Kexue) **5752**
1001-1315 Zhongguo Yixue Wenzhai (Jihua Shengyu, Fuchan Kexue) **5752**
1001-134X Zhongguo Yixue Wenzhai (Weishengxue) **7002**
1001-1358 Zhongguo Yixue Wenzhai (Erkexue) **5752**
1001-1374 Shanghai Dianqi Jishu **3113**
1001-1382 Hanjie **6342**
1001-1390 Diance yu Yibiao **4486**
1001-1412 Dizhi Zhaokuang Luncong **2732**
1001-1420 Linchuang Miniao Waike Zazhi **6271**
1001-1439 Linchuang Xinxueguanbing Zazhi **5795**
1001-1455 Baozha yu Chongji **7006**
1001-1471 Liantie **6320**
1001-148X Shangye Yanjiu **1173**
1001-1498 Linye Kexue Yanjiu **3696**
1001-151X Qilu Yuye **3605**
1001-1528 Zhongchenyao **6887**
1001-1552 Dadi Gouzao yu Chengkuangxue **2730**
1001-1560 Cailiao Baohu **3342**
1001-1579 Dianchi (Changsha) **3127**
1001-1587 Wujin Keji **6337**
1001-1595 Cehui Xuebao **2778**
1001-1609 Gaoya Dianqi **7051**
1001-1617 Yejin Nengyuan **6337**
1001-1625 Guisuanyan Tongbao **2116**
1001-1633 Jiepouxue Zazhi **680**
1001-165X Zhongguo Linchuang Jiepouxue Zazhi **928**
1001-1668 Zhongyi Zazhi **316**
1001-1692 Shiyong Zhongliu Zazhi **6034**
1001-1714 Liaoning Linye Keji **3696**
1001-1722 Liaoning Yixue Zazhi **5661**
1001-1730 Zhili **3830**
1001-1749 Wutan Huatan Jisuan Jishu **2718**
1001-1757 Dangdai Waiguo Wenxue **5282**
1001-1773 Guowai Yixue (Shengli Bingli Kexue yu Linchuang Fence)/Foreign Medical Sciences (Phisiology, Pathology & Clinic) *changed to* 1673-2588 **5622**
1001-1781 Linchuang Erbi Yanhouke Zazhi **6082**
1001-179X Dongnan Wenhua **391**
1001-1803 Riyong Huaxue Gongye **2244**
1001-182X Gongye Kongzhi Jisuanji **2460**
1001-1862 Qingdao Haiyang Daxue Xuebao/Ocean University of Qingdao. Journal *changed to* 1672-5174 **2821**
1001-1889 Zhongguo Difangbing Fangzhi Zazhi **5735**
1001-1897 Yilin **5403**
1001-1900 Zhongguo Shengwuxue Wenzhai **720**
1001-1919 Zhongguo Shuxue Wenzhai **5549**
1001-1935 Naihuo Cailiao **6327**
1001-1951 Duanya Jixie/Metalforming Machine Tools *changed to* 1672-0121 **5451**
1001-1978 Zhongguo Yaolixue Tongbao **6887**
1001-1986 Meitian Dizhi yu Kantan **2754**
1001-1994 Shuichan Keji Qingbao **3608**
1001-2001 Zhongguo Kangfu **7001**
1001-201X Dang'anxue Tongxun **5005**
1001-2028 Dianzi Yuanjian yu Cailiao **3093**
1001-2044 Shanghai Fangzhi Keji **8457**
1001-2052 Huagong Yejin/Engineering Chemistry & Metallurgy *changed to* 1009-606X **3244**
1001-2060 Reneng Dongli Gongcheng **3394**
1001-2079 Zhongguo Minhang Bao **8777**
1001-2087 Shanghai Yixue Jianyan Zazhi **5911**
1001-2095 Dianqi Chuandong **3300**
1001-2125 Shanghai Jinshu (Youse Fence) **6331**
1001-2141 Chongqing Huanjing Kexue **3410**
1001-2168 Moju Gongye **3210**
1001-2206 Shiyou Gongcheng Jianshe **6792**
1001-2214 Haihuyan yu huagong/Sea-lake Salt Industry & Chemical Engineering *changed to* 1673-6850 **3257**
1001-2222 Cheyong Fadongji **8573**
1001-2230 Zhongguo Rupin Gongye **270**
1001-2249 Tezhong Zhuzao Ji Youse Hejin **6335**
1001-2265 Zuhe Jichuang yu Zidonghua Jiagong Jishu **5462**
1001-2303 Dianhanji **6342**
1001-2311 Gangguan **6313**
1001-232X Fenxi Yiqi **4486**
1001-2346 Zhonghua Shenjing Waike Zazhi **6264**
1001-2362 Xinxi Xitong Gongcheng **2345**
1001-2397 Xiandai Faxue **4816**
1001-2400 Xi'an Dianzi Keji Daxue Xuebao *changed to* 1008-472X **8015**
1001-2435 Anhui Shida Xuebao (Zhe She Ban) **7947**
1001-2443 Anhui Shida Xuebao **7835**
1001-246X Jisuan Wuli **7019**
1001-2478 Xiandai Mianyixue **5767**
1001-2486 Guofang Keji Daxue Xuebao **6423**
1001-2494 Zhongguo Yaoxue Zazhi **6888**
1001-2516 Gongye Qiye Guanli **1748**
1001-2524 Luoji **6933**
1001-2532 Xinlixue **7415**
1001-2567 Meixue **6934**
1001-2583 Lishixue **4151**
1001-2621 Zhongguo Jindaishi **4191**
1001-263X Song Liao Jin Yuanshi **4188**
1001-2648 Shijieshi **4161**
1001-2656 Zhongguo Dili†
1001-2672 Zhongguo Xiandaishi **4191**
1001-2699 Makesi Zhuyi, Liening Zhuyi Yanjiu **7153**
1001-2702 Maozedong Sixiang Yanjiu *changed to* 1009-7570 **7153**
1001-2710 Zhexue Yuanli **6962**
1001-2729 Kexue Jishu Zhexue **6930**
1001-2737 Lunlixue **6933**
1001-2753 Sixiang Zhengzhi Jiaoyu **2913**
1001-2761 Wenyi Lilun **5245**
1001-2788 Wenhua Yanjiu **8014**
1001-2826 Zhiye Jishu Jiaoyu **3088**
1001-2834 Gaodeng Jiaoyu **2982**
1001-2842 Zhongguo Waijiao **7276**
1001-2869 Jiaoyuxue **3025**
1001-2885 Waiguo Wenxue Yanjiu (Beijing) **5396**
1001-2893 Zhongguo Gudai, Jindai Wenxue Yanjiu **5404**
1001-2907 Zhongguo Xiandai, Dangdai Wenxue Yanjiu **5404**
1001-2982 Zhongxiaoxue Jiaoyu **2929**
1001-3024 Gongye Jingji **1115**
1001-3067 Zhongguo Zhengzhi **7198**
1001-3180 Zhongguo Gongchandang **7198**
1001-3202 Guoji Gongchanzhuyi Yundong **7139**
1001-3253 Tiyu **8212**
1001-3261 Yuyan Wenzixue **5198**
1001-3334 Dang'anxue **5005**
1001-3350 Zhengzhi Jingjixue (Shehuizhuyi Bufen) *changed to* 1005-4294 **1173**
1001-3385 Jingjishi (Beijing) **1132**
1001-3407 Waimao Jingji, Guoji Maoyi **1587**
1001-3431 Shehui Kexue Zonglun **8001**
1001-344X Shehuixue **8132**
1001-3482 Shiyou Kuangchang Jixie **5459**
1001-3504 Guowai Yixue (Pifubingxue Fence) **5877**
1001-3512 Guowai Yixue (Erkexue Fence) **6092**
1001-3520 Qilu Xiangqing **3827**
1001-3539 Gongcheng Suoliao Yingyong **7092**
1001-3555 Fenzi Cuihua **7012**
1001-3563 Xuanmei Jishu **6484**
1001-358X Kuangshan Celiang **6468**
1001-3598 Tezhong Jiegou **459**
1001-3601 Guizhou Nongye Kexue **117**
1001-3644 Sichuan Huanjing **3466**
1001-3652 Tea Abstracts **3670**
1001-3679 Jiangxi Kexue **7870**
1001-3687 Jiangsu Keji Chengguo Tongbao† **8968**
1001-3695 Jisuanji Yingyong Yanjiu **2428**
1001-3709 Ranliao yu Huagong **3254**
1001-3717 Laiyang Nongxueyuan Xuebao **132**
1001-3733 Shiyong Kouqiang Yixue Zazhi **5931**
1001-3768 Juzuojia **8472**
1001-3776 Zhejiang Linye Keji **3708**
1001-3784 Fenmo Yejin Jishu **6311**
1001-3806 Jiguang Jishu **7077**
1001-3849 Diandu yu Jingshi **2113**
1001-3865 Huanjing Wuran yu Fangzhi **3486**
1001-389X Fujian Linxueyuan Xuebao **3691**
1001-3946 Kancha Kexue Jishu **6467**
1001-3954 Kuangshan Jixie **6468**
1001-3970 Fujian Dizhi **2734**
1001-3997 Jixie Sheji yu Zhizao **5454**
1001-4012 Lihua Jianyan (Wuli Fence) **6403**
1001-4020 Lihua Jianyan (Huaxue Fence) **3250**
1001-4039 Baijia Zuowen Zhidao **5098**
1001-4055 Tuijin Jishu **73**
1001-408X Hongshuihe **3162**
1001-411X Huanan Nongye Daxue Xuebao **119**
1001-4136 Zhongguo Yixue Wenzhai (Neike Xue) **5752**
1001-4152 Hulixue Zazhi **5960**
1001-4160 Jisuanji yu Yingyong Huaxue **2108**
1001-4179 Renmin Changjiang **4026**
1001-4195 Zhongguo Ganju/China Citrus *changed to* 1007-1431 **172**
1001-4209 Nuyou **8878**
1001-4217 Shantou Daxue Xuebao (Ziran Kexue Ban) **7914**
1001-4225 Shantou Daxue Xuebao (Renwen Kexue Ban) **4475**
1001-4268 Yingyong Gailu Tongji **5547**
1001-4276 Wuyi Kexue **711**
1001-4284 Kexue Zhifu yu Shenghuo **7876**
1001-4306 Gushengwuxue Wenzhai **6731**
1001-4314 Bianji Xuebao **7552**
1001-4322 Qiangjiguang yu Lizishu **3173**
1001-4330 Xinjiang Nongye Kexue **171**
1001-4357 Chaiyouji **3375**
1001-4381 Cailiao Gongcheng **50**
1001-4403 Suzhou Daxue Xuebao (Zhexue Shehui Kexue Ban) **8008**
1001-4411 Zhongguo Fuyou Baojian **6006**
1001-4438 Chu Feng **3615**
1001-4454 Zhongyaocai **5739**
1001-4462 Linye Jixie **3696**
1001-4489 Zhongguo Baoxian **4529**
1001-4497 Zhonghua Xiong-xin Xueguan Waike Zazhi **5803**

ISSN

1002-0608 Zhongguo Keji Chanye **1803**
1002-0616 Turang Feiliao **256**
1002-0640 Huoli Yu Zhihui Kongzhi **6424**
1002-0705 China University of Geosciences. Journal **2704**
1002-0721 Journal of Rare Earths **6319**
1002-0748 Wuli Jiaoxue **7046**
1002-0772 Yixue yu Zhexue **6961**
1002-0829 Shanghai Jingshen Yixue **6185**
1002-0837 Hangtian Yixue yu Yixue Gongcheng **58**
1002-0853 Feixing Lixue **55**
1002-087X Dianyuan Jishu **3300**
1002-0888 Faguo Yanjiu **7964**
1002-0918 China Auto **8523**
1002-0926 Kunchongxue Yanjiu Jikan **854**
1002-0942 Annals of Differential Equations **5471**
1002-0950 China's Tibet *see* 1002-9591 **3830**
1002-1027 Daxue Tushuguan Xuebao **5005**
1002-1051 Beijing Dang'an **4994**
1002-106X Lianyou Sheji **6777**
1002-1078 Guoyi Luntan **6845**
1002-1094 Xindianxue Zazhi **5802**
1002-1124 Huaxue Gongchengshi **3245**
1002-1167 Tushuguan Luntan **5051**
1002-1213 Xinsheng Erke Zazhi **6105**
1002-1221 Jinzhan: Guoji Maoyi yu Keji Jiaoliu **1573**
1002-1248 Nongye Tushu Qingbao Xuekan **5036**
1002-1256 Qiqiha'er Yixueyuan Xuebao **5701**
1002-1264 Chengshi Huanjing yu Chengshi Shengtai **3410**
1002-1299 Ke Xue **7875**
1002-1302 Jiangsu Nongye Kexue **125**
1002-1310 Pifubing yu Xingbing **5881**
1002-1329 Chengshi Guihua **4407**
1002-137X Jisuanji Kexue **2428**
1002-1396 Hecheng Shuzhi ji Suliao **7092**
1002-1434 Fayu Xuexi **5118**
1002-1450 China Chemical Reporter **3241**
1002-1477 Xiandai Zhong-xiaoxue Jiaoyu **2927**
1002-1493 Kexue Shehui Zhuyi **7981**
1002-1507 Liusuan Gongye **3250**
1002-1515 Guoji Jingji Hezuo **1596**
1002-1582 Guangxue Jishu **7075**
1002-1604 Journal of Earthquake Prediction Research **2785**
1002-1612 Zhongguo Shuichan Wenzhai **3614**
1002-1620 Dang'an Xue Yanjiu **5005**
1002-1639 Gongye Jiare **4119**
1002-1671 Shiyong Fangshexue Zazhi **6208**
1002-168X Shaanxi Zhongyi Xueyuan Xuebao **5712**
1002-171X Dangdai Xiju **8468**
1002-1809 Dangdai Zuojia Pinglun **5282**
1002-1841 Yibiao Jishu yu Chuanganqi **4490**
1002-185X Xiyou Jinshu Cailiao yu Gongcheng **1197**
1002-1884 Tushuguan Xuebao **5051**
1002-1892 Zhongguo Xiufu Chongjian Waike Zazhi **6263**
1002-1906 Xiangqi Yanjiu **8217**
1002-1914 Zhongwai Fuzhuang **2263**
1002-1922 Liaoning Qingnian **2199**
1002-1949 Zhongguo Jijiu Yixue **5736**
1002-1973 Luhua yu Shenghuo **3696**
1002-2007 Dongjiang Xuekan (Zhexue Shehui Kexue Ban) **7960**
1002-2031 Chengshi Wenti **7954**
1002-2058 Shaanxi Jiaoyu†
1002-2082 Yingyong Guangxue **7085**
1002-2104 Zhongguo Renkou Ziyuan yu Huanjing **7296**
1002-2139 Qingnian Wenxuejia **5356**
1002-221X Zhongguo Gongye Yixue Zazhi **6689**
1002-2236 Qilu Yiyuan **513**
1002-2260 Xin Liaozhai **5402**
1002-2287 Zhongguo Youzheng **2356**
1002-2295 Xinwen yu Xiezuo **4586**
1002-2325 Heilongjiang Dizhi **2746**
1002-2341 Daqing Shehui Kexue **7958**
1002-235X Zhongguo Tushu Pinglun **7576**
1002-2384 Zhongxiaoxue Guanli **3035**
1002-2392 Zhongyiyao Xuebao **5739**
1002-2406 Zhongyiyao Xinxi **5739**
1002-2481 Journal of Shanxi Agricultural Science **128**
1002-2511 Senlin Fanghuo **3581**
1002-252X Heilongjiang Qixiang **6353**
1002-2554 Gushi Lin **5303**
1002-2597 Dang De Shenghuo (Ha'erbin) **7128**
1002-2600 Fujian Yiyao Zazhi **6843**
1002-2619 Hebei Zhongyi **309**
1002-2627 Kongzi Yanjiu **7738**
1002-266X Shandong Yiyao **5713**
1002-2694 Zhongguo Renshou Gonghuanbing Zazhi **898**
1002-2740 Fujian Jinrong **1348**
1002-2759 Qingnian Jizhe **2209**
1002-2813 Siliao Yanjiu **275**
1002-283X Jishu Kaifa yu Yinjin† **8968**
1002-297X Jiankang **6990**
1002-2996 Dangdai Xumu **284**
1002-3054 Beijing Shehui Kexue **7950**
1002-3070 Shiyong Zhongliuxue Zazhi **6034**
1002-3089 Jiankang Shaonian Huabao **6990**
1002-3127 Weisheng Dulixue Zazhi **5729**
1002-3135 Beijing Gongshang Guanli/Beijing Industrial and Commercial Management *changed to* 1671-9557 **1066**
1002-3194 Yantai Daxue Xuebao (Shehui Kexue Ban) **8017**
1002-3208 Beijing Shengwu Yixue Gongcheng **5584**
1002-3232 Jianzhu Gongren **1017**
1002-3291 Liaoning Daxue Xuebao (Zhexue Shehui Kexue Ban) **7983**
1002-3305 Shuili Tiandi **8832**
1002-3321 Fuzhou Daxue Xuebao (Zhexue Shehui Kexue Ban) **7965**
1002-3348 Beijing Fangzhi† **8935**
1002-3356 Hebei Linye Keji **3692**
1002-3372 Riben Yixue Jieshao **5706**
1002-3429 Linchuang Wuzhen Wuzhi **5661**
1002-3461 Zhongguo Haiyang Yaowu Zazhi **6887**
1002-3488 Bingxue Yundong **8306**
1002-3631 Anquan **7508**
1002-364X Fujian Zhibu Shenghuo **7137**
1002-3674 Zhongguo Weisheng Tongji **7002**
1002-3682 Haian Gongcheng **2805**
1002-3801 Hainei yu Haiwai **3824**
1002-381X Zhongguo Nongji Tuiguang **172**
1002-3828 Guanzi Xuekan **4454**
1002-3879 Yinjin yu Zixun† **8999**
1002-3917 Jintian **3826**
1002-3933 Hebei Faxue **4686**
1002-3968 Nanfang Wenxue **5338**
1002-3976 Tianjin Shehui Kexue **8010**
1002-3984 Waixiang Jingji†
1002-4034 Duiwai Jingji Maoyi Daxue Xuebao/University of International Business and Economics. Journal *changed to* Guoji Shangwu - Duiwai Jingji Maoyi Daxue Xuebao **1568**
1002-4042 Ertong Chuangzhao **2853**
1002-4069 Haizi Tiandi **2154**
1002-4077 Yan Du **8017**
1002-4123 Zhongxue Shuxue Jiaoxue **2929**
1002-414X Beijing Chengren Jiaoyu† **8935**
1002-4158 Shizhuang **2261**
1002-4182 Guijinshu Dizhi/Journal of Precious Metallic Geology *changed to* 1671-1947 **2776**
1002-4212 Laoren Tiandi **4050**
1002-4239 Shenji Yanjiu **1301**
1002-4255 Xiandai Minhang†
1002-431X Jiankang Tiandi **6990**
1002-4360 Minsu Yanjiu **7986**
1002-4379 Zhongguo Zhongyi Yanke Zazhi **6053**
1002-4395 Riyu Xuexi yu Yanjiu **5169**
1002-4409 Gaoxiao Lilun Zhanxian **2982**
1002-4417 Zhongguo Gaodeng Jiaoyu **3011**
1002-4433 Shijie Nongye **156**
1002-4441 Zhongguo Minzheng **7198**
1002-4468 Xinwen yu Chengcai **4586**
1002-4530 Guoji Guangbo Dianshi Jishu **2322**
1002-4549 Zhongguo Jianzai **2228**
1002-4557 Zhongguo Tongji **8414**
1002-4611 Zhonghua Renmin Gongheguo Zuigao Renmin Fayuan Gongbao **4820**
1002-462X Xuexi yu Tansuo **8017**
1002-4646 Dangdai Dianying **6495**
1002-4654 Jiefangjun Shenghuo **6429**
1002-4670 Guoji Maoyi Wenti **1567**
1002-4719 Zhongguo Minzheng Yixue Zazhi/Medical Journal of Chinese Civil Administration *changed to* 1672-0369 **7547**
1002-4727 Dongfang Shaonian **2186**
1002-4743 Xiyu Yanjiu **8016**
1002-4808 Zhongguo Jiaoyu Xuekan **2928**
1002-4867 Siwang Yinshua **7328**
1002-4875 Zhongwai Faxue **4820**
1002-4883 Junshi Lishi **6430**
1002-4891 Shijie Junshi **6446**
1002-4905 Zhongguo Xiangzhen Qiye **1969**
1002-4913 Guoji Shehui Kexue Zazhi **7967**
1002-4921 Zhongguo Shehui Kexue **8019**
1002-493X Linye Jingji†
1002-4956 Shiyan Jishu yu Guanli **8438**
1002-4980 Qiushi **7175**
1002-4999 Guoji Maoyi **1567**
1002-5006 Luyou Xuekan **8731**
1002-5014 Guowai Wenxue **5303**
1002-5049 Zhongguo Shenji **1304**
1002-5081 Zhongguo Minbing **6455**
1002-5103 Zhongguo Nongye Wenzhai - Nongye Gongcheng **190**
1002-5111 Gaodeng Shifan Jiaoyu Yanjiu *changed to* 1672-5905 **2873**
1002-5154 Seedling **770**
1002-5219 Guowai Suliao **7092**
1002-5235 Guangxi Xumu Shouyi **8798**
1002-5243 Riyu Zhishi **5169**
1002-5278 Zhongguo Laonian **4058**
1002-5286 Bayi Dianying *changed to* 1007-5305 **6517**
1002-5308 Xueke Jiaoyu *changed to* 1673-1298 **2873**
1002-5332 Shixueshi Yanjiu **4161**
1002-5464 Shengwu Jishu Tongbao **770**
1002-5480 Nongyao Kexue yu Guanli **243**
1002-5502 Guanli Shijie **1749**
1002-5529 Waiguo Wenxue **5396**
1002-5545 Deyu Xuexi **5111**
1002-5553 Yingyu Xuexi **5197**
1002-5561 Guang Tongxin Jishu **2322**
1002-557X Zhongguo Zangxue **564**
1002-5588 Nongcun Caiwu Kuaiji **1297**
1002-5596 Nongye Hezuo Jingji Jingying Guanli **204**
1002-560X Banzhuren **3052**
1002-5626 Jiayong Dianqi **1890**
1002-5634 Huabei Shuili Shuidian Xueyuan Xuebao **8825**
1002-5677 Rensheng Zixun†
1002-5685 Guoji Xinwenjie **26**
1002-5723 Liaowang **3826**
1002-5731 Jiaoyu Yanjiu **2873**
1002-574X Dazhong Jiankang **6984**
1002-5766 Jingji Guanli **1762**
1002-5790 Xue Hanyu **5197**
1002-5804 Shijie Hanyu Jiaoxue **5173**
1002-5839 Jingji Kexue **1131**
1002-588X Sixiang Zhengzhike Jiaoxue **2913**
1002-5898 Jiyou Bolan†
1002-591X Zhongguo Shangye Nianjian/Almanac of China's Commerce *changed to* 1673-1158 **1434**
1002-5936 Shehuixue Yanjiu **8132**
1002-5952 Zhongguo Minzu Jiaoyu **2928**
1002-6045 Dang-jian Yanjiu **7128**
1002-6061 Hangkong Jice Jishu **57**
1002-6142 Beijing Dianying Xueyuan Xuebao **6490**
1002-6169 Dangdai Tiyu **8168**
1002-6177 Jingwu **8182**
1002-6215 Shan Hai Jing **3622**
1002-6282 Mingren Zhuanji **644**
1002-6312 Haixia **5303**
1002-6320 Nandu Xuetan **4466**
1002-6339 Jieneng Jishu **3140**
1002-6401 Gushi Daguan† **8960**
1002-641X Guowai Youtian Gongcheng **6772**
1002-6452 Guangxi Jinrong Yanjiu/Journal of Guangxi Financial Research *changed to* 1674-5477 **1163**
1002-6495 Fushi Kexue yu Fanghu Jishu **6313**
1002-655X Zhuomuniao **5405**
1002-6584 Quanguo Qinggong Xinxi† **8983**
1002-6592 China Aerospace Abstracts **76**
1002-6606 Zhongguo Hangkong Wenzhai *see* 1002-6592 **76**
1002-6630 Shipin Kexue **3663**
1002-6649 Lading Meizhou Yanjiu **7982**
1002-6665 Hangtian Jishu yu Minpin†
1002-6681 Zhongguo Shuichan **3612**
1002-6711 Zhongguo Keji Luntan **7934**
1002-6738 Shenzhou Xueren **3002**
1002-6754 Motuo Che **8265**
1002-6770 Sheying Shijie **6976**
1002-6789 Zhongguo Jiyou **6901**
1002-6819 Nongye Gongcheng Xuebao **141**
1002-6827 Nongcun Shiyong Gongcheng Jishu **141**
1002-686X Huaxi **5307**
1002-6878 Shangpin Pingjie/Review on Commodity *changed to* Target **5084**
1002-6886 Xiandai Jixie **5461**
1002-6908 Dazhong Kexue **7849**
1002-6924 Guizhou Shehui Kexue **7967**
1002-6959 Guizhou Minzu Yanjiu **550**
1002-6975 Hushi Jinxiu Zazhi **5961**
1002-7076 Kexue Jishu Yanjiu Chengguo Gongbao† **8969**
1002-7092 Guowai Keji Dongtai†
1002-7106 Quanli Kexue Wenzhai **1788**
1002-7122 Xiya Feizhou **8016**
1002-7157 Zhong Lao Nian Baojian Yixue **4058**
1002-7165 Huanqiu **7240**
1002-7173 Falu yu Shenghuo **4671**
1002-7203 Nongji Shiyan yu Tuiguang **213**
1002-7211 Renxiang Sheying **6976**
1002-7238 Renmin Tiaojie **4768**
1002-7270 Jiankang Zhinan (Zhong Lao Nan) **6990**
1002-7289 Huangpu **7970**
1002-7335 Banyuetan **5208**
1002-7343 Xiezuo **5402**
1002-736X Gaige yu Zhanlue **7966**
1002-7378 Guangxi Kexueyuan Xuebao **7859**
1002-7386 Hebei Yiyao **6846**
1002-7432 Reguxing Shuzhi **6720**
1002-7459 Shidai Jiemei **8883**
1002-753X Taigang Wenxue Xuankan **5384**
1002-7548 Zhanghui Xiaoshuo **5404**
1002-7564 Zhongguo Gushi **5404**
1002-7580 Zhongxiaoxue Yinyue Jiaoyu **6630**
1002-7629 Guangxi Wenxue **5302**
1002-7637 Dazhong Xiaoshuo **5283**
1002-7653 Fenyou **8863**
1002-767X Beifang Yinyue **6548**
1002-7742 Zhongguo Hangtian **76**
1002-7750 Jiyou Yanjiu†
1002-7777 Zhongguo Yaoshi (Beijing) **6887**
1002-7785 Nongcun Dashijie **141**
1002-7823 Guoji Laogong Tongxun **1684**
1002-7874 Riben Xuekan **1515**
1002-7904 Funu Shenghuo **8864**
1002-7912 Faxue Yicong†
1002-7920 Xiandai Fuzhuang†
1002-7963 Zhongguoshi Yanjiu **4191**
1002-7971 Zhongguoshi Yanjiu Dongtai **4191**
1002-7998 Beijing Zhibu Shenghuo **7109**
1002-8005 Zhongguo Jingjishi Yanjiu **1551**
1002-803X Fei Tian **5295**
1002-8048 Zuowen **5200**
1002-8064 Jiaoyu Kexue **2873**
1002-8072 Cai-kuai Tongxun **1323**
1002-8102 Caimao Jingji **1323**
1002-8110 Niangjiu **608**
1002-8129 Juece yu Xinxi **7149**
1002-8137 Beijiguang **5261**
1002-8145 Beijing Gongren/Beijing Workers *changed to* 1009-9166 **4595**
1002-8153 Xiaoxuesheng Zuowen Xuankan **5196**
1002-8161 Guangxi Nongye Kexue **117**
1002-8188 Laotongzhi zhi You **4050**
1002-8196 Liaoning Jiaoyu **2883**
1002-820X Chuzhongsheng Xuexi Zhidao **2837**
1002-8277 Xiaoxing Neiranji **3399**
1002-8315 Meitan Qiye Guanli **1779**
1002-8390 Jingjixue Dongtai **1132**
1002-8439 Cunzhen Jianshe† **8947**
1002-8447 China City Planning Review†
1002-8455 Chengxiang Jianshe **4407**
1002-8471 Jishui Paishui **8827**
1002-848X Jianzhu Jiegou **3273**
1002-8498 Shigong Jishu **457**
1002-8501 Nuantong Kongtiao **4124**
1002-851X Jianzhu Jingji **1131**
1002-8528 Jianzhu Kexue **3274**
1002-8536 Zhongguo Fangdi Xinxi **7616**
1002-8544 Jianzhu Zhishi **447**
1002-8587 Qingshi Yanjiu **4187**
1002-8617 Zhongguo Jiaotong Nianjian **2345**
1002-8633 Gushi Jia **5303**
1002-8668 Jingji Guanli Wenzhai **1763**
1002-8676 Guowai Shehui Kexue Lunwen Suoyin†
1002-8706 Weiqi Tiandi **8215**
1002-8714 Jiankang zhi You **8869**
1002-8722 Zhongguo Paiqiu†
1002-8730 Wushu Jianshen†
1002-8757 Wanbao Wencui **3828**
1002-879X Tiyu Huabao **8212**
1002-8803 Jian yu Mei **6990**

ISSN

1003-6555 Wenwu Chunqiu **423**
1003-6563 Guizhou Kexue **7859**
1003-6652 Sanwen Baijia **5367**
1003-6660 Hangkong Biaozhunhua yu Zhiliang **57**
1003-6679 Shidai **3828**
1003-6687 Bianji zhi You **7552**
1003-6709 Guangdong Jiage Yanjiu†
1003-6768 Zhongzhou Jingu **4035**
1003-6784 Yinyue Shijie **6629**
1003-6830 Wenxue Gang **5397**
1003-6881 Tequ Wenxue **5386**
1003-692X Yunnan Huabao **3829**
1003-6946 Shiyong Fuchanke Zazhi **6004**
1003-6962 Sichuan Wenwu **416**
1003-6970 Ruanjian **2596**
1003-7012 Manzu Wenxue **5330**
1003-7055 Kehuan Shijie **5444**
1003-7071 Hebei Xuekan **7968**
1003-708X Dangshi Yanjiu yu Jiaoxue **7128**
1003-7098 Dang'an yu Jianshe **5005**
1003-711X Nanjing Jianzhu Gongcheng Xueyuan Xuebao **450**
1003-7128 Manhua Yuekan **2201**
1003-7136 Sichuan Tushuguan Xuebao **5047**
1003-7225 Guo Moruo Xuekan **643**
1003-725X Jiangxi Tushuguan Xuekan **5019**
1003-7268 Shaanxi Dang'an **5047**
1003-7365 Hanyu Xuexi **5124**
1003-7438 Jinri Keji **7871**
1003-7446 Jixie Gongye Gao-jiao Yanjiu/Higher Education Research *changed to* 1672-0717 **2977**
1003-7470 Nongcun Jingji **204**
1003-7497 Dang De Shenghuo (Nanjing) **7128**
1003-7500 Sichuan Xiju **517**
1003-7519 Waiguo Wenxue Yanjiu (Wuhan) **5396**
1003-7527 Yang Guan *changed to* 1674-1420 **5261**
1003-7535 Zhongguo Wenxue Yanjiu **5404**
1003-7543 Gaige **7965**
1003-7551 Guangxi Wuli **7014**
1003-756X Anhui Xiaofang† **8930**
1003-7586 Zhongxue Shengwuxue **2929**
1003-7624 Touzi Yanjiu **1952**
1003-7632 Xiandai Kouqiang Yixue Zazhi **5932**
1003-7640 Wenxue Shaonian **5398**
1003-7667 Bijiao Jiaoyu Yanjiu **2831**
1003-7713 Huaxue Wuli Xuebao *changed to* 1674-0068 **7008**
1003-7721 Huang Zhong **6574**
1003-7772 Nanfang Wentan **5338**
1003-7780 Dangdai Qingnian **2185**
1003-7802 Changcheng **5272**
1003-7810 Baihuayuan **5259**
1003-7837 Guangdong Yousejinshu Xuebao/Journal of Guangdong Non-Ferrous Metals *changed to* 1673-9981 **6307**
1003-7888 Taian Shi-Zhuan Xuebao *changed to* 1672-2590 **8009**
1003-7918 Xiaoxiaoshuo Xuankan **5402**
1003-7942 Xuewu Wenhua **563**
1003-7985 Southeast University. Journal **7919**
1003-8051 Dangdai Gongren **1674**
1003-8094 Hebei Huabao **3825**
1003-8159 Minzu **3550**
1003-8213 Weixi Jiagong Jishu **3116**
1003-8248 Anhui Caikuai **1280**
1003-8280 Zhongguo Meijie Shengwuxue ji Kongzhi Zazhi **5767**
1003-8299 Xiangtu **3829**
1003-8310 Zhongguo Shiyongjun **824**
1003-8337 Dianci Bileiqi **3343**
1003-8353 Dongyue Luncong **7960**
1003-8418 Jiangsu Gaojiao **2988**
1003-8426 Renkou yu Fazhan (Chengdu)† **8985**
1003-8507 Xiandai Yufang Yixue **5732**
1003-8523 Zhongguo Yixue Wenzhai (Kouqiang Yixue) **5752**
1003-854X Jianghan Luntan **7976**
1003-8558 Dianshi Yuekan **2380**
1003-8620 Teshu Gang **6335**
1003-8639 Qiche Dianqi **3328**
1003-8663 Fazhi Yuekan **4671**
1003-8728 Jixie Kexue yu Jishu **3384**
1003-8817 Qiche Gongyi yu Cailiao **8600**
1003-8868 Yiliao Weisheng Zhuangbei **5911**
1003-8914 Guangming Zhongyi **5621**
1003-8930 Dianli Xitong Jiqi Zidong Huaxue Bao **7850**
1003-9015 Gaodeng Xuexiao Huaxue Gongcheng Xuebao **3244**
1003-9031 Hainan Jinrong **1350**
1003-904X Jinshajiang Wenyi **5313**
1003-9058 Foshan Wenyi **5297**
1003-9082 Zhongwen Xinxi **5056**
1003-9104 Yishu Baijia **528**
1003-9198 Shiyong Laonian Yixue **4056**
1003-9279 Zhonghua Shiyan he Linchuang Bingduxue Zazhi **5829**
1003-9309 Mangzhong **5330**
1003-9325 Dangdai Jingcha† **8948**
1003-9384 Jingxi Shiyou Huagong **6775**
1003-9406 Zhonghua Yixue Yichuanxue Zazhi **879**
1003-9430 Zhongguo Jiguang Yixue Zazhi **5736**
1003-9481 Yishu Shenghuo **528**
1003-952X Yixue Wenxuan *changed to* Weichuang Yixue **5751**
1003-9538 Wenyi Zhengming **5245**
1003-9562 Gu yu Guanjie Sunshang Zazhi/Journal of Bone and Joint Injury *changed to* 1672-9935 **6075**
1003-9570 Dang De Shenghuo (Zhengzhou) **7128**
1003-9589 Shandong Jingji Zhanlue Yanjiu **1721**
1003-9643 Sanjiao Zhou **5367**
1003-966X Anhui Nongcun Tongxun **91**
1003-9678 Xingxing Shikan **5438**
1003-9740 Mishu Gongzuo **1852**
1003-9767 Jisuanji Funzhu Sheji yu Tuxingxue Xuebao **2487**
1003-9783 Zhongyao Xinyao yu Lingchuang Yaoli **6888**
1003-9791 Qingdao Wenxue **5355**
1003-9821 Huanjing Daobao **3437**
1003-9856 Nanyang Wenti Yanjiu **557**
1003-9872 Kouqiang Yixue **5854**
1003-9929 Baozhuang Shijie **6708**
1003-9945 Keji yu Falu **4709**
1003-9953 Journal of Natural Gas Chemistry **6775**
1003-9961 Jibing Jiance **5819**
1004-0013 Shixue Lilun Yanjiu **4161**
1004-003X Zhenjiang Shi-Zhuan Xuebao (Shehui Kexueban) *changed to* Jiangsu Daxue Xuebao (Gao-jiao Ban) **2988**
1004-0064 Lushi Shijie **4726**
1004-0072 Wawa Huabao **2221**
1004-0080 Shaonian Kexue **2212**
1004-0145 Fengliu Yidai **2255**
1004-0153 Sheying Zhiuou **6976**
1004-017X Shanghai Huagong **3255**
1004-0218 Huangjin Shidai **3825**
1004-0242 Zhongguo Zhongliu **6037**
1004-0285 Guoji Jinrong Daokan†
1004-0293 Quanguo Zhongxue Youxiu Zuowen Xuan *changed to* Quanguo Zhongxue Youxiu Zuowen Xuan (Gaozong Ban) **5164**
1004-0293 Quanguo Zhongxue Youxiu Zuowen Xuan *changed to* Quanguo Zhongxue Youxiu Zuowen Xuan (Chuzong Ban) **2901**
1004-0307 Xiaoxuesheng Yuwen Xuexi **5196**
1004-0315 Chanye yu Huanjing/Industry and Environment *changed to* 1673-5897 **3466**
1004-0323 Yaogan Jishu yu Yingyong **2718**
1004-0358 Shanxi Yixueyuan Xuebao/Shanxi Medical College. Journal *changed to* 1007-6611 **5713**
1004-0366 Gansu Kexue Xuebao **7857**
1004-0374 Shengming Kexue **704**
1004-0404 Hubei Huagong *changed to* 1672-5425 **2064**
1004-0412 Jilin Yixue **5644**
1004-0439 Yinran Zhuji **8463**
1004-0447 Zhifu Shidai **1198**
1004-0501 Sichuan Yixue **5715**
1004-0552 Chinese Journal of Biomedical Engineering **748**
1004-0560 Shenyang Tiyu Xueyuan Xuebao **2912**
1004-0579 Beijing Institute of Technology. Journal **7839**
1004-0587 Dadi **3823**
1004-0595 Mocaxue Xuebao **7061**
1004-0609 Zhongguo Youse Jinshu Xuebao **6337**
1004-0625 China Medical Abstracts (Surgery) **5742**
1004-0633 Tianfu Xinlun **8010**
1004-0641 Nan Feng Chuang **7254**
1004-0676 Guijinshu **6314**
1004-0714 Tequ Jingji **1182**
1004-0749 Funu **8864**
1004-0765 Xiamen Wenxue **5402**
1004-0862 Huagong zhi You† **8962**
1004-0889 Shaonian Wenyi (Shanghai) **2212**
1004-0919 Shizhen Guoyao Yanjiu/Shizhen Journal of Traditional Chinese Medicine Research *changed to* 1008-0805 **6881**
1004-0935 Liaoning Huagong **3250**
1004-0951 Neimenggu Yixue Zazhi **5684**
1004-0978 Zhiwu Ziyuan yu Huanjing **824**
1004-0994 Caikuai Yuekan **1323**
1004-1060 Meishu Xuebao **505**
1004-1079 Qingshaonian Riji **2209**
1004-1109 Jiaoyu Pinglun **2873**
1004-1257 Zhiye yu Jiankang **7546**
1004-1265 Sichuan Sichou **8457**
1004-1281 Haiyang Huanjing Kexue **3436**
1004-1303 Faxue Pinlun **4671**
1004-132X Zhongguo Jixie Gongcheng **3400**
1004-1338 Cejing Jishu **6765**
1004-1389 Xibei Nongye Xuebao **171**
1004-1427 Duilian - Minjian Duilian Gushi **5286**
1004-1435 Xizang Wenxue **5402**
1004-1486 Touzi yu Jianshe†
1004-1508 Nanya Yanjiu Jikan **557**
1004-1524 Zhejiang Nongye Xuebao **172**
1004-1540 Zhongguo Jiliang Xueyuan Xuebao **7934**
1004-1648 Linchuang Shenjingbingxue Zazhi **6158**
1004-1656 Huaxue Yanjiu yu Yingyong **2064**
1004-1680 Jintu Xuekan **5020**
1004-1699 Chuan'gan Jishu Xuebao **8418**
1004-1729 Hainan Daxue Xuebao (Ziran Kexue Ban) **7859**
1004-1737 Wuhan Wenshi Ziliao **4190**
1004-1761 Menggu Yuwen **5151**
1004-1842 Heilongjiang Shangxueyuan Xuebao (Ziran Kexueban) **7861**
1004-1869 Yingshan Xuekan (Zhexue Shehui Kexue Ban) *changed to* Yingshan Xuekan (Shehui Kexue Ban) **8017**
1004-1877 Jining Shi-zhuan Xuebao *changed to* Jining Shifan Zhuanke Xuexiao Xuebao **2873**
1004-2008 Zhongguo Guoqing Guoli **1534**
1004-2024 Tiedao Zhuangxie yu Jizhuangxiang Yunshu **8626**
1004-2067 Anhui Dangshi Yanjiu *changed to* 1005-9482 **7128**
1004-2075 Fujian Yishu **8471**
1004-2083 Sichuan Pengren **4367**
1004-2105 Jingji yu Jianmei **8182**
1004-2113 Neimenggu Yixueyuan Xuebao **5684**
1004-213X Shufa Shangping **517**
1004-2164 Xiaoshuo Pinglun **5402**
1004-2172 Yinyue Tansuo **6630**
1004-2180 Linye Kancha Sheji **3696**
1004-2202 Shanghai Huabao **3827**
1004-2210 Sichuan Huabao *changed to* Sichuan Huabao - Luyou Renwen **3828**
1004-227X Diandu yu Tushi **2113**
1004-2326 Shiyan Jiaoxue yu Yiqi **2912**
1004-2369 Guowai Yixue (Neikexue Fence) **5945**
1004-2377 Zhonghua Shaonian **2224**
1004-2393 Jiankang Wenzhai†
1004-2407 Xibei Yaoxue Zazhi **6886**
1004-244X Bingqi Cailiao Kexue yu Gongcheng **6413**
1004-2458 Riben Wenti Yanjiu **559**
1004-2474 Yadian yu Shengguang **3334**
1004-2490 Haiyang Yuye **3596**
1004-2539 Jixie Chuandong **5453**
1004-2563 Funu Yanjiu Luncong **8897**
1004-258X Nanjing Daxue Xuebao (Shuxue Banniankan) **5519**
1004-2628 Yinxiang Shijie **6629**
1004-2636 Fayin **7701**
1004-2784 Heilongjiang Huabao **3825**
1004-2792 Dianzi yu Zidonghua **3093**
1004-2806 Linchuang Xueyexue Zazhi **5940**
1004-2822 Chinese Journal of Lasers *changed to* 1671-7694 **7074**
1004-2873 Gongke Wuli *changed to* 1009-7104 **7047**
1004-2881 Fojiao Wenhua **7701**
1004-2903 Diqiu Wulixue Jinzhan **2705**
1004-2911 Ningde Shi-Zhuan Xuebao (Ziran Kexueban) **7893**
1004-292X Jishu Jingji yu Guanli Yanjiu **1763**
1004-2997 Zhipu Xuebao **7085**
1004-3071 Mishu Zhi You **1852**
1004-3101 Weifang Yixueyuan Xuebao **5729**
1004-311X Shengwu Jishu **770**
1004-3217 *see* 1000-8012
1004-3225 *see* 1000-8012
1004-325X Tushuguan Jianshe **5051**
1004-3306 Baoxian Yanjiu **4494**
1004-3314 Zhongguo Siliao **305**
1004-3322 Dangdai Laonian **4043**
1004-3330 Mingqing Xiaoshuo Yanjiu **5334**
1004-3349 Shandong Huabao **3827**
1004-3365 Weidianzixue **2466**
1004-3381 Renmin Luntan **3827**
1004-342X Chengdu Daxue Xuebao (Shehui Kexue Ban) **7954**
1004-3438 Zhonghua Renmin Gongheguo Guowuyuan Gongbao **7478**
1004-3462 Zhongguo Zhexue Nianjian (Jingzhuangben) **6962**
1004-3470 Natural Disaster Reduction in China *see* 1002-4549 **2228**
1004-3489 Guoji Guanxi Xueyuan Xuebao **7239**
1004-3543 Scientia Geologica Sinica **2766**
1004-3578 Zhongguo Musilin **7717**
1004-3586 Zongheng†
1004-3594 Wujing Yixue **5732**
1004-3675 Zhongguo Qinggongye Nianjian **1198**
1004-3691 Furong **5299**
1004-3756 Journal of Systems Science and Systems Engineering **2523**
1004-3780 Qingnian Tansuo **2166**
1004-3845 Shengzhi Yixue Zazhi **6004**
1004-3861 Chinese Trade Unions **1670**
1004-3896 Gongnengxing he Liti Dingxiang Shenjing Waike Zazhi *changed to* 1008-2425 **6251**
1004-390X Yunnan Nongye Daxue Xuebao **171**
1004-3918 Henan Kexue **7861**
1004-3926 Xinan Minzu Xueyuan Xuebao (Zhexue Shehui Kexue Ban) *changed to* Xinan Minzu Daxue Xuebao (Zhexue Shehui Kexue Ban) **8016**
1004-3934 Xinxueguanbingxue Jinzhan **5802**
1004-3950 Nengyuan Gongcheng **3142**
1004-3985 Jiaoyu yu Zhiye **2943**
1004-4035 Nongji Shichang **213**
1004-4043 Renmin Jiancha **4768**
1004-4051 Zhongguo Kuangye **6484**
1004-406X Zhongguo Jizhu Jisui Zazhi **6076**
1004-4094 Suowei Jishu/Journal of Micrographics *changed to* 1672-495X **6980**
1004-4124 Zhongguo Renli Ziyuan Kaifa **1878**
1004-4167 Dianchi **5284**
1004-4213 Guangzi Xuebao **7076**
1004-4221 Zhonghua Fangshe Zhongliuxue Zazhi **6037**
1004-4248 Meitan Zhuanhua **6470**
1004-4280 Shandong Qinggongye Xueyuan Xuebao **7914**
1004-4310 Fuyang Shifan Xueyuan Xuebao (Shehui Kexueban) **7965**
1004-4337 Shuli Yiyaoxue Zazhi **6881**
1004-4353 Yanbian Daxue Xuebao (Ziran Kexue Ban) **7932**
1004-437X Henan Yixue Yanjiu **5628**
1004-4388 Youqijing Ceshi **6798**
1004-440X Zhaoming Gongcheng Xuebao **7085**
1004-4434 Xueshu Luntan **8016**
1004-4442 Dali Yixueyuan Xuebao (Yixue Ban) **5603**
1004-4469 Yanke **6053**
1004-4477 Zhonghua Chaosheng Yingxiangxue Zazhi **6210**
1004-4493 China's Refractories **6308**
1004-4523 Zhendong Gongcheng Xuebao **76**
1004-4558 Qingnian Bolan **2209**
1004-4574 Ziran Zaihai Xuebao **2229**
1004-4582 Chuangyezhe† **8941**
1004-4590 Tiyu yu Kexue **8212**
1004-4612 Xueshu Yanjiu Dongtai *changed to* 1672-2728 **1494**
1004-4620 Shandong Yejin **6331**
1004-4639 Shenyang Huagong Xueyuan Xuebao **7915**
1004-471X Shipin Gongye (Shanghai) **3663**
1004-4728 Fujian Jiancai **1008**
1004-4736 Wuhan Huagong Xueyuan Xuebao/Wuhan Institute of Chemical Technology. Journal *changed to* 1674-2869 **3257**
1004-4752 Shenjian **5371**
1004-4809 Shuhua Yishu **517**
1004-4892 Caijing Luncong **1079**
1004-4914 Jingjishi (Taiyuan) **1132**
1004-4930 Yantai Shifan Xueyuan Xuebao (Ziran Kexueban)/Yantai Normal University Journal (Natural Science Edition) *changed to* 1673-8020 **7880**
1004-4965 Redai Qixiang Xuebao **6393**
1004-4973 Qimeng **6536**
1004-499X Dandao Xuebao **6417**
1004-5007 Zhongwai Wenhua Jiaoliu *see* China & The World Cultural Exchange **3012**
1004-5015 Culture Exchange *changed to* China & The World Cultural Exchange **3012**
1004-5023 Faxian **3824**
1004-504X Daolu Jiaotong Guanli **8630**
1004-5058 Dongfang Yangsheng **6984**
1004-5074 Yishu yu Shidai *changed to* 1005-3190
1004-5104 Alabo Shijie **5092**
1004-5112 Waiyujie **5194**
1004-5120 Yinyu Zixue **5197**
1004-5139 Waiguoyu **5194**

1005-3824 Shuzi Tongxin **3113**
1005-3840 Weixing Xiaoshuo Xuankan **5397**
1005-3867 Algebra Colloquium **5468**
1005-3883 Fushun Shiyou Xueyuan Xuebao/Fushun Petroleum Institute. Journal *changed to* 1672-6952 **6777**
1005-393X Openings **3826**
1005-3956 Zajiao Shuidao **260**
1005-3980 Changjiang Luntan **7115**
1005-4014 Dalian Qinggongye Xueyuan Xuebao/Dalian Institute of Light Industry. Journal *changed to* 1674-1404 **7849**
1005-4057 Guangdong Yixueyuan Xuebao **5621**
1005-4103 Di-er Ketang *changed to* 1005-1430 **2191**
1005-4111 Chinese Rice Research Newsletter *changed to* 1672-6308 **275**
1005-4154 Wenshi Jinghua **4167**
1005-4162 Zongjiao **7697**
1005-4189 Tushuguanxue, Xinxi Kexue, Ziliao Gongzuo **5051**
1005-4235 Renkouxue yu Jihua Shengyu **7292**
1005-4243 Funu Yanjiu **8897**
1005-4251 Jingjifaxue, Laodongfaxue **4872**
1005-426X Guoji Zhengzhi **7239**
1005-4286 Lilun Jingjixue **1546**
1005-4294 Shehui Zhuyi Jingji Lilun yu Shijian **1173**
1005-4332 Chengshi Jingji, Quyue Jingji **1082**
1005-4367 Shangye Qiye Guanli **1793**
1005-4375 Caizheng yu Shuiwu **1914**
1005-4383 Jinrong yu Baoxian **1360**
1005-4405 Zhengzhixue **7197**
1005-443X Qiyejia Xinxi **1162**
1005-4448 Zhongwai Jingmao Xinxi **1589**
1005-4472 Shipin Xinxi **3663**
1005-4537 Zhongguo Fushi yu Fanghu Xuebao **6721**
1005-4545 Zhongguo Shouyi Xuebao **8815**
1005-4553 Dajia **5282**
1005-4561 Zhejiang Zhongxiyi Jiehe Zazhi **5735**
1005-4596 Jiankang Shijie **6990**
1005-4626 Wenxue Daguan **5397**
1005-4650 Nongcun Shiyong Jishu yu Xinxi **141**
1005-4669 Jiating Dianzi **3106**
1005-4715 Shiji **3828**
1005-474X Jingji Zhengce Xinxi **1132**
1005-4812 Guoji Guancha **7239**
1005-4820 Renkou yu Yousheng/Population and Better Birth *changed to* 1671-0061 **7286**
1005-4839 Ertong Xiaoshuo **2188**
1005-4847 Zhongguo Shiyan Dongwu Xuebao **969**
1005-4863 Zhongzhou Jianshe **4432**
1005-4871 Deguo Yanjiu **7230**
1005-4901 Huanqiu Shichang Xinxi Daobao **1119**
1005-491X Minhang Guanli **8548**
1005-4952 Dangdai Zhongguoshi Yanjiu **4181**
1005-4979 Kouqiang Hemian Waike Zazhi **6251**
1005-5053 Hangkong Cailiao Xuebao **57**
1005-5150 Xiaoxiliu *changed to* Xiaoxiliu (Xiaoyuan Chengzhang Ban) **5402**
1005-5169 Feixia **5295**
1005-5177 Xizang Yiyao Zazhi **5732**
1005-5185 Zhongguo Yixue Yingxiangxue Zazhi **6210**
1005-5207 Dili Jiaoyu **4004**
1005-5231 Shaonian Zuowen Fudao **5371**
1005-5282 Cuiyuan **5281**
1005-5304 Zhongguo Zhongyiyao Xinxi Zazhi **5738**
1005-5320 Weiliang Yuansu yu Jiankang Yanjiu **5729**
1005-5347 Kewai Shenghuo **2197**
1005-5371 Baojian yu Shenghuo **6982**
1005-538X E L T Newsletter *changed to* C E L E A Journal **5102**
1005-541X Linchuang Xiaohuabing Zazhi **5928**
1005-5452 Wawa Leyuan **2221**
1005-5487 Qingchun yu Jiankang/Youth and Health *changed to* 1009-9409 **6990**
1005-5509 Zhejiang Zhongyi Xueyuan Xuebao *changed to* Zhejiang Zhongyiyao Daxue Xuebao **5735**
1005-5630 Guangxue Yiqi **4487**
1005-5657 Guangdong Shipin† **8960**
1005-5673 Weishengwuxue Mianyixue Jinzhan **898**
1005-572X Jianghuai Wenshi **4184**
1005-5738 Xizang Daxue Xuebao **8016**
1005-5746 *see* 1005-5738 **8016**
1005-5819 Zhongguo Tongyi Zhanxian **6455**
1005-5835 Quanzhou Wenxue **5356**
1005-6017 Zaoqi Jiaoyu (Jiaoshi Ban) **2928**
1005-6025 Qianwei Yiyao Zazhi/Qianwei Joruna1 of Medicine *changed to* 1671-4008 **5714**
1005-6041 Tushuguan Jie **5051**
1005-605X Anhui Shixue **4179**
1005-6084 Hunan Yejin *changed to* Jinshu Cailiao yu Yejin Gongcheng **6318**
1005-6122 Weibo Xuebao **3116**
1005-6130 Chuzhongsheng Bidu **2836**
1005-6149 Anhui Jiaoyu **2826**
1005-6181 Anhui Shuiwu† **8930**
1005-6378 Hebei Daxue Xuebao (Shehui Zhexue Ban) **7968**
1005-6432 Zhongguo Shichang **1198**
1005-6483 Linchuang Waike Zazhi **6251**
1005-6505 Dangdai Shijie yu Shehui Zhuyi **7230**
1005-6548 Dianli Xuebao **3156**
1005-6556 Jing Fang **2656**
1005-6572 Lianyou Huagong Zidonghua/Automation in Refined and Chemical Industry *changed to* 1007-7324 **6792**
1005-6610 Tushuguan Gongzuo yu Yanjiu **5051**
1005-6629 Huaxue Jiaoxue **3024**
1005-6637 Shanghai Jianshe Keji **1035**
1005-6661 Zhongguo Xuexichongbing Fangzhi Zazhi **5737**
1005-6718 Chaidamu Kaifa Yanjiu **7953**
1005-6734 Zhongguo Guanxing Jishu Xuebao **3228**
1005-6777 Dianying Xinzuo **6496**
1005-6807 Daode yu Wenming **7128**
1005-684X Shidai Jianzhu **3282**
1005-6890 Jiangsu Huakan **498**
1005-6912 Guohua Jia **492**
1005-6920 Zhongguo Youhua **528**
1005-6939 Xiaoshuojia† **8999**
1005-6947 Zhongguo Putong Waike Zazhi **6263**
1005-6955 Zhongguo Manhua **528**
1005-7021 Weishengwuxue Zazhi **898**
1005-703X Zhongguo Jingji Tizhi Gaige Nianjian **1535**
1005-7064 Xinli yu Jiankang **6190**
1005-7072 Zhongguo Zhongyiyao Keji **5738**
1005-7099 Dangdai Getan **6561**
1005-7110 Dongfang Luntan **548**
1005-7145 Tianjin Zhongyi Xueyuan Xuebao *changed to* Tianjin Zhongyiyao Daxue Xuebao **5722**
1005-7153 Ertong Huabao **2187**
1005-7188 Yunnan Minzu Xueyuan Xuebao (Ziran Kexue Ban) *changed to* 1672-8513 **7933**
1005-7234 Jingyaotong Zazhi **5644**
1005-7323 Sanwen Haiwaiban **5367**
1005-7374 Shinei Sheji yu Zhuangxiu **4550**
1005-7382 Haha Huabao **2192**
1005-7471 Zaisheng Ziyuan Yanjiu/Recycling Research *changed to* 1674-0912 **3476**
1005-748X Fushi yu Fanghu **2113**
1005-751X Jiangsu Baoxian†
1005-7528 Zhongguo Yiyao Zonghe Ban†
1005-7536 Haishang Wentan† **8961**
1005-7552 Shanghai Touzi **1651**
1005-7560 Jianchuan Biaozhunhua yu Huanjing Tiaojian **8648**
1005-7595 Zhongshan **5405**
1005-7684 Eluosi Wenyi **5289**
1005-7692 Ziran yu Ren **4168**
1005-7706 Xiaoshuo Jie **5402**
1005-7722 Yishu Shijie **528**
1005-7730 Luyou Tiandi **8731**
1005-7749 Yinyue Aihaozhe **6629**
1005-7765 Shanghai Xiangqi†
1005-7781 Yuwen Yuekan **8018**
1005-7803 Jiangsu Weisheng Shiye Guanli **6990**
1005-782X Shanghai Jichuang **5459**
1005-7870 Zhongguo Daodan yu Hangtian Wenzhai **77**
1005-7889 Xiaoyishujia **527**
1005-7919 Zhongguo Xinxi Daobao/China Information Review *changed to* 1674-1544 **5056**
1005-7943 Qing Ming **5355**
1005-796X Chuangzuo Pingtan **5273**
1005-8001 Yingxiang Zhenduan yu Jieru Fangshexue **6210**
1005-8036 Zhongyang Minzu Daxue Xuebao (Ziran Kexue Ban) **7935**
1005-8060 Dongfang Qiyejia **1093**
1005-8095 Qingbao Tansuo **5041**
1005-8141 Ziyuan Kaifa yu Shichang **2634**
1005-8184 Guoji Shipin/Global Food Magazine *changed to* 1673-6745 **3656**
1005-8257 Shoudu Yiyao **5714**
1005-8273 Mao Zedong Deng Xiaoping Lilun Yanjiu **7153**
1005-829X Gongye Shui Chuli **3486**
1005-8303 Huaren Wenhua Shijie **3825**
1005-832X Kang Fu **6112**
1005-8354 Jidian Shebei **5453**
1005-8451 Tielu Jisuanji Yingyong **8626**
1005-8478 Zhongguo Jiaoxing Waike Zazhi **6076**
1005-8486 Ningxia Yixueyuan Xuebao **5687**
1005-8508 Guowai Yixue (Bingduxue Fence)/Foreign Medical Sciences (Virology) *changed to* 1673-4092 **5913**
1005-8575 Zhongyang Minzu Daxue Xuebao (Zhexue Shehui Kexue Ban) **8019**
1005-8737 Zhongguo Shuichan Kexue **3612**
1005-8796 Zhangjiakou Yixueyuan Xuebao/Zhangjiakou Medical College. Journal *changed to* 1673-1484 **5627**
1005-8850 University of Science and Technology Beijing. Journal **6483**
1005-8877 Family **5558**
1005-8885 Beijing University of Posts and Telecommunications. Journal **2313**
1005-8893 Jiangsu Shiyou Huagong Xueyuan Xuebao/Jiangsu Institute of Petrochemical Technology. Journal *changed to* Jiangsu Gongye Xueyuan Xuebao **6775**
1005-8907 Duankuai Youqitian **6767**
1005-8915 Yaowu Shengwu Jishu **6886**
1005-8923 Zhongguo Xueshu Qikan Wenzhai **18**
1005-894X Fujian Wenbo **394**
1005-8982 Zhongguo Xiandai Yixue **5737**
1005-9024 Bo **8162**
1005-9040 Chemical Research in Chinese Universities **2054**
1005-9059 Yuhua **5403**
1005-9075 Beijing Jishi **3822**
1005-9083 Dangdai Zuojia† **8948**
1005-9091 Linchuang Naodianxue Zazhi/Journal of Clinical Electroencephalogy *changed to* 1009-5934 **6158**
1005-9113 Harbin Institute of Technology. Journal **8423**
1005-9121 Zhongguo Nongye Ziyuan yu Quhua **173**
1005-913X Beifang Jingmao **1066**
1005-9156 Zhongguo Guanggao **37**
1005-9164 Guangxi Kexue **7858**
1005-9172 Shijie Wenhua **5371**
1005-9202 Zhongguo Laonianxue Zazhi **4058**
1005-9245 Xinjiang Shifan Daxue Xuebao (Zhexue Shehui Kexue Ban) **8016**
1005-9253 Dongfang Wenhua **4450**
1005-9261 Zhongguo Shengwu Fangzhi **712**
1005-930X Guangxi Yike Daxue Xuebao **5621**
1005-9318 Shanghai Gongshang **1432**
1005-9334 Hangkong Hangtian Yiyao **5623**
1005-9369 Dongbei Nongye Daxue Xuebao **105**
1005-9385 Zuopin **5405**
1005-9393 Qinghai Keji **7900**
1005-9407 Jinshan **5313**
1005-9423 Shanghai Baozhuang **6715**
1005-944X Zhongguo Dongwu Jianyi **8815**
1005-9482 Dangshi Zonglan **7128**
1005-9490 Dianzi Qijian **3092**
1005-9512 Zhengzhi yu Falu **4820**
1005-9539 Chengdu Ligong Xueyuan Xuebao/Chengdu Institute of Technology. Journal *changed to* 1671-9727 **8418**
1005-958X Jinri Zhongguo **3826**
1005-9598 Mei Huagong **3250**
1005-9628 Zhuxing Xuebao **861**
1005-9709 Linye Jingji Wenti **3696**
1005-9733 Dongfang Yishu **487**
1005-9784 Central South University of Technology. Journal **6460**
1005-9830 Nanjing Ligong Daxue Xuebao **3211**
1005-9857 Haiyang Kaifa yu Guanli **2805**
1005-9865 Haiyang Gongcheng **3194**
1005-9873 Shiyongjun Xuebao **817**
1005-9881 Xiao Mihou **2222**
1005-9903 Zhongguo Shiyan Fangjixue Zazhi **6887**
1005-9954 Huaxue Gongcheng **3245**
1005-9989 Shipin Keji **6669**
1006-0065 Renmin Ribao Suoyin **4588**
1006-0103 Huaxi Yaoxue Zazhi **6846**
1006-0111 Yaoxue Shijian Zazhi **6886**
1006-0138 Xinshiye **7197**
1006-0189 Mingzuo Xinshang **5334**
1006-0197 Beiyue Feng **5261**
1006-0235 Shi-hua Jishu **6792**
1006-0294 Dongfang Jian **5409**
1006-0375 Wenzhou Shifan Xueyuan Xuebao/Wenzhou Normal College. Journal *changed to* 1674-3563 **7928**
1006-0391 Zhongguo Dangzheng Ganbu Luntan **7198**
1006-0448 Nanchang Daxue Xuebao (Shehui Kexue Ban) **4465**
1006-0456 Nanchang Daxue Xuebao (Gongke Ban) **8432**
1006-0464 Nanchang Daxue Xuebao (Like Ban) **7885**
1006-0545 Zhongxue Keji **2929**
1006-0561 Canxue Tongxun **842**
1006-0588 Changzhi Yixueyuan Xuebao **5593**
1006-0642 Cehui Wenzhai (Cehuixue) **4035**
1006-0766 Sichuan Daxue Xuebao (Zhexue Shehui Kexue Ban) **8001**
1006-0820 Dangdai Wentan **5282**
1006-0855 Yundong Xiuxian **8217**
1006-0863 Zhongguo Xingzheng Guanli **7478**
1006-0871 Jisuanji Fuzhu Gongcheng **3292**
1006-0936 Kanshijie **3826**
1006-0995 Sichuan Dizhi Xuebao **2767**
1006-1010 Yidong Tongxin **2345**
1006-1037 Qingdao Daxue Xuebao (Ziran Kexue Ban) **7900**
1006-1088 Huadong Chuanbo Gongye Xueyuan Xuebao/East China Shipbuilding Institute. Journal *changed to* 1673-4807 **7870**
1006-1096 Jingji Jingwei **1131**
1006-1126 Guangxi Linye Kexue **3692**
1006-1169 Shijie Shizhuang Zhiyuan **8883**
1006-1207 Tiyu Keyan **6234**
1006-124X Zhongguo Gangkou **8666**
1006-1266 *see* 1000-1964 **6484**
1006-1274 Tian Feng **7777**
1006-1304 Nongye Shengwu Jishu Xuebao **141**
1006-1312 Zongjiaoxue Yanjiu **7697**
1006-1320 Shanghai Baoxian **4523**
1006-1398 Huaqiao Daxue Xuebao (Zhexue Shehui Kexue Ban) **7970**
1006-1428 Shanghai Jinrong **1383**
1006-1444 Baihua Zhou **5259**
1006-1460 Xinwen Daxue **4586**
1006-1509 Qingshaonian Fanzui Wenti **4764**
1006-1517 Shanghai Shengwu Yixue Gongcheng/Shanghai Journal of Biomedical Engineering *changed to* 1674-1242 **751**
1006-1525 Daxue Tushu Qingbao Xuekan **5005**
1006-1533 Shanghai Yiyao **5713**
1006-1576 Binggong Zidonghua **6413**
1006-1592 Xiaoxue Yuwen Jiaoshi **5196**
1006-1606 Xiaoxue Shuxue Jiaoshi **5547**
1006-1614 Kantu Shuohua **2196**
1006-1622 A B C Pinpin Dudu Huabao **2821**
1006-1630 Shanghai Hangtian **70**
1006-1649 Zhengzhi Jiaoyu *changed to* 1672-0237 **7187**
1006-169X Jinrong yu Jingji **1132**
1006-1703 Biaoji Mianyi Fenxi yu Linchuang **5755**
1006-1711 Shanghai Dianshi **2390**
1006-1738 Hanghai Jishu **8645**
1006-1746 Dahuilang Huabao **2184**
1006-1789 Dangdai Qingnian Yanjiu **2150**
1006-1878 Huagong Huanbao **3437**
1006-1908 Guangxian yu Dianlan **3309**
1006-1940 Yingju Xinzuo†
1006-2068 Shanghai Jiaoyu **2911**
1006-2076 Shandong Tiyu Xueyuan Xuebao **3081**
1006-2106 Tiedao Gongcheng Xuebao **8626**
1006-2114 Gongcheng Jixie yu Weixiu **5452**
1006-2130 Hangkong Wenzhai **76**
1006-2149 Zhongguo Hangwu Zhoukan **8666**
1006-2157 Beijing Zhongyiyao Daxue Xuebao **5584**
1006-2165 Daqing Gaodeng Zhuanke Xuexiao Xuebao **7958**
1006-2181 Shinei Sheji **4550**
1006-2211 Wenxue Yuebao *changed to* 1009-3915
1006-222X Gaokeji yu Chanyehua **8423**
1006-2238 Jiangxi Yiyao **5644**
1006-2262 Zhongguo Fangzhi Meishu/China Textiles Design *changed to* Shishang Neiyi **8457**
1006-2300 Wangqiu Tiandi **8251**
1006-2327 Fujian Re-zuo Keji **232**
1006-2335 Nongye Kaogu **408**
1006-2343 Jixie Sheji yu Yanjiu **5453**
1006-2394 Yibiao Jishu **4490**
1006-2424 Duxie Yuebao **5112**
1006-2432 Zhishi Chuang **7934**
1006-2459 Dangan Tiandi **5005**
1006-2467 Shanghai Jiaotong Daxue Xuebao **8438**
1006-2513 Zhongguo Shipin Tianjiaji **3668**
1006-2548 Beifangren **3822**
1006-2599 Guoji Zaozhi **6733**
1006-2629 Xinan Luyou **8776**
1006-2661 Jianzhu Jishu Ji Sheji **446**
1006-2696 China Oil and Gas **6766**
1006-2726 Shanghai Tongji **8399**
1006-2769 Xibei Yixue Jiaoyu **2927**
1006-2793 Guti Huojian Jishu **57**

ISSN

1007-1059 Wuliu Jishu yu Yingyong **1802**
1007-113X Luoyang University. Journal **7984**
1007-1156 Fushi Wenhua: Zhongguo Bianzhi *changed to* Zhongguo Bianzhi **2263**
1007-1172 Shanghai Jiaotong University. Journal **8438**
1007-1202 Wuhan University Journal of Natural Sciences **7930**
1007-1237 Hainan Yixueyuan Xuebao **5623**
1007-1245 Guoji Yiyao Weisheng Daobao **5622**
1007-1261 Baoji Wenli Xueyuan Xuebao (Ziran Kexue) **7839**
1007-130X Jisuanji Gongcheng yu Kexue **2473**
1007-1385 Shenyang Hangkong Gongye Xueyuan Xuebao **70**
1007-1423 Xiandai Jisuanji *changed to* Xiandai Jisuanji (Zhuanye Ban) **2441**
1007-1423 Xiandai Jisuanji *changed to* Xiandai Jisuanji (Puji Ban) **2441**
1007-1431 Zhongguo Nanfang Guoshu **172**
1007-144X Wuhan Qiche Gongye Daxue Xuebao/Wuhan Automotive Polytechnic University. Journal *changed to* Wuhan Ligong DaxueXuebao (Xinxi yu Guanligongcheng Ban) **2551**
1007-1482 Zhongguo Tishixue yu Tuxiang Fenxi **6979**
1007-1520 Zhongguo Er-Bi-Yanhou-Ludi Waike Zazhi **6086**
1007-158X Guangxi Yufang Yixue/Guangxi Journal of Preventive Medicine *changed to* Yingyong Yufang Yixue **5733**
1007-161X Dangdai Ya-Tai **547**
1007-1628 Yingyang yu Shipin Weisheng *changed to* 1674-2044 **3663**
1007-1660 Jingji Shuxue **5499**
1007-1725 Jiefangjun Yixue Gaodeng Zhuanke Xuexiao Xuebao/P L A Junior Colleges of Medicine. Journal *changed to* 1671-3826 **6431**
1007-1741 Jiangsu Ligong Daxue Xuebao (Ziran Kexue Ban)/of Jiangsu University of Science and Technology. Journal (Nature Science Edition) *changed to* 1671-7775 **7870**
1007-1784 Zhongguo Renmin Jingguan Daxue Xuebao (Ziran Kexue Ban) **7934**
1007-1792 Zhongshan Daxue Xuebao Luncong **8019**
1007-1857 Shandong Gongcheng Xueyuan Xuebao *changed to* 1672-6197 **7914**
1007-1865 Guangdong Huagong **2062**
1007-1873 Shilin **5434**
1007-1881 Zhejiang Dianli **3162**
1007-1903 Beijing Dizhi **2726**
1007-1938 Chuban yu Yinshua **7558**
1007-1954 Gandanyi Waike Zazhi **5924**
1007-1962 Lilun Qianyan **7152**
1007-1989 Zhongguo Neijing Zazhi **5736**
1007-2004 Zhongguo Gongwuyuan **7478**
1007-2012 Suxing Gongcheng Xuebao **3256**
1007-2020 Shanghai Jiaoyu Keyan **2911**
1007-2101 Hebei Jingmao Daxue Xuebao **1351**
1007-2187 Gaodeng Hanshou Xuebao (Zhexue Shehui Kexue Ban) **7966**
1007-2195 Gaige Zongheng **1541**
1007-2209 Turang Qinshi yu Shuitu Baochi Xuebao/Journal of Soil Erosion and Soil and Water Conservation *changed to* 1009-2242 **252**
1007-2225 Zaozhi Huaxuepin **6740**
1007-2268 Guanli yu Xinxi† **8960**
1007-2276 Hongwai yu Jiguang Gongcheng **58**
1007-2322 Xiandai Dianli **3162**
1007-2330 Yuhang Cailiao Gongyi **75**
1007-2349 Yunnan Zhongyi Zhongyao Zazhi **315**
1007-2365 Selected Papers of Engineering Chemistry and Metallurgy **6331**
1007-2373 Hebei Gongye Daxue Xuebao **3195**
1007-2438 Xinwenjie **4586**
1007-2489 Shuyu Biaozhunhua yu Xinxi Jishu **2550**
1007-2624 Zhongguo Tangliao **173**
1007-2640 Beijing Huagong Daxue Xuebao *changed to* 1671-4628 **7839**
1007-2659 Zhongguo Xinzang Qibo yu Xindian Shengli Zazhi **5802**
1007-2683 Haerbin Ligong Daxue Xuebao **7859**
1007-2691 Huabei Dianli Daxue Xuebao **3158**
1007-2705 Haixia Yufang Yixue Zazhi **5623**
1007-2764 Guangzhou Shipin Gongye Keji/Guangzhou Food Science and Technology *changed to* 1673-9078 **3668**
1007-2772 Xiangqi†
1007-2780 Yejing yu Xianshi **7085**
1007-2802 Kuangwu Yanshi Diqiu Huaxue Tongbao **2752**
1007-2829 Hebei Ligong Xueyuan Xuebao/Hebei Institute of Technology. Journal *changed to* Hebei Ligong Daxue Xuebao **8423**
1007-2861 Shanghai Daxue Xuebao (Ziran Kexue Ban) **7914**
1007-290X Guangdong Dianli **3158**
1007-2942 Zhongguo Gangbi Shufa **528**
1007-2985 Jishou Daxue Xuebao (Ziran Kexue Ban) **7871**
1007-3051 Jiaoyu yu Xiandaihua **2873**
1007-3124 Liuti Lixue Shiyan yu Celiang/Experiments and Measurements in Fluid Mechanics *changed to* 1672-9897 **7063**
1007-3205 Hebei Yike Daxue Xuebao **5627**
1007-3213 Guangzhou Zhongyiyao Daxue Xuebao **5621**
1007-3221 Yunchou yu Guanli **1802**
1007-323X Guangzhou Tiyu Xueyuan Xuebao **2861**
1007-3264 Xi'an Youdian Xueyuan Xuebao **2345**
1007-3280 Zhongguo Minying Keji yu Jingji **1434**
1007-3299 Zhejiang Shiyong Yixue **5735**
1007-3388 Dangyuan Wenzhai **7128**
1007-3418 Zhonghua Ganzangbing Zazhi **5949**
1007-3450 He'nan Kuchong Fenlei Quxi Yanjiu **848**
1007-3507 Baotou Yixue **5583**
1007-3515 Junwu Xitong *changed to* 1672-6472 **890**
1007-3523 Zhongguo Xingbing Aizibing Fangzhi/Chinese Journal of Prevention and Control of STD & AIDS *changed to* 1672-5662 **5828**
1007-3566 Dangdai Dangyuan **7128**
1007-3612 Beijing Tiyu Daxue Xuebao **6982**
1007-3647 Renkou Zhanxian†
1007-3698 Zhonghua Nuzi Xueyuan Xuebao **8906**
1007-3701 Hua'nan Dizhi yu Kuangchan **2746**
1007-3728 Zhongguo Teshu Jiaoyu **3049**
1007-3795 Qinghai Yiyao Zazhi **5701**
1007-3809 Gaoyuan Yixue Zazhi **5617**
1007-3817 Cehui Xinxi yu Gongcheng **4002**
1007-385X Zhongguo Zhongliu Shengwu Zhiliao Zazhi **6037**
1007-3884 Bianji Xuekan **7552**
1007-3930 Dianshi Yanjiu **2380**
1007-3949 Zhonggou Dongmai Yinghua Zazhi **5735**
1007-3957 Zhongguo Kouqiang Zhongzhixue Zazhi **5870**
1007-3981 Anhui Keji yu Qiye **8416**
1007-4066 Neimenggu Linye Keji **3698**
1007-4074 Jishou Daxue Xuebao (Shehui Kexue Ban) **7977**
1007-4112 Xi'an Gonglu Jiaotong Daxue Xuebao *changed to* 1671-8879 **8630**
1007-4139 Zhongguo Wuzi Liutong *changed to* 1671-6663 **1198**
1007-4155 Bianjiang Wenxue **5262**
1007-4244 Xiandai Funu **8892**
1007-4252 Gongneng Cailiao yu Qijian Xuebao **6314**
1007-4295 Bainianchao **4180**
1007-4325 Yingyong Huagong **3257**
1007-4333 Zhongguo Nongye Daxue Xuebao **172**
1007-4368 Nanjing Yike Daxue Xuebao (Ziran Kexue Ban) **5682**
1007-4376 Nanjing Medical University. Journal **5682**
1007-4406 Zhongguo Linchuang Yaoxue Zazhi **6887**
1007-4465 Yangzhou Daxue Shuiwu Xueyuan Xuebao **1955**
1007-449X Dianji yu Kongzhi Xuebao **3300**
1007-4546 International Journal of Plant Engineering and Management **3202**
1007-4600 Bailiu **5260**
1007-4619 Yaogan Xuebao **4034**
1007-4627 Yuanzi Hewuli Pinglun **7073**
1007-4635 Diannao yu Xinyongka/Computer & Credit Card *changed to* 1009-2056 **1392**
1007-4651 A V State of the Art **3089**
1007-4708 Jisuan Lixue Xuebao **2428**
1007-4716 Shantou Daxue Yixueyuan Xuebao **5713**
1007-4740 Medium/Small Hydro Power & Equipment **3325**
1007-4805 Meishu Qimeng† **8974**
1007-4848 Zhongguo Xiongxin Xueguan Waike Linchuang Zazhi **5802**
1007-4856 Zhongguo Zhongxiyi Jiehe Erbiyanhouke Zazhi **6086**
1007-4872 Chaye Kexue Jishu **224**
1007-4880 Ketang Neiwai (Chuzhong Ban) **2197**
1007-4899 Ketang Neiwai (Gaozhong Ban) **2197**
1007-4902 Ketang Neiwai (Xiaoxue Ban) **2197**
1007-4929 Jieshui Guan'gai **8827**
1007-5038 Dongwu Yixue Jinzhan **8796**
1007-5062 Xinfeixueguanbing Zazhi **5802**
1007-5119 Zhongguo Yancao Kexue **8489**
1007-5135 Shanghai Kuaiji **1301**
1007-5178 Tequ Jiaoyu *changed to* Tequ Xiaoxuesheng **2216**
1007-5232 Zhonghua Xiaohua Neijing Zazhi **5901**
1007-5240 Anhui Jidian Xueyuan Xuebao **3373**
1007-5305 Zhongwai Junshi Yingshi **6517**
1007-5321 Beijing Youdian Daxue Xuebao **2313**
1007-533X Jinzhou Shifan Xueyuan Xuebao (Zike Ban) *changed to* 1673-0569 **7841**
1007-5429 Gongye Gongcheng yu Guanli **3367**
1007-5437 Nanfang Gangtie *changed to* 1009-9700 **6327**
1007-5453 Hangkong Kexue Jishu **57**
1007-5461 Liangzi Dianzi Xuebao **7025**
1007-550X Fujian Qingfang **7965**
1007-5534 Huazhong Yixue Zazhi **5630**
1007-5550 Zhongguo Tupian†
1007-5615 Hebei Zhongyiyao Xuebao **5627**
1007-5666 Baoxian Yingjia **4494**
1007-5682 Xiaofei Jingji **1196**
1007-5704 Communications in Nonlinear Science and Numerical Simulation **5479**
1007-578X Zhongguo Caizheng **1955**
1007-5798 Zhongguo Minjian Liaofa **316**
1007-5828 Dazhong Wenyi **485**
1007-5836 Zhongguo Musilin (Weiwen) *see* 1004-3578 **7717**
1007-5968 Xuexiao Dangjian yu Sixiang Jiaoyu **7197**
1007-6069 Shijie Dizhen Gongcheng **3282**
1007-6093 Yunchouxue Xuebao **7933**
1007-6107 Huizhou Daxue Xuebao *changed to* 1671-5934 **7970**
1007-614X Zhongguo Xiangcun Yisheng/Chinese Rural Doctors *changed to* Zhongguo Shequ Yishi **5736**
1007-6174 Zhonghua Renmin Gongheguo Shuishou Fagui Gonggao **1956**
1007-6190 Guangdong Qixiang **6353**
1007-6220 Linfei yu Fufei **241**
1007-6239 Zhonghua Hangkong Hangtian Yixue Zazhi **5738**
1007-6255 Shijie Zongjiao Wenhua **7681**
1007-6271 Changsha Dianli Xueyuan Xuebao (Shehui Kexue Ban)/Changsha University of Electric Power. Journal (Social Science) *changed to* 1672-934X **7954**
1007-628X Zhongxue Yuwen Yuandi **5200**
1007-6298 Qingnian Shejiao **2209**
1007-6301 Dili Kexue Jinzhan **4004**
1007-631X Zhonghua Putong Waike Zazhi **5738**
1007-6417 Shanghai University. Journal **7914**
1007-6425 Xuzhou Shifan Daxue Xuebao (Zhexue Shehui Kexue Ban) **8017**
1007-6492 Zhengzhou Gongye Daxue Xuebao *changed to* 1671-6833 **3228**
1007-6514 Jiangsu Linchuang Yixue Zazhi/Journal of Jiangsu Clinical Medicine *changed to* 1672-2353 **5714**
1007-6573 Xuzhou Shifan Daxue Xuebao (Ziran Kexue Ban) **7932**
1007-6581 Jisuanji yu Nongye/Computer and Agriculture *changed to* 1672-6251 **215**
1007-659X Shandong Zhongyiyao Daxue Xuebao **5713**
1007-6611 Shanxi Yike Daxue Xuebao **5713**
1007-662X Journal of Forestry Research **3695**
1007-6638 Zhonghua Xinlu Shichangxue Zazhi **5803**
1007-6654 Liangzi Guangxue Xuebao **7025**
1007-6670 Touzi yu Zhengquan **1656**
1007-6689 Zhongguo Zhexue **6962**
1007-6697 Falixue, Fashixue **4670**
1007-6719 Waiguo Zhexue **6960**
1007-6735 Shanghai Ligong Daxue Xuebao **8438**
1007-6751 Shijie Yixue Zazhi **5713**
1007-676X Dazhong Touzi Zhinan **1620**
1007-6832 Guizhou Gongye Daxue Xuebao *changed to* 1009-0509 **7967**
1007-6867 Guoji Fangzhi Daobao **8451**
1007-6883 Hanshan Shifan Xueyuan Xuebao **7968**
1007-6948 Zhongguo Zhong-Xiyi Jiehe Waike Zazhi **6263**
1007-6964 Shijie Jingji Yanjiu **1517**
1007-7030 Yangzhou Daxue Xuebao (Renwen Shehui Kexue Ban) **8017**
1007-7065 Chinese Journal of Polar Science **2704**
1007-7073 Jidi Yanjiu **2711**
1007-7111 Chongqing yu Shijie **3823**
1007-712X Jituan Jingji Yanjiu **1132**
1007-7146 Jiguang Shengwu Xuebao **734**
1007-7162 Yangzhou Daxue Xuebao (Gao Jiao Yanjiu Ban) **3011**
1007-7219 Dongfang Nuxing **8859**
1007-7278 Nanjing Daxue Xuebao (Zhexue Renwen Shehui Kexue) **7885**
1007-7294 Chuanbo Lixue **8641**
1007-7308 Guangdong Zidonghua yu Xinxi Gongcheng/Guangdong Automation & Information Engineering *changed to* 1674-2605 **2465**
1007-7316 Dongfang Wenhua Zhoukan **486**
1007-7324 Shiyou Huagong Zidonghua **6792**
1007-7375 Gongye Gongcheng **3367**
1007-7383 Shihezi Daxue Xuebao (Ziran Kexue Ban) **7915**
1007-7391 Talents **3828**
1007-7405 Jimei Daxue Xuebao (Ziran Kexue Ban) **7871**
1007-7413 Tiyu Kexue Yanjiu **6998**
1007-7421 Fujian Caikuai *changed to* Fujian Caikuai Yanjiu **1348**
1007-7448 Jingji Dongwu Xuebao **4973**
1007-7480 Zhonghua Fengshibingxue Zazhi **6228**
1007-7537 Nanjing Huagong Daxue Xuebao/Nanjing University of Chemical Technology. Journal *changed to* 1671-7627 **3251**
1007-7561 Laingyou Shipin Keji **132**
1007-7588 Ziyuan Kexue **3477**
1007-7618 Zhongwai Keji Xinxi† **9000**
1007-7626 Zhongguo Shengwu Huaxue yu Fenzi Shengwu Xuebao **746**
1007-7634 Qingbao Kexue (Changchun) **2550**
1007-7642 Xiao Shuidian **3164**
1007-7669 Zhongguo Xinyao Yu Linchuang Zazhi **6887**
1007-7685 Jingji Zongheng **1132**
1007-7693 Zhongguo Xiandai Yingyong Yaoxue **6887**
1007-7790 Dushi *changed to* Dushi - Fanyue Rili **3824**
1007-7812 Chinese Journal of Explosives & Propellants **3241**
1007-7820 Dianzi Keji **3092**
1007-7847 Shengming Kexue Yanjiu **704**
1007-7855 Anhui Keji **7835**
1007-788X Gansu Zheng-Fa Xueyuan Xuebao **7138**
1007-791X Yanshan Daxue Xuebao **8017**
1007-7995 Zhanjiang Haiyang Daxue Xuebao *changed to* 1673-9159 **2709**
1007-8010 Chinese Academic Journals Full-Text Database. Science & Engineering, Series A **7845**
1007-8029 Chinese Academic Journals Full-Text Database. Science & Engineering, Series B **7845**
1007-8037 Chinese Academic Journals Full-Text Database. Science & Engineering, Series C **7845**
1007-8061 Chinese Academic Journals Full-Text Database. Literature, History & Philosophy **4447**
1007-807X Chinese Academic Journals Full-Text Database. Economics, Politics & Laws **7954**
1007-810X Changwai yu Changnei Yingyang **6656**
1007-8118 Zhonghua Gandan Waike Zazhi **6263**
1007-8134 Chuanranbing Xinxi **5811**
1007-8142 Dadushi **8858**
1007-8193 Aizheng Kangfu **6106**
1007-824X Yangzhou Daxue Xuebao (Ziran Kexue Ban) **7932**
1007-8274 Dangdai Yuyanxue **5110**
1007-8347 Zhongzhi yu Yangzhi **260**
1007-8355 Zhongxue Lishi Dili Jiaoxue *changed to* 1009-2978 **2929**
1007-8428 Boai **6983**
1007-8444 Huaiyin Shifan Xueyuan Xuebao (Zhexue Shehui Kexue Ban) **7970**
1007-8576 Xinjiang Caijing **1196**
1007-8592 Minzu Luntan **7155**
1007-8614 Xinjiang Nongye Daxue Xuebao **171**
1007-8622 Xibei Guofang Yixue Zazhi **5732**
1007-869X Chengshi Guidao Jiaotong Yanjiu **8493**
1007-8738 Xibao yu Fenzi Mianyixue Zazhi **5767**
1007-8746 Zhongguo Laodong **1717**
1007-8754 Guangdong Jiaoyu Xueyuan Xuebao **2861**
1007-8770 Xiandai Chuanbo **2345**
1007-8827 Xinxing Tancailiao **3257**
1007-8924 Mo Kexue Jishu **3250**
1007-8983 Sichuan Jianzhu **457**
1007-9017 Zhongguo Xingshifa Zazhi **2672**
1007-9041 Guangdong Jinrong/Guangdong Finance *changed to* Nanfang Jinrong **1369**
1007-9068 Xiaoxue Jiaoxue Cankao **2927**
1007-9084 Zhongguo Youliao Zuowu Xuebao **260**
1007-9130 Hao/How *changed to* 1674-3113 **2263**
1007-9149 Pingxiang Gaodeng Zhuanke Xuexiao Xuebao **7992**
1007-9165 Guangdong Huabao/Guangdong Pictorial *changed to* Cheng Shi Huabao **3823**
1007-9211 Zhonghua Zhiye **6740**
1007-9289 Zhongguo Biaomian Gongcheng **3228**
1007-9297 Falu yu Yixue Zazhi/Journal of Law & Medicine *changed to* 1674-1226 **4820**
1007-9327 World Journal of Gastroenterology **5932**
1007-9378 Dangdai Jingji **1090**
1007-9408 Zhonghua Weichan Yixue Zazhi **6006**
1007-9416 Dianzi yu Jin Xilie Gongcheng Xinxi/Electronics & Golden Projects Collection *changed to* Shuzi Jishu yu Yingyong **8438**
1007-9424 Zhongguo Pu-wai Jichu yu Linchuang Zazhi **6263**
1007-9432 Taiyuan Ligong Daxue Xuebao **8440**
1007-9459 Xiaoer Jijiu Yixue/Pediatric Emergency Medicine *changed to* Zhongguo Xiaoer Jijiu Yixue **6105**

ISSN

9444 1007-953X ULRICH'S PERIODICALS

1007-953X Zhongguo Weisheng Ziyuan **7547**
1007-9556 Shanxi Caijing Daxue Xuebao **1173**
1007-9564 Zhongguo Meitan Gongye Yixue Zazhi **5736**
1007-9572 Zhongguo Quanke Yixue **5736**
1007-9580 Yuye Xiandaihua **3612**
1007-9610 Waike Lilun yu Shijian **6262**
1007-9629 Jianzhu Cailiao Xuebao **1017**
1007-9688 Lingnan Xinxueguanbing Zazhi **5795**
1007-9718 Zhongguo Yaowu Yilaixing Zazhi **2700**
1007-9742 Yingguo Yixue Zazhi (Chinese Edition) **5733**
1007-9769 Hulianwang Zhoukan **2557**
1007-9777 Zhongguo Jingmao Daokan **1198**
1007-9793 Yunnan Shifan Daxue Xuebao (Ziran Kexue Ban) **7933**
1007-9831 Gao-shi Li-ke Xuekan **7857**
1007-984X Qiqihaer Daxue Xuebao (Ziran Kexue Ban) **7901**
1007-9858 Liaoning Yaowu yu Linchuang *changed to* 1673-0070 **5714**
1007-9882 Jiamusi Daxue Shehui Kexue Xuebao **4458**
1007-9912 Gansu Jiaoyu Xueyuan Xuebao (Ziran Kexue Ban)/Gansu Education College. Journal (Natural Science Edition) *changed to* 1672-691X **7857**
1007-9939 Guangdong Yaoxue/Guangdong Pharmaceutical Journal *changed to* 1674-229X **6851**
1008-0058 Changchun Kejie Daxue Xuebao/Changchun University of Science and Technology. Journal *changed to* 1671-5888 **2749**
1008-0074 Xinxueguan Kangfu Yixue Zazhi **5802**
1008-0104 Heilongjiang Yiyao Kexue **5627**
1008-0112 Guangdong Shuili Shuidian **8824**
1008-0120 Shanxi Shuitu Baochi Keji **2627**
1008-0171 Foshan Kexue Jishu Xueyuan Xuebao (Ziran Kexue Ban) **7855**
1008-018X Foshan Kexue Jishu Xueyuan Xuebao (Shehui Kexue Ban) **7965**
1008-0201 Heilongjiang Shiyou Huagong/Heilongjiang Petrochemical Technology *changed to* 1671-4962 **6777**
1008-021X Shandong Huagong **3255**
1008-0244 Dizhi Diqiu Huaxue **2731**
1008-0287 Linchuang Guke Zazhi **6066**
1008-0341 Qilu Yixue Zazhi **5701**
1008-0376 Cishan **8033**
1008-0384 Fujian Nongye Xuebao **114**
1008-0457 Shandi Nongye Shengwu Xuebao **155**
1008-049X Zhongguo Yaoshi (Wuyi) **6887**
1008-0511 Huagong Keji **1119**
1008-0562 Liaoning Gongcheng Jishu Daxue Xuebao (Ziran Kexue Ban) **7879**
1008-0570 Weijisuanji Xinxi **2573**
1008-0589 Zhongguo Yufang Shouyi Xuebao **8816**
1008-066X Ziben Shichang **1198**
1008-0678 Zhongguo Linchuang Shenjing Kexue **6191**
1008-0716 Baogang Jishu **6306**
1008-0732 Lu Ming **5328**
1008-0775 Ruanjian Gongchengshi **2596**
1008-0805 Shizhen Guoyi Guoyao **6881**
1008-0813 Yeya Qidong yu Mifeng **3365**
1008-0848 Zhongguo Nankexue Zazhi **6285**
1008-0864 Zhongguo Nongye Keji Daobao **172**
1008-0872 Zhongguo Shenjing Kexue Zazhi/Chinese Journal of Neuroscience *changed to* 1673-7067 **6169**
1008-097X Ruanjian yu Guangpan **2596**
1008-0996 Shijie Hangkong Hangtian Bolan/Aerospace World *changed to* 1674-3776 **70**
1008-1011 Huaxue Yanjiu **2116**
1008-1062 Zhongguo Linchuang Yixue Yingxiang Zazhi **6210**
1008-1070 Zhongguo Yikan **5737**
1008-1089 Zhongguo Linchuang Yisheng **5736**
1008-1127 Nongken Yixue **5687**
1008-1143 Gongye Cuihua **3367**
1008-1151 Dazhong Keji **8419**
1008-1194 Tance yu Kongzhi Xuebao **3221**
1008-1208 Beijing Guancha **7109**
1008-1267 Tianjin Huagong **1183**
1008-1275 Chinese Journal of Traumatology **6057**
1008-1321 Forestry Studies in China **3690**
1008-1372 Zhongguo Yishi Zazhi **5737**
1008-1402 Jiamusi Daxue Xuebaon (Ziran Kexue Ban) **7870**
1008-1429 Chenggong Yingxiao **1810**
1008-1534 Hebei Gongye Keji **8423**
1008-1542 Hebei Keji Daxue Xuebao **7860**
1008-1569 Dongnan Xueshu **7960**
1008-1593 Ribenxue Luntan **7998**
1008-1658 Beijing Jijie Gongye Xueyuan Xuebao (Zonghe Ban) **5449**
1008-1674 Shaoyang Shifan Gaodeng Zhuanke Xuexiao Xuebao/Shaoyang Teachers College. Journal *changed to* 1672-7010 **7914**
1008-1674 Shaoyang Shifan Gaodeng Zhuanke Xuexiao Xuebao/Shaoyang Teachers College. Journal *changed to* Shaoyang Xueyuan Xuebao (Shehui Kexue Ban) **8000**
1008-1682 Dianli Jishu Jingji **1092**
1008-1704 Ganzang **5924**
1008-1712 Guangxi Jingmao† **8960**
1008-1739 Jisuanji yu Wangluo **2359**
1008-1755 Guoji Luntan **7239**
1008-1801 Yanshi Guangxue Zazhi **6053**
1008-1836 Guangzhou Yixueyuan Xuebao **5621**
1008-1852 Zhongguo Shiyou he Huagong **6798**
1008-1895 Nanjing Nong-Zhuan Xuebao/Nanjing Agricultural Technology College. Journal *changed to* 1673-131X **7977**
1008-1917 Jiangsu Ligong Daxue Xuebao (Shehui Kexue Ban)/of Jiangsu University of Science and Technology. Journal (Social Sciences Edition) *changed to* 1671-6604 **7976**
1008-2018 Beijing Wudao Xueyuan Xuebao **2682**
1008-2050 21 Shiji Xiaoxuesheng Zuowen/21st Century Elementary School Compositions *changed to* 1673-0666 **2198**
1008-2107 Hu'nan Shangxueyuan Xuebao **1119**
1008-2174 Liaodong Xueyuan Xuebao (Ziran Kexue Ban) **7879**
1008-2190 Nantong Gongxueyuan Xuebao/Nantong Institute of Technology. Journal *changed to* Nantong Daxue Xuebao (Jiaoyu Kexue Ban) **2889**
1008-2204 Beijing Hangkong Hangtian Daxue Xuebao (Shehui Kexue Ban) **7949**
1008-2263 Shiyouku yu Jiayouzhan **6793**
1008-2271 Chengshi Guanli yu Keji **7489**
1008-228X Beijing Jiaoyu Xueyuan Xuebao **2830**
1008-2344 Shenyang Yixueyuan Xuebao **5713**
1008-2360 Henan Shiyong Shenjing Jibing Zazhi **6144**
1008-2409 Huaxia Yixue **5630**
1008-2425 Liti Dingxiang he Gongnengxing Shenjing Waike Zazhi **6251**
1008-245X Xi'an Jiaotong Daxue Xuebao (Shehui Kexue Ban) **8015**
1008-2484 Zhongwen Zixue Zhidao **5199**
1008-2506 Guangdong Shangxueyuan Xuebao **1115**
1008-2514 Guowai Yixue (Fu-you Baojian Fence) **5991**
1008-2522 Daolu Jiaotong yu Anquan **8630**
1008-2530 Tianjin Yinyue Xueyuan Xuebao (Tianlai) **6623**
1008-2565 Beijing Shiyou Huagong Xueyuan Xuebao **3236**
1008-2603 Huabei Dianli Daxue Xuebao (Shehui Kexue Ban) **7969**
1008-2611 Zhuzhou Gongxueyuan Xuebao/Zhuzhou Institute of Technology. Journal *changed to* 1673-9833 **7863**
1008-2638 Qiqihaer Daxue Xuebao (Zhexue Shehui Kexue Ban) **7994**
1008-2646 Nanjing Ligong Daxue Xuebao (Shehui Kexue Ban) **7987**
1008-2662 Shangqiu Shifan Xueyuan Xuebao **3002**
1008-2670 Shandong Caizheng Xueyuan Xuebao **1383**
1008-2689 Beijing Keji Daxue Xuebao (Shehui Kexue Ban) **7950**
1008-2700 Shoudu Jingji Maoyi Daxue Xuebao **1174**
1008-2735 Jinggangshan Yi-Zhuan Xuebao **5644**
1008-2751 Liaoning Cai-Zhuan Xuebao *changed to* 1672-8572 **7983**
1008-2751 Liaoning Cai-Zhuan Xuebao/Liaoning Financial College Journal *changed to* 1008-2174 **7879**
1008-2786 Shandi Xuebao **2767**
1008-2794 Changshu Gao-Zhuan Xuebao *changed to* Changshu Ligong Xueyuan Xuebao **8418**
1008-2859 Liaoning Shuiwu Gaodeng Zhuanke Xuexiao Xuebao **1933**
1008-2867 Kaifeng Yi-Zhuan Xuebao/Academic Journal of Kaifeng Medical College *changed to* Henan Daxue Xuebao (Yixue Kexue Ban) **5627**
1008-293X Shaoxing Weli Xueyuan Xuebao **8000**
1008-2972 Jiangxi Cai-Jing Daxue Xuebao **1131**
1008-3065 Kang'ai **6025**
1008-3073 Handan Yixue Gaodeng Zhuanke Xuexiao Xuebao† **8961**
1008-3162 Shandong Dianli Gaodeng Zhuanke Xuexiao Xuebao **3161**
1008-3243 Shenji Wenzhai **1301**
1008-3251 Gonggong Xingzheng **7439**
1008-326X Dangdai Wencui **5282**
1008-3278 Shijie Jingji *changed to* 1009-7511 **1721**
1008-3286 Tequ Jingji yu Konggaotai Jingji† **8993**
1008-3367 Beijing Shuili/Beijing Water Resources *changed to* 1673-4637 **8818**
1008-3391 Liaoning Gongxueyuan Xuebao (Shehui Kexue Ban)/Liaoning Institute of Technology. Journal (Social Science Edition) *changed to* 1674-327X **7983**
1008-3421 Fujian Shi-Da Fuqing Fenxiao Xuebao **7965**
1008-343X Kaifeng Daxue Xuebao **7981**
1008-3456 Huazhong Nongye Daxue Xuebao (Shehui Kexue Ban) **7970**
1008-3464 Guangxi Nongye Shengwu Kexue **676**
1008-3472 Lianyungang Huagong Gaodeng Zhuanke Xuexiao Xuebao/Lianyungang College of Chemical Technology. Journal *changed to* 1672-6685 **7862**
1008-3499 Huaihai Gongxueyuan Xuebao/Huaihai Institute of Technology. Journal *changed to* Huaihai Gongxueyuan Xuebao (Shexue Kexue Ban) **7969**
1008-3499 Huaihai Gongxueyuan Xuebao/Huaihai Institute of Technology. Journal *changed to* 1672-6685 **7862**
1008-3561 Chengcai zhi Lu **8573**
1008-3596 Hebei Tiyu Xueyuan Xuebao **6988**
1008-3634 Hefei Gongye Daxue Xuebao (Shehui Kexue Ban) **7968**
1008-3650 Xingshi Jishu **5917**
1008-3693 Yangzhou Zhiye Daxue Xuebao **8017**
1008-3715 Zhongzhou Daxue Xuebao **7935**
1008-374X Shenyang Shifan Xueyuan Xuebao (Ziran Kexue Ban) *changed to* 1673-5862 **7915**
1008-3758 Dongbei Daxue Xuebao (Shehui Kexue Ban) **7959**
1008-3782 Hebei Gongcheng Jishu Gaodeng Zhuanke Xuexiao Xuebao **3195**
1008-3804 Lujiang Zhiye Daxue Xuebao/Lujiang University. Journal *changed to* 1673-4432 **7930**
1008-3812 Liaoning Sheng Jiaotong Gaodeng Zhuanke Xuexiao Xuebao **2331**
1008-3839 Nanke Xuebao/Acta Andrologica Sinica *changed to* 1009-3591 **6285**
1008-3855 Jiaoyu Fazhan Yanjiu **2988**
1008-391X Liaoning Gongcheng Jishu Daxue Xuebao (Shehui Kexue Ban) **7983**
1008-3944 Pingyuan Daxue Xuebao **7992**
1008-3952 Dongfang Wawa (Youer Ban) **2150**
1008-4002 Beijing Qingnian Zhengzhi Xueyuan Xuebao **7109**
1008-4061 Zhongnan Gongye Daxue Xuebao (Shehui Kexue Ban) *changed to* 1672-3104 **8019**
1008-407X Dalian Ligong Daxue Xuebao (Shehui Kexue Ban) **7958**
1008-4096 Dongbei Cai-Jing Daxue Xuebao **1336**
1008-4142 Aba Shifan Gaodeng Zhuanke Xuexiao Xuebao **7944**
1008-4185 Hebei Jianzhu Gongcheng Xueyuan Xuebao **444**
1008-4231 Liaoning Zhongyi Xueyuan Xuebao/Liaoning College of Traditional Chinese Medicine. Journal *changed to* 1673-842X **5661**
1008-4339 Tianjin Daxue Xuebao (Shehui Kexue Ban) **8010**
1008-4355 Xi'nan Zheng-Fa Daxue Xuebao **4816**
1008-4371 Wugang Jishu **6337**
1008-438X Sichuan Qing-Huagong Xueyuan Xuebao/Sichuan Institute of Light Industry and Chemical Technology. Journal *changed to* 1673-1549 **7916**
1008-4428 Shichang Zhoukan **1173**
1008-4444 Huabei Shuili Shuidian Xueyuan Xuebao (She-ke Ban) **7969**
1008-4533 Guangdong Xingzheng Xueyuan Xuebao **7139**
1008-455X Yiyao Gongcheng Sheji **6886**
1008-4622 Huadong Zheng-Fa Xueyuan Xuebao **4688**
1008-4649 Shaanxi Guangbo Dianshi Daxue Xuebao **2364**
1008-4657 Jingmen Zhiye Jishu Xueyuan Xuebao **7977**
1008-4681 Changsha Daxue Xuebao **7953**
1008-4703 Xi'an Waiguoyu Xueyuan Xuebao **5196**
1008-472X Xi'an Dianzi Keji Daxue Xuebao (Shehui Kexue Ban) **8015**
1008-4754 Zhongguo Dongwu Baojian **8815**
1008-4762 Cangzhou Shifan Zhuanke Xuexiao Xuebao **7953**
1008-4800 Huagong Guanli **1750**
1008-4932 Jinling Zhiye Daxue Xuebao/Nanjing Polytechnic College. Journal *changed to* 1673-131X **7977**
1008-4967 Dangdai Guizhou **3824**
1008-5017 Xinmin Zhoukan **3829**
1008-5130 Jingji Yuekan **1132**
1008-5157 Yixue Qingbao Gongzuo/Medical Information Work *changed to* 1673-6036 **5832**
1008-5211 Pingdingshan Shi-Zhuan Xuebao *changed to* 1673-1670 **7992**
1008-5254 Guangxi Qingnian Ganbu Xueyuan Xuebao **2941**
1008-5327 Nantong Zhiye Daxue Xuebao **6701**
1008-5335 Sichuan Shangye Gaodeng Zhuanke Xuexiao Xuebao/Sichuan Business College Journal *changed to* 1672-0539 **7954**
1008-536X Zhejiang Shuili Shuidian Zhuanke Xuexiao Xuebao **8842**
1008-5378 Liaoning Jing-Zhuan Xuebao **4893**
1008-5424 Huanghe Keji Daxue Xuebao **7863**
1008-5432 Sichuan Pengren Gaodeng Zhuanke Xuexiao Xuebao **3664**
1008-5440 Chengdu Dianzi Jixie Gaodeng Zhuanke Xuexiao Xuebao **3184**
1008-5459 Zigong Shifan Gaodeng Zhuanke Xuexiao Xuebao/Zigong Teachers College Journal *changed to* 1672-8580 **8001**
1008-5483 Hubei Qiche Gongye Xueyuan Xuebao **3195**
1008-5513 Chuncui Shuxue yu Yingyong Shuxue **5478**
1008-5521 Deng yu Zhaoming **3298**
1008-553X Anhui Huagong **3236**
1008-5564 Xi'an Jiaoyu Xueyuan Xuebao/Xi'an College of Education. Journal *changed to* Xi'an Wenli Xueyuan Xuebao (Ziran Kexue Ban) **7931**
1008-5572 Shiyong Guke Zazhi **6073**
1008-5580 Chengdu Fangzhi Gaodeng Zhuanke Xuexiao Xuebao **8449**
1008-5629 Qinzhou Shifan Gaodeng Zhuanke Xuexiao Xuebao **7993**
1008-5688 Liaoning Shi-Zhuang Xuebao (Ziran Kexue Ban) **7879**
1008-5696 Jiaotong Keji yu Jingji **2328**
1008-5734 Yaowu Buliang Fanying Zazhi **6886**
1008-5823 Lanzhou Jiaoyu Xueyuan Xuebao **2882**
1008-5831 Chongqing Daxue Xuebao (Shehui Kexue Ban) **7954**
1008-5882 Zhongguo Linchuang Yingyang Zazhi **6671**
1008-5963 Nanping Shi-Zhuan Xuebao **2889**
1008-5971 Shiyong Xinnaofei Xueguanbing Zazhi **5799**
1008-6013 Jibing Kongzhi Zazhi *changed to* 1674-3679 **5829**
1008-6021 Anhui Guangbo Dianshi Daxue Xuebao **2375**
1008-603X Nanjing Youdian Xueyuan Xuebao (Shehui Kexue Ban) *changed to* 1673-5420 **2334**
1008-6056 Hefei Lianhe Daxue Xuebao/Hefei Union University. Journal *changed to* 1673-162X **7860**
1008-6072 Yunyang Shifan Gaodeng Zhuanke Xuexiao Xuebao **2947**
1008-6080 Guilin Luyou Gaodeng Zhuanke Xuexiao Xuebao **8717**
1008-6099 Dongnanya Yanjiu **548**
1008-6129 Xingtai Zhiye Jishu Xueyuan Xuebao **6705**
1008-617X Shanghai Yixue Yingxiang **5713**
1008-6234 China Petroleum Processing and Petrochemical Technology **6766**
1008-6285 Shanxi Gaodeng Xuexiao Shehui Kexue Xuebao **8000**
1008-6293 Chinese Academic Journals Full-Text Database. Electronic Technology & Information Science **5001**
1008-634X Xiandai Linchuang Yixue Shengwu Gongchengxue Zazhi **751**
1008-6358 Zhongguo Linchuang Yixue **5736**
1008-6374 Huabei Gongxueyuan. Ceshi Jishu Xuebao *changed to* 1671-7449 **7844**
1008-6382 Chongqing Guangbo Dianshi Daxue Xuebao **2357**
1008-6455 Zhongguo Meirong Yixue **5736**
1008-6471 Hebei Daxue Chengren Jiaoyu Xueyuan Xuebao **2941**
1008-6528 Zhongguo Meitan Gongye Nianjian **6484**
1008-6579 Zhongguo Ertong Baojian Zazhi **6105**
1008-6587 Baoshan Shi-Zhuan Xuebao **2830**
1008-6633 Huabei Meitan Yixueyuan Xuebao **5629**
1008-665X Tianjin Waiguoyu Xueyuan Xuebao **7268**
1008-6706 Zhongguo Jiceng Yiyao **5736**
1008-6722 Qiongzhou Daxue Xuebao **7993**
1008-6757 Nanchang Jiaoyu Xueyuan Xuebao **2889**
1008-6765 Xinyu Gao-Zhuan Xuebao **8016**
1008-682X Asian Journal of Andrology **5579**
1008-6838 Zhonghua Nuzi Xueyuan Shandong Fenyuan Xuebao **8906**
1008-6870 Yunnan Gongan Gaodeng Zhuanke Xuexiao Xuebao/Yunnan Public Security College. Journal *changed to* 1672-6057 **2672**
1008-6927 Hebei Nongye Daxue Xuebao (Nong Lin Jiaoyu Ban) **118**
1008-696X Nanning Shifan Gaodeng Zhuanke Xuexiao Xuebao **2889**
1008-6978 Linchuang Chaosheng Yixue Zazhi **6202**
1008-6994 Taiyuan Shifan Zhuanke Xuexiao Xuebao **2917**
1008-7044 Huaihai Yiyao **5630**
1008-7060 Cangsang **4180**
1008-7125 Weichangbingxue **5932**

1008-7133	Keji yu Guanli **1770**
1008-7141	Laiyang Nongxueyuan Xuebao (Shehui Kexue Ban) **7982**
1008-7192	Xi'an Jianzhu Keji Daxue Xuebao (Shehui Kexue Ban) **8015**
1008-7206	Zhongguo Shehui Daokan **8019**
1008-7249	Shanxi Yike Daxue Xuebao (Jichu Yixue Jiaoyu Ban) **2911**
1008-7303	Nongyaoxue Xuebao **141**
1008-7354	Nanchang Gao-Zhuan Xuebao **2889**
1008-7362	Shanxi Cai-Jing Daxue Xuebao (Gaodeng Jiaoyu Ban) **3002**
1008-7435	Zibo Xueyuan Xuebao (Shehui Kexue Ban)/Zibo University. Journal (Social Sciences) *changed to* 1672-0040 **8000**
1008-746X	Tuo Ling†
1008-7486	Guangxi Zhongyi Xueyuan Xuebao **5621**
1008-7494	Huadong Yejin Xueyuan Xuebao. Journal (Shehui Kexue Ban)/East China University of Metallurgy. Journal (Social Sciences) *changed to* 1671-9247 **7947**
1008-7532	Jiating Baishitong **4361**
1008-7575	Hunan Gongan Gaodeng Zhuanke Xuexiao Xuebao **2677**
1008-7613	Xinxiang Shifan Gaodeng Zhuanke Xuexiao Xuebao **2927**
1008-7664	Zhejiang Linchuang Yixue **5735**
1008-7710	Chizhou Shi-Zhuan Xuebao **2836**
1008-7729	Beijing Youdian Daxue Xuebao (Shehui Kexue Ban) **7950**
1008-7796	He'nan Jinrong Guanli Ganbu Xueyuan Xuebao **1118**
1008-7826	Zhangzhou Shifan Xueyuan Xuebao (Ziran Kexue Ban) **7933**
1008-7834	Luliang Gaodeng Zhuanke Xuexiao Xuebao **7984**
1008-7842	Tiedao Jiche Cheliang **8626**
1008-7850	Zhongguo Ziran Yixue Zazhi **316**
1008-7885	Putian Gaodeng Zhuanke Xuexiao Xuebao **7993**
1008-7923	Dianchi Gongye **3156**
1008-7931	Suzhou Jiaoyu Xueyuan Xuebao **2916**
1008-794X	Jieru Fangshexue Zazhi **6200**
1008-7974	Tonghua Shifan Xueyuan Xuebao **2920**
1008-8024	Xiandai Yuwen *changed to* Xiandai Yuwen (Jiaoyu Yanjiu) **5196**
1008-8024	Xiandai Yuwen *changed to* Xiandai Yuwen (Yuyan Yanjiu) **5196**
1008-8024	Xiandai Yuwen *changed to* Xiandai Yuwen (Wenxue Yanjiu) **5196**
1008-8091	Shandong Nongye Daxue Xuebao (Shehui Kexue Ban) **8000**
1008-8113	Guangxi Youjiang Minzu Shifan Gaodeng Zhuanke Xuexiao Xuebao **2861**
1008-813X	Zhongguo Huanjing Guanli Ganbu Xueyuan Xuebao **3476**
1008-8156	Zhangjiakou Zhiye Jishu Xueyuan Xuebao **8445**
1008-8164	Hubei Minzu Xueyuan Xuebao (Yixue Ban) **5630**
1008-8202	Shandong Yi-Da Jichu Xueyuan Xuebao *changed to* Shandong Daxue Jichuyixueyuan Xuebao **5712**
1008-8261	Juzhi Gongye **1139**
1008-8288	Chengdu Zhongyiyao Daxue Xuebao (Jiaoyu Kexue Ban) **2836**
1008-830X	Zhejiang Haiyang Xueyuan Xuebao (Ziran Kexue Ban) **7933**
1008-8318	Zhejiang Haiyang Xueyuan Xuebao (Renwen Shehui Kexue Ban) **4483**
1008-8423	Hubei Minzu Xueyuan Xuebao (Ziran Kexue Ban) **7863**
1008-8512	Guancha yu Sikao **7967**
1008-8520	Haerbin Shi-Wei Dangxiao Xuebao **7140**
1008-8571	Shanxi Shi-Da Tiyu Xueyuan Xuebao **6996**
1008-858X	Yanhu Yanjiu **2718**
1008-8628	Guangxi Zheng-Fa Guanli Ganbu Xueyuan Xuebao **2653**
1008-8652	Huokong Leida Jishu **6424**
1008-8717	Mudanjiang Daxue Xuebao **7883**
1008-8725	Meitan Jishu **3142**
1008-8814	Luoyang Gongye Gaodeng Zhuanke Xuexiao Xuebao **7984**
1008-8830	Zhongguo Dangdai Erke Zazhi **6105**
1008-8849	Xiandai Zhongxiyijiehe Zazhi **5732**
1008-8857	Nengyuan Yanjiu Xinxi **3142**
1008-889X	Jimei Daxue Xuebao (Zhexue Shehui Kexue Ban) **7977**
1008-8946	Shanghai Jinrong Gaodeng Zhuanke Xuexiao Xuebao **1173**
1008-9055	Tianjin Shi Cai-Mao Guanli Ganbu Xueyuan Xuebao **1797**
1008-9071	Xinjiang Shiyou Jiaoyu Xueyuan Xuebao **6798**
1008-9098	Zhongguo Fangwei/China Anti Counterfeiting *changed to* Zhongguo Pinpai yu Fangwei **6760**
1008-911X	Hebei Gongye Daxue Chengren Jiaoyu Xueyuan Xuebao **2942**
1008-9209	Zhejiang Daxue Xuebao (Nongye yu Shengming Kexue Ban) **172**
1008-9225	Shenyang Daxue Xuebao **8001**
1008-9241	Huanjing Wuran Zhili Jishu yu Shebei **3487**
1008-925X	Daguan Zhoukan **3823**
1008-9276	He'nan Zhigong Yixueyuan Xuebao **7969**
1008-9292	Zhejiang Daxue Xuebao (Yixue Ban) **5735**
1008-9306	Shanxi Caizheng Shuiwu Zhuanke Xuexiao Xuebao **1943**
1008-9322	Zhaotong Shifan Gaodeng Zhuanke Xuexiao Xuebao **2928**
1008-9357	Gongneng Gaofenzi Xuebao **3244**
1008-939X	Hu'nan Jingji Guanli Ganbu Xueyuan Xuebao **1119**
1008-942X	Zhejiang Daxue Xuebao (Renwen Shehui Kexue Ban) **8018**
1008-9446	Chengde Shiyou Gaodeng Zhuanke Xuexiao Xuebao **6765**
1008-9497	Zhejiang Daxue Xuebao (Lixue Ban) **7933**
1008-9500	Zhongguo Ziyuan Zonghe Liyong **6337**
1008-9519	Hebei Vocation-Technical Teachers College. Journal **2863**
1008-9594	Fuling Shi-Zhuan Xuebao *changed to* 1672-366X **2859**
1008-9632	Shengwuxue Zazhi **704**
1008-9659	Xinjiang Shifan Daxue Xuebao (Ziran Kexue Ban) **7932**
1008-9691	Zhongguo Zhong-Xiyi Jiehe Jijiu Zazhi **5737**
1008-9713	Shenyang Nongye Daxue Xuebao (Shehui Kexue Ban) **8001**
1008-973X	Zhejiang Daxue Xuebao (Gongxue Ban) **3228**
1008-9764	Guangdong Guangbo Dianshi Daxue Xuebao **2358**
1008-9802	Kexue yu Wushenlun **7876**
1008-9810	Fangshe Mianyixue Zazhi **5758**
1008-9845	Chongqing Shiyou Gaodeng Zhuanke Xuexiao Xuebao/Chongqing Petroleum College. Journal *changed to* 1673-1980 **7846**
1008-987X	Hubei Zhongyi Xueyuan Xuebao **310**
1008-9896	Hebei Jianzhu Keji Xueyuan Xuebao (She-ke Ban) **7968**
1008-9926	Jiefangjun Yaoxue Xuebao **6851**
1008-9969	Nanfang Huli Xuebao/Nanfang Journal of Nursing *changed to* Huli Xuebao **5960**
1008-9977	Hubei Sheng Weisheng Zhigong Yixueyuan Xuebao **5630**
1008-9985	Jiefangjun Yiyuan Guanli Zazhi **4103**
1008-9993	Jiefangjun Huli Zazhi **5963**
1009-0002	Shengwu Jishu Tongxun **770**
1009-0029	Xiaofang Kexue yu Jishu **3582**
1009-0045	Shihua Jishu Yu Yingyong **6792**
1009-007X	Baogao Wenxue (Wuhan) **5260**
1009-0126	Zhonghua Laonian Xin-Nao-Xueguanbing Zazhi **5802**
1009-0134	Zhizaoye Zidonghua **1909**
1009-0150	Shanghai Caijing Daxue Xuebao **1173**
1009-0177	Jingshui Chuli **8827**
1009-0185	Jilin Jianzhu Gongcheng Xueyuan Xuebao **447**
1009-0193	Guizhou Gongye Daxue Xuebao (Ziran Kexue Ban) **7859**
1009-0207	Xinjiang Shiyou Xueyuan Xuebao *changed to* 1673-2677 **6798**
1009-0231	Car & Motor **8571**
1009-024X	Ankang Shi-Zhuan Xuebao **2826**
1009-038X	Wuxi Qinggong Daxue Xuebao **8445**
1009-0452	Zibo Xueyuan Xuebao (Ziran Kexue yu Gongcheng Ban)/Zibo University. Journal (Natural Sciences and Engineering) *changed to* 1672-6197 **7914**
1009-0460	Linchuang Zhongliuxue Zazhi **6026**
1009-0479	Kunming Yejin Gaodeng Zhuanke Xuexiao Xuebao **6320**
1009-0509	Guizhou Gongye Daxue Xuebao (Shehui Kexue Ban) **7967**
1009-0533	Sichuan Xumu Shouyi Xueyuan Xuebao/Sichuan Institute of Animal Husbandry and Veterinary Medicine. Journal *changed to* 1672-5379 **8016**
1009-055X	Huanan Ligong Daxue Xuebao (Shehui Kexue Ban) **7970**
1009-0568	Talimu Nongken Daxue Xuebao **7922**
1009-0592	Fazhi yu Shehui **4671**
1009-0630	Plasma Science and Technology **3252**
1009-0649	Rongbaozhai **515**
1009-0657	Jilin Sheng Jingji Guanli Ganbu Xueyuan Xuebao **1762**
1009-0681	Shenyang Jianzhu Gongcheng Xueyuan Xuebao (Shehui Kexue Ban)/Shenyang Architectural and Civil Engineering University. Journal (Social Science) *changed to* 1673-1387 **457**
1009-0746	Anhui Zhengbao **7420**
1009-0770	Fangzhi Xinxi Zhoukan/Textile Information Weekly *changed to* 1674-196X **8450**
1009-0789	Zhongguo Daxue Jiaoxue **3011**
1009-086X	Xiandai Fangyu Jishu **6454**
1009-0908	Changjiang Zhigong Daxue Xuebao *changed to* 1673-0496 **2835**
1009-0940	Jiangxi Tongxin Keji **2328**
1009-1017	Guji Zhengli Yanjiu Xuekan **5011**
1009-1041	Mailei Zuowu Xuebao **242**
1009-105X	Zhongguo Kuangye Daxue Xuebao (Shehui Kexue Ban) **8018**
1009-1130	Hehai Daxue Changzhou Fenxiao Xuebao **3195**
1009-1157	Zhongguo Mafeng Pifubing Zazhi **5736**
1009-1173	Zhongguo Nongye Jiaoyu **172**
1009-122X	Zhongguo Wei Qinxi Shenjing Waike Zazhi **6263**
1009-1270	Zhengzhou Gongye Daxue Xuebao (Shehui Kexue Ban) **8018**
1009-1297	Hefei Jiaoyu Xueyuan Xuebao/Hefei Institute of Education. Journal *changed to* 1672-920X **7968**
1009-1319	Feihang Daodan **55**
1009-1327	Yingyong Fanhan Fenxi Xuebao **7073**
1009-1343	Xinwen yu Chuanbo **4586**
1009-1351	Shichang Yingxiao **1843**
1009-136X	Gonghui Gongzuo **4595**
1009-1378	Zhengquan Daokan **1198**
1009-1432	Zhuzhou Shifan Gaodeng Zhuanke Xuexiao Xuebao/Zhuzhou Teachers College. Journal *changed to* 1674-117X **7971**
1009-1459	Nanjing Guangbo Dianshi Daxue Xuebao **2360**
1009-1505	Zhejiang Sheng Zheng-Fa Guanli Ganbu Xueyuan Xuebao/Zhejiang College of Politics and Law. Journal *changed to* Zhejiang Gongshang Daxue Xuebao **1197**
1009-1513	Wuyi Daxue Xuebao (Shehui Kexue Ban) **8015**
1009-1556	Chuzhou Shi-Zhuan Xuebao *changed to* 1673-1794 **7955**
1009-1564	Tongxin Shijie **2342**
1009-1572	Guomin Jingji Guanli **1116**
1009-1580	Shangye Jingji/Commercial Economy *changed to* 1009-752X **1431**
1009-1610	Xiangzhen Qiye, Minying Jingji/Village and Township Enterprises & the Private Sector Economy *changed to* 1674-4497 **1958**
1009-1629	Keji Guanli **1770**
1009-1637	Luyou Guangli **8731**
1009-1645	Chuban Gongzuo **7558**
1009-1661	Ren yu Shengwuquan **700**
1009-1696	Shanghai Tuke **6720**
1009-1726	Shijie Redai Nongye Xinxi **156**
1009-1734	Huzhou Shifan Xueyuan Xuebao **4456**
1009-1742	Zhongguo Gongcheng Kexue **3228**
1009-1750	Zhengzhou Hangkong Gongye Guanli Xueyuan Xuebao (Shehui Kexue Ban) **8018**
1009-1793	Di-Yi Junyi Daxue Fenxiao Xuebao **5604**
1009-1807	Liang-you Jiagong yu Shipin Jixie **3654**
1009-1823	Hua'nan Redai Nongye Daxue Xuebao **119**
1009-1858	Touzi yu Licai **1656**
1009-1874	Nanjing Junyi Xueyuan Xuebao **5682**
1009-1912	Nanchang Hangkong Gongye Xueyuan Xuebao (Shehui Kexue Ban) **7987**
1009-1955	Chang'an **7429**
1009-1963	Chinese Physics (Overseas Edition) *changed to* 1674-1056 **7008**
1009-1971	Haerbin Gongye Daxue Xuebao (Shehui Kexue Ban) **7968**
1009-2013	Hunan Nongye Daxue Xuebao (Shehui Kexue Ban) **7971**
1009-2056	Zhongguo Xinyongka **1392**
1009-2099	Yunnan Jiaoyu **2928**
1009-2102	Xibei Minzu Xueyuan Xuebao (Ziran Kexue Ban) *changed to* Xibei Minzu Daxue Xuebao (Ziran Kexue Ban) **7931**
1009-2137	Zhongguo Shiyan Xueyexue Zazhi **5942**
1009-2145	Huabei Hangtian Gongye Xueyuan Xuebao **7862**
1009-2153	Qiche Zu **8600**
1009-2188	Zhongguo Xiandai Shoushuxue Zazhi **6263**
1009-220X	Guangzhou Huaxue **2062**
1009-2218	Zawen Yuekan **5246**
1009-2226	Shanghai Shehui Kexueyuan Xueshu Jikan/Shanghai Academy of Social Sciences. Quarterly Journal *changed to* 0257-5833 **8001**
1009-2242	Shuitu Baochi Xuebao **252**
1009-2250	Zhaoxiangji **6978**
1009-2269	Lanzhou Gongye Gaodeng Zhuanke Xuexiao Xuebao **7879**
1009-2307	Cehui Kexue **4002**
1009-2323	Mudanjiang Jiaoyu Xueyuan Xuebao **7986**
1009-2382	Xiandai Jingji Tantao **1551**
1009-2420	Zhong-xiao Qiye Keji **1198**
1009-2439	Shaoyang Gaodeng Zhuanke Xuexiao Xuebao/Shaoyang College. Journal *changed to* 1672-7010 **7914**
1009-2439	Shaoyang Gaodeng Zhuanke Xuexiao Xuebao/Shaoyang College. Journal *changed to* Shaoyang Xueyuan Xuebao (Shehui Kexue Ban) **8000**
1009-2447	Xibei Gongye Daxue Xuebao (Shehui Kexue Ban) **8015**
1009-2455	Gongye Yongshui yu Feishui **3506**
1009-2463	Anhui Nongye Daxue Xuebao (Shehui Kexue Ban) **7947**
1009-248X	Fujian Dili/Fujian Geography *changed to* 1673-7105 **3476**
1009-2501	Zhongguo Linchuang Yaolixue yu Zhiliaoxue **6887**
1009-2560	Ningbo Jiaoyu Xueyuan Xuebao **7989**
1009-2587	Zhonghua Shaoshang Zazhi **5883**
1009-2633	Guangxi Daxue Wuzhou Fenxiao Xuebao **7858**
1009-265X	Xiandai Fangzhi Jishu **8462**
1009-2692	Yanshan Daxue Xuebao (Zhexue Shehui Kexue Ban) **8017**
1009-2706	Fujian Waiyu **5121**
1009-2714	Hubei Shifan Xueyuan Xuebao (Ziran Kexue Ban) **7863**
1009-2757	Science in China. Series F: Information Sciences **2437**
1009-2773	Jilin Shangye Gaodeng Zhuanke Xuexiao Xuebao/Jilin Commercial College. Journal *changed to* Jilin Shanggaozhuan **1131**
1009-2781	Caijing Jie **1079**
1009-2811	Kongjun Zongyiyuan Xuebao **5658**
1009-282X	Dizhi Zhuangbei **4486**
1009-2854	Xiangfan Xueyuan Xuebao **8015**
1009-2862	Beijing Shi Renmin Zhengfu Gongbao **7422**
1009-2919	Zhongxue Shuxue Jiaoyuxue **5547**
1009-2927	Zhongxue Wuli Jiaoyuxue **7047**
1009-2935	Zhongxue Huaxue Jiaoyuxue **2084**
1009-2943	Zhongxue Waiyu Jiaoyuxue **5199**
1009-296X	Zhongxue Zhengzhi Ji Qita Geke Jiaoxue **2929**
1009-2978	Zhongxue Lishi, Dili Jiaoxue **2929**
1009-2986	Zhongxue Yuwen Jiaoyuxue **5200**
1009-301X	Jianghan Shiyou Zhigong Daxue Xuebao **6775**
1009-3044	Diannao Zhishi yu Jishu **2416**
1009-3060	Tongji Daxue Xuebao (Shehui Kexue Ban) **8010**
1009-3079	Shijie Huaren Xiaohua Zazhi **5931**
1009-3087	Sichuan Daxue Xuebao (Gongcheng Kexue Ban) **7916**
1009-3095	Zhejiang University. Journal (Science) *changed to* 1673-1581 **5735**
1009-3095	Zhejiang University. Journal (Science) *changed to* 1673-565X **7933**
1009-3117	Hong Qingting **2193**
1009-3125	Guojia Tushuguan Xuekan **5011**
1009-315X	Dalian Minzu Xueyuan Xuebao **7849**
1009-3176	Shanghai Xingzheng Xueyuan Xuebao **8000**
1009-3222	Nanjing Zhongyiyao Daxue Xuebao (Shehui Kexue Ban) **7987**
1009-3257	Hanshao Jibing Zazhi **5623**
1009-3281	Huagong Shebei yu Guandao **3245**
1009-329X	Zhongguo Sifa **4820**
1009-3311	Yanbian Daxue Xuebao (Shehui Kexue Ban) **8017**
1009-3370	Beijing Ligong Daxue Xuebao (Shehui Kexue Ban) **7950**
1009-3397	Urumqi Zhiye Daxue Xuebao **8013**
1009-3419	Zhongguo Feiyan Zazhi **6221**
1009-3427	Haijun Zongyiyuan Xuebao **5623**
1009-3443	Jiefangjun Ligong Daxue Xuebao (Ziran Kexue Ban) **7870**
1009-3486	Haijun Gongcheng Daxue Xuebao **3194**
1009-3516	Kongjun Gongcheng Daxue Xuebao (Ziran Kexue Ban) **7877**
1009-3591	Zhonghua Nankexue **6285**
1009-3613	Shenghuo yu Jiankang **6996**
1009-3621	Nanning Zhiye Jishu Xueyuan Xuebao **7987**
1009-3699	Wuhan KeJi Daxue Xuebao (Shehui Kexue Ban) **8015**
1009-3710	Dushi Zhufu **8859**
1009-3729	Zhengzhou Qinggongye Xueyuan Xuebao (Shehui Kexue Ban) **8018**
1009-3745	Zhengfa Xuekan **4819**
1009-3761	Kouqiang Hemian Xiufuxue Zazhi **5854**
1009-3796	Xiaoxuesheng Daodu **2927**

ISSN

DIRECTORY 2010 1011-5641 9447

1010-2248 Tribune de Geneve 3959
1010-2388 I L O Metal Trades Committee. Report 1686
1010-2566 Entomological Society of Southern Africa. Proceedings of the Congress 845
1010-2582 Mintek Research Digest 6473
1010-2671 Assiut University. Faculty of Science. Bulletin. Section B. Chemistry *changed to* 1687-4919 2051
1010-2728 Ergonomics S A 6676
1010-2744 Materials Research Laboratories. Bulletin of Research and Development 8431
1010-2752 Revista de Proteccion Vegetal 250
1010-2760 Revista Ciencias Tecnicas Agropecuarias 151
1010-2787 Indice des Prix a la Consommation *see* 1013-3402 2642
1010-2809 Name-Ye 'Olum-e Ejtema'i†
1010-2817 F I R T - I F T R - S I B M A S Bulletin 8470
1010-2825 Barrasiha-Ye Tarikhi†
1010-2965 Sistema de Indicadores Socio-Economicos y Educativos de la O E I 2935
1010-2973 Repertorio de Servicios IberoAmericanos de Documentacion e Informacion Educativas 5043
1010-3066 *see* 1010-3074 606
1010-3074 Office International de la Vigne et du Vin. La Lettre 606
1010-3228 Quanqiu Fangwei Zazhi 6442
1010-3465 Klasgids 5317
1010-3481 Kenya Coffee 3652
1010-3538 Veterinary Drug Registration Newsletter†
1010-3562 Pakistan Seafood Digest 3604
1010-3589 Academia de Stiinte Agricole si Silvice. Buletin Informativ 78
1010-3597 Rilke-Gesellschaft. Blaetter 5363
1010-3627 Cinema 6493
1010-3643 Cahiers Internationaux d'Histoire Economique et Sociale†
1010-3716 Kenya Review†
1010-3724 Archeion Euvoikon Meleton 2230
1010-3740 Libyan Journal of Agriculture 134
1010-3783 Rural Demography 7292
1010-3791 Jute and Jute Fabrics - Bangladesh 8454
1010-3821 Arquitectura Cuba 433
1010-3856 Kunsthistorisches Jahrbuch Graz 501
1010-3872 Ecclesia Orans 7796
1010-3961 Universite d'Abidjan. Annales. Hors Serie†
1010-397X United Nations. Economic and Social Commission for Asia and the Pacific. Natural Resources - Water Series†
1010-3996 Belaruskaya Mova 5099
1010-4003 Ndertuesi 1026
1010-4054 I P H Yearbook *changed to* 1815-669X 6734
1010-4089 Archithese 432
1010-4127 African Journal of Sociology 8086
1010-4135 The Accountant 1276
1010-4143 Asian Finance†
1010-4151 Instituto Nacional de Estadistica. Boletim Mensal de Estadistica 7481
1010-4208 Sri Lanka Journal of Tea Science 3664
1010-4224 I A G L R Program 8825
1010-4283 Tumor Biology 6035
1010-4291 Trinidad and Tobago Review 3995
1010-4402 Acta Oceanografica del Pacifico 2799
1010-4429 Caribbean Conservation News†
1010-4437 Cooperation Sud *see* 0259-3882 8096
1010-447X United Nations. International Trade Statistics Yearbook 1273
1010-450X Academia de Ciencias de Cuba. Instituto de Oceanologia. Reporte de Investigacion 2799
1010-4534 P E N International. Bulletin of Selected Books 5347
1010-4569 Aiolika Grammata 5250
1010-4615 Musica
1010-4720 Tapia 5241
1010-4852 Farhan-o-Zendegi†
1010-4976 Masa'il-i Jahan†
1010-4992 University of Ferdowsi. Faculty of Theology and Islamic Studies. Publication†
1010-5093 Ueberseeische Bahnen *changed to* 1430-6891 8617
1010-5182 Journal of Cranio-Maxillofacial Surgery 6247
1010-5220 Opuscula Zoologica Fluminensia 959
1010-5247 S T I Review†
1010-528X Cuadernos de Sociologia†
1010-5298 E S A - F (French Edition) *see* 1010-5301
1010-5301 E S A - F (English Edition)
1010-5395 Asia-Pacific Journal of Public Health 7508
1010-5409 Pharma Kritik 6867
1010-545X South Africa. Council for Geoscience. Geological Maps. Explanations 2768
1010-5492 Manuscriptum 5330
1010-5506 Anale de Istorie†
1010-5522 African Environment 3401
1010-5549 Malawian Geographer 4019
1010-559X Berner Kunstmitteilungen 478
1010-5662 Neurofibromatosis†
1010-5700 B T - L M & S 978
1010-5719 Business 1070
1010-5735 News Advertiser 4580
1010-5743 Sportswatch 8208
1010-576X Kenya Medical Research Institute. Proceedings of the Annual Medical Scientific Conference†
1010-5778 Architektur und Ladenbau 431
1010-5786 Casa†
1010-5808 Schweizer Bank 1381
1010-5832 Ethnic Studies Report 3532
1010-5913 Zambia Journal of Applied Earth Sciences 2718
1010-593X Calendar of Congresses of Medical Sciences 6278
1010-6030 Journal of Photochemistry and Photobiology, A: Chemistry 2137
1010-6049 Geocarto International 4008
1010-609X Tinplate World†
1010-6197 Organisation Maritime Internationale. Nouvelles *see* 0253-8199 8646
1010-6227 Annuarium Statisticum Ecclesiae 7697
1010-6251 Bulletin Eucarpia 782
1010-6367 Jamaican Historical Review 4298
1010-6413 Ashna'iba Kitab†
1010-6499 Negin†
1010-657X Tahqiqat e Eqtesadi (English Edition) 1181
1010-660X Medicina 5672
1010-6618 Muzah'ha 507
1010-6634 Universite d'Abidjan. Annales. Serie J. Traditions Orales 3623
1010-674X Universite d'Abidjan. Annales. Serie F: Ethnosociologie 359
1010-6960 Turkiye Entomoloji Dergisi 860
1010-7053 Safety and Health at Work†
1010-7061 Securite et Sante au Travail†
1010-7185 European Cement Association. European Annual Review 1007
1010-7193 Visindafelag Islendinga - Radstefnurit 7928
1010-7215 Lateranum 7804
1010-7304 Journal of Ethical Studies
1010-7339 Dental Journal of Zambia 5840
1010-7347 Journal of International Marketing & Marketing Research
1010-7355 Christian Nurse International *changed to* 1681-9594 7805
1010-7363 Diotima 6914
1010-7428 Union Postal Universal. Actas *see* 0252-3973 2355
1010-7924 Association of Professional Engineers of Trinidad and Tobago. Journal 3182
1010-7940 European Journal of Cardio-Thoracic Surgery 5786
1010-8017 Practical Theology in South Africa 7670
1010-8149 E S R A Newsletter†
1010-8238 Revue Juridique du Rwanda†
1010-8246 Pop Sahel 3907
1010-8289 Seoul National University Forests. Research Bulletin 3702
1010-8327 Asian Electronics Engineer 3295
1010-836X Jahrbuch Precision†
1010-8378 Durch†
1010-8386 Imagination†
1010-8394 National Mirror 2334
1010-8408 Issues in Biomedicine†
1010-8432 Rapports sur les Etudes et Recherches Entreprises dans le Bassin Lemanique 3490
1010-867X Erdem 3532
1010-8734 I F E S Review†
1010-8742 Journal de Monaco 7448
1010-8793 N A T O Advanced Science Institutes Series H: Cell Biology 835
1010-8831 Revue Internationale de Droit Economique 4774
1010-8874 Turkish Review† 8995
1010-8947 Cooperation Technique Postale†
1010-9099 World Food Programme Journal 6671
1010-9102 Programe Mundial de Alimentos *see* 1010-9099 6671
1010-9110 Programme Alimentaire Mondial. Journal *see* 1010-9099 6671
1010-9161 Tyche 4165
1010-9226 Suid-Afrikaanse Kultuurhistoriese Museum. Annale 4178
1010-9501 U D T Newsletter 5051
1010-9536 Bangladesh Institute of International and Strategic Studies Journal 7223
1010-9552 Focus on Science and Technology 7855
1010-9560 Insights†
1010-9595 Manufacture of Narcotic Drugs and Psychotropic Substances under International Control 2697
1010-9609 W H O Drug Information 7545
1010-9633 Iran Dar A'inah-i Amar 8380
1010-965X Al-Umam al-Muttahidat al-Lagnat al-Iqtisadiyyat wa-al-Igtimaiyyat li-Garbi Asiya. Dirasat al-Hisabet al-Qawmiyat *changed to* 1564-7625 1092
1010-9722 Vienna International Centre. Library Accessions List
1010-9862 Education in Asia and the Pacific: Reviews, Reports and Notes†
1010-9897 Periodicals of Asia and the Pacific†
1010-9919 Old Testament Essays 7667
1010-9935 O D T U Gelisme Dergisi 1547
1011-002X Pakistan Economic and Social Review 1603
1011-0046 *see* 1011-0054 207
1011-0054 Spore 207
1011-0070 Oesterreichische Zeitschrift fuer Soziologie 8124
1011-0089 Pro Zukunft 3461
1011-0135 Aurum†
1011-0186 Papier aus Oesterreich 6736
1011-0240 Rights†
1011-0267 Progress in Basic and Clinical Pharmacology 6876
1011-0275 Uniciencia 7925
1011-0410 Revista Peruana de Ciencias Sociales
1011-0488 The Farmer 111
1011-050X O E C D Food Consumption Statistics†
1011-0569 Catalogue of I L O Publications in Print 1220
1011-0623 Analele Universitatii Bucuresti. Drept†
1011-0844 Eurostat. ECU-EMS Information *changed to* 1024-4239 1340
1011-0984 World Bank Operations Evaluation Study 1195
1011-1077 Europaeische Integration - Auswahlbibliographie†
1011-1131 C N U C E D Bulletin *see* U N C T A D News 1585
1011-1263 Internationale Gewaesserschutzkommission fuer den Bodensee. Berichte 2615
1011-1271 Internationale Gewaesserschutzkommission fuer den Bodensee. Jahresbericht 2615
1011-128X Borehole Water 8819
1011-1301 Universal Dataflow and Telecommunications. Bulletin *see* 1010-9501 5051
1011-1344 Journal of Photochemistry and Photobiology, B: Biology 737
1011-1557 Athena 2230
1011-159X Revue Agricole pour l'Europe *see* 1011-3363 8928
1011-1603 Sea Wind
1011-1611 South African Bride to Be: First Home 5561
1011-1638 Hellenic Photography Selections†
1011-1727 Sunjet 8786
1011-1743 Periodiko 3832
1011-1883 Recherches d'Archeologie, de Philologie et d'Histoire 413
1011-1891 Routes - Roads 8634
1011-193X Elephant's Child 6523
1011-1948 Toposcope 4178
1011-1980 Southern Africa Freedom Bulletin†
1011-2006 Bulletin de Sinologie *changed to* 1021-9013 7259
1011-2030 Asian Computer Directory
1011-2189 Caijing Jishi†
1011-2200 Defence Asia - Pacific 6417
1011-2219 Zhongguo Shehui Xuekan/Chinese Journal of Sociology *changed to* Taiwan Shehui Xuekan 8142
1011-2227 Excellence Business Monthly 1107
1011-2251 Paradigma 2896
1011-226X Quest (Leiden) 6946
1011-2340 Biblioteka Bulteno
1011-2359 China Current Laws 4642
1011-2367 Asian - Australasian Journal of Animal Sciences 279
1011-2499 Information Processing in Medical Imaging 5635
1011-2529 Animal Production and Health Newsletter 6192
1011-2545 C I N D A 7048
1011-257X Guoji Yuanzineng Jigou Tongbao *see* 0020-6067 3168
1011-260X Mutation Breeding Newsletter *changed to* Plant Mutation Reports 248
1011-2618 Mutation Breeding Review 242
1011-2642 International Atomic Energy Agency. Nuclear Power Reactors in the World 3169
1011-2650 Soils Newsletter 253
1011-288X Douleur et Analgesie 5607
1011-2898 China Economic Express (Japanese Edition) 1447
1011-2901 Geriatrie fuer die Taegliche Praxis†
1011-291X Pharmacology and the Skin†
1011-2928 Lithium Therapy Monographs†
1011-3010 Gregorios O Palamas 7704
1011-3029 Journal of Pacific Studies 7979
1011-3207 World Meteorological Organization. Commission for Marine Meteorology. Abridged Final Report of the (No.) Session 6399
1011-3231 World Meteorological Organization. Executive Council Session. Abridged Final Reports with Resolutions 6399
1011-3266 I A T A - I A L Air Distances
1011-3363 Agricultural Review for Europe† 8928
1011-3436 South African Journal of Economic History 1549
1011-3487 South African Journal of Higher Education 3002
1011-3495 Daneshmand 3186
1011-3576 Organizacion Meteorologica Mundial. Reunion del Consejo Ejecutivo. Informe Abreviado y Resoluciones 6393
1011-3592 Organisation Meteorologique Mondiale. Session du Conseil Executif. Rapport Abrege et Resolutions 6393
1011-3649 I P Asia 6751
1011-3673 Vsemirnaya Meteorologicheskaya Organizatsiya. Sessiya Ispolnitel'nogo Soveta. Sokrashchennyi Otchet s Rezolyutsiyami 6397
1011-372X Catalysis Letters 2052
1011-3738 Teaching and Training in Geriatric Medicine†
1011-3797 Bulletin des Transports Internationaux Ferroviaires 8615
1011-386X Die Volkswirtschaft 1192
1011-3878 Ethics & Perspectives!†
1011-3916 Bangladesh Journal of Extension Education 94
1011-3924 Chemical Society of Ethiopia. Bulletin 2055
1011-3940 Panama Now 1431
1011-3959 Panama Hoy *see* 1011-3940 1431
1011-3983 The Article 19 Bulletin†
1011-4009 Maajan - Die Quelle 7726
1011-4033 Hong Kong Annual Digest of Statistics 7307
1011-4041 Asian Marine Biology 654
1011-4165 You 8892
1011-4181 Hellenic Stomatological Review 5846
1011-4246 E P A Newsletter 2134
1011-4289 I A E A Technical Documents Series 3168
1011-4378 Atlantic Salmon Federation. Special Publication Series†
1011-4475 W V A Informative Bulletin
1011-4521 Hong Kong (Year) 7284
1011-4548 World Competition 4944
1011-4564 Yixue Yanjiu Zazhi 5733
1011-4637 E C S C Financial Report 1921
1011-4688 Tax - Benefit Position of Production Workers *changed to* 1995-3844 1951
1011-4750 Eastern Africa Economic Review 1097
1011-4793 E S C W A Population Bulletin 7282
1011-4807 Wiener Beitraege zur Ethnologie und Anthropologie 361
1011-4831 Geriatrica†
1011-484X Revista Geografica de America Central 4027
1011-4858 Foreign Trade Statistics of Asia and the Pacific 1233
1011-4866 Carindex: Science & Technology 7936
1011-4874 Etudes Rwandaises 4175
1011-4955 Plus
1011-4963 B I T Programme des Entreprises Multinationales. Documents de Travail *see* 1011-4971 1490
1011-4971 I L O Multinational Enterprises Programme. Working Paper 1490
1011-498X O I T Programa de Empresas Multinacionales. Documentos de Trabajo *see* 1011-4971 1490
1011-4998 I A O Programm der Multinationale Unternehmen. Arbeitspapiere *see* 1011-4971 1490
1011-5048 Women in Action 8890
1011-5110 South Pacific Periodicals Index 17
1011-5129 University of the South Pacific. Publications 638
1011-5145 South Pacific Research Register 635
1011-5196 Terra Grischuna - Graubuenden 3470
1011-5218 Panorama (Duebendorf) 2895
1011-5226 Al-Barnamaj al-Amm lil-Ma'lumat - An-Nashrah al-I'lamiyyah lil-Yunisist 4988
1011-5269 European Communities. Economic and Social Consultative Assembly. Annual Report 1107
1011-5323 Islensk Fyrirtaeki 2009
1011-5331 Index to the Correspondence of the Foreign Office for the Year†
1011-5366 F A O Investment Centre Technical Paper† 8955
1011-5498 Madoqua 2618
1011-5528 Medical Technology S A 5909
1011-5536 Quarterly Countdown†
1011-5544 South African Institute of Race Relations. Update†
1011-5552 South African Institute of Race Relations. Topical Briefings†
1011-5641 Com

ISSN

DIRECTORY 2010 1013-9923 9449

1012-6821 Jingjibu Zhongyang Diszhi Diaochasuo Huikan 2749
1012-6848 Integro†
1012-6899 European Centre for Medium-Range Weather Forecasts. Technical Report† 8954
1012-6902 International Review for the Sociology of Sport 8110
1012-6910 Buvisindi *changed to* 1670-567X 119
1012-7054 Revista UNELLEZ de Ciencias y Tecnologia. Serie Produccion 250
1012-7089 Terra 4031
1012-7313 Wespennest 5245
1012-7348 I A R C Technical Reports 6021
1012-7410 Pasturas Tropicales 145
1012-7666 Register of Development Activities of the United Nations System 7262
1012-7682 Pakistan Journal of History & Culture 4468
1012-7720 I F P R A Bulletin 8318
1012-7771 Settlements Information Network Africa Newsletter 4426
1012-7801 Compendium of Social Statistics and Indicators 8082
1012-7844 Journal of Social Studies 7980
1012-7887 H K Staff 1862
1012-8026 Social Indicatior of Development (Year)†
1012-8034 Internationale Bachakademie Stuttgart. Schriftenreihe 6577
1012-8042 International Academy for the Study of Tourism. Newsletter 8723
1012-8069 I F C Discussion Paper 1597
1012-8093 Acta Criminologica 2643
1012-8107 Iles† 8963
1012-8115 Emerging Stock Markets Factbook *changed to* 1530-678X 1384
1012-8204 Complement and Inflammation†
1012-8255 Academia (Caracas) 2823
1012-8263 Transition 8011
1012-8271 Reglementation du Transport des Animaux Vivants *see* 0256-4742 8547
1012-8298 Bahrain Medical Bulletin 5583
1012-8328 I T Asia 2534
1012-8360 I C A A News 2694
1012-8387 Schweizer Zeitschriftenverzeichnis†
1012-8697 J O P S O M 7528
1012-876X I.D.A. Journal†
1012-8840 King Abdul Aziz University. Faculty of Marine Science. Journal†
1012-8875 Journal of Paediatrics, Obstetrics and Gynaecology (Hong Kong Edition) 5996
1012-8891 Lucrari de Cercetare†
1012-8905 Instituto Centroamericano de Investigacion y Tecnologia Industrial. Revista†
1012-9030 Erasmus Newsletter†
1012-9200 Diario Oficial de las Comunidades Europeas. L: Legislacion *see* Official Journal of the European Union. L Series: Legislation 7256
1012-9219 Jornal Oficial das Comunidades Europeias. L: Legislacao *see* Official Journal of the European Union. L Series: Legislation 7256
1012-9308 Theoretical and Applied Karstology†
1012-9324 Coal Information 6460
1012-9340 Graphis Design Journal *changed to* Graphis Design Annual 492
1012-9367 Pakistan Journal of Statistics 5524
1012-9405 Afrika Mathematica 5467
1012-9480 Dominican Republic. Secretariado Tecnico de la Presidencia. Boletin†
1012-9510 Banco Central de Honduras. Departamento de Estudios Economicos. Boletin Estadistico Mensual 1212
1012-9588 Melita Theologica 7662
1012-960X Academia Venezolana de la Lengua Correspondiente de la Espanola. Boletin
1012-9685 Pan American Health Organization. Proposed Program and Budget Estimates 7535
1012-9707 The Clipper 3631
1012-9790 Revista de Historia 4310
1012-9804 Himal South Asian 7140
1012-9871 New Issues in Neurosciences†
1012-9952 Bankers Handbook for Asia†
1013-0020 Competition Policy in O E C D Countries†
1013-0047 Rhinology. Supplement *see* 0300-0729 6085
1013-0055 Bank of Korea. Monthly Statistical Bulletin 1213
1013-0071 I J B - Report 5307
1013-0098 Bank of Korea. Quarterly Economic Review *changed to* 1975-4914 1441
1013-0152 Journal of Mauritian Studies 5315
1013-0241 O E C D Employment Outlook 1504
1013-0284 Statistical Trends in Transport†
1013-0322 International Institute of Tropical Agriculture. Annual Report and Research Highlights 123
1013-0349 Geologische Bundesanstalt. Jahresbericht 2741
1013-0365 World Directory of Parliaments 7194
1013-042X Financing and External Debt of Developing Countries†
1013-0519 Isis International Women's Book Series†
1013-0667 Blick 3957
1013-0691 L'Hebdo 3958
1013-0713 F B V A Berichte 3688
1013-0845 World Health Organization AIDS Technical Bulletin†
1013-087X Zhonghua Minguo Chuban Nianjian 7576
1013-0896 Freies China 3960
1013-090X Jiaoyu Ziliao yu Tushuguanxue 5019
1013-0942 Republic of China Yearbook (Year) *changed to* Taiwan Yearbook (Year) 3122
1013-0950 Agenda 8893
1013-1019 Before You Build†
1013-1108 Strategic Review for Southern Africa 7267
1013-1116 Tydskrif vir Christelike Wetenskap 7778
1013-1191 Peake Studies 5233
1013-1205 L M S 5907
1013-1221 I C A News 7240
1013-1396 Bulletin de Liaison de Demographie Africaine 7278
1013-1442 Aufklaerung - Vormaerz - Revolution 4201
1013-1450 La Restructuration 1514
1013-1469 S W S - Rundschau 7999
1013-171X African Christian Studies 7782
1013-1744 Compendium of Tourism Statistics 8778
1013-1752 English Academy Review 5289
1013-1779 I C H S Information Bulletin
1013-2147 Kneipp Magazin *changed to* Kneipp Zeitschrift 6991
1013-2198 Rubber Research Institute of Sri Lanka. Annual Review 7827
1013-2309 Dostoevsky Studies 5285
1013-2368 Revista Venezolana de Filosofia 6949
1013-2457 Journal des Communes et Regions d'Europe†
1013-2511 Issues & Studies 7246
1013-2740 Blush
1013-2791 Taniguchi Symposia on Brain Sciences†
1013-2821 Cuadernos de Historia de la Salud Publica 7513
1013-3089 Entreprise Romande 1402
1013-3097 Cancer Pain Release 6013
1013-3119 A B B Review 3293
1013-3127 Revue A B B *see* 1013-3119 3293
1013-3143 A B B Technik *see* 1013-3119 3293
1013-3151 Rivista A B B *see* 1013-3119 3293
1013-316X A B B Tidning *see* 1013-3119 3293
1013-3178 United Nations Children's Fund. Programme Division. Staff Working Papers Series 8075
1013-3186 United Nations Children's Fund. Programme Division. Conference Reports Series†
1013-3194 U N I C E F Policy Review Series
1013-3356 S A Golf Journal†
1013-3402 Eurostat Consumer Price Index (Monthly Edition) 2642
1013-3445 Zimbabwe Journal of Educational Research 2929
1013-3453 Narcotic Drugs: Estimated World Requirements for (Year) 6890
1013-3461 Pakistan Congress of Zoology. Proceedings 959
1013-350X Helvetische Muenzen-Zeitung *changed to* 1424-9383 6652
1013-3593 Chantiers *changed to* 1660-8100 991
1013-3666 S A Journal of Food Science and Nutrition†
1013-3771 Anuario del Comercio Exterior de Venezuela 1200
1013-3917 History of Oceanography 2806
1013-3933 Il-Merill 910
1013-4050 Airline Coding Directory 8536
1013-4069 Estudios del Desarrollo 8100
1013-4077 Seoul Daehag'gyo Nonghag Yeon'gu† 8988
1013-4115 Analele Universitatii Bucuresti. Geografie 3998
1013-4123 Analele Universitatii Bucuresti. Geologie 2777
1013-4247 Pontica 4254
1013-428X Apulum 4199
1013-431X Bermuda Journal of Archaeology and Maritime History 383
1013-4328 Vietnam Social Sciences 8014
1013-4344 Multilateral Interline Traffic Agreements Manual 8548
1013-4409 Modellbahnwelt 4341
1013-4425 Herpetozoa 946
1013-4468 International Council of Kinetography Laban. Proceedings†
1013-4484 Social Security Documentation: Asia and Pacific Series 4523
1013-4506 Fortschritte im Strahlenschutz 6677
1013-4549 Ministries and Communities†
1013-4573 Stilet 5377
1013-4689 I F L A Round Table on Continuing Professional Education. Newsletter 5013
1013-4700 Sport International 8204
1013-4751 I F L A Geography and Map Libraries Section. Newsletter 5013
1013-4859 Tantara 4178
1013-5081 Aqui 3802
1013-5189 International Union of Geological Sciences. United Nations Educational, Scientific and Cultural Organization. International Geological Correlation Programme. Projet 133. Bulletin de Liaison et Information 2784
1013-5278 Iasi Polytechnic Magazine 3196
1013-5294 Pharmeuropa 6875
1013-5308 *see* 1013-5294 6875
1013-5316 Science International 7910
1013-5332 Banque de la Republique du Burundi. Bulletin Mensuel 1320
1013-5340 Banque de la Republique du Burundi. Bulletin Trimestriel†
1013-5359 Banque de la Republique du Burundi. Rapport Annuel 1320
1013-5375 China Economic Express (Korean Edition) 1447
1013-543X Dhaka University Studies. Part A: Arts, Humanities, and Social Science 4449
1013-5472 Postgraduate Medical Institute. Journal 5698
1013-5529 Turkey. Turkiye Istatistik Kurumu. Bina Insaat Istatistikleri† 8994
1013-5545 Acta Cancerologica 6007
1013-5693 Botswana. Central Statistics Office. Statistical Bulletin 1215
1013-5707 Botswana. Central Statistics Office. External Trade Statistics 1215
1013-5715 Botswana. Central Statistics Office. Tourist Statistics 8778
1013-5723 Botswana. Central Statistics Office. Health Statistics Report 5741
1013-5731 Botswana. Central Statistics Office. Transport Statistics 8491
1013-574X Botswana. Ministry of Agriculture. Agricultural Statistics 176
1013-5774 Oeffentliche Finanzen der Schweiz 1937
1013-5804 Schweizerische Strassenverkehrszaehlung 8529
1013-5995 Footwear, Raw Hides and Skins, and Leather Industry in O E C D Countries†
1013-6002 Equinoxe 7961
1013-6045 K D I Quarterly Economic Outlook *changed to* K D I Gyeongje Jeonmang 1495
1013-6061 Mauritius. Central Statistical Office. Annual Digest of Statistics 1251
1013-6118 Comptes Economiques Nationaux du Rwanda 1222
1013-6150 Turkey. Turkiye Istatistik Kurumu. Turizm Istatistikleri (Year) 8781
1013-6177 Turkey. Turkiye Istatistik Kurumu. Su Urunleri Istatistikleri (Year) 3614
1013-6185 Turkey. Turkiye Istatistik Kurumu. Ticaret, Otel, Lokanta ve Hizmet Istatistikleri† 8995
1013-6193 Central Bank of the Republic of Turkey. Annual Report 1326
1013-6207 Cuba. Ministerio de Cultura. Cartelera 7127
1013-6371 La Releve *changed to* La Nouvelle Releve 7160
1013-638X Economia Andina†
1013-6444 Naturalist†
1013-6452 Innovation and Technology Transfer *changed to* 1830-4338
1013-6479 E S A - I R S News & Views
1013-655X Sidwaya 3805
1013-6606 C I C I B A Lettre d'Information†
1013-6614 L'Union 3790
1013-6657 Hafta Sonu 3962
1013-6800 Gesellschaft fuer Vergleichende Kunstforschung in Wien. Mitteilungen 6524
1013-6827 Algiers†
1013-6835 Tribune de l'Orgue 6624
1013-6843 Al-Watwan 5245
1013-6916 Zurcher Kunstgesellschaft, Kunsthaus Zurich. Jahresbericht 529
1013-6924 Revue Historique Vaudoise 414
1013-6940 Das Kunst-Bulletin 501
1013-6991 Jahrbuch fuer die Geschichte des Protestantismus in Oesterreich 7762
1013-7009 Ungyong Mulli 7044
1013-7017 Mulli Kyoyuk 7026
1013-7025 Hong Kong Physiotherapy Journal 6110
1013-7041 Entomologische Berichte Luzern *changed to* 1662-8500 844
1013-7122 Nongsa Siheom Yeon'gu Bo'go. To'yang Biryo Jagmul Boho Gyun'i/The Office of Rural Development. Research Reports. Soil Science, Fertilizer, Plant Protection and Micrology *changed to* R D A Journal of Agricultural Science 8983
1013-7181 Institutul de Geologie si Geofizica. Studii Tehnice si Economice†
1013-7289 South Africa. Statistics South Africa. Financial Statistics of Companies (Year)†
1013-7300 South Africa. Central Statistical Service. Education: Asian†
1013-7319 South Africa. Central Statistical Service. South African Life Tables†
1013-736X Libya. Census and Statistics Department. Vital Statistics of the Socialist People's Libyan Arab Jamahiriya 1249
1013-7394 Our Planet 3458
1013-7440 Price Prospects for Major Primary Commodities† 8982
1013-7459 Basler Beitraege zur Chirurgie 6237
1013-7467 Recent Achievements in Restorative Neurology†
1013-7521 Digging Stick 390
1013-7548 South African Theatre Journal 8479
1013-767X Huoyao Jishu 3246
1013-7696 Zhonghua Minguo Xiaohua Xiyi Xuehui Zazhi *changed to* Taiwan Xiaohua Xiyi Xuehui Zazhi 5931
1013-7750 African Livestock Research 277
1013-7769 Telema 7819
1013-7815 Fizik Muhendisligi 7012
1013-7823 Yachtrevue 8285
1013-7939 Academia Boliviana de Ciencias Economicas. Revista†
1013-7998 Groupe de Travail Mondial sur les Rapaces. Circulaire 908
1013-8005 The World Working Group on Birds of Prey and Owls. Newsletter 917
1013-8013 Weltarbeitsgruppe fur Greifvogel und Eulen. Rundbrief 916
1013-8056 Nutrition de Sante Publique†
1013-8064 Asian Migrant 7277
1013-8129 Diagnostic Oncology†
1013-8250 Supplement to Narcotic Drugs†
1013-8285 Public Health Nutrition†
1013-8293 Nutricion en Salud Publica†
1013-8374 Industrial Property, Statistics B. Part 1 - Patents 6760
1013-8382 Industrial Property, Statistics B. Part 2 - Trademarks and Service Marks, Utility Models, Industrial Designs, Varieties of Plants, Microorganisms 6760
1013-8390 Getaway 8713
1013-8471 Journal for Semitics 7724
1013-8641 Sahel Dimanche 3790
1013-8765 Centre de Recherches Semiologiques. Travaux 6910
1013-8919 Tiroler Heimat 4273
1013-9036 E C S L News 53
1013-9044 Reaching for the Skies
1013-9052 The Saudi Dental Journal 5864
1013-9060 Revista Nacional de Cultura 7997
1013-9087 Annals of Dermatology 5871
1013-9095 Economy†
1013-9214 Conmilit
1013-9222 International Symposia on the Pharmacology of Thermoregulation†
1013-929X Current Writing 5281
1013-9451 Nongsa Siheom Yeon'gu Bo'go. To'bi Jagbo Gyun'i Nong'ga *changed to* R D A Journal of Agricultural Science 8983
1013-9478 Gusto 4359
1013-9486 Oesterreichisches Recht der Wirtschaft 1156
1013-9516 E C E T O C Document 3496
1013-9532 World Cement Directory 1043
1013-9559 Varia Antiqua 563
1013-9567 *see* 0254-802X
1013-9591 Agroforestry Today 87
1013-9656 Chinese Journal of Psychology 7344
1013-980X Inazucar 235
1013-9818 Royal Asiatic Society. Sri Lanka Branch. Journal†
1013-9826 Key Engineering Materials 6320
1013-9834 Ciencia y Tecnica en la Agricultura. Serie: Cafe y Cacao 224
1013-9877 South Pacific Journal of Natural Science 7919
1013-9885 Iran Agricultural Research 123
1013-9915 South Pacific Commission. Information Circular *changed to* Pacific Community. Information Circular
1013-9923 Hong Kong Journal of Paediatrics 6092

ISSN

DIRECTORY 2010 1016-4731 9451

1015-0935 Natal Museum Journal of Humanities *changed to* 1681-5564 **418**
1015-0951 Amirkabir **7835**
1015-0986 Kenya Railways. Annual Report **8501**
1015-1141 Centre Protestant d'Etudes de Geneve. Bulletin **7750**
1015-1184 Sigmund Freud House Bulletin†
1015-1303 Salzburger Nachrichten **3798**
1015-1451 Outdoor Living and Sports Goods (Year)†
1015-146X Jewellery, Curios, Arts & Crafts (Year)†
1015-1516 BankArchiv **1316**
1015-1532 Who's Who in Cargo Handling **8665**
1015-1575 Emanzipation
1015-1621 Aquatic Sciences **2792**
1015-1648 Microgravity News from E S A†
1015-1753 I D F Directory†
1015-1818 Tarih Dergisi **4272**
1015-1850 Orbis Biblicus et Orientalis **2238**
1015-1885 Law of the Sea Bulletin **4970**
1015-1915 Camera Austria **6965**
1015-1990 Asian Journal of Physical Education†
1015-2008 Pathobiology **5764**
1015-2105 Selcuklu Arastirmalari Dergisi†
1015-2229 Filosofs'ka i Sotsiolohichna Dumka *changed to* 0235-7941 **6920**
1015-2261 Antilia†
1015-2288 Agronomie Africaine **88**
1015-230X Chemicals, Adhesives and Pharmaceuticals (Year)†
1015-2342 Engineer
1015-2369 National Ceramics Quarterly **537**
1015-2385 Servamus **2668**
1015-2393 Settler **3949**
1015-2415 Cuadernos Historicos
1015-2423 Oekologie und Landbau **143**
1015-2563 Centre International d'Etudes Platoniciennes et Aristoteliciennes. Serie Recherches **6910**
1015-2628 Revue Economique et Financiere Ivoirienne **1515**
1015-2636 N A G R A Technischer Bericht **3509**
1015-2687 Guoli Taiwan Daxue. Wenshi Zhexue Bao **4182**
1015-2717 National Bank of Ethiopia. Annual Report **1370**
1015-2784 Tianxia **1183**
1015-2822 Ma'arif **7713**
1015-2830 Majallah-i Bastanshinasi o Tarikh **404**
1015-2849 Majallah-i Shimi **2072**
1015-2857 Nashr-i Riyazy **5519**
1015-2873 Cyprus Diplomatist **7229**
1015-2881 The Cyprus Review **7958**
1015-3004 Synthesis **2250**
1015-3047 Ginecologia y Obstetricia **5991**
1015-3071 Eurostat. Geonomenclature **1227**
1015-3128 Asian Meetings and Incentives
1015-3225 Agroforesterie Aujourd'hui *see* 0120-2243 **95**
1015-3225 Agroforesterie Aujourd'hui *see* 1013-9591 **87**
1015-3233 Frente Maritimo **3595**
1015-3276 Transfusion Today (English Edition) **5942**
1015-3284 Transfusion Today (French Edition) *see* 1015-3276 **5942**
1015-3292 Transfusion Today (Spanish Edition) *see* 1015-3276 **5942**
1015-339X U S A C **7925**
1015-3497 Studia Friburgensia **7684**
1015-3519 Syndicat des Exportateurs et Negociants en Bois de Cote d'Ivoire. Bulletin de Liaison et d'Information **3704**
1015-3578 Memoires de Geologie Lausanne **2754**
1015-3640 Meteorology and Hydrology†
1015-3802 Urban Forum **4430**
1015-3829 *see* 0772-0394
1015-3837 Fetal Diagnosis and Therapy **5990**
1015-3845 Magnesium and Trace Elements†
1015-3918 Ankara Universitesi. Eczacilik Fakultesi. Dergisi **6820**
1015-3926 Elektrotechnik **3306**
1015-406X Das Achtzehnte Jahrhundert und Oesterreich **4196**
1015-4159 O E C D External Debt Statistics
1015-4248 Balance Financiero
1015-4256 Medical Progress (Indonesia Edition) **5670**
1015-4272 Medical Progress (Malaysia Edition) **5671**
1015-4280 Medical Progress (Pakistan Edition) **5671**
1015-4299 Medical Progress (Philippines Edition) **5671**
1015-4302 Medical Progress (Singapore Edition) **5671**
1015-4310 Medical Progress (Taiwan Edition) **5671**
1015-4329 Medical Progress (Thailand Edition) **5671**
1015-4337 Journal of Paediatrics, Obstetrics and Gynaecology (Taiwan Edition) **5996**
1015-4345 Journal of Paediatrics, Obstetrics and Gynaecology (Thailand Edition) **5996**
1015-440X Revista U N I B E de Ciencia y Cultura **7179**
1015-4442 Arab Gulf Journal of Scientific Research **7836**
1015-4523 Raydan **4324**
1015-4531 R I L E M News **1031**
1015-4639 Purchasing Power Parities and Real Expenditures **1513**
1015-468X Centre Genevois d'Anthropologie. Bulletin **332**
1015-4744 I C E S Council Meeting **3597**
1015-4760 Pharmaceutical & Cosmetic Review **596**
1015-4817 Taehan Sin'gyong Chongsin Uihak Hoeji **6187**
1015-4868 Turk Folkloru Arastirmalari **3623**
1015-4892 N A T O Handbogen **7253**
1015-4957 Whydah **7929**
1015-4965 Orienteering World **8326**
1015-5015 Yazhou Zhoukan†
1015-5023 Asiamac Journal†
1015-5031 Rapport sur un Seminaire de Politique Generale de I D E *see* 1012-490X **1096**
1015-504X Asian Manufacturers Journal **1880**
1015-5074 Instituto Interamericano de Derechos Humanos. Revista **7209**
1015-5082 Pilot (Nairobi)†
1015-5104 Aegypten und Levante **371**
1015-5287 Transport Manager's Handbook and Trucker's Guide **8676**
1015-5295 Istanbul Universitesi Fen Fakultesi Astronomi ve Fizik Dergisi
1015-5309 Strategic Briefing
1015-5376 Fichier Afrique
1015-549X Pretexts†
1015-5546 Kobus **2616**
1015-5570 Law Society of Hong Kong Gazette **4716**
1015-5589 World Safety Journal **3475**
1015-5597 A D A Magazine **426**
1015-5716 Terminologies Nouvelles **5186**
1015-5759 European Journal of Psychological Assessment **7356**
1015-5775 Cahiers de Musiques Traditionnelles **6553**
1015-5856 Zhongguo Tumu Shuili Gongcheng Xuekan **3288**
1015-5910 Mittex: Mitteilungen ueber Textilindustrie **8455**
1015-5945 Human Rights Worldwide† **8962**
1015-6070 China Steel Technical Report **6308**
1015-6119 Hafrannsoknastofnunin. Fjoelrit **3596**
1015-616X Oesterreichisches Jahrbuch fuer Internationale Politik†
1015-6178 Mila†
1015-6208 Geologische Bundesanstalt. Fuehrer zu den Arbeitstagungen **2741**
1015-6224 O P E C Papers† **8978**
1015-6275 Progress in Coal Steel and Related Social Research **6486**
1015-6305 Brain Pathology **6127**
1015-6321 Bahrain Medical Society. Journal **5583**
1015-6402 Taehan Songhyong Oekwa Hakhoe Chi **6260**
1015-647X Con-text **5277**
1015-6488 Life Cycle†
1015-6585 Trapezikos **1183**
1015-6607 China Review *changed to* 1680-2012 **3823**
1015-6704 University of Nairobi. Institute for Development Studies. Working Paper **4179**
1015-6763 International Cartographic Conference. Proceedings **4016**
1015-6798 Musik & Gottesdienst **6595**
1015-6828 The Zimbabwe Librarian **5056**
1015-6836 Asiatic Society of Bangladesh. Journal: Humanities **4443**
1015-7131 Asian Property†
1015-7174 Tea **3665**
1015-7328 Eurozoom
1015-7344 Encyclopedie Berbere **3120**
1015-7573 Paralleles **5160**
1015-7743 Energy Balance Sheets **3152**
1015-7867 Pacific Health Dialog **7534**
1015-7891 Journal of Parametrics *changed to* 1941-658X **1294**
1015-7999 South African Computer Journal **2438**
1015-8014 Compleat Golfer **8225**
1015-8073 Cargo Interchange Message Procedures Manual
1015-8138 A T A Journal **8447**
1015-8146 Genetic Counseling **868**
1015-8154 Devenir **5604**
1015-8227 Centre for Entomological Studies. Memoirs **842**
1015-8235 Centre for Entomological Studies. Miscellaneous Papers **842**
1015-8243 Priamus **857**
1015-8316 Arab Construction World International *changed to* 1990-3936 **975**
1015-8324 Arab Health International *changed to* 1990-3944 **7506**
1015-8332 Arab Water World International *changed to* 1990-3952 **8817**
1015-8340 Middle East Food International *changed to* 1990-3960 **3655**
1015-8367 Xiangjian Xiaolu **171**
1015-8383 Universitas **4480**
1015-843X Modern China **5228**
1015-8480 Cartographica Helvetica **4002**
1015-8529 Umfeld **7190**
1015-8545 Nashriyyah-i 'ilmi Sazman-i Inirzhi-i Atumi-i Iran/Atomic Energy Organization of Iran. Scientific Bulletin *changed to* 1735-1871 **7068**
1015-8553 Revista C E N I C. Ciencias Quimicas **2078**
1015-860X Zimbabwe Journal of Economics
1015-8618 African Journal of Neurological Sciences **6120**
1015-8634 Korean Mathematical Society. Bulletin **5508**
1015-8642 European Communities. Cost **1922**
1015-8650 I B S R A M Proceedings **234**
1015-8693 Socio-Economic Papers **7682**
1015-8758 Acta Theologica **7620**
1015-8782 Southern African Journal of Epidemiology and Infection **5882**
1015-8790 Umqondiso†
1015-8812 South African Journal of Economic and Management Sciences **1794**
1015-888X South African Home Owner **457**
1015-8898 R T T Review†
1015-8987 Cellular Physiology and Biochemistry **830**
1015-9118 Arhivele Olteniei **4131**
1015-9193 Beitraege zur Volkskunde†
1015-9231 Gazette du Golfe **3802**
1015-9274 Antike Welt. Sondernummer†
1015-9355 Chung Kung Yen Chiu **7116**
1015-9436 Danjiang Xuebao. Quyu Yanjiu Bumen†
1015-9568 International Navigation Congress. Papers **8647**
1015-9584 Asian Journal of Surgery†
1015-9592 Gazi Universitesi Eczacilik Fakultesi Dergisi **6843**
1015-9649 Vrye Weekblad†
1015-9657 Cardiovascular Journal of Southern Africa *changed to* 1995-1892 **5781**
1015-9746 Institut Suisse de Droit Compare. Publications **4693**
1015-9770 Cerebrovascular Diseases **6130**
1015-9797 Artium **473**
1015-9835 Assemblee de l'Union de l'Europe Occidentale. Lettre de l'Assemblee **4918**
1015-9894 Haus Tech **4120**
1015-9908 Chongbo Kwahak Hoechi **2542**
1015-9924 Eurostat Agricultural Prices. Price Indices and Absolute Prices. **108**
1015-9991 I S B N Newsletter† **8963**
1016-0019 Beihefte Zur Sydowia **778**
1016-0035 Pakphyton **807**
1016-0183 Eurostat Catalogue†
1016-0361 Staff Studies for the World Economic Outlook *see* 1729-701X **1358**
1016-0361 Staff Studies for the World Economic Outlook *see* 0256-6877 **1493**
1016-0361 Staff Studies for the World Economic Outlook *see* 0258-7440 **1358**
1016-0396 Revista de Bibliotecologia y Ciencias de la Informacion **5043**
1016-0434 W W F & C F Letter†
1016-0469 Manejo Integrado de Plagas **768**
1016-0477 I C A D T S Reporter **2694**
1016-0515 Sicherheitsmagazin **6687**
1016-0523 Zimbabwe Law Review **4820**
1016-0566 Jindai Zhongguo Shi Yanjiu Tongxun **4184**
1016-0590 Red†
1016-0698 Hueso Humero **5307**
1016-0728 Journal of Humanities **4460**
1016-0744 Koreana **554**
1016-0809 Temporale **522**
1016-1015 Zhonghua Yaoxue Zazhi (Taipei) **6888**
1016-1058 Journal of Science (National Edition) **7872**
1016-1066 Musicologica Austriaca **6594**
1016-1104 Journal of Sciences, Islamic Republic of Iran **7873**
1016-121X Options Mediterraneennes. Serie A: Seminaires Mediterraneens **144**
1016-1228 Options Mediterraneennes. Serie B: Etudes et Recherches **144**
1016-1333 Musil - Forum **5337**
1016-1384 South African Panorama (Chinese Edition)†
1016-1422 Tropical Agricultural Research **163**
1016-1430 Medical Journal of the Islamic Republic of Iran **5669**
1016-1503 The Zimbabwe Science News **7935**
1016-1511 Zimbabwe Veterinary Journal **8816**
1016-1538 Fu Jen Studies. Natural Sciences **7856**
1016-1554 A G E N Mitteilungen†
1016-1562 Schweizerische Akademie der Medizinischen Wissenschaften. Jahresbericht **5710**
1016-1597 Punjab University Journal of Zoology **961**
1016-1708 Fantasmagie†
1016-1902 Endangered Wildlife **2610**
1016-197X Nuclear Science and Applications
1016-2011 Societe Suisse de Chronometrie. Bulletin **4569**
1016-2054 Jamaican Journal of Science and Technology **7870**
1016-2070 Tourism & Hotel Security Worldwide Magazine†
1016-2127 Fuzzy Systems - Reports and Letters **5489**
1016-2135 Fiji. Mineral Resources Department. Information Notes **2734**
1016-2178 V A M A S. Bulletin **6407**
1016-2216 I S S X Newsletter **5632**
1016-2224 Taiwan Statistical Data Book **7294**
1016-2240 Review of Rural and Urban Planning in Eastern and Southern Africa†
1016-2283 Yeong'eo Yeongmunhag **5197**
1016-2291 Pediatric Neurosurgery **6173**
1016-2356 Fangshi Gongcheng **6717**
1016-2364 Journal of Information Science and Engineering **3205**
1016-2399 Zack **2224**
1016-2461 Revue Africaine de Theologie **7815**
1016-2526 Punjab University Journal of Mathematics **5526**
1016-2607 Joryu Haghoeji/Korean Journal of Phycology *changed to* 1226-2617 **774**
1016-264X Zeitschrift fuer Neuropsychologie **7416**
1016-2658 The Korea Letter
1016-2712 Jahrbuch fuer Landeskunde von Niederoesterreich **4234**
1016-281X I F L A Section on Document Delivery and Interlending. Newsletter **5014**
1016-2860 Continent Cendrars **5279**
1016-2879 Schweizer Kunst **516**
1016-3042 Jingjibu. Zhongyang Dizhi Diaochasuo. Tekan **2749**
1016-3107 The South African Criminal Law Reports **4898**
1016-3158 Eidgenoessische Forschungsanstalt fuer Wald, Schnee und Landschaft. Mitteilungen *changed to* 1424-5108 **2611**
1016-3166 Eidgenoessische Forschungsanstalt fuer Wald, Schnee und Landschaft. Berichte†
1016-3190 Ciji Yixue **5595**
1016-3255 Ulum va-Tiknuluzhi-i Pulimir **3257**
1016-3263 I U F R O World Series **3693**
1016-3271 The Korean Journal of Defense Analysis **6430**
1016-328X Bibliographie Courante de la Litterature Luxembourgeoise **618**
1016-3328 Computational Complexity **5551**
1016-3476 Journal of Mediterranean Studies **4460**
1016-359X World Link†
1016-3611 Turkish Journal of Medical & Biological Research
1016-362X L'Homme **8898**
1016-3646 Pietersburg Buyers' Guide†
1016-3654 Pretoria News **3949**
1016-3697 The Sowetan **3950**
1016-3700 The Star **3950**
1016-3735 Transvaler†
1016-3778 Comite Consultatif pour la Masse et les Grandeurs Apparentees† **8942**
1016-3816 Braby's Krugersdorp Koopgids†
1016-3905 Beeld **3947**
1016-3948 Cape Times **3948**
1016-3956 The Citizen **3948**
1016-3964 City Press **3948**
1016-3999 Lesotho Business Directory **2013**
1016-4057 Bangladesh Journal of Biological Sciences **656**
1016-4162 Kaleidoscope **5222**
1016-4170 Yishujia **528**
1016-4278 Kuwait & Gulf Economic and Financial Bulletin **1496**
1016-4286 Centre Europeen d'Etudes Bourguignonnes (XIVe-XVIe S.). Publications **4210**
1016-4359 Stellenbosch Law Review **4789**
1016-4367 Deutschunterricht im Suedlichen Afrika **5111**
1016-4383 Sarhad Journal of Agriculture **154**
1016-443X Geometric and Functional Analysis **5490**
1016-4464 Zhongguo Wenhua Yanjiusuo Xuebao **564**
1016-457X Taiwan Wen Hsien **4189**
1016-4723 International Society for Applied Cardiovascular Biology†
1016-4731 Southern Africa Report **3950**

ISSN

9452 1016-4839 ULRICH'S PERIODICALS

1016-4839 Institutul de Cercetare si Productie pentru Cultura si Industrializarea Sfeclei de Zahar si a Substantelor Dulci-Fundulea. Lucrari Stiintifice. Sfecla si Zahar **237**
1016-491X Puntos de Vista†
1016-4979 *see* 1998-1430 **2612**
1016-4987 Aschkenas **7718**
1016-4995 Droit Nucleaire **3166**
1016-5037 Dental Review
1016-5061 Ecology and Farming **106**
1016-5118 Cagdas Cerrahi Dergisi† **8939**
1016-5126 Jinekoloji ve Obstetrik Dergisi **5994**
1016-5134 Sendrom **5712**
1016-5169 Turk Kardiyoloji Dernegi Arsivi†
1016-5177 Bold (Print Edition) *changed to* Bold (Online Edition) **4041**
1016-5185 F I P L V World News **5118**
1016-524X Ingens Bulletin **794**
1016-5304 Business Korea†
1016-5312 Chequered Flag **8573**
1016-5320 Nidan **7708**
1016-5363 Industrial Policy in O E C D Countries†
1016-538X Consumer Policy in O E C D Countries†
1016-5428 European University Institute. Academic Year **2855**
1016-5444 Employment in Europe **1678**
1016-555X Samudra Report (French Edition) **3607**
1016-5568 Samudra Report (English Edition) **3607**
1016-5576 Samudra Revista **3607**
1016-5584 Journal of Coptic Studies **4322**
1016-5614 European Foundation for the Improvement of Living and Working Conditions. Annual Report **1680**
1016-572X Europa Forum **4924**
1016-5738 Europa Oggi **4924**
1016-5746 Tribuna da Europa **4942**
1016-5754 Tribuna del Parlamento Europeo **4942**
1016-5762 Eurostat Statistiques Rapides. Commerce Exterieur *see* 1024-6878 **1227**
1016-5886 Economic Accounts for Agriculture *changed to* 1816-7586 **184**
1016-5983 Conference Generale des Poids et Mesures. Comptes Rendus des Seances **6401**
1016-5991 South Africa. Council for Geoscience. Annual Technical Report **2768**
1016-605X Neue Denkschriften des Naturhistorischen Museums in Wien **7988**
1016-6106 Korea Letter (Nihonban)
1016-6130 Iranian Journal of International Affairs **7246**
1016-6262 Verhaltenstherapie **6189**
1016-6351 Roodepoort Buyers' Guide†
1016-6378 Braby's South Coast and Southern Natal Directory **1976**
1016-6416 Computaform **8289**
1016-6572 George Buyers' Guide†
1016-6602 Braby's Kimberley Buyers' Guide†
1016-6645 KwaZulu†
1016-6653 Lesotho†
1016-6734 O F S Philatelic Magazine **6897**
1016-6742 C M E **5590**
1016-6793 Phoenix - Verulam & Tongaat Buyers' Guide†
1016-6904 Springs Buyers' Guide **2029**
1016-6912 Stanger Directory†
1016-6939 Sunday Tribune **3950**
1016-6947 Asiatic Society of Bangladesh. Journal: Science **7837**
1016-6998 F I P E S O Newsletter†
1016-7048 F I P E S O. Nouvelles†
1016-7064 Swaziland†
1016-7072 Swaziland Buyers' Guide **2029**
1016-7161 Weekend Argus *see* 1017-6128 **3947**
1016-7250 Forum **3719**
1016-7277 Bursa Devlet Hastanesi Bulteni **4089**
1016-7390 Neike Xuezhi **5947**
1016-751X Studia Philosophica. Supplementum *see* 0081-6825 **6954**
1016-7536 Textile Leader **8460**
1016-7544 Nepal Rastra Bank. Annual Report **1370**
1016-7560 I F A Congress Seminar Series **1928**
1016-7587 Adevarul (Bucharest) **3932**
1016-7609 Contrapunct **4573**
1016-765X Oesterreichische Zeitschrift fuer Geschichtswissenschaften **4250**
1016-7692 Grazer Mathematische Berichte **5490**
1016-7803 Orte **5346**
1016-7846 W U F A **4190**
1016-7994 Revista Ecuatoriana de Historia Economica **1167**
1016-8087 Revista Interamericana de Educacion de Adultos **2945**
1016-8184 Daily News **3948**
1016-8192 Durban†
1016-8206 Media Focus†
1016-8222 Port Elizabeth†
1016-8257 Yachay **4482**
1016-8397 S E B E S†
1016-8400 Arzt und Praxis **5578**
1016-8478 Molecules and Cells **690**
1016-8664 Structural Engineering International **3284**
1016-8699 International Child Health: A Digest of Current Information†
1016-8737 International Economic Journal **1493**
1016-8826 African Association for Literacy and Adult Education. Journal
1016-8834 B I R D
1016-8885 Iran Exports **1572**
1016-8923 Al Magallah Al-'arabiyyah Li-l-tibb Al-nafsi **6159**
1016-8974 AIDS Analysis Africa **5808**
1016-8982 Centre International d'Etude des Textiles Anciens. Bulletin **8449**
1016-9008 Centre Gustave Glotz. Cahiers **4134**
1016-9040 European Psychologist **7356**
1016-9075 New Ground
1016-9113 Ege Tip Dergisi **5608**
1016-913X Arete **4443**
1016-9148 Espacio y Desarrollo **4451**
1016-927X Species **2628**
1016-9342 University of Sindh Arts Research Journal *changed to* International Research Journal of Arts & Humanities **497**
1016-9415 Scenes Magazine **516**
1016-9458 Litteratura **5327**
1016-9504 Cuadernos de Nuestra America **7127**
1016-9512 Cuba. Centro de Informacion y Documentacion Agropecuario. Boletin de Resenas. Serie: Mecanizacion de la Agricultura **210**
1016-9520 Memo
1016-9601 Revista de Investigacao Pesqueira **3606**
1016-9628 Pensamiento Propio **7991**
1016-9660 Cine et Media *changed to* 1726-0426 **6513**
1016-9717 Wajibu **3902**
1016-9725 Diners Club Magazin **3797**
1016-9733 Pferderevue **8296**
1016-9741 C A F R A News **8894**
1016-975X Novedades C A F R A†
1016-9776 Business China **1444**
1016-9857 Pasos **7770**
1016-9970 Pacific Impact†
1016-9989 Fiji Library Association. Journal **5009**
1016-9997 Fiji Library Association. Newsletter **5009**
1017-0324 S I D I C† **8986**
1017-0367 Museion 2000 *changed to* 1661-7924 **4247**
1017-0405 Statistica Sinica **8403**
1017-0448 Routes du Monde†
1017-0499 Studia Historiae Ecclesiasticae **7684**
1017-0510 Wirtschaftsgeographische Studien **4034**
1017-0588 Baurecht **4628**
1017-0596 Estudios Sociales **8100**
1017-060X Anjoman-i Riyazi-i Iran. Bulitan-i *see* 1018-6301 **5498**
1017-0618 South African Labour Law Reports **1708**
1017-0626 Pakistan Journal of Hydrocarbon Research **6786**
1017-0642 Instituto Nacional de Enfermedades Neoplasticas. Boletin **6022**
1017-0669 Gongye Gongcheng Xuekan **3367**
1017-0715 Mogjae Gonghag **3714**
1017-0839 T A O: Terrestrial, Atmospheric and Oceanic Sciences **2717**
1017-0855 Huawen Shijie **5125**
1017-088X Kongjian **448**
1017-0952 Afrique 2000 **7220**
1017-1118 Hong Kong Bird Report **908**
1017-1185 Jutastat's South African Statutes **4708**
1017-1193 Tax Library **1948**
1017-1207 South African Tax Library & South African Statutes on CD-ROM
1017-1215 Obzor A B B *see* 1013-3119 **3293**
1017-1304 Guoli Zhengzhi Daxue. Bianzheng Yanjiusuo Nianbao/Institute of China Border Area Studies. Bulletin *changed to* 1024-8250 **3551**
1017-1363 Computaform (Eastern Cape Edition) *see* 1016-6416 **8289**
1017-138X Geologie Africaine†
1017-1398 Numerical Algorithms **5522**
1017-141X Perspectives†
1017-1436 South Africa. Council for Geoscience. South African Committee for Stratigraphy. Lithostratigraphic Series **2768**
1017-1444 Geschichte und Gegenwart†
1017-1452 Recent Laws of Nepal **4766**
1017-1460 Boletim de Informacao Socio-Economica **1536**
1017-155X Horticultura **3737**
1017-1576 Das Tier **965**
1017-1606 I A R C Monographs on the Evaluation of Carcinogenic Risks to Humans **6021**
1017-1622 Phoenix **5351**
1017-1657 Rapport **3949**
1017-1703 Tydskrif vir Skoonlug **3491**
1017-1711 PedMed†
1017-1819 International Journal of Information and Management Sciences **2522**
1017-1827 Pakistan Entomologist **857**
1017-1983 South Pacific Commission. Annual Report **7266**
1017-2092 Il-Mument **3907**
1017-2106 In-Nazzjon Taghna **3907**
1017-2270 Industria Usoara - Pielarie, Confectii de Piele, Prelucrarea Cauciucului si a Maselor Plastice, Componente Tehnolgice si Accesorii pentru Industria Usoara†
1017-2297 Sui Yuan Wen Hsien **3566**
1017-2300 Chung-kuo Yuwen **5106**
1017-2548 Korean Chemical Society. Journal **2071**
1017-2564 Iran Statistical Yearbook **8380**
1017-2572 J A R D - Journal of Age Related Disorders†
1017-2696 Unsere Heimat **4276**
1017-270X International Production Cost Comparison **8453**
1017-2718 Gnusletter **2612**
1017-2734 *see* 0252-306X **1243**
1017-2742 Surtur **2770**
1017-2777 Buhardilla **6644**
1017-2785 C E D H U **4635**
1017-2793 Mbya Guarani **3549**
1017-2807 Menores **2174**
1017-2815 La Puerta **8881**
1017-2823 Galeria Michele Malingue. Catalogo **6524**
1017-2831 La Cour Internationale d'Arbitrage de la C C I. Bulletin *see* 1017-284X **1404**
1017-284X The I C C International Court of Arbitration Bulletin **1404**
1017-2866 Forum†
1017-2874 Changer **7226**
1017-2920 Medical Quarterly†
1017-298X Oceanographic Research Institute. Poster Series†
1017-3102 World Animal Health in (Year) **8815**
1017-317X Analytical Reporter **2050**
1017-3188 University of Salahaddin. College of Agriculture. Scientific Journal "ZANCO"
1017-3285 Fachsprache **5118**
1017-3293 Gesnerus. Supplement **5619**
1017-3323 Car and Driver **8571**
1017-3390 Dans les Media, Demain **4574**
1017-3412 *see* 0250-8613 **6021**
1017-3439 Sirenews **2627**
1017-3463 Zeitschrift fuer Verwaltung **7478**
1017-3528 Bondinn†
1017-3536 Fiskifrettir **3594**
1017-3544 Frjals Verslun **1817**
1017-3552 Gestgjafinn **4359**
1017-3560 Grodur og Gardar†
1017-3579 Ithrottabladid†
1017-3587 Mannlif **3877**
1017-3595 Nytt Lif **8878**
1017-3609 Sjavarfrettir **3608**
1017-3617 Sjonvarpsvisir **2390**
1017-3803 Computer Spectrum **2412**
1017-3862 L'Osservatore Romano (French Edition. Weekly) **7811**
1017-3900 Women's News **8891**
1017-4095 Adineh **5250**
1017-4109 Ayandeh **544**
1017-4117 Farhang **4452**
1017-4125 Faslnamah-i Tahqiqat-i Jughrafiya-i **4006**
1017-4141 Ettela'at-e Siyassi Eqtesadi **7133**
1017-415X Kelk - Mahnamah-i Farhangi va Hunari **5222**
1017-4168 Kitab-i Subh
1017-4265 Tu Cher Wen Cher Reader's Digest (Chinese Edition) **3875**
1017-4273 Estadistica Panamena. Situacion Economica. Seccion 343. Hacienda Publica **1226**
1017-4281 Estadistica Panamena. Situacion Economica. Seccion 344. Finanzas **1226**
1017-4362 Sanidad Animal Mundial en (Year) *see* 1017-3102 **8815**
1017-4397 Xingda Gongcheng Xuebao **3227**
1017-4435 The Woman **8889**
1017-4508 Environmental Research Newsletter
1017-4559 Current Legal Sociology **4822**
1017-4567 Pignus **1374**
1017-4680 Revista de Historia **4310**
1017-4753 Jamaican Geographer **4016**
1017-4796 Documentacao Europeia *see* 0251-2998 **8366**
1017-480X Documentation Europea *see* 0251-2998 **8366**
1017-4818 Documentazione Europea *see* 0251-2998 **8366**
1017-4826 Europaeisk Dokumentation *see* 0251-2998 **8366**
1017-4834 Europaika Keimena *see* 0251-2998 **8366**
1017-4842 Europaeische Dokumentation *see* 0251-2998 **8366**
1017-4850 European Documentation *see* 0251-2998 **8366**
1017-4869 Europese Documentatie *see* 0251-2998 **8366**
1017-4877 B E S T **8089**
1017-4907 Collection Abysses **2802**
1017-4966 Technobrief **7922**
1017-5156 Zimbabwe Agricultural Journal **173**
1017-5164 *see* 0038-2396 **4785**
1017-5199 China Telecommunications Construction **2366**
1017-5350 Annuaire Minas de l'Ile Maurice
1017-5415 New Contrast **5340**
1017-5423 Viet Nam Sciences Sociales *see* 1013-4328 **8014**
1017-5474 Aegyptica Helvetica **371**
1017-5504 Lavra & Oficina **4463**
1017-5547 Internationales Waffen-Magazin **8181**
1017-5571 South Africa. Council for Geoscience. South African Committee for Stratigraphy. Circular **2768**
1017-5652 Iranian Journal of Agricultural Sciences **124**
1017-5695 Finanz Journal **1347**
1017-5709 History Gazette **4296**
1017-5741 Yuanjian Zazhi **7275**
1017-5806 Eurostat Schnellberichte. Aussenhandel *see* 1024-6878 **1227**
1017-5962 Education, Formation *see* Education and Training
1017-5989 Pediatric and Adolescent Medicine **6099**
1017-6047 Centro de Documentacion y Estudios. Informativo Campesino **7279**
1017-6055 Centro de Documentacion y Estudios. Informativo Laboral **1670**
1017-6063 Centro de Documentacion y Estudios. Informativo Mujer **8855**
1017-6071 Cuaderno de Historia Obrera†
1017-611X M R C News **5663**
1017-6128 The Argus **3947**
1017-6187 African Herp News **930**
1017-6195 I C E S Cooperative Research Report **3597**
1017-6233 Brigades Bopang Botswana **8028**
1017-6268 Quarantine Advisory Leaflet **249**
1017-6276 Pest Advisory Leaflet **246**
1017-6284 Commission de Pacifique Sud. Fiche Technique *see* 1017-6276 **246**
1017-6357 Sveitarsjodareikningar **1269**
1017-6365 Verslunarskyrslur **1273**
1017-6381 Papua New Guinea. National Statistical Office. Economic Indicators†
1017-639X Papua New Guinea. National Statistical Office. Gross Domestic Product and Expenditure **1258**
1017-6403 Papua New Guinea. National Statistical Office. Domestic Factor Incomes, by Region and Province **1258**
1017-6411 Papua New Guinea. National Statistical Office. Government Finance Statistics **1258**
1017-6497 Papua New Guinea. National Statistical Office. Production Statistics†
1017-6500 Papua New Guinea. National Statistical Office. Consumer Price Index **8393**
1017-6519 Papua New Guinea. National Statistical Office. International Trade - Exports **1258**
1017-6527 Papua New Guinea. National Statistical Office. Export Price Indexes **1258**
1017-6535 Papua New Guinea. National Statistical Office. International Trade - Imports **1258**
1017-6543 Papua New Guinea. National Statistical Office. Import Price Indexes **1258**
1017-6551 Papua New Guinea International Arrivals and Departures **7313**
1017-6667 Althingiskosningar **7198**
1017-6675 Forsetakjoer **7136**
1017-6683 Landshagir **8385**
1017-6705 Energy in Europe (Multilingual Edition) **3131**

1017-6713 P +†
1017-6721 European Journal of Physical Medicine and Rehabilitation†
1017-6764 Caribbean Journal of Mathematical and Computing Sciences **5550**
1017-6772 African Development Review **1590**
1017-6780 Soziographie†
1017-6861 I I P Monitor†
1017-6993 Tutorial Texts in Optical Engineering **7085**
1017-7124 Taiwan, Republic of China. National Science Council. Proceedings. Part D: Mathematics, Science, and Technology Education†
1017-7442 UniSwa Research Journal **4479**
1017-7450 Caribbean Marine Studies **664**
1017-7469 Schweizer Wald **3701**
1017-7485 Information Update - Human Sciences Research Council†
1017-7507 Universidad Autonoma de Centro America. Actas Academicas **2306**
1017-7566 Chaillot Papers **7226**
1017-7574 Cahiers de Chaillot **7225**
1017-7604 Latvijas Preses Hronika **629**
1017-7620 ZeitSchrift fuer Kultur Politik Kirche *changed to* Reformatio **7772**
1017-7647 *see* 1018-3183 **1690**
1017-7655 Kazi Sonuclari Toplantisi **402**
1017-7663 Arastirma Sonuclari Toplantisi **374**
1017-7671 Arkeometri Sonuclari Toplantisi **380**
1017-7698 Ege University. Medical Journal *see* 1016-9113 **5608**
1017-7760 Fairuz **2254**
1017-7787 S A A O Newsletter **581**
1017-7817 Hong Kong Law Digest **4688**
1017-7825 Journal of Microbiology and Biotechnology **767**
1017-7833 Klinik Psikofarmakoloji Bulteni **6157**
1017-7841 Bank of Valletta Review **1065**
1017-7892 Dianshi Zhoukan†
1017-7981 Chinese Journal of Entomology. Special Publication *see* 0258-462X **842**
1017-8147 Die Praxis **4658**
1017-8260 Monthly Engineering Horizons **3211**
1017-8279 Mesotes†
1017-8457 Golf Revue **8232**
1017-849X Societe d'Histoire et d'Archaeologie de Geneve. Bulletin **417**
1017-8511 Societe d'Histoire et d'Archeologie. Memoires et Documents. Serie in 8 **417**
1017-8546 Hospital Nacional de Ninos Dr. Carlos Saez Herrera. Revista Medica **6092**
1017-8554 Revista Guatemalteca de Estomatologia **5864**
1017-8562 O E C D Agricultural Policies, Markets and Trade. Monitoring and Outlook *changed to* Agricultural Policies in O E C D Countries: Monitoring and Evaluation **1909**
1017-8686 Progress in Applied Microcirculation **5798**
1017-8716 China's Military: P L A in (Year)†
1017-8791 Infotheque SIDA *see* 1021-321X **5809**
1017-8856 Comentarios Economicos de Actualidad **1084**
1017-8880 Geologische Bundesanstalt. Berichte **2741**
1017-8902 Panorama Centroamericano. Reporte Politico **7163**
1017-8910 Margenes **3927**
1017-8929 Korea Economic Report **1142**
1017-8937 Anales del Caribe **4442**
1017-9011 Debate Agrario **104**
1017-9208 Southern Africa. Political and Economic Monthly **7266**
1017-9216 Institute of Postgraduate Medicine and Research. Journal **5636**
1017-9240 Commission de Pacifique Sud. Rapport de Conference *see* 0377-452X **1519**
1017-9275 Pacific Foods†
1017-9283 South Pacific Conference. Report **7266**
1017-9291 Conference de Pacifique Sud. Rapport *see* 1017-9283 **7266**
1017-9313 Skyjum Ofar†
1017-9402 O E C D Nuclear Energy Agency. Nuclear Energy Data **3173**
1017-9542 Cultura Peruana
1017-9593 Zhonghua Minguo Taiwan Diqu. Jinrong Tongji Yuebao/Financial Statistics Monthly, Taiwan District, Republic of China *changed to* Zhonghua Minguo Jinrong Tongji Yuebao **1275**
1017-9623 Zhongyang Yinhang Jikan **1392**
1017-9631 Zhongua Minguo Taiwan Diqu Jingji Tongji Tubiao† **9000**
1017-9674 Zhongyang Yinhang Nanbao **1392**
1017-9690 Guoji Jingrong Cankao Ziliao **1350**
1017-9909 Journal of Electronic Imaging **6970**
1017-9933 I C R I S A T Report **235**
1017-995X Acta Orthopaedica et Traumatologica Turcica **6054**
1018-0206 South Africa. Council for Geoscience. South African Committee for Stratigraphy. Chronostratigraphic Series **2768**
1018-0265 Austria. Statistisches Zentralamt. Baustatistik
1018-0281 Jiushi Niandai†
1018-0311 U D T Series on Data Communication Technologies and Standards for Libraries **5063**
1018-0354 Journal Ivoirien d'Oceanologie et de Limnologie **2809**
1018-0370 Ornis **912**
1018-0389 Calitatea Vietii **8092**
1018-0400 Viata Armatei **6452**
1018-0419 Moftul Roman **5228**
1018-0435 Dreptul **4661**
1018-0443 Revista Istorica **4257**
1018-0451 Tribuna Economica **1522**
1018-046X Revista Romana de Statistica **8396**
1018-0540 Curierul Romanesc **5213**
1018-0621 Peru Economico **1511**
1018-0664 Polemica **7166**
1018-0702 P N G Coffee Journal **3659**
1018-0745 South African Journal of Cultural History†
1018-0753 South African Journal of Art and Architectural History†
1018-0761 Universiteit van Stellenbosch. Annale **7926**
1018-077X Saudi Heart Journal
1018-0893 South Pacific Epidemiological and Health Information Service Annual Report **7549**
1018-0931 *see* 1027-0728 **3604**
1018-094X Regional Tuna Bulletin **3605**
1018-0958 South Pacific Economies: Statistical Summary **1266**
1018-0966 South Pacific Foods **3664**
1018-1008 Revista Olimpica *see* 0377-192X **8191**
1018-1148 Elle (Hong Kong) **8860**
1018-1172 Journal of Vascular Research **5794**
1018-1180 Pakistan Journal of Entomology **857**
1018-1210 C A R A P H I N News **98**
1018-1253 Join Us...Costa Rica Awaits You
1018-1261 Jamaica Naturalist **2615**
1018-1296 Aliments du Pacifique Sud *see* 1018-0966 **3664**
1018-130X Revista Medica Herediana **5706**
1018-1385 Power Boat and Ski†
1018-1474 S A Retail Chemist
1018-1520 Sub-Saharan Monitor†
1018-1571 I C E S Fisheries Statistics†
1018-161X Academia Economic Papers **1056**
1018-1806 Helia **234**
1018-1814 Panorama Centroamericano. Temas y Documentos de Debates **7163**
1018-1822 Panorama Centroamericano. Pensamiento y Accion **7163**
1018-1857 Archaeologie Oesterreichs
1018-189X Renwen ji Shehui Kexue Jikan **6947**
1018-192X Han'gug Dongmul Bunryu Haghoeji **945**
1018-1946 Anatolia Antiqua **542**
1018-1954 Sortenversuchsergebnisse **157**
1018-1989 Instituto de Ecologia y Sistematica. Reporte de Investigacion. Serie Zoologica†
1018-1997 Critical Reviews of Optical Science and Technology†
1018-208X Trends in Private Investment in Developing Countries **1606**
1018-2098 Cinebulletin **6493**
1018-2101 Pragmatics **5162**
1018-2136 African Urban and Regional Science Index **7936**
1018-2152 Pacific AIDS Alert Bulletin **5824**
1018-2160 J B I Quarterly **6467**
1018-2179 TransPort **8514**
1018-2217 Ivory Coast. Ministere de l'Agriculture. Annuaire des Statistiques Agricoles **183**
1018-2241 Djibouti. Ministere de l'Education Nationale. Annuaire Statistique **2932**
1018-2276 Financial Statements of the International Monetary Fund **1345**
1018-2330 Jamaican Weekly Gleaner **3542**
1018-2403 African Markets†
1018-2411 Urban Directions **4430**
1018-2438 International Archives of Allergy and Immunology **5761**
1018-2462 Natur-Museum Luzern. Veroeffentlichungen **7887**
1018-2500 Proceedings of Parasitology **895**
1018-2535 Brauerei und Getraenke-Rundschau†
1018-2888 Diagnostico **5605**
1018-2896 University of the South Pacific. Marine Studies Programme. Technical Report **966**
1018-290X Annual Report on the Environment and Natural Resources **3403**
1018-2918 Informe Anual sobre el Medio Ambiente y los Recursos Naturales *see* 1018-290X **3403**
1018-3124 *see* 1018-3183 **1690**
1018-3132 *see* 1018-3183 **1690**
1018-3140 *see* 1018-3183 **1690**
1018-3159 *see* 1018-3183 **1690**
1018-3167 *see* 1018-3183 **1690**
1018-3175 *see* 1018-3183 **1690**
1018-3183 Janus **1690**
1018-3191 *see* 1018-3183 **1690**
1018-3310 Informat (International Edition)†
1018-3337 Marine Ornithology **910**
1018-3361 Phafoga!
1018-3418 Fast Food & Family Restaurant **4385**
1018-3493 S A Barometer†
1018-3582 King Saud University Journal. Administrative Sciences **1140**
1018-3590 King Saud University Journal. Agricultural Sciences **130**
1018-3604 King Saud University Journal. Architecture and Planning **4418**
1018-3612 King Saud University Journal. Arts **500**
1018-3639 King Saud University Journal. Engineering Sciences **3207**
1018-3647 King Saud University Journal. Science **7876**
1018-3671 Caribbean Law Review **4640**
1018-3698 Haflingersport *changed to* Mensch und Pferd **8294**
1018-3736 Le Matin **3958**
1018-3795 Riderz Daidzhest **3940**
1018-3841 Renkou Zuekan **7292**
1018-3914 Studies in Language and Literature **5381**
1018-3930 Renkou Yanjiu Tongxun **7291**
1018-3949 Funu Yanjiu Tongxun/Women's Research Program. Bulletin *changed to* 1682-8607 **8897**
1018-4171 Arachnologische Mitteilungen **839**
1018-4252 Pacific Arts **510**
1018-4287 Bangladesh Journal of Obstetrics and Gynecology **5986**
1018-4295 S A B S Catalogue **6406**
1018-4406 Iranian Journal of Pediatrics **6094**
1018-4430 Salud y Familia
1018-4473 Taiwan, Republic of China. National Science Council. Proceedings. Part C: Humanities and Social Sciences†
1018-4538 T F R I Conference Proceedings **3609**
1018-4570 Wiener Sprachblaetter **5195**
1018-4619 Fresenius Environmental Bulletin **3432**
1018-4627 Medical Microbiology Letters†
1018-4775 Dongfang Xindi **3875**
1018-4783 I S S N Compact† **8963**
1018-4813 European Journal of Human Genetics **866**
1018-4864 Telecommunication Systems **2372**
1018-4902 Foreign Investment Advisory Service. Occasional Paper **1625**
1018-4910 Teacher in Zimbabwe†
1018-5011 Gripla **5302**
1018-502X F A T - Berichte *changed to* 1661-7568 **78**
1018-5089 P A S Research Paper Series **1603**
1018-5100 Tabcont
1018-5151 Urodinamica Aplicada **6275**
1018-5178 *see* 1018-5739 **8399**
1018-5259 Jahresberichte aus Augst und Kaiseraugst **400**
1018-5275 Adli Tip Dergisi† **8928**
1018-5291 Asia - Pacific Journal of Rural Development **194**
1018-5313 Analisis **3927**
1018-5321 Revista Boliviana de Nefrologia
1018-5356 Chengshi Zhoukan
1018-5445 Newton **2205**
1018-5577 Atomic and Plasma-Material Interaction Data for Fusion **7064**
1018-5593 E U R **5608**
1018-5674 Folia Amazonica **3431**
1018-5712 Instituto Interamericano de Cooperacion para la Agricultura - O E A. Documentos Oficiales†
1018-5739 Sigma **8399**
1018-5763 Revista de Interpretacion Biblica Latinoamericana **7814**
1018-578X Today's Living **4551**
1018-5852 Cement Standards of the World **990**
1018-5895 Geneva Papers on Risk and Insurance - Issues and Practice **4503**
1018-5933 European Communities. Court of Justice and Court of First Instance. Proceedings **4950**
1018-5941 I M F Working Paper **1490**
1018-595X O A P E C Monthly Bulletin **6781**
1018-5968 I S O Catalogue. Supplement **6402**
1018-5984 Icelandic Fisheries Laboratories. Report **3597**
1018-5992 Marmara University. Faculty of Dentistry. Journal† **8972**
1018-6026 Developer†
1018-6034 European Furniture **4556**
1018-6077 Kataloge des Oberoesterreichische Landesmuseums **6541**
1018-6093 Catalogus Faunae Austriae **938**
1018-6107 Burgenlaendische Heimatblaetter **4207**
1018-6174 Swara **2628**
1018-6182 Institute of Agriculture and Animal Science. Journal **8799**
1018-6190 Monticola **910**
1018-6204 Bodhi Baum†
1018-6212 Peru. Policia Nacional. Revista de la Sanidad
1018-6255 Biomethods Series *changed to* Methods and Tools in Biosciences and Medicine **689**
1018-6298 International Thermonuclear Experimental Reactor. Documentation Series **3169**
1018-6301 Iranian Mathematical Society. Bulletin **5498**
1018-631X Economic Journal of Nepal **1595**
1018-6379 Amateur Boat Builder†
1018-6409 Metamorphosis **854**
1018-6441 In die Skriflig **7761**
1018-6689 Australasian Ceramic Society. Journal **2037**
1018-6735 Villes et Ports **1586**
1018-6751 Hong Kong Economic Journal **1543**
1018-6786 Catalogue des Publications. O C D E *see* 0474-5086
1018-6999 Die Volksblad **3950**
1018-7014 Zululand Observer **3950**
1018-7049 O C D E Statistiques de la Dette Exterieure *see* 1015-4159
1018-7057 Geological Society of China. Journal **2739**
1018-7081 The J A P S **949**
1018-7138 Tannlaeknabladid **5867**
1018-7170 Guatemala. Instituto Nacional de Estadistica. Anuario Estadistico†
1018-7235 Gatekeeper Series **2612**
1018-7243 Mechanisms of B Cell Neoplasia **925**
1018-7324 Journal of Taiwan Fisheries Research **3600**
1018-7405 E B U Review. (Programmes, Administration, Law Edition)†
1018-7480 Nouvel Horizon **7160**
1018-7529 Cronica
1018-7537 Antropologia Ecuatoriana
1018-757X International Commission for the Conservation of Atlantic Tunas. Historical Statistical Bulletin *changed to* 1726-247X **3613**
1018-760X G W A **6769**
1018-7618 Oesterreichisches Getraenke Institut. Mitteilungen **608**
1018-7626 Directory of South African Publishers **7560**
1018-7634 Southern Birds **914**
1018-7677 Namibia Scientific Society. Journal **7885**
1018-7685 Namibia Scientific Society. Newsletter **7885**
1018-7871 Trinidad and Tobago National Bibliography **636**
1018-7901 Fotograf† **8957**
1018-7928 Ultrahigh and High Speed Photography, Videography and Photonics†
1018-7987 Schweizerische Zeitschrift fuer Wirtschaftsrecht **4880**
1018-8029 Plant Tissue Culture *changed to* 1817-3721 **813**
1018-810X *see* 1726-9032 **6139**
1018-8177 Dongfang Ribao **3875**
1018-8371 Automotive Industries (Year)†
1018-838X Building, Hardware and Housewares (Year)†
1018-8517 Instituto de Ecologia y Sistematica. Reporte de Investigacion. Serie Botanica†
1018-8592 Journal of African Religion and Philosophy **7654**
1018-8649 Elle (Taiwan) **8860**
1018-8657 Preparing for the Future: E S A Technology Quarterly† **8982**
1018-8665 Dermatology **5875**
1018-8673 Asia - Pacific Uplands†
1018-8681 Dusunen Adam† **8951**
1018-8770 Visual Communications and Image Processing **7085**
1018-8800 Acta Medica Peruana **5566**
1018-8819 Organisation Internationale pour l'Etude de l'Endurance des Cables. Bulletin *changed to* 1997-6461 **3273**
1018-8827 European Child & Adolescent Psychiatry **6139**
1018-8843 Gynaekologisch - Geburtshilfliche Rundschau **5992**
1018-8851 Ege Universitesi. Ziraat Fakultesi. Dergisi **106**
1018-8916 Natural Immunity†
1018-8940 Zhonghua Minguo Fangshexian Yixue Zazhi **6211**
1018-8983 Bridge†

ISSN

1020-2889 F A O Regional Conference for Latin America and the Caribbean. Report **109**
1020-2927 African Development Indicators **1435**
1020-2994 High Technology Spin-Offs: Monitor **8424**
1020-3001 Emerging Technology Series: Marine Industrial Technology **3188**
1020-3060 Regional Development Studies **1604**
1020-3079 World Employment (Year) **1716**
1020-3184 Nations Unies. Conseil de Securite. Documents Officiels *see* 0082-8416 **7271**
1020-3192 Naciones Unidas. Consejo de Seguridad. Documentos Oficiales *see* 0082-8416 **7271**
1020-3206 Organizatsiya Ob'edinennykh Natsii. Sovet Bezopasnosti. Ofitsial'nyi Otchet *see* 0082-8416 **7271**
1020-3214 Lianheguo. Anquan Lishihui. Zhengshi Jilu *see* 0082-8416 **7271**
1020-3222 Al-Umam al-Muttahidat. Maglis al-Amn. Al Wata'iq al-Rasmiyyat *see* 0082-8416 **7271**
1020-3249 F A O Computerized Information Series. Fisheries **3590**
1020-3311 The World Health Report **7545**
1020-332X *see* 1020-3311 **7545**
1020-3362 Plant Genetic Resources Newsletter **811**
1020-3397 Eastern Mediterranean Health Journal **7515**
1020-3443 F A O Aquaculture Newsletter **3590**
1020-3478 U N C R D Annual Report (English Edition) **1606**
1020-3486 U N C R D Annual Report (Nihonban) *see* 1020-3478 **1606**
1020-3508 United Nations. Human Rights Committee. Official Records **7217**
1020-3516 Studies in Trade and Investment **1180**
1020-3613 Habitat Debate **4411**
1020-3737 R E U Technical Series **149**
1020-3745 Tribunal Penal International pour l'ex-Yougoslavie. Documents de Reference† **8994**
1020-3753 World Food Programme. Annual Report **1608**
1020-3761 Programa Mundial de Alimentos. Informe Anual *see* 1020-3753 **1608**
1020-377X Programme Alimentaire Mondial. Rapport Annuel *see* 1020-3753 **1608**
1020-3796 F A O Serie Informatique. Peche *see* 1020-3249 **3590**
1020-3877 Issues in Development. Discussion Paper **1599**
1020-3907 International Criminal Tribunal for the Former Yugoslavia. Yearbook **4930**
1020-4032 Commission Oceanographique Intergouvernementale. Rapport Annuel *see* 1020-4040 **2807**
1020-4040 Intergovernmental Oceanographic Commission. Annual Report **2807**
1020-4067 Refugee Survey Quarterly **7314**
1020-4148 I T U News **2325**
1020-4199 A T A S Information Technology for Development **1589**
1020-4202 World Heritage Review **4167**
1020-4393 Estudio F A O, Riego y Drenaje **8823**
1020-4407 Annual World Bank Conference on Development Economics†
1020-4431 Forest Genetic Resources **3688**
1020-444X Recursos Geneticos Forestales *see* 1020-4431 **3688**
1020-4520 Revue du Patrimoine Mondial *see* 1020-4202 **4167**
1020-4539 Revista del Patrimonio Mundial *see* 1020-4202 **4167**
1020-4555 Integrated Crop Management **237**
1020-4598 W E S T P A C Information **2820**
1020-461X Mirovoe Mashinostroenie i Avtomatizaciya. Pokazateli i Perspektivy Gody *see* 1020-1300 **3359**
1020-4679 Gazette O M P I des Marques Internationales **6750**
1020-4687 Refworld **4939**
1020-4873 I M O, F A O, Unesco - I O C, W M O, W H O, I A E A, U N, U N E P - G E S A M P Reports and Studies **3487**
1020-492X Commodity Market Review†
1020-4989 Revista Panamericana de Salud Publica **7539**
1020-4997 W T O Annual Report **1586**
1020-5004 Organisation Mondiale du Commerce. Rapport Annuel *see* 1020-4997 **1586**
1020-5012 Organizacion Mundial del Comercio, Informe Anual *see* 1020-4997 **1586**
1020-5071 Perspectivas de la Economia Mundial *see* 0256-6877 **1493**
1020-508X *see* 0256-6877 **1493**
1020-5098 International Monetary Fund. Economic Issues **1571**
1020-5101 Fonds Monetaire International. Etudes Economiques et Financieres **1348**
1020-5144 Inversion Extranjera en America Latina y el Caribe **1599**
1020-5152 Panorama Social de America Latina (Year) **1510**
1020-5160 Social Panorama of Latin America (Year) **1517**
1020-5179 Comision Economica para America Latina y el Caribe. Serie Desarrollo Productivo **1592**
1020-5209 Emerging Technology Series: Genetic Engineering and Biotechnology **866**
1020-5225 Emerging Technology Series: Information Technology **3099**
1020-5241 Emerging Technology Series: New and Advanced Materials **3343**
1020-525X I A E A Safety Standards Series **7524**
1020-5292 F A O Technical Guidelines for Responsible Fisheries **3591**
1020-5306 F A O Directives Techniques pour une Peche Responsable *see* 1020-5292 **3591**
1020-5314 F A O Orientaciones Tecnicas para la Pesca Responsable *see* 1020-5292 **3591**
1020-5454 Global Development Finance **1596**
1020-5489 The State of World Fisheries and Aquacultures **3609**
1020-5535 UNESCO Nairobi Bulletin **7925**
1020-5543 I C O M Study Series **6525**
1020-5551 Perspectives in Health **7535**
1020-556X Perspectivas de Salud *see* 1020-5551 **7535**
1020-5578 Bulletin - Bureau de l'Unesco a Nairobi *see* 1020-5535 **7925**
1020-5586 A C G C Chemical Research Communications **2096**
1020-5705 The State of the World's Forests **3703**
1020-5772 United Nations. Economic and Social Commission for Western Asia. Review of Transport in E S C W A Member Countries **8519**
1020-5799 Trends in Europe and North America **1550**
1020-6086 Newsletter on Fisheries for the Sahel **3603**
1020-6140 World Bank. Annual Conference on Development in Latin America and the Caribbean **1607**
1020-6167 Concise International Chemical Assessment Documents **2059**
1020-6264 P C T Gazette (Bilingual Edition) **6755**
1020-6418 I C O M News (English Edition) **6525**
1020-6426 I C O M. Nouvelles *see* 1020-6418 **6525**
1020-6434 I C O M. Noticias *see* 1020-6418 **6525**
1020-6450 International Atomic Energy Agency. Safety Reports Series **3169**
1020-6469 Organismo Internacional de Energia Atomica. Coleccion de Informes de Seguridad *see* 1020-6450 **3169**
1020-6477 Agence Internationale de l'Energie Atomique. Collection Rapports de Surete *see* 1020-6450 **3169**
1020-6485 Mezdunarodnoe Agentstvo po Atomnoj Energii. Doklady po Bezopasnosti *see* 1020-6450 **3169**
1020-6507 Human Rights **7208**
1020-6515 Museum Internacional (Spanish Edition)†
1020-6558 Bibliotheque des Nations Unies. Bibliographie Mensuelle **620**
1020-6574 Silsilat Tatwir al-Ihsa'At *see* 1014-3378 **8369**
1020-6663 F A O Yearbook. Fishery Statistics. Capture Production **3613**
1020-6671 Food and Environmental Protection Newsletter **3637**
1020-6779 I M F. Economic Reviews. Press Information Notices **1490**
1020-6825 U N R I S D News **8011**
1020-6833 U N R I S D infos *see* 1020-6825 **8011**
1020-6841 U N R I S D informa *see* 1020-6825 **8011**
1020-685X Environment Matters (Print) **3422**
1020-6892 World Science Report **7930**
1020-6930 Educacion para Todos. Situation et Tendencias *see* 1020-0908 **2868**
1020-7007 Abdus Salam International Centre for Theoretical Physics. Annual Report **7002**
1020-7066 Intellectual Property Laws and Treaties†
1020-7074 W I P O Magazine **6760**
1020-721X Global Commodity Markets†
1020-7236 General Fisheries Commission for the Mediterranean **3595**
1020-7244 Commission Generale des Peches pour la Mediterrane *see* 1020-7236 **3595**
1020-7287 Disarmament Forum **7231**
1020-7333 Studies in Comparative Education **2915**
1020-7368 Bulletin on Vital Statistics in the E S C W A Region **7304**
1020-7376 I P T R I D Issues Paper **235**
1020-7392 Review of Science and Tecnology in Economic and Social Commission for Western Asia Member Countries **7903**
1020-7481 Euro Observer **7516**
1020-7511 *see* 1020-0908 **2868**
1020-7635 International Monetary Fund. Staff Papers **1358**
1020-7724 Fonds Monetaire International. Dossiers Economiques *see* 1020-5098 **1571**
1020-7813 World Commodity Survey **1587**
1020-7856 International Economic Policy Review **1599**
1020-7953 *see* 0082-8041 **7294**
1020-797X Development Outreach **1594**
1020-7988 U N C T A D Handbook of Statistics **1271**
1020-8100 F A O Bulletin of Statistics **179**
1020-8135 Disaster Risk Management Series **1739**
1020-8313 International Monetary Fund. Research Bulletin **1358**
1020-8372 Fondo Monetario Internacional. Temas de Economia *see* 1020-5098 **1571**
1020-8380 Sunduq al-Naqd al-Duwalil. Al-Qadaya al-Iqtisadiyyat *see* 1020-5098 **1571**
1020-8399 Guoji Huobi Jijin Zuzhi. Jingji Wenti *see* 1020-5098 **1571**
1020-8402 Mezhdunarodnyj Valutnyj Fond. Voprosy Ekonomiki *see* 1020-5098 **1571**
1020-8453 Etat de la Migration dans le Monde *see* World Migration **7295**
1020-8712 F A O Agricultural Information Management Series **109**
1020-8887 The Steel Market and Prospects† **8990**
1020-895X Dengue Bulletin **7513**
1020-9018 C B D News **663**
1020-9050 *see* 1020-9018 **663**
1020-9212 Forum on Crime and Society **2653**
1020-9247 Forum po Problemam Prestupnosti i Obsestva *see* 1020-9212 **2653**
1020-9255 Forum sur le Crime et la Societe *see* 1020-9212 **2653**
1020-9263 Foro Sobre el Delito y la Sociedad *see* 1020-9212 **2653**
1020-9271 Muntada Hawla al-Garimat wa-al-Mugtama' *see* 1020-9212 **2653**
1020-928X Fanzui yu Shehui Wenti Luntan *see* 1020-9212 **2653**
1020-9492 Pan American Health Organization. Scientific and Technical Publication **7535**
1020-9549 General Fisheries Commission for the Mediterranean. Studies and Reviews **3595**
1020-9956 Eastfish. Fishery Industry Profiles **3590**
1021-0024 Interjeunes *see* 0294-7579 **2223**
1021-0067 Durban Chamber of Commerce and Industry. Chamber Digest **1401**
1021-0075 Mixtura **6861**
1021-0113 The International Journal of Hematological Research **5938**
1021-0164 Revista Forestal Centroamericana†
1021-0172 *see* 0770-1683 **2893**
1021-0180 Regards sur l'Etain†
1021-0296 Revista Nicaraguense de Entomologia **858**
1021-044X Hombre y Ambiente **8105**
1021-0474 Academie Malgache. Bulletin d'Information et de Liaison **7830**
1021-0555 Oceanographic Research Institute. Special Publication **2815**
1021-058X Luxembourg. Ministere d'Etat. Bulletin d'Information et de Documentation **7451**
1021-0601 Kunststoffe - Synthetics *changed to* 1662-0739 **7100**
1021-0628 Blickpunkte
1021-0806 United Arab Emirates University. Faculty of Science. Journal **7925**
1021-0814 Insula **7973**
1021-0822 Tendencias
1021-0865 Izobreteniya **6753**
1021-0873 UniSwa Journal of Agriculture **165**
1021-0970 Sportswear International News **2249**
1021-0989 Sportswear International (European Edition) **2249**
1021-1004 Bangladesh Journal of Entomology **840**
1021-1055 South Africa. Sea Fisheries Research Institute. Research Highlights **3608**
1021-1063 Navorsingshoogtepunte **3602**
1021-108X Isalp **8319**
1021-1128 Egerton Journal **4450**
1021-1144 New I C C World Directory of Chambers of Commerce†
1021-1209 Reflexiones **7995**
1021-1225 Dynamic Nutrition Research†
1021-125X Economic Times **1101**
1021-1314 Chinamac Journal **5450**
1021-1322 China Automotive Journal **8574**
1021-1330 China Plastic and Rubber Journal **7091**
1021-1357 Majallat al-Imarat lil-'Ulum al-Zira'iyyah **135**
1021-1454 Wine **612**
1021-1497 Image & Text **495**
1021-1500 University of Transkei. Department of Information Science. Occasional Papers **2551**
1021-156X Vestigia **6960**
1021-1608 Weltbund der Partnerstadte. Mitteilungsblatt *see* United Towns News. Newsletter **7504**
1021-1616 Citta Unite. Lettera *see* United Towns News. Newsletter **7504**
1021-1624 Ciudades Unidas. Informativo *see* United Towns News. Newsletter **7504**
1021-1667 *see* Office for Official Publications of the European Union. Newsletter **7256**
1021-1675 Eur-Op News *changed to* Office for Official Publications of the European Union. Newsletter **7256**
1021-1683 *see* Office for Official Publications of the European Union. Newsletter **7256**
1021-1705 Monde des Femmes *see* 1019-1534 **8892**
1021-173X Women's Global Network for Reproductive Rights. Newsletter **8849**
1021-1748 Reseau Mondial des Femmes pour les Droits sur la Reproduction *see* 1021-173X **8849**
1021-1780 South Africa Foundation Review **1518**
1021-1802 King Abdulaziz University. Faculty of Marine Science. Journal **2810**
1021-1810 Alerta Agrario **90**
1021-1853 Iraqi Journal of Marine Science *changed to* 1815-2058 **967**
1021-1861 Pearl Oyster **3604**
1021-2000 Civil Engineering **3262**
1021-2019 South African Institution of Civil Engineering. Journal **3283**
1021-2043 Communications in Asteroseismology **573**
1021-2221 Aquarien - Terrarien - Information **3586**
1021-2256 Forum fuer Wissen **2611**
1021-2337 Graenseloese Europa *see* 1021-2353 **1566**
1021-2345 Europa ohne Grenzen *see* 1021-2353 **1566**
1021-2353 Frontier-Free Europe **1566**
1021-2361 Europa sin Fronteras *see* 1021-2353 **1566**
1021-237X Europe sans Frontieres *see* 1021-2353 **1566**
1021-2388 Europe horis Sunora *see* 1021-2353 **1566**
1021-240X Europa zonder Grenzen *see* 1021-2353 **1566**
1021-2418 Europa sem Fronteiras *see* 1021-2353 **1566**
1021-2442 Sciences & Techniques **7912**
1021-2477 Bank for International Settlements. Annual Report **1313**
1021-2485 Bank fuer Internationalen Zahlungsausgleich. Jahresbericht *see* 1021-2477 **1313**
1021-2493 Banque des Reglements Internationaux. Rapport Annuel *see* 1021-2477 **1313**
1021-2507 Banca dei Regolamenti Internazionali. Relazione Annuale *see* 1021-2477 **1313**
1021-2655 Annals of Numerical Mathematics†
1021-268X Grid **233**
1021-271X Monitor **2432**
1021-2752 A R D R I News **78**
1021-2760 Instituto de Estudios Peruanos. Boletin Argumentos†
1021-2892 Graphis Posters **492**
1021-2981 Lewende Woorde **2237**
1021-3058 Oumei Yanjiu **4307**
1021-3120 Zhonghua Mingguo Yanke Yixuehui Zazhi **6053**
1021-318X Vietnam Investment Review **1192**
1021-321X AIDS Infothek **5809**
1021-3236 C E D R E S. Revue Economique et Sociale **195**
1021-3244 Figura **8470**
1021-3279 Bangladesh Journal of Forest Science **3684**
1021-3333 Boletin Informativo U D T *see* 1010-9501 **5051**
1021-335X Oncology Reports **6030**
1021-3457 Diffusion (French Edition) **2358**
1021-3465 Diffusion (English Edition) **2358**
1021-3538 International Journal of Diabetes *changed to* 1606-7754 **5894**
1021-3570 S A Baseball Digest **8244**
1021-3589 African Entomology **837**
1021-3619 Hong Kong Journal of Social Sciences **7969**
1021-3740 Asian Air Transport **8538**
1021-3864 Politiques Energetiques des Pays de l'A I E *see* 1021-3872 **3132**
1021-3872 Energy Policies of I E A Countries **3132**
1021-4070 I F L A Section of Libraries Serving Disadvantaged Persons. Newsletter **5013**
1021-4127 Transport Europe **8514**
1021-4135 Europe Transports *see* 1021-4127 **8514**
1021-4151 Lettre Sociale Europeenne *changed to* 1811-413X **7233**
1021-416X Europe Environment *changed to* Europolitics Environment **3431**
1021-4178 Europe Environnement *changed to* 1811-4458 **3430**
1021-4186 Multinational Service†
1021-4194 Europe Entreprises *see* 0030-3593 **1484**
1021-4208 Euro-East **7233**

ISSN

1021-4216 Euro-Est *see* 1021-4208 **7233**
1021-4224 Monthly Report on Europe **7253**
1021-4232 Tech Europe **2352**
1021-4259 Europe Energy **3134**
1021-4267 European Report *changed to* Europolitics **1340**
1021-4275 Europolitique (Bruxelles) **7234**
1021-4283 European Insight **7233**
1021-4291 Lettre Europeenne *see* 1021-4283 **7233**
1021-4313 In Touch†
1021-4437 Russian Journal of Plant Physiology **816**
1021-4453 Longevity **4051**
1021-447X Journal of Energy in Southern Africa **3140**
1021-450X Gozaresh **3891**
1021-4526 Valstieciu Laikrastis **168**
1021-4534 Monthly Report on Tourism - Republic of China **8780**
1021-4577 Heneng Tiandi **3168**
1021-4712 Win!
1021-4895 Agrifokus **86**
1021-500X I S S N Register (Tape)† **8963**
1021-5042 Veterinary Review **8814**
1021-514X Haske **3920**
1021-5212 International Commission for the Conservation of Atlantic Tunas. Collective Volume of Scientific Papers **3598**
1021-5417 Excavatio **5294**
1021-5425 Eurostat Verbraucherpreisindex *see* 1013-3402 **2642**
1021-5506 Zoological Studies **970**
1021-5530 Western Cape Travel Guide†
1021-5549 Utano - Zimbabwe
1021-5573 Papers on Social Representations. Thread of Discussion **7389**
1021-559X Mosenodi **2887**
1021-5611 Hong Kong Enterprise **4060**
1021-562X I A S A Journal **8153**
1021-5646 Sveitarstjornarkosningar **7187**
1021-5697 Frauenheilkunde Aktuell†
1021-5700 European Mediafacts
1021-5719 The Bulletin†
1021-5794 O E C D Reviews of Foreign Direct Investment
1021-5808 Examens de l'O C D E sur l'Investissement Direct Etranger *see* 1021-5794
1021-5824 Zhongguo Fangzhi ji Chengyi **8463**
1021-5948 South Africa. Sea Fisheries Research Institute. Investigational Report **3608**
1021-5972 Brenner-Studien† **8937**
1021-5980 Civitas **5211**
1021-6006 Studies in English Literature and Linguistics *changed to* 1729-6897 **5277**
1021-6138 Molten Salt Forum **3251**
1021-6243 Sub-Saharan Newsbrief
1021-626X Highlife
1021-6278 Genome Priority Reports†
1021-6286 Complement Profiles†
1021-6294 Repertorio Cientifico **7902**
1021-6316 Avard Magazine **8160**
1021-6332 China Property Review **7586**
1021-6340 Analisis Internacional **7221**
1021-643X Noise - News International **3489**
1021-6472 European Billiard News
1021-6480 Pretextos **7173**
1021-6510 Film International **6499**
1021-6626 Listasafn Sigurjons Olafssonar. Arbok **6528**
1021-6642 *see* 1021-268X **233**
1021-6650 *see* 1021-268X **233**
1021-6731 South China Morning Post **3875**
1021-6758 Molecular Comparative Physiology†
1021-6790 The Ethiopian Journal of Health Development **7516**
1021-6804 Mu'tah lil-Buhuth wal-Dirasat. Al-Silsilah A: Al-'Ulum al-Insaniyyah wal-Ijtima'iyyah **4465**
1021-6812 Mu'tah lil-Buhuth wal-Dirasat. Al-Silsilah B: Al-'Ulum al-Tabi'iyyah wal-Tatbiqiyyah **7884**
1021-691X Directory of Chinese Government Organs **7434**
1021-6928 Elements de Bibliographie sur les Pays du Sahel
1021-6952 Melita Historica
1021-6987 Medifile
1021-7002 Electronic Components (American Edition)†
1021-7061 Juta's Business Law **4873**
1021-707X Hustler **6292**
1021-7150 Bleikt og Blatt *changed to* 1670-5971 **8090**
1021-7169 Eidfaxi **8290**
1021-7223 Neytendabladid **2640**
1021-724X Toelvumal **2440**
1021-7266 Morgunbladid **3877**
1021-7274 O E C S Annual Digest of Statistics **8393**
1021-7290 O E C S Statistical Pocket Digest **8393**
1021-7304 O E C S Select Bibliography **1505**
1021-7312 O E C S Current Awareness Bulletin **1505**
1021-7320 O E C S Digest of External Trade Statistics **1257**
1021-7339 O E C S National Accounts Digest **8393**
1021-7347 O E C S Energy Review **3153**
1021-7398 Mercosul: Sinopse Estatistica **1251**
1021-7401 Neuroimmunomodulation **5764**
1021-7444 Agronomia Mesoamericana **277**
1021-7460 National Botanical Institute. Annual Review **804**
1021-7509 *see* 0379-0584 **8**
1021-7592 Samuel†
1021-7762 Folia Phoniatrica et Logopaedica **6080**
1021-7770 Journal of Biomedical Science **5646**
1021-8009 Journal of Anaesthesia & Critical Care **5771**
1021-8122 Ethica - Wissenschaft und Verantwortung **7853**
1021-8130 Grenzgebiete der Wissenschaft **7858**
1021-8149 The Baltic Review **1065**
1021-8157 Progressive Racing
1021-8165 Parade†
1021-8181 Modelling and Simulation **5554**
1021-8203 Althydubladid†
1021-8254 D V **3877**
1021-8270 Faxi **3877**
1021-8327 Hus & Hibyli **4542**
1021-8351 Kirkjuritid **7763**
1021-8440 Stofnun Sigurdar Nordals - Frettabref **5178**
1021-8467 Verzlunartidindi†
1021-8505 Auto Italiana **8558**
1021-8513 New Salon
1021-8521 Needlework's Cross Stitch†
1021-8564 Rheumatology in Europe†
1021-8610 Frozen Ground **2734**
1021-8629 Imprint **495**
1021-8637 Geotechnique
1021-8858 East African Journal of Peace and Human Rights **7205**
1021-8866 Hong Kong Electronics **3101**
1021-8874 Hong Kong Garments and Accessories†
1021-8882 Hong Kong Household **1054**
1021-8912 Hong Kong Watches & Clocks **4566**
1021-8920 Hong Kong Toys **4060**
1021-8939 Hong Kong Apparel **2247**
1021-8947 Hong Kong Optical **6043**
1021-8955 Hong Kong Leather Goods and Bags **4973**
1021-9013 Perspectives Chinoises **7259**
1021-9056 Infokara **5635**
1021-9102 Aardvark **929**
1021-9137 D I Y Trade News **4438**
1021-9161 Great Photo & Video
1021-9269 Arbor **3683**
1021-9277 Niche
1021-9390 E P O Script†
1021-9498 Journal of Food and Drug Analysis **3649**
1021-9536 Business Weekly **1076**
1021-9595 Sardius†
1021-9617 Tutor **3005**
1021-9633 Alma Mater **2966**
1021-9641 Hora de Cierre **4576**
1021-9706 Cratschla **2608**
1021-9722 No D E A - Nonlinear Differential Equations and Applications **5520**
1021-9730 African Crop Science Journal **216**
1021-9749 News from I S S N *see* 1021-9757 **5014**
1021-9757 I S S N. Nouvelles **5014**
1021-9765 Hustler Humor†
1021-9773 House and Leisure **3948**
1021-9978 Der Treuhandexperte†
1021-9986 Iranian Journal of Chemistry and Chemical Engineering (International English Edition) **2066**
1021-9994 Cahiers Africains **4174**
1022-0038 Wireless Networks **2344**
1022-0046 Hustler Classics†
1022-0119 African Journal of Range & Forage Science **216**
1022-0151 European Optical Society. Annual Meetings Digest Series **7075**
1022-016X Bangladesh Chemical Society. Journal **2051**
1022-0194 Revista Peruana de Fisica **7038**
1022-0216 C R E Info†
1022-0267 AsiaLaw **4856**
1022-0356 Instituto de Estudios Peruanos. Documentos de Trabajo **7973**
1022-0364 Instituto de Estudios Peruanos. Documentos de Trabajo. Serie Antropologia **343**
1022-0372 Instituto de Estudios Peruanos. Documentos de Trabajo. Serie Documentos de Politica **7143**
1022-0380 Instituto de Estudios Peruanos. Documentos de Trabajo. Serie Etnohistoria **343**
1022-0399 Instituto de Estudios Peruanos. Documentos de Trabajo. Serie Economia **1125**
1022-0402 Instituto de Estudios Peruanos. Documentos de Trabajo. Serie Historia **4298**
1022-0410 Instituto de Estudios Peruanos. Documentos de Trabajo. Serie Linguistica **5128**
1022-0429 Instituto de Estudios Peruanos. Documentos de Trabajo. Serie Sociologia, Politica **8107**
1022-0437 Instituto de Estudios Peruanos. Documentos de Trabajo. Serie Talleres **1889**
1022-0461 The South African Journal of International Affairs **7266**
1022-0666 Zhongguo Hangkong Taikong Xuehui Xuekan/Aeronautical and Astronautical Society of the Republic of China. Transactions *changed to* 1990-7729 **57**
1022-0666 Zhongguo Hangkong Taikong Xuehui Xuekan/Aeronautical and Astronautical Society of the Republic of China. Transactions *changed to* 1990-7710 **63**
1022-0747 S C L News **5045**
1022-0771 Documentos de Literatura **5285**
1022-078X S A F T O World Trader†
1022-0798 Innovant
1022-0941 Trabajos del Colegio Andino **8010**
1022-100X I S S N Register (Microfiche)†
1022-1026 Vox Nostra **4070**
1022-1034 Vox Nostra (Ed. Espanola) **4070**
1022-1050 Rapports de Synthese sur les Themes Techniques Presentes au Comite International ou aux Commissions Regionales
1022-1069 Sarko **5367**
1022-1093 South African Commercial Fisheries Review **3608**
1022-1115 Vision of Wildlife, Ecotourism and the Environment in Southern Africa *changed to* 1814-781X **2631**
1022-1123 Analytica **2097**
1022-1220 Physiology Society of Southern Africa. Proceedings **927**
1022-1239 Iuzhna Afrika, Sega **3949**
1022-1247 The Home Handyman **4438**
1022-1255 Intertec†
1022-1263 Noord-Transvaler Metro **3949**
1022-1271 Farvis - Afangar†
1022-1301 Archivos Latinoamericanos de Produccion Animal **279**
1022-1336 Macromolecular Rapid Communications **2126**
1022-1344 Macromolecular Theory and Simulations **2126**
1022-1352 Macromolecular Chemistry and Physics **2126**
1022-1360 Macromolecular Symposia **2126**
1022-1379 Cahiers Options Mediterraneennes **99**
1022-1387 Oorsig van die Suid-Afrikaanse Kommersiele Vissery *see* 1022-1093 **3608**
1022-1492 C B N Newsletter†
1022-1506 Serie Linguistica Peruana **5173**
1022-1514 Comunidades y Culturas Peruanas **333**
1022-1522 Instituto Linguistico de Verano. Documentos de Trabajo **5128**
1022-1611 P C News **2434**
1022-1646 Critical Perspectives **2940**
1022-1751 Jasmine **8869**
1022-1778 *see* 1016-3107 **4898**
1022-1786 Die Tukkie **3005**
1022-1794 Executive Summary **4670**
1022-1808 C B E
1022-1824 Selecta Mathematica **5533**
1022-1913 S A D C C Energy Bulletin **3147**
1022-193X Dokimion **7638**
1022-2057 Information Technology Review **2423**
1022-2081 Suid-Afrikaanse Tydskrif vir Geo-inlighting†
1022-2111 Profil **3798**
1022-2138 Film-khane-ye Melli-e Iran. Name-ye†
1022-2146 Alternative Johannesburg
1022-2154 Hinduism Today (South Africa Edition) **7707**
1022-2170 Pathways to Health
1022-2189 Bahamas Journal of Science **7838**
1022-2200 Playboy (South Africa)
1022-2278 Timarit Hjukrunarfraedinga **5983**
1022-2294 Erziehung Heute **2854**
1022-2405 Burda **2252**
1022-2421 Brenthurst Archives†
1022-2456 N L P World†
1022-2464 Asian Journal of Nursing Studies **5952**
1022-2480 The Rock†
1022-2499 Rugby Review **8244**
1022-2502 The Dhaka University Journal of Science **7850**
1022-2529 Meditari **1296**
1022-2588 Vereinigung Oesterreichischer Bibliothekarinnen und Bibliothekare. Mitteilungen **5054**
1022-2596 Conciencia y Libertad
1022-2642 Mnemosyne **3551**
1022-2715 Nouvelle Bibliotheque Initiatique **4250**
1022-2782 Pacific Islands Nutrition **6668**
1022-2790 Nutrition en Oceanie *see* 1022-2782 **6668**
1022-2898 Zhongguo Caiwu Xuekan *changed to* Caiwu Jinrong Xuekan **1323**
1022-2901 Di San Bo **2589**
1022-291X C A D yu Zidonghua **3289**
1022-2928 Xing Dianzi Keji **3116**
1022-3045 Revista de la OIM sobre Migraciones en America Latina **7292**
1022-3053 Minimag **2202**
1022-3061 Hit Songs†
1022-3088 First Bite **6290**
1022-3096 Stag Sexual Forum **6300**
1022-310X African Panorama†
1022-3118 Journal of Engineering, Islamic Republic of Iran - Majallah-i Muhandisi, Jumhuri Islami Iran *changed to* 1728-144X **3201**
1022-3134 Guzarish-i Film
1022-3185 Litterae Zoologicae **954**
1022-3282 International Newsletter on Rock Art **398**
1022-3320 Tots: Quaderns d'Educacio Ambiental†
1022-3347 Australian Beacon **7624**
1022-3487 Bilanz **1442**
1022-3495 Schweizerische Akademie der Naturwissenschaften. Denkschriften **7907**
1022-355X In Print†
1022-3568 Kompass South Africa **2012**
1022-3770 Katzenauge **8260**
1022-3819 Kickoff **8236**
1022-3827 Myth & Symbol **3620**
1022-386X College of Physicians and Surgeons Pakistan. Journal **5599**
1022-3878 I J O Newsletter† **8963**
1022-3908 International Civil Defence Journal **2226**
1022-4025 European Qualifying Examination **6749**
1022-4076 *see* 0020-8442 **8622**
1022-422X Asian Law Journal†
1022-4238 The Employment Report **1680**
1022-4289 Pacific P O P I N Directory **7289**
1022-4408 L'Express **3907**
1022-4432 INFORUM **8047**
1022-4440 *see* 1022-4432 **8047**
1022-4483 Humanities and Social Sciences. Latvia **7970**
1022-4556 International Journal of Hindu Studies **7707**
1022-4564 S P C Tuna Fishery Yearbook **3606**
1022-4572 Southern African Journal of Mathematics and Science Education **5537**
1022-4599 Pool News' Good News†
1022-4610 Ord og Tunga **5158**
1022-4629 Uppeldi og Menntun **2923**
1022-4653 Chinese Journal of Electronics **3090**
1022-4734 Journal of Statistical Studies **8383**
1022-4742 Mymensingh Medical Journal **5681**
1022-4890 South African Garden Guide **3750**
1022-4920 Gedvernd **6142**
1022-4955 Hjartavernd **5789**
1022-5021 Mulathing **4246**
1022-5102 R S I Bladid **4601**
1022-5110 Uppeldi **2923**
1022-5129 Revista de Gastroenterologia del Peru **5930**
1022-5234 Farvahar
1022-5277 Positive Outlook
1022-5293 Young Custos†
1022-534X Europolis - N U R E C Working Papers **4410**
1022-5358 The P R C Employment Manual†
1022-5366 Terminating Employment†
1022-5390 Theologika **7689**
1022-5404 International Desalination and Water Reuse Quarterly **8826**
1022-5412 I O D A Journal
1022-5439 Tropical Forest Update **3705**
1022-5455 Mining Mirror **6473**
1022-5528 Topics in Catalysis **2082**
1022-5536 Journal of Orthopaedic Surgery **6065**
1022-5560 B J. Building Journal **978**
1022-5579 Construction and Contract News **994**

1022-5617 Schweizerische Aktuarvereinigung. Mitteilungen **4522**
1022-5625 Institut fuer Schweizerisches Arbeitsrecht. Mitteilungen **1688**
1022-5633 Reflections†
1022-5692 Africa 2000 **464**
1022-5706 Asian Geographer **3999**
1022-5897 Quepo **814**
1022-5919 Excelsa Taxonomic Series **787**
1022-6109 Sword Newsletter
1022-6117 Science Education International **7909**
1022-6230 Journal of Sunology **553**
1022-629X International Cotton Advisory Committee. Proceedings **8453**
1022-6303 I C A C Recorder **8452**
1022-6435 Pai Shing Semi-Monthly
1022-6451 Faslname-yi Ketab **5009**
1022-646X Majallah-i Danishkadah-i Dampizishki **8802**
1022-6478 S A Cricketer **8244**
1022-6486 Acta Patristica et Byzantina **5090**
1022-6508 Revista Iberoamericana de Educacion **2907**
1022-6559 C O R D I S Focus **8417**
1022-6583 World Trade and Arbitration Materials **1588**
1022-6605 Estadistica Panamena. Situacion Demografica. Seccion 231. Movimiento Internacional de Pasajeros **7306**
1022-663X Agrarforschung **80**
1022-6680 Advanced Materials Research **3335**
1022-6699 Sport *changed to* 1422-0644 **6232**
1022-677X Needlework's Embroidery†
1022-6788 Needlework's Needlepoint†
1022-6834 Revista Guatemalteca de Cirugia **6257**
1022-6877 European Addiction Research **2694**
1022-6915 U I T P Biblio-Express†
1022-694X Lifgeislar
1022-6958 Skak **8201**
1022-6966 Tydskrif vir Nederlands en Afrikaans **5189**
1022-6982 ADvantage **19**
1022-7040 Nuclear Waste Bulletin
1022-7091 Annals of Software Engineering†
1022-7113 Schweizer Eisenbahn Revue **8624**
1022-7202 Gardoon
1022-7288 Decisiones seu Sententiae **4655**
1022-7334 Journal pour le Transport International *see* 0020-9341 **8500**
1022-7334 Journal pour le Transport International *see* 1420-5688 **8500**
1022-744X Jahrbuch der Grillparzer-Gesellschaft **5312**
1022-7466 Bangladesh Journal of Psychology **7338**
1022-7687 Bibliotheque Nationale Suisse. Rapport Annuel (Bern, 1988) *changed to* 1660-1254 **5046**
1022-7695 Schweizerische Landesbibliothek. Jahresbericht (Bern, 1988) *changed to* 1660-1254 **5046**
1022-7709 O R L Highlights *changed to* O R L - Praxis **6083**
1022-7741 Islenskur Idnadur **4596**
1022-7768 Nashriyyah-i Shimi va-Muhandisi-i Shimi-i Iran *see* 1021-9986 **2066**
1022-7784 World Executive's Digest - China Edition **1801**
1022-7792 Rahnama-yi Siminarha-yi Iran **7901**
1022-7806 Chikidah-i Tazahha-yi Tahqiq dar Danishgahha va Marakiz-i Tahqiqati Iran **7845**
1022-7814 Chikidah-i Payan'namahha-yi Iran **2931**
1022-7822 Ettela' Resani **7853**
1022-7849 Futures Bulletin **7965**
1022-7873 Paginas **5232**
1022-789X Signos **7681**
1022-7954 Russian Journal of Genetics **878**
1022-7970 America Latina Noticias Dentales **5834**
1022-8047 Sozialversicherungsrecht - Rechtsprechung **4786**
1022-8055 Heilsa & Sport†
1022-8071 What's on
1022-811X Between the Chains **4173**
1022-8144 Psychological Studies in Africa†
1022-8152 The Shopsteward **4602**
1022-8160 Africa South & East **3947**
1022-8179 Bua†
1022-8187 Foundry & Heat Treatment S A **6342**
1022-8195 Language Matters **5141**
1022-8209 Wood Southern Africa & Timber Times **3707**
1022-8217 Fourrier Suisse
1022-8314 Intelligence **1492**
1022-8349 South African Labour Library **1708**
1022-8381 Recopilacion de la Jurisprudencia del Tribunal de Justicia y del Tribunal de Primera Instancia *see* 1605-7767 **4938**
1022-8381 Recopilacion de la Jurisprudencia del Tribunal de Justicia y del Tribunal de Primera Instancia *see* 1023-4314 **4938**
1022-8381 Recopilacion de la Jurisprudencia del Tribunal de Justicia y del Tribunal de Primera Instancia *see* 1022-842X **4922**
1022-8381 Recopilacion de la Jurisprudencia del Tribunal de Justicia y del Tribunal de Primera Instancia *see* 1605-7775 **4938**
1022-8381 Recopilacion de la Jurisprudencia del Tribunal de Justicia y del Tribunal de Primera Instancia *see* 1023-4322 **4938**
1022-839X Samling af Afgoerelser fra Domstolen og Retten i Foerste Instans *see* 1023-4322 **4938**
1022-839X Samling af Afgoerelser fra Domstolen og Retten i Foerste Instans *see* 1605-7775 **4938**
1022-839X Samling af Afgoerelser fra Domstolen og Retten i Foerste Instans *see* 1023-4314 **4938**
1022-839X Samling af Afgoerelser fra Domstolen og Retten i Foerste Instans *see* 1605-7767 **4938**
1022-839X Samling af Afgoerelser fra Domstolen og Retten i Foerste Instans *see* 1022-842X **4922**
1022-8403 Sammlung der Rechtsprechung des Gerichtshofes und des Gerichts Erster Instanz *see* 1023-4314 **4938**
1022-8403 Sammlung der Rechtsprechung des Gerichtshofes und des Gerichts Erster Instanz *see* 1022-842X **4922**
1022-8403 Sammlung der Rechtsprechung des Gerichtshofes und des Gerichts Erster Instanz *see* 1605-7767 **4938**
1022-8403 Sammlung der Rechtsprechung des Gerichtshofes und des Gerichts Erster Instanz *see* 1023-4322 **4938**
1022-8403 Sammlung der Rechtsprechung des Gerichtshofes und des Gerichts Erster Instanz *see* 1605-7775 **4938**
1022-8411 Sulloge tes Nomologias tou Dikasteriou Kai Tou Protodikeiou *see* 1023-4322 **4938**
1022-8411 Sulloge tes Nomologias tou Dikasteriou Kai Tou Protodikeiou *see* 1605-7775 **4938**
1022-8411 Sulloge tes Nomologias tou Dikasteriou Kai Tou Protodikeiou *see* 1023-4314 **4938**
1022-8411 Sulloge tes Nomologias tou Dikasteriou Kai Tou Protodikeiou *see* 1022-842X **4922**
1022-8411 Sulloge tes Nomologias tou Dikasteriou Kai Tou Protodikeiou *see* 1605-7767 **4938**
1022-842X Court of Justice and the Court of First Instance. Reports of Cases before the Court **4922**
1022-8446 Jurisprudentie van Het Hof van Justitie en van Het Gerecht van Eerste Aanleg *see* 1605-7767 **4938**
1022-8446 Jurisprudentie van Het Hof van Justitie en van Het Gerecht van Eerste Aanleg *see* 1023-4314 **4938**
1022-8446 Jurisprudentie van Het Hof van Justitie en van Het Gerecht van Eerste Aanleg *see* 1022-842X **4922**
1022-8446 Jurisprudentie van Het Hof van Justitie en van Het Gerecht van Eerste Aanleg *see* 1605-7775 **4938**
1022-8446 Jurisprudentie van Het Hof van Justitie en van Het Gerecht van Eerste Aanleg *see* 1023-4322 **4938**
1022-8454 Colectanea da Jurisprudencia do Tribunal de Justica e do Tribunal de Primeira Instancia *see* 1023-4322 **4938**
1022-8454 Colectanea da Jurisprudencia do Tribunal de Justica e do Tribunal de Primeira Instancia *see* 1605-7775 **4938**
1022-8454 Colectanea da Jurisprudencia do Tribunal de Justica e do Tribunal de Primeira Instancia *see* 1022-842X **4922**
1022-8454 Colectanea da Jurisprudencia do Tribunal de Justica e do Tribunal de Primeira Instancia *see* 1023-4314 **4938**
1022-8454 Colectanea da Jurisprudencia do Tribunal de Justica e do Tribunal de Primeira Instancia *see* 1605-7767 **4938**
1022-8527 Almanak fyrir Island **568**
1022-8632 Pistes et Recherches **2898**
1022-8659 Dolentium Hominum **7795**
1022-8667 I S M N Newsletter **6574**
1022-8675 Cultures and Faith **7636**
1022-8713 *see* 1023-425X **2323**
1022-873X Vibrations **6626**
1022-8748 *see* Office for Official Publications of the European Union. Newsletter **7256**
1022-8756 *see* Office for Official Publications of the European Union. Newsletter **7256**
1022-8764 *see* Office for Official Publications of the European Union. Newsletter **7256**
1022-8772 *see* Office for Official Publications of the European Union. Newsletter **7256**
1022-8829 Dai Doan Ket **7128**
1022-8896 Ecole et Vie **2844**
1022-9078 North Pacific Anadromous Fish Commission. Annual Report **3603**
1022-9124 Austria Innovativ **8416**
1022-9205 Biometeorology Bulletin **6347**
1022-9221 Garden to Kitchen Newsletter **6659**
1022-9272 African Journal of Health Sciences **5569**
1022-9353 Eldisfrettir
1022-9418 ecolex **4866**
1022-9426 J A P - Juristische Ausbildung und Praxis Vorbereitung **4698**
1022-9434 Recht der Medizin **4766**
1022-9442 Recht der Umwelt **4766**
1022-9450 Z E R - Zeitschrift fuer EuropaRecht *changed to* Zeitschrift fuer Europarecht, Internationales Privatrecht und Rechtsvergleichung **4818**
1022-9485 Medicina Legal de Costa Rica **4732**
1022-9493 Nationalpark-Forschung in der Schweiz **2620**
1022-9507 A V S **426**
1022-9515 South Africa Yearbook (Year) **4171**
1022-9582 Paediki Hara **2206**
1022-9671 Shiyou Jikan **6792**
1022-968X Kaifang Xitong yu Wanglu **2500**
1022-9698 0 yu 1 Byte Keji Zazhi **2494**
1022-9760 Journal of Polymer Research **7093**
1022-9825 Innovaciones Educativas **2942**
1022-9841 S C A T News **5045**
1022-985X U W I Students' Law Review **4800**
1022-9868 I F L A Section on Regional Activities: Latin America and the Caribbean. Newsletter **5014**
1022-9892 Emirates Journal for Engineering Research **3188**
1022-9906 I F L A Section on Statistics. Newsletter **5014**
1023-0068 Infomusa (French Edition) **236**
1023-0076 Infomusa (English Edition) **236**
1023-0114 Forum Logiciel **2590**
1023-0157 Abhath al-Yarmuk **5248**
1023-0203 Garment Technologies and Accessories News†
1023-0211 Gongye Qicai Zhongguoban†
1023-022X Electronics Production Equipment News†
1023-0246 Sujiao Keji†
1023-0254 Gongye Qicai **5452**
1023-0270 Kayhan Karikatur **5222**
1023-0289 Kayhan Farhangi **5222**
1023-0432 Himayat al-Milkiyyat al-Fikriyyat
1023-0440 Journal of Comparative Religion
1023-0459 Journal of Comparative Sociology and Ethics
1023-0467 Journal of International Human Resource Management
1023-0475 Journal of International Marketing Management
1023-0513 Monthly Review†
1023-0548 Psycho-analytic Psychotherapy in South Africa **7394**
1023-0564 Acta Structilia **427**
1023-0572 Execubrief (English Edition) **1108**
1023-0629 Congreso Judio Latinoamericano. Boletin Informativo O J I **3528**
1023-0645 Global Ocean Ecosystem Dynamics Special Contribution **3434**
1023-0785 Hustler Busty Beauties†
1023-0793 Family Life **3948**
1023-0807 Religion and Theology **7674**
1023-0815 Kayhan-i Hava'i **3891**
1023-0823 T R Transfer **8440**
1023-0890 Istmica **4458**
1023-0904 Journal fuer Menopause *changed to* 1997-6690 **5994**
1023-098X Research in Official Statistics†
1023-1072 Pakistan Journal of Agriculture, Agricultural Engineering and Veterinary Sciences **145**
1023-1218 E C Fisheries Cooperation Bulletin **3590**
1023-134X Universite de Lausanne. Institut de Linguistique et des Sciences du Langage. Bulletin **5191**
1023-1668 Agrarnaya Nauka **81**
1023-1706 *see* 1023-9340 **8938**
1023-1730 Alerte au S I D A Oceanie *see* 1018-2152 **5824**
1023-1757 Alternation **5251**
1023-1765 South African Journal of Environmental Law and Policy **3467**
1023-1781 South African Country Life **3949**
1023-1803 Fashion Ensemble
1023-182X Kayhan-e Bacheha **2196**
1023-1838 Iran Commerce **1405**
1023-1897 Oesterreichische Bibliographie. Reihe B: Verzeichnis der Oesterreichischen Hochschulschriften **7578**
1023-1900 Oesterreichische Bibliographie. Reihe C: Neuere Auslaendische Austriaca **7578**
1023-1935 Russian Journal of Electrochemistry **2114**
1023-1943 Frauensolidaritaet **8897**
1023-2001 International Journal of Rural Studies **8109**
1023-2028 Beitraege zur Infusionstherapie und Transfusionsmedizin†
1023-2044 Bulletin Suisse de Linguistique Appliquee **5102**
1023-2079 Kayhan Elmi **7875**
1023-2109 Taiwan Jingqi Zhibiao **1181**
1023-2141 Zhonghua Gonggong Weisheng Zazhi/Chinese Journal of Public Health *changed to* Taiwan Gonggong Weisheng Zazhi **7543**
1023-2249 Xin Shixue **4190**
1023-2427 Physics of the Alive **7033**
1023-2443 Reference Information Review Southern Africa
1023-2451 Home Owner Building & Improvements Buyers Guide **1012**
1023-2516 That **3950**
1023-2575 South East European Monitor **4266**
1023-2621 Euro Bulletin†
1023-263X Maastricht Journal of European and Comparative Law **4726**
1023-2680 Societe Suisse de Chronometrie. Actes de la Journee d'Etude **4569**
1023-2699 Societe Suisse de Chronometrie. Actes du Congres de Chronometrie **4569**
1023-2796 Journal of Marine Science and Technology **2809**
1023-294X E X S **669**
1023-2958 Obst- und Weinbau **608**
1023-2982 Short-Term Economic Indicators. Transition Economies†
1023-2990 Bulletin d'Information Penologique *see* 1028-625X **2663**
1023-3008 I & T Magazine News Review†
1023-3016 Bulletin de Jurisprudence Constitutionnelle **4846**
1023-3040 Commission of the European Communities. Erasmus and Lingua Action II. Directory **2973**
1023-3091 Vysokomolekulyarnye Soedineniya. Seriya A i Seriya B **2142**
1023-3121 African Plant Protection **774**
1023-3261 *see* 1023-327X **6402**
1023-327X I S O Catalogue (English Edition) **6402**
1023-330X Estadistica Panamena. Indicadores Sociales. Seccion 012 **8082**
1023-3318 Estadistica Panamena. Indicadores Economicos. Seccion 011 **1226**
1023-3377 T R - Wissen **8440**
1023-3385 Guyana Library Association. Bulletin **5011**
1023-3474 Review of Human Factor Studies **353**
1023-361X Banco Central de Bolivia. Memoria **1212**
1023-3679 Kenya Birds **909**
1023-3687 Kayhan Andisheh **6930**
1023-3741 Mongolian Journal of International Affairs **7253**
1023-3768 Essentials **3948**
1023-3776 Business Travel & Executive Leisure Magazine†
1023-3792 Nasionale Kultuurhistoriese Museum. Nuus†
1023-3806 Labour Law Reports **1694**
1023-3814 Constitutional Law Reports **4847**
1023-3830 Inflammation Research **6848**
1023-3857 Journal of Euromed Pharmacy **6853**
1023-3873 N E D University Journal of Research **3211**
1023-3881 Indologica Taurinensia **551**
1023-3903 Bangladesh Journal of Dermatology, Venereology and Leprology **5872**
1023-3938 Agrarwirtschaft und Agrarsoziologie **191**
1023-4039 Interchange†
1023-4047 Topics in Obstetrics and Gynaecology
1023-4055 International Council on Metals and the Environment. Newsletter *changed to* International Council on Mining and Metals. Newsletter **6316**
1023-4063 C C A M L R Science **2801**
1023-4128 Company Secretary **1734**
1023-4160 Recopilacion de Jurisprudencia. Funcion Publica *see* 1023-4209 **4669**
1023-4179 Sammlung der Rechtsprechung. Offentlicher Dienst *see* 1023-4209 **4669**
1023-4187 Samling af Afgorelser. Personalesager *see* 1023-4209 **4669**
1023-4195 Sulloge Nomologias. Upallelikes Upothedeis *see* 1023-4209 **4669**
1023-4209 European Court Reports. Reports of European Community Staff Cases **4669**
1023-4217 Recueil de Jurisprudence. Fonction Publique *see* 1023-4209 **4669**
1023-4225 Raccolta della Giurisprudenza. Pubblico Impiego *see* 1023-4209 **4669**
1023-4233 Jurisprudentie. Ambtenarenrecht *see* 1023-4209 **4669**
1023-4241 Colectanea de Jurisprudencia. Funcao Publica *see* 1023-4209 **4669**
1023-425X I & T Magazine **2323**
1023-4268 *see* 1023-425X **2323**
1023-4276 *see* 1023-425X **2323**

ISSN

Link to your serials resources and content with ulrichsweb.com

9460 1026-2296 ULRICH'S PERIODICALS

1026-2296 Russian Journal of Herpetology **962**
1026-2350 Le Courrier: Afrique - Caraibes - Pacifique - Union Europeenne *see* Magazine of A C P - E U Development Co-operation **1601**
1026-2628 The World Competitiveness Yearbook **1525**
1026-2636 Hong Kong Mathematical Society. Bulletin†
1026-2652 Asian Journal of English Language Teaching **5096**
1026-2679 Lecturas Contemporaneas **7150**
1026-2865 African Primates **2601**
1026-2881 Pachyderm **959**
1026-2911 Biocontrol **882**
1026-2938 Chernobyl Digest **7512**
1026-2946 Africa Journal of Evangelical Theology **7744**
1026-2954 Geological Survey of Namibia. Communications **2740**
1026-3012 Europe. Documents **7233**
1026-3047 Akademiai Ilmhoi Cumhurii Tocikiston. Su'bai Ilmhoi Haetsinosi. Ahbori **652**
1026-3063 TanzAffiche†
1026-3098 Scientia Iranica **7912**
1026-3241 Russian Journal of Experimental and Clinical Pharmacology†
1026-325X Jiemian Kexue Huizhi **3248**
1026-3292 Turkmenistan Ylymlar Akademiasynyn Habarlary. Biologik Ylymlaryn Seriasy **708**
1026-3306 Akademiai Ilmhoi Cumhurii Tocikiston. Silsilai Falsafa va Hukuksinosi. Ahbori **6902**
1026-3454 The International Journal of Architectural Management Practice & Research† **8966**
1026-3470 Rossiiskaya Akademiya Nauk. Izvestiya. Seriya Biologicheskaya **701**
1026-3489 Rossiiskaya Akademiya Nauk. Izvestiya. Seriya Fizicheskaya **7038**
1026-3500 Rossiiskaya Akademiya Nauk. Izvestiya. Seriya Khimicheskaya **2079**
1026-3519 Rossiiskaya Akademiya Nauk. Izvestiya. Mekhanika Tverdogo Tela **3395**
1026-3527 Rossiiskaya Akademiya Nauk. Izvestiya. Fizika Zemli **2789**
1026-3543 Morfologiya **690**
1026-3551 Maskan **1022**
1026-356X Sankt-Peterburgskii Universitet. Vestnik. Seriya 5. Ekonomika **1170**
1026-3632 Braueria
1026-3713 Dirasat. Educational Sciences **2932**
1026-3721 Dirasat. Human and Social Sciences **4449**
1026-373X Dirasat. Administrative Sciences *changed to* 1815-8633 **1774**
1026-3748 Dirasat. Sha'ria and Law Sciences **4658**
1026-3764 Dirasat. Agricultural Sciences **105**
1026-3772 Dirasat. Medical and Biological Sciences **5605**
1026-3802 Taiwan Agricultural Research Institute. Special Publication **160**
1026-3810 Academia Sinica. Institute of Zoology. Monograph Series†
1026-3829 Biological Bulletin **658**
1026-3861 Walia **3474**
1026-3950 Social Development Review **8069**
1026-4345 Speak Out! (Canterbury) **5176**
1026-4442 Taiwan Diqu Daomi Shengchanliang Diaocha Baogao *changed to* Quanguo Daomi Shengchanliang Diaocha Baogao **249**
1026-4469 Taiwan Linye Kexue **3704**
1026-4493 Soochow Journal of Social Work **8072**
1026-4825 Quality Life **4054**
1026-4892 Organohalogen Compounds
1026-4906 Oesterreichische Gesellschaft fuer Tropenmedizin und Parasitologie. Mitteilungen **5823**
1026-4914 Rostrum **858**
1026-4922 Landesmuseum Joanneum. Abteilung fuer Zoologie. Beiblaetter zu den Mitteilungen **953**
1026-4949 Biosystematics and Ecology **662**
1026-5007 Applied Entomology and Phytopathology **839**
1026-5023 Phelsuma **697**
1026-5120 Journal of Modern Literature in Chinese **5315**
1026-5139 University of Tehran. Journal of Science (International Edition) *changed to* 1607-4033 **7868**
1026-5260 Peace Brigades International. Newsletter *changed to* 1719-7155 **8063**
1026-5279 Guojia Tushuguan Guankan **5011**
1026-5414 *see* 0021-8464 **7019**
1026-5430 *see* 0731-5171 **3308**
1026-5449 *see* 0275-7540 **2056**
1026-5511 *see* 1065-5131 **3385**
1026-552X East and Central African Journal of Pharmaceutical Sciences **6837**
1026-5538 Medical Student International **5672**
1026-5619 Fauna Rossii i Sopredel'nykh Stran **943**
1026-5651 South African Yearbook of International Affairs **7266**
1026-6062 TeVeo **8885**
1026-6151 Natura 2000†
1026-6186 Information Society News **2545**
1026-6267 Bundesanstalt fuer Alpenlaendische Landwirtschaft. Bericht **98**
1026-6275 B A L Veroeffentlichungen **94**
1026-6380 Russian Conservation News **1169**
1026-6402 Visual Arts & Culture†
1026-6461 Asian Oil and Gas **6763**
1026-6496 Hayastany Guitoutyunnery Azgayin Academia Zekuyts'ner **7860**
1026-6542 Iranian Economic Review†
1026-6550 The S A I M A S **1792**
1026-6593 Labour Law Digest **1694**
1026-6690 Bangladesh Journal of Fisheries Research **3587**
1026-6704 Hong Kong Design Services†
1026-6712 Hong Kong Electronic Components and Parts **3101**
1026-6720 Hong Kong Packaging **6710**
1026-678X South Asian Studies **4188**
1026-6836 Pizhuhish'ha-yi Jughrafiyayi **4024**
1026-6887 Forest Participation Series **3689**
1026-7018 Playboy (Guoji Zhongwenban) **6298**
1026-7077 *see* 1024-123X **3209**
1026-7085 *see* 0020-7454 **6147**
1026-7107 *see* 1023-666X **3247**
1026-7115 *see* 1023-621X **5453**
1026-7158 *see* 1061-186X **6853**
1026-7166 Contemporary Theatre Review **8468**
1026-7182 Iranian Government Reports **7200**
1026-7190 The Abstract of Scientific and Technical Papers **7936**
1026-7204 Kazar Information†
1026-7212 Dissertation Abstracts of Iranian Graduates Abroad **2932**
1026-7360 *see* 0003-6811 **5471**
1026-7379 *see* 0098-6445 **3238**
1026-7417 *see* 1061-8562 **7059**
1026-7425 *see* 0020-7160 **5552**
1026-7433 *see* 0300-8207 **831**
1026-7441 *see* 0095-8972 **2068**
1026-745X *see* 0305-215X **3190**
1026-7468 *see* 0306-7319 **2101**
1026-7476 The International Journal of Environmental Studies. Section B, Environmental Science and Technology *see* 0020-7233 **3442**
1026-7484 *see* 0015-0193 **7012**
1026-7492 *see* 0308-1079 **2522**
1026-7506 *see* 0309-1929 **2781**
1026-7530 *see* 1058-4587 **3319**
1026-7573 *see* 0308-1087 **5509**
1026-7603 *see* 1061-026X **3448**
1026-7654 *see* 1048-5252 **8383**
1026-7662 *see* 0233-1934 **5523**
1026-7670 *see* 1055-6788 **5555**
1026-7689 *see* 1744-5760 **2507**
1026-7700 *see* 0141-1594 **7030**
1026-7719 *see* 1042-6507 **2117**
1026-7727 *see* 0031-9104 **7062**
1026-7735 *see* 1051-9998 **7035**
1026-7743 *see* 1040-6638 **2129**
1026-7751 *see* 0091-4037 **3247**
1026-776X *see* 1062-936X **3464**
1026-7778 *see* 0094-9655 **2443**
1026-7786 *see* 0233-1888 **8405**
1026-7794 *see* 1744-2508 **5538**
1026-7816 *see* 1061-0278 **2081**
1026-7832 *see* 0277-2248 **3502**
1026-7840 *see* 0308-1060 **8516**
1026-7867 *see* 0892-7014 **3494**
1026-7883 *see* 1543-5180 **664**
1026-7883 *see* 1541-9061 **664**
1026-7913 *see* 1940-1736 **738**
1026-793X *see* 1062-3329 **671**
1026-7964 *see* 0897-7194 **922**
1026-7980 *see* 0891-2963 **6725**
1026-8022 *see* 1042-8194 **5940**
1026-8049 *see* 1478-6419 **2074**
1026-8162 *see* 1023-6171 **879**
1026-8316 *see* 1022-6559 **8417**
1026-8324 *see* 1022-6559 **8417**
1026-8413 Architektur & Bau Forum **431**
1026-8421 Arzt und Praxis **5578**
1026-8472 International Navigation Association. Proceedings of Annual Meeting†
1026-8634 Zashchita i Karantin Rastenii **260**
1026-8731 Jaarlikse Ekonomiese Verslag - Suid-Afrikaanse Reserwebank *see* 0081-2528 **1518**
1026-8766 Listados Faunisticos de Mexico **954**
1026-8774 Revista Mexicana de Ciencias Geologicas **2764**
1026-8960 Ahwaz University of Medical Sciences. Scientific Medical Journal **5570**
1026-9029 P A Communications
1026-9126 Sister Namibia **8884**
1026-9134 Statistics of Road Traffic Accidents in Europe and North America **8530**
1026-9150 Eurostat E U External Trade Indices†
1026-9169 Studia et Documenta Historiae et Iuris **4163**
1026-9185 South African Journal of Chemical Engineering **3255**
1026-9339 V E O Journal **3333**
1026-9347 Wittgenstein Gesellschaft. Schriftenreihe *changed to* Austrian Ludwig Wittgenstein Society. Publications **6906**
1026-9428 Meditsina Truda i Promyshlennaya Ekologiya **6681**
1026-9444 Spros **2641**
1026-9452 Gosudarstvo i Pravo **4682**
1026-9487 Polis **7167**
1026-9525 Productos de Taiwan†
1026-9541 Akademiai Ilmhoi Cumhurii Tocikiston. Dokladhoi **7833**
1026-9576 Al-Majallat al-Arabiyyat lil-Uloom al-Insaniyyat **4464**
1026-969X Zhonghua Foxue Yanjiu **7703**
1026-9819 H F S P Workshop **5622**
1026-9878 Yadernyi Kontrol' *changed to* 1992-9242 **7241**
1027-0183 What Cellphone and Mobile Communications Magazine
1027-0256 Medical Biochemistry†
1027-0272 Venue†
1027-0353 African Journal of Political Science **7103**
1027-037X Pacific Journal of Theology **7668**
1027-0469 P C Format **2579**
1027-0582 I F A W P C A Information Services **1013**
1027-0590 I F A W P C A Newsletter **1013**
1027-0728 Oceanic Fisheries Programme Technical Report **3604**
1027-0868 L A N **2500**
1027-0965 World Conservation **2633**
1027-0973 Planete Conservation *see* 1027-0965 **2633**
1027-099X Conservacion Mundial *see* 1027-0965 **2633**
1027-1015 Journal of Structural Learning and Intelligent Systems *changed to* 1540-0182 **7411**
1027-1066 Open Magazine **3875**
1027-1163 Soochow Journal of Chinese Studies **560**
1027-1279 International Ombudsman Journal *changed to* 1387-1846 **4696**
1027-1368 China Enterprise
1027-1503 China Archaeology and Art Digest **387**
1027-152X Revista Chapingo. Serie Horticultura **3749**
1027-1546 Rapport General sur l'Activite de l'Union Europeenne *see* 1608-7321 **3837**
1027-1724 South Africa Survey **1177**
1027-1767 Matematicheskaya Fizika, Analiz, Geometriya *changed to* 1812-9471 **5548**
1027-1775 Eastern Africa Social Science Research Review **7960**
1027-1988 Universite du Benin. Journal de la Recherche Scientifique *changed to* Universite de Lome. Journal de la Recherche Scientifique **7926**
1027-202X South African Journal of Radiology **6208**
1027-2135 Revista Electronica Video **4472**
1027-2143 Education International Quarterly Magazine **2848**
1027-2151 Internacional de la Educacion *see* 1027-2143 **2848**
1027-216X Internationale de l'Education *see* 1027-2143 **2848**
1027-2194 E I Monthly Monitor **2843**
1027-2348 *see* 0049-0253 **2212**
1027-2569 Hypoxia Medical Journal **5906**
1027-2658 Parallel and Distributed Computing and Systems **2434**
1027-2666 I A S T E D International Conference. Applied Informatics. Proceedings **2420**
1027-2674 Enfermedades del Torax **6213**
1027-2798 (Year) Priorities and Progress under the Great Lakes Water Quality Agreement **8831**
1027-2852 *see* 0864-4551 **761**
1027-2860 Advances in Modern Biotechnology **755**
1027-2992 Cat News **2606**
1027-300X Mongolyn Anagaakh Ukhaan **5680**
1027-3077 Electronic Business Asia†
1027-3085 International Symposium on Capillary Chromatography and Electrophoresis. Proceedings†
1027-3093 Annual Bulletin of Transport Statistics for Europe and North America **8521**
1027-3107 Review of Fisheries in O E C D Countries *changed to* Review of Fisheries in O E C D Countries: : Policies and Summary Statistics **3605**
1027-3182 Berezil' **5208**
1027-3204 Ukrains'kyi Radiolohichnyi Zhurnal **6209**
1027-3212 Funktsional'nye Materialy **2110**
1027-3239 Akademiya Nauk Ukrainy. Visnyk **7834**
1027-3247 Ekotekhnologii i Resursosberezhenie **3243**
1027-3255 Budivnytstvo Ukrainy **984**
1027-3271 China Law for Business **4642**
1027-331X Sakartvelos Metsnierebata Akademia. Matsne. Istoriis Etnografiisa da Xelovnebis Istoriis Seria†
1027-3344 Eurostat Pesca. Estadisticas Anuales†
1027-3352 Schweiss- und Prueftechnik **6343**
1027-3360 Studien zum Neuen Testament und Seiner Umwelt. Serie A **7684**
1027-3379 Salzburg Studies in English Literature: Poetic Drama & Poetic Theory *changed to* Mellen Studies in Literature: Poetic Drama and Poetic Theory **5332**
1027-3417 Stellenbosch Papers in Linguistics **5178**
1027-3433 Uzbekskii Matematicheskii Zhurnal **7045**
1027-3441 Subsidia Biblica **7686**
1027-3468 Digest of South African Architecture **440**
1027-3476 South African Golfers Yearbook **8246**
1027-3514 InfoTax
1027-3603 Rossiiskaya Akademiya Nauk. Sibirskoe Otdelenie. Ob'edinennyi Institut Geologii, Geofiziki, i Mineralogii. Trudy **2765**
1027-3670 Mythosphere†
1027-3719 International Journal of Tuberculosis and Lung Disease **6215**
1027-376X International Journal of Computational Linguistics and Chinese Language Processing **5202**
1027-3948 Hong Kong Practitioner **5629**
1027-3956 Revista Mexicana de Ciencias Farmaceuticas **6879**
1027-3964 Itogi **3936**
1027-3999 Taiwan Communique **7216**
1027-4065 Rossiiskii Vestnik Perinatologii i Pediatrii **6003**
1027-4189 BeautyWorx **585**
1027-4251 Legal Forum **4720**
1027-4278 Urban Morphology **4430**
1027-4324 Management Today **1777**
1027-4332 African Sociological Review **8086**
1027-4359 Soznanie i Fizicheskaya Real'nost' **8007**
1027-4375 Mediterranean Journal of Human Rights **7212**
1027-4448 Ritmennt **5044**
1027-4472 Orbita Cientifica **5523**
1027-4502 Medicinal and Aromatic Plants **312**
1027-4510 Surface Investigation: X-Ray, Synchrotron and Neutron Techniques **3396**
1027-4529 I C C O P S Newsletter **2806**
1027-4561 Nuevo Diario **3821**
1027-4588 La Prensa **3920**
1027-4618 Journal of Law and Society **4702**
1027-4634 Matematychni Studii **5511**
1027-4642 Journal of Physical Studies **7021**
1027-4820 Association Scientifique Europeenne pour l'Eau et la Sante. Cahiers **2792**
1027-4863 Office International de la Vigne et du Vin. La Lettre Vin, Nutrition et Sante (French Edition)
1027-488X European Mathematical Society. Newsletter **5487**
1027-4928 Journal of Science and Technology **7873**
1027-4960 Malta. Central Office of Statistics. Industry Statistics **1251**
1027-5193 European Integration Online Papers **7233**
1027-5207 European Journal of Open and Distance Learning *changed to* European Journal of Open, Distance and E-Learning **3061**
1027-5487 Taiwanese Journal of Mathematics **5540**
1027-5495 Functional Materials **2110**
1027-5525 Nezavisimaya Moldova **3913**
1027-555X Sakartvelos Metsnierebata Akademia. Matsne. Biologiis Seria **702**
1027-5592 Asia - Pacific Journal of Taxation **1910**
1027-5606 Hydrology and Earth System Sciences **2795**
1027-5622 I A R C Handbooks of Cancer Prevention **6021**
1027-5649 Mitteilungen aus dem Brenner-Archiv **4465**
1027-5673 Slovo i Chas **5374**
1027-5703 Integration and Trade *see* 1026-0463 **1598**
1027-5797 Extra **109**
1027-5851 International Journal of Acoustics and Vibration **3381**
1027-5991 Blimp **6490**
1027-6289 Financial Gazette **3996**

1027-6319 Hong Kong Construction & Architecture†
1027-6327 Hong Kong Printing†
1027-6335 Hong Kong Financial Services **1351**
1027-6424 European Union. Bulletin. Supplement **1485**
1027-6432 Aussnhandel. Warenverzeichnis **1552**
1027-6505 Diario Oficial de las Communidades Europeas. S: Licitaciones y Contratos Publicos **4923**
1027-6521 Bio-Math **5476**
1027-6580 New Horizons in Therapeutics: Smith, Kline & French Laboratories Research Symposia Series **5685**
1027-6599 Neuroscience News†
1027-6661 Angiologiya i Sosudistaya Khirurgiya **6236**
1027-6726 C R E Doc†
1027-6750 Agenda Internacional **7220**
1027-6769 Pensamiento Constitucional **7164**
1027-6793 South African Mango Growers' Association Yearbook *changed to* 1814-2575 **242**
1027-6874 Men's Health (South Africa Edition) **6284**
1027-7218 Zdravookhranenie **7546**
1027-7269 Arbeits- und Sozialrechtskartei **7948**
1027-7323 The Hong Kong Journal of Sports Medicine and Sports Science *changed to* 1728-869X **6230**
1027-7331 Contacto **3906**
1027-7358 C O N C A W E Review **3408**
1027-7412 Choices (London) **7279**
1027-7420 I T U Global Directory **2325**
1027-748X European Coffee Report **3635**
1027-7595 Danishkahad-i Pizishki-i Isfahan. Majallah **667**
1027-7617 I O M News *changed to* 1813-2839 **7287**
1027-7773 Education 2000 **2846**
1027-779X Oncology Forum **6030**
1027-7811 Hong Kong College of Cardiology. Journal **5789**
1027-7862 Zambia Law Journal **4818**
1027-7978 Fanyi Xuebao **5118**
1027-8001 Direct Access to Key People in Southern Africa†
1027-801X Health Counter News
1027-8087 Translatio **5188**
1027-8117 Zhonghua Pifuke Yixue Zazhi **5883**
1027-8168 Ius et Praxis **4697**
1027-8265 Mezhdunarodnyi Zhurnal Meditsinskoi Praktiki†
1027-8303 Neue Argumente **3456**
1027-8311 Archaeologia Mosellana **375**
1027-832X Natturufraedistofnun Islands. Fjoelrit **7887**
1027-8346 Cars in Action **8573**
1027-8354 Bakkie and Recreational Vehicle *changed to* 1991-6450 **8669**
1027-8419 Selected Energy Statistics: South Africa†
1027-8508 My New English Fun Book **2204**
1027-8516 My New English Magazine **2204**
1027-8540 Caucasian Regional Studies **7114**
1027-8559 Translation Quarterly **5188**
1027-8591 Gold Bulletin **6338**
1027-8869 Monographs on Coleoptera **690**
1027-9075 Energiewende†
1027-9148 South African Journal of Anaesthesiology and Analgesia **5774**
1027-9237 Gendereview **8865**
1027-930X Infeuro **4928**
1027-9318 *see* 1027-930X **4928**
1027-9326 *see* 1027-930X **4928**
1027-9350 International Journal of Mathematical Algorithms†
1027-9369 Religion for Peace **7674**
1027-9377 Unfallstatistik *changed to* 1991-8089 **8219**
1027-961X Science Vision **7911**
1027-9644 Sport Klub **8204**
1027-9660 Temps Europeens†
1027-9725 H d A - Dokumente zur Architektur **444**
1027-975X Granma Ciencia **8423**
1027-9776 Journal of Educational Research **2876**
1028-0057 Biologicheskie Nauki **659**
1028-0227 North Pacific Anadromous Fish Commission. Newsletter **3603**
1028-0235 North Pacific Anadromous Fish Commission. Statistical Yearbook **3613**
1028-0332 Foliaca **790**
1028-0537 New Age Gaming Magazine **2478**
1028-0588 European Industrial Relations Observatory Observer†
1028-0685 Die Verwaltung der Stadt Wien *changed to* Die Leistungen der Stadt Wien **7451**
1028-0693 Becs Szamokbau *see* 1028-074X **1274**
1028-0707 Viden v Cislech *see* 1028-074X **1274**
1028-0715 Vienna in Cifre *see* 1028-074X **1274**
1028-0723 Vienna in Figures *see* 1028-074X **1274**
1028-0731 Vienne en Chiffres *see* 1028-074X **1274**
1028-074X Wien in Zahlen **1274**
1028-0790 I N A S P Newsletter **5014**
1028-0820 Namibia Holiday and Travel **8740**
1028-0839 Namibia Trade Directory **2018**
1028-0855 Boletin de Novedades Cientifico-Tecnicas **7841**
1028-088X Granma Internacional (German Edition) **7139**
1028-091X Tongxin KeJi Shangqing *see* Global Sources Telecom Products **2322**
1028-0960 Poverkhnost'. Rentgenovskie, Sinkhrotronnye i Nejtronnye Issledovaniya **7035**
1028-0979 Problemy Upravleniya i Informatiki **2463**
1028-0987 Mikrobiolohichnyi Zhurnal **892**
1028-110X Importers and Exporters in Taiwan, R.O.C. **1569**
1028-1126 Taiwan Trade Opportunities **1583**
1028-1215 Cape Business News **1080**
1028-1452 Cuba. Oficina Cubana de la Propiedad Industrial. Boletin Oficial **6748**
1028-1460 Xianggang Fangshe Jishi Zazhi **6210**
1028-1487 LernSprache Deutsch **5143**
1028-1495 Oesterreichische Namenforschung **5157**
1028-1509 Stimulus **5178**
1028-1584 Hong Kong Transportation and Communications†
1028-1592 Hong Kong Food†
1028-1606 Hong Kong for the Business Visitor†
1028-2092 Bangladesh Journal of Plant Taxonomy **778**
1028-2149 O B R A S **1027**
1028-2327 Journal fuer Hypertonie **5791**
1028-2351 Zambian Papers **4179**
1028-2580 Contemporary Justice Review **4650**
1028-2599 Combustion **7053**
1028-2637 Hong Kong Journal of Orthopaedic Surgery **6061**
1028-2831 Amemboa **652**
1028-284X Share Europe Spring Conference. Proceedings **2550**
1028-2920 Sowetan Soccer Guide **8246**
1028-2947 Wetlands International. Seaduck Specialist Group. Bulletin **917**
1028-3072 A A A. Archivos de Arquitectura Antillana **425**
1028-3153 Journal of Studies in International Education **3014**
1028-3242 Juta's Tax Law Report **1932**
1028-3307 Jobmail **6699**
1028-334X Doklady Earth Sciences **2705**
1028-3358 Doklady Physics **7010**
1028-3412 European Research on Cetaceans **3590**
1028-3420 Dugesiana **843**
1028-3455 Microscopy Society of Southern Africa. Proceedings **900**
1028-348X Eurostat International Transport by Air. Intra - and Extra - EU **8540**
1028-3498 *see* 1028-348X **8540**
1028-3552 International Technical Consultation on Veterinary Drug Registration. Proceedings†
1028-3633 E U I Papers in Political and Social Sciences **7131**
1028-365X International Association for Shell and Spatial Structures. Journal **3272**
1028-3668 European Association of Geoscientists and Engineers. Conference and Technical Exhibition **2733**
1028-3706 Nashriyyah-i Inirzhi-i Iran **3142**
1028-3781 South African Sugar Technologists' Association. Annual Congress *see* 0373-045X **254**
1028-3900 Dmitrovskii Vestnik **3935**
1028-4001 College of Surgeons Hong Kong. Annals *changed to* 1744-1625 **6260**
1028-415X Nutritional Neuroscience (Print)†
1028-432X *see* 1028-4354 **5602**
1028-4338 *see* 1028-4362 **5703**
1028-4346 *see* 1028-4370 **5826**
1028-4354 Cuba. Ministerio de Salud Publica. Unidad de Analisis y Tendencias en Salud. Reporte Semanal **5602**
1028-4362 Reporte Tecnico de Vigilancia **5703**
1028-4370 Situacion Epidemiologica Internacional **5826**
1028-4389 Silac **6258**
1028-4397 Panorama Economico Latinoamericano **1510**
1028-4427 Genii Ortopedii **6060**
1028-4435 Hong Kong Journal of Applied Linguistics **5125**
1028-4559 Taiwanese Journal of Obstetrics and Gynecology **6005**
1028-4583 Jie Di Xuekan **6927**
1028-4656 Das Recht der Arbeit **1705**
1028-4680 Africult†
1028-4753 Specialist Update
1028-4796 Revista Cubana de Plantas Medicinales **6878**
1028-4818 Multimed **5681**
1028-4885 Peace and Security **7258**
1028-5067 Telematik **2342**
1028-5083 Boletin Epidemiologico Semanal **7510**
1028-5164 Flashes from the Trade Unions **4594**
1028-5229 International Journal of Surgical Investigation†
1028-5237 *see* Office for Official Publications of the European Union. Newsletter **7256**
1028-5245 *see* Office for Official Publications of the European Union. Newsletter **7256**
1028-5288 The World of Cargo Handling *changed to* Cargo World **8641**
1028-5369 International Center for Living Aquatic Resources Management. Annual Report *changed to* WorldFish Center. Annual Report **3611**
1028-5474 Addis Tribune **3837**
1028-5636 Guoli Bingdong Keji Daxue Xuebao **7859**
1028-5679 Ruren Xuezhi. Ligong Lei **7906**
1028-5717 The Teacher **2917**
1028-5733 Mining & Business in Southern Africa **6472**
1028-5911 Tropical Disease Research News **5827**
1028-592X S A Refrigeration and Airconditioning **4126**
1028-5938 Archivos de Neurociencias **6124**
1028-5954 Euratex. Bulletin **8450**
1028-5962 European Foundation for the Improvement of Living and Working Conditions. Bulletin from the Foundation **7963**
1028-5970 Sankt-Peterburgskoe Obshchestvo Estestvoispytatelei. Trudy **703**
1028-6020 Journal of Asian Natural Products Research **311**
1028-6098 The Journal of Food Technology in Africa **3651**
1028-625X Penological Information Bulletin **2663**
1028-6276 Iranian Journal of Science and Technology. Transaction A: Science **7868**
1028-6284 Iranian Journal of Science and Technology. Transaction B: Technology **8428**
1028-6578 International Journal of Transport Phenomena **3203**
1028-6608 Civil Engineering and Environmental Systems **3262**
1028-6624 Inorganic Reaction Mechanisms **2135**
1028-6632 The International Journal of Cultural Policy **7974**
1028-6640 Kashmir Journal of Language Research **5136**
1028-6764 Quadrifina **857**
1028-6780 Jus & News **4708**
1028-6802 *see* 1022-6559 **8417**
1028-6810 *see* 1022-6559 **8417**
1028-6861 Zavodskaya Laboratoriya. Diagnostika Materialov **2107**
1028-6969 Edu-Index to South African Periodicals†
1028-7035 Directory of Iranian Periodicals and Newspapers **624**
1028-7094 Cool **3960**
1028-7108 Stabroek News **1179**
1028-7116 Sunday Stabroek *see* 1028-7108 **1179**
1028-7175 Dermatologia Peruana **5874**
1028-7221 Russian Journal of Immunology
1028-7418 Journal of Physical Education & Recreation **6991**
1028-7442 Novoe v Bukhgalterskom Uchete i Otchetnosti v Rossiiskoi Federatsii **1298**
1028-7493 Otkrytye Sistemy **2473**
1028-7531 Children's Rights **7204**
1028-7612 Chemical World **3240**
1028-7655 Journal of Science and Technology of Agriculture and Natural Resources **128**
1028-768X Acta Neurologica Taiwanica **6118**
1028-771X Buch und Co **7579**
1028-7736 Teledetection **4030**
1028-7825 Human Reproduction and Genetic Ethics **676**
1028-7957 Electrical Technology Russia **3157**
1028-8023 I S O Yearbook *see* 1607-0348 **6574**
1028-8031 Dairy Sector Indicators†
1028-8228 Policy that Works for Forests and People **3460**
1028-8341 Freedom Digest **7206**
1028-8457 African Journal of Mathematics, Science and Technology Education **5467**
1028-852X Iranian Biomedical Journal **5641**
1028-8554 Nezavisimyi Psikhiatricheskii Zhurnal **6170**
1028-8759 Droit de l'Enfant *see* 1028-7531 **7204**
1028-8767 *see* 1028-7531 **7204**
1028-8813 Journal of Eastern Caribbean Studies **7978**
1028-8821 I C H C A News and Cargo Management **8646**
1028-8880 Pakistan Journal of Biological Sciences **696**
1028-8910 Motor **8591**
1028-8945 Pharmacology Reviews and Communications†
1028-8961 Geoinfo **2781**
1028-8988 Cubalex **4653**
1028-9097 Journal of Behavioural Sciences **7369**
1028-9127 North Pacific Anadromous Fish Commission. Bulletin **959**
1028-9143 Namibia Economist **1151**
1028-9186 Tanzania Law Reports **4792**
1028-9194 *see* 1028-9186 **4792**
1028-9208 Zambia Law Reports **4818**
1028-9240 Elle Decoration **4539**
1028-9283 Contemporary Caribbean Legal Issues **4649**
1028-9291 Conference Permanente des Recteurs, des Presidents et des Vice-Presidents des Universites Europeennes Guide†
1028-9402 Kumbez **448**
1028-9445 Central Bank of Iceland. Working Papers **1325**
1028-9453 Lateinamerika Anders Panorama **7250**
1028-9623 Hong Kong Dermatology & Venereology Bulletin *changed to* 1814-7453 **5877**
1028-9674 Novosti Razvedki i Kontrazvedki **6439**
1028-9763 Matematychni Mashyny i Systemy **2462**
1028-9771 Zdravookhranenie **7546**
1028-9852 Society in Transition *changed to* South African Review of Sociology **8140**
1028-9933 Revista Informacion Cientifica **5705**
1028-995X Vek **3943**
1028-9968 R P M: Review of Popular Music **6609**
1028-9976 Neft' Rossii **2622**
1028-9984 Rossiiskii Onkologicheskii Zhurnal **6034**
1029-0109 T A P P S A Journal **6739**
1029-0249 *see* 1028-6608 **3262**
1029-0257 *see* 1061-8562 **7059**
1029-0265 *see* 0020-7160 **5552**
1029-0273 *see* 0305-215X **3190**
1029-029X *see* 0898-1507 **7080**
1029-0311 *see* 1048-5252 **8383**
1029-0338 *see* 0141-1594 **7030**
1029-0354 *see* 0308-1060 **8516**
1029-0362 *see* 1023-6244 **687**
1029-0370 *see* 0275-7540 **2056**
1029-0389 *see* 0095-8972 **2068**
1029-0397 *see* 0306-7319 **2101**
1029-0400 Environmental Studies: Sections A & B *see* 0020-7233 **3442**
1029-0419 *see* 0309-1929 **2781**
1029-0427 *see* 1061-026X **3448**
1029-0435 *see* 0892-7022 **2073**
1029-0451 *see* 0031-9104 **7062**
1029-046X *see* 1062-936X **3464**
1029-0478 *see* 1061-0278 **2081**
1029-0486 *see* 0277-2248 **3502**
1029-0516 *see* 1070-3608 **5905**
1029-0540 World Hospitals and Health Services **4113**
1029-0656 GmbH Bulletin **4869**
1029-0680 Asia Pacific Journal of Language in Education **5096**
1029-0737 Medium Aevum Quotidianum **4244**
1029-0869 Skyrslur og Reikningar Felagatal *see* 0256-8446 **5373**
1029-0877 The Iceland Reporter†
1029-0931 Antropologicas **328**
1029-0990 Strategic Studies **7267**
1029-1024 Wetlands International Cormorant Research Group Bulletin
1029-1105 Nouvelles Atlantiques *changed to* 1784-0759 **7233**
1029-1253 Af Vettvangi **1662**
1029-1261 Public Transport International (French Edition) **8509**
1029-127X Public Transport International (English Edition) *see* 1029-1261 **8509**
1029-1288 Public Transport International (Deutsche Ausgabe) *see* 1029-1261 **8509**
1029-1725 International W O C E Newsletter **6358**
1029-1733 Folia Dermatologica Peruana **5876**
1029-1768 I C H C A News and Cargo Today **8526**
1029-1776 Liechtensteinische Juristen Zeitung†
1029-1784 Earth Focus **2706**
1029-1865 Ship Year **8661**
1029-1903 Asian Affairs **7107**
1029-1962 Obstetrics & Gynaecology Forum **6001**
1029-2004 Boletin de Arqueologia PUCP **331**
1029-2020 Journal of Neuropterology **952**
1029-2039 B I V A **6347**
1029-2047 Boletin de la Vigilancia del Clima **6347**
1029-2136 Conceptual Advances in Brain Research **6133**
1029-2160 *see* 1025-3890 **5718**
1029-225X Direct
1029-2292 *see* 0897-7194 **922**
1029-2314 Cell Adhesion and Communication (Online Edition) *changed to* 1543-5180 **664**
1029-2330 *see* 1061-186X **6853**
1029-2373 *see* 1062-3329 **671**
1029-2381 *see* 0891-2963 **6725**
1029-2403 *see* 1042-8194 **5940**
1029-242X *see* 1025-5834 **5504**

9462 1029-2446 ULRICH'S PERIODICALS

1029-2446 *see* 1024-2422 **757**
1029-2454 *see* 0892-7014 **3494**
1029-2470 *see* 1071-5762 **732**
1029-2551 Agrokhimicheskii Vestnik **217**
1029-2624 Journal fuer Schulentwicklung **3025**
1029-2659 Journal of Applied Therapeutic Research **6852**
1029-2667 Adweek Asia†
1029-2756 Railways Africa **8624**
1029-2977 Archives of Iranian Medicine **5577**
1029-3019 Medisan **5676**
1029-3035 Medi Ciego **5666**
1029-3132 Asia Pacific Management Review **1725**
1029-3256 S Af AIDS News **5826**
1029-3299 Living World **687**
1029-3302 Juta's Insurance Law Bulletin **4873**
1029-3450 Avanzada Cientifica **7838**
1029-3507 Zhong-Taiwan Yixue Kexue Zazahi **5735**
1029-3523 Investment Analysts Journal **1632**
1029-3531 Methods of Functional Analysis and Topology **5517**
1029-354X European Communities. Asylum-Seekers **7233**
1029-3566 World Transport Statistics†
1029-3590 Mining World **6473**
1029-3620 Rossiiskaya Akademiya Nauk. Izvestiya. Teoriya i Systemy Upravleniya **2528**
1029-3639 External and Intra-European Union Trade. Monthly Statistics **1228**
1029-3701 Colloque Scientifique International sur le Cafe **225**
1029-371X International Organization for Standardization, International Electrotechnical Commission. Guide **6403**
1029-3736 Moskovskii Gosudarstvennyi Universitet. Vestnik. Seriya 18: Sotsiologiya i Politologiya **8121**
1029-3825 Medienimpulse **3072**
1029-3914 Mir Piva *see* 0934-9340 **600**
1029-4066 Journal for Scientific Research. Medical Sciences **5645**
1029-4139 Practical Guide to Foreign Direct Investment in the European Union - The Green Book **1645**
1029-4147 The E U Institutions' Register **1991**
1029-4309 Oil Information **6784**
1029-4325 World Development Indicators **1587**
1029-4341 Autodeterminacion **7108**
1029-4503 Finansovaya Rossiya *changed to* 1727-6349 **1346**
1029-4546 Central Bank of Kuwait. Annual Report **1325**
1029-4554 Central Bank of Kuwait. Economic Report **1446**
1029-4562 Central Bank of Kuwait. Monthly Monetary Statistics **1220**
1029-4570 Taqrir al-Iqtisadi - Bank al-Kuwayt al-Markazi *see* 1029-4554 **1446**
1029-4589 At-Taqrir as-Sanawi. Bank al-Kuwayt al-Markazi **1309**
1029-4740 Academia Sinica. Institute of Modern History. Bulletin **4128**
1029-4759 Jindai Zhongguo Funu Shi Yanjiu **4184**
1029-4805 I D N **2534**
1029-4864 South African Dental Journal **5865**
1029-4910 *see* 0233-1888 **8405**
1029-4929 *see* 1051-9998 **7035**
1029-4937 *see* 1055-6788 **5555**
1029-4945 *see* 0233-1934 **5523**
1029-4953 *see* 1042-0150 **7071**
1029-5097 Hong Kong College of Radiologists. Journal **6197**
1029-516X Ingenieria Mecanica **3379**
1029-5313 Oesterreichische Freiberufs Tierarzt **8804**
1029-5321 Vet Journal **8810**
1029-5488 Oe Z B - Oesterreichische Zeitschrift fuer Berufsbildung *changed to* 1817-4019 **3088**
1029-5828 Geo **3433**
1029-5925 The Southern African Forestry Journal *changed to* 2070-2620 **3703**
1029-5933 Ethiopian Pharmaceutical Journal **6838**
1029-6026 The Judicial Officer **4953**
1029-6069 Magallat al-Huquq **4726**
1029-6174 Benguo Yinhang Yingyun Jixiao Jibao **1321**
1029-6646 International Journal of Elevator Engineering† **8966**
1029-6670 Mekhanika Kompozitsionnykh Materialov i Konstruktsii **7061**
1029-6735 I E E E International Engineering Management Conference. Proceedings **3196**
1029-6816 Forum **8102**
1029-6832 BirdLife International. Annual Review **903**
1029-6840 Elevator Technology **1006**
1029-6891 Akademiya Agrarnykh Navuk Respubliki Belarusi. Vestsi **89**
1029-6905 Hayastani Bzhshkagitutyun **5905**
1029-7022 European Agency for Safety and Health at Work. Newsletter† **8954**
1029-7065 A C P - E C Council of Ministers. Annual Report (Year) **1589**
1029-7073 S A B R A O Journal of Breeding and Genetics **153**
1029-709X I C A E Bulletin **2942**
1029-7111 El Boletin del I C A E *see* 1029-709X **2942**
1029-712X European Journal for Sport Management†
1029-7200 Bibliotechnyi Visnyk **4995**
1029-7227 Dramaturg **8469**
1029-7456 Sankt-Peterburgskii Universitet. Vestnik. Seriya 7. Geologiya, Geografiya **2765**
1029-7774 Brides and Homes **5557**
1029-7790 Baltic 21 Series **8090**
1029-7901 Hayastany Hanrapetutyan Titutyunneri Azgayin Akademia Teghekagir. Gitutyunner Erkri Masin **7860**
1029-8010 Guoji Luntan **7239**
1029-810X Al-Majallah at-Tarbawiyah **2885**
1029-8142 Euronews on Special Needs Education **3039**
1029-8223 Otkrytaya Politika† **8979**
1029-8231 Zhonghua Minguo Chi'e Jiaozheng Xuehui Zazhi **5870**
1029-8347 Jiuye Shichang Qingshi Yuebao **1132**
1029-8428 Neurotoxicity Research **6170**
1029-8436 The International Journal of Pavement Engineering **3272**
1029-8479 The Journal of High Energy Physics (Online) **7020**
1029-8487 Vremya MN **3943**
1029-8525 International Textile Bulletin **8453**
1029-855X Arab Journal of Administrative Sciences **1725**
1029-8614 Food Additive Intake Studies **6659**
1029-8622 Food, Agriculture and the Environment **113**
1029-8630 European Social Fund. Evaluation Unit. Impact of Evaluations (Year) **8039**
1029-8649 Musicae Scientiae **6593**
1029-8657 Kazakstan Respublikasynyn Gylym Ministrligi. Gylym Akademiasynyn Khabarlary. Seriya Obshchestvennykh Nauk **7981**
1029-8681 Emerging Market Trends† **8953**
1029-8703 Ecological Economics Bulletin **3416**
1029-8711 Motorcycles, Parts & Accessories Buyers' Guide **2017**
1029-8762 Environmental Encounters **3424**
1029-8770 Khimicheskoe i Neftegazovoe Mashinostroenie **3249**
1029-8878 Cahiers du Judaisme **7719**
1029-8916 Steel R T D Newsletter **6333**
1029-8940 Natsiyanal'naya Akademiya Navuk Belarusi. Vestsi. Seryya Biyalagichnykh Navuk **692**
1029-8983 Respublika Armeniya **3792**
1029-9599 Physical Mesomechanics **7062**
1030-004X Campaign Brief (Sydney) **22**
1030-0090 Airborne (Tullamarine) **4327**
1030-0112 Australasian Journal of Special Education **3036**
1030-0139 Women - Church† **8998**
1030-0155 Access (Vermont) **4987**
1030-021X Australian Railway Enthusiast **8615**
1030-0244 New South Wales. Law Reform Commission. Reports **4744**
1030-0287 Junior Clubhouse† **8969**
1030-0295 Today (Lawson) **7777**
1030-0325 Power Farming **213**
1030-0384 Hostel Travel†
1030-0392 Garden Peskem† **8958**
1030-0406 Accommodation Directory† **8928**
1030-0481 South Australian Geographical Journal **4029**
1030-0562 A C C Touche Ross Tax Legislation Fact Papers†
1030-0724 Australia. Bureau of Statistics. Victorian Office. Local Government Finance, Victoria†
1030-0740 Red Tape **4601**
1030-0759 Commercial Vessel Yearbook **3589**
1030-0775 A C C Submission Papers†
1030-0856 Hunter Region Economic Indicators **1241**
1030-1011 Australia. Bureau of Statistics. Queensland Office. Interstate and Foreign Trade†
1030-1046 Crime and Justice Bulletin **2648**
1030-147X A C C Research Papers†
1030-1763 Labour & Industry **1694**
1030-178X A.D. Magazine†
1030-1798 A.D. Youthleader†
1030-1879 Phoenix **2228**
1030-1887 Australian Systematic Botany **777**
1030-1917 Australian Home Builder and Improver†
1030-1925 Australian Building News†
1030-1976 Australian National University. National Centre for Development Studies. Indian Ocean Policy Papers†
1030-2166 Space Association News†
1030-2379 Insurance Law Journal **4693**
1030-2425 National Marina Survey†
1030-245X Centre for South Pacific Studies. Newsletter† **8940**
1030-2646 Family Matters **8102**
1030-2662 Silicon Chip **2541**
1030-2913 Legal Aid News† **8970**
1030-3812 A S S I G Newsletter†
1030-3839 Antithesis **5206**
1030-391X Directions in Government
1030-3987 New Parent
1030-3995 Symphony Australia†
1030-407X Journal of Teaching Practice **3068**
1030-4215 C S I R O Annual Report **8417**
1030-4312 Continuum **6495**
1030-4479 Guide to Craft Supplies in New South Wales and the Australian Capital Territory†
1030-4495 Appropriate Technology Index **8446**
1030-4614 Agricultural Science **84**
1030-4649 Scitech Technology Directory†
1030-469X Wild **8341**
1030-472X National Baptist†
1030-4754 Meatworker†
1030-4770 Canberra Cyclist **8256**
1030-4908 Sounds Australian *changed to* Resonate **6611**
1030-4932 Redoubt†
1030-5009 Topics in Australasian Library and Information Studies **5050**
1030-5033 Australasian Public Libraries and Information Services **4993**
1030-536X Australia. Bureau of Statistics. Victorian Office. Labour Force, Victoria†
1030-5459 Lonely Planet Update†
1030-5467 Third Opinion†
1030-5505 Toowoomba and Golden West Tourist Region†
1030-570X Pacifica **7668**
1030-5882 Exposure Draft (Accounting Standards)†
1030-5890 Proposed Statement of Accounting Concepts
1030-5920 Australian Regional Impact Analysis Series (No.)†
1030-5947 University of Technology, Sydney. Calendar **3009**
1030-603X Exposure Draft (Auditing Practice) **1288**
1030-617X A J L **7619**
1030-6196 W.H.A.T.†
1030-6234 Australian Biologist† **8933**
1030-6560 Australian Economic Brief†
1030-6641 National Guide to Government **7156**
1030-7052 Contact (Box Hill) **7752**
1030-7168 Roadwise *changed to* 1832-9497 **8490**
1030-7222 Australian Journal of Labour Law **4857**
1030-7230 Journal of Contract Law **4700**
1030-7389 Australia. Bureau of Statistics. Queensland Office. Queensland Year Book†
1030-7451 Activnews **8023**
1030-763X Recreation and Sport in the Holidays†
1030-7699 Virgats **3571**
1030-7710 Victorian Historical Journal **4166**
1030-7745 Australian Nuclear Science and Technology Organisation - E **3165**
1030-7788 Scots Link† **8987**
1030-7915 Australian Nugget Journal†
1030-8253 S A Motor **8602**
1030-8385 T E S O L in Context **3015**
1030-8482 Mediterranean Archaeology **405**
1030-8768 Tell **2216**
1030-8954 Australian Birdkeeper Magazine **6804**
1030-8962 East Asian Library Resources Group of Australia. Newsletter (Canberra, 1978)†
1030-8970 Australia. National Drug Abuse Information Centre. Technical Information Bulletin on Drug Abuse†
1030-8989 Australia. Bureau of Statistics. Estimated Resident Population by Marital Status, Age and Sex, Australia†
1030-9039 Australia. Bureau of Statistics. Price Indexes of Materials Used in Coal Mining, Australia†
1030-9160 Printing Trades Journal†
1030-9179 Australia. Bureau of Statistics. Estimated Resident Population by Country of Birth, Age and Sex, Australia†
1030-9268 Australia. Bureau of Statistics. Queensland Office. Law and Order, Queensland, Summary†
1030-9616 Accounting Research Journal **1278**
1030-9810 Australia. Bureau of Statistics. Victorian Office. Labour Force at a Glance, Victoria†
1030-9896 Overlander 4WD Touring Guide **8597**
1030-9985 Vietnam Today†
1031-0029 Australia. Bureau of Statistics. Price Indexes of Articles Produced by Manufacturing Industry, Australia†
1031-0053 Australia. Bureau of Statistics. Perinatal Deaths, Australia†
1031-010X A H A Special Monographs†
1031-0193 Australia. Bureau of Statistics. Commercial Finance, Australia†
1031-0258 Australia. Bureau of Statistics. Employment Benefits, Australia†
1031-0282 Australia. Bureau of Statistics. Expenditure on Education, Australia†
1031-0355 Australia. Bureau of Statistics. Industrial Disputes, Australia†
1031-038X Australia. Bureau of Statistics. Labour Force, Australia, Preliminary† **8932**
1031-0460 Australia. Bureau of Statistics. Multiple Jobholding, Australia (Print) *changed to* Australia. Bureau of Statistics. Multiple Jobholding, Australia (Online) **1208**
1031-0541 Australia. Bureau of Statistics. Australia at a Glance **8348**
1031-0584 Australia. Bureau of Statistics. Average Weekly Earnings, Australia, Preliminary† **8932**
1031-0649 Australia. Bureau of Statistics. Price Indexes of Materials Used in Manufacturing Industries, Australia†
1031-0789 Australia. Bureau of Statistics. Value of Agricultural Commodities Produced, Australia†
1031-0800 Australia. Bureau of Statistics. Viticulture, Australia, Preliminary†
1031-1009 A C I A R Partners Magazine **77**
1031-1084 Australia. Bureau of Statistics. Road Traffic Accidents Involving Fatalities, Australia†
1031-1157 Aller-Gen
1031-1343 The Business Who's Who Australian Products and Tradenames Guide† **8938**
1031-1548 Australia. Bureau of Statistics. Northern Territory Office. Agriculture and Fishing, Northern Territory†
1031-1580 Commonwealth Scientific and Industrial Research Organization. Division of Animal Health. Report†
1031-1718 New England News†
1031-1939 Australia. Bureau of Statistics. South Australian Office. Agriculture, South Australia†
1031-1971 Australia. Bureau of Statistics. Queensland Office. Building Approvals: Preliminary Figures for Dwelling Units Approved†
1031-2145 Australia. Bureau of Statistics. Queensland Office. Crops and Pastures, Queensland†
1031-2153 Australia. Bureau of Statistics. South Australian Office. Deaths, South Australia†
1031-2226 Australia. Bureau of Statistics. South Australian Office. Dwelling Unit Commencements Reported by Approving Authorities, South Australia†
1031-2269 Australia. Bureau of Statistics. Queensland Office. Government Finance, Queensland†
1031-2277 Australia. Bureau of Statistics. Queensland Office. Health and Welfare Establishments, Queensland, Preliminary†
1031-2315 Business Directions
1031-2331 Indian Ocean Review† **8964**
1031-248X Australia. Bureau of Statistics. South Australian Office. Labour Force, South Australia†
1031-2498 Australia. Bureau of Statistics. South Australian Office. Livestock and Livestock Products, South Australia†
1031-2501 Australia. Bureau of Statistics. New South Wales Office. Local Government Finance, New South Wales†
1031-2528 Australia. Bureau of Statistics. Queensland Office. Local Government, Queensland†
1031-2544 Australia. Bureau of Statistics. South Australian Office. Manufacturing Establishments: Details of Operations by Industry†
1031-2617 Victorian Administrative Reports **4808**
1031-2641 Australia. Bureau of Statistics. N I F - 10S Model Data Base Manual† **8932**
1031-2714 Australia. Bureau of Statistics. Queensland Office. Mineral Production, Queensland†
1031-2730 Australia. Bureau of Statistics. Queensland Office. Motor Vehicle Registrations, Queensland†
1031-2749 Australia. Bureau of Statistics. Victorian Office. Motor Vehicle Registrations, Victoria†
1031-2765 Australia. Bureau of Statistics. Budget Related Paper: National Income and Expenditure†
1031-279X Australia. Bureau of Statistics. Queensland Office. Queensland in Relation to Australia†
1031-2803 Australia. Bureau of Statistics. Queensland Office. Road Traffic Accidents, Queensland (Quarterly)†
1031-2889 Commission for the Conservation of Antarctic Marine Living Resources. Report of the Meeting of the Scientific Committee **2802**

Link to your serials resources and content with ulrichsweb.com

DIRECTORY 2010 1034-5329 9463

1031-2900 Australia. Bureau of Statistics. Victorian Office. Tourist Accommodation, Victoria *changed to* Australia. Bureau of Statistics. Victorian Office. Tourist Accommodation, Small Area Data, Victoria **4401**
1031-2935 Australia. Bureau of Statistics. South Australian Office. Value of Agricultural Commodities Produced, South Australia†
1031-2943 Australian Religion Studies Review **7624**
1031-296X Manufacturing Report†
1031-3001 Terror Australis†
1031-301X *see* 1326-4672 **2668**
1031-3109 Accounting Guidance Release **1277**
1031-3443 Patricia Chomley Orations **5977**
1031-3613 Reproduction, Fertility and Development **700**
1031-3745 Building Construction Materials & Equipment **985**
1031-3796 Resource **2905**
1031-3893 Australia. Bureau of Statistics. Queensland Office. Road Traffic Accidents, Queensland (Annual)†
1031-3958 Lithuanian Papers **3548**
1031-4121 Australia. Department of the Treasury. Tax Expenditures Statement **1911**
1031-444X Education Australia†
1031-461X Australian Historical Studies **4132**
1031-4695 Weekly Times Technical Annual†
1031-4784 Australia. Bureau of Tourism Research. Occasional Papers *changed to* Tourism Research Australia. Occasional paper **8781**
1031-4830 Mother & Baby **4364**
1031-4881 River Watch **3463**
1031-5020 S I L - A A I B Bibliography† **8986**
1031-5187 Australian Libraries: The Essential Directory **4993**
1031-5330 Crime Prevention Series†
1031-5411 N A A T I News
1031-6264 Australia. Bureau of Statistics. Queensland Office. Estimated Resident Population: Components of Change, Queensland† **8933**
1031-6280 Donkey Digest **319**
1031-6353 What's New in Radio Communications *changed to* 1448-8906 **2362**
1031-6515 Australian Nuclear Science and Technology Organisation - M **3165**
1031-6590 Children's Court of New South Wales Information Bulletin† **8941**
1031-6655 Australian Nuclear Science and Technology Organisation. Annual Report **3165**
1031-6930 Western Australia. Department of Fisheries. Annual Report **3611**
1031-6965 Natural Therapist†
1031-704X Ministerial Document Service†
1031-7295 Australia. Bureau of Statistics. Queensland Office. Sand, Gravel and Quarry Production, Queensland†
1031-7317 S.A. & W.A. Judgments Bulletin
1031-735X Studio for Men†
1031-7368 Fishing Today **3594**
1031-7503 Mathematics Competitions **5515**
1031-7511 Psychological Test Bulletin†
1031-7627 Australia. Bureau of Statistics. Tasmanian Office. Education, Tasmania†
1031-7716 Tasmanian Index of Community Organisations†
1031-7767 Australia. Bureau of Statistics. Victorian Office. Schools, Victoria†
1031-7872 New South Wales Statutes Annotations **4824**
1031-8046 Australia. Bureau of Statistics. Retail Trade, Australia: Commodity Details† **8933**
1031-8062 Australian Museum. Technical Reports (Print) *changed to* Australian Museum. Technical Reports (Online) **935**
1031-8097 Australia. Bureau of Statistics. Queensland Office. Transport, Queensland†
1031-8151 C C H International Tax Planning Manual **1914**
1031-8194 A C I A R Monograph Series **77**
1031-8208 P C Update **2581**
1031-8216 A N S T O Technology†
1031-8240 Manufacturers' Monthly's Pulse Report *see* 0025-2530 **1898**
1031-8283 Tightrope†
1031-8364 C C H Journal of Asian Pacific Taxation†
1031-8445 Australia. Bureau of Statistics. Western Australian Office. Vehicles on Register, Western Australia†
1031-8453 A.D. 2000 **7619**
1031-8534 Australia. Bureau of Statistics. New South Wales Office. Economic Indicators, New South Wales†
1031-8569 The Law Handbook **2639**
1031-8585 Commonwealth Superannuation Administration. Annual Report **7431**
1031-8690 University of Technology, Sydney. Annual Report **3009**
1031-8844 Comite Scientifique pour la Conservation de la Faune et la Flore Marines de l'Antarctique. Rapport de la Reunion du Comite Scientifique *see* 1031-2889 **2802**
1031-8852 Comision para la Conservacion de los Recursos Vivos Marinos Antarticos. Informe de la Reunion del Comite Cientifico *see* 1031-2889 **2802**
1031-8860 Naucnyi Komitet po Sohraneniyu Morskikh Zhivykh Resursov Antarktiki. Otchet Soveshchaniya Nauchnogo Komiteta *see* 1031-2889 **2802**
1031-8968 Australia. Department of the Treasury. Economic Round-Up **1211**
1031-9115 Studio for Brides **5561**
1031-9204 Australian Academy of Science. Newsletter **7838**
1031-9344 Tournament Fisherman
1031-9379 Pacific Research†
1031-9425 National Union Catalogue of Non-Book Materials†
1031-9476 Royal Australian Historical Society. History Magazine **4194**
1031-9573 Australia. Bureau of Statistics. Tasmanian Office. Tasmanian Pocket Yearbook† **8933**
1031-9956 C S I R O Division of Fisheries. Research Report
1031-9964 C S I R O Division of Oceanography. Research Report†
1032-0229 Pride (Collingwood)†
1032-0288 Australian Construction Law Newsletter
1032-0393 Northern Territory. Department of Primary Industry and Fisheries. Technical Bulletin **142**
1032-0776 Resources - Quarry Mine & Construction News
1032-0865 Australia. Bureau of Statistics. Directory of Housing Related Statistics **4433**
1032-089X Workplace Change†
1032-1012 Venereology†
1032-1063 Australian Defence Intelligencer **6413**
1032-1233 New Scientist (Chatswood) **7892**
1032-125X Freshwater Fishing Australia Magazine **3595**
1032-1640 Idiom 23 **5424**
1032-1942 Australian Art Education **477**
1032-2019 Australia. Department of Foreign Affairs and Trade. Annual Report **1591**
1032-2167 Australian Science and Technology Newsletter†
1032-2345 Commonwealth of Australia Gazette. Special†
1032-2353 Commonwealth of Australia Gazette. Public Service (Print)†
1032-2663 Graduate Careers in Engineering†
1032-2752 The Australian Gardener†
1032-285X Taiwan Australia Business Discussion Papers†
1032-2973 T V Hits **2215**
1032-3279 Pharmacy Guild of Australia. Annual Report **6873**
1032-3317 Tracks **8338**
1032-335X Australasian Journal of Neuroscience **6125**
1032-3368 Antipodes **5255**
1032-3686 Ancient History **4130**
1032-3732 Accounting History **1278**
1032-3759 Pork Journal **296**
1032-3767 Poultry Digest **296**
1032-3899 Sound & Image **2391**
1032-4003 Australian Family and Society Abstracts†
1032-4070 Eyecare Australia†
1032-4321 Impact (Strawberry Hills) **8046**
1032-4410 Geriaction
1032-4429 Australia. Bureau of Statistics. Victorian Office. Retail Industry: Details of Operations, Victoria **1211**
1032-450X Dairy Moves†
1032-4666 Environment†
1032-500X Thai - Yunnan Project Newsletter†
1032-5077 Papers in Austronesian Linguistics **5159**
1032-5107 Papers in Papuan Linguistics **5159**
1032-5212 Neville Coleman's Underwater Geographic†
1032-5298 Food Australia **3638**
1032-5352 Australia. Bureau of Statistics. Queensland Office. Employment Injuries, Queensland†
1032-5360 Boats, Boats, Boats...†
1032-5441 Commonwealth Scientific and Industrial Research Organization. Division of Soils. Annual Report†
1032-5506 Sports Trainers Digest **8208**
1032-5662 Sport Health **6233**
1032-6138 Australia. Bureau of Statistics. Australia's Health† **8932**
1032-643X Australian Social Policy (Kensington)†
1032-6448 Showcast Casting Directory
1032-6456 Contacts & Facilities in the Australian Entertainment Industry
1032-6499 Americar Australia†
1032-6529 Fire Australia **3577**
1032-6626 Australian Equine Veterinarian **8793**
1032-6634 Policy **1160**
1032-707X Australian Collector's Quarterly†
1032-7150 Focus on Photography†
1032-7290 International Tree Crops†
1032-8149 National Union Catalogue of Library Materials for People with Disabilities†
1032-8408 Australia. Bureau of Statistics. Queensland Office. Directory of Small Area Statistics, Queensland†
1032-8599 Access (Glenside)
1032-8696 Australian Nineteenth Century Literature in Print†
1032-8882 Murray-Darling Freshwater Research Centre. Annual Report†
1032-9005 Action Network
1032-9102 Victoria, Australia. Statutory Rules **4808**
1032-9145 Among Ourselves†
1032-9234 Anglican Encounter **7745**
1032-948X Gould League Club Newsletter†
1032-9560 A M L C News†
1032-9609 Cottager† **8944**
1032-9625 Birth†
1032-9641 Political Theory Newsletter†
1032-9684 University of Western Australia. Asian Studies Centre. Monographs†
1032-996X Personal Success†
1032-9994 Directory of Australian Academic and Research Libraries†
1033-0003 Early Morn African Violet Group Newsletter **3728**
1033-0186 Lifestyles Season
1033-0216 Artwork Magazine **476**
1033-0526 C A M S Manual of Motor Sport **8164**
1033-1220 Forest Resources Series **3689**
1033-131X Australian Studies†
1033-1352 Australian Record & Music Review
1033-1425 Health at Work†
1033-1433 Tourism and Travel Management
1033-1441 *see* Australian Sentencing Judgments Bulletin
1033-1530 Cross Section **5481**
1033-1808 Celsius Journal **4117**
1033-1867 Fabrications **442**
1033-1875 Ergonomics Australia **3344**
1033-1913 Action Africa† **8928**
1033-2170 Mathematics Education Research Journal **3072**
1033-2405 Corporate and Business Law Journal†
1033-2510 Australian Folklore. Newsletter *see* 0819-0852 **3615**
1033-2596 Decisions *see* 0404-2018 **1309**
1033-2618 Australia. Bureau of Statistics. Australian National Accounts: Gross Product, Employment and Hours Worked†
1033-2626 Australasian Religion Index†
1033-2774 A M R E P Resource Politics†
1033-2839 Legal Education Review **4719**
1033-2863 I V S Annual **8816**
1033-3010 Australia. Bureau of Statistics. Australian National Accounts: Capital Stock†
1033-3096 Helix **7861**
1033-3177 South Australian Volunteering **8072**
1033-3258 The Picture **6297**
1033-3479 Paraphernalia†
1033-3525 Birds International
1033-3665 Australia. Bureau of Statistics. Victorian Office. Summary of Statistics, Victoria†
1033-3673 Australian Garden History **3723**
1033-3797 Community Visitors for the Year Ended 30th June. Intellectually Disabled Persons' Services Act 1986. Annual Report *changed to* 1833-9409 **4064**
1033-3843 Australian Gold Bulletin - Monthly Summary†
1033-3940 Australia. Bureau of Statistics. Labour Force, Australia - Preliminary Data on Floppy Disk *see* 1031-038X **8932**
1033-3975 Stages†
1033-4025 Art Monthly Australia **470**
1033-4505 Bond Law Review **4631**
1033-4513 Down Under Quilts **534**
1033-4688 Signals **6537**
1033-470X Australian Press Council News **4572**
1033-4831 Video & Music Business†
1033-4874 Australian Zoological Reviews†
1033-4890 Education Monitor†
1033-5595 Keyword *changed to* 1832-0120 **2339**
1033-5722 Australian Foreign Affairs and Trade: The Monthly Record†
1033-6060 Australian Country Style **5065**
1033-6133 Australia. Bureau of Statistics. Tasmanian Office. Employment Injuries, Tasmania†
1033-6206 Bioethics Research Notes **6908**
1033-6273 Information, Theory and Society **8107**
1033-6303 Nursing and Health Science Education **5973**
1033-6427 International Working Paper **1572**
1033-6559 Journal Review Service *see* 0817-1351 **5565**
1033-6621 Blarney **3760**
1033-6818 Australia. Bureau of Statistics. Tasmanian Office. Court Statistics, Tasmania†
1033-6826 Conscious Living Fremantle **3412**
1033-6974 A I M S Report **2799**
1033-7288 Girlfriend **2190**
1033-7466 Australian Corporations and Securities Reports **4857**
1033-7539 24 Hours†
1033-758X Stationery News **1855**
1033-7687 Gippsland Heritage Journal Index (Print) *changed to* Gippsland Heritage Journal Index (Online) **4170**
1033-7814 Hands On†
1033-7830 Ossia†
1033-7903 New Life **7768**
1033-7954 Australian and New Zealand Wine Industry Directory **598**
1033-8012 T A F E Link (Print) *changed to* T A F E Link (Online) **2946**
1033-8195 Performance Sailing
1033-8217 Networks†
1033-8284 New Woman†
1033-8330 Australian Journal of Medical Herbalism **307**
1033-8403 Australia. Bureau of Statistics. Survey of Motor Vehicle Use, Australia, Preliminary†
1033-8446 Australian National University. Centre for Resource and Environmental Studies. Working Paper
1033-8527 C S I R O Rural Sector Report†
1033-8640 Australia. Bureau of Statistics. Statistics Weekly†
1033-8713 Culture and Policy† **8947**
1033-8918 Mingay's Retail Guide
1033-9035 Accent† **8928**
1033-9280 A Q I S Bulletin **78**
1033-9957 The Independent Monthly†
1034-0084 Sydney for Parents† **8992**
1034-0785 Australian Book Collector†
1034-1021 Sunday Age *see* 0312-6307 **3793**
1034-1102 National Trust of Australia (W.A.) Annual Report **4193**
1034-1110 Commonwealth Statutes Annotations **4948**
1034-1412 University of Tasmania. Centre for Environmental Studies. Occasional Paper **3472**
1034-1471 Australian National University. National Centre for Development Studies. Reprint Series
1034-1803 Australia. Bureau of Statistics. Tasmanian Office. Tasmanian Statistical Indicators† **8933**
1034-215X Rock (Prahran) **8330**
1034-229X Legaldate (Print) *changed to* Legaldate (Online) **4721**
1034-2346 Riptide **8330**
1034-2370 Travelnews Australia **8768**
1034-2516 Radio (Year)†
1034-3016 Australian Cyclist **8253**
1034-3024 Public Law Review **4763**
1034-3040 Journal of Banking and Finance - Law and Practice **1360**
1034-3059 Australian Dispute Resolution Journal *changed to* 1441-7847 **4623**
1034-3326 Networking†
1034-3350 Journal of Higher Education
1034-3423 Audit Monograph
1034-3431 Australian Sun & Health Magazine†
1034-361X Antarctic and Southern Ocean Law and Policy Occasional Papers **4917**
1034-3695 Army Magazine† **8931**
1034-3717 Australian Accounting Standard
1034-3822 Wicks Subject Index of Commonwealth Legislation **4826**
1034-4209 C E D A Monograph Series†
1034-4233 Australian Institute for the Conservation of Cultural Material. Bulletin **477**
1034-4284 New Perspectives†
1034-4748 Australia. Bureau of Statistics. Constant Price Estimates of Manufacturing Production, Australia† **8932**
1034-4810 Journal of Paediatrics and Child Health **6094**
1034-4942 Australasian Journal of Combinatorics **5474**
1034-5043 TraveLeisure
1034-5051 Immigration Update **8377**
1034-5086 Australian Institute of Criminology. Conference Proceedings (No.)†
1034-5132 Australia. Bureau of Statistics. Queensland Office. Child Care Arrangements, Queensland†
1034-5329 Current Issues in Criminal Justice **2650**

ISSN

Link to your serials resources and content with ulrichsweb.com

1036-9201 Margaret Gee's Australian Media Guide **2015**
1036-9368 Literature and Aesthetics **5325**
1036-9449 Australia. Bureau of Statistics. Foreign Trade, Australia: Merchandise Exports (Monthly)†
1036-9457 Australian Journal of Music Therapy **6546**
1036-9503 Polemic **4758**
1036-9686 Compass **7793**
1036-9694 Defense and Aerospace Notes†
1036-9821 Farm Computing†
1036-9856 Domestic Tourism Monitor. Quarterly Reports†
1036-9864 Drugs in Society† **8951**
1036-9872 The Rangeland Journal **2625**
1036-9953 Australia. Bureau of Statistics. Tasmanian Office. Agriculture, Tasmania (Hobart, 1985)†
1037-0196 History of Economics Review **1118**
1037-0285 Practical Queensland Landscape Design, Construction and Maintenance **3748**
1037-0323 Australian Bodyboarder†
1037-0552 Australian Journal of Mining **6457**
1037-0692 Reef Research†
1037-079X About U†
1037-0838 Australian Journal of Jewish Studies **7718**
1037-1095 Climate Change Newsletter†
1037-1176 Australia. Bureau of Statistics. Northern Territory Office. Northern Territory in Focus†
1037-1397 Japanese Studies **8111**
1037-1400 Photoworld†
1037-1443 Travelweek Australia *changed to* 1833-5179 **8768**
1037-1451 Keypoints†
1037-1508 Great Barrier Reef Marine Park Authority Research Publication Series **675**
1037-1591 Australian Injury Prevention Bulletin†
1037-1648 Inside Sport **8179**
1037-1656 Rural Society **8130**
1037-1664 Top Gear† **8993**
1037-1818 University of Southern Queensland. Handbook† **8996**
1037-2040 Spectrum (Hobart) **2914**
1037-2105 Australian Journal of Otolaryngology†
1037-2245 Australia. Bureau of Statistics. Northern Territory Office. Northern Territory Business Indicators†
1037-2296 Australia. Bureau of Statistics. Foreign Trade, Australia: Merchandise Exports (Quarterly)†
1037-230X Australia. Bureau of Statistics. Foreign Trade, Australia: Merchandise Imports (Quarterly)†
1037-2334 The Green Leaf Garden Series
1037-2342 Australian Garden Guide
1037-2369 Australian Country Craft and Decorating **4532**
1037-2512 A S L Newsletter **2792**
1037-258X The Sunbird **915**
1037-2792 Friends of Lutheran Archives. Journal **7644**
1037-2911 Australian Journal of Guidance & Counselling **2829**
1037-2997 The Fossil Collector **6724**
1037-3047 A I M S Monograph Series†
1037-3314 Australian Institute of Marine Science. Annual Report **2800**
1037-3403 Aboriginal and Islander Health Worker Journal **7506**
1037-3608 Bureau of Meteorology. Annual Report **6348**
1037-3640 Architect (Perth) **428**
1037-3748 Work Boat World **8665**
1037-3780 Australian Sports Drug Agency. Annual Report *changed to* 1833-8976 **7509**
1037-390X World Cinderella News†
1037-4124 Australian Journal of Corporate Law **4857**
1037-4361 Nargun **2757**
1037-4590 Western Australian Prospect **1659**
1037-4957 Australia. Bureau of Statistics. Labour Force Status and Educational Attainment, Australia†
1037-5007 Charles Sturt University. Undergraduate Handbook *changed to* 1832-3278 **2970**
1037-5015 Charles Sturt University. Postgraduate Handbook *changed to* 1832-3278 **2970**
1037-5090 Top Dog Journal†
1037-5155 Australia. Bureau of Statistics. Foreign Trade, Australia: Merchandise Exports (Annual)†
1037-5562 Legislative Policy Discussion Paper
1037-5570 Australian Accounting Research Foundation. Accounting Research Study
1037-5678 Australia. Bureau of Statistics. Western Australian Office. Summary of Crops, Western Australia†
1037-5783 Road and Transport Research **3282**
1037-5872 U M E **459**
1037-5902 Australia. Bureau of Statistics. Foreign Trade, Australia: Merchandise Imports (Annual)†
1037-616X Information Technology, Education and Society **2866**
1037-6178 Contemporary Nurse **5956**
1037-6267 Chartac Accountancy News†
1037-6410 Bioethics Outlook **6908**
1037-6534 Asiaview **3926**
1037-6631 Current Family Law **4908**
1037-6666 Guide to Campus Recruiting **2956**
1037-6674 T A A S A Review **520**
1037-6879 Australian Bureau of Agricultural and Resource Economics. Australian Fisheries Statistics (Year) (Print)†
1037-6909 National Industrial Chemicals Notification & Assessment Scheme. Annual Report **2074**
1037-6925 Australian Prison Trends†
1037-7107 Materials Australia **6321**
1037-7131 Indian Ocean Centre for Peace Studies. Briefing Papers†
1037-728X Current Social Issues **7958**
1037-7298 Current Environmental Issues **3413**
1037-7433 Australia. Bureau of Statistics. Shearing and Wool Production Forecast, Australia†
1037-7824 Stepping Stones
1037-826X Crosslight **7753**
1037-8286 A B A R E Research Reports **1055**
1037-8480 Permaculture International Journal†
1037-8553 Graduate Destination Survey **6698**
1037-8839 Chiropractors' Association of Australia. Members' Contact Directory *changed to* Chiropractors' Association of Australia. Membership Directory **5804**
1037-888X Australia. Bureau of Statistics. Foreign Trade, Australia: Merchandise Exports, Detailed Commodity Tables†
1037-9010 Environment South Australia† **8954**
1037-9053 Australia. Bureau of Statistics. Foreign Trade, Australia: Merchandise Exports and Imports†
1037-907X Australia. Bureau of Statistics. Foreign Trade, Australia: Merchandise Imports, Detailed Commodity Classifications†
1037-9088 Australia. Bureau of Statistics. Foreign Trade, Australia: International Cargo†
1037-9096 Australia. Bureau of Statistics. Participation in Education, Australia†
1037-9118 Australia. Bureau of Statistics. New South Wales Office. Agriculture Statistics - Selected Small Area Data, New South Wales†
1037-9126 Australia. Bureau of Statistics. Victorian Office. Agriculture Statistics - Selected Small Area Data, Victoria†
1037-9142 Australia. Bureau of Statistics. South Australian Office. Agriculture Statistics - Selected Small Area Data, South Australia†
1037-9150 Australia. Bureau of Statistics. Western Australian Office. Agriculture Statistics - Selected Small Area Data, Western Australian†
1037-9169 Australia. Bureau of Statistics. Tasmanian Office. Agriculture Statistics - Selected Small Area Data, Tasmania†
1037-9177 Australia. Bureau of Statistics. Western Australian Office. Summary of Criminal Court Proceedings, Western Australia†
1037-969X Alternative Law Journal **4613**
1037-9851 Public History Review **4157**
1037-9894 Asia - Pacific Forest & Timber Bulletin†
1037-9908 National Precaster **1026**
1037-9959 Building Services & Maintenance†
1037-9967 Australian Science Fiction and Fantasy News
1038-0140 Centre for Information Studies. Occasional Monographs†
1038-0213 Family Notes†
1038-023X Birth Issues†
1038-0264 Ulitarra†
1038-0361 Australia. Air Transport Statistics. Regional Airlines Annual† **8932**
1038-0493 The Record (Darlinghurst) **7814**
1038-0507 Australian Family Briefings†
1038-0671 Australian Official Journal of Designs (Print) *changed to* 1832-9942 **6745**
1038-0701 Who's Who in Business in Australia **647**
1038-1139 Theosophy in Australia **7742**
1038-118X Oil and Gas Resources of Australia† **8978**
1038-1317 Oil & Gas Gazette **6783**
1038-1368 Directions in Education **3012**
1038-1562 Australian Journal of Language and Literacy **3017**
1038-1600 HazMat News (Box Hill) *see* 1032-6529 **3577**
1038-1635 Australian Intellectual Property Journal **6745**
1038-1643 Australian Journal of Medical Science **5581**
1038-1678 Farming Ahead **112**
1038-1856 Object **538**
1038-1953 Bulletin of Words and Phrases
1038-2046 International Research in Geographical and Environmental Education **4016**
1038-2097 Pacific Conservation Biology **2624**
1038-2135 A N A R E Reports† **8927**
1038-2224 Queen Victoria Museum and Art Gallery. Occasional Papers **6536**
1038-2232 Australian Society for Biochemistry and Molecular Biology. Proceedings†
1038-2267 International Trade Handbook for Western Australia **1572**
1038-2569 Youth Studies Australia **2172**
1038-2658 Japan Monitor†
1038-2909 Perfect Beat **6605**
1038-3395 Thorpe - R O M† **8993**
1038-3409 Kidsafe **2158**
1038-3425 Sunday Herald-Sun **3796**
1038-3433 Herald-Sun News-Pictorial **3794**
1038-3441 Griffith Law Review **4683**
1038-3514 Simply Better **5083**
1038-3859 University of New England. Centre for Water Policy Research. Discussion Papers (No.)† **8996**
1038-3875 Brother Sister
1038-3964 Centre for Legal Education. Newsletter **2971**
1038-4030 P S A Industrial Bulletin†
1038-4057 Queensland Water Management Journal and Environmental Review†
1038-4111 Asia Pacific Journal of Human Resources **1856**
1038-4162 Australian Journal of Career Development **6692**
1038-4170 One on One Basketball Magazine
1038-4286 Australia. Bureau of Statistics. Australian National Accounts: Financial Accounts *changed to* Australia. Bureau of Statistics. Australian National Accounts: Financial Accounts (Online) **1201**
1038-4359 Architectural Product News **429**
1038-4464 Voiceworks **5437**
1038-4510 Wool Monitor†
1038-4812 A S U National†
1038-4871 The Island Arc **2748**
1038-5002 Retailers Digest
1038-5231 Technical Computing† **8992**
1038-5266 Gifted **2860**
1038-5282 Australian Journal of Rural Health **7509**
1038-5355 C I S Research Reports **4999**
1038-5401 Bowls Alive *changed to* Bowls N S W Magazine **8224**
1038-5509 Newsbeat Australia **8058**
1038-5622 Legal Education Digest **2992**
1038-5657 Eidolon† **8953**
1038-5762 Perspectives in Human Biology **697**
1038-5878 Centre for Information Studies. Bibliographies and Indexes†
1038-5959 Australian Property Law Journal **4827**
1038-5967 Torts Law Journal **4843**
1038-6130 Australian Studies in Journalism† **8934**
1038-6300 Australia. Bureau of Statistics. Index to the Historical Microfiche Series - Statistical Publications Since Federation†
1038-6432 Australian Directory of Academics **2968**
1038-6750 Media Australia†
1038-6777 Law Society of South Australia. Bulletin **4717**
1038-6807 Appita Journal **6732**
1038-6920 A C I A R Proceedings **77**
1038-6963 World Acrobatics†
1038-6998 New South Wales Criminal Courts Statistics **4895**
1038-7234 Assisted Conception, Australia and New Zealand *changed to* 1832-066X **5884**
1038-7536 Queensland Chess†
1038-7544 C Q Chess News†
1038-8400 Tirra Lirra **5389**
1038-846X Craft Arts International **533**
1038-8516 Koori Mail **3546**
1038-8559 The Judicial Review **4953**
1038-8613 N S W Agriculture Today **138**
1038-8761 The Australian **3793**
1038-8796 Grains from Australia†
1038-880X Ingrained†
1038-8842 The Australian - Technology and Science†
1038-8958 Occasional Papers in Open and Distance Learning **2944**
1038-9237 Northern Territory Law Reports **4958**
1038-927X Australia. Bureau of Statistics. Australian Labour Market†
1038-9423 Black+White **6964**
1038-9563 Tourism Education Directory
1038-9601 Sportsman **8298**
1038-9652 Wilderness News **3475**
1038-9725 Woorilla **5400**
1038-9830 Primary Report†
1039-0081 Your Mortgage Magazine **1391**
1039-0170 Nexus Magazine **6742**
1039-0464 Liturgy News **7805**
1039-0537 Snowy Mountains Council. Annual Report† **8988**
1039-0553 Barb's Factory Shopping Guide **1425**
1039-0626 Australian Maritime Safety Authority. Annual Report **8639**
1039-0642 Australasian Welding Journal **6342**
1039-074X Violence Prevention Today†
1039-0871 Indian Ocean Centre for Peace Studies. Occasional Papers and Monographs†
1039-091X A G S O Research Newsletter†
1039-1010 Arena Magazine **7107**
1039-1029 Convention & Incentive Marketing **6279**
1039-1738 Australian and New Zealand Industry Defence Equipment and Capability Catalogue **6412**
1039-222X Education for Library and Information Services: Australia†
1039-2246 Video†
1039-2300 Australasian Muslim Times†
1039-2351 Sydney Restaurant Survey
1039-2610 Australia. Bureau of Statistics. Australian National Accounts: State Accounts (Quarterly)†
1039-2645 Australian Geological Survey Organisation. Bulletin **2702**
1039-2750 A B A Update *changed to* 1832-8784 **2310**
1039-2785 Australia. Bureau of Statistics. Manufacturing Industry: Summary of Operations, Australia†
1039-2831 Modern Greek Studies (Australia and New Zealand) **4245**
1039-2858 ViewPoint: On Books for Young Adults **7575**
1039-3099 Australian Fisheries Management Authority. Annual Report **3586**
1039-3145 Direction **6984**
1039-3277 Trade Practices Law Journal **4882**
1039-3285 Tort Law Review **4843**
1039-3293 Insolvency Law Journal **4693**
1039-3498 National Library of Australia Gateways (Print)† **8976**
1039-3625 Art Asia Pacific **468**
1039-3676 Annual Report by the Inspector-General in Bankruptcy on the Operation of the Bankruptcy Act 1966 **1308**
1039-382X Redress **2903**
1039-3897 Rural Business **1169**
1039-3986 Australian College of Health Service Executives. Monograph Series **4088**
1039-4184 Sunday Mail (Adelaide) **3793**
1039-4192 Advertiser (Adelaide) **3793**
1039-4354 Fellowship of Australian Composers. Journal **6566**
1039-4516 Motor Racing Australia **8188**
1039-4680 Complete Melbourne Wedding Guide **5558**
1039-4761 Survey of Australian Manufacturing†
1039-4788 People and Place **8125**
1039-4982 The Classroom Connection† **8941**
1039-5083 Australia - Japan Economic Institute. Economic Bulletin†
1039-5350 Rawlinsons Construction Cost Guide **1031**
1039-5423 Resource Sciences Interface† **8985**
1039-5466 Write On *changed to* Victorian Writer **7575**
1039-5598 Competition and Consumer Law Journal **4862**
1039-5679 Australian Geological Survey Organisation. Yearbook†
1039-5873 Australian Corporations and Securities Legislation
1039-608X National Accountant **1297**
1039-6594 Australia. Bureau of Statistics. Australian Capital Territory in Focus†
1039-6616 Australian Law Librarian **4993**
1039-6896 Australian Industrial Digest†
1039-6993 International Journal of Employment Studies **1689**
1039-7086 Math Math World **5511**
1039-7116 Australian Doctor **5581**
1039-7205 Western Australia. Department of Agriculture. Resource Management Technical Reports **259**
1039-7213 Local Government and Environmental Reports of Australia **7496**
1039-7469 General Practitioner†
1039-7523 Cotton Research and Development Corporation. Handbook *changed to* 1448-4838 **254**
1039-7779 LifeWise Magazine†
1039-7795 Jazzchord† **8967**
1039-785X Commercial Dispute Resolution Journal†

ISSN

1041-7125 Sophisticate's Hairstyle Guide **591**
1041-7141 Christian College Handbook†
1041-7176 American Lutherie **6544**
1041-7184 Brigham Young University Geology Studies **2727**
1041-7230 976 Cities Plus
1041-7249 Pulp and Paper Industry Technical Conference. Conference Record **6737**
1041-7273 Directory of Theatre Faculties in Colleges and Universities, U S & Canada†
1041-7400 Service Employees News **4602**
1041-7478 O & M Intelligence†
1041-7494 Traverso **6624**
1041-7516 Youth Markets Alert **1849**
1041-7591 Middle Eastern Dancer Magazine **2686**
1041-7648 Biostatistica
1041-7710 Fidelis et Verus **7798**
1041-7737 Special Libraries Association. Social Science Division. Bulletin **5048**
1041-7826 Advances in Small Animal Medicine and Surgery **8790**
1041-7869 Northland Business Ledger **1155**
1041-7877 County Care
1041-7893 Communication Serials **2347**
1041-7915 Computers in Libraries **2570**
1041-794X Southern Communication Journal **2339**
1041-7958 American Machinist **1879**
1041-8032 How to Find Company Intelligence in Federal Documents†
1041-8040 How to Find Company Intelligence in Libraries†
1041-8067 How to Use the Freedom of Information Act†
1041-8091 Ocean Perspectives Journal **2815**
1041-8121 Apple IIGS Buyer's Guide†
1041-8164 F.O.C. Review
1041-8172 Environmental Management Review†
1041-8199 Reality (Houston) **5863**
1041-8202 Fodor's Great Travel Values: Spain†
1041-8237 Midrange Systems†
1041-8253 Reality Now **5863**
1041-8296 Keller's Hazardous Materials Transportation Report **8672**
1041-830X Log Home Living **1021**
1041-8318 Airport Noise Report **8537**
1041-8334 Journal of Network Management
1041-8377 Imagery Today **7361**
1041-8385 Qui Parle **4471**
1041-8407 Gold Sheets **1627**
1041-844X California Business Conditions†
1041-8466 Appalachian Families†
1041-8474 T V I Report†
1041-8490 Voice of the Diabetic **4086**
1041-8504 Maledicta Monitor†
1041-8520 Network for Public Schools
1041-8644 Folklore Historian **3618**
1041-8695 West Virginia and Regional History Collection Newsletter **4167**
1041-8741 Self-Employed America **1966**
1041-875X Sino-Western Cultural Relations Journal **4161**
1041-8830 Sino - Japanese Studies **4188**
1041-8857 A A A S Report: Research and Development **7829**
1041-892X Year Book of Otolaryngology - Head and Neck Surgery **6086**
1041-9039 Philadelphia Papers†
1041-9098 Information Executive†
1041-911X Interact (Wyndmoor)†
1041-9268 Iowa Crops & Weather **182**
1041-9306 Mississippi Outdoors **2619**
1041-9314 Adventure Travel†
1041-9411 Regional Theatre Directory (Year) **8477**
1041-9462 Education Monitor†
1041-9470 Fox Magazine **6291**
1041-9489 Safety Brief **3395**
1041-9527 Women's Studies International **8905**
1041-9551 Nintendo Power **2479**
1041-956X A H A F Journal **7330**
1041-9632 Trolley Fare **6538**
1041-9756 Older Truck Blue Book **8674**
1041-9764 State University of New York. Research†
1041-9772 R V West†
1041-9802 Praxis (Medford) **1603**
1041-9918 Current Opinion in Orthopaedics *changed to* 1940-7041 **6058**
1041-9926 Potato Eyes†
1041-9934 Automotive Electronic News *changed to* 1054-4828
1041-9985 Family Letter†
1041-9993 Up Against the Wall, Mother†
1042-007X Operating Results of Mass Retail Stores - Mass Retailers' Merchandising Report - Cornell Study†
1042-0134 Left Business Observer **1144**
1042-0142 Washington Regulatory Report†
1042-0150 Radiation Effects and Defects in Solids **7071**
1042-0169 Synthesis (Asheville) **3004**
1042-0193 Abstracts in Human - Computer Interaction†
1042-0215 Who Knows About Industries and Markets†
1042-0231 Local Governmental Accounting Trends and Techniques† **8971**
1042-0282 Nashville Automotive Report **8595**
1042-0290 Resolve National Newsletter **6003**
1042-0355 The Kansas Directory of Commerce
1042-0371 Centro de Estudios Puertorriquenos. Bulletin†
1042-041X Psychiatric Abstract and Comment†
1042-0487 Pro Principal **3030**
1042-0533 American Journal of Human Biology **652**
1042-0541 Journal of Agricultural Education **2874**
1042-0592 Florida Public Employee Reporter **1682**
1042-0614 Recycling Times†
1042-0622 Hidden Pictures Magazine†
1042-0630 Solar Today **3177**
1042-0649 Soundtrack **6618**
1042-0681 Shareware Magazine
1042-0711 Advanced Imaging **2349**
1042-0746 Business Information Alert **4998**
1042-0819 Off - Road Advertiser
1042-0851 Announcer†
1042-0940 Ichnos **6725**
1042-0959 Applied Thermal Sciences *see* 0204-3602 **3394**
1042-0967 Electronic and Communications in Japan. Part 3: Fundamental Electronic Science *changed to* 1942-9533 **3096**
1042-0983 Health Law Handbook **4686**
1042-0991 Pharmacy Today **6874**
1042-1009 Heartland Boating **8276**
1042-1041 D M S - Precision Guided Munitions Market Study†
1042-105X Type & Press **7575**
1042-1068 West Coast Conference on Formal Linguistics. Proceedings **5195**
1042-1122 Ceramic Transactions **2039**
1042-1149 Orbit Video
1042-1254 Northwestern Financial Review **1372**
1042-1262 Music Research Forum **6591**
1042-1297 Conceive Magazine (California)†
1042-1319 Journal of Information Technology Management **2548**
1042-1335 Golf Book of Records†
1042-1394 Alcoholism & Drug Abuse Weekly **2691**
1042-1440 The Natural Gas Yearbook†
1042-1459 Archives and Museum Informatics Technical Report†
1042-1491 Woman of Mystery
1042-1521 Your Patient & Fitness in Rheumatology **6228**
1042-153X Consultants Directory for Business and Industry†
1042-1564 The Maryland Report **7452**
1042-1572 World News Digest
1042-1610 S R C Brown Book of 5-Trend O T C Charts†
1042-1629 Educational Technology Research & Development **3059**
1042-1653 Accountants Microcomputer News†
1042-1661 Southern Saltwater†
1042-1696 Veterinary Management Update†
1042-1726 Journal of Computing in Higher Education **2949**
1042-1734 U.S. Library of Congress. Accessions List: Brazil and Uruguay. Annual List of Serials†
1042-1807 Rabbinical Council of America. Sermon Anthology† **8984**
1042-1858 Georgetown International Environmental Law Review **3433**
1042-1866 Seminars Directory†
1042-1882 Johns Hopkins Medical Letter Health after 50 **4048**
1042-1904 C C T V Applications & Technology
1042-1912 Public Gaming International **8194**
1042-1920 Naval History **6438**
1042-1939 Energy and Engineering Science Series
1042-1955 Male - Female Roles†
1042-1963 Employee Assistance†
1042-1998 Between C and D†
1042-2021 Advanced Development **7331**
1042-2048 Helicopter Safety *changed to* 1934-4015 **8533**
1042-2080 Stagecoach†
1042-2099 Dis - Ability Law Briefs†
1042-2137 Spectrum (Sacramento) **4056**
1042-2145 Floral and Nursery Times†
1042-217X Resources (Lake Oswego)†
1042-2196 Cancer Cells (Monthly)†
1042-2234 Bridges (Monkton) **6908**
1042-2250 Contemporary Urology *changed to* Urology Times: The Urology Times Clinical Edition **6276**
1042-2420 Directory of Women Entrepreneurs
1042-2455 Today in Medicine. Cardiovascular Disease†
1042-2471 Ancient Controversy
1042-2501 Midatlantic Antiques Magazine **367**
1042-251X E I Digest **3505**
1042-2528 Focus on Ohio Dentistry *changed to* 1536-1683 **5857**
1042-2579 Physical Therapy Today†
1042-2587 Entrepreneurship: Theory and Practice **1960**
1042-2633 Who's Who in Live Animal Trade & Transport†
1042-2757 Sensor's Buyers Guide **4490**
1042-2781 Health News Daily **5625**
1042-2803 Take One Production
1042-2838 Today in Medicine. Diabetology and Endocrinology **5900**
1042-2846 Today in Medicine. Respiratory Disease **6220**
1042-2889 University of Nebraska. Agricultural Research Division. Research Bulletin **167**
1042-2951 Blue Mesa Review **5264**
1042-296X I E E E Transactions on Robotics and Automation *changed to* 1552-3098 **2584**
1042-2986 Jewish Community Voice (Cherry Hill) **7722**
1042-2994 Symposium on Small Computers in the Arts. Proceedings
1042-3036 Tant†
1042-3044 Schoolhouse Magazine **2962**
1042-3052 Radcliffe News†
1042-3060 The Crimean Review
1042-3079 Oakley's Aggressive Stock Alert†
1042-3087 Personal Investing News†
1042-3109 Solstice
1042-3133 Game Player's†
1042-3141 Association Meetings **6278**
1042-315X Chemical Dependency†
1042-3168 Tennessee Environmental Law Letter
1042-3176 Professional Reader
1042-3192 Studies in Qualitative Methodology **8008**
1042-3230 Society Farsarotul Newsletter **3565**
1042-3249 Monthly Planet†
1042-3257 Nashville Visitor's Guide
1042-3281 Canales†
1042-329X Black Health (Madison)
1042-3311 Ward Foundation News **6540**
1042-332X Index of Model Periodicals†
1042-3346 Independent Investor†
1042-3435 Specialization Update **4786**
1042-3443 Musical America†
1042-346X Journal of Laser Applications **7078**
1042-3494 The Catholic World†
1042-3524 P G R S A Quarterly **806**
1042-3540 MuniWeek†
1042-3575 P C Digest Ratings Report†
1042-3591 Directory of Foreign Trade Organizations in Eastern Europe†
1042-363X Progress in AIDS Pathology†
1042-3664 Inside Texas Running **8318**
1042-3672 C V: The College Magazine†
1042-3680 Neurosurgery Clinics of North America **6252**
1042-3699 Oral and Maxillofacial Surgery Clinics of North America **6255**
1042-3737 E P S I G News **7560**
1042-3745 Glos Nauczyciela **2860**
1042-3834 Society of Basque Studies in America. Journal **4265**
1042-3850 Means Plumbing Cost Data **4128**
1042-3869 N C A A Men's and Women's Illustrated Basketball Rules **8239**
1042-3877 N C A A Men's and Women's Basketball Rules and Interpretations **8239**
1042-3907 J. Paul Getty Trust. Report
1042-3915 Journal of Fire Protection Engineering **3579**
1042-3931 Journal of Invasive Cardiology **5793**
1042-394X Sports Illustrated for Kids **2214**
1042-4016 Greyhound Review **8176**
1042-4032 The International Journal of Humanities and Peace **4457**
1042-4067 Journal of Gynecologic Surgery **5995**
1042-4075 The M A Report **5763**
1042-413X Initiatives (Louisville)†
1042-4172 Directory of State Court Clerks & County Courthouses (Year) **4950**
1042-4199 Black Heritage Unveiled Newsletter
1042-4229 Washington View **3572**
1042-4245 School Library Media Folders of Ideas for Library Excellence†
1042-4261 The Hulbert Financial Digest **1629**
1042-4296 Intelligence **2423**
1042-4326 Newspaper Investor† **8977**
1042-4334 I H N News **4066**
1042-4423 Abstracts of Clinical Care Guidelines† **8927**
1042-4431 Journal of International Financial Markets, Institutions & Money **1362**
1042-444X Journal of Multinational Financial Management **1769**
1042-4482 Professional, Sales & Technical Remuneration, Canada† **8982**
1042-4563 I E E E Workshop on Languages for Automation (Proceedings)†
1042-4601 Practical Homeowner Magazine†
1042-461X Virginia Employment Law Letter **4809**
1042-4628 Classics in the History and Philosophy of Science
1042-4636 Research and Bibliographical Guides in Criminal Justice† **8985**
1042-4652 The Exchange (San Francisco)†
1042-4687 Applications of Digital Image Processing **7073**
1042-4768 The Dirty Goat **5421**
1042-4784 AIDS Update (Washington)†
1042-4822 P S A **5347**
1042-4865 Pacific - Mountain Oil Directory **2023**
1042-4873 Coral Springs Monthly
1042-5055 The Journal of Chiropractic Education **5806**
1042-508X Compoundings **6766**
1042-511X Winging It **917**
1042-5128 The Washington Times Index **4588**
1042-5152 WordPerfect Magazine†
1042-5179 D N A Sequence *changed to* 1940-1736 **738**
1042-5195 Incentive **1820**
1042-5209 Environmental Lab†
1042-5217 Business & Management Education Funding Alert†
1042-5233 American CattleWoman **277**
1042-5276 Sophisticate's Black Hair **591**
1042-5284 Wrestling Superstars†
1042-5292 Boxing (Year) **8162**
1042-5314 Gold Belt Wrestling
1042-5330 Ideas Plus† **8963**
1042-5357 Mark Twain Circular **5331**
1042-5381 Heaven Bone **5423**
1042-5446 State Backgrounder **7185**
1042-5632 Thoroughbred Racing Action†
1042-5667 Amaryllis **3721**
1042-5675 Professional Lawyer **4762**
1042-5721 Journal of C Language Translation†
1042-5772 Stockholders and Creditors News Service Concerning L T V Corporation, et al†
1042-5799 Stockholders and Creditors News Service Concerning the Public Service Company of New Hampshire†
1042-5845 Aggressive Tax Avoidance for Real Estate Investors **7581**
1042-587X Berkshire Magazine†
1042-590X Florida Business **1110**
1042-5926 Delaware Keystone Motorist *changed to* 1523-9403 **8553**
1042-5934 Domestic Relations Journal of Ohio **4909**
1042-5942 Criminal Law Journal of Ohio†
1042-5985 American University Studies. Series 27. Feminist Studies **8893**
1042-6027 State Fiscal Capacity and Effort **1944**
1042-606X News Network International†
1042-6086 CommunicationsWeek International†
1042-6094 Weekend Woodworking Projects†
1042-6167 Catalog Handbook **1979**
1042-6175 Business Opportunities Handbook **1958**
1042-6205 Auto Price Almanac†
1042-6213 The Americas Review (Houston)†
1042-6221 Aquaculture Situation & Outlook Report†
1042-6256 N S A A News†
1042-6299 Fisheries Review†
1042-6302 FoxTalk†
1042-6329 Audiotex Directory & Buyer's Guide **2365**
1042-6337 Journal of Business & Entrepreneurship **1133**
1042-6345 Vision Care Assistant†
1042-6388 Student Assistance Journal **2699**
1042-6418 The Business Review of Northeast Ohio
1042-6442 Cleanfax Magazine **2242**
1042-6450 Gun Tests **8316**
1042-6493 Radiation Effects and Defects in Solids Bulletin†
1042-6507 Phosphorus, Sulfur and Silicon and the Related Elements **2117**

1042-6531 West's South Eastern Reporter **4814**
1042-654X H B S Catalog of Teaching Materials†
1042-6566 New Age Retailer **6646**
1042-6590 Partnerships in Education Journal
1042-6604 Southern Reader
1042-6647 Ex Libris (Concord) *changed to* 1932-8206 **7568**
1042-6655 Syntax in the Schools *changed to* Assembly for the Teaching of English Grammar Journal **3051**
1042-671X Barton County Genealogical Society. Quarterly†
1042-6736 B M I: Music World **6547**
1042-6795 Western Blue Chip Economic Forecast **1524**
1042-6833 Societe Americaine de Philosophie de Langue Francaise. Bulletin *changed to* 1936-6280 **6928**
1042-6841 National Underwriter. Property & Casualty - Risk & Benefits Management Edition *changed to* 1940-1353 **4516**
1042-6884 Will - Grundy Counties Genealogical Society News **3788**
1042-6914 Materials & Manufacturing Processes **3389**
1042-6922 Lens and Eye Toxicity Research†
1042-6965 America Oggi **3518**
1042-7015 B N A Special Report Series on Work & Family†
1042-704X Orthopedic Products News†
1042-7104 Black Arts Annual†
1042-7120 Community Associations Institute. Board Briefs†
1042-7139 Bread Pudding Update **4353**
1042-7147 Polymers for Advanced Technologies **7099**
1042-7155 Symmetry†
1042-7163 Heteroatom Chemistry **2116**
1042-7201 Forensic Science Review **4676**
1042-721X Federal Computer Market Report **2513**
1042-7252 Software Industry Report **2597**
1042-7260 Journal of Zoo and Wildlife Medicine **8802**
1042-7279 Dissertation Abstracts International. Section C: Worldwide **4484**
1042-7309 Journal of Management Science & Policy Analysis **1768**
1042-7325 Reseller Management†
1042-7341 "Check the Oil!" Magazine **4331**
1042-735X Trikone Magazine **4379**
1042-7392 Antique Power **209**
1042-7481 Electricity Yearbook
1042-749X Chinese Journal of Biotechnology†
1042-7562 In-Site **3738**
1042-7589 Adolescent Counselor Magazine *changed to* Adolescent Magazine
1042-7597 Viet Nam Generation†
1042-7643 Weavers†
1042-7678 Met Golfer **8238**
1042-7694 Video Investor†
1042-7848 Civilian Career Guide **6695**
1042-7899 Unknown *changed to* Doe **5069**
1042-7937 Passenger Train Annual†
1042-7953 Teenage†
1042-7961 Journal of Women's History **8900**
1042-7988 International Journal of Computer Aided V L S I Design†
1042-8011 World Resource Review **3475**
1042-802X Plastics News **7097**
1042-8038 Oahu Update†
1042-8046 Hawaii: The Big Island Update **8717**
1042-8119 Ohio Realtor **7603**
1042-8127 Today's Investor **1655**
1042-8194 Leukemia and Lymphoma **5940**
1042-8216 Primary Sources & Original Works†
1042-8232 Journal of Progressive Human Services **8050**
1042-8267 America's Best Colleges **2953**
1042-8275 Oceanography **2815**
1042-8399 England on Fifty Dollars a Day **8701**
1042-8461 Horizon (Chicago) **7648**
1042-8623 CD-ROM EndUser†
1042-864X Camoes Center Quarterly†
1042-8658 GamePro **2476**
1042-8712 Frommer's Touring Guides. Amsterdam **8711**
1042-878X Track and Field and Cross Country Rules Book **8337**
1042-8801 Tennessee Business Directory **2030**
1042-8836 C B M R Monographs **6552**
1042-8879 Payments Monthly†
1042-895X Gastroenterology Nursing **5925**
1042-8976 Oklahoma Grocers Journal **3680**
1042-9018 Association for Supervision and Curriculum Development. Yearbook†
1042-9034 The Brooklyn Museum Report†
1042-9042 Child Welfare League of America. Directory of Member Agencies†
1042-9050 Moxie†
1042-9085 Rental Management **1839**
1042-9115 Corporate Real Estate Executive†
1042-9123 Food Arts **4386**
1042-9166 Emerald City Comix & Stories†
1042-9239 Earnshaw's Plus Sizes†
1042-9247 Engineering Management Journal **3190**
1042-9271 Atlanta Kids
1042-9379 The Peanut Grower **245**
1042-9387 Hoop Basketball Yearbook **8235**
1042-9409 Stage & Studio **6619**
1042-9417 Bestsellers†
1042-9476 Consumer Reports Used Car Buying Guide **8576**
1042-9522 Angeles†
1042-9549 Colorado Woman News†
1042-9565 Advancing Clinical Care†
1042-9573 Journal of Financial Intermediation **1545**
1042-9662 Sports Car International **8604**
1042-9670 Academic Psychiatry **6118**
1042-9719 Washington History **4317**
1042-976X Study of Federal Tax Law. Taxation of Income†
1042-9778 Annual Obituary (Year)†
1042-9808 Latin American Art†
1042-9832 Random Structures & Algorithms **5528**
1042-9840 The Wall Street Journal Index **1274**
1042-993X Bare Knuckles†
1042-9948 Comstock Quarterly†
1042-9972 Weekend Gardener†
1042-9980 Louisiana Life **3980**
1043-0075 Blk†
1043-0083 P J G†
1043-0121 A 2 L A (Year) Annual Report **1970**
1043-013X Methane Recovery from Landfill Yearbook **3509**
1043-0164 The Turkish Times **3569**
1043-0210 Penthouse Forum **6297**
1043-0253 Fodor's United States of America† **8957**
1043-0261 (Year) V I P Address Book **36**
1043-027X Nichols Nostalgia **3777**
1043-0342 Human Gene Therapy **871**
1043-0490 Wisconsin Lawyer **4815**
1043-0547 Bankruptcy Law Review†
1043-0555 Anesthesia Today **5769**
1043-0628 New York Civil Motion Citator **4839**
1043-0636 New York Matrimonial Case Citator **4913**
1043-0652 American Gas **6762**
1043-0660 Clinical Consultations in Obstetrics and Gynecology†
1043-0679 Seminars in Thoracic and Cardiovascular Surgery **6258**
1043-0695 Communique (Columbus, 1967) **1734**
1043-0709 Student Traveler†
1043-0768 Acknowledge the Window Letter **2570**
1043-0792 Compute's Amiga Resource†
1043-0806 Buried Treasure
1043-0814 Poetics†
1043-0865 Satellite Business News **2389**
1043-092X National Directory of Art Internships **508**
1043-0946 Search (Devon)†
1043-0962 Asphalt **8629**
1043-0989 Conference on Artificial Intelligence Applications. Proceedings†
1043-0997 Science Weekly. Level F **2212**
1043-1012 Decisions in Imaging Economics *changed to* Imaging Economics **6198**
1043-1020 Journal of Artificial Intelligence in Education†
1043-1039 Live Animal Trade & Transport Magazine†
1043-1047 Taekwondo World†
1043-108X I E E E Mining Industry Technical Conference. Conference Record†
1043-1195 Official Guide to American Historic Inns **8744**
1043-1241 C B M R Digest **6552**
1043-125X Renewal News†
1043-1268 Big Hammer
1043-1357 Fielding's Budget Europe†
1043-1365 International Social Movement Research *see* 0163-786X **8128**
1043-1373 A I C P A Professional Standards†
1043-139X Current Veterinary Therapy. Food Animal Practice†
1043-142X Joke in the Box Newsletter *changed to* 1046-5588
1043-1470 Third Circuit Digest **4966**
1043-1489 Seminars in Colon and Rectal Surgery **6258**
1043-1497 Sycamore Review **5384**
1043-1535 The World Almanac of U.S. Politics†
1043-1543 AIDS Clinical Care **5808**
1043-1578 Social Justice **7265**
1043-1640 Japanese Sword Society of the U S Bulletin **366**
1043-1659 Arizona Facts **3118**
1043-1667 The Estimate **6420**
1043-1675 Commercial Property News **7587**
1043-1683 Asbestos Monitor†
1043-1705 Workshop by and for Teachers
1043-1721 Society for Health Systems. Journal **6687**
1043-1780 Ophthalmic Drug Facts **6047**
1043-1802 Bioconjugate Chemistry **726**
1043-1810 Operative Techniques in Otolaryngology - Head and Neck Surgery **6083**
1043-1837 Medical Virology†
1043-1888 Credit Union Financial Profiles **1333**
1043-190X Barron's Guide to Graduate Business Schools **1065**
1043-1918 V A S Newsletter†
1043-2035 Professional Boatbuilder **8280**
1043-2043 Directory of World Leaders & Factbook (Year)
1043-2051 Professional Licensing Report **4762**
1043-2086 Campus - Free College Degrees **2970**
1043-2094 Against the Grain **4987**
1043-2167 National Forum of Special Education Journal **3044**
1043-2175 Seismic Interpretation Series **2789**
1043-2205 Critical Care Choices *see* 0744-6314 **5974**
1043-2213 *see* 1538-4608 **4218**
1043-2221 New Women, New Church **7666**
1043-223X La Red - The Net Hotline†
1043-2256 California Dental Association. Journal **5837**
1043-2264 New Federalist **1501**
1043-2280 The Mature Traveler†
1043-2299 Micropendium†
1043-2302 Texas Printer†
1043-237X Library Talk *changed to* 1542-4715 **5028**
1043-240X Humor and Cartoon Markets†
1043-2418 Super Group Magazine (English Edition)
1043-2450 North American Fisherman **8325**
1043-2485 Fire Protection Contractor **3577**
1043-2523 Historical Harpsichord Series **6573**
1043-254X Journal of Dental Hygiene **5851**
1043-2558 Fluid - Particle Separation Journal **3244**
1043-2590 Mustang! (Rollingstone)†
1043-2604 Dermatology Clinical Digest Series†
1043-2639 Mayberry Gazette
1043-268X Report on Defense Plant Waste†
1043-2701 Rugging Room Bulletin†
1043-2752 Regulatory Affairs†
1043-2760 Trends in Endocrinology and Metabolism **5900**
1043-2779 Healthy Harvest†
1043-2795 National Jewish News **7727**
1043-2809 The Appalachian Reader **3403**
1043-2841 PreShipment Testing **6714**
1043-2906 Growing Edge Magazine **3735**
1043-2981 Infectious Disease and Therapy Series **5817**
1043-3031 Clinical Abstracts - Current Therapeutic Findings†
1043-3074 Head & Neck **6245**
1043-3082 Executive Action Report†
1043-3104 Dealer Progress† **8949**
1043-3120 The ArmBender **8159**
1043-3163 Recovery Now†
1043-3198 Clinical Practice of Gynecology†
1043-321X Breast Diseases: A Year Book Quarterly **5987**
1043-3260 Whitney Museum of American Art. Biennial Exhibition *changed to* Whitney Biennial **526**
1043-3287 Current Research on Occupations and Professions **8097**
1043-3309 Journal of Agricultural Economics Research†
1043-3317 Ars Ceramica **364**
1043-3325 Parting Gifts **5429**
1043-3333 The Evergreen Chronicles†
1043-3341 Echoes (Caribou)
1043-335X Quaternary Sciences Center Technical Report **7901**
1043-3384 O C L C Participating Institutions. Arranged by Institution Name **5037**
1043-3473 Mystery Readers Journal **5414**
1043-3503 Haunts **5443**
1043-352X Augsburg Fortress Book Newsletter†
1043-3546 Dairy, Food and Environmental Sanitation *changed to* 1541-9576 **3641**
1043-3686 After Hours†
1043-3694 InfoText **2368**
1043-3724 NewsLinks **3014**
1043-3732 Bad Haircut†
1043-3740 Fair News **6523**
1043-3783 Haiti Observateur **3874**
1043-3805 Kansas Working Papers in Linguistics **5136**
1043-383X Cabirion: Gay Books Bulletin **4371**
1043-3848 Ars Lyrica **6546**
1043-3856 Report on Guatemala **7262**
1043-3945 The Real Ghostbusters Magazine†
1043-3953 Physician's Drug Handbook **6875**
1043-3996 Contemporary Topics in Pure and Applied Condensed Matter Science
1043-4038 Audio Video Review Digest†
1043-4046 Advances in Physiology Education **918**
1043-4054 Transportation Builder **8636**
1043-4062 Constitutional Political Economy **4847**
1043-4070 Journal of the History of Sexuality **8116**
1043-4100 International Contract Design **4544**
1043-4119 Plastic Surgery News **6255**
1043-4186 Sorrow's Reward†
1043-4216 Media Update (Print) *changed to* Media Update (Online) **6587**
1043-4224 Scientific Sleuthing Review **5916**
1043-4232 Professional Cleaning Journal
1043-4275 Florida State University Research in Review **7855**
1043-4364 Peak Performance Selling†
1043-4445 Data News Weekly **3529**
1043-4488 Country America†
1043-4526 Advances in Food and Nutrition Research **6654**
1043-4534 Harvard Papers in Botany **792**
1043-4542 Journal of Pediatric Oncology Nursing **6025**
1043-4631 Rationality and Society **7995**
1043-464X Fire Resistant Materials and Products: Patents and Abstracts†
1043-4658 Technique (San Diego) **707**
1043-4666 Cytokine **865**
1043-4674 The New Biologist†
1043-4771 Paintball†
1043-4852 Catalog of New Foreign and International Law Titles†
1043-4879 Van & Truck Digest†
1043-4895 Central Virginia Heritage **3761**
1043-4933 Yellow Sheet (Ballwin)
1043-4976 S I M Industrial Microbiology News **770**
1043-500X Journal of Offender Monitoring **2657**
1043-5026 Folk Art Messenger **490**
1043-5034 Spaniels in the Field **6815**
1043-5050 Pacific Review (San Bernardino) **5232**
1043-5085 Aspen Magazine **3969**
1043-5158 Southeastern College Art Conference Review **518**
1043-5174 Barley Genetics Newsletter
1043-5212 Pacific Northwest Executive†
1043-5239 Textile Topics (Print) *changed to* Textile Topics (Online) **8461**
1043-5247 Context (Boston) **388**
1043-5328 Sacred Dance Guild Journal **2687**
1043-5336 Business Today (St. Paul)
1043-5379 The A M I C A News Bulletin **6541**
1043-5441 Railmodel Journal† **8984**
1043-5468 Beautiful Glass for Home & Office†
1043-5492 Bowhunting World **8306**
1043-5506 Labor Relations Reference Manual **1693**
1043-5514 Labor Arbitration Reports *see* Labor Relations Reporter. Labor Arbitration and Dispute Settlements **1693**
1043-5522 Biblical Preaching Journal **7627**
1043-5565 Noise Regulation Report **3489**
1043-5573 World Tables†
1043-5646 Allstate Motor Club Fishing Hotspots. Wisconsin
1043-5662 International Trade Reporter. Import Reference Manual **1572**
1043-5670 International Trade Reporter Export Reference Manual **1572**
1043-5689 Labor Relations Reporter. Wage and Hour Cases **1693**
1043-5700 Environmental Hazards†
1043-5727 Sociocriticism: Literature, Society, and History **5374**
1043-5735 Hermeneutic Commentaries†
1043-5743 Irish Studies **4232**
1043-5751 Studies in Gerard Manley Hopkins†
1043-576X The Enlightenment: German and Interdisciplinary Studies†
1043-5778 Ars Interpretandi **5257**
1043-5786 Studies in European Thought **4270**
1043-5794 Studies in Italian Culture: Literature in History **5381**
1043-5808 New German-American Studies **4466**
1043-5816 Emory Studies in Early Christianity†
1043-5824 Allstate Motor Club R V Sales, Rental and Service Directory
1043-5859 Allstate Motor Club R V Park and Campground Directory†
1043-5905 Pharmaceutical Activities Index - Directory†
1043-5913 Libanun Niyuz†

ISSN

ISSN

1046-5472 As I See It Today†
1046-5480 All About Business in Hawaii **1436**
1046-5545 Seneca Searchers **3782**
1046-557X Pirandellian Studies†
1046-5588 Laughter Prescription Newsletter
1046-560X Journal of Science Teacher Education **2878**
1046-5634 Mas†
1046-5642 Voice (Ft. Lauderdale) **6117**
1046-5715 Advances in Accounting. Supplement **1279**
1046-5723 Advances in Solid-State Chemistry†
1046-5782 International Journal of Roofing Technology†
1046-5847 Advances in Financial Planning and Forecasting. Supplement **1724**
1046-5901 Charbonneau Connection†
1046-591X The Wine Spectator's Great Restaurant Wine Lists Dining Guide *see* 0193-497X **613**
1046-5928 Protein Expression and Purification **743**
1046-6053 Maine (Auburn)
1046-607X Video Software Magazine†
1046-6150 Report on Literacy Program†
1046-6193 Teacher Magazine **3084**
1046-6282 Hostile Environments and High Temperature Measurements†
1046-6312 Beautiful Homes† **8935**
1046-6339 Trees from the Grove **3786**
1046-6355 Mainstream News **4075**
1046-638X Manual of Oncologic Therapeutics
1046-6444 Casualty Actuarial Society. Discussion Paper Program **4498**
1046-6487 Casualty Actuarial Society. Forum **4498**
1046-6495 Stone Drum
1046-6517 A N A Communique†
1046-6614 Image File **4297**
1046-6657 Development Education Annual†
1046-6665 Equipment Leasing Today **5451**
1046-6673 American Society of Nephrology. Journal **6265**
1046-669X Journal of Marketing Channels **1825**
1046-6789 Society for Experimental Mechanics. Annual Proceedings **3357**
1046-6819 Learning Disabilities (Pittsburgh) **3043**
1046-6959 Developments in Cardiology†
1046-7041 A B N F Journal **5949**
1046-705X Food Structure†
1046-7092 Shepard's New York Miscellaneous Case Names Citator **4963**
1046-7157 Tire Retreading - Repair Journal **7827**
1046-7203 Who's Who in American Education **646**
1046-7211 International New Product Newsletter
1046-7238 Developing the World Class Information Systems Organization†
1046-7262 Dial-A-Fax Directory **1984**
1046-7378 Ancestors - Descendants of Futral - Clifford, Watkins - Wood **3758**
1046-7386 Cytometry. Supplement *see* 1552-4922 **831**
1046-7394 South Carolina Nurse†
1046-7408 American Journal of Reproductive Immunology **5754**
1046-7416 *see* 0022-4790 **6250**
1046-7491 Journal of Employee Ownership Law and Finance **4701**
1046-7548 W H Y†
1046-7599 Human Communication and Its Disorders†
1046-7602 College Alumni and Military Publications **2278**
1046-7696 AIDS Update (New York)†
1046-7734 Swords and Ploughshares **7268**
1046-7874 The Formalist **5422**
1046-7882 Bibliographies and Indexes in Ethnic Studies† **8936**
1046-7890 The Journal of Clinical Ethics **5647**
1046-7912 Lies of Our Times†
1046-7947 Agricultural Building Cost Guide (Year)†
1046-8021 E **3414**
1046-8064 Research in the Social Scientific Study of Religion **7676**
1046-8110 Hudson's Subscription Newsletter Directory†
1046-8129 North Dakota Business Directory **2021**
1046-8188 A C M Transactions on Information Systems **1413**
1046-8196 C H F Newsbriefs **4405**
1046-8234 Income - Expense Analysis: Conventional Apartments **7595**
1046-8242 Best in Advertising†
1046-8250 Jobson's Liquor Handbook†
1046-8331 Wisconsin Facts **3122**
1046-834X Kentucky Facts **3120**
1046-8358 Bridges **8894**
1046-8366 The International Permaculture Solutions Journal **2615**
1046-8374 Criminal Law Forum **4887**
1046-8390 University of Kansas. Paleontological Contributions. New Series **6731**
1046-8471 Art Issues†
1046-8684 New Media News†
1046-8749 Washington Park Arboretum Bulletin **3753**
1046-8773 Mutual Fund Performance Report†
1046-8781 Simulation & Gaming **2518**
1046-8862 National Survey of Professional, Administrative, Technical, and Clerical Pay. Private Nonservice Industries†
1046-8897 Chiron Review **5419**
1046-896X Advances in the Study of Entrepreneurship, Innovation, and Economic Growth. Supplement *see* 1048-4736 **1435**
1046-8986 American Photo **6963**
1046-9001 Visual Resources Association Bulletin **525**
1046-9036 The Selling Advantage **1172**
1046-9060 North Carolina Business Directory **2021**
1046-9079 Military & Aerospace Electronics **66**
1046-9087 Contemporary Print Portfolio **483**
1046-9109 Michigan Employment Law Letter **4733**
1046-9176 U C L A Latin American Studies **4315**
1046-9206 Ohio Employment Law Letter **4751**
1046-9214 Texas Employment Law Letter **4794**
1046-9249 Portage County Legal News **4759**
1046-9265 Port of New Orleans Record *changed to* Port Record **8657**
1046-9389 The North Stone Review **5343**
1046-9397 Aquatic Plant News **776**
1046-9427 Twin Plant News **1585**
1046-9486 Coal Transportation Statistics **6460**
1046-9494 North Carolina Manufacturing Firms Directory†
1046-9508 C U P A - Journal *changed to* C U P A - H R Journal **2970**
1046-9516 N I D A Research Monograph **2697**
1046-9524 Management Consulting†
1046-9559 The Connection (Washington) **8856**
1046-9567 Series in Representation and Reasoning
1046-9575 Business N H Magazine **1426**
1046-9613 Tribe
1046-9621 Moscow International Business
1046-9648 Inside Microsoft Works (Macintosh Edition)†
1046-9656 Inside WordPerfect†
1046-9699 Craft Marketing News†
1046-9702 Residential and Commercial Sunspaces†
1046-9761 Lilacs Quarterly Journal **3742**
1046-9818 Computer-Assisted Anthropology News **333**
1046-9826 5 AM **5439**
1046-9834 Afghanistan Studies Journal†
1046-9885 Ventura Professional†
1046-9958 Ingram's **1123**
1046-9966 Real Estate / Environmental Liability News **4765**
1046-9974 Times: in Harness **8299**
1047-0034 High Tech Lifestyles
1047-0042 Research in Urban Sociology **8128**
1047-0077 Yesteryears Trails **3788**
1047-0093 Wayne County Historian **4317**
1047-0158 Hubbub **5424**
1047-0166 Tennessee Pharmacist **6882**
1047-0204 Favonius†
1047-0239 Propaganda Review†
1047-0298 Grassroots Motorsports **8583**
1047-031X Alabama Living **2634**
1047-0328 Christmas: Year Round Needlework & Craft Ideas **6637**
1047-0344 Compensation in Manufacturing **1671**
1047-0352 B L S Update **1212**
1047-0387 Attention and Performance **7337**
1047-0425 Fire Protection Equipment Directory **3577**
1047-0441 Food Cost Review **198**
1047-0476 Joe Franklin's Nostalgia†
1047-0530 Tokyo Business Month†
1047-059X Employment, Hours, and Earnings: United States†
1047-0719 Focus (San Francisco) **5814**
1047-0735 Develop†
1047-0743 California Bankruptcy Journal **4859**
1047-076X Edmund's Car Savvy†
1047-0816 Women's Policy Research Conference. Proceedings *changed to* Institute for Women's Policy Research. Conference Proceedings **8899**
1047-0840 Highways (Region 2 Southwest Edition) **8317**
1047-0859 Highways (Region 3, 4 Central Edition) **8317**
1047-0867 Highways (Region 5 Northeast Edition) **8317**
1047-0875 Highways (Region 6 Southeast Edition) **8317**
1047-0905 Perspectives on Social Problems†
1047-0913 Van Hoc **5394**
1047-0999 Almanac of the Unelected **7104**
1047-1006 Comparative State Politics **7118**
1047-1057 Koinonia **7763**
1047-1073 Canadian - American Public Policy **7225**
1047-1111 World Currency Monitor Annual. U.S. Dollar†
1047-1189 Criminal Law Advocacy Reporter **4887**
1047-1227 Seminars in Chiropractic†
1047-126X Research in Asian Economic Studies **1165**
1047-1286 Resources (New York) **634**
1047-1308 Circle Y of Yoakum **1882**
1047-1324 Congress and the Nation **7118**
1047-1367 TechNotes - dBASE IV†
1047-1375 TechNotes - Framework III†
1047-1383 TechNotes - Graphics†
1047-1391 TechNotes - Word Publishing†
1047-1405 Haiti Progres **3536**
1047-1413 Charlotte County Florida Land Owner *changed to* 1053-3060
1047-143X Figment: Tales from the Imagination
1047-1480 Modern Millionaire
1047-1618 The Special Educator **3047**
1047-1634 Quiltmaker **6641**
1047-1642 Youth Ministry Quarterly (Saint Louis)†
1047-1669 Competition Angler†
1047-1693 Digital Directions Report†
1047-1707 Promo **33**
1047-1715 Who's Where in the American Theatre†
1047-1731 On Watch **6440**
1047-1790 Michigan Business Directory **2016**
1047-1820 Magazette (Birmingham)†
1047-1863 Medicare Compliance Alert **4514**
1047-1871 Topps†
1047-1901 Stage Directions **8479**
1047-191X Future Choices†
1047-1979 International Journal of Clinical Acupuncture **310**
1047-1987 Political Analysis **7168**
1047-2002 Advances in Social Science Methodology **7945**
1047-2061 AutoGlass **2037**
1047-2134 Virginia Trial Lawyers Association. Journal **4809**
1047-2207 Rhododendron
1047-2215 Sensible Agriculture†
1047-2223 Body Boarding†
1047-224X Qualified Retirement and Other Employee Benefit Plans *changed to* Employment Law Series. Qualified Retirement Plans **1860**
1047-2258 Birmingham Poetry Review **5417**
1047-2312 Jobber Executive†
1047-2320 Good News (New Berlin) **7645**
1047-2339 Word & Witness **7780**
1047-2347 Independent Business†
1047-2363 InMusic†
1047-2398 Nova (New Berlin) **7809**
1047-2436 Stocks, Bonds, Bills and Inflation (Year) Yearbook **1654**
1047-2444 Billiards: The (Year) Official B C A Rules & Records Book **8223**
1047-2452 Computer-Assisted Composition Journal†
1047-255X Family Business **1960**
1047-2576 Academic Year Abroad **3011**
1047-2592 Upscale **3570**
1047-2622 Straight Ahead†
1047-2665 Vivarium
1047-2711 Virginia Business Directory **2033**
1047-2746 New Age Encyclopedia†
1047-2754 Knife & Fork†
1047-2770 Bucks County Genealogical Society. Newsletter **3760**
1047-2789 Carolina Literary Companion†
1047-2797 Annals of Epidemiology **7507**
1047-2827 Europe 1992: Law & Strategy†
1047-2843 Tennessee Illustrated†
1047-2908 Inside Market Data **1393**
1047-2916 Your Family†
1047-2924 V L A News
1047-2932 University of Nevada. Basque Studies Program Newsletter **3570**
1047-2967 Manufactured Home Merchandiser **4419**
1047-2975 Hotels **4390**
1047-3025 Transactions of the North American Manufacturing Research Conference. Proceedings **3224**
1047-3033 T A P P I Polymers, Laminations & Coatings Conference. Proceedings (Year) **6739**
1047-3068 Old News **4155**
1047-3076 A M S A T Journal **2356**
1047-3084 Cubs Vine Line **8226**
1047-3130 Who's Who in H R *see* 1047-3149 **1862**
1047-3149 H R Magazine **1862**
1047-3157 H R News **1862**
1047-3181 Minnesota Business Directory **2017**
1047-3203 Journal of Visual Communication and Image Representation **2488**
1047-3211 Cerebral Cortex **6130**
1047-322X Applied Occupational and Environmental Hygiene *changed to* 1545-9624 **6680**
1047-3297 Arts & Culture Funding Report **474**
1047-3300 Minority Funding Report†
1047-3378 Cruise Industry News Annual **8696**
1047-3394 State and Local Statistics Sources†
1047-3408 International Annual of Oral History† **8965**
1047-3416 Archives Accessions Annual†
1047-3440 Template Directory for Libraries†
1047-3564 European Deal Review
1047-3572 American Enterprise *changed to* 1932-8117 **7104**
1047-3645 Advances in Carbocation Chemistry†
1047-367X Miniature Gazette **4340**
1047-3688 The Report on Library Cooperation **5043**
1047-3718 Board and Administrator: Association Edition **1728**
1047-3726 Punto 7 Review **7993**
1047-3777 In View†
1047-3785 Connections (Knoxville)†
1047-3793 Physician's Weekly **5696**
1047-3815 Pet Care Report†
1047-3823 Dental Health Adviser†
1047-3831 Big Picture (Knoxville)†
1047-384X Pre-Parent Adviser†
1047-3874 Campus Voice (Knoxville)†
1047-3882 Best of Business Quarterly†
1047-3920 Health Digest†
1047-3955 Country Sampler **532**
1047-3963 Fox Valley Living†
1047-3971 The Second Stone
1047-398X Issues in Mathematics Education **5498**
1047-4013 Personal Workstation†
1047-4048 Consumer Reports News Digest†
1047-4064 Lithuanian Physics Journal†
1047-4110 San Francisco Performing Arts Library and Museum Journal†
1047-417X News Library News **5036**
1047-4250 Tawagoto **7687**
1047-4269 King's Coal Export Report **6468**
1047-4315 Dirty Linen **6562**
1047-4331 Hawaii Pacific Review **5304**
1047-4374 Industrial Machine Trader **5453**
1047-4404 Car Trader†
1047-4412 Journal of Educational and Psychological Consultation **2875**
1047-4420 Vintage Fashions†
1047-4447 Workplace Trends†
1047-4463 Gauntlet **5217**
1047-451X 24 Hours†
1047-4528 Puncture† **8983**
1047-4544 S I G Forth†
1047-4552 Mediterranean Quarterly **7252**
1047-4625 Country Folk Art Magazine†
1047-4633 North Carolina Environmental Law Letter
1047-4668 Recommended Country Inns: New England **8750**
1047-4692 Senior Media Directory **2338**
1047-4757 N A S N Newsletter *changed to* 1942-602X **5970**
1047-4781 AgExporter (Print Edition)†
1047-4811 Galilean Electrodynamics **7014**
1047-482X International Journal of Osteoarchaeology **343**
1047-4838 J O M **6318**
1047-4862 Abstracts in Social Gerontology **4058**
1047-4951 Vineyard and Winery Management **257**
1047-496X BoCoEx Index†
1047-4978 Grain & Feed Marketing *changed to* Grain & Feed Manager **272**
1047-4986 Soil Science Society of America Book Series **253**
1047-4994 Art of the West **470**
1047-5001 Bus Operator†
1047-5028 Inflammatory Disease and Therapy **5927**
1047-5079 The A I C P A's Uniform C P A Exam† **8927**
1047-5109 Court Rules Pamphlet(s). Pennsylvania Rules of Court, State and Federal **4949**
1047-5125 Autonomic Nervous System **920**
1047-5141 First Things **7643**
1047-515X Black Ice **5264**
1047-5168 Chief Counsel for Advocacy on Implementation of the Regulatory Flexibility Act. Annual Report **4847**
1047-5176 The Alaska Angler **8302**

ISSN

DIRECTORY 2010 1051-1032 9477

1050-2688 Emerging Food R & D Report **3634**
1050-270X McMahon Heavy Construction Cost Guide†
1050-2742 Religious Conference Manager **7675**
1050-2769 Prentice-Hall Signal Processing Series **3393**
1050-2823 Washington Peace Letter **7273**
1050-2831 Real Life in a Big City
1050-2882 In-Side Harlem
1050-2939 Frommer's Mid-Atlantic States **8711**
1050-2947 Physical Review A (Atomic, Molecular and Optical Physics) **7032**
1050-2955 Cornell East Asia Series **547**
1050-2998 Single Today **7944**
1050-3005 Central New York Business Journal **1446**
1050-3021 California Population Characteristics (Year)†
1050-303X California County Projections (Year) **1217**
1050-3048 C++ Journal†
1050-3056 Legal Researcher's Desk Reference **4720**
1050-3102 U S S R Calendar of Events Annual†
1050-3145 Alternative Energy Digests†
1050-3153 Waste Information Digests†
1050-320X Corporate Growth Report **1619**
1050-3218 Directory of Institutional Investment Funds **1987**
1050-3242 Federal Assistance Monitor *changed to* 1934-5054 **4672**
1050-3293 Communication Theory **5107**
1050-3307 Psychotherapy Research **7401**
1050-3331 National Mortgage News **1370**
1050-3366 Florida Communication Journal **2321**
1050-3374 Clinical Surveys in Endocrinology **5885**
1050-3390 Astronomical Society of the Pacific. Conference Proceedings **6278**
1050-3404 Journal of Biblical Ethics in Medicine
1050-3412 Continental Philosophy **6912**
1050-3420 Electromagnetic Applications Series†
1050-3471 Armenian International Magazine **3519**
1050-351X China Statistical Abstract **8363**
1050-3536 P3: Planet Three†
1050-3633 T V Station & Cable Ownership Directory†
1050-365X Sports Card Trader†
1050-379X Louisiana Banker **1366**
1050-3811 C D - Housing Register **4405**
1050-382X Selling to Seniors **1843**
1050-3838 Scotland County Genealogical Society. Quarterly Newsletter **3782**
1050-3900 Guide to International Arbitration and Arbitrators (Year)†
1050-3919 Contemporary Dramatists **8468**
1050-3935 Mid Atlantic Bulletin of Korean Studies **555**
1050-3943 Studies of High Temperature Superconductors **2115**
1050-3978 Resolution†
1050-4028 International Defense Images†
1050-4036 American Trapper **4972**
1050-4060 Construction Injury Liability Monthly†
1050-4109 American Review of International Arbitration **4916**
1050-4125 Christian Studies **7792**
1050-415X The New Delta Review **5340**
1050-4230 E R I S A: The Law and the Code **1676**
1050-4265 T A P P I Finishing and Converting Conference. Proceedings (Year) **6738**
1050-4273 Issues in Applied Linguistics **5130**
1050-4281 Journal of Chemical Education: Software. Series A†
1050-429X Journal of Chemical Education: Software. Series B†
1050-4303 Journal of Chemical Education: Software. Series C†
1050-4338 Jeffers Directory of Law Enforcement Officials†
1050-4362 Emerson Society Papers **5289**
1050-4427 The Beverage Journal **599**
1050-4435 Traditional Quiltworks *changed to* Quiltworks Today **6642**
1050-4443 Year Book of Ultrasound†
1050-4451 Optometry†
1050-4524 The Southern Collegiate Accountant†
1050-4605 Environmental Compliance
1050-4613 Connecticut Facts - Rhode Island Facts **3119**
1050-4621 Campus Marketplace **1809**
1050-463X Family Health Adviser†
1050-4648 Fish and Shellfish Immunology **943**
1050-4672 A P S Observer **7330**
1050-4680 North Bi Northwest **4377**
1050-4699 Broder New York Tort Reporter†
1050-4729 I E E E International Conference on Robotics and Automation. Proceedings **2460**
1050-4745 Torah U - Madda Journal **7730**
1050-4753 Behavioral Research in Accounting **1281**
1050-4818 Global Volcanism Network. Bulletin **2745**
1050-4826 Money Laundering Law Report **4876**
1050-4834 Office of Thrift Supervision Journal†
1050-4842 Museum of Natural Science. Occasional Papers **957**
1050-4850 Current World Affairs†
1050-4877 The Review of Archaeology **413**
1050-4885 Renew America Report†
1050-494X Home Magazine's Best Kitchen & Bath **1011**
1050-4958 Sprinkler Quarterly **3581**
1050-4966 Optics Education†
1050-4974 Pensions & Investments **1644**
1050-5067 Public Perspective†
1050-5075 Country Yossi Family Magazine **3528**
1050-5121 Bowling Magazine†
1050-513X K C T S - Nine **2384**
1050-5156 Copyright Directory: Attorneys, Professors, Government Agencies, Congressional Committees, Searchers, Clearinghouses, Hotlines & Associations, (Year)†
1050-5164 Annals of Applied Probability **5470**
1050-5229 Society of Real Estate Appraisers. Directory of Designated Members†
1050-5237 A P N A News **5950**
1050-5245 Aerospace Propulsion†
1050-527X Trainers' Forum
1050-5326 Energy & Consciousness **7354**
1050-5334 Xenophilia†
1050-5342 Probate Law Journal of Ohio **4905**
1050-5350 Journal of Gambling Studies **6152**
1050-5415 Used Car Prices†
1050-5466 International Directory of Importers: North America **2007**
1050-5504 Past Times: The Nostalgia Entertainment Newsletter **6509**
1050-5520 The International Directory of Importers: Africa **2007**
1050-5539 International Directory of Importers: Asia - Pacific **2007**
1050-5547 The International Directory of Importers: South - Central America **2007**
1050-5555 International Directory of Importers: Europe **2007**
1050-5563 The International Directory of Importers: Middle East **2007**
1050-558X Trackside Magazine **8212**
1050-5628 Metric Today **6404**
1050-5636 Report on Medical Guidelines & Outcomes Research *changed to* 1531-5681 **4092**
1050-5644 Campus Watch†
1050-5652 Money Maker's Monthly **1964**
1050-5660 Solar Industry Journal†
1050-5695 American Academy of Medical Acupuncture Review *changed to* 1933-6586 **312**
1050-5717 Shooting Sportsman **8332**
1050-5725 A S C P Update **6818**
1050-5741 Bit and Bridle (National Edition) **8288**
1050-5830 National Directory of Catalogs **631**
1050-5857 National Underwriter Profiles. Life Insurers†
1050-5873 Colby Quarterly **5275**
1050-5881 The Prostate. Supplement *see* 0270-4137 **6273**
1050-6004 Public Access Computer Systems News **5063**
1050-6039 A M E Christian Recorder **7743**
1050-6098 A R L **4986**
1050-6101 Human Genome News†
1050-6152 Tourism's Top Twenty†
1050-6160 Training Directors' Forum Newsletter†
1050-6179 Notiziario degli Standard I E E E *see* I E E E StandardsWire **6402**
1050-6187 I E E E Normen Nachrichten *see* I E E E StandardsWire **6402**
1050-6195 I E E E Nouvelle des Normes *see* I E E E StandardsWire **6402**
1050-6209 I E E E Standards Bearer (British Edition) *see* I E E E StandardsWire **6402**
1050-6217 Nursery Business Grower†
1050-6233 AIDS Summary
1050-6268 516 Magazine
1050-6306 Sociological Practice Review†
1050-6357 National Underwriter Profiles. Health Insurers†
1050-6365 National Underwriter Profiles. Property - Casualty Insurers†
1050-6411 Journal of Electromyography & Kinesiology **754**
1050-642X Clinical Journal of Sport Medicine **6229**
1050-6438 Neurosurgery Quarterly **6253**
1050-6519 Journal of Business and Technical Communication **1133**
1050-6527 I S A Analysis Division Symposium. Proceedings (Print) *changed to* 5617-1099 **4487**
1050-6551 Investment Performance Digest **1130**
1050-656X Mutual Fund Advisor **1641**
1050-6586 American Journal of Rhinology *changed to* 1945-8924 **6077**
1050-6594 Game Times†
1050-6608 Game Researcher's Notes†
1050-6616 Gunmaker **1887**
1050-6667 Online Alert†
1050-6675 East Texas Medicine†
1050-6691 Breakthroughs in Health & Science†
1050-6802 Hippo†
1050-6918 Optometry Clinics†
1050-6926 Journal of Geometric Analysis **5503**
1050-6934 Journal of Long-Term Effects of Medical Implants **6248**
1050-6942 Journal of Chemical Education: Software. Special Issue Series†
1050-6977 Progress in Probability **5526**
1050-7027 Deathrealm
1050-7035 Wittenberg Review†
1050-7051 Journal of Hospitality & Leisure Marketing *changed to* 1936-8623 **4392**
1050-7078 Skybox†
1050-7086 Calliope (Peru) **4134**
1050-7116 Texas Energy†
1050-7159 College Preview **2973**
1050-7167 First Opportunity (Hispanic Students' Edition) *see* First Opportunity **2857**
1050-7175 First Opportunity (Black Students' Edition) *see* First Opportunity **2857**
1050-7221 Visions (Kansas City) **3571**
1050-723X Journey (Kansas City)†
1050-7256 Thyroid **5900**
1050-7264 Optical Science and Engineering Series **7082**
1050-7299 Adult's Health Adviser†
1050-7302 Parent's Health Adviser†
1050-7310 Language of Defense†
1050-7361 Yellowed Pages
1050-7418 Pet Veterinarian†
1050-7434 A D A Courier **6654**
1050-7442 A R L Preservation Statistics **5056**
1050-7604 Hands On Language†
1050-7612 Office Dealer **1853**
1050-7671 American Trucking Associations. Current Economic Bulletin†
1050-7698 South Carolina Business **1177**
1050-7760 Tiny Toon Adventures Magazine†
1050-7779 European Community Law and Business Reporter†
1050-785X Bass Player **6548**
1050-7868 E Q (New York) **8152**
1050-7914 Reunion Talks on Risleys **3780**
1050-7922 Risley Record **3780**
1050-7965 A I Directory†
1050-799X Simmons Study of Media & Markets (Year) **2338**
1050-8015 Simmons Study of Media and Markets. Technical Guide **2338**
1050-8031 Trilogy†
1050-8112 Computerization and Networking of Materials Databases†
1050-8147 School of Library and Information Science. Occasional Papers Series†
1050-8171 Assembly (Oak Brook) **3182**
1050-821X K I N D News Jr. **320**
1050-8236 Euromedia Regulation†
1050-8244 Illinois Archaeology **397**
1050-8252 Design Spirit†
1050-8309 Academic Press Geology Series **2722**
1050-8376 International Brands and Their Companies†
1050-8384 International Companies and Their Brands†
1050-8392 Journal of Research on Adolescence **2156**
1050-8406 Journal of the Learning Sciences **2879**
1050-8414 The International Journal of Aviation Psychology **8546**
1050-8422 Ethics & Behavior **7355**
1050-8430 Genome Analysis†
1050-8481 International Economic Insights†
1050-8538 Modern Warfare†
1050-8600 Club Director **2265**
1050-8619 The International Journal for the Psychology of Religion **7650**
1050-8694 Directory of Foreign Investment in the U S†
1050-8791 Physician's Payment Advisory *changed to* 1055-629X
1050-8813 A Q P Report†
1050-8864 Yivo Annual†
1050-8902 D M S World Military Avionics Inventory & Forecast†
1050-8910 World Helicopter Inventory & Forecast†
1050-8929 World Ordnance Inventory & Forecast
1050-8953 Inform Special Reports **3439**
1050-897X Mealey's European Environmental Law Report†
1050-8996 H B O's Guide to Movies on Videocassette and Cable TV **6502**
1050-9003 Executive Search Review **1743**
1050-9011 Bob Nurock's Advisory†
1050-9046 Frontiers in Communications **2321**
1050-9062 A I P Translation Series **7002**
1050-9070 International Spectrum **2493**
1050-9089 Rogerian Nursing Science News†
1050-9127 D G Review†
1050-9135 Healthcare Informatics **5830**
1050-9143 U.S. Department of Agriculture. Situation & Outlook Report. Feed†
1050-9208 Quarterly Review of Film and Video **6510**
1050-9232 Risk & Insurance **4521**
1050-9267 Lasers in Surgery and Medicine. Supplement *see* 0196-8092 **6251**
1050-9410 Market: Europe **1577**
1050-9453 New York International Law Review **4936**
1050-9461 Roger Tory Peterson Institute's Field Guide to Natural History **7904**
1050-9496 Advances in Telematics†
1050-9518 Old-Time Crochet†
1050-9526 Southwest Stockman **301**
1050-9542 K I N D News Sr. **320**
1050-9585 European Romantic Review **5293**
1050-9607 Contemporary Management in Internal Medicine†
1050-9615 Contemporary Management in Obstetrics and Gynecology†
1050-9623 Contemporary Management in Critical Care†
1050-9631 The Hippocampus **5628**
1050-964X The Report on Pediatric Infectious Diseases†
1050-9658 Laboratory Medicine Abstract and Comment†
1050-9674 Journal of Offender Rehabilitation **2657**
1050-9690 Society of Flight Test Engineers. Annual Symposium Proceedings **70**
1050-9712 Backwoods Home Magazine **3970**
1050-9720 New England Theatre Journal **8474**
1050-9739 Studies in Medieval and Renaissance Teaching **5381**
1050-9755 Purdue University. Cooperative Extension Service. H E **149**
1050-9771 Fodor's Barbados **8704**
1050-9836 Worker's Compensation Law Review†
1050-9852 National Directory of Corporate Giving **8083**
1050-9860 Aberdeen's Concrete Sourcebook†
1050-9887 C M A Matters **6552**
1050-9917 Nomad†
1050-995X Year Book of Health Care Management†
1050-9992 Cancer Therapy Reports†
1051-0036 Briefly... (LeRoy)†
1051-0192 Preservation Progress (Crownsville)†
1051-0214 National Ground Water Association. Briefings†
1051-0230 Spectator (Los Angeles, 1987) **6513**
1051-0257 Washington International **8773**
1051-0303 Aperiodicity and Order†
1051-0311 Harvard Contemporary China Series **4182**
1051-032X California Series on Social Choice & Political Economy **7112**
1051-0346 Studies in French Civilization†
1051-0354 Comparative Studies on Muslim Societies **7710**
1051-0362 Topics in Philosophy **6957**
1051-0427 Better Homes and Gardens Home Products Guide **982**
1051-0435 American Association of Blood Banks. Membership Directory (Print Edition) *changed to* American Association of Blood Banks. Membership Directory (Online Edition) **5571**
1051-0443 Journal of Vascular and Interventional Radiology **6201**
1051-0478 E P R I-NP **3301**
1051-0508 Iron & Steel Society. Transactions†
1051-0532 E P R I-EA **3301**
1051-0559 Transforming Anthropology **358**
1051-0575 Cross Roads†
1051-0583 Water Farming Journal†
1051-0613 Safe Cycling **8267**
1051-0621 Hawaiian Express Magazine†
1051-063X Sailorman Star Magazine†
1051-0761 Ecological Applications **3416**
1051-077X Current Obstetric Medicine†
1051-0788 Willem Mengelberg Society. Newsletter†
1051-0834 Journal of Applied Communications **127**
1051-0842 A C A S Bulletin **4172**
1051-0869 The Appraisers Standard **467**
1051-0923 Surveillant†
1051-094X Business People **1074**
1051-0974 Communication Studies **8094**
1051-1032 Screenplay†

ISSN

Link to your serials resources and content with ulrichsweb.com

DIRECTORY 2010 1052-7117 9479

1051-9173 I E E E Symposium on Mass Storage Systems. Digest of Papers **2421**
1051-919X Oklahoma Directory of Manufacturers and Processors **2022**
1051-9211 D R I - McGraw-Hill Automotive Review
1051-9246 Introducing Computers: Concepts, Systems, and Applications **2427**
1051-9254 World Agriculture Regional Supplement: Middle East and North Africa†
1051-9335 Travelin' Magazine†
1051-9394 Health Labor Relations Alert
1051-9416 Directory of International Library Education Experience†
1051-9521 StraightTalk **1519**
1051-953X Multimedia Computing & Presentations†
1051-9548 International Directory of Interactive Multimedia Producers†
1051-9556 Vue
1051-9602 Nonprofit Management Strategies†
1051-9629 C E News **3261**
1051-9637 3 Tech **2541**
1051-9688 Transgenica†
1051-9696 Paradox Developer's Journal†
1051-9718 Artists and Issues in the Theatre **8465**
1051-9726 Health Watch†
1051-9734 Inside Microsoft Windows†
1051-9793 Aerospace & Defense Science
1051-9815 Work **6688**
1051-9831 Recycled Paper News **3510**
1051-984X Medical Design and Material†
1051-9939 S & L - Savings Bank Financial Quarterly **1169**
1051-998X Objectivity†
1051-9998 Plasma Devices and Operations **7035**
1052-0007 Baran's Tech Letter†
1052-0023 New Hampshire Rules of Evidence **4957**
1052-0031 Directory of Foreign Manufacturers in the U S†
1052-0066 W A A C Newsletter **525**
1052-0082 Behavior Analysis Digest **7338**
1052-0112 C O S L A Directory **4999**
1052-0139 CryoGas International **3375**
1052-0147 Qualitative Report **7994**
1052-018X Maine Scholar *changed to* Southern Maine Review
1052-0228 Fluid Measurements and Instrumentation Forum†
1052-0236 American Corporate Identity **21**
1052-0279 World Agricultural Production **170**
1052-0287 AIDS Bibliography (Bethesda)†
1052-0295 Biotechnic and Histochemistry **898**
1052-0309 Diplomatic Record†
1052-0341 Upside†
1052-0384 Nonviolent Sanctions **7255**
1052-0406 Nineteenth-Century Prose **5342**
1052-0449 Frontiers of Anthropology†
1052-0457 Research in Accounting Regulation **1299**
1052-0465 Advances in Eating Disorders†
1052-049X Networking Management†
1052-0503 Studies in Evangelicalism **7742**
1052-0511 Theater Three†
1052-0554 Advances in Contemporary Educational Thought Series **2824**
1052-0597 The Educated Traveler†
1052-0600 Journal of Mathematical Systems, Estimation and Control†
1052-0627 Clinician Reviews **5598**
1052-0678 Annual Editions: Canadian Politics **7106**
1052-0686 Fodor's Bed & Breakfast Guide†
1052-0775 Quser News†
1052-0791 Negotiations Proposals to Achieve - Avoid†
1052-0805 Doll Artistry†
1052-0848 Vacation Industry Review **8771**
1052-0899 The Wrestler **8216**
1052-0929 British Car **8570**
1052-0953 Membrane Quarterly **3250**
1052-0961 Mini Truckin' **8673**
1052-097X Hobson's Choice **5443**
1052-0996 Baltimore - Annapolis (Year)†
1052-1011 Caribbean Travel + Life **8692**
1052-1054 Albert Einstein Institution. Monograph Series **7104**
1052-1135 Comparative Studies in Religion & Society **7634**
1052-1151 Religion and American Culture **7674**
1052-1216 University of Virginia. Center for Oceans Law and Policy. Annual Seminar† **8996**
1052-1232 National Sports Daily†
1052-1372 P & T **6865**
1052-1380 Prince George's County Genealogical Society. Bulletin **3780**
1052-1437 U.S. Library of Congress. Period Subdivisions under Names of Places†
1052-1445 U.S. Library of Congress. Free - Floating Subdivisions: An Alphabetic Index **637**
1052-1496 Journal of New York Taxation†
1052-150X Business Ethics Quarterly **6909**
1052-1569 The Bridge (Oak Park) **5418**
1052-1577 The Harvard Health Letter **6987**
1052-1615 The Travelin' Talk Newsletter†
1052-164X N B R Analysis **7254**
1052-1674 Acquisition Issues†
1052-1682 Boomerang! **2180**
1052-1690 D R I - McGraw-Hill Cost and Price Review: International Focus
1052-1712 Modern Arts Criticism†
1052-1747 Cash Management Performance Report†
1052-1755 Green Market Alert†
1052-1763 Women's Recovery Network†
1052-1798 D I M A C S Series in Discrete Mathematics and Theoretical Computer Science **5481**
1052-181X Martin Luther King, Jr. Memorial Studies in Religion, Culture and Social Development **7662**
1052-195X Datapro Software Finder. Complete ed.†
1052-1976 C A Selects. Oleochemicals Containing Nitrogen **2089**
1052-1984 C A Selects. Omega-3 Fatty Acids & Fish Oil†
1052-2018 New York State Museum. Circular **7892**
1052-2077 Advances in Cycloaddition†
1052-2131 European Packaging Newsletter and World Report†
1052-2158 Journal of Family Social Work **8049**
1052-2166 Gene Expression **867**
1052-2174 Video Journal of Echocardiography†
1052-2182 Video Journal of Color Flow Imaging†
1052-2204 The Rockwell Lecture Series†
1052-2212 What Do I Read Next? **639**
1052-2220 The Awards Almanac†
1052-2255 Agri-Topics **82**
1052-2263 Journal of Vocational Rehabilitation **7381**
1052-2271 Moody†
1052-231X Adult Basic Education *changed to* 1934-2322 **2937**
1052-2379 California Lawyers *changed to* 1932-0515 **4636**
1052-2433 Today in Mississippi **3161**
1052-2468 U.S. Environmental Protection Agency. Ecological Research Series **708**
1052-2484 Urban Forests†
1052-2522 73 Amateur Radio Today†
1052-262X Advances in Library Resource Sharing†
1052-2654 How to Find Financial Information about Companies **1351**
1052-2662 Inside 1-2-3 Release 3 (3.1 & 3.4)†
1052-2670 Almanac of the Christian World
1052-2689 Violence Update†
1052-2697 Small Press Book Review Annual†
1052-2727 Alaska's Wildlife†
1052-2794 Federal Sentencing Guidelines Manual **4889**
1052-2824 M A S B Journal **3027**
1052-2840 Emory International Law Review **4924**
1052-2859 Journal of Dispute Resolution **4701**
1052-2867 Michigan Journal of International Law **4935**
1052-2891 New Directions for Adult and Continuing Education **2944**
1052-2921 California Real Property Journal **7586**
1052-293X Arkansas Law Notes **4621**
1052-2964 Employment Law Counselor **1679**
1052-2972 Law Department Management Adviser†
1052-3057 Journal of Stroke & Cerebrovascular Diseases **5794**
1052-3073 Journal of Financial Counseling and Planning **1361**
1052-309X National Medical-Legal Journal *changed to* 1533-9564 **5915**
1052-3103 C A C D Journal **7342**
1052-3111 Herold's Comparative Appraisal Reports - Sector 3
1052-3138 The Business Television Directory†
1052-3146 Hospital Pharmacist Report **6846**
1052-3154 Bakunin†
1052-3162 Without Halos†
1052-3170 Turok's Choice **6625**
1052-3189 Geborener Deutscher **3767**
1052-3227 Software Directory. Industry Specific Applications†
1052-3235 Software Directory. Manufacturing and Engineering†
1052-3251 Turning Wheels **8609**
1052-3324 Drums & Drumming†
1052-3359 Chest Surgery Clinics of North America *changed to* 1547-4127 **6261**
1052-3413 Natural Gas Lawyer's Journal
1052-3421 Wisconsin Women's Law Journal *changed to* 1943-1600 **4815**
1052-343X South Texas Law Review **4785**
1052-3472 Olderr's Young Adult Fiction Index for (Year)†
1052-3545 Dowline†
1052-3561 Midrange Computing†
1052-3588 Executive Business Tools
1052-3650 *see* 0195-6310 **8095**
1052-3693 Advances in Chinese Industrial Studies **3365**
1052-3723 Beam's Directory of International Tourist Events†
1052-3774 Legacy (Fort Collins) **3450**
1052-3782 News About Adult Services†
1052-3790 Covenant Discipleship Quarterly *changed to* Covenant Discipleship Connection **7753**
1052-3804 Discipulos Responsables† **8950**
1052-3812 Society of Exploration Geophysicists. Expanded Abstracts with Biographies *changed to* Society of Exploration Geophysicists. S E G Technical Program Expanded Abstracts **2790**
1052-3839 Berklee Today **6549**
1052-3855 Trucking Digest†
1052-3898 Fare Share, the Food Letter and Cookbook News **4358**
1052-3928 Journal of Professional Issues in Engineering Education and Practice **3276**
1052-3944 Postal Watch†
1052-3979 Charitable Organizations of the U S†
1052-4002 Current Problems in Geriatrics†
1052-4010 Current Problems in Urology†
1052-4029 Collection Agency Report **1327**
1052-4037 Who's Who in Photography†
1052-4053 Disc Magazine†
1052-407X Car Dealer Insider **8572**
1052-4088 Restaurant Management Insider†
1052-4096 National Gardening **3744**
1052-4134 Who Knows about Foreign Industries and Markets†
1052-4142 Minilab Developments **6971**
1052-4150 Robotics and Manufacturing†
1052-4169 Beauty Education Journal†
1052-4207 AIDS Treatment News **5809**
1052-4215 Nashville Business and Lifestyles **1152**
1052-4231 Virginia Medical Quarterly†
1052-4282 MarineFacts†
1052-4304 Construction Contracting Alert†
1052-4355 Ohio Environmental Law Letter†
1052-4363 Pennsylvania Employment Law Letter **4756**
1052-4371 Kentucky Employment Law Letter **4709**
1052-438X On!†
1052-4436 Current Critical Problems in Vascular Surgery†
1052-4533 The Studia Philonica Annual **7730**
1052-4568 M V R Book **8589**
1052-4592 Delaware Valley
1052-4622 Real Estate Securities & Capital Markets†
1052-4630 Gourmet News **3678**
1052-4649 Law Reporter **4716**
1052-4681 A Brief Relation **6521**
1052-469X Montana Land Magazine **7600**
1052-4703 Homes & Real Estate Magazine - Billings, Montana†
1052-4711 Homes & Real Estate Magazine - Great Falls, Montana†
1052-472X I M S A Arrow†
1052-4746 The Hunting Report for Big Game Hunters **8318**
1052-4770 Planned Giving Today **8062**
1052-4789 Dusty Dog Chapbook Series†
1052-4800 Journal on Excellence in College Teaching **2991**
1052-4819 Stern's SourceFinder **1268**
1052-4851 Poetry Criticism **5431**
1052-4894 Medical Office Manager **1779**
1052-4908 Plastics Recycling Update **3510**
1052-4924 Medical Records Briefing **4106**
1052-4940 Beam (Boalsberg)†
1052-4959 Women's Caucus for Art. National Update **527**
1052-5017 Transformations (Wayne) **8144**
1052-5025 Seconds Magazine **5369**
1052-5033 Audio Carpetorium†
1052-5068 European Television† **8955**
1052-5076 S O F's Combat Weapons *changed to* 0887-2546
1052-5092 Dividend Reinvestment Plans†
1052-5106 American Bar Association. Family Law Section. Annual Meeting Compendium†
1052-5149 Neuroimaging Clinics of North America **6203**
1052-5157 Gastrointestinal Endoscopy Clinics of North America **5925**
1052-5165 Great Plains Research **7858**
1052-5173 G S A Today **2734**
1052-522X Albertsen's - International Edition†
1052-5238 U S and Foreign Diplomatic Contacts†
1052-5254 The Perryman Texas Letter **1510**
1052-5327 The Iowa Lawyer **4697**
1052-536X U.S. National Agricultural Library. Reference Section. Special Reference Briefs **164**
1052-5378 U.S. National Agricultural Library. Quick Bibliography Series **164**
1052-5386 A R S†
1052-5394 Journal for Hawaiian and Pacific Agriculture **125**
1052-5416 Floriculture Indiana **3729**
1052-5467 California Highways†
1052-5505 Tribal College **3005**
1052-5521 The Quarterly Byte†
1052-5548 Comics Interview†
1052-5572 Newspapers & Technology **4581**
1052-5580 Pipers Magazine **68**
1052-5629 Journal of Management Education **1768**
1052-5645 Shepard's District of Columbia Case Names Citator **4961**
1052-5653 Shepard's Colorado Case Names Citator **4960**
1052-5661 Shepard's Connecticut Case Names Citator **4960**
1052-567X Shepard's Arizona Case Names Citator **4960**
1052-5688 Shepard's Arkansas Case Names Citator **4783**
1052-5696 Shepard's Alaska Case Names Citator **4960**
1052-570X Shepard's Alabama Case Name Citator **4960**
1052-5726 Progressive Librarian **5040**
1052-5742 Serials Holdings in the Linda Hall Library†
1052-5769 Renovated Lighthouse†
1052-5777 Government Contract Costs, Pricing & Accounting Report **4682**
1052-5785 Martha's Vineyard Magazine **3981**
1052-5823 California Coast & Ocean **2605**
1052-5882 Cellular and Molecular Mechanisms of Inflammation†
1052-5920 Shepard's Hawaii Case Name Citator **4961**
1052-5947 Shepard's Iowa Case Names Citator **4961**
1052-5963 Shepard's Kentucky Case Names Citator **4961**
1052-598X Shepard's Maryland Case Names Citator **4962**
1052-6099 Journal of the International Academy of Hospitality Research **4392**
1052-6102 Air & Waste Management Association. Meeting Proceedings† **8929**
1052-6153 Biotechnology Handbooks **761**
1052-6161 The Maryland Grapevine **3743**
1052-6188 Journal of Machinery Manufacture and Reliability **5454**
1052-6234 S I A M Journal on Optimization **5531**
1052-6242 Virtual Reality Report†
1052-6250 A T T W Bulletin **3050**
1052-6277 Shepard's Oklahoma Case Names Citator **4963**
1052-6307 Shepard's Nevada Case Names Citator **4962**
1052-6315 Shepard's Nebraska Case Names Citator **4962**
1052-6323 Shepard's Mississippi Case Names Citator **4962**
1052-6358 Workers' Compensation Outlook **4528**
1052-6366 Access to Wang†
1052-6463 Hardware
1052-6471 FedWatch†
1052-648X Short Story **5239**
1052-6498 Local 11. Noticias **4598**
1052-6536 Florida Geological Survey. Biennial Report **2734**
1052-6579 P C Sources†
1052-6587 The Press (Overland Park)†
1052-6609 Dalton's New York Metropolitan Directory: Business - Industry **1983**
1052-6641 Shepard's Puerto Rico Case Names Citator **4964**
1052-665X Shepard's South Carolina Case Names Citator **4964**
1052-6668 Shepard's Tennessee Case Names Citator†
1052-6676 Shepard's Virginia Case Names Citator **4964**
1052-6684 Shepard's West Virginia Case Names Citator **4964**
1052-6692 Progress in Computer-Aided V L S I Design†
1052-6722 Northwest Mileposts†
1052-6730 Ocean and Coastal Law Memo†
1052-6765 T D & T **8480**
1052-6773 National Cancer Institute. Journal. Monographs **6028**
1052-6781 S A A S Bulletin. Biochemistry and Biotechnology **744**
1052-6838 Annual Advanced Research Techniques Forum **1805**
1052-6846 Journal of School Leadership **2878**
1052-6862 Ships & Shipwrecks **8662**
1052-6994 Stone World **6480**
1052-7001 Journal of Housing Research **4417**
1052-7036 Foreign Policy Bulletin **7235**
1052-7060 Professions Education Researcher Quarterly **2998**
1052-7095 Community College Exemplary Instructional Programs **2973**
1052-7109 The M Street Journal **2360**
1052-7117 The M Street Radio Directory **2360**

Link to your serials resources and content with ulrichsweb.com

ISSN

9480 1052-7184 ULRICH'S PERIODICALS

1052-7184 American Sociological Association. Biographical Directory of Members **8087**
1052-7206 Business and the Environment **3407**
1052-7214 Intelligent Software Strategies†
1052-729X Urban Perspectives **4430**
1052-7346 Optometric Economics†
1052-7354 Who's Who Among Hispanic Americans†
1052-7362 C P A Firm Practice Manual (Year)†
1052-7494 Death Row (Year)†
1052-7524 Transportation Research Forum. Proceeding†
1052-7532 Annual Editions: Public Administration **7420**
1052-7605 The Inside Word (P C Edition - Microsoft Word 5.5 & 6.0)†
1052-7613 Aquatic Conservation **2602**
1052-7656 Community Alternatives†
1052-7664 Looking for Employment in Foreign Countries†
1052-7672 Kalamazoo Valley Heritage **3772**
1052-7737 Directory of Selected Research and Policy Centers Working on Women's Issues†
1052-7753 Tackett Family Journal **3784**
1052-7761 Mexico Watch (Washington, 1990)†
1052-7788 Research in Financial Services **1378**
1052-7842 The World Satellite Annual **2345**
1052-7877 Thesaurus of Metallurgical Terms **6335**
1052-7893 A S C P Washington Report on National and State Issues†
1052-7915 Quilting International†
1052-794X The Innkeepers' Register **8721**
1052-7958 The American Psychoanalyst **7333**
1052-7974 Albemarle **3969**
1052-8008 Marketing Education Review **2993**
1052-8067 Vintage Motorsport **8215**
1052-8083 Princeton Series in Physics **7036**
1052-813X B N A California - Environment Reporter†
1052-8164 Constructive Criticism
1052-8245 Grants and Appropriations†
1052-8415 Otterwise†
1052-8423 S E P M Midyear Meeting. Abstracts **6730**
1052-8555 Genesis (New York)†
1052-8571 Microsoft Networking Journal†
1052-858X Ohio Genealogical Society. Newsletter *changed to* O G S Genealogy News **3777**
1052-8725 Real-Time Systems Symposium **2524**
1052-875X Star (Boca Raton) **3989**
1052-8768 Rockin' Records **6612**
1052-8776 World Gas Intelligence **6797**
1052-8822 Northern California Business Directory and Buyers Guide **2021**
1052-8849 Country Extra **5068**
1052-8857 Inside Michigan Politics **7446**
1052-8873 The MacNeil - Lehrer Newshour†
1052-8881 Rockefeller Foundation. Annual Report **8066**
1052-889X Passager **4053**
1052-8938 Horace **3064**
1052-8989 The Active Window†
1052-9063 National Library of Medicine. Current Bibliographies in Medicine **5749**
1052-9128 MacTech Journal†
1052-9152 Medical Research Funding News†
1052-9179 Consumer Guide to Home Energy Savings†
1052-9187 International Contributions to Labour Studies†
1052-9225 China Statistical Yearbook **8363**
1052-9233 Surveys in Differential Geometry **5540**
1052-9241 Journal of Culinary Practice†
1052-9268 International Video Journal of Engineering Research†
1052-9276 Reviews in Medical Virology **895**
1052-9284 Journal of Community & Applied Social Psychology **7371**
1052-9292 International Petroleum Abstracts†
1052-9411 Quality Assurance†
1052-9438 New York Review of Science Fiction **5445**
1052-9470 Inside HyperCard†
1052-9551 Diagnostic Molecular Pathology **5605**
1052-9578 Market Share Reporter **1251**
1052-9586 Guide to International Education in the United States†
1052-9608 Space Station Directory & Program Guide†
1052-9624 Circle Track **8166**
1052-9640 Pension Fund Litigation Reporter† **8980**
1052-9705 Europe America Series†
1052-9756 The Fordham Corporate Law Institute Annual Proceedings *changed to* The Fordham Competition Law Institute. Annual Proceedings **4868**
1052-9977 Picture Framing Magazine **538**
1052-9985 Parking Security Report†
1053-0010 North South Trader's Civil War **4306**
1053-0029 Products Liability Law Reporter **4762**
1053-0053 Condition of Teaching†
1053-0126 Connecticut Family†
1053-0177 Romantic Traveling **8753**
1053-0193 Oshkaabewis Native Journal **6636**
1053-0223 Stockholders & Creditors News Service Re: Federated Department Stores†
1053-0266 Securities Litigation Reporter†
1053-0274 Wrongful Discharge Report†
1053-0347 Cash Flow Enhancement Report†
1053-0355 Annual and Cumulative Field and Operator Production. Area, New Mexico. Product, Southeast Crude†
1053-0363 Human Resource Manager's Legal Reporter **1685**
1053-0398 Comics Scene†
1053-0401 Action Wheels Presents†
1053-041X T V Wrestlers† **8992**
1053-0452 Clinics in Applied Nutrition†
1053-0460 Clearinghouse Directory†
1053-0479 Journal of Psychotherapy Integration **6156**
1053-0487 Journal of Occupational Rehabilitation **6680**
1053-0495 Journal of Inorganic and Organometallic Polymers *changed to* 1574-1443 **2124**
1053-0509 Journal of Fluorescence **2117**
1053-0525 Recycling Related Newsletters, Publications, Periodicals **3511**
1053-0533 Florida Geological Survey. Report of Investigations **2734**
1053-055X T H - Ers Express†
1053-0576 Annual and Cumulative Field and Operator Production. Area, New Mexico. Product, Northwest Crude†
1053-0584 Aspects (Encino)†
1053-0606 Advances in Long-Term Care† **8928**
1053-0614 Across the Border **3757**
1053-0703 Mail: The Journal of Communication Distribution **2354**
1053-0738 Wing Beats of the American Mosquito Control Association **861**
1053-0754 The Responsive Community†
1053-0762 Home Ground **4412**
1053-0770 Journal of Cardiothoracic and Vascular Anesthesia **5792**
1053-0789 Journal of Social Distress and the Homeless†
1053-0797 Dreaming **7353**
1053-0800 Journal of Child and Adolescent Group Therapy†
1053-0819 Journal of Behavioral Education **2874**
1053-0827 K M T: A Modern Journal of Ancient Egypt **402**
1053-0886 N C A A Manual†
1053-0894 The A I D S Reader **5807**
1053-0908 Bowser Directory of Small Stocks **1613**
1053-0967 American College of Physicians. Membership Directory†
1053-1092 Allergic Disease and Therapy **5753**
1053-1106 C D I A C Communications **6348**
1053-1173 I R S Practice Alert†
1053-1181 Civil War News **4288**
1053-1203 N A F A Fleet Executive **8505**
1053-122X Current Topics in Photovoltaics **3126**
1053-1297 New England Review **5340**
1053-1343 Businessmac†
1053-1378 Educational Rankings Annual†
1053-1386 Counterpoint (Horsham) **3038**
1053-1424 Consumers Reference Disc†
1053-1467 Inside Quattro Pro†
1053-1696 The San Francisco Almanac **1966**
1053-170X Creative Training Techniques **2840**
1053-1750 International Education Forum†
1053-1793 Writer's Guidelines Magazine **4585**
1053-1807 Journal of Magnetic Resonance Imaging **6200**
1053-1831 Color Wheel **5419**
1053-184X Advances in Information Storage Systems†
1053-1858 Journal of Public Administration Research and Theory **7448**
1053-1866 Contributions in Asian Studies† **8943**
1053-1874 Job Hunter's Sourcebook **6699**
1053-1890 Child and Youth Care Forum **2147**
1053-1912 E T Ideas†
1053-1920 Postmodern Culture **4156**
1053-1963 Private Banking Report†
1053-1998 Travel Review†
1053-2013 Craft Related Newsletters, Periodicals & Publications **533**
1053-2021 Bargain Hunters & Budgeteers Opportunity Newsletter **4352**
1053-2064 Rod & Custom **8602**
1053-2137 Journal of Human Muscle Performance†
1053-2153 Solid Freeform Fabrication Symposium Proceedings **3395**
1053-2161 Stress and Emotion **7410**
1053-220X Chilton's Electronic Engine Controls Manual. General Motors Cars and Light Trucks **8574**
1053-2285 Cakelele: Maluku Research Journal **7952**
1053-234X FAXreporter†
1053-2366 North American Masonry Conference. Proceedings **1027**
1053-2404 Atlantic Trade Report & Global Defense Industry **1552**
1053-2447 Frommer's Comprehensive Travel Guide. Morocco **8711**
1053-248X The Unofficial Guide to Disneyland **8770**
1053-2498 The Journal of Heart and Lung Transplantation **6248**
1053-251X Christian Science Quarterly. Bible Lessons (Full Text Edition) *changed to* 1938-6184 **7734**
1053-2528 Annual Review of Sex Research **7335**
1053-2544 Equities **1622**
1053-2552 Used Cars Insider
1053-2579 Financial & Accounting Systems†
1053-2587 Innovating **1753**
1053-2617 New England Garden History Society. Journal **3744**
1053-2633 Cowboy Magazine **8289**
1053-2641 Street & Smith's Pro Football **8247**
1053-2676 The Reporter (New York, 1966) **7728**
1053-2692 Ag Executive **191**
1053-2749 Minorities and Women in Business
1053-2811 Chamber Insider **1398**
1053-2838 Life & Health Insurance Sales *changed to* 1524-7589
1053-2854 Directory of Fine Art Representatives and Corporations Collecting Art†
1053-296X Our Stories **4377**
1053-2986 Residential Building Cost Guide (Year) *changed to* Residential Cost Handbook **1033**
1053-2994 Dodge Square Foot Cost Data†
1053-301X Dodge Unit Cost Data†
1053-3060 Florida Land Owner
1053-3087 Blitz Chess **8162**
1053-332X Main Event†
1053-3338 N A V A News **3775**
1053-3435 State of the State Banking System **1384**
1053-3605 Buzz (Los Angeles)†
1053-3648 Supermarket Strategic Alert **3682**
1053-3699 Discount & Wholesale Printing Newsletter **7319**
1053-3745 HomeWork†
1053-3818 Drug and Alcohol Abuse Reviews†
1053-3826 Keller's Industrial Safety Report *changed to* 1931-7638 **6680**
1053-3842 Punch in International Travel and Entertainment Magazine **8749**
1053-3877 Arthurian Yearbook†
1053-3893 Black BottomLine
1053-3907 Searching for Scruggs **3782**
1053-3915 American Artist. Watercolor **465**
1053-4083 Action Alert (Washington, 1980) **4609**
1053-4113 Emunah **7721**
1053-4156 Artists Resource Guide to New England Galleries, Grants and Services†
1053-4202 Anthropology of Consciousness **327**
1053-4237 Ukrainian Business Digest
1053-4245 Journal of Exposure Analysis and Environmental Epidemiology *changed to* 1559-0631 **3447**
1053-4261 Advanced Labanotation†
1053-4296 Seminars in Radiation Oncology **6034**
1053-4318 Auto Service Insider
1053-4326 Only the Best†
1053-4385 Bulletin for the History of Chemistry **2052**
1053-4407 Field Guide to Estate Planning, Business Planning & Employee Benefits **4502**
1053-4423 Mawewi†
1053-4474 Brunner / Mazel Integrative Psychotherapy Series†
1053-4490 Advances in Applied Biotechnology Series†
1053-4512 Intervention in School and Clinic **3042**
1053-4571 Digest for Home Furnishers
1053-4628 Journal of Clinical Pediatric Dentistry **5851**
1053-4636 Bibliographies and Indexes in Science Fiction, Fantasy, and Horror† **8936**
1053-4644 Motion Control *changed to* 0737-7908
1053-4652 Federal Staffing Digest†
1053-4660 International Merger Law: Events and Commentary†
1053-4695 Small Business Forum†
1053-4768 Exceptional Human Experience **6645**
1053-4776 Wine on Line **613**
1053-4806 Korea Briefing **1601**
1053-4822 Human Resource Management Review **1864**
1053-4857 Investing in Art
1053-4881 North American Pylon **8595**
1053-4903 Utility Fleet Management **8678**
1053-492X Worksite Wellness Works *changed to* The Well Workplace Newsletter **7545**
1053-4938 California Water Law & Policy Reporter **4637**
1053-4962 Full Disclosure
1053-4970 Directory of Psychology Internships: Programs Offering Behavioral Training†
1053-4997 Japan Notebook†
1053-5012 Provincetown Arts **513**
1053-5020 The Round Table (Beloit) **2299**
1053-5330 Journal of Cardiovascular Management **5792**
1053-5357 Journal of Socio-Economics **1546**
1053-5365 Brong's Business Success News†
1053-5373 B N A's Employee Relations†
1053-5381 International Journal of Offshore and Polar Engineering **3383**
1053-5454 Dancing U S A **2685**
1053-5462 Global Shareholder†
1053-5489 Corporate Governance Bulletin **4864**
1053-5500 Case Management Advisor **5592**
1053-5527 Gary North's Remnant Review **1113**
1053-556X Risk & Benefits Journal (Marina del Rey) **1791**
1053-5586 Infant - Toddler Intervention†
1053-5594 Data Resource Management†
1053-5608 American Heartworm Society. Symposium Proceedings **8791**
1053-5616 Arizona Jewish Post **7718**
1053-5802 World Cogeneration **3150**
1053-5829 Donald R. Morris Newsletter **7231**
1053-5845 Solid Value **1652**
1053-587X I E E E Transactions on Signal Processing **3316**
1053-5888 I E E E - Signal Processing Magazine **7087**
1053-5934 Reinsurance Educator **4520**
1053-5950 Fodor's San Diego **8708**
1053-5969 Basic U C C Skills. Article 4A **4628**
1053-5977 Digest of Chinese Studies **5006**
1053-6051 Robotics Abstracts Annual†
1053-6086 Farm Income Tax Manual **198**
1053-6108 Cut Your Own Taxes and Save (Year)
1053-6175 Unit Investment Trusts
1053-6191 Indiana Employment Law Letter **4691**
1053-623X Athens Magazine **3969**
1053-6256 Vizions
1053-6345 Nevada Beverage Analyst **608**
1053-6361 Bluff City
1053-637X Walkerana **967**
1053-6388 Journal of Medical and Applied Malacology **952**
1053-640X European Faculty Directory†
1053-6434 Private Placement Alert **1645**
1053-6477 University of Michigan. Museum of Zoology. Special Publications **966**
1053-6493 T-Shirt Business Info Mapping Newsletter **1968**
1053-6507 Clothing for Less Newsletter **2636**
1053-6523 Coupon Treasure Hunt Newsletter **2637**
1053-6531 Be Somebody, Be Yourself Poetry Newsletter **5417**
1053-654X Jobs in Recessionary Times Possibility Newsletter **6700**
1053-6558 The New Catholic Miscellany **7809**
1053-6582 Arkansas Business Journal **1061**
1053-6639 New Hampshire Life†
1053-6698 Texas Business Directory **2030**
1053-6728 Technology and Learning **2951**
1053-6736 Duke Journal of Comparative and International Law **4923**
1053-6752 Automatic Musical Instrument Collectors Association. Membership Directory
1053-6809 Northwest High Tech on the Web *see* Northwest High Tech Database **2494**
1053-6833 Directory of Consultants and Translators for Engineered Materials **1986**
1053-685X Dalton's Philadelphia Metropolitan Directory: Business - Industry **1983**
1053-6884 Jukebox Collector **4337**
1053-6949 L N G Observer†
1053-699X The Journal of Jewish Thought and Philosophy **7725**
1053-7007 Trade Union Handbook **4603**
1053-7015 3X - 400 Information Management†
1053-7023 Labor News (New York) **4597**
1053-7031 Photographic Art Market: Auction Prices (Year) **6974**
1053-704X Black Employment and Education
1053-7066 California City and County Rankings†
1053-7090 Footnotes from the Arid Zone†
1053-7163 Initial Public Offerings Annual†
1053-7171 Recipe Greetings Update **4366**

Link to your serials resources and content with ulrichsweb.com

DIRECTORY 2010 1054-5484 9481

1053-7201 Remark (New York)†
1053-721X Travel Consultants Directory
1053-7252 California Economic Growth (Year) **1217**
1053-7287 Journal of Global Business **1136**
1053-7465 Developments in Nanotechnology
1053-7473 Church Computing News†
1053-749X Complications in Surgery
1053-7503 Recharger **1854**
1053-752X Communal Computing News **2570**
1053-7651 Today in Medicine. Obstetrics & Gynecology **6005**
1053-7694 C A S Journal **6552**
1053-7724 Public Affairs Video Archives. Catalog
1053-7740 States in Profile†
1053-7791 Song Hits' Heartbreakers†
1053-783X International Public Works Review†
1053-7864 In Perspective of the Black American Veteran
1053-7899 M S W Management **3508**
1053-7929 A C's Tech for the Commodore Amiga†
1053-7937 Writing about Women: Feminist Literary Studies **5401**
1053-7988 Super Cracked
1053-8003 Cracked Collectors Edition
1053-802X Zoological Record Search Guide **969**
1053-8062 Corporate and Communications Design Annual†
1053-8100 Consciousness and Cognition **7348**
1053-8119 NeuroImage **6165**
1053-8127 Journal of Back and Musculoskeletal Rehabilitation **6063**
1053-8135 NeuroRehabilitation **6168**
1053-8151 Journal of Early Intervention **3042**
1053-816X Urologic Nursing **6276**
1053-8186 Harvard Law Bulletin **2286**
1053-8194 International Co-Productions†
1053-8259 Journal of Experiential Education **3067**
1053-8305 N R C A Membership Directory **2018**
1053-8313 Euro Cable T V Programming **2380**
1053-8321 MediaWatch **4579**
1053-8348 Behavior and Philosophy **7338**
1053-8356 American Journal of Numismatics **6648**
1053-8364 Journal of Philosophical Research **6929**
1053-8372 Journal of the History of Economic Thought **1546**
1053-8402 A M S Office Professional and Data Processing Salaries Report†
1053-8445 Journal of Progressive Legal Thought† **8968**
1053-8526 O S A Proceeding Series **7081**
1053-8534 Space Science Series **582**
1053-8542 Insight Magazine (Chicago) **1290**
1053-8569 Pharmacoepidemiology and Drug Safety **6871**
1053-8577 Prism (Boston) **1786**
1053-8607 American Statistical Association. Stats **8344**
1053-8615 Anthology of New England Writers **5416**
1053-8623 African Farmer†
1053-8631 Basta!†
1053-8658 The Bond Buyer's Municipal Marketplace **1976**
1053-8712 Journal of Child Sexual Abuse **8049**
1053-8720 Journal of Gay & Lesbian Social Services **8049**
1053-8739 Journal of College & University Foodservice†
1053-8747 Popular Culture in Libraries†
1053-8755 Journal of Ministry in Addiction & Recovery *changed to* 1550-4247
1053-8763 Africa Investment Monitor
1053-8801 Publishing Research Quarterly **7571**
1053-881X Integrative Physiological and Behavioral Science *changed to* 1932-4502 **6146**
1053-8828 Inside P R†
1053-8844 Clinical Anesthesia Updates **5770**
1053-8852 Environtech†
1053-8860 Technical Brief **8481**
1053-8941 Association of Jesuit Colleges and Universities and Jesuit Secondary Education Association Directory **2968**
1053-8984 Perspectives on Medical Research†
1053-8992 Louisiana Manufacturers Register **2013**
1053-900X Text Technology **7580**
1053-9018 Chalcedon Report **7630**
1053-9026 Cable Contacts (Year)†
1053-9107 A B C Dialogue **1956**
1053-9115 Sensations Magazine **5434**
1053-9182 Flea Market†
1053-9204 Vermont Philatelist **6901**
1053-9212 The Big Bopper *changed to* 8750-7242 **2180**
1053-9247 Painted Hills Review†
1053-9263 Central Business Review
1053-931X Landmark Studies
1053-9344 Literary Griot **5224**
1053-9360 Travel Agent **8765**
1053-9379 Utility Environment Report†
1053-9395 Who's Who (Year) **646**
1053-9409 Craftsmen Review†
1053-9433 Communications Quarterly **2357**
1053-945X Tiananmen Notes
1053-9492 Albanica†
1053-9506 Advances in Regulation of Cell Growth Series†
1053-9514 International Productivity Journal†
1053-9530 Roster & Government Guide **7180**
1053-9573 Dusty Dog Reviews†
1053-9603 Agriview **86**
1053-9611 Cancer Economics **6012**
1053-9638 WordPerfect Report
1053-9662 Hawaii Health Messenger
1053-9697 Clinical Dermatology†
1053-9700 Caribbean Perspectives†
1053-9751 Public Pulse **1838**
1053-976X Monographs on the Fine Arts **506**
1053-9816 History of Neuroscience†
1053-9832 Nonwovens Market and Fiber Structures Report†
1053-9859 World Geophysical News **6797**
1053-9867 Federal Sentencing Reporter **2652**
1053-9905 Consolidated Treaties & International Agreements: United States Current Document Service **4922**
1053-9948 Ernst Krenek Archive. Newsletter **6565**
1054-0008 T V Times (St. Paul)
1054-0040 Montessori Life **3073**
1054-0067 The Earth Care Annual†
1054-0083 Foreign Policy Briefing **7235**
1054-0105 The Journal of the Association of Graduate Near Eastern Students *changed to* 1930-9643 **3544**
1054-013X N I S T Technical Notes **6404**
1054-0156 Pro Football Illustrated (Year)†
1054-0164 Football Preview (Year)†
1054-0202 Marriage & Family Living†
1054-0210 A S A E Monograph Series†
1054-0229 I T E A Journal of Test and Evaluation **8425**
1054-0288 Animal Transportation Association. International Conference. Proceedings **8490**
1054-0326 New York State Bar Association. Business Law Section. Newsletter **4877**
1054-0407 Circuits Assembly **3091**
1054-0415 Computer Publishing Magazine†
1054-0423 Beverage Industry News **599**
1054-058X Austrian Culture **4202**
1054-0598 Photobulletin Daily **6973**
1054-0644 Golf Course News *changed to* Golf Course Industry **8231**
1054-0679 International Review
1054-0695 ShareDebate International **8000**
1054-0709 Archives Sharing Bulletin†
1054-0725 Emergency Medicine News **6059**
1054-0733 Insurance & Technology **4531**
1054-075X Orgonomic Functionalism **6172**
1054-0768 Food Free or Cheap Newsletter **4358**
1054-0784 Windows Watcher†
1054-0814 The D B S Report† **8947**
1054-0830 Journal of Regression Therapy **7379**
1054-0857 Hellenistic Culture & Society **2235**
1054-0873 The New Historicism: Studies in Cultural Poetics **5340**
1054-089X Journal of Data and Computer Communications†
1054-0946 Guide to Social Science and Religion **7698**
1054-0954 Advances in Molecular Modeling†
1054-0962 Veteran's View **6452**
1054-1039 Muhlenberg County Heritage **4304**
1054-1055 Ejournal **2497**
1054-1098 Research in Economic History. Supplement†
1054-1136 Timber Frame Homes *changed to* Timber Home Living **1040**
1054-1144 Children's Ministry **2149**
1054-1195 Structural Mover **3284**
1054-1209 Cal - O S H A Reporter **6675**
1054-1241 Conservation Aeronautics **3412**
1054-1365 Chicago Jewish Star **7720**
1054-1373 Illness, Crisis, and Loss **8107**
1054-1381 Icarus (New York)†
1054-139X Journal of Adolescent Health **5645**
1054-1403 Studies on Cervantes and His Times **5382**
1054-1411 Alateen Talk **2175**
1054-142X Al-Anon in Institutions†
1054-1438 Inside Al-Anon†
1054-1446 Al-Anon Speaks Out **2690**
1054-1500 Chaos **7008**
1054-1527 Southwest Crafts†
1054-1551 Cross Stitch Sampler†
1054-1578 English Leadership Quarterly **3061**
1054-1624 Ethnomusicology Research Digest **337**
1054-1632 Snail's Pace Review†
1054-1675 P H R Record **7213**
1054-1756 Forging **6312**
1054-1802 Journal of Urban and Cultural Studies **8116**
1054-1829 Friends of the Earth **3432**
1054-187X Pediatric Pulmonology. Supplement *see* 8755-6863 **6101**
1054-1888 Advances in Health Economics and Health Services Research. Supplement†
1054-1942 Telecommunications Reports International **2341**
1054-1950 From the Gym to the Jury **8174**
1054-1969 Women of Color and Southern Women†
1054-1985 Progressive Periodicals Directory†
1054-2027 A S F A Marine Biotechnology Abstracts (Print)†
1054-2035 A N A Resource Directory†
1054-2043 T D R **8480**
1054-206X University of Chicago. Geography Research Papers **4032**
1054-2086 Pediatric Hematology - Oncology Series **6032**
1054-2116 Soybean Genetics Newsletter (Print Edition) *changed to* 1930-8981 **878**
1054-2159 The State of Working America **1519**
1054-2175 The Hoosier Genealogist **3771**
1054-2183 The Show
1054-2191 Don Heinrich's College Football **8226**
1054-2205 The National Sports Review
1054-2213 Dick Vitale's Basketball
1054-2221 Don Heinrich's Pro Preview
1054-2248 Bill Mazeroski's Baseball
1054-2256 Radio Control Action Series†
1054-2280 Rehabilitation Today†
1054-2337 Hispanic Outlook in Higher Education **2985**
1054-2361 Ohio Sourcebook (Year)
1054-2388 Marketing Executive Report†
1054-240X National Undersea Research Program. Research Report **2813**
1054-2426 The Catalog of Funeral Home Supplies **1979**
1054-2434 Artes Graficas **7318**
1054-2493 Tulsa Daily Commerce & Legal News **1185**
1054-2523 Medicinal Chemistry Research **5673**
1054-254X Knoxville Automotive Report **8588**
1054-2558 Memphis Automotive Report **8590**
1054-2604 State Environment Report†
1054-2639 M U S E, MUsic SEarch **6631**
1054-2655 Mad River†
1054-2663 Mexico Business Monthly†
1054-2698 Superconductivity Review†
1054-2701 Supreme Court Yearbook† **8991**
1054-2728 Catholic Courier **7788**
1054-2744 Jawetz, Melnick & Adelberg's Medical Microbiology **888**
1054-2760 Boardwatch (Print Edition) *changed to* Boardwatch (Online Edition)
1054-2779 Annual Editions: World History **4130**
1054-2825 Inside Hollywood†
1054-2841 Kentucky Checklist of State Publications **628**
1054-2868 Kids Discover **2197**
1054-2884 Philosophical Inquiries
1054-2892 Insurance Collision Report Passenger Cars, Cargo Vans, Pickups, and Utility Vehicles† **8965**
1054-2914 U.S. Nuclear Regulatory Commission. Title List of Documents Made Publicly Available†
1054-2957 Health and Sexuality **6988**
1054-3007 Journal of Construction Accounting and Taxation **1294**
1054-3023 Journal of Legal Economics **1545**
1054-3031 Silver & Blue **2301**
1054-3066 Medical News Report **1834**
1054-3082 Directory of High Volume Independent Drug Stores (Year)†
1054-3090 Freedom Review†
1054-3120 Studies on the Shoah†
1054-3139 I C E S Journal of Marine Science **2806**
1054-3155 Country Stitch **6637**
1054-3201 Paso Fino Horse World **8295**
1054-3287 National Environmental Scorecard **3454**
1054-3368 Real Estate West†
1054-3376 E L F†
1054-3406 Journal of Biopharmaceutical Statistics **6889**
1054-3414 Polymer Reaction Engineering *changed to* 0360-2559 **2129**
1054-3430 Cross-Stitch Plus†
1054-3465 Reflex Magazine†
1054-3481 United States Anti-Apartheid Newsletter **7218**
1054-352X Association Contact **2827**
1054-3589 Advances in Pharmacology **6819**
1054-3619 Academy of Accounting Historians. Directory†
1054-3635 First Amendment Law Handbook **4848**
1054-3724 Laserjet Journal
1054-3732 The Indiana Lawyer **4692**
1054-3775 N C L C Reports: Bankruptcy & Foreclosures **4737**
1054-3791 News Bureau Contacts (Year)†
1054-3805 Savings Banks of America†
1054-3821 Campus Crime†
1054-3848 Property Management Monthly
1054-3902 Symantec **2599**
1054-3910 Politics of Education Association. Yearbook **3030**
1054-3929 Paradigm Shift (Boston)†
1054-3937 Exit 13 Magazine **5294**
1054-3996 CD - MARC Bibliographic†
1054-4011 Pen - Based Computing†
1054-402X Wiley Employment Law Update on CD-ROM†
1054-4054 Law Firms Yellow Book **4715**
1054-4062 Municipal Yellow Book **7498**
1054-4070 Associations Yellow Book **1973**
1054-4089 Best Bed & Breakfast in England, Scotland & Wales **8687**
1054-4143 Perspectives in Physics **7029**
1054-4178 The Guinness Book of Sports Records†
1054-4186 Guide Magazine (Seattle)†
1054-4208 Focus (Burbank)†
1054-4216 Business Espionage Report **1554**
1054-4232 Sanyo P C Hackers Newsletter†
1054-4240 Feature News Publicity Outlets
1054-4259 T V & Cable Publicity Outlets - Nationwide
1054-4267 Technology Alert†
1054-4275 Management Matters†
1054-4283 Voices of the African Diaspora†
1054-4305 Cryonics **5904**
1054-4313 World Bank Watch†
1054-433X Cover Story Index†
1054-4445 C J F Annual Report†
1054-4550 *see* 1938-6184 **7734**
1054-4607 Amerikai Magyar Levelestar **4197**
1054-4623 New Jersey Lake Survey Fishing Maps Guide†
1054-4631 AmigaWorld Tech Journal†
1054-4666 Architectus†
1054-4674 Gauer Distinguished Lecture in Law and Public Policy **4679**
1054-4682 Journal of Home & Consumer Horticulture†
1054-4712 Medical Psychiatric Practice†
1054-4720 The Anthropology of East Europe Review **327**
1054-4747 Ideas Unlimited **4576**
1054-4763 Washington Letter on Puerto Rico†
1054-4828 Automotive Electronics Journal†
1054-4836 Men's Health (United States Edition) **6285**
1054-4887 Applied Computational Electromagnetics Society Journal **7051**
1054-4941 Chemical Industry Sourcebook and Strategic Overview
1054-495X D R I - McGraw-Hill Cost and Price Review: Utility Focus†
1054-4984 Membrane Technology Reviews **768**
1054-5034 Tim Bell's Alaska Travel Guide **8761**
1054-5050 Road Work Safety Report†
1054-5085 Price Waterhouse - Review†
1054-5115 World Fence News **1043**
1054-5123 Pig Tale Times **6813**
1054-514X T E Notes **646**
1054-5174 Command Post
1054-5182 Atlanta's Business Makers and Shakers. Volume I - Atlanta's Top Decision Makers†
1054-5190 New Jersey Media Guide **2020**
1054-5220 The P R S Group. Country Reports: Algeria **1505**
1054-5239 The P R S Group. Country Reports: Argentina **1505**
1054-5271 The P R S Group. Country Reports: Bolivia **1506**
1054-528X The P R S Group. Country Reports: Brazil **1506**
1054-5298 The P R S Group. Country Reports: Bulgaria **1506**
1054-5301 The P R S Group. Country Reports: Cameroon **1506**
1054-5328 The P R S Group. Country Reports: Chile **1506**
1054-5336 The P R S Group. Country Reports: China **1506**
1054-5344 The P R S Group. Country Reports: Colombia **1506**
1054-5352 The P R S Group. Country Reports: Costa Rica **1506**
1054-5387 The P R S Group. Country Reports: Dominican Republic **1506**
1054-5395 The P R S Group. Country Reports: Ecuador **1506**
1054-5476 In Vitro Cellular & Developmental Biology - Plant **793**
1054-5484 The P R S Group. Country Reports: Egypt **1506**

ISSN

Link to your serials resources and content with ulrichsweb.com

9482 1054-5492 ULRICH'S PERIODICALS

1054-5492 The P R S Group. Country Reports: El Salvador **1506**
1054-5522 The P R S Group. Country Reports: Gabon **1506**
1054-5549 The P R S Group. Country Reports: Guatemala **1507**
1054-5557 The P R S Group. Country Reports: Guinea **1507**
1054-5565 The P R S Group. Country Reports: Haiti **1507**
1054-5573 The P R S Group. Country Reports: Honduras **1507**
1054-5581 The P R S Group. Country Reports: Hong Kong **1507**
1054-559X The P R S Group. Country Reports: Hungary **1507**
1054-5603 The P R S Group. Country Reports: India **1507**
1054-5611 The P R S Group. Country Reports: Indonesia **1507**
1054-562X The P R S Group. Country Reports: Iran **1507**
1054-5638 The P R S Group. Country Reports: Iraq **1507**
1054-5662 The P R S Group. Country Reports: Israel **1507**
1054-5670 The P R S Group. Country Reports: Cote d'Ivoire **1506**
1054-5689 The P R S Group. Country Reports: Jamaica **1507**
1054-5700 The P R S Group. Country Reports: Kenya **1507**
1054-5719 The P R S Group. Country Reports: Libya **1507**
1054-5727 The P R S Group. Country Reports: Malaysia **1508**
1054-5735 The P R S Group. Country Reports: Mexico **1508**
1054-5743 The P R S Group. Country Reports: Morocco **1508**
1054-576X The P R S Group. Country Reports: Nigeria **1508**
1054-5786 The P R S Group. Country Reports: Nicaragua **1508**
1054-5808 The P R S Group. Country Reports: Oman **1508**
1054-5824 Clapper **6556**
1054-5859 Government and Politics Alert†
1054-5891 New Korea **3554**
1054-5913 A A P P O Journal (American Association of Preferred Provider Organizations) *changed to* 1085-1089
1054-5948 A D A Compliance Guide **8022**
1054-5956 Fund Action **1348**
1054-5999 Appraiser News (Print Edition)†
1054-6006 Fisheries Oceanography **3592**
1054-6014 Fugue (Moscow) **5299**
1054-6022 Seventeenth Century Music **6616**
1054-6030 The P R S Group. Country Reports: Pakistan **1508**
1054-6049 The P R S Group. Country Reports: Panama **1508**
1054-6057 The P R S Group. Country Reports: Peru **1508**
1054-6065 The P R S Group. Country Reports: Philippines **1508**
1054-6073 The P R S Group. Country Reports: Poland **1508**
1054-6103 The P R S Group. Country Reports: Romania **1508**
1054-6111 The P R S Group. Country Reports: Saudi Arabia **1508**
1054-612X The P R S Group. Country Reports: Singapore **1508**
1054-6138 The P R S Group. Country Reports: South Africa **1509**
1054-6146 The P R S Group. Country Reports: South Korea **1509**
1054-6162 The P R S Group. Country Reports: Sri Lanka **1509**
1054-6170 The P R S Group. Country Reports: Sudan **1509**
1054-6197 The P R S Group. Country Reports: Syria **1509**
1054-6200 The P R S Group. Country Reports: Taiwan **1509**
1054-6219 The P R S Group. Country Reports: Thailand **1509**
1054-6227 The P R S Group. Country Reports: Tunisia **1509**
1054-6235 The P R S Group. Country Reports: Turkey **1509**
1054-6251 The P R S Group. Country Reports: United Arab Emirates **1509**
1054-6286 The P R S Group. Country Reports: Uruguay **1509**
1054-6294 The P R S Group. Country Reports: Venezuela **1509**
1054-6308 Political Risk Services. Country Reports: Yugoslavia†
1054-6324 The P R S Group. Country Reports: Zambia **1510**
1054-6332 The P R S Group. Country Reports: Zimbabwe **1510**
1054-6340 The Pittsburgh Quarterly (Pittsburgh, 1991) **5351**
1054-6359 North Carolina Employment Law Letter **4748**
1054-6367 Minnesota Employment Law Letter **4734**
1054-6375 Missouri Employment Law Letter **4735**
1054-6456 InCider - A Plus†
1054-6464 E & P Environment†
1054-6480 Oakland University Magazine **2294**
1054-6553 West Virginia Beverage Journal **612**
1054-6561 Virginia Beverage Journal **612**
1054-657X North Carolina Beverage Journal **608**
1054-660X Laser Physics **7080**
1054-6618 Pattern Recognition and Image Analysis **5524**
1054-6626 Public Opinion in the Soviet Union: Statistics and Analysis†
1054-6634 Mathematical Modeling **5554**
1054-6693 Sensors and Actuators **3395**
1054-6707 Dream Network Journal **6644**
1054-674X Fitness Plus†
1054-6790 Contributions in Latin American Studies **4290**
1054-6812 Sales & Use Tax Alert†
1054-6863 Kennedy Institute of Ethics Journal **5657**
1054-6936 Economic Development Monitor
1054-6995 Briefings on J C A H O *changed to* 1941-5877 **4089**
1054-7002 KidSports†
1054-7053 I S S A Today **7524**
1054-7126 Youth Ministry Quarterly (New Hampton)†
1054-7150 Southern Shipper **8663**
1054-7207 Crawl Out Your Window†
1054-724X Text and Presentation **8481**
1054-7304 Credit Union Technology **1392**
1054-7371 Agency†
1054-7444 N R C FM Radio Log†
1054-7460 Presence **2489**
1054-7479 American Periodicals **5252**
1054-7495 The Hymnology Annual **6574**
1054-7584 East Asia High Tech Review
1054-7606 Vinyar Tengwar **5395**
1054-7614 Loyola **2290**
1054-7665 Vision Monday **6053**
1054-7673 N C R T L Special Report†
1054-7681 Handbook of Comparative Economic Policies† **8961**
1054-7711 Allure **8851**
1054-772X Year Book of Clinical Microbiology†
1054-7738 Clinical Nursing Research **5955**
1054-7797 Convenience Store Decisions **3677**
1054-7894 Selected Readings for C P As in Industry†
1054-7908 Mechanical Engineering Systems†
1054-8017 Environmental Finance†
1054-8033 Home School Researcher **2864**
1054-8084 Exotic Cars Quarterly **8580**
1054-8122 Ellery Queen's Mystery Magazine (Print Edition) **5413**
1054-8165 Herald Tribune Crosswords & Other Word Games
1054-8238 The National Yellow Book of Funeral Directors **2019**
1054-8246 Treasure Facts†
1054-8289 The Future of Children **2153**
1054-8297 Environmental Law Anthology†
1054-8300 Louisiana State University, Rice Research Station. Annual Research Report **134**
1054-8351 Virginia Facts **3122**
1054-8378 Theatre Topics **8483**
1054-8386 Semiotics and the Human Sciences **5173**
1054-8408 Journal of Travel & Tourism Marketing **8726**
1054-8491 Simpsons Illustrated†
1054-8513 Physical Therapy Practice†
1054-8521 Today in Medicine. Family Practice **5722**
1054-853X International Journal of Energy, Environment and Economics **3139**
1054-8548 In Toon!†
1054-8564 Conference on Hazardous Waste Research. Proceedings **3495**
1054-8637 World Trade *changed to* 1949-9140 **1588**
1054-8645 A I Review of Products, Services and Research†
1054-867X P C Advisor†
1054-8688 Current Thoughts & Trends†
1054-8696 Intelligent Systems Report **2450**
1054-8718 Oh|! Zone†
1054-8726 Family Dynamics of Addiction Quarterly†
1054-8734 Journal of Urogenital Pathology†
1054-8742 Global Trade White Pages†
1054-8777 Dickens' Universe†
1054-8793 N F P A Journal **3580**
1054-8807 Cardiovascular Pathology **5781**
1054-8823 World Letter†
1054-8874 Chronicle of Latin American Economic Affairs†
1054-8890 SourceMex **1518**
1054-8912 Muscle Mustangs & Fast Fords **8594**
1054-898X Footwear Plus **7941**
1054-9048 Radio Week **2363**
1054-9064 Country Folks of Pennsylvania **102**
1054-9072 The Ukrainian News **3569**
1054-9080 Classical Chinese Furniture Society. Journal†
1054-9102 Bibliographies and Indexes in Latin American and Caribbean Studies† **8936**
1054-9110 Reference Guides to Archival and Manuscript Sources in World History† **8984**
1054-9153 Magnolia (Winston-Salem) **3742**
1054-917X Currents in Emergency Cardiovascular Care **5785**
1054-9196 Facility Strategies†
1054-9234 Who's Who in Congress†
1054-9293 A R R L - D X X C Countries List **2356**
1054-9390 I S L A: A Journal of Micronesian Studies†
1054-9404 Literati Internazionale
1054-9447 Nuclear Plant Maintenance Newsletter†
1054-9463 Bankruptcy Yearbook and Almanac **1319**
1054-9471 National Directory of Courts of Law†
1054-948X Human Rights Watch World Report **7209**
1054-9552 Rocky Mountain Gardener **3757**
1054-9560 Bushong Bulletin **3761**
1054-9587 Today's Woman
1054-9595 American Woman (New York, 1991)†
1054-9609 Diagnostics Intelligence **6833**
1054-9633 Humanist News & Views **6924**
1054-9641 NatureSouth†
1054-9668 Microelectronics Manufacturing Technology†
1054-9676 Library Mosaics†
1054-9714 Journal of Phase Equilibria *changed to* 1547-7037 **6319**
1054-9757 Best Vacation Rentals. Caribbean†
1054-979X TechScan Newsletter **1421**
1054-9811 Journal of Sustainable Forestry **3695**
1054-982X Textile Financial Outlook
1054-9919 O E R I Bulletin†
1054-9943 New Home†
1054-9994 Cash Rich Companies†
1055-0070 Standard & Poor's Financial Institutions Ratings. Europe, Asia, Oceania **1652**
1055-0100 Baldwin's Ohio School Law Journal **4626**
1055-0119 Southwest Business Review†
1055-0143 Psycoloquy (Print) *changed to* Psycoloquy (Online)
1055-0208 Quantum P C Report for C P As **1299**
1055-0216 Building Products†
1055-0259 Powder Coating **3215**
1055-0267 The Video Annual†
1055-0305 Wound Ballistics Review **5917**
1055-033X Hack'd **8259**
1055-0364 Decoy Magazine **4333**
1055-0461 College Broadcaster†
1055-047X Northwest Construction Weekly†
1055-0496 American Journal on Addictions **2691**
1055-050X Journal of Psychotherapy Practice and Research†
1055-0518 Child Assessment News
1055-0550 Black History is No Mystery **3522**
1055-0569 The D O S Authority†
1055-0577 Inside QuickBasic†
1055-0607 Dairy Field *changed to* 0888-0050 **3633**
1055-0623 Corporate Giving Directory **8035**
1055-064X Music & Computers†
1055-0666 Consumer Media Tech†
1055-0674 American Bungalow **427**
1055-0712 Perio Reports **5861**
1055-0763 New Hampshire Genealogical Record **3776**
1055-081X Film Composers Guide **1993**
1055-0828 Television Directors Guide **2030**
1055-0836 Film Actors Guide **6498**
1055-0852 Who Is Who in Service to the Earth†
1055-0860 Education in the Public Eye†
1055-0879 Best Places to Stay in Mexico **8687**
1055-0887 Journal of Addictive Diseases **2695**
1055-0895 Random Lengths Yardstick **3709**
1055-0925 Journal of Economics and Finance **1135**
1055-100X Word & Image†
1055-1018 Campbell Contacts in America **3761**
1055-1042 Soviet Perspectives†
1055-1077 American Banker. Consumer Survey†
1055-1093 Keystone A A A Motorist *changed to* 1523-9403 **8553**
1055-1158 Research in Religion and Family: Black Perspectives **7676**
1055-1166 Wild Earth **2632**
1055-1190 Oye! *changed to* 0033-5940 **5164**
1055-1220 Copains *changed to* 0006-7121 **5101**
1055-1247 Agenda (New York)†
1055-128X Law Office Computing†
1055-1336 Our Gifted Children **2163**
1055-1344 Siberian Advances in Mathematics **5536**
1055-1352 Current Issues in Exercise Science†
1055-1360 Journal of Linguistic Anthropology **345**
1055-1387 Journal of Tree Fruit Production *changed to* 1553-8362 **237**
1055-145X The Social Contract **8132**
1055-1468 Foreign Trade†
1055-1476 Images (Pensacola) *changed to* 1546-0843 **5967**
1055-1492 Quarry Farm Papers **5356**
1055-1565 Vault of Horror
1055-1603 Physician Manager†
1055-1638 American International Checkers Society Newsletter
1055-1670 Poet's Handbook†
1055-1689 N A M B L A Bulletin **4377**
1055-1697 Healthcare Employment News
1055-1700 Cycle Projections **1334**
1055-1743 F Y I - I M†
1055-176X MediaWeek **30**
1055-1778 Official City Guide **8744**
1055-1859 West European Program†
1055-1913 Texas Criminal Law & Motor Vehicle Handbook **4794**
1055-193X Building Permits Law Bulletin **4405**
1055-2006 Shelby County Historical Society. The Quarterly **4312**
1055-2278 Vestnik (Baltimore)†
1055-2286 Art and Design News†
1055-2340 Spray Technology & Marketing **6715**
1055-2367 Full-Time Dads†
1055-2413 Ukrainski Visti **3569**
1055-2421 Faulkner & Gray's European Business Directory†
1055-2456 Tax Penalties†
1055-2464 Studies in Anthropology and History
1055-2561 Texas Industry Environmental Alert
1055-257X Louisiana Industry Environmental Alert **3451**
1055-2634 N F O Reporter **138**
1055-2685 Goldmine **6570**
1055-2723 Syndicated Columnist Contacts (Year)†
1055-2774 Step-by-Step Electronic Design *changed to* 1536-1594 **7580**
1055-2782 Drinking Water & Backflow Prevention **3265**
1055-2790 Camp Chase Gazette **6414**
1055-2804 Intercultural Studies†
1055-2839 European Home Video†
1055-2847 Vignettes†
1055-2855 Chicora Foundation Research **4288**
1055-2863 Records of Wills, Surrogates Court Staten Island, New York **3780**
1055-2871 The Cross Stitcher **6638**
1055-2936 Concrete Repair Bulletin **993**
1055-2944 Texas Hispanic Magazine **3568**
1055-2979 Stallion Directory **8298**
1055-3029 Impact (Augusta) **1405**
1055-3037 The Public Policy & Aging Report **4054**
1055-3088 Journal of Nursing Jocularity
1055-3096 Journal of Information Systems Education **2950**
1055-3134 Tennessee Nurse **5982**
1055-3169 Today's Family†
1055-3177 Novon **806**
1055-3207 Surgical Oncology Clinics of North America **6035**
1055-3223 Feed & Grain **271**
1055-3231 Plumbing, Heating, Piping†
1055-3258 The Microcomputer Trainer **2572**
1055-3266 Civil War Regiments†
1055-3290 Association of Nurses in AIDS Care. Journal **5810**
1055-3339 Color Business Report **2483**
1055-3371 Global Connector
1055-3398 Best of Health
1055-3444 ProSales **1030**
1055-3479 Custom Home **1000**
1055-3495 Hazardous Waste Management & Business Opportunities Newsletter†
1055-3509 Agglomerations **1879**
1055-355X Florida Mosquito Control Association. Journal†
1055-3568 Business Speaker's Digest†
1055-3576 Parish Directory
1055-3584 Siteworld†
1055-3649 International Parallels†
1055-3665 Libraries and Information Services Today†
1055-3703 Response (Los Angeles) **7728**
1055-3746 E I T F Abstracts **1287**
1055-3754 Israeli - Palestinian Digest
1055-3762 S A E A M S Index **3218**
1055-3797 Compensation of Industrial Engineers†
1055-3827 Read More about It - Book of Days†
1055-3835 Journal of Addictions & Offender Counseling **7368**
1055-3851 M R I Bankers' Guide to Foreign Currency **1366**
1055-3894 La Verne Magazine **2308**
1055-3916 Information Searcher **2558**
1055-3932 Emily Dickinson International Society Bulletin **5421**
1055-3940 Global Communique **1235**
1055-3967 Hobo Times
1055-3983 Word Progress **4845**
1055-3991 Document Assembly and Practice Systems Report†
1055-4009 Business Lawyer's Computer News **4844**
1055-4017 A B A - UNIX - Group Newsletter **4844**
1055-4033 Law Practice Today†
1055-4041 Leadership and Management Directions **4718**
1055-4076 Lawyering Skills Bulletin **4718**
1055-4084 Litigation Applications **4845**
1055-4157 Early Childhood Law and Policy Reporter **3058**
1055-4165 Metropolitan New York Business and Market Guide
1055-4173 University Press Books for Public and Secondary School Libraries *changed to* 1537-5218 **5060**
1055-4181 Technology and Disability **4070**
1055-422X San Joaquin Agricultural Law Review **4778**
1055-4238 Colorado. Division of Wildlife. Terrestrial and Aquatic Wildlife Research. Research Review **3589**

DIRECTORY 2010 1056-3210 9483

1055-4262 Medical Equipment Designer **4489**
1055-436X The Thistle & Shamrock **6623**
1055-4408 Aberdeen's Magazine of Masonry Construction *changed to* Masonry Construction **1022**
1055-4440 Modern Woodworking **4560**
1055-4505 Dwelling Construction under the Uniform Mechanical Code† **8951**
1055-4513 Journal of Translation and Textlinguistics†
1055-4610 Viet Nam Hthmai Ngoai†
1055-4629 Shepard's Wisconsin Express Citations *changed to* 0730-4552 **4964**
1055-4653 Shackelford Newsletter†
1055-4696 Mortgage and Consumer Loan Disclosure Handbook **1369**
1055-4718 System Link *changed to* 1535-7937 **1359**
1055-4726 The Battalion **2274**
1055-4742 Book Links **2146**
1055-4750 Second Language Instruction - Acquisition Abstracts†
1055-4785 Disc Golf Journal
1055-484X Tricycle **7702**
1055-4890 Sommers Letter†
1055-4998 Foundation Reporter **8041**
1055-5099 Hazardous Waste Case Law Update
1055-5145 Grand Rapids Magazine **3976**
1055-5153 Grand Rapids Parent **2154**
1055-520X Individuals with Disabilities Education Law Report **3041**
1055-5242 Indoor Air Bulletin **3487**
1055-5269 Surface Science Spectra **7042**
1055-5277 F J C Directions
1055-5293 U F P S S Friendship
1055-5307 E R I S A Litigation Reporter **2555**
1055-5323 Frommer's Budget Travel Guide. Madrid on ... Dollars a Day **8711**
1055-5331 Frommer's Budget Travel Guide. London on ... Dollars a Day **8711**
1055-5374 Frommer's Comprehensive Travel Guide. Bangkok **8711**
1055-5447 Frommer's Comprehensive Travel Guide. The Virgin Islands **8711**
1055-5455 Annual Editions: Business Ethics **1060**
1055-5463 Living Faith **7805**
1055-548X Global Pesticide Campaigner **3497**
1055-5498 Major Tax Planning **1934**
1055-5536 U.S. Library of Congress. Music Catalog on Microfiche†
1055-5552 Slim Fast Magazine†
1055-5579 MarketSource†
1055-5609 One Meadway **5232**
1055-5625 Bahamas (Year) Including Turks & Caicos **8685**
1055-5633 Acapulco (Year) **8680**
1055-5641 Cancun, Cozumel, and Isla Mujeres **8691**
1055-565X Spain (Year) **8757**
1055-5668 Portugal (Year) **8748**
1055-5676 Ixtapa & Zihuatanejo (Year) **8725**
1055-5684 Bermuda (Year) **8687**
1055-5722 JazzSouth†
1055-5773 Super Collider News†
1055-5862 Municipal Liability Litigation Reporter†
1055-5897 Cancer Prevention†
1055-5900 Current Issues in Cancer Nursing Practice†
1055-5919 Military Advisor **4339**
1055-5935 Abortion and Family Planning Bibliography†
1055-596X Guide to Federal Funding for Governments and Nonprofits **7493**
1055-5978 Corporate Cleveland
1055-6060 Video Prophiles†
1055-6133 DisClosure (Lexington) **7959**
1055-6168 B O C A National Energy Conservation Code **3124**
1055-6176 B O C A National Private Sewage Disposal Code†
1055-6192 B O C A National Property Maintenance Code **978**
1055-6257 Annual A C M Symposium on Computational Geometry. Proceedings **5550**
1055-6273 M R (San Francisco)†
1055-6281 Drug Detection Report†
1055-629X Physician's Payment Update†
1055-6338 A C M SIGACT-SIGMOD-SIGART Symposium on Principles of Database Systems. Proceedings **2528**
1055-6370 Worcester Medicine **5731**
1055-6400 O O P S Messenger†
1055-6532 Great Plains Game & Fish **8316**
1055-6540 Mid-Atlantic Game & Fish **8322**
1055-6575 Slide Atlas of Current Ophthalmology (Year)†
1055-6583 Slide Atlas of Current Orthopaedics (Year)†
1055-663X Network News (New York)
1055-6656 Cleft Palate - Craniofacial Journal **6239**
1055-6699 Journal of Health Education *changed to* 1932-5037 **3050**
1055-6710 Directory of Professional Genealogists (Year) **3764**
1055-6729 Creative Woodworks & Crafts **1049**
1055-6737 American Angler **8303**
1055-677X Computational Fluid Dynamics
1055-6788 Optimization Methods and Software **5555**
1055-6796 Astronomical and Astrophysical Transactions **569**
1055-6818 Nursing Quality Connection†
1055-6826 Bio-Bibliographies in Art and Architecture† **8936**
1055-6850 Touring America†
1055-6877 I E E E - L T S: The Magazine of Lightwave Telecommunications Systems†
1055-6885 S P I E Publications Index†
1055-6893 The Green Book: Environmental Resource Directory†
1055-6915 Magnetic and Electrical Separation *changed to* 1478-6478 **7032**
1055-6931 H D World Review†
1055-6990 Annual Editions: Nutrition **6655**
1055-7008 Amanecer
1055-713X Progress in Neural Networks†
1055-7148 International Journal of Network Management **2327**
1055-7180 International Studies in Global Change
1055-7199 Hoover's Handbook of World Business **2004**
1055-7202 Hoover's Handbook of American Business **2004**
1055-730X Premises Liability Report **4760**
1055-7334 Confluence (Belpre) **5211**
1055-7342 Connecticut Technology Resource Guide (Year)†
1055-7369 Legal Malpractice Report **4720**
1055-7415 Drummer **4372**
1055-7423 Ridge Till Hotline†
1055-7431 D B†
1055-744X Gulf Reconstruction Report†
1055-7466 Health Systems Review†
1055-7490 International Journal of Mathematical and Statistical Sciences **5496**
1055-7512 Journal of Individual Employment Rights *changed to* 1938-4998 **1691**
1055-7520 Glimmer Train **5301**
1055-7601 Anesthesia & Pain Control in Dentistry†
1055-7628 American Salaries and Wages Survey **1200**
1055-7644 Temporary Culture†
1055-7660 Bryn Mawr Classical Review (Print Edition)†
1055-7679 Writers' Bar-B-Q†
1055-7717 Practical Accountant Alert†
1055-7725 Road and Rec *changed to* 1938-3932 **6454**
1055-7814 Citizen Participation **7489**
1055-7857 Wake Treasures **3787**
1055-7881 Who Trades Where?†
1055-789X Journal of Technology in Mathematics†
1055-7903 Molecular Phylogenetics and Evolution **875**
1055-7911 Yoga International *changed to* 1935-2158 **6648**
1055-792X Award-Winning Books for Children and Young Adults†
1055-7954 Ukrainian Biochemistry†
1055-7970 Economics Working Papers: Bibliography†
1055-8020 Sports Market Place **8208**
1055-808X Advances in Gastrointestinal Radiology†
1055-8136 Developments **4409**
1055-8152 Children and the Law†
1055-8195 Federal Circuit Bar Journal **4672**
1055-8217 Business Concepts†
1055-8225 Credit & Finance†
1055-8233 Motor World†
1055-8241 Health Diet & Nutrition†
1055-825X Government Programs†
1055-8268 National Auctions & Sales†
1055-8276 U S Immigration†
1055-8284 Economic Home Owner†
1055-8292 Current Employment†
1055-8306 American Senior†
1055-8314 Ideal Traveller†
1055-8349 A A C N Nursing Scan in Critical Care†
1055-8365 Export Yellow Pages **1564**
1055-8411 Earth First! **2609**
1055-842X Nihilistic Review†
1055-8438 Cat Lovers†
1055-8446 Santa Fe Literary Review†
1055-8454 Telecommunications Directory **2030**
1055-8462 International Journal of Systems Automation, Research & Applications†
1055-8489 Maxine's Pages
1055-8527 Financial Cycles **566**
1055-856X Michigan Feminist Studies **8875**
1055-8586 Seminars in Pediatric Surgery **6258**
1055-8616 American Society for Philatelic Pages and Panels. Page & Panel Journal **6891**
1055-8632 Nuggets from Paradise **3777**
1055-8659 Whetstone (Barrington) **5245**
1055-8675 Financial Leadership Speaks†
1055-8683 Educational I R M Quarterly†
1055-8756 Andean Past **373**
1055-8780 Black Face
1055-8799 Southwestern Entomologist. Supplement **859**
1055-887X Radio Fun
1055-8896 Journal of Educational Multimedia and Hypermedia **2469**
1055-890X Parking Technology†
1055-8942 Kansas Journal of Law & Public Policy **4709**
1055-8993 F. Paul Pacult's Spirit Journal **603**
1055-9000 Inside the Independents **2368**
1055-9027 Inside the R H C's†
1055-9035 The Thomas J. Herzfeld Encyclopedia of Closed-End Funds **1655**
1055-906X Sorkins Directory of Business & Government (Chicago Edition) **1904**
1055-9078 Animal Tales†
1055-9094 Applied H.R.M. Research **7335**
1055-9116 Taiwan Product Guide (Year) **2029**
1055-9124 Mexican Product Guide **2016**
1055-9140 Drinking Water Research **8821**
1055-9175 Oil Spill U S Law Report†
1055-9191 American Holiday and Life†
1055-9205 Asphalt Contractor **976**
1055-9221 Child, Youth, and Family Futures Clearinghouse†
1055-923X National Consumers League Bulletin **2640**
1055-9248 GamePlan Pro Football Annual Preview **8230**
1055-9256 GamePlan College Football Annual Preview **8230**
1055-9299 InterAmerican Opportunities Briefing†
1055-9337 High-Yield Bonds **1628**
1055-937X Seminars in Avian and Exotic Pet Medicine *changed to* 1557-5063 **8800**
1055-9434 The P R S Group. Country Reports: Kuwait **1507**
1055-9469 California Construction Law Reporter **989**
1055-9477 Bankruptcy Practice Series. Chapter 11 Update†
1055-9493 Asbestos Regulatory Reporter - New York Edition†
1055-9523 National Business Employment Weekly†
1055-9558 Checklists and Illustrative Financial Statements for Corporations **1284**
1055-9612 Drug Design and Discovery†
1055-9620 Technology for Critical Care Nurses†
1055-9639 Comic Relief†
1055-9663 Maintenance Executive
1055-9671 Global Market Perspective **1626**
1055-9701 Color Publishing†
1055-9779 Disability Compliance Bulletin **4065**
1055-9809 In Depth (Washington)†
1055-9833 American Dream Cars†
1055-985X European Textiles *see* 1092-5511 **8449**
1055-9868 New Myths
1055-9884 Heaven Earth
1055-9914 Research in Contemporary and Applied Geography: A Discussion Series **4026**
1055-9922 Remote Sensing of Earth Resources: A Quarterly Bibliography†
1055-9949 Feminist Majority Report **8896**
1055-9965 Cancer Epidemiology, Biomarkers & Prevention **6012**
1056-0009 International Information Systems†
1056-0017 A P I C S - The Performance Advantage *changed to* 1946-0384 **1722**
1056-0025 Paul Edwards' Travel Confidential **8747**
1056-005X Kosmas: Czechoslovak and Central European Journal **4238**
1056-0106 Washington - Oregon Game & Fish **8340**
1056-0114 Rocky Mountain Game & Fish **8331**
1056-0122 California Game & Fish **8307**
1056-0173 Turnaround Letter **1656**
1056-0297 Esperanto U S A **5116**
1056-0300 Social Studies and the Young Learner **3082**
1056-0319 American Jails **2643**
1056-0327 Laughing Bear Newsletter
1056-0335 Councilor **2839**
1056-0351 Crafting Today†
1056-0378 O'Lochlainns Irish Family Journal **3778**
1056-0386 Microleads Vendor Directory
1056-0505 Teen Beat AllStars†
1056-0513 Teen Beat†
1056-053X Diabetes Prevention and Therapy†
1056-0548 Insights (Austin) **7761**
1056-0556 Windows **7780**
1056-0572 Checklists and Illustrative Financial Statements for Credit Unions **1284**
1056-0580 Checklists and Illustrative Financial Statements for Finance Companies† **8941**
1056-0793 RadTech Report **2078**
1056-0815 Housewife - Writer's Forum
1056-0831 Top Producer **163**
1056-0866 Life Science Lab Products†
1056-0912 Starting Line†
1056-1021 Southwestern Archivist **5048**
1056-103X Out in Video†
1056-1072 Contention†
1056-1080 AIDS Research Reviews†
1056-1218 Eldercare - Law Newsletter†
1056-1293 Administrative Focus **3016**
1056-1331 Checklist Supplement and Illustrative Financial Statements for Construction Contractors **1284**
1056-1374 Hogs Today† **8962**
1056-1382 Dairy Today **263**
1056-1390 Beef Today **280**
1056-1439 New People
1056-1455 Motorcycle Road Racer Illustrated
1056-1463 Circus Fanfare **8468**
1056-148X Earth (Waukesha)†
1056-1528 California Libraries **5000**
1056-1536 Impact Pump News and Patents **5452**
1056-1544 Impact Valves News and Patents **5452**
1056-1595 Okay America
1056-1617 Athlon's Southeastern Football **8221**
1056-1625 Athlon's Big Ten Football **8221**
1056-1633 Athlon's Pac Ten Football **8221**
1056-1641 Athlon's Baseball **8221**
1056-165X Grammy Magazine **8153**
1056-1714 Nutz & Boltz Newsletter *changed to* MotorWatch **8594**
1056-1722 C F A Candidate Study and Examination Program Review†
1056-1730 Athlon's Western Football **8221**
1056-1749 Athlon's Eastern Football **8221**
1056-1757 Athlon's Atlantic Coast Conference Football **8221**
1056-1862 Official Hotel Guide *changed to* Official Hotel Guide Worldwide
1056-1919 Fort Worth Magazine **1403**
1056-1951 Digest of Geriatrics†
1056-196X *see* 1081-258X **4720**
1056-2036 C Q Researcher **7111**
1056-2044 Infectious Agents and Disease†
1056-2060 Western English World†
1056-2079 Silky Terrier Quarterly†
1056-2168 Alabama Facts **3117**
1056-2176 Dynamic Systems and Applications **3187**
1056-2184 Southern Law Journal **4786**
1056-2192 The Greenwood Educators' Reference Collection **2860**
1056-2230 D O J Alert **4950**
1056-2354 Ethiopian Review†
1056-2400 Bison World **281**
1056-2435 Northeast Ohio Avenues
1056-2451 Adventure Games for Microcomputers†
1056-2478 Journal of Medical Education Technologies†
1056-2559 Fashion Jewelry Plus†
1056-2583 International Accounting Summaries†
1056-2591 The Sagarin Review **5366**
1056-2613 Oxygen **5347**
1056-263X Journal of Developmental and Physical Disabilities **4067**
1056-2656 Education Grants Alert **3021**
1056-2699 Tech Market South
1056-2729 Automotive History Review **8565**
1056-2761 F A A Aviation Safety Journal **8540**
1056-277X Careers and the Disabled **4064**
1056-2818 Journal of Military Preparatory School Education†
1056-2826 Metal Revolution **6587**
1056-2850 C A Services Today†
1056-2877 Monthly Music Report
1056-2966 Mopar Muscle **8591**
1056-2974 Chevy Action **8573**
1056-3008 Executive Women International. Pulse **1108**
1056-3024 Issues in International Business **1573**
1056-3059 Legal Backgrounder **4719**
1056-3105 Gulf Reconstruction Business Guide
1056-3121 J.K. Lasser's Monthly Tax Letter **1931**
1056-3164 Environmental Regulatory Advisor *changed to* 1935-0309 **3506**
1056-3199 Focus (Washington, D.C. 1976) **2284**
1056-3210 Farmlife†

ISSN

1057-2643 Late Model Digest **8185**
1057-2651 Investor Guide†
1057-266X Journal for Preachers **7762**
1057-2678 St. Lawrence County Agricultural News **154**
1057-2708 Seafood Trend Newsletter **3607**
1057-2732 Advances in Magnetic and Optical Resonance **7004**
1057-2740 Clinical Correlations in the Head and Neck†
1057-2759 Food, Drug, Cosmetic, and Medical Device Law Digest†
1057-2813 Valve Magazine **5461**
1057-2821 Wonder: Observing & Confronting the Enigmas That Surround Us
1057-2848 Big Bond Book†
1057-2856 Michigan Hunting & Fishing†
1057-2864 Design Firm Management & Administration Report **1738**
1057-2880 National Teaching & Learning Forum **2995**
1057-2899 M L A Directory of Scholarly Presses in Language and Literature **2993**
1057-2902 Observations **5522**
1057-2961 Religious Leaders of America† **8985**
1057-2988 University of Kentucky. College of Agriculture. Cooperative Extension Service. H O **3753**
1057-302X Michigan Upper Peninsula Region Business Register†
1057-3062 Michigan Central Region Business Register†
1057-3070 Michigan Thumb Region Business Register†
1057-3143 Michigan Kent County Business Register†
1057-316X Michigan Macomb County Business Register†
1057-3208 Michigan Western Wayne County Business Register†
1057-3224 Longwood Graduate Program Seminars **800**
1057-3232 Progress in Poultry "Through Research" **297**
1057-3321 Journal of Chronic Fatigue Syndrome† **8968**
1057-3356 Successful Payroll Management†
1057-3372 Countryside†
1057-3399 Frommer's Comprehensive Travel Guide. San Francisco **8711**
1057-3429 Southern Living House Plans **457**
1057-3445 Patterson People **3779**
1057-3453 Culinary Trends **4384**
1057-3534 Dentistry **5842**
1057-3569 Reading and Writing Quarterly **3045**
1057-3577 Cyanosis
1057-3623 State Rankings **4436**
1057-3631 Journal of Nursing Care Quality **5966**
1057-364X Survivalist S I G Newsletter
1057-378X Massage **6112**
1057-3801 Doing Business in South Africa **1562**
1057-381X Doing Business in Zimbabwe **1562**
1057-3852 Doing Business in the United Kingdom **1093**
1057-3879 Doing Business in Malaysia **1562**
1057-3887 Doing Business in Spain **1093**
1057-3909 Doing Business in Singapore **1562**
1057-3925 Doing Business in Japan **1093**
1057-3941 Minnesota Mediterranean and East European Monographs **3550**
1057-3968 National Tropical Botanical Garden. Bulletin†
1057-3984 Human Resources Outlook†
1057-4026 Frommer's Comprehensive Travel Guide. England & Scotland **8711**
1057-4042 The Ballroom Dancer's Rag **2682**
1057-4050 Idaho Supreme Court Report and Idaho Court of Appeals Report **4952**
1057-4123 Anesthesia ComputerFile†
1057-4131 Analgesia ComputerFile†
1057-414X Honolulu Weekly **3977**
1057-4190 The Council Chronicle **3055**
1057-4204 Council-Grams (Print) *changed to* Council-Grams (Online) **3055**
1057-4212 Access (Chicago, 1990)† **8928**
1057-4239 Black Arts New York
1057-4263 International Journal of Arts Medicine†
1057-428X Continuing Care News **4091**
1057-4298 Environmental Protection **3427**
1057-4492 Geo-Monitor†
1057-4522 Integrated Circuits: Interface **3104**
1057-4530 Integrated Circuits: Digital† **8965**
1057-4549 Massachusetts Voter **7154**
1057-4565 Directory of New Mexico Manufacturers
1057-4581 Naval Institute Guide to Combat Fleets of the World **6438**
1057-4735 Berlitz Travellers Guide to England & Wales†
1057-4794 Legal Reporter **4720**
1057-4816 Leadership (Fairfield) **1772**
1057-4824 Income Taxation of Natural Resources
1057-4832 Successful Estate Planning: Ideas and Methods
1057-493X Guidance and Control **57**
1057-4956 European Electro-Optics
1057-4999 Global 500 Directory†
1057-5022 The Harvard Mental Health Letter **6144**
1057-5030 The Beverage Marketing Directory (Year) **599**
1057-5057 Harvard Human Rights Journal **7207**
1057-5073 Journal of Health Care Benefits†
1057-5111 Directory of United States Importers **1561**
1057-5200 Midnight Express†
1057-5219 International Review of Financial Analysis **1359**
1057-5227 Spark! (Cincinnati)†
1057-5235 International Communicator **5848**
1057-5243 Nevada Industrial Directory **2020**
1057-5251 Martha Stewart Living **4363**
1057-526X Private Equity Analyst **1645**
1057-5286 Directory of Engineering and Engineering Technology Undergraduate Programs **3187**
1057-5316 Frohlinger's Marketing Report†
1057-5332 Mediation News **4912**
1057-5367 Medieval Perspectives **4153**
1057-5375 Fiber Optics Business†
1057-5391 Wireless Telecommunications *changed to* Wireless L A N **2344**
1057-5405 Glass Factory Directory of North America and U.S. Industry Factbook **1997**
1057-5413 ArtWorld Hotline
1057-5456 Independent Auditors' Report on General Purpose Financial Statements - Kosrae†
1057-5480 Clinical Dental Briefings†
1057-5537 Airport Operations *changed to* 1934-4015 **8533**
1057-5545 Human Factors & Aviation Medicine *changed to* 1934-4015 **8533**
1057-5553 Cabin Crew Safety *changed to* 1934-4015 **8533**
1057-5561 Accident Prevention *changed to* 1934-4015 **8533**
1057-557X Flight Safety Foundation News†
1057-5588 Flight Safety Digest *changed to* 1934-4015 **8533**
1057-5618 En Route Technology†
1057-5642 America's Finest Companies **1972**
1057-5677 International Criminal Justice Review **4891**
1057-5723 Psychoanalysis and Psychotherapy **7395**
1057-5758 Energy-Related Laboratory Equipment Catalog†
1057-5766 F C C Record **2320**
1057-5774 List of Parties Excluded from Federal Procurement and Nonprocurement Programs **7451**
1057-5782 D O E This Month **3126**
1057-5790 U.S. Department of Energy. Energy Information Administration. Weekly Petroleum Status Report (Print)†
1057-5820 Job Safety and Health Quarterly†
1057-5839 A W I S Magazine **8850**
1057-5847 Journal of Court Reporting **4701**
1057-5863 Weekly Commercial News and Shipping Guide **8665**
1057-5871 N I H Record **5682**
1057-5987 U.S. Centers for Disease Control and Prevention. Morbidity and Mortality Weekly Report. Recommendations and Report **7544**
1057-6002 Telecom Calendar **2340**
1057-6010 Reynolds Records **3780**
1057-6037 Language and Literature†
1057-607X *see* Biotechnology Citation Index **713**
1057-6088 *see* Chemistry Citation Index **2093**
1057-6096 *see* Neuroscience Citation Index **5749**
1057-610X Studies in Conflict and Terrorism **7267**
1057-6185 Southeast Sourcebook
1057-6223 F D A Veterinarian **8797**
1057-624X Serono Symposia Series: Advances in Experimental Medicine†
1057-6258 Tracer (Fairview Park) **3785**
1057-6282 Advances in Artificial Intelligence in Software Engineering†
1057-6290 Advances in Medical Sociology **8085**
1057-6355 Bookways†
1057-6398 Indians Ink **8236**
1057-641X Doing Business in Hungary **1562**
1057-6428 Field & Stream Deer Hunter's Guide
1057-6533 *see* Wilson Business Abstracts **1274**
1057-6576 Current Topics in Plant Physiology†
1057-6592 Advances in Neuropsychiatry and Psychopharmacology†
1057-6606 Bristol-Myers Squibb - Mead Johnson Nutrition Symposia†
1057-6614 Feline Practice†
1057-6622 Canine Practice†
1057-6649 American Feed Industry Association. Annual and Semiannual Meetings of the Nutrition Council. Proceedings **278**
1057-6681 Montana Manufacturers Directory **2017**
1057-6703 Fund Watch†
1057-6711 Investor's Digest†
1057-6851 Tennis Illustrated (New York) **8248**
1057-686X Westchester County Business Journal **1524**
1057-6878 Directory of United States Exporters **1561**
1057-6886 National Patterns of R & D Resources **7887**
1057-6991 Alabama Cooperative Extension Service. Circular A N R **89**
1057-7017 Council for Agricultural Science and Technology. Task Force Reports **102**
1057-7025 Mandate Monitor†
1057-7041 Silicon Graphics World *changed to* Professional Graphics World
1057-705X State-by-State Biotechnology Directory†
1057-7076 Crochet World Specials†
1057-7122 I E E E Transactions on Circuits and Systems Part 1: Fundamental Theory and Applications *changed to* 1549-8328 **3102**
1057-7130 I E E E Transactions on Circuits and Systems Part 2: Analog and Digital Signal Processing *changed to* 1549-7747 **3102**
1057-7149 I E E E Transactions on Image Processing **2486**
1057-7157 I E E E Journal of Microelectromechanical Systems **3312**
1057-7246 White Buffalo Tales **3787**
1057-7262 Equipment World **1007**
1057-736X Children's Voice **8033**
1057-7378 Cable Avails†
1057-7386 Dimensions Magazine **8858**
1057-7408 Journal of Consumer Psychology **27**
1057-7416 Media Studies Journal†
1057-7459 Fairfax Magazine **5295**
1057-7475 Keltic Fringe **3546**
1057-7521 Defaulted Bonds Newsletter **1620**
1057-7629 U.S. National Center for Health Statistics. Vital and Health Statistics. Series 21. Data on Natality, Marriage, and Divorce **7549**
1057-7645 Frommer's Comprehensive Travel Guide. New Orleans **8711**
1057-7769 Intercultural Communication Studies **8108**
1057-7785 Food News for Consumers†
1057-7793 U.S. Department of Agriculture. Accepted Meat and Poultry Equipment†
1057-7882 U.S. Department of Agriculture. National Agricultural Statistics Service. Potato Stocks **189**
1057-7890 Economic Indicators of the Farm Sector. Costs of Production. Major Field Crops†
1057-7912 U.S. Department of Agriculture. National Agricultural Statistics Service. Noncitrus Fruits and Nuts **188**
1057-7920 U.S. Department of Agriculture. National Agricultural Statistics Service. Rice Stocks (Print)†
1057-7939 Information Technology Newsletter **2546**
1057-7971 Lady's Circle Patchwork Quilts Presents Quilt Craft†
1057-798X Software Directory. Master Index†
1057-7998 Americas Review (Berkeley)
1057-8005 Talking Stick†
1057-8048 Fodor's Healthy Escapes **8706**
1057-8056 Corporate Finance (New York, 1982)†
1057-8064 Commission on Preservation & Access. Annual Report (Year)†
1057-8080 Lifestyle Zip Code Analyst
1057-8153 Accident Reconstruction Journal **4608**
1057-8188 R S A P Newsletter **634**
1057-8218 Graham Group **3769**
1057-8250 Video Shopper†
1057-8269 Fine Art Index
1057-8277 Designers World
1057-8307 Journal of Military Aviation†
1057-8323 Nursing Staff Development Insider†
1057-834X Electronic Public Information Newsletter†
1057-8358 Journal of Asian Martial Arts **553**
1057-8374 Cognizer Report
1057-8404 State Tax Notes **1944**
1057-8439 Arkansas Catholic **7784**
1057-8447 U.S. Department of Agriculture. Situation & Outlook Report. Agricultural Resources†
1057-8501 Hunter & Sport Horse **8293**
1057-8536 Home Automation News **2460**
1057-8544 Wine Business Insider **613**
1057-8641 Brookings Papers on Economic Activity: Microeconomics†
1057-8684 Doing Business in the United States **1093**
1057-8714 Global Guaranty's Credit Enhancement and Financial Guaranty Directory†
1057-8765 U.S. Imports of Merchandise (CD-ROM)† **8995**
1057-8773 U.S. Exports of Merchandise (CD-ROM)† **8995**
1057-8919 Antitrust Report **4619**
1057-8943 Advances in Biophysical Chemistry†
1057-8951 Advances in Molecular Electronic Structure Theory†
1057-896X J C T **3066**
1057-8994 Perspectives in Personality†
1057-9036 Lace & Crafts†
1057-9168 Dodgers Dugout Newsmagazine **8226**
1057-9192 Soap Opera Magazine†
1057-9214 Journal of Multi-Criteria Decision Analysis **1769**
1057-9222 Companies Participating in the Department of Defense Subcontracting Program
1057-9230 Health Economics **5625**
1057-9249 Psycho-Oncology **6033**
1057-9273 Health & Healing **6987**
1057-929X Catholic Heritage† **8940**
1057-932X The Coast **5275**
1057-9354 Medicine, Exercise, Nutrition and Health†
1057-9397 F D A Enforcement Report (Print Edition)†
1057-9400 N C R R Reporter **5682**
1057-9427 Celebrity Access: The Directory (Year)†
1057-9435 Carolina Herald and Newsletter **3761**
1057-9478 Computing and Musicology **6633**
1057-9494 Report on Office Personnel Remuneration
1057-9540 Reds Report **8243**
1057-9613 Utah Index **4806**
1057-9621 Notices to Airmen **67**
1057-963X Airman's Information Manual **46**
1057-9648 F A A Aviation News **8540**
1057-9656 Census and You† **8940**
1057-9664 N O A A National Weather Service. Climate Analysis Center. Monthly and Seasonal Weather Outlook†
1057-9680 U.S. Merchandise Trade. F T 925, Exports, General Imports, and Imports for Consumption - Standard International Trade Classification Revision 3 - Commodity by Country† **8995**
1057-9699 Current Governments Reports: Quarterly Summary of Federal, State, and Local Tax Revenue†
1057-9737 Heat Treatment Yearbook†
1057-9745 Minerals Today†
1057-9796 Networking Directory†
1057-9834 Rand McNally World Facts & Maps† **8984**
1057-9893 On the Air Magazine†
1057-9958 U.S. Bureau of Alcohol, Tobacco and Firearms. Quarterly Bulletin **2670**
1057-9966 Commodity Classification under the Harmonized System Handbook **1556**
1057-9990 U.S. Department of State. Standardized Regulations (Government Civilians, Foreign Areas) **4800**
1058-0018 U.S. Department of State Indexes of Living Costs Abroad, Quarters Allowances, and Hardship Differentials **1272**
1058-0069 Annual and Cumulative Field and Operator Production. Area, South Louisiana Onshore. Product, Gas†
1058-0077 Annual and Cumulative Field and Operator Production. Area, Louisiana Offshore. Product, Gas†
1058-0123 Special Warfare **6447**
1058-0131 General - Flag Officer Worldwide Roster **6422**
1058-0158 D C A A Offices. Directory **1919**
1058-0190 Insurance Law Review
1058-0212 Mobile Beat **6588**
1058-0271 Front Lines (Portland) **2638**
1058-0344 Infomercial Marketing Report **1821**
1058-0360 American Journal of Speech - Language Pathology **4072**
1058-0379 Electronic Document Management Systems Journal†
1058-0417 Quality Quips Newsletter **1788**
1058-045X S P I E Holographics International Directory and Resource Guide†
1058-0468 Journal of Assisted Reproduction and Genetics **5995**
1058-0476 Journal of Family and Economic Issues **7373**
1058-0484 Cascade Cattleman **283**
1058-0506 International Employment Gazette **1688**
1058-0530 Information Systems Management **5061**
1058-0557 Trade Union Advisor **4603**
1058-059X Yesterday Today in New Jersey **4319**
1058-062X Northrop Frye Newsletter **5231**
1058-0638 Singles Choice
1058-0646 The Well Service Market Report **6797**
1058-0654 Blue Ryder
1058-0751 Amazing Stories†
1058-076X D C A A Contract Audit Manual **1919**

1058-9406 The Report (Eugene)†
1058-9430 Annual and Cumulative Field and Operator Production. Area, Federal Offshore. Product, Crude†
1058-9449 Annual and Cumulative Field and Operator Production. Area, Federal Offshore. Product, Gas†
1058-9457 Ecology Digest **3418**
1058-949X Lambda Update **4376**
1059-9503 3 D Artist **2490**
1058-9562 Foundations of Human Behavior *changed to* Evolutionary Foundations of Human Behavior **7356**
1058-9627 Northwest Dispatch†
1058-9643 Studies in New England Thought and Literature†
1058-9651 Studies in African Health & Medicine†
1058-966X Studies in African Economic & Social Development†
1058-9678 Recording Engineering Production†
1058-9694 Offshore Contractors and Equipment Worldwide Directory†
1058-9759 Nondestructive Testing and Evaluation **3355**
1058-9805 African Wildlife Update **2601**
1058-9813 Progress in Pediatric Cardiology **5798**
1058-9848 Rock Beat†
1058-9856 Teen Set†
1058-9937 McCutcheon's Functional Materials (International Edition) **2127**
1058-9945 A C A Newsletter *changed to* 1933-2785 **2108**
1058-997X Studies in Modern Art **520**
1059-0005 A A H A Dialogue **7329**
1059-0013 Financial Privacy Report **1344**
1059-0064 Orangeburgh German-Swiss Newsletter **3778**
1059-0137 Entrepreneurship, Innovation and Change†
1059-0145 Journal of Science Education and Technology **7873**
1059-0153 Biomimetics†
1059-0161 Journal of Archaeological Research **400**
1059-017X Washington Bond & Money Market Report†
1059-0234 Wine Industry Phone Book **613**
1059-0277 Handling Corporate Employment Problems **4870**
1059-0307 Today's Facility Manager **1855**
1059-0382 Dance Research **2688**
1059-048X Journal of Bankruptcy Law and Practice *changed to* Norton Journal of Bankruptcy Law and Practice **4749**
1059-0498 Guide to Resources on Women and AIDS†
1059-0501 Journal of Environmental Science and Health. Part C: Environmental Carcinogenesis & Ecotoxicology Reviews **3499**
1059-0528 Tree Care Industry **3704**
1059-0536 Perspectiva Monthly *changed to* 1097-1343
1059-0544 Broadband Networking News *changed to* Broadband Business Forecast (Print Edition)
1059-0560 International Review of Economics & Finance **1493**
1059-065X G L B Ames Newsletter **4373**
1059-0684 Quilt† **8983**
1059-0714 Wrestling Fury†
1059-0749 Matrix News **2564**
1059-0757 Beta Phi Mu Newsletter **4994**
1059-0803 Family Tree Quarterly **3766**
1059-0846 Futurebus plus Design†
1059-0870 Pediatric Emergency & Critical Care†
1059-0889 American Journal of Audiology **4072**
1059-0919 Gale Environment Sourcebook†
1059-0927 Revolution†
1059-0935 Wisconsin Newmonth **3993**
1059-0943 P B E Spectrum†
1059-096X Physical Therapy Products **6114**
1059-0994 Veterinary Medical Review **8813**
1059-1001 Autocephalous Orthodox Churches†
1059-101X Cracking the A C T **2975**
1059-1028 Wired **8147**
1059-1052 Southern Orthopaedic Association. Journal *changed to* 1548-825X **6066**
1059-1125 O A H Newsletter **4306**
1059-1133 Approaches to Teaching World Literature **2967**
1059-1168 Early Drama, Art, and Music Reference Series† **8952**
1059-1176 Forest World†
1059-1184 Studies in Renaissance Literature **5381**
1059-1192 MemberNet **2534**
1059-1222 Tarih†
1059-1265 Doing Business in Cyprus **1562**
1059-1273 Doing Business in Argentina **1561**
1059-1311 Seizure - European Journal of Epilepsy **6184**
1059-132X Columbian (Indianapolis) **2265**
1059-1419 Morningstar Closed-End Funds **1641**
1059-1427 Morningstar Mutual Funds Ondisc **1641**
1059-1435 Morningstar Variable Annuity Performance Report *changed to* 1075-5179
1059-1443 Morningstar Mutual Funds **1641**
1059-146X Equal Means†
1059-1478 Production and Operations Management **1786**
1059-1494 American Journal of Pain Management **5573**
1059-1516 Orthopaedic Physical Therapy Clinics of North America†
1059-1524 Molecular Biology of the Cell **834**
1059-1540 Advances in Neuroscience†
1059-1591 International Integrated Services Digital Networks Conference & Exposition. Proceedings†
1059-163X Directory of Executive Recruiters (Corporate Edition)†
1059-1664 Gleanings (Keokuk) **3769**
1059-1680 Preview Pro Football†
1059-1702 Small Corporation Update†
1059-1710 The Boston Parents' Paper **2146**
1059-1729 I R & R News Report **4689**
1059-1737 Petersen's Annual Hunting **8328**
1059-1753 A O T A Self Study Series **6672**
1059-1761 Petersen's Preview Pro Basketball†
1059-177X XXIst Century†
1059-180X Federal Sentencing Guidelines Handbook: Text, Analysis, Case Digest **2652**
1059-1818 New York Amsterdam News **3554**
1059-1931 World & Science†
1059-194X Soldiers Today†
1059-1958 Situations Digest†
1059-2032 P B C Federal Tax Guide†
1059-2091 Innovations & Ideas†
1059-2113 Analog Science Fiction & Fact **5439**
1059-2121 Hellenic Times **3537**
1059-2156 Lippincott's Reviews. Radiology **6202**
1059-2210 Sidewalks
1059-2237 The Business Partner†
1059-2350 Pearls of Wisdom **7669**
1059-2385 University of Texas. M.D. Anderson Cancer Center. Cancer Bulletin†
1059-2423 C J Europe†
1059-2458 Asian Americans Information Directory†
1059-2466 Treasures in Needlework†
1059-2504 Iowa State University. Center for Agricultural and Rural Development. Staff Report **8111**
1059-2539 Living Better **4363**
1059-2547 Oklahoma State University. Cooperative Extension Service. Forestry Extension Report **3699**
1059-2555 Clemson University. Cooperative Extension Service. H E Leaflet **4354**
1059-2563 Grower *changed to* Yankee Grower **259**
1059-2571 Petersen's Preview College Football†
1059-261X Motor Trend's Road Tests†
1059-2636 San Francisco Daily Journal **4778**
1059-2644 Beltwide Cotton Conferences. Proceedings **221**
1059-2679 Checklists and Illustrative Financial Statements for Nonprofit Organizations **1285**
1059-2725 The Online Journal of Current Clinical Trials†
1059-2733 The Living Pulpit **7661**
1059-2741 I O M A's Report on Managing 401k Plans **1865**
1059-275X Market: Asia Pacific **1577**
1059-2784 C A Selects. Molecular Modeling (Biochemical Aspects) **2088**
1059-2792 Kraft Recovery Operations Short Course **6735**
1059-2822 Spirit of Massachusetts Guidebook†
1059-2873 Bankruptcy Evidence Manual **4626**
1059-289X The Energy Newsbrief†
1059-292X Technology Commercialization - North America Edition **8442**
1059-2997 Anvil Magazine **6305**
1059-3055 Cleveland Enterprise **1083**
1059-3071 National Housing Register†
1059-308X School Community Journal (Print) *changed to* The School Community Journal (Online) **2909**
1059-311X Orthopedic Network News **6070**
1059-3128 Integrated Circuits: Linear†
1059-3144 Opus Dei Awareness Network **7668**
1059-3152 Journal of Sung-Yuan Studies **553**
1059-3160 Gas & Liquid Chromatography Literature - Abstracts & Index†
1059-3195 Letter to Libraries Online **5062**
1059-3454 Garland Reference Library of the Humanities **4453**
1059-3470 Client - Server Computing†
1059-3489 Implant Society†
1059-3497 American Counselor†
1059-3535 Major Concepts in Politics and Political Theory **7153**
1059-3551 The Reshaping of Psychoanalysis **7403**
1059-3624 Orlando **8745**
1059-3632 Alabama Cooperative Extension Service. Circular C R D **8086**
1059-3659 American City & County Directory of Administrative Service†
1059-3667 Facility Management Journal **1744**
1059-3691 The Snow Lion Buddhist News & Catalog **7702**
1059-3705 Morris Members **3775**
1059-3713 Murphy Mates **3775**
1059-3721 Home Textiles International†
1059-3772 Specialty References. Application Notes† **8989**
1059-3802 Cancer Watch **6014**
1059-3837 Hunting Horizons†
1059-3918 Quality Briefing†
1059-3950 Financial Women Today **1346**
1059-3977 Buckeye Pietenpol Association Newsletter **50**
1059-3985 Easy Fast 'n' Fun Crosswords *changed to* 1944-4222 **4333**
1059-4019 Stewart Connection
1059-4051 Franklintonian **3767**
1059-406X C B R Construction Business Review **988**
1059-4094 School Law Reporter **4780**
1059-4116 Mealey's Litigation Report: Lead **4836**
1059-4124 Paleoanthropology Annuals†
1059-4132 MacArtist
1059-4140 New Miami
1059-4167 The Journal of Workers Compensation **4510**
1059-4191 Playboy's Book of Lingerie **6298**
1059-4221 International Educator (Washington) **3013**
1059-4248 Case Citations†
1059-4256 Advances in Silicon Chemistry **2115**
1059-4272 Westchester Connections **3787**
1059-4280 Albany Law Journal of Science and Technology **4826**
1059-4299 Transition (Year)
1059-4329 Journal of Supreme Court History **4953**
1059-4337 Studies in Law, Politics, and Society **4790**
1059-4388 Jewish Thought†
1059-4396 Wright Angles **461**
1059-440X Asian Cinema Journal **6490**
1059-4418 U S and Asia Statistical Handbook **1271**
1059-4434 Architecture - Georgia
1059-4450 Systems Building Review†
1059-4523 Oklahoma Manufacturers Register **2022**
1059-4531 Materials Management in Health Care **4106**
1059-454X Technology for Emergency Care Nurses†
1059-4566 National Museum of Natural History Quest **7887**
1059-4620 Mississippi Construction†
1059-4655 Veale Heritage†
1059-468X Hazardous Waste Strategies Update†
1059-4752 Karate International†
1059-4760 Oggi 7†
1059-4779 Raivaaja **3560**
1059-4809 Live Wire†
1059-4817 Shout†
1059-485X Scream Factory†
1059-4892 Electric Pages†
1059-4906 Researching Law **4769**
1059-5031 Beethoven Forum† **8935**
1059-504X Colorado Employment Law Letter **4645**
1059-5058 Louisiana Employment Law Letter **4725**
1059-5066 Wisconsin Employment Law Letter **4815**
1059-5074 Illinois Environmental Law Letter†
1059-5082 Tennessee Law Enforcement Bulletin
1059-5090 Tennessee Real Estate Law Letter **4794**
1059-5155 Boating World **8273**
1059-518X Anderson's Ohio Case Locator **4615**
1059-5201 Special Report†
1059-521X Living Bird **910**
1059-5228 Official International Wrestling Insider
1059-5244 Chiron Rising **4372**
1059-5252 Today's Family Home Plans **459**
1059-5295 The Fisherman (Florida Edition) **8313**
1059-5317 Computer Security Buyer's Guide **2512**
1059-5325 Solstice **5537**
1059-5341 Southwest Publishing Market Place†
1059-535X Orange County Magazine
1059-5368 Mustang & Fords *changed to* 1944-9887 **367**
1059-5406 A M S Studies in Nineteenth-Century Literature and Culture **5247**
1059-5414 California Environmental Law and Regulation Reporter
1059-5422 Competitiveness Review **1556**
1059-5511 In Context (Crownsville) **4297**
1059-552X Real-Time Interface
1059-5635 R S Wavelength†
1059-5651 Command Magazine†
1059-5805 Petersen's College Basketball†
1059-5813 Energy, Economics and Climate Change†
1059-5856 Careers & Majors†
1059-5872 Sarmatian Review **4160**
1059-5899 Rip Photo Special
1059-5902 New Direction **4377**
1059-5910 Info-South Abstracts†
1059-5945 Key Note
1059-5953 The Traditional MusicLine†
1059-5988 Global Studies: Japan and the Pacific Rim **7238**
1059-6003 Oil and Gas Accounting
1059-6011 Group & Organization Management **2861**
1059-6038 HRfocus **1863**
1059-6054 Gospel Music Connection
1059-6097 Perspective (Cleveland)†
1059-6100 Unique Opportunities **5726**
1059-6119 Freelance Graphics Report†
1059-6143 Green Car Journal **3136**
1059-6216 Walk Away†
1059-6224 The Guardian (Los Angeles) **7139**
1059-6232 Asbestos M D L 875 Update†
1059-6240 Verses **5395**
1059-6259 Sober Times†
1059-6267 The Working Border Collie **6817**
1059-6275 Florida Jury Verdict Reporter **4675**
1059-6305 The Rural Virginia Voice
1059-6348 Turf Central **3752**
1059-6372 Freedom Writer†
1059-6399 Rapid Prototyping Report†
1059-6402 Enlace (Washington, 1975) **7232**
1059-6445 Now Hiring **6701**
1059-6518 Wilderness Medicine Newsletter **5731**
1059-6569 Compiler **2647**
1059-6585 Lawyers' Committee on Nuclear Policy. Newsletter **4971**
1059-6593 Life-Line **6158**
1059-6623 Conscious Consumer†
1059-6631 E M F Keeptrack†
1059-6674 Smart Investing†
1059-6763 Anglican Advance **7745**
1059-6771 Lhasas Unlimited†
1059-6798 Hustler Busty Beauties *changed to* Busty Beauties **6287**
1059-6828 Federal Court Appointments Report†
1059-6852 Faxon Guide to Serials†
1059-6879 The Emily Dickinson Journal **5421**
1059-6887 The U S Beer Market: Impact Databank Review and Forecast **611**
1059-695X Newcomen Publication **1153**
1059-6976 The Sutler **3784**
1059-6992 World Silver Survey (Year) **6484**
1059-7050 Local Climatological Data. Middletown Harrisburg International Airport. Monthly Summary **6377**
1059-7069 Journal of Technology and Teacher Education **2950**
1059-7077 Orange County Business and Industrial Directory
1059-7093 Contra Costa County Commerce and Industry Directory
1059-7107 Current Issues in Middle Level Education **2840**
1059-7123 Adaptive Behavior **2445**
1059-7131 Cheri **6287**
1059-7190 A B A's Financial Services Industry Trends *changed to* A B A Trust & Investments **1304**
1059-7239 Practices **453**
1059-7255 A M S Studies in Religious Tradition **7619**
1059-728X Studies in Symbolic Interaction. Supplement *see* 0163-2396 **8142**
1059-7298 Fire and Arson Investigator **2652**
1059-7352 Biotechnology Directory (Year) *changed to* Nature Biotechnology Directory (Year) **2019**
1059-7417 Educational Facility Planner **2850**
1059-7425 A I M **1803**
1059-7468 Static Line **6447**
1059-7484 New Alaska Outdoors
1059-7492 Storyboard **5435**
1059-7506 Missouri Record **4075**
1059-7530 Methods in Computational Chemistry **2108**
1059-7573 Benchmarks (Manhasset) *see* 1539-7343 **2510**
1059-7573 Benchmarks (Manhasset) *see* 1066-7598
1059-759X In the Wind **8259**
1059-7670 Nordstjernan **3555**
1059-7700 Journal of Genetic Counseling **7374**
1059-7727 Nebraska Manufacturers Register **2019**
1059-7743 I E A Reporter (Year) **2865**
1059-7786 Liturgical Ministry **7805**
1059-7794 Human Mutation **872**
1059-7816 International Offshore Oil Company Directory **6774**
1059-7840 Association of Ancient Historians. Publications **4201**

ISSN

DIRECTORY 2010 1061-754X 9489

1060-8982 A S C B Newsletter 826
1060-9075 Recording Industry Sourcebook†
1060-9105 EuroScope†
1060-913X Progress in Liver Disease†
1060-9148 Black Authors & Published Writers Directory 641
1060-9164 Colonial Latin American Review 4289
1060-9180 Beverage Aisle†
1060-9202 *see* Arts & Humanities Citation Index (Online) 529
1060-9202 *see* 0162-8445
1060-9237 Fitness 6986
1060-9253 Healthcare Human Resources†
1060-9288 Pigulki 5233
1060-9296 Growing for Market 3735
1060-930X Work-Family Roundtable†
1060-9369 Epilepsy U S A 6138
1060-9393 Russian Education and Society 2908
1060-9415 Aikido Today Magazine 8157
1060-9458 The S L S Report *changed to* 1553-7080 6251
1060-9504 High - Scope Buyer's Guide to Children's Software†
1060-9520 I R S Research Bulletin (Print) *changed to* I R S Research Bulletin (Online) 1928
1060-9563 Rodale's Scuba Diving *changed to* 1553-7919 8332
1060-9598 Ladies' Home Journal Parent's Digest
1060-9644 Pondscapes Magazine
1060-9741 World Agriculture†
1060-9792 C A N A, Inc. (Print Edition)†
1060-9814 Kids Count Data Book 2158
1060-9857 Symposium on Reliable Distributed Systems. Proceedings 2525
1060-989X Wall Street & Technology 1394
1060-9903 Louis Rukeyser's Wall Street 1637
1060-9911 Soccer Jr.†
1060-992X Optical Memory & Neural Networks 7082
1060-9962 Landscape Architect & Specifier News 3741
1060-9970 Trading Cards 4349
1060-9997 Star Guide (Year) 6514
1061-0014 Statutes and Decisions: The Laws of the U S S R & Its Successor States 4788
1061-0022 St. Petersburg Mathematical Journal 5532
1061-0057 American Drama 8465
1061-009X Braswell Branches 3760
1061-0103 World Explorer 8776
1061-0154 Sociological Research 8137
1061-0251 Occupational Hygiene†
1061-026X Journal of Marine Environmental Engineering 3448
1061-0278 Supramolecular Chemistry 2081
1061-0308 Animation Journal 6489
1061-0324 International Observer 7244
1061-0367 Laughter Works†
1061-0383 Contemporary Oncology†
1061-0405 Journal of Russian and East European Psychology 7379
1061-0413 Journal of Russian and East European Psychiatry†
1061-0421 Journal of Product and Brand Management 1826
1061-0448 Judaica News†
1061-0464 Logic Programming 2454
1061-0510 Print Buyers Review†
1061-0553 DePaul Journal of Art & Entertainment Law *changed to* DePaul Journal of Art, Technology & Intellectual Property Law 4656
1061-0723 Dun's Regional Business Directory. Alabama Area 1989
1061-0731 Dun's Regional Business Directory. Tennessee Metros Area 1991
1061-074X Dun's Regional Business Directory. Chicago Metropolitan Area 1989
1061-0758 Dun's Regional Business Directory. Columbus Area 1989
1061-0774 Dun's Regional Business Directory. New England Area 1990
1061-0782 Dun's Regional Business Directory. Norfolk - Richmond Area 1990
1061-0790 Dun's Regional Business Directory. Oklahoma - Arkansas Area 1990
1061-0804 Dun's Regional Business Directory. Northern New York State Area 1990
1061-0812 Dun's Regional Business Directory. San Antonio Area 1990
1061-0820 Dun's Regional Business Directory. Central Pennsylvania Area 1989
1061-0855 Standard & Poor's Ratings Handbook†
1061-088X Micronesian Educator 2886
1061-0901 Hastings Women's Law Journal 4685
1061-0987 Minnesota Guidebook to State Agency Services 7453
1061-1010 Picking the "Right" Bible Study Program†
1061-1053 The WordPerfectionist†
1061-1118 Design Net†
1061-1126 Dun's Regional Business Directory. Central Indiana Area 1989
1061-1134 Dun's Regional Business Directory. Charlotte - Greensboro Area 1989
1061-1142 Dun's Regional Business Directory. Denver Area 1989
1061-1150 Dun's Regional Business Directory. Iowa Metros and Omaha, Nebraska Area 1989
1061-1169 Dun's Regional Business Directory. Kentucky Metros (including Evansville, IN) 1990
1061-1177 Dun's Regional Business Directory. Michigan Metros (excluding Detroit) Area 1990
1061-1185 Dun's Regional Business Directory. Northern California Area 1990
1061-1193 Dun's Regional Business Directory. Orlando - Jacksonville Area 1990
1061-1207 Dun's Regional Business Directory. Georgia (excluding Atlanta) Area 1989
1061-1215 Dun's Regional Business Directory. South Carolina Area 1991
1061-1231 The Dispatch (Midland) 53
1061-1258 Who Owns Corporate America†
1061-1266 Major Donors†
1061-1274 Corporate and Foundation Grants†
1061-1304 The P R S Group. Country Reports: Ukraine 1509
1061-1347 Dun's Regional Business Directory. Oregon Area 1990
1061-1355 Dun's Regional Business Directory. St. Louis Area 1990
1061-1371 Ad Business Report†
1061-138X Commercial Inc. 7586
1061-1428 Russian Social Science Review 7181
1061-1444 W B F In Action 4527
1061-1452 Progress in Paper Recycling 6737
1061-1495 Better Teaching *changed to* 1556-9861 3052
1061-1495 Better Teaching *changed to* 1556-987X 3052
1061-1517 Police Forum 2663
1061-155X The Environmental Contract Opportunity Report 7435
1061-1568 Women's Sports Experience 8216
1061-1576 Compensation and Benefits Alert†
1061-1711 International Journal of Angiology†
1061-1797 Automatic Merchandiser 1806
1061-1800 Monad†
1061-1827 American Society of Agricultural Engineers. Comprehensive Index of Publications†
1061-1835 Directory of Associations for Women Lawyers 4658
1061-186X Journal of Drug Targeting 6853
1061-1878 Jeffersoniana 7870
1061-1886 Morningstar Japan†
1061-1924 Middle East Policy 7252
1061-1932 Chinese Education and Society 2836
1061-1940 Russian Politics and Law 4777
1061-1959 Anthropology and Archeology of Eurasia 326
1061-1967 Russian Studies in Philosophy 6950
1061-1975 Russian Studies in Literature 5365
1061-1983 Russian Studies in History 4159
1061-1991 Problems of Economic Transition 1161
1061-2025 Harris National Manufacturers Directory. Midwest Edition (Year) *changed to* Harris Directory. U.S. Midwest Manufacturing 2002
1061-2033 Harris National Manufacturers Directory. Southeast Edition (Year) *changed to* Harris Directory. U.S. Southeast Manufacturing 2002
1061-2041 Harris National Manufacturers Directory. Northeast Edition (Year) *changed to* Harris Directory. U.S. Northeast Manufacturing 2002
1061-2076 Harris U.S. Manufacturers Directory - National Edition 2003
1061-2114 American Wholesalers and Distributors Directory 1972
1061-2122 Environmental Industries Marketplace†
1061-2130 Journal of Optimal Nutrition†
1061-2181 Southern California Business Directory 2028
1061-219X American Manufacturers Directory 1972
1061-2203 Instrument Business Outlook 4487
1061-2327 HolQeD 6502
1061-2335 Drug G M P Report 6835
1061-2343 Transitions Abroad 8765
1061-2386 Magic Realism
1061-2416 Strong Coffee†
1061-2424 Sporting Clays 8205
1061-2467 Searchnotes 3782
1061-2491 Brides Today†
1061-2548 The Uppercrust†
1061-2556 Employee Fringe and Welfare Benefit Plans 1677
1061-2610 Michigan Insurance Handbook
1061-2688 Sys Admin†
1061-2726 News Record 4599
1061-2785 Clinical Cardiology Monographs†
1061-2793 Current Endocrinology†
1061-2831 Global Studies: Latin America 7238
1061-2858 Straightalk 7730
1061-2890 Investor's Business Daily 1633
1061-2947 Annual Status Report on Minorities in Higher Education 2966
1061-2963 Architecture in Perspective (No.) 430
1061-2971 Restoration Ecology 3463
1061-3013 Skin Art 518
1061-3056 Directory of Aging Resources†
1061-3064 Craftmaster News 533
1061-3072 G P L L A Newsletter 5010
1061-3080 Boston Literary Review†
1061-3099 CyberEdge Journal†
1061-3153 Federal Regional Yellow Book 7437
1061-3234 Simply Cross Stitch 6642
1061-3269 Advance for Health Information Professionals 5568
1061-3285 Job Seeker's Guide to Private and Public Companies†
1061-3293 Inside dBASE†
1061-3315 Atlas of the Oral and Maxillofacial Surgery Clinics of North America 5835
1061-3323 Dive Training 8169
1061-3331 University of San Francisco Maritime Law Journal 4971
1061-3358 Directory of MasterCard & VISA Credit Card Sources 1336
1061-3412 Fort Lauderdale Magazine
1061-3420 Microbeam Analysis†
1061-3439 I S S X Proceedings†
1061-3447 Stanford Law Alum
1061-3455 Journal of Questioned Document Examination 2658
1061-348X MidLife Woman†
1061-3501 Windows Tech Journal†
1061-3544 Great Golf Resorts of the World 8234
1061-3579 Sandhills Review 5367
1061-3609 The Informed Librarian 5058
1061-365X California Environmental Law Reporter 3408
1061-3692 Improved Recovery Week 3137
1061-3749 Journal of Nursing Measurement 5966
1061-3773 Computer Applications in Engineering Education 3289
1061-3781 Bulletin of American Odonatology 841
1061-382X Restaurant Finance Monitor 4396
1061-3846 Marketing Management 1832
1061-3862 International Journal of Self-Propagating High-Temperature Synthesis 7055
1061-3889 Backgrounder (Washington, DC) 7278
1061-3900 California Republic†
1061-3927 Miracles Magazine†
1061-3943 Inside Waste
1061-396X Better World†
1061-3994 Neil Sperry's Gardens 3744
1061-4036 Nature Genetics 876
1061-4044 Who's Who Worldwide Registry (Platinum Edition)†
1061-4079 Houseplant Magazine
1061-4095 Ukraine Update†
1061-4125 Personal Health Reporter 5695
1061-4141 Animal Guardian 317
1061-4176 Turnarounds & Workouts - Europe†
1061-4184 Turnarounds & Workouts - Survey†
1061-4192 Medical Record Risks: Claims & Litigation†
1061-4230 America's Censored Newsletter†
1061-4249 Board Leadership 1728
1061-4303 Water Environment Research 3493
1061-4338 A S O R N News†
1061-4362 Therapists Report 7412
1061-4389 Turnarounds & Workouts - Supplement†
1061-4397 Menopause News 8847
1061-4427 South Dakota Hall of Fame 4313
1061-4435 Ennaanin Etto 392
1061-446X Community News (Washington, DC) 2279
1061-4494 Inside Flyer (Americas Edition) 8544
1061-4524 S T N
1061-4621 O & P Almanac 6068
1061-4648 Treasure Found
1061-4656 Office Technology Management†
1061-4699 Yankee Traveler†
1061-4737 Model Call 6701
1061-4753 Nursing Homes *changed to* 1940-9958 5969
1061-480X Inside Indiana 8236
1061-4885 International Risk Management Advisor†
1061-4982 Indiana International & Comparative Law Review 4928
1061-5008 Education Technology News†
1061-5091 The Boston Irish Reporter 3523
1061-5121 Times (Bethlehem) 4428
1061-5202 A D L on the Frontline 7201
1061-5210 Religion and the Social Order 7674
1061-5229 Hazard Communication Handbook 3507
1061-5245 Rocky Mountain Coal Mining Institute. Proceedings 6478
1061-5261 Praeger Series in Transformational Politics and Political Science 7173
1061-5288 Corporate Library Update†
1061-5296 Misnomer†
1061-5342 C A Selects. Bismuth Chemistry 2085
1061-5369 Neural, Parallel & Scientific Computations 2455
1061-5377 Cardiology in Review 5780
1061-5415 Birnbaum's Montreal & Quebec City†
1061-544X Birnbaum's Washington D.C.†
1061-5466 Birds of North America†
1061-5474 Down Memory Lane
1061-558X MacGuide Report
1061-5709 Signature (Nashville)
1061-5741 Television & Cable Action Update (Print Edition) *changed to* Television & Cable Action Update (Online Edition)
1061-575X Progress in Veterinary Neurology†
1061-5792 Intimate Fashion News
1061-5806 Anxiety, Stress and Coping 7335
1061-5822 Georgia Magazine 3976
1061-5857 Log Cabin News 1021
1061-5865 Inside P C Tools†
1061-5873 Inside Microsoft Works for Windows†
1061-5903 Comparative Studies of Health Systems & Medical Care 5599
1061-5938 Epigraphic Society. Occasional Papers 392
1061-5954 Contemporary Neuroscience 6133
1061-6012 Plattsburgh Studies in the Humanities 4469
1061-6055 Berkeley Models of Grammar†
1061-6071 Monographs in P - M Series 6326
1061-6098 Emerging Pharmaceuticals†
1061-6101 Pakistan 4187
1061-611X Gamer's Connection 8174
1061-6136 Stephen Crane Studies 5435
1061-6152 Refrigerated and Frozen Foods 3662
1061-6160 Spectrum (Wheaton) 7775
1061-6187 Viewpoint (New York, 1972) 1800
1061-6292 Oughtred Society. Journal 5523
1061-6365 Texture 5436
1061-642X Bay Food
1061-6500 Bibliographies of the Presidents of the United States 7199
1061-656X R C D A *changed to* 2150-0274 7673
1061-6578 Hastings Communications and Entertainment Law Journal 4685
1061-6616 Nextworld†
1061-6640 Playboy's Playmate Review 6298
1061-6748 Savannah Magazine 3988
1061-6756 Sampler & Antique Needlework Quarterly 6642
1061-6829 Apparel Marketing Digest†
1061-6845 Defense Intelligence Journal *changed to* 1940-4042 7254
1061-6861 Rapport 7572
1061-687X SportsTurf 8247
1061-6934 Sport Marketing Quarterly 8204
1061-6950 State of the States†
1061-6977 Future Sex 7943
1061-6993 Nebraska English Journal†
1061-7000 The Atrocity 5207
1061-7027 Radio Guide 2362
1061-7094 Handbook of U S Government and Federal Agency & Related Money Market Instruments†
1061-7159 Marketer's Guide to Media 29
1061-7167 Sbornik 7215
1061-7191 Recovery Today 2698
1061-7205 Radio Control Model Cars and Trucks†
1061-7264 Fortran Forum 2506
1061-7272 Lawyer's Register International by Specialties and Fields of Law Including a Directory of Corporate Counsel 4718
1061-7280 Cato Institute. Briefing Papers 7114
1061-7361 Journal of Social and Evolutionary Systems†
1061-737X Clutch†
1061-7426 O C International†
1061-7434 Citations for Serial Literature 5057
1061-7469 Geographic Reference Report (Year) 1861
1061-754X Microwave Product Digest 3325

ISSN

Link to your serials resources and content with ulrichsweb.com

DIRECTORY 2010 1063-4665 9491

1062-645X E D I Monthly Report†
1062-6484 P M A Update **8656**
1062-6492 Directory of Building and Equipment Grants **8037**
1062-6506 C I B Daily Maritime Newsletter **8640**
1062-6514 A A C O G Region **7486**
1062-6549 Cistercian Studies Quarterly **7633**
1062-6581 Lepidoptera News **854**
1062-6611 State Bar of New Mexico. Bar Bulletin **4788**
1062-6646 The Texas Music Industry Directory **2030**
1062-6700 Westminster Magazine **2309**
1062-6727 Cole Papers **8418**
1062-6743 C T D News **6675**
1062-676X World Citizen News†
1062-6778 The Capstone (Washington, DC) **2276**
1062-6808 Electrical Contacts: I E E E Holm Conference on Electrical Contacts. Proceedings **3302**
1062-6859 Barnes Bulletin 2.0 **3759**
1062-6883 C D Guide **6552**
1062-6956 Play (Boca Raton) **2165**
1062-6964 Comic Art Studies†
1062-6999 The Robert Frost Review **5363**
1062-709X Mountain Bike Action Buyer's Guide†
1062-7111 Mountain Bike Action Accessory Guide
1062-7146 International Saddlery and Apparel Journal†
1062-7197 Educational Assessment **2849**
1062-7200 The Highwayman†
1062-7219 The Goose†
1062-7243 Opera America Newsline **6601**
1062-726X Journal of Public Relations Research **27**
1062-7324 Foodservice Yearbook International **1995**
1062-7332 Menopause Management **8847**
1062-7359 Dovetail (Print Edition) *changed to* Dovetail (Online Edition) **3530**
1062-7375 Journal of Global Information Management **1766**
1062-7391 Journal of Mining Science **6467**
1062-7413 The Barnstormer†
1062-7421 Law and Politics Book Review **4714**
1062-7464 Wicked Mystic **5438**
1062-7472 Focus: Carrying Capacity Selections†
1062-7510 Gaitway Magazine†
1062-7537 Med-Surg Nursing Quarterly†
1062-7561 The Best American Short Plays (Year) **5262**
1062-7626 Pulse! (West Sacramento)†
1062-7634 Voyageur **4317**
1062-7650 The Workstation Report **1855**
1062-7723 How on Earth!
1062-7774 Board Report for Graphic Artists†
1062-7812 American Girl **2176**
1062-7820 Timmons Family Newsletter **3785**
1062-7855 Pollock Potpourri **3779**
1062-7863 Critique of Trade Union Rights in Countries Affiliated with the League of Arab States **4592**
1062-7901 Phase Transitions and Critical Phenomena† **8980**
1062-791X G I S Newsletter **2707**
1062-7928 Out **4377**
1062-7952 N F A I S Yearbook of the Information Industry (Year)†
1062-7960 Maryland Environmental Law
1062-7987 European Review **7853**
1062-7995 Progress in Photovoltaics **3145**
1062-8029 Doing Business in Paraguay **1562**
1062-8061 Nursing History Review **5973**
1062-8088 Journal of the Coin Laundry and Drycleaning Industry **2243**
1062-8096 Hazardous Emergency Response†
1062-810X Colorado Springs Business Journal **1084**
1062-8150 Clinical Microbiology Reports†
1062-8169 Coin Dealer Newsletter **6650**
1062-8193 California Therapist *changed to* 1540-2770 **7412**
1062-8207 Creative Outlets **534**
1062-8258 Guide to the Nursing Home Industry†
1062-8266 Trends Magazine **8809**
1062-8274 Nebraska Cattleman **294**
1062-8312 Artworld Europe **476**
1062-8339 United States Importers Product Guide **2032**
1062-8355 Small Diesel Engine Service Manual
1062-8371 The Courier (Brockton) **4332**
1062-855X The Flora-Line†
1062-8576 Experimental Rocket Flyer **54**
1062-8592 Sports Medicine and Arthroscopy Review **6073**
1062-8606 American Journal of Medical Quality **5572**
1062-8630 Pittsburgh Engineer **3215**
1062-8649 Pennsylvania Architect
1062-8657 Place **453**
1062-8665 The Food Channel **3638**
1062-8681 C A Selects. Metallic Glasses†
1062-869X C A Selects. Shape Memory Alloys†
1062-8711 Tzivos HaShem Children's Newsletter **3569**
1062-872X Central Massachusetts Business Digest
1062-8738 Russian Academy of Sciences. Bulletin. Physics **7038**
1062-8746 Wireline (Dallas) **5869**
1062-8770 Writing Right†
1062-8800 The Engineering Documentation Advisor†
1062-8835 Directory of Nurse-Midwifery Practices (Year) **5957**
1062-8886 The Last Leaf **4301**
1062-8983 Tennessee Farm Bureau News **161**
1062-8991 Workforce Strategies†
1062-9017 The Mathematics Educator **3072**
1062-9025 Hardy Enough
1062-9068 Embassy's Marine Marketplace†
1062-9084 Affordable Caribbean†
1062-9130 S A L - News†
1062-922X I E E E International Conference on Systems, Man, and Cybernetics. Conference Proceedings†
1062-9238 Getting the Lowdown on Employers and a Leg Up on the Job Market
1062-9246 Sing Tao Daily **3564**
1062-9254 Hospitality Design **4542**
1062-9327 Blue Chip Job Growth Update **1442**
1062-9351 Tech Directions **3085**
1062-936X S A R and Q S A R in Environmental Research **3464**
1062-9408 The North American Journal of Economics and Finance **1502**
1062-9416 D E O S News†
1062-9424 EFFector **7205**
1062-9459 Art on Screen†
1062-9483 Transit Research Abstracts **8531**
1062-9491 Inner Voice *changed to* Forest Magazine **3689**
1062-9505 Latvian Dimensions **3547**
1062-9548 Cheap Relief†
1062-9629 Sport Compact Car **8604**
1062-9645 E T Cetera **1850**
1062-967X Science and Technology of Building Seals, Sealants, Glazing, and Waterproofing†
1062-9696 ShopNotes **1051**
1062-9726 Greenwood Historical Encyclopedia of the World's Political Parties† **8960**
1062-9769 The Quarterly Review of Economics and Finance **1163**
1062-9807 New Mexico State University. Cooperative Extension Service. Guide D **294**
1062-9823 New Mexico State University. Cooperative Extension Service. Guide G **4365**
1062-9831 New Mexico State University. Cooperative Extension Service. Guide F **4365**
1062-9858 New Mexico State University. Cooperative Extension Service. Guide E **4365**
1062-9866 New Mexico State University. Cooperative Extension Service. Guide Z **204**
1062-9882 New Mexico State University. Cooperative Extension Service. Guide C **4365**
1062-9890 New Mexico State University. Cooperative Extension Service. Guide H **3745**
1062-9939 Index: Foreign Broadcast Information Service Daily Reports. Central Eurasia†
1062-9963 Writer's Chapbook Series†
1063-0023 Complete Directory for People with Disabilities **4064**
1063-0082 Federal Rules of Civil Procedure (Year) **4951**
1063-0104 C S W S Review†
1063-0120 Ag Facts **80**
1063-018X Pesticide Information Program Information Sheet **246**
1063-0198 HortTechnology **3738**
1063-0244 AudioFile **5258**
1063-0287 Accounting and Tax Index (Print Edition) **1199**
1063-0333 International Tennis
1063-0368 Austin Report **7108**
1063-0376 Texas Finance Report **1386**
1063-0406 Texas Pollution Report **3491**
1063-0414 Power Equipment Trade **5458**
1063-0503 3 W Register of Chinese Business
1063-0589 Equal Time
1063-0619 Advances in Detailed Reaction Mechanisms†
1063-0627 Harvard AIDS Institute Series on Gene Regulation of Human Retroviruses
1063-0635 Dun & Bradstreet Comments on the Economy†
1063-0643 Dialog Docket†
1063-0651 Journal of Physical and Chemical Reference Data. Monograph **2068**
1063-0686 Wiley Librarians' Newsletter **7576**
1063-0724 North Carolina Literary Review **5231**
1063-0732 Journal of Urban Technology **8429**
1063-0740 Russian Journal of Marine Biology **702**
1063-0775 Caribbean Digest
1063-0821 Court Management & Administrative Report **4948**
1063-083X International Enforcement Law Reporter **4930**
1063-0848 Minas Tirith Evening Star
1063-0864 C R I S Newsletter
1063-0902 A F S World†
1063-0929 Barnwood†
1063-0953 Arkansas Wildlife **2603**
1063-097X Employee Terminations Law Bulletin **1860**
1063-1011 B R E **2357**
1063-1054 Marriage Magazine **5560**
1063-1100 Engineering Simulation *changed to* 1687-5591 **3109**
1063-1119 Society and Animals **321**
1063-1135 International Construction Directory. International Section†
1063-1151 Agricultural & Environmental Biotechnology Abstracts (Print)†
1063-116X Environmental Viewpoints†
1063-1178 Medical & Pharmaceutical Biotechnology Abstracts (Print)†
1063-1186 Heartland Critiques **5410**
1063-1267 The Free Press **5216**
1063-1283 Rap Pages **6609**
1063-1321 Expose†
1063-1348 Audiotex News *changed to* 1527-3539 **2368**
1063-1372 Treasure Cache **4349**
1063-1399 Nelson's Directory of 'Neglected Stock' Opportunities†
1063-1410 A C H Participant Directory **1970**
1063-1488 Microsystems Handbook **2572**
1063-1518 The Puck Stops Here
1063-1526 Austin Lawyers Journal **4623**
1063-1585 Hawaii Bar Journal **4685**
1063-1593 Atlanta Homes and Lifestyles **4532**
1063-1607 Interior Landscape **3739**
1063-1615 Building Environment Report
1063-1623 Kansas Optometric Journal **6045**
1063-1631 Observer (Rock Island) **2294**
1063-1658 Immigration and Nationality Laws of the United States *changed to* Martin, Aleinikoff, Motomura, and Fullerton's Forced Migration: Law and Policy **4935**
1063-1682 Playboy Playmate Desk Calendar
1063-1690 Statistical Abstract of the United States (Large Print Edition) **8403**
1063-1720 Comparative Performance of U.S. Hospitals: The Sourcebook **4091**
1063-1739 Publicity and Media Resources for Book Publishers†
1063-1763 The Mid-Atlantic Almanack **8121**
1063-1771 Publications Newsletter†
1063-178X Playboy Playmate Calendar
1063-1801 Configurations **5277**
1063-181X Electronic Product Review†
1063-1836 Chaucer Yearbook†
1063-1917 S E R America **1874**
1063-2042 Simone de Beauvoir Studies **5372**
1063-2069 Tax Management Transfer Pricing Report **1948**
1063-2085 The Source (New York, 1988) **6618**
1063-2107 Cosmetics Counter Update
1063-214X Sistersong†
1063-2158 Human Evolution, Behavior, and Intelligence **871**
1063-2166 Journal of Biblical Counseling **7654**
1063-2190 North American Religion†
1063-2220 Clark's Bank Deposits and Payments Monthly **1327**
1063-2239 Journal of End User Computing *changed to* 1546-2234 **2571**
1063-2255 Advances in Online Public Access Catalogs **5060**
1063-2409 Stochastic Optimization and Design†
1063-2425 Metro Golf **8238**
1063-245X C N S Meeting Reports†
1063-2468 Cardiovascular Meeting Reports†
1063-2476 Pension Benefits **1702**
1063-2506 Disability Law Compliance Report **4065**
1063-2565 S S S A Special Publication **251**
1063-2581 Current Topics in General Thoracic Surgery† **8947**
1063-2611 Secular Humanist Bulletin **7680**
1063-2700 MacAuthority Software Connection†
1063-2719 WordPerfect Software Connection†
1063-2727 Inside WordPerfect for Windows†
1063-2778 Stanford **2301**
1063-2808 Adrian Day's Investment Analyst†
1063-2816 The Nonprofit Board Report **1154**
1063-2875 North Carolina Magazine **1431**
1063-2883 Total T V
1063-2913 Arts Education Policy Review **475**
1063-2921 Journal of Arts Management, Law, and Society **4700**
1063-293X Concurrent Engineering: Research and Applications **2470**
1063-2948 Bryn Mawr Classical Review **2231**
1063-3006 Corporate Legal Times *changed to* 1930-6393 **4870**
1063-3014 Illinois Legal Times†
1063-3111 B N A's Americans with Disabilities Act Manual. Newsletter **4968**
1063-312X Computer Artist†
1063-3146 Inside O S - 2†
1063-3189 American Association of Retired Persons. Public Policy Institute. Issue Brief **8024**
1063-3197 Bio-Bibliographies in Economics† **8936**
1063-3200 Payroll Practitioner's Compliance Handbook **1298**
1063-3286 *see* 0006-3053 **648**
1063-3308 Social Sciences Index (WilsonDisc) *see* 0094-4920 **8021**
1063-3332 Prehospital Care Reports†
1063-3340 Think Tank Directory **7188**
1063-3359 Salamander **5238**
1063-3383 Buzz (Rochester) **1809**
1063-3391 Pleiades **5352**
1063-3405 Acquisition
1063-3413 Dayton Business Reporter
1063-3421 Forever Alive
1063-343X Journal of Business and Economic Studies **1133**
1063-3448 World Aquatic News & Travel
1063-3561 Bootstrappin' Entrepreneur **1957**
1063-357X Risk Retention Reporter **4522**
1063-3588 N D T Update *changed to* N D T Update News
1063-3596 Bioethics Bulletin **4630**
1063-3677 Methods in Toxicology†
1063-3685 Narrative **5338**
1063-3707 Akcens†
1063-3715 Alaska Industry Occupation Outlook to (Year)†
1063-3723 Alaska Occupational Supply & Demand (Year)†
1063-3758 Alaska Wage Rates (Year) **1662**
1063-3766 Alaska Career Guide†
1063-3774 Directory of Licensed Occupations in Alaska (Year)†
1063-3782 Alaska Employment and Earnings Report **1199**
1063-3790 Alaska Population Overview **7276**
1063-3812 Unemployment Insurance Actuarial Study & Financial Handbook (Year) **1712**
1063-3820 Occupational Injury & Illness Information **6691**
1063-3928 I E E E Particle Accelerator Conference. Conference Record **3313**
1063-3987 Archives of Family Medicine†
1063-3995 Clinical Psychology & Psychotherapy **7345**
1063-4053 Auditor-Trak†
1063-4061 Health Law Week **4686**
1063-407X Systems Integration Business†
1063-4088 Scientific and Applied Photography†
1063-4134 Toward Freedom **7216**
1063-4142 Knarr, Knerr, Knorr Family Newsletter **3773**
1063-4177 Northern California Business Directory **2021**
1063-4185 News and Views (Gaithersburg) **5857**
1063-4215 The Carolinas Golf Reporter Newspaper
1063-4231 Guitar Buyer's Guide *see* 1045-6295 **6571**
1063-4258 Atomic Energy **3164**
1063-4266 Journal of Emotional and Behavioral Disorders **6151**
1063-4274 Management and Avoidance of Complications of Eyelid Surgery†
1063-4282 Interventional Cardiology Newsletter†
1063-4290 Real Estate Workouts and Asset Management
1063-4304 J R A - The Supplementary Series **399**
1063-4339 Steel Industry Update **6333**
1063-4371 Service Quality Connection **4111**
1063-4398 I H S Primary Care Provider **8045**
1063-441X Payment Systems Newsletter†
1063-4428 Bank Network News†
1063-4444 Contra Costa Lawyer **4650**
1063-4525 The U.P. Catholic **7821**
1063-4541 St. Petersburg University. Vestnik. Mathematics **5532**
1063-455X Journal of Water Chemistry and Technology **8827**
1063-4568 Ukrainian Chemistry Journal†
1063-4576 Journal of Superhard Materials **7023**
1063-4584 Osteoarthritis and Cartilage **6225**
1063-4614 Jewish Denominations in America **3542**
1063-4622 Primary Care Rheumatology†
1063-4630 Filipinas **3533**
1063-4649 Ohio Records & Pioneer Families **3777**
1063-4657 Men's Journal **6295**
1063-4665 Key of Kappa Kappa Gamma **2267**

ISSN

1064-2536	American Society for Photogrammetry and Remote Sensing. Fall Convention. Technical Papers†
1064-2552	Center for Parent Education Newsletter†
1064-2560	I M S A Journal **8631**
1064-2587	Maine Policy Review **8054**
1064-2684	G L Q **4373**
1064-2714	D I P P R Data Series **3242**
1064-2765	Pro Bike News†
1064-2781	Childworld **2149**
1064-2811	Consulting Services **2059**
1064-301X	Biblion†
1064-3028	Washington Journal of Modern China **7272**
1064-3087	Outreach (New York) **7705**
1064-3095	Decorating Digest Craft & Home Projects **4537**
1064-3133	John A. Pugsley's Journal†
1064-3184	Aura Wealth Newsletter **1438**
1064-3389	Critical Reviews in Environmental Science & Technology **3485**
1064-3427	Frommer's Comprehensive Travel Guide. Barcelona **8711**
1064-3605	Senior Observer **5082**
1064-3621	Outstate Business **1505**
1064-3699	News Dimensions
1064-3737	Resources (Dayton) *see* The Influential Executive **26**
1064-3745	Methods in Molecular Biology **689**
1064-3761	Quality Assurance Institute. Journal **6405**
1064-3818	Air Traffic Control Quarterly **8534**
1064-3826	International Directory of Primatology **948**
1064-3834	American Fastener Journal **3373**
1064-3842	O R L - Head and Neck Nursing **6083**
1064-3869	Haiti en Marche **3536**
1064-3877	Atlanta Tribune: The Magazine **3521**
1064-3893	The Marketing Report **1833**
1064-3907	Communications Standards Review†
1064-3915	Creative New Jersey **23**
1064-3923	Internet World (West Port)†
1064-3958	Duke Environmental Law & Policy Forum **4661**
1064-4016	Human Rights & Peace Law Docket **4849**
1064-4024	Surry County Genealogical Association. Journal **3784**
1064-4032	Douglasia **786**
1064-4059	Quest Magazine
1064-4067	Virginia Agriculture Commodity Newsletter **168**
1064-4075	Virginia Fruit and Vegetable Bulletin **208**
1064-4083	Virginia Fruit and Vegetable Market Information **257**
1064-4148	Report on Medical Guidelines and Outcomes Research. Annotated Directory of Medical Practice Guidelines†
1064-4156	Trenchless Technology **3224**
1064-4164	Old Toy Soldier **368**
1064-4180	Biomedical Market Newsletter **1807**
1064-4210	A A - B A Newsletter
1064-4253	The Moving World† **8975**
1064-4296	Packer Plus **8242**
1064-430X	Business and Incentive Strategies†
1064-4318	Brandweek **22**
1064-4326	Interpersonal Computing and Technology†
1064-4350	Plastic Figure and Playset Collector†
1064-4377	Grants for Women and Girls **3024**
1064-4431	Independent Newspaper from Russia†
1064-444X	Nezavisimaya Gazeta†
1064-4458	Jack Anderson First Confidential†
1064-4482	C O S M E P Newsletter†
1064-4504	Street Sheet **8073**
1064-4555	Audacity†
1064-4563	Physician Compensation and Production Survey **5750**
1064-4571	Cost Survey **5743**
1064-458X	System for Information on Grey Literature in Europe
1064-4601	Chemical Information Alert†
1064-461X	South Carolina Employment Law Letter **4785**
1064-4628	Truck, Van, 4 x 4 Prices, New & Used†
1064-4660	P A I S International on SilverPlatter *see* 1051-4015 **7200**
1064-4679	Congressional Masterfile 2 *see* 0007-8514 **7479**
1064-4687	Dissertation Abstracts on Disc **4484**
1064-4695	*see* 0091-1658 **8344**
1064-4709	American Academy of Insurance Medicine. Transactions†
1064-4768	Virginia Aquaculture Market News Report†
1064-4776	Lesbian Contradiction
1064-4814	National Fire and Arson Report†
1064-4849	Child Health Alert **6089**
1064-4857	Research in Global Strategic Management **1789**
1064-4865	Tilt-Up†
1064-4873	The Helper **5814**
1064-4903	Connecticut Employment Law Letter **4648**
1064-4938	Recycling Sourcebook†
1064-4997	Wonderful World of Flying **75**
1064-5012	Widener Journal of Public Law *changed to* 1548-4076 **4853**
1064-5020	E M F: Studies in Early Modern France **5287**
1064-5063	Viewpoints (Macon)
1064-5071	Violent Kin **2671**
1064-508X	Journal of Correctional Training
1064-5098	Pen Fancier's Magazine†
1064-5101	Topics in Veterinary Medicine **8808**
1064-5128	Means Site Work and Landscape Cost Data (year) **1023**
1064-5136	Crisis Intervention and Time-Limited Treatment *changed to* 1532-5024 **7376**
1064-5144	Bibliography of Native North Americans on Disc†
1064-5276	Frommer's Comprehensive Travel Guide. New York State **8711**
1064-5349	American Bankers Association Key to Routing Numbers **1307**
1064-5373	Utility Forecaster
1064-539X	County Business Patterns (CD-ROM)† **8946**
1064-5454	Managed Care Quarterly *changed to* 0896-6567 **4513**
1064-5462	Artificial Life **2446**
1064-5497	Healthy Home & Workplace†
1064-5500	S R D S Media and Market Planner. Architectural and Construction Markets†
1064-5543	Call Center Magazine *changed to* Customer Management Insight (Print) **8947**
1064-5551	Leaves of Grass†
1064-556X	Latin Mass **7804**
1064-5578	Visitor Studies **7414**
1064-5586	Millennium Film Journal **6507**
1064-5594	Cucurbit Genetics Cooperative. Report **227**
1064-5616	Sbornik: Mathematics **5533**
1064-5624	Doklady Mathematics **5484**
1064-5632	Izvestiya: Mathematics **5499**
1064-5675	Minnesota Historical Society. Member News *changed to* 1931-8197 **4296**
1064-5691	Virginia (Berryville)†
1064-5713	S R D S Media and Market Planner. Health, Beauty and Fashion Markets†
1064-573X	Sports Advantage†
1064-5764	MediaScope: Market and Media Planner. Chicago†
1064-5772	MediaScope: Media Sourcebook. Southern California†
1064-5853	Blade **4330**
1064-587X	Radio Ink **2362**
1064-590X	Food and Drug Law Journal **4676**
1064-5926	N A C C A S Review **589**
1064-5942	New Jersey Economic Indicators **1501**
1064-5950	L G S N: Lesbian and Gay Studies Newsletter†
1064-5969	Slide Atlas of Current Cardiology†
1064-5993	Windows & D O S Users' Guide†
1064-6000	Advances in Structural Biology **651**
1064-6051	Writing on the Edge **5401**
1064-6086	Maine Genealogist **3774**
1064-6094	Turkey Call **915**
1064-6108	A R C News **4036**
1064-6167	Family Life Matters†
1064-6175	Howard Journal of Communications **2323**
1064-6191	Dramascope **7352**
1064-6205	U C S D Guardian **2304**
1064-6221	Baja Explorer†
1064-6299	Oasis (Largo) **5344**
1064-6345	International Journal of Flexible Automation and Integrated Manufacturing†
1064-6361	Networking Management Europe†
1064-637X	Russia and Commonwealth Business Law Report **4777**
1064-640X	Contact Sheet **6966**
1064-6418	Twine Line **2819**
1064-6442	Miami Hurricane **2292**
1064-6493	News and Issues **8058**
1064-6507	Sport Karate International **8204**
1064-6515	Dance / U S A Journal **2685**
1064-6620	ArtSource Quarterly
1064-6647	Journal of Actuarial Practice **4510**
1064-6655	Journal of Orofacial Pain **5853**
1064-6663	Elementa†
1064-6671	S P E Drilling & Completion **6791**
1064-6795	Government Contracts and Subcontracts Leads Directory **1886**
1064-6833	Independent Television
1064-6868	V P I's Imprintables Today†
1064-6892	Hockey Magazine†
1064-6906	Island Home
1064-6914	Southwest Contractor **1036**
1064-7031	E E O BiMonthly†
1064-7120	Ready, Set, Go! In-Depth
1064-721X	Sports Eye **8207**
1064-7317	The Spokesman Review
1064-7406	Facial Plastic Surgery Clinics of North America **6243**
1064-7414	The Right Guide **2026**
1064-7449	Infectious Diseases in Obstetrics and Gynecology **5993**
1064-7473	American Small Farm Magazine *changed to* 1543-1487 **91**
1064-7481	American Journal of Geriatric Psychiatry **4040**
1064-749X	Directory of the Wood Products Industry†
1064-7503	Prevention's Quick & Healthy Low-Fat Cooking
1064-7554	Journal of Mammalian Evolution **951**
1064-7562	Journal of Materials Synthesis and Processing†
1064-7570	Journal of Network and Systems Management **2500**
1064-7597	Inside Edge for Men
1064-7627	Floor Focus **4540**
1064-7635	Q W†
1064-7678	Earnings Guide†
1064-7686	Port of Houston **8657**
1064-7716	Belarusian Review **1066**
1064-7767	S L D
1064-7953	Face Magazine (Malibu) **3533**
1064-797X	Pharmacy Cadence **6873**
1064-7988	Quality of Life†
1064-8011	Journal of Strength and Conditioning Research **6231**
1064-8046	Ergonomics in Design **3191**
1064-8070	Color Life!†
1064-8089	For the Bride by Demetrios **5558**
1064-8097	A G A News **5919**
1064-8127	Business and Finance Career Directory†
1064-8143	Diseased Pariah News†
1064-8186	Light **5323**
1064-8194	Law Marketing Exchange **4715**
1064-8208	The Electrochemical Society Interface **2113**
1064-8275	S I A M Journal on Scientific Computing **5532**
1064-8291	Solar Letter
1064-8399	I A C InfoTrac **8**
1064-8402	Nowy Dziennik **3555**
1064-8429	World Wastes†
1064-8488	Literary Gazette International†
1064-8496	Directory of Health Care Group Purchasing Organizations **1986**
1064-8542	Applied Clinical Trials **5576**
1064-8569	To Us†
1064-8585	Working Together (Seattle) **2672**
1064-8615	Critical Studies in Education and Culture **2840**
1064-8682	You!†
1064-8720	Colors
1064-8739	Co-Op America's National Green Pages **3411**
1064-881X	Tabletalk **7776**
1064-8852	Green Alternatives†
1064-8860	Softwatch†
1064-8887	Russian Physics Journal **7038**
1064-8933	The Volunteer Choir **6627**
1064-8941	The Choir Herald†
1064-8968	Oklahoma Living **3984**
1064-8992	Bay Journal **8818**
1064-900X	Glass **2041**
1064-9050	Freelance Writer's Newsletter†
1064-9085	American Banker's Banking Factbook†
1064-9131	Diabetes Care. Supplement **5887**
1064-9263	Trade Policy Agenda and Annual Report of the President of the United States on the Trade Agreements Program **1433**
1064-9336	Wolgan K'oria
1064-9352	Terrorism: Documents of International and Local Control. Second Series **2228**
1064-9409	N C S A Access
1064-9476	Bond Counsel†
1064-9484	Bank Stock Analyst†
1064-9492	Banking Attorney†
1064-9506	Behavior and Social Issues **7339**
1064-9557	Variety and Daily Variety Television Reviews **2398**
1064-9638	Institute of Paper Science and Technology. Graphic Arts Bulletin†
1064-9670	California Agriculture Export Bulletin and Statistical Appendix (Year)†
1064-9689	Magnetic Resonance Imaging Clinics of North America **6202**
1064-9697	Russian Oil & Gas Guide†
1064-9719	Chip's Closet Cleaner **5210**
1064-9727	Thing†
1064-9735	Panamerican Mathematical Journal **5524**
1064-9778	S P E Computer Applications†
1064-9824	Divulgacion Martiana†
1064-9867	Journal of Pastoral Theology **7655**
1064-9913	National Trade Data Bank **1407**
1064-993X	Newspaper Abstracts Ondisc *see* Newspaper Abstracts **4587**
1065-0008	Responsive Philanthropy **8065**
1065-0024	History Notes†
1065-0067	Foodtalk†
1065-0075	Positive Alternatives **7172**
1065-0105	International Career Employment Opportunities *changed to* International Career Employment Weekly **6699**
1065-0113	Ethics & Policy **8100**
1065-0121	Opportunities in Public Affairs **6702**
1065-0148	Microtimes†
1065-0229	Music Video Magazine
1065-0245	Miniature Quilts **6640**
1065-0296	Collegiate Trends **1811**
1065-0334	Directory of Law - Related CD-ROMs **4845**
1065-0342	Borderlands (Austin) **5418**
1065-0377	The Limbaugh Letter **7152**
1065-0393	Information Marketplace Directory **7563**
1065-0407	Tax Facts on Life Insurance (Student Edition)
1065-0555	Advanced Packaging **3089**
1065-058X	Turning Wheel **7702**
1065-0709	Prison Life Magazine†
1065-0733	Woman's Own **8890**
1065-0741	Campus Wide Information Systems **2495**
1065-075X	O C L C Systems & Services **5037**
1065-0768	1-2-3 Software Connection†
1065-0776	D O S Software Connection†
1065-0784	Windows Software Connection†
1065-0792	Auto Sound & Security†
1065-0830	German Shorthaired Pointer News **6808**
1065-0849	Resorts & Parks Purchasing Guide **4396**
1065-0857	Camp Directors Purchasing Guide **4976**
1065-0938	Convene **1735**
1065-0970	Federal Employees News Digest **7436**
1065-0989	Topics in Health Information Management†
1065-0997	The WorldPaper **7275**
1065-1004	Banking Law Briefs†
1065-1020	Comedy U S A Industry Guide†
1065-1039	Inside - Outside†
1065-108X	Pumps and Systems **3394**
1065-1098	Worldwide Government Report†
1065-1101	At the Museum *changed to* 1555-8185 **476**
1065-1136	Journal of Aviation-Aerospace Education & Research **63**
1065-1160	The E R I C Review†
1065-1217	The Sonoma Searcher **3783**
1065-1241	*see* 0009-563X **7734**
1065-1284	Pediatric Report's Child Health Newsletter†
1065-1330	Garment Manufacturer's Index **2247**
1065-1349	International Perspectives in Software Engineering
1065-1357	Taber's Cyclopedia Medical Dictionary **5719**
1065-1365	Index to United Nations Documents and Publications **7200**
1065-1381	SciDex Cumulative Index†
1065-1403	Health Care State Rankings **7521**
1065-1411	Borderlines (Silver City)†
1065-1438	Journal of Medical Speech - Language Pathology **6082**
1065-1497	Food Insight **3639**
1065-1500	International Examiner **3540**
1065-1519	Movement Theatre Quarterly **8474**
1065-1535	Destination Discovery **2380**
1065-1543	Artspeak
1065-1594	Pacific Coast Journal (Carlsbad) **5429**
1065-1640	G M P Horizons **4594**
1065-1659	Philanthropic Trends Digest†
1065-1667	Alternative Press **6543**
1065-1675	I F C O News **8045**
1065-1683	Florida Nurseryman†
1065-1691	Cultivar **103**
1065-1713	Textile Manufacturing†
1065-173X	Federal Technology Transfer†
1065-1756	Country Folks Grower **3727**
1065-1772	Automatome **4844**
1065-1799	Journal of Pharmaceutical Care in AIDS - HIV Treatment†
1065-1829	Science Fiction Age†
1065-1853	The Journal of Financial and Strategic Decisions†
1065-1896	Regulatory Update **7099**
1065-190X	Atlantic Bakers News†

ISSN

1066-288X Critical Matrix **8895**
1066-2898 Super Snack News†
1066-2936 Undersea & Hyperbaric Medicine **5726**
1066-2944 A W H O N N Newsletter†
1066-3029 Cheklist **1327**
1066-3037 B B I's Monitor of Technology Assessment and Reimbursement†
1066-3061 Check Collector **6649**
1066-3347 Now (Longview) **2294**
1066-341X School Scene **2910**
1066-3428 TechnoScene†
1066-3487 The Florida Tax Review **4676**
1066-3517 Fanlight News†
1066-3584 A N E R A Newsletter **7219**
1066-3622 Radiochemistry **2140**
1066-3630 Readerly - Writerly Texts **5358**
1066-3657 International Review of Psychiatry **6148**
1066-3681 Tringa Press Monograph Series†
1066-369X Russian Mathematics **5531**
1066-3754 Southern Business Review and Forecast†
1066-3762 Viajero V I P†
1066-3797 Bodywise
1066-3843 Delphi Workflow Report†
1066-3851 Seminars for Nurse Managers†
1066-3878 A B Q Correspondent **8415**
1066-3894 Pacific Telecommunications Review **2370**
1066-3916 Milwaukee Undergraduate Review
1066-3940 Industrial Fire Chief†
1066-3959 Master's Seminary Journal **7766**
1066-3967 Police Career Digest
1066-3991 Outerwear **2249**
1066-405X Aggies Illustrated **8220**
1066-4068 Blues Access†
1066-4092 InLine†
1066-4106 Remineralize the Earth†
1066-4114 Capsules & Comments in Oncology Nursing†
1066-4122 Hat Life Directory **2247**
1066-4130 V H L Family Forum **6189**
1066-4157 Journal of Chemical Education: Software. Series D†
1066-4173 Art Materials Today†
1066-4742 Grasslands Review **5302**
1066-4769 Booklist's Guide to the Year's Best Books†
1066-4793 Fodor's Great Travel Values: Canada†
1066-4807 The Family Journal **7357**
1066-4815 Capsules & Comments in Critical Care Nursing†
1066-484X Year Book of Chiropractic†
1066-4858 Zarubezhnaya Periodicheskaya Pechat' na Russkom Yazyke **18**
1066-4890 Shoptalk (Englewood) **321**
1066-4920 Considerations†
1066-4947 Sierra Leone Digest
1066-4971 C C T E Studies **5102**
1066-503X F A C T **6768**
1066-5048 I C E **3379**
1066-5056 Dementia Reviews†
1066-5072 Techniques in Diagnostic Pathology†
1066-5099 Stem Cells **706**
1066-5102 Country Sampler's Decorating Ideas† **8946**
1066-5129 Playboy's Blondes, Brunettes, Redheads **6298**
1066-5137 Playboy's Wet & Wild Women **6298**
1066-5145 Aeon **7945**
1066-5218 Inside Quattro Pro for Windows†
1066-5226 Sweepstakes Magazine
1066-5234 The Journal of Eukaryotic Microbiology **889**
1066-5277 Journal of Computational Biology (Print)† **8968**
1066-5285 Russian Chemical Bulletin **2079**
1066-5293 The Librarian's Yellow Pages **2563**
1066-5307 Mathematical Methods of Statistics **5513**
1066-5315 Chemical Heritage **2054**
1066-5331 Post Network News *changed to* 1559-629X **5697**
1066-534X I V U N News *changed to* 1559-4947 **5728**
1066-5358 Exploring Ireland **8702**
1066-5382 On the Ramage Trail **3778**
1066-5439 Emerge PlayCouple **4977**
1066-5447 The Score **6615**
1066-5463 Sales and Marketing Strategies & News†
1066-5471 Firsts **7561**
1066-551X Collector's Mart Magazine *changed to* 1533-3000
1066-5552 U.S. Bureau of Mines. Report of Investigations†
1066-5595 National Directory of Law Enforcement Administrators and Correctional Institutions **2661**
1066-5633 Independent Scholar **2986**
1066-5641 BioVenture Stock Report†
1066-5684 Equity & Excellence in Education **2853**
1066-5730 C A Selects. Geochemistry†
1066-5757 Wood Design Focus **3718**
1066-5773 Electronic Distribution Today **3095**
1066-5870 C R O W Quarterly Review†
1066-5897 Packer - Shipper†
1066-5935 Regional Plan Association. Working Paper
1066-5943 P I M E World **7811**
1066-596X Windy City Bowling News **8251**
1066-601X Think On **3785**
1066-6028 S O S S I Journal **6899**
1066-6036 F A D Magazine **3975**
1066-6044 Plastic Tower **5430**
1066-6060 Racer **8195**
1066-6095 Daily Washington Law Reporter **4654**
1066-6168 Bulletin of Tall Timbers Research **3685**
1066-6176 The Heartlands Today *changed to* Heartlands **5304**
1066-6192 Euromicro Workshop on Parallel and Distributed Processing **2466**
1066-6257 Judo Journal **8183**
1066-6265 Fiero Owner
1066-6281 Classic Amusements
1066-6311 Hon Viet Magazine **3538**
1066-6346 Events - U S A
1066-6389 Golf Lessons **8232**
1066-6419 Cross Sales Report *changed to* 1535-5918 **1839**
1066-6451 Decisions of the Nebraska Court of Appeals **4655**
1066-646X Small Business Profiles (Washington, D.C.) **1967**
1066-6494 N A D A Official Heavy Duty Truck Guide **8673**
1066-6516 Architronic **432**
1066-6559 Caribbean Historical & Genealogical Journal **4287**
1066-677X Clinical Practice Guidelines **5597**
1066-6958 View Camera **6978**
1066-7024 Market: Latin America
1066-7032 Family Counseling and Therapy†
1066-7083 Imprinting Business **2247**
1066-713X Optometry Today†
1066-7148 Bowhunting News†
1066-7156 Pueblo Business Journal†
1066-7210 Humanitas **4455**
1066-7245 Country Sampler's West†
1066-7296 Fishhead's Children†
1066-730X A2 - Central
1066-7318 Script - Central
1066-7326 TimeOut - Central
1066-7334 Studio City for the II GS
1066-7377 Laubach Literacy International. Annual Report *changed to* ProLiteracy Worldwide. Annual Report **2945**
1066-7385 Green Egg†
1066-7466 Highway Loss Data Institute. Vehicle Descriptions **4505**
1066-7474 Interphex U S A. Proceedings of the Technical Program **6850**
1066-7490 *see* The Serials Directory **635**
1066-7504 Design Technologies†
1066-758X American Patchwork & Quilting **6636**
1066-7598 Computer Retail Week†
1066-7601 Who's Who Electronics Buyers Guide - Midwestern Edition†
1066-761X Who's Who Electronics Buyers Guide - Northeastern Edition†
1066-7628 Who's Who Electronics Buyers Guide - Southeastern Edition†
1066-7636 Who's Who Electronics Buyers Guide - Western Edition†
1066-7644 Who's Who Electronics Buyers Guide - Southwestern Edition†
1066-7660 Synergist (Fairfax) **6687**
1066-7679 Guide to Unique Meeting and Event Facilities **8717**
1066-7717 Maro Polymer Notes
1066-7741 The Rx Consultant **6879**
1066-7776 Out & About **8745**
1066-7784 High-Tech Marketing News†
1066-7814 Canadian Journal of Applied Physiology *changed to* 1715-5312 **6228**
1066-7857 Materials Technology **6322**
1066-7865 Journal of Clinical Research and Drug Development†
1066-7873 P R I S M (Chicago) **4518**
1066-7881 Global Ocean Ecosystems Dynamics Report Series **3434**
1066-7911 Smart Access† **8988**
1066-792X School & Home Office Products†
1066-7938 Corporate Environmental Strategy†
1066-8098 Rotor & Wing **69**
1066-8160 The Bull Bulletin **2459**
1066-8187 Oxalis†
1066-8195 The Yellow Sheet (Print)† **8999**
1066-8209 Recent Researches in the Oral Traditions of Music **6609**
1066-8217 Music of the United States of America **6591**
1066-8268 Vibrations **3359**
1066-8322 Frontiers in Headache Research **5616**
1066-8357 Nor'easter (Narragansett)†
1066-8446 McClain County Oklahoma Historical and Genealogical Society. Quarterly **3775**
1066-8454 J I S Computerized Bibliography **628**
1066-8527 Process Safety Progress **3253**
1066-8632 Pacific Rim Law & Policy Journal **4755**
1066-8675 Industrial Cleaning Contractor†
1066-8683 Cogeneration and Competitive Power Journal *changed to* 1545-3669 **3126**
1066-8691 Association Source **1063**
1066-8721 Arshile **5257**
1066-873X Federal Technology Report†
1066-8756 Wisconsin Land Information Newsletter†
1066-8772 American Paleontologist **6723**
1066-8829 L C Cataloging Newsline **5024**
1066-8837 Buffalo Environmental Law Journal **4633**
1066-8888 The V L D B Journal **2532**
1066-8918 N A F T A Report **2018**
1066-8926 Community College Journal of Research and Practice **2974**
1066-8934 Gale Directory of Databases **2530**
1066-8950 Journal of Fuzzy Mathematics
1066-8969 International Journal of Surgical Pathology **6246**
1066-9116 Viewpoint Sweden **3957**
1066-9205 Forbes F Y I *changed to* ForbesLife **5071**
1066-9221 Die Cast Digest **4333**
1066-9264 C D A / Wiesenberger Mutual Funds Update†
1066-937X The Menninger Letter†
1066-9396 Black Literary Players **641**
1066-9434 Contemporary Impressions **483**
1066-9450 Journal of Oregon Ornithology **909**
1066-9531 Cities International Newsletter†
1066-9558 The Forum for Advancing Basic Education and Literacy†
1066-9612 Russian Fiber Optics and Telecommunications Business
1066-9701 Shopping Center Directory **2027**
1066-9728 Real Estate Directory of Major Investors, Developers and Brokers†
1066-9744 Directory of M & A Intermediaries **1987**
1066-9817 The Journal of Manual & Manipulative Therapy **6111**
1066-9825 Business & Legal CD-ROMS in Print
1066-9833 Inside Out†
1066-9868 Journal of East - West Business **1544**
1066-9884 Psychoanalytic Abstracts (Print) *changed to* PsycSCAN: Psychoanalysis (Online) **7417**
1066-9914 A Contemporary Journal to Self-Discovery
1066-9922 Critique *changed to* 1943-6149 **555**
1066-9957 Annual Advanced Antitrust Seminar **4855**
1066-9965 World Wastes - International Edition†
1066-999X Russian Life **8753**
1067-0017 San Francisco State University Series in Philosophy **6951**
1067-0025 California Studies in German and European Romanticism and in the Age of Goethe **5269**
1067-0041 Wedding Gown Guide†
1067-005X Your Prom†
1067-0084 Luz en Arte y Literatura
1067-0114 Literacy Advocate **2944**
1067-0149 Rio Bravo†
1067-0181 The C M T A Report **6129**
1067-019X Native American Law Digest **6635**
1067-0246 Mealey's Litigation Report: Breast Implants†
1067-0297 Transit California **8513**
1067-0394 Researching Markets, Industries, and Business Opportunities **1165**
1067-0408 Latin American Markets: A Guide to Company and Industry Information Sources **1575**
1067-0432 Treasury & Risk Management *changed to* 1935-7214 **1656**
1067-0440 Show Technology Magazine†
1067-0483 Repetitive Stress Injury Litigation Reporter† **8985**
1067-0521 Registry Review **7610**
1067-0548 Bay Sports Review†
1067-0564 Journal of Contemporary China **4184**
1067-0599 Georgia Automotive Business
1067-0629 Kurenai: Japanese Embroidery Journal†
1067-0637 Wings (Granada Hills) **75**
1067-0653 Military Review (Portuguese Edition) *see* 0026-4148 **6436**
1067-0661 Michigan Overseas Veteran **6434**
1067-067X Talking to the Boss **1181**
1067-0696 International Union of Crystallography. Newsletter **2110**
1067-0718 AIDS Targeted Information†
1067-0734 Marine Safety Report **8277**
1067-0769 Washington Job Source **6705**
1067-0777 Hillary Clinton Quarterly†
1067-0793 What's on Satellite **2344**
1067-0807 National Golf Course Directory
1067-0815 Document Delivery World†
1067-0823 Studies in Shakespeare **5382**
1067-0831 Animerica **466**
1067-084X U. S. Geological Survey Circular **2771**
1067-0882 Medical Liability Week†
1067-0904 Rental Product News **1902**
1067-0912 Antiquing America†
1067-0920 Coonhound Bloodlines **8310**
1067-0947 The Pointing Dog Journal **8329**
1067-098X Disabled Outdoors Magazine **8311**
1067-0998 P C Upgrade†
1067-1005 Blank Gun Silencer†
1067-1013 E & P Health, Safety and Environment
1067-1021 Gas Processing and Pipelining†
1067-103X Offshore Technology†
1067-1048 Airpower **46**
1067-1056 N N & I - E S R D Product and Service Directory†
1067-1064 Wood Technology†
1067-1072 Directory of Computer and Consumer Electronics Retailers **2494**
1067-1080 The Swiss Connection **3784**
1067-1110 The Paint Dealer **6719**
1067-1161 National Character Laboratory Newsletter **7386**
1067-1293 Software Engineering Strategies†
1067-1323 Voz y Datos†
1067-1331 Object Lesson
1067-134X The Best Men's Stage Monologues **8466**
1067-1358 Mutual Fund Buyer's Guide†
1067-1412 Texarkana U S A Quarterly *changed to* 1549-6317 **3785**
1067-1439 Today's Astrologer **567**
1067-1455 Florida Shipper **8644**
1067-1463 Arts & Crafts Retailer†
1067-151X American Academy of Orthopaedic Surgeons. Journal **6055**
1067-1587 Charleston Jewish Journal *changed to* 1537-0976 **7719**
1067-1595 InfoWorld Direct†
1067-1609 Orders and Medals Society of America. Journal **4342**
1067-1641 S R D S The Bullet† **8986**
1067-1692 Pendragon†
1067-1714 A W H P Action **6981**
1067-1722 G C Government Communications **4575**
1067-1803 Community College Journal **2973**
1067-182X S R D S Lifestyle Market Analyst (Print) *changed to* S R D S Lifestyle Market Analyst (Online) **1261**
1067-1846 Fairs and Festivals (Year)†
1067-1897 Frontiers in Biomedicine and Biotechnology **6843**
1067-1919 Journal of Urologic Pathology†
1067-1927 Wound Repair and Regeneration **6075**
1067-1951 Food History News **3639**
1067-1986 The Fertilizer & Ag-Chemical Digest *changed to* 1536-8815 **242**
1067-2036 Laparoscopic Surgery Update†
1067-2052 Cracking the English Achievements *changed to* 1944-379X **2976**
1067-2060 Skin Art Presents†
1067-2079 Long Island Update†
1067-2095 Wildlife: The Artist's View†
1067-2117 Cracking the Math Achievements *changed to* 1556-7095 **2976**
1067-2206 Physician Office Lab News **5910**
1067-2222 P - Form†
1067-2249 Piecework **6641**
1067-2257 Planning for Aging or Incapacity† **8981**
1067-2338 Illinois Workers' Compensation Law Bulletin **4505**
1067-2346 Ophthalmology Resident†
1067-2354 New Dentist†
1067-2362 Resident in Pediatrics†
1067-2370 Hem-Onc Annals†
1067-2389 Methods in Molecular Genetics†
1067-2400 Personal Injury Reporter **4757**
1067-2419 Dollars & Cents of Small Town - Nonmetropolitan Shopping Centers **7589**
1067-2427 Personal Injury Verdict Reviews **4757**
1067-2451 Specifier Reports **1037**

ISSN

1070-2202 Journal of Oromo Studies **5135**
1070-2210 Financial Manager's Report on Cost Cutting†
1070-2342 Chamber Executive Network **1398**
1070-2377 Eagle Investigators' News†
1070-2385 I E E E Conference on Visualization **2449**
1070-2415 The Winning Edge **4605**
1070-2423 A R R S Memo *changed to* 1936-2234 **6198**
1070-2431 Home Health Products *changed to* 1940-6479 **5622**
1070-244X Quest (Boston) **7672**
1070-2504 Environmental Laboratory Washington Report **5905**
1070-2512 The Woodwind Quarterly *changed to* The Journal of Musical Instrument Technology **6581**
1070-2644 Consumers' Guide to Hospitals **2637**
1070-2733 Cornell Magazine *changed to* 1548-8810 **2279**
1070-2792 Monitor (Brookeville) **2572**
1070-2814 Tennis Match Magazine†
1070-2873 North Dakota. Geological Survey. Field Study **2759**
1070-289X Identities **3538**
1070-2911 Spider **2214**
1070-2938 The Los Angeles Letter
1070-2954 NetTeach News†
1070-2962 Really, a Free Newsletter†
1070-3004 Emergency Radiology **6195**
1070-3047 Alternatives (Washington, D.C. Print Edition)†
1070-308X A W H O N N Women's Health Nursing Scan†
1070-3160 Cultural Diversity at Work **1859**
1070-3179 The Towers Club U S A Info Marketing Report **1846**
1070-3187 California Fairways†
1070-3241 The Joint Commission Journal on Quality Improvement *changed to* 1553-7250 **4103**
1070-3268 Volt **5396**
1070-3284 Russian Journal of Coordination Chemistry **2079**
1070-3322 Professional and Occupational Licensing Directory†
1070-3365 Americans Traveling Abroad: What You Should Know before You Go **8682**
1070-3411 The Remington Report **5703**
1070-3519 Alaska Court Rules, State and Federal **4946**
1070-3586 School Transportation News **2910**
1070-3608 Diagnostic and Therapeutic Endoscopy **5905**
1070-3624 Puppetry Yearbook **8477**
1070-3632 Russian Journal of General Chemistry **2079**
1070-3667 Protein Profile†
1070-3683 New Telecom Quarterly†
1070-3705 Water Technology News†
1070-3713 Howard Scroll *changed to* Human Rights & Globalization Law Review **4689**
1070-3756 Civil War Chronicles†
1070-3829 Interdisciplinary Studies Forum
1070-3837 Journal of Heart Failure†
1070-3845 Tampa Bay Magazine **5084**
1070-3861 Globe Union†
1070-3896 WordPerfect for the Law Office†
1070-390X Blades on Ice **8162**
1070-3926 Fast Track News
1070-3950 Directory of Computer and High Technology Grants
1070-4019 Diamond (Scottsdale)
1070-4027 E M F Health Report **6676**
1070-4043 Mealey's Litigation Report: Patents **6754**
1070-4094 The Hook (Marshfield) **4336**
1070-4140 Holarctic Lepidoptera **848**
1070-4272 Russian Journal of Applied Chemistry **3255**
1070-4280 Russian Journal of Organic Chemistry **2130**
1070-4329 J M N R **5963**
1070-4337 The Value Line Mutual Fund Survey **1658**
1070-437X Journal of Turfgrass Management††
1070-4418 Educational Testing Service Annual Report **2979**
1070-4434 Olympia Review
1070-4442 Washington State Grange News **169**
1070-4450 Perspectives in General and Laparoscopic Surgery†
1070-4493 The Newbery and Caldecott Awards†
1070-4531 Construction Products†
1070-454X Transputer Communications†
1070-4604 Gypsy Lore Society. Newsletter **340**
1070-4639 The (Year) Information Please Business Almanac & Desk Reference **1123**
1070-4655 Arizona Environmental Compliance Update†
1070-4671 Supernatural Magazine
1070-468X North Carolina Naturalist **6534**
1070-4698 Electromagnetic Waves **7051**
1070-4701 Vibe **6626**
1070-4728 Commercial Builder **992**
1070-4752 High-Tech Hot Sheet†
1070-4779 Circuits Assembly Asia† **8941**
1070-4795 Searcher (Medford) **2532**
1070-4809 Family Tree **3766**
1070-4817 Elder Law Attorney **4664**
1070-4825 Elder Law Advisory **4664**
1070-4833 Journal of Natural Resources & Environmental Law **3448**
1070-485X The Leading Edge (Tulsa) **2786**
1070-4868 The Resources of International Permaculture **700**
1070-4906 Federal Immigration Laws and Regulations **4672**
1070-4949 Psychotronic Video **2403**
1070-4965 Journal of Environment & Development **3444**
1070-4973 U S - Iran Review
1070-5007 Wildlife Worldwide **720**
1070-5031 The Nose **5231**
1070-5066 Colorado Expression **3973**
1070-5104 Modern Screen's Country Music†
1070-5112 Alzheimer's Care Guide **4040**
1070-5163 Jacksonville Magazine **5074**
1070-5171 Real Estate Entrepreneur†
1070-521X Journal of Public and International Affairs (Princeton) **1600**
1070-5244 High Power Rocketry **4336**
1070-5252 Lutheran Historical Society of Eastern Pennsylvania. Periodical **7766**
1070-5287 Current Opinion in Pulmonary Medicine **6213**
1070-5295 Current Opinion in Critical Care **6058**
1070-5309 Social Work Research **8071**
1070-5317 Social Work Abstracts **8084**
1070-5325 Numerical Linear Algebra with Applications **5522**

1070-535X Seminars in Radiologic Technology *changed to* 1543-3544 **6194**
1070-5376 Year Book of Pain†
1070-5384 Advances in Clinical Ophthalmology†
1070-5392 Advances in Obstetrics and Gynecology†
1070-5422 Journal of Community Practice **8049**
1070-5430 White Crane **4380**
1070-5465 Palaeoslavica **5348**
1070-549X Feminism in Social Sciences **7964**
1070-5503 International Journal of Behavioral Medicine **7364**
1070-5511 Structural Equation Modeling **7410**
1070-552X Regional Technology Guide - New England†
1070-5538 Regional Technology Guide - New York Metro†
1070-5546 Regional Technology Guide - New Jersey and Delaware Valley†
1070-5554 Regional Technology Guide - Mid-Atlantic†
1070-5562 Regional Technology Guide - Southeast U S†
1070-5570 Regional Technology Guide - Midwest†
1070-5589 Regional Technology Guide - Great Lakes†
1070-5597 Regional Technology Guide - Eastern Lakes†
1070-5600 Regional Technology Guide - Central U S†
1070-5619 Regional Technology Guide - Northwest U S†
1070-5627 Regional Technology Guide - Southern California†
1070-5635 Regional Technology Guide - Northern California†
1070-5643 Regional Technology Guide - Southwest U S†
1070-5708 Mortgage Originator† **8975**
1070-5767 Rehabilitation Nursing Research†
1070-5848 Jewish News of Greater Phoenix **7723**
1070-5864 Latin American Studies. Volume 1 **4170**
1070-5872 Latin American Studies. Volume 2 **4171**
1070-5880 Scholastic News en Espanol. Edicion 1 **3080**
1070-5945 Diabetes Care and Education Newsletter **5887**
1070-6003 Washington State Agriculture Export Bulletin and Statistical Appendix (Year)†
1070-6011 Oregon Agriculture Export Bulletin and Statistical Appendix (Year)†
1070-6070 Inside Triathlon **8318**
1070-6127 Southwest Journal on Aging **4056**
1070-6143 Better Homes and Gardens Craft and Wear†
1070-6232 S W E **3218**
1070-6259 *see* 1466-5026 **888**
1070-6275 *see* 1092-2172 **892**
1070-6313 *see* 0019-9675 **5816**
1070-6321 *see* 0022-538X **890**
1070-633X *see* 0095-1137 **5647**
1070-6364 Court Rules Pamphlet(s). New Jersey Rules of Court, State and Federal **4949**
1070-6380 Fodor's U S & British Virgin Islands **8710**
1070-6399 Fodor's Miami & the Keys **8707**
1070-6410 Frommer's Comprehensive Travel Guide. Denver, Boulder & Colorado Springs *changed to* Frommer's Denver, Boulder & Colorado Springs **8711**
1070-6437 Miami Daily Business Review **1149**
1070-6461 Synthetic Rubber Manual **7827**
1070-6488 International Institute of Synthetic Rubber Producers. Proceedings Annual General Meeting **7825**
1070-6496 Focus on Privatization: The Russian Perspective†
1070-6526 Bus Conversions **8491**
1070-6534 Insider (Los Angeles) **2288**
1070-6593 Land Mobile Radio News†
1070-6623 Scientific Evidence Review **4960**
1070-6631 Physics of Fluids **7033**
1070-664X Physics of Plasmas **7033**
1070-6658 Toybox Magazine†
1070-6674 Pelizza's Positive Principles for Better Living **7389**
1070-6704 Real Estate Transactions **1941**
1070-6763 American Water Resources Association Technical Publication Series **8817**
1070-6771 Changing Medical Markets†
1070-6836 Aladdin's Window **6302**
1070-6844 Expanse
1070-6852 Cross-Talk†
1070-6860 Buffaloon Newsletter
1070-6887 Fodor's Hong Kong **8706**
1070-6895 Fodor's China **8705**
1070-6917 Kagan's Media Trends **2384**
1070-6925 Medical Malpractice Defense and Health Care Counsel Directory†
1070-695X Trotter Review **3569**
1070-700X The A B A A Newsletter **7550**
1070-7158 Guide to the Managed Care Industry†
1070-7204 Coal Tech International†
1070-7212 A S G E Clinical Update **5919**
1070-7220 Disability Resources Monthly **4065**
1070-7247 Tattoos For Men **521**
1070-7255 Who Cares†
1070-728X Computing and Software Design Career Directory
1070-7298 Mental Health and Social Work Career Directory **7531**
1070-7352 American Currents **931**
1070-7379 New Teacher Advocate **2891**
1070-7409 Delaney Report **24**
1070-7417 Communication Technology Update (Year)†
1070-7425 Macintosh Tips & Tricks **2577**
1070-7549 Four Directions **394**
1070-7573 Screen **2389**
1070-7581 Polish Digest†
1070-7611 Bank Director **1312**
1070-762X The Networker (Asheville)
1070-7719 State House Watch **7470**
1070-7727 New Unionist **4599**
1070-7735 Fulton County Images **3767**
1070-7778 Hughston Health Alert **6061**
1070-7794 G I A Quarterly **6568**
1070-7808 The Gilcrease Journal **4293**
1070-7964 Guide to Private Fortunes†
1070-8014 Native North American Almanac **6635**
1070-8022 Journal of Neuro-Ophthalmology **6045**
1070-8030 Journal of Bronchology *changed to* 1944-6586 **6215**
1070-8049 The Otolaryngology Journal Club Journal†
1070-8057 Police and Security News **2663**
1070-812X Northbound **3457**
1070-8146 Chaos Network†

1070-8170 Sheriff Magazine **2668**
1070-8200 Guidepoints **6109**
1070-8251 Country Dance & Song Society News **2683**
1070-826X Creative Exhibiting Techniques†
1070-8286 Journal of Criminal Justice and Popular Culture **2656**
1070-8375 Inside P C Tools for Windows†
1070-8464 Louis L'Amour Western Magazine†
1070-8499 New Novel Review **5340**
1070-8510 Studies in Jewish Civilization **4271**
1070-8588 Software Development *changed to* 1044-789X **2589**
1070-8618 Earthsong **6523**
1070-8634 The Houston JobBank† **8962**
1070-8642 Fodor's Acapulco, Ixtapa, Zihuatanejo **8704**
1070-8677 Northern Arizona Genealogical Society. Bulletin **3777**
1070-8855 Travel & Tourism Executive Report **8766**
1070-8928 The Electricity Daily **3157**
1070-8952 The Job Seeker **6699**
1070-8987 Late Editions†
1070-9029 Federal Physician **7517**
1070-9061 Successful Fund Raising **8073**
1070-9096 U S Ad Review **36**
1070-910X Harvard Women's Health Watch **8845**
1070-9169 A C C R A Cost of Living Index **1199**
1070-9185 Survey of East European Law **4941**
1070-9231 Economic Analysis of United States Ski Areas **8311**
1070-9282 Countdown (New York) **5885**
1070-9290 Classic Boating **8274**
1070-9304 H - Scoop†
1070-9312 N C L C Energy & Utility Update **4737**
1070-9320 Positively Pasta†
1070-9371 Indiana English **5308**
1070-9401 A. Magazine: Inside Asian America†
1070-9428 Journal of Hymenoptera Research **852**
1070-9436 Daily Tar Heel **2281**
1070-9444 Contributions **8035**
1070-9479 Porthole **8748**
1070-955X Comparative Cultures and Literature **5277**
1070-9568 International Figure Skating **8180**
1070-9576 Current Clinical Trials: Oncology **5743**
1070-9592 Adhesives & Sealants Industry **3235**
1070-9622 Shock and Vibration **7089**
1070-9657 Student Leader **2302**
1070-9673 Secretary: F Y I†
1070-9681 Caregiving†
1070-969X Quake†
1070-9711 Classical Russia **5274**
1070-972X The Silver Age **5372**
1070-9738 Policy Line: Current Issues in Health Care†
1070-9754 Soccer Magazine†
1070-9762 Journal of Optical Technology **7079**
1070-9789 Journal of Advanced Materials (Covina) **3349**
1070-986X I E E E MultiMedia Magazine **2486**
1070-9878 I E E E Transactions on Dielectrics and Electrical Insulation **3314**
1070-9908 I E E E Signal Processing Letters **3313**
1070-9932 I E E E Robotics and Automation Magazine **2584**
1070-9967 Law Enforcement Legal Review **2659**
1070-9983 Annals of Earth **3403**
1071-0035 Animal People **318**
1071-0043 Raven: A Journal of Vexillology **3780**
1071-006X Report on Healthcare Information Management **5703**
1071-0124 Studies in Nineteenth-Century British Literature **5436**
1071-0191 Music Box Society International. News Bulletin **6590**
1071-0213 C C H Pulse†
1071-0248 News India-Times **3554**
1071-0272 Wyoming Agriculture **171**
1071-0353 Austin Lawyer **4623**
1071-0426 Legacies **1963**
1071-0469 Ductile Iron Pipe News **4118**
1071-0485 Workshop on Future Trends of Distributed Computing Systems. Proceedings **2525**
1071-0523 Bush - Meeting Dutch **3761**
1071-0566 Texas Veterinarian **8808**
1071-0590 Grassroots Economic Organizing Newsletter **6698**
1071-0639 A C M R Newsletter *changed to* A C M R Reports **6541**
1071-0655 Aircraft Value News **8535**
1071-0698 Multimedia Monitor†
1071-0728 Inside Auto C A D **2591**
1071-0752 International Annals of Adolescent Psychiatry†
1071-0892 Conservation (Los Angeles) **483**
1071-0922 Society for Information Display. Journal **2490**
1071-0949 Operative Techniques in Plastic and Reconstructive Surgery **6254**
1071-099X American Cost of Living Survey†
1071-1007 Foot & Ankle International **6060**
1071-1023 Journal of Vacuum Science and Technology. Part B. Microelectronics and Nanometer Structures **7023**
1071-1090 World Beer Review†
1071-1112 Hood County Genealogical Society Newsletter **3771**
1071-1198 L N G Express *changed to* 1944-5881 **6798**
1071-1201 National Guide to Funding in Health **5683**
1071-1279 Auburn Plainsman **2273**
1071-1295 Document Imaging Report **2533**
1071-1309 Scholastic Girl†
1071-1376 Law Review Access
1071-1384 A W I Quarterly **317**
1071-1554 Workman Branches† **8999**
1071-1570 European Media Business & Finance†
1071-1627 The Michigan Optometrist **6046**
1071-1686 N Y C Poetry Calendar†
1071-1732 Public Employment Law Notes **1704**
1071-1740 Market Charts (Print Edition) *changed to* Market Charts (Online Edition) **1638**
1071-1767 W F S Quarterly **3582**
1071-1791 Chamber Music **6555**
1071-1813 Human Factors and Ergonomics Society Annual Meeting. Proceedings **3195**
1071-1864 Tradition **6624**
1071-1902 Gridiron Coach **8234**
1071-1937 Madison County Musings **3774**
1071-1945 Quality Abstracts†
1071-1996 Criminal Procedure Checklists **4888**

1074-1518 Tomart's Disneyana Update 4061
1074-1542 Journal of Chemical Crystallography 2111
1074-1550 Chemical Physics Reports *changed to* 1479-4810 7019
1074-1593 Timelines *changed to* Compassion and Choices Magazine 5599
1074-164X Mediterranean Studies 4323
1074-1658 Russia & Eurasia Facts & Figures Annual 7200
1074-1674 N T I S Alerts: Business & Economics 1252
1074-1690 New Steel†
1074-1712 Faith and Fellowship 7757
1074-1720 K C P T Magazine *changed to* 1942-4132 6505
1074-1739 Minnesota Christian Chronicle 7663
1074-1755 Bird Populations 903
1074-1763 Nantucket Magazine†
1074-1844 Annual Editions: Physical Anthropology 325
1074-1887 Coverage 4500
1074-1895 Good Old Days Specials *changed to* 1938-0569 5327
1074-1917 Harvard Journal of Hispanic Policy 3536
1074-195X Hip Mama 5219
1074-1984 M S D S Software Report 3482
1074-200X Beatlick News 5417
1074-2026 Anterior Poetry Monthly†
1074-2042 Anterior Fiction Quarterly†
1074-2174 Ethos (Ames) 2283
1074-2247 Bolivian Studies *changed to* Bolivian Studies Journal 4286
1074-2255 Israel Faxx 3541
1074-2271 Time of Singing 5436
1074-228X Industrial Computing *changed to* 1538-2893 4488
1074-2301 Advance for Respiratory Care Practitioners 6211
1074-2336 Cracking the T O E F L 2976
1074-2360 Active Voice 7102
1074-2441 Fiction Writer's Guideline
1074-2476 South Carolina Manufacturers Register 2028
1074-2484 Journal of Cardiovascular Pharmacology and Therapeutics 6852
1074-2670 Carlyle Studies Annual 641
1074-2689 American Morris Newsletter†
1074-2727 Federal Advisory Directory†
1074-2778 Northwest Indiana Catholic 7809
1074-2816 Current Cancer Therapeutics 6017
1074-2824 Physical Sciences Career Directory 7898
1074-2859 Film and Video Career Directory†
1074-2883 AIDS & T B Weekly Article Summaries†
1074-2891 AIDS & T B Weekly Abstracts from Conference Proceedings 5740
1074-2921 Vaccine Weekly 6884
1074-2956 Beyond Behavior 3037
1074-2972 Water Environment Laboratory Solutions 3492
1074-3006 Tyme Management 1876
1074-3057 NewsNet 4248
1074-3065 Spokane Business Interaction 1410
1074-3154 Third World Resource Directory 7188
1074-3219 Journal of Cranio-Maxillofacial Trauma†
1074-3227 Theory & Practice of Object Based Systems†
1074-3235 Country Weekly 6559
1074-3251 Jack Mackerel Magazine 5424
1074-326X ParentLife 7770
1074-3286 Military Sources, Queries and Reviews† 8974
1074-3308 Datapro Directory of Microcomputer Hardware†
1074-3375 An Gael 3534
1074-3472 International Defense Electronics Systems Handbook
1074-3502 Kashrus Magazine 3652
1074-3510 Miss Information's Automotive Calendar of Events 367
1074-3529 Contemporary Economic Policy 1086
1074-357X Mid-South Farmer 203
1074-360X Gochiso-sama!†
1074-3634 The Beltane Papers 8853
1074-3642 The Caretaker Gazette 6695
1074-3650 Wild Forest Review
1074-3693 River Oak Review 5433
1074-3715 Integrated Resource Planning Report†
1074-3723 Gas Utility Report 6770
1074-3774 VideoGames
1074-3804 American Association of Gynecologic Laparoscopists. Journal *changed to* 1553-4650 5995
1074-3871 Nurse Practitioners' Prescribing Reference 6864
1074-388X Physician Assistants' Prescribing Reference 6875
1074-3898 Managing Litigation Costs†
1074-3936 Community Cable Letter†
1074-3944 Advances in Blood Disorders†
1074-3995 Microcomputer Abstracts *changed to* 1529-7705
1074-4002 Securities Industry Management†
1074-4061 Auction Magazine
1074-407X Microlithography World 3109
1074-4142 Fodor's Euro Disney 8705
1074-4266 Balanced Reading Instruction 3052
1074-4274 House 3977
1074-4312 Airline & Commercial Aircraft Report International†
1074-4320 Airways 8537
1074-438X Smith University Funding Report
1074-4398 Smith Medical Funding Report
1074-4444 Managed Health Care Overview†
1074-4525 The Oxford American 5347
1074-4584 Cape Cod Travel Guide 8691
1074-4606 Tell (New York)†
1074-4614 KnowHow†
1074-4665 Historic Traveler†
1074-469X Beijing Spring 7203
1074-472X Healing Light Journal†
1074-4746 Karma Lapel
1074-4754 State Health Watch 7542
1074-4762 Voices from the Middle 3087
1074-4770 Health Management Technology 5830
1074-4797 Journal of Healthcare Risk Management 4104
1074-4819 Medical Imaging News†
1074-4827 Human Ecology Review 8106
1074-4843 Brahms Studies 6551
1074-4851 Technology Connection†
1074-4916 Embedded Systems Programming Product News† 8953
1074-5009 Illinois PressLines 4576
1074-5017 N A E D A Equipment Dealer 212
1074-5238 Heritage Quest Magazine 3770
1074-5246 Genre Magazine† 8959
1074-5254 Emphasis 2853
1074-5270 Basketball America 8222
1074-5297 Shoot 35
1074-5351 International Journal of Communication Systems 3320
1074-5378 Shutterbug Buying Guide 6977
1074-5408 Harvard Middle Eastern and Islamic Review 4321
1074-5424 I A A O Opportunities for Education and Employment 7594
1074-5475 Jobs in Higher Education
1074-5505 Human Gene Mapping (Year)†
1074-5521 Chemistry & Biology 2056
1074-553X Lake Home 7597
1074-5572 Current Opinion in Pediatrics. Current World Literature *see* 1040-8703 6090
1074-5599 Taiwan Studies†
1074-5610 Cold Fusion
1074-5629 Yefief 527
1074-5734 The Hearing Review 6080
1074-5807 Journal for Minority Medical Students 5645
1074-5815 World Christian News
1074-5823 Teletimes 2373
1074-5831 Vitality 6999
1074-584X Otto Scott's Compass 3984
1074-5890 Watercraft Philately 6901
1074-5904 S N L Quarterly Bank Digest *changed to* 1555-810X
1074-5920 S N L Quarterly Thrift Digest *changed to* 1555-810X
1074-598X The Greenwood Press "Literature in Context" Series 5302
1074-5998 Censored: The Project Censored Yearbook†
1074-6005 International Workshop in Rapid System Prototyping. Proceedings 2593
1074-6072 Biotechnology in the U.S. Pharmaceutical Industry†
1074-6110 Beer Cans & Brewery Collectibles 4330
1074-6188 State A D M Report†
1074-6196 Astro Digest
1074-6226 American Bar Association. Section of Public Utility, Communications and Transportation Law. News *changed to* 1097-251X 4692
1074-6315 Pangolin Papers 5233
1074-634X Compensation and Benefits in Engineering Firms in the Geotechnical Field *changed to* Compensation in Engineering Firms in the Geotechnical Field 1671
1074-6374 Nuclear Energy†
1074-6404 Relational Database Journal†
1074-6420 Electronic Contracting Law†
1074-6498 S C O R Report 1648
1074-6544 Henderson Electronic Market Forecast 3100
1074-6560 The Efficient Banker 1337
1074-6609 The S N L Financial Services Daily (Print) *changed to* The S N L Financial Services Daily (E-mail) 1649
1074-6714 Lead Detection and Abatement Contractor
1074-6749 Studies in Church History 7685
1074-6757 Belgian Francophone Library 5261
1074-6765 Studies in Ethnolinguistics 5182
1074-6773 Nuestra Voz (New York) 5344
1074-6781 Contemporary Critical Concepts and Pre-Enlightenment Literature 5278
1074-6803 Rocky Mountain Oil Journal 6790
1074-6846 Demokratizatsiya 7129
1074-6900 Breast Cancer†
1074-6978 C M J New Music Monthly 6553
1074-7001 Disorient Journalzine†
1074-7184 Contemporary Austrian Studies 4448
1074-7214 Heat Exchanger Design Update 3195
1074-7257 Page P C†
1074-7354 Hogan's Alley 493
1074-7419 Magazine Dimensions 7567
1074-7427 Neurobiology of Learning and Memory 6164
1074-7443 Chinese Journal of Advanced Software Research†
1074-746X Billboard International Latin Music Buyer's Guide 6549
1074-7494 Teen Voices 8885
1074-7516 Europe TravelBook 8702
1074-7532 Advances in Expert Systems for Management†
1074-7540 Advances in Entrepreneurship, Firm Emergence and Growth 1724
1074-7575 Advances in Neural Science†
1074-7583 Journal of Agricultural Safety and Health 126
1074-7613 Immunity 5759
1074-7648 Real Living with Diabetes 5899
1074-7737 Home & Community Health Special Interest Section Newsletter *changed to* 1093-7218 7524
1074-777X Dog Industry Newsletter†
1074-7788 Cat Industry Newsletter†
1074-7796 Veterinary Industry Newsletter†
1074-780X International Pet Industry News 6810
1074-7818 Verbal Abuse 5244
1074-7877 International Research in the Business Disciplines 1129
1074-7885 American Institute for Conservation of Historic and Artistic Works. Directory 465
1074-7931 The Neurologist 6166
1074-794X Letras Hispanas (Edinburg) 5144
1074-7966 Craft - Crafts
1074-7990 Advances in Chiropractic†
1074-8016 Volta Voices 4077
1074-8067 Notes from a Beadworker's Journal†
1074-8083 The McGruffletter (National Edition) 2660
1074-8091 West Virginia Nurse 5984
1074-8105 Dispute Resolution Journal 1675
1074-8121 On the Horizon 2996
1074-813X Window Technology
1074-8148 Slick Times†
1074-830X Muae†
1074-8350 American Shipper 8638
1074-8369 Advanced Seminar on Copyright Law 6744
1074-8407 Journal of Family Nursing 5965
1074-8520 Annual Editions: International Business 1552
1074-8547 Athletes in Action 8159
1074-858X Nursing Spectrum - Greater Philadelphia - Tri-State Edition 5975
1074-8601 A C O G Patient Education 5984
1074-861X A C O G Committee Opinions 5984
1074-8652 Right-to-Know Planning Guide Report 3463
1074-8687 Uro-Gram 6275
1074-875X C C D Astronomy†
1074-8792 Gale State Rankings Reporter†
1074-8806 Bailliere's Clinical Psychiatry†
1074-8822 Asian Fortune 3520
1074-8849 Facts about Family Practice† 8955
1074-8857 American Folklore Society News 3614
1074-889X Personal 401 (K) Advisor†
1074-8903 I O M A's Report on Managing Credit, Receivables and Collections 1352
1074-8911 Digital Unix News†
1074-8970 International Conference on Computer Languages. Proceedings†
1074-9004 Community Media Review 8095
1074-9039 Mind, Culture, and Activity 7986
1074-9055 I I 7240
1074-9098 Chemical Health and Safety *changed to* 1871-5532 3498
1074-9144 21st Century Afro Review†
1074-9209 The Caller 2605
1074-9233 Ohio Biological Survey. Miscellaneous Contributions 695
1074-9276 Crittenden Golf Inc. 8226
1074-9292 The Parker School Journal of Foreign and Comparative Law *changed to* 1941-8930 4933
1074-9314 U S F A National Newsletter (Print) *changed to* U S F A National Newsletter (Email) 8214
1074-9357 Topics in Stroke Rehabilitation 5801
1074-9403 College Theology Society. Annual Publication 7793
1074-9446 Burrelle's Media Directory. Vol 1, Newspapers & Related Media† 8938
1074-9462 Burrelle's Media Directory. Vol 3, Broadcast & Related Media† 8938
1074-9527 Whisper
1074-9535 Ethereal Dances
1074-9551 A A C E Careers Update 2937
1074-956X J O B 7494
1074-9624 Eastern Pennsylvania Business Journal 1097
1074-9632 Doody's Health Sciences Book Review Annual†
1074-9683 Occupational Therapy Forum
1074-9942 National Biotech Register 768
1074-9969 Glass Cherry†
1075-0045 New Energy News 3142
1075-0053 Insider Alert†
1075-0126 Quartz Hill Journal of Theology 7772
1075-0169 Healthy Weight Journal *changed to* 1708-5926 6660
1075-0185 ChiMe 2265
1075-0207 Applied Microwave & Wireless†
1075-0223 W G & L Tax Journal Digest 1954
1075-0274 Means Concrete and Masonry Cost Data 1023
1075-0282 Warehousing - Distribution Directory 8678
1075-0320 96 Inc 5406
1075-0347 The Journal of Biblical Storytelling 7654
1075-0355 American Careers 6692
1075-0371 Browbeat†
1075-038X Hart's 21st Century Fuels†
1075-041X Mediations 7154
1075-0436 Adirondack Journal of Environmental Studies 3401
1075-0487 Alimentos Balanceados para Animales†
1075-0576 Vital Signs (Years) 3473
1075-0592 Private Power Executive 3145
1075-0649 California International Practitioner 4919
1075-0665 Lead Poisoning Report†
1075-0711 Fodor's Virginia & Maryland 8710
1075-0754 Issues in Psychoanalytic Psychology 7367
1075-0789 Means Facilities Construction Cost Data 1023
1075-0797 Hawk 6292
1075-0800 High Society 6292
1075-0819 Celebrity Skin 6287
1075-0851 Echoes & Mirrors 6496
1075-086X Azerbaijan International 7222
1075-0886 A R L Proceedings of the Meetings 4986
1075-0894 Artist's and Graphic Designer's Market 473
1075-0924 Methods of Logic in Computer Science†
1075-0967 Tercer Milenio
1075-1017 Xavier 2310
1075-1041 M I D I
1075-1084 National Referral Roster 7601
1075-1165 Sarah Lawrence Review 5238
1075-1173 Film Crew Magazine
1075-1211 Annals of Behavioral Science and Medical Education 2826
1075-122X The Breast Journal 5987
1075-1262 The Soviet and Post Soviet Review 4266
1075-1300 Cross Currents (Los Angeles) 8096
1075-1319 Hand Papermaking Newsletter 6734
1075-1327 Binders' Guild Newsletter 7553
1075-1351 Appalachian Trail Data Book 8683
1075-136X Aviation Telephone Directory. Western & Northcentral States 8538
1075-1378 Aviation Telephone Directory. Eastern, Western, Southwestern and North Central States 8538
1075-1386 Sonoran Quarterly 818
1075-1416 Accounting Historians Notebook 1278
1075-1424 Midwest Hospitality†
1075-1467 IdeaSource†
1075-1491 Renaissance (Cambridge)†
1075-1580 Inside Microsoft Excel 2591
1075-1629 Advances in Metal and Semiconductor Clusters 2049
1075-1653 Different Drummer Magazine†
1075-1742 Air Cargo Report†
1075-1815 Barbara Brabec's Self Employment Survival Letter†
1075-1823 Satellite Choice 2389
1075-2021 Venezuelan Literature and Arts Journal
1075-203X Corrections Alert 2647
1075-2099 Advances in the Use of Synthons in Organic Chemistry†
1075-2110 The Medieval & Renaissance Times
1075-2188 Home Health Focus†

ISSN

1076-254X Network (Rockville) **30**
1076-2612 Forerunners **6895**
1076-2671 West's Alaska Reporter **4812**
1076-268X West's Alabama Reporter **4812**
1076-2701 Sport Rocketry **4347**
1076-2752 Journal of Occupational and Environmental Medicine **5653**
1076-2787 Complexity **5480**
1076-2809 Alternative & Complementary Therapies **306**
1076-2825 Ecosystem Health *changed to* 1612-9202 **3416**
1076-2833 Quintessence†
1076-285X Journal for a Just and Caring Education†
1076-2906 C R B Commodity Yearbook **1614**
1076-2922 The Classicist **437**
1076-2930 Ultimate Sports Pro Football **8250**
1076-2949 Hawes Fantasy Football Guide **8235**
1076-2957 Reed Read Reid Roots† **8984**
1076-2981 West's Delaware Report *changed to* Delaware Reporter **4655**
1076-3163 U.S. Government Periodicals Index (Print)†
1076-3198 Plumpers and Big Women
1076-3279 Tissue Engineering *changed to* 1937-3341 **751**
1076-3279 Tissue Engineering *changed to* 1937-3368 **708**
1076-3279 Tissue Engineering *changed to* 1937-3384 **708**
1076-3295 Naturally **5078**
1076-3309 Keep Up to Date on Payroll **1295**
1076-3333 Resource (Niles) **250**
1076-3406 Strategic Alliance Alert†
1076-3430 Earth Observation Magazine (Print Edition) *changed to* Earth Observation Magazine (Online Edition) **2706**
1076-3457 Tea Talk **3666**
1076-3465 Sugah
1076-3503 New England Folk Almanac†
1076-3511 The Health Care M & A Report **5624**
1076-3600 The Merger Yearbook† **8974**
1076-3635 Talking Leaves (Eugene) **707**
1076-3651 Cobras†
1076-366X Smart Electronics†
1076-3678 Custom Rodder† **8947**
1076-3732 I E E E Newsletter†
1076-3856 F M R A News **197**
1076-3872 Veterinary Clinical Nutrition†
1076-3910 Financial Statistics of Major U.S. Publicly Owned Electric Utilities (Year) (Print Edition)†
1076-3929 Grain: World Markets and Trade **1997**
1076-3937 Platt's Metals Week **6476**
1076-3945 U.S. Department of Agriculture. National Agricultural Statistics Service. Chickens and Eggs **187**
1076-3961 Foundation News & Commentary **8041**
1076-4046 Stanford Synchrotron Radiation Laboratory. Activity Report **7063**
1076-4119 Folk Era Today! **6567**
1076-4135 Fund Directions **1625**
1076-4143 Internet Homesteader. Series A: Library and Information Science **5019**
1076-4216 Kaleidoscope of Carolina†
1076-4224 In Motion (Daytona Beach) **2287**
1076-4240 Wireless Design and Development **3334**
1076-4275 U S P Dictionary of U S A N and International Drug Names **6884**
1076-433X The Best Toys, Books & Videos for Kids (Year)†
1076-4356 Collectible Newspapers†
1076-4429 Real-Time Engineering **2468**
1076-4437 Visions (Moorpark)†
1076-450X The Sondheim Review **8479**
1076-4542 Plot Magazine†
1076-4550 See†
1076-4577 Virginia CapitolConnections **7476**
1076-4607 Veterinary & Comparative Ophthalmology†
1076-4623 C A P Sule (Levittown) **4042**
1076-4658 Rampant Lion **4256**
1076-4674 Current Topics in Wetland Biogeochemistry **2730**
1076-4682 Agente de Viajes al Dia†
1076-4704 Hoofcare & Lameness **8798**
1076-4712 Illinois Natural History Survey. Biological Notes **677**
1076-4755 Who's Who in Washington Nonprofit Groups† **8998**
1076-4941 F & S Index. United States (Annual) **1228**
1076-4968 Acres U S A **215**
1076-500X The Mini-Annals of Improbable Research **7882**
1076-5123 Harris Texas Manufacturers Directory *changed to* Harris Directory. Texas Manufacturing **2002**
1076-5174 Journal of Mass Spectrometry **2102**
1076-5204 International Journal for Computers and Their Applications **2424**
1076-5301 Cracking the French Achievement *changed to* Cracking the S A T French Subject Test **2976**
1076-531X Cracking the S A T II. Chemistry Subject Test *changed to* 1556-844X **2976**
1076-5336 Cracking the S A T II. Biology Subject Test *changed to* 1556-8431 **2976**
1076-5344 The Princeton Review Student Access Guide to Paying for College *changed to* 1944-3781 **2997**
1076-5352 Cracking the G E D **2975**
1076-5360 Cracking the S A T II. Physics Subject Test *changed to* 1558-0067 **2976**
1076-5387 Cracking the S A T II. Math Subject Tests *changed to* 1556-7095 **2976**
1076-5395 Cracking the S A T II. English Subject Tests *changed to* 1944-379X **2976**
1076-5425 Front Lines Research **972**
1076-5441 Speaking of Fire **3581**
1076-5476 *see* 1542-9040 **7479**
1076-5476 *see* C S A Worldwide Political Science Abstracts **7199**
1076-5484 America, History and Life on Disc *see* 0002-7065 **4168**
1076-5492 Inquisitor **3978**
1076-5506 Tick, Tick, Tick...
1076-5514 Studies in Psychoanalytic Theory†
1076-5522 The Connection **994**
1076-5549 Asia - Pacific Observer†
1076-5557 Bay & Delta Yachtsman **8272**
1076-5638 Comprehensive Accreditation Manual for Hospitals **4091**
1076-5670 Advances in Imaging and Electron Physics **3294**
1076-5697 Focus on Literatur *changed to* Focus on German Studies **5297**
1076-5700 Optics Report†
1076-5719 Travel Companions **8766**
1076-5743 Assisted Living Today *changed to* 1553-8281 **4041**
1076-5778 Aspire†
1076-5859 Life and Work Pathways: Bible Studies for Adults 70 & Up†
1076-5867 Life and Work Ventures: Bible Studies for Adults 55-69†
1076-5883 Life and Work Pursuits: Bible Studies for Adults 35-54†
1076-5891 Life and Work Directions: Bible Studies for Early Adulthood (18-24)†
1076-5905 Life and Work Directions: Bible Studies for Young Adults (25-34)†
1076-5913 Life and Work Ventures and Pathways: Teacher Edition†
1076-5921 Life and Work Pursuits: Teacher Edition†
1076-593X Life and Work Directions: Teacher Edition†
1076-5972 Briefings on Hospital Safety **4089**
1076-5980 Briefings on Credentialing **4089**
1076-5999 Briefings on Subacute Care *changed to* Executive Briefings Digest (Email) **4093**
1076-6006 Briefings on Practice Management†
1076-6014 Briefings on Long-Term Care Regulations *changed to* 1937-2728 **4089**
1076-6022 Medical Staff Briefing **4107**
1076-6030 Respiratory Care Manager†
1076-6081 Card Talk **23**
1076-609X SpaceWatch **72**
1076-6138 Estep Family Journal†
1076-6200 Cracking the S A T II. Spanish Subject Test *changed to* 1558-3406 **2976**
1076-6286 Biomaterials Science and Engineering†
1076-6294 Microbial Drug Resistance **5679**
1076-6332 Academic Radiology **6191**
1076-6405 Travel Notes **8767**
1076-6413 Potpourri **5234**
1076-6421 Re-Publish†
1076-643X Red Herring Mystery Magazine†
1076-6456 IntlEc CD-ROM†
1076-6480 A & E Magazine **462**
1076-6502 R & R† **8983**
1076-660X Modern Accounting and Auditing Checklists **1297**
1076-6677 Rider University Magazine **2299**
1076-6693 A C & Y H S News **8614**
1076-6715 The Columbia Journal of European Law **4921**
1076-6758 Image (Studio City)
1076-6766 Let's Find Out (Spanish Edition) **3070**
1076-6987 Servant Life†
1076-7029 The Gentle Survivalist†
1076-7037 *see* 0006-3177 **713**
1076-7045 *see* 0006-7326 **5209**
1076-7053 *see* 0007-6961 **1216**
1076-707X *see* 0013-1385 **2932**
1076-7088 *see* 0014-083X **5407**
1076-7096 *see* 0162-1963 **7937**
1076-7118 *see* 1079-4719 **4822**
1076-7169 Modern Reformation **7768**
1076-7207 TurfGrass Trends **3752**
1076-7223 Minority Nurse **6701**
1076-7231 Advanced Practice Nurse†
1076-7258 Directory World†
1076-7274 Federal Assistance Directory†
1076-7282 Country Sampler's Country Business **4059**
1076-7290 *see* 0004-3222 **529**
1076-7339 Letter Arts Review **502**
1076-7460 American Journal of Geriatric Cardiology **5776**
1076-7517 Illinois Legislative Service **4690**
1076-755X Directory of Shrimp Farming in the Western Hemisphere†
1076-7568 Shrimp News International **3608**
1076-7681 *see* 0082-9072 **6707**
1076-769X National Prison Project Journal **2661**
1076-7762 Current Issues in Public Health†
1076-7843 (Year) Directory of Conventions. Southeast Convention Guide†
1076-7851 (Year) Directory of Conventions. West Convention Guide†
1076-786X (Year) Directory of Conventions. Central Convention Guide†
1076-7878 (Year) Directory of Conventions. Northeast & Mid-Atlantic Convention Guide†
1076-7886 International String Figure Association. Bulletin **8181**
1076-7924 International Airborne Remote Sensing Conference and Exhibition. Proceedings **3199**
1076-7967 I Hate Computers **2421**
1076-7975 Electronic Green Journal **3419**
1076-7991 Eldritch Tales **5442**
1076-8017 C L E A R News (Print) *changed to* C L E A R News (Online) **7510**
1076-8025 C L E A R Exam Review **7510**
1076-8033 *see* 0898-3720 **8152**
1076-8084 National Hospital Discharge Survey **7548**
1076-8092 Try It Yourself Hair **592**
1076-8106 Inside Microsoft PowerPoint **2591**
1076-8114 The Magic Carpet Bag†
1076-8149 Beverage World en Espanol **599**
1076-819X Estate Planner's Alert **4902**
1076-8262 Scholastic News en Espanol. Edicion 3 **3080**
1076-8270 Vertical Application Reseller†
1076-8289 MicroComputer Journal **2572**
1076-8300 Global Investment Magazine†
1076-8343 International Instrumentation & Controls†
1076-8351 Asian Industrial Reporter†
1076-836X *see* 1063-5157 **707**
1076-8386 Instrumentos y Controles Internacionales **3246**
1076-8424 I D B Projects **1352**
1076-8483 Small Business Profiles (Farmington Hills)†
1076-8491 Municipal Issuers Registry **1641**
1076-8548 Inclusive Education Programs *changed to* 1934-5704 **3043**
1076-8572 The Scottish Rite Journal of Freemasonry Southern Jurisdiction U S A **2270**
1076-8599 Sun Valley Magazine **3989**
1076-8645 Covert Intelligence Letter **6417**
1076-8653 Exegy†
1076-8661 Indiana Legislative Insight **7445**
1076-867X Indiana Gaming Insight **8179**
1076-8769 Jamail Center for Legal Research Annual Report *changed to* 1935-1453 **5043**
1076-884X Generic Line **6844**
1076-8858 Aviation History **48**
1076-8866 American History (Leesburg) **4282**
1076-8890 babysue **5417**
1076-8971 Psychology, Public Policy, and Law **7400**
1076-898X Journal of Experimental Psychology: Applied **7373**
1076-8998 Journal of Occupational Health Psychology **6680**
1076-9005 Journal of Buddhist Ethics **7701**
1076-9021 Approved Variety Puzzles Plus Crossroads
1076-9080 I F S Newsletter **3168**
1076-9110 Slap Skateboard Magazine *changed to* Slap **8201**
1076-9242 Dyslexia **3038**
1076-9293 Intermodal Shipping†
1076-9307 International Journal of Finance & Economics **1357**
1076-9382 Pharmaceutical Ventures
1076-9412 Forward Motion†
1076-9447 Odyssey (Lexington) **2996**
1076-9471 Murder is Academic **5414**
1076-9668 Christian Counseling Today **7631**
1076-9676 Debt-Free and Prosperous Living **1334**
1076-9684 Dynamic Chiropractic **5805**
1076-9722 New Member Round Table Footnotes **5035**
1076-9757 The Journal of Artificial Intelligence Research **2453**
1076-9765 *see* 0191-0574 **8020**
1076-9773 Index to Scientific & Technical Proceedings CD-ROM *see* 0149-8088 **7937**
1076-979X Substance Abuse Letter
1076-9803 The New York Journal of Mathematics **5520**
1076-9838 Professional Speaker *changed to* 1934-9076 **5176**
1076-9854 Terry Tracings† **8993**
1076-9897 Teen Life†
1076-996X The Harness Shop News *changed to* 1547-0121 **4975**
1076-9986 Journal of Educational and Behavioral Statistics **2934**
1077-0003 Angel Times†
1077-0097 Advances in Competitiveness Research **1551**
1077-0186 Francophone Cultures and Literatures **5298**
1077-0194 The Literature and Poetry of Exile **5325**
1077-0216 Many Voices: Ethnic Literatures of the Americas **5330**
1077-0232 F P A News
1077-0283 Connecticut Warbler **905**
1077-0305 Association for Child Psychoanalysis. Newsletter **2144**
1077-0313 O-Hayo Sensei **3014**
1077-0402 White Press†
1077-0445 Consumer Lending News **1329**
1077-0453 Kansas Living **130**
1077-0461 Farm and Ranch Tax Letter **198**
1077-0526 Conference Board. Corporate Contributions **1085**
1077-0550 The Journal of Educational Issues of Language Minority Students **2875**
1077-0577 DanceView **2685**
1077-0615 Public Interest Law Journal **4763**
1077-0704 Southern California Interdisciplinary Law Journal **4786**
1077-0712 10 Percent†
1077-0739 Who Got In? **3010**
1077-0747 On the Brain **6171**
1077-0755 Journal of International Agricultural and Extension Education **127**
1077-0887 Singles & Leaders Newsletter†
1077-0933 Movement Research Performance Journal **2687**
1077-095X California Central Coast Genealogical Society. Bulletin **3761**
1077-0968 Cherokee Observer **3526**
1077-0984 Earshot Jazz **6564**
1077-1018 Historical Gamer
1077-1093 Arriving†
1077-1131 Babybug **2177**
1077-114X Asia - Pacific Exchange Journal **2967**
1077-1158 Journal of Applied Management and Entrepreneurship **1763**
1077-1166 Beyond the Counter†
1077-1212 (Year) Index of Social Health **7548**
1077-1271 The Solution†
1077-128X World Business Solution†
1077-1298 Solution Internationale†
1077-131X Georgia Health Law Update†
1077-1328 Illinois Health Law Update†
1077-1344 New York Health Law Update **7533**
1077-1352 Encyclopedia of Endangered Species **2610**
1077-1360 Statistical Abstract of the World†
1077-145X W I D Bulletin **7218**
1077-1514 Women's Environment and Development Organization News & Views **8891**
1077-1557 Subscription Marketing **7574**
1077-1573 A M R's C I M Strategies†
1077-1581 Road King **8675**
1077-162X A E G I S News†
1077-1646 Ancient American **373**
1077-1719 Hospital and Health Administration Index†
1077-1808 Go Magazine (Charlotte) **8714**
1077-1816 Plan Sponsor **1703**
1077-1824 G M H C Treatment Issues *changed to* 1948-0687 **5807**
1077-1840 LottoWorld†
1077-1867 Texas Construction **1040**
1077-1921 The Earth Times†
1077-193X Challenge (Atlanta) **3526**
1077-1948 Pun American Newsletter **5355**
1077-1956 Excellence in Service†
1077-1972 Professional Telephone Selling†
1077-1999 Philosophy in the Contemporary World **6943**
1077-2014 Real-Time Imaging† **8984**
1077-2081 Oregon Employment Law Letter **4754**
1077-209X Continuing Medical Education Directory† **8943**
1077-2197 Violence & Abuse Abstracts **8151**
1077-2243 The Market Data Industry†

ISSN

DIRECTORY 2010 1081-3284 9509

1080-2657 Compliance Engineering (European Edition) **3091**
1080-2711 The Journal of Electronic Publishing **7580**
1080-2754 Synthesis (Knoxville) **5384**
1080-2797 Integrated System Design†
1080-2800 Construction & Aggregates Machinery en Espanol **5450**
1080-2819 Arkansas United Methodist **7746**
1080-2843 The Antitrust Counselor **4856**
1080-286X Information Management *changed to* Information Technology Management **1753**
1080-2924 Laboratory Hematology **5939**
1080-3009 Breakthrough News **7224**
1080-3017 Radio Resource Magazine *changed to* 1544-9556 **2360**
1080-3025 Radio Resource International **2363**
1080-305X A G U Reference Shelf Series **2776**
1080-3076 Natural Pet Magazine†
1080-3157 Stock Summary (Monthly Edition) **1653**
1080-3165 Stock Summary (Semi-annual Edition) *see* 1080-3157 **1653**
1080-3203 Purchasing Management Bulletin **1839**
1080-3211 Labor Relations Bulletin *changed to* 1069-921X **4670**
1080-3238 International Practitioners' Workshop Series **4932**
1080-3262 Spiritual Massage Ministry Newsletter†
1080-3297 The Journal of Legal Nurse Consulting **5965**
1080-3432 What is Enlightenment? *changed to* 1946-0805 **7640**
1080-3467 Harris New England Manufacturers Directory *changed to* Harris Directory. New England Manufacturing **2001**
1080-3521 Educational Synopses in Anesthesiology and Critical Care Medicine **5608**
1080-353X P M Engineer **4124**
1080-3548 International Journal of Occupational Safety and Ergonomics **6679**
1080-3564 Early Childhood NEWS **2151**
1080-3572 Jazz Improv **6578**
1080-3769 Salt of the Earth†
1080-3793 Star Trek Communicator **2391**
1080-3807 N A N N Central Lines *changed to* 1554-3382 **5970**
1080-384X Plastic Canvas Crafts†
1080-3858 Infusion (Alexandria) **6022**
1080-3874 Metrolina Golf Magazine **8238**
1080-3912 The Irwin Investor's Handbook **1634**
1080-3920 American Foreign Policy Interests **7220**
1080-398X Do It With Microsoft Office
1080-4080 China Business Update. Automotive *changed to* 1548-1166 **8574**
1080-4153 Global Studies: India and South Asia **550**
1080-4161 Health & Environment in America's Top-Rated Cities: A Statistical Profile (Years)† **8961**
1080-4188 Guide to Dividend Reinvestment Plans†
1080-4293 Advanced Practice Nursing Quarterly†
1080-4455 Couloir *changed to* 1083-5350 **8305**
1080-4463 Idaho Catholic Register **7800**
1080-4471 P C Gamer **2579**
1080-4498 Best of Genesis†
1080-4501 Girls - Girls†
1080-451X Style 1900 **369**
1080-4625 European Cellular Mobile Communications Directory†
1080-4633 Chemical Processing. Environment *see* 0009-2630 **3239**
1080-4730 Home School Market Guide†
1080-4757 APStracts†
1080-4781 National Cooperative Highway Research Program. Legal Research Digest **8505**
1080-4889 Federal Claims Reporter. Bound Volumes *see* 1067-4934 **4951**
1080-4919 Carroll's Federal Directory **7429**
1080-4927 Interactive Age†
1080-5060 Daily Bruin **2280**
1080-5109 Integrated Photonics Research **3319**
1080-5222 Straub Foundation. Proceedings **5718**
1080-5230 Journal of Functional and Logic Programming **2508**
1080-5249 Wireless: For the Corporate User†
1080-5354 Advances in Analytical Geochemistry†
1080-5370 G P S Solutions **4007**
1080-5389 American Liberal Religious Thought **7621**
1080-5397 Studies in Composition and Rhetoric **5381**
1080-5400 Taboo **2917**
1080-5494 Sociolinguistics in Deaf Communities **4076**
1080-5516 Federal Criminal Code and Rules **4889**
1080-5540 Fuel Magazine†
1080-5575 Federal Grant Deadline Calendar **7492**
1080-5583 Federal Grant Deadline Calendar. A Supplement to the Guide to Federal Funding for Education **3022**
1080-5621 Pain Medicine Journal Club Journal†
1080-563X C N S Drug Reviews *changed to* 1755-5930 **6827**
1080-5664 Great Lakes Environmental Directory **2612**
1080-5699 Business Communication Quarterly **1729**
1080-5702 Consequences **3412**
1080-5729 B M W - O N **8254**
1080-580X Taking Sides: Clashing Views on Controversial Political Issues **7187**
1080-5826 Drug Benefit Trends **6833**
1080-5885 Executive Denver Corporate Connection
1080-6032 Wilderness and Environmental Medicine **5730**
1080-6040 Emerging Infectious Diseases (Print) **7515**
1080-6059 Emerging Infectious Diseases (Online) **7515**
1080-6121 Mining Voice†
1080-6180 Dr. Marcus Laux's Naturally Well *changed to* Dr. Marcus Laux's Naturally Well Today **308**
1080-6318 Funding Sources for Community and Economic Development **8103**
1080-6377 *see* 0002-9327 **5468**
1080-6385 Journal for the Professional Counselor **2874**
1080-6393 Surgical Physician Assistant **6260**
1080-6431 National Council for Geocosmic Research. Memberletter **567**
1080-6458 Safety Resources†
1080-6474 Many Mountains Moving **5330**
1080-6490 *see* 0003-0678 **4442**
1080-6504 *see* 0004-0975 **2230**
1080-6512 *see* 0161-2492 **5269**
1080-6520 *see* 1063-1801 **5277**
1080-6539 *see* 0300-7162 **5284**
1080-6547 *see* 0013-8304 **5286**
1080-6555 *see* 0273-0340 **5305**
1080-6563 *see* 0147-2593 **5323**
1080-6571 *see* 0278-9671 **5325**
1080-658X *see* 0026-7724 **5335**
1080-6598 *see* 0026-7910 **5149**
1080-6601 *see* 1071-6068 **4153**
1080-661X *see* 0028-6087 **5340**
1080-6628 *see* 0048-7511 **4310**
1080-6679 Greenhouse Management & Production **3734**
1080-6687 Journal of International Law and Policy **4701**
1080-6695 Nursery Management & Production **3745**
1080-675X The Federal Lawyer **4673**
1080-6776 Military Life†
1080-6784 Modern Ferret†
1080-6792 Public Relations Tactics **33**
1080-6814 The Daily Barometer **2977**
1080-6873 Terminal Fright **5448**
1080-6903 The Tracking Angle†
1080-692X Boston University Conference on Language Development. Proceedings **5101**
1080-6954 Journal of Chinese Political Science **7146**
1080-6970 Schwann Artist† **8987**
1080-6989 W D A Journal **5869**
1080-7039 Human and Ecological Risk Assessment **3437**
1080-7063 Profiles of Worldwide Government Leaders **7173**
1080-7152 New York School Boards **3028**
1080-7241 DoubleTake *changed to* 1558-4828 **5286**
1080-725X Ukrainian Economic Review **1186**
1080-7268 Stage of the Art† **8990**
1080-7284 Advances in Clinical Pharmacology†
1080-7349 Common Sense
1080-742X GenBank†
1080-7446 Professional Animal Scientist **8805**
1080-7489 Meeting & Conference Executives Alert†
1080-7535 Pittsburgh International News **3557**
1080-7543 School Nurse News **5981**
1080-7578 Federal Civil Judicial Procedure and Rules **4830**
1080-7586 The Typhooner **8283**
1080-7594 Dogtown Territorial Quarterly *changed to* California Territorial Quarterly **4287**
1080-7608 Christianity and the Arts†
1080-7659 Complete Directory for People with Chronic Illness **5599**
1080-7675 Internet White Pages
1080-7683 Journal of Ocular Pharmacology and Therapeutics **6045**
1080-7705 The Value Line Investment (Expanded Edition) **1658**
1080-7713 Federation News (Wilton)†
1080-7799 Site Selection **1903**
1080-787X Current Opinion in Cardiology, with Evaluated MEDLINE *see* 0268-4705 **5784**
1080-7950 World Magazine Bank† **8999**
1080-8019 Hydrogen & Fuel Cell Letter **2116**
1080-8027 The Pyrotechnic Reference Series **3254**
1080-8078 Current Opinion in Anesthesiology, with Evaluated MEDLINE *see* 0952-7907 **5771**
1080-8086 Current Opinion in Otolaryngology & Head and Neck Surgery, with Evaluated MEDLINE *see* 1068-9508 **6079**
1080-8094 *see* 0963-0643 **6267**
1080-8116 Current Opinion in Pediatrics, with Evaluated MEDLINE *see* 1040-8703 **6090**
1080-8132 Current Opinion in Ophthalmology, with Evaluated MEDLINE *see* 1040-8738 **6041**
1080-8167 Current Opinion in Gastroenterology, with Evaluated MEDLINE *see* 0267-1379 **5922**
1080-8175 Current Opinion in Rheumatology, with Evaluated MEDLINE *see* 1040-8711 **6223**
1080-8183 *see* 1070-5295 **6058**
1080-8191 Current Opinion in Psychiatry, with Evaluated MEDLINE *see* 0951-7367 **6135**
1080-8205 Current opinion in Endocrinology & Diabetes, with Evaluated MEDLINE *see* 1752-296X **5885**
1080-8221 Current Opinion in Nephrology & Hypertension, with Evaluated MEDLINE *see* 1062-4821 **6266**
1080-823X Current Opinion in Lipidology, with Evaluated MEDLINE *see* 0957-9672 **5784**
1080-8256 Current Opinion in Obstetrics & Gynecology, with Evaluated MEDLINE *see* 1040-872X **5988**
1080-837X T T R A News **8759**
1080-8388 Research Communications in Alcohol & Substances of Abuse **6878**
1080-8434 V B Tech Journal†
1080-8493 Internet Connection (Little Falls) **2560**
1080-8558 Compensation in Nonprofit Organizations **1671**
1080-8582 University of Memphis Law Review **4804**
1080-8590 Idaho Economics **119**
1080-8604 Blueprints for Economic Development **4404**
1080-8620 Real Estate Economics **7608**
1080-8639 AgLetter **80**
1080-8698 Figurines & Collectibles (Livonia)†
1080-8914 Techniques in Protein Chemistry **2131**
1080-8930 Baltimore Alternative **4371**
1080-8949 Action Figure News & Toy Review *changed to* 1545-0651 **4060**
1080-8965 Choirboy Notes†
1080-9015 I D (New York) *changed to* 1541-8235
1080-9058 Culture Wars Magazine **7794**
1080-9198 Applied Physics **7005**
1080-9201 World Investor **1660**
1080-9317 Woolf Studies Annual **5400**
1080-9368 Poetry in Motion Magazine
1080-9392 Mitchell Imported Cars, Light Trucks & Vans Service & Repair **8591**
1080-9414 U.S. Export Directory **1585**
1080-9422 Jay Abraham's Business Breakthroughs
1080-9449 Lubes 'n' Greases **6777**
1080-9457 Courtroom Handbook on Federal Evidence **4949**
1080-9570 Private Cable & Wireless Cable *changed to* 1539-8803 **2375**
1080-9619 Appendx **427**
1080-9724 Issues in Education†
1080-9775 Biomedical Safety & Standards **5586**
1080-9805 Genesee Country **4293**
1080-9813 Financial Times Global Investors' Digest†
1080-983X Master Type Locator **3108**
1080-9864 Peace Watch **7259**
1080-9910 DargonZine **5441**
1080-9929 MotoRacing **8593**
1081-0064 M D R's Canadian School Directory†
1081-0072 Writers' International Forum†
1081-0102 *see* 0001-1452 **40**
1081-0161 A G Bulletin **4607**
1081-0218 V S O Newsletter **915**
1081-0226 Review of Ophthalmology **6051**
1081-0374 Business Products Update **1850**
1081-0390 West's Tax Law Dictionary **1955**
1081-0463 Harvard Journal of African American Public Policy **7443**
1081-0587 Stedman's Wordwatcher†
1081-0595 Micro†
1081-0625 InterJournal **2987**
1081-0706 Annual Review of Cell and Developmental Biology **827**
1081-0714 Journal of Innovative Management **1766**
1081-0722 Primary Care Weekly†
1081-0730 Journal of Health Communication **5649**
1081-0749 Terra Nova *changed to* The New Earth Reader **6936**
1081-0765 Rock Garden Quarterly **3749**
1081-079X United Methodist Life **7778**
1081-0846 Wages and Cost of Living†
1081-0919 The Official Bed & Breakfast Guide for the United States, Canada & the Caribbean **8744**
1081-0927 Internet Connection (Tampa)†
1081-0943 Seminars in Urologic Oncology *changed to* 1078-1439 **6036**
1081-0951 Cutting Horse Chatter **8290**
1081-1028 Deaf Rochester†
1081-1044 Science and Engineering Network News **3219**
1081-1052 European Union Business Law. Sourcebook
1081-1109 Tri-City Computing Magazine **2440**
1081-1117 Britain by Britrail **8688**
1081-1133 Small Publisher **7574**
1081-1206 Annals of Allergy, Asthma, & Immunology **5754**
1081-1214 Northern New Jersey Business **1502**
1081-1257 South Carolina Business Vision **1177**
1081-1273 Hydrogen Today **3163**
1081-129X Special Situations Newsletter **1652**
1081-1311 The Extreme†
1081-132X Nash
1081-1346 Classified Communication
1081-1354 Directory of Contract Electronics Manufacturers. North American Edition (Print Edition)†
1081-1400 Who's Who Among African Americans **646**
1081-1419 Lingo **5425**
1081-1451 The International Journal of Virtual Reality
1081-1478 N S S News Bulletin **507**
1081-1494 D V M Management Consultants Reports†
1081-1540 Today's Father†
1081-1575 Construccion del Norte
1081-1613 Guide to Nontraditional Engagements **4683**
1081-1621 The Plantagenet Connection **4254**
1081-1672 Journal of Clinical Ligand Assay **5762**
1081-1680 Communication Law and Policy **4646**
1081-1702 Creative Options for Business and Annual Reports†
1081-1710 Journal of Vector Ecology **685**
1081-1753 Journal of African American Men *changed to* 1559-1646 **6302**
1081-1788 Fan Club Directory†
1081-180X The Harvard International Journal of Press / Politics *changed to* 1940-1612 **4577**
1081-2024 Directory of Online Services† **8950**
1081-2059 Chevy Truckin' **8573**
1081-2075 Euro Sport Car†
1081-2121 Card Trade **4331**
1081-2229 The Roundup Magazine **5365**
1081-2288 Any Amsbaugh Ancestors? **3758**
1081-230X The B Q R Yearbook **8221**
1081-2326 Hot Calaloo **5219**
1081-2334 Tidewater Parent **2169**
1081-2350 Lott Lineages **3774**
1081-2393 Training Research Journal†
1081-2431 Personal Injury Institute Annual **4840**
1081-2520 Info Technology†
1081-2539 World's Best Money Managers **1660**
1081-2555 Movie Advertising Collector†
1081-258X The Legal Publisher **4720**
1081-2598 More than Money **1641**
1081-2628 Siberian Journal of Differential Equations†
1081-2636 Current Blackjack News **8168**
1081-2644 America at the Polls **5205**
1081-2695 Folk Dance Phone Book and Group Directory (Year) **2686**
1081-2717 Faxnewz **2677**
1081-275X I D Systems European Edition†
1081-2776 Kosciuszko Foundation Newsletter **3546**
1081-2792 Foundation & Corporate Funding Advantage **8041**
1081-2865 Mathematics and Mechanics of Solids **7026**
1081-2911 Information Technology Report **826**
1081-292X Biological Science Report **658**
1081-2989 Environmental Management Information Systems Report **3481**
1081-3004 Journal of Adolescent & Adult Literacy **3025**
1081-3055 The Electronic Journal of Virtual Culture **2556**
1081-3098 Traditions **2304**
1081-3101 The Nursing Spectrum - Greater New York/New Jersey Metro Edition **5975**
1081-311X Bank Lawyer Liability†
1081-3160 Costa Rica Adventure & Business†
1081-3179 Global Connection†
1081-3187 Cisco World†
1081-3209 Book / Mark **4997**
1081-3217 Lesbian Connection **4376**
1081-3225 Blind Horse Review **5418**
1081-325X Explorations (Juneau) **5294**
1081-3268 Derivatives Quarterly†
1081-3284 World Business Review **1587**

ISSN

Link to your serials resources and content with ulrichsweb.com

ISSN

DIRECTORY 2010 1085-5386 9513

1084-533X Directory of Discount and General Merchandise Stores (Year) *changed to* 1937-4240 **1986**
1084-5356 Texas Town & City **7472**
1084-5402 Ranch & Rural Living Magazine **297**
1084-5429 Inside Nonprofit Accountability†
1084-5437 American Society of Legislative Clerks and Secretaries. Journal **7420**
1084-5445 Men's Perspective
1084-5453 Environmental History **4138**
1084-547X Journal of Experimental Fiction **5314**
1084-5496 The Forestry Source **3690**
1084-550X Time Out New York **3990**
1084-5518 A D D - up
1084-5526 Lagniappe Monthly on Latin American Projects & Finance†
1084-5569 Forensic Examiner **5913**
1084-5577 The Servants' Quarters
1084-5593 Keltria†
1084-5666 The Princeton Papers **4324**
1084-5720 Teens in Motion News **2216**
1084-5747 Colorado Evidence Courtroom Manual **4947**
1084-5771 Hermaphrodites with Attitudes **4374**
1084-5798 The Internet Resource Directory for K-12 Teachers and Librarians **2561**
1084-5844 Masala†
1084-5852 V G S Newsletter **3786**
1084-5968 Brain Injury Update†
1084-600X A P P R† **8927**
1084-6050 Caveat Lector **5419**
1084-6093 Response (Seattle) **2298**
1084-6190 Mother Baby Journal†
1084-6204 Development Director's Letter†
1084-628X Home Care Provider†
1084-6379 The RastaMon Times **6609**
1084-6506 Escene (Year)†
1084-6522 N C S S S M S T Journal **2888**
1084-6565 The Maverick Press†
1084-659X Infusion (Cambridge) **7142**
1084-6603 The Journal of Early Education and Family Review *changed to* 1550-0128 **2875**
1084-662X George†
1084-6654 Journal of Experimental Algorithmics **2508**
1084-6700 A D A†
1084-6743 Current Contents. Engineering, Computing & Technology with Abstracts *see* 1079-1450 **3229**
1084-676X Virginia Museum of Fine Arts Calendar **6539**
1084-6778 Fabricare **2243**
1084-6786 Population Briefs **7289**
1084-6832 Citizen (Colorado Springs) **7955**
1084-6905 Physician **5695**
1084-6913 The Personnel Legal Alert **1872**
1084-693X Campus Magazine **2970**
1084-7111 Barnabe Mountain Review **5260**
1084-7138 Trends in Amplification **6085**
1084-7146 Disease Management News **4092**
1084-7197 Talebones **5448**
1084-7219 Journal of Baccalaureate Social Work **8048**
1084-7243 American Society for Composites Technical Conference. Proceedings **3336**
1084-7278 Product Design and Development **3216**
1084-7316 Subject to Debate **2669**
1084-7340 Not Bored **3984**
1084-7480 Review of Heterodox Economics **1548**
1084-7529 Optical Society of America. Journal A: Optics, Image Science, and Vision **7082**
1084-7553 International Journal of Tantric Studies **6926**
1084-7561 Electronic Journal of Vedic Studies **549**
1084-7588 State & Local Taxes **1944**
1084-760X Shepard's Vermont Case Names Citator **4964**
1084-7650 Modern Dad
1084-7707 Folk on the Delaware General Corporation Law: Fundamentals **4868**
1084-7790 Software Digest†
1084-7820 Denver Bar Association. Docket **4656**
1084-7847 Shepard's Utah Case Names Citator **4964**
1084-7855 Wildlife Art **526**
1084-7898 Federal Acquisition Regulation (Chicago) **6421**
1084-7979 Shepard's Rhode Island Case Names Citator **4964**
1084-7987 Shepard's Ohio Unreported Appellate Citations **4963**
1084-8002 Signature Bride
1084-8045 Journal of Network and Computer Applications **2500**
1084-8053 Criminal Politics **1620**
1084-807X Shepard's Wyoming Case Names Citator†
1084-8142 The Journal of African Communications **3544**
1084-8185 Health News Naturally†
1084-8223 Home Health Care Management and Practice **4098**
1084-8231 Split Shift
1084-824X Journal of Women's Imaging† **8969**
1084-8258 Cardiovascular and Thoracic Anesthesia Journal Club Journal†
1084-8266 C L F Newsletter†
1084-8282 Illinois Dental News **5847**
1084-8320 Tri-State Letter Plus†
1084-8339 Multichannel News International†
1084-841X Composites Fabrication *changed to* Composites Manufacturing **7091**
1084-8436 Orlie's Lowriding **8597**
1084-8452 The Sodus News†
1084-8479 Defense & Security Electronics†
1084-8568 Journal of Quality Management†
1084-8592 Molecular Diagnosis *changed to* 1177-1062 **5680**
1084-8614 Encyclopedia of Global Industries **1992**
1084-8657 Gestalt Review **7358**
1084-8665 Creative Screenwriting **6495**
1084-8746 Bio-Med Technology Alert
1084-8770 The European Legacy **6918**
1084-8878 Directory of Drug Store and H B C Chains (Year) **1986**
1084-8916 Shepard's South Dakota Case Names Citator†
1084-8975 Gesneriad Journal†
1084-8983 Job Line and News from C P R S **4978**
1084-9041 The Nurturing Parent†
1084-9076 Digital Age†
1084-922X Weekly News Update on the Americas **3821**
1084-9238 Scale Steam Pictorial
1084-9246 Business Russia (Chicago)†
1084-9262 Camp Management†
1084-9289 The Vegan News **6670**
1084-9319 The Poetry Project **5431**
1084-9343 Club Z! **2183**
1084-9394 Air Quality Data Management Software Report **3481**
1084-9432 Trans: Arts Cultures Media **522**
1084-9459 Developing Indicators for Academic Library Performance†
1084-9467 Journal of Developmental Entrepreneurship **1962**
1084-9475 (Year) World Guide to Television† **8999**
1084-9483 Public Sector Contracting Report†
1084-9513 Israel Studies **7976**
1084-9521 Seminars in Cell and Developmental Biology **836**
1084-953X Workplace Ergonomics†
1084-9548 Florida Construction News Weekly Covering Miami & Vicinity† **8956**
1084-9556 Tennessee Construction News Weekly. Nashville & Vicinity **1040**
1084-9564 Florida Construction News Weekly Covering West Palm Beach and Vicinity **1008**
1084-9572 Tennessee Construction News Weekly. Memphis & Vicinity **1040**
1084-9580 Tennessee Construction News Weekly. Knoxville & Vicinity **1040**
1084-9599 Safety Library on C D *changed to* 1936-6752 **6686**
1084-9610 Boxing Almanac and Book of Facts **8162**
1084-9696 Construction Data & News Covering Sacramento†
1084-970X Daily Pacific Builder **1001**
1084-9718 Dodge Construction News Green Sheet **4409**
1084-9769 Slugfest, Ltd.†
1084-9785 Cancer Biotherapy & Radiopharmaceuticals **6011**
1084-9793 State Bar of New Mexico. Bar Journal **4788**
1084-9904 U-direct
1084-9912 E-Scape **5442**
1084-9971 DesignMart†
1085-0058 Individual Employment Rights† **8964**
1085-0082 Ken Blanchard's Profiles of Success **8116**
1085-0139 Andrews Foreign Assets Litigation Reporter†
1085-0171 Interactive Travel Report **8723**
1085-0287 Inkwell **5309**
1085-0295 Child and Adolescent Psychopharmacology News **6131**
1085-0309 Nursing Home Statistical Yearbook **5974**
1085-0317 Managed Medicare & Medicaid News
1085-0325 Guide to Government Information Available on the Internet **7443**
1085-0333 Cartoon Times **6522**
1085-035X Annual. Volume 1: Training *changed to* The (Year) Pfeiffer Annual. Training **1785**
1085-0368 Annual. Volume 2: Consulting *changed to* The (Year) Pfeiffer Annual. Consulting **1785**
1085-0376 Journal of Copyright Information†
1085-0422 Desktop Engineering **3290**
1085-0430 Family Preservation Journal **8040**
1085-0449 Northeast Corridor **5231**
1085-0473 Wireless Week **2345**
1085-049X Neurology Report *changed to* 1557-0576 **6154**
1085-0503 Feed and Grain - para America Latina†
1085-0554 Glacial Geology and Geomorphology†
1085-0619 Grand Tour†
1085-0635 Best Practices and Benchmarking in Healthcare†
1085-066X Modern American History: the United States Since 1865 **4304**
1085-0678 History of Schools and Schooling **4145**
1085-0716 C Q Contest **2357**
1085-0724 Instruction Section Newsletter **5018**
1085-0732 New York - New Jersey Environmental Compliance Update†
1085-0767 Chicago Computer Guide
1085-0821 Tomorrow's Morning Classroom Edition†
1085-0856 E A P Association Exchange *changed to* 1544-0893 **6700**
1085-0872 Latin American Energy Alert†
1085-0880 Dr. Andrew Weil's Self Healing **308**
1085-0902 Home Equity News **1351**
1085-0910 Latin American Power Watch **3160**
1085-0953 Update to A Selective History of the Crego Family **3786**
1085-1003 New Choices†
1085-1011 Safari Times **8331**
1085-1038 O R - M S Today **7894**
1085-1046 Virginia Economic Journal **1192**
1085-1089 Health Care Innovations†
1085-1151 International Private Sewage Disposal Code **1016**
1085-1232 Microsoft Magazine†
1085-1240 Directory of Trust Banking **1988**
1085-1267 Tam Kernewek **3567**
1085-1321 Direct Response **1814**
1085-1348 Facts & Faith†
1085-1437 Georgia Bar Journal **4680**
1085-1453 The Multimedia Directory†
1085-1461 Journal of Artists' Books **498**
1085-147X Chisholm Trail **3762**
1085-150X Shepard's California Federal Citations†
1085-1534 Better Homes and Gardens Christmas Cookies **4353**
1085-1542 360 Degrees: Art & Literary Review
1085-1712 Track and Field Coaches Review *changed to* Coaches Review **8309**
1085-1852 Construction News Weekly, Covering Southern Wisconsin **997**
1085-1860 F.W. Dodge Construction News Weekly, Covering Northeast Wisconsin - Upper Peninsula **1004**
1085-1879 Chicago Metro Construction News Weekly (Engineering Edition) **991**
1085-1887 Chicago Metro Construction News Weekly (General Building Edition) **991**
1085-1895 Detroit Metro Construction News Weekly **1002**
1085-1909 F.W. Dodge Construction News Weekly, Covering Western Pennsylvania **1004**
1085-1941 Northwest Illinois Construction News Weekly **1027**
1085-195X F.W. Dodge Construction News Weekly, Covering Central and Southern Illinois **1003**
1085-1968 Epoche **6916**
1085-1976 Florida Media Quarterly†
1085-1984 The Basement Magazine **6548**
1085-1992 I E E E Conference on Control Applications. Proceedings **2460**
1085-2026 Postcard History Society **4343**
1085-2042 News from Nowhere (Ukiah)†
1085-2077 Food & Drug Packaging *changed to* 1941-8531 **6710**
1085-2115 Marketing Educators' Journal **1831**
1085-2166 *see* 0046-2284 **3426**
1085-2174 A W H P's Worksite Health†
1085-2182 Carolina Construction News Weekly Covering Winston - Salem - Greensboro†
1085-2190 Carolina Construction News, Covering Asheville-Charlotte, Greenville†
1085-2212 Carolina Construction News Covering South Carolina†
1085-2239 Florida Construction News Covering Orlando & Vicinity **1008**
1085-2255 Florida Construction News Covering Northwest Florida **1008**
1085-2271 Carolina Construction News Covering Columbia - Charleston†
1085-228X Hope Magazine†
1085-2301 World Wide Web Journal†
1085-2352 Journal of Prevention and Intervention in the Community **7417**
1085-2360 Clinical Excellence for Nurse Practitioners **5955**
1085-2395 E N T (Online) **2589**
1085-2417 The CyberSkeptic's Guide to Internet Research **2554**
1085-2425 Saint Louis - Warsaw Transatlantic Law Journal† **8986**
1085-2468 CompressorTech Two **5450**
1085-2484 Suitcase **5241**
1085-2492 Ohio Journal of the English Language Arts **5157**
1085-2522 Touro International Law Review†
1085-2549 Colorado Language Arts Society. Statement **3055**
1085-2565 German Genealogical Digest
1085-2573 Resorts & Great Hotels **8752**
1085-2581 *see* 0899-6180 **5518**
1085-259X Directory of Building Products & Hardlines Distributors **1985**
1085-2603 Minnesota Women's Press **8875**
1085-2700 South Pacific Handbook **8757**
1085-2727 Oyster Boy Review *changed to* Oyster Boy **5347**
1085-2751 GroundWork **3436**
1085-276X Hispanic Resource Directory **3537**
1085-2859 Blue Stocking
1085-2875 Avery Index to Architectural Periodicals **462**
1085-2972 Securities Handbook Series. Proxy Rules Handbook **1650**
1085-3103 Executive Report on Integrated Care and Capitation†
1085-3111 Employers' Managed Healthcare Benefits Advisor†
1085-3146 Printer's Northwest Trader **7326**
1085-3170 The Trustee **5051**
1085-3200 Do It With Lotus 1-2-3 for Windows†
1085-3235 Agility and Global Competition†
1085-3278 Land Degradation & Development **2712**
1085-3286 Journal of Asian and Asian American Theology **7654**
1085-3332 Nebraska Employment Law Letter **4740**
1085-3375 Abstract and Applied Analysis **5463**
1085-3391 Artnoir Showcase **474**
1085-3464 Journal of Financial Statement Analysis†
1085-3499 Point of Contact **5352**
1085-3502 Medicine on the Net **4114**
1085-3529 Intuition
1085-3545 Democracy & Education **2841**
1085-3596 The Foreign-Born Parent Network
1085-3634 Albany Law Environmental Outlook†
1085-3677 Muslim Sunrise **7715**
1085-3693 The M & A Tax Report **1933**
1085-3707 The Prospector **3780**
1085-410X Culinary Sleuth **4355**
1085-4169 New York International Chapter News **4936**
1085-4185 Pharmaceutical Industry Guide†
1085-4193 New York Litigator **4895**
1085-4274 Preston Pipe & Tube Report **6789**
1085-4363 Chicago Home & Garden **3972**
1085-4401 Community Policing Exchange **2647**
1085-4428 Purdue Retailer†
1085-4452 E B R I Notes **1676**
1085-4525 Plazm **512**
1085-4541 Early American Literature and Culture Through the American Renaissance **5287**
1085-455X Bishop Museum Technical Report **7841**
1085-4568 Frontiers (Carlisle) **3012**
1085-4576 Fourteen Hills **5297**
1085-4630 Journal of the Assembly for Expanded Perspectives on Learning **5136**
1085-4681 Judicial Review **4954**
1085-469X Comprehensive Accreditation Manual for Pathology and Clinical Laboratory Services *changed to* 1550-3569 **5599**
1085-4908 Education and Culture (Ashland) **2846**
1085-4924 Legal Eagle Eye Newsletter for the Nursing Profession **5969**
1085-4975 Center for Rural Affairs Newsletter **100**
1085-5009 Point of Purchase Magazine†
1085-5017 The Optimist (St. Louis) **2268**
1085-5041 Indian Artist†
1085-5068 Online Tactics†
1085-5092 B H A Bibliography of the History of Art **529**
1085-5149 Futon Life **4557**
1085-5181 Eli's Rehab Report **4093**
1085-5211 A I M **5204**
1085-522X Early Childhood Connections **2151**
1085-5254 Harlan Mountain Roots **3769**
1085-5262 Cold Facts **7053**
1085-5289 Relocation Journal & Real Estate News **7610**
1085-5300 Research in the Schools **2904**
1085-5351 Hard Row to Hoe **5303**
1085-5386 N O R M Report **2757**

ISSN

Link to your serials resources and content with ulrichsweb.com

1086-4903	Wireless Business & Technology†
1086-4946	Italian Politics **1130**
1086-4997	Journal of Asset Protection (New York)†
1086-508X	American Journal of Electroneurodiagnostic Technology **6121**
1086-5101	Pharmaceutical Management†
1086-5152	Junior Golf Magazine
1086-5195	I E E E Communications Theory Mini-Conference. Proceedings **2323**
1086-5217	The Bond Markets†
1086-5241	The Regional Alliance Construction News Weekly **1032**
1086-539X	Masterworks in the Western Tradition **5331**
1086-5462	Medicine and Health - Rhode Island **5674**
1086-5470	Edmund's New Cars **8578**
1086-5519	International Journal of Wilderness **2615**
1086-5543	Interior Decorators' Handbook **4543**
1086-5551	Not-For-Profit Financial Strategies†
1086-5586	Model Railroad Planning **4341**
1086-5624	Gerbil **4374**
1086-5632	A T V Magazine **8554**
1086-5675	T V International Daily (Print) **2393**
1086-5683	Environmental & Nutritional Interactions†
1086-5691	Internet Medicine *changed to* 1531-5681 **4092**
1086-5721	Matriarch's Way†
1086-5837	Rural Migration News **7292**
1086-5845	*see* 1086-5837 **7292**
1086-5853	Purchasing Today *changed to* 1538-733X **1821**
1086-5896	Research Nurse *changed to* 1528-0330 **5910**
1086-590X	Merchandising & Operating Results of Retail Stores†
1086-5985	Rockrgrl **6612**
1086-6051	Mommy and I Are One
1086-6078	Main Line Today **5076**
1086-6108	Construction News Weekly Covering Western Oklahoma **998**
1086-6116	F.W. Dodge Construction News Weekly Covering Eastern Oklahoma **1003**
1086-6124	Construction News Weekly, Covering Southern Mississippi **997**
1086-6132	Construction News Weekly, Covering Northern Mississippi **997**
1086-6140	Construction News Weekly, Covering the State of Mississippi **998**
1086-6159	F.W. Dodge Construction News Weekly Covering Houston **1003**
1086-6175	Construction News Weekly, Covering Shreveport & Vicinity **997**
1086-6183	F.W. Dodge Construction News Weekly, Covering Dallas & Vicinity **1003**
1086-6191	Construction News Weekly, Covering New Orleans & Vicinity **997**
1086-6221	Construction News Weekly, Covering the Rio Grande Valley **998**
1086-623X	F.W. Dodge Construction News Weekly Covering Greater Kansas City **1003**
1086-6248	Construction News Weekly, Covering Western Missouri **998**
1086-6280	International Business and Trade Directories **2006**
1086-6353	R S O Magazine **6684**
1086-6388	*see* 0011-3409 **715**
1086-6396	*see* 1079-1450 **3229**
1086-640X	*see* 0092-6361 **7417**
1086-6426	*see* 0163-2574 **2094**
1086-6450	Current Contents for Windows. Engineering, Computing & Technology *see* 1079-1450 **3229**
1086-6507	Progressive Dentistry†
1086-6523	Milton Review **5334**
1086-6531	SpaceViews†
1086-6558	Spaceviews Update†
1086-6582	Lindy's A C C Basketball†
1086-6647	InLine Hockey News†
1086-6655	Mathematical Physics Electronic Journal **5514**
1086-6671	Music K-8 **6591**
1086-671X	Mobilization **8121**
1086-6728	Mercator's World *changed to* Exploring Mercator's World
1086-6795	The Maturing Marketplace†
1086-6809	Studies in Theoretical and Applied Ethics **6955**
1086-6957	C P A Review. Business Law *changed to* 1547-8092 **1283**
1086-7015	Advanced Psychology Texts **7331**
1086-704X	Store Windows **35**
1086-7058	Artforum International **472**
1086-7074	Crain's Small Business (New York)†
1086-7139	Year Book of Nephrology, Hypertension, and Mineral Metabolism†
1086-7147	FranchiseWise
1086-7155	Rethinking Childhood **2167**
1086-7201	American Legacy **3518**
1086-721X	Cross Stitch and Needlework†
1086-7260	Higher Education Report Card (Year)†
1086-7325	Romance Writers' Report **5412**
1086-7341	Trade Fax† **8994**
1086-7376	Studies in Economics and Finance **1385**
1086-7449	The Lighthouse Electronic Magazine
1086-7570	Battelle Solutions Update **8416**
1086-7589	New Hampshire Employment Law Letter **4741**
1086-7597	Vermont Employment Law Letter **4808**
1086-7600	The Handmaiden **7704**
1086-7643	Physical Therapy in Perspective†
1086-7651	Journal of Graphics Tools **2487**
1086-7678	New Millennium Writings **5230**
1086-7686	*see* 0084-2729 **7576**
1086-7694	*see* 0006-3223 **6126**
1086-7716	Cellular Integration **2366**
1086-7732	Journal of Singing **6581**
1086-7821	Tele.com†
1086-7872	University of Pennsylvania. Journal of International Economic Law *changed to* 1938-0283 **4944**
1086-7899	Government Recreation & Fitness **4978**
1086-7929	Sursum Corda†
1086-7937	The DeWeese Report **7130**
1086-7945	C A A S Urban Policy Series **3524**
1086-8046	Northern Virginia Home - Garden News Magazine
1086-8062	Illinois Country Living **3978**
1086-8089	Society of Laparoendoscopic Surgeons. Journal **6259**
1086-8143	Moose Bound Press Newsletter
1086-8151	Island Business†
1086-8178	Inside Microsoft Office 95†
1086-8208	S R D S Consumer Magazine Advertising Source **39**
1086-8259	Journal of New Energy **3140**
1086-8283	Business Products Professional
1086-8291	Association Leadership **6277**
1086-8313	A M I News **5564**
1086-8380	Delaware Today **3974**
1086-847X	P W C Magazine†
1086-8488	Business Statistics of the United States **1076**
1086-8518	Mythos Journal **3620**
1086-8542	Electronic Commerce Report†
1086-8690	Firestation Management Advisor†
1086-8704	Textos **5387**
1086-8720	Shelby Exchange **3782**
1086-878X	Drug Topics Redbook *changed to* 1556-3391 **6877**
1086-881X	A S - 400 Systems Management†
1086-8828	K E T C Guide **3979**
1086-8852	California Education Funding Alert†
1086-8925	Heather Notes **3736**
1086-900X	Field Analytical Chemistry and Technology†
1086-9085	The Brightstar Bulletin
1086-9093	The Droplet Journal
1086-9123	Global MarketPlace
1086-914X	The I P Litigator **6751**
1086-9174	Eritrean Studies Review **3532**
1086-9263	U.S. Library of Congress. Classification Plus†
1086-9379	Meteoritics and Planetary Science **578**
1086-9417	RoadSmart†
1086-9468	Focus on Cumulation. Sports Science & Medicine *see* 1069-7004 **5746**
1086-9506	Adhesion Society. Annual Meeting. Proceedings **3235**
1086-9557	Daily Bread Magazine **8310**
1086-9581	I O M A's Pay for Performance Report *changed to* I O M A's Complete Guide to Best Practices in Performance Management **1865**
1086-9611	X C P: Cross-Cultural Poetics **5246**
1086-9638	Digital Systems Report *changed to* 0045-7841 **2412**
1086-9751	Virginia Libraries **5054**
1086-976X	Shepard's Labor Law Citations **1707**
1086-9808	Science & Spirit *changed to* 1943-1848 **7680**
1086-9824	Might†
1086-9832	Corporate Counsel's Annual Review **4863**
1086-9905	American Renaissance **3518**
1086-9956	Neuroscience-net **6169**
1087-0024	The Journal of Investigative Dermatology Symposium Proceedings **5879**
1087-0032	Inside Private School Management **3025**
1087-0059	The Learning Assistance Review **3070**
1087-0075	Spelunker Flophouse
1087-0083	Gardening How-To **3732**
1087-0091	Public Administration and Management **7461**
1087-0113	S M E Resource Guide **6478**
1087-0148	Valuation Insights and Perspectives **7614**
1087-0156	Nature Biotechnology **768**
1087-027X	Physician's Managed Care Report†
1087-0288	Hospice Management Advisor **4099**
1087-0296	Patient Education Management **5694**
1087-030X	Disease State Management†
1087-0350	Outpatient Benchmarks **5691**
1087-0377	Subacute Care Management†
1087-0385	Home Care Education Management†
1087-0393	Home Care Case Management†
1087-0407	Home Care Quality Management†
1087-0415	*see* 1081-0730 **5649**
1087-0458	Hart's Gas - L P G Markets†
1087-0466	Shakers World Magazine **3563**
1087-0474	CrossConnect **5280**
1087-0512	Shockwaves (Campbell)†
1087-0547	Journal of Attention Disorders **6149**
1087-0571	Journal of Biomolecular Screening **735**
1087-0601	Chain Store Age **1809**
1087-061X	Chef **3630**
1087-0644	Cost Management in Cardiac Care†
1087-0652	Hospital Case Management **4100**
1087-0695	Research Communications in Biological Psychology and Psychiatry *changed to* Research Communications in Biological Psychology, Psychiatry and Neurosciences **7403**
1087-0717	Directory of Consultants and Contractors Active in Latin America and the Caribbean†
1087-0725	Directory of Consultants and Contractors Active in the United States and Canada†
1087-075X	Directory of Consultants and Contractors Active in the Middle East and Africa†
1087-0768	Directory of Consultants and Contractors Active in the Far East†
1087-0792	Sleep Medicine Reviews **6186**
1087-0830	Umbr(a) **7413**
1087-0849	Transmission & Distribution World **3161**
1087-0857	Latin Trade **1575**
1087-0865	Complementary Medicine for the Physician†
1087-0873	Hazardous Waste Regulatory Analysis Service†
1087-089X	Air Pollution Regulatory Analysis Service†
1087-092X	Michigan Construction News Weekly, Covering the Southern Peninsula Beyond Detroit **1024**
1087-0946	Weekly Construction News, Covering Youngstown & Vicinity **1043**
1087-0954	Weekly Construction News, Covering Toledo & Vicinity **1043**
1087-0970	F.W. Dodge Weekly Construction News, Covering Columbus & Vicinity **1005**
1087-0989	F.W. Dodge Weekly Construction News, Covering Dayton & Vicinity **1005**
1087-0997	F.W. Dodge Weekly Construction News, Covering Cincinnati & Vicinity **1005**
1087-1004	Weekly Construction News, Covering Western Kentucky **1043**
1087-1012	F.W. Dodge Weekly Construction News, Covering Eastern Kentucky **1005**
1087-1020	F.W. Dodge Weekly Construction News, Covering Lexington & Vicinity **1005**
1087-108X	C U E S - For Your Information **1323**
1087-1101	Research Communications in Pharmacology and Toxicology **6878**
1087-111X	Research Communications in Biochemistry and Cell & Molecular Biology **744**
1087-1128	Missouri Realtor **7600**
1087-1209	Human Dimensions of Wildlife **3438**
1087-1268	Shepard's Intellectual Property Law Citations **4783**
1087-1276	Game Bird and Conservationists Gazette **287**
1087-1306	Journal of Sudden Infant Death Syndrome and Infant Mortality†
1087-1357	Journal of Manufacturing Science and Engineering **3385**
1087-139X	Mealey's Emerging Insurance Disputes **4514**
1087-1403	Technical Literature Abstracts: Petroleum Refining and Petrochemicals (Print)†
1087-1411	Technical Literature Abstracts: Health and Environment (Print)†
1087-142X	Technical Literature Abstracts: Transportation and Storage (Print)†
1087-1438	Technical Literature Abstracts: Petroleum Substitutes (Print)†
1087-1446	Technical Literature Abstracts: Catalysts - Zeolites (Print)†
1087-1454	Technical Literature Abstracts: Fuel Reformulation **2096**
1087-1462	Technical Literature Abstracts: Tribology **2096**
1087-1470	Technical Literature Abstracts: Oilfield Chemicals (Print)†
1087-1500	Blue Violin **5418**
1087-1527	String Figure Magazine **8210**
1087-1578	Quest (Tucson) **6180**
1087-1586	Healing Ministry **7646**
1087-1624	Journal for Christian Theological Research **7653**
1087-1640	Motor Control **6113**
1087-1659	Sport History Review **8204**
1087-1667	Today's Surgical Nurse†
1087-1756	Down Syndrome Quarterly **6137**
1087-1764	The World Almanac for Kids **2222**
1087-1837	Graphic Arts Blue Book. Texas - Central Edition **7322**
1087-1845	Fungal Genetics and Biology **790**
1087-1861	Path-Cyclopedia†
1087-1896	Delaware Manufacturers Register **1983**
1087-1950	Orchids **3746**
1087-1985	Chiropractic Economics **5803**
1087-2000	Coach and Athletic Director **8166**
1087-2019	Life Link†
1087-2027	Lost Worlds **5444**
1087-2043	Lakewood Report on Technology for Learning Newsletter†
1087-2094	Single File Magazine
1087-2108	Dermatology Online Journal **5875**
1087-2124	Decorative Home†
1087-2132	Tinfish **5436**
1087-2140	Megawatt Markets **3160**
1087-2159	Public Interest Law Reporter **4763**
1087-2175	Manifest Reader†
1087-2183	Direction (Allendale) **24**
1087-2191	International Computer Performance and Dependability Symposium **2591**
1087-2302	*see* 1066-3878 **8415**
1087-2310	Huna Work **6924**
1087-2353	Headway†
1087-2418	Current Opinion in Organ Transplantation **5602**
1087-2434	Clinical Asthma Reviews†
1087-2469	Monitors†
1087-2531	Angiology (Spanish Edition) *see* 0003-3197 **5777**
1087-2558	Securities Pro Newsletter **3563**
1087-2604	The Catholic Moment **7789**
1087-2620	*see* 1528-7394 **3499**
1087-2647	Casino Player **8165**
1087-268X	L B J Journal of Public Affairs **7982**
1087-2698	SkyPower
1087-2701	Airborne Log†
1087-2728	Baltimore County Muster†
1087-2744	Progression **6608**
1087-2760	Northwest Fishing Holes **8325**
1087-2809	Administrative Eyecare **6037**
1087-2817	In-Plant Graphics **7323**
1087-2825	Portable Buyer's Guide
1087-2833	CommonQuest†
1087-2906	Antisense and Nucleic Acid Drug Development *changed to* 1545-4576 **877**
1087-2914	AIDS Patient Care and S T Ds **5809**
1087-2922	Tax Management Financial Products Report† **8992**
1087-2949	S P A N Connection **7572**
1087-2957	Progress in Cell Cycle Research **836**
1087-2965	Explore the Net with Internet Explorer - M S N†
1087-2981	Medical Education Online **5668**
1087-299X	Sunwear **6052**
1087-3007	John Lyons' Perfect Horse **8294**
1087-3104	Traumatic Stress Points Newsletter **6188**
1087-3112	Acquisition Review Quarterly *changed to* 1553-6408 **6418**
1087-3163	On-Campus Hospitality **2295**
1087-3201	Journal of Gender, Culture, and Health†
1087-3244	American Journal of Health Behavior **6981**
1087-3252	Bank Card Industry Survey Report *changed to* 1555-9416 **1304**
1087-3260	Professional Car Washing & Detailing **8599**
1087-3295	Advances in Molecular Structure Research†
1087-3309	Science & Medicine **5911**
1087-3325	Standard & Poor's Security Dealers of North America **1653**
1087-335X	Smoky Mountain Historical Society Journal and News Letter **3783**
1087-3384	W E F Highlights **3474**
1087-3414	California School Psychologist **7343**
1087-3430	Electronic Journal of Science Education **2852**

9516 1087-3481 ULRICH'S PERIODICALS

1087-3481 Shepard's Atlantic Reporter Case Names Citator†
1087-349X Shepard's Employment Law Citations **1707**
1087-3503 Image (Seattle) **7649**
1087-3562 Earth Interactions **2706**
1087-3570 Millenium Medicine†
1087-3678 Healthplan *changed to* 1551-8442 **4490**
1087-3708 Sweet Annie & Sweet Pea Review **5436**
1087-3732 Journal of Aging & Identity†
1087-3821 Sports Traveler
1087-3864 Marine News **8651**
1087-3872 A P S A Survey of Political Science Departments **7101**
1087-3899 Black Parenting Today
1087-3945 The Value Line Options Survey **1658**
1087-3953 Five Thousand Personalities of the World† **8956**
1087-3961 Two Thousand Notable American Women **646**
1087-397X International Book of Honor† **8965**
1087-3988 International Directory of Distinguished Leadership† **8965**
1087-3996 Five Hundred Leaders of Influence† **8956**
1087-4038 The Catholic Faith† **8940**
1087-4046 Embroidery Business News†
1087-4054 Inside Self-Storage **1962**
1087-4089 International Symposium on Parallel Architectures, Algorithms, and Networks **2522**
1087-4097 Workshop on Parallel and Distributed Simulation. Proceedings **2468**
1087-4151 Countertrade & Offset **1619**
1087-4194 Mobile Communications Report†
1087-4208 Journal of Neurotherapy **6155**
1087-4224 New Hampshire Golf **8240**
1087-4275 International Monetary Fund. Selected Decisions and Selected Documents of the International Monetary Fund **1358**
1087-433X Washington Telecom Newswire **3992**
1087-4399 WorldLinks U S A *changed to* 1533-1504 **4337**
1087-4402 The Pyrotechnic Literature Series **3254**
1087-4410 The American Forecaster Newsletter **1436**
1087-450X American Butterflies **838**
1087-4542 New Netherland Connections **3776**
1087-4550 Genealogical Society of Vermont. Newsletter **3768**
1087-4593 Dark Night: Field Notes **7205**
1087-4615 Crain's Small Business†
1087-4658 Virtual City
1087-4704 Business Examiner **1072**
1087-4720 Earth Science Software Directory **6488**
1087-4755 Corporate University Review†
1087-4763 Stanford Report (Print) *changed to* Stanford Report (Online) **2302**
1087-4798 Better Communication†
1087-481X Michigan ComputerUser Magazine†
1087-4852 I E E E International Workshop on Memory Technology, Design and Testing **2540**
1087-4879 Farandula Internacional **6566**
1087-4895 Carisma y Vida Cristiana **7630**
1087-4925 Chicago Books in Review **7558**
1087-4933 Systems & Network Management Report *changed to* Systems & Network Management Journal **2504**
1087-495X Essential Psychopharmacology **6139**
1087-4976 Evermore **5293**
1087-4992 Multimedia Telecommunication News†
1087-500X World Stock Exchange Fact Book **1660**
1087-5026 Special Places **2628**
1087-5034 Ed Hitzel's Restaurant Newsletter **4385**
1087-5050 Natural Living Today **5078**
1087-5093 Journal of East Asian Libraries **5020**
1087-5107 Korean Philately **6896**
1087-5174 Warren's Telecom Regulation Monitor†
1087-5220 Property Insurance Report **4519**
1087-5263 Mass. Transit News†
1087-5298 Heroes from Hackland **5410**
1087-5301 Internet Reference Services Quarterly **5019**
1087-5433 Metis (San Francisco) **8874**
1087-5441 Cosmetic - Personal Care Packaging **593**
1087-5549 Journal of Poverty **8050**
1087-5557 Interdisciplinary Journal for Germanic Linguistics and Semiotic Analysis **5128**
1087-5565 Journal for the Critical Study of Religion *changed to* Journal for the Scientific Examination of Religion **7653**
1087-5581 Biblio†
1087-5638 San Francisco Downtown **3987**
1087-5654 Space, Energy and Transportation
1087-5662 BrewPub†
1087-5670 Journal of Neurovascular Disease†
1087-5743 M S W Solutions **3509**
1087-6103 Fluid Transients†
1087-6111 Mecklermedia's Official Internet Yellow Pages†
1087-6146 Algorithms for Synthetic Aperture Radar Imagery **7073**
1087-6154 Jack Benny Times **2267**
1087-6197 California Family Law First Alert **4907**
1087-6200 Court Companion (Year) **4908**
1087-6278 Next Step **1153**
1087-6286 The Code Authority **3184**
1087-6294 The MOOsletter **4342**
1087-6316 The SandMUtopian Guardian **4982**
1087-6324 Video Eyeball Magazine
1087-6359 Index Magazine **3978**
1087-6367 Software & CD-ROM Reviews on File†
1087-6391 On the Mark **1782**
1087-643X Berkshire News, Chester White Journal, Poland China Advantage, Spotted News **280**
1087-6456 Telicom **6956**
1087-6464 Canadian Farmers' Almanac **3119**
1087-6502 Chicago District Golfer **8225**
1087-6510 Macomb Dental Society. Journal **5855**
1087-6537 *see* 0197-2243 **2545**
1087-6545 *see* 0883-9514 **2445**
1087-6553 *see* 0196-9722 **2526**
1087-6596 Glass Physics and Chemistry **2042**
1087-6626 Ohio Ecological Food and Farm Association News **244**
1087-6677 Employment & Labor Lawcast **4664**
1087-6685 Intellectual Property Lawcast **4694**
1087-6693 New Jersey Lawcast **4743**
1087-6707 Corporate Counsel Lawcast **4651**
1087-6715 N E M L A Italian Studies **5337**
1087-674X Mystery Scene **5414**
1087-6758 History Computer Review†
1087-6766 Noticias para los Californianos **3555**
1087-6839 What's Working in Vehicle Management†
1087-6847 Time Machine†
1087-6871 International Index to Music Periodicals **6631**
1087-688X Gulf of Mexico Science **2805**
1087-6944 Java Developer's Journal **2507**
1087-6952 Middle School Companion
1087-6995 Journal of Technology Law & Policy **6753**
1087-7045 Pacific Northwest Golfer **8242**
1087-7088 Q B R: The Black Book Review
1087-7096 Midwest Dairybusiness **267**
1087-7118 Compensation & Benefits Software Census **1415**
1087-7126 Radio and Communications Technology†
1087-7142 The Journal of Film Music **6580**
1087-7185 B N A's Health Law & Business Series **4088**
1087-7207 Kansas Legislative Handbook **7495**
1087-7215 American Institute of Aeronautics and Astronautics. Meeting Papers on Disc **46**
1087-7223 Internet Lawyer **2561**
1087-7231 I O M A's Medical Laboratory Management Report†
1087-724X Public Works Management & Policy **7463**
1087-7304 Bankcheck†
1087-7347 E D Legal Letter **4662**
1087-7398 Junior Storyteller **2196**
1087-7436 Lies†
1087-7444 Federal Tort Claims Act News†
1087-7509 The Licking River Review **5322**
1087-7525 Connecticut Wildlife **2607**
1087-755X Story Rhyme Newsletter for Schools **2215**
1087-7614 Clay Times **532**
1087-7649 Tightwad Living†
1087-7703 Internet Law Researcher **2561**
1087-7770 Gloria Pitzer's Secret Recipes Newsletter†
1087-7835 Health Care Fraud **7521**
1087-7843 The Electronic Marketplace (Year) **2556**
1087-7983 The Physician Recruiter **6702**
1087-8025 Live Turkeys†
1087-8114 Franklin Flyer **4293**
1087-8122 Camerawork **6965**
1087-8149 Leader to Leader **1772**
1087-8157 Jinhua Yuekan **3543**
1087-8181 Convivium **4354**
1087-8238 Aftermarket Today†
1087-8262 Beethoven Journal **6548**
1087-8270 I E E E Virtual Reality Annual International Symposium **2465**
1087-8343 North Dakota Manufacturers Register **2021**
1087-8378 The Quality Assurance Journal **5701**
1087-8440 U S T A Top Spin†
1087-8459 Studies in Religion, Politics, and Public Life **7685**
1087-8467 Newcomer's Handbook for Minneapolis and Saint Paul *changed to* 1930-6296 **7602**
1087-8475 Receptors and Signal Transduction†
1087-8483 The Bitter Oleander **5417**
1087-8491 Central Atlantic Environmental Directory **2606**
1087-853X Keller's Compliance Focus **6680**
1087-8564 G L S G American Musicological Society. Newsletter *changed to* 1556-0406 **4370**
1087-8572 Strategy & Leadership **1795**
1087-8599 Health Governance Report **4096**
1087-8629 Union Membership and Earnings Data Book **4604**
1087-867X Curve **4372**
1087-8718 The Nilson Report **1372**
1087-8734 The Equine Trade Journal **8290**
1087-8785 Southcon Conference Record **3395**
1087-8807 Sonoma County Physician **5716**
1087-8823 Am Law Tech† **8929**
1087-8874 Hart's Gulf States Petroleum Directory†
1087-8955 Entrepreneurial Executive **1741**
1087-8963 Cooking on the Edge†
1087-8971 Entertainment Magazine On-line **6565**
1087-8998 Local Competition Report† **8971**
1087-903X The Perl Journal (Print Edition) *changed to* 1545-7567
1087-9048 Texas Petroleum and C-Store Journal **6794**
1087-9064 Global Studies: Russia, the Eurasian Republics, and Central - Eastern Europe **7238**
1087-9110 Forest Landowner **3689**
1087-9153 The Gospel Voice **6570**
1087-917X Government Video **2401**
1087-9226 Inside Netscape Navigator†
1087-9269 American Writers Review **4571**
1087-9293 New Scholars, New Visions in Canadian Studies **7158**
1087-9366 Silver Sentinel
1087-9382 Visions (Tallahassee) **2925**
1087-9404 The Maccabean **7251**
1087-9412 Construction Data & News Covering Oregon†
1087-9447 Medical Electronics Manufacturing **3108**
1087-9471 Franchise Times (New York)†
1087-9501 Le Cygne **5282**
1087-951X Earthsongs†
1087-9528 Conde Nast House & Garden *changed to* 1522-0273
1087-9560 Engineering I D E A S†
1087-9595 Academy of Entrepreneurship Journal **1722**
1087-9617 Obituaries in the Performing Arts **8475**
1087-9641 Research Business Report **1840**
1087-965X Technotrends Newsletter **8442**
1087-9749 Climate *changed to* N W Florida's Business Climate **1151**
1087-979X 50 Plus Senior News **4058**
1087-9803 S & D Reflector **3781**
1087-982X I F T Insight **2865**
1087-9862 Interlocking Concrete Pavement Magazine **1015**
1087-9870 Intersociety Conference on Thermal Phenomena in Electronic Systems. Proceedings **2466**
1087-9889 Common Ground (Washington, DC) **388**
1087-9900 Development Anthropologist†
1087-9935 Case Reports of the Mormon Alliance **7733**
1087-996X Wealth Building†
1087-9978 The American Gardener **3722**
1088-0038 Journal of Small Exotic Animal Medicine†
1088-0054 Devo'Zine **7754**
1088-0070 Yahoo! Internet Life†
1088-016X Advance (San Francisco)
1088-0178 *see* 1548-520X **4704**
1088-0194 Amernick Market Report **1610**
1088-0208 UnDiscovered Stocks **1657**
1088-033X Society of Composers Newsletter **6617**
1088-0348 American Physical Society. Membership Directory **7005**
1088-0364 Power Tool (Year) **5458**
1088-0402 American Zoo and Aquarium Association. Regional Conference Proceedings **932**
1088-0429 Brassey's Mershon American Defense Annual†
1088-0585 Score (Moscow) **5434**
1088-0593 Cyberspace Lawyer **2554**
1088-0666 Internet InfoScavenger
1088-0712 Asthma Magazine†
1088-0755 Journal of Credibility Assessment and Witness Psychology **7372**
1088-0763 Psychoanalysis, Culture & Society **7395**
1088-0860 The American Sentinel
1088-0909 Glow Magazine†
1088-0941 Jamaica Handbook *changed to* Moon Handbooks: Jamaica **8738**
1088-0992 Visual Developer Magazine†
1088-1018 Mineral Resources Data System **6470**
1088-1034 Little Green Men†
1088-1093 *see* 1538-8999 **5056**
1088-1166 L G N Y **4376**
1088-128X Failure & Lessons Learned in Information Technology Management†
1088-1425 F.W. Dodge Weekly Construction News, Covering Cleveland, Akron, Canton **1005**
1088-1441 New Life **6646**
1088-1468 T R C Spectral Data - 1 H Nuclear Magnetic Resonance **2106**
1088-1476 T R C Spectral Data - Mass **2106**
1088-1484 T R C Spectral Data - Raman **2106**
1088-1492 T R C Spectral Data - Ultraviolet **2106**
1088-1506 T R C Spectral Data - 13 C Nuclear Magnetic Resonance **2106**
1088-1514 Live!†
1088-1557 V-Twin **8270**
1088-1611 Super L C C S **5049**
1088-1697 Journal of Solid Waste Technology and Management **3508**
1088-1727 Dealer's Edge **8577**
1088-1735 Warranty Dollars & Sense for GM Dealers **8611**
1088-1743 Warranty Dollars & Sense for Ford Dealers **8611**
1088-1751 Miniatura†
1088-176X 350 F†
1088-1778 Studio†
1088-1824 The Vision Maker **2398**
1088-1840 Southern Voice **4379**
1088-1913 Environmental Quality Management **3428**
1088-1980 Journal of Industrial Ecology **3447**
1088-2081 I G C C Policy Papers†
1088-2103 A T C C Connection†
1088-2111 The Monitor **6862**
1088-2340 Title and Registration Text Book **8607**
1088-2359 What's Working for American Companies in International Sales & Marketing†
1088-2448 In the Flesh†
1088-2456 Tattoos For Women **521**
1088-2642 Medicaid Managed Care Currents **4514**
1088-2677 Mailing Systems Technology **2354**
1088-274X 78†
1088-2758 Evo†
1088-2766 10x†
1088-2782 Esalen Catalog **7354**
1088-2839 Monitor (St. Paul) **2292**
1088-2847 Standard & Poor's Industry Reports† **8990**
1088-2898 State Income Tax Alert (Atlanta) **1944**
1088-291X Property Tax Alert **1940**
1088-2936 Better Homes and Gardens Holiday Cooking **3671**
1088-2952 Remodeling Ideas for Your Home *changed to* 1935-0678 **455**
1088-2979 Better Homes and Gardens Kitchen Planning Guide **4533**
1088-2995 Better Homes and Gardens Holiday Celebrations **4353**
1088-3002 Better Homes and Gardens Holiday Appetizers **4353**
1088-3029 Catfish Guide **8308**
1088-3118 Journal of Dental Technology **5851**
1088-3142 *see* 0036-0775 **7264**
1088-3150 The Almanac of American Employers **1662**
1088-3177 Garden Shed **3731**
1088-3207 Drag Racing Monthly†
1088-3223 What's Working in Human Resources **1877**
1088-324X Expressive Spirals†
1088-3339 Shopping Center Business **7612**
1088-3347 Graywolf Forum
1088-3371 Disease Management and Clinical Outcomes†
1088-3452 Hispanic Engineer & Information Technology **3195**
1088-3460 Pictorial Directory of Spokane Physicians **5696**
1088-3487 Journal of Therapeutic Horticulture **3740**
1088-3495 Solo *changed to* 1931-3713 **5435**
1088-3517 I O M A's Mail Center Management Report†
1088-3541 Dodge Custom Newsletter Covering Wal Mart **1004**
1088-355X Dodge Daily Bulletin. Northwest and West Texas†
1088-3576 Focus on Autism and Other Developmental Disabilities **6141**
1088-3622 Interweave Knits **6639**
1088-3665 Clackamas Literary Review **5211**
1088-3673 Dodge Daily Bulletin. Central Pennsylvania†
1088-369X Dodge Daily Bulletin. Baltimore†
1088-3711 F.W. Dodge Construction News Weekly Covering Long Island
1088-3886 The Dental Assistant **5839**
1088-3894 America's Top Jobs for People Without College Degrees *changed to* 1931-017X **6692**

1088-3924 America's Top Jobs for College Graduates *changed to* America's Top 101 Jobs for College Graduates **6692**
1088-3932 Dodge Daily Bulletin. Five Boros†
1088-3940 Dodge Daily Bulletin. Baltimore - Delaware†
1088-3959 Dodge Daily Bulletin. Connecticut†
1088-3967 Dodge Daily Bulletin. Eastern Massachusetts†
1088-3975 Dodge Daily Bulletin. Long Island†
1088-3983 Dodge Daily Bulletin. Maine - New Hampshire - Vermont†
1088-3991 Dodge Daily Bulletin. Westchester†
1088-4009 Dodge Daily Bulletin. Northern New Jersey†
1088-4017 Dodge Daily Bulletin. Rhode Island†
1088-4025 Dodge Daily Bulletin. Western Massachusetts†
1088-4033 Dodge Daily Bulletin. Southern New Jersey and Philadelphia Housing†
1088-4041 Dodge Daily Bulletin. Manhattan†
1088-405X Dodge Daily Bulletin. Nassau - Suffolk†
1088-4068 Dodge Daily Bulletin. Four Boros†
1088-4076 Dodge Daily Bulletin. Philadelphia Housing†
1088-4084 Dodge Daily Bulletin. Washington and Vicinity†
1088-4106 Sport Pilot & Ultralights†
1088-4114 Rod Action†
1088-4122 The Bagpipe **280**
1088-4157 Pacific Tourism Review *changed to* 1544-2721 **8764**
1088-4165 Representation Theory **5528**
1088-4173 Conformal Geometry and Dynamics **5481**
1088-4246 Journal of Porphyrins and Phthalocyanines **2068**
1088-4254 International Journal of Land Management†
1088-4300 Agnieszka's Dowry **5416**
1088-4319 Megawatt Daily **3160**
1088-4335 Synthesis C E **7776**
1088-4343 Getting Results ... for the Hands-On Manager†
1088-4378 Viewpoint *changed to* 1933-2513 **3162**
1088-4416 The Northern Light **2268**
1088-4440 Bond Fund Report†
1088-4491 Crime in America's Top-Rated Cities (Years)† **8947**
1088-4548 Checklists and Illustrative Financial Statements for Defined Benefit Pension Plans **1285**
1088-4564 Theatre World **8483**
1088-4572 Shepard's Northwestern Reporter Case Names Citator **4963**
1088-4580 Seed and Crops Digest†
1088-4602 Journal of Addictions Nursing **5964**
1088-467X Intelligent Data Analysis **2450**
1088-484X Journal of Precision Teaching and Celeration **2877**
1088-4874 The Edge City Review **5288**
1088-4955 Symposium on the Frontiers of Massively Parallel Processing. Proceedings **2599**
1088-4963 *see* 0048-3915 **7165**
1088-4971 No Depression†
1088-498X Contemporary Argumentation and Debate **2839**
1088-5161 Hoover Digest **7141**
1088-5188 Leadership Journal†
1088-520X The Physician's Personal Advisory **4109**
1088-5218 The Physician's Advisory **4109**
1088-5331 Pasta Press†
1088-5382 Stygian Articles†
1088-5412 Allergy and Asthma Proceedings **5753**
1088-5447 Drug Development Pipeline **6834**
1088-5455 *see* 0894-9301 **1414**
1088-5471 Lippincott's Primary Care Practice†
1088-548X Mac Addict *changed to* 1935-4010 **2576**
1088-5501 Best American Gay Fiction **4371**
1088-5625 George Mason Law Review **4679**
1088-5676 Advance for Medical Laboratory Professionals **5902**
1088-5765 Walworth County Genealogical Society. Newsletter **3787**
1088-5803 Speech Technology (Lexington) **2339**
1088-5811 Property Digest and Economic Development Magazine **7605**
1088-5870 PsyArt **7394**
1088-5889 Aging America **4039**
1088-5900 Facilities Engineering Journal **3192**
1088-5935 H R Advisor: Legal & Practical Guidance **1862**
1088-5943 Iowa Heritage Illustrated **4298**
1088-5951 Cityscape (Des Moines) **4407**
1088-5994 U.S. Master Employee Benefits Guide **1712**
1088-6141 American Foreign Policy and Treaty Index†
1088-6168 Hardware Age Home Improvement Market†
1088-6176 Catholic Spirit (Wheeling) **7790**
1088-6192 Crank!†
1088-6222 Tennessee Medicine **5721**
1088-6273 Hydroworld Alert **3163**
1088-6281 Binocular Vision & Strabismus Quarterly **6039**
1088-6362 International Journal of Cognitive Ergonomics†
1088-6397 Mailbox Bookbag **3071**
1088-6419 The Practical Nomad **8748**
1088-6451 Mountain Living **4981**
1088-6508 Chicagoland Gardening **3726**
1088-6672 Marathon & Beyond **8186**
1088-6699 Respiratory Reviews†
1088-6710 International Journal of Psychopathology, Psychopharmacology, and Psychotherapy **7365**
1088-6737 Intelligent Gamer†
1088-677X Container Recycling Report†
1088-6796 Missouri Library World†
1088-680X Newsline (Jefferson City) **5036**
1088-6826 *see* 0002-9939 **5469**
1088-6834 *see* 0894-0347 **5469**
1088-6842 *see* 0025-5718 **5516**
1088-6850 *see* 0002-9947 **5469**
1088-6869 Ward's Engine and Vehicle Technology Update **8611**
1088-6877 Ward's Automotive International. Focus on China†
1088-6923 Affirmation & Critique **7620**
1088-6931 Global Business & Finance Review **1567**
1088-7008 Hem Aware **5937**
1088-7067 D V D Report *changed to* Digital Content Delivery Report
1088-7091 Cartoonist and Comic Artist Magazine **481**
1088-7105 Chelonian Research Monographs **938**
1088-713X Nerve Cowboy **5339**
1088-7156 The Psychologist-Manager Journal **7398**
1088-7180 Cardiovascular Pathobiology†
1088-7237 *see* 1088-680X **5036**
1088-7245 Carolina Fairways†
1088-7253 A F E Newsline **3179**
1088-727X Lottery & Casino News
1088-730X Bank Investment Marketing *changed to* 1543-2068 **1611**
1088-7326 International Policy Review **7244**
1088-7350 A U A News **6264**
1088-7385 U S African Voice **3569**
1088-7393 A M A Alliance Today *changed to* Connection (Chicago) **5600**
1088-7423 Current Research in Social Psychology **7350**
1088-7458 Midwesterner†
1088-7482 So Young! **6997**
1088-7539 Source Book on Collective Bargaining†
1088-7563 Sex Crimes Digest†
1088-7571 Philadelphia Magazine's Elegant Wedding **5561**
1088-7601 New Mexico Manufacturers Register **2020**
1088-761X Rhode Island Manufacturer's Register **2026**
1088-7628 South Dakota Manufacturers Register **2028**
1088-7679 Homicide Studies **2654**
1088-7733 The Farmer's Exchange **111**
1088-7776 Machete **5329**
1088-7806 Magnet **6586**
1088-7857 Business Cycle Indicators **1444**
1088-7881 Evolutionary Programming
1088-7911 Complexity and Chaos in Nursing **5956**
1088-7954 Pedal Steel Newsletter **6604**
1088-7989 T R C Spectral Data - Infrared **2106**
1088-8004 National Singles Register†
1088-8063 Springhouse Nurse's Drug Guide *changed to* 1941-739X **6864**
1088-8071 Vacation Ownership World **7614**
1088-8128 International Society of Air Safety Investigators. Forum **61**
1088-8136 Estafeta **7232**
1088-8152 The Shape of Enrichment **321**
1088-8179 Scottsdale Scene Magazine†
1088-8195 A Moving Journal **5336**
1088-8217 Speak†
1088-8276 Delmar's Drug Guide for Nurses†
1088-8349 Communities Directory **5068**
1088-8357 *see* 0038-1527 **7682**
1088-8373 Standard & Poor's 500 Indexes of the Securities Markets - Flash Report **1652**
1088-8438 Scientific Studies of Reading **2910**
1088-8497 Global Insecticide Directory **233**
1088-8500 Five Points **5296**
1088-8535 *see* 0003-6900 **3228**
1088-8586 *see* 0001-2505 **4116**
1088-8594 Complete Book of Colleges **2974**
1088-8683 Personality and Social Psychology Review **7390**
1088-8691 Applied Developmental Science **7335**
1088-8705 Journal of Applied Animal Welfare Science **320**
1088-8713 Family Futures†
1088-8802 Animal Law **317**
1088-8845 Rural Cooperatives **153**
1088-890X Standard & Poor's Trendline Current Market Perspectives **1653**
1088-8934 Global Mobile **2322**
1088-8969 Pension & Benefits Week **1702**
1088-8977 Red Book Credit Services **3661**
1088-9000 Defense Communities **6418**
1088-9027 Spa Finder *changed to* 1553-0698 **6992**
1088-9051 Genome Research **870**
1088-906X Renaissance Magazine **4257**
1088-9108 University of Illinois at Chicago. College of Dentistry. Alumni Report **2306**
1088-9159 Miller G A A S Guide **1296**
1088-9191 Spirit and Life **7818**
1088-9280 Shepard's Environmental Law Citations (Federal) **4961**
1088-9299 Bipolar - B I C M O S Circuits and Technology Meeting. Proceedings **3090**
1088-937X Polar Geography **4024**
1088-9434 Peterson's Graduate Programs in the Biological Sciences **2961**
1088-9442 Peterson's Graduate and Professional Programs: Business, Education, Health, Information Studies, Law, and Social Work **2961**
1088-9469 Drugs in Litigation: Damage Awards Involving Prescription and Nonprescription Drugs **6836**
1088-9477 *see* 0002-9920 **5469**
1088-9485 *see* 0273-0979 **5469**
1088-9523 Sales and Marketing Jobs Report **6703**
1088-9531 Finance and Accounting Jobs Report **6697**
1088-9590 Funny Business **1747**
1088-9612 Trialogue (Contoocook) **7575**
1088-9752 The New York Environmental Lawyer **3456**
1088-9779 Martindale-Hubbell International Law Digest **4728**
1088-985X WebINK†
1088-9868 Bioremediation Journal **3483**
1088-9922 Inside Employee Rights Litigation† **8964**
1088-9981 E M **3505**
1089-0017 The Good Society **7138**
1089-0025 International Journal of Applied Science & Computations **7867**
1089-0076 Long Riders **8260**
1089-019X Computing News & Review **2529**
1089-0343 A B C News Transcripts **4570**
1089-0408 Asia Pacific Economic Review
1089-0432 Pillsbury Classic Cookbooks **4365**
1089-0475 The Foundation Piecer *changed to* 1543-1606 **6641**
1089-0599 Thomson National Directory of Mortgage Brokers†
1089-0645 Studies in Biblical Literature (New York) **7685**
1089-0661 C P A Review. Tax-Man-Gov *changed to* 1547-8092 **1283**
1089-0785 I E E E - E M C Society Newsletter **3311**
1089-0793 OffLead **6812**
1089-084X *see* 0164-2006 **3312**
1089-0882 Mealey's Emerging Toxic Torts **3509**
1089-0955 Bass West
1089-0971 Bacon's International Media Directory†
1089-098X Bacon's Media Calendar Directory **1974**
1089-1013 Peterson's Grants for Graduate & Postdoctoral Study (Year)†
1089-1080 The Arbitrageur **1308**
1089-1102 Harvard Men's Health Watch **6284**
1089-1145 The Clinical Letter for Nurse Practitioners†
1089-1196 Princeton Arts Review **5432**
1089-1277 Whiskey Island Magazine **5398**
1089-1307 Epiphany International **7640**
1089-1374 Hemp Times
1089-1404 The Physician Medical Group Acquisition Report† **8981**
1089-1412 The Senior Care Acquisition Report **1172**
1089-1447 The Jewish Star **3543**
1089-148X Health and Stress **5624**
1089-1617 Environmental Management Today†
1089-1668 A S A Newsletter **463**
1089-1722 Deaf - Hard of Hearing Yellow Book **4073**
1089-1749 Hoover's Directory of Human Resources Executives†
1089-1765 Oil Market Intelligence **6801**
1089-182X Griffith's 5 Minute Clinical Consult *changed to* The 5-Minute Clinical Consult **5739**
1089-1862 Journal Francais *changed to* 0747-2757 **3534**
1089-1870 U S A Table Tennis Magazine **8250**
1089-1900 Quality Customer Service†
1089-1919 Cost Control Strategies for Health Care Providers†
1089-1927 Technology News and Trends†
1089-201X Comparative Studies of South Asia, Africa and the Middle East **4181**
1089-2028 U A News†
1089-2044 Card Player **8164**
1089-2141 Guidelines Letter **444**
1089-2176 TechKnow Times **2567**
1089-2230 Quick & Healthy†
1089-232X Environmental Technology† **8954**
1089-2362 New Product News (New York)
1089-2397 Mealey's International Arbitration Report **4935**
1089-2435 All About Women Consumers **1804**
1089-246X Peterson's Learning Adventures Around the World†
1089-2516 Techniques in Vascular and Interventional Radiology **6209**
1089-2524 New Medicine **5685**
1089-2532 Seminars in Cardiothoracic and Vascular Anesthesia **5799**
1089-2540 (Year) Interactive Sourcebook **2498**
1089-2559 Behavioral Health Treatment†
1089-2575 Corrections Journal **2647**
1089-2591 Journal of Lower Genital Tract Disease (Print) **5995**
1089-2605 U C L A Journal of International Law and Foreign Affairs **4943**
1089-2613 New Hampshire Government Register **7455**
1089-2664 The Complete Gift Basket Industry Reference Directory **1958**
1089-2680 Review of General Psychology **7403**
1089-2699 Group Dynamics **7359**
1089-2745 Cyberhound's Guide to People on the Internet†
1089-2753 Cyberhound's Guide to Companies on the Internet†
1089-2788 Videre†
1089-2869 10 Things Jesus Wants You to Know†
1089-2877 Teaching in the Community Colleges Journal
1089-2907 Harvard BlackLetter Law Journal **4832**
1089-2931 Cyberhound's Guide to Internet Discussion Groups†
1089-2990 Iniciativas en Politicas sobre la Salud Reproductiva *see* 1086-4350 **8846**
1089-3032 Electronic Journal of Geotechnical Engineering **3266**
1089-3059 Electronic Commerce Advisor
1089-3075 Parents Make the Difference! (School Readiness Edition) **2896**
1089-313X Journal of Dance Medicine & Science **6111**
1089-3148 Black Renaissance **3523**
1089-3199 Dayspa **587**
1089-3202 Mosby's Medical Drug Reference **6862**
1089-3253 U S Offshore Oil Company Contact List **6796**
1089-3261 Clinics in Liver Disease **5921**
1089-327X Corporate Finance Review **1329**
1089-3288 A M S - I P Studies in Advanced Mathematics **5463**
1089-3326 The Paleontological Society. Papers **6729**
1089-3334 Waste Manifest Software Report **3482**
1089-3342 Peterson's U.S. & Canadian Medical Schools†
1089-3350 Computer Science & Electrical Engineering Programs†
1089-3385 T A F C S Research Journal **4368**
1089-3393 Techniques in Hand & Upper Extremity Surgery **6261**
1089-344X Exploring Oracle D B M S *changed to* 1098-4755
1089-3466 Country's Best Log Homes **1000**
1089-3504 Psoriasis Forum **5881**
1089-3520 Gambit Weekly **3976**
1089-3539 International Test Conference. Proceedings **2427**
1089-3547 Intersociety Energy Conversion Engineering Conference. Proceedings†
1089-3555 I E E E Neural Networks for Signal Processing *changed to* 1551-2541 **2454**
1089-361X Northern Kentucky Zine
1089-3687 Cracking the G R E Biology Test **2975**
1089-3695 P C Games **2479**
1089-3709 Vision Systems Design **3226**
1089-3733 The Complete Organ **6558**
1089-3741 Dimension & Diversity **6561**
1089-375X Bucina **6552**
1089-4012 Illinois Golfer's Travel Guide†
1089-4020 Indiana Golfer's Travel Guide†
1089-4039 Michigan Golfer's Travel Guide†
1089-4047 New York Golfer's Travel Guide†
1089-4055 Ohio Golfer's Travel Guide†
1089-4063 Pennsylvania Golfer's Travel Guide†
1089-4071 Minnesota - Wisconsin Golfer's Travel Guide†
1089-408X Cardiology Clinics: Annual of Drug Therapy†
1089-4098 *see* 1073-8584 **6169**
1089-411X Shepard's Federal Statute Citations **4783**
1089-4128 Cyberhound's Guide to Publications on the Internet†
1089-4136 Psi Chi Journal of Undergraduate Research **7392**
1089-4160 Journal of Lesbian Studies **4375**
1089-4179 Journal of Nutraceuticals, Functional & Medical Foods *changed to* 1939-0211 **6853**

1090-3933 Standard & Poor's Institutional Equity Research **1653**
1090-3941 Surgical Technology International **6260**
1090-3968 Roger Williams University Law Review **4776**
1090-3976 Global Economic Trends **1567**
1090-3984 Law Librarian's Bulletin Board **4715**
1090-3992 N A C A News **6811**
1090-400X Underground Focus **1041**
1090-4018 International Journal of Listening **4457**
1090-4034 Real (Kansas City) **2210**
1090-4085 Daily Nebraskan **2280**
1090-4115 The Double Dealer Redux **5286**
1090-4123 Futures & Derivatives Law Report **4678**
1090-4190 S N L Real Estate Securities Daily (E-mail) *changed to* Real Estate Daily: North America Edition **1647**
1090-4220 Employee Benefits and Executive Compensation Counselor† **8953**
1090-4247 The Early America Review **4291**
1090-4255 Media Computing **2564**
1090-431X The D L A Financial
1090-4395 Health Care Strategist†
1090-4409 Pharmaceutical Strategic Alliances†
1090-4417 Start-Up **5717**
1090-4484 La Cucina Italiana **4355**
1090-476X Inside Microsoft Word **2591**
1090-4859 Hillel Guide to Jewish Life on Campus (Year)†
1090-4867 Institute on Telecommunications Policy and Regulation. Annual **2368**
1090-4875 (Year) Federal Tax Course **1923**
1090-4905 Control of Communicable Diseases Manual **5812**
1090-4964 Transplant News **5949**
1090-4972 Dialogo **8098**
1090-4999 Journal of Regional Analysis & Policy **1138**
1090-5073 South Central High Technology Directory **2028**
1090-5103 Zweig Performance Ratings Report†
1090-5138 Evolution and Human Behavior **942**
1090-5197 Eclipse
1090-5251 *see* 0882-3723 **7206**
1090-5278 Thomas Jefferson Law Review **4899**
1090-5413 Maine History **4302**
1090-5529 MaMaMedia **2201**
1090-5553 Making the Most of Microsoft Money†
1090-560X Worm Digest **968**
1090-5634 Copyrights Newsletter†
1090-5642 Asbury Theological Journal *changed to* The Asbury Journal **7746**
1090-5693 New York Economic Review **1501**
1090-5707 Hip Magazine†
1090-6215 Hearing Loss **4074**
1090-641X Tips & Tricks *changed to* 1941-3327 **2481**
1090-6460 *see* 1063-7834 **7033**
1090-6479 *see* 1063-7826 **7039**
1090-6487 J E T P Letters Online *see* 0021-3640 **7019**
1090-6509 *see* 1063-7761 **7020**
1090-6517 *see* 1063-777X **7055**
1090-6525 *see* 1063-7842 **7042**
1090-6533 *see* 1063-7850 **7042**
1090-655X Journal of Outcome Measurement†
1090-6568 Pastor's Family†
1090-6576 Genetic Testing *changed to* 1945-0265 **869**
1090-6584 Slate on Paper *see* 1091-2339 **5239**
1090-6649 Healthinform's Resource Guide to Alternative Health
1090-6738 International Journal of Auditing **1292**
1090-6754 Southern Africa Investor†
1090-6797 The Nuclear Review **3172**
1090-6827 Water Gardening **3754**
1090-6851 Education about Asia **549**
1090-6878 Young Lawyer **4817**
1090-6924 Journal of Cave and Karst Studies **2749**
1090-6975 Mobil Travel Guide. Mid-Atlantic **8737**
1090-7009 *see* 0162-5748 **3000**
1090-7017 TidBits (Issaquah) **2567**
1090-7025 Journal of Hazardous Substance Research **3499**
1090-7033 Consumer Connections **5600**
1090-7076 American Canada Watch
1090-7122 Maryland Sports, Health & Fitness Magazine **6992**
1090-7130 Council on East Asian Libraries Directory **5004**
1090-7157 Malachite & Agate†
1090-7165 AIDS & Behavior **5752**
1090-7173 Gay and Lesbian Medical Association. Journal†
1090-7211 The Left Guide **2013**
1090-7238 Inside Golf†
1090-7270 Publishing Entrepreneur†
1090-7327 The Final Call **7710**
1090-7475 FacilityCare **4093**
1090-7491 Cancer Case Presentations: The Tumor Board†
1090-7505 Women and Music **6628**
1090-7718 Youth Disciple Leader's Packet†
1090-7807 Journal of Magnetic Resonance **7020**
1090-798X Year Book of Obstetrics, Gynecology, and Women's Health **6006**
1090-8188 I P News (Print Edition)†
1090-820X Aesthetic Surgery Journal **6235**
1090-8218 Government Performance Report†
1090-8234 Reference Guides to the World's Cinema **6511**
1090-8307 Romance Forever†
1090-8366 InTents **8453**
1090-8420 Electronic Banking Law and Commerce Report **2556**
1090-8447 Business Crimes Bulletin **4885**
1090-8471 Human Factors and Ergonomics in Manufacturing **3367**
1090-8498 Black Diaspora **3970**
1090-851X Ohio's Last Frontier **3778**
1090-8579 Snap B M X *changed to* 1078-0084 **8267**
1090-8595 C S S Journal†
1090-8625 Immunotherapy Weekly **5760**
1090-8633 Sex Weekly Plus†
1090-8706 Hart's Energy Markets† **8961**
1090-8722 The Missouri JobBank†
1090-8730 Entertainment, Arts and Sports Law Journal **4666**
1090-879X Litigation Docket **4724**
1090-8811 Performance Improvement **3076**
1090-8862 The Rail Splitter **4309**
1090-8919 Michigan Journal of Economics **1149**
1090-896X Music Paper
1090-901X M C A T Comprehensive Review **2993**
1090-9214 Massachusetts Beverage Business **607**
1090-9222 Alternative Therapies in Clinical Practice†
1090-9389 Integrated Design and Process Technology **3199**
1090-9443 Research in Economics **1165**
1090-9451 *see* 1090-9443 **1165**
1090-9486 Sport Utility Buyer's Guide†
1090-9508 Journal of Human Virology†
1090-9516 Journal of World Business **1574**
1090-9524 Race and Society†
1090-9540 Journal of Psychotic Disorders Reviews & Commentaries†
1090-9591 Spectacle
1090-963X On the Water **8326**
1090-9648 American Trucker (Badger Edition) **8666**
1090-9656 American Trucker (Buckeye Edition) **8667**
1090-9664 American Trucker (California Edition) **8667**
1090-9672 American Trucker (Cascade Edition) **8667**
1090-9680 American Trucker (Central States Edition) **8667**
1090-9699 American Trucker (Florida Edition) **8667**
1090-9702 American Trucker (Illinois Edition) **8667**
1090-9710 American Trucker (Indiana Edition) **8667**
1090-9729 American Trucker (Kentucky / Tennessee Edition) **8667**
1090-9737 American Trucker (Metro East Edition) **8667**
1090-9745 American Trucker (Michigan Edition) **8667**
1090-9753 American Trucker (Mid Atlantic Edition) **8668**
1090-9761 American Trucker (Minnesota / Dakota Edition) **8668**
1090-977X American Trucker (Mountain America Edition) **8668**
1090-9788 American Trucker (New England Edition) **8668**
1090-9796 American Trucker (New York / Pennsylvania Edition) **8668**
1090-980X American Trucker (South Central Edition) **8668**
1090-9818 American Trucker (Southern Edition) **8668**
1090-9931 Preservation **454**
1090-994X Panorama (New York) **6972**
1090-9966 *see* 0735-9462 **3459**
1090-9982 C A R L Newsletter (Print) *changed to* C A R L Newsletter (Online) **4999**
1091-0050 I E E E Southeastcon. Proceedings **3313**
1091-014X A S B O Accents (Print Edition) *changed to* A S B O Accents (Email Edition) **3016**
1091-0212 Windows NT Systems†
1091-0220 Mayo Clinic Women's HealthSource **8846**
1091-0239 New Nietzsche Studies **6936**
1091-0263 Paludicola **6729**
1091-0271 Mode†
1091-028X Journal of Porous Media **3350**
1091-0301 Pacific Northwest Environmental Directory **2624**
1091-031X Fashion Almanac **2254**
1091-0344 Machining Science and Technology **3352**
1091-0387 Parenting's Healthy Pregnancy **6001**
1091-0441 Camcorder & ComputerVideo **2400**
1091-045X A T H S Show Time **8666**
1091-0492 Latin America in Graphs
1091-0506 H M O *changed to* 1551-8442 **4490**
1091-0638 M R O Today **1146**
1091-0646 Coal Age **6460**
1091-0786 *see* 1070-9762 **7079**
1091-0808 Information Outlook **5016**
1091-0832 Signs of the Times & Screen Printing en Espanol **7328**
1091-0840 Aircraft Interiors
1091-0883 Orpheus Grid
1091-0905 The Catholic Social Science Review **7790**
1091-0956 Electrical World Directory of Electric Power Producers in Canada **3157**
1091-1006 Taking Sides: Clashing Views on Controversial Issues in Business Ethics and Society **1181**
1091-109X Leasing Professional Newsletter **1963**
1091-1197 Brilliant Corners (Williamsport) **5266**
1091-1200 State Profiles: Financing Public Higher Education. Rankings†
1091-1219 State Profiles: Financing Higher Education. Trend Data†
1091-126X In Process **5308**
1091-1332 Journal of Maintenance in the Addictions† **8968**
1091-1340 Journal of Segmentation in Marketing†
1091-1359 Journal of Human Behavior in the Social Environment **8050**
1091-1367 Journal of Internet Cataloging *changed to* 1938-6389 **2563**
1091-1375 Global Fungicide Directory **233**
1091-1405 Web Marketing Update **1847**
1091-1421 Public Finance Review **1941**
1091-1464 Adolescent Cultures, School and Society **2143**
1091-1480 Phati-tude Literary Magazine **5350**
1091-1553 N B A A Digest **66**
1091-1596 The N S A Practitioner **1297**
1091-1626 24x7 **4112**
1091-1669 Mobile Computing & Communications†
1091-1677 District 725 Aeronaut **4593**
1091-1707 Utah Business **1190**
1091-1766 Gestalt! **7358**
1091-1812 Healthcare Practice Management News†
1091-1820 I T Cost Management Strategies **2536**
1091-1847 Moderna†
1091-1863 The Charleston Report **5001**
1091-1898 Seybold Publications. Bulletin **7580**
1091-1936 Ticker (New York, 1996) **1655**
1091-1952 Embroidery / Monogram Business†
1091-1960 The Prager Perspective **7728**
1091-1979 Blue Water Sailing **8272**
1091-2061 Online Pioneers†
1091-2177 Country Victorian Decorating Ideas
1091-2193 I C H P E R - S D Journal *changed to* 1930-4595 **6989**
1091-2339 Slate **5239**
1091-2347 Focus On: Psychopharmacology†
1091-2436 RailNews†
1091-2460 Stamping Journal **6333**
1091-2479 The Tube & Pipe Journal **6336**
1091-2487 Club Connection†
1091-2495 Zoetrope **5405**
1091-2533 Inside Tracks (Greenwich) **8179**
1091-255X Journal of Gastrointestinal Surgery **6248**
1091-2622 Education Update (Alexandria) **2849**
1091-2703 Curriculum - Technology Quarterly†
1091-2711 American Society for Church Growth. Journal **7621**
1091-272X Young Conservative Letter
1091-2851 International Journal of Self-Help and Self-Care **7366**
1091-2886 Nebraska Life **3982**
1091-2894 B N A's SafetyNet **6674**
1091-2908 National Guide to Funding in Higher Education†
1091-2983 Journal of Ophthalmic Prosthetics **6045**
1091-3092 Fleet Maintenance & Safety Report **8581**
1091-3114 Cosmic Current News†
1091-3173 Parent Pages **2164**
1091-3181 Paginas para los Padres y Madres **2164**
1091-3211 The Journal of Hospitality Financial Management **4392**
1091-322X Berks County Genealogical Society. Journal **3760**
1091-3238 Branches of Berks **3760**
1091-3297 European Law Reports **4830**
1091-3408 Access Review†
1091-3416 Newsweek en Espanol **3910**
1091-3424 Oil Spill Law Information Service†
1091-3521 Kids' Wall Street News†
1091-3556 netWorker **2502**
1091-3580 Creating Keepsakes **534**
1091-3602 Whitechapel Journal **2672**
1091-3610 International Journal of Scholarly Academic Intellectual Diversity **2871**
1091-3637 International Wealth Success Newsletter **1572**
1091-3653 Reading Man Quarterly†
1091-3661 Dinosaur World **6724**
1091-367X Measurement in Physical Education and Exercise Science **6992**
1091-3696 Diesel Progress International Edition **3376**
1091-370X Diesel Progress North American Edition **3376**
1091-3718 Assembly (Notre Dame) **7623**
1091-3734 Online Journal of Issues in Nursing **5976**
1091-3742 Judicial Staff Directory **4954**
1091-3777 The Volunteer Management Report **8077**
1091-3823 H M E News **4047**
1091-3866 Under the Sun **5243**
1091-3939 Biography Today Scientists & Inventors Series **641**
1091-3947 Biography Today Artists Series **640**
1091-3963 Mprove **3551**
1091-4021 B N A's Health Care Daily Report **4088**
1091-4056 Welfare Bulletin **4826**
1091-4099 School-to-Work Reporter **2945**
1091-4153 Technology Century **3222**
1091-4188 The Beckett Football Card Price Guide **4329**
1091-4250 Megawatt Week **3160**
1091-4269 Depression and Anxiety (Hoboken) **7351**
1091-4358 Journal of Mental Health Policy and Economics (Print Edition) **7376**
1091-4439 Cyberhound's Guide to Internet Databases†
1091-4498 Health Grants Funding Alert **4096**
1091-4552 The Grindstone Magazine†
1091-4587 Development in Supportive Cancer Care†
1091-4609 Environmental Cost Estimating Software Report **3481**
1091-4684 Impaired Driving Update **8585**
1091-4706 Reaching Today's Youth†
1091-4714 Armenian Forum **8089**
1091-4722 Family Business Professional†
1091-4781 Psych Discourse **7394**
1091-479X Georgia Food Connection **3678**
1091-482X American Runner **8303**
1091-4846 Association for Death Education & Counseling. Forum Newsletter **7337**
1091-4862 Gold Newsletter **1350**
1091-4927 The WEB Magazine†
1091-5001 Austin Homes & Living *changed to* 1521-9585 **4532**
1091-5044 Shape Cooks†
1091-5168 Osstium **5860**
1091-5176 *see* 1091-5168 **5860**
1091-5184 Laboratory Digest **5855**
1091-5222 Signature (Mahwah) **5865**
1091-5281 I E E E Instrumentation and Measurement Technology Conference. Proceedings **4487**
1091-5354 SportsTravel **8208**
1091-5362 Molecular Urology†
1091-5397 A C S M's Health & Fitness Journal **6981**
1091-546X Exploring for Older Children†
1091-5478 Exploring for Younger Children†
1091-5486 Exploring for Leaders†
1091-5508 Business Valuation by Industry Review Series **1977**
1091-5516 Fathering Magazine **2152**
1091-5540 Book Lovers **7554**
1091-5583 P R Watch **32**
1091-5680 Managing Menopause **5997**
1091-5710 International Journal for Human Caring **5961**
1091-5753 Wadabagei **3571**
1091-5788 Lake Country Journal **3979**
1091-5818 International Journal of Toxicology **3498**
1091-5885 El Restaurante Mexicano **3662**
1091-5915 Strategic Orthopaedics†
1091-5923 A W H O N N Lifelines *changed to* 1751-4851 **8847**
1091-594X America at Work†
1091-6083 EuroPhonics **7075**
1091-6121 Path†
1091-613X Annual Editions: Anthropology **325**
1091-6148 California Educator **2970**
1091-6172 Southwest Senior†
1091-6199 Waste News *changed to* Waste & Recycling News **3513**
1091-6202 Weekly Bookmark Standard
1091-6237 Law Firm Partnership and Benefits Report **4714**
1091-630X Hoffman Heart Institute of Connecticut. Journal **5789**
1091-6318 Gender & Psychoanalysis **7358**
1091-6369 Underwater World Resource Directory **8214**
1091-6377 Cats†
1091-6385 Banking Strategies (Print)† **8934**
1091-644X Financial Consultant†
1091-6458 Historical Geography **4014**
1091-6466 Petroleum Science and Technology **3214**

ISSN

1092-6771 Journal of Aggression, Maltreatment & Trauma **7368**
1092-6798 Journal of Emtional Abuse *changed to* 1092-6771 **7368**
1092-6801 Journal of Pharmaceutical Marketing Practice†
1092-6836 Inside Microsoft Office 97†
1092-6844 Inside Microsoft Planning Tools†
1092-6895 Elderhostel: International Catalog **8700**
1092-6909 American Windsurfer **8303**
1092-6917 Business Rules Alert!†
1092-6984 Jump†
1092-7018 Journal of Computational Intelligence in Finance†
1092-7026 Systems Research and Behavioral Science **2525**
1092-7042 Asthma and Allergy Exchange
1092-7085 Third Century Methodism **7777**
1092-7131 A L N Magazine†
1092-7174 Explore the Bible: Adult Commentary **7757**
1092-7190 Explore the Bible. Adult Teacher *changed to* 1930-5877 **7757**
1092-7239 C B A Marketplace *changed to* 1941-9600 **7557**
1092-728X Naughty Neighbors **6296**
1092-731X Home Theater Buyer's Guide **3101**
1092-7328 California Thoroughbred **8288**
1092-7336 Ethnomusicology Online **6565**
1092-7352 Screaming in Digital **6615**
1092-7360 Network Science **7891**
1092-7395 Dealer & Applicator† **8948**
1092-7417 Union Craftsman **4604**
1092-7441 World Libraries **5055**
1092-7506 Hastings Historian **4294**
1092-7514 Food Quality **3641**
1092-7530 Ocean Drive **5079**
1092-7549 Native American Report†
1092-7565 Mealey's Daubert Report **4836**
1092-7603 Large Animal Practice†
1092-7670 Environmental Compliance Auditing Software Report **3481**
1092-7697 International Journal of Historical Archaeology **398**
1092-7735 Short Stories for Students **5371**
1092-776X Annual Editions: Economics **1060**
1092-7786 Power Generation Technology & Markets **3145**
1092-7794 On Design **4548**
1092-7816 McBroom's Camera Bluebook **6971**
1092-7824 Military Vehicles Magazine **6436**
1092-7840 Health Plan Business Advisor†
1092-7859 Health Network Letter†
1092-7867 Cooking Contest Chronicle **3632**
1092-7875 Maternal and Child Health Journal **5998**
1092-7891 Biography (New York) **2375**
1092-793X Gilbert Law Summaries. Future Interests and Perpetuities **4681**
1092-7964 Cleaning Business **1958**
1092-7972 Martial Arts Legends Presents **8186**
1092-8014 The Customer Service Advantage **1812**
1092-8022 Union News†
1092-8049 Westsylvania **3992**
1092-8057 Cost Management **1087**
1092-8073 Distribution Sales & Management *changed to* 1931-8278 **6736**
1092-8081 I E E E Lasers and Electro-Optics Society. Annual Meeting **7076**
1092-8111 Daedalian **6913**
1092-812X Canfield Family Association. Publication†
1092-8197 Golda Meir Library Newsletter **5011**
1092-8219 Boating Life **8273**
1092-8235 *see* 1939-5256 **2500**
1092-8286 Online Journal of Ethics†
1092-8316 The Runner's Schedule **8198**
1092-8367 Laubach LitScape **2943**
1092-8456 Smart Wine†
1092-8464 Current Treatment Options in Cardiovascular Medicine **5785**
1092-8472 Current Treatment Options in Gastroenterology (Print)† **8947**
1092-8480 Current Treatment Options in Neurology **6135**
1092-8529 C N S Spectrums **6129**
1092-8545 National Farmers Union News **138**
1092-8618 Scrap **3512**
1092-8626 North Carolina State Bar Journal **4748**
1092-8634 Underground Construction **6796**
1092-8650 Focus on Members *changed to* 1542-1678 **2848**
1092-8669 International Conference on Indium Phosphide and Related Materials. Proceedings **7077**
1092-8707 *see* Humanities Abstracts Full Text **4484**
1092-8707 *see* Humanities Abstracts **4484**
1092-8723 Verge†
1092-874X *see* 1091-5818 **3498**
1092-8758 Environmental Engineering Science (Print)† **8954**
1092-8774 M I S A H A Newsletter†
1092-8782 Western Places **4318**
1092-8839 School Reform News **2910**
1092-8847 Rotation†
1092-8898 Marshland to Heartland **3774**
1092-8928 *see* 0884-2914 **3350**
1092-8987 Issues in Ecology **3444**
1092-8995 BioTech Navigator **1612**
1092-9088 Computer Aided Surgery **6240**
1092-910X Advances in Nonlinear Variational Inequalities **5467**
1092-9126 Pediatric Cardiac Surgery Annual of the Seminars in Thoracic and Cardiovascular Surgery **5797**
1092-9134 Annals of Diagnostic Pathology **5575**
1092-9150 British Ideas and Issues, 1660-1820 **4206**
1092-9185 Inside Aviation/Aerospace I T **60**
1092-9207 Lady Like **5075**
1092-9223 People, Places & Plants **3747**
1092-924X Annual Editions: Multicultural Education **3011**
1092-9320 X-Ray Magazine (Print) *changed to* X-Ray Magazine (Online) **7580**
1092-9347 Authorship **5259**
1092-9487 Hustler's Hometown Girls **6293**
1092-9495 Hustler's Leg World **6293**
1092-9525 Journal of Ministry & Theology **7655**
1092-9533 WeMedia Magazine **4070**
1092-9541 American Sportswear & Knitting Times†
1092-9576 Electronic Journal of Africana Bibliography **4170**
1092-9592 Technician News & Satellite Journal **3115**
1092-9614 Performance Horse **296**
1092-9630 California Landscaping **3726**
1092-9649 Golf Course Turf & Irrigation **8231**
1092-9711 Venture Capital and Health Care *changed to* 1550-3224 **1658**
1092-9770 C A R A Catholic Ministry Formation Directory **7787**
1092-9789 Maxim (Print) **6295**
1092-9819 *see* 0278-6680 **1492**
1092-9851 African Profiles U S A **3516**
1092-9886 The Voice **7615**
1092-9894 Idaho Bankruptcy Court Report **4952**
1093-0019 Journal of Border Health† **8968**
1093-0051 Newspeak **2293**
1093-0078 E H E News **6644**
1093-0116 American Venture **1610**
1093-0159 I E E E Conference on Computational Complexity. Proceedings **5491**
1093-0167 I E E E - V L S I Test Symposium **2540**
1093-0175 Conference on Software Engineering Education and Training. Proceedings **2588**
1093-023X Journal of Interactive Learning Research **2950**
1093-0248 BioSupplyNet Source Book **661**
1093-0272 Biomedical Therapy *changed to* Journal of Biomedical Therapy **5646**
1093-0337 Home Accents Today **4541**
1093-0418 *see* 1553-6408 **6418**
1093-0426 E R I C / E E C E Newsletter (Online Edition)†
1093-0442 Parent News (Champaign)†
1093-054X Poetry International **5431**
1093-0566 Yankee Magazine's New England Bed & Breakfast and Inn Directory **4400**
1093-0574 Pennsylvania Angler & Boater **8328**
1093-0647 X X L **6629**
1093-0655 I M Advantage (Print) *changed to* I M Advantage Papers (Online) **5945**
1093-0736 Delaware Capitol Review (Print)†
1093-0930 Food Writer **4575**
1093-0949 Forza **8581**
1093-0957 Health Care Business Digest
1093-0973 Tradicion Revista **522**
1093-099X U.S. - Cuba Policy Report **7269**
1093-1007 Conserve Wildlife Newsletter **2608**
1093-1082 Inquiry (Upper Montclair)† **8964**
1093-1104 Inter-State High Way **6645**
1093-1139 Academic Physician and Scientist **6691**
1093-1163 Controller's Cost and Profit Report
1093-118X Photographer's Almanac of the Sun & Moon (Year) **579**
1093-121X Fashion Reporter
1093-1228 Office Number One **5345**
1093-1244 Financial Service OnLine†
1093-1252 Mortgage Servicing News **1369**
1093-1260 Collections and Credit Risk **1327**
1093-1279 Card Technology†
1093-1295 A S U Research **2822**
1093-135X Fauna **942**
1093-1376 I C H F Newsletter **7524**
1093-1627 Pakn Treger **7727**
1093-1643 Arts (New Brighton) **474**
1093-1716 VIA (San Francisco) **8771**
1093-1724 Cal - Tax Digest **1914**
1093-1767 Region Focus **1513**
1093-1783 Outcomes Management for Nursing Practice *changed to* 1063-8628 **4110**
1093-1791 Pulmonary Infections Forum
1093-1805 Surgical Infections Forum†
1093-1821 Health Data Directory†
1093-1880 American Statistical Association. Section on Statistics and the Environment. Proceedings *changed to* 1543-3218 **8344**
1093-2054 Carroll's Municipal - County Directory (Year) Annual†
1093-2062 Carroll's Military Facilities Directory†
1093-2070 Carroll's State Directory (Year) Annual **7489**
1093-2216 Selling Power **1843**
1093-2275 Barthmes Family Association Newsletter **3759**
1093-2356 Multimedia Entertainment & Technology Report†
1093-2372 Hare Krishna World **7736**
1093-2402 Networking Solutions†
1093-2453 Editorial Cartoons by Kids†
1093-2518 Drip Investor **1621**
1093-2534 Family Practice Alert (Atlanta, 1997)†
1093-2607 Human Antibodies **5758**
1093-2615 U U & Me! *changed to* 1532-7450 **7742**
1093-2658 African Studies Quarterly **7945**
1093-2666 Emerging Markets Quarterly† **8953**
1093-2682 The Journal of Oncology Index & Reviews†
1093-2763 American Statistical Association. Biometrics Section. Proceedings *changed to* 1543-3218 **8344**
1093-278X Annual Editions: Global Issues **3998**
1093-2801 No Salt Week **4365**
1093-281X The Silver Sheet **5715**
1093-2844 Wingspan (Cheyenne) **2310**
1093-2879 A R T Newsletter *changed to* 1546-3125 **5032**
1093-2909 About This Particular Macintosh **2574**
1093-2925 Bread Pudding Recipe Exchange **4353**
1093-2941 International Symposium on Discharges and Electrical Insulation in Vacuum. Proceedings **3321**
1093-2984 Russian Polymer News **7099**
1093-3174 N C A A Division I Manual **8189**
1093-3182 Ultimate Audio **8155**
1093-3190 Crossings (Binghamton) **5281**
1093-3247 C O B R A Advisory **4089**
1093-3255 The M & A Lawyer **2564**
1093-3263 Journal of Molecular Graphics and Modelling **2108**
1093-328X Ink World **7323**
1093-3301 Essential Ecology, Zoology & Plant Science Abstracts†
1093-331X *see* 0002-662X **4571**
1093-3328 Sociofile *changed to* Sociological Abstracts **8150**
1093-3344 Essential Wildlife & Conservation Biology Abstracts **2634**
1093-3484 American Statistical Association. Epidemiology Section. Proceedings *changed to* 1543-3218 **8344**
1093-3514 Buffalo Criminal Law Review *changed to* 1933-4192 **4894**
1093-3557 Women's Resources International *changed to* Women's Studies International (Baltimore) **8906**
1093-3565 *see* 0888-8027 **5201**
1093-3581 Coast to Coast **8494**
1093-359X Residential Architect **455**
1093-3611 High Temperature Material Processes **2135**
1093-3670 RANGE (Carson City) **5081**
1093-3689 Libros en Venta en Hispanoamerica y Espana **629**
1093-3700 Oceanographic & Marine Resources†
1093-376X Nutshell (Etters) **3745**
1093-3824 Detwiler's Directory of Health and Medical Resources (Year) **5744**
1093-3859 Networking in New Jersey **2019**
1093-3875 Exposure! (Yakima)
1093-3964 Seedsman N W†
1093-3980 The Tomato Magazine **255**
1093-4030 Inside Mortgage Finance's Inside B&C Lending **1354**
1093-4049 Inside Mortgage Technology **1354**
1093-4081 V G Classics†
1093-412X Active Server Developer's Journal†
1093-4162 Property/Casualty Insurance *changed to* 1931-7727 **4505**
1093-4170 Smart Computing **2583**
1093-4189 Woodall's Northeast Outdoors **8342**
1093-4200 Independent Adviser for Vanguard Investors **1629**
1093-4227 Strength Magazine†
1093-4243 I A E E Newsletter *changed to* 1944-3188 **3137**
1093-4391 Integrative Biology†
1093-4421 Harvard Design Magazine **444**
1093-4510 History of Psychology **7360**
1093-4529 Journal of Environmental Science and Health. Part A: Toxic Hazardous Substances and Environmental Engineering **3499**
1093-4537 International Journal of Organization Theory and Behavior **7447**
1093-4545 Nutrition Forum **6665**
1093-4618 Cedarville Torch **7750**
1093-4677 Crayon **5279**
1093-4715 *see* 1093-9946 **5616**
1093-474X American Water Resources Association. Journal **8817**
1093-4758 Brain Injury Association. T B I Challenge! **6057**
1093-4782 Aero Safety & Maintenance†
1093-4804 Engineering, Construction, and Operations in Space **53**
1093-4812 D & B Million Dollar Directory **1983**
1093-4987 Visual J Plus Plus Developer's Journal†
1093-5029 The Meeting Professional *changed to* 1943-1864 **6282**
1093-5045 O S H A Required Training for Supervisors **3457**
1093-5061 The Managed Care Payment Advisor†
1093-507X Disease Management *changed to* 1942-7891 **5697**
1093-5126 China Watch† **8941**
1093-5134 West's Federal Taxation: Introduction to Business Entities *changed to* 1544-3590 **4883**
1093-5169 Living Buddhism **7701**
1093-5193 M Web Magazine **2508**
1093-5207 I V D Technology **5632**
1093-5231 Consumer Electronics Vision **3091**
1093-5266 Pediatric and Developmental Pathology **6100**
1093-5282 California Workplace Monitor†
1093-5355 Alzheimer's Disease Review†
1093-5371 R L G DigiNews **5042**
1093-538X Boating for Women†
1093-5398 Afro-Latin/American Research Association. Publication **3517**
1093-5401 America's Pharmacist **6820**
1093-541X Licensure Exchange **3208**
1093-5428 Trend Letter **1522**
1093-5460 Talking River Review **5385**
1093-5479 HomeGirl Press†
1093-5568 U S Markets Regional Review. Midwestern State Focus **1907**
1093-5630 Capital Growth Interactive **1615**
1093-5657 Gig Magazine† **8959**
1093-5665 Hypothesis **5012**
1093-5681 Philips Graduate Institute. Progress **8062**
1093-569X Madison Review (Madison) **5426**
1093-5738 N S E E Quarterly **6701**
1093-5746 E R I C / E E C E Newsletter (Print Edition)†
1093-5770 Journal of Accounting and Finance Research **1293**
1093-5789 Ballast Quarterly Review **5208**
1093-5797 Inside AutoC A D Collection CD *see* 1071-0728 **2591**
1093-5908 Mom Guess What Newspaper **4376**
1093-5924 This Week in Cleveland **8760**
1093-5940 Stargreen **6619**
1093-5975 Prohibition History Notes **4309**
1093-6017 Mealey's Insurance Law Weekly†
1093-6025 Glossen **5301**
1093-6076 P G A Tour Partners **8242**
1093-6092 Leadership in Action **1772**
1093-6106 The Asian Journal of Mathematics **5474**
1093-6114 Executive Advantage **1743**
1093-622X Hotbox **4336**
1093-6238 Tomorrow's Christian Graduate **6704**
1093-6262 Computer & Net Player†
1093-6270 Directory of California Wholesalers and Service Companies **1985**
1093-6327 Compendium of Veterinary Products **8795**
1093-6467 Missouri Court Rules **4956**
1093-6483 Concrete Openings **993**
1093-6491 Savage Underground **6511**
1093-6513 Black Book Illustration **478**
1093-6564 World Authors **648**
1093-6580 W E F A Industrial Monitor **1192**
1093-6602 New York Golf **8240**
1093-6629 Catia Solutions **2409**
1093-667X DeafNation **4073**
1093-6696 A T M World **2495**
1093-6785 The State and Local Tax Lawyer **4788**

ISSN

1094-608X Journal of Convention & Exhibition Management *changed to* 1547-0148 **6280**
1094-6098 American Journal of Pastoral Counseling *changed to* 1934-9637 **7381**
1094-6136 Journal of Scheduling **2593**
1094-6144 North American Swans **911**
1094-6152 F.W. Dodge Construction News Weekly Covering the State of Georgia *changed to* 1551-0115 **998**
1094-6160 F.W. Dodge Construction News Weekly Covering the State of Alabama *changed to* 1551-0107 **998**
1094-6187 Montana Living **3982**
1094-6195 Balance (Alexandria) **4041**
1094-6209 Studies in European Union (New York) **7187**
1094-6217 Patristic Studies **7669**
1094-6225 Politics, Media, and Popular Culture **8125**
1094-6233 Women in German Literature **8890**
1094-6349 Inside Microsoft Publisher†
1094-6438 The Dow Jones Guide to the World Stock Market **1621**
1094-6470 S P E Reservoir Evaluation and Engineering **6791**
1094-656X P E L Plastics Update **7095**
1094-6616 Refractive Eyecare for Ophthalmologists *changed to* 1931-7905 **6050**
1094-6624 National Association of Student Affairs Professionals Journal **3028**
1094-6632 Creation Matters **7636**
1094-6640 Furniture Style **4557**
1094-6683 Official U.S. PlayStation Magazine (Print Edition)†
1094-6705 Journal of Service Research **1826**
1094-673X Tech Capital **1394**
1094-6748 Slant (Philadelphia)
1094-6810 Cosmetic Surgery Times **6240**
1094-6829 Ambulatory Outreach†
1094-6853 Shop Owner†
1094-687X I E E E Engineering in Medicine and Biology Society. International Conference *changed to* 1557-170X **5830**
1094-6950 Journal of Clinical Densitometry **5647**
1094-6969 I E E E Instrumentation and Measurement Magazine **6402**
1094-6977 I E E E Transactions on Systems, Man and Cybernetics, Part C: Applications and Reviews **2526**
1094-6985 Who's Who in the Media and Communications†
1094-7019 Poetry for Students **5431**
1094-7027 Corrections Technology & Management **2648**
1094-7094 Stoic Academy of Research Scholars. Journal
1094-7116 I E E E International Conference on Innovative Systems in Silicon **2520**
1094-7124 Fodor's Pocket London **8708**
1094-7132 Joy of Collecting†
1094-7159 Neuromodulation **6166**
1094-723X The Federal Investigator **2652**
1094-7256 International Conference on High-Performance Computing. Proceedings **2467**
1094-7264 Paroles Gelees **5349**
1094-7329 Upper South Carolina Genealogy & History **4316**
1094-7337 Daily Free Press **2280**
1094-7361 AmericasTrade†
1094-7450 Food Logistics **3640**
1094-7531 Taking Sides: Clashing Views on Controversial Issues in Health and Society **7543**
1094-754X Taking Sides: Clashing Views on Controversial Issues in World Politics **7268**
1094-7566 Taking Sides: Clashing Views on Controversial Issues in Drugs and Society **2700**
1094-7604 Taking Sides: Clashing Views on Controversial Moral Issues **7411**
1094-7612 Taking Sides: Clashing Views on Controversial Economic Issues **1521**
1094-771X Environment Library on CD *changed to* 1932-5142 **3422**
1094-7760 Exponent II **8862**
1094-7809 B N A's Employee Benefits Library on CD† **8934**
1094-7868 More (New York) **8876**
1094-7876 Inside Lotus SmartSuite†
1094-7914 Aqua†
1094-7965 Bathtub Gin **5260**
1094-799X Journal of Burma Studies **4184**
1094-8007 Communication Booknotes Quarterly **2347**
1094-8015 Independent Sawmill & Woodlot Management **1752**
1094-8074 Palaeontologia Electronica **6728**
1094-8104 T W 3 **5384**
1094-8112 Web Marketing Today **1847**
1094-8120 American Diplomacy **7104**
1094-8198 The Northern Colorado Business Report **1431**
1094-8201 American Italian Heritage Association Newsletter **3518**
1094-8228 Fresh Cup Magazine **603**
1094-8260 Y E S Magazine†
1094-8309 Nutrition Focus **2163**
1094-8317 Readings from the Midwest Poetry Festival **5433**
1094-8325 Science Frontiers **7909**
1094-8341 Physiological Genomics **742**
1094-8384 The Best American Mystery Stories **5413**
1094-8392 Rhetoric & Public Affairs **5362**
1094-8406 *see* 1094-8414 **4469**
1094-8414 Post Identity **4469**
1094-8449 Columbia Journal of Asian Law **4645**
1094-8473 Detroit Baptist Seminary Journal **7754**
1094-8481 L A E Journal **4893**
1094-8503 MetroKids **2161**
1094-8562 Acts & Facts **7620**
1094-8570 Research Conference Report **1840**
1094-8597 Catering Service Idea Newsletter **3630**
1094-8635 Vision Enhancement (Online Edition)†
1094-8651 Conquistador **8289**
1094-866X The National Jurist **4739**
1094-8686 The Design Firm Directory - Product Design Edition **1984**
1094-8724 California Labor News **4591**
1094-8732 American Cake Decorating **3670**
1094-8759 The Public Eye (Somerville) **7174**
1094-8848 Journal of Transportation and Statistics†
1094-8864 LatinCom (Print Edition)†
1094-8902 California Public Finance†
1094-8910 N C U A Watch *changed to* 1540-4528 **1333**
1094-8937 Credit Union Accountant†
1094-8945 High Yield Report **1351**
1094-8988 Emerging Markets Debt Report†
1094-8996 Private Placement Report **1376**
1094-9011 Web Commerce Today **1193**
1094-902X The North Star (Rochester) **3555**
1094-9046 Knowledge Quest **5023**
1094-9054 Reference and User Services Quarterly **5042**
1094-9119 Law Books in Print **4823**
1094-9143 Low-Fat & Fast
1094-9194 Veterinary Clinics of North America: Exotic Animal Practice **8812**
1094-9224 A C M Transactions on Information and System Security **2511**
1094-9232 Drama for Students **8469**
1094-9313 CyberPsychology & Behavior **2554**
1094-9399 Struggle **5240**
1094-9410 Lexicon (Jackson) **3773**
1094-9445 Wisconsin State Genealogical Society Newsletter **3788**
1094-9453 The Asian Reporter **3520**
1094-9488 Jam Rag **6578**
1094-9518 Corrections Caselaw Quarterly **2647**
1094-9542 I D C Quarterly **4689**
1094-9631 Home Schooling Laws and Resource Guide for All Fifty States†
1094-9666 Multistate Sales Tax Review **1935**
1094-9682 Tournament Variety Puzzles
1094-9704 Golfing†
1094-9828 Idaho Wool Growers Bulletin **288**
1094-9860 Natural Areas News **3455**
1094-9917 Personal Transformation†
1094-9968 Journal of Interactive Marketing **1824**
1095-0419 Friends (Winter Park) *changed to* 1554-1614 **4047**
1095-0427 Catholic Cemetery **3719**
1095-0435 Bowlers Journal International **8162**
1095-0443 Mekeel's and Stamps Magazine **6897**
1095-0591 F.W. Dodge Construction News Weekly Covering Eastern Missouri **1003**
1095-0605 International Bluegrass **6576**
1095-0613 Veterinary Economics Firstline†
1095-063X Mac@Home†
1095-0656 The Scientific Review of Alternative Medicine and Aberrant Medical Practices **314**
1095-0664 Hart's Asian Petroleum News **6772**
1095-0672 Institutional Trading Technology†
1095-0680 The Journal of Electroconvulsive Therapy **6151**
1095-0710 City-Smart Guidebook: San Antonio *changed to* City-Smart: San Antonio **8941**
1095-0729 Commercial Mortgage Insight **7587**
1095-0737 Consortium Coleopterorum. Occasional Papers **938**
1095-0753 *see* 1095-0761 **5467**
1095-0761 Advances in Theoretical and Mathematical Physics **5467**
1095-080X The Edge (McLean) **1287**
1095-0826 F.W. Dodge Construction News Weekly Covering Northern Indiana **1004**
1095-0885 F.W. Dodge Construction News Weekly Covering North and South Dakota *changed to* 1550-0888 **997**
1095-0915 Construction News Weekly, Covering the State of Vermont **998**
1095-0923 F.W. Dodge Construction News Weekly Covering the State of Maine **1004**
1095-094X F.W. Dodge Construction News Weekly Covering Baltimore, Maryland **1003**
1095-0958 F.W. Dodge Construction News Weekly Covering Southern New Jersey and Delaware **1004**
1095-0966 F.W. Dodge Construction News Weekly Covering the South Shore, Massachusetts **1004**
1095-0974 F.W. Dodge Construction News Weekly Covering Central New Jersey **1003**
1095-0982 F.W. Dodge Construction News Weekly Covering the State of New Hampshire **1004**
1095-0990 F.W. Dodge Construction News Weekly Covering Norfolk & Vicinity **1004**
1095-1008 F.W. Dodge Construction News Weekly Covering Richmond, Virginia and Vicinity **1004**
1095-1016 Construction News Weekly, Covering Roanoke, Virginia and Vicinity **997**
1095-1024 F.W. Dodge Construction News Weekly Covering Eastern Massachusetts **1003**
1095-1032 F.W. Dodge Construction News Weekly Covering Western Massachusetts **1004**
1095-1040 F.W. Dodge Construction News Weekly Covering Northern New Jersey **1004**
1095-1075 Flight Journal **55**
1095-1083 Brown University Long-Term Care Quality Advisor†
1095-1091 Yachts International **8286**
1095-113X The Writer's Block (Whitewater)
1095-1180 Nevada Web Pages **2565**
1095-1253 Solid Solutions **3512**
1095-1318 Materials Issues in Art and Archaeology **504**
1095-1342 Orthopaedic Medline on CD-ROM **6069**
1095-1350 Working Conference on Reverse Engineering. Proceedings **2600**
1095-1377 Computer Currents. Atlanta† **8942**
1095-1415 Advanced Fuel Cell Technology **3235**
1095-1423 Chasidic Historical Review†
1095-1431 F.W. Dodge Construction News Weekly Covering Metropolitan Philadelphia and Delaware **1003**
1095-144X F.W. Dodge Construction News Weekly Covering Rochester, New York and Vicinity **1004**
1095-1458 F.W. Dodge Construction News Weekly Covering Syracuse, New York & Vicinity **1004**
1095-1466 F.W. Dodge Construction News Weekly Covering the North Shore, Massachusetts **1004**
1095-1474 F.W. Dodge Construction News Weekly Covering the Hudson Valley, New York **1004**
1095-1482 F.W. Dodge Construction News Weekly Covering Buffalo, New York and Vicinity **1003**
1095-1490 F.W. Dodge Construction News Weekly Covering Washington D.C. **1004**
1095-1520 Visual Proceedings†
1095-1539 Journal of Environmental Medicine†
1095-1555 Undercurrent **8214**
1095-158X Psychiatric Rehabilitation Journal **6176**
1095-1598 Clinical Geriatrics **4043**
1095-161X The International Directory of Agents, Distributors & Wholesalers **2006**
1095-1644 News from the Republic of Letters **5341**
1095-1695 English Digest
1095-1717 One
1095-1776 Assisted Living Business Report†
1095-1938 Inspirational Crafts **6639**
1095-1962 Journal for the Study of Peace and Conflict **7247**
1095-2020 I E E E International Symposium on Electronics and the Environment **3102**
1095-2055 International Conference on Computer Communications and Networks. Proceedings **2498**
1095-2063 Wetland Journal†
1095-2071 Andrews Insurance Coverage Litigation Report *changed to* 1557-024X **4492**
1095-208X Andrews Latex Allergy Litigation Reporter **4616**
1095-2098 Andrews Managed Care Litigation Reporter **4617**
1095-2101 Andrews Health and Life Insurance Litigation Reporter **4616**
1095-2136 Impressions (New York) **495**
1095-2160 Planning & Action Journal **8062**
1095-2179 School Technology Market Report†
1095-2187 Professional Publishing Report **7570**
1095-2195 Roundup†
1095-2624 R U S A Update **5042**
1095-2675 Fodor's Australia (Year) **8704**
1095-2721 Michigan Journal of Race & Law **3550**
1095-273X Ohio Civil War Genealogy Journal **3777**
1095-2756 The Judkins Journal†
1095-2799 Chinese Journal of Coffee Research **3631**
1095-2802 The Saint-Domingue Newsletter **3781**
1095-2829 Online Banking Report **1373**
1095-2853 Young Horizons Indigo†
1095-2861 Arizona Informant **3519**
1095-2896 U.S. Department of Health and Human Services. Indian Health Service. Trends in Indian Health **6636**
1095-2926 Fair Housing - Fair Lending† **8955**
1095-3000 Association for Social Anthropology in Oceania. Newsletter **329**
1095-323X I E E E Aerospace Conference. Proceedings **59**
1095-3248 Label & Narrow Web **2563**
1095-3256 Managers Handbook†
1095-3302 Estylo **3532**
1095-3337 Recruit! **4520**
1095-3647 xChange **2374**
1095-3655 ThriftInvestor (Print) *changed to* ThriftInvestor (E-mail) **1655**
1095-3698 Bank Investor†
1095-371X VideoHound's Golden Movie Retriever (Year) **6516**
1095-3876 Fodor's Santa Fe, Taos, Albuquerque **8708**
1095-3884 A V M A Directory and Resource Manual **8790**
1095-3914 Fodor's Los Angeles **8707**
1095-3922 Fodor's Vienna and the Danube Valley *changed to* 1554-5857 **8710**
1095-3965 Lockergnome's Free Windows 95 - N T E-Zine **2594**
1095-3973 The Internet Writing Journal **5310**
1095-4120 Evidence Based Practice **5612**
1095-4155 C V D Prevention
1095-4171 Your World of Birds†
1095-4201 Journal of Eye Trauma†
1095-421X Postacute Payment Report†
1095-4244 Wind Energy **3178**
1095-4317 Airline Pilot Careers **45**
1095-4333 *see* 1051-2004 **3093**
1095-4341 Orthopaedics Today International *changed to* 1942-6275 **6069**
1095-4376 Fodor's Exploring Japan **8705**
1095-4775 Arcade (Seattle) **428**
1095-483X Regional Differences in Indian Health **8064**
1095-4872 C S A Newsletter **436**
1095-4902 Medico-Legal Watch†
1095-4929 Fitness Product News **6986**
1095-4961 Inside Illustrator†
1095-4996 Crochet with Heart **534**
1095-5046 Journal of Radio Studies *changed to* 1937-6529 **2359**
1095-5054 Stanford Encyclopedia of Philosophy **6953**
1095-5062 Parking Today **8508**
1095-5070 P C Portables Magazine†
1095-5100 The Prostate Journal†
1095-5127 The Journal of Biolaw and Business **766**
1095-5143 Sexuality & Culture **8132**
1095-5216 The Green Bag **4682**
1095-5224 Works + Conversations **527**
1095-5305 Chicago Philanthropy Magazine†
1095-5615 B N A's Intellectual Property Library on C D **6746**
1095-5623 *see* 0010-0285 **7347**
1095-5631 B N A's Labor & Employment Law Library on CD *see* 1527-7356 **5024**
1095-564X *see* 0012-1606 **668**
1095-5658 Vantage Point **5911**
1095-5674 Torrey Botanical Society. Journal **820**
1095-5992 Medical Immunology **5763**
1095-6239 Human Resources Report **1685**
1095-6247 Integration Management†
1095-6263 Card Marketing
1095-6298 Academy of Marketing Studies Journal **1803**
1095-6328 Academy of Educational Leadership Journal **3050**
1095-6336 Natural Medicine Law **4739**
1095-6395 U S Social Policy Shareholder Resolutions in (Year) **1657**
1095-6433 Comparative Biochemistry and Physiology. Part A: Molecular & Integrative Physiology **921**
1095-6441 Global Power Report **3136**
1095-6654 Comparative Labor Law & Policy Journal **1671**
1095-6670 Journal of Biochemical and Molecular Toxicology (Print Edition) **681**
1095-6727 Tundra **5437**

9524 1095-6808 ULRICH'S PERIODICALS

1095-6808 *see* 0091-3022 **5893**
1095-6824 Passport Newsletter **8747**
1095-6840 *see* 0016-6480 **5893**
1095-6859 *see* 0090-8258 **5992**
1095-6867 *see* 0018-506X **5894**
1095-7073 Oxygen **8847**
1095-7103 *see* 0021-9797 **2136**
1095-7111 *see* 0097-5397 **5555**
1095-712X *see* 0036-1399 **5531**
1095-7138 *see* 0363-0129 **5531**
1095-7146 *see* 0895-4801 **5531**
1095-7154 *see* 0036-1410 **5531**
1095-7162 *see* 0895-4798 **5531**
1095-7170 *see* 0036-1429 **5531**
1095-7189 *see* 1052-6234 **5531**
1095-7197 *see* 1064-8275 **5532**
1095-7200 *see* 0036-1445 **5532**
1095-7219 *see* 0040-585X **5541**
1095-7227 *see* 0147-5967 **1134**
1095-7235 *see* 0022-0531 **1545**
1095-7243 *see* 0047-259X **5506**
1095-7251 *see* 0092-6566 **7379**
1095-726X *see* 0022-4596 **2138**
1095-7286 PassageMaker **8280**
1095-7294 Wall Street Companion†
1095-7308 Index of Economic Freedom **7142**
1095-7316 Broadband Systems & Design†
1095-7332 InTheater†
1095-7340 Journal of Surgical Outcomes†
1095-7359 Washington Law & Politics **4810**
1095-7367 G A M A International Journal **4503**
1095-7375 American Bicyclist **8253**
1095-7863 I E E E Nuclear Science Symposium Conference Record **6198**
1095-7898 Hosteur **4389**
1095-791X W E S C O N Conference Proceedings†
1095-7960 New Labor Forum **4599**
1095-7979 Bicyclist†
1095-7987 City-Smart Guidebook: Calgary *changed to* City-Smart: Calgary **8941**
1095-807X International Journal of Environmentally Conscious Design and Manufacturing **3442**
1095-8096 A A T T Bulletin **5088**
1095-8118 Quinlan Law Bulletin on Police Immunity†
1095-8134 La Voz Newsmagazine **3571**
1095-8169 Cornell Daily Sun **2279**
1095-8258 Fantasy & Science Fiction **5442**
1095-8274 *see* 1075-9964 **880**
1095-8282 *see* 0003-3472 **932**
1095-8290 *see* 0305-7364 **775**
1095-8304 *see* 0195-6663 **6655**
1095-8312 *see* 0024-4066 **687**
1095-8320 *see* 1045-1056 **659**
1095-8339 *see* 0024-4074 **800**
1095-8347 *see* 0890-8389 **1282**
1095-8355 *see* 1065-6995 **829**
1095-8363 *see* 0885-2308 **2506**
1095-8371 Judicial - Legislative Watch Report **4704**
1095-841X Ekphrasis **5421**
1095-8452 Telecom Market Report: Latin America & the Caribbean
1095-8525 The E C S Industry Report on Supervisory Management Compensation *changed to* 1930-4277 **1796**
1095-8533 *see* 1045-926X **5203**
1095-8541 *see* 0022-5193 **685**
1095-855X *see* 0747-7171 **5553**
1095-8568 *see* 0022-460X **7088**
1095-8576 *see* 0095-4470 **5135**
1095-8584 *see* 0022-2828 **5794**
1095-8592 *see* 1084-8045 **2500**
1095-8606 *see* 0047-2484 **874**
1095-8614 *see* 0305-7488 **4017**
1095-8622 *see* 0889-9746 **3205**
1095-8630 *see* 0301-4797 **3446**
1095-8649 *see* 0022-1112 **951**
1095-8657 *see* 1047-8477 **684**
1095-8673 *see* 0022-4804 **6250**
1095-8681 *see* 0889-1583 **1574**
1095-8711 Income Taxation Fiduciaries and Beneficiaries **1929**
1095-8754 Southern Living Recipes†
1095-8762 *see* 1067-151X **6055**
1095-8835 Michigan Journal of Gender & Law **4733**
1095-8843 Amazonian Literary Review **5251**
1095-8878 Colonial Mexico Handbook† **8942**
1095-8886 Archaeological Mexico **8683**
1095-8924 Discover en Espanol **7851**
1095-8932 Environmental Design + Construction **1007**
1095-8940 Journal of Health & Population in Developing Countries **7529**
1095-8975 International Cemetery and Funeral Management *changed to* 1936-2099 **3719**
1095-905X The Nebraska Lawyer Magazine **4740**
1095-9068 *see* 0094-1190 **1138**
1095-9076 *see* 1047-3203 **2488**
1095-9084 *see* 0001-8791 **7381**
1095-9092 Cat Watch **6805**
1095-9114 *see* 0895-3996 **7023**
1095-9122 *see* 0023-9690 **2882**
1095-9130 *see* 1046-2023 **738**
1095-9149 *see* 0026-265X **899**
1095-9157 *see* 0896-8411 **5762**
1095-9165 The Ride Magazine *changed to* 1933-222X **8255**
1095-9173 Telephone Nursing Telezine†
1095-9203 *see* 0036-8075 **7908**
1095-922X *see* 0140-1963 **4016**
1095-9238 *see* 0305-4403 **400**
1095-9254 *see* 0140-1971 **2156**
1095-9262 *see* 1756-0616 **4695**
1095-9270 *see* 1057-2414 **398**
1095-9289 *see* 1054-3139 **2806**
1095-9297 *see* 1057-2317 **5018**
1095-9300 *see* 1071-5819 **2527**
1095-9319 *see* 0026-2862 **5795**
1095-9327 *see* 1044-7431 **6161**
1095-936X Small Business Times *changed to* 1946-8482 **1068**
1095-9475 Latin American Private Equity Analyst **1637**
1095-9513 *see* 1055-7903 **875**
1095-953X *see* 0969-9961 **6164**
1095-9564 *see* 1074-7427 **6164**
1095-9572 *see* 1053-8119 **6165**
1095-9726 Insurance Meetings Management *changed to* 1931-9975 **6280**
1095-9742 Portland Best Places *changed to* Best Places Portland **8687**
1095-9815 Working at Home (New York)†
1095-9823 American Tanka **5253**
1095-9858 The Burning Cloud Review
1095-9882 Cuizine Magazine *changed to* Fervor Magazine **3975**
1095-9890 *see* 0147-619X **698**
1095-9904 *see* 0090-3752 **3171**
1095-9912 *see* 1068-5200 **7082**
1095-9920 *see* 0749-5978 **1784**
1095-9939 *see* 0048-3575 **246**
1095-9947 *see* 1050-4648 **943**
1095-9955 *see* 1045-2354 **1286**
1095-9963 *see* 0733-5210 **273**
1095-9971 *see* 0195-6698 **5487**
1095-998X *see* 0195-6671 **2705**
1095-9998 *see* 0740-0020 **886**
1096-0007 *see* 0014-4835 **6041**
1096-0015 *see* 0272-7714 **2804**
1096-0023 *see* 1043-4666 **865**
1096-0031 *see* 0748-3007 **666**
1096-0058 Instinct **4375**
1096-0104 Journal of Clinical Psychiatry (Audiograph Series) *see* 0160-6689 **6150**
1096-0120 Skin & Aging **4056**
1096-0155 Sexual Assault Report **2668**
1096-0260 *see* 0091-7435 **5699**
1096-0279 *see* 1046-5928 **743**
1096-0287 *see* 0033-5894 **2763**
1096-0295 *see* 0273-2300 **3500**
1096-0309 *see* 0003-2697 **722**
1096-0317 *see* 0049-089X **8004**
1096-0325 *see* 0040-5809 **707**
1096-0333 *see* 0041-008X **3502**
1096-0341 *see* 0042-6822 **897**
1096-035X *see* 0003-4916 **7005**
1096-0384 *see* 0003-9861 **723**
1096-0406 Science and Technology in Congress (Print Edition)†
1096-0430 *see* 0021-9045 **5501**
1096-0449 *see* 0095-0696 **3445**
1096-0457 *see* 0022-0965 **7373**
1096-0465 *see* 0022-1031 **7373**
1096-0473 *see* 1042-9573 **1545**
1096-0481 *see* 0889-1575 **3650**
1096-0546 Standards for Long Term Care Subacute Programs, and Dementia Special Care Units **8073**
1096-0651 Winter Sports Business†
1096-0678 Mealey's Litigation Report: Attorney Fees†
1096-0708 Pathfinders Travel **8747**
1096-0716 Technical Computing Report†
1096-0724 Seed Technology **155**
1096-0740 Digital Television **2380**
1096-0759 The Royal Spaniels **6814**
1096-0783 *see* 0022-1236 **5503**
1096-0791 *see* 1051-1377 **4417**
1096-0805 *see* 0022-2011 **951**
1096-0813 *see* 0022-247X **5505**
1096-0821 *see* 0749-596X **5134**
1096-083X *see* 0022-2852 **7078**
1096-0848 *see* 0743-7315 **2429**
1096-0856 *see* 1090-7807 **7020**
1096-0880 *see* 0022-2496 **7376**
1096-0899 *see* 0097-3165 **5501**
1096-0902 *see* 0095-8956 **5501**
1096-0910 *see* 0161-7346 **6209**
1096-0929 *see* 1096-6080 **3502**
1096-0937 *see* 1087-1845 **790**
1096-0945 *see* 0014-4800 **5612**
1096-0953 *see* 0013-9351 **3428**
1096-0961 *see* 1079-9796 **5934**
1096-0996 PanGaia **7740**
1096-1003 InfoAdvantage Internet Guide†
1096-102X Mentor & Protege†
1096-1046 Research Advisor **5043**
1096-1054 Quinnipiac Probate Law Journal **4764**
1096-1127 L W T - Food Science and Technology *see* L W T- Food Science and Technology **3653**
1096-1135 *see* 0024-2829 **800**
1096-1151 *see* 0048-721X **7674**
1096-1178 *see* 0885-5765 **808**
1096-1186 *see* 1043-6618 **6872**
1096-1194 *see* 0890-8508 **5909**
1096-1208 *see* 0882-4010 **5823**
1096-1216 *see* 0888-3270 **3389**
1096-1224 *see* 1044-5005 **1296**
1096-1232 Reading Online **2903**
1096-1291 Pacific Review of Ethnomusicology **6604**
1096-1372 Women Alive **8848**
1096-1453 Academic Exchange Quarterly **3050**
1096-1461 Louis Navellier's Blue Chip Growth Letter **1637**
1096-1488 Country Western Corner **6560**
1096-1526 Metalforming Technology†
1096-1577 Baking Management **3671**
1096-1585 S I Review **1874**
1096-1623 JBuilder Developer's Journal†
1096-1658 *see* 0022-314X **5506**
1096-1712 Continental Newstime **3973**
1096-1747 Intermarket Review **1821**
1096-1763 Dredging Contract News†
1096-1801 Medical Design Technology (Print)† **8973**
1096-1828 Fatigue and Fracture Mechanics **3192**
1096-1844 New Urban News **4420**
1096-1860 The American Journal of Managed Care **5572**
1096-1879 Multinational Finance Journal **1393**
1096-1887 San Diego Lawyer **4778**
1096-1941 Sand Sports Magazine **8603**
1096-1968 Portable Computing Direct Shopper†
1096-1976 Vermont Outdoors Magazine *changed to* 1931-8294 **8327**
1096-1984 Ad Power
1096-2115 Bird Breeder On-Line†
1096-2123 The Journal of Library Services for Distance Education **5022**
1096-214X Sleep Research (Los Angeles, 1998) **928**
1096-2174 Colombia Bulletin
1096-2182 Unzipped Monthly **6301**
1096-2190 Integrative Medicine†
1096-2220 Cost Control Strategies for Financial Institutions†
1096-2247 Air & Waste Management Association. Journal **3503**
1096-2298 Wild Garden
1096-231X Frontiers in Health Policy Research (Print)† **8958**
1096-2336 Writers' Intl. Forum for Young Authors†
1096-2344 Black Dirt†
1096-2409 Professional School Counseling **2900**
1096-2492 Arizona Journal of Hispanic Cultural Studies **8088**
1096-2506 Young Exceptional Children **3049**
1096-2514 *see* 0884-5891 **2814**
1096-2522 Ocean Drilling Program. Proceedings. Initial Reports *changed to* 1930-1022 **2807**
1096-2581 Rice Farming **275**
1096-2638 Trading Technology Week *changed to* 1744-0416 **1392**
1096-2719 Brookings Papers on Education Policy (Year) **3018**
1096-2816 Wood Carving Illustrated **541**
1096-2832 Teen People†
1096-2867 Clinical Techniques in Small Animal Practice *changed to* 1938-9736 **8808**
1096-2875 Operative Techniques in Oculoplastic, Orbital and Reconstructive Surgery†
1096-2883 Techniques in Gastrointestinal Endoscopy **5931**
1096-2921 The Journal of Community Association Law **4417**
1096-2956 New York Stories **5341**
1096-2964 Surgical Infections **6260**
1096-3014 Shenandoah Valley Folk Art and Heritage Center Newsletter **3782**
1096-3057 Poultry (Chicago) **296**
1096-3065 Home Theater **2382**
1096-3235 Oil Price Information Service's Petroleum Terminal Encylopedia **6785**
1096-326X Drag News Magazine **8170**
1096-3278 The Decorative Painter **534**
1096-3308 Briefings on Accreditation & Certification for Physician Organizations†
1096-3316 Directory of Environmental Websites on the Internet **3414**
1096-3324 Mathematica in Education and Research†
1096-3367 Journal of Public Budgeting, Accounting & Financial Management **7448**
1096-3375 Investment Policy
1096-3480 Journal of Hospitality & Tourism Research **4392**
1096-3553 Integrated Solutions **2423**
1096-357X Market Study of Restaurant Technology *changed to* 1527-0777 **1831**
1096-3588 Directory of Physicians in the United States†
1096-360X Taunton's Fine Homebuilding **1039**
1096-3618 *see* 1044-5323 **5766**
1096-3626 *see* 0021-9614 **2136**
1096-3634 *see* 1084-9521 **836**
1096-3642 *see* 0024-4082 **953**
1096-3650 *see* 1044-579X **928**
1096-3669 *see* 0734-242X **3513**
1096-3677 *see* 0749-6036 **2081**
1096-3685 Academy of Accounting and Financial Studies Journal **1276**
1096-3707 Journal of Healthcare Safety, Compliance & Infection Control†
1096-3758 Journal of Hospitality & Tourism Education **4392**
1096-3766 Wearables Business **2250**
1096-3782 Crusade Magazine **8096**
1096-3790 Unknown Magazine **6744**
1096-3839 InSync **4566**
1096-3901 Open Spaces **3984**
1096-391X The Muslim Magazine **7714**
1096-3936 S I G C S E Bulletin Inroads **2951**
1096-3944 Great Scale Modeling (Year) **4335**
1096-3995 Union Contract Law Bulletin **1712**
1096-4037 Clinical Child and Family Psychology Review **7345**
1096-4045 Journal of Immigrant Health *changed to* 1557-1912 **5650**
1096-4053 Journal of Radiosurgery†
1096-4096 Designer/Builder **440**
1096-4126 The Informed Outlook† **8964**
1096-4142 S M T International Asia Pacific Edition†
1096-4207 Annual Editions: Criminology **2644**
1096-4215 Annual Editions: Developing World **3998**
1096-4231 Annual Editions: Geology†
1096-424X Annual Editions: Macroeconomics **1717**
1096-4258 Annual Editions: Microeconomics **1535**
1096-4266 Annual Editions: Teaching English as a Second Language†
1096-4274 Annual Editions: Violence and Terrorism **2225**
1096-4282 Annual Editions: Accounting **1280**
1096-4290 International Journal of R F and Microwave Computer-Aided Engineering (Print) **3292**
1096-4304 E D Nursing **5957**
1096-4320 Insider (Rosemead) **6575**
1096-4339 Diggin' for Davises **3764**
1096-4371 Courtroom Handbook on Georgia Evidence **4949**
1096-441X Variety Junior†
1096-4479 Year 2000 Practitioner†
1096-4495 Java Pro **2507**
1096-4533 F.W. Dodge Construction News Weekly Covering the State of Kansas, Excluding Kansas City *changed to* 1550-8684 **997**
1096-4568 Cost Control Strategies for Manufacturing Executives **1736**

DIRECTORY 2010 1097-4180 9525

1096-4649 *see* 1064-6175 **2323**
1096-4657 *see* 0361-073X **7356**
1096-4665 *see* 0739-9332 **8846**
1096-4673 *see* 0161-2840 **5963**
1096-4681 *see* 0146-8030 **7075**
1096-4738 International Journal of Applied Quality Management (Oxford)†
1096-4746 Andrews Telecommunications Industry Litigation Reporter *changed to* 1555-8908 **2312**
1096-4762 Thunderbird International Business Review **1183**
1096-4789 International Conference on Integrated Circuits Yields. Proceedings **2465**
1096-4835 Snack Food & Wholesale Bakery **3675**
1096-4886 Western Criminology Review **2671**
1096-4908 NetBits†
1096-4924 Electronic Journal of Cognitive and Brain Sciences†
1096-4959 Comparative Biochemistry and Physiology. Part B: Biochemistry & Molecular Biology **729**
1096-4991 Mind - Body Health Newsletter†
1096-5076 Jeffers Studies **5424**
1096-5254 Soft Dolls & Animals **539**
1096-5289 Mary Engelbreit's Home Companion **537**
1096-5297 The Journal of Gift Planning **8050**
1096-5408 Knit 'n Style **6639**
1096-5424 Remote Gas Strategies *changed to* 1930-0646 **6770**
1096-5467 Glue†
1096-5513 Oregon Manufacturers Register
1096-5572 The Journal of Private Equity **1635**
1096-5599 SearchLites **581**
1096-5645 Managed Care Interface **4106**
1096-5688 The Stampers' Sampler **540**
1096-5718 Journal of the Lincoln Assassination
1096-5726 Nerium News **3744**
1096-5750 People en Espanol **3985**
1096-5807 OfficePro **1782**
1096-5823 Somerset Studio **540**
1096-5858 The Motorist *changed to* 1539-7696 **8701**
1096-5882 Selecta **5082**
1096-5890 Latin America Evangelist **7764**
1096-5904 Veterinary Heritage **8812**
1096-5939 Sacred Journey **7679**
1096-5955 Perspectives (Baltimore, 1999) **8125**
1096-5971 Progressive Populist **7174**
1096-598X Compound Semiconductor† **8942**
1096-603X *see* 1063-5203 **5472**
1096-6080 Toxicological Sciences **3502**
1096-6099 *see* 1094-2025 **1514**
1096-6102 New York Manufacturers Register **2020**
1096-6196 Dollars & Cents of Multifamily Housing **7589**
1096-620X Journal of Medicinal Food **5652**
1096-6218 Journal of Palliative Medicine **5653**
1096-6269 Advance for Directors in Rehabilitation **5568**
1096-6277 Advance for Administrators of the Laboratory **5901**
1096-6293 Advance for Nurse Practitioners **5950**
1096-6307 Advance for Managers of Respiratory Care **6211**
1096-6315 Advance for Physician Assistants **5568**
1096-6323 Recycling Today **3511**
1096-6374 Growth Hormone & IGF Research **5893**
1096-6501 Capital Style†
1096-651X Prism(s) **5354**
1096-6625 Take Pride! Community Magazine **3567**
1096-6668 Manufacturing Science and Engineering **1898**
1096-6757 Genealogia **3767**
1096-6781 Nutrition in Clinical Care†
1096-6803 Best's Insurance Reports: Life Health United States *changed to* 1550-0152 **4495**
1096-682X S I G U C C S User Services Conference. Proceedings **2436**
1096-6838 East Asia **4181**
1096-6919 Chicago Reader **3972**
1096-6927 Paint & Decorating Retailer **4548**
1096-701X Central PA **2378**
1096-7028 International Journal of Intensive Short Term Dynamic Psychotherapy†
1096-7079 Lexicon **6584**
1096-7095 Design - Build **3264**
1096-7117 NeighborWorks Journal **4420**
1096-7133 *see* Harrison's Principles of Internal Medicine **5945**
1096-7176 Metabolic Engineering **750**
1096-7184 *see* 1096-7176 **750**
1096-7192 Molecular Genetics and Metabolism **739**
1096-7206 *see* 1096-7192 **739**
1096-7214 Real Estate Weekly **7610**
1096-7230 Federal Electronic Commerce Report†
1096-7249 University of North Carolina School of Law Banking Institute **4804**
1096-7303 Connections (Sausalito)†
1096-7451 *see* 0884-5891 **2814**
1096-746X The Medieval Review **4243**
1096-7494 International Public Management Journal **7447**
1096-7508 International Food and Agribusiness Management Review **200**
1096-7516 The Internet and Higher Education **2560**
1096-7524 Dental Liability Alert **4830**
1096-7567 Data Communications Management **2533**
1096-7575 Data Base Management **2529**
1096-7583 E D P Auditing **2536**
1096-7699 The Guttmacher Report on Public Policy **972**
1096-7702 Rick Steves' Best of Europe **8752**
1096-7729 Global Wireless (Print Edition)†
1096-7745 *see* 1083-2289 **1949**
1096-7788 Mobil Travel Guide: Florida **8737**
1096-7796 Mobil Travel Guide: Southern California **8737**
1096-7850 Workers' Compensation Monitor† **8999**
1096-7893 Systems Development Management **2525**
1096-7907 Data Security Management **2513**
1096-7923 Bird Times **6804**
1096-7966 The Ministry Magazine *changed to* 1938-1921 **7663**
1096-8024 Information Management (Washington) **2537**
1096-8148 The Madison Business Journal†
1096-8156 I D E A Health & Fitness Source *changed to* 1548-419X **6989**
1096-8261 Cable T V Magazine†
1096-830X Pottery Making Illustrated **2044**
1096-8342 Journal of Insurance Coverage†
1096-8377 F.W. Dodge Construction News Weekly Covering Western North Carolina **1004**
1096-8431 Marketplace (Menasha) **1147**
1096-8474 Antique Doll Collector **363**
1096-8490 Corrections Management Quarterly **2647**
1096-8504 Oklahoma Criminal Justice Research Consortium. Journal **2662**
1096-8520 Print on Demand Business†
1096-8547 Dictionary of Literary Biography **642**
1096-858X *see* 1059-6879 **5421**
1096-8598 *see* 1097-2129 **8111**
1096-8636 Business Courier **1071**
1096-8644 *see* 0002-9483 **324**
1096-8652 *see* 0361-8609 **5933**
1096-8660 Washington Journey **8773**
1096-8733 Crime & Justice International **2648**
1096-8741 The International Student Handbook of U.S. Colleges *changed to* 1536-9439 **2972**
1096-8857 Cognitive Neuroscience Society *see* 0898-929X **6151**
1096-8865 The Journal of Cardiac Arrhythmias, Index & Reviews†
1096-8903 Information Security **2514**
1096-8911 Play and Culture Studies **5351**
1096-8954 Primary Care Case Reviews† **8982**
1096-8970 U S A F Weapons Review
1096-8997 Orient Magazine†
1096-9012 Journal of Healthcare Management **4104**
1096-9020 ChildArt **481**
1096-9071 *see* 0146-6615 **5652**
1096-9098 *see* 0022-4790 **6250**
1096-9101 *see* 0196-8092 **6251**
1096-9144 Orion Afield†
1096-9160 HealthCare Distributor **6846**
1096-9179 Community Pharmacist **6829**
1096-9195 Oil, Gas and Energy Quarterly **1937**
1096-9209 New York Runner **8190**
1096-9268 T P A Speedletter **6882**
1096-9365 Meat & Seafood Merchandising **3655**
1096-9411 Dental Anthropology **335**
1096-942X Alternative Medicine Alert **306**
1096-9446 Issues and Answers in Sales Management† **8967**
1096-9489 Harris Minnesota Directory of Manufacturers *changed to* Harris Directory. Minnesota Manufacturing **2000**
1096-9519 I D E A Fitness Edge†
1096-9624 Records & Information Management Report†
1096-9705 Annual Editions: Astronomy†
1096-9713 Annual Editions: Women's Health **8843**
1096-973X Best Practices in H R **1857**
1096-9764 PC / 104 & Small Form Factors **2509**
1096-9772 Spin to Win Rodeo **8298**
1096-9837 *see* 0197-9337 **2732**
1096-9845 *see* 0098-8847 **3266**
1096-9853 *see* 0363-9061 **3272**
1096-9861 *see* 0021-9967 **6151**
1096-987X *see* 0192-8651 **2068**
1096-9888 *see* 1076-5174 **2102**
1096-9896 *see* 0022-3417 **5653**
1096-9918 *see* 0142-2421 **2106**
1096-9934 *see* 0270-7314 **1635**
1096-9969 InternetWeek†
1096-9985 California Notary Law Primer **4637**
1096-9993 ElectriCity **7051**
1097-0002 Advances in X-Ray Analysis **7004**
1097-0010 *see* 0022-5142 **128**
1097-0029 *see* 1059-910X **900**
1097-0037 *see* 0028-3045 **5555**
1097-0045 *see* 0270-4137 **6273**
1097-0053 *see* 1044-8136 **1294**
1097-0061 *see* 0749-503X **823**
1097-007X *see* 0098-9886 **3320**
1097-0088 *see* 0899-8418 **6357**
1097-0096 *see* 0091-2751 **6200**
1097-0118 *see* 0364-9024 **5504**
1097-0126 *see* 0959-8103 **7099**
1097-0134 *see* Proteins: Structure, Function, and Bioinformatics **743**
1097-0142 *see* 0008-543X **6010**
1097-0150 *see* 1092-9088 **6240**
1097-0169 *see* 0886-1544 **829**
1097-0177 *see* 1058-8388 **668**
1097-0193 *see* 1065-9471 **6145**
1097-0207 *see* 0029-5981 **3200**
1097-0215 *see* 0020-7136 **6022**
1097-0223 *see* 0197-3851 **6002**
1097-0231 *see* 0951-4198 **2104**
1097-024X *see* 0038-0644 **2598**
1097-0258 *see* 0277-6715 **5751**
1097-0266 *see* 0143-2095 **1795**
1097-0274 *see* 0271-3586 **6672**
1097-0282 *see* 0006-3525 **2120**
1097-0290 Biotechnology and Bioengineering (Online) *see* 0006-3592 **760**
1097-0312 *see* 0010-3640 **5480**
1097-0339 *see* 8755-1039 **832**
1097-0347 *see* 1043-3074 **6245**
1097-0355 *see* 0163-9641 **6093**
1097-0363 *see* 0271-2091 **3362**
1097-0525 The Middle East Women's Studies Review **8901**
1097-0568 Western New York Heritage **4317**
1097-0614 Drum! (San Jose) **6562**
1097-069X Models of Care **4107**
1097-0800 Thomas M Cooley Journal of Practical and Clinical Law **4795**
1097-0819 The Healthcare Strategist **4098**
1097-0843 Solar & Renewable Energy Outlook†
1097-0878 Life and Learning **6932**
1097-0924 A M A A News **7703**
1097-0975 Military Training Technology **6436**
1097-1009 S E I U Action **4601**
1097-1041 Military Information Technology **6435**
1097-1068 Peterson's Graduate Programs in Engineering & Applied Sciences **3214**
1097-1076 Peterson's Graduate Programs in the Humanities, Arts, and Social Sciences **4469**
1097-1165 Coastal Living **5068**
1097-1181 Studio Photography & Design *changed to* Studio Photography **6977**
1097-119X Team Marketing Report **1845**
1097-1254 Transitions (Print) *changed to* Transitions (Washington, D.C.) (Online) **2170**
1097-1262 Christian Library Journal **5002**
1097-1327 R S F Newsletter **3748**
1097-1343 El Puente†
1097-1394 Pittsburgh Business Times **1159**
1097-1408 J O O P†
1097-1424 Allergy and Clinical Immunology International† **8929**
1097-1440 The Journal of Combinatorics **5501**
1097-1467 Contemporary Chinese Thought **6911**
1097-1475 The Chinese Economy **1083**
1097-1505 N F P A Update† **8975**
1097-1521 International Software Process Workshop. Proceedings **2592**
1097-1548 Aullwood Notes **2603**
1097-1572 Hidden San Francisco & Northern California **8718**
1097-1599 International Sports Directory **8181**
1097-1653 The Sonography Letter†
1097-167X A 2 C 2 *changed to* 1556-9268 **3366**
1097-1726 W C & P International **8835**
1097-1734 E Commerce Alert†
1097-1742 1394 Newsletter *changed to* Plastic Optical Fiber Newsletter **2371**
1097-1769 Journal of Unification Studies **7738**
1097-1807 West's Federal Taxation: Advanced Taxation *changed to* 1544-3582 **4883**
1097-1823 Strategic Environmental Management†
1097-184X Men and Masculinities **6303**
1097-1874 Delaware Law Review **4655**
1097-1904 Ohio Biological Survey Notes **695**
1097-198X Journal of Global Information Technology Management **2429**
1097-1998 E S P N The Magazine **8170**
1097-2021 I O M A's Report on Managing Logistics†
1097-203X The Japanese Economy **1131**
1097-2102 Journal of Technology Computer Aided Design†
1097-2129 Journal of Asian American Studies **8111**
1097-2137 Conference on Optoelectronic and Microelectronic Materials and Devices. Proceedings **7074**
1097-2218 Signs & Screen em Portugues†
1097-2226 Preparing for the California Notary Public Exam **4760**
1097-2277 Export Reference Guide on CD *changed to* Export Reference Library on CD **1564**
1097-2420 HomeBusiness Journal **1961**
1097-2447 Aquaculture News **3585**
1097-2501 InfoStor **2546**
1097-251X Infrastructure (Chicago) **4692**
1097-2552 Guide to Architecture Schools **444**
1097-2560 Vincentian Chair of Social Justice. Presentations **8077**
1097-2641 I E E E International Performance, Computing, and Communications Conference. Proceedings **2534**
1097-2668 Regulatory Affairs Focus *changed to* Regulatory Focus **5703**
1097-2676 STIHL Post **3703**
1097-2692 Horse Connection†
1097-2714 Washington Native Plant Society. Occasional Papers **822**
1097-2730 Jp Magazine **8587**
1097-2757 Cracking the A P U.S. Government and Politics Exam **2975**
1097-2765 Molecular Cell **835**
1097-2803 Parallel and Distributed Computing Practices *changed to* 1535-6698 **2425**
1097-2838 Inter-American Trade Report **4929**
1097-2854 Dreams of Decadence **5286**
1097-2862 Individual Investor's Guide to Computerized Investing **1629**
1097-2900 Rattle **5357**
1097-2943 Bow Masters†
1097-296X Whitetail Journal **8341**
1097-2978 Southern Sporting Journal **8335**
1097-2986 EyeNet **6042**
1097-2994 Foodservice Equipment & Supplies **4386**
1097-3052 Reaching Out **4069**
1097-3087 Cultural Logic **5213**
1097-3133 Air Shows **45**
1097-3141 Today's Home Healthcare Provider†
1097-315X International Socialist Review **7144**
1097-3206 Wideband Magazine†
1097-3230 Historical Miniature **4336**
1097-3389 Practice Builder Association's What's Working†
1097-3435 Psychiatric Rehabilitation Skills *changed to* 1548-7768 **6121**
1097-3494 Discoveries (Columbus) **4214**
1097-3508 Dream/Girl
1097-3540 Quick Print Products†
1097-3702 Hugoye: Journal of Syriac Studies **551**
1097-3710 In Visible Culture **496**
1097-3729 *see* 0040-165X **8442**
1097-3761 Quick and Easy Painting **4344**
1097-3923 Journal of Public Economic Theory **1545**
1097-394X GameWEEK†
1097-3958 Journal of Surfactants and Detergents **2125**
1097-3982 Directory of Consultants and Contractors Active in Europe†
1097-4008 Cicada (Peru) **2182**
1097-4059 Apartment Finance Today **7582**
1097-4067 *see* 1068-9613 **5486**
1097-4105 Sci-Fi Teen†
1097-4121 Journal of Critical Pedagogy†
1097-4156 Keep On Truckin' Re-Visited **8116**
1097-4164 *see* 1097-2765 **835**
1097-4172 *see* 0092-8674 **828**
1097-4180 *see* 1074-7613 **5759**

ISSN

9526 1097-4199 ULRICH'S PERIODICALS

1097-4199 *see* 0896-6273 **6167**
1097-430X Independent Rowing News **8179**
1097-4377 Operating Results of Independent Supermarkets
1097-4458 Insulation Outlook **1015**
1097-4466 Internet Gaming International†
1097-4482 Export Sales and Marketing Manual (Year) **1564**
1097-4490 Standard & Poor's Stock Reports **1653**
1097-4539 *see* 0049-8246 **2107**
1097-4547 *see* 0360-4012 **6155**
1097-4555 *see* 0377-0486 **2103**
1097-458X *see* 0749-1581 **2103**
1097-4598 *see* 0148-639X **5681**
1097-4601 *see* 0538-8066 **2136**
1097-461X *see* 0020-7608 **2065**
1097-4628 *see* 0021-8995 **3248**
1097-4644 *see* 0730-2312 **735**
1097-4652 *see* 0021-9541 **923**
1097-4660 *see* 0268-2575 **767**
1097-4679 *see* 0021-9762 **7370**
1097-4687 *see* 0362-2525 **683**
1097-4717 Sex & Health†
1097-4725 The Wrestling Analyst **8216**
1097-4741 Architectural West **430**
1097-4768 Journal of Health Care Law & Policy **4701**
1097-4814 Limousine & Chauffeured Transportation **8589**
1097-4873 The P R S Group. Country Reports: Myanmar **1508**
1097-4881 Electronic Business†
1097-4903 Communications Supplies Weekly **7329**
1097-4911 Professional Development **8063**
1097-4938 University of Pennsylvania. Journal of Labor and Employment Law *changed to* 1940-8064 **8996**
1097-4938 University of Pennsylvania. Journal of Labor and Employment Law *changed to* 1945-2934 **4882**
1097-4946 The Jeffries Letter **2499**
1097-4954 Global Business & Economics Review **1114**
1097-4997 Latin American Political Yearbook **7150**
1097-5039 Internet Search Advantage†
1097-5047 I O M A's Marketing Department Management Report†
1097-511X Best Practices in Compensation *changed to* Best Practices in Compensation & Benefits **1857**
1097-5128 Vehicle Thermal Management Systems Conference Proceedings **3359**
1097-5136 V T M S Conference Proceedings on CD-ROM *see* 1097-5128 **3359**
1097-5152 Storage Management Solutions **2438**
1097-5209 Heterogeneous Computing Workshop. Proceedings **2466**
1097-5233 Bank Technology News International
1097-5241 Mechanical Solutions†
1097-5268 Whole Earth†
1097-5276 Inside Microsoft FrontPage†
1097-5314 Professional Jeweler Magazine **4569**
1097-5322 Whole Dog Journal **6817**
1097-5349 Gaming Law Review & Economics **4679**
1097-5411 Medical School Admissions Adviser *changed to* Get into Medical School **2982**
1097-5438 University of Illinois at Urbana-Champaign. College of Commerce and Business Administration. Office of Research. Results **1188**
1097-5454 Florida Notary Law Primer **4675**
1097-5462 Texas Notary Law Primer **4795**
1097-5497 Mealey's Litigation Report: Fen-Phen - Redux **6860**
1097-5535 C P A Internet Connection†
1097-5594 Global I T Consulting Report†
1097-5659 I E E E National Radar Conference. Proceedings **3313**
1097-5667 Solutions Integrator†
1097-5756 GreatLife
1097-5764 I E E E Radar Conference. Proceedings **59**
1097-5772 Inside QuarkXPress†
1097-5837 Access: Paris **8680**
1097-5845 Taiwan Literature English Translation Series **5384**
1097-5926 Digital Graphics Magazine **530**
1097-5950 Off-Price Apparel **2249**
1097-5977 Studies in Penderecki **6621**
1097-5985 Showcase Stock Premier Illustration†
1097-6035 The Tennessee Williams Annual Review **5385**
1097-6043 Snowbound **5447**
1097-6051 I Am Nation News **6645**
1097-6108 American Southwest Travel-Smart† **8929**
1097-6116 Loss Prevention†
1097-6205 Medicina y Cultura **5673**
1097-6213 Biomedicina **5586**
1097-6221 Employee Assistance Report **1860**
1097-6256 Nature Neuroscience **6162**
1097-6280 Transportation Management Today **8676**
1097-6299 Steinbeck Yearbook **5377**
1097-6337 California Journal of Health - System Pharmacy **6827**
1097-6345 San Francisco **3987**
1097-6353 A-E-C Systems†
1097-640X Digital Production Executive†
1097-6418 Guide to Your Career **6698**
1097-6426 National Consumer Phone Book†
1097-6450 Telecom Business†
1097-6493 Ohio Lawyer **4751**
1097-6566 Stone-Campbell Journal **7776**
1097-6574 I R S Practice Adviser Report **1928**
1097-6612 Thiagi GameLetter†
1097-6647 Journal of Cardiovascular Magnetic Resonance **5792**
1097-6671 University Business **3008**
1097-6736 New Directions for Evaluation **7988**
1097-6744 *see* 0002-8703 **5776**
1097-6752 *see* 0889-5406 **5834**
1097-6760 *see* 0196-0644 **6055**
1097-6779 *see* 0016-5107 **5925**
1097-6787 *see* 0190-9622 **5871**
1097-6795 *see* 0894-7317 **5776**
1097-6809 *see* 0741-5214 **6250**
1097-6817 *see* 0194-5998 **6083**
1097-6825 *see* 0091-6749 **5762**
1097-6833 *see* 0022-3476 **6095**
1097-6841 *see* 0022-3913 **5853**
1097-685X *see* 0022-5223 **6250**
1097-6868 *see* 0002-9378 **5985**
1097-6892 Collectors' Eye **365**
1097-6949 Horse Journal **8292**
1097-6957 Vulcan Historical Review **4166**
1097-6981 Utility Business†
1097-699X Glamour en Espanol *changed to* 1556-2131 **8866**
1097-7023 Directory of Department Stores **1986**
1097-7066 4 Wheel Drive & Sport Utility **8613**
1097-7104 International Journal of Environmental Studies **3442**
1097-7139 Physician's Money Digest†
1097-7155 Wire & Cable Technology International **2399**
1097-7201 BioCentury: The Bernstein Report on BioBusiness **1067**
1097-7236 Copper State Journal† **8944**
1097-7260 On Production†
1097-7279 T V Entertainer†
1097-7309 Executive Report on Physician Organizations **4502**
1097-7341 ArtByte†
1097-7384 Black Dates **4371**
1097-7465 Bimmer **8569**
1097-7481 Liturgical Catechesis†
1097-7538 Sacramento Business Journal **1170**
1097-7589 Safety Alert **3395**
1097-7848 Country Marketplace† **8944**
1097-7929 Log Home Design Ideas *changed to* 1931-955X **1021**
1097-7961 H S R: Health Supplement Retailer *changed to* Natural Products Marketplace **6664**
1097-797X Orthodontic Products **5859**
1097-7988 Classic Trucks **8575**
1097-8003 Journal of Prenatal & Perinatal Psychology & Health **5996**
1097-8011 Bulgaria Press **3524**
1097-8038 Coastal Charts for Cruising Guide to Western Florida **8694**
1097-8054 Wood Strokes & Woodcrafts *changed to* 1544-7022
1097-8062 Apparel Specialty Stores *see* 1092-4442 **1985**
1097-8135 Life Science Journal **5661**
1097-8143 ToyFare **4062**
1097-8194 Quality (New York) **7291**
1097-8216 The White Paper *changed to* 1553-6645 **2677**
1097-8224 Product Data Management Report†
1097-8275 Optical Networks / W D M Newsletter **2370**
1097-8283 Asia - Pacific Telecom Newsletter **2365**
1097-8291 Internet World (New York)†
1097-8356 The Welfare Reporter (Arlington)†
1097-8372 Fidelity Investor **1623**
1097-8380 Icelandic Horse and Travel Magazine **8293**
1097-847X Computer Currents. Dallas - Ft. Worth† **8942**
1097-850X Powersports Business **8329**
1097-8526 Latin American Business Review **1575**
1097-8534 Devil Shat **3974**
1097-8550 Weil's Hawaii Government Register **7476**
1097-8569 Tax Management Tax Practice Plus for Windows (CD-ROM) *changed to* 1944-4923 **1949**
1097-8577 Hollywood Scriptwriter **6502**
1097-8585 International Workshop on Research Issues in Data Engineering. Proceedings **2547**
1097-864X *see* 0362-6830 **7482**
1097-8658 A C U T A Journal of Telecommunications in Higher Education **2964**
1097-8674 Inside Auto C A D - L T†
1097-8690 Internal Medicine News **5946**
1097-8704 Quality Manager's Alert **1788**
1097-8739 I T Performance Improvement†
1097-8755 A A A Mid-Atlantic Motorist *changed to* 1523-9403 **8553**
1097-8771 Sacramento Lawyer **4778**
1097-8836 Maghreb Weekly Monitor *changed to* 1097-8844 **1154**
1097-8844 The North Africa Journal **1154**
1097-8879 Stata Technical Bulletin *changed to* 1536-867X **8403**
1097-8895 Cable Program Investor (Print) *changed to* Cable Program Investor (Online) **2378**
1097-8917 Chicago Wilderness **2606**
1097-9131 Drovers **285**
1097-9190 Electronic Publishing†
1097-9220 Laces & Embroidery Directory Annual **8454**
1097-9255 Embroidery News **8450**
1097-9298 Stefan University Press Series on Achievements in Physics **7041**
1097-9328 Toledo Journal of Great Lakes' Law, Science & Policy **4797**
1097-9336 In Vitro & Molecular Toxicology†
1097-945X A T S D R's Toxicological Profiles on CD-ROM **3493**
1097-9530 Patient-Focused Care and Satisfaction†
1097-9638 Catholic Education **2835**
1097-9700 Link (Baltimore) **503**
1097-9743 A S E P Newsletter **918**
1097-9751 Journal of Exercise Physiology - Online **924**
1097-9778 Meridian (Raleigh) **2950**
1097-9867 *see* 1083-7450 **6868**
1097-9883 *see* 0360-2532 **5607**
1097-9891 *see* 0095-2990 **2691**
1097-9905 Bank Investment Services Report†
1097-9913 Environment of Care News **4093**
1097-9921 Health Care Fraud and Abuse Newsletter†
1097-993X Lundellia **800**
1097-9980 Fence **5295**
1098-0008 Internet Telephony Magazine **2369**
1098-0083 Metro (Torrance) *changed to* Metro Magazine **8504**
1098-0105 COALDAT Marketing Report
1098-0113 Credit Union Executive Journal†
1098-0121 Physical Review B (Condensed Matter and Materials Physics) **7032**
1098-0202 Keep Up to Date on Accounts Payable **1295**
1098-0229 Backyard Bird News **902**
1098-0261 Corporate Counsel's Records Retention Report **4864**
1098-0407 Entrepreneur's Home Office **1960**
1098-0415 Private Banking & Money Management in Latin America **1376**
1098-0423 A T V 4-Wheel Action **8554**
1098-0431 Christie's Great Estates **7586**
1098-044X Aroma-Chology Review†
1098-0458 The Pipings **3779**
1098-0490 Airline Pilot Job Monthly **45**
1098-0520 Macromedia Interactive Designer†
1098-0539 Guinea Pig Zero **6845**
1098-0571 Briefings On Coding Compliance Strategies **4089**
1098-0636 Florida International Magazine **3975**
1098-0660 Beauty Store Business **585**
1098-0784 Virginia Civil Benchbook for Judges and Lawyers **4843**
1098-0806 *see* 1098-0814 **3022**
1098-0814 eSchool News **3022**
1098-0857 Advances in Performance Analysis
1098-0865 Women's Health in Primary Care†
1098-0873 Reflexiones (Year) **3560**
1098-089X Catering Magazine **3630**
1098-0903 Direction (Alexandria) **8670**
1098-092X Gender Issues **8898**
1098-0938 Contact Kids†
1098-0946 Chilton's Eyewear
1098-0989 Kagan's Radio Financial Databook† **8969**
1098-0997 *see* 1064-7449 **5993**
1098-1004 *see* 1059-7794 **872**
1098-1012 Diagnostic Insight **5605**
1098-1039 Spirit (Joplin) **7775**
1098-1063 *see* 1050-9631 **5628**
1098-1071 *see* 1042-7163 **2116**
1098-108X *see* 0276-3478 **6660**
1098-1098 *see* 0899-9457 **7017**
1098-1101 *see* 0733-2459 **5939**
1098-111X *see* 0884-8173 **2451**
1098-1128 *see* 0198-6325 **6861**
1098-1136 *see* 0894-1491 **6143**
1098-1144 Harvard China Review **1117**
1098-1152 Pacific Russia Oil and Gas Report **6786**
1098-1179 Nutritional Outlook **6667**
1098-1187 Cooking Pleasures **4354**
1098-1195 I F A R Journal **494**
1098-1217 The Journal of Markets & Morality **1137**
1098-1241 Systems Engineering **3396**
1098-1381 Grrowl! Ezine **8866**
1098-1489 A S I S Dynamics **1722**
1098-1497 The Future of IT
1098-1519 Roofing Contractor **1034**
1098-1594 Executive's Tax & Management Report **1923**
1098-1608 Journal of At-Risk Issues **8048**
1098-1616 Risk Management and Insurance Review **4521**
1098-1632 Stefan University. Bulletin **7920**
1098-1667 Call Center Product News†
1098-173X Mealey's Managed Care Liability Report **4731**
1098-1748 Orphic Chronicle†
1098-1772 The Associate†
1098-1799 Pediatric Coding Alert **4518**
1098-1837 Investment News **1633**
1098-1845 Modern Physician **5680**
1098-1853 Pharmacy Society of Wisconsin. Journal **6874**
1098-1861 Wisconsin Medical Journal **5731**
1098-1942 North American Wetlands Conservation Act Progress Report **2623**
1098-2051 Roads to Adventure **8510**
1098-2108 America's Favorite Inns, B & Bs & Small Hotels: The South **4381**
1098-2140 American Journal of Evaluation **7946**
1098-2191 America's Favorite Inns, B & Bs & Small Hotels: The Middle Atlantic **4381**
1098-2205 America's Favorite Inns, B & Bs & Small Hotels: The West Coast **4381**
1098-2221 Directory of Retirement Facilities†
1098-2264 *see* 1045-2257 **868**
1098-2272 *see* 0741-0395 **869**
1098-2280 *see* 0893-6692 **866**
1098-2299 *see* 0272-4391 **6834**
1098-2302 *see* 0012-1630 **668**
1098-2329 *see* 0730-6679 **7090**
1098-2337 *see* 0096-140X **7332**
1098-2345 *see* 0275-2565 **931**
1098-2353 *see* 0897-3806 **5596**
1098-2361 *see* 0733-3188 **969**
1098-237X *see* 0036-8326 **7909**
1098-2396 *see* 0887-4476 **6187**
1098-240X *see* 0160-6891 **5980**
1098-2418 *see* 1042-9832 **5528**
1098-2426 *see* 0749-159X **5522**
1098-2434 Fantasy Sports **4335**
1098-2442 Young Rider **8300**
1098-2485 Sporting Goods Intelligence Asia **1178**
1098-2515 Las Vegas Life Monthly **3979**
1098-2523 D V D News **2400**
1098-2639 Dog Watch **8796**
1098-2736 *see* 0022-4308 **7872**
1098-2744 *see* 0899-1987 **6028**
1098-2752 *see* 0738-1085 **6252**
1098-2760 *see* 0895-2477 **7080**
1098-2787 *see* 0277-7037 **7080**
1098-2795 *see* 1040-452X **740**
1098-2825 *see* 0887-8013 **5907**
1098-2876 The W R E N Magazine **3162**
1098-2892 Lucero **5328**
1098-2922 Transnational Law Exchange†
1098-2957 The Securitization Conduit
1098-2973 Real Florida *changed to* 1946-9918 **8704**
1098-3007 Journal of Positive Behavior Interventions **7378**
1098-3015 Value in Health **6884**
1098-304X Tourism, Culture & Communication **8763**
1098-3058 Information Technology & Tourism **2546**
1098-3066 I O M A's Shipping Manager's Report†
1098-3104 Fork, Fingers, & Chopsticks†
1098-3163 500 Notable Women **648**
1098-3171 Millennium Hall of Fame **644**
1098-3287 Russian Forward **3562**
1098-3333 International Information Directory† **8966**
1098-3341 Fetish
1098-3376 Bookforum **5209**
1098-3392 H R Practitioners Guide **1863**
1098-3430 The Women's Law Journal **4815**

1100-4096	Nordic Journal of Freshwater Research†
1100-4274	Dagens Lantbruk†
1100-4290	Studies in Philosophy **6955**
1100-4312	Hassela Solidaritet **2694**
1100-4681	Vaerldarnas Moete **7743**
1100-4738	Modern Banking **1367**
1100-4746	Palestina Nu **4177**
1100-4800	Kulturmiljoevaard†
1100-4843	Det Baesta **3954**
1100-4894	Fackligt Aktuellt†
1100-4924	KonferensVaerlden **1142**
1100-4959	Kina-nytt **1574**
1100-5114	Miljoe & Utveckling **3453**
1100-5149	Affarsresenaren **8681**
1100-5165	Hjulet **8618**
1100-522X	Nordisk Kriminalpolis†
1100-5327	Foereningen Ordfronts Aarsskrift†
1100-5416	Det Svenska Motor-Magasinet **8606**
1100-5491	Soedok Nyfoervaervslista†
1100-5580	Baatar til Salu **8271**
1100-5815	Sveriges Riksbank. Penning- och valutapolitik **1385**
1100-5874	Finland Levererar *changed to* 1653-7351 **1403**
1100-6145	Madame†
1100-620X	J U S E K Tidningen **4698**
1100-6331	Foeretag & Naeringsliv†
1100-6447	Nyliberalen **7160**
1100-6854	Duoddaris **3616**
1100-7028	Umeaa Universitet. Institutionen foer Arkeologi och Samiska Studier. Studia Archaeologica Universitatis Umensis **421**
1100-7087	Bergslagsarkiv *changed to* 1653-2848 **4204**
1100-7303	Idrottens Affaerer†
1100-7362	Filmkonst **6500**
1100-7435	Maskin och Transport†
1100-7559	Nordic Economic Outlook **1154**
1100-7605	Z **5246**
1100-763X	Nisse Hult **7159**
1100-7761	Juridisk Tidskrift vid Stockholms Universitet **4705**
1100-780X	Boecker, Bilder och Saant **2180**
1100-7818	Sweden. Konjunkturinstitutet. Working Papers **1905**
1100-7931	Studia Graeca et Latina Lundensia **2240**
1100-8105	Signal Processing Report **3331**
1100-8164	Poesijournalen **5430**
1100-8172	Till Skogs†
1100-8245	Foersvarets Forum **6421**
1100-8466	Szocialdemokrata Szemle†
1100-8679	Sveriges Lantbruksuniversitet. International Rural Development Centre. Working Papers *changed to* 1402-3237 **137**
1100-911X	Affaers - Sverige†
1100-9144	Nordisk Golfguide†
1100-9233	Journal of Vegetation Science **799**
1100-9373	Sweden. Statistiska Centralbyraan. Statistiska Meddelanden. Serie Se, Servicenaeringar **1269**
1100-9381	Sweden. Statistiska Centralbyraan. Statistiska Meddelanden. Serie Uh, Utrikeshandel **1269**
1100-9403	Sweden. Ministry of Finance. Revised Budget Statement **1946**
1100-9438	Svensk Vaegtidning†
1100-9535	Miljoemedicin†
1100-956X	New Scandinavian Technology†
1100-9586	Tillslaget **420**
1100-9632	Marinarkeologisk Tidskrift **405**
1100-9667	Stockholm Studies in the History of Ideas **6953**
1100-9691	Kreativ Pedagogik **2881**
1100-9721	Ridsport Special **8298**
1100-9748	Faaglar i Oestra Smaaland **906**
1100-9799	Haest- och Ponnyboken
1100-9802	Skada och Ersaettning†
1100-9837	Svensk Flyghistorisk Tidskrift **72**
1100-9861	Doktorand†
1101-0002	Verkstadskontakt **3359**
1101-0010	Laetta Lastbilar **8672**
1101-0193	Laeget i Vaerlden **7250**
1101-0207	Modelltaag **4342**
1101-0568	Energi och Miljoe **3419**
1101-0630	Russi **4159**
1101-1165	Spraak och Stil **5177**
1101-122X	Reflexer†
1101-1262	European Journal of Public Health **7516**
1101-1408	Divan **7352**
1101-1416	Svenska Macpressen *changed to* 0284-3005 **2577**
1101-1432	Baatbranschen **8271**
1101-1491	Bjoernhunden **6804**
1101-198X	Svensk Hjortavel **301**
1101-2005	Lund Studies in Legal History **4726**
1101-2013	Klinisk Kemi i Norden **5658**
1101-2021	Cafe **3955**
1101-2226	Who Sells What?
1101-2277	Ledarskap†
1101-2331	Brottsforebyggande Raadet. B R AA-Report **2645**
1101-2412	Svenska Dagbladet **3957**
1101-2447	Dagens Nyheter **3955**
1101-2633	Laerarnas Tidning **2881**
1101-2706	S D I - Scandinavian Dairy Information†
1101-2714	Phonum **5161**
1101-2722	Vi Skogsaegare **3707**
1101-2765	Crafoord Lectures **1736**
1101-2854	Arabhaestinformation†
1101-2897	Anarkistisk Tidskrift **7106**
1101-2927	Oevergrepp†
1101-3273	Bowlaren Magazinet **8224**
1101-3354	Skogsindustrierna *changed to* 1654-8523 **3715**
1101-3915	Flygledaren **56**
1101-3923	Scandinavian Journal of Plastic and Reconstructive Surgery and Hand Surgery. Supplement **6258**
1101-4032	Foeretagsprofilen†
1101-4059	Foeretaget och Framtiden†
1101-4067	Naeringslivets Foeretagsekonomi†
1101-4148	Universidad de Gotumburgo. Instituto Ibero Americano. Anales **4315**
1101-4245	Miljoerapporten **3453**
1101-4253	Baatracing **8272**
1101-4369	Liv i Sverige-Bladet
1101-4423	Djurtidningen Djurskyddet *changed to* 1651-4505 **319**
1101-4431	Informationsbulletinen†
1101-4539	Medienotiser fraan NORDICOM-Sverige **8120**
1101-4571	Bygd och Natur (Skriftserie) **4207**
1101-4601	X-Men† **8999**
1101-4628	Gryps **4225**
1101-4709	Sparoeversikt **1519**
1101-4733	Forests, Trees and People Newsletter†
1101-492X	Modern Industri
1101-4946	Aktuellt i Vaesterbotten†
1101-4954	Foeretagarjournalen†
1101-5004	Katten Din†
1101-5152	S A - Sound Affects†
1101-5179	Nordic Road & Transport Research **8633**
1101-5187	Kvinnovett **8900**
1101-5268	Bakgrund **7065**
1101-5284	Jernkontorets Bergshistoriska Utskott. H **6467**
1101-5314	Faaglar i Soedra Aelvsborg
1101-5527	Daphne **785**
1101-5578	Industriell Foernyelse†
1101-5772	Sweden Business†
1101-5810	Golfkalendern†
1101-5888	Vael & Ve†
1101-6345	Current Sweden **3955**
1101-6396	Moderna Tider†
1101-6469	Svensk Tennis *changed to* 1653-2546 **8249**
1101-6590	Foeretagsaffaerer†
1101-6698	Audiovisuella Medier†
1101-6817	Svenska Narkotikapolisfoereningen. Publikation **2669**
1101-6868	Byahornet **5267**
1101-6892	Idrottslaeraren **8235**
1101-6930	Working Environment†
1101-704X	Lund Publications in Physical Geography†
1101-7104	Information fraan Laekemedelsverket **6848**
1101-7139	Shambala†
1101-7260	School of Business, Economics and Law, Goeteborg University. Department of Human and Economic Geography. Occasional Papers **4028**
1101-7341	Enviro *changed to* 6209-9450
1101-7430	Studia Uralica Upsaliensia **5181**
1101-7473	Foeretagsminnen **4220**
1101-7546	Alla Bilar **8555**
1101-7597	Sveamaal **7187**
1101-7643	Malmoe Hoegskola. Laerarutbildningen. Rapporter om Utbildning **2885**
1101-7686	Didaktisk Tidskrift (Print) *changed to* Didaktisk Tidskrift (Online) **2842**
1101-7848	Laborativ Arkeologi *changed to* 1650-1519 **399**
1101-7880	Tommy Iseskogs Arbetsraettliga Nyhetsbrev **4603**
1101-7953	Short Stories of Crime, Detection & Mystery **5415**
1101-7961	Marknadstendenser†
1101-8003	Skog & Saag **3715**
1101-8259	Arbetsterapeuten Publicerar Sig **6106**
1101-8267	Renewable Energy for Development **3146**
1101-8429	Acta Regiae Societatis Scientiarum et Litterarum Gothoburgensis. Biomedica **650**
1101-8437	Byggfakta Projektnytt **988**
1101-8550	Gloed **8042**
1101-8623	Konsttidningen **500**
1101-8658	Fogningsteknik **6342**
1101-8704	Ingenjoeren **3198**
1101-878X	Studia Biblica Upsaliensia **7684**
1101-881X	Ny Kultur†
1101-8968	Microsoft Magazine *changed to* 1650-2507
1101-9093	Oerebro Universitet. Centrum foer Stadsmiljoeforskning. Rapport *changed to* 1653-1531 **4421**
1101-9107	Teatertidningen **8480**
1101-914X	Trots Allt **5243**
1101-9182	Vaensterpress **7191**
1101-9190	Betong **982**
1101-9212	Box†
1101-9301	Museum of National Antiquities. Monographs **6531**
1101-9417	B U D - Information†
1101-9506	Skog och Forskning *changed to* 1653-6568 **3702**
1101-9522	Skaanekuriren **7183**
1101-9565	Sweden. Statistiska Centralbyraan. Arbetssjukdomar och Arbetsolyckor **4524**
1101-9581	Hennes Serier **3955**
1101-9611	Vaegledaren i Utbildning och Arbetsliv **6704**
1101-9654	Lantmaeteritidsskriften *changed to* Lantmaetaren **4018**
1101-9670	Kyrkokoerjournalen **6583**
1101-9727	Smalspaarsinform **8625**
1101-9948	Lund Monographs in Social Anthropology **7984**
1102-0024	Fastighetsvaerlden **7590**
1102-0105	Hela Jorden **7647**
1102-0180	Civil **2225**
1102-0199	Vegetar†
1102-030X	Svenskt Naeringsliv och Naeringspolitik†
1102-0423	Svensk Racing†
1102-0458	Studies in Research Ethics **6955**
1102-0814	Danstidningen **2685**
1102-0822	Populaer Historia **4156**
1102-0938	Tomorrow **3470**
1102-0970	Statens Jordbruksverks Foerfattningssamling *changed to* 1652-3040 **319**
1102-1187	Skolbarn *changed to* 1652-7844 **2861**
1102-1217	Jaktkamraten **8320**
1102-1276	Specialpedagogen *changed to* 1650-7231 **3047**
1102-1322	Skogsvetenskap†
1102-1330	Svensk Foersaekring **4524**
1102-1349	Faaglar i Stockholmstrakten **906**
1102-1764	Goeteborgs Universitet. Department of Oceanography. Report†
1102-1802	Arauco Documentos†
1102-1853	Polisrapport†
1102-187X	Riksantikvarieambetet. Arkeologiska Undersoekningar. Skrifter **414**
1102-1934	Affaersbilen†
1102-1969	Fakta. Traedgaard - Fritid **3729**
1102-1993	Svensk Danssport *changed to* 1651-7946
1102-2043	Comprehensive Summaries of Uppsala Dissertations from the Faculty of Arts **483**
1102-2191	Konstmagasinet†
1102-2272	Baat-Revyn†
1102-2329	Klenoder **4237**
1102-2353	Familjefoereningen foer Internationell Adoption **8040**
1102-2388	Ladysport Magazine†
1102-2671	Kryss foer Alla†
1102-2752	Tidskrift foer Sveriges Domarefoerbund **4796**
1102-2892	Elbogen (Aarskrift) **4217**
1102-2922	Ekonomi & Styrning†
1102-2930	Mersmak **2640**
1102-3007	Statens Jordbruksverk. Rapport **158**
1102-3104	Empati **6137**
1102-3252	Aftonbladet Kultur†
1102-3384	Marknadsjournalen†
1102-3414	Haestar och Ridsport†
1102-3449	Bon Appetit†
1102-3511	Fast Food **4385**
1102-3597	Tema Arkiv **1797**
1102-3619	Svenskans Beskrivning **5184**
1102-3821	Foer **7643**
1102-3902	Statens Invandrarverks Foerfattningssamling *changed to* 1650-2515 **7287**
1102-397X	Extreme Survival†
1102-4038	Copyright†
1102-416X	European Journal of Surgery. Supplement†
1102-4291	Akademiker†
1102-4321	Kvinnovetenskapliga Studier **8900**
1102-4356	Konsumentnytt†
1102-4712	Lund Dissertations in Sociology **8119**
1102-4739	Befolkningsstatistik. Del 2, Inrikes och Utrikes Flyttningar **7303**
1102-4747	Befolkningsstatistik. Del 3, Folkmangden efter Kon, Alder och Medborgarskap M M **7303**
1102-4941	Royal Swedish Academy of Sciences. Beijer International Institute of Ecological Sciences. Discussion Paper Series **3490**
1102-500X	Logopednytt **6159**
1102-5026	Jaktdebatt **8320**
1102-5212	Samlarboken **368**
1102-5298	Aecklet†
1102-5425	Skattelagstiftning **4784**
1102-5441	MediaCom†
1102-5530	Svensk Fonogramfoerteckning†
1102-5565	Adomus†
1102-5581	Management of Technology **1776**
1102-5786	Stora Skatteboken†
1102-5824	Nordisk Arkitekturforskning **451**
1102-593X	A S U Newsletter **2505**
1102-5956	Kretslopp **3488**
1102-5964	Encordado **6564**
1102-6014	Kultura *changed to* 1654-6555 **96**
1102-6103	I A T U L News **5012**
1102-6111	Vaare Rovdjur **966**
1102-6138	Integral Psykoanalys†
1102-6146	Tandhygienist Tidningen **5867**
1102-626X	V T I Saertryck **8636**
1102-6324	Officeren†
1102-6472	Utbildning och Demokrati **2924**
1102-6499	Pequod **5350**
1102-6502	Folkens Museum - National Museum of Ethnography **339**
1102-6510	Scandinavian Journal of Nutrition. Supplement†
1102-6596	Globala Affaerer†
1102-6634	Provning och Forskning *changed to* 1654-6342 **3222**
1102-6642	Teknisk Tidskrift (Stockholm)†
1102-6758	Ekologiskt Lantbruk **107**
1102-6804	Goda Grannar **1009**
1102-6812	Ornis Svecica **912**
1102-6901	Amatoerastronomen *changed to* 1651-6346 **582**
1102-7053	Stockholm Water Front **8832**
1102-7207	Amningsnytt **5985**
1102-7355	Current Swedish Archaeology **389**
1102-7428	O J **6600**
1102-7460	Finansinspektionens Foerfattningssamling **7437**
1102-7495	Elektroniktidningen **3098**
1102-769X	Lund Studies in Ethics and Theology **7661**
1102-7878	Uppsala Studies in Faith and Ideologies **7692**
1102-7908	Kulturella Perspektiv **346**
1102-7940	Suecoromana **4271**
1102-7967	Teknik, Kommunikation och Handikapp **4070**
1102-8025	Jordbruksinformation **125**
1102-8033	Farmacifacket **6841**
1102-8254	Ingenjoersvetenskapsakademien. I V A - M **8426**
1102-8610	Veteranposten **8076**
1102-8629	Nya Cykeltidningen **8265**
1102-8882	Handels Utredningsinstitut. Forskningsrapport **1818**
1102-9021	Oberoende **2697**
1102-9056	K S L A Nytt **129**
1102-9137	Tidningen Fastighetsfoervaltaren **7613**
1102-917X	Handeln i Sverige **1719**
1102-9218	Svensk Fastighetsindikator **7613**
1102-9722	St. Petersburg News **8785**
1103-0011	Corporate Computing†
1103-0100	Papers in Museology **6535**
1103-0615	Nytt om Niotusen *changed to* Nytt om 9000 & 14000 **6405**
1103-0836	Movium Bulletin **4419**
1103-0844	Snowmobile **8334**
1103-0895	Kreditguide **1365**
1103-0968	Melos **6587**
1103-114X	Loener foer Sveriges Olika Yrkesgrupper†
1103-1239	Pro Hockey **8194**
1103-1247	Vind†
1103-1255	A A F - Tidningen†
1103-1263	Africa Info **4172**
1103-1484	Landstingens Ekonomi *changed to* 1653-0853 **1921**
1103-1522	Kristdemokratisk Debatt *changed to* 1652-5728 **7116**
1103-1727	Praktikan **5699**
1103-1832	Heterogenesis **493**
1103-1875	Definitioner av Strukturbegreb inom Varuhandeln **24**

ISSN

9530 1103-1905 ULRICH'S PERIODICALS

1103-1905 Kostnads- och Effektivitetsdata **1247**
1103-1948 Shamansk Aarsbok†
1103-1999 Somalia News Update†
1103-2391 Nyfoeretagaren *changed to* 1653-4816 **1740**
1103-2472 Fantomen-Kroenika **2188**
1103-2618 Oerebro Universitet. Centrum foer Feministiska Samhaellsstudier. Skriftserie **8902**
1103-2650 Rak Vaenster†
1103-2669 Briefing fraan Utriksdepartementet†
1103-2731 Jaktvapenguiden **8320**
1103-2855 Cirkulation **8820**
1103-291X All Vaerldens Kvinnor **8850**
1103-2928 Cupido†
1103-2944 Elektronik i Norden **3098**
1103-3037 Skattehandbok foer Chefer **1943**
1103-3088 Young **2172**
1103-3096 Kurdistan Rapport†
1103-3126 Kvinnotryck **4710**
1103-3142 Koepmannen Vaest **1430**
1103-3177 Fotografi *changed to* 1404-0212
1103-3363 Sveriges Geologiska Undersoekning. Serie Ca. Avhandlingar och Uppsatser i Kvarto **2770**
1103-3371 Sveriges Geologiska Undersoekning. Serie C. Forskningsrapporter **2770**
1103-341X I T M Rapport **3438**
1103-3568 Close-Up Magazine **6557**
1103-3614 Proffs **8508**
1103-3665 Daeck-Profil†
1103-3738 Skattebok foer Dig†
1103-3754 Bygg och Jaernhandeln *changed to* 1651-7326 **1823**
1103-3762 Golf Digest **8231**
1103-3878 Loenner i Sverige†
1103-3991 Scan AOPA Newsletter†
1103-4009 SD-Kuriren **7182**
1103-4092 R V F Rapport *changed to* 1654-5303 **3504**
1103-4246 Sportfack **8205**
1103-4270 Royal Institute of Technology. Department of Structural Engineering. Trita - B K N. Bulletin **3282**
1103-4289 Kungliga Tekniska Hoegskolan. Institutionen foer Byggkonstruktion. Trita-B K N. Rapport **3277**
1103-4297 Kungliga Tekniska Hoegskolan. Institutionen foer Byggkonstruktion. Trita-B K N. Examensarbete **3277**
1103-4386 F A Rs Regelsamling *changed to* 1653-591X **4630**
1103-4386 F A Rs Regelsamling *changed to* 1653-5898 **4806**
1103-4386 F A Rs Regelsamling *changed to* 1653-5901 **4626**
1103-4424 Mur och Puts†
1103-470X Trita-F K T *changed to* 1651-7660 **69**
1103-4777 Havsfiskelaboratoriet. Meddelande **3596**
1103-4793 En Vaerld†
1103-4904 Roeda Korsets Tidning *changed to* Henry **8044**
1103-4920 Beckerell **477**
1103-4955 Tuberkulos i Sverige **5828**
1103-503X Incitament **5633**
1103-5285 Skandinavisk Underhaallsmarknad†
1103-5757 Lund Studies in Psychology of Religion **7661**
1103-5765 B F N Informerar **1281**
1103-582X Cykelkalendern *changed to* 1651-162X **8269**
1103-5897 G F F **2734**
1103-5935 Skatteinformation **1943**
1103-6060 Jakthunden†
1103-6133 Foeretagarna i Skaane†
1103-6206 Saendaren **7773**
1103-6516 Etnologiska Skrifter **338**
1103-6575 Allt om Traedgaard **3721**
1103-6591 Barbar
1103-6931 Naetverk och Kommunikation *changed to* 1654-2002 **2504**
1103-7334 Nostalgia Motor Magazine *changed to* 1650-8947 **368**
1103-7415 Allt om Vin *changed to* 1653-3925 **4351**
1103-7652 Svensk Idrottsmedicin **6234**
1103-8063 Allt om Hjaelpmedel **4063**
1103-8128 Scandinavian Journal of Occupational Therapy **5710**
1103-8152 Nordisk Museologi **6534**
1103-8233 Aarsbok foer Riksarkivet och Landsarkiven **4986**
1103-8527 Miljoeforskning (Solna) **3453**
1103-8578 Pop†
1103-8764 Kult (Stockholm) **4150**
1103-8799 Alhambras Litteraera Magasin†
1103-8802 Elle Interioer **4556**
1103-8977 Tjeckiska och Slovakiska Roester **7268**
1103-9000 Aftonbladet **3954**
1103-9019 Alingsaas Tidning - Elfsborgs Laens Tidning **3954**
1103-9027 Arbetarbladet **3954**
1103-9051 Avesta Tidning **3954**
1103-906X Barometern *changed to* Barometern Oskarshamnstidningen **3954**
1103-9086 Blekinge Laens Tidning **3954**
1103-9094 Blekingeposten **3954**
1103-9108 Bohuslaeningen **3955**
1103-9159 Dagbladet **3955**
1103-9183 Dalademokraten **3955**
1103-9205 Elfsborgs Laens Allehanda **3955**
1103-9221 Eskilstuna-Kuriren **3955**
1103-923X Expressen **3955**
1103-9302 Gefle Dagblad **3955**
1103-9329 Gotlands Tidningar **3955**
1103-9345 Goeteborgs - Posten **3955**
1103-9353 Hallands Nyheter **3955**
1103-937X Haparandabladet **3955**
1103-940X Hudiksvalls Tidning **3956**
1103-9469 Joenkoepingsposten **3956**
1103-9523 Kristianstadsbladet **3956**
1103-9892 Post- och Inrikes Tidningar (Print) *changed to* 1654-0816 **1160**
1103-9914 Sala Allehande **3956**
1104-005X Sundsvalls Tidning **3925**
1104-0084 Soedermanlands Nyheter **3956**
1104-0114 Trelleborgs Allehanda **3957**
1104-0122 Trollhaettans Tidning **3957**
1104-0173 Upsala Nya Tidning **3957**
1104-0246 Vaesterbottens - Kuriren **3957**
1104-0327 Ystads Allehanda **3957**
1104-0556 Tidskrift foer Litteraturvetenskap **5389**
1104-067X Medier & Kommunikation **30**
1104-0688 Socialfoersaekring **4523**
1104-0696 Reumatikertidningen **6226**
1104-0807 Uppsala North American Studies Series **4316**
1104-0939 Met-Aviisi **3549**
1104-0963 Grana. Supplement **791**
1104-1099 C A P & Design **7579**
1104-1102 Svensk Periodicafoerteckning (Print edition) *changed to* Svensk Periodicafoerteckning. (Online) **636**
1104-1242 Astronomi och Rymdfart†
1104-1250 Medicinsk Vetenskap & Praxis **5675**
1104-1315 Afrikagruppernas Aarskroenika†
1104-1382 Sveriges Rikes Lag CD-ROM†
1104-1412 Ungdom foer Djurens Raett *changed to* 1651-5528 **321**
1104-1420 Socialvetenskaplig Tidskrift **8071**
1104-1560 Studia Statistica Upsaliensia **8407**
1104-1722 Bindu **6643**
1104-196X Ariel **3954**
1104-2060 Alla Ledare **7745**
1104-232X Comprehensive Summaries of Uppsala Dissertations from the Faculty of Science and Technology **7936**
1104-2370 Medicinskt Forum (Print) *changed to* Medicinskt Forum (Online) **5675**
1104-2400 Papper & Kontor **1854**
1104-2435 Parkinson-Journalen **6173**
1104-2516 Uppsala Dissertations from the Faculty of Science and Technology **7927**
1104-2842 Systems Ecology Contributions†
1104-2974 Alla Tiders Boecker **7551**
1104-2982 Nytt fraan Revisorn **1298**
1104-3121 Archaeology and Natural Science†
1104-3180 Klassiker **2236**
1104-3199 Documenta Mundi **4321**
1104-327X Goeteborgs Universitet. Centrum foer Forskning om Offentlig Sektor. Rapport (Print Edition) *changed to* 1653-1264 **7439**
1104-3369 S C A Investor Report†
1104-3377 S C A Investor Report **6738**
1104-3385 Goal **8230**
1104-3431 Acta Sueco-Polonica **3515**
1104-3490 Bra Korsord **4330**
1104-3520 Umeaa Universitet. Institutionen foer Arkeologi och Samiska Studier. Arkeologiska Studier **421**
1104-358X Folkhaelsoinstitutet. Rapport *changed to* 1651-8624 **7542**
1104-3695 Faaglar i NV-Skaane **906**
1104-3822 Medicinsk Vetenskap **5675**
1104-4195 University of Stockholm. Institute for International Economic Studies. Annual Report **1189**
1104-4233 Mynttidningen **6651**
1104-4403 Environmental Policy and Society. Research Report **3427**
1104-4446 Acta Americana **322**
1104-4551 Alternativ
1104-4616 Dialaesen **6267**
1104-4632 Karolina **5656**
1104-4675 Brand News **6746**
1104-4721 Geologiskt Forum **2742**
1104-4969 Kroenika **7659**
1104-5035 Kvinnor & Fundamentalism **8870**
1104-5191 Svarta Fanor†
1104-5205 Glaenta **5218**
1104-5256 Nordiska Afrikainstitutet - Annual Report **4177**
1104-5337 Oeppet Hus **4421**
1104-5477 Svensk Tidskrift foer Medicinsk Akupunktur **315**
1104-5515 Studia Celtica Upsaliensia **4269**
1104-5523 Praxis†
1104-5558 Foto **6967**
1104-5701 Master of Public Health Essay **7531**
1104-5825 Bildteknik *changed to* 1651-8705 **4018**
1104-5957 Stobaeana **964**
1104-5965 Soedra Afrika **7266**
1104-5981 Byggindustrin **988**
1104-618X Raettsfall fraan Foersaekringsoeverdomstolen†
1104-6376 Socialpolitik **8071**
1104-6481 Uppsala Studies on Eastern Europe **4276**
1104-6503 Fjaellet **8313**
1104-6546 Aeldreomsorg *changed to* 1403-7025 **8074**
1104-6570 Praktik & Teori **2898**
1104-6627 Kvinnosyn†
1104-6678 Skogsindustriernas Aarsskrift **3715**
1104-6686 Skogsindustrierna. Annual Publication *see* 1104-6678 **3715**
1104-6694 Skogsindustrierna. Rapport Annuel *see* 1104-6678 **3715**
1104-6708 Skogsindustrierna. Jahresschrift *see* 1104-6678 **3715**
1104-6856 Svenska Friidrottsforbundets Tidning Friidrott†
1104-6899 Journal of Forest Economics **3694**
1104-7267 V T I Konferens **8636**
1104-7313 Sveriges Lantbruksuniversitet. Institutionen foer Jordbrukets Biosystem och Teknologi. Rapport **160**
1104-7321 Sveriges Lantbruksuniversitet. Institutionen foer Jordbrukets Biosystem och Teknologi. Specialmeddelande *changed to* 1104-7313 **160**
1104-7348 Finansmarknadet **1347**
1104-7356 Swedish Financial Market *see* 1104-7348 **1347**
1104-7402 Special Features in Vegetation Science *see* 1100-9233 **799**
1104-7410 Miljoe Eko **3453**
1104-7488 Dagens Medicin **5603**
1104-7739 K A M E D O *changed to* 1652-6775 **8052**
1104-7860 Shetlandsponnyn **8298**
1104-800X Arbetsmarknaden **1664**
1104-8077 87: an Axelsson **5247**
1104-8123 Jaernaffaerer med Bygg-och Faergaktuellt *changed to* 1651-7326 **1823**
1104-8158 Evolution **3377**
1104-8166 Evolution (English Edition) *see* 1104-8158 **3377**
1104-8174 Evolution (German Edition) *see* 1104-8158 **3377**
1104-8182 Evolution (Spanish Edition) *see* 1104-8158 **3377**
1104-8190 Evolution (French Edition) *see* 1104-8158 **3377**
1104-8204 Evolution (Italian Edition) *see* 1104-8158 **3377**
1104-8247 Artes International†
1104-828X Skandinavisk Dyk-Guide **8201**
1104-8301 T S Tidskriftsbok (Year)†
1104-8387 Svensk Kaernbraenslehantering. S K B R D & D-Programme *see* 1104-8395 **3512**
1104-8395 Svensk Kaernbraenslehantering. S K B F U D-Program **3512**
1104-8417 Nordiska Afrikainstitutet. Discussion Papers **1602**
1104-8425 Nordiska Afrikainstitutet. Research Report **4177**
1104-8565 Kommunernas Ekonomiska Laege *changed to* 1653-0853 **1921**
1104-8646 Loenejournalen
1104-8891 Entreprenoer **1960**
1104-8999 Stjaernurmakaren **4569**
1104-9006 Rikslarm
1104-9022 Tidskriften foer Medicin och Haelse†
1104-909X Se & Hoer **2364**
1104-9111 Haelsinglands Tidning **3955**
1104-9154 F O A - R *changed to* 1650-1942 **6420**
1104-957X Musik†
1104-9650 Advokatnytt **4611**
1104-9723 Symfo'ni **6622**
1104-9804 Telekom Idag **2342**
11046414 Sveriges Riksdag. Utredningar *changed to* 1653-0942 **7471**
1105-0004 Annales Geologiques des Pays Helleniques **2724**
1105-008X Aristotelion Panepistemion Thessalonikes. Theologike Schole. Epistemonike Epeteris
1105-0136 Balkanika Symmeikta **4202**
1105-0144 Andriaka Chronika **4130**
1105-0225 Hiaka Khronika **4227**
1105-0462 Chronika Aisthetikes **6910**
1105-0519 Bank of Greece. Monthly Statistical Bulletin **1213**
1105-0527 Bank of Greece. Report of the Governor **1314**
1105-073X Platon **2239**
1105-0888 Episteme kai Tehnologia Galaktos **264**
1105-0950 Arhaiologike Efemeris **380**
1105-0969 Archailogike Hetaireia en Athenais. Praktika **378**
1105-1019 Mnemosyne **4245**
1105-1213 Agroticos Synergatismos **1421**
1105-1280 4 Trochoi **8613**
1105-1299 2 Trochoi **8270**
1105-1302 Echos kai Hi Fi **6564**
1105-1310 Ptisi kai Diastima **6442**
1105-1329 4 Trochoi Test **8613**
1105-1345 Stereofonia & Mousike **6619**
1105-140X Ellenike Nefrologia **6267**
1105-1469 Komix **2198**
1105-1477 Praktiki **8880**
1105-1493 Gynaika **8866**
1105-1531 Geografikes Uperesias Stratou. Deltio **4009**
1105-1582 Skepsis **6952**
1105-1590 The European Review of Public Law **4669**
1105-1930 Elektron **3097**
1105-2139 Kleronomia **7704**
1105-2147 Greece. National Statistical Service. Quarterly National Accounts of Greece **1235**
1105-2155 Anthropos: Yearbook in Anthropology **328**
1105-2163 Horos
1105-221X Fondation de Recherche et d'Editions de Philosophie Neohellenique. Serie Recherches **6920**
1105-2325 Paidiatrike Boreiou Ellados **6099**
1105-2333 Psuhiatrike **6175**
1105-235X Philosophical Inquiry **6940**
1105-2414 Gefsi **3644**
1105-2430 Metalleiologika-Metallourgika Hronika **6324**
1105-2503 Epilogi **1338**
1105-2511 Balance Sheets **1212**
1105-252X Economic Review of the Year - The Greek Economy **1480**
1105-2554 American School of Classical Studies at Athens. Newsletter **372**
1105-2783 Eikastika†
1105-3208 Sughrona Bemata **7819**
1105-3992 Arheia Ellenikes Iatrikes **5577**
1105-4069 Epitheoresis Klostoufantourgias **8450**
1105-4204 Norwegian Institute at Athens. Papers **2238**
1105-4263 Bibliophilia **4204**
1105-4964 Guide of Consumer Goods in Greece **1818**
1105-4972 Self Serbis **1843**
1105-4999 Pharmakeftiki
1105-5049 Bios **661**
1105-5162 Studies in Locational Analysis **4428**
1105-5219 Pontiake Hestia **4254**
1105-5421 Egnatia **4216**
1105-5464 Computer gia Olous **2411**
1105-5472 P C Master **2580**
1105-5480 Pixel†
1105-5502 Information **1752**
1105-5901 Balkan Bibliography†
1105-5936 Archeion Thessalikon Meleton **4199**
1105-6770 Amaltheia **4197**
1105-7181 O Mentor **405**
1105-7726 Edessaika Chronika **4216**
1105-7785 Bibliotheke tes en Athenais Archailogikes Hetaireias **384**
1105-7858 Amuna kai Diplomatia **7105**
1105-8269 Fauna Graeciae **942**
1105-8390 Index Hellas†
1105-8439 Europe Sud-Est†
1105-8536 Athens Financial Gazette **1063**
1105-8579 Nomismatika Khronika **6652**
1105-8919 Spoudai **1178**
1105-8986 Energeia **3128**
1105-9176 Eurobalkans **4219**
1105-9419 Aristoteles **4201**
1105-9664 Nea Oikologia **3456**
1105-9729 Bank of Greece. Economic Bulletin **1314**
1105-9745 Politika Themata **7171**
1105-9893 Paidi kai Nei Gonis **2164**
1106-0077 C A D - C A M & Computer Graphics **3288**
1106-0115 Ta Athenaika **4201**

DIRECTORY 2010 1110-4929 9531

1106-0247 Aristoteleion Panepistemion Thessalonikes. Philosophike Schole. Ereterida - Periodos Beta: Tmema Gallikes Glossas kai Philologias **4201**
1106-1391 Almanako **2175**
1106-1405 Charoumenes Istories **2182**
1106-1502 Greece. National Statistical Service. Statistiques du Travail **1235**
1106-1553 Greece. National Statistical Service. Environmental Statistics **3479**
1106-1936 Oikonomikos Tahudromos **1156**
1106-2134 Elleniko Zoologiko Arheio **941**
1106-2606 Studies in Regional and Urban Planning **4428**
1106-2738 Imaging Pro†
1106-2878 Astrolabos **5474**
1106-2975 F I T C E Forum **3308**
1106-3076 Aktines **7620**
1106-3718 Trofima kai Pota **611**
1106-3734 Galaktomia *see* 1106-3718 **611**
1106-4226 B M J (Greek Edition) *see* 0959-535X **5582**
1106-4641 Alieftika Nea **3583**
1106-4838 Aristoteleion Panepistemion Thessalonikes. Philosophike Schole. Epistomonike Ereterida - Periodos Beta: Teuchos Thematos Philologias **4200**
1106-5028 B M J (Middle East Edition) *see* 0959-535X **5582**
1106-5109 Pharmakeftikon Deltion (Regular Edition)†
1106-5524 Cosmopolitan (Athens) **8856**
1106-5605 Neusis **7891**
1106-5737 Psuhologia **7394**
1106-6040 Athens News **3873**
1106-6571 Commercial Bank of Greece. Economic Review **1328**
1106-658X Emporike Trapeza tes Ellados. Oikonomiko Deltio **1483**
1106-661X Tekmeria (Print) *changed to* Tekmeria (Online) **4164**
1106-6776 Auto Motor & Sport **8559**
1106-7829 Demosiografiki **4574**
1106-8299 New Europe **1501**
1106-8590 Diakopes **8698**
1106-8892 Sea & Yachting **8282**
1106-983X Petalon **4156**
1107-0129 Greece. National Statistical Service. Agricultural and Livestock Production (Year) **181**
1107-0625 Balkan Union of Oncology. Journal **6009**
1107-065X Monitor P C **2578**
1107-1141 Balkan Journal of Stomatology **5836**
1107-311X Gaia **2735**
1107-356X Games **2477**
1107-3721 Benakeio Futopathologico Instituoto. chorika *see* 0365-5814 **122**
1107-3748 Greek Travel Pages **8715**
1107-3756 International Journal of Molecular Medicine **5639**
1107-5287 Bank of Greece. Bulletin of Conjunctural Indicators **1314**
1107-5392 Filologos **2234**
1107-714X Playboy (Athens)
1107-7999 Thesis **7268**
1107-8421 Tile Kontrol **2397**
1107-8588 Status **6300**
1107-8618 Ram **2435**
1107-8642 Stigmes **3874**
1108-1279 Ellenike Orthodontike Epitheorese **5843**
1108-1430 Hellenic Journal of Nuclear Medicine **5627**
1108-149X The Danish Institute at Athens. Proceedings **389**
1108-1503 The Danish Institute at Athens. Monographs **389**
1108-2682 Haema **5936**
1108-2690 Bank of Greece. Monetary Policy **1536**
1108-2712 Nautica **8279**
1108-2992 Series in Economics, Business and the Environment **1172**
1108-3115 National Geographic Ellada **4020**
1108-3417 B S A Newsletter **383**
1108-3794 Monografies Thalassion Epistemon **2813**
1108-393X Mediterranean Marine Science **2812**
1108-4081 Anistoriton **4130**
1108-4146 Contributions to the Zoogeography and Ecology of the Eastern Mediterranean Region **2608**
1108-4707 Graecolatinitas Nostra - Fonti **2234**
1108-5037 Difono **6561**
1108-5045 Metal Hammer & Heavy Metal **6587**
1108-5673 7 Meres T V **2399**
1108-569X Ego **8859**
1108-5991 E Y *changed to* E Y Z H N **3874**
1108-6033 Vita **6999**
1108-6041 Marie Claire **8873**
1108-6122 Hitech **3101**
1108-6130 Market Hitech **3108**
1108-6173 Gamos **5558**
1108-6181 Tahudromos **3874**
1108-622X To Paidi Mou Kai Ego **2164**
1108-6289 Men **6295**
1108-636X Formula 1 **8173**
1108-6653 Vogue **2262**
1108-6661 Focus **7855**
1108-6866 Kafenio **2563**
1108-7048 Alpha Guide **4381**
1108-7366 I C U s and Nursing Web Journal **5961**
1108-7471 Annals of Gastroenterology **5920**
1108-7609 H E R M I S **5552**
1108-7641 Connecting **2367**
1108-7684 Auto Triti Aggelies **8561**
1108-7714 Best Tips & Praxis **2408**
1108-7773 Chip **2410**
1108-779X Auto Triti **8560**
1108-7803 Auto Triti Test Book **8561**
1108-7811 Auto Triti Touring **8561**
1108-782X Auto Katalog **8558**
1108-7838 Auto Accessories **8557**
1108-7846 Moto Accessories **8261**
1108-7854 Moto Triti **8261**
1108-8028 Exodos **3874**
1108-8036 Sok **3874**
1108-8044 Diva **8858**
1108-8060 Astrologos **565**
1108-8087 Penthouse **6297**
1108-8095 Metro **5227**
1108-8192 InLife **2558**
1108-8230 Geuse Kouzina **4359**
1108-8508 Traveler National Geographic **8768**
1108-8613 PlayStation Tips **2481**
1108-863X GamePro Greece **2476**
1108-8648 Computer Games Magazine **2475**
1108-8699 Ethnos **3874**
1108-8907 Elle (Greek Edition) **8860**
1108-961X Mediterranean Archaeology and Archaeometry **405**
1109-1584 Oikonomike Biomehanike Epitheorese **1900**
1109-1681 Ankyra **4130**
1109-1789 Computer Games Magazine Collection **2475**
1109-1797 PlayStation Tips Collection **2481**
1109-1800 PlayStation Magazine Collection **2480**
1109-1819 GamePro Collection **2476**
1109-2483 About Thessaloniki **3873**
1109-2580 Agricultural Economics Review **192**
1109-2734 W S E A S Transactions on Circuits and Systems **3115**
1109-2742 W S E A S Transactions on Communications **2344**
1109-2750 W S E A S Transactions on Computers **2441**
1109-2769 W S E A S Transactions on Mathematics **5546**
1109-2777 W S E A S Transactions on Systems **5546**
1109-2858 Operational Research **1783**
1109-3099 Hormones **5894**
1109-3501 Glamour (Athens) **8865**
1109-3552 About Thessaloniki Geusis tis Polis **3873**
1109-4028 Chemistry Education: Research and Practice in Europe *changed to* 1756-1108 **2057**
1109-4486 To Vima tou Asklipiou **5728**
1109-5202 Forma **8845**
1109-6020 Athletike Psuhologia **7337**
1109-6535 Cancer Genomics & Proteomics **6012**
1109-7035 Sport Auto **8604**
1109-7647 *see* 1109-7655 **6020**
1109-7655 Gastric and Breast Cancer **6020**
1109-8597 S E E J E **1516**
1109-9445 W S E A S Transactions on Electronics **3115**
1109-9518 W S E A S Transactions on Biology and Biomedicine **711**
1109-9526 W S E A S Transactions on Business and Economics **1193**
1109-9577 W S E A S Transactions on Acoustics and Music **6627**
1110-0001 Bibliotheque d'Etudes Coptes **7703**
1110-001X Textes et Traductions d'Auteurs Orientaux† **8993**
1110-0028 Communications in Science and Development Research† **8942**
1110-0036 Alexandria. High Institute of Public Health. Bulletin **7506**
1110-0044 Egyptian Journal of Plastic and Reconstructive Surgery
1110-0052 Bulletin of Pharmaceutical Sciences **6827**
1110-0060 Alexandria Medical Journal **5571**
1110-0133 The Medical Research Institute. Journal **5671**
1110-0141 Mansoura Engineering Journal **3209**
1110-015X Alexandria Dental Journal **5834**
1110-0168 Alexandria Engineering Journal **3180**
1110-0176 Alexandria Science Exchange **7834**
1110-0184 Aswan Science and Technology Bulletin **7837**
1110-0192 Egyptian Journal of Food Science **3634**
1110-0206 Egyptian Journal of Horticulture
1110-0214 Egyptian Journal of Physics **7010**
1110-0222 Egyptian Journal of Veterinary Science
1110-0230 Egyptian Journal of Phytopathology **786**
1110-0257 Minia Journal of Agricultural Research and Development
1110-0265 Minufiya Journal of Agricultural Research **137**
1110-0303 Egyptian Journal of Radiation Sciences & Applications **6195**
1110-032X Journal of Agricultural Research **126**
1110-0338 Zagazig Journal of Agricultural Research **171**
1110-0346 Mansoura University Journal of Agricultural Sciences **136**
1110-0354 National Institute of Oceanography and Fisheries. Bulletin *changed to* 1687-4285
1110-0362 Egyptian National Cancer Institute. Journal **6018**
1110-0397 Ain Shams Science Bulletin **7833**
1110-0400 Al Azhar Medical Journal† **8934**
1110-0419 Annals of Agricultural Science, Moshtohor **91**
1110-0435 Geological Survey of Egypt. Annals
1110-0451 Arab Journal of Nuclear Sciences and Applications **3164**
1110-046X Arab Roads **8629**
1110-0486 Assiut Journal of Agricultural Sciences **93**
1110-0494 Assiut Medical Journal **5580**
1110-0532 The Egyptian Academy of Sciences. Proceedings† **8953**
1110-0540 The Egyptian Journal of Medical Sciences **5608**
1110-0559 The Egyptian Journal of Histology **832**
1110-0583 Egyptian Society of Parasitology. Journal **5813**
1110-0591 National Research Centre. Bulletin **7887**
1110-0613 Mathematical and Physical Society of Egypt. Proceedings
1110-0664 Maritime Research Journal **8653**
1110-0672 Journal of Arab Child **6094**
1110-077X Sahara Review
1110-0834 University of Alexandria. Faculty of Medicine. Bulletin **5727**
1110-0877 Egyptian Society of Cardiology. Bulletin *changed to* 1110-2608 **5785**
1110-0885 Entomological Society of Egypt. Bulletin. Economic Series **845**
1110-0915 Assiut University. Faculty of Engineering. Bulletin *changed to* 1687-0530 **3205**
1110-0931 Cairo University. Faculty of Pharmacy. Bulletin **6827**
1110-0958 Assuit University. Faculty of Science. Bulletin: A. Physics *changed to* 1687-4900 **7006**
1110-0966 Cairo University. Faculty of Science. Bulletin **7843**
1110-0974 The Nutrition Institute of the Arab Republic of Egypt. Bulletin† **8978**
1110-0982 Ophthalmological Society of Egypt. Bulletin†
1110-0990 Civil Engineering Research Magazine† **8941**
1110-1008 Ain Shams University. Economic and Business Review **1057**
1110-1024 Miki **2202**
1110-1067 The Egyptian Journal of Haematology **5936**
1110-1075 The Egyptian Journal of Mental Health **6137**
1110-1083 The Egyptian Journal of Neurology, Psychiatry, and Neurosurgery **6137**
1110-1105 The Egyptian Journal of Psychiatry **6137**
1110-1121 The Egyptian Journal of Surgery **6242**
1110-113X Egyptian Journal of Wildlife and Natural Resources† **8953**
1110-1148 Egyptian Orthopaedic Journal **6058**
1110-1156 The Egyptian Population and Family Planning Review **972**
1110-1164 The Egyptian Rheumatologist **6223**
1110-1199 Ittihad al-Sinaat al-Misriyah. Year Book† **8967**
1110-1237 Magallat Kulliyyat al-Tarbiyyat Gami'at Tanta **2884**
1110-1245 Egyptian Society of Endocrinology, Metabolism and Diabetes. Journal **5890**
1110-1253 Egyptian Society of Engineers. Journal **3188**
1110-127X Egyptian Society of Toxicology. Journal **3496**
1110-1288 Egyptian Veterinary Medical Association. Journal **8797**
1110-1318 Mansoura Journal of Pharmaceutical Sciences
1110-1326 Mansoura Science Bulletin *changed to* 1687-5109 **7881**
1110-1334 Mental Peace **6160**
1110-1342 Dirasat Sukkaniyyat
1110-1350 Zoological Society A.R. Egypt. Proceedings *changed to* 1110-6344 **941**
1110-1369 Helwan University. Science & Arts. Research Studies **5304**
1110-1377 The Review of the Faculty of Commerce **1432**
1110-1385 Ain Shams University. Scientific Bulletin of the Faculty of Engineering **3180**
1110-1415 Tanta Medical Journal **5720**
1110-1431 Zagazig University Medical Journal **5734**
1110-144X The Zoological Society of Egypt *changed to* 1110-6344 **941**
1110-1458 Zagazig Veterinary Journal **8815**
1110-1466 Egyptian Mineralogist **6461**
1110-1482 Mansoura Dental Journal†
1110-1547 Al Dirasat wa-al-Buhuth al-Tigariyyat **1092**
1110-1555 Zagazig University. Faculty of Science. Bulletin **7933**
1110-1563 Al Azhar Journal of Agricultural Research *changed to* 1687-8698 **89**
1110-1571 Egyptian Journal of Applied Science **106**
1110-158X The Directory of Egyptian Research Periodicals (D E R P) **624**
1110-1601 Al Azhar Journal of Microbiology† **8934**
1110-161X Egyptian Rheumatology and Rehabilitation **6223**
1110-1644 Al Azhar Journal of Pharmaceutical Sciences **6824**
1110-1776 Applied Endocrinology in Egypt *changed to* 1110-7812 **5890**
1110-1792 Alexandria Journal of Pharmaceutical Sciences **6819**
1110-1814 The Egyptian Military Medical Journal
1110-1822 The Arab Journal of Laboratory Medicine **5902**
1110-1849 Egyptian Journal of Anaesthesia **5771**
1110-1865 The Egyptian Journal of Community Medicine
1110-1881 Egyptian Journal of Occupational Medicine **5609**
1110-1903 Journal of Engineering and Applied Science **3204**
1110-192X Journal of Environmental Sciences **3447**
1110-1946 New Egyptian Journal of Medicine **5685**
1110-2004 Egyptian Journal for Remote Sensing *changed to* 1110-9823 **2707**
1110-2039 The Medical Journal of Teaching Hospitals & Institutes **4106**
1110-2047 Alexandria Journal of Veterinary Sciences **8790**
1110-2055 Center Papyrological Studies. Bulletin† **8940**
1110-208X Benha Medical Journal **5584**
1110-2098 Menoufia Medical Journal **5678**
1110-211X Mansoura Medical Journal
1110-2195 Scientific Journal of Faculty of Science, Minoufia University
1110-225X Magallat al-Buhuth al-Idariyyat **7452**
1110-2276 Magallat al-Buhuth al-Tigariyyat al-Mu'asirat
1110-2284 Al Magallat al-Misriyyat lil-Dirasat al-Tigariyyat
1110-2322 Zagazig Medical Association Journal *changed to* 1110-1431 **5734**
1110-2330 Engineering Research Bulletin *changed to* 1110-5615 **3190**
1110-2381 The Scientific Journal of Al-Azhar Medical Faculty, Girls **5711**
1110-2411 Magallat Kulliyyat al-Tarbiyyat bi-Banha **2993**
1110-242X Minia University. Faculty of Engineering & Technology. Bulletin
1110-2446 El-Minia Medical Bulletin
1110-2454 Al Minia Science Bulletin. Section Botany
1110-2462 Al Minia Science Bulletin. Physics Section
1110-2489 Bulletin d'Information Archeologique
1110-2497 Etudes Urbaines
1110-2519 Tabbin Institute for Metallurgical Studies. Bulletin **6480**
1110-2527 Sedimentology of Egypt **2766**
1110-2535 Al-Azhar Bulletin of Science **7949**
1110-2543 Journal of Productivity and Development **1890**
1110-256X Egyptian Mathematical Society. Journal **5485**
1110-2578 Nashrat Buhuth al-Iqtisad al-Manzili **4364**
1110-2586 Egyptian Computer Science Journal **2417**
1110-2594 Egyptian Journal of Rabbit Science **941**
1110-2608 The Egyptian Heart Journal **5785**
1110-2624 Al Azhar Dental Journal *changed to* 1110-6751 **8934**
1110-2675 Arab Universities Journal of Agricultural Sciences **92**
1110-2861 Magallat al-Muhandisin **3209**
1110-2918 Assiut Journal of Environmental Studies, Overview Series **3405**
1110-2977 Al-Ahram Weekly **3835**
1110-3248 Magallat Rabitat al-Tarbiyyat al-Hadithat **2884**
1110-3809 Majallat al-Dirasat al-Qanuniyyah **4727**
1110-4562 Mansoura Science Bulletin. A, Chemistry *changed to* 1687-5060 **2072**
1110-4570 Mansoura Science Bulletin. B, Biology *changed to* 1687-5087 **687**
1110-4589 Mansoura Science Bulletin. C, Natural Sciences *changed to* 1687-5095 **7881**
1110-4678 Al-Ahram ar-Riyadi
1110-4708 Al-Bitrul
1110-4929 Water Science **8840**

ISSN

9532 1110-502X ULRICH'S PERIODICALS

1110-502X Serket
1110-5089 Zagazig Journal of Pharmaceutical Sciences 6886
1110-5097 Egypte - Monde Arabe 7132
1110-5313 Cancer Molecular Biology† 8939
1110-5321 Egyptian German Society for Zoology. Journal. A, Comparative Zoology 941
1110-533X Egyptian German Society for Zoology. Journal. B, Anatomy and Embryology 941
1110-5348 Egyptian German Society for Zoology. Journal. C, Histology and Histochemistry 941
1110-5356 Egyptian German Society for Zoology. Journal. D, Invertebrate Zoology and Parasitology 941
1110-5364 Egyptian German Society for Zoology. Journal. E, Entomology 941
1110-5372 Journal of Union of Arab Biologists Cairo. A. Zoology 952
1110-5437 Mansoura Journal of Forensic Medicine and Clinical Toxicology
1110-5585 Journal of the Advances in Agricultural Research 128
1110-5593 Egyptian Journal of Medical Laboratory Sciences 5905
1110-5607 Scientific Medical Journal 5711
1110-5615 Engineering Research Journal 3190
1110-5623 Egyptian Poultry Science 285
1110-5690 Middle East Fertility Society Journal 5998
1110-5704 African Journal of Urology 6264
1110-5712 Egyptian Journal of Urology 6267
1110-5747 Biological Current Content of Egypt† 8936
1110-5879 The African Journal of Mycology and Biotechnology 755
1110-5925 Ain Shams University. Current Psychiatry
1110-600X Egyptian Journal of Textile & Polymer Science & Technology 8450
1110-6093 Egyptian Journal of Biotechnology 763
1110-6107 Assiut University Bulletin for Environmental Researches 3405
1110-6131 Egyptian Journal of Aquatic Biology and Fisheries 670
1110-614X South Valley University. Faculty of Arts. Bulletin 5375
1110-6158 Egyptian Journal of Agronematology 106
1110-628X Magallat al-Muhasabt wa-al-Idarat wa-al-Ta'min 1296
1110-6298 Suez Canal Veterinary Medicine Journal 8807
1110-631X Journal of Hepatology, Gastroenterology, Infectious Diseases 5820
1110-6328 Maritime Technology 8653
1110-6336 Egyptian Journal of Agricultural Research *changed to* 1687-837X 106
1110-6344 Egyptian Journal of Zoology 941
1110-6360 Egyptian Journal of Nutrition and Feed 6658
1110-6379 Egyptian Journal of Biomedical Sciences 5905
1110-6409 Al Azhar University Engineering Journal *changed to* 1687-8418 3180
1110-6425 Advances in Agricultural Research in Egypt† 8928
1110-6433 Journal of Arab Academy for Science, Technology & Maritime Transport *changed to* Scientific Journal of Arab Academy for Science, Technology & Maritime Transport
1110-6468 The Journal of Legal Medicine Forensic Sciences 5915
1110-6506 Journal of Petroleum and Mining Engineering
1110-6565 Egyptian Journal of Biophysics 753
1110-6573 The Egyptian Hospitals Association. Bulletin† 8953
1110-6581 Banha Veterinary Medical Journal 8794
1110-6603 Port - Said Engineering Research Journal 3215
1110-6611 Cairo University. Faculty of Physical Therapy. Bulletin 6107
1110-662X International Journal of Photoenergy 2136
1110-6638 Egyptian Paediatric Association. Gazette 6091
1110-6670 Egyptian Journal of E N T and Allied Sciences 6079
1110-6751 Al Azhar Journal of Dental Science† 8934
1110-6778 Statistics, Computer Science and Operations Research. Annual Conference 1179
1110-6816 Al-Ahram 3835
1110-6859 Egyptian Journal of Biology 670
1110-6867 Egyptian Journal of Natural History 670
1110-6875 Arab Journal of Biotechnology 756
1110-6964 Al-Magallat al-Qanuniyyat al-Iqtisadiyyat 4726
1110-6972 National Radio Science Conference. Proceedings† 8976
1110-6999 Suez Canal University Medical Journal 5718
1110-7162 Entomological Society of Egypt. Bulletin 845
1110-7219 Journal of Veterinary Medical Researches 8801
1110-7227 Ain Shams University. Faculty of Arts. Annals 5250
1110-7243 Journal of Biomedicine and Biotechnology 5646
1110-7251 *see* 1110-7243 5646
1110-7278 Egyptian Journal of Schistosomiasis and Infectious and Endemic Diseases
1110-7308 Journal of Pest Control and Environmental Sciences 3499
1110-7324 Magallat Gam'iyyat al-Muhandisin al-Mikanikiyin al-Misriyyat
1110-7332 Assiut University. Faculty of Science. Bulletin. Section C. Mathematics *changed to* 1687-4897 5474
1110-7340 Assiut University. Faculty of Science. Bulletin. Section D. Botany *changed to* 1687-4927 777
1110-7359 Assiut University. Faculty of Science. Bulletin: E. Zoology *changed to* 1687-4935 934
1110-7367 Assiut University. Faculty of Science. Bulletin. Section F. Geology *changed to* 1687-4943 2725
1110-743X Journal of Union of Arab Biologists. Microbiology and Viruses 890
1110-7448 Journal of Union of Arab Biologists. Physiology and Algae 925
1110-7456 Journal of Union of Arab Biologists. Cytogenetics, Ecology and Toxonomy 834
1110-7499 Cataract and Cornea 6039
1110-7502 Population Sciences
1110-7510 Egyptian Society of Pharmacology and Experimental Therapeutics. Journal 6837
1110-7529 South Valley Medical Journal *changed to* 1687-8353 5716
1110-7537 Egyptian Journal of Comparative Pathology and Clinical Pathology 5608
1110-7545 Beni Suef Veterinary Medical Researches *changed to* 1687-7926 8794
1110-757X Journal of Applied Mathematics 5501
1110-7588 Magallat Kuliyyat al-Tigarat lil-Buhuth al-'Ilmiyat 1774
1110-760X Psychiatry Update† 8983
1110-7626 Ain Shams University. Faculty of Education. Journal. Education and Psychology 2825
1110-7634 Ain Shams University. Faculty of Education. Journal. Scientific Section 7833
1110-7642 Ain Shams Dental Journal 5833
1110-7650 Egyptian Journal of Dermatology and Andrology 5875
1110-7669 Egyptian Society of Ultrasonics in Medicine. Journal† 8953
1110-7685 Business Today 1076
1110-7707 International Congress for Statistics, Computer Science† 8965
1110-7731 Gami'at al-Zagazig. Magallat al-Buhuth al-Tigariyyat 1113
1110-7774 Al Azhar Journal of Pediatrics 6088
1110-7782 The Egyptian Journal of Internal Medicine 5945
1110-7790 Fayoum Journal of Agricultural Research and Development 112
1110-7804 Ulum wa-Funun al-Musiqa 6625
1110-7812 Egyptian Journal of Applied Endocrinology 5890
1110-7820 The Medical Journal of Ahmed Maher Teaching Hospital
1110-7987 Ruh al-Qawanin
1110-8525 Egyptian Journal of Biophysics & Biomedical Engineering
1110-8657 Eurasip Journal on Applied Signal Processing *changed to* 1687-6172 2470
1110-8673 Alif 5416
1110-9777 Majallat Kulliyyat al-Tarbiyyat Bil-Mansura
1110-9823 Egyptian Journal of Remote Sensing and Space Sciences 2707
1111-0015 Revue de l'Information Scientifique et Technique 2907
1111-0171 Algerie Actualite
1111-0287 El Moudjahid 3790
1111-0333 El Watan 3790
1111-035X Annuaire Statistique de l'Algerie 8345
1111-0368 Algeria. Office National des Statistiques. Annuaire Statistique des Wilayate de l'Ouest 8344
1111-0376 Algeria. Office National des Statistiques. Annuaire Statistique des Wilayate du Centre 8344
1111-0384 Algeria. Office National des Statistiques. Statistiques (Revue Trimestrielle) 8344
1111-0392 Algeria. Office National des Statistiques. Collections Statistiques 8344
1111-0902 Technologies Avancees 2439
1111-1100 Le Matin
1111-4398 Revue Maghrebine de Mathematiques 5529
1111-4797 Societe Algerienne de Chimie. Journal 2080
1111-5556 Universite de Sidi Bel Abbes. Annales de Mathematiques 5544
1111-5696 Algeria. Office National des Statistiques. Bulletin de Statistiques Courantes 8344
1111-5939 Algeria. Office National des Statistiques. Donnees Statistiques 8344
1111-7001 Algeria. Office National des Statistiques. Informations Statistiques sur la Conjoncture 8344
1111-7680 Algeria. Office National des Statistiques. Annuaire Statistique des Wilayate de l'Est 8344
1112-5152 Bien-Etre 6983
1112-5209 Journal of Electrical Systems 3322
1113-1292 Turjuman 5189
1113-2175 Morocco. Direction de la Statistique. Indice du Cout de la Vie 1252
1113-531X Katab: Index Analytique Bibliographique 1247
1113-7207 Morocco. Direction de la Statistique. Bulletin Statistique 8389
1113-738X Reperes Statistiques 1514
1113-9048 Conjoncture: Evolutions et Perspectives 8364
1113-9536 Activite, Emploi et Chomage 8023
1114-0097 Les Indicateurs Sociaux (Year) 1490
1114-3800 Physical & Chemical News 2139
1114-6834 Institut Scientifique. Bulletin. Section Sciences de la Terre 2710
1114-8500 Institut Scientifique. Bulletin. Section Sciences de la Vie 678
1114-8802 e - T I 2417
1115-0017 Issues in Nigerian Development Series 3920
1115-0335 Borno Museum Society. Newsletter 6521
1115-0351 Tortoise 3470
1115-0521 Orient Journal of Medicine 5691
1115-232X Ogbomoso Journal of Theology 7769
1115-2613 Nigerian Journal of Medicine 5686
1115-2788 Journal of Aquatic Sciences 3599
1115-4322 Research in Yoruba: Language & Literature 5166
1115-8832 The Catholic Ambassador 7788
1115-8891 *see* 1013-0322 123
1116-1027 Nigeria Industrial Directory 2021
1116-1043 Journal of Medical Laboratory Science 5907
1116-2775 Journal of Mining and Geology 6467
1116-4077 African Journal of Medicine & Medical Sciences (New Series) 5570
1116-4689 Ife Journal of History 4175
1116-4875 African Journal of Economic Policy 1057
1116-7157 The News (Lagos) 3920
1117-0603 Nigeria. National Universities Commission. Statistical Digest 2934
1117-0611 Nigeria. National Universities Commission. Convocation Speeches of Nigerian Universities 2996
1117-062X Nigeria. National Universities Commission. Annual Report 2996
1117-0638 Nigeria. National Universities Commission. Research Bulletin 2996
1117-1073 E C W A Theological Seminary. Journal 7638
1117-1421 I F E PsychologIA 7361
1117-1936 The Nigerian Postgraduate Medical Journal 5686
1117-272X African Journal of International Affairs & Development 7219
1117-370X Africa Geoscience Review 2723
1117-4315 African Journal for Physical, Health Education, Recreation and Dance 6981
1117-7322 Gender & Behaviour 7358
1117-9686 West African Journal of Nursing 5983
1118-0579 Global Journal of Pure and Applied Sciences 7858
1118-1028 Journal of Pharmaceutical Research and Development *changed to* Journal of Phytomedicine and Therapeutics 6856
1118-146X Glendora Review 5301
1118-1737 University of Lagos. Law Society. Law Journal†
1118-2733 Nigerian Journal of Horticultural Science 3745
1118-3713 L B S Management Review 1771
1118-4035 Nigerian Journal of Clinical and Counselling Psychology 7388
1118-4485 B M J (Nigerian Edition) *see* 0959-535X 5582
1118-4841 African Journal of Reproductive Health 8843
1118-5570 Journal of Technology and Education in Nigeria 212
1118-6267 Nigerian Journal of Natural Products and Medicine 6864
1118-7387 Prison Watch 2666
1118-8561 Sahel Medical Journal 5708
1119-1716 Nigerian Infection Control Association. Journal 5823
1119-2712 Journal of Nomadic Studies 345
1119-2984 B M J (West African Edition) *see* 0959-535X 5582
1119-3077 Nigerian Journal of Clinical Practice 5686
1119-3999 Journal of Medicine and Medical Sciences 5652
1119-409X Mary Slessor Journal of Medicine 5822
1119-5096 African Journal of Biomedical Research 5569
1119-7048 International Journal of Emotional Psychology and Sport Ethics 7364
1119-7056 African Journal of Cross-Cultural Psychology and Sport Facilitation 7332
1119-8362 Journal of Applied Sciences and Environmental Management 3488
1120-0030 Cholesterol News
1120-009X Journal of Chemotherapy 6024
1120-012X Office Layout 1853
1120-0138 Office Automation 1853
1120-0146 Microbiologia Medica 5679
1120-0200 Journal of Paleopathology 6726
1120-0227 Surfing† 8991
1120-0251 Il Ferroviere† 8956
1120-0405 Giornale di Chirurgia Plastica Ricostruttiva ed Estetica†
1120-0413 Altreltalie 7276
1120-0421 C I - Cardiovascular Imaging†
1120-0499 Giornale Internazionale di Dermatologia Pediatrica†
1120-0588 Economia Aziendale†
1120-0650 Passato e Presente 4253
1120-0669 Storia e Critica 4268
1120-0677 Storia delle Relazioni Internazionali†
1120-0863 Livres et Revues d'Italie *see* 0024-2683 7566
1120-0979 Universita degli Studi di Bologna. Istituto di Entomologia Guido Grandi. Bollettino *changed to* 1721-8861 841
1120-1177 Studi Storici Meridionali
1120-1371 Revue Valdotaine d'Histoire Naturelle 7904
1120-1622 Accademia delle Scienze di Torino. Memorie. Classe di Scienze Morali, Storiche e Filologiche 4440
1120-1630 Accademia delle Scienze di Torino. Memorie. Classe di Scienze Fisiche, Matematiche e Naturali 7831
1120-1657 Difesa Oggi†
1120-1665 Defence Today†
1120-1681 Protec† 8983
1120-172X Le Industrie Italiane per la Protezione Civile e Ecologia. Annuario† 8964
1120-1762 Ragiusan 7538
1120-1770 Italian Journal of Food Science 3649
1120-1789 Parts 8598
1120-1797 Physica Medica 5695
1120-1819 Edizioni per la Conservazione 3418
1120-1894 Istituto di Tecnologia della Pesca e del Pescato. Note Tecniche e Reprints
1120-1908 Alta Frequenza Rivista di Elettronica†
1120-1932 MediaplusNews† 8973
1120-1959 Lady Moda†
1120-1967 Moda In Collezioni†
1120-1975 Collezioni Donna 2252
1120-1983 Collezioni Bambini 2252
1120-1991 Collezioni Accessori 2252
1120-2009 Cucina Naturale 4355
1120-2017 Guide A P A†
1120-2033 Collezioni Uomo 2253
1120-205X A F T 6963
1120-222X Tutto Casalinghi & Ferramento†
1120-2238 L'Altro Piemonte. Valle d'Aosta†
1120-2246 Euro Power Transmission†
1120-2254 N P S†
1120-2262 Il Gommone e la Nautica per Tutti 8276
1120-2343 Rassegna Bagno Cucina†
1120-2351 Contatto Elettrico 3298
1120-236X Habitat Ufficio 4541
1120-2386 Office Furniture 4548
1120-2394 Keramikos International Ceramics Magazine†
1120-2440 C I L E A. Bollettino 2408
1120-2459 Artista 473
1120-2467 Quaderni Petrarcheschi 5356
1120-2513 O P D Restauro 509
1120-2521 A I B Notizie 4985
1120-253X Sfoglialibro 7573
1120-2556 Perspectives in E.N.T. - Immunology†
1120-2564 Giovani Amici† 8959
1120-2602 Lettera della Nutrizione†
1120-2637 Porte e Cancelli†
1120-267X Teologia 7688
1120-2688 Systema Naturae
1120-270X Petit Rapporteur
1120-2718 Chiaroscuro
1120-2726 Rivista di Linguistica 5169
1120-2742 Bollettino di Archeologia 384
1120-2750 Rivista Medica Italiana di Psicoterapia ed Ipnosi 7405
1120-2777 Arpel 4972
1120-2858 Microcomputer & Software†
1120-2874 Anthropotes 328
1120-2890 Economia Politica 1098
1120-2955 Il Perito Agrario 146
1120-2963 Trombosi & Aterosclerosi†
1120-298X Nomos. Le Attualita del Diritto 4747
1120-3005 Vita in Campagna 5086

1120-303X Pandora 5693
1120-3064 Moda e Bijoux†
1120-3072 18 Karati Gold & Fashion 4570
1120-3080 Istituto di Idrobiologia e Acquacoltura G. Brunelli. Quaderni† 8967
1120-3226 Verona Illustrata 8771
1120-3323 Lunarionuovo
1120-3382 In Oltre† 8963
1120-3420 Rivista di Studi Canadesi† 8986
1120-3455 L'Otorinolaringologia Pediatrica
1120-3471 Lettera di Urologia 6271
1120-348X Autotech†
1120-3501 Arpel Fur 4972
1120-351X Prime Note 7501
1120-3536 Journal of Gynaecological Endocrinology†
1120-3544 Paesaggio Urbano 4422
1120-3560 Giornale Italiano di Riflessoterapia ed Agopuntura† 8959
1120-3579 Rivista di Studi Pompeiani 415
1120-3587 Logistica Management 1773
1120-3595 Sistemi Software†
1120-3633 Attivita Fisica e Sport†
1120-3714 Adolescenza†
1120-3749 Giornale Italiano di Farmacia Clinica 6844
1120-3757 Gastroenterologia Clinica† 8958
1120-3765 Journal of Immunological Research†
1120-3773 Medicina e Informatica†
1120-3781 Prospettive Psicoanalitiche nel Lavoro Istituzionale†
1120-379X Ricerca & Pratica 6116
1120-3854 Methodologia 5151
1120-3889 Agrinform†
1120-3900 Camera di Commercio, Industria, Artigianato e Agricoltura di Ferrara. Listino dei Prezzi all'Ingrosso 1398
1120-3919 Prezzi dei Materiali e delle Opere Edili in Ferrara 1409
1120-3927 Rassegna Stampa†
1120-3943 Camera di Commercio, Industria, Artigianato e Agricoltura di Ferrara. Notiziario Mensile
1120-3951 Elenco Ufficiale dei Protesti Cambiari†
1120-396X Ferrara Economica
1120-4001 Annali di Storia dell'Esegesi 7783
1120-4036 Rivista di Studi Politici 7179
1120-4095 Libri per Bambini e Ragazzi 7566
1120-415X La Motorizzazione 8505
1120-4176 La Patente di Guida 8598
1120-4206 Storia e Problemi Contemporanei 4268
1120-4214 Airline†
1120-4281 Sala Bano 4562
1120-4311 La Lettera di Broncopneumologia
1120-432X Amica 8851
1120-4346 Anna (Italian Edition) 8851
1120-4362 Brava Casa 6637
1120-4389 Domenica Quiz 4334
1120-4397 Elle (Milan) 8860
1120-4400 Elle Decor 4556
1120-4419 Linus 5224
1120-4427 Insieme 8868
1120-4435 Max 3897
1120-4443 Novella 2000 3898
1120-4451 Piu Bella *changed to* 1970-6898 8935
1120-446X Salve 8848
1120-4486 Visto 3899
1120-4516 Spazio Casa 4562
1120-4540 Amadeus 6543
1120-4559 Archeo 378
1120-4567 Natura Oggi
1120-4575 Pratica† 8982
1120-4583 Speak Up 5176
1120-4591 Vitality 6670
1120-4621 La Cartellina 6554
1120-4648 Tribuna Biologica e Medica 708
1120-4699 State Archives of Assyria Bulletin 418
1120-4737 Paragone. Arte†
1120-4745 Paragone. Letteratura†
1120-4761 Model Time 4341
1120-4788 Spaziolegno† 8989
1120-4826 Minerva Biotecnologica 768
1120-4834 Surgery and Immunity†
1120-4885 Centro Documentazione e Ricerche Economico-Sociali. Quaderni
1120-4923 Erba d'Arno. Quaderni 5290
1120-4931 Il Nuovo Club 6994
1120-494X Auto Oggi 8559
1120-4958 100 Cose *see* 1124-1713 2396
1120-4958 100 Cose *see* 1120-4982 3896
1120-4958 100 Cose *see* 0391-6855 1150
1120-4958 100 Cose *see* 1126-4497 4555
1120-4958 100 Cose *see* 1120-5261 9000
1120-4958 100 Cose *see* 1120-5016 6984
1120-4958 100 Cose *see* 1120-5296 3899
1120-4974 Confidenze 8856
1120-4982 Corriere della Sera 3896
1120-5016 Corriere Salute 6984
1120-5024 Donna Moderna 8859
1120-5032 Economia & Management 1740
1120-5059 Fortune†
1120-5067 La Gazzetta dello Sport 8174
1120-5083 Il Giallo Mondadori
1120-5105 Giornale delle Assicurazioni 4504
1120-5113 Grazia 8866
1120-5121 Guida T V†
1120-513X Guidacucina†
1120-5156 Marie Claire 8873
1120-5164 Ministeismi†
1120-5180 La Gazzetta dello Sport. I Quaderni 8174
1120-5199 I Romanzi
1120-5237 Secondamano (Parma) 35
1120-5245 Secondamano (Piacenza) 35
1120-5253 Segretissimo 5412
1120-5261 7† 9000
1120-527X Starbene 6997
1120-5288 Urania 5448
1120-5296 Vivimilano 3899
1120-5318 Rivista della Borsa†
1120-5334 Tecnologie Alimentari 3666
1120-5377 G T Il Giornale del Termoidraulico 4119
1120-5393 L'Educazione dei Sordi 4074
1120-5407 Bagno e Cucina. Architettura e Interior Design *changed to* 1591-7193 8934
1120-5415 Allure 592
1120-5458 Bucher und Zeitschriften Italiens *see* 0024-2683 7566
1120-5490 Libros y Revistas de Italia *see* 0024-2683 7566
1120-5504 Vita Italiana. Temi† 8997
1120-5512 Vita Italiana. Speciale. Istituzioni e Comunicazione† 8997
1120-5520 Vita Italiana. Speciale† 8997
1120-5555 E N E A (Rapporti Tecnici) R T - AMB 3166
1120-5571 E N E A (Rapporti Tecnici) R T - GEN 3166
1120-558X E N E A (Rapporti Tecnici) R T - I N N 3166
1120-5598 E N E A (Rapporti Tecnici) R T - NUCL 3166
1120-5636 Accademia Italiana della Cucina. Rivista *changed to* Civilta della Tavola 3631
1120-5679 Sahara 4178
1120-5695 Rivista Internazionale di Diritto Comune 4841
1120-5741 Recercare 6609
1120-575X Tramonti per Emigrati
1120-5776 Ippologia 8799
1120-5784 Media Production
1120-5822 D'A† 8948
1120-5830 Commercio Bomboniera Italiana†
1120-5857 Suedtiroler Landwirt 159
1120-5865 Windsurf Italia 8285
1120-5873 Tutto Mountain Bike 8269
1120-592X Doctor
1120-5962 Meditime
1120-5989 Urodinamica
1120-6020 Avvenire 3896
1120-6039 Ristorazione Collettiva 4397
1120-6055 Gazzettino dell'Economia†
1120-6101 La Madre 8873
1120-611X Topolino 2218
1120-6144 Ristorazione Piu†
1120-6195 Il Giornale della Musica 6569
1120-6268 Italian Design Fashion
1120-6276 Ondaverde 8633
1120-6330 Accademia Nazionale dei Lincei. Atti. Matematica e Applicazioni. Rendiconti 5464
1120-6349 Accademia Nazionale dei Lincei. Atti. Scienze Fisiche e Naturali. Rendiconti 7831
1120-6373 Giornale Italiano di Allergologia e Immunologia Clinica 5758
1120-6381 La Casa sui Campi†
1120-639X Collettivita - Convivenze
1120-6403 Medit *changed to* 1594-5685 140
1120-6462 Ius Ecclesiae 7801
1120-6500 Spiragli
1120-6519 Il Naturalista Valtellinese 692
1120-656X Grotta della Vipera†
1120-6578 Etnie
1120-6659 Giornale della Lamiera News†
1120-6667 Medicina 7†
1120-6683 Talento 4477
1120-6705 Ethology Ecology & Evolution. Special Issue 942
1120-6721 European Journal of Ophthalmology 6041
1120-6756 Caleidoscopio Letterario 5269
1120-6772 Abitare con Arte
1120-6861 Archeologia e Calcolatori 425
1120-687X Archivio della Nuova Procedura Penale 4884
1120-6888 Argomenti di Gerontologia†
1120-690X Induzioni 8378
1120-6934 Vaccari Magazine 6901
1120-6942 Detergo 2243
1120-6977 Istituto Italiano di Navigazione. Atti 61
1120-6993 Progetto (Rome)
1120-7000 Hip International 5628
1120-706X Bonsai & News 3725
1120-7086 Buon Gusto
1120-7094 Comparatistica 5211
1120-7108 Diagnosis†
1120-7116 Car Stereo & F M
1120-7140 Doctor Os 5842
1120-7159 Scuola Superiore della Pubblica Amministrazione. Bollettino. Documenti e Informazioni† 8987
1120-7183 Rendiconti di Matematica e delle Sue Applicazioni 5528
1120-7302 Materials Engineering†
1120-7353 Il Mondo della Bibbia 7808
1120-737X Mondo della Tecnica e della Chimica Conciaria†
1120-7493 Pagine SudNord
1120-7507 Pediatrics (Italian Edition) 6102
1120-7558 Rivista Italiana di Chirurgia Maxillo-Facciale 5864
1120-7612 Syrinx 6622
1120-7639 Veneto: Ieri, Oggi, Domani
1120-7647 Videotecnica† 8997
1120-7655 Auto In†
1120-7663 Yacht Capital 8285
1120-7698 Petria 807
1120-7728 Casa Vogue Antiques†
1120-7760 Uomo Vogue 2262
1120-7779 Vanity Fair. Italia†
1120-7787 Vogue Bambini 2263
1120-7795 Vogue Pelle 2263
1120-7809 Vogue Sposa 5561
1120-7817 Vogue Gioiello 4570
1120-7825 La Sapienza della Croce 7816
1120-7876 S E C Serramenti e Componenti *changed to* 1824-4696 1055
1120-7884 Tile Italia 4551
1120-7892 Giornale Italiano dell'AIDS†
1120-7914 Alfa Romeo World†
1120-7957 Cinologia
1120-7965 Diritto e Pratica del Lavoro 4866
1120-799X Il Giornale delle Barche a Motore 8276
1120-8031 Luogo Comune
1120-804X Meridiani 8733
1120-8066 P C World Italia 2581
1120-8120 Q†
1120-8163 Telecom†
1120-8198 Vera
1120-8260 Le Fonti Musicali in Italia†
1120-8287 Il Giornale del Meccanico 8582
1120-8309 Unione Matematica Italiana. Bollettino. Sezione C: Analisi Funzionale e Applicazioni†
1120-8333 Ricerche Teologiche 7678
1120-8376 Laboratorio 2000 2103
1120-8414 800 Italiano†
1120-8422 Istituto Universitario Orientale di Napoli. Dipartimento di Studi dell'Europa Orientale. Sezione Storico - Politico - Sociale 4148
1120-8457 R C I. Riscaldamento Climatizzazione Idronica 3217
1120-8465 Macintosh Magazine† 8972
1120-849X Achab (Rome) 5408
1120-8554 Costruire il Mobile†
1120-8619 Guida al Software†
1120-8635 Argomenti di Cardiologia
1120-8643 Argomenti di Chemioantibioticoterapia†
1120-8651 Argomenti di Gastroenterologia Clinica 5920
1120-866X Argomenti di Neurologia
1120-8678 Bollettino di Farmacosorveglianza† 8937
1120-8694 Diseases of the Esophagus 6079
1120-8724 Optolaser†
1120-8740 American Journal of Orthodontics and Dentofacial Orthopedics: Edizione Italiana†
1120-8767 Imballaggio e Movimentazione
1120-8848 Rivista Giuridica del Molise e del Sannio 4776
1120-8856 Rivista Pascoliana 4473
1120-8899 Tutto Strumenti
1120-8902 Politecnico†
1120-8910 Journal of Prosthetic Dentistry (Edizione Italiana)†
1120-8953 Italy. Istituto Nazionale di Statistica. Collana d'Informazione 8381
1120-9135 Annali di Igiene, Medicina Preventiva e di Comunita 7507
1120-9151 Rivista Italiana di Acquacoltura 3606
1120-916X Strolic Furlan 3622
1120-9178 Quaderni di Lingue e Letterature 5356
1120-9216 Museo Civico di Storia Naturale di Venezia. Quaderni 690
1120-9224 Quaderni di Archeologia del Veneto 412
1120-9232 Quaderni Emiliani
1120-9283 Plot
1120-9364 Atque 6906
1120-9372 Immediati Dintorni†
1120-9380 La Pratica Analitica 7391
1120-9402 Stomatologia Mediterranea
1120-9410 Sanita, Scienza e Storia
1120-9445 Imprese e Storia†
1120-9453 Banca Impresa Societa 1310
1120-9461 Finanza Imprese e Mercati†
1120-947X Lavoro e Diritto 4598
1120-9488 Polis 7167
1120-9496 Politica Economica 1511
1120-950X Politica in Italia 7167
1120-9518 Rapporto sull'Economia del Mezzogiorno 1164
1120-9526 Ricerche di Storia Politica 4159
1120-9534 Rivista Economica del Mezzogiorno 1168
1120-9542 Rivista Giuridica del Mezzogiorno 4776
1120-9550 Sistemi Intelligenti 2456
1120-9593 Economia Marche†
1120-9607 Materiali per una Storia della Cultura Giuridica 4955
1120-9720 Design Diffusion News 440
1120-9739 OFX Office International *changed to* 1827-6547 452
1120-9747 Giornale Italiano di Suicidologia
1120-9755 Padova e il Suo Territorio 510
1120-9860 Civilta del Mediterraneo 7955
1120-9879 High Blood Pressure & Cardiovascular Prevention
1120-9887 Professional
1120-9895 Tecnologia della Deformazione
1120-9909 Symphonia† 8992
1120-9968 La Matematica e la sua Didattica 5510
1120-9976 Rivista di Neuroradiologia *changed to* 1971-4009 6204
1120-9992 Basic and Applied Myology 656
1121-0001 Hotel Domani 4389
1121-0028 Osteoporosis News
1121-0036 Estetica (Bologna)†
1121-0052 Il Fauno
1121-0095 A I D A Informazioni 4985
1121-0206 La Buona Cucina 4353
1121-0303 Geschichte und Region 4223
1121-0311 Il Delfino 2693
1121-0338 La Citta di Riga
1121-0346 Fotologia 6968
1121-0419 Fidia Research Series†
1121-0435 Quaderni di Cooperazione Sanitaria 5825
1121-0516 Materia 449
1121-0524 Arte Documento 472
1121-0532 Il Territorio 3899
1121-0621 Studi Italiani 5378
1121-063X Stampi 8439
1121-0656 Laser and Technology†
1121-0664 Il Sogno della Farfalla 6186
1121-0680 Ventesimo Secolo 4276
1121-0745 Reggio Calabria. Dipartimento Patrimonio Architettonico e Urbanistico. Rivista Semestrale 455
1121-0753 Letteratura Italiana. Aggiornamento Bibliografico 629
1121-0761 Rivista della Scuola 3030
1121-0788 Amministrazione e Management†
1121-0796 Ceramic World Review 2039
1121-0958 Cause di Morte 7304
1121-1008 Statistiche della Sanita 7549
1121-1059 Quaderni Tecnici di Acquacoltura
1121-1067 Quaderni di Henoch *see* 0393-6805 7721
1121-1148 Sociologia e Ricerca Sociale 8136
1121-1288 Stop 3899
1121-1318 Consigli Pratici
1121-1342 Societa Medico-Chirurgica della Provincia di Cremona. Bollettino† 8989

ISSN

ISSN

ISSN

1130-9113 Publicaciones de Biologia. Serie Botanica **814**
1130-9121 Revista de la Economia Social y de la Empresa **1167**
1130-9148 Formacion de Seguridad Laboral **2677**
1130-9180 Alerta de Farmacovigilancia *see* 0212-9450 **6826**
1130-9210 Diario Oficial de Galicia (Galician Edition) **4657**
1130-9229 Diario Oficial de Galicia (Spanish Edition) **4658**
1130-9407 Dermatologia Practica **5874**
1130-9431 Gastroenterologia Practica **5924**
1130-9458 Diseno Interior **4538**
1130-9466 Situacion Latinoamericana† **8988**
1130-9512 Revista de Psiquiatria Infanto-Juvenil **6182**
1130-9571 Equipos Productos Industriales **1885**
1130-958X Revista Forestal Espanola **3700**
1130-961X Scriptura **5368**
1130-9644 R D M. Revista de Minas **6477**
1130-9717 N A C C Bioloxia **691**
1130-9776 Verdolay **6539**
1130-9784 Coyuntura Economica de Navarra
1130-9849 Fundacion la Caixa. Panorama **6524**
1130-9857 *see* 1130-9849 **6524**
1130-9865 *see* 1130-9849 **6524**
1130-9881 Retema **3463**
1130-989X Larouco **403**
1130-9903 Endodoncia **5843**
1130-9946 Actualidad Administrativa (Weekly Edition) **1661**
1130-9954 P C Actual **2579**
1130-9970 Journal of Esthetic Dentistry (Spanish Edition)
1131-0111 Semana Medica†
1131-1673 Unifarma†
1131-2386 A E F A Informa†
1131-3587 Revista Espanola de Cardiologia. Suplemento **5799**
1131-3978 Guia Puntex. Anuario Hospitalario Espanol **5621**
1131-4044 Revista Espanola de Anestesiologia y Reanimation. Suplemento *see* 0034-9356 **5774**
1131-4168 Nefrologia. Suplemento *see* 0211-6995 **6271**
1131-4648 Practica Diaria†
1131-494X Athena†
1131-5016 Tierra y Tecnologia **2771**
1131-5040 Real Observatorio de la Armada. Boletin†
1131-5172 Revista Espanola de Defensa **6443**
1131-5199 Archivos de Flora Iberica **776**
1131-527X Sociedad Espanola de Malacologia. Noticiario **818**
1131-5288 I Love English Junior **2193**
1131-5326 Revista de Fisica **7037**
1131-5350 Sancho el Sabio **354**
1131-5369 Aranzadi Social **4620**
1131-5423 Zubia. Monografico **7935**
1131-5490 Boletin de Economia de Navarra†
1131-5571 Revista de la Inquisicion **7814**
1131-558X Revista de Antropologia Social **353**
1131-5598 Arte, Individuo y Sociedad **472**
1131-5601 E I **3094**
1131-5628 Azara†
1131-5660 Fruticultura Profesional **232**
1131-5679 Viticultura Enologia Profesional **257**
1131-5768 Revista de Medicina Familiar y Comunitaria **5705**
1131-5776 Freudiana **6142**
1131-5814 Antropologia
1131-5903 Institut Agricola Catala de Sant Isidre. Butlleti†
1131-5954 Infancia y Sociedad†
1131-5989 Minius **4465**
1131-5997 Vino y Gastronomia **611**
1131-6047 Calidad, Gestion y Tecnica
1131-6128 Canarias Pediatrica **6089**
1131-6144 Investigacion y Marketing **1823**
1131-6225 Revista de Psicologia Social Aplicada **8129**
1131-6233 Update†
1131-6284 Revista Espanola del Pacifico **4158**
1131-6357 Periodistas†
1131-6411 Album, Letras y Artes **464**
1131-6438 Los Complementarios **5211**
1131-6454 Noticias de la Economia Publica, Social y Cooperativa **1502**
1131-6470 B I A **434**
1131-6489 Notas y Estudios Filologicos **5156**
1131-6497 Critica **5212**
1131-6500 C O A G - Informa†
1131-6519 Encrucillada **7640**
1131-6551 Empresario **1104**
1131-656X Tapia **4792**
1131-6632 Estudios de Ciencias Sociales **7962**
1131-6640 Euridice **6918**
1131-6713 Report to the Congress and Senate - Consejo de Seguridad Nuclear†
1131-6756 Instituto de Investigacion Textil y de Cooperacion Industrial. Boletin Intexter **8453**
1131-6837 Cuadernos de Gestion **1737**
1131-6861 Anuari de Filologia. Seccio A, Filologia Anglesa i Alemana **5094**
1131-687X Anuari de Filologia. Seccio B, Estudis Arabs **5094**
1131-6888 Anuari de Filologia. Seccio C, Llengua i Literatura Catalanes **5094**
1131-6896 Anuari de Filologia. Seccio D, Studia Graeca et Latina **5094**
1131-690X Anuari de Filologia. Seccio F, Estudios de Lengua y Literatura Espanola **5095**
1131-6918 Anuari de Filologia. Seccio G, Filologia Romanica **5095**
1131-6950 Excerpta e Dissertationibus in Philosophia **6919**
1131-6977 Entre Estudiantes **5070**
1131-6985 Cuadernos de Estudios Empresariales **1959**
1131-6993 Complutum **4212**
1131-7027 Isidorianum **7801**
1131-7108 Cell Biology Reviews†
1131-7140 Sport Auto
1131-7167 Especial Autocares
1131-7396 Rivasgodaya†
1131-7515 Plast 21 **7096**
1131-7612 Revista d'Historia Medieval **4158**
1131-768X Espacio, Tiempo y Forma. Serie IV. Historia Moderna **4139**
1131-7698 Espacio, Tiempo y Forma. Serie I. Prehistoria y Arqueologia **392**
1131-7736 Veintiuno† **8997**
1131-7744 Cuadernos Republicanos **7432**
1131-7833 Alternativas de Marketing†
1131-785X Motociclismo Catalogo **8262**
1131-7884 Hoteles de Espana **4390**
1131-7957 Revista de Enfermeria **5980**
1131-7965 Investigacion Agraria. Sistemas y Recursos Forestales **3694**
1131-8066 Revista de Economia Aplicada e Historia Economica **1548**
1131-8074 Cuadernos de Grado Medio **2840**
1131-8163 Faro de Vigo **3952**
1131-8597 Anuari de Filologia. Seccio E, Estudis Hebreus i Arameus **5095**
1131-8635 Cuadernos de Relaciones Laborales **1674**
1131-866X Acacia **8085**
1131-8694 Comercio e Industria de la Madera **3710**
1131-8783 R E D† **8983**
1131-8821 Periodoncia
1131-883X Revista d'Arqueologia de Ponent **413**
1131-8848 Florentia Iliberritana **2234**
1131-8872 Centro de Profesores de Albacete. Programas **2835**
1131-8910 Investigacion Clinica y Bioetica **6850**
1131-897X Maderpress†
1131-8988 Phytoma Espana **247**
1131-9054 European Journal of Gerontology†
1131-9062 Cuadernos de Filologia Clasica. Estudios Latinos **5109**
1131-9070 Cuadernos de Filologia Clasica. Estudios Griegos e Indoeuropeos **5109**
1131-9097 Analisis Financiero Internacional **1610**
1131-9100 Mapping **2712**
1131-9208 Kantil†
1131-9240 Mar (Madrid, 1965) **2811**
1131-9267 Papers d'Art **511**
1131-9321 Epsilon **5486**
1131-933X Zapateri **861**
1131-9364 L'Esmalt **2040**
1131-9372 Nosferatu (Spanish Edition)† **8977**
1131-9380 Nosferatu (Basque Edition) *see* 1131-9372 **8977**
1131-9518 Diario de Mallorca **3951**
1131-9526 Residuos
1131-9577 Revista del Centro de Estudios Merindad de Tudela **4472**
1131-9593 Catalogo Bicisport **8256**
1131-9615 Trabajadores de la Ensenanza **2920**
1131-9674 R E D E N **4309**
1131-9712 Bio-Reguladores†
1131-9879 Cuadernos de Estudios del Siglo XVIII **5281**
1131-995X Aula de Innovacion Educativa **3051**
1132-0044 Revista Juridica del Notariado **4773**
1132-0052 Spain. Ministerio de Economia y Hacienda. Boletin de Informacion Trimestral **1519**
1132-0095 Actualizaciones en Anestesiologia y Reanimacion **5768**
1132-0109 Annals of Oncology (Spanish Edition) **6008**
1132-0117 Ideal (Granada Edition) **3952**
1132-0125 Ideal (Jaen Edition) **3952**
1132-0133 Ideal (Almeria Edition) **3952**
1132-0176 Distribucion y Consumo **105**
1132-0214 Linguistica **5146**
1132-0249 Revista Iberoamericana de Fertilidad y Reproduccion Humana **6003**
1132-0257 Actualidad Juridica Aranzadi **4609**
1132-0265 Philologia Hispalensis **5160**
1132-0273 Cuadernos de Medicina Psicosomatica *changed to* 1695-4246 **6134**
1132-032X Revista Ibero-Latinoamericana de Enfermedades de Transmision Sexual
1132-0346 Tratamientos Termicos **6335**
1132-0354 Moldes **6326**
1132-0362 Fundidores **6313**
1132-0389 Campitur **8308**
1132-0427 Bibliografia Dieciochista **5406**
1132-0451 Iberlex B O E - Boletin Oficial del Estado **4849**
1132-0516 Instituto Nacional de Estadistica. Boletin Mensual de Estadistica **8379**
1132-0559 Intervencion Psicosocial **7366**
1132-0591 La Palabra **7811**
1132-0605 Cuadernos de Trabajo de Flora Micologica Iberica **785**
1132-0621 Fundacion Archivo Manuel de Falla. Boletin **6568**
1132-0702 Litterae Vasconicae **5326**
1132-0729 Etniker Bizkaia **338**
1132-080X Idatz & Mintz **5308**
1132-0869 Real Sociedad Espanola de Historia Natural. Memorias **7902**
1132-0877 Telos **6956**
1132-0931 Moda en Espana **2258**
1132-0958 Tempus **4273**
1132-1156 Macworld Espana **2577**
1132-1164 Legislacion de las Comunidades Europeas *changed to* 1135-5425 **4801**
1132-1202 Poligonos **4156**
1132-127X Comunicacion y Estudios Universitarios† **8943**
1132-1296 Index de Enfermeria **7525**
1132-130X Studia Lulliana **4269**
1132-1369 Cromatografia y Tecnicas Afines **2122**
1132-1466 Ferronoticias **3378**
1132-1474 Neumaticos y Accesorios **7825**
1132-1490 Recambio Libre **8600**
1132-1660 Coloquios de Paleontologia **6723**
1132-1717 Fundamentos de Antropologia† **8958**
1132-175X Direccion y Organizacion **1739**
1132-1873 Revista General de Informacion y Documentacion **5043**
1132-189X Historia Urbana **444**
1132-1911 Revista Sindrome de Down **6103**
1132-192X Acciones e Investigaciones Sociales **7945**
1132-1946 Archivos de Cirugia Vascular **5777**
1132-1954 Tecnicas Quirurgicas en Ortopedia y Traumatologia **6073**
1132-1989 Cuadernos de Bioetica **5601**
1132-2012 60 y Mas **8079**
1132-2047 Radio Plans Electronica†
1132-2063 Maquetren **4339**
1132-2098 Delek Elektor Electronics Espana
1132-2179 Belarra **778**
1132-2217 Munibe Antropologia - Arkeologia **348**
1132-2233 Teatro **8481**
1132-2292 Aranzadiana **7836**
1132-2306 Boletin de Astronomia **572**
1132-2330 Revista M E I
1132-2365 Lactarius **799**
1132-2373 Tropelias **5390**
1132-239X Revista de Psicologia del Deporte **7404**
1132-2446 Investigaciones Arqueologicas† **8966**
1132-2462 Habilidad Motriz **6229**
1132-2470 Gala (Sant Feliu De Codines) **395**
1132-2527 Comunidad Europea *changed to* 1579-0452 **4801**
1132-256X Catalan Working Papers in Linguistics *changed to* 1695-6885 **5105**
1132-2640 Papeles de Trabajo **1785**
1132-2675 Eurocarne **3634**
1132-273X Revista del Area de Sanidad, Consumo y Calidad de la Vida **3501**
1132-2799 Revista Galega de Economia **1515**
1132-2950 Horticultura **3737**
1132-3094 Ciutat **7955**
1132-3132 Economia y Finanzas†
1132-3191 Livius **5327**
1132-3213 Clara **8855**
1132-3272 Lecturas. Especial Recetas Cocina *see* 0047-4304 **3952**
1132-3272 Lecturas. Especial Recetas Cocina *see* 1132-3280 **2257**
1132-3280 Lecturas. Especial Moda **2257**
1132-3310 Francofonia **5298**
1132-3329 Fragmentos de Filosofia **6921**
1132-3337 Bolsa de Barcelona. Informe Anual **1613**
1132-3485 Instituto Egipcio de Estudios Islamicos en Madrid. Revista **7711**
1132-3493 Arquitectura del Paisaje **3723**
1132-3701 Sociedad Oftalmologica de Madrid. Boletin **6052**
1132-4287 Medicina Intensiva. Suplemento *see* 0210-5691 **5673**
1132-4791 Urgencias
1132-6107 D C I D O B **7229**
1132-6123 Koiunturaz **1546**
1132-6204 Justidata **4708**
1132-6239 Tarbiya **2917**
1132-6255 Asociacion Espanola de Especialistas en Medicina del Trabajo. Revista **6673**
1132-631X S E L I M **5171**
1132-6336 Revista Espanola de Trasplantes **6257**
1132-6360 Academia de Ciencias Exactas, Fisicas, Quimicas y Naturales de Zaragoza. Monografias **7829**
1132-6409 A + T **425**
1132-6506 Tabula **5050**
1132-6581 Revista d'Etnologia de Catalunya **353**
1132-6751 Duoda **8895**
1132-6824 Cosmos *see* 0037-6604 **581**
1132-6840 Red de Bibliotecas Universitarias† **8984**
1132-6875 Hispania Epigraphica **4227**
1132-6891 Archaeofauna **375**
1132-7030 Zahora **5198**
1132-7170 Revista de Estudios Europeos **4771**
1132-7200 Revista de Historia Industrial **8436**
1132-7294 Humana Iura **7209**
1132-7308 Fidelium Iura **4674**
1132-7359 Cardiologia Practica **5779**
1132-7502 Carlsberg Meridian Catalogue la Palma†
1132-7510 Informe Tecnico de la Pesqueria de la Anchoa **3613**
1132-7545 Boletin Informativo de Lenguas **5265**
1132-7553 Cuadernos de Estudios Medievales y Ciencias y Tecnicas Historiograficas† **8947**
1132-7669 Societat Catalana de Lepidopterologia. Butlleti **859**
1132-7685 Ciencias de la Tierra **784**
1132-7707 Puertanueva **2901**
1132-7715 Puertanueva. Anexo **2901**
1132-7723 Excerpta Philologica **2234**
1132-7731 El Mundo de Tu Bebe **2203**
1132-7790 Compas de Letras†
1132-7839 Revista Espanola de Estudios Canadienses **7997**
1132-7863 Spain. Ministerio del Interior. Revista de Documentacion **4786**
1132-7944 Amadeus
1132-7952 Asmoz Ta Jakitez **329**
1132-8029 Sociedad Espanola de Briologia. Boletin **818**
1132-8037 Fin de Siglo **5296**
1132-8096 Kalium **3249**
1132-810X Georgica **115**
1132-8177 Laguna **6931**
1132-8231 Asparkia **8894**
1132-8304 Cuadernos de Ilustracion y Romanticismo **5409**
1132-8312 Revista Complutense de Historia de America **4310**
1132-8428 Atlantica Internacional **476**
1132-8436 Al Dia **3402**
1132-8444 Aula Verde **3405**
1132-8460 Revista Espanola de Enfermedades Metabolicas Oseas **5807**
1132-8479 Estudios de Pedagogia y Psicologia **2854**
1132-8568 Jurisprudencia Tributaria (Bi-weekly Edition) **1932**
1132-8576 Quincena Fiscal **1941**
1132-8584 Revista de Trabajo y Seguridad Social†
1132-8592 Ciencia y Tecnologia de los Materiales **6308**
1132-8851 Movimiento Natural de la Poblacion Espanola. Tomo II. Resultados por Comunidades Autonomas. Volumen 17, La Rioja†
1132-8886 Pagina Abierta **8124**
1132-8916 Centro de Salud
1132-8924 Somontano **4162**
1132-8940 Paremia **3621**
1132-8975 Ius Fugit **4234**
1132-9041 Viridiana† **8997**
1132-9319 Arxius de les Seccions de Ciencies **7837**
1132-9327 A T. Actualidad Tecnologica **8415**
1132-9386 Cuadernos de Informacion Economica **1089**
1132-9432 Revista Internacional de Filosofia Politica **6949**

ISSN

DIRECTORY 2010 1136-1956 9541

1134-4881 Horticultura Internacional **3737**
1134-4903 Instituto de Recursos Naturales y Agrobiologia de Sevilla. Memoria **122**
1134-5047 Spain. Direccion General del Servicio Juridico del Estado. Anales *changed to* 1695-2626 **4608**
1134-5160 Hiades **5960**
1134-5187 Circulation (Spanish Edition)†
1134-5209 Noticias Paleontologicas **6727**
1134-5225 Clara. Especial Belleza *see* 1132-3213 **8855**
1134-5233 Resena Biblica **7676**
1134-5284 Biomedicina Veterinaria **5586**
1134-5292 Cuadernos de Lazarillo **5109**
1134-5381 Referata
1134-5535 Alquibla **2792**
1134-5543 G I A M. Boletin **907**
1134-556X Spain. Instituto Nacional para la Conservacion de la Naturaleza. Monografias
1134-5578 Parc Natural del Delta de l'Ebre. Butlleti **2624**
1134-5608 Peluquerias de Gran Seleccion **590**
1134-5616 Peluquerias. Suplemento Informativo *see* 1134-5608 **590**
1134-5624 Priceski *see* 1134-5608 **590**
1134-5632 Mathware and Soft Computing **5554**
1134-5640 Dulces Noticias ... y Algo Mas **3673**
1134-5764 T O P **5540**
1134-5837 Anuario de Migraciones **7296**
1134-587X Quaderns de Medi Ambient **3461**
1134-5934 Psiquiatria Biologica **6175**
1134-5993 Foto **6967**
1134-6019 Boletin del Centro de Documentacion en Ocio (A D O Z) **7951**
1134-6035 Gestion y Analisis de Politicas Publicas **7439**
1134-6094 Sociedad Entomologica Aragonesa. Boletin **859**
1134-6108 Catalogus de la Entomofauna Aragonesa **842**
1134-6272 Voice **6627**
1134-6302 Diablotexto **5284**
1134-6396 Arenal **8893**
1134-6469 Editur **8700**
1134-654X Microcirugia Ocular **6046**
1134-6574 Temas para el Debate **7188**
1134-6582 El Pais (Madrid Edition) **3953**
1134-6590 El Pais Semanal **3953**
1134-6612 Por la Danza **2687**
1134-6620 Bibliografia Espanola. Publicaciones Periodicas† **8936**
1134-6760 Dirigentes
1134-6795 Secuencias **6512**
1134-6884 G Q (Spanish Edition) **6291**
1134-7074 Mundo Negro **7664**
1134-7147 Zerbitzuan **8079**
1134-7198 Revista de Derecho y Genoma Humano **4771**
1134-7252 Todo Perros **6816**
1134-7317 Oferta Inmobiliaria **4421**
1134-7368 Revista Espanola de Antropologia Biologica **353**
1134-7376 Repertorio Mensual de Jurisprudencia **4768**
1134-7457 Cuadernos de Jazz **6560**
1134-749X Real Academia de Farmacia de Catalunya. Revista **6877**
1134-7627 Mar Oceana **4152**
1134-7643 Assaig de Teatre **8466**
1134-7686 Revista de Derecho de Sociedades **4880**
1134-7708 Law and the Human Genome Review *see* 1134-7198 **4771**
1134-7724 Llengua i Us **5148**
1134-7759 Gestion de Hoteles y Empresas Turisticas *changed to* 1887-4533 **4387**
1134-7783 Sessio Conjunta d'Entomologia† **8988**
1134-7872 Cuadernos de Artroscopia **6241**
1134-7880 Dialogos (El Mansou, Barcelona) **2940**
1134-7937 Ansiedad y Estres **6123**
1134-7988 Revistart **515**
1134-8046 Sociedad Espanola del Dolor. Revista **5774**
1134-8100 Alimarket. Alimentacion Perecedera **3626**
1134-8119 Alimarket. Alimentacion no Perecedera **3676**
1134-8127 Alimarket. Bebidas **597**
1134-8135 Alimarket. Distribucion **1804**
1134-8151 Alimarket Revista **3626**
1134-816X Alimarket **3626**
1134-8232 Formacio†
1134-8259 Huarte de San Juan. Geografia e Historia **4014**
1134-8275 Huarte de San Juan. Sociologia y Trabajo Social **8105**
1134-8291 Revista Asturiana de Economia† **8985**
1134-8445 Volubilis **4166**
1134-8496 Encuentros en la Biologia **671**
1134-8577 Novedades y Perspectivas Terapeuticas *see* 0214-0934 **6836**
1134-8615 Quodlibet **6608**
1134-8755 Lateral **5320**
1134-8887 Lecturas. Especial Decoracion *see* 1132-3280 **2257**
1134-8887 Lecturas. Especial Decoracion *see* 0047-4304 **3952**
1134-8984 Documentos de Trabajo Biltoki **8367**
1134-9018 Teoria Critica **5386**
1134-9123 Boletin del Real Patronato. Cuaderno de Documentacion **4064**
1134-914X Informe de Salud Publica **7525**
1134-9247 D E P A N A en Accio **4449**
1134-9255 Avance Normativo Fiscal **1911**
1134-9263 Treballs d'Arqueologia **421**
1134-928X Gerokomos **4046**
1134-9468 Cuadernos Cervantes de la Lengua Espanola **5109**
1134-9670 Cuadernos de Derecho Judicial **4949**
1134-9883 Las Pensiones de la Seguridad Social, en la C A V **8061**
1134-9905 El Extramundi y los Papeles de Iria Flavia **5294**
1134-9913 Medicina Aerospacial y Ambiental† **8973**
1134-993X Boletin de la Asociacion Internacional de Derecho Cooperativo **4630**
1134-9999 Area 3 (Print) *changed to* 1886-6530 **7948**
1135-0067 Turismo Rural y Agroturismo en la Comunidad Valenciana† **8994**
1135-0105 Scripta Musei Geologici Seminarii Barcinonensis **6730**
1135-0253 Alcuza **218**
1135-0261 Sociedad "Puig Adam" de Profesores de Matematicas. Boletin **5536**
1135-0407 Byte Espana **2408**
1135-0482 El Europeo de las Cuatro Estaciones† **8955**
1135-0504 Papers on Joyce **5348**
1135-0520 Scripta Fulgentina **7680**
1135-0628 Spain. Ministerio Fiscal. Revista **4786**
1135-0652 Banca & Finanzas **1310**
1135-0679 Catedra Fadrique Furio Ceriol. Cuadernos Constitucionales **4847**
1135-0695 A L I Base Informatica **2405**
1135-0733 Limpieza Inform **2243**
1135-0814 Cauces de Intercomunicacion **7630**
1135-0946 Inflamacion y Regulacion del Crecimiento Celular†
1135-0970 Cuadernos de Medicina Reproductiva **5601**
1135-108X Gold & Time **4566**
1135-1152 Oficio y Arte **538**
1135-1225 Revista Catalana de Micologia **700**
1135-1268 Societat Valenciana de Psicologia. Anuari de Psicologia **7409**
1135-1349 Sorites **6953**
1135-1438 U T **2921**
1135-1608 Cuadernos de Cultura **4448**
1135-1624 Despacho de Abogados **4657**
1135-1667 Sibila **4475**
1135-1675 Sibila (Book Edition) *see* 1135-1667 **4475**
1135-1683 Sibila (Original Edition) *see* 1135-1667 **4475**
1135-1772 Matador **5227**
1135-1853 Museo Nacional de Antropologia. Anales **348**
1135-1896 Revista de Filologia Valenciana **5167**
1135-2167 Imatge **6503**
1135-2183 *see* 1134-4792 **2438**
1135-2191 *see* 1134-4792 **2438**
1135-2205 Biomecanica†
1135-2299 Revista de Estudios Ibericos **413**
1135-2337 Eubalaena. Suplemento *see* 1132-970X **3590**
1135-2388 Farmaceuticos
1135-2469 *see* 0214-9958 **1178**
1135-2523 Investigaciones Europeas de Direccion y Economia de la Empresa **1762**
1135-2582 Systemica **6116**
1135-2663 Recerques del Museu d'Alcoi **413**
1135-2760 Anales de Cirugia Cardiaca y Cirugia Vascular **5777**
1135-2779 La Cana de Flamenco† **8939**
1135-2817 Futbol Cuadernos Tecnicos **8229**
1135-2841 Medicina Preventiva **5947**
1135-2876 Universo **583**
1135-2949 Gaceta Dental **5845**
1135-2957 Ferre Press **3378**
1135-2981 Catedra Nova **2835**
1135-304X Hieronymus Complutensis **5305**
1135-3058 Barcelona - Quaderns d'Historia **4203**
1135-3074 Revista Espanola de Nutricion Comunitaria **6669**
1135-3171 Revista de Psicoanalisis (Madrid) **7404**
1135-3384 N A: Nueva Architectura con Arcilla Cocida **450**
1135-3503 Cuadernos de Bibliografia de las Artes Escenicas **8468**
1135-3511 Fiapas **4074**
1135-366X Jardin Botanico de Cordoba. Monografias **795**
1135-3716 Scire **5046**
1135-3775 Surf a Vela **8336**
1135-3805 Dealer World Spain **2492**
1135-3848 Revista Iberoamericana de Diagnostico y Evaluacion Psicologica **7404**
1135-4011 Ciudad de Melilla. Boletin Oficial **4642**
1135-4089 Aplausos **279**
1135-4127 Cuadernos de Gestion para el Profesional de Atencion Primaria† **8947**
1135-416X Quaderns de Filologia. Estudis Linguistics **5164**
1135-4178 Quaderns de Filologia. Estudis Literaris **5356**
1135-4267 Boletin **2832**
1135-4356 Avances Informativos. Especial **4624**
1135-4410 Pediatria Rural y Extrahospitalaria **6099**
1135-450X Mi Bebe y Yo **2161**
1135-4534 Dental Economics† **8949**
1135-4542 Pediatria Integral **6099**
1135-4704 R E A **699**
1135-4712 'Ilu **7649**
1135-4895 Acero Inoxidable **6303**
1135-5123 Informacion Civil **4833**
1135-5220 Legislacion de Aragon **4721**
1135-5239 Legislacion de Extremadura **4721**
1135-5247 Legislacion de Galicia **4721**
1135-5255 Legislacion de la Region de Murcia **4722**
1135-5263 Legislacion de la Rioja **4722**
1135-5271 Legislacion de Castilla - La Mancha **4721**
1135-528X Legislacion del Pais Vasco **4722**
1135-5298 Legislacion del Principado de Asturias **4722**
1135-5301 Legislacion de la Comunidad de Madrid **4721**
1135-531X Legislacion de Canarias **4721**
1135-5328 Legislacion de Cataluna **4721**
1135-5336 Legislacion de Navarra **4722**
1135-5344 Legislacion de Andalucia **4721**
1135-5352 Legislacion de la Comunidad Autonoma de las Islas Baleares **4721**
1135-5360 Legislacion de Cantabria **4721**
1135-5379 Legislacion de la Comunidad Valenciana **4722**
1135-5387 Legislacion de Castilla y Leon **4721**
1135-5417 Real Academia Gallega de Ciencias. Revista **7902**
1135-5425 Union Europea. Indice Anual **4801**
1135-5441 Especial Directivos. Coyuntura Empresarial **1540**
1135-545X Especial Directivos. Management **1742**
1135-5468 Especial Directivos. Estrategias **1105**
1135-5700 Revista de Estudios Asiaticos†
1135-5727 Revista Espanola de Salud Publica **7539**
1135-5832 Reptilia (Spanish Edition) **961**
1135-5840 Cinemania **6494**
1135-5891 Perspectives **1408**
1135-5948 Procesamiento del Lenguaje Natural **5163**
1135-5956 Ciencia Psicologica **7345**
1135-6103 Anuario de los Hechos **3951**
1135-6146 Memoria de Proyectos **449**
1135-6286 Boletin Epidemiologico Semanal **7510**
1135-6308 Eufonia **6565**
1135-6316 Revista Integral†
1135-6332 Gaceta Internacional **3952**
1135-6340 Supernet Magazine **2599**
1135-6359 Franquicias Hoy **1428**
1135-6391 Ihitza **3439**
1135-6405 Cultura y Educacion **2840**
1135-6421 Usus Iuris **4806**
1135-6472 Recopilacion de Doctrina Legal†
1135-6588 Etologuia†
1135-660X Guia Deusto Laboral† **8960**
1135-6618 Revista de Estudios Cooperativos **7997**
1135-6677 Saturnia **858**
1135-6782 Panoramica de la Edicion Espanola de Libros **3953**
1135-6855 R E M A **5527**
1135-6863 Edafologia **106**
1135-6871 Republica de las Letras. Informes - Estudios **5359**
1135-6901 El Nino **7388**
1135-691X Revista Murciana de Antropologia **354**
1135-6936 Boletin Aceprensa **4445**
1135-7029 Mail Marketing **28**
1135-7088 Informe Semanal de Politica Exterior **7242**
1135-7096 Anuario Juridico de La Rioja **4619**
1135-710X Meridiano C E R I **7252**
1135-7118 Anuario del Seminario Permanente Sobre Derechos Humanos **7202**
1135-7134 C D Compact **8152**
1135-7509 Estudios del Ministerio Fiscal **1922**
1135-755X Psicologia Educativa **7393**
1135-7606 Cuadernos de Medicina Forense **5912**
1135-7665 Societat Paleontologica d'Elx. Seccion Paleontologica. Revista **6730**
1135-7673 Seminarios Complutenses de Derecho Romano **4842**
1135-7681 Nickel Odeon **6508**
1135-7789 S E D E R I **5170**
1135-7924 Guineana **791**
1135-7983 Baluarte **3521**
1135-7991 Cuadernos de Informacion y Comunicacion **2318**
1135-8009 Revista de Psicologia del Lenguaje†
1135-8122 Ciencia y Tecnologia Alimentaria *changed to* 1947-6337 **3629**
1135-819X La Revista Economica de Catalunya **1515**
1135-8246 Base de Datos Aranzadi. Jurisprudencia Social† **8935**
1135-8289 Banco de Bilbao. Agenda Financiera† **8934**
1135-8408 Polen **813**
1135-8491 Instituto Espanol de Oceanografia. Microfichas *changed to* 1578-410X **2807**
1135-8505 *see* 0029-7437 **6000**
1135-8513 Anuario del Instituto Ignacio de Loyola **7784**
1135-8521 Quark **7901**
1135-8599 Cuestiones de Fisioterapia **6108**
1135-8629 Educacion Social **2845**
1135-8637 Cuadernos de Filologia Francesa **5109**
1135-867X Espanol Actual **5115**
1135-8793 Redes (Barcelona) **7402**
1135-8831 Pediatria Catalana **6099**
1135-8920 Viceversa **5193**
1135-9099 Infomarine **4969**
1135-9137 Cairon **2683**
1135-9145 Legislacion Fiscal **1933**
1135-9196 Mon Juridic **4736**
1135-9250 Edutec **2852**
1135-934X Quaderns d'Historia de l'Ingenyeria **3216**
1135-9420 C I E M A T. Informes Tecnicos **3166**
1135-9536 Editur Catalunya **8700**
1135-9552 El Podologo **6071**
1135-9692 Revista Internacional de Protocolo **8129**
1135-9714 Revista de Derecho Civil Aragones **4841**
1135-9722 Locus Armoenus **537**
1135-9730 Quaderns d'Italia **5164**
1135-9773 Correo Bibliotecario **5004**
1135-9811 Cresol **5109**
1135-9838 Panoptico **5233**
1135-9846 Anuario Estadistico de Andalucia **7296**
1135-9854 Nuevo Diccionario de Legislacion. Tabla de Puesta al Dia. Apendice 1975-85 **4750**
1135-9994 Correo de la Construccion **1000**
1136-0062 Tectonica **1039**
1136-0089 Casa Moda **4535**
1136-0143 A B C **3950**
1136-0208 A B C (Sevilla Edition) **3951**
1136-0267 Institut d'Estudis Empordanesos. Annals **4231**
1136-0275 Boletin Fiscal **1913**
1136-0283 Avance Normativo Laboral y Seguridad Social **4624**
1136-0291 Estudios Migratorios **8100**
1136-0313 Vela Major† **8997**
1136-0429 Anuario Alimentacion, Equipos y Tecnologia **3627**
1136-0496 Grama y Cal **5123**
1136-0593 Fuzzy Economic Review **1112**
1136-0607 Pasarelas Internacionales **2259**
1136-0623 S I C - Seguridad en Informatica y Comunicaciones **2516**
1136-0666 Unidad de Estudiod Biograficos. Boletin *changed to* 1696-9863 **644**
1136-0828 Huarte de San Juan. Psicologia y Pedagogia **7360**
1136-0968 R E T Revista de Toxicomanias **2698**
1136-1034 Revista de Psicodidactica **2906**
1136-1182 Clarin **5274**
1136-1239 Bravo por Ti **2180**
1136-131X Informe Comunidades Autonomas **4833**
1136-1336 La Alimentacion en Espana **6654**
1136-1433 Ventas de Perfumeria y Cosmetica† **8997**
1136-1581 Espai de Llibertat† **8954**
1136-1611 Espana en Cifras **7306**
1136-1700 Historia, Antropologia y Fuentes Orales **4142**
1136-1794 Fish and Fisheries Research
1136-1867 P H. Boletin del Instituto Andaluz del Patrimonio Historico **4252**
1136-193X Instituto Canario de Ciencias Marinas. Informes Tecnicos **2807**
1136-1956 Sociedad Valenciana de Patologia Digestiva. Revista **5931**

ISSN

9542 1136-2006 ULRICH'S PERIODICALS

1136-2006 Arte y Parte 472
1136-2049 Antilia 653
1136-2057 Opto† 8979
1136-2065 I C E Revista de Instrumentacion, Componentes y Equipos Electronicos† 8963
1136-2073 I C R: The International Cookbook Revue 4361
1136-2111 *see* 1135-9773 5004
1136-2243 Documentos Enfermeria 5957
1136-2308 Siglo Diecinueve 5173
1136-2448 El Carabo
1136-2464 Panta Rei 4155
1136-2642 Anuario de Gaita 6545
1136-2847 Hot Shareware
1136-288X Informatica y Derecho 4845
1136-3010 Revista Tecnica de Distribucion, Mantenimiento y Limpiezas 2244
1136-3053 Infopack E & E 6710
1136-3169 Philologica Canariensia 5160
1136-3177 Proyecto Hombre 2698
1136-3312 Boletin Oficial de la Propiedad Industrial. 4: Resumenes de Patentes 6746
1136-3495 Estadistica de la Produccion Editorial de Libros 5058
1136-3630 Ninsmoda 2259
1136-3649 Benestar y Proteccion Infantil† 8935
1136-3703 Manuscrt.cao† 8972
1136-3711 Ars Brevis 4131
1136-3738 Jurisprudencia Constitucional 4850
1136-3819 Trabajo 1711
1136-3894 Seminario Iberoamericano de Matematicas. Publicaciones 5534
1136-3916 Que Leer 5235
1136-3967 Sentencias de Tribunales Superiores de Justicia y Audiencias Provinciales y Otros Tribunales (Bi-weekly Edition) 4782
1136-3991 Fantastic Magazine†
1136-4025 Flumen 2857
1136-4076 Contrastes 6912
1136-4327 Boletin de Informacion Dental
1136-4343 Torre de los Lujanes 7189
1136-4351 Fotogramas y Video 6501
1136-4645 Guardia Civil. Cuadernos 6423
1136-4696 Enigmas 53
1136-470X Ano Cero 7836
1136-4769 P C Week 2581
1136-4815 Alimentacion, Nutricion y Salud 6654
1136-4831 Papel Alpha 6972
1136-4890 European Journal of Anatomy 5611
1136-4939 Melomano 6587
1136-4963 Itsas Memoria 680
1136-5080 Frecuencia L 5120
1136-517X Auditoria Publica 7421
1136-5234 Ars Sacra 434
1136-5277 Universidad de Alcala de Henares. Departamento de Geografia. Serie Geografica 4032
1136-5331 Balanza de Pagos de Espana *changed to* 1698-2487 1912
1136-534X Pediatric Dermatology (Spanish Edition) 5880
1136-5390 Espejo de Paciencia 488
1136-5420 Revista de Psicopatologia y Psicologia Clinica 7404
1136-548X La Revista Espanola de Sexologia 8129
1136-5536 Cuadernos de Musica Iberoamericana 6560
1136-5544 Super Foto Practica 6977
1136-5552 The First Word Bulletin 2611
1136-5560 Revista de Serveis Personals Locals 8065
1136-5633 Instituto Nacional de Estadistica. Encuesta de Poblacion Activa. Tablas Anuales†
1136-5773 Anuario Lope de Vega 5095
1136-5781 Lectora 6931
1136-5943 Iberoamerican Journal of Hypertension† 8963
1136-5951 Area† 8931
1136-601X Museo 6530
1136-6141 Spain. Ministerio de Fomento y Ministerio de Medio Ambiente. Revista *changed to* 1577-4589 3467
1136-6273 Doce Notas 6562
1136-629X Patrimonio Cultural 4469
1136-6389 Encuentro de la Cultura Cubana 7961
1136-6427 Acuario Practico 4326
1136-6524 Andalucia Costa del Sol 5064
1136-6532 Medicina Maritima 5673
1136-6664 A V E P A. Actualidad 8790
1136-6834 Vasconia 4166
1136-6877 Huelva en Su Historia 4231
1136-7016 Aena Arte 464
1136-7091 Padres Caracola *see* 0214-2872 2181
1136-7105 Pares Cucafera 4365
1136-7172 Urologia Integrada y de Investigacion 6275
1136-7180 Neuropsychologia Latina†
1136-7210 Boina Negra 6413
1136-7342 Revista de Medicina y Practica Clinica
1136-7385 Filmhistoria 6500
1136-7458 Catalunya Musica 6554
1136-7539 CONECtronica 3185
1136-7547 *see* 1134-4261 3953
1136-7563 Catalogo de Revistas Culturales de Espana 622
1136-758X Loggia 449
1136-7652 Stony Thursday Book: Cuaderno de Madrid
1136-7679 T K 5049
1136-7717 Primeras Noticias. El Periodico Juvenil 2899
1136-7733 Primeras Noticias. Comunicacion y Pedagogia 2899
1136-7806 Seguridad Nuclear *changed to* 1888-8925 3180
1136-8071 Revista de Hispanismo Filosofico 6948
1136-811X Cuenta y Razon del Pensamiento Actual *changed to* 1889-1489 8096
1136-8144 Boletin Academia 6491
1136-8187 Seminario de Arqueologia y Etnologia Turolense. Revista 416
1136-8195 Arqueologia Espacial 381
1136-8217 Autoridades de la Biblioteca Nacional de Espana en CD-ROM† 8934
1136-8489 Noveldiana 5344
1136-8527 Revista Catalana de Sociologia 8128
1136-8632 AgentTravel 8682
1136-8780 Travesias 8011
1136-8861 Asociacion Proyecto Hombre. Memoria 2692
1136-8985 Nosocomio 5971
1136-906X T C. Tribuna de la Construccion 1039
1136-9221 Economia, Trabajo y Sociedad 1676
1136-9345 Guia Puntex. Anuario Espanol de Veterinaria 8798
1136-9353 Guia Polibea de la Discapacidad 4066
1136-954X Non Food Alimarket 4061
1136-9647 2 G 461
1136-9698 Bibliografia Nacional Espanola† 8936
1136-9922 Contrastes. Suplemento 6912
1137-005X The Grove 5123
1137-0157 Guia de Fundidores 6314
1137-0270 *see* 1136-3738 4850
1137-0572 Kalakorikos 4236
1137-0602 Cuadernos Azafea *see* 0213-3563 6907
1137-0734 Historia y Comunicacion Social 2323
1137-0823 Comunidad Escolar†
1137-084X Noticiero Textil 8456
1137-0882 Cirugia Mayor Ambulatoria 6239
1137-0912 Revista de Ciencias Juridicas 4770
1137-1021 Inversion y Capital *changed to* 1698-1952 1639
1137-1056 Emblemata 3765
1137-1064 Spanish Balance of Payments *changed to* 1698-8566 1944
1137-1099 Faro de Vigo (Pontevedra Edition) 3952
1137-1102 Zer 4586
1137-1110 E G M - El Gran Musical†
1137-1145 Revista Espanola de Psiquiatria Forense, Psicologia Forense y Criminologia† 8985
1137-1153 Asociacion de Autocontrol de la Publicidad 21
1137-1234 Sociologica†
1137-1250 Union Libre 3954
1137-1404 El Mundo. Anuario 3953
1137-1455 Guia Practica de Legislacion Laboral 4848
1137-1676 Anuario de Estadisticas Laborales y de Asuntos Sociales 1200
1137-1951 Eleria 4664
1137-196X Current Problems in Cancer (Spanish Edition) 6018
1137-2001 Sileno 517
1137-2044 Hostelmarket 4388
1137-2079 Scope†
1137-2176 Cuadernos de Anuario Filosofico 6912
1137-2192 Polibea 4069
1137-2230 Training & Development Digest 1876
1137-2273 Ciencia Ginecologika†
1137-2281 Nomina del Personal Academico y Anuario de la Corporation 7893
1137-2311 Trans 5188
1137-232X Spain in Figures *see* 1136-1611 7306
1137-2338 L'Espagne en Chiffres *see* 1136-1611 7306
1137-2346 Moenia 5152
1137-2354 Guaraguao 5218
1137-2397 Iacobus 4146
1137-2427 Boletin Criminologico 2645
1137-2435 Iuris 4697
1137-2443 Lecturas. Cocina Facil *see* 0047-4304 3952
1137-2443 Lecturas. Cocina Facil *see* 1132-3280 2257
1137-2516 Guia Practica del Mar 8645
1137-2702 Universidad de Leon. Facultad de Derecho. Anales 4801
1137-2729 Revista Iberoamericana de Ingenieria Mecanica 3394
1137-2818 Faro de Vigo (Vilagarcia de Arousa Edition) 3952
1137-2834 Medicina Oral *changed to* 1698-4447 5855
1137-2885 Nuclear Espana 3171
1137-2982 Repertorio de Jurisprudencia Tributaria 4768
1137-2990 Folia Clinica en Obstetricia y Ginecologia 5991
1137-3148 Revista Electronica de Psiquiatria 6182
1137-3156 Guia de Distribuidores *see* 1137-3164 1972
1137-3164 Anuario Distribucion 1972
1137-3210 Lecturas. Alta Costura *see* 1132-3280 2257
1137-3210 Lecturas. Alta Costura *see* 0047-4304 3952
1137-3350 A tu Salud 2823
1137-3520 Estudios de Derecho Judicial 4950
1137-3601 Inteligencia Artificial 2450
1137-3636 Revista Anthropos 4472
1137-3911 Auditoria Interna 1281
1137-4063 *see* 0214-0241 4835
1137-4128 Fomento del Trabajo. Horizonte Empresarial 1487
1137-4144 Con Ene 3528
1137-4241 Cuadernos de Pedagogia (CD-ROM Edition) 2840
1137-439X Zainak 361
1137-4403 Ondare 510
1137-4411 Formula 2062
1137-442X Azkoaga 1064
1137-4438 Ikusgaiak 6503
1137-4446 Ikastaria 2865
1137-4454 Oihenart 5345
1137-4462 Mediatika 8120
1137-4470 Musiker 6596
1137-4489 Isturitz 399
1137-4640 Techno Hotel 8760
1137-4683 Cuadernos Editur 8696
1137-4705 Estudios de Gestion Turistica 8701
1137-4713 Mini Guias Editur 8736
1137-4764 Las Guias de Editur 8716
1137-4772 Economia Exterior 1718
1137-4802 Trama y Fondo 4478
1137-4829 Los Cuadernos de Editur. Tecno Hosteleria 8696
1137-4837 Los Cuadernos de Editur. Tecno Agencias 8696
1137-4888 Bidebarrieta 5100
1137-5019 Cybermetrics 5004
1137-5051 Revista de Hacienda Local† 8985
1137-5345 Repertorio de Consultas Tributarias 4768
1137-5434 Real Academia de Cultura. Serie Literaria 5358
1137-5523 Magazine 3952
1137-5647 *see* 1137-5655 3953
1137-5655 Regio 7 3953
1137-5671 Qurtuba 3560
1137-5868 Spain. Ministerio de Trabajo y Asuntos Sociales. Revista 1708
1137-5892 Sistema Tributario. Avance Mensual 1943
1137-6228 Informe Espana 3952
1137-6341 Doctrina 4950
1137-6368 Universidad de Zaragoza. Departamento de Filologia Inglesa y Alemana. Miscelanea 4316
1137-6384 El Exportador 1564
1137-6430 C D - Cibepat 6747
1137-6546 Imagenes de Actualidad 6503
1137-6619 Laboratorio y Clinica 6931
1137-6627 Anales del Sistema Sanitario de Navarra 7507
1137-6651 Salina 5366
1137-6821 Emergencias 6059
1137-6848 Papeles de Historia 4253
1137-6856 Herramientas 1685
1137-6864 Papers del Montgri 6535
1137-6880 Nexo 2891
1137-6945 Tempos Novos 3954
1137-7038 Arxius de Sociologia 8089
1137-7127 Revista Juridica de Andalucia 4772
1137-7186 Papeles de Trabajo. Economia 1510
1137-7194 Papeles de Trabajo. America Latina 4307
1137-7224 Papeles de Trabajo. Administracion Publica 7459
1137-7232 Papeles de Trabajo. Historia Contemporanea 4155
1137-7240 Papeles de Trabajo. Arqueologia†
1137-7259 Papeles de Trabajo. Relaciones Internacionales 7257
1137-7275 Entre Lineas (Madrid) 2853
1137-7283 Papeles de Trabajo. Estudios Europeos 7257
1137-7402 Via Arquitectura 460
1137-7518 *see* 0038-822X 8207
1137-7550 Estudios Penales y Criminologicos
1137-7615 Mercadocontinuo† 8974
1137-7623 Educacion Canaria 2845
1137-7631 Actualidad Administrativa. Legislacion 4846
1137-7682 Temas de Psicoanalisis 7411
1137-781X Progresos de Obstetricia y Ginecologia. Suplemento *see* 0304-5013 6002
1137-7968 E D N A 5113
1137-8042 Industria y Mineria 6465
1137-8069 Initium 4692
1137-814X Anales del Sistema Sanitario de Navarra. Suplemento 7507
1137-8174 A E L F A. Boletin 6076
1137-8204 A Parte Rei 6938
1137-8247 Don Balon 8226
1137-8263 Tribunales Superiores de Justicia y Audiencias Provinciales *changed to* 1697-3666 4668
1137-831X Anuari Ornitologic de les Balears 901
1137-8360 Alfa 6903
1137-8417 Studium (Teruel) 4477
1137-8484 Revista de Estudios Empresariales 1966
1137-8492 Revista Electronica de Psicologia 7404
1137-8573 Heuresis 3063
1137-859X Jentilbaratz 3619
1137-8603 Naturzale 693
1137-8611 Relaciones Laborales. Normativa Laboral y de Seguridad Social 1705
1137-8654 Revista Espanola de Educacion Comparada 2906
1137-8700 Galemys 944
1137-8778 Aula de Encuentro 2828
1137-8875 Revista Espanola de Desarrollo y Cooperacion 4772
1137-8883 D A U 439
1137-8905 Revista de Poetica Medieval 5433
1137-9022 Revista de Gestion Publica y Privada 7466
1137-9030 Anuario de Drogueria y Perfumeria 592
1137-9537 Universidad Nacional de Educacion a Distancia. Ciencias 7926
1137-9669 Semata 4474
1137-9685 Psychology in Spain 7399
1137-9960 Ciclos 3410
1138-011X S D. Revista Medica Internacional sobre la Sindrome de Down (Catalan Edition) 6183
1138-0187 Dimension Humana 5605
1138-0322 Actividad Dietetica 6654
1138-0357 Revista Anthropos. Extra 4472
1138-0381 Haematologica 5936
1138-039X Universidade da Coruna. Facultade de Dereito. Anuario 4802
1138-0462 Memoria sobre la Actividad de la Central de Anotaciones en Cuenta y de los Mercados de la Deuda Publica *changed to* 0210-3737 1440
1138-0470 Archivos de la Fotografia 6964
1138-0489 Demografia y Salud† 8949
1138-0810 Urban 4429
1138-0853 Psicologia Politica 7393
1138-0861 BIME. Bibliografia Musical Espanola 6631
1138-1043 B I T - Boletin de Informacion Farmacoterapeutica de Navarra 6824
1138-1094 Sal Terrae 7816
1138-1140 Mercurio 1148
1138-123X Ilustre Consejo General de Colegios de Ondotologos y Estomatologos de Espana. Revista 5847
1138-1299 Cuadernos de Restauracion 484
1138-1310 Tiempos de America 4315
1138-1434 National Geographic Espanol 4020
1138-1442 Revista Espanola de Investigacion de Marketing 1841
1138-1477 Novedades Electronicas† 8978
1138-154X Boletin Internacional de Lenguas y Culturas Amerindias 331
1138-1566 Estadistica de Huelga y Cierres Patronales 1226
1138-1663 Revista Galego-Portuguesa de Psicoloxia e Educacion 2907
1138-1728 Cultura de los Cuidados 5602
1138-1868 Anesthesia & Analgesia (Spanish Edition) 5769
1138-1922 Exemplaria (Huelva) *changed to* 1699-3225 5294
1138-1981 Banda Aparte† 8934
1138-2074 S D. Revista Medica Internacional sobre el Sindrome de Down (Spanish Edition) *see* 1138-011X 6183
1138-2139 Caritas 8031
1138-2171 Volver a Ser 8077
1138-218X Entre Culturas 8038
1138-221X Boletin Mensual de Coyuntura† 8937
1138-2333 Revista de Antiguos Alumnos 1167
1138-2414 Real Academia de Doctores. Anales 5702

Link to your serials resources and content with ulrichsweb.com

1146-5530 P A S C A L. E 65: Psychologie, Psychopathologie, Psychiatrie†
1146-5549 P A S C A L. E 68: Genetique Humaine†
1146-5557 P A S C A L. E 71: Ophtalmologie†
1146-5565 P A S C A L. E 72: Otorhinolaryngologie. Stomatologie. Pathologie Cervicofaciale†
1146-5573 P A S C A L. E 73: Dermatologie. Maladies Sexuellement Transmissibles†
1146-5581 P A S C A L. E 74: Pneumologie†
1146-559X P A S C A L. E 75: Cardiologie et Appareil Circulatoire†
1146-5603 P A S C A L. E 76: Gastroenterologie, Foie, Pancreas, Abdomen†
1146-5611 P A S C A L. E 77: Nephrologie. Voies Urinaires†
1146-562X P A S C A L. E 78: Neurologie†
1146-5638 P A S C A L. E 79: Pathologie et Physiologie Osteoarticulaires†
1146-5646 P A S C A L. E 80: Hematologie†
1146-5662 P A S C A L. E 82: Gynecologie, Obstetrique, Andrologie†
1146-5670 P A S C A L. E 83: Anesthesie et Reanimation†
1146-5689 P A S C A L. E 84: Genie Biomedical. Informatique Biomedicale†
1146-5697 P A S C A L. E 89: Cancer†
1146-5786 Courants†
1146-5794 Esthetica Professionnel† 8954
1146-5948 Paris Transcontinental†
1146-609X Acta Oecologica 650
1146-6227 Harvest 3345
1146-6316 La Revue du Courtage 4521
1146-6480 Lidil†
1146-6537 Revue du Cardiologue Praticien†
1146-6804 Cardinale changed to 1960-1646 5779
1146-7282 Academie des Sciences et Lettres de Montpellier. Bulletin Mensuel 7830
1146-7673 Nouveaux Actes Semiotiques 5156
1146-8599 La Champagne Economique changed to 1629-3576 1400
1147-1948 Cinematographe†
1147-1999 Bottin Administratif 7423
1147-2081 Croyants en Liberte†
1147-2138 Hotellerie. Resto Flash†
1147-3797 Cahiers du Leopard d'Or 4208
1147-3991 Espaces Tropicaux 4005
1147-436X Temoins de Notre Histoire 4273
1147-5161 Asie et Monde Insulindien 5096
1147-5358 Centre de Recherches Archeologiques. Monographie 386
1147-6702 Guide des Prix Litteraires†
1147-6753 Caravelle 4446
1147-7105 Homme et l'Architecture†
1147-727X Ecrire Aujourd'hui changed to 1631-462X 4574
1147-7563 Horizons Centre Ile-de-France (Edition Seine-et-Marne) 119
1147-758X Horizons Centre Ile-de-France (Edition Loir-et-Cher) 119
1147-7598 Horizons Centre Ile-de-France (Edition Eure et Loir) 119
1147-7717 Marches Arabes 1577
1147-7776 Direct†
1147-7806 Science et Changements Planetaires - Secheresse 3465
1147-7814 Repertoire des Banques de Donnees Professionnelles† 8985
1147-8209 Repertoire International des Seiziemistes 4257
1147-8217 Repertoire d'Annuaires Francais changed to 1242-4315
1147-9213 Hydroecologie Appliquee 3163
1147-9558 Repertoire des Geographes Francais (Year)†
1147-9604 Tourisme Marketing et Communication†
1148-0483 La Revue des Montres 4569
1148-0858 Detours en France (Sainte-Genevieve) 8698
1148-0904 Otrante 5446
1148-1331 Eurotechnologie†
1148-1757 Echos de l'Exportation† 8952
1148-1978 Banques des Professionnels 1321
1148-1994 Montres Magazine†
1148-201X Cheval Star 8289
1148-2168 France. Ministere de l'Agriculture et de la Foret. Bulletin Technique d'Information†
1148-2230 Hotels et Restauration Magazine†
1148-2648 Qantara 4471
1148-2664 Confluences Mediterranee 7228
1148-3121 Avenir Agricole et Rural de la Haute Marne 94
1148-3202 Les Carnets de l'Exotisme 4446
1148-3326 Maisons Cote Sud 4546
1148-3652 L'Archer 8158
1148-4012 Informatique U.S. en Direct†
1148-425X Maintenant†
1148-4330 Moniteur Vinicole†
1148-4446 Profils I F P 6789
1148-4519 Perspectives Documentaires en Education 2897
1148-4624 Liaisons Juridiques et Fiscales†
1148-4675 Decision Micro 2570
1148-5493 European Cytokine Network (Print)†
1148-5531 Bulletin Europeen du Moniteur 987
1148-554X Journal du Chauffage et du Sanitaire 1018
1148-5566 Espace Bureau†
1148-5833 Societes en Mouvement 8135
1148-6198 Memoires de la Delegation Archeologique Francaise en Iran 405
1148-6201 Bibliographies Francaises de Sciences Sociales. Guides de Recherches†
1148-6228 Orphelinat Mutualiste changed to 1769-0129
1148-6244 Repertoire des Disques Compacts†
1148-6252 G E O S. Circular on Eclipsing Binaries 574
1148-6503 Revue du Rosaire 7815
1148-6716 Bulletin des Etudes Karaites†
1148-6740 Electro†
1148-7305 Bureaux d'Etudes†
1148-7488 Paysan du Midi 146
1148-7941 Realites Industrielles 6477
1148-7968 Societe de l'Histoire de Paris et de l'Ile-de-France. Bulletin 4264

1148-8085 Societe Historique et Archeologique de Pontoise, du Val d'Oise et du Vexin. Memoires 4265
1148-8115 Medecine d'Urgence 6067
1148-8204 Formation Professionnelle Continue 2941
1148-8247 Agriculteur de l'Aisne 82
1148-8549 Societe des Amis du Vieux Toulon et de sa Region. Bulletin 4264
1148-8565 Societe d'Etude des Sciences Naturelles de Vaucluse. Bulletin 7918
1148-862X Societe J.K. Huysmans. Bulletin 5239
1148-9006 Marie Claire Maison 4546
1148-9227 Kairos 6930
1148-9286 Tonus Dentaire†
1148-9502 Psychologie & Education 2901
1148-9634 Challenges Haute-Marne 1426
1148-9979 Arachnides†
1149-0039 Cahiers de Rheologie 7007
1149-0209 Gulliver
1149-0349 Academie Nationale de Metz. Memoires 4440
1149-0411 Groupe de Recherches Socio-Economiques. Papiers†
1149-1566 Vocal†
1149-1590 France. Caisse Nationale des Allocations Familiales. Recherches et Previsions 8041
1149-2767 Tout Lyon et le Moniteur Judiciaire Reunis changed to 1772-3124 4797
1149-4670 Societe Archeologique de Touraine. Memoires 417
1149-5758 Visions Internationales†
1149-6452 Journal de l'Assurance
1149-6525 Cahiers d'Etudes Hongroises 4208
1149-6576 Epilepsies 6138
1149-6630 Tsafon 7731
1149-6851 L'Orgue Dossier 6603
1149-8315 Vingtieme Siecle Federaliste†
1149-8633 Cahiers Leon Bloy
1149-9877 Le Marin 3601
1150-1367 Raisons Pratiques 7994
1150-1448 Reunion. Direction de l'Agriculture et de la Foret. Agreste. Donnees, Bulletin de Statistique Agricole Reunion†
1150-1456 Reunion. Direction de l'Agriculture et de la Foret. Agreste. Donnees, Annuaire de Statistique Agricole Reunion†
1150-1502 Service Traiteur† 8988
1150-1553 Uranie 5394
1150-160X Distribution R H F†
1150-1634 Les Cahiers de la Securite Interieure changed to 1774-475X 2676
1150-1944 Societes Contemporaines 8135
1150-255X Lecteurs en Herbe 2199
1150-3696 Esthetique & Politique 6916
1150-4447 Maghreb Confidentiel 7251
1150-4706 La Lettre d'Activites en Pays Basque† 8971
1150-4919 Virages† 8997
1150-5028 Federation Nationale de l'Industrie Laitiere. Bulletin d'Information†
1150-5273 Profession Marketing†
1150-5567 Participer†
1150-5958 Museart†
1150-644X Argus Machine - Outil
1150-6652 Revue Internationale de Psychopathologie†
1150-6709 Preferences
1150-6954 Voyager Magazine changed to 1622-874X 8931
1150-708X Guepard†
1150-7454 Croissance†
1150-7608 Fichier Banque Afrique 1565
1150-7683 Produits de la Mer
1150-7691 Sites Commerciaux†
1150-7772 Juridisque Formulaire Social Commente 4705
1150-8019 Picoti 2207
1150-8116 Nouvel Hospitalier 4108
1150-8809 Les Cahiers Scientifiques du Transport see 0564-1373 8518
1150-9694 Annuaire des Serveurs Temps Partage†
1151-0080 see 1959-920X 7583
1151-0218 Annuaire Birkner France†
1151-0285 Journal International des Sciences de la Vigne et du Vin 125
1151-0358 C N C Info changed to 1952-3866 6491
1151-0854 Alpes Magazine (Toulouse) 3997
1151-1109 Viticulture en Val de Loire 258
1151-1397 Marine 6432
1151-1737 Societe d'Ethnozootechnie. Lettre 963
1151-177X Les Saisons de la Danse†
1151-2288 Lettre d'Information Trimestrielle changed to 1950-8387 5322
1151-2385 Revue Francaise de Droit Constitutionnel 4852
1151-3365 Scouts Avenir† 8987
1151-3470 Music and Business†
1151-4051 Signes Musiques 6616
1151-4787 Securite Echos† 8987
1151-5430 Annales de la Voirie 4617
1151-5708 Juris-Classeur Numerique. Concurrence Consommation see 0153-775X 4873
1151-843X Societes Arabes et Musulmanes 4325
1151-9037 Histoire Economique et Financiere de la France. Recueils de Documents 1542
1151-941X Parlanghe 5349
1152-3263 Impulsion 1405
1152-3336 Empan 8038
1152-4952 Collection Conjoncture 1447
1152-5096 Institut International d'Administration Publique. Dossiers et Debats 7446
1152-5428 see 0990-0632 8805
1152-6351 Cote 3840
1152-6564 European Oil & Gas Management Directory†
1152-6653 Vivre Ensemble 3049
1152-7137 Top Sante 6998
1152-8729 Quotidien du Tourisme 8750
1152-880X Agro-Distribution 193
1152-8885 Collector (Paris)† 8942
1152-9172 Revue des Affaires Europeennes 4939
1152-9563 Sport et Vie 8203

1152-9776 France. Institut National de la Statistique et des Etudes Economiques. Conjoncture in France 1233
1153-0642 Praxipharm
1153-0758 Minzhu Zhongguo†
1153-1134 Grand J†
1153-1401 France Boxe changed to 1958-7023 8162
1153-1444 Nouvelles du Marketing (Print) changed to 1961-8417 1836
1153-2254 Institut des Actuaires Francais. Bulletin Trimestriel†
1153-2521 Societe Archeologique de Touraine. Bulletin 417
1153-2599 Bulletin Historique et Scientifique de l'Auvergne 4207
1153-2785 Banque de France. Comite des Etablissements de Credit et des Entreprises d'Investissements. Rapport 1319
1153-3277 Societe d'Histoire et d'Archeologie de Vichy et des Environs. Bulletin 417
1153-4540 Euro C E Magazine
1153-5903 La Jurisprudence Automobile†
1153-7787 Tribune Graphologique†
1153-8236 Revue Culinaire 3662
1153-950X L'Eclaireur des Coiffeurs 587
1154-0842 Bulletin des Opportunites d'Alsace† 8938
1154-1105 Caoutchoucs et Plastiques 7824
1154-1342 Revue Archeologique de Bordeaux
1154-2594 Academie d'Histoire. Cahiers†
1154-2721 Flux 7855
1154-2829 Systeme D Pratique
1154-354X Infotecture Europe†
1154-3590 Bibliographie de la Litterature Francaise see 0035-2411 5362
1154-4724 Lettre d'Excel†
1154-516X Courrier International 3840
1154-5232 Gestalt 309
1154-5305 Commerce et Franchise
1154-5399 Euro Pop†
1154-5720 AutoFace Ink 6546
1154-5763 Autrement. Serie Morales changed to 1770-7625 6935
1154-5992 Today in English 2217
1154-6123 Journal du Bois 3713
1154-6433 Maintenance and Entreprise 1774
1154-6646 G R A L. Bulletin 395
1154-7472 Societe des Sciences Historiques & Naturelles de la Corse. Bulletin 7918
1155-1569 Lettre de Paradox†
1155-1585 Decision Environnement†
1155-1704 Journal de Therapie Comportamentale et Cognitive 6149
1155-1852 Guide National de Prescription des Medicaments changed to 1769-5406 6837
1155-1917 Encyclopedie Medico-Chirurgicale. Nephrologie - Urologie changed to 1762-0945 6267
1155-1925 Encyclopedie Medico-Chirurgicale. Toxicologie - Pathologie Professionelle changed to Encyclopedie Medico-Chirurgicale. Pathologie Professionnelle et de l'Environnement 3496
1155-1941 Encyclopedie Medico-Chirurgicale. Endocrinologie - Nutrition (Print) changed to Encyclopedie Medico-Chirurgicale. Endocrinologie - Nutrition 5890
1155-195X Encyclopedie Medico-Chirurgicale. Pneumologie 6213
1155-1968 Encyclopedie Medico-Chirurgicale. Gastro-Enterologie 5923
1155-1976 Encyclopedie Medico-Chirurgicale. Hepatologie 5923
1155-1984 Encyclopedie Medico-Chirurgicale. Hematologie 5936
1155-2069 Moto Legende 8261
1155-2093 Composants Instrumentation Electroniques changed to 1957-5580 3094
1155-2239 Etudes Schweitzeriennes† 8954
1155-2492 Realites Therapeutiques en Dermato-Venerologie 5881
1155-2506 La Feuille et l'Aiguille 3688
1155-2549 D E C Professionnel†
1155-3197 Catholic International see 0012-4613 7795
1155-3219 Geneses 7966
1155-3316 Apocrypha 7622
1155-3464 Je Chante! 6580
1155-3839 Abstract Hopital†
1155-4339 Journal de Physique IV changed to 1951-6355 7012
1155-4363 Alizes 5092
1155-4452 Revue de Neuropsychologie 6182
1155-4495 France. Ministere de l'Agriculture et de la Peche. Agreste Commerce Exterieur Bois et Derives†
1155-5408 Feux Croises 5296
1155-5645 Paediatric Anaesthesia 5773
1155-8709 Bateaux 8272
1155-8938 Unite Stenographique†
1156-0428 Journal des Anthropologues 344
1156-1602 Top Cultures†
1156-1661 Medias†
1156-1874 Vente Equipements Menagers†
1156-2935 Revue de Jurisprudence de Droit des Affaires 1791
1156-296X Revue Marivaux† 8985
1156-3141 see 0035-1563 6330
1156-377X Magazine de Midi-Pyrenees†
1156-4865 Route Actualite 8634
1156-4954 France Tennis de Table Journal 8229
1156-5209 Fab†
1156-5233 Journal de Mycologie Medicale 5761
1156-5802 Informatique et Sante†
1156-5977 Jericho†
1156-6183 U N E T A R†
1156-6272 Marches Graphiques†
1156-6477 Lettre de Word†
1156-6647 Video Pratique†
1156-7104 Centraliens 8417
1156-7198 Archeologie Islamique†
1156-7635 Beaute Service changed to 1620-2716
1156-8380 Centre de Prevision de l'Expansion. Tableau de Bord 1446
1156-8461 Paysan Breton (Edition Morbihan) 146
1156-8496 France Eco - Peche 3595
1156-8968 Techno-Transfert†
1156-962X Recyclage Recuperation 3510
1156-9638 Vie Economique Newsletter†

1165-8568 Technologies Internationales **8442**
1165-8606 Decisions Medias†
1165-9394 La Lettre du Cadre Territorial
1165-9823 *see* 0012-2467 **1002**
1165-9890 *see* 1161-2436 **4593**
1166-0422 Ailes Magazine† **8929**
1166-0732 Cahiers d'Archeologie Aveyronnaise **386**
1166-1011 Annuaire des Industries Charcutieres *changed to* 1967-7170 **295**
1166-1232 Enquete sur l'Histoire†
1166-2212 Recherches Interdisciplinaires sur les Textes Modernes
1166-2344 Paris Capitale **8746**
1166-2654 Andrologie **5574**
1166-3057 E D I Europe†
1166-3081 Journal of Applied Non-Classical Logics **2453**
1166-3235 Anda† **8930**
1166-3243 Narrativa **5338**
1166-3294 Les Nouvelles Publications Economiques et Juridiques **1155**
1166-3413 L'Aide Soignante **5950**
1166-3502 Centre de Documentation et d'Etudes Sociales. La Lettre - Toulouse *changed to* 1959-5093 **7106**
1166-4231 Contacts A V A† **8943**
1166-4398 Double Liaison **6717**
1166-4568 Encyclopedie Medico-Chirurgicale. Cardiologie **5786**
1166-4770 S V M Mac **2583**
1166-486X Revue du Nord. Archeologie **4258**
1166-5025 Ballet 2000 **2682**
1166-5742 Relief **7291**
1166-5785 Bulletin Bourse et Produits Financiers **1614**
1166-6609 Sonovision Qui Fait Quoi? **2028**
1166-7087 Progres en Urologie **6273**
1166-7095 Pentecote **7812**
1166-7419 Le Guide des Metiers **2861**
1166-7648 C E A Technologies **7065**
1166-7664 A F C E T Interflash
1166-7699 Cahiers d'Etudes et de Recherches Francophones. Agricultures **99**
1166-7729 Agro Magazine *changed to* 1951-0594 **86**
1166-8237 Medecine et Maladies Infectieuses. Supplement *see* 0399-077X **5822**
1166-8261 Revue Archeologique de l'Ouest. Supplement **414**
1166-8296 Scope Newsletter **3255**
1166-8385 Techniques Hospitalieres **4112**
1166-8598 Encyclopedie Medico-Chirurgicale. Maladies Infectieuses **5813**
1166-8636 Revue des Systemes de Decision *changed to* 1246-0125 **2523**
1166-8687 I R I S A Publication Interne **3196**
1166-9632 Revue d'Ecologie Alpine†
1166-9829 Anamneses†
1166-9993 Presence de Gabriel Marcel **6945**
1167-0991 D L R Magazine† **8948**
1167-1114 Cahiers de la Formation† **8939**
1167-1122 European Journal of Dermatology **5876**
1167-1793 Ingenierie International **3198**
1167-2196 Enjeux les Echos **1105**
1167-2420 Gynecologie Internationale†
1167-2846 Trafic **6515**
1167-296X Repreneur
1167-301X Citrouille **5274**
1167-3559 Freeway Magazine **8259**
1167-3656 Rhone Metiers **6703**
1167-3702 C F C A Actualites *changed to* 1951-4492 **102**
1167-4024 Bulletin Mensuel de Theodore Champion **6892**
1167-4075 Cyclo Magazine†
1167-4326 A G E F I. Cahiers†
1167-4571 Jardin des Dragons†
1167-4687 Retraite et Societe **1705**
1167-4733 Chroniques Allemandes **5273**
1167-4849 La Tribune des Metaux **6336**
1167-4849 La Tribune des Metaux *changed to* 1624-5326 **6335**
1167-4865 Etudes et Recherches des Laboratoires des Ponts et Chaussees. Serie Sciences de l'Ingenieur **3191**
1167-489X Techniques et Methodes des Laboratoires des Ponts et Chaussees. Methode **3285**
1167-492X Prehistoire Anthropologie Mediterraneennes **352**
1167-4946 Banque & Marches **1320**
1167-5101 Genesis **5299**
1167-5128 Banque de France. Analyses Comparatives **1319**
1167-5187 C N R S Litterature **5268**
1167-5381 Ports & Mouillages
1167-539X Produits Frais†
1167-5438 Les Idees en Mouvement **3840**
1167-6205 La Feuille d'info de Naturellement **3431**
1167-654X Lettre de Windows†
1167-6817 Campus Stellae **4209**
1167-7287 Industries **1889**
1167-7422 Prescrire International **6876**
1167-7619 Cuisines du Bout du Monde *changed to* 1289-2246
1167-7848 R F Conseil **1789**
1167-816X Utinam **360**
1167-8224 Le Journal de Coelio-Chirurgie **6247**
1167-8550 Telex Laiterie -Boissons **269**
1167-8569 Telex Mecanique Chaudronnerie **3223**
1167-8577 Telex Bois **3716**
1167-864X Reponses Photo **6976**
1167-9468 F B I: Fortnightly Bulletin on Interactivity†
1167-9638 Historica **6423**
1167-9689 East Asian Affairs (English Edition)†
1167-9786 Association des Naturalistes des Yvelines. Bulletin **7837**
1167-9883 Les Cles de l'Actualite **2182**
1167-993X Mouv'A N C E†
1168-0377 Banques des Entreprises **1321**
1168-0733 L'Esprit du Temps **2854**
1168-1098 Actualites Nephrologiques Jean Hamburger **6264**
1168-1128 A C T U A R† **8927**
1168-1446 Sciences de la Societe **7999**
1168-2957 Arts - Sciences - Techniques
1168-3015 Le Courrier de l'Environnement *changed to* 1969-9468 **3430**
1168-3155 Bourse de Paris. Actions† **8937**
1168-3201 Reseau Femmes Ruptures. Bullletin *changed to* 1769-924X **8882**
1168-3430 Marine Life **955**
1168-3597 Association Entomologique d'Evreux. Bulletin de Liaison **840**
1168-3651 Revue d'Ecologie. Supplement **3463**
1168-4917 Etudes Britanniques Contemporaines **5292**
1168-5344 Commerce Exterieur des Produits de la Mer *changed to* 1293-7746 **3589**
1168-5476 Endo†
1168-5638 Therese de Lisieux **7820**
1168-5751 *see* 1162-6208 **7250**
1168-609X Motocross Magazine†
1168-6944 Tribune Desfosses **1184**
1168-7509 Je Lis des Histoires Vraies **2195**
1168-9498 L'Erckmann - Chatrian *changed to* 1279-7367 **8971**
1168-9501 Cahiers F. Schubert **6553**
1168-9897 Les Cahiers de la Sous-Traitance Electronique *changed to* 1774-5438 **3297**
1168-9951 Faxmedia†
1168-996X La Lettre R C E C G T *see* 1633-3284 **1698**
1169-0682 Actualites Vasculaires Internationales†
1169-0704 Le Courrier du Meuble et de l'Habitat **4555**
1169-176X Bibliotheque de France. Lettre d'Information†
1169-1808 Provence Genealogie **3780**
1169-2014 Academie Nationale de Medecine. Annuaire **5565**
1169-2111 Q - W - E - R - T - Y† **8983**
1169-212X Societe Litteraire de la Poste et de France Telecom. Missives **5239**
1169-2294 La Gazette de l'Hotel Drouot **491**
1169-2537 Sevres **539**
1169-2936 Sources Classiques **5375**
1169-2944 Romantisme et Modernites **5364**
1169-2952 Litterature de Notre Siecle **5327**
1169-2979 Champion-Varia **4210**
1169-3029 La Tribune Ukrainienne
1169-3363 Ukrainske Slovo
1169-3630 La Lettre des Bornes Interactives†
1169-4475 Annuaire des Docteurs en Sciences Economiques **1060**
1169-4882 Freeway Magazine. Hors Serie *see* 1167-3559 **8259**
1169-5293 Lettre du Multimedia†
1169-5498 Myoline **5681**
1169-6168 Annuaire de la Recherche Geographique Francophone†
1169-6176 Repertoire International des Banques de Donnees Biomedicales†
1169-6737 Guide de la Telematique Vocale†
1169-6931 Administration des Directions Regionales de l'Industrie, de la Recherche et de l'Environnement. Annuaire **3123**
1169-7768 Encyclopedie Medico-Chirurgicale. Traite de Radiodiagnostic: Coeur - Poumon *changed to* Encyclopedie Medico-Chirurgicale. Radiologie et Imagerie Medicale. Cardiovasculaire - Thoracique - Cervicale **6196**
1169-7954 Revue des Composites et des Materiaux Avances **3357**
1169-8152 Natation **8189**
1169-8217 Le Mouvement Hotelier et Touristique **4394**
1169-8330 Revue du Rhumatisme (French Edition) **6226**
1169-8446 Revue du Rhumatisme (English Edition)†
1169-8462 Banque de France. Comite de la Reglementation Bancaire et Financiere. Rapport† **8935**
1169-8489 Banque de France. Comite Consultatif. Rapport† **8934**
1169-8683 Scenes et Pistes†
1169-873X L'Industrie Ceramique et Verriere **2043**
1169-8837 Observatoire de Strasbourg. Centre de Donnees Astronomiques de Strasbourg. Information Bulletin†
1169-9019 Catacombes†
1169-9604 Centre de Documentation et d'Information sur le Laos. Bulletin d'Information
1170-0009 Wairarapa Times-age **3919**
1170-0025 Ashburton Guardian **3916**
1170-0041 Auckland City Harbour News **3916**
1170-005X The Chronicle *changed to* The Bay Chronicle **3916**
1170-0068 Bay of Plenty Times **3916**
1170-0092 Cambridge Edition **3916**
1170-0130 Central Leader **3916**
1170-0181 Clutha Leader **3916**
1170-019X Coastal News **3916**
1170-0246 Daily News *changed to* 1176-7596 **3919**
1170-0254 The Daily Post **3917**
1170-0335 Eastern Courier **3917**
1170-036X The Ensign **3917**
1170-0408 Feilding Herald **3917**
1170-0416 Franklin County News **3917**
1170-0424 The Riversider† **8986**
1170-0491 Hamilton Press **3917**
1170-0513 Hauraki Herald **3917**
1170-0564 Hutt News **3917**
1170-0580 Kaikoura Star **3917**
1170-0599 Kapi-Mana News **3917**
1170-0602 Kapiti Observer **3917**
1170-0610 Katikati Advertiser **3917**
1170-067X Wanganui Chronicle **3920**
1170-0688 Waikato Times **3919**
1170-0696 Manukau Courier **3917**
1170-070X The Marlborough Express **3917**
1170-0718 Matamata Chronicle **3917**
1170-0769 Northern Advocate **3918**
1170-0777 New Zealand Herald **3918**
1170-0793 The Oamaru Mail **3918**
1170-0823 Nor'West News Brief *changed to* Nor'West News **3918**
1170-084X The Christchurch Star *changed to* Star **3919**
1170-0882 Sunday News **3919**
1170-0920 Timaru Herald **3919**
1170-0939 The Tribune **3919**
1170-0947 Upper Hutt Leader **3919**
1170-0998 Northern News **3918**
1170-103X Piako Post **3918**
1170-1072 Taupo Times **3919**
1170-1099 Te Awamutu Courier **3919**
1170-1102 Te Puke Times **3919**
1170-1145 Western Leader **3920**
1170-1226 North Shore Times Advertiser *changed to* North Shore Times **3918**
1170-1242 South Waikato News **3919**
1170-1250 Turangi Chronicle **3919**
1170-1277 Christchurch Mail† **8941**
1170-1293 Saturday Express **3919**
1170-1331 Taieri Herald **3919**
1170-1366 Taupo Weekender **3919**
1170-1374 Thermalair **8760**
1170-1447 Wanganui Midweek **3920**
1170-151X North Taranaki Midweek **3918**
1170-1560 Rotorua Review **3919**
1170-1595 Star *changed to* South Taranaki Star **3916**
1170-1684 Ruapehu Press **3919**
1170-1749 Flowers New Zealand† **8957**
1170-1927 Pharmacy Today (Auckland) **6874**
1170-1978 Wellington Working Papers in Linguistics **5194**
1170-229X Drugs & Aging **6836**
1170-2540 New Zealand Identicar **8595**
1170-280X Vetscript New Zealand **8814**
1170-2915 The New Zealand Angus Cattleman **294**
1170-3075 H E R A Annual Report **3194**
1170-3105 Lymphoma / Leukaemia Review **5940**
1170-3121 Next **8877**
1170-3202 Hepatitis Research Review **5926**
1170-3253 Service (Christchurch)†
1170-327X New Zealand General Practice, Business Management†
1170-3369 New Zealand Science Monthly†
1170-3415 Rehabilitation Research Review **6115**
1170-344X Reserve Bank of New Zealand. Corporate Plan†
1170-3709 Threatened Species Occasional Publication **3470**
1170-3776 The T V Guide **2392**
1170-3784 Equal Employment Opportunities Plan†
1170-3806 Threatened Species Recovery Plan Series **3470**
1170-4195 Health Research Council of New Zealand Newsletter *changed to* 1178-9565 **7520**
1170-4306 New Zealand Computer Scene†
1170-4411 Army News *changed to* 1170-8859 **6437**
1170-4527 Building Industry News
1170-4810 Pantograph **8621**
1170-4829 Reserve Bank of New Zealand. Monetary Policy Statement **1514**
1170-4861 B E R L Forecasts **1439**
1170-487X University of Waikato. Department of Computer Science. Working Paper Series (Print) *changed to* 1177-777X **2440**
1170-4918 Leading Light **6527**
1170-5256 Arts Horizon† **8931**
1170-5663 Waimakariri District Council. Draft Annual Plan and Budget *changed to* Waimakariri District Council. Long Term Council Community Plan **7505**
1170-5884 Vocation - The Who's Who of Human Resources†
1170-6031 Cranwell's Constructor†
1170-6058 Healthy Options **6988**
1170-6139 Kiwi Surf **8320**
1170-6244 Current†
1170-6325 Tirohia†
1170-6775 Quality New Zealand†
1170-7240 Children **8033**
1170-7321 Transearch *changed to* 1174-0523 **3279**
1170-747X New Zealand. Statistics New Zealand. Consumer Expenditure **1254**
1170-7569 New Zealand Nursery Register **3757**
1170-7607 Lincoln University. Agribusiness and Economics Research Unit. Discussion Paper† **8971**
1170-7623 Property Investor Weekly **7605**
1170-7682 Lincoln University. Agribusiness and Economics Research Unit. Research Report **202**
1170-7690 PharmacoEconomics **6871**
1170-7992 Network†
1170-800X Tokelau National Bibliography **636**
1170-8352 New Zealand Marine Sciences Society Review **693**
1170-8859 N Z Army News **6437**
1170-893X National Museum of New Zealand Miscellaneous Series†
1170-9154 New Zealand Annual Mining Review†
1170-9332 New Zealand Classic Car **8595**
1170-9758 Shadows **6208**
1170-9898 Water & Wastes in NZ *changed to* 1177-1313 **8829**
1170-9928 Airborn **8157**
1170-9960 Jewellery Time **4567**
1171-0179 Directions **3917**
1171-0187 Manu Rere *changed to* 1176-9904 **8077**
1171-0195 New Zealand Journal of Medical Laboratory Science **5909**
1171-0241 New Zealand. House of Representatives. Journals *changed to* 0113-1176 **7456**
1171-039X Waimakariri District Council. Annual Plan and Budget **7505**
1171-042X Victoria University of Wellington Law Review **4808**
1171-0462 New Zealand Journal of Occupational Therapy **5686**
1171-0705 University of Canterbury. Department of Economics. Discussion Paper† **8996**
1171-0772 Dairying Today **263**
1171-1159 Homoeopathy NewZ **5805**
1171-1337 New Zealand Cartography and Geographic Information Systems† **8977**
1171-140X Cookia **939**
1171-1418 N Z T B Visitor Statistics Research Series†
1171-1426 Connect (Christchurch)† **8943**
1171-1744 Wool Report†
1171-1884 New Zealand Resource Management Appeals **4421**
1171-2031 Programme Profiles - New Zealand Official Development Assistance† **8982**
1171-2163 New Zealand. Statistics New Zealand. Business Activity Statistics† **8977**
1171-283X New Zealand. Statistics New Zealand. Labour Market Statistics **1255**
1171-2937 N Z T B International Visitors Research Series†
1171-2961 Trans Tasman **7189**
1171-302X New Zealand Institute of Public Administration. Research Papers **7456**

ISSN

DIRECTORY 2010 1175-897X 9549

1174-2216 Log Illustrated† **8971**
1174-2267 Sound Ideas (Print) *changed to* Sound Ideas (Online) **6618**
1174-2380 Landscan **2617**
1174-250X Inspiration Input *changed to* 1177-2131 **8964**
1174-2542 Massey University. Department of Applied and International Economics. Discussion Paper **1147**
1174-2631 N I W A Technical Report **3602**
1174-2666 New Zealand Outside **8324**
1174-2704 Southern Med Review **6881**
1174-2720 Farm Trader **210**
1174-2747 Motorcycle Trader & News **8263**
1174-2755 Australian Women's Weekly **8852**
1174-3166 Road Safety New Zealand *changed to* 1176-841X **8977**
1174-3174 Annual Report on the Microbiological Quality of Drinking-Water in New Zealand *changed to* 1176-9424 **3483**
1174-3352 Bella New Zealand†
1174-3484 New Zealand. Parliamentary Counsel Office. Departmental Forecast Report *changed to* 1176-3884 **7456**
1174-3506 M I S New Zealand *changed to* 1174-992X **1415**
1174-3530 Rainbow News **314**
1174-3581 Pet New Zealand *changed to* 1177-7737 **6813**
1174-3654 New Zealand Customs Service. Annual Report **7455**
1174-3719 New Zealand Reseller News **2493**
1174-3727 Electoral Commission. Report *changed to* 1177-956X **7159**
1174-3735 AgVetLink **217**
1174-3913 Journal of Te Ao Marama† **8968**
1174-3921 Royal Philatelic Society of New Zealand. Bibliographic Series **6901**
1174-3948 Antarctica New Zealand. Annual Report **7420**
1174-3972 Equestrian N Z *changed to* 1177-1410 **8295**
1174-4030 The Pander† **8980**
1174-4065 New Zealand Industry Outlook *changed to* 0113-1680 **1721**
1174-4243 Yearbook of New Zealand Jurisprudence **4817**
1174-4464 Novachem Manual *changed to* 1178-3184 **243**
1174-4502 New Ethicals Journal *changed to* 1176-5844 **6859**
1174-4537 The Energy File **3131**
1174-460X Pulp **2209**
1174-4618 A P Bulletin *changed to* 1177-4762 **7517**
1174-4707 Australasian Journal of Disaster and Trauma Studies **6056**
1174-474X Massey University. Centre for Applied Economics and Policy Studies. Discussion Paper in Natural Resource and Environmental Economics **1498**
1174-4758 New Zealand. Securities Commission. Bulletin **1642**
1174-491X Kiwi Motorcycle Rider *changed to* 1177-0023 **8260**
1174-4960 New Zealand G P†
1174-5096 Forest Research Bulletin **3689**
1174-5177 University Graduate Destinations *changed to* 1177-4045 **1701**
1174-5177 University Graduate Destinations *changed to* 1177-3782 **1701**
1174-5177 University Graduate Destinations *changed to* 1177-2220 **1701**
1174-5223 New Zealand WineGrower **243**
1174-5266 Reserve Bank of New Zealand. Financial Statistics†
1174-5339 New Zealand Management **1781**
1174-5428 N Z Radiator Magazine **8594**
1174-5622 Dive New Zealand **8169**
1174-5703 Naku **2661**
1174-5878 Paediatric Drugs **6866**
1174-5886 Drugs in R & D **6837**
1174-5894 Paediatrics Today **6098**
1174-5908 C N S Disorders Today **6129**
1174-5916 Cancer Today **6014**
1174-5924 Anti-Infectives Today **6821**
1174-5967 Research in Anthropology & Linguistics **353**
1174-6017 New Zealand Road Safety Research **8506**
1174-6106 Civil Aviation Authority of New Zealand. Review *changed to* 1173-9614 **74**
1174-6114 Unitec Institute of Technology. Research and Development Report *changed to* 1176-7391 **2965**
1174-6122 New Zealand Research in Early Childhood Education **2162**
1174-6157 Accounting, Corporate and Tax Alert *changed to* 1178-2277 **1302**
1174-6165 Catering Plus **3630**
1174-619X Electricity Engineers' Association of New Zealand. Annual Conference Proceedings *changed to* 1177-5432 **3304**
1174-6327 Food to Go **4386**
1174-6424 Urbis **460**
1174-6599 Autofacts *changed to* Autofile New and Used Annual **8934**
1174-6610 Wellington Occasional Papers in Applied Linguistics **5194**
1174-6769 Hi-Tech N Z†
1174-6793 Caritas Update **8031**
1174-6920 C C H Guide to Tax *changed to* 1177-4363 **4760**
1174-6920 C C H Guide to Tax *changed to* 1177-4134 **4793**
1174-6998 Older and Bolder (Christchurch Edition) **4052**
1174-7366 Unlimited **1799**
1174-748X A C E Papers **2822**
1174-7579 The Dissector **5957**
1174-7676 Asian Studies Institute. Translation Paper **5096**
1174-7846 Dairy Connection *changed to* 1177-4762 **7517**
1174-7935 New Zealand Truck and Driver Magazine **8673**
1174-7943 Reserve Bank of New Zealand Bulletin **1379**
1174-7986 New Zealand Journal of Forestry **3698**
1174-8052 Pacific Wings **67**
1174-8133 Sponsors' Update *changed to* 1176-9068 **2647**
1174-8265 New Zealand Health Information Service. Selected Morbidity Data for Publicly Funded Hospitals **4114**
1174-8362 Energy Matters New Zealand†
1174-8435 Monarchy New Zealand **7453**
1174-8451 Infoyouthaffairs *changed to* 1177-2379 **7478**
1174-8486 She†
1174-8540 Concrete **992**
1174-863X New Zealand Home & Entertaining *changed to* 1178-4148 **1012**
1174-8656 Weekend Gardener **3754**
1174-8729 Gallery News *changed to* 1177-4614 **6535**
1174-8737 New Zealand Fishing News. Map Guide Annual *changed to* 1177-6463 **8336**
1174-8915 New Zealand Journal of Asian Studies **557**
1174-9075 Executive Health & Wealth *changed to* 1177-6846 **2639**
1174-9210 Sportscience **8208**
1174-9334 Funding Hamilton *changed to* 1176-9599 **8041**
1174-9369 S A F E Magazine **321**
1174-9385 Curriculum Update† **8947**
1174-9423 Property Business†
1174-9482 Star *changed to* 1176-6670 **3576**
1174-9768 E E O Trust Diversity Index *changed to* 1176-8045 **1676**
1174-9776 New Zealand Law Commission. Study Paper **4746**
1174-9784 Vision† **8997**
1174-9792 Hawke's Bay Today **3917**
1174-9857 New Zealand Society for Earthquake Engineering. Bulletin **3279**
1174-9865 New Zealand Laboratory News **3251**
1174-992X C I O New Zealand **1415**
1174-9946 University of Auckland Business Review **1188**
1174-9970 Work and Progress **3049**
1175-0057 Kitchens and Bathrooms†
1175-009X Interior Detail(s)†
1175-0162 Alfresco **3721**
1175-0200 Current Directory of International Chambers of Commerce and Industry† **8947**
1175-0219 New Zealand Trade Directory† **8977**
1175-0278 Young Country Newsletter **171**
1175-0286 Foodtown Magazine **3643**
1175-0545 The Cut **8226**
1175-0561 American Journal of Clinical Dermatology **5871**
1175-0642 Heartland Sheep **117**
1175-0693 Golf Leisure & Lifestyle† **8960**
1175-0782 Main Report (Agriculture Edition) *changed to* 1177-939X **135**
1175-0790 Artscape† **8931**
1175-0855 Law Diary **4714**
1175-0928 Healthcare Review Online: Experience in Practice **4098**
1175-107X New Zealand Journal of Speech-Language Therapy **6083**
1175-1088 N Z Rugby World **8239**
1175-1258 The Weekly Samoa Post *changed to* 1177-1712 **3919**
1175-1355 New Zealand Hydrological Society. Current **2797**
1175-1371 Te Puna CD-ROM†
1175-1444 Resource Management Journal **4879**
1175-1487 New Zealand. Patent Office. Journal (CD-ROM) **6755**
1175-1576 Galaxy† **8958**
1175-1649 New Zealand Guns & Hunting **8324**
1175-1681 Apparel Trade Directory **1972**
1175-1738 Massey University. Department of Information Systems. Technical Report† **8973**
1175-1827 New Zealand 4 W D Magazine **8506**
1175-1908 Motor Equipment News **8592**
1175-1916 Southern Bird **914**
1175-1932 e.Office (Year)† **8952**
1175-1975 I P S Policy Newsletter *changed to* 1176-8797 **7166**
1175-2025 E.nz Magazine **3187**
1175-2033 Asia New Zealand Foundation. Review†
1175-2076 Regional Outlook *changed to* 1176-9416 **1524**
1175-2203 American Journal of Pharmacogenomics *changed to* 1177-1062 **5680**
1175-2238 Horticulture Facts & Figures *changed to* 1177-2190 **3755**
1175-2416 CounterAction†
1175-2459 Tone (Auckland) **3115**
1175-2742 Grower (Wellington) **116**
1175-2750 New Zealand Kennel Gazette *changed to* N Z Dog World **6811**
1175-2777 Research Letters in the Information and Mathematical Sciences (Print) *changed to* 1177-6994 **5529**
1175-2807 N G V Worldwide† **8976**
1175-2831 Alcohol.org.nz **2690**
1175-2874 Massey University. School of Accountancy. Discussion Paper Series **1296**
1175-2904 New Zealand Nursing Review **5971**
1175-2955 Arable Monitoring Report *changed to* 1178-2757 **200**
1175-2963 Horticulture Monitoring Report *changed to* 1178-2757 **200**
1175-3099 Journal of Maori and Pacific Development **1600**
1175-3277 American Journal of Cardiovascular Drugs **5776**
1175-3374 New Zealand Fishing World **8324**
1175-3390 Lifestyle Farmer **134**
1175-3420 Electrical Technology *changed to* 1177-2123 **2460**
1175-3455 New Zealand Bioethics Journal *changed to* 1176-7529 **4460**
1175-3501 About Kids†
1175-3722 Horizons.mw. Annual Report *changed to* 1176-9548 **7494**
1175-3781 Parenting with Confidence *changed to* 1176-8541 **2164**
1175-3811 Internet Magazine† **8966**
1175-3862 Fiction-plus† **8956**
1175-3994 New Zealand Fire Service Commission. Research Report **3580**
1175-4117 Reserve Bank of New Zealand. Discussion Paper Series (Print) *changed to* 1177-7567 **1379**
1175-4141 Asthma and Respiratory News **6211**
1175-4370 Pacific MotorYacht **8279**
1175-4486 Communication Journal of New Zealand **2315**
1175-4591 Stout Research Centre. Treaty of Waitangi Research Unit. Occasional Papers Series *changed to* 1177-2077 **7216**
1175-4621 Food New Zealand **3640**
1175-4702 N Z Woodturner *changed to* 1177-2697 **4555**
1175-477X Enterprise Networkz *changed to* 1177-875X **1885**
1175-5040 Code Word **1733**
1175-5164 Public Health Intelligence Occasional Bulletin **7537**
1175-5180 Essentially Food **4357**
1175-5202 S P A N Z **7773**
1175-5229 Culture and Heritage *changed to* 1177-0430 **8932**
1175-5245 DayStar **7637**
1175-5253 Sojourney† **8989**
1175-530X Tourism Satellite Account **8764**
1175-5326 Zootaxa **971**
1175-5334 *see* 1175-5326 **971**
1175-5393 M I S New Zealand. New Zealand's 100 Biggest I T Users *changed to* 1177-9233 **2531**
1175-5407 New Zealand Journal of Human Resources Management **1870**
1175-5520 Archives New Zealand. Departmental Forecast Report *changed to* 1175-8686 **7420**
1175-5636 Applied Bioinformatics†
1175-5644 Applied Genomics and Proteomics†
1175-5652 Applied Health Economics and Health Policy **5577**
1175-5687 Clinical Trials Insight Classics. Neurological Disorders†
1175-5717 Clinical Trials Insight Classics. Hypertension†
1175-5725 Clinical Trials Insight Classics. Antibacterials†
1175-5733 Clinical Trials Insight Classics. PharmacoEconomics†
1175-5741 Clinical Trials Insight Classics. Hyperlipidaemia†
1175-575X Clinical Trials Insight Classics. Heart Failure†
1175-5768 Clinical Trials Insight Classics. Diabetes†
1175-5776 Clinical Trials Insight Classics. Ischaemic Heart Disease†
1175-5784 Clinical Trials Insight Classics. Obstructive Airways Disease†
1175-5792 Clinical Trials Insight Classics. Antithrombotics†
1175-5806 Clinical Trials Insight Classics. Cancer Chemotherapy†
1175-5814 Clinical Trials Insight Classics. Pain Control†
1175-5822 Clinical Trials Insight Classics. Antivirals†
1175-5830 Clinical Trials Insight Classics. Rheumatic Disease†
1175-5849 Clinical Trials Insight Classics. Arrhythmias†
1175-5857 Clinical Trials Insight Classics. Peptic Ulcer Disease *changed to* 1176-5763
1175-5865 Clinical Trials Insight Classics. Immunotherapeutics. Transplant Rejection†
1175-5873 Clinical Trials Insight Classics. Immunotherapeutics. Vaccines†
1175-5881 Clinical Trials Insight Classics. Obesity†
1175-589X Clinical Trials Insight Classics. Women's Health†
1175-5970 Organic N Z **245**
1175-6012 N Z InfoTech *changed to* 1175-9488 **3917**
1175-6020 Touchstone **7777**
1175-6136 New Zealand Armed Forces Law Review **4972**
1175-6322 New Zealand Grapegrower **243**
1175-6349 Treatments in Endocrinology (Print Edition)†
1175-6357 American Journal of Cancer†
1175-6365 American Journal of Respiratory Medicine *changed to* 1176-3450
1175-639X Player†
1175-6438 Heartland Beef **117**
1175-6446 Mainland Beef *see* 1175-6926 **103**
1175-6519 D O C Science Internal Series *changed to* 1176-8886 **2608**
1175-6632 Skill New Zealand. Insight *changed to* 1176-3590 **8972**
1175-6799 Artists Alliance *changed to* 1177-2964 **468**
1175-6829 OnHoliday
1175-6918 Country-Wide (Northern Edition) **103**
1175-6926 Country-Wide (Southern Edition) **103**
1175-7108 Veterinary Council of New Zealand. Handbook & Code of Professional Conduct *changed to* 1176-0028 **8812**
1175-7124 Environment B O P. Guideline *changed to* 1177-2174 **3421**
1175-7213 Pacific Yachting† **8979**
1175-7248 Housing New Zealand Corporation. Annual Report **4413**
1175-7272 New Zealand Forest Industries *changed to* 1176-9785 **3713**
1175-7329 Discovery **2609**
1175-737X Mainland Sheep *see* 1175-6926 **103**
1175-7388 Driver **8578**
1175-7507 CAP Online **7319**
1175-7515 *see* 1176-8169 **2257**
1175-7523 Economic Service. Publication *changed to* 1176-824X **203**
1175-754X *see* 0369-3902 **140**
1175-7655 Global Issues **7966**
1175-7663 Dev-zine *changed to* 1176-8185 **8052**
1175-771X Marine Biodiversity Biosecurity Report *changed to* 1176-9440 **3456**
1175-7752 Engineering Dimension **3189**
1175-7787 Royal New Zealand Foundation for the Blind. Outlook *changed to* 1177-052X **4084**
1175-7930 Asia Info *changed to* 1178-1122 **556**
1175-7965 Tourism News **8763**
1175-8066 New Zealand's Best Employers in Work & Life *changed to* 1178-2781 **1676**
1175-8104 Effective Youth Transitions *changed to* 1176-3590 **8972**
1175-8147 University of Otago Magazine **2307**
1175-8171 New Zealand Property Journal *changed to* 1834-5662 **7583**
1175-8228 New Dialogue (Wellington, 2002. Print)†
1175-8279 F M C G **3677**
1175-8295 New Zealand. Education Review Office. Statement of Intent **7456**
1175-8376 Consumer Gardening† **8943**
1175-8384 New Zealand Industries and Regions *changed to* 0113-1680 **1721**
1175-8430 FitnessLife **6986**
1175-8457 University of Auckland. Department of Geography and Environmental Science. Occasional Publication **4032**
1175-8503 New Zealand. Ministry of Education. Research Section Report Series **2891**
1175-8570 Staples' Tax Guide **1944**
1175-8619 The Open Society **6937**
1175-8686 Archives New Zealand. Statement of Intent **7420**
1175-8708 English Teaching: Practice and Critique **2853**
1175-8716 New Zealand Medical Journal (Online) **5686**
1175-8724 International Visitor Arrivals to New Zealand **8779**
1175-8953 Juice **6224**
1175-897X New Zealand. Land Transport Safety Authority. Road Safety Issues *changed to* New Zealand. Land Transport NZ. Road Safety Issues **8506**

ISSN

Link to your serials resources and content with ulrichsweb.com

ISSN

1177-8482 see 1177-8474 8103
1177-8504 see 1176-1024 8632
1177-8512 see 1177-7796 78
1177-8539 New Zealand History Teachers' Association. Journal 4154
1177-8571 Kea Conservation Trust. Newsletter 2616
1177-858X Info Direct 3197
1177-8598 see 1177-858X 3197
1177-861X see 1177-8628 7254
1177-8628 N Z A I Regional Analysis 7254
1177-8644 see 1174-7943 1379
1177-8652 Hospital Throughput (Online)† 8962
1177-8660 see 1176-659X 7506
1177-8679 see 1176-6670 3576
1177-8687 see 1176-8533 120
1177-8695 see 1175-9917 8134
1177-8717 see 1177-1119 4418
1177-8725 see 1176-4295 4418
1177-8733 Conquest 5068
1177-875X Enterprise Matters 1885
1177-8768 see 1177-875X 1885
1177-8776 see 1175-7329 2609
1177-8784 see 1173-762X 259
1177-8806 see 1175-8295 7456
1177-8814 see 1177-4762 7517
1177-8822 Massey University. Centre for Public Health Research. Quarterly Monitoring Report changed to 1173-6437 7531
1177-8830 see 1173-6437 7531
1177-8849 Balanced Nutrition Index 6655
1177-8881 Drug Design, Development and Therapy 5607
1177-889X Patient Preference and Adherence 5694
1177-8903 Nanotechnology, Science and Applications 7027
1177-8911 New Scouting News 2204
1177-8946 U N O (Wellington Edition) 5085
1177-8970 Urban 8146
1177-9004 see 1174-2380 2617
1177-9012 see 1175-7752 3189
1177-9020 Student Direct 3221
1177-9039 Engineering Direct 3189
1177-9047 see 1176-2667 1150
1177-9055 New Zealand Society on Large Dams. Newsletter 3363
1177-9063 Pasifika Interactions Project. Working Paper 7164
1177-908X see 1176-9289 4420
1177-9101 see 1178-4997 6160
1177-9136 see 1170-4829 1514
1177-9144 see 1176-6786 1379
1177-9152 see 0110-7070 1379
1177-9179 see 1177-6986 8792
1177-9187 Profitable Transport & Logistics 8508
1177-9209 New Zealand Transport & Logistics Business Week (Online) see 1177-9187 8508
1177-9233 M I S 100 2531
1177-9284 see 1172-4005 3422
1177-9292 University of Auckland. School of Business Papers 1188
1177-9306 see 1176-8886 2608
1177-9314 Clinical Medicine: Oncology 6016
1177-9322 Bioinformatics and Biology Insights 825
1177-9349 Neuseeland News 8741
1177-939X Main Report's Profitable Agri-Business 135
1177-9403 see 1177-6072 7430
1177-9411 Civil Aviation Authority of New Zealand. Statement of Intent 8539
1177-942X see 1177-9411 8539
1177-9438 Her Magazine 8867
1177-9446 Otago Climate and Pasture Update 6393
1177-9454 see 1177-9446 6393
1177-9462 see 1174-3948 7420
1177-9470 see 1171-8722 3017
1177-9497 see 1175-8686 7420
1177-9500 see 1176-3124 7511
1177-9519 see 1176-2659 7512
1177-9527 see 1176-0516 7512
1177-9535 see 1171-7467 7489
1177-9543 Network News 8057
1177-9551 see 1177-956X 7159
1177-956X New Zealand. Electoral Commission, Te Kaitiaki Taki Kowhiri. Annual Report 7159
1177-9578 see 1175-2831 2690
1177-9586 Asia New Zealand Foundation. Review (Online) 7222
1177-9608 see 1177-2859 8061
1177-9616 Organic Update 144
1177-9624 MetaMoreTalk 6646
1177-9659 Cancer Control Council of New Zealand. Mapping Progress 7511
1177-9667 Cancer Control Council of New Zealand. Summary Mapping Progress 7511
1177-9675 see 1177-9659 7511
1177-9691 see 1171-3224 7489
1177-9705 Property Focus 7605
1177-9713 Who's Who 2035
1177-9748 see 1171-039X 7505
1177-9756 see 1177-1593 4406
1177-9764 see 1173-6771 3489
1177-9799 see 1172-0638 2647
1177-9837 see 1172-4382 7183
1177-9853 see 1176-8126 7456
1177-987X see 1176-9165 2965
1177-9934 Public Health Advice 7537
1177-9942 see 1177-9934 7537
1177-9977 see 1175-7248 4413
1178-0126 Coffee Culture Handbook 3631
1178-0193 see 1179-1098 5999
1178-0207 see 1179-0849 4394
1178-0231 see 1179-0881 1048
1178-024X see 1179-0903 1899
1178-0274 New Zealand. Statistics New Zealand. External Migration changed to 1179-0954 7288
1178-0282 see 1179-092X 3658
1178-0304 New Zealand. Statistics New Zealand. Local Authority Statistics (Online) 8390
1178-0320 see 1179-1020 1579
1178-0355 see 1179-1128 1255
1178-0371 see 1179-1144 1048
1178-038X see 1179-1101 1255
1178-0401 see 1179-1268 608
1178-041X see 1179-1071 1254
1178-0436 see 1179-0873 7288
1178-0444 see 1179-089X 1254
1178-0460 see 1179-1187 1254
1178-0479 see 1179-1152 1254
1178-0487 see 1179-0946 1700
1178-0495 see 1179-1632 2444
1178-0517 see 1179-0989 1700
1178-0525 see 1179-0970 1700
1178-0568 see 1179-1292 1255
1178-0576 see 1179-1012 7288
1178-0614 see 1179-2221 1255
1178-0622 see 1179-1055 1255
1178-0630 see 1179-1772 1899
1178-0649 see 1179-111X 1255
1178-0673 see 1179-1233 7288
1178-0843 Lincoln University. Research Profile 7880
1178-1076 New Zealand Physical Educator 3074
1178-1122 N Z A I Bulletin 556
1178-1149 Clinical Medicine: Arthritis and Musculoskeletal Disorders 5944
1178-1157 Clinical Medicine: Circulatory, Respiratory and Pulmonary Medicine 6213
1178-1165 Clinical Medicine: Cardiology 5783
1178-1173 Clinical Medicine: Endocrinology and Diabetes 5885
1178-1181 Clinical Medicine: Pathology 5597
1178-119X Clinical Medicine: Gastroenterology 5921
1178-122X Virology: Research and Treatment 897
1178-1238 Retrovirology: Research and Treatment 5825
1178-1254 Weekend 8773
1178-1289 see 1177-3545 8123
1178-1297 New Zealand Institute. Discussion Paper 1153
1178-1300 see 1176-5860 1500
1178-1319 see 1174-0922 253
1178-1327 see 1176-9068 2647
1178-1335 see 1174-5703 2661
1178-1343 see 1174-7676 5096
1178-1351 see 0111-1957 7834
1178-1394 see 1177-2085 3134
1178-1483 see 0111-3895 7905
1178-1521 New Zealand Crime Statistics 2675
1178-153X Northland District Crime Statistics 2675
1178-1548 Waitemata District Crime Statistics 2675
1178-1556 Auckland District Crime Statistics 2672
1178-1564 Counties / Manukau District Crime Statistics 2673
1178-1572 Waikato District Crime Statistics 2675
1178-1580 Bay of Plenty District Crime Statistics 2673
1178-1599 Eastern District Crime Statistics 2674
1178-1602 Central District Crime Statistics 2673
1178-1610 Wellington District Crime Statistics 2675
1178-1629 Tasman District Crime Statistics 2675
1178-1637 Canterbury District Crime Statistics 2673
1178-1645 Southern District Crime Statistics 2675
1178-1653 The Patient 5694
1178-1661 see 1178-1653 5694
1178-1696 see 1177-9667 7511
1178-170X see 1175-9348 3638
1178-1807 Info-Link Hardware+ 1054
1178-1831 Everyday Healthy Food 4357
1178-1912 Pacific Human Rights Issues Series 7213
1178-1920 see 1178-1912 7213
1178-1998 Clinical Interventions in Aging (Online) 4043
1178-2005 The International Journal of Chronic Obstructive Pulmonary Disease (Online) 5790
1178-2013 International Journal of Nanomedicine (Online) 6849
1178-2021 Neuropsychiatric Disease and Treatment (Online) 6167
1178-203X Therapeutics and Clinical Risk Management (Online) 6882
1178-2048 Vascular Health and Risk Management (Online) 5801
1178-217X Clinical Medicine: Geriatrics 4043
1178-220X Clinical Medicine: Pediatrics 6090
1178-2218 Substance Abuse: Research and Treatment 2699
1178-2226 Biomedical Informatics Insight 5586
1178-2234 Breast Cancer 6009
1178-2242 Palliative Care: Research and Treatment 5977
1178-2269 Clinical Medicine: Blood Disorders 5944
1178-2277 Taxation Today 1302
1178-2293 see 0111-1760 1189
1178-2390 Journal of Multidisciplinary Healthcare 5653
1178-2439 Museums Aotearoa. Directory 6532
1178-2463 New Zealand. Maori Broadcasting Funding Agency. Annual Report see Te Mangai Paho. Annual Report 2340
1178-2501 The Best of New Zealand 3916
1178-2528 see 0113-8596 6508
1178-2536 Where to Live in Auckland 8147
1178-2560 see 0114-2720 4877
1178-2587 MindNet.org.nz 6161
1178-2595 Pharmaceutical Medicine 6869
1178-2706 New Zealand Energy Quarterly 3153
1178-2714 see 1178-2706 3153
1178-2722 see 1175-5040 1733
1178-2730 New Zealand. Ministry of Justice. Annual Report 7456
1178-2749 see 1178-2730 7456
1178-2757 Horticulture and Arable Monitoring Report 200
1178-2765 see 1178-2757 200
1178-2773 New Zealand Computer Club. Newsletter 2572
1178-2781 E E O Trust Work & Life Awards (Series) 1676
1178-2811 see 1178-3281 1966
1178-282X Microscopy in Focus (Online) 900
1178-2986 see 0111-5715 408
1178-3028 Te Kairangahau 8116
1178-3052 see 1176-4007 7456
1178-3079 New Zealand. Law Commission. Annual Report see 1172-174X 4746
1178-3141 see 1172-6210 7295
1178-3184 New Zealand Novachem Agrichemical Manual 243
1178-3192 University of Otago. Department of Computer Science. Technical Report 2440
1178-3206 see 1176-3388 8058
1178-3222 see 1176-6352 1698
1178-3265 The Source 8400
1178-3273 see 1178-3265 8400
1178-3281 S M Es in New Zealand 1966
1178-329X E E L Research Report 1676
1178-3303 see 1178-329X 1676
1178-332X International Accreditation New Zealand. Technical Guide 4488
1178-3338 Development West Coast. Group Annual Report (Print) 1883
1178-3346 Development West Coast. Group Annual Report (Online) see 1178-3338 1883
1178-3354 see 1174-748X 2822
1178-3362 see 1176-211X 2287
1178-3370 see 1177-2379 7478
1178-3389 see 1175-9895 7456
1178-3397 see 1170-7240 8033
1178-3400 see 1176-8096 4418
1178-3419 see 1172-269X 686
1178-3427 New Zealand. Law Commission. Statement of Intent 4746
1178-3435 see 1178-3427 4746
1178-3451 New Zealand. Ministry of Maori Development. Statement of Intent (Online) 7456
1178-346X ACCtive 4490
1178-3478 see 1178-346X 4490
1178-3486 Stitch Innovation Series 1904
1178-3494 see 1178-3486 1904
1178-3508 see 1178-1122 556
1178-3516 Panui Whainga 7459
1178-3524 C I T R - T R 2409
1178-3532 The Wine Science Press 613
1178-3540 C D M T C S Research Report Series 5476
1178-3559 see 1173-0889 5545
1178-3567 see 1173-5627 7432
1178-3575 Food Service 3642
1178-3583 Network (Auckland) 2293
1178-3591 Retirement Policy and Research Centre Working Paper 4054
1178-3605 see 1175-8147 2307
1178-3648 see 1175-3994 3580
1178-3656 Institute of Policy Studies. Working Paper 7143
1178-3680 see 0111-0136 3225
1178-3702 see 1173-9614 74
1178-3710 see 1176-2306 5034
1178-3753 New Dialogue (Wellington, 2007. Print) 8058
1178-377X see 1176-2128 7455
1178-3885 see 0112-0328 8103
1178-3893 see 0114-7870 5999
1178-3907 see 1176-4112 2610
1178-3923 Heart to Heart 5410
1178-3958 see 1172-9139 2622
1178-3982 see 1177-6315 1593
1178-413X see 1177-1593 4406
1178-4148 Home New Zealand 1012
1178-4210 see 1176-0567 2708
1178-4229 Used Car Safety Ratings (Online) 8609
1178-4237 Catapult 5001
1178-4245 see 1174-6017 8506
1178-4253 see 1176-3949 8527
1178-4261 see 1176-4473 6162
1178-4296 see 1176-5259 2669
1178-4407 Journal of Health Informatics in Developing Countries 5649
1178-4423 Information and Communication Technology in New Zealand 2347
1178-4431 see 1178-4423 2347
1178-4601 Environmental Performance of the Electricity Commission changed to 1173-8839 3147
1178-4652 see 1177-147X 8058
1178-4997 Mental Health Newsletter 6160
1178-5012 Brookers Medical Law Handbook 4632
1178-5098 see 1176-8282 3147
1178-511X see 1176-9467 8104
1178-5136 Environment Waikato Regional Council. Policy Effectiveness Paper 2610
1178-5144 see 1178-5136 2610
1178-5179 see 1175-7655 7966
1178-5195 see 1172-2584 4716
1178-5403 Alive 5064
1178-5454 M S R Youth† 8972
1178-5462 see 1175-1444 4879
1178-5527 Aotearoa New Zealand Social Work Review 8025
1178-5608 International Journal on Smart Sensing and Intelligent Systems 2452
1178-5616 University of Canterbury. Department of Economics. Working Paper 1188
1178-5624 University of Canterbury. Computer Science and Software Engineering. Technical Report 2599
1178-5632 N C R E Working Paper 7254
1178-5640 N C R E Online Papers 4247
1178-5721 see 1174-6793 8031
1178-5802 Beautynz 585
1178-5896 see 1177-2247 2291
1178-5934 Human Interface Technology Laboratory New Zealand. Technical Report 2448
1178-6086 Cardiology Research Review 5780
1178-6094 Colorectal Oncology Research Review 6016
1178-6108 Dental Research Review 5841
1178-6116 Diabetes and Obesity Research Review 5886
1178-6124 G P Research Review 5617
1178-6132 HIV/AIDS Research Review 5815
1178-6140 Internal Medicine Research Review 5946
1178-6159 Neurology Research Review 6166
1178-6167 Pacific Health Review 7534
1178-6175 Pharmacy Research Review 6874
1178-6183 Psychiatry Research Review 6178
1178-6191 Maori Health Review 7531
1178-6205 Respiratory Research Review 6219

ISSN

ISSN

1200-247X Prairie Renovation Markets†
1200-2488 Ontario Renovation Markets†
1200-2496 Quebec Renovation Markets†
1200-2569 Canada. Canadian Heritage. Annual Report on the Operation of the Canadian Multiculturalism Act **7426**
1200-2852 Biological Survey of Canada. Taxonomic Series **841**
1200-3336 Transmontanus **3568**
1200-3387 Northstar Compass **7159**
1200-3557 Canada. Department of Finance. Annual Financial Report of the Government of Canada **1914**
1200-3654 Television and the House of Commons **7471**
1200-3964 AIDS **5808**
1200-4057 Bankruptcy Law Update **4857**
1200-409X Inclusion News **3041**
1200-4189 Pages *changed to* 1719-9603 **7238**
1200-4227 Canada. Statistics Canada. Health Statistics Division. Therapeutic Abortions†
1200-4537 First Nations Policing Update *changed to* 1914-4067 **2643**
1200-5223 Canada. Statistics Canada. Analytical Studies Branch. Research Paper Series (Print Edition) *changed to* Canada. Statistics Canada. Analytical Studies Branch. Research Paper Series **1079**
1200-5460 *see* 1198-8819 **1957**
1200-5495 Wedding Bells (Ottawa Edition) *see* 1707-3987 **5562**
1200-5495 Wedding Bells (Ottawa Edition) *see* 1715-9792
1200-5517 Wedding Bells (Atlantic Canada Edition) *see* 1715-9792
1200-5517 Wedding Bells (Atlantic Canada Edition) *see* 1707-3987 **5562**
1200-5525 Wedding Bells (Saskatchewan Edition) *see* 1707-3987 **5562**
1200-5525 Wedding Bells (Saskatchewan Edition) *see* 1715-9792
1200-5533 Old Age Security, Child Tax Benefit, Children's Special Allowances and Canada Pension Plan. Report **8060**
1200-5649 Royal Gazette. Part 1 **3817**
1200-5657 National Pollutant Release Inventory. Summary Report *changed to* 1492-4730 **3478**
1200-569X Quebec. Commission des Valeurs Mobilieres. Rapport Annuel *changed to* 1710-7725 **1646**
1200-5800 Index of Airworthiness Directives Applicable in Canada **76**
1200-5835 Canadian Circumpolar Library. Occasional Publications Series†
1200-670X Vecteur Environnement **3473**
1200-6866 *see* 0821-8110 **7421**
1200-751X O S M T Advocate **5910**
1200-7676 Atlantic Canada Oil Works Magazine **6763**
1200-7900 National Edition of Notices to Mariners *changed to* 1714-0196 **8655**
1200-7935 Ecrits **5287**
1200-8001 AgriView **86**
1200-815X S A S C A Newsletter **2299**
1200-8168 You (Toronto)
1200-8184 Quarterly Regional Statistics **1259**
1200-8222 New City Magazine†
1200-8540 Scott's Directories - Western Industrial Manufacturers **2027**
1200-8591 Canada. Department of Finance. Government of Canada Tax Expenditures *changed to* 1495-6489 **1914**
1200-8710 Ordre Professionnel des Travailleurs Sociaux du Quebec. Bulletin de Nouvelles *changed to* 1716-3706 **8060**
1200-8923 Signs Canada *changed to* 1718-3006 **530**
1200-9059 Oilweek Magazine **6785**
1200-9679 Canadian Journal of Women's Health Care for Physicians Addressing Women's Health Issues†
1200-9954 Theatrum's Stage†
1201-0154 International Journal of Comparative Sociology and Anthropology†
1201-0162 International Journal of Comparative African and Asian Studies†
1201-026X McGill Journal of Medicine **5665**
1201-0278 Legal Aid in Canada: Description of Operations **8053**
1201-0383 C I H I Directions **7510**
1201-0421 Bulletin d'Histoire Politique **4286**
1201-0472 Access **4987**
1201-057X Canada. Statistics Canada. Capital Expenditures by Type of Asset **1045**
1201-060X Aboriginal Voices†
1201-0766 Questions de Patrimoine *see* 1198-2454 **4295**
1201-0790 Forensic Scientist **5913**
1201-1223 R E M: The Real Estate Magazine **7606**
1201-1541 Pipeline Safety Reflexions *changed to* 1499-2450 **8636**
1201-169X *see* 0704-5603 **7427**
1201-1770 C N T C News† **8938**
1201-1835 The Write File Quarterly†
1201-1916 New Media Canada†
1201-2459 Early Modern Literary Studies **5421**
1201-2475 Informed **5635**
1201-2491 Sprinter†
1201-2882 Graffito *changed to* Spire **5435**
1201-303X Access to Canadian Commodity Taxes†
1201-3072 Anglo-Celtic Roots **3758**
1201-3080 Water Quality Research Journal of Canada **3493**
1201-3307 Journal of Professional Studies *changed to* 1708-2749 **2898**
1201-3315 EnviroMation **3485**
1201-3390 Dynamics of Continuous, Discrete and Impulsive Systems. Series A: Mathematical Analysis **5484**
1201-3447 Scandinavian Press **3562**
1201-3501 Canada. Statistics Canada. Adult Criminal Court Statistics **2673**
1201-3595 Quebec. Ministere de la Culture et des Communications. Rapport Annuel *changed to* 1703-9193 **7439**
1201-3633 British Columbia Financial and Economic Review (Print Edition) *changed to* British Columbia Financial and Economic Review (Online Edition) **1215**
1201-401X Afterthoughts†
1201-4087 Business Events Guide (Year) **6278**
1201-4184 Municipal Pension Plan Annual Report **1641**
1201-4192 Public Service Pension Plan Annual Report **1646**
1201-4710 Histoire Quebec **4295**
1201-4826 Between the Lines **6549**
1201-4834 *see* 1201-4826 **6549**
1201-4907 Germs and Ideas†
1201-5059 Crop Protection **226**
1201-530X Canadian Healthcare Source Book **5591**
1201-5326 The Sponsorship Report **8073**
1201-5407 L'Escale Nautique **8275**
1201-558X Forum Focus **7644**
1201-5598 D I Y Boat Owner **8275**
1201-561X Theory and Applications of Categories **5541**
1201-5679 Canadian Grains Industry Statistical Handbook **177**
1201-5741 Mixtures **6588**
1201-5989 Skin Therapy Letter **5882**
1201-6144 Avante† **8934**
1201-6179 Voyageur (Woodbridge) **2270**
1201-6195 Quebec International (Montreal)†
1201-6284 Canada. Statistics Canada. Public Sector Finance *changed to* 1494-5797 **1218**
1201-6292 Insights On **1243**
1201-6381 In 2 Print **5308**
1201-639X Association of Universities and Colleges in Canada. Research File **2968**
1201-6624 Fermata *changed to* 1711-9235 **6594**
1201-673X Canadian Wildlife **2605**
1201-7094 Bottin du Pouvoir a Quebec *changed to* 1491-6983 **7443**
1201-7302 Cursus **5004**
1201-737X Poets' Podium **5432**
1201-7582 Industrial Monitor on CD-ROM **1242**
1201-7647 Resource Links **2210**
1201-7817 Management Matters **1776**
1201-7892 The Activist **7202**
1201-821X GlennGould† **8959**
1201-8325 Extraction System of Agricultural Statistics **179**
1201-8384 The Sustainable Times **1709**
1201-8481 Canada. Statistics Canada. Public Sector Employment and Wages and Salaries *changed to* 1494-5797 **1218**
1201-8538 Wireless Telecom **2345**
1201-8783 Monetary Policy Report **1499**
1201-8791 The Communicator
1201-8996 Broken Pencil **5209**
1201-9313 Farm Operations Cost Guide **198**
1201-9364 C M Magazine **7557**
1201-950X Quebec. Bulletin Regional sur le Marche du Travail *changed to* 1912-6603 **1669**
1201-9569 Student Traveller **8758**
1201-9607 International Journal of Comparative Criminology **2655**
1201-9712 International Journal of Infectious Diseases **5818**
1201-9828 Heart Disease and Stroke in Canada **5788**
1201-9984 British Columbia Hydro. Corporate Review **8819**
1202-0206 Annotated Canada Labour Code **4617**
1202-0249 Studio†
1202-0265 FishBoats **8275**
1202-0974 Dalhousie University. Department of Oceanography. Biennial Report **2803**
1202-1156 Roncarelli Report on the Computer Animation Industry **2489**
1202-3116 Northern Horse Review **8295**
1202-3302 Gazeta Montrealska
1202-3329 Mutual Fund Monitor†
1202-3337 Natural Gas Hedger *changed to* 1491-2279 **6780**
1202-3930 Freedom to Read Week *changed to* 1711-9367 **2858**
1202-4562 Atlantic Review†
1202-4651 Autoroute†
1202-5879 C S C News **6491**
1202-5925 Award Magazine **977**
1202-6298 Get a Life! **8104**
1202-6328 Usine
1202-6379 Budget Speech **7425**
1202-6395 Accommodation and Campground Guide **8680**
1202-6891 Travel Exclusive **8766**
1202-6913 Legislation Canadienne en Propriete Intellectuelle **4722**
1202-7383 C P F National News **5102**
1202-7405 Investment Executive **1632**
1202-7472 Menz Magazine **6295**
1202-7480 Lethbridge Living **5075**
1202-7545 Welcome to Vancouver Gastronomic
1202-7553 Celtic Heritage **3526**
1202-757X Halton-Peel News Letter *changed to* 1719-4474 **3769**
1202-7588 Kids Creations **2248**
1202-7596 Agent Canada Magazine†
1202-7707 Yardstick **3718**
1202-807X Consolidated Federal Employment and Labour Statutes and Regulations **4649**
1202-8991 Boer Country†
1202-9114 Compendium of Nonprescription Products *changed to* 1703-2563 **6830**
1202-9262 The FundLetter **1625**
1202-9408 Maple Ridge, Pitt Meadows Times **3813**
1202-9459 Liezhiwen Shi Bao **3548**
1202-9718 Canadian Healthcare Manager **4090**
1203-0287 Ralph **5433**
1203-0325 Wedding Bells (British Columbia Edition) *see* 1707-3987 **5562**
1203-0325 Wedding Bells (British Columbia Edition) *see* 1715-9792
1203-0333 Wedding Bells (Calgary Edition) *see* 1715-9792
1203-0333 Wedding Bells (Calgary Edition) *see* 1707-3987 **5562**
1203-0341 Wedding Bells *changed to* 1707-3987 **5562**
1203-035X Wedding Bells (Edmonton Edition) *see* 1707-3987 **5562**
1203-035X Wedding Bells (Edmonton Edition) *see* 1715-9792
1203-0368 Wedding Bells (Hamilton - Niagara Edition) *see* 1715-9792
1203-0368 Wedding Bells (Hamilton - Niagara Edition) *see* 1707-3987 **5562**
1203-0376 Wedding Bells (London, Ontario Edition) *see* 1707-3987 **5562**
1203-0376 Wedding Bells (London, Ontario Edition) *see* 1715-9792
1203-0384 Wedding Bells (Montreal Edition) *see* 1715-9792
1203-0384 Wedding Bells (Montreal Edition) *see* 1707-3987 **5562**
1203-0392 Wedding Bells (Toronto Edition) *see* 1707-3987 **5562**
1203-0392 Wedding Bells (Toronto Edition) *see* 1715-9792
1203-0996 Bulletin Infoaction **7425**
1203-1151 Human Resources Advisor Newsletter (Ontario Edition) **1864**
1203-1178 Canadian Western Geographical Series **4001**
1203-1267 Exit **5422**
1203-1372 Camauto Plus *changed to* 1912-3132 **8571**
1203-1488 A R Q **426**
1203-1496 The Charlton Standard Catalogue of Royal Doulton Beswick Storybook Figurines **6649**
1203-1542 Journal of Hebrew Scriptures **7725**
1203-1569 Zen Views
1203-1607 Ontario. Ministry of Agriculture, Food and Rural Affairs. Dairy Report†
1203-1666 Edmonton Public Library. The Source **5008**
1203-1771 Canadian Locksmith **1053**
1203-1887 Rights Canada **7572**
1203-1925 International Health News **5637**
1203-214X B C Pharmacy **6824**
1203-2255 Quebec (Province). Ministere des Ressources Naturelles. Rapport Annuel *changed to* 1910-7005 **3145**
1203-2395 Black Cat 115†
1203-2433 Legislation Quebecoise en Droit des Institutions Financieres **4874**
1203-2549 Conspiracy!
1203-2743 Construction Innovation **996**
1203-2778 Quetico Provincial Park *changed to* 1710-6370 **2625**
1203-2816 Contemporary Canadian Authors **5278**
1203-2832 Canadian Dental Directory **1978**
1203-3103 Habitabec Plus Montreal
1203-3111 Habitabec Plus Quebec†
1203-3154 The Miser's Gazette **4364**
1203-3243 Infertility Helper†
1203-3308 Research Matters **2904**
1203-3421 Ontario Association of Social Workers. Newsmagazine **8060**
1203-3634 Who's Who in International Development **1607**
1203-3642 Qui Fait Quoi en Developpement International *see* 1203-3634 **1607**
1203-3669 Sante et Services Sociaux au Quebec **7541**
1203-3774 Worksite News **6689**
1203-3901 Vox Feminarum **8888**
1203-3995 Ontario Insects **856**
1203-4142 SchoolNet *changed to* 1494-7331 **2951**
1203-4533 Canada. Statistics Canada. Canada's Culture, Heritage and Identity: a Statistical Perspective *changed to* 1496-418X **7479**
1203-4606 Finances of the Nation **1924**
1203-4657 B N A Portraits **6892**
1203-4754 Journal of Cutaneous Medicine and Surgery **5878**
1203-4789 College Canada **2972**
1203-5025 *see* 0843-8994 **4789**
1203-5149 Alberta Business Directory **1971**
1203-5157 Atlantic Provinces Business Directory **1973**
1203-5165 British Columbia Business Directory **1977**
1203-522X Manitoba Business Directory **2015**
1203-5238 Saskatchewan Business Directory **2026**
1203-5246 Ontario Business Directory **2022**
1203-5564 Harbour Authorities Forum **8645**
1203-5629 Theatre News
1203-5696 O S/2 e-Zine! **2595**
1203-5769 Legacy (Edmonton) **5224**
1203-5793 Rugby Catalogue of Information Sources **8244**
1203-5874 African Access Magazine†
1203-5912 Ecocycle **3416**
1203-5920 *see* 1203-5912 **3416**
1203-6056 British Columbia. Ministry of Health and Ministry Responsible for Seniors. Annual Report *changed to* 1499-0350 **7510**
1203-6463 Bottin des Communications du Quebec **2313**
1203-6528 Annual Production of Soft Drinks **597**
1203-6595 Poemata **5430**
1203-6692 Blizzart **479**
1203-6706 InsuranceWest **4509**
1203-6765 Pain Research & Management **6173**
1203-6838 Canadian Pizza Magazine **3629**
1203-6927 Anglo-Celtic Annals†
1203-7109 Personal Finance **1374**
1203-7125 Outpost (Toronto) **8746**
1203-7796 The Canadian Journal of Rural Medicine **5592**
1203-7990 Model Forest Network. Year in Review **3697**
1203-8016 YES Mag **2223**
1203-8032 Journal of Law and Social Work **4702**
1203-8261 Gift and Collectibles Retailer†
1203-8393 Justice as Healing **4708**
1203-8407 Journal of Advanced Oxidation Technologies **2136**
1203-844X Canadian Journal of Allergy and Clinical Immunology *changed to* 1710-1484 **5753**
1203-858X Gardening Life **3732**
1203-8601 Silicon Valley North *changed to* 1910-992X **1152**
1203-8660 Canadian Criminal Law Review **4885**
1203-8946 Prieres Missionnaires **7813**
1203-8954 Provenance
1203-9012 Technology Overview **5720**
1203-9195 British Columbia. Ministry of Employment and Investment. Annual Report *changed to* 1496-9939
1203-9209 Canadian Association of Radiologists. Forum **6193**
1203-9241 Former "State Socialist" World **7136**
1203-9268 Canada. Governor General. Speech from the Throne to Open the Session of Parliament **7113**
1203-9438 Politique et Societes **7171**
1203-9586 FreeFall **5216**
1203-9667 It's a Bunny **5312**
1204-041X Ontario Casino Corporation. Annual Report *changed to* 1499-4887 **7458**
1204-0592 *see* 1188-665X **3125**
1204-072X W C R A News **8627**
1204-1335 Canadian Resources†
1204-136X Canadian Flight Annual†
1204-1645 Turtle Island News **3569**
1204-2277 C I S S Bulletin **7224**
1204-2390 National Council of Welfare. Poverty Profile **8057**
1204-2579 Dundas Star *changed to* 1707-1364 **3809**

ISSN

1207-0513 On the Administration of the Access to Information Act and the Privacy Act. Annual Reports (Print) *changed to* 1910-3506 **7534**
1207-0661 Review of O H & S Legislation in (Year)†
1207-0750 Dossier Chiropratique *see* 0836-1444 **5804**
1207-0998 Memorial University of Newfoundland. Institute of Social and Economic Research. Bibliography† **8974**
1207-1226 Nova Scotia Employment Program for Students Job Catalogue *changed to* 1719-4180 **6704**
1207-1463 Canadian Traveller (Vancouver) **8691**
1207-1846 B C L A Reporter **4993**
1207-1978 C A H S Journal **50**
1207-2222 Pets Quarterly **6813**
1207-2478 Coup de Pouce Cuisine **3632**
1207-2591 Alberta Venture **1058**
1207-2842 Orthoscope **6070**
1207-3016 Canada. Statistics Canada. National Tourism Indicators. Historical Estimates **8778**
1207-3423 East York Mirror **3809**
1207-3644 Directory of Canadian Search and Rescue Organizations **8037**
1207-4195 Alberta Financial Services Corporation. Annual Report **218**
1207-4845 Migration Highlights **7312**
1207-4888 Earnings and Employment Trends **1225**
1207-4977 Alberta Community Development. Annual Report **7946**
1207-5272 N S S B A Matters! **3028**
1207-5361 Virtual Physics
1207-5469 Pioneer†
1207-5639 The O S L A Connection†
1207-5647 Aviso (Ottawa) **4088**
1207-5825 *see* 1207-5833 **5903**
1207-5833 Canadian Journal of Medical Laboratory Science **5903**
1207-5841 British Columbia. Ministry of Finance and Corporate Relations. Budget Reports *changed to* 1705-6071 **7424**
1207-621X Canada. Agriculture & Agri-Food Canada. Policy Branch. Bi-Weekly Bulletin **99**
1207-652X National Plumbing Code of Canada **1026**
1207-6600 Exclaim! **6566**
1207-7011 National Farm Building Code of Canada **1026**
1207-7062 Prince George Free Press **3816**
1207-7267 Directory of Disability Organizations in Canada **4064**
1207-7585 D A I S†
1207-7798 Canadian Journal of Educational Administration and Policy **3019**
1207-7933 Oilweek **6785**
1207-8166 Ottawa Business Journal **1157**
1207-8190 T D Quarterly Economic Report†
1207-8409 Miramichi City & Area Directory *changed to* 1493-6208 **3813**
1207-8514 Canadian Climate Summary **6348**
1207-8603 Electronic Information Partnerships **2530**
1207-9030 Canadian Centre on Substance Abuse. Action News **2692**
1207-909X Survey of Mutual Funds†
1208-011X Canadian International Development Agency. Development Information Program. Guidelines for Submitting Proposals *changed to* 1707-7168 **1592**
1208-0608 Red Book **8064**
1208-0721 McMichael Canadian Art Collection. Annual Report **6529**
1208-0845 B C R Group of Companies. Annual Report *changed to* 1713-2738 **8615**
1208-0888 Prince Edward Island. Department of Education. Annual Report **2899**
1208-0985 *see* 0832-9257 **4822**
1208-1167 Indian Life **7707**
1208-123X Wildlife Watchers Report on Monitoring **2632**
1208-171X Directory of Courses and Materials for Training in Distance Education **2842**
1208-2163 Tenant†
1208-2260 GEOtext **2708**
1208-2325 Solicitor's Journal **4784**
1208-2473 The Disseminator **5007**
1208-2937 Yukon Exploration and Geology **2775**
1208-3143 Annual Report on Organized Crime in Canada (Print Edition) **2644**
1208-3453 Canadian Maturity†
1208-3488 Landmark†
1208-3658 Bulla Gymnasia Virtualis
1208-4484 Canada. Department of Finance. Fiscal Reference Tables **1217**
1208-4581 Caledon Profiles. Real Leaders *see* 1912-225X **8881**
1208-5308 Magazine P M E *changed to* 1491-221X **1965**
1208-5499 Institute of Chartered Accountants of British Columbia. Beyond Numbers **1291**
1208-5855 Nonferrous Metals Outlook **6327**
1208-5995 Independent & Free Press **3811**
1208-6002 *see* 0829-8211 **725**
1208-6010 *see* 0008-3674 **2703**
1208-6029 *see* 0315-1468 **3261**
1208-6037 *see* 0045-5067 **3685**
1208-6045 *see* 0008-4204 **7007**
1208-6053 *see* 1181-8700 **3428**
1208-6460 *see* 1207-8603 **2530**
1208-6495 Clinical Handbook of Psychotropic Drugs **6829**
1208-669X Infotox† **8964**
1208-6878 Annuel de Peche **8304**
1208-6924 Polski Instytut Naukowy w Kanadzie i Biblioteka Polska im. Wandy Stachiewicz. Biuletyn **4469**
1208-7009 North American Food Processing Directory†
1208-7068 Coverings **4536**
1208-7661 Regie Regionale de la Sante et des Services Sociaux de la Cote-Nord. Rapport Annuel *changed to* 1719-8577 **7506**
1208-7777 The Afro News **3517**
1208-7920 British Columbia. Office of the Auditor General. Annual Report **7424**
1208-8110 Focus on Children and Youth *changed to* VocalPoint **8077**
1208-865X Canadian Pacific Railway News *changed to* 1709-870X **8620**
1208-8676 Nova Scotia Open to the World **1155**
1208-8722 Freshwater Fishing Regulations Synopsis **8315**
1208-8765 Saskatchewan Drama Association. Newsletter **3079**
1208-9087 Curling News†
1208-9125 Ambassador Newfoundland and Labrador *changed to* 1912-6565 **1425**
1208-9230 Charlton Standard Catalogue of Canadian Country Store Collectables **532**
1208-9400 Safety Digest (Ottawa) **6444**
1208-9427 Electronic Graffito†
1208-9435 *see* 1719-8224 **4607**
1208-9982 Economic Review **1480**
1209-0174 Hunting and Trapping Regulations Synopsis **2614**
1209-0182 Doings Online **574**
1209-0409 Alberta Law Reform Institute. Report **4613**
1209-0670 B C A Emerging Markets Analyst†
1209-0689 Animus **6904**
1209-0727 Wilderness Activist *changed to* 1717-8894 **2605**
1209-0891 Annuaire Municipal de l'Ontario *see* 1198-824X **7458**
1209-1235 Quarterly Demographic Statistics *changed to* 1911-0928 **7278**
1209-1278 Science Statistics (Online Edition) **7938**
1209-1286 *see* 0848-5216 **1217**
1209-1316 Canada. Statistics Canada. Rail in Canada **8523**
1209-1367 Health Reports (Online) **7523**
1209-1375 Rapports sur la Sante (Online) *see* 1708-7694 **7541**
1209-1375 Rapports sur la Sante (Online) *see* 1209-1367 **7523**
1209-2053 MSCommunique **7532**
1209-2428 Canadian Plastics Technology Showcase†
1209-2800 Alberta Education. Annual Report and Annual Results Report *changed to* 1715-3492 **2966**
1209-2800 Alberta Education. Annual Report and Annual Results Report *changed to* 1715-4391 **2825**
1209-322X Western Canada Stallion Directory *changed to* 1914-0835 **8300**
1209-336X Canada. Treasury Board. Program Expenditure Detail: A Profile of Departmental Spending **7428**
1209-3459 Canada. Statistics Canada. Police Personnel and Expenditures in Canada (Print Edition) *changed to* 1493-5090
1209-3696 Lumen **4152**
1209-3718 L C B O Annual Report *changed to* 1713-0514 **7451**
1209-3955 The Rider *changed to* 1910-2275 **8298**
1209-3963 Canadian Capital Cost Allowance Guide†
1209-4617 Family Chronicle **3765**
1209-465X The Wick **7694**
1209-4730 Communication Research Center. Business Plan *changed to* 1491-6851 **2314**
1209-5176 Manitoba Dentist **5855**
1209-5206 Co-operatives in Canada - (Year) Data **4643**
1209-5281 Agence Canadienne de Developpment International. Marches de Services et Lignes de Credit *changed to* 1709-853X **1589**
1209-5400 Business Development Bank of Canada. Annual Report **1322**
1209-5478 Life Insurance Companies, Property and Casualty Insurance Companies. Summary Financial Data **4512**
1209-5559 Parks & Recreation Canada **4981**
1209-5591 Fleming's Canadian Legislatures **4674**
1209-563X Senate of Canada. Subcommittee on Transportation Safety. Proceedings **8510**
1209-5648 Senate of Canada. Subcommittee on Communications. Proceedings **2338**
1209-5966 Swim News **8210**
1209-6008 Petroleum Land Journal
1209-6083 Canadian Toy & Decoration Fair Guide & Membership Directory **1978**
1209-6245 B C Coach's Perspective **8160**
1209-6539 Canadian Directory of Search Firms **1857**
1209-6563 Annotated Employment Insurance Statutes **4617**
1209-6571 Pacific Forestry Centre. Technology Transfer Note **3699**
1209-7136 Architecture Canada (Ottawa) **430**
1209-7195 O A L A Membership Directory *changed to* 1912-0214 **452**
1209-7209 Canada. Statistics Canada. Prosecutions Resources, Expenditures and Personnel *changed to* 1706-8177
1209-7330 Canada. Citizenship and Immigration Canada. Annual Immigration Plan *changed to* 1497-9284 **7289**
1209-7411 Solas
1209-8221 Canadian Recycling Resoucedisk *see* 1196-7382 **3504**
1209-8345 Seniors Advisory Council for Alberta. Update *changed to* 1912-6999 **8068**
1209-8558 Guide Complet de Prix Autos, Fourgonnettes et Camions Usages *changed to* 1719-7112 **8583**
1209-8558 Guide Complet de Prix Autos, Fourgonnettes et Camions Usages *changed to* 1719-7104 **8583**
1209-8590 Canadian Environmental Protection **3409**
1209-8965 Strengthening Farming **159**
1209-9392 Women in Judaism **7731**
1209-9481 Northern Life (North Bay) **3814**
1209-9945 Members' Dialogue *changed to* 1715-8966 **5662**
1210-0048 Kardiologia **5794**
1210-0250 Teorie Vedy **7923**
1210-0366 EuroRehab†
1210-0390 Ceskoslovenski Vybor pro Spolupraci s F A O. Bulletin†
1210-0404 Sestra **5981**
1210-0420 Thaiszia **820**
1210-0455 Prague Economic Papers **1160**
1210-0471 Vysoka Skola Banska - Technicka Univerzita Ostrava. Sbornik Vedeckych Praci: Rada Strojni **3399**
1210-048X Vysoka Skola Banska - Technicka Univerzita Ostrava. Sbornik Vedeckych Praci: Rada Elektrotechnicka **3334**
1210-0552 Neural Network World **2455**
1210-0641 Novohradske Noviny **3946**
1210-065X Erica **671**
1210-0668 Endocrine Regulations **5891**
1210-0684 Chip **2410**
1210-0714 Ekonom **1102**
1210-0811 Cizi Jazyky **2837**
1210-0889 Elektro **3305**
1210-0935 I T News†
1210-0943 Nova Sloboda
1210-096X Knihovnice a Informacie†
1210-1060 Vyber Kulturnich Vyroci (Print) *changed to* 1803-6953 **638**
1210-1079 P C World (Print)† **8979**
1210-1087 AutoTip **8567**
1210-1141 Dopravni Noviny **8495**
1210-1168 Mlada Fronta Dnes **3832**
1210-132X Cinema **6493**
1210-1346 Signalni Informace ze Sveta Zemedelstvi†
1210-1389 Vytapeni, Vetrani, Instalace **4127**
1210-1419 Motocykl **8262**
1210-1583 Medzinarodne Otazky *changed to* 1337-5482 **7243**
1210-1761 Matematika, Fyzika, Informatika **2885**
1210-1893 Pritel'†
1210-1931 Rheumatologia **6226**
1210-1982 Knizna Revue **7565**
1210-2008 Sekretarska a Manazerska Praxe
1210-2040 Plus 7 Dni **3946**
1210-2245 Domino **2186**
1210-2261 From the Logical Point of View†
1210-2512 Radioengineering **2363**
1210-2687 Obchodni Vestnik **1156**
1210-2695 Geologica Carpathica - Clays†
1210-2709 Acta Polytechnica **3179**
1210-2717 Inzenyrska Mechanika *changed to* 1802-1484 **7058**
1210-2741 New Glass Review†
1210-3055 Human Affairs **7970**
1210-3195 Tatra Mountains Mathematical Publications **5540**
1210-3209 Oecologia Montana **695**
1210-3306 Listy Cukrovarnicke a Reparske **3654**
1210-3349 Biologie, Chemie, Zemepis **2831**
1210-3543 Metrologie: Vedecka, Legalni, Prakticka†
1210-356X T Z B **4127**
1210-3640 Religio **7674**
1210-3683 Hudebni Vychova **2864**
1210-3691 Vytvarna Vychova **2925**
1210-3721 Computer Index†
1210-3756 Strategie **1180**
1210-3772 Czechoslovak Industry†
1210-3934 The Prague Post **3832**
1210-4019 Auto (Year) (Prague)† **8934**
1210-406X Food Service **3642**
1210-4078 Textil Zurnal **2250**
1210-4086 Maso **3655**
1210-4094 Moderni Obchod **1780**
1210-4108 Folia Heyrovskyana **848**
1210-4132 J A M A (Czech and Slovak Edition) **5642**
1210-4353 Koktejl **4018**
1210-4566 Ohlasene Knihy **633**
1210-471X Divadelni Noviny **8469**
1210-4728 Eko. Ekologie a Spolecnost **670**
1210-4817 Pravni Radce **4760**
1210-4825 Stavitel **458**
1210-4922 Odpady **3509**
1210-5120 T V Magazin **2393**
1210-5333 Blesk **3832**
1210-5341 Blesk Magazin **3832**
1210-5430 Yazzyk†
1210-5538 Zpravy Pamatkove Pece **6540**
1210-5600 Zahranicni Politika Ceske Republiky. Dokumenty **7275**
1210-5759 European Journal of Entomology **847**
1210-5848 Pudoznalectvi a Meliorace†
1210-6097 Historicky Obzor
1210-6100 Klapalekiana **853**
1210-616X Technik **8441**
1210-6283 Czech Republic. Urad pro Technickou Normalizaci, Metrologii a Statni Zkusebnictvi. Vestnik†
1210-6313 Ceskoslovenska Fyziologie **920**
1210-6410 Pravni Rozhledy **4760**
1210-6488 Trafika† **8994**
1210-6550 Cesky Statisticky Urad. Zpravodaj **8362**
1210-6798 Ikarie **5443**
1210-6801 Filips† **8956**
1210-6860 Moderni Dejiny **4245**
1210-695X Cesky Instalater **3184**
1210-7026 Stereo & Video† **8990**
1210-7050 Soudobe Dejiny **4266**
1210-7077 Reader's Digest Vyber **3832**
1210-7085 Bezpecnost Jaderne Energie
1210-7441 AutoProfi **8566**
1210-7506 Informatorium **2866**
1210-762X Perspectives **7259**
1210-7654 Muj Dum **1025**
1210-7689 Telesna Vychova a Sport Mladeze **8211**
1210-7697 Uhli - Rudy - Geologicky Pruzkum **6482**
1210-7727 The Heart of Europe *see* 1211-9296 **5220**
1210-7743 Data a Fakta†
1210-7778 Central European Journal of Public Health **7512**
1210-7816 Ceska a Slovenska Farmacie **6828**
1210-7824 Ceska a Slovenska Gastroenterologie *changed to* 1213-323X **5921**
1210-7832 Ceska Gynekologie **5988**
1210-7840 Hygiena†
1210-7859 Ceska a Slovenska Neurologie a Neurochirurgie **6131**
1210-7867 Otorinolaryngologie a Foniatrie **6084**
1210-7875 Cesko-Slovenska Patologie a Soudni Lekarstvi **5593**
1210-7883 Ceska Radiologie **6193**
1210-7905 Ceska Revmatologie **6222**
1210-7913 Epidemiologie, Mikrobiologie, Imunologie **885**
1210-7921 Klinicka Biochemie a Metabolismus† **8969**
1210-8049 Journal of Nannoplankton Research **2809**
1210-8057 Penthouse†
1210-8189 Film News†
1210-8197 Czech Geological Society. Journal *changed to* 1802-6222 **2750**
1210-8235 Zena a Zivot **8892**
1210-8294 Media Tarif† **8973**
1210-8308 Realit **7610**
1210-8383 Sport **8203**
1210-8480 Elle (Prague) **8860**
1210-8499 Historica. Historical Studies in the Czech Republic. Series Nova **4228**

ISSN

1220-7586 Bursa **1322**
1220-7799 National **3933**
1220-7853 Viata Capitalei†
1220-7888 Albina **3932**
1220-8019 Libertatea **3933**
1220-8140 Satul Romanesc **154**
1220-8167 Tomis **3934**
1220-8248 Gazeta Sporturilor **8174**
1220-8272 *see* 0304-3517 **3933**
1220-840X Revue Roumaine de Physiologie *changed to* 1223-4974 **927**
1220-8620 Anticipatia **5439**
1220-8655 Telecomunicatii **2341**
1220-8671 Revista Transporturilor. Auto, Drumuri, Navigatie†
1220-868X Revista Cailor Ferate Romne†
1220-871X Analele Universitatii Bucuresti. Chimie **2049**
1220-8795 East European Medical Journal†
1220-8825 Probleme de Pedagogie Contemporana **2900**
1220-8841 Romanian Neurosurgery†
1220-9376 Nine O'Clock **3933**
1220-9554 Calende **3932**
1220-9597 Curierul de Vilcea **3932**
1220-9821 Adevarul Literar si Artistic **5205**
1220-9864 Contemporanul Ideea Europeana **3932**
1220-9880 Erdeyi Figyelo **3932**
1221-0110 Gazeta de Transilvania **3932**
1221-0684 Montana **8737**
1221-0692 Romania Pitoreasca **8752**
1221-079X Studia Universitatis "Babes-Bolyai". Geographia **4030**
1221-0803 Studia Universitatis "Babes-Bolyai". Geologia **2770**
1221-0935 Catalogul Cartilor Straine Intrate in Bibliotecile din Romania **622**
1221-1249 Transylvanian Review **4274**
1221-1265 Universitatea din Oradea. Analele. Fascicula Matematica **2343**
1221-1273 Universitatea din Oradea. Analele. Fascicula Geografie **4032**
1221-1451 Romanian Report in Physics **7038**
1221-146X Romanian Journal of Physics **7038**
1221-1680 Technologii Educationale Moderne *see* 0034-8678 **2906**
1221-1745 *see* 0304-3517 **3933**
1221-180X Bibliografia Nationala Romana. Publicatii Seriale **617**
1221-2229 Revista de Medicina si Farmacie **5705**
1221-2369 Arges (Pitesti) **3932**
1221-2520 Revista de Igiena si Sanitate Publica **7539**
1221-3055 Dilema **4214**
1221-3152 Capital **1080**
1221-3349 Sport Magazin **8204**
1221-3365 Rumynskaya Panorama **3933**
1221-3489 Liceul George Bacovia. Bacau. Anuarul†
1221-356X Romanian Journal of Endocrinology *changed to* 1841-0987 **5883**
1221-3705 Institutul de Istorie "A.D. Xenopol". Anuarul **398**
1221-4035 O.K. Week-end Magazin *see* 1221-4051
1221-4051 Renasterea Banateana
1221-4167 Romanian Journal of Gastroenterology **5930**
1221-4191 Muzeul Militar National. Revista **4247**
1221-437X Automation Computers Applied Mathematics **2458**
1221-454X Universitatea "Dunarea de Jos" din Galati. Analele. Fascicula III. Electrotehnica, Electronica, Automatica, Informatica **3115**
1221-4566 Universitatea "Dunarea de Jos" din Galati. Analele. Fascicula V. Tehnologii in Constructia de Masini **3398**
1221-4612 Universitatea "Dunarea de Jos" din Galati. Analele. Fascicula X. Mecanica Aplicata **3359**
1221-4620 Universitatea "Dunarea de Jos" din Galati. Analele. Fascicula XI. Constsructii Navale **3225**
1221-4663 Romanian Journal of Tectonics and Regional Geology **2765**
1221-4779 Bibliografia Geologica si Geofizica a Romaniei **2719**
1221-4914 Viata Libera **3934**
1221-5023 General Mathematics **5490**
1221-5163 Studia Judaica **7730**
1221-5244 Societatea Lepidopterologica Romana. Buletin de informare **859**
1221-5252 Romanian Chemical Quarterly Reviews†
1221-5309 Bibliografia Nationala Romana. Publicatii Oficiale†
1221-5317 Agricultura **82**
1221-5341 Universitatea "Al. I. Cuza" din Iasi. Analele Stiintifice. Chimie **2083**
1221-5503 Cercetari Metalurgice si de noi Materiale **2040**
1221-5732 Kozoktatas **2881**
1221-5775 Agenda **3932**
1221-5805 Anunt de la A la Z **21**
1221-5813 Ateneu **3932**
1221-6445 T V Cablu *see* 1221-6453 **2394**
1221-6453 T V Satelit **2394**
1221-650X Historia Urbana **4142**
1221-6518 Studii si Comunicari de Etnologie - Sibiu†
1221-678X Analele Banatului. Arheologie-Istorie **373**
1221-6844 Industria Lemnului & Mobila **3693**
1221-6860 Repertoriul Colectiv al Periodicelor Straine Intrate in Bibliotecile din Romania **634**
1221-6909 Science and Technology of Environmental Protection **3465**
1221-6984 Destin Romanesc **4214**
1221-6992 I M A S Bulletin **1820**
1221-7034 Rumania. Comisia Nationala pentru Statistica. Buletin Statistic Trimestrial **8397**
1221-7050 Rumania. Comisia Nationala pentru Statistica. Buletin Statistic de Preturi **1261**
1221-7069 Romania. National Commission for Statistics. Monthly Statistical Bulletin *see* 1223-7507 **8397**
1221-7867 Jurnalul National **3933**
1221-7956 Allgemeine Deutsche Zeitung fuer Rumaenien **3932**
1221-8103 Studia Universitatis "Babes-Bolyai". Biologia **706**
1221-8111 Studia Universitatis "Babes-Bolyai". Psychologia - Paedagogia **2915**
1221-8138 Studia Universitatis "Babes-Bolyai". Philosophia **6954**
1221-8286 Astra **5207**
1221-8421 Universitatea "Al. I. Cuza" din Iasi. Analele Stiintifice. Matematica **5544**
1221-8448 Universitatea "Al. I. Cuza" din Iasi. Analele Stiintifice. Lingvistica **5191**
1221-8456 Universitatea "Al. I. Cuza" din Iasi. Analele Stiintifice. Literatura **5392**
1221-8464 Universitatea "Al. I. Cuza" din Iasi. Analele Stiintifice. Stiinte Juridice **4802**
1221-8618 Revista de Medicina Legala **5916**
1221-8685 Universul Cartii **3934**
1221-9088 Magazin International **3933**
1221-9118 Chirurgia **6239**
1221-9126 Bibliografia Nationala Romana. Carti. Albume. Harti **617**
1221-9134 Bibliografia Nationala Romana. Note Muzicale. Discuri. Casete **617**
1221-9975 Analele Bucovinei **4130**
1222-006X Agenda Magazin **3932**
1222-1201 Universitatea din Baia Mare. Buletin Stiintific. Seria B. Fascicula Matematica-Informatica *changed to* 1584-2851 **5477**
1222-1732 Catavencu **5210**
1222-1775 Intamplari Adevarate **3933**
1222-1910 Cimbora
1222-328X Evenimentul Zilei **3932**
1222-3891 Romanian Archives of Microbiology and Immunology **896**
1222-4189 Computerworld Romania **2414**
1222-4715 Informatia Zilei **3933**
1222-5126 Revista de Medicina Militara†
1222-5347 Industria Textila **8452**
1222-5428 Revista Romana de Turism† **8985**
1222-5517 Universitatea din Oradea. Analele. Fascicula Mecanica. Sectiunea Mecanisme, Organe de Masini, Tribologie, Mecanica Fina, Roboti, Desen **7064**
1222-5525 Universitatea din Oradea. Analele. Fascicula Mecanica. Sectiunea Masini Hidraulice, Masini Termice si Termotehnice **7063**
1222-5533 Universitatea din Oradea. Analele. Fascicula Mecanica. Sectiunea Masini Unelte, Roboti Industriali si Sisteme Flexibile de Prelucrare **7063**
1222-5541 Universitatea din Oradea. Analele. Fascicula Mecanica. Sectiunea Mecanica, Vibratii, Rezistenta, Materialelor **3359**
1222-555X Universitatea din Oradea. Analele. Fascicula Mecanica. Sectiunea Tehnologii in Constructia de Masini **3286**
1222-5606 Glasul Bucovinei **4454**
1222-5630 Arhiva Genealogica **3759**
1222-5657 Octogon Mathematical Magazine **5522**
1222-569X Universitatea din Oradea. Analele. Stiinte Economice **1187**
1222-5703 Bucuresti - What, Where, When **8689**
1222-5835 B M J (Romanian Edition) *see* 0959-535X **5582**
1222-5940 Jurnal Bihorean **3933**
1222-5959 Jurnalul de Dimineata **3933**
1222-6084 Europa XXI **4219**
1222-6734 Bihari Naplo **3932**
1222-7013 Rebusache **4345**
1222-7129 G Info - Gazeta de Informatica **1417**
1222-7633 Sanatatea†
1222-7994 A Het **3932**
1222-8338 Korunk **3619**
1222-8346 Knijevni Jivot **5318**
1222-8354 Karpatenrundschau **3545**
1222-894X Lucrari de Muzicologie **6585**
1222-9016 Mathematica **5512**
1222-9024 Revue d'Analyse Numerique et de Theorie de l'Approximation **5529**
1222-9849 Modelism International **4341**
1223-043X Ziua **3934**
1223-0502 Rumania. Comisia Nationala pentru Statistica. Buletin Statistic Industrie **1261**
1223-0510 Rumania. Comisia Nationala pentru Statistica. Buletin Statistic de Comert Exterior **1261**
1223-057X Electromotion **3157**
1223-1088 Institutul de Cercetari Socio-Umane -Sibiu. Anuarul **7973**
1223-1118 Romanian Journal of Meteorology **6394**
1223-1193 Euresis - Cahiers Roumains d'Etudes Litteraires **5292**
1223-1479 Lumea Femeilor **8872**
1223-1576 Contrafort **5279**
1223-1908 Romanian Civilization Studies **4260**
1223-2254 Museum National d'Histoire Naturelle "Grigore Antipa". Travaux **691**
1223-3056 Pneumofitziologia†
1223-4737 Szabadsag **3934**
1223-494X Universitatea Agronomica Ion Ionescu de la Brad. Lucrari Stiintifice. Seria Agronomie **165**
1223-4958 Universitatea Agronomica Ion Ionescu de la Brad. Lucrari Stiintifice. Seria Horticultura **3753**
1223-4974 Romanian Journal of Physiology **927**
1223-5083 Institutul Politehnic din Iasi. Buletinul. Sectia 7: Hidrotehnica **2795**
1223-5180 Impozite si Taxe **1929**
1223-5229 Derby *see* 1222-5940 **3933**
1223-5334 Universitatea "Al. I. Cuza" din Iasi. Analele Stiintifice. Geografie **4032**
1223-5342 Universitatea "Al. I. Cuza" din Iasi. Analele Stiintifice. Geologie **2772**
1223-5377 Casa Lux **4535**
1223-5636 Comertul Exterior al Romaniei **1221**
1223-6578 Universitatea "Al. I. Cuza" din Iasi. Analele Stiintifice. Biologie Vegetala **821**
1223-6772 Auto Pro **8560**
1223-6799 Oradeanul **3933**
1223-6837 Romanian Business Journal **1168**
1223-6934 Universitatea din Craiova. Analele. Seria: Matematica, Informatica **5544**
1223-7027 Polytechnical University of Bucharest. Scientific Bulletin. Series A: Applied Mathematics and Physics **5525**
1223-7485 Bibliografia Nationala Romana. Teze de Doctorat **617**
1223-7507 Rumania. Comisia Nationala pentru Statistica. Buletin Statistic Lunar **8397**
1223-7515 Turismul in Romania **8781**
1223-7531 Agricultura si Silvicultura Romaniei in Profil Teritorial†
1223-7566 Household Labour Force Survey **8376**
1223-7728 Buletin Oficial de Proprietate Industriala. Sectiunea Desene si Modele Industriale **6747**
1223-8120 Institutul Politehnic din Iasi. Buletinul. Sectia 6: Constructii, Arhitectura **1014**
1223-8139 Institutul Politehnic din Iasi. Buletinul. Sectia 3: Electrotehnica, Energetica, Electronica **3319**
1223-8147 Institutul Politehnic din Iasi. Buletinul. Sectia 2: Chimie **2065**
1223-8546 Tribuna **3934**
1223-9631 Transylvania University of Brasov. Bulletin. Series A **3397**
1223-964X Transylvania University of Brasov. Bulletin. Series B **5542**
1223-9844 Tele Cablu **2395**
1224-0184 Revista Bibliotecii Nationale a Romaniei **5043**
1224-0346 Famila Moderna **8862**
1224-0761 International Studies
1224-0869 Studia Universitatis "Babes-Bolyai". Theologia Orthodoxa **7706**
1224-0923 Jurnalul de Calarasi **3933**
1224-094X Institutul de Cercetare si Projectare pentru Electrotehnica. Lucrarile **3319**
1224-1261 Universitatea din Oradea. Analele. Fascicula Energetica **3149**
1224-1342 In Review **1122**
1224-1784 Universitatea "Ovidius" Constanta. Analele. Seria Matematica **5544**
1224-1903 Luxury House *see* 1223-5377 **4535**
1224-2594 Entomologica Romanica **844**
1224-2780 Balkan Journal of Geometry and Its Applications **5475**
1224-2888 Anuarul Demografic al Romaniei†
1224-290X Romania. National Commission for Statistics. National Accounts **1261**
1224-3086 British and American Studies **5101**
1224-3183 Revista de Ecologie Industriala **3463**
1224-3450 Fundeni Hospital. Annals **5617**
1224-3809 Central European Issues. Romanian Foreign Affairs Review **7225**
1224-3957 Duelul Mintii **2187**
1224-4376 Avantaje **8852**
1224-452X Prelucrari la Cald **6329**
1224-5097 Universitatea din Oradea. Analele. Fascicula Fizica **7044**
1224-5119 Universitatea din Oradea. Analele. Fascicula Biologie **709**
1224-581X Universitatea "Al. I. Cuza" din Iasi. Analele Stiintifice. Biologie Animala **966**
1224-600X Universitatea Politehnica din Timisoara. Buletinul Stiintific. Seria Automatica si Calculatoare **2464**
1224-6018 Universitatea Politehnica din Timisoara. Buletinul Stiintific. Seria Chimie si Ingineria Mediului **3257**
1224-6026 Universitatea Politehnica din Timisoara. Buletinul Stiintific. Seria Constructii Arhitectura **1041**
1224-6034 Universitatea Politehnica din Timisoara. Buletinul Stiintific. Seria Electronica, Electrotehnica si Telecomunicatii **3225**
1224-6042 Universitatea Politehnica din Timisoara. Buletinul Stiintific. Seria Hidrotehnica **2799**
1224-6069 Universitatea Politehnica din Timisoara. Buletinul Stiintific. Seria Matematica, Fizica **5544**
1224-6077 Universitatea Politehnica din Timisoara. Buletinul Stiintific. Seria Mecanica **3398**
1224-6085 Universitatea Politehnica din Timisoara. Buletinul Stiintific. Seria Stiinte Socio-Umane. Limbi Moderne. Educatia Fizica **4480**
1224-6271 Martor **347**
1224-645X Jurnalul de Arges **3933**
1224-6492 Mami **5997**
1224-6689 The Guide - Bucuresti **8716**
1224-6808 Geoecomarina **2736**
1224-6832 Universitatea Petrol - Gaze din Ploiesti. Seria Stinte Economice. Buletinul **1799**
1224-6891 Auto Mondial **8160**
1224-7154 Studia Universitatis "Babes-Bolyai". Chemia **2081**
1224-7170 Analele Universitatii Bucuresti. Matematica-Informatica **5469**
1224-7359 Universitatea "Ovidius" Constanta. Analele. Serie Educatie Fizica si Sport **8214**
1224-7448 Philobiblon **5039**
1224-7626 Universitatea din Oradea. Analele. Fascicula Chimie **2083**
1224-7685 Studies and Researches in Veterinary Medicine†
1224-7774 Universitatea de Stiinte Agronomice si Medicina Veterinara. Lucrari Stiintifice. Seria F, Biotehnologii **771**
1224-807X Info Satelit *see* 1221-6453 **2394**
1224-810X Invest Romania Magazine **1631**
1224-8134 Povestea Mea **3933**
1224-8169 Estetica *see* 1224-4376 **8852**
1224-8177 Social Situation and Economy of Romania **8399**
1224-8339 Agenda Zilei **3932**
1224-8398 Cognitie, Creier, Comportament **7346**
1224-869X Studia Universitatis "Babes-Bolyai". Informatica **5049**
1224-8703 Studia Universitatis "Babes-Bolyai". Sociologia **8141**
1224-8711 Studia Universitatis "Babes-Bolyai". Politica **7186**
1224-872X Studia Universitatis "Babes-Bolyai". Ephemerides **7186**
1224-8738 Studia Universitatis "Babes-Bolyai". Negotia **1180**
1224-8746 Studia Universitatis "Babes-Bolyai". Studia Europaea **8008**
1224-8754 Studia Universitatis "Babes-Bolyai". Theologia Catholica **7819**
1224-8797 Tom si Jerry **2217**
1224-9262 Revista Romana de Sociologie **8129**
1224-9351 Universitatea "Dunarea de Jos" din Galati. Analele. Fascicula I. Economie **1550**
1224-9483 Pro T V **2388**
1224-9513 West University of Timisoara. Annals. Series of Chemistry **2084**
1224-967X Universitatea de Vest din Timisoara. Analele. Seria Stiinte Filologice **5191**
1224-970X Universitatea de Vest din Timisoara. Analele. Seria Matematica - Informatica **5544**

ISSN

ISSN

1237-9115 see 0046-0192 5886
1237-9263 Finnish Institute of Occupational Health. Reviews 6677
1237-9530 see Kelan Sanomat 4511
1237-9700 see 0023-4281 4362
1238-0261 Finland. Tilastokeskus. Luonnonvarat ja Ymparisto 3479
1238-0288 Riistantutkimuksen Tiedote 3606
1238-0466 HELECON Nordic†
1238-0474 HELECON International†
1238-0482 Hanasaari Meny changed to 1795-8830 7239
1238-0679 see 0358-1705 3838
1238-0814 Socius 8072
1238-1136 Mikrobiologian Julkaisuja 892
1238-125X Kuntatekniikka 4418
1238-1594 Alula 901
1238-1683 Suomen Pankki. Tutkimuksia. Sarja A 1385
1238-1691 Suomen Pankki. Tutkimuksia. Sarja E 1385
1238-1837 Astra Nova 8852
1238-2086 Nordia Geographical Publications 4022
1238-223X Monumenta Cartographica Septentrionalia 4019
1238-2388 Vaisala News 6397
1238-2574 Sukeltajan Maailma 8210
1238-2582 Finland. Tilastokeskus. Finland's Natural Resources and the Environment see 1238-0261 3479
1238-2620 Tyottomyyspaivarahat 8075
1238-268X Nauta 294
1238-2728 Finland. Tilastokeskus. Kuntafakta 7480
1238-2760 Z changed to 1797-2760 4380
1238-3104 Nordinfo - Rapport†
1238-3325 Kala- ja Riistaraportteja 3600
1238-3503 Bibliotheca Historica 4204
1238-3546 Finland. Tilastokeskus. Kuntapuntari 8370
1238-3724 Jaakartta 2784
1238-3759 Moro see 0355-6913 3838
1238-3783 Lappeenrannan Teknillinen Korkeakoulu. Koulutus- ja Kehittamiskeskus. Julkaisu changed to 1459-3025 2992
1238-4100 Kuvataiten Keskusarkisto 502
1238-4135 Avain Suomen Metsateollisuuteen 3684
1238-4143 Facts and Figures changed to 1796-8933 3688
1238-4178 Key to the Finnish Forest Industry 3695
1238-4283 Valmentaja 6999
1238-4569 Socius Finland 8072
1238-4623 Finland. Tilastokeskus. Rakennus- ja Asuntotuotanto 1046
1238-4704 Finland Tilastokeskus. Teollisuuden, Rakennusalan ja Liikenteen Tyontekijoiden Palkat changed to 1797-0776 1232
1238-4747 Tampereen Teknillinen Korkeakoulu. Energia- ja Prosessitekniikka. Raportti changed to 1459-3440 3397
1238-4755 see 0744-5105 6993
1238-4895 Kauppalehti Optio see 0451-5560 1139
1238-4895 Kauppalehti Optio see 1795-3030 1139
1238-4909 Finland. Tilastokeskus. Kuntayhtymien Talous 7480
1238-5018 Manuscripta Orientalia 555
1238-5050 Sosiaali- ja Terveysturvan Tutkimuksia 8005
1238-5069 Sosiaali- ja Terveysturvan Katsauksia 8005
1238-5328 Meri - Report Series of the Finnish Institute of Marine Research 2813
1238-5387 Poliisi & Oikeus 2664
1238-5484 Sophia 4171
1238-5654 Glorian Antiikki 366
1238-5700 Humanistisen Tiedekunnan Jatkotutkinto-Opas changed to 1796-3176 2986
1238-5913 Teatterikorkeakoulu. Acta Scenica 8481
1238-5980 Merkurius-Kirjakerho 2202
1238-6022 Logistiikka 8503
1238-6111 Finland. Tilastokeskus. Julkisyhteisojen Alijaama ja Bruttovelka EMU-Kriteerien Mukaisina (Print) changed to Finland. Tilastokeskus. Julkisyhteisojen Alijaama ja Bruttovelka EMU-Kriteerien Mukaisina (Online) 1231
1238-6170 Finland. Tilastokeskus. Naturresurserna och Miljoen see 1238-0261 3479
1238-6715 see 0049-1349 8072
1238-6944 University of Joensuu. Department of Computer Science. Dissertations changed to 1796-8100 2440
1238-7118 Vaasan Yliopiston Julkaisuja. Selvityksia ja Raportteja 1550
1238-7150 Finland. Tilastokeskus. Matkailutilasto 8779
1238-7169 Finland. Tilastokeskus. Matkailutilasto 8779
1238-7312 Suomen Ymparisto 3468
1238-7584 see 0359-4947 2583
1238-7606 see 0359-4947 2583
1238-8424 Suomen Maksutase. Vuositilasto 1904
1238-8629 Vaasan Yliopisto. Julkaisuja. Tutkimuksia. Sosiaali- ja Terveyshallinto 2671
1238-8785 European Forest Institute. Research Reports 3687
1238-9064 Finland. Tilastokeskus. Oulun Aluepalvelu. Pohjois-Suomen Katsaus 7480
1238-9315 Suomen Kaukolampo ry L. Raportti changed to Energiateollisuus ry L. Raportti 3128
1238-9544 W I D E R Angle 1607
1238-9587 Apaja 3584
1238-9838 Nyt 3839
1238-9889 Suomen Siipikarja 301
1238-9978 Lento 8784
1239-0143 S M L Info 1842
1239-0291 Ilmastokatsaus†
1239-0429 K M Vet 129
1239-0518 Acta Polytechnica Scandinavica. C H. Chemical Technology Series 2048
1239-0690 F 1 - Maailma†
1239-0992 Agricultural and Food Science in Finland changed to 1459-6067 83
1239-1085 Advokaatii 4611
1239-1204 Rytmi 6614
1239-1409 Yleisradio. Yleisotutkimus. Tutkimuksia 2399
1239-162X Tampereen Teknillinen Korkeakoulu. Automaatiotekniikan Osasto. Automaatio- ja Saatotekniikan Laitos. Raportti changed to 1459-3505 2464
1239-1638 Finland. Eduskunnan Kanslia. Julkaisu 7437
1239-1735 Suomen Standardisoimisliitto. S F S - Luettelo 6407
1239-1743 see 1239-1735 6407
1239-1875 Boreal Environment Research. Monographs 3483
1239-193X International Institute of Applied Aesthetics. Series 497
1239-1948 Konsainvalinen Soveltavan Estetiikan Instituutti. Raportteja 500
1239-1980 Finland. Tilastokeskus. Kuntien Talous ja Toiminta 1231
1239-257X see 0355-2047 3838
1239-2669 Finland. Tilastokeskus. Suomen Lahialueet 1232
1239-2685 Electronic Journal of Business Ethics and Organization Studies 1104
1239-2847 Finland. Tilastokeskus. Prices and Wages Review†
1239-3177 Geologian Tutkimuskeskus. Kertomus Toiminnasta 2737
1239-3401 Ptah 454
1239-3614 Informaatiotutkimus 5015
1239-3843 Kultaneito 3619
1239-3975 Finland. Tilastokeskus. Tuottavuuskatsaus 1232
1239-4327 Report Series in Physical Sciences 7037
1239-4335 Vaasan Yliopisto. Julkaisuja. Tutkimuksia. Julkisoikeus 4853
1239-4378 see 0359-1255 6688
1239-4386 African Newsletter on Occupational Health and Safety - Online see 0788-4877 6672
1239-4505 Kudos 4462
1239-4602 Alimenta 90
1239-4645 see 1795-2484 3692
1239-467X Finland. Tilastokeskus. SijoittumisCD 2933
1239-4963 Didacta Varia 2842
1239-5773 Glossolalia 5301
1239-6044 Liiketalous 1144
1239-6052 Sahkoalan Palveluhakemisto changed to 1797-2485 3330
1239-6095 Boreal Environment Research 3483
1239-629X Annales Academiae Scientiarum Fennicae. Mathematica 5470
1239-6303 Annales Academiae Scientiarum Fennicae. Mathematica Dissertationes 5470
1239-6311 Annales Academiae Scientiarum Fennicae. Chemica 2050
1239-632X Annales Academiae Scientiarum Fennicae. Geologica-Geographica 2724
1239-6427 Dimensio 486
1239-6494 see 0785-5540 1977
1239-6540 see 0781-7916 7923
1239-6753 Tampereen Teknillinen Korkeakoulu. Mittaus- ja Informaatiotekniikka. Raportti changed to 1459-3297 3332
1239-6826 Lifelong Learning in Europe 2944
1239-6982 Annales Academiae Scientiarum Fennicae. Series Humaniora 4443
1239-7342 Finland. Tilastokeskus. Suomalaisten Matkailu 8779
1239-7407 Finland. Tilastokeskus. Europarlamenttivaalit, Ennakkotilasto 7199
1239-7415 Finland. Tilastokeskus. Europarlamenttivaalit 7199
1239-7466 Finland. Tilastokeskus. Ita-Suomen Katsaus 7480
1239-7474 Finland. Tilastokeskus. Etela-Suomen Katsaus 7480
1239-7482 Finland. Tilastokeskus. Lansi-Suomen Katsaus 7480
1239-7504 KotiPC†
1239-758X Teknologiakatsaus changed to 1797-7339 72
1239-7911 Elakevaen Ristikot Extra changed to 1459-1626 8185
1239-8179 Finland. Tilastokeskus. Kuntien Kuukausipalkat Ammateittain changed to 1459-6377 1231
1239-8306 Etela-Karjalan Ammattikorkeakoulu. Julkaisuja. Sarja A, Raportteja ja Tutkimuksia 2980
1239-8314 Etela-Karjalan Ammattikorkeakoulu. Julkaisuja. Sarja B, Oppimateriaaleja 2980
1239-8322 Etela-Karjalan Ammattikorkeakoulu. Julkaisuja. Sarja C, Opinnaytteita 2980
1239-8411 Elamanhalu changed to 1459-2312
1239-856X Hevoset ja Ratsastus 8291
1239-8950 Ilmansuojeluyhdistys 3487
1239-9035 Slammer 8334
1239-906X Ammattina Kauneus†
1239-9132 Tietolinja 5050
1239-9329 Suomen Pankki. Vuosikertomus 1385
1239-9337 Finlands Bank. Aarsberaettelse 1347
1239-9345 Bank of Finland. Annual Report 1314
1239-9469 Helsingin Yliopisto. Biocentri Viikki Universitatis Helsingiensis. Dissertations changed to 1795-7079 676
1239-9663 Finland. Tilastokeskus. Ulkomaalaiset ja Siirtolaisuus 7306
1239-9736 International Journal of Circumpolar Health 5637
1239-9744 International Journal of Circumpolar Health. Supplement 5638
1240-0068 Charlie Hebdo 5210
1240-0866 Pharmaceutiques 6870
1240-1153 Reperes Ocean 2817
1240-1307 Natures - Sciences - Societes 2714
1240-1439 Etudes Ecossaises 5292
1240-2001 Ecrans d'Afrique†
1240-2044 Jazzman 6579
1240-2346 Charge Utile Magazine 8669
1240-2419 Revue d'Histoire de Bayonne, du Pays Basque et du Bas - Adour 4258
1240-2427 M Scope Revue†
1240-3113 Air & Cosmos - Aviation Magazine International 44
1240-3156 Chirurgie Endoscopique 5594
1240-3237 F A C E 5612
1240-3318 Cardiologie Pratique. Supplement 5779
1240-3946 Productique - Affaires†
1240-4292 Journal of High Temperature and Chemical Processes†
1240-4489 Union Genealogique du Centre. Informations Genealogiques du Centre†
1240-4535 Advances in Modelling & Analysis. C: Systems Analysis, Control & Design 5550
1240-4543 Advances in Modelling & Analysis. B: Signals, Information, Data, Patterns 5550
1240-4551 Modelling, Measurement & Control. D: Manufacturing, Management, Human and Socio-Economic Problems 5555
1240-456X Talents†
1240-4640 R F Paye 1789
1240-5205 Juris-Classeur Divorce 4911
1240-5248 Figaro Etudiant Grandes Ecoles Universites (Daily Edition) changed to 1950-1919 2981
1240-6309 Aeroports de Paris. Trafic des Principaux Aeroports Mondiaux 8533
1240-6813 Banque de France. Report 1320
1240-747X France. Service d'Etude des Strategies et des Statistiques Industrielles. Les Chiffres Cles de l'industrie dans les Regions
1240-8093 Economie Internationale 1562
1240-8255 Aeroports de Paris. Rapport Annuel 8520
1240-8409 France. Parlement. Assemblee Nationale. Bulletin des Commissions†
1240-8751 L'Officiel du Cycle et de la Moto 8265
1240-8964 Carnet de Provence 3840
1240-9367 Vie a Defendre 4605
1240-9782 Revue de Medecines et Pharmacopees Africaines
1240-9863 Meilleures Adresses des Traitements de Surface†
1240-9987 A R L I T & Cie 5204
1241-1337 Rock Sound 6612
1241-2767 Societe Philomatique Vosgienne. Bulletin changed to 1626-5238 4244
1241-3496 Histoire Economique et Financiere de la France. Etudes et Documents 1542
1241-3623 Musique et Sciences Humaines. Documents de Recherches† 8975
1241-3992 Courrier de l'Environnement de l'I N R A 103
1241-4727 Journal d'Obstetrique et de Gynecologie†
1241-5286 Graphe 7646
1241-5294 Monde Arabe Maghreb - Machrek changed to 1762-3162 7153
1241-5650 Centrale du Transport Routier
1241-6290 Maniere de Voir 7153
1241-7068 Habitat 4411
1241-7076 Chorus 6556
1241-7696 Le Matricule des Anges 5331
1241-8218 Encyclopedie Medico-Chirurgicale. Traite de Radiodiagnostic: Urologie - Gynecologie changed to Encyclopedie Medico-Chirurgicale. Radiologie et Imagerie Medicale. Genito-Urinaire - Gyneco-Obstetricale - Mammaire 6196
1241-8226 Encyclopedie Medico-Chirurgicale. Techniques Chirurgicales. Thorax 6242
1241-8234 Encyclopedie Medico-Chirurgicale. Urgences 6059
1241-8625 Where Paris 8788
1241-8986 Trajets 7821
1241-9257 Centre Pierre Leon d'Histoire Economique et Sociale. Bulletin†
1241-9648 Vous et Votre Sante†
1242-0018 Realites Ophtalmologiques 6050
1242-014X Auto Infos
1242-0492 Le Mensuel du Cinema†
1242-1316 Le Gymnaste 8176
1242-1367 Archimag. Hors-Serie 4990
1242-1383 Acta Endoscopica. Supplement 5919
1242-1472 Amities Spirituelles 7621
1242-1626 Ingenieurs de la Vie changed to 1951-0594 86
1242-1693 Centre Regional d'Information et de Prevention du S I D A. Lettre d'Information 5811
1242-1898 Focales† 8957
1242-2347 Annuaire General de la Publicite et de la Communication†
1242-3912 La Lettre Clandestine
1242-3947 Recherches Marines†
1242-4315 Francais Repertoire des Annuaires Professionnels Francais
1242-5028 Collection Tests Psychologiques
1242-6121 Hypotheses 7361
1242-6326 Philosophie 6941
1242-6652 Cribles
1242-8671 C N R S Sociologie 8091
1242-8809 De l'Allemagne 335
1242-9198 Connaissance des Arts. Numero Hors - Serie see 0293-9274 483
1242-9554 Racines & Modeles
1242-9945 L'Homme et la Societe (Paris, 1993) 8105
1243-0587 Colloques, Congres et Conferences sur la Renaissance 4211
1243-0617 Manuscrits 5330
1243-1923 Cahiers pour l'Histoire de la Recherche 7843
1243-3306 Anciens des Forces Francaises en Allemagne et en Autriche. Ceux 6410
1243-3470 La Gestion en Resumes†
1243-3853 Karate, Bushido 8183
1243-3918 Cahiers Francais de Electricite. Industrie†
1243-4019 View on Colour changed to 1762-4576 7318
1243-4167 L'Entreprise 1741
1243-4442 Museum National d'Histoire Naturelle. Memoires 7884
1243-4450 Cle...s a Venir† 8941
1243-4477 Protection Sociale Informations 1162
1243-5066 Filigrana changed to 1770-9571 5268
1243-5082 Le Guide des Assurances Sociales 8043
1243-5139 Du Theatre†
1243-5201 C E D R E. La Lettre (Print) changed to 1961-9553 3484
1243-549X Tumultes 8144
1243-5554 Snow Surf 8334
1243-5619 Revue de la Gendarmerie Nationale†
1243-6003 Autrement dit 7949
1243-6070 Gala 8865
1243-6267 Rebondir 6703
1243-6852 Les Cahiers de l'Animation, Vacances, Loisirs 3053
1243-6933 Actualites Reproduction Humaine†
1243-7492 Revue des Telecommunications changed to 1960-7636 2367
1243-7581 La Lettre de l'Internat 5661
1243-7751 Minute
1243-8642 Le Magazine des Professionnels du Cable et du Satellite changed to 1248-3222
1243-8650 Avions 8539
1243-8804 La S H M C. Bulletin see 0048-8003 4159
1243-8863 Institut Pasteur. Lettre 5635
1243-9193 Credit Agricole Magazine 196
1243-9681 Filiere Gourmande 3673
1243-969X Acquisition et Interaction en Langue Etrangere 5089

1255-250X Societe Francaise d'Histoire des Hopiteaux. Revue **5716**
1255-2917 Le Guide du Travail **1862**
1255-3034 Ligue Urbaine et Rurale. Cahiers *changed to* 1761-5534 **3459**
1255-3239 Cinethique†
1255-3468 Images Documentaires **6503**
1255-6270 France. Ministere de la Culture. Lettre d'Information **5010**
1255-7196 Ubu **8484**
1255-765X C D - R A M A†
1255-8001 Le Fil (Ivry-sur-Seine)†
1255-8591 Maisons et Bois International†
1256-544X Fruitrop (French Edition) **3730**
1256-5458 Fruitrop (English Edition) *see* 1256-544X **3730**
1256-5482 Entreprise et Ethique†
1256-6128 Journal de Parodontologie et d'Implantologie Orale **5850**
1256-6276 EssOr Contacts. L'Electricite et l'Electronique†
1256-737X Guitar Part **6571**
1256-7531 Encadrement Decoration†
1256-7590 Revue de Droit Commercial, Maritime, Aerien et des Transports
1256-7779 Dumerilia†
1256-7809 Arkeo Junior **2176**
1256-9747 A Cheval *changed to* 1951-4115 **8291**
1256-9917 Lamy Transport. Tome 1 **4934**
1256-9941 Xoana† **8999**
1256-9976 Societe de Linguistique de Paris. Memoires (Nouvelle Serie) **5175**
1257-001X France. Centre d'Etudes de l'Emploi. Lettre†
1257-0273 Lusotopie† **8972**
1257-032X Societe des Antiquaires de l'Ouest et des Musees de Poitiers. Memoires **4265**
1257-0702 Notre Foret Region Centre *changed to* 1953-1923 **3699**
1257-0907 Dictionnaire Permanent: Bioethique et Biotechnologies **763**
1257-1008 Instantanes Techniques **3199**
1257-127X Chretiens et Societes XVIe-XXe Siecles **8093**
1257-144X Bourbonnais Rural **97**
1257-1512 Ecrivain Magazine† **8952**
1257-1652 Lamy Social **4712**
1257-1660 Lamy Droit du Financement **1365**
1257-1709 Lamy Droit Immobilier **7597**
1257-1792 Lamy Transport. Tome 2 **4934**
1257-1822 Lamy Assurances **4512**
1257-2187 La Cote des Vins **602**
1257-2330 Vigie. Environnement†
1257-2349 Vigie. Opto-Electronique†
1257-2357 Vigie. Energie-Globe†
1257-2365 Vigie. Medecine & Pharmacie†
1257-2373 Vigie. Agronomie & Industrie Alimentaire†
1257-2381 Vigie. Materiaux Avances†
1257-2489 Technologies France†
1257-2551 La Revue Salon Equip'Hotel *changed to* 1637-2808 **8985**
1257-273X Vigie. Technologies de l'Information†
1257-2748 Vigie. Informatique Appliquee†
1257-2829 Guide des Revetements et des Finitions *see* 1162-3497 **4562**
1257-3833 Blanchisserie, Location, Textiles Professionnels **2242**
1257-4627 Les Dossiers de l'Environnement de l'I N R A **106**
1257-5011 World Rabbit Science **968**
1257-5143 Encyclopedie Medico-Chirurgicale. Traite de Radiodiagnostic: Squelette Normal - Neuroradiologie - Appareil Locomoteur *changed to* Encyclopedie Medico-Chirurgicale. Radiologie et Imagerie Medicale. Musculosquelettique - Neurologique - Maxillofaciale **6196**
1257-5151 Ateliers Proteges†
1257-5496 Biologie et Evolution des Insectes
1257-6360 Annuaire de la Marine Marchande **8638**
1257-7537 Musurgia **6597**
1257-8002 L'Odyssee du Sang† **8978**
1257-8223 Bottin de la Sante†
1257-8576 Surfer's Journal **8336**
1257-8894 Archimag. Guide d'Achat†
1257-9068 C N R S Langage **5102**
1257-9114 Collection Cursus. Serie Litterature **5275**
1257-9149 Bibliotheque Jungienne **7340**
1257-9343 Empreintes de l'Homme **336**
1257-9629 J'Apprends a Dessiner **2195**
1257-9947 Chemins de l'Ethnologie **333**
1258-0104 Logiques Sociales. Serie Theories Sociologiques **8119**
1258-0147 P I R Ville. Cahiers **8124**
1258-116X Histoire des Sciences **7861**
1258-1402 Collection Histoires Graphiques **5275**
1258-195X Universites **3007**
1258-2697 Hommes de Dieu et Revolution **7648**
1258-3421 Anejos de Criticon
1258-3804 Documents et Recherches sur le Monde Byzantins, Neohellenique et Balkanique **4215**
1258-3901 Maritimes **4152**
1258-4711 Visite Actuelle **6885**
1258-5769 Advances in Modelling & Analysis. A: General Mathematical and Computer Tools **5550**
1258-6307 Representants Commerciaux et V R P†
1258-6447 Mon Quotidien **2203**
1258-6900 DAFSA des Administrateurs† **8948**
1258-732X Annuaire General des Cooperatives Francaises et de leurs Fournisseurs (Print) *changed to* Annuaire Cooperatives Francaises **1425**
1258-780X Metiers de la Petite Enfance **2161**
1258-8075 Annuaire du Tabac *changed to* 1964-4108 **8487**
1258-8210 Oleagineux Corps Gras Lipides (Print)† **8978**
1258-8342 U N I T. Le Journal *changed to* 1958-136X **7614**
1258-8555 Scoot'n Scoot **8268**
1258-9543 Defense et Armement International†
1258-9977 Carta de Taize *see* 0750-3695 **7804**
1258-9985 Brief aus Taize *see* 0750-3695 **7804**
1258-9993 Letter from Taize *see* 0750-3695 **7804**
1259-0312 Figurines **4335**
1259-0614 L'Afrique Politique (Revue) *changed to* 1778-266X **4174**
1259-0657 Ceramagazine† **8940**
1259-069X Sedimagazine **214**
1259-1130 Ecole Nationale Superieure des Sciences de l'Information et des Bibliotheques. Revue des Sommaires† **8952**
1259-1556 Cahiers du Jazz†
1259-1734 Annales Mathematiques Blaise Pascal **5470**
1259-2099 I N S E R M. Atelier **5632**
1259-2242 Pretentaine **8126**
1259-2439 L'Officiel des Transporteurs **8674**
1259-346X Le Cuisinier **4384**
1259-4261 France. Institut National de la Statistique et des Etudes Economiques. Recueil d'Etudes Sociales **1541**
1259-4415 Le Regne Mineral **2764**
1259-4482 Les Dix-huitiemes Siecles **4215**
1259-4490 Textes de Litterature Moderne et Contemporaine **5387**
1259-458X European Bibliography of Slavic and East European Slavonic Studies **4170**
1259-4792 Soins Pediatrie - Puericulture **5981**
1259-4962 Annuaire de Droit Maritime et Oceanique **4969**
1259-5020 Leather Markets†
1259-5098 Annales du Monde Anglophone†
1259-5225 Marie France **8874**
1259-5314 Ecologie **3417**
1259-542X La Lettre du Disque† **8971**
1259-5969 Modelling, Measurement & Control. B: Solid & Fluid Mechanics & Thermics, Mechanical Systems **5554**
1259-5977 Modelling, Measurement & Control. C: Energetics, Chemistry, Earth, Environmental & Biomedical Problems **5554**
1259-5985 Modelling, Measurement & Control. A: General Physics, Electronics, Electrical Engineering **5554**
1259-6094 Association Francaise de Lutte Antirhumatismale. Journal *changed to* 1959-285X **6222**
1260-0199 Rythmes†
1260-0849 Sesame Bulletin†
1260-0938 Terre Provencale†
1260-0970 Republique Internationale des Lettres†
1260-1063 Bourgogne Aujourd'hui **600**
1260-156X Vamos **5193**
1260-1578 Ready for English **5165**
1260-1586 Azzurro **5098**
1260-1640 Metal Industries
1260-1705 Revue Internationale de Psychosociologie **8130**
1260-1799 Reussir Bovins - Viande **298**
1260-237X L'Aventure Humaine†
1260-3775 Lamy Protection Sociale **4873**
1260-433X Laboratoire d'Informatique pour la Mecanique et les Sciences de l'Ingenieur. Scientific Report **3208**
1260-4755 Lettera da Taize *see* 0750-3695 **7804**
1260-4763 Brief uit Taize *see* 0750-3695 **7804**
1260-4984 Systemes d'Information et Management **1796**
1260-4992 Mythologie Francaise **3620**
1260-5646 Filieres Avicole **286**
1260-5875 Revue Internationale de Geomatique **2524**
1260-5999 Journal Francais de Psychiatrie **6149**
1260-8556 L A T E C. Document de Travail **1496**
1260-8599 Comite Consultatif National d'Ethique pour les Sciences de la Vie et de la Sante. Les Cahiers **6911**
1260-8718 Congres National des Societes Historiques et Scientifiques. Actes. Section de Geographie Physique et Humaine **4003**
1260-8726 Congres National des Societes Historiques et Scientifiques. Actes. Section d'Archeologie **388**
1260-8971 Institut Universitaire d'Etudes du Developpement. Les Nouveaux Cahiers **1598**
1260-9447 Dizajn (Print) *changed to* 1760-8325 **486**
1260-9978 Aromes Ingredients Additifs **3627**
1261-0208 Reussir Vigne **250**
1261-0402 Les Cahiers du Management Technologique **1732**
1261-0410 Guitar Collector's **6571**
1261-0666 Choisir†
1261-0674 50 Titres Sur... **7317**
1261-1522 Generiques†
1261-3347 Les Cles de l'Actualite Junior **2182**
1261-3436 Gibier et Chasse **287**
1261-3665 Rail Passion **8622**
1261-3797 I N S E E Picardie Premiere **1241**
1261-3800 Entrevue Hors Serie **6288**
1261-4319 Reussir Aviculture **298**
1261-4327 Reussir Porcs **298**
1261-467X Caravane Magazine *changed to* 1638-3494 **8322**
1261-4858 Dada **2184**
1261-5102 Avenir Agricole (Laval) **94**
1261-6818 Aquitaine Ocean **2800**
1261-694X Archives des Maladies du Coeur et des Vaisseaux - Pratique **5777**
1261-6990 Sequence†
1261-7458 Club de Reflexion des Cabinets et Groupes d'Hepato-Gastroenterologie. Lettre **5921**
1261-7709 Lettres Internationales du Marketing Bancaire†
1261-7733 Systemes de Paiement† **8992**
1261-825X Point de Vue **3801**
1261-8373 Annuaire des Operations de Terrain en Milieu Urbain **374**
1261-9086 Les Guides des Grossistes Informatiques *see* 0757-309X **2492**
1261-9515 Marketing Magazine **1832**
1261-9523 Marketing Direct **1831**
1262-0092 Regards (Paris) **5236**
1262-022X Revue d'Histoire des Mathematiques **5529**
1262-0289 Prestige Audio Video *changed to* 1766-4098 **8152**
1262-0378 Magic! **6586**
1262-0386 Les Cahiers de la Shoah **4208**
1262-0424 L'Art du Cinema **6489**
1262-0955 Bulletin du Droit de l'Environnement Industriel **3407**
1262-1137 L'Objet **2433**
1262-1196 Ingenieurs I.N.P.G., Reussir Grenoble†
1262-1218 Causes Communes **7225**
1262-1277 Marseille. Recueil des Actes Administratifs **7497**
1262-1676 Pole Sud **7166**
1262-1692 L'Ordinaire Latinoamericain **7161**
1262-2583 Agriculture Dromoise **85**
1262-2753 Bibliotheque Nationale de France. Actualites†
1262-2788 Comptabilite Controle Audit **1285**
1262-2842 Textes de la Renaissance **4273**
1262-2850 Bibliotheque de Litterature Generale et Comparee **5263**
1262-2869 Le Savoir de Mantice **4261**
1262-2966 Societes & Representations **8005**
1262-3261 Electronic Journal on Networks and Distributed Processing **2497**
1262-3318 *see* 1292-8100 **5485**
1262-3350 Association pour la Promotion de la Protection des Invertebres. Cahiers **840**
1262-3377 Control Optimisation and Calculus of Variations Online *see* 1292-8119 **5485**
1262-3490 Carrefours de l'Education **2835**
1262-3598 Dix-Neuf-Vingt† **8951**
1262-3636 Diabetes & Metabolism **5886**
1262-3857 C C E International **1592**
1262-4055 Preventique Securite **2679**
1262-4586 Ortho Magazine **5910**
1262-4705 Poesie 1, Vagabondages **5430**
1263-1973 France. Direction de l'Animation de la Recherche, des Etudes et des Statistiques. Dossiers **1233**
1263-2325 Notes du Centre de Prospective et de Veille Scientifique. Equipement **7457**
1263-3879 France. Delegation Generale a la Langue Francaise et aux Langues de France. Rapport Annuel *changed to* 1957-1615 **5120**
1263-5251 Le Journal du Multimedia et des Nouvelles Technologies **2487**
1263-5456 Export Services†
1263-5618 Equipement, Transport et Services Infos **8495**
1263-5782 Pratique des Arts **512**
1263-8072 Acoustique et Techniques **3482**
1263-8730 Pays du Nord **4023**
1263-8935 Mediterranees **8120**
1263-8978 Mediterranee (Paris, 1994) **3841**
1263-946X Apocryphes **7622**
1264-0441 Interlangues
1264-0999 C N R S Ethnologie **331**
1264-157X Essentialis **7355**
1264-174X Patrimoine de la Mediterranee **4253**
1264-188X Pratique du Marketing Direct **1838**
1264-2010 Perspectives Germaniques **5350**
1264-3025 Dossiers Pedagogiques **3058**
1264-3238 Bibliotheque Hispanique **4445**
1264-3688 Porphyre (Collection) **6875**
1264-4102 Departements **8697**
1264-5044 Detours en France (Paris) **4003**
1264-532X Le Horla **5306**
1264-5834 Bibliotheque Italienne **4445**
1264-6253 Info Buro Mag. **1851**
1264-6520 Medecine Therapeutique **5666**
1264-6539 International Cosmetique News **589**
1264-6806 Le Sport **8203**
1264-7020 Musique, Images, Instruments **6597**
1264-7527 Hematologie **5937**
1264-8809 Realites en Gynecologie-Obstetrique **6002**
1264-9120 Bulletin Europeen et International† **8938**
1264-9147 Ingenieries **121**
1264-935X P C Team† **8979**
1265-0080 Monsieur **6296**
1265-0692 Figures de l'Art **489**
1265-129X Cinema 9†
1265-1362 Educations **3060**
1265-1397 Genie Logiciel† **8959**
1265-1664 Contre Bande **6495**
1265-2067 Sud Nord **8008**
1265-230X Champagne - Ardenne Guide de l'Exportateur† **8940**
1265-2571 Museart. Hors - Serie†
1265-2903 Ateliers **4443**
1265-3292 Europe Locale **7492**
1265-356X M6 Dance **6586**
1265-3578 Tetu **4379**
1265-485X Chant Choral Magazine†
1265-4876 Solaris Information Communication **5063**
1265-4906 Hernia **6245**
1265-499X International Journal of Information Sciences for Decision Making (Online) *see* 1290-2942 **8966**
1265-5287 Bourgogne Magazine *changed to* 1968-908X **4034**
1265-5449 Psychologie Clinique et Projective **7397**
1265-5538 Le Moniteur Fiscal plus Social *changed to* 1955-9267 **1150**
1265-5627 Mobilis†
1265-5635 Maisons a Vivre **4546**
1265-5651 Massif Central **4019**
1265-566X Massif Central. Hors Serie *see* 1265-5651 **4019**
1265-5678 Massif Central. Hors Serie Balades *see* 1265-5651 **4019**
1265-616X Confederation des Industries Ceramiques de France. Annuaire† **8943**
1265-6240 Actualite des Religions *changed to* 1763-3346 **7808**
1265-6534 Revue de l'Electricite et de l'Electronique **3329**
1265-6739 Lettre d'Information Juridique **4955**
1265-7034 Le Visiteur **460**
1265-7131 Engadine†
1265-9576 Observatoire Francais des Conjonctures Economiques. Revue **1156**
1265-9983 Pages d'Archeologie Medievale en Rhone - Alpes **410**
1266-0078 Revue d'Ethique et de Theologie Morale **7677**
1266-0167 Le Vide: Science, Technique et Applications†
1266-1341 Pays Comtois **4023**
1266-1791 Exploitant Agricole du Gard **109**
1266-2089 Batirama, le Batisseur Europeen **979**
1266-2550 C I E S Food Business News **3629**
1266-2585 Mer et Littoral **3489**
1266-3697 Realites Pediatriques **6103**
1266-3840 Alcatel Telecom Rundschau†
1266-4006 Equus les Chevaux *changed to* 1961-6937 **488**
1266-4081 Pays de Bretagne† **8980**

ISSN

1297-4773 Cosmetique Hebdo **586**
1297-4781 Cosmetique Magazine **587**
1297-5060 Cent Idees Jardin **3726**
1297-5354 Le Journal des Professionnels de l'Enfance **6094**
1297-5516 Reponse a Tout! Jeux **3842**
1297-6253 Quoi de Neuf? *changed to* 1966-6144 **1406**
1297-7551 Clivages†
1297-7659 Societe Herpetologique de France. Bulletin de Liaison *see* 0754-9962 **963**
1297-8019 Revue Europeenne de Management du Sport (Print) *changed to* 1961-912X **8196**
1297-8094 Anatolia Moderna **542**
1297-8183 La Nouvelle Lettre Internationale†
1297-8604 C'Est Quoi? **4447**
1297-8671 Mes Premiers J'aime Lire **2202**
1297-8736 Volumes **5413**
1297-9066 Le Bac en Tete. Sciences Economiques et Sociales **2830**
1297-9511 Juridisque Cour de Justice des Communautes Europeennes **4934**
1297-9562 I T B M - R B M *changed to* 1959-0318 **765**
1297-9570 I T B M - R B M News *changed to* 1959-7568 **770**
1297-9589 Gynecologie Obstetrique et Fertilite **5992**
1297-9597 Juris-Classeur Numerique. Administratif *see* Juris-Classeur Administratif **4706**
1297-9600 Juris-Classeur Numerique. Bail a Loyer *see* 0750-8328 **4706**
1297-9635 Documents Scientifiques et Techniques - I R D **2803**
1297-966X Annals of Forest Science Online *see* 1286-4560 **3683**
1297-9678 *see* 0044-8435 **839**
1297-9686 *see* 0999-193X **870**
1297-9716 *see* 0928-4249 **8814**
1297-9937 Juris-Classeur Numerique. Encyclopedie des Huissiers de Justice *see* 0750-8638 **4706**
1298-0013 Top Famille Magazine† **8993**
1298-0129 Lamy Droit des Medias et de la Communication **4712**
1298-0137 Electronic Journal of Evolutionary Modeling and Economic Dynamics **1104**
1298-0285 *see* 1951-8366 **4873**
1298-0358 The Asianists' Asia **544**
1298-0382 Lamy Droit des Personnes et de la Famille **4912**
1298-0455 Guide du Dirigeant d'Entreprise *changed to* 1779-3831 **4873**
1298-0463 *see* 0335-1793 **3841**
1298-048X Juris-Classeur Numerique. Civil *see* 0448-0732 **4833**
1298-1133 La Vie Financiere **1434**
1298-115X La Revue du Son & du Home Cinema **8154**
1298-1168 Universite de Marne-la-Vallee. Travaux et Recherches **4480**
1298-2032 Essais **5291**
1298-2113 Crea-Deco **533**
1298-227X Universites. Informatique **2440**
1298-2628 Atlas des Guerres **4131**
1298-2938 Mineraux et Fossiles. Hors-Serie *see* 0335-6566 **6726**
1298-4701 Cosinus **2184**
1298-5619 Fan 2 **2188**
1298-5708 Neurofibromatoses **6164**
1298-6046 Cahiers du Genre **8092**
1298-6704 Points & Commentaires en Radioprotection†
1298-6895 Ideal Patisserie **4361**
1298-728X Le Dalloz **4654**
1298-7387 Geriatries *changed to* 1767-803X **4054**
1298-7638 Fashion Daily News **2254**
1298-8510 Debats Philosophiques **6913**
1298-8723 Asie Orientale **4180**
1298-9428 Biotechnologies & Finances *changed to* 1779-4633 **759**
1298-9800 La Revue pour l'Histoire du C N R S **7903**
1298-9851 Les Cahiers de Linguistique de l'I N A L C O **5103**
1299-006X Photo Plus† **8981**
1299-0094 Agence Francaise de Developpement. Rapport Annuel **1421**
1299-1929 Neuf Mois Magazine **5999**
1299-2518 Pratiques Medicales et Therapeutiques†
1299-2585 Campagne Decoration **4534**
1299-2798 Point Banque **1375**
1299-2968 Vertical, Roc *changed to* 1764-6243 **8339**
1299-3166 Psychanalyse Magazine *changed to* 1778-7793 **8988**
1299-3174 Banque Magazine *changed to* 1772-6638 **1377**
1299-3573 Cote Femme† **8944**
1299-3867 La Lettre du Heron *see* 0399-1040 **908**
1299-5495 Cites **6910**
1299-5606 Cahiers d'Economie Politique **1536**
1299-6599 Login. Hors-Serie† **8971**
1299-6793 Liquides & Conditionnement **606**
1299-9180 Mixte **8875**
1299-9547 I T - Expert (Print) *changed to* 1961-9855 **2544**
1299-9695 Figaro Etudiant Grandes Ecoles-Universites (Weekly Edition) *changed to* 1950-1919 **2981**
1299-992X Maisons Cote Est **4546**
1300-0012 Agri **6120**
1300-0039 Turk Kutuphaneciligi
1300-008X Turkish Journal of Botany **821**
1300-0098 Turkish Journal of Mathematics **5542**
1300-0101 Turkish Journal of Physics **7044**
1300-011X Turkish Journal of Agriculture and Forestry **163**
1300-0128 Turkish Journal of Veterinary and Animal Sciences **8809**
1300-0144 Turkish Journal of Medical Sciences **5725**
1300-0152 Turkish Journal of Biology **708**
1300-0160 Turkish Journal of Engineering and Environmental Sciences **3224**
1300-0179 Turkish Journal of Zoology **965**
1300-0292 Turkiye Klinikleri Tip Bilimleri Dergisi **5725**
1300-0306 Turkiye Klinikleri Jinekoloji Obstetrik **6005**
1300-0438 Jinekoloji ve Obstetrik Bulteni† **8968**
1300-0527 Turkish Journal of Chemistry **2083**
1300-0535 Turkey. Turkiye Istatistik Kurumu. Istatistik Gostergeler (Year) **8410**
1300-0551 Spor Hekimligi Dergisi **6233**
1300-056X Gazi Medical Journal **5618**
1300-0578 Anestezi Dergisi **5769**
1300-0586 Kitap-lik **5222**
1300-0632 Turkish Journal of Electrical Engineering and Computer Sciences **2440**
1300-0659 Turk Oftalmoloji Gazetesi **6052**
1300-0667 Noropsikiyatri Arsivi **6171**
1300-0675 Klinik Gelisim **5658**
1300-0683 Annals of Medical Sciences **5575**
1300-0691 Romatoloji ve Tibbi Rehabilitasyon Dergisi **6227**
1300-0705 Ulusal Cerrahi Dergisi **6262**
1300-0713 Istanbul Universitesi. Fen Fakultesi. Matematik Dergisi† **8967**
1300-0721 Turkish Daily News **3963**
1300-073X Turkish Probe **3963**
1300-0802 Turkey. Turkiye Istatistik Kurumu. Aylik Dis Ticaret Ozeti† **8994**
1300-0861 Ankara Universitesi Veteriner Fakultesi Dergisi **8792**
1300-090X Turkey. Turkiye Istatistik Kurumu. Donemler Itibariyle Imalat Sanayii: Istihdam - Odemeler - Uretim Egilim (Gecici Sonuclar)†
1300-0934 Cumhuriyet **3962**
1300-0942 Turkish Association of Petroleum Geologists. Bulletin **6795**
1300-0985 Turkish Journal of Earth Sciences **2717**
1300-0993 Turkey. Turkiye Istatistik Kurumu. Milli Egitim Istatistikleri Orgun Egitim **2936**
1300-1000 Turkey. Turkiye Istatistik Kurumu. Kabotaj ve Uluslararasi Deniz Tasimasi Istatistikleri† **8995**
1300-1019 Turkey. Turkiye Istatistik Kurumu. Ulastirma Istatistikleri Ozeti (Year) **8532**
1300-1027 Turkey. Turkiye Istatistik Kurumu. Milli Egitim Istatistikleri; Yaygin Egitim (Year) **2936**
1300-1035 Turkey. Turkiye Istatistik Kurumu. Perakende Fiyat Istatistikleri† **8995**
1300-1043 Turkey. Turkiye Istatistik Kurumu. Kamu Kurumu ve Kuruluslari Hizmet Oncesi ve Hizmet Ici Egitim Istatistikleri† **8995**
1300-106X Turkey. Turkiye Istatistik Kurumu. Motorlu Kara Tasitlari Istatistikleri (Year) **8532**
1300-1086 Turkey. Turkiye Istatistik Kurumu. Evlenme Istatistikleri (Year) **5563**
1300-1094 Turkey. Turkiye Istatistik Kurumu. Maden Istatistikleri† **8995**
1300-1108 Turkey. Turkiye Istatistik Kurumu. Gevre Istatistikleri - Hava Kirliligi† **8994**
1300-1116 Turkey. Turkiye Istatistik Kurumu. Gaz ve Su Istatistikleri† **8994**
1300-1124 Turkey. Turkiye Istatistik Kurumu. Sirket Kooperatifl ve Ticaret Unvanli Isyeri Istatistikleri (2007) **1271**
1300-1140 Turkey. Turkiye Istatistik Kurumu. Toptan Fiyat Istatistikleri **1271**
1300-1159 Turkey. Turkiye Istatistik Kurumu. Intihar Istatistikleri (Year) **7317**
1300-1167 Turkey. Turkiye Istatistik Kurumu. Kultur Istatistikleri (Year) **8410**
1300-1175 Turkey. Turkiye Istatistik Kurumu. Trafik Kaza Istatistikleri; Karayolu (Year) **8532**
1300-1183 Turkey. Turkiye Istatistik Kurumu. Bosanma Istatistikleri **5563**
1300-1191 Turkey. Turkiye Istatistik Kurumu. Olum Istatistikleri; Il ve Ilce Merkezlerinde (Year) **7317**
1300-1205 Turkey. Turkiye Istatistik Kurumu. Butceler - Belediyeler, Il Ozel Idarler ve Koyler (Year) **7485**
1300-1213 Turkey. Turkiye Istatistik Kurumu. Tarim Istatistikleri Ozeti (Year) **187**
1300-1221 Turkey. Turkiye Istatistik Kurumu. Kesin Hesaplar - Belediyeler ve Il Ozel Idareleri (Year) **7485**
1300-123X Turkey. Turkiye Istatistik Kurumu. Ciftcinin Eline Gecen Fiyatlar† **8994**
1300-1248 Turkey. Turkiye Istatistik Kurumu. Adalet Istatistikleri **4825**
1300-1264 Turkey. Turkiye Istatistik Kurumu. Turkiye Ekonomisi Istatistik ve Yorumlar† **8995**
1300-1337 Egitim ve Bilim **2852**
1300-1361 Ekoloji **3419**
1300-1396 Banka ve Ticaret Hukuku Dergisi **4626**
1300-1450 Karinca **1424**
1300-1477 Cooperation in Turkiye **1423**
1300-1515 Pendik Veteriner Mikrobiyoloji Dergisi **8804**
1300-1612 Eurasian Studies **1106**
1300-1698 Turkey. Turkiye Istatistik Kurumu. Deniz Tasitlari Istatistikleri (18 ve Daha Yukari Gros Tonilatoluk) **8531**
1300-1728 Varlik **5394**
1300-1809 Turkish Yearbook of Human Rights **7216**
1300-1833 Gazi Universitesi Fen Gilimler Enstitusu Dergisi *changed to* 1303-9709 **7857**
1300-1876 G E F A D **2859**
1300-1884 Gazi Universitesi Muhendislik Mimarlik Fakultesi Dergisi **3193**
1300-199X Erciyes Tip Dergisi **5610**
1300-2082 Savunma ve Havacilik **6445**
1300-2155 Turk Dili Dil ve Edebiyat Dergisi **5391**
1300-2163 Turk Psikiyatri Dergisi **6189**
1300-2260 Turkey **1185**
1300-2481 Yaklasim† **8999**
1300-2511 Samanyolu **7716**
1300-2899 Inonu Universitesi. Egitim Facultesi. Dergisi **2867**
1300-2945 Dicle Tip Dergisi **5605**
1300-2996 Ondokuz Mayis Universitesi Tip Dergisi **5690**
1300-3372 Turk Kulturu **562**
1300-3399 Tesisat Muhendisligi **1040**
1300-3402 Muhendis ve Makina **3390**
1300-3410 Endustri Muhendisligi Dergisi **3377**
1300-3437 Yapi
1300-3453 Teknik Dergi **3285**
1300-3542 Dil Dergisi **5112**
1300-3550 Turk Ortodonti Dergisi **5868**
1300-3666 Istanbul Ticaret Gazetesi
1300-3704 Ekonomik Rapor *see* 1300-3712
1300-3712 Istanbul Chamber of Commerce. Economic Report
1300-3720 I C O C
1300-3984 Milli Folklor **3620**
1300-3992 Turkey. Turkiye Istatistik Kurumu. Tasimacelik Acisindan Turkiye'nin Dis Ticaeti† **8995**
1300-4077 Turkiye Istatistik Dernegi Istatistik Dergisi **8410**
1300-4093 Journal of Neonatology
1300-4182 F A B A D Farmasotik Bilimler Dergisi **6840**
1300-4212 Mimarlik Dergisi **450**
1300-4220 Anatolia Turizm ve Cevre Kulturu Dergisi **8683**
1300-4263 Hacettepe Fen ve Muhendislik Bilimleri Dergisi. Seri B: Matematik ve Istatistik *changed to* 1303-5010 **5505**
1300-4271 Hacettepe Fen ve Muhendislik Bilimleri Dergisi. Seri C: Kimya, Fizik ve Muhendislik†
1300-428X Edebiyat ve Elestiri **5288**
1300-4301 Turkish Journal of Dermatopathology
1300-431X Istatistiklerle Turkiye (Year) **8381**
1300-4328 Turkey in Statistics (Year) **8410**
1300-4360 Tanisal ve Girisimsel Radyoloji *see* 1305-3825 **6195**
1300-4433 Turk Psikoloji Dergisi
1300-4565 Turkiye Cumhuriyet Merkez Bankasi. Aylik Bulten **1387**
1300-4824 Metalurji **6325**
1300-4905 Selcuk Universitesi. Fen-Edebiyat Fakultesi. Fen Dergisi **7913**
1300-4921 Selcuk Universitesi Fen-Edebiyat Fakultesi Edebiyat Dergisi **5369**
1300-4948 The Turkish Journal of Gastroenterology **5932**
1300-5030 Turkish Defence & Aerospace Update† **8995**
1300-5057 Selcuk Universitesi Ilahiyat Fakultesi Dergisi **7716**
1300-5227 Cerrahpasa Tip Dergisi **5593**
1300-526X Goztepe Tip Dergisi **5620**
1300-5278 Spor ve Tip† **8989**
1300-5286 Turkish Journal of Rheumatology **6227**
1300-5340 Hacettepe Egitim Dergisi **2862**
1300-5464 Ankara Medical School. Journal **5574**
1300-5529 Maison Francaise **4546**
1300-5588 Hey Girl **2192**
1300-5596 Milliyet Kardes **2202**
1300-5618 Formsante **309**
1300-5715 Turk Dili ve Edebiyatii Arastiirmalarii Dergisi
1300-574X Ege Ingiliz ve Amerikan Incelemeleri Dergisi **5113**
1300-5804 Turk Uroloji Dergisi **6275**
1300-5820 Elele **3962**
1300-5847 Ekonomist
1300-5855 Blue Jean **6550**
1300-5863 Auto Show **8560**
1300-588X Tempo **3963**
1300-5901 Atlas **8684**
1300-591X Focus **3962**
1300-5928 Marie Claire **8873**
1300-5936 Art Decor† **8931**
1300-5952 Klips **3962**
1300-5960 Capital **1080**
1300-6150 P C World Turkey **2582**
1300-6169 Macworld Turkey **2577**
1300-638X Acta Pharmaceutica Turcica *changed to* 1307-2080 **6818**
1300-6436 Tekstil Maraton **2250**
1300-6444 Lykia **404**
1300-6487 Bilgisayarli Tomografi Bulteni **6193**
1300-6606 J A S T **4298**
1300-6614 Fizik Tedavi Rehabilitasyon Dergisi **6109**
1300-6622 Dokuz Eylul Universitesi Tip Fakultesi Dergisi **5606**
1300-6711 Byte Tuerkiye **2570**
1300-6738 Ulusal Travma Dergisi **4112**
1300-6746 Turkey. Turkiye Istatistik Kurumu. Gap Il Istatistikleri† **8994**
1300-6754 Turkey. Turkiye Istatistik Kurumu. Donemlere Gore Bina Insaati Maliyet Endeksi (Year) **1049**
1300-6827 Geological Bulletin of Turkey **2738**
1300-686X Mathematical & Computational Applications **5554**
1300-6983 Donald Amca **2186**
1300-7025 Toplumsal Tarih **4325**
1300-7122 Turkish Journal of Marine Sciences *changed to* Journal of the Black Sea / Mediterranean Environment **2810**
1300-7173 Turkey. Turkish Statistical Institute. Census of Industry and Business Establishments - 1st Stage Results† **8994**
1300-7386 Psikiyatri, Psikoloji ve Psikofarmokoloji Dergisi. Ek
1300-7580 Tarim Bilimleri Dergisi **160**
1300-7777 Turkish Journal of Haematology **5942**
1300-8013 Burda **2251**
1300-8021 Oto Haber **8597**
1300-8048 Aktuel **3962**
1300-8056 Home Art **4541**
1300-8064 P C Magazine Turkiye **2434**
1300-8072 Cosmopolitan (Istanbul) **8857**
1300-8099 Esquire **6289**
1300-8110 Gelin **5558**
1300-8153 Power **1160**
1300-8161 Sinema **6513**
1300-8552 Dilbilim Arastirmalari **5112**
1300-8641 Perceptions **7165**
1300-865X Adli Tip Bulteni **5912**
1300-8757 Fizyoterapi Rhabilitasyon **6109**
1300-8773 Yeni Symposium **6190**
1300-879X P **510**
1300-8838 Turkey. Turkiye Istatistik Kurumu. Il ve Bolge Istatikleri† **8994**
1300-9052 Ataturk Universitesi. Turkiyat Arastirmalari Enstitusu Dergisi **5258**
1300-9265 Economic Indicators of Turkey **1718**
1300-9354 Toplum ve Bilim **8144**
1300-9419 Chip **2410**
1300-9583 Bogazici Journal: Review of Social, Economic and Administrative Sciences **7951**
1300-963X Turkey. Turkiye Istatistik Kurumu. Tarimsal Yapi; Uretim, Fiyat, Deger (Year) **187**
1300-9672 Suleyman Demirel Universitesi Ilahiyat Fakultesi Dergisi **7686**
1300-9818 Firat Tip Dergisi **5614**
1300-9974 Konfeksiyon Teknik **2248**
1300-9982 Tekstil & Teknik **8458**
1301-0026 Yapi Malzeme & Teknik **1055**
1301-0034 Medikal & Teknik **5675**
1301-0085 Pamukkale Universitesi Egitim Fakultesi Dergisi **2895**
1301-0093 Bebegim ve Biz **1065**

ISSN

1310-0831 Standartizatsia, Metrologia, Sertifikatsia **6406**
1310-1331 Bulgarska Akademiya na Naukite. Dokladi **7842**
1310-1722 Meditsinski Pregled. Radiatsiia i Meditsina†
1310-182X Obshchestveno Zdraveopazvane†
1310-2028 E K **3805**
1310-2230 Matematika i Informatika **5511**
1310-2311 Demokraticheski Pregled **7129**
1310-2443 Muzika Vcera, Dnes i Utre **6597**
1310-2699 Biologia, Ekologia i Biotekhbologii **758**
1310-2818 Biotechnology and Biotechnological Equipment **760**
1310-3067 Bulgarian National Bank. Monthly Bulletin **1322**
1310-3393 Sport i Nauka **8204**
1310-3415 Minalo **4153**
1310-3423 Filosofski Vestnik **4452**
1310-3571 Andromeda **568**
1310-392X Bio-Medical Reviews **827**
1310-3970 Balkanistic Forum **4202**
1310-3989 Evropa 2001 **3837**
1310-4047 Vsichko za Knigata **7575**
1310-4284 Anesteziologiia i Intensivno Lechenie **5769**
1310-4314 Balon **3962**
1310-4586 Bulgarian Journal of Plant Physiology *changed to* 1312-8183 **3733**
1310-4772 Balkan Tribological Association. Journal **7057**
1310-5213 Bulgarska Etnologiia **331**
1310-5825 Veterinarna Meditsina **8811**
1310-5914 Acta Entomologica Bulgarica **837**
1310-6236 East Journal on Approximations **5485**
1310-6511 Kula **500**
1310-6600 Serdica **5534**
1310-6716 Khimiya i Industriya **2070**
1310-683X Zhelezoputen Transport **8628**
1310-6848 Putishta **8633**
1310-6988 Lettre International **4463**
1310-7283 Tsenitel **522**
1310-7364 Statisticheski Godishnik na Narodna Republika Bulgaria **8405**
1310-7410 Spisanie Statistika **8402**
1310-7496 Meditsinski Pregled. Sestrinsko Delo **5969**
1310-7615 Sofiiski Universitet Sv. Kliment Ohridski. Biologicheski Fakultet. Godishnik. Kniga 4. Biohimiya, Biofizika, Molekulyarna Biologiya i Genetika, Mikrobiologiya i Fiziologiya **745**
1310-7771 Phytologia Balcanica **809**
1310-7798 Molekuliarna Meditsina†
1310-7917 Literaturen Glas **5326**
1310-8085 Severniak **5370**
1310-8131 Endokrinologiya **5892**
1310-814X Universitet po Arhitektura, Stroitelstvo i Geodezia. Godisnik **460**
1310-8255 Complex Control Systems **2519**
1310-8328 Darba **5283**
1310-8360 Journal of Culture Collections **889**
1310-8441 Vitamin B **5437**
1310-8611 Atelie 16 **6964**
1310-8727 B A D. Dokladi **3165**
1310-8751 Posoki **3077**
1310-8840 Advances in Amphibian Research in the Former Soviet Union **930**
1310-8972 Liubopitko **2200**
1310-8999 Meditsinski Pregled. Savremenna Stomatologia **5855**
1310-9057 Meditsinski Pregled. Immunni Defitsiti†
1310-9081 Stranitsa **5378**
1310-9146 Chuzhdestranni Periodichni Izdaniia v Bulgaria **7936**
1310-9154 Diskografia **6631**
1310-9332 Infobusiness - Economic News of Bulgaria **1405**
1310-9499 Archaeology in Bulgaria **378**
1310-9537 Archaeologia Bulgarica **375**
1310-9561 Literaturen Vestnik **5326**
1310-9626 New Rhythm **6599**
1310-9901 Sedmichen Zakonnik **1301**
1311-0098 Bulgarski Mesechnik **3804**
1311-0144 Istoricheskо Budeshte **4233**
1311-0160 Balkan Journal of Medical Genetics **863**
1311-0209 Sveta Gora **5383**
1311-0276 Etno Reporter **7206**
1311-0454 Fractional Calculus and Applied Analysis **5488**
1311-0489 Journal of Mountain Agriculture in the Balkans **128**
1311-0527 Journal of Balkan Ecology **3444**
1311-0640 Zharava **8892**
1311-0829 Tehniceskia Universitet Sofiya. Godisnik **3397**
1311-0845 Auditorium **2828**
1311-0918 Ethnologia Bulgarica **3616**
1311-0950 Zhazhda **5404**
1311-0993 Dzhipsi Rai **3530**
1311-1108 Krug **2198**
1311-1450 Galeria Izkustvo i Kultura **490**
1311-1477 Bulgarian Journal of Veterinary Medicine **8794**
1311-1493 Information & Security **2677**
1311-1515 Muzika Viva **6597**
1311-1620 Zhitan **3573**
1311-1663 Bulgarian Chemistry and Industry **2052**
1311-1728 International Journal of Applied Mathematics **5495**
1311-1817 Obshta Meditsina **5689**
1311-2198 Bulgaria Dnes **3804**
1311-2244 Biudzheti na Domakinstvata v Republika Bulgaria **8358**
1311-2252 Iznos i Vnos **8381**
1311-2260 Vunshna Turgovia na Republika Bulgaria **8413**
1311-2287 Dochodi, Raschodi i Potreblenie na Domakinstvata **8366**
1311-2309 Zaetost i Bezrabotitsa **8414**
1311-2325 Mestni Organi na Upravlenie **8388**
1311-2341 Naselenie i Demografski Protsesi **8389**
1311-235X Oblasti i Obshchini v Republika Bulgaria **8393**
1311-2368 Okolna Sreda **8393**
1311-2376 Ikonomika i Finansi **8377**
1311-2422 Sotsialni Tendentsii **8399**
1311-2449 Tekushta Stopanska Koniunktura **8408**
1311-2457 Tseni, Indeksi na Tsenite i Inflatsia **1270**
1311-266X Andral **3518**
1311-2759 Meditsinski Pregled. Akupunktura **312**
1311-2872 International Journal of Differential Equations and Applications **5496**
1311-2880 Vurkhoven Kasatsionen Sud na Republika Bulgaria. Bulletin **4967**
1311-3127 P C World Bulgaria **2581**
1311-3151 NetworkWorld Bulgaria **2502**
1311-3178 Foto Oko **6967**
1311-3364 Bulgaria: Sotsialno-Ikonomichesko Razvitie **8359**
1311-3879 Teleskop **582**
1311-4360 Academic Open Internet Journal **7830**
1311-4573 Meditsinski Pregled. Klinichna Onkologiia *changed to* 1312-1111 **6027**
1311-4824 Commercial Banks in Bulgaria **1328**
1311-5030 Meditsinski Pregled. Gastroenterologiia **5929**
1311-5065 Journal of Environmental Protection and Ecology **3446**
1311-509X Meditsinski Pregled. Klinika i Predklinika *changed to* 1312-2193 **5749**
1311-5162 Farma News **6840**
1311-6584 Meditsinski Pregled. Nevrologiia i Psichiatriia **6159**
1311-6770 Meditsinski Pregled. Prakticheska Meditsina **7531**
1311-6789 International Journal of Computational and Numerical Analysis and Applications **5495**
1311-6851 Experimental Pathology and Parasitology **885**
1311-7149 Bulgarski Vekove **4207**
1311-753X Bulgarian Geophysical Journal **2778**
1311-7629 University of Chemical Technology and Metallurgy. Journal **3257**
1311-7785 Health Tourism†
1311-8080 International Journal of Pure and Applied Mathematics **5497**
1311-8706 Silva Balcanica **3702**
1311-8773 Acta Morphologica et Anthropologica **650**
1311-8803 Bibliosphere **4994**
1311-9109 Propagation of Ornamental Plants **814**
1311-9702 Cybernetics and Information Technologies **2526**
1312-0069 Playboy (Sofia) **6298**
1312-0328 Scripta Periodica **5711**
1312-0336 Meditsinski Pregled. Meditsinski Menidzhment i Zdravna Politika **7548**
1312-076X Ecology and Future **3418**
1312-0832 Clinical Application of Immunology **5756**
1312-1111 Meditsinski Pregled. Onkologiia i Radiologiia **6027**
1312-1537 W.I.T.C.H. **2220**
1312-1723 Trakia Journal of Sciences **7924**
1312-2193 Meditsinski Pregled **5749**
1312-238X Scripta & e-Scripta **4263**
1312-2711 Energetika & Biznes **3128**
1312-2754 Spectacular Spider-Man **2214**
1312-3548 Cosmopolitan (Sofia) **8857**
1312-4129 Sofia University St. Kliment Ohridski. Faculty of Biology. Annual. Book 2. Botany **705**
1312-5192 Journal of Geometry and Symmetry in Physics **5503**
1312-6164 Advances in Bulgarian Science **7833**
1312-7586 International Journal of Contemporary Mathematical Sciences **5496**
1312-7594 International Mathematical Forum **5497**
1312-8183 General and Applied Plant Physiology **3733**
1312-8221 *see* 1312-8183 **3733**
1312-885X Applied Mathematical Sciences **5472**
1312-8868 International Journal of Algebra **5495**
1312-8876 International Journal of Mathematical Analysis **5496**
1313-1311 Advanced Studies in Theoretical Physics **7003**
1313-2970 *see* 1313-2989 **969**
1313-2989 ZooKeys **969**
1313-8006 Journal of International Research Publications: Economy & Business **1137**
1313-8014 Journal of International Research Publications: Materials, Methods & Technologies **8429**
1315-0006 Espacio Abierto **8100**
1315-0049 Universidad Central de Venezuela. Instituto de Estudios Hispanoamericanos. Anuario **4315**
1315-0138 Salud de los Trabadores **7540**
1315-0162 Saber **702**
1315-0588 Revista Bigott **4472**
1315-0855 Vision Tecnologica **6796**
1315-1762 Educacion y Ciencias Humanas **2846**
1315-1789 Federacion Medica Venezolana. Revista **5613**
1315-2068 Divulgaciones Matematicas **5484**
1315-2076 Universidad del Zulia. Facultad Experimental de Ciencias. Ciencias **7926**
1315-2378 Reforma y Democracia **7465**
1315-2467 Revista Economia **1167**
1315-2556 Sociedad Venezolana de Microbiologia. Boletin *changed to* Sociedad Venezolana de Microbiologia. Revista **896**
1315-267X Manongo
1315-3013 Agenda Academica **2966**
1315-3072 Instituto de Filosofia del Derecho Dr. Jose Manuel Delgado Ocando. Cuaderno de Trabajo **4693**
1315-3269 Instituto de Filosofia del Derecho Dr. Jose Manuel Delgado Ocando. Boletin **4693**
1315-3617 Revista Venezolana de Analisis de Coyuntura **1515**
1315-3854 Notitarde **3994**
1315-401X Accion Pedagogica **2823**
1315-4079 Encuentro Educacional **2853**
1315-4125 Asociacion Matematica Venezolana. Boletin **5474**
1315-4176 Cuadernos Latinoamericanos **7957**
1315-4192 Universitas 2000 **3007**
1315-4915 Medico de Familia **5675**
1315-5792 Guia Maritima, Portuaria y de la Industria Naval de Venezuela **1998**
1315-6268 Fronesis **6921**
1315-6284 Anales de Botanica Agricola **91**
1315-6411 Revista Venezolana de Economia y Ciencias Sociales **1167**
1315-642X Anartia **652**
1315-8589 Actual **5249**
1315-8597 Gaceta Laboral **4678**
1315-883X Laurus **2882**
1315-8856 Ominia **2893**
1315-9453 Contexto (San Cristobal) **5278**
1315-9518 Revista de Ciencias Sociales **7996**
1315-9984 Revista Venezolana de Gerencia **1791**
1316-0087 Investigaciones y Postgrado **7975**
1316-0354 Agroalimentaria **8086**
1316-0486 Relea **1514**
1316-0664 Banco Central de Venezuela. Anuario de Estadisticas: Precios y Mercado Laboral **1212**
1316-0680 Banco Central de Venezuela. Informe Semestral **1311**
1316-0923 Revista de Psicologia **7404**
1316-1164 Revista Propiedad Intelectual **4880**
1316-1296 Debates I E S A **7958**
1316-1547 Plantula **813**
1316-1857 Presentia **4470**
1316-2012 Materials Science and Technology **3354**
1316-3337 Clinica Medica H.C.C. **5595**
1316-3361 Bioagro **96**
1316-3701 Revista Venezolana de Estudios de la Mujer **8902**
1316-371X Ciencias de Gobierno **7430**
1316-4090 Revista Venezolana de Ciencias Sociales **7998**
1316-4821 Universidad, Ciencia y Tecnologia **3225**
1316-4880 Myceteae **802**
1316-4899 Lichens **800**
1316-4910 Educere **2852**
1316-4945 Instituto de Investigaciones Literarias. Anuario **5309**
1316-4988 Petroleum **6786**
1316-5003 Temas de Coyuntura **8009**
1316-5216 Utopia y Praxis Latinoamericana **6959**
1316-5232 Acentos **2264**
1316-5399 Docencia, Investigacion, Extension **2842**
1316-5437 Geografia **4009**
1316-5852 Instituto de Derecho Comparado. Anuario **4693**
1316-5917 Revista Ciencias de la Educacion **2905**
1316-6077 Geoensenanza **2859**
1316-6204 Escritos **488**
1316-6212 Educare **2846**
1316-6689 Lingua Americana **5144**
1316-6727 Aldea Mundo **7946**
1316-6883 Revista Tachirense de Derecho **4773**
1316-693X Logoi **6932**
1316-7138 Universidad de Carabobo. Facultad de Ciencias. Revista **5726**
1316-7162 Anuario Social y Politico de America Latina y el Caribe **7948**
1316-7219 Tropicos **7413**
1316-7480 Extramuros **7964**
1316-7553 Apuntes de Filosofia **6904**
1316-7790 Agora Trujillo **7946**
1316-8533 Actualidad Contable Faces **1279**
1316-9505 Revista de Teoria y Didactica de las Ciencias Sociales **7997**
1316-9688 Informe Medico **5635**
1317-0570 Telos **4477**
1317-102X Unica **5392**
1317-1070 Objeto Visual **6509**
1317-1798 Akademos **2825**
1317-2255 Multiciencias **7883**
1317-5262 Entomotropica **847**
1317-5734 Cayapa **8092**
1317-5815 Sapiens **355**
1317-5823 Revista Latinoamericana de Ortodoncia y Odontopediatria **5864**
1317-5904 Revistas Otras Miradas **7998**
1317-6099 Compendium **7956**
1317-8245 Ciencia Odontologica **5838**
1317-8822 Vision Gerencial **1800**
1317-9152 U D O Agricola. Revista Cientifica **163**
1317-9535 Provincia **7174**
1317-987X Vitae **5728**
1317-9888 Guia de Productos Terapeuticos **5621**
1318-007X Piranesi **453**
1318-0177 Litterae Slovenicae **5326**
1318-0185 Acta Histriae **4196**
1318-0207 Acta Chimica Slovenica **2048**
1318-0320 Dnevnik **3947**
1318-0339 Nedeljski Dnevnik **3947**
1318-0347 Zdravniski Vestnik **5734**
1318-0614 Nase Nebo **578**
1318-072X Bank of Slovenia. Annual Report **1315**
1318-0746 Kranjcan **7495**
1318-1025 Podjetnik **1159**
1318-1092 J A M A (Slovenian Edition) **5642**
1318-1483 Solski Razgledi **2913**
1318-1866 Koroski Vestnik
1318-1874 Psiholoska Obzorja **7394**
1318-1882 Uporabna Informatika **2440**
1318-1998 Acta Entomologica Slovenica **837**
1318-2099 Radiology and Oncology **6207**
1318-2269 Kinesiologia Slovenica **6991**
1318-2277 Javna Uprava **4698**
1318-2358 Ambient **4531**
1318-2498 Zgodovina za Vse **4280**
1318-2803 I B Revija **1489**
1318-2951 Obzornik Zdravstvene Nege *changed to* 1854-4754 **5976**
1318-296X Moj Pes **6811**
1318-3109 Revija o Konjih **298**
1318-3222 Javnost **7976**
1318-3362 Phainomena **6939**
1318-3664 Exuviae **847**
1318-3680 Apokalipsa **5256**
1318-3745 Slovenia v Stevilkah **8399**
1318-3818 Ekonomsko Ogledalo **1482**
1318-3826 Slovenian Economic Mirror **1517**
1318-3834 Jesensko Porocilo **1719**
1318-3842 Autumn Report **1717**
1318-3850 Pomladansko Porocilo **1720**
1318-3869 Spring Report **1721**
1318-3877 Informacije Z P M S† **8964**
1318-4458 Acta Dermatovenerologica Alpina, Pannonica et Adriatica **5870**
1318-4598 Grand Prix Magazine
1318-461X Joker **2478**
1318-4636 Modna Jana **2259**
1318-4717 Geografija v Soli **4009**

ISSN

9578 1318-5284 ULRICH'S PERIODICALS

1318-5284 Banka Slovenije. Letno Porocilo **1316**
1318-5403 Statisticni Letopis Republike Slovenije **8405**
1318-5411 Falco **907**
1318-5454 Organizacija **1870**
1318-5497 Emzin **487**
1318-5640 Slovenska Bibliografija (CD-ROM Edition)†
1318-5748 Slava. Posebna Izdaja **5174**
1318-5764 Viceversa **6189**
1318-6701 Porocilo o Raziskovanju Paleolita Neolita in Eneolita v Sloveniji **411**
1318-6728 Solska Kronika **2913**
1318-6833 Mini Skandi **4340**
1318-7031 Lady **8871**
1318-7163 Univerza v Ljubljani. Veterinarska Fakulteta. Zbornik. Suplement†
1318-721X Mesecni Agrometeoroloski Bilten†
1318-7279 Ventil **7064**
1318-735X Glasba v Soli **2860**
1318-8038 Smrklja **8884**
1318-8828 Poligrafi **5352**
1318-8917 Grif
1318-9131 Znanstveno Raziskovalno Sredisce. Glasnik **4483**
1318-9239 Moj Dom *see* 1318-0320 **3947**
1318-9328 Bozje Okolje **7786**
1319-0067 Saudi Arabia. Ministry of Education. Educational Documentation **2909**
1319-0148 Al Darat **7849**
1319-0164 Saudi Pharmaceutical Journal **6879**
1319-0210 Al-Yawm
1319-0229 Al-Nadwah **3944**
1319-0237 Al-Madinah **3944**
1319-0245 Al-Bilad **3944**
1319-0253 Al-Jazirah **3944**
1319-0261 Al-Massaiyah **3944**
1319-027X Riyadh Daily **3944**
1319-0288 Al-Riyadh **3944**
1319-0296 Al-Yamamah **3944**
1319-0318 Okaz **3944**
1319-0326 Saudi Gazette **3944**
1319-0342 Al-Manhal **5226**
1319-0547 Al-Qafilah (Dhahran)
1319-0725 Akhbar al-A'alam al-Islami **7708**
1319-0768 Saudi Arabia. Wizarat al-Ma'arif. Al-Istikhlasat Al-Tarbawiyyah **2935**
1319-0806 Iqraa **3944**
1319-0814 Al-Sharq al-Awsat **3912**
1319-0822 Al-Riyadiyyah **8197**
1319-0830 Al-Iqtisadiyyah **1359**
1319-0849 Basem **2178**
1319-0865 Majallat al-Sharq al-Awsat **3912**
1319-0881 Aalam ar-Riyadah **8156**
1319-089X Arrajol **6286**
1319-0903 Hiya **8867**
1319-1128 Al-Muslimun **7715**
1319-1314 Islamic Development Bank. Annual Report **1359**
1319-1403 Tilivisyon al-Khalij **2397**
1319-1543 Ahlan wa-Sahlan **8782**
1319-156X Arabian Sun
1319-1578 King Saud University Journal. Computer and Information Sciences **2430**
1319-1594 Al-Suqur
1319-1616 Islamic Economic Studies **7712**
1319-1845 At-Taqrir as-Sanawi - S A M A *see* 0558-7220 **1942**
1319-2388 Saudi Aramco Journal of Technology **8437**
1319-2434 Da'wat al-Haqq **7710**
1319-2442 Saudi Journal of Kidney Diseases and Transplantation **6274**
1319-2655 Al-Haras al-Watani **3944**
1319-304X Majallat al-Dirassat al-Diblomasiyah **7251**
1319-3287 Urdu News **3944**
1319-3449 Al-Aswaq **1063**
1319-3767 The Saudi Journal of Gastroenterology **5930**
1319-4607 Sehhatuk Alyoum **5711**
1319-5166 Arab Journal of Mathematical Sciences **5473**
1319-5913 Al-Mustaqbal al-Islami (Riyad) **7708**
1319-6103 Saudi Chemical Society. Journal **2080**
1319-6138 Neurosciences **6169**
1319-6618 King Saud University Journal. Language and Translation **5137**
1319-7266 Al-Sukkaryoun **5900**
1319-8025 Arabian Journal for Science and Engineering. Section B: Engineering **3181**
1319-8947 Adumatu **371**
1319-9226 *see* 0256-4947 **5576**
1320-0100 Building Industry Connection *changed to* Building Connection **985**
1320-0593 Hazard **7520**
1320-0615 Rolling Stone **6613**
1320-0682 Complexity International†
1320-0941 Australian Style (Macquarie) **5097**
1320-0968 The Australian Feminist Law Journal **8894**
1320-1115 Monument **450**
1320-1220 Live To Ride **8260**
1320-1263 Hospital and Healthcare *changed to* 1835-663X **4099**
1320-1492 H R Report **1863**
1320-159X Journal of Law and Medicine **4702**
1320-1867 Quality Time† **8983**
1320-2073 Australian Auto Action **8159**
1320-2103 Australian Motorcycle News **8253**
1320-212X Cricketer†
1320-2251 Australian Language Matters *changed to* 1449-3659
1320-243X Australian Academy of the Humanities. Lecture Series (No.) **4443**
1320-2464 Animals Today **318**
1320-2472 Australian Chamber of Manufactures. Bulletin *changed to* A I G Bulletin
1320-2480 Australian and New Zealand Student Services Association. Journal **2828**
1320-2545 Australian Defence Force Journal **6413**
1320-2677 Museum Matters **6531**
1320-2839 Fishing World **3594**
1320-2871 Child Abuse Prevention **8032**
1320-2944 E Q Australia **3058**
1320-2960 Regional Policy and Practice†
1320-3185 Australian Nursing Journal **5952**
1320-3274 Australia. Air Transport Statistics. General Aviation **8521**
1320-3584 Women in Welfare Education (Print) *changed to* 1834-4941 **8078**
1320-3606 Electronic Antiquity **2233**
1320-3843 Australian College of Health Service Executive. Annual Report **4088**
1320-3851 Footnotes to South Australian History and Literature **4192**
1320-3878 WALIS News **208**
1320-3924 Western Fisheries **3611**
1320-3940 Warm Earth **3753**
1320-3975 F M - Facility Management **1851**
1320-4181 The Moving Image **6508**
1320-4300 Building Cost Guide. Housing. New South Wales **985**
1320-4319 Cordell's Building Cost Guide. Commercial and Industrial **1000**
1320-4424 Diggings Journal **390**
1320-4653 Cordell's Building Cost Guide. Housing, Queensland **1000**
1320-4823 Australian Family Tree Connections **3759**
1320-4912 Directions (North Adelaide) *see* 0158-099X **2200**
1320-5102 Softlink Times **5063**
1320-5323 The Australasian Journal of Natural Resources Law and Policy **2603**
1320-5331 Lakes and Reservoirs: Research and Management **8828**
1320-5358 Nephrology **6272**
1320-5455 Journal of Quality in Clinical Practice†
1320-5463 Pathology International **5694**
1320-5609 New Librarian†
1320-5692 Literacy Learning: The Middle Years **3070**
1320-5773 Australian Triathlete **8160**
1320-5870 Flightpath **55**
1320-6133 Australian Entomologist **840**
1320-6176 Melbourne's Child **2161**
1320-6184 Australia. Bureau of Statistics. Public Sector Financial Assets and Liabilities, Australia†
1320-6346 Direct Link **4658**
1320-6435 Red Politics **7176**
1320-6494 Australia. Bureau of Statistics. Population Survey Monitor†
1320-6524 Australasian Drilling **8818**
1320-6567 Arena Journal **7107**
1320-6648 Australian Research in Early Childhood Education **2829**
1320-6680 A B I X: Australasian Business Intelligence†
1320-6702 Canberra Law Review **4640**
1320-6915 Interlogue†
1320-7091 Australian Children's Rights News **7202**
1320-7105 Australian Journal of Administrative Law **4846**
1320-7156 International Journal of Business Studies **1127**
1320-7199 Journal of Arabic, Islamic and Middle Eastern Studies† **8968**
1320-7229 Reserve Bank of Australia. Research Discussion Paper **1378**
1320-744X Australia. Air Transport Statistics. Digest of Statistics† **8932**
1320-7458 Hyper **2477**
1320-7873 Communal - Plural†
1320-7881 Nursing Inquiry **5974**
1320-811X Australia. Bureau of Statistics. Australian Business Expectations†
1320-8403 Lighting **3324**
1320-8616 Election Funding Authority of New South Wales. Annual Report **7435**
1320-8632 Brotherhood Comment **8028**
1320-9019 Clematis†
1320-9272 Law Association for Asia and the Pacific. Legal Education Standing Committee. Newsletter **2992**
1320-9302 Theatre Australasia†
1320-9337 FreeXpresSion **5298**
1320-9345 Poetrix **5430**
1320-9426 Tax Week
1320-9450 Dutch Weekly† **8951**
1320-9507 The Greyhound Recorder **6809**
1320-954X Q H A Review **4396**
1320-9582 Australian Veterinary Association. Annual Report **8793**
1320-9647 Australian Environmental Law News *changed to* 1445-405X **4738**
1320-968X Ecodate (Print) *changed to* Ecodate (Online) **1097**
1320-9698 Geodate (Print) *changed to* Geodate (Online) **4008**
1320-9701 Nutridate (Print) *changed to* Nutridate (Online) **6665**
1320-971X Businessdate (Print) *changed to* Businessdate (Online) **1731**
1320-9736 Australian Nature Conservation Agency. Annual Report† **8933**
1320-9825 Independent Education **2986**
1320-9914 New & Used 4 W D Buyers Guide *changed to* 1832-7575 **8556**
1320-9981 Juice†
1321-0122 International Journal of Transpersonal Studies **7366**
1321-0157 Stock and Land **158**
1321-0165 Good Fruit & Vegetables **233**
1321-0238 Tasmanian Rail News **8625**
1321-0262 Australian Tennis Magazine **8221**
1321-0335 A M B A Journal
1321-0408 Asian Journal of Mining **6457**
1321-0564 Airnews **46**
1321-0599 V E Bulletin **6959**
1321-067X Cordell's Building Cost Guide. Commercial Industrial. Queensland **1000**
1321-0696 Building Materials. Price Index. New South Wales **986**
1321-0823 Advocate Weekender†
1321-0971 The Examiner **3794**
1321-103X Research Studies in Music Education **6611**
1321-1072 James Cook University Law Review **4698**
1321-1080 Australia-India Council. Annual Report **7222**
1321-1099 Heritage N S W **444**
1321-120X Onwood *changed to* 1832-2425
1321-1269 Australian and New Zealand Citator to UK Reports **4821**
1321-1455 Australia. Bureau of Statistics. Australia's Welfare† **8932**
1321-1617 Australia. Bureau of Statistics. Australian Housing in Brief† **8932**
1321-1641 Australia. Bureau of Statistics. Queensland Office. Building Approvals and Dwelling Unit Commencements: Small Area Statistics, Queensland†
1321-1668 North Queensland Register **3795**
1321-1676 Neos Kosmos **3553**
1321-1781 Australia. Bureau of Statistics. Australian Social Trends **8019**
1321-1838 Criminal Law News **4887**
1321-1870 Pedal Update **8266**
1321-1919 Stock Journal **301**
1321-196X C I R C M E Lecture Series **6552**
1321-1986 Queensland Graingrower† **8983**
1321-1994 Queensland Farmer *changed to* 1321-1668 **3795**
1321-2036 Australian Surf Lifesaver† **8934**
1321-2133 Australian Journal of Intelligent Information Processing Systems **2446**
1321-2249 Southern Fisheries **3609**
1321-2354 Heritage Highlights†
1321-2613 University of New England. Information Technology Services News†
1321-2664 Brisbane's Child **2146**
1321-2753 Monash Bioethics Review **6935**
1321-2923 Russia, Siberia, Mongolia and North Korea Travel News†
1321-3067 W I S E R† **8998**
1321-3075 Spectrum (Collingwood) **6208**
1321-3512 Australia. Bureau of Statistics. International Merchandise Trade, Australia† **8932**
1321-3660 Deakin Law Review **4655**
1321-3679 Table & Kitchen†
1321-3822 Australian Topical Law Journal
1321-3830 Gold Coast Bulletin **3794**
1321-3881 Italian Historical Society Journal **4233**
1321-3903 Australian Clay Target Shooting News **8160**
1321-4012 Australian Aerospace Industry Capability Directory†
1321-408X Franchising **1961**
1321-4217 Australian Open Official Tournament Magazine **8221**
1321-4446 Australian Human Rights Law Journal
1321-4454 Australian Banking Law Journal
1321-4462 Australian Accounting Law Journal
1321-4470 Australian Telecommunications Law Journal
1321-4489 Australian Administrative Law Journal **4856**
1321-4497 Australian Judiciary Law Journal **4946**
1321-4500 Australian Crime Prosecution Law Journal **4885**
1321-4764 Official Directory of the Catholic Church in Australia **7667**
1321-4799 RealTime **8477**
1321-4853 Didaskalia **2233**
1321-5175 Business Law Update **4859**
1321-5221 Harden Murrumburrah Express **3794**
1321-5272 Port Lincoln Times **3796**
1321-5353 The Gympie Times **3794**
1321-537X Merredin-Wheatbelt Mercury **3795**
1321-554X Great Lakes Advocate **3794**
1321-5779 Australian Tax Planning Law Journal
1321-5787 Australian Small Business Law Journal
1321-5795 Australian Social Engineering Law Journal
1321-5914 Australian Snowboarder Magazine **8304**
1321-5930 Australian Parliamentary Law Journal **4846**
1321-5949 Australian Family Law Journal **4907**
1321-5957 Australian Employment Law Journal **1666**
1321-5965 Stage Whispers **8479**
1321-6015 Food Management News *changed to* 1833-5098 **3637**
1321-6163 Proceedings of the Legislative Assembly for the Australian Capital Territory. Digest **7460**
1321-618X Australian Insolvency Law Journal **4827**
1321-6279 Owner - Driver **8674**
1321-6287 Benchmarking H R **1856**
1321-6376 Australian Photography Photo-Directory†
1321-6481 Imago: New Writing†
1321-6554 Geo Australasia†
1321-6562 Australian Criminal Law Journal
1321-6597 Journal of International Communication **8114**
1321-6627 Rural Social Work *changed to* 1833-3060 **8066**
1321-6880 Memoir Geology **2754**
1321-7003 Powderhound **8329**
1321-7054 Patent Abridgements Supplement to the Australian Official Journal of Patents†
1321-7062 Annual Record of Patent Office Proceedings†
1321-7070 Annual Record of Trade Marks Office Proceedings†
1321-7089 Annual Record of Designs Office Proceedings†
1321-7267 Quality Certification News *changed to* 1447-364X
1321-7348 Asian Review of Accounting **1280**
1321-747X Australian Corporations Law Journal **4857**
1321-7488 Australian Taxation Law Journal **1911**
1321-7496 Australian Legal Profession Law Journal
1321-7526 Farm Weekly **111**
1321-764X Australia. Bureau of Statistics. Tourist Accommodation, Australian Capital Territory†
1321-7690 That's Life! **8885**
1321-7763 Soccer International **8245**
1321-7771 Australasian Taekwondo Magazine **8159**
1321-7844 Australian Bureau of Agricultural and Resource Economics. Australian Commodities **194**
1321-8166 Queensland Review **4194**
1321-8247 eLaw Journal **4663**
1321-828X Geological Survey of New South Wales. 1:250000 Geological Sheets Series. Explanatory Notes **2740**
1321-8301 Native Title News **4739**
1321-8476 N T E U Advocate *changed to* 1329-7295 **2965**
1321-8697 Clearing House† **8941**
1321-8719 Psychiatry Psychology and Law **6177**
1321-8727 Practical Hydroponics and Greenhouses **3748**
1321-8794 Proctor **4761**
1321-8824 Slimming *changed to* Slimming & Health **6669**

Link to your serials resources and content with ulrichsweb.com

1321-9065 Australia. Bureau of Statistics. Motor Vehicles in Australia†
1321-9324 Case Studies†
1321-9545 Proactive 7291
1321-9553 Safety W A 6686
1321-9715 Monash University. Development Studies Centre. Monash - Melbourne Joint Project on Comparative Australian - Asian Development. Working Paper†
1321-9758 Australian Prescription Products Guide 6824
1321-9812 Australian Business Monthly†
1321-9820 H Q†
1321-9839 Woman's Day 8889
1321-9847 People 6297
1322-0179 Australia. Bureau of Statistics. New South Wales Office. Labour Force, New South Wales and Australian Capital Territory†
1322-0187 Changing Education (Geelong)† 8940
1322-0314 Ngulaig†
1322-0446 Watershed Magazine changed to 1447-1655
1322-0594 Disney Adventures 2185
1322-0659 Every Child 2856
1322-0683 Australian Financial Review Quarterly on CD-ROM see 0404-2018 1309
1322-0705 Zadok Papers 7696
1322-0756 Infogram†
1322-0829 Phycological Research 808
1322-1159 Australian Patchwork and Quilting 6637
1322-1337 Asia Pacific Journal of Transport 8490
1322-168X A S S E S S†
1322-1833 Agenda 1909
1322-2368 Australia. Bureau of Statistics. Queensland Office. Regional Statistics, Queensland (Print) changed to Australia. Bureau of Statistics. Queensland Office. Regional Statistics, Queensland (Online) 8933
1322-2481 Principal Matters 3030
1322-2775 Modern Phytotherapist† 8975
1322-2872 Australian Leisure†
1322-2945 N T E U Frontline 2994
1322-3267 Competitions and Financial Opportunities for Artists 483
1322-3712 Australian P C User 2574
1322-3895 Periodicals in Print: Australia, New Zealand & Papua New Guinea changed to 1444-5980
1322-400X Benchmark†
1322-4018 Aid Watch 1590
1322-4301 Hot Topics 4688
1322-4417 New Zealand Journal of Taxation Law and Policy 1937
1322-4611 Legal Practice Briefing changed to 1448-4803 4719
1322-4875 Handbook of Records and Results 8219
1322-4883 Sportdiving Magazine 8335
1322-4891 Fastlane†
1322-5103 Fusions 2041
1322-5235 The Courier-Mail 3794
1322-5243 Sunday Mail 3796
1322-5464 Australian Stitches 6637
1322-6479 Seatalk 6445
1322-6525 Archaeological Diggings 376
1322-6622 Hockey Circle†
1322-6754 Building in Australia 985
1322-6762 Long Term Forecasts (Year) 1145
1322-6916 Culture Mandala (Print)† 8947
1322-6975 Environmental Manager 3426
1322-705X Electronic Publishing Australia†
1322-7084 Animal Health in Australia 8792
1322-7114 International Journal of Nursing Practice 5962
1322-7130 Australian Journal of Grape and Wine Research 598
1322-7157 Aboriginal and Torres Strait Islander Studies Unit Research Report Series 3515
1322-7181 Electrical Inspections 3303
1322-7254 Money Management 1368
1322-7351 Australian Jeweller changed to Jeweller 4567
1322-7386 Carnet Austral 5271
1322-7610 New South Wales State Emergency Services. Annual Report 2227
1322-7645 Brolga 2683
1322-7696 Collegian 5955
1322-770X Sydney Bride 5561
1322-7785 Better Photography 6964
1322-7971 ConVivio† 8944
1322-8064 The British White Bulletin 282
1322-8099 The Australian Women's Weekly Handmade†
1322-8242 Aviation Trader 48
1322-8269 Directory of Higher Education Nursing Courses†
1322-8307 Australian Ironman 6982
1322-8587 The Cairns Post 3793
1322-8633 Australia. Bureau of Statistics. New South Wales Office. Principal Agricultural Commodities, New South Wales, Preliminary†
1322-865X Australia. Bureau of Statistics. Agriculture, Australia (Print) changed to Australia. Bureau of Statistics. Agriculture, Australia (Online) 175
1322-8668 Australia. Bureau of Statistics. Queensland Office. Agriculture, Queensland†
1322-8676 The Australian Electronic Journal of Nursing Education† 8933
1322-8692 Australia. Bureau of Statistics. Marriages and Divorces, Australia†
1322-8765 Australia. Bureau of Statistics. Migration, Australia (Print) changed to Australia. Bureau of Statistics. Migration, Australia (Online) 7299
1322-8803 Australian Journal of Holistic Nursing†
1322-9060 Law Text Culture 4717
1322-9214 Australasian Historical Archaeology 382
1322-9230 Desktop 7579
1322-9397 Quality of Australian Canola (Years) 249
1322-9400 Journal of Family Studies 5559
1322-9559 Australian Style (Cottesloe)†
1322-9796 Marron Growers Bulletin 3601
1322-9869 A I A L Forum 4607
1322-9974 Home Economics Institute of Australia. Journal 4360
1322-9982 Success Review Magazine†
1323-000X Artswest†
1323-0026 Blue 4371

1323-0069 C A D User South East Asia 3289
1323-0077 Aqua Australis 8818
1323-0190 Friends of Libraries Australia. News Update 5010
1323-0360 Australia. Bureau of Statistics. Western Australian Office. Price Index of Western Australian Produced Hardwoods†
1323-0417 Five Bells 5422
1323-0425 Asia - Pacific Constitutional Yearbook† 8931
1323-0514 Master Builder (Melbourne) 1022
1323-0670 Fantastic Bear Patterns
1323-0824 Australian Health and Medical Industry Guide changed to 1444-4399
1323-1197 National Water Polo News† 8976
1323-1316 Psychiatry and Clinical Neurosciences 6177
1323-1413 Science Spectra†
1323-1650 Marine & Freshwater Research 2811
1323-1685 International Review of Women and Leadership 8899
1323-1715 International Arms & Military Collector
1323-191X CultureScope 7957
1323-207X Paper Wasp 5348
1323-2118 National Parks & Wildlife News†
1323-2266 Just Policy 8052
1323-2347 Federal Court Digest†
1323-238X Australian Journal of Human Rights 7203
1323-2495 Primary Intention changed to Wound Practice & Research 6075
1323-2649 Monash University. Development Studies Centre. Occasional Papers† 8975
1323-2681 Geelong Bird Report 907
1323-2770 The Australasian Professional Legal Education Directory (Print) changed to The Australasian Professional Legal Education Directory (Online) 2968
1323-3009 New Office World
1323-3122 Australia. Bureau of Statistics. Tasmanian Office. Agriculture, Tasmania (Hobart, 1987)†
1323-3270 Commonwealth Legislation on CD-ROM†
1323-3289 High Court and Federal Court Decisions† 8962
1323-3297 Family Court and A A T Decisions†
1323-3408 CAMERA Photographer's Handbook 6965
1323-3475 Australasian Journal of Ecotoxicology 3494
1323-3580 Astronomical Society of Australia. Publications (Print)†
1323-367X Architectural Review Australia 430
1323-3890 Australian Gold Annual†
1323-4021 H E R D S A Gold Guide Series† 8960
1323-4382 Informatics in Heathcare Australia† 8964
1323-4528 Australia. Bureau of Statistics. New Motor Vehicle Registrations, Australia, Preliminary†
1323-4536 V I M P Report 2773
1323-4552 Artonview 6520
1323-4595 Motoring Directions 8505
1323-4633 De Proverbio 3616
1323-4846 Federal Judgments Bulletin
1323-4854 Feathers & Fur 8312
1323-4943 Baptist Union of Victoria. Yearbook 7624
1323-4951 Weekly Industrial Register†
1323-5060 Bride to Be 5557
1323-5109 Transplant Nurses Journal 5983
1323-5192 National Gallery of Australia. Annual Report 6534
1323-5257 Phantom 7570
1323-5494 W E L Read
1323-5761 Political Crossroads 7260
1323-577X Educational Practice and Theory 3059
1323-5818 Molluscan Research 955
1323-5850 Australia. Bureau of Statistics. National Public Health Expenditure Report†
1323-5869 Liquor Retailing Handbook† 8971
1323-5885 Artworker 6520
1323-5966 Australia. Bureau of Statistics. Historical Publications on CD-ROM†
1323-6032 Myrmecia 855
1323-6040 Tempus 358
1323-6164 Costs Watch 1286
1323-6210 Hinzmusic Arrangements Series†
1323-6229 Western Australian Research Activities 2821
1323-627X V I E R Bulletin†
1323-6342 The Manufacturing and Logistics Software Buyers Guide†
1323-6377 Uniting Church Studies 7778
1323-6490 Mathematics Contests 5515
1323-661X Textile and Apparel of Australasia 8464
1323-675X Ovulation Method Research and Reference Centre of Australia. Bulletin 973
1323-6822 Public Library News 5040
1323-6903 Journal of Contemporary Issues in Business and Government 1494
1323-7136 Academy of the Social Sciences in Australia. Occasional Paper Series 7945
1323-7292 Australian Music Calendar 6546
1323-7349 Queensland Environmental Practice Reporter 4764
1323-7454 Australian Doll Digest
1323-7462 Bear Facts Review
1323-7640 The Australian Journal of Mineralogy 6457
1323-7721 The Write Stuff 5400
1323-7756 Australian Indigenous Law Reporter changed to 1835-0186 7202
1323-7799 Respirology 6219
1323-7969 World Patrol and Rescue Craft changed to 1440-3307
1323-8086 Australian Drama Education Magazine 2828
1323-8175 Victorian and Tasmanian Retail Directory 2033
1323-8418 Sensibilities 5369
1323-8558 Modern Building and Architecture and Engineering in Australia
1323-8663 University of New England. Department of Marketing and Management. Working Papers†
1323-8884 National Housing Action†
1323-8922 The Australian Journal of Rehabilitation Counselling 3036
1323-8930 Allergology International 5753
1323-8949 University of New South Wales. School of Economics. Discussion Paper 1189
1323-8965 Simbeef 300
1323-8973 Rubicon†

1323-9163 Third Sector Review 8010
1323-9236 Australia. Bureau of Statistics. Heart, Stroke and Vascular Diseases Australian Facts 5740
1323-9376 What's New in W W W Social Sciences Newsletter 4485
1323-9546 Australia. Department of the Treasury. Treasury Research Papers 1438
1323-9589 Worldwide Attitudes Electronic Journal†
1323-9686 Australasian Journal of Gifted Education 2828
1323-9708 Australian Country Collections 4553
1323-9767 Equity Network
1323-9791 The Technology Directory of Australia†
1324-0307 Victoria, Australia. Geological Survey. Technical Record 2773
1324-034X Australian Law Book Review
1324-048X Tasmanian Historical Studies 4194
1324-0625 Hypermedia Joyce Studies 5307
1324-0633 The Studio (Oatley) 3083
1324-0749 Australian Options†
1324-0781 E-Journal of Instructional Science and Technology changed to 1449-5554 3051
1324-0935 Australasian Journal of Regional Studies 1438
1324-1117 Australia. Bureau of Statistics. Release Advice†
1324-1125 International Employment Relations Review 1688
1324-1141 Alternative Plans & Products Catalogue
1324-1265 Local Government Law Journal 4725
1324-1427 Lawyers' Admission Handbook 4718
1324-1435 Australian and New Zealand Nuclear Medicine 5581
1324-1486 Australian Journal of Outdoor Education 2829
1324-1540 The Australian Journal of Emergency Management 2225
1324-1583 Australian Journal of Water Resources 8818
1324-1591 Transport Engineering in Australia 3285
1324-1605 Journal of Project & Construction Management 3206
1324-1613 Australian Creative 21
1324-1702 International Studies in Educational Administration 3013
1324-2008 Spatial Business Newsletter 4037
1324-2083 S A R D I Research Report Series 153
1324-2113 Graduate Women 2982
1324-2288 FlyLife 8314
1324-230X AusIndustry Magazine†
1324-2326 Independence 2866
1324-2342 The Electronic Journal of Australian and New Zealand History 4191
1324-2385 Australian Seafood Industry Directory (Year) 3587
1324-2598 Nature Australia changed to 1833-752X 7854
1324-2652 Victorian G U M News 3786
1324-2962 Certified Male Magazine 6287
1324-3209 Australian and New Zealand Academy of Management. Journal changed to 1833-3672 1767
1324-3268 Maritime Workers' Journal 8653
1324-3276 Industrial Relations and Management Letter† 8964
1324-3667 Australia. Bureau of Statistics. South Australian Office. Sales of Goods and Services by Businesses Involved in Water Related Activity in South Australia (Print) changed to Australia. Bureau of Statistics. South Australian Office. Sales of Goods and Services by Businesses Involved in Water Related Activity in South Australia (Online) 1210
1324-3853 South East Fishing changed to South East & West Fishing 8335
1324-4027 H R Monthly 1862
1324-4043 Waterline 8665
1324-4094 The Australian Worker (Sydney) 4590
1324-4175 Ceramics Technical 2040
1324-4183 Australia. Auditing and Assurance Standards Board. Auditing Standard
1324-4272 Microbiology Australia 892
1324-4361 Parkwatch 2624
1324-437X The Police Journal 2663
1324-454X Psyche (Print)†
1324-4558 Limina 4193
1324-4795 Y A C V Bits†
1324-504X Western Australia. Geological Survey. Annual Review 2774
1324-5074 Australia. Air Transport Statistics. International Scheduled Air Transport† 8932
1324-5139 Action Abroad changed to 1833-8666 8045
1324-5155 Analysis (Melbourne) 7334
1324-5295 Super Review 1385
1324-5309 Beef Improvement News 280
1324-5333 Catholic Education Circular 2835
1324-535X Marie Claire 8873
1324-5643 Outdoor Australia 8326
1324-5686 Tawantinsuyu 357
1324-5724 Melbourne Anglican 7767
1324-5740 Greener Times 2613
1324-5767 Mercantile Agent†
1324-5848 Deep Surfing Magazine†
1324-5864 Journal of International Marketing and Exporting 1825
1324-5945 InformationAge 2498
1324-5961 Practically Primary 3077
1324-6011 LEAD Action News 7530
1324-6038 Noetica† 8977
1324-6046 Bride to Be's Wedding Cakes 3672
1324-6216 Geelong Advertiser 3794
1324-6240 Australasian Institute of Mining and Metallurgy Publications 6457
1324-6283 Australian Gas Association. Research Paper 6763
1324-6399 Drug Wise
1324-6534 Australian A P E C Studies Centre. Issues Paper (Print) changed to 1832-9306 1553
1324-6542 L O T L 8870
1324-6550 A D M 6408
1324-6577 Australia's Economic Objectives and Management††
1324-6798 House & Home 4438
1324-6879 Catholic Social Justice Series 7203
1324-7077 Breast News 6010
1324-7271 Art + Law 4621
1324-7425 Australia. Bureau of Statistics. Western Australian Office. Dwelling Unit Commencements Reported by Approving Authorities, Western Australia†

1327-8746 Australasian Victorian Studies Association. Journal (Print) *changed to* Australasian Journal of Victorian Studies **4443**
1327-8800 Educare News *changed to* 1449-9274 **2917**
1327-8835 Australasian Epidemiologist **5810**
1327-8983 Reed's Print Production Directory†
1327-8991 Your Home **4431**
1327-9041 Craft and Decorating with Tracy Marsh
1327-905X Nordic Notes† **8977**
1327-9289 Australian Sugar Industry Handbook **220**
1327-9343 A M C Solutions and Statistics (Year) *changed to* A M C Solutions and Statistics (Year) (Middle Primary Upper Primary) **5463**
1327-9343 A M C Solutions and Statistics (Year) *changed to* A M C Solutions and Statistics (Year) (Junior Intermediate Senior) **5463**
1327-9408 World Fast Ferry Market **8665**
1327-9432 Digital Photography + Design **6966**
1327-9491 Therapeutic Guidelines. Neurology **6187**
1327-9505 Therapeutic Guidelines. Endocrinology **5900**
1327-9513 Therapeutic Guidelines. Cardiovascular **5800**
1327-9548 International Education - ej†
1327-9556 Text **5386**
1327-9599 Physiotherapy Moves†
1327-9858 Strehlow Research Centre. Occassional Papers **3566**
1328-0201 Print Asia Pacific *changed to* 1446-6554 **7325**
1328-021X Hospitality **4388**
1328-0228 Waste Management & Environment
1328-0384 Australasian Chiropractic and Osteopathy *changed to* 1746-1340 **5803**
1328-0503 Vietnamese Studies Review†
1328-0694 Australasian Journal of Podiatric Medicine†
1328-1046 Australian Nursery Manager **3723**
1328-1089 InSite
1328-1143 Australian Journal of Labour Economics **1666**
1328-1720 Medical History Australia *changed to* Medical History Newsletter **5669**
1328-1801 Kanu Culture **8277**
1328-1879 Australian Coal Review†
1328-1976 Call Link
1328-2115 Asia Pacific Channels **2682**
1328-214X Opera - Opera† **8979**
1328-2174 Family History Netletter **8102**
1328-2204 Postgraduate Review *changed to* Plane Tree **2998**
1328-2344 Central Coast Campus Working Paper Series **5060**
1328-2360 Open Learning Deferred Payment Scheme†
1328-2409 Discovery **2731**
1328-2484 Tax Guide (Glen Waverley)
1328-2573 Australian Printer **7318**
1328-259X Australian Business News *changed to* Business Connect Magazine **1881**
1328-2727 Wartime **6453**
1328-2778 Australia. Bureau of Statistics. International Trade in Goods and Services, Australia (Print) *changed to* Australia. Bureau of Statistics. International Trade in Goods and Services, Australia (Online) **1207**
1328-2786 Australia. Bureau of Statistics. Publications and Products Released in (Month)†
1328-2883 Australian Society of Soil Science. Profile **220**
1328-3049 AppleSauce† **8930**
1328-3057 AppleSauce (Online) **2574**
1328-3154 Global Journal of Engineering Education **3193**
1328-3219 University of Western Australia. Department of Organisational and Labour Studies. Discussion Paper **1713**
1328-3308 Dance Forum†
1328-3340 Altair†
1328-3359 Click it @ R A C P† **8941**
1328-3464 Water and the Environment† **8998**
1328-3588 The Sport Educator†
1328-3626 Australasian Journal of Emergency Care†
1328-3774 Australian Financial Review Magazine **1064**
1328-3847 Packaging **6712**
1328-3901 Australasian Corrosion Association. Annual Conference Proceedings **2112**
1328-3952 Activate†
1328-4045 C I O **1414**
1328-4193 Europe Business Review†
1328-4207 Clinical Psychologist **7345**
1328-4312 Health & Healing **309**
1328-4541 Rainbowfish On-Line†
1328-4681 Easy Feng Shui **4539**
1328-4711 Ideas Magazine
1328-4738 Kompass Agribusiness, Food and Beverage†
1328-4754 Kompass Business and Transport Services†
1328-4762 In-Tax **1929**
1328-4908 Copyright Updates **6748**
1328-5092 Mediterranean Archaeology. Supplement *see* 1030-8482 **405**
1328-5335 Roundtable† **8986**
1328-5475 Indigenous Law Bulletin **4692**
1328-5548 Victoria. Department of Natural Resources and Environment. Marine and Freshwater Resources Institute. Report **710**
1328-5661 The Pregnancy Book **6002**
1328-5742 Geekgirl **8865**
1328-5947 Academy of the Social Sciences in Australia. Annual Report **7945**
1328-598X Crops†
1328-6021 Australian Educator **2828**
1328-6196 The Australian Holstein Journal **261**
1328-6218 Electronics Australia with Professional Electronics and E T I *changed to* Electronics Australia Today
1328-6226 Urban Cinefile **6516**
1328-6404 Dickson Precinct Community Group. Newsletter **5006**
1328-6498 Australasian Flowers **3755**
1328-6544 A L F A Lotfeeding **270**
1328-6609 Beef†
1328-6617 Wool†
1328-665X University of New South Wales. Faculty of Applied Science Handbook†
1328-6692 Extra Extra **5009**
1328-6749 Backpacker Essentials **8685**
1328-679X Autumn School of Studies on Alcohol & Drugs. Proceedings of Seminars
1328-682X S P E L D Bulletin **3046**
1328-6854 Australian Mountain Bike **8253**
1328-6889 Australian Association of Jewish Studies. Newsletter (Print) *changed to* Australian Association of Jewish Studies. Newsletter (Online) **7718**
1328-7133 A C H P E R Active and Healthy Magazine **6980**
1328-715X ProPhoto **6976**
1328-7176 Knowit **5023**
1328-7192 Aircargo Asia - Pacific **8535**
1328-7206 A R R B Transport Research. Briefing **8629**
1328-7214 National Accommodation Guide **8740**
1328-7265 Journal of Systems and Information Technology **2549**
1328-732X Commonwealth Budget Submission for Older Australians *see* 1325-4359 **4056**
1328-7435 Globe† **8959**
1328-7451 Plastics News International **7097**
1328-7540 WellBeing Magazine **7000**
1328-7567 Asia - Pacific Magazine†
1328-7621 Languages Victoria **5142**
1328-7699 A C M Bulletin *changed to* A I G Bulletin
1328-7761 Anxiety Disorders Foundation of Australia NSW Branch Inc. Newsletter†
1328-7842 Bikwil **5263**
1328-7850 Experience Victoria **8702**
1328-7982 Australian Journal of Structural Engineering **3259**
1328-8032 Australia's Mining Monthly **6458**
1328-8040 Australasian College of Nutritional and Environmental Medicine. Journal **5580**
1328-8067 Pediatrics International **6102**
1328-8229 R M I T Publishing News†
1328-8318 Alpacas Australia **277**
1328-8369 News Vein
1328-8431 Massage Australia **6112**
1328-8466 F Y I **5009**
1328-8911 Design Computing Newsletter **2447**
1328-9039 FoodService News **3643**
1328-9071 Australian Occupational Health & Safety File **6673**
1328-9128 Croquet Australia **8226**
1328-9187 Templer Record **7688**
1328-9225 Vive **8887**
1328-925X Online Journal of Veterinary Research **8804**
1328-9292 University of Technology, Sydney. Faculty of Design Architecture and Building Handbook *changed to* University of Technology, Sydney. Handbook **2923**
1328-9306 University of Technology, Sydney. Faculty of Business Handbook *changed to* University of Technology, Sydney. Handbook **2923**
1328-9330 Plaintiff *changed to* 1449-7719 **4760**
1328-9454 Clinical Update **6016**
1328-9756 Screening the Past **516**
1328-9780 Queensland Teachers Union Professional Magazine *see* 0033-6238 **2902**
1329-0223 P C Week Australia†
1329-0258 The Australian Direct Marketing Directory†
1329-0320 University of technology, Sydney. Faculty of Science Handbook *changed to* University of Technology, Sydney. Handbook **2923**
1329-0436 Australian Viticulture **598**
1329-0460 Pig Meat Zine **6605**
1329-0517 Arts Access News **4063**
1329-0533 Audio Yearbook *changed to* 1442-2824 **8153**
1329-0622 School of Languages Postgraduate Research Papers on Language and Literature *changed to* School of Languages and Linguistics Postgraduate Research Papers on Language and Literature **5367**
1329-0762 Public Works Engineering Australia
1329-0940 Secretariat **6184**
1329-1130 Ad News Promotional Products Directory **1970**
1329-1149 E D A P Joint Policy Studies† **8952**
1329-1203 Tax Specialist **1950**
1329-1254 Architect Victoria **428**
1329-1270 C A E R Working Paper **1077**
1329-1351 Australia. Bureau of Statistics. Western Australian Office. Western Australia at a Glance *changed to* Australia. Bureau of Statistics. Western Australian Office. Western Australia at a Glance (Online) **8355**
1329-1408 Australian Journal of Academic Dissent†
1329-1440 Learning Communities†
1329-1475 Street Commodores **8605**
1329-1645 UniServe Science News (Online) **7925**
1329-184X Reform (Kingston)† **8984**
1329-1874 Best Practice **5584**
1329-1920 Australia. Bureau of Statistics. Mining, Electricity and Gas Operations, Australia, Preliminary†
1329-1947 Australian Endodontic Journal **5835**
1329-1955 A M A List of Medical Services and Fees **5564**
1329-2048 Positively Aging†
1329-2056 Australia. Bureau of Statistics. Apparent Consumption of Foodstuffs, Australia†
1329-2277 *see* 1329-2285 **3066**
1329-2285 Issues of Teaching and Learning **3066**
1329-234X Queensland Board of Senior Secondary School Studies. Publication List
1329-2366 *see* 1323-0077 **8818**
1329-2447 Australian Property Investor **7583**
1329-2463 Play and Folklore **3621**
1329-2641 A U S O M News **2574**
1329-2676 Centre for Labour Market Research. Discussion Paper Series **1670**
1329-2811 Aussie Post†
1329-2978 Australian P C Authority **2574**
1329-3052 News of the Day† **8977**
1329-3079 Men's Health **6284**
1329-3346 Queensland Court of Appeal Headnotes **4824**
1329-3389 Land and Water Link†
1329-3443 Australia. Bureau of Statistics. Telecommunication Services, Australia†
1329-3532 P C Magazine Australia *changed to* 1445-8675 **8992**
1329-3583 Dog's Life **6807**
1329-3737 Southern Cross University Law Review **4786**
1329-3745 Labor Review **7150**
1329-3907 Australia. Bureau of Statistics. Housing Occupancy and Costs, Australia *changed to* Australia. Bureau of Statistics. Housing Occupancy and Costs, Australia (Online) **4433**
1329-4016 Cream Magazine **6560**
1329-4059 Australia. Bureau of Statistics. Tasmanian Office. Population by Age and Sex, Tasmania†
1329-4091 Australia. Bureau of Statistics. New South Wales Office. Population by Age and Sex, New South Wales†
1329-4105 Australia. Bureau of Statistics. Victorian Office. Population by Age and Sex, Victoria†
1329-4113 Australia. Bureau of Statistics. Queensland Office. Population by Age and Sex, Queensland†
1329-4121 Australia. Bureau of Statistics. South Australian Office. Population by Age and Sex, South Australia†
1329-413X Australia. Bureau of Statistics. Western Australian Office. Population by Age and Sex, Western Australia†
1329-4148 Australia. Bureau of Statistics. Northern Territory Office. Population by Age and Sex, Northern Territory†
1329-4156 Australia. Bureau of Statistics. Population by Age and Sex, Australian Capital Territory†
1329-4164 Australia. Bureau of Statistics. New South Wales Office. Population, New South Wales†
1329-4172 Australia. Bureau of Statistics. Victorian Office. Population, Victoria†
1329-4180 Australia. Bureau of Statistics. Queensland Office. Population, Queensland†
1329-4199 Australia. Bureau of Statistics. South Australian Office. Population, South Australia†
1329-4202 Australia. Bureau of Statistics. Western Australian Office. Population, Western Australia†
1329-4210 Australia. Bureau of Statistics. Tasmanian Office. Population, Tasmania†
1329-4229 Australia. Bureau of Statistics. Northern Territory Office. Population, Northern Territory†
1329-4237 Australia. Bureau of Statistics. Populations, Australian Capital Territory†
1329-430X Australian Occupational Health & Safety Yearbook† **8933**
1329-4326 Retirement & Estate Planning Bulletin **4905**
1329-4474 Internet Directory†
1329-4539 Leading and Managing **2882**
1329-458X Litigation Notes **4724**
1329-4660 Australian Classic Car **8556**
1329-4709 Riptide. Photo Annual *see* 1034-2346 **8330**
1329-4741 Australia. Bureau of Statistics. Manufacturing, Australia† **8932**
1329-4857 Space Industry News† **8989**
1329-5039 Therapeutic Guidelines. Antibiotic **5721**
1329-5160 University of Technology, Sydney. U T S Faculty of Humanities and Social Sciences Handbook *changed to* University of Technology, Sydney. Handbook **2923**
1329-5179 University of Technology, Sydney. U T S Institute for International Studies Handbook *changed to* University of Technology, Sydney. Handbook **2923**
1329-5195 Border Watch **4572**
1329-5713 C S I R O Land and Water. Position Papers†
1329-5780 H M A A Q News **4387**
1329-5799 Higher Education Contribution Scheme *changed to* 1449-8588 **2986**
1329-6221 P A C E - Process & Control Engineering **3251**
1329-6647 The Australian's Review of Books *see* 1038-8761 **3793**
1329-6671 C S I R O Tropical Agriculture. Tropical Agriculture Technical Memorandum†
1329-6701 Secondary Schools Network, Catholic Curriculum Coordinators. Newsletter†
1329-6868 Board of Vocational Education and Training. Annual Report **2831**
1329-6884 Australian Council on Smoking and Health Newsletter†
1329-6906 E F A News† **8952**
1329-7074 Arts Alive **474**
1329-7147 International Journal of Design Computing†
1329-7236 Land Rights Queensland† **8970**
1329-7295 Advocate **2965**
1329-7538 Opinion Adelaide **3075**
1329-7651 Gourmet Vegetarian†
1329-7686 Australian Guitar Magazine **6546**
1329-7724 UniServe Science News† **8996**
1329-7783 G T A V News **4007**
1329-7902 Western Australia. Fisheries Department. Fisheries Management Report **3611**
1329-7945 Birds Australia Report **903**
1329-7961 Manifest **2660**
1329-8100 Institute of Public Affairs. Review **1125**
1329-8356 Local-Link **5030**
1329-8402 N A Q S News *changed to* 1033-9280 **78**
1329-8526 Flexible Online Learning
1329-8755 Emergency Support† **8953**
1329-878X Media International Australia Incorporating Culture and Policy **8120**
1329-881X The Weaver **2925**
1329-9069 Global Telecommunications Strategies
1329-9220 Studies of Society and Environment Magazine **2916**
1329-9360 Australian Infection Control *changed to* 1835-5617 **5814**
1329-9409 Swag of Yarns†
1329-9441 Melbourne Art Journal **505**
1329-9484 Australian Macworld **2574**
1329-9549 Foreign Affairs and Trade Record† **8957**
1329-9581 Weekly Tax Bulletin **1954**
1329-9735 Internet Law Bulletin **2561**
1329-9778 The Asian Studies W W W Monitor **564**
1329-9980 Australian Defence Business Review **6412**
1330-0008 Fizika A **7012**
1330-0016 Fizika B **7012**
1330-0024 Acta Historico-Oeconomica **1535**
1330-0059 Napredak **2889**
1330-0067 Informatologia **5017**
1330-0075 Acta Pharmaceutica **6818**
1330-0083 Hrvatski Meteoroloski Casopis **6356**
1330-0091 Gynaecologia et Perinatologia **5992**

ISSN

1334-2576 see 0543-5846 6325
1334-2584 see 0543-5846 6325
1334-2606 see 1330-9862 764
1334-2630 Elmar Proceedings 3099
1334-2762 see 1330-1012 2421
1334-3327 Fantom Slobode 7561
1334-3386 Moj Lijepi Vrt. Specijalno Izdanje see 1334-1448 3743
1334-3416 T V Story changed to 1845-7061 2391
1334-3432 National Geographic Hrvatska 4021
1334-417X see 0011-1643 2059
1334-4366 Acta Medico-Historica Adriatica 5567
1334-4676 see 1334-4684 3440
1334-4684 Interdisciplinary Description of Complex Systems 3440
1334-5230 see 1334-4684 3440
1334-5605 Signa Vitae 6104
1334-5966 Ogranak Matice Hrvatske Slavonski Brod. Godisnjak 4251
1334-5982 Sveuciliste u Zadru. Strueni Odjel za Izobrazbu Ueitelja i Odgojitelja Predskolske Djece. Zbornik Radova 2916
1334-6253 see 1334-4366 5567
1334-6598 Dnevnik changed to 1845-576X 3831
1334-6768 Relations 5359
1334-6857 see 1330-7193 6910
1334-7144 Moj Stan 4547
1334-7640 Men's Health 6284
1334-7799 Chica 2182
1334-8043 Bob the Builder 2179
1334-8531 National Geographic Junior 4021
1334-8671 Kvartal 502
1334-9090 see 0022-9830 3249
13346938 see 0507-1925 5054
1335-0013 Klinicka Imunologia a Alergologia 5763
1335-0102 Slovenska Archeologia 416
1335-0226 P C Revue 2580
1335-048X International Journal of Forest Genetics 3694
1335-0544 Slovak Review 5373
1335-0552 Geologica Carpathica 2737
1335-0560 Medicinska Etika a Bioetika 5675
1335-0617 Vlakna a Textil 8462
1335-0668 Organon F 6937
1335-0684 Trend 1184
1335-0838 Detsky Lekar 6091
1335-0846 Inzinierske Stavby 3273
1335-096X Slovak Geological Magazine 2716
1335-1214 Entomofauna Carpathica 941
1335-1230 A S B 425
1335-1257 Asian and African Studies 543
1335-1303 Slovensky Narodopis 355
1335-1400 Lisiak
1335-1583 Poradca 1160
1335-1710 Kritika a Kontext 5223
1335-177X Zo Sudnej Praxe 4968
1335-1788 Acta Montanistica Slovaca 2723
1335-2008 Obchod 1155
1335-2016 Strategie 1180
1335-2040 Slovensky Jazyk a Literatura v Skole 3082
1335-2180 Projekt 454
1335-2202 Slovenska Narodna Bibliografia† 8988
1335-2458 Slovenska Hudba 6617
1335-2555 Acta Technologica Agriculturae 79
1335-2563 Acta Horticulturae et Regiotecturae 3721
1335-2571 Acta Oeconomica et Informatica 191
1335-258X Acta Fytotechnica et Zootechnica 216
1335-2776 Markiza 3946
1335-2806 Slovak Academy of Sciences. Geophysical Institute. Contributions to Geophysics and Geodesy 2789
1335-2830 Acta Geologica Universitatis Comenianae 2723
1335-289X Kacer Donald (Slovak Edition) 2196
1335-2938 Strojarstvo 3220
1335-3268 Arch 428
1335-339X Slovensky Hydrometeorologicky Ustav. Meteorologicky Casopsis 6395
1335-342X Ekologia 670
1335-3535 Natura Carpatica 2713
1335-3608 Clovek a Spolocnost 8094
1335-3632 Journal of Electrical Engineering 3322
1335-3683 Slovak Journal of Animal Science 300
1335-3853 Slovgas 6793
1335-387X Profipredaj 1162
1335-4000 Quark 7901
1335-4116 Ethnologia Slovaca et Slavica 3616
1335-4140 Hudobny Zivot 6574
1335-4159 1000 Rieseni 1199
1335-4205 Komunikacie 2331
1335-4221 Prakticka Gynekologia 6002
1335-4353 Pamiatky a Muzea 4252
1335-440X Sme 3947
1335-4418 see 1335-440X 3947
1335-4426 Domino Forum changed to 1337-6772 8954
1335-4442 T H - Extra 3947
1335-4477 Zdravotnicke Noviny 7546
1335-4523 Pekne Byvanie 4548
1335-4531 Trucker (Prague) 8677
1335-4566 Korzar 3946
1335-4604 Urob si Sam 4551
1335-4620 Profit 1646
1335-4639 Rodina changed to 1336-586X 8881
1335-4655 Novy Cas 3946
1335-4671 Narodna Obroda† 8976
1335-4701 Hospodarske Noviny 1119
1335-4787 Infoware 2423
1335-5074 Etnologicke Rozpravy 338
1335-5554 Kvety a Zahrada 3741
1335-5651 Kysucke Noviny 3946
1335-5899 Entomological Problems 844
1335-5902 Moj Dom 4547
1335-6119 Ponuka Prace 1837
1335-6127 Zakony 4818
1335-6259 Slovak Foreign Policy Affairs changed to 1337-5482 7243
1335-6372 Biologia. Section Botany 779
1335-6380 Biologia. Section Zoology 936
1335-6399 Biologia. Section: Cellular and Molecular Biology 726
1335-6828 Tatry 3469
1335-6836 Rehotnik 3947
1335-7026 Kniznica 7565
1335-7034 Dane a Uctovnictvo v Praxi 1334
1335-7042 Vasarnap 3947
1335-7050 Uj Szo 3947
1335-7107 Emma 8861
1335-7522 Folia Faunistica Slovaca 944
1335-7662 P C Bazar & Mobilmania 2434
1335-7697 Svadba 5561
1335-7778 Pes a Macka 6812
1335-7972 Vyrobne Inzinierstvo 3372
1335-8049 P C Space 2434
1335-8200 H N Reality 7592
1335-8235 Investor 1633
1335-8251 Bratislava In Your Pocket 8688
1335-8286 Film.sk 6499
1335-8359 Interna Medicina 5945
1335-8367 Smer Magazin 3947
1335-8375 Nitrianske Noviny 3946
1335-8863 Building Research Journal 986
1335-8871 Measurement Science Review 5517
1335-8987 Powder Metallurgy Progress 6329
1335-9053 Materials Science and Technology 3389
1335-9061 Telemagazin 2396
1335-910X T V Oko 2393
1335-9150 Computing and Informatics 2447
1335-9444 Sestra 5981
1335-9584 Psychiatria pre Prax 6176
1335-9592 Neurologia pre Prax 6165
1335-9614 Plynar - Vodar - Kurenar & Klimatizacia 4125
1335-9630 Dane, Uctovnictvo - Vzory a Pripady 1287
1335-9843 The Slovak Spectator 5239
1335-9878 Liecive Rastliny 800
1336-0019 Krizovy Manazment 2679
1336-0043 Zilinske Noviny 3947
1336-0051 Nasa Orava 3946
1336-006X Novy Vpred Zurnal 3946
1336-0078 Liptov 3946
1336-0191 Stavebnictvo a Byvanie 1037
1336-0256 Extra Plus 3946
1336-0329 see 1210-0668 5891
1336-037X Poradca Extra. Podvojne Uctovnictvo see 1335-1583 1160
1336-0388 Poradca Extra. Jednoduche Uctovnictvo see 1335-1583 1160
1336-0396 Poradca Extra. Verejna Sprava see 1335-1583 1160
1336-040X see 0323-0465 7003
1336-0426 Diabetik 5889
1336-0612 Slovenske Lesokruhy changed to 1337-088X 3703
1336-0876 Auto Aktual 8557
1336-0965 see 1335-7026 7565
1336-0973 see 0231-6676 8884
1336-099X Aspekt 8852
1336-1066 Dobre Jedlo 4356
1336-1228 Profesia 6702
1336-1279 Art Expo 469
1336-1457 Brejk 6287
1336-1473 Gastroenterologia pre Prax 5924
1336-149X Studies of the University in Zilina. Mathematical Series 5539
1336-1996 see 1335-4701 1119
1336-2038 Auto Motor a Sport 8559
1336-2119 see 1335-7050 3947
1336-2151 see 1210-2040 3946
1336-2305 see 0001-723X 880
1336-2364 see 0037-6787 5175
1336-2372 see 1335-8049 2434
1336-2429 see 1210-0048 5794
1336-2437 Sport Magazin changed to 1337-1827 8203
1336-247X see 1210-1982 7565
1336-2615 see 0044-1953 7001
1336-2623 see 1335-4523 4548
1336-2631 see 1335-7107 8861
1336-264X see 0862-5565 3754
1336-2674 eTrend see 1335-0684 1184
1336-2712 see 1335-8286 6499
1336-2844 see 1335-2776 3946
1336-2925 Rande Extra 7943
1336-300X Acta Facultatis Ecologiae, Zvolen 3400
1336-3085 see 1336-1457 6287
1336-3107 see 1335-8235 1633
1336-314X see 1335-4655 3946
1336-3166 see 1336-1228 6702
1336-3190 Sarm 8882
1336-331X Enduro Aktual 8258
1336-3360 Svadba.sk 5561
1336-3425 Gynekologia pre Prax 5992
1336-3433 Kardiologia pre Prax 5794
1336-3654 Novy Cas pre Zeny 8878
1336-3999 see 0139-6323 8893
1336-4006 Eurotelevizia 2381
1336-4332 HoReCa 4388
1336-4375 Tuzolto 3581
1336-4529 see 1335-7522 944
1336-4561 Wood Research 3718
1336-4693 Muzeum.sk 6533
1336-4790 Via Practica 5728
1336-4871 Kompendium Mediciny 5658
1336-4928 Icko 2287
1336-4979 see 1336-3190 8882
1336-4987 see 1336-3654 8878
1336-5266 Folia Oecologica 3688
1336-5312 Vyber z Rozhodnuti Sudneho Dvora Europskych Spolocenstiev 4967
1336-5452 Acta Regionalia et Environmentalica 3400
1336-5614 Bajecna Zena 8852
1336-5622 My Ziara 3946
1336-5630 Dnesok 3946
1336-5649 Spex 5240
1336-5746 Tyzden na Pohroni 3947
1336-5754 Digi Revue 6966
1336-586X Rebecca 8881
1336-6041 Stavebne Hmoty 1037
1336-6092 Sekretariat pod Lupou 1793
1336-6556 Ostium 6937
1336-6572 Mininvazivna Chirurgia a Endoskopia, Chirurgia Sucasnosti 6252
1336-6599 Jasnovidka 566
1336-6602 Sarmantna Zena 8882
1336-6750 Ambulantna Terapia 5571
1336-6882 In 2194
1336-7102 Multimedia 2385
1336-7218 Zahranicna Politika 7275
1336-7269 Mamina 2160
1336-7277 Playboy (Slovakia) 6298
1336-7293 Lekarsky Kurier 5661
1336-7307 Partitura 5349
1336-7404 Sarmantne Dievca 2260
1336-7455 Svet Zdravia changed to 1336-8745 7001
1336-7463 Novy Cas Nedel'a 3946
1336-7579 Klinicka Urologia 6271
1336-7587 Novy Cas Special. Krizovky 8191
1336-7617 Stavebne Materialy 1037
1336-7633 Skaut Explorer (Print Edition) changed to 1336-9792 2168
1336-7668 Prakticka Prirucka pre Bezpecnostnych Technikov 6684
1336-7781 Novy Cas L'udia† 8978
1336-7803 Autotuning Autohifi changed to 1337-0987 8554
1336-782X S K A S E Journal of Theoretical Linguistics 5171
1336-7900 Auto Zurnal 8561
1336-7919 Spravca Bytovych Domov 1037
1336-796X Marketing Inspirations 1832
1336-7986 Dane, Uctovnictvo, Odvody bez Chyb, Pokut a Penale 1919
1336-8001 Geo 4007
1336-8044 Hudba 6574
1336-8109 Medical Practice 5670
1336-8133 Kremnicky Rumaj changed to 1337-0618 4238
1336-8168 Pediatria pre Prax 6099
1336-8176 Onkologia 6031
1336-8184 Familia 3946
1336-8257 Auto Filter 8558
1336-8273 InEnergoEco 1014
1336-8281 Posta, Telekomunikacie a Elektronicky Obchod 1420
1336-8346 see 1336-7668 6684
1336-8362 Osvetlenie Info 4561
1336-8370 Elektronicky Pravnik 4845
1336-8400 Aktualne Vzorove Zmluvy a Pravne Podania 4854
1336-8575 Excel v Prikladoch 2589
1336-8613 see 0049-1225 8135
1336-8621 Neurologia 6165
1336-863X Pediatria 6099
1336-8648 Rodinne Krizovky 8197
1336-8664 Ellen 8845
1336-8672 Journal of Food and Nutrition Research 6661
1336-8745 Zdravie.sk 7001
1336-8761 Euro-Atlantic Quarterly 7233
1336-8796 Euroreport Plus 1564
1336-8834 Magicke Obrazky 8186
1336-8842 Novy Cas Byvanie 8878
1336-8877 E-Poradca 1096
1336-8893 Eruditio - Educatio 2853
1336-8915 Socialna a Charitativna Sluzba 8071
1336-894X Big Interview 3946
1336-8958 Security Magazine 2516
1336-8990 Inzinierska Pedagogika 2988
1336-9059 Senior.sk 4055
1336-9067 see 1336-4928 2287
1336-9075 see 0366-6352 2054
1336-9083 see 0440-6605 945
1336-9091 Rossica Nitriensia 5365
1336-9105 Ekonomicke Spektrum 1103
1336-913X Uniform Distribution Theory 5543
1336-9148 Acta Historica Neosoliensia 4129
1336-9164 Najlepsia Gazdinka 4364
1336-9172 Ftip.sk 3946
1336-9210 Echoviny 3946
1336-9237 Slovenske Lesokruhy & Les changed to 1337-088X 3703
1336-9245 see 1335-258X 216
1336-9253 see 1336-5452 3400
1336-9261 see 1335-2571 191
1336-9318 I T Profesia 6698
1336-9369 T V Svet 2394
1336-9431 Nehnutel'nosti a Byvanie 1026
1336-944X see 1336-9431 1026
1336-9512 T V Max 2393
1336-9539 Epicure 4357
1336-9563 see 0006-3088 657
1336-9571 Forum Seniorov 4045
1336-958X Magazin 3278
1336-9628 Magicka Vestiaren 566
1336-9679 Socialna Prevencia 8071
1336-9687 Moja Kariera 6701
1336-9717 Security Revue 2680
1336-9776 Plus Jeden Den 3946
1336-9792 Skaut 2168
1336-9822 Dia Spektrum 5886
1336-9849 Manazment Skoly v Praxi 3027
1336-9865 Hlavicka 2193
1336-9903 N S C Revue 8189
1336-9911 Moderna Zena 8875
1336-9989 O Laske 8878
1337-0006 Medialne 1834
1337-0049 Istropolitan 3946
1337-012X Moj Interier 4547
1337-0138 Doprava a Logistika 1884
1337-0146 Financie
1337-0170 Pravny Kurier per Skoly 2898
1337-0197 Uctovnictvo R O P O a Obci v Praxi 1799
1337-0219 Aktualne.sk 3946
1337-0227 see 1336-9792 2168

ISSN

DIRECTORY 2010 1344-8455 9585

1342-1689 Kobe Shoin Joshi Gakuin Daigaku, Kobe Shoin Joshi Gakuin Tanki Daigaku. Gakujutsu Kenkyukai. Kenkyu Kiyo. Jinbun Kagaku, Shizen Kagaku-hen 4462
1342-1751 Clinical and Experimental Nephrology 6266
1342-176X Kanagawa-ken Suisan Sogo Kenkyujo. Kenkyu Hokoku 3600
1342-2022 Iyakuhin Fukusayo Bunken Sokuho 6851
1342-2030 Iyakuhin Fukusayo Bunken Johoshu. Shorokushu-hen 6889
1342-2049 Iyakuhin Fukusayo Bunken Johoshu. Yakkobetsu Fukusayo Ichiran-Hen 6851
1342-2154 Rinsho Koketsuatsu 5799
1342-2189 3 D Eizo 2399
1342-2308 Nihon Ongakushi Kenkyu 6599
1342-2340 Tokyo - Mitsubishi Review 1386
1342-2367 Taxa 965
1342-2510 Jozo Kenkyujo Hokoku 605
1342-2804 Research Reports on Mathematical and Computing Sciences. Series B, Operations Research 2550
1342-2812 Research Reports on Mathematical and Computing Sciences. Series C, Computer Sciences 2550
1342-3037 Gekkan Eko Indasutori 3433
1342-3053 SPring-8 Annual Report *changed to* 1347-104X 7072
1342-310X Taisekigaku Kenkyu 2770
1342-3215 Nihon Seiri Jinrui Gakkaishi 926
1342-3258 University of Osaka Prefecture. Bulletin. Series A: Engineering and Natural Sciences 3225
1342-338X Productivity Statistics 1259
1342-3428 High Performance Computing in R I K E N 2471
1342-3495 Nihon Sogai Kotei, Kotsu Encho Gakkai Zasshi 6068
1342-3681 Nihon Hansenbyo Gakkai Zasshi 5823
1342-369X France Japon Eco 1403
1342-3789 Nikkei Senior Business
1342-3800 Japan Meteorological Agency. Report of Magnetic Pulsations 2784
1342-3819 Research Reports on Information Science and Electrical Engineering 3329
1342-3967 Men'eki, Shuyo Kakuigaku†
1342-4033 N I P R Arctic Data Reports 2713
1342-4092 Gunma Museum of Natural History. Bulletin 7859
1342-4149 Kindai 6505
1342-4181 Sessile Organisms 2818
1342-422X Asia Electronics Industry 3295
1342-4327 Hozen Seitaigaku Kenkyu 2613
1342-436X Bunshi Kokyukibyo 6212
1342-4521 Bank of Japan. Price Indexes Annual 1213
1342-4580 Plant Biotechnology 810
1342-4599 Material Flow 5456
1342-4645 Wakayama Daigaku Kyoikugakubu Kiyo. Shizen Kagaku 7928
1342-4718 Seikei-geka Kango 5981
1342-4815 Biocontrol Science 656
1342-4904 Complication 5944
1342-5447 Shinkenchiku 457
1342-5552 Gunzo 5303
1342-5641 Yuriika: Shi to Hihyo 5438
1342-5668 Shisutemu Seigyo Joho Gakkai Ronbunshi 3220
1342-5684 Kenshin Jiho 2786
1342-5757 Norin Tokei Chosa 184
1342-6095 Bigaku Geijutsugaku Kenkyu 4445
1342-6133 Japanese Journal of Zoo and Wildlife Medicine 8800
1342-6230 Journal of Signal Processing 2330
1342-6311 Microbes and Environments 891
1342-6338 Helicobacter (Japanese Edition) *see* 1083-4389 887
1342-6478 J A 446
1342-6591 Heart View 5788
1342-6648 National Institute of Agro-Environmental Sciences. Annual Report *changed to* National Institute for Agro-Environmental Sciences. Annual Report 138
1342-6680 Nihon Bacharu Riariti Gakkaishi 2433
1342-6753 Nihon Shoni Rinsho Yakuri Gakkai Zasshi 6864
1342-6826 Japan Pharmaceutical Report
1342-6893 Eizou Joho Media Gakkai Gijutsu Hokoku 2319
1342-6907 Eizo Joho Media Gakkaishi 2319
1342-7016 Foreign Correspondent 2189
1342-7067 Yokufukai Chosa Kenkyu Kiyo†
1342-7121 Shimane University. Faculty of Science and Engineering. Memoirs. Series B, Mathematical Science 5535
1342-7504 Tokushu Kyoiku Kenkyu Shisetsu Kenkyusei Kenkyu Hokoku *changed to* 1346-910X 2920
1342-7709 Hyogo Kenritsu Kogyo Gijutsu Senta. Sen'i Kogyo Shidosho. Kenkyu hokoku/Technical Center for Textiles, Hyogo Prefectural Institute of Industrial Research. Reports *changed to* Hyogo Prefectural Institute of Technology. Technical Support Center for Textiles Industries. Reports 8452
1342-7776 Undo Ryoho to Butsuri Ryoho 5726
1342-7784 Higashi Nihon Seikei Saigai Geka Gakkai Zasshi 6061
1342-8047 East Asian Review 548
1342-8144 Paleontological Research 6729
1342-8284 Chromatography 2099
1342-8349 Nihon Butsuri Gakkai Koen Gaiyoshu 7028
1342-8551 Kochi Rihabiriteshon Gakuin Rigaku Ryoho Gakka Sotsugyo Kenkyu Ronbunshu 6112
1342-8616 Nihon Daigaku. Keizaigaku Kenkyukai.Kenkyu Kiyo. Ippan Kyoiku, Gaikokugo, Hoken Taiiku 2892
1342-8675 Onsei Kenkyu 5158
1342-8810 Journal of Medical and Dental Sciences 5651
1342-8853 Kwansei Gakuin University Humanities Review 4462
1342-8861 Kwansei Gakuin University Social Sciences Review 7982
1342-8993 Kanagawa-kenritsu Hakubutsukan Shiryo Mokuroku. Shizen Kagaku 7874
1342-9248 Nihon Rimpa Monaikei Gakkai Kaishi 5687
1342-9272 Shiga Daigaku Kyoiku Gakubu Kiyo. Shizen Kagaku 7915
1342-9280 Shiga Daigaku Kyoiku Gakubu Kiyo. Kyoiku Kagaku 2912
1342-9329 Nagoya City University. Institute of Natural Sciences. Annual Review (Year) 7885
1342-937X Gondwana Research 2709
1342-9574 National Science Museum Monographs 7887
1342-9590 Josai University. Science Bulletin. Special Issue *changed to* 1344-7777 5499
1342-9612 Nihon Suimon Kagaku Kaishi 2797
1342-9825 Kensa Gijutsu 3207
1342-9892 Shinryo Naika 6185
1342-999X Chikyu Kankyo 3410
1343-0068 Chuo Daigaku Rikogaku Kenkyujo Ronbunshu 7846
1343-0130 Journal of Advanced Computational Intelligence and Intelligent Informatics 2548
1343-0254 Sentairui Kenkyu 816
1343-0289 Miruku Saiensu 267
1343-0297 University of Tokyo. Institute for Solid State Physics. Neutron Scattering Laboratory. Activity Report on Neutron Scattering Research 7073
1343-0637 Wakayama University. Faculty of Economics. Annals 1193
1343-0742 Kokuritsu Shakai Hosho, Jinko Mondai Kenkyujo Nenpo 7286
1343-0823 J I M S T E F News 2808
1343-0831 Derma 5874
1343-084X Nihonkai Chiiki no Shizen to Kankyo 3456
1343-0874 Plankton Biology and Ecology *changed to* 1880-8247 2816
1343-0874 Plankton Biology and Ecology 697
1343-0882 Chonai Saikingaku Zasshi 784
1343-0920 Sapporo Ika Daigaku Igakubu Jinbun Shizen Kagaku Kiyo 4474
1343-0955 Ibaraki University. Natural History Bulletin 7864
1343-0971 Idenshi Igaku 872
1343-1196 Nipponia 3900
1343-1420 Journal of Medical Investigation 5907
1343-1633 Niigata Daigaku Rigakubu Fuzoku Sado Rinkai Jikkenjo Kenkyu Hokoku 694
1343-1846 Eizou Joho Media Gakkai Nenji Taikai Koen Yokoshu 2319
1343-2036 The Circulation Frontier 5782
1343-2060 Tokyo Les Nouvelles Municipales *see* 0916-7951 7504
1343-2079 Tokyoto News *see* 0916-7951 7504
1343-2443 Soki Daichogan 6034
1343-2583 Juiekigaku Zasshi 8802
1343-2745 Nihon Daigaku Bunrigakubu Shizen Kagaku Kenkyujo Kenkyu Kiyo. Chikyu System Kagaku 2714
1343-2761 Seishin Kango 6184
1343-2826 Kitakanto Medical Journal 5658
1343-3490 Nihon Kokyuki Gakkai Zasshi 6217
1343-3547 *see* K E K News 7023
1343-3563 Genshiryoku Eye 3167
1343-3636 Ibaraki University. Mathematical Journal 5492
1343-3644 Shimane Daigaku Seibutsu Shigen Kagakubu Kenkyu Hokoku 3466
1343-3873 Hokkaido Seikei Saigai Geka Gakkai Zasshi 6061
1343-3881 Dekomisshoningu Giho 3166
1343-3946 Kyoto Furitsu Daigaku Gakujutsu Hokoku. Jimbun Shakai 4462
1343-3954 Kyoto Furitsu Daigaku Gakujutsu Hokoku. Ningen Kankyogaku, Nogaku/Kyoto Prefectural University. Scientific Reports: Agriculture *changed to* 1882-6946 3449
1343-4144 No no Kagaku 6864
1343-4152 Mammal Study 954
1343-4179 Gunma Hokengaku Kiyo 5621
1343-4284 Antarctic Meteorite Research *changed to* 1873-9652 2715
1343-4292 Kokuritsu Iyakuhin Shokuhin Eisei Kenkyujo Hokoku 7530
1343-4330 S E I Tekunikaru Rebyu 3330
1343-4349 S E I Technical Review 3329
1343-4373 Advances in Mathematical Sciences and Applications
1343-4446 Genshiryoku Bakku Endo Kenkyu 3167
1343-4500 Information 7865
1343-4535 Theoretical and Applied Lingusitics at Kobe Shoin 5187
1343-4594 Shishitsu Eiyougaku 6669
1343-4608 Furuido Pawa Shisutemu/Japan Hydraulics Pneumatics Society. Journal *changed to* 1346-7719 3361
1343-4934 Journal of Oral Science 5852
1343-4969 Jishin, Kazan Geppo. Katarogu-hen (Print) *changed to* 1349-8320 2784
1343-4977 Jishin, Kazan Geppo. Bosai-hen 2784
1343-5566 Ryutsu Netto Wakingu 1841
1343-7674 Yuki 3227
1343-7844 Shoku ni Kansuru Josei Kenkyu Chosa Hokokusho 6669
1343-828X Saitama Daigaku Kyoikugakubu Chikyu Kagaku Kansoku Jikkenshitsu Kenkyu Hokoku 2716
1343-8492 Dynamis: Language and Culture 5113
1343-8530 Gengo to Bunka (Nishinomiya) 5121
1343-8565 Maikuromekatoronikusu 2572
1343-8670 Kyushu Institute of Technology. Bulletin: Pure & Applied Mathematics 5508
1343-8719 Tokyo Kogyo Daigaku Seimitsu Kogaku Kenkyujo Yoran 5460
1343-8743 Tokyo Metropolitan University. Graduate School of Engineering. Memoirs 3223
1343-8786 Entomological Science 845
1343-8794 Japanese Journal of Entomology. New Series 851
1343-8808 Global Environmental Research 3434
1343-8832 Earth, Planets and Space 2706
1343-8875 Journal of Visualization 7060
1343-8921 Ibaraki-ken Shizen Hakubutsukan Kenkyu Hokoku 6525
1343-8964 R I S T News 7901
1343-9006 Asia - Pacific Review 7222
1343-9294 Haigan no Rinsho/Japanese Journal of Lung Cancer Clinics *changed to* Mook: Haigan no Rinsho 6028
1343-9383 Hypertension Frontier 5789
1343-943X Plant Production Science 812
1343-9502 Food Style 21 3642
1343-9529 Matsushita Technical Journal 3325
1343-9677 Erekutoronikusu Jisso Gakkaishi 6709
1343-9693 Nihon Yougo Kyouyu Kyouiku Gakkaishi 3044
1343-9936 Shokubai Toronkai, Toronkai A Yokoshu 2141
1343-9944 Nippon Dental University. Journal†
13436589 Japan Research Review *changed to* 1880-3482 1070
1344-008X Ryukyu Mathematical Journal 5531
1344-011X Nihon Bacharu Riariti Gakkai Ronbunshi 2432
1344-0241 Orthodontic Waves 5860
1344-0306 Akamata†
1344-0446 Nihon Tokei Kyokai. Sekai No Tokei (Year) 8391
1344-0616 Shakai to Rinri 6951
1344-0640 I P S J Symposium Series 2536
1344-1051 Chromosome Science 830
1344-1256 Okinawa Kenritsu Chubu Byoin Zasshi 5689
1344-1272 Japanese Physical Therapy Association. Journal 6110
1344-1299 K E K High Energy Accelerator Research Organization. Annual Report 7023
1344-1418 Gengo Bunka 5121
1344-168X Kita Nihon Kango Gakkaishi 5968
1344-1698 Resource Geology 2764
1344-1817 Tenri Igaku Kiyo 5721
1344-1922 Sei Roka Kango Gakkaishi 5981
1344-2139 Hirosaki University. Faculty of Science and Technology. Bulletin 7861
1344-2554 Hokkaido Kyoiku Daigaku Kiyo. Kyoiku Kagaku-Hen 2864
1344-2562 Hokkaido Kyoiku Daigaku Kiyo. Jimbun Kagaku, Shakai Kagaku-Hen 4455
1344-2570 Hokkaido Kyoiku Daigaku Kiyo. Shizen Kagaku-hen 7862
1344-2929 University of Tokyo. School of Engineering. Journal 3225
1344-2988 Steel Today and Tomorrow†
1344-3062 Kaigai Shakai Hosho Kenkyu 4511
1344-316X Radiology Frontier 6207
1344-3194 Polar Geoscience *changed to* 1873-9652 2715
1344-3399 Shokaki Gazo 6208
1344-3437 Polar Meteorology and Glaciology *changed to* 1873-9652 2715
1344-3542 Electrochemistry 2113
1344-3631 Saikuru†
1344-3755 Oyo Seitai Kogaku 3459
1344-3879 R I K E N - A F - N P 7071
1344-3909 Shakai Gengo Kagaku 5173
1344-3941 Animal Science Journal 278
1344-3992 Anthropological Science. Japanese Series 326
1344-4050 Daizu Tampakushitsu Kenkyu 6657
1344-4174 Shinrin Kenkyu 3702
1344-4239 Saikuru Kiko Giho†
1344-4271 K D D R & D Report†
1344-4425 Nihon Gazo Gakkaishi 6971
1344-4468 Kogakkan Daigaku Bungakubu Kiyo 5318
1344-4611 Yokohama Kokuritsu Daigaku Kyoiku Ningen Kagakubu Kiyo. I, Kyoiku Kagaku 2927
1344-462X Yokohama Kokuritsu Daigaku Kyoiku Ningen Kagakubu Kiyo. II, Jimbun Kagaku 4483
1344-4638 Yokohama Kokuritsu Daigaku Kyoiku Ningen Kagakubu Kiyo. III, Shakai Kagaku 8017
1344-4646 Yokohama Kokuritsu Daigaku Kyoiku Ningen Kagakubu Kiyo. IV, Shizen Kagaku 7932
1344-4697 Denshi Jouhou Tsuushin Gakkai Rombunshi. B 2318
1344-4743 Adikushon to Kazoku 2690
1344-4751 P C World Japan 2581
1344-4786 Gekkan Medikaru & Fain
1344-4867 Tokyo Toritsu Sangyo Gijutsu Kenkyujo Kenkyu Hokoku 8443
1344-4891 Nihon P D A Gakujutsushi GMP to Barideshon 6864
1344-4905 Nihon Reito Kucho Gakkai Rombunshu 4124
1344-4964 The Japanese Journal of Thoracic and Cardiovascular Surgery *changed to* 1863-6705 6244
1344-4980 Jomyaku, Keicho Eiyo 6661
1344-5871 Nisseki Mitsubishi Rebyu 6781
1344-6223 Legal Medicine 5915
1344-6231 Polar Bioscience *changed to* 1873-9652 2715
1344-6304 Japanese Journal of Infectious Diseases 5643
1344-6320 Photon Factory Activity Report. Part A. High Lights and Facility Report 7030
1344-6339 Photon Factory Activity Report. Part B. Users' Report 7030
1344-6401 Toyama Daigaku Kyouikugakubu Kenkyuroshu 2920
1344-641X Toyama Daigaku Kyouikugakubu Kiyo 2920
1344-6460 Nihon Koku Uchu Gakkai Rombunshu 67
1344-6495 Jitsumu Tembo *changed to* 1880-7283 5450
1344-6541 Nihon Yakkyokuho Foramu 6864
1344-6606 Food Science and Technology Research 3642
1344-6703 Nihon Naishikyo Geka Gakkai Zasshi 6253
1344-672X Ochanomizu Ongaku Ronshu 6600
1344-6835 Annals of Cancer Research and Therapy 6008
1344-6924 Seitaibunsi Kaiseki Kenkyu Senta Dayori 745
1344-6932 Arerugi, Men'eki 5754
1344-6940 Ketsueki Furontia 5939
1344-7084 Kyoryo & Toshi Project 3277
1344-722X C D N L A O Newsletter (Online Edition) 4999
1344-7238 National Diet Library. Newsletter 5034
1344-7297 Japan Mission Journal 7652
1344-753X Bunsoku. Energi, Genshiryoku Kogaku-Hen 3228
1344-7556 Sake, Masu Shigen Kanri Senta Kenkyu Hokoku 3607
1344-7610 Breeding Science 97
1344-7629 Ikushugaku Kenkyu 677
1344-7645 Rikkyo Daigaku Genshiryoku Kenkyujo Genshiro Riyo Jisseki Hokoku 3174
1344-7653 J S M E International Journal. Series C, Mechanical Systems, Machine Elements and Manufacturing 3384
1344-770X Journal of Economics, Business and Law 1135
1344-7777 Josai Mathematical Monographs 5499
1344-7882 Journal of Applied Glycoscience 3649
1344-7904 Shinseiki 7182
1344-7912 J S M E International Journal. Series A: Solid Mechanics and Material Engineering 3384
1344-8013 Ningen Bunka Ronso 4467
1344-8293 Ganka Kea 6042
1344-8404 Kaigo Shien Semmon'in 5968
1344-8412 Biburosu (Online) 4997
1344-8439 Global Outsourcing Review 5620
1344-8455 Kansai University Review of Business and Commerce 1430

ISSN

ISSN

DIRECTORY 2010 1351-8836 9589

1350-9438 Family Law Directory†
1350-9446 Family Law Tax Guide†
1350-9462 Progress in Retinal and Eye Research **6050**
1350-9497 The Fitzhugh Directory of N H S Trusts. Financial Information†
1350-9500 B C I S Guide to House Rebuilding Costs **977**
1350-956X Mini Micro Systems†
1350-9624 B B C Top Gear **8568**
1350-9667 Audio Journal of Oncology **6009**
1350-9683 The Countryman's Weekly **8310**
1350-9713 Journal of Orthotics and Prosthetics **5853**
1350-9756 Family Mediation **8040**
1350-9829 PrintWeek **7327**
1350-9837 Grasslands and Forage Abstracts **181**
1350-9845 Best Practice Report Series†
1350-9853 Organizational Excellence Newsletter†
1350-9888 Cabling World *changed to* 0013-4414 **3304**
1350-9896 Royal College of Psychiatrists. Psychotherapy Section. Behavioural Cognitive Bulletin†
1350-990X E L SNews **2447**
1350-9942 Social Attitudes in Northern Ireland **4264**
1350-9969 Packaging Technology International (Year)†
1351-0002 Redox Report (Print)†
1351-0029 Sports, Exercise and Injury†
1351-007X Counselling at Work **7349**
1351-0088 Endocrine - Related Cancer **5891**
1351-010X Building Acoustics **7087**
1351-0126 Journal of Psychiatric and Mental Health Nursing **6156**
1351-0142 Cycling Today **8257**
1351-0193 Mojo **6588**
1351-0207 Your Complete Guide to Pregnancy & Birth **8849**
1351-0223 Emile Zola Society. Bulletin **5289**
1351-024X Language Forum†
1351-0304 Pingu **2207**
1351-0347 Democratization **7230**
1351-0355 Dialogos†
1351-0371 Education in Russia, the Independent States and Eastern Europe **2848**
1351-0487 Constellations **7119**
1351-0495 Arab - British Trade **1395**
1351-0525 Surface World *changed to* 1743-4033 **2106**
1351-0541 Alcoholism *changed to* 1752-4725 **2691**
1351-055X Employee Development Bulletin **1860**
1351-0592 Gloucestershire & Avon Life
1351-0614 Personnel Assistant's Handbook Bulletin **1872**
1351-0657 R S S News **8395**
1351-0711 Occupational and Environmental Medicine **6682**
1351-072X Production Pharmafile *changed to* Supply Chain Pharmafile **6882**
1351-0746 International Property **7596**
1351-0754 European Journal of Soil Science **229**
1351-0762 European Baker **3673**
1351-0819 Business Tax Planning
1351-086X Reportback† **8985**
1351-0878 Liverpool Studies in Language and Discourse†
1351-0886 Journal of Intellectual Disability Research. Supplement *see* 0964-2633 **6152**
1351-0894 Management Consultants News **1775**
1351-0924 Management Consultancy **1775**
1351-0959 Consensus Forecasts - U S A **1883**
1351-0967 Asia Pacific Consensus Forcasts **1437**
1351-0983 Foreign Exchange Consensus Forecasts **1348**
1351-1009 Justis Celex **4823**
1351-1114 Electronic Author†
1351-1203 Classic Car Mart **8574**
1351-1211 Jane's Transport Finance **1359**
1351-122X Dinosaurs!
1351-1297 European Journal of Clinical Hypnosis **5943**
1351-1386 Environmental Sensors†
1351-1491 Environmental Issues Newsletter†
1351-1599 European Railway Review **8617**
1351-1610 Innovation (Abingdon) **7972**
1351-1637 U S A and Europe in Business **1585**
1351-1645 Scottish Drama **8478**
1351-1653 Peace & Freedom (Spalding) **5350**
1351-1696 Colourama **308**
1351-170X Restitution Law Review **4879**
1351-1718 Stubbs Gazette. Northern Ireland (Print) *changed to* 1756-9214 **1795**
1351-1742 Land Rover Owner International **8588**
1351-1890 The Musgrave Papers **5414**
1351-2013 Radio Times (Yorkshire/Tyne Tees Edition) *changed to* 1754-8667 **2388**
1351-2021 Gainsborough's House Review **490**
1351-2145 Employment Policy Institute Economic Report
1351-2447 Black Country Bugle Annual **3615**
1351-251X D P A News **1983**
1351-2625 Batman - Judge Dredd **2178**
1351-2676 Young Archaeologist **424**
1351-2684 Leicestershire Now!
1351-2714 Puzzle Selection **4344**
1351-2781 Property News Midlands **7605**
1351-301X Tanker News†
1351-3095 English Place-Name Society. Journal **4005**
1351-3109 Future and the Inventor **6750**
1351-3117 School Library 2000†
1351-3133 Snacks Magazine **3681**
1351-3176 O E Report and Fibre News **8456**
1351-3214 Cellular Pharmacology†
1351-3222 Document Manager **2535**
1351-3249 Natural Language Engineering **2509**
1351-3362 The Bunker News Directory of International Bunker Suppliers, Traders & Brokers **1553**
1351-3397 Live and Kicking *changed to* 1476-5225
1351-346X International Pesticide Directory **237**
1351-3478 Shephard's Unmanned Vehicles Handbook **70**
1351-3540 P C Gamer **2479**
1351-3591 Second Shift† **8987**
1351-3621 Economic & Financial Review **1099**
1351-3680 Business & Technology Magazine **1413**
1351-3702 Clinica Factbook *see* 0144-7777 **5595**
1351-3737 Tate (London) *changed to* 1743-8853 **521**
1351-3818 Irish Journal of American Studies **5130**
1351-3877 Coach & Bus Week **8493**
1351-3885 Target Europe. Case Studies Newsletter†
1351-3893 Video Home Entertainment **2403**
1351-3915 Who Owns Who in Mining **6483**
1351-3958 Asian Economic Journal **1535**
1351-4091 Studies in Modern Languages Education **3083**
1351-4105 The Living Tradition **6585**
1351-4113 Information U K Outlooks†
1351-4121 Photo Technique†
1351-4180 Focus on Catalysts **2094**
1351-4199 Focus on Paper Chemicals†
1351-4202 Focus on Solvents
1351-4210 Focus on Surfactants **2094**
1351-4261 Bridge Magazine **8163**
1351-427X New Telecom Networks†
1351-4288 Social Housing **4427**
1351-4385 Joseph Rowntree Foundation. Briefings **8048**
1351-4407 Airfinance Journal Business Handbook *see* 0143-2257 **8535**
1351-4504 Labour Market Bulletin **1248**
1351-4512 Institute of Engineers & Technicians Journal†
1351-4520 Brazil Business Brief **8688**
1351-4555 Incentive Today (London, 1993) *changed to* 1752-766X **1820**
1351-4571 Americas Review **1436**
1351-458X Asia & Pacific Review **1437**
1351-4598 Institute of Public Relations. Handbook (Year) **27**
1351-4601 Export Handbook (Year) **1402**
1351-4636 All U.K. Agents Handbook (Year)†
1351-4660 School Management Handbook (Year) **3032**
1351-4709 New Arabian Studies **4324**
1351-4717 Middle East Review **1499**
1351-4725 World Business and Economic Review†
1351-4733 Wanderlust **8773**
1351-4768 Watching and Waiting **7779**
1351-4784 World Telecom Daily
1351-4792 Workers' Health International Newsletter **6689**
1351-4822 Franchise Networks **8581**
1351-5047 Antiques Fairs Guide **363**
1351-5101 European Journal of Neurology **6139**
1351-5136 Chemistry Factsheets **2057**
1351-5195 F X & M M **1341**
1351-5217 The Zone **5449**
1351-525X Nitric Oxide
1351-5268 Activin and Inhibin†
1351-5276 Eating Disorders†
1351-5284 Helicobacter (Sheffield)
1351-5292 Mycobacteria
1351-5306 Catecholamines and Adrenergic Receptors
1351-5314 Cell Contact and Communication†
1351-5322 Lysosomes and Endocytosis
1351-5330 Oxytocin and Vasopressin†
1351-5349 Scottish Episcopal Church Review **7774**
1351-5373 *see* 1355-2384 **2579**
1351-542X International Human Rights Reports **7210**
1351-5500 Client Server News **2496**
1351-5535 The U K Tourist: Statistics (Year) **8781**
1351-5543 Banking Automation Bulletin for Europe *changed to* 1748-5304 **1317**
1351-5551 Juke Blues **6581**
1351-5578 Nurse Researcher **5972**
1351-5586 Social Services Research **8070**
1351-5608 New Zealand Concise Stamp Catalogue†
1351-5667 British Association for Canadian Studies. Newsletter **7951**
1351-5691 Hollis Sponsorship & Donations Yearbook **26**
1351-5896 Which Business CD-ROM†
1351-590X Synchro World
1351-5993 European Law Journal **4925**
1351-6027 Lines of Communication†
1351-6043 Seafood Processing & Packaging International *see* 0268-1293 **3607**
1351-6140 Marketeer
1351-6183 Parliamentary Monitor **7459**
1351-6272 Celtic Connections Magazine **532**
1351-6337 Pharmaceutical Science Communications†
1351-6345 Medical Law Monitor **4731**
1351-6361 Coal in the U.K.†
1351-6388 Green†
1351-640X Dream World Cruise Destinations **8642**
1351-6442 Fighting Back†
1351-6477 Sew Today **6642**
1351-6515 Mobile and Cellular Magazine
1351-6531 Development. Supplement *see* 0950-1991 **668**
1351-6566 British Society for Plant Growth Regulation. Monographs **223**
1351-6620 The European Journal **7134**
1351-6647 European Journal of Oriental Medicine **309**
1351-668X Facilities Management **1851**
1351-6736 British Journal of Optometry and Dispensing†
1351-6752 Country Risk Service. Algeria **1471**
1351-6760 Country Risk Service. Angola **1471**
1351-6779 Country Risk Service. Argentina **1471**
1351-6787 Country Risk Service. Australia **1471**
1351-6809 Country Risk Service. Bangladesh **1471**
1351-6817 Country Risk Service. Bolivia **1471**
1351-6825 Country Risk Service. Brazil **1471**
1351-6833 Country Risk Service. Bulgaria **1471**
1351-6841 Country Risk Service. Cameroon **1471**
1351-685X Country Risk Service. Chile **1471**
1351-6868 Country Risk Service. China **1471**
1351-6876 Country Risk Service. Colombia **1471**
1351-6884 Country Risk Service. Congo **1472**
1351-6892 Country Risk Service. Costa Rica **1472**
1351-6906 Country Risk Service. Cote d'Ivoire **1472**
1351-6914 Country Risk Service. Cyprus **1472**
1351-6922 Country Risk Service. Czech Republic **1472**
1351-6930 Country Risk Service. Dominican Republic **1472**
1351-6949 Country Risk Service. Ecuador **1472**
1351-6957 Country Risk Service. Egypt **1472**
1351-6965 Country Risk Service. El Salvador **1472**
1351-6973 Country Risk Service. Gabon **1472**
1351-6981 Country Risk Service. Ghana **1472**
1351-699X Country Risk Service. Greece **1472**
1351-7007 Country Risk Service. Guatemala **1472**
1351-7015 Country Risk Service. Honduras **1472**
1351-7023 Country Risk Service. Hong Kong **1472**
1351-7031 Country Risk Service. Hungary **1472**
1351-704X Country Risk Service. India **1472**
1351-7058 Country Risk Service. Indonesia **1472**
1351-7066 Country Risk Service. Iran **1472**
1351-7074 Country Risk Service. Iraq **1473**
1351-7082 Country Risk Service. Israel **1473**
1351-7090 Country Risk Service. Jamaica **1473**
1351-7104 Country Risk Service. Jordan **1473**
1351-7112 Country Risk Service. Kazakhstan **1473**
1351-7120 Country Risk Service. Kenya **1473**
1351-7139 Country Risk Service. Kuwait **1473**
1351-7147 Country Risk Service. Libya **1473**
1351-7155 Country Risk Service. Malawi **1473**
1351-7163 Country Risk Service. Malaysia **1473**
1351-7171 Country Risk Service. Mexico **1473**
1351-718X Country Risk Service. Morocco **1473**
1351-7198 Country Risk Service. Namibia **1473**
1351-7201 Country Risk Service. New Zealand **1473**
1351-721X Country Risk Service. Nicaragua **1473**
1351-7228 Country Risk Service. Nigeria **1473**
1351-7236 Country Risk Service. Pakistan **1474**
1351-7244 Country Risk Service. Panama **1474**
1351-7252 Country Risk Service. Papua New Guinea **1474**
1351-7260 Country Risk Service. Paraguay **1474**
1351-7279 Country Risk Service. Peru **1474**
1351-7287 Country Risk Service. Philippines **1474**
1351-7295 Country Risk Service. Poland **1474**
1351-7309 Country Risk Service. Portugal **1474**
1351-7317 Country Risk Service. Romania **1474**
1351-7325 Country Risk Service. Russia **1474**
1351-7333 Country Risk Service. Saudi Arabia **1474**
1351-7341 Country Risk Service. Senegal **1474**
1351-735X Country Risk Service. Singapore **1474**
1351-7368 Country Risk Service. Slovenia **1474**
1351-7376 Country Risk Service. South Africa **1474**
1351-7384 Country Risk Service. South Korea **1474**
1351-7392 Country Risk Service. Spain **1474**
1351-7406 Country Risk Service. Sri Lanka **1474**
1351-7414 Country Risk Service. Sudan **1475**
1351-7422 Country Risk Service. Syria **1475**
1351-7430 Country Risk Service. Taiwan **1475**
1351-7449 Country Risk Service. Thailand **1475**
1351-7457 Country Risk Service. Trinidad and Tobago **1475**
1351-7465 Country Risk Service. Tunisia **1475**
1351-7473 Country Risk Service. Turkey **1475**
1351-7481 Country Risk Service. Ukraine **1475**
1351-749X Country Risk Service. United Arab Emirates **1475**
1351-7503 Country Risk Service. Uruguay **1475**
1351-7511 Country Risk Service. Venezuela **1475**
1351-752X Country Risk Service. Yemen **1475**
1351-7546 Country Risk Service. Zaire **1475**
1351-7554 Country Risk Service. Zambia **1475**
1351-7562 Country Risk Service. Zimbabwe **1475**
1351-7570 Education Law Reports **4663**
1351-7597 Spotlight on Presenters **8479**
1351-7716 Timber Trades Address Book. Shipping Marks - Softwood†
1351-7791 Swimming Pool News **1039**
1351-7848 International Journal of Vehicle Design. Heavy Vehicle Systems *changed to* 1744-232X **8499**
1351-7937 European Economic Perspectives **1541**
1351-7945 Catholic Times **7790**
1351-802X North Sea Rig Forecast **3143**
1351-8046 The Journal of Slavic Military Studies **6429**
1351-8062 Currency Manager
1351-8070 Ethnic Minorities Directory **3532**
1351-8097 Hobsons I T Casebook **1887**
1351-8143 Fireplace Yearbook *changed to* Essential Fireplace Book **4539**
1351-8178 C A S A F A Report Series
1351-8186 Tourism Marketplace†
1351-8216 Haemophilia **5937**
1351-8275 European Book World **7560**
1351-8305 Country and Distance Rider **8289**
1351-8313 Land Rover World **8588**
1351-833X Race Walking Record **8330**
1351-8348 Business Travel World **8689**
1351-8372 The Journal of Dementia Care **6151**
1351-8402 The Diplomate†
1351-8429 North American Register†
1351-8453 Furthering Education
1351-847X The European Journal of Finance **1339**
1351-8488 Tumor Targeting†
1351-8518 Justis CD-ROM Official Journal. C Series **4934**
1351-8534 JUSTIS Weekly Law Reports *see* 0019-3518 **4811**
1351-8542 International Journal of Insurance Law†
1351-8569 Oasis **1602**
1351-8615 New Impact **6701**
1351-864X N S P C C News **8056**
1351-8704 Country Forecast. New Zealand **7122**
1351-8712 Country Forecast. Czech Republic **7120**
1351-8720 Country Forecast. Russia **7122**
1351-8747 Country Profile. Madagascar† **8945**
1351-8763 Business Eastern Europe **1444**
1351-878X East European Industrial Monitoring Service. Agriculture and Food†
1351-8798 East European Industrial Monitoring Service. Automotive and Transport†
1351-8801 East European Industrial Monitoring Service. Chemical Industry†
1351-881X East European Industrial Monitoring Service. Construction†
1351-8828 East European Industrial Monitoring Service. Consumer Goods†
1351-8836 East European Industrial Monitoring Service. Drinks and Tobacco†

ISSN

ISSN

ISSN

1359-835X Composites Part A: Applied Science and Manufacturing **3342**
1359-8368 Composites Part B: Engineering **3185**
1359-8384 Current Medical Literature. Epilepsy Monitor†
1359-8392 Current Medical Literature. Focus on Intravenous Anaesthesia†
1359-8414 Stroke Review†
1359-8422 Current Medical Literature. Anaesthesiology - Peer Selected Citations†
1359-8449 Current Medical Literature. Infectious Diseases - Peer Selected Citations†
1359-8457 Current Medical Literature. Neurology & Neurosurgery - Peer Selected Citations†
1359-8465 Current Medical Literature. Psychiatry - Peer Selected Citations†
1359-8473 Current Medical Literature. The Year in Heart Failure†
1359-8481 Current Medical Literature. The Year in Hypertension†
1359-8511 O P C S Monitor. MB1: Registrations of Cancer Diagnosed in ... England & Wales
1359-852X Franchising Research *changed to* 0736-3761 **1823**
1359-8546 Supply Chain Management **1796**
1359-8554 Virtual Prototyping Journal†
1359-8570 Tetrahedron Alert†
1359-866X Asia - Pacific Journal of Teacher Education **3051**
1359-8678 Nonlinear Studies **5521**
1359-8716 Current Medical Literature. Kardiologie *see* 1354-0122 **5784**
1359-8724 Current Medical Literature. Cardiologia *see* 1354-0122 **5784**
1359-8929 Art East **469**
1359-9011 Current Medical Literature. Psychiatrie (German Edition) *see* 0957-770X **6134**
1359-9011 Current Medical Literature. Psychiatrie (German Edition) *see* 1507-7535
1359-9046 Statistics of Education. Schools in England **2936**
1359-9054 New Zealand Intellectual Property Journal **6755**
1359-9089 Community and Organisational Psychology Research Group. Occasional Papers **7348**
1359-9127 Croner's Employment Case Law Index **1674**
1359-9151 London School of Economics and Political Science, Financial Markets Group. Special Paper **1366**
1359-9178 Goodtimes **4978**
1359-9224 International Healthcare News†
1359-9291 Sudan Democratic Gazette **7187**
1359-9313 Safety Express **6686**
1359-9364 Occupational Ergonomics **6682**
1359-9372 Technology, Law and Insurance†
1359-9380 Young Writer **2223**
1359-9461 Family History Monthly **3765**
1359-9488 Pregnancy Plus†
1359-9496 Golf Owners, Operators and Developers Directory **8232**
1359-9755 Multi-Skills†
1359-978X Computers in Africa *changed to* 1746-1510 **2415**
1360-0095 International Management†
1360-0168 Medicine On-Line **5674**
1360-0176 Family Medical Practice On-Line **5613**
1360-0257 The Annual Practice† **8930**
1360-032X Key Note Market Review: Retailing in the U K†
1360-0419 The British Rifleman **8163**
1360-0443 *see* 0965-2140 **2689**
1360-0451 *see* 0954-0121 **5807**
1360-046X *see* 0268-8697 **6238**
1360-0478 *see* 0958-3157 **221**
1360-0486 *see* 0305-0068 **2838**
1360-0494 *see* 0954-0091 **2447**
1360-0508 *see* 0968-7599 **4077**
1360-0516 *see* 0954-0253 **2859**
1360-0524 *see* 0966-369X **8898**
1360-0532 *see* 0266-4763 **8382**
1360-0540 *see* 0260-7476 **2875**
1360-0559 *see* 0964-0568 **3446**
1360-0567 *see* 0963-8237 **6152**
1360-0583 *see* 0269-7459 **4423**
1360-0591 *see* 0034-3404 **4425**
1360-063X *see* 0042-0980 **4430**
1360-0648 *see* 0790-0627 **8826**
1360-0699 Workbox **6643**
1360-0729 Current Affairs†
1360-0737 Research Report - Transport Research Laboratory†
1360-0745 Natural History Museum. Biennial Report for Science†
1360-0796 Journal of Applied Management Studies†
1360-080X Journal of Higher Education Policy and Management **2990**
1360-0818 Oxford Development Studies **1603**
1360-0826 Global Society **7238**
1360-0834 Information and Communications Technology Law **2325**
1360-0869 International Review of Law, Computers & Technology **4845**
1360-0885 Isis Cumulative Bibliography†
1360-0923 Brushstrokes **545**
1360-0958 Fashion Index **2254**
1360-0982 Index Islamicus **3574**
1360-1083 Moving Pictures Television **6508**
1360-1105 International History of Nursing Journal†
1360-1164 Biodiversity News **656**
1360-1245 Plastics and Rubber Asia **7096**
1360-127X Journal of Semitic Studies. Monograph *see* 0022-4480 **5135**
1360-1326 Web Journal of Current Legal Issues **4811**
1360-1334 Redland Papers *changed to* 1754-1204 **2891**
1360-1369 Network Briefing **2370**
1360-1385 Trends in Plant Science **820**
1360-1431 Journal of Design & Technology Education **3067**
1360-144X International Journal for Academic Development **2868**
1360-1504 Flour Milling and Baking Abstracts *changed to* 1751-973X **179**
1360-1539 Standards and Technology Update **3396**
1360-1563 Pan **6604**
1360-1644 Asia Environmental Review **3404**
1360-1652 Legal Semiotics Monographs **4720**
1360-1679 Aerospace Review **43**
1360-1733 Harpers Dispatches†
1360-1741 Living Earth **241**
1360-175X Lloyd's Inactive Vessels†
1360-1784 Infrastructure in the U K **1429**
1360-1792 Medical Interface†
1360-1830 Public Sector Procurement and Finance†
1360-1865 Key Note Market Review: U K D I Y & Home Improvements *changed to* 1478-8535 **4536**
1360-1881 Key Note Market Report: Broadcasting in the U K *changed to* Key Note Market Report: Digital Broadcasting **1894**
1360-192X Travel Retailer International Yearbook *see* 1357-3489 **1846**
1360-1938 Today's Emergency **6074**
1360-1954 Interactive **2949**
1360-1962 Vet On-Line **8810**
1360-1997 V - T V†
1360-2004 Journal of Muslim Minority Affairs **7713**
1360-2020 Labour Studies Working Papers **1695**
1360-208X Animation UK *changed to* 1755-0718 **6503**
1360-2098 Railway Bylines **8623**
1360-2187 Justis Family Law *see* 0261-4375 **4910**
1360-2241 *see* 0143-6597 **1606**
1360-2276 Tropical Medicine & International Health **5827**
1360-2322 Journal of Applied Research in Intellectual Disabilities **6149**
1360-2357 Education and Information Technologies **3059**
1360-2365 The Journal of Architecture **447**
1360-2381 Asia Pacific Business Review **1061**
1360-2438 Discussion Paper in Economics **1092**
1360-2659 Quick and Easy Cross Stitch *changed to* 1753-2213 **6641**
1360-2772 Sunday Life **3871**
1360-2861 Sounds Great! **6618**
1360-3051 One Up **7667**
1360-306X Intensive Care Monitor **5636**
1360-3086 David Hall's Advanced Carp Fishing **8310**
1360-3108 Perspectives (London, 1997) **2997**
1360-3116 International Journal of Inclusive Education **2870**
1360-3124 International Journal of Leadership in Education **2870**
1360-3132 Civil Service Pensioner **4043**
1360-3140 ManuScript **5330**
1360-3175 PlayStation Plus†
1360-3183 Beautiful Stitches†
1360-323X Link (London, 1966) **4067**
1360-3450 New Buckinghamshire Countryside **3869**
1360-3485 V R News **2490**
1360-3507 Ride **8267**
1360-3566 Construction Manager **997**
1360-3701 Hair & Beauty **588**
1360-3728 Naturally Speaking **2621**
1360-3736 International Journal of Training & Development **1867**
1360-3876 Transgressions **4428**
1360-3930 P A W 2 - Asia Pacific†
1360-399X E E C S Newsletter† **8952**
1360-4074 Power in Latin America **3160**
1360-4082 Irish Sea Forum. Seminar Report **2808**
1360-4171 E-Med News†
1360-418X Complementary Care Journal **8095**
1360-4341 Airport World **8537**
1360-4384 New Review (London, 1979) **3142**
1360-4392 European Potato Markets Monthly **197**
1360-4414 Key Note Market Report: Betting & Gaming **1893**
1360-4422 Peak District Journal of Natural History and Archaeology **411**
1360-4430 British Interdisciplinary Journal of Childhood†
1360-4511 Microbiology Newsletter **892**
1360-4619 O T C LatinA **6865**
1360-4635 Air Navigation International **44**
1360-466X Dress, Body, Culture **335**
1360-4678 C I B News **1323**
1360-4724 I D S Policy Briefing **1597**
1360-4732 The Brief
1360-4740 Fraud Report **1348**
1360-4791 Biotechnology and Biological Sciences Research Council. Annual Report **760**
1360-4813 City **4407**
1360-4937 Business Monitor SDQ11 - The U.K. Service Sector **7479**
1360-4953 International Equity Review **1631**
1360-497X Rosemary Conley Diet & Fitness **6996**
1360-4988 The Drum **7320**
1360-5062 Readers' Wives Bumper Video Pack **6299**
1360-5178 Astonishing Spiderman **2176**
1360-5186 Essential X-Men **2188**
1360-5208 Spectacular Spider-Man **2214**
1360-5305 *see* 1360-5313 **6294**
1360-5313 Marquis **6294**
1360-5372 Computer Arts **2484**
1360-5518 Synergy **6209**
1360-5526 Aviation Modeller International **4328**
1360-5550 Tayside and Fife Archaeological Journal **420**
1360-5682 Jane's Armour and Artillery Upgrades **6426**
1360-5720 Routledge Studies in Information and Library Management Systems *changed to* Routledge Research in Information Systems **5063**
1360-5739 Corporate Systems† **8944**
1360-5798 Jockey Slut† **8968**
1360-5801 European Journal of Cancer Care. Supplement *see* 0961-5423 **6019**
1360-5844 C M L R Antitrust Reports **4859**
1360-5860 Focus on Biopesticides Plus
1360-5879 Focus on Organic Dyes and Colours
1360-5941 Dental Business **5839**
1360-6050 Wine & Spirit International **613**
1360-6069 European Card Review *changed to* 1759-829X **1374**
1360-6255 Directory of Employers Associations, Trade Unions, and Other Employees' Associations **1675**
1360-6352 Journal of Cognitive Education†
1360-6360 Paper Finder†
1360-6387 Airlines International **8536**
1360-6441 Journal of Sociolinguistics **5135**
1360-6530 Cult Times **2379**
1360-6603 G S M Quarterly **2321**
1360-6689 The Guide to the Executive Agencies **7443**
1360-6719 Managing Leisure **4980**
1360-6727 Bernoulli News **5475**
1360-6743 English Language and Linguistics **5115**
1360-6786 Document Management Update **2530**
1360-6875 Cafe Magazine **2553**
1360-6913 Dive International **8169**
1360-6956 Inline Skatermag†
1360-7103 Site Safe News **6687**
1360-7162 Las Vegas & Nevada Holiday & Travel Guide **8728**
1360-7189 Tennessee Holiday Guide & Travel Planner **8760**
1360-7197 Natchez Holiday & Travel Guide **8740**
1360-7219 Discover the Lee Island Coast Holiday & Travel Guide **8698**
1360-7243 North Carolina Holiday & Visitors Guide **8742**
1360-7251 The Best of Florida **8687**
1360-726X Georgia Holiday Guide **8713**
1360-7278 Essential Guide to the New England States **8701**
1360-7286 The Regulator and Professional Conduct Quarterly **4767**
1360-7391 WorldFish Report **3612**
1360-7413 Genes and Function†
1360-7456 Asia Pacific Viewpoint **1591**
1360-7766 Golf Days. Golf Courses in Ireland **8714**
1360-7782 Scottish Law & Practice Quarterly **4780**
1360-7804 Sociological Research Online **8137**
1360-7863 Aging & Mental Health **4039**
1360-788X Total Sport **8212**
1360-7898 Social Research Update **8003**
1360-7995 World Drinks Report **614**
1360-8037 Water Management International†
1360-8185 Apoptosis **827**
1360-8215 Retail Week **1841**
1360-8223 Asian Commercial Law Review† **8931**
1360-8274 Multimedia Futures **2334**
1360-8282 Packaging Business **6712**
1360-8347 The Mundi Club. Special Publications **3454**
1360-8371 Stroke News **6116**
1360-841X European Business Locations
1360-8436 British Toys & Hobbies Briefing **4059**
1360-8460 Office Products International **1853**
1360-8487 Bibliography of Nautical Books† **8936**
1360-8495 Alzheimer Insights†
1360-8525 Nuclear Forum†
1360-8568 Emerald, the Guide†
1360-8584 Travel Britain
1360-8592 Journal of Bodywork and Movement Therapies **6111**
1360-8606 European Pharmaceutical Review **6839**
1360-8711 I R S Pay Intelligence **1751**
1360-8738 M A I L†
1360-8746 South European Society & Politics **7266**
1360-8762 Crossword Collection
1360-8924 V J M's Jazz & Blues Mart **6626**
1360-9009 Cross & Cockade International **6417**
1360-9033 Cambridge University Library. Readers' Newsletter **5000**
1360-9165 Windows on Finance†
1360-922X Billing Systems Review *changed to* 1467-2782 **1281**
1360-9327 Inside Out (Edinburgh) *see* 1357-0595 **4378**
1360-9335 Baltimore Studies in Nationalism and Internationalism† **8934**
1360-936X Management Issues in Social Care **7531**
1360-9378 Healthcare Market News **4097**
1360-9408 R I B International **8281**
1360-9416 AutoAsia **8561**
1360-9505 Flexible Working **1746**
1360-9513 Golf Enterprise Europe **8231**
1360-9599 Resourcing R E
1360-9939 International Journal of Law, Policy and the Family **4911**
1360-9947 Molecular Human Reproduction **5999**
1361-0104 Environmental Taxation and Accounting **1922**
1361-0120 International Food Abstracts. Science and Technology Disk **3670**
1361-0139 International Food Abstracts. Market Intelligence Disk **3670**
1361-0155 International Food Abstracts. Bakery Disk **3670**
1361-0163 International Food Abstracts. Food Safety Disk **3670**
1361-018X International Food Abstracts. Functional Foods Disk **3670**
1361-0198 International Food Abstracts. Dairy Disk **182**
1361-021X C T I Centre for Nursing and Midwifery. Newsletter **5954**
1361-0465 B A D **5259**
1361-1240 Charles Christian's Legal Technology Insider *changed to* 1740-5033 **4845**
1361-1267 Mentoring & Tutoring **3072**
1361-1305 I R R V Insight **7594**
1361-1429 Together with Children **7777**
1361-1445 Country Report. Myanmar **1458**
1361-147X Country Report. Kazakhstan **1456**
1361-1526 European Human Rights Law Review **4830**
1361-1585 The International in Britain
1361-1593 Investment Adviser **1632**
1361-1623 Film Extrusion Materials and Markets Bulletin **6709**
1361-1631 Self-Adhesive Materials and Markets Bulletin **7099**
1361-164X Corrugated and Carton Bulletin **6709**
1361-1658 Flexpack Materials & Markets Bulletin **6710**
1361-1666 Panel Industry Monitor **1029**
1361-1674 Plastics Packaging Monitor
1361-1682 Transactions in G I S **4031**
1361-1720 Packaging Focus **6713**
1361-1798 Central European Handbook†
1361-1836 Theme **4399**
1361-1879 The Journal of Performance Enhancing Drugs†
1361-1917 Rubber Statistics Yearbook (Year) **7828**
1361-1933 Bete Noire **5262**
1361-1941 Window Fabricator and Installer **1043**
1361-1968 Male View Magazine *changed to* 1745-9257 **6294**
1361-2026 Journal of Fashion Marketing and Management **1824**
1361-2042 Mathematics Today **5516**
1361-2050 Image (London) **6969**

ISSN

1362-5098 Alien Encounters **5439**
1362-511X *see* 0957-4166 **2131**
1362-5187 The European Journal of Contraception and Reproductive Health Care **972**
1362-5241 The Guide to the House of Lords **7443**
1362-5276 Modern English Professional **3073**
1362-5306 Trends in Urology, Gynaecology & Sexual Health **6275**
1362-5403 Energy & Power Risk Management *changed to* 1742-4305 **1337**
1362-5411 Nutraceuticals International **6864**
1362-5462 C A D D. Computer Aided Draughting and Design *changed to* 1471-5082 **3388**
1362-5519 Wax **6627**
1362-5551 Parents News **2165**
1362-5640 Bike Trader **8255**
1362-5667 Classics from the Comics **2182**
1362-5845 Inside Cornwall **8721**
1362-6035 Equilibrium†
1362-6094 Bournemouth University. School of Conservation Sciences. Occasional Paper **2604**
1362-6183 Scottish Abstract of Statistics†
1362-6299 Natural Stone Directory **1054**
1362-6302 North West Labour History **4249**
1362-6337 Obstetric Ultrasound† **8978**
1362-6396 Key Note Market Review: U K Defence Industry *changed to* 1741-7821 **6418**
1362-6450 Disarmament Diplomacy **2651**
1362-654X Warmer Bulletin **3513**
1362-6558 Warwick Papers on Education Policy **2925**
1362-6620 Soundings **5239**
1362-6647 Central Bureau News **3012**
1362-671X Internet Journal of Vibrational Spectroscopy **2065**
1362-6752 Sheffield Archaeological Monographs **416**
1362-6779 Travel Media Directory†
1362-6787 Opinion: Specialist Reviews of Key Papers in GUM - AIDS†
1362-6809 Opinion: Specialist Reviews of Key Papers in Microbiology
1362-6825 Scrip O T C News
1362-7015 Citizens Advice Notes Service **4642**
1362-704X Fashion Theory **489**
1362-7147 Chronicles of Disorder
1362-7163 Vista **2671**
1362-7171 Vehicle Technology **8610**
1362-7198 The Ship Supplier **8661**
1362-7252 Mini Magazine **8590**
1362-7295 G L P†
1362-7325 International Living **8724**
1362-7368 International Journal of Computer Algebra in Mathematics Education *changed to* 1744-2710 **5552**
1362-7511 The Financial Regulator **1345**
1362-7562 Oulu Port Handbook *changed to* 1755-8751 **8657**
1362-7627 Cambridge International Documents Series† **8939**
1362-7635 Cambridge International Series on Parallel Computation **2409**
1362-7651 Cambridge Studies in Medical Anthropology **332**
1362-766X Cargo Systems **8493**
1362-7686 S I S Internet Digest† **8986**
1362-7767 London Monitor†
1362-7783 Sell's Marine Industry Buyers' Guide† **8987**
1362-7856 *see* 1359-1193 **7928**
1362-7902 Symbiosis **5384**
1362-7937 Gothic Studies **5301**
1362-7996 Sci-Journal **7907**
1362-8089 A A B's British Bibliography of Rare and Out-of-Print Titles Available **5056**
1362-8283 Just Criss-Cross **4337**
1362-8321 Harold Recorder **3866**
1362-8364 Chelsea **8225**
1362-8496 Hair Now **588**
1362-8534 A A B's British Bibliography of Rare & Out of Print Publications Reported Available For Sale This Week By the Legitimate Owners. By Subjects. Special Issue **7577**
1362-8607 Prima Baby *changed to* 1749-4346 **2166**
1362-8674 PlayStation Power **2481**
1362-8690 Disney's Big Time **2185**
1362-914X Closer to God **7752**
1362-9255 International Turfgrass Bulletin **8181**
1362-928X Fun to Learn - Barney **2189**
1362-9360 Water and Environment Manager *changed to* 1746-028X **8837**
1362-9387 The Journal of North African Studies **4176**
1362-9395 Mediterranean Politics **7252**
1362-9417 The Journal of Algerian Studies†
1362-9484 Classic and Vintage Commercials **8574**
1362-9506 The Central Government Grants Guide **8031**
1362-9557 Child Support Handbook **4908**
1362-9603 Aberystwyth Economic Research Papers **1056**
1362-962X Advanced Software Development Series **2587**
1362-9662 Advances in Population†
1362-9670 Advances in Reproductive Endocrinology
1362-9778 Key Note Market Report: Giftware **4060**
1362-9786 Scottish Banker *changed to* 1759-9520 **1326**
1362-9859 Psychology and Health Series†
1362-9905 SiF News **6721**
1362-9921 The Parliamentary Policy Forum **7164**
1362-9948 C R I Proceedings Series **7425**
1362-9980 Oxford Psychiatry Series† **8979**
1363-0059 Social Work Monographs **8071**
1363-0105 Research Matters **8065**
1363-013X Quaker Studies **7740**
1363-0148 Hot Dip Galvanizing **6314**
1363-0164 Classics of Espionage Series **7227**
1363-0199 Digital Broadcasting Europe
1363-0202 D V D and Future C D
1363-027X Progress in Preterm†
1363-0296 *see* 1350-4630 **3565**
1363-030X *see* 1036-1146 **7108**
1363-0377 P F I Intelligence Bulletin (Private Finance Initiative) *changed to* 1752-7007 **1938**
1363-0393 Health on the Internet **5625**
1363-0407 Inside Cosmetics†
1363-0520 Warwick Business School Research Papers **1193**
1363-0539 Journal of Financial Services Marketing **1824**
1363-0601 B W P Update†
1363-0687 University of Manchester. S P A Working Paper **4032**
1363-0695 Great Britain. Health & Safety Executive. Technology and Health Sciences Division. Specialist Inspector Reports **7519**
1363-0814 Modern Cartography **4037**
1363-0865 Key Note Market Report: Stationery (Personal & Office) **1852**
1363-0911 Property Investment
1363-092X In-Flight Entertainment International **8784**
1363-0938 Oxford Handbooks in Emergency Medicine **6070**
1363-0946 Oxford Biogeography Series **696**
1363-0954 Key Note Market Report: Timber & Joinery **1895**
1363-1004 Armourer **6411**
1363-1039 Medical Device Business News†
1363-1063 In Brief† **8963**
1363-1160 Voice Plus Asia Pacific†
1363-1225 War Studies Journal **6453**
1363-1268 Key Note Market Assessment. Opticians and Optical Goods **1892**
1363-1349 McDonald Institute Monographs **405**
1363-1411 On Course **8879**
1363-1454 Lloyd's Greek Maritime Directory
1363-1462 New Local Government Area Monitor **7312**
1363-1667 The New Writer **5341**
1363-1780 Trusts & Trustees **4906**
1363-1829 *see* 0962-9483 **330**
1363-1888 Charity Finance Yearbook **1616**
1363-1942 Computing for Insurance† **8943**
1363-1950 Current Opinion in Clinical Nutrition and Metabolic Care **6657**
1363-1993 A A B's Guide to Private English Language Schools in the U.K. for Overseas Students **2953**
1363-2043 Lloyd's Cruise International **8731**
1363-206X Key Note Market Report: Further and Higher Education **2992**
1363-2094 Child Health Dialogue† **8941**
1363-2108 Cross-Link†
1363-2175 Journal of Financial Management of Property and Construction **7596**
1363-2191 Food Patents Bulletin *changed to* 1478-792X **6750**
1363-2205 D & B Business Register. South Yorkshire, Humberside *changed to* 1748-8044 **1983**
1363-2213 D & B Business Register. West Yorkshire **1983**
1363-2221 D & B Business Register. Durham, Cleveland, North Yorkshire **1982**
1363-2329 Cass Series on Security Studies
1363-2353 C M I Technology Watch, Data Warehousing **2529**
1363-2434 School Leadership & Management (Print) **3032**
1363-2450 Biopolicy Journal *changed to* 0717-3458 **763**
1363-2469 Journal of Earthquake Engineering **3275**
1363-2507 Ulster Business **1186**
1363-254X Journal of Communication Management **1765**
1363-2647 Envirotec **3430**
1363-2655 U K Directory of Property Developers, Investors & Financiers **7614**
1363-2736 Hereford's Global Update
1363-2752 Emotional and Behavioural Difficulties **3039**
1363-2779 I M Industrial Minerals Directory **6464**
1363-2914 I J A S†
1363-2922 Internet for Business†
1363-2949 S S S I Monitoring Report Series **3464**
1363-2965 British Ornithologists' Club. Occasional Publications† **8937**
1363-2981 N R A Research & Development Report†
1363-299X Birds of Spurn **904**
1363-3015 English Nature Science **2610**
1363-304X Chapman & Hall Ecotoxicology Series†
1363-3082 Birds in the Sheffield Area **904**
1363-3090 Conservation Biology Series **2607**
1363-3198 Amateur Entomologists' Society. Pamphlet **838**
1363-3201 Oxford Ornithology Series **913**
1363-3244 Europa†
1363-3260 Key Note Market Report: Stockbroking†
1363-3279 Key Note Market Report: Electricity Industry **3159**
1363-3287 Key Note Market Report: Men's Magazines†
1363-3295 Key Note Market Report: Packaging (Food & Drink) *changed to* 1743-4882 **6712**
1363-3368 Psittascene **913**
1363-3376 British Simuliid Group. Bulletin **841**
1363-3422 Signet
1363-3554 History Workshop Journal **4146**
1363-3589 Corporate Reputation Review **1736**
1363-3740 Middle East Business Review **1499**
1363-3759 Library of Holocaust Testimonies **4151**
1363-3775 F W **2254**
1363-4127 Information Security Technical Report **2514**
1363-4186 Forecourt Trader Supplier Guide *changed to* 1477-769X **1995**
1363-4216 Selden Society, London. Lectures **4781**
1363-4224 Selden Society, London. Supplementary Series **4782**
1363-4313 Derwent Directory. Supplementary Protection Certificates. Great Britain **6832**
1363-4321 Hockey Sport† **8962**
1363-4380 Tyto **915**
1363-4402 Papers in Linguistics from the University of Manchester **5159**
1363-4410 The Chichester Leaflet *changed to* 1750-8479 **7750**
1363-4496 Kemps Film, TV & Video Handbook (UK Edition) *changed to* 1754-8489 **6505**
1363-4518 Survey Methods Centre. Newsletter **8008**
1363-4534 International Journal of Gastroenterology†
1363-4542 European Trade Mark Reports **6749**
1363-4550 Chichester Magazine **7750**
1363-4577 Professional Negligence and Liability Reports **4762**
1363-4585 Public and Social Policy **7174**
1363-4593 Health **7520**
1363-4607 Sexualities **7408**
1363-4615 Transcultural Psychiatry **6188**
1363-464X Society for Companion Animal Studies. Journal **322**
1363-4666 Country Profile. Yugoslavia (Serbia-Montenegro), Macedonia *changed to* 1462-6780 **8945**
1363-4674 Ace (London) *changed to* 1750-4996 **8220**
1363-4682 Mental Health Occupational Therapy **7385**
1363-4801 I F P O Journal **3579**
1363-4844 Northamptonshire Bird Report **911**
1363-5247 Worldviews **3475**
1363-5387 Internet Archaeology **399**
1363-5409 Financial Survey. Printers **1994**
1363-545X Revs†
1363-5530 New, Rare and Unusual Plants *changed to* 1474-4953 **3728**
1363-5565 Airbrush Art & Action **464**
1363-5662 Kids Alive **7763**
1363-5700 Birds and Wildlife in Cumbria **903**
1363-5808 Offshore International†
1363-5832 Ports International
1363-5905 Chartered Secretary **1733**
1363-5921 R I C S Research Findings **3281**
1363-6057 Forty and Over **6291**
1363-6073 Top Heavy Video Special† **8993**
1363-6235 Potters Monthly *changed to* 1752-8534 **8247**
1363-6383 Electronics and Beyond **3096**
1363-6588 Fferm a Thyddyn **4219**
1363-660X Health Law for Healthcare Professionals **4686**
1363-6669 Review of Development Economics **1604**
1363-6804 Conspectus **1735**
1363-6820 Journal of Vocational Education and Training **2943**
1363-6847 Diabetes Reviews International†
1363-6952 I P A Magazine **1686**
1363-7029 Economic Issues **1539**
1363-7045 The European Union Encyclopedia and Directory (Year) **7234**
1363-7088 Key Note Market Report: Horticultural Retailing **3740**
1363-7096 Key Note Market Report: Baths & Sanitaryware **589**
1363-710X Business & Technology
1363-7134 Asian Environmental Technology **3404**
1363-7169 Commonwealth Human Rights Law Digest **7204**
1363-7177 University of Leicester Discussion Papers in Politics **7191**
1363-7185 University of Leicester Discussion Papers in Mass Communications **8145**
1363-7207 University of Leicester. Department of Geography. Faculty of Social Sciences. Discussion Papers in Geography **4032**
1363-7258 Hospitality Matters **4388**
1363-7274 Franchise International **1817**
1363-7282 World of Information Business Intelligence Reports. Bulgaria **1587**
1363-7290 World of Information Business Intelligence Reports. Poland **1531**
1363-7320 Ecotheology *changed to* 1749-4907 **7653**
1363-7339 Current Medical Literature. Psychiatry Reviews†
1363-7355 Indonesia Handbook **8721**
1363-7363 Malaysia and Singapore Handbook **8732**
1363-7371 South Africa Handbook (Year) **8756**
1363-738X Peru Handbook **8747**
1363-7398 Ecuador and Galapagos Handbook **8700**
1363-7401 Brazil Handbook **8688**
1363-741X Chile Handbook **8693**
1363-7428 Thailand Handbook **8760**
1363-7436 Myanmar Burma Handbook **8739**
1363-7444 Vietnam Handbook **8772**
1363-7452 Laos Handbook **8728**
1363-7460 Cambodia Handbook†
1363-7479 Morocco Handbook **8739**
1363-7487 Tunisia Handbook **8769**
1363-7495 Namibia Handbook **8739**
1363-7517 Andalucia Handbook **8683**
1363-7525 Tibet Handbook **8761**
1363-755X Developmental Science **7352**
1363-7576 OneStop **7325**
1363-7681 International Journal of C O M A D E M **8426**
1363-7746 *see* 0956-1382 **3871**
1363-7797 Group Leisure **4978**
1363-7800 Discussion Papers in Diplomacy **7231**
1363-7827 Socialist History Working Papers **4161**
1363-7959 Key Note Market Report: Automotive Services **8588**
1363-7975 Sri Lanka Handbook **8758**
1363-7983 Egypt Handbook **8700**
1363-7991 Pakistan Handbook **8746**
1363-8106 Timber Floors **4563**
1363-8203 Discussion Papers in Management Studies *changed to* 1461-6017 **1739**
1363-8211 University of Leicester. Centre for European Economic Studies. Discussion Papers in European Economic Studies **1188**
1363-822X Discussion Papers in Public Sector Economics **1092**
1363-8289 Xpose **6517**
1363-8300 Landwards **133**
1363-8327 Health Which?†
1363-8378 *see* 1361-6153 **2440**
1363-8491 Pediatric Rehabilitation *changed to* 1751-8423 **6108**
1363-8912 Financial Survey. Fruit, Flower & Vegetable Merchants **1994**
1363-8947 Financial Survey. Textile Rental, Launderers and Dry Cleaners **1994**
1363-8971 Motorhome Monthly **8505**
1363-898X Breakthrough†
1363-9005 Financial Services in Leeds **1345**
1363-9056 Financial Survey. The Hand and Small Tool Industry **1994**
1363-9064 Strategic Communication Management **1795**
1363-9072 E T H O S Newsletter **2350**
1363-9080 Journal of Education and Work **3067**
1363-9099 World of Information Business Intelligence Reports. Algeria **1587**
1363-9102 World of Information Business Intelligence Reports. Croatia **1527**
1363-9110 World of Information Business Intelligence Reports. Czech Republic **1587**

ISSN

DIRECTORY 2010 1365-4632 9599

1364-6303 World of Information Business Intelligence Reports. Thailand **1533**
1364-6311 World of Information Business Intelligence Reports. Tunisia **1533**
1364-632X World of Information Business Intelligence Reports. Turkey **1533**
1364-6338 World of Information Business Intelligence Reports. Uganda **1533**
1364-6346 World of Information Business Intelligence Reports. United Kingdom **1533**
1364-6354 World of Information Business Intelligence Reports. United Arab Emirates **1533**
1364-6362 World of Information Business Intelligence Reports. Uruguay **1533**
1364-6370 World of Information Business Intelligence Reports. United States **1533**
1364-6389 World of Information Business Intelligence Reports. Vietnam **1534**
1364-6397 World of Information Business Intelligence Reports. Democratic Republic of Congo **1527**
1364-6400 World of Information Business Intelligence Reports. Zambia **1534**
1364-6419 World of Information Business Intelligence Reports. Zimbabwe **1534**
1364-6559 Crops **227**
1364-6575 *see* 0967-0335 **2102**
1364-6591 Compound Semiconductor Newsletter
1364-6613 Trends in Cognitive Sciences **7413**
1364-6737 Lottery Monitor *changed to* 1478-3452 **8039**
1364-6745 Neurogenetics **876**
1364-6753 *see* 1364-6745 **876**
1364-6826 Journal of Atmospheric and Solar - Terrestrial Physics **2784**
1364-6869 F E D A Bulletins†
1364-6885 *see* 1360-0869 **4845**
1364-6893 *see* 0144-3615 **5996**
1364-6907 *see* 1359-0847 **6662**
1364-6915 *see* 1360-7863 **4039**
1364-694X Information for Social Change†
1364-6974 Institute of Health Record Information & Management. Journal **5635**
1364-7075 Current Medical Literature. Respiratory Medicine - Peer Selected Citations†
1364-7180 *see* 0332-4095 **3232**
1364-7245 Tracks Catalogue
1364-727X International Journal of Dairy Technology **266**
1364-7369 Country Profile. Ethiopia† **8945**
1364-7393 B B C Learning Is Fun **2177**
1364-7407 E U Dairy Monitor **264**
1364-7431 New Statesman **5230**
1364-7512 International Guide to the Coalfields **6466**
1364-7768 P F I Report *changed to* 1742-0334 **1377**
1364-7776 New Media Age **2335**
1364-7784 B P I News **6964**
1364-7814 Confectionery Industry Bulletin *changed to* 1478-7873 **3673**
1364-7822 Euromoney Bank Register (Year)
1364-7830 Combustion Theory and Modelling **7053**
1364-7970 Key Note Market Report: Fish & Fish Products **1894**
1364-7989 Key Note Market Report: Household Appliances (Brown Goods) **3107**
1364-7997 Key Note Market Report: Mixed Retail Businesses†
1364-8004 Key Note Market Report: Pensions **1895**
1364-8128 Financial Products **1345**
1364-8152 Environmental Modelling & Software **3482**
1364-8160 N I S W Briefing†
1364-8187 Global Healthcare†
1364-8233 International Journal of Geriatric Psychopharmacology†
1364-8284 Electronic Library Research†
1364-8314 Property Preview **7605**
1364-8330 Ground Handling International **8497**
1364-8470 Anthropology & Medicine **327**
1364-8497 Health Service Risks. Special Report **4096**
1364-8500 New Scientist: Planet Science *see* 1356-1766 **7892**
1364-8500 New Scientist: Planet Science *see* 0262-4079 **7891**
1364-8535 Critical Care (Print Edition)†
1364-8543 Toxicology and Ecotoxicology News / Reviews†
1364-856X Mineral Markets International
1364-8594 *see* 0003-4983 **5810**
1364-8764 Dirt **8257**
1364-8861 E S A Directory **3505**
1364-9027 International Journal of Pharmaceutical Medicine *changed to* 1178-2595 **6869**
1364-906X Intellectual Property Quarterly **6752**
1364-9094 D F N I Guide to New Airline Listings *see* 1357-7077 **8783**
1364-9159 Global Banking & Financial Policy Review (Years) **1349**
1364-9167 International Oil & Gas Finance Review (Year) **6774**
1364-9175 Management Skills and Development†
1364-9205 The International Trade Law Reports **4932**
1364-9213 *see* 0961-4524 **1594**
1364-9221 *see* 1355-2074 **8897**
1364-9353 Emulsion Polymer Technologies *changed to* 1750-2438 **6717**
1364-9485 Inside Energy **3159**
1364-9493 Employers Law **1860**
1364-9507 Drinks International Bulletin *changed to* 1477-8017 **602**
1364-9515 Farmland Market **112**
1364-9590 Football Europe†
1364-9604 Country Profile. Thailand† **8946**
1364-9620 Scottish Drugs Forum. Policy Statement **2699**
1364-9639 Stuff **5084**
1364-9647 Jane's High-Speed Marine Transportation **8648**
1364-9698 Shephard's Police Aviation Handbook *changed to* Shephard's Public Service Aviation Handbook **8551**
1364-971X International Journal of Iberian Studies **4232**
1364-9752 Ageing and Health **4038**
1364-9809 Edinburgh Law Review **4924**
1364-985X The Australian Journal of Agricultural and Resource Economics **194**
1364-9876 World Casualty Statistics **8533**
1364-9892 Advance I T Directory
1364-9922 Esprit **593**
1364-9957 What's New in Process & Control **3257**
1365-0092 Club On **5068**
1365-0157 100 Arrows **4351**
1365-0165 Pocket Arrows†
1365-0483 Lakeland Walker **4018**
1365-0513 Translation Theories Explained **5189**
1365-0556 Progress in Structural Engineering and Materials *changed to* 1545-2255 **7041**
1365-0564 Business & Finance in Scotland **1070**
1365-0572 Gardens of England and Wales Open for Charity (Year) **3732**
1365-0580 Political Violence **7260**
1365-0629 The Pharmacy Assistant†
1365-0637 Dialogism†
1365-067X Digital Publishing Technologies **7579**
1365-0734 Knave Penpower **6293**
1365-0831 Major Companies of Central & Eastern Europe and the Commonwealth of Independent States **2014**
1365-1005 Macroeconomic Dynamics **1720**
1365-1455 Thurrock Recorder **3872**
1365-1501 International Journal of Psychiatry in Clinical Practice **6147**
1365-1528 Performance Chemicals News Bulletin **2075**
1365-1560 Business in Africa International Magazine **1072**
1365-1609 International Journal of Rock Mechanics and Mining Sciences **6466**
1365-1617 Geomechanics Abstracts **2719**
1365-1773 New T C S & D **3658**
1365-182X H P B **5926**
1365-1846 D & B Business Register. London. S W, S E **1982**
1365-1854 D & B Business Register. London. W C, E C, E, N **1982**
1365-1862 D & B Business Register. London. N W, W **1982**
1365-1870 D & B Business Register. Nottinghamshire, Lincolnshire **1982**
1365-1889 D & B Business Register. Wales **1983**
1365-1897 D & B Business Register. Middlesex, Buckinghamshire **1982**
1365-1900 D & B Business Register. Bedfordshire, Hertfordshire **1089**
1365-1935 Training Technology and Human Resources *changed to* 1753-7746 **1863**
1365-1951 U.A. International **459**
1365-196X Polymer Curing Technologies **7098**
1365-1978 B B C on Air **2357**
1365-2028 African Journal of Ecology Online **651**
1365-2036 *see* 0269-2813 **5920**
1365-2044 *see* 0003-2409 **5768**
1365-2052 *see* 0268-9146 **862**
1365-2060 *see* 0785-3890 **5902**
1365-2079 *see* 0954-1020 **653**
1365-2095 *see* 1353-5773 **3585**
1365-2109 *see* 1355-557X **3585**
1365-2117 Basin Research (Online) **2702**
1365-2125 *see* 0306-5251 **6826**
1365-2133 *see* 0007-0963 **5872**
1365-2141 *see* 0007-1048 **5935**
1365-2168 *see* 0007-1323 **6238**
1365-2184 *see* 0960-7722 **830**
1365-2192 *see* 0193-6484 **2057**
1365-2206 Child & Family Social Work Online **8032**
1365-2214 *see* 0305-1862 **6089**
1365-2222 *see* 0954-7894 **5756**
1365-2230 *see* 0307-6938 **5873**
1365-2249 *see* 0009-9104 **5756**
1365-2257 Clinical and Laboratory Haematology (Online) *changed to* 1751-553X **5938**
1365-2265 *see* 0300-0664 **5885**
1365-229X *see* 0009-9260 **6194**
1365-2303 *see* 0956-5507 **832**
1365-2311 Ecological Entomology Online **843**
1365-232X *see* 0969-9988 **1006**
1365-2338 *see* 0250-8052 **228**
1365-2346 *see* 0265-0215 **5771**
1365-2354 European Journal of Cancer Care Online **6019**
1365-2362 *see* 0014-2972 **5611**
1365-2389 *see* 1351-0754 **229**
1365-2397 First Break Online **2780**
1365-2400 Fisheries Management & Ecology Online **3592**
1365-2419 Fisheries Oceanography Online **3592**
1365-2427 Freshwater Biology Online **674**
1365-2435 *see* 0269-8463 **2612**
1365-2443 *see* 1356-9597 **868**
1365-2451 Geology Today Online **2742**
1365-246X *see* 0956-540X **2782**
1365-2478 *see* 0016-8025 **2782**
1365-2486 *see* 1354-1013 **675**
1365-2494 *see* 0142-5242 **116**
1365-2516 Haemophilia Online **5937**
1365-2524 Health and Social Care in the Community (Online) **7521**
1365-2540 *see* 0018-067X **871**
1365-2559 *see* 0309-0167 **6021**
1365-2567 *see* 0019-2805 **5760**
1365-2575 Information Systems Journal Online **2521**
1365-2583 *see* 0962-1075 **849**
1365-2591 International Endodontic Journal Online **5848**
1365-2605 *see* 0105-6263 **6269**
1365-2613 *see* 0959-9673 **5638**
1365-2621 International Journal of Food Science & Technology Online **3648**
1365-263X International Journal of Paediatric Dentistry (Online) **5849**
1365-2648 *see* 0309-2402 **5964**
1365-2656 *see* 0021-8790 **680**
1365-2664 *see* 0021-8901 **680**
1365-2672 *see* 1364-5072 **888**
1365-2699 *see* 0305-0270 **4017**
1365-2702 *see* 0962-1067 **5964**
1365-2710 *see* 0269-4727 **6852**
1365-2729 *see* 0266-4909 **2469**
1365-2745 *see* 0022-0477 **682**
1365-2753 Journal of Evaluation in Clinical Practice Online **5649**
1365-2761 Journal of Fish Diseases Online **3599**
1365-277X *see* 0952-3871 **6661**
1365-2788 *see* 0964-2633 **6152**
1365-2796 *see* 0954-6820 **5946**
1365-2818 *see* 0022-2720 **899**
1365-2826 *see* 0953-8194 **6153**
1365-2834 *see* 0966-0429 **5966**
1365-2842 *see* 0305-182X **5852**
1365-2850 Journal of Psychiatric and Mental Health Nursing Online **6156**
1365-2869 Journal of Sleep Research Online **5654**
1365-2885 Journal of Veterinary Pharmacology and Therapeutics Online **6857**
1365-2893 *see* 1352-0504 **5928**
1365-2907 Mammal Review Online **954**
1365-2915 Medical & Veterinary Entomology Online **5667**
1365-2923 *see* 0308-0110 **5668**
1365-2931 *see* 1364-5706 **5679**
1365-294X *see* 0962-1083 **893**
1365-2958 *see* 0950-382X **893**
1365-2966 *see* 0035-8711 **580**
1365-2982 Neurogastroenterology and Motility Online **5929**
1365-2990 *see* 0305-1846 **6167**
1365-3008 *see* 0030-6053 **959**
1365-3016 Paediatric and Perinatal Epidemiology (Online) **6098**
1365-3024 *see* 0141-9838 **5824**
1365-3032 Physiological Entomology Online **857**
1365-3040 *see* 0140-7791 **697**
1365-3059 *see* 0032-0862 **811**
1365-3067 *see* 1750-4740 **899**
1365-3075 *see* 0033-4545 **2077**
1365-3083 *see* 0300-9475 **5765**
1365-3091 Sedimentology Online **2766**
1365-3113 Systematic Entomology Online **860**
1365-3121 Terra Nova Online **2717**
1365-313X *see* 0960-7412 **811**
1365-3148 *see* 0958-7578 **5942**
1365-3156 *see* 1360-2276 **5827**
1365-3164 *see* 0959-4493 **8812**
1365-3180 *see* 0043-1737 **258**
1365-3199 D & B Business Register. Avon, Somerset, Dorset *changed to* 1748-8001 **1983**
1365-3237 D & B Business Register. Scotland. South. Strathclyde, Borders, Dumfries & Galloway *changed to* 1748-765X **1982**
1365-3245 D & B Business Register. Scotland. North. Lothians, Fife, Tayside, Grampian, Central, Highlands & Islands *changed to* 1748-7668 **1982**
1365-3288 Cable Talk **3297**
1365-330X Cancer Epidemiology
1365-3318 Cystic Fibrosis
1365-3326 Osteoporosis
1365-3342 D & B Business Register. Leicestershire, Northamptonshire, Cambridgeshire **1982**
1365-3350 D & B Business Register. Norfolk, Suffolk **1982**
1365-3369 D & B Business Register. Essex **1982**
1365-3377 D & B Business Register. Oxfordshire, Berkshire, Wiltshire **1982**
1365-3385 D & B Business Register. Surrey **1983**
1365-3407 D & B Business Register. Lancashire **1982**
1365-3415 D & B Business Register. Greater Manchester, Merseyside *changed to* 1755-3369 **1982**
1365-3423 D & B Business Register. Cheshire **1981**
1365-3431 D & B Business Register. East & West Sussex **1982**
1365-344X D & B Business Register. Kent **1982**
1365-3458 D & B Business Register. Devon, Cornwall, Isles of Scilly, Channel Isles **1982**
1365-3466 D & B Business Register. Hampshire, Isle of Wright **1982**
1365-3482 D & B Business Register. Northumberland, Tyne & Wear, Cumbria, Isle of Man **1982**
1365-3520 D & B Business Register. Birmingham **1981**
1365-3539 D & B Business Register. Shropshire, Hereford & Worcester, Gloucestershire **1982**
1365-3547 D & B Business Register. Derbyshire, Staffordshire **1982**
1365-3555 D & B Business Register. West Midlands, Warwickshire **1983**
1365-3563 Viewpoints (Birmingham) **7779**
1365-358X The Big Cheese **6287**
1365-3598 Weddings Annual **5562**
1365-3636 U K E R N A News (United Kingdom Education and Research Network Association) *changed to* 1755-2397 **2988**
1365-3725 Malacological Society of London. Bulletin **954**
1365-3733 Cummings Center Series **4213**
1365-3741 English Language Teacher Education and Development **3061**
1365-3881 Assemblage **381**
1365-3970 International Water Power and Dam Construction Yearbook **3163**
1365-3989 Country Report. European Union **1454**
1365-4004 The Complete A-Z of PlayStation Games†
1365-4039 On the Ball **8241**
1365-4055 Kent Archaeological Rescue Unit. Special Subject Series **402**
1365-4101 Engineering Integrity **3190**
1365-411X Essential PlayStation **2476**
1365-4179 Jane's Defence Upgrades *changed to* 1476-2129 **6427**
1365-4187 Jane's Missiles and Rockets **6427**
1365-4284 Post Magazine - The Insurance Weekly **4519**
1365-4292 Furniture & Cabinetmaking **1050**
1365-4314 L N G Journal **3141**
1365-4322 Centres, Bureaux & Research Institutes **1979**
1365-4357 Medicine (CD-ROM Edition) **5674**
1365-439X Internet World **2562**
1365-4543 Key Note Market Report: Milk & Dairy Products **1895**
1365-4578 Business Ratio Report: Food Processing & Packaging Machinery†
1365-4586 Winning Business†
1365-4632 *see* 0011-9059 **5877**

ISSN

9600 1365-4667 ULRICH'S PERIODICALS

1365-4667 Pike & Predators **8219**
1365-4675 Electronics World **3097**
1365-4691 Health & Ageing **4047**
1365-4756 Country Risk Service. Bahrain **1471**
1365-4764 Country Risk Service. Oman **1473**
1365-4772 Country Risk Service. Qatar **1474**
1365-4802 Improving Schools **3024**
1365-4845 Major Companies of Africa South of the Sahara (Year) **2014**
1365-4861 Records Management Society of Great Britain. Newsletter
1365-490X Grove Biblical Series **7759**
1365-4926 S P C Asia **596**
1365-4969 Mobile Choice **2369**
1365-4977 *see* 1355-7602 **2564**
1365-5000 Event Magazine
1365-5086 Alabama Holiday & Travel Planner **8682**
1365-5094 Colorado Holiday Planner **8694**
1365-5108 Chicago & Illinois Travel Guide **8693**
1365-5302 Xnet†
1365-5485 Tyneside Supermart **8609**
1365-5531 Cleanroom Technology **3184**
1365-5590 Tolley's Payroll Handbook **1876**
1365-5604 British Journal of Renal Medicine **6266**
1365-5639 The Major Companies Guide†
1365-5647 Changing Eastern Europe **7226**
1365-5671 Building Services Journal *changed to* 2040-0500 **4116**
1365-5671 Building Services Journal *changed to* 1759-846X **989**
1365-5701 Readings in Mind and Language†
1365-571X Potato Markets Weekly **147**
1365-5728 Knowledge, Identity and School Life Series†
1365-5760 Business Information Searcher **4998**
1365-5817 The Publican Newspaper **609**
1365-5825 I F A Now **1352**
1365-585X Antiques Info Magazine **363**
1365-5868 Air Pollution International Conference **3482**
1365-5884 I D Weekly Highlights†
1365-5949 Great Britain. Department of Trade and Industry. Energy Paper **1428**
1365-5965 Irrigation Management Network. Network Paper†
1365-6058 Conference Calendar (Print) *changed to* Conference Calendar (Online) **6279**
1365-6090 Biblical Studies Bulletin **7748**
1365-6112 O A G Rail Guide **8621**
1365-6155 Key Note Market Report: Steel Industry†
1365-6236 Questions of Maths and Science†
1365-6309 Housing Today **4414**
1365-6325 Information Strategy (London)†
1365-6368 Business Computer World **2408**
1365-6414 Radioactivity in Food and the Environment **3510**
1365-649X Shephard's Civil Helicopter Handbook **8551**
1365-6546 Shephard's Regional Aviation Handbook *changed to* 1753-1845 **8548**
1365-6597 Shephard's Air Ambulance Handbook *changed to* Shephard's Public Service Aviation Handbook **8551**
1365-6600 Shephard's Military Helicopter Handbook **8551**
1365-6619 Document Systems Outlook **2530**
1365-6708 Key Note Market Report: Building Societies *changed to* Key Note Market Assessment. Customer Services in Financial Organisations **1827**
1365-6716 Key Note Market Report: Builders' Merchants **1019**
1365-6740 Key Note Market Report: Design Consultancies **1894**
1365-6775 European Packaging & Waste Law *changed to* 1750-0079 **3506**
1365-6813 S T P Magazine **1381**
1365-6821 Nikon Pro **6972**
1365-6864 Now **8878**
1365-6872 Golf Xtreme†
1365-6929 Application Guide - Transport Research Laboratory **8629**
1365-6937 Filtration Industry Analyst **3367**
1365-6945 Loughborough University. Department of Economics. Economic Research Papers *changed to* Loughborough University. Department of Economics. Economic Research Paper **1145**
1365-6953 Commodities Now **1617**
1365-697X Conference Blue and Green (CD-ROM) *see* 1756-1140 **6278**
1365-697X Conference Blue and Green (CD-ROM) *see* 1756-1159 **6278**
1365-6988 *see* 0966-3371 **2384**
1365-702X International Journal of Facilities Management†
1365-7062 Technology in Practice **8442**
1365-7070 Good Health†
1365-7119 Bulk Solids Today **3236**
1365-7127 International Journal of Evidence & Proof **4891**
1365-7186 Town Hall **7504**
1365-7216 Neon **6508**
1365-7267 Financial Stability Review *changed to* 1751-7044 **1345**
1365-7291 Hellenic Medical Journal **5627**
1365-7305 Aquaculture Economics & Management **3585**
1365-7356 European Packaging Price Trends†
1365-7402 Help the Aged News **8044**
1365-7410 Jazz Rag **6579**
1365-7453 U K Airprox (P) Involving Commercial Air Transport **8552**
1365-7496 New Nation (London) **4580**
1365-7518 Burns Chronicle **5267**
1365-7542 Maritime Review **8653**
1365-7585 Waterlog **8340**
1365-7623 Lab Africa **2071**
1365-7690 Bank of England. Monetary and Financial Statistics **1314**
1365-7712 Key Note Market Assessment. Working Women **8870**
1365-7798 Trent Geographical Papers **4031**
1365-781X Ground Improvement *changed to* 1755-0750 **3271**
1365-7836 Jane's Airports and Handling Agents. United States and Canada **8547**
1365-7852 Prostate Cancer and Prostatic Diseases **6033**
1365-7879 Black Media Journal†
1365-7887 Problems of Capitalism and Socialism **7173**
1365-8018 Landlord & Tenant Law Review **7598**
1365-8050 Discrete Mathematics and Theoretical Computer Science (Online Edition) **5483**
1365-8077 X X L Basketball **8252**
1365-8123 Key Note Market Report: Computer Hardware **2540**
1365-8131 Key Note Market Report: Defence Equipment **6430**
1365-8190 Make†
1365-8255 Logic Problems Annual **4338**
1365-8263 Hot! **2382**
1365-8298 Simpsons Comics **2213**
1365-8557 Teazer Just 18 **6300**
1365-862X Cult Times Special **2379**
1365-876X Net Profit *changed to* 1476-8380
1365-8778 Baking and Confectionery International†
1365-8808 Practical Office†
1365-8816 International Journal of Geographical Information Science **4037**
1365-8824 *see* 1365-8816 **4037**
1365-8859 Information Technology Law Reports **4870**
1365-8867 Bio-Science Law Review **4858**
1365-8875 Nips **6812**
1365-8913 Journal of Fertility Counselling **5649**
1365-893X Journal of Interactive Media in Education **2950**
1365-9049 Key Note Market Report: Electrical Contracting **3323**
1365-9073 International Who's Who of Corporate Immigration Lawyers **4696**
1365-909X Account Management Series. Safeway plc†
1365-9138 Fireplace Specialist **1008**
1365-9146 North West Nature **2623**
1365-9189 Creative Crafts for the Home **534**
1365-9200 A E S I E A P Goldbook (Year) **7051**
1365-9235 The Art of Bonsai†
1365-9375 D N A (London) **4372**
1365-9421 Internet Today†
1365-9537 Classic Cars **8574**
1365-9677 Burgundy Book of European Broadcasting **1977**
1365-9693 South East Business **1433**
1365-9774 O A G Air Cargo Guide with Rates **8549**
1365-9782 O A G Executive Flight Planner: Asia, Pacific **8549**
1365-9804 International Financial Law Review Weekly Fax
1365-9812 L G C Law and Administration *see* 0024-5534 **7496**
1365-9820 Welfare World **8078**
1365-9839 Outcomes in Community Care Practice **8061**
1365-9863 The Seed Search **816**
1365-9898 Keele Papers in Geriatric Medicine and Gerontology **4050**
1366-0004 Isle of Wright Ornithological Group. Bird Report **909**
1366-0012 Jane's Police and Security Equipment (Years) *changed to* Jane's Police and Homeland Security Equipment (Years) **2678**
1366-0063 Fawcett Library Newsletter **5009**
1366-0071 Acute Pain **5567**
1366-008X O A G World Airways Guide - Trade Edition†
1366-0101 Horizons (Newport) **7284**
1366-0233 Biosafety Journal *changed to* 0717-3458 **763**
1366-0276 Asia Cover **4493**
1366-0284 O T C Yearbook **6865**
1366-0314 Aberdeen Studies in Politics **7219**
1366-0357 Multimedia Silicon
1366-0365 Hull Strategy Papers **2226**
1366-042X Key Note Market Report: Aerospace **64**
1366-0551 Chartered Association of Certified Accountants. Research Report *changed to* A C C A Research Report **1275**
1366-056X Auden Studies† **8932**
1366-0675 Cambria **3862**
1366-0691 Medieval Sermon Studies **5332**
1366-0756 International Journal of Health Care Quality Assurance *changed to* 1751-1879 **4105**
1366-0799 British Association of Teachers of the Deaf. Magazine **4072**
1366-0802 Shipcare **8661**
1366-0853 Insurance International Outlook† **8965**
1366-0950 Current Advances in Mechanical Design and Production **3375**
1366-0969 Accordia Specialist Studies on Italy **370**
1366-0977 Farm Trader†
1366-106X Best of Tots TV†
1366-1108 Forever Friends†
1366-1302 Take a Break's Code Breakers **4348**
1366-1523 The Acronym **7219**
1366-1531 Centre for Resarch in Economic Development and International Trade. Research Paper **1081**
1366-1582 Community Development Foundation. Research and Policy Papers **7117**
1366-1647 Employment Audit
1366-1752 Trace (London) **6624**
1366-185X Advances in Veterinary Dermatology
1366-1922 Key Note Market Report: Exhibitions & Conferences **1894**
1366-1930 Key Note Market Report. Clothing Manufacturing **2248**
1366-1949 Key Note Market Report: Networks†
1366-1957 F T Food Business *changed to* 0955-5404 **3634**
1366-1965 Institution of Occupational Safety and Health. Journal *changed to* 1477-3996 **6684**
1366-1981 Hydraulics & Pneumatics **3362**
1366-199X Private Finance Initiative Journal **1940**
1366-2031 Reach Newsletter **3045**
1366-2120 Technical Tips Online **707**
1366-2163 The International Journal of Project & Business Risk Management†
1366-2295 All about Making Money **1804**
1366-2392 Local Government Management†
1366-2406 Exporter **1565**
1366-2473 I C H A Buyers' Guide to Manufacturers (Year) **8646**
1366-2511 Mining History **6473**
1366-2538 Great Britain. Office for National Statistics. Consumer Trends **1115**
1366-2546 Social Science Working Paper **1549**
1366-2554 Manchester Sociology Occasional Papers **8119**
1366-2627 Home Office Circular **7444**
1366-2651 Publications of the Newton Institute† **8983**
1366-2678 The Surfer's Path **8336**
1366-2694 Linacre Lectures **8632**
1366-2716 Industry and Innovation **1123**
1366-2724 The Sculpture Journal **530**
1366-2821 Internet Business **2560**
1366-283X The European Mergers & Acquisitions Handbook (Years) **1107**
1366-2856 Tolley's Health and Safety at Work Handbook **6688**
1366-2864 Discussion Papers in Economic and Social History **1092**
1366-302X Education Parliamentary Monitor **2848**
1366-3135 Total Film **6515**
1366-3143 Developing World Telecommunications†
1366-3151 Telecoms Tariffs Innovation
1366-3186 Liquid Foods International
1366-3216 Datasite CD-ROM **2349**
1366-3224 Computer Software and Services CD-ROM **2588**
1366-3232 *see* 0950-9879 **2351**
1366-3267 Contact Girls **6288**
1366-3372 Mourne Observer & County Down News **3894**
1366-350X Advanced Cordless Communications†
1366-3534 My Beautiful Horses†
1366-3631 Two Blue Couples **6301**
1366-3666 Working with Older People **8078**
1366-3798 The Environment in Your Pocket **3421**
1366-3852 Airport Equipment and Services Review **8537**
1366-3992 Journal of Viral Hepatitis. Supplement *see* 1352-0504 **5928**
1366-400X Country Report. Bulgaria **1451**
1366-4018 Country Report. Albania **1449**
1366-4026 Country Report. Costa Rica **1452**
1366-4034 Country Report. Panama **1459**
1366-4042 Country Report. Czech Republic **1453**
1366-4050 Country Report. Slovakia **1461**
1366-4077 Country Report. Azerbaijan **1450**
1366-4085 Country Report. Papua New Guinea *changed to* 1753-1721 **1459**
1366-4131 Country Report. Slovenia **1461**
1366-4158 Country Report. Uzbekistan **1463**
1366-4166 Country Profile. Bulgaria† **8944**
1366-4174 Country Profile. Albania† **8944**
1366-4182 Country Profile. Costa Rica† **8945**
1366-4190 Country Profile. Panama† **8946**
1366-4204 Country Profile. Czech Republic† **8945**
1366-4212 Country Profile. Slovakia† **8946**
1366-4239 Country Profile. Azerbaijan† **8944**
1366-4255 Country Profile. Slovenia† **8946**
1366-4271 Country Profile. Uzbekistan† **8946**
1366-4328 Country Risk Service. Uzbekistan **1475**
1366-4360 Estate Agency News **7589**
1366-4409 M P S Casebook **5663**
1366-4417 Green Futures **3435**
1366-4425 Shetland Fishing News **3608**
1366-4433 Justis European Commentaries *see* European Update **1922**
1366-4476 Personal Communications Newsletter†
1366-4484 Telecoms Standards Monitor
1366-4492 Interactive Video Newsletter
1366-4522 Blag **6490**
1366-4530 Teacher Development **3084**
1366-4557 Links (Tunbridge Wells)†
1366-459X Monitor, Population and Health. MB2 **7287**
1366-4646 Contacts **8468**
1366-4697 The Journal of Maxillofacial Prosthetics and Technology **5852**
1366-4727 Space & Communications
1366-4786 Journal of Memetics - Evolutionary Models of Information Transmission **6929**
1366-5030 New Network Operator†
1366-5057 R I B A Connect†
1366-5073 Key Note Market Report: Toys & Games **1895**
1366-5081 International Appliance Manufacturing **1889**
1366-5103 Jane's Mines and Mine Clearance **6427**
1366-5138 Sightseeing in the U K (Year)†
1366-5146 Antibiotics Chemotherapy **5576**
1366-5189 Consulting Engineer† **8943**
1366-5251 University of Hertfordshire. Numerical Optimisation Centre. Technical Report **5545**
1366-5278 Health Technology Assessment **5830**
1366-5324 What Digital Camera **6978**
1366-5456 Journal of Education & Christian Belief **7655**
1366-5510 Microstructure of High Temperature Materials **6326**
1366-5545 Transportation Research. Part E: Logistics and Transportation Review **8517**
1366-5553 Environmental Products **3427**
1366-5588 British Nursing Index **5741**
1366-5626 Journal of Workplace Learning **1868**
1366-5650 Business Standards **1075**
1366-5715 Foundations **8083**
1366-5804 *see* 1354-750X **5585**
1366-5812 *see* 0010-7514 **7009**
1366-5820 *see* 0020-7179 **3200**
1366-5839 *see* 0022-0272 **3067**
1366-5847 *see* 0014-0139 **3191**
1366-5855 *see* 0267-8292 **2111**
1366-5863 *see* 0967-0874 **237**
1366-5871 *see* 0953-7287 **3293**
1366-588X *see* 0020-7543 **1889**
1366-5898 *see* 0951-8398 **2870**
1366-5901 *see* 0143-1161 **2710**
1366-591X *see* 0144-235X **2136**
1366-5928 *see* 0049-8254 **746**
1366-5944 Air Ambulance†
1366-6029 International Regulatory Update
1366-6045 Messaging Newsletter
1366-610X Practical Pre-School **2898**
1366-6193 Key Note Market Report: The Take Home Trade **1895**
1366-6207 Key Note Market Report: Cable & Satellite T V **2384**
1366-6215 Canada Travel Planner **8691**
1366-6223 Capital Region U S A Holiday Guide **8691**
1366-6266 Nintendo 64 Magazine **2479**
1366-6282 A Life in the Day **8054**
1366-6339 International Airport Review **8545**

9602 1367-7810 ULRICH'S PERIODICALS

1367-7810 Northumbria University. Division of Geography and Environmental Management. Departmental Occasional Papers 4022
1367-7845 Association of Chartered Physiotherapists in Women's Health. Journal 6106
1367-7853 Adhesives and Sealants Directory *changed to* British Adhesives and Sealants Association. Handbooks 1977
1367-787X Rising East†
1367-7969 National Freight & Transport Industry Review
1367-806X Where to Buy Chemicals, Plant and Services 1848
1367-8086 Asset Finance International† 8931
1367-8116 Big Ones International 6287
1367-8140 European Construction Institute. Publication 1007
1367-8213 Senior Life 8067
1367-8272 International Arbitration Law Review 4694
1367-8302 Soft Drinks International 610
1367-8329 Practical Arbitration Journal†
1367-8361 Journal of Turfgrass Science *changed to* 1478-548X 8968
1367-8388 Great Britain. Energy Technology Support Unit. Energy and the Environment Programme. Unit J. Report 3136
1367-8396 Fish & Fisheries 3591
1367-8418 Combat Aircraft 51
1367-8426 A N T E Plus†
1367-8531 Business Crime 4885
1367-8620 Research Papers in Media and Cultural Studies 2337
1367-8728 Croner's Reference Book for Employers - Magazine 1859
1367-8779 International Journal of Cultural Studies 8109
1367-8809 Classic Ford 8575
1367-8817 Time to Cook 4368
1367-8825 Literacy Today 3071
1367-8841 European Logistics Directory
1367-885X A B Europe 4975
1367-8868 Human Resource Development International 1863
1367-8876 Country Report. United States of America 1463
1367-8922 C P D Rheumatology 6222
1367-8930 C P D Bulletin. Clinical Biochemistry 727
1367-8949 C P D Bulletin. Immunology and Allergy 5755
1367-8957 C M E Orthopaedics 6057
1367-899X C E Optometry 6039
1367-9007 C M E Bulletin. Haematology *changed to* 1743-0313 5935
1367-9015 C M E Journal. Gastroenterology, Hepatology, and Nutrition 5921
1367-9031 C M E Bulletin Oncology *changed to* 1475-8075 6010
1367-9082 Harpers 604
1367-9090 Harpers Wine and Spirit Directory 604
1367-9120 Journal of Asian Earth Sciences 2749
1367-9163 Register of Ships. Supplement & New Entries†
1367-9198 Wales Council for Voluntary Action. Report Series 8077
1367-9279 Star Performers 2029
1367-9341 H C B International Drum and I B C Guide 6710
1367-9368 Risk Financier†
1367-9414 O A G Air Cargo Rules 8549
1367-9430 Animal Conservation 2602
1367-9546 International Quilting Times†
1367-9643 Computer Contractor 2494
1367-966X Infomatics Digest 2537
1367-9678 Network Solutions 2501
1367-9708 Your Health
1367-9759 The Stakeholder 7185
1367-9813 Business Ratio Report: Process Plant Industry†
1367-9856 A C T T News 8415
1367-9880 Peacekeeping 7259
1367-9899 Abstracts in New Technologies and Engineering 8446
1367-9929 Directory of U K Importers†
1367-9937 Directory of U K Exporters†
1367-9996 European Communications 2320
1368-0005 Syntax 5184
1368-0021 Jazzwise 6580
1368-0080 Good Practice Case Study 1009
1368-0099 Global Ceramic Review 2042
1368-0145 A Guide to Major Trusts (Year) 8043
1368-0234 Cambridge Insider 3862
1368-0269 Paribas Central Bank and Ministry of Finance Yearbook (Year) 1374
1368-0293 British Institute of International and Comparative Law. Director's Report 1282
1368-0439 German Investment World
1368-051X The Company Financial and Insolvency Law Review†
1368-0668 Accounting, Auditing and Accountability Journal 1277
1368-0684 Vacuum Solutions†
1368-0722 Uncut 6625
1368-0773 Adventure Travel 8681
1368-0900 AgraFood Latin America 3625
1368-0919 Modern Astronomer 578
1368-0978 Campden Food and Drink Research Association. Technical Memorandum *changed to* Campden & Chorleywood Food Research Association. Technical Memorandum 3629
1368-1095 Gravesiana 5302
1368-1109 Journal of Diabetes Nursing 5964
1368-1184 Bag
1368-1249 Ophthalmic Nursing 5977
1368-132X Human Rights Centre. Occasional Papers 7208
1368-1427 Merseyside Business Prospect 1498
1368-1435 Advances in Architecture 427
1368-1451 Key Note Market Report: Paper & Board Manufacturing 1895
1368-1486 World Graphic Arts Technology†
1368-1494 Dams & Reservoirs 3264
1368-1532 Key Note Market Report: Short Break Holidays 8727
1368-1559 Telecoms World
1368-1583 National Museums & Galleries of Wales. Annual Report 6534
1368-1613 Information Research 5016
1368-1818 Cross Stitch Gallery 6638
1368-2016 Historical Research. Special Supplement†
1368-2105 Speech & Language Therapy in Practice 3047
1368-2148 International Journal of Manufacturing Technology and Management 3382
1368-2156 International Journal of Healthcare Technology and Management 5831
1368-2164 Brunel University. Vice-Chancellor's Report to Court (Year) 2969
1368-2172 Performance Chemicals International *changed to* 1469-3011 2075
1368-2199 The Imaging Science Journal 6969
1368-2229 Transport Economist 8514
1368-2237 Game Conservancy Trust. Review 907
1368-2288 Applying G A A P 1280
1368-230X Unit Costs of Health & Social Care 8075
1368-2318 Applied Accounting Research Series 1280
1368-2326 University of Wales. Welsh Institute of Rural Studies. Working Paper 8145
1368-2423 Northumbrian Holdings. Annual Report 8830
1368-2431 Arts News *changed to* N C A News 507
1368-244X Great Britain. Department for Work and Pensions. Social Research Branch. In-House Report 8042
1368-2539 Environmental Modeling Series 3482
1368-2547 B†
1368-2628 E L Gazette 5113
1368-2660 Local Government I T in Use 2549
1368-2679 International Journal of Francophone Studies 7974
1368-275X International Journal of Entrepreneurship and Innovation Management 1757
1368-2768 Feminist Praxis†
1368-2784 Opinion: Specialist Reviews of Key Papers in General & Elderly Medicine
1368-2792 Euromoney Derivatives Handbook (Year) 1622
1368-2822 International Journal of Language and Communication Disorders 6081
1368-2865 Post Express 2355
1368-2938 Breakthru 6551
1368-2954 A P E 7550
1368-3020 Focus on Plastics Additives 7092
1368-3047 Measuring Business Excellence 1779
1368-3098 The International Travel Law Journal 4696
1368-3128 International Who's Who of Product Liability Defence Lawyers 4872
1368-3136 Competition 4647
1368-3160 Farm and Country Retailer 110
1368-3179 R C Scale International 4344
1368-3225 Popular Arrowords†
1368-3233 Connexions†
1368-325X Chartered Institute of Public Finance and Accountancy. Waste Collection & Disposal Statistics. Actuals 3478
1368-3276 Key Note Market Report: Housebuilding 1019
1368-3284 Cognitive Neuropsychology Reviews 7347
1368-3454 Country Risk Service. Cuba 1472
1368-3497 Journal of Natural Medicine 312
1368-3500 Current Issues in Tourism 8696
1368-3713 Key Note Market Report: Sports Equipment 8184
1368-373X Key Note Market Report: Agricultural Machinery†
1368-3748 Key Note Market Report: Consumer Magazines 1893
1368-3993 The Best of Big & Black 6286
1368-4027 Golf International 8232
1368-4043 Key Note Market Report: Mortgage Finance†
1368-4051 Key Note Market Report: Fruit Juices & Health Drinks 606
1368-406X British Crop Protection Council. Symposium Proceedings 223
1368-4124 Howard League Handbooks† 8962
1368-4175 The Boutonneur 4330
1368-4213 Association Manager *changed to* 1754-2391 1779
1368-4221 The Econometrics Journal 1097
1368-423X *see* 1368-4221 1097
1368-4264 Bolivia Handbook 8688
1368-4272 Goa Handbook 8714
1368-4280 Israel Handbook 8724
1368-4299 Nepal Handbook 8741
1368-4302 Group Processes & Intergroup Relations 8105
1368-4310 European Journal of Social Theory 8101
1368-440X Journal of Veterinary Pharmacology and Therapeutics. Supplement *see* 0140-7783 6857
1368-4477 Country Profile. European Union† 8945
1368-4574 Social Psychology 7409
1368-4604 Lancashire History Quarterly 4239
1368-4671 Engineering Trends *changed to* 1472-3913 3190
1368-4736 Cytokines, Cellular & Molecular Therapy (Print Edition)†
1368-4752 The Router 1051
1368-4795 Israeli History, Politics and Society 7246
1368-4809 Cheshire Bride & Home 5557
1368-485X World Directory of Leisure Aviation 75
1368-4868 Teaching Theology and Religion 7687
1368-4892 International Journal of Business Performance Management 1755
1368-4965 European Paper Analyst†
1368-4973 Sexually Transmitted Infections 5881
1368-5015 New Journal News 7568
1368-5023 Scintilla 5368
1368-5031 International Journal of Clinical Practice 5638
1368-504X International Journal of Clinical Practice. Supplement *see* 1368-5031 5638
1368-5163 Elgar Society. News 6564
1368-518X Local Government Voice†
1368-5201 Journal of Money Laundering Control 1362
1368-5236 Visiting Arts 524
1368-5295 Linguistics Abstracts Online 5201
1368-5317 Ultimate P C 2482
1368-5325 S M T 2679
1368-5392 Writer's Bulletin†
1368-5449 Parkes-Wiener Series on Jewish Studies 7727
1368-5503 I G E R Innovations 235
1368-552X European Automotive Design 8579
1368-5538 The Aging Male 6283
1368-5562 Bank of England. Working Paper Series 1314
1368-5589 Criminal Law Week 4888
1368-5597 Studies in Air Power 6448
1368-5732 Food Marketing and Manufacturing 3640
1368-5902 Y Llyfr Yng Nghymru 7566
1368-5929 Middle East Grocer 3680
1368-5937 Middle East Paediatrics *changed to* 1755-3172 6098
1368-5945 Middle East Pharmacy 6861
1368-597X Conde Nast Traveller 8694
1368-5988 Key Note Market Report: Training 1895
1368-5996 Key Note Market Report: Sports Clothing and Footwear 2248
1368-6100 Commerce Business Directories. Black Country 1980
1368-6194 Pregnancy *changed to* 1750-4880 8880
1368-6232 Best of Thomas the Tank Engine†
1368-6267 The Art Book 468
1368-6321 Key Note Market Report: Windows & Doors 1896
1368-6348 Cultural Trends in Scotland 484
1368-6356 L S E Health Discussion Paper 7530
1368-6364 Carousel 2181
1368-6402 Touchline 8212
1368-6429 Lloyd's Electronic Law Reports *see* 0024-5488 4724
1368-6437 Lloyd's Electronic Maritime Directory *see* 0268-327X 8650
1368-6445 Promoting Health 7537
1368-6453 Horse Magazine 8292
1368-6534 Culture and Cosmos 565
1368-6542 The Journal of Housing Law 4417
1368-6550 Measurement Good Practice Guide 7026
1368-6607 B R A D Media Ownership Directory 1974
1368-6615 B R A D Inserts Guide
1368-6623 B R A D Recruitment Media 21
1368-6666 In Focus (Sudbury) *see* 0140-8534 6678
1368-6720 Health Economics Research Group. Research Report 4096
1368-6739 Home - Grown Cereals Authority. Project Report 234
1368-6747 H H S C Handbook 3436
1368-6828 H S E Contract Research Report† 8961
1368-6836 Huguenot Society New Series 3771
1368-6909 Eastern European Newsletter 7131
1368-6917 International Library of Macroeconomic and Financial History† 8966
1368-6925 International Library of Critical Writings in Business History 1129
1368-6933 International Library of Critical Writings in Economics 1129
1368-700X X-Files Magazine 2399
1368-7018 Babylon 5: The Offical Magazine 5440
1368-7123 Car Ad 8571
1368-731X Cardio-Vascular Clinical Trials
1368-7360 Association of Paediatric Chartered Physiotherapists. Journal 6106
1368-7417 Network (London, 1922)†
1368-7425 F S U Energy 3135
1368-7433 Argus Global Markets 6762
1368-7506 Journal of Digital Information 2548
1368-7638 Advances in High Performance Computing 3288
1368-7646 Drug Resistance Updates 5607
1368-7727 Golf Management Europe 8232
1368-776X U H S L Newsletter†
1368-7808 International Trade Law Quarterly†
1368-7867 P A W 5 - Eastern Europe†
1368-7913 Poetry Monthly (Print) *changed to* 1750-8509 5432
1368-8022 Boobs 6287
1368-8030 New Talent Video Special 6296
1368-8081 Needlecraft Magic 6640
1368-8111 Marvel Heroes Reborn 2201
1368-8200 Spice 2214
1368-8286 University of Essex. Department of Accounting and Financial Management. Working Paper Series 1303
1368-8340 European Venture Capital Association. Yearbook 1622
1368-8359 Jane's International Defence Directory 6427
1368-8375 Oral Oncology 6032
1368-8391 Environmental Health Series†
1368-8421 European Cycle Routes 8258
1368-843X Great Britain. Energy Technology Support Unit. Energy and the Environment Programme. Unit B-CR. Report 3136
1368-8456 House of Commons. Library. Research Paper 7444
1368-8529 Drugs Quarterly† 8951
1368-8642 Monographs in Supramolecular Chemistry 2127
1368-8766 I G B P Book Series 2746
1368-8774 International Journal of Nematology 948
1368-8790 Postcolonial Studies 4156
1368-8804 Media History 8120
1368-8812 G O - M I N I S†
1368-8901 J S B Journal 4953
1368-8944 E N T News 6079
1368-8952 Eye News 6042
1368-8960 Urology News 6276
1368-8979 Cardiology News 5780
1368-9002 Flying Scale Models 4335
1368-9029 League Cricket Review 8237
1368-9037 Logistics Europe Yearbook 8502
1368-9053 Legal Experts 4720
1368-9061 Plumbing, Heating & Air Movement News 4125
1368-907X E U Focus 1562
1368-9088 Company Law Newsletter 4647
1368-9118 International Rig Report 6774
1368-9126 Dancing Year Book *changed to* Dance International 2684
1368-9207 Contemporary Psychology Series†
1368-9223 Cognitive Science Research Papers 7347
1368-924X U K Environment News 3491
1368-9290 International Journal of Non-Equilibrium Processing 6317
1368-9312 Pinturas y Tintas 6720
1368-9320 Getting Paid 2638
1368-9339 Network World (London)
1368-9355 Journal of Practical Ecology & Conservation. Special Publication 684
1368-9371 @Eco.News 3405
1368-9444 Insurance Direct International†
1368-9460 C D M A Spectrum *changed to* 1467-1034 2366
1368-9584 I E A Studies on the Environment 3438
1368-9592 I E E Electrical Measurement Series *changed to* I E T Electrical Measurement Series 3317
1368-9657 Cover Magazine
1368-9665 Jane's Defence†

Link to your serials resources and content with ulrichsweb.com

ISSN

1392-1746	Bibliografijos Zinios. Straipsniai **618**
1392-1754	Bibliografijos Zinios. Serialiniai Leidiniai **618**
1392-1762	Bibliografijos Zinios. Lituanika **618**
1392-1916	Dialogas **2842**
1392-2114	Ultragarsas **6209**
1392-2130	Veterinarija ir Zootechnika **967**
1392-2327	Donaldas ir Kiti **2186**
1392-2343	Lithuanian Historical Studies **4240**
1392-2351	Lietuvos Rytas **3905**
1392-2475	Zuvininkyste Lietuvoje **3612**
1392-2637	Pinigu Studijos **1375**
1392-2645	Tom & Jerry† **8993**
1392-267X	Terminologija **5186**
1392-2785	Inzinerine Ekonomika **1130**
1392-2807	Verslo Zinios **3906**
1392-2831	Tautosakos Darbai **3623**
1392-3137	Tiltai **3005**
1392-3161	Lietuvos Respublikos Mokejimu Balansas **1365**
1392-3358	Sociologija. Mintis ir Veiksmas **8005**
1392-3463	Genocidas ir Rezistencija **4223**
1392-3498	Kompiuterija **2430**
1392-3536	Barbe **2177**
1392-3730	Journal of Civil Engineering and Management **3274**
1392-4028	Lietuvos Etnologija **346**
1392-4044	Lietuvos Mokslas **4463**
1392-4338	Mike Pukuotukas **2202**
1392-4559	Valstybes Zinios **7191**
1392-4656	Balance of Payments of the Republic of Lithuania *see* 1392-3161 **1365**
1392-4699	Lietuvos Bankas. Metu Ataskaita **1365**
1392-4702	Bank of Lithuania. Annual Report **1315**
1392-5113	Nonlinear Analysis **5520**
1392-5156	Veidas **4481**
1392-5326	Muziejininkystes Biuletenis **6533**
1392-5504	Lithuanian Foreign Policy Review **7251**
1392-5520	Archaeologia Baltica **375**
1392-5628	Humanistica **4455**
1392-5873	Respublika **3906**
1392-592X	Vilniaus Gedimino Technikos Universitetas. Filologija *changed to* 1822-430X **5171**
1392-6195	Jurisprudencija **4707**
1392-6276	Aviacija *changed to* 1648-7788 **48**
1392-6292	Mathematical Modelling and Analysis **5513**
1392-639X	Ugdymo Psichologija **7413**
1392-6748	Archaeologia Lituana **375**
1392-687X	Lietuvos Bankas. Banku Statistikos Metrastis **1365**
1392-7086	Fizikos ir Matematikos Fakulteto Mokslinio Seminaro Darbai *changed to* 1822-511X **5536**
1392-737X	Archivum Lithuanicum **4131**
1392-740X	Environmental and Chemical Physics **7010**
1392-7450	Soter **7682**
1392-7647	Musu Praeitis **4154**
1392-8589	Stomatologija **5866**
1392-8600	Zmogus ir Zodis **5200**
1392-8619	Ukio Technologinis ir Ekonominis Vystymas **1186**
1392-902X	Belaruski Histarychny Ahliad **4204**
1392-9313	Lietuvos Muzikologija **6584**
1392-9321	Lithuanian Political Science Yearbook **7152**
1392-9739	Lithuanian Business Review **1144**
1393-0311	The Irish Family **3893**
1393-0397	Local Authority News **7496**
1393-046X	Westmeath Independent **3895**
1393-0478	Offaly Independent **3894**
1393-0486	Funds International **1349**
1393-0583	Ireland. Central Statistics Office. Annual Services Inquiry **1244**
1393-0591	P C Live! **1420**
1393-0605	Veterinary Bulletin
1393-063X	La Cometa **5107**
1393-0710	Autumn Home **4532**
1393-0729	Environmental Management Ireland **3426**
1393-0737	Irish Chemical & Processing Journal
1393-0753	ShelfLife **3663**
1393-0826	Licensing World **606**
1393-0869	Breaking the Mould
1393-0974	Communique (Dublin) **2647**
1393-1415	Patents Office Journal **6756**
1393-1792	Medico-Legal Journal of Ireland **5915**
1393-1849	Your New Baby **2172**
1393-2047	Ireland. Central Statistics Office. National Income and Expenditure. First Results **1245**
1393-211X	Irish Music **6578**
1393-2152	Drystock Farmer **285**
1393-2470	Gorey Guardian **3893**
1393-2489	Enniscorthy Guardian *see* 1393-2470 **3893**
1393-2497	Wexford People **3895**
1393-2616	Buy & Sell (Munster Edition) *see* 0791-5446 **1977**
1393-2667	Ireland. Central Statistics Office. Meat Supply Balance **182**
1393-2683	The Shooting News (Curragh)
1393-273X	Spirituality **7818**
1393-2764	Ireland. Central Statistics Office. Agricultural Labour Input **182**
1393-2772	Irish Wedding and New Home **5559**
1393-290X	D C U B S Research Papers **1089**
1393-2950	Practice and Procedure
1393-2985	Cyphers **5213**
1393-2993	Decision **1738**
1393-3019	Beyond The Hall Door **4533**
1393-3043	House and Home **4542**
1393-306X	Irish Journal of Feminist Studies†
1393-3167	dot.ie **2555**
1393-3191	Boyzone†
1393-3213	Conveyancing and Property Law Journal **4650**
1393-3221	Political and Economic Review†
1393-3280	Ireland. Central Statistical Office. Agricultural Land Sales **182**
1393-3310	Ireland. Central Statistics Office. Milk and Milk Products Supply Balance **182**
1393-3337	The Tillage Farmer - Incorporating Biatas†
1393-3418	Carlow People **3892**
1393-3426	The Bar Review **4627**
1393-3582	Eisteach **6137**
1393-3701	Foinse† **8957**
1393-3825	Ireland. Central Statistics Office. Cereals Supply Balance **182**
1393-3841	Irish Farmhouse Bed and Breakfast†
1393-4120	Ireland's Horse Review **8293**
1393-4171	Irish Musical Studies **6578**
1393-4201	N E S F Forum Opinion **1500**
1393-421X	N E S F Forum Report **1500**
1393-4317	Irish Intellectual Property Review†
1393-4384	Exporting Today **1565**
1393-4406	Image Interiors **4543**
1393-4414	Metre (Dublin) **5427**
1393-4457	U C D Connections **2304**
1393-4635	Food & Wine Magazine **4358**
1393-4643	Marine Resource Series **3601**
1393-4783	Irish Insurance Law Review *changed to* 1649-0363
1393-4791	Ireland. Central Statistics Office. Regional Accounts. GDP by Region *changed to* 1649-1866 **1244**
1393-4805	Contact News
1393-4813	InTouch **2988**
1393-483X	Slainte **7542**
1393-4945	The Irish Journal of Social Work Research **7976**
1393-4996	Irish Tyre Trade Journal **8586**
1393-5011	Irish 4 X 4 & Off Road **8586**
1393-5062	Medicine Weekly **5675**
1393-5100	Ireland. Central Statistics Office. Agricultural Price Indices **182**
1393-5119	Ireland. Central Statistics Office. Livestock Slaughterings **182**
1393-5127	Ireland on Sunday *changed to* 1752-1696 **3893**
1393-5143	Ireland. Central Statistics Office. Earnings and Hours Worked in Construction **1047**
1393-516X	Ireland. Central Statistics Office. Milk Statistics **182**
1393-5178	Ireland. Central Statistics Office. Index of Employment in Construction **1047**
1393-5232	Kilkenny People **3893**
1393-5259	Chronicon **4135**
1393-5283	Living Space **4545**
1393-5305	Ireland. Central Statistics Office. Vehicles Licensed for the First Time (Month) **1245**
1393-533X	Irish Van & Truck **8586**
1393-5364	Ireland. Central Statistics Office. External Trade **1244**
1393-5372	Basketball Ireland **8222**
1393-5402	The Cookbook **4354**
1393-5453	Ireland. Central Statistics Office. Earnings of Agricultural Workers **182**
1393-5461	The Echo (Ballyfermot Edition) *changed to* 1649-962X **3892**
1393-5461	The Echo (Ballyfermot Edition) *changed to* 1649-9638 **3894**
1393-547X	The Echo (Clondalkin Edition) *changed to* 1649-962X **3892**
1393-547X	The Echo (Clondalkin Edition) *changed to* 1649-9638 **3894**
1393-5488	The Echo (Lucan Edition) *changed to* 1649-962X **3892**
1393-5488	The Echo (Lucan Edition) *changed to* 1649-9638 **3894**
1393-5526	Ireland. Central Statistics Office. Agricultural Price Indices. Preliminary Estimates **182**
1393-5534	Six Mag **3894**
1393-5542	Ireland. Central Statistics Office. Live Register Area Analysis *changed to* 1649-8011 **1245**
1393-5550	Ireland. Central Statistics Office. Live Register Flow Analysis *changed to* 1649-8011 **1245**
1393-5577	Ireland. Central Statistics Office. Output, Input and Income in Agriculture. Advance Estimate **182**
1393-5585	Ireland. Central Statistics Office. Trade with Non - E U Countries **1245**
1393-5593	Ireland. Central Statistics Office. Population and Migration Estimates **7310**
1393-5615	Ireland. Central Statistics Office. Live Register Age by Duration Analysis *changed to* 1649-8038 **7310**
1393-5623	Westmeath Examiner **3895**
1393-5631	Ireland. Central Statistics Office. Tourism and Travel **8779**
1393-5674	Ireland. Central Statistics Office. Fishery Statistics **3613**
1393-5682	Kerry's Eye **3893**
1393-5712	Business Plus **1075**
1393-5747	Ireland. Central Statistics Office. Industrial Stocks **1244**
1393-5755	Ireland. Central Statistics Office. Capital Assets in Industry **1244**
1393-581X	Limerick Papers in Criminal Justice **4893**
1393-5941	Trinity College Law Review **4798**
1393-595X	Western People **3895**
1393-614X	Minerva **6934**
1393-6158	Highball **8235**
1393-6190	Institute of Public Administration, Dublin. Discussion Paper **7446**
1393-6212	Irish Practice in Engineering **3203**
1393-6220	Irish Business Law **4697**
1393-6492	Land Registry and Registry of Deeds. Information Guide **4834**
1393-6530	Country Music Plus
1393-6689	Ireland. Central Statistics Office. Crops and Livestock Survey - Final Estimates **182**
1393-6719	Irish Construction Times **1017**
1393-6832	Irish Catholic **7801**
1393-6867	Ireland. Central Statistics Office. Area, Yield and Production of Crops **182**
1393-6875	Ireland. Central Statistics Office. Quarterly National Household Survey **1245**
1393-6905	Ireland. Central Statistics Office. Output, Input and Income in Agriculture. Preliminary Estimate **182**
1393-6913	Ireland. Central Statistics Office. Census of Industrial Production. Provisional Results **1244**
1393-6948	Ireland. Central Statistics Office. Output, Input and Income in Agriculture **182**
1393-6956	Law Society of Ireland. Gazette **4716**
1393-7065	Fragments of Fingal **4221**
1393-7073	Irish Journal of Family Law **4911**
1393-7081	Ireland. Central Statistics Office. Vehicles Licensed for the First Time (Year) **8527**
1393-709X	Ireland. Central Statistics Office. Pig Survey - June **182**
1393-7103	Ireland. Central Statistics Office. Census of Building and Construction **1047**
1393-7197	Mathematical Proceedings of the Royal Irish Academy **5514**
1393-7200	The Echo (Enniscorthy) **3892**
1393-7235	Wexford Echo **3895**
1393-726X	Women's Studies Review *changed to* 1649-6825 **8899**
1393-7278	Ireland. Central Statistics Office. Crops and Livestock Survey, June - Provisional Results **182**
1393-7359	Moving In **4547**
1393-7391	Rugby Ireland International **8244**
1393-7413	Distribution Management Briefing *changed to* 1393-9580 **1817**
1393-743X	Export Ireland Services to Irish Exporters Guide **1564**
1393-7472	Activities of Irish Psychiatric Services (Year) **6119**
1393-7545	CompuSchool **2948**
1393-7634	Auto Woman **8561**
1393-7642	Roscommon Herald **3894**
1393-7669	Ireland. Office of the Directory of Telecommunications Regulation. Annual Report and Accounts *changed to* 1649-3117 **2328**
1393-7804	Ireland. Department of Foreign Affairs. International Covenant on Civil and Political Rights **7210**
1393-7855	Irish Theatre Magazine **8472**
1393-8061	Zentrum fuer Deutsch-Irische Studien. Jahrbuch **5199**
1393-8088	The World of Irish Nursing *changed to* The World of Irish Nursing & Midwifery **5984**
1393-8096	Ireland. Central Statistics Office. Size of Herd **182**
1393-8126	Classical Ireland†
1393-8207	Heartwise **5788**
1393-8401	The Argus Weekender **3892**
1393-8517	Spokeout **4078**
1393-8576	Drive! **8577**
1393-8584	Ireland. Central Statistics Office. Irish Babies' Names **2174**
1393-8592	Irish Journal of Anthropology **343**
1393-8614	Key Irish Enterprises
1393-8665	Galway Now **3893**
1393-872X	Irish Construction Arbitration Newsletter *changed to* Irish Construction Insight Newsletter **1016**
1393-8738	Dairy & Food Industries Magazine **262**
1393-8746	Dairy & Food Industries Yearbook **262**
1393-8797	Business Health **6674**
1393-8800	Sligo Weekender **3894**
1393-8843	The Clare Champion **3892**
1393-8916	Enter **4977**
1393-8940	Hibernian Law Journal **4687**
1393-9076	Nationalist and Munster Advertiser **3894**
1393-9084	Tipperary Star **3895**
1393-9122	Backspin **8221**
1393-9130	The Mayo News **3894**
1393-9165	Golf Ireland **8232**
1393-9211	RoadRunner **8267**
1393-922X	Ultimate Health **7544**
1393-9289	Kompass Ireland (Year) **2011**
1393-9335	Environmental Studies Research Series Working Papers **3429**
1393-9424	Institute of Public Administration, Dublin. Research Report **7446**
1393-9475	T V Now **2393**
1393-9491	Wild Ireland **2632**
1393-9505	Ireland. Central Statistics Office. Public Sector Employment Earnings **1245**
1393-9521	Sporting Press **8206**
1393-9580	Financial Services Distribution **1817**
1393-9599	PlayStation Official Magazine Ireland **2481**
1393-967X	Business Travel **8689**
1393-9742	No Limits **2162**
1393-9890	Wine Ireland **613**
1393-9947	Student Xpress **2915**
1394-0546	Malaysia. Department of Statistics. Malaysian Economy in Brief **1250**
1394-1070	Computimes Shopper Malaysia **2415**
1394-1291	Malaysia Source Book for Architects and Designers (Year) *changed to* Malaysia Source Book for Architects, Designers & Building Contractors **2015**
1394-1321	Times Business Directory of Malaysia (Year) **2030**
1394-1712	Malaysian Journal of Science. Series A: Life Sciences **687**
1394-178X	Asian Defence and Diplomacy **6412**
1394-195X	Malaysian Journal of Medical Science **5664**
1394-2204	Journal of Tropical Forest Products†
1394-3065	Malaysian Journal of Science. Series B: Physical & Earth Sciences **7025**
1394-4444	Arrows for Change **8852**
1394-4924	Malaysia. Department of Statistics. Annual Statistics of Manufacturing Industries, Malaysia - Part A **1250**
1394-4983	Palm Oil Technical Bulletin **3144**
1394-5076	Malaysian Minerals Yearbook **6469**
1394-5084	The Gombak Review **5301**
1394-5130	Serangga **858**
1394-5599	Indexes on CD-ROM†
1394-5602	Malaysian National Bibliography (CD-ROM Edition) **630**
1394-5610	Buletin Nuklear Malaysia **3165**
1394-5629	Journal of Industrial Technology **8429**
1394-6048	Malaysia. Department of Statistics. Annual Statistics of Manufacturing Industries, Malaysia - Part B **1250**
1394-6234	Malaysian Journal of Library and Information Science **5031**
1394-7338	Malaysia's Best Restaurants **4393**
1394-7346	Couture **2253**
1394-7354	Malaysia Tatler **3907**
1394-7591	Cleo **8855**
1394-7680	I I U M Journal of Economics and Management **1751**
1394-8393	Menmode **2258**
1394-9829	Journal of Tropical Agriculture and Food Science **128**
1395-0045	Froedi **3837**
1395-0061	Skulabladid **2913**
1395-0118	l'Afrika **4175**
1395-0150	Geologisk Tidsskrift **2742**
1395-0320	A F A Specialkatalog **6891**

ISSN

DIRECTORY 2010 1399-7394 9613

1397-7989 Vegetaren **6670**
1397-7997 Byggeri **988**
1397-8209 Denmark. Ministeriet for Foedevarer, Landbrug og Fiskeri. Danmarks JordbrugsForskning. Beretning†
1397-8365 Danish Meteorological Institute. Magnetic Results - Brorfelde, Qeqertarsuaq, Qaanaaq and Narsarsuaq Observatories (Print edition) *changed to* Denmark. Danmarks Meteorologiske Institut. Magnetic Results - Brorfelde, Qeqertarsuaq, Qaanaaq and Narsarsuaq Observatories (Online edition) **2779**
1397-8497 *see* 1396-6588 **1593**
1397-8586 Godt i Gang **2860**
1397-873X Statens Regnskab†
1397-8799 Antik & Auktion **362**
1397-887X Denmark. Biblioteksstyrelsen. Rapport **5005**
1397-8985 Denmark. Risoe National Laboratory. Condensed Matter Physics and Chemistry Department. Annual Progress Report
1397-9272 Tidningsteknik (Copenhagen)† **8993**
1397-9329 Denmark. Ministeriet for Foedevarer, Landbrug og Fiskeri. Danmarks JordbrugsForskning. Forskningsrapport†
1397-9345 Danmarks Tekniske Universitet. Institute of Hydrodynamics and Water Resources. Series Paper†
1397-9353 Kunstmagasinet 1%†
1397-9418 D S B i Dag **8494**
1397-9426 Teatermagasinet ARTE Nyt† **8992**
1397-9507 Virtuelt Center for Sundhedsinformatik. Technical Report **5728**
1397-9523 Foresty Discussion Paper
1397-985X Groen Viden, Markbrug **116**
1397-9868 Groen Viden, Husdyrbrug **116**
1397-9892 Denmark. Ministeriet for Foedevarer, Landbrug og Fiskeri. Rapport. Husdyrbrug **285**
1398-0017 Nordic Statistical Yearbook **8391**
1398-0300 Danish Polar Center. Publication **4191**
1398-0440 Nyhedsmagasinet Danske Kommuner **7500**
1398-0459 Net Prima Vista *see* 0108-1594 **633**
1398-0548 Pluk **7992**
1398-0580 Aktive Kvinder **8850**
1398-0599 Foedevarenyt†
1398-067X Handelshoejskolen i Aarhus. Institut for Informationsbehandling. Working Papers
1398-0742 STRIP! **519**
1398-0769 Immunological Reviews. Supplement *see* 0105-2896 **5759**
1398-0777 Denmark. Danmarks Statistik. Danmarks Vareimport og -Eksport *changed to* 1902-8628 **1224**
1398-0823 Biozoom **727**
1398-1005 The Copenhagen Post **3833**
1398-1056 Faellesskrift **2856**
1398-1080 Denmark. Styrelsen for Statens Uddannelsesstoette. Haandbog om SU til Ungdomsuddannelser **3020**
1398-1099 Eurowoman **3833**
1398-1161 Eksport Kontakt *changed to* 1602-7191 **1883**
1398-1293 Review of Greenland Activities *changed to* 1603-9769 **2764**
1398-1315 Nordic Directory of Dissertation Projects in Asian Studies **564**
1398-1390 Nye Veje†
1398-1420 Kommunerne & Europa† **8969**
1398-1609 Statens Museum for Kunst. Journal *changed to* 1604-9853 **516**
1398-1714 Reviews in Immunogenetics†
1398-1862 Studies in 20th and 21st Century European History **4270**
1398-1951 Regnskabsstatistik for Oekologisk Jordbrug **205**
1398-201X Denmark. Ministeriet for Foedevarer, Landbrug og Fiskeri. Danmarks JordbrugsForskning. Aarsberetning **285**
1398-2133 *see* 1395-4660 **8031**
1398-2176 Kig Ind **3834**
1398-2184 *see* 1395-8054 **4067**
1398-2265 Pediatric Transplantation. Supplement *see* 1397-3142 **6101**
1398-2273 Transplant Infectious Disease **6261**
1398-2362 Nyhedsbrev om Islam og Kristendom *changed to* 1902-5823 **7690**
1398-2370 D S I. Aarsberetning *changed to* 1902-8121 **4092**
1398-2451 Vedligehold Drift og Teknologi **1042**
1398-2567 Ridehesten, Hippoloisk Junior *changed to* 1903-7880 **8298**
1398-2842 Community Dentistry and Oral Epidemiology. Supplement *see* 0301-5661 **5838**
1398-2966 Scandinavian Journal of Sexology†
1398-3091 Folk og Musik *changed to* 1902-8539 **8986**
1398-3105 Socialsektor. Nyhedsbrev *changed to* 1902-1682 **8997**
1398-313X Nordic Institute of Asian Studies. Report Series **557**
1398-3172 Denmark. Ministeriet for Foedevarer, Landbrug og Fiskeri. Strukturdirektoratet. Kortlaegning **105**
1398-3180 Pohjoismainen Kuurosokeiden Henkiloestoen Koulutuskeskus. Uutislehti *see* 0902-7890 **8059**
1398-3202 Nordic Staff Training Center for Deafblind Services. N U D News Bulletin *see* 0902-7890 **8059**
1398-3237 Nordisk Uddannelsescenter for Doevblindepersonle. Arbejdstekst **8059**
1398-3245 Pohjoismainen Kuurosokeiden Henkiloestoen Koulutuskeskus. Tyoeteksti *see* 1398-3237 **8059**
1398-330X Aarhus Universitet. Virksomhedsregnskab *changed to* 1901-0656 **2964**
1398-3393 European Journal of Oral Sciences. Supplement (CD-ROM Edition)†
1398-3458 Nordic Labour Journal **1700**
1398-3563 *see* 0107-7902 **7659**
1398-3598 Denmark. Undervisningsministeriet. Nyhedsbrev *changed to* Nyheder fra uvm.dk **2892**
1398-3644 *see* 0902-5456 **4118**
1398-3830 *see* 1397-4017 **1334**
1398-3849 *see* 1397-520X **1334**
1398-3857 *see* 0107-1289 **1334**
1398-3865 *see* 0011-6149 **1334**
1398-3873 *see* 0902-6681 **7433**
1398-392X Graf *changed to* 1903-4644 **5377**
1398-3938 Haandsretning **2862**
1398-4349 *see* 0907-2675 **6766**
1398-4357 *see* Denmark's Oil and Gas Production **6766**
1398-4403 Socialreformen **8135**
1398-4411 Danhostel, Danmarks Vandrerhjem **4384**
1398-4586 Kirkegaarden **3720**
1398-4810 Danske Skattelove **1919**
1398-490X Denmark. Danmarks Meteorologiske Institut. Danmarks Klimacenter. Rapport **6352**
1398-4977 Denmark. Folketinget. Ombudsmanden. Summary Annual Report **4847**
1398-5027 Eltra Magasinet *changed to* 1901-1989 **3326**
1398-5043 Akademiet for de Tekniske Videnskaber. Aarsberetning *changed to* 1901-8444 **8415**
1398-5116 Bureauoversigt **22**
1398-5213 Golfmagasinet **8233**
1398-523X Politologiske Studier *changed to* 1604-0058 **7171**
1398-5299 Forsikring og Pension i Danmark†
1398-5310 Jernbanefritid **4337**
1398-5523 JydskeVestkysten **3834**
1398-554X Denmark. Ministeriet for Foedevarer, Landbrug og Fiskeri. Foedevareministeriets Aarsrapport **196**
1398-5558 *see* 1398-554X **196**
1398-5566 Denmark. Ministeriet for Foedevarer, Landbrug og Fiskeri. Plantedirektoratet. Beretning *see* 0909-1378 **227**
1398-5574 *see* 0107-1181 **6882**
1398-5590 Home-Entertainment + Videotraileren **2382**
1398-5604 Gravid **5991**
1398-5647 Bipolar Disorders **6127**
1398-585X *see* 0419-9480 **1476**
1398-6023 In Vitro Befrugtning **5633**
1398-6147 I F L A Danida Newsletter†
1398-6163 Centre for Analytical Finance. Working Papers Series **1326**
1398-6244 Loenmagasin† **8971**
1398-6562 Sentura **6512**
1398-7038 Denmark. Ministeriet for Foedevarer, Landbrug og Fiskeri. Danmarks Jordbrugsforskning. Ramme- og Aktivitetsplan (Online Edition) **105**
1398-7127 Alt om Net *changed to* 1602-1495
1398-7135 P C Pro *changed to* 1602-1495
1398-7143 Dansk Center for Byokologi. Medlemsblad *changed to* 1901-4422 **3405**
1398-7224 Privat Computer *changed to* 0109-2847 **2535**
1398-7461 Copenhagen Business School. Department of Industrial Economics and Strategy. Working Papers† **8944**
1398-7526 *see* 0904-4760 **8085**
1398-7763 Semikolon **7680**
1398-7801 Drift **7353**
1398-8697 *see* 0070-3583 **8366**
1398-8700 World Catalogue of Insects **861**
1398-8980 Etnologiske Studier **338**
1398-8999 Kontor & IT†
1398-9014 Lastbil Aarbogen **8672**
1398-9073 Bornholms Museum, Bornholms Kunstmuseum **6521**
1398-9103 Denmark. Danmarks Statistik. Konjunkturstatistik **1223**
1398-9111 Denmark. Danmarks Statistik. Konjunkturstatistik. Supplement **8366**
1398-9154 Ingelise **4361**
1398-9219 Traffic **837**
1398-9308 Denmark. Oekonomi- og Erhvervsministeriet. Energistyrelsen. Energy in Denmark **3127**
1398-9480 Handelshoejskolen i Koebenhavn. Department of Operations Management. Working Paper **1749**
1398-9553 Denmark. Biblioteksstyrelsen. Vejledning **5006**
1398-9626 Denmark. Finanstilsynet. Fondsmaeglerselskaber **1335**
1398-9855 Tidens Mand *changed to* T M **6300**
1398-9898 *see* 0901-7003 **6891**
1398-9995 *see* 0105-4538 **5753**
1399-0004 *see* 0009-9163 **864**
1399-0012 *see* 0902-0063 **6240**
1399-0020 *see* 0901-5027 **5849**
1399-0039 *see* 0001-2815 **5722**
1399-0047 *see* 0907-4449 **2109**
1399-0160 Ny Viden fra Miljoestyrelsen†
1399-0179 Geografisk Tidsskrift. Special Issue **4009**
1399-0616 *see* 0900-0801 **162**
1399-0659 Denmark. Danmarks Statistik. Sociale Forhold, Sundhed og Retsvaesen (Print) *changed to* 1601-0973 **8082**
1399-0667 Denmark. Danmarks Statistik. Generel Erhvervsstatistik (Print) *changed to* 1601-0884 **1223**
1399-0683 Denmark. Danmarks Statistik. Transport. (Print) *changed to* 1601-0981 **8778**
1399-0691 Denmark. Danmarks Statistik. Nationalregnskab og Betalingsbalance (Print) *changed to* 1601-0930 **1223**
1399-0705 Denmark. Danmarks Statistik. Offentlige Finanser (Print) *changed to* 1601-0949 **1223**
1399-0713 Denmark. Danmarks Statistik. Industristatistik *changed to* 1603-9181 **1223**
1399-0721 Denmark. Danmarks Statistik. Byggeri og Boligforhold (Print) *changed to* 1601-0876 **1045**
1399-0772 Ny Viden **2996**
1399-0888 M T F-Nyt *changed to* 0018-4934 **4074**
1399-0896 Markedsoversigten Erhvervsejendom *changed to* 1604-5602 **7589**
1399-1183 Web Ecology **3474**
1399-1256 Arbejdsmarkedsrapport **1664**
1399-1337 Sigma-Serien **5372**
1399-1353 Transfiguration **522**
1399-1361 Bibliana **7627**
1399-137X Udtryk **3048**
1399-1388 *see* 0906-897X **6351**
1399-140X Nordisk Tidsskrift for Selskabsret **1154**
1399-1426 List of Mineral and Petroleum Licenses in Greenland *see* 1399-5340 **6777**
1399-1442 Tidsskrift for Arbejdsliv **1710**
1399-1574 SiD Fiskeren *changed to* 1901-6654 **4606**
1399-1698 Liver. Supplement *see* 1478-3223 **5928**
1399-1701 Spektakel *changed to* 1902-5076 **8478**
1399-1779 Handelshoejskolen i Koebenhavn. Institut for Informatik. Working Paper **1749**
1399-1949 *see* 0905-3263 **6351**
1399-1957 *see* 1398-490X **6352**
1399-199X Historisk Aarbog for Bov og Holboel Sogne **6525**
1399-2023 Danmarks Nationalbank. Danish Government Borrowing and Debt **1334**
1399-204X Aatsitassarsiorneq Pillugu Nalunaarusiaq **6456**
1399-2058 Annual Report on Mineral and Petroleum Activities *see* 1399-204X **6456**
1399-2112 Denmark. Forbrugerstyrelsen. Ren Besked† **8949**
1399-2139 Facts and Figures, Agriculture in Denmark *changed to* 1902-0279 **174**
1399-2236 *see* 0106-2840 **3166**
1399-2260 Denmark. Undervisningsministeriet. Uddannelsesstyrelsen. Haandbogsserie **2841**
1399-2279 Denmark Undervisningsministeriet. Uddannelsesstyrelsen. Temahaefteserie **2841**
1399-2317 Viborg Stifts Bog **7779**
1399-2406 Bipolar Disorders. Supplement *see* 1398-5647 **6127**
1399-2503 Aalborg University. Department of Mathematical Sciences. R **3294**
1399-2554 Dansk Oplagsbulletin **4574**
1399-2570 Tilskud til Miljoeaktiviteter i Oesteuropa *changed to* 1603-0389 **3453**
1399-2589 *see* 1399-5979 **3423**
1399-2686 Aarhus Studies in Mediterranean Antiquity **2229**
1399-2805 Hoejskolernes Faelleskatalog *changed to* 1902-1283 **2942**
1399-2813 Film **6498**
1399-2864 Vmax **8611**
1399-3003 *see* 0903-1936 **6214**
1399-3011 Journal of Peptide Research (Online) *changed to* 1747-0285 **728**
1399-302X *see* 0902-0055 **894**
1399-3038 *see* 0905-6157 **6099**
1399-3046 *see* 1397-3142 **6101**
1399-3054 *see* 0031-9317 **808**
1399-3062 Transplant Infectious Disease Online **6261**
1399-3089 *see* 0908-665X **6262**
1399-3356 Denmark. Det Danske Filminstitut. Katalog. Supplement **6495**
1399-3658 Medier i Norden†
1399-3666 Medier i Norden **8120**
1399-3836 Informationsspecialisten **5017**
1399-3941 *see* 1399-2023 **1334**
1399-4050 Haandvaerksraadet. Nyhedsbrev **1961**
1399-4069 Syddansk Universitet. Virksomhedsregnskab *changed to* 1901-2756 **3004**
1399-4093 Det Blaa Danmark (Online) **8639**
1399-4174 *see* 0041-5782 **5725**
1399-4409 Journey through the History of the English Language in England and America **5136**
1399-445X FotoGuiden† **8957**
1399-4549 Forum for Koen og Kultur **8897**
1399-4638 D O N G Magasinet *changed to* 1902-777X **6793**
1399-4689 Kraks Indkoebsboeger. Transport og Emballage *changed to* 1603-7812 **8970**
1399-4751 Skov & Land **3703**
1399-4786 Handicaphistorisk Tidsskrift **4066**
1399-4859 This is Greenland (Print) *changed to* This is Greenland (DVD) **1433**
1399-5022 Oelentusiasten **608**
1399-5146 *see* 0902-0152 **8421**
1399-5200 *see* 0105-7480 **6832**
1399-5219 Danske Busvognmaend **8577**
1399-5308 Copenhagen Studies in Indo-European **5108**
1399-5332 Statsbiblioteket. Arbejdspapirer **5049**
1399-5340 List of Mineral and Petroleum Licenses in Greenland **6777**
1399-543X Pediatric Diabetes **6100**
1399-5448 Pediatric Diabetes Online **6100**
1399-5456 Danish Environment **3413**
1399-5472 *see* 0905-5991 **3453**
1399-5510 Outlines **8124**
1399-557X Denmark. Danmarks Statistik. Indkomster **1223**
1399-560X Insect Systematics & Evolution **849**
1399-5618 Bipolar Disorders Online **6127**
1399-5820 Selskabet til Historiske Kildeskrifters Oversaettelse **4161**
1399-5855 Raad og Vink fra Biblioteksstyrelsen **5042**
1399-5863 European Journal of Dental Education. Supplement *see* 1396-5883 **5843**
1399-5979 Environmental Assistance to Eastern Europe **3423**
1399-5987 Revisorhaandbogen, Revision **1300**
1399-5995 Revisorhaandbogen, Regnskab **1300**
1399-6010 Natura Jutlandica. Occasional Papers **692**
1399-6142 Diamanten **5006**
1399-6215 Udlaendinge i Danske Kommuner og Amtskommuner *changed to* 1603-6727 **7286**
1399-6290 *see* 0006-2537 **3833**
1399-6444 S A S Magasinet† **8986**
1399-6460 *see* 0909-816X **3834**
1399-6525 *see* 1604-0570 **2853**
1399-6576 *see* 0001-5172 **5768**
1399-669X *see* 0011-6238 **8168**
1399-6703 Fyns Amts Avis **3833**
1399-6711 *see* 1399-6703 **3833**
1399-6738 Clinical Transplantation. Supplement *see* 0902-0063 **6240**
1399-6789 *see* 1398-6163 **1326**
1399-6975 Transplant Infectious Disease. Supplement *see* 1398-2273 **6261**
1399-7114 *see* 0106-2557 **3127**
1399-7149 *see* 0106-1062 **347**
1399-7327 *see* 1395-5403 **221**
1399-7335 Denmark. Miljoe- og Energiministeriet. Miljoestyrelsen. Arbejdsrapport **3413**
1399-7343 *see* 0900-3738 **3413**
1399-7351 *see* 0107-2722 **3458**
1399-7386 *see* 1399-2279 **2841**
1399-7394 *see* 1399-2260 **2841**

ISSN

1402-5701 Teknik & Vetenskap **7922**
1402-5728 Nordic Journal of Building Physics **1027**
1402-5744 Personal & Ledarskap, P & L **1871**
1402-5787 Meddelanden fraan Parasitologen **8803**
1402-5965 Fickdata **1924**
1402-6104 Studenthandboken **3003**
1402-6139 P C foer Alla **2579**
1402-6309 *see* 0348-6567 **3955**
1402-6597 Revisorn Informerar **1300**
1402-6600 Oft Cavum **5858**
1402-6651 S I K A Rapport **8510**
1402-6783 Dialekt-, Ortnamns- och Folkminnesarkivet i Umeaa. Skrifter, Serie E, Vaextnamm **5111**
1402-7003 Jaernvaegar *changed to* 1652-4373 **8522**
1402-7135 Handledarskap i Foerskolan *changed to* 1652-8409 **2857**
1402-7151 Blickpunkt Bygg & Fastighet **982**
1402-7402 HemmaBio **6502**
1402-7429 *see* 1400-5360 **2692**
1402-7496 Stockholm New **3957**
1402-7542 Miljoeaktuellt Plus **3453**
1402-7631 Monographs on Teacher Education and Research *changed to* 1651-0127 **2887**
1402-7852 Metro (Stockholm) **3834**
1402-7984 Aorta **5255**
1402-800X Tjustbygden **421**
1402-8069 Stockholmstidningen **7186**
1402-8085 Gris **287**
1402-8115 Marinmuseum. Skrifter **6432**
1402-8182 Oestran/Nyheterna **3956**
1402-8239 Riksdagens Ledamoeter **7179**
1402-8298 Mission (Uppsala) *see* 1651-405X **7659**
1402-8530 Viikkoviesti *changed to* 1652-1234
1402-8557 Yrkeslaeraren - Ret-info **2947**
1402-859X Arbete, Maenniska, Miljoe & Nordisk Ergonomi†
1402-8603 Perspektiv paa Arbetslivet†
1402-8638 Tidskriften Kuba **4315**
1402-8743 Mac Magazine†
1402-893X *see* 0280-1981 **8563**
1402-9235 Argaladei **8304**
1402-9251 Journal of Nonlinear Mathematical Physics **7021**
1402-9324 Veterinaermoetet *changed to* 1654-9848 **8810**
1402-9375 Femina **8862**
1402-9596 Naettidningen Roetter **3776**
1402-974X Matmagasinet **4363**
1402-9839 Spraak- och Folkminnesinstitutet. Dialektenheten i Uppsala. Skrifter. Ser. D *changed to* 1651-1204 **5177**
1402-9871 Svensk Medicinhistorisk Tidskrift **5719**
1402-9928 *see* 1403-8285 **1170**
1403-0004 Sveriges Riksbank. Financial Market Report *changed to* 1404-2207 **1345**
1403-0047 Vagabond (Stockholm) **8771**
1403-011X Svensk Handelstidning Justitia. Aarsfakta **1946**
1403-0217 T F S Pack + Plast *changed to* 1602-1436 **6712**
1403-0349 Konsultguiden **1771**
1403-0454 J I B S. Working Paper Series **1762**
1403-0462 J I B S. Research Reports **1131**
1403-0470 J I B S. Dissertation Series **1130**
1403-0497 Kosmetik **595**
1403-0586 Oerebro Universitet. Institutionen foer Ekonomi, Statistik och Informatik. Working Paper Series **1156**
1403-0640 Komputer foer Alla *changed to* 1652-3407 **2408**
1403-0667 Roya†
1403-1000 Disney's Nalle Puh Magasinet **2186**
1403-1035 Svensk Medicinhistorisk Tidskrift. Supplement *see* 1402-9871 **5719**
1403-1043 Beredskap *changed to* 1651-5420 **2227**
1403-1094 Nyans **3956**
1403-1108 N O R D I C O M Review **8122**
1403-1248 Mission i Stockholm **8055**
1403-1302 Sveriges Lantbruksuniversitet. Institutionen foer Jordbruksvetenskap Skara. Serie A, Husdjursproduktion. Rapport *changed to* 1652-2885 **301**
1403-1310 Swedish Critical Art Magazine†
1403-1442 Fredstidningen Pax **7236**
1403-1515 Corpus Troporum **7635**
1403-1698 Maestarkryss **4339**
1403-1744 Fakta. Jordbruk **110**
1403-1760 Sic!†
1403-1922 S I D A Evaluations Newsletter **1605**
1403-2031 Electronic News Journal on Reasoning about Actions and Change **2447**
1403-204X *see* 1403-2031 **2447**
1403-2082 Nordisk Geriatrik **4052**
1403-2147 International Journal of Low Energy and Sustainable Buildings **3272**
1403-2252 Gaesthamnsguiden **8275**
1403-2279 Humanetten **5307**
1403-2309 PatentEye **6756**
1403-2457 Sandebudet **7773**
1403-2465 *see* 1403-2473 **1171**
1403-2473 School of Business, Economics and Law, Goeteborg University. Working Papers in Economics **1171**
1403-252X Allers Traedgaard **3721**
1403-2716 *see* 1403-1094 **3956**
1403-2740 Scouting Spirit **2168**
1403-2759 Dagens Handel **1427**
1403-2864 Handelshoegsskolan vid Goeteborgs Universitet. Ekonomisk-Historiska Institutionen. Meddelanden **1116**
1403-297X Res Forum **8751**
1403-2988 Trafik Forum **8513**
1403-3070 Handledarskap i Aeldre och Handikappomsorg **8043**
1403-3194 Baltic Sea Dialogue **2939**
1403-3216 Nordisk Kulturpolitisk Tidskrift **4467**
1403-3313 Biblis **7553**
1403-3402 Agrarhistoria **80**
1403-3526 *see* 1403-3534 **2448**
1403-3534 Electronic Transactions on Artificial Intelligence **2448**
1403-3569 Metro (Goeteborg) **3956**
1403-3585 Sylwan **7574**
1403-3755 New Routes **7255**
1403-3860 Research Institute of Industrial Economics. Working Papers **1165**
1403-4026 Hemma Baest†
1403-4042 Sweden. Socialstyrelsen. Foerteckning oever Sveriges Legitimerade Laekare **5719**
1403-4182 Aktuell FoU **2966**
1403-4336 Svenska PlayStation Magasinet†
1403-4387 Ljud och Bild *changed to* 1653-9907 **2332**
1403-4433 S S E/E F I Working Paper Series in Business Administration **1170**
1403-4530 Africa Forum **7276**
1403-476X Polishoegskolan. Forskningsrapport **7460**
1403-4905 V T I EC Research **8636**
1403-4948 Scandinavian Journal of Public Health **5710**
1403-4956 Scandinavian Journal of Public Health. Supplement **5710**
1403-4964 In Situ **397**
1403-4972 Stockholm Studies of Curriculum Studies **2915**
1403-5057 Korrschack **8184**
1403-543X Herman Hedning **2192**
1403-5472 Postverksamhet **2348**
1403-5502 Moderna Laekare **4599**
1403-5561 *see* 1403-5502 **4599**
1403-5685 Oestersjoejudiskt Bulletin **4251**
1403-5693 Nu *changed to* 1650-4224 **1797**
1403-5715 S T M-online *see* 0081-9816 **6621**
1403-5758 Kriminalwaarden. Kriminalwaardens Redovisning om Drogsituationen **2696**
1403-591X Svenska P C Format†
1403-6010 Sport foer Alla†
1403-6096 Housing, Theory and Society **4414**
1403-6142 Germanistische Schlaglichter **5122**
1403-6169 Umeaa Universitet. Pedagogiska Institutionen. Pedagogiska Rapporter **2921**
1403-6304 Currents **104**
1403-6398 Skog & Trae **3702**
1403-6525 Humanistica Oerebroensia. Artes et Linguae **4455**
1403-6592 Foeretagaren **1960**
1403-6606 Evolution (Chinese Edition) *see* 1104-8158 **3377**
1403-6746 Tidskriften Bioenergi **3223**
1403-6967 Allt om Resor **8682**
1403-7025 Tidningen Aeldreomsorg **8074**
1403-7076 Tidskriften Alphaomega†
1403-7203 Reports on Business and Informatics **1165**
1403-7211 Ikoner **5014**
1403-722X Vin och Mat *changed to* 1653-3925 **4351**
1403-7262 Svenska Handelsbanken. Interim Report **1385**
1403-7300 Fiskejournalen **8313**
1403-7467 Paulus **7812**
1403-7505 Aktuellt i Politiken **7104**
1403-7599 Oerebro Universitet. Centrum foer Feministiska Samhaellsstudier. Arbetsrapport **8902**
1403-7785 MacGregor News **8651**
1403-7858 Fakta om Sveriges Skatter *changed to* 1404-0883
1403-7912 Transporter och Kommunikationer **8517**
1403-7963 Presens **8476**
1403-8064 Hennes **8867**
1403-8099 Karlstad University Studies **3956**
1403-8196 Advances in Physiotherapy **6106**
1403-8234 Naturvaardsverkets Foerfattningssamling **2622**
1403-8285 S S E/E F I Working Paper Series in Economics and Finance **1170**
1403-8293 Gotarc. Serie A **395**
1403-8331 Konjunkturinstitutet. K I Dokument *changed to* 1650-996X **1896**
1403-8366 News from the Nordic Africa Institute **4177**
1403-848X Institutet for Metalfarskning. Forskningsrapport **6316**
1403-8498 Dagens Media **1813**
1403-8668 Hygiea Internationalis **7524**
1403-8722 Europaraettslig Tidskrift **4668**
1403-8943 Genus **8898**
1403-9052 RetorikMagasinet **5360**
1403-9427 Tidningen G **1798**
1403-9605 Svensk Papperstidning *changed to* 1651-9981 **6738**
1403-9605 Svensk Papperstidning *changed to* 1651-9515 **6735**
1403-9656 *see* 1103-9000 **3954**
1403-9699 Foersaekringsboken **4503**
1403-9710 Du & Jobbet **6676**
1403-9842 Pejling fraan Svensk Mjoelk **268**
1403-9850 Morgonbris **8876**
1404-0050 Springtime med Runner's World *changed to* 1654-7837 **8198**
1404-0069 Monitor **2334**
1404-0212 Bild†
1404-0344 Svensk Kaernbraenslehantering. Technical Report **3175**
1404-0360 The Royal Institute of Technology. Department of Aeronautics. Report *changed to* 1651-7660 **69**
1404-0581 Marinmuseum. Aarsbok **6528**
1404-0638 Din Traedgaard *changed to* 1652-8824 **4538**
1404-0662 Acta Bibliothecae Universitatis Oerebroensis **4440**
1404-0670 Evidensbaserad Sjukgymnastisk Behandling **5612**
1404-0700 I U I Dissertation Series (Year) **1751**
1404-0743 Reports on Asian and African Studies **5166**
1404-0883 Fakta om Skatter†
1404-0891 Magisteruppsats i Biblioteks- och Informationsvetenskap vid Bibliotekshoegskolan-Biblioteks- och Informationsvetenskap (Print) *changed to* 1654-0247 **5031**
1404-0956 Kriminalvaardsverkets Administrative Foereskrifter *changed to* 1653-6657 **2659**
1404-0980 rfv.se *changed to* 1652-9472 **8036**
1404-1022 Svensk Aakeritidning **8675**
1404-1049 Minerals & Energy **1601**
1404-1227 Fakta om Loener & Arbetstider **1681**
1404-1553 Prinsessan **2209**
1404-157X Botilda **8894**
1404-1634 Journal of Intercultural Communication **8114**
1404-1650 Social Insurance in Sweden *see* 1403-9699 **4503**
1404-1804 Plan **3173**
1404-1863 Bidrag till Kungliga Musikaliska Akademiens Historia **6549**
1404-2029 U V Vaest Rapport **421**
1404-207X Nu†
1404-2134 S I W I Proceedings **8831**
1404-2169 Current Issues **335**
1404-2177 Kadenz **3956**
1404-2185 Evangelisk-Luthersk Barntidning Droppen *changed to* 1654-9457 **7755**
1404-2193 Finansiell Stabilitet **1346**
1404-2207 Financial Stability Report **1345**
1404-224X R F M A Debatt†
1404-2339 Sveriges Lantbruksuniversitet. Institutionen foer Ekologi och Vaextproduktionslaera. Rapport **160**
1404-2347 Ecology and Crop Production Science **106**
1404-2487 The Nordic Textile Journal **8456**
1404-2576 Statens Institutionsstyrelse. Forskningsrapport **8073**
1404-2584 Statens Institutionsstyrelse. Allmaen SiS-Rapport **8073**
1404-2614 Fronesis **7137**
1404-2924 Diakonivetenskapliga Institutet. Skriftserie **7637**
1404-2959 Nordisk Interioer **4547**
1404-2991 Datateknik 3.0 *changed to* 1651-3169
1404-3181 Vaara Katter **6816**
1404-3386 Visuellt **525**
1404-3467 Faerghandel **6717**
1404-3769 Sesam paa Laett Svenska *changed to* 1651-1190 **3955**
1404-3815 International Society for the History and Bibliography of Herpetology. Newsletter and Bulletin *changed to* 1653-3798 **936**
1404-3858 Journal of Scandinavian Studies in Criminology and Crime Prevention **2658**
1404-3874 Karavan **5317**
1404-4013 *see* 1403-8668 **7524**
1404-4056 Psoriasistidningen **5881**
1404-4110 Fiskeriverket Rapport†
1404-4188 Integration i Fokus†
1404-4218 Anfang **4571**
1404-4307 Acta Wexionensia **7832**
1404-4358 Postbulletinen **2355**
1404-4412 Lantliv **5075**
1404-4447 Spider-Man
1404-4595 On **2370**
1404-4625 Vaegtrafikskador **8532**
1404-4757 Spraak- och Folkminnesinstitutet. Dialekt-, Ortnamns- och Folkminnesarkivet i Umeaa. Skrifter. Serie C, Folkminnen och Folkliv **3622**
1404-4870 Statens Historiska Museums Utstaellningskatalog **6537**
1404-4900 Energivaerlden **3129**
1404-5052 S C O R E Rapportserie **7181**
1404-5346 I V L - Nyheter (Print Edition) *changed to* I V L - Nyheter (Online Edition) **3438**
1404-5591 I Luften **59**
1404-5648 Sweden. Riksfoersaekringsverket. Vaegledning *changed to* 1653-3232 **4524**
1404-5672 Arbetet Ny Tid†
1404-5699 Metro (Skaane) **3834**
1404-5834 Sweden. Statistiska Centralbyraan. Statistiska Meddelanden. Serie JO, Jordbruk, Skogsbruk och Fiske **186**
1404-5893 Sweden. Statistiska Centralbyraan. Statistiska Meddelanden. Serie Uf, Utbildning och Forskning **2936**
1404-594X Tynglyftaren **8213**
1404-5974 Sveriges Lantbruksuniversitet. Faeltforskningsenheten. Rapport **159**
1404-6091 Central Asia and the Caucasus **7115**
1404-6105 Spraak- och Folkminnesinstitutet. Dialekt-, Ortnamns- och Folkminnesarkivet i Goeteborg. Smaaskrifter **3622**
1404-6113 Handledarskap i Skolan *see* 1652-7844 **2861**
1404-6555 Svenska Blodhunden **6815**
1404-6768 Sveriges Riksbank. Economic Review *see* 1100-5815 **1385**
1404-6822 Offside **8241**
1404-6857 I & M **7284**
1404-7187 S O K Magasin *changed to* 1654-4625 **8191**
1404-7225 Oerebro Universitet. Institutionen foer Teknik. Studies **3213**
1404-7314 F O V U Dialog **2941**
1404-7322 Haestmagasinet **8291**
1404-7365 Saekerhet & Sekretess **2516**
1404-7586 Nobel Museum. Archives **4467**
1404-7659 Tidskrif foer Laerarutbildning och Forskning **2919**
1404-7667 Stockholm University. Department of Economics. Working Papers **1179**
1404-773X Vaexjoe University. School of Management and Economics. Working Paper Series *changed to* 1653-638X **1191**
1404-7845 Globala Studier **1114**
1404-7853 Nysvensk Tidende **7160**
1404-790X Working Life Research in Europe. Report **1716**
1404-8051 Nya Dagen **3956**
1404-823X 00tal **5405**
1404-8280 Tidsperspektiv **420**
1404-837X Hemkundskap i Skolan *changed to* 1651-0992 **4361**
1404-8426 Arbetsliv i Omvandling **1664**
1404-8434 Akila **8302**
1404-8469 Plastforum Nordica *changed to* 1653-557X **7096**
1404-8477 Packmarknaden Nordica **6714**
1404-8507 F F-Tidningen
1404-854X S I K A Statistik **8397**
1404-8590 Fiskeriverket Informerar (Online Edition) **3594**
1404-8647 N P. Nationellt Pistolskytte **8189**
1404-8868 Alla **8024**
1404-8876 Aentligen Hemma *changed to* 1652-8824 **4538**
1404-8892 Residence **4549**
1404-8906 Depaa *changed to* 1652-5949 **364**
1404-8914 Sjoefart och Sjoefoersvar†
1404-8922 Teknik & Maenniska **6515**
1404-8965 Barn **8027**
1404-9007 Forum foer Migration och Kultur **7283**
1404-9023 Magisteruppsats i Pedagogik **2884**
1404-904X Nordiska Hoegskolan foer Folkhaelsovetenskap. Thesis **7534**
1404-918X Julia **2195**
1404-921X Magasinet Vildmark **8321**
1404-9341 Kultursmocken **6583**

ISSN

9616 1404-9430 ULRICH'S PERIODICALS

1404-9430 *see* 0015-7813 **394**
1404-9465 Power *changed to* 1653-2902 **8210**
1404-9538 Oerebro Universitet. Pedagogiska Institutionen. Arbetsrapporter **2893**
1404-9546 Goeteborgs Stadsmusei Skriftserie **3955**
1404-9562 S I D A Studies **1605**
1404-9570 Oerebro Studies in Education **2893**
1404-9597 Paa Kryss **8279**
1404-966X Chalmers Tekniska Hoegskola. Vatten Miljoe Transport. Rapport **8819**
1404-9783 On Demand (Malmoe) *changed to* 0347-9846 **7318**
1404-983X Laerarhoegskolan i Stockholm. Institutionen foer Individ, Omvaerld och Laerande. Forskning **2881**
1404-9848 Area†
1404-9899 Dokumenterat **6562**
1404-9902 Kommuniket†
1405-0056 Anestesia en Mexico **5769**
1405-0099 Cirujano General (Print Edition) *changed to* Cirujano General (Online Edition) **5595**
1405-0145 Informacion Dinamica de Consulta **4870**
1405-0242 Artemisa **5740**
1405-0269 Ciencia Ergo Sum **4447**
1405-0315 Revista Mexicana de Enfermeria Cardiologica **5799**
1405-0439 DeDiseno **7319**
1405-0471 Madera y Bosques **3713**
1405-0560 Poliester **512**
1405-0595 Inversion y Finanzas **1631**
1405-0625 Cirugia Plastica **6239**
1405-0676 Ingenierias **7866**
1405-0749 Revista de Enfermedades Infecciosas en Pediatria **6103**
1405-0811 Inversionista Mexicano **1631**
1405-0927 Historia y Grafia **4142**
1405-0935 Juridica **4705**
1405-0943 Psicologia Iberoamericana **7393**
1405-0951 Prometeo (Mexico City)†
1405-096X Sociologia y Politica†
1405-0994 Enfermedades Infecciosas y Microbiologia **5813**
1405-1001 Trauma **6074**
1405-101X Revista Iberolatinoamericana de Cuidados Intensivos†
1405-1036 La Experiencia Literaria **5294**
1405-1060 Politica y Gobierno **7460**
1405-1079 Gestion y Politica Publica **7138**
1405-1109 Psicologia y Salud **7393**
1405-1117 Estudios del Hombre **336**
1405-1168 Practica Pediatrica **6103**
1405-1303 Hospital Infantil del Estado de Sonora. Boletin Clinico **5629**
1405-1435 Convergencia **7432**
1405-1443 Calidad Ambiental **3408**
1405-1559 Manufactura **1898**
1405-1648 Revista Medica de Aguascalientes **5706**
1405-1680 Puentelibre **513**
1405-1699 Alergia, Asma e Inmunologia Pediatricas **5752**
1405-1710 Centro Dermatologico Pascua. Revista **5873**
1405-1745 Red-Mat **5528**
1405-1923 Archivos Hispanoamericanos de Sexologia **7336**
1405-1966 Cuadernos del Sur **7957**
1405-2040 Desde el Sur **2977**
1405-2059 Revista Mexicana de Astronomia y Astrofisica Serie de Conferencias **580**
1405-2075 Educacion 2001 **2845**
1405-2091 Salud en Tabasco **7540**
1405-213X *see* 0037-8615 **5536**
1405-2210 Estudios sobre las Culturas Contemporaneas **4451**
1405-2229 Nueva Cardiologia **5796**
1405-2253 America Latina en la Historia Economica. Boletin de Fuentes **4168**
1405-230X Bolsa Mexicana de Valores. Resumen Bursatil **1215**
1405-2342 *see* 1560-7348 **2974**
1405-2466 Estudios Agrarios (Mexico, D.F.) **108**
1405-2687 Revista de Literatura Mexicana Contemporanea **5361**
1405-2768 Polibotanica **813**
1405-2849 Gaceta Ecologica **3432**
1405-2938 Neumologia y Cirugia de Torax **6252**
1405-2946 S I D A - E T S
1405-2962 Revista Mexicana del Caribe **7997**
1405-3020 Cuadernos de Derecho **4653**
1405-3136 A B Z
1405-3195 Agrociencia **87**
1405-3322 Sociedad Geologica Mexicana. Boletin **2767**
1405-3500 Carrizos **5271**
1405-3543 Revista Internacional de Ciencias Sociales y Humanidades **7997**
1405-3551 Instituto Nacional de Investigaciones Forestales, Agricolas y Pecuarias. Boletin Tecnico **850**
1405-356X Instituto Nacional de Investigaciones Forestales, Agricolas y Pecuarias. Boletin Divulgativo **850**
1405-3578 Instituto Nacional de Investigaciones Forestales, Agricolas y Pecuarias. Publicacion Especial **850**
1405-3586 Ciencia Forestal en Mexico **3686**
1405-4167 Revista de Humanidades **4472**
1405-4558 Metapolitica **7154**
1405-4574 Hitos de Ciencias Economico Administrativas **1750**
1405-4604 Travelers Guide to Mexico **8786**
1405-4787 Educar **2846**
1405-4817 Boletin La Pintura Prehispanica en Mexico **384**
1405-5082 Psicologia y Ciencia Social **7393**
1405-5163 Universidad Veracruzana. Gaceta **3007**
1405-5406 Tiempo Libre **3911**
1405-5546 Computacion y Sistemas **2410**
1405-602X Istmo **3909**
1405-6550 Ciencia **7846**
1405-6658 Sputnik **2567**
1405-6666 Revista Mexicana de Investigacion Educativa **2907**
1405-6690 Universidad de la Salle. Centro de Investigacion. Revista **4479**
1405-6763 Revista Medica La Salle **5706**
1405-7107 Caleidoscopio **7952**
1405-7247 Foresta Veracruzana **3690**
1405-7255 Ethos Educativo **2855**
1405-7425 Papeles de Poblacion **7289**
1405-7697 G C D: La Revista de la Seguridad **7438**
1405-7743 Ingenieria, Investigacion y Tecnologia **3198**
1405-776X Dimension Antropologica **335**
1405-7786 Alquimia **6963**
1405-7840 *see* 1606-5913 **5224**
1405-7867 Vertientes **5728**
1405-7980 Investigacion en Salud **5641**
1405-8111 Bon Vivant **5066**
1405-8251 Revista Mexicana de Estudios Canadienses **4311**
1405-8421 Economia, Sociedad y Territorio **7960**
1405-8626 Quivera **3461**
1405-8723 Scientiae Naturae **7912**
1405-8790 Revista Mexicana de Medicina Fisica y Rehabilitacion **6116**
1405-888X Tip **746**
1405-8901 Bitacora. Revista de Arquitectura **435**
1405-8928 Trayectorias **8011**
1405-8960 Acta Medica de Sonora **5566**
1405-9282 Revista Mexicana de Agronegocios **1791**
1405-9525 Revista Internacional de Estudios en Educacion **2907**
1405-9657 Archivos de Medicina Familiar **5577**
1405-9940 Archivos de Cardiologia de Mexico **5777**
1406-0000 Studia Philosophica **6954**
1406-0078 Tallinn **3567**
1406-0086 Estonian Academy of Sciences. Proceedings. Physics. Mathematics **7011**
1406-0124 Estonian Academy of Sciences. Proceedings. Chemistry **2061**
1406-0132 Estonian Academy of Sciences. Proceedings. Geology *changed to* 1736-4728 **2733**
1406-0140 Papers on Anthropology **351**
1406-0175 Estonian Academy of Sciences. Proceedings. Engineering **3191**
1406-023X Estonian Marine Institute. Report Series **2804**
1406-0388 Eesti Rahva Muuseumi Aastaraamat **336**
1406-0477 Eesti Naine **8859**
1406-0515 Loomingu Raamatukogu **5225**
1406-0582 Kroonika **3836**
1406-0612 Luup **3836**
1406-0639 Estonian Legislation in Translation **4667**
1406-0701 Interlitteraria **5309**
1406-0760 Eesti Ajalooarhiivi Toimetised **4216**
1406-0779 Eesti Paevaleht **3836**
1406-0795 Vanavaravedaja **3623**
1406-0914 Estonian Academy of Sciences. Proceedings. Biology. Ecology **671**
1406-0922 Trames **8010**
1406-0949 Folklore **3617**
1406-0957 *see* 1406-0949 **3617**
1406-0965 Keskkond **3449**
1406-0981 Postimees **3836**
1406-099X Baltic Journal of Economics **1065**
1406-1015 Naedal **8877**
1406-1023 Teleleht **3837**
1406-1074 Juridica **4705**
1406-1082 Juridica International **4705**
1406-1112 Anne **8851**
1406-1171 Tallinn This Week **3837**
1406-1244 Sporditaht **3837**
1406-1252 Arielu **1061**
1406-1392 Eesti Pank. Bulletin **1337**
1406-1783 Eesti Statistika Aastaraamat **8367**
1406-2062 Hirundo **908**
1406-2119 Kodukiri **3836**
1406-216X Pere ja Kodu **3836**
1406-2178 Stiil **2261**
1406-2208 City Paper - The Baltic States **8693**
1406-2232 Estonia **3836**
1406-2240 Vesti Nedelja Plus **3837**
1406-2283 Acta et Commentationes Universitatis Tartuensis de Mathematica **5464**
1406-2585 Aripaev **3836**
1406-2593 Delovye Vedomosti **1091**
1406-2690 Tallinn In Your Pocket **8759**
1406-2739 Barbie **2177**
1406-278X Abiks Loodusvaatlejale **2601**
1406-2801 Dissertationes Scientiarum Naturalium Universitatis Agriculturae Estoniae **105**
1406-2860 Kunstiteaduslikke Uurimusi **501**
1406-2925 Acta Historica Tallinnensia **4129**
1406-2933 Eesti Arheoloogia Ajakiri **391**
1406-2984 Maaleht **3836**
1406-300X Tervis Pluss **6998**
1406-3018 Stiina **8884**
1406-3034 Tom ja Jerry **2217**
1406-3085 Seltskond **3837**
1406-3328 Riigi Teataja. I Osa **4775**
1406-3433 Eesti Putukate Levikuatlas **843**
1406-3530 Acta Bibliothecae Nationalis Estoniae **615**
1406-3786 Tanapaeva Folkloorist **3623**
1406-3859 Ajalooline Ajakiri **4197**
1406-3867 Muinasaja Teadus **406**
1406-4030 Tuna **4274**
1406-4049 Eesti Pollumajandusulikooli. Teadustoode Kogumik **106**
1406-4243 Sign Systems Studies **5174**
1406-4332 Parnu In Your Pocket **8746**
1406-4499 Eesti Majanduse Teataja **1102**
1406-4774 Tallinn Technical University. Theses **3256**
1406-4804 Saladused **8882**
1406-4812 EuroUniversity. Series. International Relations **7234**
1406-4979 A D A C Special Auto **8554**
1406-5053 Folia Baeriana **673**
1406-5266 Elukiri **3836**
1406-5304 Looduseuurija Kasiraamatud **7880**
1406-5428 Paar Sammukest **5347**
1406-5495 *see* 1406-1074 **4705**
1406-5509 *see* 1406-1082 **4705**
1406-5967 University of Tartu. Faculty of Economics and Business Administration. Working Paper Series **1189**
1406-6173 S L Ohtuleht **3836**
1406-6203 Studia Humaniora Tartuensia **4476**
1406-6238 Maamajandus **135**
1406-7099 Rahvusvahelise Eduard Tubina Uhingu Aastaraamat **6609**
1406-7110 Eesti Tootervishoid **6676**
1406-8834 Karupoeg Puhh **2196**
1406-894X Agronomy Research **88**
1406-9490 Music in Estonia **6591**
1406-992X Maetagused **3620**
1406-9938 *see* 1406-992X **3620**
1406-9954 Metsanduslikud Uurimused **3696**
1406-9962 Pro Ethnologia *changed to* 1736-6518 **3619**
1407-0049 Latvijas Prese (Year) **629**
1407-0081 Latvijas Zinatnu Akademijas Vetis. A Dala. Humanitaras Zinatnes **4463**
1407-009X Latvian Academy of Sciences. Section B. Natural Sciences. Proceedings **7879**
1407-0332 Gramatu Apskats†
1407-0391 Latvijas Vestnesis **3904**
1407-0464 Dambo **2185**
1407-0863 Tom & Jerry **2217**
1407-0944 Baltic Journal of Laboratory Animal Science†
1407-1010 Latvijas Ekonomist **1144**
1407-1398 Latvijas Korespondencsahs
1407-1525 Donalds Daks **2186**
1407-1584 Santa **3905**
1407-1592 *see* 1407-1584 **3905**
1407-1614 Mans Mazais **2161**
1407-1649 Klubs **6583**
1407-1657 Chas **3904**
1407-1894 Barbie **2177**
1407-2033 Ieva **8868**
1407-2300 The Baltic Times **3904**
1407-2319 E-tbt *see* 1407-2300 **3904**
1407-2335 Riga In Your Pocket **8752**
1407-2343 *see* 1407-2335 **8752**
1407-2629 Lyublyu! **8872**
1407-3005 R A U Scientific Reports (Online)†
1407-3021 Biznes i Baltiya **1068**
1407-3269 Copes Lietas **8310**
1407-3331 Lauku Avize *changed to* Latvijas Avize **3904**
1407-3358 Praktiskais Latvietis **3905**
1407-3390 Vinnijs Puks **2219**
1407-3412 *see* Latvijas Avize **3904**
1407-3617 S **3031**
1407-4311 Privata Dzive **3905**
1407-5806 Computer Modelling and New Technologies **2412**
1407-6632 *see* 1407-2629 **8872**
1407-6640 *see* 1407-1657 **3904**
1407-7027 Deko **4537**
1407-7183 C A D / C A M / C A E Observer **3288**
1407-7299 e-Pasaule **2417**
1407-7604 Princeses **2208**
1407-768X Baltic Journal of Psychology **7338**
1407-7841 Cels **7630**
1407-8619 Baltic Journal of Coleopterology **840**
1407-8953 Acta Biologica Universitatis Daugavpiliensis **772**
1407-9283 Avene **2177**
1408-0109 *see* 0032-9088
1408-0133 Moj Hobi **4438**
1408-0192 Brat Francisek **7786**
1408-032X Anthropological Notebooks **325**
1408-0419 Acta Historiae Artis Slovenica **463**
1408-0877 T V Special **2394**
1408-0893 K I H Zima *see* 0353-3522 **4337**
1408-0907 K I H Poletje *see* 0353-3522 **4337**
1408-1121 Knjiznica Annales **5023**
1408-1482 Metodolosko Gradivo **8388**
1408-1547 Knjiznica Sigma **7024**
1408-1687 Oskar **6509**
1408-1741 Onkologija **6031**
1408-192X Statisticne Informacije **8405**
1408-1970 Katalog Statisticnih Publikacij†
1408-239X K I H Pomlad *see* 0353-3522 **4337**
1408-2403 Muska **6597**
1408-2497 Pilot R T V *see* 1318-0339 **3947**
1408-2500 CESTAT Statistical Bulletin *changed to* CANSTAT Statistical Bulletin
1408-2527 Smrklja Roman **5374**
1408-2616 Slovenski Jezik **5175**
1408-2640 Tehnika in Narava **214**
1408-2799 *see* 0005-4631 **1311**
1408-2942 Socialna Pedagogika **8134**
1408-3108 Vase Najlepse Ljubezenske Zgodbe **5412**
1408-340X University of Ljubljana. Biotechnical Faculty. Research Reports *changed to* 1581-9175 **216**
1408-3744 P C Format **2359**
1408-3760 Delo + Varnost **1674**
1408-4295 Lord **6811**
1408-4937 Hopla **3947**
1408-5038 Snopje z Domacih in Tujih Njiv Krscanske Misli†
1408-533X Znanstveno Raziskovalno Sredisce Republike Slovenije. Annales. Series Historia Naturalis **712**
1408-5348 Znanstveno Raziskovalno Sredisce Republike Slovenije. Annales. Series Historia et Sociologia **4168**
1408-5593 Koledarcek **2198**
1408-5763 Skrjancek **2371**
1408-6271 Studia Mythologica Slavica **3566**
1408-6980 Journal of International Relations and Development **7248**
1408-7952 Svet & Ljudje **8759**
1408-8347 Non-Stop **8325**
1408-8606 Statisticna Sporocila **8405**
1408-8681 Nekateri Pomembnejsi Podatki o Republiki Sloveniji†
1408-869X Kakovostna Starost **4050**
1408-8754 *see* 1318-1092 **5642**
1408-9114 Klasifikacije **8384**
1409-0015 *see* 1022-9485 **4732**
1409-0090 Acta Pediatrica Costarricense **6087**
1409-0112 Pensamiento Actual **4469**
1409-018X Costa Rica. Direccion General de Estadistica y Censos. Estadisticas Vitales **8365**

DIRECTORY 2010 1417-3980 9617

1409-0198 Costa Rica. Direccion General de Estadistica y Censos. Encuesta de Hogares de Propositos Multiples Modulo de Empleo **1222**
1409-0201 Costa Rica Calculo de Poblacion **7305**
1409-0279 Revista del Archivo Nacional **5043**
1409-0724 Revista de Ciencias del Ejercito y la Salud **8196**
1409-1259 Gestion **8042**
1409-1429 Revista Costarricense de Salud Publica **7539**
1409-150X Revista Crisol **7903**
1409-1941 Costa Rica. Instituto Nacional de Estadistica y Censos. Anuario Estadistico **8365**
1409-214X AmbienTico **3402**
1409-2158 Ciencias Ambientales **3410**
1409-2433 Revista de Matematicas: Teoria y Aplicaciones **5529**
1409-2441 Ingenieria **3197**
1409-245X Estudios de Linguistica Chibcha **336**
1409-3871 Lankesteriana **799**
1409-4002 Revista Espiga **2906**
1409-4142 Revista Costarricense de Cardiologia **5799**
1409-4185 Adolescencia y Salud **5567**
1409-424X Letras **5321**
1409-438X Revista de Agricultura Tropical **151**
1409-4568 Enfermeria Actual en Costa Rica **5958**
1409-4592 Actualidad Tributaria **1909**
1409-469X Dialogos **4137**
1409-4703 Revista Electronica Actualidades Investigativas en Educacion **2906**
1409-4746 Intersedes **2871**
1409-4851 Geobuzon **2735**
1409-6048 Energetika **3128**
1409-8695 Makedonsko Farmacevtski Bilten **6859**
1409-8709 *see* 1409-9454 **7157**
1409-9454 New Balkan Politics **7157**
1409-9721 Mathematica Macedonica **5512**
1410-0886 Media Akuntansi **1296**
1410-5217 Journal of Coastal Development **8827**
1410-6817 Jurnal Riset Akuntansi Indonesia **1295**
1410-7767 Critical Care and Shock **5601**
1410-8860 Indonesian Physical Society. Physics Journal **7016**
1411-7959 Latitudes **8649**
1411-982X Indonesian Journal of Agricultural Science **236**
1412-2073 A S E A N Journal on Hospitality and Tourism **8680**
1412-4963 Chip **2410**
1412-6796 Level **2478**
1413-0025 Contos do Folclore Colore para Ler e Colorir **2183**
1413-0033 Contos de Fadas Colore para Ler e Colorir **2183**
1413-0130 Revista Brasileira de Ciencia Veterinaria **8806**
1413-0149 Relacoes Internacionais **7262**
1413-0270 Infanto **6093**
1413-0351 Urologia Contemporanea **6275**
1413-0378 Terceira Margem **4477**
1413-0394 Aletheia **7332**
1413-0556 Psicanalise e Universidade **7392**
1413-0920 Mesoterapia Actual†
1413-0939 Estudos Linguisticos (Sao Paulo) **5116**
1413-1153 Trekking
1413-1412 Nautica Magazine **8279**
1413-1439 Revista de Direito Ambiental **4771**
1413-1536 Conjuntura & Planejamento **1448**
1413-2060 Doxa **2843**
1413-2095 Cadernos de Arquitetura e Urbanismo **436**
1413-2117 Novos Estudos Juridicos **4749**
1413-2478 Revista Brasileira de Educacao **2905**
1413-2575 Paparazzi **6972**
1413-2591 Revista Alcance (Print) *changed to* 1983-716X **150**
1413-2672 C A Design **3289**
1413-2702 Moda Moldes Especial Lingerie *see* 0104-1983 **6640**
1413-2796 Dirt Action **8258**
1413-2907 Interacoes **7363**
1413-294X Estudos de Psicologia (Natal) **7355**
1413-2982 Literatura e Sociedade **5325**
1413-3024 Locus **4302**
1413-3067 Moda Moldes Especial Homem *see* 0104-1983 **6640**
1413-3075 Querida Especial **2209**
1413-3083 Moda Moldes Especial Tamanhos Grandes *see* 0104-1983 **6640**
1413-3091 Moda Moldes Especial Maios e Biquinis *see* 0104-1983 **6640**
1413-3202 B I T. Design **434**
1413-3350 Spawn **2214**
1413-3415 Revista Brasileira de Saude Escolar **7538**
1413-3482 Revista Brasileira de Atividade Fisica & Saude **6996**
1413-3490 Faca Facil Especial. Papel Vegetal **4357**
1413-3547 Universidade de Alfenas. Revista **8012**
1413-3555 Revista Brasileira de Fisioterapia **6115**
1413-4063 Psicologia Revista **7393**
1413-4128 CEPE. Estudos **1446**
1413-4152 Engenharia Sanitaria e Ambiental **3188**
1413-4225 Destino Edicao Especial **566**
1413-4403 Chiroptera Neotropical **938**
1413-4411 Edentata **2609**
1413-4438 Sociedade Psicanalitica de Porto Alegre. Revista de Psicanalise **7409**
1413-4543 Revista de Direito Imobiliario **4841**
1413-4608 Ceramica Industrial **2039**
1413-4705 Neotropical Primates **958**
1413-4780 Arquivos de Dermatologia†
1413-4853 Boletim de Ciencias Geodesicas **572**
1413-5388 Revista Brasileira de Implantodontia **5863**
1413-5507 Animais e Cia **6803**
1413-5736 Episteme **6916**
1413-5787 Phoinix **4308**
1413-585X Organizacoes & Sociedade **4468**
1413-6090 Economia em Revista **1479**
1413-6163 Metal Head **6587**
1413-6538 Revista Brasileira de Educacao Especial **3046**
1413-6554 Revista Pescador **8330**
1413-6597 Arquivo Edgard Leuenroth. Cadernos **7948**
1413-666X Imaginario **7361**
1413-7054 Ciencia e Agrotecnologia **101**
1413-7100 Instituto de Pesquisa e Estudos. Revista **4693**
1413-7232 Fotografe Melhor **6968**
1413-7313 Colloquium **7847**
1413-733X Brincadeiras do Jarbas **2181**
1413-7372 Psicologia em Estudo **7393**
1413-7615 Arquivos de Geriatria e Gerontologia **4041**
1413-7704 Tempo **4314**
1413-7739 Revista Brasileira de Oceanografia **2817**
1413-7747 Universidade de Sao Paulo. Instituto Oceanografico. Relatorios Tecnicos **2820**
1413-7852 Acta Ortopedica Brasileira **6054**
1413-7879 Revista de Fisioterapia da Universidade de Sao Paulo **6115**
1413-8042 AnaMaria **8851**
1413-8050 Revista de Economia Aplicada **1167**
1413-8093 Ethica **6917**
1413-8123 Ciencia & Saude Coletiva **7513**
1413-8255 Cuadernos de Recienvenido **5281**
1413-8271 Psico-USF **7392**
1413-828X Gestao e Desenvolvimento **1747**
1413-8557 Psicolgia Escolar e Educacional **7392**
1413-8670 The Brazilian Journal of Infectious Diseases **5810**
1413-8913 Racing **8195**
1413-893X Thot **6957**
1413-8999 Revista Ciencias Sociais **7996**
1413-9049 Guia do Turista **8715**
1413-9111 Motus Corporis **5681**
1413-9138 Hypnos **6924**
1413-9308 Autoesporte **8562**
1413-9324 Scientia Forestalis **3701**
1413-9367 P C World Brazil **2581**
1413-9456 Design Grafico **486**
1413-9596 Brazilian Journal of Veterinary Research and Animal Science **8794**
1413-9626 Farmacoterapeutica
1413-9871 Academia Brasileira de Ciencias Morais e Politicas. Revista **6901**
1413-9936 Perspectivas em Ciencia da Informacao **5039**
1413-9979 Diagnostico & Tratamento **5944**
1414-0055 Revista de Historia Regional **4310**
1414-008X C E J. Revista **4635**
1414-0144 Estudos de Sociologia **8100**
1414-0284 Glossarium Oncologia **6844**
1414-0330 Glossarium Cardiologia **6844**
1414-0349 Glossarium Dermatologia **6844**
1414-0365 Revista Brasileira de Neurologia e Psiquiatria **6181**
1414-039X Revista Brasileira de Horticultura Ornamental **3749**
1414-0438 Guia Maritimo **6423**
1414-0454 Agora (Santa Cruz do Sul) **3997**
1414-0543 Revista Mediacoes **7997**
1414-0594 Revista A C B **5043**
1414-1833 U F O **73**
1414-1868 Mente Social **7385**
1414-1906 Pandaemonium Germanicum **5348**
1414-1922 Guia de Fornecedores Hospitalares **4047**
1414-2139 Informacao & Informacao (Print) *changed to* 1981-8920 **5015**
1414-218X Saude, Etica & Justica **5709**
1414-221X Caros Amigos **3803**
1414-2791 Anuario Brasileiro da Industria Grafica **7318**
1414-2937 Caderno Cientifico do Maestrado e Doutorado em Direito **4635**
1414-3038 Empresa Brasileira de Pesquisa Agropecuaria. Centro Nacional de Pesquisa de Florestas. Documentos *changed to* 1517-526X **3687**
1414-3046 Empresa Brasileira de Pesquisa Agropecuaria. Centro Nacional de Pesquisa de Florestas. Circular Tecnica **3687**
1414-3283 Interface **2868**
1414-3410 Associacao Brasileira de Medicina Psicossomatica. Revista **5580**
1414-3429 Iris
1414-3461 Guia de Fornecedores Municipais **7443**
1414-3534 Go Atual **5991**
1414-3690 Cerebro e Mente **6130**
1414-3755 Sala do Artista Popular
1414-381X R B R H **3364**
1414-3828 P C Master **2580**
1414-4018 *see* 1414-3690 **6130**
1414-4077 Avaliacao **2968**
1414-414X Brasil em Exame **1069**
1414-4336 Colore Atividade Brincar **2183**
1414-4425 S O B E C C. Revista **5980**
1414-4972 Manequim Ponto Cruz **6640**
1414-4980 Revista Katalysis **8065**
1414-5111 Ciencia & Ensino **7846**
1414-512X Multitemas **2994**
1414-5235 Anuario de Literatura **5255**
1414-5243 Claritas **5106**
1414-526X Cadernos de Traducao **5103**
1414-5472 Bons Fluidos **5066**
1414-6142 H B Cientifica **5622**
1414-6231 Revista Brasileira de Terapia Floral **314**
1414-6304 Revista Multipla **7997**
1414-6347 Biotecnologia Ciencia & Desenvolvimento **761**
1414-6398 Backstage **6547**
1414-6894 Claudia Cozinha **4354**
1414-7106 Redes **7261**
1414-7149 A D A P E C. Arquivos **7829**
1414-7327 Concilium (Brazilian Edition) **7634**
1414-753X Ambiente & Sociedade **7946**
1414-7637 Faculdade de Odontologia. Revista **5844**
1414-7653 Fantasia Disney **2188**
1414-8595 Pesquisa Naval **3605**
1414-8633 Fluxo **4452**
1414-8889 A B O P. Revista **6691**
1414-9494 Fragmentos de Cultura **4453**
1415-0158 Brazilian Journal of Population Studies **7278**
1415-0549 Faculdade dos Meios de Comunicacao Social. Revista **7964**
1415-0646 Geonotas **4013**
1415-0654 Molde e Cia **2259**
1415-0778 Milton Campos. Faculdade de Direito. Revista **4734**
1415-0980 Floresta e Ambiente **3431**
1415-1111 Geodesia Online **2736**
1415-1138 Psyche **7394**
1415-1359 Marvel **2201**
1415-1863 Motociclismo Magazine **8262**
1415-1928 Linguagem & Ensino **5145**
1415-1979 Sociedade Brasileira de Economia Politica. Revista **7184**
1415-2061 Centro de Ciencias da Economia e Informatica. Revista **2542**
1415-2134 Automacao **1880**
1415-2649 Global **1428**
1415-2800 Estudos Leopoldenses. Serie Educacao **2854**
1415-2819 Estudos Leopoldenses. Serie Historia **4139**
1415-2827 Calliostoma **937**
1415-2983 Revista Brasileira de Toxicologia **3501**
1415-3211 Scientia Sexualis **7407**
1415-3270 Info Exame **2422**
1415-3971 Guia da Carga Aerea **8543**
1415-4129 Brazil. Centro Nacional de Pesquisa de Milho e Sorgo. Boletim de Pesquisa **222**
1415-4250 Instituto de Pesquisa Economica Aplicada. Boletim Conjuntural **1125**
1415-4366 Revista Brasileira de Engenharia Agricola e Ambiental **151**
1415-4544 J A M A Brasil†
1415-4668 Ideacao **6924**
1415-4676 Pensar a Pratica **8193**
1415-4706 Ethnos **3532**
1415-4714 Revista Latinoamericana de Psicopatologia Fundamental **6182**
1415-4757 Genetics and Molecular Biology **869**
1415-4846 J B P **5850**
1415-5206 Voce S.A. **3804**
1415-5273 Revista de Nutricao **6668**
1415-5311 Veja Kid Mais **2219**
1415-5400 Revista Brasileira de Ciencias Criminais **4897**
1415-5419 Revista Dental Press de Ortodontia e Ortopedia Facial **5863**
1415-5494 Epoca **3803**
1415-5788 Producao & Sociedade **3371**
1415-5796 Revista de Ciencias Medicas (Campinas) **5705**
1415-5907 Estudos de Cinema **6497**
1415-6229 Tecno Logica **2082**
1415-6393 Turismo (Print)† **8994**
1415-6423 Vamos Brincar com as Palavras Cruzadas **2219**
1415-6431 Vamos Brincar com os Passatempos **2219**
1415-644X Almanaque Vamos Brincar Baratinho **2176**
1415-6555 Revista de Administracao Contemporanea **1790**
1415-6725 Sociedade Brasileira de Cancerologia. Revista **6034**
1415-689X Sexta Feira **355**
1415-6938 Ensaios e Ciencia **7852**
1415-7004 Brazilian Journal of Materials Science and Engineering **3342**
1415-7314 Engevista **8100**
1415-7403 Confluencia **5277**
1415-7659 Jornal do Commercio **3804**
1415-7683 Instituto dos Advogados de Sao Paulo. Revista **4693**
1415-7705 Revista de Direito do Consumidor **4771**
1415-7713 Revista Transportes **8510**
1415-790X Revista Brasileira de Epidemiologia **7538**
1415-7942 Brasil Nuclear **3165**
1415-8124 Direito Tributario Atual **1920**
1415-8280 Centro de Pesquisas Biomedicas Gonzaga da Gama Filho. Revista Cientifica **5593**
1415-8426 Revista Brasileira de Cineantropometria & Desempenho Humano **6996**
1415-8566 Sociedade e Cultura **8005**
1415-8582 Manequim. Faca e Venda **2258**
1415-8876 Ambiente Construido **975**
1415-8884 Solutions Integrator **2494**
1415-899X Ultimo Andar **7691**
1415-9031 Gamers Pro Dicas **2476**
1415-9104 Universidade de Sao Paulo. Revista de Terapia Ocupacional **6117**
1415-9538 Electronic Musicological Review **6564**
1415-9848 Rivista de Economia Contemporanea **1548**
1415-9856 Galileu **3803**
1415-9945 Dialogos (Maringa) **4290**
1416-0161 *see* 1215-4504 **7963**
1416-020X Tuzok **915**
1416-1346 Uj Dunataj **7504**
1416-2792 Molnarok Lapja **274**
1416-3586 Ungarische Wirtschaft **1847**
1416-3799 Film, Szinhaz, Muzsika, Kultura†
1416-3837 Periodica Polytechnica. Social and Management Sciences **1785**
1416-4906 Nepszabadsag Online **3876**
1416-5414 Magyar Nemzeti Bibliografia. Periodikumok **630**
1416-6194 Az Europai Unio Agrargazdasaga **108**
1416-6461 Listak Konyve *see* 1219-1841 **1069**
1416-7263 Acta Universitatis Szegediensis. Acta Hispanica **5249**
1416-7336 Mediafigyelo **1834**
1416-7913 Romanc, Armany es Szerelem **8882**
1416-7921 Noi Magazin Onagysaga **8878**
1416-8510 Archaeolingua. Studien zur Eisenzeit im Ostalpenraum **329**
1416-8537 Fotografia†
1416-8650 Komarom-Esztergom Megyei 24 Ora **3876**
1417-0132 M M Muszaki Magazin **5455**
1417-1015 Foglalkozas-Egeszsegugy **6677**
1417-1406 Veteran Auto es Motor **8610**
1417-1597 Tajekoztato az ... Gazdasagi Folyamatokro†
1417-1902 Ugyes **4350**
1417-2518 Joy **8869**
1417-2542 Cosmopolitan (Budapest) **8856**
1417-3085 Figyelo Pesti Tozsdek **1109**
1417-3255 Agro Naplo **86**
1417-3875 Electronic Journal of Qualitative Theory of Differential Equations **5486**
1417-393X *see* 0040-3717 **7923**
1417-3948 *see* 0865-5243 **2412**
1417-3980 *see* 0133-1906 **3876**

ISSN

1421-7082 Endocrine Development **5890**
1421-7171 Anlagefonds *see* 0015-220X **1624**
1421-718X Invest-Immobilien *see* 0015-220X **1624**
1421-7228 Schweizerisches Arbeitsrecht - Rechtsprechung†
1421-7236 Schweizer Familie **3959**
1421-7252 Portfolio *see* 0015-220X **1624**
1421-7384 Federation de l'Industrie Horlogere Suisse. Annual Report **4566**
1421-7430 Neue Luzerner Zeitung **3958**
1421-7899 Sapheneia **2240**
1421-7902 German-Australian Studies **5300**
1421-7910 Perspectivas Hispanicas **5350**
1421-8089 Lebensmittel - Revue - Alimentaire **3653**
1421-8208 Internationale Georg-Lukacs-Gesellschaft. Jahrbuch **6926**
1421-8488 Motorsport Aktuell **8264**
1421-8593 Schweizer Holz Revue **3715**
1421-8615 Wasser - Boden - Luft Umweltschutz **3474**
1421-864X Einkauf - Materialwirtschaft - Logistik **1815**
1421-8747 Sankt Galler Beitraege zum Tourismus und zur Verkehrswirtschaft: Reihe Verkehrswirtschaft†
1421-8763 Rote Revue **7180**
1421-8909 Revue Schweiz Suisse Svizzera **3959**
1421-8925 Swissmechanic **5460**
1421-8976 Freie Fahrt†
1421-9158 Recht und Politik des Wettbewerbs **4879**
1421-9166 Commerce Exterieur Suisse†
1421-9352 Switzerland. Directorate General of Customs. Schweizerische Aussenhandelsstatistik. Jahresstatistik **1269**
1421-9468 Switzerland. Directorate General of Customs. Annual Report **1269**
1421-9581 Jahrbuch Schweiz-Dritte Welt *see* 0256-5382 **1590**
1421-9662 *see* 0001-5792 **5933**
1421-9670 *see* 0250-8095 **6265**
1421-9689 *see* 0301-3006 **7334**
1421-9697 *see* 0250-6807 **6655**
1421-9700 *see* Audiology and Neurotology **6078**
1421-9735 *see* 0253-5068 **5934**
1421-9743 *see* 0006-8977 **6127**
1421-9751 *see* 0008-6312 **5779**
1421-976X *see* 0008-6568 **5837**
1421-9778 *see* 1015-8987 **830**
1421-9786 *see* 1015-9770 **6130**
1421-9794 *see* 0009-3157 **6828**
1421-9824 *see* 1420-8008 **6136**
1421-9832 *see* 1018-8665 **5875**
1421-9859 *see* 0378-5866 **6136**
1421-9867 *see* 0012-2823 **5922**
1421-9875 *see* 0257-2753 **5922**
1421-9883 *see* 0253-4886 **6241**
1421-9891 *see* 1022-6877 **2694**
1421-9913 *see* 0014-3022 **6140**
1421-9921 *see* 0014-312X **6243**
1421-993X *see* 0302-2838 **6268**
1421-9956 Experimental Nephrology *changed to* 1660-2129 **6252**
1421-9964 *see* 1015-3837 **5990**
1421-9972 *see* 1021-7762 **6080**
1421-9980 *see* 0015-5713 **944**
1422-0059 Infomed Screen **5635**
1422-0067 International Journal of Molecular Sciences (Online) **2124**
1422-0113 *see* 1422-0059 **5635**
1422-0466 ClingKlong **6557**
1422-0482 G D I Impuls **1112**
1422-0644 Schweizerische Zeitschrift fuer Sportmedizin und Sporttraumatologie **6232**
1422-0660 Schweizer Lehrerinnen- und Lehrerzeitung **2910**
1422-0857 Crime, Histoire et Societes **2648**
1422-0873 Zeichnen und Gestalten†
1422-0970 Fuer Uns Vita Sana **6986**
1422-1098 Media-Expert **6971**
1422-1144 Schweizerische Zeitschrift fuer Forstwesen. Beihefte **3701**
1422-1187 Textilarbeit und Werken **2919**
1422-1268 Tele Online **2395**
1422-1454 German Linguistic and Cultural Studies **5122**
1422-1462 S Z V Bulletin†
1422-1691 Detail **4565**
1422-1705 *see* 1422-1691 **4565**
1422-1896 Logistik *changed to* 1661-674X **1897**
1422-2086 V S A O Journal **5727**
1422-2132 Current Directions in Autoimmunity **5757**
1422-2140 Progress in Respiratory Research **6217**
1422-2159 Impressum - Schweizerisches Medienhandbuch **4587**
1422-2183 Impressum 2 - Cartoonisten, Illustratoren, Archive†
1422-2205 Impressum Bulletin **4587**
1422-2213 The Journal of World Intellectual Property **6753**
1422-2248 The Geneva Post Quarterly **7237**
1422-2337 Fruit World International **3644**
1422-2426 A K **4370**
1422-2620 U B S Publications on Business, Banking and Monetary Problems
1422-2698 Montres Passion **4568**
1422-2701 Uhrenwelt **4570**
1422-2728 Webdo **2568**
1422-2795 Community Genetics *changed to* 1662-4246 **877**
1422-2825 Congres Europeen de Chronometrie. Actes **3375**
1422-2868 Skin Pharmacology and Applied Skin Physiology *changed to* 1660-5527 **6881**
1422-2876 Merkblatt fuer die Praxis **2618**
1422-3090 Interlabor News *changed to* 1661-6545 **3648**
1422-3430 Textilpflege Schweiz **2244**
1422-3481 Archiv fuer Schweizerisches Abgaberecht **1910**
1422-3511 Oberflaechen **6719**
1422-3597 Materials Science Foundations **3354**
1422-3619 Terre & Nature **161**
1422-3694 Bern Universitaet. Seminar fuer Klassische Archeologie. Beiheft **383**
1422-3740 *see* 1021-9056 **5635**
1422-3902 Die Banken in der Schweiz **1316**
1422-4135 Sound and Vision†
1422-4178 Nova **5971**
1422-4186 D M V - Seminar *changed to* 1661-237X **5522**
1422-4194 Applica **6716**
1422-4208 Bioelectrochemistry: Principles and Practice **726**
1422-4380 Freiburger Zeitschrift fuer Philosophie und Theologie. Oekumenische Beihefte *changed to* 1662-6540 **7818**
1422-4399 Orbis Biblicus et Orientalis. Series Archaeologica **409**
1422-4410 Praktische Theologie im Dialog **7671**
1422-4429 Religion - Politik - Gesellschaft in der Schweiz **7675**
1422-4437 Res Socialis **6947**
1422-4445 Scrinium Friburgense **4262**
1422-4453 Studia Ethnographica Friburgensia **357**
1422-4496 Ethik und Politische Philosophie **6918**
1422-4526 Die Schweizer Hebamme *changed to* Hebamme.ch **5960**
1422-4658 Finance et Bien Commun **1343**
1422-4674 Schweizer Musikzeitung **6615**
1422-4704 P C Tip **2580**
1422-4720 Medkalender **5677**
1422-4917 Zeitschrift fuer Kinder- und Jugendpsychiatrie und Psychotherapie **6190**
1422-5107 Motorfahrzeuge in der Schweiz. Eingefuehrte Motorfahrzeuge **8527**
1422-5182 Revue Historique Neuchateloise **4258**
1422-5239 Cahiers Psychiatriques
1422-5271 Bauernzeitung Zentralschweiz Aargau **95**
1422-5298 Schweizerische Nationalbank. Statistisches Monatsheft **1382**
1422-5417 Archi **428**
1422-5581 Cahiers d'Humanisme et Renaissance **5268**
1422-5662 SWITCH-Journal **2567**
1422-5778 Anwaltsrevue / Revue de l'Avocat **4619**
1422-5786 Camping-Revue **8308**
1422-5794 Info S O L O G **6424**
1422-5840 Bioethica Forum *changed to* 1662-6001 **6907**
1422-5883 Vivant Univers. Edition Suisse *changed to* 1379-4205 **7232**
1422-5980 Alma **2272**
1422-6073 Arbeiten zur Editionswissenschaft **5256**
1422-6111 C H - Lit **5268**
1422-6243 New York Contemporary Art Report **508**
1422-6251 Key Issues in Human Genetics *changed to* Monographs in Human Genetics **875**
1422-6367 Fauna Helvetica **847**
1422-6375 Journal of Metastable and Nanocrystalline Materials *see* 0255-5476 **7026**
1422-6383 Results in Mathematics **5529**
1422-6405 Cells, Tissues, Organs **5593**
1422-6421 *see* 1422-6405 **5593**
1422-6472 Sandorama (German-French Edition)† **8987**
1422-6553 S B B Zeitung **8624**
1422-6561 Courrier C F F *see* 1422-6553 **8624**
1422-6588 Corriere F F S *see* 1422-6553 **8624**
1422-6618 Managed Care *changed to* 1662-5404 **5592**
1422-6634 Management und Qualitaet **6403**
1422-6820 Oltner Tagblatt **3958**
1422-6928 Journal of Mathematical Fluid Mechanics **7021**
1422-6944 Physics in Perspective **7033**
1422-6952 *see* 1422-6928 **7021**
1422-6960 *see* 1422-6944 **7033**
1422-7320 French Studies of the Eighteenth and Nineteenth Centuries **5298**
1422-7339 Switzerland. Directorate General of Customs. Quarterly Statistics **1269**
1422-7371 Dissonanz **6562**
1422-7401 Dissonance *see* 1422-7371 **6562**
1422-7517 Univeristaetsbibliothek Basel. Schriften **5052**
1422-7584 Nestle Nutrition Workshop Series Clinical and Performance Programme **6664**
1422-7606 Recherches et Rencontres. Publications de la Faculte des Lettres de l'Universite de Geneve **5358**
1422-7622 Das Goetheanum **3958**
1422-7681 Swissboat *see* 1422-7703 **8283**
1422-7703 Swissboat - Yachting **8283**
1422-7746 Progress in Inflammation Research **5700**
1422-7762 Fullsize **6291**
1422-7797 Augusta Raurica **382**
1422-7851 Mobile **2887**
1422-7878 *see* 1422-7851 **2887**
1422-7894 *see* 1422-7851 **2887**
1422-7924 Repere Social **7995**
1422-8084 Buendner Wald **3685**
1422-8122 Mayer **504**
1422-8165 Laborscope **5909**
1422-8327 Studien zur Zeitgeschichte und Sicherheitspolitik **7267**
1422-8408 Key Issues in Plastic and Cosmetic Surgery†
1422-8459 Wohnmobil & Caravan **8342**
1422-8467 Das Einfamilienhaus **1006**
1422-8475 Maisons & Ambiances **4546**
1422-8483 Haeuser Modernisieren **1010**
1422-8491 Raum und Wohnen **4549**
1422-8521 Acta Historica Astronomiae **568**
1422-8556 Yabyum **3959**
1422-8599 Molbank **2073**
1422-8610 *see* 1422-8629 **5984**
1422-8629 www.PrInterNet.info **5984**
1422-8696 Le Romantisme et Apres en France **5364**
1422-8777 B A B Working Paper **4169**
1422-8823 M S M **5455**
1422-8866 Der Unternehmer **1425**
1422-8890 *see* 1019-6781 **1815**
1422-8947 P M E Magazine **1785**
1422-8955 Banque Assurance **4494**
1422-8963 Schweizer Versicherung **4522**
1422-8971 HandelsZeitung **1117**
1422-8998 Religions and Discourse **7675**
1422-9005 Modern French Identities **5335**
1422-9137 Ferrum **6312**
1422-9188 Shape **8848**
1422-9196 Dermatology and Psychosomatics†
1422-9277 Informationsblatt Forschungsbereich Landschaft *changed to* 1661-5824 **2614**
1422-9307 Schweizer Uhrenjournal **4569**
1422-9315 Swiss Watch Journal **4569**
1422-9323 Journal Suisse d'Horlogerie **4567**
1422-9331 Electronic Journal of Organizational Virtualness **2556**
1422-9366 Swiss Sectoral Trends **1385**
1422-9528 Heart Drug *changed to* 0008-6312 **5779**
1422-9609 Visicom **7328**
1422-9846 L'Europe et les Europes **4219**
1422-9986 Facts **3958**
1422-9994 Tages-Anzeiger **3959**
1423-0003 *see* 0304-324X **4046**
1423-0011 *see* 1018-8843 **5992**
1423-002X *see* 0378-7346 **5992**
1423-0054 *see* 0018-716X **5630**
1423-0062 *see* 0001-5652 **872**
1423-0070 *see* 1420-326X **5760**
1423-0097 *see* 1018-2438 **5761**
1423-0100 *see* 0300-5526 **888**
1423-0127 *see* 1021-7770 **5646**
1423-0135 *see* 1018-1172 **5794**
1423-0143 *see* 1420-4096 **6270**
1423-0151 *see* 1011-7571 **5670**
1423-0194 *see* 0028-3835 **5898**
1423-0208 *see* 0251-5350 **6164**
1423-0216 *see* 1021-7401 **5764**
1423-0224 *see* 0302-282X **6168**
1423-0232 *see* 0030-2414 **6030**
1423-0240 *see* 0378-584X **6031**
1423-0259 *see* 0030-3747 **6048**
1423-0267 *see* 0030-3755 **6048**
1423-0275 *see* 0301-1569 **6083**
1423-0291 *see* 1015-2008 **5764**
1423-0305 *see* 1016-2291 **6173**
1423-0313 *see* 0031-7012 **6872**
1423-0321 *see* 0031-8388 **5161**
1423-033X *see* 0254-4962 **6179**
1423-0348 *see* 0033-3190 **6180**
1423-0356 *see* 0025-7931 **6218**
1423-0372 *see* 1011-6125 **6259**
1423-0380 *see* 1010-4283 **6035**
1423-0399 *see* 0042-1138 **6275**
1423-0402 *see* 1016-6262 **6189**
1423-0410 *see* 0042-9007 **5767**
1423-0445 *see* 0937-7409 **2121**
1423-0526 Artibus Asiae Supplementum **473**
1423-0534 Archives Heraldiques Suisses **3759**
1423-0658 Tec (German Edition)†
1423-1018 Association Jean-Jacques Rousseau. Bulletin **5258**
1423-1387 Geneve. Office Cantonal de la Statistique. Bulletin Statistique Mensuel **8373**
1423-1697 Concast Standard News **6309**
1423-1956 Drehpunkt†
1423-2456 Wald und Holz **3717**
1423-2707 Transport Rundschau **8676**
1423-3215 Interavia **60**
1423-3789 Schweizerische Nationalbank. Quartalsheft **1382**
1423-3797 Banque Nationale Suisse. Bulletin Trimestriel **1320**
1423-3967 Le Temps **3959**
1423-3983 Italique **5424**
1423-4017 Neujahrsblatt der G G G **4248**
1423-4092 Physiotherapie *changed to* 1660-5209 **6109**
1423-4211 Medecine Psychosomatique et Psychosociale†
1423-4319 Swiss Camion **8625**
1423-4688 Steuerbelastung in der Schweiz - Kantonshauptorte, Kantonsziffern **1945**
1423-4696 Steuerbelastung in der Schweiz - Natuerliche Personen nach Gemeinden **1268**
1423-5110 Marmite **3655**
1423-5129 Natuerlich **8324**
1423-5137 Fit for Life **8313**
1423-5277 Bau- und Wohnbaustatistik in der Schweiz **1044**
1423-5471 S V S Journal **8659**
1423-5528 Kardiovaskulaere Medizin **5795**
1423-5536 Gesundheit-SprechStunde **6987**
1423-5587 European Semiotics **5117**
1423-5595 S A B Info **5044**
1423-5633 Jardin Romand **3739**
1423-5765 Medical Prescription of Narcotics†
1423-646X Windows-Guide Schweiz *changed to* 1424-4055 **2423**
1423-6478 Windows Guide *changed to* 1424-4055 **2423**
1423-6486 P C Guide *changed to* 1424-4055 **2423**
1423-6494 Ideales Heim **4542**
1423-6508 Umbauen und Renovieren **4551**
1423-6516 Einfamilienhaeuser **4539**
1423-6532 Ideales Heim. Sonderpublikation **4542**
1423-6540 Bibliotheca Bodmeriana. Textes **4169**
1423-6559 Bibliotheca Bodmeriana. Catalogues **4169**
1423-6567 Bibliotheca Bodmeriana. Papyri **4169**
1423-6664 M **7567**
1423-6729 Seemeile **8282**
1423-6818 Schweizerische Saengerzeitung†
1423-6826 Unsere Welt **7272**
1423-6834 Schweizer Hunde Magazin **6815**
1423-6869 Katzen Magazin **6810**
1423-6885 ComTexte *see* 1423-6893 **2367**
1423-6893 ComText **2367**
1423-6931 Eu Z - Zeitschrift fuer Europarecht **4668**
1423-6958 E T H - Bibliothek. A: Wissenschaftsgeschichte **7852**
1423-6966 E T H - Bibliothek. B: Bibliothekswesen **5057**
1423-7008 Armee-Logistik **6411**
1423-7016 Papeterie und Buero **6736**
1423-7377 Atrium **4532**
1423-8705 Webdo Mag **2568**
1423-9531 Social Strategies **8134**
1423-9787 Melting Pot **5227**
1423-9825 Occasional Papers in Swiss Studies **5157**
1424-0025 Steuer Revue **1945**
1424-0041 Spuren **6647**
1424-0092 Gartenidee **3733**
1424-0106 Bauen und Wohnen Heute **979**
1424-0114 Maisons d'Aujourd'hui **4546**
1424-0130 Auto Illustrierte **8558**

ISSN

1428-4707 Komputer w Firmie *see* 1230-2856 **1161**
1428-4839 Claudia. Numer Specjalny *see* 1230-8609 **8855**
1428-5487 Flex (Polish Edition) *see* 8750-8915 **6986**
1428-5673 Polonia Sacra **7812**
1428-5851 Nadcisnienie Tetnicze **5796**
1428-5894 Kawaii **2478**
1428-5983 RUaH **6613**
1428-5991 Problemy Oswiaty i Wychowania **2900**
1428-6327 Nowy Filomata **2238**
1428-6394 T A S K Quaterly **2504**
1428-6564 Nafta & Gaz Biznes **6779**
1428-6793 *see* 0006-1093 **617**
1428-6998 Biblioteka Tradycji Literackich **5263**
1428-7005 Nowy Czas Krakowski†
1428-7218 Uniwersytet Opolski. Wydzial Teologiczny. Studia Biblijne. Scriptura Sacra **7692**
1428-7382 Koszty **1142**
1428-7439 Bardziej Kochani **3037**
1428-7501 Gazeta Ubezpieczeniowa **4503**
1428-7617 Przewodnik Twojego Biznesu **1162**
1428-8060 Nowe Ubezpieczenia **4517**
1428-8176 Rachunkowosc Budzetowa **1299**
1428-8184 Jak Prowadzic Ksiege Przychodow i Rozchodow? **1293**
1428-8257 Gazeta Samorzadu i Administracji **7438**
1428-8664 Uniwersytet Slaski w Katowicach. Prace Naukowe. Psychologia. Badania i Aplikacje **7414**
1428-8842 Polish Culture **5234**
1428-8931 Plama **512**
1428-9512 Annales Universitatis Mariae Curie-Sklodowska. Sectio K. Politologia **7106**
1429-0022 Medicina Sportiva **6231**
1429-009X Geopolitical Studies **4013**
1429-0359 Wiadomosci - Wlokno, Odziez, Skora *changed to* 1731-8645 **8456**
1429-0502 Kurenda†
1429-0693 Lekarz **5661**
1429-1096 Nowe Powisle Dabrowskie **5231**
1429-1290 Mare Articum **6528**
1429-1568 Samo Zdrowie **6996**
1429-2009 Przyjaciolka Poleca **8881**
1429-2173 Neofilolog **5154**
1429-2335 Sea Fisheries Institute. Bulletin†
1429-2416 Studia nad Rodzina **7818**
1429-2548 Gazeta w Toruniu **3929**
1429-2556 Gazeta w Bydgoszczy **3929**
1429-2629 Dysonanse **6563**
1429-2866 Lubie Gotowac **4363**
1429-2955 Journal of Theoretical and Applied Mechanics **3351**
1429-303X Annual Review of Agricultural Engineering **209**
1429-3056 Rachunkowosc z Komentarzem **1299**
1429-320X Glos Tymbarku **5218**
1429-3226 Dobre Wnetrze **4538**
1429-3447 Automatyka **2458**
1429-3471 Prawo i Gospodarka†
1429-3625 Magazyn Rynku Komputerowego†
1429-3803 Jus Matrimoniale **7802**
1429-3862 Plant Breeding and Seed Science **147**
1429-4168 Acta Universitatis Wratislaviensis. Wroclawskie Studia Wschodnie **4196**
1429-4966 Medycyna Praktyczna. Ultrasonografia **6203**
1429-5415 Woman *changed to* 1643-8264 **8858**
1429-6462 Kubus Puchatek **2199**
1429-6586 Szafa **5241**
1429-6675 Polityka Energetyczna **3144**
1429-6829 Encyklopedia Mamo to Ja *see* 1233-7366 **2160**
1429-6950 Olivia **8879**
1429-7027 O S K a **8878**
1429-7132 Europa XXI **7283**
1429-7248 Inzynieria Biomaterialow **749**
1429-740X Orzecznictwo Sadowe *see* 1427-3594 **4710**
1429-7426 Journal of Water and Land Development **240**
1429-7507 Architectus **431**
1429-7698 Brac Lowiecka **8306**
1429-799X Uniwerstytet Slaski w Katowicach. Prace Naukowe. Landform Analysis **2799**
1429-8171 Teksty Jednolite Aktow Prawnych *see* 1427-3594 **4710**
1429-8198 Murator Numer Specjalny *see* 0239-6866 **450**
1429-8538 Psychoonkologia **6178**
1429-8597 Raptularz Kulturalny **5236**
1429-9089 Wokol Plytek Ceramicznych **2046**
1429-9321 Management **1774**
1429-9496 Mandragora **5226**
1429-9585 Jagiellonian University. Yearbook of Labour Law **4698**
1429-964X Action Plus **2474**
1429-9968 Wynagrodzenia **4816**
1430-0060 Mystery **5414**
1430-0079 Mystery Gruselbox **5414**
1430-0095 Europaeische Migrationsforschung **7283**
1430-0117 F-40 **6420**
1430-0133 Koelnische Geschichtsverein. Veroeffentlichungen **4150**
1430-015X Beitraege zur Bayerischen Entomofaunistik **840**
1430-0168 Humboldt-Universitaet zu Berlin. Wissenschaftliche Zeitschrift: Geistes- und Sozialwissenschaften†
1430-0192 D C C - Camping Fuehrer Europa **8696**
1430-0214 Sondersprachenforschung **5176**
1430-0265 Epidemiologisches Bulletin **5813**
1430-032X Ideal - Gesuender Leben†
1430-0532 Linguistic Typology **5146**
1430-0540 Colloques Phytosociologiques **784**
1430-0613 Traditionsverband Ehemaliger Schutz- und Ueberseetruppen. Mitteilungsblatt **4274**
1430-0672 Rheinisch-Pfaelzische Hotels and Gaststaetten **4397**
1430-0680 Asia Minor Studien **4320**
1430-0702 T.akt **3858**
1430-0729 Auto Motor und Sport Spezial Gebrauchtwagen - Sonderheft **8559**
1430-0931 Tuebinger Schriften zur Ur- und Fruehgeschichtlichen Archaeologie **421**
1430-0966 D C C - Caravan und Motorcaravan Modellfuehrer **8576**
1430-0974 European Packaging *changed to* 0342-3743 **1837**
1430-1008 Sport-Welt **8205**
1430-1016 Missionsgeschichtliches Archiv **4245**
1430-1024 I F O Japan Branchendienst. Automobil und -zulieferer†
1430-1067 Sportiv **8206**
1430-1091 R K I - Schriften **5702**
1430-1121 Imaging und Foto-Contact **6970**
1430-1172 *see* 1430-0265 **5813**
1430-1229 Shomingeki **6513**
1430-1253 Bibliographia Mesostigmatologica *changed to* 1618-8977 **649**
1430-144X European Transactions on Electrical Power **3308**
1430-1474 Media Facts† **8973**
1430-1695 Statistisches Landesamt Saarland. Statistische Berichte B *changed to* 1864-2268 **7483**
1430-1709 Statistisches Landesamt Saarland. Statistische Berichte C *changed to* Statistisches Amt Saarland. Statistische Berichte C **7484**
1430-1717 Statistisches Landesamt Saarland. Statistische Berichte D *changed to* Statistisches Amt Saarland. Statistische Berichte D **7484**
1430-1725 Statistisches Landesamt Saarland. Statistische Berichte E *changed to* Statistisches Amt Saarland. Statistische Berichte E **7484**
1430-1733 Statistisches Landesamt Saarland. Statistische Berichte F *changed to* 1864-2276 **7484**
1430-1741 Statistisches Landesamt Saarland. Statistische Berichte G *changed to* Statistisches Amt Saarland. Statistische Berichte G **7484**
1430-175X Internationale Politik **7246**
1430-1784 Statistisches Landesamt Saarland. Statistische Berichte H *changed to* Statistisches Amt Saarland. Statistische Berichte H **7484**
1430-1792 Statistisches Landesamt Saarland. Statistische Berichte J *changed to* Statistisches Amt Saarland. Statistische Berichte J **7484**
1430-1806 Statistisches Landesamt Saarland. Statistische Berichte K *changed to* Statistisches Amt Saarland. Statistische Berichte K **7484**
1430-1814 Statistisches Landesamt Saarland. Statistische Berichte L *changed to* 1864-2608 **7484**
1430-1822 Statistisches Landesamt Saarland. Statistische Berichte M *changed to* Statistisches Amt Saarland. Statistische Berichte M **7484**
1430-1830 Statistisches Landesamt Saarland. Statistische Berichte N *changed to* Statistisches Amt Saarland. Statistische Berichte N **7484**
1430-1849 Statistisches Landesamt Saarland. Statistische Berichte P *changed to* 1864-2616 **7484**
1430-1857 Statistisches Landesamt Saarland. Statistische Berichte Q *changed to* Statistisches Amt Saarland. Statistische Berichte Q **7484**
1430-1873 Rettungs-Magazin **6071**
1430-189X Journal of Automata, Languages and Combinatorics **2453**
1430-1911 Pro Alter **4053**
1430-192X Berliner Slawistische Arbeiten **5099**
1430-1938 Aethiopica **4172**
1430-2209 Archive in der Bundesrepublik Deutschland, Oesterreich und der Schweiz **4200**
1430-2225 Deutsche Vereinigung fuer Sportwissenschaft. Schriften **8169**
1430-225X Taschenlexikon Schul- und Hochschulrechtlicher Entscheidungen **2917**
1430-2438 Feuerungstechnik, Energie & Umwelt†
1430-2446 Z S W - Zucker- und Suesswaren Wirtschaft†
1430-2519 George-Jahrbuch **5300**
1430-2527 Shakespeare Jahrbuch **5370**
1430-2535 Anna Spitzenhaekeln **6637**
1430-2659 Cottbuser Studien zur Geschichte von Technik, Arbeit und Umwelt **4212**
1430-2667 Jugend - Religion - Unterricht **7657**
1430-2675 Lernen fuer Europa **2883**
1430-2683 Studium im Alter **2946**
1430-2713 A F Z - Der Wald **3682**
1430-2721 E D V und Kommunikation fuer das Handwerk **2417**
1430-2748 Gebaeude Management† **8958**
1430-2756 Weserlotse-Logistik
1430-2772 *see* 0340-0727 **7396**
1430-2780 Universitaets- und Stadtbibliothek Koeln. Kleine Schriften **5052**
1430-2918 Artist Window **473**
1430-2926 BauTrend **2898**
1430-2977 Paedagogische Psychologie und Entwicklungspsychologie **2895**
1430-3345 Yoga und Ganzheitliche Gesundheit **7001**
1430-3418 Experimental Biology Online†
1430-3426 Rundbrief Frauen in der Literaturwissenschaft **5365**
1430-3442 Materialhefte zur Archaeologie in Baden-Wuerttemberg **405**
1430-3469 Erratica **2733**
1430-3663 GeoBIT *changed to* G I S Business **2722**
1430-3671 Forum **2858**
1430-368X *see* 0341-9363 **5406**
1430-3906 Rendsburger Jahrbuch
1430-3922 Horizonte (Tuebingen) **5306**
1430-3965 Akademie Verlag Series in Optical Metrology
1430-3981 Prinz **5080**
1430-399X Prinz (Koeln) *see* 1430-3981 **5080**
1430-4023 Seminar Hausarztpraxis **5712**
1430-4031 Kosmetische Medizin **5659**
1430-4082 Stores & Shops **1179**
1430-4104 Friseurwelt **587**
1430-4139 Stauffenburg Linguistik **5178**
1430-4147 Prinz (Stuttgart) *see* 1430-3981 **5080**
1430-4155 Prinz (Frankfurt) *see* 1430-3981 **5080**
1430-4163 Prinz (Bremen) *see* 1430-3981 **5080**
1430-4171 The Chemical Educator **2054**
1430-4201 Skyweek† **8988**
1430-421X VergabeNews **4843**
1430-4503 Prinz (Berlin) *see* 1430-3981 **5080**
1430-4511 Hideaways **8718**
1430-4546 Kulturland Oldenburg **4238**
1430-4554 G Z M **5845**
1430-4627 Prinz (Muenchen) *see* 1430-3981 **5080**
1430-4635 Handbuch der Universitaeten und Fachhochschulen Deutschland, Oesterreich, Schweiz **2983**
1430-4783 Zeitschrift fuer Qigong Yangsheng **316**
1430-4791 Sued-Afrika **8758**
1430-483X Grundwasser **8824**
1430-4899 Studien zur Reiseliteratur- und Imagologieforschung **5380**
1430-5208 IT.Services *changed to* 1617-5794 **1751**
1430-5224 Berichte aus der Sportwissenschaft **8161**
1430-5267 Scriptum **2716**
1430-5275 Prinz (Ruhrgebiet) *see* 1430-3981 **5080**
1430-5283 Fachhochschule des Bundes fuer Oeffentliche Verwaltung. Mitteilungen†
1430-5321 Aesthetik und Naturwissenschaften **6902**
1430-5348 Photon **3177**
1430-5372 Kierkegaard Studies **6930**
1430-5437 International Vergleichende Schriften zur Personaloekonomie und Arbeitspolitik **1690**
1430-5496 Anzeiger des Germanischen Nationalmuseums **4199**
1430-5704 P C Video **2402**
1430-5712 Aspekte *changed to* AXA Konzern Magazin **4494**
1430-5755 Feine Adressen Bodensee **3847**
1430-5763 Prinz (Duesseldorf) *see* 1430-3981 **5080**
1430-5771 Prinz (Hannover) *see* 1430-3981 **5080**
1430-5828 Public Relations†
1430-5887 Elektro Automation **3305**
1430-5895 Behinderung und Dritte Welt **3037**
1430-5968 Zivil **7219**
1430-6336 Guetertransport im Land-, See- und Luftverkehr *changed to* 1861-0986 **8645**
1430-6344 Hamburg-Bibliographie **626**
1430-6352 Beitraege zur Deutschen Kolonialgeschichte **4203**
1430-6360 Spektrum Freizeit
1430-6387 Zeitschrift fuer Politikwissenschaft **5246**
1430-6395 Applied Rheology **7057**
1430-645X Agrarmarkt
1430-6468 Informationen zur Beruflichen Bildung†
1430-6646 OekologiePolitik **2623**
1430-6891 Fern Express **8617**
1430-6905 Erfurt Electronic Studies in English **5290**
1430-6921 International Journal of Practical Theology **7650**
1430-6999 B B A Bau - Beratung - Architektur **977**
1430-7235 ProLibris **5040**
1430-726X Bus-Tourist International *changed to* 1610-3882 **8689**
1430-7278 G K S S Forschungszentrum. Jahresbericht **7856**
1430-7308 Haus- und Grundbesitz *changed to* 1860-8450 **7592**
1430-7537 Volkskunde in Sachsen **4278**
1430-7561 RegulationsMedizin **5702**
1430-7715 Haeuser Heute **1010**
1430-7731 Powder & Bulk Solids Yearbook & Directory **8435**
1430-7774 TexDecor *changed to* 1612-5096 **8460**
1430-7820 Zeitschrift fuer Theologie und Gemeinde **7697**
1430-788X Holzpraxis Exklusiv **1050**
1430-7901 Darmstaedter Forschungsberichte fuer Konstruktion und Fertigung *changed to* Innovation Fertigungstechnik **3270**
1430-7928 Wer Leitet - die Fuehrungskraefte der Oesterreichischen Wirtschaft
1430-7936 Instant Time Book
1430-7987 Weltwunder der Kinematographie **6516**
1430-7995 Das Branchen Forum **6805**
1430-810X Business Traveller (German Edition) **8689**
1430-8223 Einkaufen auf dem Bauernhof in Deutschland **107**
1430-8274 Eurolaser **3366**
1430-8312 SteuerBrief Touristik *changed to* 1613-0782 **1945**
1430-8320 Historia Scientiarum **4142**
1430-8339 Deutsche Gesellschaft fuer Geschichte der Nervenheilkunde. Schriftenreihe **6136**
1430-8355 Prima mit Carina†
1430-8460 Lebensmittel Zeitung Spezial **3654**
1430-8495 Infodienst Reisemedizin Aktuell **5635**
1430-855X Aerztlicher Ratgeber fuer Junge Eltern†
1430-8576 Conflicts, Options, Strategies in a Threatened World† **8943**
1430-8614 I A F - Informationen **8868**
1430-8630 H C I Letters†
1430-8681 Umweltmedizin in Forschung und Praxis **5726**
1430-8711 Anno Domini **4199**
1430-8762 Weinwirtschaft **612**
1430-8770 Muenchener Beitraege zur Interkulturellen Kommunikation **3014**
1430-8819 Avifaunistischer Informationsdienst Bayern **902**
1430-886X M I B A - Die Eisenbahn im Modell **4339**
1430-8886 Podologie **6255**
1430-9017 Jahrbuch fuer Wissenschaft und Ethik **7870**
1430-9084 Der Pruefingenieur **3281**
1430-9092 Mission Weltweit **7767**
1430-9122 Top Hair International **591**
1430-9211 Argonautenschiff **5206**
1430-9254 Aufatmen **7746**
1430-9262 Immissionsschutz (Berlin. Zeitschrift) **3487**
1430-9270 Cavallo **8289**
1430-9351 Mein Geheimnis **8874**
1430-9459 Award Winning Architecture International Yearbook†
1430-9467 Magazin Junger Medienmacher **2201**
1430-953X Medicinal Plant Conservation† **8973**
1430-9572 Scottish Studies International **4262**
1430-9602 Advances in Spatial Science **568**
1430-9734 Leipziger Juristische Studien. Oeffentlich-Rechtliche Abteilung **4722**
1430-9769 Guitar **6571**
1430-9777 Beschreibende Sortenliste Kartoffeln **270**
1430-9858 Biomedical Ethics†
1430-9874 Wireless†
1430-9939 Beratungsbrief fuer Produktmanager und Marketingleiter *changed to* 1619-2753 **1837**
1430-9947 F K T **6497**
1430-9971 La Gazzetta **6569**
1431-0554 Kunststoff-Magazin **7094**
1431-0635 Documenta Mathematica **5484**
1431-0643 *see* 1431-0635 **5484**
1431-0651 Extremophiles **764**

ISSN

1431-0678 Deutsche Erbrechtszeitschrift **1920**
1431-0694 Frankreich-Zentrum. Veroeffentlichungen **4221**
1431-0775 Stadt Duisburg. Programm-Informations-Dienst. Foerderprogramme **7483**
1431-0821 Classics in Mathematics **5478**
1431-0880 B M F T Risiko- und Sicherheitsforschung†
1431-1062 U T A International† **8995**
1431-1097 Lena **6640**
1431-1119 Franz-Fischer-Jahrbuecher **6921**
1431-1399 Symbolic Computation†
1431-1550 Algorithms and Computation in Mathematics **5468**
1431-1798 Notes Magazin *changed to* 1861-5597 **2589**
1431-1933 Contributions to Economics **1086**
1431-1992 Blickpunkt Gemeinde† **8937**
1431-200X Theologisches Gespraech **7689**
1431-2018 Von B bis Y
1431-2158 D D S **3019**
1431-2174 Hydrogeology Journal **2794**
1431-2271 F B - I E **1744**
1431-231X Heimat-Chronik - Komotauer Zeitung **3536**
1431-2379 Welt und Umwelt der Bibel **7694**
1431-2433 E S O Astrophysics Symposia **574**
1431-2468 Current Issues in Toxicology†
1431-2492 Environmental Engineering **3424**
1431-2530 Island-Berichte **3850**
1431-2549 V E D D Forum **7778**
1431-2840 Kunstzeitung **502**
1431-2921 DStR-CD *see* 0949-7676 **1920**
1431-293X Beck'sches Nachschlagewerk der Entscheidungen des Bundesfinanzhofs†
1431-3006 European and Transatlantic Studies **1106**
1431-3022 Spektrum der Psychiatrie, Psychotherapie und Nervenheilkunde†
1431-3049 Studien und Texte zur Keltologie **5181**
1431-312X Universitaet Konstanz. Personal- und Vorlesungsverzeichnis **2962**
1431-3510 Textile Forum (Deutsche Ausgabe) **8459**
1431-3529 Textile forum (English edition) *see* 1431-3510 **8459**
1431-357X Frontiers of Virology **886**
1431-3626 Focus on Cancer†
1431-3669 Relationen **7262**
1431-3677 Armband Uhren **4564**
1431-3707 D S W '12 Nachrichten **8168**
1431-374X Rock & Pop Single - Preiskatalog **6612**
1431-3790 Informationsdienst F I Z Technik. Industrieroboter und Handhabungssysteme **3230**
1431-3863 Der Platow Brief **1511**
1431-3928 B F H - P R **1911**
1431-3936 Deutsche Bilanzierungs-Richtlinien **1920**
1431-3995 M F I **4339**
1431-4096 Deutschland Spezial Ost **1920**
1431-4177 Handbuch der Helmholtz-Zentren†
1431-4355 Didaktik Deutsch **5112**
1431-4428 Getraenke! Technologie und Marketing **604**
1431-4436 JAVA Spektrum **2507**
1431-4452 Waxmann Studies **8014**
1431-4576 Ratgeber Bauen **1031**
1431-4584 Umweltprobenbank des Bundes **3472**
1431-4614 Z M P Bilanz Forst und Holz *changed to* Z M P Marktbilanz Forst und Holz **3708**
1431-4649 Zeitschrift fuer Lebensmittel-Untersuchung und -Forschung B *changed to* 1438-2377 **3669**
1431-472X Informatik Aktuell **2422**
1431-4746 I S W Forschung und Praxis **5452**
1431-4800 Jugendrotkreuz† **8969**
1431-4819 Descriptions of Ectomycorrhizae **785**
1431-4932 Katholischer Digest *changed to* 1619-2001 **7633**
1431-4975 Drama und Theater in Suedasien **548**
1431-4983 Turkic Languages **5189**
1431-5025 B Z B Sachmagazin fuer Buerokommunikation, Bueroeinrichtung, Bueroumwelt†
1431-5041 Scientia Poetica **5368**
1431-5084 Geologisches Jahrbuch. Reihe G: Informationen aus den Bund - Laender-Arbeitsgruppen der Geologischen Dienste **2742**
1431-5092 Geologisches Jahrbuch. Reihe H: Wirtschaftsgeologie, Berichte zur Rohstoffwirtschaft **2742**
1431-5157 Molecules (Print Archive Edition) **690**
1431-5165 *see* 1420-3049 **2127**
1431-5211 B m K - Bauen mit Kunststoffen und Neuen Baustoffen†
1431-522X Brauwelt - Brevier (Year) **600**
1431-5254 A T W - Internationale Zeitschrift fuer Kernenergie **3164**
1431-5262 Medienwissenschaft **2385**
1431-5335 H L Z - Zeitschrift der G E W Hamburg **2861**
1431-553X Logistikwelt **3352**
1431-5548 Marburger Literatur-Almanach **5330**
1431-5556 Seibt Verpackungstechnik **6715**
1431-5602 Biologische Zahnmedizin†
1431-5610 Schaefereikalender **299**
1431-5637 Kirchenbote **7803**
1431-5726 Zeitschrift fuer Japanisches Recht **4968**
1431-5734 I F O Japan Branchendienst. Elektrotechnik und Elektronik†
1431-5777 *see* 0340-0131 **6679**
1431-5890 *see* 0931-7597 **2093**
1431-5971 Review of Information Science†
1431-6005 Microeconomic Studies†
1431-6072 Gelbe Liste Pharmindex. Internisten **6844**
1431-6250 Environmental Science **3428**
1431-6463 Versicherungsrecht Schriftenreihe **4527**
1431-6579 Old Herborn University Seminar Monograph **5930**
1431-6684 Siegener Beitraege **4263**
1431-6706 Fruehgeschichtliche und Provinzialroemische Archaeologie **394**
1431-6714 Die Zuckerrueben Zeitung **261**
1431-6730 Biological Chemistry **727**
1431-6757 Juedische Kultur **4236**
1431-679X Environmental and Safety Technology†
1431-6811 Principles of Pediatric Neurosurgery†
1431-6854 Perspectives in Neural Computing **2456**
1431-6900 Monographs in Computer Science **2432**
1431-7079 Immobilienmakler *changed to* Haufe Immobilien-Makler Office **4412**
1431-7087 Konstanzer Schriften zum Verwaltungsrecht und zur Rechtstatsachenforschung **4710**
1431-7125 N A T O Advanced Sciences Institutes Series. Series I. Global Environmental Change†
1431-7133 Ernst Schering Research Foundation Workshop. Supplement *see* 0947-6075 **731**
1431-7168 Supervision **1709**
1431-7184 Umwelt - Kommunale Oekologische Briefe *changed to* 1866-0037 **3472**
1431-7281 Moraltheologie - Anthropologie - Ethik **6935**
1431-729X Kieler Werkstuecke. Reihe E: Beitraege zur Sozial- und Wirtschaftsgeschichte **4237**
1431-7303 Kieler Werkstuecke. Reihe G: Beitraege zur Fruehen Neuzeit **4237**
1431-7419 Universitaet Mannheim. Vorlesungsverzeichnis **3034**
1431-7451 Zeitspruenge **4280**
1431-7540 Research in Criminology†
1431-7613 Theory in Biosciences **707**
1431-7664 Filmforum **6500**
1431-7737 Advances in Food Sciences **3625**
1431-7990 Tarantulas of the World **964**
1431-8016 Mathematische Geologie **2754**
1431-8024 Capri **4372**
1431-8059 Innovation (English Edition) **7077**
1431-8067 Die Blaue Reihe **3018**
1431-8172 Zeitschrift fuer Klinische Psychologie, Psychiatrie und Psychotherapie *changed to* 1661-4747 **6190**
1431-8202 Progress in Biomedical Research† **8982**
1431-8253 Kommunale Entsorgung **7495**
1431-827X H F Report
1431-8318 Oper Aktuell **6601**
1431-8407 D M K - Die Moderne Kueche **4555**
1431-8598 Springer Series in Operations Research *changed to* Springer Series in Operations Research and Financial Engineering **2438**
1431-8822 Studies in Economic Ethics and Philosophy **6955**
1431-8857 Pflanzenbauwissenschaften **3747**
1431-8997 Reptilia **961**
1431-9055 Der Vermieter-Brief **7615**
1431-9136 P V - Report **4395**
1431-9152 Mystery Thriller **5414**
1431-9268 Chemtracts **2093**
1431-9276 Microscopy and Microanalysis **900**
1431-9292 Zeitschrift fuer Arznei- und Gewuerzpflanzen **6887**
1431-9306 Series in Broadband Communications **2338**
1431-9314 Topics in Atmospheric and Oceanographic Sciences†
1431-9349 Texts and Monographs in Economics and Mathematical Systems†
1431-9489 Psychotherapeuten Forum *changed to* 1860-7357 **7357**
1431-9543 Familie & Co. **6092**
1431-9551 Kutter und Kueste **8321**
1431-956X Deutsches Steuerrecht - Entscheidungsdienst **1920**
1431-9691 Werk und Zeit. Brief *changed to* 1617-058X **461**
1431-9705 Mediengeschichtliche Veroeffentlichungen **7567**
1431-9721 Insecta **849**
1431-9810 Der ImmobilienVerwalter **7595**
1431-9845 Aufwaerts (Giessen) **7623**
1431-9918 Tanzwissenschaft **2688**
1431-9969 Forensia Jahrbuch†
1431-9993 Forum Suevicum **4221**
1432-0002 Disorders of Human Learning, Behavior, and Communication†
1432-0010 I L S I Monograph **6660**
1432-010X *see* 0947-3602 **3293**
1432-0142 Korea **7149**
1432-0169 Technische Universitaet Muenchen. Lehrstuhl fuer Rechnertechnik und Rechnerorganisation. Research Report Series **2439**
1432-0258 Erziehung, Schule, Gesellschaft **2152**
1432-0266 Ethno-Islamica **549**
1432-0274 Literatura **5324**
1432-0282 Nachrichten aus dem Martin-von-Wagner-Museum **407**
1432-0290 Politik und Gesellschaft. Wuerzburger Universitaetsschriften **7171**
1432-0304 Religion in der Gesellschaft **7675**
1432-0312 Spektrum Philosophie **6953**
1432-0320 Wuerzburger Forschungen zur Altertumskunde **424**
1432-0339 Wuerzburger Rechtswissenschaftliche Schriften **4816**
1432-038X Kommunale Fahrzeuge **7495**
1432-0401 Conferencing
1432-041X *see* 0949-944X **668**
1432-0428 *see* 0012-186X **5890**
1432-0436 *see* 0301-4681 **669**
1432-0444 *see* 0179-5376 **5483**
1432-0452 *see* 0178-2770 **2417**
1432-0460 *see* 0179-051X **6079**
1432-0479 *see* 0938-2259 **1540**
1432-0487 *see* 0948-7921 **3303**
1432-0495 *see* 0943-0105 **2733**
1432-0509 *see* 0942-8925 **5919**
1432-0517 *see* 0949-1775 **2096**
1432-0525 *see* 0001-5903 **2541**
1432-0533 *see* 0001-6322 **6118**
1432-0541 *see* 0178-4617 **2406**
1432-055X *see* 0003-2417 **5769**
1432-0576 *see* 0992-7689 **2777**
1432-0584 *see* 0939-5555 **5933**
1432-0592 *see* 0570-1864 **1060**
1432-0606 *see* 0095-4616 **5472**
1432-0614 *see* 0175-7598 **756**
1432-0622 *see* 0938-1279 **5550**
1432-0630 *see* 0947-8396 **7005**
1432-0649 *see* 0946-2171 **7005**
1432-0657 *see* 0003-9519 **7836**
1432-0665 *see* 0933-5846 **5473**
1432-0673 *see* 0003-9527 **5473**
1432-0681 *see* 0939-1533 **3182**
1432-069X *see* 0340-3696 **5871**
1432-0703 *see* 0090-4341 **3494**
1432-0711 *see* 0932-0067 **5986**
1432-072X *see* 0302-8933 **881**
1432-0738 *see* 0340-5761 **3494**
1432-0746 *see* 0004-6361 **570**
1432-0754 *see* 0935-4956 **571**
1432-0762 *see* 0340-5443 **3406**
1432-0770 *see* 0340-1200 **825**
1432-0789 *see* 0178-2762 **221**
1432-0800 *see* 0007-4861 **3494**
1432-0819 *see* 0258-8900 **2778**
1432-0827 *see* 0171-967X **5884**
1432-0835 *see* 0944-2669 **5477**
1432-0843 *see* 0344-5704 **6011**
1432-0851 *see* 0340-7004 **6012**
1432-086X *see* 0174-1551 **6193**
1432-0878 *see* 0302-766X **829**
1432-0886 *see* 0009-5915 **864**
1432-0894 *see* 0930-7575 **6349**
1432-0916 *see* 0010-3616 **7008**
1432-0924 *see* 0178-7675 **5551**
1432-0932 *see* 0940-6719 **6243**
1432-0940 *see* 0176-4276 **5481**
1432-0959 *see* 0935-1175 **7053**
1432-0967 *see* 0010-7999 **2730**
1432-0975 *see* 0722-4028 **2803**
1432-0983 *see* 0172-8083 **865**
1432-0991 *see* 0343-8651 **883**
1432-1009 *see* 0364-152X **3426**
1432-1017 *see* 0175-7571 **753**
1432-1033 European Journal of Biochemistry (Online) *changed to* 1742-4658 **732**
1432-1041 *see* 0031-6970 **6838**
1432-1068 *see* 1633-8065 **6060**
1432-1076 *see* 0340-6199 **6091**
1432-1084 *see* 0938-7994 **6196**
1432-1092 *see* 0531-7479 **7012**
1432-1106 *see* 0014-4819 **6140**
1432-1114 *see* 0723-4864 **3377**
1432-1122 *see* 0949-2984 **1343**
1432-1157 *see* 0276-0460 **2735**
1432-1165 *see* 1430-483X **8824**
1432-1173 Elektronische Ausgabe *see* 0017-8470 **5877**
1432-1181 *see* 0947-7411 **7054**
1432-119X *see* 0948-6143 **833**
1432-1203 *see* 0340-6717 **871**
1432-1211 *see* 0093-7711 **872**
1432-122X *see* 0170-6012 **3291**
1432-1238 *see* 0342-4642 **5636**
1432-1246 *see* 0340-0131 **6679**
1432-1254 *see* 0020-7128 **6357**
1432-1262 *see* 0179-1958 **6246**
1432-1270 *see* 0020-7276 **5496**
1432-1289 *see* 0020-9554 **5946**
1432-1297 *see* 0020-9910 **5498**
1432-1300 *see* 1432-5012 **5062**
1432-1319 *see* 0342-7188 **124**
1432-1327 *see* 0949-8257 **2117**
1432-1335 *see* 0171-5216 **6024**
1432-1343 *see* 0176-4268 **5020**
1432-1351 *see* 0340-7594 **924**
1432-136X *see* 0174-1578 **924**
1432-1378 *see* 0933-2790 **5502**
1432-1386 *see* 0936-9937 **1545**
1432-1394 *see* 0949-7714 **2785**
1432-1416 *see* 0303-6812 **683**
1432-1424 *see* 0022-2631 **834**
1432-1432 *see* 0022-2844 **874**
1432-1440 *see* 0946-2716 **5653**
1432-1459 *see* 0340-5354 **6154**
1432-1467 *see* 0938-8974 **7021**
1432-1475 *see* 0933-1433 **7286**
1432-1564 Koelner Informations Management **2531**
1432-1661 Alsterverein Jahrbuch **4197**
1432-1696 Museum fuer Naturkunde Chemnitz. Veroeffentlichungen **691**
1432-170X Bodenschutz Zeitschrift **2604**
1432-1750 *see* 0341-2040 **6216**
1432-1769 *see* 0932-8092 **2527**
1432-1777 *see* 0938-8990 **875**
1432-1785 *see* 0025-2611 **5510**
1432-1793 *see* 0025-3162 **688**
1432-1807 *see* 0025-5831 **5516**
1432-1815 *see* 0720-728X **5517**
1432-1823 *see* 0025-5874 **5517**
1432-1831 *see* 0300-8584 **5763**
1432-184X *see* 0095-3628 **891**
1432-1858 *see* 0946-7076 **2473**
1432-1866 *see* 0026-4598 **2755**
1432-1882 *see* 0942-4962 **2488**
1432-1890 *see* 0940-6360 **803**
1432-1904 *see* 0028-1042 **7890**
1432-1912 *see* 0028-1298 **6863**
1432-1920 *see* 0028-3940 **6204**
1432-1939 *see* 0029-8549 **695**
1432-1955 *see* 0932-0113 **894**
1432-1963 *see* 0172-8113 **5693**
1432-1971 *see* 0172-0643 **5797**
1432-198X *see* 0931-041X **6273**
1432-1998 *see* 0301-0449 **6205**
1432-2013 *see* 0031-6768 **5695**
1432-2021 *see* 0342-1791 **6476**
1432-203X *see* 0721-7714 **811**
1432-2048 *see* 0032-0935 **813**
1432-2056 *see* 0722-4060 **698**
1432-2064 *see* 0178-8051 **5526**
1432-2072 *see* 0033-3158 **6876**
1432-2080 *see* 0935-6185 **6179**
1432-2099 *see* 0301-634X **754**
1432-2102 *see* 0033-832X **6206**
1432-2110 *see* 0934-9847 **3217**
1432-2129 *see* 0932-433X **5710**
1432-2137 *see* 0037-1912 **5533**
1432-2145 *see* 0934-0882 **817**

ISSN

1434-8128 Regulierungsbehoerde fuer Telekommunikation und Post. Amtsblatt **2355**
1434-825X Computerpraxis, Telekommunikation *changed to* 1613-9364 **2351**
1434-8268 Elektromaschinenbau *changed to* 1613-6918 **3306**
1434-8330 Kindschaftsrechtliche Praxis *changed to* 1861-6631 **4915**
1434-8411 A E Ue: International Journal of Electronics and Communication **2310**
1434-8454 Deutsches Zentrum fuer Luft- und Raumfahrt. Forschungsberichte **53**
1434-8489 Documenta Orthographica **5112**
1434-8500 Haushaltstechnik **4558**
1434-8578 Pirckheimer Jahrbuch fuer Renaissance- und Humanismusforschung **4253**
1434-8802 Computerrecht Intern *changed to* 1617-1527 **2514**
1434-8853 E P I Information **6749**
1434-8888 Zeitschrift fuer Zivilprozess International **4945**
1434-8942 Pharma und Food **6868**
1434-8950 Der Hausarzt **5623**
1434-8977 Therapie Kreativ **7412**
1434-9051 Springer Praxis und Recht **4787**
1434-906X Springers Handbuecher der Rechtswissenschaft **4787**
1434-9078 Texte zur Rechtspolitik **4795**
1434-9086 Frauenheilkunde Plus
1434-9132 Kleintier Konkret **8802**
1434-9140 Tuebinger Texte **421**
1434-9272 Neue Zeitschrift fuer Gesellschaftsrecht **4741**
1434-9302 Aufbereitungs-Technik - Mineral Processing **6457**
1434-9329 Rma.de **3856**
1434-9442 Der Vermieter **7615**
1434-9582 Bundesamt fuer Bauwesen und Raumordnung. Arbeitspapiere **4405**
1434-9590 Informationen aus der Forschung des B B R *changed to* 1868-0089 **4404**
1434-9604 *see* 1434-9329 **3856**
1434-9728 Technische Ueberwachung **6688**
1434-9817 Lernchancen **3070**
1434-9825 Desktop Dialog Special *see* 0936-8833 **2570**
1434-9892 Betriebswirtschaftliche Studien Marketing, Organisation, Rechnungslegung **1067**
1434-9922 Studies in Fuzziness and Soft Computing **2456**
1434-9949 *see* 0770-3198 **6223**
1434-9957 *see* 1359-4338 **2490**
1435-0017 Orthopaedie und Rheuma **6069**
1435-0092 SchulVerwaltung. Ausgabe Schleswig-Holstein, Hamburg, Bremen *changed to* 1618-9167 **3032**
1435-0122 Praxis Steuerstrafrecht **1940**
1435-0130 *see* 0930-343X **6243**
1435-0157 *see* 1431-2174 **2794**
1435-0211 Journal of Wood Science **3713**
1435-0246 B A P - Betriebliche Ausbildungspraxis†
1435-0343 The Coach†
1435-0408 Automobil Entwicklung **8563**
1435-0475 T & E Sport und Medizin†
1435-0491 Universitaet Kiel. Walter-Schuecking-Institut fuer Internationales Recht. Veroeffentlichungen **4944**
1435-0556 Muensteraner Schriften zur Volkskunde - Europaeischen Ethnologie **348**
1435-0629 *see* 1432-9840 **3418**
1435-0645 *see* 0002-1962 **88**
1435-0653 *see* 0011-183X **226**
1435-0661 *see* 0361-5995 **253**
1435-0920 Zuerich Club Communique **1661**
1435-0939 New Yorker Beitraege zur Literaturwissenschaft **5341**
1435-0955 Familienmosaik fuer Mecklenburg-Vorpommern **3765**
1435-0963 Recht in Afrika **4766**
1435-098X Romania Judaica **7729**
1435-1013 Forst und Technik **3691**
1435-103X KuechenWelt† **8970**
1435-1048 Stauffenburg Medien **2339**
1435-1080 Aerztliche Praxis. Urologie, Nephrologie *changed to* 1436-266X **6264**
1435-1102 *see* 1434-1816 **8843**
1435-1145 C E Markt **3090**
1435-1196 Digital World†
1435-1218 Report Naturheilkunde **314**
1435-1250 *see* 0340-1855 **6228**
1435-1269 *see* 0948-6704 **4057**
1435-1277 *see* 0930-9225 **5802**
1435-1358 Jahrbuch fuer Universitaetsgeschichte **4234**
1435-1420 *see* 0175-3851 **5636**
1435-1463 *see* Journal of Neural Transmission **6153**
1435-1528 *see* 0035-4511 **7062**
1435-1536 *see* 0303-402X **2122**
1435-1544 *see* 0938-7412 **5789**
1435-165X *see* 1018-8827 **6139**
1435-1714 Bau (Berlin) **979**
1435-1730 New World† **8977**
1435-1803 *see* 0300-8428 **5778**
1435-1854 Bauelemente Bau **979**
1435-1889 Advances in Materials Research **3335**
1435-1900 Medizin Report†
1435-1935 Mitteilungen aus dem Museum fuer Naturkunde in Berlin - Zoologische Reihe *changed to* Zoosystematics and Evolution **971**
1435-1943 Mitteilungen aus dem Museum fuer Naturkunde in Berlin - Geowissenschaftliche Reihe **2713**
1435-1951 Mitteilungen aus dem Museum fuer Naturkunde in Berlin - Deutsche Entomologische Zeitschrift **855**
1435-1978 Karrierefuehrer Hochschulen **6700**
1435-1994 B L N - Bayerische Luftsport-Nachrichten
1435-2028 Eltern for Family **2151**
1435-2176 Waegen, Dosieren und Mischen **6407**
1435-2206 Nord Oe R **7213**
1435-2214 Deutsches Entertainment Magazin **6496**
1435-2230 Die Johanniter **8048**
1435-2249 Z N T - Zeitschrift fuer Neues Testament **7696**
1435-2273 Patientenforum Homoeopathie†
1435-2311 Kolam **5318**
1435-232X *see* 1434-5161 **874**
1435-2443 Langenbecks Archives of Surgery **6251**
1435-2451 *see* 1435-2443 **6251**
1435-246X Central European Journal of Operations Research **2409**
1435-2508 ZahnRat **5870**
1435-2516 Neue Saechsische Lehrerzeitung **2890**
1435-2524 Network Computing **2501**
1435-2567 Hygiene und Desinfektion **3246**
1435-2591 P C Player Plus†
1435-2664 Rueckblick **4260**
1435-2745 I F O Studien zur Bau- und Wohnungswirtschaft **1013**
1435-2788 N f Z Werkstatt **8673**
1435-2842 Immunologie und Impfen†
1435-2850 Sueddeutsche Wohnwirtschaft *changed to* 1861-0773 **4414**
1435-2869 South East Europe Review **8006**
1435-2982 Image Home Entertainment **3104**
1435-3040 Leipziger Studien zur Erforschung von Regionenbezogenen Identifikationsprozessen **7983**
1435-3067 Viszeralchirurgie **6262**
1435-3121 Kalaschnikow **5222**
1435-3199 V G B PowerTech *see* 0372-5715 **3333**
1435-3253 Europa Blaetter† **8954**
1435-3261 Karrierefuehrer Finanzdienstleistungen **6700**
1435-327X Karrierefuehrer Bauingenieure **6700**
1435-3288 Z E I Discussion Paper **7275**
1435-330X Teamwork (German Edition) **5867**
1435-3326 Kran-Magazin *changed to* 1861-1036 **1020**
1435-3369 GmbH-Tip **1927**
1435-3385 Autoforum†
1435-3407 PraxisNetz†
1435-3415 Logische Philosophie **6932**
1435-3423 Lebensmittel Zeitung Direkt **3654**
1435-3458 Gruener Anzeiger **3735**
1435-3474 GoingPublic **1627**
1435-3504 Wassersport im Westen *changed to* 1861-6534 **8284**
1435-3547 Verbraucher Konkret **2642**
1435-3571 Getraenke-Ring Aktiv **604**
1435-3601 Die Privatbrauerei†
1435-3644 Diabetesprofi *changed to* 1614-6476 **5887**
1435-3660 Natalie†
1435-3679 Julia Saison **5410**
1435-3695 Julia Special† **8969**
1435-3717 E-Card Business†
1435-3725 European Physical Journal Direct **7011**
1435-375X Deutsches Handwerksblatt. Ausgabe Bielefeld *see* Deutsches Handwerksblatt **1675**
1435-3768 Deutsches Handwerksblatt. Ausgabe Dortmund *see* Deutsches Handwerksblatt **1675**
1435-3776 Deutsches Handwerksblatt. Ausgabe Koeln *see* Deutsches Handwerksblatt **1675**
1435-3784 Deutsches Handwerksblatt. Ausgabe Koblenz *see* Deutsches Handwerksblatt **1675**
1435-3806 Deutsches Handwerksblatt. Ausgabe Muenster *see* Deutsches Handwerksblatt **1675**
1435-3814 Deutsches Handwerksblatt. Ausgabe Pfalz *see* Deutsches Handwerksblatt **1675**
1435-3822 Deutsches Handwerksblatt. Ausgabe Duesseldorf *see* Deutsches Handwerksblatt **1675**
1435-3830 Deutsches Handwerksblatt. Ausgabe Rheinhessen *see* Deutsches Handwerksblatt **1675**
1435-3849 Deutsches Handwerksblatt. Ausgabe Saarbruecken *see* Deutsches Handwerksblatt **1675**
1435-3857 Deutsches Handwerksblatt. Ausgabe Trier *see* Deutsches Handwerksblatt **1675**
1435-3865 Deutsches Handwerksblatt. Ausgabe Arnsberg *see* Deutsches Handwerksblatt **1675**
1435-3873 Deutsches Handwerksblatt Magazin. Ausgabe Cottbus *see* Deutsches Handwerksblatt Magazin **1675**
1435-3881 Deutsches Handwerksblatt Magazin. Ausgabe Frankfurt am Oder *see* Deutsches Handwerksblatt Magazin **1675**
1435-389X Deutsches Handwerksblatt Magazin. Ausgabe Ostmecklenburg-Vorpommern *see* Deutsches Handwerksblatt Magazin **1675**
1435-3903 Deutsches Handwerksblatt Magazin. Ausgabe Potsdam *see* Deutsches Handwerksblatt Magazin **1675**
1435-4039 Germany. Deutscher Bundestag. Wissenschaftliche Dienste. Aktuelle Bibliographien der Bibliothek **625**
1435-4217 Pflegefreund **8062**
1435-4233 Paediatrische Allergologie in Klinik und Praxis **5764**
1435-4365 Angewandte Sprachwissenschaft **5093**
1435-4373 *see* 0934-9723 **885**
1435-439X Z Eu S - Zeitschrift fuer Europarechtliche Studien **4945**
1435-4438 Kit *changed to* 1619-5582 **4337**
1435-4438 Kit *changed to* 1619-5574 **4337**
1435-4446 *see* 1433-5883 **5504**
1435-4454 Autotuning **8567**
1435-4578 J U V E Rechtsmarkt **4698**
1435-4594 Jahrbuch Grundschulforschung **3066**
1435-4616 Welt der Frau†
1435-4659 Forschungen **4410**
1435-4683 Budo, Karate **8163**
1435-4691 Zeitschrift fuer Audiologie **7090**
1435-4705 Fruehe Kindheit **2153**
1435-4721 Kinder- und Jugendkultur, -literatur und -medien **5317**
1435-4853 Katalog Distributor **2010**
1435-4918 Germany. Deutscher Bundestag. Wissenschaftliche Dienste. Laenderbibliographien der Bibliothek
1435-4934 E-Journal of Nondestructive Testing & Ultrasonics **3343**
1435-5043 Branchenfuehrer Galvanotechnik **1976**
1435-5078 Europarecht. Beiheft *see* 0531-2485 **4924**
1435-5167 Unicum Abi **2174**
1435-5175 Women & Work
1435-5213 Auto Bild Spezial **8557**
1435-5264 European Promotional Products Industry **25**
1435-5272 Transkript **751**
1435-5280 Studien zum Physiklernen **7041**
1435-5337 *see* 0933-7741 **5488**
1435-5345 *see* 0075-4102 **5500**
1435-5361 Das Hauseigentum **4412**
1435-5396 Monatsschrift Magazin fuer den Gartenbauprofi **3743**
1435-5418 Unternehmensberater† **8996**
1435-5434 Textil-Wirtschaft Sports†
1435-5469 Spanish Economic Review **1519**
1435-5477 *see* 1435-5469 **1519**
1435-5507 Gyn-Depesche **5992**
1435-5515 Neuro-Depesche **6163**
1435-5558 Cognition, Technology and Work **7346**
1435-5566 *see* 1435-5558 **7346**
1435-5574 C R M - Handbuch zur Reisemedizinischen Beratung *changed to* C R M - Handbuch Reisemedizin **5590**
1435-5590 Intercultural Music Studies **6576**
1435-5604 *see* 0914-8779 **5895**
1435-5655 *see* 0951-5666 **2444**
1435-5663 *see* 0177-0667 **3291**
1435-5671 *see* 0947-3580 **2460**
1435-568X *see* 0932-4194 **3370**
1435-571X Gegenworte **7857**
1435-5744 HiFi Mobil†
1435-5809 Computer@Produktion **3290**
1435-5914 *see* 0911-0119 **5552**
1435-5922 *see* 0944-1174 **5927**
1435-5930 Journal of Geographical Systems **4037**
1435-5949 *see* 1435-5930 **4037**
1435-5957 *see* 1056-8190 **7991**
1435-6007 Ullmann's Encyclopedia of Industrial Chemistry **2083**
1435-604X *see* 0268-8921 **5660**
1435-6066 *see* 0934-9839 **3217**
1435-6074 A E P **8554**
1435-6104 Economics of Governance **1101**
1435-6112 Das Collegmagazin Zahnarzt *changed to* 1617-5077 **5870**
1435-6139 Implantologie Journal **5847**
1435-6147 Laser Journal **5855**
1435-6163 International Journal for Ion Mobility Spectrometry **2101**
1435-6201 Agrarwissenschaftliche Forschungsergebnisse **81**
1435-6228 Oeko-Management **1782**
1435-6236 Schriften zum Betrieblichen Rechnungswesen und Controlling **1792**
1435-6244 Schriften zur Konzernsteuerung **1381**
1435-6260 Forschungsergebnisse zur Informatik **1417**
1435-6279 Studien zur Datenbankforschung **2532**
1435-6287 Forschungsergebnisse Programmentwicklung **2506**
1435-6295 Studien zur Wirtschaftsinformatik **1421**
1435-6309 Hippokrates **5628**
1435-6317 Studien zur Schizophrenieforschung **6187**
1435-6376 Ostfriesland-Magazin **3854**
1435-6406 Archiv fuer Hydrobiologie. Supplement Volumes, Monographic Studies **654**
1435-6422 I P A Aktuell **2654**
1435-6430 Bauen Mit Textilien†
1435-6465 Lebens- und Glaubenswelten **7659**
1435-649X Das Deutsche Hunde Magazin **6806**
1435-6503 Studien zur Psychiatrieforschung **6187**
1435-6511 Naturwissenschaftliche Forschungsergebnisse **7890**
1435-652X Studien zur Erwachsenenbildung **2946**
1435-6538 Studien zur Schulpaedagogik **2915**
1435-6546 Schriften zur Sportwissenschaft **8199**
1435-6554 Poetica (Hamburg) **5352**
1435-6562 Orbis **8124**
1435-6570 Philologia **5160**
1435-6589 Schriften zur Kulturwissenschaft **7999**
1435-6597 Boethiana **6908**
1435-6600 Studien zur Geschichtsforschung des Altertums **4163**
1435-6619 Studien zur Geschichtsforschung des Mittelalters **4163**
1435-6627 Studien zur Geschichtsforschung der Neuzeit **4163**
1435-6635 Studien zur Zeitgeschichte (Hamburg) **4163**
1435-6643 Politica **7167**
1435-6651 Socialia **8134**
1435-666X Psychologische Forschungsergebnisse **7398**
1435-6678 Feminat **8896**
1435-6694 Hannoversche Berichte zum Qualitaetsmanagement **1887**
1435-6775 Studien zur Familienforschung **8141**
1435-6783 Forschungsergebnisse zur Sexualpsychologie **7357**
1435-6791 Studien zur Kindheits- und Jugendforschung **2168**
1435-6805 Studien zur Stressforschung **7410**
1435-6813 Studien zur Gerontologie **4056**
1435-6821 Studien zur Rechtswissenschaft **4790**
1435-683X Wirtschaftsrechtliche Forschungsergebnisse **1195**
1435-6848 Arbeitsrechtliche Forschungsergebnisse **1664**
1435-6856 Technische Forschungsergebnisse **8441**
1435-6864 Theos **7690**
1435-6872 Volkswirtschaftliche Forschungsergebnisse **8014**
1435-6880 Volkswirtschaften der Welt **1524**
1435-6899 Euro-Wirtschaft **1563**
1435-6902 Institut fuer Rehabilitationsmedizin und Balneologie Bad Wildungen. Wissenschaftliche Schriftenreihe **5635**
1435-6910 Hamburger Beitraege zur Geschichte des Oestlichen Europas **4225**
1435-6929 Greifswalder Historische Studien **4225**
1435-6937 Stiftung Herzogtum Lauenburg. Schriftenreihe **4268**
1435-6945 Europaeischer Arbeitskreis fuer Prae- und Postnatale Entwicklungsforschung. Schriftenreihe **5989**
1435-6953 Ulmer Sprachstudien **5190**
1435-7003 Tele-Satellite International **2395**
1435-702X *see* 0721-832X **6043**
1435-7054 I T - Sources **1417**
1435-7135 Aachener Finanzwirtschaftliche Studien **1056**
1435-7151 Nichtlineare und Stochastische Physik **7028**
1435-7216 Immobilien Vertraulich **7595**
1435-7259 Diabetes Newsletter **5888**
1435-7267 RechtsBrief Touristik *changed to* 1613-0782 **1945**
1435-7305 Bellevue Guide Mallorca
1435-7356 Iwalewa Forum†
1435-7402 Im Focus Onkologie **6021**
1435-7445 Antiquitates **374**
1435-7518 KursKontakte **6645**
1435-7607 B I T Online **5060**
1435-7720 Der Erfolgreiche Verkaufsprofi
1435-7941 Organ **6602**
1435-795X Signifikation **8132**
1435-800X Aerztliches Journal Reise und Medizin **5569**
1435-8018 Apotheken Journal Reise und Pharmazie **6821**
1435-8034 Aktuell Informiert **8024**
1435-8042 *see* 0934-9340 **600**

ISSN

1437-000X Universitaet Bremen. Arbeitsbereich Nachrichtentechnik. Forschungsberichte 2343
1437-0069 Gruener Markt 3735
1437-0093 Natuschutz und Landschaftspflege Baden-Wuerttemberg 2622
1437-0115 Naturschutz-Spectrum 2621
1437-0336 Taxi 8606
1437-0379 Springer Series in Photonics 7085
1437-0387 Springer Series in Advanced Microelectronics 3114
1437-0433 Saxonia 4261
1437-0441 Vermoegen & Steuern 1389
1437-045X Literaturnyj Evropeec 5225
1437-062X InFo Neurologie und Psychiatrie 6145
1437-0735 Natuerlich Vegetarisch 6664
1437-0751 see 0178-7667 7357
1437-0808 Deutsches Gewaesserkundliches Jahrbuch. Kuestengebiet der Nordsee†
1437-0824 Bauen und Renovieren 4437
1437-0867 Angewandte Carabidologie 838
1437-0875 Games and More 2477
1437-0980 see 0171-5445 980
1437-0999 see 0932-8351 981
1437-1006 see 0005-9900 982
1437-1022 see 1432-3427 1023
1437-1030 see 1438-7778 1001
1437-1049 see 0038-9145 3283
1437-1057 Spa
1437-1065 MedAmbiente 4106
1437-1073 Cardio News 5779
1437-109X Top Magazin Dortmund - Recklinghausen 3858
1437-1103 Spot On 8758
1437-1146 Gehet Hin! - Missionsblatt 7759
1437-1162 Auto-Service-Praxis 8560
1437-1200 Akademie fuer Migration und Integration. Beitraege 7276
1437-1340 Art Journal†
1437-1359 Creative Journal 484
1437-1367 Pablo Journal 510
1437-1375 Marketing Musing on Art 504
1437-1383 Weekly Work 526
1437-1472 Advances in Laser Medicine† 8928
1437-1499 Freie Universitaet Berlin. Osteuropa-Institut. Arbeitspapiere. Bereich Geschichte und Kultur 4140
1437-1502 Freie Universitaet Berlin. Osteuropa-Institut. Arbeitspapiere. Bereich Recht und Wirtschaft 4678
1437-1545 Z E I - Report†
1437-1588 see 1436-9990 7510
1437-160X see 0172-8172 6227
1437-1618 see 0935-7335 6918
1437-1634 Bio- und Gentechnik 863
1437-1693 Wirtschaftspaedagogische Studien zur Individuellen und Kollektiven Entwicklung 1195
1437-1707 Freiburger Beitraege zur Archaeologie und Geschichte des Ersten Jahrtausends 394
1437-1731 Deutsche Cichliden-Gesellschaft. Region Berlin. Jahresbericht† 8949
1437-1782 Paediatrie Hautnah 6098
1437-1790 KiTa KinderTageseinrichtungen Aktuell. Ausgabe Hessen, Rheinland-Pfalz, Saarland 2159
1437-1812 S I P - Siebdruck Infopost 7327
1437-1898 Info3 7736
1437-2002 Wortlaut.de 5400
1437-2029 Advances in Statistical Software†
1437-2053 Metaphysica 6934
1437-2096 see 0936-5214 2131
1437-210X see 0039-7881 2131
1437-2177 Nachrichten aus Niedersachsens Urgeschichte. Beiheft see 0342-1406 407
1437-2185 Walt Disney's Micky Maus 2221
1437-2193 Orthopaedische Nachrichten 6069
1437-2207 Card-Forum 1392
1437-2223 L S K - stud.†
1437-2231 Ag V Forum†
1437-224X Produktionsmenge und Produktionswert der Verpackungsindustrie in der Bundesrepublik Deutschland
1437-2320 see 0344-5607 6253
1437-2355 Kunstrecht und Urheberrecht 6754
1437-2444 KommunalPraxis. Ausgabe Brandenburg, Mecklenburg-Vorpommern, Sachsen, Sachsen-Anhalt, Thueringen, Berlin† 8969
1437-2479 Goldschmiede Zeitung - European Jeweler 4566
1437-2533 Umrisse *changed to* Baukultur 980
1437-255X Trainer 6998
1437-2592 Professional System 1420
1437-2703 Universitaet Augsburg. Institut fuer Europaeische Kulturgeschichte. Mitteilungen 8012
1437-2711 Deutsche Angst-Zeitschrift 7351
1437-2827 S E F News 1605
1437-2835 see 1437-2827 1605
1437-286X Body Life 6983
1437-2878 C I M - Conference and Incentive Management 1731
1437-2916 Grimme 2382
1437-2940 Z f F - Zeitschrift fuer Familienforschung 8148
1437-2959 Braunschweigisches Jahrbuch fuer Landesgeschichte 4206
1437-3033 Medusa-Medias 5332
1437-3084 Advoice 4611
1437-3106 S A Z Sport 1841
1437-3114 S A Z Sportsfashion Magazin 2260
1437-3157 Foreign Language Teaching in Europe 2858
1437-3181 Beratung Aktuell (Internet)†
1437-319X Grundschule Sachunterricht - Themenheft 3063
1437-322X Forschungszentrum Rossendorf. Wissenschaftlich-Technische Berichte 7855
1437-3246 Koelner Forum fuer Geologie und Palaeontologie 2752
1437-3254 International Journal of Earth Sciences 2748
1437-3262 see 1437-3254 2748
1437-3270 Anno Domini Jahrbuch 4199
1437-3327 Freiburger Archaeologische Studien 394
1437-3335 Bochumer Beitraege zur Semiotik 5264
1437-3343 Schuetzenwarte 8199
1437-3475 Berliner Kurier 3844
1437-3599 S T - Computer 2481
1437-3688 Asien und Pazifik 544
1437-3718 Sergej 4379
1437-3785 Horticultural Industry *changed to* 1617-2000 3734
1437-3831 K U L I M U 5316
1437-3866 Pferdebetrieb 8296
1437-3890 Hallesche Schriften zur Sprechwissenschaft und Phonetik 5124
1437-398X P O S - Manager Technology 3681
1437-4013 KiTa Spezial 2159
1437-4021 Gottes Volk Sonderband see 0946-8943 7799
1437-403X Ti Geschaeftsreise†
1437-4056 Wave†
1437-4064 Diabetes Voice 5889
1437-4196 Berliner Statistik. Statistische Monatsschrift 7479
1437-4234 D U Z *changed to* 1613-1290 2977
1437-4250 Trade Fairs International 6283
1437-4293 Telemann Beitraege see 0541-8968 6586
1437-4315 see 1431-6730 727
1437-4323 see 0006-8055 780
1437-4331 see 1434-6621 729
1437-434X see 0018-3830 3712
1437-4358 see 0340-0204 7055
1437-4382 F G G B Rundbriefe 6894
1437-4439 Informationsdienst Europa Kompakt†
1437-448X Edition Globale - Lokale Sportkultur 8171
1437-451X Informationsdienst F I Z Technik. Kalt- und Warmmassivumformung 6339
1437-4641 Religion and Society in Transition 7674
1437-4692 Informationen aus Politik und Wirtschaft†
1437-4722 Diskussion Musikpaedagogik 6562
1437-4730 Praxishandbuch Geldanlage 1940
1437-4765 F M T 4334
1437-4781 Forest Pathology 3689
1437-482X Funkschau Handel 2350
1437-4854 Aquaristik - Fachmagazin 3586
1437-4927 Z N N - Zahnaerztliche Nachrichten Niedersachsen *changed to* Z K N - Mitteilungen 5869
1437-4935 Werbetechnik 37
1437-4943 Der Anaesthesist. Supplement 5769
1437-4951 Photographie 6974
1437-5001 frauennews 8864
1437-5028 see 1436-6444 2384
1437-5095 Schlesischer Kulturspiegel 3856
1437-5230 Krankenversicherungs- und Sozialrecht *changed to* 1439-8893 7519
1437-529X Leipziger Skripten 5143
1437-5370 Religion and Society 7674
1437-5435 Automation & Qualitaet 2458
1437-5443 Bochumer Italien-Studien 5264
1437-5532 Business Geomatics 4001
1437-5559 Kraftverkehrsrecht von A-Z† 8970
1437-5567 Suchtmedizin in Forschung und Praxis 2699
1437-5605 Journalismus und Geschichte 4578
1437-5699 P M A Production Management 8154
1437-5842 Informationen fuer die Fischwirtschaft aus der Fischereiforschung *changed to* 1860-9902 3597
1437-5850 Bundesamt fuer Bauwesen und Raumordnung. Research News 4405
1437-5923 D A V Panorama 8310
1437-5958 Kultur News 500
1437-5974 Stadt und Raum 4427
1437-6016 A P R International
1437-6032 Potsdamer Altertumswissenschaftliche Beitraege 2239
1437-6059 Frankfurter Beitraege zur Biologischen Bildung 673
1437-6083 Konflikte und Kultur 4238
1437-6091 Brennpunkt Lateinamerika (Print Edition) *changed to* 1862-3352 7236
1437-6105 Arbeitsmaterialien Wirtschaftsgeographie Regensburg 3999
1437-6113 Beitraege zur Wirtschaftsgeographie Regensburg 4000
1437-613X Leipziger Juristische Studien. Strafrechtliche Abteilung 4722
1437-6199 Hannover-Journal 1429
1437-6229 N K W - Partner 8673
1437-6237 Nobilis 5078
1437-644X Ju S - Basis†
1437-6482 Computer Bild 2411
1437-6547 Voix du Diabete see 1437-4064 5889
1437-6555 Voz de Diabetes see 1437-4064 5889
1437-6571 Epigraphische Forschungen auf der Arabischen Halbinsel 392
1437-6636 Octopus†
1437-6644 Online Today†
1437-6660 Verein fuer Geschichte an der Universitaet G H Paderborn. Mitteilungen 4276
1437-6873 Pharmacology Fast 6872
1437-6881 Politische Philosophie und Oekonomie 6944
1437-6903 Konturen 2696
1437-7012 Protozoological Monographs 698
1437-7071 Wirtschaft in Mittelfranken 1412
1437-708X Kaese und Wein 605
1437-711X Unternehmensfuehrung und Logistik 1908
1437-7128 Cognitive Strategy Concepts 1733
1437-7152 Offenbacher Wirtschaft 1408
1437-7160 Zeitschrift fuer Paedagogik und Theologie 2928
1437-7195 FlaechenRecycling GeoProfit†
1437-7217 Mein Schicksal 8874
1437-7233 Snow 8201
1437-7276 Weinwelt 612
1437-7306 Freshmen *changed to* Dreamboys 4372
1437-7330 Stadt Herne. Arbeitsmarktbericht 7503
1437-7357 Herne in Zahlen. Vierteljahresberichte 1236
1437-7365 Herne in Zahlen. Jahrbuch (Year) 1236
1437-7373 Medicus Plus†
1437-7462 klettern 8320
1437-7470 Hochzeitsplaner 5559
1437-7500 Gewaesserguetebericht 8824
1437-7543 Robin Wood Magazin 3464
1437-7667 Berichte aus dem Apparatebau 3374
1437-7772 International Journal of Clinical Oncology (Online) 6023
1437-7780 see 1341-321X 6853
1437-7799 see 1342-1751 6266
1437-7802 Rostocker Beitraege zu Controlling und Rechnungswesen 1791
1437-7810 Universitaet Landau. Neurowissenschaftliches Seminar 6189
1437-7829 Kolloquium Fremdsprachenunterricht 5137
1437-7837 Herodot 340
1437-7845 Studien zur Stadt- und Verkehrsplanung 4428
1437-7853 Universitaet Bielefeld. Institut fuer Anwalts- und Notarrecht. Schriftenreihe 4802
1437-7861 Lebenserinnerungen 4239
1437-787X Innovative Betriebswirtschaftliche Forschung und Praxis 1753
1437-790X S E M A - Rezensionen in Sachen Kommunikation†
1437-7942 I S Report 1417
1437-7993 Topics in Biological Inorganic Chemistry 746
1437-8027 see 0340-255X 2139
1437-8086 Feuerwehr Aktuell 3576
1437-8094 V B B Magazin 6451
1437-8140 Rock Hard 6612
1437-8175 Bayer Report 6825
1437-8183 see 1437-8175 6825
1437-8191 see 1437-8175 6825
1437-8213 see 0948-4280 2809
1437-8337 Behoerden Spiegel 7488
1437-8353 Berliner Behoerden Spiegel 7488
1437-8477 Rheinisch-Westfaelische Technische Hochschule Aachen. Lehrstuhl und Institut fuer Wasserbau und Wasserwirtschaft. Mitteilungen 2797
1437-8639 Astronomie und Raumfahrt im Unterricht 570
1437-8809 Unicum Beruf 2305
1437-8841 Duerrnberg-Forschungen 391
1437-8965 Netiva 4248
1437-8981 Finanz Betrieb 1347
1437-9023 Concrete Plant International 993
1437-904X Concilium Medii Aevi 4136
1437-9058 see 1437-904X 4136
1437-9066 see 1437-904X 4136
1437-9074 see 1437-9082 4140
1437-9082 G F A 4140
1437-9090 see 1437-9082 4140
1437-9112 Der Ertrag-Steuer-Berater 1922
1437-9147 Praxis Aktuell. Ausgabe Bayern 8063
1437-9155 Praxis Aktuell. Ausgabe Berlin 8063
1437-9171 Praxis Aktuell. Ausgabe Bremen und Bremerhaven 8063
1437-918X Praxis Aktuell. Ausgabe Hessen 8063
1437-9228 Praxis Aktuell. Ausgabe Schleswig-Holstein 8063
1437-9244 Praxis Aktuell. Ausgabe Westfalen-Lippe 8063
1437-9279 Praxis Aktuell. Ausgabe Rheinland 8063
1437-9287 Praxis Aktuell. Ausgabe Rheinland-Pfalz 8063
1437-9376 Anschauliche Wissenschaft 6904
1437-9406 Arbeitskreis Bild - Druck - Papier 7551
1437-949X Die Fleischmehl-Industrie *changed to* Tierische Nebenprodukte Nachrichten 3513
1437-9546 Acta Ethologica Online 649
1437-9619 Internet Journal of Public Health Education 7527
1437-9643 Gelaendewagen Magazin Testjahrbuch†
1437-9708 Opel Club und Trend†
1437-9716 Saechsische Akademie der Wissenschaften, Leipzig. Technikwissenschaftliche Klasse. Sitzungsberichte 8437
1437-9767 Bike Sport News 8255
1437-9813 see 0179-0358 6255
1437-983X G D S - Magazin 4594
1437-9856 B B W Magazin 7488
1437-9864 B D Z Magazin 1911
1437-997X V B O B Magazin 7475
1437-9996 Frankfurt Geht Aus! (Year) 4386
1438-0005 Frankfurt Kauft Ein! 5071
1438-0056 see 1437-8175 6825
1438-0099 G D L Magazin Voraus 8617
1438-0102 CyberKoch 4356
1438-0153 Success in Soccer 8247
1438-0161 Dent-Online 2554
1438-0196 Interkulturelle Bildungsgaenge 8108
1438-0218 CyberKino 6495
1438-0226 Filmstar 6501
1438-0250 T V und Serien 2395
1438-0307 Fundus (Goettingen)† 8958
1438-0374 Eisenbahner-Rundschau *changed to* 1861-4809 1682
1438-0420 Der Eisstocksport 8171
1438-0439 Tag der Juristischen Fakultaet 4792
1438-0501 Kieferorthopaedie Journal 5854
1438-0552 Altertumswissenschaftliches Kolloquium 2229
1438-0595 Deutscher Museumsbund. Bulletin 6523
1438-0609 Series in Microsystems 7039
1438-0617 Stiftung & Sponsoring 8073
1438-0625 Learning Technology 2950
1438-0633 D P V Kom Magazin 2354
1438-0692 Universitaet Hamburg. Institut fuer Rechtsmedizin. Forschungsergebnisse 5727
1438-0714 Technik in Hessen *changed to* 1611-5546 3222
1438-0897 Mediations - Report 4731
1438-0900 Forum der Medizin-Dokumentation und Medizin-Informatik 5615
1438-0919 P C Magazin 2580
1438-0978 Fliegerkalender 55
1438-1168 see 0930-0708 6471
1438-1303 Computerwoche Young Professional 2414
1438-1397 D J G Magazin 4654
1438-1435 see 1070-3004 6195
1438-146X D B B Regional-Magazin 4592
1438-1478 Arbeiten zur Angewandten Linguistik 5096
1438-1656 Advanced Engineering Materials 3180
1438-1680 Sprache und Literatur 5177
1438-1753 Novum 31
1438-1818 Email 1006
1438-1907 SchulVerwaltung Spezial 3032
1438-2083 Tattoo Scene Live 521
1438-2091 see 1868-9426 5254
1438-213X Neulateinisches Jahrbuch 2238

1439-3875 Technische Universitaet Braunschweig. Institut fuer Baustoffe, Massivbau und Brandschutz. Materialpruefanstalt fuer das Bauwesen. Schriftenreihe **1039**
1439-3964 *see* 0172-4622 **6230**
1439-3999 *see* 0023-2165 **6045**
1439-4049 *see* 1432-2625 **5619**
1439-4057 Sozialmarkt Aktuell **1794**
1439-4073 Bochum Publications in Evolutionary Cultural Semiotics **5264**
1439-4081 *see* 1434-0275 **6158**
1439-409X Besser Lackieren **6716**
1439-4162 Essener Studien zur Semiotik und Kommunikationsforschung **5116**
1439-4197 *see* 0932-8122 **5993**
1439-4200 *see* 0020-0336 **5848**
1439-4227 ChemBioChem **728**
1439-4235 ChemPhysChem **2133**
1439-4243 Imaging & Microscopy **899**
1439-4251 ReinRaumTechnik **3371**
1439-4286 *see* 0018-5043 **5893**
1439-4294 *see* 0014-0082 **5610**
1439-4308 *see* 0935-0853 **5807**
1439-4340 Frankfurter Frauenschule. Materialienband **8897**
1439-4359 *see* 0415-6412 **5604**
1439-4367 Figurationen **5296**
1439-4413 *see* 3002-1472 **5744**
1439-4413 *see* 0012-0472 **5604**
1439-4421 Das Gesundheitswesen (Online) **7519**
1439-4456 *see* 1438-8871 **5832**
1439-4472 A I N S Supplement *see* 0939-2661 **5767**
1439-4499 Wege mit Franziskus **7822**
1439-4618 Archaeologie in Sachsen-Anhalt **377**
1439-4650 Snudebiller **858**
1439-4693 Management & Training†
1439-474X Publikationen der G K S S **7900**
1439-4766 Ideenmanagement **1752**
1439-4847 Das Neurophysiologie - Labor **5796**
1439-4871 Urologische Nachrichten **6276**
1439-488X Paediatrische Nachrichten† **8979**
1439-4898 Gynaekologische Nachrichten **5992**
1439-491X Neuro-Psychiatrische Nachrichten† **8976**
1439-5037 Life & Style†
1439-5088 J M F - Der Metalltechniker
1439-5134 Arbeitspapiere - Distribution & Handel **1879**
1439-5142 Balint-Journal **6126**
1439-5215 Denk-Schriften **7010**
1439-5223 Deutsche Dissertationen **5284**
1439-524X Der Turnermusiker **6625**
1439-5258 Personalwirtschaft (Hamburg) **1872**
1439-5266 Finanzmanagement **1347**
1439-5274 Innovation und Technik **7324**
1439-5312 Der Absolvent **6691**
1439-5355 Vollstreckung effektiv **4810**
1439-538X CYbiz.de **1416**
1439-5398 Hockey Training **8235**
1439-5444 *see* 0289-0771 **950**
1439-5452 Brewing and Beverage Industry Espanol **601**
1439-5517 Das T A S P O Magazin **3751**
1439-5533 Die Dorflinde **3846**
1439-5541 Konkreter Erfolg *changed to* 1864-1350 **587**
1439-5592 Sueddeutsches Baumagazin *changed to* 1610-3785 **980**
1439-5606 Baustoff Partner **981**
1439-5703 Druck & Medien Magazin **7319**
1439-5770 Der Gefahrgut-Beauftragte **8497**
1439-5800 *see* 0723-7065 **6204**
1439-5819 Nebenwerte-Journal **1642**
1439-586X Zeitschrift fuer Tagesmuetter und -vaeter **2173**
1439-5894 Im Medium Fremder Sprachen und Kulturen **5126**
1439-5908 Z T R - Zeitschrift fuer Tarif-, Arbeits- und Sozialrecht des Oeffentlichen Dienstes **1955**
1439-5916 Beratung Aktuell **7340**
1439-5967 Stp - Digest **8439**
1439-6041 E P D Medien **2319**
1439-6092 Organisms Diversity & Evolution **696**
1439-6165 Communio **7793**
1439-619X Zeitschrift fuer Altorientalische und Biblische Rechtsgeschichte. Beihefte **564**
1439-6262 International Journal of Communications Law and Policy **2424**
1439-6319 European Journal of Applied Physiology **922**
1439-6327 *see* 1439-6319 **922**
1439-6343 D I F U - Berichte **4409**
1439-6351 Neue Zeitschrift fuer Baurecht und Vergaberecht **1026**
1439-6378 Inside Wohn-Markt-Magazin **4559**
1439-6416 L W - Landwirtschaftliches Wochenblatt Hessen, Rheinland-Pfalz. Hessenbauer (Ausgabe Nord) **132**
1439-6424 L W - Landwirtschaftliches Wochenblatt Hessen, Rheiland-Pfalz. Hessenbauer (Ausgabe Sued) **132**
1439-6432 L W Pfaelzer Bauer - Der Landbote **241**
1439-6440 Wein und Markt **612**
1439-6491 Beitraege zur Hagiographie **7624**
1439-653X Eurogay† **8954**
1439-6556 Auto & Elektronik **8557**
1439-6564 Wasserversorgungs- und Abwassertechnik. Band 1: Rohrnetztechnik
1439-6610 CYbiz† **8947**
1439-667X Form & Werkzeug **5452**
1439-6688 Berliner Arbeiten zur Bibliothekswissenschaft **4994**
1439-670X Zeitschrift fuer Wundheilung *changed to* Wundmanagement **6075**
1439-6777 Der Umsatz-Steuer-Berater **1953**
1439-6912 *see* 0209-9683 **5479**
1439-6955 Personal-Profi *changed to* Arbeit und Arbeitsrecht fuer den Personal-Profi **1663**
1439-7064 Rechtsformen der Wirtschaft **4879**
1439-7080 Men's Fashion International *changed to* 1614-4872 **8955**
1439-717X Forum Hals-, Nasen-, Ohrenheilkunde **6080**
1439-7242 Forum Wohneigentum **7591**
1439-7250 Hideaways Beauty Special **8718**
1439-7277 Proteome†
1439-7285 Proteome Online†
1439-7358 Lecture Notes in Computational Science and Engineering **2473**
1439-7420 Pflegemagazin *changed to* Pflege und Gesellschaft **7535**
1439-748X Communicatio (Hamburg) **2315**
1439-7528 Schriften zur Politischen Oekonomik **1582**
1439-7536 Eleusis **6915**
1439-7544 Reinigungs Markt **1854**
1439-7552 Beitraege zur Archaeologie in Niedersachsen **383**
1439-7560 Wuerzburger Arbeiten zur Praehistorischen Archaeologie **424**
1439-7595 Modern Rheumatology **6225**
1439-7609 *see* 1439-7595 **6225**
1439-7617 *see* 1439-8516 **5464**
1439-7625 Innovatives Dienstleistungsmanagement **1753**
1439-7633 *see* 1439-4227 **728**
1439-7641 *see* 1439-4235 **2133**
1439-765X Wittgenstein-Jahrbuch† **8998**
1439-7668 Wittgenstein Studien *changed to* 1868-7431 **6961**
1439-7676 C O S S M A **593**
1439-7684 Platow Boerse **1644**
1439-7706 Betonwerk International **982**
1439-7722 I T & Production **1417**
1439-779X Koralle **2810**
1439-7803 *see* 0044-2771 **5932**
1439-782X Schriften zur Saechsischen Geschichte und Volkskunde **4262**
1439-7846 Beitraege zur Geschichte der Stadt Bad Salzuflen **4203**
1439-7854 M M I Interaktiv **2454**
1439-7870 Kompass Arbeits- und Sozialrecht CD
1439-7889 Schriften der Internationalen Arnim-Gesellschaft **5368**
1439-7943 Young Look **8079**
1439-7986 Nailpro Europe *changed to* 1614-0834 **593**
1439-8036 Braunschweiger Beitraege zur Geschichte der Deutschen Sprache und Literatur **5265**
1439-8044 The History Journals News **4145**
1439-8052 Dreamcast Magic†
1439-8079 L I M P A C T **3488**
1439-8168 Draco **940**
1439-8176 Goettinger Forschungen zur Landesgeschichte **4225**
1439-8206 Informationsdienst F I Z Technik. Nachrichtenleitungen und Antennen **2348**
1439-829X Unsere Wirtschaft **1411**
1439-832X Kleine Schriften zur Celler Stadtgeschichte **4237**
1439-8338 Kulturlandschaft Schaumburg **4238**
1439-8443 Internationale Politik - Transatlantic Edition *see* 1430-175X **7246**
1439-8516 Acta Mathematica Sinica **5464**
1439-8575 Incentive Congress Journal *changed to* 1862-8672 **1819**
1439-8583 Materialen zur Regionalgeschichte **4242**
1439-8591 Quellen zur Regionalgeschichte **4256**
1439-8605 Quellen und Forschungen zur Lingener Geschichte **4255**
1439-8613 Vesti **3570**
1439-8621 Limnology **2797**
1439-863X *see* 1439-8621 **2797**
1439-8672 Net-Business†
1439-8702 RadZeit **8266**
1439-8710 T3†
1439-8753 Religion in der Geschichte **7674**
1439-8761 Heresbach Stiftung Kalkar. Schriften **4226**
1439-880X Zeitschrift fuer Wirtschafts- und Unternehmensethik **1197**
1439-8834 Deutsche Sprachwelt. Ausgabe fuer Deutschland *see* 1606-0008 **5111**
1439-8893 Gesundheitspolitik, Management, Oekonomie **7519**
1439-8907 K W I - Gutachten **7449**
1439-8931 Psychotraumatologie **6180**
1439-8990 *see* 1438-2563 **5803**
1439-9008 *see* 1439-5142 **6126**
1439-9016 Aseptica **5903**
1439-913X *see* 1438-7026 **6179**
1439-9148 *see* 0044-166X **5869**
1439-9156 Deutsche Gesellschaft fuer Angiologie, Gesellschaft fuer Gefaessmedizin. Mitteilungen† **8949**
1439-9229 *see* 1433-6251 **5734**
1439-9326 Sozialer Sinn **8140**
1439-9350 Germany. Bundesanstalt fuer Arbeit. Foerderung der Beruflichen Weiterbildung **3063**
1439-9458 My Lady Royal **5411**
1439-9482 Historical Special **5410**
1439-9490 Tiffany Sexy **5412**
1439-9504 Bianca Baby†
1439-9512 Bianca Arztroman† **8935**
1439-9563 Savoir-Vivre **3662**
1439-9571 Computer Bild Spiele **2475**
1439-958X Fortschritt-Berichte V D I. Reihe 22: Mensch - Maschine - Systeme **3193**
1439-9598 Nachrichten aus der Chemie **2074**
1439-9733 Open Automation **2463**
1439-9776 International Journal of Fluid Power **3362**
1439-9849 Logos and Language† **8971**
1439-9857 Pallas Athene **7991**
1439-989X *see* 1439-9903 **2699**
1439-9903 Suchttherapie **2699**
1439-9938 Prophylaxe Impuls **5862**
1439-9962 Blumen Worldwide† **8937**
1440-0022 mETAphor **3072**
1440-0057 Harness Racing Weekly **8291**
1440-0073 Topics in Australian Teacher Librarianship **5050**
1440-0278 Question Book, Income Tax Law for Accountants, Income Tax Law for Tax Agents **1941**
1440-0286 Answer Book, Income Tax Law for Accountants, Income Tax Law for Tax Agents **1910**
1440-0405 Journal of Australian Taxation **1931**
1440-0502 Science (Wayville) **2910**
1440-0510 Mathematics **2885**
1440-0529 Languages **2882**
1440-0545 Health and Personal Development Learning Area Manual (Year) **2862**
1440-0669 Humanities Research **4456**
1440-0693 Soap World **2390**
1440-0731 Advances in Technology of Materials and Materials Processing Journal **3335**
1440-0952 *see* 0812-0099 **2726**
1440-0960 *see* 0004-8380 **5872**
1440-1134 Birds Australia Monograph **903**
1440-1320 International Artist **496**
1440-1460 Natural Resources Management†
1440-1541 Nuritinga **5971**
1440-1584 *see* 1038-5282 **7509**
1440-1592 *see* 1323-8930 **5753**
1440-1614 *see* 0004-8674 **6125**
1440-1630 *see* 0045-0766 **6107**
1440-1665 *see* 1039-8562 **6125**
1440-1681 *see* 0305-1870 **921**
1440-169X *see* 0012-1592 **668**
1440-1703 *see* 0912-3814 **670**
1440-1711 *see* 0818-9641 **5760**
1440-172X *see* 1322-7114 **5962**
1440-1738 *see* 1038-4871 **2748**
1440-1746 *see* 0815-9319 **5928**
1440-1754 *see* 1034-4810 **6094**
1440-1770 *see* 1320-5331 **8828**
1440-1789 *see* 0919-6544 **6167**
1440-1797 *see* 1320-5358 **6272**
1440-1800 *see* 1320-7881 **5974**
1440-1819 *see* 1323-1316 **6177**
1440-1827 *see* 1320-5463 **5694**
1440-1835 *see* 1322-0829 **808**
1440-1843 *see* 1323-7799 **6219**
1440-1991 Australasian Pentecostal Studies **7733**
1440-2009 Australia. Department of the Parliamentary Library. Information and Research Services. Current Issues Brief *changed to* 1834-9854 **7421**
1440-2076 Connections Newsletter **2839**
1440-2173 Australian Fisheries Management Authority. Corporate Plan **3586**
1440-2386 Credit Transfer and Learning Pathways **2976**
1440-2408 Electricity Week's Energy Risk (Print) *changed to* Electricity Week's Energy Risk Weekly **3128**
1440-2440 Journal of Science and Medicine in Sport **6230**
1440-2807 Journal of Astronomical History and Heritage **576**
1440-2971 A E U S A Branch Journal **2822**
1440-2998 South Australian Geographer **4029**
1440-3064 Australian Yearbook of Music and Music Education†
1440-3307 World Patrol and Rescue Craft Yearbook†
1440-3358 F H M (Australia) **6289**
1440-3382 Houses **445**
1440-3846 A C A Connections†
1440-3900 Outdoor Showman **8327**
1440-396X Regional Review (Online) **150**
1440-3994 Australasian Rehabilitation Nurses Association. Official Journal **6107**
1440-4125 Agriculture Victoria Rutherglen Research Report
1440-432X Aiming Higher†
1440-4389 Asia Pacific Public Relations Journal **7107**
1440-4397 Australian Landcare **220**
1440-4508 Australasian Coin and Banknote Magazine **6649**
1440-4532 Employment Law Bulletin **4867**
1440-4540 The A D R Bulletin **4826**
1440-4559 Constitutional Law & Policy Review **4847**
1440-4575 Australian Robotics and Automation Association. Newsletter
1440-4737 Jacket **5424**
1440-4788 Queensland Museum. Memoirs. Cultural Heritage Series **4471**
1440-4842 Australian Social Monitor **7949**
1440-4877 School Magazine. Touchdown **2211**
1440-4885 School Magazine. Blast Off! **2211**
1440-4893 School Magazine. Orbit **2211**
1440-4907 School Magazine. Countdown **2211**
1440-4982 Australian Journal of Legal Philosophy **4624**
1440-5059 Murdoch University. Department of Economics. Working Paper Series **1151**
1440-5113 Journal of Battlefield Technology **6429**
1440-5202 Journal of Australian Indigenous Issues **344**
1440-5210 Australian Athlete†
1440-5229 Runner's World **8198**
1440-5342 Bairnsdale Advertiser **5208**
1440-5377 International Journal of Organisational Behaviour **7365**
1440-5423 Australia. Bureau of Statistics. Use of the Internet by Householders, Australia†
1440-5466 Austr@alien Mag@zine **5097**
1440-5520 Australian Net Guide **2552**
1440-5628 The Animist†
1440-5636 Management Today **1777**
1440-5873 Youth Options†
1440-6004 Language, Gender & Sexism†
1440-6047 *see* 0964-7058 **6655**
1440-6055 *see* 1326-6756 **840**
1440-611X Australia. Bureau of Statistics. Manufacturing Production, Commodities Produced, Australia†
1440-6357 Therapeutic Guidelines. Dermatology **5882**
1440-6365 A S A N S W Update *changed to* Australian Society of Archivists. New South Wales Branch. Newsletter **4993**
1440-6381 Australasian Journal on Ageing **4041**
1440-6500 Vogue Entertaining + Travel **4984**
1440-656X Concrete in Australia **993**
1440-673X Bankruptcy and Insolvency Law Library on CD-ROM†
1440-7019 Building Australia†
1440-7221 The Inside Running†
1440-723X Education Horizons **2848**
1440-7256 Natural Heritage **2620**
1440-7485 The Bulletin with Newsweek† **8938**
1440-7515 Insurance and Financial Services Remuneration Review **1866**
1440-7582 Electricity Week Queensland **3157**
1440-7701 Life Spirit Magazine†
1440-7795 G Q Australia **6291**

ISSN

1443-2250 Online Journal of Bioinformatics 826
1443-2269 see 0313-1971 5034
1443-2285 Online Journal of Pharmacokinetics 6865
1443-2307 Police Association Victoria. Journal 2663
1443-2374 Online Journal of Physiology 5690
1443-2447 Journal of Population Research 7286
1443-2471 Preview 2788
1443-265X Online Journal of Immunology 5764
1443-2676 ARTicle 3051
1443-2730 E F A Update 2417
1443-2838 Modern Boating 8278
1443-2943 University of South Australia. Centre of Business Analysis and Research. Working Paper (Online)† 8996
1443-3117 About the House 7418
1443-3435 University of New England. Teaching & Learning Centre. Updates† 8996
1443-3591 Chisholm Health Ethics Bulletin 5594
1443-3605 A Q (Balmain) 7101
1443-3680 Inspirasi 496
1443-3710 Women in Australia 8906
1443-4059 Senses of Cinema 6512
1443-4253 First Priority Now 7643
1443-430X Medicine Today 5674
1443-4318 Australian and New Zealand Journal of Art 477
1443-4342 The Black Book Directory 8090
1443-4350 In Style 3794
1443-4482 CAL-Laborate 7843
1443-4490 see 1443-4482 7843
1443-458X Journal of Research and Practice in Information Technology 2429
1443-4628 Australia.edu 2828
1443-4636 International Hospital & Aged Care Journal†
1443-4792 Australian Homespun 4352
1443-4814 Western Australia. Recreational Fishing Advisory Committee. Paper 8341
1443-4873 Australian and New Zealand Journal of Audiology 4072
1443-5012 Darwin Gay and Lesbian Newsletter
1443-508X Art & Design Education Resource Guide 2953
1443-5144 Open Museum Journal† 8979
1443-5292 University of Queensland. Calendar Series. Vol.2: Undergraduate Handbook†
1443-5306 University of Queensland. Calendar Series. Vol.3: Postgraduate Handbook†
1443-5349 The Wiggles 2221
1443-5373 CREArTA 484
1443-5381 The Gazette 3767
1443-5454 Appita. Annual Conference Proceedings 6732
1443-5489 Recruitment Journal 1873
1443-5527 Federal Cases (Disk 1)† 8956
1443-5535 Federal Cases (Disk 2)† 8956
1443-5713 A S J (Kent Town) 8301
1443-5756 Journal of Inequalities in Pure and Applied Mathematics 5504
1443-5764 see R G M I A Research Report Collection 5527
1443-5993 Anglican Historical Society (Diocese of Sydney). Journal 7745
1443-6027 World of Antiques and Art 369
1443-6345 Council of Financial Regulators. Annual Report† 8944
1443-6671 Australia. Productivity Commission. P C Update 1439
1443-6892 Australian Station
1443-6914 Melbourne Papers in Linguistics and Applied Linguistics†
1443-7023 UltiBASE Journal† 8995
1443-7058 Australian Military Medicine 5581
1443-7155 Australia. Bureau of Statistics. Australia's Environment: Issues and Trends 3477
1443-7171 A I R S Resources Bulletin changed to 1449-3659
1443-7201 Inside Football
1443-721X State of the Arts 6537
1443-7295 Carter's Antiques & Collectables†
1443-735X Christian Teachers Journal 2836
1443-7368 Nurture 2892
1443-7619 Contretemps 6912
1443-7651 see 1443-766X 3567
1443-766X Tap San Tu Tuong 3567
1443-7678 Australian Academy of the Humanities. Occasional Papers 4444
1443-8070 Australia. Bureau of Statistics. Victorian Office. Regional Statistics, Victoria (Print) changed to Australia. Bureau of Statistics. Victorian Office. Regional Statistics, Victoria (Online) 8355
1443-8267 Australia. Department of Industry, Science and Resources. Annual Report changed to 1836-3083 1911
1443-833X see 0816-9020 2948
1443-8356 Nuance
1443-8364 Misli 7807
1443-8445 Aboriginal and Torres Strait Islander Commission. Annual Report†
1443-8550 Anglo-Australian Observatory. Annual Report 568
1443-8577 C S I R O Entomology. Report of Research 841
1443-8631 Local Government and Environmental Law Library 7496
1443-8844 Safety Science Monitor 6686
1443-8976 The Pacific Studies W W W Monitor†
1443-9018 Centre for Studies in Australian Music. Review 6555
1443-9255 Electronic Journal of Structural Engineering 3266
1443-9344 Zeitgeist Gazette†
1443-9506 Heart, Lung and Circulation (Print) 5788
1443-9549 Commercial Notes 4861
1443-9565 Surgical News (Online) 3004
1443-9573 Chinese Journal of Digestive Diseases Online changed to 1751-2980 5927
1443-9611 Chinese Journal of Digestive Diseases changed to 1751-2972 5927
1443-9638 Master Builder 1022
1443-9646 Brain Impairment 6127
1443-9697 The Australian Journal of Counselling Psychology 7338
1443-9778 Australian Cotton Outlook 220
1443-9832 O H S Bulletin 6682
1443-9905 Journal of Applied Management Accounting Research 1294
1443-9913 see 1443-9905 1294
1443-993X Australia. Bureau of Statistics. Western Australian Office. Western Australian Statistical Indicators (Print) changed to Australia. Bureau of Statistics. Western Australian Office. Western Australian Statistical Indicators (Online) 8355
1444-0148 Choice Travel†
1444-0199 C M S Checkpoint 7749
1444-0288 National Register of Independent Schools of Australia 2960
1444-061X Electronics Australia changed to Electronics Australia Today
1444-0628 E A: Electronics Australia changed to Electronics Australia Today
1444-0717 Internet and Online Market
1444-075X Wireless Market changed to Global Mobile Communications Market 8959
1444-0865 Australian Geodynamic Cooperative Research Centre. Annual Report
1444-0873 Australian Geodynamic Cooperative Research Centre. Annual Report (Online Edition)
1444-0903 Internal Medicine Journal (Print) 5946
1444-0938 see 0816-4622 6040
1444-0989 Australia. Bureau of Statistics. South Australian Office. Regional Statistics, South Australia (Print) changed to Australia. Bureau of Statistics. South Australian Office. Regional Statistics, South Australia (Online) 8354
1444-1063 University of Technology, Sydney. U T S Information Technology Handbook changed to University of Technology, Sydney. Handbook 2923
1444-1128 Housing 1012
1444-1160 Altitude 8086
1444-1187 Gardens & Outdoor Living†
1444-1241 WebBusiness†
1444-1551 Australian Society of Archivists. Queensland Branch. Newsletter 4993
1444-156X see 1444-1551 4993
1444-1586 Geriatrics & Gerontology International 4045
1444-1594 Thylazine 522
1444-1632 Virgin Blue Voyeur 8786
1444-1683 Asia Pacific Family Medicine (Print) 5579
1444-1810 Floriculture News 3756
1444-1861 Momentum†
1444-190X Australian Accounting Standards Board. Urgent Issues Group. Abstract changed to 1449-8316 1303
1444-2094 Balayi 5260
1444-2213 The Asia Pacific Journal of Anthropology 329
1444-2248 Business Life changed to Xpress 1413
1444-2477 Telecommunications Industry, Australia changed to Telecoms Industry Australia. Analyses 2372
1444-2477 Telecommunications Industry Australia 2372
1444-2493 Telco Company Profiles Australia 2504
1444-2515 Regulatory and Competition Australia
1444-2531 Girlz Klub changed to 1446-5507
1444-2647 Security Electronics Magazine changed to Security Electronics & Networks 2516
1444-271X Friday Magazine†
1444-2752 Radiation Protection in Australasia 7538
1444-2817 Dotlit 5286
1444-2841 Clean Air and Environmental Quality 3484
1444-2892 Heart, Lung & Circulation (Online)†
1444-2906 see 0919-9268 3593
1444-2957 The College of Law Practice Papers 4644
1444-2973 A F L Record 8220
1444-3058 Journal of Australian Studies 4192
1444-3163 Overland Express see 0030-7416 5232
1444-3171 M L A Annual Report 292
1444-3244 A N Z S L A Commentator 4608
1444-3635 View (Sydney) 8887
1444-3775 Transformations 8011
1444-383X Post-Script 2998
1444-3902 Australia. Bureau of Statistics. Environment Expenditure, Local Government, Australia (Print) changed to Australia. Bureau of Statistics. Environment Expenditure, Local Government, Australia (Online) 3477
1444-3961 Botanical Pathways 307
1444-4003 V 8 Bathurst Magazine 8214
1444-402X B M W Magazine 8568
1444-4046 Living Planet 2617
1444-4062 Business Asia 1554
1444-4178 Missionaries of the Sacred Heart. Annals Australasia 7807
1444-4399 Australian Health and Medical Exports†
1444-4429 Australian Multiples Magazine 2144
1444-4437 Australia. Bureau of Statistics. South Australian Office. South Australia: A Statistical Profile†
1444-4496 E A Journal 5113
1444-4976 Asia Pacific Shipping changed to Ships and Shipping 8661
1444-4984 Asset 1309
1444-5026 Australian Innovation Magazine† 8933
1444-5093 B - H E R T News 1064
1444-5212 Environmental Health (Print Edition) changed to 1832-3367 3425
1444-531X 4 W D Australia† 9000
1444-5344 M I M S Hospital Equipment & Supplies Directory 4105
1444-5352 Cruzin 8576
1444-5379 Crime Factory† 8947
1444-5409 Australian Journal of Irish Studies 3521
1444-5417 Hearing Matters 4074
1444-5468 Australian Bureau of Agricultural and Resource Economics. Australian Crop Report (Online) 194
1444-5530 The Journal of Educational Enquiry 2875
1444-5603 Christian Woman 7632
1444-5743 Campaign Brief 22
1444-5980 Periodicals in Print: Australia, New Zealand & the South Pacific (Year)†
1444-6154 Australian Government Solicitor. Annual Report 4624
1444-6162 Weed Biology and Management 258
1444-6219 Money Magazine 1368
1444-6359 Journal of Research for Consumers 2639
1444-6545 Living Ethics 6932
1444-6839 National Relay Service Provider Performance Report changed to 1833-0754 2370
1444-6855 Murdoch University. Asia Research Centre. Working Paper 556
1444-691X 3rd Muse Poetry Journal 5439
1444-6936 Avmedia changed to 1449-3764 5581
1444-6995 Safety at Work 6685
1444-7037 Classroom Focus 2837
1444-710X Australia. Bureau of Statistics. Prisoners in Australia†
1444-7134 bizreview.com.au† 8936
1444-7150 see 1320-2545 6413
1444-7320 Ministry changed to 1447-4182
1444-738X Channel X Australia† 8940
1444-741X Ejournalist 2320
1444-7614 Keeping Good Companies 1770
1444-8068 Esky†
1444-8157 see 1325-6459 5028
1444-8467 see 0725-7066 7542
1444-8505 Australian and New Zealand Institute of Insurance and Finance. Journal 4493
1444-8599 Autoengineer Australasia 8562
1444-8602 Melbourne Journal of International Law 4935
1444-8610 see 1444-8602 4935
1444-8637 Australia. Bureau of Statistics. Australian Industry (Print) changed to Australia. Bureau of Statistics. Australian Industry (Online) 1201
1444-8718 Build Home (Victoria) 4534
1444-8807 Open Road 8597
1444-8998 Atomic Maximum Power Computing 2574
1444-9064 Gas Week (Email) 6770
1444-9102 Water Report changed to 1833-5047 8841
1444-9552 Computer Craft† 8942
1444-965X Australia. Department of Family and Community Services. Occasional Paper Series changed to 1833-4415 8026
1444-9668 Better Digital 6964
1444-9803 Reportage Media Magazine 4583
1444-9862 see 0067-1924 777
1444-9889 Mundaring Magazine changed to Swan Magazine 3796
1444-9900 see 0404-2018 1309
1445-0038 see 0004-9425 2051
1445-0089 Southern Cross 7775
1445-0143 Modelart Australia 7095
1445-0232 Asia Pacific Digestive News 5920
1445-0291 E R P Software Selection Guide (CD-ROM) 2417
1445-0445 Outskirts (Online) 5232
1445-0682 Mania 3795
1445-0801 M H D Supply Chain Solutions 1773
1445-1255 Pregnancy & Birth 6002
1445-1344 Protecting the Border changed to 1449-6461 7286
1445-1387 see 1444-691X 5439
1445-1425 see 1445-0232 5920
1445-1433 A N Z Journal of Surgery 6234
1445-1565 Bega District News 3793
1445-159X D E 2379
1445-1808 Youth Research News 2223
1445-209X Pharmaceutical and Healthcare Industry Remuneration Review 1872
1445-2197 see 1445-1433 6234
1445-2227 Energy News 3132
1445-2278 A A S Newsletter 322
1445-2294 N J Drama Australia Journal 8474
1445-2308 Australian Journal of Parapsychology 6741
1445-243X see A F F H O Newsflash 3757
1445-2561 Police Journal 2663
1445-2634 Australian Journal of Construction Economics and Building changed to 1835-6354 977
1445-2715 World of Alpacas Directory 304
1445-2723 Active State 8156
1445-2766 Centre for Law and Genetics. Occasional Paper 4641
1445-2774 Sensitivity Matters 5766
1445-2847 Australian Fluoridation News 8818
1445-2901 Australian T3 8416
1445-2928 Australian Journal of Middle Schooling 2829
1445-310X Muse changed to 1833-752X 7854
1445-3118 see 1322-7084 8792
1445-3215 Perth Woman 8880
1445-3312 Journal of Information Warfare 1766
1445-3347 see 1445-3312 1766
1445-3592 Dawsons Venue Selections 8697
1445-3789 Australia. Bureau of Statistics. Western Australian Office. Estimated Stocks of Dwellings, Western Australia† 8933
1445-386X Macquarie Law Journal 4726
1445-3894 Commonwealth of Australia Gazette. Public Service (Online) changed to 1835-2480 7418
1445-405X National Environmental Law Review 4738
1445-4270 The Grapeline 3769
1445-4300 Asia Today International 1062
1445-4319 Australian Science Fiction Bullsheet 5440
1445-4327 see 1445-4319 5440
1445-4335 Local Government Manager 7497
1445-436X Domestic Violence and Incest Resource Centre. Newsletter changed to 1834-366X 8036
1445-4386 Australian Journal of Midwifery changed to 1871-5192 6006
1445-4408 Functional Plant Biology 790
1445-4416 see 1445-4408 790
1445-4475 Alcohol Studies Bulletin 2691
1445-4610 Beat Magazine 6548
1445-470X Carrier Aviation News 51
1445-4866 see 1447-4514 5812
1445-5072 Music Teacher changed to Music Teacher International 6592
1445-5080 Vocal Journal 6705
1445-5218 Eras 4139
1445-5226 Invertebrate Systematics 949
1445-5269 Australasian Dental Practice 5835
1445-5382 M I S (Australian Edition) 1773
1445-5439 see Random Sampling
1445-5781 Reproductive Medicine and Biology 5703
1445-5838 Transparency (Print)†

ISSN

1447-6770	Journal of Hospitality and Tourism Management†
1447-6959	Anatomical Science International **653**
1447-7076	What's New in Waste Technology *changed to* 1834-917X **3512**
1447-7297	University of New South Wales Law Journal Forum *see* 0313-0096 **4804**
1447-7483	Anex Bulletin **7507**
1447-8277	Safety Solutions **6686**
1447-8366	A B A R E Farm Surveys Report (Year) (Online) **190**
1447-8447	Contemporary Architecture **438**
1447-8501	The River News **3796**
1447-8552	School of Development Studies, Melbourne University Private. Working Paper Series **1605**
1447-8595	International Visitors in Australia (Online) **8779**
1447-8722	Australia. Department of Health and Ageing. Annual Report **7421**
1447-8986	Association for the Study of Australian Literature. Journal **5257**
1447-9079	Poisoning in South Australia **5916**
1447-9109	Bridal Style **5067**
1447-9125	Australasian Parliamentary Review **7421**
1447-915X	Clumbers **6806**
1447-9168	The Veterinarian **8811**
1447-9184	*see* 1446-8719 **1137**
1447-9249	Extreme *changed to* 1834-5107 **8580**
1447-9265	MedicSA **5675**
1447-9273	The Golfer (Victoria & Tasmania Edition) *see* 1835-1336 **8233**
1447-9281	The Golfer (Queensland & Northern Territory Edition) *see* 1835-1336 **8233**
1447-9338	Innovation: Management, Policy & Practice **1753**
1447-9494	The International Journal of Learning **2870**
1447-9508	International Journal of the Humanities **4458**
1447-9516	International Journal of the Book **2327**
1447-9524	International Journal of Knowledge, Culture and Change Management **1128**
1447-9532	The International Journal of Diversity in Organisations, Communities and Nations **3540**
1447-9540	*see* 1447-9494 **2870**
1447-9559	*see* 1447-9508 **4458**
1447-9575	*see* 1447-9524 **1128**
1447-9583	*see* 1447-9532 **3540**
1447-963X	*see* 1447-8552 **1605**
1447-9710	Australian Resources and Energy Law Journal **6457**
1447-9818	Fishing Future **3593**
1447-9850	Funtime with Friends **2190**
1447-9915	Cabling Connection **2314**
1448-000X	Writing Edge *changed to* 1833-1734 **5087**
1448-0107	Australian Field Ornithology **902**
1448-0131	Australian and New Zealand Continence Journal **6265**
1448-0220	International Journal of Training Research **2871**
1448-0271	*see* 0310-057X **5768**
1448-0352	Western Australia. Department of Agriculture. Bulletin *changed to* 1833-7236 **170**
1448-0387	Meat & Livestock Weekly **293**
1448-0395	Built Environment & Manufacturing Innovation†
1448-0417	Ozco News *changed to* 1834-1500 **472**
1448-0581	infLect **5308**
1448-0662	The Rhododendron **3749**
1448-0980	Qualitative Research Journal **7994**
1448-1014	Stamp News Australasia **6900**
1448-1065	What's New in Laboratory Technology **7929**
1448-1316	Annual Statistical Publication†
1448-1324	Ethos (Carlton) **3061**
1448-1332	Directory of Internships Available in Victorian Hospitals† **8950**
1448-1421	Iris **2236**
1448-1537	Leading the Way **1869**
1448-1642	Foodweek **3678**
1448-1871	Libraries Alive **5025**
1448-1901	*see* 1325-8109 **1211**
1448-2010	C X **8152**
1448-2037	Australian Academy of Science. Annual Report **7838**
1448-207X	Pharmacy News **6873**
1448-210X	Australian Fabian News **7108**
1448-2177	Geoscience Australia. Record **2743**
1448-2215	PlayStation 2 Cheats **2480**
1448-238X	The Naturalist News **7888**
1448-2398	eJournal of Tax Research **1921**
1448-241X	Australian Meat News **3627**
1448-2452	F H M Collections† **8955**
1448-2517	Environmental Chemistry (Print)†
1448-2649	Modern Hair + Beauty **8875**
1448-2673	The Knowledge Tree **2880**
1448-2843	Australian Army Journal **6412**
1448-3254	R + B Inside *changed to* 1832-116X **8983**
1448-3300	U.S. Lamb Market Update **302**
1448-3319	History Matters (Adelaide)† **8962**
1448-336X	Earthmatters **2732**
1448-3467	Australian Sports Foundation. Newsletter **8160**
1448-3475	Australian Institute of Sport Alumni News **2968**
1448-3483	*see* 1448-3475 **2968**
1448-3599	E S D Report Series **3590**
1448-3610	Northern Territory Government. Department of Business, Industry and Resource Development. Technical Publications Catalogue *changed to* 1833-4156 **148**
1448-3610	Northern Territory Government. Department of Business, Industry and Resource Development. Technical Publications Catalogue *changed to* 1833-4148 **3593**
1448-3645	Golden Dolphin Video C D Magazine **2804**
1448-3653	*see* 1448-3645 **2804**
1448-3696	The E B E Journal **1096**
1448-3734	Sydneyeats **4399**
1448-384X	Queensland Street Car **4344**
1448-3858	Australian Garden History. Studies **3723**
1448-3882	Telecommunications Technology Handbook
1448-3939	Australian & New Zealand Handgun **8159**
1448-3971	Basic Digital
1448-4005	Southern Queensland Forestry News **3703**
1448-4129	Multicultural Libraries† **8975**
1448-4145	Accord **4077**
1448-4161	I F A **1629**
1448-4374	International Journal of Forensic Psychology **5914**
1448-4390	Quest (Canberra City) **2945**
1448-4404	Prism **32**
1448-4455	Delicious **4356**
1448-448X	Australasian Journal of Economics Education **2968**
1448-4498	*see* 1448-448X **2968**
1448-451X	*see* 1320-7091 **7202**
1448-4528	Life Writing **5322**
1448-4749	Common Ground **8034**
1448-4803	Legal Briefing **4719**
1448-4838	Spotlight (Narrabri) **254**
1448-4846	Australian Journal of Mechanical Engineering **3374**
1448-4862	Australasian Toy-Maker **4328**
1448-4900	Verandah Literary Journal **5244**
1448-4919	Luxury Car Tax Determination **1933**
1448-4951	Magazine of Engineers Australia (General Edition) **3209**
1448-496X	Magazine of Engineers Australia (Civil Edition) *see* 1448-4951 **3209**
1448-5028	Sexual Health **5826**
1448-5052	The Australasian Journal of Logic **6906**
1448-5176	Synergy **5049**
1448-532X	*see* 1442-939X **1378**
1448-5494	*see* 1035-3712 **968**
1448-5508	*see* 0727-3061 **7861**
1448-5516	*see* 1049-8001 **3579**
1448-5540	*see* 0158-4197 **906**
1448-5699	The Australian Writer's Marketplace **1973**
1448-5702	The Bridal DVD **8854**
1448-5842	The V I F M Review **5917**
1448-5869	International Journal of Hybrid Intelligent Systems **2451**
1448-5915	Australian N S P Survey National Data Report **5810**
1448-5923	A R C S Australia. Newsletter **7829**
1448-5990	*see* 1031-3613 **700**
1448-6032	*see* 0815-3191 **777**
1448-6040	Queensland Grains Outlook **275**
1448-6059	*see* 1323-1650 **2811**
1448-6083	Astronomical Society of Australia. Publications (Online) **569**
1448-6156	Spreadsheets in Education **2914**
1448-6261	Inherit **3771**
1448-6288	R + B Outside *changed to* 1832-116X **8983**
1448-6296	*see* 1448-6261 **3771**
1448-6326	Australian Ejournal of Theology **7785**
1448-6563	Australasian Journal of Environmental Management **3405**
1448-6733	PlayStation 2 *changed to* 1834-3805 **2480**
1448-675X	*see* 1449-0161 **7290**
1448-6830	Dairy Australian (Farm Edition) **262**
1448-6849	Dairy Australia **262**
1448-6873	Queensland. Department of Industrial Relations. Annual Report **1704**
1448-6881	Research Matters **7292**
1448-6954	Legislation Review Digest **4722**
1448-7039	James Cook University. Student Handbook *changed to* James Cook University. Course and Subject Handbook **2988**
1448-7047	*see* James Cook University. Course and Subject Handbook **2988**
1448-708X	The Dairy Australian (International Edition) **263**
1448-7128	Australian Graduate School of Entrepreneurship Research Report Series **1064**
1448-7136	Design Philosophy Papers **440**
1448-7195	Monitor (Online) **2385**
1448-7209	Fair Trading - Serving Consumers and Traders in N S W **1109**
1448-7330	Australian Anthill **1064**
1448-7446	C P T E D Journal **3408**
1448-7519	Country Collections Home Series† **8944**
1448-7527	Australian Journal of Primary Health **5581**
1448-7535	A C O R N **4086**
1448-756X	Fishing Victoria Annual **8313**
1448-7608	The PricewaterhouseCoopers Excellence in Franchising Awards **1161**
1448-7616	Drags Magazine *changed to* Drags & Pro Street Magazine **8170**
1448-7683	Queensland Business Review **1163**
1448-7780	Australasian Computer Music Conference. Proceedings **2495**
1448-7837	Awareness **3504**
1448-7985	Krash **2198**
1448-8140	A C S S A Briefing Papers *changed to* 1833-1483 **8850**
1448-8213	Carbon Week **3126**
1448-8272	Australian Midwifery *changed to* 1871-5192 **6006**
1448-8299	Question: Research@U N S W Magazine *changed to* Research @ U N S W **2904**
1448-8310	Pacific Linguistics **5159**
1448-8345	Macquarie Journal of International and Comparative Environmental Law **4935**
1448-8353	Australian Journal of Civil Engineering **3259**
1448-837X	Australian Journal of Electrical and Electronic Engineering **3296**
1448-8388	Australian Journal of Multi-Disciplinary Engineering **3182**
1448-8469	In Quest **4691**
1448-8728	South Australia. Department of Human Services. Annual Report (Online Edition) *changed to* 1832-8938 **8072**
1448-8825	Australian GamePro† **8933**
1448-8841	Blue's Country Magazine **1068**
1448-8906	Radio Comms Asia-Pacific **2362**
1448-9015	The Australian Retailer Magazine **1806**
1448-9023	Tasmania. Department of Premier and Cabinet. Annual Report **7471**
1448-9031	*see* 1448-9023 **7471**
1448-9066	Tasmania. Office of the State Service Commissioner. Annual Report **7471**
1448-9074	*see* 1448-9066 **7471**
1448-9120	ENGINESonblue (Year) **8275**
1448-9295	Fiend **6566**
1448-9392	Australian Dairy Industry In Focus **261**
1448-9538	Contractor (Leederville) **999**
1448-9546	Super Food Ideas **3665**
1448-9716	Marketing Insights **1832**
1448-9759	Pro Utilitate **7536**
1448-9791	Australian Life Scientist **7838**
1448-9937	Tourism Victoria. Annual Report **8764**
1448-997X	Australian Association of Massage Therapists. Journal **6107**
1449-0102	Justice Review **4708**
1449-0161	Population Projections to 2051, Queensland and Statistical Divisions **7290**
1449-020X	Jewellery Making Ideas† **8967**
1449-0269	Macquarie Journal of Business Law **4875**
1449-034X	Fashion Capital **2254**
1449-0374	Church Guardian (Print) *changed to* The Anglican Guardian (Online) **7745**
1449-0404	Canberra's Child **2146**
1449-0412	*see* 1449-0404 **2146**
1449-0471	Philament **4469**
1449-048X	Sacred Space **7679**
1449-0587	Directory of Services for People with a Disability **4064**
1449-0633	University of New England. School of Economic Studies, Econometrics Discipline. Working Papers in Econometrics and Applied Statistics (Online) **8413**
1449-0684	Moto Manual† **8975**
1449-0706	Australian Journal of Emerging Technologies and Society *changed to* 1835-8780 **7867**
1449-0854	History Australia (Print) **4192**
1449-0927	Journeys† **8969**
1449-1168	Road Deaths Australia **8634**
1449-1192	China Wool Facts & Figures **1083**
1449-1370	Irrigation & Water Resources **8826**
1449-1389	Fluid News **231**
1449-1397	Vegenotes **257**
1449-1427	Tourism Forecasting Council. Forecast *changed to* 1832-598X **8710**
1449-1443	Fibreculture Journal **2321**
1449-1532	Sheep's Back to Mill **8457**
1449-1559	Commercial Property Gazette **1734**
1449-1583	Product Grant and Benefit Ruling **1703**
1449-1613	Australian Bus & Commercial Vehicle Heritage **8490**
1449-1672	M E R I T Annual Report **2660**
1449-1710	Australia. Bureau of Statistics. Measuring Australia's Economy (Online) **1208**
1449-1796	West Wimmera Landcare News **3474**
1449-1818	Scan (Sydney) **8131**
1449-1834	International Market Overview **1822**
1449-1850	Australian Bureau of Agricultural and Resource Economics. Australian Forest and Wood Products Statistics **3708**
1449-1907	International Journal of Medical Sciences **5639**
1449-1923	Gambling Matters **6142**
1449-2016	Queensland Resources Council. Annual Report **6477**
1449-2040	China Connections *changed to* Australia China Connections **1063**
1449-2199	*see* The U N E Law Journal **4799**
1449-2210	Farm Policy Journal **111**
1449-2288	International Journal of Biological Sciences **678**
1449-2407	Weekly Book Newlsetter Media Extra† **8998**
1449-2490	Portal **4469**
1449-2555	Reflections (Lakemba) **7715**
1449-2601	Caves Australia **2728**
1449-2679	African Journal of Information and Communication Technology **2311**
1449-2733	Good Practice Guide **1289**
1449-275X	Journal Australian Ceramics **536**
1449-2806	Australian Judges' Associates Handbook **4624**
1449-2822	Seeing Red **7182**
1449-2873	Windows XP **2600**
1449-2938	Contract Management in Practice **4650**
1449-2946	Around the Globe **7221**
1449-2997	Winning Homes Queensland **1043**
1449-3012	Reel Women **8330**
1449-3063	Touch Text†
1449-3071	Hunter Gatherer **3646**
1449-308X	Acumen **1723**
1449-3098	Australasian Journal of Educational Technology (Print)†
1449-311X	Australian Law Students' Competitions Handbook **4624**
1449-3225	O2+ **4548**
1449-3535	The Accredited Pharmacist **6818**
1449-3551	Bhavan's News Australia *changed to* Bhavan Australia **7707**
1449-3659	Australian Language & Literacy Matters†
1449-3705	Precision Agnews **148**
1449-3764	Australasian Society of Aerospace Medicine. Journal **5581**
1449-387X	Journal of Business and Policy Research **1133**
1449-3918	A C H S E Health Manager†
1449-3942	Organisations, Institutes and Research Centres, Asia-Australasia **2023**
1449-4035	Policy & Society **7166**
1449-4043	Museums Australia Magazine **6532**
1449-4116	The Australian Fundraising Magazine **1309**
1449-4183	The Great Ideas Letter **1115**
1449-4205	E B C Business Benchmarking Guide Update for Car Dealers: New & Used **1094**
1449-4213	E B C Business Benchmarking Guide Update for Cabinet Makers **1094**
1449-4221	E B C Business Benchmarking Guide Update for Butchers **1094**
1449-423X	E B C Business Benchmarking Guide Update for Bus & Coach Operators **1093**
1449-4248	E B C Business Benchmarking Guide Update for Building Contractors **1093**
1449-4264	E B C Business Benchmarking Guide Update for Auto Electricians **1093**
1449-4272	E B C Business Benchmarking Guide Update for Auto Accessories & Spare Parts Retailers **1093**
1449-4280	E B C Business Benchmarking Guide Update for Architects *changed to* E B C Business Benchmarking Guide Update for Architectural Practices **1093**
1449-4299	E B C Business Benchmarking Guide Update for Tyre Dealers **8495**
1449-4302	E B C Business Benchmarking Guide Update for Computer and Phone Sales & Repair **1094**

ISSN

9640 1462-6772 **ULRICH'S PERIODICALS**

1462-6772 Country Profile. Yugoslavia Serbia-Montenegro *changed to* 1756-4352 **8946**
1462-6772 Country Profile. Yugoslavia Serbia-Montenegro *changed to* 1756-4344 **8945**
1462-6780 Country Profile. Macedonia† **8945**
1462-6799 Country Profile. Estonia† **8945**
1462-6802 Country Profile. Latvia† **8945**
1462-6810 Country Profile. Lithuania† **8945**
1462-6829 Country Profile. Bosnia-Hercegovina† **8944**
1462-6837 Country Profile. Croatia† **8945**
1462-6853 Country Profile. Turkmenistan† **8946**
1462-7132 Puzzles
1462-7264 Discrete Mathematics and Theoretical Computer Science (Print Edition)†
1462-7272 Education Review **2979**
1462-7302 Biscuit World **3672**
1462-7337 Barbie Special **2178**
1462-7345 Disney's Princess **2186**
1462-7582 Euromoney Japanese Digest†
1462-7639 Star Trek Fan Club **2391**
1462-7663 Sexual Health Agenda *changed to* 1749-8325 **973**
1462-7825 Euromoney Global M & A Handbook **1338**
1462-7973 European Pensions News **4502**
1462-8007 Rapport **8064**
1462-8074 Scripophily **368**
1462-8112 Space Business International **70**
1462-8120 Caribbean Health **7512**
1462-8201 Conveyancers' Yearbook **4650**
1462-821X Shaw's Local Government Directory **7502**
1462-8252 Frontier Brands **1818**
1462-8260 Healthy Minds **2154**
1462-8333 Project Finance Sector Report. Commercial **1512**
1462-8341 Project Finance Sector Report. Industry **1512**
1462-835X Project Finance Sector Report. Natural Resources **1513**
1462-8368 Project Finance Sector Report. Energy - Power **1512**
1462-8376 Project Finance Sector Report. Infrastructure **1512**
1462-8384 Dairy Industry Bulletin†
1462-8465 Accounting Technician **1279**
1462-8546 National Housing Federation Directory of Members **8057**
1462-8597 Pharmafile International **6874**
1462-8600 U K Space Index **73**
1462-866X Finance Director Europe **1343**
1462-8708 Scottish Transport Review **8510**
1462-8732 Journal of Commercial Biotechnology **767**
1462-8783 C M E Bulletin. Gynaecology†
1462-8791 C M E Bulletin Palliative Medicine *changed to* 1475-8075 **6010**
1462-8813 Pet Power **6813**
1462-8848 International Journal of Cardiovascular Interventions (Print Edition) *changed to* 1748-2941 **5775**
1462-8856 New Media Investor **1642**
1462-8902 Diabetes, Obesity and Metabolism **5888**
1462-8910 Colorectal Disease **5921**
1462-9011 Environmental Science & Policy **3428**
1462-9089 International Who's Who of Insolvency and Restructuring Lawyers **4871**
1462-9178 Retail Warehouse Park Development Master List†
1462-9194 Shop Expansion Plans†
1462-9240 Shopping Centres in the Pipeline (Print) *changed to* 1741-7724
1462-9259 The Wire (Maresfield) **2344**
1462-9283 Der Syndikus
1462-9291 International Who's Who of Capital Markets Lawyers **4871**
1462-9410 Evidence - Based Healthcare *changed to* 1744-2249
1462-9488 Traffic Report†
1462-9526 Equestrian Trade News **8290**
1462-9607 Total Style
1462-964X The Agents News **1425**
1462-9704 Queen's Awards Magazine **1580**
1462-9720 Energy Information Centre. CentreNews **1483**
1462-9755 Nationalism and Ethnicity†
1462-9836 Latin Insurance **4512**
1462-9860 British Music Society News **6552**
1462-9933 Social Services Parliamentary Monitor **8070**
1462-995X The Mirror **3869**
1462-9976 The European Biotechnology Directory (Year) **763**
1463-001X Journal of Corporate Real Estate **7596**
1463-0036 Harpsichord and Fortepiano **6572**
1463-0095 Paediatric and Perinatal Drug Therapy *changed to* 0003-9888 **6088**
1463-0109 *see* 1528-3119 **8485**
1463-0117 The Newspaper Index **4587**
1463-015X MacUser's Mac Sources *see* 0269-3275 **2577**
1463-0184 Crystal Engineering†
1463-0192 Intervention†
1463-0257 Yes! Magazine **4070**
1463-0311 Baby's Best Buys
1463-032X T T J - Timber and Wood Products *changed to* 1740-701X **3716**
1463-0354 The Irish Franchise Magazine **1823**
1463-0397 Key Note Market Report: Videoconferencing **1896**
1463-0435 Employment Lawyer **1860**
1463-046X C P D Bulletin. Psychiatry†
1463-0486 C M E Bulletin. Cardiology **5778**
1463-0605 200 Crosswords†
1463-0613 200 Wordsearch†
1463-0656 Take a Break's Picture Arrowwords **4348**
1463-0664 Adsmart **3861**
1463-0702 Best of Readers' Wives **6286**
1463-080X Lab South America **5908**
1463-0877 Market Leader **1147**
1463-0931 Foreign Companies in Argentina Yearbook **1995**
1463-094X Foreign Companies in Brazil Yearbook **1995**
1463-0958 Foreign Companies in China Yearbook **1995**
1463-0966 Foreign Companies in Egypt Yearbook **1996**
1463-0974 Foreign Companies in Hong Kong Yearbook **1996**
1463-0982 Foreign Companies in Indonesia Yearbook **1111**
1463-0990 Foreign Companies in Malaysia Yearbook **1996**
1463-1008 Foreign Companies in Mexico Yearbook **1996**
1463-1016 Foreign Companies in Russia Yearbook **1996**
1463-1024 Foreign Companies in Saudi Arabia Yearbook **1996**
1463-1032 Foreign Companies in Singapore Yearbook **1996**
1463-1040 Foreign Companies in South Africa Yearbook **1996**
1463-1059 Foreign Companies in United Arab Emirates Yearbook **1996**
1463-1180 Family & Community History **4139**
1463-1202 Land Rover Monthly **8588**
1463-1245 Pharmaceutical Manufacturing & Packing Sourcer **6869**
1463-1253 Technology in Banking and Finance†
1463-1318 Colorectal Disease Online **5921**
1463-1326 Diabetes, Obesity and Metabolism Online **5888**
1463-1350 Crimewave **5413**
1463-1369 Asian Ethnicity **3520**
1463-1377 Post-Communist Economies **1547**
1463-1415 International Journal of Call Centre Management **1755**
1463-1458 Hampshire Life **3866**
1463-1555 International Tug and Salvage **8647**
1463-1652 International Journal of Systematic Theology **7651**
1463-1679 Guide to the Economic Regulation of the Gas Industry **6771**
1463-1687 Guide to Price Reviews at the M M C **3136**
1463-1695 Guide to the Economic Regulation of the Energy Industries in the European Union **3136**
1463-1725 Archeology International **379**
1463-1741 Noise & Health **6083**
1463-1776 E N D S Environment Daily *changed to* 1751-0376 **3415**
1463-1830 Property Forecast (London) **4762**
1463-1849 African Energy **3123**
1463-1857 World Automotive Manufacturing **8612**
1463-1911 Money Management **1368**
1463-2098 Art of Fishing†
1463-2101 Noah's Island Adventures†
1463-211X Good Cooking with Gary Rhodes†
1463-2411 Computers & Finance†
1463-242X Tunnel Management International† **8994**
1463-2438 EuroWire **3366**
1463-2446 Enterprise and Innovation Management Studies†
1463-3523 Project Finance News (London, 1997)†
1463-3647 Coatings Agenda New Products **6716**
1463-3655 Property Broker **7605**
1463-371X International Journal of Public - Private Partnerships†
1463-3817 Irish Nurse **5963**
1463-385X Eastern Art Report Online *see* 0269-8404 **487**
1463-3906 Computer Trade Shopper†
1463-3914 Cable Guide†
1463-3922 I T Directory **1629**
1463-3930 Al-Aqsa **7104**
1463-3949 F H M Collections **2254**
1463-4198 (Year) Who's Who of Executive Heads: Vice-Chancellors, Presidents, Principals, Rectors *changed to* Association of Commonwealth Universities. Who's Who (Year) **2968**
1463-4201 International Journal of Computerized Dentistry **5848**
1463-4236 Primary Health Care Research and Development **5699**
1463-4295 Neftepanorama **6780**
1463-4309 Sevashram News **5238**
1463-435X Howard League Magazine *changed to* 1753-7134 **2654**
1463-4376 HIV & AIDS
1463-4406 Project Finance Report. B O O & B L T Projects **1376**
1463-4414 Project Finance Report. B O O & B O O T Projects **1377**
1463-4422 Project Finance Report. Privatisation **1377**
1463-4430 Project Finance Report. D B F O, D B O, D B O T and Turnkey Projects **1377**
1463-4449 Participation & Empowerment†
1463-4473 Landlord & Tenant Reports **7598**
1463-4562 Food Law International Bulletin **4926**
1463-4988 Aquatic Ecosystem Health & Management **776**
1463-4996 Anthropological Theory **326**
1463-5003 Ocean Modelling **2814**
1463-5011 *see* 1463-5003 **2814**
1463-5038 Ocean and Atmospheric Data Management†
1463-5062 Durlacher A I M Bulletin *changed to* 1750-4147 **1609**
1463-5089 Real Time Gross Settlement Report
1463-5097 International Investment Review *changed to* International Investment and Securities Review **1631**
1463-5216 Veterinary Ophthalmology **8813**
1463-5224 *see* 1463-5216 **8813**
1463-5240 International Journal of Health Promotion and Education **6990**
1463-5364 Take a Break's Fiction Feast **5415**
1463-5461 Jane Greenoff's Cross Stitch **6639**
1463-5674 Football Magic **8228**
1463-5771 Benchmarking **1727**
1463-578X Journal of Property Investment & Finance **7596**
1463-5801 Design Optimization†
1463-581X O S J. Offshore Support Journal **8655**
1463-5828 I P Asia Law Reports **4689**
1463-5968 International Who's Who of Corporate Tax Lawyers **4871**
1463-5992 Baring Asset Management Top 3000 Charities (Year) *changed to* 1470-7845 **8075**
1463-6204 Journal of Spanish Cultural Studies **3545**
1463-6212 Down Syndrome News and Update *changed to* 0968-7912 **6137**
1463-6255 I G E R Annual Report & Accounts **235**
1463-6263 Station†
1463-6298 Air Power Review **6409**
1463-6344 I T S International **8498**
1463-6395 Acta Zoologica Online **930**
1463-6409 *see* 0300-3256 **969**
1463-659X Key Note Market Report: Dry Cleaning & Laundry Services **2243**
1463-662X InterChange (Swindon) **2558**
1463-6646 The British Journal of Forensic Practice **5912**
1463-6662 Old Age Psychiatrist **6171**
1463-6689 Foresight (Cambridge) **8422**
1463-6697 Info (Bingley) **2325**
1463-6778 New Genetics and Society **876**
1463-6786 The Manchester School **1546**
1463-6875 Computer Music **2495**
1463-7006 Intellectual Property and Information Technology Law **6752**
1463-7057 Loaded Fashion *changed to* 1751-1410
1463-7073 Education (Crediton) **3020**
1463-7081 Managing Education Matters **3027**
1463-7146 Biblio Tech Review **5060**
1463-7154 Business Process Management Journal **1730**
1463-7200 Play Guitar **6606**
1463-8029 The ScrollSaw **4562**
1463-8274 Journal of the M D U **5655**
1463-8452 Windows Expert **2583**
1463-8460 The Directory of the Turf (Year) **8290**
1463-8932 Aircraft Interiors International **45**
1463-9068 Walking Abroad†
1463-9076 Physical Chemistry Chemical Physics **2139**
1463-9084 P C C P Online *see* 1463-9076 **2139**
1463-9092 U K Shipping Contacts **2032**
1463-9106 Women's Health (London, 1998)†
1463-9122 Belly **6286**
1463-922X Theoretical Issues in Ergonomics Science **3223**
1463-9238 Medical Informatics and the Internet in Medicine *changed to* 1753-8157 **5831**
1463-9246 Journal of Automated Methods & Management in Chemistry **2101**
1463-9254 Aviation Strategy **8538**
1463-9262 Green Chemistry **2062**
1463-9270 *see* 1463-9262 **2062**
1463-9319 World Gold **6337**
1463-9327 World Gold Analyst **6337**
1463-9335 Noticiero de Tortugas Marinas *see* 0839-7708 **955**
1463-9394 Educational Technology Research Papers Series **2852**
1463-9416 Educational Technology Technical Report Series **2852**
1463-9424 *see* 1463-9416 **2852**
1463-9440 Self Service and Interactive Kiosk Review
1463-9491 Contemporary Issues in Early Childhood **2149**
1463-9505 R I B A Journal **455**
1463-9599 The Maritime Advocate **4970**
1463-9610 Mental Health Act Commission. Biennial Report **8055**
1463-9629 B I L D Seminar Papers **6125**
1463-9661 Global Gypsum **1009**
1463-9688 Puppy in My Pocket and Friends **2209**
1463-9696 European Race Bulletin **3533**
1463-9718 Rangers **8243**
1463-9785 Organisations Concerned with Health and Safety Information **2022**
1463-9793 Great Britain. Department of the Environment, Transport and the Regions. Advisory Committee on Releases to the Environment Guidance Note **3434**
1463-9807 The Psychology of Education Review **2901**
1463-9947 Contemporary Buddhism **7701**
1463-9955 Implicit Religion **7649**
1463-9963 Interfaces and Free Boundaries **2517**
1463-9971 *see* 1463-9963 **2517**
1463-998X Institute for Animal Health **320**
1464-0015 Scotland for Fishing
1464-0058 International Aquafeed **3598**
1464-0066 European Packaging Strategy
1464-0082 International Food Ingredients & Analysis Directory *changed to* 1753-450X **2009**
1464-0090 Who's Who in the Water Industry **8842**
1464-0104 Wood Equipment News Buyers Guide
1464-0120 International Cleaning Review†
1464-0147 International Milling Directory **273**
1464-0155 Bulk Handling International Directory
1464-0163 Who's Who in Bulk Handling *changed to* 1479-5833
1464-0171 Finishing Industry Yearbook **1995**
1464-018X International Aquafeed Directory & Buyers Guide **2006**
1464-0287 Current Medical Literature. Parkinson's Disease†
1464-0309 International Hydrocarbon **6774**
1464-0317 Classic Railways† **8941**
1464-0325 Journal of Environmental Monitoring **2102**
1464-0333 *see* 1464-0325 **2102**
1464-0414 East Asia Journal **336**
1464-0430 C L A S S - Cocktail Liqueur and Specialty Spirt *changed to* CLASS **601**
1464-052X Literacy Time Years 3/4 **3070**
1464-0570 Microbiology Today **892**
1464-0589 Astrology Quarterly **565**
1464-0597 *see* 0269-994X **7336**
1464-0600 *see* 0269-9931 **7346**
1464-0619 *see* 1354-6805 **7347**
1464-0627 *see* 0264-3294 **6133**
1464-0635 *see* 0954-1446 **7355**
1464-0643 *see* 1359-432X **7356**
1464-0651 *see* 0165-0254 **7364**
1464-066X *see* 0020-7594 **7365**
1464-0678 *see* 1357-650X **6158**
1464-0686 *see* 0965-8211 **7384**
1464-0694 *see* 0960-2011 **6168**
1464-0708 *see* 1354-6783 **7412**
1464-0716 *see* 1350-6285 **7414**
1464-0732 *see* 0169-0965 **5139**
1464-0805 Jane's Underwater Technology *changed to* Jane's Underwater Security Systems & Technology **2809**
1464-0813 British School at Athens. Supplementary Volume **385**
1464-0899 Local Governance *changed to* 1946-0171 **7127**
1464-0902 Complementary Medicine Bulletin **5804**
1464-0996 AgBiotechNet *see* 0954-9897 **712**
1464-1011 Asia Risk **1308**
1464-102X Consumer Goods Europe **1811**
1464-1038 Prosper **1965**
1464-1046 Soviet Maritime Newsletter **8663**
1464-1054 Homebuilding & Renovating **1012**
1464-1089 Image Processing Europe *changed to* 1089-3709 **3226**
1464-1119 E Banker
1464-1186 Key Note Market Report: Packaging (Paper & Board) **1895**
1464-1194 Countryside Recreation **4977**
1464-1224 Organic Farming **144**
1464-1259 Key Note Market Report: Computer Software **2593**
1464-1313 Machinery Outlook Europe **5456**
1464-133X Hunting with Country Illustrated **5073**

ISSN

9644 1467-5986 ULRICH'S PERIODICALS

1467-5986	Intercultural Education **8108**
1467-6222	C C H Tax Handbook **1914**
1467-6281	*see* 0001-3072 **1275**
1467-629X	*see* 0810-5391 **1277**
1467-6303	*see* 0155-9982 **1277**
1467-6311	Long-Term Health Management†
1467-632X	Business Law International **4858**
1467-6338	*see* 0044-6483 **7102**
1467-6346	*see* 0001-9852 **1435**
1467-6370	International Journal of Sustainability in Higher Education **2987**
1467-6419	*see* 0950-0804 **1135**
1467-6427	*see* 0163-4445 **6151**
1467-6435	*see* 0023-5962 **8117**
1467-6443	*see* 0952-1909 **8113**
1467-6451	*see* 0022-1821 **1136**
1467-646X	*see* 0954-1314 **1362**
1467-6478	*see* 0263-323X **4702**
1467-6486	*see* 0022-2380 **1768**
1467-6494	*see* 0022-3506 **7377**
1467-6648	Stitch With The Embroiderers Guild **6642**
1467-6656	European Copyright and Designs Report **6749**
1467-6664	Forage Maize Variety Leaflet†
1467-6672	Grasses and Herbage Legumes Variety Leaflet **273**
1467-6680	International Sports Law Review **8181**
1467-6702	Professional Agronomy **249**
1467-680X	Buffy The Vampire Slayer (U.K. Edition) **2377**
1467-6818	Xena Warrior Princess†
1467-6907	Cross Stitch Crazy **6638**
1467-6915	P A D I Member News **8192**
1467-6923	H M V Choice **6572**
1467-6958	Archives of Ibadan Medicine **5577**
1467-7016	T V Choice (Central Edition) *changed to* 1758-4124 **2392**
1467-7059	T V Choice (Ulster Edition) *see* 1758-4124 **2392**
1467-7083	T V Choice (Scotland Edition) *see* 1758-4124 **2392**
1467-7113	P C Friendly **2434**
1467-7288	Thomas & Friends **2216**
1467-7334	Mining (London, 1999) **6472**
1467-7415	Scotland in Business **1171**
1467-7423	Tweenies Magazine **2218**
1467-744X	European Competition Law Annual **4669**
1467-758X	Campaign Media Business *changed to* 1473-4613
1467-7644	Plant Biotechnology Journal **810**
1467-7652	*see* 1467-7644 **810**
1467-7660	*see* 0012-155X **1593**
1467-7679	*see* 0950-6764 **1594**
1467-7687	*see* 1363-755X **7352**
1467-7695	*see* 0392-1921 **7959**
1467-7709	*see* 0145-2096 **4137**
1467-7717	*see* 0361-3666 **1594**
1467-7784	U K Competition Law Reports **4799**
1467-7792	Japanese Performance **8587**
1467-7806	Liner Register *changed to* 1750-3752 **8641**
1467-7873	Geochemistry: Exploration, Environment, Analysis **2735**
1467-7881	Obesity Reviews **6667**
1467-789X	*see* 1467-7881 **6667**
1467-7946	Harpers on Retail
1467-7954	Journal of Conflict and Security Law **4933**
1467-7962	*see* 1467-7954 **4933**
1467-8039	Arthropod Structure & Development **839**
1467-8047	Performance Measurement and Metrics **5039**
1467-825X	*see* 0001-9844 **7102**
1467-8268	*see* 1017-6772 **1590**
1467-8276	*see* 0002-9092 **193**
1467-8284	*see* 0003-2638 **6904**
1467-8292	*see* 1370-4788 **1422**
1467-8306	*see* 0004-5608 **3999**
1467-8314	*see* 0066-3832 **4199**
1467-8322	*see* 0268-540X **327**
1467-8330	*see* 0066-4812 **3998**
1467-8349	*see* 0309-7013 **6906**
1467-8357	*see* 1368-6267 **468**
1467-8365	*see* 0141-6790 **469**
1467-8373	*see* 1360-7456 **1591**
1467-8381	*see* 1351-3958 **1535**
1467-839X	*see* 1367-2223 **7337**
1467-8403	*see* 1035-7823 **4180**
1467-8411	*see* 0818-9935 **1200**
1467-842X	*see* 1369-1473 **8356**
1467-8438	*see* 0814-723X **8089**
1467-8446	*see* 0004-8992 **1536**
1467-8454	*see* 0004-900X **1064**
1467-8462	*see* 0004-9018 **1064**
1467-8489	*see* 1364-985X **194**
1467-8497	*see* 0004-9522 **7108**
1467-8500	*see* 0313-6647 **7421**
1467-8519	*see* 0269-9702 **6907**
1467-8527	*see* 0007-1005 **2832**
1467-8535	*see* 0007-1013 **3053**
1467-8543	*see* 0007-1080 **1668**
1467-8551	*see* 1045-3172 **1729**
1467-856X	*see* 1369-1481 **7110**
1467-8578	*see* 0952-3383 **3037**
1467-8586	*see* 0307-3378 **1070**
1467-8594	*see* 0045-3609 **1070**
1467-8608	*see* 0962-8770 **1072**
1467-8616	*see* 0955-6419 **1730**
1467-8624	*see* 0009-3920 **2147**
1467-8640	*see* 0824-7935 **2410**
1467-8659	*see* 0167-7055 **2484**
1467-8667	*see* 1093-9687 **3289**
1467-8675	*see* 1351-0487 **7119**
1467-8683	*see* 0964-8410 **1087**
1467-8691	*see* 0963-1690 **1088**
1467-8705	*see* 0011-1562 **5280**
1467-8713	*see* 1479-7585 **4459**
1467-8721	*see* 0963-7214 **7350**
1467-873X	*see* 0362-6784 **3057**
1467-8748	*see* 1355-4905 **785**
1467-8764	World Insurance Policy Guide **4528**
1467-8799	The Conflict, Security & Development Group. Working Papers **6416**
1467-8802	Conflict, Security & Development **7227**
1467-8837	Cave Archaeology & Palaeontology Research Archive **386**
1467-887X	Business Ratio. Clothing Manufacturers **2245**
1467-8888	Business Ratio. Clothing Retailers **2245**
1467-890X	Business Ratio Plus: Food Processors **3629**
1467-8918	Business Ratio. Periodical Publishers **7556**
1467-8926	Business Ratio. Retail and Wholesale Chemists **6827**
1467-8950	Business Ratio. Stationery Distributors **1850**
1467-8969	Business Ratio. Stationery Manufacturers **1850**
1467-8985	Business Ratio. Chemical Distributors **2052**
1467-9027	The Good Skiing and Snowboarding Guide *changed to* 1750-7103 **8316**
1467-9051	Optometry in Practice **6050**
1467-906X	Automotive Aftermarket World Buyers' Guide **8564**
1467-9086	Axis† **8934**
1467-9108	Business Ratio. Joinery Manufacturers **1049**
1467-9116	Business Ratio. Market Research Agencies **1808**
1467-9175	Casino International **8165**
1467-9183	Business Ratio. Mining & Quarrying **6459**
1467-9191	*see* 0031-806X **6940**
1467-9205	*see* 0190-0536 **6940**
1467-9213	*see* 0031-8094 **6941**
1467-9221	*see* 0162-895X **7168**
1467-923X	*see* 0032-3179 **7169**
1467-9248	*see* 0032-3217 **7169**
1467-9256	*see* 0263-3957 **7170**
1467-9264	Aristotelian Society. Proceedings (Online) **6905**
1467-9272	*see* 0033-0124 **4025**
1467-9280	*see* 0956-7976 **7397**
1467-9299	*see* 0033-3298 **7461**
1467-9302	*see* 0954-0962 **7462**
1467-9310	*see* 0033-6807 **1788**
1467-9329	*see* 0034-0006 **6946**
1467-9337	*see* 0952-1917 **4765**
1467-9361	*see* 1363-6669 **1604**
1467-937X	*see* 0034-6527 **1166**
1467-9388	*see* 0962-8797 **3463**
1467-9396	*see* 0965-7576 **1166**
1467-940X	*see* 0917-0553 **1604**
1467-9418	*see* 1350-7303 **7677**
1467-9434	*see* 0036-0341 **4260**
1467-9442	*see* 0347-0520 **1171**
1467-9450	*see* 0036-5564 **7406**
1467-9469	*see* 0303-6898 **8398**
1467-9477	*see* 0080-6757 **7181**
1467-9485	*see* 0036-9292 **1172**
1467-9493	*see* 0129-7619 **4028**
1467-9507	*see* 0961-205X **8133**
1467-9515	*see* 0144-5596 **8069**
1467-9523	*see* 0038-0199 **8136**
1467-9531	*see* 0081-1750 **8136**
1467-954X	*see* 0038-0261 **8137**
1467-9558	*see* 0735-2751 **8137**
1467-9566	*see* 0141-9889 **8138**
1467-9574	*see* 0039-0402 **8403**
1467-9582	*see* 0039-3193 **5180**
1467-9590	*see* 0022-2526 **5539**
1467-9604	*see* 0268-2141 **3047**
1467-9612	*see* 1368-0005 **5184**
1467-9620	*see* 0161-4681 **2918**
1467-9639	*see* 0141-982X **2936**
1467-9647	*see* 1368-4868 **7687**
1467-9655	*see* 1359-0987 **354**
1467-9663	*see* 0040-747X **4031**
1467-9671	*see* 1361-1682 **4031**
1467-968X	*see* 0079-1636 **5161**
1467-9698	*see* 0265-9484 **1391**
1467-9701	*see* 0378-5920 **1196**
1467-971X	*see* 0883-2919 **5196**
1467-9728	*see* 0950-1029 **6797**
1467-9736	*see* 0044-0124 **5246**
1467-9744	*see* 0591-2385 **7697**
1467-9752	*see* 0309-8249 **6929**
1467-9760	*see* 0963-8016 **6929**
1467-9779	*see* 1097-3923 **1545**
1467-9787	*see* 0022-4146 **4417**
1467-9795	*see* 0384-9694 **7656**
1467-9809	*see* 0022-4227 **7656**
1467-9817	*see* 0141-0423 **2878**
1467-9833	*see* 0047-2786 **6929**
1467-9841	*see* 1360-6441 **5135**
1467-985X	*see* 0964-1998 **8397**
1467-9868	*see* 1369-7412 **8397**
1467-9876	*see* 0035-9254 **8397**
1467-9892	*see* 0143-9782 **8383**
1467-9906	*see* 0735-2166 **4417**
1467-9914	*see* 1121-7081 **1693**
1467-9922	*see* 0023-8333 **5141**
1467-9930	*see* 0265-8240 **4714**
1467-9957	*see* 1463-6786 **1546**
1467-9965	*see* 0960-1627 **1367**
1467-9973	*see* 0026-1068 **6934**
1467-9981	*see* 0815-0796 **7882**
1467-999X	*see* 0026-1386 **1149**
1468-0009	*see* 0887-378X **7154**
1468-0017	*see* 0268-1064 **6934**
1468-0025	*see* 0266-7177 **7664**
1468-0033	*see* 1350-0775 **6531**
1468-005X	*see* 0268-1072 **1699**
1468-0068	*see* 0029-4624 **6937**
1468-0084	*see* 0305-9049 **1157**
1468-0092	*see* 0262-5253 **410**
1468-0106	*see* 1361-374X **1510**
1468-0114	*see* 0279-0750 **6938**
1468-0122	*see* 0264-3944 **2896**
1468-0130	*see* 0149-0508 **7258**
1468-0149	*see* 0031-8051 **6963**
1468-0173	Journal of Social Work **8051**
1468-0181	Global Social Policy **8042**
1468-0238	The English Home **4539**
1468-0254	*see* 0963-9462 **4216**
1468-0262	*see* 0012-9682 **1097**
1468-0270	*see* 0265-0665 **1098**
1468-0289	*see* 0013-0117 **1539**
1468-0297	*see* 0013-0133 **1100**
1468-0300	*see* 0391-5026 **1100**
1468-0319	*see* 0140-489X **1480**
1468-0327	*see* 0266-4658 **1100**
1468-0335	*see* 0013-0427 **1101**
1468-0343	*see* 0954-1985 **1540**
1468-0351	*see* 0967-0750 **1540**
1468-036X	*see* 1354-7798 **1339**
1468-0378	*see* 0966-8373 **6918**
1468-0386	*see* 1351-5993 **4925**
1468-0394	*see* 0266-4720 **2448**
1468-0408	*see* 0267-4424 **1924**
1468-0416	*see* 0963-8008 **1344**
1468-0424	*see* 0953-5233 **4140**
1468-0432	*see* 0968-6673 **1747**
1468-0440	*see* 1018-5895 **4503**
1468-0459	*see* 0435-3676 **4009**
1468-0467	*see* 0435-3684 **340**
1468-0475	*see* 1465-6485 **1488**
1468-0483	*see* 0016-8777 **5300**
1468-0491	*see* 0952-1895 **7138**
1468-0610	Business Ratio. Confectionery Manufacturers **3672**
1468-0629	Road Materials and Pavement Design **3282**
1468-0777	Feminist Media Studies **8896**
1468-0785	Business Ratio. Engineering Distributors **3183**
1468-0831	Business South East **1075**
1468-0874	International Journal of Engine Research **3382**
1468-0971	Content Creation Europe
1468-098X	S T B News **5045**
1468-1099	Japanese Journal of Political Science **7145**
1468-1102	Shares **1651**
1468-1137	International Journal of Engineering Simulation **3201**
1468-1153	The Sandhurst Conference Series **7264**
1468-117X	Company Accountant **1285**
1468-1188	Animation U K (Quarterly edition) *changed to* 1748-1244 **6503**
1468-1196	Retail Finance Strategies **1379**
1468-120X	Business India Intelligence **1073**
1468-1218	Nonlinear Analysis: Real World Applications **5520**
1468-1250	D V D Buyer **2400**
1468-1293	*see* 1464-2662 **5815**
1468-1315	Dining Out (Leeds) **4384**
1468-1331	*see* 1351-5101 **6139**
1468-1366	Pedagogy, Culture and Society **3076**
1468-1412	Asia Pacific Coatings Journal **6716**
1468-1498	Business Eye **1072**
1468-1544	Dunstaffnage Marine Laboratory and Scottish Association for Marine Science. Centre for Coastal and Marine Sciences. Report and Accounts *changed to* Scottish Association for Marine Science. Report and Accounts **2817**
1468-1609	Who's Who in Charities **8078**
1468-1625	Impact (Milton Keynes) **5014**
1468-1641	Field Mycology **787**
1468-165X	C P D. Dentistry *changed to* 1479-1900 **5842**
1468-1668	C P D Infection **5590**
1468-1714	Computer & Communications Security Abstracts **2442**
1468-1722	*see* 1468-1714 **2442**
1468-1730	Play and Learn - Thomas & Friends **2207**
1468-1749	*see* 1468-1994 **7407**
1468-179X	*see* 0960-7439 **5849**
1468-1811	Sex Education **2911**
1468-1838	World Economics **1195**
1468-1846	The Egypt Report†
1468-1870	Asia-Pacific Insurance **4493**
1468-1927	Key Note Market Report. New Media Marketing **2330**
1468-1935	Key Note Market Report: Rugby Clubs & Finance **8236**
1468-1994	Sexual and Relationship Therapy **7407**
1468-2044	*see* 0003-9888 **6088**
1468-2052	e A D C - F & N *see* 1359-2998 **5986**
1468-2060	A R D Online *see* 0003-4967 **6221**
1468-2079	B J O Online *see* 0007-1161 **6039**
1468-2087	T H M C F Technical Report **2628**
1468-2095	I W M Scientific & Technical Review (Institute of Wastes Management) *changed to* 1754-5714 **3505**
1468-215X	Medical Humanities **5669**
1468-2168	North East Corporate Finance Directory *changed to* 1749-4028 **1354**
1468-2176	Major Pharmaceutical Companies of the World (Year) *changed to* 1742-8408 **2015**
1468-2184	Major Information Technology Companies of the World (Year) **8431**
1468-2206	Major Employers of Europe (Year) - The Job Finder's Directory **2014**
1468-2230	*see* 0026-7961 **4735**
1468-2249	*see* 0262-5245 **6589**
1468-2257	*see* 0017-4815 **1887**
1468-2265	*see* 0018-1196 **7647**
1468-2273	*see* 0951-5224 **2984**
1468-2281	*see* 0950-3471 **4143**
1468-229X	History Online *see* 0018-2648 **4145**
1468-2303	*see* 0018-2656 **4145**
1468-2311	*see* 0265-5527 **2654**
1468-232X	*see* 0019-8676 **1687**
1468-2338	*see* 0019-8692 **1688**
1468-2346	*see* 0020-5850 **7243**
1468-2354	*see* 0020-6598 **1126**
1468-2362	*see* 1367-0271 **1356**
1468-2370	*see* 1460-8545 **1759**
1468-2389	*see* 0965-075X **1867**
1468-2397	*see* 1369-6866 **8047**
1468-2400	*see* 1463-1652 **7651**
1468-2419	*see* 1360-3736 **1867**
1468-2427	*see* 0309-1317 **4416**
1468-2435	*see* 0020-7985 **7285**
1468-2443	*see* 1369-412X **1358**
1468-2451	*see* 0020-8701 **7975**

DIRECTORY 2010 1471-1370 9647

1470-1316 see 1084-8770 **6918**
1470-1324 see 1360-144X **2868**
1470-1332 see 0951-2748 **7257**
1470-1340 see 1461-6688 **8763**
1470-1367 see 0957-4042 **8904**
1470-1375 see 0043-8243 **424**
1470-1391 Information Research Watch International **5016**
1470-143X Ore & Alloys for the Global Steel Industry changed to 1750-6573 **6311**
1470-143X Ore & Alloys for the Global Steel Industry changed to 1741-6167 **6323**
1470-1448 World Wide Words **5196**
1470-1456 Armed Forces Medical Developments†
1470-1472 Current Medical Literature. Dermatologie see 1361-4215 **5873**
1470-1537 see 0969-7667 **5815**
1470-1545 see 0272-2631 **5183**
1470-1553 see 1060-1503 **5395**
1470-160X Ecological Indicators **3417**
1470-1626 Reproduction **700**
1470-1669 Human Rights Law Reports - UK Cases **7208**
1470-174X see 0307-5079 **3003**
1470-1804 Pergamon Materials Series **3356**
1470-1847 Journal of Iberian and Latin American Studies **4299**
1470-1863 Mantex Newsletter **2469**
1470-1952 L M **7150**
1470-1995 D P I C T†
1470-2002 see 1463-578X **7596**
1470-2029 Journal of Visual Art Practice **499**
1470-2037 Eastern Angle **6894**
1470-2045 The Lancet Oncology **6026**
1470-2061 Avian and Poultry Biology Reviews changed to 1758-1559 **935**
1470-2118 Clinical Medicine **5597**
1470-2126 EuroWired **1743**
1470-2266 Global Networks (Oxford) **8104**
1470-2282 Barts and the London Chronicle **4088**
1470-2290 Logistics Services (Year) **3680**
1470-2320 London School of Economics and Political Science. Development Studies Institute. Working Paper Series **1601**
1470-2355 Ballooning U K
1470-2401 Sondheim News **6617**
1470-241X D R A M **1983**
1470-2436 Defence Studies **6418**
1470-2517 Harpers on Trade
1470-2525 Civil Procedure News **4947**
1470-2541 Scottish Geographical Journal **4028**
1470-2584 Activity Time (Exeter)†
1470-2673 Pilot's Learn to Fly Guide **68**
1470-2681 Parliamentary I T Briefing changed to 1754-3479 **4997**
1470-269X The Pharmacogenomics Journal **6871**
1470-2711 British Postmark Society. Quarterly Bulletin changed to 1753-0717 **6892**
1470-272X Go Girl **2191**
1470-2738 J E C H Online see 0143-005X **5648**
1470-2754 Big Print Codebreakers **4330**
1470-2851 Tough Puzzles
1470-3114 U K Newspaper Directory **4584**
1470-3122 U K Business & Professional Magazines Directory **1185**
1470-3130 U K Consumer Magazines Directory changed to U K Consumer Directory **7579**
1470-3149 U K Freelance Directory **4584**
1470-3157 U K Broadcast Media **2398**
1470-3165 O E N Dealer changed to 1467-0593 **4555**
1470-3203 Journal of the Renin-Angiotensin-Aldosterone System **5655**
1470-3254 Human Rights Alerter **7208**
1470-3289 M Q R. Mining Quarrying & Recycling changed to 1753-6804 **6473**
1470-3297 Innovations in Education and Teaching International (Print) **3065**
1470-3300 Innovations in Education and Teaching International (Online) **3064**
1470-3343 Business Ratio. Building & Civil Engineering. Major **3261**
1470-3351 Business Ratio. Building & Civil Engineering. Intermediate **3261**
1470-336X Business Ratio. Contract Cleaners **2242**
1470-3394 Business Ratio. Mail Order & Catalogue Houses **1808**
1470-3416 Business Ratio. Paper Merchants **6732**
1470-3424 Business Ratio. Printers. Intermediate **7318**
1470-3432 Business Ratio. Printers. Major **7318**
1470-353X Donegal Democrat **3892**
1470-3548 Donegal People's Press **3892**
1470-3556 Advances in Mind - Body Medicine (Print Edition) changed to 1532-1843 **5568**
1470-3572 Visual Communication **2343**
1470-3610 see 1352-7258 **4147**
1470-3629 see 1360-4813 **4407**
1470-3637 see 0376-835X **1594**
1470-3696 Integrated Coastal Zone Management **3440**
1470-3726 Getting Married in Northern Ireland **5558**
1470-3742 Cheltenham Racecourse **8289**
1470-3807 Landlines Tech **3741**
1470-3815 P C Gameplay **2479**
1470-3904 Electronic Commerce Briefing **1416**
1470-3947 Endocrine Abstracts **5744**
1470-3955 Chamber **1398**
1470-398X Key Note Market Report. Electrical Wholesale **3323**
1470-4005 International Securities Finance **1359**
1470-4056 Aromatherapy†
1470-4064 Racing Days **8297**
1470-4129 Journal of Visual Culture **4461**
1470-4188 Internet Broadcaster **2560**
1470-4234 Linux Format **2594**
1470-434X EuroPetroleum **6768**
1470-4366 Repair & Reconstruction†
1470-4382 3 D World **2490**
1470-4390 Business 2.0†
1470-4439 Environmental Hazards Briefing **6676**
1470-451X Pop **2260**
1470-4528 The UK Motor Industry Directory (Year) **8609**
1470-4552 Fine Food Digest **3677**
1470-4560 Life Science Today **6858**
1470-4625 Fuels International†
1470-4692 British Journal of Engineering Education† **8937**
1470-4730 Nutrition in Practice **6666**
1470-482X International Relations of the Asia-Pacific **7245**
1470-4838 see 1470-482X **7245**
1470-4862 International Schools, the Database **2957**
1470-4897 see 1470-4862 **2957**
1470-5001 The Journal of Corporate Citizenship **1765**
1470-515X Dipterists Forum Occasional Publication **843**
1470-5176 Asia Monitor. Indian Subcontinent changed to 1479-5744 **1437**
1470-5184 Asia Monitor. China & North Asia changed to 1474-5615 **1437**
1470-5206 Grand Rounds **5814**
1470-5249 Skydive **8334**
1470-5257 Public Service Review. Central Government **7463**
1470-5281 Building and Facilities Management **4405**
1470-5303 All England Law Reports. Commercial Cases **4946**
1470-5346 Billing Plus changed to 1752-5543 **2387**
1470-5427 Journal of Germanic Linguistics **5133**
1470-5648 Consciousness, Literature and the Arts **4448**
1470-5656 Craft Business **533**
1470-5680 International Pension Funds and Their Advisors **1631**
1470-5699 Central and South Eastern Europe **7114**
1470-5702 Eastern Europe, Russia and Central Asia (Year) **7131**
1470-5710 Wholeness†
1470-5761 Tomorrow's Pharmacist **6883**
1470-5788 Asian Woman & Bride changed to 1473-4141 **3520**
1470-5788 Asian Woman & Bride changed to 1473-4133
1470-5842 Corporate Watch **7120**
1470-5885 Cleaning Matters **2242**
1470-5931 Marketing Theory **1833**
1470-594X Politics, Philosophy & Economics **7171**
1470-5958 International Journal of Cross Cultural Management **1867**
1470-5966 Enlargement **7232**
1470-6008 Packaging Today International changed to 1747-7468 **6714**
1470-6059 P S Pro†
1470-6067 International Journal of Electronic Business **1418**
1470-6075 International Journal of Technology Transfer and Commercialisation **8428**
1470-6105 Teaching Thinking Magazine **3085**
1470-6121 P E & Sport Today **3075**
1470-6237 What Cellphone changed to 1745-9885
1470-6326 Management Information Systems **2549**
1470-634X see 0893-133X **6168**
1470-6423 International Journal of Consumer Studies **2638**
1470-6431 see 1470-6423 **2638**
1470-6660 Automotive World **8566**
1470-6717 Journal of Alternative Dispute Resolution, Mediation and Negotiation **1690**
1470-6784 International Policing Technology **2678**
1470-6806 Business Ratio. Bus and Coach Operators **8492**
1470-6814 Business Ratio. Constructional Steelwork Manufacturers **987**
1470-6822 Business Ratio. The Footwear Industry **7940**
1470-6830 Business Ratio. Commercial Horticulture & Garden Centres **3726**
1470-6849 Business Ratio. The Lighting Equipment Industry **4534**
1470-6857 Business Ratio. Meat Processors **282**
1470-6865 Business Ratio. Meat Wholesalers **282**
1470-6873 Business Ratio. The Rubber and Tyre Industry **1881**
1470-689X Business Ratio. Book Publishers **7556**
1470-6911 Business Ratio. Paper and Board Manufacturers **6732**
1470-692X Business Ratio. Poultry Processors **282**
1470-6938 Business Ratio. The Agricultural Equipment Industry **5450**
1470-6946 Business Ratio. Antiques and Fine Art Dealers and Auctioneers **364**
1470-7004 Business Ratio. The Fire Protection Equipment Industry **3576**
1470-7012 Business Ratio. Pharmaceutical Manufacturers & Developers **6827**
1470-7047 Business Ratio. Travel Agents & Tour Operators **8689**
1470-7055 Business Ratio. Wine & Spirit Merchants **601**
1470-7063 Business Ratio. The Film and Television Industry **6491**
1470-7071 Business Ratio. Grocery Wholesalers **3676**
1470-708X Business Ratio. Advertising Agencies **22**
1470-7098 Business Ratio. Public Relations Consultancies **22**
1470-711X E-Executive†
1470-7152 Business Ratio. The Optical Industry **7074**
1470-7160 Business Ratio. The Toiletries & Cosmetics Industry **593**
1470-7209 Ireland's Homes, Interiors and Living **4544**
1470-7268 The Training Manager's Yearbook **1799**
1470-7330 Cancer Imaging **6012**
1470-7349 Saudi Arabia Quarterly Forecast Report changed to 1745-0683 **1516**
1470-7357 Turkey Quarterly Forecast Report changed to 1745-0748 **1522**
1470-7365 Egypt Quarterly Forecast Report changed to 1744-8840 **1482**
1470-7373 United Arab Emirates Quarterly Forecast Report changed to 1744-8859 **1522**
1470-7381 China Quarterly Forecast Report changed to 1744-8778 **1447**
1470-739X Malaysia Quarterly Forecast Report changed to 1744-8794 **1497**
1470-7403 Indonesia Quarterly Forecast Report changed to 1745-0586 **1490**
1470-7411 Brazil Quarterly Forecast Report changed to 1744-8875 **1443**
1470-742X Mexico Quarterly Forecast Report changed to 1744-8891 **1498**
1470-7438 Argentina Quarterly Forecast Report changed to 1745-0462 **1437**
1470-7446 Russia Quarterly Forecast Report changed to 1744-8824 **1516**
1470-7527 Japanese Puzzles changed to 1746-1219 **8176**
1470-7799 Professional Business & Technical Management **1787**
1470-7810 Asia Monitor. South East Asia **1437**
1470-7837 Food Business changed to 0955-5404 **3634**
1470-7845 Top 3000 Charities (Year) **8075**
1470-7853 International Journal of Market Research **1821**
1470-7888 Smarthouse changed to 1748-331X **4562**
1470-7926 O E M Online see 1351-0711 **6682**
1470-7950 European Rental News changed to 1749-5040 **1890**
1470-8078 Max Weber Studies **7984**
1470-8086 Journal of Obligations & Remedies **4833**
1470-8159 Consumer Sciences Today† **8943**
1470-8175 Biochemistry and Molecular Biology Education **725**
1470-8213 Personal Care **590**
1470-823X Wool Record Weekly Market Report (Print) changed to Wool Record Weekly Market Report (Email) **8462**
1470-8272 The Journal of Asset Management **1635**
1470-8302 Green's Scottish Human Rights Journal **7207**
1470-8310 Hospitality Briefing **4388**
1470-8361 Parking News **8633**
1470-8396 Law, Probability and Risk **4716**
1470-840X see 1470-8396 **4716**
1470-8442 see 0305-5736 **7166**
1470-8477 Language and Intercultural Communication **5139**
1470-8493 Candelabrum Poetry Magazine **5419**
1470-8515 L S E Gender Institute. New Working Paper Series **8900**
1470-8531 Grove Renewal Series **7759**
1470-854X Grove Ethics Series **6922**
1470-8558 Journal of Disability and Oral Health **4067**
1470-8566 European Journal of Neuroscience. Supplement **6139**
1470-8582 Lancet Neurology Network **6158**
1470-8590 Heart Failure Monitor **5788**
1470-8612 Women's Business **1195**
1470-8647 Montessori International **3073**
1470-8728 see 0264-6021 **724**
1470-8736 see 0143-5221 **5597**
1470-8744 see 0885-4513 **760**
1470-8752 see 0300-5127 **725**
1470-8817 Manga Max **504**
1470-8884 Bare†
1470-8914 Contemporary Political Theory **7119**
1470-9023 Clinical Governance Bulletin **4090**
1470-9031 Breast Cancer Online **6010**
1470-9120 Body, Space & Technology **479**
1470-918X U K and Irish Dividend & Interest Record **1387**
1470-921X Internet Markets changed to 1750-3906 **2317**
1470-9236 Quarterly Journal of Engineering Geology and Hydrogeology **3281**
1470-9260 Hotdog **6503**
1470-9279 The European Lawyer **4925**
1470-9325 see 0269-0942 **1145**
1470-9465 Clinical Microbiology and Infection. Supplement see 1198-743X **5597**
1470-949X International Journal of Mobile Communications **2327**
1470-9503 International Journal of Networking and Virtual Organisations **2499**
1470-9511 International Journal of Automotive Technology and Management **8586**
1470-9570 German as a Foreign Language **5122**
1470-9597 Face-Off **8172**
1470-9600 Retail Interiors†
1470-9848 Association of Christian Teachers. Digest
1470-9856 see 0261-3050 **7951**
1470-9872 Locum Destination Review **8731**
1470-997X Education Law Update **3021**
1470-9988 Convenience Retailing **3677**
1471-003X Nature Reviews. Neuroscience **6162**
1471-0048 see 1471-003X **6162**
1471-0056 Nature Reviews. Genetics **876**
1471-0064 see 1471-0056 **876**
1471-0072 Nature Reviews. Molecular Cell Biology **893**
1471-0080 see 1471-0072 **893**
1471-0153 Eating Behaviors **7353**
1471-0188 International Ocean Systems **2808**
1471-0226 International Journal of Vehicle Autonomous Systems **8499**
1471-0234 International Journal of Alternative Propulsion **3138**
1471-0242 International Journal of Vehicle Information and Communication Systems **8500**
1471-0277 Encounters Series **5114**
1471-0307 International Journal of Dairy Technology Online **1127**
1471-0315 The Facilities Business
1471-0358 Journal of Agrarian Change **201**
1471-0366 see 1471-0358 **201**
1471-0374 see 1470-2266 **8104**
1471-0463 H S M **6677**
1471-0498 University of Oxford. Department of Economics. Discussion Paper Series **1189**
1471-0528 see 1470-0328 **5986**
1471-0552 see 1351-5101 **6139**
1471-0641 I D J **6574**
1471-0668 Rail Technology Magazine **8622**
1471-0676 Platinum Metals Review (Online) **6329**
1471-0684 Theory and Practice of Logic Programming **2510**
1471-0692 Bliss for Brides **5556**
1471-082X Statistical Modelling **5538**
1471-0846 Refocus changed to 1755-0084 **3146**
1471-0854 All Ireland Journal of Nursing and Midwifery **5951**
1471-0927 Broadband Media changed to 1750-3906 **2317**
1471-0994 Legal Profession **4720**
1471-1044 V N Times **8810**
1471-1052 Modern Simulation and Training **6437**
1471-1060 Bus & Coach Preservation **8491**
1471-1079 SelfBuild & Design **1051**
1471-115X Industrial Vehicle Technology International **8671**
1471-1184 Digital Photography Made Easy **6980**
1471-1192 P 2 **2479**
1471-1222 Litigation. An International Who's Who of Commercial Litigators **4724**
1471-1230 Mergers & Acquisitions (Year) **4733**
1471-1370 Inland Waterways Handbook **8646**

Link to your serials resources and content with ulrichsweb.com

ISSN

1472-2240 The Ultrasound Review of Obstetrics and Gynecology†
1472-2275 Insurance Brokers' Monthly **4506**
1472-2402 B A F M Newsletter & Museum Visitor *changed to* 1755-2656 **6520**
1472-2445 Advances in Sepsis **5808**
1472-2488 World Mission *changed to* 1756-2481 **7755**
1472-2526 The Insurance Insider **4507**
1472-2542 The Official M B A Handbook (Year) **1156**
1472-2569 Hi-Fi News **6573**
1472-2607 L A P V. Local Authority Plant & Vehicles **7495**
1472-2674 New Design **8433**
1472-2739 *see* 1472-2747 **5468**
1472-2747 Algebraic & Geometric Topology **5468**
1472-2860 Euromoney Foreign Exchange and Treasury Management Handbook **1338**
1472-2879 Subject Magazine **6300**
1472-2895 New Technologies / New Cultures **7989**
1472-2909 Global Sport Cultures **8175**
1472-2925 M T N Week *changed to* 0952-7036 **1340**
1472-2984 Nuffield Institute for Health Service Studies. Working Papers
1472-3018 British Exports **1977**
1472-3034 Industrial Automation Insider (E-mail) **2461**
1472-3042 Fund Strategy **1625**
1472-3085 EnterText **4451**
1472-3107 Cookbook **4354**
1472-3123 Official U K PlayStation 2 Magazine **2479**
1472-3166 D & B Europa **1812**
1472-3247 Mortgage Edge **1369**
1472-3263 S T I Online *see* 1368-4973 **5881**
1472-3336 The Offshore & International Taxation Review **1937**
1472-3352 *see* 1754-8675 **2332**
1472-3395 Public Service Review. European Union **7463**
1472-3409 *see* 0308-518X **4410**
1472-3417 *see* 0265-8135 **4410**
1472-3433 *see* 0263-7758 **4410**
1472-3441 *see* 0018-1544 **7054**
1472-3484 Local Government Executive **7496**
1472-3514 The Journal of Drug Evaluation: Cardiovascular Medicine *changed to* 1479-1137
1472-3522 The Journal of Drug Evaluation: Respiratory Medicine *changed to* 1479-1137
1472-3530 The Journal of Drug Evaluation: Oncology *changed to* 1479-1137
1472-3549 The Journal of Drug Evaluation: Rheumatology *changed to* 1479-1137
1472-3557 The Journal of Drug Evaluation: Obstetrics and Gynecology *changed to* 1479-1137
1472-3581 Coloration Technology **2242**
1472-3611 Which Camera? Digital **6980**
1472-362X Centre for Monetary and Financial Economics. Discussion Papers **1326**
1472-3638 FibreSystems Europe **2350**
1472-3646 Archaea **881**
1472-3654 *see* 1472-3646 **881**
1472-3662 The Pink Paper (Print) *changed to* The Pink Paper (Online) **4378**
1472-376X B A S E E F A List **3296**
1472-3808 Royal Musical Association Research Chronicle **6613**
1472-3824 Arkleton Research Papers **8088**
1472-3867 Voluntary Sector *changed to* 1759-9911 **8038**
1472-3891 Journal of Public Affairs **7448**
1472-3913 Engineering Outlook **3190**
1472-3921 Immunotherapeutics Quarterly **5760**
1472-4022 The Journal of Drug Evaluation: Gastroenterology *changed to* 1479-1137
1472-4049 Journal of Ecotourism **8725**
1472-409X Waitrose Food Illustrated **3667**
1472-4103 Emerging Europe Monitor. Russia, C I S & Baltics *changed to* 1742-8890 **1482**
1472-4146 J C P Online *see* 0021-9746 **5647**
1472-4359 Diesel Car *changed to* 1753-0334 **8612**
1472-4367 Customer Management *changed to* 1757-3688 **1859**
1472-4375 The British Journal of Teaching Physical Education†
1472-4391 Personal Loans **1374**
1472-4421 *see* 0957-5146 **3058**
1472-443X The Wire (London, 1963) **7273**
1472-4472 Current Opinion in Investigational Drugs **6831**
1472-4499 E C & T **2948**
1472-4502 Tax Adviser **1947**
1472-4529 International Energy: Law and Taxation Review *changed to* 1757-4404 **3138**
1472-4537 Engineering Distributor *changed to* 0019-8277 **1820**
1472-4545 Running Fitness **6996**
1472-4596 Card Collectors News **4331**
1472-4642 *see* 1366-9516 **669**
1472-4669 *see* 1472-4677 **2735**
1472-4677 Geobiology **2735**
1472-4715 Drug Delivery Systems and Sciences **6834**
1472-4782 Asian Business & Management **1726**
1472-4790 Comparative European Politics **7227**
1472-4839 Able Magazine **4063**
1472-4855 Durham Working Papers in Linguistics **5112**
1472-4863 HIV Treatment Bulletin **5816**
1472-4944 Family Law Journal **4910**
1472-5037 Croner's Environment Magazine **3412**
1472-5053 Regeneration & Renewal **4425**
1472-5061 Adult Learning Yearbook (Year) **2938**
1472-5177 Working with Parents **3088**
1472-5215 Evening Standard (West End Final Edition) **3865**
1472-5223 Evening Standard (City Prices) **3865**
1472-5231 Evening Standard (Late Prices Extra Edition) **3865**
1472-524X Evening Standard (News Extra Edition) **3865**
1472-5266 Leisure & Hospitality Business *changed to* 1741-6647 **4980**
1472-5274 Postal Technology International **2355**
1472-5290 Employment Law & Litigation **4867**
1472-5312 Opinion. Specialist Reviews of Key Topics in Haematology
1472-5339 Professional Photographer **6976**
1472-5347 *see* 0143-7739 **1772**
1472-5401 Healthcare Equipment Supplies International† **8961**
1472-5428 Rail Business Intelligence **8622**
1472-5495 Ethnic Interiors *changed to* 1742-030X **4561**
1472-5762 Chilli Magazine **3631**
1472-5770 Private Hospital Healthcare Europe **4109**
1472-5797 Classic Record Collector **6557**
1472-5819 Ends and Means **6915**
1472-5843 African Identities **3516**
1472-5851 *see* 1472-5843 **3516**
1472-586X Visual Studies **8146**
1472-5878 *see* 1472-586X **8146**
1472-5886 Journal of Modern Jewish Studies **4460**
1472-5894 *see* 1472-5886 **4460**
1472-5908 Primary Care Management *changed to* 1479-2818 **5698**
1472-5967 Journal of Facilities Management **1766**
1472-6033 *see* 1467-2715 **7228**
1472-6041 Scottish Labour History **1707**
1472-6092 Jane's Asian Infrastructure *changed to* 1742-9943 **8490**
1472-6165 Glamour (London) **8865**
1472-6297 It's on the Net
1472-6300 Geophilos† **8959**
1472-6459 Family Court Reports **4909**
1472-6475 Trusts & Estates **4906**
1472-6483 Reproductive BioMedicine Online **6002**
1472-6491 *see* 1472-6483 **6002**
1472-6564 Career Research & Development **6695**
1472-667X What Van? Fleet **8679**
1472-6696 Legal Information Management **5025**
1472-6726 Business Ratio Report. Plastics Processors (Year) **7091**
1472-6750 B M C Biotechnology **756**
1472-6769 B M C Chemical Biology **724**
1472-6785 B M C Ecology **655**
1472-6793 B M C Physiology **920**
1472-6807 B M C Structural Biology **655**
1472-6815 B M C Ear, Nose and Throat Disorders **6078**
1472-6823 B M C Endocrine Disorders **5884**
1472-6831 B M C Oral Health **5836**
1472-684X B M C Palliative Care **5582**
1472-6874 B M C Women's Health **8844**
1472-6882 B M C Complementary and Alternative Medicine **307**
1472-6890 B M C Clinical Pathology **5934**
1472-6904 B M C Clinical Pharmacology **6824**
1472-6920 B M C Medical Education **5582**
1472-6939 B M C Medical Ethics **5582**
1472-6947 B M C Medical Informatics and Decision Making **5829**
1472-6955 B M C Nursing **5952**
1472-6963 B M C Health Services Research **5582**
1472-698X B M C International Health and Human Rights **7509**
1472-7110 Holiday Guide. Winter **8718**
1472-7161 Extradition (London) *changed to* 1476-6019 **2687**
1472-7188 Bluetooth World **2313**
1472-7226 Wireless Evolution **2504**
1472-7234 *see* 0007-4918 **1443**
1472-7323 Business Ratio Report. Housebuilders. Intermediate (Year) **987**
1472-7463 Current Drug Discovery **6830**
1472-751X Business Ratio Report. Freight Forwarders **8492**
1472-7544 ELLEgirl†
1472-7609 Lingerie Buyer **2248**
1472-7641 Big Blue Book **982**
1472-765X *see* 0266-8254 **890**
1472-7676 Business Ratio Report. Housebuilders. Major (Year) **987**
1472-7684 Business Ratio Report. Printed Circuit Manufacturers (Year) **3090**
1472-7692 Business Ratio Report. Management Consultancies (Year) **1730**
1472-7706 Business Ratio Report. Industrial Chemical Manufacturers **2052**
1472-7773 Journal of the Chemical Society. Dalton Transactions *changed to* 1477-9226 **2115**
1472-782X Mary Seacole Research Center. Research Papers **5969**
1472-7862 Journal of Supramolecular Chemistry† **8968**
1472-7889 Handbooks in Transport **8497**
1472-7978 Journal of Computational Methods in Sciences and Engineering **5502**
1472-8028 Forest, Trees and Livelihoods **3690**
1472-8117 The International Journal of Management Education **1759**
1472-8168 Best Practice Measurement Strategies **2313**
1472-8206 *see* 0767-3981 **6843**
1472-8214 Expert Opinion on Emerging Drugs **6839**
1472-8222 Expert Opinion On Therapeutic Targets **6840**
1472-8249 International Journal of Applied Marketing (Print)
1472-8923 International Journal of Energy Technology and Policy **3139**
1472-8931 Business Ratio Report. Heating and Ventilating Equipment Manufacturers (Year) **4117**
1472-9016 Charities Management Outlook† **8940**
1472-9245 Business Ratio Report. Plant Hire (Year) **1857**
1472-9288 Thalamus and Related Systems† **8993**
1472-9296 *see* 0022-1856 **1690**
1472-9342 Oxford University Commonwealth Law Journal **4754**
1472-9377 P C First Aid **2579**
1472-9490 Journal of Personal Injury Law **4833**
1472-9679 Journal of Adventure Education and Outdoor Learning **8320**
1472-9695 Classic Tractor **210**
1472-9725 Clinical and Experimental Allergy Reviews **5756**
1472-9733 *see* 1472-9725 **5756**
1472-9741 Internal Communication **1754**
1472-9768 Ingenia **3197**
1472-9776 French Magazine **5071**
1472-9792 Tuberculosis **6220**
1472-9806 Sales Rewards **1707**
1472-9814 Engineering Rewards **1680**
1472-9822 Arbitration Law Monthly **4917**
1472-9849 Finance Rewards **1682**
1472-9857 I T Rewards **1686**
1472-9881 Marketing Rewards **1696**
1472-9911 Business Ratio Report. Mechanical Power Transmission Equipment Manufacturers (Year) **3375**
1472-992X Business Ratio Report. The New Car Industry (Year) **8570**
1472-9970 Business Ratio Report. Non-ferrous Founders (Year) **6307**
1473-0065 E-Commerce (London, 2000) **4662**
1473-0111 International Journal for Mathematics Teaching and Learning **5495**
1473-012X AIDS & Hepatitis Digest **5808**
1473-0189 *see* 1473-0197 **2071**
1473-0197 Lab On a Chip **2071**
1473-0227 The Book *changed to* 1752-573X **8646**
1473-0235 Electronic Business Law Reports **4664**
1473-0367 Commercial Property (Bristol) **4861**
1473-0383 Cake Craft & Decoration **3672**
1473-0391 Fashion Business International **2247**
1473-0413 Financial Times Expat **1346**
1473-0480 B J S M Online *see* 0306-3674 **6229**
1473-0502 Transfusion and Apheresis Science **5941**
1473-0529 A X M (Print) *changed to* A X M (Online) **4370**
1473-0537 Salaries and Staff Issues in I T. Business Report *changed to* 1745-8129 **6693**
1473-0693 UnixNT **2599**
1473-0766 *see* 0951-3590 **5893**
1473-0782 *see* 1362-5187 **972**
1473-0790 *see* 1368-5538 **6283**
1473-0804 *see* 1369-7137 **8844**
1473-0901 Current Medical Literature. Lysosomal Storage Disease **5885**
1473-0928 Herpetological Bulletin **946**
1473-0952 Planning Theory **4423**
1473-0960 Infoconomist **1491**
1473-0979 Student Accountant **1302**
1473-0987 Entertainment Law†
1473-1045 Business Ratio Report. Compound Animal Feedstuffs **270**
1473-1053 Business Ratio Report. Employment Agencies (Year) **6693**
1473-1061 Business Ratio Report. Design Consultancies (Year) **480**
1473-107X Business Ratio Report. Department & Variety Stores **1808**
1473-1096 Business Ratio Report. Electrical Contractors (Year) **3296**
1473-1118 Business Ratio Report. Motor Component & Accessory Manufacturers (Year) **5450**
1473-1134 Business Ratio Report. Iron Founders (Year) **6307**
1473-1142 Business Ratio Report. The Greeting Card Industry **4059**
1473-1150 *see* 1470-269X **6871**
1473-124X Health Development Today† **8961**
1473-1525 *see* 1460-0781 **1534**
1473-1533 *see* 1464-2948 **6867**
1473-1576 *see* 1462-656X **6827**
1473-1800 Farm Animal Voice **319**
1473-1819 Digital Music Maker **6633**
1473-1827 Journal of Renovascular Disease **5794**
1473-1894 Briefings In Real Estate Finance **7584**
1473-1940 Global Cement and Lime Magazine **1009**
1473-2114 Nurse 2 Nurse **5971**
1473-2130 Journal of Cosmetic Dermatology **5878**
1473-2165 *see* 1473-2130 **5878**
1473-2173 Finance on Windows **1393**
1473-219X Imperium **8107**
1473-2246 Skyview (Analogue) **2390**
1473-2254 Youth Justice **2672**
1473-2262 European Cells & Materials **731**
1473-2297 Journal of Integrated Care Pathways *changed to* 2040-4026 **4509**
1473-2300 *see* 0300-0605 **5650**
1473-2343 Telecoms Law Today **4793**
1473-2408 Jaguar **8586**
1473-2866 Ephemera **7961**
1473-2963 Medical China Update **5667**
1473-2998 Document Skateboard Magazine **8170**
1473-3021 Men's Health Journal **6285**
1473-3099 The Lancet Infectious Diseases **5821**
1473-3145 Counselling and Psychotherapy Research **7349**
1473-3153 EuroHedge **1622**
1473-3161 AsiaHedge **1610**
1473-3250 Qualitative Social Work **8064**
1473-3269 *see* 1461-6718 **4410**
1473-3277 *see* 1473-3285 **7344**
1473-3285 Children's Geographies **7344**
1473-3315 International Journal of Ventilation **4122**
1473-3323 Financial Regulation International **1345**
1473-3374 Lab Magazine **502**
1473-3382 Frozen Food Europe **3678**
1473-3404 The Women's Oncology Review†
1473-3420 Cartel Regulation **4860**
1473-348X *see* 0950-3110 **7714**
1473-3498 Privacy & Data Protection **2515**
1473-3536 Journal of Romance Studies **5135**
1473-3579 World Data Protection Report **2569**
1473-3625 Lara Croft Tomb Raider **502**
1473-3633 Farscape **2381**
1473-3811 Curtido y Calzado **4973**
1473-3870 Business Ratio Report. The Food Ingredients Industry (Year) **3629**
1473-3897 World of Wine **614**
1473-3919 Business Ratio Report. Distillers (Year) **601**
1473-3943 Business Ratio Report. The Sports Equipment Industry (Year) **8164**
1473-3986 Anglia Property Guide **7582**
1473-4087 Key Note Market Report: Slimming Market *changed to* 1478-9795 **1893**
1473-4095 Business Ratio Report. Textile Rental, Launderers & Dry Cleaners (Year) **2242**
1473-4133 Asian Woman
1473-4141 Asian Bride **3520**
1473-4192 *see* 0802-6106 **5129**
1473-4222 The Cerebellum **6130**
1473-4230 *see* 1473-4222 **6130**

ISSN

1474-3779 Food & Drink Industry Bulletin *changed to* 1479-537X **4676**
1474-3841 Kennedy's Confection **3674**
1474-385X ArtsProfessional **475**
1474-3884 *see* 1468-1838 **1195**
1474-3892 American Communist History **4282**
1474-3906 *see* 1474-3892 **4282**
1474-4260 Waterstone's Books Quarterly **5245**
1474-4368 World of Information Business Intelligence Reports. Macedonia **1530**
1474-4376 World of Information Business Intelligence Reports. Federal Republic of Yugoslavia *changed to* 1744-6317 **1532**
1474-4384 World of Information Business Intelligence Reports. Trinidad and Tobago **1533**
1474-4422 The Lancet Neurology **6158**
1474-4457 *see* 1473-3099 **5821**
1474-4465 *see* 1474-4422 **6158**
1474-449X *see* 0955-7571 **7225**
1474-452X Tip Station **2481**
1474-4600 Moving Worlds **5336**
1474-4740 Cultural Geographies **3413**
1474-4902 The Anglican Peacemaker **7746**
1474-4945 Talisman **2946**
1474-4953 Dirk van der Werff's Plants **3728**
1474-4996 International Cement and Lime Journal **2043**
1474-5003 The New Review of Applied Expert Systems and Emerging Technologies†
1474-5054 EcoTech *see* 0958-6407 **431**
1474-5127 E.Learning Age **1416**
1474-5143 Archbold Criminal Appeal Cases Index **4884**
1474-5151 European Journal of Cardiovascular Nursing **5958**
1474-5178 Living Well *changed to* 1752-007X **4067**
1474-5186 Mental Health Today **6160**
1474-5232 The Fish Industry **3592**
1474-547X *see* 0140-6736 **5660**
1474-5488 *see* 1470-2045 **6026**
1474-5615 Asia Monitor. China & North East Asia **1437**
1474-5666 Planet Wireless†
1474-5747 Key Note Market Report. Debt Management (Commercial & Consumer) **1364**
1474-5755 Maxim Fashion†
1474-5771 E-commerce Law Reports **1096**
1474-5798 Charity Finance **1616**
1474-6085 Emerald Management Reviews (Print)†
1474-6174 Competition Law Monitor **4647**
1474-6239 European Legal Business **4867**
1474-6247 Optician Directory **6049**
1474-6298 RussiaMoney **1381**
1474-6506 Freight Transport Review **8671**
1474-6514 The British Journal of Diabetes and Vascular Disease **5884**
1474-6549 G T Purely Porsche **8582**
1474-6689 South Asian Popular Culture **356**
1474-6697 *see* 1474-6689 **356**
1474-6700 Theology and Science **7689**
1474-6719 *see* 1474-6700 **7689**
1474-6743 International Development Planning Review **4416**
1474-6778 International Journal of Environment and Sustainable Development **3441**
1474-6824 Global Built Environment Review **3433**
1474-6832 *see* 1474-6824 **3433**
1474-6883 Digital Photo **6979**
1474-7030 Mercedes Enthusiast **8590**
1474-7049 Evolutionary Psychology **7356**
1474-7065 Physics and Chemistry of the Earth (Print) **2714**
1474-709X Plastic Cards in Europe **1375**
1474-7138 N L K Monitor. Market Pulp **1899**
1474-7146 All England Legal Opinion **4613**
1474-7197 Interior Design (Watford) **4543**
1474-7332 International Journal of Revenue Management **1357**
1474-7359 HIV Nursing **5960**
1474-7456 World Trade Review **1588**
1474-7464 Social Policy and Society **8133**
1474-7472 Journal of Pension Economics and Finance **1868**
1474-7480 Institute of Mathematics of Jussieu. Journal **5494**
1474-7596 Genome Biology (Print)† **8959**
1474-760X Genome Biology (Online) **675**
1474-7669 The Follies Journal **442**
1474-7677 Public Service Review. Department of Transport, Local Government and the Regions *changed to* 1478-2200 **7501**
1474-7685 Forum: for Promoting 3-19 Comprehensive Education **3023**
1474-7731 Globalizations **7858**
1474-774X *see* 1474-7731 **7858**
1474-7758 Practical Neurology **6174**
1474-7766 *see* 1474-7758 **6174**
1474-7782 Ankara Papers†
1474-7790 The International Journal of Pain Medicine and Palliative Care†
1474-7863 Advances in Program Evaluation **3050**
1474-7871 Advances in Management Accounting **1279**
1474-7952 R O S P A Occupational Safety & Health Journal **6684**
1474-7979 Advances in International Marketing **1804**
1474-8029 Public Service Review. Department of Trade and Industry **7463**
1474-8177 Developments in Environmental Science **3414**
1474-8185 *see* International Journal of Performance Analysis in Sport **8180**
1474-8193 m.logistics **2369**
1474-8231 Advances in Health Care Management **5568**
1474-8436 R M Report
1474-8460 London Review of Education **2884**
1474-8479 *see* 1474-8460 **2884**
1474-855X Peru Quarterly Forecast Report *changed to* 1745-0640 **1511**
1474-8606 Automotive Digest†
1474-8657 Butterworths Local Government Reports **4634**
1474-8665 Autonomic & Autacoid Pharmacology **6824**
1474-8673 Autonomic & Autacoid Pharmacology Online **6824**
1474-8754 U K Irrigation **8833**
1474-8789 Conscience Update **7204**
1474-8797 Japan Christian Link News **7652**
1474-8800 Private Equity International **1376**
1474-8843 European Update†
1474-8851 European Journal of Political Theory **7134**
1474-8916 Digital Display Printing *changed to* Screen Process & Digital Imaging **7327**
1474-8932 Bronte Studies **5266**
1474-9009 Institute of Materials, Minerals and Mining. Transactions. Section A: Mining Technology **6465**
1474-9025 Personal Injury Law Journal **4757**
1474-9041 European Educational Research Journal **2855**
1474-905X Photochemical & Photobiological Sciences **2075**
1474-9092 *see* 1474-905X **2075**
1474-9114 The Journal of Family Health Care **5965**
1474-9173 Catalysts & Catalysed Reactions **2093**
1474-9181 *see* 1474-9173 **2093**
1474-919X *see* 0019-1019 **908**
1474-9203 Microwave Engineering **3109**
1474-9335 Teaching Citizenship **7188**
1474-9408 Foundation of Nursing Studies Newsletter **5959**
1474-9475 Holy Land Studies **7648**
1474-9602 I M I†
1474-9610 Medical Device Developments **6860**
1474-9629 Dod's European Companion *changed to* Eurosource **624**
1474-9661 I P Wireline and Wireless Week **2324**
1474-967X Broadcasting Strategy and Finance Week
1474-9718 Aging Cell **827**
1474-9726 *see* 1474-9718 **827**
1474-9734 *see* 0266-8734 **7395**
1475-0104 Country Profile. Cote d'Ivoire† **8945**
1475-0171 Screen Digest **2390**
1475-018X L T World **5062**
1475-0198 *see* 0158-7919 **2940**
1475-0279 British Journal of Community Justice **2645**
1475-0309 K S L **7149**
1475-0376 International Financial Adviser
1475-0384 The Drug and Alcohol Professional *changed to* 1745-9265 **2693**
1475-0449 Alpine Gardener **774**
1475-0457 Key Note Market Report: The Offshore Oil & Gas Industry **6776**
1475-0538 Digital Camera Buyer **6966**
1475-0686 Dairy Markets **263**
1475-0708 Therapy **5911**
1475-0724 Healthcare Counselling and Psychotherapy Journal **4097**
1475-0759 C M Focus *changed to* Ei Magazine **2556**
1475-0791 Resource Management and Recovery **3511**
1475-0805 Middle East Health **7531**
1475-0902 Institution of Mechanical Engineers. Proceedings. Part M: Journal of Engineering for the Maritime Environment **8646**
1475-0910 Press **7329**
1475-0929 Brand **6708**
1475-0945 B R A T Series in Clinical Psychology **7338**
1475-0961 Clinical Physiology and Functional Imaging **5597**
1475-097X *see* 1475-0961 **5597**
1475-1062 Vienna Music **6626**
1475-1097 Key Note Market Assessment. Small Office Home Office (SoHo) - Consumer **1963**
1475-1119 Key Note Market Assessment. Small Office Home Office (SoHo) - Products **1963**
1475-1127 The Internet Directory of the Turf *see* 1463-8460 **8290**
1475-116X Ag **6963**
1475-1232 Circuit News *changed to* 1478-3916 **8166**
1475-1283 Journal of Finance and Management in Public Services **1294**
1475-1305 *see* 0039-2103 **3358**
1475-1313 *see* 0275-5408 **6047**
1475-1321 Country by Country **1449**
1475-1364 T S Today **1845**
1475-1380 Practical Web Projects **2566**
1475-1399 Cube **2475**
1475-1410 P D A Essentials *changed to* 1754-2693 **2582**
1475-1429 X B M **2482**
1475-1453 C M E Journal. Geriatric Medicine **5590**
1475-1461 Socio-Economic Review **1517**
1475-147X *see* 1475-1461 **1517**
1475-1488 Advances in Accounting Behavioral Research **1279**
1475-1534 *see* 1471-4418 **6217**
1475-1542 Key Note Market Assessment. Supermarket Services **3679**
1475-1550 Birdwatch **904**
1475-1585 Journal of English for Academic Purposes **3067**
1475-1704 F S T Journal **7854**
1475-1712 Key Note Market Report: Newspapers **4579**
1475-1739 British Myriapod and Isopod Group. Bulletin **937**
1475-1763 North & West London Journal of General Practice **5688**
1475-1798 Defence and Security Analysis **6417**
1475-1801 *see* 1475-1798 **6417**
1475-1887 Tolley's Company Law & Insolvency **4882**
1475-1984 Internal Auditing & Business Risk *changed to* 1757-0999 **1291**
1475-2174 Conflict Assessments† **8943**
1475-2255 Key Note Market Assessment. Financial Services Marketing to A Bs **1364**
1475-2298 Transport Research Foundation. Fellowship Lecture **8636**
1475-2301 Nottingham Today
1475-2336 Dance Today! **2685**
1475-2352 Tolley's Practical Tax Newsletter **1952**
1475-2409 Journal of Research in International Education **3014**
1475-2441 Kinoeye†
1475-245X Financial Technology **1345**
1475-2484 Occasional Papers in Educational Evaluation†
1475-262X Middle Eastern Literatures (Print) **5333**
1475-2638 Middle Eastern Literatures (Online) **5333**
1475-2654 *see* 1466-2523 **8792**
1475-2662 *see* 0007-1145 **6656**
1475-2670 *see* 0007-4853 **841**
1475-2689 *see* 1054-5476 **793**
1475-2697 *see* 0022-149X **5820**
1475-2700 *see* 0954-4224 **6666**
1475-2719 *see* 0029-6651 **6667**
1475-2727 *see* 1368-9800 **6668**
1475-2735 *see* 0960-2585 **251**
1475-2743 *see* 0266-0032 **253**
1475-2832 Annals of General Hospital Psychiatry *changed to* 1744-859X **6123**
1475-2840 Cardiovascular Diabetology **5884**
1475-2859 Microbial Cell Factories **834**
1475-2867 Cancer Cell International **6011**
1475-2875 Malaria Journal **5822**
1475-2891 Nutrition Journal **6666**
1475-2999 *see* 0010-4175 **8095**
1475-3006 *see* 1473-5504 **678**
1475-3014 *see* 1470-5427 **5133**
1475-3022 *see* 1474-7472 **1868**
1475-3030 *see* 1474-7480 **5494**
1475-3049 *see* 0261-4448 **5201**
1475-3057 *see* 0032-2474 **4024**
1475-3065 *see* 0036-9306 **7680**
1475-3073 *see* 1474-7464 **8133**
1475-3081 *see* 1471-0684 **2510**
1475-3138 *see* 1474-7456 **1588**
1475-3162 *see* 0003-4878 **6672**
1475-3219 International Journal of Critical Infrastructures **3139**
1475-3294 Training Magazine *changed to* 1751-0805 **1876**
1475-3308 Serials (Online) **5047**
1475-3324 Food Science & Technology **3642**
1475-3332 I T Reseller **2493**
1475-3375 Postgraduate U K *changed to* 1750-6964 **2985**
1475-3405 Model Aircraft Monthly **4340**
1475-3413 The Vegetarian **6670**
1475-3480 C M E Breast **5987**
1475-3502 *see* 0025-1003 **5130**
1475-3553 The Review of International Affairs†
1475-357X Child and Adolescent Mental Health **7344**
1475-3588 Child and Adolescent Mental Health (Online) *see* 1475-357X **7344**
1475-3618 Primary Headship **3030**
1475-3626 Psychodynamic Practice (Online) **6178**
1475-3634 Psychodynamic Practice (Print) **6178**
1475-3669 Higher Quality **2863**
1475-3685 Review of Middle East Economics and Finance (Print)† **8985**
1475-3693 Review of Middle East Economics and Finance (Online) **1166**
1475-3723 The Ghosts & Scholars M R James Newsletter **5443**
1475-3731 Furniture News **4557**
1475-3812 N O D A National News **8474**
1475-3820 Bulletin of Spanish Studies **5267**
1475-3839 Bulletin of Hispanic Studies (Print Edition. Liverpool, 2002) **5267**
1475-388X EurOhs **6676**
1475-3898 Quality and Safety in Health Care **5701**
1475-3901 Q S H C Online *see* 1475-3898 **5701**
1475-3928 Journal of Customer Behavior **1824**
1475-3995 *see* 0969-6016 **2427**
1475-4053 Displays Europe†
1475-4061 I S P World **2558**
1475-4126 Clinica's Device and Diagnostic Daily *see* 0144-7777 **5595**
1475-4266 Cancer Nursing Practice **5954**
1475-4320 International Technology Law Review **4932**
1475-4347 International Financial Law Review 1000 **4931**
1475-4355 Red Hot Penny Shares **1647**
1475-4363 Bake & Take **3671**
1475-4398 Strategic H R Review **1875**
1475-4517 *see* 0017-8160 **7646**
1475-4533 *see* 0040-5574 **8483**
1475-4541 *see* 0364-0094 **7717**
1475-455X Aluminium International Today **6304**
1475-4584 Journal of Pipeline Integrity *changed to* 1753-2116 **6776**
1475-4703 Interplay **2155**
1475-472X International Journal of Aeroacoustics **7088**
1475-4738 Noise Notes **7089**
1475-4754 *see* 0003-813X **378**
1475-4762 *see* 0004-0894 **3999**
1475-4770 Liberal Aerogramme *changed to* 1754-1964 **7151**
1475-4819 *see* 0021-0862 **552**
1475-4835 Journal of Human Rights **7211**
1475-4843 *see* 1475-4835 **7211**
1475-4894 Families in Business *changed to* Campden F B **1732**
1475-4916 Homeopathy (Print) **5805**
1475-4924 *see* 1478-5854 **681**
1475-4932 *see* 0013-0249 **1100**
1475-4959 *see* 0016-7398 **4010**
1475-4967 *see* 1061-1924 **7252**
1475-4975 *see* 0363-6550 **6934**
1475-4983 *see* 0031-0239 **6728**
1475-4991 *see* 0034-6586 **1721**
1475-5122 *see* 1362-5241 **7443**
1475-519X Latin America Financial Alert **1496**
1475-5203 Asia Weekly Financial Alert **1438**
1475-5211 Middle East & Africa Financial Alert **1499**
1475-5270 History Scotland **4230**
1475-5297 *see* 0952-8822 **522**
1475-5319 The Supply Line *see* 0009-3068 **2057**
1475-5327 Journal of Forest Policy **3694**
1475-5335 Law, Science and Policy **686**
1475-5351 Frontiers (Brighton) **6214**
1475-536X Wenner - Gren International Symposium Series **7928**
1475-5416 40up **6302**
1475-5424 Teen Angels **6300**
1475-5505 Scotland Magazine **3870**
1475-5564 Archaeology & History in Lebanon **378**
1475-5610 Culture and Religion **7636**
1475-5629 *see* 1475-5610 **7636**
1475-5661 Electronic Transactions *see* 0020-2754 **4015**
1475-5696 *see* 0965-7517 **7164**

ISSN

1476-6884 Understanding Children's Social Care **2170**
1476-6930 Journal of Revenue and Pricing Management **1295**
1476-699X Mediation Matters **8055**
1476-7058 The Journal of Maternal - Fetal & Neonatal Medicine **5995**
1476-7104 *see* 1326-7612 **7261**
1476-7120 Cardiovascular Ultrasound **6193**
1476-7155 Scottish Golf **8245**
1476-7163 Solids & Bulk Handling **5459**
1476-7171 Library and Information Update **5027**
1476-718X Journal of Early Childhood Research **6094**
1476-7244 *see* 0811-1146 **4430**
1476-7309 Journal of Conflict Processes and Change
1476-7333 Action Learning **2824**
1476-7341 *see* 1476-7333 **2824**
1476-7376 HazardEx **3436**
1476-7392 *see* 1606-6359 **2689**
1476-7414 Integrated Contact Centres†
1476-7422 Exam.net **672**
1476-7430 Journal of Critical Realism **6928**
1476-7481 Key Note Market Report: Air Freight **8547**
1476-7503 Action Research **5567**
1476-7546 Journal of International Commercial Law†
1476-7589 Music Week International Directory **1578**
1476-7600 G A (London) **2734**
1476-766X News on the Block **7602**
1476-7724 Globalisation, Societies and Education **2860**
1476-7732 *see* 1476-7724 **2860**
1476-7783 Urbio **2630**
1476-7791 Gardens Monthly **3732**
1476-7848 E E Times U K **3094**
1476-7864 Hospice Information Bulletin **4099**
1476-7910 Rating Appeals
1476-7937 *see* 8756-6583 **4230**
1476-7953 *see* 1463-9947 **7701**
1476-7961 Clinical and Molecular Allergy **5756**
1476-8062 International Journal of Art & Design Education **3065**
1476-8070 *see* 1476-8062 **3065**
1476-8127 Corporate Governance (London) **4864**
1476-816X For the Record **365**
1476-8186 International Journal of Automation and Computing **2461**
1476-8259 *see* 1025-5842 **825**
1476-8267 *see* 1024-2694 **6417**
1476-8275 *see* 0300-4430 **2151**
1476-8291 *see* 1065-2469 **5494**
1476-8305 Nutritional Neuroscience (Online) **6171**
1476-8321 *see* 0887-0446 **7398**
1476-8364 *see* 1043-8599 **8420**
1476-8380 Reconnaissance
1476-8429 Investing for Growth **1631**
1476-8518 Journal of Immune Based Therapies and Vaccines **5762**
1476-8569 Active Travel *changed to* 1745-0438 **8253**
1476-8690 Journal for the Study of the Historical Jesus **7653**
1476-8720 Mardek Guide to U K Convenience Retailing†
1476-8739 F 1 News International† **8955**
1476-8747 Motorcycle Fashion **8263**
1476-8844 *see* 0307-1766 **1346**
1476-8917 Progress in Industrial Ecology **3461**
1476-8941 GEO: Connexion *changed to* 1748-5487 **4037**
1476-9018 Journal of Integrated Care **8050**
1476-9026 Hertfordshire Life **3866**
1476-9085 Competition Law Journal **4647**
1476-914X International Journal of Nuclear Desalination **8826**
1476-9158 Electronic Journal of Contemporary Japanese Studies **549**
1476-9212 Muso **6597**
1476-9255 Journal of Inflammation **6248**
1476-9263 Psychotherapy and Politics International **6179**
1476-9271 Computational Biology and Chemistry **2107**
1476-928X *see* 1476-9271 **2107**
1476-9328 *see* 1472-4782 **1726**
1476-9336 *see* 1470-8914 **7119**
1476-9344 *see* 0960-085X **2543**
1476-9352 I A O R Online *see* 0020-580X **2443**
1476-9360 *see* 0160-5682 **2433**
1476-9433 Medical Immunology **5763**
1476-945X Ecological Complexity **3416**
1476-9581 The Sustainable World **3469**
1476-9646 Streetwise Profits *changed to* 1748-5177 **1844**
1476-9662 Sherlock†
1476-9670 Journal of Multilingual Communication Disorders *changed to* 0269-9206 **6132**
1476-9700 Research Bibliographies and Checklists **5408**
1476-9808 British Journal of Educational Psychology. Monograph Series II. Psychological Aspects of Education - Current Trends **7342**
1476-9840 *see* 1476-945X **3416**
1476-9883 Primary Leadership **3077**
1476-9905 Trade International Digest **1584**
1476-9913 Antiques Diary **363**
1476-993X Currents in Biblical Research **7636**
1476-9948 Black Theology **7628**
1476-9964 G K T Gazette **4093**
1477-0024 Journal of International Trade Law & Policy **4933**
1477-0075 Travel Industry Rewards **1711**
1477-0202 Retail Express **1965**
1477-0229 U K Economic Brief (Print) *changed to* 1749-5474 **1522**
1477-027X *see* 1464-9934 **8126**
1477-0288 *see* 0309-1325 **4025**
1477-0296 *see* 0309-1333 **4025**
1477-030X *see* 0269-2163 **5693**
1477-0318 *see* 0968-1302 **5692**
1477-0326 *see* 0267-6583 **5172**
1477-0334 *see* 0962-2802 **8404**
1477-0342 *see* 1471-082X **5538**
1477-0350 *see* 1460-4086 **6074**
1477-0369 *see* 0142-3312 **4487**
1477-0377 *see* 1358-863X **5421**
1477-0385 *see* 0968-3445 **6453**
1477-0393 *see* 0748-2337 **3502**
1477-0415 Reproduction. Supplement **927**
1477-044X BioMagnetic Research and Technology **727**
1477-0520 Organic & Biomolecular Chemistry **2127**
1477-0539 *see* 1477-0520 **2127**
1477-0571 International Journal of Business Continuity Management†
1477-0628 Retail Directory of Europe (Year) (Print)†
1477-0660 Key Note Market Assessment. Over-40s Consumer **1892**
1477-0806 Key Note Market Assessment. Men & Women's Buying Habits **1827**
1477-0814 Journal of Comparative Law **4700**
1477-0830 Rent and Yield Monitor†
1477-0849 *see* 0143-6244 **986**
1477-0857 *see* 1471-4175 **996**
1477-0865 *see* 0265-6590 **3037**
1477-0873 *see* 0269-2155 **6107**
1477-0881 *see* 1474-4740 **3413**
1477-089X *see* 0266-3554 **4223**
1477-0903 *see* 0960-3271 **3497**
1477-0911 *see* 0959-6836 **3437**
1477-092X *see* 1078-1552 **6855**
1477-0938 *see* 1477-1535 **3324**
1477-0946 *see* 0265-5322 **5141**
1477-0954 *see* 1362-1688 **5141**
1477-0962 *see* 0961-2033 **6224**
1477-0970 *see* 1352-4585 **6162**
1477-0989 *see* 0969-7330 **5973**
1477-111X *see* 0267-6591 **5797**
1477-1128 *see* 1463-4236 **5699**
1477-1217 O R C A **2623**
1477-1276 Vintage Spirit **4277**
1477-1314 Kiteworld **8320**
1477-1500 *see* 0306-8374 **543**
1477-1535 Lighting Research and Technology **3324**
1477-1594 The Erotic Review **6289**
1477-1705 Lloyd's Law Reports Citator *see* 0024-5488 **4724**
1477-1721 Digital Camera **6979**
1477-1756 Think (London) **6957**
1477-1896 Hospital Pharmacy Europe **6846**
1477-1969 Overseas Diplomat **7257**
1477-1993 Key Note Market Assessment. Customer Relationship Management **1891**
1477-2000 Systematics and Biodiversity **707**
1477-2019 Journal of Systematic Palaeontology **2751**
1477-2035 Key Note Market Assessment. Small Businesses & Banks **1963**
1477-206X I F R I C Update **1290**
1477-2205 *see* 1061-5806 **7335**
1477-2213 *see* 1028-6020 **311**
1477-2221 *see* 1024-5294 **1085**
1477-223X *see* 1025-3866 **1718**
1477-2248 *see* 1028-2580 **4650**
1477-2256 *see* 0749-4467 **6558**
1477-2264 *see* 1026-7166 **8468**
1477-2280 *see* 0703-6337 **7263**
1477-2299 *see* 0895-7959 **7059**
1477-2337 Target City & Finance **7503**
1477-2388 I Love Pop *changed to* I Love Stars **2193**
1477-2396 Iran Focus *changed to* 1751-4614 **1493**
1477-2426 Nigeria Focus **1501**
1477-2434 Libya Focus **1497**
1477-2442 Algeria Focus **1436**
1477-2450 Brazil Focus **1443**
1477-2493 B M X Rider†
1477-2566 *see* 1465-3249 **5936**
1477-2574 *see* 1365-182X **5926**
1477-2612 *see* 0275-7206 **341**
1477-2620 *see* 0734-1512 **4145**
1477-2639 *see* 1025-6016 **2066**
1477-2655 *see* 1023-8166 **7067**
1477-2663 *see* 0890-5495 **5341**
1477-2671 *see* 1058-9759 **3355**
1477-268X *see* 1029-8436 **3272**
1477-2701 *see* 1560-2214 **6873**
1477-271X *see* 1561-4263 **2664**
1477-2728 *see* 1043-9463 **2664**
1477-2736 Journal of Policy Reform (Online) *changed to* 1748-7889 **1765**
1477-2744 *see* 1068-316X **7399**
1477-2760 *see* 1475-9551 **7957**
1477-2809 *see* 0197-3762 **525**
1477-2817 *see* 1745-039X **8793**
1477-2833 *see* 1028-6632 **7974**
1477-285X *see* 1053-699X **7725**
1477-2906 *see* 0323-5408 **92**
1477-2922 World Online Gambling Law Report **8216**
1477-2930 *see* 1477-2922 **8216**
1477-3015 The Guide to Local Authorities **7443**
1477-3023 The Directory of U K Parliaments and Assemblies **7434**
1477-3120 Great Britain. Home Office. Development and Practice **7442**
1477-3155 Journal of Nanobiotechnology **767**
1477-3163 *see* 0974-6773 **6024**
1477-3171 Advising Business **1956**
1477-3201 Manufacturer **1898**
1477-3236 Lloyd's Register Fairplay World Shipping Directory **8650**
1477-3325 Muse *changed to* 1755-6112 **3036**
1477-3368 Dermatological Nursing **5875**
1477-3503 The Business Magazine. Solent & South Central **1074**
1477-3554 Nursery Market News *changed to* 1747-5147 **1900**
1477-3635 Journal for Lacanian Studies **7367**
1477-3643 Leeds International Classical Studies **2237**
1477-366X I Can **6021**
1477-3708 European Journal of Criminology **2651**
1477-3724 Embroidery **6638**
1477-3759 Verification Yearbook **7272**
1477-3783 Psoriasis in Practice **5881**
1477-3805 *see* 0307-1235 **3864**
1477-3848 *see* 0743-4618 **5580**
1477-3880 International Review of Economics Education **1130**
1477-3996 Policy and Practice in Health and Safety **6684**
1477-4003 *see* 1477-3996 **6684**
1477-4038 The Official Harley-Davidson Collection†
1477-4054 *see* 1467-5463 **825**
1477-4062 *see* 1473-9550 **864**
1477-4143 Funland Nursery Rhyme Time
1477-416X Vegetable Handbook **257**
1477-4259 I T in Manufacturing **1417**
1477-4437 Showroom Management†
1477-4445 Dealership Management†
1477-4496 Retail Directory of the UK (Year) *changed to* 1753-1918 **1840**
1477-450X *see* 0142-6001 **5095**
1477-4526 *see* 0951-0893 **5113**
1477-4534 *see* 0013-8266 **4217**
1477-4542 *see* 0269-1191 **4222**
1477-4550 *see* 0017-3835 **2234**
1477-4569 *see* 1363-3554 **4146**
1477-4577 *see* 0950-3846 **5129**
1477-4585 *see* 0002-7189 **7620**
1477-4593 *see* 0167-5133 **5203**
1477-4607 *see* 0022-5185 **7657**
1477-4615 *see* 0268-1145 **5203**
1477-4623 *see* 0269-1205 **5325**
1477-4631 *see* 0027-4224 **6589**
1477-464X *see* 0031-2746 **4155**
1477-4658 *see* 0269-1213 **4158**
1477-4666 *see* 0951-631X **5715**
1477-4674 *see* 0955-2359 **4274**
1477-4739 The Communications Network. Journal *changed to* 1755-9278 **2368**
1477-4747 *see* 0032-4728 **7291**
1477-4755 Antiquarian Book Review *changed to* 1746-7101 **7572**
1477-478X Early Music Performer **6563**
1477-481X Patient Centre Care **4109**
1477-4860 Wellcome History **5729**
1477-4968 The Irish in Britain Business Yearbook **3541**
1477-5085 Journal of Sport Tourism *changed to* Journal of Sport and Tourism **4978**
1477-5115 What Home Cinema **3116**
1477-5131 Journal of Pediatric Urology **6270**
1477-5174 Campaign (London) **4077**
1477-5190 M C C *changed to* 1476-9018 **8050**
1477-5212 International Journal of Internet Marketing and Advertising **2559**
1477-528X Kompass Product Locator **2011**
1477-5360 International Journal of Integrated Supply Management **1821**
1477-5395 Offshore Vessel Register **8656**
1477-5557 Educate~ **2979**
1477-5700 Comparative American Studies **7956**
1477-5751 Journal of Negative Results in BioMedicine **684**
1477-576X Topic (Cambridge) **5242**
1477-5883 Community Safety Journal *changed to* 1757-8043 **2228**
1477-5956 Proteome Science **743**
1477-5964 Intranet Strategist *changed to* Ei Magazine **2556**
1477-6006 *see* 0308-0226 **5589**
1477-6111 West Midland Bird Club. Bulletin **916**
1477-6162 Irish Pages **5311**
1477-6200 Civil Service Rewards **1670**
1477-6219 Cost of Living Regional Comparisons **1222**
1477-6227 London Secretarial and Clerical Rewards **1696**
1477-6235 Research and Development Rewards **1705**
1477-6243 Employee Benefits Report **1677**
1477-6294 Textiles That Changed the World **8461**
1477-6332 Public Sector Director *changed to* 1755-9464 **1780**
1477-6340 Health Director (Manchester) **4096**
1477-6375 7 Update *changed to* 1479-7380 **6626**
1477-6421 *see* 1475-3928 **1824**
1477-6456 Performance Apparel Markets **2249**
1477-6545 International Journal of Low Radiation **3443**
1477-657X *see* 1476-6930 **1295**
1477-6588 Bees for Development Journal **95**
1477-6650 Digital Photographer **6980**
1477-6707 Total Digital Photography **6980**
1477-674X *see* 0030-9230 **2895**
1477-6804 Clinical Radiology Extra† **8941**
1477-691X Bollywood **6491**
1477-6928 Fun to Learn - Discovery **2189**
1477-7029 Electronic Journal of Business Research Methods **1741**
1477-7053 *see* 0017-257X **7138**
1477-7061 Emerging Europe Financial Alert **1337**
1477-7118 The International Who's Who of Corporate Governance Lawyers **4871**
1477-7169 Key Note Market Review: The Energy Industry **3141**
1477-7185 The Waterlow Stock Exchange Yearbook **1659**
1477-7266 Journal of Health, Organization and Management **4104**
1477-7274 Clinical Governance **5596**
1477-7282 Development and Learning in Organizations **1859**
1477-738X Event **6279**
1477-7398 Plastics Board Industries Federation Magazine† **8981**
1477-741X The E S H R E Monographs **921**
1477-7428 I T and E-Business Management Briefing **1417**
1477-7487 Surveillance & Society **8008**
1477-7495 The Drinks Business **602**
1477-7509 Clinical Ethics **5596**
1477-7517 Harm Reduction Journal **7520**
1477-7525 Health and Quality of Life Outcomes **7521**
1477-7541 Broadband Markets *changed to* 1750-3906 **2317**
1477-7606 Progress in Rubber, Plastics and Recycling Technology **3254**
1477-7622 Astropolitics **572**
1477-769X Forecourt Trader Business Directory **1995**
1477-7800 International Seminars in Surgical Oncology **6023**
1477-7819 World Journal of Surgical Oncology **6036**
1477-7827 Reproductive Biology and Endocrinology **5899**
1477-7835 Management of Environmental Quality **3451**
1477-7843 D A O L **5110**
1477-7894 Crackin'†
1477-7975 Curriculum Briefing **3056**
1477-7991 Mix Fashion *changed to* 1751-0422 **2258**
1477-7991 Mix Fashion *changed to* 1751-0430 **2258**
1477-8017 Drinks Bulletin **602**

ISSN

1479-8336 Electronics Systems & Software *changed to* 1750-9637 **3189**
1479-8344 Power Engineer *changed to* 1750-9637 **3189**
1479-8352 Communications Engineer *changed to* 1750-9637 **3189**
1479-8360 Museum & Society **6531**
1479-8387 Research Methodology in Strategy and Management **1790**
1479-8409 Journal of Financial Econometrics **1361**
1479-8417 *see* 1479-8409 **1361**
1479-8425 *see* 1446-9235 **5715**
1479-8441 Information Scotland **5017**
1479-862X Continuity Insurance & Risk **4500**
1479-8727 *see* The Review of Economic Theory
1479-8751 Royal Institution of Naval Architects. Transactions. Part A. International Journal of Maritime Engineering **8659**
1479-9022 *see* 0459-7222 **6435**
1479-9154 Attractions Management **4976**
1479-9200 S C Magazine (UK/Europe Edition) **2516**
1479-9219 Trust and Estate Practitioner *changed to* 1754-095X **4905**
1479-9413 Golf **8230**
1479-9448 The Party Magazine **3870**
1479-9499 Conservation Land Management **2607**
1479-9634 Retour **5043**
1479-9669 NatWest S B R T Quarterly Survey of Small Business in Britain *changed to* NatWest / S E R Team Quarterly Survey of Small Business in Britain **1964**
1479-9693 E S R C Research Group on Wellbeing in Developing Countries. Newsletter **8038**
1479-9723 Chronic Respiratory Disease **6212**
1479-9731 *see* 1479-9723 **6212**
1479-974X I D S Research Direct†
1479-9766 Television in Central and Eastern Europe to the Year... **2397**
1479-9774 Information Security Management **1418**
1479-9782 Electronic Design Europe **3095**
1479-9855 Asian Security **2676**
1479-9863 Tolley's Construction Newsletter *changed to* 1746-7624 **1041**
1479-9995 Advances in Gastrointestinal Cancers **5919**
1480-0039 Network (Winnipeg) **8847**
1480-0268 Agrivision **86**
1480-042X Canadian Mennonite **7733**
1480-0462 The Herald (Hamilton) **4294**
1480-0551 Key Student Outcomes Indicators for B.C. College and Institutions. Analysis by Institution **2934**
1480-0675 Words of Life **7823**
1480-0764 Quarterly Agri-Food Trade Highlights **149**
1480-0780 Rapport Trimestriel Sur le Commerce Agroalimentaire, Faits Saillants *see* Michigan Constructor **1024**
1480-0926 Sidney Journal **5372**
1480-1132 S Q R M. Cahiers **6614**
1480-1167 Nature's Resources **2621**
1480-1248 Annotated British Columbia Residential Tenancy Act **4403**
1480-1361 Independent Times
1480-1434 RealScreen **1164**
1480-1574 Bottin des Services et d'Expertise-Conseil **1069**
1480-1698 Fraternite 299 *changed to* 1719-5985 **4594**
1480-1744 Wiccan Candles **6744**
1480-1752 Control and Intelligent Systems **2459**
1480-1760 Canadian Financial Services Policy Report†
1480-1876 Reproductive Health, Pregnancy Outcomes, Alberta *changed to* 1712-0780 **5985**
1480-1930 Professional Lighting **2336**
1480-2147 Nickle's New Technology Magazine **6780**
1480-2171 Annotated British Columbia Municipal Act†
1480-2201 Ontario Petroleum Institute. Newsletter **6785**
1480-221X Hospital Quarterly *changed to* 1710-2774 **5626**
1480-2333 Symposium: Canadian Journal of Continental Philosophy **6956**
1480-2422 Journal of New Materials for Electrochemical Systems **2114**
1480-2538 Montreal Review of Books **7568**
1480-266X B T M P†
1480-2821 The Sources HotLink **35**
1480-2996 Manufacturing Automation **3370**
1480-302X Smoke
1480-3119 Osteoporosis Update **6225**
1480-3127 Point sur L'Osteoporose *see* 1480-3119 **6225**
1480-3151 Albertaviews **5205**
1480-3194 Fire Services Journal *changed to* 1488-0865 **3576**
1480-3275 *see* 0008-4166 **882**
1480-3283 *see* 0008-4301 **937**
1480-3291 *see* 0008-4042 **2052**
1480-3313 *see* 0008-4077 **2703**
1480-3321 *see* 0831-2796 **870**
1480-3445 Annotated British Columbia Human Rights Code **7202**
1480-3453 Dart: British Columbia Civil Practice (CD-ROM Edition) *changed to* Dart: British Columbia Annual Practice (Print Edition) **4830**
1480-347X AutoService Quarterly **8566**
1480-3534 Humanities and Social Sciences Federation of Canada. Annual Report†
1480-3666 Critical Issues Bulletin **1593**
1480-3682 *see* 1480-3666 **1593**
1480-3690 *see* 0827-7893 **1487**
1480-3763 British Columbia Environmental Law Digest†
1480-3801 Science & the Environment Bulletin **3465**
1480-3844 Health Authority Business Plan and Annual Report Requirements *changed to* 1910-1597 **7520**
1480-4085 The Canadian Postal Code Directory **2353**
1480-4131 Dart International **485**
1480-4336 Maple Leaf **6432**
1480-445X Dart: British Columbia Statute Service **4950**
1480-4549 Annotated British Columbia Mineral Tenure Act **4946**
1480-4557 Dart: British Columbia Employment Standards†
1480-4565 Alberta Decisions - Civil and Criminal Cases. Monthly Headnotes **4613**
1480-4573 Saskatchewan Decisions - Civil and Criminal Cases. Monthly Headnotes **4779**
1480-4581 Manitoba Decisions - Civil and Criminal Cases. Monthly Headnotes
1480-4638 Leadership Montreal **1406**
1480-4980 British Columbia. Children's Commission. Annual Report *changed to* 1716-6144 **7430**
1480-5065 Dart: British Columbia Labour Decisions **1674**
1480-5073 Dart: National Decisions†
1480-5162 N A S L I N E **8188**
1480-5189 Scott's Government Index **7468**
1480-5456 Dart: Ontario Criminal Decisions†
1480-5464 Dart: The Charter†
1480-5472 C **480**
1480-5502 Labour Force Historical Review **1694**
1480-5545 Visual Convergence **2404**
1480-5642 *see* 1203-2743 **996**
1480-5669 Abraxis†
1480-5707 Ontario. Workplace Safety and Insurance Appeals Tribunal. Annual Report **4753**
1480-5731 W S I A T in Focus **1714**
1480-6290 Manitoba Gardener *changed to* 1914-5519 **3742**
1480-6339 Innovations (Calgary) **7142**
1480-6355 Seminars in Hypertension Management†
1480-6363 *see* 0575-9455 **1218**
1480-638X Innuvelle **3539**
1480-6401 Ygdrasil **5438**
1480-655X Toronto Police Association. Tour of Duty **2670**
1480-6622 *see* 1204-5675 **3421**
1480-6681 Teen Tribute **2216**
1480-6800 Arab World Geographer **3999**
1480-6886 Workplace Gazette **1716**
1480-6894 Gazette du Travail (Hull) *see* 1480-6886 **1716**
1480-6908 Collective Bargaining Bulletin **1670**
1480-6924 Heritage (Ottawa) **4294**
1480-7076 Dart: Western Decisions **4655**
1480-7084 Annotated Alberta Franchises Act **4855**
1480-7092 Annotated British Columbia Legal Profession Act **4617**
1480-7165 *see* 1480-784X **8081**
1480-7289 Bulletin 41-42 **5101**
1480-7378 *see* 0008-5391 **622**
1480-7467 *see* 0380-7894 **1219**
1480-7475 *see* 0318-8809 **1045**
1480-7483 *see* 0068-7057 **8523**
1480-7599 *see* 1206-5064 **177**
1480-7815 Wapahke **6636**
1480-784X Canada. Statistics Canada. Family Violence in Canada, a Statistical Profile **8081**
1480-7858 Violence Familiale au Canada, Un Profil Statistique *see* 1480-784X **8081**
1480-7866 British Columbia. Ministry of Human Resources. Annual Report†
1480-7912 Eldercare Quarterly **4044**
1480-8161 The Brazilianist **1553**
1480-8382 Services Indicators (Online Edition) **1432**
1480-8684 *see* 0824-0310 **7854**
1480-8692 Canada. Statistics Canada. Criminal Prosecutions, Expenditures and Personnel (Print Edition) *changed to* 1706-8177
1480-8900 Alberta Environmental Law Digest†
1480-8919 British Columbia Assessment Appeal Decisions†
1480-8943 Journal of Geographic Information and Decision Analysis†
1480-8986 International Journal of Arts Management **497**
1480-9206 The Annihilation Fountain†
1480-9214 *see* 0705-5900 **6347**
1480-9222 Biological Procedures Online **658**
1480-932X Fine F A C T A **2857**
1480-9591 Canada. Statistics Canada. Economic Overview of Farm Incomes **177**
1480-9745 Saguenay-St. Lawrence Marine Park Bulletin **2626**
1480-9826 Army Doctrine and Training Bulletin *changed to* 1713-773X **6415**
1481-028X Canadian Journal of Clinical Medicine† **8939**
1481-0425 Canada Asia Commentary **1079**
1481-0433 *see* 1481-0425 **1079**
1481-0468 Journal of Comparative International Management **1765**
1481-0565 Victoria Genealogical Society. Journal **3786**
1481-0581 La Rotonde **2299**
1481-0719 *see* 0829-8947 **8678**
1481-0794 The McMaster Journal of Theology and Ministry (Online) **7662**
1481-0816 GirlsCan Magazine†
1481-0999 Network News (Ottawa) **6029**
1481-1006 British Columbia Business Legislation *changed to* 1492-6385
1481-1626 *see* 1201-0278 **8053**
1481-1634 *see* 0831-5698 **7304**
1481-1642 *see* 0831-5701 **7316**
1481-1715 The Canadian Journal of Adlerian Psychology **7343**
1481-1782 Teacher Librarian **2918**
1481-1804 Mi Gente **3550**
1481-1901 Defiance!†
1481-1952 Quotes, Notes & Anecdotes on CD-ROM **5357**
1481-2002 I E E E Canadian Review **3311**
1481-2029 Annotated British Columbia Company Act *changed to* Annotated British Columbia Business Corporations Act **4855**
1481-2185 The Corporate Executive **1087**
1481-2258 Preview **6536**
1481-2282 Good Tidings **7736**
1481-2428 WatchDog Newsletter **5245**
1481-2436 Ontario Agri-food Exporter *changed to* 1719-4113 **109**
1481-2495 *see* 1496-3922 **8376**
1481-2703 Internationaliste Canadien *see* 1484-8678 **3012**
1481-3122 The Journal of Addiction and Mental Health *changed to* 1706-9548 **2692**
1481-3254 Le Journal de Toxicomanie et de Sante Mentale *see* 1706-9548 **2692**
1481-3440 AnthroGlobe Journal **325**
1481-3556 Canadian Tourism Commission. Annual Report **8691**
1481-3793 Alberta. Ministry of Science, Research and Information Technology. Annual Report *changed to* 1497-0732 **7419**
1481-3807 Vintage Muskoka **4350**
1481-4064 *see* 1483-2615 **2022**
1481-4072 E T F O Voice **2844**
1481-4218 Canada. Statistics Canada. Oil and Gas Extraction **6799**
1481-4234 Natural Gas Transportation and Distribution **6800**
1481-4374 C L C Web: Comparative Literature and Culture **5268**
1481-4390 Canada. Statistics Canada. Electric Power Generation, Transmission and Distribution (Print) *changed to* 1703-2636 **3151**
1481-4404 Canada. Statistics Canada. Coal Mining **6485**
1481-4412 Embrace the Spirit **7640**
1481-4420 Administration Publique au Quebec **7419**
1481-4439 Bibliotheques et Centres de Documents **4997**
1481-4447 Organismes Communautaires du Quebec (Year) **8060**
1481-4463 Canadian Health Facilities Directory **4090**
1481-4722 Quebec. Conseil des Aines *changed to* 1913-3960 **4043**
1481-4900 Financial Post Markets Canadian Demographics **1817**
1481-4919 F P Survey - Industrials **1623**
1481-4935 Summit **7471**
1481-4943 Vernissage **6539**
1481-5133 The Gig **5423**
1481-5184 Canada. Statistics Canada. Metal Mines (Online Edition) *changed to* 1708-6299 **6485**
1481-5311 *see* 0380-6898 **1037**
1481-5389 Canada. Statistics Canada. Police Personnel and Expenditures in Canada (Online Edition) *changed to* 1488-867X **2673**
1481-5400 Canada. Statistics Canada. Crime and Police Resources in Canadian Municipalities (Online Edition) *changed to* 1488-867X **2673**
1481-5532 Occupational Therapy Now **6113**
1481-5567 O E E News **3143**
1481-5575 Bulletin de l'OEE *see* 1481-5567 **3143**
1481-5761 WeddingBells (U.S. General Edition) *changed to* 1715-9792
1481-5842 Journal of Social and Political Thought **7148**
1481-5869 Globe (Montreal) **4294**
1481-5923 Actualites Ergotherapiques **6106**
1481-594X Corporate Travel Management **6279**
1481-5974 Ethnologies **3616**
1481-6180 Dragon Soup Quarterly **5442**
1481-6202 I S L C Newsletter *changed to* 1488-1322 **5199**
1481-6229 Canada. Statistics Canada. Production and Value of Honey and Maple (Online Edition) **177**
1481-6253 Canadian Screenwriter **5270**
1481-6857 British Columbia Decisions - Criminal Cases. Monthly Headnotes **4885**
1481-6881 Canadian Journal of Infertility Awareness *changed to* 1715-9504 **5885**
1481-6962 Leadership Times
1481-708X FaceOff
1481-7152 British Columbia. Ministry of Energy and Mines. Annual Report *changed to* 1705-9275 **7424**
1481-7284 Environmental Trends in British Columbia **3429**
1481-7357 Small Business Canada Magazine **1967**
1481-7586 Canadian Business and Current Affairs Education **2931**
1481-7934 Give 'Em the Old Razzle Dazzle†
1481-8027 Child Care Bridges **2147**
1481-8035 C J E M **6057**
1481-8043 *see* 1481-8035 **6057**
1481-8132 Legal Aid in Canada: Resource and Caseload Statistics **4823**
1481-8175 Today's Grandparent†
1481-8248 Ivey Business Journal (Print Edition) *changed to* Ivey Business Journal (Online Edition) **1762**
1481-8256 Notos **5156**
1481-8280 on site review **452**
1481-8345 Advanced Manufacturing **1879**
1481-837X Quebec. Ministere de la Famille et de l'Enfance. Rapport Annuel *changed to* 1912-0931 **6703**
1481-840X Nineteenth-Century Feminisms†
1481-8515 Audio Programmers' Database **6546**
1481-8523 *see* 0228-8699 **5944**
1481-8531 *see* 1188-4169 **7511**
1481-854X *see* 0228-8702 **5947**
1481-8582 Commission Canadienne du Tourisme. Communique *changed to* Tourisme (Online) **8764**
1481-868X Canadian Journal of Applied Linguistics **5104**
1481-8868 Forest Health in Canada **3689**
1481-9112 Journal of Aboriginal Economic Development **1132**
1481-9120 *see* 1481-9112 **1132**
1481-9155 Southern California's Divorce Magazine **8140**
1481-9163 Chicago's Divorce Magazine *changed to* 1492-2045 **8106**
1481-9171 New York / New Jersey Divorce Magazine *changed to* 1719-363X **4908**
1481-9244 Living with Christ Complete - American Edition **7805**
1481-9287 Print Action **512**
1481-9309 PrintAction National Directory of Services & Equipment for the Trade **2024**
1481-9384 Perspectives Interdisciplinaires sur le Travail et la Sante **7535**
1481-9406 Curriculum Handbook for Parents. Senior High School (Catholic School Version) **3057**
1481-9643 Canadian Journal of Nursing Leadership *changed to* 1910-622X **5974**
1481-9708 Print on Demand *changed to* 1481-9287 **512**
1481-9724 Canada. Statistics Canada. Rubber and Plastic Products Industries (Online) **7827**
1481-9805 Canada. Statistics Canada. Fabricated Metal Products Industries (Online) **6338**
1481-9848 Chemical and Chemical Products Industries (Online Edition) **2053**
1481-9856 Industries Chimiques *see* 1481-9848 **2053**
1481-9864 Whispers Online Magazine for Women
1481-9945 RicePaper **5362**
1481-9988 Alberta R N **5950**
1482-0455 Action Nouvelles **2689**
1482-0978 Sailing Directions: Detroit River, Lake St. Clair, St. Clair River **8659**
1482-1168 *see* 0849-7818 **1422**

ISSN

1502-2730 Norges Bank. Inflation Report *changed to* 1504-8470 **1502**
1502-2749 Norges Bank. Financial Stability **1372**
1502-2765 Norges Bank. Finansiell Stabilitet *see* 1502-2749 **1372**
1502-2781 *see* 0802-6602 **7265**
1502-2803 K - Serien *changed to* 0809-7488 **2670**
1502-2897 Topp **2218**
1502-2900 Liberal.no *changed to* 1504-7431 **7151**
1502-2927 Innsikt *changed to* 1504-4297 **4600**
1502-3028 National Geographic Norge **4021**
1502-3133 Norway. Olje- og Energidepartementet. Fakta (Bokmaal) **6781**
1502-3400 Environment (Oslo) **3420**
1502-3524 Nansenskolen. Skriftserie **3924**
1502-3567 Kognitiv Terapi i Norge *changed to* 1504-3142 **7412**
1502-3583 Eureka-Nytt *changed to* 1504-8276 **8433**
1502-3648 National Geographic Sverige **4021**
1502-3664 Norway. Norges Vassdrags- og Energidirektorat. Haandbok **3163**
1502-3680 *see* 0333-2306 **3924**
1502-3710 Media i Skole og Samfunn *changed to* 1502-2471 **2919**
1502-3842 Salg og Suksess *changed to* 1890-1360 **1843**
1502-3850 *see* 0001-6357 **5833**
1502-3869 *see* 0001-6993 **8085**
1502-3877 Hoegskolen i Stavanger. Doktor Ingenioer-Avhandling *changed to* 1890-1387 **3225**
1502-3885 *see* 0300-9483 **2726**
1502-3923 *see* 0020-174X **6925**
1502-3931 *see* 0024-1164 **6726**
1502-394X *see* 0803-8740 **8901**
1502-4008 Norsk Tidsskrift for Migrasjonsforskning **7288**
1502-4156 Perspektiv: A5 **8125**
1502-4288 Servicehandelen *changed to* 1502-9557 **3679**
1502-430X Utemiljoe†
1502-4334 Appetitt **4352**
1502-4350 Emissions and Discharges from the Norwegian Petroleum Industry *changed to* 1890-2200 **3428**
1502-4377 Industridata *changed to* 1504-6184 **2458**
1502-4385 Plast†
1502-4458 Norway. Fiskedirektoratet. Oekonomiske Analyser. Fiskeopdrett *changed to* 1890-5447 **3603**
1502-4717 *see* 0332-5865 **5155**
1502-4725 *see* 0803-9488 **6171**
1502-475X Temamagasinet for Foraeldre om... *changed to* 0801-1346 **7383**
1502-4873 Fauna Norvegica **942**
1502-4911 Energi & Ledelse **3307**
1502-4946 F O U - Rapport **5959**
1502-5039 Aarbok for Nordisk Skatteforskning *changed to* 1890-3029 **1955**
1502-5101 Diakonos Magasin *see* 0333-4589 **7637**
1502-5195 *see* 1502-1521 **8901**
1502-5292 *see* 0029-1951 **4022**
1502-5314 Universitetet i Oslo. Senter for Studier i Vikingtid og Nordisk Middelalder. Skriftserie *changed to* 0809-8646 **4246**
1502-5322 *see* 0029-196X **2759**
1502-5373 Den Norske Atlanterhavskomite. Internett Tekster **7255**
1502-5381 Monitor 21 **3453**
1502-542X Vaaronnavisa Nordpaa *changed to* 1504-5706 **168**
1502-5446 Norway. Olje- og Energidepartementet. Facts **6781**
1502-5462 *see* 0801-5775 **5126**
1502-5519 University of Bergen. Reports in Meteorology and Oceanography **6397**
1502-5527 Den Norske Kreftforening. D N K-Rapport *changed to* 1504-2553 **6026**
1502-556X Telecom (Oslo) *changed to* 0809-9030 **2318**
1502-5578 Kulturliv *changed to* 1504-6591 **8117**
1502-5624 Agenda 3:16 **7744**
1502-5683 Samfunnsoekonomisk Debatt **1170**
1502-573X Havne@visen *changed to* 1504-7601 **8649**
1502-5780 Norges Bank. Working Papers **1372**
1502-5853 Her og Na **3923**
1502-5985 Convenience & Fastfood **3632**
1502-6108 Oekonomisk Forum *changed to* 1890-5250 **1170**
1502-6507 Elektro *changed to* 1503-8246 **3115**
1502-6809 *see* 1501-0333 **2501**
1502-685X Tidsskrift for Strafferett **4899**
1502-6973 Julia **2196**
1502-699X Rettshistoriske Studier **4769**
1502-7112 Agenda *changed to* 1504-601X **1695**
1502-7120 Norsk Traverstambok for Kaldblodshester *changed to* 1504-4351 **8295**
1502-7147 Sondreposten *changed to* 1504-789X **4077**
1502-7198 Universitetet i Oslo. InterMedia. Rapport **8145**
1502-7244 *see* 0901-8328 **7679**
1502-7287 Intrafish **1572**
1502-7384 Norsk Bokfortegnelse. Nyhetsliste (Online) **632**
1502-7414 Hytte og Fritid **1013**
1502-7465 Ukeavisen Ledelse og Naeringsliv *changed to* 1503-6200 **1908**
1502-7473 Tidsskrift for Kulturforskning **358**
1502-7511 Universitetet i Oslo. Senter for Barne- og Ungdomspsykiatri. Monografiserien *changed to* 1504-2537 **6189**
1502-7554 W.I.T.C.H. **2220**
1502-7570 Journal of Military Ethics **6429**
1502-7589 *see* 1502-7570 **6429**
1502-7678 *see* 0029-3652 **408**
1502-7686 *see* 0036-5513 **5910**
1502-7694 N J E S (Print) *changed to* 1654-6970 **5153**
1502-7708 *see* 0036-5521 **5930**
1502-7716 *see* 0346-8755 **4160**
1502-7724 *see* 0281-3432 **5710**
1502-7732 *see* 0300-9742 **6227**
1502-7740 *see* 0301-3847 **6227**
1502-7759 Tidsskrift for Ungdomsforskning **2169**
1502-7783 Kingsize **6582**
1502-7791 *see* 0039-338X **7684**
1502-7805 *see* 0039-7679 **2241**
1502-783X Kontur *changed to* Negotia **4599**
1502-7848 Vaar Energi **3162**
1502-7902 Rapport om Arbeidsmarkedet *changed to* 1504-8217 **1663**
1502-8054 Musee d'Alta. Brochures *see* 0805-9128 **4197**
1502-8143 *see* 1502-5780 **1372**
1502-8232 Smaabedrifter i Fokus **1966**
1502-8283 *see* 1502-1424 **5886**
1502-8313 Kloekt **1770**
1502-8356 *see* 0807-6375 **7749**
1502-8410 Facsimilia Bibliothecae Universitatas Nidrosiensis **3922**
1502-8658 Monster *changed to* 1890-5838 **6600**
1502-878X Hotell-, Institusjons- og Restaurantguiden *changed to* 1503-4704 **4390**
1502-8860 Lydskrift **6585**
1502-8879 Det Nye MakeUp og Har *changed to* Det Nye MakeUp **595**
1502-8933 Eureka *changed to* 0809-8026 **2855**
1502-8933 Eureka *changed to* 0809-8034 **2855**
1502-9026 *see* 1502-5381 **3453**
1502-9085 Nasjonalt Formidlingssenter i Geriatri. Undervisningssykehjem. Rapport **4052**
1502-9247 Nasjonalt Formidlingssenter i Geriatri. Geritri Norge. Rapport **4052**
1502-9425 Nordic Innovation *changed to* 1503-9676 **8426**
1502-9557 Handelsbladet F K **3679**
1502-9727 Det Norske Videnskaps-Akademi. II. Hist.-Filos. Klasse. Skrifter og Avhandlinger **4467**
1502-9778 Utdanning **2924**
1502-9794 N I B R-Rapport **4420**
1502-9808 Fiskeriteknisk Fagblad **3594**
1502-9824 Forbundsnytt **4594**
1502-9832 Utdanningsforbundet. Hefteserie **2924**
1502-9867 Petromagasinet *changed to* 1890-2707 **6786**
1502-9964 Eksportaktuelt.no **1563**
1503-0075 Universitetet i Oslo. Institutt for Kriminologi og Rettssosiologi. Skriftserie *changed to* 0809-7488 **2670**
1503-0180 Drift og Vedlikehold *changed to* 0800-7713 **987**
1503-0237 Svin **301**
1503-0245 Klartekst **7565**
1503-0261 Alternativt Nettverk *changed to* 0809-8565 **315**
1503-030X Elmagasinet **3307**
1503-0318 Norway. Norges Vassdrags- og Energidirektorat. Oppdragsrapport. A **3163**
1503-0628 Idrett & Anlegg **8178**
1503-0741 Norges Bank. Doctoral Dissertations in Economics **1372**
1503-0792 Universitetet i Oslo. Kulturhistoriske Museer. Skrifter *changed to* 1504-3258 **422**
1503-0814 Norsk Utemiljoe **3745**
1503-0849 Aldring og Livsloep **4040**
1503-0857 Report on Science & Technology Indicators for Norway **8396**
1503-0938 Mat & Pack *changed to* 0013-6581 **6709**
1503-0946 Rokkansenteret-Notat **7998**
1503-111X *see* 0800-3831 **7945**
1503-1233 Jakt **8319**
1503-1276 Norway. Fiskeridirektoratet. Fiskefartoey og Fiskarar, Konsesjoner og Aarlege Deltakaradgangar **3604**
1503-1330 Nordem Report **7213**
1503-1349 Universitetet i Oslo. Institutt for Menneskerettigheter. Research Notes *changed to* 1504-0062 **7218**
1503-1403 Norway. Nasjonalt Folkehelseinstitutt. Rapport **8059**
1503-1438 International Journal of Disaster Medicine **5638**
1503-1519 Mamma **2160**
1503-1535 Norway. Central Bureau of Statistics. Economic Survey (Online) *see* 0800-4110 **1502**
1503-1543 Odd **509**
1503-1551 *see* 1503-4712 **1256**
1503-1640 I T- Karriere **2494**
1503-1667 Universitetet for Miljoe- og Biovitenskap. Doctor Philosophia Thesis **165**
1503-1705 Norut I T. I T-Rapport *changed to* 1890-5226 **8123**
1503-1748 Fagbladet Bygning *changed to* 1504-4696 **4591**
1503-1780 Helse **8044**
1503-1810 Baby, Hobby, Leketoey **4059**
1503-1853 Norway. Norges Vassdrags- og Energidirektorat. Oppdragsrapport *changed to* 1503-0318 **3163**
1503-1918 Norway. Nasjonalt Folkehelseinstitutt. Nytt†
1503-1950 Park og Anlegg **3747**
1503-1993 Fiskets Gang (Online Edition) **3594**
1503-2086 *see* 0809-1668 **5342**
1503-2108 Norske Insekttabeller **856**
1503-2175 D B E - Aktuelt *changed to* 1503-7843 **2228**
1503-2310 Norsk Shakespeare og Teater-Tidsskrift **5342**
1503-2337 Barne- og Ungdomslitteratur (year) **2178**
1503-2361 R O S - Info **6180**
1503-2442 Kunst†
1503-2507 Aarringer **4402**
1503-2523 Trondhjems Turistforening. Aarbok *changed to* 1503-7460 **8769**
1503-2566 Beredskapsnytt *changed to* 1503-7843 **2228**
1503-2701 Geografi i Bergen **7966**
1503-2728 Bloeder-Nytt **8028**
1503-2841 Dagens Medier **4574**
1503-2868 S I U *changed to* 1503-2876 **3000**
1503-2876 S I U. Publikasjoner **3000**
1503-2892 Dagsavisen **3922**
1503-2914 Fokus *changed to* 1503-4399 **6420**
1503-2965 Tidsskrift for Familierett, Arverett og Barnevernrettslige Spoergsmaal **4914**
1503-2981 Acta Ibseniana **5249**
1503-3066 N I J O S. Rapport *changed to* 1890-159X **3707**
1503-3163 Al Farah Magasinet **2682**
1503-318X Autofil **8562**
1503-3201 *see* 1502-7198 **8145**
1503-3228 C M I Policy Brief *changed to* 0809-6732 **7224**
1503-3244 Tidsskrift for Jordmoedre **6005**
1503-3341 N G H - Nytt **294**
1503-3414 *see* 1503-3341 **294**
1503-3422 *see* 1503-9498 **294**
1503-3430 *see* 1503-9498 **294**
1503-3449 Personal og Ledelse **1785**
1503-352X Tall og Fakta **6882**
1503-3791 Norsk Revmatikerforbund. Temahefte **8059**
1503-3821 Utslipp fra Olje- og Gassvirksomheten **3473**
1503-3953 Nordic Navigation *changed to* 1571-473X **8954**
1503-4003 *see* 1503-1330 **7213**
1503-4119 Norway. Statistisk Sentralbyraa. Overnattingsstatistikk **8780**
1503-416X Norges Teknisk- Naturvitenskapelige Universitet. Institutt for Datateknikk og Informasjonsvitenskap. I D I - Rapport **2433**
1503-4224 Det Norske Videnskaps-Akademi. Senter for Grunnforskning. Informasjonsblad **4467**
1503-4232 Det Norske Videnskaps-Akademi. Senter for Grunnforskning. Newsletter **4467**
1503-4283 Vaaronnavisa *changed to* 1504-5706 **168**
1503-4364 Norway. Statistisk Sentralbyraa. Strukturstatistikk for Samfersel og Reiseliv **8528**
1503-4380 Notat **7666**
1503-4399 F F I - Fokus **6420**
1503-4402 *see* 1503-4399 **6420**
1503-4445 Norway. Statistisk Sentralbyraa. Innenlandske Transportytelser **8528**
1503-4488 D V D og Hemmekino *changed to* 1890-0291 **8153**
1503-4585 Alt om Haandarbeide **4351**
1503-4593 Palmebladet **807**
1503-4674 Norway. Statistisk Sentralbyraa. Kvartalsvis Investeringsstatistikk - Industri, Bergverksdrift og Kraftforsyning *changed to* 0809-6023 **1256**
1503-4682 Farlig Gods-Info **2226**
1503-4704 Hotell **4390**
1503-4712 Norway. Statistisk Sentralbyraa. Arbeidsundersoekelsen **1256**
1503-4801 Under Utdanning **2922**
1503-4879 Verdensmagasinet X **7192**
1503-4917 Racingavisa *changed to* 1503-8696 **8195**
1503-4925 Norsk Varemerketidende (Online) **6755**
1503-4933 Norsk Patenttidende (Online) **6755**
1503-4992 Programbladet *changed to* 1890-0488 **2392**
1503-5034 Norsk Tidsskrift for Ernaering **6664**
1503-5093 Norges Handelshoeyskole. Institutt for Strategi og Ledelse. Discussion Paper **1782**
1503-5107 Nemi **2204**
1503-514X Tilstanden i Finansmarkedet **1386**
1503-5158 N I N A Fakta **2619**
1503-5220 Vaaler og Svinndal Historielag. Aarbok **4276**
1503-5360 Paidos **6099**
1503-5425 Foretaksnytt *changed to* 1890-1581 **8044**
1503-5433 Egenmeldingen *changed to* 1890-1581 **8044**
1503-5654 Doktor i Nord **4593**
1503-5662 MiRA-Senteret. Temahefte **8875**
1503-5751 Gamlebyen Historielag. Skriftserie **4222**
1503-576X I Tavisen Business *changed to* 0809-9030 **2318**
1503-5808 Norsk Designtidende **6755**
1503-5883 Arbeidsrett **4620**
1503-5891 Market Excellence **1830**
1503-5921 Transport Inside **8515**
1503-5972 Norway. A B M - Utvikling. A B M-Skrift **5036**
1503-6065 Moving Bodies **6993**
1503-6073 V A-Nytt **8835**
1503-6170 Fugler i Aust-Agder **907**
1503-6189 C I O Business Standard Norway *changed to* 1504-064X **1414**
1503-6200 Ukeavisen Ledelse **1908**
1503-6391 Tjenestemannsbladet **1710**
1503-6405 *see* 0801-2482 **4597**
1503-6480 Nordisk Tidsskrift for Menneskerettigheter **7213**
1503-6529 Seniormagasinet *changed to* 1504-324X **8131**
1503-6553 Sykkelmagasinet **8269**
1503-6650 Classification News **8641**
1503-6669 *see* 0333-3205 **8139**
1503-6707 Tidsskrift for Psykisk Helsearbeid **6188**
1503-6782 Tidsskrift for Erstatningsrett **4881**
1503-6944 Fagbladet **7492**
1503-6960 Horeca Storkjoekken, Menu *changed to* 1504-2073 **4388**
1503-6979 Kjoepmann†
1503-6987 Salg og Markedsfoering *changed to* 1890-1360 **1843**
1503-7088 Sexologi **355**
1503-7096 Mandag Morgen Norge **1778**
1503-7258 Baatforeningen **8272**
1503-7304 Kjedebutikken *changed to* 1504-1271 **1963**
1503-7312 Goavddis **4224**
1503-7320 Kjoettsamvirket *changed to* 1504-6524 **142**
1503-7436 Riss (Bergen) **414**
1503-7444 Flymagasinet **56**
1503-7460 Tur-Glede **8769**
1503-7797 Europower Nytt *changed to* 1503-9013 **3135**
1503-7835 D! **8858**
1503-7843 Samfunnssikkerhet **2228**
1503-7878 *see* 1503-7843 **2228**
1503-7959 Credimus **7794**
1503-7991 Melhusbyggen **4244**
1503-8068 H O R N Skriftserie **4095**
1503-8076 *see* 1502-2013 **2823**
1503-8122 C! **3922**
1503-8149 *see* 1503-352X **6882**
1503-819X Auto Motor og Sport **8559**
1503-8211 Oaidnil **5688**
1503-822X *see* 1503-8211 **5688**
1503-8246 Volt **3115**
1503-8254 Oslo School of Architecture. CON-TEXT, Skrift **452**
1503-8262 Samspill *changed to* 1504-6915 **4467**
1503-8270 *see* 0805-1232 **4926**
1503-8289 *see* 0800-7853 **4725**
1503-8297 *see* 0333-0753 **4851**
1503-8319 Innovista†
1503-8343 *see* 1503-0245 **7565**
1503-8386 Utveier **7191**
1503-8408 P C World Norge Ekstra **2493**
1503-8505 Forsvarsforum **6421**
1503-8572 Memento *changed to* 1504-520X **6532**
1503-8572 Memento *changed to* 1504-4645 **4221**
1503-8580 Jordmora **5994**
1503-8599 *see* 0332-7531 **5156**

ISSN

1503-867X *see* 1503-5360 **6099**
1503-8696 Racing **8195**
1503-8718 Prosessindustrien **3216**
1503-8726 *see* 1504-0895 **5785**
1503-8742 *see* 0333-0761 **4851**
1503-8750 Familia (Online) **8039**
1503-8769 Rygge Museum. Tidsskriftserie **4261**
1503-8815 *see* 0332-5598 **1374**
1503-8831 *see* 0029-1676 **1501**
1503-8858 *see* 1502-2749 **1372**
1503-8866 *see* 0807-8521 **1501**
1503-8947 Teknisk Nytt *changed to* 1504-7776 **2457**
1503-8955 Automasjon *changed to* 1504-7776 **2457**
1503-8998 Q Katolsk Ungdom **7813**
1503-9013 Europower **3135**
1503-9056 Sunnmoersposten **3925**
1503-9064 *see* 1503-9056 **3925**
1503-9196 Norges Landbrukshoegskole. Institutt for Tekniske Fag. I M T - Rapport *changed to* Universitetet for Miljoe- og BioVitenskap. Institutt for Matematiske Realfag og Teknologi. I M T- Rapport **7926**
1503-9250 N A F Guide Europe **8739**
1503-9358 Statsnoekkelen (Year) **7470**
1503-9390 Working Papers ISK **5196**
1503-9404 Seniorpolitikk.no **8068**
1503-9412 *see* 1503-9404 **8068**
1503-9439 I N A Fagreport **2614**
1503-9447 Norway. Statistisk Sentralbyraa. Lastebilstatistikk **8528**
1503-9463 Nerven **8057**
1503-948X Digital World **2485**
1503-9498 N G H-Genviten **294**
1503-9501 Miljoeguide *see* 0807-1268 **3489**
1503-9528 TradeWinds Today *see* 0803-9364 **8664**
1503-9536 *see* 1503-2507 **4402**
1503-9544 Nasjonalt Kunnskapssenter for Helsetjenesten. Rapport **4107**
1503-9552 Scandinavian Journal of Forensic Science **5916**
1503-9579 *see* 1503-9552 **5916**
1503-9595 Roest **1168**
1503-9609 Diabetesforum **5889**
1503-9625 *see* 1503-9609 **5889**
1503-9633 Telemarksmagasinet **4273**
1503-9676 Innovate **8426**
1503-9692 Mea Nytt (Print) *changed to* 1504-7466 **3601**
1503-9714 Norges Bank. Staff Memo **1372**
1503-9803 For Velferdsstaten. Skriftserie **8041**
1503-9811 U B A S, Hovedfag/Master **421**
1503-9838 Livsglede *changed to* 1504-789X **4077**
1503-9862 Kirkens Noedhjelp Magasinet **8052**
1503-9927 Hardanger Fartoeyvernsenter. Rapport **8645**
1503-996X *see* 1503-8246 **3115**
1503-9986 Ukeavisa Ny Tid **3925**
1504-0003 *see* 0806-7066 **3110**
1504-0062 Universitetet i Oslo. Norsk Senter for Menneskerettigheter. Research Notes **7218**
1504-0070 *see* 1504-0062 **7218**
1504-0100 F H M (Norway) **6289**
1504-0119 Hytte-Fritid *changed to* 1890-1573 **1013**
1504-0127 Norway. Utlendingsdirektoratet. Tall og Fakta **7288**
1504-0216 Flyktningsregnskapet **7283**
1504-0534 Tungvekter'n **8608**
1504-0577 *see* 0802-7188 **1502**
1504-0623 Fuglevennen **907**
1504-0631 S M B - Data† **8986**
1504-064X C I O Computerworld **1414**
1504-0666 *see* 0800-7713 **987**
1504-0674 Bolig, Hytte og Fritid *changed to* 1504-4483 **982**
1504-0704 Fedayie **4321**
1504-0712 Universitetet i Oslo. Kulturhistoriske Museer. Fornminneseksjonen. Varia *changed to* 1504-3266 **4275**
1504-0755 Universitetet i Bergen. Institutt for Medievitenskap. Publikasjon *changed to* 1504-1697 **8145**
1504-078X Norway. Statistisk Sentralbyraa. Utdanningsbarometeret **2934**
1504-0798 Utrop **3925**
1504-0828 Norges Teknisk-Naturvitenskapelige Universitet. Institutt for Historie og Klassiske Fag. Forum for Kunnskapshistorie. Publikasjon **7893**
1504-0887 N I F U S T E P. Arbeidsnotat *changed to* 1504-1824 **4465**
1504-0895 Ductus **5785**
1504-0917 Kunstkritikk.no **501**
1504-0925 *see* 1504-0917 **501**
1504-0984 The Financial Market in Norway (Year) **1344**
1504-1166 Paa Flukt Aktuelt **7289**
1504-1174 Tromsoe Geophysical Observatory. Reports **6397**
1504-1182 Billy **2179**
1504-1204 Misjonshoegskolen. Ressursserie **7663**
1504-1271 Kjedemagasinet **1963**
1504-1301 Bulk Carrier Update **8640**
1504-1441 N OE F Info **2661**
1504-145X *see* 1504-1441 **2661**
1504-1468 Norsk Sokkel **6781**
1504-1484 Columna **5804**
1504-1530 Bedre Barnehager Skriftserie **2830**
1504-1549 Meteorologisk Institutt. Met.no-Report, Klima **6391**
1504-1573 J K **7652**
1504-1611 Voices **6627**
1504-1697 Universitetet i Bergen. Institutt for Informasjons- og Medievitenskap. Rapport **8145**
1504-1700 Bygdo **3922**
1504-1743 Bli Med Ut! **663**
1504-1751 Universitetet i Oslo. Institutt for Helseledelse og Helseoekonomi. Rapport **4112**
1504-1786 *see* 0801-6003 **7506**
1504-1808 Malegleder *changed to* 1890-2928 **534**
1504-1824 N I F U S T E P. Rapport **4465**
1504-1832 N I F U S T E P. Skriftserie†
1504-1840 Norges Teknisk-Naturvitenskapelige Universitet. Institutt for Sosialt Arbeid og Helsevitenskap. Rapportserie **8059**
1504-1891 Foerste Steg **2858**
1504-1905 Yrke (Oslo, 2004) **2927**
1504-1913 Fortid **4140**
1504-1921 Fett **8897**
1504-1972 Namaste *changed to* 1504-4548 **6648**
1504-1980 E B L Forum **3157**
1504-1999 E B L Forum, Euro-Nytt *see* 1504-1980 **3157**
1504-2006 Ratatosk **5357**
1504-2022 Norske Moebler **4561**
1504-2030 Eksportstatistikk **3613**
1504-2065 Norwegian Continental Shelf **6781**
1504-2073 Horeca **4388**
1504-2103 United Nations Development Programme. Oslo Governance Centre. Update **4943**
1504-2111 *see* 0802-0477 **6800**
1504-2146 B Vpraxis **2144**
1504-2154 Faghefte **1960**
1504-2162 *see* 0807-4763 **1256**
1504-2170 *see* 0078-1916 **1256**
1504-2189 *see* 0550-0400 **8219**
1504-2235 *see* 0809-201X **1256**
1504-2251 *see* 0809-4527 **3613**
1504-226X Laering & Kompetanse†
1504-2316 Norway. Statistisk Sentralbyraa. Sosialhjelp, Barnevern og Familievern **8150**
1504-2324 *see* 1504-2316 **8150**
1504-2340 *see* 1504-1743 **663**
1504-2391 *see* 0550-032X **7313**
1504-2405 Norway. Statistisk Sentralbyraa. Utenrikshandel (Online) **1256**
1504-2502 Woman **8889**
1504-2510 Magasinet Treindustrien **4545**
1504-2529 Container Ship Update **8641**
1504-2537 Universitetet i Oslo. Sogn Senter for Barne- og Ungdomspsykiatri. Monografiserien **6189**
1504-2545 Towards Inclusion **3048**
1504-2553 Kreftforeningen. Rapport **6026**
1504-2561 *see* 0333-3728 **3614**
1504-257X *see* 1504-5404 **184**
1504-2596 *see* 1503-9714 **1372**
1504-2618 Betwixt & Between **330**
1504-2685 Eva
1504-2707 Regionsnytt (Ski) **8064**
1504-2715 Fylkesnytt (Greaaker) *changed to* 1504-2707 **8064**
1504-2723 Norway. Norad. Evalueringsrapport **7255**
1504-2774 Kunsthoegskolen i Oslo. Aarbok **501**
1504-2804 Aeksj'n *changed to* 1504-7415 **2202**
1504-2855 Forum 18 News Service **7206**
1504-2871 *see* 1501-0074 **1161**
1504-288X *see* 0809-2044 **5342**
1504-2898 *see* 0802-7285 **350**
1504-291X *see* 0040-716X **8010**
1504-2928 *see* 0804-0486 **8139**
1504-2936 *see* 0801-1745 **7159**
1504-2944 *see* 0018-263X **4144**
1504-2952 *see* 0040-7194 **7777**
1504-2960 *see* 0332-5024 **6620**
1504-2979 *see* 0029-2176 **7666**
1504-2987 *see* 0029-2052 **2892**
1504-2995 *see* 0901-8050 **2892**
1504-3002 *see* 0023-186X **7658**
1504-3010 *see* 1503-6707 **6188**
1504-3029 *see* 0023-5415 **501**
1504-3037 *see* 0333-1342 **8059**
1504-3045 *see* 0805-083X **1511**
1504-3053 *see* 0800-336X **7160**
1504-3061 *see* 0024-6980 **4725**
1504-307X *see* 1503-6480 **7213**
1504-3088 *see* 1503-5883 **4620**
1504-3096 *see* 0040-7143 **4796**
1504-310X *see* 0333-2810 **4784**
1504-3118 *see* 0028-0887 **7889**
1504-3126 *see* 0022-6971 **4708**
1504-3134 Beta (Online Edition) **1728**
1504-3142 Tidsskrift for Kognitiv Terapi **7412**
1504-3223 Norges Handikapforbund. Oslofjord Vest.Medlemsnytt *changed to* 0809-6457 **8059**
1504-324X Senior **8131**
1504-3258 Universitetet i Oslo. Kulturhistorisk Museum. Skrifter **422**
1504-3266 Universitetet i Oslo. Kulturhistorisk Museum. Fornminneseksjonen. Varia **4275**
1504-3304 Teknologi & Verkstedindustri **3371**
1504-3355 La Ventana **3570**
1504-3363 Budstikken **6414**
1504-338X Budstikken (Haerens Sambands Kameratforening) *changed to* 1504-3363 **6414**
1504-3398 Norway. Olje- og Energidepartementet. Fakta (Nynorsk) **6781**
1504-3401 Studiehefte i Landbrukspolitikk **159**
1504-3428 PasOpp-Rapport **5693**
1504-3436 Fronsbygdin. Aarbok **4222**
1504-3452 Baatfolkets Aarbok **8271**
1504-3460 Universitetet i Bergen. Filosofisk Institutt. Filosofiske Smuler **6959**
1504-3487 Truckers Guide **8678**
1504-3495 Tidsskrift for Eiendomsrett **4905**
1504-3576 Klinisk Sykepleie **5968**
1504-3584 Universitetet for Miljoe- og BioVitenskap. Institutt for Plante- og Miljoevitenskap. Rapport **256**
1504-3606 Saerpublikasjon **3701**
1504-3665 4x4guiden **8614**
1504-3673 Tilsynsinfo (Print) *changed to* 1504-4718 **4969**
1504-369X Popular Science (Bergen) **8435**
1504-3703 Helse i Vest **8044**
1504-3711 *see* 1504-3703 **8044**
1504-372X Tall og Fakta. Kortversjon *changed to* 1890-6192 **6858**
1504-3762 Hoegskolan i Soer-Troendelag. Avdeling for Helse- og Sosialfag og Avdeling for Sykepleie. Hist-A H S/A S P **8044**
1504-3789 Lev Landlig **3923**
1504-3843 Firdaposten. Aarbok **3922**
1504-3878 VestBio **3611**
1504-3908 Baatliv **8272**
1504-3975 Vakre Hjem & Interioer **4551**
1504-4017 Bladet Norsk Transport **8669**
1504-4025 Jeger & Fisker **8320**
1504-4092 Oilinfo News **6785**
1504-4114 Miljoejournalen **3453**
1504-4130 *see* 1503-8068 **4095**
1504-4157 Norske Boligbyggelags Landsforbund. Aarsstatistik (Year) **4436**
1504-4165 Sopp- og Nyttevekster **818**
1504-4181 Dakota Norway **8540**
1504-4203 Normtallsundersoekelsen **7578**
1504-4211 Mandag Morgen Norge. Rapporter *see* 1503-7096 **1778**
1504-4246 Tekstilkunst **522**
1504-4254 N O P E F Aktuelt *changed to* 1890-4815 **4596**
1504-4262 Galdu Cala **7207**
1504-4270 *see* 1504-4262 **7207**
1504-4289 *see* 1504-4262 **7207**
1504-4297 Parat **4600**
1504-4327 N A F K A M. Skriftserie **313**
1504-4343 Acem-Magasinet **6643**
1504-4351 Norsk-Svensk Traverstambok for Kaldblodshester **8295**
1504-436X Nytt Paradigme **7160**
1504-4386 Ett Trykk **6650**
1504-4408 Business Q4 **1881**
1504-4483 Boligfakta **982**
1504-4548 Yoga - Nytt **6648**
1504-4556 NorDiNa **7893**
1504-4564 Naturfag **3074**
1504-4610 Norway. Norad. Study **8123**
1504-4645 Fortidsvern **4221**
1504-4696 Byggfagbladet **4591**
1504-470X *see* 0332-7221 **988**
1504-4718 Tilsynsinfo (Online) **4969**
1504-4750 Madagaskar Forum **4176**
1504-4769 *see* 1504-4750 **4176**
1504-4777 Roedt! **7180**
1504-4785 *see* 1504-4777 **7180**
1504-4831 Seminar.net **2911**
1504-4858 Moebel & Interioer **4560**
1504-4882 *see* 0804-7545 **7855**
1504-4920 Norsk Bufe. Aarsskrift **295**
1504-4939 Universitetet i Stavanger. Notater **3225**
1504-4971 Skadedyr **3750**
1504-498X Karriere **6700**
1504-4998 Totalregnskap for Reindriftsnaeringen **1905**
1504-5021 Nordisk Musikkpedagogisk Forskning **6600**
1504-503X Norges Teknisk-Naturvitenskapelige Universietet. Vitenskapsmuseeet. Seksjon for Naturhistorie. Zoologisk Notat **958**
1504-5048 Norges Forskningsraad. HOEYKOM-Rapport **2502**
1504-5056 Norway. Vegdirektoratet. Vegteknisk Avdeling. Publikasjon *changed to* 1504-5064 **3279**
1504-5064 Norway. Vegdirektoratet. Teknologiavdelingen. Publikasjon **3279**
1504-5072 Utviklingen i Norsk Kosthold **6670**
1504-5129 *see* 0078-1185 **1372**
1504-5137 *see* 0800-8507 **1372**
1504-5145 Aarbok om Menneskerettigheter i Norge (Year) **7201**
1504-5153 *see* 1504-5145 **7201**
1504-5161 Flomsonekart **8823**
1504-517X Europa *changed to* 1890-5668 **4936**
1504-5188 Ren Idrett **8196**
1504-520X Museumsnytt **6532**
1504-5226 S OE F Rapport **1170**
1504-5242 Nytt fra U K F *changed to* 1504-5250 **8024**
1504-5250 Afrodite **8024**
1504-5277 Spinalkanalen *changed to* 1504-1484 **5804**
1504-5307 Dictum **5213**
1504-5323 Cosmopolitan (Oslo) **8857**
1504-5374 Vett **4944**
1504-5404 Norway. Statistisk Sentralbyraa. Boendenes Inntekt og Formue (Oslo, 2001) **184**
1504-5471 *see* 1504-0216 **7283**
1504-551X Ledernett.no **1772**
1504-5528 Aquanews **3585**
1504-5536 Hoegskolan i Soer-Troendelag. Avdeling for Mat- og Medisinsk Teknologi. HiST/AMMT-Notat **3923**
1504-5544 Estetisk Forum **2980**
1504-5560 Asias Millioner **7746**
1504-5595 Reiki **314**
1504-5625 *see* 0800-4110 **1502**
1504-5641 Strandsitteren **4268**
1504-5676 Funksjonaeren-Kontur *changed to* Negotia **4599**
1504-5684 Museo di Alta. Opuscoli *see* 0805-9128 **4197**
1504-5706 Vaaronnavisa for Nord-Norge **168**
1504-5749 G E C H S Report **3432**
1504-579X Monitor **2334**
1504-5943 Vellum **4276**
1504-5994 *see* 1504-579X **2334**
1504-6001 Jaroey Skattelovsamling **1931**
1504-601X Lederne (Oslo) **1695**
1504-6028 Trevennen **3752**
1504-615X Vi Menn Bat **8284**
1504-6184 Automatisering & Industridata **2458**
1504-6222 Rapport fra Skogforskningen *changed to* 1890-1662 **3691**
1504-6311 *see* 0800-2088 **6672**
1504-6338 *see* 1504-5749 **3432**
1504-6346 Seher.no *see* 0809-4519 **3924**
1504-6370 Biofokus-Rapport **657**
1504-6427 Marg **3923**
1504-6494 Hoeyremagasinet **7140**
1504-6524 Norturamagasinet **142**
1504-6532 Defence and Security Studies **2226**
1504-6575 *see* 0332-7590 **4707**
1504-6591 Kultmag **8117**
1504-6605 Norsk Tidsskrift for Misjonsvitenskap **7666**
1504-6729 *see* 1504-8217 **1663**
1504-6753 Oslo Files on Defence and Security **2228**
1504-6796 FriProg-Magasinet **2590**
1504-680X *see* 1504-6796 **2590**
1504-6869 Arkeologiske Rapporter **380**

1504-6893 FoU i Praksis **2858**
1504-6907 University of Oslo. ARENA - Centre for European Studies. RECON Online Working Paper **7191**
1504-6915 Nytt om E U-Forskningen **4467**
1504-6923 Amnestymagasinet **7221**
1504-6931 Forvaltning, Drift, Vedlikehold **1746**
1504-694X Vitenskapskomiteen for Mattrygghet. Rapport **8077**
1504-6958 S I N T E F Byggforsk. Prosjektrapport **1034**
1504-6966 Resursoversikt fra Skog og Landskap **3700**
1504-7180 *see* 1890-2707 **6786**
1504-7342 The Scorpion Files **963**
1504-7415 Miljoeagent-Rapporten **2202**
1504-7431 Liberal **7151**
1504-744X *see* 1504-7431 **7151**
1504-7466 Mea (Print) **3601**
1504-7512 Gro **2191**
1504-7547 *see* 1890-3517 **1502**
1504-7563 Global Knowledge **2982**
1504-758X H L-Senteret. Temahefte **4225**
1504-7598 *see* 1890-3541 **1372**
1504-7601 Knutepunkt **8649**
1504-7628 Arkitektur N **433**
1504-7776 Amnytt Magazine **2457**
1504-7814 Ikon **3923**
1504-7822 Og Bedre Skal Det Bli! **8060**
1504-789X Armer & Bein **4077**
1504-7903 Mur + Betong **450**
1504-7989 Soekelys paa Arbeidslivet *see* 1504-8004 **1707**
1504-7997 *see* 0804-6832 **8149**
1504-8004 Soekelys paa Arbeidslivet **1707**
1504-8136 Klima **6359**
1504-8152 *see* 0807-3139 **8012**
1504-8217 Arbeid og Velferd **1663**
1504-8225 F U G E - Funksjonell Genomforskning *changed to* 1504-8241 **741**
1504-8241 Nytt fra F U G E **741**
1504-825X *see* 1504-8241 **741**
1504-8276 Nytt fra Eureka **8433**
1504-8284 Nytt fra Eureka *see* 1504-8276 **8433**
1504-8446 International Journal of Social and Management Sciences **7974**
1504-8462 100 Noekkeltal for Helse- og Sosialsektoren **8084**
1504-8470 Norges Bank. Monetary Policy Report **1502**
1504-8497 *see* 1504-8470 **1502**
1504-9272 University of Agder. Doctoral Dissertations **8012**
1504-9310 S A M-U N I F O B Rapport **3491**
1504-937X Golfposten **8233**
1504-9558 Fishfarming Xpert **3593**
1504-9922 Acta Didaktica Norge **2823**
1505-0297 Electronic Journal of Polish Agricultural Universities **7852**
1505-0440 W U G **6483**
1505-0505 Komentarze do Obowiazujacych Aktow Prawnych *see* 1427-3594 **4710**
1505-0572 Nowy Swiat Ciszy *changed to* 1509-5436 **4076**
1505-0580 Archives of Perinatal Medicine **5986**
1505-0610 Archives of Perinatal Medicine. Supplement *see* 1505-0580 **5986**
1505-0882 Voyage **8773**
1505-1013 Technical University of Lodz. Scientific Bulletin. Physics **7042**
1505-1099 Sredzki Kwartalnik Kulturalny **5240**
1505-1161 Rubikon **7998**
1505-1196 Lotnictwo Wojskowe *changed to* 1732-5323 **65**
1505-1250 Molecular Physics Reports **7068**
1505-1269 Ceramika. Materialy Ogniotrwale *changed to* 1644-3470 **2044**
1505-1676 Pobocza **5352**
1505-1773 Polish Journal of Veterinary Sciences **8805**
1505-1943 Gazeta Przedsiebiorczych **1113**
1505-1951 Krynytsya **3546**
1505-2095 Politechnika Lodzka. Zeszyty Naukowe. Inzynieria Chemiczna i Procesowa **3252**
1505-2192 Athenaeum **5207**
1505-2249 Polish Journal of Ecology **3460**
1505-232X Oceanological Studies *changed to* 1730-413X **2815**
1505-2575 A T R Express **209**
1505-2753 Okulistyka **6047**
1505-277X Jacwiez **5221**
1505-3016 Dom dla Kowalskich **1005**
1505-3261 Polski Cement *changed to* 1644-745X **984**
1505-3601 Podroze **8748**
1505-3695 Inzynieria i Ochrona Srodowiska **3443**
1505-3768 Medycyna Rodzinna **5678**
1505-3954 Hydraulika i Pneumatyka **3362**
1505-4454 Antyfon **7703**
1505-456X Computer World Top 200 **2413**
1505-4578 She **8848**
1505-4594 Dialogikon **6914**
1505-4667 Natural Sciences *changed to* 1643-9953 **7898**
1505-4675 Technical Sciences **8441**
1505-4683 Economic Sciences **1101**
1505-5337 *see* 1985-4668 **6660**
1505-6155 Kwartalnik Wrzesinski **5223**
1505-6562 C K M **6287**
1505-6732 Onkologia Polska **6031**
1505-6783 Poland. Glowny Urzad Statystyczny. Ceny w Gospodarce Narodowej **1258**
1505-6988 Mieszkaj **4546**
1505-7038 Maszyny, Technologie, Materialy **3209**
1505-7216 Annals of Agricultural Sciences. Series E. Plant Protection **218**
1505-7429 Wiadomosci Psychiatryczne **6189**
1505-7453 Bukiety **3755**
1505-7895 *see* 0033-2518 **634**
1505-8328 Gutenberg **7323**
1505-8808 Terazniejszosc, Czlowiek, Edukacja **2919**
1505-9057 Acta Universitatis Lodziensis: Folia Litteraria Polonica **5249**
1505-9065 Acta Universitatis Lodziensis: Folia Litteraria Romanica **5249**
1505-9294 Vita **6999**
1505-9405 Telekomunikacja Cyfrowa **2373**
1505-943X Current Medical Literature. Urologia†
1505-9448 Current Medical Literature. Okulistyka†
1505-9634 Pastores **7812**
1506-0403 Dobre Rady. Horoskop **566**
1506-0632 Poland. Glowny Urzad Statystyczny. Rocznik Statystyczny Rzeczypospolitej Polskiej **8394**
1506-090X Urzad Regulacji Energetyki. Biuletyn **3149**
1506-1426 Kurier Dembudu **1424**
1506-168X Folia Universitatis Agriculturae Stetinensis. Piscaria **3595**
1506-1698 Folia Universitatis Agriculturae Stetinensis. Zootechnica **287**
1506-1817 Czasopismo Prawa Karnego i Nauk Penalnych **4888**
1506-1949 Instytut Odlewnictwa. Biuletyn *changed to* 1730-2250 **6328**
1506-1965 Folia Universitatis Agriculturae Stetinensis. Oeconomica **7964**
1506-1973 Folia Universitatis Agriculturae Stetinesis. Agricultura **231**
1506-221X Viva! Wydanie Specjalne *see* 1426-9554 **3930**
1506-2546 Zabawy i Marzenia z Barbie **2224**
1506-2899 Nieruchomosci **7602**
1506-3267 Ladny Dom **448**
1506-3682 Nowa Okolica Poetow **5428**
1506-4026 Komputer Swiat **2430**
1506-4077 Medycyna Intensywna i Ratunkowa **6067**
1506-4832 Unia & Polska **7270**
1506-4883 The Warsaw Voice I S O Almanac (Year) **2033**
1506-4891 The Warsaw Voice Tourism Guide **8773**
1506-4956 *see* 1427-3594 **4710**
1506-5693 Current Medical Literature. Leczenie Zywieniowe†
1506-5774 Informator I T **1418**
1506-5855 Nieruchomosci Stoleczne **7602**
1506-588X Uniwersytet Opolski. Biblioteka Glowna. Rocznik **5054**
1506-5901 Tom i Jerry Czyli Kot i Mysz *changed to* 1897-3264 **2217**
1506-5928 Archivolta **432**
1506-6398 Sport (Warsaw) **8203**
1506-6428 Kino Domowe **2402**
1506-6444 Dom (Warsaw, 1994) **1005**
1506-7629 Folia Malacologica **944**
1506-7637 Optimum **1157**
1506-7904 Poland. Glowny Urzad Statystyczny. Pracujacy w Gospodarce Narodowej **1259**
1506-8161 Current Medical Literature. Neurologia†
1506-8331 Obyczaje **3930**
1506-915X Akademia Rolnicza im. Hugona Kollataja w Krakowie. Zeszyty Naukowe. Seria: Hodowla i Biologia Zwierzat†
1506-9168 Akademia Rolnicza im. Hugona Kollataja w Krakowie. Zeszyty Naukowe. Seria: Rolnictwo Swiatowe†
1506-9184 Podatki i Prawo Gospodarcze Unii Europejskiej **4758**
1506-9427 Vegetable Crops Research Bulletin **257**
1506-9575 Informator Uslug Budowlanych **1014**
1506-9680 Nuclear Medicine Review **6204**
1506-9729 Studia Judaica **4269**
1506-9796 Claudia Rodzice **2149**
1507-0042 Wierntnictwo, Nafta, Gaz **6797**
1507-0360 Journal of Applied Computer Science **2428**
1507-0840 Poster Motomagazyn **8599**
1507-1308 Rejs **8281**
1507-1367 Reports on Practical Oncology and Radiotherapy **6033**
1507-174X Media & Marketing Polska **2332**
1507-2789 Budujemy Dom **984**
1507-3149 Polska Gospodarka **1511**
1507-3157 Polish Economic Outlook **1511**
1507-3939 Ladnie Mieszkac **4545**
1507-4137 Foto Pozytyw **6967**
1507-4145 Folia Cardiologica *changed to* 1897-5593 **5780**
1507-4161 Ogrody, Ogrodki, Zielence **3746**
1507-5524 Chirurgia Polska **6239**
1507-5532 Pediatria Wspolczesna **6099**
1507-5540 Polski Przeglad Kardiologiczny **5797**
1507-5966 National Geographic Polska **4021**
1507-6164 Case Reports & Clinical Practice Review *changed to* 1941-5923 **5571**
1507-6407 Politechnika Poznanska. Zeszyty Naukowe. Architektura i Urbanistyka **453**
1507-6563 Edukacja Ustawiczna Doroslych **2940**
1507-7063 Jan Pawel II Kolekcja†
1507-7519 Current Medical Literature. Onkologia†
1507-7527 Current Medical Literature. Pediatria†
1507-7535 Current Medical Literature. Psychiatria†
1507-7640 P C World Komputer Extra *see* 1232-3004 **2581**
1507-8078 Current Medical Literature. Ginekologia i Poloznictwo†
1507-8558 P C World Komputer Special *see* 1232-3004 **2581**
1507-9600 Poland. Glowny Urzad Statystyczny. Uzytkowanie Gruntow, Powierzchnia Zasiewow i Poglowie Zwierzat Gospodarskich **185**
1507-9716 Current Medical Literature. Alergologia†
1507-9791 Polish Geological Institute. Special Papers **2762**
1508-0447 Arkadia **5207**
1508-0560 Rachunkowosc. Poradnik Praktyczny **1299**
1508-1109 Acta Chiropterologica **929**
1508-1354 Studia Choreologica **2688**
1508-1834 Patos **6938**
1508-1850 Swiat Medycyny i Farmacji **6882**
1508-2083 M jak Mieszkanie **4545**
1508-2121 Polska Medycyna Rodzinna *changed to* 1734-3402 **5613**
1508-2334 Krakow In Your Pocket **8728**
1508-2806 Computer Science **2542**
1508-4221 Current Medical Literature. Anestezjologia†
1508-4280 Komputer Swiat Biblioteczka **2430**
1508-4868 *see* 1505-0580 **5986**
1508-5104 Besida **3522**
1508-5287 Czlowiek i Ruch *changed to* 1732-3991 **6989**
1508-5791 *see* 0029-5922 **3173**
1508-5813 Christianitas **7792**
1508-6143 Poradnik Plantatora Buraka Cukrowego **248**
1508-6593 Gazeta Szkolna **2859**
1508-681X Current Medical Literature. Dermatologia *changed to* 1895-2348
1508-6976 Zadra **8892**
1508-7719 Elpis **7704**
1508-8081 Urzadzamy z Muratorem **4551**
1508-8618 Linux Plus Extra! *see* 1427-5562 **2594**
1508-9746 Twoj Magazyn Medyczny **6883**
1508-9851 Upper Silesian Museum. Monographs **6539**
1509-0108 Undergrunt **5243**
1509-0213 P C World Komputer na Gwiazdke *see* 1232-3004 **2581**
1509-0558 Click! **2475**
1509-1066 Przez Czern **5235**
1509-1317 Czestochowski Magazyn Numizmatyczny **6650**
1509-1503 Burda Special. Bluzki, Spodnie, Spodnice **2252**
1509-1600 Neuroskop **5685**
1509-1619 Acta Neophilologica **5090**
1509-1732 Architekt (Warsaw) **431**
1509-2046 Archives of Psychiatry and Psychotherapy **6124**
1509-2178 Uniwersytet Opolski. Zeszyty Naukowe. Prace Germanistyczne **5394**
1509-2305 Diagnostyka Laboratoryjna **5605**
1509-3018 Uniwersytet Warminsko-Mazurski w Olsztynie. Rozprawy i Monografie **7927**
1509-3077 Stosunki Miedzynarodowe (Warsaw, 1999) **7266**
1509-3298 Twist **2218**
1509-3360 Stronica Snieznicka **5240**
1509-3492 Ortopedia, Traumatologia, Rehabilitacja **6070**
1509-409X Acta of Bioengineering and Biomechanics **746**
1509-412X Rzeczy Teatralne **8477**
1509-4251 Kontaktologia i Optyka Okulistyczna **6045**
1509-4308 Antena Krzyku **6545**
1509-4537 *see* 0001-7051 **930**
1509-4553 Journal of Telecommunications and Information Technology **2330**
1509-4987 Ogolnopolski Klub Milosnikow Opery Trubadur. Biuletyn *changed to* 1642-3399 **6624**
1509-5304 Uniwersytet Warminsko-Mazurski. Prace Jezykoznawcze **5192**
1509-5436 Swiat Ciszy **4076**
1509-572X *see* 1641-4640 **6141**
1509-5738 *see* 1232-7174 **5940**
1509-5754 *see* 0024-0745 **5661**
1509-5770 *see* 0587-4254 **7003**
1509-6033 Dobre Rady. Kwiaty w Domu **3728**
1509-6378 Labuz **5223**
1509-6602 Prawo Pracy i Prawo Socjalne. Przeglad Orzecznictwa **1703**
1509-6653 Current Medical Literature. Gastroenterologia†
1509-6858 Dobre Rady. Fryzury **587**
1509-6866 Burda. Szycie Krok po Kroku **2252**
1509-6874 Auto Testy **8560**
1509-6882 Digit **2485**
1509-7013 Politechnika Lodzka. Zeszyty Naukowe. Chemia Spozywcza i Biotechnologia **2129**
1509-7021 Moj Piekny Ogrod Extra **3743**
1509-7269 .net†
1509-7935 Ksiezniczka **2198**
1509-8117 Polish Journal of Chemical Technology **2076**
1509-8680 Current Medical Literature. Geriatria†
1509-8699 Postepy Fitoterapii **6876**
1509-8710 Windsurfing **8342**
1509-877X Kwartalnik Prawa Podatkowego **1932**
1509-8834 Shape **8848**
1509-9156 Uniwersytet Jagiellonski. Instytut Botaniki. Prace Botaniczne **821**
1509-9407 Discussiones Mathematicae. Differential Inclusions, Control and Optimization **5483**
1509-9415 Discussiones Mathematicae. General Algebra and Applications **5483**
1509-9423 Discussiones Mathematicae. Probability and Statistics **5483**
1509-9628 Fotografia **6968**
1509-9849 B.E.S.T. **2273**
1509-9857 B.E.S.T. Plus *see* 1509-9849 **2273**
1509-9873 Echa Przeszlosci **4216**
1510-0804 Relevamientos de Biodiversidad **3462**
1510-0839 Agrociencia **87**
1510-091X Canopus **573**
1510-0960 Revista Uruguaya de Derecho Internacional Privado **4939**
1510-1061 Todovida **315**
1510-1835 Lazos **2290**
1510-2718 Archivos del Instituto de Neurologia **6124**
1510-3218 Sociedad Uruguaya de Egiptologia. Revista **416**
1510-3625 Infopesca Internacional **3597**
1510-3749 Diario Oficial de la Republica Oriental del Uruguay **4658**
1510-4427 Revista de Tecnica Forense **5916**
1510-5148 Propuesta **609**
1510-5172 Revista de Derecho **4770**
1510-6888 Electromagazine **3304**
1510-7353 Museo Nacional de Historia Natural y Antropologia. Publicacion Extra **6530**
1510-7701 Revista Uruguaya de Epilepsia **6182**
1510-8031 Universidad de la Republica. Estadisticas Basicas **8413**
1510-804X *see* 1510-8031 **8413**
1511-0095 Day & Night **3906**
1511-0117 Kuntum **2199**
1511-0125 Flavours **4358**
1511-0133 Galaxie **3907**
1511-1768 Journal of Rubber Research **7825**
1511-2780 Journal of Oil Palm Research **128**
1511-3248 F H M (Malaysia) **6289**
1511-3388 Malaysia. Department of Statistics. Framework for the Development of Environment Statistics (F D E S) in Malaysia **3480**
1511-3396 Malaysia. Department of Statistics. Compendium of Environment Statistics, Malaysia **3480**
1511-3701 Pertanika Journal of Science and Technology **7897**
1511-404X P C World Malaysia **2581**
1511-5631 Eh! **8859**
1511-564X NuYou **8878**

ISSN

DIRECTORY 2010 1520-1872 9667

1517-3011 Annual Review of Biomedical Sciences (Print) *changed to* 1806-8774 **5576**
1517-3151 Revista Brasileira de Engenharia Biomedica **5704**
1517-3267 Sociedade Brasileira de Agroinformatica **157**
1517-3348 Historia & Estorias das Palavras **5125**
1517-3585 CD-ROM Facil **2575**
1517-3747 Embrapa Gado de Corte. Documentos **286**
1517-3801 Datagramazero **5005**
1517-4115 Revista Brasileira de Estudos Urbanos e Regionais **456**
1517-4522 Sociologias **8136**
1517-4840 Charuto et Cia **8485**
1517-526X Embrapa Florestas. Documentos **3687**
1517-5308 Jornal Brasileiro de Fonoaudiologia **6081**
1517-5316 Pulsional Revista de Psicanalise **7402**
1517-5359 Nattereria **910**
1517-5545 Revista Brasileira de Terapia Comportamental e Cognitiva **5704**
1517-5693 Jornal Brasileiro de Reproducao Assistida **734**
1517-5863 Fides Reformata **7758**
1517-588X *see* 0100-381X
1517-5901 *see* 0104-8015 **1703**
1517-5928 Textos sobre Envelhecimento **4057**
1517-6088 Intersecoes **7975**
1517-610X Academica **1722**
1517-6290 Revista de Direito Privado **4841**
1517-6363 Revista Ceciliana **4472**
1517-6398 Pesquisa Agropecuaria Tropical **146**
1517-6770 Revista Brasileira de Zoociencias **961**
1517-6851 Revista Direito Mackenzie **4772**
1517-6878 Brazilian Journal of Urology *changed to* 1677-5538 **6269**
1517-6916 Caos **7953**
1517-6932 Endocrinologia e Diabetes Clinica e Experimental **5891**
1517-6975 Convenit Internacional **5108**
1517-7017 Opus **6602**
1517-7076 Materia (Rio de Janeiro) **3352**
1517-7130 Espaco para a Saude **7516**
1517-7246 Carta de Conjuntura **1446**
1517-7262 Carta de Conjuntura F E E **1446**
1517-7599 Per Musi **6604**
1517-7807 Itaici Revista de Espiritualidade Inaciana **7801**
1517-7823 Epistemologiques **6916**
1517-784X Archives of Veterinary Science **8793**
1517-7874 G E L N E. Revista **5121**
1517-7912 Administracao On Line **1723**
1517-798X Piadas Coloridas **4982**
1517-8048 Revista Tecnologica **8437**
1517-8382 Brazilian Journal of Microbiology **882**
1517-8595 Revista Brasileira de Produtos Agroindustriais **151**
1517-8668 Revista Brasileira de Analise Transacional **7403**
1517-8692 Revista Brasileira de Medicina do Esporte **6232**
1517-8854 Edutran 2000 **8495**
1517-8900 Faces **1744**
1517-8935 Cavalos de Raca *changed to* Cavalos de Raca e Esporte **8289**
1517-9443 Revista Brasileira de Herbicidas (Online) **250**
1517-9664 Biosaude **661**
1517-9702 Educacao e Pesquisa **2845**
1517-9869 Educacao (Rio Claro) **2845**
1517-9877 Brasil Alimentos **3628**
1518-0158 Estudos de Literatura Brasileira Contemporanea **5291**
1518-0212 *see* 0009-0905 **280**
1518-0352 Revista Ciencias Exactas e Naturais **7903**
1518-0360 Ambito Juridico **4614**
1518-0557 *see* 1517-5693 **734**
1518-0581 Associacao Brasileira de Estudos Irlandeses. Journal **5257**
1518-1219 Meridiano 47 **7252**
1518-1243 Iniciacao Cientifica CESUMAR **7866**
1518-1359 Mathesis **2885**
1518-1561 Revista www.com.br **2566**
1518-1634 Holos **3269**
1518-1812 B I S **5582**
1518-1944 Revista Eletronica de Enfermagem **5980**
1518-2355 Revista Brasileira de Saude da Familia **7538**
1518-2630 A B E M. Revista **6541**
1518-2703 Revista de Direito Bancario e do Mercado de Capitais **4771**
1518-2711 Revista Tributaria e de Financas Publicas **4773**
1518-272X Revista de Direito Constitucional e Internacional **4852**
1518-2797 Ciencia Animal Brasileira **284**
1518-2819 Associacao Brasileira de Radiologia Odontologica. Revista **5835**
1518-2924 Encontros Bibli **5008**
1518-2932 Economia & Energia **1098**
1518-3327 Arquivos Brasileiros de Psiquiatria, Neurologia e Medicina Legal **6124**
1518-3483 Revista Dialogo Educacional **2906**
1518-3564 Associacao Brasileira de Direito Tributario. Revista **4622**
1518-367X Linhas **2883**
1518-3963 Bike Action **8255**
1518-4684 Revista de Ciencias Humanas (Federico Westphalen) **2905**
1518-4919 Textura **2919**
1518-5192 Visao Academica **6885**
1518-5303 Boletim de Iniciacao Cientifica em Psicologia **7341**
1518-5532 A N G R A D Revista **1722**
1518-5540 Revista Technologia **8437**
1518-5648 Olhar de Professor **3075**
1518-5923 Psicologia **7392**
1518-594X Revista IMES. Direito **4772**
1518-6091 O Mundo da Usinagem **1054**
1518-6113 Revista Fronteiras **2337**
1518-6148 Revista Mal-Estar e Subjetividade **7404**
1518-6385 Edubase **2845**
1518-6393 Teoria e Pratica na Engenharia Civil **3285**
1518-6490 Embrapa Trigo. Circular Tecnica Online **229**
1518-6520 Analecta **2826**
1518-658X Conta Mais **3803**
1518-6660 Politica Externa **7260**
1518-6776 Revista de Administracao Mackenzie (Print)† **8985**
1518-7012 Interacoes (Campo Grande) **7973**
1518-7322 Cadernos de Pos-Graduacao em Administracao de Empresas **1732**
1518-7470 Revista Mackenzie de Engenharia e Computacao **3218**
1518-7586 Centro de Ciencias Agrarias. Anuario **100**
1518-7632 Linguagem em (Dis)curso **5145**
1518-7853 Crop Breeding and Applied Biotechnology **762**
1518-8191 Sociedade Brasileira de Biomecanica **3395**
1518-8353 *see* 0100-1965 **5002**
1518-8647 Passos *see* 1128-9333 **7690**
1518-8698 Revista Brasileira de Ortopedia Pediatrica **6072**
1518-8744 C E N D O T E C Dossier **8417**
1518-8787 *see* 0034-8910 **7539**
1518-8795 *see* 1518-9384 **7868**
1518-904X Cadernos de Pos-Graduacao em Engenharia Eletrica **3297**
1518-9058 Cadernos de Pos-Graduacao em Comunicacao e Letras **5268**
1518-9384 Investigacoes em Ensino de Ciencias **7868**
1518-9724 Hermeneutica **7647**
1518-9791 Colofao **5276**
1519-0099 Educere **2852**
1519-0129 Gazeta Mercantil (International Edition) **1113**
1519-0307 Cadernos de Pos-Graduacao em Disturbios do Desenvolvimento **6129**
1519-0501 Pesquisa Brasileira em Odontopediatria e Clinica Integrada **5861**
1519-0617 Ciberlegenda **2315**
1519-0862 Expedicao Eco Turismo Especial **8702**
1519-1125 Scientia Agraria **155**
1519-1397 Phyllomedusa **960**
1519-1540 Revista Brasileira de Geomorfologia **2715**
1519-1567 Rap Brasil Especial **514**
1519-1974 Revista de Ciencias Humanas (Vicosa) **7996**
1519-1982 Biologia Geral e Experimental **657**
1519-2407 Anuario de Jornalismo **1663**
1519-2512 Cinergis **6984**
1519-3268 Viaje Mais por Menos **8772**
1519-3403 Jornal Brasileiro de Dependencias Quimicas **2695**
1519-3527 Ultra Jovem **2219**
1519-3810 Boletim dos Procuradores da Republica **4630**
1519-3829 Revista Brasileira de Saude Materno Infantil **2167**
1519-3993 P U C - Campinas. Revista de Educacao **2894**
1519-4108 Revista Brasindoor **3463**
1519-4442 Stomatos **5866**
1519-5228 Revista de Biologia e Ciencias de la Terra **700**
1519-5287 Evidencia **764**
1519-5538 Campos **332**
1519-566X Neotropical Entomology **855**
1519-5708 Geo.br **2735**
1519-5716 Geo.br (English Edition) *see* 1519-5708 **2735**
1519-5899 Espaco Juridico **4667**
1519-5902 Revista Brasileira de Historia de Educacao **2905**
1519-6089 Civitas **7955**
1519-6186 Espaco Academico **4451**
1519-6984 Brazilian Journal of Biology **663**
1519-7077 Revista Contabilidade & Financas **1167**
1519-7522 Revista Brasileira de Hipertensao **5798**
1519-7530 Revista Brasileira de Paleontologia **6730**
1519-7654 Com Ciencia **4573**
1519-7727 Oculum Ensaios **452**
1519-776X Cadernos de Pos-Graduacao em Educacao, Arte e Historia da Cultura **4446**
1519-8227 Contrapontos **2839**
1519-8421 *see* 1519-8634 **3437**
1519-8464 Pensar **4757**
1519-8499 Revista do DVD **2403**
1519-8529 Colabor@ **2837**
1519-8634 Holos Environment **3437**
1519-874X U S P. Geologia. Serie Cientifica **2771**
1519-888X International Journal of Ornithology *changed to* 1676-6180 **687**
1519-9053 Brathair **5265**
1519-9088 Fitness & Performance Journal **6986**
1519-9185 P C Brasil **2579**
1519-9339 Politeia **4156**
1519-9452 Tellus **358**
1519-955X Revista Brasileira de Historia da Matematica **5529**
1519-9657 Revista Mackenzie **5237**
1519-9681 C L E e-prints **6909**
1519-9843 Historia & Educacao Matematica **5491**
1519-9940 Revista Brasileira de Saude e Producao Animal **961**
1520-0124 Doing Business in Bahrain **1561**
1520-0175 The Fritz **6568**
1520-0191 Forest Chemicals Review **6733**
1520-0221 Documentary Credit World **1092**
1520-0256 Econoguide: Las Vegas, Reno, Laughlin, Lake Tahoe *changed to* 1544-8436 **8700**
1520-0272 Catholic Campaign for America. Campaign Update **7788**
1520-0310 What Helen Heard **4380**
1520-0345 Black Book. Official Motorcycle Value Guide *changed to* 1935-7028 **1975**
1520-0361 Journal of Retirement Planning **1769**
1520-037X Preventive Cardiology **5798**
1520-0388 Cruising Rider†
1520-0396 Snowboarding Business
1520-040X National E-mail and Fax Directory **2018**
1520-0426 *see* 0739-0572 **6358**
1520-0434 *see* 0882-8156 **6398**
1520-0442 *see* 0894-8755 **6358**
1520-0469 *see* 0022-4928 **6359**
1520-0477 *see* 0003-0007 **6346**
1520-0485 *see* 0022-3670 **2810**
1520-0493 *see* 0027-0644 **6391**
1520-0558 Directory of Chemical Producers - Europe **2060**
1520-0639 Conservation Voices *changed to* 0022-4561 **2616**
1520-0663 Country Review. Vanuatu **1471**
1520-0671 Country Review. Vietnam **1471**
1520-0698 Country Review. Yemen **1471**
1520-0701 Country Review. Zambia **1471**
1520-071X Country Review. Zimbabwe **1471**
1520-0736 Country Review. Swaziland **1470**
1520-0744 Country Review. Seychelles **1469**
1520-0752 Country Review. Lesotho **1467**
1520-0760 Country Review. Liberia **1467**
1520-0779 Country Review. Libya **1468**
1520-0787 Country Review. Liechtenstein **1468**
1520-0795 Country Review. Lithuania **1468**
1520-0809 Country Review. Luxembourg **1468**
1520-0817 Country Review. Macedonia **1468**
1520-0825 Country Review. Madagascar **1468**
1520-0833 Country Review. Malawi **1468**
1520-0841 Country Review. Malaysia **1468**
1520-085X Country Review. Maldives **1468**
1520-0868 Country Review. Mali **1468**
1520-0876 Country Review. Malta **1468**
1520-0884 Country Review. Venezuela **1471**
1520-0892 Country Review. Marshall Islands **1468**
1520-0906 Country Review. Mauritania **1468**
1520-0914 Country Review. Mauritius **1468**
1520-0922 Country Review. Mexico **1468**
1520-0930 Country Review. Morocco **1468**
1520-0949 Country Review. Micronesia **1468**
1520-0957 Country Review. Moldova **1468**
1520-0965 Country Review. Mongolia **1468**
1520-0973 Country Review. Monaco **1468**
1520-0981 Country Review. Mozambique **1468**
1520-099X Country Review. Myanmar **1468**
1520-1007 Country Review. Namibia **1468**
1520-1015 Country Review. Nauru **1468**
1520-1023 Country Review. Nepal **1468**
1520-104X Country Review. Netherlands **1468**
1520-1058 Country Review. New Zealand **1468**
1520-1066 Country Review. Nicaragua **1468**
1520-1074 Country Review. Niger **1468**
1520-1082 Country Review. Nigeria **1469**
1520-1090 Country Review. Norway **1469**
1520-1104 Country Review. Oman **1469**
1520-1112 Country Review. Palau **1469**
1520-1120 Country Review. Panama **1469**
1520-1139 Country Review. Papua New Guinea **1469**
1520-1147 Country Review. Paraguay **1469**
1520-1155 Country Review. Peru **1469**
1520-1163 Country Review. Philippines **1469**
1520-1171 Country Review. Poland **1469**
1520-118X Country Review. Portugal **1469**
1520-1198 Country Review. Qatar **1469**
1520-1201 Country Review. Romania **1469**
1520-121X Country Review. Russia **1469**
1520-1228 Country Review. Rwanda **1469**
1520-1236 Country Review. Saint Kitts Nevis **1469**
1520-1244 Country Review. Saint Lucia **1469**
1520-1252 Country Review. Sain Vicent and the Grenadines **1469**
1520-1260 Country Review. San Marino **1469**
1520-1287 Country Review. Saudi Arabia **1469**
1520-1295 Country Review. Senegal **1469**
1520-1309 Country Review. Serbia and Montenegro **1469**
1520-1317 Country Review. Sierra Leone **1469**
1520-1325 Country Review. Singapore **1883**
1520-1333 Country Review. Slovakia **1469**
1520-1341 Country Review. Slovenia **1470**
1520-135X Country Review. Solomon Islands **1470**
1520-1368 Country Review. Somalia **1470**
1520-1376 Country Review. South Africa **1470**
1520-1384 Country Review. Spain **1470**
1520-1392 Country Review. Sri Lanka **1470**
1520-1406 Country Review. Sudan **1470**
1520-1414 Country Review. Suriname **1470**
1520-1422 Country Review. Sweden **1470**
1520-1430 Country Review. Switzerland **1470**
1520-1449 Country Review. Syria **1470**
1520-1457 Country Review. Tajikistan **1470**
1520-1465 Country Review. Tanzania **1470**
1520-1473 Country Review. Togo **1470**
1520-1481 Country Review. Tonga **1470**
1520-149X Country Review. Trinidad and Tobago **1470**
1520-1503 Country Review. Tunisia **1470**
1520-1511 Country Review. Turkey **1470**
1520-152X Country Review. Turkmenistan **1470**
1520-1538 Country Review. Tuvalu **1470**
1520-1546 Country Review. Uganda **1470**
1520-1554 Country Review. Ukraine **1470**
1520-1562 Country Review. United Arab Emirates **1470**
1520-1570 Country Review. United Kingdom **1470**
1520-1589 Country Review. United States **1470**
1520-1597 Country Review. Uruguay **1471**
1520-1600 Country Review. Uzbekistan **1471**
1520-1619 Country Review. Kenya **1467**
1520-1627 Country Review. Kiribati **1467**
1520-1635 Country Review. North Korea **1469**
1520-1643 Country Review. South Korea **1470**
1520-1651 Country Review. Kuwait **1467**
1520-166X Country Review. Kyrgyzstan **1467**
1520-1678 Country Review. Laos **1467**
1520-1686 Country Review. Latvia **1467**
1520-1694 Country Review. Lebanon **1467**
1520-1708 Country Review. Ecuador **1466**
1520-1716 Country Review. Egypt **1466**
1520-1724 Country Review. El Salvador **1466**
1520-1732 Country Review. Eritrea **1466**
1520-1740 Country Review. Estonia **1466**
1520-1759 Country Review. Equatorial Guinea **1466**
1520-1767 Country Review. Ethiopia **1466**
1520-1775 Country Review. Fiji **1466**
1520-1783 Country Review. Finland **1466**
1520-1791 Country Review. France **1466**
1520-1805 Country Review. Gabon **1466**
1520-1821 Country Review. Georgia **1466**
1520-183X Country Review. Germany **1466**
1520-1848 Country Review. Ghana **1466**
1520-1856 Country Review. Greece **1466**
1520-1864 Country Review. Grenada **1466**
1520-1872 Country Review. Guatemala **1467**

ISSN

DIRECTORY 2010 1521-8198 9669

1520-9385 Motor Age 8592
1520-944X Ocular Surgery News (Latin America Edition) 6047
1520-9474 Troubled Company Reporter 1184
1520-9482 Troubled Company Reporter - Asia Pacific 1184
1520-9512 Sleep and Breathing 6185
1520-9601 Exotic Market Review
1520-9679 The Oswald Review 5346
1520-9695 Game Buyer 2476
1520-9717 P S I Global Abstracts†
1520-9733 Annual Review of Development Effectiveness 1590
1520-9830 m i n's b2b 7567
1520-9857 Modern Chinese Literature and Culture 348
1520-9865 Internet Media Investor†
1520-9873 The Driftwood 5286
1521-0081 see 0031-6997 6872
1521-009X see 0090-9556 6835
1521-0103 see 0022-3565 6855
1521-0111 see 0026-895X 6862
1521-012X Adventure Journal 8681
1521-0138 Guns & Gear 8316
1521-0189 A C O N A Outdoor Adventure 8301
1521-0200 Aluminum Transactions 6305
1521-0227 Interdisciplinary Environmental Review 3440
1521-0235 Willamette Journal of International Law and Dispute Resolution 4944
1521-0251 Journal of College Student Retention: Research, Theory & Practice 2989
1521-0278 Infinity†
1521-0383 see 0192-6187 7333
1521-0391 see 1055-0496 2691
1521-0413 see 1066-8926 2974
1521-0421 see 0892-0753 2802
1521-043X see 0146-0862 5963
1521-0448 see 0149-5933 7118
1521-0456 see 0163-9625 8098
1521-0464 see 1071-7544 6834
1521-0472 see 0360-1277 4044
1521-0480 see 0891-6152 7054
1521-0499 see 0190-2148 6214
1521-0529 see 0149-0451 886
1521-0537 see 0145-7632 3245
1521-0545 see 0885-3908 1572
1521-0553 see 0894-1939 6248
1521-0561 see 0885-0607 7243
1521-057X see 0194-7648 5651
1521-0588 see 0149-0400 4980
1521-060X see 0149-0419 4019
1521-0618 see 1064-119X 2812
1521-0626 see 1040-7790 3392
1521-0634 see 1040-7782 3391
1521-0642 see 0090-8320 2814
1521-0650 see 1072-0537 7371
1521-0669 see 0888-0018 6101
1521-0685 see 0270-2711 2903
1521-0693 see 1057-3569 3045
1521-0707 see 0273-2173 8137
1521-0715 see 0092-623X 7380
1521-0723 see 0894-1920 3466
1521-0731 see 1057-610X 7267
1521-074X see 0149-5739 3387
1521-0758 see 0191-3123 6036
1521-0898 Applied Occupational and Environmental Hygiene changed to 1545-9632 6680
1521-0901 American Law Yearbook 4615
1521-091X Voice Coil 3115
1521-0928 Great American Crafts†
1521-0960 Multicultural Perspectives 3073
1521-0987 Care Management Journals 5954
1521-1029 Journal of Forensic Neuropsychology† 8968
1521-1037 Journal of Religion & Abuse† 8968
1521-1118 Ahimsa 6654
1521-1169 New Single Copy 7568
1521-1185 No Quarter Given 5411
1521-1231 Sophia (Virginia) 7682
1521-1258 Gay Theological Journal 4374
1521-1274 Marketing with Honors 1834
1521-1290 Cavalcade of Acts & Attractions† 8940
1521-1304 Directory of North American Fairs, Festivals and Expositions† 8950
1521-1320 Public Human Services Directory (Year) 8064
1521-1363 Exotic D V M 8797
1521-1398 Journal of Computational Analysis and Applications 5501
1521-1401 Journal of Applied Psychoanalytic Studies†
1521-1428 Archi-Tech 428
1521-1436 Satellite Today 2338
1521-1444 Detroit Lutheran 7754
1521-1452 Annual Survey of Eastern Europe and the Former Soviet Union 7221
1521-1495 Transportation Watch†
1521-1525 Perspectives in Supramolecular Chemistry 2112
1521-1568 The Hill 7444
1521-1606 Art Lies 470
1521-1673 Carroll's Defense Industry Charts 6415
1521-1681 Carroll's Defense Organization Charts 6415
1521-169X Carroll's Federal Organization Charts 7429
1521-1703 Social Security Plus changed to Social Security Excellence (LawDesk) 4523
1521-1738 Stick It 6619
1521-1746 see 0278-808X 5668
1521-1754 N R B Magazine 2386
1521-1843 see 1060-6696 3217
1521-186X see 0197-8462 752
1521-1878 see 0265-9247 657
1521-1886 see 1080-5370 4007
1521-1916 Rainbow Reflections 6743
1521-1924 Living with Crystals 6646
1521-1932 This Is True 4584
1521-1975 Romantic Russia 5364
1521-2076 Medscape Women's Health 8847
1521-2106 N H F Head Lines 6162
1521-2114 Sports Etc 8335
1521-2149 Symposion 6956
1521-219X Online Journal of Clinical Innovations 5976
1521-2211 The Mentor (University Park) 2993
1521-2254 see 1099-498X 873
1521-2300 Kairos 3069
1521-236X Home Networking News 1119
1521-2459 Sotheby's International Realty Domain† 8989
1521-2483 Rattapallax DVD 5357
1521-2491 Archives of Facial Plastic Surgery 6237
1521-2548 Managing Accounting Systems and Technology†
1521-2815 Belize First Magazine 8686
1521-2823 University of Pennsylvania. Journal of Constitutional Law 4853
1521-2831 School Policy Legal Insider†
1521-284X Medicare Compliance and Reimbursement & Winners & Losers
1521-2904 Taste for Life 5084
1521-2912 D M Review changed to Information Management (Brookfield) 2531
1521-2939 Asian Enterprise 1956
1521-298X Dissolution Technologies 6833
1521-303X Topics in Diagnostic Radiology and Advanced Imaging†
1521-3110 Premise Wiring 2352
1521-3137 I S P Business Monthly Newsletter 2368
1521-3145 Advanced Materials and Composites News†
1521-320X see 0084-9499 642
1521-3250 Emergence (Mahwah, Print Edition) changed to Emergence: Complexity and Organization 1741
1521-3269 Media Psychology 7384
1521-3277 Youth Crime Alert†
1521-3285 Business Law Adviser†
1521-3307 C E Pro 3090
1521-3323 I E E E Transactions on Advanced Packaging 3314
1521-3331 I E E E Transactions on Components and Packaging Technology 3314
1521-334X I E E E Transactions on Electronics Packaging Manufacturing 3315
1521-3366 Pacific Seabird Group. Technical Publication 913
1521-3374 Education Statistics Quarterly (Print)†
1521-3420 Mountain Sports and Living†
1521-3447 Contemporary Long-Term Care Payment and Regulatory Alert†
1521-3455 Water Law Review 8837
1521-3471 Atlantic City Insider 8159
1521-3536 Church Business changed to Church Solutions 1733
1521-3544 Casino Journal's National Gaming Summary†
1521-3579 Fingerstyle Guitar 6567
1521-3595 Journal Watch Dermatology 5879
1521-3609 Journal Watch Infectious Diseases 5748
1521-3617 Journal Watch Psychiatry 5748
1521-3641 The Oxfordian 5428
1521-3668 Journal of Social Work Research and Evaluation†
1521-3676 Buffy: The Vampire Slayer†
1521-3684 Vacuum & Thinfilm†
1521-3706 San Francisco Review†
1521-3730 see 0944-5846 2057
1521-3749 see 0044-2313 2084
1521-3757 see 0044-8249 2050
1521-3765 see 0947-6539 2056
1521-3773 see 1433-7851 2050
1521-3781 see 0009-2851 2055
1521-379X see 0038-9056 2130
1521-3811 see 0937-1478 3654
1521-3854 see 1439-9598 2074
1521-3862 see 0948-1907 2109
1521-3870 see 0942-5616 5513
1521-3889 see 0003-3804 7005
1521-3900 see 1022-1360 2126
1521-3919 see 1022-1344 2126
1521-3927 see 1022-1336 2126
1521-3935 see 1022-1352 2126
1521-3943 see 0031-9252 7034
1521-3951 see 0370-1972 7031
1521-3978 see 0015-8208 7013
1521-3986 see 0863-1042 7009
1521-3994 see 0004-6337 570
1521-4001 see 0044-2267 5547
1521-401X Acta Hydrochimica et Hydrobiologica (Online Edition) changed to 1863-0669 8820
1521-4028 see 0233-111X 888
1521-4036 see 0323-3847 660
1521-4052 see 0933-5137 6322
1521-4079 see 0232-1300 2110
1521-4087 see 0721-3115 3254
1521-4095 see 0935-9648 3335
1521-4109 see 1040-0397 2100
1521-4117 see 0934-0866 7029
1521-4125 see 0930-7516 3238
1521-4141 see 0014-2980 5758
1521-415X see 0045-205X 659
1521-4176 see 0947-5117 6321
1521-4184 see 0365-6233 6822
1521-4206 Southern Jewish History 7729
1521-4230 Optometric Education (Print)†
1521-4249 Souvenirs, Gifts, and Novelties 4061
1521-4273 Daughters 2150
1521-4281 Marvels & Tales 3620
1521-4303 Computer Bits 2411
1521-4400 see 0148-0375 6774
1521-446X Handbook of Natural Toxins†
1521-4478 Advances in Nitrogen Heterocycles†
1521-4486 Antioxidants in Health and Disease†
1521-4494 Corrosion Technology 6309
1521-4524 American Nutraceutical Association. Journal 6655
1521-4591 Electronics and Biotechnology Advanced. Forum Series 763
1521-4605 Methods in Physiology Series 925
1521-4613 B E D Series 747
1521-4621 Toxicity Report Series 3501
1521-463X Organized Assemblies in Chemical Analysis†
1521-4648 American Chemical Society. Division of Fuel Chemistry. Preprints of Symposia 6762
1521-4664 Molecular and Supramolecular Photochemistry†
1521-4672 Informing Science 5017
1521-4680 see 1051-4775 1715
1521-4699 see 1049-7986 5583
1521-4710 Journal Watch Women's Health 8850
1521-4818 Business Finance (Print) 1730
1521-4826 Controversia 3055
1521-4842 Journal of Real Estate Practice and Education 7597
1521-4893 The Best of Golf Tips (Year) Instruction Annual changed to 1557-2358 8223
1521-4990 P P S Alert For Long Term Care 4109
1521-5016 Yadkin County Historical Society. Journal 3788
1521-5105 Credit Union Journal 1333
1521-5156 Fancy Food & Culinary Products 3677
1521-5202 Technology Meetings 8442
1521-5210 Arthur Frommer's Budget Travel 8684
1521-5237 Ob-Gyn Coding Alert 4517
1521-5261 Restoration (Corvallis, OR) 3605
1521-5288 see 1072-1967 1856
1521-5296 Assisted Living Executive Report†
1521-5318 Futures Magazine 5299
1521-5326 Managing Employees Under F M L A and A D A 1869
1521-5350 B N A's Health Law Reporter (Online) 4625
1521-5369 see 1068-1213 7509
1521-5385 Twentieth-Century China 4189
1521-5482 Tulsa Jewish Review 7731
1521-5512 Real Estate Software Guide 7619
1521-5571 Security Intelligence Report†
1521-5636 Beckett Baseball Card Alphabetical Checklist 4329
1521-5644 The Offshore Journal†
1521-5768 see 1531-0035 6255
1521-5806 Holiday Decorating 536
1521-5822 Journal Watch Cardiology 5748
1521-5865 Footsteps†
1521-5873 see MoXie (Berkeley) 8876
1521-5881 Competitive Intelligence Magazine 1734
1521-5962 Journal of Property Tax Management changed to 1538-2338 1931
1521-5970 Hunter Education Journal changed to Hunter & Shooting Sports Education Journal 8317
1521-5997 C Q Weekly 7112
1521-6039 Polish Music Journal 6606
1521-6055 Global Journal of Classical Theology 7645
1521-6071 Pogonip 5352
1521-611X License! changed to 1936-4989 1829
1521-6136 Sociology of Crime, Law and Deviance 2668
1521-6160 Plunkett's Entertainment and Media Industry Almanac 2387
1521-6381 A S P C A Animal Watch†
1521-6497 Bench & Bar 4628
1521-6519 Italia Magazine†
1521-6535 Journal Watch Emergency Medicine 6066
1521-6543 I U B M B Life 733
1521-6551 see 1521-6543 733
1521-6578 Hustler's Brown Sugar 6293
1521-6586 Hustler's Asian Fever 6292
1521-6594 Hustler's Honey Buns 6293
1521-6616 Clinical Immunology 5756
1521-6683 Major Marketing Campaigns Annual 28
1521-6764 see 1521-6772 3329
1521-6772 Retail Wheeling & Restructuring Report 3329
1521-6802 Farmer's Market Online 112
1521-690X Best Practice & Research: Clinical Endocrinology & Metabolism 5884
1521-6918 Best Practice & Research: Clinical Gastroenterology 5920
1521-6926 Best Practice & Research: Clinical Haematology 5934
1521-6934 Best Practice & Research: Clinical Obstetrics & Gynaecology 5986
1521-6942 Best Practice & Research: Clinical Rheumatology 6222
1521-6950 see 1093-7404 3499
1521-6985 Flying Solo 5009
1521-7000 Texas Construction News Weekly Covering Fort Worth and Vicinity 1040
1521-7027 Business Solutions 1850
1521-7035 see 1521-6616 5756
1521-7043 Editorial Strategies 4574
1521-7183 New York Business Law Journal 4744
1521-7205 AnimeFantastique 6489
1521-7256 Intellectual Property Today 1570
1521-7264 C S G State Directory. Directory III, Administrative Officials 7425
1521-7272 C S G State Directory. Directory I. Elective Officials 7425
1521-7299 The Southwest's Best Bed & Breakfasts 8757
1521-7310 Organized Crime Digest 2662
1521-7329 Oiwi 8124
1521-7337 Review of National Literatures and World Report†
1521-7361 Flyfishing & Tying Journal 8314
1521-737X Heart Disease† 8961
1521-7388 see 0278-6826 2049
1521-740X C M S Workshop Lectures 6459
1521-7418 Pathology and Laboratory Medicine 5910
1521-7434 Education Technology Literature Review 3021
1521-7523 Texas Press Messenger 4584
1521-7574 Uncompahgre Valley Chronicle 3786
1521-7590 Research Department Report 1840
1521-7639 Hazmat 5304
1521-7760 see 1063-2069 1948
1521-7779 Journal of Children's Literature 2156
1521-7795 P C Accelerator†
1521-7922 Art on Paper 470
1521-8007 Cuaderno Internacional de Estudios Humanisticos y Literatura 334
1521-8031 National Floor Trends 4547
1521-804X Portuguese Literary & Cultural Studies 5353
1521-8066 Supervisors Legal Update 1795
1521-8112 Machinist's Workshop 5456
1521-8120 Heritage Southwest Jewish Press
1521-8139 Bonkers!†
1521-8171 Construction Distribution 995
1521-8198 York County Genealogical Society. Journal 3788

ISSN

DIRECTORY 2010 1523-5890 9671

1522-6689 Massachusetts Civil Service Reporter 4728
1522-6735 Pharmaceutical News Daily 6869
1522-6751 Writers in Paradise 5401
1522-6786 Washington Semesters and Internships 2925
1522-6794 Smile†
1522-6808 Pocket World in Figures 1159
1522-6840 Voice (Sioux Center) 2308
1522-6859 Fossil News 6724
1522-6867 The P C I A Washington Bulletin 2335
1522-6883 Online Journalism Review 4581
1522-6891 E-Tailer's Digest 1815
1522-6999 Savoy Magazine†
1522-7057 see 1522-6328 2920
1522-7200 see 1523-908X 3446
1522-7219 see 1522-7227 7362
1522-7227 Infant and Child Development 7362
1522-7235 Luminescence 2138
1522-7243 see 1522-7235 2138
1522-726X see 1522-1946 5781
1522-7278 Environmental Toxicology (Online Edition) see 1520-4081 3496
1522-7294 Midwest Construction 1024
1522-7316 Low Fat - No Fat Cooking
1522-7340 Essays in the Philosophy of Humanism 6916
1522-7383 Cutter I T Journal 2506
1522-7448 Route Driver and Service Technician 8510
1522-7464 Music in Art 6591
1522-7472 Cardiology Coding Alert 4498
1522-7480 Internal Medicine Coding Alert 4509
1522-7502 Composition Forum 2838
1522-7510 In Touch (Melville) 6022
1522-7529 Journal of Clinical Problem-Based Learning 2874
1522-7553 Animal Welfare Information Center Bulletin 318
1522-7588 Q V Magazine 3559
1522-7634 Telecom A.M. 2340
1522-7731 The Home Business Files 1961
1522-7758 Stires Family Newsletter 3784
1522-7782 Webmasters Journal
1522-7863 National Directory of Fire Chiefs & E M S Administrators 3580
1522-7871 The Parts Manager changed to DealersEdge Parts Manager 8577
1522-788X Auto Retailing on the Web†
1522-7898 Printwear 2249
1522-7928 Idaho Cities Focus 7494
1522-7952 Pediatric Pathology & Molecular Medicine (Print Edition) changed to 1551-3815 6092
1522-7979 Student Companion to Classic Writers 5378
1522-7987 Environmental Epidemiology and Toxicology changed to 1438-4639 7526
1522-8002 NeoPlasia 6029
1522-8010 Fordham Business Review 1111
1522-8037 Current Gastroenterology Reports (Print)†
1522-8053 Journal of Information Technology Cases and Applications changed to Journal of Information Technology Case and Application Research 2429
1522-8118 Orthopedic Technology Review†
1522-8185 Information Technology in Childhood Education Annual†
1522-8223 Journal of Undergraduate Nursing Scholarship 5967
1522-8290 Washington Business Forward 1193
1522-8304 P R B Reports on America 7289
1522-8339 Native Plants Journal 804
1522-8363 Applied and Computational Control, Signals, and Circuits 2532
1522-8398 Journal of Business and Public Affairs (Murray) 1133
1522-8401 Clinical Pediatric Emergency Medicine 6090
1522-8436 Natural Horse 321
1522-8452 Collective Bargaining Bulletin 4592
1522-8460 Junior Baseball 8236
1522-8495 Pre-Columbiana 352
1522-8517 Neuro-Oncology 6029
1522-8584 Oracle Internals 2532
1522-8606 Journal of Continuing Education Topics & Issues 2874
1522-8614 XY Magazine 4380
1522-8649 Bulletin of Anesthesia History 5770
1522-8665 Schwing!†
1522-8681 International Symposium on Advanced Research in Asynchronous Circuits and Systems 3105
1522-869X Conference on Advanced Research in V L S I. Proceedings 2539
1522-8703 First Hold 587
1522-8711 The Supervisor's Guide to O S H A Regulations 6687
1522-8746 Journal of Performance Measurement 1635
1522-8789 SeaWIFS Postlaunch Technical Report Series 2817
1522-8797 see 0037-0665 4781
1522-8800 see 0092-6884 1919
1522-8819 see 0891-4141 1693
1522-8835 Journal of Technology in Human Services 8151
1522-8851 Small Fruits Review changed to 1553-8362 237
1522-886X Journal of New Seeds 239
1522-8878 Psychoanalytic Social Work 8063
1522-8886 Slavic & East European Information Resources 5048
1522-8894 Harrington Lesbian Fiction Quarterly changed to 1556-9225 8961
1522-8908 International Journal of Police Negotiations and Crisis Management†
1522-8916 Journal of African Business 1133
1522-8924 Critical Strategies: Psychotherapy in Managed Care†
1522-8932 Journal of Forensic Psychology Practice 7374
1522-8940 Journal of Herbal Pharmacotherapy changed to 1939-0211 6853
1522-8959 Public Services Quarterly 5041
1522-8967 Journal of Religion, Disability & Health 7656
1522-8983 America's Horse 8287
1522-8991 see 1522-8835 8151
1522-9025 see 1522-886X 239
1522-9033 see 1522-8878 8063
1522-9041 see 1522-8886 5048
1522-9076 see 1522-8916 1133
1522-9092 see 1522-8932 7374
1522-9114 see 1522-8959 5041
1522-9122 see 1522-8967 7656
1522-9149 Los Angeles Magazine 3980
1522-9270 see 0039-3657 5381
1522-9289 Indianagram 3024
1522-936X AgBioforum 191
1522-9483 Courtside 8225
1522-9491 Giftware Business†
1522-9564 Potentials changed to 1042-5195 1820
1522-9572 Gun-Knife Show Calendar 366
1522-9580 Journal of Psychotherapy in Independent Practice changed to 1540-1383 7372
1522-9602 see 0092-8240 663
1522-9610 see 0272-4944 7373
1522-9629 see 1094-5539 6218
1522-9645 European Heart Journal (Online) 5786
1522-9653 see 1063-4584 6225
1522-9688 A Penny Saved 2634
1522-9726 Rider 8267
1522-9734 The N A M T A Journal 2888
1522-9742 North & South 4305
1522-9777 Desert Golf Magazine 8226
1522-9823 Alternative Currents 1307
1522-9882 Financial Focus 1623
1522-9920 Writers Ask 5401
1522-9971 Trips†
1522-998X PRINTthoughts 7327
1523-0023 Bloomberg Personal Finance†
1523-0031 Warbirds International 74
1523-0104 Tomas Rivera Policy Institute. Policy Brief 3568
1523-018X A L C T S Newsletter Online 4985
1523-0309 Multilingual Computing and Technology changed to 1931-9428 2432
1523-0325 Organic Pages 3659
1523-0384 BiblioData's Price Watcher†
1523-0392 Beverage Dynamics 599
1523-0406 Cartography and Geographic Information Science 4002
1523-0422 Long Distance Competition Report 2571
1523-0430 Arctic, Antarctic, and Alpine Research 7836
1523-0465 Performance and Practices of Successful Medical Groups 5695
1523-0473 Health Products Business†
1523-0481 see 1523-9225 596
1523-049X O E M Worldwide 213
1523-0708 I O M A's Report on Hourly Compensation†
1523-0767 see Images Inscript 5220
1523-0864 Antioxidants & Redox Signaling 5576
1523-0872 Mystical Sacrifice†
1523-0880 The Larcom Review 5223
1523-0899 Clinical Implant Dentistry and Related Research 5838
1523-0902 Inside Personal Finance with Ric Edelman 1630
1523-0910 College Planning and Management 2973
1523-0937 Disputatio 4214
1523-0953 Fodor's Pocket Puerto Rico 8708
1523-0996 see 0730-2126 4963
1523-1003 Diabetes Interview changed to 1936-9522 5887
1523-1011 see 0730-403X 4962
1523-102X see 0730-3971 4961
1523-1038 see 0730-4145 4962
1523-1054 see 0730-4552 4964
1523-1062 see 0730-4358 4963
1523-1070 see 0730-4528 4964
1523-1216 Cyberjournal for Pentecostal-Charismatic Research 7636
1523-1224 Esoterica 6644
1523-1232 Make-Up Artist Magazine 589
1523-1267 see 1089-3075 2896
1523-1275 Parents Make the Difference! (Elementary Edition) 2896
1523-1283 see 1071-5118 2896
1523-1291 see 1523-2395 2896
1523-1305 see 1523-2360 2895
1523-1313 see 1523-2379 2895
1523-1321 see 1523-2387 2895
1523-133X see 1523-2417 2894
1523-1437 Parker's California Code of Civil Procedure 4840
1523-1461 Water Gardens†
1523-1496 Heat Transfer - Asian Research (Online Edition) 3379
1523-1518 The Public Purchaser
1523-1585 G w D†
1523-1615 Current Issues in Comparative Education (CISE) 2840
1523-1623 Chemical Journal on Internet 2054
1523-1631 Interactive Global News 1570
1523-1712 see Idea (Chicago) 7971
1523-1720 Ciberletras 5274
1523-1739 see 0888-8892 2607
1523-1747 see 0022-202X 5879
1523-1755 see 0085-2538 6271
1523-1771 Journal of Geosciences of China†
1523-178X Auto Restorer 8560
1523-1828 401(k) Answer Book: Forms & Worksheets 1661
1523-1852 Lindy's Big 12 Football Annual 8237
1523-1879 Ice Fishing Guide 8318
1523-1887 Mary Beth's Beanie World for Kids†
1523-1917 see 0163-3155 4484
1523-231X U S A - Bericht
1523-2344 C W R U Magazine changed to 1547-5360 2277
1523-2360 Los Padres Hacen la Diferencia! 2895
1523-2379 Los Padres Hacen la Diferencia! (Elementary Edition) 2895
1523-2387 Los Padres aun Hacen la Diferencial (Escuela Intermedia) 2895
1523-2395 Parents Still Make the Difference! (High School Edition) 2896
1523-2409 Journal of Supply Chain Management 1827
1523-2417 Los Padres aun Hacen la Diferencia! (Escuela Secundaria) 2894
1523-2425 A H I M A Advantage 4086
1523-2433 Managed Care and Medical Cost Containment in Worker's Compensation 4513
1523-2492 Player (Boston)
1523-2522 Dayton Art Institute. Member Quarterly 485
1523-2611 Practical Latin American Tax Strategies 1939
1523-262X International Securitization & Structured Finance Report 1571
1523-2638 Practical U.S. / International Tax Strategies 1939
1523-2670 Finance and Treasury's International Reports 1343
1523-2689 Pro Video Review 2402
1523-2727 Future Drive†
1523-2816 see 1098-4240 1572
1523-2824 see 0003-6021 4855
1523-2832 see 1095-6239 1685
1523-2859 see 0025-732X 6860
1523-2867 A C M / S I G P L A N Notices 2504
1523-2883 Positively Aware 5824
1523-293X Transgender Community News 4379
1523-2956 Better Homes and Gardens Traditional Style 4533
1523-3057 Small Business Computing & Communications 2583
1523-3081 E C N†
1523-3146 Oakland County Legal News 4750
1523-3154 Crop Science, Soil Science, Agronomy News changed to 1529-9163 223
1523-3359 American Health†
1523-3367 Database Marketer 1813
1523-3375 Women's Health Advocate changed to 1529-532X 5660
1523-3383 Financial Advisor Pro†
1523-343X Stocks, Bonds, Bills and Inflation Yearbook (Valuation Edition) 1654
1523-3472 Gaseous Dielectrics 7051
1523-3502 Family Digest (Daville) 3533
1523-360X Journal of Applied Medical Polymers
1523-3693 Value Retail News 1847
1523-3766 The Dental Practice Acquisition Report 5841
1523-3774 Current Rheumatology Reports (Print)†
1523-3782 Current Cardiology Reports (Print) 5784
1523-3790 Current Oncology Reports (Print)†
1523-3804 Current Atherosclerosis Reports 5784
1523-3812 Current Psychiatry Reports 6135
1523-3820 Current Treatment Options in Infectious Diseases†
1523-3839 Current Interventional Cardiology Reports† 8947
1523-3847 Current Infectious Disease Reports 5757
1523-3855 Current Anesthesiology†
1523-388X Abstract Bulletin of Paper Science and Technology 6740
1523-3952 see 0017-260X 1684
1523-3960 Western Wood Products Association. Statistics for Analysis 3717
1523-3979 Practitioner's Trademark Manual of Examining Procedure 6757
1523-4002 Femspec 8863
1523-4045 Mary Dee's Quick and Tasty Recipes 4363
1523-410X The Black Flame 7733
1523-4126 Rails to Trails Magazine 8330
1523-4142 Sleeper News 3783
1523-4207 Aula 434
1523-4215 Good Stuff (Malvern) 1115
1523-4223 Advances in Developing Human Resources 1855
1523-4231 Ultimate Black Hair Guide 592
1523-424X Famous Salons Presents 587
1523-4266 Industrial Laser Solutions for Manufacturing 3197
1523-4282 The Milken Institute Review 1499
1523-4320 School Library Media Research 5046
1523-4371 Engineered Casting Solutions 6311
1523-4401 Heard Museum Journal 6525
1523-4479 International Conference on Software Engineering: Education and Practice. Proceedings† 8965
1523-4487 Chemical Specialties 3240
1523-4495 Palms 807
1523-4533 Food Safety Report† 8957
1523-4614 Manufacturing and Service Operations Management 1778
1523-4665 Premier Hospital Services Report (Print) changed to 1538-2710
1523-4681 see 0884-0431 6063
1523-469X I O M A's Report on Managing Design Engineering†
1523-4762 580 Split 5439
1523-4770 Tooele Valley Magazine 8761
1523-4800 Technical Guide to Visual Programming†
1523-4819 G B U Reporter 4503
1523-4835 E D Coding Alert 4501
1523-4843 Ophthalmology Coding Alert 4517
1523-4851 Sound Collector 6618
1523-486X American Spa 585
1523-4967 Preservation Tips 6536
1523-5033 The Daily Northwestern 2280
1523-5092 Natural Cat 6811
1523-5106 Marine Fish & Reef U S A 6811
1523-519X Business Trucking†
1523-5238 Philadelphia County Dental Society. Journal 5861
1523-5262 CandyBusiness 3672
1523-5270 I O M A's Report on Managing the General Ledger†
1523-5289 Wall and Window Trends†
1523-5327 On Investing†
1523-536X see 0730-7659 5986
1523-5378 see 1083-4389 887
1523-5386 The Astrophysicist's Tango Partner Speaks 5417
1523-5394 Cancer Practice Online†
1523-5432 Bride Again 8854
1523-5475 Journal of Agricultural and Urban Entomology 851
1523-5491 Buffalo Women's Law Journal† 8937
1523-5521 Inside Business 1124
1523-553X I E E E International Symposium on Semiconductor Manufacturing Conference Proceedings 2471
1523-5610 M I N D Institute Newsletter†
1523-5661 see 1098-5190 4830
1523-567X see 0148-8155 1737
1523-5688 see 0010-6836 1673
1523-5696 see 0014-9063 7436
1523-570X Money & Politics Report 7453
1523-5718 Pension & Benefits Daily 1702
1523-5726 Flaunt 5071
1523-5734 The Bryn Mawr Review of Comparative Literature 5266
1523-5742 Woman Motorist 8612
1523-5858 Loving More Magazine 5076
1523-5866 see 1522-8517 6029
1523-5882 Bilingual Research Journal 2831
1523-5890 see 1523-5882 2831

ISSN

9672 1523-5971 **ULRICH'S PERIODICALS**

1523-5971 Newport's RoadStar† **8977**
1523-5998 Primary Care Companion to the Journal of Clinical Psychiatry **6174**
1523-6005 A L A Washington News **4985**
1523-6064 The Internet Journal of Advanced Nursing Practice **5962**
1523-6072 Chicago Art Journal **481**
1523-6161 Reviews in Urology **6274**
1523-617X Quality Whitetails **2625**
1523-6196 Successful Officer Call Strategies **1385**
1523-6226 National Geographic Adventure **8323**
1523-6250 Practical Tax Strategies **1939**
1523-6269 The Value Line Special Situations Service **1658**
1523-6277 AutoGraphics† **8934**
1523-6307 Dell Pocket Word Search *changed to* 1944-4303 **4344**
1523-6315 Facilities and Destinations **1744**
1523-6323 Senior Living Exec.†
1523-6331 Minnesota Conservation Volunteer **2619**
1523-634X Family Urology **6268**
1523-6358 St. Charles County Business Record **1179**
1523-6366 ColoradoBiz **1447**
1523-6390 Press (Harrisburg) **4582**
1523-6412 Northern Pilot *changed to* 1099-8160 **8747**
1523-6420 Connecticut Golf **8167**
1523-6471 The Best Children's Books of the Year **2179**
1523-648X Journal Watch. Audio *see* Journal Watch General Medicine **5748**
1523-651X *see* International Conference on Offshore Mechanics and Arctic Engineering. Proceedings **3381**
1523-6528 *see* 1080-2924 **5939**
1523-6536 *see* 1083-8791 **5934**
1523-6587 Poetry Super Highway **5431**
1523-6625 Canine Times **6805**
1523-6773 3rd Bed **5439**
1523-6781 Business People Vermont **1074**
1523-679X Recreational Sports and Fitness†
1523-6803 Journal of Public Affairs Education **7448**
1523-6838 *see* 0272-6386 **6265**
1523-6889 *see* 0730-4706 **4963**
1523-6900 Shepard's Citations. Illinois Official, Illinois Statutes *see* 0730-3904 **4961**
1523-6919 Journal of Cotton Science **239**
1523-6951 Zopilote **5247**
1523-6986 El Norte **3555**
1523-7036 The Journal of Gender-Specific Medicine†
1523-7052 *see* 1523-7060 **2128**
1523-7060 Organic Letters **2128**
1523-7079 The New York Times Almanac **3121**
1523-7117 Pets†
1523-7125 Kagan's Media Mergers & Acquisitions **2330**
1523-7168 Inspection Trends **6343**
1523-7184 Semiconductor Business News† **8987**
1523-7222 A S H R A E Handbook. Fundamentals (Inch-Pound Edition) **4115**
1523-7230 A S H R A E Handbook. Fundamentals (S I Edition) **4115**
1523-7249 Harvey
1523-7273 Teen en Espanol
1523-729X Student Press Review **4584**
1523-7303 Fabrics and Furnishings International **4539**
1523-7370 The Brayer **8288**
1523-7419 White Eagle **4278**
1523-7443 York County Genealogical and Historical Society. Quarterly **3788**
1523-7451 Readers Speak Out! **5358**
1523-746X Al Jadid **3541**
1523-7486 Gaming Industry Weekly Report **8174**
1523-7516 Games Business† **8958**
1523-7524 Publishing for Professional Markets **7571**
1523-7559 Wireless Technology International†
1523-7575 Healthcare Life Safety Compliance **4097**
1523-7605 Wildfowl Carving Magazine **4350**
1523-763X Mobile Electronics **2334**
1523-7656 Response Magazine **34**
1523-7672 Jewish Women's Literary Annual **3543**
1523-7729 *see* 0731-0781 **6569**
1523-780X Personal Fitness Professional **6994**
1523-7834 Association of Genetic Technologists. Journal **863**
1523-8024 Edmund's Used Cars & Trucks, Prices & Ratings **8578**
1523-8083 Museletter **4154**
1523-8091 Friends of the Amherst College Library. Newsletter **5010**
1523-8105 Memory Magic†
1523-8202 Christian School Education **3019**
1523-8253 ChoiceReviews.online **7558**
1523-8261 Safe Ride News **2211**
1523-8288 Symposium on Foundations of Computer Science. Annual Proceedings **2438**
1523-8334 Insiders' Guide to Charlotte **8721**
1523-844X Digital Camera **6966**
1523-8504 Elder's Advisor *changed to* 1935-7958 **4904**
1523-8555 Hooked on the Outdoors†
1523-8644 C F & Y's Foodservice Information Systems Report **2535**
1523-8652 Compendium's Standards of Care: Emergency and Critical Care Medicine **8795**
1523-8679 Employment Law Update (New York) **4665**
1523-8695 Corporate Counsel's Primers **4864**
1523-8709 The Strand Magazine (Birmingham) **5415**
1523-8717 Hermenaut **6923**
1523-8776 Fodor's Oregon **8708**
1523-8806 Joint Commission Benchmark **4103**
1523-8822 Intelligence Magazine†
1523-8857 The Horse, Backstreet Choppers **8259**
1523-8865 *see* 0011-3409 **715**
1523-889X *see* 0163-2574 **2094**
1523-8903 Current Contents Desktop. Engineering, Computing & Technology *see* 1079-1450 **3229**
1523-9004 Heart Advisor **5788**
1523-9012 Literary Imagination **5224**
1523-9047 Contractor Tools and Supplies **999**
1523-9055 Township Perspective **7504**
1523-9063 International Journal of Condensed Matter Research and Internet Reviews **2110**
1523-908X Journal of Environmental Policy and Planning **3446**
1523-9101 ColdFusion Developer's Journal **2588**
1523-9225 Soap and Cosmetics **596**
1523-9233 Prairie Pioneer **3779**
1523-939X A A B B News (Print Edition) *changed to* A A B B News (Online Edition) **5563**
1523-9403 A A A World (York) **8553**
1523-9411 P D R Family Guide to Prescription Drugs **6866**
1523-9454 G M High Tech Performance **8581**
1523-9470 Global Cosmetic Industry **594**
1523-9497 Honduras and the Bay Islands **8719**
1523-9543 New Literacies and Digital Epistemologies **2891**
1523-9551 Higher Ed **2984**
1523-9705 Careers and the International M B A† **8940**
1523-9721 Public Finance and Management **1940**
1523-973X Journal of Power and Ethics **7448**
1523-9748 International Journal of Economic Development **1493**
1523-9756 Global Virtue Ethics Review **7439**
1523-9764 German Policy Studies **7439**
1523-9829 Annual Review of Biomedical Engineering **653**
1523-9845 Rehab Report *changed to* 1530-0420
1523-9888 Studies in Contemporary Islam **7716**
1523-9896 Techniques in Shoulder and Elbow Surgery **6261**
1523-9926 Technology Interface **3222**
1524-0010 Weekend Web Picks **2569**
1524-007X Agenda (Memphis) **1394**
1524-0096 Go figure! **4335**
1524-010X Food & Water Journal *changed to* Wild Matters **2642**
1524-0134 Advanced Rescue Technology **6055**
1524-0193 Phenomenology and Literature **6939**
1524-0207 Journal Watch Neurology **5748**
1524-0215 Journal of Biomolecular Techniques **767**
1524-0258 Facilities and Event Management **1744**
1524-0274 The Internet Journal of Thoracic and Cardiovascular Surgery **6247**
1524-0304 G-Two Compliance Report **4678**
1524-0339 H X Magazine† **8961**
1524-0355 Great Lakes Angler **8316**
1524-0371 Wrestling Digest **8216**
1524-038X Megawatt Daily's Generation Week†
1524-0398 Gas Daily's Gas Transportation & Storage Week **6770**
1524-0428 Repair Shop Product News **8601**
1524-0436 U.S. Army Medical Department. Journal **5725**
1524-0452 The Federation Flash **6645**
1524-0460 Medical Computing Today†
1524-0487 Journal of Critical Inquiry Into Curriculum and Instruction†
1524-0509 Deanotations†
1524-0517 U W M Post **2305**
1524-0541 U L I Market Profiles (Year): North America†
1524-055X U L I Market Profiles (Year): Europe†
1524-0568 U L I Market Profiles (Year): Pacific Rim†
1524-0576 Home Systems
1524-0606 Employee Assistance *changed to* 1945-3469 **1878**
1524-0657 Studies in Gender and Sexuality **8142**
1524-0703 Graphical Models **2485**
1524-0711 *see* 1524-0703 **2485**
1524-0754 N H S A Dialog **3044**
1524-0770 American Journal of Italian Studies **5252**
1524-0827 American Public Health Association. Annual Meeting and Exposition. Final Program **7507**
1524-0835 American Public Health Association. Annual Meeting. Abstracts **7507**
1524-0851 Let's Go: Turkey (Year) **8730**
1524-086X Let's Go: Greece (Year) **8729**
1524-0886 American Banker's Financial Modernization Report **1307**
1524-0916 Nebraska Criminal and Traffic Law Manual **4894**
1524-0924 Wyoming Criminal and Traffic Law Manual **4900**
1524-0932 Eye (Greensboro)†
1524-0940 Lincoln Center Theater Review **8473**
1524-0991 Sports Medicine Reports†
1524-1009 Trucking Technology **8678**
1524-1033 Workforce Professional **1716**
1524-1041 Industry Focus (Yorba Linda) **1851**
1524-105X Action Line (Sacramento) **2643**
1524-1068 The Healthcare Registration **1749**
1524-1084 The Richard Wilbur Society Newsletter **5363**
1524-1114 Q E C E†
1524-1122 Men of Integrity **7662**
1524-1130 The Catbird Seat **5419**
1524-1149 Flesh and Blood **5442**
1524-1165 Nuclear Weapons & Materials Monitor **3509**
1524-119X N O B S Newsletter **4342**
1524-1211 Computer Link Magazine **2553**
1524-1297 Hidden Montana **8718**
1524-1343 Freeze†
1524-1394 One Trick Pony **5428**
1524-1467 Metroparent (Wauwatosa) **2161**
1524-1521 Research in Healthcare Financial Management **4110**
1524-153X Operative Techniques in General Surgery **6254**
1524-1548 International Journal for Manufacturing Science & Technology **3368**
1524-1556 The Leibniz Review **6932**
1524-1580 Payroll Administration Guide Newsletter **1702**
1524-1599 Payroll Administration Guide **1702**
1524-1602 Strength and Conditioning Journal **6997**
1524-1610 Perdido **1159**
1524-1629 El Nuevo Patria **3555**
1524-1637 Aging Arkansas **4039**
1524-1645 P C I Journal **5880**
1524-1688 Current Politics and Economics of Russia, Eastern and Central Europe **7229**
1524-1696 P R Week (US Edition) **32**
1524-1734 Reflections (Cambridge) **1789**
1524-1750 Nylon **8878**
1524-1777 Young Romantic **5413**
1524-1815 Jesuit Bulletin **7802**
1524-1823 Massachusetts Bar Association Lawyers Journal **4728**
1524-1866 *see* 1523-4533 **8957**
1524-1904 Applied Stochastic Models in Business and Industry **5473**
1524-1912 Transportation Alternatives **8636**
1524-1939 Foreign Policy in Focus **7236**
1524-1971 Emergency Medicine Practice **5609**
1524-198X Life Extension **312**
1524-2021 Journal of Modeling and Simulation of Microsystems **2517**
1524-2110 Indiana University. Working Papers in Linguistics **5127**
1524-2196 American Journal of Medicine and Sports†
1524-220X Mask Lore
1524-2218 Latingirl†
1524-2226 Journal of Popular Music Studies **6581**
1524-2242 Outdoor Explorer†
1524-2269 Janus Head (Print) **4458**
1524-2293 Booktech, the Magazine *changed to* 1558-9889 **7554**
1524-2315 Hill Country Sun **8718**
1524-234X Florida Estimates of Population (Year) **7307**
1524-2439 Directory of Scholarly Electronic Journals and Academic Discussion†
1524-2471 Silicon Magazine *changed to* Polygon **2481**
1524-248X New Mexico Business Weekly **1153**
1524-251X Mundi Medicina **7664**
1524-2536 Home Health Care Dealer/Provider *changed to* 1936-2102 **4095**
1524-2579 Mountainfreak **8323**
1524-2609 Web Guide **2568**
1524-2706 Verbatim (Mahwah) **5869**
1524-2730 Haunted Attraction Magazine **3618**
1524-2749 Two Rivers Review **5437**
1524-2757 The Revised Uniform Partnership Act **4879**
1524-2765 Special Education Technology Practice **3047**
1524-279X Hispanic Today **3537**
1524-2803 Prensa Latina **1512**
1524-2838 Stuff **6300**
1524-2854 Golf Today **8233**
1524-2870 Geriatric Care **4045**
1524-2889 Activity Director's Guide *changed to* 1932-8729 **4043**
1524-2897 Remembering Yesterday **4054**
1524-2900 Nurse Aide - V I P **4052**
1524-2919 Volunteer and Vistors' Guide **4057**
1524-2927 Alzheimer's Home Companion *changed to* 1070-5112 **4040**
1524-2943 Many Happy Returns **8186**
1524-3168 Eastmans' Hunting Journal **8311**
1524-3176 Car Toy Collectibles **4331**
1524-3222 Perimeter Star
1524-3230 Juvenile Justice (Print)†
1524-3249 Commercial Investment Real Estate **7586**
1524-3257 Working America **4605**
1524-3265 House of Roses **6292**
1524-3273 Policy Evaluation†
1524-3303 *see* 1523-6919 **239**
1524-3435 Education Reform News†
1524-3559 Foxfire News **3062**
1524-3567 Pocket Games **2481**
1524-3575 D C M *changed to* D C M Magazine **2475**
1524-3583 Business Entities **1913**
1524-3613 Nanotech Alert **8433**
1524-3621 Intelligent Enterprise (Print)†
1524-3648 Harris Directory. U.S. Electronics Manufacturers Database†
1524-3672 Windows NT Administrator Report **2510**
1524-377X Oregon Vital Statistics Annual Report **7548**
1524-3796 Oregon Vital Statistics County Data **7549**
1524-3877 Jane's Terrorism Watch Report **7247**
1524-3885 Intelligence Watch Report **7242**
1524-394X Education Statistics of the United States **2932**
1524-3958 State Profiles **8403**
1524-3974 Georgetown Journal on Poverty Law and Policy **8042**
1524-4040 *see* 0148-396X **6170**
1524-4059 Component Advisor *changed to* Databased Advisor Magazine **2554**
1524-4113 Journal of Jewish Education **2876**
1524-4121 Beckett Sci-Fi Collector†
1524-4156 New Mexico Museum of Natural History and Science. Bulletin **6727**
1524-4172 Perihelion **5429**
1524-4180 Manhattan Arts International **504**
1524-4210 A B A Trust Letter **1305**
1524-4253 Schwann D V D Advance **6512**
1524-427X Holidays & Seasonal Celebrations. Grades 1-3†
1524-4377 Vinegar Connoisseurs International. Newsletter **4369**
1524-4385 N C G A Golf **8189**
1524-4423 International Journal of Geomagnetism and Aeronomy **2784**
1524-4466 Stitcher's World *changed to* 1932-2720 **6638**
1524-4474 Dance Teacher **2685**
1524-4539 *see* 0009-7322 **5782**
1524-4547 I E E E International Workshops on Enabling Technologies: Infrastructure for Collaborative Enterprises. Proceedings **3312**
1524-4563 *see* 0194-911X **5789**
1524-4571 *see* 0009-7330 **5782**
1524-4628 *see* 0039-2499 **5800**
1524-4636 *see* 1079-5642 **5777**
1524-4652 International Journal of Volleyball Research **8236**
1524-4679 Discovery Trails†
1524-4695 Waterbirds **916**
1524-4725 Dermatologic Surgery Online **6241**
1524-4733 *see* 1098-3015 **6884**
1524-4741 *see* 1075-122X **5987**
1524-475X *see* 1067-1927 **6075**
1524-4776 Journal of Caribbean Archaeology **400**
1524-4814 Franchising World **1817**
1524-4830 States of Health **4056**
1524-4849 Server - Workstation Expert†
1524-4857 *see* 0190-1052 **3181**
1524-4938 N D A Journal†
1524-4946 Briefings on Health Information Security†
1524-4997 Brazzil (Print)†
1524-5004 Social Marketing Quarterly **1844**

1524-5012 The Ochsner Journal 5689
1524-5039 Early Childhood Research & Practice 2844
1524-5047 J C R Science Edition 7869
1524-5055 J C R Social Sciences Edition 8020
1524-5071 Timber Creek Review 5389
1524-508X Corporate Compass 7588
1524-511X Journal of Wide Bandgap Materials†
1524-5160 Tower Investor 2343
1524-5187 C I R A Bulletin changed to 1525-9307 7147
1524-525X U S A Cycling 8269
1524-5268 Midwest Traveler 8590
1524-5306 Solimar 5083
1524-5314 Bitch 8894
1524-5322 Display Development News 3093
1524-5330 Drug Discovery & Technology News changed to Nano-Bio Convergence News
1524-5349 Fuel Cell Technology News 7014
1524-5365 Prosodia 5432
1524-5381 The Elementary School Library Collection†
1524-539X Disney's Animal Kingdom
1524-5470 Gravity (Scottdale) 5423
1524-5489 The Business Press 1075
1524-5519 Harvard Management Communication Letter† 8961
1524-5578 Jewish Business Quarterly 1131
1524-5586 Journal of Forensic Accounting 1295
1524-5594 Girl Talk Magazine 5072
1524-5608 International Journal of Heat Exchangers 4122
1524-5624 Word (Waldport) 5400
1524-5748 Journal of Practical Estate Planning 4903
1524-5756 Orthopedic Coding Alert 4518
1524-5772 Contents†
1524-5780 C A Selects. Detergents, Soaps, & Surfactants 2086
1524-5799 C A Selects. Fungicides 176
1524-5802 C A Selects. Herbicides 176
1524-5810 C A Selects. Insecticides 176
1524-5829 Local Climatological Data. Grand Forks, North Dakota. Monthly Summary 6370
1524-5837 Local Climatological Data. Grand Forks, North Dakota. Annual Summary with Comparative Data 6370
1524-5845 International Journal for Computational, Civil & Structural Engineering 3272
1524-5853 Manual of Credit and Commercial Laws 1366
1524-587X Country Home Antiques Extra†
1524-5896 Today's Child 2169
1524-5942 Spa Business Monthly†
1524-5977 Hidden Maui 8718
1524-6000 Psoriasis Resource†
1524-6035 The Journal of Investment Consulting 1635
1524-6043 Blue Book of Gun Values 8162
1524-6094 Journal of Women's Health and Gender-Based Medicine changed to 1540-9996 8846
1524-6132 The Trumpeter (Westbrook) 8483
1524-6159 E-Business Strategies and Solutions 1416
1524-6175 Journal of Clinical Hypertension 5793
1524-6205 Cerebrum 6131
1524-6272 Alternate Music Press 6543
1524-6310 Catahoula Ezine 6805
1524-6337 Readio 3986
1524-6345 Radical Pedagogy 3078
1524-6353 Web Informant (Port Washington) 2568
1524-6388 Advisor Expert: Lotus Notes and Domino Administration† 8928
1524-6396 Advisor Expert: Lotus Notes & Domino R5† 8928
1524-6418 Income - Expense Analysis: Shopping Centers, Open and Enclosed 7595
1524-6426 Income - Expense Analysis: Federally Assisted Apartments 7595
1524-6493 Currents in Electronic Literacy 2415
1524-6515 Euronomics 1106
1524-6558 Storage Inc† 8991
1524-6566 Beverage Retailer Magazine 599
1524-6582 PetLife†
1524-6655 The Female Patient 8845
1524-668X Ezine Seek Informer
1524-671X Dark Matter Chronicles 5441
1524-6728 Any Swing Goes 6545
1524-6744 The Cortland Review 5420
1524-6752 see 1522-8436 321
1524-6795 Fodor's Exploring Ireland 8705
1524-6817 Adultspan Journal 7331
1524-6957 International Space Industry Report†
1524-6965 International Society for Magnetic Resonance in Medicine. Scientific Meeting and Exhibition. Proceedings 6199
1524-7112 Romance Review 5364
1524-7120 Anotherealm 5439
1524-7147 Poets on the Line†
1524-7244 A A C E Bonus Briefs 2937
1524-7252 Academy of Information and Management Sciences Journal 2519
1524-7260 Academy for Studies in Business Law Journal changed to 1544-0036 4703
1524-7287 Journal of the American Society of Questioned Document Examiners 5915
1524-7317 The Clinical Advisor 5955
1524-7341 Today's Librarian†
1524-7368 Delaware Law Weekly 4655
1524-7430 Journal of Clinical Research Practice changed to 1528-0330 5910
1524-7449 I O M A's Business Tax News Bulletin changed to 1527-9294
1524-7473 The Next Step Magazine 6701
1524-7511 The Pacesetter changed to 1931-6658 4604
1524-7538 Salt Lake 3987
1524-7589 Financial Services Advisor†
1524-7597 Corporate Counsel (New York) 4863
1524-7651 Family Focus (New York) 6268
1524-766X I E E E International Symposium on V L S I Technology, Systems and Applications. Proceedings of Technical Papers changed to 1930-8868 2465
1524-7686 Information Systems Spending changed to 1943-8672 2537
1524-7716 B N A's Federal Environment & Safety Regulatory Monitoring Report 3405
1524-7759 Digestive Health & Nutrition 5922
1524-7767 S A P Professional Journal 2436
1524-7775 Holidays & Seasonal Celebrations. Preschool - Kindergarten†
1524-7783 Global Media News 8104
1524-7791 eBay Magazine†
1524-7805 Latin America: Interdisciplinary Studies 5320
1524-7821 Framing Film 6501
1524-783X Drug Discovery & Development 6834
1524-7848 C C M Magazine† 8938
1524-7856 Better Homes and Gardens Hometown Cooking†
1524-7864 Water Garden News 3754
1524-7899 Mystery Buff Magazine 5414
1524-7902 Securities Law Daily 1650
1524-7910 Computer Grants Alert† 8942
1524-7929 Annals of Long-Term Care 4040
1524-7961 Farm Smart 215
1524-797X Singles Network Newsletter 7944
1524-8011 The New Jersey JobBank† 8976
1524-8267 Single Shot Rifle Journal 8201
1524-8275 Foodservice Research International (Print Edition) changed to 1748-0140 3651
1524-833X Strategic Finance 1302
1524-8348 University of the Sciences in Philadelphia. Bulletin 6884
1524-8372 Journal of Cognition and Development 7370
1524-8380 Trauma, Violence & Abuse 6074
1524-8399 Health Promotion Practice 7523
1524-8402 Food & Service News changed to 1555-5968 4386
1524-8429 Interdisciplinary Literary Studies 5309
1524-8453 Hawaii Westways 8717
1524-847X Rutgers Race and the Law Review 4777
1524-8488 Angus Beef Bulletin 278
1524-8631 Amy Love's Real Sports 8158
1524-8666 Military Heritage 6435
1524-8704 Celebrity Website and E-mail Directory 6492
1524-8755 Saint Louis Homes and Lifestyle 4550
1524-8771 InnSights†
1524-878X Safe Schools, Safe Students 2909
1524-881X Women's Health Advisor 8849
1524-8860 Ed Hitzel's Restaurant Magazine 4385
1524-8879 Human Rights Review 7209
1524-8887 Advisor Expert: Microsoft S Q L Server† 8928
1524-8895 Advisor Expert: Microsoft Visual Basic Web Development†
1524-8909 e-biomed†
1524-900X Fire Protection Engineering 3577
1524-9018 Industrial-Utility Vehicle & Mobile Equipment Magazine 3379
1524-9034 The Pastel Journal 511
1524-9042 Pain Management Nursing 5773
1524-9050 I E E E Transactions on Intelligent Transportation Systems 8498
1524-9174 Fodor's Caribbean 8705
1524-9204 Women's Basketball 8252
1524-9212 D S P Engineering changed to D S P - F P G A.com 3091
1524-9212 D S P Engineering Magazine changed to D S P & F P G A Product Resource Guide 2416
1524-9220 Psychology of Men & Masculinity 7399
1524-9492 3 G Mobile changed to 1751-4797 2346
1524-9522 Protection News 2679
1524-9549 University of Pennsylvania. Working Papers in Linguistics 5192
1524-9557 Journal of Immunotherapy 5763
1524-9573 Mealey's Emerging Drugs & Devices 4875
1524-9581 Art Papers Magazine 471
1524-9719 Produce Concepts 4396
1524-9743 D & B Consultants Directory 1983
1524-9778 Video Journal of Orthopaedics 6075
1524-9840 World Refining†
1524-9859 Bobbitt's Manufactured Structures Newsletter 982
1524-9956 African Language Teacher's Association. Journal 5091
1524-9999 Colorado Manufacturers Directory 1980
1525-0008 Infancy 2155
1525-0016 Molecular Therapy 6028
1525-0024 see 1525-0016 6028
1525-0741 Nylink Connection 5037
1525-075X see 1525-0741 5037
1525-0814 Missouri Life 3982
1525-0849 Utah Preservation 8076
1525-0857 Working Together 1877
1525-0873 Dartnell's Teamwork 1859
1525-0881 Dartnell's Team Leader†
1525-089X Dartnell's Successful Supervisor 1737
1525-0903 Dartnell's Getting Along 1859
1525-0911 Dartnell's First Line Supervisor† 8948
1525-0946 Dartnell's Successful Closing Techniques†
1525-0954 Dartnell's Sales and Marketing Executive Report†
1525-0962 Dartnell's Salesmanship 1813
1525-0989 Dartnell's Overcoming Objections†
1525-1012 Dartnell's Quality First changed to Inside Out
1525-1039 Effective Telephone Techniques 1740
1525-1047 Customers First 1737
1525-1071 Justice Research and Policy (Print) changed to 1942-8022 2658
1525-1098 West Virginia Criminal and Traffic Law Manual 4900
1525-1195 Window & Door 1043
1525-1217 Western Farm Press 170
1525-1233 Endangered Peoples of the World† 8953
1525-125X M A C L A S Latin American Essays 5328
1525-1268 Natural Golfer 8240
1525-1284 Fons and Porter's Love of Quilting 6639
1525-1292 The New York Times Upfront (Student Edition) 2205
1525-1314 see 0263-4929 2750
1525-1330 Aluminum Now 6304
1525-1357 Hospitalist & Inpatient Management Report†
1525-139X see 0894-0959 6274
1525-1403 see 1094-7159 6166
1525-142X Evolution & Development Online 672
1525-1438 see 1048-891X 5993
1525-1446 see 0737-1209 5979
1525-1470 see 0736-8046 5880
1525-1489 see 0885-0666 5650
1525-1497 see 0884-8734 5946
1525-1543 Opportunity Journal 3556
1525-1578 The Journal of Molecular Diagnostics 5653
1525-1594 see 0160-564X 5903
1525-1624 Damon Women's Traveller 8696
1525-1667 Every Second Counts† 8955
1525-1748 Focus on the Family: Life Wise†
1525-1756 Oracle Professional 2532
1525-1764 Official Sega Dreamcast Magazine†
1525-1772 Art World News 471
1525-1799 Rebecca's Garden†
1525-1810 Journal of Special Education Leadership 3026
1525-1829 Fodor's San Francisco 8708
1525-1918 Street Trucks 8605
1525-2019 Journal of Interactive Advertising 27
1525-2027 G3: Geochemistry, Geophysics, Geosystems 2707
1525-2035 Knowledge Management†
1525-2051 Peterson's Job Opportunities. Business†
1525-206X Peterson's Job Opportunities. Health and Science†
1525-2078 Peterson's Job Opportunities. Engineering and Computer Science†
1525-2140 Lummox Journal 5426
1525-2159 Allen Letter 1058
1525-2167 European Journal of Echocardiography 5786
1525-2191 see 0002-9440 5573
1525-2205 see 0148-7973 3484
1525-2213 see 0011-1341 4887
1525-2221 Annuity Market News changed to Retirement Income Reporter 1647
1525-2272 Class Action Reporter 4643
1525-2299 Educause Monograph Series 2949
1525-2329 Marketing to Women 1833
1525-2418 Federal Labor Relations Advisor 1681
1525-2469 Conference on Applied Natural Language Processing. Proceedings of the Conference 5202
1525-2477 International Conference on Computational Linguistics. Proceedings 2424
1525-2531 EContent 2556
1525-2647 Comparative Parasitology 938
1525-2671 The Rejected Quarterly 5359
1525-2736 Employment Practice Liability Verdicts and Settlements 1679
1525-2833 Housing Facts & Findings 4412
1525-2930 21st Century Adventures 8777
1525-2973 Frontiers in Political Communication 7137
1525-3120 Enculturation 8099
1525-3163 see 0021-8812 291
1525-3171 see 0032-5791 297
1525-318X see 1080-7446 8805
1525-3198 see 0022-0302 266
1525-3236 D I S A M Journal see 1532-0359 7251
1525-3244 see 0006-3568 661
1525-3252 see 0899-8280 5584
1525-3260 see 0187-7372 4007
1525-3279 Alzheimer's Care Quarterly changed to 1936-3001 6121
1525-3309 Animal Fair 6803
1525-3325 Nocturnes 5342
1525-3430 Theoretical Aspects of Rationality and Knowledge 2456
1525-3449 Construction News Weekly Covering Central Pennsylvania 997
1525-3503 Ordained Servant 7769
1525-3511 I E E E Wireless Communications and Networking Conference. Proceedings 2324
1525-3562 Guitar One† 8960
1525-3589 Today's O E A 2920
1525-3708 North American Birds 911
1525-3775 Stamping Arts & Crafts changed to 1545-6315 539
1525-3813 Colleges for Students with Learning Disabilities or A D D 2954
1525-383X Multinational Business Review 1578
1525-3864 Plugged In (Colorado Springs) 2165
1525-3880 A V N Online Magazine 2552
1525-3899 Insider Viewpoint of Las Vegas 8179
1525-3902 The Wishing Well 4380
1525-3937 Axe Factory 5259
1525-3945 Snapshot Memories†
1525-3961 J A R O 6081
1525-3996 Artemis 569
1525-4003 see 1525-4011 5061
1525-4011 The Charleston Advisor 5061
1525-4054 Idaho Manufacturers Directory 2005
1525-4062 Wyoming Manufacturers Directory 2036
1525-4070 Arizona Manufacturers Directory 1973
1525-4097 Oregon Manufacturers Directory 1900
1525-4100 Washington Manufacturers Directory 2033
1525-4119 Utah Manufacturers Directory 2033
1525-4135 J A I D S 5819
1525-4194 El Andar (Print Edition) changed to El Andar (Online Edition) 3518
1525-4208 Children's Book and Play Review 7558
1525-4216 Children's Book and Play Review Online 7558
1525-4267 The Open Space Magazine 6601
1525-4275 Corrugating International 6733
1525-4283 Townsend Letter for Doctors & Patients changed to 1940-5464 315
1525-4313 College Spotlight 2954
1525-4321 Consulting Magazine 1735
1525-4399 Economics of T V Programming & Syndication 2380
1525-4429 Peterson's Colleges in the Middle Atlantic States (Year) 2961
1525-4453 Specialty Lender Quarterly changed to Specialty Finance Quarterly 1384
1525-4488 West Africa Review 4179
1525-4496 Association of Jewish Libraries. Proceedings of the Annual Convention (Print Edition) changed to Association of Jewish Libraries. Proceedings of the Annual Convention (Online Edition) 4992
1525-450X Insurance Investor†
1525-4534 CompuNotes

ISSN

1526-5439 Family Bible Studies: Life Truths Leader Guide *changed to* 1557-475X **7625**
1526-5447 *see* 0041-1655 **8517**
1526-5455 *see* 1047-7039 **1784**
1526-5463 *see* 0030-364X **2433**
1526-5471 *see* 0364-765X **2431**
1526-548X *see* 0732-2399 **1833**
1526-5498 *see* 1523-4614 **1778**
1526-5501 *see* 0025-1909 **1776**
1526-551X *see* 0092-2102 **1754**
1526-5528 *see* 1091-9856 **2421**
1526-5536 *see* 1047-7047 **2545**
1526-5560 F B S. Older Youth Learner Guide *changed to* 1557-4938 **7626**
1526-5609 Eli's Medicare Risk *changed to* 1547-9315 **4515**
1526-5641 Classroom Notes Plus **3054**
1526-5668 Family Bible Study: Bible Teaching for 3rd and 4th Graders Leader Guide *changed to* 1557-4377 **7626**
1526-5676 Family Bible Study: Bible Teaching for 3rd and 4th Graders Learner Guide *changed to* 1557-4318 **7626**
1526-5781 Juluka **8726**
1526-5803 N A B C O Breast Cancer Resource List **6028**
1526-5838 Christian Science Quarterly Weekly Bible Lessons *changed to* 1938-6176 **7734**
1526-5854 Family Bible Study: Single Adult Learner Guide†
1526-5900 The Journal of Pain **6155**
1526-5919 Dunnan's Guide to Your Investments **1621**
1526-5927 Cases in Corporate Acquisitions, Buyouts, Mergers & Takeovers† **8940**
1526-5943 The Journal of Risk Finance **1636**
1526-6028 Journal of Endovascular Therapy **6247**
1526-6052 e-Healthcare Market Reporter **1096**
1526-6125 Journal of Manufacturing Processes **1890**
1526-6133 Journal of Electronic Commerce Research (Online Edition) **3106**
1526-6230 The Compassionate Shopper **319**
1526-632X *see* 0028-3878 **6166**
1526-6346 Elysian Fields Quarterly **8227**
1526-6397 Nick Jr. *changed to* 1540-9333 **8977**
1526-6540 Fluid Handling Systems†
1526-6559 The Transcendental Friend **5437**
1526-6575 Quodlibet Online Journal of Christian Theology and Philosophy†
1526-6702 *see* 0730-2347 **5800**
1526-6753 Greater New York and New Jersey Regional Industrial Buying Guide
1526-6915 E-Gear **5070**
1526-7040 *see* 1085-0171 **8723**
1526-7059 *see* 1548-9973 **8766**
1526-7148 This Active Life **4057**
1526-7164 I O M A's Report on Managing Training & Development **1865**
1526-7202 Women in the Life **8890**
1526-7431 Journal of Family Communication **8113**
1526-744X Nephrology Nursing Journal **5971**
1526-7474 EcoFlorida **8699**
1526-7482 Quaker Theology **7740**
1526-7512 Transfer and Mortgage Recording Taxes in New York Title Closings
1526-7539 International Symposium on Modeling, Analysis, and Simulation of Computer and Telecommunication Systems. Proceedings **2472**
1526-7555 Communications in Information and Systems **2410**
1526-7598 *see* 0003-2999 **5769**
1526-7822 Africa Update (New Britain) **4172**
1526-7857 Animals Exotic and Small *changed to* 1048-986X **6814**
1526-8004 Seminars in Reproductive Medicine **5900**
1526-8012 Seminars in Neurosurgery†
1526-8047 *see* 1526-7822 **4172**
1526-8055 Noon **5342**
1526-811X Oklahoma Publisher **7569**
1526-8179 Football Player† **8957**
1526-8195 Cancer Pain Forum†
1526-8209 Clinical Breast Cancer **6016**
1526-8217 Women in the Outdoors **8890**
1526-8233 Journal of Multicultural Nursing and Health† **8968**
1526-8241 Grayson Report **594**
1526-8268 Soundings (Essex) **8283**
1526-8322 Terrain (Berkeley) **3470**
1526-839X Global Technology Business **2534**
1526-8403 Indoor Environment Connections **3439**
1526-8411 Family Bible Study. Access Leader Pack *changed to* 1557-3869 **7620**
1526-8519 Go Boating **8276**
1526-8527 Compensation and Benefits Library **4647**
1526-8535 Intellectual Property Library **4694**
1526-8578 The Chicken Soup Report†
1526-8616 El Visitante de Puerto Rico **7822**
1526-8632 Three Rivers Chronicle **4315**
1526-8667 Exegesis **5294**
1526-8675 Asian Pages **543**
1526-8721 The Endeavor (Gettysburg) **4074**
1526-8748 Neurology & Clinical Neurophysiology (Online) *changed to* 1933-1266 **6166**
1526-8896 N B C Soaps in Depth†
1526-8934 Collision Parts Journal **8575**
1526-8942 Clearing **3054**
1526-8977 Expedition News **8702**
1526-8985 Indian Crusader **6635**
1526-9051 Powder and Bulk Dot Com Newsletter **3356**
1526-9175 Vermont Manufacturers Directory *changed to* Harris Directory. Vermont Manufacturing **8961**
1526-9191 Dam Safety (Year). Annual Conference Proceedings **3264**
1526-9248 Progress in Transplantation **6256**
1526-9256 Helping Children Learn (School Readiness English Edition) **2863**
1526-9264 Helping Children Learn (Elementary School Edition) **2863**
1526-9272 Helping Students Learn (Middle School English Edition) **2863**
1526-9280 Helping Students Learn (High School English Edition) **2863**
1526-9299 Ayudando a los Ninos a Aprender (Preparacion para la Escuela) **2829**
1526-9302 Ayudando a los Ninos a Aprender (Escuela Primaria) **2829**
1526-9310 Ayudando a los Estudiantes a Aprender (Escuela Intermedia) **2829**
1526-9329 Ayudando a los Estudiantes a Aprender (Escuela Secundaria) **2829**
1526-9388 Windows Professional **2600**
1526-9396 Office and Emergency Pediatrics†
1526-9426 Bryant Literary Review **5209**
1526-9469 Offender Employment Report **2662**
1526-9477 Inside Corel WordPerfect Suite†
1526-9507 Criminal Justice Research Reports **2649**
1526-9515 Correctional Mental Health Report **2647**
1526-9523 Journal of Midwifery & Women's Health **5995**
1526-954X Genesis: The Journal of Genetics and Development **868**
1526-9574 AccessWorld (Online Edition) **4079**
1526-9582 AccessWorld (Print Edition)†
1526-9620 Y B News *changed to* 1944-1126 **3719**
1526-9655 Clinical Lymphona *changed to* 1557-9190 **6016**
1526-968X *see* 1526-954X **868**
1526-9744 Contacto (Northbrook) **5742**
1526-9841 Deaf - Blind Perspectives **4081**
1526-985X American Blood Resources Association. Journal†
1526-9884 Film Journal International **6499**
1526-9892 Infotech Trends **2493**
1526-9906 NeoReviews.org **6097**
1526-9914 Journal of Applied Clinical Medical Physics **5906**
1526-999X Research for Nursing Practice **5980**
1527-0009 Graduate Research in Nursing Education **5959**
1527-0025 Journal of Sports Economics **1138**
1527-0106 A C R L New England Chapter Newsletter **4985**
1527-0157 The Bookdragon Review **5209**
1527-0246 Billing Alert For Long-Term Care **4088**
1527-0270 Inside Web Design **2507**
1527-0289 The Clinical Journal of Women's Health†
1527-0297 High Altitude Medicine and Biology **5628**
1527-0351 Travel Guide International **8766**
1527-0378 Creativity Plus **7126**
1527-0408 Tax Foundation. Background Papers **1947**
1527-0424 Vogue en Espanol *changed to* 1556-2123 **2263**
1527-0637 Historical Highlights **7760**
1527-067X Dagobert's Revenge (Print Edition) *changed to* Dagobert's Revenge (Online Edition) **2265**
1527-0718 Classic Trains **8616**
1527-0777 Market Study of Retail Technology **1831**
1527-0793 *see* 1042-1068 **5195**
1527-0807 Parker's California Family Code **4914**
1527-0815 Economics of Neuroscience *changed to* T E N **6187**
1527-084X Men's Health Advisor **6285**
1527-0858 Nepantla: Views from South†
1527-0874 Studies in Intelligence **7267**
1527-0904 Western North American Naturalist **967**
1527-1005 *see* 1526-9256 **2863**
1527-1021 *see* 1526-9272 **2863**
1527-1048 *see* 1526-9299 **2829**
1527-1056 *see* 1526-9302 **2829**
1527-1064 *see* 1526-9310 **2829**
1527-1072 *see* 1526-9329 **2829**
1527-1080 *see* 1527-4306 **2852**
1527-1099 American Cynic **5205**
1527-1129 Coatings World **6716**
1527-1188 Insiders' Guide to Cincinnati **8721**
1527-1315 *see* 0033-8419 **6206**
1527-1323 *see* 0271-5333 **6206**
1527-1366 International Conference on Automated Software Engineering. Proceedings *changed to* 1938-4300 **2590**
1527-1390 r.w.t.†
1527-1404 Journal of Sedimentary Research **2711**
1527-1439 Texas Workers' Comp Advisor **1710**
1527-1447 Florida Worker's Comp Advisor†
1527-1455 California Worker's Comp Advisor
1527-1463 Ohio's Worker's Comp Advisor **4517**
1527-1471 Technology Investor (Print) *changed to* Technology Investor (Online) **1655**
1527-1501 National Driller **8829**
1527-1536 Tango Developer's Journal†
1527-1544 Policy, Politics & Nursing Practice **5978**
1527-1560 Journal Watch Oncology and Hematology **6025**
1527-1579 Journal Watch Gastroenterology **5748**
1527-1722 Mennonite Directory **7738**
1527-1730 Oil Market Outlook: Short Term Focus *changed to* 1549-2931 **6771**
1527-1803 Techniques **2918**
1527-1811 The Jewish Star *changed to* New Jersey Jewish News, Jewish Federation of Greater Middlesex County Edition **7727**
1527-1862 Cider Press Review **5419**
1527-1870 Advisor Expert: Microsoft Outlook & Exchange†
1527-1889 *see* 1040-0656 **8901**
1527-1897 *see* 0022-4529 **8115**
1527-1900 *see* 0018-2168 **4295**
1527-1919 *see* 0018-2702 **1542**
1527-1927 *see* 0361-6878 **5649**
1527-1935 *see* 1047-4552 **7252**
1527-1943 *see* 0026-7929 **5335**
1527-1951 *see* 0164-2472 **8134**
1527-196X *see* 0161-0775 **8481**
1527-1978 *see* 0001-9887 **7102**
1527-1986 *see* 1040-7391 **8895**
1527-1994 *see* 0935-560X **4145**
1527-2001 *see* 0887-5367 **8898**
1527-201X *see* 1084-9513 **7976**
1527-2028 *see* 0021-6704 **7724**
1527-2036 *see* 1042-7961 **8900**
1527-2044 *see* 0034-5210 **5360**
1527-2052 *see* 0042-5222 **4481**
1527-2060 *see* 0021-3667 **2876**
1527-2079 *see* 0031-8213 **6943**
1527-2087 *see* 0009-7101 **6493**
1527-2095 *see* 0049-2426 **5383**
1527-2109 *see* 0742-5457 **8466**
1527-2117 *see* 0002-9831 **5252**
1527-2125 *see* 0065-9142 **5252**
1527-2133 *see* 0003-1283 **5092**
1527-2141 *see* 0190-3659 **5265**
1527-2168 Vegetarian Nutrition & Health Letter†
1527-2206 Health Notes Review of Complementary and Integrative Medicine **309**
1527-2214 Radio Control Microflight **4345**
1527-2222 *see* 1527-2214 **4345**
1527-2303 School Superintendent's Insider†
1527-2311 Tax Credit Housing Management Insider **1947**
1527-2338 Radiology Administrator's Compliance & Reimbursement Insider **4110**
1527-2346 The MacGuffin **5329**
1527-2370 Vision (Milwaukee) **7822**
1527-2451 Tissue Engineering Intelligence Unit **751**
1527-2478 P / M Science & Technology Briefs **6328**
1527-2486 Biostatistics **5587**
1527-2494 International Nonwovens Journal†
1527-2508 Webbound
1527-2524 Positive Teens **2165**
1527-2532 Theory Into Practice - Digital *see* 0040-5841 **2919**
1527-2575 A A A Journeys **8679**
1527-2613 Interactive Healthcare Report
1527-2648 *see* 1438-1656 **3180**
1527-2672 Broker/Dealer Compliance Report (Online) **1614**
1527-2729 Current Treatment Options in Oncology **6018**
1527-2737 Current Urology Reports **6267**
1527-2753 Floral Retailing *changed to* Super Floral Retailing **3757**
1527-277X Plastics Machining & Fabricating **7097**
1527-2958 El Cuento en Red **5281**
1527-2966 *see* 0099-1767 **5964**
1527-2974 The Dollar Stretcher **1336**
1527-2982 Banyan Quarterly **5260**
1527-3024 Interactive Designer†
1527-3032 The Telecom Manager's Voice Report **2372**
1527-3059 Beckett Sports Collectibles†
1527-3148 *see* Employment Guide **1678**
1527-3172 M E D I C C Review **5662**
1527-3288 *see* 0147-9563 **5959**
1527-3296 *see* 0196-6553 **5809**
1527-330X *see* 1090-820X **6235**
1527-3326 *see* 0926-2040 **2105**
1527-3334 Downtown (Charlotte) **3974**
1527-3342 I E E E Microwave Magazine **3312**
1527-3350 *see* 0270-9139 **5926**
1527-3369 Newborn and Infant Nursing Reviews **5971**
1527-3512 U.S. Notary Reference Manual **4800**
1527-3520 Law Technology News **4717**
1527-3539 Infotech Industry News **2368**
1527-3555 Meridian (Charlottesville) **5333**
1527-358X Historical Society of Frederick County. Journal **4296**
1527-3660 Human Factors and Ergonomics Society Bulletin **3196**
1527-3733 Mozart Society of America. Newsletter **6589**
1527-3741 American Pomological Society. Journal **3722**
1527-3776 Studies in Slavic Cultures **4271**
1527-3784 Wine X Magazine†
1527-3792 *see* 0022-5347 **6270**
1527-3806 Talk†
1527-3814 Jewish Voice & Opinion **7724**
1527-3849 The Irascible Professor **2871**
1527-3946 Journal of Cognitive Liberties **7371**
1527-3954 Clinical Leadership & Management Review **5904**
1527-3962 Street of Dreams *changed to* 1540-7683 **975**
1527-3970 Annual Review of Adult Learning and Literacy *changed to* 1930-854X **2945**
1527-3989 Queens County Dental Society. Bulletin **5862**
1527-4047 Essential Assistant
1527-4055 H P A C Engineering **4119**
1527-408X Revolver **6611**
1527-411X Volunteer Leadership **8077**
1527-4136 Golob's Environmental Business Report **3506**
1527-4144 The Portable Bankruptcy Code & Rules **1375**
1527-4160 Journal of Psychiatric Practice **6156**
1527-4209 Lowrider Arte **503**
1527-4217 Lowrider Bicycle†
1527-4225 Lowrider Euro *changed to* 1555-5682
1527-4233 Trends and Issues in Elementary Language Arts†
1527-4241 Trends and Issues in Postsecondary English Studies† **8994**
1527-4268 Contemporary Spine Surgery **6240**
1527-4306 Educator's Notebook on Family Involvement **2852**
1527-4314 Journal of Microfinance *changed to* 1932-9075 **1336**
1527-4381 Complete Guide to Kayak Touring **8274**
1527-439X Blueprint (Washington, D.C.) **7110**
1527-4446 Taking Stock†
1527-4470 Field Force Automation *changed to* 1547-4828 **2369**
1527-4519 A S H R A E. I A Q Applications **4115**
1527-4578 Pop Culture Collecting†
1527-4608 Model Cars Magazine **4340**
1527-4640 Advances in Strained and Interesting Organic Molecules†
1527-4667 Ft. Worth Business Press **1112**
1527-4675 Mergent Unit Investment Trusts **1639**
1527-4683 Mergent's Industry Review **1252**
1527-4705 Tea & Harrisburg Champion *changed to* 1931-8863 **3972**
1527-4756 The Catholic New World **7789**
1527-4764 Television & New Media **2396**
1527-4772 Clinical Practice of Alternative Medicine†
1527-4799 Chemical Innovation†
1527-4829 Fodor's Morocco **8707**
1527-4985 Kayak Magazine **8277**
1527-5027 Strictly Slots **8209**
1527-5035 Track Magazine **8299**
1527-5051 New Hampshire Government Directory **7455**
1527-5167 Children's Writing Update **5273**
1527-5221 Safe Schools Today **3031**

ISSN

DIRECTORY 2010 1529-4552 9677

1528-5855 A I S E Steel Technology changed to 1547-0423 6317
1528-588X Intuitive Flash 2710
1528-591X Graduate Programs in Arts and Architecture 2956
1528-5960 Graduate Programs in Physical Sciences 2956
1528-5979 Graduate Programs in Psychology 7359
1528-5987 Graduate Programs in Social Sciences 2956
1528-6002 JobWatch 6852
1528-610X Intersections in Communications and Culture 8110
1528-6118 Critical Cultural Communications Studies 8096
1528-6193 Limn 503
1528-6223 Graduate Programs in Engineering and Computer Science 2419
1528-6258 Bildhaan 4173
1528-6274 Geo World 4037
1528-6290 Taijiquan Journal 8211
1528-6312 Controls Intelligence & Plant Systems Report 2539
1528-6320 The Boulder County Business Report 1425
1528-6363 Frontline Solutions†
1528-638X G P Solo 4678
1528-6398 Veterinary Practice News 8813
1528-6428 Advertising & Marketing Review 20
1528-6436 Tennessee Archivist 5050
1528-6479 Lifeline (Syracuse) 3773
1528-6487 Avalanche Review 2702
1528-6509 Journal of Ecological Anthropology 344
1528-6533 International Folkloristics 3618
1528-6584 Time for Kids Big Picture (Grades K-1) 2217
1528-6592 Civil War Book Review (Print) changed to Civil War Book Review (Online) 4288
1528-6606 C A E L Forum and News 2939
1528-6681 U S A Deaf Sports Federation Bulletin 4076
1528-6703 Auction Bytes - Update 4327
1528-6746 AltFuels Advisor 8555
1528-6827 Small Flows Quarterly 7542
1528-6916 see 0885-4726 6991
1528-6924 see 1047-7845 7656
1528-6932 see 1097-8526 1575
1528-6940 see 1059-9231 1573
1528-6959 see 1066-9868 1544
1528-6967 see 1049-6483 1824
1528-6975 see 0891-1762 1824
1528-6983 see 0897-4438 202
1528-6991 see 0897-5930 1574
1528-7033 see 0738-0569 2948
1528-7068 see 0896-1530 1825
1528-7084 Brookings-Wharton Papers on Urban Affairs (Year) 8091
1528-7092 Southeastern Naturalist 818
1528-7106 A A C E International Transactions 3179
1528-7122 see 1528-7130 1636
1528-7130 The Kiplinger Letter 1636
1528-7165 The World's Water 8842
1528-7181 Educators for Urban Minorities 3531
1528-7211 The International Abraham Lincoln Journal 7242
1528-7254 Judicial Division Record 4953
1528-7335 New England Travel & Life 5078
1528-7351 A S D S O Newsletter 3258
1528-7386 Internet Healthcare Strategies†
1528-7394 Journal of Toxicology and Environmental Health. Part A 3499
1528-7416 Local Climatological Data. Dallas, Texas. Dallas Love Field. Monthly Summary 6367
1528-7424 Local Climatological Data. Seattle Sand Point, Washington. W S F O Seattle Sand Point 6385
1528-7440 Local Climatological Data. Austin City, Texas. Camp Mabry Army National Guard. Annual Summary with Comparative Data 6362
1528-7459 Local Climatological Data. Austin-Bergtrom, Texas. Austin-Bergstrom International Airport. Annual Summary with Comparative Data 6362
1528-7475 Food & Fitness Advisor 3975
1528-7483 Crystal Growth & Design 2109
1528-7505 see 1528-7483 2109
1528-7521 Broadcast Law Report
1528-753X New York Family Law Monthly 4913
1528-7548 Fuel Cell Industry Report 3135
1528-7556 O A G Flight Guide. North America 8549
1528-7564 O A G Pocket Flight Guide. Latin American - Caribbean changed to 1541-373X 8549
1528-7572 Urology Coding Alert 4526
1528-7580 Physical Medicine & Rehab Coding Alert 4519
1528-7602 Solidsurface changed to 1931-826X 4551
1528-7610 Fleet Maintenance Supervisor 8496
1528-7637 Briefings on Patient Safety 4089
1528-767X see 1048-3306 1949
1528-7815 Washington Techway† 8998
1528-7831 Berlitz Southern Caribbean Pocket Guide 8687
1528-7858 Residential Systems 3112
1528-7971 Shelflife (Princeton) 5173
1528-8005 Forensic Science Communications 5913
1528-8013 Workplace Ergonomics News 6689
1528-8099 see 1524-7716 3405
1528-8129 Romantic Circles Praxis Series 5364
1528-8161 Global Business Magazine 1114
1528-817X Journal of Islamic Law & Culture 7713
1528-820X A S T C Dimensions 7829
1528-8226 e-Service Journal 2543
1528-8234 see 1528-8226 2543
1528-8242 The Internet Journal of Surgery 6246
1528-8250 The Internet Journal of Law, Healthcare and Ethics 5914
1528-8269 The Internet Journal of Ophthalmology and Visual Science 6044
1528-8277 The Internet Journal of Pain, Symptom Control and Palliative Care 5771
1528-8285 The Internet Journal of Neurosurgery 6246
1528-8293 The Internet Journal of Plastic Surgery 6246
1528-8307 The Internet Journal of Pathology 5640
1528-8315 The Internet Journal of Health 7527
1528-8323 The Internet Journal of Gastroenterology 5927
1528-8331 The Internet Journal of Oncology 6023
1528-834X The Internet Journal of Cardiology 5790
1528-8358 The Internet Journal of Family Practice 5946
1528-8366 The Internet Journal of Infectious Diseases 5640
1528-8374 The Internet Journal of Pediatrics and Neonatology 6093
1528-8382 The Internet Journal of Internal Medicine 5946
1528-8390 The Internet Journal of Urology 6269
1528-8404 The Internet Journal of Radiology 6199
1528-8412 The Internet Journal of Rheumatology 6224
1528-8420 The Internet Journal of Otorhinolaryngology 6081
1528-8439 The Internet Journal of Gynecology and Obstetrics 5994
1528-8447 see 1526-5900 6155
1528-8463 Hospital Law's Regan Report 4100
1528-8471 Medical Law's Regan Report 5669
1528-848X Nursing Law's Regan Report 5974
1528-8528 Nanoparticle News 7027
1528-8552 Physicians & Surgeons Directory 2023
1528-8560 Luxury Golf Homes & Resorts†
1528-8609 Lodging F & B 4393
1528-8625 Michigan Telecommunications & Technology Law Review 4734
1528-8838 Teen Style
1528-8870 The Cambridge Yearbook of European Legal Studies 4919
1528-8889 see 0094-4289 3349
1528-8897 see 0742-4787 6776
1528-8900 see 0889-504X 3387
1528-8919 see 0742-4795 3385
1528-8927 see 1048-9002 3387
1528-8935 see 1087-1357 3385
1528-8943 see 0022-1481 3385
1528-8951 see 0148-0731 5646
1528-896X see 0892-7219 3386
1528-8978 see 0094-9930 3386
1528-8986 see 0199-6231 3176
1528-8994 see 0195-0738 3140
1528-9001 see 1050-0472 3386
1528-901X see 0098-2202 3363
1528-9028 see 0022-0434 3349
1528-9036 see 0021-8936 3385
1528-9044 see 1043-7398 3106
1528-9079 The Scholarship Book 3031
1528-9117 The Cancer Journal 6013
1528-9168 Journal of Infant, Child and Adolescent Psychotherapy 7375
1528-9176 Heads Up News†
1528-9257 see 1522-4228 3405
1528-9273 Siliconeer 3564
1528-9303 Inform (Champaign) 2065
1528-9370 The Paumanok Review 5350
1528-9435 see 1528-2953 5626
1528-9494 Transforming Traditional Libraries
1528-9508 Strategy Corner
1528-9648 Seminars in Vascular Medicine changed to 0094-6176 5941
1528-9664 Rain Crow 5357
1528-9672 The Modernist Revolution in World Literature 5336
1528-9702 S A E Off-Highway Engineering 8602
1528-9729 Kiplinger's Personal Finance 1364
1528-9753 Kiplinger's Personal Finance Retirement Planning 1636
1528-9796 Journal for the Study of Food and Society changed to 1552-8014 4358
1528-9826 Ferrets (Print) changed to Ferrets Magazine 6808
1528-9850 Let's Go: South Africa (Year) 8730
1528-9877 Berks County Living 5066
1528-9885 Nuts & Volts 3110
1528-9923 Chemical Abstracts Service. Registry Handbook - Common Names†
1528-9931 Seminars in Cerebrovascular Diseases and Stroke†
1529-0018 Business Finance (Online) 1730
1529-0077 eCommerce Business†
1529-0115 Class Action Litigation Report 4643
1529-0131 see 0004-3591 6222
1529-0212 Satellite Transponder Guide 2389
1529-0298 Family Tree Magazine 3766
1529-0409 Website Success Monthly 2569
1529-0506 A A A Going Places (Buffalo) 8679
1529-0522 F R A Bulletin 3688
1529-0646 Home Planners Presents: Vacation & Second Homes 4541
1529-0654 Ruminator Review†
1529-0662 Biography for You†
1529-0689 Women, Girls & Criminal Justice 2672
1529-0697 Sex Offender Law Report 4898
1529-0719 Journal of Women's Cancer 6025
1529-0751 G A A P Handbook of Policies and Procedures 1289
1529-0778 Kiplinger's Stocks†
1529-0816 Chicago Journal of International Law 4920
1529-0824 Journal of Dance Education 2686
1529-0840 Lapis (Print Edition)†
1529-0999 Jubilat 5424
1529-1006 Psychological Science in the Public Interest 7397
1529-1014 ADDitude 4063
1529-1049 Clinical and Applied Immunology Reviews 5755
1529-1154 Time Almanac 3122
1529-1170 Mr. Cheap's New York† 8975
1529-1189 Global Foodservice 1997
1529-1197 Journal of Men's Health†
1529-1227 Journal of Social Structure 7980
1529-126X Cosmic Mailbox from Circles of Light 565
1529-1278 Astrosolutions 565
1529-1294 The Armchair Astronomer 569
1529-1332 Community Banker (Washington, 1880) 1328
1529-1340 The Hearing Professional 4074
1529-1367 North American Financial Institutions Directory 2021
1529-1391 Broadband World 2495
1529-1456 see 0162-4962 640
1529-1464 see 0022-281X 5315
1529-1472 Science Week 7911
1529-1480 see 0741-5842 5371
1529-1499 see 1098-7371 7554
1529-1502 see 0048-7384 5360
1529-1510 see 0270-5346 6491
1529-1529 see 0145-840X 554
1529-160X Schooldays†
1529-1634 Philosophia Christi. Series 2 6940
1529-1669 The Voice of Agriculture 169
1529-1677 Poultry U S A 297
1529-1715 HomeCare Magazine 5960
1529-174X Insiders' Guide to the Florida Keys and Key West 8722
1529-1774 see 1087-0024 5879
1529-1804 Office Solutions 1853
1529-1820 The American Journal of Transportation 8490
1529-1839 Optometry - Journal of the American Optometric Association 6050
1529-1863 C O R Healthcare Market Strategist changed to 1931-9894 4097
1529-1898 see 0031-8221 6943
1529-1944 The International Electronic Journal of Health Education 6989
1529-2053 Safety Connection changed to 1949-548X 4101
1529-207X Research on Accounting Ethics changed to 1574-0765 1299
1529-2088 Current Topics in Management 1737
1529-2096 Research in Ethical Issues in Organizations 1789
1529-210X Studies in Educational Ethnography†
1529-2126 Advances in Gender Research 8893
1529-2134 Advances in Austrian Economics 1057
1529-2142 Advances in the Economics of Sport†
1529-2169 Advances in Global High-Technology Management†
1529-2177 eDigitalPhoto.com†
1529-2193 Biota of South Carolina 662
1529-2266 Primeros 12 Meses 2166
1529-2282 California Payroll Compliance Report 1669
1529-2290 Payroll Practitioner's State Tax Alert 1938
1529-2304 Atlanta Goodlife 5065
1529-2312 Happy Halloween Magazine†
1529-2339 Tech Finance News†
1529-2347 Money Management Letter 1640
1529-2355 Foundation & Endowment Money Management 1625
1529-2371 Advances in Pacific Basin Financial Markets 1306
1529-2401 see 0270-6474 6154
1529-241X Popular Politics and Governance in America 7172
1529-2428 Popular Culture and Everyday Life 8126
1529-2444 Studies in Crime and Punishment 2669
1529-2460 The Dietary Supplement 6833
1529-2487 Jewish World Review 7724
1529-2509 Caspian Investor 1882
1529-2517 I E E E Radio Frequency Integrated Circuits Symposium. Digest of Papers 2465
1529-2525 Tort Law Desk Reference 4797
1529-2541 The A L P C A Register changed to 1554-6896 4343
1529-255X L O H A S Journal 1143
1529-2584 The Brown University Geriatric Psychopharmacology Update 4042
1529-2622 The African Connection 2143
1529-2673 Family Matters! 2152
1529-2703 see 1073-8886 4111
1529-272X Carve Magazine 5271
1529-2746 Troubled Company Reporter - Latin America 1184
1529-2754 Troubled Company Reporter - Europe 1184
1529-2789 Museums Washington 6532
1529-2819 Tzemach News Service 7731
1529-2908 Nature Immunology 5764
1529-2916 see 1529-2908 5764
1529-2924 Endarch 7133
1529-2983 Quarter Horses U S A 8297
1529-3009 Work at Home Parents E-Zine 1969
1529-3017 Telecommuting Today 1710
1529-3041 Journal of Mundane Behavior†
1529-3181 Association for Information Systems. Communications 2542
1529-3203 Doctor Ebiz 1959
1529-3254 Lollypops 6294
1529-3262 Gastronomica 7966
1529-3459 The Insiders' Guide to Tucson 8723
1529-353X Journal of Space Commerce 63
1529-367X College Admissions Index of Majors & Sports changed to 1550-3186 2954
1529-3688 see 1076-1659 6713
1529-370X Prevention en Espanol 6995
1529-3734 see 0899-188X 5119
1529-3742 Biography Today Sports Series 641
1529-3750 Arkansas Preservation Digest 4284
1529-3769 New York State Bar Association. Journal 4745
1529-3777 A I: Performance for the Planet 463
1529-3785 A C M Transactions on Computational Logic 2405
1529-3963 Performance Computing†
1529-398X Journal of Law & Family Studies 4702
1529-3998 Latino Leaders 3547
1529-4013 see 1528-6312 2539
1529-4021 Tailgate† 8992
1529-4064 Tempus changed to 1538-3105 5223
1529-4129 Journal of Imago Relationship Therapy 7375
1529-4137 Journal of Developmental and Learning Disorders changed to 1944-4133 7372
1529-4145 Neuro-Psychoanalysis 6163
1529-4153 W T O Reporter 1587
1529-4161 Managed Care Law Strategist 4727
1529-4188 International Workshop on Database and Expert Systems Applications 2523
1529-4196 Advances in Lung Cancer 6007
1529-4234 Kagan European Sports†
1529-4242 see 0032-1052 6255
1529-4250 Defence Daily International 6418
1529-4285 B.Smith Style†
1529-4323 N G S News Magazine 3775
1529-4331 World of Drug Information 6886
1529-434X Nanny Fanny 5427
1529-4366 Oil Daily (Online) 6784
1529-4374 Gallaudet Today. Newsletter 2982
1529-4420 Today's Grocer 3682
1529-4455 Nerve (Print)†
1529-4552 Syncopated Perfs 6900

ISSN

1530-3896 Trusts and Estates Law Section Newsletter **4906**
1530-390X Torts, Insurance & Compensation Law Section Journal **4797**
1530-3918 N.Y. Real Property Law Journal **7601**
1530-3926 Health Law Journal **4686**
1530-3934 Bright Ideas (Albany) **4632**
1530-3942 Government, Law and Policy Journal **4682**
1530-3950 L & E Newsletter **4710**
1530-3969 Municipal Lawyer (Albany) **4737**
1530-3977 Construction & Surety Law Newsletter **4649**
1530-3985 *see* 1933-8457 **4798**
1530-4035 California C P A **1284**
1530-4043 Commercial and Federal Litigation Section *see* 1933-8570 **4645**
1530-4086 Annals of Ophthalmology **6038**
1530-4159 Training and Simulation Journal **6449**
1530-4213 Music Express! Primary **6590**
1530-4280 Working Smarter with WordPerfect **2601**
1530-4299 Working Smarter with Microsoft Word **2601**
1530-4302 Working Smarter with Windows 95†
1530-4310 Working Smarter with Windows 98†
1530-4329 Working Smarter with Office 2000 **2600**
1530-4337 Working Smarter with Microsoft Excel **2600**
1530-4345 Working Smarter with Microsoft PowerPoint† **8999**
1530-4353 Working Smarter with Microsoft Access **2600**
1530-4361 Working Smarter on the Internet†
1530-437X I E E E Sensors Journal **4487**
1530-4388 I E E E Transactions on Device and Materials Reliability **3103**
1530-440X Evidence Report - Technology Assessment (Summary) **5612**
1530-4426 Wildlife Conservation Society. Working Paper **3707**
1530-4507 Simplicity **2249**
1530-4515 Surgical Laparoscopy, Endoscopy and Percutaneous Techniques **6260**
1530-4604 Guide to Choosing Retirement Plans for Small Businesses **1684**
1530-4698 Dolls in Print **4334**
1530-4701 ePlant **1105**
1530-4736 Journal of Spatial Hydrology **2712**
1530-4744 Employment Law Week†
1530-4981 The Sedona Conference Journal **4781**
1530-499X Banking & Financial Services Policy Report **1317**
1530-5007 Flight Simulator World **2476**
1530-5015 Better Homes and Gardens Living Room† **8935**
1530-5058 International Journal of Testing **7366**
1530-5147 Schuylkill (Online Edition) **5368**
1530-5228 The Journal for Cultural and Religious Theory **7653**
1530-5309 Dwell **441**
1530-5333 Let's Go: China **8729**
1530-535X Crosstimbers **5281**
1530-5430 Marriage & Family: A Christian Journal **7806**
1530-5449 Loyola Consumer Law Review **4726**
1530-5473 Sociocultural Studies in Educational Policy Formation and Appropriation **3033**
1530-549X Beckett Digimon Collector **4329**
1530-5538 Journal of Jungian Theory and Practice **7375**
1530-5546 Mississippi Economics Review & Outlook **1499**
1530-5627 Telemedicine Journal and e-Health *changed to* Telemedicine and e-Health **5832**
1530-5643 Health Care Program Compliance Guide Monthly Focus **4095**
1530-5678 World Journal of Orthodontics **5869**
1530-5686 Jenda **8899**
1530-5767 Advances in Hepatitis C†
1530-5813 Fund$Raiser Cyberzine **8041**
1530-5821 Saudi Aramco World **4324**
1530-597X Dietary Supplement & Food Labeling News†
1530-5988 The Design Authority *changed to* 1550-4352 **2484**
1530-6003 Hearing Products Report **4074**
1530-6011 Staffing Success **1875**
1530-602X P C Chronicles **2579**
1530-6097 Southeast Real Estate Business **7612**
1530-6100 Christian Media Journal†
1530-6119 Catholic University Law Review **7790**
1530-6127 Fundraising for Small Groups Newsletter *see* 1530-5813 **8041**
1530-6143 Fundraising Providers and Suppliers Newsletter *see* 1530-5813 **8041**
1530-616X The Brandweek Directory **1976**
1530-6194 The Gold Sheet **6844**
1530-6208 The Green Sheet (Chevy Chase) **6844**
1530-6216 Cincinnati Medicine Digest **5595**
1530-6224 Contract **4535**
1530-6232 Pharmaceutical Approvals Monthly **6868**
1530-6240 The Pink Sheet **6875**
1530-6267 Business Woman Magazine **8854**
1530-6283 eWEEK **2557**
1530-6399 e-learning *changed to* 1544-645X
1530-6402 Treating Tobacco Use and Dependence **2700**
1530-6410 Research News & Opportunities in Science and Theology **7902**
1530-6429 Sampling Theory in Signal and Image Processing **2538**
1530-647X Consumer Reports Guide to Online Shopping **2637**
1530-6526 Plumbing & Heating Contractor **4124**
1530-6542 Davison's Gold Book **8463**
1530-6550 Reviews in Cardiovascular Medicine **5798**
1530-6569 *see* 0897-6368 **6085**
1530-6585 Computing Reviews Online *see* 0010-4884 **2415**
1530-6607 Briefings On A P Cs **4089**
1530-6623 Exchange & Outlook†
1530-6631 Journal of School Improvement†
1530-6666 Emergency Response Guidebook **7515**
1530-6747 Federal Workers' Compensation Update†
1530-678X Standard & Poor's Emerging Stock Markets Factbook **1384**
1530-6801 Egypt Revealed†
1530-6860 *see* 0892-6638 **672**
1530-695X Fables **5442**
1530-6984 Nano Letters **3355**
1530-6992 *see* 1530-6984 **3355**
1530-7026 Cognitive, Affective, & Behavioral Neuroscience **7346**
1530-7034 Websphere Advisor *changed to* Databased Advisor Magazine **2554**
1530-7069 Human Ecology (Ithaca) **7970**
1530-7077 Garden State Woman **8865**
1530-7085 Pain Practice **6173**
1530-7107 Genome Technology **764**
1530-7131 *see* 1531-2542 **5039**
1530-7190 *see* 0042-5206 **5437**
1530-7220 Azizah **7709**
1530-7247 International Journal of Applied Economics and Econometrics†
1530-7271 Dentist's Money Digest†
1530-745X State-by-State Health Care Collection Laws and Regulations **4788**
1530-7484 Mealey's International Arbitration Quarterly Law Review **4956**
1530-7530 Charleston Regional Business Journal **1082**
1530-7638 Journal of Integer Sequences **5504**
1530-7646 The Drunken Boat (Farmington) **5421**
1530-7719 Florida Statutes & Rules. Civil **4831**
1530-7743 Sm@rt Partner†
1530-7824 Organic Style†
1530-7832 Hedge Fund Alert **1628**
1530-7859 The Journal of Science Education for Persons with Disabilities **2878**
1530-7867 Voices (Washington) **8077**
1530-7905 Cardiovascular Toxicology **5781**
1530-7913 ChemCite Research Suite **3410**
1530-7921 *see* 1056-7895 **3346**
1530-793X *see* 0021-9983 **3349**
1530-7964 *see* 0731-6844 **3351**
1530-7972 *see* 1099-6362 **3351**
1530-7980 *see* 0892-7057 **7094**
1530-7999 *see* 0021-955X **7093**
1530-8006 *see* 0095-2443 **7093**
1530-8014 *see* 8756-0879 **7093**
1530-8022 *see* 0885-3282 **6247**
1530-8030 *see* 0883-9115 **734**
1530-8049 *see* 0734-9041 **3349**
1530-8057 *see* 1528-0837 **8454**
1530-812X *see* 0069-4770 **6889**
1530-8138 *see* 1045-389X **3349**
1530-8154 Retail Merchandiser **1840**
1530-8162 S R D S Hispanic Media & Market Source **39**
1530-8170 The Business Journal (Kansas City) **1073**
1530-8197 Auto Interiors†
1530-8200 International Journal of Cosmetic Surgery and Aesthetic Dermatology†
1530-8219 The Mentor (Fayetteville) **2993**
1530-8227 Ornamental Outlook **3757**
1530-8235 Let's Go: Ireland (Year) **8729**
1530-8251 Let's Go: Europe (Year) **8729**
1530-826X Let's Go: Eastern Europe (Year) **8729**
1530-8278 Let's Go: Southeast Asia (Year)† **8971**
1530-8286 Management Report (Online Edition) **1696**
1530-8375 City-Smart: Portland† **8941**
1530-8391 Travel Weekly's Official Cruise Guide†
1530-8405 Let's Go: Germany (Year) **8729**
1530-8413 Let's Go: Paris (Year) **8730**
1530-8421 Consumer Goods Technology **1735**
1530-8448 America's 1st Freedom **5206**
1530-8472 Export Today's Global Business **1564**
1530-8480 Golf World Business **8233**
1530-8502 South Dakota Genealogical Society. Quarterly **3783**
1530-8561 Clinical Chemistry Online *see* 0009-9147 **5904**
1530-8669 Wireless Communications and Mobile Computing **2344**
1530-8677 *see* 1530-8669 **2344**
1530-8731 Dahesh Voice **4449**
1530-874X Senior Market Advisor **1843**
1530-8774 Duke Gifted Letter **2843**
1530-8839 Employment in the Mainstream **7206**
1530-888X *see* 0899-7667 **2455**
1530-8898 *see* 0898-929X **6151**
1530-891X Endocrine Practice **5891**
1530-8995 *see* 1081-0706 **827**
1530-9118 Girl
1530-9134 *see* 1058-6407 **1545**
1530-9142 *see* 0034-6535 **1166**
1530-9150 *see* 0024-3892 **5145**
1530-9169 *see* 0022-1953 **4149**
1530-9177 *see* 0163-660X **7273**
1530-9185 *see* 1064-5462 **2446**
1530-9207 Lawyer Referral Directory **4718**
1530-9274 *see* 1063-6145 **7897**
1530-9282 *see* 0024-094X **502**
1530-9290 *see* 1088-1980 **3447**
1530-9304 *see* 1063-6560 **2418**
1530-9312 Computational Linguistics (Online) **5202**
1530-9320 Accounting and the Public Interest **1277**
1530-9339 Aero - News Network **42**
1530-9436 MonsterZine **6507**
1530-9495 Open (Acton) **2595**
1530-9568 Cultural Critique (New York) **7957**
1530-9576 Public Performance and Management Review **7462**
1530-9681 *see* 1531-0043 **6240**
1530-9819 The American Muse†
1530-9827 Journal of Computing and Information Science in Engineering **3385**
1530-9932 A A P S PharmSciTech **6817**
1531-0027 Vascular Surgery and Endovascular Therapy Outlook **5751**
1531-0035 Perspectives in Vascular Surgery and Endovascular Therapy **6255**
1531-0043 Clinics in Colon & Rectal Surgery **6240**
1531-006X Trade Services Directory & Guide **1584**
1531-0078 Official Export Guide: Country Trade Sourcebook **1579**
1531-0086 U.S. Custom House Guide: U.S. Harmonized Tariff Schedule **1585**
1531-0094 Official Export Guide: U.S. Export Regulations **1579**
1531-0108 U.S. Custom House Guide: Ports of Entry and U.S. Import Regulations **1585**
1531-0132 MedGenMed *changed to* 1934-1997 **5677**
1531-0167 Hispanic Poetry Review **5423**
1531-0183 Brandeis Law Journal *changed to* University of Louisville Law Review **4915**
1531-023X Kritika (Bloomington) **4238**
1531-0256 Hedge *changed to* 1558-8645 **1638**
1531-0264 M A R *changed to* 1558-8645 **1638**
1531-0353 Irrigation and Drainage **124**
1531-0361 *see* 1531-0353 **124**
1531-037X CareManagement **4090**
1531-0388 Mosaic Literary Magazine **7568**
1531-0434 Satellite Broadband†
1531-0442 La Herencia **3537**
1531-0450 Fodor's New Zealand **8707**
1531-0477 The Finnish Update *changed to* 1557-1815 **3558**
1531-0485 Journal for Early Modern Cultural Studies **7977**
1531-0558 The R M A Journal **1377**
1531-0612 E-Merging Business **1959**
1531-0671 Nutraceuticals World **6664**
1531-0752 Information Finance & Services U S A†
1531-0809 World of Physics **7046**
1531-0868 Latina Style **3547**
1531-0914 American Society for Surgery of the Hand. Journal **6236**
1531-0930 Gaming Research & Review Journal *changed to* 1535-7589 **8213**
1531-0949 Pennsylvania Economic Review **1159**
1531-0965 Financial Crime Review **1344**
1531-0981 The Journal of E-Business and Information Technology **1419**
1531-1015 Digital Coast Reporter **2554**
1531-1074 Astrobiology **654**
1531-1082 Trauma Reports **6074**
1531-1120 Historical Abstracts **4170**
1531-118X Xi Psi Phi Fraternity Quarterly **5869**
1531-1198 M X Racer† **8972**
1531-1228 Java Enterprise Developer† **8967**
1531-1309 I E E E Microwave and Wireless Components Letters **3312**
1531-1341 Digitrends†
1531-135X *see* 1530-7026 **7346**
1531-1376 Mobile Bay Monthly **5228**
1531-1406 Leisure Group Travel **8728**
1531-1430 Cabinet **480**
1531-1627 Worldmark Encyclopedia of the States **4034**
1531-1635 Worldmark Encyclopedia of the Nations **4034**
1531-1651 Music Express! Intermediate **6590**
1531-1732 Michigan Links Magazine **8238**
1531-1767 Country Discoveries† **8944**
1531-1848 Community Mental Health Report **8035**
1531-1864 Journal of Organizational Excellence *changed to* 1932-2054 **1748**
1531-1872 E-Drive Magazine **3376**
1531-1902 P I M A's Asia Pacific Papermaker **6735**
1531-1929 *see* 1069-5648 **5613**
1531-1937 *see* 0897-1900 **6856**
1531-2003 *see* 1063-293X **2470**
1531-2046 I T E Letters on Batteries, New Technologies & Medicine (with News) *changed to* I T E - I B A Letters on Batteries, New Technologies & Medicine (with News for Research) **7051**
1531-2054 International Journal of Yoga Therapy **6990**
1531-2097 Ancient America **4283**
1531-2135 Pharmaceutical Formulation & Quality **6869**
1531-2178 Casino Crime Digest *changed to* 1553-2909 **2661**
1531-2208 Weil's Arkansas Government Register **7476**
1531-2216 I E E E International Conference on Networks. Proceedings *changed to* 1556-6463 **2498**
1531-2267 *see* 1094-8341 **742**
1531-2291 *see* 0890-5339 **6065**
1531-2356 Florida Grower **113**
1531-2380 Dogs in Review **6807**
1531-2445 Family Court Review **4909**
1531-2453 *see* 1531-2461 **4692**
1531-2461 Insights on Law & Society **4692**
1531-2488 California Journal of Science Education **7843**
1531-250X Expedia Travels†
1531-2518 Easy Internet†
1531-2542 Portal **5039**
1531-2569 Key Readings in Social Psychology **7382**
1531-2615 C V Surgery Online†
1531-2623 Motor Boating **8278**
1531-2712 Standards Manual for Hospice *changed to* 1555-9890 **7542**
1531-2720 Standards Manual for Home Health, Personal Care, Support Services *changed to* 1555-9890 **7542**
1531-2739 Standards Manual for Home Medical Equipment, Respiratory Therapy, Rehabilitation Technology *changed to* 1940-4581 **4111**
1531-2739 Standards Manual for Home Medical Equipment, Respiratory Therapy, Rehabilitation Technology *changed to* 1940-4573 **4111**
1531-2763 The International Social Studies Forum†
1531-2828 Research on Sociocultural Influences on Motivation and Learning **2904**
1531-2909 Headquarters U S A **2004**
1531-2933 The Internet Journal of Healthcare Administration **4102**
1531-2941 The Internet Journal of Mental Health **7366**
1531-295X The Internet Journal of Neurology **6148**
1531-2968 The Internet Journal of Orthopedic Surgery **6062**
1531-2976 The Internet Journal of Pharmacology **6850**
1531-2984 The Internet Journal of Pulmonary Medicine **6215**
1531-2992 The Internet Journal of Rescue and Disaster Medicine **6062**
1531-300X The Internet Journal of Neuromonitoring **6148**
1531-3018 The Internet Journal of Dermatology **5878**
1531-3026 The Internet Journal of Perfusionists **5790**
1531-3034 Sleep Review **7408**
1531-3042 Rink (Ambler) **8197**
1531-3069 Medicine of the Americas†
1531-3085 dotCEO **1740**
1531-314X *see* 1046-4883 **447**
1531-3174 Leadership (Sacramento) **2882**

ISSN

ISSN

1533-7731 American Indian and Alaska Native Mental Health Research (Online Edition) **6634**
1533-7790 *see* 0070-3370 **7281**
1533-7812 Academic Leadership (Hernando) **2823**
1533-7820 Journal Watch Online *see* Journal Watch General Medicine **5748**
1533-7839 *see* 1521-5822 **5748**
1533-7847 *see* 1521-3595 **5879**
1533-7855 *see* 1521-3617 **5748**
1533-7871 *see* 1521-3609 **5748**
1533-788X *see* 1524-0207 **5748**
1533-7898 *see* 1527-1579 **5748**
1533-7901 *see* 0749-6427 **6636**
1533-791X *see* 1091-6687 **7805**
1533-7928 Journal of Machine Learning Research (Online) **2454**
1533-7944 *see* 1521-4710 **8850**
1533-7952 *see* 1521-6535 **6066**
1533-7960 Novell Connection **2502**
1533-7979 *see* 1040-1628 **1753**
1533-7995 *see* 1062-7375 **1766**
1533-8010 *see* 1063-8016 **2531**
1533-8029 S R D S Community Publication Advertising Source **39**
1533-8037 Off the Beaten Path: Vermont **8744**
1533-8053 Bodhi **7700**
1533-824X Prose Ax **5432**
1533-8290 *see* 0002-1482 **83**
1533-8304 The Week **4585**
1533-8312 *see* 0730-7829 **6591**
1533-8320 *see* 0742-9797 **4464**
1533-8339 *see* 0195-6167 **6592**
1533-8347 *see* 0277-9269 **6581**
1533-8363 *see* 1053-9867 **2652**
1533-8371 *see* 0888-3254 **7131**
1533-838X *see* 0004-4687 **7107**
1533-8401 HopeDance **3437**
1533-841X Gothic Beauty **6570**
1533-8428 Garden Compass Magazine **3731**
1533-8436 Southeastern Biology **706**
1533-8444 Language Perils **4512**
1533-8460 Mealey's Litigation Report: Mold **4836**
1533-8487 P P S Alert for Inpatient Rehab†
1533-8509 Eureka Studies on Teaching Short Fiction **5292**
1533-8525 *see* 0038-0253 **8137**
1533-8533 *see* 0037-7791 **8134**
1533-8541 *see* 0734-8584 **5168**
1533-855X *see* 0734-6018 **4472**
1533-8568 *see* 1052-1151 **7674**
1533-8576 *see* 0272-3433 **4157**
1533-8584 *see* 0030-8684 **4307**
1533-8592 *see* 0094-0798 **4155**
1533-8606 *see* 0148-2076 **6599**
1533-8614 *see* 0377-919X **4322**
1533-8622 *see* 1529-3262 **7966**
1533-8630 *see* 0015-1386 **6499**
1533-8665 *see* 0195-6086 **8008**
1533-8673 *see* 0731-1214 **8137**
1533-869X Journal of Experimental Therapeutics and Oncology Online **6024**
1533-8711 Metal Roofing **1023**
1533-8746 InfoCommerce Report **1418**
1533-8762 Teen Hairstyles & Trends **591**
1533-8770 Extreme Collector's Guide **4334**
1533-8789 Hollywood Worldwide Black Hairstyles & Trends **589**
1533-8797 Celebrity Cuts Hairstyles & Trends **586**
1533-8800 Black Hair & Braids **586**
1533-8819 Ignite **6574**
1533-8827 Kid Power! **2197**
1533-8835 Belle Armoire **4564**
1533-8886 Different Kind of Parenting **7352**
1533-8916 New Directions for Youth Development **2162**
1533-8924 Moon Handbooks: Dominican Republic **8737**
1533-8932 The Gardener (Torrington) **3732**
1533-8975 MiBiz West *changed to* 1933-0618 **1149**
1533-8983 Enterprise Systems **2536**
1533-9009 Inside Adobe InDesign **2591**
1533-9017 Focus on Imaging†
1533-9025 Dell All Easy Crosswords *changed to* 1944-4214 **4333**
1533-9041 The Sinatra Health Report *changed to* 1554-2467 **5627**
1533-905X Journal of Injection Molding Technology **7093**
1533-9084 Michaels Create!†
1533-9114 The Journal of Comparative Asian Development **1599**
1533-9122 Mac Administration†
1533-9149 M Magazine **2200**
1533-9165 Technology Electronic Reviews **5063**
1533-9211 The Seybold Report **7580**
1533-9238 Loop†
1533-9254 Southern California Physician **5717**
1533-9300 Managed Healthcare Executive **4106**
1533-936X Strategic Investor Relations†
1533-9440 Journal of Mine Action **8050**
1533-9459 6 Poets X 6 Pages **5439**
1533-9475 Media **4579**
1533-9556 Trends (Chicago) **4975**
1533-9564 Legal Nurse Consulting Ezine **5915**
1533-9610 International Conference on Distributed Computing Systems Workshop. Proceedings **2521**
1533-967X C B S Soaps in Depth **2377**
1533-9769 Friends and Alumni of Indo-European Studies Bulletin **5121**
1533-9793 Polygraph **5234**
1533-9866 *see* 0029-7828 **6000**
1533-9882 Karst Chronicle **2751**
1533-9890 Adolescent & Family Health† **8928**
1533-9939 Internet Banking Growth Strategies **1393**
1534-0139 Children's Magic Window Magazine†
1534-0295 A List Apart **2488**
1534-0333 Trauma and Loss: Research and Interventions **7413**
1534-0341 Just Labs **6810**
1534-035X Transworld B M X *changed to* 1078-0084 **8267**
1534-0384 Molecular Interventions **6862**
1534-0392 Communications on Pure and Applied Analysis **5480**
1534-0406 Emergency, Fire/Rescue & Police Product Review Magazine **7515**
1534-0414 The N A W W Writer's Guide **5337**
1534-0422 International Journal of Hybrid Systems *changed to* 1751-570X **2433**
1534-0473 Women's Policy Journal of Harvard **8905**
1534-052X Moon Handbooks: Hawaii **8737**
1534-0554 Blender (New York, 1994)† **8937**
1534-0562 Consulting Alert **1735**
1534-0589 Pennsylvania Outdoor Times **8328**
1534-0627 *see* 1069-0697 **4477**
1534-0635 *see* 1520-5479 **1553**
1534-0643 *see* 0748-4321 **5320**
1534-0686 Off the Beaten Path: Maine **8743**
1534-0708 *see* 0008-8080 **7789**
1534-083X Embedded Linux Journal†
1534-0937 Cites & Insights. Crawford at Large **5002**
1534-1003 Drug-Induced Nutrient Depletion Handbook **6835**
1534-1178 Forum Geometricorum **5488**
1534-1267 Explorations in Early American Culture *changed to* 1543-4273 **4291**
1534-1410 KotaPress Journals Online *changed to* 1931-342X **5425**
1534-1453 *see* 0163-6545 **4157**
1534-1461 *see* 0038-4291 **5375**
1534-147X *see* 0012-8163 **5287**
1534-1488 *see* 1068-8218 **4475**
1534-150X *see* 0027-4380 **5033**
1534-1518 *see* 0003-5491 **325**
1534-1550 Tax Management Weekly State Tax Report **1949**
1534-1585 Information Plus Reference Series. Energy **3138**
1534-1631 Information Plus Reference Series. Growing Up in America **8107**
1534-164X Information Plus Reference Series. The American Family† **8964**
1534-1712 Reader's Digest Your Family†
1534-1828 *see* 0095-182X **6634**
1534-1836 *see* 0098-9355 **5217**
1534-1844 *see* 1188-9330 **8240**
1534-1852 C - C++ Coder Magazine **2505**
1534-1895 Borough News *changed to* 1940-5774 **7500**
1534-1909 Information Plus Reference Series. Gun Control **2655**
1534-1917 Wisconsin Law Journal **4815**
1534-1925 National Slovak Society of the United States of America. National News **3553**
1534-200X Fellowship of Catholic Scholars Quarterly **7797**
1534-2042 Early American Life **4556**
1534-2093 Renovation Style **1032**
1534-2107 Truck & S U V Performance **8677**
1534-2115 Print Media Magazine *changed to* 1558-9641 **7571**
1534-2158 Oncology Spectrums†
1534-2166 Insiders' Guide to Denver **8721**
1534-2174 Arise Magazine **3519**
1534-2182 Commercial Floor Care†
1534-2204 Nurseweek California **5972**
1534-2212 To Your Health **6998**
1534-228X Cefiro **5271**
1534-2301 Job Choices in Science, Engineering, and Technology (Year) **6699**
1534-2336 *see* 1527-8611 **1073**
1534-2360 Meat Processing Global *changed to* 0892-6077 **3655**
1534-2379 Sufism **7410**
1534-2395 Shutterbug's Outdoor & Nature Photography†
1534-2425 Tools of the Trade **1041**
1534-2441 Radiology on CD-ROM *see* 1534-4363 **6206**
1534-245X Baker's Clinical Neurology on CD-ROM *changed to* Baker and Joynt's Clinical Neurology on CD-ROM **6126**
1534-2530 World Dentistry **5869**
1534-2549 Wilderness Road **3788**
1534-2557 The Wyoming Business Report **1196**
1534-2581 Micologia Aplicada International **801**
1534-259X R E C Focus **7772**
1534-2611 The Community Tax Law Report **1917**
1534-262X Julia **5425**
1534-2719 J C K **4567**
1534-2743 Lenswork **6970**
1534-276X Classical Singer **6557**
1534-2778 CurtinCalls **5956**
1534-2794 The Birmingham Times **3522**
1534-2808 eXtreme teaching **3062**
1534-2816 Complicated Conversation **2838**
1534-2832 Transform† **8994**
1534-2840 Communications Convergence† **8942**
1534-2948 Forum News (Washington, D C) **6524**
1534-2956 Vancouver Business Journal **1191**
1534-3030 On Tap (Alexandria) **5079**
1534-3049 Big 6 eNewsletter **3052**
1534-3057 Journal of Biblical Studies **7654**
1534-3081 *see* 1531-3433 **6135**
1534-309X Current Treatment Options in Gastroenterology (Online) *see* 1092-8472 **8947**
1534-3111 *see* 1522-6417 **5784**
1534-312X Current Gastroenterology Reports (Online) **5922**
1534-3138 *see* 1092-8480 **6135**
1534-3146 *see* 1523-3847 **5757**
1534-3170 Current Cardiology Reports (Online) **5784**
1534-3189 *see* 1092-8464 **5785**
1534-3219 21st-century Music **6631**
1534-3227 Where Chicago **8786**
1534-3359 Damron Men's Travel Guide **8696**
1534-3383 North Carolina Criminal and Traffic Law Manual **4895**
1534-3499 Arts and Learning Research **474**
1534-3502 Official Guide to A B A-Approved Law Schools **4751**
1534-3529 Hi-Torque's R/C Car **4336**
1534-3588 Export America†
1534-3618 Intellectual Property and Technology Law Journal **6752**
1534-3642 P D R for Nutritional Supplements **6668**
1534-3650 Harris Georgia Services Directory **2003**
1534-3820 Plainsongs **6606**
1534-3855 The African American HealthLink **8024**
1534-3871 Points North (Cumming) **3985**
1534-388X Currents: International Trade Law Journal **4922**
1534-3901 Progressive Railroading's Car & Locomotive Yearbook & Buyers' Guide **8622**
1534-391X Industry Norms and Key Business Ratios. Desk-top Edition **1491**
1534-4002 Inside Project Management†
1534-410X Texas Monthly Biz†
1534-4282 Kiteboarding **8320**
1534-4320 I E E E Transactions on Neural Systems and Rehabilitation Engineering **749**
1534-4363 Radiology **6206**
1534-4371 Turnstile's Golf & Travel†
1534-438X Bankruptcy Law Daily **4626**
1534-4398 Telecommunications Monitor **2341**
1534-4401 Chemical Regulation Daily **3484**
1534-441X Federal Contracts Daily **7436**
1534-4428 International Business & Finance Daily **1126**
1534-4436 *see* 1081-1206 **5754**
1534-4541 WagTeen†
1534-455X Corporate Counsel's Licensing Letter **6748**
1534-4568 Corporate Counsel's Web Site Review† **8944**
1534-4606 Comics & Games Retailer† **8942**
1534-4673 *see* 0897-1617 **4864**
1534-4681 *see* 1068-9265 **6236**
1534-4711 Dealerscope **3091**
1534-4746 Anderson's Ohio Law on Disc† **8930**
1534-4754 Ritmo Beat
1534-4789 Patient Care Staffing Report *changed to* 1933-3293
1534-4797 International Conference on Autonomous Agents. Proceedings **2450**
1534-4800 Let's Go: U S A (Year) **8730**
1534-4827 Current Diabetes Reports **5885**
1534-4835 Business Security Advisor *changed to* Boomer Advisor **4042**
1534-4843 Human Resource Development Review **1864**
1534-4878 Mantram **1147**
1534-4908 *see* 1530-4515 **6260**
1534-4916 *see* 1050-6438 **6253**
1534-5025 Proud Parenting†
1534-505X Center for the Study of National Reconnaissance. Bulletin *changed to* 1557-0304 **6438**
1534-5084 Assessment for Effective Intervention **3036**
1534-5130 Bill Dance's Fishing
1534-5157 *see* 0018-1498 **2863**
1534-5165 *see* 0882-8539 **7729**
1534-5173 Cycle World's Motorcycle Travel & Adventure **8257**
1534-5181 Joint Commission Perspectives on Patient Safety **4103**
1534-519X Supply Strategy†
1534-5203 *see* 0882-4371 **334**
1534-522X Arkansas Criminal And Traffic Manual *changed to* 1545-4983 **4884**
1534-5238 *see* 1094-8392 **5362**
1534-5297 National Apostolate for Inclusion Ministry. Quarterly Publication†
1534-5300 Parker's California Labor Code **1702**
1534-5351 European Conference on Software Maintenance and Reengineering. Proceedings **2589**
1534-5378 Star Wars Gamer **8209**
1534-5440 Georgia Workers' Compensation Laws, Rules & Regulations Annotated **1683**
1534-5459 Aquatic Therapy Journal **6106**
1534-5467 ArcUser **2587**
1534-5483 E D N Europe **3093**
1534-5491 DebtSmart **1334**
1534-553X Martha Stewart Weddings **5560**
1534-5548 Rhode Island Workers' Compensation Law **1706**
1534-5637 Black Book. Official Dollar Residual Value Guide **1975**
1534-5653 Group Facilitation **7359**
1534-5661 Clear **2252**
1534-5726 Drive America **8699**
1534-5785 Technology Grant News **8074**
1534-5807 Developmental Cell **832**
1534-5815 *see* 1092-3977 **350**
1534-5823 Behavioral & Cognitive Neuroscience Reviews†
1534-5874 Current Women's Health Reports†
1534-5955 Frontiers of Theoretical Economics *changed to* 1935-1704 **1536**
1534-5963 Advances in Theoretical Economics *changed to* 1935-1704 **1536**
1534-5971 Contributions to Theoretical Economics *changed to* 1935-1704 **1536**
1534-598X Topics in Theoretical Economics *changed to* 1935-1704 **1536**
1534-6056 Vive **8887**
1534-6080 *see* 0041-1337 **6261**
1534-6102 Journal of Higher Education Outreach and Engagement **2990**
1534-6188 *see* 0030-8870 **7896**
1534-6242 *see* 1523-3804 **5784**
1534-6269 Current Oncology Reports (Online) **6018**
1534-6277 *see* 1527-2729 **6018**
1534-6285 *see* 1527-2737 **6267**
1534-6293 *see* 1528-4042 **6134**
1534-6307 Current Rheumatology Reports (Online) **6223**
1534-6315 *see* 1529-7322 **5757**
1534-6331 *see* 1040-8800 **6065**
1534-648X Journal of Housing and Community Development **4417**
1534-6501 Clinical Case Studies **6131**
1534-6528 New Hampshire Selected Motor Vehicle, Boating and Related Laws Annotated **8595**
1534-6536 The Journal of Accelerated Learning and Teaching **2874**
1534-6587 Lunar and Planetary Information Bulletin **577**
1534-6617 *see* 0018-7143 **871**
1534-665X Review of Business Information Systems **1300**
1534-6668 Journal of Applied Finance **1360**
1534-6676 Moon Handbooks: Virgin Islands **8738**
1534-6714 *see* 0799-0537 **5239**
1534-6722 The Dog Lover's Companion to Seattle† **8951**
1534-6749 On-math **5523**
1534-6765 Portrait of Health in the United States **7536**
1534-6781 Ius Gentium **4698**
1534-6803 Manufacturing I T **2524**

ISSN

1535-7155 Florida Monthly **5071**
1535-7163 Molecular Cancer Therapeutics **6027**
1535-718X Mealey's Litigation Report: Cyber Tech & E-Commerce **4875**
1535-7228 *see* 0002-953X **6122**
1535-7260 Homeschooler's Guide to Free Teaching Aids **3064**
1535-7295 Garden & Deck Design *changed to* 1550-6371 **3732**
1535-7309 The Spear Report **1652**
1535-7325 N I D A Notes **2697**
1535-7414 Alcohol Research & Health **2691**
1535-7430 Moon Handbooks: Southern California **8738**
1535-7449 Indicators (Armonk)†
1535-7465 ELLEgirl†
1535-7511 *see* 1535-7597 **6138**
1535-752X Yard Style **3573**
1535-7589 U N L V Gaming Research & Review Journal **8213**
1535-7597 Epilepsy Currents **6138**
1535-7635 Bamboo Science & Culture **778**
1535-7716 *see* 1535-7325 **2697**
1535-7732 *see* 1051-0443 **6201**
1535-7740 T+ D **1876**
1535-7783 International Tax Monitor **1930**
1535-7805 Fairways & Greens (Nevada Edition) **8227**
1535-7813 New York Archives **5035**
1535-7821 *see* 1090-7033 **5600**
1535-7848 Free Online Scholarship Newsletter *changed to* 1546-7821 **3000**
1535-7937 InTouch (Jackson) **1359**
1535-7945 A P C Answer Letter **4087**
1535-7953 Voices from the Earth **3473**
1535-7988 Salud Plus **3987**
1535-8100 Fun with the Family in Missouri **8712**
1535-8143 E X P N Magazine†
1535-8232 Shifra Stein's Day Trips from Austin **8756**
1535-8283 *see* 0066-8435 **381**
1535-8313 Off the Beaten Path: Hawaii **8743**
1535-8364 Blues Buster† **8937**
1535-8402 Women Writers **5400**
1535-847X Strategies For Nurse Managers **5982**
1535-850X S N L Daily EnergyWatch **1649**
1535-8534 Newcomer's Almanac **3983**
1535-8593 The Review of Communication **2337**
1535-864X Intel Technology Journal **2423**
1535-9069 Cycling Utah **8257**
1535-9158 Beckett Golf Collector†
1535-9174 Beckett Baseball Card Plus **4329**
1535-9190 Harris Directory of Nevada Businesses **2001**
1535-9379 Charitable Gift Planning News **1916**
1535-9409 Ag Equipment Power **209**
1535-9433 Photo Industry Reporter **6973**
1535-9468 The Global Community **4927**
1535-9476 Molecular and Cellular Proteomics **739**
1535-9484 *see* 1535-9476 **739**
1535-9492 W L T Magazine *changed to* 0196-3570 **5400**
1535-9573 Class Action Law Monitor **4643**
1535-9581 WebLogic Developer's Journal **2510**
1535-962X Corporate Executive **1087**
1535-9646 Xtreme R C Cars **4350**
1535-9670 Stern's Guide to the Cruise Vacation **8758**
1535-9689 Annual Review of Developments in Business and Corporate Litigation **4855**
1535-9727 Print Solutions Magazine **7326**
1535-9778 Eukaryotic Cell (Print)†
1535-9786 Eukaryotic Cell (Online) **885**
1535-9794 Globalization **7967**
1535-9883 Advance for Imaging and Radiation Therapy Professionals **6192**
1535-9891 Ziff Davis Smart Business (Print Edition)†
1535-9948 L P N/L V N State-Approved Schools of Nursing†
1535-9980 Progress in Oncology **6032**
1536-0024 (Year) Oncology Nursing Drug Handbook **5976**
1536-0032 W D M Solutions†
1536-0040 S I A M Journal on Applied Dynamical Systems **5531**
1536-0067 *see* 1535-2188 **6258**
1536-0075 *see* 1526-5161 **862**
1536-0083 *see* 1535-3516 **1062**
1536-0091 *see* 1526-3800 **3434**
1536-0105 *see* 1526-3819 **444**
1536-0121 *see* 1535-3508 **835**
1536-013X *see* 0162-2870 **509**
1536-0148 *see* 1524-1734 **1789**
1536-0172 *see* 0146-7891 **5342**
1536-0199 *see* 0163-0350 **6584**
1536-0210 *see* 0020-9996 **6199**
1536-0229 *see* 0363-9762 **6194**
1536-0237 *see* 0883-5993 **6201**
1536-0245 *see* 1084-824X **8969**
1536-0253 *see* 0894-8771 **6210**
1536-0261 P E N America **5347**
1536-0288 Journal of Pain & Palliative Care Pharmacotherapy **6855**
1536-0326 Cemetery Directory **3719**
1536-0334 *see* 0160-9009 **8897**
1536-0342 *see* 0011-1589 **5280**
1536-0369 Hotline (Cumming) **4120**
1536-0431 Athletic Insight **7337**
1536-0474 The Ohio Family Physician **5689**
1536-0490 Filson History Quarterly†
1536-0539 *see* 1536-0288 **6855**
1536-0547 Planetizen Newswire **4423**
1536-0555 Storytelling **5378**
1536-0636 Techniques in Knee Surgery **6261**
1536-0644 Techniques in Foot & Ankle Surgery **6260**
1536-0652 Journal of Spinal Disorders & Techniques (Print) **6065**
1536-0687 *see* 1086-4822 **2965**
1536-0695 *see* 0164-7970 **2995**
1536-0717 *see* 1052-2891 **2944**
1536-0725 *see* 1041-6099 **2967**
1536-0733 *see* 0194-3081 **2995**
1536-0741 *see* 0271-0560 **2995**
1536-075X *see* 0271-0579 **2995**
1536-0768 *see* 0271-0633 **2995**
1536-0792 American Brewer and Distiller **597**
1536-0903 Advances in Neonatal Care **6087**
1536-0911 *see* 1536-0903 **6087**
1536-1004 *see* 0899-3459 **6209**
1536-1012 Forum Journal **442**
1536-1020 The Senior Executive Report **1382**
1536-1039 PackagePrinting **7325**
1536-1047 Briefings on Managed Care Credentialing†
1536-1055 Fusion Science and Technology **3167**
1536-108X O G *changed to* Organic Gardening **3746**
1536-1098 Tree-Ring Research **820**
1536-111X Community News Reporter **7720**
1536-1179 E O S O A A Option Alert *changed to* 1931-2768 **1639**
1536-1225 I E E E Antennas and Wireless Propagation Letters **2323**
1536-1233 I E E E Transactions on Mobile Computing **2421**
1536-1241 I E E E Transactions on NanoBioscience **749**
1536-125X I E E E Transactions on Nanotechnology **2571**
1536-1268 I E E E Pervasive Computing **2420**
1536-1276 I E E E Transactions on Wireless Communications **2324**
1536-1284 I E E E Wireless Communications Magazine **2324**
1536-1349 Advance for Imaging and Oncology Administrators *changed to* 1941-3610 **6196**
1536-1357 HealthLeaders **4098**
1536-1365 Advanced Nonlinear Studies **5465**
1536-1438 Harp **6572**
1536-1454 Africa (Year) **1551**
1536-1519 306090 **462**
1536-1527 HIV Nutrition Update **5815**
1536-1535 *see* 1536-1527 **5815**
1536-156X Korean Quarterly **3546**
1536-1594 S B S Digital Design **7580**
1536-1632 Molecular Imaging and Biology **6203**
1536-1675 Miami Metro *changed to* 1538-229X **3981**
1536-1683 O D A Today **5857**
1536-173X Lighthouse **7152**
1536-1772 Acceso. Revista Puertorriquena de Bibliotecologia y Documentacion **4986**
1536-1802 *see* 1521-4281 **3620**
1536-1810 *see* 1522-5321 **4450**
1536-1837 Delaware Review of Latin American Studies **5283**
1536-1888 Planet **5080**
1536-1896 Expert Evidence Report **4670**
1536-190X *see* 1536-1896 **4670**
1536-1977 Privacy Law Watch **4761**
1536-1993 Union County Heritage **3786**
1536-2019 *see* 0525-2156 **1857**
1536-2027 Journal of Vertebral Subluxation Research (Online Edition) **5806**
1536-206X Journal of Law and Border Studies **7249**
1536-2078 Western Wood Products Association. Import Report **3717**
1536-2213 International Energy Conservation Code (Year) **1016**
1536-223X American Spirit (Nashville) **4282**
1536-2256 Darwin (Print Edition)†
1536-2272 Adweek Magazines' Technology Marketing *changed to* 1064-4318 **22**
1536-2302 Cloning and Stem Cells **864**
1536-2310 O M I C S: A Journal of Integrative Biology **876**
1536-2329 The Pure Fundamentalist **1377**
1536-2388 Catholic Quote **7789**
1536-2426 Advances in the History of Rhetoric **5250**
1536-2434 The A M S S Bulletin **7708**
1536-2442 Journal of Insect Science **852**
1536-2531 P C Teach It
1536-2558 Heat Treating Progress **6314**
1536-2582 P C Create It **6980**
1536-2612 S Q L Server Solutions **2509**
1536-2620 Photoshop Fundamentals *changed to* 1094-0774 **2487**
1536-2671 Rhode Island Criminal and Traffic Law Manual **4897**
1536-2698 E-Commerce Law & Strategy **2555**
1536-2779 Placebo Journal **5697**
1536-2922 Journal of Trauma Practice *changed to* 1092-6771 **7368**
1536-2949 Journal of Immigrant & Refugee Services (Print Edition) *changed to* 1556-2948 **7248**
1536-2965 Exchange & Outlook Administrator (Print) *changed to* Exchange & Outlook Pro V I P **8955**
1536-3007 Rocky Mountain Rider Magazine **8298**
1536-3031 Issues in Teacher Education **3066**
1536-3066 I S A News **59**
1536-3090 Pepperdine Dispute Resolution Law Journal **4757**
1536-3112 Keyframe Magazine **2488**
1536-3155 Black Camera **6490**
1536-3201 Oregon Home **3984**
1536-3244 Medical Office Billing and Collections Alert **4514**
1536-3252 Log & Timber Style† **8971**
1536-3341 *see* 1536-3376 **1872**
1536-335X *see* Personnel Software Census. Vol. 2: Human Resource Information Systems **1872**
1536-3376 Personnel Software Census. Vol. 1: Departmental Software **1872**
1536-3384 *see* Personnel Software Census. Vol. 2: Human Resource Information Systems **1872**
1536-3414 Let's Go: Boston **8729**
1536-3430 iC3d **2486**
1536-3465 Let's Go: Washington, D.C. (Year) **8730**
1536-349X To the Trade†
1536-3562 Dub Magazine **8578**
1536-3570 Off the Beaten Path: Chicago **8743**
1536-3589 Day Trips from Columbus **8697**
1536-3600 The Messenger Magazine *changed to* 1096-6625 **3567**
1536-3619 Clinical Updates in Women's Health Care **8845**
1536-3678 *see* 1077-4114 **6025**
1536-3686 *see* 1075-2765 **5573**
1536-3694 *see* 0163-4356 **6882**
1536-3708 *see* 0148-7043 **6236**
1536-3724 *see* 1050-642X **6229**
1536-3732 *see* 1049-2275 **6247**
1536-3759 Christian Higher Education **7632**
1536-3775 S R D S International Media Guide. Business Publications. The Americas **34**
1536-383X Fullerenes, Nanotubes, and Carbon Nanostructures **2135**
1536-3856 E-Scrap News **3505**
1536-3929 American Nursing Student **5951**
1536-3937 Practicing Oil Analysis **6789**
1536-3953 The Pro Rider **8329**
1536-4003 University of California, Berkeley. Center for Slavic & East European Studies. Newsletter **4275**
1536-4046 *see* 1536-383X **2135**
1536-4097 Busy Marketing Tips **1808**
1536-4100 ROTH Teien Journal of Japanese Gardening *changed to* 1942-4094 **3751**
1536-4135 Racquet Tech *changed to* Racquet Sports Industry **8243**
1536-4240 Dialogue: A Journal for Writing Specialists†
1536-4321 Slate & Style **4085**
1536-4445 A L I - A B A Business Law Course Materials Journal **4607**
1536-4550 Nasaba Magazine **3552**
1536-4569 Journal of Islamic Philosophy **6928**
1536-4585 American Journal of Undergraduate Research **7834**
1536-4623 Politics in Minnesota **7170**
1536-464X Indiana Workers' Compensation Laws and Rules Annotated **1687**
1536-4666 C S G State Directory. Directory II, Legislative Leadership, Committees & Staff **7112**
1536-4674 Linux Magazine **2508**
1536-4682 Tucumcari Literary Review **5390**
1536-4704 Tax-Exempt Organization Alert! **1947**
1536-4739 Early Developments **2151**
1536-4755 *see* 1536-4569 **6928**
1536-4771 North Carolina Mental Health, Developmental Disabilities and Substance Abuse Laws **6171**
1536-4798 *see* 0277-3740 **6040**
1536-4801 *see* 0277-2116 **6662**
1536-481X *see* 1057-0829 **6044**
1536-4828 *see* 0885-3177 **5898**
1536-4844 *see* 1078-0998 **5927**
1536-4925 C B R Magazine **8256**
1536-5018 Journal of the Philosophy of Surgery and Medicine **6250**
1536-5026 Nursing Education Perspectives **5973**
1536-5042 Contexts **8095**
1536-5050 Medical Library Association. Journal **5669**
1536-5077 Georgetown Journal of Law & Public Policy **4679**
1536-5107 U C L A Journal of Islamic and Near Eastern Law **4799**
1536-5166 *see* 1070-8022 **6045**
1536-5190 Information Plus Reference Series. Prisons and Jails *changed to* 1938-890X **2655**
1536-5212 Information Plus Reference Series. Water **8825**
1536-5220 Information Plus Reference Series. Illegal Drugs *changed to* 1938-8896 **2695**
1536-5239 Information Plus Reference Series. Alcohol and Tobacco *changed to* 1938-8896 **2695**
1536-5247 Information Plus Reference Series. Transportation† **8964**
1536-5255 Information Plus Reference Series. Nutrition†
1536-5263 Information Plus Reference Series. Immigration and Illegal Aliens **7241**
1536-5298 Crowd Magazine (Print Edition) *changed to* Crowd Magazine (Online Edition) **484**
1536-531X King **6293**
1536-5328 Smart Homeowner (Print)† **8988**
1536-5336 Customer Contact Management Report **1737**
1536-5379 Journal of Optical Networking *changed to* 1943-0620 **7079**
1536-5387 Elite Traveler **8700**
1536-5395 *see* 0275-665X **5772**
1536-5409 *see* 0749-8047 **6131**
1536-5433 Management Research **1776**
1536-5492 Succes d'Estime **8885**
1536-5506 Mande Studies **5330**
1536-5514 Ghana Studies **5300**
1536-5522 Mealey's Litigation Report: California Insurance **4836**
1536-5557 Florida Fossil Invertebrates **944**
1536-5565 Diversity and the Bar **4660**
1536-5581 Conflict Resolution Quarterly **7348**
1536-5603 Harris Directory of Delaware Businesses **2001**
1536-5611 Harris Directory of Maine Businesses (Print) *changed to* Harris Directory of Maine Businesses (Online) **2001**
1536-5638 Harris Directory of New Hampshire Businesses (Print) *changed to* Harris Directory of New Hampshire Businesses (Online)
1536-5646 Harris Directory of North Dakota Businesses (Print) *changed to* Harris Directory of North Dakota Businesses (Online) **2001**
1536-5654 Harris Directory of South Dakota Businesses (Print) *changed to* Harris Directory of South Dakota Businesses (Online) **2001**
1536-5662 Harris Directory of Washington, D.C. Businesses **2001**
1536-5689 Harris Directory of Montana Businesses (Print) *changed to* Harris Directory of Montana Businesses (Online) **2001**
1536-5727 Harris Connecticut Services Directory **1999**
1536-5751 Loyola of Los Angeles Entertainment Law Review **4726**
1536-576X Parker's California Uniform Commercial Code **4878**
1536-5778 Loyola Journal of Public Interest Law **7451**
1536-5786 Michie's Alabama Motor Vehicle Laws Annotated with Commentaries **8504**
1536-5840 Visible Human Journal of Endosonography *changed to* 1559-4017 **5949**
1536-5875 TaxPro Journal **1951**
1536-593X *see* 1091-5397 **6981**
1536-5948 *see* 1076-2752 **5653**
1536-5956 *see* 1068-0640 **6213**
1536-5964 *see* 0025-7974 **5674**
1536-5980 Delicious Living **5069**
1536-6006 Journal of Historical Research in Music Education **6580**
1536-6162 Fun with the Family in Maine **8712**
1536-6189 Off the Beaten Path: New Mexico **8743**
1536-6197 Off the Beaten Path: Pennsylvania **8744**

9686 1536-6200 ULRICH'S PERIODICALS

1536-6200 Daytrips and Getaway Weekends in Connecticut, Rhode Island, and Massachusetts† 8948
1536-626X Best Business Schools changed to Best Business Schools 2954
1536-6324 In Sight (Charleston)†
1536-6340 Bergen Health & Life 3970
1536-6359 see 1536-6367 5517
1536-6367 Measurement 5517
1536-6421 Parker's California Business & Professions Code 4878
1536-6502 Consumer Dimensions 2636
1536-6510 Electronics Industry Year Book 3096
1536-6553 Photo Imaging News 6973
1536-6766 Colorado School of Mines Quarterly Review 1447
1536-6847 Housing Bond Report† 8962
1536-6863 Property Compliance Report 1940
1536-6871 see 1536-6863 1940
1536-691X Social Work Forum 8070
1536-6936 Meridians 8901
1536-7002 Paint Decor 4548
1536-7037 Andrews E-Business Law Bulletin changed to 1555-5941 8930
1536-7096 Gospel Entertainment Magazine 6570
1536-710X Journal of Social Work in Disability & Rehabilitation 8051
1536-7118 see 1536-710X 8051
1536-7150 see 0002-9246 1059
1536-7185 see 0039-6206 5751
1536-7207 Translation Journal 5188
1536-7290 see 1746-1391 8171
1536-7304 Pentagon Brief - Deutsche Ausgabe see 1551-6679 6441
1536-7312 see 0196-206X 6094
1536-7355 see 1076-1608 6224
1536-7371 see 1541-0668 4486
1536-738X Construction Contracts Law Report 4649
1536-7398 Ink Reader†
1536-7428 The Health Care Services Acquisition Report 1117
1536-7452 Harris Massachusetts Services Directory 2003
1536-7495 Genomics & Proteomics 764
1536-7509 Cell Biology Education changed to 1931-7913 828
1536-7517 Long Term Care Litigation† 8971
1536-7533 Seattle Theology and Ministry Review 7680
1536-755X iSeries News changed to 1933-1738 2541
1536-7568 C P U 2409
1536-7657 Foundation Giving Trends 8082
1536-7673 Small Times 2573
1536-7738 Oklahoma Native Plant Record 806
1536-7827 Japanese Language and Literature 5131
1536-7851 My Evil Twin Sister 5228
1536-786X Bandwidth Investor†
1536-7878 Latin American Broadband Markets 2384
1536-7886 Media Money 2333
1536-7967 Journal of Access Services 5062
1536-7975 see 1536-7967 5062
1536-7983 Journal of High Technology Law 4701
1536-7991 Cheri XXX Hardcore 6287
1536-8017 New England Journal of Traditional Chinese Medicine 313
1536-805X see 1525-4097 1900
1536-8165 L J N's Equipment Leasing Newsletter 4710
1536-8270 Pain Management Coding Alert† 8979
1536-8297 Allergy Coding Alert† 8929
1536-8300 D Home and Garden 3727
1536-836X Nephrology Self-Assessment Program 6272
1536-8378 Electromagnetic Biology and Medicine 753
1536-8386 see 1536-8378 753
1536-8491 Broadband Cable Financial Databook 2375
1536-8505 Southwest Fly Fishing 8335
1536-8513 General Aviation News 56
1536-8580 Insiders' Guide to Santa Barbara 8722
1536-8599 Hybridoma and Hybridomics changed to 1554-0014 8962
1536-867X The Stata Journal 8403
1536-8734 see 1536-867X 8403
1536-8742 Medieval Feminist Forum 8901
1536-8815 Nebraska Agri-Business Digest 242
1536-8823 Automotive Design & Production 8564
1536-8890 C L I R Annual Report 4999
1536-8904 Unleashed 5085
1536-898X Fun for Kidz 2189
1536-9013 Fun with the Family in Las Vegas 8712
1536-9056 Zhongguo Jing Ji Ping Lun 1588
1536-9064 Miller's Pond† 8974
1536-9102 Northwest Public Health 7534
1536-9110 see 1536-9102 7534
1536-9129 Communication, Journalism Education Today 2837
1536-9153 see 1551-6679 6441
1536-9161 Hampton Roads Military History†
1536-9323 Association of Information Systems. Journal 2542
1536-9420 Harris Directory. San Diego County Commerce and Industry Directory 2002
1536-9439 The College Board International Student Handbook 2972
1536-9455 Off the Beaten Path: Puerto Rico 8744
1536-9471 Exploratorium (San Francisco)†
1536-9501 The Undying Fire 5392
1536-9536 Art of Angling Journal 8304
1536-9609 Hampton Roads International Security Quarterly 7239
1536-9617 see 0020-8167 6044
1536-9633 City (New York) 5068
1536-9935 Journal of Gynecologic Oncology Nursing 6024
1536-9943 see 1056-9103 5634
1537-0011 European Broadband 2381
1537-002X Visual Studio Magazine 2441
1537-0038 Taste of Home's Light & Tasty changed to 1942-5988 3665
1537-0046 Pro Lights & Staging News 3328
1537-0127 DuPage County (IL) Genealogical Society. The Review 3764
1537-0135 Today's Christian Teen 7690
1537-0186 A I A A Annual Report see 0740-722X 42
1537-0216 Briefings On H I P A A 4089
1537-0224 A H R Q Research Activities 4087
1537-0240 M G M A Connexion 5663
1537-0259 Transportation Management & Engineering 8516
1537-0275 Solutions! changed to 1933-3684 6736
1537-0291 V B Net Advisor changed to Databased Advisor Magazine 2554
1537-0305 Unicenter Advisor† 8996
1537-0364 Backpacking.com see 1550-4417 8305
1537-0410 The Music Index (Online) 6632
1537-0429 Journal of Industrial Technology (Online Edition) 8429
1537-0437 see 1056-6171 291
1537-0453 Wired Art From Wired Hearts 5399
1537-0461 Cemetery & Funeral Business & Legal Guide 3719
1537-0496 The Dark Man: The Journal of Robert E. Howard Studies 5409
1537-050X Off the Beaten Path: Alaska 8742
1537-0518 Fun with the Family in Florida 8712
1537-0526 Off the Beaten Path: Texas 8744
1537-064X Journal of Applied Research 5646
1537-0658 Impact (Westport)†
1537-0747 SpeciaLiving Magazine 4078
1537-0755 Electronic Device Failure Analysis 2485
1537-0798 Sound & Vision Buyers' Guide 8155
1537-0844 see 1043-1543 5808
1537-0852 Linguistic Discovery 5145
1537-0968 U S A Equestrian changed to 1548-873X 8290
1537-0976 Charleston Jewish Voice 7719
1537-0992 Pacific Voices Talk Story 8124
1537-1093 Community Association Management Insider 4647
1537-1107 Private School Director's Legal Guide 4761
1537-1166 Better Homes & Gardens Single-Level House Plans 4533
1537-1239 Best Practices 1066
1537-1247 The Patent Journal†
1537-1301 Lubricants World†
1537-131X N C S E E News changed to 1543-0006 3016
1537-1328 Pharmaceutical Innovation changed to 1176-3469
1537-1336 Diagnostic Innovation changed to 1176-3469
1537-1344 eDesign 8421
1537-1352 see 1535-2722 744
1537-1360 Stem Cell Week 5717
1537-1379 see 1537-1360 5717
1537-1409 Medical Devices & Surgical Technology Week 5668
1537-1417 see 1537-1409 5668
1537-1425 Diabetes Week 5889
1537-1433 see 1537-1425 5889
1537-145X S A P Insider 2436
1537-1476 Exempt Organizations Report 4670
1537-1484 Black Book News 7553
1537-1506 Chinese Business Review 1555
1537-1549 Motor Vehicle Laws of North Carolina 8504
1537-1603 see 0736-0258 6150
1537-1611 see 1522-0443 5647
1537-162X see 0362-5664 6829
1537-1646 Journal of Microlithography, Microfabrication, and Microsystems changed to 1932-5150 7078
1537-1697 A B A Installment Credit Survey Report 1304
1537-1700 Installment Credit Survey Report changed to 1537-1697 1304
1537-1719 see 0737-4038 689
1537-1727 General Anthropology 340
1537-1735 Nutritional Anthropology†
1537-1743 see 1098-3392 1863
1537-1751 see 1077-5714 354
1537-1794 Motion System Design 3390
1537-1816 Journal of Financial Service Professionals 1361
1537-1824 Iowa Journal of Communication 5130
1537-1832 Technology in Practice†
1537-1891 Vascular Pharmacology 6884
1537-1905 see 0363-471X 5767
1537-1913 see 0020-5907 5771
1537-1921 see 0898-4921 5772
1537-1948 see 0025-7079 5667
1537-1956 A T V Illustrated 8253
1537-1999 O S H A Environmental Compliance Handbook 3457
1537-2014 Windows Developer Magazine changed to 1543-6454 8998
1537-2065 Mealey's Asbestos Bankruptcy Report 4835
1537-2073 International Journal of M S Care 6146
1537-209X Journal of Swine Health and Production 8801
1537-2103 Profiles in Diversity Journal 7214
1537-2111 S R D S International Media Guide. Newspapers Worldwide 39
1537-2197 see 0002-9122 774
1537-226X see 1537-2278 4301
1537-2278 Lincoln Editor 4301
1537-2286 California Song 6553
1537-2294 Disaster Safety Review 7514
1537-2308 Optimize changed to 8750-6874 2531
1537-2421 X M L Developer† 8999
1537-2456 International Journal on E-learning 2560
1537-2537 see 0047-2425 3446
1537-2553 GameNow†
1537-260X Academy of Management Learning and Education 1723
1537-2618 see 1531-3468 1124
1537-2634 Frontiers in Health Policy Research (Online) changed to 1558-9544 7518
1537-2642 see 0889-3365 1720
1537-2650 see 0892-8649 1949
1537-2677 see 0740-9303 6048
1537-2693 see 1085-7117 716
1537-2707 see 0735-0015 1247
1537-2715 see 1061-8600 5502
1537-2723 see 0040-1706 3222
1537-2731 see 0003-1305 8344
1537-274X see 0162-1459 8344
1537-2758 Outreach 7770
1537-2766 Marine Business Journal 8277
1537-2774 Office Technology†
1537-288X Techlinks 8440
1537-2898 Drug Delivery Technology 6834
1537-291X Fun with the Family in Massachusetts 8712
1537-2944 Managing Accounts Payable Europe†
1537-2960 Arthritis & Rheumatology 6222
1537-2995 see 0041-1132 5723
1537-3010 Expression (San Diego) 488
1537-3053 Genome Letters (Print Edition) changed to 1551-7551 874
1537-3061 Geonome Letters (Online Edition) changed to 1551-756X 874
1537-3088 Warren's Consumer Electronics Daily 8445
1537-310X Fodor's Washington, D.C. with Kids 8710
1537-3118 Metro.pop 5077
1537-3126 The Whitetail Fanatic 8341
1537-3193 Smooth 5083
1537-3207 International Journal of Coatings Science 2124
1537-3231 Bucks County Writer 5266
1537-3320 Guide to the National Park Areas: Eastern States 8717
1537-3339 Guide to the National Park Areas: Western States† 8960
1537-3347 S R D S International Media Guide. Business Publications. Asia-Pacific/Middle East/Africa 39
1537-3355 S R D S International Guide. Business Publications. Europe 39
1537-3363 S R D S International Media Guide. Consumer Magazines Worldwide 39
1537-3371 College of Aerospace Doctrine. Research and Education. Papers 6416
1537-338X BizEd 2969
1537-3428 Weiss Ratings' Guide to Common Stocks changed to 1935-0031 1655
1537-3460 see 1056-8158 4498
1537-3495 see 1529-840X 1679
1537-3525 Fun with the Family in Tennessee 8712
1537-3592 Health Care Employment Law Letter† 8961
1537-3606 The Manufacturer†
1537-3649 International Journal of Gastrointestinal Cancer changed to 1941-6628 5896
1537-3657 Advances in Service Learning 2824
1537-3703 Language, Literacy, and Learning 5141
1537-3711 The Handbook of Research in Middle Level Education 2862
1537-3738 Research and Theory in Educational Administration 3030
1537-3797 Research in Science Education 7902
1537-405X The Scholar: St. Mary's Law Review on Minority Issues 4779
1537-4238 Taxation of Exempts 1950
1537-4246 OnEarth 3458
1537-4254 The Business Review 1075
1537-4394 Women's Health Wisdom 8849
1537-4416 Journal of Clinical Child and Adolescent Psychology 7370
1537-4424 see 1537-4416 7370
1537-4475 Windows & .Net Magazine changed to 1552-3136 2525
1537-4483 Windows Scripting Solutions changed to Scripting Pro V I P 2503
1537-4505 see 1531-7129 6084
1537-4513 see 1524-9557 5763
1537-4521 see 0148-5717 5881
1537-453X see 0277-3732 6007
1537-4564 Mises Review 1546
1537-4661 Sociological Studies of Children and Youth 2168
1537-4688 100 Show†
1537-4696 Rural Policy Matters 2908
1537-4699 see 1535-2757 759
1537-4726 Journal of American and Comparative Culture changed to 1542-7331 4459
1537-4866 City and Town Government Winning Legal Strategies Report†
1537-4874 Briefings on Local Government Immunity changed to 1537-4866
1537-4947 Alaska Journal of Commerce 1425
1537-4955 Journal of Alaska Business and Commerce changed to 1537-4947 1425
1537-5013 Mind Freedom Journal 6161
1537-5048 Bellevue Literary Review 5208
1537-5080 U S D L A Journal†
1537-5099 Digital Discovery & e-Evidence 4844
1537-5102 Corporate Practice Library (Online) 4864
1537-5110 Biosystems Engineering 222
1537-5129 see 1537-5110 222
1537-5137 Journal for Advancement of Marketing Education 1823
1537-5218 University Press Books Selected for Public and Secondary School Libraries 5060
1537-5269 see 0022-1376 2750
1537-5277 see 0093-5301 1823
1537-5285 see 0022-2186 4702
1537-5293 see 1522-2152 960
1537-5307 see 0734-306X 1691
1537-5315 see 1058-5893 795
1537-5323 see 0003-0147 652
1537-5331 see 0033-362X 7174
1537-534X see 0022-3808 1138
1537-5358 see 0022-2801 4149
1537-5366 see 0047-2530 4703
1537-5382 see 0011-3204 335
1537-5390 see 0002-9602 8087
1537-5404 see 0037-7961 8069
1537-5463 Anabolic Insider†
1537-5498 see 1531-4340 1279
1537-5609 Fodor's Kenya & Tanzania 8707
1537-5617 Fodor's Holland 8706
1537-5749 District Administration 3058
1537-5781 see 1533-8916 2162
1537-5838 Sound & Vision 8155
1537-5846 Contemporary Ophthalmology 6040
1537-5897 Seminars in Pain Medicine 6185
1537-5900 Jitanjafora 5313
1537-5919 The N D T Technician (TNT) 3454
1537-5927 Perspectives on Politics 7165
1537-5935 see 1049-0965 7163
1537-5943 see 0003-0554 7105
1537-5951 Value Line Insight†

1537-5978 Mathematical Sciences Research Journal 5514
1537-6052 see 1536-5042 8095
1537-6079 ProteoMonitor 770
1537-6125 Zine Guide 7577
1537-6133 Fun & Amusement Resources 1997
1537-615X No Limits 2163
1537-6168 Mammography Regulation Report changed to 1554-3285 4106
1537-6176 Ursus 966
1537-6206 Plastics Auxiliaries & Machinery changed to Plastics Machinery & Auxiliaries
1537-6230 Sports Illustrated Women†
1537-6249 School Counselor Magazine 3046
1537-6370 French Politics, Culture & Society 7137
1537-6389 Wage, Hour & Leave Report 1714
1537-6443 Refractories Applications and News 2045
1537-6478 Good Housekeeping Annual Recipes 4359
1537-6494 Mechanics of Advanced Materials and Structures 3354
1537-6516 Toxicology Mechanisms and Methods 3503
1537-6524 see 1537-6516 3503
1537-6532 see 1537-6494 3354
1537-6583 Early Pregnancy (Online Edition)†
1537-6591 see 1058-4838 5811
1537-6605 see 0002-9297 862
1537-6613 see 0022-1899 5820
1537-6656 Experience Life 6985
1537-6664 Chapman Family Association Quarterly 3762
1537-6680 Fathering 8102
1537-6699 see 1523-5998 6174
1537-6796 S I M P L E, S E P, and S A R S E P Answer Book 1706
1537-6869 Smart Tips and Quick Tricks for Microsoft Word 2597
1537-6877 Smart Tips and Quick Tricks for Microsoft Excel 2597
1537-6885 Smart Tips and Quick Tricks for Microsoft Access 2597
1537-6893 Smart Tips and Quick Tricks for Microsoft Powerpoint†
1537-6907 Smart Tips and Quick Tricks for Microsoft FrontPage†
1537-6923 Smart Tips and Quick Tricks for Microsoft Office 2000†
1537-6931 Smart Tips and Quick Tricks for Microsoft Windows 2000†
1537-6958 Smart Tips and Quick Tricks for Microsoft Windows N T†
1537-6966 Smart Tips and Quick Tricks for Adobe Photoshop 2597
1537-6974 Smart Tips and Quick Tricks for Adobe PageMaker†
1537-6982 Smart Tips and Quick Tricks for Adobe Illustrator†
1537-6990 Smart Tips and Quick Tricks for Adobe InDesign†
1537-7008 Smart Tips and Quick Tricks for QuarkXPress†
1537-7016 Smart Tips and Quick Tricks for AutoCAD†
1537-7032 West's Federal Appendix 4967
1537-7040 Beckett Football Card Plus 4329
1537-7199 Studies in Venetian Art and Conservation 520
1537-7342 The Journal of East European Law changed to 1941-8930 4933
1537-7342 The Journal of East European Law changed to Columbia Journal of East European Law 4645
1537-7385 see 0894-9115 6106
1537-7393 see 1533-0397 8768
1537-744X The Scientific World Journal 7913
1537-7628 Model and Talent 2259
1537-7679 Carnegie 481
1537-7695 AIDS Therapies & Vaccines 5809
1537-7709 see 1537-7695 5809
1537-7814 Journal of the Gilded Age and Progressive Era 4300
1537-7822 Intermarium 4232
1537-7830 Journal of Electronic Resources†
1537-7849 see 1537-7830
1537-7857 Journal of Political Marketing 7148
1537-7865 see 1537-7857 7148
1537-7873 Cultural Analysis 3616
1537-7881 Journal of Industrial Hemp† 8968
1537-7903 Journal of Applied School Psychology 3042
1537-7911 see 1537-7903 3042
1537-7938 Journal of Ethnicity in Criminal Justice 2657
1537-7946 see 1537-7938 2657
1537-7989 American Jewish Archives Journal (Online Edition) 7717
1537-8004 Library Resource Guide 5029
1537-8020 Journal of Foodservice Business Research 4392
1537-8039 see 1537-8020 4392
1537-8055 Current Politics and Economics of Asia changed to Current Politics and Economics of Asia and China 7127
1537-8225 Cuisine at Home 4355
1537-825X Windows Web Solutions†
1537-8276 Current Psychiatry 6135
1537-8292 Resonancias 6611
1537-8349 Motor Carrier Permit & Tax Bulletin 8673
1537-8373 Miller Not-For-Profit Reporting 1297
1537-8462 M I N Magazine 7567
1537-8497 i Q: 2558
1537-8551 Foghorn Outdoors. Washington Camping changed to 1557-7236 8323
1537-8721 U Maine Today 2921
1537-8748 Mealey's Product Liability & Risk 4837
1537-8853 Heart Healthy Cooking 4360
1537-890X Current Sports Medicine Reports 6229
1537-8918 see 1537-890X 6229
1537-8926 images.MD 5633
1537-9000 New Architect†
1537-9019 Expert Witnesses & Consultants. Directory (Mid-Atlantic Edition) changed to 1559-6796 4607
1537-9132 see 1537-9140 6093
1537-9140 The Internet Guide to Baby Health 6093
1537-9310 Advanced Topics in End User Computing changed to 1935-309X 2406
1537-937X Annals of Cases on Information Technology changed to 1548-7717 1770
1537-940X see 1537-9418 2156
1537-9418 Journal of Child Custody 2156
1537-9426 Journal of Gay & Lesbian Politics†
1537-9434 see 1537-9426
1537-9477 see 1520-281X 8475
1537-9485 Family Foundation Advisor 4671
1537-9493 Estate Tax Planning Advisor†

1537-9574 C C H Analysis of Top Tax Issues for (Year) changed to 1933-1657 1952
1537-9582 see 1081-3810 5485
1537-9752 see 0032-0919 812
1537-9892 P D R Monthly Prescribing Guide† 8979
1537-9922 F I / C O Expert changed to 1554-365X 2524
1538-0033 Directions in Science 7850
1538-005X see 0898-5669 6101
1538-0084 Absolute Advantage 7506
1538-0130 Roofing Materials and Systems Directory 1034
1538-019X Learning by Design 1020
1538-0254 see 0739-1102 735
1538-0378 Journal of Eurasian Research 4460
1538-053X Foghorn Outdoors. Northern California Cabins & Cottages changed to 1557-2579 8738
1538-0661 H-Net Reviews in the Humanities and Social Sciences 4454
1538-067X see 1092-1095 5955
1538-0688 see 0190-535X 5976
1538-0696 Southern Online Journal of Nursing Research 5982
1538-0726 W O R L D 8848
1538-0742 A N J E C Report 2601
1538-0777 J O F A Journal 7722
1538-0874 FORENSICnetBASE 5913
1538-0920 Thomson World Bank Directory. 1-Vol Edition changed to World Bank Directory 2035
1538-0963 Today's Insurance Professionals 4525
1538-1072 The Drug Advisor†
1538-1102 Foodsafety Magazine 3643
1538-1145 see 1527-4160 6156
1538-1196 Moon Handbooks: British Columbia 8737
1538-120X Moon Handbooks: Arizona 8737
1538-1218 Wheelin' Sportsmen 8341
1538-1242 Surveying and Land Information Science 4030
1538-1439 Kentucky Business Organizations Laws and Rules 4873
1538-1501 Journal of HIV - AIDS & Social Services 8050
1538-151X see 1538-1501 8050
1538-1617 Notre Dame Philosophical Reviews 6937
1538-165X see 0032-3195 7169
1538-1692 Pharmaceutical and Medical Device Law Bulletin†
1538-1730 Business 2.0†
1538-1757 Daily Business Review (Broward Edition) 1090
1538-1811 Deluxe Celebrity Address List 24
1538-1838 The Times-Independent (Moab) 3990
1538-1862 Screen & Display Graphics† 8987
1538-1897 I E E E Workshop Content - Based Access of Image and Video Libraries 2544
1538-1927 Journal of Hispanic Higher Education 2991
1538-1935 see 1536-0636 6261
1538-1943 see 1536-0644 6260
1538-1951 see 1062-8592 6073
1538-196X Vaccinate Women 8848
1538-1978 see 1538-196X 8848
1538-201X California Nuts† 8939
1538-2052 Adolescence and Education 2824
1538-2060 Disability, Culture and Education† 8950
1538-2079 Eurotuner 8579
1538-2273 Biotechnology and Molecular Biology Reviews 760
1538-229X Miami Metro City Guide 3981
1538-2311 Daily Business Review (Palm Beach Edition) 1090
1538-2338 Journal of Property Valuation and Taxation 1931
1538-2354 I E E E L E O S Newsletter changed to 1949-128X 7076
1538-2362 Science Fiction and Fantasy Writers of America. Bulletin 5447
1538-2443 see 1355-0284 6155
1538-263X Electronic Journal of Mathematical and Physical Sciences 5485
1538-2656 Maryland Medicine 5665
1538-2680 Voices (Arlington) 360
1538-2710 Premier Hospital Services Report (Online)†
1538-2745 Oregon Camping changed to 1557-2587 8738
1538-2834 Journal of Northwest Anthropology 345
1538-2842 O P B Member Guide changed to 1949-3827 2387
1538-2869 Lawyers Journal 4718
1538-2885 Country Living Holidays 532
1538-2893 InTech with Industrial Computing 4488
1538-2907 Teach 2917
1538-2931 C I N: Computers, Informatics, Nursing 5829
1538-2982 see 1056-6163 5847
1538-2990 see 0002-9629 5573
1538-3008 see 0091-6331 6229
1538-3059 Harris Directory of Kansas Businesses (Print) changed to Harris Directory of Kansas Businesses (Online) 2001
1538-3083 Contemporary Oral Hygiene† 8943
1538-3105 Lake Effect (Erie) 5223
1538-313X M X Machine Magazine 8260
1538-3180 Peterson's Colleges in New England 2961
1538-3199 see 1538-5442 6091
1538-3202 The Special Ed Advocate Newsletter 4069
1538-327X Stem Cell Research News 878
1538-3296 Current Biography International Yearbook 642
1538-330X Healthcare Resources 5747
1538-3318 Electronic Journal of Mathematical and Physical Sciences. Conference and Seminar Edition 5485
1538-3326 see 1538-263X 5485
1538-3334 see 1538-263X 5485
1538-3423 Privacy & Security Law Report 4761
1538-3431 see 1538-3423 4761
1538-3458 Directory of Steel Foundries and Buyer's Guide 1988
1538-3490 The American Quarter Horse Journal 8286
1538-3512 International Directory of Refrigerated Warehouses and Distribution Centers changed to 1942-7557 4121
1538-3555 see 0037-3222 5370
1538-3571 Journal Watch Pediatrics & Adolescent Medicine 6095
1538-358X see 1538-3571 6095
1538-3598 see 0098-7484 5642
1538-3601 see 0003-9950 6038
1538-361X see 0886-4470 6077
1538-3628 see 1072-4710 6088
1538-3636 see 0003-990X 6124
1538-3644 see 0004-0010 6237

1538-3652 see 0003-987X 5872
1538-3660 see 1521-2491 6237
1538-3679 see 0003-9926 5944
1538-3687 see 0003-9942 6124
1538-3695 Sendero 5369
1538-3792 Real Estate Taxation 7610
1538-3873 see 0004-6280 570
1538-3881 see 0004-6256 569
1538-3911 Country Style Homes, Plans and Designs† 8946
1538-3938 Peterson's Colleges in the Midwest (Year) 2961
1538-4047 Cancer Biology & Therapy 6011
1538-4098 Neurology & Clinical Neurophysiology (Print)†
1538-4101 Cell Cycle 829
1538-4144 Parker's California Civil Code 4840
1538-4209 Legal Resources 4824
1538-4357 see 0004-637X 571
1538-4365 see 0067-0049 572
1538-439X Journal of Christianity and Foreign Languages 5133
1538-4578 see 0961-754X 6911
1538-4586 see 0022-5053 6930
1538-4594 see 0968-8005 6929
1538-4608 Essays in Medieval Studies 4218
1538-4616 see 0022-2879 1362
1538-4632 see 0016-7363 4010
1538-4640 see 0022-1546 2990
1538-4667 see 0196-0202 6079
1538-4683 see 1061-5377 5780
1538-4705 e-Pro Magazine†
1538-4721 Brachytherapy 6009
1538-4748 RoadBike 8267
1538-4756 see 0741-9325 3046
1538-4764 see 0022-4669 3043
1538-4772 see 1098-3007 7378
1538-4780 see 0022-2194 3042
1538-4799 see 1063-4266 6151
1538-4802 see 1044-2073 4067
1538-4810 see 1053-4512 3042
1538-4829 see 1088-3576 6141
1538-4837 see 1525-7401 3038
1538-4845 see 0271-1214 3048
1538-4853 see 0034-3552 4069
1538-4918 Daily News Bulletin changed to J T A World Report (Print Edition)
1538-4934 I O M A's Report on Customer Relationship Management† 8963
1538-4950 Quilting Arts 6641
1538-4977 Harris Arizona Services Directory 1999
1538-4985 Scientific Review of Mental Health Practice 7407
1538-4993 Shifra Stein's Day Trips from Kansas City 8756
1538-5000 see 1531-023X 4238
1538-5027 The Dog Lover's Companion to New York City 8699
1538-5043 Central Eurasian Studies Review 4181
1538-5108 I S P O R Connections 6847
1538-5132 Journal of Planning History 4417
1538-5159 see 0017-9078 5626
1538-5175 Contemporary Psychiatry†
1538-5183 Contemporary Oncology† 8943
1538-5191 Scholastic Administr@tor 3031
1538-5213 A Marmac Guide to Fort Worth and Arlington 8732
1538-5248 Queen 4471
1538-5264 Journal of Lutheran Ethics 7762
1538-5329 U.S. Master Estate and Gift Tax Guide†
1538-5337 Injury Facts (Year) 7525
1538-537X Women Who Rock 6628
1538-5396 Journal of Pharmaceutical Finance, Economics & Policy† 8968
1538-5442 Current Problems in Pediatric and Adolescent Health Care 6091
1538-5485 Off the Beaten Path: Maryland and Delaware 8743
1538-5604 Business Resources 1216
1538-5612 Anew changed to 1934-4317 8844
1538-5620 Promowear 2249
1538-5671 Rhythm changed to 1553-9814 6569
1538-568X International Conference on Knowledge-Based Intelligent Engineering Systems & Allied Technologies. Proceedings†
1538-5701 see 1538-537X 6628
1538-5728 Bio - I T World 757
1538-5744 Vascular and Endovascular Surgery 6262
1538-5876 The Journal of Law in Society 4703
1538-5906 Pro A V 2336
1538-5914 Phi Kappa Phi Forum 2296
1538-5930 I T Contractor 2493
1538-599X Microsoft Office Solutions changed to 1544-1660 8988
1538-6007 Crafty Kids†
1538-6252 Surfacing Solutions 7100
1538-6279 Centro 4446
1538-6309 Nations in Transit (Year) 8122
1538-6341 Perspectives on Sexual and Reproductive Health 6001
1538-6414 Internet Electronic Journal of Molecular Design 734
1538-6430 Public Accommodations Under the Americans With Disabilities Act 4763
1538-6473 Criminology and Public Policy 2650
1538-6570 F.W. Dodge Southeast Construction changed to 1546-9808 1036
1538-6589 Seton Hall Journal of Diplomacy and International Relations changed to 1936-3419 7273
1538-6597 Boston Theological Institute. Bulletin 7628
1538-6600 Venture Reporter 1658
1538-6619 Y C - Young Children 3088
1538-6627 Information Plus Reference Series. Profile of the Nation† 8964
1538-6643 Information Plus Reference Series. Abortion 972
1538-6651 Information Plus Reference Series. Garbage and Other Pollution† 8964
1538-6678 Information Plus Reference Series. Capital Punishment 2655
1538-6686 Information Plus Reference Series. Growing Old in America 4047
1538-6724 see 0031-9023 6113
1538-6732 Wall Street Journal (Classroom Edition) 1193
1538-6740 see 1534-5491 1334

ISSN

DIRECTORY 2010 1540-3335 9689

1539-5693 University of the District of Columbia Law Review **4805**
1539-5715 Off the Beaten Path: West Virginia **8744**
1539-5758 The Wooden O Symposium. Journal **8484**
1539-5863 Travel Tips†
1539-5898 The Journal of Vascular Technology (Online Edition) *changed to* 1544-3175 **5791**
1539-591X *see* 1523-9896 **6261**
1539-6002 Guide to Wealth Protection Strategies **1350**
1539-6045 Biscayne Magazine **5066**
1539-6053 Gothic.net **5443**
1539-607X Limnology and Oceanography Bulletin **2811**
1539-6088 *see* 1539-607X **2811**
1539-6096 Common Ground (Fort Kent) **3411**
1539-6142 Keep on Truckin' News **8671**
1539-6150 Science of Aging Knowledge Environment† **8987**
1539-6177 Mealey's Litigation Report: Copyright **6754**
1539-6185 Mealey's Litigation Report: Baycol *changed to* 1936-7422 **4731**
1539-6207 New Hampshire For-Profit and Non-Profit Business Laws Annotated with Forms **4877**
1539-624X Buyer's Guide **8570**
1539-6282 Plains Song Review **5351**
1539-6304 *see* 1088-5412 **5753**
1539-6339 Carroll's Federal Regional Directory (Year) Annual **7429**
1539-6355 Mergent Municipal and Government Manual **1639**
1539-6444 Mergent Bank and Finance Manual **1367**
1539-6487 Report on Patient Privacy **4110**
1539-6495 G T I Journal†
1539-6509 Discovery Medicine **763**
1539-6533 Reiki News Magazine **314**
1539-6541 Arizona Game and Fish Laws and Rules
1539-655X New Hampshire Court Rules Annotated **4957**
1539-6584 Insiders' Guide to Yellowstone and Grand Teton **8723**
1539-6614 Off the Beaten Path: Colorado **8743**
1539-6630 *see* 1532-687X **4466**
1539-6746 Communications in Mathematical Sciences **5479**
1539-6754 Chinese Public Administration Review **7430**
1539-6797 Chemical Engineering Buyers' Guide **2054**
1539-6827 Conservation In Practice *changed to* 1936-2145 **2607**
1539-6843 Mergent O T C Industrial Manual and News Reports **1639**
1539-6851 Lymphatic Research and Biology **6026**
1539-6924 *see* 0272-4332 **5530**
1539-6932 Off the Beaten Path: Nebraska **8743**
1539-6975 *see* 0022-4367 **4510**
1539-6983 The Healing Muse **5304**
1539-6991 Smooth Jazz Travel Guide *changed to* 1557-3400 **6617**
1539-7025 Tea Room Guide & Digest **3666**
1539-7033 Off the Beaten Path: Montana **8743**
1539-7114 Value Line 600 **1657**
1539-7130 Dig **390**
1539-7149 Registered Rep **1647**
1539-7157 Fired Arts & Crafts **535**
1539-7203 Fundamentals of Antitrust Law **4678**
1539-7262 *see* 0022-2275 **736**
1539-7289 Emerging Industries in the United States **1104**
1539-7319 Connecticut Opinions *see* 0198-0289 **4649**
1539-7343 C R N **2510**
1539-736X *see* 0022-3018 **6153**
1539-7378 Insiders' Guide to Savannah and Hilton Head **8722**
1539-7386 E P M Entertainment Marketing Sourcebook **1815**
1539-7424 Maintaining Safe Schools **3027**
1539-7432 Farming Magazine **112**
1539-7467 Japan Travel View **8725**
1539-7505 The Recorder (San Francisco) **4767**
1539-7521 A C M S I G S O F T International Symposium on the Foundations of Software **2504**
1539-7637 The American Beagler **6802**
1539-7653 Healthcare Information Security†
1539-7661 HazMat Transportation News **8498**
1539-767X *see* 0031-8248 **7898**
1539-7696 EnCompass **8701**
1539-7718 *see* 0033-5770 **699**
1539-7734 Mechanics Based Design of Structures and Machines **3389**
1539-7742 *see* 1539-7734 **3389**
1539-7750 Golfscape Resources†
1539-7769 Off the Beaten Path: North Carolina **8743**
1539-7777 Stratos **8786**
1539-7785 Explorations in Media Ecology **7964**
1539-7858 *see* 0093-1896 **5212**
1539-7890 A B A Bank Marketing **1304**
1539-7904 San Diego International Law Journal **4940**
1539-8072 Sino - U S English Teaching **5174**
1539-8080 U S - China Foreign Language **5190**
1539-8099 Readings in Financial Planning **1377**
1539-8102 Off the Beaten Path: Tennessee **8744**
1539-8110 Off the Beaten Path: Virginia **8744**
1539-8129 Off the Beaten Path: Missouri **8743**
1539-8137 Network Magazine *changed to* 1557-2145
1539-8196 Off the Beaten Path: Ohio **8743**
1539-8250 Philosophia Africana **6940**
1539-8269 Old-House Interiors Design Center Sourcebook **4561**
1539-8285 Journal of Consumer Health on the Internet **2562**
1539-8293 *see* 1539-8285 **2562**
1539-8323 The Journals of Legal Scholarship. Issues in Legal Scholarship **4704**
1539-834X SkillsU S A Champions **2913**
1539-8358 G.K. Hall Bibliographic Guide to Latin American Studies†
1539-8366 AggMan *changed to* 1552-3071 **975**
1539-8412 Journal of Geriatric Physical Therapy **4049**
1539-851X African Diaspora Journal of Mathematics **5467**
1539-8528 Arkansas Nursing News **5952**
1539-8595 Psyche (Staten Island) **5355**
1539-8609 Caregiving! **4042**
1539-8625 DataLink **5005**
1539-8633 Italian Cooking & Living **4391**
1539-8641 Off the Beaten Path: Connecticut **8743**
1539-865X Supply Chain Systems Magazine *changed to* E R I Journal
1539-8684 Pennsylvania Health & You†
1539-8706 *see* Journal of International Women's Studies **8899**
1539-8714 Journal of Articles in Support of the Null Hypothesis **7872**
1539-8730 Fun with the Family Pennsylvania **8712**
1539-8773 Clifford the Big Red Dog **2183**
1539-8803 Broadband Properties **2375**
1539-8978 Wiley C P A Examination Review. Business Law and Professional Responsibilities *changed to* 1930-9090 **4883**
1539-8978 Wiley C P A Examination Review. Business Law and Professional Responsibilities *changed to* 1930-7489 **1303**
1539-9036 Buffalo Intellectual Property Law Journal **4633**
1539-9044 Fun with the Family in North Carolina **8712**
1539-9079 Hunting & Fishing Collectibles **8318**
1539-9087 A C M Transactions on Embedded Computing Systems **2405**
1539-9184 Gulf Coast Business Review **1115**
1539-9192 *see* 1051-2144 **5891**
1539-9273 S C S I Safety Monitor **6685**
1539-946X Smart Tips and Quick Tricks for Microsoft Office X P†
1539-9508 Popstar! **6607**
1539-9532 Tomorrow's Technician **8607**
1539-9583 F Y E *changed to* 1545-5742 **2978**
1539-9591 Twin Cities Jewish Life **7731**
1539-9664 Education Next **3021**
1539-9672 *see* 1539-9664 **3021**
1539-9699 International Country Risk Guide Annual. Vol. 1, The Americas **1492**
1539-9710 Points of Entry *changed to* 1558-4828 **5286**
1539-9788 International Country Risk Guide Annual. Vol. 2, Europe (European Union) **1492**
1539-9796 International Country Risk Guide Annual. Vol. 3, Europe (Non-European Union) **1492**
1539-9818 International Country Risk Guide Annual. Vol. 5, Sub-Saharan Africa **1492**
1539-9826 International Country Risk Guide Annual. Vol. 6, Asia & the Pacific **1492**
1539-9834 International Country Risk Guide Annual. Vol. 7, Risk Ratings & Statistics **1492**
1539-9885 Security Resources **2516**
1539-9893 *see* 1539-9273 **6685**
1539-9907 Joint Commission International Accreditation Standards for Clinical Laboratories **4103**
1539-9915 Karen Brown's U.S.A.: Pacific Northwest **8727**
1539-9923 Insiders' Guide to California Wine Country **8721**
1539-9958 Concepts in Modern Optics *changed to* 1543-0537 **7081**
1539-9966 Ear Piece *changed to* 1546-735X **4463**
1539-9990 Parks & Rec Business **8327**
1540-0018 Federal Personnel Guide on LAN *see* 0163-7665 **1861**
1540-0026 Direct Instruction News **3058**
1540-0034 Homes of Color **4360**
1540-0050 W W D Children's Business *changed to* 1554-2122
1540-0069 *see* 1028-6578 **3203**
1540-0077 Journal of Direct Instruction **3067**
1540-0085 Expressions Maghrebines **5294**
1540-0093 Ultimate Marvel **2219**
1540-0107 Undiplomatic Times **7270**
1540-0123 Human Rights Dialogue **7208**
1540-0158 FightSport **8173**
1540-0166 *see* 1540-0123 **7208**
1540-0174 *see* 1540-0182 **7411**
1540-0182 Technology, Instruction, Cognition and Learning **7411**
1540-0190 *see* 1540-0204
1540-0204 Synchrotron Radiation International†
1540-0212 *see* 1540-0220 **4395**
1540-0220 Philadelphia Restaurateur **4395**
1540-0298 Internships†
1540-0344 Association for the Advancement of Automotive Medicine. Conference Proceedings *changed to* 1943-2461 **5575**
1540-0352 Clinical Prostate Cancer *changed to* 1558-7673 **6016**
1540-0360 Association for the Advancement of Automotive Medicine. Annual Proceedings *changed to* 1943-2461 **5575**
1540-0492 *see* 1538-9006 **5056**
1540-0514 *see* 1073-2322 **5714**
1540-0565 Scrye **4346**
1540-0573 Cherokee Phoenix and Indian Advocate **3526**
1540-0581 Military Trader **4340**
1540-059X Cotton & Quail Antique Gazette† **8944**
1540-0603 Internet Travel Planner **8724**
1540-0611 Hiking Rocky Mountain National Park **8718**
1540-0638 Rental and Staging Systems **2025**
1540-0697 H F M A Wants You to Know **6698**
1540-0719 2.5 G-3 G **2346**
1540-0735 Endocrine Today **5891**
1540-0786 Cuaderno de Investigacion en la Educacion **2840**
1540-0794 Brazil Country Report† **8937**
1540-0816 Honorbound Magazine for Men **7760**
1540-0824 Broker Magazine **1614**
1540-0867 Lehigh Valley Style **3980**
1540-0875 Susquehanna Style **3990**
1540-0891 Cyber-Crime Fighter **2512**
1540-0913 Qualified Retirement Plans **1704**
1540-0921 Alaska Criminal and Traffic Law Manual **4883**
1540-0948 Ethics, Law, and Aging Review†
1540-1014 Business Scene **1075**
1540-1022 Los Servicios Sociales Para Las Personas Mayores En Iberoamerica **8068**
1540-1065 The C A A S Research Report **7203**
1540-1073 *see* 1540-1065 **7203**
1540-1081 Lightning Bug **2199**
1540-1111 *see* 1936-248X **1658**
1540-1197 Off the Beaten Path: Arizona **8743**
1540-1200 American Academy of Business, Cambridge. Journal **1058**
1540-1286 Rundt's World Business Intelligence **1581**
1540-1324 African American Yearbook **6692**
1540-1340 Off the Beaten Path: Iowa **8743**
1540-1383 Journal of Creativity in Mental Health **7372**
1540-1391 *see* 1540-1383 **7372**
1540-1405 Journal of the National Comprehensive Cancer Network **6025**
1540-1413 *see* 1540-1405 **6025**
1540-1421 Nonlinearity in Biology, Toxicology and Medicine†
1540-143X Nonlinearity in Biology, Toxicology, Medicine *changed to* 1559-3258 **5606**
1540-1448 9 Magazine **8614**
1540-1456 Let's Go: Western Europe **8730**
1540-1480 Georgia Environmental Action Report†
1540-1499 Public Policy & Practice **7174**
1540-1502 DiversityInc **4866**
1540-1510 Fun with the Family in Indiana **8712**
1540-1529 Romantic Days and Nights in New Orleans **8753**
1540-1537 Off the Beaten Path: New Hampshire **8743**
1540-1545 Quick Escapes: Boston **8749**
1540-1650 Chinese Journal of International Law **4920**
1540-1669 The Industrial Geographer **4015**
1540-1677 Communications in Theriogenology **8795**
1540-1707 Complete Book of Business Schools *changed to* Best Business Schools **2954**
1540-1758 Insiders' Guide to the Monterey Peninsula **8723**
1540-1766 Advanced Metallization Conference. Proceedings **6304**
1540-1774 Noodle **4377**
1540-1847 The Business Journal (Minneapolis - St. Paul) **1073**
1540-1855 Journal of Integrative Psychology **7375**
1540-1863 Psych Thoughts **7394**
1540-1871 Terminus **5386**
1540-188X N E C Digest†
1540-1960 M I S Quarterly Executive **1145**
1540-1979 *see* 1540-1960 **1145**
1540-1995 Articles, Abstracts, Documents, Papers, Reports and Literature Resources **2552**
1540-2002 Behavioral Sleep Medicine **7339**
1540-2010 *see* 1540-2002 **7339**
1540-2088 Zuri
1540-2096 Quick Escapes: Los Angeles **8749**
1540-210X Off the Beaten Path: Southern California **8744**
1540-2118 E B N†
1540-2126 Journal of Hate Studies **7979**
1540-2134 Off the Beaten Path: Wisconsin **8744**
1540-2142 Off the Beaten Path: Quebec **8744**
1540-2150 Fun with the Family in Utah *changed to* Fun with the Family Utah **8712**
1540-2169 Fun with the Family in Connecticut **8711**
1540-2185 Paraglider **8192**
1540-2193 Stock Car REV† **8990**
1540-2207 Warzones† **8998**
1540-2215 Teen Vogue **2262**
1540-2274 M D R's New Mexico School Directory **2957**
1540-2282 M D R's Oregon School Directory **2957**
1540-2290 M D R's Rhode Island School Directory **2957**
1540-2304 M D R's South Carolina School Directory **2960**
1540-2312 M D R's Tennessee School Directory **2960**
1540-2320 M D R's Virginia School Directory **2960**
1540-2347 *see* 1527-5256 **5507**
1540-2355 Managed Care Pharmacy Update **6860**
1540-2428 Nature Conservancy **2621**
1540-2436 Step Inside Design† **8990**
1540-2452 *see* 1535-5535 **2584**
1540-2460 Laparoscopy and S L S Report *changed to* 1553-7080 **6251**
1540-2479 Health in Action†
1540-2487 Disaster Management & Response **5957**
1540-2495 *see* 1540-2487 **5957**
1540-2525 The Journal of Technology, Learning, and Assessment **2430**
1540-2584 The Internet Journal of Alternative Medicine **311**
1540-2592 The Internet Journal of Cardiovascular Research **5790**
1540-2606 The Internet Journal of Endocrinology **5895**
1540-2614 The Internet Journal of Epidemiology **7527**
1540-2622 The Internet Journal of Forensic Sciences **5914**
1540-2630 The Internet Journal of Genomics and Proteomics **766**
1540-2649 The Internet Journal of Hematology **5939**
1540-2657 The Internet Journal of Medical Simulation and Technology *changed to* 1559-4734 **5640**
1540-2665 The Internet Journal of Nephrology **6269**
1540-2673 The Internet Journal of Space Medicine†
1540-2681 The Internet Journal of Tropical Medicine **5819**
1540-269X The Internet Journal of World Health and Societal Politics **7527**
1540-2711 H R Department Benchmarks and Analysis **1862**
1540-2770 The Therapist **7412**
1540-2800 Power Electronics Technology **3111**
1540-2827 W W E Raw *changed to* 1933-4524 **8215**
1540-2886 Jazz Education Journal† **8967**
1540-2916 American Medical Association. Council on Ethical and Judicial Affairs. Code of Medical Ethics. Current Opinions with Annotations **5573**
1540-2967 Black Tech **2408**
1540-2975 *see* 1540-2967 **2408**
1540-2991 MWorld **1780**
1540-3009 Dao **6913**
1540-3025 Clinical Perspectives on Lysosomal Storage Disorders **5597**
1540-3033 1000 World Leaders of Scientific Influence **648**
1540-305X Fun with the Family in Northern California **8712**
1540-3068 Blackbird **5264**
1540-3084 American Literary Realism **5406**
1540-3092 N F L Insider Magazine†
1540-3106 Paste **6604**
1540-3114 REALbasic Developer **2509**
1540-3122 *see* 1540-3114 **2509**
1540-3149 Military Aerospace Technology† **8974**
1540-3246 Los Angeles Loyolan **2290**
1540-3270 The Minnesota Journal of Business Law and Entrepreneurship **4876**
1540-3297 Smock **518**
1540-3300 The Dog Lover's Companion to Washington D.C. & Baltimore **8699**
1540-3327 CryptoRights Journal **2512**
1540-3335 *see* 1540-3327 **2512**

ISSN

DIRECTORY 2010 **1541-8243** **9691**

1541-0625 Healthcare Security and Disaster Alert *changed to* 1543-7280
1541-0668 BioResearch Monitoring Alert **4486**
1541-0692 Focus Magazine (San Jose) **3023**
1541-0706 *see* 1540-3416 **5922**
1541-0714 *see* 1540-3408 **5935**
1541-0757 *see* 1541-0765 **4883**
1541-0765 Aele Law Enforcement Legal Center. Monthly Law Summaries **4883**
1541-0773 The Insurance Coverage Law Bulletin **4507**
1541-0803 Journal of Taxation of Corporate Transactions **1932**
1541-0889 Journal of Gay & Lesbian Issues in Education *changed to* 1936-1653 **2876**
1541-0935 The Community College Enterprise **2973**
1541-0943 D V **2379**
1541-0951 Vida Actual **3992**
1541-0978 The Best American Magazine Writing (Year) **5262**
1541-0986 *see* 1537-5927 **7165**
1541-1036 Organizational Intersections in Healthcare, Business and Policy **5691**
1541-1052 Healthcare Benchmarks and Quality Improvement **4097**
1541-1087 *see* 0731-5724 **6654**
1541-1095 *see* 0361-526X **5047**
1541-1109 *see* 0194-262X **5046**
1541-1117 *see* 0276-3877 **5042**
1541-1125 *see* 0737-7797 **5043**
1541-1141 Inventory Management Report **1851**
1541-115X Accounting Department Management Report **1277**
1541-1168 End-of-Life Choices *changed to* Compassion and Choices Magazine **5599**
1541-1184 Africa & the Middle East Telecom **2365**
1541-1192 *see* 1541-1184 **2365**
1541-1206 Fixed Wireless Monthly Newsletter **2557**
1541-1214 *see* 1541-1206 **2557**
1541-1222 Gigabit / A T M **2497**
1541-1249 Internet Business Newsletter **2368**
1541-1257 *see* 1541-1249 **2368**
1541-1265 Latin American Telecom **2331**
1541-1273 *see* 1541-1265 **2331**
1541-1281 Mobile Internet **2564**
1541-129X *see* 1541-1281 **2564**
1541-132X The Review of Policy Research **7177**
1541-1338 *see* 1541-132X **7177**
1541-1354 I E E E International Conference on Personal Wireless Communications. Proceedings **2359**
1541-1389 Peer Review **2997**
1541-1397 Best Easy Day Hikes: Sequoia and Kings Canyon National Parks **8687**
1541-1419 Columbia Journal of American Studies **4289**
1541-1427 *see* 1541-1419 **4289**
1541-1443 ReVista (Cambridge) **4310**
1541-1451 *see* 1541-1443 **4310**
1541-1478 Vocational and Technical Schools. East **2963**
1541-1508 *see* 1536-5581 **7348**
1541-1524 Contemporary Hispanic Biography **642**
1541-1532 C P A's Guide to Management Letter Comments **1283**
1541-1540 *see* 0161-6846 **5041**
1541-1559 Psychological Services **7397**
1541-1567 Miller G A A P Practice Manual **1296**
1541-1591 College Money Handbook (Year) **2954**
1541-163X Coptica **7704**
1541-1656 The Journal of Cost Analysis & Management **1294**
1541-1672 I E E E Intelligent Systems **2471**
1541-1796 The Teaching Artist Journal **521**
1541-180X *see* 1541-1796 **521**
1541-1834 S R O *changed to* 1559-2359 **8473**
1541-1915 X M L & Web Services Magazine†
1541-1931 KoreAm Journal **3546**
1541-1974 The Courier **4290**
1541-1982 Immigration Business News & Comment **4928**
1541-1990 Knit It! **6639**
1541-2008 Southern Farmer **158**
1541-2016 Applied Immunohistochemistry & Molecular Morphology **723**
1541-2040 Youth Violence and Juvenile Justice **2672**
1541-2075 Reflections (Baltimore) **5358**
1541-2083 Facts & Findings **4670**
1541-2261 Hotel Amerika **5219**
1541-2407 Plant Safety & Maintenance **6684**
1541-2415 F & M **6311**
1541-244X Asian-Pacific Law & Policy Journal **4622**
1541-2458 Diagnostic Imaging Intelligence Report **6195**
1541-2474 The Valuation Report† **8997**
1541-2490 Homecare Administrator **5960**
1541-2512 Mealey's Emerging Securities Litigation **4731**
1541-2520 *see* 1526-6753
1541-2555 C O P D **6212**
1541-2563 *see* 1541-2555 **6212**
1541-258X All-Time Favorites: Slow Cooker **4351**
1541-2601 *see* 1535-685X **4713**
1541-2628 Carolina - Virginia Farmer **224**
1541-2679 Motion Picture Editors Guild Magazine **6507**
1541-2733 Medical Design News *changed to* Medical Design **3210**
1541-2741 African American Golfer's Digest **8220**
1541-275X Foster Electric Report **3158**
1541-2768 Farm and Home Research **110**
1541-2776 Men's Fitness **6284**
1541-2784 Treatment Guidelines from The Medical Letter **5724**
1541-2792 *see* 1541-2784 **5724**
1541-2806 Sloan-C View **3082**
1541-2814 Mealey's Litigation Report: Thimerosal & Vaccines **6860**
1541-2849 .Net Developer's Journal **2509**
1541-2911 Fodor's Martha's Vineyard and Nantucket *changed to* 1934-5569 **8705**
1541-2938 Patient Safety Monitor **7535**
1541-2946 Home Care Connection†
1541-2989 U.S. Library of Congress. Bibliographic Products & Services *changed to* 1541-2997 **637**
1541-2997 U.S. Library of Congress. Product Catalog **637**
1541-3004 Baseline (New York) **2408**
1541-3020 Bartow Access Magazine **3970**
1541-308X Physics of Wave Phenomena **7034**
1541-3098 *see* 0738-0577 **5689**
1541-3101 *see* 0164-212X **6171**
1541-3136 One2One Living **7943**
1541-3144 *see* 0194-2638 **6102**
1541-3152 *see* 0270-3181 **4053**
1541-3160 Napa Valley **4304**
1541-3233 North America Executive Flight Guide *changed to* O A G Pocket Flight Guide. North America Edition **8549**
1541-3241 International Journal of Information Technology Policy and Practice†
1541-325X Import Racer *changed to* 1559-8837
1541-3268 The Microenterprise Journal **1963**
1541-3284 M B A Jungle **1145**
1541-3306 V O D & I T V Investor **1657**
1541-3322 Nordic Reach **3555**
1541-3357 National Geographic Explorer **4020**
1541-3403 Creativity **23**
1541-3446 Journal of Transformative Education **2879**
1541-3500 Cracking the G R E Literature in English Subject Test *changed to* Cracking the G R E Literature Test **2975**
1541-3519 *see* 0272-684X **7527**
1541-3527 *see* 0091-2174 **6147**
1541-3535 *see* 0091-4150 **4048**
1541-3543 *see* 0197-6931 **408**
1541-3551 Human Resources Outsourcing Today **1865**
1541-356X *see* 1541-3551 **1865**
1541-3675 Budget Living†
1541-3705 Jabberwock Review **5312**
1541-3721 *see* 1047-6938 **7083**
1541-373X O A G Executive Flight Guide. Latin American - Caribbean **8549**
1541-3764 *see* 0030-2228 **7388**
1541-3772 *see* 1048-2911 **6681**
1541-3780 *see* 0047-2816 **2879**
1541-3802 *see* 0047-2433 **3447**
1541-3810 *see* 0047-2395 **2949**
1541-3888 Advising Start-Up & Emerging Companies **4854**
1541-3934 *see* 1095-905X **4740**
1541-3969 Value Line Industry Watch†
1541-3977 Executive Compensation (Bryn Mawr) **1681**
1541-4019 Westchester Life **3992**
1541-4094 Focus (Arlington, 2003) **6141**
1541-4108 *see* 1541-4094 **6141**
1541-4140 *see* 0735-6331 **2949**
1541-4159 *see* 0047-2379 **2695**
1541-4167 *see* 1521-0251 **2989**
1541-4183 *see* 1044-4300 **3579**
1541-4221 Ave Maria Law Review **4624**
1541-4248 Manhattan Literary Review **5226**
1541-4272 X X vs. X Y **4057**
1541-4280 *see* 1541-4272 **4057**
1541-4302 Young Adult Library Services **5055**
1541-4329 Journal of Food Science Education **3651**
1541-4337 Comprehensive Reviews in Food Science and Food Safety **3632**
1541-437X Firm, Fair & Consistent **2857**
1541-4434 Handbook for Military Life **6423**
1541-4450 *see* 1091-2851 **7366**
1541-4469 *see* 0020-7314 **7526**
1541-4477 *see* 0276-2366 **7362**
1541-4485 *see* 1535-6523 **4047**
1541-4493 *see* 0276-2374 **487**
1541-4507 American Writers Classics **5253**
1541-454X Insiders's Guide to Williamsburg and Virginia's Historic Triangle **8723**
1541-4566 Developmental Policy **7129**
1541-4574 Power Daily Midwest **3144**
1541-4612 Nurse Leader **5972**
1541-4620 *see* 1541-4612 **5972**
1541-4639 Insiders' Guide to Berkeley and the East Bay **8721**
1541-4647 Streams of William James **6953**
1541-4671 Ramp **6299**
1541-468X Telemedium *changed to* 1944-4982 **8114**
1541-4728 Frontiers in Genomic Medicine†
1541-4744 Innovations in End-of-Life Care **8047**
1541-4760 Questions **6946**
1541-4795 Antique Map Price Record (Macintosh) **3998**
1541-4817 Newtype U S A **508**
1541-4892 Advance for Nurses, Serving the Greater Philadelphia/Tri-State Metro Area *changed to* 1941-3750 **5950**
1541-4914 Journal of Interactive Online Learning **3068**
1541-4922 I E E E Distributed Systems Online **2520**
1541-4949 Wiley C P A Examination Review. Auditing *changed to* 1549-0041 **1303**
1541-4957 Cracking the G R E Math Test **2975**
1541-5007 Inside Lacrosse **8179**
1541-5015 The Interdisciplinary Journal of Problem-Based Learning **2867**
1541-5031 Atlantis Rising **7838**
1541-5066 2 Year Colleges **2963**
1541-5112 Susquehanna Heritage **4314**
1541-5120 Fredericksburg History and Biography **4293**
1541-5139 *see* 1540-8418 **2629**
1541-5147 The International Journal of Nursing Terminologies and Classifications **5962**
1541-5163 Women & Success **8890**
1541-518X J D Jungle *changed to* Jungle Law **4705**
1541-5198 Quick Escapes: Washington, D. C. **8750**
1541-5201 Off the Beaten Path: Washington, D. C. **8744**
1541-521X Tin House **5242**
1541-5228 U S A Today Sports Weekly **8250**
1541-5244 Privacy, Security & Trust Report **2515**
1541-5252 Today's Officer (Alexandria) **6449**
1541-5260 H I P A A @ I T Monthly Update
1541-5279 *see* 1541-5260
1541-5309 Bird Watcher† **8936**
1541-5325 International Archives of Bioscience
1541-5392 Web Ad Monthly **2567**
1541-5414 Creative Machine Embroidery **6637**
1541-5457 The Iowa Orthopaedic Journal **6062**
1541-5473 Puerto Rico Report **7214**
1541-5562 Visit Detroit **8772**
1541-5570 Power Daily's Generation Markets Week **3145**
1541-5597 Insiders' Guide to Jacksonville **8722**
1541-5600 Mammoth Monthly **3981**
1541-5619 Cataract & Refractive Surgery Today **6039**
1541-5694 Venture (Cambridge) **1658**
1541-5775 Neurosciencenetbase **5685**
1541-5783 Contemporary Optometry (Hagerstown) **6040**
1541-5791 Contemporary Dermatology† **8943**
1541-583X Workshop on Computers in Power Electronics. Record *changed to* 1541-5848 **2474**
1541-5848 Workshop on Computers in Power Electronics. Proceedings **2474**
1541-5856 Limnology and Oceanography: Methods **2811**
1541-5864 Highend Magazine (Henderson) **2486**
1541-5872 The Inside Scoop **2194**
1541-5910 J O Y **6645**
1541-5929 F B S. All Youth Learner Guide H C S B *changed to* 1557-4725 **7625**
1541-5945 F B S. Adult Learner Guide H C S B *changed to* 1557-4741 **7625**
1541-5961 E Z Tech Guides **2417**
1541-597X The Upland Almanac **8339**
1541-5988 Practical Pain Management **5698**
1541-5996 U P **8552**
1541-6003 Journal of Undergraduate Chemistry Research **2069**
1541-602X Lay Witness **7804**
1541-6038 The Justice Express **2658**
1541-6062 Power Daily Northeast **3144**
1541-6070 Coastal Woman **3973**
1541-6089 ArtsHouston **475**
1541-6100 *see* 0022-3166 **6661**
1541-6135 Asian Long-Term Outlook **1552**
1541-6143 Herald (Independence) **7736**
1541-6151 Anthropology News **327**
1541-6178 Journal of Medical Advances **5651**
1541-6216 New York Discrimination Law Bulletin **4744**
1541-6224 Journal of Women in Educational Leadership **2879**
1541-6259 Successful Hunter **8336**
1541-6275 I E E E International Carcas Conference on Devices Circuits and Systems. Proceedings **3101**
1541-6321 Military Classics Illustrated†
1541-6518 Organization Management Journal **1784**
1541-6542 Studies in Democratization **7187**
1541-6569 Atomica **3970**
1541-6577 Research and Theory for Nursing Practice **5979**
1541-6607 Drug Industry Daily **6835**
1541-6615 Off the Beaten Path: Georgia **8743**
1541-6704 West Virginia Children, Youth and Family Laws Annotated **4915**
1541-681X Building Materials Directory **986**
1541-6887 Moon Handbooks: Honduras **8737**
1541-6895 TourBook: Southern California and Las Vegas **8762**
1541-6933 Neurocritical Care **5685**
1541-6976 Better Homes and Gardens Perennials **3725**
1541-7069 Journal of Children's Health†
1541-7107 Atlanta Woman **8852**
1541-7115 Urban Habitats **710**
1541-7131 The Captain's Log **8539**
1541-7158 Econoguide Walt Disney World, Universal Orlando **8700**
1541-7166 Quiet Flyer Magazine *changed to* 1941-3467 **4344**
1541-7182 Let's Go: San Francisco (Year) **8730**
1541-7379 Manager's Security Alert **1778**
1541-7387 Plate **3660**
1541-7395 R V America **8329**
1541-7409 International Humanitarian Affairs **7210**
1541-745X Individual Differences Research **7362**
1541-7476 ChesapeakeHome **4555**
1541-7484 Places (Carrboro) **5080**
1541-7492 Resort Living **7611**
1541-7506 Archery Focus **8304**
1541-7514 Sculptural Pursuit **516**
1541-7549 Let's Go: Egypt **8729**
1541-7557 Georgia Journal of Professional Counseling **7358**
1541-7603 Plastic Canvas Today *changed to* 1556-8113 **8930**
1541-7611 Nanotech Business Update **1780**
1541-7646 Getting Paid in Behavioral Healthcare **6143**
1541-7662 Campus Safety & Student Development **3018**
1541-7689 Current Methods **3264**
1541-7719 International Enterprise Distributed Object Computing Conference. Proceedings **2521**
1541-7727 Joint Commission International Accreditation Standards for Medical Transport Organizations **4103**
1541-7735 CustomRetailer **1089**
1541-7786 Molecular Cancer Research **6027**
1541-7794 The Structural Design of Tall and Special Buildings **3284**
1541-7808 *see* 1541-7794 **3284**
1541-7824 Florida Curiosities **8703**
1541-7840 Chief Counsel Advice Service **1917**
1541-7867 Beckett Hockey Card Plus **8161**
1541-7875 Beckett Yu-Gi-Oh Collector **2474**
1541-7883 Beckett Dealer Direct **4329**
1541-7891 Cardiopulmonary Physical Therapy Journal **6107**
1541-7905 Healthcare Design **4097**
1541-7913 Private Air† **8982**
1541-7921 Insiders' Guide to Portland, Oregon **8722**
1541-7948 Electric Transmission Week **3128**
1541-7956 Embedded Systems Development
1541-7980 B/I Te (Online Edition) **4993**
1541-8057 E P R **7131**
1541-8073 The Medical Technology Acquisition Record **1367**
1541-809X Dream Trains
1541-8111 Boston Magazine's Concierge **3971**
1541-8138 Palabras Pastorales **7668**
1541-8162 Poesy **5430**
1541-8170 Ultimate Athlete **8214**
1541-8197 L A B I Enterprise **1430**
1541-8219 Asian Information - Science - Life *changed to* Asia Pacific Journal of Life Sciences **543**
1541-8235 I D Sales Pro†
1541-8243 *see* 0038-4348 **5717**

ISSN

Link to your serials resources and content with ulrichsweb.com

1542-4790 The A I S Report on Blue Cross and Blue Shield Plans **4490**
1542-4804 Off the Beaten Path: Michigan **8743**
1542-4812 Proud (El Paso) **3559**
1542-4863 *see* 0007-9235 **6010**
1542-4898 G. K. Hall's Women's Studies Index†
1542-4901 Insurance Networking News **4531**
1542-4928 Native American Times **6635**
1542-4952 Student Discipline Law Bulletin **3033**
1542-4960 Manufactured Home Managers' Law Bulletin†
1542-4987 Public Employment Compliance Law Bulletin†
1542-4995 Special Education Law Bulletin **3047**
1542-5002 Legal Briefings for Fire Chiefs **3580**
1542-5010 Landlord's 'Bottom Line' Bulletin **7598**
1542-5045 Brujula **4445**
1542-5061 Plunkett's Energy Industry Almanac **3144**
1542-5088 Harvard Law Today **4685**
1542-5134 Advance for Audiologists **5567**
1542-5150 Let's Go: Amsterdam **8729**
1542-5169 Day Trips from New Orleans **8697**
1542-5177 North Carolina Journal of Law & Technology **4748**
1542-5185 *see* 1542-5177 **4748**
1542-5193 Insiders' Guide to the Great Smoky Mountains **8722**
1542-5223 Industrial Machinery Digest **3368**
1542-524X CleanRooms Master Source Guide *see* 1043-8017 **3366**
1542-5266 Luxury Business **1829**
1542-5274 Asphalt (Redondo Beach) **8253**
1542-5312 Internet Newsroom **2561**
1542-5320 Marine Safety Update **7531**
1542-5339 Dog Days of Denver **6807**
1542-5347 Cultural Events of New Jersey **6523**
1542-5355 MitoMatters **834**
1542-5363 *see* 0010-0447 **6650**
1542-5371 Muslim Kid's Journal†
1542-538X *see* 0744-6020 **5977**
1542-5401 Dungeon†
1542-5436 *see* 1542-5355 **834**
1542-5444 *see* 1542-5320 **7531**
1542-5525 Quick Escapes: St. Louis **8750**
1542-5533 Off the Beaten Path: Maritime Provinces **8743**
1542-5541 Adventure Sports Magazine **8157**
1542-555X Desire **5283**
1542-5568 Marine Digest *changed to* 1944-3323 **8640**
1542-5576 Language Magazine **5141**
1542-5592 The Harvard Mosaic **3536**
1542-5606 Journal of Agricultural Lending **1360**
1542-5657 Sangbad Bichitra **3562**
1542-5665 Global H R Report **1861**
1542-5673 N J L L A In-Site **4737**
1542-5681 *see* 0163-7169 **1555**
1542-569X Broadband Access Report **2553**
1542-5703 Educational Sales and Marketing Insider (Print)†
1542-5711 Educational Sales and Marketing Insider (Online) **2851**
1542-5738 Notre Dame Studies in Theology **7809**
1542-5762 The New York Sun **3983**
1542-5800 The Windmill Clipper **6540**
1542-5843 The Scots Record **635**
1542-5894 Composition Studies **3055**
1542-5908 *see* 1542-8060 **2450**
1542-5932 Responder Safety *changed to* Responder Safety **7538**
1542-5940 Lindy's National College Football Annual **8237**
1542-5967 Off the Beaten Path: Boston **8743**
1542-5983 Journal of Pelvic Medicine and Surgery **6249**
1542-5991 *see* 1542-5983 **6249**
1542-6009 Network Technology Report **2502**
1542-6041 Bowker's Audio & Video Database†
1542-6092 Nightingale's Healthcare News **4747**
1542-6122 Transportation Watch **8517**
1542-6130 Mission Update **7807**
1542-6149 Archives of Inequalities and Applications **5473**
1542-6157 International Journal of Technology and Management†
1542-6165 *see* 1542-6157
1542-6181 *see* 1542-6149 **5473**
1542-619X Trailhead **4983**
1542-6262 Off the Beaten Path: Wyoming **8744**
1542-6270 *see* 1060-0280 **6820**
1542-6289 Fun with the Family in Iowa **8712**
1542-6297 Journal of International Accounting Research **1295**
1542-6300 Sociation Today **8135**
1542-6319 BioProcess International **661**
1542-636X Wastewater Professional **3514**
1542-6378 Medieval Studies **4153**
1542-6394 Rocky Mountain Communication Review **2337**
1542-6408 Embedded Computing Design **2418**
1542-6416 Clinical Proteomics **729**
1542-6424 Divide **5285**
1542-6432 Journal of Religion and Spirituality in Social Work **8051**
1542-6440 *see* 1542-6432 **8051**
1542-6459 *see* 1542-6408 **2418**
1542-6572 Bioentrepreneur **757**
1542-6580 International Journal of Chemical Reactor Engineering **3247**
1542-6599 Harvard Working Papers in Linguistics **5124**
1542-6602 Gilbert! **5300**
1542-6610 Vapors **3991**
1542-6629 *see* 1056-6171 **291**
1542-6637 Homecoming Magazine **7648**
1542-6661 *see* 1523-8695 **4864**
1542-6696 Bowker - Whitaker Global Books in Print on Disc *changed to* Bowker's Global Books in Print on Disc **621**
1542-6718 Company Data **1415**
1542-6823 Rhapsoidia **5362**
1542-6866 Lange Smart Charts: Pharmacology **6858**
1542-6963 Xantippe **5402**
1542-6971 Case In Point **5592**
1542-7072 Episteme **6916**
1542-7080 The Vocabula Review **5194**
1542-7099 Stanford Social Innovation Review **1179**
1542-7102 Journal of Environmental Monitoring and Restoration **3446**
1542-7218 Books in Print with Book Reviews on Disc **620**
1542-7234 Books in Print Plus (Canadian Edition) *changed to* Canadian Books in Print on Disc **622**
1542-7242 Economic Database. Household Database **1099**
1542-7307 Indigo (New York) **3539**
1542-7315 Nova et Vetera (English Edition) **7666**
1542-7331 Journal of American Culture **4459**
1542-734X *see* 1542-7331 **4459**
1542-7358 Journal of Culture and Its Transmission in the African World **344**
1542-7366 Family Bible Study. Life Ventures Learner Guide *changed to* 1557-4776 **7748**
1542-7374 Family Bible Study: Life Ventures Leader Guide *changed to* 1557-492X **7748**
1542-7390 Space Weather **582**
1542-7404 Insiders' Guide to Kansas City **8722**
1542-7412 *see* 0737-0806 **8800**
1542-7420 Insiders' Guide to the Jersey Shore **8722**
1542-7447 Comic Art **482**
1542-7528 Journal of Crop Improvement **239**
1542-7536 *see* 1542-7528 **239**
1542-7544 Analisis **8025**
1542-7560 The Journal of Behavioral Finance **7369**
1542-7579 *see* 1542-7560 **7369**
1542-7587 Critical Inquiry in Language Studies **5109**
1542-7595 *see* 1542-7587 **5109**
1542-7609 Research in Human Development **7403**
1542-7617 *see* 1542-7609 **7403**
1542-7625 *see* 1057-2252 **3085**
1542-7641 Trailer Life Campgrounds, R V Parks & Services Directory *changed to* Trailer Life R V Parks, Campgrounds & Services Directory **4983**
1542-7706 Reglas Firmes, Justas y Constantes **2904**
1542-7714 *see* 1542-3565 **5921**
1542-7730 A C M Queue **2587**
1542-7749 *see* 1542-7730 **2587**
1542-7811 *see* 0027-9013 **7499**
1542-782X Ann Arbor Magazine **3969**
1542-7838 Dimensions of Dental Hygiene **5842**
1542-7854 *see* 1048-6682 **1781**
1542-7862 *see* 1061-4249 **1728**
1542-7870 Generation Speed **8175**
1542-7919 *see* 1542-7838 **5842**
1542-7935 Positive Magazine **8748**
1542-7951 Internet Mathematics **2561**
1542-8044 *see* 1542-8052 **6661**
1542-8052 Journal of Culinary Science & Technology **6661**
1542-8060 International Journal of Computational Cognition **2450**
1542-8079 Debating Historical Issues in the Media of the Time **4290**
1542-8087 Food Through History **3643**
1542-8109 Precursors & Aftermaths *changed to* 1551-9309 **5376**
1542-8117 A I H A Journal *changed to* 1545-9624 **6680**
1542-8141 Diabetes Health Monitor **5887**
1542-815X Family Care Health Monitor **5613**
1542-8168 Una Vida Saludable con Diabetes **5901**
1542-8184 Health Monitor Allergies & Asthma **6214**
1542-8192 Senior Life Health Monitor **4055**
1542-8206 Cancer Care Health Monitor **6011**
1542-8214 Digestion & Diet Health Monitor **6657**
1542-8311 Heartland Real Estate Business **7592**
1542-8389 A L S Connect (Print) *changed to* A L S Connect (Online) **4986**
1542-8397 International Abstracts of Human Resources **1243**
1542-8400 *see* 1542-8397 **1243**
1542-8419 Bruce Hopkins' Nonprofit Counsel **4632**
1542-8427 *see* 1542-8419 **4632**
1542-8435 Addiction Professional **2689**
1542-8443 *see* 0030-8900 **8656**
1542-8451 Insiders' Guide to Memphis **8722**
1542-846X Insiders' Guide to San Antonio **8722**
1542-8559 The Best Christian Writing **7625**
1542-8567 Staffing Industry Supplier Directory & Buyers Guide *changed to* 1553-8168 **1875**
1542-8583 Family Bible Study: Younger & Older Youth Leader Guide *changed to* 1557-5020 **7748**
1542-8591 *see* 0745-5100 **8534**
1542-8672 Joint Commission: The Source **4103**
1542-8680 Joint Commission International Newsletter† **8968**
1542-8699 Internet Dimensions **2561**
1542-8710 Academy of Business and Economics. Journal **1551**
1542-8737 S N P Tech Reporter **6879**
1542-8745 The American Journal of Urology Review **6265**
1542-8788 Traffic East **3991**
1542-8818 Journal of Microbiology and Biology Education **889**
1542-8826 Topics in HIV Medicine **5827**
1542-8877 Ophthalmic Surgery, Lasers and Imaging **6254**
1542-8885 The Gallup Poll Tuesday Briefing *changed to* 1930-224X **7137**
1542-8907 Army Chaplaincy **6411**
1542-8915 *see* 1542-8907 **6411**
1542-8923 Tech Decisions for Insurance **4531**
1542-8931 Powertrain International **3216**
1542-894X Industrial Engineer **3197**
1542-8958 Digital Journal of Ophthalmology **6041**
1542-8974 Alabama Business **1058**
1542-8990 Focus on Your Child's Early Stages **2153**
1542-9008 Family Bible Study. Younger Youth Leader Pack *changed to* 1557-3850 **7625**
1542-9040 C S A Political Science & Government **7479**
1542-9059 Woman Dentist Journal†
1542-9164 T V Station Deals & Finance Databook **2394**
1542-9172 Research Alert Yearbook **1840**
1542-9180 Journal of Student Research **5316**
1542-9199 C S A Journal (Denver) **4042**
1542-9210 Focus on Microbiology Education **886**
1542-9229 Transworld Skateboarding Business *changed to* 1552-227X **1183**
1542-9253 American Railway Engineering and Maintenance-of-Way Association. Annual Conference. Proceedings **8614**
1542-9261 *see* 1091-9988 **3423**
1542-930X Illinois Domestic Relations and Related Laws Annotated **4911**
1542-9326 Mergent's Handbook of N A S D A Q Stocks **1639**
1542-9334 Berks County Newcomer **5066**
1542-9415 World Harp Congress Review **6629**
1542-9423 Journal of Aerospace Computing, Information, and Communication **63**
1542-9431 Preclinica† **8982**
1542-944X V W Tuner†
1542-9466 Active Trader **1609**
1542-9520 The American Journal of Oncology Review *changed to* 1939-6163 **6008**
1542-9547 Pharmaceutical Law & Industry Report **6869**
1542-9555 *see* 1542-9547 **6869**
1542-9563 Corporate Accountability Report **4651**
1542-9571 *see* 1542-9563 **4651**
1542-9601 Ristorante! **4397**
1542-961X Reviews in Analgesia **5773**
1542-9628 Union Labor Report Newsletter **4604**
1542-9636 *see* 1542-9628 **4604**
1542-9660 Habitation **3645**
1542-9679 Simple Scrapbooks **4347**
1542-9687 Grace Woman Magazine†
1542-9695 Intersection **7651**
1542-9709 Perspectives (Skokie) **7728**
1542-9717 Instructional Leadership Abstracts (Print Edition) *changed to* 1551-7756 **2942**
1542-9733 Birth Defects Research. Part B: Developmental and Reproductive Toxicology **5587**
1542-9741 *see* 1542-9733 **5587**
1542-975X Birth Defects Research. Part C: Embryo Today Reviews **5587**
1542-9768 *see* 1542-975X **5587**
1542-9776 Above and Beyond **2175**
1542-9784 Think & Discover **2216**
1542-9792 Arms Sales Monitor **6411**
1542-9806 Children and Libraries **5001**
1542-9814 Hospital Recruiting Update†
1542-9822 E D Documentation and Coding Update†
1542-9830 H I P A A Regulatory Alert **4504**
1542-9903 Private Secondary Schools **2962**
1542-9938 Argonaut (San Francisco) **5206**
1542-9954 The C L M P Directory of Literary Magazines and Presses *changed to* The Literary Press and Magazine Directory **5407**
1542-9962 O P Magazine *changed to* 1551-5001 **7561**
1543-0006 A G E L E News **3016**
1543-0014 Bell'Italia **8686**
1543-0154 *see* 0885-8195 **6023**
1543-0197 Oklahoma Music Magazine **6601**
1543-0219 The Insiders' Guide to Louisville and Southern Indiana† **8964**
1543-0235 Marcato **5031**
1543-0243 Bioterrorism Watch (Print Edition) *changed to* Bioterrorism Watch (Online Edition) **7509**
1543-0359 M H S L A News **5030**
1543-0367 *see* 1080-0727 **4691**
1543-0375 *see* 0002-726X **4071**
1543-0383 *see* 0039-3738 **5183**
1543-0391 *see* 1068-2090 **5135**
1543-0413 *see* 0737-7037 **3619**
1543-0421 *see* 0040-5841 **2919**
1543-043X Journal of Writing Assessment **5316**
1543-0448 S D M S Sound News **6208**
1543-0464 Journal of Economics and Finance Education **1361**
1543-0499 Shifra Stein's Day Trips from Phoenix, Tucson, and Flagstaff **8756**
1543-0529 American School of Prehistoric Research Monograph Series **372**
1543-0537 Nonlinear Optics, Quantum Optics **7081**
1543-0723 *see* 1543-1258 **5330**
1543-0731 *see* 0722-5741 **956**
1543-0790 Clinical Advances in Hematology & Oncology **5935**
1543-0804 Allergy & Asthma Today **5753**
1543-0812 Inside Microsoft Windows X P **2591**
1543-0820 Logos (Midland Park) **8119**
1543-0855 Proudflesh **3559**
1543-091X Scribendi **2300**
1543-0928 Cerca Magazine **3972**
1543-0960 D V 8 **6561**
1543-1002 Nineteenth-Century Art Worldwide **509**
1543-1010 Securities Class Action Reporter **1650**
1543-1029 Minority and Small Business Review **1149**
1543-1061 Fodor's Great American Vacations **8706**
1543-1088 S C I Psychosocial Process **7406**
1543-110X Inside Gymnastics **8179**
1543-1134 Smart Tips and Quick Tricks for Microsoft Windows X P†
1543-1142 Smart Tips and Quick Tricks for S Q L Server Solutions†
1543-1150 Seminars in Integrative Medicine **5712**
1543-1169 *see* 1543-1150 **5712**
1543-1177 Asia Policy Calendar **7222**
1543-1185 Asia Policy Weekly **7222**
1543-1215 The New Atlantis **7157**
1543-1231 Fun with the Family in Colorado **4977**
1543-124X Clean Air Compliance Solutions **3484**
1543-1258 March Magazine **5330**
1543-1274 Day Trips from Raleigh-Durham **8697**
1543-1282 Hardcore Delphi† **8961**
1543-1304 Safundi (Online Edition) **4178**
1543-1312 Miller Governmental G A A P Guide **1297**
1543-1347 The Philip Roth Society Newsletter **5350**
1543-1371 Corporate Accountability & Fraud Daily **4863**
1543-138X Pierce Law Review **4758**
1543-1398 C F A Magazine **1323**
1543-1401 Advertising Law **4610**
1543-1428 Speed Style & Sound **8604**
1543-1436 The Vital Record **3786**
1543-1487 American Small Farm **91**
1543-1495 De Christian Science Heraut *see* 0146-7174 **8962**
1543-1495 De Christian Science Heraut *see* 1520-7072 **7736**
1543-155X Moon Handbooks: South Korea **8738**
1543-1606 Quilts with Style **6641**

ISSN

1543-9143	*see* 1543-9135 **6014**
1543-916X	Library of Congress Changed Subject Heading Subdivisions **5028**
1543-9313	Vadeboncoeur Collection of Images **524**
1543-933X	The Art & Law Electronic Journal **4621**
1543-9348	*see* 0737-0741 **6899**
1543-9356	China Report **1555**
1543-9364	*see* 1543-9356 **1555**
1543-9372	Critical Social Work **8036**
1543-9380	Der Ahnenforscher **3758**
1543-9399	Journal of Game Development **2478**
1543-9445	The Wharf Lane Newsletter **3787**
1543-950X	C A A Reviews **480**
1543-9518	The Sport Journal **8204**
1543-9526	Native American Law Report†
1543-9542	*see* 0022-2402 **2809**
1543-9585	Network Chicago Guide **2386**
1543-9607	Pharmacy Careers *see* 0003-0627 **6874**
1543-9607	Pharmacy Careers *see* Generic Rx Product Report **6844**
1543-9720	CircuiTree Profiles *see* 1059-843X **3090**
1543-9852	*see* 0886-3547 **1655**
1543-9860	Oregon Review of International Law **4937**
1543-9879	Bone & Joint *changed to* Lippincott's Bone and Joint Newsletter **6066**
1543-9887	Power Daily North America *changed to* 1556-6943 **3144**
1543-9895	Sales & Use Tax Monitor **1942**
1543-9925	Antiphon **7784**
1543-9941	Ancient Mediterranean and Medieval Texts and Contexts. Medieval Philosophy, Mathematics and Science **4198**
1543-995X	Ancient Mediterranean and Medieval Texts and Contexts. Studies in Philo of Alexandria and Mediterranean Antiquity *changed to* 1875-029X **6955**
1543-9968	Literature as Windows to World Cultures **5325**
1543-9976	Review of the Electronic and Industrial Distribution Industries **3112**
1543-9984	Virginia Living **3992**
1543-9992	LifeCoach Magazine†
1544-0001	Women's Faith & Spirit **8891**
1544-001X	Better Homes and Gardens Quick & Easy Decorating **4554**
1544-0028	Journal of Commercial Banking and Finance *changed to* 1939-2230 **1305**
1544-0036	Journal of Legal, Ethical and Regulatory Issues **4703**
1544-0044	*see* 1544-0036 **4703**
1544-0060	S G I A News **7327**
1544-0079	Florida Studies Weekly. 3rd Grade *changed to* 1556-3553 **2926**
1544-0214	Science Studies Weekly, 3rd Grade *changed to* 1933-3110 **7911**
1544-0222	Journal of International Business Research **1574**
1544-0230	*see* 1544-0222 **1574**
1544-0370	Freire Online **2858**
1544-0389	Journal of College Teaching and Learning **2989**
1544-046X	*see* 1544-0478 **273**
1544-0478	Journal of Natural Fibers **273**
1544-0494	Family Bible Study. Music for Kindergarten *changed to* 1557-4059 **7748**
1544-0508	Journal of Organizational Culture, Communications and Conflict **1769**
1544-0516	Television Week (Print)† **8992**
1544-0524	Police Fleet Manager **2663**
1544-0532	A A M C Medical Reporter **5563**
1544-0540	*see* 1544-0532 **5563**
1544-0567	Interlochen Review **5309**
1544-0575	Benefits Practice Center **1856**
1544-0583	Movieline's Hollywood Life *changed to* 1557-7228 **6502**
1544-0591	*see* 0022-0345 **5851**
1544-0702	Frommer's London with Kids **8711**
1544-0729	The B'nai B'rith I J M *changed to* 1549-4799 **7719**
1544-0737	*see* 0895-9374 **5833**
1544-0745	Custom Gift Retailer† **8947**
1544-0761	*see* 0090-4600 **1948**
1544-077X	*see* 0148-8295 **1948**
1544-0788	*see* 0747-8607 **1797**
1544-0796	*see* 8755-0628 **7613**
1544-0869	Idebate **3064**
1544-0885	Sankofa **2167**
1544-0893	Journal of Employee Assistance **6700**
1544-0907	Yoga for EveryBody **7000**
1544-0915	Best of Veggie Life†
1544-0923	Holiday Painting†
1544-0958	*see* 1544-0869 **3064**
1544-0974	Haiku Society of America. Member's Anthology **5423**
1544-1008	The Powhatan Review **5353**
1544-1016	*see* 1059-9630 **7055**
1544-1024	*see* 1059-9495 **3350**
1544-1059	Handbook on Injectable Drugs **6845**
1544-1229	Fun with the Family in Ohio **4977**
1544-1237	Radiology Department Compliance Manual **7538**
1544-1245	Seattle Journal for Social Justice **7215**
1544-1253	Green Seattle **7139**
1544-1261	Practicing Planner (Chicago) **4424**
1544-127X	Groupwise Advisor *changed to* Databased Advisor Magazine **2554**
1544-1377	Paradise Family Guides: Maui **8746**
1544-1407	Paradise Family Guides: Kauai **8746**
1544-144X	Mima'amakim **7727**
1544-1458	Academy of Strategic Management Journal **1723**
1544-1547	Administrative & Regulatory Law News **4610**
1544-158X	Catalyst (Dublin) **1284**
1544-161X	Multistate Corporate Tax Guide Mid-Year Supplement *see* 1051-1555 **1935**
1544-1644	Corn and Soybean Digest **225**
1544-1660	Smart Solutions† **8988**
1544-1687	Government Security **2677**
1544-1709	Annals of Family Medicine **5575**
1544-1717	*see* 1544-1709 **5575**
1544-1725	Austin Golf†
1544-1733	*see* 1522-3868 **5297**
1544-175X	Family Bible Study. Music for 3's-Pre-K *changed to* 1557-4032 **7748**
1544-1849	River Teeth **5363**
1544-1857	Burn Support News **6057**
1544-1865	Current Prostate Reports **6267**
1544-1873	Current Osteoporosis Reports (Print)†
1544-1881	I M S Bulletin **5492**
1544-1911	Internet Law & Strategy **2561**
1544-2160	B R†
1544-2217	*see* 0300-9858 **8813**
1544-2225	Utne *changed to* Utne Reader **3991**
1544-2233	Geriatric Times†
1544-2241	Current Osteoporosis Reports (Online) **6058**
1544-225X	*see* 1544-1865 **6267**
1544-2306	Prostate Bulletin **6273**
1544-2314	P T I Journal (Phoenix) **3356**
1544-2322	Foreign-Trade Zones Board. Annual Report to Congress **1566**
1544-2330	Four-Year Colleges **2955**
1544-2519	Family Bible Study. Music for Babies, 1's & 2's *changed to* 1557-4040 **7748**
1544-2632	Managing the Margin **4106**
1544-2640	Insiders' Guide to Civil War Sites in the Southern States† **8964**
1544-2659	Antiques Roadshow Insider **363**
1544-2667	Executive Insights *changed to* 1934-7103 **4112**
1544-2691	Plunkett's Companion to the Almanac of American Employers: Mid-Size Firms **1703**
1544-2721	Tourism Review International **8764**
1544-273X	Tourism in Marine Environments **8763**
1544-2748	Kagan's Latin American Broadband **2534**
1544-2756	Broadband Wireless Data Review **2533**
1544-2802	The-hold.com **5387**
1544-2837	Employee Benefits in Mergers and Acquisitions **4866**
1544-2861	Filter Magazine **6567**
1544-2896	Journal of Undergraduate Neuroscience Education **6157**
1544-2950	ReadyMade **4562**
1544-3000	Shooting Illustrated **8332**
1544-3027	At Play **5258**
1544-3035	Best's Key Rating Guide: Property - Casualty United States Edition *changed to* 1554-9127 **4495**
1544-3043	*see* 0042-4161 **4316**
1544-306X	Fourth Circuit Criminal Reporter **4890**
1544-3159	Culture, Society & Praxis **7957**
1544-3167	Journal for Vascular Ultrasound (Print Edition) **5791**
1544-3175	Journal for Vascular Ultrasound (Online Edition) **5791**
1544-3183	Corvette Enthusiast **8168**
1544-3191	American Pharmacists Association. Journal **6820**
1544-3221	Inside Energy **3138**
1544-3353	Telecom Policy Report (Print)†
1544-337X	Central Valley Homes & Lifestyles Magazine **5067**
1544-3418	White House Historical Association. Newsletter **4318**
1544-3434	The Ave **3521**
1544-3450	*see* 1544-3191 **6820**
1544-3531	Vision (Dearborn)† **8997**
1544-354X	Bead Style **531**
1544-3558	A C M Transactions on Applied Perception **2405**
1544-3566	A C M Transactions on Architecture and Code Optimization **2466**
1544-3574	Computers in Entertainment **2413**
1544-3582	West Federal Taxation: Advanced Business Entity Taxation **4883**
1544-3590	West Federal Taxation: Taxation of Business Entities **4883**
1544-3655	Arthur Rackham Society. Journal **472**
1544-3736	CitySlicker Entertainment Magazine **6556**
1544-3817	Adventure Guide to the Cayman Islands **8681**
1544-3833	Monthly Outlook. Asia and Oceania *changed to* 1553-7048 **1150**
1544-3884	Chronicle (Jackson) **4288**
1544-3930	Design & Architecture (Arizona Edition) **439**
1544-3965	*see* 1544-3558 **2405**
1544-3973	*see* 1544-3566 **2466**
1544-3981	*see* 1544-3574 **2413**
1544-399X	*see* 0018-7895 **5307**
1544-4015	Insiders' Guide to Myrtle Beach and the Grand Strand **8722**
1544-4023	Insiders' Guide to Glacier National Park **8722**
1544-404X	Glossos **5122**
1544-4058	Ohio Valley History **4307**
1544-4090	Eastman's Online Genealogy Newsletter **3764**
1544-418X	R C Driver **4344**
1544-4236	Retail Traffic **1841**
1544-4287	Moon Handbooks: New Zealand **8738**
1544-4333	The Mail Research Society. Journal *changed to* 1557-1297 **364**
1544-4341	Texas Workers' Comp Reporter **4881**
1544-4368	*see* 0192-4788 **4038**
1544-4376	*see* 0364-3107 **8023**
1544-4384	CompScope Benchmarks. Multistate Comparisons *changed to* 1558-8505 **1673**
1544-449X	*see* 1544-466X **7177**
1544-4503	Mustang Enthusiast **8594**
1544-4511	LinuxWorld (Print)† **8971**
1544-452X	*see* 1092-6755 **8023**
1544-4538	*see* 0734-7324 **2691**
1544-4546	*see* 0163-9269 **4994**
1544-4554	*see* 0163-9374 **5001**
1544-4600	Harris Directory. Georgia Manufacturing **1999**
1544-4627	Annual Review of Banking and Financial Law *changed to* Review of Banking and Financial Law **1379**
1544-466X	Research U S A **7177**
1544-4694	Oil & Gas Journal Petroleum Software & Technology Guide *see* 0030-1388 **6783**
1544-4708	American Musicological Society. Bulletin *changed to* 0003-0139 **6544**
1544-4716	Linea (New York) **503**
1544-4724	*see* 1083-7345 **1948**
1544-4732	Additional Earnings and Union Membership Data *see* 1087-8629 **4604**
1544-4759	Journal of Investigative Psychology and Offender Profiling **7375**
1544-4767	*see* 1544-4759 **7375**
1544-4775	Haute Doll **4336**
1544-4813	Custom Classic Trucks **8670**
1544-4848	Columbia Journal of Law & the Arts **482**
1544-4856	Road to Emmaus **7678**
1544-4872	Securitization News *changed to* 1938-7504 **1386**
1544-4902	Philadelphia Magazine's Home & Garden *changed to* 1942-1435 **4549**
1544-4910	*see* 0038-3139 **5717**
1544-4929	The W A C Journal **3087**
1544-4945	A C T E C Journal **4900**
1544-4953	The Journal of Caribbean Ornithology **909**
1544-497X	CarbHealth Magazine **6656**
1544-5003	*see* 0037-0193 **2668**
1544-5011	*see* 8755-8297 **3031**
1544-5038	*see* 8755-8300 **2644**
1544-5046	*see* 0271-5228 **7598**
1544-5054	*see* 1542-5002 **3580**
1544-5135	Beyond Pinstripes **1067**
1544-5151	*see* 8755-8289 **2661**
1544-516X	Grants for Cities and Towns (E-Mail Edition) **7493**
1544-5178	*see* 1079-297X **3023**
1544-5186	Nursing Made Incredibly Easy! **5974**
1544-5208	Web Exclusives **7545**
1544-5216	Popular Mechanics en Espanol **8435**
1544-5232	U S Insurance News *changed to* Cyber Insurance News **4500**
1544-5275	Earthhuman **3974**
1544-5321	Ferrari Guides' Men's Travel in Your Pocket
1544-5429	Natural Resource Year in Review **2621**
1544-5437	*see* 1544-5429 **2621**
1544-5488	Coping with Cancer **6017**
1544-5496	Let's Go: Thailand **8730**
1544-5542	Atomic Magazine†
1544-5615	I E E E International Fuzzy Systems Conference. Proceedings **2449**
1544-5801	Carologue **4287**
1544-581X	*see* 0148-916X **5818**
1544-5836	*see* 0514-7905 **7616**
1544-5844	*see* 0748-7878 **1715**
1544-5933	General Requirements for Applications in Commercial Offset Lithography *see* 1047-9325 **7322**
1544-5976	*see* 1540-9589 **2473**
1544-5992	G.K. Hall Bibliographic Guide to Slavic, Baltic, and Eurasian Studies†
1544-600X	G.K. Hall Bibliographic Guide to Dance†
1544-6093	OurPC Magazine **2434**
1544-6107	Catalina **3525**
1544-6115	Statistical Applications in Genetics and Molecular Biology **878**
1544-6123	Finance Letters *changed to* Finance Research Letters **1343**
1544-6131	*see* Finance Research Letters **1343**
1544-614X	Road Runner Motorcycle Cruising & Touring *changed to* 1939-7976 **8267**
1544-6158	Dolls Beautiful **534**
1544-6212	Riverwind **5433**
1544-6301	Journal of Cancer Integrative Medicine *changed to* 1715-894X **6034**
1544-6344	Thomas Food and Beverage Market Place *changed to* 1936-2501 **1995**
1544-6360	Pennsylvania Legacies **4308**
1544-6395	Everyday Food **3635**
1544-6409	Investigative Stops Law Bulletin **2656**
1544-6417	*see* 1544-6409 **2656**
1544-6425	*see* 1075-900X **2663**
1544-645X	Learning & Training Innovation†
1544-6476	Oklahoma Country **144**
1544-6484	Quick Answers for Microsoft PowerPoint†
1544-6492	Quick Answers for Microsoft Windows 2000†
1544-6506	Quick Answers for Microsoft Office 2000†
1544-6514	Quick Answers for Web Design†
1544-6522	Quick Answers for A S P†
1544-6530	Quick Answers for Microsoft FrontPage†
1544-659X	Fish & Hunt *changed to* 1931-6267 **8324**
1544-6751	Odyssey (Washington, D.C.) **3044**
1544-6778	Genomic Proteomic Technology† **8959**
1544-6794	The Journal of Supportive Oncology **6025**
1544-6808	C T B S S P Synthesis Reports **8669**
1544-6816	G M R†
1544-6824	The Newport Papers **6439**
1544-6921	Export Aerospace News **54**
1544-693X	*see* 1544-6921 **54**
1544-6956	Environmental Export News **1563**
1544-6980	Journal of Air Transportation **8501**
1544-6999	The Next American City **4421**
1544-7022	Weekend Woodcrafts†
1544-7057	National Export Strategy Annual Report
1544-709X	Catfish In-Sider. Guide **8309**
1544-7227	G E D Basics **2941**
1544-726X	Rodziny **3781**
1544-7278	*see* Gallup Management Journal **1747**
1544-7308	Search and Rescue **7541**
1544-7316	*see* 1544-7308 **7541**
1544-7324	Projection Monthly *changed to* 1937-9870 **2384**
1544-7375	Billing World and O S S Today *changed to* 2150-508X **2366**
1544-7413	Off the Beaten Path: Philadelphia **8744**
1544-743X	Latitudes (Los Angeles) **5024**
1544-7464	Smart Supervision **1793**
1544-7480	Pacific Coast Sportfishing **8327**
1544-7502	Himalayan Linguistics **5124**
1544-7529	Information Technologies and International Development **2545**
1544-7537	*see* 1544-7529 **2545**
1544-7545	Acumen Journal of Sciences†
1544-7596	Alternative Investment News **1610**
1544-7731	Who's Who Among American High School Students. Sports Edition **2926**
1544-7774	Locating Gold, Gems, & Minerals **6468**

ISSN

1545-617X Federal Employment Law Insider **4848**
1545-6188 Probiotics and Prebiotics†
1545-6196 Wagadu **8904**
1545-6285 Greenwood Introduces Literary Masterpieces **5302**
1545-6315 Scrap & Stamp Arts **539**
1545-6366 Wellness Foods *changed to* 0015-6523 **3640**
1545-6420 *see* 1532-5555 **8009**
1545-6439 Properties (New York) **7604**
1545-6447 Texas Estate Planning Statutes **4905**
1545-6463 Tall Magazine **3990**
1545-6471 The Catholic Pharmacist **6828**
1545-648X Insiders' Guide to Grand Canyon *changed to* Insiders' Guide to Grand Canyon and Northern Arizona **8722**
1545-6498 Fun with the Family Arizona **8711**
1545-6501 Essential Teacher **5116**
1545-651X Retirement Places Rated **4425**
1545-6536 Inspired House†
1545-6579 Cable T V Investor. Deals & Finance **1615**
1545-6609 Tennis Life **8248**
1545-6633 Arizona Curiosities **8683**
1545-6668 A M F News **7619**
1545-6676 The Episcopal Evangelical Journal **7756**
1545-6684 Illinois Journal of Technology Education **8425**
1545-6692 Planet Capoeira **8193**
1545-6706 The Arabian Horse Newspaper **8287**
1545-6714 Gay Parent **2153**
1545-6781 Practice Matters **8062**
1545-682X *see* 1532-8759 **8033**
1545-6838 *see* 1070-5309 **8071**
1545-6846 *see* 0037-8046 **8070**
1545-6854 *see* 0360-7283 **8044**
1545-6870 Atlantic Journal of Communication **8089**
1545-6889 *see* 1545-6870 **8089**
1545-6900 Better Homes and Gardens Home Planning Ideas *changed to* 1935-2972 **4364**
1545-6927 *see* 0084-0416 **526**
1545-6935 *see* 0018-2710 **7647**
1545-6943 *see* 0097-9740 **8903**
1545-6951 *see* 0026-8232 **5152**
1545-696X *see* 0897-6546 **4714**
1545-6978 *see* 0022-2968 **401**
1545-6986 *see* 0021-9371 **4235**
1545-6994 *see* 0021-1753 **7868**
1545-7001 *see* 0020-7071 **5129**
1545-701X *see* 0010-4086 **2838**
1545-7028 C N A Training Advisor **5954**
1545-7036 H2Nation **3162**
1545-7117 Woman's Day Weekend Crafts†
1545-7133 Caring with Confidence **8031**
1545-7176 Living Forge **5327**
1545-7206 *see* 0033-3182 **6179**
1545-7214 *see* 1064-7481 **4040**
1545-7222 *see* 0895-0172 **6154**
1545-7230 *see* 1042-9670 **6118**
1545-7249 *see* 0039-8322 **5185**
1545-7257 Allergy Nursing Newsletter†
1545-7311 Call to Unity **7629**
1545-732X Keep Up to Date on Family Medicine Coding & Reimbursement **4511**
1545-7338 Society for the Study of Metaphysical Religion. Journal **6953**
1545-7346 The Hazen Road Dispatch **4294**
1545-7354 Hydrogen **3137**
1545-7362 International Journal of Web Services Research **2560**
1545-7419 *see* 0038-1128 **3512**
1545-7427 *see* 8756-0054 **5969**
1545-7435 *see* 0009-8620 **3484**
1545-7443 *see* 0275-3758 **8627**
1545-7451 *see* 0272-4561 **995**
1545-746X *see* 1064-0401 **4418**
1545-7516 International Gestalt Journal **7364**
1545-7532 Analytic Separations News **2097**
1545-7540 Biomolecular Diagnostics News†
1545-7559 Tampa Bay Illustrated **3990**
1545-7567 The Perl Journal (Online Edition)†
1545-7575 *see* 1545-3669 **3126**
1545-7605 North Coast Review *changed to* 1930-5559 **5428**
1545-7621 Fun with the Family in New Mexico **8712**
1545-763X Gospel Voice (Sugarland) **6570**
1545-7648 Maritime Museum News **8652**
1545-7656 Welcome Home (Des Moines) **4552**
1545-7664 Gentry Magazine **3976**
1545-7672 C A P S T Journal **3524**
1545-7699 R M A Annual Statement Studies **1377**
1545-7737 *see* 1541-437X **2857**
1545-7745 *see* 1542-7706 **2904**
1545-7818 Shonen Jump **517**
1545-7869 *see* 0276-2897 **3509**
1545-7877 Penn State Law Review **4756**
1545-7885 *see* 1544-9173 **696**
1545-7893 Natural Gas & Electricity **6779**
1545-7907 *see* 1545-7893 **6779**
1545-7915 California Home and Design **436**
1545-8067 G.K. Hall Bibliographic Guide to Art and Architecture†
1545-8075 Corporate Accountability Alert†
1545-8083 Current Psychosis & Therapeutics Reports **6135**
1545-8091 *see* 1545-8083 **6135**
1545-8105 Kitchen & Cook **4362**
1545-8113 Water Strategist **8841**
1545-813X Ink Maker† **8964**
1545-8210 HazMat Transport News **3507**
1545-8229 *see* 1545-8210 **3507**
1545-8261 Headache & Pain **6144**
1545-830X The Daily Deal **1090**
1545-8318 *see* 1541-9878 **1090**
1545-8415 The Dante Society of America. Electronic Bulletin **5283**
1545-8490 Decision Analysis **1738**
1545-8504 *see* 1545-8490 **1738**
1545-8512 Report of Human Relief and Protection Series
1545-8520 Digital Photo Pro **6966**
1545-8539 Consultant for Pediatricians **6090**
1545-8547 Zebrafish **968**
1545-858X Tribology & Lubrication Technology **3398**
1545-8601 *see* 1057-5987 **7544**
1545-861X *see* 0149-2195 **7530**
1545-8628 O C L C Reports **5037**
1545-8636 *see* 1546-0738 **5663**
1545-8644 Cyber Therapy **6135**
1545-8709 The Mutual Fund Service Guides **1641**
1545-8717 *see* 1545-8725 **6983**
1545-8725 Californian Journal of Health Promotion **6983**
1545-8733 N C Boating Lifestyle† **8975**
1545-8741 Amber Waves **90**
1545-8822 *see* 0737-0652 **7020**
1545-8830 *see* 0740-817X **3367**
1545-892X Jacob's Well Professional Newsletter **7801**
1545-8970 Japanese Guide to Hawaii **8725**
1545-8997 Woodall's Eastern America Campground Directory **8342**
1545-9020 Screen World **6512**
1545-9039 G P S User Magazine **3193**
1545-9047 Annual Editions: Homeland Security **7507**
1545-9055 E-Journal of Teaching and Learning in Diverse Settings **2843**
1545-9063 The Global Sourcing Guide **3378**
1545-9071 Town Hall Journal **8075**
1545-911X *see* 0899-6563 **1342**
1545-9136 Outpatient Department E M T A L A Handbook **6070**
1545-9144 Journal of Investment Management **1362**
1545-9152 *see* 1545-9144 **1362**
1545-9217 Travel Savvy†
1545-9225 Great Minds of the 21st Century **642**
1545-9241 *see* 1063-097X **1860**
1545-925X *see* 1542-5010 **7598**
1545-9268 *see* 1096-3995 **1712**
1545-9276 Fire / E M S Product News **3577**
1545-9284 Transformations (Atlanta) **4485**
1545-9292 Building Women **987**
1545-9306 Esopus **5215**
1545-9330 International Coated Papers (Year)
1545-9462 *see* 1542-4995 **3047**
1545-9470 *see* 1542-4952 **3033**
1545-9489 Fire Code Inspections Law Bulletin **4674**
1545-9497 *see* 1545-9489 **4674**
1545-9500 Municipal Planning - Land Use Bulletin **7498**
1545-9519 *see* 1545-9500 **7498**
1545-9527 G I Jobs **6697**
1545-9535 Information Technology in Hospitality **2546**
1545-9616 Journal of Drugs in Dermatology **5879**
1545-9624 Journal of Occupational and Environmental Hygiene (Print) **6680**
1545-9632 Journal of Occupational and Environmental Hygiene (Online) **6680**
1545-9683 Neurorehabilitation and Neural Repair **6168**
1545-9691 The World of Welding **6345**
1545-9705 New Products Magazine **3657**
1545-9845 A B A / B N A Lawyers' Manual on Professional Conduct *see* 0740-4050 **4606**
1545-9896 Oncology Nutrition Connection **6030**
1545-9985 *see* 1545-9993 **693**
1545-9993 Nature Structural and Molecular Biology **693**
1546-0002 Health Imaging & I T **6197**
1546-0037 South Magazine (Jackson)
1546-007X The Steinbeck Review **5377**
1546-0096 Pediatric Rheumatology Online Journal **6225**
1546-010X Sea Tow Lifelines **8282**
1546-0118 *see* 0199-8595 **3131**
1546-0126 *see* 1048-5236 **3148**
1546-0134 The Complete Investor **1618**
1546-0169 Leadership Compass **3026**
1546-0185 Journal of Directed Energy **3140**
1546-0193 P R News **31**
1546-0371 American Academy of Psychoanalysis and Dynamic Psychiatry. Journal **7332**
1546-0525 Wage & Hour†
1546-055X Armchair General **639**
1546-0592 Servo **2586**
1546-0606 B **2251**
1546-0622 Old Timers' Bulletin *changed to* 1937-1810 **4326**
1546-0630 Over the Back Fence **3984**
1546-0657 Bookmarks **7555**
1546-0673 Geographic Report on Sales and Marketing Personnel Compensation *changed to* Survey Report on Marketing Personnel Compensation **1709**
1546-0673 Geographic Report on Sales and Marketing Personnel Compensation *changed to* Survey Report on Sales Personnel Compensation **1709**
1546-072X *see* 0009-837X **2232**
1546-0738 M M W R. Surveillance Summaries **5663**
1546-0762 2e: Twice-Exceptional Newsletter (Print)†
1546-0835 V Man **6301**
1546-0843 Journal of Radiology Nursing **5967**
1546-086X Rime Magazine **5081**
1546-0886 Truckin's S U V†
1546-0894 Figure **2255**
1546-0924 Journal of Worry and Affective Experience *changed to* 1931-5694 **7399**
1546-1017 Accreditation Process Guide for Behavioral Health Care **4087**
1546-1025 Accreditation Process Guide for Ambulatory Care **4087**
1546-1033 Accreditation Process Guide for Laboratories **5901**
1546-1130 Chimera†
1546-1254 European Homes & Gardens†
1546-1270 Control Solutions International†
1546-1408 Ohio Genealogical Society. Quarterly **3777**
1546-1440 American College of Radiology. Journal **6192**
1546-1483 Cardozo Public Law, Policy & Ethics Journal **4640**
1546-1696 *see* 1087-0156 **768**
1546-170X *see* 1078-8956 **5684**
1546-1718 *see* 1061-4036 **876**
1546-1726 *see* 1097-6256 **6162**
1546-184X Ensemble (Montvale) **4539**
1546-1955 Journal of Computational and Theoretical Nanoscience **7019**
1546-1963 *see* 1546-1955 **7019**
1546-1971 *see* 1546-198X **3330**
1546-198X Sensor Letters **3330**
1546-1998 Journal of Low Power Electronics **3106**
1546-2005 *see* 1546-1998 **3106**
1546-203X Nanotechnology Law & Business **4738**
1546-2048 Mechanics & Chemistry of Biosystems *changed to* 1556-5297 **750**
1546-2072 Dude Ranch Vacations & Horseback Adventures **8699**
1546-2080 *see* 1546-203X **4738**
1546-2218 Computers, Materials & Continua **2413**
1546-2226 *see* 1546-2218 **2413**
1546-2234 Journal of Organizational and End User Computing **2571**
1546-2250 Children, Youth and Environments **2148**
1546-2323 Applied Research in Coaching and Athletics Annual **8158**
1546-2331 Basic Communication Course Annual **2313**
1546-234X International Journal of Sport Management **1761**
1546-2366 San Francisco Estuary and Watershed Science **8831**
1546-2501 Sexuality, Reproduction & Menopause **6004**
1546-251X Annual Editions: World Religions **7621**
1546-2552 G.K. Hall Bibliographic Guide to East Asian Studies†
1546-2595 American Public Warehouse Register **8490**
1546-2609 Review of Business Research **1581**
1546-2617 Planned Giving Mentor **8062**
1546-2625 Online Cl@ssroom **2950**
1546-2633 *see* 0190-3373 **361**
1546-2757 The Dog Lover's Companion to Boston **8698**
1546-2765 Portland Monthly **3985**
1546-2781 Alabama Counseling Association. Journal **6692**
1546-279X AIDScience† **8929**
1546-2803 Oeconomicus **1547**
1546-2811 Musclecar Enthusiast **8188**
1546-282X Buckaroo Scene **8163**
1546-2838 NewWitch **6742**
1546-3087 Intranets **1419**
1546-3095 The Journal of Applied Research in Clinical Dentistry **5850**
1546-3109 *see* 1430-144X **3308**
1546-3117 Car Design News **8572**
1546-3125 Metropolitan Archivist **5032**
1546-3133 Insiders' Guide to Pittsburgh **8722**
1546-3141 *see* 0361-803X **6192**
1546-3206 Journal of Urban Education **2879**
1546-3214 International Journal of Applied Aviation Studies **61**
1546-3222 American Thoracic Society. Proceedings **6236**
1546-3257 B G C World *changed to* 1945-9696 **7752**
1546-3273 U N L V Journal of Hospitality, Tourism & Leisure Science **4399**
1546-3281 The South Carolina Modern Language Review **5176**
1546-329X Insiders' Guide to Charleston **8721**
1546-3303 Fun with the Family in Illinois **8712**
1546-3427 Penn State Environmental Law Review **4756**
1546-3435 Penn State International Law Review **4937**
1546-3443 P D R Drug Guide for Mental Health Professionals **6172**
1546-346X R S N A News **6205**
1546-3516 From the Other Shore **5298**
1546-3664 C M B S World **1323**
1546-3826 The Yale - China Health Journal **5732**
1546-3958 Inside the G S E s **1354**
1546-3966 D & O Advisor **4865**
1546-3974 Law Firm Inc. **4874**
1546-4032 Let's Go: Central America (Year) **8729**
1546-4075 Let's Go: New Zealand, Including Fiji (Year) *changed to* 1930-7497 **8730**
1546-4105 Bank Fraud and I T Security Report **2511**
1546-4121 *see* 1080-0344 **2104**
1546-4148 Harley Hahn's Internet Yellow Pages **2557**
1546-4156 *see* 0893-0341 **6121**
1546-4202 Cal P E R S Watch **1615**
1546-4229 Pennsylvania Labor History Journal **1702**
1546-4261 Computer Animation and Virtual Worlds **2484**
1546-427X *see* 1546-4261 **2484**
1546-4288 Learning Series **2431**
1546-4296 DCWatch **7128**
1546-4385 Black Elected Officials (Statistical Summary) (Print Edition) *changed to* Black Elected Officials (Statistical Summary) (CD-ROM) **7423**
1546-4423 Hudson Valley Review **1119**
1546-4431 S G I A Journal **7327**
1546-4466 The Michigan Front Page **3550**
1546-4504 Blackgirl Magazine
1546-4598 Textile World Asia **8461**
1546-4636 MultiMedia & Internet@Schools **2950**
1546-4652 Hastings Race and Poverty Law Journal **4849**
1546-4660 Joint Commission International Accreditation Standards for the Care Continuum **7447**
1546-4679 Job Safety 21 **6679**
1546-4687 Car and Driver Ultimate Road Test Comparisons **8571**
1546-4709 Martha Stewart Kids† **8972**
1546-4717 Zink **2264**
1546-4725 Marr's Field Journal **5331**
1546-4776 A C C Docket **4854**
1546-4792 American Ship Review *see* 1066-2774 **8657**
1546-4806 American Yacht Review **8271**
1546-4814 Ocean Voyager **8279**
1546-5004 *see* 1545-7362 **2560**
1546-5012 Journal of Organizational and End User Computing (Online) *see* 1546-2234 **2571**
1546-5020 Northwest Education **2892**
1546-5047 Motley Fool Income Investor **1641**
1546-5055 *see* 1546-5047 **1641**
1546-508X Eyes on the I C C **4926**
1546-5098 Fish Physiology **943**
1546-5101 Computer Games **2475**
1546-5306 *see* 1083-7310 **7533**
1546-5314 California Workers' Comp Law Bulletin **1669**
1546-5322 *see* 1546-5314 **1669**
1546-5330 Army History **6412**
1546-5381 Journal of Martial Arts & Healing **6991**

ISSN

1547-4992 *see* 1547-5476 **2520**
1547-500X The Journal of Educators Online **2876**
1547-5042 Jobsite. Tools, Materials & Equipment for the H V A C R Professional **4122**
1547-5069 *see* 1527-6546 **5966**
1547-5085 Today's Christian **3991**
1547-5093 *see* 1547-5085 **3991**
1547-5115 Healing Lifestyles & Spas **6110**
1547-5131 NurseWeek (South Central Edition) *see* 1534-2204 **5972**
1547-514X Neopets **8190**
1547-5158 T V P P A News **3332**
1547-5166 CoDe (Houston) **2505**
1547-5174 Kids' Pages **2158**
1547-5263 Coping with Heart Conditions†
1547-5271 Heart Rhythm **5788**
1547-5298 S O L G A Newsletter **354**
1547-5360 Case Magazine **2277**
1547-5379 SmackDown! Magazine *changed to* 1933-4524 **8215**
1547-5425 Ethics and Critical Thinking Journal **6917**
1547-5441 Language Learning and Development **5141**
1547-545X New York Construction **1027**
1547-5476 Defense A T & L **2520**
1547-5514 Solid State Technology Resource Guide *see* 0038-111X **3114**
1547-5522 Music Library Association - Southern California Chapter. Newsletter **5033**
1547-5530 Tarab **6622**
1547-5565 Workforce Management **1877**
1547-562X Harper's Illustrated Biochemistry **733**
1547-5638 Men's Health en Espanol **5076**
1547-5646 *see* 1547-5654 **6249**
1547-5654 Journal of Neurosurgery: Spine **6249**
1547-5662 Digital Buying Guide **2576**
1547-5689 Kitchen Makeovers **4560**
1547-5719 Additions & Decks **975**
1547-5727 The Village Rambler Magazine *changed to* 1557-5322 **5357**
1547-5735 *see* 1547-5743 **3570**
1547-5743 Vanderbilt e-Journal of Luso-Hispanic Studies **3570**
1547-5778 Journal of Transnational Management **1574**
1547-5786 *see* 1547-5778 **1574**
1547-5808 International Sephardic Journal **3540**
1547-5816 Journal of Industrial and Management Optimization **1766**
1547-5840 Issues in Informing Science & Information Technology **8428**
1547-5859 *see* 1547-5840 **8428**
1547-5867 *see* 1547-5840 **8428**
1547-5875 Gobshite Quarterly **5301**
1547-5905 *see* 0001-1541 **3234**
1547-5913 *see* 1066-8527 **3253**
1547-5972 Cold Mountain Review **5275**
1547-5999 *see* 1546-4148 **2557**
1547-6006 Ask Harley **3969**
1547-6014 Harley Hahn's Tidbits **3977**
1547-6022 The Harley Hahn Experience **3977**
1547-6030 Harley Hahn's Internet Insecurity **2513**
1547-6049 Harley Hahn's Internet Advisor **2557**
1547-6057 Harley Hahn's Guide to Muds **2477**
1547-6065 The Little Nipper's Internet Clubhouse **2200**
1547-6073 Learning Through History **4151**
1547-6189 Photography in New York International *changed to* 1544-9084 **6974**
1547-6251 V O N Magazine **2567**
1547-6278 Organogenesis **926**
1547-6286 R N A Biology **744**
1547-6294 Annexins†
1547-6308 Plunkett's Food Industry Almanac **3660**
1547-6340 Woodall's North America Campground Directory **8342**
1547-6375 H E P Express **7520**
1547-6383 Dermatology Business Management **1738**
1547-6391 Pristine Processing **2077**
1547-6405 Adopting Today†
1547-6413 Lubrication & Fluid Power *changed to* 1941-4447 **3352**
1547-6502 Robb Report Worth *changed to* 1931-9908 **1660**
1547-6510 *see* 1040-8347 **2099**
1547-6529 *see* 1088-9868 **3483**
1547-6537 *see* 1064-3389 **3485**
1547-6545 *see* 0191-9512 **3251**
1547-6553 *see* 1064-1262 **3605**
1547-6561 *see* 1040-8436 **7009**
1547-657X *see* 1040-6026 **4666**
1547-6669 Hopekeepers **7648**
1547-6693 S C Magazine (US Edition) **2516**
1547-6707 Satellite Business Solutions **2389**
1547-6715 Labor: Studies in Working-Class History of the Americas **1693**
1547-6723 Utility Automation & Engineering T&D **3149**
1547-6731 Manufacturing I T (Carol Stream) **2549**
1547-6804 Fun with the Family in Vermont and New Hampshire *changed to* Fun with the Family Vermont and New Hampshire **8712**
1547-6863 Federal Reserve Bulletin. Statistical Supplement† **8956**
1547-688X The New Educator **2890**
1547-6898 *see* 1040-8444 **3495**
1547-6901 *see* 1547-691X **5763**
1547-691X Journal of Immunotoxicology **5763**
1547-6952 Patient Drug Facts†
1547-6979 Tracks **6624**
1547-6987 No Compromise **321**
1547-7002 Journal of Medical Risk†
1547-7010 Jewish Review **7724**
1547-7029 Journal of Failure Analysis and Prevention **6319**
1547-7037 Journal of Phase Equilibria and Diffusion **6319**
1547-7045 *see* 0049-7878 **8905**
1547-7061 Mosaic (Newton) **2887**
1547-7088 American Art Collector (Scottsdale) **465**
1547-7150 Anthurium **3519**
1547-7185 *see* 0022-2429 **1825**
1547-7193 *see* 0022-2437 **1825**
1547-7207 *see* 0743-9156 **1826**
1547-7215 *see* 1069-031X **1825**
1547-7223 Cable FAX's Cable WORLD *changed to* 1931-7697
1547-724X *see* 0889-8480 **7287**
1547-7304 *see* 0141-1896 **6581**
1547-7355 Journal of Homeland Security and Emergency Management **2678**
1547-7363 *see* 0094-9000 **5541**
1547-7371 *see* 1061-0022 **5532**
1547-738X *see* 0077-1554 **5518**
1547-7398 *see* 0012-7094 **5484**
1547-7401 *see* 0882-7508 **6326**
1547-741X *see* 0882-2840 **3049**
1547-7428 E H S Assist **3414**
1547-7444 *see* 0305-0629 **7243**
1547-7460 Complete Catalog of Plays **8468**
1547-7487 *see* 1071-4421 **2315**
1547-7568 Day Trips from Indianapolis **8697**
1547-7584 Corporate Dealmaker **1619**
1547-7592 MaryJanesFarm **136**
1547-7681 A S A Professional **7581**
1547-769X Forensic Science, Medicine, and Pathology **5913**
1547-7703 Wagon Tracks **4317**
1547-7800 *see* 0892-9882 **7908**
1547-7827 Cracking the A C T, with Practice Tests on CD-ROM *changed to* Cracking the A C T with Sample Tests on CD-ROM **2975**
1547-7878 Technology Leadership News (Online) **2951**
1547-7908 Catechetical Leader **7787**
1547-8092 C P A Review. Regulation **1283**
1547-8165 Microsoft Windows Server 2003 Solutions **2508**
1547-8181 *see* 0018-7208 **3195**
1547-819X The Internet Review of Science Fiction **5443**
1547-8335 Mergent's Dividend Achievers **1639**
1547-8343 Mergent's Handbook of Common Stocks **1639**
1547-8416 Hiram Poetry Review **5423**
1547-8424 *see* 1536-6936 **8901**
1547-8432 Cargo†
1547-8440 Ninth Letter **5342**
1547-8459 E M S Management Journal **7514**
1547-8475 P S M. 100% Independent P S 2 & PlayStation Magazine *changed to* 1941-5303 **2480**
1547-8483 I E E E Power Electronics Specialists Conference. Conference Proceedings *changed to* I E E E Power Electronics Specialists Conference. Proceedings **59**
1547-8521 Biotech Law Weekly **4630**
1547-853X *see* 1547-8521 **4630**
1547-8548 Porcupine Literary Arts Magazine **5353**
1547-8556 The Dualist (Online) **6915**
1547-8572 Preventive Medicine Week **5699**
1547-8580 *see* 1547-8572 **5699**
1547-8599 Bioterrorism Week (Online) *see* 1547-8602 **7223**
1547-8602 Bioterrorism Week **7223**
1547-8610 Digital Document Quarterly **2571**
1547-8769 Insiders' Guide to the N A S C A R Tracks† **8964**
1547-8777 Quick Escapes: Minneapolis-St. Paul **8749**
1547-8785 Airways Classics **8538**
1547-8793 Iconofile **494**
1547-8807 Austin - Healey Magazine **8556**
1547-8823 The Women's Health Activist **8849**
1547-8874 The Guide (San Francisco) **2322**
1547-8890 Contact in Context **573**
1547-8904 C P M Global Assurance **1731**
1547-8912 MicroTEC†
1547-8920 Southern California Curiosities **8757**
1547-8939 Insiders' Guide to the Maine Coast **8723**
1547-898X Committee on Corporate Counsel. Newsletter *changed to* 1937-2442 **4691**
1547-8998 Current Rheumatology Diagnosis and Treatment **6223**
1547-9064 American Journal of Diabetes **5883**
1547-9072 Mohawk Valley History **3775**
1547-9080 Newman Studies Journal **7809**
1547-9102 Law Practice **4716**
1547-9129 Common Ground Journal **7634**
1547-9137 Country Commerce. Germany **1558**
1547-9153 *see* 1547-9064 **5883**
1547-9196 Country Commerce. Hong Kong **1558**
1547-920X Country Commerce. Brazil **1557**
1547-9218 Country Commerce. Colombia **1557**
1547-9226 Country Finance. New Zealand **1331**
1547-9234 Country Commerce. Indonesia **1558**
1547-9242 Country Finance. Germany **1330**
1547-9250 Country Commerce. Israel **1558**
1547-9285 Vital Woman Magazine **7779**
1547-9307 The Mower's Tree **5336**
1547-9315 Medicine & Health's Managed Care Report **4515**
1547-9323 Country Commerce. Canada **1557**
1547-9331 Country Commerce. Hungary **1558**
1547-934X Country Finance. China **1330**
1547-9382 Punitive Damages (Eagan) **4840**
1547-9463 The Wide - Format Imaging **7329**
1547-9498 Consumer Guide to Homeowners Insurance *changed to* 1934-4368 **4525**
1547-9579 Glimpse Quarterly *changed to* 1932-9407
1547-9587 Laws of Virginia Related to Financial Institutions **4874**
1547-9595 Blanket Statements **6637**
1547-9617 Graphic & Design Business **491**
1547-9641 Journal of Undergraduate Research **2991**
1547-965X Western Real Estate Business **7616**
1547-9676 Marine Safety and Security Council. Proceedings **6432**
1547-9684 *see* 1521-4672 **5017**
1547-9692 *see* 1521-4672 **5017**
1547-9706 *see* 1539-3585 **3067**
1547-9714 *see* 1539-3585 **3067**
1547-9803 Davison's Box & Carton Blue Book **6709**
1547-9811 The Advertising Red Books. International Advertisers & Agencies **1971**
1547-982X Lute Society of America. Quarterly **6585**
1547-9838 Thalia (Woodland Hills)†
1547-9846 Foundations and Trends in Microeconomics **1541**
1547-9854 *see* 1547-9846 **1541**
1547-9943 Vertical Systems Reseller **1847**
1547-9951 Seminars in Anesthesia, Perioperative Medicine and Pain **5774**
1547-9986 Executive Traveler **8702**
1547-9994 Pharma Market Research Report **6867**
1548-0003 International Journal of Applied Economics **1571**
1548-002X Supervisor Safety Alert **6687**
1548-0046 *see* 0272-6351 **3251**
1548-0119 *see* 1548-0593 **5349**
1548-0135 Zoning Practice **4432**
1548-0216 Journal of Plastic Surgery
1548-0399 Photoshop Fix **6975**
1548-0410 U S Markets Metro Economies. South **1907**
1548-0488 Eurekah Bioscience†
1548-050X L J N's Legal Tech Newsletter **4710**
1548-0518 Journal of Leadership and Organizational Studies **1767**
1548-0569 *see* 0272-8397 **7098**
1548-0585 *see* 1083-5601 **7094**
1548-0593 Paradox **5349**
1548-0607 Chlenskii Zhurnal **5273**
1548-0615 *see* 1548-0623 **1418**
1548-0623 International Journal of Cases on Electronic Commerce **1418**
1548-0631 International Journal of Business Data Communications and Networking **2534**
1548-064X *see* 1548-0631 **2534**
1548-0658 *see* 1548-0666 **1758**
1548-0666 International Journal of Knowledge Management **1758**
1548-0704 Professional Studies Review **6702**
1548-0712 Journal of Catholic Social Thought **7802**
1548-0755 Planning & Environmental Law **7604**
1548-0828 N M T C Monthly Report *changed to* 1941-482X **1937**
1548-095X Country Commerce. Pakistan **1559**
1548-0968 Country Commerce. Spain **1559**
1548-0976 Country Commerce. United Kingdom **1560**
1548-0984 Country Commerce. Mexico **1558**
1548-0992 I E E E America Latina. Revista **3362**
1548-100X Country Commerce. Japan **1558**
1548-1018 Country Commerce. Nigeria **1559**
1548-1026 Country Commerce. Kenya **1558**
1548-1085 The Heirloom Gardener Magazine **3736**
1548-1093 International Journal of Web-Based Learning and Teaching Technologies **2469**
1548-1107 *see* 1548-1093 **2469**
1548-1115 International Journal of Enterprise Information Systems **2522**
1548-1123 *see* 1548-1115 **2522**
1548-1131 International Journal of E-Business Research **1418**
1548-114X *see* 1548-1131 **1418**
1548-1166 China Automotive Review **8574**
1548-1174 HomePlanners Ultimate Home Plan Collection *changed to* 1930-6466 **435**
1548-1263 Cracking the S A T II. Biology E/M Subject Test *changed to* 1556-8431 **2976**
1548-1336 *see* 0160-6972 **5852**
1548-1352 *see* 0091-2131 **337**
1548-1360 *see* 0886-7356 **334**
1548-1379 *see* 0892-8339 **349**
1548-1395 *see* 1055-1360 **345**
1548-1409 *see* 1559-9167 **326**
1548-1417 *see* 0883-024X **327**
1548-1425 *see* 0094-0496 **324**
1548-1433 *see* 0002-7294 **324**
1548-1441 Sizzle **4367**
1548-145X International Jew's Harp Society. Journal **6576**
1548-1468 Art Premium Puerto Rico *changed to* 1559-825X **474**
1548-1476 *see* 1388-0292 **3448**
1548-1492 *see* 0161-7761 **326**
1548-1506 List Insider **1829**
1548-1514 2Wheel Tuner **8270**
1548-159X Dynamics of Partial Differential Equations **5484**
1548-1603 GIScience and Remote Sensing **4013**
1548-1611 Fidelity & Surety Digest **4674**
1548-1654 Contact (New York) **3528**
1548-1689 Journal of Vegetable Science *changed to* 1931-5260 **237**
1548-1743 Georgia Administrative Law Digest of Environmental Decisions **4680**
1548-176X The Korea Society Quarterly **7250**
1548-1778 Private Practice Success†
1548-1786 Group Practice Solutions **4094**
1548-1824 HomePlanners Outdoor Living **3736**
1548-1840 Feature Edition **2283**
1548-1859 Business Journal for Entrepreneurs **1073**
1548-1867 Journal of African American History **3544**
1548-1875 Environmental Health News **3425**
1548-1921 Mars **577**
1548-1956 Christian History and Biography† **8941**
1548-1964 E A P S U Online **5113**
1548-2030 Take-Care Connections†
1548-2057 Conversations **7635**
1548-209X *see* 0196-6197 **5875**
1548-212X Best Life **6283**
1548-2197 Zeichner Risk Assessment **7546**
1548-2200 *see* 1548-2197 **7546**
1548-2219 ElderCare **4044**
1548-2227 Horizons (Metuchen) **5629**
1548-2243 Physician Forum **5696**
1548-2251 Women's Health Resource Guide **8849**
1548-226X *see* 1089-201X **4181**
1548-2278 *see* 0022-037X **1599**
1548-2286 The Electronic Proceedings of Undergraduate Mathematics Day **5486**
1548-2324 *see* 0363-6445 **819**
1548-2367 Country Finance. Indonesia **1330**
1548-2375 Country Finance. Hong Kong **1330**
1548-2383 Country Finance. India **1330**
1548-2391 Country Finance. Poland **1331**
1548-2405 Country Finance. France **1330**
1548-2413 Her Sports *changed to* Her Sports + Fitness **8177**
1548-2421 Scratch Magazine *changed to* X X L Presents: Scratch **6629**
1548-243X Eleven Eleven **487**

ISSN

ISSN

1551-5265 see 1551-5257 5694
1551-5273 Cancer Law Weekly 6013
1551-5281 see 1551-5273 6013
1551-529X Physician Law Weekly 4758
1551-5303 see 1551-529X 4758
1551-5311 see 1551-532X 6835
1551-532X Drug Law Weekly 6835
1551-5338 Hospital Law Weekly 4100
1551-5346 see 1551-5338 4100
1551-5354 Law & Health Weekly 4713
1551-5362 see 1551-5354 4713
1551-5370 Health Insurance Law Weekly 4504
1551-5389 see 1551-5370 4504
1551-5397 Food & Drug Law Weekly 6842
1551-5400 see 1551-5397 6842
1551-5486 New York Journal of American History 4305
1551-5494 Telemedicine Law Weekly 4793
1551-5508 see 1551-5494 4793
1551-5516 Healthcare Finance, Tax & Law Weekly 1351
1551-5524 see 1551-5516 1351
1551-5532 see 1551-5540 6867
1551-5540 Pharma Investments, Ventures and Law Weekly 6867
1551-5559 Medical Verdicts & Law Weekly 4732
1551-5567 see 1551-5559 4732
1551-5575 Surgery Litigation & Law Weekly 6259
1551-5583 see 1551-5575 6259
1551-5591 see 1551-5605 4788
1551-5605 State & Local Health Law Weekly 4788
1551-5613 Medicine & Law Weekly 5674
1551-5621 see 1551-5613 5674
1551-563X Pharma Law Weekly 6867
1551-5648 see 1551-563X 6867
1551-5672 Yard 527
1551-5680 The Looking Glass 5328
1551-5796 Luxury Log Homes & Timber Frame changed to 1943-6610 1001
1551-5826 Crimespree Magazine 5413
1551-5869 Opolis 4421
1551-6067 see 1545-7699 1377
1551-6083 Speedworld Magazine 8202
1551-6091 Diagnostic & Invasive Cardiology 6195
1551-6105 Acuity Care Technology 5567
1551-6113 Boatworks for the Hands-On Sailor changed to Boatworks 8640
1551-6237 I E E E International Conference on Mobile Data Management. Mobile Data Management changed to 1551-6245 2350
1551-6245 I E E E International Conference on Mobile Data Management. Proceedings 2350
1551-6253 American Bar Association. Antitrust Law Section. Annual Meeting 4854
1551-6342 Shehui Kexue Yanjiu (Zhongwen Ban) 8001
1551-6393 International Conference on Scientific and Statistical Database Management. Proceedings 2591
1551-644X Cracking the New S A T changed to 1934-239X 2976
1551-6458 Cracking the New S A T with Practice Tests on CD-ROM changed to 1936-4091 2976
1551-6490 Construction Pro
1551-6512 Creative Knitting 6637
1551-6598 Housing for Seniors Report 4412
1551-6628 Coalbed Natural Gas Report changed to 1938-2596 6796
1551-6679 Pentagon Brief 6441
1551-6709 see 0364-0213 7347
1551-6741 U S A Hockey Magazine 8213
1551-6776 Journal of Pediatric Pharmacology and Therapeutics 6095
1551-6822 Quick Escapes: Las Vegas 8749
1551-6830 Quick Escapes: Pittsburgh† 8983
1551-6849 International Management Review 1762
1551-6857 A C M Transactions on Multimedia Computing Communications and Applications 2532
1551-6865 see 1551-6857 2532
1551-6881 Strategic R M 4524
1551-689X H D R I 3 D 2486
1551-6911 T M T Advisor 2340
1551-692X Prosper 1162
1551-6962 Literal 5224
1551-6970 A S H E Higher Education Report Series 2964
1551-6989 see 1550-624X 3385
1551-6997 A I S Tech (Year) Conference Proceedings 6303
1551-7004 A R K I V O C 2048
1551-7012 see 1551-7004 2048
1551-711X Cityland 4642
1551-7136 Heart Failure Clinics 5788
1551-7144 Contemporary Clinical Trials 5904
1551-7268 Voices (Schenectady) 3623
1551-7322 America's Best Value Colleges 2953
1551-7411 Research in Social and Administrative Pharmacy 6878
1551-742X Harris Directory. New Jersey Manufacturing 2001
1551-7489 Journal of Opioid Management 5653
1551-7497 I E E E Computational Systems Bioinformatics Conference. Proceedings changed to 1752-7791 2409
1551-7519 R W P 5357
1551-7551 Journal of Genome Science and Technology (Print Edition) 874
1551-756X Journal of Genome Science and Technology (Online Edition) 874
1551-7616 A I P Conference Proceedings 7002
1551-7624 Pacific Journal of Science and Technology (Hilo) 7896
1551-7667 see 1551-6997 6303
1551-7683 The Dramatist 8469
1551-773X Andrews Litigation Reporter: Patent 4855
1551-7748 see 1552-8073 1641
1551-7756 Instructional Leadership Abstracts (Online Edition) 2942
1551-7772 Woodworking for Women†
1551-7853 European Diabetes Nursing 5958
1551-7861 see 1551-7853 5958
1551-787X Hawaii Library Association Newsletter (Online) 5011
1551-7888 Substance Abuse Funding Week changed to 1934-4848 8073
1551-7896 Disability Funding Week changed to 1933-3854 8037
1551-7918 Insurance Journal. Southeast Edition 4507
1551-7977 Year Book of Hand and Upper Limb Surgery 6263
1551-7985 Iowa Curiosities 8724
1551-8000 Damron Road Atlas 8696
1551-8027 Town & Country Travel 8765
1551-806X Psychoanalytic Perspectives 7395
1551-8159 Country Finance. Mexico 1331
1551-8167 see ExtremeTech 2418
1551-8175 Cloth Paper Scissors 532
1551-8183 Country Finance. Japan 1330
1551-8213 Shaadi Style†
1551-8221 American Medical Women's Association. Journal (Online)†
1551-823X American Anthropological Association. Archaeological Papers 372
1551-8248 see 1551-823X 372
1551-8264 News from the South Carolina Library Association 5036
1551-8272 U.S. National Toxicology Program. Report on Carcinogens 6036
1551-8280 see 1551-8272 6036
1551-8329 Ivy Cottage Scrapbook Trends Magazine 536
1551-8396 The Hopkins HIV Report 5816
1551-840X A H P Journal 8022
1551-8418 The Director (Cincinnati) 5957
1551-8426 DePaul Journal of Health Care Law 4656
1551-8442 A H I P Coverage 4490
1551-8450 Waterweek changed to 1946-7141 8817
1551-8515 Cocoaroma 3631
1551-8612 Marketing y Medios 29
1551-8620 Scale Auto Contest Cars 4346
1551-8647 E-MainStream changed to 1946-7141 8817
1551-8647 E-Mainstream see 0273-3218 8927
1551-8655 N J P A Real Estate Journal changed to 1945-8053 7599
1551-8663 see 1365-7305 3585
1551-868X Southwestern Directory of Expert Witnesses & Consultants changed to 1931-5767 4608
1551-8701 see 0149-8029 3214
1551-871X P F S Advisor (Patient Financial Services) changed to 1933-3307 4109
1551-8817 Mealey's Mass Tort Pleadings (Print) changed to Mealey's Mass Tort Pleadings (Online) 4731
1551-8833 American Water Works Association. E-Journal see 0003-150X 8817
1551-8841 The Women's Health Data Book 8849
1551-885X HIV Clinician 5815
1551-8868 see H R S A CareAction 5814
1551-8876 Survival News 5827
1551-8884 Mealey's Litigation Report: Welding Rods 4837
1551-8892 Midwifery Today 5998
1551-8906 Healthcare Leadership Report 7523
1551-8914 see 1551-8876 5827
1551-8922 U.S. Department of Health and Human Services. National Center for Health Statistics. National Vital Statistics Reports 7317
1551-8930 see 1551-8922 7317
1551-8949 Journal of Dentistry for Children (Print Edition) changed to 1935-5068 5851
1551-8965 N I H Guide for Grants and Contracts (Online) 8056
1551-8973 U P S Teamster 8678
1551-9023 Access Management Journal 4087
1551-904X Guideposts Sweet 16 2191
1551-9066 HIV Inside 5815
1551-9074 SIDAhora†
1551-9104 C A R I N G 5953
1551-9147 Acute Care Perspectives 6106
1551-9155 Wild Ones Journal 3754
1551-9171 A C E P News 6054
1551-9236 see 1056-6139 4457
1551-9252 International Country Risk Guide Annual. Vol. 4, The Middle East & North Africa 1492
1551-9287 Boomer Market Advisor 1807
1551-9295 Microscopy Today 900
1551-9309 The Space Between 5376
1551-9325 E-quality 7639
1551-9589 Chinascope 7226
1551-9627 Transit 4274
1551-9783 The Journal of Structured Finance 1363
1551-9791 see 1551-6881 4524
1551-9805 see 1551-6881 4524
1551-983X The Grove Review 5302
1551-9880 Journal of Social and Ecological Boundaries 4461
1551-9899 Ad-Hoc & Sensor Wireless Networks 5465
1551-9902 Motley Fool Inside Value 1641
1552-0633 see 1551-9899 5465
1552-1222 Scientific Inquiry 7912
1552-1249 Savings Bond Alert 1649
1552-1281 Compact Equipment 5450
1552-146X see 0093-0334 5623
1552-1907 see Ohio Criminal Law Handbook 2662
1552-1915 see 1552-1923 4974
1552-1923 Leather Times 4974
1552-1990 Cook's Country 4355
1552-2016 One (New York) 7810
1552-2024 D O C News† 8948
1552-2032 see 1544-5186 5974
1552-2059 Northeast Ohio Journal of History 4306
1552-2148 see 1551-5869 4421
1552-2202 Time Out Chicago 3990
1552-2210 Interdisciplinary Journal of Knowledge and Learning Objects 5018
1552-2229 see 1552-2210 5018
1552-2237 see 1552-2210 5018
1552-2245 Foundations and Trends in Economic Theory changed to 1547-9846 1541
1552-227X Transworld Business 1183
1552-2288 Plunkett's Consulting Industry Almanac 2024
1552-2326 Business Integration Journal 1073
1552-2466 Life Science Weekly 686
1552-2474 see 1552-2466 686
1552-2482 Cardiovascular Device Liability Week 5780
1552-2490 see 1552-2482 5780
1552-2504 Cardiovascular Business Week 1080
1552-2512 see 1552-2504 1080
1552-2520 Medical Device Business Week 1148
1552-2539 see 1552-2520 1148
1552-2547 Genetics & Environmental Health Week 869
1552-2555 see 1552-2547 869
1552-2563 Nursing Home & Elder Business Week 5974
1552-2571 see 1552-2563 5974
1552-258X Aging & Elder Health Week 4039
1552-2598 see 1552-258X 4039
1552-2733 iSixSigma Magazine 1762
1552-2814 Federal Reserve Bank of Boston. Research Review 1486
1552-2822 see 1552-2814 1486
1552-2830 Better Homes and Gardens Santa Claus (Year) 532
1552-2903 Journal of International Business Strategy 1574
1552-2946 Making Music 6586
1552-2962 D K World Soccer Yearbook 8226
1552-3004 Plunkett's Automobile Industry Almanac 8598
1552-3020 see 0886-1099 8024
1552-3039 see 0095-3997 7418
1552-3047 see 0741-7136 2938
1552-3055 see 1523-4223 1855
1552-3063 How2 5424
1552-3071 Aggregates Manager 975
1552-3098 I E E E Transactions on Robotics 2584
1552-3136 Windows I T Pro 2525
1552-3152 Nouvelles Etudes Francophones 3555
1552-3160 Bound & Lettered 479
1552-3233 Innovate (North Miami) 2867
1552-325X Academic.Writing 5248
1552-3268 Edwardsville Journal of Sociology†
1552-3276 see 0194-9543 278
1552-3284 see 0161-3626 2465
1552-3330 Refrigerated and Frozen Foods Retailer 3662
1552-3349 see 0002-7162 7104
1552-3357 see 0275-0740 7419
1552-3365 see 0363-5465 6228
1552-3373 see 1532-673X 7105
1552-3381 see 0002-7642 7946
1552-3411 Emergency Number Operations changed to 1553-4995 7515
1552-3470 Small Firm Business 1967
1552-3489 see 1073-1911 7337
1552-3497 see 0146-6216 7336
1552-3519 see 0013-161X 3021
1552-3527 see 0013-1601 2932
1552-3535 see 0013-1245 2847
1552-3543 see 0891-2424 1539
1552-356X see 1532-7086 5281
1552-3578 see 1069-3971 7957
1552-3586 see 0887-4034 4886
1552-3594 see 0093-8548 2649
1552-3608 Crossroads (Dublin) 5004
1552-3624 see 1054-0725 6059
1552-3721 Sustainable Development Law & Policy 3468
1552-373X see 1552-3721 3468
1552-3748 Manage (Online) 1774
1552-3799 see 1054-7738 5955
1552-3802 see 1534-6501 6131
1552-3810 see 0093-6502 8094
1552-3829 see 0010-4140 7117
1552-3837 see 0886-3687 1671
1552-3845 see 1533-2101 308
1552-3861 see 0011-0000 7349
1552-387X see 0011-1287 2648
1552-3888 see 0013-1644 7353
1552-3896 see 0895-9048 3022
1552-390X see 0013-9165 8100
1552-3918 see 0163-2787 5612
1552-3926 see 0193-841X 7963
1552-3934 see 1077-727X 4357
1552-3942 see 1531-2445 4909
1552-3950 see 1066-4807 7357
1552-3969 see 1525-822X 339
1552-3977 see 0891-2432 8104
1552-3993 see 1059-6011 2861
1552-4078 Data Link (Online) 3290
1552-4124 Roundtables in Spine Surgery 6257
1552-4167 see 0145-4455 7339
1552-4175 see 1099-8004 5953
1552-4183 see 0270-4676 7842
1552-4191 see 1080-5699 1729
1552-4205 see 0007-6503 1070
1552-4256 Journal of Social Work in End-of-Life & Palliative Care 7380
1552-4264 see 1552-4256 7380
1552-4272 Woman International 8889
1552-440X see Casino City's Casino Vendors Guide 8164
1552-4450 Nature Chemical Biology 2074
1552-4469 see 1552-4450 2074
1552-4477 Taking Sides: Clashing Views on Controversial Issues in Management 1797
1552-4485 see 0033-569X 5527
1552-4523 see 0733-4648 4049
1552-4531 see 0748-7304 6149
1552-454X see 1087-0571 735
1552-4558 see 0095-7984 7369
1552-4566 see 0021-9347 7978
1552-4574 see 1050-6519 1133
1552-4582 see 0021-9436 1764
1552-4590 see 1069-0727 7369
1552-4604 see 0091-2700 6852
1552-4612 see 0196-8599 8112
1552-4647 Inside Weddings 5559
1552-4701 Queer Ramblings 4378
1552-4728 Land Development Today changed to 1938-1050 1038
1552-4736 see 1938-1050 1038
1552-4744 Canadian Benefits & Compensation Reporter 4638
1552-4752 see 1552-4744 4638
1552-4809 Journal of System-on-Chip 3117
1552-4817 see 1552-4809 3117

DIRECTORY 2010 1553-0671 9705

1552-4825 American Journal of Medical Genetics. Part A **862**
1552-4833 *see* 1552-4825 **862**
1552-4841 American Journal of Medical Genetics. Part B: Neuropsychiatric Genetics **862**
1552-485X *see* 1552-4841 **862**
1552-4868 American Journal of Medical Genetics. Part C: Seminars in Medical Genetics **862**
1552-4876 *see* 1552-4868 **862**
1552-4884 The Anatomical Record. Part A: Discoveries in Molecular, Cellular, and Evolutionary Biology *changed to* 1932-8486 **652**
1552-4906 The Anatomical Record. Part B: The New Anatomist *changed to* 1932-8486 **652**
1552-4922 Cytometry. Part A **831**
1552-4930 Cytometry. Part A (Online Edition) *see* 1552-4922 **831**
1552-4949 Cytometry. Part B: Clinical Cytometry **831**
1552-4957 *see* 1552-4949 **831**
1552-4965 *see* 1549-3296 **766**
1552-4973 Journal of Biomedical Materials Research. Part B: Applied Biomaterials **766**
1552-4981 *see* 1552-4973 **766**
1552-499X Journal of Experimental Zoology. Part A: Comparative Experimental Biology (Online Edition) *changed to* 1932-5231 **950**
1552-5007 Journal of Experimental Zoology. Part B: Molecular and Developmental Evolution **951**
1552-5015 *see* 1552-5007 **951**
1552-5023 Concepts in Magnetic Resonance. Part A (Online) *see* 1546-6086 **6194**
1552-5031 Concepts in Magnetic Resonance. Part B: Magnetic Resonance Engineering **6194**
1552-504X Concepts in Magnetic Resonance. Part B: Magnetic Resonance Engineering (Online) *see* 1552-5031 **6194**
1552-5112 Kritikos **4462**
1552-5120 New York Insurance Law and Litigation Alert **4516**
1552-5139 California Insurance Law & Litigation Alert **4497**
1552-5147 Texas Insurance Law & Litigation Alert **4525**
1552-5155 Journal of Counterterrorism & Homeland Security International **2678**
1552-518X Florida Community Studies Weekly *changed to* 1556-3553 **2926**
1552-5244 I E E E International Conference on Cluster Computing. Proceedings **2497**
1552-5260 Alzheimer's & Dementia **6121**
1552-5279 *see* 1552-5260 **6121**
1552-5287 Beckett Got Sports for Kids†
1552-5295 *see* 1552-5309 **4099**
1552-5309 Hospital & Nursing Home Week **4099**
1552-5341 Visual Basic Developer† **8997**
1552-5384 Health Insurance Week **4505**
1552-5392 *see* 1552-5384 **4505**
1552-5406 *see* 1043-9862 **4892**
1552-5414 *see* 0891-2416 **8112**
1552-5422 *see* 0022-0221 **7372**
1552-5430 *see* 8756-4793 **6200**
1552-5449 *see* 0272-4316 **2156**
1552-5457 *see* 0075-4242 **5133**
1552-5465 *see* 1070-4965 **3444**
1552-5473 *see* 0363-1990 **8113**
1552-5481 *see* 0192-513X **8113**
1552-549X *see* 1074-8407 **5965**
1552-5503 Club Industry's Fitness Business Pro **6984**
1552-5511 Fiberoptic Technology†
1552-5546 Visual Studio .NET Developer *changed to* Visual Studio Developer **2510**
1552-5597 Medical Patent Business Week **6754**
1552-5600 *see* 1552-5597 **6754**
1552-5619 Medical Patent Week **6755**
1552-5627 *see* 1552-5619 **6755**
1552-5635 Oncology Business Week **6030**
1552-5643 *see* 1552-5635 **6030**
1552-5651 Genetics & Environmental Business Week **1113**
1552-566X *see* 1552-5651 **1113**
1552-5678 Managed Care Business Week **1146**
1552-5686 *see* 1552-5678 **1146**
1552-5694 Animal Lab News **8792**
1552-5708 *see* 0891-9887 **4049**
1552-5716 *see* 1538-1927 **2991**
1552-5724 *see* 0898-0101 **5965**
1552-5732 *see* 0890-3344 **5995**
1552-5767 The Permanente Journal **5695**
1552-5775 *see* 1552-5767 **5695**
1552-5783 *see* 0146-0404 **6044**
1552-5791 Journal of G X P Compliance **4701**
1552-5821 Applied Turfgrass Science **654**
1552-5856 The Biodefense Funding Report **757**
1552-5864 Journal of Middle East Women's Studies **8900**
1552-5929 Rock & Sling **5363**
1552-5937 Appliance Design **3295**
1552-5996 A C M / I E E E Joint Conference on Digital Libraries. Proceedings **4985**
1552-6011 Medicare Drug Watch **4107**
1552-6097 Western New York **8774**
1552-6100 Journal of Green Building **1018**
1552-6119 *see* 1077-5595 **2148**
1552-6127 *see* 1090-1981 **7522**
1552-6178 Vestal Review **5395**
1552-6194 Nor'Easter (Duluth) **4305**
1552-6208 The Advocate (Alexandria) **7332**
1552-6224 Business Puerto Rico **1075**
1552-6240 Idaho Magazine **3978**
1552-6259 *see* 0003-4975 **6237**
1552-6283 International Journal on Semantic Web and Information Systems **2547**
1552-6291 *see* 1552-6283 **2547**
1552-6305 Family Caregiver Magazine **4044**
1552-6313 U S Business Review **1185**
1552-6364 *see* 0739-9863 **7360**
1552-6372 *see* 1524-8399 **7523**
1552-6380 Healthcare Mergers, Acquisition and Ventures Week **4097**
1552-6399 Medical Imaging Business Week **1148**
1552-6402 Telemedicine Week **1182**
1552-6410 Disease Prevention Week **5606**
1552-6429 *see* 1552-6410 **5606**
1552-6437 *see* 1552-6402 **1182**
1552-6445 *see* 1552-6399 **1148**
1552-6453 *see* 1552-6380 **4097**
1552-6461 Lab Business Week **1143**
1552-647X *see* 1552-6461 **1143**
1552-6496 *see* 1532-4516 **2547**
1552-650X *see* 0022-1678 **7375**
1552-6518 *see* 0886-2605 **2657**
1552-6526 *see* 0261-927X **7375**
1552-6534 *see* 0276-1467 **1825**
1552-6542 *see* 1056-4926 **1768**
1552-6550 *see* 0273-4753 **1825**
1552-6569 *see* 1051-2284 **6153**
1552-6577 *see* 0739-456X **4417**
1552-6585 *see* 1538-5132 **4417**
1552-6593 *see* 0885-4122 **4417**
1552-6607 *see* 1549-3636 **2428**
1552-664X Summer Jobs in the USA†
1552-6658 *see* 1052-5629 **1768**
1552-6674 I E E E International High-Level Design Validation and Test Workshop. Proceedings **2471**
1552-6712 *see* 1534-4843 **1864**
1552-6720 *see* 1088-7679 **2654**
1552-6739 *see* 1084-8223 **4098**
1552-6763 *see* 0047-2875 **8726**
1552-6771 *see* 0096-1442 **4150**
1552-678X *see* 0094-582X **7982**
1552-6798 *see* 0893-3189 **1775**
1552-6801 *see* 1077-5587 **7548**
1552-681X *see* 0272-989X **5667**
1552-6828 *see* 1097-184X **6303**
1552-6836 *see* 0097-7004 **4186**
1552-6844 *see* 1545-9683 **6168**
1552-6879 *see* 0021-8863 **7368**
1552-6887 *see* 0898-2643 **4048**
1552-6895 *see* 0743-5584 **7368**
1552-6909 *see* 0884-2175 **5966**
1552-6917 *see* 1055-3290 **5810**
1552-6925 *see* 0160-0176 **7975**
1552-6933 *see* 0306-624X **2655**
1552-6941 *see* 1534-7346 **5639**
1552-695X *see* 1534-7354 **6022**
1552-6968 *see* 1054-1373 **8107**
1552-6976 Fed Tech Magazine **7486**
1552-6992 Halliwell's Film Guide **6502**
1552-7042 Human Rights Watch. D† **8962**
1552-7077 *see* 1552-7093 **7580**
1552-7085 *see* 1552-7093 **7580**
1552-7093 Free E-Book About Free E-Books **7580**
1552-7204 Explore the Bible. Leader Quicksource *changed to* 1557-4350 **7748**
1552-7212 Explore the Bible: Adult Study Guide Discovery **7757**
1552-7239 Inside Public Accounting **1290**
1552-7247 Insiders' Guide to Fairfield County **8722**
1552-7255 Syngas Refiner **3256**
1552-7263 *see* 1552-7255 **3256**
1552-731X *see* 0022-4278 **2658**
1552-7379 *see* 1094-6705 **1826**
1552-7395 *see* 0899-7640 **8059**
1552-7409 *see* 0894-3184 **5975**
1552-7417 *see* 1086-0266 **6684**
1552-7425 *see* 1094-4281 **1784**
1552-7433 *see* 0146-1672 **7390**
1552-7441 *see* 0048-3931 **7992**
1552-745X *see* 1098-6111 **4896**
1552-7468 *see* 1527-1544 **5978**
1552-7476 *see* 0090-5917 **7169**
1552-7514 *see* 0032-3292 **7170**
1552-7522 *see* 0032-8855 **2666**
1552-7530 *see* 1091-1421 **1941**
1552-7549 *see* 1087-724X **7463**
1552-7557 *see* 1049-7323 **5701**
1552-7565 *see* 1077-8004 **7994**
1552-7573 *see* 0164-0275 **4054**
1552-7581 *see* 1049-7315 **8128**
1552-759X *see* 0734-371X **7466**
1552-7638 *see* 0193-7235 **8182**
1552-7646 Ghost! Magazine **6741**
1552-7662 Ptrint **5355**
1552-7743 Nursing Programs **5975**
1552-7751 Peterson's Professional Degree Programs in the Visual and Performing Arts **511**
1552-7794 *see* 1527-0025 **1138**
1552-7808 *see* 1028-3153 **3014**
1552-7816 *see* 0022-4871 **2878**
1552-7824 *see* 0092-0703 **1803**
1552-7832 *see* 1043-6596 **5967**
1552-7840 *see* 1541-3446 **2879**
1552-7891 Special Operations Technology **6447**
1552-7905 Military Geospatial Technology **6435**
1552-793X Summer Jobs for Students (Year) *changed to* 1552-664X
1552-8006 Feasting with Fiction **5295**
1552-8014 Food, Culture, and Society **4358**
1552-8022 Native America Yesterday and Today **4304**
1552-8030 Journal of Religion, Spirituality & Aging **4049**
1552-8049 *see* 1552-8030 **4049**
1552-8065 Diabetic Living **5889**
1552-8073 Motley Fool Rule Your Retirement **1641**
1552-8081 The Architect's Newspaper (New York Edition) **429**
1552-8103 Handheld Computing†
1552-812X Retinal Physician **6051**
1552-8138 International Handwriting Analysis Review **7364**
1552-8162 Financial Institutions Compensation Survey. Report on Commercial Banking Positions *changed to* 1933-4400 **1709**
1552-8200 Food in American History **3639**
1552-8243 Disease-Specific Care Certification Manual **4092**
1552-8251 *see* 0162-2439 **7911**
1552-826X *see* 1046-8781 **2518**
1552-8278 *see* 1046-4964 **7408**
1552-8286 *see* 0894-4393 **2951**
1552-8294 *see* 0049-1241 **8137**
1552-8308 *see* 1206-3312 **4029**
1552-8316 *see* 1527-4764 **2396**
1552-8324 *see* 1524-8380 **6074**
1552-8332 *see* 1078-0874 **4429**
1552-8340 *see* 0042-0859 **2924**
1552-8359 Frets† **8958**
1552-8367 *see* 0009-8604 **6460**
1552-8383 Southwest Hydrology **2798**
1552-8391 Journal of Applied Research for Business Instruction **3067**
1552-8448 *see* 1077-8012 **8146**
1552-8456 *see* 0193-9459 **5984**
1552-8464 *see* 0730-8884 **8147**
1552-8472 *see* 0741-0883 **2345**
1552-8499 *see* 0044-118X **2172**
1552-8502 *see* 0486-6134 **1548**
1552-8510 Mealey's Litigation Report: Arthritis Drugs **4836**
1552-8529 Indigenous Nations Studies Journal **6635**
1552-8545 *see* 1075-5470 **8131**
1552-8588 Financial Institutions Compensation Survey. Report on Trust and Investment Services Positions *changed to* 1936-9506 **1654**
1552-8596 Patient Safety Advisory *changed to* 1941-7144 **7535**
1552-8618 *see* 0730-7268 **3497**
1552-8642 H. P. Lovecraft's Magazine of Horror **5443**
1552-8650 Women and Mathematics Education Newsletter **2926**
1552-8677 Remodeling Magazine **1032**
1552-8685 North Carolina Builder **1027**
1552-8693 Georgia Builder†
1552-8707 Ohio Builder **1028**
1552-8715 Virginia Builder **1042**
1552-8723 Mississippi Builder **1024**
1552-8731 Louisiana Builder **1021**
1552-874X Oregon Builder **1028**
1552-8766 *see* 0022-0027 **7978**
1552-8774 College Athletics and the Law **2972**
1552-8812 M D Week **5662**
1552-8820 *see* 1552-8812 **5662**
1552-8855 Association for Vascular Access. Journal **5778**
1552-8901 National Journal of Sexual Orientation Law **4377**
1552-8952 Handicrafts Through World History **535**
1552-8960 Chicago CAREgiver **4090**
1552-9029 Edutopia **2852**
1552-9045 Journal of Leadership Education **2877**
1552-9053 Hospital Business Week **4100**
1552-9061 *see* 1552-9053 **4100**
1552-907X Physician Business Week **5696**
1552-9088 *see* 1552-907X **5696**
1552-9096 Mental Health Business Week **6160**
1552-910X *see* 1552-9096 **6160**
1552-9118 Fitness and Wellness Business Week **6986**
1552-9126 *see* 1552-9118 **6986**
1552-9215 *see* 1553-3697 **4069**
1552-9282 Paradise Family Guides: Big Island of Hawaii **8746**
1552-9290 The Sporting News Fantasy Football **8246**
1552-9304 The Sporting News Fantasy Baseball **8246**
1552-9312 Electrical Contracting Products **3303**
1552-9355 Medical Imaging Week **6203**
1552-9363 *see* 1552-9355 **6203**
1552-941X ArtMatters! **474**
1552-9428 *see* 1552-941X **474**
1552-9495 Davison's Fence Blue Book **1001**
1552-9533 Minnesota Journal of Law, Science & Technology **4734**
1552-9541 *see* 1552-9533 **4734**
1552-9568 Mid-Columbian **5077**
1552-9576 Pink Magazine **8880**
1552-9592 Conversations on Philanthropy **8035**
1552-9606 Democracy at Large **7129**
1552-9657 The Online Journal of Bass Research **6601**
1552-9665 University of California, Berkeley. Center for Latin American Studies. Policy Papers **7271**
1552-9711 M A E S **3208**
1552-972X *see* 1552-9711 **3208**
1552-9738 Gamestar†
1552-9746 Restaurant Startup & Growth **4397**
1552-9827 Abundant Wellness **6643**
1552-9886 Web3D (Year) Symposium. Proceedings **2490**
1552-9894 Products Liability (Wayne) **4762**
1552-9924 *see* 0091-6765 **3425**
1552-9932 Country Finance. Brazil **1330**
1552-9975 Inside Wisconsin Sports **8179**
1552-9983 Chronicle (Radford) **5440**
1553-0116 Big **6964**
1553-0124 Pragmatic Case Studies in Psychotherapy **7391**
1553-0159 Concept **4535**
1553-0175 Fierce **8863**
1553-0205 *see* 1043-254X **5851**
1553-0213 Food & Wine Annual Cookbook **4358**
1553-0256 Lasting Moments **537**
1553-0280 Best's Financial Suite. P / C, US *changed to* 1942-8642 **4495**
1553-0302 Findings Brief **7517**
1553-0337 Clinical Coding and Reimbursement **4499**
1553-0396 International Journal of Microwave and Optical Technology **7077**
1553-040X Geosphere **2744**
1553-0418 Natural Home and Garden *changed to* 1933-1134 **4364**
1553-0426 *see* 0037-7317 **8068**
1553-0469 Baylor Journal of Theatre and Performance *changed to* 1942-4558 **8470**
1553-0582 L P N (Year) **5968**
1553-0590 *see* 1553-0582 **5968**
1553-0604 *see* 0021-6682 **7723**
1553-0612 *see* 1090-7505 **6628**
1553-0620 *see* 0275-1275 **4300**
1553-0639 *see* 0018-2176 **5125**
1553-0663 *see* 1553-0949 **8080**
1553-0671 L D I Issue Brief **7530**

ISSN

1553-8273 V P Magazine **1191**
1553-8281 Assisted Living Executive **4041**
1553-829X The Chesapeake Bay Book **8693**
1553-8311 Profiles of Governmental Excellence **7461**
1553-832X Inside Microsoft Windows Server Security†
1553-8338 *see* 1553-8605 **7375**
1553-8346 Journal of HIV - AIDS Prevention in Children & Youth **5820**
1553-8362 International Journal of Fruit Science **237**
1553-8370 Current Essentials of Surgery **6241**
1553-8389 Cardiovascular Revascularization Medicine **5781**
1553-8397 Auto Aficionado **8557**
1553-8419 Benefits Cost Control Advisor **1856**
1553-8443 Life Insurers Fact Book **4513**
1553-8486 Annual Gulf and Caribbean Fisheries Institute. Proceedings **3584**
1553-8516 Celebrated Living **5067**
1553-8591 Aerospace Daily & Defense Report **43**
1553-8605 Journal of L G B T Issues in Counseling **7375**
1553-8613 *see* 1553-8346 **5820**
1553-8621 *see* 1553-8362 **237**
1553-8656 Neale Sourna's North Coast Academies Diary **5338**
1553-8664 E D P Weekly **2536**
1553-8710 New York Moves **5078**
1553-877X I E E E Communications Surveys and Tutorials **2323**
1553-8796 *see* 1553-7625 **1641**
1553-8818 The Rational Investor **1647**
1553-8907 Psychopharmacology Educational Update **6877**
1553-8915 *see* 1553-8907 **6877**
1553-8923 Magazine Americana **8119**
1553-8931 Americana (Hollywood) **8087**
1553-894X *see* 1553-8958 **1704**
1553-8958 Quinlan's H R Compliance Law Bulletin **1704**
1553-8966 *see* 1553-8974 **4528**
1553-8974 Workers' Comp Bottom Line **4528**
1553-9032 Casino City's Nevada Gaming Almanac **8165**
1553-9040 *see* 1553-9032 **8165**
1553-9059 Offspring†
1553-9075 Foghorn Outdoors. Washington Hiking **8314**
1553-9083 China Medical Device Manufacturer **4486**
1553-9105 Journal of Computational Information Systems **2548**
1553-9121 Test Critiques†
1553-913X Chemical Engineering Faculty Directory **3238**
1553-9148 Idaho Issues Online **4297**
1553-9156 Rose Croix Journal **4473**
1553-9164 Fodor's Belgium **8704**
1553-9202 Grand Magazine **2154**
1553-9318 Teaching Exceptional Children Plus **3048**
1553-9431 Cheer Biz News **8165**
1553-944X T3 - Technical Textile Technology **8458**
1553-9490 Hamodia (Weekend Edition) **3536**
1553-9555 Law Officer **2659**
1553-9563 International Journal of Business Strategy **1755**
1553-9571 Government Leasing News *changed to* 1931-1974 **7596**
1553-958X A FalconGuide to the Mount Baker-Mount Shuksan Area **8312**
1553-9598 A FalconGuide to Everglades National Park and the Surrounding Area **8680**
1553-9601 Virtual Journal of Ultrafast Science **7046**
1553-961X Virtual Journal of Quantum Information **7051**
1553-9628 Virtual Journal of Biological Physics Research **7046**
1553-9636 Virtual Journal of Applications of Superconductivity **7046**
1553-9644 Virtual Journal of Nanoscale Science & Technology **7046**
1553-9652 Family Reformation **7643**
1553-9695 *see* 1527-2338 **4110**
1553-9709 *see* 1533-5453 **4106**
1553-9717 *see* 1522-533X **4105**
1553-9725 *see* 1551-2258
1553-9733 *see* 1556-1089
1553-9768 Journal of Special Operations Medicine **6429**
1553-9784 Advances in Financial Education **2824**
1553-9814 Global Rhythm **6569**
1553-9822 Vitals Woman†
1553-9938 Absolute†
1553-9946 WebMD the Magazine **5729**
1553-9962 Religion and Society in Central and Eastern Europe **7674**
1553-9989 24/7 Magazine **3993**
1554-0014 Hybridoma (Print)† **8962**
1554-0030 Daily International Pharma Alert†
1554-0049 F D A News Nutraceutical Weekly Bulletin **6840**
1554-0057 The New York Dog†
1554-0073 Energybiz **3134**
1554-0103 Taste of Home's Diabetic Cookbook **4368**
1554-0111 Taste of Home's Favorite Brand Name Recipes **4368**
1554-0138 PsycCRITIQUES (Online) **7394**
1554-0146 Undersea Warfare **6450**
1554-0170 *see* 0268-1102 **1598**
1554-0189 Competition Policy International **4647**
1554-0278 Tango **5084**
1554-0294 Ink & Ashes **5309**
1554-0359 Credentialing & Peer Review Legal Insider (Online) **4091**
1554-0448 *see* 1531-6009 **7522**
1554-0464 Effective Practices for Academic Leaders **3022**
1554-0472 *see* 1554-0464 **3022**
1554-0480 Public Justice Report (Online) **7261**
1554-0499 *see* 1554-7787 **5783**
1554-0502 The Non-GMO Report *changed to* The Organic & Non-G M O Report **244**
1554-0545 Inspired Living Magazine **5074**
1554-0561 Information Age Warfare Quarterly **6424**
1554-057X Foundations and Trends in Networking **2497**
1554-0588 *see* 1554-057X **2497**
1554-0626 Quarterly Journal of Political Science **7175**
1554-0634 *see* 1554-0626 **7175**
1554-0642 Foundations and Trends in Accounting **1289**
1554-0650 *see* 1554-0642 **1289**
1554-0669 Foundations and Trends in Information Retrieval **2530**
1554-0677 *see* 1554-0669 **2530**
1554-0766 Journal of Burns and Wounds *changed to* 1937-5719 **5913**
1554-0774 *see* 0361-0128 **2732**
1554-0790 Integral Leadership Review **1754**
1554-0839 Claremont Review of Books **5211**
1554-0847 Northeast Real Estate Business **7602**
1554-0871 G C New England **4678**
1554-091X Survey Report on Expatriate Compensation, Policies and Practices **1875**
1554-0936 H R Hero's Hiring & Firing **1862**
1554-1010 Journal of Information Assurance and Security **2515**
1554-1029 *see* 1554-1010 **2515**
1554-1045 International Journal of Information Technology and Web Engineering **2559**
1554-1053 *see* 1554-1045 **2559**
1554-1134 International Journal of Cancer Prevention **6022**
1554-1142 Academic Review *changed to* 1942-5074 **1738**
1554-1185 Grace Ormonde Wedding Style **5558**
1554-1215 Plunkett's Airline, Hotel & Travel Industry Almanac **8748**
1554-1282 Natural Health Retailer **1835**
1554-1312 Theoria (Denton) **6623**
1554-1339 Business Jet Traveler **8539**
1554-1355 Co-Inquiry Journal **2837**
1554-1363 First Aid for the U S M L E Step 3 **5614**
1554-138X The Photography Show **6975**
1554-1398 Executive Legal Summaries on CD-ROM *see* 0898-9931 **4867**
1554-141X CompScope Benchmarks for California (Print) *changed to* Baselines for Evaluating the Impact of the Reforms in California **1666**
1554-1452 CompScope Benchmarks for Louisiana **1672**
1554-1460 *see* 1554-1452 **1672**
1554-1479 CompScope Benchmarks for Massachusetts **1673**
1554-1487 *see* 1554-1479 **1673**
1554-1495 CompScope Benchmarks for North Carolina **1673**
1554-1509 *see* 1554-1495 **1673**
1554-1517 CompScope Benchmarks for Pennsylvania **1673**
1554-1525 *see* 1554-1517 **1673**
1554-1533 CompScope Benchmarks for Tennessee (Print) *changed to* Baselines for Evaluating the Impact of the Reforms in Tennessee **1666**
1554-155X CompScope Benchmarks for Texas (Print) *changed to* Baselines for Evaluating the Impact of the Reforms in Texas **1666**
1554-1576 CompScope Benchmarks for Wisconsin **1673**
1554-1584 *see* 1554-1576 **1673**
1554-1614 H2U **4047**
1554-1657 Corporate Governance Library (Online Edition) **4651**
1554-169X Biotechnology Healthcare **761**
1554-1711 CompScope Benchmarks. Technical Appendix **1673**
1554-172X *see* 1554-1711 **1673**
1554-1770 Theme **3568**
1554-1851 CompScope Benchmarks. Databook **1672**
1554-186X *see* 1554-1851 **1672**
1554-1878 Construction Supervisor's Safety Bulletin **6675**
1554-1886 The Green Magazine (New York) **8234**
1554-1894 ePregnancy **5989**
1554-1908 Journal of Emerging Technologies in Accounting **1294**
1554-1940 Current Trends in Psychoanalysis and Psychotherapy **7350**
1554-1959 Dental Clinics of North America. C M E Supplement *see* 0011-8532 **5839**
1554-2009 Event D V **2557**
1554-2033 Athletic Management **3017**
1554-2092 Michigan Entomological Society. Newsletter **854**
1554-2106 First Glimpse **3099**
1554-2122 Children's Business†
1554-2130 A A A Living (Michigan Edition) **8679**
1554-2149 Power Cruising **8280**
1554-2157 Directory of Periodicals ONLINE: Science and Technology **7936**
1554-2165 Directory of Periodicals ONLINE: Humanities and Religion **4484**
1554-2173 Directory of Periodicals ONLINE: Medical and Pharmaceutical **5744**
1554-2181 International Observer Political Report **7244**
1554-219X Terror Response Technology Report (Print) *changed to* Terror Response Technology Report (Email) **2228**
1554-2211 Get in the Game **8315**
1554-222X Sex, Love and Psychology **7407**
1554-2238 Abnormal Psychology **7330**
1554-2246 Insite (Colorado Springs) **8319**
1554-2254 Cleveland Art **482**
1554-2262 Journal of Education for International Development **3013**
1554-2270 The F T E Guide to Theological Education **7642**
1554-2327 Moon Handbooks: Hudson River Valley **8737**
1554-2408 Ecological and Environmental Anthropology **336**
1554-2416 Scuola Calcio Coaching Magazine **8245**
1554-2432 *see* 1046-0462 **3522**
1554-2440 Scholastic News. Grade 5/6 Edition **3080**
1554-2459 The Wittenburg Door† **8998**
1554-2467 Heart, Health & Nutrition **5627**
1554-2475 The Door Magazine *changed to* 1554-2459 **8998**
1554-2483 Implant News & Views **5847**
1554-2491 *see* 1554-2483 **5847**
1554-2505 *see* 1555-385X **6408**
1554-2513 Business Review, Washtenaw Livingston *changed to* 1932-2712 **1059**
1554-2548 Early Childhood and Elementary Literacy **2844**
1554-2556 Annual Editions: Labor-Management Relations **1663**
1554-2564 Prep Traveler **8748**
1554-2602 A A A Living (Wisconsin Edition) **8679**
1554-2610 New Jersey Motor Truck Association. Bulletin **8673**
1554-2629 GolfStyles **8234**
1554-2645 Everton's Genealogical Helper **3765**
1554-267X The Courant **5004**
1554-2688 *see* 1554-267X **5004**
1554-2769 *see* 0003-8504 **429**
1554-2785 Mealey's Litigation Report: Antidepressant Drugs **4731**
1554-2807 *see* International Association of Culinary Professionals Food Forum Quarterly **3648**
1554-2815 *see* 1520-765X **5786**
1554-2823 Dialysis Reimbursement and Quality Advisor†
1554-2858 Anti-Money Laundering Update *changed to* 1943-0973 **1310**
1554-2866 Anderson's (Year) Ohio Insurance Law Handbook **4492**
1554-2904 Petroleum Accounting and Financial Management Journal **6787**
1554-2947 Anderson's Ohio Civil Procedure *changed to* 1938-999X **4844**
1554-2998 Journal of School Counseling **3068**
1554-303X Montague Institute Review **5032**
1554-3048 Vision Update **6053**
1554-3110 D C Plan News & Analysis **1334**
1554-3137 The Ocean and Coastal Conservation Guide **3457**
1554-3145 International Journal of Leadership Studies **8109**
1554-3188 Business Review Western Michigan **1075**
1554-3196 First Aid for the Orthopaedic Boards **6060**
1554-3218 Taking Sides: Clashing Views and Controversial Issues in 20th Century American History **4314**
1554-3226 Taking Sides: Clashing Views and Controversial Issues in Classroom Management **3083**
1554-3234 The Homeland Security Review **7444**
1554-3242 *see* 1554-3234 **7444**
1554-3277 Knucklebones **8184**
1554-3285 Mammography Regulation and Reimbursement **4106**
1554-3293 Electronic Health Records Briefing **4114**
1554-3315 Louisiana Levant Magazine **3451**
1554-3323 One Magazine (Antioch) **7769**
1554-3358 Cuerpo **3529**
1554-3366 A G A Perpectives **5919**
1554-3374 Sructure and Dynamics **356**
1554-3382 N A N N Central **5970**
1554-3404 Manufacturing Business Technology **1898**
1554-3412 Studio/Monthly **2490**
1554-3439 International Fire Service Journal of Leadership and Management **3579**
1554-3447 Fodor's Prague **8708**
1554-3455 Fodor's Budapest **8704**
1554-348X Instore Buyer **3647**
1554-3498 Food Business News **3638**
1554-351X Behavior Research Methods **7339**
1554-3528 *see* 1554-351X **7339**
1554-3536 The S R C Red Book of 21-Month Charts **1649**
1554-3544 The S R C Industry Book of 12-Year Charts **1649**
1554-3617 Human Security & Development **3196**
1554-3625 Journal of Human Security and Development *see* 1554-3617 **3196**
1554-3641 *see* 1546-9239 **7834**
1554-365X S A P Financials Expert **2524**
1554-3684 Child Protection Law Report†
1554-3730 Network Support **2501**
1554-3749 Studies on Asia (Online) **561**
1554-3765 Lindy's Fantasy Baseball **8237**
1554-3781 Family Bible Study: Bible Teaching for 3rd and 4th Graders. Teaching Pictures *changed to* 1558-8289 **7626**
1554-379X Family Bible Study. Bible Teaching for 3rd and 4th Graders. Leader Pack *changed to* 1557-3915 **7626**
1554-382X Family Bible Study: Bible Teaching for 1st and 2nd Graders Teaching Pictures *changed to* 1558-8270 **7626**
1554-3838 Family Bible Study: Bible Teaching for 1st and 2nd Graders. Leader Pack *changed to* 1557-3893 **7626**
1554-3846 Family Bible Study: Bible Teaching for Grades 1 to 3 and 4 to 6. Leader Pack *changed to* 1557-3931 **7626**
1554-3862 Daily Variety (Gotham Edition) *see* 0011-5509 **2379**
1554-3870 Rick Steves' Prague & the Czech Republic **8752**
1554-3897 African Journal of Criminology and Justice Studies **2643**
1554-4052 Andrews Litigation Reporter: Intellectual Property **1552**
1554-4060 Andrews Litigation Reporter: Antitrust **4854**
1554-4079 How to Pay for Your Degree in Business & Related Fields **3024**
1554-415X Layers **2488**
1554-4168 The Journal of N A E T Energetics and Complementary Medicine **5763**
1554-432X *see* 0007-666X **1071**
1554-4338 JazzWeek **6580**
1554-4370 In Tune Monthly **6575**
1554-4389 Recreation† **8984**
1554-4419 Muslim World Journal of Human Rights **7212**
1554-4451 Simply Perfect Kids' Parties *changed to* 1938-4963 **8969**
1554-4494 Advancing Suicide Prevention **6120**
1554-4508 *see* 1554-4494 **6120**
1554-4516 Advances in Planar Lipid Bilayers and Liposomes **651**
1554-4567 International Commentary on Evidence **4953**
1554-4583 Connected Newsletter† **8943**
1554-4710 Latino Future Magazine **3547**
1554-4753 Magnet Status Advisor *changed to* 1939-5671 **5959**
1554-477X Journal of Women, Politics & Policy **7148**
1554-4788 *see* 1554-477X **7148**
1554-4796 University of Maryland Law Journal of Race, Religion, Gender and Class **4804**
1554-480X Pedagogies **3076**
1554-4818 *see* 1554-480X **3076**
1554-4842 Specialty Law Digest: Environmental Law **3467**
1554-4893 Journal of Early and Intensive Behavior Intervention **7372**
1554-4931 Texas Poetry Journal **5436**
1554-4958 Fourth Quarterly **7758**
1554-4974 Mosquito and Vector Control Association of California. Proceedings and Papers of the Annual Conference **7532**
1554-5008 Georgia Voyager Magazine **2190**
1554-5016 Ash Breeze **531**
1554-5156 Florida Civil Procedure **4831**
1554-5180 *see* 1554-5199 **4835**
1554-5199 LexisNexis AnswerGuide New York Civil Litigation **4835**
1554-5210 International Journal of Progressive Education **2870**
1554-5229 For Me†
1554-5253 F G B G **2188**
1554-527X *see* 0736-0266 **6064**
1554-530X Bundle†

ISSN

1555-2713 *see* 1552-3004 **8598**
1555-2721 *see* 1534-6528 **8595**
1555-2748 Heritage News (Washington, D.C.) **4295**
1555-2756 Fabric Trends **8450**
1555-2764 *see* 1479-9855 **2676**
1555-2780 Florida Travel & Life **5071**
1555-2810 *see* 1550-9702 **749**
1555-2853 *see* 1555-2861 **204**
1555-2861 National Honey Report **204**
1555-287X *see* 1555-2888 **2648**
1555-2888 Crime and the Nation's Households (Year) **2648**
1555-2896 Poker Pro **8193**
1555-2934 *see* 1081-6976 **352**
1555-2942 Vintage Bicycle Quarterly *changed to* 1941-8809 **8254**
1555-2993 The Lookout (Cincinnati) **7765**
1555-3094 Family Bible Study: Kindergarten Connection Learner Guide *changed to* 1557-4490 **7626**
1555-3108 Estudios Biblicos LifeWay para Adultos. Manual para el Lider **7756**
1555-3248 HygieneTown **5846**
1555-3264 Groovest†
1555-3310 Barron's How to Prepare for the A P Advanced Placement Exam. Calculus *changed to* 1940-3089 **5475**
1555-3310 Barron's How to Prepare for the A P Calculus Advanced Placement Examination. Calculus *changed to* 1940-3119 **5475**
1555-3337 *see* 0731-7131 **5050**
1555-3353 Journal of Business Case Studies **1764**
1555-3396 International Journal of Healthcare Information Systems and Informatics **2522**
1555-340X *see* 1555-3396 **2522**
1555-3418 New Perspectives in Criminology and Criminal Justice **2662**
1555-3426 Communications Business Daily† **8942**
1555-3434 Journal of Cognitive Engineering and Decision Making **7371**
1555-3469 Town & Country Weddings *see* 0040-9952 **3991**
1555-3531 N C A A Men's and Women's Lacrosse Records Book. Official Records **8189**
1555-354X *see* 1555-3531 **8189**
1555-3566 Winnetka Magazine **5087**
1555-3604 I O M A's Report on Managing Accounts Payable **1290**
1555-3744 Hoover's Handbook of Private Companies **2004**
1555-3787 Kahani **2196**
1555-3795 Bulk Transporter **8669**
1555-3817 *see* 1555-3825 **6409**
1555-3825 Air & Space Power Journal in Portuguese **6409**
1555-3833 Air & Space Power Journal Espanol **6409**
1555-3841 *see* 1555-3833 **6409**
1555-385X The Air & Space Power Journal **6408**
1555-3868 Air & Space Power Journal bil-'Arabiya **6409**
1555-3876 *see* 1542-961X **5773**
1555-3884 *see* 1052-2166 **867**
1555-3892 *see* 0963-6897 **830**
1555-3906 *see* 0965-0407 **6031**
1555-3914 Identity (Coral Springs) **3978**
1555-3922 New York Spaces (New Jersey Edition) **4547**
1555-3930 I E E E Computer Society Bioinformatics Conference. Proceedings *changed to* 1752-7791 **2409**
1555-4007 Northern California Curiosities **8742**
1555-4015 European Journal of Management **1742**
1555-404X Dentaltown **5842**
1555-4058 Studies in Cistercian Art and Architecture **520**
1555-4082 Oil & Gas Financial Journal **6783**
1555-4120 Games and Culture **8174**
1555-4139 *see* 1555-4120 **8174**
1555-4147 Letter & Spirit **7804**
1555-4155 Journal for Nurse Practitioners **5963**
1555-4163 *see* 1555-404X **5842**
1555-421X *see* Missouri Estate Planning, Will Drafting and Estate Administration Forms **4904**
1555-4236 Looking Good Now!†
1555-4309 Contrast Media & Molecular Imaging **6194**
1555-4317 *see* 1555-4309 **6194**
1555-4325 Performance Business **8598**
1555-4406 Andrew's Litigation Reporter: Tobacco Industry **4617**
1555-4473 *see* 0300-838X **717**
1555-4481 *see* 0300-8398 **717**
1555-449X *see* 0301-2328 **717**
1555-4503 C S A Neurosciences Abstracts (Online) **5742**
1555-4511 Nucleic Acids Abstracts (Online) **717**
1555-452X *see* 0748-1489 **2720**
1555-4538 C S A Oncogenes and Growth Factors Abstracts **5742**
1555-4546 *see* 0032-3624 **3480**
1555-4554 *see* 0896-5919 **720**
1555-4562 *see* 0140-5365 **3481**
1555-4570 *see* 0896-5900 **7050**
1555-4589 Journal of Cases in Educational Leadership **3025**
1555-4619 Seek (Grantham) *changed to* 1940-2937 **7761**
1555-4627 One Less **5346**
1555-4635 Reviews for Primary Care **5703**
1555-466X Hidden Philadelphia & the Amish Country **8718**
1555-4686 Windows I T Security *changed to* Security Pro V I P **2516**
1555-4694 Sly **6300**
1555-4708 Celebrity Living†
1555-4716 S P A R Q Magazine **8198**
1555-4775 Natural Philosophy Alliance. Proceedings **6935**
1555-4791 Measure (Evansville) **5427**
1555-4856 S A P Netweaver **2524**
1555-4864 Road Biking Colorado's Front Range **8267**
1555-4880 Nanoscience **8433**
1555-4902 A FalconGuide to Saguaro National Park & the Santa Catalina Mountains Guide Book **8680**
1555-4953 Cosmetic Packaging & Design *changed to* 1931-8308 **1807**
1555-4961 Finanzmarkt und Portfolio Management *changed to* 1934-4554 **1623**
1555-497X *see* 1934-4554 **1623**
1555-4996 Syracuse Science & Technology Law Reporter **4792**
1555-502X Write Now! **527**
1555-5054 Physician Advocate **5696**
1555-5062 International Journal of Education Policy and Leadership **3025**
1555-5070 International Law & Management Review **4931**
1555-5089 Progress in Complexity, Information and Design **3216**
1555-5100 Journal of Philosophy & Scripture **7655**
1555-5119 Tobacco Abstracts **8489**
1555-5135 M E M S: Micro-Electromechanical Systems **8431**
1555-5194 *see* 1550-5952 **6177**
1555-5240 Journal of Workplace Behavioral Health **1868**
1555-5259 *see* 1555-5240 **1868**
1555-5267 *see* 1555-5275 **3423**
1555-5275 Environmental Bioindicators **3423**
1555-5372 *see* 1554-9372 **4895**
1555-5380 Jewel (New York) **3542**
1555-5399 Journal of Digital Business **1134**
1555-550X The Strange Fruit†
1555-5534 Progress in Physics **7036**
1555-5542 Biological Theory **659**
1555-5550 *see* 1555-5542 **659**
1555-5569 *see* 1543-1215 **7157**
1555-5615 *see* 1555-5534 **7036**
1555-5623 Politics & Policy **7170**
1555-5631 Journal of Northern European Studies **4236**
1555-564X The Jackson Letter **1634**
1555-5658 Advising Boomers **1609**
1555-5674 Hopegivers Journal **7736**
1555-5682 Lowrider Edge†
1555-5720 Andrews Litigation Reporter: Privacy **4846**
1555-5739 Andrews Litigation Reporter: Gun Industry **4616**
1555-5747 Andrews Litigation Reporter: Utilities Industry **4617**
1555-5763 History of Meteorology **6353**
1555-578X Surveys in Approximation Theory **5540**
1555-5798 I E E E Pacific Rim Conference on Communications, Computers and Signal Processing. Conference Proceedings **2350**
1555-5860 *see* 1741-9166 **7129**
1555-5879 Review of Law & Economics **4879**
1555-5887 P L o S Clinical Trials **5910**
1555-5895 Arizona Education Review **2827**
1555-5925 AlwaysOn **1725**
1555-5933 Andrews Litigation Reporter: Construction Defect & Mold **4616**
1555-5941 Andrews Litigation Reporter: E-Business Law Bulletin† **8930**
1555-595X Andrews Litigation Reporter: Professional Liability **4617**
1555-5968 Food for Thought (Austin) **4386**
1555-5976 Baking & Snack International **3628**
1555-6026 Symposium on the Art of Scientific Glassblowing. Proceedings **2046**
1555-6042 Cutthroat **5281**
1555-6069 The Business Publisher **7556**
1555-6077 Advanced Polymers Abstracts **2085**
1555-6085 Agricultural & Environmental Biotechnology Abstracts (Online) **173**
1555-6093 *see* 1470-1391 **5016**
1555-6107 *see* 1757-1820 **2129**
1555-6115 *see* 1066-0623 **6338**
1555-6123 *see* 1560-0904 **2076**
1555-6131 *see* 0301-8695 **712**
1555-614X *see* 1811-2382 **2076**
1555-6158 *see* 0263-5534 **8842**
1555-6166 A S F A Aquaculture Abstracts (Online) **3612**
1555-6174 *see* 0031-0301 **6729**
1555-6182 A S F A Marine Biotechnology Abstracts (Online) **712**
1555-6190 *see* 0031-918X **6328**
1555-6204 *see* 0140-5373 **2634**
1555-6212 *see* 1054-6618 **5524**
1555-6220 *see* 0140-5381 **8842**
1555-6239 *see* 0965-5441 **6787**
1555-6247 *see* 1045-6031 **3477**
1555-6255 *see* 0869-5733 **6325**
1555-6263 *see* 0869-5938 **2769**
1555-6271 BioEngineering Abstracts (Online) **713**
1555-628X *see* 0001-4338 **6394**
1555-6298 Calcium and Calcified Tissue Abstracts (Online) **714**
1555-6301 *see* 0040-6015 **3397**
1555-6336 Journal of International Finance and Economics **1362**
1555-6344 Behold (Inver Grove Heights) **478**
1555-6395 Compliance Solutions Advisor *changed to* Databased Advisor Magazine **2554**
1555-6409 Ceramic Abstracts / World Ceramic Abstracts **2047**
1555-6417 Chemoreception Abstracts (Online) **2093**
1555-6433 Composites Industry Abstracts **7101**
1555-6441 *see* 0191-9776 **2442**
1555-645X *see* 0016-7932 **2781**
1555-6468 *see* 0162-704X **6283**
1555-6476 *see* 1075-7015 **6463**
1555-6484 *see* 0010-9339 **3229**
1555-6492 *see* 1019-3316 **7906**
1555-6506 *see* 1069-3513 **2789**
1555-6514 *see* 0143-3296 **3478**
1555-6522 *see* 0364-1074 **3478**
1555-6549 *see* Electronics and Communications Abstracts Journal **2347**
1555-6557 *see* 1064-2269 **2329**
1555-6565 The Bonefolder **4997**
1555-6581 *see* 0013-8924 **715**
1555-659X Environmental Engineering Abstracts (Online Edition) **3479**
1555-6603 *see* 0016-674X **716**
1555-6611 *see* 1054-660X **7080**
1555-662X Health and Safety Science Abstracts (Online) **7548**
1555-6638 *see* 1061-9208 **7038**
1555-6646 Immunology Abstracts (Online) **5747**
1555-6654 *see* 0006-3509 **752**
1555-6662 *see* 0965-5425 **5480**
1555-6670 *see* 0020-5842 **76**
1555-6689 *see* 0013-8738 **845**
1555-6719 Digital Cinematography **6496**
1555-6727 Specialty Pharma **6881**
1555-6735 *see* 1555-6727 **6881**
1555-676X Historic Main Street St. Charles, Missouri **4296**
1555-6794 The Journal of Germanic Mythology and Folklore **7737**
1555-6808 *see* 1555-6794 **7737**
1555-6816 Mealey's Litigation Report: Insurance Broker Liability **4875**
1555-6824 International Journal of Play Therapy **7365**
1555-6832 Texas Theatre Journal **8481**
1555-6840 Moorpark Review **5336**
1555-6867 Hemmings Sports & Exotic Car **8177**
1555-6875 M (The Colony) **6294**
1555-6891 Ephemera News **4334**
1555-7030 Avenues to Marketing Success **1806**
1555-7057 Italian Academy Lectures **5311**
1555-7065 Literary Conversations Series **5323**
1555-7073 Native Americans of the Northeast **6635**
1555-7154 *see* The Organic & Non-G M O Report **244**
1555-7162 *see* 0002-9343 **5572**
1555-7200 MountainRise **2887**
1555-7235 Leonard Maltin's Movie Guide **6506**
1555-7278 The S B L Forum **7678**
1555-7286 LexisNexis Answerguide New York Real Property **7598**
1555-7294 *see* 1555-7286 **7598**
1555-7308 Mind, Mood & Memory **7385**
1555-7332 Rocky Mountain Geology **2765**
1555-7340 *see* 1555-7332 **2765**
1555-7359 Journal of Politics & Society **7979**
1555-743X Rock Island County Illinois Genealogical Society Quarterly Journal **3780**
1555-7448 The American Directory of Writer's Guidelines **7551**
1555-7464 Consumer Reports S U V's, Wagons, Minivans, Trucks **8576**
1555-7480 The Manager as... **1777**
1555-7502 *see* 1554-3366 **5919**
1555-7561 *see* 1933-6837 **1550**
1555-7596 Divergencias **5285**
1555-7669 *see* 1545-0791 **4110**
1555-7715 International Journal of Business Studies **1571**
1555-7774 Iran Analysis Quarterly **4322**
1555-7839 Studies in Twentieth and Twenty-First Century Literature **5382**
1555-7847 The O. Henry Prize Stories **5344**
1555-7855 International Journal of Behavioral and Consultation Therapy **7364**
1555-7863 Watcher Junior **3010**
1555-788X Vanderbilt Undergraduate Research Journal **4481**
1555-7901 China - USA Business Review **1555**
1555-7960 *see* 1527-3172 **5662**
1555-7979 Inside Dentistry **5848**
1555-8037 *see* 1551-4897 **3106**
1555-8053 American Casebook Series **4614**
1555-810X S N L Quarterly Bank & Thrift Digest†
1555-8142 James MacGregor Burns Lectureship in Leadership Studies and Biography **4148**
1555-8150 Vitals Man†
1555-8185 At L A C M A **476**
1555-8193 Baker Studies in Biblical Archaeology†
1555-824X *see* 1062-8606 **5572**
1555-8282 Truckers News en Espanol *changed to* 1934-3264 **8676**
1555-8304 E S P N Sports Almanac (Year) **8170**
1555-8339 Meat & Deli Retailer **3655**
1555-8347 Jonesreport Plus **1823**
1555-8436 Risk Abstracts (Online) **3481**
1555-8444 Materials Business File **6340**
1555-8452 *see* 1063-7311 **3232**
1555-8460 Medical & Pharmaceutical Biotechnology Abstracts (Online) **5749**
1555-8479 *see* 0026-0924 **6340**
1555-8509 Buyers Guide for the Health Care Market
1555-8533 *see* 1555-855X **2368**
1555-855X Frecuencia Latinoamerica **2368**
1555-8568 *see* 1555-855X **2368**
1555-8576 *see* 1538-4047 **6011**
1555-8584 *see* 1547-6286 **744**
1555-8592 *see* 1547-6278 **926**
1555-8614 Translation **5188**
1555-8622 Archaeologies **377**
1555-8630 Inked **496**
1555-8681 Frank M. Covey, Jr., Loyola Lectures in Political Analysis **7137**
1555-8703 S N L Renewable Energy Week **3147**
1555-8711 Communication for Development and Social Change **8094**
1555-872X International Forum of Teaching and Studies **2868**
1555-8797 Arizona Notary Law Primer **4621**
1555-8800 Official Media Guide of the Senior P G A Tour *changed to* Official Champions Tour Guide **8241**
1555-8819 Alarm **6543**
1555-8908 Andrews Litigation Reporter: Telecommunications Industry **2312**
1555-8916 Andrews Litigation Reporter: Drug Recall **4616**
1555-8924 New York State School Counseling Journal **7388**
1555-8932 Genes & Nutrition **868**
1555-8959 Washington Gardener **3753**
1555-8967 Democratic Communique **7958**
1555-8975 Best Practices for Hospital & Health-System Pharmacy **6825**
1555-8983 Plunkett's Renewable, Alternative & Hydrogen Energy Industry Almanac **3144**
1555-8991 The Air Force Civil Engineer **3259**
1555-9009 *see* 1555-8991 **3259**
1555-9033 International Journal for Service Learning in Engineering **3200**
1555-9041 American Society of Nephrology. Clinical Journal **6265**
1555-905X *see* 1555-9041 **6265**
1555-9068 Foresight **1746**
1555-9092 L I S Programs and Faculty in the United States and Canada. Directory **5024**
1555-9173 Texas Real Estate Business **7613**
1555-9203 Evidence - Based Ophthalmology **6041**
1555-9211 *see* 1555-9203 **6041**
1555-922X Global Gaming Business **8175**
1555-9262 The Journal of Conscious Evolution **7371**
1555-9327 The White Pages Business Directory **2034**

ISSN

DIRECTORY 2010 1557-2358 9711

1556-6463 I E E E International Conference on Networks. Proceedings **2498**
1556-6471 Weinstein's Evidence Manual **4812**
1556-6501 *see* 1042-1629 **3059**
1556-6544 Journal of Biopharmaceutics and Biotechnology **6852**
1556-6552 *see* 1556-6544 **6852**
1556-6560 Journal of Biobased Materials and Bioenergy **766**
1556-6579 *see* 1556-6560 **766**
1556-6587 Journal of Autonomic and Trusted Computing **2537**
1556-6595 *see* 1556-6587 **2537**
1556-6609 Hyperbaric Medicine Product & Resource Guide **5631**
1556-6641 Modern Intellectual and Political History in the Middle East **4323**
1556-665X McGraw-Hill Series in Developmental Psychology **7384**
1556-6676 *see* 0748-9633 **7372**
1556-6706 Scientia Magna **7912**
1556-6714 Naptural Roots **590**
1556-6765 EDge (Bloomington) **3059**
1556-6781 American Art Collector (Berkeley) **465**
1556-679X Clinical and Vaccine Immunology (Online) **5756**
1556-6803 Journal of Women's Health Physical Therapy **8846**
1556-6811 Clinical and Vaccine Immunology (Print)†
1556-682X Native American Rights Fund. Annual Report **6635**
1556-6838 Ferrari Guides' Women's Travel in Your Pocket: U S A and Worldwide
1556-6900 Safety Compliance Letter **6685**
1556-6927 Pediatrics On Call **6102**
1556-6935 *see* 1040-9289 **2844**
1556-6943 Power Daily **3144**
1556-6978 *see* 0011-0035 **2839**
1556-7001 *see* 1556-701X **5345**
1556-701X On the Page Magazine **5345**
1556-7036 Energy Sources. Part A. Recovery, Utilization, and Environmental Effects **3133**
1556-7095 Cracking the S A T Math 1 & 2 Subject Tests **2976**
1556-7125 *see* 1535-3141 **5814**
1556-7168 Four Windows **4410**
1556-7206 I P Magazine **4689**
1556-7230 Energy Sources. Part A. Recovery, Utilization, and Environmental Effects (Online Edition) *see* 1556-7036 **3133**
1556-7249 Energy Sources. Part B. Economics, Planning, and Policy **3133**
1556-7257 *see* 1556-7249 **3133**
1556-7265 Nanoscale & Microscale Thermophysical Engineering (Print) **7056**
1556-7273 Nanoscale & Microscale Thermophysical Engineering (Online) **7056**
1556-7281 Journal of Digital Forensic Practice **2678**
1556-7303 I F I Insurance Investment Resource Guide *see* 1529-6636 **4507**
1556-7338 Billboard Radio Monitor *changed to* 1076-6502 **8983**
1556-7346 *see* 1556-7281 **2678**
1556-7370 Rail Teamster **4601**
1556-7389 Morningstar GrowthInvestor **1641**
1556-7397 Quick & Simple† **8983**
1556-7400 The Environmental Communication Yearbook *changed to* 1752-4032 **3423**
1556-7419 *see* 0147-4642 **5276**
1556-7427 New York Negligence **4745**
1556-7443 Intravenous Medications **6850**
1556-7486 Escapees **8579**
1556-7516 United States at War
1556-7524 Nineteenth Century Gender Studies **8901**
1556-7532 *see* 1068-5308 **6877**
1556-7540 *see* 1529-2584 **4042**
1556-7559 *see* 1040-6328 **2692**
1556-7567 *see* 1527-8395 **6089**
1556-7575 *see* 1058-1073 **2146**
1556-7583 *see* 1058-1103 **7385**
1556-7591 *see* 1042-1394 **2691**
1556-763X Forum on Public Policy **7965**
1556-7648 Trash Talk **3513**
1556-7702 Moon Handbooks: Las Vegas **8738**
1556-777X Vault Guide to the Top 25 Tech Consulting Firms **1191**
1556-7915 SELECT Journal **2532**
1556-7931 Perioperative Nursing Clinics **5977**
1556-7966 *see* 1556-7486 **8579**
1556-8016 Massachusetts Super Lawyers **4730**
1556-8024 Family Tree Magazine: Yearbook (Year)† **8955**
1556-8032 EnergyWashington Week **3307**
1556-8105 Urbanite (Baltimore) **5086**
1556-8113 Annie's Plastic Canvas† **8930**
1556-8121 Homeland Response *changed to* Responder Safety **7538**
1556-813X Business Performance Management **1730**
1556-8164 *see* 1556-8105 **5086**
1556-8172 O K! **5079**
1556-8180 Journal of Multidisciplinary Evaluation **8115**
1556-8237 Cognitive Science (Hauppauge) **7347**
1556-8253 Breastfeeding Medicine **920**
1556-8318 International Journal of Sustainable Transportation **8499**
1556-8326 Tech Confidential **1386**
1556-8334 *see* 1556-8318 **8499**
1556-8342 *see* 1556-8253 **920**
1556-8369 A S A - S I A M Series on Statistics and Applied Probability **5463**
1556-8431 Cracking the S A T Biology E/M Subject Test **2976**
1556-844X Cracking the S A T Chemistry Subject Test **2976**
1556-8482 SAT Subject Test: World History **4160**
1556-8490 Envy Man **4373**
1556-8504 In War and in Peace: U.S. Civil-Military Relations **6424**
1556-8512 Understanding Our Government **7190**
1556-8520 Journal of International Agricultural Trade and Development **202**
1556-8539 Journal of Stem Cells **5907**
1556-8547 Magic, Ritual, and Witchcraft **6742**
1556-8555 Bible Standard **7625**
1556-8563 Perspectives Online *see* 1940-8048 **4156**
1556-8571 A C C Cardiosource Review Journal† **8927**
1556-858X Ultrasound Clinics **6209**
1556-8598 P E T Clinics **6205**
1556-8601 *see* 1548-0755 **7604**
1556-8652 Campaigns and Commanders **4287**
1556-8687 Ruckus **6614**
1556-8717 M D T V Retailer *changed to* 1930-1642 **2382**
1556-8733 The Journal of Sexual Offender Civil Commitment, Science and the Law **2658**
1556-875X Journal of International Media & Entertainment Law **4701**
1556-8768 O'Connor's Property Code Plus **4751**
1556-8830 Andrews Litigation Reporter: Derivatives **4616**
1556-8849 SafetyLit Injury Prevention Literature Update **7540**
1556-8865 *see* 1556-8881 **4457**
1556-8873 *see* 1556-8881 **4457**
1556-8881 International Journal of Doctoral Studies **4457**
1556-889X China Media Research **4573**
1556-8903 Opium Magazine.print **5346**
1556-8911 Global Studies: Islam and the Muslim World **7710**
1556-8962 Opium Magazine.com *see* 1556-8903 **5346**
1556-8970 Suffolk Alumni Magazine **2916**
1556-8997 The Organized Executive **1784**
1556-9039 Journal of Medical Toxicology **6854**
1556-9047 Global Antiviral Journal **5814**
1556-9055 *see* 1556-9047 **5814**
1556-9101 Studies in American Literature and Culture: Literary Criticism in Perspective **5380**
1556-9128 The Series on Social Emotional Learning **2911**
1556-9152 *see* 1467-0100 **6240**
1556-9160 *see* 0954-0350 **7341**
1556-9187 *see* 1742-3341 **7364**
1556-9195 *see* 1476-9263 **6179**
1556-9217 Rural Realities **8130**
1556-9225 Harrington Lesbian Literary Quarterly† **8961**
1556-9241 Harrington Gay Men's Literary Quarterly† **8961**
1556-925X *see* 1556-9241 **8961**
1556-9268 Controlled Environments **3366**
1556-9276 Muzyka **6598**
1556-9330 *see* 1541-2040 **2672**
1556-9349 Healthcare Market Strategist *changed to* 1931-9894 **4097**
1556-9357 Refiner **6790**
1556-9411 Studies in German Thought and History **3566**
1556-942X Voices of Twentieth Century Conflict **8146**
1556-9519 *see* 1556-3650 **6829**
1556-9527 Cutaneous and Ocular Toxicology **6832**
1556-9535 *see* 1556-9527 **6832**
1556-9543 Toxin Reviews **6883**
1556-9551 *see* 1556-9543 **6883**
1556-956X On Scene (Lakewood) **7534**
1556-9756 Artifax **381**
1556-9764 Hot Rod's Bikeworks *changed to* 1939-7968 **8259**
1556-9780 Living Well **4051**
1556-9799 Virginia Sports and Entertainment Law Journal **4809**
1556-9829 Ocean (Corona Del Mar) **2259**
1556-9837 Foundations (Crestwood) **7704**
1556-9845 Innovations (Philadelphia) **5790**
1556-9861 Better Teaching (Elementary Edition) **3052**
1556-987X Better Teaching (Secondary Edition) **3052**
1556-990X Upholstery Manufacturing (Mt. Morris) **4563**
1556-9934 *see* 1556-9861 **3052**
1556-9942 *see* 1556-987X **3052**
1556-9950 Andrews Litigation Reporter: Class Action **4616**
1556-9969 Andrews Litigation Reporter: Bankruptcy **1307**
1556-9977 Andrews Litigation Reporter: Aviation **4616**
1556-9985 Andrews Litigation Reporter: Asbestos **4616**
1556-9993 Andrews Litigation Reporter: Nursing Home **5951**
1557-0002 Andrews Litigation Reporter: Health Law **4826**
1557-0010 Andrews Litigation Reporter: Bank & Lender Liability **4616**
1557-0029 Andrews Litigation Reporter: Entertainment Industry **4616**
1557-0037 Andrews Litigation Reporter: Toxic Torts **4617**
1557-0045 Andrews Litigation Reporter: White-Collar Crime **2643**
1557-0061 G C California **4678**
1557-0150 Andrews Litigation Reporter: Franchise & Distribution **4855**
1557-0169 Andrews Litigation Reporter: Computer & Internet **2490**
1557-0177 New York Outdoor News **8324**
1557-0185 Andrews Litigation Reporter: Medical Devices **5574**
1557-0193 Uptime (Fort Myers) **5461**
1557-0207 Edwards County Historical Society. Quarterly **4291**
1557-0215 Acoustics Today **7086**
1557-0223 *see* 1557-0215 **7086**
1557-024X Andrews Litigation Reporter: Insurance Coverage **4492**
1557-0258 Andrews Litigation Reporter: Sexual Harassment **4827**
1557-0266 Globality Studies Journal **4140**
1557-0274 The Review of Faith & International Affairs **7677**
1557-0282 Variety / Variedad **2671**
1557-0290 *see* 0069-6412 **5276**
1557-0304 National Reconnaissance **6438**
1557-0312 Library and Information Problem-Solving Skills Series **5026**
1557-0320 Libraries Unlimited Library Management Collection **5026**
1557-0371 *see* 1557-0282 **2671**
1557-0444 A A A S Annual Meeting **7935**
1557-0452 Andrews Litigation Reporter: Automotive **4616**
1557-0460 Andrews Litigation Reporter: Insurance Bad Faith **4855**
1557-0479 Andrews Litigation Reporter: Software Law Bulletin **2587**
1557-0487 Andrews Litigation Reporter: Delaware Corporation Law Update **4855**
1557-0495 Andrews Litigation Reporter: Mergers & Acquisitions **4855**
1557-0509 Andrews Litigation Reporter: Disability **4855**
1557-0517 Andrews Litigation Reporter: Employment **4616**
1557-0525 Andrews Litigation Reporter: Delaware Corporate **4855**
1557-0533 Andrews Litigation Reporter: Securities Litigation & Regulation **4617**
1557-0541 Progress in Community Health Partnerships **8126**
1557-055X *see* 1557-0541 **8126**
1557-0576 Journal of Neurologic Physical Therapy **6154**
1557-0584 *see* 1557-0576 **6154**
1557-0606 A S H P Midyear Clinical Meeting Symposium Highlights **6818**
1557-0614 Design Management Review **1738**
1557-0630 The Bead Release *changed to* 1945-8045 **2042**
1557-0657 *see* 1049-8931 **6147**
1557-0681 *see* 1478-2189 **6225**
1557-069X *see* 1464-3154 **4073**
1557-0703 *see* 0966-7903 **6683**
1557-0711 *see* 0960-5290 **5942**
1557-0738 Association for Library and Information Science Education. Membership Directory **4992**
1557-0746 Blackacre **4630**
1557-0762 Cards & Payments **1325**
1557-0843 Insulin **5894**
1557-0851 Feminist Criminology **2652**
1557-086X *see* 1557-0851 **2652**
1557-0878 *see* 1098-2140 **7946**
1557-0886 *see* 1545-1097 **5818**
1557-0983 Xerolage **5438**
1557-1009 Andrews Litigation Reporter: Corporate Officers & Directors Liability **4854**
1557-1017 International Journal of Pharmacy Education **6850**
1557-1025 Georgia Law Advocate **2285**
1557-1033 *see* 1557-1025 **2285**
1557-105X *see* 1475-9861 **5698**
1557-1076 Insurance Directory **4507**
1557-1114 Moon Handbooks: Illinois **8737**
1557-1211 *see* 0149-2063 **1767**
1557-1246 *see* 1087-0547 **6149**
1557-1254 John Bollinger's Capital Growth Letter **1634**
1557-1262 *see* 1557-1254 **1634**
1557-1289 *see* 1552-8855 **5778**
1557-1297 The Armour Research Society. Journal **364**
1557-1300 *see* 1543-7760 **1180**
1557-1319 Journal of Information, Information Technology, and Organizations **5021**
1557-1327 *see* 1557-1319 **5021**
1557-1335 *see* 1557-1319 **5021**
1557-136X Emerging Investments *changed to* 1934-6239 **1637**
1557-1394 Immigration Monthly **4849**
1557-1459 Bariatric Nursing and Surgical Patient Care **5952**
1557-1467 *see* 1557-1459 **5952**
1557-1475 The Anatomy of Workers' Compensation Medical Costs and Utilization in California **1662**
1557-1483 *see* 1557-1475 **1662**
1557-1491 The Anatomy of Workers' Compensation Medical Costs and Utilization in Florida **1662**
1557-1505 *see* 1557-1491 **1662**
1557-1513 The Anatomy of Workers' Compensation Medical Costs and Utilization in Louisiana **1662**
1557-1521 *see* 1557-1513 **1662**
1557-153X The Anatomy of Workers' Compensation Medical Costs and Utilization in Massachusetts **1662**
1557-1548 *see* 1557-153X **1662**
1557-1556 The Anatomy of Workers' Compensation Medical Costs and Utilization in North Carolina **1662**
1557-1564 *see* 1557-1556 **1662**
1557-1572 The Anatomy of Workers' Compensation Medical Costs and Utilization in Pennsylvania **1662**
1557-1580 *see* 1557-1572 **1662**
1557-1599 The Anatomy of Workers' Compensation Medical Costs and Utilization in Texas **1663**
1557-1602 *see* 1557-1599 **1663**
1557-1610 The Anatomy of Workers' Compensation Medical Costs and Utilization in Tennessee **1662**
1557-1629 *see* 1557-1610 **1662**
1557-1637 The Anatomy of Workers' Compensation Medical Costs and Utilization in Wisconsin **1663**
1557-1645 *see* 1557-1637 **1663**
1557-170X I E E E Engineering in Medicine and Biology Society. Conference Proceedings **5830**
1557-1718 Rubber Directory and Buyers Guide (Year) **7826**
1557-1734 *see* 0364-4324 **8839**
1557-1742 *see* 0364-4324 **8839**
1557-1785 Neteffect Series **2995**
1557-1815 Pohjois Amerikan Uutiset **3558**
1557-1823 Surveying the Digital Future **2567**
1557-1831 Arizona Agriculture **93**
1557-184X P G A Tour†
1557-1858 Food Biophysics **753**
1557-1866 *see* 1557-1858 **753**
1557-1874 International Journal of Mental Health and Addiction **7365**
1557-1882 *see* 1557-1874 **7365**
1557-1890 Journal of Neuroimmune Pharmacology **6854**
1557-1904 *see* 1557-1890 **6854**
1557-1912 Journal of Immigrant and Minority Health **5650**
1557-1920 *see* 1557-1912 **5650**
1557-1939 Journal of Superconductivity and Novel Magnetism **7023**
1557-1947 *see* 1557-1939 **7023**
1557-1955 Plasmonics **7035**
1557-1963 *see* 1557-1955 **7035**
1557-2013 Teaching and Learning in Nursing **5982**
1557-2021 The Latin Americanist **4151**
1557-203X *see* 1557-2021 **4151**
1557-2064 Sensing and Imaging **4489**
1557-2072 *see* 1557-2064 **4489**
1557-2099 Morningstar DividendInvestor **1641**
1557-2102 Legal Alert for Supervisors **1869**
1557-2145 I T Architect†
1557-2153 Methods in Pharmacology and Toxicology **6861**
1557-2196 *see* 1098-4321 **3440**
1557-2218 Kids on Wheels (Parents' Edition) **2158**
1557-2250 The S R C A D R Book of 12-Year Charts **1649**
1557-2285 Journal of Maritime Archaeology **401**
1557-2293 *see* 1557-2285 **401**
1557-2315 C I O Today **1415**
1557-2323 NewsFactor Magazine **2432**
1557-2331 Y'All **3993**
1557-234X Review of Human Factors and Ergonomics **6685**
1557-2358 The Best of Golf Tips **8223**

ISSN

1557-8232 see 0749-0704 5601
1557-8240 see 0031-3955 6100
1557-8259 see 0030-6665 6083
1557-8275 see 0033-8389 6206
1557-8283 Flyy Girl 8863
1557-8313 C G S Journal of Research 2833
1557-8321 see 1557-8313 2833
1557-833X Policy Today 7167
1557-8348 Hybridoma (Online) 733
1557-8364 see 1094-9313 2554
1557-8399 see 0065-3527 880
1557-8410 see 0065-2601 8085
1557-8429 see 0065-2725 2119
1557-8437 see 0065-7743 6821
1557-8445 see 0065-2776 5752
1557-850X see 1538-7135 758
1557-8518 see 1540-4196 5897
1557-8526 see 1545-4576 877
1557-8534 see 1547-3287 5941
1557-8542 see 1545-8547 968
1557-8550 see 1549-5418 6205
1557-8577 see 1549-1684 4054
1557-8585 see 1539-6851 6026
1557-8593 see 1520-9156 5889
1557-8607 see 0889-8561 5760
1557-8615 see 0883-9441 6063
1557-8623 see 0749-0690 4043
1557-8666 Journal of Computational Biology (Online) 682
1557-8674 see 1096-2964 6260
1557-8682 see 1527-0297 5628
1557-8704 see 0730-031X 761
1557-8771 International Journal of Construction Education and Research (Print) 1016
1557-8852 see 1084-9785 6011
1557-8917 see 0898-8838 2115
1557-8925 see 1054-3589 6819
1557-8933 see 0070-2153 667
1557-8941 see 0065-3233 722
1557-8976 see 0882-8245 5766
1557-8992 see 1044-5463 6150
1557-900X see 0892-7790 6270
1557-9018 Environmental Engineering Science (Online) 3424
1557-9034 see 1092-6429 6248
1557-9042 see 0897-7151 6064
1557-9077 see 1050-7256 5900
1557-9085 see 1076-2809 306
1557-9123 F H I Chicago 8862
1557-914X Human Security Report 2677
1557-9158 Soft Targets 5239
1557-9190 Clinical Lymphoma & Myeloma 6016
1557-9220 Rum & Reggae's Puerto Rico, Culebra & Vieques 8753
1557-9247 Rum & Reggae's Grenadines 8753
1557-9263 see 0273-8570 909
1557-9271 see 1530-9576 7462
1557-928X see 0742-1222 2548
1557-9298 see 0012-8775 1097
1557-9301 see 1086-4415 1418
1557-931X see 1061-1991 1161
1557-9328 see 0020-7411 7365
1557-9336 see 0020-7659 8109
1557-9387 see 1045-1870 6104
1557-9395 see 1043-1810 6083
1557-9409 see 1092-440X 6254
1557-9441 see 1527-6805 2541
1557-945X see 1529-3785 2405
1557-9468 see 1071-9040 5471
1557-9476 A C M S I G Ada Ada Letters 2504
1557-9484 see 0163-5999 2474
1557-9522 Supply Chain Strategy 1796
1557-9530 see 1557-9522 1796
1557-9573 S I A M News 5532
1557-9581 see 1527-3342 3312
1557-959X see 0885-8985 3101
1557-9603 see 0018-9251 3314
1557-9611 see 0018-9316 2382
1557-9638 see 0018-9359 3314
1557-9646 see 0018-9383 3103
1557-9654 see 0018-9448 2544
1557-9662 see 0018-9456 6402
1557-9670 see 0018-9480 3315
1557-9700 see 1075-2730 6176
1557-9743 A I M S Magazine 2822
1557-9751 Suffering 7686
1557-976X see 1557-9751 7686
1557-9778 see 1557-9751 7686
1557-9786 see 1064-9689 6202
1557-9794 see 1060-1872 6232
1557-9808 see 1089-2516 6209
1557-9816 see 0955-470X 6261
1557-9824 see 0891-5520 5817
1557-9832 see 0272-2712 5904
1557-9840 see 0095-5108 5988
1557-9859 see 0025-7125 5667
1557-9867 see 1052-5149 6203
1557-9875 see 0733-8619 6165
1557-9883 American Journal of Men's Health 6283
1557-9891 see 1557-9883 6283
1557-9913 Newcomer's Handbook for Moving to and Living in Washington D C 8741
1557-9921 Newcomer's Handbook for Moving to and Living in the San Francisco Bay Area 8741
1557-9948 see 0278-0046 3103
1557-9956 see 0018-9340 2421
1557-9964 see 1545-5963 825
1557-9972 see 1521-3331 3314
1557-9980 see 1521-3323 3314
1557-9999 see 1063-8210 2521
1558-0008 see 0733-8716 2323
1558-0016 see 1524-9050 8498
1558-0032 see 1089-7771 765
1558-0040 see 0018-9391 3315
1558-0059 see 0885-8969 3159

1558-0067 Cracking the S A T Physics Subject Test 2976
1558-0121 Journal of Diversity Management 1868
1558-0148 Vascular Specialist 6262
1558-0156 Thoracic Surgery News 6261
1558-0164 Clinical Endocrinology News 5885
1558-0172 Advanced Studies in Nursing 5950
1558-0180 see 1558-0172 5950
1558-0199 Advanced Studies in Ophthalmology 6037
1558-0202 see 1558-0199 6037
1558-0210 see 1534-4320 749
1558-0229 see 0163-5840 2550
1558-030X RestoreUS.org 5081
1558-0318 Fantasy Magazine (Print) changed to Fantasy Magazine (Online) 5442
1558-0326 Fretboard Journal 6568
1558-0334 see 1530-3004 5568
1558-0342 Advanced Studies in Pharmacy 6819
1558-0350 see 1558-0342 6819
1558-0407 see 0009-4633 4135
1558-0415 see 1061-0405 7379
1558-0423 see 1060-9393 2908
1558-0431 see 1061-1967 6950
1558-0466 see 1547-9951 5774
1558-0474 see 0889-8545 6001
1558-0482 see 1041-7826 8790
1558-0490 see 1056-4993 6089
1558-0504 see 0094-1298 6240
1558-0512 see 0011-8532 5839
1558-0520 see 0733-8635 5874
1558-0539 see 0733-8627 6059
1558-0563 see 0741-3106 3101
1558-0571 see 1545-598X 3311
1558-0598 see 1077-2618 3311
1558-0628 Technical Quarterly & the M B A A Communicator 611
1558-0644 see 0196-2892 3315
1558-0660 see 1536-1233 2421
1558-0679 see 0885-8950 3159
1558-0687 see 1536-1284 2324
1558-0733 Survey Report on Technician & Skilled Trades Personnel Compensation 1876
1558-0741 see 1071-0949 6254
1558-075X see 0146-0005 6104
1558-0768 see 1085-5629 5881
1558-0776 see 1071-9091 6185
1558-0792 see 1053-5888 7087
1558-0806 see 1549-8328 3102
1558-0814 see 0018-9162 2411
1558-0822 see 1521-334X 3315
1558-0830 see 1531-636X 2465
1558-0857 see 0090-6778 2324
1558-0865 see 1063-6536 3314
1558-0881 see 1061-1983 4159
1558-0903 see 1061-0014 4788
1558-0911 see 0020-8825 1762
1558-092X see 1061-1959 326
1558-0938 see 1540-496X 1563
1558-0946 see 1536-5433 1776
1558-0954 see 1097-1475 1083
1558-0962 see 1061-1940 4777
1558-0970 see 0891-1916 7144
1558-0989 see 1099-9922 7462
1558-0997 see 1097-1467 6911
1558-1004 see 0009-4625 8093
1558-1047 Chilton European Service Manual changed to 1557-2781 8574
1558-1071 S I G I T E Newsletter 3079
1558-108X see 0146-4116 2457
1558-1098 see 1544-8118 2518
1558-1101 see 1530-1591 2416
1558-111X see 1533-4678 3105
1558-1128 see 1078-2192 2570
1558-1179 see 1096-3936 2951
1558-1187 see 1558-2337 4071
1558-1195 see 1049-3301 2405
1558-1209 see 1534-4797 2450
1558-1217 see 0736-6906 8151
1558-1225 see 0270-5257 2591
1558-1349 see 1042-3680 6252
1558-1357 see 0029-6465 5973
1558-1365 see 1042-3699 6255
1558-1373 see 0030-5898 6069
1558-1381 see 1047-9651 6113
1558-139X see 0010-6720 995
1558-1403 see 0192-3978 995
1558-1411 see 1047-9325 7322
1558-142X see 0888-0050 3633
1558-1454 see 1547-6715 1693
1558-1462 see 0094-033X 4466
1558-1470 see 0031-8108 6941
1558-1489 see 0577-5132 1082
1558-1497 see 0197-4580 925
1558-1500 see 0361-1434 3316
1558-1519 see 1058-9813 5798
1558-1527 see 1529-1839 6050
1558-1551 see 0888-6008 5987
1558-156X see 0890-8044 2498
1558-1578 see 0018-9499 3315
1558-1586 see 0161-1194 2512
1558-1608 Industrial Buying Guide. Southern California see 1063-5424 2025
1558-1632 Florida Construction Law Manual 1008
1558-1683 see 1541-4922 2520
1558-1691 see 0364-9059 3312
1558-1713 see 0018-9197 3102
1558-1721 see 0018-9529 3316
1558-173X see 0018-9200 3312
1558-1748 see 1530-437X 4487
1558-1756 see 0272-1716 2486
1558-1764 see 1531-1309 3312
1558-1772 see 0278-6648 3313
1558-1780 see 1530-1877 2471
1558-1829 Today's SurgiCenter changed to 1946-0783 4112

1558-1837 Discover Horses 8290
1558-1845 U S A Today Now Personal Technology 3115
1558-1853 Cooking with Paula Deen 4354
1558-187X see 0018-9375 3103
1558-1896 see 0163-6804 3311
1558-1918 see 0740-7475 2471
1558-1926 see 1064-7406 6243
1558-1934 see 1083-7515 6060
1558-1942 see 0889-8553 5924
1558-1950 see 1052-5157 5925
1558-1969 see 0749-0712 6061
1558-1977 see 0889-8588 6021
1558-2027 Journal of Cardiovascular Medicine (Hagerstown) 5792
1558-2035 see 1558-2027 5792
1558-2159 Journal of School Choice 2957
1558-2167 see 1558-2159 2957
1558-2183 see 1045-9219 2467
1558-2191 see 1041-4347 3315
1558-2205 see 1051-8215 3102
1558-2213 see 0733-8724 7078
1558-2221 see 0018-926X 3314
1558-223X see 1070-9932 2584
1558-2248 see 1536-1276 2324
1558-2256 see 0018-9219 3319
1558-2264 see 0733-8651 5779
1558-2272 see 1938-9736 8808
1558-2299 see 1526-0046 5598
1558-2302 see 1559-6486 6057
1558-2310 see 1522-8401 6090
1558-2337 Accessibility and Computing 4071
1558-2345 see 0894-6507 3316
1558-2361 see 1070-9908 3313
1558-2426 see 1083-4427 2526
1558-2442 see 1094-6977 2526
1558-2477 Innovations (Cambridge) 7486
1558-2485 see 1558-2477 7486
1558-2493 Embedded Systems Design 2470
1558-2507 see 1558-2493 2470
1558-2515 see 1051-8223 3102
1558-2523 see 0018-9286 3314
1558-2531 see 0018-9294 749
1558-254X see 0278-0062 6198
1558-2558 see 1089-7798 2323
1558-2566 see 1063-6692 2497
1558-2574 see 1530-4388 3103
1558-2590 see 1536-1268 2420
1558-2612 see 1525-3511 2324
1558-2639 see 1536-1241 749
1558-268X Journal of Schenkerian Studies 6581
1558-271X Stockholm International Arbitration Review 4941
1558-2760 Fiber Optics Forecast changed to Broadband Business Forecast (Online Edition) 2495
1558-2809 I E E E International Workshop on Imaging Systems and Techniques 2420
1558-2868 see 1046-8188 1413
1558-2876 see 0892-5046 3185
1558-2892 see 1520-9385 8592
1558-2906 see 0747-2536 3660
1558-2957 see 0032-082X 3215
1558-2965 see 0276-8593 2385
1558-2973 Learning Inquiry 2882
1558-2981 see 1558-2973 2882
1558-299X see 0095-4543 5699
1558-304X C R M Expert 1078
1558-3058 International Journal of Architectural Heritage 446
1558-3066 see 1558-3058 446
1558-3090 see 1539-364X 2423
1558-3112 Cracking the S A T II. U.S. and World History Subject Tests changed to 1558-3120 2976
1558-3120 Cracking the S A T U.S. & World History Subject Tests 2976
1558-3147 see 0193-953X 6176
1558-3155 see 1078-5337 6218
1558-3163 see 0889-857X 6226
1558-3171 see 0039-6109 6259
1558-318X see 0094-0143 6276
1558-3384 The International Radioactive Exchange 3508
1558-3392 see 0163-6006 2591
1558-3406 Cracking the S A T Spanish Subject Test 2976
1558-3430 see 1530-0226 5202
1558-3449 see 1072-5520 2507
1558-3465 see 1539-9087 2405
1558-3473 see 1091-3556 2502
1558-3481 see 0899-5885 5956
1558-349X see 1546-1440 6152
1558-352X see 1527-3369 5971
1558-3570 Brand Packaging 6708
1558-3589 see 1558-3570 6708
1558-3597 see 0735-1097 5776
1558-3635 see Society for Neuroscience. Abstract Viewer & Itinerary Planner 6186
1558-366X see 1521-9615 7050
1558-3708 Studies in Nonlinear Dynamics and Econometrics 5539
1558-3716 see 1558-3724 2129
1558-3724 Polymer Reviews 2129
1558-3759 Fleet Administrator Safety Report 8581
1558-3767 see 1540-7985 7015
1558-3775 see 1553-619X 5754
1558-3783 see 1545-5955 3314
1558-3791 see 1549-7747 3102
1558-3805 see 1050-1797 3319
1558-3821 Vocabula Bound Quarterly see 1542-7080 5194
1558-383X see 1524-153X 6254
1558-3848 see 1048-6666 6068
1558-3856 see 0896-1549 6048
1558-3872 see 1938-4300 2590
1558-3880 see 1530-1052 2484
1558-3899 see 1548-3746 2466
1558-3910 see 1553-345X 3402
1558-4046 see 1540-7993 2513
1558-4062 Economic Outlook Update as of (Year) 1480
1558-4070 Building Safety Journal 986

ISSN

1559-0143 Honors in Practice 3064
1559-0151 National Collegiate Honors Council. Journal 2889
1559-016X Octopus 509
1559-0178 see 1559-016X 509
1559-0186 M (Lebanon) 3071
1559-0194 see 1559-0186 3071
1559-0240 Part B Insider 4518
1559-0259 see 1530-7905 5781
1559-0267 see 1080-0549 5756
1559-0275 see 1542-6416 729
1559-0283 see 1085-9195 829
1559-0291 see 0273-2289 723
1559-0305 see 1073-6085 768
1559-0313 Military Review (Arabic Edition) see 0026-4148 6436
1559-0321 Hudson's Childrenswear Review 2256
1559-0348 Long Island Pulse 3980
1559-0356 Prep Audio 6103
1559-0364 see 1559-0356 6103
1559-0372 Travel & Leisure the Best of the World's Greatest Hotels, Resorts + Spas 8766
1559-0380 Ecological Home Ideas 3417
1559-0399 Naturopathy Digest (Print)† 8976
1559-0402 Naturopathy Digest (Online) 313
1559-0410 Journal of Quantitative Analysis in Sports 8182
1559-0429 Leonardo Reviews 4485
1559-047X Journal of Burn Care & Research 5646
1559-0488 see 1559-047X 5646
1559-0518 I A N Inside Products 4487
1559-0534 Retail Construction Magazine 1033
1559-0542 The Eleventh Muse 5421
1559-0585 Current Clinical Neurology 6134
1559-0631 Journal of Exposure Science and Environmental Epidemiology 3447
1559-064X see 1559-0631 3447
1559-0682 see 0024-2594 5029
1559-0704 Subtropics 5383
1559-0720 see 0163-4984 727
1559-0747 see 1094-6950 5647
1559-0755 see 0257-277X 5759
1559-078X Fodor's Great Places to Escape to Nature without Roughing It 8706
1559-0798 Fodor's Maui with Molokai and Lanai 8707
1559-0801 Fodor's Montana & Wyoming 8707
1559-081X Fodor's Belize 8704
1559-0836 Metal Ions in Life Sciences 2127
1559-0879 see 1556-9845 5790
1559-0887 see 0195-7678 5276
1559-0895 see 1543-4273 4291
1559-0909 see 0161-4622 5311
1559-095X Natural Animal Connections see 1933-9291 6811
1559-0968 Asia Policy 7222
1559-0984 Journal of Health Administration Ethics 4104
1559-1018 see 1559-0984 4104
1559-1042 Red Hat Society Lifestyle 8882
1559-1131 A C M Transactions on the Web 2552
1559-114X see 1559-1131 2552
1559-1158 Science Magazine's State of the Planet 3465
1559-1166 see 0895-8696 6153
1559-1174 see 1535-1084 6167
1559-1182 see 0893-7648 739
1559-1190 see 0098-8243 5599
1559-1247 NanoBiotech News†
1559-1255 see 0033-2704 6176
1559-1263 see 0029-8182 2815
1559-128X Applied Optics 7074
1559-1298 The Survey of Academic Libraries 1845
1559-131X see 1357-0560 6027
1559-1360 Bentson Clark Resource 1066
1559-1409 Columbia Series in Science and Religion 7848
1559-1417 S I L Electronic Survey Reports 5171
1559-1425 Advertising Forecasts 20
1559-1468 P W Booklife 7569
1559-1476 see 0145-482X 4082
1559-1492 Community Greening Review 3727
1559-1506 Garden Chic 3731
1559-1549 SAT Subject Test: Spanish 5171
1559-1557 SAT Subject Test: Chemistry 2080
1559-1565 Situations 5239
1559-1573 The Crisis 3528
1559-159X The Mobility Forum 6437
1559-1603 New Crisis changed to 1559-1573 3528
1559-1611 Bright Ideas (Washington, D.C.) 4405
1559-162X Armed Forces Journal 6411
1559-1638 The Freeman 7207
1559-1646 Journal of African American Studies 6302
1559-1662 Mobile Computing and Communications Review 2333
1559-1697 Spenser Review 5376
1559-176X see 1548-5390 5502
1559-1778 Moon Outdoors: Take A Hike Seattle 8739
1559-1786 see 1085-4908 2846
1559-1816 see 0021-9029 7369
1559-1824 Law Library Benchmarks 5024
1559-1883 West's Missouri Jury Verdict Reporter changed to 1932-2828 4707
1559-1905 The Objective Standard 6937
1559-1913 see 1559-1905 6937
1559-193X DramaBiz Magazine 8469
1559-1948 Journal of Applied Functional Analysis 5500
1559-1956 see 1559-1948 5500
1559-1999 Bible Teaching for Kids: Babies Leader Pack 7626
1559-2014 Bible Teaching for Kids: 1s & 2s Leader Pack 7626
1559-2022 Bible Teaching for Kids: Kindergarten Leader Pack 7626
1559-2030 see 1551-7144 5904
1559-2073 The P E R M Quarterly† 8979
1559-2081 Application Trends 2529
1559-212X Tea Time (Birmingham) 611
1559-2146 Bible Teaching for Kids: 1s & 2s Leader Guide 7626
1559-2154 Bible Teaching for Kids: 3s-Pre-K. Leader Guide 7626
1559-2162 Family Bible Study: Bible Teaching for Kindergarten 7758
1559-2189 Texas Journal of Oil, Gas & Energy Law 4881
1559-2200 Form and Style 2255
1559-2243 see 1558-7894 1573
1559-2278 Jewelers Quarterly 4567
1559-2294 Epigenetics 866
1559-2308 see 1559-2294 866
1559-2316 Plant Signalling & Behavior 812
1559-2324 see 1559-2316 812
1559-2332 Simulation in Healthcare 4111
1559-2340 Review of International Business Research 1581
1559-2359 Live Design 8473
1559-2367 Greenwood Guides to Business and Economics 1115
1559-2375 American Subcultures 8087
1559-243X Perspectives in Peer Programs 8061
1559-2448 see 1096-7508 200
1559-2480 Truck Safety Manager Report 8677
1559-2510 Rum & Reggae's Costa Rica 8753
1559-2537 MOMsense 2161
1559-2553 Government Health I T 7519
1559-2618 Arizona-Sonora Desert Museum Studies in Natural History 934
1559-2634 Ad Feminam 5249
1559-2642 Taking Sides: Clashing Views in Lifespan Development 7411
1559-2650 Construction Today 998
1559-2669 Interior Landscape Business†
1559-2715 see 0013-8339 5290
1559-2723 Estuaries and Coasts 671
1559-2731 see 1559-2723 671
1559-2766 Journal on Alternative Schooling 3069
1559-2774 N I S O Newsline 5033
1559-2804 Doctoral Forum 2978
1559-2812 Classics and Contemporary Thought 5274
1559-2863 see 0361-7734 5859
1559-2871 Heart-Healthy Living 6660
1559-288X S L A B 5366
1559-2898 Lifewriting Annual 5323
1559-2928 see 1072-902X 2162
1559-2936 Textual Cultures 5387
1559-2944 University of Chicago Oriental Institute Seminars 422
1559-2960 see 1559-0968 7222
1559-2979 L J N's Franchising Business & Law Alert 4834
1559-3002 Columbia Critical Guides 5276
1559-3053 Journal of Physics Teacher Education Online 3068
1559-3061 Journal of Ethics & Social Philosophy 6928
1559-3096 Plagiary 4582
1559-310X The Fourth River 5297
1559-3126 see 1095-158X 6176
1559-3134 Online Publishing 7569
1559-3142 see 1559-3134 7569
1559-3150 The Power of Travel changed to 1935-3286 8764
1559-3169 see 1096-7494 7447
1559-3185 White Collar Crime Report 2671
1559-3193 Gary Life 5072
1559-3207 see 1559-3185 2671
1559-3215 see 0068-6506 966
1559-3223 see 0068-645X 2718
1559-3231 see 0068-6484 5191
1559-324X see 0068-6417 860
1559-3258 Dose-Response 5606
1559-3320 The Metals Directory 2117
1559-3339 Rurals 153
1559-3355 Journal of Business and Leadership 1764
1559-3371 Moon Outdoors: Take a Hike New York City 8739
1559-338X Vault Guide to the Top Telecom Employers 1713
1559-3398 West's Jury Verdicts. Iowa Reports 4813
1559-3428 Agent@Home 8681
1559-3452 see 1559-3533 3566
1559-3479 Moon Handbooks: Montreal & Quebec City 8738
1559-3509 News & Notes 3326
1559-3533 Spoken Magazine 3566
1559-3541 Fresh Paint 2858
1559-355X Vault Guide to the Top Tech Employers 1713
1559-3568 Synchronized Skating Magazine 8337
1559-3576 Value Engineering Today† 8997
1559-3584 see 0028-1425 3212
1559-3606 Hospitalist Management Advisor 4101
1559-3622 Vault Guide to the Top Media & Entertainment Employers 1713
1559-3630 Vault Guide to the Top Health Care Employers 1713
1559-3649 Vault Guide to the Top Retail Employers 1713
1559-3665 Vault Guide to the Top Consumer Products Employers 1713
1559-3673 Vault - S E O Guide to Investment Bank Diversity Programs 6705
1559-3681 Vault - INROADS Guide to Diversity Internship, Co-op and Entry-Level Programs 6705
1559-369X American Libraries Direct 4988
1559-3703 Anthology 3051
1559-3711 Review Americana 5360
1559-372X Journal of Vietnamese Studies 553
1559-3738 see 1559-372X 553
1559-3754 Anointed Magazine 7621
1559-3770 Casino Enterprise Management 1732
1559-3789 Plunkett's Outsourcing & Offshoring Industry Almanac 1901
1559-3797 Frommer's Cruises & Ports of Call 8711
1559-3800 StyleCity Paris 8758
1559-3819 Going Places: Alaska and the Yukon for Families 8714
1559-3827 Adventure Guide. Paris & Ile-de-France 8681
1559-3835 Frommer's Walt Disney World & Orlando with Kids 8711
1559-3851 The Hudson Valley and Catskill Mountains 8720
1559-386X Journal of Human Thermodynamics 3140
1559-3894 International Journal of Modern Mathematics 5497
1559-3908 see 1524-1971 5609
1559-3916 The Internet Journal of Toxicology 6850
1559-3924 The National Infectious Disease Directory changed to 1939-4047 5823
1559-3959 Journal of Mechanics of Materials and Structures 3206
1559-3967 The Journal of Trading 1636
1559-3975 H D I Support World 2419
1559-3983 see 1559-3975 2419
1559-3991 Heart of New Hampshire Magazine 8718
1559-4009 see 1559-3991 8718
1559-4017 Visible Human Journal of Endoscopy 5949
1559-4041 Constancea 784
1559-4068 A H R Q Publications Catalog 7505
1559-4076 A M I A Annual Symposium. Proceedings 5829
1559-4084 Aromatherapy Journal 307
1559-4092 Chiropractic Wellness and Fitness Magazine 5804
1559-4106 see 1934-8630 7841
1559-4114 Schizophrenia Digest (U.S. Edition) see 1198-4104 6184
1559-4122 Perspectives in Health Information Management changed to 1944-4907 5649
1559-4130 Privacy and Human Rights 4761
1559-4165 Chosen Words 3527
1559-4173 Moore's Index to Playboy Magazine see 0032-1478 6297
1559-419X A C M Workshop on Next-Generation Residential Broadband Challenges. Proceedings 2405
1559-4211 Report on the Implementation of the Charter for the Protection of Children and Young People 2167
1559-422X International Code Interpretations 4694
1559-4238 Travel Weekly. U.S. Travel Industry Survey see 0041-2082 8768
1559-4246 The Best Test Preparation for the C L E P. Introductory Psychology 2969
1559-4262 Survey of Pharmacy Law (CD-ROM) 6882
1559-4289 Mallorca Directions 8732
1559-4297 Metal Maniacs† 8974
1559-4300 Compendium of Selected Publications 5988
1559-4319 Current Practice Guidelines in Primary Care (Year) 5602
1559-4343 Ethical Human Psychology and Psychiatry 6139
1559-4351 Folio Physician Directory with Healthcare Facilities. New York City and Long Island 5615
1559-436X Folio Physician Directory with Healthcare Facilities. New York Upstate 5615
1559-4378 Forensic Nurse†
1559-4386 The N S D U H Report 2697
1559-4394 see N C I Cancer Bulletin 6028
1559-4408 Military Medical/N B C Technology changed to Military Medical/C B R N Technology 5679
1559-4432 see 1559-4440 2990
1559-4440 Journal of Higher Education Ethics 2990
1559-4459 A C M Workshop on Security of Ad Hoc and Sensor Networks. Proceedings 2405
1559-4475 The Caregiver Resource Guide 8030
1559-4491 The Wilson Journal of Ornithology 917
1559-4521 Better Grades (High School Edition) 3052
1559-453X see 1559-4521 3052
1559-4548 Better Grades (Intermediate Edition) 3052
1559-4556 see 1559-4548 3052
1559-4564 Journal of the Cardiometabolic Syndrome 5794
1559-4572 see 1559-4564 5794
1559-4599 ImmunoFacts Vaccines & Immunologic Drugs 6847
1559-4602 International Journal of Applied Research in Veterinary Medicine 8799
1559-4610 The Internet Journal of Medical Technology 8428
1559-4629 The Internet Journal of Parasitic Diseases 5819
1559-4637 Issues in Urology 6269
1559-4645 Mammography Centers Directory 4106
1559-4653 Nursing Spectrum - D.C. - Maryland - Virginia Edition 5975
1559-4661 Unified Agenda of Federal Regulatory and Deregulatory Actions 7473
1559-467X United States Government Policy and Supporting Positions 7474
1559-4688 National Survey on Drug Use & Health. Results 7533
1559-4696 Review of Refractive Surgery changed to 1081-0226 6051
1559-470X see 1559-4602 8799
1559-4718 Bottom Line / Natural Healing 307
1559-4734 The Internet Journal of Medical Simulation 5640
1559-4742 Informational Guide to Passover Medicines & Cosmetics and Star-K Passover Directory 3539
1559-4750 Institute on Computer & Internet Law. Annual 2558
1559-4769 West's Wisconsin Criminal Law 4900
1559-4777 Washington Weddings 5561
1559-4785 Fordham Environmental Law Review 3431
1559-4807 The Shield of Freedom 6446
1559-4815 HarrisMartin Columns. Silica 4684
1559-4823 International Workshop on Autonomous Decentralized System. Proceedings 2523
1559-484X Telehealth Practice Report† 8992
1559-4866 In Touch (Moorestown) 3539
1559-4882 The A F J M H Newsletter changed to 1559-4866 3539
1559-4890 Popular Pets Series 6814
1559-4904 Yavapai Magazine 3993
1559-4912 The Toxicology Forum. Winter Meeting 3502
1559-4920 U R A C Directory of Accredited Organizations and Resource Guide 7544
1559-4939 E N Today 6079
1559-4947 Ventilator-Assisted Living 5728
1559-4955 Well Being Journal 7000
1559-4963 Anamesa 5254
1559-4971 Green Builder Magazine 1010
1559-498X see 1559-4971 1010
1559-5005 Electronic Magazine of Multicultural Education changed to 1934-5267 2870
1559-5013 Red Book Update†
1559-503X Inside G N S S 2383
1559-5048 International Journal of Marketing Research 1821
1559-5064 Grief Digest 7359
1559-5072 A K C Family Dog 6802
1559-5080 Backwards City Review 5259
1559-5102 Inside A S H E 4102
1559-5110 Today's Diet & Nutrition 6669
1559-5145 (Re)-turn 7402
1559-5153 America's Top Doctors 5573
1559-5161 Consumer Products Buyer 1811
1559-5188 Drafting Fundamental Estate Planning Documents† 8951

ISSN

9718 1561-2023 ULRICH'S PERIODICALS

1561-2023 Pravda - Piat' (Weekly) **3939**
1561-2074 South African Food & Beverage Manufacturing Review *changed to* 1726-0280 **3664**
1561-2082 Centre International de Rencontres Mathematiques. Publications **7557**
1561-2104 International Paper History *changed to* Paper History **6736**
1561-2120 European Communities. European Environment Agency. Annual Report **3430**
1561-2147 Fonds de Cohesion. Rapport Annuel *see* 1680-2187 **1083**
1561-2155 Findings **1596**
1561-2341 mitbestimmung **1697**
1561-2384 Revista Mexicana de Seguros Fianzas y Finanzas **1380**
1561-2406 Jiashi Yuan **8587**
1561-2430 Natsiyanal'naya Akademiya Navuk Belarusi. Vestsi. Seryya Fizika-Matematychnykh Navuk **7028**
1561-2716 Novaya Literatura po Sotsial'nym i Gumanitarnym Naukam. Yazykoznanie **5201**
1561-2767 Understanding Unit Trusts *changed to* Profile's Unit Trusts and Collective Investments **1646**
1561-2775 Journal of Clinical and Basic Cardiology†
1561-2783 Travel Africa **8765**
1561-2805 African Development Bank. Selected Statistics on African Countries **1199**
1561-2813 African Development Bank. Compendium of Statistics on Bank Group Operations **1199**
1561-2848 Quasigroups and Related Systems **5527**
1561-2880 *see* 1024-9435 **5565**
1561-2899 *see* 1013-2821 **7513**
1561-2902 *see* 0864-2141 **5704**
1561-2945 *see* 0034-7493 **6256**
1561-2953 *see* 0864-4462 **5900**
1561-2961 *see* 0864-0319 **5980**
1561-297X *see* 0034-7507 **5863**
1561-2988 *see* 0034-7515 **6878**
1561-2996 *see* 0864-0289 **5941**
1561-3003 *see* 0253-1151 **7539**
1561-3011 *see* 0864-0300 **700**
1561-302X *see* 0034-7523 **5704**
1561-3038 *see* 0864-2125 **5704**
1561-3046 *see* 0138-6557 **5704**
1561-3054 *see* 0375-0760 **5825**
1561-3062 *see* 0138-600X **6003**
1561-3070 *see* 0864-2176 **6051**
1561-3097 *see* 0864-3784 **5863**
1561-3100 *see* 0864-215X **6072**
1561-3119 *see* 0034-7531 **6103**
1561-3127 *see* 0864-3466 **7539**
1561-3135 *see* 1025-6539 **5581**
1561-3178 Revista Peruana de Neurologia **6182**
1561-3186 *see* 0864-3210 **5566**
1561-3305 S A Holsteiner **299**
1561-333X Energy Management News **3132**
1561-3410 Lebanese Science Journal **7879**
1561-347X Kommersant **1141**
1561-3488 Pinakoteka **512**
1561-3496 Letapis Druku Belarusi. Letapis Chasopisnykh Artykulau **629**
1561-350X Letapis Druku Belarusi. Letapis Gazetnykh Artykulau **629**
1561-3550 NetMag **2501**
1561-3569 *see* 1561-3550 **2501**
1561-4026 South African Journal of Surveying and Geo-Information†
1561-4034 Euro-Mediterranean Statistics **1227**
1561-4042 Computer Science Journal of Moldova **2588**
1561-4085 Nonlinear Phenomena in Complex Systems **7028**
1561-4190 Hayastani Chimikakan Handes **2063**
1561-4247 The Hong Kong Court of Final Appeal Reports **4687**
1561-4255 Comments on Astrophysics and Space Based Sciences†
1561-4263 Police Practice and Research **2664**
1561-4301 The Dairy Mail **263**
1561-4395 Iranian Hospital. Medical Journal **5641**
1561-4417 Clean Air†
1561-4425 Cuba. Ministerio de Salud Publica. Direccion Nacional de Estadisticas. Anuario Estadistico **5743**
1561-4433 *see* 1561-4425 **5743**
1561-4506 Europaeiske Centralbank. Arsberetning *see* 1561-4573 **1339**
1561-4514 Europaike Kentrike Trapeza. Etesia Ekthese *see* 1561-4573 **1339**
1561-4522 Banco Central Europeo. Informe Anual *see* 1561-4573 **1339**
1561-4530 Banca Centrale Europea. Rapporto Annuale *see* 1561-4573 **1339**
1561-4549 Banco Central Europeu. Relatorio Anual *see* 1561-4573 **1339**
1561-4557 Europeiska Centralbanken. Arsrapport *see* 1561-4573 **1339**
1561-4565 Europaeische Zentralbank. Jahresbericht *see* 1561-4573 **1339**
1561-4573 European Central Bank. Annual Report **1339**
1561-4581 Banque Centrale Europeenne. Rapport Annuel *see* 1561-4573 **1339**
1561-459X Europese Centrale Bank. Jaarverslag *see* 1561-4573 **1339**
1561-4603 Euroopan Keskuspankki. Vuosikertomous *see* 1561-4573 **1339**
1561-4832 Eurostat Statistik Kurz Gefasst. Industrie, Handel und Dienstleistungen **1227**
1561-4840 Eurostat Statistics in Focus. Industry, Trade and Services **1227**
1561-4859 Eurostat Statistiques en Bref. Industrie, Commerce et Services **1228**
1561-4867 Eurostat Statistik Kurz Gefasst. Allgemeine Statistik *see* 1561-4875 **1227**
1561-4875 Eurostat Statistics in Focus. General Statistics **1227**
1561-4883 Eurostat Statistiques en Bref. Statistiques Generales *see* 1561-4875 **1227**
1561-5006 Noticias S I D A **5823**
1561-5235 Jatros Dermatologie **5878**
1561-5243 Jatros Medizin fuer die Frau **8846**
1561-5251 Jatros Vaccines **6851**
1561-526X Urologik **6276**
1561-5324 Intellectual News *changed to* 1749-6977 **4147**
1561-5359 Iskustvennyi Intellekt **2452**
1561-5405 Izvestiya Vysshikh Uchebnykh Zavedenii. Elektronika **3105**
1561-5413 Hong Kong Journal of Nephrology **6268**
1561-5499 Migration in the C I S *changed to* New Challenges for Migration Policy in Central & Eastern Europe **7288**
1561-5502 World Migration Report *changed to* World Migration **7295**
1561-5529 *see* 0029-7054 **1504**
1561-5936 Remedium **5703**
1561-6169 Panorama Mensuel des Entreprises Europeennes *see* 1561-6177 **1578**
1561-6177 Monthly Panorama of European Business **1578**
1561-6185 Monatliches Panorama Europaeischer Unternehmen *see* 1561-6177 **1578**
1561-7343 Asian Brand News **1805**
1561-7408 Vestnik Molodych Uchenych. Tekhnicheskiye Nauki **8445**
1561-7424 *see* 1561-7432 **4953**
1561-7432 Jones & Buckle: The Civil Practice of the Magistrates' Courts in South Africa **4953**
1561-7467 *see* 1561-7475 **4950**
1561-7475 Erasmus: Superior Court Practice **4950**
1561-7564 The International Guide to Universities & 4-year Colleges in the U S A **2957**
1561-7637 Delovaya Moskva **1959**
1561-7645 Journal of Agriculture, Science and Technology **127**
1561-7718 Oesterreichische Polizei-Zeitung **2662**
1561-7807 Savannah Flames **5367**
1561-7823 Lloyd's Freight Transport Buyer Asia **8502**
1561-8048 Italian Labour Law e-Journal **4697**
1561-8307 Tamsui Oxford University Journal of Mathematical Sciences **5540**
1561-8323 Natsiyanal'naya Akademiya Navuk Belarusi. Doklady **7887**
1561-8331 Natsiyanal'naya Akademiya Navuk Belarusi. Vestsi. Seryya Khimichnykh Navuk **2074**
1561-834X Belorusskii Gosudarstvennyi Universitet. Vestnik. Seriya 1. Fizika, Matematika, Informatika **5475**
1561-8358 Natsiyanal'naya Akademiya Navuk Belarusi. Vestsi. Seryya Fizika-Technichnykh Navuk **7028**
1561-8366 A G E F I Luxembourg **1305**
1561-8374 Instituto Medico Sucre. Revista **7866**
1561-8382 Evaluating Eden Series **5293**
1561-8439 South-East Europe **1519**
1561-8455 Eurostat Statistiques en Bref. Agriculture et Peche **179**
1561-8463 Mir Istorii **4245**
1561-8625 Asian Journal of Control **2519**
1561-8633 Natural Hazards and Earth System Sciences **2787**
1561-882X Wulfenia **823**
1561-8927 Labyrinth **6931**
1561-896X Southern African Business Review (Print) *changed to* 1998-8125 **1177**
1561-9060 Naval Digest **6438**
1561-9087 Prikladnaya Gidromekhanika **7062**
1561-9125 Uspekhi Gerontologii **4057**
1561-9133 Inostranets **3936**
1561-9214 Medical Focus International
1561-9273 European Venture Capital Association. Directory **1992**
1561-9508 Water 21 **3492**
1561-9818 Conflict Trends Magazine **8035**
1561-9958 Avian Ecology and Behaviour **655**
1561-9982 *see* 1562-3181 **6467**
1561-9990 Zhongguohua *see* 1562-1138 **29**
1562-0085 Journal of Ethiopian Medical Practice **5648**
1562-0093 Semeinyi Doktor **5712**
1562-0204 Golos Armenii **3792**
1562-0395 L G dos'e **5223**
1562-0433 Vita. Traditsii, Meditsina, Zdorov'e **5728**
1562-0506 International Journal of Curriculum and Instruction *changed to* 1993-7660
1562-0808 Kul'tura Narodov Prichernomor'ya **5223**
1562-0859 La Revue Francaise **5168**
1562-1103 Journal of the Documentation and Humanities Research Centre **4461**
1562-1138 Media **29**
1562-1146 Ukrains'kyi Medychnyi Chasopys **5725**
1562-1154 International Journal of Radiation Medicine *see* Mezhdunarodnyi Zhurnal Radiatsionnoi Meditsiny **6203**
1562-1162 Ukrains'kyi Khimioterapevtychnyi Zhurnal **2083**
1562-1227 Call **2366**
1562-1286 Pakistan Journal of Marine Biology **696**
1562-1324 Eurostat Statistics in Focus. Transport **8524**
1562-1340 Eurostat Statistics in Focus. Agriculture and Fisheries **179**
1562-1359 Eurostat Statistik Kurz Gefasst. Landwirtschaft und Fischerei **179**
1562-1391 Voprosy Filologii **5194**
1562-1413 Mir Biblii **7663**
1562-1421 Stranitsy. Bogoslovie, Kul'tura, Obrazovanie **7818**
1562-143X Jatros Diabetes und Stoffwechsel **5895**
1562-1774 Onkologiya **6031**
1562-1987 Moskovskii Komsomolets **3937**
1562-2312 R T O Educational Notes
1562-2339 R T O Lecture Series
1562-2436 L'Emploi en Europe *see* 1016-5444 **1678**
1562-2479 International Journal of Fuzzy Systems **2522**
1562-2495 Sotsiologicheskii Zhurnal **8140**
1562-2703 International Journal Automation Austria **2461**
1562-2770 Gami'at Qatar. Kulliyyat al-Insaniyyat Wa-al-'ulum al-Igtima'iyyat. Magallat **4453**
1562-2878 Klagenfurter Beitraege zur Sprachwissenschaft **5137**
1562-2916 Iranian Journal of Fisheries Science **3599**
1562-2975 The World Journal of Biological Psychiatry **6189**
1562-2991 Elektromagnitnye Yavleniya **7051**
1562-3009 Fitosanidad **231**
1562-3041 Eurostat Geld, Finanzen und der Euro: Statistiken **1227**
1562-3084 Eurostat Statistiques en Bref. Environnement et Energie *see* 1562-3106 **3479**
1562-3092 Eurostat Statistik Kurz Gefasst. Umwelt und Energie *see* 1562-3106 **3479**
1562-3106 Eurostat Statistics in Focus. Environment and Energy **3479**
1562-3181 Jutastat Mining and Minerals Library **6467**
1562-3238 Kino-Teatr **6506**
1562-3297 Centro de Informacion y Gestion Tecnologica. Avances **7844**
1562-3335 Klassnyi Zhurnal **2198**
1562-3610 F I B Bulletin **1007**
1562-3629 International Journal on Immunorehabilitation **5761**
1562-3750 Personal Finance (Cape Town) **1644**
1562-3815 Panorama Stolitsy **3939**
1562-3823 Revista Boliviana de Fisica **7037**
1562-384X Sincronia **8132**
1562-3920 Eurasian Chemico-Technological Journal **2061**
1562-4021 Zeitschrift fuer Gemeinwirtschaft **1197**
1562-4072 Argos **5256**
1562-4226 Internationale Freimaurer-Forschung **2267**
1562-4293 Mobil'nye Telekommunikatsii **2334**
1562-4374 Namaste *changed to* 0256-0356 **6937**
1562-4382 Article 40 **4907**
1562-4528 Holiday Asia
1562-4692 F H M (South Africa) **6290**
1562-4722 Building Review **986**
1562-4730 Biblios **4994**
1562-5028 Kacike **345**
1562-5087 Cosmopolitan (Moscow) **8857**
1562-5095 Harper's Bazaar **8867**
1562-5117 Men's Health **6284**
1562-5125 Domashnii Ochag **4356**
1562-5141 Marie Claire **8873**
1562-5206 Tuna Fisheries Assessment Report **3610**
1562-5257 V A S S A Journal **460**
1562-5265 Timbila (Elim Hospital) **5436**
1562-5273 Annals of the Eastern Cape Museums **7835**
1562-5311 *see* 1562-3041 **1227**
1562-5338 Cool Toys **2183**
1562-5427 *see* 1562-5435 **4597**
1562-5435 Labor Magazine **4597**
1562-5443 *see* 1562-5435 **4597**
1562-5451 *see* 1562-5435 **4597**
1562-546X *see* 1562-5435 **4597**
1562-5702 K Z N Industrial & Business News **1430**
1562-5915 Lingnan Journal of Chinese Studies†
1562-5958 Zimbabwe Human Rights Bulletin **7219**
1562-6121 Journal of Civil Engineering *changed to* 1729-5769 **3274**
1562-6369 Wirtschafts Ausblick *see* 0304-3274 **1159**
1562-6369 Wirtschafts Ausblick *see* 0474-5574 **1502**
1562-6865 *see* 1063-7710 **7086**
1562-6873 *see* 1063-7737 **571**
1562-6881 *see* 1063-7729 **571**
1562-689X *see* 1063-7745 **2110**
1562-6903 *see* 1028-3358 **7010**
1562-6911 *see* 0030-400X **7083**
1562-692X *see* 1063-7788 **7071**
1562-6938 *see* 1063-780X **7035**
1562-6997 African Journal on Conflict Resolution **7220**
1562-7012 Wineland **259**
1562-7020 African Zoology **931**
1562-7128 Sistemy Bezopasnosti **2516**
1562-7144 Tekhnologii i Sredstva Svyazi **2340**
1562-7241 Visnyk Farmatsii **6885**
1562-725X Klinichna Farmatsiya **6857**
1562-7314 Carbon Dioxide Emissions from Fuel Combustion **3484**
1562-7462 A i F. Na Dache **3934**
1562-7470 A i F. Lyubov' **6285**
1562-7489 A i F. Dochki-Materi **8850**
1562-7497 A i F. Ya Molodoi *changed to* 1727-2076 **2175**
1562-7535 A i F. Subota - Voskresenie *changed to* 1727-2084 **3934**
1562-756X Doberman **6806**
1562-7586 Money Marketing **1368**
1562-7969 Earthquake Engineering and Engineering Seismology **2732**
1562-8019 On Station† **8978**
1562-8264 Southern African Journal of Critical Care *see* 1608-9677 **5896**
1562-8264 Southern African Journal of Critical Care *see* 0038-2329 **6005**
1562-8264 Southern African Journal of Critical Care *see* 1608-9685 **6186**
1562-8264 Southern African Journal of Critical Care *see* 1607-0658 **6669**
1562-8264 Southern African Journal of Critical Care *see* 0256-9574 **5708**
1562-8264 Southern African Journal of Critical Care *see* 1995-1892 **5781**
1562-8272 Die Rampe **5357**
1562-8353 Nonlinear Dynamics and Systems Theory **5520**
1562-8434 Interpol†
1562-8515 Arion **5206**
1562-8582 L'Egalite des Chances pour les Femmes et les Hommes dans l'Union Europeenne *see* 1680-2381 **1680**
1562-8639 European Industrial Relations Observatory. Annual Review **1681**
1562-8884 Commerce Exterieur et Intra-Union Europeenne. Annuaire Statistique *see* 1606-3481 **1228**
1562-9023 Journal of Chinese Clinical Medicine **5646**
1562-9120 The Fishing Journal **8313**
1562-9147 Skate Extension **1651**
1562-9163 Capital Markets Eurasia **1615**
1562-9171 *see* 1562-9163 **1615**
1562-918X East Asian Science, Technology, and Medicine **548**
1562-9279 Buchforschung **7556**
1562-9392 National Library of South Africa. Quarterly Bulletin **5034**
1562-9414 Joannea Botanik **796**
1562-9430 Joannea Zoologie **949**
1562-9449 Joannea Geologie und Palaeontologie **2749**

1562-9619 Mining Weekly 6473
1562-9627 Khanya 2880
1563-0102 Arheologiya, Etnografiya i Antropologiya Evrazii 380
1563-0110 Archaeology, Ethnology & Anthropology of Eurasia 378
1563-0129 The Buyer's Guide changed to 1995-5111 6212
1563-0447 O E C D Agricultural Outlook 143
1563-0455 O C D E Perspectives Agricoles see 1563-0447 143
1563-0579 see 1563-0587 4868
1563-0587 Foodstuffs, Cosmetics and Disinfectants Act, Regulations and Standards 4868
1563-0846 Gesellschaft der Geologie- und Bergbaustudenten in Oesterreich. Mitteilungen 2744
1563-0889 O E C D. Wirtschaftsberichte see 0376-6438 1502
1563-0889 O E C D. Wirtschaftsberichte see 0304-3363 1502
1563-0927 Developments in Steelmaking Capacity of Non-O E C D Countries changed to Developments in Steelmaking Capacity of Non-O E C D Economies 6310
1563-0935 Bank Profitability (Bilingual Edition)
1563-1036 Social Justice 355
1563-129X Eat In 4356
1563-1400 Beitraege zur Entomofaunistik 840
1563-194X V K S S Connect 2343
1563-1958 Connect! Mir Svyazi 2317
1563-227X Kontinent 3936
1563-258X see 0043-5341 5730
1563-2628 PapierRestaurierung changed to 1868-0860 499
1563-2717 C I E S M Workshop Series changed to 1726-5886 2801
1563-275X Itogi Nauki i Tekhniki. Seriya Elektronika i ee Primenenie†
1563-2857 Crossing Borders 8096
1563-2865 The Youth Times 2223
1563-2873 Journal fuer Ernaehrungsmedizin 6661
1563-311X Current Opinion in Clinical Experimental Research 5905
1563-3128 Heilsuhringurinn 309
1563-3144 Les Dossiers du C A D see 1816-8124 1602
1563-3152 D A C Journal changed to 1816-8124 1602
1563-3233 Glos Znad Niemna 3800
1563-3276 Stability and Control: Theory and Applications 5538
1563-3403 Journal of Psychology in Chinese Societies 7379
1563-3632 I C S S P E Bulletin (Print) changed to 1728-5666 6997
1563-3675 Aktuelle Steuer News 1909
1563-3772 Journal of Geospatial Engineering 3275
1563-3799 Austrian Politicians, Parties and Mayors Index 7198
1563-3802 Austrian Journalists and P R Index 4586
1563-3810 Chastnaya Zhizn' 5068
1563-3829 Ochnaya Stavka 4751
1563-3845 Tainaya Vlast' 6744
1563-3861 Pole Chudes 4982
1563-390X Zhivotnye Strasti 6817
1563-3934 African Journal of Social Work 8024
1563-4159 L'Environnement pour les Europeens see 1563-4183 3421
1563-4167 Medio Ambiente para los Europeos see 1563-4183 3421
1563-4175 Umwelt fur Europaer see 1563-4183 3421
1563-4183 Environment for Europeans 3421
1563-4191 L'Ambiente per gli Europei see 1563-4183 3421
1563-423X O C D E. Estudios Economicos see 0304-3363 1502
1563-423X O C D E. Estudios Economicos see 0376-6438 1502
1563-4302 O E C D Development Centre Studies
1563-4310 Etudes du Centre de Developpement see 1563-4302
1563-4329 O E C D Development Centre Seminars
1563-4337 Seminaires du Centre de Developpement see 1563-4329
1563-440X Migration and Diffusion 7985
1563-4477 Razgadai! 8196
1563-4604 Der Oeffentliche Sektor 1372
1563-4612 eCommerce World†
1563-4914 Reviews of National Policies for Education 3030
1563-4922 Examens des Politiques Nationales d'Education see 1563-4914 3030
1563-5031 see 0882-7516 3294
1563-504X see 0003-6811 5471
1563-5074 see 1065-5131 3385
1563-5104 see 0308-1079 2522
1563-5112 see 0015-0193 7012
1563-5120 see 1023-6198 5502
1563-5139 see 0308-1087 5509
1563-5147 see 1024-123X 3209
1563-5163 see 0094-9655 2443
1563-5171 see 1065-514X 2474
1563-5201 see 0098-6445 3238
1563-521X see 0010-2202 2134
1563-5228 see 0731-5171 3308
1563-5236 see 1042-0940 6725
1563-5244 see 0883-0185 5761
1563-5260 see 0167-7063 6153
1563-5279 see 0020-7454 6147
1563-5325 see 1042-6507 2117
1563-5333 see 1040-6638 2129
1563-5341 see 1023-666X 3247
1563-535X see 0091-4037 3247
1563-5430 see 1560-6155 3798
1563-5457 see Kleine Zeitung 3797
1563-5473 Salzburger Nachrichten Online 3798
1563-5503 see 1028-9143 1151
1563-552X see 1023-7607 3947
1563-5570 Daily Mail and Guardian see Mail & Guardian 3949
1563-5600 see 1028-1215 1080
1563-5686 The Independent (Boroko, Online) 3927
1563-5694 Papua New Guinea Post-Courier (Online) 3927
1563-5775 see 1015-0706 1071
1563-5783 see 1027-6874 6284
1563-5848 Le Matinal 3802
1563-5929 see Oman Daily Observer 3926
1563-5953 SoirInfo 3899
1563-5961 L'Inter 3899
1563-6003 Liechtenstein News 3905
1563-6011 see 1818-9202 3905
1563-602X see Liechtensteiner Volksblatt 3905
1563-6038 see Telecran 2396
1563-6070 see Tageblatt 3906
1563-616X see 1017-3862 7811
1563-6178 L'Osservatore Romano (English Edition. Weekly) 7811
1563-6186 see 1563-6178 7811
1563-6194 L'Osservatore Romano (Portuguese Edition. Weekly) 7811
1563-6208 see 1563-6194 7811
1563-6216 L'Osservatore Romano (Spanish Edition. Weekly) 7811
1563-6224 see 1563-6216 7811
1563-6232 L'Osservatore Romano (Italian Edition. Weekly) 7811
1563-6240 see 1563-6232 7811
1563-6259 see 0391-688X 7811
1563-6267 L'Osservatore Romano (Polish Edition. Monthly) 7811
1563-6275 see The Moscow Times 3937
1563-6283 see 1563-6291 3941
1563-6291 The St. Petersburg Times 3941
1563-6321 see 1563-6593 3940
1563-6348 see 1560-1005 3938
1563-6372 see 0233-4194 3936
1563-6380 see 1561-347X 1141
1563-6399 Pravda (Online) 3939
1563-6429 see Kyiv Post 3964
1563-647X see 1605-5330 8562
1563-6518 see 1810-6617 2410
1563-6593 The Russia Journal 3940
1563-6712 Advances in Biopesticide Research
1563-6968 see Tiroler Tageszeitung 3798
1563-700X Tabasco Hoy 3911
1563-7018 Mexico Hoy 3909
1563-7026 Campeche Colonial 23
1563-7123 Gorkhapatra 3913
1563-7131 Janmabhoomi†
1563-7166 see Saptahik 3914
1563-7182 Pingguo Ribao Wangluo see Pingguo Ribao 3875
1563-7263 see 1563-8642 3911
1563-7271 Express en linea 3908
1563-7328 El Heraldo de Leon 3909
1563-7336 El Siglo de Durango 3911
1563-7344 El Siglo de Torreon 3911
1563-7352 see 0185-0601 1556
1563-7387 see 1563-7506 3908
1563-7395 Esto 3908
1563-7417 El Cotidiano en Linea see 0186-1840 3908
1563-7433 see 0185-2728 1885
1563-7441 see El Financiero International Edition 1346
1563-745X see El Heraldo de Mexico 3909
1563-7468 Federacion. Diario Oficial (Online Edition) 7436
1563-7476 La Jornada (Online Edition) 3909
1563-7484 see Libertas 2992
1563-7492 Machetearte 5226
1563-7506 La Cronica de Hoy 3908
1563-7522 see 0186-1395 7154
1563-7530 Milenio.com 3909
1563-7549 Milenio Semanal 3909
1563-7565 see Mundo Ejecutivo 1151
1563-7573 see Golf Tournament 8233
1563-7581 Mexico Alternativo 3909
1563-7611 Cine Alternativo 6492
1563-762X see 0185-1535 7989
1563-7638 see 0188-2856 3910
1563-7638 see 0188-2856 3910
1563-7638 see 1563-7654 3909
1563-7654 The News 3909
1563-7662 La Prensa 3910
1563-7670 see 0185-1632 3910
1563-7689 reforma.com see 1563-7697 3910
1563-7697 Reforma 3910
1563-7727 see Epoca (Mexico D.F.) 3908
1563-7735 El Informador (Online) see El Informador (Print) 3909
1563-7743 mural.com see 1563-7751 3909
1563-7751 Mural 3909
1563-776X Publi.com see 1563-7778 3910
1563-7778 Publico 3910
1563-7786 see 1563-7794 3909
1563-7794 El Imparcial (Hermosillo) 3909
1563-7808 see 1018-7529
1563-7816 see La Hora 3874
1563-7824 see 0185-0784 5239
1563-7859 ElNorte.com see 1563-7867 3910
1563-7867 El Norte 3910
1563-7875 El Porvenir 3910
1563-7883 see Diario de Yucatan 3908
1563-7891 see 1563-7905 3911
1563-7905 La Revista Peninsular 3911
1563-7913 La Voz de Michoacan 3912
1563-7921 palabra.com see 1563-793X 3910
1563-793X Palabra (Saltillo) 3910
1563-7948 Vanguardia 3911
1563-7956 see 1563-7964 3908
1563-7964 Cronica de Baja California 3908
1563-7972 see 1563-7980 3911
1563-7980 Siete Dias 3911
1563-7999 El Debate 3908
1563-8049 see Amandala 7419
1563-8057 see Belize Times 7109
1563-8065 see Reporter 3802
1563-8081 El Deber Digital 3802
1563-809X El Mundo 3802
1563-812X see Pelita Brunei 7460
1563-8170 Zhonshi Dianzi Bao see Zhonggo Shibao 3960
1563-8200 Los Tiempos 3803
1563-8219 Bolivian Times 3802
1563-8227 see 0254-7457 3802
1563-8243 La Razon 3803
1563-8251 see Nhan Dan 3994
1563-826X El Economista de Cuba 1102
1563-8278 see 0017-3223 3831
1563-8286 see 0864-4616 7139
1563-8294 see 0864-4624 7139
1563-8308 see 0864-4640 7139
1563-8316 see 0864-4632 7139
1563-8324 see 1028-088X 7139
1563-8332 see 0864-1609 7189
1563-8340 Cuba Rebelde Digital see 0864-1412 2157
1563-8367 Trabajadores Digital see 0864-0432 1711
1563-8375 see The Chronicle 3995
1563-8391 see Diario de Centro America 7433
1563-8405 Guatemala Flash 3874
1563-8413 see Prensa Libre 3874
1563-8480 see 1563-8499 3905
1563-8499 Al-Anwar 3905
1563-8545 see 1563-8553 3905
1563-8553 As-Safir 3905
1563-8588 see 1563-8596 3903
1563-8596 Al Siyasat 3903
1563-8642 El Sur de Campeche 3911
1563-8723 Ruznamah-i Jang 3926
1563-8812 Thoi Bao Kinh Te Vietnam Online 1182
1563-8820 Tu Van Tieu Dung Online 3994
1563-8839 The Guide Online 8716
1563-8847 see 1420-2573 1192
1563-8855 see 0259-1642 3914
1563-8898 La Prensa on the Web 3821
1563-8901 see Tiempo 3875
1563-891X see Honduras This Week 3875
1563-8936 Diario Digital 3908
1563-8944 El Diario Digit@al. Chihuahua 3908
1563-8952 see El Heraldo de Chihuahua 3909
1563-8960 Tiempo (Chihuahua) 3911
1563-8979 see Imagen 3909
1563-8987 La Region 3910
1563-9002 see 1020-6558 620
1563-907X W T O Focus (Print) changed to 1563-9088 1586
1563-9088 W T O Focus (Online) 1586
1563-9193 see 1020-3907 4930
1563-9282 The Independent 3799
1563-9320 Borneo Bulletin 3804
1563-9339 see 0014-7591 1485
1563-9436 Business Recorder 1444
1563-9479 The News International (Karachi, 199?) 3926
1563-9533 The Taiwan Economic News 1181
1563-9614 Zimbabwe Mirror 3996
1563-9622 Douze 8170
1563-9630 L'Union Edition Web see 1013-6614 3790
1563-969X Saigon Times Daily 3994
1563-9770 Kantipur Online 3913
1563-9827 Sunday Post (Online Edition) see 1563-9770 3913
1563-986X see 1017-6128 3947
1563-9967 see 1025-854X 3966
1564-0027 International Society for Environmental Ethics. Newsletter 6926
1564-0035 Iran Weekly Press Digest (Online) 3891
1564-0051 see 1564-0361 7366
1564-0094 see 0926-4981 2350
1564-0175 see 1028-5474 3837
1564-0183 see 1022-4408 3907
1564-023X see 1024-1418 3902
1564-0256 Daily Nation on the Web see 1025-1227 3902
1564-0264 Kuwait Times 3903
1564-0272 Coastweek (Online edition) 3902
1564-0302 see 0301-3529 3905
1564-0345 see 1025-3556 3906
1564-0353 see 1564-068X 3963
1564-0361 International Psychoanalysis 7366
1564-0442 see 1027-6289 3996
1564-0469 see 0255-6227 3996
1564-0477 Zimbabwe Independent Online see 1564-0698 3996
1564-0493 Ivoir'soir 3899
1564-0507 Le Jour 3899
1564-0523 Les Echos 3907
1564-0531 see 1560-6023 3913
1564-0604 see 0042-9686 5731
1564-0620 Desastres. Preparativos y Mitigacion en las Americas 7514
1564-0639 see 1564-0620 7514
1564-0655 Progress in Human Reproduction Research 6002
1564-068X The Monitor 3963
1564-0698 Zimbabwe Independent 3996
1564-0701 Disasters. Preparedness and Mitigation in the Americas 7514
1564-071X see 1564-0701 7514
1564-0728 Vaccine and Immunization News 5828
1564-0779 Polio News 5765
1564-0787 see 1564-0795 5801
1564-0795 World Diabetes 5801
1564-0809 see 1020-3131 7545
1564-0825 see 1564-0833 5824
1564-0833 Pan American Health Organization. Expanded Program on Immunization. Measles Surveillance in the Americas. Bulletin 5824
1564-0841 see 1564-085X 5824
1564-085X Pan American Health Organization. Expanded Program on Immunization. Poliomyelitis Surveillance in the Americas. Bulletin 5824
1564-0884 see 0252-7987 3480
1564-0930 see 1020-5551 7535
1564-0949 see World Health Organization. Fact Sheet 7545
1564-0965 see World Health Organization. Press Release 7545
1564-1104 see 1014-952X 6004
1564-1120 W H O Pharmaceuticals Newsletter 6885
1564-1201 Revue de l'Ocean Indien. Madagascar 3789
1564-121X see 1015-0919 6838
1564-1546 Compte a Rebours 2838
1564-1554 see 1564-1562 2843
1564-1562 E F A - 2000 2843
1564-1805 Rapport Mondial sur la Science see 1020-6892 7930
1564-1813 Intergovernmental Oceanographic Commission. Reports of Governing and Major Subsidiary Bodies 1126
1564-2054 Iran Weekly Press Digest (Print) 3891
1564-2119 see 0309-068X 7221
1564-2356 I I E P Newsletter 2865
1564-2364 see 1564-2356 2865
1564-2585 Insect and Pest Control Newsletter 3246
1564-264X see 1564-1562 2843

ISSN

1567-0333 Netherlands. Centraal Bureau voor de Statistiek. Verkiezingen (Year)
1567-0341 Netherlands. Centraal Bureau voor de Statistiek. Gemeenten in Nederland. Historisch Overzicht†
1567-0392 N B T Magazine **3657**
1567-0422 *see* 1386-0240 **2056**
1567-0988 Aandeelhoudersnieuws *changed to* 1874-0472 **1928**
1567-1143 Tiengemeten Nieuws *changed to* 1871-9252 **8993**
1567-133X Gene Expression Patterns **867**
1567-1348 Infection, Genetics and Evolution **5634**
1567-1356 F E M S Yeast Research **886**
1567-1364 Federation of European Microbiological Societies Yeast Research Online *see* 1567-1356 **886**
1567-1739 Current Applied Physics **7009**
1567-178X Missieinteractie *changed to* 1874-5873 **7663**
1567-181X Automobiel Klassiek en Exclusief *changed to* 1572-2392 **364**
1567-1828 Laboratorium Magazine **5908**
1567-1844 Landwerk **241**
1567-1852 Eisma's Schildersblad **6717**
1567-1860 Interface
1567-1917 Business in Office **1850**
1567-200X Semeia Studies **7680**
1567-2018 Current Drug Delivery **6830**
1567-2026 Current Neurovascular Research **6134**
1567-2034 Medicinal Chemistry Reviews Online†
1567-2042 Frontiers in Medicinal Chemistry **5616**
1567-2050 Current Alzheimer Research **6134**
1567-2069 Strength, Fracture and Complexity **7063**
1567-2190 Foundations and Trends in Communications and Information Theory **2350**
1567-2298 Nederlandse Jurisprudentie Feitenrechtspraak **4740**
1567-2328 *see* 1567-2190 **2350**
1567-2336 The Medieval Chronicle **5332**
1567-2344 *see* 0889-3675 **7378**
1567-2352 Medicine and Science in Tennis **6231**
1567-2379 Journal of Molecular Histology **834**
1567-2387 *see* 1567-2379 **834**
1567-2417 Updatebulletin Flexibiliteit in Arbeidsrelaties **1713**
1567-245X M K B-Nederland - N I P O Ondernemerspanel *changed to* 1872-9258 **1720**
1567-2468 Annals of Bioethics **6904**
1567-2557 A S A Bulletin **4915**
1567-2573 Inspectie van het Onderwijs. Onderwijsverslag **2867**
1567-2581 Strafblad **4898**
1567-259X Tekst en Toelichting Wet Werk en Bijstand **1710**
1567-2654 Pensioen Monografieen **1702**
1567-2697 Drug Design Reviews Online†
1567-2700 Vascular Disease Prevention **5801**
1567-2719 Handbook of Magnetic Materials **6314**
1567-2743 Nederlands Tijdschrift voor Diabetologie **5898**
1567-2778 Checklist Ondernemen **1718**
1567-2786 H R Management **1684**
1567-2794 Social Sciences in Asia **560**
1567-2808 Texts and Studies on the Quran **7716**
1567-2883 Management Trends **1869**
1567-2891 BNSPnieuws
1567-2905 CosmoGirl! **3914**
1567-293X Koninklijke Bibliotheek. Hoofdafdeling Research en Development. Jaaroverzicht **5023**
1567-3073 Research World **1840**
1567-3189 Dagbladen *changed to* 1874-8007 **4580**
1567-3200 Remote Sensing and Digital Image Processing **2489**
1567-3499 Tijdschrift Geestelijke Verzorging **6188**
1567-3502 Leven **6663**
1567-3618 De Basisschool *changed to* 1574-1435 **2899**
1567-3642 De Beste I C T-Bedrijven om Voor te Werken *changed to* 1876-3545 **2494**
1567-3804 Lopende Zaken **8321**
1567-3812 Oog & Oor *changed to* 1571-0475 **4978**
1567-3863 Pensioen Actief **1702**
1567-4045 Vlees Plus *changed to* 1871-739X **303**
1567-4215 Journal of Heart Failure. Supplement *see* 1388-9842 **5786**
1567-4223 Electronic Commerce Research and Applications **2543**
1567-424X Clinical Neurophysiology. Supplement **6132**
1567-4258 European Journal of Cardio-Thoracic Surgery. Supplements *see* 1010-7940 **5786**
1567-4274 Netherlands. Centraal Bureau voor de Statistiek. Verzorgingshuizen
1567-4649 Amsterdamse Cahiers voor Exegese van de Bijbel en zijn Tradities **7621**
1567-4703 Effectengids **1621**
1567-4738 Qvijver *changed to* 1876-2085 **3030**
1567-4762 E T F R N Series **3687**
1567-4843 Arbo Jaarboek **6673**
1567-4916 Adfo Direct Jaarboek *changed to* 1570-176X **1807**
1567-4924 Gelijke Behandeling **1683**
1567-5017 Dangerous Substances CD **7433**
1567-5025 Europese Gemeenschap Recht CD **4926**
1567-5114 Baby
1567-5157 Sensory Neuron†
1567-5238 Polsslag **6441**
1567-5343 Koppeling *changed to* 1567-6110 **8995**
1567-536X International Criminal Law Review **4891**
1567-5394 Bioelectrochemistry **726**
1567-553X Finance & Control **1342**
1567-5599 O N - W I J S† **8978**
1567-567X Journal of Pharmacokinetics and Pharmacodynamics **6855**
1567-5688 Atherosclerosis. Supplement **5778**
1567-5726 De Wereld Achter de Cijfers *changed to* 1872-1184 **1288**
1567-5734 Publieke Zaken *changed to* 1872-1184 **1288**
1567-5769 International Immunopharmacology **6849**
1567-5793 Homepages *changed to* 1572-4018 **7574**
1567-5815 V M B O - Reeks **2924**
1567-5882 Geomatics World **4013**
1567-5947 OndernemersZaken Signaal *changed to* 1574-7743 **1782**
1567-5963 I T Beheer **2421**
1567-5998 Business Process Magazine **2459**
1567-6056 Linux Magazine **2594**
1567-6110 Ugo Krant† **8995**
1567-6471 NEN Nieuwsbrief. K A M-Management *changed to* 1871-787X **1771**
1567-6587 Maatwerk **8054**
1567-6617 L1 Educational Studies in Language and Literature **2881**
1567-6633 Neerlandistiek **5154**
1567-6668 Vereniging van Vrouwen met Hogere Opleiding. Nieuwsbrief **2308**
1567-6897 Fiscaal Rendement **1925**
1567-6951 African Sources for African History **4172**
1567-7052 I H E Delft Lecture Note Series **3362**
1567-7095 Journal of Cognition and Culture **7370**
1567-7109 Pedagogiek **2896**
1567-7117 Tijdschrift voor Humanistiek **5242**
1567-7125 Non-State Actors and International Law *changed to* 1871-9740 **4930**
1567-7133 European Journal of Transport and Infrastructure Research **8422**
1567-7141 *see* 1567-7133 **8422**
1567-715X KronoScope (Print)† **8970**
1567-7184 Research Profiles in Aging **4054**
1567-7192 Handbook of Analytical Separations **2100**
1567-7230 Water, Air & Soil Pollution: Focus **3492**
1567-7249 Mitochondrion **893**
1567-7257 *see* 1567-1348 **5634**
1567-7346 Issues in the Practice of Psychology **7367**
1567-7370 C D A Krant *changed to* 1871-6733 **7114**
1567-7419 Environmental Fluid Mechanics (Dordrecht, 2001) **2707**
1567-7427 Management Select *changed to* 1571-862X **1775**
1567-7443 NeuroImmune Biology **925**
1567-7559 The International Sports Law Journal **4696**
1567-7575 Plenum Series in Rehabilitation and Health **6114**
1567-7605 Nieuwsbrief StAB *changed to* 1573-806X **4427**
1567-7613 Cricket Magazine *changed to* 0927-7021 **8251**
1567-763X Rendemens *changed to* 1874-2742 **1856**
1567-7753 World Gastroenterology News **5932**
1567-7761 Aansprakelijkheid, Verzekering & Schade **4826**
1567-777X MuziekGroep Nederland Info *changed to* 1574-7662 **6599**
1567-7818 Natural Computing **2432**
1567-7842 De Academische Boekengids **7550**
1567-7923 De Architect. Interieur *see* 0044-8621 **428**
1567-7974 Plenum Series in Computer Science *changed to* Series in Computer Science **2437**
1567-7982 Advances in Archaeological and Museum Science **371**
1567-7990 Non-destructive Evaluation Series **3355**
1567-8016 Prevention in Practice Library **5699**
1567-8032 Handbook of Petroleum Exploration and Production **6772**
1567-8040 Fundamental Issues in Archaeology **394**
1567-813X Indigenous Languages of Latin America **5127**
1567-8164 Jurisprudentie Geneesmiddelenrecht **4707**
1567-8202 Natural Language Processing **5154**
1567-8237 Nijgh Hout in de Bouw **3714**
1567-830X Fundamental Materials Research **3345**
1567-8318 Max Plank Series on Asian Intellectual Property Law **6754**
1567-8326 The Journal of Logic and Algebraic Programming **2508**
1567-8385 Bibliotheca Humanistica & Reformatorica **7627**
1567-8393 Medieval and Early Modern Science **7882**
1567-8466 BioComplexity†
1567-8474 Nin†
1567-8571 I & O†
1567-858X Kunstblad *changed to* 0929-1032 **368**
1567-8598 Politiek! *changed to* 1872-0862 **7151**
1567-861X Technologie in de Gezondheidszorg *changed to* 1873-8877 **1744**
1567-8628 T M (Amsterdam) **8480**
1567-8644 J G Z **6094**
1567-8717 The Hoogsteder Journal **493**
1567-8725 Veiligheid Voorop **8636**
1567-8822 Cardiovascular Engineering **5781**
1567-892X N E R G **2334**
1567-8962 Bieb† **8936**
1567-8989 Interne Rapportenreeks Communicatie Research en Semiotiek **8110**
1567-9063 Studio (Hilversum) *changed to* 1872-4655 **2384**
1567-908X Draf en Rensport **8290**
1567-9195 Ontmoetingen *changed to* 1574-9193 **7644**
1567-9241 Wie Werkt Waar bij Adverteerders (Diskette) *see* 1387-2907 **1848**
1567-9268 Wie Werkt Waar in de Media (Diskette) *see* 1387-2915 **1848**
1567-9381 Building Business **1729**
1567-9764 International Environmental Agreements: Politics, Law and Economics **3441**
1567-9799 Roundabout **3919**
1567-9837 Hunch **445**
1567-9896 Aries **6643**
1568-0037 Doe een Wens Krant *changed to* 1874-6845 **3035**
1568-0045 De DonderbergGroep. Nieuwsbrief *changed to* 1871-6245 **453**
1568-0053 Current Drug Targets. Infectious Disorders *changed to* 1871-5265 **5634**
1568-0061 Current Drug Targets. Cardiovascular & Hematological Disorders *changed to* 1871-529X **5780**
1568-007X Current Drug Targets. C N S & Neurological Disorders *changed to* 1871-5273 **6129**
1568-0088 Current Drug Targets. Immune, Endocrine & Metabolic Disorders *changed to* 1871-5303 **5757**
1568-0096 Current Cancer Drug Targets **6017**
1568-010X Current Drug Targets. Inflammation & Allergy *changed to* 1871-5281 **5761**
1568-0118 Current Medicinal Chemistry. Anti-Cancer Agents *changed to* 1871-5206 **6008**
1568-0126 Current Medicinal Chemistry. Anti-Infective Agents *changed to* 1871-5214 **6821**
1568-0134 Current Medicinal Chemistry. Immunology, Endocrine and Metabolic Agents *changed to* 1871-5222 **5894**
1568-0142 Current Medicinal Chemistry. Anti-Inflammatory & Anti-Allergy Agents *changed to* 1871-5230 **6821**
1568-0150 Current Medicinal Chemistry. Central Nervous System Agents *changed to* 1871-5249 **6130**
1568-0169 Current Medicinal Chemistry. Cardiovascular & Hematological Agents *changed to* 1871-5257 **5780**
1568-0185 Rijksarchief in Friesland. Nieuwsbrief *changed to* 1871-966X **5025**
1568-0193 De Oanbring *changed to* 1871-966X **5025**
1568-0258 *see* 1570-5854 **7259**
1568-0266 Current Topics in Medicinal Chemistry **5603**
1568-0495 Thema *changed to* 1574-339X **7354**
1568-0584 European Journal of East Asian Studies **549**
1568-0703 Markassiet **6754**
1568-0851 Non-Hodgkin Contactblad *changed to* 1871-7314 **5896**
1568-0908 Facto Magazine **1745**
1568-0924 Teletubbies Tijdschrift **2169**
1568-0975 Sign+ *changed to* 1871-6741 **7328**
1568-0991 Apotheekmanagement.online **6821**
1568-1009 Stadler Genetics Symposium. Series **878**
1568-1076 Studiereeks Nederlands-Antilliaans en Arubaans Recht **4941**
1568-1114 Praktijkonderzoek voor de Akkerbouw en de Vollegrondsgroenteteelt. Rassenbulletin†
1568-1130 F A Rendement **1288**
1568-1181 Intersections **4148**
1568-1203 African Social Studies Series **8086**
1568-1238 N A T O Science Series. Series IV: Earth and Environmental Sciences **2713**
1568-1254 Cell and Molecular Responses to Stress **727**
1568-1297 The British Institute of Human Rights Library **7203**
1568-1300 Information Science and Knowledge Management **5016**
1568-1319 Managing Forest Ecosystems **3451**
1568-1335 Allen and Overy Legal Practice **4613**
1568-1467 Annual Review of Language Acquisition†
1568-1475 Gesture **8104**
1568-1483 Linguistic Variations Yearbook **5146**
1568-1491 E U R O S L A Yearbook **5113**
1568-1505 Arbo Informatie *changed to* 1876-4223 **6684**
1568-1513 Arbo Actueel **6673**
1568-1548 International Institute of Sociology. Annals (New Series) **8108**
1568-1602 Genus: Gender in Modern Culture **8104**
1568-1637 Ageing Research Reviews **4039**
1568-1645 Multilingualism and Linguistic Diversity†
1568-1718 National Geographic Nederland - Belgie **4021**
1568-1777 African Dynamics **4172**
1568-1785 Humanistisch Erfgoed **6924**
1568-184X F H M (Netherlands) **6289**
1568-1858 European Studies **7234**
1568-1963 Document Design Companion Series **2319**
1568-2021 Club Business Update. Manager *changed to* 1572-7599 **8173**
1568-203X Club Business Update. Instructor *changed to* 1572-7599 **8173**
1568-2072 Utrechtse Historisch-Kartografische Studies **4033**
1568-2129 NEA News (Nederlandse Editie) *changed to* 1875-421X **8506**
1568-2358 Multimedia Systems and Applications Series **2432**
1568-2366 Developments in Fullerene Science **2134**
1568-2455 Tijdschrift Luchtrecht *changed to* 1569-6855 **63**
1568-2498 Nederlands Tijdschrift voor Allergie **5764**
1568-2536 Studies in Employment and Social Policy **8073**
1568-2552 Studies in Overseas History **4271**
1568-2587 Genetic Algorithms and Evolutionary Computation *changed to* 1932-0167 **868**
1568-2609 N A T O Science Series. Series II: Mathematics, Physics and Chemistry **5519**
1568-2625 Neurobiological Foundation of Aberrant Behaviors **6163**
1568-2633 Advances in Information Security **2511**
1568-2684 Computational Biology **825**
1568-2692 Proceedings in Marine Science **2816**
1568-2706 Studies in Narrative **5183**
1568-2714 Jazz **6578**
1568-2722 Interdisciplinary Contributions to Archaeology **398**
1568-2730 Archis (English Edition) *changed to* 1574-9401 **460**
1568-2749 Immigration and Asylum Law and Policy in Europe **4849**
1568-2803 Rond de Sjprung
1568-2897 Boekblad Magazine **7553**
1568-296X Comparative Environmental Law & Policy Series **4647**
1568-2986 All'Art *changed to* 1570-7989 **6583**
1568-301X Pactnieuws *changed to* 1871-2878 **4596**
1568-3109 101 Woonideeen **4370**
1568-3184 Cosun in Business† **8944**
1568-3443 Pericope **7669**
1568-3478 Mensen in Nood Nieuws **1601**
1568-3494 Verademing *changed to* 1871-8264 **5576**
1568-3524 Familie Vereniging "Van Engelenburg". Familieblad *changed to* 1572-5405 **3765**
1568-3532 Ancient Narrative **5254**
1568-3540 *see* 1568-3532 **5254**
1568-3540 *see* 1574-5066 **5254**
1568-3672 Infosecurity.nl (Haarlem)
1568-3788 Rioleringswetenschap **3512**
1568-4008 Elsevier Food International† **8953**
1568-4121 Notariaat Magazine **4749**
1568-4156 International Journal of Integrated Care **4102**
1568-4318 Osteoporose Journaal **6225**
1568-4474 International Comparative Social Studies **7974**
1568-4539 Fuzzy Optimization and Decision Making **2448**
1568-4555 Language Policy **5141**
1568-461X Comprehensive Series in Photosciences **3242**
1568-4628 Salaris en Benefits *changed to* 1872-5686 **1684**
1568-4849 Asian Journal of Social Science **7948**
1568-4857 Review of Rabbinic Judaism **7728**
1568-4946 Applied Soft Computing **2587**
1568-4997 Handbooks in Finance **1351**
1568-5004 Studies in European Judaism *changed to* 1874-9895 **7730**
1568-5012 Tijdschrift voor Omgevingsrecht **3470**
1568-5020 Leiderschap in Zorg *changed to* 1876-0171 **1728**

ISSN

1569-9838	see 0957-6851 **5132**
1569-9846	see 1566-5844 **5133**
1569-9854	see 1566-5852 **5133**
1569-9862	see 1569-2159 **5134**
1569-9870	see 0920-9034 **5135**
1569-9889	see 0272-2690 **5141**
1569-9897	see 1387-6759 **5142**
1569-9900	see 1568-1483 **5146**
1569-9919	see 0929-7332 **5147**
1569-9927	see 0378-4169 **5147**
1569-9935	see 1387-6740 **5338**
1569-9943	see 0929-0907 **5204**
1569-9951	see 0925-4757 **5359**
1569-996X	Sign Language and Linguistics (Online) **5173**
1569-9978	see 0378-4177 **5182**
1569-9986	see 0924-1884 **5185**
1569-9994	see 0929-9971 **5186**
1570-0011	School en Wet **3031**
1570-0194	European Executive Education Directory (Print Edition) changed to European Executive Education Directory (Online Edition) **1742**
1570-0208	Asia Pacific Executive Education Directory (Print Edition) changed to Asia Pacific Executive Education Directory (Online Edition) **1725**
1570-0224	American Executive Education Directory (Print) changed to American Executive Education Directory (Online) **2966**
1570-0232	Journal of Chromatography. B, Analytical Technologies in the Biomedical and Life Sciences **2067**
1570-0267	see 1345-711X **874**
1570-0291	Indigenous Knowledge Worldwide **1598**
1570-0399	Cainozoic Research **2727**
1570-0461	Large Marine Ecosystems **2811**
1570-0534	Verzuim en Reintegratie changed to 1876-4223 **6684**
1570-0542	The Atlantic World **4131**
1570-0577	see 0929-077X **4179**
1570-0585	see 0570-5398 **542**
1570-0593	see 1567-9896 **6643**
1570-0607	see 0043-2539 **7717**
1570-0615	see 1568-0584 **549**
1570-0631	see 0047-2212 **7725**
1570-064X	see 0085-2376 **5314**
1570-0658	see 1385-3783 **4149**
1570-0666	see 0022-4200 **7737**
1570-0674	see 1380-7854 **7726**
1570-0682	see 0943-3058 **7663**
1570-0690	see 0014-9527 **7571**
1570-0704	see 1568-4857 **7728**
1570-0720	see 0042-6032 **7692**
1570-0739	see 0044-3441 **7697**
1570-0747	see 0272-0965 **7770**
1570-0755	Quantum Information Processing **2456**
1570-0763	Leadership and Policy in Schools **3026**
1570-078X	Jerusalem Studies in Religion and Culture **7737**
1570-0852	Treasury Affairs **1303**
1570-0860	SITED **2550**
1570-095X	Philo of Alexandria Commentary Series **6939**
1570-1166	Journal of Mathematical Modelling and Algorithms **5505**
1570-1247	Onderneming en Financiering **4752**
1570-1255	Information Polity **5061**
1570-1263	Web Intelligence and Agent Systems **2457**
1570-1328	Tijdschrift over Angst en Depressie changed to 1872-4396 **6185**
1570-1336	Studies in the Aramaic Interpretation of Scripture **7730**
1570-1344	China Studies **4181**
1570-1395	F N V Bouw Magazine **4594**
1570-145X	Power Technology and Engineering **3281**
1570-1468	see 1570-145X **3281**
1570-1484	Sir Henry Wellcome Asian Studies **560**
1570-1522	Historical Materialism Book Series **7140**
1570-1530	MSC Ph.D.-Thesis Series **5519**
1570-1581	I J S Studies in Judaica **7722**
1570-159X	Current Neuropharmacology **6134**
1570-1603	Current Pharmacogenomics changed to 1875-6921 **6831**
1570-1611	Current Vascular Pharmacology **5785**
1570-162X	Current H I V Research **5812**
1570-1638	Current Drug Discovery Technologies **6830**
1570-1646	Current Proteomics **730**
1570-1719	Kwartaalbericht Detailhandel **1248**
1570-1727	Journal of Academic Ethics **2989**
1570-176X	Branchebijlage **1807**
1570-1786	Letters in Organic Chemistry **2126**
1570-1794	Current Organic Synthesis **2122**
1570-1808	Letters in Drug Design & Discovery **6858**
1570-1816	Nieuwsbrief Cultureel Erfgoed changed to 1871-6571 **4144**
1570-1824	Statistics Education Research Journal **8406**
1570-1867	Historiography East and West†
1570-193X	Mini - Reviews in Organic Chemistry **2127**
1570-1972	Global Perspectives on Biblical Scholarship **7645**
1570-1980	Academia Biblica **7619**
1570-1999	Studies in Biblical Literature (Atlanta) **7685**
1570-2057	Ellips **7640**
1570-2081	Educational Research for Policy and Practice **2851**
1570-212X	Food Trends. Distributie changed to 1574-4655 **3677**
1570-2154	Dutch Classics on History of Science **7851**
1570-2162	Bibliotheca Bibliographica Neerlandica **619**
1570-2170	Hes Studia Historica **4141**
1570-2189	Studia Bibliothecae Wittockianae **7574**
1570-2197	Advances in Electromagnetic Fields in Living Systems **751**
1570-2227	Internationale Christelijke Ambassade Jeruzalem. Nieuwsbrief changed to 1871-8248 **7639**
1570-226X	Bonsai Europe (Netherlands Edition) changed to 1874-6896 **3725**
1570-2278	Bonsai Europe (English Edition) changed to 1876-6137 **3725**
1570-2294	Electronic Communication Law Review **2533**
1570-2456	Geistliche Literatur der Barockzeit **5299**
1570-2464	Studies in Logic and Practical Reasoning **5539**
1570-2693	SynthesHis **5719**
1570-2782	Information Technology and Law Series **2422**
1570-2820	Journal of Numerical Mathematics **5553**
1570-2855	Controleprotocol PO changed to 1873-8915 **1285**
1570-2952	Doomse Krant De Kaap changed to 1871-6458 **3915**
1570-3215	International Banking, Finance and Economic Law **1570**
1570-3258	Klokhuis Magazine **2570**
1570-3363	Raadsleden Nieuws **7501**
1570-3460	I O A W - I O A Z - W I K changed to 1573-2339 **4505**
1570-3460	I O A W / I O A Z / W I K (Wet Inkomensvoorziening Oudere en gedeeltelijk Arbeidsongeschikt Werkloze Werknemers / Wet Inkomensvoorziening Oudere en Gedeeltelijk Arbeidsongeschikte Gewe en Zelfstandigen / Wet Inomensvoorziening Kunstenaars) changed to 1871-8396 **4528**
1570-3487	Memo Beslagrecht **4837**
1570-3517	W O Z Zakboekje changed to 1573-9864 **1390**
1570-3517	W O Z Zakboekje changed to 1573-9856 **1390**
1570-3584	Insolventierecht (Nijmegen) **4693**
1570-3592	Vraagbaak Rechtspositie en Arbeidsvoorwaarden bij de Overheid changed to 1872-4191 **4810**
1570-3606	De Sociale Staat van Nederland **8071**
1570-3649	Handboek Europa **8717**
1570-3754	Islam in Africa **7712**
1570-3827	Elsevier Pensioen Almanak **1677**
1570-3894	Financiele Gegevens van de Pensioenfondsen† **8956**
1570-3940	Banketbakkerijen changed to 1871-4803 **8937**
1570-3975	Onderzoek en Netwerkinformatie changed to 1567-293X **5023**
1570-405X	Resource changed to 1874-2475 **2308**
1570-4114	Traiteur changed to 1382-3345 **3664**
1570-4149	Zorg Administratie en Informatie **5739**
1570-4173	P C Plus (Haarlem) **2580**
1570-4181	Open (Amsterdam) **510**
1570-4416	S D V Communicatief changed to 1572-3054 **6242**
1570-4475	Nieuw Vuur changed to 1875-2578 **7738**
1570-4580	Op Ruwe Planken **5346**
1570-4599	Inzet Insight†
1570-4602	Sportfacilities. Club changed to 1871-434X **8205**
1570-4629	W I S E/N I R S Nuclear Monitor **3175**
1570-4645	InScope Magazine changed to 1568-0908 **1745**
1570-4653	Metaalbewerking changed to 1571-9405 **3214**
1570-4688	Accounting† **8928**
1570-470X	Ronduit Insite **7773**
1570-4858	Regio Valkenswaard changed to 1872-0331 **1721**
1570-4866	Materialen en Processen changed to 1872-5929
1570-4874	Foam **6967**
1570-5188	Pro en Contra changed to 1574-2733 **7180**
1570-520X	VAKnieuws **7942**
1570-5218	M L D S Newz changed to 1874-0278 **5932**
1570-5250	Recherche Magazine changed to 1871-4307 **4630**
1570-5285	Girlz! **2191**
1570-5293	N E N Nieuwsbrief. Bouwnormalisatie changed to 1871-6199 **1026**
1570-5331	M I C E. Meetings Incentives Congressen Exhibitions changed to 1574-7921 **6280**
1570-5366	Voor Elkaar changed to 1875-1164 **8044**
1570-5463	Chief Financial Officer **1733**
1570-5587	De Salarisadviseur changed to 1872-5686 **1684**
1570-5595	see 1461-0213 **5088**
1570-5684	Communicatiedesk. Interne Communicatie **23**
1570-579X	Studies in Computational Mathematics **5539**
1570-5811	Advanced Studies in Theoretical and Applied Econometrics **1535**
1570-5838	Applied Ontology **7335**
1570-5846	see 0010-437X **5480**
1570-5854	Perspectives on European Politics and Society **7259**
1570-5870	Cellular Oncology **830**
1570-5986	Archaeology and Biblical Studies **378**
1570-5994	The New Testament in the Greek Fathers **7739**
1570-6001	see 1387-6732 **5196**
1570-6192	Amnesty in Actie **7220**
1570-6222	Biology of Growing Animals **936**
1570-6257	Ros Paardenmagazine **8298**
1570-6303	Rehabilitatie **6180**
1570-632X	SURF (Utrecht) **2567**
1570-6338	Woon Journaal **4563**
1570-6346	Boot Journaal **8273**
1570-6354	Horsimo **8293**
1570-6362	Jet Residence **8547**
1570-6370	Dier Journaal **6806**
1570-6389	Uniekum **3034**
1570-6397	Retail Manager **1840**
1570-6443	Journal of Hydro-Environment Research **2796**
1570-6451	International Relations Studies Series **7245**
1570-646X	Energy Efficiency **3131**
1570-6478	see 1570-646X **3131**
1570-6486	Actueel Nieuws H R M
1570-6494	Voorwaarts Mars **583**
1570-6613	T O P. Tijdschrift voor de Ondernemingsrechtpraktijk **4792**
1570-6621	Architectuur N L **976**
1570-663X	SURF Special changed to 1570-632X **2567**
1570-6656	Regelingen Omgevingsrecht **4767**
1570-6672	Journal of Transportation Systems Engineering and Information Technology see 1009-6744 **8632**
1570-6680	Tijdschrift Voor Orthomoleculaire Geneeskunde **6669**
1570-677X	Economics and Human Biology **7961**
1570-6893	Late Antique Archaeology **4322**
1570-6990	Thuiswinkel Nieuwsbulletin changed to 1871-8140 **1846**
1570-7008	Writings from the Ancient World **7695**
1570-7024	Crustaceana Monographs **939**
1570-7075	Research on Language and Computation **5166**
1570-7113	At the Interface/Probing the Boundaries **4443**
1570-7121	On the Boundary of Two Worlds **7990**
1570-7156	Quantitative Marketing and Economics **1163**
1570-7202	Kunstagenda **501**
1570-7210	Kamer van Koophandel voor Veluwe en Twente. Kamerkrant (Veluwe/Stendriehoek Edition) changed to 1875-8002 **1720**
1570-7245	Planbureaustudies changed to 1871-0298 **3476**
1570-7253	Thamyris / Intersecting **8009**
1570-7261	Tussen Duin en Dijk **821**
1570-7296	Badkamer Studio **4554**
1570-7318	European Association for Animal Production. Technical Series **286**
1570-7350	The History of Christian-Muslim Relations **7647**
1570-7385	Journal of International Entrepreneurship **1574**
1570-7458	see 0013-8703 **844**
1570-7512	Yearbook of Women's Rights **8906**
1570-7520	International Yearbook of Minority Issues **7210**
1570-7539	Applied Herpetology† **8930**
1570-7555	Animal Biology **932**
1570-7563	see 1570-7555 **932**
1570-7571	Muslim Minorities **7714**
1570-761X	Bulletin of Earthquake Engineering **2778**
1570-7628	Women and Gender: The Middle East and the Islamic World **8147**
1570-7741	Antitrust Developments in Europe changed to 1947-6175 **4643**
1570-7814	PropertyNL Research Quarterly changed to 1871-9120 **7605**
1570-7822	International Journal of I T in Architecture, Engineering and Construction (Print Edition)†
1570-7830	International Journal of I T in Architecture, Engineering and Construction (Online Edition) see 1570-7822
1570-7830	International Journal of I T in Architecture, Engineering and Construction (Online Edition) changed to 1874-4753 **2548**
1570-7865	European Yearbook of Minority Issues **3533**
1570-7873	Journal of Grid Computing **2508**
1570-7938	Tijdschrift voor Onderneming en Strafrecht changed to 1574-7913 **1951**
1570-7946	Computer - Aided Chemical Engineering **3289**
1570-7954	Handbook of Algebra **5491**
1570-7989	Kunstzone **6583**
1570-7997	Jewish Identities in a Changing World **3542**
1570-8187	Kamerkrant voor de Ondernemende Regio Zwolle changed to 1875-0001 **1720**
1570-8233	Kamerkrant voor Ondernemend Limburg-Noord changed to 1876-2980 **1719**
1570-8233	Kamerkrant voor Ondernemend Limburg-Noord changed to 1876-3006 **1719**
1570-825X	VrouwenMode **2263**
1570-8268	Journal of Web Semantics **2563**
1570-8276	De Opticien **6049**
1570-8284	De Juwelier **4567**
1570-8306	Nederlands Tijdschrift voor Klinische Chemie en Laboratoriumgeneeskunde **2074**
1570-8349	Kamerkrant voor Ondernemend Twente changed to 1875-8002 **1720**
1570-8357	Kamerkrant voor Ondernemend Veluwe/Stedendriehoek changed to 1875-8002 **1720**
1570-842X	Kamerkrant voor Ondernemend Gooi- en Eemland changed to 1877-3478 **1406**
1570-8438	Kamerkrant voor Ondernemend Flevoland changed to 1877-3478 **1406**
1570-8470	Staatsalmanak **7469**
1570-8578	Praktijkkompas Varkens changed to 1574-1575 **303**
1570-8586	Praktijkkompas Rundvee changed to 1574-1575 **303**
1570-8659	Handbook of Numerical Analysis **5491**
1570-8667	Journal of Discrete Algorithms changed to 0196-6774 **5553**
1570-8683	Journal of Applied Logic **6928**
1570-8691	see 1570-8683 **6928**
1570-8705	Ad Hoc Networks **2495**
1570-8713	see 1570-8705 **2495**
1570-8721	Sources for African History **4178**
1570-8764	Journaal Milieu Agrarische Sector changed to 1570-6656 **4767**
1570-8799	Marketing International **1832**
1570-8802	Journaal Milieu changed to 1570-6656 **4767**
1570-9124	E A U Update Series (European Association of Urology) changed to 1871-2592 **6267**
1570-9132	OK Magazine changed to 1872-6712 **6254**
1570-9159	De Nederlandsche Bank. Occasional Studies **1936**
1570-9175	Internet Tips & Trucs† **8966**
1570-9183	C I O **2408**
1570-9205	Studiefinancieringsschijf **3003**
1570-9213	Fries Ondernemers Contact changed to 1871-2886 **1782**
1570-9256	see 0922-2936 **7655**
1570-9264	Bond voor Materialenkennis. Nieuwsbrief changed to 1872-5929
1570-9310	Afrika-Studiecentrum Series **4173**
1570-9337	G **7518**
1570-9361	Tijdschrift voor Openbare Financien (Print) changed to 1875-8401 **1905**
1570-9434	Numen Book Series **7667**
1570-9612	Tijdschrift voor Veiligheid en Veiligheidszorg changed to 1872-7948 **2681**
1570-9639	B B A - Proteins and Proteomics **723**
1570-9663	Milieutijdingen changed to 1872-3446 **2629**
1570-9930	Storage Magazine **2541**
1571-0017	Benelux Tekeningen- of Modellenblad (CD-ROM) **6746**
1571-0068	International Journal of Science and Mathematics Education **7868**
1571-0122	R O M **3461**
1571-0351	AmericA **8682**
1571-0475	H E T **4978**
1571-053X	Mondhygienisten Vademecum **5856**
1571-0564	Keesing's Journal of Documents changed to 1871-272X **2515**
1571-0629	Vastgoed Fiscaal en Civiel **1954**
1571-0645	Physics of Life Reviews **697**
1571-0653	Electronic Notes in Discrete Mathematics **5486**
1571-0661	Electronic Notes in Theoretical Computer Science **2600**
1571-0718	Spanish in Context **5376**
1571-0726	see 1571-0718 **5376**
1571-0734	S C R O L L **5366**
1571-0785	The Chemical Physics of Solid Surfaces **2133**
1571-0831	Studies in Multidisciplinarity **7920**
1571-0866	Developments in Quaternary Science **2731**
1571-0882	CoDesign **437**
1571-0912	Women's Care changed to 1873-1287 **8844**

1572-431X Okki. Groep 3 **2205**
1572-4328 Okki. Groep 4 *changed to* 1872-0293 **2195**
1572-4336 Jurisprudentie Wet Werk en Bijstand (Print)† **8969**
1572-4344 Nature, Culture and Literature **5338**
1572-4352 Developments in Clay Science **2730**
1572-4379 World Crop Pests **259**
1572-4387 Transportation Research, Economics and Policy **8516**
1572-4395 Law and Philosophy Library **4714**
1572-4409 Process Metallurgy **6329**
1572-4417 Manufacturing Research and Technology **1898**
1572-4433 Fundamental Studies in Engineering **3193**
1572-4441 I C C A Congress Series **4870**
1572-4492 E-AMDAR Quality Evaluation on AMDAR Data. Quarterly Reports **6352**
1572-4514 Bedrijfseconomische Kerncijfers van Gespecialiseerde Bedrijven in de Bouw **3260**
1572-459X Social and Critical Theory **6952**
1572-4603 Accountantspraktijk† **8928**
1572-4638 International Corporate Rescue **4871**
1572-4646 Traffic in the Netherlands. Key Figures **8635**
1572-4727 Journaal Bouw en Infra *changed to* 1570-6656 **4767**
1572-4778 Cheminformatics **2107**
1572-4794 The Future of Learning **2859**
1572-4840 OR Rendement **6702**
1572-4859 Dislocations in Solids **7010**
1572-4875 European Journal of Traditional Chinese Medicine **309**
1572-4913 Pauline Studies **7669**
1572-493X Andere Tijden **4198**
1572-4956 Tortuca Cahier **5389**
1572-4964 Nieuwsbrief Gemeentelijke Activering **8058**
1572-4980 Machinebouw **2462**
1572-4999 European Company Law **4867**
1572-5030 Nederlands Tijdschrift voor Coaching *changed to* 1877-0959 **1798**
1572-5049 Zorg Rond de Pasgeborene† **9000**
1572-5057 Theologisch Debat **7689**
1572-5103 Koster Service Schrift **4511**
1572-5111 K M P Pensioen Perspectief **4511**
1572-5138 *see* 1476-7430 **6928**
1572-5162 Vast Werken **6451**
1572-5200 Hollandiai Magyar Hirek **3538**
1572-5219 Klachtenmanagement **4709**
1572-5227 Communicatie Memo **8094**
1572-5243 Feedback†
1572-5251 Werkvloer **169**
1572-526X S T I N Journaal *changed to* 1572-5278 **5789**
1572-5278 I C D Journaal **5789**
1572-5286 Discrete Optimization **5552**
1572-5294 De Verpakkingskrant
1572-5324 The I P L O C A Yearbook **6773**
1572-5391 Praaiberichten **3779**
1572-5405 De Engelenbrug **3765**
1572-5421 EstateTip Review **4902**
1572-543X *see* 0166-2740 **7642**
1572-5448 *see* 1387-6988 **7448**
1572-5456 Voorwaarts! (Print) *changed to* Voorwaarts! (Online) **7192**
1572-5472 Tiem **1798**
1572-5480 Developments in Marine Geology **2730**
1572-5499 Studiepockets Privaatrecht *changed to* 1573-9791 **4736**
1572-557X Advances in Phytomedicine **6819**
1572-560X Advances in Tourism Research **8681**
1572-5642 Plenum Series on Human Exceptionality **7391**
1572-5960 Real-Time Safety Critical Systems **2468**
1572-5979 Process Measurement & Control **3253**
1572-5987 Science & Technology Education Library **5046**
1572-5995 Studies in Natural Products Chemistry **2081**
1572-6061 Plasma Technology **7035**
1572-610X Annals of Oncology. Supplement *see* 0923-7534 **6008**
1572-6126 Trends in Logic - Studia Logica Library **6958**
1572-6207 Monitoring Zoete Rijkswateren **7453**
1572-624X Penny **8296**
1572-6258 Teksten Financiering en Planning Gezondheidszorg *changed to* 1874-8201 **4781**
1572-6304 Studies in Writing **5382**
1572-6320 Joint Institute for V L B I in Europe. Annual Report **576**
1572-6401 C E D L A Latin America Studies **7951**
1572-641X Agrapower **209**
1572-6487 The Hogendorp Papers **4849**
1572-6525 Fossilium Catalogus: Animalia **6724**
1572-6541 Cosun Magazine **225**
1572-6622 Paleo-aktueel **6728**
1572-6649 Studies in Spirituality Supplements **7686**
1572-6657 Journal of Electroanalytical Chemistry **2102**
1572-6681 Symposium on Information Theory in the Benelux. Proceedings **2551**
1572-6991 The Medieval Franciscans **7806**
1572-7106 Mushroom Business *see* 1380-359X **3747**
1572-7238 Auto & Tuning **8558**
1572-7335 *see* 1380-2879 **264**
1572-7343 *see* 1380-2879 **264**
1572-7459 Diacoon **7754**
1572-7475 F C *changed to* 1872-0269 **8250**
1572-7483 Meridian *changed to* Meridian Travel **8733**
1572-7521 Vonk *changed to* 1574-2725 **7693**
1572-7599 Fitness Update **8173**
1572-7610 Vakblad Natuur Bos Landschap **3707**
1572-7742 Landscape Series **3741**
1572-7807 Nederlands Tijdschrift voor Handelsrecht **4740**
1572-7815 Topological Fixed Point Theory and its Applications **5542**
1572-7858 Info Regio (Dutch Edition) **3915**
1572-7874 S O A Bulletin *changed to* 1573-6369 **5765**
1572-7904 Veenkoloniale Volksalmanak **4033**
1572-7939 Navenant **8740**
1572-7947 LeukoNieuws **6026**
1572-7971 Flits *changed to* 1873-118X **3035**
1572-7998 Hervormd Kerkblad **7760**
1572-8005 Fanmail **2358**
1572-8013 Stichting Geestelijk-Wetenschappelijk Genootschap "De Eeuw van Christus". Donateursblad **7741**
1572-8056 Doorgeefbrief **7638**
1572-8080 *see* 0929-5585 **2460**
1572-8099 *see* 0015-2684 **3578**
1572-8102 *see* 0925-9856 **2520**
1572-8110 *see* 1381-2416 **5203**
1572-8129 *see* 1068-9605 **2327**
1572-8137 *see* 1569-8025 **2428**
1572-8145 *see* 0956-5515 **2453**
1572-8153 *see* 1383-469X **2501**
1572-817X *see* 0306-8919 **7081**
1572-8188 *see* 1387-974X **7030**
1572-8196 *see* 1022-0038 **2344**
1572-820X Holland Real Estate Yearbook **7592**
1572-8315 *see* 1573-3750 **2657**
1572-8331 Werk en Handicap **1714**
1572-834X *see* 0929-6212 **2365**
1572-8358 *see* 0001-5342 **649**
1572-8366 *see* 0889-048X **85**
1572-8374 *see* 0920-427X **6905**
1572-8382 *see* 0924-8463 **4622**
1572-8390 Axiomathes (Online) **6907**
1572-8404 *see* 0169-3867 **660**
1572-8420 *see* 0165-0106 **6916**
1572-8439 *see* 1388-1957 **5008**
1572-8447 *see* 1386-2820 **6917**
1572-8455 *see* 0966-3622 **4673**
1572-8463 *see* 1386-4238 **2062**
1572-8471 *see* 1233-1821 **7856**
1572-8498 *see* 0956-2737 **4094**
1572-8501 *see* 0167-9848 **6924**
1572-851X *see* 0163-8548 **6923**
1572-8536 *see* 0019-7246 **551**
1572-8544 *see* 1570-1727 **2989**
1572-8552 *see* 1383-4924 **5133**
1572-8560 *see* 0925-8558 **5133**
1572-8579 *see* 0334-701X **7723**
1572-8587 *see* 0925-4560 **7871**
1572-8595 *see* 1383-875X **5793**
1572-8609 *see* 1382-4554 **6928**
1572-8617 *see* 0957-8536 **4713**
1572-8625 *see* 0144-932X **4724**
1572-8633 *see* 1386-7423 **5674**
1572-8641 *see* 0924-6495 **2454**
1572-865X *see* 0925-854X **5154**
1572-8668 *see* 0028-2677 **5339**
1572-8676 *see* 1568-7759 **6939**
1572-8684 *see* 0020-7047 **7650**
1572-8692 *see* 1356-4765 **6947**
1572-8706 *see* 1570-7075 **5166**
1572-8714 *see* 0304-3487 **5170**
1572-8722 *see* 0952-8059 **4694**
1572-8730 *see* 0039-3215 **6954**
1572-8749 *see* 0167-7411 **6957**
1572-8757 *see* 0929-5607 **3235**
1572-8773 *see* 0966-0844 **727**
1572-8781 *see* 1387-2176 **5586**
1572-879X *see* 1011-372X **2052**
1572-882X *see* 0969-0239 **2121**
1572-8838 *see* 0021-891X **2114**
1572-8854 *see* 1074-1542 **2111**
1572-8862 *see* 1040-7278 **2067**
1572-8889 *see* 0892-7553 **852**
1572-8897 *see* 0259-9791 **5505**
1572-8900 *see* 1566-2543 **2125**
1572-8927 *see* 0095-9782 **2138**
1572-8935 *see* 1022-9760 **7093**
1572-8943 *see* 1388-6150 **2138**
1572-896X *see* 1388-0764 **7021**
1572-8986 *see* 0272-4324 **3252**
1572-8994 *see* 1569-0660 **2118**
1572-9001 *see* 1040-0400 **2081**
1572-901X *see* 0340-4285 **6335**
1572-9028 *see* 1022-5528 **2082**
1572-9036 *see* 0167-8019 **5464**
1572-9044 *see* 1019-7168 **5549**
1572-9052 *see* 0020-3157 **5494**
1572-9060 *see* 0232-704X **5471**
1572-9079 *see* 1386-923X **5468**
1572-9087 *see* 0252-9602 **5464**
1572-9095 *see* 0927-2852 **5550**
1572-9109 *see* 0862-7940 **5471**
1572-9125 *see* 0006-3835 **2505**
1572-9141 *see* 0011-4642 **5481**
1572-915X *see* 1386-1999 **8369**
1572-9168 *see* 0046-5755 **5490**
1572-9176 *see* 1072-947X **5490**
1572-9184 *see* 1570-7873 **2508**
1572-9192 *see* 0925-9899 **5500**
1572-9206 *see* 1521-1398 **5501**
1572-9214 *see* 1570-1166 **5505**
1572-9222 *see* 1040-7294 **5503**
1572-9230 *see* 0894-9840 **5507**
1572-9249 *see* 1380-7870 **8385**
1572-9265 *see* 1017-1398 **5522**
1572-9273 *see* 0167-8094 **5523**
1572-9281 *see* 1385-1292 **5525**
1572-929X *see* 0926-2601 **5525**
1572-9303 *see* 1382-4090 **5527**
1572-9311 *see* 1387-0874 **5538**
1572-9338 *see* 0254-5330 **2406**
1572-9346 *see* 1381-298X **5551**
1572-9354 *see* 1383-7133 **2447**
1572-9362 *see* 1389-5753 **2556**
1572-9389 *see* 1386-9620 **4095**
1572-9397 *see* 1381-1231 **2453**
1572-9400 *see* 1387-3741 **5626**
1572-9419 *see* 1387-3326 **2545**
1572-9427 *see* 1566-113X **2518**
1572-9435 *see* 0049-4488 **8515**
1572-9443 *see* 0257-0130 **3328**
1572-9451 *see* 1018-4864 **2372**
1572-946X *see* 0004-640X **572**
1572-9478 *see* 0923-2958 **573**
1572-9494 *see* 0253-6102 **7008**
1572-9508 *see* 0922-6435 **574**
1572-9516 *see* 0015-9018 **7013**
1572-9532 *see* 0001-7701 **7014**
1572-9540 *see* 0304-3843 **7015**
1572-9567 *see* 0195-928X **7055**
1572-9575 *see* 0020-7748 **7018**
1572-9583 *see* 0925-8531 **5134**
1572-9591 *see* 0164-0313 **3170**
1572-9613 *see* 0022-4715 **7022**
1572-963X *see* 1385-3457 **1767**
1572-9648 *see* 0025-6455 **7060**
1572-9656 *see* 1385-0172 **7026**
1572-9672 *see* 0038-6308 **582**
1572-9680 *see* 0167-4366 **87**
1572-9699 *see* 0003-6072 **756**
1572-9702 *see* 0168-8162 **942**
1572-9710 *see* 0960-3115 **2604**
1572-9729 *see* 0923-9820 **3504**
1572-9737 *see* 1566-0621 **865**
1572-9753 *see* 1366-638X **852**
1572-9761 *see* 0921-2973 **3450**
1572-9788 *see* 1380-3743 **801**
1572-9796 *see* 1567-7818 **2432**
1572-980X *see* 1568-7767 **808**
1572-9818 *see* 0735-9640 **742**
1572-9826 *see* 1569-1705 **770**
1572-9834 *see* 0923-4861 **8842**
1572-9842 *see* 0263-0338 **371**
1572-9850 *see* 1046-8374 **4887**
1572-9869 *see* 0928-1371 **2651**
1572-9877 *see* 1205-8629 **2674**
1572-9885 *see* 0168-6577 **7306**
1572-9893 *see* 0343-2521 **4012**
1572-9907 *see* 0926-2644 **1748**
1572-9915 *see* 0300-7839 **341**
1572-994X *see* 0920-8569 **897**
1572-9958 *see* 0217-4561 **1725**
1572-9966 *see* 1043-4062 **4847**
1572-9974 *see* 0927-7099 **1415**
1572-9982 *see* 0013-063X **1102**
1572-9990 *see* 0929-1261 **1107**
1573-000X EMBASE. Drugs & Pharmacology **6889**
1573-0158 Exameneisen V W O-H A V O **3022**
1573-0166 Zwei Oder Drei **7697**
1573-0182 Kluwer Tarievenboek **1932**
1573-0190 Schoolmanagers V O *changed to* 1873-1163 **3035**
1573-0212 Teksten Kwaliteit Gezondheidszorg en Patientenrechten *changed to* 1874-8201 **4781**
1573-0220 Campergids Facile-en-Route **8307**
1573-0255 *see* 0268-0556 **4619**
1573-0263 F M N Almanak **1744**
1573-0298 Toeractief **8761**
1573-0352 *see* 0925-9880 **4769**
1573-0379 The Amsterdam Review **5416**
1573-0387 *see* 0022-5010 **685**
1573-0395 *see* 0022-1791 **6928**
1573-0409 *see* 0921-0296 **2453**
1573-0417 *see* 0921-2728 **6726**
1573-0433 *see* 0022-3611 **6929**
1573-0441 *see* 0895-562X **1769**
1573-045X *see* 0895-5638 **7597**
1573-0468 *see* 0922-680X **1546**
1573-0476 *see* 0895-5646 **1546**
1573-0484 *see* 0920-8542 **2430**
1573-0492 *see* 0022-5363 **6930**
1573-0514 *see* 0920-3036 **5507**
1573-0522 *see* 0167-5249 **4713**
1573-0530 *see* 0377-9017 **7025**
1573-0549 *see* 0165-0157 **5147**
1573-0557 *see* 1388-3690 **2486**
1573-0565 *see* 0885-6125 **2454**
1573-0573 *see* 0922-6567 **5204**
1573-0581 *see* 0025-3235 **2812**
1573-059X *see* 0923-0645 **1832**
1573-0611 *see* 1387-2842 **6912**
1573-062X Urban Water Journal **8834**
1573-0638 *see* 0020-8566 **2871**
1573-0646 *see* 0167-6997 **6851**
1573-0654 *see* 0168-6291 **212**
1573-0662 *see* 0167-7764 **2066**
1573-0670 *see* 0168-7433 **2453**
1573-0689 *see* 0092-0606 **753**
1573-0697 *see* 0167-4544 **1134**
1573-0700 *see* 0168-7034 **2639**
1573-0719 *see* 0169-3816 **4049**
1573-0727 *see* 0923-8174 **3322**
1573-0735 *see* 0920-8550 **1361**
1573-0751 *see* 0925-4994 **2648**
1573-076X *see* 0165-005X **335**
1573-0778 *see* 0920-9069 **832**
1573-0786 *see* 0304-4092 **335**
1573-0794 *see* 0167-9295 **574**
1573-0816 *see* 0013-1954 **5485**
1573-0824 *see* 0923-6082 **2524**
1573-0832 *see* 0301-486X **803**
1573-0840 *see* 0921-030X **2713**
1573-0859 *see* 0167-806X **5154**
1573-0867 *see* 1385-1314 **244**
1573-0875 *see* 0169-6149 **696**
1573-0883 *see* 0031-8116 **6941**
1573-0891 *see* 0032-2687 **7166**
1573-0905 *see* 0922-4777 **5165**
1573-0913 *see* 0921-898X **1967**
1573-0921 *see* 0303-8300 **8150**
1573-093X *see* 0038-0938 **581**
1573-0948 *see* 0925-9392 **7187**
1573-0956 *see* 0169-3298 **2790**
1573-0964 *see* 0039-7857 **6956**
1573-0972 *see* 0959-3993 **771**
1573-1111 *see* 1388-3127 **2136**
1573-1200 *see* 1386-7415 **5721**

ISSN

1573-6490 E L S A Leiden Magazine **4924**
1573-6547 *see* 0278-095X **7378**
1573-6555 *see* 0090-6905 **5135**
1573-6563 *see* 0894-9085 **7379**
1573-6571 *see* 0022-4197 **7656**
1573-6598 *see* 0894-9867 **7381**
1573-6601 *see* 0047-2891 **2157**
1573-661X *see* 0147-7307 **4713**
1573-6628 *see* 1092-7875 **5998**
1573-6644 *see* 0146-7239 **7386**
1573-6652 *see* 1090-0578 **7388**
1573-6660 *see* 1040-7308 **6168**
1573-6679 *see* 0031-2789 **7389**
1573-6687 *see* 0190-9320 **7168**
1573-6695 *see* 1389-4986 **5825**
1573-6709 *see* 0033-2720 **6176**
1573-6717 *see* 0146-1044 **5712**
1573-6725 *see* 0885-7466 **8133**
1573-6741 *see* 0002-9548 **7333**
1573-675X *see* 1360-8185 **827**
1573-6768 *see* 1389-5729 **4041**
1573-6776 *see* 0141-5492 **761**
1573-6792 *see* 0896-0267 **6128**
1573-6806 *see* 1567-8822 **5781**
1573-6814 *see* 1389-9333 **828**
1573-6822 *see* 0742-2091 **3495**
1573-6830 *see* 0272-4340 **6130**
1573-6849 *see* 0967-3849 **728**
1573-6857 *see* 0016-6707 **869**
1573-6873 *see* 0929-5313 **6151**
1573-6881 *see* 0145-479X **735**
1573-689X *see* 0148-5598 **5832**
1573-6903 *see* 0364-3190 **6164**
1573-6911 *see* 0340-8744 **1483**
1573-6938 *see* 1386-4157 **1541**
1573-6946 *see* 1387-2834 **1392**
1573-6962 *see* 1389-6563 **7526**
1573-6970 *see* 0927-5940 **1930**
1573-6989 *see* 1387-6996 **681**
1573-6997 *see* 0885-2545 **1544**
1573-7012 *see* 1566-1679 **1137**
1573-7020 *see* 1381-4338 **1544**
1573-7039 *see* 1083-3021 **924**
1573-7047 *see* 0892-9912 **8429**
1573-7055 *see* 1064-7554 **951**
1573-7071 *see* 1385-9587 **2501**
1573-708X *see* 0923-7992 **1547**
1573-7098 *see* 1566-7170 **1787**
1573-7101 *see* 0048-5829 **1162**
1573-711X *see* 1570-7156 **1163**
1573-7128 *see* 0889-3047 **1548**
1573-7136 *see* 1380-6653 **1300**
1573-7144 *see* 1380-6645 **1379**
1573-7152 *see* 1569-5239 **1166**
1573-7160 *see* 0889-938X **1548**
1573-7179 *see* 0924-865X **1300**
1573-7187 *see* 0040-5833 **8009**
1573-7209 *see* 0969-6970 **6008**
1573-7217 *see* 0167-6806 **6010**
1573-7225 *see* 0957-5243 **6011**
1573-7233 *see* 0167-7659 **6011**
1573-7241 *see* 0920-3206 **5781**
1573-7276 *see* 0262-0898 **6015**
1573-7284 *see* 0393-2990 **5611**
1573-7292 *see* 1389-9600 **6019**
1573-7322 *see* 1382-4147 **5788**
1573-7330 *see* 1058-0468 **5995**
1573-7349 *see* 1570-7385 **1574**
1573-7357 *see* 0022-2291 **7055**
1573-7365 *see* 0885-7490 **5678**
1573-7373 *see* 0167-594X **6025**
1573-739X *see* 0928-1231 **6874**
1573-7403 *see* 1386-341X **5898**
1573-742X *see* 0929-5305 **5794**
1573-7438 *see* 0049-4747 **8809**
1573-7446 *see* 0165-7380 **8814**
1573-7454 *see* 1387-2532 **2447**
1573-7462 *see* 0269-2821 **2446**
1573-7470 *see* 1012-2443 **2445**
1573-7497 *see* 0924-669X **2446**
1573-7500 *see* 1389-0166 **4990**
1573-7527 *see* 0929-5593 **2584**
1573-7535 *see* 0928-8910 **2446**
1573-7543 *see* 1386-7857 **2496**
1573-7551 *see* 0925-9724 **2412**
1573-756X *see* 1384-5810 **2530**
1573-7578 *see* 0926-8782 **2530**
1573-7586 *see* 0925-1022 **5482**
1573-7594 *see* 0924-6703 **2517**
1573-7608 *see* 1360-2357 **3059**
1573-7616 *see* 1382-3256 **2589**
1573-7624 *see* 1384-6175 **2722**
1573-7632 *see* 1389-2576 **2448**
1573-7640 *see* 0885-7458 **2507**
1573-7659 *see* 1386-4564 **2545**
1573-7667 *see* 1385-951X **1851**
1573-7675 *see* 0925-9902 **2453**
1573-7683 *see* 0924-9907 **5553**
1573-7691 *see* 0885-7474 **7940**
1573-7705 *see* 1064-7570 **2500**
1573-7713 *see* 1387-5841 **5517**
1573-7721 *see* 1380-7501 **2488**
1573-773X *see* 1370-4621 **2455**
1573-7748 *see* 1092-7697 **398**
1573-7756 *see* 1059-0161 **400**
1573-7764 *see* 1072-5369 **400**
1573-7772 *see* 1566-4910 **4417**
1573-7780 *see* 1389-4978 **7374**
1573-7799 *see* 0748-4518 **2658**
1573-7802 *see* 0892-7537 **401**
1573-7810 *see* 0199-0039 **7391**
1573-7829 *see* 0167-5923 **7290**
1573-7837 *see* 0162-0436 **8127**
1573-7845 *see* 0033-5177 **8150**
1573-7853 *see* 0304-2421 **8143**
1573-7861 *see* 0884-8971 **8136**
1573-7888 *see* 0957-8765 **8077**
1573-8051 Freight Transport in the Netherlands. Key Figures **8496**
1573-806X StAB **4427**
1573-8086 Reviews in Fluorescence **2105**
1573-8094 Premsela Nieuwsbrief *changed to* 1874-4605 **512**
1573-8140 Nationale Monitor Geestelijke Gezondheid **6162**
1573-8159 *see* 1381-1118 **7336**
1573-8175 *see* 1672-4070 **5470**
1573-8183 *see* 0003-6838 **723**
1573-8191 *see* 0571-7256 **572**
1573-8205 *see* 1063-4258 **3164**
1573-8221 *see* 0007-4888 **663**
1573-8248 *see* 1386-6141 **841**
1573-8256 *see* 0006-3398 **5585**
1573-8264 *see* 0006-3134 **779**
1573-8302 *see* 0002-5232 **5467**
1573-8310 *see* 0009-3092 **6765**
1573-8329 *see* 0009-2355 **3238**
1573-8337 *see* 1060-0396 **2526**
1573-8345 *see* 0010-5082 **3241**
1573-8353 *see* 0009-3122 **2121**
1573-837X *see* 1046-283X **5551**
1573-8388 *see* 0009-3130 **2121**
1573-8469 *see* 0929-1873 **787**
1573-8477 *see* 0269-7653 **3431**
1573-8485 *see* 0016-2663 **5488**
1573-8493 *see* 0015-0541 **8451**
1573-8507 *see* 0015-4628 **7058**
1573-8515 *see* 0361-7610 **2041**
1573-8582 *see* 1063-7095 **3346**
1573-8604 *see* 0164-0291 **948**
1573-8620 *see* 0021-8944 **3349**
1573-8647 *see* 0021-9037 **7077**
1573-8663 *see* 1385-3449 **3349**
1573-868X *see* 0916-8370 **2809**
1573-8698 *see* 1079-2724 **3369**
1573-8701 *see* 1569-1721 **1494**
1573-871X *see* 1062-0125 **3205**
1573-8736 *see* 1062-7391 **6467**
1573-8744 *see* 1567-567X **6855**
1573-8760 *see* 1071-2836 **3206**
1573-8779 *see* 0022-4766 **2069**
1573-8795 *see* 1072-3374 **5505**
1573-8809 *see* 0927-7544 **7597**
1573-8825 *see* 0363-1672 **5509**
1573-8841 *see* 1569-1713 **3347**
1573-885X *see* 1068-820X **3353**
1573-8876 *see* 1067-9073 **5530**
1573-8892 *see* 0026-0894 **6325**
1573-8906 *see* 0543-1972 **6404**
1573-8922 *see* 0191-5665 **3250**
1573-8973 *see* 0026-0673 **6323**
1573-8981 *see* 1520-7439 **6474**
1573-899X *see* 0097-0549 **6169**
1573-9007 *see* 0090-2977 **6167**
1573-9031 *see* 0091-150X **6868**
1573-904X *see* 0724-8741 **6870**
1573-9058 *see* 0300-3604 **807**
1573-9066 *see* 1068-1302 **6329**
1573-9090 *see* 0033-1538 **2900**
1573-9104 *see* 0921-9668 **6668**
1573-9120 *see* 0033-8443 **3112**
1573-9139 *see* 1083-4877 **2045**
1573-9147 override
1573-9171 *see* 1066-5285 **2079**
1573-9228 *see* 1064-8887 **7038**
1573-9252 *see* 1387-5868 **7409**
1573-9260 *see* 0037-4466 **5536**
1573-9279 *see* 0038-0741 **3283**
1573-9295 *see* 1094-429X **1797**
1573-9325 *see* 0039-2316 **3358**
1573-9333 *see* 0040-5779 **7043**
1573-935X *see* 0040-5760 **2082**
1573-9368 *see* 0962-8819 **879**
1573-9376 *see* 0041-5995 **5543**
1573-9406 Vestigia Rapporten **423**
1573-9414 Economic Change and Restructuring **1479**
1573-9422 Rechtspraak Arbeidsrecht **4959**
1573-9511 Netherlands. Ministerie van Verkeer en Waterstaat, Rijkswaterstaat. Adviesdienst Verkeer en Vervoer. Kerncijfers Infrastructuur **8506**
1573-952X Infrastructure in the Netherlands. Key Figures **8499**
1573-9538 Purinergic Signalling **699**
1573-9546 *see* 1573-9538 **699**
1573-9597 Bibliotheek **4996**
1573-9619 Info Regio (Editie Kennemerland en de IJmond) **3915**
1573-9627 Info Regio (Editie De Meerlanden) **3915**
1573-9643 Reinwater **3490**
1573-9651 Feiten over Verpleegkundige en Verzorgende Beroepen in Nederland **5959**
1573-966X *see* 1083-0898 **1126**
1573-9678 *see* 0197-4254 **1063**
1573-9686 *see* 0090-6964 **5575**
1573-9775 Tijdschrift voor Taalbeheersing **5187**
1573-9791 Monografieen Privaatrecht **4736**
1573-9805 Jaaruitgave Inkoop van Energie **3140**
1573-9813 Gids Bedrijfshulpverlening **6677**
1573-983X Zakboek Proces-Verbaal *changed to* 1876-2409 **2672**
1573-9848 Mededingingsrecht **4875**
1573-9856 W O Z Zakboekje. Wetgeving **1390**
1573-9864 W O Z Zakboekje. Jurisprudentie **1390**
1573-9880 K A N Vastgoedrapportage **4418**
1573-9902 Wooninnovatie Reeks **1043**
1573-9910 Tijdschrift Aanbestedingsrecht **7614**
1573-9929 Amsterdam **4129**
1573-9945 Jaarboek Flexibiliteit in Arbeidsrelaties **1690**
1573-9953 Miscellanea Malacologica **955**
1573-9961 Maranatha Kalender *changed to* 1573-997X **7661**
1573-997X Maranatha **7661**
1574-0005 Handbook of Game Theory and Economic Applications **1542**
1574-0013 Handbook of Defense Economics **7443**
1574-0021 Handbook of Computational Economics **1542**
1574-003X Handbook of Population and Family Economics **7284**
1574-0048 Handbook of Macroeconomics **1719**
1574-0056 Handbook of Income Distribution **1542**
1574-0064 Handbook of Health Economics **4095**
1574-0072 Handbook of Agricultural Economics **199**
1574-0080 Handbook of Regional and Urban Economics **4412**
1574-0099 Handbook of Environmental Economics **3436**
1574-0102 Handbook of the Economics of Finance **1350**
1574-0110 Handbook of Social Choice and Welfare **8043**
1574-0129 Frontiers of Family Economics **1112**
1574-0137 Computer Science Review **2412**
1574-0153 Cancer Biomarkers **6011**
1574-017X Mobile Information Systems **2334**
1574-0196 European Constitutional Law Review **4848**
1574-020X Language Resources and Evaluation **4485**
1574-0218 *see* 1574-020X **4485**
1574-0226 Platform (Amsterdam) **3558**
1574-0250 Creatief met Kaarten **534**
1574-0269 Vermogensrechtelijke Annotaties **4882**
1574-0277 *see* 1573-9414 **1479**
1574-0307 Externe Veiligheid (Alphen aan den Rijn) *changed to* 1876-6188 **2679**
1574-0323 Grand Slam Darts Magazine **8175**
1574-0374 Circumpolar Studies **4002**
1574-0382 Microsoft.NET Magazine **2431**
1574-0404 Computing Letters†
1574-0412 Schriftuur **5368**
1574-0447 Fundamental and Applied Catalysis **3244**
1574-0463 I F S R International Series on Systems Science and Engineering **2521**
1574-0471 Issues in Clinical Child Psychology **7367**
1574-051X Monografieen Sociaal Recht **4838**
1574-0552 Scholen en Bouwen an de Toekomst. Basis Onderwijs **456**
1574-0609 Auditing in de Praktijk **1280**
1574-0617 Journal of Satisfiability, Boolean Modeling and Computation **2429**
1574-0625 Bouwkrant Hanzelijn **8615**
1574-0641 Handai Nanophotonics **7014**
1574-065X Universiteit van Amsterdam. Duitsland Instituut Amsterdam. Forschungsberichte **4275**
1574-0668 Journal of Cardiothoracic-Renal Research **5792**
1574-0684 Handbook of Economic Growth **1568**
1574-0706 Handbook of Economic Forecasting **1116**
1574-0757 Journal of Dermatological Science. Supplement **5879**
1574-0765 Research on Professional Responsibility and Ethics in Accounting **1299**
1574-0773 Journal of Conflict Archaeology† **8968**
1574-079X Constante† **8943**
1574-0803 Rechtspraak Familierecht **4914**
1574-0811 Het Goede Leven **5072**
1574-082X Friesch Dagblad **3914**
1574-0846 C T I T Workshop Proceedings Series **2409**
1574-0854 Het Vrije Woord† **8998**
1574-0862 *see* 0169-5150 **192**
1574-0870 Advances in Organic Synthesis **2119**
1574-0889 Frontiers in Drug Design and Discovery **6843**
1574-0897 Frontiers in Natural Product Chemistry **2062**
1574-0900 Frontiers in Organic Chemistry **2123**
1574-0919 Advances in Global Change Research **7833**
1574-0927 Levend Erfgoed **3619**
1574-0935 Natuurplanbureau. Vestiging Wageningen. Planbureaurapporten *changed to* 1871-028X **3474**
1574-0943 De Limit† **8971**
1574-0951 *see* 0167-6768 **4936**
1574-096X *see* 1389-1359 **4945**
1574-1001 Longitudinal Research in the Social and Behavioral Sciences **7983**
1574-101X Developments in Integrated Environmental Assessment **3414**
1574-1028 Topics in Applied Chemistry **2082**
1574-1044 Mag het Wat Minder Zijn? **2640**
1574-1060 Serie Onderneming en Recht **4782**
1574-1079 Journaal Stoffen en Preparaten **2066**
1574-1087 AutoConnect (Dutch Edition) **2313**
1574-1095 ConneXie (Dutch Edition for Belgium and Luxembourg) **2317**
1574-1109 Zorgmanagement Tools *changed to* 1876-0171 **1728**
1574-1125 W A A P Book of the Year **303**
1574-1141 Lekker Amsterdam **4393**
1574-115X L A N Magazine **2500**
1574-1176 T V Film **2392**
1574-1184 Journaal Bestuursrecht **4850**
1574-1192 Pervasive and Mobile Computing **2435**
1574-1206 Journaal Insolventie, Financiering en Zekerheden *changed to* Tijdschrift Financiering, Zekerheden en Involventiepraktijk **4882**
1574-1214 International Conference on Grey Literature. Conference Memorandum† **8965**
1574-1230 Information and Communication Technologies and the Knowledge Economy **2544**
1574-1273 Beauty Xpert† **8935**
1574-1281 Digital Movie **2401**
1574-1303 Checklist Financieel *changed to* 1875-9483 **1284**
1574-1311 I S Y P Journal on Science and World Affairs **7241**
1574-132X Jurisprudentie Aansprakelijkheid **4510**
1574-1338 Jurisprudentie Personen- en Familierecht **4912**
1574-1346 SpecialBite **4398**
1574-1370 Henri Frankfort Foundation. Publications†
1574-1389 Damon Boekenmagazine† **8948**
1574-1397 V P B Gids **1954**
1574-1419 Dossier F A Rendement **1287**
1574-1427 Snow **8334**
1574-1435 Primair Onderwijs **2899**
1574-1443 Journal of Inorganic and Organometallic Polymers and Materials **2124**
1574-1451 *see* 1574-1443 **2124**

ISSN

9730 1575-1937 ULRICH'S PERIODICALS

1575-1937 Pasajes. Arquitectura y Critica 452
1575-1996 Juguetes y Juegos de Espana Express 4060
1575-2011 Cruz Roja 8036
1575-2054 Union Europea y de la Competencia. Gaceta Juridica 4801
1575-2224 Tecno Energia 3148
1575-2232 Jardineros 3739
1575-2240 Prosign 7327
1575-2259 Pasajes 7164
1575-2275 Digithum 7959
1575-2437 Anales de Documentacion 4989
1575-2445 Historiar 4143
1575-2453 Hostelmarket Revista 4389
1575-2607 Mi Jardin Extra 3743
1575-2615 Casa y Campo Extra 4535
1575-2623 Guia Prevenir *changed to* 1888-0991 6987
1575-2631 On Off Extra *see* 1575-1686 3110
1575-2712 El Ecologista 3417
1575-2747 HoReCo 4388
1575-2836 Foc Nou 7643
1575-2879 Avances Informativos. Administrativo 4624
1575-2895 Avances Informativos. Penal 4885
1575-3018 Revista de Oncologia *changed to* 1699-048X 6015
1575-3026 Avances Informativos. Civil 4827
1575-3166 Geriatrianet.com 4045
1575-3247 Fundamentos 4848
1575-3298 Spain. Ministerio del Interior. Direccion General de Trafico. Anuario Estadistico de Accidentes 8530
1575-3360 D T - DownTown 6288
1575-3395 Spain. Ministerio del Interior. Direccion General de Trafico. Anuario Estadistico General 8530
1575-3409 Ciencia y Tecnologia Pharmaceutica†
1575-3417 Real Sociedad Espanola de Quimica. Anales 2078
1575-3433 *see* 1575-3247 4848
1575-3565 Cachorros y Mascotas Extra
1575-3638 Electrodomesticos de Alimarket 4357
1575-3646 Alimarket. Comerciales 1804
1575-3654 Hostelmarket. Anuario de la Hosteleria 2004
1575-3662 PuntoMarket 6714
1575-3840 Estudios sobre Patrimonio, Cultura y Ciencias Medievales 4451
1575-3956 Leo Leo. Extra 2199
1575-3964 Editur Latinoamerica 8700
1575-3980 Editur Online 8700
1575-3999 *see* 1575-3964 8700
1575-4014 Libro Electronico Aranzadi. Formularios Aranzadi 4723
1575-4022 Revista de Derecho y Proceso Penal 4897
1575-409X Formacion Continuada en Nutricion y Obesidad *changed to* 1696-6112 6669
1575-4146 Enfermeria en Cardiologia 5958
1575-4227 Quorum 7175
1575-4316 Meridiano Dos Mil†
1575-4367 *see* 0210-1521 1130
1575-443X Annals of Tourism Resarch en Espanol 8683
1575-4677 *see* 0025-7753 5673
1575-4723 Enfermedades Emergentes 5609
1575-474X Manicomic 504
1575-4812 Cuadernos de Derecho y Comercio 4653
1575-4847 Fisioterapia y Calidad de Vida 6109
1575-4995 On Off Guia *see* 1575-1686 3110
1575-5045 Aurora 6906
1575-524X Cepco-Magazine 3262
1575-5266 Analisis Local 7420
1575-5290 *see* 1130-9210 4657
1575-5371 Salud Total de la Mujer† 8986
1575-5460 Qualitative Theory of Dynamical Systems 5527
1575-5479 Viajes National Geographic 8772
1575-5533 Estudios de Fonetica Experimental 5116
1575-5622 Revista de Biomecanica 750
1575-5886 B i D. Textos Universitaris de Biblioteconomia i Documentacio 4993
1575-5940 Diario Juridico Aranzadi 4657
1575-5959 *see* 1132-0257 4609
1575-5967 Cuadernos de Psiquiatria y Psicoterapia del Nino y del Adolescente 6134
1575-605X Rect@ 5528
1575-6068 *see* 1575-5371 8986
1575-6092 Monografias I N I A. Agricola 3697
1575-6106 Monografias I N I A. Forestal 137
1575-6130 Gigatronic 3193
1575-6157 Dentum 5842
1575-6343 Contributions to Science 7848
1575-6386 Anuario de Pedagogia 2826
1575-6440 Central de Balances. Resultados Trimestrales de las Empresas no Financieras 1326
1575-6483 Intersubjetivo 6148
1575-6548 Revista Espanola de Ciencia Politica 7178
1575-6661 A B C Toledo *changed to* 1696-9111 3951
1575-6688 *see* 1139-966X 8005
1575-6793 Ciencia Forense 5912
1575-6823 Araucaria 7948
1575-6866 Logos. Anales del Seminario de Metafisica 6932
1575-7005 Soziologiazko Euskal Koadermoak 8141
1575-7048 Lan Harremanak 1695
1575-7056 Estudios Internacionales de la Complutense 7232
1575-7072 Fuentes 2859
1575-720X Revista Juridica de Estudiantes 4773
1575-734X Alergologia e Inmunologia Clinica 5752
1575-7382 Revista Telematica de Filosofia del Derecho 4773
1575-7447 Construccion Alimarket 994
1575-7641 Debates Constitucionales 4847
1575-7730 Alergologia e Inmunologia Clinica. Extraordinario *see* 1575-734X 5752
1575-8079 Cocina Ligera y Vida Sana 4354
1575-8087 Boletin de Informacion Terapeutica 6826
1575-8133 Relaciones Economicas Internacionales 7262
1575-8141 Prosopopeya 5163
1575-8214 Informe Anual del Sector Agrario en Andalucia 200
1575-8281 ChaletDeco 4535
1575-8362 Derecho y Medio Ambiente† 8949
1575-8400 Superficies 6334
1575-8427 Universidad Autonoma de Madrid. Facultad de Derecho. Anuario 4801
1575-8435 *see* 1575-734X 5752
1575-8443 Perspectivas Bioeticas 7991
1575-8478 Revista de Derecho y Proceso Penal. Monografia 4897
1575-8516 Metas de Enfermeria. Suplemento *see* 1138-7262 5970
1575-8621 Nerter 5339
1575-8834 La Opinion de Tenerife 3953
1575-8842 Faro de Vigo (Deza-Tabeiros Edition) 3952
1575-8923 Revista Juridica del Deporte 4773
1575-9059 Revista Espanola de Historia Militar 6443
1575-9105 Metodologia de las Ciencias del Comportamiento†
1575-9237 Ganar.com 1113
1575-9245 *see* 1575-9237 1113
1575-9377 Mujeremprendedora 8876
1575-9563 L E E M E. Revista Electronica 6584
1575-9687 *see* 1131-9518 3951
1575-9725 *see* 1133-3030 2485
1575-9733 *see* 1133-3030 2485
1575-9776 New Left Review (Spanish Edition) 5230
1575-9784 Plantas en Casa
1576-0154 Agenda de la Empresa Andaluza 1724
1576-0162 Revista de Economia Mundial 1515
1576-0251 *see* 1576-026X 4496
1576-026X Boletin Informativo de la Seguridad Social. Gestion Economica 4496
1576-0316 Puesta al Dia en Urgencias, Emergencias y Catastrofes 6071
1576-0324 Revisiones en Ginecologia y Obstetricia
1576-0332 La Actualidad en Cirugia Oral y Maxilofacial 6235
1576-0359 Archivos de Psiquiatria. Suplementos *see* 1576-0367 6124
1576-0367 Archivos de Psiquiatria 6124
1576-0421 Casas de Siempre
1576-0464 Filomusica 6567
1576-0529 Cuadernos de Gobierno y Administracion 7432
1576-0545 Revista Espanola de Ecografia Digestiva 5930
1576-0588 Ars et Sapientia 4443
1576-0642 Transporte y Logistica Terrestre 8517
1576-0650 Medio Ambiente Canarias 3452
1576-0839 Gastroenterologia Integrada 5924
1576-0952 Revista de Fitoterapia 6879
1576-1118 C I C. Centro Informativo de la Construction 989
1576-1126 La Rioja. Boletin Oficial 4775
1576-1185 Revista de Neurologia Clinica 6182
1576-1266 La Situacion en el Mundo 1517
1576-141X Fisioterapia Actual 6109
1576-1444 Ban y Coc† 8934
1576-1452 Pinker Moda 8456
1576-1487 Guia Puntex. Anuario Espanol de Analitica 5945
1576-1495 Barbie 2178
1576-1509 Guia Puntex. Anuario Dental Espanol 5846
1576-1533 Guia Puntex. Anuario Espanol de E F P y Parafarmacia 6845
1576-1584 Guia Puntex. Anuario Espanol de Enfermeria 5959
1576-1622 Guia Puntex. Anuario Espanol de Ortopedia y Gerontologia 6061
1576-1649 Guia Puntex. Anuario Espanol de Podologia 6061
1576-1657 Guia Puntex. Anuario Espanol de Protesis Dental 5846
1576-169X Revista de Justicia Laboral 1705
1576-1746 CodeXXI 6557
1576-1789 Universidad Europea de Madrid. Boletin Juridico 4802
1576-1908 R J D Jurisprudencia 4765
1576-1959 Prevencion del Tabaquismo 6217
1576-1967 *see* 0304-5412 5674
1576-2025 Cirugest Archivos de Cirugia General y Digestiva 6239
1576-2033 R C E. Revista de Contratacion Electronica 4764
1576-2521 Ideas y Trabajos Odontoestomatologicos 5847
1576-2564 Gerion. Anejos 4140
1576-2610 Fuera de Serie *see* 1576-3323 1108
1576-2807 Brico 4533
1576-2890 *see* 0214-7092 423
1576-2912 *see* 0210-5810 7947
1576-2947 Cooperacion Espanola 1593
1576-3013 Anuario Espanol de Mantenimiento y Limpieza 2242
1576-3048 La Mirada 3952
1576-3056 Hygia de Enfermeria 5961
1576-3080 Medicina Naturista 5806
1576-3110 *see* Anuario Espanol de la Seguridad 2676
1576-3196 Medio Ambiente & Derecho 3452
1576-3234 Guia Puntex. Anuario Espanol de Optica y Audioprotesis 5621
1576-3323 Expansion de la Actualidad Economica Diaria 1108
1576-3358 Brico. Bricolage y Decoracion. Extra 4533
1576-3366 Pe.i 4756
1576-351X Esteticistas, Federacion Nacional 594
1576-3633 La Poesia, Senor Hidalgo 5430
1576-3749 *see* 1134-6582 3953
1576-3757 El Pais Digital *see* 1134-6582 3953
1576-3765 El Pais (Barcelona Edition) 3953
1576-3986 *see* 1139-1847 3951
1576-3994 *see* 1576-3765 3953
1576-4044 Dezeme 4137
1576-4079 Linux Magazine 2508
1576-4087 Archaia 378
1576-4133 Revista de Informacion Fiscal 4771
1576-4141 Informacion Fiscal *changed to* 1576-4133 4771
1576-4168 Faro del Silencio 4074
1576-4184 Res Publica 6947
1576-4214 Revista Espanola de Motivacion y Emocion 7404
1576-429X Bike a Fondo 8255
1576-4400 Arian 8159
1576-4435 *see* 1576-4885 1821
1576-4494 Alea 6903
1576-4729 Historia Constitucional 4849
1576-4737 Circulo de Linguistica Aplicada a la Comunicacion 5106
1576-4745 Revista Espanola de Sistemas† 8985
1576-4826 Conecta 7848
1576-4869 Spain. Ministerio de Agricultura Pesca y Alimentacion. Secretaria General Tecnica. Anuario de Estadistica Agroalimentaria 186
1576-4885 Interactiva 1821
1576-4982 Senda Senior 5082
1576-4990 Interactive Educational Multimedia 3065
1576-5032 Temas Tributarios de Actualidad Fiscal 1951
1576-5059 E L I A 5113
1576-5113 Mania 6933
1576-5148 Psicologia Practica 7393
1576-5172 Geotemas 2744
1576-5199 Educacion y Futuro 2846
1576-5237 Informe del Consejo de Seguridad Nuclear al Congreso de los Diputados y al Senado 3168
1576-5385 Revista Electronica de Informatica en Terapia Ocupacional 6115
1576-5490 Silueta de Mujer 8848
1576-5520 Enfermeria Oncologica 5958
1576-5547 Caracola. Extra *see* 0214-2872 2181
1576-558X Revista de Derecho Maritimo 4971
1576-5873 Punto de Cruz 6641
1576-5954 Capsa 2232
1576-5962 Revista de Psicologia del Trabajo y de las Organizaciones 7404
1576-6063 Distribucion Actualidad 1814
1576-6136 Nox 6296
1576-625X La Fertilidad de la Tierra 113
1576-6357 Journal of English Studies 5133
1576-6411 Suplementos de Revista de Neurologia *see* 0210-0010 6182
1576-6462 Medio Ambiente y Comportamiento Humano 7384
1576-6500 Papeles del Este 7163
1576-6543 Vivir Feliz
1576-6578 *see* 0210-0010 6182
1576-6888 El Mundo del Siglo Veintiuno, El Dia de Baleares 3953
1576-6969 elmundo.es *see* 1134-4261 3953
1576-6977 El Mundo Andalucia 3953
1576-7000 Guia del Marketing 1818
1576-7108 Estudios de Construccion y Transportes 8495
1576-7124 R E D I 4765
1576-7132 *see* 1134-6582 3953
1576-7167 Cosas de Casa 4355
1576-7280 La Pluma y el Tiempo 5352
1576-7329 Revista Internacional de Psicologia Clinica y de la Salud *changed to* 1697-2600 7364
1576-7418 Estudios de Sociolinguistica *changed to* 1750-8649 5175
1576-754X Terra Incognita 5241
1576-7566 Seshat 416
1576-771X Playboy (Spain) 6298
1576-7787 Sociedad Espanola de Italianistas. Revista 4475
1576-7868 *see* 1133-0422 524
1576-7914 Cuadernos Dieciochistas 4448
1576-7930 REDMarket 2566
1576-7965 European Journal of Obstetrics and Gynecology and Reproductive Biology (Spanish Edition) 5990
1576-8074 *see* 1134-816X 3626
1576-8082 C G A C. Revista 480
1576-8252 Consultorio Inmobiliario 4901
1576-8260 *see* 0004-0614 6265
1576-8341 Habitania 4541
1576-8384 *see* 1576-1126 4775
1576-8511 Destino Cuba 8698
1576-852X *see* 1134-5160 5960
1576-8570 *see* 1134-5160 5960
1576-8589 Tectonica (English Edition) *see* 1136-0062 1039
1576-8597 *see* 0211-2159 7393
1576-8929 Saber Vivir 8882
1576-8937 Cocina Ligera Especial *changed to* 1697-5111 4354
1576-8945 Embarazo Sano Extra 5989
1576-8953 Extra Cuerpo de Mujer
1576-9127 O.R.L. Aragon 6083
1576-9216 Tenzone 5386
1576-933X Resenas Malacologicas 815
1576-9372 Suhayl 7921
1576-9380 Revista de Urbanismo y Edificacion 4425
1576-9402 Applied General Topology 5472
1576-9445 B M J (Spanish Edition)†
1576-9496 Anales de Derecho 4615
1576-950X *see* 0214-0896 669
1576-9518 Revista de Aracnologia 961
1576-9526 Sociedad Entomologica Aragonesa. Manuales and Tesis 859
1576-9550 Societat Paleontologica d'Elx. Seccion Vertebrados Actuales. Revista 6730
1576-9712 Estudios, Informes y Dictamenes 4668
1576-9720 Barbastella 935
1576-9763 Revista de Derecho Penal 4897
1576-9798 *see* 0210-2145 1006
1576-9879 Europea de Derecho. Avance Normativo 4950
1576-9887 Vacunas 5766
1576-9968 Revista de Urbanismo y Edificacion. Monografia *see* 1576-9380 4425
1577-0079 Revista de Estudios Orteguianos 6948
1577-0265 D P A 439
1577-0338 Pulso 2901
1577-0346 *see* 1577-0567 6910
1577-0354 Revista Internacional de Medicina y Ciencias de la Actividad Fisica y del Deporte 6232
1577-0451 Fundacion Puigvert. Boletin Informativo 5617
1577-0567 La Caverna de Platon 6910
1577-0664 El Correo Digital 3951
1577-0834 Tandem 6998
1577-094X Bergueda Setmana *see* 1137-5655 3953
1577-1156 *see* 0213-6562 4883
1577-1261 Debate y Perspectivas 7849
1577-1342 Directorio de Unidades de Actividad Economica de la Comunidad de Madrid† 8950
1577-1350 The Region of Madrid in Figures 8396
1577-1369 Contabilidad Regional de la Comunidad de Madrid 1448
1577-1377 Los Transportes y los Servicios Postales 8517
1577-1385 Actualizaciones en Dolor†
1577-161X Communidad de Madrid Datos Basicos 8364
1577-1628 Region of Madrid Data Guide 8396
1577-1687 Bases de Datos C S I C 7839

1577-1806 Universidad Autonoma de Madrid. Coleccion de Estudios **2922**
1577-1865 Agencia d'Avaluacio de Tecnologia i Recerca Mediques. Informatiu **5570**
1577-208X *see* 1139-2819 **4959**
1577-239X R I P S. Revista de Investigaciones Politicas y Sociologicas **7175**
1577-242X S E M A P. Revista **5980**
1577-2721 Exit, Imagen y Cultura **488**
1577-2802 Asociacion Primatologica Espanola. Boletin **934**
1577-2845 Merida Ciudad y Patrimonio **4153**
1577-3167 Monografias I N I A. Ganadera **293**
1577-3256 Migraciones y Exilios **7287**
1577-3272 *see* 0210-5233 **8129**
1577-3388 Iberoamericana America Latina - Espana - Portugal **5220**
1577-3396 Revista Medica **5705**
1577-3434 Ex Libris **5422**
1577-3558 Gestion y Evaluacion de Costos Sanitarios **3506**
1577-3566 Asociacion Espanola de Reumatologia. Seminarios **6222**
1577-3698 *see* 1579-2242 **5799**
1577-3698 *see* 0300-8932 **5799**
1577-3760 Textos de la CiberSociedad **2439**
1577-3787 Hibris **7562**
1577-4015 Apunts. Educacion Fisica y Deportes **8158**
1577-4163 Revista Valenciana de Economia y Hacienda **1380**
1577-4260 Optronica *see* 0300-3787 **3109**
1577-4368 Cronica de Albacete **3951**
1577-4430 Revista Juridica de Economia Publica, Social y Cooperativa **4773**
1577-4511 Avances Informativos. Mercantil **4624**
1577-4589 Spain. Ministerio de Fomento. Revista (Madrid, 2001) **3467**
1577-4643 *see* 1577-2802 **934**
1577-4929 *see* 1577-4589 **3467**
1577-5003 Troianalexandrina **5390**
1577-5097 E L C V I A **2417**
1577-5119 Huerta de San Vicente. Cuadernos **5307**
1577-533X Cursos de Derecho Internacional y Relaciones Internacionales de Vitoria-Gasteiz **4922**
1577-5380 Anuario Social de Espana **7296**
1577-5399 *see* 1577-5380 **7296**
1577-5593 Collegi Oficial de Metges de la Provincia de Girona. Butlleti de Illustre **5599**
1577-5615 Aula de Infantil **2828**
1577-5623 Guix d'Infantil *see* 1577-5615 **2828**
1577-5739 Propiedad Horizontal *changed to* 1886-9033 **7612**
1577-578X *see* 0105-4538 **5753**
1577-5984 Revista de Filologia Romanica. Anejos **5167**
1577-631X Mini Auto **4340**
1577-6395 El Ebro **8099**
1577-6700 Espana Desconocida **8701**
1577-6719 R C Model *changed to* 1578-4630 **4344**
1577-6719 R C Model *changed to* 1578-4649 **4344**
1577-6883 Mundo Linux **2432**
1577-6921 Tonos Digital **5389**
1577-693X *see* 1132-2063 **4339**
1577-7057 Revista Internacional de Psicologia y Terapia Psicologica **7404**
1577-7103 Carta Tributaria. Al Dia **1916**
1577-7189 Nuevo Estilo. Ambientes Vivos y Personales **4561**
1577-7200 Frenia **6142**
1577-7243 *see* 1133-9934 **7296**
1577-7804 Nueva Empresa.com **1155**
1577-7898 Hot English Magazine **5125**
1577-7928 Guia Practica de Seguridad Social **8043**
1577-8029 Industria & Diseno **496**
1577-8037 Grafica y Diseno **491**
1577-8045 Medio Ambiente. Castilla y Leon **3452**
1577-8223 D M D. Documentacion en Medicina del Deporte *changed to* 1888-7546 **6232**
1577-8517 The International Journal of Digital Accounting Research **1292**
1577-8533 Osasunaz **5691**
1577-855X Cuentas de las Administraciones Publicas de Madrid† **8947**
1577-8576 *see* Asociacion Nacional de Porcinocultura Cientifica (A N A P O R C). Revista **279**
1577-8681 *see* 0212-033X **7469**
1577-872X Donde Exportar†
1577-8819 Papers de la Catedra UNESCO **7991**
1577-9068 Dietas **6657**
1577-9076 Cocina con Truco **4354**
1577-9084 El Mundo de los Astros **566**
1577-9297 Quaderns de la Mediterrania **352**
1577-9378 International Nursing Review en Espanol *see* 0020-8132 **5962**
1577-9424 Gogoa **6922**
1577-9572 Revista de Salud Ambiental **7539**
1577-9858 *see* Construinter **999**
1578-0007 Aracne **4036**
1578-0023 Chest (Spanish Edition) *see* 1970-4917 **6212**
1578-0023 Chest (Spanish Edition) *see* 0012-3692 **6212**
1578-0201 Conarquitectura **438**
1578-0236 Portularia **8062**
1578-0619 Alcazar de Sevilla. Apuntes **372**
1578-0678 Informativo Ensenanza Andaluza **2866**
1578-0716 Pedologia Clinica **6071**
1578-0732 Economia Agraria y Recursos Naturales **106**
1578-0740 Matronas Profesion **5998**
1578-0872 *see* 1137-5868 **1708**
1578-0910 Acto **464**
1578-102X Timely Topics in Medicine. Enfermedades Cardiovasculares **5800**
1578-1194 Comunicaciones Hoy **2317**
1578-1224 Tecno Roca **1039**
1578-1232 Actual Bebe **2142**
1578-1259 Acta Dental Internacional **5833**
1578-1267 *see* 0301-0546 **5753**
1578-1275 *see* 0212-6567 **5580**
1578-1283 *see* 0213-9111 **7518**
1578-1291 *see* 1130-2399 **5958**
1578-1305 'Ilu. Anejos **7649**
1578-1410 Okapi **2205**
1578-1453 *see* 0304-5013 **6002**
1578-147X *see* 0009-739X **6239**
1578-1518 Aquila Legionis **4130**
1578-1542 *see* 0034-947X **6103**
1578-1550 Gastroenterologia y Hepatologia Continuada **5924**
1578-1569 *see* 0212-047X **6865**
1578-1615 *see* 1576-0839 **5924**
1578-1631 *see* 0210-1637 **5860**
1578-164X *see* 1134-928X **4046**
1578-1666 Sociedad Andaluza de Entomologia. Boletin **859**
1578-1674 *see* 1136-1956 **5931**
1578-1712 *see* 0214-4603 **6084**
1578-1747 *see* 0211-139X **4054**
1578-1755 J A M A. Journal of the American Medical Association (Spanish Edition)†
1578-1763 Eslavistica Complutense **5115**
1578-178X *see* 0033-8338 **6206**
1578-1844 *see* 1132-8460 **5807**
1578-1852 *see* 0213-005X **5813**
1578-1860 *see* 0014-2565 **5704**
1578-1879 *see* 0214-9168 **5782**
1578-1941 *see* 1138-6045 **6115**
1578-1968 *see* 0213-4853 **6165**
1578-1992 Legislacion Laboral y de Seguridad Social **1695**
1578-200X *see* 0212-6982 **6207**
1578-2034 Drug R & D Backgrounders **6836**
1578-2050 *see* 1578-2069 **5959**
1578-2069 Fisioterapia. Monografico **5959**
1578-2107 *see* 0211-5638 **5959**
1578-214X Creatividad y Sociedad (Print) *changed to* 1887-7370 **7956**
1578-2158 *see* 0214-8919 **4094**
1578-2190 *see* 0001-7310 **5871**
1578-2425 Construccion Alimarket. Informe Anual. Distribucion de Materiales **994**
1578-2433 Campo de Agramante **5270**
1578-2492 *see* 1130-9229 **4658**
1578-2506 S.I.D.A. *see* 1130-1597 **5826**
1578-2549 *see* 1138-9672 **6673**
1578-2603 Antropo **328**
1578-262X Trastornos Adictivos. Monografico **2700**
1578-2638 *see* 1575-0973 **2700**
1578-2646 *see* 1578-262X **2700**
1578-2700 Revista Latina de Cardiologia† **8985**
1578-2719 *see* 1578-2700 **8985**
1578-2735 *see* 1139-9287 **6119**
1578-2824 Revista Espanola de Sociologia **8129**
1578-3081 Today I Love English **5187**
1578-3103 Agathos **7506**
1578-3138 Anuario Espanol de Derecho Internacional Privado **4917**
1578-3154 Djovenes del Siglo XXI **2842**
1578-3162 Anuario de Justicia Alternativa: Derecho Arbitral **4619**
1578-3278 *see* 0048-7120 **6115**
1578-3456 Empresa Global **1741**
1578-3499 Muy Extra **3953**
1578-3502 *see* 1578-3499 **3953**
1578-3642 Anuario Bibliografico Cervantino **5406**
1578-3804 Societas & Lex† **8989**
1578-3820 Odisea **5157**
1578-3855 El Cuaderno de los Padres **4355**
1578-410X Instituto Espanol de Oceanografia. Tesis Doctorales **2807**
1578-4118 *see* 1135-6405 **2840**
1578-4126 *see* 0210-3702 **2866**
1578-4282 Revista de Antropologia Experimental **353**
1578-4312 Letras Libres **5321**
1578-4398 El Valor de la Palabra **5244**
1578-4460 Estudios Economicos Regionales y Sectoriales **1484**
1578-4479 Estudios Economicos de Desarrollo International **1484**
1578-4487 Applied Econometrics and International Development **7106**
1578-4517 MHNH **566**
1578-4541 AquaTIC **3586**
1578-4576 Foro Interno **7964**
1578-4630 R C Model Auto **4344**
1578-4649 R C Model Aero **4344**
1578-4789 *see* 1139-6407 **8364**
1578-486X Skribuak **2913**
1578-4878 Infanciaenur-ro-pa (Spanish Edition) **2866**
1578-4886 Infanciaaeu-ro-pa (Catalan Edition) *see* 1578-4878 **2866**
1578-4967 Control **23**
1578-5130 Litterae **4463**
1578-5157 Geofocus **4008**
1578-5211 Revista Manresa *see* 1137-5655 **3953**
1578-522X Negocis *see* 1137-5655 **3953**
1578-5297 Revista Catalana de Musicologia **6611**
1578-5319 Salud y Drogas **2698**
1578-5386 Palaeohispanica **4252**
1578-5483 Constructiva **438**
1578-5564 *see* 1139-5680 **5212**
1578-5637 Xeografica **4034**
1578-5769 Detail (Spanish Edition) **440**
1578-5777 T S T. Transportes, Servicios y Telecomunicaciones **8512**
1578-5874 Community of Madrid in Figures *changed to* 1577-1350 **8396**
1578-598X Evidence - Based Medicine (Ed. Espanola) **5612**
1578-5998 Fabrikart **489**
1578-6072 Anuario de Investigacion en Literatura Infantil y Juvenil **5255**
1578-6099 Matematicas en Breve **5510**
1578-6153 Tecnologia del Vino *changed to* 1887-2794 **611**
1578-6420 Revista Juridica de la Comunidad Valenciana **4773**
1578-6579 Dialogo Mediterraneo **1561**
1578-6587 *see* 1578-6579 **1561**
1578-665X Animal Biodiversity and Conservation **932**
1578-6676 Estudios Nietzsche **6917**
1578-6730 Nomadas **8123**
1578-6749 *see* 0210-5691 **5673**
1578-6846 Yerba *see* 0362-630X **5073**
1578-696X Produccion Profesional **2388**
1578-7001 Estudios Sobre Educacion **2854**
1578-701X La Brujula de Papel **2833**
1578-7044 International Journal of English Studies **5129**
1578-7168 Ager **1435**
1578-7206 Arte Heladero **261**
1578-7214 Saber y Sabor **4398**
1578-7265 Papeles Salmantinos de Educacion **2895**
1578-7303 Real Academia de Ciencias Exactas, Fisicas y Naturales. Revista. Serie A, Matematicas **7902**
1578-746X *see* 1578-7478 **3953**
1578-7478 El Periodico de Catalunya **3953**
1578-7486 Revista de Estudios Latinos **5167**
1578-7559 Revista Tradumatica **5168**
1578-7567 B y N Dominical†
1578-7575 *see* 1578-1550 **5924**
1578-7680 Revista de la Educacion a Distancia **2906**
1578-7729 Fomento de la Produccion. Espana 30000 **1886**
1578-8008 *see* 1135-9846 **7296**
1578-8393 Area Abierta **1805**
1578-8423 Cuadernos de Psicologia del Deporte **7350**
1578-858X Salud Publica y Educacion para la Salud† **8986**
1578-8601 Conductas Adictivas **6830**
1578-861X Equinus **286**
1578-8768 Revista de Climatologia **6394**
1578-8822 *see* 0304-5412 **5674**
1578-8830 *see* 0213-9251 **5881**
1578-8865 *see* 1138-3593 **5708**
1578-8946 Athenea Digital **7949**
1578-8962 *see* 1134-5934 **6175**
1578-8989 *see* 0025-7753 **5673**
1578-9047 Descubrir el Arte **485**
1578-9098 *see* 0210-220X **5643**
1578-9349 *see* 0210-573X **5988**
1578-942X Anuario Estadistico de la Banca en Espana **1308**
1578-9438 Estudios Filologicos Alemanes **5116**
1578-9519 *see* 0210-5705 **5924**
1578-9543 *see* 0213-9324 **6841**
1578-956X Actualidad Juridica Uria & Menendez **4609**
1578-9594 Cuadernos de Psiquiatria Comunitaria **6134**
1578-9705 *see* 1695-9752 **4199**
1578-9853 Revista de Filoloxia Asturiana **5167**
1578-9926 Resena† **8985**
1578-9969 Convertronic **3186**
1579-0185 Redes **7995**
1579-0207 EduPsykhe **2852**
1579-0266 Poblacion de los Municipios Espanoles **7314**
1579-0363 Genomics - Based Drug Data Report Regenerative Therapy **871**
1579-0452 Union Europea Aranzadi **4801**
1579-0622 Clinica y Pensamiento *changed to* 1888-279X **7408**
1579-0681 Heteropterus **848**
1579-0789 Timely Topics in Medicine. Cardiovascular Diseases **5800**
1579-1475 Economic Analysis Working Papers **1479**
1579-1513 Revista Electronica de Ensenanza de las Ciencias **2906**
1579-1610 *see* 1579-0363 **871**
1579-1726 Retos **8196**
1579-1734 Higiene y Sanidad Ambiental **7524**
1579-1750 Anuario de Derecho Europeo **4917**
1579-1785 Estadisticas del Movimiento Natural de la Poblacion de la Comunidad de Madrid. Nacimientos, Matrimonios, Defunciones, Mortalidad Segun Causas Multiples *changed to* 1696-0432 **8954**
1579-1785 Estadisticas del Movimiento Natural de Poblacion de la Comunidad de Madrid. Nacimientos, Matrimonios, Defunciones, Mortalidad Segun Causas Multiplas *changed to* 1696-0459 **7306**
1579-1785 Estadisticas del Movimiento Natural de Poblacion de la Comunidad de Madrid. Nacimientos, Matrimonios, Defunciones, Mortalidad Segun Causas Multiplas *changed to* 1696-0440 **8954**
1579-1785 Estadisticas del Movimiento Natural de Poblacion de la Comunidad de Madrid. Nacimientos, Matrimonios, Defunciones, Mortalidad Segun Causas Multiples *changed to* 1696-0467 **8954**
1579-1793 Drug Data Report **6833**
1579-1807 *see* 1053-0894 **5807**
1579-1920 Oncologia. Suplemento *see* 0378-4835
1579-1971 Revista de Oncologia. Suplemento *see* 1699-048X **6015**
1579-2013 *see* 1130-8621 **5958**
1579-2021 *see* 1575-0922 **5891**
1579-203X Motociclismo **8262**
1579-2048 Soldados y Estrategia **4347**
1579-2072 Grupo I C O. Memoria **1927**
1579-2080 American Academy of Orthopaedic Surgeons. Journal (Spanish Edition) **6055**
1579-2099 *see* 1575-1813 **5608**
1579-2102 Instituto de Credito Oficial. Annual Report **1929**
1579-2129 *see* 0300-2896 **6211**
1579-2242 Revista Espanola de Cardiologia (Online) **5799**
1579-2250 *see* 1131-3587 **5799**
1579-2277 I N E. Cifras **8377**
1579-234X Trofeo Todo Caballo **8299**
1579-2390 Neumaticos & Mecanica Rapida **8595**
1579-2404 Recambios & Accesorios **8600**
1579-248X Defunciones Segun la Causa de Muerte (Optical Disk Edition)†
1579-2528 *see* 1351-5101 **6139**
1579-2617 Ensenanza de las Ciencias Sociales **7961**
1579-2641 Materia (Barcelona) **504**
1579-2722 *see* 0066-5177 **8379**
1579-2803 *see* 1695-7229 **7150**
1579-282X Nayade **4466**
1579-3036 Contratacion Administrativa Practica **4862**
1579-3044 *see* 1579-3036 **4862**
1579-3133 Indivisa Revista **2866**

ISSN

1586-4944 Men's Fitness 6284
1586-5223 see 1585-7379 8848
1586-5339 Beau Monde 8853
1586-5355 see 1215-1068 3876
1586-5363 Argus 2511
1586-5584 see 1419-2489 6287
1586-5908 Mai Ez a Divat 2258
1586-6513 Nograd Megyei Hirlap Gratisz see 1215-9042 3876
1586-7811 Praehistoria 4156
1586-7897 see 1586-4197 7115
1586-8591 Reumainfo changed to 1789-6894 5666
1586-8850 Mathematical Notes changed to 1787-2405 5518
1586-894X Magyar Gyomkutatas es Technologia 241
1586-9016 see 1416-8650 3876
1586-9024 see 1215-9042 3876
1586-9032 see 0133-235X 3877
1586-9040 see 0865-9125 3877
1586-9059 see 0865-915X 3877
1586-930X Fragmenta Paleontologica Hungarica 6724
1586-9733 Southeast European Politics Online†
1586-9792 see 1216-8890 477
1587-0596 Burda Finomsagok changed to 1785-184X 4357
1587-1037 see 1217-8977 2776
1587-1320 see 0133-0950 3877
1587-1444 see 1585-7972 4438
1587-1606 O E C D Kornyezeti Adattar see 1015-0293 3457
1587-1878 Figyelo Trend 1109
1587-1908 Natura Somogyiensis 692
1587-2025 Blikk 3876
1587-2084 Ara 8851
1587-2238 Burda Viragoskert 3726
1587-2378 Tirana In Your Pocket 8761
1587-2440 see 0374-0676 575
1587-3145 Terefere 8885
1587-3552 see 1217-0771 3876
1587-3765 see 0324-5853 3252
1587-379X see 0324-6051 3392
1587-4168 Tema 3666
1587-4206 Tele Szuper changed to 1785-6744 2375
1587-4621 Intelligens Epuelet 1015
1587-4648 Gepgyartas 5452
1587-5598 Burda Special. Boldog Karacsonyt 2252
1587-5601 Burda Gyerekdivat 2252
1587-6578 see 0374-0676 575
1587-8600 W.I.T.C.H. 2220
1587-9089 Kulugyi Szemle 7250
1588-0230 see 0133-5596 5779
1588-0265 see 0237-7837 2414
1588-0540 see 0015-3257 7013
1588-0672 see 0324-7627 4230
1588-0818 see 1215-5233 2872
1588-0974 see 0039-8071 6758
1588-1318 see 0238-2865 5294
1588-1415 see 0027-5336 6597
1588-2039 Chronica 4210
1588-2519 see 1585-1923 5089
1588-2527 see 0238-0161 78
1588-2535 see 0139-3006 3625
1588-2543 see 0044-5975 2229
1588-2551 see 0001-5210 370
1588-256X see 0236-5383 649
1588-2578 see 0236-6495 772
1588-2586 see 1216-9803 322
1588-2608 see 0001-5830 463
1588-2616 see 1216-2574 4609
1588-2624 see 1216-8076 5090
1588-2632 see 0236-5294 5464
1588-2640 see 1217-8950 880
1588-2659 see 0001-6373 1056
1588-2667 see 0001-6446 541
1588-2683 see 0231-424X 918
1588-2691 see 0238-1249 773
1588-2705 see 0236-6290 8790
1588-2713 see 0002-1873 87
1588-2721 see 0865-9303 3016
1588-273X see 0133-3852 5470
1588-2748 see 0003-567X 2230
1588-2756 see 1585-8553 784
1588-2764 see 0013-9661 1007
1588-2772 see 0236-6568 4456
1588-2780 see 0236-5731 2102
1588-2799 see 0025-0279 7384
1588-2802 see 0027-5247 507
1588-2810 see 0324-4652 5339
1588-2829 see 0031-5303 5524
1588-2837 see 0133-1736 2140
1588-2861 see 0138-9130 7913
1588-2888 see 1788-6244 6620
1588-2896 see 0081-6906 5538
1588-290X see 0039-3363 5181
1588-2918 see 0231-2522 8143
1588-3264 see 1419-0109 3877
1588-3280 Magyar Immunologia 5763
1588-3531 Wellness 8848
1588-385X Acta Biologica Szegediensis 649
1588-3884 Kreativ Intern changed to 1785-8100 1821
1588-4082 see 1588-385X 649
1588-418X Best 8853
1588-5518 Praktika 8880
1588-5909 Uzlet & Siker 1190
1588-6735 European Integration Studies 7963
1588-7154 Libri Historiae Medicae 5661
1588-7235 Kozlekedesi Ertesito 1142
1588-7855 Foreign Policy Review see 1587-9089 7250
1588-9025 Business Studies 1076
1588-970X see 1588-9726 1176
1588-9726 Society and Economy 1176
1588-9734 Tarsadalom es Gazdasag† 8992
1589-0309 Gyermekorvos Tovabbkepzes 6092
1589-1410 Food Service changed to 1589-6382 3642
1589-1623 Applied Ecology and Environmental Research 3403
1589-3014 13 2224
1589-3383 Jegyzo es Koezigazgatas 4698
1589-3464 I T - Business 1417
1589-3596 Fejlesztes es Finanszirozas see 1589-3820 1335
1589-3669 National Geographic Magyarorszag 4021
1589-3820 Development and Finance 1335
1589-4592 Hercegnok 2192
1589-486X see 0003-8032 375
1589-5254 Journal of Cultural and Evolutionary Psychology changed to 1789-2082 7373
1589-5297 see 1215-6043 6493
1589-6382 Food Service Trend 3642
1589-6560 Formula changed to 1785-9484 8160
1589-7397 see 1789-2082 7373
1589-780X Elelmiszer-biztonsag 3634
1589-9284 Kepes Sport 8184
1589-9535 Acta Physica Hungarica. B. Quantum Electronics changed to 1434-6001 7065
1589-9802 Nok Lapja Konyha Plusz 8878
1590-0088 Guida Pratica del Lavoro 1684
1590-0223 Contrappunti 6133
1590-0266 L'Esperto Risponde† 8954
1590-0282 Guida al Diritto 4683
1590-0304 Guida Normativa 1115
1590-069X Politiche Sanitarie 7535
1590-0908 Nuovo Totoguida Sport 8191
1590-0916 Totoguida Scommesse 8212
1590-0924 Totoguida Super Lotto 8212
1590-0932 see 1123-2536 5521
1590-1009 Office Journal changed to Office Magazine 2595
1590-1157 Annuario Sanita Italia 7507
1590-1254 Ambiente e Sviluppo (Milan)† 8929
1590-1262 see 1124-4909 6137
1590-1505 Kosmetica 595
1590-1602 L'Opinione (Rome, 1949)†
1590-1653 Totoguida Super Lotto Mese see 1590-0924 8212
1590-1726 Panificazione e Pasticceria 3659
1590-1785 Azienditalia Finanza e Tributi 1911
1590-1807 Snippets 5175
1590-1831 Palomar 4468
1590-1874 Neurological Sciences 6165
1590-301X Le Riviste Database 634
1590-3044 D V D Magazine
1590-3052 Arte Musica Spettacolo 5257
1590-3206 Scuola dell'Infanzia 2910
1590-3478 see 1590-1874 6165
1590-3575 Men's Health 6284
1590-3583 La Pesca Mosca e Spinning 8328
1590-3605 Chip 2410
1590-3699 Farmacia News 6841
1590-3729 see 0939-4753 6666
1590-3796 Supplementi all'Italian Heart Journal see 1827-6806 5787
1590-3907 Journal of Mountain Ecology 3448
1590-413X Cavallo Magazine 319
1590-4261 Annals of Microbiology 722
1590-4601 Sette e Religioni 7681
1590-4733 Comuni in Rete† 8943
1590-492X Encyclopaideia 2853
1590-4970 Il Nuovo Leopardi†
1590-5128 Mercato Concorrenza Regole 1148
1590-5268 Zjarri 3573
1590-5705 Bollettino di Microbiologia ed Indagini di Laboratorio News 882
1590-5837 Studi sulla Questione Criminale 2669
1590-5896 Nexus Network Journal 451
1590-5942 Aspenia 5207
1590-6353 Lucina 5997
1590-6388 Museo Regionale di Scienze Naturali Torino. Guide 7884
1590-6515 Italian Food and Beverage Technology 3649
1590-6647 Scienza della Riabilitazione 6116
1590-6663 Giudice di Pace Oggi 4831
1590-6833 Hermeneutica 7647
1590-685X Il Filugello†
1590-6876 Rivista dell'Esecuzione Forzata 4776
1590-6957 Ragionamenti sui Fatti e le Immagini della Storia
1590-7031 La Societa degli Individui 4475
1590-7058 Il Progetto (Rome, 1998) 454
1590-7090 Pesaro Citta e Conta 4253
1590-7120 International Journal of Clinical Investigation 5638
1590-7198 Journal of Agriculture and Environment for International Development 126
1590-7341 L'Umanita†
1590-7430 Analecta Orientalia 542
1590-7449 Orientalia Christiana Analecta 558
1590-749X Rassegna Tributaria 1941
1590-7651 L'Energia Elettrica 3307
1590-7716 Lo Scarpone 8332
1590-7880 Coaching & Sport Science Journal 8167
1590-7929 Nuova Rivista di Letteratura Italiana 5344
1590-7953 Rivista Italiana di Letteratura Comparata† 8986
1590-8011 Bollettino Archivio Pace Diritti Umani see 0394-7440 7213
1590-8100 Corriere Tributario 1087
1590-8399 Museo Civico di Storia Naturale di Verona. Bollettino. Botanica Zoologia 802
1590-8402 Museo Civico di Storia Naturale di Verona. Bollettino. Geologia Paleontologia Preistoria 2756
1590-8410 Magic Patch 6640
1590-8461 Evo 8579
1590-8577 Journal of the Pancreas 5928
1590-864X La Comunicazione 2317
1590-8658 Digestive and Liver Disease 5922
1590-8909 Foro e Cassazione Civile see 0015-783X 4677
1590-900X Corriere della Pesca e dell'Acquacoltura† 8944
1590-9018 Iniziativa Pesca†
1590-9093 Istituto Universitario Navale. Facolta di Scienze Nautiche, Naples. Annali changed to Universita degli Studi di Napoli Parthenope. Facolta di Scienze e Tecnologie. Annali 7926
1590-9107 Istituto Universitario Navale. Facolta di Economia Marittima, Napoli. Annali†
1590-9131 Almanacco Navale 8638
1590-9158 PharmacoEconomics. Italian Research Articles see 1170-7690 6871
1590-9212 Gazzetta Giuridica Giuffre. Italia Oggi†
1590-9247 Diritto e Giustizia (Print)†
1590-9255 Diritto e Giustizi@ 4659
1590-9271 Internal Medicine. Clinical and Laboratory 5946
1590-9514 Barche
1590-9522 Natura Nascosta 2713
1590-959X Magnesium Industry
1590-9603 Aluminium Extrusion
1590-9611 Il Giornale del Serramentista e delle Costruzioni in Alluminio† 8959
1590-9638 E F F 5070
1590-9921 Journal of Orthopaedics and Traumatology 6065
1590-9999 see 1590-9921 6065
1591-0067 PROtech 5862
1591-0075 Area Pediatrica 6088
1591-0083 Facts, News & Views 6140
1591-0237 Come Fare† 8942
1591-0261 Molossi 6811
1591-0288 Coupe & Cabrio† 8946
1591-0318 Software World 2598
1591-0326 Quale Computer 2582
1591-0342 Societa Storica Valtellinese. Bollettino 4161
1591-0458 Fuoricasa 3730
1591-0598 Pol.it Psychiatry Online Italia 6174
1591-0628 Amici di Casa 6803
1591-0660 Filosofia e Questioni Pubbliche 6919
1591-0725 see 0563-3745 820
1591-0733 see 0394-3054 6924
1591-0989 Journal of Functional Syndromes† 8968
1591-1047 Jack 6293
1591-1071 Aerei nella Storia 4327
1591-1160 Cucina Creativa† 8947
1591-1195 Sport Cardiology 6233
1591-1209 Psiche Donna 6175
1591-1349 Il Passatempo 2896
1591-1489 Artroscopia 6237
1591-173X In Sella 8259
1591-1764 Business 2.0†
1591-1772 Tattoo One 521
1591-1853 Ras. Rassegna Amministrativa della Scuola
1591-2000 see 1591-2019 4877
1591-2019 Notariato 4877
1591-2027 Sociologia e Politiche Sociali 8136
1591-2086 see 0394-2740 4867
1591-2094 Le Societa 8135
1591-2108 see 1591-2094 8135
1591-2205 Artu 4352
1591-2361 see 1724-2541 500
1591-237X Acqua & Aria 3400
1591-240X Motor 8548
1591-2507 Pokemon World changed to 1827-1553 2208
1591-2515 Pagine Web Facile 2565
1591-2523 Fotografia Digitale Facile 6980
1591-254X Eurocalcio 8171
1591-2701 Toscana Qui† 8993
1591-2736 Oasis† 8978
1591-2787 Orizzonti 409
1591-2795 Psicoanalisi Forense 6175
1591-2922 Rivista di Filologia e Letterature Ispaniche 5169
1591-2930 Rivista di Arte e Critica
1591-2965 Studi Zancan 8007
1591-3007 see 0391-8157 4440
1591-3031 Eserciti nella Storia 6420
1591-3082 Ciao Amici 2182
1591-3090 Medico e Bambino 6096
1591-3163 La Piscina 453
1591-3341 Case al Mare 437
1591-3392 Why? Perche? changed to 1592-0011 462
1591-3503 Associazione Italiana Protezione contro le Radiazioni. Bolletino†
1591-3511 Global Electric
1591-3643 Annuario del Pesce e della Pesca 3584
1591-3694 Arte Stampa† 8931
1591-3775 P S 2† 8979
1591-3783 La Macchina del Tempo 7880
1591-3961 G T 1926
1591-397X see 1591-3961 1926
1591-4135 Activa Design Management 427
1591-4178 Il Lavoro nella Giurisprudenza 1695
1591-4194 La Legge 4721
1591-4216 see 0024-1598 4723
1591-4232 Il Corriere Giuridico 4651
1591-4267 Maltrattamento e Abuso all'Infanzia 2160
1591-4291 Lotus Navigator
1591-4305 Bollettino Sistematico di Filosofia Politica 7110
1591-4348 Vernissage see 0394-0543 491
1591-4798 Popolazione e Storia 7289
1591-4844 G Baby 2190
1591-4941 Digimon Magazine† 8950
1591-5204 Modus Vivendi 3453
1591-528X Enti Non Profit 1922
1591-5344 I Quaderni de il Fracastoro 5701
1591-5484 see 1123-5047 1086
1591-559X Giornale di Diritto Amministrativo 4681
1591-5603 see 1591-559X 4681
1591-5611 Diritto Penale e Processo 4889
1591-562X see 1591-5611 4889
1591-5883 see 0017-0631 4831
1591-5921 see 0436-0230 4831
1591-612X Impresa Artigiana 1121
1591-6243 Industria & Distribuzione† 8964
1591-6553 Crociere see 1120-7663 8285
1591-6596 Cipria 586
1591-6693 Statistica e Metrica Italiana 8403
1591-6707 Harmony Temptation 5410
1591-6715 Il Corriere dei Concorsi 2839
1591-6723 Cerca Lavoro 1670
1591-6901 Aves Ichnusae
1591-6928 Idee per la Casa† 8963

ISSN

1594-5812	Alternative/i†	8929
1594-5936	Orologi & Market†	8979
1594-6061	Comunicazione Politica	2317
1594-6193	Salute & Benessere†	8986
1594-6517	Linguistica e Filologia	5146
1594-672X	Campus Web	2276
1594-6738	Luna	8872
1594-6754	Class	1858
1594-6762	Case & Country	4555
1594-6770	Milano Finanza	1639
1594-7041	Macchine Edili	1021
1594-7068	Sacra Doctrina	7679
1594-7084	B C S P	383
1594-719X	Dimagrire	6657
1594-7580	Equilibri	3430
1594-7637	Servizi	
1594-7920	ManiTese	8055
1594-8072	Poetica	5430
1594-8137	Progettare (Milan)	454
1594-8161	Il Commercio Edile	992
1594-8528	Disegno Industriale Industrial Design†	8950
1594-901X	Cronaca Numismatica	6650
1594-9060	Macrame	537
1594-9168	Timer Magazine†	8993
1594-9184	P C Photo	6972
1594-9230	Play Nation 2 Magazine†	8981
1594-9281	Genesis	8865
1594-9311	Il Giornale del Colore changed to 1825-1196	6720
1594-9389	Nintendo	2478
1594-9532	Grand Tour Cult	8714
1594-9540	Archaedilia	976
1594-9613	Pagine Aperte	
1594-9745	Anima Mundi	4443
1594-9893	Reset	3898
1594-9974	Quaderni di Storia della Fisica	7036
1594-9982	Societa Italiana di Fisica. Nuovo Cimento B. Basic Topics in Physics	7040
1595-0956	Journal of Cultural Studies	7978
1595-1103	Nigerian Journal of Surgical Research	6253
1595-2304	PhAction	274
1595-5125	Journal of Environmental Extension	3445
1595-6121	Nigerian Journal of Soil and Environmental Research	140
1595-6180	Ethiope Research	7962
1595-689X	African Journal of Clinical and Experimental Microbiology	880
1595-7470	Journal of Agriculture and Social Research	126
1595-7632	Supreme Court of Nigeria. Monthly Judgments	4965
1595-8272	Nigerian Journal of Health and Biomedical Sciences	5686
1595-8922	Journal of Librarianship and Information Science in Africa	5021
1595-9716	International Journal of Agriculture and Rural Development	123
1596-0749	Humanities Review Journal	4456
1596-0862	Nigeria Journal of Pure and Applied Physics	7028
1596-2393	Journal of Experimental and Clinical Anatomy	924
1596-2407	Highland Medical Research Journal	5628
1596-2903	Global Journal of Agricultural Sciences	115
1596-2911	Global Journal of Medical Sciences	5620
1596-292X	Global Journal of Engineering Research	3194
1596-3233	Journal of Applied Science, Engineering and Technology	3204
1596-3497	Journal of Modeling, Design and Management of Engineering Systems	3206
1596-3519	Annals of African Medicine	5575
1596-4019	African Journal of Livestock Extension	277
1596-5031	Lagos Historical Review	4176
1596-5996	see Tropical Journal of Pharmaceutical Research	6883
1596-6194	Global Journal of Environmental Sciences	3434
1596-6208	Global Journal of Mathematical Sciences	5490
1596-6216	Global Journal of Social Sciences	7967
1596-6224	Global Journal of Educational Research	2860
1596-6232	Global Journal of Humanities	4454
1596-6798	Global Journal of Geological Sciences	2745
1596-6844	Genevieve	3920
1596-6941	Journal of Medicine and Biomedical Research	5652
1596-7689	City Post	3920
1596-7808	Business Opportunities	1957
1596-7891	Marine Business International	8651
1596-8499	Journal of Pharmaceutical and Allied Sciences	6855
1596-9487	Lagos Journal of Library and Information Science	5024
1596-9819	see 1596-9886	5639
1596-9886	International Journal of Health Research	5639
1597-0043	Journal of Biomedical Investigation	5907
1597-0752	Corporate Standard	1087
1597-3522	Journal of International Politics and Development	7248
1597-376X	Our Daily Manna	7668
1597-4030	Pharmascope	6874
1597-488X	Inter-World Journal of Science and Technology	7867
1597-5282	Nuggets	7705
1597-5355	J A E E T	124
1597-6343	Science World Journal	7911
1598-0073	International Journal of Reliability and Applications	3202
1598-1037	Asia Pacific Education Review	2827
1598-1398	Yeong'eohag	5197
1598-141X	Ocean and Polar Research	2814
1598-1657	Journal of Semiconductor Technology and Science	3323
1598-1681	Journal of Korean Law	4701
1598-2041	International Journal of Korean History	4184
1598-2092	Journal of Power Electronics	3107
1598-2254	The Plant Pathology Journal	812
1598-2262	Sigmulbyeong Yeon'gu	817
1598-2351	International Journal of Steel Structures	1016
1598-2408	Journal of East Asian Studies	553
1598-2467	Journal of Bacteriology and Virology	888
1598-2602	K I E E International Transactions on Electrical Machinery and Energy Conversion Systems changed to 1975-0102	3322
1598-2610	K I E E International Transactions on Electrophysics and Applications changed to 1975-0102	3322

1598-2688	Asian Journal of Quality	1880
1598-2750	Journal of the Korean Economy	1138
1598-2874	Daehan Ganho Haghoeji	5956
1598-2920	Cheyug Gwahag Yeon'gu	8166
1598-2939	International Journal of Applied Sports Sciences	8180
1598-2998	Cancer Research and Treatment	6014
1598-3269	19 Se'gi Yeong'eo'gwon Munhag	5405
1598-3579	International Journal of Industrial Entomology	850
1598-4249	K I E E International Transactions on Power Engineering changed to 1975-0102	3322
1598-4613	Chongi ui Segye	3297
1598-4818	Gugje Jeongchi Nonchong	7239
1598-5032	Macromolecular Research	2126
1598-5245	Ko M C I Journal	5748
1598-5865	Journal of Applied Mathematics and Computing	5501
1598-6217	see 1225-4568	3396
1598-6225	see 1226-6116	3287
1598-6233	see 1229-9367	6333
1598-6357	see 1011-8934	5650
1598-6365	Sigmul Saengmyeong Gong Haghoeji	770
1598-6381	Journal of Universal Language changed to Journal of Language & Translation	5134
1598-642X	Han'gug Mi'saengmul Saengmyeong Gong Haghoeji	886
1598-6446	International Journal of Control, Automation and Systems	2461
1598-6462	Corrosion Science and Technology	3343
1598-706X	Han'gug Jujo Gong Haghoeji	6314
1598-723X	Korean Journal of Thinking and Problem Solving changed to The International Journal of Creativity & Problem Solving	7364
1598-7264	Kushiro Kogyo Koto Senmon Gakko Kiyo	8430
1598-7477	see 1226-4806	2708
1598-7876	see 1225-8245	6158
1598-8074	Development and Society	7282
1598-818X	see 1598-8198	992
1598-8198	Computers and Concrete	992
1598-9100	Intestinal Research	5927
1598-9429	Han'gug Dongmul Jawon Gwahag Hoeji	288
1598-9461	K I E T San'eob Gyeongje	1139
1598-947X	K I E T Industrial Economic Review	1139
1598-9623	Metals and Materials International	6325
1598-9992	Korean Journal of Gastroenterology	5928
1599-046X	Ingu Dongtae Tong'gye Yeonbo. Chong'gwal Chulsaeng Sa'mang Pyeon	7309
1599-0478	Ingu Dongtae Tong'gye Yeonbo. Hon'in Ihon Pyeon	7309
1599-0486	Sa'mang Won'in Tong'gye Yeonbo	7292
1599-0605	Sa'eobche Gicho Tong'gye Jo'sa Bo'go'seo. Jeon'gug Pyeon	1261
1599-063X	Unsu'eob Tong'gye Jo'sa Bo'go'seo	8532
1599-0907	Han'gug ui Sahoe Ji'pyo	7307
1599-0958	see 0075-6873	7307
1599-1180	Saenghwal Si'gan Jo'sa Bo'go'seo. Je 1 Gwon, Saenghwal Si'ganlyang Pyeon	7314
1599-1199	Saenghwal Si'gan Jo'sa Bo'go'seo. Je 2 Gwon, Si'gan Dae'byeol Haengwija Biyul Pyeon	7292
1599-1229	see 1599-063X	8532
1599-1237	see 1599-1407	1046
1599-1369	Gwang Gong'eob Tong'gye Jo'sa Bo'go'seo. Jiyeog Pyeon	6485
1599-1407	Geonseol'eob Tong'gye Jo'sa Bo'go'seo	1046
1599-1717	In'gu Jutaeg Chong Jo'sa Jamjeong Bo'go'seo	7309
1599-2152	Jeon'gug Ju'min Deunglog In'gu Tong'gye	7311
1599-3361	Saengmyeong Pyo	7314
1599-4384	Janglae In'gu Chu'gye	7311
1599-4473	Eoeob Chong Jo'sa Bunseog Bo'go'seo	3613
1599-4481	Nong'eob Chong Jo'sa Bunseog Bo'go'seo	184
1599-5194	Do So'maeeob Tong'gye Jo'sa Bo'go'seo	1224
1599-6484	Janglae Ga'gu Chu'gye	7311
1599-7731	Elle Girl	8861
1599-9505	Ju'gan Han'gug	3902
1600-0048	see 0905-815X	3413
1600-0110	Dialogos Latinoamericanos	4291
1600-0196	A O F Perspektiv changed to 1604-4703	
1600-0293	Social- & Sundhedssektorens Haandbog	8069
1600-0315	Ekko changed to 1903-4075	6500
1600-0366	Denmark. Undervisningsministeriet. Uddannelsesstyrelsen. Beretning om Gymnasiet og H F	2841
1600-0374	see 1600-0366	2841
1600-0390	see 0065-101X	370
1600-0404	see 0001-6314	6118
1600-0412	see 0001-6349	5985
1600-0420	Acta Ophthamologica Scandinavica (Online) changed to 1755-3768	6037
1600-0439	see 0001-6438	541
1600-0447	see 0001-690X	6119
1600-0455	see 0284-1851	6192
1600-0463	see 0903-4641	650
1600-0471	Arabian Archaeology and Epigraphy Online	374
1600-048X	see 0908-8857	909
1600-0498	see 0008-8994	7844
1600-0501	see 0905-7161	5838
1600-051X	see 0303-6979	5851
1600-0528	Community Dentistry and Oral Epidemiology Online	5838
1600-0536	see 0105-1873	5873
1600-0560	see 0303-6987	5878
1600-0579	European Journal of Dental Education Online	5843
1600-0587	see 0906-7590	3416
1600-0609	see 0902-4441	5936
1600-0617	see 0905-9180	6214
1600-0625	Experimental Dermatology Online	5876
1600-0633	see 0906-6691	941
1600-0641	see 0168-8278	5928
1600-065X	see 0105-2896	5759
1600-0668	Indoor Air Online	7525
1600-0684	see 0047-2565	952
1600-0706	see 0030-1299	3458
1600-0714	see 0904-2512	5852
1600-0722	European Journal of Oral Sciences Online	5844

1600-0730	see 0105-7510	5346
1600-0757	Periodontology 2000 Online	5861
1600-0765	see 0022-3484	5853
1600-0781	Photodermatology, Photoimmunology & Photomedicine Online	5880
1600-079X	see 0742-3098	6156
1600-0803	see 0106-2301	6184
1600-0811	see 0035-3906	5168
1600-082X	see 0080-6765	5172
1600-0838	see 0905-7188	6232
1600-0846	see 0909-752X	5882
1600-0854	see 1398-9219	837
1600-0862	Reviews in Immunogenetics Online†	
1600-0870	see 0280-6495	6396
1600-0889	see 0280-6509	6396
1600-0897	American Journal of Reproductive Immunology Online	5754
1600-0927	Ridehesten	8297
1600-1087	V V S & El Guiden†	
1600-1273	Kinabladet	3826
1600-1281	MusikBIB	5033
1600-146X	Taenk + Test changed to 1604-6307	2641
1600-1621	Kommunale Sundhedsordninger. Hjemmesygeplejen	8053
1600-1664	Fiske-Feber (Copenhagen)	8313
1600-1729	Dansk Flygtningehjaelp	8036
1600-1974	Sats	6951
1600-2008	Samfund & Forskning†	
1600-2350	Danmarks Tekniske Universitet. Institut for Baerende Konstruktioner og Materialer. Serie†	8948
1600-2482	Vi Foraeldre	2170
1600-2490	Kongelige Veterinaer- og Landbohoejskole. De Studerendes Raad. Tvaerfagligt Rusudvalg. Brugsanvisning i KVL†	8970
1600-2555	Rationrl Farmakoterapi	6877
1600-2717	GameZone changed to 0109-2847	2535
1600-2768	Hjemmevaernsbladet changed to 1902-3391	6423
1600-2822	P C World†	8979
1600-2865	Journal of Clinical Periodontology. Supplement see 0303-6979	5851
1600-2962	Grafguide	7321
1600-3020	Statistics Across Borders†	8990
1600-3039	Woman	8889
1600-3179	Miljoeberetning changed to 1901-6476	3419
1600-3373	Nyhedsbrev om Ulykkesforskning & Forebyggelse	7534
1600-3411	L O-Dokumentation	4597
1600-3489	Dansk Glaucom Forening Informerer changed to 1901-774X	6042
1600-3543	Acta Jutlandica. Universitetshistorisk Serie	3833
1600-3578	Danmarks Tekniske Universitet. Virksomhedsregnskab changed to 1603-1784	8419
1600-3586	Inseminoeren	289
1600-3616	I T Branchen†	8963
1600-3748	Produktions Guiden†	
1600-3888	Vismandsrapport	2631
1600-3934	see 1600-3888	2631
1600-3993	Ark.byg changed to 1901-4457	439
1600-4094	Elektronik Nyt	3098
1600-4116	see 0107-7902	7659
1600-4167	Tegn	2918
1600-4310	Tissue Antigens. Supplement see 0001-2815	5722
1600-4396	see 0909-4288	3264
1600-440X	Laengden af Offentlige Veje (Online Edition)	8632
1600-4469	Dental Traumatology	5841
1600-4485	EU-Information	1563
1600-4558	Dansk Karate Forbund†	8948
1600-4590	see 0106-1046	2754
1600-4604	Retail Focus	1432
1600-4760	Vejledning i Oekologisk Jordbrugsproduktion	168
1600-499X	see 0105-0982	8970
1600-5031	see 0907-9300	8059
1600-5163	Danmarks Tekniske Universitet. Institut for Fysik. Teknisk Rapport†	
1600-5341	see 1902-7915	1662
1600-5368	Acta Crystallographica. Section E: Structure Reports Online	2109
1600-5449	see 0065-1427	6118
1600-5465	see Acta Ophthalmologica. Supplementum	6037
1600-5473	see 0065-1591	6119
1600-549X	see 0108-1675	5754
1600-5503	see 0903-465X	648
1600-5562	see 0906-5784	6099
1600-5643	Nyt fra det Dansk Bibelselskab changed to 1902-4746	7667
1600-5724	Acta Crystallographica. Section A: Foundations of Crystallography. Online see 0108-7673	2108
1600-5740	Acta Crystallographica. Section B: Structural Science. Online see 0108-7681	2109
1600-5759	see 0108-2701	2109
1600-5767	see 0021-8898	2111
1600-5775	see 0909-0495	7068
1600-583X	Legenda	5321
1600-6038	Danske Talesprog	5110
1600-6100	I T University. Technical Report Series	2422
1600-6135	American Journal of Transplantation	6235
1600-6143	American Journal of Transplantation (Online)	6236
1600-6208	National Geographic Danmark	4020
1600-6216	Ny Sociallovgivning changed to 1901-0400	4969
1600-6275	Clinical Oral Implants Research. Supplement see 0905-7161	5838
1600-633X	Institut for Graenseregionsforskning. Working Papers	7973
1600-6356	Geologi - GEUS-imit Nutaariassat	
1600-6364	Denmark. Ministeriet for Foedevarer, Landbrug og Fiskeri. Foedevaredirektoratet. Pesticidrester i Foedevarer	227
1600-6380	see 1600-6364	227
1600-6526	Witherloese	4279
1600-6585	Miljoebistand i Oesteuropa changed to 1603-0389	3453
1600-6704	Nyhedsbrev om Etniske Minoriteter changed to 1603-435X	
1600-6801	Denmark. Danmarks Statistik. Landbrug	179

ISSN

1602-7051 Hvidovre Lokalhistorie **4231**
1602-706X K R I F A *changed to* 1901-5291 **4597**
1602-7094 K R I F A A-Kasse† **8969**
1602-7183 Visitor **4400**
1602-7191 Dansk Export **1883**
1602-7213 D S-Bladet **6309**
1602-7248 Dansk Center for Byoekologi. Nyhedsbrev (Online) *changed to* 1902-4789 **3431**
1602-7272 Denmark. Danmarks Statistik. Prisstatistik (Online) **1224**
1602-7361 Focus Denmark (Japanese edition) *see* 1601-9776 **1487**
1602-7450 Froeavleren **232**
1602-7469 The Seed Grower *see* 1602-7450 **232**
1602-7493 Grafisk Haandbog **7321**
1602-7574 Normtal for Sportsbranchen i Danmark **8191**
1602-7787 Indikation **5634**
1602-7795 *see* 1602-7787 **5634**
1602-7841 Redegoerelse om Jordforurening **3511**
1602-785X Design† **8949**
1602-7930 *see* 1902-2255 **5236**
1602-7949 Isabellas **3834**
1602-799X eDanmak **2319**
1602-8031 Danish Genocide Studies Series **2650**
1602-8074 Boern og Unge† **8937**
1602-8155 Skolen i Norden (Online) **2913**
1602-8171 Greenland Mineral Resources. Fact Sheet **6464**
1602-818X Geology and Ore **2742**
1602-8554 *see* 0905-3549 **8642**
1602-8589 Denmark. Indenrigs- og Sundhedsministeriet. Indenrigs- og Sundhedsministeriets Afgoerelser og Udtalelser om Kommunale Forhold† **8949**
1602-8740 Tennismagasinet† **8993**
1602-8910 Medicinpriser **6861**
1602-9038 Byplan Nyt **4405**
1602-9313 Vand & Data **2820**
1602-9348 Assurandoer Nyt *changed to* 1902-9519 **4493**
1602-9372 Aestetik og Kulturs Nyhedsbrev *changed to* 1901-0559
1602-9402 Arken Bulletin **467**
1602-9585 Lige Nu! **5030**
1602-9968 Erhvervspsykologi **7354**
1602-9992 Dansk Annoncoerforening. Annoncoerguide **24**
1603-015X Aabne Doere **7619**
1603-0338 Theses and Other Publications of the University of Copenhagen **636**
1603-0362 Brandvaesen **3575**
1603-0370 Mandat†
1603-0389 Miljoestoette til Oesteuropa **3453**
1603-0494 Oscar Yankee **67**
1603-0680 Denmark. Finanstilsynet. Beretning **1335**
1603-0699 *see* 1603-0680 **1335**
1603-0702 Denmark. Finanstilsynet. Aarsrapport **1335**
1603-0850 Nomos **5342**
1603-0885 Danish Offshore Industry **6766**
1603-0893 Brand og Sikring **3575**
1603-0907 Baadnyt **8271**
1603-1059 Designmatters **8420**
1603-1083 A G I **7318**
1603-1121 E U Baggrund **7231**
1603-1156 Boerne- og Juniorbladet Konrad *changed to* 1902-4193 **7763**
1603-1482 Den Danske Skoleaarbog **2841**
1603-1601 moMentum *see* 0906-7043 **125**
1603-1784 Danmarks Tekniske Universitet. Aarsrapport **8419**
1603-1806 Proces-Teknik **3216**
1603-2322 You Know How **6760**
1603-2454 Danske Golfbaner **8226**
1603-2551 On Edge **2549**
1603-2586 Denmark. Risoe National Laboratory. Radiation Research Department. Annual Report† **8949**
1603-2861 Aktuel Arkaeologi† **8929**
1603-2985 Nippon Kitte Nyt **6897**
1603-3078 A T V Nyt (Online) **8415**
1603-3280 Agora **6902**
1603-3345 Bips **982**
1603-337X Aarhus Universitet. Det Teologiske Facultet. Aarsskrift **7688**
1603-3388 Hest **288**
1603-3485 Imarsiornermik Quppersagaq **3597**
1603-3493 Forbindelser **8102**
1603-3523 Denmark. Forbrugerstyrelsen. Forbrugerredegoerelsen **2637**
1603-3558 Baltic Development Forum. Report *changed to* 1902-6080 **1064**
1603-3566 E U **1097**
1603-3574 Denmark. Transport- og Energiministeriet. Vejdirektoratet. Aarsrapport **8630**
1603-3620 P C Gaming World† **8979**
1603-3639 Automatik, Teknisk Udvikling *changed to* 1902-0228 **2458**
1603-3663 Carl Nielsen Studies **6554**
1603-3736 F H M (Denmark)† **8955**
1603-3744 Nyt om Biler† **8978**
1603-3914 Nordiske GENressurser **876**
1603-3922 Nordic GENEresources *see* 1603-3914 **876**
1603-3930 Pohjolan GEENIvarat *see* 1603-3914 **876**
1603-3957 *see* 1397-5307 **8149**
1603-4058 Sociologisk Tidende **8138**
1603-4120 Danish Exporters **1561**
1603-4236 LandbrugsAvisen **133**
1603-4279 *see* 1603-1482 **2841**
1603-4309 *see* 1603-4120 **1561**
1603-435X Etcetera†
1603-4406 Lettre Internationale†
1603-4546 A B L O Nyt† **8927**
1603-4597 Sejleravisen *changed to* 1902-4665 **8271**
1603-4635 Scandinavian Brewers' Review **610**
1603-4791 Produktionsoekonomi, Svin **205**
1603-483X Forsvaret **6421**
1603-4880 Medicon Valley **3250**
1603-5003 Morada Internacional **5228**
1603-5011 Abroad **5204**
1603-5194 16:9 **6517**
1603-5259 Kompass (Print) *changed to* 1902-7001 **2011**
1603-5267 Bygningskulturens Dag **436**
1603-5305 Zoom paa Arbejdsmarkedet **1717**
1603-5313 Journal of the David Collection **6526**
1603-5348 Danmarks Paedagogiske Universitet. Aarsberetning **2841**
1603-5550 Styrelsen *changed to* 1902-598X **7445**
1603-5593 F A O S Information **1681**
1603-5607 Social Service *changed to* 1902-8571 **8069**
1603-5704 Filmmagasinet Mifune *changed to* 1903-4075 **6500**
1603-5712 Fokus paa Kraeft og Sygepleje **6020**
1603-5860 Guld, Soelv, Ure *changed to* 1604-9659 **4564**
1603-5925 Tidsskrift for Sprogforskning **5187**
1603-595X T3 **8440**
1603-6026 Afhaengig - og Hvad Saa? **2690**
1603-6042 Nye Film i Skolekataloget *see* 1602-5008 **6499**
1603-6050 Graphikos **7322**
1603-6182 Fordeling og Levevilkaar **1682**
1603-6379 Kvaeg **291**
1603-6565 SEE-J. Hiphil Old Testament **7680**
1603-6581 Svin **301**
1603-6670 The Gaia Guardian† **8958**
1603-6689 Nyt fra Danske Soemands- og Udlandskirker **7667**
1603-6727 Kommunale Noegletal om Udlaendinge **7286**
1603-6735 Proever, Evaluering, Undervisning **3030**
1603-6778 Ledelse **1772**
1603-6794 Mark **242**
1603-6816 Giv det Stoerste til de Mindste **7759**
1603-6824 *see* 0041-5782 **5725**
1603-6832 Focus Kontakt†
1603-6913 H V A C Magasinet **4120**
1603-7146 Hjaelpemidlet *changed to* 1902-9136 **3048**
1603-7170 The Journal of Music and Meaning **6580**
1603-726X Looks†
1603-7383 Metro Nyt **8620**
1603-7480 Notat **7255**
1603-7618 ErhvervNord **1483**
1603-7707 M S Bladet *changed to* 1903-4954 **7219**
1603-7812 Kraks Transport og Emballage† **8970**
1603-7820 Krakteknik **5454**
1603-7898 Planer og Budget **4253**
1603-7936 Medicinsk Teknologi *changed to* 1901-4465 **5675**
1603-7979 Spindet **5177**
1603-7995 H K-Merkur *changed to* 1901-9254 **4595**
1603-8002 Dyrlaegemagasinet for Praktiserende Dyrlaeger **8797**
1603-8037 Center for Ledelse. Aarsrapport **1732**
1603-8282 Orienteringsloeb.dk *changed to* 1901-3825 **8192**
1603-8347 Bilarbogen **8569**
1603-8398 Tidsskrift for Miljoe **4796**
1603-8401 Kongres for Svineproducenter **291**
1603-8444 Bio-Etik i Praksis **6907**
1603-8509 Res Cogitans **6947**
1603-855X International WasteNews *see* 1601-2852 **3508**
1603-8630 Kontor/papir **1852**
1603-8665 Raastofproduktion i Danmark, Havomraadet (Online) **2763**
1603-8843 Ny Viden fra Miljoestyrelsen *changed to* 1603-9254 **7882**
1603-8886 F S F - Tidindi **8227**
1603-8967 Textuelt Monthly† **8993**
1603-9092 Kunstuff **536**
1603-9106 Prent† **8982**
1603-9173 Denmark. Danmarks Statistik. Industri (Print) *changed to* 1603-9181 **1223**
1603-9181 Denmark. Danmarks Statistik. Industri (Online) **1223**
1603-9203 Psykologi **7401**
1603-9254 Miljoenyt.dk **7882**
1603-9408 Kernekraft og Nuklear Sikkerhed **3207**
1603-9491 Dansk Landbrugsraadgivning. Dansk Kvaeg. Rapport, Dansk Kvaeg† **8948**
1603-9610 Boligliv **4353**
1603-9629 Danish Medical Bulletin (Online) **5603**
1603-9661 Sadolin & Albaek. Newsletter **7612**
1603-967X *see* 1603-9661 **7612**
1603-970X Autobranchen *changed to* 1903-4695 **8561**
1603-9726 Mama *changed to* 1903-0770 **2153**
1603-9742 Denmark. Forbrugerstyrelsen. Forbrugerjura **2637**
1603-9769 Review of Survey Activities **2764**
1603-9939 Biotech Medical *changed to* 1902-7818 **759**
1603-9947 Kapital† **8969**
1603-9955 Kapital Nyt **1363**
1604-0023 Panbladet† **8980**
1604-0058 Politik **7171**
1604-0163 Elforbrugeren *changed to* 1902-5696 **3158**
1604-0295 Handikids Sport *changed to* 1902-1666 **8342**
1604-0414 Behandlerbladet **5884**
1604-049X Musikbladet **6596**
1604-0503 *see* 1397-6109 **7898**
1604-0511 Q **3834**
1604-0538 Foedevaremagasinet Koedbranchen *changed to* 1902-4509 **3636**
1604-0570 Erhvervsskolen.dk **2853**
1604-0597 Energibladet† **8953**
1604-0708 D I Business **1883**
1604-0821 Skandinavisk Oekonomi *changed to* 1902-3685 **1154**
1604-0864 Nyhedsorientering *changed to* 1902-3146 **1797**
1604-0899 Menighedsfakultetets Venneblad *changed to* 1604-911X **7661**
1604-0961 K O M Magasinet **4597**
1604-0988 Udspil **8214**
1604-1089 Flyvesikkerhedsmaessige Begivenheder Indrapporteret til SLV *changed to* 1604-9020 **8539**
1604-1232 D T U Avisen **8419**
1604-1259 Mejeri **267**
1604-1267 & Maelk **268**
1604-1380 Maelkeproducent Nyt **266**
1604-1550 Ekstra *changed to* 1901-3272
1604-1623 Scandinavian Outlook *changed to* 1902-4355 **1501**
1604-1704 Windows X P Magasinet **2600**
1604-1712 Produktionsoekonomi, Kvaeg **205**
1604-1720 Konjunkturundersoegelse af Vognmandserhvervet i Danmark **8672**
1604-178X Leder i Skolen *changed to* 1902-438X **3033**
1604-1984 Dansk Landbrugs Grovvareselskab. Aarsrapport **104**
1604-2050 Stork **2915**
1604-2069 Oekonomisk Fokus **1505**
1604-2115 Oelkassen **608**
1604-2220 Kommunale Noegletal om Udlaendinge *see* 1603-6727 **7286**
1604-231X Landbrugs-Nyt **133**
1604-2344 Hafnarposturinn† **8961**
1604-2603 Berlingske Nyhedsmagasin **1066**
1604-2646 HTS Oekonomiske Prognose *changed to* 1902-5831 **1408**
1604-2859 Daylight *changed to* 1901-0982 **439**
1604-3006 *see* 1395-4873 **5170**
1604-3014 *see* 0908-8865 **5386**
1604-3022 *see* 1601-3476 **7992**
1604-3049 *see* 1399-1353 **522**
1604-3081 Banestyrelsen. Aarsrapport *changed to* 1604-309X **8615**
1604-309X Banedanmark. Aarsrapport **8615**
1604-3189 Trygd & Trivni **7543**
1604-3472 Computerworld, Top 100 **2492**
1604-3480 Computerworld, Aarsnummer **2492**
1604-3561 *see* 1603-8444 **6907**
1604-360X *see* 1603-8037 **1732**
1604-3618 *see* 1603-9769 **2764**
1604-3634 *see* 1604-1984 **104**
1604-3707 L D+ *changed to* 1902-3650 **8319**
1604-4037 Kvinna **8870**
1604-4134 Ledelse og Uddannelse **4105**
1604-4177 *see* 1603-9408 **3207**
1604-4371 *see* 1601-7196 **8408**
1604-4509 Det Nordiske Samarbejde i EU **4249**
1604-4517 *see* 1604-4509 **4249**
1604-4657 Praxis Oekonomi **5699**
1604-4703 Perspektiv†
1604-4843 *see* 0036-5602 **5045**
1604-486X Danfoss. Aarsrapport **3360**
1604-4878 Landbohistorisk Tidsskrift **4239**
1604-4886 Holbo Herreds Kulturhistoriske Centre, Gilleleje og Omegns Museumsforening, Arkiv- og Museumsforeningen i Helsinge. Aarbog **4230**
1604-4959 Greenland. Groenlands Statistik. Udenrigshandel **1567**
1604-5076 Refleks† **8984**
1604-5157 Lilleskolenyt *changed to* 1902-6501 **8971**
1604-5203 Udvalgene Vedroeende Videnskabelige Uredelighed. Aarsberetning **6958**
1604-5262 Hairstyle & Beauty **588**
1604-5394 Aarhus Universitet. Institut for Sprog, Litteratur og Kultur. Prepublications **5089**
1604-5505 Erhvervsskolelaereren *changed to* 1903-7139 **2921**
1604-5599 Julemaerker Norden **6896**
1604-5602 Erhvervsejendom **7589**
1604-5645 Kapital Nyt†
1604-5807 Visit Denmark **8772**
1604-5815 Historisk Samfund for Hoeje-Taastrup Kommune. Medlemsblad *changed to* 1901-8274 **4230**
1604-5858 Formidl† **8957**
1604-5874 S P F-Sundhedsregler for S P F-Besaetninger **299**
1604-6048 Nyt fra Biblioteksstyrelsen *changed to* 1903-0819 **5037**
1604-6110 Doevblevne.info† **8951**
1604-6307 Taenk **2641**
1604-6528 Domino **7735**
1604-6595 Digetale Medier *changed to* 1902-6757 **7579**
1604-6641 Det Danske Proust-Selskab. Bulletin *changed to* 1902-424X **5355**
1604-665X S D A Nyt (Farum, 2005) *changed to* 1902-4959 **394**
1604-6676 Akvakultur Magasinet *changed to* 1902-276X **3590**
1604-6765 Det Frie Forskningsraad. Aarsrapport **7856**
1604-6781 Fagbladet 3F **4594**
1604-6803 Testnyt **1797**
1604-6811 Nyt om Excellence *changed to* 1901-659X **1743**
1604-6838 F A O S. Beretning **1681**
1604-6935 Geoviden **2709**
1604-7117 *see* 1603-1784 **8419**
1604-729X *see* 1602-9585 **5030**
1604-7400 *see* 1602-799X **2319**
1604-7591 Bordtennisguiden† **8937**
1604-763X *see* 1603-0893 **3575**
1604-7672 *see* 1603-6050 **7322**
1604-7680 He **6292**
1604-7729 *see* 1603-6735 **3030**
1604-7761 Askov Hoejskole og Efterskole. Aarsskrift **2938**
1604-7796 Dansk Fjernvarme. Statistik *changed to* 1902-4258 **4128**
1604-780X *see* 1603-3574 **8630**
1604-7842 Slagteriernes Forskningsinstitut **3664**
1604-7869 Dansk Biblioteksforskning **5005**
1604-7877 Dynamo **7852**
1604-7885 *see* 1604-7877 **7852**
1604-7982 Game Studies **2476**
1604-8016 Glas **2041**
1604-8024 Dansk Fjernvarme. Aarsberetning **4118**
1604-8156 *see* 1811-4598 **2740**
1604-8164 Arkfokus **432**
1604-8172 *see* 1604-6935 **2709**
1604-8202 Nordisk Exlibris Tidsskrift **7569**
1604-8229 Sygehusstatistik (Year) **4114**
1604-8237 *see* 1604-8229 **4114**
1604-8318 Jurainformation. Socialsektor. Nyhedsbrev *changed to* 1902-1682 **8997**
1604-8318 Jurainformation. Socialsektor. Nyhedsbrev *changed to* Voksne (Online) **7545**
1604-8326 Jurainformation. Aeldre- og Handicappedesektor. Nyhedsbrev *changed to* Handicappede, Sindslidende, Aeldre (Online) **8043**
1604-8326 Jurainformation. Aeldre- og Handicapsektor. Nyhedsbrev *changed to* 1902-1704 **8961**
1604-8334 Jurainformation. Dagtilbud for Boern og Unge. Nyhedsbrev *changed to* 1902-1690 **8937**
1604-8431 *see* 0909-9093 **5023**
1604-844X *see* 1600-888X **8075**

ISSN

1604-8504 Olivia 2206
1604-8555 Statistik Nyt fra Dansk Landbrug† 8990
1604-8644 Gerontologi 4046
1604-8660 Alt om Gymnastik 8157
1604-875X Egmont Foundation. Annual Report 4450
1604-8997 see 1604-6765 7856
1604-9020 B L 8-10 Aarsrapport 8539
1604-911X M F Bladet 7661
1604-9136 Dragonen 6419
1604-9381 see 1902-4959 394
1604-9411 see 0106-5815 2232
1604-9500 see 1604-911X 7661
1604-9659 AuClock 4564
1604-9667 H S D 5124
1604-9764 Foodculture 1423
1604-9780 Geological Survey of Denmark and Greenland Map Series 4012
1604-9853 S M K Art Journal 516
1604-9896 Danish Yearbook of Musicology 6561
1604-990X Forskerhistorier 8422
1604-9942 Landbrugsraadet. Aarsberetning 133
1605-0045 Renaissance 7715
1605-0088 see 1560-0459 3790
1605-010X see Le Patriote 3899
1605-0134 see Al- Ba'ath 3960
1605-0193 see 0864-0777 3831
1605-0207 CubAhora 3831
1605-0312 Noroeste 3910
1605-0339 see 1605-0347 3910
1605-0347 El Orbe 3910
1605-0355 Cuarto Poder 1476
1605-0363 Zeta 7197
1605-0371 El Imparcial 3909
1605-038X Noticias (Oaxaca) 3910
1605-0398 Oaxaca Times 3910
1605-0401 El Sur 3911
1605-041X see 1605-0428 3910
1605-0428 Pulso 3910
1605-0436 see Adelante 3907
1605-0444 Ocho Columnas 3910
1605-0452 Este Sur 3908
1605-0460 see 1605-0479 3911
1605-0479 La Republica en Chiapas 3911
1605-0487 see La Opinion 3910
1605-0495 El Mercurio de Tamaulipas 3909
1605-0509 Noti Arandas 3910
1605-0517 see 1605-0525 3908
1605-0517 see 1605-0509 3910
1605-0525 Expia 3908
1605-0533 see Noticias 3910
1605-0541 see Tribuna (Ciudad Obregon) 3911
1605-055X see 1605-0568 3908
1605-0568 Diario de Morelia 3908
1605-0576 see 1405-4558 7154
1605-0606 see Diario de Nuevo Laredo 3908
1605-0614 see 1027-4561 3821
1605-0622 see 1027-4588 3920
1605-0630 see 1605-0649 3821
1605-0649 Tiempos del Mundo. Nicaragua 3821
1605-0657 see La Tribuna 3821
1605-0665 see Panama America 3927
1605-0681 El Siglo Digital see El Siglo 3927
1605-069X Prensa Web see La Prensa 3927
1605-0703 see 1018-5313 3927
1605-072X Guadalajara Reporter 3909
1605-0738 see Dia 1092
1605-0746 A B C Digital see 1605-5705 3927
1605-0754 see 1605-0762 3927
1605-0762 Noticias 3927
1605-0770 see 1605-0789 3803
1605-0789 Tiempos del Mundo. Bolivia 3803
1605-0797 Tiempos del Mundo. Guatemala 3874
1605-0835 see 1605-0843 3911
1605-0843 Tiempos del Mundo. Mexico 3911
1605-0851 see 1605-086X 3927
1605-086X Tiempos del Mundo. Paraguay 3927
1605-0924 see 1605-0932 3927
1605-0932 Enfoques & Imagen 3927
1605-0959 see 1605-0967 1085
1605-0967 Confidencial 1085
1605-0975 La Noticia Digital 3821
1605-0983 El Universal en Linea 3927
1605-0991 see 1605-3001 8223
1605-1041 see 0049-4623 1184
1605-1092 see T V Media 2393
1605-1114 see Format 3797
1605-1122 see 1605-4598 6507
1605-1157 see Augustin 3797
1605-1165 see Woche Bildpost 3798
1605-1203 Auf - Info Online 8852
1605-122X see Reise Aktuell 8751
1605-1238 see Das Gruene Haus 8845
1605-1289 see Tele 2395
1605-1300 see 1605-4652 314
1605-1319 see 24 Stunden fuer Wien 3150
1605-1335 see 1560-9162 8215
1605-1343 see Schuh-Revue und Lederwaren 7941
1605-136X see WirtschaftsBlatt 1194
1605-1408 Rbxpress 5081
1605-1416 m@il
1605-1513 Wienerin 3798
1605-1653 Oesterreichische Zeitschrift fuer Vermessung und Geoinformation 4023
1605-1823 El Diario de Hoy 3821
1605-1831 Guanaquin On Line 3821
1605-184X Hablemos Online 3821
1605-1858 Planeta Alternativo 3836
1605-1866 Vertice 3836
1605-1882 see El Faro 3836
1605-1904 see 1605-1912 3836
1605-1912 La Prensa Grafica 3836
1605-1920 see 1605-1939 7179

1605-1939 Revista Probidad 7179
1605-2048 Balance 8852
1605-2099 Vestnik Molodych Uchenych. Prikladnaya Matematika i Mekhanika 5546
1605-2277 see 0864-0467 7116
1605-2471 Taiwan Nongye Huaxue yu Shipin Kexue 3665
1605-2528 Ecologia en Bolivia 669
1605-2536 Immolex 4832
1605-2544 Oesterreichisches Anwaltsblatt 4751
1605-2579 Jordan Journal of Applied Science. Humanities 4459
1605-2587 Jordan Journal of Applied Science. Natural Science 7871
1605-2730 Materials Physics and Mechanics 3353
1605-2935 EUROSTAT. European Union Direct Investment. Yearbook 1622
1605-2986 Obozrenie 350
1605-3001 El Bocon 8223
1605-3036 see 1605-3044 1081
1605-3044 Caretas 1081
1605-3052 see 0010-2253 1426
1605-3060 Cronica Viva 3927
1605-3109 see 1606-1055 3928
1605-3109 see 1605-3117 3927
1605-3109 see 1606-1047 3928
1605-3117 Expreso 3927
1605-3125 see 1605-3133 3927
1605-3133 Gente 3927
1605-3141 Gestion 3927
1605-315X see 1605-3168 3927
1605-3168 Cosas 3927
1605-3176 see 1605-3184 7586
1605-3184 Casas 7586
1605-3192 see 1605-3206 4365
1605-3206 Padres 4365
1605-3273 La Republica (Online) 3928
1605-3281 La Republica (Print) 3928
1605-329X see 1605-3273 3928
1605-329X see 1605-3303 3927
1605-3303 Domingo 3927
1605-3311 Andares see 1605-3273 3928
1605-3311 Andares see 1605-332X 3927
1605-332X Andares 3927
1605-3338 see 1605-3273 3928
1605-3338 see 1605-3346 3928
1605-3346 V S D 3928
1605-3362 TeleVicio†
1605-3435 see 0250-9806 7175
1605-3540 La Industria Digital see La Industria de Chiclayo 3927
1605-3559 see 1605-3567 3927
1605-3567 Lundero 3927
1605-3575 see 1605-3583 3927
1605-3583 Dominical 3927
1605-3656 Hoy 3835
1605-3664 Listin Digital 3835
1605-3672 El Domingo 3835
1605-3680 see 1605-3699 3835
1605-3699 El Nacional 3835
1605-3702 Rumbo 3835
1605-3710 El Siglo 3835
1605-377X see 1605-3788 3926
1605-3788 Takbeer 3926
1605-3842 Crisol Virtual 3908
1605-3931 Xianggang Jianzhu Zhinan (Zhongguo Ban) see Hong Kong Builder Directory (Hong Kong Edition) 1012
1605-3958 Contractors Plant & Equipment Catalogue 1981
1605-3966 Architects & Designers Catalogue changed to Hong Kong Source Book for Architects, Designers & Building Contractors 1012
1605-3974 Journal of Water Supply Research and Technology. Aqua Online see 1606-9935 8828
1605-4024 La Nueva Cubana 3831
1605-4032 see 0188-3615 3911
1605-4040 see 0186-2863 3006
1605-4059 see 0188-6630 3006
1605-4067 see 0185-1330 2922
1605-4075 see Revista Red 2503
1605-4083 see 0187-8190 2337
1605-4091 see Rompan Filas 2908
1605-4105 Skene 8478
1605-4113 see P C Semanal 2580
1605-4121 see 0188-6959 342
1605-413X see 1405-5406 3911
1605-4148 see 0187-1560 8733
1605-4156 see 1605-4164 3910
1605-4164 Novedades Quintana Roo (Online) 3910
1605-4172 Novedades Acapulco (English Edition) (Online) 3910
1605-4180 Novedades Acapulco (Spanish Edition) (Online) 3910
1605-4210 Enlace 8100
1605-4229 Expresion 2980
1605-4237 see 1605-4245 3005
1605-4245 Transferencia 3005
1605-4504 see News 3797
1605-4547 Elektronik Aktuell
1605-4555 Beauty Life 585
1605-4563 see 1605-4555 585
1605-4598 Media Biz 6507
1605-4628 Ecosophia 1006
1605-4636 Forum Archaeologiae 394
1605-4652 Pulsar 314
1605-4709 Austrian Economic Quarterly 1439
1605-4717 see 1011-5641
1605-4768 see 0185-464X 1028
1605-4776 see 1405-1559 1898
1605-4792 see 1405-0145 4870
1605-4806 Razon y Palabra 8127
1605-4822 see 1405-0439 7319
1605-4873 Cuarto Poder de Michoacan 1476
1605-4881 AgroCultura 87
1605-4903 Cuarto Oscuro 6966
1605-4911 Cyber Periodico 2000 2977
1605-4954 Diario Olmeca 3908
1605-4970 see Dimension Optica 6041

1605-4989 see Manana (Reynosa) 3909
1605-5055 Seti i Sistemy Svyazi 2338
1605-5276 Wuff 6817
1605-5284 Besser Wohnen 7583
1605-5330 Autocentre 8562
1605-5470 Korporativnye Sistemy 1393
1605-5519 Globalizacion 1488
1605-5543 Novedades de Tabasco 3910
1605-5551 see 0188-932X 2503
1605-5616 see 1605-5624 433
1605-5624 Arquine 433
1605-5632 Arquitectura y Humanidades 434
1605-5640 Architecture and Humanities 430
1605-5659 see Gente Sur 1488
1605-5675 Momento Economico. Boletin Electronico see 0186-2901 1149
1605-5683 Revista Morelia 8243
1605-5691 see Motor a Diesel 3390
1605-5705 A B C Color 3927
1605-5713 Mundo Minero en Linea see Revista Mundo Minero 6477
1605-5721 see Neo 1835
1605-573X see 0187-7542 8075
1605-5780 Virtualia 2440
1605-5810 Crime Research in South Africa 2649
1605-5888 see Ciencias Pedagogicas 2837
1605-6035 Cinetext 6494
1605-6108 see 1562-3750 1644
1605-6213 see 1862-7560 5870
1605-6221 see 1862-7137 5568
1605-6272 Leadership Magazine Online see Leadership Magazine 5224
1605-6353 see 1018-9564 2436
1605-6442 Sailing 8281
1605-6523 Windows Middle East 2583
1605-6582 see 1560-8034 7051
1605-671X see Falter 3797
1605-6728 Pacific Islands Communication Journal 2335
1605-6736 Heureka! 6741
1605-6779 see 0018-3784 3712
1605-6906 Taipei Journal changed to Taiwan Journal 3960
1605-699X Auto Trader Interactive see 1019-2093 8604
1605-7031 see 1729-3456 3799
1605-718X Jatros Haematologie und Onkologie 5939
1605-7333 see 1562-8515 5206
1605-7422 Progress in Biomedical Optics and Imaging 7084
1605-7430 Conocimiento 5108
1605-7597 Inter@ctive Week changed to 1815-1590 2427
1605-7678 Russkoe Entomologicheskoe Obshchestvo. Trudy 858
1605-7724 Revista de Investigacion de Fisica 7038
1605-7759 Saltwater Girl 8331
1605-7767 Raccolta della Giurisprudenza della Corte e del Tribunale di Primo Grado. Parte 1. Corte di Giustizia 4938
1605-7775 Raccolta della Giurisprudenza della Corte e del Tribunale di Primo Grado. Parte 2. Tribunale di Primo Grado 4938
1605-7783 Unione Europea. Bollettino see 1025-4005 1485
1605-7872 see 1024-1922 6966
1605-7953 Sankt-Peterburgskii Universitet. Vestnik. Seriya 8. Menedzhment 1792
1605-8054 see 1606-4550 431
1605-8070 Rossiiskii Fond Fundamental'nykh Issledovanii. Vestnik 1169
1605-8089 Winduz see 1605-6523 2583
1605-8119 see 1605-2730 3353
1605-8127 Reviews on Advanced Materials Science 3356
1605-816X see Music Manual 6591
1605-8186 see 0304-8713 3797
1605-8232 see Osttiroler Bote 3798
1605-8445 see 1019-2158 435
1605-8488 Historische Sozialkunde 4228
1605-8585 Feinspitz 3636
1605-8844 Vremya Novostei 3943
1605-9018 Lig see L I G 7764
1605-9042 Invasor Digital see 0864-1110 7144
1605-9050 see 0864-1277 7133
1605-9069 Giga Online 1886
1605-9077 see 0864-1706 5344
1605-9085 see 1025-3084 6535
1605-9115 see 0864-0521 2224
1605-9131 see 0449-4555 8429
1605-914X see 0864-0513 5210
1605-9204 European Journal of Underwater and Hyperbaric Medicine† 8955
1605-9239 Opinion 3802
1605-9255 see 1012-9804 7140
1605-9263 Shangri-la 8785
1605-9298 Cyber Post†
1605-9395 Sci-Tech Focus 7907
1605-9468 Peningamal 1374
1605-9581 N E A News 3171
1605-959X A E N Infos see 1605-9581 3171
1605-9786 The African Finance Journal 1306
1605-9840 see Der Grazer 3797
1605-9921 see 1606-1330 7972
1606-0008 Deutsche Sprachwelt 5111
1606-0180 see 1563-311X 5905
1606-0229 Enterprise Partner 2589
1606-0237 Telesport 8211
1606-027X Vietnam Review see 0866-806X 3995
1606-0512 La Nacion 3927
1606-0563 Bioingenieria y Fisica Medica Cubana 747
1606-0784 see 1026-6062 8885
1606-0792 La Pesca Europea (Spanish Edition) see Fisheries and Aquaculture in Europe 3592
1606-0806 Europaeisk Fiskeri see Fisheries and Aquaculture in Europe 3592
1606-0814 Fischerei in Europa see Fisheries and Aquaculture in Europe 3592
1606-0822 Fishing in Europe changed to Fisheries and Aquaculture in Europe 3592

1606-0830 TopTeen **2218**
1606-0849 La Peche Europeenne *see* Fisheries and Aquaculture in Europe **3592**
1606-0857 La Pesca Europea (Italian Edition) *see* Fisheries and Aquaculture in Europe **3592**
1606-0865 Visserij in Europa *see* Fisheries and Aquaculture in Europe **3592**
1606-0873 Kalastus Euroopassa *see* Fisheries and Aquaculture in Europe **3592**
1606-0881 Europeiskt Fiske *see* Fisheries and Aquaculture in Europe **3592**
1606-089X A Pesca na Europa *see* Fisheries and Aquaculture in Europe **3592**
1606-0903 E Europaike Alieia *see* Fisheries and Aquaculture in Europe **3592**
1606-0911 A I A **426**
1606-0962 Profile's J S E Results & Earnings *changed to* Profile's Results & Earnings **1646**
1606-0997 Journal of Health Population and Nutrition **5748**
1606-1020 *see* 1017-2092 **3907**
1606-1047 Soluciones **3928**
1606-1055 El Navegante **3928**
1606-1063 *see* Guatemala News Watch **3874**
1606-1128 Morgunbladid a Netinu *see* 1021-7266 **3877**
1606-1136 Iceland Business (Online)†
1606-1160 Institut Oceonographique. Bulletin. Numero Special **2807**
1606-1187 *see* 1028-0790 **5014**
1606-1276 Reflections **4471**
1606-1330 Informatsionnoe Obshchestvo **7972**
1606-1438 *see* 1561-7637 **1959**
1606-1446 Biznes i Kriminal **1068**
1606-1454 Marketing i Praktika Predprinimatel'stva **1832**
1606-1462 Nalogi i Biznes **1935**
1606-1470 Novye Tekhnologii **8433**
1606-1489 Moskva: Mer i Biznes **7454**
1606-1497 Torgovaya Nedelia **1433**
1606-1500 Rossiya Vybirayet **7180**
1606-1519 Novosti Sistemy M M Ts **1836**
1606-1527 Vesti Otechestva **3943**
1606-1535 Novosti Malogo Biznesa **1964**
1606-1543 Rossiiskiye Politicheskiye Portrety **7180**
1606-1551 Biznes dlya Vsekh **1068**
1606-156X Novosti e-Kommertsii **1420**
1606-1578 Biznes za Rubezhom **1553**
1606-1616 Vneshneekonomicheskoye Obozreniye **1586**
1606-1756 *see* Yuwamanch **2224**
1606-2000 The Courier. Africa - Caribbean - Pacific - European Union *changed to* Magazine of A C P - E U Development Co-operation **1601**
1606-2019 La Situation de l"Agriculture dans l"Union Europeenne. Rapport... *see* 1025-6660 **85**
1606-2043 A Situacaco da Agricultura na Uniao Europeia. Relatorio... *see* 1025-6660 **85**
1606-206X La Situazione dell'Agricoltura nell'Unione Europea. Relazione... *see* 1025-6660 **85**
1606-2078 Die Lage der Landwirtschaft in der Europaeischen Union. Bericht... *see* 1025-6660 **85**
1606-2086 La Situacion de la Agricultura en la Union Europea. Informe de... *see* 1025-6660 **85**
1606-2191 Uniao Europeia. Boletim *see* 1025-4005 **1485**
1606-2205 Europaeische Union. Bulletin *see* 1025-4005 **1485**
1606-2213 Union Europea. Boletin *see* 1025-4005 **1485**
1606-2221 Europaeiske Unie. Bulletin *see* 1025-4005 **1485**
1606-223X Europese Unie. Bulletin *see* 1025-4005 **1485**
1606-2248 Europaikes Enoses. Deltio *see* 1025-4005 **1485**
1606-2256 *see* 1027-930X **4928**
1606-2264 *see* 1027-930X **4928**
1606-2272 *see* 1027-930X **4928**
1606-2280 *see* 1027-930X **4928**
1606-2299 *see* 1027-930X **4928**
1606-2302 *see* 1027-930X **4928**
1606-2310 *see* 1027-930X **4928**
1606-2329 *see* 1027-930X **4928**
1606-2418 Commerce Exterieur et Intra-Union Europenne. Statistiques Mensuelles *see* 1029-3639 **1228**
1606-2426 Aussen- und Intrahandel der Europaeischen Union. Monatliche Statistiken *see* 1029-3639 **1228**
1606-2663 Southern African Review of Books
1606-3457 Europeisk Dokumentation *see* 0251-2998 **8366**
1606-3465 *see* 1028-348X **8540**
1606-3473 Aussen- und Intrahandel der Europaeischen Union. Statistisches Jahrbuch *see* 1606-3481 **1228**
1606-3481 External and Intra-European Union Trade. Statistical Yearbook **1228**
1606-3546 *see* 1606-3562 **3925**
1606-3562 Al-Ayyam **3925**
1606-3678 Al-Quds **3559**
1606-3708 Al-Sabbar **3896**
1606-3740 Rapport du Directeur sur l'Activite et la Gestion du Bureau International des Poids et Mesures **6405**
1606-3759 Comite International des Poids et Mesures. Comite Consultatif de l'Acoustique, des Ultrasons et des Vibrations† **8942**
1606-3775 *see* 1606-3783 **3895**
1606-3783 Fasl Al-Maqal **3895**
1606-3791 Kull Al-Arab **3895**
1606-4097 *see* Krymskaya Pravda **3964**
1606-4224 Northwest Atlantic Fisheries Organization Convention **3603**
1606-4305 Proizvodstvo i Realizatsiya Morozhenogo i Bystrozamorozennykh Produktov **4125**
1606-4313 Mezhdunarodnaya Akademiya Kholoda. Vestnik **4123**
1606-4321 Zwischenwelt **5405**
1606-4372 E E F - N E T **7639**
1606-4380 *see* 1606-4372 **7639**
1606-447X *see* 1015-2784 **1183**
1606-4550 Architektur **431**
1606-4577 *see* Al- Sharq **3932**
1606-4615 *see* 0131-0097 **5232**
1606-4879 Publications et Bases de Donnees **1259**
1606-4925 *see* 0864-4659 **5002**
1606-4933 Eurostat Veroeffentlichungen und Datenbanken *see* 1606-4879 **1259**
1606-4941 Eurostat Publications and Databases *see* 1606-4879 **1259**
1606-5131 *see* 1605-8127 **3356**
1606-5239 De Ware Tijd **3954**
1606-5271 *see* 0204-0476 **3934**
1606-531X *see* 1562-1987 **3937**
1606-5344 *see* Sovetskaya Rossiya **3941**
1606-5395 Segodnya **3965**
1606-5468 *see* 0868-4855 **5374**
1606-5484 Rossiiskaya Gazeta Online **3940**
1606-5581 Revista Cubana de Reumatologia **6226**
1606-559X *see* Kievskie Novosti **3964**
1606-5727 Formosan Journal of Medical Humanities **4453**
1606-5913 Letras Libres **5224**
1606-6243 Wink Up **3960**
1606-6286 *see* 1606-6294 **6324**
1606-6294 Metall Ukrainy **6324**
1606-6316 The Metal Business *see* 1606-6294 **6324**
1606-6340 Euroabstracts **8446**
1606-6359 Addiction Research and Theory **2689**
1606-6464 Komp'yuternaya Gazeta **2430**
1606-6758 *see* 1012-9324 **6460**
1606-6766 *see* 1606-8424 **3157**
1606-6898 *see* 1563-0935
1606-6979 Instituto Nacional de Salud. Boletin **5636**
1606-6995 F H M (Taiwan) **6290**
1606-7010 Muzykal'naya Gazeta **6598**
1606-7037 *see* Metal Music Magazine **6587**
1606-7053 *see* Stroitel'stvo i Nedvizhimost' **1038**
1606-724X *see* Kangjian Zazhi **6991**
1606-7290 *see* 1606-7304 **2070**
1606-7304 Khimiya Ukrainy **2070**
1606-7312 *see* Cuestion **3908**
1606-7347 Angel de Puebla **3907**
1606-7363 El Dictamen **3908**
1606-7479 Vulture News **916**
1606-7509 Tushu Zixum Xuekan **5051**
1606-7657 *see* Tribuna **3911**
1606-7754 International Journal of Diabetes and Metabolism **5894**
1606-7789 Iskusstvo Upravlenia **1762**
1606-7800 *see* 1606-7819 **1514**
1606-7819 Reporte Politico Policiaco **1514**
1606-7851 Homopolitan **4375**
1606-7886 Debate Legislativo **4655**
1606-7908 Proyecciones **2998**
1606-7916 *see* 0036-3634 **7540**
1606-7932 Ceiberweiber **8855**
1606-8092 Schrift/zeichen **7573**
1606-8106 Zhonghua Zhongxiyi Zazhi **5738**
1606-8122 Another Day in Paradise **3908**
1606-8149 *see* 0186-8470 **1098**
1606-8165 Investigacion y Desarrollo **7868**
1606-8181 Psihofarmakologia i Biologiceskaa Narkologia **6876**
1606-819X Negocios (Veracruz) **1152**
1606-822X Yuyan Ji Yuyangxue **5198**
1606-8378 *see* 1607-6788 **660**
1606-8424 Electricity Information **3157**
1606-8459 Gestion y Estrategia. Edicion para Internet *see* 0188-8234 **7439**
1606-8521 Revista Electronica de Literatura Mexicana **5361**
1606-8610 Hong Kong Journal of Sociology **8105**
1606-8726 Liza. Goroskop **566**
1606-8734 Liza. Moi Rebenok **2160**
1606-8742 Cool Poster **2183**
1606-8769 Liza. Krossvordy **8186**
1606-8793 African Markets Overview **1609**
1606-8823 *see* 1422-9188 **8848**
1606-8823 *see* 1585-7379 **8848**
1606-8823 *see* 0744-5121 **8848**
1606-8963 The European Union Review **7234**
1606-9269 Directorio de Exportadores de la Republica de Cuba (Year) **1984**
1606-9331 Journal of Nephrology, Urology, and Transplantation **6270**
1606-951X Lichnost', Kultura, Obshchestvo **7983**
1606-9536 Knowledge Bridge **7877**
1606-9609 Liza. Tsvety v Dome **3742**
1606-9749 Water Science and Technology: Water Supply **8840**
1606-9781 Entomologische Arbeitsgemeinschaft Salzkammergut. Mitteilungen **846**
1606-9935 Journal of Water Supply: Research and Technology. AQUA **8828**
1607-0046 Rossiiskaya Akademiya Nauk. Izvestiya. Seriya Matematicheskaya **5530**
1607-0062 La Palabra del Beni **3802**
1607-0135 *see* 1025-3858 **8116**
1607-0313 Diario de Morelos **3908**
1607-0321 El Diario de Tampico **3908**
1607-0348 I S O Journal **6574**
1607-050X Desacatos **335**
1607-0526 *see* AsiaMoney **1308**
1607-0615 Ekonomika i Zhizn' **1103**
1607-0623 Monthly Statistics of International Trade **1252**
1607-0631 Asian Affairs Online **7107**
1607-0658 S A J C N **6669**
1607-0704 International Journal of Business and Economics **1127**
1607-0798 *see* 1606-9749 **8840**
1607-0852 *see* Al- Ittihad **3966**
1607-1042 Frontera **3909**
1607-1069 College of the Bahamas Research Journal **4447**
1607-1093 *see* Infochannel **2558**
1607-1115 *see* 0027-7509 **7156**
1607-1123 Zona Libre **7198**
1607-1220 *see* Origina **7325**
1607-1239 La Republica **3911**
1607-1247 *see* Examen **7135**
1607-1255 *see* 0188-8013 **8517**
1607-1263 Voz Publica **3912**
1607-128X *see* 1405-6658 **2567**
1607-1395 7 Dias **3821**
1607-1425 Angel de la Guarda **8025**
1607-1433 *see* 1607-1425 **8025**
1607-1484 European Central Bank. Occasional Papers **1339**
1607-1751 *see* P C World Malta **2581**
1607-1891 Ekspress K Online **3902**
1607-2006 Pakistan Journal of Radiology **6205**
1607-2081 Afaq al-Taqafah Wa-al-Turath **7945**
1607-209X Magallat Kulliyyat al-Dirasa al-Islamiyyat wa-al-Arabiyyat **5149**
1607-2286 Chinese Journal of the Practical Chinese with Modern Medicine **5594**
1607-2308 Agrarstatistik. Vierteljahresbulletin **81**
1607-2375 Global Insight **7238**
1607-2421 Zhongguo Yiyao Kexue Zazhi/Journal of Chinese Medical Sciences *changed to* 1029-3507 **5735**
1607-2499 Klinicheskaya Gerontologiya **4050**
1607-2510 Applied Mathematics E - Notes **5472**
1607-2650 Le Carcan **3907**
1607-2715 University of KwaZulu-Natal. School of Development Studies. Policy Brief **1607**
1607-2820 New Agenda **1153**
1607-2863 Cocuyo **7847**
1607-2871 Freenews Marketineras **1817**
1607-3088 Lignes Directrices pour les Essais de Produits Chimiques **3500**
1607-310X O E C D Guidelines for the Testing of Chemicals (Online) **3500**
1607-324X Condensed Matter Physics **7009**
1607-3304 Soundscape **3491**
1607-3312 *see* 1450-1147 **6210**
1607-338X I O M Migration Research Series **7284**
1607-3401 El Chino **3927**
1607-3428 El Nuevo Fenix Digital **3831**
1607-3509 *see* 0250-4189 **7909**
1607-3606 Quaestiones Mathematicae **5527**
1607-3614 Southern African Linguistics and Applied Language Studies **5176**
1607-3649 Commission Internationale pour la Protection du Rhin. Rapport d'Activite **2606**
1607-3657 Internationale Kommission zum Schutze des Rheins. Taetigkeitsbericht **2615**
1607-3762 Daily News (Harare) **3996**
1607-3894 Iraqi Journal of Veterinary Sciences **8800**
1607-3983 ART Chronika **469**
1607-4033 Iranian International Journal of Science **7868**
1607-4041 Revista Electronica de Investigacion Educativa **3000**
1607-4106 Journal of Tropical Microbiology *changed to* 1814-7593 **890**
1607-4165 Zhongyang Ribao **3960**
1607-419X Arterial'naya Gipertenziya **5777**
1607-4327 L'Express de Madagascar **3906**
1607-4343 The China Post **3960**
1607-4866 *see* 1018-8177 **3875**
1607-4874 Taiyang Wang *see* 1560-3342 **3875**
1607-4920 *see* 1608-0459 **3943**
1607-4939 *see* 1812-1896 **1108**
1607-4947 *see* 1727-7981 **1347**
1607-503X O P C W Annual Report **7160**
1607-5242 Neft' Priob'ya **6780**
1607-5420 *see* Samarskie Izvestiya **3941**
1607-5471 *see* 1025-1189 **3942**
1607-551X Kaohsiung Journal of Medical Sciences **5656**
1607-5560 Industrial Commodity Statistics Yearbook **1242**
1607-5579 Zeitschrift fuer Schriftpsychologie und Schriftvergleichung†
1607-5617 Instituto Geologico Minero y Metalurgico. Boletin. Serie D. Estudios Regionales **6466**
1607-5684 Ciencia en Accion **7847**
1607-5692 *see* 1607-5684 **7847**
1607-5722 National Taiwan Museum Special Publication Series **7887**
1607-5889 *see* 1816-3831 **4932**
1607-5900 Vanguardia Web *see* 0864-098X **7191**
1607-6079 Revista Digital Universitaria **2566**
1607-6087 C E N D A **7557**
1607-6273 Revista Cubana del Arroz **250**
1607-629X Transversal **7731**
1607-6370 Revista Cine Cubano *see* 0009-6946 **6492**
1607-6389 *see* 0864-1641 **7103**
1607-6397 *see* 0864-0505 **2207**
1607-6400 *see* 0864-0564 **2168**
1607-6524 Current Opinion in European Medicine **5602**
1607-6680 Central Bank of Iceland. Monetary Bulletin **1325**
1607-6729 Doklady Biochemistry and Biophysics **731**
1607-6788 Biomedicas **660**
1607-7016 Cheers **1670**
1607-7334 Bezopasnost' Evrazii **7223**
1607-7393 Reef Resources Assessment and Management. Technical Paper **3605**
1607-7482 Huanbao Chanye **3437**
1607-7938 *see* 1027-5606 **2795**
1607-7946 *see* 1023-5809 **2787**
1607-7962 Geophysical Research Abstracts **2719**
1607-7970 Technichna Elektrodynamika **3332**
1607-8047 Kuwait Medical Journal **5659**
1607-8055 World Leisure Journal **4984**
1607-8063 African Development Report (Year) **1590**
1607-8071 Journal fuer Urologie und Urogynaekologie. Ausgabe Schweiz *see* 1023-6090 **6270**
1607-842X *see* 0891-6934 **5755**
1607-8438 *see* 0300-8207 **831**
1607-8454 *see* 1024-5332 **5937**
1607-8462 *see* 0894-8569 **6244**
1607-8470 *see* 1028-6624 **2135**
1607-8489 *see* 1058-4587 **3319**
1607-8586 Transgenics (Lausanne. Online) *see* 1023-6171 **879**
1607-8616 Geneva Reports on the World Economy **1488**
1607-8810 C N N Interactive English Magazine **5102**
1607-8829 Journal of Thermoelectricity **3159**
1607-887X *see* 1026-0226 **7851**
1607-8888 *see* 1025-3890 **5718**

ISSN

DIRECTORY 2010 1613-3692 9743

1612-2569 eCompany **1416**
1612-2577 Kieferorthopaedie Nachrichten **5854**
1612-2607 I T Qualifikation **1417**
1612-2631 Schriften zur Pflegewissenschaft **5981**
1612-2690 Schriften zum Internationalen Management **1792**
1612-2763 ThyssenKrupp Techforum **8443**
1612-2771 ThyssenKrupp Techforum (English Edition) **8443**
1612-278X Bibliographie zur Geschichte und Kultur des Weines **599**
1612-2909 Notes on Numerical Fluid Mechanics and Multidisciplinary Design **3363**
1612-2941 Marburg Journal of Religion **7661**
1612-295X Intercultural Pragmatics **5128**
1612-3093 E R A Forum **4924**
1612-3166 Heidegger-Jahrbuch **6922**
1612-3174 German Medical Science **5619**
1612-3360 W & S **2671**
1612-3433 Welding and Cutting **6344**
1612-3441 Der Schweisser **6344**
1612-3557 Der Arzt - Zahnarzt und Sein Recht *changed to* 1864-354X **5578**
1612-3565 R W I: Discussion Papers†
1612-3573 R W I: Materialien **7994**
1612-3654 Grundlagen der Rechtsphilosophie **4683**
1612-3743 Die Sparkassen-Zeitung **1384**
1612-3859 Essen und Trinken fuer Jeden Tag **4357**
1612-3867 Angewandte Carabidologie. Supplement *see* 1437-0867 **838**
1612-3980 Ausbildung Pruefung Fortbildung (Baden-Wuerttemberg Edition) **7421**
1612-412X Zitteliana. Reihe A. Mitteilungen der Bayerischen Staatssammlung fur Palaontologie und Geologie **6731**
1612-4138 Zitteliana. Reihe B: Abhandlungen der Bayerischen Staatssammlung fuer Palaeontologie und Geologie **6731**
1612-4162 Olms Forum **6601**
1612-4243 Eur U P **4924**
1612-4340 Begegnungen **7719**
1612-4375 Ambulante Chirurgie **6235**
1612-443X Trends in Medieval Philology **5390**
1612-4545 KlostermannSeminar *changed to* KlostermannRoteReihe **7981**
1612-460X Medical Tribune Klinik **5672**
1612-4642 European Journal of Wildlife Research **319**
1612-4669 European Journal of Forest Research **3688**
1612-4677 *see* 1612-4669 **3688**
1612-4758 Journal of Pest Science **852**
1612-4766 *see* 1612-4758 **852**
1612-4774 Sicherheitshalber **1174**
1612-4782 Cognitive Processing **7347**
1612-4790 *see* 1612-4782 **7347**
1612-4804 International Economics and Economic Policy **1570**
1612-4812 *see* 1612-4804 **1570**
1612-4820 *see* 0172-9179 **2707**
1612-4847 Digital World† **8950**
1612-4855 Der Personalleiter **1871**
1612-4863 Fraunhofer Series in Information and Communication Technology **2543**
1612-4898 Spin Report **751**
1612-4928 Auftragsberater fuer Architekten und Ingenieure **434**
1612-4952 Computer-Guide† **8942**
1612-5010 Zeitschrift fuer Sportpsychologie **7416**
1612-5096 Textile Network **8460**
1612-510X Landslides **2786**
1612-5118 *see* 1612-510X **2786**
1612-5134 Verkehrspolitik in Forschung und Praxis **7475**
1612-5142 Gender Studies **8104**
1612-5177 Vita **6285**
1612-524X Bilanzierungs-Richtlinien Special **1913**
1612-5282 Milchwoche **3656**
1612-5428 V M B G - Mitteilungen (Ausgabe N M B G) *changed to* 1866-7201 **1425**
1612-5460 Ausgabe Technik - I T fuer Finanzdienstleister **1392**
1612-5479 Smart Investor **1651**
1612-5584 Hamotherapie, Beitrage zur Transfusionsmedizin (Bayern Edition) *see* Hamotherapie, Beitrage zur Transfusionsmedizin **5937**
1612-5592 Hamotherapie, Beitrage zur Transfusionsmedizin (Baden-Wurttemberg, Hessen Edition) *see* Hamotherapie, Beitrage zur Transfusionsmedizin **5937**
1612-5606 Hamotherapie, Beitrage zur Transfusionsmedizin (Nordrhein-Westfalen, Rheinland-Pfalz, Saarland Edition) *see* Hamotherapie, Beitrage zur Transfusionsmedizin **5937**
1612-5614 Hamotherapie, Beitrage zur Transfusionsmedizin (Bremen, Niedersachsen, Sachsen-Anhalt, Thuringen Edition) *see* Hamotherapie, Beitrage zur Transfusionsmedizin **5937**
1612-5622 Hamotherapie, Beitrage zur Transfusionsmedizin (Hamburg, Schleswig-Holstein Edition) *see* Hamotherapie, Beitrage zur Transfusionsmedizin **5937**
1612-5630 Hamotherapie, Beitrage zur Transfusionsmedizin (Mecklenburg-Vorpommern Edition) *see* Hamotherapie, Beitrage zur Transfusionsmedizin **5937**
1612-5649 Hamotherapie, Beitrage zur Transfusionsmedizin (Berlin, Brandenburg Edition) *see* Hamotherapie, Beitrage zur Transfusionsmedizin **5937**
1612-5657 Hamotherapie, Beitrage zur Transfusionsmedizin (Sachsen Edition) *see* Hamotherapie, Beitrage zur Transfusionsmedizin **5937**
1612-5681 Journal of Politeness Research **5135**
1612-5746 Beitraege zur Stadtgeschichte und Urbanisierungsforschung **4404**
1612-5835 Donauschwaben-Zeitung **4215**
1612-5940 Historisches Forum **4144**
1612-5959 Zahnarzt und Praxis International *changed to* 1863-7965 **5870**
1612-5983 Rotary Magazin **2269**
1612-6033 Zeithistorische Forschungen **4280**
1612-6041 *see* 1612-6033 **4280**
1612-6068 Journal of International Biotechnology Law **4701**
1612-6076 *see* 1612-6068 **4701**
1612-6327 KoCa - Konditorei und Cafe **3674**
1612-6386 Schriftenreihe Reaktorsicherheit und Strahlenschutz (Online) **3174**
1612-6475 Automation **2458**
1612-6572 Interaktionistischer Konstruktivismus **6925**
1612-6599 Rollladen - Tore - Sonnenschutzsysteme **1034**
1612-6602 Potsdamer Beitrage zur Sozialforschung **7993**
1612-6734 Schriftenreihe der A M L **8131**
1612-6769 Approaches to Applied Semiotics **5095**
1612-6777 Bibliotheca Academica. Reihe Kunst und Altertumswissenschaft **478**
1612-6890 Ballettanz **2682**
1612-7013 *see* 1610-7780 **7276**
1612-703X *see* 0084-5310 **4818**
1612-7048 *see* 0340-2479 **4819**
1612-7056 *see* 1439-1589 **4657**
1612-7064 *see* 0022-6920 **4707**
1612-7110 Profits **1162**
1612-7137 Rechtsdepesche fuer das Gesundheitswesen **5702**
1612-7226 K E M **3206**
1612-7307 PraxisMagazin **5806**
1612-734X Zeitschrift fuer das Gesamte Medizin- und Gesundheitsrecht **5734**
1612-7358 Com! **2553**
1612-7390 Cosmetic Dentistry **5839**
1612-7420 Berichte aus der Fachhochschule **1066**
1612-7501 *see* 1610-241X **1078**
1612-7552 Scientific and Technical Information (CD-ROM) *changed to* reSolution **7084**
1612-7587 Transplantation Aktuell **6261**
1612-7617 Springer Series on Chemical Sensors and Biosensors **2081**
1612-765X S I F A Tipp **6685**
1612-7668 Pressesprecher **32**
1612-7676 Pharma Kodex. Band 1: Arzneimittelsicherheit **6867**
1612-7684 Pharma Kodex. Band 2: Arzneimittelmarkt, Werbung und Information **6867**
1612-7692 Pharma Kodex. Band 3: Europa **6867**
1612-7714 Frankfurter Bibliotheksschriften **5010**
1612-7722 Martin-Heidegger-Gesellschaft. Schriftenreihe **6933**
1612-7730 Studien zu Policey und Policeywissenschaft **4790**
1612-7749 International Poster Journal of Dentistry and Oral Medicine **5849**
1612-7757 Banken und Partner **1316**
1612-779X J u S - Magazin *see* 0022-6939 **4707**
1612-7803 InfrastrukturRecht **4692**
1612-7889 Das Personalvermoegen **1374**
1612-7919 Geist, Erkenntnis, Kommunikation **6921**
1612-8001 Samples **6614**
1612-8060 Orthopedic Trauma Directions **6070**
1612-8087 *see* 1612-8060 **6070**
1612-8133 55plus *changed to* LebensLauf **7764**
1612-8141 Klaex **2198**
1612-815X Language Testing and Evaluation **5142**
1612-8168 Joyce **8869**
1612-8257 Yaez **2222**
1612-8354 Laborjournal **5909**
1612-8419 Trierer Beitraege zum Diversity Management **1876**
1612-8427 Narratologia **5338**
1612-8583 Notfall und Hausarztmedizin. Fokus auf Hausarztmedizin *changed to* 1865-0791 **6068**
1612-8591 Notfall und Hausarztmedizin. Fokus auf Notfallmedizin *changed to* 1865-0791 **6068**
1612-8664 Pflegen Intensiv **5978**
1612-8702 Linguistik - Impulse und Tendenzen **5147**
1612-8753 ProjektArbeit **2900**
1612-880X C E S - I F O Research Reports **1078**
1612-8842 Bericht zum Redaktionsdatenschutz **4572**
1612-8850 Plasma Processes and Polymers **7035**
1612-8869 *see* 1612-8850 **7035**
1612-9008 Totalitarismus und Demokratie **4274**
1612-9059 Esophagus **5923**
1612-9067 *see* 1612-9059 **5923**
1612-9199 *see* 0003-9098 **279**
1612-9202 EcoHealth **3416**
1612-9210 *see* 1612-9202 **3416**
1612-9229 G P R - Zeitschrift fuer Gemeinschaftsprivatrecht **4678**
1612-9237 *see* 0173-783X **8485**
1612-9245 Netzwirtschaften und Recht **4740**
1612-927X Life and Science **6700**
1612-9296 Schriften zur Europapolitik **7265**
1612-930X Forschungsarbeiten und Ergebnisse aus der Psychosomatischen Medizin und Psychotherapie **6141**
1612-9393 Mundo **7883**
1612-9407 Engagiert **7796**
1612-9482 G Ä M **443**
1612-9520 *see* 0028-3517 **7665**
1612-9555 Verband der Privaten Bausparkassen. Jahrbuch **1042**
1612-9563 Rolling Stone **6613**
1612-9571 Starflash† **8990**
1612-958X Jolie **8869**
1612-961X *see* 0949-9571 **7696**
1612-9660 Institut fuer Landes- und Stadtentwicklungsforschung und Bauwesen des Landes N R W. Journal **4416**
1612-9687 Streiflichter (Karben) **4268**
1612-9741 Akademische Blaetter **5205**
1612-9768 *see* 1430-6921 **7650**
1612-9776 *see* 0943-7592 **7696**
1612-9792 *see* 1430-5372 **6930**
1612-9806 *see* 0933-9906 **8893**
1612-9830 Journal of Agriculture and Rural Development in the Tropics and Subtropics **126**
1612-9873 Miteinander (Wuerzburg) **5680**
1612-989X Freiberger Beitraege zur Interkulturellen und Wirtschaftskommunikation **7965**
1612-9938 Bayreuth Evangelisch **7748**
1612-9954 Abenteuer Archaeologie *changed to* 1865-5718 **392**
1613-0006 Anwaltspraxis Wirtschaftsrecht† **8930**
1613-0014 Pet in Europe *changed to* Pet Worldwide **6813**
1613-009X *see* 0044-2615 **7696**
1613-0103 *see* 0044-2526 **7696**
1613-012X Weltengarten **5245**
1613-0138 Technology Review **7922**
1613-0235 KommJur **4710**
1613-026X I D R - Journal of International Dispute Resolution *changed to* 0340-7926 **4938**
1613-0405 *see* 0019-7262 **5127**
1613-0413 *see* 0080-3898 **5170**
1613-0421 *see* 0003-5696 **2230**
1613-0464 *see* 0014-6242 **3617**
1613-0472 Internationales Jahrbuch des Deutschen Idealismus **6926**
1613-0480 *see* 1613-0472 **6926**
1613-060X R V G - Letter†
1613-0626 *see* 0301-3294 **5199**
1613-0642 *see* 0003-7982 **5256**
1613-0650 *see* 0003-9101 **6905**
1613-0669 MedienWirtschaft **2360**
1613-0685 Sabrina - Filetove Hackovani† **8986**
1613-0693 Deutschmagazin **5111**
1613-0707 Sozialwirtschaft **8072**
1613-0723 *see* 0022-7498 **2236**
1613-0731 Dream-Machines Harley-Davidson **8258**
1613-0766 Jungle World **3851**
1613-0782 Steuer- und RechtsBrief Touristik **1945**
1613-0790 *see* 0342-1422 **6936**
1613-0804 *see* 0079-4848 **412**
1613-0812 *see* 0071-9706 **4222**
1613-0820 K f W - Publikationen zu Gruendung und Mittelstand **1139**
1613-0863 Bewegungstherapie und Gesundheitssport **6229**
1613-0871 Procycling **8266**
1613-0901 Praxis Fremdsprachenunterricht **5163**
1613-0928 *see* 0021-1818 **7711**
1613-0952 Studien zum Zivilrecht **4790**
1613-0979 Studien zum Voelker- und Europarecht **4941**
1613-0987 Studien zum Internationalen Privat- und Zivilprozessrecht sowie zum U N Kaufrecht **4941**
1613-0995 Studien zum Familienrecht **4914**
1613-1002 Studien zum Verwaltungsrecht **4790**
1613-107X Digitales Handbuch zur Geschichte und Kultur Russlands **4214**
1613-1096 Strassenverkehrsrecht **4789**
1613-1118 Eurolinguistische Arbeiten **5117**
1613-1134 *see* 0022-8877 **6930**
1613-1142 *see* 1430-9017 **7870**
1613-1150 *see* 0084-5299 **424**
1613-1185 Studien zur Musikwissenschaft (Hamburg) **6621**
1613-1215 Detail. Bauten und Produkte **440**
1613-1223 Sicher ist Sicher - Arbeitsschutz Aktuell **6687**
1613-1266 Interkulturell und Global **2868**
1613-1274 Spass mit Musik *changed to* 1862-2488 **6606**
1613-1290 D U Z Magazin **2977**
1613-1304 D U Z Nachrichten *changed to* 1867-9595 **2977**
1613-138X Schriften zur Kunstpaedagogik und Aesthetischen Erziehung **516**
1613-1460 P F A D **2163**
1613-1479 Schriften zur Sozialisationsforschung **8131**
1613-1606 Last und Kraft **8672**
1613-1770 Mosty **5228**
1613-186X EyeBizz **6042**
1613-1878 Gender Forum **4374**
1613-2009 F F† **8955**
1613-2033 Linux Journal†
1613-2041 Monatsschrift fuer Brauwissenschaft (Online) **614**
1613-2068 Heritage **4226**
1613-2076 Gynecological Surgery **6244**
1613-2084 *see* 1613-2076 **6244**
1613-2092 FibrinolyseNews **5905**
1613-2122 Friedrich-Alexander-Universitaet Erlangen-Nuernberg. Lehrstuhl Qualitaetsmanagement und Fertigungsmesstechik. Berichte **1886**
1613-2130 Praxis Ethnologie **352**
1613-2238 *see* 0943-1853 **7546**
1613-2246 *see* 0021-5155 **6044**
1613-2254 *see* 1346-4523 **7088**
1613-2319 Automatisierungstechnische Praxis International **4486**
1613-2351 Schriftenreihe Rechtswissenschaft **4780**
1613-236X Bestseller† **8935**
1613-2394 World of Metallurgy - Erzmetall **6337**
1613-2408 World of Mining - Surface & Underground **6483**
1613-2483 A D A C Special Gebrauchtwagen Test **8554**
1613-2505 T V P - Fachzeitschrift fuer Textilveredlung und Promotion **8458**
1613-2548 European Company and Financial Law Review **4867**
1613-2556 *see* 1613-2548 **4867**
1613-2599 Schriften zum Versicherungs-, Haftungs- und Schadensrecht **4780**
1613-267X Gesellschaft fuer Umweltrecht. Tagungen **3433**
1613-2696 Food & Hygiene **3637**
1613-2718 Food Ingredients & Sensorik **3639**
1613-2831 Schriften zum Medienrecht **2338**
1613-3110 Berater-Brief Vermoegen *changed to* Berater-Brief Erben und Vermoegen **1912**
1613-3161 Audio Video Foto Bild **2400**
1613-317X Barlach-Journal **5208**
1613-3218 Diana - Detska Sita Moda† **8950**
1613-3226 Diana - Hackovani Special **6638**
1613-3269 *see* 1613-0863 **6229**
1613-3277 Blickwechsel **7950**
1613-3331 Bus Blickpunkt **8491**
1613-3358 Bau im Norden *changed to* 1860-1790 **979**
1613-3382 Soil Biology **896**
1613-3390 Russlandanalysen **7264**
1613-3412 European Clinics in Obstetrics and Gynaecology†
1613-3544 Wissen und Lernen in Organisationen **2926**
1613-3625 *see* 1612-1783 **5599**
1613-3633 InFo Onkologie **6022**
1613-3641 *see* 0936-5907 **5106**
1613-365X *see* 1612-295X **5128**
1613-3668 *see* 0165-2516 **5130**
1613-3676 *see* 0167-6318 **5146**
1613-3684 *see* 0167-8507 **5153**
1613-3692 *see* 0037-1998 **5173**

ISSN

1623-6718 Les Enjeux du L A B O†
1623-6742 Syntaxe & Semantique **5184**
1623-6955 Texnews by France Textile
1623-7080 Sageret. Nord *changed to* 1967-5917 **1034**
1623-7153 Sageret. Sud *changed to* 1967-5917 **1034**
1623-7382 T C M **4975**
1623-8397 Droit-Eco-Gestion **2978**
1623-8613 Tresors du Bouddhisme **7702**
1623-9083 Archives des Maladies du Coeur et des Vaisseaux - Infirmiere Pratique† **8931**
1623-944X A E F A. Association des Entraineurs Francais d'Athletisme **8156**
1624-0014 Africa Mining Intelligence (French Edition) **6456**
1624-0022 Africa Mining Intelligence (English Edition) **6456**
1624-0693 Reanimation **5773**
1624-074X Journees de Medecine Orthopedique et de Reeducation **6111**
1624-0898 T H S la Revue des Addictions **5827**
1624-1789 Universites. Lettres Classiques **5393**
1624-1940 Les Cahiers Magellanes **842**
1624-2165 Cahier des Sciences Morales et Politiques
1624-365X Revue du Droit de l'Union Europeenne **1581**
1624-3765 Profession Fonctionnaire. Hors Serie
1624-4710 P S M 2 **2480**
1624-5326 La Tribune de la Suderurgie **6335**
1624-5636 Office National de la Chasse. Fiche Technique *see* 1626-6641 **943**
1624-5687 Douleurs **5607**
1624-5709 Banque de France. La Situation des Entreprises Industrielles† **8935**
1624-5849 Encyclopedie Medico-Chirurgicale. Techniques Chirurgicales. Tete et Cou **6242**
1624-5857 Encyclopedie Medico-Chirurgicale. Techniques Chirurgicales. Gynecologie **6242**
1624-5865 Encyclopedie Medico-Chirurgicale. Traite de Radiodiagnostic: Principes et Techniques *changed to* Encyclopedie Medico-Chirurgicale. Radiologie et Imagerie Medicale. Principes et Techniques - Radioprotection **6196**
1624-6039 *see* 1625-8312 **8511**
1624-6179 Le Guide de la Protection de l'Enfance **8043**
1624-6209 *see* 1624-0014 **6456**
1624-6217 *see* 1624-0022 **6456**
1624-6837 F 1 Magazine **8172**
1624-6853 L'Officiel de l'Artisan Rural†
1624-6934 Reserve de Biosphere Transfrontaliere Vosges du Nord - Pfalzerwald. Annales Scientifiques
1624-6969 Audit **1280**
1624-7396 Centre d'Etudes Techniques Maritime et Fluviales. Revue Technique† **8940**
1624-7701 France. Ministere de l'Agriculture et de la Peche. Agreste Conjoncture Aviculture†
1624-7949 Le Monde de l'Inconnu†
1624-8228 Euro T B Newsletter **5813**
1624-8570 Kiteboarder **8320**
1624-8597 Phytotherapie **6114**
1624-8694 Maison Creative **4546**
1624-8813 Geo Hors-Serie *see* 0220-8245 **4007**
1624-8953 Pharmacien Manager **6871**
1624-9011 France. Ministere de l'Agriculture et de la Peche. Agreste. Chiffres et Donnees. Agriculture **199**
1625-1180 European Practice in Gynaecology and Obstetrics **5990**
1625-211X Amis de Saint Jacques en Alsace. Le Bulletin *changed to* 1774-5268 **7623**
1625-2721 College de 'Pataphysique. Carnets Trimestriels *changed to* 1965-1244 **6912**
1625-2780 Imaginaires (Villeneuve d'Ascq)
1625-3310 Economies Plurielles **1102**
1625-4104 Le Bulletin Juridique du Praticien Hospitalier **5589**
1625-449X Jeux Video **2478**
1625-4759 Moi Je Lis **2203**
1625-5437 Transversal (Montgeron)†
1625-5771 C N E S Magazine (English Edition) *changed to* 1283-9817 **50**
1625-5925 Techniques de l'Ingenieur. Environnement. La Lettre *changed to* 1957-2891 **3371**
1625-6433 France - Photographie **6968**
1625-6484 Pedagogie Medicale **2997**
1625-6581 Historia Thematique **4142**
1625-6778 Maison Bricolage *changed to* 1766-4381 **4546**
1625-7456 Architectures a Vivre **431**
1625-7464 Vermeil† **8997**
1625-7553 Messages *changed to* 1961-7070 **5709**
1625-8266 Pays de Lunel *changed to* 1774-5462 **7490**
1625-8312 Supply Chain Forum **8511**
1625-8738 Sciences de la Musique **6615**
1625-8851 Autrement Junior. Serie Societe **2177**
1625-9297 Bibliotheque Nordique **4445**
1625-9548 Lamy Produits et Biens de Grande Consommation **132**
1625-9572 *see* 1762-0589 **7488**
1625-9602 Lamy Droit de la Responsabilite **4834**
1625-967X *see* 0248-1294 **3730**
1625-9734 *see* 1166-7648 **7065**
1625-9777 Qui Transporte **8509**
1625-9785 Lamy Logistique **8502**
1625-9793 Juridisque Transport Jurisprudence **4706**
1625-9823 Lyon Pharmaceutique (Online)†
1625-9963 *see* 0153-4092 **7899**
1626-0082 Bibliographie Nationale Francaise. Livres, Publications en Serie et Documents Electroniques† **8936**
1626-0104 Bibliographie Nationale Francaise. Livres (Online Edition) **7577**
1626-0112 Bibliographie Nationale Francaise. Publications en Serie **618**
1626-0163 CD-ROM Electre† **8940**
1626-0198 C E A Annual Report (Year) **7842**
1626-0228 Juris-Classeur Numerique. Protection Sociale Traite *see* 1623-4774 **4706**
1626-0244 Juris-Classeur Numerique. Responsabilite Civile et Assurances *see* 0750-8301 **4706**
1626-0252 Nuevo Mundo - Mundos Nuevos **4306**
1626-0279 Lamy Negociation Collective **4873**
1626-0384 Societe Francaise de Parasitologie. Bulletin **896**
1626-0457 Juris-Classeur Numerique. Banque Credit Bourse *see* 1761-290X **4872**
1626-0465 Juris-Classeur Numerique. Copropriete *see* 0750-8573 **4873**
1626-0473 Juris-Classeur Numerique. Divorce *see* 1240-5205 **4911**
1626-0481 Juris-Classeur Numerique. Environnement *see* 1163-0949 **4706**
1626-049X Juris-Classeur Numerique. Rural *see* 0750-831X **4706**
1626-1429 MediaMorphoses **7985**
1626-1437 Caucesť **8940**
1626-1607 Annales de l'I S U P **5548**
1626-1682 Revue Internationale de l'Economie Sociale **1424**
1626-1844 Le Geste et l'Outil **535**
1626-3162 Marges Linguistiques†
1626-3219 *see* 1270-9638 **43**
1626-3375 Revue Francophone du Stress et du Trauma
1626-4142 Ragga *changed to* Reggae Vibes **6610**
1626-4207 Comprendre† **8942**
1626-4428 L'Argus de L'Assurance **4493**
1626-5238 Memoire des Vosges **4244**
1626-5246 Horizons Banquaires **200**
1626-5394 W A D **2220**
1626-5734 Neuronale **6167**
1626-598X Alafolie *changed to* 1964-9169 **8879**
1626-6641 Faune Sauvage **943**
1626-6838 Eurovin - News **109**
1626-715X Playbox† **8981**
1626-7370 Champs Libres **4447**
1626-7680 Legalis.net **2431**
1626-7745 Etudes Kurdes **3532**
1626-8210 Auto Moto *changed to* 1762-9314 **8555**
1627-0274 Initiatives Magazine *changed to* 1955-9631 **1964**
1627-0452 Pianiste **6605**
1627-0541 Celtics
1627-0711 C L E I R P P A. Documents. Cahier **4042**
1627-0983 PlayStation 2 Magazine **2480**
1627-1009 P C Jeux. Hors-Serie **2479**
1627-1041 Terre de Provence **8760**
1627-2676 Dental Dialogue (French Edition) *see* 1825-2206 **5840**
1627-2676 Dental Dialogue (French Edition) *see* 1697-3879 **5840**
1627-2676 Dental Dialogue (French Edition) *see* 1862-3743 **5840**
1627-2757 Correspondances en Pelvi-Perineologie† **8944**
1627-3052 Girl! Hors-Serie *see* 1286-577X **2191**
1627-3184 Armes de Chasse **8304**
1627-3346 Prevalence **5699**
1627-3486 Composites International **7091**
1627-3516 Centre de Coservation et d'Etude des Collections. Cahiers Scientifiques **7844**
1627-3583 Animal Research *changed to* 1751-7311 **932**
1627-4040 Collection Versions Francaises **5276**
1627-430X Frontieres **8103**
1627-4512 Une Histoire pour l'Histoire **5306**
1627-4571 Crimes & Mysteres **5413**
1627-4784 *see* 1625-6484 **2997**
1627-4792 Management **1774**
1627-4830 N P G - Neurologie Psychiatrie Gerontologie **6162**
1627-4857 L'A G E F I Actifs **1609**
1627-4873 Geocarrefour **4008**
1627-4911 La Geographie **4011**
1627-492X Coaching†
1627-4970 Livraisons d'Histoire de l'Architecture **449**
1627-5977 Droits et Procedures **4661**
1627-623X S N E T A C. Journal *changed to* 1761-6425 **1034**
1627-7112 Textes et Contre-Textes **5187**
1627-7244 Solutions Reseaux **2503**
1627-8283 Secrets d'Artisans **539**
1627-9158 Bottin Entreprises (Paris, 2000) **1069**
1627-9395 Loft Story **2384**
1627-9433 Association Francaise de la Gestion Financiere. Annuaire **1611**
1628-0229 B@ti-Com **978**
1628-0482 Histoire Urbaine **4227**
1628-0695 Ideal Broderie† **8963**
1628-0741 Medecine du Sud Est†
1628-1241 Le Journal des Telecoms **2369**
1628-1276 Banque de France. Recueil des Textes Relatifs a l'Exercice des Activites Bancaires et Financieres *changed to* 1955-0502 **1319**
1628-1306 Infos - U N S A Education†
1628-1616 Revue Economique Franco Suisse **1409**
1628-1632 Micro Dingo **2578**
1628-1829 Ideal Coiffure **589**
1628-2124 Maximoto **8260**
1628-2205 Bulletin Infermier du Cancer **6010**
1628-2329 College de France. La Lettre **4447**
1628-3368 Developpeur Reference **2506**
1628-3376 P C Utilities **2581**
1628-3384 Rap U S *see* 1966-6748 **6609**
1628-3392 Recording Musicien **8154**
1628-3414 M6 Tomb Raider **2478**
1628-3457 P C Driver **2579**
1628-464X Les Dossiers de Spirale **7352**
1628-4658 Chemins Noirs **5413**
1628-4771 Les Cahiers de la Nature **307**
1628-5263 Reference Artisan **539**
1628-5735 Cahiers de Cantercel **436**
1628-5921 Idees et Modeles **536**
1628-6073 Gestion Publique **7439**
1628-6332 R H Territoriales *changed to* 1958-1254 **8984**
1628-6731 Les Cahiers A L H I M **3524**
1628-674X La Nouvelle Vie Ouvriere **4600**
1628-6847 La Phytotherapie Europeenne **6875**
1628-7657 Correspondances en Neurologie Vasculaire **5784**
1628-7711 La Lettre de la Region - Conseil Regional Provence-Alpes-Cote d'Azur *changed to* 1779-1561 **4981**
1628-8319 Le Courrier de la Transplantation **6240**
1628-8556 Online Gamer **2479**
1628-870X D V D Magazine **2400**
1628-8890 Games Collector **2477**
1628-8971 Pages Web Pratiques **2565**
1628-9595 Pierre Actual **6476**
1628-9676 Imaginaire & Inconscient **7361**
1628-9706 Wood Surfer **461**
1629-1212 Alimentation et Precarite **6654**
1629-1603 Protection Individuelle & Collective **1704**
1629-2472 Maison Passion Creation† **8972**
1629-2715 Croire Aujourd'hui Jeunes Chretiens *changed to* 1778-994X **8947**
1629-3576 Champ'eco **1400**
1629-436X Le Point Eco **1408**
1629-4475 Photoniques **7084**
1629-4793 Logiques Sociales. Serie Sociologie de la Modernite **8119**
1629-4939 Documents Mathematiques **5484**
1629-5560 I N S E E Resultats **1241**
1629-5781 Danse (Paris, 2001) **2685**
1629-6583 Droit, Deontologie et Soin **5607**
1629-6966 Muteen **2204**
1629-7121 Enquete - Ecole des Hautes Etudes en Sciences Sociales **336**
1629-7199 L'Esprit de la Creation **4451**
1629-7830 Cooperation Internationale **7120**
1629-825X Societes Bresiliennes† **8989**
1629-8640 Le Grand Livre P N P *changed to* 1764-6499 **8960**
1629-8888 Politique
1629-9213 Musiciens Magazine† **8975**
1629-9248 Asset Management Magazine **1610**
1629-9655 Revue - Toxibase†
1629-9744 D Lire **2184**
1630-0165 Universites. Statistiques Sciences Humaines **8084**
1630-019X Guide Rouge **4359**
1630-0211 Universites. Mathematiques Appliquees **5545**
1630-0246 Autrement Junior. Serie Histoire **2177**
1630-1412 La Gazette du Groupe d'Etude en Orthopedie Pediatrique†
1630-1633 Le Bulletin de Phyllie *changed to* 1777-6198 **841**
1630-2206 Actualite Juridique. Famille **4906**
1630-3164 Juris-Classeur Numerique. Brevets *see* 0181-446X **4706**
1630-3482 La Synthese - A E F *changed to* 1779-0875 **2996**
1630-3555 Federation Hospitaliere de France. La Lettre **4093**
1630-3792 La Volonte des P M E **1434**
1630-3903 W A D. Hors-Serie **2220**
1630-4101 Activeto **8790**
1630-4578 Strasbourg In Your Pocket **8758**
1630-4586 Le Journal de la Renaissance **4235**
1630-4799 Office National Interprofessionnel des Produits de la Mer et de l'Aquaculture. Rapport Annuel **3604**
1630-487X Maison & Jardin Passion† **8972**
1630-4969 Le Mans Racing **8186**
1630-4977 Biblia **7627**
1630-5078 Fondation de la France Libre **6421**
1630-5159 Drummer *changed to* 0981-8936 **6548**
1630-5639 Recherche et Pratique dans la Maladie d'Alzheimer *see* 1284-8360 **4054**
1630-5752 Itineraires du Savoir **6927**
1630-649X Information Interaction Intelligence **2545**
1630-7062 Electronic Auto Volt **8578**
1630-7267 International Journal of Design Sciences & Technology **8427**
1630-7356 Actes de l'Histoire de l'Immigration (Print Edition) **7276**
1630-7364 Tabularia **4272**
1630-7380 Vigilances **5728**
1630-7399 L'Hemovigilance **5938**
1630-7445 Alizes **4282**
1630-800X Assistante Plus *changed to* 1959-7606 **1853**
1630-8174 L'Annuaire des Laboratoires d'Analyses de Biologie Medicale **5902**
1630-8255 *see* 1624-8228 **5813**
1630-9553 Electronic Banking News† **8953**
1630-9782 Logiciels & Services† **8971**
1631-0438 Outre-Mers. Revue d'Histoire **4155**
1631-0675 Dictionnaire Permanent: Recouvrement des Creances et Procedures d'Execution **1287**
1631-0683 Academie des Sciences. Comptes Rendus. Palevol **6722**
1631-0691 Academie des Sciences. Comptes Rendus. Biologies **649**
1631-0705 Academie des Sciences. Comptes Rendus. Physique **2132**
1631-0713 Academie des Sciences. Comptes Rendus. Geoscience **7830**
1631-0721 Academie des Sciences. Comptes Rendus. Mecanique **3372**
1631-073X Academie des Sciences. Comptes Rendus. Mathematique **5464**
1631-0748 Academie des Sciences. Comptes Rendus. Chimie **2048**
1631-1035 A D D X **8554**
1631-1132 La Revue de l'Atelier **1432**
1631-1353 Cancer Futures **6012**
1631-2864 Fleuristerie **3756**
1631-4271 Mythes, Croyances et Religions†
1631-462X Ecrire Magazine **4574**
1631-4786 Francophonies du Sud **5120**
1631-5227 Mickey Parade Geant **2202**
1631-7696 Syndicat des Enseignants Bourgogne *changed to* 1774-4741 **4593**
1631-7904 Twenty†
1631-8102 Astro Revue **565**
1631-963X Pas a Pas **3747**
1631-9737 Sciences Politiques
1631-9761 Coming Next **2506**
1631-994X Le Bac en Tete. Sciences de la Vie et de la Terre **2830**
1632-0654 Stuff **2438**
1632-0700 Special Derniere - Le Meilleur **8298**
1632-0859 Histoire Antique **4141**
1632-0948 Les Medailles du C N R S *changed to* 1777-0378 **7844**
1632-0948 Les Medailles du C N R S *changed to* 1777-9251 **7844**
1632-1049 Titres Infos **1846**
1632-2274 L'Internet Agricole *changed to* 1950-1390 **85**

ISSN

1640-7598 Wyszsa Szkola Pedagogiczna im. Komisji Edukacji Narodowej w Krakowie. Rocznik Naukowo-Dydaktyczny. Prace z Edukacji Obronnej *changed to* 1734-9133 **2225**
1640-7601 Warsaw University of Technology. Institute of Aeronautics and Applied Mechanics. Research Bulletin†
1640-7776 P C Format **2579**
1640-842X Echo Peryferii **2979**
1640-8497 Diabetologia Praktyczna **5890**
1640-8632 Annual of Navigation **3998**
1640-873X Polska 2000 Plus **8125**
1640-8993 13 **2224**
1640-9280 Policja **2664**
1640-9930 Practyczny Poradnik Ksiegowego **1299**
1641-0106 Body Life **586**
1641-0440 Naj Poleca *see* 1232-7654 **8877**
1641-0777 Wskazniki, Stawki, Dokumenty **1304**
1641-0785 Serwis Nieruchomosci Administracji i Zarzadzania **7612**
1641-0793 Personel i Zarzadzanie **1872**
1641-0874 Zarzadzanie Zasobami Ludzkimi **1878**
1641-0882 Human Resource Management *see* 1641-0874 **1878**
1641-1005 Informator Instalacyjny **4121**
1641-1021 Obywatel **3930**
1641-1196 Forum Teologiczne **7644**
1641-1307 Dendrobiology **785**
1641-148X *see* 0867-3764 **4237**
1641-1706 Takie jest Zycie! **8885**
1641-2168 Akademia Ekonomiczna w Poznaniu. Zeszyty Naukowe **1058**
1641-2389 Klub dla Ciebie **4979**
1641-2575 Internet Standard **2562**
1641-2613 Perspectives in Environmental Sciences **3459**
1641-3474 Lodzka Szkola Diabetologii. Dziennik **5896**
1641-3490 Alter Ego **5205**
1641-3628 Uniwersytet Slaski w Katowicach. Prace Naukowe. Fizyka i Chemia Materialow†
1641-3970 Bunt Mlodych Duchem **5209**
1641-4233 International Studies **7975**
1641-4608 Kazimierz **3930**
1641-4616 *see* 1641-4608 **3930**
1641-4640 Folia Neuropathologica **6141**
1641-5280 Inwestor Finansowy **1634**
1641-5558 Studia Quaternaria **2770**
1641-5566 Boss Gospodarka **194**
1641-5574 Boss Business News Poland **1068**
1641-5639 Akademia Pedagogiczna im. Komisji Edukacji Narodowej w Krakowie. Rocznik Naukowo-Dydaktyczny. Prace Ekonomiczno-Spoleczne†
1641-5701 Boss Rolnictwo **97**
1641-5973 Archeus **329**
1641-6007 Sen **7407**
1641-6279 Nowosci Neurologiczne *see* 0741-4234 **6166**
1641-6554 Kolposkopia *changed to* 1731-8602 **6002**
1641-6759 R jak Remont **4549**
1641-6961 Bialostockie Archiwum Jezykowe **5099**
1641-7046 Katedra **8900**
1641-7291 Geological Quarterly **2738**
1641-7348 Ogolnopolski Przeglad Medyczny **5689**
1641-7445 Polish Entomological Monographs **857**
1641-7453 Ha!art **5219**
1641-750X Ekonomia On-line **1225**
1641-7844 *see* 0079-2993 **7391**
1641-7968 Orzecznictwo Podatkowe. Przeglad **1938**
1641-8077 Organizacja i Zarzadzanie w Regionie Nadmorskim **1431**
1641-8190 Polish Botanical Journal **813**
1641-8204 Current Medical Literature. Laryngologia†
1641-8611 Kompozyty **7094**
1641-876X International Journal of Applied Mathematics and Computer Science **2472**
1641-9103 Ochrona Srodowiska. Przeglad **3457**
1641-9162 Maxim **6294**
1641-9251 International Maritime Health **5819**
1641-9367 Profit *changed to* 1733-7291 **1110**
1641-9561 Instytut Pamieci Narodowej. Biuletyn **4232**
1641-9715 Modus **506**
1641-9758 Studia Kognitywne **5180**
1642-0136 Fizjoterapia Polska **6109**
1642-0489 Studia Informatica **2464**
1642-0853 Gosciniec **8714**
1642-1027 Teaching English with Technology **2951**
1642-168X Argumenta Oeconomica Cracoviensia **1061**
1642-2104 Dobra Gra **2475**
1642-2309 Informator Kulturalny Miasta Katowice **5221**
1642-2473 Studia Psychologica **7410**
1642-2503 Polska Akademia Umiejetnosci i Polska Akademia Nauk w Krakowie. Biblioteka Naukowa. Rocznik **5039**
1642-2945 Swiat Filmu D V D. Kino **2403**
1642-2953 Swiat Filmu D V D. Fantastyka **2403**
1642-2961 Swiat Filmu D V D. Komedia **2403**
1642-316X Neurologia Praktyczna **6165**
1642-3178 Ortopedia Szczekowa i Ortodoncja†
1642-3305 Akademia Pedagogiczna im. Komisji Edukacji Narodowej w Krakowie. Rocznik Naukowo-Dydaktyczny. Prace Geograficzne†
1642-3399 Trubadur **6624**
1642-3402 Annals of Animal Science **318**
1642-3593 Ecohydrology & Hydrobiology **2793**
1642-395X Postepy Dermatologii i Alergologii **5881**
1642-4026 Filipinka Wydanie Specjalne *see* 0426-1216 **2188**
1642-4042 Sports Illustrated. Swimsuit Edition **8207**
1642-4069 Polski Przeglad Dyplomatyczny **7260**
1642-4204 *see* 1643-7721 **1259**
1642-431X Reproductive Biology **700**
1642-4441 Indeks O T C **6847**
1642-445X A B C Apteki **6817**
1642-4670 Praca, Zdrowie, Bezpieczenstwo **6684**
1642-5308 Archiwum Odlewnictwa *changed to* 1897-3310 **6305**
1642-557X Studia Wschodnioslowianskie **5181**
1642-5626 Gala **8865**
1642-5650 Studia Bobolanum **7818**
1642-5758 Anaesthesiology Intesive Therapy **5768**
1642-6231 Swiat Filmu D V D. Kino Artystyczne **2403**
1642-624X Swiat Filmu D V D. Akcja **2403**
1642-6606 Politechnika Poznanska. Zeszyty Naukowe. Maszyny Robocze i Transport **3393**
1642-6770 Business Week **1076**
1642-7602 2 + 3 D **7329**
1642-8080 Nowosci Ginekologiczne *see* 0743-8354 **6000**
1642-8188 C X O *changed to* 1734-9478 **1414**
1642-8412 Meble **5227**
1642-8463 Operomania **6602**
1642-8471 Current Medical Literature. Kardiologia†
1642-8951 Cybiz **1416**
1642-9249 Polish Construction Review **1644**
1642-9303 Foundations of Civil and Environmental Engineering **3267**
1642-9478 Zdrowie Seniora **4057**
1642-9893 Bohemistyka **5265**
1642-9974 Burda. Wydanie Specjalne **2252**
1643-0360 Evropa **7234**
1643-0379 The Polish Foreign Affairs Digest **7259**
1643-0867 Dobre Rady. Piekna i Zdrowa **8858**
1643-0905 *see* 0867-3217 **3480**
1643-112X Cyber Mycha Extra *see* 1640-307X **2184**
1643-1278 Czarodziejki W.I.T.C.H. **2184**
1643-1588 Chwila na 100 Panoramicznych **8166**
1643-1618 Drogi i Mosty **3265**
1643-2053 Murator Wielkopolski *see* 0239-6866 **450**
1643-2061 Murator Malopolski *see* 0239-6866 **450**
1643-207X Murator Lodzki *see* 0239-6866 **450**
1643-2088 Murator Pomorski *see* 0239-6866 **450**
1643-2096 Murator Slaski *see* 0239-6866 **450**
1643-210X Murator Dolnoslaski *see* 0239-6866 **450**
1643-2118 Murator Mazowiecki *see* 0239-6866 **450**
1643-2444 Keryks **7803**
1643-2762 Studia Oecumenica **7684**
1643-3289 Ksiezniczka. Wydanie Specjalne *see* 1509-7935 **2198**
1643-3319 Przeglad Muzykologiczny **6608**
1643-3750 *see* 1234-1010 **5671**
1643-4439 Journal of Apicultural Science **127**
1643-5664 Poland. Ministerstwo Zdrowia. Dziennik Urzedowy *changed to* 1643-5672 **7434**
1643-5672 Dziennik Urzedowy Ministra Zdrowia **7434**
1643-6202 Dobre Rady. Diety Odchudzajace **6657**
1643-6520 Annales Academiae Paedagogicae Cracoviensis. Studia Romanica **5094**
1643-6539 Annales Academiae Paedagogicae Cracoviensis. Studia ad Bibliothecarum Scientiam Pertinentia **4989**
1643-6547 Annales Academiae Paedagogicae Cracoviensis. Studia Historica **4130**
1643-6555 Annales Academiae Paedagogicae Cracoviensis. Studia Mathematica **5470**
1643-6911 Krakowskie Studia Malopolskie **4238**
1643-7306 Magazyn Przemyslu Miesnego **3655**
1643-7365 Przy Stoliku **3681**
1643-7373 W Akcji **3582**
1643-7381 Laboratorium **5908**
1643-742X Poland Monthly **1160**
1643-7446 Humanizacja Pracy **1685**
1643-7489 Malzenstwo i Rodzina **8119**
1643-7721 Poland. Glowny Urzad Statystyczny. Rocznik Statystyczny Handlu Zagranicznego **1259**
1643-8191 Klio **4237**
1643-8256 Komputerowa Gratka **2198**
1643-8264 Dobre Rady **8858**
1643-8388 Forum Iuridicum **7798**
1643-8590 Wedrowiec **6628**
1643-8876 Przeglad Menopauzalny **6002**
1643-8949 Information Technology for Economics & Management **2423**
1643-9252 Nature Conservation **2621**
1643-9279 Postepy w Chirurgii Glowy i Szyi **6256**
1643-9953 Polish Journal of Natural Sciences **7898**
1643-9988 Cukiernictwo i Piekarstwo **3673**
1644-0625 Acta Scientiarum Polonorum. Agricultura **79**
1644-0633 Acta Scientiarum Polonorum. Architectura **427**
1644-0641 Acta Scientiarum Polonorum. Biologia **650**
1644-065X Acta Scientiarum Polonorum. Biotechnologia **755**
1644-0668 Acta Scientiarum Polonorum. Geodesia et Descriptio Terrarum **3997**
1644-0676 Acta Scientiarum Polonorum. Medicina Veterinaria **8790**
1644-0684 Acta Scientiarum Polonorum. Technica Agraria **209**
1644-0692 Acta Scientiarum Polonorum. Hortorum Cultus **3721**
1644-0706 Acta Scientiarum Polonorum. Piscaria **3582**
1644-0714 Acta Scientiarum Polonorum. Zootechnica **277**
1644-0722 Acta Scientiarum Polonorum. Silvarum Colendarum Ratio et Industria Lignaria **3682**
1644-0730 Acta Scientiarum Polonorum. Technologia Alimentaria **3625**
1644-0749 Acta Scientiarum Polonorum. Administratio Locorum **4402**
1644-0757 Acta Scientiarum Polonorum. Oeconomia **1056**
1644-0765 Acta Scientiarum Polonorum. Formatio Circumiectus **3400**
1644-0919 Krytyka Polityczna **5223**
1644-115X Polska Medycyna Paliatywna *changed to* 1898-0678 **5678**
1644-1664 Current Medical Literature. Reumatologia *changed to* 1895-2356
1644-1869 Annales Academiae Paedagogicae Cracoviensis. Studia ad Calculum Probabilitatis Eiusque Didacticam Pertinentia **5470**
1644-1877 Annales Academiae Paedagogicae Cracoviensis. Studia Linguistica **5094**
1644-1885 Annales Academiae Paedagogicae Cracoviensis. Studia Historicolitteraria **5255**
1644-1893 Annales Academiae Cracoviensis. Studia Zoologica **933**
1644-2296 Journal of Elementology **736**
1644-2911 Dziennik Urzedowy Ministra Edukacji Narodowej *changed to* 1644-292X **2843**
1644-292X Dziennik Urzedowy Ministra Edukacji Narodowej i Sportu **2843**
1644-3101 *see* 1428-5851 **5796**
1644-3306 *see* 1641-6007 **7407**
1644-3349 *see* 1507-5524 **6239**
1644-3381 Nowa Wies Europejska **143**
1644-3470 Materialy Ceramiczne **2044**
1644-3586 Uniwersytet Jagiellonski. Instytut Geografii i Gospodarki Przestrzennej. Prace Geograficzne **4033**
1644-3608 Central European Journal of Physics **7007**
1644-3616 *see* 1895-1074 **5477**
1644-3624 *see* 1895-1066 **2053**
1644-3632 *see* 1895-104X **665**
1644-3640 *see* 1895-1058 **5593**
1644-387X Dental and Medical Problems **5839**
1644-3888 Artifex **473**
1644-3985 Drewno **1050**
1644-4019 Zgrzewanie Metali i Tworzyw w Praktyce *changed to* 1732-1425 **6344**
1644-4116 *see* 1429-8538 **6178**
1644-4124 *see* 1426-3912 **5755**
1644-4345 *see* 1506-9680 **6204**
1644-4477 *see* 1640-8497 **5890**
1644-4493 *see* 1898-0678 **5678**
1644-4841 Controlling i Rachunkowosc Zarzadcza **1286**
1644-485X Nefrologia i Nadcisnienie Tetnicze **6271**
1644-4906 Strzal **8210**
1644-5198 Emerging Europe Market Review **1621**
1644-5392 *see* 0867-339X **5806**
1644-6496 Nowa Miss *changed to* 1733-1951 **8854**
1644-6658 Impuls
1644-7298 Ecological Questions **3417**
1644-7387 Nowosci w Chorobach Infekcyjnych *see* 0739-7348 **5817**
1644-745X Budownictwo, Technologie, Architektura **984**
1644-7700 Biological Letters **658**
1644-7921 Annales Academiae Paedagogicae Cracoviensis. Studia Politologica **7106**
1644-793X Annales Academiae Paedagogicae Cracoviensis. Studia Philosophica **6904**
1644-9274 I T & Telecoms Monitor **2325**
1644-9665 Archives of Civil and Mechanical Engineering **3374**
1645-0086 Psicologia, Saude e Docencas **7393**
1645-0523 Revista Portuguesa de Ciencias do Desporto **8196**
1645-0639 Cidades - Comunidades e Territorios **4407**
1645-1384 Curriculo sem Fronteiras **2976**
1645-2194 Intervir **2871**
1645-2259 Revista da Historia da Sociedade e da Cultura **4472**
1645-2453 Revista Estudos - Patrimonio **4257**
1645-2844 Universidade Tecnica de Lisboa. Faculdade de Arquitectura. Cadernos **459**
1645-3530 Estudos do Seculo XX **4218**
1645-4537 Journal of Portuguese Linguistics **5135**
1645-5681 Media e Jornalismo **4579**
1645-5797 J A M A (Portuguese Edition) *see* 0098-7484 **5642**
1645-6432 E-journal of Portuguese History **4174**
1645-6726 Revstat Statistical Journal **8396**
1645-6971 Peninsula (Porto) **5160**
1645-7250 Revista Lusofona de Educacao **2907**
1645-779X Babilonia **5098**
1645-9199 Relacoes Internacionais **7262**
1645-9261 Revista Turismo & Desenvolvimento **8752**
1645-9350 Confluencias **5107**
1645-958X E-topia **5287**
1645-9652 Via Panoramica **5395**
1645-9911 Tekhne **8443**
1646-0758 *see* 0870-399X **5566**
1646-1223 Enterprise and Work Innovation Studies **7961**
1646-1509 Wildlife Biology in Practice **968**
1646-2335 Interaccoes **4457**
1646-2742 *see* 1646-1509 **968**
1646-3153 Prisma.com **2336**
1646-365X Jornal de Ciencias Cognitivas **7367**
1646-3714 Cuadernos de Sociomuseologia **6522**
1646-4001 Revista Lusofona de Ciencia das Religioes **7677**
1646-401X *see* 1645-7250 **2907**
1646-4729 Spaces of Utopia **5376**
1646-5237 Laboreal **7982**
1646-6500 Sisifo **2912**
1646-7698 Carnets **5104**
1646-8880 E - Fabulations **5286**
1648-0627 Verslas **1800**
1648-0635 Property Management *changed to* 1648-715X **7596**
1648-1143 *see* 0258-0802 **5324**
1648-276X Mergaite **2202**
1648-2824 Kalbu Studijos **5136**
1648-3073 Reklama *changed to* 1822-1904 **3906**
1648-3219 Lithuanian Music Review **6585**
1648-3480 *see* 1648-4142 **8514**
1648-3537 *see* 1392-1630 **4431**
1648-3804 Ieva **2256**
1648-3898 Journal of Baltic Science Education **2874**
1648-4142 Transport **8514**
1648-4444 Acta Linguistica Lithuanica **5090**
1648-4460 Transformations in Business & Economics **1183**
1648-4517 Lietuvos Trombozes Hemostazes Zurnalas **5795**
1648-4789 Socialinis Darbas **8005**
1648-4886 Bank of Lithuania. Banking Statistics Yearbook **1315**
1648-5289 Lietuvos Oftalmologija **6046**
1648-5475 *see* 0258-0802 **5324**
1648-5831 Informatics in Education **2461**
1648-6897 Journal of Environmental Engineering and Landscape Management **3445**
1648-7109 Lietuvos Muziejai **6528**
1648-715X International Journal of Strategic Property Management **7596**
1648-7788 Aviation **48**
1648-8016 Lietuvos Metine Strategine Apzvalga **6431**
1648-8024 Lithuanian Annual Strategic Review **6431**
1648-8504 Lithuanian Journal of Physics **7025**
1648-858X *see* 0067-3064 **2726**
1648-861X *see* 1392-687X **1365**
1648-8946 *see* 1648-4886 **1315**
1648-8970 *see* 1392-2637 **1375**
1648-8997 *see* 1392-0413 **1365**
1648-9020 *see* 1392-4699 **1365**

ISSN

1650-0172 Naturlaekemedel **6863**
1650-0245 Sweden. Statens Folkhaelsoinstitut. Alkoholstatistik **614**
1650-0326 Dialekt-, Ortnamns- och Folkminnesarkivet i Umeaa. Skrifter. Seroe F, Musikliv **3616**
1650-0342 Fjaerran Vatten **3594**
1650-0504 Finansplan och Sammandrag **1924**
1650-0598 Laga Mat†
1650-0652 Oerebro Universitet. Pedagogiska Institutionen. Rapporter **3075**
1650-0725 Kemivaerlden *changed to* 1653-5596 **2070**
1650-0776 Svenska Kyrkan. Bestaemmelser (Print) *changed to* Svenska Kyrkan. Bestaemmelser (Online) **7687**
1650-0873 Lifestyle (Stockholm) **5075**
1650-089X Rumba **6614**
1650-0946 Haelge **2192**
1650-0962 Skogshistoriska Saellskapet. Aarsskrift **3702**
1650-1225 Sweden. Migrationsverket. Statistik **7316**
1650-1306 Datormagazin **2416**
1650-1446 Sveriges Lantbruksuniversitet. Institutionen foer Biometri och Informatik. Rapport *changed to* 1652-3253 **706**
1650-1519 J O N A S **399**
1650-1594 Redo foer Scouting *changed to* 1654-1278 **2212**
1650-1594 Redo foer Scouting *changed to* 1654-1286 **2212**
1650-1632 Oerebro Studies in Political Science **7160**
1650-1748 Umeaa Studies in Philosophy **6958**
1650-1837 Forum Navales Skriftserie **6421**
1650-1942 F O I - R **6420**
1650-1969 Journal of Rehabilitation Medicine. Supplement†
1650-1977 Journal of Rehabilitation Medicine **8051**
1650-2019 Africa & Asia **5250**
1650-2035 Uppsala Peace Research Papers **7272**
1650-2159 Blekinge Institute of Technology. Dissertation Series *changed to* 1653-2090 **8417**
1650-2280 International Utblick. Loener och Arbetskraftskostnader **1690**
1650-2302 Coniunctio **7348**
1650-2345 Aktiemarknaden *changed to* Kapitalmarknaden **1363**
1650-2353 Sjoebefael **8662**
1650-2361 Naturvaardsverket. Handbok **3455**
1650-2418 Oerebro Studies in History **4155**
1650-2426 Faarskoetsel **286**
1650-2507 OneMagazine†
1650-2515 Migrationsverkets Foerfattningssamling **7287**
1650-2523 Diakonivetenskapliga Institutet. Temabok **7637**
1650-2531 Oerebro Studies in Sociology **8124**
1650-254X Umeaa Studies in Linguistics **5190**
1650-2671 Framsyn **6421**
1650-2949 Minaret **7714**
1650-3104 V I N N O V A Rapport **1800**
1650-3112 V I N N O V A Meddelande *changed to* 1650-3104 **1800**
1650-3139 V I N N O V A Debatt *changed to* 1651-3541 **1800**
1650-3147 V I N N O V A Innovation i Fokus *changed to* 1651-355X **1799**
1650-3163 Arbetsmiljoeverkets Foerfattningssamling **6673**
1650-3201 F O I Informerar om **6420**
1650-3341 *see* 1101-7880 **4603**
1650-3465 Televerksamhet **2349**
1650-349X I T P S S **1241**
1650-3600 Res (Stockholm, 1995)†
1650-3627 Skaanska Jaernvaegar **8625**
1650-3643 Linkoepings Universitet. Institutionen foer Beteendevetenskap **7383**
1650-3732 Haelsahoegskolan i Joenkoeping. Avdelingen foer Rehabilitering. Forskningsrapport **6109**
1650-3767 Botaniska Notiser (Lund, 2001) **3407**
1650-3929 Plaza Kvinna **8880**
1650-3953 Foerbundet foer Musikterapi i Sverige **6109**
1650-402X Grafiskt Forum **7321**
1650-4038 Dokumentation av Faeltarbetsfasen **390**
1650-4143 Chalmers Tekniska Hoegskola. Institutionen foer Vatten Miljoe Transport. Doktorsavhandlingar och Licentiatuppsatser **3360**
1650-4224 Tempo (Stockholm) **1797**
1650-4607 S T F I Report. PUB **6738**
1650-4704 Grus & Guld **1350**
1650-4747 Musikmagasin Evterpe *changed to* 1653-3348 **6582**
1650-4801 Umeaa Universitet. Institutionen foer Kultur och Medier. Rapportserien **36**
1650-4925 Miljoeforskning (Stockholm) **1024**
1650-4984 Snabba Koep **3681**
1650-5077 Svensk Gris med Knorr **301**
1650-5085 Haro! **8105**
1650-5131 Nordiska Medieforskare Reflekterar **2335**
1650-5174 Naturmedicinaren *changed to* 1651-9809 **5807**
1650-5298 Eidos **487**
1650-5468 Pengar **1374**
1650-5670 Digimon **2185**
1650-5719 Spraak- och Folkminnesinstitutet. Dialektavdelingen. Skrifter. A **5177**
1650-5743 Willy Brandt Series of Working Papers in International Migration and Ethnic Relations **7295**
1650-576X Swedish Research for Sustainability *changed to* 1654-8329 **3491**
1650-5786 M3 **2572**
1650-5840 Oerebro Studies in Literary History and Criticism **5345**
1650-5891 Journal of Nordregio **1890**
1650-5913 Bilboersen **8569**
1650-593X Recycling och Miljoeteknik *changed to* 1653-5588 **3510**
1650-6065 Malmoe Hoegskola. Odontologiska Fakulteten. Odontological Dissertations **5855**
1650-6073 Cognitive Behaviour Therapy **7346**
1650-6359 Forskning Paagaar *changed to* 1651-6745
1650-6707 Cosmopolitan (Stockholm) **8857**
1650-6812 Allt om Flugfiske **8302**
1650-710X Ethos (Print Edition)†
1650-7177 Populaer Astronomi **580**
1650-7215 Amos **7621**
1650-7231 Specialpedagogik **3047**
1650-7320 Baatmarknaden **8272**
1650-7398 Psykoanalytisk Tid/skrift **7401**
1650-7479 W.I.T.C.H. **2220**
1650-7541 Acta Agriculturae Scandinavica. Section C. Food Economics **190**
1650-755X Studia Historica Lundensia **4163**
1650-7606 Tidskrift foer Amfibiekaaren **6449**
1650-7711 Bon **2251**
1650-772X Staalbyggnad **1037**
1650-7770 I G B P Science **7971**
1650-7789 Stat och Kommuninformation *changed to* 1653-3674 **7458**
1650-7819 Byggare Bob Magasin **2181**
1650-7878 Spraak- och Folkminnesinstitutet. Namnavdelingen. Skrifter. Serie A, Sveriges Ortnamn **4029**
1650-7924 Byraaboken **22**
1650-8017 Ottar (Stockholm, 2001) **8124**
1650-8033 Foer Alla **4066**
1650-8092 Tidningen Skogsteknik **3704**
1650-8114 Ingelise *changed to* 1653-8080 **4351**
1650-8122 Malmoe Kulturmiljoe. Rapport **4242**
1650-8211 Aktuellt fraan Centrum foer Danmarksstudier **4197**
1650-8335 Kriminalvaardsstyrelsen. Rapport *changed to* Kriminalvaarden. Rapport **2659**
1650-8394 Tidskrift (Kalmar) *changed to* 1653-7742 **422**
1650-8424 Gamepro Sweden†
1650-8432 Ekeloefet **5289**
1650-8475 PrioriteringsCentrum. Rapport **7536**
1650-8580 Oerebro Studies in Technology **8434**
1650-8718 Studier av Inter-Religioesa Relationer **7685**
1650-8726 Plaza Stockholm **5080**
1650-8793 Oerebro Studies in Biology **695**
1650-8882 Nya Svenska Filmvaagen **6509**
1650-8947 Nostalgia **368**
1650-9382 Handbollsmagasinet **8235**
1650-9544 European Journal of Spatial Development **4410**
1650-9579 Stockholms Stadsmuseum. Kulturmiljoeavdelingen. Arkeologisk Rapport **418**
1650-9692 Aarsbok fraan Groenkoepings Veckoblad **5204**
1650-9730 Transport iDag och i Trafik *changed to* 1654-2118 **8514**
1650-9730 Transport iDag och i Trafik *changed to* 1654-2150 **1773**
1650-9781 Working Life†
1650-9811 Malmoe Museer. Skriftserie **6528**
1650-9951 Konjunkturbarometern. Maanad **1896**
1650-996X Konjunkturinstitutet. Specialstudier **1896**
1651-0003 Chalmers Tekniska Hoegskola. Department of Materials Science and Engineering. Diploma Work *changed to* 1652-8913 **8418**
1651-002X S I K A Statistiska Meddelanden **8398**
1651-0038 Vaexjoe University. School of Industrial Engineering. Reports *changed to* 1652-8433 **8444**
1651-0127 Monographs on Journal of Research in Teacher Education **2887**
1651-0194 Royal Institute of Technology. Department of Infrastructure. Transactions **4027**
1651-0224 Maenniskors Vaerde, Haelsa och Vitaliserande Processer **8054**
1651-0380 Construction Management Publications **997**
1651-050X Loenebildningen **1696**
1651-0534 Barnlaekaren **8027**
1651-0674 Svenskt Vatten **8832**
1651-0682 Verkstaederna **5461**
1651-0690 Tidningen Tennis *changed to* 1653-2546 **8249**
1651-0755 Nyckeln till Svenska Kyrkan **7667**
1651-095X Inkomstskattelagen **1929**
1651-0992 Hushaalsvetaren **4361**
1651-1085 Finans Vision†
1651-114X Sveriges Lantbruksuniversitet. Institutionen foer Skogens Produkter och Marknader. Uppsats **3704**
1651-1190 Goeteborgs Fria Tidning **3955**
1651-1204 Spraak- och Folkminnesinstitutet. Dialektavdelingen. Skrifter. Ser. D **5177**
1651-1263 Forskning & Medicin **5615**
1651-1328 Oerebro Studies in Psychology **7388**
1651-1425 Sweden. Integrationsverket. Skriftserie **7294**
1651-145X Oerebro Studies in Social Work **8060**
1651-1484 Justitia **1363**
1651-1611 Camping & Fritid **4976**
1651-162X Svenska Cykelfoerbundets Officiella Kalender **8269**
1651-1638 Forskning och Haelsa *changed to* 1653-9753 **5787**
1651-1662 Rapport Integration **7291**
1651-1670 Stockholm Lectures in Educology **2915**
1651-1778 Kemivaerlden. Biotech *changed to* 1653-5596 **2070**
1651-1808 Utblick Folkhaelsa†
1651-1891 *see* 0282-7581 **3701**
1651-1905 *see* 1403-4948 **5710**
1651-1913 *see* 0906-4710 **216**
1651-1948 *see* 1403-8196 **6106**
1651-1972 *see* 0906-4702 **277**
1651-1980 *see* 0036-5548 **5826**
1651-1999 *see* 0803-7051 **5778**
1651-2006 *see* 1401-7431 **6257**
1651-2014 *see* 1103-8128 **5710**
1651-2022 *see* 1401-5439 **6082**
1651-2030 *see* 0346-1238 **4522**
1651-2049 *see* 0017-3134 **791**
1651-2065 *see* 0036-5599 **6274**
1651-2073 *see* 0284-4311 **6257**
1651-2081 *see* 1650-1977 **8051**
1651-2170 Bolaget **3628**
1651-2227 *see* 0803-5253 **6086**
1651-2235 *see* 0891-060X **5822**
1651-226X *see* 0284-186X **6007**
1651-2278 *see* 1403-6096 **4414**
1651-2286 *see* 1404-1049 **1601**
1651-2294 *see* 0023-3609 **500**
1651-2308 *see* 0039-3274 **5180**
1651-2316 *see* 1650-6073 **7346**
1651-2324 *see* 0803-706X **7363**
1651-2340 *see* 1404-3858 **2658**
1651-2464 *see* 0365-5237 **6076**
1651-2480 *see* 0803-8023 **5778**
1651-2499 *see* 1100-1704 **6007**
1651-2510 *see* 1401-7458 **5799**
1651-2553 *see* 0001-6489 **6076**
1651-2650 Acta Orthopaedica Scandinavica. Supplementum (Online Edition) *changed to* 1745-3704 **6054**
1651-2715 Sjukhuslaekaren **5715**
1651-2731 Linneavhandlingar i Nytryck **800**
1651-2804 Sveriges Lantbruksuniversitet. Institutionen foer Jordbruksvetenskap. Teknisk Rapport *changed to* 1652-2826 **159**
1651-2820 Efs.nu **7755**
1651-288X *see* 1650-7541 **190**
1651-2936 Malmoe University. Faculty of Odontology. Annual Publications **5855**
1651-2960 Amphioxnytt *see* 1653-9796 **2993**
1651-2995 Nordisk Papper & Massa **6735**
1651-3037 *see* 1503-1438 **5638**
1651-3053 Mitrania **5445**
1651-3118 C I O Sweden **2553**
1651-3169 Nyhetsbrevet Datateknik
1651-324X Biotech Sweden **662**
1651-3363 Nyheter & Debatt **2996**
1651-3401 Movium Rapport **4419**
1651-3495 Katalogaktuellt *changed to* 1653-2341 **2024**
1651-3525 Vuollerim 6000 Aar. Arkeologiska Rapporter **423**
1651-3541 V I N N O V A Forum **1800**
1651-355X V I N N O V A Analys **1799**
1651-3568 V I N N O V A Policy **1800**
1651-3762 B R I S Tidningen Barn och Ungdom **2144**
1651-3770 Tidskriften Opera **6623**
1651-3789 Socialfoersaekringen Aarsredovisning foer Budgetaaret (Year) *changed to* 1653-5774 **4524**
1651-3835 *see* 1651-386X **6078**
1651-386X Audiological Medicine **6078**
1651-4025 Uti var Hage **2219**
1651-405X Kyrkans Tidning **7659**
1651-4084 Placeringsguiden **1644**
1651-4270 Oerebro Studies in Chemistry **2075**
1651-4289 School of Business, Economics and Law, Goeteborgs University. Economic Studies **1171**
1651-4297 *see* 1651-4289 **1171**
1651-436X World Maritime University. Journal of Maritime Affairs **8665**
1651-4408 Kaernfullt fraan Svensk Mjoelk **266**
1651-4416 Svensk Kaernbraenslehantering. S K B P **3512**
1651-4459 Magasinet Fotboll **8238**
1651-4491 Oerebro Universitet. Skriftserie **4467**
1651-4505 Djurskyddet **319**
1651-4521 Tidningen C **7189**
1651-453X Texter fraan Migrations- och Etnicitetsseminariet **8143**
1651-4564 Sweden. Statens Konstraad. Katalog **520**
1651-4750 Wage Formation **1714**
1651-4777 Uppsala Studies in Media and Communication **8146**
1651-4785 Oerebro Studies in Media and Communication **8124**
1651-4890 Skoter Racing *changed to* 1652-9154 **8334**
1651-4963 Chalmers University of Technology. School of Computer Science and Engineering.Technical report. L *changed to* 1652-876X **2539**
1651-5080 Nyhetsbrev. S A F Tidningen Naeringsliv *changed to* 1104-8891 **1960**
1651-5099 F 1 Racing **8172**
1651-5110 Entreprenoer.se *see* 1104-8891 **1960**
1651-5161 Tidskriften Doktorn **5722**
1651-5242 Goeteborg University. School of Public Administration. S P A Working Papers **7439**
1651-5285 Dixi *changed to* 1654-2592 **4481**
1651-5307 Allt om DVD *changed to* 1654-4994 **6489**
1651-5374 Maritime Skrifter **6432**
1651-5420 Krisberedskap **2227**
1651-5447 Biblioteksbladet **4995**
1651-5471 Reflex **6180**
1651-5528 Raedda Djuren! **321**
1651-5706 Laensmuseet Halmstad. Skriftserie **6527**
1651-5838 Designmagasinet Forum *changed to* 1653-8218 **4540**
1651-5870 Sweden. Statens Konstraad. Catalogue *see* 1651-4564 **520**
1651-6028 International Clearinghouse on Children, Youth and Media. Yearbook **8108**
1651-6036 Nordisk Tidskrift foer Hoersel- och Doevundervisning NTD
1651-6095 Fraan Schlyters Lustgaard **4677**
1651-6249 Sveriges Riksdag. Sveriges Riksdag **7187**
1651-6265 The Hugo Valentin Lectures **4231**
1651-6273 Sveriges Riksdag. The Swedish Parliament *see* 1651-6249 **7187**
1651-6281 Sverigs Riksdag. Le Parlement Suedois *see* 1651-6249 **7187**
1651-629X Sveriges Riksdag. Der Schwedische Reichstag *see* 1651-6249 **7187**
1651-6303 Sveriges Riksdag. Parlamento de Suecia *see* 1651-6249 **7187**
1651-6311 Sveriges Riksdag. Svedskij Parlament *see* 1651-6249 **7187**
1651-6346 Telescopium **582**
1651-646X Plaza Magazine International **5080**
1651-6540 Endangered Languages and Cultures **8099**
1651-6567 Kooperativ Horisont **1424**
1651-6583 Alltid Scout†
1651-6605 Expo & Profil *changed to* 1652-0602 **25**
1651-6648 Litholund Theses **2752**
1651-6710 Vaelfaerd **7485**
1651-6745 Samspel†
1651-680X Social Insurance Studies **4523**
1651-6818 N T T Saag & Trae **3714**
1651-6826 Film International **6499**
1651-6885 Utredningar fraan Riksdagsfoervaltningen **7475**
1651-6923 Marginal **5226**
1651-694X Animagi **6489**
1651-7059 Blickpunkt Soedra Afrika **4173**
1651-7229 Stockholm Environmental Institute. Report Series **3148**
1651-727X Svenska Finlandsfrivilligas Minnesfoerening. Tidning
1651-7326 Jaern, Bygg, Faerg **1823**
1651-7350 Vetenskapsraadet. Rapportserie **4481**
1651-7393 Frontiers of Research in International Marketing **1566**
1651-7466 Digitala Tankar **2842**

DIRECTORY 2010 1660-2137 9755

1653-428X Myndigheten foer Sveriges Naetuniversitet. Rapport *changed to* 1654-1715 2994
1653-4298 Golfbladet 8233
1653-431X Kalmar Studies in Archaeology 402
1653-4328 Stockhom Environment Institute. EcoSanRes Programme. Publications Series 3468
1653-4360 International Journal of Public Information Systems 2426
1653-4379 Djurskyddssamyndigheten. Foereskriftsmotiv 319
1653-4492 Bergslagsforskning 8090
1653-4522 Sudoku Frossa
1653-4573 U C D P Papers 8144
1653-4581 Hoegskolan Vaest. Arbetsrapport 2985
1653-459X Hoegskolan Vaest. Forskningsrapport 2985
1653-4654 Foerhandlingsguiden 4868
1653-4816 Eget Foeretag 1740
1653-4859 Stockholm Cinema Studies 6514
1653-4905 F A R Skatt & Redovisning (Online Edition) 1288
1653-4964 Polhem 8434
1653-4999 Boggi 210
1653-5014 Edge Magazine (Stockholm) 8171
1653-5022 Hundstallsnytt 8798
1653-5081 Jessy 2195
1653-509X F A Rs Normsamling foer den Offentliga Sektion 1288
1653-5103 Diego 3955
1653-5154 Norra Skogsmagasinet 3698
1653-5197 Uppsala Studies in History of Ideas 4481
1653-5219 Royalty Digest Quarterly 645
1653-5235 Svensk Biblioteksforskning (Online) 5049
1653-526X Resurs 6443
1653-5294 Vaexjoe Universitet, Institutionen foer Vaardvetenskap och Socialt Arbete. Rapportserie i Vaardvetenskap 5728
1653-5316 I N A H T A Briefs 5632
1653-5332 Forum foer Levande Hisoria. Skriftserie 4140
1653-5367 Energigas 6767
1653-5405 Elle Interioer Sommarstaellet 4556
1653-5413 Djurskyddsmyndigheten. Rapport 319
1653-5464 Uppsala Stadsarkiv. Skriftserie 4276
1653-5502 Ansvarskommitten. Skriftserie 8025
1653-5545 Saellskapet Artur Lundkvists Vaenner. Aarsskrift 5366
1653-5553 Glid. Laangfaerdsskridskor 8315
1653-5561 Conditions of Democracy 7118
1653-557X Plastforum 7096
1653-5588 Recycling 3510
1653-5596 Kemivaerlden, Biotech, Kemisk Tidskrift 2070
1653-5618 Borzoi-Ringen 6804
1653-5642 First Poker 8173
1653-5774 Sweden. Foersaeksringskassan. Aarsredovisning 4524
1653-5804 Fysioterapi 5617
1653-5898 Vaerdepapper 4806
1653-5901 Bank & Foersaekring 4626
1653-591X Boers 4630
1653-5952 Kroenikan 5024
1653-5960 Plaza Watch 4569
1653-610X University of Stockholm. Institute for International Economic Studies. Seminar Papers 1586
1653-6169 Kriminalteknik 2659
1653-6215 Modellvision 2259
1653-6266 Plaza Stora Koek & Badguiden 4549
1653-6339 Sthlm Fest & Moeten 4367
1653-6355 Anpere 325
1653-638X Vaexjoe University. Centre for Labour Market Policy Research. Working Paper Series 1191
1653-6460 Eldrimner. Nyhetsblad 3634
1653-6533 Skriftserie i Vaardvetenskap 5981
1653-6541 Elektronikvaerlden *changed to* 1653-9907 2332
1653-6568 Skogsliv 3702
1653-6606 Malmoe Hoegskola. Konst, Kultur och Kommunikation. Dissertations in Arts and Coummunication 8119
1653-6614 Globale Roester 1596
1653-6657 Kriminalvaardens Administrative Foereskrifter 2659
1653-6665 Kriminalvaardens Foerfattningssamling 2659
1653-6703 Allt om Villor & Hus 4553
1653-6754 Finyar 7643
1653-6762 Glamour (Stockholm) 8866
1653-6800 M K G Rapport 3508
1653-6851 Drustveno Glasilo 3530
1653-6886 Design paa Chalmers 8420
1653-6916 Allt om Energi 3123
1653-6959 Allt om Hotell & Resor 8682
1653-7009 *see* 1654-8507 7414
1653-7084 Allt om Klockor & Smycken 4564
1653-7122 Bad- & Koekguiden 4554
1653-7254 Sjoestaden 3956
1653-7351 Forum Finland 1403
1653-7408 Kulturmiljoevaard Maelardalen. Rapport 403
1653-7467 *see* 1652-2915 7529
1653-7505 S C O R E Arbetsrapporter *see* 1404-5052 7181
1653-7548 *see* 1652-0432 7264
1653-7599 Level 2478
1653-7602 Journal Chocolat 4361
1653-7629 Antikvaerlden 362
1653-7742 Urminne 422
1653-7750 Shortcut 6703
1653-7793 Sko & Mode 7942
1653-784X Kalmar Studies in Humanities and Social Sciences 4461
1653-8021 C F K- Kortrapport 1809
1653-8080 Allt om Handarbete 4351
1653-8129 South Asian Studies 561
1653-8137 Naeringsvaert 6664
1653-820X Statens Raad foer Kaernavfallsfraagor. Rapport 3512
1653-8218 Forum A I D 4540
1653-8307 I Tjaenst foer Riksdagen 7141
1653-8315 Swedish University of Agricultural Sciences. Department of Biomedical Sciences and Veterinary Public Health. Report 160
1653-8358 Goeteborgs Universitet. Foervaltningshoegskolan. Avhandlingsserie 1748
1653-8447 Skatteaktuellt 1943
1653-8498 Situne Dei 4161
1653-851X Stockholm Studies in Ethnology 8141
1653-8595 Elvis 2187
1653-8625 Passion 3956
1653-8684 Statens Energimyndighet. Energimarknadsinspetion. Aarsrapport 3148
1653-9044 Teknisk Design *changed to* 1653-6886 8420
1653-9109 Foeraeldrakraft 8040
1653-9117 Anglo Nytt 8287
1653-9141 *see* 0281-3343 6642
1653-9192 Forum Sveaskog 3691
1653-9206 Elle Mat & Vin 3634
1653-9249 S A D E V. Report 1605
1653-9257 S A D E V Policy Brief 1605
1653-9265 Forsknings- och Utvecklingsenheten. Skriftserie (Region Skaane) 5615
1653-932X Medmaensklighet 1601
1653-9400 Go Retro! 3955
1653-9419 Cap & Design Proffsfoto 2483
1653-9443 Kvartalsbrev fraan Fotosekretariatet 6970
1653-9451 Intelligent Logistik 1754
1653-9583 Xbox 360 2482
1653-9656 Samlarguiden 4345
1653-9753 Forskning foer Haelsa 5787
1653-9796 Medicor Magasin 2993
1653-9907 Ljud & Bild i Elektronikvaerlden 2332
1654-0050 Swedish Film 6515
1654-0131 Forskningstemat Maenniska, Haelsa, Samhaelle 8102
1654-0247 Magisteruppsats i Biblioteks- och Informationsvetenskap vid Institutionen Biblioteks- och Informationsvetenskap (Online) 5031
1654-031X Din Teknik 8420
1654-0328 Nordisk Energi 3143
1654-045X S A D E V. Working Papers 1605
1654-0549 Sametinget. Foerfattningssamling 4852
1654-0565 Sveriges Lantbruksuniversitet. Institutionen foer Stad och Land. Rapporter 520
1654-059X Roomservice Pro 1034
1654-0654 Jazz Facts 6578
1654-0700 S I I A Papers 7264
1654-0816 Post- och Inrikes Tidningar (Online) 1160
1654-0824 Institutet foer Naeringslivsforskning. Aarsbok 1889
1654-0905 Bilwaerlden 8569
1654-0980 Donationsraadet Rekommenderar 6242
1654-1049 Penningpolitisk Rapport 1374
1654-109X *see* 1402-2001 776
1654-1103 *see* 1100-9233 799
1654-1243 Allt om Moebler 4553
1654-1251 Allt om Drycker 4351
1654-1278 Scoutmagasinet 2212
1654-1286 Scouten 2212
1654-1421 Klinisk Patientnaera Forskning 5658
1654-1618 Lyztran 6646
1654-1707 *see* 0347-7193 8408
1654-1715 Myndigheten foer Naetverk och Samarbete inom Hoegre Utbildning. Rapport 2994
1654-1855 Goeteborg Gender Studies 8898
1654-2002 Techworld 2504
1654-2118 Transport iDag 8514
1654-2150 Logistik iDag 1773
1654-2169 Referee 8330
1654-2207 Medievaerlden 4580
1654-2282 Camino 3125
1654-2290 Nordic Research Programme 2005-2008. Report 4421
1654-2363 Studies in Osteology 419
1654-238X Umeaa Working Papers in Political Science 7190
1654-2398 Umeaa Working Papers in Peace and Conflict Studies 7190
1654-2495 Medievarlden *see* 1654-2207 4580
1654-2541 Global Challenge. Report 1596
1654-2568 Umeaa Studies in Cognitive Science 5190
1654-2576 Hem & Hyra 4412
1654-2592 Uppsala Papers in History of Ideas 4481
1654-3734 Klavernytt 6583
1654-398X Nordisk Industri 3213
1654-4250 Critical Currents 7229
1654-4277 Arbetarskyddsregler foer Byggsektorn 6673
1654-4293 Idag.se 1888
1654-4307 *see* 1654-4293 1888
1654-4463 Archeology@Lund 380
1654-4544 Market 1830
1654-4587 Dagens Ledare 1737
1654-4625 O S Magasinet 8191
1654-4846 Brandmanager 6747
1654-4927 Arkeologiska Rapporter 380
1654-4951 Ethics & Global Politics 7133
1654-4994 Allt om Film 6489
1654-5079 Opera Mycologica 806
1654-5087 Avfall och Miljoe 3504
1654-5303 Avfall Sverige Utveckling. Rapport 3504
1654-5354 Hagstroemerbibliotekets Skriftserie 5622
1654-5370 Biz&Art 8090
1654-5443 Tidskrift foer Genusforskning 8903
1654-5613 Plus Sverige 8880
1654-5753 Genusstudier vid Mittuniversitetet 8104
1654-5788 Magasinet Existera 7661
1654-5915 Journal of Northern Studies 8115
1654-594X *see* 1404-2207 1345
1654-6040 SiS i Fokus 8068
1654-6172 Global Utmaning. Rapport 1596
1654-6342 Teknik & Forskning 3222
1654-6350 Restaurangvaerlden 4396
1654-6369 *see* 1654-4951 7133
1654-6393 Sveriges Mjoelkboender 269
1654-6458 Guinness World Records 3120
1654-6512 Flerskrovsbladet 8275
1654-6555 Biodynamisk Odling 96
1654-661X *see* 1654-6628 6659
1654-6628 Food & Nutrition Research 6659
1654-6709 N A I Policy Dialogue *see* 1654-9090 1603
1654-6792 International Journal of Feminist Technoscience 8899
1654-6806 Svenskarna och Internet 2567
1654-6946 Miljoeaktuellt 3453
1654-6970 N J E S (Online) 5153
1654-7063 Resistance Studies Magazine 7214
1654-7098 S V A. Rapportserie 8807
1654-7128 Perspektiv 6441
1654-7209 Ambio Journal Online *see* 0044-7447 3402
1654-7322 Research Paper Series 7676
1654-7373 Kommuner och Landsting 7450
1654-7403 High School Musical 2192
1654-7489 Claude Ake Memorial Papers 7227
1654-7837 Runner's World 8198
1654-7934 Svensk Vindkraft 3178
1654-7985 Glocal Times 8104
1654-8043 Samhaellsforsksning 3174
1654-8167 *see* 1654-0050 6515
1654-8221 Skriftserie foer Funktionshinder 4069
1654-8264 S I P R I Update 7264
1654-8329 Sustainability 3491
1654-8345 Oldtimer Hockey 8191
1654-8361 Kommuninfo Obiz 7450
1654-8388 Forkirurgisk Tidskrift 6060
1654-8507 Vaara Tonaaringar 7414
1654-8523 Skog & Industri 3715
1654-871X Kriminalvaarden. Aarsbok 8117
1654-8744 C E M U S. Skriftserie 7951
1654-8752 Almegatidningen 1879
1654-8809 Elektor 3097
1654-8825 Evidens 8039
1654-9090 Policy Dialogue 1603
1654-9260 Byggvaerlden 988
1654-9457 Droppen 7755
1654-9589 ForetagsInspiration 1817
1654-9597 *see* 1654-9589 1817
1654-9694 World Health Design 4112
1654-9848 Veterinaerkongressen 8810
1654-9880 Global Health Action 5620
1655-1516 Philippine Review of Economics 1159
1655-1524 Social Science Diliman 8003
1655-1532 Humanities Diliman 4455
1655-1702 Philippine Journal of Counseling Psychology 7391
1655-2245 Igorota 8868
1655-5104 Bangko Sentral ng Pilipinas. Inflation Report 1065
1655-5112 Bangko Sentral ng Pilipinas. Annual Report 1312
1655-5236 E R D Technical Note Series 1478
1655-5252 E R D Working Paper Series 1478
1655-8049 Philippine Population Review 7289
1655-8561 Smart Parenting 2168
1656-152X Kritika Kultura 5137
1657-0790 Profile 3078
1657-1959 Revista de la Propriedad Inmaterial 4880
1657-2416 Zona Proxima 2929
1657-3242 Artes. La Revista 472
1657-3498 Universidad Tecnologica del Choco. Revista 8444
1657-4206 Ecos de Economia 1481
1657-4249 Uni-pluriversidad 2922
1657-4583 Revista U I S Ingenierias 3282
1657-4680 Revista Bioanalisis 896
1657-477X Catedra Corona 1732
1657-480X Observatorio Colombiano de Energia. Boletin 3143
1657-5083 Palimpsestus 7991
1657-5636 Epiciclos 3191
1657-5946 Economia, Gestion y Desarrollo 1479
1657-5997 Aquichan 7948
1657-6276 Pensamiento & Gestion 1785
1657-6772 Revista de Investigacion 7997
1657-7027 Revista Gerencia y Politicas de Salud 4110
1657-7205 Carta Petrolera 6765
1657-7558 Observatorio de Analisis de los Sistemas Internacionales 7256
1657-7663 Avances en Sistemas e Informatica 2519
1657-8031 El Agora U S B 6902
1657-8236 Gerencia Tecnologica Informatica 2419
1657-8651 Observatorio de Politicas, Ejecucion y Resultados de la Administracion Publica 7458
1657-8856 Selecciones de Bioetica 6951
1657-8961 Pensamiento Psicologico 7390
1657-9119 Maxim en Espanol 6295
1657-9267 Universitas Psychologica 7413
1657-9534 Colombia Medica (Online Edition) 5599
1657-9550 Biosalud 5587
1657-9763 Apuntes 427
1658-2489 Saudi German Hospitals Medical Journal 5709
1658-3558 *see* 1013-9052 5864
1658-3876 Hematology - Oncology and Stem Cell Therapy 5937
1659-0201 Poblacion y Salud en Mesoamerica 7289
1659-0430 Derecho y Tecnologias de Informacion y Comunicaciones 5006
1659-0732 Zeledonia 917
1659-097X MHSalud 6231
1659-1046 Odovtos 5858
1659-1119 Girasol 2982
1659-1933 Revista de Lenguas Modernas 5167
1659-2069 Revista de Derecho Electoral 7178
1659-2182 Metodos en Ecologia y Sistematica 689
1659-2751 Tierra Tropical 3470
1659-3049 *see* 1659-2182 689
1660-0088 Publikationen zur Zeitschrift fuer Germanistik 5355
1660-0339 Arbeitsrecht 1664
1660-0347 Forum of Nutrition 6659
1660-0436 Swiss Medical Informatics 5832
1660-0673 Vereinigung Pro Sihltal. Jahrheft 4277
1660-0835 Podologie Schweiz 6256
1660-0851 N Z Z am Sonntag 3958
1660-0878 Rotblau 8244
1660-1149 InfoWeek.ch. Special 2423
1660-1254 Schweizerische Landesbibliothek. Jahresbericht (Bern, 2001) 5046
1660-1262 Kochen 4362
1660-1505 Liminaires 5323
1660-1769 Journal of Object Technology 2508
1660-1890 Issues in Infectious Diseases 5819
1660-2110 Nephron Clinical Practice 6252
1660-2129 Nephron Experimental Nephrology 6252
1660-2137 Nephron Physiology *see* 1660-8151 6272

ISSN

1662-3797 see 1660-9263 **870**
1662-3800 see 0074-1132 **4048**
1662-3819 see 1660-1890 **5819**
1662-3827 see 0077-0809 **5680**
1662-3835 see Monographs in Human Genetics **875**
1662-3843 see 0077-0892 **5856**
1662-3851 see 0077-0965 **893**
1662-386X see 1422-7584 **6664**
1662-3878 see 1661-6677 **6664**
1662-3886 see 1017-5989 **6099**
1662-3894 see 1017-8686 **5798**
1662-3908 see 1011-0267 **6876**
1662-3916 see 0079-6263 **6032**
1662-3924 see 0079-6492 **6174**
1662-3932 see 1422-2140 **6217**
1662-3940 see 1024-2651 **6256**
1662-3959 see 0080-2727 **6226**
1662-3967 see 0253-200X **2132**
1662-3975 see 0084-2230 **6671**
1662-4025 Obesity Facts **6667**
1662-4033 see 1662-4025 **6667**
1662-405X Translational Research in Biomedicine **771**
1662-4068 see 1662-405X **771**
1662-4246 Public Health Genomics **877**
1662-4505 see 1662-2685 **6161**
1662-4548 Frontiers in Neuroscience **6142**
1662-4874 Key Issues in Mental Health **6157**
1662-4882 see 1662-4874 **6157**
1662-5099 Frontiers in Molecular Neuroscience **6142**
1662-5102 Frontiers in Cellular Neuroscience **6142**
1662-5110 Frontiers in Neural Circuits **6142**
1662-5129 Frontiers in Neuroanatomy **6142**
1662-5137 Frontiers in Systems Neuroscience **6142**
1662-5145 Frontiers in Integrative Neuroscience **6142**
1662-5153 Frontiers in Behavioral Neuroscience **6142**
1662-5161 Frontiers in Human Neuroscience **6142**
1662-5188 Frontiers in Computational Neuroscience **6142**
1662-5196 Frontiers in Neuroinformatics **6142**
1662-5218 Frontiers in Neurorobotics **6142**
1662-5250 Journal of Nano Research **7021**
1662-5404 Care Management **5592**
1662-5412 see 1662-5404 **5592**
1662-5544 International Journal of Internet Science **2559**
1662-5579 Margini **5150**
1662-6001 Bioethica Forum **6907**
1662-601X see 1662-6001 **6907**
1662-6079 S G B E Bulletin changed to 1662-6001 **6907**
1662-6257 Synapse **5719**
1662-6273 PrimaryCare (French Edition) see 1424-3776 **5699**
1662-629X see 1423-5528 **5795**
1662-632X see 1661-0903 **5916**
1662-6540 Studia Oecumenica Friburgensia **7818**
1662-6567 Case Reports in Dermatology **5872**
1662-6575 Case Reports in Oncology **6015**
1662-6664 Viszeralmedizin **5932**
1662-6672 see 1662-6664 **5932**
1662-680X Case Reports in Neurology **6130**
1662-8063 see 1662-4246 **877**
1662-811X Journal of Innate Immunity **889**
1662-8128 see 1662-811X **889**
1662-8500 Entomo Helvetica **844**
1662-8691 Edelweiss Men **2254**
1662-8993 see 1662-1018 **767**
1662-9558 Megalink **2352**
1662-9647 GeroPsych **4046**
1662-971X see 1662-9647 **4046**
1662-9981 Journal of Pseudo-Differential Operators and Applications **5506**
1662-999X see 1662-9981 **5506**
1663-0114 Else Kroener-Fresnius-Symposia **763**
1663-2818 Hormone Research in Paediatrics **5894**
1663-2826 Hormone Research in Paediatrics (Online) see 1663-2818 **5894**
1665-014X Administracion y Organizaciones **1723**
1665-0204 Revista Iberoamericana de Tecnologia Postcosecha **151**
1665-0441 Ra Ximhai **7994**
1665-0557 Revista Panamericana de Pedagogia **2907**
1665-0565 Espiral **7133**
1665-0824 Tiempo de Educar **2919**
1665-1103 Avatares **6906**
1665-1146 see 0539-6115 **4100**
1665-1200 Topicos del Seminario **5188**
1665-1219 Aportes **1437**
1665-1316 Signos Linguisticos **5174**
1665-1324 Signos Filosoficos **6952**
1665-143X Oral Dos Mil 4 **5859**
1665-1685 Arqui Tectonica **433**
1665-1707 Foreign Affairs en Espanol see 0015-7120 **7235**
1665-1839 Hospitalidad E S D A I **8719**
1665-1995 Revista de Educacion Bioquimica **744**
1665-2118 Anales de Radiologia de Mexico **6192**
1665-2436 Revista Latinoamericana de Investigacion en Matematica Educativa **5529**
1665-2533 Inventario Antropologico see 0188-7017 **323**
1665-2681 Annals of Hepatology **5933**
1665-2738 Revista Mexicana de Ingenieria Quimica **2079**
1665-3254 Plasticidad y Restauracion Neurologica **6174**
1665-3521 Superficies y Vacios **3358**
1665-3572 Revista de Educacion y Desarrollo **2906**
1665-4390 Dermatologia Cosmetica, Medica y Quirurgica **5874**
1665-4412 Investigacion y Ciencia **7975**
1665-4420 Signos Historicos **4161**
1665-4862 AlterTexto **5251**
1665-5044 Revista Mexicana de Neurociencia **6182**
1665-5060 Revista del Climaterio **5705**
1665-5125 Nutricion Clinica **5948**
1665-529X Ingenieria **3197**
1665-5745 E-gnosis **7852**
1665-5796 Medicina Universitaria **5673**
1665-6180 Apertura **2826**
1665-6423 Journal of Applied Research and Technology **8428**
1665-7330 Revista de Especialidades Medico-Quirurgicas **6256**

1665-7381 Ingenieria Mecanica, Tecnologia y Desarrollo **3379**
1665-7446 Desicio **2940**
1665-8027 Liminar **4301**
1665-8140 Espacios Publicos **7133**
1665-8906 Migraciones Internacionales **7985**
1665-9201 Gaceta Mexicana de Oncologia **6020**
1665-983X Tecnointelecto **7922**
1666-0056 Asociacion Argentina para el Estudio del Climaterio. Revista **5986**
1666-017X Revista Argentina de Agrometeorologia **6394**
1666-0226 Living Especial see 1514-6073 **4545**
1666-0234 Coleccionables Living see 1514-6073 **4545**
1666-0390 B A G. Journal of Basic and Applied Genetics **863**
1666-0404 Escribas **5290**
1666-0501 Especial Autodefinidos Pocket **4334**
1666-0536 see 0327-9383 **955**
1666-0706 Claves de Odontologia **5838**
1666-1044 Buenos Aires Herald **3791**
1666-1079 J A I I O. A S A I. Anales **2452**
1666-1087 J A I I O. A S S E. Anales **2593**
1666-1095 J A I I O. A S T. Anales **2427**
1666-1109 J A I I O. S I D. Anales **2515**
1666-1117 J A I I O. S I O. Anales **2428**
1666-1125 J A I I O. S I S. Anales **5831**
1666-1133 J A I I O. W A I T. Anales **2547**
1666-1141 J A I I O Anales **2428**
1666-115X Universidad Nacional de Rosario. Instituto de Fisiografia y Geologia. Boletin **4032**
1666-1222 Cuadernos Templarios **3763**
1666-1680 Tecnica Administrativa **1182**
1666-2105 Intersecciones en Antropologia **343**
1666-2121 Glandulas Tiroides y Paratiroides **5893**
1666-2156 Conexion Abierta **2974**
1666-2288 Somos†
1666-244X Subjetividad y Procesos Cognitivos **7410**
1666-2687 Asociacion Medica Argentina. Boletin **5579**
1666-2830 Revista Theomai **3463**
1666-292X Cuentistas Rosarinos **2976**
1666-2938 Palabra Clave **5039**
1666-3020 Nueva **3791**
1666-3276 see 1666-3020 **3791**
1666-3438 Paparazzi **5079**
1666-3519 Discurso.org **5112**
1666-3535 Encuentro (Buenos Aires) **7132**
1666-3543 Actas - Jornadas Investigaciones en la Facultad de Ciencias Economicas y Estadistica changed to 1668-5008 **8369**
1666-3659 Medicina Antropologica **5673**
1666-3845 E-Commentarii Aplicandae Mathematicae. LN. Lecture Notes **5484**
1666-3934 Sociedad Argentina de Educacion Matematica. Boletin **5536**
1666-3993 Business and Natural Environment **3407**
1666-4035 Comunicaciones Cientificas Tecnologicas Anuales **438**
1666-4094 Boletin Agrometeorologico del Centro Sur de la Provincia de Buenos Aires **97**
1666-4612 see 1515-1557 **859**
1666-485X Topicos **6957**
1666-4884 Universidad de Buenos Aires. Centro de Estudios de Sociologia del Trabajo. Documentos de Trabajo **8145**
1666-4892 see 1666-4884 **8145**
1666-504X Anuario de Estudios de Turismo **8683**
1666-5112 C I M B A G E. Cuadernos **1731**
1666-5139 Revista Argentina de Osteologia **6071**
1666-5171 see 0327-1218 **7847**
1666-5392 Boletin de Novedades Fruticolas **222**
1666-5481 I R A M. Boletin **6402**
1666-552X Estacion Experimental Agropecuaria El Colorado. Boletin de Divulgacion **108**
1666-5678 see 0328-607X **4848**
1666-5732 Energeia **6915**
1666-5740 see 0325-6081 **4990**
1666-5880 E-Commentarii Aplicandae Mathematicae. NN. Notes & News **5484**
1666-5899 E-Commentarii Aplicandae Mathematicae. TD. Thesis & Dissertations **5484**
1666-5902 E-Commentarii Aplicandae Mathematicae. Working Papers **5484**
1666-5910 E-Commentarii Aplicandae Mathematicae. PN. Pedagogic Notes **5484**
1666-6038 see 1666-6046 **2428**
1666-6046 Journal of Computer Science and Technology **2428**
1666-6097 Hoja Informativa Electronica **118**
1666-6143 Electronic Journal of Endodontics Rosario **5843**
1666-6178 E-Commentarii Aplicandae Mathematicae **5484**
1666-6577 Red Agronomica de Administracion de Recursos. Boletin de Divulgacion Tecnica **150**
1666-6607 Comunicar **102**
1666-6704 Buenas y Nuevas **762**
1666-6739 Cuadernos Profesionales **1089**
1666-6836 Centro de Estudios Historicos Profesor Carlos S.A. Anuario **4134**
1666-7050 Transoxiana **562**
1666-714X Antecedentes Parlamentarios **4618**
1666-7166 Agenda Impositiva, Laboral, Previsional y Societaria **7419**
1666-7573 Actas de la Academia Luventicus **7832**
1666-7581 see 1666-7573 **7832**
1666-7719 F A V E. Seccion Ciencias Agrarias **109**
1666-7727 Aportes Pedagogicos para Carreras de Disciplinas Tecnologicas **2827**
1666-7743 Ordia Prima **4468**
1666-7832 DavarLogos **7637**
1666-7883 Revista S A A P **7179**
1666-7948 Quimica Viva **744**
1666-8227 Albeiteria Argentina **8790**
1666-8979 Argumentos **8088**
1666-8987 El Derecho **4656**
1666-938X F A V E. Seccion Ciencias Veterinarias **8797**
1666-9398 Federacion Argentina de Sociedades de Otorrinolaringologia. Revista **6080**
1666-9606 e-l@tina **7960**

1667-1090 Asociacion Civil Argentina de Auditoria Odontologica. Revista **5835**
1667-1635 see 0329-9368 **4137**
1667-2003 Dialogos Pedagogicos **2842**
1667-4162 Revista Escuela de Historia **4311**
1667-4901 Archives of Internal Medicine (Spanish Edition) see 0003-9926 **5944**
1667-4944 Aristas **4131**
1667-5002 Reportes Tecnicos en Ingenieria del Software **2596**
1667-5061 Academia Luventicus Reportes **6902**
1667-5088 see 1667-5061 **6902**
1667-5738 Revista Argentina de Cirugia Cardiovascular **5798**
1667-5746 see 0327-9545 **827**
1667-5762 Saber Vivir. Especial see 1514-3384 **8882**
1667-6351 Centro de Estudios sobre Bibliotecologia. Boletin Informativo Electronico **5001**
1667-782X Ecologia Austral (Online Edition) **669**
1667-7838 see 1667-782X **669**
1667-8370 Contratiempo **5279**
1667-8613 see 1515-5390 **1437**
1667-8982 Salud(i)Ciencia **5709**
1667-8990 see 1667-8982 **5709**
1667-9008 S I I Csalud **5708**
1667-9059 Coleccion Trabajos Distinguidos. Serie Cardiologia **5783**
1667-9067 Coleccion Trabajos Distinguidos. Serie Infectologia **5811**
1667-9075 Coleccion Trabajos Distinguidos. Serie Urologia **6266**
1667-9083 Coleccion Trabajos Distinguidos. Serie Gastroenterologia **5921**
1667-9091 Coleccion Trabajos Distinguidos. Serie Clinica Medica **5598**
1667-9105 Coleccion Trabajos Distinguidos. Serie Salud Mental **6133**
1667-9121 Coleccion Trabajos Distinguidos. Serie Cirugia **6240**
1667-913X Coleccion Trabajos Distinguidos. Serie Obstetricia y Ginecologia **5988**
1667-9148 Coleccion Trabajos Distinguidos. Serie Pediatria **6090**
1667-9156 Coleccion Trabajos Distinguidos. Serie Alergia e Inmunologia **5756**
1667-9164 Coleccion Trabajos Distinguidos. Serie Osteoporosis y Osteopatias Medicas **6058**
1667-9172 Coleccion Trabajos Distinguidos. Serie Medicina Farmaceutica **6829**
1667-9180 Coleccion Trabajos Distinguidos. Serie Factores de Riesgo **5598**
1667-9202 Antiguo Oriente **542**
1667-9261 Revista Argentina de Sociologia **8128**
1668-0030 CTS - Ciencia, Tecnologia y Sociedad **7849**
1668-0553 Informe de Inflacion **1491**
1668-0561 see 1668-0553 **1491**
1668-091X R E T E L **7538**
1668-1002 Everba **4452**
1668-1444 Business & Sustainability **1071**
1668-1541 Cuspide **5839**
1668-1584 Cuestiones de Sociologia **8097**
1668-1754 P I N A C O. Programa de Investigaciones sobre Antropologia Cognitiva **351**
1668-1924 Revista Argentina de Cirugia Cardiovascular (Separata) see 1667-5738 **5798**
1668-1940 Revista de Ciencias Agrarias y Tecnologia de los Alimentos (Online) **151**
1668-1967 Revista Argentina de Documentacion Biomedica **5043**
1668-2610 Journal of Latin American Hermeneutics **7762**
1668-298X see 0327-6244 **86**
1668-3145 Ambiente y Sociedad **3402**
1668-3498 see 1514-6634 **8799**
1668-3501 see 0325-0075 **6088**
1668-3633 Telar **4477**
1668-3870 Psicoanalisis: Ayer y Hoy **6175**
1668-396X Boletin de Estabilidad Financiera **1321**
1668-3978 see 1668-396X **1321**
1668-4125 Gabo **6291**
1668-4753 Educacion, Lenguaje y Sociedad **2845**
1668-4826 FTV Mag **2255**
1668-4834 Revista Veterinaria **8806**
1668-4869 see 0326-1638 **657**
1668-5008 Facultad de Ciencias Economicas y Estadisticas. Actas de las Jornadas Anuales Investigaciones **8369**
1668-5024 Hologramatica **2323**
1668-5180 Geografica Digital see 0325-4097 **4009**
1668-5415 Revista Argentina de Neuropsicologia **6181**
1668-5458 Poblacion de Buenos Aires **7289**
1668-5628 La Trauma de la Comunicacion **2343**
1668-5695 Coleccion la Biblioteca Escolar en la Escuela de Hoy **2837**
1668-7027 see 0325-8203 **7363**
1668-7116 see 1515-4467 **7358**
1668-740X see 1666-5481 **6402**
1668-7515 Astrolabio **8089**
1668-7620 Cuadernos de Critica **5212**
1668-8090 see 0327-1676 **324**
1668-8104 see 0327-1471 **8012**
1668-8309 see 1514-514X **5015**
1668-8708 see 1669-7634 **1800**
1668-8910 C E T. Revista de Ciencias Exactas e Ingenieria **7842**
1668-9070 Investigaciones y Ensayos Geograficos **4016**
1668-9151 Revista Argentina de Neurocirugia **6181**
1668-9178 see 1668-8910 **7842**
1668-950X Instituto de Historia Argentina. Anuario **4298**
1669-0990 see 0325-6669 **355**
1669-1555 Revista Argentina de Humanidades y Ciencias Sociales (Online) **7996**
1669-1571 Arte Decorativo **531**
1669-1830 see 1666-5112 **1731**
1669-2314 see 0325-8718 **149**
1669-2381 Salud Colectiva **7540**
1669-2411 Asociacion Medica Argentina de Anticoncepcion. Revista **971**
1669-2438 Revista de Psicologia **7404**
1669-2721 see 1514-6006 **2980**
1669-3795 Uno Mismo **7414**

ISSN

1673-1697 Banna **5260**
1673-1727 Zhonghua Zhongyiyao Zazhi **6888**
1673-1751 Henan Gongye Daxue Xuebao (Shehui Kexue Ban) **7968**
1673-1794 Chuzhou Xueyuan Xuebao **7955**
1673-1875 Hunan Zhongxue Wuli **7015**
1673-1883 Xichang Xueyuan Xuebao (Shehui Kexue Ban) **8016**
1673-1891 Xichang Xueyuan Xuebao (Ziran Kexue Ban) **7931**
1673-1905 Optoelectronics Letters **7083**
1673-193X Zhongguo Anquan Shengchan Kexue Jishu **6689**
1673-1948 Yulei Jishu **6455**
1673-1980 Chongqing Keji Xueyuan Xuebao (Ziran Kexue Ban) **7846**
1673-1999 Chongqing Keji Xueyuan Xuebao (Shehui Kexue Ban) **7954**
1673-2006 Suzhou Xueyuan Xuebao **7921**
1673-2022 Hebei Ruanjian Zhiye Jishu Xueyuan Xuebao **7860**
1673-2049 Jianzhu Kexue yu Gongcheng Xuebao **446**
1673-2057 Taiyuan Keji Daxue Xuebao **7922**
1673-2138 Dangdai Jiangxi **3824**
1673-226X Dongbei Cehui/Northeast Surveying and Mapping *changed to* 1672-5867 **4002**
1673-2340 Nantong Daxue Xuebao (Ziran Kexue Ban) **7886**
1673-2359 Nantong Daxue Xuebao (Shehui Kexue Ban) **7987**
1673-2383 Henan Gongye Daxue Xuebao (Ziran Kexue Ban) **7861**
1673-2405 Dangdai Jinrongjia **1334**
1673-2421 Hangtian Dianzi Duikang **6423**
1673-2545 Yiyuan **528**
1673-2553 Shishang Xiansheng **6300**
1673-2561 Dangzhibu Shuji **7128**
1673-2588 Guoji Bingli Kexue yu Linchuang Zazhi **5622**
1673-2669 Xizang Fazhan Luntan **7197**
1673-2677 Xinjiang Shiyou Tianranqi **6798**
1673-2774 Chengshi Dangbao Yanjiu **7115**
1673-2855 Zhipin Shenghuo **3830**
1673-2871 Zhongguo Gua-cai **172**
1673-2928 Anyang Gongxueyuan Xuebao **8416**
1673-2944 Shaanxi Ligong Xueyuan Xuebao (Ziran Kexue Ban) **7914**
1673-2995 Jilin Yiyao Xueyuan Xuebao **5644**
1673-307X Shanghai Shibo **1173**
1673-310X Nongcun Shiyong Jishu **141**
1673-3134 Mazui yu Zhentong **5772**
1673-3185 Zhongguo Jianchuan Yanjiu **8666**
1673-3193 Zhongbei Daxue Xuebao (Ziran Kexue Ban) **8446**
1673-324X Shanghai Shangxueyuan Xuebao **1173**
1673-3274 Duzhe. Yuanchuang Ban **5286**
1673-3339 Kexue Zhong Yang **7876**
1673-3347 Jiefangjun Lilun Xuexi **7145**
1673-3371 Xinfaxian **7931**
1673-3401 Frontiers of History in China **4182**
1673-341X Frontiers of Education in China **2858**
1673-3428 Frontiers of Law in China **4678**
1673-3436 Frontiers of Philosophy in China **6921**
1673-3444 Frontiers of Economics in China **1112**
1673-3452 Frontiers of Mathematics in China **5488**
1673-3460 Frontiers of Electrical and Electronic Engineering in China **3308**
1673-3479 Frontiers of Mechanical Engineering in China **3378**
1673-3487 Frontiers of Physics in China **7013**
1673-3495 Frontiers of Chemistry in China **2062**
1673-3509 Frontiers of Biology in China **674**
1673-3517 Frontiers of Forestry in China **3691**
1673-3525 *see* 1673-3401 **4182**
1673-3533 *see* 1673-341X **2858**
1673-3541 *see* 1673-3428 **4678**
1673-355X *see* 1673-3436 **6921**
1673-3568 *see* 1673-3444 **1112**
1673-3576 *see* 1673-3452 **5488**
1673-3584 *see* 1673-3460 **3308**
1673-3592 *see* 1673-3479 **3378**
1673-3606 *see* 1673-3487 **7013**
1673-3614 *see* 1673-3495 **2062**
1673-3622 *see* 1673-3509 **674**
1673-3630 *see* 1673-3517 **3691**
1673-3649 Banyue Xuandu **5208**
1673-3657 Daxue Suzhi Jiaoyu Tongshike Xilie Jiaocai **3057**
1673-3770 Shandong Daxue Erbihouyan Xuebao **6085**
1673-3789 Fengdu **6290**
1673-3851 Zhejiang Ligong Daxue Xuebao **8463**
1673-3916 Zhongguo Fuchanke Linchuang Zazhi **6006**
1673-3940 Beida Ban Xin Yidai Duiwai Hanyu Jiaocai. Shangwu Hanyu Jiaocheng Xilie **5098**
1673-3959 Xiandai Chuban Xue - 21 Shiji Xinwen yu Chuanboxue Xilie Jiaocai **7576**
1673-4084 Chinese Science Abstracts *see* 1005-8923 **18**
1673-4092 Guoji Bingduxue Zazhi **5913**
1673-4130 Guoji Jianyan Yixue Zazhi **5622**
1673-422X Guoji Zhongliuxue Zazhi **6020**
1673-4246 Guoji Zhongyi Zhongyao Zazhi **5622**
1673-4432 Xiamen Ligong Xueyuan Xuebao **7930**
1673-4467 Beida Ban Xin Yidai Duiwai Hanyu Jiaocai. Kouyu Jiaocheng Xilie **5098**
1673-4475 Beida Ban Xin Yidai Duiwai Hanyu Jiaocai. Jichu Jiaocheng Xilie **5098**
1673-4483 Beida Ban Xin Yidai Duiwai Hanyu Jiaocai. Shiyong Hanyu Jiaocheng Xilie **5098**
1673-4602 Qingdao Ligong Daxue Xuebao **7900**
1673-4610 Xiandai Shipin yu Yaopin Zazhi/Journal of Modern Food and Pharmaceuticals *changed to* 1674-229X **6851**
1673-4629 Longyan Xueyuan Xuebao **7880**
1673-4637 Beijing Shuiwu **8818**
1673-4661 Fazhi Rensheng **4671**
1673-4734 Caikuai Xuexi **1283**
1673-4769 Yinxiang Gaizhuang Jishu **3116**
1673-4793 Zhongguo Chuanmei Daxue (Ziran Kexue Ban) **7934**
1673-4807 Jiangsu Keji Daxue Xuebao (Ziran Kexue Ban) **7870**
1673-4831 Shengtai yu Nongcun Huanjing Xuebao **3466**
1673-4904 Zhongguo Yishi Jinxiu Zazhi **5737**
1673-5005 Zhongguo Shiyou Daxue Xuebao (Ziran Kexue Ban) **6798**
1673-5021 Zhongguo Caodi Xuebao **260**
1673-5056 Chuan Ting **8641**
1673-5099 Duzhe. Xiangturenwen Ban **5286**
1673-5102 Zhiwu Yanjiu **824**
1673-5110 Zhongguo Shiyong Shenjing Jibing Zazhi **6191**
1673-5188 Z T E Communications **2374**
1673-5196 Lanzhou Ligong Daxue Xuebao **7879**
1673-520X Fenzi Xiabao Shengwu Xuebao **832**
1673-5226 Beijing Fuzhuang Fangzhi *changed to* 1674-3105 **2261**
1673-5269 Zhonghua Zhongliu Fangzhi Zazhi **6037**
1673-5374 Neural Regeneration Research **6163**
1673-5412 Zhongliu Jichu yu Linchuang **6037**
1673-5420 Nanjing Youdian Daxue Xuebao (Shehui Kexue Ban) **2334**
1673-5439 Nanjing Youdian Daxue Xuebao (Ziran Kexue Ban) **7886**
1673-5609 Guangxi Caijing Xueyuan Xuebao **1115**
1673-5641 Chanye yu Keji Luntan **1082**
1673-565X Zhejiang University. Journal (Science A) **7933**
1673-5668 Kexue Guancha **7876**
1673-5692 Zhongguo Dianzi Kexue Yanjiuyuan Xuebao **3116**
1673-5730 Wangkuan Shidai† **8998**
1673-579X Zhongwai Nengyuan **3150**
1673-5854 Shengwuzhi Huaxue Gongcheng **3255**
1673-5862 Shenyang Shifan Daxue Xuebao (Ziran Kexue Ban) **7915**
1673-5897 Shengtai Duli Xuebao **3466**
1673-601X Chang'an Daxue Xuebao (Diqiu Kexue Ban) *changed to* 1672-6561 **2705**
1673-6036 Yixue Xinxixue Zazhi **5832**
1673-6079 Riyong Dianqi **4366**
1673-6273 Progress in Modern Biomedicine **5700**
1673-6311 Dushi Xinqing **8859**
1673-632X Dangdai Nong-ji **210**
1673-6338 Cehui Kexue Jishu Xuebao **4002**
1673-6532 Jinchukou Jingliren **1573**
1673-6567 Zhongguo Shangcan Yixue **6076**
1673-6613 Shijie ZhongXiyi Jiehe Zazhi **5713**
1673-6737 Beifang Shuidao **270**
1673-6745 Meishi yu Meijiu **3656**
1673-677X Zhonghua Yixue Jiaoyu Zazhi **5738**
1673-6796 Xinli Yuekan **7415**
1673-6834 Zhongguo Shangwu Nianjian *see* 1673-6842 **1082**
1673-6842 China Commerce Yearbook **1082**
1673-6850 Yanye yu Huangong **3257**
1673-6974 Huaxia Dili **4014**
1673-7008 Beijing Daxue Zhongguo Yuyan Wenxue Jiaocai Xilie **5098**
1673-7040 Zhongguo Meirong Zhengxing Waike Zazhi **6263**
1673-7067 Neuroscience Bulletin **6169**
1673-7091 Fengshangzhi **2255**
1673-7105 Yaredai Ziyuan yu Huanjing Xuebao **3476**
1673-7113 Yueji **8892**
1673-7172 Dangdai Qiche **8577**
1673-7180 Zhongguo Keji Lunwen Zaixian **7934**
1673-7253 Kuaile Yingyu **5137**
1673-7318 Frontiers of Literary Studies in China **5298**
1673-7326 Frontiers of Business Research in China **1112**
1673-7334 Frontiers of Agriculture in China **114**
1673-7342 Frontiers of Medicine in China **5616**
1673-7350 Frontiers of Computer Science in China **2418**
1673-7369 Frontiers of Chemical Engineering in China **3244**
1673-7377 Frontiers of Materials Science in China **3345**
1673-7385 Frontiers of Earth Science in China **2707**
1673-7393 Frontiers of Energy and Power Engineering in China **3158**
1673-7407 Frontiers of Architecture and Civil Engineering in China **443**
1673-7415 Frontiers of Environmental Science & Engineering in China **3193**
1673-7423 *see* 1673-7318 **5298**
1673-7431 *see* 1673-7326 **1112**
1673-744X *see* 1673-7334 **114**
1673-7458 *see* 1673-7342 **5616**
1673-7466 *see* 1673-7350 **2418**
1673-7474 *see* 1673-7369 **3244**
1673-7482 *see* 1673-7377 **3345**
1673-7490 *see* 1673-7385 **2707**
1673-7504 *see* 1673-7393 **3158**
1673-7512 *see* 1673-7407 **443**
1673-7520 *see* 1673-7415 **3193**
1673-7563 Xin Tansuo **8445**
1673-7717 Zhonghua Zhongyiyao Xuekan **5738**
1673-7784 Baixing Shenghuo **3822**
1673-7830 Shoudu Gonggong Weisheng **7542**
1673-8004 Chongqing Wenli Xueyuan Xuebao (Shehui Kexue Ban) **7954**
1673-8012 Chongqing Wenli Xueyuan Xuebao (Ziran Kexue Ban) **7846**
1673-8020 Ludong Daxue Xuebao (Ziran Kexue Ban) **7880**
1673-8039 Ludong Daxue Xuebao (Zheshe Ban) **7984**
1673-8098 Jiaotong Jianshe yu Guanli **8632**
1673-8160 Shangye Gushi **1173**
1673-8225 Zhongguo Zuzhi Gongcheng yu Linchuang Kangfu **6117**
1673-825X Chongqing Youdian Xueyuan Xuebao (Ziran Kexue Ban) *changed to* Chongqing Youdian Daxue Xuebao (Ziran Kexue Ban) **7846**
1673-8268 Chongqing Youdian Daxue Xuebao (Shehui Kexue Ban) **7954**
1673-8306 Dongfang Shanglu **8783**
1673-8330 Beifang Faxue **4628**
1673-8403 Caoye yu Xumu **283**
1673-842X Liaoning Zhongyiyao Daxue Xuebao **5661**
1673-8519 Minying Jingji yu Zhongxiao Qiye Guanli/Non-State Owned Economy & Small Business Management *changed to* 1674-4497 **1958**
1673-8527 Journal of Genetics and Genomics **874**
1673-8551 Shangwu Luxing **8755**
1673-8659 Shiyou Huagong Anquan Huanbao Jishu **6792**
1673-8705 Zhonghua Linchuang Mianyi he Biantai Fanying Zazhi **5767**
1673-8837 China Economist **1082**
1673-8845 Diangong Wenzhai **3229**
1673-8888 Junsao **6430**
1673-9027 An **8851**
1673-9078 Xiandai Shipin Keji **3668**
1673-9140 Dianli Kexue yu Jishu Xuebao **7850**
1673-9159 Guangdong Haiyang Daxue Xuebao **2709**
1673-9221 Changjiang Xueshu **5272**
1673-9280 Qinghua Faxue **4764**
1673-9434 Huwai Zhuangbei **8318**
1673-9485 Huanjing yu Shenghuo **3437**
1673-9531 Xueqian Kecheng Yanjiu **3088**
1673-9582 Xin Kecheng Daoxue **3088**
1673-9590 Dalian Jiaotong Daxue Xuebao **7849**
1673-9647 Huaxue Gongye **3245**
1673-9663 Shuyuan **8883**
1673-9728 Danjian yu Zhidao Xuebao **52**
1673-9752 Zhonghua Xiaohua Waike Zazhi **5933**
1673-9760 Gaojiao Tansuo **2859**
1673-9833 Hunan Gongye Daxue Xuebao **7863**
1673-9841 Xi'nan Daxue Xuebao (Shehui Kexue Ban) **8016**
1673-9892 Dianzi Yuanqijian Zixun **3093**
1673-9981 Cailiao Yanjiu yu Yingyong **6307**
1674-0009 Dianwang yu Shuili Fadian Jinzhan/Advances of Power System & Hydroelectric Engineering *changed to* 1674-3814 **3127**
1674-0068 Chinese Journal of Chemical Physics **7008**
1674-0297 Chongqing Jiaotong Daxue Xuebao (Shehui Kexue Ban) **7115**
1674-0416 Liaoning Yixueyuan Xuebao (Shehui Kexue Ban) **7983**
1674-0424 Liaoning Yixueyuan Xuebao **7879**
1674-0432 Jilin Nongye **125**
1674-0440 Guoji Yaoxue Yanjiu Zazhi **6845**
1674-0475 Yingxiang Kexue yu Guanghuaxue **6978**
1674-0483 Dongfang Fengqing **8783**
1674-0629 Nanfang Dianwang Jishu **3160**
1674-0696 Chongqing Jiaotong Daxue Xuebao (Ziran Kexue Ban) **8493**
1674-070X Hunan Zhongyiyao Daxue Xuebao **5631**
1674-0742 Zhongwai Yiliao **5739**
1674-0750 Fudan Journal of the Humanities and Social Sciences **4453**
1674-0769 Virologica Sinica **897**
1674-0777 Jinri Yishu **498**
1674-0823 Shenyang Gongye Daxue Xuebao (Shehui Kexue Ban) **8001**
1674-0831 Shiyou Shihua Wuzi Caigou **6792**
1674-0858 Huanjing Kunchong Xuebao **849**
1674-0904 Zhongliu Yufang yu Zhiliao **6037**
1674-0912 Zaisheng Ziyuan yu Xunhuan Jingji **3476**
1674-0947 Shandong Yixue Gaodeng Zhuanke Xuexiao Xuebao **5712**
1674-0963 Zhongguo Zhongxing Zhuangbei **5462**
1674-1013 Chengse **3823**
1674-1048 Liaoning Keji Daxue Xuebao **6320**
1674-1056 Chinese Physics B **7008**
1674-1064 Keji Shangpin **3107**
1674-1129 Shiyan yu Jianyan Yixue **5911**
1674-1137 Chinese Physics C, High Energy Physics and Nuclear Physics **7065**
1674-1145 Xiandai Qiye Wenhua **1196**
1674-1161 Nongye Keji yu Zhuangbei **213**
1674-117X Hunan Gongye Daxue Xuebao (Shehui Kexue Ban) **7971**
1674-1188 Zhejiang Shiyongjun **823**
1674-1196 Xiandai Suzhou **3829**
1674-1226 Zhengju Kexue **4820**
1674-1242 Shengwu Yixue Gongchengxue Jinzhan **751**
1674-1250 Kaoshi yu Zhaosheng **2879**
1674-1285 Xinxi Tongxin Jishu **2345**
1674-1293 Shiyong Pifubingxue Zazhi **5882**
1674-1315 Guanggaozhu Shichang Guancha **26**
1674-1323 Shetuan Guanli Yanjiu **8068**
1674-1331 Ningxia Shifan Xueyuan Xuebao **7989**
1674-1382 Changchun Gongye Daxue Xuebao (Gaojiao Yanjiu Ban) **2971**
1674-1390 Tezhong Shebei Anquan Jishu **6688**
1674-1404 Dalian Gongye Daxue Xuebao **7849**
1674-1420 Beifang Zuojia **5261**
1674-1455 Fazhi Yanjiu **4671**
1674-1528 Jundui Dangde Shenghuo **6430**
1674-1536 Jiaoyu Celiang yu Pingjia **2873**
1674-1544 Zhongguo Keji Ziyuan Daokan **5056**
1674-1560 Tongqu **2218**
1674-1579 Kongjian Kongzhi Jishu yu Yingyong **64**
1674-1609 Xiaoxuesheng Shenghuo **2222**
1674-1625 Guangdong Jinrong Xueyuan Xuebao **1350**
1674-1641 Jinshu Jiagong. Lengjiagong **6318**
1674-165X Jinshu Jiagong. Rejiagong **6318**
1674-1668 Renkou yu Fazhan (Beijing) **7291**
1674-1749 Huanqiu Zhongyiyao **5630**
1674-1757 Dianli Dianrongqi yu Wugong Buchang **3127**
1674-1765 Shanghai Haiguan Xueyuan Xuebao **1582**
1674-179X Xueyuan Jiaoyu **2927**
1674-1803 Zhongguo Meitan Dizhi **6484**
1674-1838 Huanqiu Cishan **8045**
1674-1870 Guoji Fuchan Kexue Zazhi **5991**
1674-1889 Guoji Shengzhi Jiankang / Jihua Shengyu Zazhi **972**
1674-1897 Guoji Yixue Fangshexue Zazhi **6197**
1674-1900 Jushe **4544**
1674-1943 Liangyou Cangchu Keji Tongxun **3654**
1674-1951 Huadian Jishu **3137**
1674-196X Fangzhi Fuzhuang Zhoukan **8450**
1674-2001 Particuology **7029**
1674-2028 Zhonghua Renmin Gongheguo Guojia Fazhan he Gaige Weiyuanhui Wengao **7478**
1674-2036 Xinxi Fanglue **1421**
1674-2044 Shijing **3663**
1674-2052 Molecular Plant **801**
1674-2087 Dangdai Jiaoshi Jiaoyu **2940**
1674-2095 Chaosheng **5272**
1674-2117 Zhongguo Xinxi Jishu Jiaoyu **2928**
1674-2125 Yunzhong Wanglai **8789**
1674-2133 Jianzhu Jiandu Jiance yu Zaojia **1017**

ISSN

1678-8931 Revista Virtual de Estudos da Linguagem - ReVEL **5168**
1678-8982 Economia & Gestao **1479**
1678-9180 *see* 1678-9199 **952**
1678-9199 Journal of Venomous Animals and Toxins Including Tropical Diseases **952**
1678-9547 Revista Brasileira de Direito Constitucional **4852**
1678-9563 *see* 1677-1168 **7393**
1678-9741 *see* 0102-7638 **5798**
1678-9849 *see* 0037-8682 **5826**
1678-9865 *see* 1415-5273 **6668**
1678-9873 *see* 0104-4478 **8129**
1678-9946 *see* 0036-4665 **5818**
1679-0073 Natureza & Conservacao **3455**
1679-0499 Flash **3803**
1679-0731 Revista Brasileira de Financas **1380**
1679-0995 Semiosfera†
1679-1010 Sociedade Brasileira de Clinica Medica. Revista **5716**
1679-1045 Revista de Direito Electronico **4771**
1679-1363 Revista da Ajuris **4770**
1679-1541 Cadernos de Pos - Graduacao em Letras **5268**
1679-1797 *see* 1678-7137 **6256**
1679-1851 Revista Factus **7997**
1679-1991 Revista Capital Cientifico **7996**
1679-2041 Textos & Contextos **8074**
1679-2211 Design Magazine **2485**
1679-2343 Revista Brasileira de Biociencias **700**
1679-3005 Tropical Oceanography **708**
1679-3013 *see* 1679-3005 **708**
1679-3390 Revista Brasileira de Orientacao Profissional **6703**
1679-3560 Carangos Especiais **8572**
1679-3838 Informativo Tecnico **8426**
1679-3919 *see* 0104-5687 **6084**
1679-396X Marine Systems & Ocean Technology **3209**
1679-4427 Mental **7384**
1679-4435 Revista Brasileira de Medicina do Trabalho **5704**
1679-4508 Einstein **5609**
1679-4575 Educ@cao **2845**
1679-5008 P S World **2480**
1679-5237 Veterinaria em Foco **8810**
1679-5350 U N I M E P. Revista de Administracao **1799**
1679-5377 Fronteira **7236**
1679-5636 Cadernos de Historia **4133**
1679-5954 A B E N O. Revista **5832**
1679-6225 Neotropical Ichthyology **958**
1679-6454 Visao Juridica **4809**
1679-6462 Revista de Arbitragem e Mediacao **4770**
1679-6888 Revista Escrita **5361**
1679-7140 Revista Panamericana de Infectologia **7539**
1679-7361 Acta Scientiarum. Human and Social Sciences *changed to* 1983-4675 **7945**
1679-7817 Latin American Journal of Solids and Structures **3278**
1679-7825 *see* 1679-7817 **3278**
1679-7930 Revista Brasileira de Ciencias do Envelhecimento Humano **4054**
1679-8368 Cultura Homeopatica (Print) *changed to* 1982-6206 **5639**
1679-8678 *see* 1677-7360 **6231**
1679-8759 Brazilian Journal of Oceanography **2800**
1679-8953 Revista Brasileira de Ultra - Sonografia **6207**
1679-902X Revista Brasileira de Gerenciamento de Projetos **1790**
1679-9216 *see* 1678-0345 **8790**
1679-9275 Acta Scientiarum. Agronomy **79**
1679-9283 Acta Scientiarum. Biological Sciences **650**
1679-9291 Acta Scientiarum. Health Sciences **5567**
1679-9615 Horizonte **7648**
1680-0001 El Combatiente **6416**
1680-0095 The C S I Handbook **1615**
1680-0338 Ingenieria Hidraulica y Ambiental **3362**
1680-0370 Council for Geoscience of South Africa. Bulletin **2730**
1680-0516 Enterprise Europe **1483**
1680-0788 Energypress.com **3134**
1680-0826 Protistology **698**
1680-0893 Chinese Journal of Mechanics. Series A *changed to* 1727-7191 **3350**
1680-0907 Zhonghua Minguo Lixue Xuehui Qikan. Xilie B†
1680-0982 International Journal of Arabic-English Studies **5310**
1680-1059 International Navigation Association. Bulletin *changed to* On Course **8656**
1680-1156 C R I Annual Report **3629**
1680-1180 Black Business Quarterly **1068**
1680-1202 Achiever **2937**
1680-144X International Journal of Science and Technology of the University of Kashan **7868**
1680-1466 Endokrynolohiya **5892**
1680-1555 ITWeb Brainstorm **1762**
1680-1687 Economic Portrait of the European Union **1423**
1680-1857 Flamingo Specialist Group Newsletter **2611**
1680-1865 Comma†
1680-1938 Muratho **5153**
1680-1970 Psychosocial Notebook **7400**
1680-2012 The China Review **3823**
1680-2136 Gleichstellung von Frauen und Mannern *see* 1680-2144 **8865**
1680-2144 Gender Equality Magazine **8865**
1680-2152 Magazine Egalite entre Femmes et Hommes *see* 1680-2144 **8865**
1680-2179 South African Actuarial Journal **4524**
1680-2187 Cohesion Fund. Annual Report (Year) **1083**
1680-2209 Fondo de Cohesion. Informe Anual *see* 1680-2187 **1083**
1680-2217 Tameiou Sunohes. Etesia Ekthese *see* 1680-2187 **1083**
1680-2225 Fundo de Coesao. Relatorio Anual *see* 1680-2187 **1083**
1680-2233 Biblio International (Print) *changed to* Biblio International (Online) **616**
1680-2314 Keji Fazhan Biaogan **7875**
1680-2373 Litasfera **2752**
1680-2381 Equal Opportunities for Women and Men in the European Union **1680**
1680-2721 Aktual'nye Problemy Sovremennoi Nauki **7834**
1680-2799 Horizon **7862**
1680-2829 E F-Sortsmyndigheden. Aarsrapport *see* 1680-2845 **3411**
1680-2837 Gemeinschaftliches Sortenamt. Jahresbericht *see* 1680-2845 **3411**
1680-2845 Community Plant Variety Office. Annual Report **3411**
1680-2853 Oficina Comunitaria de Variedades Vegetales. Informe Anual *see* 1680-2845 **3411**
1680-2861 Yhteison Kasvilajikevirasto. Vuosikertomus *see* 1680-2845 **3411**
1680-287X Office Communautaire des Varietes Vegetales. Rapport Annuel *see* 1680-2845 **3411**
1680-2888 Koinotiko Grafeio Thutikon Poikilion. Etesia Ekthese *see* 1680-2845 **3411**
1680-2896 Ufficio Comunitario delle Varieta Vegetali. Relazione Annuale *see* 1680-2845 **3411**
1680-290X Instituto Comunitario das Variedades Vegetais. Relatorio Anual *see* 1680-2845 **3411**
1680-2918 Gemenskapens Vaxtsortsmyndighet. Aarsrapport *see* 1680-2845 **3411**
1680-2942 Communautair Bureau voor Plantenrassen. Jaarverslag *see* 1680-2845 **3411**
1680-3043 Idees **4361**
1680-3051 *see* 1562-1146 **5725**
1680-3310 Dilovyi Visnyk **1092**
1680-3469 Commission of the European Communities. Investment in the Community Coal Mining and Iron and Steel Industries. Report on the Survey **6461**
1680-3671 Fortegnelse Over alle Institutioner. Hvem er Hvem i Den Europaeiske Union? *see* 1680-3698 **643**
1680-368X Interinstitutionelles Verzeichnis. Who's Who in der Europaischen Union? *see* 1680-3698 **643**
1680-3698 Interinstitutional Directory. Who's Who in the European Union? **643**
1680-3701 Anuario Interinstitucional. Quien es Quien en la Union Europea *see* 1680-3698 **643**
1680-371X Toimielinhakemisto. Kuka Kukin on Euroopan Unionissa? *see* 1680-3698 **643**
1680-3728 Annuaire Interinstitutionnel. Qui Fait Quoi dans l'Union Europeenne? *see* 1680-3698 **643**
1680-3736 Diorganikos Katalogos. Poios Kanei ti Oten Europaike Enon *see* 1680-3698 **643**
1680-3744 Annuario Interistituzionale. Who's Who nell'Unione Europea *see* 1680-3698 **643**
1680-3752 Interinstitutioneel Jaarboek. Wie is Wie in de Europese Unie *see* 1680-3698 **643**
1680-3760 Anuario Interinstitucional. Quem e Quem na Uniao Europeia? *see* 1680-3698 **643**
1680-3779 Institutionskatalog. Vem gor Vad i Europeiska Unionen? *see* 1680-3698 **643**
1680-3809 The European Ombudsman. Annual Report **4669**
1680-3817 Consensus **7956**
1680-3922 *see* 1680-3809 **4669**
1680-4023 Mekong Development Series **8829**
1680-4325 Sotsionika, Mentologiya i Psikhologiya Lichnosti **8140**
1680-4333 European Political Science **7134**
1680-4465 Pakistan Journal of Library and Information Science **5039**
1680-449X Palitra Pedagoga **2895**
1680-4724 China Hand **1083**
1680-4864 Independent Financial Advice *changed to* 1728-5976 **4502**
1680-4953 *see* 1024-6991 **4738**
1680-5011 Ligestilling Mellem Maend og Kvinder i den Europaiske Union *see* 1680-2381 **1680**
1680-502X Chancengleichheit fuer Frauen und Manner in der Europaischen Union *see* 1680-2381 **1680**
1680-5038 Igualdad de Oportunidades entre Mujeres y Hombres en la Union Europea *see* 1680-2381 **1680**
1680-5046 Naisten ja Miesten Yhtalaiset Mahdollisuuet Euroopan Unionissa *see* 1680-2381 **1680**
1680-5054 Pari Opportunita tra Donne e Uomini nell'Unione Europea *see* 1680-2381 **1680**
1680-5062 Gelijke Kansen voor Vrouwen en Mannen in de Europese Unie *see* 1680-2381 **1680**
1680-5070 Lika Mojligheter for Kvinnor och Man i Euopeiska Unionen *see* 1680-2381 **1680**
1680-5089 Ises Eukairies gia tis Gunaikes kai tous Andres oten Europaike Enose *see* 1680-2381 **1680**
1680-5135 Igualdade de Oportunidades entre Mulheres e Homens na Uniao Europeia *see* 1680-2381 **1680**
1680-5194 Pakistan Journal of Nutrition **6668**
1680-5291 Aerokosmicheskii Kur'er **42**
1680-5348 *see* 1020-4989 **7539**
1680-5356 International Coronelli Society. News **4016**
1680-5550 Jiaoyu yu Shehui Yanjiu **2873**
1680-5593 Journal of Animal and Veterinary Advances **8800**
1680-581X Hi-Fi & Music **6573**
1680-5968 Mir Razvlechenii **6295**
1680-5976 O M **6296**
1680-6077 Staroe Literaturnoe Obozrenie **5240**
1680-6190 Inter-Forum Newsletter **3835**
1680-6387 Natsiyanal'naya Akademiya Navuk Belarusi. Vestsi. Seryya Medyka-Biyalagichnykh Navuk **5684**
1680-6433 Iranian Journal of Reproductive Medicine **5994**
1680-645X Esli **5442**
1680-6492 Zeitschrift fuer Vergaberecht und Beschaffungspraxis **7478**
1680-6603 Namibia Business Climate Survey **1500**
1680-6905 African Health Sciences **5569**
1680-6921 Fizika Soznaniya i Zhyzni, Kosmologiya i Astrofizika **7013**
1680-7057 Physics of Consciousness and Life, Cosmology and Astrophysics *see* 1680-6921 **7013**
1680-7073 Journal of Agricultural Science and Technology **126**
1680-7316 Atmospheric Chemistry and Physics **6347**
1680-7324 *see* 1680-7316 **6347**
1680-7340 Advances in Geosciences **2701**
1680-7359 *see* 1680-7340 **2701**
1680-7367 Atmospheric Chemistry and Physics Discussions **6347**
1680-7375 *see* 1680-7367 **6347**
1680-743X Journal of Data Science **8382**
1680-7650 Taiwan Kunchong **860**
1680-7677 Infomed, Anuario Estadistico **5747**
1680-7820 100% Zdorov'ya†
1680-8096 I S O Management Systems (Swiss Edition) **6402**
1680-810X I S O Management Systems (French Edition) *see* 1680-8096 **6402**
1680-810X I S O Management Systems (French Edition) *see* 1681-6552 **6402**
1680-8177 Direktor Informacionnoj Sluzby **1416**
1680-8185 Socionics, Mentology and Personality Psychology *see* 1680-4325 **8140**
1680-8207 Pakistan Journal of Agronomy *changed to* 1812-5379 **127**
1680-8398 C I M E L **5590**
1680-8428 Zixun Shehui Yanjiu **2569**
1680-8959 *see* 1609-0144 **2760**
1680-9289 Estomatologia Integrada **5843**
1680-9297 Time Out Dubai **3967**
1680-936X *see* 1024-0098 **5791**
1680-9378 *see* 1028-2327 **5791**
1680-9408 *see* 1023-7763 **734**
1680-9424 *see* 1023-6090 **6270**
1680-9432 *see* 1563-2873 **6661**
1680-9440 *see* 1608-1587 **6149**
1680-9521 Novyi Krokodil **5231**
1680-9742 Annual Report on Human Rights **4917**
1680-9882 Focus (Houghton) **7136**
1681-0031 Akademiya Nauk Vysshei Shkoly. Sibirskoe Otdelenie. Doklady *changed to* 1727-2769 **7834**
1681-0090 *see* 1681-0155 **6676**
1681-0104 *see* 1681-0155 **6676**
1681-0120 *see* 1681-0155 **6676**
1681-0139 *see* 1681-0155 **6676**
1681-0155 European Agency for Safety and Health at Work. Annual Report **6676**
1681-0163 *see* 1681-0155 **6676**
1681-0171 *see* 1681-0155 **6676**
1681-018X *see* 1681-0155 **6676**
1681-0198 *see* 1681-0155 **6676**
1681-0201 *see* 1681-0155 **6676**
1681-0228 *see* 1681-0155 **6676**
1681-0279 *see* 1564-4235 **1594**
1681-0384 *see* 0257-2184 **1480**
1681-0392 *see* 0257-2176 **1484**
1681-0406 Entomologica Austriaca **844**
1681-0597 Economic Survey of Latin America and the Caribbean. Summary **1480**
1681-0600 *see* 1681-0597 **1480**
1681-066X I U S T International Journal of Engineering Science **3196**
1681-0678 Central Library European Commission. Activity Report **5001**
1681-0686 Bibliotheque Centrale Commission Europeenne. Rapport d'activite *see* 1681-0678 **5001**
1681-1070 Diani yu Fengzhuang **6709**
1681-1178 Rossiiskii Zhurnal Nauk o Zemle (Print) **2715**
1681-1186 *see* 1561-2120 **3430**
1681-1194 Rossiiskii Zhurnal Nauk o Zemle (Online) **2715**
1681-1208 Russian Journal of Earth Sciences *see* 1681-1194 **2715**
1681-1232 Pain Medicine **6172**
1681-1240 *see* 1681-1232 **6172**
1681-1267 Beschaeftigung in Europa *see* 1016-5444 **1678**
1681-1399 Wireless Asia **2344**
1681-1577 Artes en Santo Domingo **472**
1681-164X Beschreibung der Sozialen Lage in Europa *see* 1681-1658 **8134**
1681-1658 The Social Situation in the European Union **8134**
1681-1666 La Situation Sociale dans l'Union Europeenne *see* 1681-1658 **8134**
1681-181X Telecom Asia **2372**
1681-1941 Sankt-Peterburgskii Universitet **3031**
1681-1968 *see* 1681-1941 **3031**
1681-1984 *see* 1608-0254
1681-1992 *see* 1608-0203 **1582**
1681-200X *see* 1608-022X **1383**
1681-2018 Source O E C D. National Accounts & Historical Statistics **1263**
1681-2026 Source O E C D. Insurance Statistics **4530**
1681-2050 Panorama of European Business **1580**
1681-2085 *see* 1681-2123 **6676**
1681-2093 *see* 1681-2123 **6676**
1681-2107 *see* 1681-2123 **6676**
1681-2115 *see* 1681-2123 **6676**
1681-2123 European Agency for Safety and Health at Work. Facts **6676**
1681-2131 *see* 1681-2123 **6676**
1681-214X *see* 1681-2123 **6676**
1681-2158 *see* 1681-2123 **6676**
1681-2166 *see* 1681-2123 **6676**
1681-2174 *see* 1681-2123 **6676**
1681-2182 *see* 1681-2123 **6676**
1681-2239 *see* 1681-2123 **6676**
1681-228X *see* 1605-9581 **3171**
1681-2395 *see* 0108-9927 **342**
1681-2395 *see* 0105-4503 **342**
1681-2557 Medychna Khimiya **2072**
1681-2611 *see* 1681-0155 **6676**
1681-2743 National Library of South Africa. Annual Report **5034**
1681-2824 The Iranian Journal of Nuclear Medicine **6199**
1681-2875 I C C S Contact *changed to* 1681-2883 **4289**
1681-2883 Contact I C C S - C I E C **4289**
1681-293X Protecting the Community's Financial Interests and the Fight against Fraud **4897**
1681-3162 Liza **8872**
1681-3170 Burda **8854**
1681-3219 Otdokhni! **3965**
1681-3456 Fizioterapiya, Bol'neologiya i Reabilitatsiya **6109**
1681-3464 Liza. Modnye Pricheski **589**
1681-3529 Atmosfera **5065**
1681-3561 Zhengce Yanjiu Xuebao **7478**
1681-3618 Gazeta **3935**
1681-3871 *see* 1681-3618 **3935**
1681-4363 Social Evolution & History **8133**

Link to your serials resources and content with ulrichsweb.com

9764 1681-4371 ULRICH'S PERIODICALS

1681-4371 *see* 1681-4398 **6676**
1681-438X *see* 1681-4398 **6676**
1681-4398 European Agency for Safety and Health at Work. Forum **6676**
1681-4401 *see* 1681-4398 **6676**
1681-4444 *see* 1681-4398 **6676**
1681-4487 Fifteen **8228**
1681-4525 Pakistan Journal of Biochemistry and Molecular Biology **741**
1681-4703 The F E S P A Magazine *see* F E S P A World **7320**
1681-4738 Vodolaznoe Delo **8215**
1681-4746 *see* 1681-4738 **8215**
1681-4754 Commercial Diving *see* 1681-4738 **8215**
1681-4789 Eurostat Yearbook **8368**
1681-4835 The Electronic Journal of Information Systems in Developing Countries **2417**
1681-4894 Rubber Industry Report **7826**
1681-5092 Ezhenedel'nyi Zhurnal (Print Edition)†
1681-5157 Drugs in Focus **2693**
1681-5173 Aeromekhanika i Gazovaya Dinamika **42**
1681-5297 Al Fikr al-Surti **2652**
1681-5319 *see* 1608-0149 **206**
1681-5327 *see* 1608-0165 **2914**
1681-5335 *see* 1608-0173 **1176**
1681-5343 *see* 1608-0181 **1708**
1681-5351 *see* 1608-019X **3147**
1681-536X *see* 1608-0211 **3467**
1681-5378 Source O E C D. General Economies & Future Studies *see* 1684-3134
1681-5378 Source O E C D. General Economies & Future Studies *see* 1608-0238 **1177**
1681-5386 *see* 1608-0246 **1177**
1681-5394 *see* 1681-2018 **1263**
1681-5408 *see* 1608-0262 **3174**
1681-5424 *see* Source O E C D. Social Issues/Migration/ Health **8006**
1681-5432 Source O E C D. Statistics Sources & Methods (Online)
1681-5467 *see* 1608-0157
1681-5475 *see* 1608-0327
1681-5556 African Invertebrates **931**
1681-5564 Southern African Humanities **418**
1681-5602 Horitzo **2709**
1681-5653 *see* 1022-6508 **2907**
1681-5726 Alfa - Redi **4844**
1681-5947 Neilreichia **804**
1681-6013 Delovaya Panorama **1091**
1681-6048 Systemni Doslidzhennya ta Informatsiini Tekhnologii **8440**
1681-6099 South Africa. Council for Geoscience. Memoir **2768**
1681-6102 Nasha Sprava **1642**
1681-6110 *see* 1681-6102 **1642**
1681-6307 Las Drogas en el Punto de Mira *see* 1681-5157 **2693**
1681-6315 Fokus paa Narkotika (Danish Edition) *see* 1681-5157 **2693**
1681-6323 Drogen im Blickpunkt *see* 1681-5157 **2693**
1681-6331 Ta Narkotika sto Proskenio *see* 1681-5157 **2693**
1681-634X Objectif Drogues *see* 1681-5157 **2693**
1681-6358 Focus sulle Droghe *see* 1681-5157 **2693**
1681-6366 Drugs in Beeld *see* 1681-5157 **2693**
1681-6374 As Drogas em Destaque *see* 1681-5157 **2693**
1681-6382 Fokus paa Narkotika (Norwegian Edition) *see* 1681-5157 **2693**
1681-6390 Teemana Huumeet *see* 1681-5157 **2693**
1681-6404 Fokus paa Narkotika (Swedish Edition) *see* 1681-5157 **2693**
1681-6439 Salzburger Beitraege zur Sprach- und Kulturwissenschaft **5171**
1681-6536 *see* 1681-0155 **6676**
1681-6552 I S O Management Systems (Spanish Edition) **6402**
1681-696X International Addiction†
1681-7001 Journal fuer Begabtenfoerderung **3042**
1681-701X Wiener Zeitschrift zur Geschichte der Neuzeit **4278**
1681-7028 Journal fuer Lehrerinnen- und Lehrerbildung **3067**
1681-715X *see* 1682-024X **5692**
1681-7230 Sciendo **7912**
1681-7265 *see* 0233-4305 **5225**
1681-7559 Vostochnaya Kollektsiya **563**
1681-7575 *see* 0026-1394 **6404**
1681-7842 Catauro **386**
1681-7907 Delovaya Khronika **1091**
1681-8865 Chuanbo yu Guanli Yanjiu **2315**
1681-9292 Regionen: Statistisches Jahrbuch (Year) **8396**
1681-9306 Regions: Statistical Yearbook (Year) **8396**
1681-9314 Regions: Annuaire Statistique (Year) **8396**
1681-9357 Europaeische Sozialistik. Sozialschutz. Ausgaben und Einnahmen *see* 1681-9365 **8082**
1681-9365 European Social Statistics. Social Protection. Expenditure and Receipts **8082**
1681-9373 Statistiques Sociales Europeennes. Protection Sociale. Depenses et Recettes *see* 1681-9365 **8082**
1681-9594 Link International **7805**
1681-9616 Cyberbanking & Law **1334**
1681-9721 Sociedad Peruana de Medicina Interna. Revista **5948**
1681-9942 *see* 0864-1269 **7128**
1681-9977 *see* 0864-0572 **7104**
1681-9985 *see* 0011-2593 **7229**
1681-9993 Prisma **1901**
1682-0002 *see* 0864-3598 **7570**
1682-0037 Revista Cubana de Angiologia y Cirugia Vascular **5799**
1682-0045 *see* 1025-6512 **8131**
1682-0053 Iranian Journal of Electrical and Computer Engineering **2472**
1682-024X Pakistan Journal of Medical Sciences **5692**
1682-0614 Burrell's Intellectual Property Law Library (Online Edition) *see* Burrell's Intellectual Property Law Reports **6747**
1682-0622 Constitutional Library **4847**
1682-0630 Index to the Government Gazettes of South Africa *see* Juta - State Library Index to the Government Gazette **7481**
1682-0649 Indexes to the South African Law Reports **4691**
1682-0657 Juta's Daily Law Reports **4708**
1682-0703 *see* 1025-983X **4954**
1682-0711 *see* 1560-8468 **4873**
1682-072X Labour Library *see* 1022-8349 **1708**
1682-0738 Occupational Health and Safety Library **1701**
1682-0746 Road Traffic and Transport Library **8634**
1682-0754 South African Appellate Division Reports 1910 to Date **4965**
1682-0762 *see* 0038-2396 **4785**
1682-0770 *see* 1016-3107 **4898**
1682-0789 *see* 1017-1185 **4708**
1682-0789 *see* Statutes of South Africa (Print) **4789**
1682-0797 *see* 1017-1193 **1948**
1682-0800 European Competitiveness Report **1107**
1682-0908 *see* 0252-0257 **1515**
1682-0983 *see* 1680-4333 **7134**
1682-1009 *see* 1024-6991 **4738**
1682-1017 Case Law of Zimbabwe **4641**
1682-1033 Statutes of Zimbabwe **4789**
1682-1041 *see* 1028-9186 **4792**
1682-105X *see* 1028-9208 **4818**
1682-1068 Motor Industry Bargaining Council Consolidated Agreements **4736**
1682-1130 Agricultural Engineering International **83**
1682-1238 The Emirates Lecture Series **7232**
1682-1246 The Emirates Occasional Papers **4321**
1682-1319 ITWeb Corporate I T Training Guide *changed to* ITWeb Corporate I T C Training Guide **2495**
1682-170X Morgen **3797**
1682-1750 International Archives of the Photogrammetry, Remote Sensing and Spatial Information Sciences **4016**
1682-1769 European Surgery. Supplement *see* 1682-8631 **6243**
1682-1777 *see* 1682-1750 **4016**
1682-1963 The Bride's Diary **5557**
1682-2390 Avto Stil' **8567**
1682-2404 Seventeen (Russia Edition) **2212**
1682-2412 Men's Fitness **6284**
1682-2463 Calle B **7952**
1682-2587 International Journal of Transportation, Privatization & Public Policy **8499**
1682-2609 Auto Online **8559**
1682-2676 Ezhenedel'nyi Zhurnal (Online Edition) **3935**
1682-2722 Cuba. Ministerio de la Industria Ligera. Info **3186**
1682-2765 Journal of Research in Health Sciences **7529**
1682-2773 Aarsrapport om Narkotikasituasjonen i Den Europeiske Union *see* 1609-6150 **2699**
1682-296X Biotechnology **760**
1682-2978 *see* 1682-296X **760**
1682-3001 Campus de San Marcos **2970**
1682-3079 Cathedra **4641**
1682-3087 *see* 1561-0888 **2733**
1682-3141 Journal of Nursing Research **5966**
1682-3206 Education as Change **2847**
1682-3265 Gendernye Issledovaniya **340**
1682-3273 *see* 1682-3265 **340**
1682-3281 Taiwan Jiating Yixue Zazhi **5720**
1682-3419 Revista de Investigaciones Veterinarias del Peru **8806**
1682-3451 Higher Education Management and Policy **2984**
1682-346X Politiques et Gestion de l'Enseignement Superieur†
1682-3532 Journal on Composite Mechanics and Design **7060**
1682-3559 Russian Journal of Theriology **816**
1682-3915 Asian Journal of Information Technology **2407**
1682-3974 Asian Journal of Plant Sciences **777**
1682-4016 European Surgery Online **6243**
1682-4296 Kazakstan Respublikasyny Gylym Akademiasynyn Baandamalary **7875**
1682-430X Bolsa de Valores de Lima. Boletin Diario **1613**
1682-4318 Informe Bursatil **1630**
1682-4326 Estados Financieros Comparados **1622**
1682-4334 *see* Vademecum Bursatil **1657**
1682-4342 Economia y Sociedad **1479**
1682-4350 Diagnostico y Propuesta **1092**
1682-4393 Kazakhstan Respublikasy Gylym Zane Zogary Bilim Ministrliginin. Kazakhstan Respublikasy Ulttyk Gylym Akademiasynyn Khabarlary. Seriya Biologicheskaya i Meditsinskaya **685**
1682-4407 Analisis & Propuestas **7947**
1682-4474 Journal of Medical Sciences **5652**
1682-4482 Southern African Journal of Demography **7293**
1682-4539 North-West. Provincial Gazette
1682-458X Cuadernos de Antropologia **334**
1682-4636 China Coatings Journal **6716**
1682-4830 Boletin Crecer *changed to* 1682-4849 **2832**
1682-4849 Boletin UMC **2832**
1682-4857 Oficina de Cooperacion Internacional. Boletin Informativo **7256**
1682-4873 U N E B I Boletin **3015**
1682-4946 *see* Amauta **2825**
1682-4962 Mejoramiento de la Calidad de la Educacion. Documento de Trabajo **2886**
1682-5055 African Journal of Nursing and Midwifery **5985**
1682-5063 Heart **5787**
1682-5071 S L **2908**
1682-5098 Luyou Guanli Yanjiu **8731**
1682-5136 Popular Mechanics (South Africa Edition) **8435**
1682-5187 *see* 1682-5195 **4708**
1682-5195 Juta's South African Regulations **4708**
1682-5519 Ferrantia **7854**
1682-5675 Technische Universitaet Graz. Foschungsjournal **8441**
1682-5853 Obiter **4750**
1682-6000 Personal Miks **1785**
1682-6027 Pakistan Journal of Information & Technology *changed to* 1812-5638 **2423**
1682-6108 Southern African Journal of Child and Adolescent Mental Health *changed to* 1728-0583 **6150**
1682-6183 *see* 1024-946X **6614**
1682-6485 Taiwan Shouyixue Zazhi **8808**
1682-6574 Cahiers de l'Orient Chretien **7629**
1682-6655 Regionarnoe Krovoobrashchenie i Mikrotsirkulyatsiya **5941**
1682-6736 Ateneo *see* 1607-9582 **5577**
1682-6744 Trade Negotiations Insights **1584**
1682-6760 Revista Cubana de Genetica Medica **878**
1682-6779 Universo Diagnostico **5727**
1682-6876 M K Voskresen'ye **3937**
1682-6892 Al Dia **5570**
1682-6906 *see* 1682-6876 **3937**
1682-6914 *see* 1028-5083 **7510**
1682-6930 M K Bul'var **3937**
1682-6957 Iranian Journal of Physics Research **7018**
1682-6973 *see* 1682-6930 **3937**
1682-6981 Rossiiskaya Okhotnich'ya Gazeta **8331**
1682-699X *see* 1682-6981 **8331**
1682-7031 Innsbrucker Beitraege zur Kulturwissenschaft. Germanistische Reihe **5309**
1682-7090 M K Zdorov'ye **6992**
1682-7201 M Kmobil' **2332**
1682-7368 *see* 1682-2463 **7952**
1682-7384 Novaya Gazeta **3938**
1682-7449 European Court of Human Rights. Reports of Judgements and Decisions **7206**
1682-7538 *see* 1609-0233 **3297**
1682-7546 Jornada Electrotecnica **3322**
1682-7570 Zambia Museums Journal **361**
1682-7783 Social Agenda **1707**
1682-7791 Agenda Social *see* 1682-7783 **1707**
1682-7805 Sozial Agenda *see* 1682-7783 **1707**
1682-8356 International Journal of Poultry Science **289**
1682-8607 Funu yu Xingbie Yanjiu Tongxun **8897**
1682-8615 Textes et Etudes sur l'Orient Chretien **7688**
1682-8631 European Surgery **6243**
1682-8658 Eksperimental'naya i Klinicheskaya Gastroenterologiya **5922**
1682-8666 Blue Chip **1612**
1682-8917 Novosti Iskustvennogo Intellekta **2455**
1682-8941 E D U News† **8952**
1682-8976 Maxim **6294**
1682-900X East African Journal of Human Rights and Democracy **7205**
1682-9042 Clinical Trials Reporter†
1682-9298 I R E Network News†
1682-9344 Problems of Atomic Science and Technology. Series: Plasma Physics **7071**
1682-9743 Liza. Dobrye Sovety **8872**
1682-993X *see* 0256-6915 **3602**
1683-0121 B I S Quarterly Review **1310**
1683-0202 Lenau-Jahrbuch **5321**
1683-0296 Indilinga **5015**
1683-0350 *see* 1016-8664 **3284**
1683-0555 I T E R - C T A Newsletter **3168**
1683-0733 Research Reporter **5806**
1683-089X Kexue Yanxi **2880**
1683-1373 Journal on Applied Information Technology **2549**
1683-1470 Data Science Journal **2530**
1683-1489 M R C Technical Paper **3601**
1683-1691 Cape Etc. **5067**
1683-1713 Reknuus **1299**
1683-1764 Tehran University Medical Journal **5720**
1683-2302 Source O C D E. Agriculture et Alimentation
1683-2310 Source O C D E. Enseignement et Competences
1683-2329 Source O C D E. Economies Emergentes
1683-2337 Source O C D E. Emploi
1683-2345 Source O C D E. Energie
1683-2353 Source O C D E. Industrie, Services et Echanges
1683-2361 Source O C D E. Environnement et Developpement Durable
1683-237X Source O C D E. Finance et Investissement / Assurance et Retraites **1383**
1683-2388 Source O C D E. Gouvernance **1176**
1683-2396 Source O C D E. Developpement
1683-240X Source O C D E. Energie Nucleaire
1683-2418 Source O C D E. Science et Technologies de l'Information **2550**
1683-2426 Source O C D E. Questions Sociales/Migrations/ Sante **8006**
1683-2434 Source O C D E. Fiscalite **1943**
1683-2442 Source O C D E. Economie Territoriale *changed to* 1729-0635 **1176**
1683-2450 Source O C D E. Economies en Transition
1683-2469 Source O C D E. Transports **8511**
1683-2477 Source O C D E. Comptes Nationaux et Statistiques Retrospectives
1683-2566 Advocate **4610**
1683-2582 Jamaican Law Reports **4698**
1683-2604 Eastern Cape Provincial Legislation Library **4663**
1683-2612 Free State Provincial Legislation Library **4677**
1683-2620 Gauteng Provincial Legislation Library **4679**
1683-2639 KwaZulu-Natal Provincial Legislation Library **4710**
1683-2647 Mpumalanga Provincial Legislation Library **4736**
1683-2655 Northern Cape Provincial Legislation Library **4748**
1683-2698 North West Provincial Legislation Library **4748**
1683-2701 Western Cape Provincial Legislation Library **4812**
1683-2728 The State Trials **4965**
1683-2841 Avtotrio **8568**
1683-3082 Yishu: Journal of Contemporary Chinese Art (Diancang Guoji Ban) **528**
1683-3198 The International Arab Journal of Information Technology **2424**
1683-3236 *see* 0873-5379 **2693**
1683-3252 *see* 0873-5379 **2693**
1683-3414 Vladikavkazskii Matematicheskii Zhurnal **5546**
1683-3457 On the Implementation of the European Commission's External Assistance (Year). Annual Report **1602**
1683-3473 Sur la Mise en Oeuvre de l'Aide Exterieure de la Commission Europeenne. Situation au (Annee). Rapport Annuel *see* 1683-3457 **1602**
1683-3511 Applied and Computational Mathematics **5472**
1683-4097 Russian Mining **6478**
1683-4119 Zagorodnaya Zhizn' *changed to* 1813-8926 **4558**
1683-4151 Sarie Bruid **5561**
1683-4178 Fairlady Bride **5558**
1683-4224 All About Dogs in South Africa **6802**
1683-4240 *see* World Energy Statistics and Balances
1683-4259 *see* 1029-4309 **6784**
1683-4267 *see* 1995-3933 **6779**

Link to your serials resources and content with ulrichsweb.com

1683-4275 *see* 1012-9324 **6460**
1683-4283 *see* 1606-8424 **3157**
1683-4291 *see* 1562-7314 **3484**
1683-4313 Sdelai Pauzu **5082**
1683-4321 *see* 1683-626X **3137**
1683-4321 *see* 0256-2332 **3133**
1683-4577 S A Fruit Journal **3749**
1683-4593 Shop! **8883**
1683-4704 E S A - H S R
1683-478X Asian Anthropology **329**
1683-4798 ChemieReport.at **2056**
1683-4844 Majallah - 'i Ghudad - i Darun'riz va Mitabulism - i Iran **5897**
1683-4852 Nuxue Xuezhi **8902**
1683-4917 *see* 1017-7566 **7226**
1683-4925 *see* 1017-7574 **7225**
1683-4976 *see* 1608-5000 **7234**
1683-4984 Quad S A **8266**
1683-5042 Candidate Countries Eurobarometer **7279**
1683-5476 *see* 1683-4844 **5897**
1683-5506 Neurobiology of Lipids **925**
1683-5654 Daily Sun **3948**
1683-5905 Yongxu Chanye Fazhan **3476**
1683-6162 Chimurenga **3948**
1683-6197 Libros & Artes **7983**
1683-626X I E A Energy Prices and Taxes (Online) **3137**
1683-6316 News in Medical Products **5686**
1683-6707 Journal of Modern Pharmacy **6854**
1683-6804 Zhongxi Wenhua Yanjiu **5405**
1683-6936 Oesterreichische Sektion der Internationalen Liga gegen Epilepsie. Mitteilungen **6171**
1683-6979 *see* 1681-1557 **472**
1683-7444 S A Mountain Magazine **8331**
1683-7452 Instituto Nacional de Salud. Documento Tecnico **5636**
1683-7460 Azarbaycan Metabolizm Jurnali **5884**
1683-7479 *see* 1683-7452 **5636**
1683-7487 *see* 1606-6979 **5636**
1683-7584 S A Journal of Human Resource Management **1874**
1683-7673 Terminometro. Hors-Serie **5186**
1683-7681 Terminometro (CD-ROM) **5186**
1683-805X Fizicheskaya Mezomekhanika **7058**
1683-8548 A B C Interactive English Magazine **5088**
1683-8602 *see* 1680-743X **8382**
1683-870X Soffeh **457**
1683-8831 Pakistan Journal of Social Sciences (Faisalabad) **7991**
1683-8882 La Polilla **5039**
1683-8890 *see* 1683-8882 **5039**
1683-8904 Cub@: Medio Ambiente y Desarrollo **3412**
1683-8920 Medioambiente.cu **3452**
1683-8939 *see* 0006-1727 **4445**
1683-8947 *see* 0006-176X **4995**
1683-9145 Laissez - Faire **1546**
1683-9501 Finansovyi Direktor **1110**
1683-9730 Amanzi (Print Edition) *changed to* 1816-7985 **2792**
1683-9749 Guoli Chengda Lishi Xuebao **4182**
1683-979X Pediatria **6099**
1683-9803 *see* 1683-979X **6099**
1683-9919 Asian Journal of Animal and Veterinary Advances **8793**
1683-9986 C F O China **1078**
1684-0011 I C E S Newsletter *changed to* 1995-7815 **2806**
1684-0038 *see* 1560-5744 **100**
1684-0046 Red de Desarrollo Tecnologico de Frutales. Hoja Divulgativa **150**
1684-0054 Institute of Bankers. Journal. **1354**
1684-0070 *see* 1026-9487 **7167**
1684-0135 Digital Camera. Photo & Video **3093**
1684-0240 Faslnamah-i Giyahan-i Daruyi **309**
1684-0283 *see* 1605-8844 **3943**
1684-0291 Annals of Disaster Medicine **5575**
1684-033X European Economy. Special Report *see* 0379-0991 **1484**
1684-0348 *see* 0251-2920 **1445**
1684-0399 NewmusicSA **6599**
1684-0437 Insurance Journal **4507**
1684-0917 J R C Annual Report *see* 0376-5482 **7134**
1684-0925 BioFormosa **657**
1684-0933 Revista de Comunicacion **2337**
1684-1107 Zagotovitel'nye Proizvodstva v Mashinostroenii **5461**
1684-1115 Dianzi Gongcheng Zhuanji. China **3187**
1684-1131 Dianzi Gongcheng Zhuanji. Taiwan **3187**
1684-1158 Baoxian Shiwu yu Zhidu **4494**
1684-1182 Journal of Microbiology, Immunology and Infection **889**
1684-1298 Gruzovik & **8497**
1684-1301 Polet **68**
1684-1360 European Journal of Legal Education† **8954**
1684-1476 A I C M A R Bulletin **7732**
1684-1557 Mors'kyi Ekolohichnyi Zhurnal **2813**
1684-1573 Ukrainian Journal of Radiology *see* 1027-3204 **6209**
1684-1581 *see* 1562-2495 **8140**
1684-162X Public and Community Libraries Directory **5040**
1684-1638 Public and Community Libraries Inventory of South Africa (Online) *see* 1684-162X **5040**
1684-1670 Public and Community Libraries Inventory of South Africa (CD-ROM) *see* 1684-162X **5040**
1684-1700 Health and Human Rights Publication Series **7520**
1684-1786 Infocusco.com **3927**
1684-1794 *see* 1605-5055 **2338**
1684-1859 Revista Cubana de Informatica Medica **5832**
1684-193X *see* 1684-0291 **5575**
1684-1999 Acta Commercii **1723**
1684-2413 Centro Cultural Pablo de la Torriente Brau. Memoria **481**
1684-2421 *see* 1684-2413 **481**
1684-2472 Elektrika **3157**
1684-2499 Tekhnologiya Metallov **6334**
1684-2561 Remont, Vosstanovlenie, Modernizatsiya **5459**
1684-257X Proizvodstvo Prokata **6330**
1684-2588 Telekommunikatsii **2373**
1684-2596 National Agricultural Marketing Council. Annual Report **203**
1684-260X E S R Review **7205**
1684-2618 Voprosy Gumanitarnykh Nauk **4482**
1684-2626 Estestvennye i Tekhnicheskie Nauki **7853**
1684-2642 Big Issue Namibia **3913**
1684-2847 Progress (Johannesburg) **2625**
1684-2952 *see* 1683-2302
1684-2960 *see* 1683-2310
1684-2979 *see* 1683-2329
1684-2987 *see* 1683-2337
1684-2995 *see* 1683-2345
1684-3002 *see* 1683-2353
1684-3010 *see* 1683-2361
1684-3029 *see* 1683-237X **1383**
1684-3037 *see* 1683-2388 **1176**
1684-3045 *see* 1683-2396
1684-3053 *see* 1683-240X
1684-3061 *see* 1683-2418 **2550**
1684-307X *see* 1683-2426 **8006**
1684-3088 *see* 1683-2434 **1943**
1684-310X *see* 1683-2450
1684-3118 *see* 1683-2469 **8511**
1684-3126 *see* 1683-2477
1684-3134 Source O C D E. Economie Generale et Etudes Prospectives
1684-3142 Source O C D E. Statistiques: Sources et Methodes **8400**
1684-3428 *see* 0304-3363 **1502**
1684-3436 *see* 0304-3274 **1159**
1684-3592 *see* 1682-346X
1684-3681 *see* 1607-3088 **3500**
1684-3703 Quality Technology and Quantitative Management **1902**
1684-3762 O I E Boletin (French Edition) *see* 1684-3770 **8803**
1684-3770 O I E Bulletin (English Edition) **8803**
1684-3789 O I E Boletin (Spanish Edition) *see* 1684-3770 **8803**
1684-3916 Mini **2258**
1684-4130 Smithiana Bulletin **963**
1684-4149 Smithiana. Special Publication **963**
1684-4173 *see* 1027-1775 **7960**
1684-4432 B A M Asia **8491**
1684-4637 eurozine **7963**
1684-4866 Evraziatskii Entomologicheskii Zhurnal **847**
1684-4904 Lexikos **5144**
1684-498X Interim **8426**
1684-4998 Journal for New Generation Science **7871**
1684-5285 Upgrade (English Edition) **8444**
1684-5307 Journal of South Pacific Law **4704**
1684-5315 African Journal of Biotechnology **755**
1684-5358 African Journal of Food, Agriculture, Nutrition and Development **6654**
1684-5374 *see* 1684-5358 **6654**
1684-5781 Elektrometallurgiya **6311**
1684-579X Materialovedenie **3370**
1684-5900 Rolling Inspiration **4078**
1684-6052 African Capacity Building Foundation. Annual Report **1590**
1684-6060 *see* 1684-6052 **1590**
1684-6079 A C B F Newsletter **1589**
1684-6087 *see* 1684-6079 **1589**
1684-6133 Art South Africa **471**
1684-6184 Contours **8695**
1684-6192 *see* 1684-6184 **8695**
1684-6206 Quest **7672**
1684-6338 A I F. Dolgozhitel' **4037**
1684-6400 Informatsionnye Tekhnologii **2546**
1684-6486 Zhonghua Minguo Taimin Diqu Yuye Tongji Nianbao **3614**
1684-6680 King Edward Medical College. Lahore. Annals **5657**
1684-6826 R E C I D T **8436**
1684-7008 T3 **2439**
1684-7067 VISI Colour *changed to* 1994-148X **6720**
1684-7075 Pharmeuropa Bio **6875**
1684-7091 Globe Studies **4013**
1684-7725 Avtostroenie za Rubezhom **8568**
1684-7806 *see* 1609-9648 **5250**
1684-7822 Veritas **2924**
1684-8020 *see* 1560-098X **1347**
1684-8209 Jatros Radiologie **6199**
1684-8349 The Mannequin **2258**
1684-8462 Journal of Food Technology **3651**
1684-8799 *see* 1726-2135 **3482**
1684-8845 Comite International des Poids et Mesures. Comite Consultatif des Longueurs (Rapport et Annexes)† **8942**
1684-9078 Ecoloc. Gerer l'Economie Localement en Afrique. Evaluation et Prospective†
1684-9434 Tax Administration Review **1946**
1684-9507 Magallat Kulliyyah al-Tarbiyah **2884**
1684-9515 Zambia Library Association. Newsletter
1684-9787 I P R I Journal **7141**
1684-9809 *see* 1684-9787 **7141**
1684-9833 Inter-American Center of Tax Administrators. Informativo - Newsletter **1929**
1684-9965 Advances in Radio Science - Kleinheubacher Berichte **2356**
1684-9973 *see* 1684-9965 **2356**
1684-9981 *see* 1561-8633 **2787**
1685-2508 Chip **2410**
1685-6465 Penthouse **6297**
1685-7240 Room **4549**
1686-0527 H W M (Thailand) **2539**
1686-4360 Computer-Aided Design and Applications **3289**
1686-5138 Couture Thailand **2253**
1686-6525 M M - The Industrial Magazine **5455**
1686-6576 International Journal of Geoinformatics **4016**
1687-0042 *see* 1110-757X **5501**
1687-0247 *see* 1073-7928 **5498**
1687-0409 *see* 1085-3375 **5463**
1687-0425 *see* 0161-1712 **5497**
1687-0530 Journal of Engineering Sciences (J E S) **3205**
1687-0689 Jami'at al-Azhar. Kulliyyat al-Lughah al-Arabiyyah bil-Zagazig. Majallah
1687-0980 Journal of Astronomy and Astrophysics
1687-0999 Journal of Geophysics **2785**
1687-1014 Egypt. Meteorological Authority. Meteorological Research Bulletin **6352**
1687-1189 Minufiya Journal of Electronic Engineering Research
1687-1197 *see* 1687-1200 **5473**
1687-1200 Applied Mathematics Research eXpress **5473**
1687-1235 Egyptian Journal of Nutrition *changed to* 1110-6360 **6658**
1687-1278 Egyptian Medical Journal of the National Research Center **5609**
1687-1308 International Mathematics Research Surveys **5498**
1687-1324 *see* 1687-1308 **5498**
1687-1472 EURASIP Journal on Wireless Communications and Networking **2350**
1687-1499 *see* 1687-1472 **2350**
1687-1502 The Egyptian Journal of Biochemistry & Molecular Biology *changed to* 1012-554X **731**
1687-1510 Service des Antiquites de l'Egypte. Annales† **8988**
1687-1537 Egyptian Women's Dermatological Society. Journal **5876**
1687-1634 *see* 1020-3397 **7515**
1687-1804 *see* 1110-1849 **5771**
1687-1812 *see* 1687-1820 **5488**
1687-1820 Fixed Point Theory and Applications **5488**
1687-1839 Advances in Difference Equations **5466**
1687-1847 *see* 1687-1839 **5466**
1687-2177 *see* 1048-9533 **5501**
1687-2215 Cybrarians Journal **5004**
1687-2762 Boundary Value Problems **5476**
1687-2770 *see* 1687-2762 **5476**
1687-2789 Eurasip Book Series on Signal Processing and Communications **3307**
1687-2797 *see* 1687-2789 **3307**
1687-3017 International Mathematical Research Papers *changed to* 1073-7928 **5498**
1687-3831 Egyptian Dermatology Online Journal **5875**
1687-3955 Eurasip Journal on Embedded Systems **2350**
1687-3963 *see* 1687-3955 **2350**
1687-4099 Differential Equations and Nonlinear Mechanics **5482**
1687-4102 *see* 1687-4099 **5482**
1687-4110 Journal of Nanomaterials **7021**
1687-4129 *see* 1687-4110 **7021**
1687-4145 Eurasip Journal on Bioinformatics and Systems Biology **825**
1687-4153 *see* 1687-4145 **825**
1687-4161 Eurasip Journal on Information Security **2513**
1687-417X *see* 1687-4161 **2513**
1687-4188 International Journal of Biomedical Imaging **5637**
1687-4196 *see* 1687-4188 **5637**
1687-420X Journal of Nuclear and Radiation Physics **7067**
1687-4285 Egyptian Journal of Aquatic Research
1687-4714 Eurasip Journal on Audio, Speech, and Music Processing **8152**
1687-4722 *see* 1687-4714 **8152**
1687-4757 P P A R Research **741**
1687-4765 *see* 1687-4757 **741**
1687-479X *see* 1565-3633 **2115**
1687-4897 Assiut University Journal of Mathematics and Computer Science **5474**
1687-4900 Assiut University Journal of Physics **7006**
1687-4919 Assiut University Journal of Chemistry **2051**
1687-4927 Assiut University Journal of Botany **777**
1687-4935 Assiut University Journal of Zoology **934**
1687-4943 Assiut University Journal of Geology **2725**
1687-5060 Mansoura Journal of Chemistry **2072**
1687-5079 Mansoura Journal of Mathematics **5510**
1687-5087 Mansoura Journal of Biology **687**
1687-5095 Mansoura Journal of Physics **7881**
1687-5109 Mansoura Journal of Geology and Geophysics **7881**
1687-5125 Al Minia Science Bulletin. Zoology Section
1687-5133 Al Minia Science Bulletin. Geology Section
1687-5141 Al Minia Science Bulletin. Mathematics Section
1687-515X Al Minya Science Bulletin. Computer Science Section
1687-5176 Eurasip Journal on Image and Video Processing **2401**
1687-5214 Experimental Diabetes Research **5892**
1687-5249 Journal of Control Science and Engineering **2473**
1687-5257 *see* 1687-5249 **2473**
1687-5265 Computational Intelligence and Neuroscience **2447**
1687-5273 *see* 1687-5265 **2447**
1687-5281 *see* 1687-5176 **2401**
1687-529X *see* 1110-662X **2136**
1687-5303 *see* 1687-5214 **5892**
1687-5338 The Egyptian Journal of Hypertension and Cardiovascular Risk **5786**
1687-5370 International Journal of Plant Genomics **873**
1687-5389 *see* 1687-5370 **873**
1687-5397 Texture, Stress and Microstructure **2771**
1687-5400 *see* 1687-5397 **2771**
1687-5443 *see* Neural Plasticity **6163**
1687-5486 *see* 0793-0291 **2103**
1687-5591 Modelling and Simulation in Engineering **3109**
1687-5605 *see* 1687-5591 **3109**
1687-563X Advances in OptoElectronics **7073**
1687-5648 *see* 1687-563X **7073**
1687-5656 Molecular and Supramolecular Materials **2127**
1687-5664 *see* 1687-5656 **2127**
1687-5680 Advances in Multimedia **2349**
1687-5699 *see* 1687-5680 **2349**
1687-5702 International Journal of Vehicular Technology **3383**
1687-5710 *see* 1687-5702 **3383**
1687-5788 Tanta Medical Sciences Journal **5720**
1687-5826 International Journal of Microwave Science and Technology **3321**
1687-5834 *see* 1687-5826 **3321**
1687-5869 International Journal of Antennas and Propagation **3320**
1687-5877 *see* 1687-5869 **3320**
1687-5893 Advances in Human - Computer Interaction **2445**
1687-5907 *see* 1687-5893 **2445**
1687-5915 Advances in Tribology **3373**
1687-5923 *see* 1687-5915 **3373**
1687-5966 International Journal of Aerospace Engineering **61**
1687-5974 *see* 1687-5966 **61**
1687-5990 International Journal of Navigation and Observation **4037**
1687-6008 *see* 1687-5990 **4037**

ISSN

1700-0823 *see* 1200-3964 **5808**

1700-0912 Titre Aborigene, la Decision de la Cour Supreme du Canada dans Delgamuukw c. Colombie-Britannique *see* Aboriginal Title: The Supreme Court of Canada Decision in Delgamuukw v. British Columbia **4608**

1700-0947 *see* 1482-6852 **2620**

1700-0955 Fuel **2189**

1700-0963 Parcours *see* 1700-0971 **6022**

1700-0971 In Stride **6022**

1700-1005 Verve (Toronto) **2219**

1700-103X Info F C D P *changed to* 1912-032X **7206**

1700-1188 *see* 1910-7757 **4107**

1700-1315 Senate of Canada. Standing Senate Committee on Human Rights. Proceedings **7215**

1700-1323 *see* 1700-1315 **7215**

1700-1439 Multi-Unit Report *changed to* 1712-140X **4406**

1700-1536 Monitor *changed to* 1499-321X **7165**

1700-1625 Region de la Capitale-Nationale. Bulletin Regional sur le Marche du Travail *changed to* 1912-6603 **1669**

1700-1706 ForexCast. Quarterly Strategy Outlook *changed to* 1910-1953 **1566**

1700-1714 ForexCast. Special Alert *changed to* 1910-7617 **1566**

1700-1846 ForexCast. Weekly Bulletin *changed to* 1910-1961 **1566**

1700-1862 U S Equity Sector Strategist *changed to* 1912-4287 **1657**

1700-1870 U S Equity Sector Strategy *changed to* 1912-4287 **1657**

1700-1889 Canadian Vending and Office Coffee Service Magazine **3676**

1700-1919 *see* 1912-1687 **4069**

1700-1935 *see* 0842-7038 **1590**

1700-1943 *see* 0842-7046 **1590**

1700-2001 Industry Canada Research Series **1630**

1700-201X Documents de Recherche d'Industrie Canada *see* 1700-2001 **1630**

1700-2567 Alberta Finance Ministry. Activity Report **1058**

1700-2729 C I N D E Journal **3342**

1700-2796 Analyse du Marche de la Revente du Quebec Metropolitain (Print Edition) *changed to* 1912-2322 **7581**

1700-3288 *see* 1189-7716 **4851**

1700-3334 *see* 0835-3638 **4130**

1700-3504 Compliance Assessment and Enforcement Activities. Annual Report *changed to* 1912-8339 **3412**

1700-4012 Standing Senate Committee on Defence and Security. Proceedings *changed to* 1702-0921 **7469**

1700-411X International Abstracts. Alzheimer's Disease & Other Dementias **5747**

1700-5043 Canadian Florist **3755**

1700-5086 *see* 1487-7554 **2483**

1700-5132 *see* 0316-3083 **2378**

1700-5159 *see* 1497-1518 **2370**

1700-5353 Canada. Commission for Public Complaints Against the R C M P. Annual Report **7426**

1700-5361 *see* 1700-5353 **7426**

1700-5531 *see* 1208-3143 **2644**

1700-5876 *see* 1184-0471 **7113**

1700-6120 *see* 1493-4086 **4714**

1700-6627 Canada. Military Police Complaints Commission. Annual Report **2646**

1700-6929 *see* 1181-6244 **2646**

1700-7003 *see* 1491-896X **1084**

1700-7496 *see* 0700-1576 **1926**

1700-7593 Lemon-Aid New Cars and Minivans **8589**

1700-8476 Natural Health Products Canada B2B Industry Guide *changed to* 1912-0192 **2019**

1700-8492 Canadian Biotechnology **1978**

1700-8506 *see* 1910-104X **5743**

1700-9510 Canada. Passport Office. Annual Report *changed to* 1719-914X **7257**

1700-9758 *see* 1494-1791 **8083**

1700-9782 Intentions d'Achat des Consommateurs. Region Metropolitaine de Montreal *changed to* 1912-7200 **1430**

1700-9839 Intentions d'Achat des Consommateurs. Vancouver *changed to* 1912-7243 **1430**

1700-9995 Art in Profile Series **470**

1701-0004 Northern Lights Series **7894**

1701-0039 Canada Pension Plan Investment Board. Annual Report **1615**

1701-0128 Canada. Department of Fisheries and Oceans. Administration and Enforcement of the Fish Habitat Protection and Pollution Prevention Provisions of the Fisheries Act. Annual Report **4969**

1701-0438 S I R C Report *changed to* 1912-1598 **7264**

1701-0632 Canada. Statistics Canada. Wood Industries (Online Edition)†

1701-073X Canadian Institutes of Health Research. Performance Report **7428**

1701-0748 *see* 1701-073X **7428**

1701-0764 Canadian Nuclear Safety Commission. Performance Report **7428**

1701-0772 *see* 1701-0764 **7428**

1701-0802 O S F I Annual Report **7458**

1701-0810 *see* 1701-0802 **7458**

1701-0853 *see* 1701-0861 **271**

1701-0861 Canadian Grain Commission. Performance Report **271**

1701-087X Commission Canadienne des Grains. Rapport sur le Rendement *see* 1701-0861 **271**

1701-0950 Collection Fiscale *changed to* 1719-2587 **1914**

1701-1132 Canadian Cowboy Country **5067**

1701-1248 Saskatchewan. Medical Services Branch. Annual Statistical Report **5709**

1701-1299 Illinois Public Sector *changed to* 1938-4890 **7445**

1701-1388 Canada. Statistics Canada. Leather and Allied Products Industries (Online Edition)†

1701-1701 Canada. Statistics Canada. Non-Metallic Mineral Products Industries (Online)†

1701-1809 The Federal Lobbyists **4673**

1701-1868 Machinery Industries, except Electrical Machinery **5455**

1701-1876 Industries de la Machinerie, sauf Electrique *see* 1701-1868 **5455**

1701-1884 Lemon-Aid S U Vs, Vans and Trucks **8589**

1701-2031 Canada. Statistics Canada. Primary Metal Industries (Online) **6307**

1701-2163 Journal of Obstetrics and Gynaecology Canada **5996**

1701-2279 S I R C Annual Report *changed to* 1701-2287 **7264**

1701-2287 S I R C Report **7264**

1701-2473 The Link **5928**

1701-2783 S I H R Plus Newsletter *changed to* 1910-1414 **8202**

1701-2864 *see* 1193-3550 **1968**

1701-3674 C A R P Fifty Plus **4042**

1701-3690 Biotechnology Resource & Recruitment Guide *changed to* 1910-2739 **1857**

1701-4018 Saskatchewan Culture, Youth and Recreation. Annual Report **7467**

1701-4158 *see* 1488-1926 **5815**

1701-4247 *see* 0706-943X **6406**

1701-428X *see* 0703-6639 **1817**

1701-4468 SaskBusiness **1171**

1701-4522 *see* 1207-9030 **2692**

1701-4530 *see* 1482-0455 **2689**

1701-4697 I R S S T. Activity Report *see* 1701-4700 **6679**

1701-4700 Institut de Recherche en Sante et Securite du Travail. Rapport d'Activite **6679**

1701-5367 Aboriginal Head Start on Reserve Program. National Annual Report **7418**

1701-5413 *see* 0821-8110 **7421**

1701-5979 *see* 1494-6785 **7464**

1701-6029 Info-Tech - Informatique et Technologies pour la P M E

1701-6517 *see* 1191-7245 **8531**

1701-6622 *see* 1482-6992 **7549**

1701-6649 *see* 0706-9413 **3693**

1701-6908 Lemon-Aid Used Cars and Minivans **8589**

1701-7106 C A C P / A C C P Newsletter *changed to* 1719-6310 **2645**

1701-7173 Course Conductor News **6984**

1701-719X Annual Review of Civil Litigation **4618**

1701-7254 *see* 1483-0116 **4691**

1701-7440 Royal Canadian College of Organists. Yearbook & Directory of Members **6613**

1701-7688 Cottage Magazine **3808**

1701-7769 This is Manitoba, Fishing and Hunting Adventures *changed to* 1704-6718 **8732**

1701-7793 Perspectives Sectorielles du Marche du Travail au Quebec *changed to* 1719-9069 **1696**

1701-8382 Memorial University of Newfoundland. Public Policy Research Centre. Annual Report *changed to* 1910-6890 **7451**

1701-8439 ElectronicHealthcare **5830**

1701-8587 Canadian Art Teacher **2834**

1701-8773 Sailing Directions: Cape Canso to Cape Sable, including Sable Island **8659**

1701-879X Sailing Directions: Cape North to Cape Canso, including Bras d'Or Lake **8659**

1701-8811 Sailing Directions: Gulf of Maine and Bay of Fundy **8659**

1701-9036 *see* 0382-2281 **7428**

1701-9079 Canada's Missing Children. Annual Report **8030**

1701-9109 *see* 1701-9079 **8030**

1701-9125 Pulsepoint **249**

1701-9222 *see* 1702-2363 **5591**

1701-9230 *see* 1702-2363 **5591**

1701-9583 Welcome to the C I H R - Rx & D Progress Report (Year) **6885**

1701-9680 Journal of Business Administration and Policy Analysis **1764**

1701-9818 Canadian Orchestras, Ensembles, Music Organizations Directory *changed to* 1705-2807 **6602**

1702-0042 Manitoba Vacation Guide **8732**

1702-0425 The Computer Paper (Eastern Edition) *changed to* 1710-0186 **2420**

1702-0468 Canadian Venture Exchange. Review *changed to* 1704-9962 **1656**

1702-062X Canadian Camera Magazine **6965**

1702-0646 *see* 1702-2819 **4406**

1702-0921 Standing Senate Committee on National Security and Defence. Proceedings **7469**

1702-093X *see* 1702-0921 **7469**

1702-1138 *see* 1494-3409 **1682**

1702-1359 Natural Sciences and Engineering Research Council of Canada. Annual Report **7888**

1702-1367 Relance a l'Universite, Baccalaureat, Maitrise et Doctorat, le Placement des Personnes Diplomees *changed to* 1719-3877 **2999**

1702-1626 Planning for Profits Magazine **1644**

1702-2363 Canadian Institutes of Health Research. Annual Report **5591**

1702-2509 Le Contact *changed to* 1719-8542 **8047**

1702-2673 Radio Aids to Marine Navigation. Pacific and Western Arctic **2362**

1702-269X *see* 1702-2673 **2362**

1702-2746 National Directory of Services and Programs for Men Who Are or Have Been Victims of Violence **4107**

1702-2770 *see* 1498-8356 **2362**

1702-2819 Canada. Innovations and Solutions Program. Annual Report **4406**

1702-3017 Science and Technology for Sustainable Development. Annual Report *changed to* 1702-3025 **7468**

1702-3025 Science and Technology for Sustainable Development. 5NR Biennial Report **7468**

1702-3114 Directory of Editors **7559**

1702-3300 Carrieres d'Avenir **6695**

1702-3483 Pacific - Prairie Restaurant News **4395**

1702-3599 Defence R & D Canada. Annual Report **6418**

1702-3602 *see* 1702-3599 **6418**

1702-3785 C I P Magazine

1702-4188 I.E. Global **1568**

1702-4218 Canadian Studies Program Applicants' Guide **4287**

1702-4390 At Your Library *changed to* 1719-6329 **5055**

1702-4404 Optimale (French Edition) *see* 1702-4412 **6285**

1702-4412 Optimale (English Edition) **6285**

1702-5206 Trade Update *changed to* 1914-9956 **1554**

1702-5524 Trade Policy Research **1584**

1702-5540 *see* 1702-5524 **1584**

1702-5966 New Brunswick. Department of Agriculture, Fisheries and Aquaculture. Annual Report *changed to* 1913-7737 **139**

1702-5966 New Brunswick. Department of Agriculture, Fisheries and Aquaculture. Annual Report *changed to* 1913-7931 **3602**

1702-627X Des Affaires Boeuf **3633**

1702-6431 *see* 1490-7291 **1912**

1702-6598 *see* 1498-9972 **4971**

1702-6601 Medical & Assistive Devices & Diagnostics Canada Industry & Buyers Guide **2016**

1702-6660 *see* 1704-1368 **1583**

1702-7756 Annual Academic Report *changed to* 1910-2755 **3008**

1702-8264 Fonds d'Indemnisation des Services Financiers. Rapport Annuel *changed to* 1710-7725 **1646**

1702-8299 Horse Canada **8292**

1702-8396 Glow **6987**

1702-8590 Today's Parent, Pregnancy & Birth **6005**

1702-8701 Manuel d'Instructions, Patients en Traitement pour l'Insuffisance Renale Chronique *see* 1498-8100 **6269**

1702-8957 Lessons Learned **7451**

1702-9228 Canadian Journal of Law and Technology **4639**

1702-9279 *see* 1704-1244 **7453**

1702-9295 Ontario Birchbark **3556**

1702-9503 *see* 0839-8194 **3429**

1702-9554 Lloydminster Sask/Alta Meridian Booster *changed to* Lloydminster Meridian Booster **3812**

1703-0005 Wynterblue Thunder *changed to* 1719-573X **5437**

1703-0021 Lands and People Chronicle *changed to* 1703-8553 **3450**

1703-0056 Maisonneuve **3813**

1703-0072 C I O Governments' Review **7485**

1703-0080 CxO **2496**

1703-0102 O N S A. Bulletin **3556**

1703-0935 W H M I S at Work **6688**

1703-1826 Africa: Missing Voices Series **4172**

1703-2016 Corporate Knights **1736**

1703-2121 Canadian Journal of Midwifery Research and Practice **5988**

1703-2563 Compendium of Self-Care Products **6830**

1703-2598 Teaching & Learning **2918**

1703-2636 Canada. Statistics Canada. Electric Power Generation, Transmission and Distribution **3151**

1703-2652 Canada. Statistics Canada. Criminal Prosecutions: Personnel and Expenditures (Online Edition) **4821**

1703-289X Journal of Religion and Popular Culture **7656**

1703-2911 Canadian Poultry Magazine **283**

1703-2997 Journal of Law & Equality **4850**

1703-3047 *see* 1702-9228 **4639**

1703-3381 International Journal of Disability, Community & Rehabilitation **3041**

1703-3675 Farmers' Independent Weekly *changed to* 0025-2239 **136**

1703-3802 British Columbia. Ministry of Water, Land and Air Protection. Annual Report *changed to* 1705-9089 **2604**

1703-3985 British Columbia. Ministry of Transportation. Annual Report *changed to* 1705-8929 **7424**

1703-4566 Indigenous Law Journal **4692**

1703-4574 Alberta. Ministry of Energy. Annual Report **3123**

1703-4604 Quebec (Province). Ministere des Ressources Naturelles. Rapport Annuel de Gestion *changed to* 1910-7005 **3145**

1703-4906 Canada. Statistiques Canada. Statistiques sur le Secteur Public **1219**

1703-4930 Canada. Statistics Canada. Oil and Gas Extraction **6799**

1703-5031 British Columbia. Ministry of Finance. Annual Report *changed to* 1708-0266 **7424**

1703-5295 Canadian Winds **6554**

1703-5465 Quarterly Labour Market and Income Review **1873**

1703-5775 Canada. Statistics Canada. Human Activity and the Environment: Annual Statistics **3409**

1703-5783 *see* 1703-5775 **3409**

1703-5961 El Gazet di Torronto **5217**

1703-6305 Alberta Cancer Board. Business Plan **1058**

1703-7603 Islam & Science **7712**

1703-762X *see* 1703-7603 **7712**

1703-7646 Alberta Senior Annual Report **4039**

1703-7697 National Aboriginal Health Organization. Annual Report **7533**

1703-7700 Arragutamat Titirarksimajuliunguvaktut *see* 1703-7697 **7533**

1703-7700 Arragutamat Titirarksimajuliunguvaktut *see* 1703-7719 **7534**

1703-7719 Organisation Nationale de la Sante Autochtone. Rapport Annuel **7534**

1703-7921 *see* 0702-8997 **326**

1703-7956 Perspectives **2565**

1703-812X Modern Dog **6811**

1703-8138 *see* 0034-379X **1705**

1703-8189 Music Scene *see* 1486-0317 **6615**

1703-8294 Quebec Province. Centre de Recouvrement. Rapport Annuel de Gestion *changed to* 1912-0931 **6703**

1703-843X Edmonton's Media Magazine **7560**

1703-8448 Spirit Magazine **3566**

1703-8510 Alberta Transportation. Annual Report (Year) *changed to* 1715-5029 **8489**

1703-8553 Lands and People **3450**

1703-8618 Bluprint Magazine **2274**

1703-8634 Alberta. Ministry of Sustainable Resource Development. Annual Report **7419**

1703-8839 Drogues, Sante et Societe **2693**

1703-907X Microcosm - I I I **5823**

1703-9088 *see* 1703-907X **5823**

1703-9096 Microcosme - I M I I *see* 1703-907X **5823**

1703-9193 Gestion du Ministere de la Culture et des Communications du Quebec. Rapport Annuel (Year) **7439**

1703-9290 Patient Management Problems in Clinical Oncology **6032**

1703-9347 Learning with Canadian Information *changed to* 1910-7242 **3082**

ISSN

1703-9363 Comparable Health Indicators, Canada, Provinces and Territories **7547**
1703-9371 Indicateurs de la Sante Comparables, Canada, Provinces et Territoires *see* 1703-9363 **7547**
1703-9401 Plaintes de la Regie Regionale de l'Outaouais et du Reseau Regional de la Sante et des Services Sociaux. Rapport Annuel *changed to* 1910-9229 **8025**
1704-0507 Journey *changed to* 1910-0140 **8690**
1704-0639 Cape Dorset Annual Print Collection **481**
1704-0825 Ontario Family Law Rules Annotated (Year) **4914**
1704-1082 Shareowner **1651**
1704-1244 Meteorological Service of Canada. Annual Report **7453**
1704-1333 Team Canada Inc. Achievements Report *changed to* 1704-1368 **1583**
1704-1341 Team Canada Inc. Business Plan *changed to* 1704-1368 **1583**
1704-1368 Team Canada Inc. Annual Report **1583**
1704-1600 *see* 1486-8628 **5755**
1704-2070 Domaine Anglophone **1814**
1704-2461 *see* 0847-0464 **2653**
1704-2518 Alberta Rural Reminder *changed to* 1716-9356 **206**
1704-2526 Alberta, Evocations Rurales *changed to* 1716-2866 **197**
1704-2631 *see* 1205-5549 **3510**
1704-2666 Yukon Agricultural Research and Demonstration Report *changed to* 1714-5244 **171**
1704-3697 Building Aboriginal Economies *changed to* 1706-3388 **1069**
1704-3727 Family Camping Magazine *changed to* 1718-2913 **4977**
1704-3816 C C N Matthews C C E Directory **22**
1704-3999 Housing Now. New Brunswick (Online Edition) *changed to* 1719-7058 **4413**
1704-4014 Actualites Habitation (Nouveau-Brunswick) *changed to* 1719-7066 **4402**
1704-4057 Housing Now. Newfoundland and Labrador *changed to* 1719-7058 **4413**
1704-4065 Actualites Habitation (Terre-Neuve et Labrador) *changed to* 1719-7066 **4402**
1704-4073 Housing Now. Prince Edward Island *changed to* 1719-7058 **4413**
1704-4081 Actualites Habitation (Ile-du-Prince-Edouard) *changed to* 1719-7066 **4402**
1704-4286 Indian and Northern Affairs Canada. Update **8046**
1704-5061 Eagle Feather **3531**
1704-5193 Inside Entertainment **3811**
1704-5592 C N S C Annual Report **7425**
1704-5630 Canadian Tourism Commission. Corporate Plan Summary **8691**
1704-6203 Farm Credit Canada Annual Report **1341**
1704-653X National Film Board of Canada *changed to* 1704-6548 **6518**
1704-6548 National Film Board of Canada. Resource Catalogue **6518**
1704-6610 Provincial Auditor Saskatchewan. Report of the Provincial Auditor to the Legislative Assembly of Saskatchewan **1940**
1704-667X *see* 1493-0447 **1669**
1704-6696 Fashion *changed to* 1714-9835 **2254**
1704-6718 Manitoba. Fishing & Hunting Adventures **8732**
1704-6866 *see* 1910-8443 **8031**
1704-6939 Canada. Statistics Canada. Help-Wanted Index **1217**
1704-698X Code Criminel Annote (Year) **4886**
1704-7234 Vault Magazine (Canadian Edition) *changed to* 1707-2832
1704-7242 Vault Magazine (American Edition) *changed to* 1707-2859
1704-7315 *see* 1704-4286 **8046**
1704-7900 The Ansul **2272**
1704-8060 Alberta South Vacation Guide *changed to* 1910-0043 **8698**
1704-8079 Official Alberta South Vacation Guide *changed to* 1910-0043 **8698**
1704-8125 Guide to Canadian Heritage Financial Support Programs **8043**
1704-8176 Financial Consumer Agency of Canada. Annual Report **7437**
1704-8249 Canada. Statistics Canada. International Travel **8778**
1704-8389 Elections Manitoba. Annual Report **7132**
1704-8478 Science Council of British Columbia. Annual Report *changed to* 1911-0553 **8416**
1704-8532 The Electronic Journal of Academic and Special Librarianship **5008**
1704-927X Canada. Parliament. House of Commons. Standing Committee on Aboriginal Affairs, Northern Development and Natural Resources. Minutes of Proceedings **6634**
1704-9377 Law Matters **4715**
1704-9962 TSX Venture Exchange. Review **1656**
1705-0022 Patient Management Problems in Trauma and Critical Care **6070**
1705-0154 *see* 0705-3436 **4980**
1705-0189 *see* 0835-9148 **1220**
1705-0316 Quebec Province. Securite du Revenu. Rapport Annuel de Gestion *changed to* 1912-0931 **6703**
1705-0456 Perfect Match Mariage **8880**
1705-0650 Quebec (Province). Ministere des Affaires Municipales et de la Metropole. Rapport Annuel de Gestion *changed to* 1719-8631 **7464**
1705-0715 Open Spaces Series **5346**
1705-0804 Edifice Magazine *changed to* 1914-119X **4539**
1705-0839 The Corner Stone **438**
1705-1290 Financial System Review **1345**
1705-1436 Just Labour **7981**
1705-1452 Institute for Canadian Music. Newsletter **6575**
1705-1460 *see* 1705-1452 **6575**
1705-1584 M D Canada†
1705-2017 Quebec. Curateur Public. Rapport Annuel de Gestion
1705-2165 Revue UniRcoop **7998**
1705-2211 Jour - Arts **5314**
1705-222X *see* 1705-2211 **5314**
1705-2327 Topics in European Studies **1584**
1705-2394 Oncology Exchange **6030**
1705-2548 Traveller Accommodation Survey, a Report **8768**
1705-2556 *see* 1716-9070 **4410**
1705-2688 Active Woman Canada† **8928**
1705-2807 Orchestras Canada. Membership Directory **6602**
1705-3498 Canadian Journal of Quantuum Economics **7952**
1705-3668 *see* 1203-4606 **1924**
1705-3773 The Renewal Times **6647**
1705-4192 Voices across Boundaries **7743**
1705-4842 Clinical & Surgical Ophthalmology **6040**
1705-4850 Clinical & Refractive Optometry **6040**
1705-4966 *see* 1705-4974 **82**
1705-4974 Agri-Info **82**
1705-4990 *see* 1705-4974 **82**
1705-5040 Maclean's Guide to Canadian Universities **2960**
1705-5105 International Journal of Numerical Analysis and Modeling **5497**
1705-5423 Post - Scriptum.org **5353**
1705-5989 Streamline **3468**
1705-5997 *see* 1705-5989 **3468**
1705-6063 British Columbia. Ministry of Finance. Budget Speech **7424**
1705-6071 British Columbia. Ministry of Finance. Budget and Fiscal Plan **7424**
1705-625X Relational Child & Youth Care Practice **2166**
1705-6322 Annales de Biologie Clinique du Quebec **5902**
1705-6411 International Journal of Baudrillard Studies **5310**
1705-7043 Production Canadienne de Pommes de Terre *see* 0835-3255 **224**
1705-7051 *see* 0844-5621 **5954**
1705-7299 Assurances et Gestion des Risques **4493**
1705-7329 Alpha-Lien **2938**
1705-7337 *see* 1705-7329 **2938**
1705-7345 C A S C O N Proceedings **2408**
1705-7574 Sustainable Forest Management Network. Research Program *changed to* 1718-0163 **3704**
1705-7809 Canadian Children's Book News **7557**
1705-7841 Primatisiwin **7536**
1705-8422 *see* 0713-8083 **4231**
1705-8546 Intermedialites **496**
1705-8619 Toronto Working Papers in Linguistics (Print) *changed to* 1718-3510 **5188**
1705-866X Ecole Polytechnique. Rapport Annuel **2979**
1705-8724 Canadian Commission for Unesco. Annual Report of the Secretary-General **4920**
1705-8848 Alzheimer Groupe Inc **8024**
1705-8929 British Columbia. Ministry of Transportation. Annual Service Plan **7424**
1705-9089 British Columbia. Ministry of Water, Land and Air Protection. Annual Service Plan Report **2604**
1705-9097 British Columbia. Ministry of Education. Annual Service Plan Report **3018**
1705-9100 Postcolonial Text **5162**
1705-9232 Journal of Knowledge Management Practice **6928**
1705-9275 British Columbia. Ministry of Energy and Mines. Annual Service Plan Report **7424**
1705-933X *see* 0318-9201 **5395**
1705-9348 British Columbia. Agricultural Land Commission. Annual Service Plan Report **7423**
1705-9658 Latest Developments in the Canadian Economic Accounts **1248**
1705-9666 Les Nouveautes en Matiere de Comptes Economiques Canadiens **1155**
1705-9844 Comatose Rose Magazine **5441**
1705-9992 Alpha Link **2938**
1706-0346 Ontario Securities Commission. Annual Report **4753**
1706-0362 *see* 1719-9034 **4650**
1706-046X Canadian Home & Country **4534**
1706-0532 *see* 1704-8176 **7437**
1706-0745 Faze Magazine **2188**
1706-0982 Business in Calgary and Calgary Commerce Magazine *changed to* 1707-2247 **1072**
1706-1105 Wild Oats Grain Market Advisory (Alberta Edition) *see* 1185-2194 **276**
1706-1121 Canadian Retail Hardware Association. Communicator†
1706-1571 Les Tarifs d'Honoraires des Medecins. Canada. Rapport **1710**
1706-161X Report. United Western Communications *changed to* 1707-0090 **3807**
1706-1806 Report of the Ethics Counsellor on the Activities of the Office of the Ethics Counsellor **7465**
1706-2675 Manitoba. Office of the Auditor General. Operations of the Office **7452**
1706-3035 Canada. Department of Finance. Economic and Fiscal Update **1914**
1706-3043 Canada. Ministere des Finances. Mise a Jour Economique et Financiere **1915**
1706-3078 Quarterly Presentation of Financial Transactions *changed to* 1718-8369 **1935**
1706-3086 Canadian Institutes of Health Research. Institute of Aging. Annual Report of Activities **8092**
1706-3094 Canada's Poultry and Egg Industry **282**
1706-3108 Communication Canada. Performance Report **2315**
1706-3124 Canada. Indian and Northern Affairs Canada. Alberta Region Year in Review **7426**
1706-3183 Toronto Life. Kids and Parents Guide *changed to* 1912-2810 **2158**
1706-3302 Canada. Parliament. House of Commons. Standing Committee on Transport and Government Operations. Minutes of Proceedings *changed to* 1912-1342 **8492**
1706-3302 Canada. Parliament. House of Commons. Standing Committee on Transport and Government Operations. Minutes of Proceedings *changed to* 1707-8369 **7427**
1706-3353 Canada's Greenhouse Gas Inventory *changed to* 1910-7048 **3454**
1706-3361 Inventaire Canadien des Gaz a Effet de Serre *changed to* 1910-7056 **3462**
1706-3388 Building Aboriginal and Northern Economies **1069**
1706-340X Facts and Figures (Year), Statistical Overview of the Temporary Resident and Refugee Claimant Population **7283**
1706-3426 Indian Oil and Gas Canada. Annual Report (Print) **6773**
1706-3434 Petrole et Gaz des Indiens du Canada. Rapport Annuel *see* 1706-3426 **6773**
1706-3825 *see* 1912-1342 **8492**
1706-3922 Canada. Ship-Source Oil Pollution Fund. Administrator's Annual Report **3484**
1706-3930 *see* 1707-8369 **7427**
1706-4503 Revue de Psychoeducation **2907**
1706-5380 British Columbia Market Share of United States Imports *see* 1483-8095 **1228**
1706-581X The Aging Brain **6120**
1706-6131 Treasury Board. Estimates. Part III, Report on Plans and Priorities **1952**
1706-6166 Canada. Treasury Board Secretariat. Estimates. Part III: Report on Plans and Priorities **7428**
1706-6204 New Brunswick Telegraph Journal *changed to* 1910-8001 **3818**
1706-7022 Guide Aubrey des Meilleurs Vins et Spiritueux *changed to* 1912-7650 **614**
1706-8037 C N S C Staff Annual Report for (Year) on the Canadian Nuclear Power Industry *changed to* 1912-6840 **3173**
1706-8045 Personnel de la C C S N sur les Centrales Nucleaires au Canada. Rapport Annuel†
1706-8053 P R H A Community Links **8061**
1706-8142 Crux Mathematicorum with Mathematical Mayhem **5481**
1706-8177 Canada. Statistics Canada. Criminal Prosecutions: Personnel and Expenditures (Print Edition)†
1706-8266 Statistics Canada. Health Statistics Division. Births *changed to* 1710-5285 **8358**
1706-8452 Radiodiffusion et Telecommunications **2348**
1706-8568 Automotive Trade **1211**
1706-8827 Quebec Province. Ministere de la Famille et de l'Enfance. Rapport Annuel de Gestion *changed to* 1912-0931 **6703**
1706-8827 Quebec Province. Ministere de la Famille et de l'Enfance. Rapport Annuel de Gestion *changed to* 1718-0392 **8064**
1706-8932 Quebec. Inspecteur General des Institutions Financieres. Rapport Annuel de Gestion *changed to* 1710-7725 **1646**
1706-9297 Commission des Droits de la Personne et des Droits de la Jeunesse. Rapport d'Activites et de Gestion, Quebec **7204**
1706-936X Geological Association of Canada. Miscellaneous Publication **2708**
1706-9440 Dalhousie University. School of Library and Information Studies. Inform *changed to* 1912-0079 **5005**
1706-9548 CrossCurrents (Toronto) **2692**
1706-9580 Quebec Province. Ministere de l'Emploi et de la Solidarite Sociale. Rapport Annuel de Gestion *changed to* 1718-0392 **8064**
1706-9637 Scott's Canadian Pharmacists Directory **2027**
1706-9750 Conseil du Statut de la Femme. Rapport Annuel de Gestion Quebec **7204**
1706-9904 Global Economic Justice Report *changed to* 1910-4332 **7238**
1707-0090 Citizens Centre Report **3807**
1707-0104 Vie et Vieillissement **4057**
1707-0198 Quebec. Centre de Recouvrement. Rapport de Gestion *changed to* 1912-0931 **6703**
1707-0732 U S Equity Sector Strategy. Weekly Bulletin *changed to* 1912-4295 **1657**
1707-0740 Code Criminel et Lois Connexes Annotes **4886**
1707-0813 *see* 1912-6263 **7611**
1707-0848 Understanding Financial Information *changed to* 1719-8275 **4910**
1707-0945 *see* 1912-3477 **7607**
1707-097X College of Medical Radiation Technologists and Therapists of Alberta. Journal *changed to* 1711-1439 **6210**
1707-1151 Emploi - Quebec. C A M O - P I. Rapport Annuel *changed to* 1910-6866 **6696**
1707-1283 Water Professional **8838**
1707-1364 Dundas Star News **3809**
1707-1445 Repertoire Industriel du Quebec *changed to* 1714-6607 **2027**
1707-1895 Empire Club Addresses *see* 0316-0548 **4138**
1707-2034 C O P A Flight **50**
1707-2247 Business in Calgary **1072**
1707-2271 Quebec. Ministere de l'Education. Rapport Annuel de Gestion *changed to* 1715-8818 **2902**
1707-2298 *see* 1484-3773 **1079**
1707-2476 *see* 1912-3701 **2681**
1707-2689 Wild Oats Grain Market Advisory (Winnipeg Edition) *see* 1185-2194 **276**
1707-2832 Offshore Finance Canada†
1707-2859 Offshore Finance U.S.A.†
1707-3022 Natural Sciences and Engineering Research Council of Canada. Program Guide for Students and Fellows **2995**
1707-3049 S A Y Magazine **3562**
1707-3960 Canadian Council of Teachers of English Language Arts. News Update **3053**
1707-3987 Weddingbells (Regional Ontario Edition) **5562**
1707-4533 Export Development Canada. Annual Report (Print Edition) **1564**
1707-5025 Northwest Territories (Year) by the Numbers **8391**
1707-5270 Les Logements Locatifs. Edmonton. Rapport *see* 1912-5208 **7607**
1707-5386 Edinfo **2940**
1707-5491 NightViews *changed to* Ryerson Free Press **2299**
1707-553X Stoney Creek News (Stoney Creek, 1948) *changed to* 0834-7433 **3818**
1707-5548 News Serving Stoney Creek and Saltfleet *changed to* 0834-7433 **3818**
1707-5599 Canadian Hydrographic Service. Annual Report
1707-6374 Canadian Association of Chiefs of Police. Membership Directory **2646**
1707-6633 Province of Ontario Annual Report and Financial Statements **7461**
1707-7168 Canadian International Development Agency. Mass Media Initiative. Development Information Program. Guidelines for Submitting Proposals **1592**
1707-7702 Solicitor General on the Administration of the Firearms Act. Registrar's Report **2668**

ISSN

ISSN

1719-4318	College of Nurses of Ontario. Membership Statistics Report **5955**
1719-4326	M C D A Magazine **3451**
1719-4334	A Message from the Middle **2886**
1719-4393	British Columbia Family Practice Manual **4907**
1719-4407	Women in Canada (Online) **8890**
1719-4415	*see* 1495-5962 **8863**
1719-4423	Housing Information Monthly **4413**
1719-4466	Toronto Life Learning Guide *see* 0049-4194 **3818**
1719-4474	Halton-Peel KINnections **3769**
1719-4482	Magazine du Nouvel Arrivant au Canada **8054**
1719-4490	Centre de Sante et de Services Sociaux de la Pointe-de-l'Isle. Rapport Annuel d'Activites *changed to* 1912-4066 **7512**
1719-4504	Association des Archivistes du Quebec. Rapport Annuel **4992**
1719-4512	Middlesex, We're on the Way! **8736**
1719-4520	Research Matters (Burnaby) **3000**
1719-4539	Canadian Hearing Report. Corporate Profiles *changed to* 1718-1860 **4072**
1719-4555	Home & Building Automation Quarterly *changed to* 1719-4563 **3318**
1719-4563	iHomes & Buildings **3318**
1719-4571	Housing Market Outlook. Charlottetown (Online) **7593**
1719-458X	Perspectives du Marche de l'Habitation. Charlottetown *changed to* 1719-8151 **4422**
1719-4644	Townies **5085**
1719-4652	Housing Market Outlook. Gatineau **7593**
1719-4660	Perspectives du Marche de l'Habitation. Gatineau **4422**
1719-4679	Housing Market Outlook. Hamilton **7593**
1719-4687	Perspectives du Marche de l'Habitation. Hamilton **4422**
1719-4695	Housing Market Outlook. Kelowna **7593**
1719-4709	Perspectives du Marche du Logement. Kelowna *changed to* 1719-4717 **4422**
1719-4717	Perspectives du Marche de l'Habitation. Kelowna **4422**
1719-4725	Housing Market Outlook. Kitchener C M A **7593**
1719-4733	Perspectives du Marche de l'Habitation. R M R de Kitchener **4422**
1719-4741	Housing Market Outlook. London **7593**
1719-475X	Perspectives du Marche de l'Habitation. London **4422**
1719-4768	*see* 1713-4129 **7593**
1719-4776	Perspectives du Marche du Logement. Agglomeration de Victoria *changed to* 1719-4784 **4422**
1719-4784	Perspectives du Marche de l'Habitation. Agglomeration de Victoria **4422**
1719-4792	Housing Market Outlook. Oshawa **7593**
1719-4806	Perspectives du Marche de l'Habitation. Oshawa **4422**
1719-4814	Housing Market Outlook. Quebec **7594**
1719-4822	Perspectives du Marche de l'Habitation. Quebec **4422**
1719-4830	Housing Market Outlook. Regina **7594**
1719-4849	Perspectives du Marche de l'Habitation. Regina **4422**
1719-4857	Housing Market Outlook. Saguenay **7594**
1719-4865	Perspectives du Marche de l'Habitation. Saguenay **4422**
1719-4873	Housing Market Outlook. Saskatoon **7594**
1719-4881	Perspectives du Marche de l'Habitation. Saskatoon **4422**
1719-489X	Civil Rules **4829**
1719-4903	Canadian Patient Safety Institute. Annual Report **7511**
1719-4911	Housing Market Outlook. Sherbrooke **7594**
1719-492X	Perspectives du Marche de l'Habitation. Sherbrooke **4422**
1719-4938	Housing Market Outlook. St. Catharines - Niagara C M A **7594**
1719-4946	Perspectives du Marche de l'Habitation. R M R de St. Catharines - Niagara **4422**
1719-4954	Guide du Locataire **4411**
1719-4962	Housing Market Outlook. St. John's (Online) **7594**
1719-4970	Perspectives du Marche de l'Habitation. St. John's *changed to* 1719-8259 **4422**
1719-4989	Housing Market Outlook. Trois-Rivieres (Online) **7594**
1719-4997	Perspectives du Marche de l'Habitation. Trois Rivieres **4422**
1719-5004	*see* 1713-4102 **7594**
1719-5012	Perspectives du Marche du Logement. Vancouver *changed to* 1719-5020 **4422**
1719-5020	Perspectives du Marche de l'Habitation. Vancouver **4422**
1719-5039	Housing Market Outlook. Windsor (Online) **7594**
1719-5047	Perspectives du Marche de l'Habitation. Windsor **4422**
1719-5055	Housing Market Outlook. Winnipeg **7594**
1719-5063	Perspectives du Marche de l'Habitation. Winnipeg **4422**
1719-5071	Peterborough Centennial Museum and Archives. Annual Report **6535**
1719-5101	*see* 1495-3129 **7594**
1719-511X	Actualites Habitation. London **4402**
1719-5128	Housing Now. Northern Ontario **7594**
1719-5136	Actualites Habitation. Nord de l'Ontario **4402**
1719-5144	Housing Now. Windsor *see* 1495-3226 **7594**
1719-5152	Actualites Habitation. Windsor **4402**
1719-5179	State of Safety Report **7542**
1719-5187	Government On-Line **7440**
1719-5195	*see* 1719-5187 **7440**
1719-5209	Collection Langue Francaise en Amerique du Nord **5002**
1719-525X	Collection Amaryllis **5598**
1719-5268	Commission Speciale sur la Loi Electorale. Journal des Debats **7430**
1719-5276	Residential Assessment Manual **4425**
1719-5284	Quebec. Services Documentation Multimedia. Choix Jeunesse. Livres de Langue Francaise **634**
1719-5314	Canadian Council on Social Development. Board of Governors and Executive Committee *changed to* 1719-5330 **8030**
1719-5322	The World of Lubavitch **3573**
1719-5330	Canadian Council on Social Development. Board of Governors **8030**
1719-5349	Adorable au Summum **6285**
1719-5365	Ontario Sheep Marketing Agency. Annual Report **295**
1719-5381	Housing Market Outlook. Calgary (Online) **7593**
1719-539X	Perspectives du Marche du Logement. Calgary **7603**
1719-5403	Housing Market Outlook. Edmonton **7593**
1719-5411	Perspectives du Marche du Logement. Edmonton **7603**
1719-542X	Housing Market Outlook. Montreal (Online) **7593**
1719-5438	Perspectives du Marche du Logement. Montreal *changed to* 1719-5446 **7603**
1719-5446	Perspectives du Marche de l'Habitation. Montreal **7603**
1719-5454	Housing Market Outlook. Ottawa **7593**
1719-5462	Perspectives du Marche du Logement. Ottawa *changed to* 1719-5470 **7603**
1719-5470	Perspectives du Marche de l'Habitation. Ottawa **7603**
1719-5489	Housing Market Outlook. Toronto **7594**
1719-5497	Perspectives du Marche du Logement. Toronto *changed to* 1719-5500 **7603**
1719-5500	Perspectives du Marche de l'Habitation. Toronto **7603**
1719-5519	Repertoire des Colleges Prives du Quebec **2904**
1719-5527	Adnews On-line Daily (Online) **19**
1719-5535	At a Glance **5580**
1719-5543	Tableau Synthese sur les Professions et Metiers en Demande **6704**
1719-5551	P M R A List of Formulants **3251**
1719-556X	*see* 1716-3129 **3250**
1719-5586	I N R S - E T E. Rapport Annuel **3438**
1719-5616	Bilan Annuel d'Emploi - Quebec en Monteregie **1667**
1719-5624	Le Partenaire **7535**
1719-5632	Panorama (Online) **2895**
1719-5659	Calgary Chapter Newsletter **5000**
1719-5667	List of Designations of National Historic Significance *changed to* Directory of Designations of National Historic Significance **4137**
1719-5675	Repertoire des Designations d'Importance Historique Nationale *see* Directory of Designations of National Historic Significance **4137**
1719-5683	Entreprises de Transformation du Bois de l'Abitibi - Temiscamingue, Repertoire **3687**
1719-5691	Ave. *see* 1497-9195 **5065**
1719-5705	L M A P D Report **4067**
1719-5713	Puppy & Dog Basics **6814**
1719-573X	W T - Blue Sky Region **5437**
1719-5748	Housing Market Outlook. Northern Ontario **7593**
1719-5756	Perspectives du Marche de l'Habitation. Nord de l'Ontario **7603**
1719-5764	Housing Market Outlook. Saint John, Moncton and Fredericton **7594**
1719-5772	Perspectives du Marche de l'Habitation. Saint John, Moncton et Fredericton *changed to* 1719-8240 **7604**
1719-5780	Centre de Sante et de Services Sociaux de la Petite Patrie et Villeray. Rapport Annuel d'Activites **7512**
1719-5802	Guide des Programmes Federaux d'Aide Financiere a l'Industrie du Film et de la Video **6502**
1719-5810	National Grouping System Categories Report, Canada **5683**
1719-5829	Les Categories du Systeme de Groupement National, Canada. Rapport *see* 1719-5810 **5683**
1719-5837	*see* 1489-8934 **4110**
1719-5845	*see* 1709-5298 **4110**
1719-5853	*see* 1180-3223 **6521**
1719-5861	I C C. Bulletin **4297**
1719-587X	Cloverdale Reporter Newsmagazine *changed to* 1719-5888 **3807**
1719-5888	Cloverdale Reporter News **3807**
1719-590X	Horticultural Forum **3737**
1719-5918	Motor Vehicle Collision Information **7532**
1719-5926	*see* 1487-9409 **8586**
1719-5942	Le Guide de Cotation des Artistes d'Art Zoom **492**
1719-5950	Quebec Province. Ministere des Finances. Budget in Brief *see* 1719-5969 **1941**
1719-5969	Quebec Province. Ministere des Finances. Budget en Bref **1941**
1719-5985	Fraternite **4594**
1719-5993	It's Here **497**
1719-6000	Nos Services Educatifs **2892**
1719-6027	An English Speaker's Guide to Life in the Eastern Townships **8100**
1719-6043	Colloque Regional sur la Production Laitiere **262**
1719-606X	Pour Mieux Comprendre le Mode de Tarification au Taux Personnalise **7536**
1719-6078	Ontario Association of Landscape Architects. Membership Resource Guide *changed to* 1912-0214 **452**
1719-6086	Le Saint-Jerome **3817**
1719-6094	Arts Ottawa East. Annual Report **475**
1719-6108	*see* 1714-1524 **5425**
1719-6116	Canadian HIV - AIDS Legal Network. Annual Report **4639**
1719-6132	Reseau Juridique Canadien VIH-Sida. Rapport Annuel **4769**
1719-6140	Index des Periodiques de Musique Canadiens **5058**
1719-6159	Droits de Scolarite Supplementaires des Etudiants Canadiens Non-residents et des Etudiants Etrangers **2843**
1719-6167	A V Preservation Trust of Canada. Annual Report **6488**
1719-6175	Trust pour la Preservation de l'A V.C.A. Rapport Annuel *see* 1719-6167 **6488**
1719-6183	Focus on Safety and Environment **3497**
1719-6191	*see* 1716-4230 **3436**
1719-6205	*see* 0846-7986 **7428**
1719-6213	Secretariat des Conferences Intergouvernementales Canadiennes. Rapport aux Gouvernements *see* 0846-7986 **7428**
1719-6221	Nos Racines **3777**
1719-6256	Auditor General. Report to the House of Assembly on the Operations of the Office of the Auditor General **7421**
1719-6264	Auditor General, Report to the House of Assembly. (Summary). **7421**
1719-6299	Semaine Quebecoise des Personnes Handicapees. Rapport d'Evaluation **4069**
1719-6302	C L T A Newsletter **4999**
1719-6310	C A C P Bulletin **2645**
1719-6329	What's New @ St. Catharines Public Library **5055**
1719-6337	Humanist Perspectives **6924**
1719-6353	Visions sur l'Art Quebec Inc. Rapport Annuel *see* 1719-6361 **4086**
1719-6361	Visions sur l'Art Quebec Inc. Annual Report **4086**
1719-6388	Horizons (Winnipeg) **288**
1719-640X	Parenthese **3557**
1719-6426	Centre de Sante et de Services Sociaux de l'Ouest-de-l'Ile. Rapport Annuel *see* 1719-6434 **7512**
1719-6434	Centre de Sante et de Services Sociaux de l'Ouest-de-l'Ile. Annual Report **7512**
1719-6442	Most Fuel-efficient Vehicles **8591**
1719-6450	Vehicules les Plus Econergetiques *see* 1719-6442 **8591**
1719-6469	Canada. Public Service Integrity Office. Annual Report to Parliament **7427**
1719-6477	Canada. Bureau de l'Integrite de la Fonction Publique. Rapport Annuel au Parlement *see* 1719-6469 **7427**
1719-6485	*see* 1484-5830 **7908**
1719-6493	Donnees en Sciences et Technologie *see* 1484-5830 **7908**
1719-6507	Bank of Canada. Annual Report (Online Edition) **1313**
1719-6515	*see* 1704-5630 **8691**
1719-6523	Commission Canadienne du Tourisme. Sommaire du Plan d'Entreprise *see* 1704-5630 **8691**
1719-6531	Ontario Professional Surveyor **3280**
1719-6558	Canadian National Institute for the Blind. Saskatchewan Division. Annual Report *changed to* 1719-6574 **8030**
1719-6566	Canadian National Institute for the Blind. Manitoba Division. Annual Report *changed to* 1719-6574 **8030**
1719-6574	Canadian National Institute for the Blind, Manitoba - Saskatchewan Division. Annual Review **8030**
1719-6582	British Columbia Real Estate Practice Manual **7584**
1719-6612	Recommandations et Guides de Pratique en Medecine Transfusionnelle **5941**
1719-6663	Winnipeg Men **6302**
1719-6671	Prince Albert Parkland Regional Health Authority. Annual Report **7536**
1719-668X	Defined Benefit Monitor *see* 1191-0763 **1856**
1719-6698	Defined Contribution Monitor *see* 1191-0763 **1856**
1719-6701	Clinical Bulletin of the Developmental Disabilities Division **4064**
1719-6752	NETendances (Version Abregee) *see* 1719-6760 **2564**
1719-6760	NETendances (Version Integrale) **2564**
1719-6892	Registered Nurses Association of Ontario. Annual Report (Online) **5979**
1719-6906	Solidarity Fund Q F L. Annual Report **4602**
1719-6949	Enquete sur les Terrains Residentiels Vacants en Milieu Urbain, Mise a Jour **4410**
1719-6973	Professional Association of Canadian Theatres. Annual Report **8476**
1719-699X	Multiple Sclerosis Society of Canada. Alberta Division. Consolidated Annual Report **6162**
1719-7015	*see* 1203-5564 **8645**
1719-7023	Forum des Administrations Portuaires **3595**
1719-7031	Housing Now. Charlottetown **4413**
1719-704X	Actualites Habitation. Charlottetown **4402**
1719-7058	Housing Now. Atlantic Canada **4413**
1719-7066	Actualites Habitation. Canada Atlantique **4402**
1719-7074	The Bridge **2969**
1719-7082	Le Bois et sa Sous - Traitance **3710**
1719-7104	Guide Complet des Prix, Automobiles Usagees **8583**
1719-7112	Guide Complet des Prix, Fourgonnettes, V U S et Camions Usages **8583**
1719-7139	Canadian Machine Tool Dealer *see* 0383-090X **6326**
1719-7147	Peace Brigades International *changed to* 1719-7155 **8063**
1719-7155	Presence (Toronto) **8063**
1719-7236	B C Hospitality Industry Membership Directory **4382**
1719-7260	*see* 1704-8125 **8043**
1719-7279	Guide des Programmes d'Appui Financier du Patrimoine Canadien (En Ligne) **8043**
1719-7287	Language Rights. Annual Report **4712**
1719-7295	Equality Rights. Annual Report **8100**
1719-7309	Droits a l'Egalite. Rapport Annuel *see* 1719-7295 **8100**
1719-7376	Profiles of Ethnic Communities in Canada **3559**
1719-7384	Profils de Communautes Ethniques au Canada *see* 1719-7376 **3559**
1719-7392	Office des Personnes Handicapees du Quebec. Plan Strategique **4068**
1719-7406	L'Office des Personnes Handicapees du Quebec. Plan d'Action **4068**
1719-7414	Housing Now. British Columbia **4413**
1719-7422	Actualites Habitation. Colombie-Britannique **4402**
1719-7449	Le Flash Herbe a Poux **7517**
1719-7457	Actualites Habitation. Kitchener **4402**
1719-7465	Housing Now. Saint John, Moncton and Fredericton **4413**
1719-7473	Actualites Habitation. Saint John, Moncton et Fredericton **4432**
1719-7481	Housing Now. St. John's **4413**
1719-749X	Actualites Habitation (St. John's) *see* 1719-8003 **4432**
1719-7511	Housing Now. Gatineau **4413**
1719-752X	Actualites Habitation. Gatineau **4402**
1719-7546	Actualites Habitation (Province de l'Ontario) *changed to* 1496-1121 **4402**
1719-7554	Housing Now. Ontario **4413**
1719-7562	Housing Now. Quebec **4413**
1719-7570	Actualites Habitation. Quebec **4432**
1719-7589	A Selective Listing of Learning Resources **2911**
1719-7597	Housing Now. Saguenay **4413**
1719-7600	Actualites Habitation. Saguenay **4432**
1719-7619	Prix Emile - Ollivier **5163**
1719-7627	Housing Now. Saskatoon **4413**
1719-7635	Conseil des Arts et des Lettes du Quebec. Plan Strategique **483**
1719-7643	Actualites Habitation. Saskatoon **4432**
1719-766X	Hepatitis C **7548**
1719-7678	*see* 1719-7694 **8639**
1719-7678	*see* 1714-0218 **8655**
1719-7686	Northwest Territories Human Rights Commission. Annual Report **4839**
1719-7694	Avis aux Navigateurs. Publication (Edition de l'Est) **8639**
1719-7708	*see* 1714-0196 **8655**
1719-7716	Avis aux Navigateurs (Edition de l'Est) *see* 1719-7694 **8639**

ISSN

1719-7732 Plan d'Action Favorisant l'Integration des Personnes Handicapees **4069**
1719-7740 Canada. Department of Finance. Budget (Online Edition) **1914**
1719-7759 Canada. Ministere des Finances. Le Budget *see* 1719-7740 **1914**
1719-7767 *see* 1719-9786 **1915**
1719-7775 *see* 1183-0840 **3771**
1719-7805 PreserVision *see* 1719-7813 **5040**
1719-7813 PreserVision **5040**
1719-7821 *see* 0827-1046 **3783**
1719-783X Saskatchewan. Vital Statistics. Annual Report **7541**
1719-7848 Transportation of Dangerous Goods Act. Annual Report **8516**
1719-7856 Camauto Plus (Edition Annuel) *see* 1912-3132 **8571**
1719-7864 Artists' Workshops and Performances **8465**
1719-7872 Spectacles et Ateliers d'Artistes *see* 1719-7864 **8465**
1719-7902 Canada-Manitoba Economic Partnership Agreement. Annual Progress Report **1426**
1719-7929 Calendar of Events **8467**
1719-7945 C C H Financial Planning **1322**
1719-797X Pacific Folkore Studies **3621**
1719-7996 Housing Now. Province of Quebec **4413**
1719-8003 Actualites Habitation. Province de Quebec **4432**
1719-8011 Housing Now. Regina **4413**
1719-802X Actualites Habitation. Regina **4432**
1719-8038 Housing Now. Sherbrooke **4413**
1719-8046 Actualites Habitation (Sherbrooke) *see* 1719-8003 **4432**
1719-8054 Housing Now. Trois-Rivieres **4413**
1719-8062 Actualites Habitation (Trois-Rivieres) *see* 1719-8003 **4432**
1719-8100 I M G Magazine **5307**
1719-8119 *see* 1484-8619 **8091**
1719-8127 A C T Newsletter **5807**
1719-8151 Perspectives du Marche du Logement. Charlottetown **4422**
1719-8186 U R B - Info **4429**
1719-8194 AIDS Committee of Toronto. Annual Report *changed to* 1719-8208 **8024**
1719-8208 AIDS Committee of Toronto Report to Donors **8024**
1719-8216 Arctic Future **2827**
1719-8224 A D R Forum **4607**
1719-8232 Centre Regional de Services aux Bibliotheques Publiques de l'Outaouais. Rapport Annuel **5001**
1719-8240 Perspectives du Marche du Logement. Saint John, Moncton et Fredericton **7604**
1719-8259 Perspectives du Marche du Logement. St. John's **4422**
1719-8275 Financial Issues in Family Law **4910**
1719-8283 Handling Provincial Offence Cases in Ontario (Year) **4684**
1719-8291 Eat Your Way to Health **6657**
1719-8313 Labour Force Data, Historical, Revised Series **1694**
1719-8321 B C Crime Prevention Pages, Directory of Services **2644**
1719-833X Get Connected **8042**
1719-8348 L'Injecteur **2695**
1719-8356 Resultats de l'Enquete sur la Remuneration Globale au Quebec **1705**
1719-8364 *see* 1716-4990 **2314**
1719-8372 Realisations du C R T C *see* 1716-4990 **2314**
1719-8380 C R T C 3-year Work Plan (Online Edition) **2314**
1719-8399 C R T C Plan de Travail Triennal *see* 1719-8380 **2314**
1719-8402 *see* 1709-0709 **7511**
1719-8410 *see* 1709-0717 **7525**
1719-8429 Canadian Academy of Child and Adolescent Psychiatry. Journal **6129**
1719-8437 L'Echo de Saint-Francois de-la-Riviere-du-Sud **3809**
1719-850X Calendar of Public Activities at the Grande Bibliotheque *changed to* 1912-7987 **5000**
1719-8518 National Day of Healing and Reconciliation **7213**
1719-8526 Journee Nationale de la Guerison et de la Reconciliation *see* 1719-8518 **7213**
1719-8534 University of Manitoba Libraries. Annual Report **5053**
1719-8542 L'Inter-action **8047**
1719-8577 Agence de Developpement de Reseaux Locaux de Services de Sante et de Services Sociaux de la Cote-Nord. Rapport Annuel **7506**
1719-8585 Budgets de Grandes Cultures **195**
1719-8593 Agence de Developpement de Reseaux Locaux de Services de Sante et de Services Sociaux de la Capitale Nationale. Rapport Annuel de Gestion **8024**
1719-8607 Quebec. Ministere du Developpement Durable, Environnement et Parcs. Rapport Annuel de Gestion **7464**
1719-8631 Quebec (Province). Ministere des Affaires Municipales et des Regions. Rapport Annuel de Gestion **7464**
1719-864X La Revue **3816**
1719-8658 Eglise Catholique. Diocese de Gaspe. Annuaire **7796**
1719-8674 Shriners Year Book and Masonic Directory **2270**
1719-8690 Sanagan's Encyclopedia of Words and Phrases, Legal Maxims **4778**
1719-8712 Home Makeover **1011**
1719-8747 La Presse Quebecoise **4582**
1719-8755 The Annual Real Estate Law Summit **7582**
1719-8763 Y Y Z Lifestyle Magazine **5087**
1719-8771 Home and Garden *see* 0049-4194 **3818**
1719-8798 British Columbia Practice **4827**
1719-8828 La C S S Q Vous Informe **5811**
1719-8836 Canadian Labour Arbitration **4591**
1719-8844 Royal Canadian Military Institute. Members' News **6444**
1719-8879 Baie - James, Nord-du-Quebec *changed to* 1719-8895 **8685**
1719-8895 Baie - James **8685**
1719-8909 James Bay *see* 1719-8895 **8685**
1719-8917 St. John's Rehabilitation Hospital. Community Report **5717**
1719-8933 Standing Orders of the House of Commons Including the Conflict of Interest Code for Members **4852**
1719-8941 Conservation Report **2607**
1719-8968 *see* 1719-8941 **2607**
1719-8976 Bloc Quebecois **3806**
1719-8984 Communist Party of Canada **7117**
1719-9034 Convention Against Torture and Other Cruel, Inhuman or Degrading Treatment or Punishment. Report of Canada **4650**
1719-9042 Convention Contre la Torture et Autres Peines ou Traitements Cruels, Inhumains ou Degradants. Rapport du Canada *see* 1719-9034 **4650**
1719-9050 Quebec. Ministere du Developpement Economique, de l'Innovation et de l'Exportation. Rapport Annuel de Gestion **1513**
1719-9069 Le Marche du Travail et l'Emploi Sectoriel au Quebec **1696**
1719-9077 Activate Quarterly *changed to* 1719-9085 **24**
1719-9085 eCatalyst **24**
1719-9093 Institute for Research on Public Policy. Annual Report **7446**
1719-9107 New Books Service. New this Month **632**
1719-9115 Service des Nouveaux Livres. Nouveautes du Mois *see* 1719-9107 **632**
1719-9123 Housing Market Outlook. Canada **7593**
1719-9131 Perspectives du Marche de l'Habitation. Canada **7603**
1719-914X Passport Canada. Annual Report **7257**
1719-9158 Passeport Canada. Rapport Annuel *see* 1719-914X **7257**
1719-9166 Judgments of the Supreme Court of Canada **4850**
1719-9174 Jugements de la Cour Supreme du Canada *see* 1719-9166 **4850**
1719-9182 A L A R M Course Syllabus **5985**
1719-9190 Le Programme du Cours Gesta *see* 1719-9182 **5985**
1719-9204 Apna Roots **3519**
1719-9212 Canadian Council for Donation and Transplantation. Annual Report **5591**
1719-9220 Conseil Canadien pour le Don et la Transplantation. Rapport Annuel *see* 1719-9212 **5591**
1719-9239 Alberta College of Medical Diagnostic & Therapeutic Technologists. Annual Report **5570**
1719-9247 Le Journal Agricole **125**
1719-9255 Northern Experience Magazine **8742**
1719-9263 La Sante C'est Alimentaire **6669**
1719-928X The Wire Artist Jeweller†
1719-9298 Canada Labour Code **4860**
1719-9301 Debt Litigation **4655**
1719-931X Ontario Occupational Health & Safety Act **6684**
1719-9328 Centre of the City† **8940**
1719-9344 *see* 1490-8514 **7534**
1719-9352 Air Travel Complaints Report (Print) **8535**
1719-9379 Air Travel Complaints Report (Online) **8535**
1719-9387 Plaintes Relatives au Transport Aerien. Rapport *see* 1719-9379 **8535**
1719-9395 Administration of Income Tax **1909**
1719-9409 Contaminated Sites Division. Annual Report **3412**
1719-9417 Division des Lieux Contamines. Rapport Annuel *see* 1719-9409 **3412**
1719-9425 Activate (Print) *changed to* 1719-9085 **24**
1719-9433 Directory and Product Source Guide **3711**
1719-9484 Law of Real Property **4874**
1719-9506 Steel, Tubular Products and Steel Wire **1904**
1719-9514 Acier, Produits Tubulaires et Fil d'Acier **1878**
1719-9522 Occupational Health and Safety in Ontario Health Care **6683**
1719-9530 Ontario Safe Water Legislation & Commentary **3458**
1719-9549 Collection en Bref **5275**
1719-9565 A Survey of Creators **520**
1719-959X Y-go **7695**
1719-9603 The Global Educator **7238**
1719-9611 The Link **2992**
1719-962X Huronia Business Times **1489**
1719-9638 Canadian Diamonds **6459**
1719-9670 A Noter Annotez **2964**
1719-9689 Alberta and Territories Tax Reporter **1910**
1719-9697 Centre Points **5955**
1719-9700 Management's Discussion and Analysis **1296**
1719-9719 Institut Canadien des Comptables Agrees. Le Rapport de Gestion **1291**
1719-9727 Challenging Destiny **5440**
1719-9735 The Innisfil Enterprise **3811**
1719-9743 Solutions **1176**
1719-9751 *see* 1719-9743 **1176**
1719-976X Canadian Metalworking **5450**
1719-9778 Law of Publication Bans, Private Hearings and Sealing Orders **4715**
1719-9786 Canada. Ministere des Finances. Le Budget. Apercu **1915**
1719-9794 Vancouver Official Meeting Planner's Guide **6283**
1719-9808 Canada Music Fund. Annual Report **6553**
1719-9816 Fonds de la Musique du Canada. Rapport Annuel *see* 1719-9808 **6553**
1719-9824 Numbers and Issues **5037**
1719-9832 Periodiques en Revue **633**
1719-9867 C A B News **2314**
1719-9883 C F E Newsletter **6491**
1719-9891 C I F E J Info **6491**
1720-0024 Life
1720-0113 Rivista Storica del Sannio **4159**
1720-0121 T P M. Testing Psicometria Metodologia **1876**
1720-0180 Quaderni del '900 **5356**
1720-0296 A G U I News **5984**
1720-030X Prostata News **6273**
1720-0318 Psichiatria e Pratica Medica
1720-0342 D'A. D'Architettura **439**
1720-0350 Biotecnologie 2000 **761**
1720-0768 *see* 1120-6330 **5464**
1720-0776 *see* 1120-6349 **7831**
1720-0903 Musica Theorica. Spectrum
1720-0989 PlayStation 2 Magazine Ufficiale
1720-1004 Le Dimore Storiche **441**
1720-1608 La Rivista del Trekking **8752**
1720-1624 Gente Viaggi Collection **8713**
1720-1632 *see* 1722-8093 **7395**
1720-1691 Oikonomia **7990**
1720-1713 *see* 1720-0350 **761**
1720-1721 Istituto Universitario Orientale di Napoli. Annali **5131**
1720-1772 Speciale Molossi **6815**
1720-1845 Essere & Benessere† **8954**
1720-190X Storia e Furturo **4162**
1720-1969 Il Cane† **8939**
1720-2310 Working Papers in Linguistics **5196**
1720-2337 Parlamenti Regionali† **8980**
1720-2353 Studi Orientali e Linguistici **5179**
1720-2396 Ragion Pratica **6946**
1720-240X Previsioni Macroeconomiche e Tendenze dell'Industria **1512**
1720-2647 Universita degli Studi di Napoli "Federico II" Portici. Facolta di Agraria. Annali **165**
1720-2671 Diritto & Formazione†
1720-268X LEXfor **4723**
1720-2809 Piroga
1720-2892 Mezzocielo **7985**
1720-3503 Trattori **214**
1720-3635 *see* 1720-2809
1720-3694 Rivista di Diritto Romano **4841**
1720-3708 Mots Palabras Words **5153**
1720-3716 Leitmotiv **502**
1720-3929 Scienze Regionali **1549**
1720-3988 Pesci & Pesca Mare† **8980**
1720-4003 Pharmachem **6871**
1720-4011 NutraCos **3658**
1720-402X Quaderni Satyagraha **7261**
1720-4097 Parlamento†
1720-4135 Annali dell' Istruzione *changed to* 1971-5420 **3050**
1720-4240 1989. Rivista di Diritto Pubblico e Scienze Politiche† **9000**
1720-4291 Diritto e Pratica delle Societa **4866**
1720-4305 Diritto Privato
1720-4313 Diritto Pubblico Comparato ed Europeo **4866**
1720-4321 Giornale di Diritto del Lavoro e di Relazioni Industriali **1684**
1720-433X Diritto, Immigrazione e Cittadinanza **4659**
1720-4348 Il Giudice di Pace **4831**
1720-4356 Giurisprudenza Annotata di Diritto Industriale **4869**
1720-4380 Giurisprudenza Piemontese **4681**
1720-4445 Il Diritto dell'Agricoltura **105**
1720-4453 Il Diritto Industriale **4866**
1720-4518 Questione Giustizia **4764**
1720-4526 Diritto Amministrativo **4659**
1720-4542 Europa e Diritto Privato **4924**
1720-514X Cultura Tedesca **4448**
1720-5301 Login **2563**
1720-531X *see* 1720-5301 **2563**
1720-5395 L'Illuminista **4456**
1720-562X Rivista del Diritto della Sicurezza Sociale **4776**
1720-6553 The Plan **453**
1720-6561 Rivista Italiana di Ossigeno - Ozono Terapia *changed to* 1972-3539 **310**
1720-6588 *see* 1720-6952 **3673**
1720-6642 Progettare per la Sanita **1030**
1720-6952 Cioccolata & C. **3673**
1720-7088 Cucina No Problem **4355**
1720-7134 Ambiente (Milan) *changed to* 1826-7939 **3402**
1720-7495 Dimensione Lavoro† **8950**
1720-7525 PsychNology **7394**
1720-7649 P C Soluzioni† **8979**
1720-7665 Il Grande Cinema su D V D
1720-7681 Giornale Italiano di Psicologia dell'Orientamento **7358**
1720-7835 *see* 1124-6332 **5042**
1720-7959 Shopping Milano† **8988**
1720-7983 Casa D **4534**
1720-7991 Avantgarde Design Selection Koeln **4532**
1720-8017 Luce International† **8972**
1720-8025 Cucine International **4536**
1720-8041 Italian Design Selection Milano **4544**
1720-8084 La Sicilia **3898**
1720-8300 *see* 0392-3002 **5570**
1720-8319 *see* 1594-0667 **4039**
1720-8327 *see* 1592-842X **5779**
1720-8335 *see* 0394-901X **5886**
1720-8378 *see* 1122-8601 **5791**
1720-8386 *see* 0391-4097 **5896**
1720-8394 *see* 1127-4123
1720-8416 *see* 1120-5989
1720-8424 The Italian Journal of Pediatrics (Print)† **8967**
1720-8521 Cantus Planus
1720-8564 Rivista di Ippiatria e Ippologia† **8986**
1720-898X Mondo Digitale **2432**
1720-9196 Farevideo
1720-9331 Lingue e Linguaggio **5145**
1720-9439 Lazio Ieri, Oggi, Domani†
1720-9471 Famiglia Oggi **3897**
1720-951X Analisi Giuridica dell'Economia **1059**
1720-9676 Estetica U.K. **587**
1720-996X L'Integrazione Scolastica e Sociale **2867**
1720-9986 Scienza e Conoscenza **7913**
1721-0135 Psicoterapia Psicoanalitica **6175**
1721-0143 Interazioni **7363**
1721-0151 Ciclo Evolutivo e Disabilita **6131**
1721-0178 L'Arco di Giano†
1721-0208 Medici Oggi **5672**
1721-0321 Psicologia della Salute **7393**
1721-0380 Erasmo†
1721-081X Il Foro Toscano. Toscana Giurisprudenza **4677**
1721-1026 *see* 1972-8425 **1086**
1721-1301 *see* 1124-5468 **2506**
1721-1395 Steel Art **4348**
1721-1549 Atomo e Industria News
1721-1786 Ora Locale **5346**
1721-2154 Telecamere Digitali† **8992**
1721-2162 Video Digitale Facile **6980**
1721-2170 Peach Girl
1721-2189 PlayStation 2 Strategy Magazine Ufficiale
1721-2227 Art Kid's† **8931**
1721-2308 Viaggi Speciali *changed to* 1826-1000 **8997**
1721-2529 Implantologia **5847**
1721-2545 Fox Uomo **6291**
1721-2553 Subito Pronto in Cucina **4367**
1721-2588 Ortopedia e Traumatologia† **8979**

1721-2596 Acta Vulnologica **5919**
1721-2812 Fondazione Liberal† **8957**
1721-3134 Universita di Lecce. Dipartimento di Scienze Pedagogiche Psicologiche e Didattiche. Studi e Ricerche **7413**
1721-3363 Europe and the Balkans International Network **7233**
1721-3444 Speciale Gatto Magazine **6815**
1721-3673 Fictions **5296**
1721-369X Harmony Oasi Donna† **8961**
1721-3932 La Mia 4 x 4 **8590**
1721-4114 L'Eco del Chisone **3897**
1721-4149 Lavoro Sociale **8053**
1721-4157 Handicap Grave **4066**
1721-419X Tennis Oggi **8249**
1721-4890 *see* 0392-3789 **983**
1721-4971 La Romagna Agricola e Zootecnica
1721-5072 Meridiani Montagne **8321**
1721-5366 Igiene Alimenti. Disinfestazione & Igiene Ambientale **7524**
1721-5463 Il Giornale dell'Architettura **443**
1721-5471 The Suffering Child **6104**
1721-5579 Dolce Attesa† **8951**
1721-5641 Cooperative e Consorzi **1918**
1721-5676 Erboristeria Domani **6658**
1721-5714 I Romanzi Proibiti di Confessioni Donna† **8986**
1721-5757 Bibliografia Italiana di Storia della Scienza† **8936**
1721-5803 Museo di Storia Naturale di Livorno. Quaderni. Supplemento *see* 0393-3377 **7883**
1721-6281 Rassegna di Archeologia *changed to* 1721-6303 **413**
1721-629X Rassegna di Archeologia Preistorica e Protoistorica **413**
1721-6303 Rassegna di Archeologia Classica e Postclassica **413**
1721-6427 Urania Collezione **5448**
1721-6664 Rivista Italiana di Gruppoanalisi **7405**
1721-6672 Il Gazzettino della Pesca **3595**
1721-6702 Fardase. Casa Fai da Te **4438**
1721-6729 Fai da Te Facile **4438**
1721-6869 Casa Deco. Serie Oro† **8940**
1721-6885 *see* 1721-4114 **3897**
1721-6893 Digital Camera Magazine **6979**
1721-6990 Onco Gyn News
1721-7008 P O News Psicooncologia
1721-7016 S I G O Notizie **6004**
1721-7121 Battle Royale
1721-7180 Chi **3896**
1721-7199 DiPAV Quaderni **335**
1721-7202 Universita degli Studi di Verona. Istituto di Psicologia. Annali *changed to* 1721-7199 **335**
1721-758X Tecnologie e Trasporti Mare **8663**
1721-7598 *see* 1721-758X **8663**
1721-7679 Agricommercio e Garden Center **191**
1721-7709 *see* 1824-7121 **6925**
1721-7741 Livornocronaca il Vernacoliere **5225**
1721-8039 GeoActa **2707**
1721-8098 Teoria di Diritto e dello Stato **4794**
1721-8187 I Nostri Dolci† **8977**
1721-8322 I Capolavori **6637**
1721-8861 Bulletin of Insectology **841**
1721-8985 Diritto Pubblico **4659**
1721-9450 E M Linea Ecologica
1721-9612 Costruzioni Psicoanalitiche **6133**
1721-9655 Italy. Istituto Nazionale di Statistica. Statistiche delle Amministrazioni Pubbliche (Year) **7481**
1721-9736 *see* 1123-8534 **2510**
1721-9809 m@gm@ **7984**
1722-0025 Geologia Tecnica & Ambientale **2737**
1722-0262 Bollettino Linguistico Campano **5101**
1722-0270 Konsequenz **6583**
1722-0300 D V D Review Presenta **2401**
1722-0416 Salute e Benessere. Il Tuo Bambino† **8987**
1722-0637 AsteCasa **7583**
1722-0696 *see* 0066-4545 **8345**
1722-070X Harmony Intrigue† **8961**
1722-0734 Flair (Italian Edition) **5071**
1722-1137 Rivista Italiana di Politiche Pubbliche **7179**
1722-1862 P C Tutor
1722-2206 Medicina & Storia **5673**
1722-2222 Gentleman **6291**
1722-2397 Il Foro Amminstrativo T A R **4677**
1722-2400 Il Foro Amministrativo C d S **4677**
1722-2702 Marie Claire Maison **4546**
1722-2737 Amnesia Vivace **466**
1722-2958 G D C. Il Giornale dei Dottori Commercialisti
1722-3083 Motociclismo Fuoristrada **8262**
1722-3377 Donna e Societa
1722-3407 Treatment Guidelines (Italian Edition) **6883**
1722-344X Rivivere la Storia† **8986**
1722-3644 Costruire Impianti **1000**
1722-3741 *see* 0416-0371 **7130**
1722-3792 Disciplina del Commercio e dei Servizi **1427**
1722-3954 Ad Parnassum **6542**
1722-3962 Quaderni de gli Argonauti *see* 0391-7274 **6124**
1722-4020 Gazzetta d'Alba **3897**
1722-4071 Autismo e Disturbi dello Sviluppo **6125**
1722-408X Educazione Interculturale **3012**
1722-4322 BuonGusto Italiano† **8938**
1722-4365 Politica Agricola Internazionale **147**
1722-4705 *see* 0394-9397 **7675**
1722-4969 Bazmavep
1722-5183 Nuovo Bullettino Archeologico Sardo **409**
1722-5345 Piante di Casa† **8981**
1722-5523 Provincia Nuova **7461**
1722-5531 Letteratura & Societa **5321**
1722-5655 Diritto del Turismo **4923**
1722-5728 Il Commercio con l'Estero dei Prodotti Agroalimentari **196**
1722-5825 Sane e Belle† **8987**
1722-5884 Angelo di Fuoco† **8930**
1722-5906 Rivista Internazionale di Tecnica della Traduzione **5169**
1722-6104 For Men Magazine **6290**
1722-6139 Guida al Benessere (Year) *see* 1722-6147 **5084**
1722-6147 Suite Benessere **5084**
1722-6155 Ricerca di Senso **6183**
1722-6163 Linux Pro **2594**
1722-618X Universita degli Studi di Perugia. Dipartimento di Economia. Quaderni *changed to* 1825-0211 **1187**
1722-6546 Car Design **8572**
1722-6570 Nuove Tendenze della Psicologia *changed to* 1971-3711 **2900**
1722-6686 La Mia Videoteca
1722-6759 Dibattito **5957**
1722-6899 Journal of Applied Biomaterials and Biomechanics **766**
1722-6902 Alp Wall *changed to* 1972-683X **8302**
1722-6996 Agro Food Industry Hi-Tech **86**
1722-7097 Quaderni di Filologia Romanza **5164**
1722-7119 Rassegna di Diritto Pubblico Europeo **4765**
1722-7194 Sanita Pubblica e Privata **7541**
1722-7399 Energia&reti†
1722-7402 Luce e Design **3324**
1722-7666 Diritti Lavori Mercati **1675**
1722-7690 Effective Health Care (Italian Edition)† **8953**
1722-7828 Alp G M **8302**
1722-7860 *see* 1120-6020 **3896**
1722-7879 *see* 1120-6020 **3896**
1722-7895 Wound Care Times **5731**
1722-7917 L I L T **6026**
1722-7984 I Romanzi d'Amore di Confessioni Donna† **8986**
1722-8093 Psychofenia **7395**
1722-8107 Japan Car Magazine **8587**
1722-8115 *see* 1722-8107 **8587**
1722-8352 Ars Interpretandi **4621**
1722-8360 Diritto della Banca e del Mercato Finanziario **1336**
1722-8387 Studium Iuris **4791**
1722-8395 Studium Educationis **3033**
1722-8530 Giornale Italiano di Psicologia dello Sport **6229**
1722-8891 Portatile & Wireless† **8982**
1722-9383 Economy **1102**
1722-943X Etudes Arabes **7710**
1722-9480 Contributi alla Storia dell'Universita di Padova **2974**
1722-9995 Corriere dell'Allergia† **8944**
1723-0047 Il Nuovo Riformista **3898**
1723-0284 Agalma **6902**
1723-0330 Anestesia Pediatrica e Neonatale **5769**
1723-0667 Quaderni di Archeologia del Mantovano **412**
1723-0683 Il Mio Palmare **2572**
1723-1191 Photografare in Digitale **6980**
1723-1205 HotDog Magazine **6503**
1723-137X Mondo Lavoro **1698**
1723-1582 Jacques e i suoi Quaderni **5312**
1723-1604 Adrian **4564**
1723-168X Scuola Officina **8438**
1723-1906 Opere **452**
1723-2007 Blood Transfusion **5934**
1723-2155 Strade & Autostrade **3283**
1723-2163 *see* 1723-2155 **3283**
1723-2430 Rivista Italiana di Diritto Pubblico Comunitario. Quaderni **4776**
1723-2538 NEU **5971**
1723-2724 Natural Style **8877**
1723-3348 Videogiochi (Milan, 2003)† **8997**
1723-3437 Mediares **4731**
1723-3488 Horror Cult **2402**
1723-3585 Bibliographia Franciscana **7698**
1723-3658 La Mia Barca **8278**
1723-3674 Bey Blade
1723-3801 *see* 1594-6770 **1639**
1723-3844 Psicomotricita **7393**
1723-3933 H C - Home Cinema
1723-3941 I Filmissimi in D V D
1723-3976 *see* 1127-6339 **5707**
1723-4026 Cucina Popolare Italiana† **8947**
1723-4042 eSamizdat **5290**
1723-4107 Yachtsman **8286**
1723-4174 Convegni Incentive & Comunicazione **6279**
1723-4182 Turismo d'Affari **8769**
1723-4190 Incentivare **1866**
1723-4263 Fiscalita Internazionale **1925**
1723-4409 Biblioteca della Ricerca. Testi Stranieri **5262**
1723-4433 Biblioteca di Studi Antichi **2231**
1723-4549 Automobilismo d'Epoca **8564**
1723-4611 Frontiera d'Europa **4222**
1723-4670 Io Cucino **4361**
1723-5065 Sicurezza Digitale† **8988**
1723-5227 Bagno Design **4532**
1723-5804 Archaeologiae **375**
1723-5812 Top Guide **2482**
1723-6118 Il Fotografo Digitale Annual **6968**
1723-6568 Tecnica Sanitaria†
1723-6673 Vanity Fair **8887**
1723-6800 Annuario Orologi **4564**
1723-7041 Open Source† **8979**
1723-7092 Filiera Pesca e Acquacoltura **1885**
1723-7319 Prevenzione Respiratoria **6217**
1723-7432 T & T. Trasporti e Territorio
1723-7599 Il Risveglio **3898**
1723-7769 Quintessenza Odontotecnica **5862**
1723-7777 Ortodonzia **5860**
1723-7785 Progress in Orthodontics **5861**
1723-7793 Quintessenza Internazionale **5862**
1723-7807 Italian Journal of Public Health **7528**
1723-7815 *see* 1723-7807 **7528**
1723-803X DecArt **485**
1723-8080 *see* 1723-0047 **3898**
1723-8617 World Psychiatry **6190**
1723-9214 *see* 1827-2908 **4174**
1723-9400 Museo Stibbert Firenze **6530**
1723-9427 Salute e Societa **7181**
1723-9451 Musicalia (Rome) **6594**
1723-946X Art'e' *changed to* 1970-7789 **487**
1723-9524 Ad Quintum **371**
1723-9761 Bollettario **5265**
1723-9834 Idea Cucina **4361**
1723-9869 *see* 1723-9524 **371**
1723-9877 R U. Risorse Umane nella Pubblica Amministrazione **7501**
1724-0425 *see* 1121-9114 **2777**
1724-045X *see* 1721-3673 **5296**
1724-0476 *see* 1120-690X **8378**
1724-0492 *see* 1129-4981 **5321**
1724-0506 *see* 0024-1350 **5322**
1724-0514 *see* 1122-5521 **629**
1724-0522 *see* 0392-6915 **5146**
1724-0530 *see* 1128-6326 **5336**
1724-0565 Annali Benacensi **373**
1724-0573 *see* 0393-0149 **410**
1724-059X *see* 0394-4131 **6938**
1724-0603 *see* 1591-2795 **6175**
1724-062X *see* 0035-6085 **2240**
1724-0638 *see* 0392-825X **5363**
1724-0646 *see* 1592-1328 **5169**
1724-0727 Marie Claire 2 **2258**
1724-0751 Psichiatria di Comunita **7392**
1724-0794 Sud. Il Sole 24 Ore **3899**
1724-0824 Orobie **4468**
1724-0956 Humanistica (Rome) **4455**
1724-0972 Diritto Internazionale e Ordine Mondiale **4923**
1724-0980 Il Diritto Privato nella Giurisprudenza **4866**
1724-0999 Il Diritto Privato Oggi **4866**
1724-1006 I Dizionari dell'Arte **486**
1724-1014 Edizione Nazionale dei Testi Mediolatini **2233**
1724-1049 Trattato di Diritto Privato **4882**
1724-1073 Biblioteca di Testi e Studi **4445**
1724-1103 Storia e Diritto. Studi **4162**
1724-1111 Universita degli Studi di Verona. Facolta di Giurisprudenza. Pubblicazioni **4802**
1724-1138 Universita degli Studi di Trieste. Facolta di Scienze Politiche. Quaderni Giuridici **4802**
1724-1197 Cosa & Come. Leggi e Formulari **4651**
1724-1200 Cosa & Come. Diritto & Pratica Professionale **4651**
1724-1219 Confronta **4136**
1724-1278 Biblioteca di Medioevo Latino **4204**
1724-1294 Le Frontiere del Diritto **4678**
1724-1316 Istituzioni e Societa† **8967**
1724-1340 Laboratorio di Storia **4150**
1724-1359 Storia Universale dell'Arte **519**
1724-1367 Storia. Contributi **4162**
1724-1375 Societa Italiana di Medicina Generale **5716**
1724-1383 *see* 1724-1375 **5716**
1724-1391 Il Corriere Ortodontico **5839**
1724-1405 *see* 1724-1391 **5839**
1724-1499 Diritti Sociali dalla A alla Z **4659**
1724-1502 *see* 1594-1000 **5433**
1724-1510 *see* 1128-6377 **7998**
1724-1537 *see* 1128-6369 **5169**
1724-1545 I Quaderni di Confessione Donna. Il Punto Croce† **8983**
1724-1553 I Quaderni di Confessione Donna. La Maglia† **8983**
1724-1561 I Quaderni di Confessione Donna. Il Filet *changed to* 1826-1035 **8992**
1724-157X I Quaderni di Confessione Donna. I Lavori di Casa† **8983**
1724-1588 *see* 0585-492X **5378**
1724-1596 *see* 1121-0621 **5378**
1724-160X *see* 0394-3569 **5179**
1724-1650 *see* 0392-4432 **5476**
1724-1669 *see* 0390-2412 **5126**
1724-1677 *see* 0391-3368 **5311**
1724-1685 *see* 1594-5359 **5323**
1724-1693 *see* 0392-6338 **2237**
1724-1707 *see* 0390-0711 **5150**
1724-1758 Italiani nel Mondo **3897**
1724-1782 *see* 1123-4660 **4477**
1724-1790 *see* 0392-0437 **4268**
1724-1804 *see* 0303-4615 **5379**
1724-1812 *see* 1123-4938 **6953**
1724-1847 *see* 1121-9122 **7999**
1724-1855 *see* 0390-3877 **415**
1724-1863 *see* 0392-4866 **560**
1724-1871 *see* 0033-9571 **2903**
1724-1898 *see* 1720-0180 **5356**
1724-1901 *see* 0033-4987 **2239**
1724-191X *see* 1120-1797 **5695**
1724-1928 *see* 1128-6342 **4324**
1724-1936 *see* 1591-2787 **409**
1724-1944 *see* 1593-7577 **5157**
1724-1952 Best Travel *changed to* 1828-0811 **8684**
1724-2037 Valori **6959**
1724-2045 *see* 1724-2037 **6959**
1724-207X Comune di Sassuolo **7490**
1724-210X Terzo Settore **1182**
1724-2118 *see* 1592-6117 **191**
1724-2126 *see* 0391-2493 **5118**
1724-2150 *see* 1123-9883 **4244**
1724-2169 *see* 1122-8792 **1542**
1724-2185 *see* 0303-5247 **8499**
1724-2215 Colleziona i Grandi Capolavori in Miniatura **365**
1724-2274 *see* 1723-5804 **375**
1724-2347 Ateneo di Scienze, Lettere ed Arti di Bergamo. Atti **4443**
1724-2355 Fonti **7855**
1724-2363 Ateneo di Scienze, Lettere ed Arti di Bergamo. Quaderni **7837**
1724-2371 Ateneo di Scienze, Lettere ed Arti di Bergamo. Album **7837**
1724-2401 Studi Pucciniani **6620**
1724-2487 Fiati **6566**
1724-2533 Conservatorio di Musica Giuseppe Verdi di Milano. Annuario† **8943**
1724-2541 Kronos **500**
1724-2622 Dinosauri†
1724-2630 Tutto Treno Tema **4350**
1724-2649 Tutto Treno Modellismo **4350**
1724-2657 Tutto Treno & Storia **4350**
1724-2665 Tutto Aerei **4350**
1724-2789 Easy Tech **3094**
1724-2908 Giornale Italiano di Conservativa **5845**
1724-2959 I Nostri Amici Cavalli **8295**

ISSN

9778 1724-3114 ULRICH'S PERIODICALS

1724-3114 La Torre di Babele **5188**
1724-3653 Studi (e Testi) Italiani **4476**
1724-3971 T C News† **8992**
1724-3998 Punto Croce Facile e Veloce **6641**
1724-4021 Alberi e Territorio **3683**
1724-417X Quality in Anaesthesia
1724-4188 Cardiovascular Therapy and Prevention
1724-4560 Corpus Vasorum Antiquorum Italia. **388**
1724-4625 Polena **7166**
1724-4692 Web Designer Magazine **2568**
1724-4781 *see* 0391-9838 **2736**
1724-4838 Edizione Nazionale dei Testi Mediolatini. Serie I **2233**
1724-4900 La Rivista dei Maghi e delle Streghe† **8986**
1724-4919 Psichiatria e Psicoterapia (Rome) **6175**
1724-4927 Cognitivismo Clinico **6133**
1724-4935 Clinical Neuropsychiatry **6132**
1724-5230 Studi Lingustici e Filologici Online **5179**
1724-5311 Onlinegaming **2479**
1724-532X Guide Pocket **2477**
1724-5346 Harmony Premium **5410**
1724-5354 Harmony History Special **5410**
1724-5389 La Rivista delle Politiche Sociali **7998**
1724-5524 Concorsi **2839**
1724-5575 *see* 1126-3504 **810**
1724-5702 Focus Junior **2189**
1724-5761 Win Magazine Extra
1724-594X Tecnologia & Difesa **8443**
1724-5974 *see* 0394-9362 **6268**
1724-5982 *see* 1828-6232 **6667**
1724-6008 *see* 0393-6155 **678**
1724-6016 *see* 1120-6721 **6041**
1724-6024 *see* 1722-6899 **766**
1724-6032 *see* 1129-7298 **5794**
1724-6040 *see* 0391-3988 **5637**
1724-6059 *see* 1121-8428 **6270**
1724-6067 *see* 1120-7000 **5628**
1724-6075 *see* 0391-5603 **6275**
1724-6083 *see* 0393-974X
1724-6091 Archaeologia Maritima Mediterranea **375**
1724-6105 Contemporanea **5278**
1724-6113 Filologia Italiana **5118**
1724-6121 Historia Philosophica **6923**
1724-613X Letteratura & Arte **5321**
1724-6148 Sardinia, Corsica et Baleares Antiquae **415**
1724-6156 Studi di Egittologia e di Papirologia **4325**
1724-6164 Studi Rinascimentali **5379**
1724-6172 *see* 1128-7209 **2236**
1724-6385 Maecenas **2237**
1724-6768 Ri - Vista. Ricerche per la Progettazione del Paesaggio **456**
1724-6776 La Rivista Italiana di Ginecologia e Ostetricia **6003**
1724-6792 La Meta Rugby **8238**
1724-7292 *see* 0015-7856 **4677**
1724-7322 Rivista di Diritto dell'Economia, dei Trasporti e dell'Ambiente **4776**
1724-742X Export Magazine - Beauty Distributor **594**
1724-7446 *see* 1825-5132 **4268**
1724-7756 *see* 1971-3002 **438**
1724-7764 *see* 1971-3002 **438**
1724-8191 Il Crotonese **3896**
1724-8205 *see* 1724-8191 **3896**
1724-8213 Quaderni di Semitistica **5164**
1724-8221 *see* 1724-8213 **5164**
1724-8574 Ming Qing Yanjiu **4186**
1724-8698 Linguae & **5145**
1724-8884 *see* 1724-9007 **3897**
1724-8892 Rassegna Medica Felina† **8984**
1724-8914 Clinical Cases in Mineral and Bone Metabolism **5804**
1724-8922 Ricerche in Psichiatria **6183**
1724-8949 Statistica del Turismo†
1724-9007 Informa Sicilia **3897**
1724-904X Agri Centuriati **371**
1724-9058 Dante **5283**
1724-9074 La Lingua Italiana **5145**
1724-9090 Medioevo Letterario d'Italia **5332**
1724-9104 Musiva & Sectilia **450**
1724-9112 Sicilia Antiqua **416**
1724-9120 Workshop di Archeologia Classica **424**
1724-9155 Quaderni di Semitistica. Materiali *see* 1724-8213 **5164**
1724-9163 Kuma **8117**
1724-9171 Biblioteca Essenziale. Storia Contemporanea **4133**
1724-9244 Fantasia in Cucina† **8955**
1724-9279 Fiori e Piante Special† **8956**
1724-9317 Medioevalia **4243**
1724-9392 100 Anni di Italia in Automobile **8614**
1724-9449 Targets in Heterocyclic Systems. Chemistry and Properties **2131**
1724-9473 Collana Storica della Liguria Orientale **4211**
1724-9562 Home Entertainment
1724-9570 Win Magazine Giochi
1724-9597 Total Computer **2440**
1724-966X Campi Immaginabili **4446**
1724-9686 Restauro Archeologico **413**
1724-9767 Dislessia **4081**
1724-9821 Acta Photographica **6963**
1724-9953 I Classici del Fantasy **5441**
1725-0056 EUROSTAT. Methods and Nomenclatures **1227**
1725-0099 Methodology of Short-Term Business Statistics **1498**
1725-0463 International Journal of Spatial Data Infrastructures Research **2426**
1725-1370 Asia Urbs Magazine **1591**
1725-1621 Key Data on Education in Europe **2934**
1725-2423 Official Journal of the European Union **7256**
1725-275X Panorama of Transport **8528**
1725-2806 European Central Bank. Working Papers (Online) **1339**
1725-2822 *see* 1561-0136 **1339**
1725-2865 *see* 1561-4573 **1339**
1725-2970 *see* 1561-0268 **1311**
1725-4159 Diario Oficial de la Union Europea **4923**
1725-485X Quarterly Panorama of European Business Statistics **1259**
1725-6534 *see* 1607-1484 **1339**
1725-8111 Eurostatistics. Data for Short Term Economic Analysis **1228**
1725-9312 European Central Bank. Convergence Report **1339**
1725-9525 *see* 1725-9312 **1339**
1726-0000 Nikkei Electronics China *changed to* Electronic Design & Application World - Nikkei Electronics **3095**
1726-0280 South African Food Review **3664**
1726-037X Journal of Dynamical Systems and Geometric Theories **5503**
1726-0396 Grassroots **4182**
1726-040X Cine and Media *changed to* 1726-0426 **6513**
1726-0418 Cine y Medios *changed to* 1726-0426 **6513**
1726-0426 Signis Media **6513**
1726-0531 Journal of Engineering, Design and Technology **3205**
1726-0604 *see* 0007-8506 **3375**
1726-0620 E P D A Focus† **8952**
1726-0698 Vrouekeur **3950**
1726-0787 South Pacific Journal of Natural Science (Online) **7919**
1726-0841 Guia Maritima **8645**
1726-085X *see* 1726-0841 **8645**
1726-0868 Liza. Moi Liubimye Zhivotnye **6811**
1726-0876 T V 7 **2391**
1726-0892 Dom v Sadu **3728**
1726-1368 *see* 0258-7696 **8010**
1726-1406 Tuin Paleis **4368**
1726-152X *see* 1682-6744 **1584**
1726-2038 Collection and Research **6522**
1726-2135 Journal of Environmental Informatics **3482**
1726-2208 Revista Peruana de Quimica e Ingenieria Quimica **2079**
1726-2216 Ecologia Aplicada **3416**
1726-2224 International Dialogue on Migration **7285**
1726-2240 Dilmun **390**
1726-2364 Dianzi Shangwu Yanjiu **1092**
1726-247X International Commission for the Conservation of Atlantic Tunas. Statistical Bulletin **3613**
1726-3182 Winay Yachay **7929**
1726-3247 Ekonomicheskaya Sotsiologiya **1102**
1726-3255 Algebra and Discrete Mathematics **5467**
1726-3328 Journal of Probability and Statistical Science **8383**
1726-3522 *see* 0507-5386 **2510**
1726-3700 *see* 1012-1080 **8051**
1726-4170 Biogeosciences **657**
1726-4189 *see* 1726-4170 **657**
1726-426X *see* South African Family Practice **5716**
1726-4529 International Journal of Simulation Modelling **2472**
1726-4634 Revista Peruana de Medicina Experimental y Salud Publica **5910**
1726-4642 *see* 1726-4634 **5910**
1726-4677 Universitas **3007**
1726-4901 Chinese Medical Association. Journal **5594**
1726-507X Surveys, Analysis, Modelling and Mapping Research Programme. Occasional Paper **4030**
1726-5282 Sreda **2339**
1726-5479 Sensors & Transducers **3357**
1726-569X *see* 0717-5906 **5565**
1726-5878 World Bank Working Paper **1608**
1726-5886 C I E S M Workshop Monographs **2801**
1726-5894 Foret Mediterraneenne. Hors - Serie *see* 0245-484X **3691**
1726-5991 Sawubona **8785**
1726-6009 The Journal of Engineering Research **3322**
1726-6092 Zeitzoo **5404**
1726-6122 Rossiiskii Vestnik Akushera-Ginekologa **6003**
1726-6173 Aviapanorama **48**
1726-6580 *see* 1816-0247 **3462**
1726-670X tripleC **2551**
1726-6742 *see* 1726-6009 **3322**
1726-6777 *see* 0203-4646 **2803**
1726-6882 *see* 1735-0328 **6851**
1726-6890 *see* 1735-0328 **6851**
1726-7277 Al-Majdal **7212**
1726-7498 *see* 0367-3294 **7013**
1726-7544 Iranian Journal of Diabetes & Lipid Disorders **5895**
1726-7552 *see* 1726-7544 **5895**
1726-7587 Zhonghua Xiandai Linchuang Yixue Zazhi **5738**
1726-7692 Termoelektrichestvo *see* 1607-8829 **3159**
1726-7692 Termoelektrichestvo *see* 1726-7714 **3161**
1726-7714 Termoelektryka **3161**
1726-7757 *see* 1726-7277 **7212**
1726-801X *see* 1011-3924 **2055**
1726-8494 Critical Dialogue **7127**
1726-8710 Pakistan Psychiatric Society. Journal **6173**
1726-9032 Liste d'Abreviations de Mots de Titres. Titres de Publications en Serie et Autres Ressources en Continu **630**
1726-9091 *see* 0379-0622 **8018**
1726-913X International Journal of Endocrinology and Metabolism **5895**
1726-9148 *see* 1726-913X **5895**
1726-9164 Africa Wild **8681**
1726-930X *see* 0474-5523 **1504**
1726-9326 *see* 0257-7801 **1941**
1726-9415 Revista Peruana de Psicologia **7405**
1726-9679 Annals of D A A A M & Proceedings **3365**
1726-9687 D A A A M International Scientific Book **3366**
1726-9709 Human Sciences Research Council Review **8106**
1726-9725 Journal of Maltese Education Research **2877**
1726-9865 Rossiiskaya Akademiya Meditsinskikh Nauk. Rossiiskii Onkologicheskii Nauchnyi Tsentr imeni N. N. Blokhina. Vestnik **6034**
1727-0286 I C I D C A. Sobre los Derivados de la Cana de Azucar **235**
1727-0456 Rechts- und Finanzierungspraxis der Gemeinden *changed to* 1993-8098 **7501**
1727-0561 Wagnis **7576**
1727-057X Migralex **4734**
1727-0618 Lebanon Opportunities **1144**
1727-0626 *see* 1727-0618 **1144**
1727-0634 Zhurnal Issledovanii Sotsial'noi Politiki **8019**
1727-0669 Blickpunkt der Mann **6284**
1727-0707 Current European Issues **7432**
1727-0847 Klinichna Anatomiya ta Operatyvna Hhirurhiya **6251**
1727-155X I H D P Update **7971**
1727-1878 Taiwan Journal of Anthropology **3567**
1727-2076 A i F. Tvoi Kurs **2175**
1727-2084 A i F. Superzvezdy **3934**
1727-2114 Majallat Jami'at an-Nagah al-Abhath. A, Al-'ulum al-Tabi'iyyat **7881**
1727-2130 Elle Girl **2187**
1727-2327 Structural Statistics for Industry and Services *changed to* 1996-2517 **1268**
1727-2483 Naturwissenschaftlich - Medizinischen Vereins in Innsbruck. Berichte. Supplementum *see* 0379-1416 **693**
1727-2548 Iliria **397**
1727-2769 Akademiya Nauk Vysshei Shkoly Rossii. Doklady **7834**
1727-2874 Hong Kong Pharmaceutical Journal **6846**
1727-3048 Journal of Biological Sciences **681**
1727-3080 Ganzao Jishu yu Shebei **2135**
1727-3307 Who's Who (Year) **6628**
1727-3358 TechSmart **2439**
1727-3366 Competition Law Reports **4862**
1727-3382 Inwater **8319**
1727-3781 Potchefstroom Electronic Law Journal **4759**
1727-4613 *see* 1727-0669 **6284**
1727-4761 International Textile Manufacturers Federation. Annual Conference Report (Year) **8453**
1727-480X Architektur & Bau News **431**
1727-4907 Problemy Programmirovaniya **2509**
1727-5148 Taiwan Review **3960**
1727-5199 *see* 1727-5148 **3960**
1727-5431 Ahlan! **3966**
1727-5539 Okhota i Rybalka XXI Vek **8326**
1727-558X Horizonte Medico **5629**
1727-5644 *see* 0260-3055 **2724**
1727-5652 *see* 0022-1430 **2750**
1727-5792 Harmonikales Denken **6572**
1727-6349 Finans. **1346**
1727-6454 *see* 1816-9031 **1256**
1727-6519 *see* 1727-155X **7971**
1727-6853 Aktual'nye Problemy Aviatsionnykh i Aerokosmicheskikh Sistem: Protsessy, Modeli, Eksperiment **46**
1727-687X Problemy Nelineinogo Analiza v Inzhenernykh Sistemakh **7900**
1727-6993 *see* 0038-8483 **5377**
1727-7051 Problems & Perspectives in Management **1786**
1727-7140 Commonwealth Youth and Development **2149**
1727-7191 Journal of Mechanics **3350**
1727-7345 *see* 1814-3881 **1191**
1727-7434 Chelyabinskii Nauchnyi Tsentr. Izvestiya **7845**
1727-7574 *see* 1727-6349 **1346**
1727-7914 Union Newsletter (English Edition) **6220**
1727-7922 Union Newsletter (French Edition) **6220**
1727-7930 Union Newsletter (Spanish Edition) **6221**
1727-7981 Finansovaya Gazeta **1347**
1727-8015 Finansovaya Gazeta. Regional'nyi Vypusk **1347**
1727-8023 Finansovaya Gazeta. Ekspo **1924**
1727-8058 Auditorskie Vedomosti **1281**
1727-8082 *see* 1727-7981 **1347**
1727-8147 Hong Kong Journal of Modern Chinese History **4183**
1727-8309 Journal of Independent Studies and Research *changed to* 1998-4162 **1762**
1727-835X Heoloh Ukrainy **2746**
1727-8376 I E E E - A C M - S I G G R A P H Symposium on Volume Visualization and Graphics. Proceedings **2486**
1727-8449 Majallat Jami'at an-Nagah al-Abhath. B, al-'ulum al-Inssaniyyat **4464**
1727-8457 Avis d'Invasion *see* 1727-8473 **246**
1727-8473 Pest Alert **246**
1727-8589 Mina **8875**
1727-8627 Taiwan Jingji Lunheng **1181**
1727-897X Medisur **5676**
1727-9232 Corporate Ownership & Control **4864**
1727-9321 *see* 0254-6299 **818**
1727-933X *see* 1607-3606 **5527**
1727-9364 *see* 1608-5914 **651**
1727-9380 *see* 1022-0119 **216**
1727-9445 *see* 1608-5906 **5808**
1727-9461 *see* 1607-3614 **5176**
1727-947X *see* 0030-6525 **913**
1727-9933 *see* 1561-0837 **701**
1728-015X *see* 0378-8652 **4250**
1728-0311 Munhwao Haksup **5153**
1728-0540 *see* 0723-791X **695**
1728-0583 Journal of Child and Adolescent Mental Health **6150**
1728-0591 *see* 1728-0583 **6150**
1728-1431 International Journal of Engineering. Transactions A: Basics **3201**
1728-144X International Journal of Engineering. Transactions B: Applications **3201**
1728-1660 Badil Resource Center for Palestinian Residency & Refugee Rights. Working Papers **7203**
1728-1679 Survey of Palestinian Refugees and Internally Displaced Persons **7216**
1728-1865 Chetver **5210**
1728-189X Fotodelo **6968**
1728-1997 Iranian Journal of Veterinary Research **8800**
1728-2020 *see* 1562-4382 **4907**
1728-2047 International Journal of Electronic Business Management **1756**
1728-2179 International Transportation Magazine **8500**
1728-2233 Explore South Africa **8702**
1728-239X Paediatrica **6098**
1728-2403 *see* 1728-239X **6098**
1728-2810 Sotsiologiya Meditsiny **5716**
1728-2918 Molekulyarnaya Meditsina **740**
1728-2977 *see* 1605-7724 **7038**
1728-2985 Urologiya **6276**
1728-2993 Problemy Tuberkuleza i Boleznei Legkikh **6217**
1728-3043 Iranian Journal of Biotechnology **766**
1728-3051 *see* 1727-5431 **3966**
1728-3086 Xtreme Machines **8613**
1728-3124 *see* 0084-0084 **6961**
1728-3213 Development Bank of Southern Africa. Annual Report **1920**

Link to your serials resources and content with ulrichsweb.com

1728-3558 *see* 1728-1865 **5210**
1728-3574 European Cigar Cult Journal **8486**
1728-3892 Chemical Disarmament **7115**
1728-3906 *see* 1728-3892 **7115**
1728-4414 Vienna Yearbook of Population Research **7295**
1728-4457 *see* 0098-7921 **7289**
1728-4465 *see* 0039-3665 **7294**
1728-4554 Iranian Journal of Radiation Research **6199**
1728-4562 *see* 1728-4554 **6199**
1728-5070 Voz Portuguesa **3571**
1728-5291 Pacific Pest Info **245**
1728-5305 *see* 1728-4414 **7295**
1728-5666 Sport Science & Physical Education Bulletin **6997**
1728-5860 Revista Peruana de Reumatologia **6226**
1728-5879 *see* 1727-7914 **6220**
1728-5887 *see* 1727-7922 **6220**
1728-5895 *see* 1727-7930 **6221**
1728-5917 *see* 1018-8800 **5566**
1728-5925 Revista Peruana de Cardiologia **5799**
1728-5976 F A News **4502**
1728-6107 Health Policy and Development **7522**
1728-6263 Journal fuer Gastroenterologische und Hepatologische Erkrankungen **5927**
1728-6271 *see* 1728-6263 **5927**
1728-6301 World Research Journal of Schistosomology **5731**
1728-631X Morphoparasitic Spectrum International. Proceedings **5680**
1728-6328 The International Journal of Wild Life and Environmental Research **3694**
1728-645X Shijie Zongjiao Xuekan **7681**
1728-7715 Journal of Research in Architecture and Planning **447**
1728-7731 *see* 1726-4901 **5594**
1728-774X African Safety Promotion **8024**
1728-791X Electronic Journal of Natural Sciences **7852**
1728-7928 Liza. Dobrye Sovety **8872**
1728-8673 International Journal of Business and Information **1127**
1728-869X Journal of Exercise Science and Fitness **6230**
1728-8762 Global Standards **6402**
1728-8789 Taste **4368**
1728-8800 Kardiovaskulyarnaya Terapiya i Profilaktika **5795**
1728-8843 Voprosy Filologicheskikh Nauk **5194**
1728-8878 Voprosy Ekonomicheskikh Nauk **1192**
1728-8894 Pedagogicheskie Nauki **2896**
1728-9130 Muscle Evolution **6993**
1728-9246 W T O World Tourism Barometer **8781**
1728-9254 O M T. Barometro del Turismo Mundial **8780**
1728-9262 Barometre OMT du Tourisme Mondial **8778**
1728-9416 The Veterinary Practice **8813**
1728-9424 Veterinary Science. Proceedings **8814**
1728-9432 Veterinary Medicine. Proceedings **8813**
1728-9440 The Veterinary Medicine **8813**
1728-9459 Veterinary Medical Society. Record **8813**
1728-9467 Hematology. Proceedings **5938**
1728-9475 Journal of Hematological Research **5939**
1728-9483 The Journal of Hematology and Hemoparasitic Diseases Research **5939**
1728-9491 Physiology. Proceedings **927**
1728-9505 Animal Husbandry. Proceedings **317**
1728-9513 Diagnosticians. Proceedings **5605**
1728-9521 Animal Health. Proceedings **8792**
1728-9750 The Journal of Dairy Sciences **266**
1729-0104 Seventeen (South Africa Edition) **2212**
1729-0333 Profile's Offshore Investing **1646**
1729-0376 Sahara J **5826**
1729-0503 *see* 1680-6905 **5569**
1729-0619 Source O E C D. Urban, Rural and Regional Development **1177**
1729-0627 *see* 1729-0619 **1177**
1729-0635 Source O C D E. Developpement Urbain, Rural et Regional **1176**
1729-0643 *see* 1729-0635 **1176**
1729-0732 Eastlex **1921**
1729-0902 Enter **2418**
1729-0996 Infomusa (Spanish Edition) **236**
1729-1429 Kuwait Top List **2012**
1729-2042 Signos Vitales **5715**
1729-214X *see* 1018-130X **5706**
1729-2638 Doing Business In (Year) **1092**
1729-2840 Fine Living Namibia **5071**
1729-3405 Asian Counsel **4622**
1729-3456 Gulf Daily News **3799**
1729-3561 A E M I Journal **7276**
1729-3618 O E C D Journal of Business Cycle Measurement and Analysis *changed to* 1995-2805 **1155**
1729-3782 E A R Se L eProceedings **2705**
1729-4274 Social Geography **8002**
1729-4312 *see* 1729-4274 **8002**
1729-441X Images in Paediaric Cardiology **6092**
1729-4649 Taiwan Journal of Linguistics **5185**
1729-4827 Liberabit **7383**
1729-4991 Urban Health and Development Bulletin **7544**
1729-5017 Tvoi Malysh **2170**
1729-5068 Sistemy Upravleniya i Informatsionnye Tekhnologii **2437**
1729-5254 Electronic Journal of Theoretical Physics **7010**
1729-5416 *see* 0078-3579 **409**
1729-5440 Matematika v Vysshem Obrazovanii **5511**
1729-5459 Nauchnye Tsentry Chernomorskogo Ekonomicheskogo Sotrudnichestva. Ekologicheskii Vestnik **3456**
1729-5769 Journal of Civil Engineering Research and Practice **3274**
1729-6277 *see* 1023-0076 **236**
1729-6285 *see* 1023-0068 **236**
1729-6293 *see* 1729-0996 **236**
1729-6455 Middle East Journal of Emergency Medicine *changed to* 1999-7086 **5946**
1729-6579 Golden Myanmar **3966**
1729-6897 Concentric **5277**
1729-6935 *see* 0138-645X **5739**
1729-701X International Monetary Fund. Global Financial Stability Report **1358**
1729-7516 Natsional'nyi Yadernyi Tsentr Respubliki Kazakhstan. Vestnik **7069**
1729-7885 *see* 1729-7516 **7069**
1729-7893 Bangladesh Journal of Veterinary Medicine **8794**
1729-8156 P D A User **2582**
1729-8571 Creating Homes *changed to* 1816-840X **4547**
1729-8644 Glamour (Moscow) **8865**
1729-8709 I S O Focus (English Edition) **6402**
1729-8725 G W W Aktuell **6769**
1729-8806 International Journal of Advanced Robotic Systems **2585**
1729-8814 *see* 1729-8806 **2585**
1729-9101 U F S Aktuell **1953**
1729-9713 Masala! **3967**
1729-973X SoccerLife **8246**
1729-9756 Jiuzhou Xuelin **4459**
1729-9772 Portfolio. Municipalities in South Africa **7501**
1729-9802 Central Asia **546**
1729-9810 S Q U Journal for Scientific Research: Medical Sciences *see* 1029-4066 **5645**
1730-0010 *see* 1730-0029 **5998**
1730-0029 Menopauza **5998**
1730-0703 Magazyn Autostrady **3278**
1730-1270 HIV & AIDS Review **5815**
1730-1912 Pielegniarstwo XXI Wieku **5978**
1730-2250 Odlewnictwo. Nauka i Praktyka **6328**
1730-2668 Matematyka Stosowana **5511**
1730-2781 Glamour (Warsaw) **8866**
1730-2803 Rosliny Ozdobne **3749**
1730-2854 13. Wydanie Specjalne *see* 1640-8993 **2224**
1730-2897 Biuletyn Finansow Publicznych **1913**
1730-315X Dental Tribune **5841**
1730-3427 Miedzynarodowy Przeglad Polityczny **5227**
1730-413X Oceanological and Hydrobiological Studies **2815**
1730-4237 Folia Oeconomica Stetinensia **1110**
1730-4288 GameStar **2477**
1730-508X *see* 1234-9496 **5825**
1730-5241 Survival **8336**
1730-6264 *see* 0065-1036 **5464**
1730-6280 *see* 1233-7234 **5471**
1730-6299 *see* 0137-6934 **5475**
1730-6302 *see* 0010-1354 **5479**
1730-6329 *see* 0016-2736 **5489**
1730-6337 *see* 0039-3223 **5538**
1730-7201 Dermatologia Kliniczna **5874**
1730-7503 Acta Neuropsychologica **6119**
1730-8801 *see* 0732-183X **6024**
1731-0377 *see* 0090-4295 **6276**
1731-0539 Reader's Digest (Polish Edition) **3930**
1731-1136 Agro Chemia Technika *changed to* 1732-2634 **88**
1731-2302 Hereditary Cancer in Clinical Practice **6021**
1731-2450 *see* 1426-6911 **5857**
1731-2469 *see* 0860-6196 **5697**
1731-2477 *see* 1509-8699 **6876**
1731-2485 *see* 1233-5991 **5688**
1731-2493 *see* 1428-1848 **6097**
1731-2507 *see* 1427-0994 **5685**
1731-2523 *see* 1505-3768 **5678**
1731-2531 *see* 1642-5758 **5768**
1731-2922 P H P Solutions **2595**
1731-2930 *see* 1731-7150 **2513**
1731-4577 *see* 1731-2922 **2595**
1731-4585 *see* 1731-2922 **2595**
1731-4593 *see* 1731-2922 **2595**
1731-4682 Ceramika Budowlana **991**
1731-5530 Kardiochirurgia i Torakochirurgia Polska **5794**
1731-6332 Linguodidactica **5147**
1731-6383 Acta Toxicologica **6818**
1731-6677 Seksuologia Polska **5711**
1731-7037 *see* 1731-7150 **2513**
1731-7045 *see* 1731-7150 **2513**
1731-7150 Hakin 9 **2513**
1731-7533 Research in Language **5166**
1731-8068 Wiadomosci Zootechniczne **967**
1731-8165 Monitor Prawa Pracy **4599**
1731-8289 Dziennik Wschodni Lubelski **3929**
1731-8602 Przeglad Ginekologiczno-Polozniczy **6002**
1731-8645 Przeglad Wlokienniczy - Wlokno, Odziez, Skora **8456**
1731-8890 Czesc! **2184**
1731-9404 Alergologia, Immunologia **5752**
1732-0747 Poznan Studies in Contemporary Linguistics **5162**
1732-078X Budownictwo Okretowe **8640**
1732-0895 Konsyliarz **6991**
1732-1085 Annales Academiae Paedagogicae Cracoviensis. Studia Psychologica **7334**
1732-1352 Annales Universitatis Mariae Curie-Sklodowska. Sectio L. Artes **466**
1732-1360 Annales Universitatis Mariae Curie-Sklodowska. Sectio AI. Informatica **2406**
1732-1425 Spajanie Metali i Tworzyw w Praktyce **6344**
1732-1719 Technika Rolnicza, Ogrodnicza, Lesna **214**
1732-1999 Weterynaria w Praktyce **8815**
1732-2138 Noddy **2205**
1732-2189 Studia Humanistyczne **4476**
1732-2200 .psd **6980**
1732-2421 *see* 0567-7920 **6722**
1732-2634 Agrotechnika **88**
1732-2642 Psychogeriatria Polska **4053**
1732-2693 *see* 0032-5449 **5697**
1732-3681 Linux Plus DVD *see* 1427-5562 **2594**
1732-3762 Zoom **6980**
1732-3991 Human Movement **6989**
1732-4009 Ogolnopolska Gazeta Przemyslu Drzewnego *changed to* 1732-4017 **3712**
1732-4017 Gazeta Przemyslu Drzewnego **3712**
1732-4246 Biuletyn Geograficzny *changed to* 1732-4254 **4001**
1732-4254 Bulletin of Geography **4001**
1732-5153 Transport Miejski i Regionalny **8636**
1732-5323 Lotnictwo **65**
1732-5617 C F O **1078**
1732-6273 Kardiolog.pl **5794**
1732-6281 Radiolog.pl **6206**
1732-629X Chirurg.pl **6239**
1732-6508 *see* 1505-6783 **1258**
1732-6702 Gornictwo i Geoinzynieria **6463**
1732-6729 The New Educational Review **2890**
1732-7032 *see* 1361-4487 **8172**
1732-7083 *see* 1427-5562 **2594**
1732-7113 *see* 1427-5562 **2594**
1732-7857 Zoom (Lublin) **6630**
1732-7938 Chip Foto-Video Digital **6979**
1732-7970 Tan Biz **591**
1732-8160 Studies in Polish Linguistics **5183**
1732-8470 Monitor Prawny Dyrektora. Miesiecznik Dyrektora Szkoly **3027**
1732-8489 Monitor Prawny Dyrektora. Miesiecznik Dyrektora Przedskola **3027**
1732-8985 *see* 0239-7269 **5524**
1732-9132 Miscellanea Historico-Iuridica **4734**
1732-9442 Lesne Prace Badawcze **3695**
1732-9841 Psychiatria **6176**
1732-9876 Apteka Plus Prawo **6822**
1733-0297 Biuletyn Edukacji Medialnej **2313**
1733-1331 Polish Journal of Microbiology **895**
1733-134X Polish Journal of Radiology **6205**
1733-1757 Investigationes Linguisticae (Online Edition) **5130**
1733-1951 Boutique **8854**
1733-2001 Apteka Plus *changed to* 1732-9876 **6822**
1733-2095 *see* 1731-7150 **2513**
1733-2109 *see* 1731-2922 **2595**
1733-2346 Choroby Serca i Naczyn **5782**
1733-2745 *see* 1732-2200 **6980**
1733-3040 A B C Przeziebienia **5807**
1733-3490 Archives of Metallurgy and Materials **6305**
1733-4012 Studia Classica et Neolatina **2240**
1733-4101 Leczenie Ran **6066**
1733-4160 Komputerowa Gratka. Wydanie Specjalne *see* 1643-8256 **2198**
1733-4276 *see* 1733-2346 **5782**
1733-4292 Manager Magazin (Edycja Polska) **1777**
1733-4594 *see* 1732-9841 **6176**
1733-5566 Diametros **6914**
1733-6651 C I O **1414**
1733-7178 Central European Journal of Energetic Materials **2121**
1733-7186 Hakin 9 **2513**
1733-7291 Forbes **1110**
1733-7593 *see* 1731-8602 **6002**
1733-7607 *see* 1733-4101 **6066**
1733-8026 The Old and New Concepts of Physics **7029**
1733-8077 Qualitative Sociology Review **8127**
1733-8387 Geochronometria **7857**
1733-9499 Chip Komputer Test **2410**
1733-9707 Mathematical Economics **1147**
1733-9952 C M O Magazine **1809**
1734-042X Krakowsko-Wilenskie Studia Slawistyczne **5137**
1734-1140 Pharmacological Reports **6872**
1734-1515 *see* 0137-1592 **929**
1734-1531 Pediatria & Medycyna Rodzinna **6099**
1734-154X *see* 0001-527X **721**
1734-1566 Logo **6294**
1734-1922 Archives of Medical Science **5577**
1734-1981 Disney i Ja **2185**
1734-2228 Moj Kucyk Pony **2203**
1734-2260 *see* 1429-0022 **6231**
1734-2392 A B C Alergii **5752**
1734-2929 Hot Moda & Shopping **2256**
1734-3038 Experimental & Clinical Hepatology **5923**
1734-3321 Endokrynologia, Otylosc i Zaburzenia Przemiany Materii **5892**
1734-3402 Family Medicine & Primary Care Review **5613**
1734-3542 Onkologia w Praktyce Klinicznej **6031**
1734-3917 Software Developer's Journal **2597**
1734-3925 *see* 1734-3917 **2597**
1734-3933 *see* 1734-3917 **2597**
1734-428X Twoj Maluszek **2170**
1734-4417 Tips & Tricks **2583**
1734-4492 International Journal of Applied Mechanics and Engineering **3381**
1734-4506 Swiat Farmacji **6882**
1734-4948 Advances in Rehabilitation *see* 0860-6161 **6115**
1734-4956 Physical Education and Sport *see* 0043-9630 **3088**
1734-5332 Feniks **8863**
1734-5456 Magazyn Eden **6992**
1734-5960 Leczenie Zywieniowe i Metaboliczne **6663**
1734-6460 *see* 1734-3542 **6031**
1734-7416 Przedszkolak **2166**
1734-8412 Journal of Achievements in Materials and Manufacturing Engineering **3204**
1734-8463 Teletubbies **2216**
1734-8803 *see* 1473-7175 **6840**
1734-8927 Mechanics **3389**
1734-9044 *see* 1734-3321 **5892**
1734-9133 Annales Academiae Paedagogicae Cracoviensis. Studia ad Educationem Defensoriam Pertinentia **2225**
1734-915X *see* 0065-1710 **930**
1734-9168 *see* 0015-5497 **673**
1734-9338 Postepy w Kardiologii Interwencyjnej **5797**
1734-946X C S O **2512**
1734-9478 C E O **1414**
1734-9664 Nailpro **595**
1734-9885 Archives of Materials Science *changed to* Archives of Materials Science and Engineering **3341**
1735-0328 Iranian Journal of Pharmaceutical Research **6851**
1735-0344 Tanaffos **6220**
1735-0611 Journal of Basic Science **7872**
1735-0808 Iranian Journal of Materials Science and Engineering **3203**
1735-1065 Iranian Journal of Radiology **6199**
1735-1243 International Journal of Hematology-Oncology and Bone Marrow Transplantation **5938**
1735-1308 Urology Journal **6276**
1735-1383 Iranian Journal of Immunology **5761**
1735-1391 Shiraz E Medical Journal **5714**
1735-143X Hepatitis Monthly **5926**
1735-1472 International Journal of Environmental Science and Technology **3442**

1740-5556 *see* 1473-7795 **4921**
1740-5564 *see* 1461-4529 **3426**
1740-5572 *see* 1365-7127 **4891**
1740-5580 *see* 0022-0183 **4892**
1740-5599 *see* 0032-258X **2663**
1740-5610 *see* 1740-5629 **7355**
1740-5629 European Journal of Developmental Psychology **7355**
1740-5734 Home D I Y†
1740-5777 The Source *changed to* 1753-8637 **6579**
1740-5807 Crisis States Programme Working Papers. (Print Edition *changed to* 1749-1797 **7228**
1740-5815 Crisis States Programme Working Papers (Online Edition) *changed to* 1749-1800 **7228**
1740-5823 Programa Crisis de los Estados Documentos de Trabajo **7260**
1740-5831 *see* 1740-5823 **7260**
1740-5858 Little Girls (London) **2200**
1740-5866 Learning and Teaching in the Social Sciences *changed to* 1755-2273 **7983**
1740-5904 Critical Discourse Studies **7956**
1740-5912 *see* 1740-5904 **7956**
1740-5998 No. 10 **6701**
1740-6013 Region in Figures. East† **8984**
1740-6021 Region in Figures. East Midlands† **8984**
1740-6048 Region in Figures. North East† **8984**
1740-6056 Region in Figures. South East† **8984**
1740-6064 Region in Figures. South West **7314**
1740-6072 Region in Figures. West Midlands† **8984**
1740-6080 Region in Figures. North West† **8984**
1740-6099 Region in Figures. Yorkshire and the Humber† **8984**
1740-6129 Region in Figures. London (Online) **7314**
1740-6307 Workplace Report **1716**
1740-6315 Home Cultures **7969**
1740-6331 D & B Business Register. Munster, Connaught & Border Regions **1982**
1740-6471 International Optical Communications **2327**
1740-648X Audio Pro *changed to* 1750-4198 **6586**
1740-6501 Furnaces International **6313**
1740-6595 Engie Benjy **2187**
1740-6609 Milkshake! **2202**
1740-6641 Restorative & Aesthetic Practice *changed to* 1754-1581 **5833**
1740-6641 Restorative & Aesthetic Practice *changed to* 1754-159X **5847**
1740-6749 Drug Discovery Today: Technologies **6835**
1740-6757 Drug Discovery Today: Disease Models **6835**
1740-6765 Drug Discovery Today: Disease Mechanisms **6834**
1740-6773 Drug Discovery Today: Therapeutic Strategies **6835**
1740-679X Spaces **4550**
1740-701X T T J **3716**
1740-7036 Society for Medieval Archaeology Newsletter **417**
1740-7052 Information Economics Journal **1752**
1740-7125 Comparative Islamic Studies **7710**
1740-7133 Popular Music History **6607**
1740-7141 Journal of Adult Theological Education **7653**
1740-7192 Fiber Systems. America & Asia **7075**
1740-7206 Construction Industry **996**
1740-7443 Custom P C **2575**
1740-7494 Electronic Government **7485**
1740-7508 *see* 1740-7494 **7485**
1740-7516 International Journal of Automation and Control **2461**
1740-7524 *see* 1740-7516 **2461**
1740-7540 Product Id **1901**
1740-7567 R I C S Foundation. Research Papers **3281**
1740-7621 C I L I P in Yorkshire & Humberside **4999**
1740-7729 The Handbook of Competition Enforcement Agencies **4684**
1740-7737 Snapshots (Secondary Editon) **2913**
1740-7745 Clinical Trials **5904**
1740-7753 *see* 1740-7745 **5904**
1740-7788 HeliData News & Classified **58**
1740-7818 Park & Ride Great Britain **8508**
1740-7826 Gas Regulation **4679**
1740-7834 *see* 1361-4533 **5035**
1740-7842 *see* New Review of Hypermedia and Multimedia **2488**
1740-7869 *see* 1361-4576 **2502**
1740-7885 *see* 1361-4541 **5341**
1740-7923 *see* 1740-0309 **2386**
1740-7931 *see* 0141-6200 **7628**
1740-7990 Terneuzen-Vlissingen Port Handbook *changed to* 1751-2298 **8666**
1740-8008 International Journal of Accounting, Auditing and Performance Evaluation **1292**
1740-8016 *see* 1740-8008 **1292**
1740-8032 Developing Mental Health **6136**
1740-8075 U K Housing Review **4429**
1740-8083 V E R T I C Brief **7272**
1740-8105 Mediactive **8120**
1740-8148 Fun to Learn - Ladybird Magazine **2190**
1740-8210 Inside Business. Petersborough **1124**
1740-8253 Deli & Good Food Directory *see* 1359-0693 **4385**
1740-8253 Deli & Good Food Directory *see* 0959-1915 **3868**
1740-8261 *see* 1058-8183 **8813**
1740-8296 International Journal of Media and Cultural Politics **2327**
1740-8326 Country Profile. Cambodia† **8944**
1740-8334 Country Profile. Laos† **8945**
1740-8342 Country Profile. Eritrea† **8945**
1740-8350 Country Profile. Somalia† **8946**
1740-8369 Country Profile. Djibouti† **8945**
1740-8377 Country Profile. Namibia† **8945**
1740-8385 Country Profile. Swaziland† **8946**
1740-8393 Country Profile. Rwanda† **8946**
1740-8407 Country Profile. Burundi† **8944**
1740-8415 Country Profile. Togo† **8946**
1740-8423 Country Profile. Benin† **8944**
1740-8466 *see* 1740-5033 **4845**
1740-8474 *see* 1740-5033 **4845**
1740-8512 Zoo Weekly **6302**
1740-8547 Working With English **5400**
1740-8660 What Hi-Fi? Sound and Vision. Ultimate Guide *see* 1474-2764 **8155**
1740-8695 Maternal and Child Nutrition **6663**
1740-8709 *see* 1740-8695 **6663**
1740-8776 Management & Organization Review **1775**
1740-8784 *see* 1740-8776 **1775**
1740-8806 *see* 1356-0654 **1390**
1740-8822 International Journal of Innovation and Sustainable Development **1758**
1740-8830 *see* 1740-8822 **1758**
1740-8849 International Journal of Services and Standards **1129**
1740-8857 *see* 1740-8849 **1129**
1740-8865 International Journal of Intelligent Systems Technologies and Applications **2451**
1740-8873 *see* 1740-8865 **2451**
1740-8911 *see* 1356-6644 **1882**
1740-8938 International Journal of Work Organisation and Emotion **1867**
1740-8946 *see* 1740-8938 **1867**
1740-8989 Physical Education and Sport Pedagogy **3076**
1740-9004 Computer Arts Projects **2484**
1740-9071 Middle East Electricity Buyers Guide **3160**
1740-9209 Satellite & Digital Choice *changed to* 1744-8034 **8950**
1740-925X Neuron Glia Biology† **8976**
1740-9292 Contemporary French and Francophone Studies **5278**
1740-9306 *see* 1740-9292 **5278**
1740-9314 *see* 1444-2213 **329**
1740-942X *see* 0265-9816 **5439**
1740-9446 *see* 1356-6709 **1881**
1740-9462 *see* 1356-6660 **1881**
1740-9470 Country Profile. South Korea† **8946**
1740-9489 Country Profile. North Korea† **8946**
1740-9527 The Global Pedagogy Journal **2860**
1740-9624 Country Profile. Israel† **8945**
1740-9632 Country Profile. The Palestinian Territories† **8946**
1740-9640 Country Profile. Mauritius† **8945**
1740-9659 Country Profile. Seychelles† **8946**
1740-9667 Country Profile. Belarus† **8944**
1740-9675 Country Profile. Moldova† **8945**
1740-9683 Country Profile. Dominican Republic† **8945**
1740-9691 Country Profile. Haiti† **8945**
1740-9705 Significance **8399**
1740-9713 *see* 1740-9705 **8399**
1740-9721 Bullet (Wylam) **6552**
1740-973X The International Meccanoman **4337**
1740-9772 Chinese Military Update **6416**
1740-9802 Old Tractor **213**
1741-0002 Country Profile. Georgia† **8945**
1741-0010 Country Profile. Armenia† **8944**
1741-0029 Country Profile. Kyrgyz Republic† **8945**
1741-0037 Country Profile. Tajikistan†
1741-0045 Country Profile. Trinidad and Tobago† **8946**
1741-0053 Country Profile. Guyana† **8945**
1741-0061 Country Profile. Suriname† **8946**
1741-007X Country Profile. Cyprus† **8945**
1741-0088 Country Profile. Malta† **8945**
1741-0096 Country Profile. Malaysia† **8945**
1741-0126 Protein Engineering Design and Selection **743**
1741-0134 Protein Engineering Design and Selection (Online) **743**
1741-0142 Country Profile. Pakistan† **8946**
1741-0150 Country Profile. Afghanistan†
1741-0169 Country Profile. Cameroon† **8944**
1741-0177 Country Profile. Central African Republic† **8945**
1741-0185 Country Profile. Chad† **8945**
1741-0193 Country Profile. Tanzania† **8946**
1741-0207 Country Profile. Comoros† **8945**
1741-0215 Country Profile. Guinea† **8945**
1741-0223 Country Profile. Sierra Leone† **8946**
1741-0231 Country Profile. Liberia† **8945**
1741-024X Country Profile. Hong Kong† **8945**
1741-0258 Country Profile. Macau† **8945**
1741-0266 Country Profile. Sao Tome and Principe† **8946**
1741-0274 Country Profile. Guinea-Bissau† **8945**
1741-0282 Country Profile. Cape Verde† **8944**
1741-0290 Country Profile. Botswana† **8944**
1741-0304 Country Profile. Lesotho† **8945**
1741-0312 Country Profile. Gabon† **8945**
1741-0320 Country Profile. Equatorial Guinea† **8945**
1741-0339 Country Profile. Nepal† **8946**
1741-0347 Country Profile. Mongolia† **8945**
1741-0355 Country Profile. Bhutan† **8944**
1741-0363 Country Profile. The Gambia† **8946**
1741-0371 Country Profile. Mauritania† **8945**
1741-038X Journal of Manufacturing Technology Management **3292**
1741-0398 Journal of Enterprise Information Management **5021**
1741-0401 International Journal of Productivity and Performance Management **1760**
1741-041X Country Profile. Burkina Faso† **8944**
1741-0428 Country Profile. Niger† **8946**
1741-0436 Country Profile. Mali† **8945**
1741-0444 *see* 0140-0118 **826**
1741-0533 Neuron Glia Biology (Online) **6167**
1741-0541 Personalized Medicine **5695**
1741-0630 Dispute Resolution **4660**
1741-0754 Against All Reason **7332**
1741-0789 *see* 0950-2378 **5229**
1741-0797 *see* 1362-6620 **5239**
1741-0851 Sports & Activities Guide Scotland **8206**
1741-0916 Sport Commerce and Culture **8203**
1741-0932 Old Cornwall **4251**
1741-0983 *see* 1472-5967 **1766**
1741-1009 International Journal of Knowledge and Learning **1758**
1741-1017 *see* 1741-1009 **1758**
1741-1025 International Journal of Electronic Marketing and Retailing **1821**
1741-1033 *see* 1741-1025 **1821**
1741-1041 International Journal of Public Sector Performance Management **7447**
1741-105X *see* 1741-1041 **7447**
1741-1068 International Journal of Embedded Systems **2425**
1741-1076 *see* 1741-1068 **2425**
1741-1084 International Journal of Wireless and Mobile Computing **2351**
1741-1092 *see* 1741-1084 **2351**
1741-1106 International Journal of Web and Grid Services **2559**
1741-1114 *see* 1741-1106 **2559**
1741-1122 Journal of Policy and Practice in Intellectual Disabilities **4067**
1741-1130 *see* 1741-1122 **4067**
1741-1149 P A 2 **6865**
1741-1157 *see* 1741-1149 **6865**
1741-1165 Journal of Marine Science & the Environment *changed to* 1755-876X **2809**
1741-1173 Binley's Guide to the New N H S *changed to* 1742-7916 **4088**
1741-1343 Journal of Generic Medicines **6853**
1741-1416 *see* 0001-6810 **7101**
1741-1424 Intellectual Asset Management **1754**
1741-1432 Educational Management, Administration & Leadership (Print) **3021**
1741-1440 Educational Management, Administration & Leadership (Online) *see* 1741-1432 **3021**
1741-1475 Goodie Bag Mag **2191**
1741-1483 X P Essentials *changed to* Windows X P Made Easy **2583**
1741-1491 What M P V and 4 x 4? *changed to* 1745-4700 **8613**
1741-1513 Iraq Focus **1493**
1741-1548 Studies in European Cinema **6514**
1741-1564 Spanish Magazine **8757**
1741-1572 The Pantaneto Forum **7897**
1741-1580 Journal for Crime, Conflict and Media Culture **4699**
1741-1629 *see* 0968-7769 **2964**
1741-1645 International Journal of Therapy and Rehabilitation **6110**
1741-1696 Key Note Market Report: Cooking Sauces & Food Seasonings **1828**
1741-1718 Ab:UK **1878**
1741-1726 Clothing & Footwear Industry **2246**
1741-1742 Key Note Market Assessment. Personal Banking **1364**
1741-1750 Drug Delivery & Commerce **6834**
1741-1874 International Journal of Virtual Technology and Multimedia **2351**
1741-1882 *see* 1741-1874 **2351**
1741-1912 Ethnomusicology Forum **6565**
1741-1920 *see* 1741-1912 **6565**
1741-2005 *see* 0028-4289 **7809**
1741-2021 *see* 1472-6696 **5025**
1741-203X *see* 1041-6102 **6148**
1741-2188 Info Point† **8964**
1741-2234 *see* 1741-2242 **7930**
1741-2242 World Review of Science, Technology and Sustainable Development **7930**
1741-2358 *see* 0734-0664 **5845**
1741-2390 Reptile Care *changed to* Reptile & Exotic Animal Care **6814**
1741-2420 *see* 1601-6335 **5860**
1741-2439 The Journal of Database Marketing & Customer Strategy Management (Print) **1419**
1741-2447 The Journal of Database Marketing & Customer Strategy Management (Online Edition) **1419**
1741-2471 I E E Proceedings - Systems Biology *changed to* 1751-8849 **825**
1741-2544 E M I S E-Law Service **4950**
1741-2552 *see* 1741-2560 **2454**
1741-2560 Journal of Neural Engineering **2454**
1741-2609 *see* 1477-3708 **2651**
1741-2617 *see* 1476-7503 **5567**
1741-2625 *see* 1469-7874 **2965**
1741-2633 *see* 1059-7123 **2445**
1741-2641 *see* 1463-4996 **326**
1741-265X *see* 1474-0222 **4443**
1741-2668 *see* 0956-4748 **4572**
1741-2676 *see* 1477-5700 **7956**
1741-2684 *see* 1471-3012 **6135**
1741-2692 *see* 1363-2752 **3039**
1741-2706 *see* 1468-7968 **7962**
1741-2714 *see* 1466-1381 **337**
1741-2722 *see* 1461-9571 **393**
1741-2730 *see* 1474-8851 **7134**
1741-2749 *see* 1356-336X **3061**
1741-2757 *see* 1465-1165 **7234**
1741-2765 *see* 0014-4851 **3344**
1741-2773 *see* 1464-7001 **8897**
1741-2803 *see* 1468-0181 **8042**
1741-2811 *see* 1460-4582 **5830**
1741-282X *see* 0018-7267 **7970**
1741-2838 *see* 1470-5958 **1867**
1741-2846 *see* 1094-3420 **2592**
1741-2854 *see* 0020-7640 **6147**
1741-2862 *see* 0047-1178 **7245**
1741-2870 *see* 0266-2426 **1962**
1741-2889 *see* 1367-4935 **6094**
1741-2897 *see* 1468-795X **8112**
1741-2900 *see* 1469-5405 **2639**
1741-2919 *see* 1468-7984 **2875**
1741-2927 *see* 1476-718X **6094**
1741-2943 *see* 1475-2409 **3014**
1741-2951 *see* 1469-6053 **401**
1741-296X *see* 1468-0173 **8051**
1741-2978 *see* 1440-7833 **8116**
1741-2986 *see* 1077-5463 **7088**
1741-2994 *see* 1470-4129 **4461**
1741-3001 *see* 1464-8849 **4577**
1741-301X *see* 1470-5931 **1833**
1741-3028 *see* 1081-2865 **7026**
1741-3036 *see* 0027-9501 **1152**
1741-3044 *see* 0170-8406 **7990**
1741-3052 *see* 1473-0952 **4423**
1741-3060 *see* 1470-594X **7171**
1741-3079 *see* 0264-5505 **2666**
1741-3087 *see* 0305-7356 **6608**
1741-3095 *see* 1462-4745 **2666**
1741-3109 *see* 1468-7941 **7994**
1741-3117 *see* 1473-3250 **8064**
1741-3125 *see* 0306-3968 **3560**
1741-3133 *see* 0037-5497 **3220**
1741-3141 *see* 0262-7280 **560**

ISSN

1742-2582 A S D A Solutions **4351**
1742-2590 International Journal of Applied Management (Online) **1755**
1742-2604 International Journal of Applied H R M **1867**
1742-2612 International Journal of Applied Marketing (Online) **1821**
1742-2620 International Journal of Applied Sustainable Development **1755**
1742-2639 International Journal of Applied Management Education and Development **3025**
1742-2647 International Journal of Applied Quality Management (Doncaster) **1755**
1742-2655 International Journal of Applied Public Sector Management **1755**
1742-271X Ultrasound **6209**
1742-2795 Documents International **7319**
1742-2825 Marine Propulsion & Auxiliary Machinery **8652**
1742-2876 Digital Investigation **5913**
1742-2906 Linguistics and the Human Sciences **4463**
1742-2914 Landscape **448**
1742-2930 Durham Anthropological Journal **335**
1742-2981 Sustainable Business Investor - Worldwide **1654**
1742-3015 U K Police Directory (Year) **2670**
1742-3074 The Year in Heart Failure **5802**
1742-3082 The Year in Renal Medicine **6277**
1742-3090 The Year in Osteoporosis **6227**
1742-3104 The Year in Post-Menopausal Health (Year) **6006**
1742-3139 Accommodation Management **4351**
1742-3155 Retro Gamer **2481**
1742-3260 Orthodontics†
1742-3279 Perio **5861**
1742-3287 Oral Biosciences & Medicine **5859**
1742-3295 Dental Team Journal†
1742-3341 The International Journal of Applied Psychoanalytic Studies **7364**
1742-3406 *see* 0144-8420 **7072**
1742-3422 *see* 1473-6691 **7066**
1742-3430 Headache Care **6144**
1742-3457 Benn's Media: North America **4572**
1742-3600 Episteme **6916**
1742-3651 Register of Stunt - Action Co-ordinators and Performers **8477**
1742-3716 Green Places **443**
1742-3724 Green Places News **443**
1742-3775 Subject Matters **2339**
1742-3783 Advances in Electrical Engineerings and Electromagnetics **3294**
1742-3791 World Pharmaceutical Frontiers **6886**
1742-3899 Bar Guide to Glasgow & Edinburgh *see* 1359-0693 **4385**
1742-3899 Bar Guide to Glasgow & Edinburgh *see* 0959-1915 **3868**
1742-3937 P C C Bulletin *changed to* 1751-0406 **1684**
1742-3945 Manchester Journal of International Economic Law **1577**
1742-3953 Chronic Illness **5595**
1742-4070 Investor Guide (London)
1742-4100 Oil Regulation **4752**
1742-4119 O K! **8878**
1742-4143 Y S G Magazine *changed to* 1751-505X **4754**
1742-416X M A D E **449**
1742-4186 International Journal of Nuclear Governance, Economy and Ecology **3169**
1742-4194 *see* 1742-4186 **3169**
1742-4208 International Journal of Mass Customisation **1889**
1742-4216 *see* 1742-4208 **1889**
1742-4224 International Journal of Electronic Democracy **7143**
1742-4232 *see* 1742-4224 **7143**
1742-4240 International Journal of Technology Policy and Law **4871**
1742-4259 *see* 1742-4240 **4871**
1742-4267 International Journal of Powertrain **8619**
1742-4275 *see* 1742-4267 **8619**
1742-4305 Energy Risk **1337**
1742-433X *see* 1471-3322 **1350**
1742-4372 Nefte Compass (Online) **6780**
1742-447X Supply Chain Europe **1845**
1742-4542 eSharp **4451**
1742-464X The F E B S Journal **732**
1742-4658 The F E B S Journal (Online) **732**
1742-4682 Theoretical Biology and Medical Modelling **707**
1742-4690 Retrovirology **5825**
1742-4755 Reproductive Health **5703**
1742-4801 International Wound Journal **6062**
1742-481X *see* 1742-4801 **6062**
1742-4909 *see* 0950-3153 **8062**
1742-4933 Immunity & Ageing **5759**
1742-4941 Journal of Islamic State Practices in International Law **4933**
1742-495X European Mobile Communications Report
1742-5247 Expert Opinion on Drug Delivery **6839**
1742-5255 Expert Opinion on Drug Metabolism & Toxicology **6839**
1742-5263 International Journal of Applied Health Studies **5637**
1742-5271 International Journal of Applied Public - Private Partnerships **1127**
1742-528X International Journal of Applied Finance For Non-Financial Managers **1755**
1742-531X O P D Reference Book & Buyers Guide **1853**
1742-5336 Dental Practice Management Update†
1742-5360 International Journal of Entrepreneurial Venturing **1757**
1742-5379 *see* 1742-5360 **1757**
1742-5395 Supplementary Prescribing in Practice **6882**
1742-5468 Journal of Statistical Mechanics: Theory and Experiment **7060**
1742-5476 Telematics & Mobile Data Guide **2373**
1742-5549 International Journal of Human Factors Modelling and Simulation **3292**
1742-5557 *see* 1742-5549 **3292**
1742-5573 Epidemiologic Perspectives & Innovations **7516**
1742-5581 Biomedical Digital Libraries **5585**
1742-5662 *see* 1742-5689 **7873**
1742-5689 Journal of the Royal Society. Interface **7873**
1742-5786 *see* 1740-8989 **3076**
1742-5824 International Journal of Applied Entrepreneurship **1127**
1742-5964 Studying Teacher Education **2916**
1742-5972 *see* 1742-5964 **2916**
1742-6014 Take a Break's Special Series **3872**
1742-6200 Smallville (London) **2390**
1742-6316 *see* 0391-9714 **676**
1742-6405 AIDS Research and Therapy **5752**
1742-6413 *see* 0974-5963 **831**
1742-6456 British Journal of Anaesthetic & Recovery Nursing **5953**
1742-6464 Journal of Psychiatric Intensive Care **6156**
1742-6545 *see* 1355-2600 **7380**
1742-6588 Journal of Physics: Conference Series (Print)†
1742-6596 Journal of Physics: Conference Series (Online) **7022**
1742-660X *see* 0014-7281 **4909**
1742-6618 *see* 1358-8184 **4908**
1742-6723 Emergency Medicine Australasia (Online) **6059**
1742-6731 Emergency Medicine Australasia (Print) **6059**
1742-674X Managing Safety & Health (at Work)†
1742-6758 International Journal of Product Sound Quality **8153**
1742-6766 *see* 1742-6758 **8153**
1742-6774 B M J Career Focus (Online) **6692**
1742-6812 Journal of International Banking Law and Regulation **4872**
1742-6847 Infosecurity Today *changed to* 1754-4548 **2514**
1742-6855 *see* 0218-8791 **2827**
1742-6928 Health & Safety at Work in S A **6678**
1742-6936 Computers + Telecommunications in Africa *changed to* 1746-1510 **2415**
1742-6952 International Journal of Electronic Transport **8499**
1742-6960 *see* 1742-6952 **8499**
1742-6979 African Journal of Ecology. Supplement *see* 0141-6707 **651**
1742-7002 Drugs in Context. Part A. Cardiovascular Medicine 1 *changed to* 1745-1981 **5812**
1742-7010 Drugs in Context. Part B. Cardiovascular Medicine 2 *changed to* 1745-1981 **5812**
1742-7029 Drugs in Context. Part C. Psychiatry and Neurology *changed to* 1745-1981 **5812**
1742-7037 Drugs in Context. Part D. Endocrinology and Gastroenterology *changed to* 1745-1981 **5812**
1742-7045 Drugs in Context. Part E. Respiratory Medicine and Infections *changed to* 1745-1981 **5812**
1742-7053 Drugs in Context. General Medicine *changed to* 1745-1981 **5812**
1742-7061 Acta Biomaterialia **755**
1742-710X Aspire **4382**
1742-7150 Leadership **4463**
1742-7169 *see* 1742-7150 **4463**
1742-7185 International Journal of Computational Science and Engineering **2472**
1742-7193 *see* 1742-7185 **2472**
1742-7207 International Journal of Cognitive Perfomance Support **1867**
1742-7215 *see* 1742-7207 **1867**
1742-7223 International Journal of Sustainable Manufacturing **3383**
1742-7231 *see* 1742-7223 **3383**
1742-7355 International Journal of Economic Theory **1543**
1742-7363 *see* 1742-7355 **1543**
1742-7371 International Journal of Pervasive Computing and Communications **2426**
1742-738X *see* 1742-7371 **2426**
1742-7398 Digital Photography User† **8950**
1742-7509 International Journal of Electronic Governance **7446**
1742-7517 *see* 1742-7509 **7446**
1742-7525 International Journal of Electronic Trade **1128**
1742-7533 *see* 1742-7525 **1128**
1742-7541 International Journal of Trade and Global Markets **1762**
1742-755X *see* 1742-7541 **1762**
1742-7568 International Journal of Satellite Communications Policy and Management **2327**
1742-7576 *see* 1742-7568 **2327**
1742-7584 International Journal of Tropical Insect Science **850**
1742-7592 *see* 1742-7584 **850**
1742-7606 Oil & Gas (London) **6783**
1742-7622 Emerging Themes in Epidemiology **7515**
1742-7665 Global Media and Communication **2321**
1742-7673 *see* 1742-7665 **2321**
1742-7703 AccountAbility Forum **1276**
1742-7800 What Video and Widescreen T V *changed to* 1752-0215 **2404**
1742-7827 I C T for Education **3064**
1742-7835 Basic & Clinical Pharmacology & Toxicology **6824**
1742-7843 Basic & Clinical Pharmacology & Toxicology Online **6824**
1742-7851 Basic & Clinical Pharmacology & Toxicology. Supplement (Print) **6824**
1742-786X Basic & Clinical Pharmacology & Toxicology. Supplement (Online) **6824**
1742-7878 Cinema Business **6493**
1742-7908 International Rugby News **8236**
1742-7916 Binley's N H S Guide **4088**
1742-7924 *see* 1742-7932 **5963**
1742-7932 Japan Journal of Nursing Science **5963**
1742-7959 Offshore Marine Monthly **8656**
1742-7967 International Journal of Logistics Systems and Management **1758**
1742-7975 *see* 1742-7967 **1758**
1742-8009 Oncology Times (U.K. Edition) **6031**
1742-8025 Rooms, Rooms, Rooms†
1742-8084 Inside Edge *changed to* 1756-896X **8179**
1742-8130 Cellscience Reviews **665**
1742-8149 *see* 1464-7273 **5993**
1742-8173 Philosophical Practice **6941**
1742-8181 *see* 1742-8173 **6941**
1742-819X *see* 1740-9527 **2860**
1742-8254 Regions and Regionalism in History **4257**
1742-8262 Journal of Building Appraisal **1018**
1742-8297 International Journal of Exergy **3201**
1742-8300 *see* 1742-8297 **3201**
1742-8378 Air Traffic Management Directory **8534**
1742-8408 Major Pharmaceutical and Biotechnology Companies of the World (Year) **2015**
1742-8432 Kemps Film, Television, Commercials (UK Edition) *changed to* 1754-8489 **6505**
1742-8440 P C Retail **2493**
1742-853X Animation Directory *changed to* 1755-0718 **6503**
1742-8548 Key Note Market Review: Insurance Industry **1896**
1742-8556 Key Note Market Assessment. Marketing in the Digital Age **1892**
1742-8734 Construction Industry Trade Surveys **996**
1742-8777 Countryside Voice **2608**
1742-8858 Nuts **6296**
1742-8882 Emerging Europe Monitor. Russia, Ukraine & Baltics *changed to* 1746-0735 **1482**
1742-8882 Emerging Europe Monitor. Russia, Ukraine & Baltics *changed to* 1746-0743 **1482**
1742-8890 Emerging Europe Monitor. Eurasia **1482**
1742-8920 International Dividend & Interest Record *changed to* 1743-0259 **1630**
1742-8947 Update for Primary Care **5727**
1742-8955 Regulatory Rapporteur **1164**
1742-9129 Spy Master **7266**
1742-9137 Translation Studies Abstracts Online *see* 1460-3063 **5202**
1742-9145 Journal of Plant Interactions **798**
1742-9153 *see* 1742-9145 **798**
1742-917X Oxford University History Society. Journal **4252**
1742-9234 Cyfrwng **2318**
1742-9277 Chemical Safety Briefing **3240**
1742-9293 Facilities Management Update **1744**
1742-9307 Education Management Update **3021**
1742-9315 Food Hygiene and Safety Briefing **3639**
1742-9404 Maritime Risk International **4514**
1742-9412 Advances in Art & Urban Futures **8085**
1742-9501 European Venture Capital & Private Equity Journal **1622**
1742-9536 *see* 0004-9530 **7338**
1742-9544 *see* 0005-0067 **7338**
1742-9552 *see* 1328-4207 **7345**
1742-9579 European Electronics Engineer **3099**
1742-9595 Journal of Cosmetic and Laser Therapy. Supplement *see* 1476-4172 **5878**
1742-9609 What Plasma and L C D - T V **2398**
1742-9692 *see* 1467-3584 **8763**
1742-9773 Small Enterprise Research Report **1967**
1742-9781 Key Note Market Review: Leisure & Recreation Market *changed to* Key Note Market Review. Leisure in the Home **1896**
1742-9781 Key Note Market Review: Leisure & Recreation Market *changed to* Key Note Market Review: Leisure Outside the Home **4979**
1742-9943 Asian Infrastructure **8490**
1742-9994 Frontiers in Zoology **944**
1743-0003 Journal of NeuroEngineering and Rehabilitation **6153**
1743-0127 Packaging Technology
1743-016X Public Service Review. Construction **7463**
1743-0178 *see* 0035-9149 **7904**
1743-0259 International Dividend & Interest Service **1630**
1743-0283 National Deaf Children's Society. Omnidirectory†
1743-0313 C P D Journal in Haematology **5935**
1743-0372 Earthmovers **5451**
1743-0402 C I P D Policies and Proceedures for People Managers **1857**
1743-0429 Organic & Natural Business **3681**
1743-0437 Sport in Society **8204**
1743-0445 *see* 1743-0437 **8204**
1743-047X Key Note Market Review: The Catering Market **4392**
1743-0488 U K Income Tax Service **1953**
1743-0526 The Journal of Children's Literature Studies **5314**
1743-0534 The Journal of Reading, Writing and Literacy **2877**
1743-0550 Advances in Schizophrenia and Clinical Psychiatry **6120**
1743-0585 Archives of Disease in Childhood. Education and Practice Edition **6088**
1743-0593 *see* 1743-0585 **6088**
1743-0607 Foreign Exchange Rates Record *changed to* 1743-114X **1348**
1743-0615 Fieldwork in Religion **7643**
1743-0623 *see* 1743-0615 **7643**
1743-0666 *see* 0890-5762 **5360**
1743-0712 Practical Poultry **297**
1743-0801 Clash Magazine **6556**
1743-0836 Capital Gains Tax Service. Stubbs Securities Taxation **1916**
1743-0895 Developing Secondary R E **3057**
1743-0941 Friends News Letter *changed to* 1748-5312 **514**
1743-0968 Golf Punk (U K Edition) **8232**
1743-1026 Outlooks on Pest Management (Print) **245**
1743-1034 Outlooks on Pest Management (Online) **245**
1743-1050 Journal of Experimental & Clinical Assisted Reproduction **5995**
1743-1131 *see* 1750-791X **3531**
1743-114X Foreign Exchange Rates Service **1348**
1743-1166 *see* 0034-5326 **2935**
1743-1301 *see* 0031-0328 **410**
1743-131X *see* 1368-2199 **6969**
1743-1328 *see* 0161-6412 **6165**
1743-1336 *see* 1364-0461 **6316**
1743-1344 *see* 1742-271X **6209**
1743-1352 Food Trades Directory of Europe *changed to* 1746-112X **3645**
1743-1514 British Life **5067**
1743-1638 *see* 1740-7125 **7710**
1743-1646 *see* 1740-7133 **6607**
1743-1654 *see* 1740-7141 **7653**
1743-1662 *see* 1742-2906 **4463**
1743-1670 *see* 1476-9948 **7628**
1743-1697 *see* 1463-9955 **7649**
1743-1700 *see* 0952-7648 **401**
1743-1719 *see* 1462-317X **7670**
1743-1727 *see* 1462-2459 **7673**
1743-1735 *see* 1528-0268 **7670**
1743-1743 *see* 1479-7887 **5132**

ISSN

1744-0564 *see* 0144-0365 **4149**
1744-0572 Global Crime **7237**
1744-0580 *see* 1744-0572 **7237**
1744-0610 N P L Report on D Q L - O R **7027**
1744-0645 Environment (London, 2004) **3420**
1744-0661 What Digital Camcorder **2404**
1744-0696 Place Branding *changed to* 1751-8040 **32**
1744-0734 Africa Week **7103**
1744-0742 *see* 1744-0734 **7103**
1744-0807 Literary London **5324**
1744-0874 Caterfile Market Report **1882**
1744-0904 Gig **6569**
1744-0963 Music Archive Publications. Series A, Chant (Eastern and Western) **6590**
1744-0971 Music Archive Publications. Series C, Renaissance Vocal and Instrumental Music **6590**
1744-1005 New Zealand Conveyancing and Property Reports **4877**
1744-1013 *see* 1744-1005 **4877**
1744-1021 *see* 1461-7781 **7208**
1744-1048 Journal of Private International Law **4933**
1744-1056 European Competition Journal **4669**
1744-1145 British Journal of Play Therapy **7342**
1744-1153 Furniture & Furnishings Directory†
1744-1161 *see* 0261-5614 **6656**
1744-117X Comparative Biochemistry and Physiology. Part D: Genomics and Proteomics **729**
1744-1250 Mobile Handset Analyst **2334**
1744-1269 *see* 1744-1250 **2334**
1744-1331 Health Economics, Policy and Law **5625**
1744-134X *see* 1744-1331 **5625**
1744-1358 *see* 0071-1365 **731**
1744-1366 Ecclesiology **7639**
1744-1374 Journal of Institutional Economics **1137**
1744-1382 *see* 1744-1374 **1137**
1744-1439 *see* 0067-8694 **724**
1744-1463 *see* Minerva Journal of Women and War **6437**
1744-148X The Employer (Howe) **1860**
1744-1560 Chemical Technology **2055**
1744-1579 *see* 1744-1560 **2055**
1744-1595 International Journal of Evidence-Based Healthcare **5638**
1744-1609 *see* 1744-1595 **5638**
1744-1625 Surgical Practice **6260**
1744-1633 *see* 1744-1625 **6260**
1744-165X Seminars in Fetal & Neonatal Medicine **6004**
1744-1684 *see* 0032-3497 **7172**
1744-1692 Global Public Health **5620**
1744-1706 *see* 1744-1692 **5620**
1744-1714 *see* 0002-7766 **4854**
1744-1722 *see* 0896-5811 **4703**
1744-1730 Asian Population Studies **7277**
1744-1749 *see* 1744-1730 **7277**
1744-1765 International Journal of Information and Computer Security **2514**
1744-1773 *see* 1744-1765 **2514**
1744-1781 Public Servant **7463**
1744-179X Public Service Review. Intenational Development **1604**
1744-1854 Comparative Critical Studies **5277**
1744-1870 Women's Health Medicine†
1744-1889 The Foundation Years **5616**
1744-1919 Smartphone *changed to* 1745-9885
1744-196X Updates in Lymphomatous Meningitis† **8996**
1744-2117 Research in Competence-Based Management **1789**
1744-2192 *see* 1742-6456 **5953**
1744-2222 Latin American and Caribbean Ethnic Studies **5320**
1744-2230 *see* 1744-2222 **5320**
1744-2249 Evidence - Based Healthcare and Public Health†
1744-2281 Railway Interiors International **8623**
1744-2303 International Journal of Information and Operations Management Education **1757**
1744-2311 *see* 1744-2303 **1757**
1744-232X International Journal of Heavy Vehicle Systems **8499**
1744-2370 International Journal of Services and Operations Management **1761**
1744-2389 *see* 1744-2370 **1761**
1744-2397 The Mediterranean Journal of Computers & Networks **2431**
1744-2400 The Mediterranean Journal of Electronics & Communications **3108**
1744-2435 Plan B Magazine† **8981**
1744-2508 Stochastics **5538**
1744-2516 *see* 1744-2508 **5538**
1744-2532 Africa Renaissance **7102**
1744-2567 Script-ed **4781**
1744-2583 *see* 1744-2591 **3204**
1744-2591 Journal of Building Physics **3204**
1744-2605 Helicopter World. Special Report **8544**
1744-2621 International Journal of Metadata, Semantics and Ontologies **2559**
1744-263X *see* 1744-2621 **2559**
1744-2648 Evidence and Policy **7964**
1744-2656 *see* 1744-2648 **7964**
1744-2664 Industrial Inkjet (Print) *changed to* 1756-9001 **7323**
1744-2710 The International Journal for Technology in Mathematics Education **5552**
1744-277X Rhinegold Guide to Music Education (Years) *changed to* 1758-3667 **6552**
1744-2796 International Journal of Aviation Management and Logistics **8546**
1744-280X *see* 1744-2796 **8546**
1744-2818 *see* 1350-6129 **6221**
1744-2826 *see* 1359-3714 **3153**
1744-2850 *see* 1744-2869 **2351**
1744-2869 International Journal of Mobile Network Design and Innovation **2351**
1744-2893 Earth & E-nvironment **2706**
1744-3091 Acta Crystallographica. Section F: Structural Biology and Crystallization Communications Online **2109**
1744-3121 International Journal of Immunogenetics **873**
1744-313X *see* 1744-3121 **873**
1744-3210 *see* 0958-8221 **2468**
1744-3237 Morning Advertiser Directory *changed to* 1751-6323 **1974**
1744-3377 Fundamental & Clinical Pharmacology. Supplement *see* 0767-3981 **6843**
1744-3415 Suffolk Jumbo Free Ads **3968**
1744-3423 Camping in France *changed to* 1749-8465 **8311**
1744-3547 e-Business Process† **8951**
1744-3563 *see* 0263-8762 **3239**
1744-3571 *see* 0960-3085 **764**
1744-358X *see* 0260-9576 **3250**
1744-3598 *see* 0957-5820 **3253**
1744-3601 eStrategies. Central & Eastern Europe **2320**
1744-3687 International Journal of Design & Dynamics *changed to* 1755-7437 **3200**
1744-3806 *see* 1462-6268 **2485**
1744-3857 Journal of Stevenson Studies **5316**
1744-3865 British Journal of Cancer Management **6010**
1744-3873 *see* 1226-508X **7138**
1744-3881 Complementary Therapies in Clinical Practice **5956**
1744-3970 Retail & Shopping Centre Directory (Year) **2026**
1744-411X *see* 1380-3395 **7387**
1744-4128 *see* 1382-5585 **7387**
1744-4136 *see* 0929-7049 **7387**
1744-4144 *see* 1385-4046 **7387**
1744-4152 *see* 0165-0424 **839**
1744-4160 *see* 1381-3455 **919**
1744-4179 *see* 0929-1016 **658**
1744-4187 *see* 1380-3611 **2851**
1744-4195 *see* 1380-3603 **5595**
1744-4243 *see* 1382-5577 **5293**
1744-4292 Molecular Systems Biology **690**
1744-4357 R F I D Solutions **3217**
1744-4381 PaperCraft Inspirations **538**
1744-4411 Emerging Bahrain **1482**
1744-442X Annual Business, Economic and Political Review. Bahrain *see* 1744-4411 **1482**
1744-4438 *see* 1744-4551 **1482**
1744-4446 Annual Business Economic and Political Review. Egypt *see* 1744-456X **1482**
1744-4454 *see* 1744-4578 **1482**
1744-4462 *see* 1744-4586 **1482**
1744-4470 *see* 1744-4594 **1482**
1744-4489 Emerging Oman **1482**
1744-4497 Annual Business, Economic and Political Review. Oman *see* 1744-4489 **1482**
1744-4500 *see* 1744-4608 **1483**
1744-4519 *see* 1744-4616 **1483**
1744-4527 *see* 1744-4624 **1483**
1744-4535 *see* 1744-4632 **1483**
1744-4543 *see* 1744-4640 **1483**
1744-4551 Emerging Bulgaria **1482**
1744-456X Emerging Egypt **1482**
1744-4578 Emerging Jordan **1482**
1744-4586 Emerging Lebanon **1482**
1744-4594 Emerging Morocco **1482**
1744-4608 Emerging Qatar **1483**
1744-4616 Emerging Romania **1483**
1744-4624 Emerging Syria **1483**
1744-4632 Emerging Tunisia **1483**
1744-4640 Emerging Turkey **1483**
1744-4667 *see* 1467-2561 **6001**
1744-4721 J-tuner **8586**
1744-4772 Elle (U K Travel Edition) **8860**
1744-4918 Private Hospital Healthcare Europe. I T & Communications and Radiology & Imaging **4109**
1744-5019 *see* 0360-5310 **5652**
1744-5027 *see* 0929-8215 **2495**
1744-5035 *see* 0929-6174 **5203**
1744-5043 *see* 1570-0763 **3026**
1744-5051 *see* 1387-3954 **5554**
1744-506X *see* 0165-8107 **6163**
1744-5078 *see* 0927-3948 **6047**
1744-5086 *see* 0928-6586 **6047**
1744-5094 *see* 1381-6810 **6047**
1744-5108 *see* 0167-6830 **6050**
1744-5116 *see* 1388-0209 **6868**
1744-5124 *see* 0924-3453 **2909**
1744-5132 *see* 0927-3972 **6052**
1744-5140 *see* 0165-0521 **964**
1744-5159 *see* 0042-3114 **3399**
1744-5167 *see* 1388-235X **4086**
1744-5175 *see* 0899-3408 **2948**
1744-5183 *see* 0020-7144 **5943**
1744-5191 *see* 1049-4820 **2949**
1744-5205 *see* 0882-0538 **6051**
1744-5213 *see* 0964-704X **6157**
1744-5248 The Sports Market **1904**
1744-5280 Carp Addict **8308**
1744-5302 Ships and Offshore Structures **8661**
1744-537X Birding Asia **903**
1744-5396 Public Policy Research (Print) **1547**
1744-540X Public Policy Research (Online) **1547**
1744-5434 Lloyd's Law Reports: Insurance & Reinsurance **4513**
1744-5450 Kid's Nutrition Report **6662**
1744-5485 International Journal of Bioinformatics Research and Applications **826**
1744-5493 *see* 1744-5485 **826**
1744-5515 *see* 1574-0196 **4848**
1744-5523 International Journal of Law in Context **4695**
1744-5531 *see* 1744-5523 **4695**
1744-5647 Journal of Maps **2711**
1744-5655 Energy Sourcebook **6768**
1744-568X Radio-Controlled Spitfire **4345**
1744-5760 International Journal of Parallel, Emergent and Distributed Systems **2507**
1744-5779 *see* 1744-5760 **2507**
1744-5787 Medieval Clothing and Textiles **2258**
1744-5809 *see* 0264-6196 **4080**
1744-5833 Understanding Faith **7691**
1744-5876 Cultures of Consumption Series **8097**
1744-6155 *see* 1539-0136 **5963**
1744-6163 *see* 0031-5990 **5977**
1744-6171 *see* 1073-6077 **5964**
1744-618X *see* 1541-5147 **5962**
1744-6198 *see* 0029-6473 **5973**
1744-6295 Journal of Intellectual Disabilities **3042**
1744-6309 *see* 1744-6295 **3042**
1744-6317 World of Information Business Intelligence Reports. Serbia and Montenegro **1532**
1744-6392 Client Report **4860**
1744-6406 *see* 0031-8019 **6940**
1744-6414 Journal of Competition Law and Economics **4700**
1744-6422 *see* 1744-6414 **4700**
1744-6465 Labour and Employment Benefits (Year) **1693**
1744-6473 *see* 1744-6465 **1693**
1744-6503 International Journal of Educational Advancement **2869**
1744-6511 International Journal of Educational Advancement (Online) **2869**
1744-6570 *see* 0031-5826 **7390**
1744-6619 The Journal of Credit Risk **1360**
1744-6635 International Journal of Business Forecasting and Market Intelligence **1821**
1744-6643 *see* 1744-6635 **1821**
1744-6651 Expert Review of Endocrinology & Metabolism **5892**
1744-666X Expert Review of Clinical Immunology **5758**
1744-6708 Westminster Papers in Communication and Culture **2344**
1744-6716 *see* 1744-6708 **2344**
1744-6767 African and Middle East Textiles **8447**
1744-683X Soft Matter **2080**
1744-6848 *see* 1744-683X **2080**
1744-6872 Pharmacogenetics and Genomics **877**
1744-6880 *see* 1744-6872 **877**
1744-6961 Grassland Science **116**
1744-697X *see* 1744-6961 **116**
1744-6988 What Franchise **1969**
1744-7143 Journal of Multicultural Discourses **5134**
1744-716X Essential Brass **6565**
1744-7178 Vacher's Quarterly **7475**
1744-7267 Mountain Biking World **8265**
1744-7305 Creative Scrapbooking **534**
1744-7348 *see* 0003-4746 **653**
1744-7356 International Concertina Association. Papers **6576**
1744-7364 *see* 1744-7356 **6576**
1744-7380 Bulb **2181**
1744-7402 *see* 1546-542X **3246**
1744-7410 *see* 1077-8306 **948**
1744-7429 *see* 0006-3606 **662**
1744-750X Blueprint Broadside **435**
1744-7534 Inflight Hospitality *changed to* Onboard Hospitality **4395**
1744-7542 England's Equestrian **8290**
1744-7550 International Journal of Postharvest Technology and Innovation **201**
1744-7569 *see* 1744-7550 **201**
1744-7593 *see* 1742-5247 **6839**
1744-7607 *see* 1742-5255 **6839**
1744-7623 *see* 1472-8214 **6839**
1744-7631 *see* 1472-8222 **6840**
1744-764X *see* 1474-0338 **6839**
1744-7658 *see* 1354-3784 **6839**
1744-7666 *see* 1465-6566 **6839**
1744-7674 *see* 1354-3776 **6839**
1744-7682 *see* 1471-2598 **5612**
1744-7720 Street Machine & American Car World *changed to* 0969-3726 **8490**
1744-7895 Oral Oncology. Supplement **6032**
1744-7909 *see* 1672-9072 **797**
1744-7917 *see* 1672-9609 **849**
1744-7933 News@nature.com **7892**
1744-7941 *see* 1038-4111 **1856**
1744-795X *see* 0255-7614 **6577**
1744-7976 *see* 0008-3976 **195**
1744-7984 *see* 0077-5762 **2890**
1744-7992 *see* 0950-1045 **3143**
1744-8026 Research Information **7902**
1744-8034 Digital Satellite Choice† **8950**
1744-8042 *see* 1462-2416 **6871**
1744-8069 Molecular Pain **5680**
1744-8158 Auf Wiedersehen Pet **2375**
1744-8182 International Journal of Applied Operations Management **1755**
1744-8190 International Journal of Applied Management of Change **1755**
1744-8204 International Journal of Applied Strategic Management **1755**
1744-8212 International Journal for the Applied Study of Public Order **7974**
1744-828X *see* 1741-0541 **5695**
1744-8298 *see* 1479-6678 **5787**
1744-8301 *see* 1479-6694 **6020**
1744-831X *see* 1475-0708 **5911**
1744-8328 *see* 1473-7140 **6840**
1744-8336 *see* 1478-7210 **6109**
1744-8344 *see* 1477-9072 **5787**
1744-8352 *see* 1473-7159 **6840**
1744-8360 *see* 1473-7175 **6840**
1744-8379 *see* 1473-7167 **6840**
1744-8387 *see* 1478-9450 **732**
1744-8395 *see* 1476-0584 **5758**
1744-8409 *see* 1744-666X **5758**
1744-8417 *see* 1744-6651 **5892**
1744-8581 *see* 0024-2160 **5026**
1744-859X Annals of General Psychiatry **6123**
1744-8603 Globalization and Health **7519**
1744-8689 Journal of Civil Society **7146**
1744-8697 *see* 1744-8689 **7146**
1744-8700 Senses and Sensibilities†
1744-8719 Asian Cinema **6490**
1744-8727 Sikh Formations **7741**
1744-8735 *see* 1744-8727 **7741**
1744-8778 The China Business Forecast Report **1447**
1744-8786 The India Business Forecast Report **1122**
1744-8794 The Malaysia Business Forecast Report **1497**
1744-8808 The Thailand Business Forecast Report **1522**

ISSN

1744-8824	Russia Business Forecast Report **1516**
1744-8840	The Egypt Busniness Forecast Report **1482**
1744-8859	The U A E Business Forecast Report **1522**
1744-8867	The Iran Business Forecast Report **1493**
1744-8875	Brazil Business Forecast Report **1443**
1744-8883	Venezuela Business Forecast Report **1523**
1744-8891	Mexico Business Forecast Report **1498**
1744-8921	Blinds and Shutters Buyers Guide **1975**
1744-893X	Materials Handling & Distribution Services Directory
1744-8948	International Directory of Power Generation and Distribution **2008**
1744-8964	Conservatory Industries **2040**
1744-8980	*see* 1573-2479 **3220**
1744-8999	*see* 1573-2487 **3260**
1744-9006	*see* 1573-062X **8834**
1744-9014	*see* 1031-2943 **7624**
1744-9049	Respiratory Medicine Extra *changed to* 1755-0017 **6218**
1744-9057	Ethnopolitics **7133**
1744-9065	*see* 1744-9057 **7133**
1744-9081	Behavioral and Brain Functions **6126**
1744-9200	International Journal of Prisoner Health **7527**
1744-9219	*see* 1744-9200 **7527**
1744-9294	Feed Compounder. Pet Food Supplement **6808**
1744-9324	*see* 0008-4239 **7113**
1744-9359	Management & Organizational History **1775**
1744-9367	*see* 1744-9359 **1775**
1744-9375	HealthEX Specialist **6988**
1744-9383	SportEX Dynamics **6233**
1744-9413	Collingwood and British Idealism Studies **6911**
1744-9421	Hospital Healthcare Europe. Clinical Nutrition **4100**
1744-9480	Accounting in Europe **1278**
1744-9499	*see* 1744-9480 **1278**
1744-9537	Caves of China **2728**
1744-9545	*see* 1742-8262 **1018**
1744-9561	Biology Letters **660**
1744-957X	*see* 1744-9561 **660**
1744-9618	C W 3 Journal **5268**
1744-9626	Journal of Global Ethics **7979**
1744-9634	*see* 1744-9626 **7979**
1744-9642	Ethics and Education **8100**
1744-9650	*see* 1744-9642 **8100**
1744-9685	Lifestyle (Devizes) **5075**
1744-9855	Journal of Postcolonial Writing **5315**
1744-9863	*see* 1744-9855 **5315**
1744-9871	Journal of Research in Nursing **5967**
1744-988X	*see* 1744-9871 **5967**
1744-9898	Outdoor Enthusiast **8327**
1744-9901	Talking Images **6515**
1744-9928	International Journal of Green Economics **1128**
1744-9936	*see* 1744-9928 **1128**
1744-9944	International Journal of Forensic Engineering **3201**
1744-9952	*see* 1744-9944 **3201**
1744-9960	Supply Chain Business **1796**
1744-9979	Therapeutic Apheresis and Dialysis **6275**
1744-9987	*see* 1744-9979 **6275**
1744-9995	Norfolk Journal & East Anglian Life *changed to* 1751-3278 **4981**
1745-0004	American Journal of Reproductive Immunology. Supplement **5754**
1745-0012	*see* 1745-0004 **5754**
1745-0039	International Journal of Collaborative Engineering **3200**
1745-0047	*see* 1745-0039 **3200**
1745-0055	International Journal of Materials and Structural Integrity **3202**
1745-0063	*see* 1745-0055 **3202**
1745-0071	International Journal of Transitions and Innovation Systems **2462**
1745-008X	*see* 1745-0071 **2462**
1745-0101	Mobilities **7287**
1745-011X	*see* 1745-0101 **7287**
1745-0128	Vulnerable Children and Youth Studies **2171**
1745-0136	*see* 1745-0128 **2171**
1745-0144	Twenty - First Century Society **8011**
1745-0152	*see* 1745-0144 **8011**
1745-0179	Clinical Practice and Epidemiology in Mental Health **7345**
1745-0217	Cartoon Network
1745-0276	Statewatch European Monitor (Online) **7215**
1745-0322	Centre for Education in the Built Environment. Transactions **437**
1745-0330	A P T Aluminium News **6303**
1745-039X	Archives of Animal Nutrition **8793**
1745-0438	Active Travel News **8253**
1745-0446	*see* 1745-0438 **8253**
1745-0454	Respiratory Medicine: C O P D Update **6218**
1745-0462	Argentina Business Forecast Report **1437**
1745-0500	Chile Business Forecast Report **1447**
1745-0519	Colombia Business Forecast Report **1447**
1745-0543	East Caribbean Business Forecast Report **1097**
1745-0578	Hungary Business Forecast Report **1489**
1745-0586	Indonesia Business Forecast Report **1490**
1745-0640	Peru Business Forecast Report **1511**
1745-0659	Philippines Busniess Forecast Report **1511**
1745-0667	Poland Business Forecast Report **1511**
1745-0683	Saudi Arabia Business Forecast Report **1516**
1745-0713	South Africa Business Forecast Report **1518**
1745-0748	Turkey Business Forecast Report **1522**
1745-0764	Vietnam Business Forecast Report **1524**
1745-0772	West Caribbean Business Forecast Report **1524**
1745-0837	Clinical Focus: Obstetrics & Gynaecology **5988**
1745-0918	*see* 1745-0926 **5370**
1745-0926	Shakespeare **5370**
1745-0934	Student & Graduate Magazine **3331**
1745-0942	*see* 1745-0934 **3331**
1745-0950	Professional Security Magazine **2666**
1745-1000	Marine Biology Research **688**
1745-1019	*see* 1745-1000 **688**
1745-1027	*see* 1057-0314 **5195**
1745-1035	*see* 1051-0974 **8094**
1745-1043	*see* 0893-4215 **5107**
1745-1108	Puzzler Christmas Annual **4344**
1745-1140	Emerging Markets Report **1104**
1745-1167	*see* 1024-1221 **2072**
1745-1175	Disability Product News **4065**
1745-1205	Infant **6093**
1745-1264	Data Strategy **1737**
1745-1299	Microsoft Windows X P: The Official Magazine **2595**
1745-1302	*see* 1052-7036 **7235**
1745-1329	*see* 1097-4954 **1114**
1745-1337	*see* 0916-8508 **3103**
1745-1345	*see* 0916-8516 **2324**
1745-1353	*see* 0916-8524 **3103**
1745-1361	*see* 0916-8532 **2544**
1745-137X	Cambridgeshire Journal & East Anglian Life *changed to* 1750-9971 **4976**
1745-1388	Suffolk Journal & East Anglian Life *changed to* 1751-3294 **4983**
1745-1396	Essex Magazine and East Anglian Life *changed to* 1753-6790 **5070**
1745-1434	Reveal **3870**
1745-1450	National Joint Registry for England and Wales. Annual Report **4107**
1745-1590	The International Journal of Biodiversity Science & Management **2615**
1745-1604	*see* 1745-1590 **2615**
1745-1701	*see* 0586-7614 **6184**
1745-1744	*see* 0003-598X **374**
1745-1809	International Journal of Management and Sustainable Development†
1745-1817	*see* 1745-1809
1745-1825	Freedom of Information **4678**
1745-1876	Grow Your Own **3735**
1745-1981	Drugs in Context (International Edition) **5812**
1745-2007	Architectural Engineering and Design Management **429**
1745-2058	Nuclear Future **3213**
1745-2244	Inside Business. Chelmsford **1124**
1745-2414	The Offset Guidelines Quarterly Bulletin **2534**
1745-2422	*see* 1743-4440 **5905**
1745-2457	Trends and Statistics *changed to* 1759-8044 **4382**
1745-2473	Nature Physics **7028**
1745-2481	*see* 1745-2473 **7028**
1745-249X	Americas Plural **5253**
1745-2503	Scarlet **8882**
1745-2538	*see* 0021-9096 **8112**
1745-2546	Journal of Developing Societies (Online) **7978**
1745-2554	*see* 0020-7152 **8108**
1745-2627	*see* 1350-4509 **3443**
1745-2635	*see* 0885-4300 **7183**
1745-2651	*see* 0340-0352 **5013**
1745-266X	X P How To **2441**
1745-2759	Virtual and Physical Prototyping **3399**
1745-2767	*see* 1745-2759 **3399**
1745-2775	Climb Magazine **8309**
1745-2848	Your Environment **3476**
1745-2864	Health & Safety @ Work **6677**
1745-2899	World Grain Markets Report **276**
1745-2902	World Grain Markets Report Online *see* 1745-2899 **276**
1745-2937	Potato Processing International **3660**
1745-2961	Worshipful Company of Goldsmith's. Technical Report **4570**
1745-297X	*see* 1745-2961 **4570**
1745-2988	*see* 1745-2961 **4570**
1745-3011	*see* 1501-7419 **4069**
1745-3046	Foodservice Director **3643**
1745-3054	Journal of Visual Communication in Medicine **5655**
1745-3062	Journal of Visual Communication in Medicine (Online) **5655**
1745-3127	Agenda for Local Economic Development† **8928**
1745-3143	International Journal of Enterprise Systems Integration and Interoperability **1757**
1745-3151	*see* 1745-3143 **1757**
1745-316X	Scrapbook Magic **4346**
1745-3194	International Journal of Vehicle Performance **8586**
1745-3208	*see* 1745-3194 **8586**
1745-3216	International Journal of Radio Frequency Identification Technology and Applications **2359**
1745-3224	*see* 1745-3216 **2359**
1745-3232	International Journal of Intelligent Enterprise **1128**
1745-3240	*see* 1745-3232 **1128**
1745-3259	Country Report. Israel **1456**
1745-3372	L N G Focus **6776**
1745-3380	*see* 1745-3372 **6776**
1745-3410	British Origami **532**
1745-350X	*see* 1362-3435 **4585**
1745-3518	The Matron **2161**
1745-3534	Web Designer **2568**
1745-3542	Advances in Hospitality and Leisure **8681**
1745-3585	Golf Course Architecture **443**
1745-364X	Diplo Magazine **5214**
1745-3674	Acta Orthopaedica (Print) **6054**
1745-3682	Acta Orthopaedica (Online) **6054**
1745-3690	Acta Orthopaedica. Supplementum (Print Edition) **6054**
1745-3704	Acta Orthopaedica. Supplementum (Online Edition) **6054**
1745-3739	I D S Pay Report **1686**
1745-3755	*see* 1571-0882 **437**
1745-3771	Energy in East Europe (Online) **3158**
1745-3798	Bookselling Essentials **7555**
1745-3836	Advances in Electronics Manufacturing Technology†
1745-3925	Royal Astronomical Society. Monthly Notices. Letters (Print)†
1745-3933	Royal Astronomical Society. Monthly Notices. Letters (Online) **580**
1745-3984	*see* 0274-838X **2872**
1745-3992	*see* 0731-1745 **2850**
1745-4298	Accommodation Management Buyers Guide **4351**
1745-4360	Journal of eLiteracy **5020**
1745-4468	Acoustic **6542**
1745-4484	Map **504**
1745-4506	Foodservice Research International (Online Edition) *changed to* 1748-0159 **3651**
1745-4514	*see* 0145-8884 **3650**
1745-4522	*see* 1065-7258 **3650**
1745-4530	*see* 0145-8876 **3650**
1745-4549	*see* 0145-8892 **3650**
1745-4557	*see* 0146-9428 **3651**
1745-4565	*see* 0149-6085 **3651**
1745-4573	*see* 1046-0756 **3651**
1745-4581	*see* 1060-3999 **890**
1745-459X	*see* 0887-8250 **6157**
1745-4603	*see* 0022-4901 **3652**
1745-4611	Structured Products **1654**
1745-462X	*see* 1745-4611 **1654**
1745-4700	4 x 4 & M P V Driver **8613**
1745-4824	Feedback (Wembley) **2321**
1745-4832	International Journal of Art Therapy **6110**
1745-4840	*see* 1745-4832 **6110**
1745-493X	*see* 1523-2409 **1827**
1745-4980	Sport and Exercise Psychology Review **7409**
1745-4999	Research in Comparative and International Education **3015**
1745-5014	Scottish Review of Books **5238**
1745-5030	Waves in Random and Complex Media **7046**
1745-5049	Waves in Random and Complex Media (Online) **7046**
1745-5057	Women's Health (London, 2005) **8849**
1745-5065	*see* 1745-5057 **8849**
1745-509X	Aging Health **4039**
1745-5103	*see* 1745-509X **4039**
1745-5111	Pediatric Health **6101**
1745-512X	*see* 1745-5111 **6101**
1745-5170	*see* 1355-8358 **7690**
1745-5189	*see* 0966-7350 **8896**
1745-5197	*see* 1476-8690 **7653**
1745-5200	*see* 1476-993X **7636**
1745-5219	*see* 0020-157X **7800**
1745-5227	*see* 1477-8351 **7622**
1745-5235	*see* 0953-9468 **7685**
1745-5243	*see* 1740-4681 **6929**
1745-5251	*see* 0966-7369 **7762**
1745-526X	*see* 0033-6882 **5164**
1745-5278	*see* 1740-3553 **7762**
1745-5286	*see* 0951-8207 **7653**
1745-5294	*see* 0142-064X **7653**
1745-5308	*see* 0014-5246 **7642**
1745-5316	*see* 1744-1366 **7639**
1745-5332	Fun to Learn - Bag-o-Fun Magazine **2189**
1745-5391	*see* 1002-0071 **7900**
1745-5405	Light & Easy **4363**
1745-5413	The Quarterly Global Chrome Review **6330**
1745-5448	D A T A Practice **3057**
1745-5456	Fairplay **8643**
1745-5642	*see* 1090-1027 **2990**
1745-5693	The Beany **477**
1745-5731	International Journal of Applied Training and Development **1755**
1745-574X	International Journal of Applied International Management **1755**
1745-5758	Imaging and Machine Vision Europe **3367**
1745-5782	S C O N U L Focus **5059**
1745-5790	*see* 1745-5782 **5059**
1745-5855	Construction Products (London) **998**
1745-5863	Geographical Research **4011**
1745-5871	*see* 1745-5863 **4011**
1745-5898	Machinery World **5456**
1745-5944	PrintMedia Management **7570**
1745-5960	P C Upgrade *changed to* 1746-5028 **2413**
1745-5995	Truck Trader *changed to* 1745-624X **8677**
1745-6061	Country Report. Ethiopia **1454**
1745-6088	Country Report. Tanzania **1462**
1745-610X	Country Report. Mauritius **1458**
1745-6118	Country Report. Trinidad & Tobago **1463**
1745-6134	Country Report. Laos **1457**
1745-6142	Country Report. Cambodia **1451**
1745-6150	Biology Direct **660**
1745-6215	Trials **5801**
1745-624X	Truck & Plant Trader **8677**
1745-6320	Policy World **8062**
1745-6347	R I B A Sector Review. Government and Public **455**
1745-6355	Airline Yearbook (Year) **8536**
1745-641X	Work Organisation, Labour & Globalisation **1715**
1745-6436	International Journal of Vehicle Systems Modelling and Testing **8586**
1745-6444	*see* 1745-6436 **8586**
1745-6452	Journal of Banking Regulation **1360**
1745-6495	Crosswords (Redhill, 2005)
1745-6509	Clutter **2183**
1745-6541	An Essex Wedding **5556**
1745-655X	*see* 0197-5897 **7529**
1745-6584	*see* 0017-467X **2794**
1745-6592	*see* 1069-3629 **2794**
1745-6606	*see* 0022-0078 **2639**
1745-6614	*see* 1052-6773 **6028**
1745-6622	*see* 1078-1196 **1360**
1745-6673	Journal of Occupational Medicine and Toxicology (London) **5653**
1745-6681	R I H S C. Working Papers on Community Engagement **8127**
1745-669X	*see* 1745-6681 **8127**
1745-6819	Plastic Packaging Innovation News **6714**
1745-6916	Perspectives on Psychological Science **7390**
1745-6924	*see* 1745-6916 **7390**
1745-7238	China Law Review† **8941**
1745-7254	*see* 1671-4083 **6818**
1745-7262	*see* 1008-682X **5579**
1745-7270	*see* 1672-9145 **721**
1745-7289	Journal of Elections, Public Opinion, and Parties **7147**
1745-7297	*see* 1745-7289 **7147**
1745-7300	International Journal of Injury Control and Safety Promotion **2638**
1745-7319	*see* 1745-7300 **2638**
1745-7491	Freehouse Owner **4386**
1745-7564	The Hiltonian **5305**
1745-7580	Immunome Research **887**
1745-7599	*see* 1041-2972 **5951**
1745-7645	International Journal of Operational Research **1760**
1745-7653	*see* 1745-7645 **1760**

ISSN

1747-9541 International Journal of Sports Science and Coaching **8180**
1747-9681 *see* 0265-2897 **7700**
1747-9746 Undergraduate Courses & Funding Guide **2962**
1747-9789 Communities Today†
1747-9800 Independent Nurse **5961**
1747-9886 The British Journal of Leadership in Public Services *changed to* 1754-8187 **7447**
1747-9894 International Journal of Migration, Health and Social Care **8047**
1747-9924 Key Note Market Report: The Chemical Industry **3249**
1747-9959 Dentistry Scotland **5842**
1747-9967 Key Note Market Assessment. Pensions **1892**
1747-9975 The lawyer. The hot 100 *see* 0953-7902 **4717**
1747-9991 Philosophy Compass **6943**
1748-0035 Anaesthesia Product News **5768**
1748-0043 Tide Tables **8663**
1748-006X Institution of Mechanical Engineers. Proceedings. Part O: Journal of Risk and Reliability **3199**
1748-0078 *see* 1748-006X **3199**
1748-0094 Hong Kong Legends **6503**
1748-0116 Romantic Textualities **5364**
1748-0132 Nano Today **750**
1748-0140 Journal of Foodservice (Print Edition) **3651**
1748-0159 Journal of Foodservice (Online Edition) **3651**
1748-0221 Journal of Instrumentation **4488**
1748-0248 I E E Proceedings - Intelligent Transport Systems *changed to* 1751-956X **8498**
1748-0264 Financial Reporting Council. Annual Report **1288**
1748-0272 Wood Material Science and Engineering **3718**
1748-0280 *see* 1748-0272 **3718**
1748-0329 The Journal of Viral Entry **5821**
1748-0361 *see* 0890-765X **5654**
1748-0485 The International Communication Gazette **2326**
1748-0493 The International Communication Gazette (Online) **2326**
1748-0507 Annual Business Economic and Political Review. Algeria *see* 1755-2737 **1884**
1748-0574 Carpet & Flooring Review **4554**
1748-0612 Methodological Innovations Online **7985**
1748-0647 The Pinsent Masons Company Guide **1375**
1748-0671 International Journal of System of Systems Engineering **3202**
1748-068X *see* 1748-0671 **3202**
1748-0698 International Journal of Signal and Imaging Systems Engineering **3321**
1748-0701 *see* 1748-0698 **3321**
1748-071X Classics Monthly **8575**
1748-0736 B F I Film Handbook (Year) **6490**
1748-0817 European Rail Timetable **8495**
1748-0825 Investment & Savings Handbook **1632**
1748-0833 Natural Health & Beauty **6993**
1748-085X Electrical Products and Applications **3303**
1748-0876 Pig Market Trends **296**
1748-0884 *see* 1748-0876 **296**
1748-0922 *see* 0319-485X **7699**
1748-0930 International Journal of Mining, Reclamation and Environment **6466**
1748-0949 *see* 1748-0930 **6466**
1748-0981 I D S Pensions Bulletin **1686**
1748-1074 International Journal of Jaina Studies **7736**
1748-1090 *see* 0074-9664 **948**
1748-1104 The Coaching Psychologist **7346**
1748-1147 Immigration Practitioners Bulletin **4849**
1748-1201 The Greenhouse Yearbook & Buyer's Guide **3734**
1748-121X *see* 0261-3875 **4720**
1748-1244 Imagine **6503**
1748-1252 International Journal of Enterprise Network Management **1757**
1748-1260 *see* 1748-1252 **1757**
1748-1279 International Journal of Sensor Networks **2499**
1748-1287 *see* 1748-1279 **2499**
1748-1317 International Journal of Low-Carbon Technologies **3443**
1748-1325 *see* 1748-1317 **3443**
1748-135X Policy & Practice **1603**
1748-1414 New Bulletin (London) **4068**
1748-1422 Readers' Review *changed to* 1752-9433 **7573**
1748-1465 *see* 0957-2724 **9**
1748-1473 North West plc. **2021**
1748-1708 Acta Physiologica (Print) **918**
1748-1716 Acta Physiologica (Online) **918**
1748-2321 Progress in Neurotherapeutics and Neuropsychopharmacology **6174**
1748-233X *see* 1748-2321 **6174**
1748-2410 Captive & A R T Review *changed to* 1757-1251 **4498**
1748-250X Jane's Unmanned Aerial Vehicles and Targets **63**
1748-2518 Jane's World Airlines **8547**
1748-2526 Jane's World Air Forces **6428**
1748-2534 Jane's Aero-Engines **62**
1748-2542 Jane's Helicopter Markets and Systems **62**
1748-2550 Jane's Marine Propulsion **8648**
1748-2569 Jane's Electronic Mission Aircraft **62**
1748-2577 Jane's Amphibious and Special Forces **6426**
1748-2585 Jane's World Insurgency and Terrorism **2678**
1748-2593 Jane's World Defence Industry **1131**
1748-2607 Jane's World Armies **6428**
1748-2623 International Journal of Qualitative Studies on Health and Well-Being **5639**
1748-2631 *see* 1748-2623 **5639**
1748-2682 Quick123 **3968**
1748-2747 *see* 1477-6456 **2249**
1748-2763 Studies in International Financial, Economic and Technology Law **4941**
1748-2798 Journal of Children and Media **8112**
1748-2801 *see* 1748-2798 **8112**
1748-2828 I D S Employment Law Brief **1685**
1748-2852 Learning Disability Bulletin **6158**
1748-2895 G Q Style **2255**
1748-2909 Fall Line Skiing **8172**
1748-2941 Acute Cardiac Care (Print Edition) **5775**
1748-295X Acute Cardiac Care (Online Edition) **5775**
1748-2968 Amyotrophic Lateral Sclerosis **6122**
1748-2976 Scandinavian Journal of Food and Nutrition *changed to* 1654-6628 **6659**
1748-2992 The International Journal of Meteorology **6358**
1748-3018 Journal of Algorithms & Computational Technology **5500**
1748-3026 *see* 1748-3018 **5500**
1748-3050 Journal of Design Research **8429**
1748-3085 Mining (London, 2005) **6472**
1748-3093 *see* 1748-3085 **6472**
1748-3107 Disability and Rehabilitation: Assistive Technology **6108**
1748-3115 *see* 1748-3107 **6108**
1748-3131 *see* 1832-8105 **1438**
1748-3182 Bioinspiration & Biomimetics **747**
1748-3190 *see* 1748-3182 **747**
1748-331X Smart Life International **4562**
1748-3328 Journal of Arabic and Islamic Studies (Print Edition) **5132**
1748-3387 Nature Nanotechnology **7028**
1748-3395 *see* 1748-3387 **7028**
1748-3492 Grove Youth Series **7759**
1748-3506 Digital Video Techniques **2401**
1748-3530 Power Electronics Europe **3111**
1748-3565 C International Photo Magazine (English-Chinese Edition) **6965**
1748-3654 The Health and Social Care Yearbook **7521**
1748-3689 *see* 1479-117X **3432**
1748-3700 *see* 1479-1196 **3432**
1748-3719 *see* 1479-120X **3432**
1748-3727 Nineteenth Century Theatre and Film **8474**
1748-3735 International Journal of Older People Nursing **5962**
1748-3743 *see* 1748-3735 **5962**
1748-4472 China Telecommunications Report **2315**
1748-4618 The Israel Telecommunications Report **2328**
1748-4995 Annals of Actuarial Science **4492**
1748-5002 *see* 1748-4995 **4492**
1748-5037 International Journal of Industrial and Systems Engineering **3368**
1748-5045 *see* 1748-5037 **3368**
1748-5053 Dirt M X Magazine **8258**
1748-5088 Spirit of the Season **7818**
1748-5096 *see* 1748-5088 **7818**
1748-5177 Streetwise Confidential **1844**
1748-5185 Pool & Spa Industry **8329**
1748-5193 Pool & Spa Lifestyle **8329**
1748-5207 International Public Policy Review **7144**
1748-5266 Computer Video Editing† **8942**
1748-5290 Maintenance & Asset Management **3209**
1748-5304 Banking Automation Bulletin **1317**
1748-5312 R W A Friends Magazine **514**
1748-5363 Beautiful Cards **4329**
1748-538X Journal of Scottish Historical Studies **7980**
1748-541X Public Affairs News **7461**
1748-5436 Ultimate D V D Solo **6516**
1748-5452 Animal Defender & Campaigner **317**
1748-5460 *see* 0022-2151 **6081**
1748-5487 GEO (Godmanchester) **4037**
1748-5495 Taste Cornwall Magazine *see* 1362-5845 **8721**
1748-5533 Academy Exchange **2965**
1748-5541 *see* 1748-5533 **2965**
1748-5592 Therapy Weekly†
1748-5622 Total Sudoku
1748-5673 International Journal of Data Mining and Bioinformatics **2546**
1748-5681 *see* 1748-5673 **2546**
1748-569X International Journal of Internet Technology and Secured Transactions **2559**
1748-5703 *see* 1748-569X **2559**
1748-5711 International Journal of Machining and Machinability of Materials **5453**
1748-572X *see* 1748-5711 **5453**
1748-5770 News. Arab Horse Society **8295**
1748-5800 U K - Ability Magazine **4070**
1748-5819 *see* 0740-770X **8484**
1748-5827 *see* 0022-4510 **8801**
1748-5835 Reeds Oki Nautical Almanac *changed to* 1753-139X **8658**
1748-5851 *see* 1125-0003 **949**
1748-5878 Poetry Nottingham **5431**
1748-5886 PubChef **4396**
1748-5894 Hedge Fund Manager **1628**
1748-5908 Implementation Science **5633**
1748-5959 *see* 0018-2680 **2864**
1748-5967 *see* 1738-2297 **844**
1748-5975 Fulfilment & e.logistics **1818**
1748-5983 Regulation & Governance **4767**
1748-5991 *see* 1748-5983 **4767**
1748-6025 Geomechanics and Geoengineering **3267**
1748-6033 *see* 1748-6025 **3267**
1748-6041 Biomedical Materials (Bristol) **5586**
1748-605X *see* 1748-6041 **5586**
1748-6173 R T E House Hunters in the Sun **7606**
1748-6181 *see* 0075-1634 **5311**
1748-619X *see* 0261-4340 **4234**
1748-6203 Bank of England. Monetary Policy Committee. External M P C Unit. Discussion Paper (No.) **1314**
1748-6297 Digital Battlespace **6419**
1748-6327 The P E File **3075**
1748-6467 Book Trusted News **2180**
1748-6483 Aesthetic & Implant Dentistry *changed to* 1754-159X **5847**
1748-6483 Aesthetic & Implant Dentistry *changed to* 1754-1581 **5833**
1748-6645 Journal of Neuropsychology **6154**
1748-6653 *see* 1748-6645 **6154**
1748-670X Computational and Mathematical Methods in Medicine **5599**
1748-6718 *see* 1748-670X **5599**
1748-6815 Journal of Plastic, Reconstructive & Aesthetic Surgery (Print Edition) **6249**
1748-6823 Fertilizer Industry Directory **230**
1748-6831 Journal of Comparative Social Welfare **8049**
1748-684X *see* 1748-6831 **8049**
1748-6858 *see* 0034-6705 **7178**
1748-6866 Florida & Caribbean **8703**
1748-6874 Australia & New Zealand **8684**
1748-6912 Environment Review (Edinburgh) **3422**
1748-6947 Link-up **5969**
1748-6963 *see* 1743-5889 **5683**
1748-6971 *see* 1479-6708 **6142**
1748-7005 American Journal of Roentgenology (Chinese Selected Articles Edition) **6192**
1748-7048 Stroke (Selected Articles Edition) *see* 0039-2499 **5800**
1748-7161 Scoliosis **6072**
1748-717X Radiation Oncology **6033**
1748-7188 Algorithms for Molecular Biology **862**
1748-720X *see* 1073-1105 **4703**
1748-7285 A P S C C Yearbook **2311**
1748-7307 *see* 1748-7285 **2311**
1748-7331 Leonardo Supplemental Issue *see* 0961-1215 **6584**
1748-7331 Leonardo Supplemental Issue *see* 0024-094X **502**
1748-7382 *see* 1354-8565 **2379**
1748-7420 Mayfair Summer Special (Year) **6295**
1748-7625 Education Parliamentary Monitor (Online) *see* 1366-302X **2848**
1748-765X D & B Business Register. Glasgow & South of Scotland **1982**
1748-7668 D & B Business Register. Edinburgh & North of Scotland **1982**
1748-7692 *see* 0824-0469 **955**
1748-7706 C P D in Practice **5837**
1748-7714 Tripscope Newsletter **8769**
1748-7781 Independent Financial Advisors **1353**
1748-7811 Journal of Hellenic Religion **2236**
1748-7838 *see* 1001-0602 **665**
1748-7846 Therapy Today **7412**
1748-7870 Journal of Economic Policy Reform **1765**
1748-7889 Journal of Economic Policy Reform (Online) **1765**
1748-7900 C I M A Insight **1283**
1748-7919 Escort Swingmag.co.uk **6289**
1748-8001 D & B Business Register. Somerset, Dorset, Bath & Bristol **1983**
1748-8028 He@lthychurch.mag.uk **7647**
1748-8036 D & B Business Register. Manchester & Merseyside *changed to* 1755-3369 **1982**
1748-8044 D & B Business Register. South Yorkshire, East Yorkshire & North East Lincolnshire **1983**
1748-8117 Radio User **2363**
1748-8141 Biology Image Library **660**
1748-8168 Preventive Dentistry **5861**
1748-8176 *see* 0017-8969 **7522**
1748-8230 Dierenvriendjes
1748-8249 Private Laboratory **5861**
1748-8303 O P I Policy Briefs **8060**
1748-8311 O P I Issues Notes **8060**
1748-8435 Datasheet **389**
1748-8451 Airframer **45**
1748-8567 *see* 0967-0335 **2102**
1748-8575 Architect's Journal Specification **429**
1748-8583 *see* 0954-5395 **1864**
1748-8591 Girl Talk Extra **2190**
1748-8605 *see* 0301-7605 **7127**
1748-8613 *see* 1748-8621 **342**
1748-8621 Identity, Self & Symbolism **342**
1748-8753 Sumdoku
1748-880X *see* 0007-1285 **6193**
1748-8818 *see* 0965-6812 **6198**
1748-8826 Italy Pharmaceuticals & Healthcare Report **6851**
1748-8842 Aircraft Engineering and Aerospace Technology **45**
1748-8869 C International Photo Magazine (Spanish-Japanese Edition) **6965**
1748-8885 International Journal of Speech, Language and the Law **4695**
1748-8893 *see* 1748-8885 **4695**
1748-8907 Primary Leadership Today *changed to* 2040-1310 **2909**
1748-8923 Citizenship News **7116**
1748-8931 *see* 1748-8923 **7116**
1748-8958 Criminology & Criminal Justice (Print) **2650**
1748-8966 *see* 1748-8958 **2650**
1748-8982 Real People **3870**
1748-8990 Designer (Middle East Edition) **4538**
1748-9024 Life & Pensions **1637**
1748-9032 *see* 1748-9024 **1637**
1748-9105 The L I P **8117**
1748-913X The Chronicle (Buckhurst Hill) **2265**
1748-9148 The Rothschild Archive **3781**
1748-9156 *see* 1748-9148 **3781**
1748-9164 The Reuter Lecture **5360**
1748-9172 European Retail Finance **1340**
1748-9180 *see* 0262-2750 **5298**
1748-9199 Spectrum (London) **6703**
1748-9202 Mint (London) **6701**
1748-9237 Energy Materials **3132**
1748-9245 *see* 1748-9237 **3132**
1748-930X Imagine F X **2487**
1748-9326 Environmental Research Letters **3428**
1748-9377 Cost of Living Ireland Report **1222**
1748-9385 U K Writer **5391**
1748-944X Entertainment and Sports Law Journal **4666**
1748-9466 *see* 1749-088X **1794**
1748-9474 Borthwick Texts and Studies **4206**
1748-9482 Key Skills Support Programme News **3069**
1748-9539 Evidence-Based Communication Assessment and Intervention **5612**
1748-9547 *see* 1748-9539 **5612**
1748-961X Country Report. Mali **1458**
1748-9628 Arts News **8465**
1748-9636 Country Report. Burkina Faso **1451**
1748-9725 Journal of Location Based Services **2500**
1748-9733 *see* 1748-9725 **2500**
1748-9741 Timber Building **1052**
1748-975X Argentina Autos Report **8556**
1748-9768 Australia Autos Reports **8556**
1748-9776 Bahrain Autos Report **8568**
1748-9784 Brazil Autos Report **8570**
1748-9792 Bulgaria Autos Report **8570**

ISSN

1749-4923 Corporate Scotland 1087
1749-4931 Corporate Northern Ireland 1087
1749-494X T S W Holistic Health & Medicine 315
1749-4958 T S W Development & Embryology 707
1749-5008 Spark (London) 4427
1749-5016 Social Cognitive and Affective Neuroscience (Print)† 8988
1749-5024 Social Cognitive and Affective Neuroscience (Online) 6186
1749-5032 Corpora 5108
1749-5040 International Rental News 1890
1749-5059 see 1749-5040 1890
1749-5075 University of Surrey. Department of Economics. Discussion Papers in Economics (Online) 1189
1749-5083 E I P R Practice Series see 0142-0461 6749
1749-5148 International Heat Treatment and Surface Engineering 6316
1749-5156 see 1749-5148 6316
1749-5180 Shopping Centre Ireland 1432
1749-5296 Climate Change Management. e-Bulletin 3485
1749-5318 see 1473-7604 2057
1749-5326 see 0013-1350 2061
1749-5393 International Futures & Options Databook (Online) 1631
1749-5458 I S B I Schools† 8963
1749-5466 Campaign News (Online) 8029
1749-5474 U K Economic Brief (Online) 1522
1749-5482 Journal of Primehe 5654
1749-5504 D & B Business Register. Dublin 1982
1749-5512 D & B Business Register. Leinster 1982
1749-5571 European Plastics and Rubber Directory 7092
1749-558X Hospice and Palliative Care Directory 4099
1749-5598 Journal of Rural Enterprise and Management 128
1749-5652 Kingston University Research & Innovation Reports 2563
1749-5679 International Political Sociology 8110
1749-5687 see 1749-5679 8110
1749-5717 RealAdviser 1647
1749-5725 Connect (Lympstone) 3967
1749-5733 The U K Consumer Marketplace (Year)† 8995
1749-5784 Public Sector Review (Macclesfield) 7463
1749-5954 The Thirsk Weekly News 3968
1749-5962 The Easingwold Advertiser and Weekly News 3967
1749-5989 Dental Protection Ltd. Annual Review 5841
1749-5997 The Epoch Times (UK Edition) 3967
1749-6004 O see 0029-7712 3869
1749-6020 Critical Studies in Television 2379
1749-6039 see 1749-6020 2379
1749-6055 British Journal of Home Healthcare 4089
1749-6071 Bank of England. Centre for Central Banking Studies. Prospectus 1314
1749-608X see 1749-6071 1314
1749-6098 School Health 3031
1749-6101 Cardiff Economics Working Papers 1080
1749-611X Global Arbitration Review 4869
1749-6160 Editors Media Directories. Vol.4: Consumer & Leisure Magazines 1991
1749-6209 Plant Viruses 813
1749-625X see 0307-0131 4208
1749-6268 see 1741-6124 6411
1749-6276 see 1366-0691 5332
1749-6284 see 0959-3683 5289
1749-6292 see 0305-5477 460
1749-6306 see 0590-8876 2253
1749-6314 see 1461-4103 392
1749-6322 see 0305-8034 4241
1749-6497 Inside United 8236
1749-6500 Dynamic Soil, Dynamic Plant 228
1749-6535 Ethics and Social Welfare 8039
1749-6543 see 1749-6535 8039
1749-6632 see 0077-8923 7892
1749-6772 The Journal of Modern Craft 499
1749-6780 see 1749-6772 499
1749-6802 Country Report. Namibia 1458
1749-6896 Education, Knowledge & Economy 2848
1749-690X see 1749-6896 2848
1749-6942 Canals & Rivers 8274
1749-6977 Intellectual History Review 4147
1749-6985 see 1749-6977 4147
1749-7108 C L S Briefings 8091
1749-7116 see 1749-7108 8091
1749-7140 Food 3637
1749-7191 Vortex 5413
1749-7221 Journal of Brachial Plexus and Peripheral Nerve Injury 6150
1749-723X Hanburyana 792
1749-7345 see 0893-8849 2821
1749-7426 Risk Management Module 5864
1749-7701 International Journal of Urological Nursing 5962
1749-771X see 1749-7701 5962
1749-7728 Education for Chemical Engineers 3242
1749-7787 Cell Signalling Biology 665
1749-7833 Who's Who Legal U S A. Corporate Governance 4883
1749-785X International Journal of Surface Science and Engineering 3348
1749-7868 see 1749-785X 3348
1749-7884 Editors Media Directories. Vol.6: Freelancers and Writers' Guilds 1991
1749-7892 Biopack News 6708
1749-7922 World Journal of Emergency Surgery 6262
1749-7930 Hong Kong Family Law Reports 4911
1749-799X Journal of Orthopaedic Surgery and Research 6065
1749-8023 International Journal of Magnetic Resonance Imaging 6198
1749-8031 see 1749-8023 6198
1749-8090 Journal of Cardiothoracic Surgery 6247
1749-8104 Neural Development 6163
1749-8155 Reviews in History 4158
1749-8171 Religion Compass 7674
1749-818X Language and Linguistics Compass 5139
1749-8198 Geography Compass 4012
1749-8244 Super Six 2215
1749-8295 Kick (London) 2197
1749-8325 Sex Talk 973
1749-8341 see 1749-8430 5476
1749-8430 British Society for the History of Mathematics. Bulletin 5476
1749-8465 Destination France 8311
1749-8473 W P T Poker 8215
1749-8503 InAVate 2325
1749-8511 see 1749-8503 2325
1749-8546 Chinese Medicine 5594
1749-8716 Particip@tions 8125
1749-8724 Asiaint's China Watch Monthly Review 1062
1749-8732 see 1749-8724 1062
1749-8783 Food Pack India 3640
1749-8791 Cosmetics & Pharma Pack India 593
1749-8805 Beverage Pack India 599
1749-8902 Insight (London, 2006) 4082
1749-8929 see 1749-8902 4082
1749-8937 see 1749-8902 4082
1749-8945 see 1749-8902 4082
1749-8988 Icon News 2614
1749-8996 Desertification Indicator System For Medeterranean Europe 1091
1749-9003 Sudoku Pro
1749-9054 Country Report. Jamaica 1456
1749-9135 see 1368-5562 1314
1749-9143 Findings (York) 4410
1749-9151 International Journal of Teaching and Case Studies 2871
1749-916X see 1749-9151 2871
1749-9186 Digital Printer 7329
1749-9216 Journal of Business Continuity & Emergency Planning 1764
1749-9224 see 1749-9216 1764
1749-9275 World Business† 8999
1749-9321 Country Profile. Belize† 8944
1749-933X Country Report. Dominican Republic 1453
1749-9488 Mobile Choice for Business 2369
1749-9518 Georisk 2743
1749-9526 see 1749-9518 2743
1749-9542 Emigrate New Zealand 8700
1749-9550 Emigrate Australia 8700
1749-9577 Emigrate Canada 8700
1749-9585 Emigrate South Africa 8700
1749-9593 Emigrate America 8700
1749-9607 Property France 7605
1749-9755 Cultural Sociology 8097
1749-9763 see 1749-9755 8097
1749-9771 Forum (Edinburgh) 490
1750-0028 International Journal of Intercultural Information Management 2547
1750-0036 see 1750-0028 2547
1750-0044 Engineering Education 3189
1750-0052 see 1750-0044 3189
1750-0079 European Environment & Packaging Law Weekly 3506
1750-0087 see 1750-0079 3506
1750-0095 see 0264-2875 2684
1750-0109 see 1744-1854 5277
1750-0117 see 1742-3600 6916
1750-0125 see 1474-9475 7648
1750-0133 see 1355-5502 4236
1750-015X RoboZak 2586
1750-0176 see 0264-8334 5349
1750-0184 see 0001-9720 4172
1750-0192 see 1354-991X 5364
1750-0206 see 0264-2824 4155
1750-0214 see 0968-1361 5188
1750-0222 see 0036-9241 4160
1750-0230 see 1354-9901 7686
1750-0443 Micro and Nano Letters 3210
1750-0478 The International Journal of Regional and Local Studies 4232
1750-0486 Hurlingham 8235
1750-0494 see 1750-0486 8235
1750-0567 Covert Policing Review 2676
1750-0591 International Journal of Manufacturing Research 3382
1750-0605 see 1750-0591 3382
1750-0621 Cardiometabolic Risk and Weight Management 5780
1750-0664 International Journal of Electronic Customer Relationship Management 1756
1750-0672 see 1750-0664 1756
1750-0680 Carbon Balance and Management 6348
1750-0699 The Journal of Mental Health Workforce Development changed to 1755-6228 6152
1750-0729 Asiaint's China Watch Weekly Briefing 1062
1750-0753 Retinoids & Other Treatments in Clinical Dermatology changed to 1750-306X 5873
1750-0796 B a T M L Publications 935
1750-080X Eastern Eye Scotland 3531
1750-0818 see 1750-080X 3531
1750-0826 Homes 24 7593
1750-0974 The Yorkshire and Humber Regional Review 8017
1750-0982 Journal of Contemporary Politics 7146
1750-0990 see 1750-0982 7146
1750-1024 Construction Bulletin changed to 1752-8720 1031
1750-1059 Panel & System Building 3327
1750-1164 Annals of Surgical Innovation and Research 6236
1750-1172 Orphanet Journal of Rare Diseases 5948
1750-1210 The Guide to Scotland's 6 Cities 8717
1750-1229 Innovation in Language Learning and Teaching 5127
1750-1237 see 1750-1229 5127
1750-1245 Word Structure 5195
1750-1253 I H M F News 5816
1750-1261 see 1750-1253 5816
1750-127X British Baker Directory 3672
1750-1288 Meat Trades Journal Directory (Year) 3656
1750-1326 Molecular Neurodegeneration 6161
1750-1407 Policy and Practice in Health and Social Care 5697
1750-1601 Wine & Spirit 612
1750-1679 Journal of Care Services Management 4103
1750-1687 see 1750-1679 4103
1750-1733 The Network 8506
1750-1784 World Communications Regulation Report 2345
1750-1792 see 1750-1784 2345
1750-1806 Journal of Payments Strategy & Systems 1362
1750-1814 see 1750-1806 1362
1750-1849 see 1525-6995 5322
1750-1911 Epigenomics 6196
1750-192X see 1750-1911 6196
1750-1938 Journal of Airport Management 8547
1750-1946 see 1750-1938 8547
1750-1954 Papers on Surrealism 511
1750-2063 Total Konzai
1750-2071 see 1745-6452 1360
1750-208X see 1478-5315 1871
1750-2098 see 1479-1110 7597
1750-2144 Caucasus Business Forecast Report 1081
1750-2152 The Lithuania Business Forecast Report 1144
1750-2187 Journal of Molecular Signaling 924
1750-2217 Evangelical Review of Society and Politics 7735
1750-2225 see 1750-2217 7735
1750-2241 Deleuze Studies 5283
1750-2284 Global Plant Letters 791
1750-2292 Japanese Journal of Plant Science 795
1750-2330 International Clinical Trials 6849
1750-2403 ArtSEEN Journal 475
1750-2411 Brazilian Meat Monitor 281
1750-242X see 1750-2411 281
1750-2438 Dispersion Polymers 6717
1750-2446 English Heritage. Research News 4217
1750-2462 Handy Arrowords
1750-2519 C M E Journal. Radiology Update 6193
1750-2551 Wedding 5561
1750-256X Travolution 8769
1750-2624 Global Food Contact News 6710
1750-2640 Influenza and Other Respiratory Viruses 5817
1750-2659 see 1750-2640 5817
1750-2683 Food Manufacturing Efficiency 3640
1750-2691 see 1750-2683 3640
1750-2705 The Cambridge Classical Journal 2231
1750-2799 Nature Protocols (Online) 692
1750-2837 see 0358-5522 1549
1750-290X European Daily Carbon Markets 3134
1750-2942 Retro Ford 8601
1750-2977 Journal of Intervention and Statebuilding 7248
1750-2985 see 1750-2977 7248
1750-3000 The Maintenance Engineer 3388
1750-3027 Finance, Secured Lending changed to 1756-5855 1343
1750-306X Clinical Dermatology (London) 5873
1750-3132 Studies in Russian and Soviet Cinema 6514
1750-3159 Studies in Musical Theatre 8480
1750-3175 Studies in Australasian Cinema 6514
1750-323X Barbour Compendium 4532
1750-3264 AsPerceived 3967
1750-3280 Studies in Documentary Film 6514
1750-3426 Learn with Toybox
1750-3469 Psychology Review 7400
1750-3477 Your Sussex Wedding 5562
1750-3523 see 1758-1206 3200
1750-354X Asiaint's China Watch Quarterly Forecasts 1062
1750-3558 Foodies 3678
1750-3639 see 1015-6305 6127
1750-368X Studies in Pragmatics 5183
1750-3698 Bristol Review of Books 7556
1750-371X Project Control Professional 3371
1750-3736 Scottich Raptor Monitoring Report 914
1750-3752 The Containership Register (London, 2002) 8641
1750-3841 see 0022-1147 3651
1750-385X International Journal of Management in Education 3013
1750-3868 see 1750-385X 3013
1750-3906 Converging Media 2317
1750-3914 see 1750-3906 2317
1750-3930 The Communicator (Inverness) 2149
1750-3949 see 1750-3930 2149
1750-3973 Country Report. Cameroon 1451
1750-3981 The Sign Language Translator and Interpreter 5174
1750-399X The Interpreter and Translator Trainer 5130
1750-4015 Financial i 1344
1750-4023 Fish Update 8313
1750-4074 The Art of Rubber Stamping 470
1750-4090 International Journal of Tourism Policy 8723
1750-4104 see 1750-4090 8723
1750-4139 PrintBuyer changed to 1350-9829 7327
1750-4147 A I M Bulletin 1609
1750-4171 Loughborough University. Department of Economics. Discission Paper Series 1145
1750-4198 M I Pro 6586
1750-4279 Primary G & T Update 3045
1750-4317 Kemp News 4834
1750-4384 Action Learning News 3011
1750-4392 see 1750-4384 3011
1750-4554 African Journal of Business and Economic Research 1057
1750-4562 see 1750-4554 1057
1750-4589 Journal of Perioperative Practice 5967
1750-4635 Serbia and Montenegro changed to 1756-4344 8945
1750-4635 Serbia and Montenegro changed to 1756-4352 8946
1750-4686 see 1684-1360 8954
1750-4708 Negotiation and Conflict Management Research 8122
1750-4716 see 1750-4708 8122
1750-4732 Osteopathic Medicine and Primary Care 5806
1750-4740 Infocus Magazine 899
1750-4813 Discourse & Communication 2319
1750-4821 see 1750-4813 2319
1750-4880 Pregnancy, Baby & You 8880
1750-4902 Holocaust Studies 4146
1750-4910 Nurse Author and Editor (Online) 4581
1750-497X Multicultural Educational & Technology Journal 2888
1750-4996 Ace Tennis 8220
1750-5003 Bulgaria Information Technology Report see Business Monitor International. Information Technology Country Reports 2491
1750-5011 China Information Technology Report see Business Monitor International. Information Technology Country Reports 2491

ISSN

1751-2948 P E I Asia **1373**
1751-2964 *see* 1448-4528 **5322**
1751-2972 Journal of Digestive Diseases (Print) **5927**
1751-2980 Journal of Digestive Diseases (Online) **5927**
1751-3030 Philica **7898**
1751-3057 Journal of International and Intercultural Communication **8114**
1751-3065 *see* 1751-3057 **8114**
1751-309X Argus Freight **8639**
1751-3197 Pocket Phone Guides *see* 1365-4969 **2369**
1751-3227 International Journal of Information Systems and Management **2547**
1751-3235 *see* 1751-3227 **2547**
1751-3278 Norfolk Journal **4981**
1751-3286 Essex Magazine *changed to* 1753-6790 **5070**
1751-3294 Suffolk Journal **4983**
1751-3421 New Law Journal. Charities Appeals Supplement *see* 0306-6479 **4744**
1751-343X Tractor **214**
1751-3472 Journal of Mathematics and the Arts **5505**
1751-3480 *see* 1751-3472 **5505**
1751-3758 Journal of Biological Dynamics **681**
1751-3766 *see* 1751-3758 **681**
1751-3782 The Year in Lipid Disorders (Year) **5802**
1751-3804 Current Medical Literature. Pain Medicine **6058**
1751-3812 *see* 1463-1180 **4139**
1751-3901 Preview **512**
1751-391X NGamer **2478**
1751-3928 *see* 1344-1698 **2764**
1751-3952 The Zone **5200**
1751-4088 International Journal of Electric and Hybrid Vehicles **3159**
1751-4096 *see* 1751-4088 **3159**
1751-4185 Cooler Innovation **602**
1751-4193 The Soundtrack **6513**
1751-4207 *see* 1751-4193 **6513**
1751-4223 Institution of Civil Engineers. Proceedings. Energy **3138**
1751-4231 *see* 1751-4223 **3138**
1751-4258 Current Opinion in Supportive and Palliative Care **5602**
1751-4266 *see* 1751-4258 **5602**
1751-4304 Institution of Civil Engineers. Proceedings. Management, Procurement and Law **3271**
1751-4312 *see* 1751-4304 **3271**
1751-4339 Economic Focus **1562**
1751-4487 The Miniature Clock Collection **4568**
1751-4495 S P E E D **1381**
1751-4517 Photography and Culture **6974**
1751-4525 *see* 1751-4517 **6974**
1751-4584 n - Revolution **8189**
1751-4614 Iran Strategic Focus **1493**
1751-4622 Sahara Focus **1516**
1751-4649 Caspian Focus **1446**
1751-4673 Benedictine Culture **7785**
1751-469X R S P C A Science Group Review **321**
1751-4746 European Tax Service **1922**
1751-4762 The Golf Plus *changed to* 1751-4770 **8610**
1751-4770 V W Golf + **8610**
1751-4797 3 G Wireless Broadband **2346**
1751-4800 *see* 1751-4797 **2346**
1751-4819 Mobile Communications Europe **2333**
1751-4827 *see* 1751-4819 **2333**
1751-4851 Nursing for Women's Health **8847**
1751-486X *see* 1751-4851 **8847**
1751-4886 South AfricaHedge **1652**
1751-4894 *see* 1751-4886 **1652**
1751-4991 e - S P E N **6657**
1751-505X P Q E **4754**
1751-5114 T 3 Home **3114**
1751-5254 European Journal of Industrial Engineering **3366**
1751-5262 *see* 1751-5254 **3366**
1751-5270 Spider Man and Friends **2214**
1751-5300 Wear Valley Mercury **3968**
1751-5327 Benchmark of I T Spending (Year) **1880**
1751-5408 Uni **8270**
1751-5483 Wipes Innovation News **2244**
1751-5513 Oil Review Africa **6785**
1751-5521 International Journal of Laboratory Hematology (Print) **5938**
1751-553X International Journal of Laboratory Hematology (Online) **5938**
1751-5602 C I W M. the Journal for Waste & Resource Management Professionals **3504**
1751-5637 Business Strategy Series **1730**
1751-5645 *see* 1751-5637 **1730**
1751-570X Nonlinear Analysis: Hybrid Systems **2433**
1751-5793 Nature China **7889**
1751-5823 *see* 0306-7734 **8379**
1751-5831 Tribology (Leeds) **6335**
1751-584X *see* 1751-5831 **6335**
1751-5858 International Journal of Intelligent Information and Database Systems **2531**
1751-5866 *see* 1751-5858 **2531**
1751-5874 International Journal of Design Engineering **3201**
1751-5882 *see* 1751-5874 **3201**
1751-5947 The Bulletin **7749**
1751-6048 International Journal of Internet Manufacturing and Services **2559**
1751-6056 *see* 1751-6048 **2559**
1751-6129 National Council for Palliative Care. Information Exchange *changed to* 1755-7402 **5635**
1751-6153 Shopping Centre Parking **8511**
1751-6161 Journal of the Mechanical Behavior of Biomedical Materials **834**
1751-617X Research Africa **4177**
1751-6188 *see* 1751-617X **4177**
1751-6218 I G I V Insights & Viewpoints **5938**
1751-6234 Journal of Asian Public Policy **1133**
1751-6242 *see* 1751-6234 **1133**
1751-6323 The Big Red Book **1974**
1751-6404 Series on Advances in Bioinformatics and Computational Biology **826**
1751-6447 Afro-Asian Journal of Finance and Accounting **1279**
1751-6455 *see* 1751-6447 **1279**
1751-648X International Journal of Innovative Computing and Applications **2451**
1751-6498 *see* 1751-648X **2451**
1751-6528 International Journal of High Performance Systems Architecture **2467**
1751-6536 *see* 1751-6528 **2467**
1751-6552 *see* 0967-0335 **2102**
1751-6560 Environment (London, 2006) **3420**
1751-6579 *see* 1751-6560 **3420**
1751-6587 *see* 1751-6560 **3420**
1751-665X *see* 1470-2541 **4028**
1751-6714 30up **6302**
1751-6757 European Journal of International Management **1742**
1751-6765 *see* 1751-6757 **1742**
1751-679X Road Goods Vehicles Travelling to Mainland Europe (Online) **8529**
1751-6803 Ofcom Broadcast Bulletin **2387**
1751-6838 *see* 1469-0667 **2100**
1751-6943 Active Travel Cymru News **8253**
1751-6951 *see* 1751-6943 **8253**
1751-696X Time and Mind **420**
1751-6978 *see* 1751-696X **420**
1751-7044 Financial Stability Report **1345**
1751-7052 *see* 1751-7044 **1345**
1751-7087 Your Berks & Bucks Wedding **5562**
1751-7095 Your Surrey Wedding **5562**
1751-7117 *see* 0889-7204 **5798**
1751-7125 *see* 1540-9740 **8988**
1751-7133 *see* 1527-5299 **5783**
1751-7141 *see* 1520-037X **5798**
1751-715X *see* 1076-7460 **5776**
1751-7168 *see* 1541-9215 **5776**
1751-7176 *see* 1524-6175 **5793**
1751-7192 Green Chemistry Letters and Reviews **2062**
1751-7214 Obstetrics, Gynecology and Reproductive Medicine **6001**
1751-7222 Paediatrics and Child Health **6098**
1751-7257 Northern Golfer†
1751-7311 Animal **932**
1751-732X *see* 1751-7311 **932**
1751-7362 The I S M E Journal **887**
1751-7370 *see* 1751-7362 **887**
1751-7419 *see* 1362-704X **489**
1751-7427 *see* 1740-6315 **7969**
1751-7435 *see* 1743-2197 **7127**
1751-7443 *see* 1552-8014 **4358**
1751-7575 Enterprise Information Systems **2543**
1751-7583 *see* 1751-7575 **2543**
1751-7605 *see* 0951-7197 **975**
1751-7613 Geosynthetics International (Online) **8451**
1751-763X *see* 0024-9831 **1021**
1751-7648 *see* 1464-4177 **3283**
1751-7656 *see* 0016-8505 **3268**
1751-7664 *see* 1478-4637 **3270**
1751-7672 *see* 0965-089X **3270**
1751-7680 *see* 1478-4629 **3270**
1751-7699 *see* 0965-0903 **3271**
1751-7702 *see* 0965-0911 **3271**
1751-7710 *see* 0965-092X **3271**
1751-7729 *see* 1741-7589 **3271**
1751-7737 *see* 1741-7597 **3271**
1751-780X Hazardous Area International **3436**
1751-7818 *see* 1751-780X **3436**
1751-7834 Screen Decades **6512**
1751-7850 Health and Safety Newsletter **7521**
1751-7877 *see* 0162-9778 **4235**
1751-7885 Early Intervention in Psychiatry **6137**
1751-7893 *see* 1751-7885 **6137**
1751-7915 *see* Microbial Biotechnology **768**
1751-7931 Windows Vista **2600**
1751-7974 Journal of African Media Studies **8111**
1751-7990 The Journal of Gambling Business and Economics **1136**
1751-8008 *see* 1751-7990 **1136**
1751-8040 Place Branding and Public Diplomacy **32**
1751-8059 *see* 1751-8040 **32**
1751-8113 Journal of Physics A: Mathematical and Theoretical **7022**
1751-8121 *see* 1751-8113 **7022**
1751-8202 The Journal of Business and Retail Management Research **1764**
1751-8229 International Journal of Zizek Studies **8110**
1751-8253 *see* 1751-7192 **2062**
1751-8326 Economic & Labour Market Review **1676**
1751-8334 *see* 1751-8326 **1676**
1751-8342 *see* 1743-2200 **7662**
1751-8350 *see* 1475-9756 **8459**
1751-8369 *see* 0800-0395 **7898**
1751-8377 Contaminated Land Bulletin **3485**
1751-8393 National Horsemart **8295**
1751-8423 Developmental Neurorehabilitation **6108**
1751-8431 Developmental Neurorehabilitation (Online) *see* 1751-8423 **6108**
1751-8520 *see* 1476-8186 **2461**
1751-8539 *see* 0956-618X **7755**
1751-8563 *see* 1353-2618 **3271**
1751-858X I E T Circuits, Devices and Systems **3316**
1751-8598 *see* 1751-858X **3316**
1751-8601 I E T Computers and Digital Techniques **2540**
1751-861X *see* 1751-8601 **2540**
1751-8628 I E T Communications **3316**
1751-8636 *see* 1751-8628 **3316**
1751-8644 I E T Control Theory and Applications **2460**
1751-8652 *see* 1751-8644 **2460**
1751-8660 I E T Electric Power Applications **3317**
1751-8679 *see* 1751-8660 **3317**
1751-8687 I E T Generation, Transmission and Distribution **3317**
1751-8695 *see* 1751-8687 **3317**
1751-8709 I E T Information Security **3317**
1751-8717 *see* 1751-8709 **3317**
1751-8725 I E T Microwaves Antennas & Propagation **3317**
1751-8733 *see* 1751-8725 **3317**
1751-8741 I E T Nanobiotechnology **765**
1751-875X *see* 1751-8741 **765**
1751-8768 I E T Optoelectronics **7076**
1751-8776 *see* 1751-8768 **7076**
1751-8784 I E T Radar, Sonar and Navigation **3317**
1751-8792 *see* 1751-8784 **3317**
1751-8806 I E T Software **2590**
1751-8814 *see* 1751-8806 **2590**
1751-8822 I E T Science, Measurement and Technology **3318**
1751-8830 *see* 1751-8822 **3318**
1751-8849 I E T Systems Biology **825**
1751-8857 *see* 1751-8849 **825**
1751-8962 3 D Vis A Bulletin **529**
1751-8970 *see* 1751-8962 **529**
1751-9004 Social and Personality Psychology Compass **7408**
1751-9020 Sociology Compass **8138**
1751-908X *see* 1639-4488 **2744**
1751-9098 Air Transport **8535**
1751-911X International Journal of Electronic Security and Digital Forensics **2514**
1751-9128 *see* 1751-911X **2514**
1751-9136 The Yearbook of Consumer Law (Year) **2642**
1751-9152 Bad Idea **5259**
1751-9160 Annual Business Economic and Political Review. South Africa **1060**
1751-9179 Annual Business Economic and Political Review. Dubai **1060**
1751-9284 Global Sources Electronics **3100**
1751-9292 *see* 0020-8345 **7200**
1751-9322 Brit Chopper Magazine **8255**
1751-9330 *see* 1751-9322 **8255**
1751-9381 Aviation Intelligence **8538**
1751-939X Journal of Horror Studies **5444**
1751-9411 Journal of Arab & Muslim Media Research **8111**
1751-9489 Performance G T I French Cars **8598**
1751-9535 In the Know†
1751-956X I E T Intelligent Transport Systems **8498**
1751-9578 *see* 1751-956X **8498**
1751-9624 Kiteboard Pro World Tour Mag **8184**
1751-9632 I E T Computer Vision **3291**
1751-9640 *see* 1751-9632 **3291**
1751-9659 I E T Image Processing **3317**
1751-9667 *see* 1751-9659 **3317**
1751-9675 I E T Signal Processing **3318**
1751-9683 *see* 1751-9675 **3318**
1751-9721 *see* 0393-2729 **7245**
1751-973X Developments in Milling and Baking **179**
1751-9853 Aesthesis **1724**
1751-9861 *see* 1071-2089 **7369**
1751-9918 Primary Care Diabetes **5899**
1752-007X Learning Disability Today **4067**
1752-0118 *see* 0265-9883 **6128**
1752-0169 English Heritage Historical Review **4217**
1752-0215 What Video & High-Definition T V **2404**
1752-0223 Creative Beading & Jewellery Design **4333**
1752-0320 Edinburgh Bibliographical Society. Journal **624**
1752-0363 Biomarkers in Medicine **5585**
1752-0371 *see* 1752-0363 **5585**
1752-0401 *see* 0021-9118 **553**
1752-0452 International Journal of Economic Policy and Emerging Economies **1599**
1752-0460 *see* 1752-0452 **1599**
1752-0479 International Journal of Monetary Economics and Finance **1357**
1752-0487 *see* 1752-0479 **1357**
1752-0509 B M C Systems Biology **655**
1752-0533 InfoChem **2065**
1752-0541 *see* 1752-0533 **2065**
1752-0606 *see* 0194-472X **7376**
1752-0630 Mini Expert *see* 1362-7252 **8590**
1752-0665 Parent's Pocketbook **2165**
1752-0673 Alimentos y Bebidas Latinoamerica **3626**
1752-0681 Alimentos e Bebidas America Latina **3626**
1752-069X *see* 0966-6494 **5718**
1752-0738 *see* 1357-4175 **4256**
1752-0754 *see* 0311-5518 **6722**
1752-0762 *see* 1010-6049 **4008**
1752-0819 B C **1064**
1752-0843 Macroeconomics and Finance in Emerging Market Economies **1720**
1752-0851 *see* 1752-0843 **1720**
1752-0894 Nature Geoscience **2757**
1752-0908 *see* 1752-0894 **2757**
1752-0924 Emerald Management First **1226**
1752-0932 Active Sports and Bodywear **2245**
1752-0983 The Drinks Network **602**
1752-1270 International Journal of Chinese Culture and Management **8108**
1752-1289 *see* 1752-1270 **8108**
1752-1378 Cambridge Journal of Regions, Economy and Society **7113**
1752-1386 *see* 1752-1378 **7113**
1752-1394 I E T Synthetic Biology **749**
1752-1408 *see* 1752-1394 **749**
1752-1416 I E T Renewable Power Generation **3318**
1752-1424 *see* 1752-1416 **3318**
1752-1440 Law and Financial Markets Review **4874**
1752-1467 Legisprudence **4722**
1752-1475 *see* 1752-1467 **4722**
1752-1483 Law and Humanities **4713**
1752-1491 *see* 1752-1483 **4713**
1752-1505 Conflict and Health **7513**
1752-153X Chemistry Central Journal **2057**
1752-1580 Rosetta **415**
1752-167X B C N **6708**
1752-1688 *see* 1093-474X **8817**
1752-1696 The Irish Mail on Sunday **3893**
1752-1718 *see* 0379-0312 **8065**
1752-1726 *see* 0379-0282 **7975**
1752-1734 *see* 0250-605X **4521**
1752-1807 *see* 1350-293X **2855**

ISSN

1752-8933	International Journal of Nano and Biomaterials **7867**
1752-8941	*see* 1752-8933 **7867**
1752-8976	*see* 1470-3203 **5655**
1752-8984	*see* 1479-1641 **5886**
1752-9034	European Renal & Genito-Urinary Disease **6268**
1752-9042	*see* 1752-9034 **6268**
1752-9131	International Journal of Computational Vision and Robotics **2585**
1752-914X	*see* 1752-9131 **2585**
1752-9174	Payroll & Human Resources **1871**
1752-9182	*see* 1477-9757 **7390**
1752-928X	Journal of Clinical Forensic and Legal Medicine **5914**
1752-9298	Space Research Today **71**
1752-9328	The Muriel Spark Society Newsletter **5337**
1752-9360	The Otorhinolaryngologist **6084**
1752-9379	*see* 1752-9360 **6084**
1752-9433	The Self Publishing Magazine **7573**
1752-9441	Lunar Jim **2200**
1752-9476	Prison Break **2388**
1752-959X	Tax **1946**
1752-9603	*see* 1752-959X **1946**
1752-962X	Rouleur **8267**
1752-9638	Journal of Urban Regeneration and Renewal **4418**
1752-9646	*see* 1752-9638 **4418**
1752-9719	International Theory **7245**
1752-9727	*see* 1752-9719 **7245**
1752-9794	European Cardiovascular Disease **5786**
1752-9816	Journal of Nursing and Healthcare of Chronic Illness **5966**
1752-9824	*see* 1752-9816 **5966**
1752-9867	*see* 1674-2052 **801**
1752-9921	Journal of Plant Ecology **798**
1752-993X	*see* 1752-9921 **798**
1752-9956	Square Mile Magazine **5083**
1752-9972	The Horror Collection **6503**
1753-0032	Primary Choice *changed to* 1756-6509 **3084**
1753-0059	Expert Opinion on Medical Diagnostics **5612**
1753-0067	*see* 1753-0059 **5612**
1753-0180	Advances in Mental Health and Learning Disabilities **6120**
1753-0229	O P E C Energy Review **6782**
1753-0237	*see* 1753-0229 **6782**
1753-0245	Slim at Home **6669**
1753-0296	International Journal of Business Science and Applied Management **1755**
1753-0318	How to Draw **493**
1753-0334	What Diesel Car **8612**
1753-0350	Journal of Cultural Economy **7978**
1753-0369	*see* 1753-0350 **7978**
1753-0377	*see* 0892-7936 **933**
1753-0385	University of London. Institute of Education. Occasional Papers in Work-Based Learning **2923**
1753-0393	Journal of Diabetes **5895**
1753-0407	*see* 1753-0393 **5895**
1753-0458	Perfect Wedding **5561**
1753-0474	Norway Oil & Gas Report **6781**
1753-0490	F.O. Licht's World Biodiesel Price Report **732**
1753-0563	International Journal of Applied Cryptography **2514**
1753-0571	*see* 1753-0563 **2514**
1753-0598	Low-Fare & Regional Airlines **8547**
1753-0660	International Journal of Innovation and Regional Development **1599**
1753-0679	*see* 1753-0660 **1599**
1753-0717	British Postmark Society. Journal **6892**
1753-0725	The Leisure Review **4980**
1753-0768	Music, Sound and the Moving Image **6592**
1753-0776	*see* 1753-0768 **6592**
1753-0784	N D T Plus **6271**
1753-0792	*see* 1753-0784 **6271**
1753-0806	International Journal of Indian Culture and Business Management **1757**
1753-0814	*see* 1753-0806 **1757**
1753-0822	International Journal of Services, Economics and Management **1761**
1753-0830	*see* 1753-0822 **1761**
1753-0849	Childhoods Today **2148**
1753-0857	Argus Russian Coal **3124**
1753-0911	Your Herts and Beds Wedding **5562**
1753-1039	International Journal of Mechatronics and Manufacturing Systems **3382**
1753-1047	*see* 1753-1039 **3382**
1753-1055	Journal of Eastern African Studies **7978**
1753-1063	*see* 1753-1055 **7978**
1753-125X	Size 16up **6300**
1753-1330	S R I Papers **3464**
1753-1381	C F S R **8091**
1753-139X	Reeds Nautical Almanac **8658**
1753-1403	Asian Social Work and Policy Review **7949**
1753-1411	*see* 1753-1403 **7949**
1753-1446	International Journal of Services Sciences **1761**
1753-1454	*see* 1753-1446 **1761**
1753-1497	Powder Injection Moulding International **6329**
1753-1586	British Journal of Healthcare Assistants **5953**
1753-1594	Journal of Children's and Young People's Nursing† **8968**
1753-1608	Lazer **2199**
1753-1632	Cardiff Marketing and Strategy Working Papers **1732**
1753-1705	Britain Today *changed to* 1756-0578 **7951**
1753-1721	Country Report. Papua New Guinea, Timor-Leste **1459**
1753-1780	Journal of Securities Compliance *changed to* 1758-0013 **1636**
1753-1799	*see* 1758-0013 **1636**
1753-1802	Journal of Securities Operations & Custody **1363**
1753-1810	*see* 1753-1802 **1363**
1753-1829	Cardiff Logistics and Operations Management Working Papers **1732**
1753-1837	Cardiff Human Resource Management Working Papers **1858**
1753-1845	Low-Fare and Regional Aviation **8548**
1753-1918	The Retail Directory (UK Edition) **1840**
1753-1926	The Retail Directory. Year Book (Year) **2026**
1753-1934	Journal of Hand Surgery (European Volume) **6248**
1753-1942	International Journal of Technological Learning, Innovation and Development **8427**
1753-1950	*see* 1753-1942 **8427**
1753-1969	International Journal of Behavioural Accounting and Finance **1292**
1753-1977	*see* 1753-1969 **1292**
1753-2000	Child and Adolescent Psychiatry and Mental Health **6131**
1753-2086	The Brewer & Distiller International **600**
1753-2116	The Journal of Pipeline Engineering **6776**
1753-2167	*see* 0957-1736 **5141**
1753-2183	The Edge *changed to* 1758-2121 **8005**
1753-2213	Quick and Easy Stitch & Craft **6641**
1753-2280	Who's Who Legal. Banking **4883**
1753-2310	System and Information Sciences Notes *changed to* 1757-4439 **2542**
1753-2337	Health Foods and Snacks **3646**
1753-2396	Journal of Irish and Scottish Studies **4235**
1753-240X	The International Journal of Inclusive Democracy **7143**
1753-2434	Monocle (London) **3968**
1753-2469	Hornby Magazine **4336**
1753-2507	International Journal of Nanoparticles **766**
1753-2515	*see* 1753-2507 **766**
1753-2523	African Historical Review **4129**
1753-2531	*see* 1753-2523 **4129**
1753-2574	Journal of Corporate Treasury Management **1360**
1753-2582	*see* 1753-2574 **1360**
1753-2744	Landlord *changed to* 1757-7950 **7598**
1753-2787	Time Out London for Visitors **8761**
1753-2809	Endo **5843**
1753-2817	*see* 1753-2809 **5843**
1753-2825	Sustainable Building **3148**
1753-2833	*see* 1753-2825 **3148**
1753-2906	H R Yorkshire & Humber **1863**
1753-2973	M A D E **3352**
1753-3015	Arts & Health **5578**
1753-3023	*see* 1753-3015 **5578**
1753-3031	Journal of Management & Marketing in Healthcare **5651**
1753-304X	*see* 1753-3031 **5651**
1753-3066	Ophthalmology Times Europe **6048**
1753-3074	*see* 1041-2573 **5294**
1753-3090	Britain at War Magazine **6414**
1753-3104	Electronic Journal of Sustainable Development **3419**
1753-3139	Okido **2205**
1753-3155	Corel Painter Official Magazine **2484**
1753-3171	Safundi (Print Edition) **4178**
1753-3198	Dental Products Report Europe **8419**
1753-3309	International Journal of Oil, Gas and Coal Technology **6774**
1753-3317	*see* 1753-3309 **6774**
1753-3333	Racing and Football Outlook Jumps Guide
1753-3341	Racing & Football Outlook Football Guide (Years) **8195**
1753-3422	Time Out Fly Europe **8761**
1753-3465	International Journal of Computational Materials Science and Surface Engineering **3346**
1753-3473	*see* 1753-3465 **3346**
1753-3546	European Journal of Glass Science and Technology. Part A. Glass Technology **2040**
1753-3562	European Journal of Glass Science and Techology. Part B. Physics and Chemistry of Glasses **2041**
1753-3589	The Probe **5861**
1753-3600	International Journal of Sustainable Strategic Management **1761**
1753-3619	*see* 1753-3600 **1761**
1753-3627	International Journal of Business and Globalisation **1127**
1753-3635	*see* 1753-3627 **1127**
1753-3740	Best Practice & Research: Clinical Anaesthesiology **5770**
1753-3775	Shop Spec **4550**
1753-3783	The Journal of Invasive Fungal Infections **5879**
1753-3805	Advances in Pain Management **6055**
1753-3813	Hotel Spec **4390**
1753-3821	Smile (Orpington) **5865**
1753-3910	Nuclear Energy (London) **3171**
1753-3929	*see* 1753-3910 **3171**
1753-3937	Hospital Engineering & Facilities Management **4100**
1753-3945	*see* 1753-3937 **4100**
1753-3953	European Neurological Disease **6140**
1753-3961	*see* 1753-3953 **6140**
1753-397X	European Endocrine Disease **5892**
1753-3988	*see* 1753-397X **5892**
1753-4011	U S Oncological Disease **6036**
1753-402X	*see* 1753-4011 **6036**
1753-4054	*see* 1752-9794 **5786**
1753-4062	U S Endocrine Disease **5901**
1753-4070	*see* 1753-4062 **5901**
1753-4089	U S Respiratory Disease **6220**
1753-4097	*see* 1753-4089 **6220**
1753-4100	European Oncological Disease **6019**
1753-4119	*see* 1753-4100 **6019**
1753-4143	U S Musculoskeletal Review **6074**
1753-4151	*see* 1753-4143 **6074**
1753-4224	H P S Weekly Report (Online) **5814**
1753-4259	Innate Immunity **5894**
1753-4305	*see* 1474-6514 **5884**
1753-4313	*see* 0969-6113 **5778**
1753-4445	Windscreen **4350**
1753-450X	International Food Ingredients Directory **2009**
1753-4534	*see* 1528-817X **7713**
1753-4593	Epping Forest Guardian **3967**
1753-4631	Nonlinear Biomedical Physics **754**
1753-4658	Therapeutic Advances in Respiratory Disease **6220**
1753-4666	*see* 1753-4658 **6220**
1753-4887	*see* 0029-6643 **6666**
1753-4895	Let's Knit **6640**
1753-495X	Obstetric Medicine **6000**
1753-4968	*see* 1753-495X **6000**
1753-4976	The Computer Active Ultimate Guide to... **2411**
1753-4992	In the Night Garden **2194**
1753-5069	Urban Research & Practice **7475**
1753-5077	*see* 1753-5069 **7475**
1753-5115	Look **3968**
1753-5123	Reviews in Aquaculture **2817**
1753-5131	*see* 1753-5123 **2817**
1753-5174	Archives of Drug Information **6822**
1753-5190	Journal of Writing in Creative Practice **4577**
1753-5212	International Journal of Digital Culture and Electronic Tourism **2425**
1753-5220	*see* 1753-5212 **2425**
1753-5239	International Journal of Electronic Banking **1357**
1753-5247	*see* 1753-5239 **1357**
1753-5255	International Journal of Technology Enhanced Learning **3065**
1753-5263	*see* 1753-5255 **3065**
1753-528X	*see* 0075-4358 **2236**
1753-5352	*see* 0068-113X **2231**
1753-5360	*see* 1013-1752 **5289**
1753-5379	*see* 0250-0167 **8094**
1753-5387	*see* 0256-4718 **5315**
1753-5395	*see* 1022-8195 **5141**
1753-5409	*see* 1812-5441 **5369**
1753-5476	Country Risk Service Serbia **1474**
1753-5514	Dream Italian Weddings **5558**
1753-5522	*see* 1350-5033 **388**
1753-5530	*see* 1465-5187 **412**
1753-5557	*see* 1066-7857 **6322**
1753-5638	Mortgage Distributor† **8975**
1753-5654	Journal of Modern Chinese History **4184**
1753-5662	*see* 1753-5654 **4184**
1753-5689	National Health Professional **5683**
1753-5794	49th Parallel **4319**
1753-5859	European Pensions **1622**
1753-5921	*see* 1814-6627 **2966**
1753-593X	*see* 1812-5980 **6597**
1753-5956	Learning for Life **2882**
1753-5964	African Performance Review **8464**
1753-5972	*see* 1022-3827 **3620**
1753-5980	Attachment **7337**
1753-6006	Country Risk Service. Austria **1088**
1753-6022	Country Risk Service. Finland **1088**
1753-6065	Country Risk Service. Japan **1088**
1753-6146	International Musculoskeletal Medicine **6062**
1753-6154	*see* 1753-6146 **6062**
1753-6162	N A T E Classroom **5153**
1753-6200	Spotlight Dancers **2687**
1753-6219	International Journal of Business and Emerging Markets **1127**
1753-6227	*see* 1753-6219 **1127**
1753-6235	International Journal of Private Law **4695**
1753-6243	*see* 1753-6235 **4695**
1753-6383	Epping Forest Guardian (Loughton, Buckhurst Hill, Chigwell and Waltham Abbey Edition) *changed to* 1753-4593 **3967**
1753-6405	*see* 1326-0200 **7508**
1753-6421	Journal of Adaptation in Film and Performance **8472**
1753-6561	B M C Proceedings **7838**
1753-657X	I C P Advanced Texts in Mathematics **5491**
1753-6693	T V Film Memorabilia **4348**
1753-6707	Blue Tattoo **5264**
1753-6715	International Journal of Managerial and Financial Accounting **1292**
1753-6723	*see* 1753-6715 **1292**
1753-6790	Essex Style **5070**
1753-6804	Mining Quarrying & Recycling **6473**
1753-6855	Amgola Business Forecast Report Annual **1059**
1753-6871	The Cote d'Ivoire Business Forecast Report Annual **1088**
1753-688X	The Ethiopia Business Forecast Report Annual **1106**
1753-6952	Buy-Side Technology **1414**
1753-7118	Insider. Midlands Business Insider **1753**
1753-7134	The Howard **2654**
1753-7150	Dare (London, 2007) **2253**
1753-7169	International Journal of Decision Sciences, Risk and Management **1756**
1753-7177	*see* 1753-7169 **1756**
1753-7185	Takeovers **4881**
1753-7193	*see* 1753-7185 **4881**
1753-7231	In Style (Travel Edition) **8868**
1753-724X	Berg New Media Series **2313**
1753-7274	*see* 1818-6874 **4175**
1753-7355	Pathfinder Business **1158**
1753-741X	Journal of Literary Disability (Online) *changed to* 1757-6458 **3042**
1753-7444	Interactive Data Credit Ratings. International **1355**
1753-7452	*see* 1753-7444 **1355**
1753-7460	Interactive Data Credit Ratings. Emerging Markets **1355**
1753-7576	Bioenergy Business **6764**
1753-7584	*see* 1753-7576 **6764**
1753-7606	*see* 0968-7912 **6137**
1753-7703	International Journal of Information and Coding Theory **2514**
1753-7711	*see* 1753-7703 **2514**
1753-7746	Human Capital Management **1863**
1753-7762	Manchester Papers in Economic and Social History **7984**
1753-7770	*see* 1753-7762 **7984**
1753-7878	Pharmaceutical Executive Europe (Print)† **8980**
1753-7967	Pharmaceutical Technology Europe **6870**
1753-7983	Education, Business and Society **2847**
1753-7991	*see* 1753-7983 **2847**
1753-8041	People, Place and Policy Online **8125**
1753-805X	Pinstripping & Kustom Graphics Magazine **8598**
1753-8068	Journal of Communication in Healthcare **5647**
1753-8076	*see* 1753-8068 **5647**
1753-8106	Airline Fleet & Network Management **8536**
1753-8122	A I M & P L U S Newsletter **1609**
1753-8157	Informatics for Health and Social Care **5831**
1753-8165	*see* 1753-8157 **5831**
1753-822X	Let's Grow Veg **3742**
1753-8254	Indian Growth and Development Review **1122**
1753-8262	*see* 1753-8254 **1122**

ISSN

ISSN

1762-4185 E M C - Radiologie†
1762-4193 E M C - Medecine†
1762-4207 E M C - Rhumatologie - Orthopedie†
1762-4215 E M C - Veterinaire†
1762-4223 E M C - Pneumologie†
1762-4231 E M C - Neurologie (Print) *changed to* 1778-6959 **6137**
1762-4487 Banque de France. Selected French Banking and Financial Regulations **1320**
1762-4576 Bloom **7318**
1762-5092 Groupe de Recherche en Economie Financiere et Gestion des Entreprises. Cahiers de Recherche *changed to* 1960-2782 **1326**
1762-5254 L'Espace Alpin (Edition Alpes-de-Haute-Provence) *changed to* 1772-3574 **108**
1762-5653 E M C - Endocrinologie†
1762-5688 E M C - Oto-Rhino-Laryngologie†
1762-5696 E M C - Dermatologie Cosmetologie†
1762-570X E M C - Chirurgie†
1762-5718 E M C - Psychiatrie (Print) *changed to* E M C - Psychiatrie (Online) **6137**
1762-584X E M C - Ophtalmologie†
1762-5858 E M C - Toxicologie Pathologie†
1762-5912 Banque de France. Enquete Mensuelle de Conjoncture (Online) **1441**
1762-598X Creolica **5109**
1762-6013 E M C - Pediatrie†
1762-6110 Asterion **6906**
1762-6137 E M C - Cardiologie Angeiologie†
1762-6145 E M C - Gynecologie Obstetrique†
1762-6153 La Revue L I S A **6949**
1762-7907 Centre de Musique Baroque de Versailles. Anthologies **6555**
1762-7915 Monumentales **6588**
1762-8407 Actualite Juridique. Penal **4883**
1762-8717 Techniques de l'Ingenieur. Analyse et Caracterisation **3256**
1762-8733 Techniques de l'Ingenieur. Materiaux Metalliques **3358**
1762-8792 Sante et Systemique *changed to* 1960-8748 **5709**
1762-8830 France Nature **309**
1762-9055 Perspectives (Cherbourg) **1408**
1762-9314 Action Auto Moto **8555**
1762-9330 Les P'tites Princesses **2209**
1763-1203 Societe d'Archeologie et d'Histoire du Pays de Lorient. Bulletin **4264**
1763-1254 Feminin Cuisine **4358**
1763-1548 Nutritions et Facteurs de Risque *changed to* 1953-695X **5898**
1763-2234 Les Dossiers du J F P *see* 1260-5999 **6149**
1763-2552 Eyrolles Pratique **4438**
1763-3346 Le Monde des Religions **7808**
1763-3818 Magic Art **504**
1763-3850 Medecine Therapeutique - Endocrinologie & Reproduction *changed to* 1774-640X **5897**
1763-4229 Savoirs **2945**
1763-4237 Conso C E *changed to* 1771-0375 **1874**
1763-4474 Chambre de Commerce et d'Industrie d'Auxerre. Action economique *changed to* 1774-1262 **1413**
1763-4776 Dessins & Peintures **486**
1763-4881 Stiletto **2261**
1763-5179 L'Espace Alpin (Edition Hautes-Alpes) *changed to* 1772-3574 **108**
1763-5411 Revue Dermatologique du Cheveu **5881**
1763-5535 Ski **8332**
1763-5551 L'Ecole Globale **2844**
1763-5640 Tele 2 Semaines **2395**
1763-5853 L'Heritage **7140**
1763-590X Observatoire des Deplacements a Paris. Bulletin **8507**
1763-5985 Memoires **6159**
1763-6191 Les Etudes de la Documentation Francaise **1484**
1763-6876 Art Price Annual† **8931**
1763-7023 France. Ministere de l'Agriculture et de la Peche. Agreste. L'Agriculture, la Foret et les Industries Agroalimentaires **114**
1763-7155 Occasions Mag **8596**
1763-7384 Electronic Product News **3096**
1763-7570 Journal de l'Afrique en Expansion **1494**
1763-7708 Collection Magazine *changed to* 1954-1074 **4332**
1763-7716 Qualite Construction **1031**
1763-7864 Netsuds **2335**
1763-8038 Magic Loisir **537**
1763-8321 T L Catho **2215**
1763-8666 Serial Fan *changed to* 1775-0113 **6557**
1763-8682 Ivoire **8784**
1763-8739 Enfants Creatifs *changed to* 1768-4013 **536**
1763-9816 Humus, Subjectivite et Lien Social **7361**
1763-9867 Secrets d'Ateliers **539**
1764-0555 Dictionnaire Joly Concurrence **1092**
1764-0563 Juri-Dictionnaire Joly. Bourse et Produits Financiers **1636**
1764-0660 Strategie†
1764-0709 Reflets et Nuances **1032**
1764-1020 Societe Prehistorique Ariege - Pyrenees. Bulletin **417**
1764-1144 Declic **4064**
1764-1489 European Annals of Allergy and Clinical Immunology **5758**
1764-1616 Macworld France *changed to* 1767-4085 **8996**
1764-1756 Sport† **8989**
1764-1934 Equilibre **8171**
1764-1977 Afrique & Histoire **4173**
1764-2507 Le Temps des Medias **2342**
1764-2558 Altercatif **3180**
1764-2817 Energie & Developpement Durable Magazine **3129**
1764-3678 Spasmagazine *changed to* 1961-3768 **5709**
1764-3716 Espaces Politiques
1764-4283 Le Miroir des Humanistes **4465**
1764-4372 Solutions Unix-Linux **2598**
1764-4666 Les Carnets de la Forme **6983**
1764-5476 Knowledge, Work & Society **2881**
1764-5549 Bodyboard Magazine **8306**
1764-5719 Digital World **2576**
1764-5743 Correspondances en Risque Cardiovasculaire **5784**
1764-6243 Vertical **8339**
1764-6308 Materiaux Orthopteriques et Entomocenotiques **854**
1764-6340 Techniques de l'Ingenieur. Risques Industriels. La Lettre *changed to* 1957-2891 **3371**
1764-6499 Guide P N P† **8960**
1764-6510 L'Informateur Economique du Choletais† **8964**
1764-7185 Actualite et Droit International **4916**
1764-7193 Amnis **324**
1764-7223 Sciences et Technologies de l'Information et la Communication pour l'Education et la Formation **2437**
1764-9137 Pratiques du Soignant† **8982**
1764-9250 Cahiers de l'Admin **2519**
1764-9587 Le Regard Sociologique **8127**
1764-9943 Acces Libre **2587**
1765-0259 Bulletin de l'Antiquaire et du Brocanteur *changed to* 1765-0267 **364**
1765-0267 Bulletin de l'Antiquaire, du Brocanteur, et des Galleries d'Art Moderne et Contemporain **364**
1765-0828 Batailles & Blindes **6413**
1765-0887 Distances et Savoirs **2842**
1765-0917 Mutualistes **8055**
1765-1336 C S O **2511**
1765-1565 Stargate Magazine *changed to* 1779-4676 **6950**
1765-2022 Acteurs Publics **7102**
1765-2030 A F E I Newsletter *changed to* 1961-7038 **1608**
1765-2235 Autorite des Marches Financiers. Revue *changed to* 1767-848X **1611**
1765-2464 Going Out Magazine **3840**
1765-2480 Musee des Beaux-Arts de Lyon. Cahiers **6529**
1765-2553 Carnets de Geologie (CD-ROM) *see* 1634-0744 **2728**
1765-2723 Activites **7331**
1765-2766 Transatlantica **8010**
1765-2839 *see* 1292-3818 **6030**
1765-2847 *see* 1624-8597 **6114**
1765-2855 *see* 0759-2280 **6252**
1765-288X Bibliographie Nationale Francaise. Musique (Online Edition) **6631**
1765-2952 *see* 0990-7440 **3586**
1765-2960 *see* 1296-2139 **3389**
1765-2979 *see* 1240-1307 **2714**
1765-3053 Horizons & Conseils. Mensuel **1629**
1765-3061 Horizons & Conseils. Bi-Hebdomadaire **1629**
1765-307X *see* 0993-8516 **5103**
1765-3096 Loxias (Online Edition) **5328**
1765-3118 *see* 0992-1893 **5282**
1765-3134 *see* 0240-642X **5919**
1765-3193 EMednews **5609**
1765-3711 Arts Magazine **475**
1765-4602 Etiquettes Plus **6733**
1765-4629 Ethique & Sante **6985**
1765-4750 I Love English **2193**
1765-4866 Pelerin **7669**
1765-5579 La Lettre du Naturopathe **312**
1765-582X Intelligence & Strategie **7242**
1765-6206 La Librairie des Humanites **4463**
1765-6370 Societe des Explorateurs Francais **4029**
1765-6400 Entretiens **7354**
1765-6710 Collection Lusotopie **4447**
1765-6826 Anthropologie Philosophique
1765-7210 C'Est la Vie Aussi **2147**
1765-7601 Au Pied du Mur **434**
1765-7865 Le Philosophe **6939**
1765-8071 Mythes, Imaginaires, Religions **7664**
1765-8101 Collection Dicologie Didactique **5107**
1765-8195 Correspondances en Nerf & Muscle **5601**
1765-8888 Seve **5712**
1766-0181 Collection Paroles de Musicien **6557**
1766-0246 Generation **3535**
1766-0327 *see* 1264-7527 **5937**
1766-0343 *see* 1631-0675 **1287**
1766-0351 *see* 0153-4092 **7899**
1766-036X *see* 1638-2242 **1920**
1766-0734 *see* 1635-4273 **4841**
1766-2389 Revue du Soignant en Sante Publique **7540**
1766-2826 Guide International des Fournisseurs de la Beaute† **8960**
1766-2842 Feeries **339**
1766-3067 Figures Normaliennes **4452**
1766-3792 Parc Naturel Regional de Corse. Travaux Scientifiques
1766-4098 Audio Video Prestige **8152**
1766-4314 Le Journal de la Cuisine *changed to* 1777-2303
1766-4381 Maison Bricolage et Decoration **4546**
1766-4705 R P F - M A D *changed to* 1959-4747 **4125**
1766-6317 Burda Patchwork **6637**
1766-6562 Afrik Etudiant **3516**
1766-7305 Pratiques en Nutrition **6668**
1766-7313 Revue du Podologue **6072**
1766-7658 Mises au Point Cliniques d'Endocrinologie, Nutrition et Metabolisme
1766-7771 Guide de la Chimie **2062**
1766-7895 Les Cahiers de l'Humanisme **4446**
1766-8034 Annuaire des Liens Financiers **1307**
1766-8255 Transports Internationaux & Logistique **8518**
1766-8328 R M S **5527**
1766-8476 Batiment - Entretien **3405**
1766-8832 Purple Fashion **3842**
1766-8840 Purple Journal **4471**
1766-9057 Temps Course Mag **8337**
1766-9413 Sortir & Choisir Autrement
1766-9553 Moto Kids **8261**
1766-9634 Le Lien **7804**
1766-9693 La Revue Litteraire **5237**
1766-974X Docteurs & Co. **5606**
1766-9766 Les Annonces de l'Optique **6038**
1767-0187 La Decroissance **7128**
1767-0519 T V Grandes Chaines **2392**
1767-0799 Cine Films *changed to* 1957-2360 **6500**
1767-1302 Domaines Anglophones **5285**
1767-1558 Best of **2505**
1767-1841 Basic Bien-Etre **585**
1767-2163 Libelles **6932**
1767-266X Collection Cursus. Psychanalyse **7348**
1767-3143 Psychanalyse, Medecine et Societe **6175**
1767-3194 Ecrire l'Afrique **5287**
1767-3356 Connaissance de l'Emploi **6696**
1767-3623 Anuario Americanista Europeo **4284**
1767-3631 Netchercheur **5035**
1767-3844 La Soeur de l'Ange **6953**
1767-4034 Fightsport **8173**
1767-4085 Univers Mac† **8996**
1767-4328 Dimag **7588**
1767-4417 Pratique Vet des Animaux de Compagnie **8805**
1767-4433 Batailles **4203**
1767-4751 Etapes: International **7320**
1767-4883 L'Essentiel de la Moto **8258**
1767-5162 Consensus Cardio pour le Praticien **5783**
1767-5200 Le Guide des Piscines et des Spas *changed to* 1770-1759 **4977**
1767-5448 Recherches en Psychanalyse **7402**
1767-5863 Creatif Special Cartes 3 D **4333**
1767-5936 A B C Neurologies **6117**
1767-6312 La Lettre de la Justice Administrative **4850**
1767-6320 Revue Historique du Centre Ouest **4258**
1767-641X Energy & Sustainable Development Magazine **3130**
1767-6436 Exchange Magazine **2497**
1767-6509 Kompass Regional. Pays de la Loire **1142**
1767-6916 Ordre des Experts-Comptables Bourgogne - Franche-Comte. Annuaire *changed to* 1774-735X **1288**
1767-7157 Choc **3840**
1767-7254 La Lettre des Observatoires **4835**
1767-803X Reperes en Geriatrie **4054**
1767-8277 Annuaire Europeen du Froid et du Conditionnement d'Air **4116**
1767-848X Autorite des Marches Financiers. Revue Mensuelle **1611**
1767-8560 Burda Travaux Manuels **4437**
1767-8765 Champs de Bataille **6415**
1767-8862 International Justice Tribune (French Edition) **4931**
1767-8889 International Justice Tribune (English Edition) **4931**
1767-9370 Teranga **8786**
1767-9419 Traitement des Surfaces de l'Anticorrosion et des Traitements Thermiques **6721**
1767-9567 Passion du Patchwork† **8980**
1767-9915 L'Horticulture Francaise **3737**
1767-9966 Superfoot Mag **8248**
1768-0433 Le Foot Marseille **8228**
1768-0611 France. Ministere de l'Emploi, du Travail, et de la Cohesion Sociale. Bulletin Officiel† **8958**
1768-0700 Batterie Magazine **6548**
1768-0735 Bulletin Quotidien d'Afrique†
1768-1367 Suisse Magazine **5084**
1768-1456 Tribu Rock **6624**
1768-2088 Lettres et Civilisations Italiennes
1768-2428 Questions d'Ados **2166**
1768-2436 Mondes Hispanophones **5336**
1768-2959 Revue d'Etudes Tibetaines **354**
1768-3114 *see* 0369-8114 **5693**
1768-3130 *see* 1169-8330 **6226**
1768-3149 *see* 1877-0320 **5765**
1768-3165 DesignFlux **2485**
1768-3181 *see* 0003-3928 **5777**
1768-319X *see* 0294-1260 **6236**
1768-322X *see* 0248-4900 **828**
1768-3238 *see* 1631-0691 **649**
1768-3254 *see* 0223-5234 **731**
1768-3378 *see* 0003-4401 **8930**
1768-3572 Societe Geologique de Normandie et des Amis du Museum du Havre. Bulletin **2767**
1768-4013 Hobby Decoration **536**
1768-4080 Mobile Business Magazine **2333**
1768-4099 Revue Lamy Droit Civil **4841**
1768-4412 Solidarite Internationale
1768-4455 Oxyjen Magazine **3907**
1768-4463 Curie@ctu **6017**
1768-5109 Medecine & Sciences Humaines **5666**
1768-546X Ilot **5308**
1768-5605 Trait pour Trait **522**
1768-6008 Jouets de Collection **4337**
1768-6520 Parlements **7163**
1768-6563 Muze **3841**
1768-658X Terres Cathares *changed to* 1774-9689 **4002**
1768-6814 Etudes Marnaises **4451**
1768-7411 Une Memoire **4244**
1768-7985 Noir Urbain **5342**
1768-8116 Architecte Logiciel **2505**
1768-9155 *see* 0012-2483 **105**
1768-9171 *see* 0758-7309 **1738**
1768-9260 Revue des Etudes Augustiniennes et Patristiques **7677**
1768-9791 Revue Francaise de Photogrammetrie et de Teledetection **4027**
1769-0021 Vivre Ma Maison (Edition Gard Herault) **1042**
1769-0072 L'Auxiliaire Veterinaire **8793**
1769-0129 Le Magazine d'Orpheopolis
1769-0277 Beyond Beauty Mag **586**
1769-0552 La Gazette Sante Social **8042**
1769-0765 Artravel International **4531**
1769-101X Les Nouveaux Dossiers de l'Audiovisuel† **8978**
1769-1036 Revue Droit & Sante **4774**
1769-1265 Le Foot Saint-Etienne **8228**
1769-1389 France.Office National d'Etudes et de Recherches Aerospatiales. Scientific and Technical Activities *see* 1770-4448 **67**
1769-1397 Petites Histoires pour les Tout Petits **2206**
1769-1400 Rando Pyrenees **8330**
1769-1893 La Collection de YOE **5275**
1769-2067 Socioanthropologie **356**
1769-2598 Recettes Vegetariennes du Monde **4366**
1769-292X C F I Focus **2357**
1769-3128 Diaspora le Lien *changed to* 1772-0664 **3548**
1769-3519 Le Magazine du Piegeur *changed to* 1957-6455 **8321**
1769-3780 Chien Magazine *changed to* 1776-1182 **6806**
1769-3977 Regal **4366**
1769-4450 S A C D. Journal des Auteurs **8477**
1769-4566 Rapport d'Activite et de Developpement Durable **8550**
1769-4612 Inculte **5308**

ISSN

1773-4258 Le Guide de l'Emploi Associatif dans les Alpes de Haute-Provence **1489**
1773-4266 Le Commissaire aux Comptes et le Passage aux I F R S **4646**
1773-4282 Donnees d'Usinage **1005**
1773-4304 Le Guide des Ressources Humaines **1861**
1773-4312 Convention Collective Nationale de Travail des Etablissements et Service pour Personnes Inadaptees et Handicapees du 15 Mars 1966 **1673**
1773-4339 Contrats et Documents Types Loi M O P **4650**
1773-4371 Legislation Professionnelle. Pharmacie Hospitaliere **4722**
1773-438X Gestion des Plantes Exotiques Envahissantes **3433**
1773-4398 Conduite de Projet **1734**
1773-4746 Amour et Mystere *changed to* 1778-5936 **5411**
1773-4754 Passion Intense **5412**
1773-4878 Plaisirs Nature **3747**
1773-5424 Collection Chaudiere **5275**
1773-5440 Societes en Changement **8135**
1773-570X Rock One **6612**
1773-5858 Rap Mag **6609**
1773-5920 Les Aventures de Bibounet et Patagloum **2177**
1773-6064 Micro Actuel **2431**
1773-6145 PlayStation Portable **2481**
1773-6730 Petite Etoile **2206**
1773-6773 Revue Archeologique de l'Est. Supplement
1773-6781 Les Petits Guides des Paresseuses **3121**
1773-6889 Labo Numerique **6970**
1773-6897 Les Dossiers Mon Jardin et Ma Maison **3728**
1773-7257 Histoire des Bibliotheques Medievales **5012**
1773-729X L'Essentiel sur... **5008**
1773-7710 Litteratures de Langue Allemande
1773-7753 Trente Journees Qui Ont Fait la France *changed to* 1776-6400 **4236**
1773-7931 G R H I S. Cahiers **340**
1773-7974 Paris Projet **4422**
1773-8083 Nous, les Sans-Philosophie **6937**
1773-8156 Epanouissement Personnel et Professionnel **7354**
1773-8164 Vivre en Famille **7414**
1773-8490 Collection Archives of Twentieth-Century Interior Architecture *see* 1770-8095 **4535**
1773-8911 Une, Deux, Trois Belles Histoires **2219**
1773-8954 Les Bouquins Fusion **7841**
1773-9004 Collection Danses du Monde **2683**
1773-9209 Francophonie dans le Monde **8103**
1773-9241 Planete Paix **7165**
1773-9284 Maison Creamania **4546**
1773-9357 International Journal of Electrical Engineering in Transportation **3321**
1773-9578 Concurrences **4862**
1773-9837 Idees Creations Bijoux et Perles† **8963**
1774-024X EuroIntervention **6242**
1774-0398 Le Guide du Kokin **6292**
1774-0401 L'Histoire de la Marine† **8962**
1774-0436 Eh! Lisez-moi **5288**
1774-0444 Centre d'Etudes et de Recherches Economiques et Sociales de Picardie. Cahiers† **8940**
1774-0452 Gib'Echos **7439**
1774-0487 De Garches a Rueil... **7491**
1774-0711 Le Nouveau Musicien **6600**
1774-0746 Agronomy for Sustainable Development **217**
1774-0789 La Lettre du Psychiatre **6158**
1774-0800 Planete Japon **351**
1774-0835 Reverse **8243**
1774-0924 Agra Alimentation **80**
1774-1262 Yonne Eco **1413**
1774-1319 Cuisine et Salle de Bains Concept **1000**
1774-1505 Hors-Bord Magazine **8276**
1774-2994 Clitopile Pruineux **482**
1774-3044 Collection Mythes et Legendes **5275**
1774-3060 Clef des Champs **482**
1774-3079 Faits Divers **489**
1774-3184 Il Etait une Fois **4139**
1774-3621 Memoire des Nations **4153**
1774-3796 Collection Volubile **5409**
1774-3834 Collection Cursus. Langues **5107**
1774-3869 Ville & Transports **8520**
1774-4059 Bloc Notes 54 **2831**
1774-4199 Dimension Villes & Territoires **4409**
1774-4466 Seizieme Siecle **5369**
1774-4539 Exo **1288**
1774-4644 C G T. Transports. Alpes du Nord **4591**
1774-4679 Le Biblionaute **4994**
1774-4687 Dechaine ton Corps **4592**
1774-4717 Cent pour Cent Etudiant† **8940**
1774-4741 L'Enseignant de Bourgogne **4593**
1774-475X Les Cahiers de la Securite **2676**
1774-4784 Artisanat Magazine Yvelines **1956**
1774-4792 Le Gourmand **4387**
1774-4814 Barbouille **2178**
1774-4830 La Gazette des Amis de la Lecture **2190**
1774-4865 H@nd Ouest **8234**
1774-4873 Akkro Magazine **8157**
1774-489X Apozeme† **8930**
1774-492X Bulletin de Liaison Cleophas **7111**
1774-4938 Histoire et Patrimoine de Villers-Semeuse **4227**
1774-4946 La Gazette du Groupe Naturaliste de Franche-Comte **3433**
1774-4954 Info Ressources Humaines **1688**
1774-4970 Horizon Ouest **7444**
1774-5004 C G A's News Report† **8938**
1774-5012 Humacoop Infos **8045**
1774-5047 Les Chroniques de Spawn **482**
1774-5071 C V C **4117**
1774-508X Dech'Infos† **8949**
1774-5098 Dracenie Point Communication *changed to* 1957-6234 **7434**
1774-5160 Etapes: **7320**
1774-5187 Evo **8172**
1774-5195 Destination Culture **4003**
1774-5225 Les Chroniques du G E M M **4210**
1774-5233 Cent pour Cent Exclusif†
1774-525X C I R D D 37 **2692**
1774-5268 Association Les Amis de Saint Jacques. Bulletin **7623**
1774-5276 Cheval Fan **8289**
1774-5306 Heterite **7360**
1774-5314 Approche Centree sur la Personne **7336**
1774-5349 Entreprendre Placements **1622**
1774-5357 Le Grand Saint-Barthelemy **7442**
1774-5365 Dimag - Hors-Serie *see* 1767-4328 **7588**
1774-5373 Annales d'Histoire Caledonienne **4191**
1774-5381 Avertissements Agricole. Champagne-Ardenne. Pommes de Terre **94**
1774-5411 Archivistorique **4990**
1774-5438 Les Cahiers de l'Industrie Electronique & Numerique **3297**
1774-5462 Communaute de Communes du Pays de Lunel. Bulletin **7490**
1774-5470 Connaissance de Barres **5278**
1774-5853 Ada **8893**
1774-640X Medecine Therapeutique Medecine de la Reproduction **5897**
1774-6701 Argos Spine News *changed to* 1957-7729 **6056**
1774-6760 Visite Deco **4552**
1774-6779 Vivre a Table†
1774-6787 Tennis Revue **8249**
1774-6965 La Revue des Notaires **4774**
1774-7007 En Jeux Sport **8171**
1774-7155 Visit Africa **8786**
1774-7201 Closer **8856**
1774-7252 Service d'Assistance Technique aux Exploitants de Stations d'Epuration. Bilan d'Activite
1774-7287 Aftermarket News (English Edition) *see* 1774-7295 **975**
1774-7295 Aftermarket News (French Edition) **975**
1774-7309 L'Alibi du Colibri **2175**
1774-7341 Flash (Pace)† **8956**
1774-735X Les Experts-Comptables de Bourgogne-France-Comte **1288**
1774-7376 Chef d'Entreprise Magazine **1958**
1774-7414 Alternatibaz **1422**
1774-7422 Au Fil de l'Hers **8818**
1774-7465 Decouverte les Sables d'Olonne **4003**
1774-7473 En Arrivant† **8953**
1774-7503 La Semaine Juridique. Social **4782**
1774-7554 Annuaire de la Boulangerie et de la Boulangerie-Patisserie **3670**
1774-7570 Bulletin du Batonnier† **8938**
1774-7589 La Bretagne Agricole **97**
1774-7600 Couleurs Catalogne **4003**
1774-7821 Entreprendre. Carriere **6697**
1774-847X Habitat Naturel **1010**
1774-8488 Shopping Magazine† **8988**
1774-8747 Medecine Therapeutique Cardio **5795**
1774-8828 Patient Reported Outcomes Newsletter **5694**
1774-8917 Transport Info Hebdo **8515**
1774-8984 Creation d'Entreprise Magazine **1959**
1774-9271 Dessilogique Facile *changed to* 1961-0823 **8949**
1774-9298 Bulletin Climatologique Mensuel. Deux Sevres **6348**
1774-9409 Caen Parler? **2970**
1774-9425 Cahiers Claude Simon **5268**
1774-9484 Le Guide Annuel des Deplacements Professionnels **8716**
1774-9514 Le Fil Dentaire **5844**
1774-9565 Global **3840**
1774-9581 La Croisade d'Alice† **8947**
1774-959X Entr'actes **5609**
1774-9611 Infos I N A P O R C **289**
1774-9670 R E A A P du Douaisis. Bulletin d'Information
1774-9689 Cathares Espace & Patrimoine **4002**
1774-9700 Chasse Info 03 **8309**
1774-9719 Association Amicale des Anciens Combattants du 8e Regiment de Cuirassiers. Bulletin Trimestriel **2264**
1774-9743 Reliance **6115**
1774-9751 Anamnese **5254**
1774-9816 Bibliotheque Departementale de Pret. La Lettre d'Information **4996**
1774-9832 Les Cahiers de Droit de la Sante du Sud-Est **7511**
1774-9840 C O D E R P A du Nord *changed to* 1953-6828 **8029**
1774-9883 Cap Quartiers **7429**
1774-9921 L'Etat en Vendee *changed to* 1969-6027 **7451**
1774-9972 La Bazarette **4404**
1774-9999 Aerospace Insider **43**
1775-0008 Forum (Paris, 2005)† **8957**
1775-0040 Coulisses† **8944**
1775-0067 Booster & B W's *see* 1258-8555 **8268**
1775-0105 Communaute de Communes de la Haute Sevre. Bulletin d'Information **7490**
1775-0113 Club Rythm' and Blues **6557**
1775-0121 Harmonicas de France Federation magazine **6572**
1775-013X Eglise dans les Hautes-Alpes **7796**
1775-0253 La Sauvagine **8332**
1775-0318 Journal des Professionnels de la Sante au Travail **6679**
1775-0326 Ile-de-France Regards sur... **8377**
1775-0733 P D A & Smartphones Magazine **2434**
1775-0970 Les Essais du Sport **8171**
1775-0997 Elles et Eux **4138**
1775-1055 Collection S 2 P **2183**
1775-111X Les Grands Hommes d'Etat **7139**
1775-1128 Du Bonheur Sinon Rien **3119**
1775-1136 Carres de Jardin **436**
1775-1152 Collection L'Oeil du Souffleur **8468**
1775-1179 Collection Plenitude **3119**
1775-1187 Genealogies de la Psychologie **7358**
1775-1195 Guide du Debutant **2419**
1775-1233 Collection Histoire **4135**
1775-125X Collection Art et Connaissance **482**
1775-1268 Collection Coureurs des Mers **8274**
1775-1284 Collection Poussiere d'Etoiles **5441**
1775-1314 Comedie Romantique **5276**
1775-1322 Cent Une Astuces **4331**
1775-1349 Du Reel-Fiction **5286**
1775-1373 Encore un mot! **5289**
1775-1403 Collection Sante **5598**
1775-1411 L'Histoire a l'Oeuvre **4141**
1775-142X Faceties **5295**
1775-1454 Les Conferences de la J P A **2183**
1775-1462 Anthony Burgess Centre Series **5255**
1775-1470 Collection Classiques Etrangers pour Tous **5275**
1775-1489 Chemin Faisant **1858**
1775-1497 Cent Reponses sur... **3840**
1775-1519 Les Cahiers de l'As de Trefle **7112**
1775-1527 Collection Ensemble Baroque de Limoges **6557**
1775-1535 Collection Horizons Litteraires **5275**
1775-1543 Idees Minute **536**
1775-1616 Ecologie et Politique **7131**
1775-1640 La Voix de l'Inde **5395**
1775-1993 Papers Creatifs **538**
1775-2523 Fonderie sous Pression International **6312**
1775-2531 Diac'Infos **5785**
1775-2698 France Horizon, Le Cri du Rapatrie
1775-2744 Guide Pratique des Medicaments **5621**
1775-2760 L'Avenir Ensemble **7488**
1775-2892 Association Le Faubourg. Banque de Projets† **8931**
1775-2906 Les Chiffres Cles du Transport en Alsace **8493**
1775-2981 Universite de Nantes. Centre de Recherches en Histoire Internationale et Atlantique. Enquetes et Documents **4275**
1775-304X Fluides & Transmissions **3361**
1775-6464 Collection Cote Pratique **3119**
1775-6472 Musees de Macon. Les Cahiers d'Inventaire **507**
1775-6502 Chemin de Croix **7791**
1775-6561 Collection Chaos International **7117**
1775-657X Les Ecrits **5287**
1775-6618 Comprendre (Paris, 2005) **7348**
1775-6723 Citadelle **4135**
1775-6820 Histoire, Memoire et Patrimoine **4227**
1775-6871 Association Lacanienne Internationale. Cahiers **7337**
1775-7258 Memoires & Archives **4244**
1775-7266 Monde Imparfait **7155**
1775-7290 Construire les Alternatives **7119**
1775-7630 Roman **5363**
1775-7819 Inf'eau Lys **3439**
1775-7878 Communaute de Communes de l'Arentele, Durbion, Padozel. Bulletin **7490**
1775-7894 C A N A R E P Infos Retraites **1857**
1775-7924 Golf Driver Mag **8231**
1775-7959 Comite Departemental des Retraites et Personnes Agees. Bulletin *changed to* 1959-0601 **8028**
1775-7967 Le Forum des Medecins Generalistes **5615**
1775-8017 Business News **1074**
1775-8076 France Energie Avenir **1596**
1775-8084 La Lettre Sentinel **5224**
1775-8114 Contact Elevage **8289**
1775-8122 Bulletin Franco-Hellenique **3524**
1775-8130 Bulletin Climatologique Mensuel. 84 Vaucluse **6348**
1775-8149 Bulletin Climatologique Mensuel. 05 Haute Alpes **6348**
1775-8157 Bulletin Climatologique Mensuel. 34 Herault **6348**
1775-8165 Bulletin Climatologique Mensuel. 66 Pyrenees-Orientales **6348**
1775-8173 Bulletin Climatique Mensuel Sud-Est Cigale **6348**
1775-819X Cyclo Sante **6229**
1775-8246 Bretons: Societe, Culture, Musique **3840**
1775-8289 Fichenn Deknikel† **8956**
1775-8297 A H F Huntington France **6117**
1775-8343 Galopin. Hors-Serie **8291**
1775-8351 F N A D E P A Express **8039**
1775-8394 60 Grilles de Mots Fleches† **9000**
1775-8602 Micro Portable Magazine **2578**
1775-8785 Archives des Maladies Professionnelles et de l'Environnement **6673**
1775-8882 Societe Historique de Meaux et sa Region. Bulletin **4265**
1775-9196 Fiches Pratiques du Droit de la Sante **7517**
1775-920X Guide du Budget **4094**
1775-9226 Conditions d'Homologation et Procedures d'Exploitation des Aerodromes **51**
1775-9234 Dictionnaire Permanent Transactions Immobilieres **7588**
1775-9269 Audit et Autoevaluation **1805**
1775-9277 Gestion Pratique d'un C E **1683**
1775-9285 Gestion du Personnel Methodes et Outils **1861**
1775-9293 Guide Pratique et Reglementaire des Interventions et des Aides Sociales **4094**
1775-9315 Guide de la Remuneration et de la Paie des Personnels Medicaux et Hospitaliers **4094**
1775-9331 Collectivites Territoriales. Guide de la Remuneration **6696**
1775-934X Guide Pratique de l'Intendant **4683**
1775-9412 L'Exploitation Vitivinicole **109**
1775-9439 Guide du Management des Competences **1749**
1775-9455 Guide de Controle des Mutuelles du Code de la Mutualite Assumant un Risque d'Assurance **4504**
1775-9463 Guide de l'Accueil Temporaire **4066**
1775-9471 Encyclopedie des Collectivites Locales **7435**
1775-9498 Formulaire Batiment **1008**
1775-9501 L'Europe **4668**
1775-9528 Formulaires et Outils Qualite **1746**
1775-9536 Le Guide Juridique de l'Elu Local **7443**
1775-9587 Guide d'Application de l'A D R **8497**
1775-9595 Soins et Prevention en Entreprise **6687**
1775-9609 Les Conges **1673**
1775-9633 4 X 4 Story. Special Jeep *see* 1771-432X **8614**
1775-965X La Girafe **8497**
1775-9668 Force & Passion **114**
1775-9706 Syndicat Intercommunal du Loir. Bulletin d'Information **7503**
1775-9749 Le Droit Individuel a la Formation **1859**
1775-979X Les Voies de la Communication **1714**
1775-9846 Le C E et la Formation Professionnelle **1857**
1776-016X Techniques de l'Ingenieur. Physique-Chimie **3256**
1776-0178 Techniques de l'Ingenieur. Materiaux Fonctionnels **3222**
1776-0186 Techniques de l'Ingenieur. Maintenance **3222**
1776-0259 Chroniques Slaves **5273**
1776-0283 L'Officiel Voyage **8745**
1776-0550 Revue du Cadre de Sante *changed to* 1962-2287 **5716**
1776-064X *see* 1955-0960 **5079**
1776-0674 Nouvelles de la Boulangerie - Patisserie **3675**

ISSN

1779-4374 Langage et Inconscient
1779-4390 Vegetable **168**
1779-4633 Biotech Finances **759**
1779-4676 Sacree Planete **6950**
1779-4684 Cahiers d'Etudes Hispaniques Medievales **5103**
1779-4692 *see* 1288-7013 **4415**
1779-4811 A I M. Bulletin **7781**
1779-482X Impulser **1752**
1779-4838 Les Cahiers Pratiques **4353**
1779-4994 Les Cahiers de Champs Visuels†
1779-5095 Rest'ho News **4397**
1779-515X La Revue des Initiatives **7405**
1779-5281 Cheval Arabe Sport *changed to* 2103-3137 **8289**
1779-5486 Supermoto One **8268**
1779-5567 Eveil & Evolution **6918**
1779-5672 Eco Immobilier **1097**
1779-5761 Elus *changed to* 1779-577X **7502**
1779-577X Revue des Collectivites Locales **7502**
1779-6261 Mode de Recherche **2259**
1779-627X International Journal for Simulation and Multidisciplinary Design Optimization **3200**
1779-6288 *see* 1779-627X **3200**
1779-6326 Memento Pratique Francis Lefebvre. Union Europeenne **4935**
1779-6334 Memento Pratique Francis Lefebvre. Urbanisme, Construction **7599**
1779-6342 Memento Pratique Francis Lefebvre. Gestion Immobiliere **7599**
1779-6431 Association Departementale de Developpement Culturel (A D D C) **4976**
1779-6733 Le Bulletin des Gazons **3726**
1779-6903 Revue des Loyers, de la Copropriete et des Fermages **4425**
1779-6911 Electronique International **3097**
1779-7179 Revue Europeenne de Mecanique Numerique **3357**
1779-7217 Logiques Sociales. Serie Sociologies Europeennes **8119**
1779-7225 Logiques Sociales. Serie Sociologie des Arts **8119**
1779-7284 Universite de Provence. Arts. Histoire des Arts **523**
1779-7322 Giallo Polar **5300**
1779-7381 Croq'temps **5280**
1779-739X Rayon Noir **5358**
1779-7551 Pensee Africaine **351**
1779-7594 Mes P'tits Bobos **2202**
1779-7713 Centre Francais de Droit Compare **4641**
1779-7748 Collection Management Social **1734**
1779-7799 Le Scribe Cosmopolite **5368**
1779-7837 Les Cahiers de Scrap **532**
1779-7861 Collection Theatre et Connaissances **8468**
1779-787X Architectures Elementaires **431**
1779-7985 Histoires de Sciences **7861**
1779-8051 Nos Coups de Coeur **8742**
1779-8213 Les Cahiers d'Histoire de la Philosophie **6909**
1779-8337 Le Philologue **5161**
1779-8418 Cendrier du Voyage **5271**
1779-8450 Cafe Psycho **7343**
1779-8469 Quelle Sante **314**
1779-8671 Couleurs du Temps, Couleurs du Fleurissement **3727**
1779-8701 Genealogie Facile **3768**
1779-871X Empreintes **3419**
1779-8876 Cheval Attitude **8289**
1779-8884 Les Nouvelles Esthetiques Spa **590**
1779-8973 C'est a Vous **1082**
1779-9163 French Annual Review **8291**
1779-9171 Mederic Infos Sante **4514**
1779-9325 Futuremaison.com **443**
1779-9546 Le Fil d'I R I S **5758**
1779-9651 Peches et Bateaux **8328**
1779-9708 Diriger un Service des Affaires Culturelles **7434**
1779-9805 Social Batiment **1874**
1779-9813 Techniques Documentaires **2551**
1779-9848 Pratique d'Oracle **2503**
1779-9929 Emotion Spa **308**
1780-0005 Elle Belgique *see* 1379-9991 **8861**
1780-0838 La Libre Essentielle Homme **6294**
1780-1044 Textielreiniging *changed to* 1780-1052 **2244**
1780-1052 Textielverzorging **2244**
1780-1273 Het Laatste Nieuws **3801**
1780-1311 Studies in Afrotropical Zoology **964**
1780-1788 Royals Hors Serie **3781**
1780-2393 J B R - B T R **6199**
1780-3160 *see* 0020-7950 **4170**
1780-3179 *see* 0020-7950 **4170**
1780-3187 Food & History **3637**
1780-3756 Natagora **910**
1780-3837 De Leeswolf **2199**
1780-4159 Technique et Management *changed to* 1780-4175 **1752**
1780-4167 Industrie Technisch Management *see* 1780-4175 **1752**
1780-4175 Industrie Technique et Management **1752**
1780-4515 Comparatisme et Societe **7956**
1780-4582 Corpus Christianorum. Series Latina **7793**
1780-5414 Regards sur l'International **7261**
1780-5848 Geopolitique et Resolution des Conflits **7237**
1780-5910 Brepols Essays in European Culture **4206**
1780-6496 La Libre Essentielle Voyage **8730**
1780-678X Image & Narrative **4456**
1780-6895 Glam - It **588**
1780-6941 Delta **2977**
1780-7212 Gentse Bijdragen tot de Interieurgeschiedenis **491**
1780-7220 Veilig Bouwen *changed to* 1780-7875 **7532**
1780-7239 Securite Construction *changed to* 1780-7867 **6675**
1780-7603 A Magazine **2258**
1780-7611 Euredia - Revue Europeene de Droit Bancaire et Financier **1338**
1780-7867 C N A C Info **6675**
1780-7875 N A V B Info **7532**
1780-874X A N P I Magazine (Dutch Edition) **3575**
1780-9231 Negociations **7988**
1780-9665 College of Europe Studies **7227**
1780-9738 Film - DVD - Video *changed to* 1782-6756 **6500**
1781-0930 Eastern Christian Art **391**
1781-1317 Res Antiquae **4158**
1781-1392 A R P E N T **1722**
1781-2534 Khil'a **8454**
1781-2631 Info Accueillant(e)s **2866**
1781-3816 A View from Brussels **7272**
1781-3867 Etudes Canadiennes **7962**
1781-3875 Annales de Medecine Veterinaire (Online Edition) **8792**
1781-4456 H R Magazine (French Edition) **1862**
1781-5231 Vita Latina **5194**
1781-5827 Mens & Molecule **2073**
1781-5967 Corpus Christianorum. Series Graeca **7635**
1781-6718 CAP **8288**
1781-6858 European View **7234**
1781-7595 E J H P Science **6837**
1781-782X B - E N T **6078**
1781-7838 Studia Rosenthaliana **7730**
1781-877X Store Check Foodgids **3681**
1781-8818 Codex Arbeidsrecht **1670**
1781-8869 Snoecks Almanak (Jaar) **3122**
1781-8907 Store Check Guide Food **3681**
1781-8974 F W D Home Entertainment Magazine **2381**
1781-989X Tijdschrift voor Bouwrecht en Onroerend Goed **1040**
1781-9989 E J H P Practice **6837**
1782-0154 De Kers *see* 1782-0162 **6656**
1782-0162 La Cerise **6656**
1782-0642 Europe's World **7134**
1782-0715 Politiecodex **2664**
1782-0723 Code de la Police *see* 1782-0715 **2664**
1782-0758 Imagine Demain le Monde **1598**
1782-0871 Bewaking en Beveiliging **4885**
1782-0901 Nest (French Edition) *see* 1378-7101 **3801**
1782-1185 Bouwkundige Richtlijnen bij het Ontwerpen van een Brandveilig Gebouw **4496**
1782-1193 Codex Openbare Hulpverlening. Preventie **7430**
1782-1207 Codex Openbare Hulpverlening. Hulpdiensten **7430**
1782-1215 Codex Openbare Hulpverlening. Interventie **7430**
1782-1266 De Barema's voor het Notariaat **4627**
1782-138X *see* 0002-0478 **7220**
1782-1398 *see* 1372-8202 **7343**
1782-1401 *see* 1370-074X **7343**
1782-141X *see* 0577-148X **7126**
1782-1428 *see* 1373-847X **2848**
1782-1436 *see* 0027-2841 **4246**
1782-1444 *see* 0302-3052 **1601**
1782-1452 *see* 1780-9231 **7988**
1782-1479 *see* 1376-0963 **8125**
1782-1487 *see* 1245-2092 **7401**
1782-1495 *see* 0770-4518 **1164**
1782-1509 *see* 0034-2971 **1164**
1782-1517 *see* 1245-4060 **1515**
1782-1525 *see* 1010-8831 **4774**
1782-1533 *see* 1370-0731 **7263**
1782-1541 *see* 1378-1863 **6233**
1782-155X *see* 0765-3697 **8135**
1782-1568 *see* 0247-106X **6232**
1782-1576 *see* 0082-6049 **5189**
1782-1592 Recherches Sociologiques et Anthropologiques **8127**
1782-1843 O M D Actualites **7458**
1782-1851 W C O News **7476**
1782-1908 Codex O C M W - Wetgeving **8034**
1782-2041 Bulletin d'Analyse Phenomenologique **6909**
1782-2173 Codex van de Architect **438**
1782-4389 Auto Max (French Edition) **8559**
1782-4397 Auto Max (Dutch Edition) **8559**
1782-4613 Cool & Comfort (Dutch Edition) **4118**
1782-4621 Cool & Comfort (French Edition) **4118**
1782-4907 Caeculus **385**
1782-4931 Georges Pompidou - Etudes **4223**
1782-5156 Special Serres & Veranda's **1036**
1782-6454 Special Badkamers & Keukens **1036**
1782-6756 Filmmagie **6500**
1782-7183 Viking and Medieval Scandinavia **4277**
1782-740X Ik Ga Bouwen *changed to* 1782-7426 **990**
1782-7418 Je Vais Construire *changed to* 1782-7434 **990**
1782-7426 Casas (Dutch Edition) **990**
1782-7434 Casas (French Edition) **990**
1782-799X *see* 1782-8007 **1947**
1782-8007 Tax Audit & Accountancy **1947**
1782-9747 Journal des Juges de Paix **4699**
1782-9755 Journal des Juges de Police **4699**
1783-0710 Georges Pompidou - Archives **4223**
1783-094X Contextes **5278**
1783-1180 Terra Incognita **420**
1783-1199 *see* 1783-1180 **420**
1783-1326 *see* 1378-4641 **373**
1783-1334 *see* 0066-1619 **2230**
1783-1342 *see* 0959-4213 **4319**
1783-1350 *see* 0515-0361 **4493**
1783-1369 *see* 0165-9367 **385**
1783-1377 *see* 0006-2278 **6907**
1783-1385 *see* 0037-9069 **5175**
1783-1393 *see* 1782-4907 **385**
1783-1407 *see* 0771-6524 **5127**
1783-1415 *see* 1781-0930 **391**
1783-1423 *see* 0013-9513 **7796**
1783-1431 *see* 1370-0049 **6917**
1783-144X *see* 0778-6069 **6918**
1783-1458 *see* 1370-5954 **7797**
1783-1466 *see* 1780-7212 **491**
1783-1474 *see* 1370-6020 **7648**
1783-1482 *see* 0021-0870 **399**
1783-1490 *see* 0019-0810 **8425**
1783-1504 *see* 0021-762X **553**
1783-1512 *see* 1016-5584 **4322**
1783-1520 *see* 1783-1555 **7737**
1783-1539 *see* 1370-7205 **7979**
1783-1555 The Journal of Eastern Christian Studies **7737**
1783-1563 *see* 0453-3429 **402**
1783-1571 *see* 1781-2534 **8454**
1783-158X *see* 0771-6494 **556**
1783-1598 *see* 0024-1482 **5144**
1783-1601 *see* 0222-9838 **5127**
1783-161X *see* 0024-6964 **7805**
1783-1628 *see* 0575-1330 **4321**
1783-1636 *see* 0167-5257 **5154**
1783-1644 *see* 0078-463X **5157**
1783-1652 *see* 0774-2827 **7667**
1783-1660 *see* 0030-4379 **5158**
1783-1679 *see* 0085-4522 **558**
1783-1695 *see* 0295-1630 **5352**
1783-1709 *see* 0774-5524 **7673**
1783-1717 *see* 1370-7493 **7673**
1783-1725 *see* 0034-4567 **6963**
1783-1733 *see* 0035-1849 **414**
1783-1741 *see* 0080-2549 **4324**
1783-175X *see* 0484-8616 **7729**
1783-1768 *see* 0035-3841 **6949**
1783-1776 *see* 0038-7479 **5376**
1783-1784 *see* 0221-5004 **561**
1783-1792 *see* 1781-7838 **7730**
1783-1806 *see* 0926-2326 **7685**
1783-1814 *see* 0926-6453 **7685**
1783-1822 *see* 0082-6847 **562**
1783-1830 *see* 1781-5231 **5194**
1783-1970 I T Professional (Dutch Edition) *see* 1783-1989 **2544**
1783-1989 I T Professional (French Edition) **2544**
1783-2446 *see* 1783-2454 **7641**
1783-2454 European Society of Women in Theological Research. Journal **7641**
1783-3019 Equilibre **5610**
1783-3086 Gentleman (Dutch Edition) **6291**
1783-3094 Gentleman (French Edition) **6291**
1783-323X Dentist News (French Edition) *changed to* 1783-3264 **5842**
1783-3248 Dentist News (Dutch Edition) *changed to* 1783-3256 **5842**
1783-3256 Dentist News & Tandartsenwereld **5842**
1783-3264 Dentist News & le Monde Dentaire **5842**
1783-3639 A C E **1722**
1783-3914 European Journal of Oncology Pharmacy **6019**
1783-4341 Chiffres & Tarifs **1917**
1783-4384 Dokadi (Dutch Edition) **2186**
1783-4392 Dokadi (French Edition) **2186**
1783-4635 Wet & Werk *see* 1783-4880 **1869**
1783-4880 Loi & Emploi **1869**
1783-5402 Finance Management **1745**
1783-578X Documents pour l'Histoire des Francophonies. Europe **4215**
1783-5917 Competition and Regulation in Network Industries **4862**
1783-6883 Les Cahiers du C E P E S S **7225**
1783-6891 *see* 1783-6883 **7225**
1783-7014 Human Rights and International Legal Discourse **7208**
1783-7677 Journal on Multimodal User Interfaces **2549**
1783-8363 Ancient West & East **2230**
1783-8398 *see* 1783-8363 **2230**
1783-8401 *see* 0080-2654 **7815**
1783-8452 L'Ecole et la Ville *changed to* 1783-8460 **3058**
1783-8460 Dossier. L'Ecole et la Ville **3058**
1783-8479 Les Kurdes **346**
1783-8509 Le Courrier du Musee et de ses Amis **6522**
1783-8517 Chocolaterie (Dutch Edition) **3631**
1783-8525 Chocolaterie (French Edition) **3673**
1783-8738 *see* 1783-7677 **2549**
1783-8819 Precis de TVA **1940**
1783-8835 Codex Sociale Zekerheid **8034**
1783-8940 The New Social Europe **7158**
1783-8959 *see* 1783-8940 **7158**
1783-8967 *see* 1783-8940 **7158**
1783-8983 Jurisprudence en Droit des Societes Commerciales. Recueil Annuel **4873**
1783-8991 Marketing Services Yearbook **1833**
1783-9025 Journal of Inner Asian Art and Archaeology **499**
1783-9831 Wijntrends **612**
1783-984X Tendances Vin **611**
1784-0104 Special Verandas & Orangeries **1036**
1784-0112 Special Cuisines & Salles de Bain **1036**
1784-0171 Agence Federale de Controle Nucleaire. Rapport Annuel **7064**
1784-018X Federaal Agentschap voor Nucleaire Controle. Jaarverslag **7066**
1784-0376 Milo **8875**
1784-0686 The European Academy of Sciences. Annals **7853**
1784-0732 E-Newsletter for Science and Technology **7852**
1784-0759 Europe. Diplomatie & Defense **7233**
1784-0783 Windows Vista Magazine **2600**
1784-1240 C S C - Educ **4591**
1784-133X Gimik **5072**
1784-1410 Institut pour l'Egalite des Femmes et des Hommes. Rapport d'Activites **8868**
1784-150X Plus Woman (Dutch Edition) **8880**
1784-1518 Plus Woman (French Edition) **8880**
1784-1976 A B D **5883**
1784-2344 Global Focus **1748**
1784-2417 A G A B **2722**
1784-2808 Francais 2000 **5120**
1784-2816 Histocar Revue **366**
1784-2980 Belgian Motor Sport (French Edition) **8161**
1784-2999 Belgian Motor Sport (Dutch Edition) **8161**
1784-3227 Acta Gastro-Enterologica Belgica **5919**
1784-3243 Gastromania **4386**
1784-3251 *see* 1784-3243 **4386**
1784-3286 Acta Clinica Belgica **5565**
1784-3308 Omertaa **351**
1784-3405 Badje Info **8027**
1784-3413 Nouvelles Comptables **1297**
1784-3421 Acta Chirurgica Belgica **6234**
1784-3472 *see* 1784-3499 **1841**
1784-3480 Store et Showroom *changed to* 1784-3499 **1841**
1784-3499 Retail Update Magazine **1841**
1784-357X *see* 1784-0686 **7853**
1784-3685 Africalia the Newsletter **464**
1784-3693 *see* 1784-3685 **464**
1784-3707 *see* 1784-3685 **464**
1784-3847 Le Bulletin des Militants **7111**
1784-4037 PoloniaNet - Decom **3558**

1793-6799 *see* 0219-4937 **8407**
1793-6802 *see* 0219-5259 **7833**
1793-6810 *see* 0219-5194 **683**
1793-6829 *see* 0219-4988 **5500**
1793-6837 *see* 0217-5908 **1174**
1793-6845 *see* 0219-6220 **2547**
1793-6853 *see* 0192-415X **5740**
1793-6861 *see* 0219-5305 **5469**
1793-687X *see* 1609-9451 **1018**
1793-6888 *see* 0219-6336 **2108**
1793-6896 *see* 0219-6867 **1890**
1793-690X *see* 0219-6913 **5497**
1793-6918 *see* 0219-7499 **7017**
1793-6926 *see* 0219-6492 **5021**
1793-6942 *see* 0219-8436 **2585**
1793-6950 *see* 0219-8770 **3201**
1793-6969 *see* 0219-8762 **5495**
1793-6977 *see* 0219-8878 **7016**
1793-6985 *see* 0219-8789 **2426**
1793-6993 *see* 0219-8916 **5504**
1793-7000 *see* 0219-8711 **1676**
1793-7019 *see* 0217-5959 **2407**
1793-7027 *see* 1793-0057 **5520**
1793-7035 *see* 1793-0480 **7006**
1793-7043 *see* 0256-7679 **2121**
1793-7051 *see* 0219-6077 **7009**
1793-706X *see* 1084-9467 **1962**
1793-7078 *see* 1793-2068 **2436**
1793-7094 *see* 1793-2920 **3211**
1793-7108 *see* 1793-351X **2426**
1793-7116 *see* 1793-4311 **2711**
1793-7132 *see* Biomedical Engineering: Applications, Basis and Communications **748**
1793-7159 *see* 1793-5245 **5495**
1793-7167 *see* 1793-5253 **2330**
1793-7175 *see* 1793-5369 **3180**
1793-7183 *see* 1793-5571 **5473**
1793-7191 *see* 1230-1612 **2524**
1793-7205 *see* 1793-5458 **6044**
1793-7213 *see* 1793-6047 **7856**
1793-7221 *see* 1793-6187 **3404**
1793-7299 Kinki University Series on Quantum Computing **2430**
1793-7310 *see* 1793-0421 **5497**
1793-7434 *see* 1793-7442 **5481**
1793-7442 Confluentes Mathematici **5481**
1793-7469 Agriculture and Food **85**
1793-771X Advances in Environmental Research and Development **3401**
1793-8031 *see* 1793-771X **3401**
1793-8155 Frontiers of Statistics **5488**
1793-8503 Advances in Computational Fluid Dynamics **3180**
1793-8570 Mathematical Olympiad Series **5514**
1794-0915 Ornitologia Colombiana **912**
1794-1113 Observatorio de Economia y Operaciones Numericas **1156**
1794-1237 Escuela de Ingenieria de Antioquia. Revista **3191**
1794-2489 Tabula Rasa **4477**
1794-4449 Revista Lasallista de Investigacion **151**
1794-4724 Avances en Psicologia Latinoamericana **7338**
1794-5216 Universitas Estudiantes **4802**
1794-5240 *see* 0121-0319 **5672**
1794-5887 Revista Co-herencia **4472**
1794-6190 Earth Sciences Research Journal **2780**
1794-631X Revista de Investigaciones **7903**
1794-6670 Cuadernos de Musica, Artes Visuales y Artes Escenicas **6560**
1794-7111 Kepes **4544**
1794-7715 Cuadernos del C I P E **7957**
1794-9165 Ingenieria y Ciencia **3198**
1794-9998 Diversitas **7352**
1795-0015 Enermail (Finnish Edition) **3134**
1795-0023 Enermail (English Edition) **3134**
1795-0031 Enermail (Swedish Edition) **3134**
1795-004X Enermail (German Edition) **3134**
1795-0058 Enermail (French Edition) **3134**
1795-0546 Turbo **8608**
1795-0570 *see* 1795-0589 **2863**
1795-0589 Helsingin Yliopisto. Viikin Normaalikoulu. Julkaisu **2863**
1795-0813 Savonia-Ammattikorkeakoulu. Julkaisu. A **3001**
1795-0821 Savonia-Ammattikorkeakoulu. Julkaisu. B **3001**
1795-083X Savonia-Ammattikorkeakoulu. Julkaisu. C **3001**
1795-0848 Savonia-Ammattikorkeakoulu. Julkaisu. D **3001**
1795-1178 Ilta-Sanomat T V *see* 0355-2055 **3838**
1795-1496 *see* 1796-9905 **4890**
1795-150X Metlan Tyoraportteja **3696**
1795-1631 Systeri **2215**
1795-1739 Kulttuuripoliittisen Tutkimuksen Edistamissaatio. Cuporen Julkaisuja **7450**
1795-1798 Ilta-Sanomat Plussa *see* 0355-2055 **3838**
1795-1828 Helsingin Kauppakorkeakoulu. W. Working Papers (Online) **1118**
1795-1887 Finland. Tilastokeskus. Vaestorakenne ja Vaestonmuutokset Kunnittain **7306**
1795-1895 Agricultural and Food Science (Online) *see* 1459-6067 **83**
1795-1909 Kotu-Tutkimuksia *changed to* 1797-0466 **8052**
1795-1917 Kotunet (Online) *changed to* 1797-0474 **6157**
1795-2050 Finland. Tilastokeskus. Rahalaitokset **1231**
1795-2131 Katsaus **5222**
1795-2158 Helsingin Yliopisto. Soveltavan Kasvatustieteen Laitos. Tukimuksia **2863**
1795-2476 Persona Grata **7390**
1795-2484 The Griffin **3692**
1795-2492 *see* 1795-2484 **3692**
1795-2506 *see* 1795-2484 **3692**
1795-2514 *see* 1795-2484 **3692**
1795-2808 Universitas Chydenius **3007**
1795-2824 Tampereen Teknillinen Yliopisto. Opetusmoniste **3221**
1795-3030 Kauppalehti Presso **1139**
1795-3049 *see* 1795-3030 **1139**
1795-3340 *see* 0788-5008 **1191**
1795-3359 *see* 0788-5016 **1191**
1795-3405 Helsingin Yliopisto. Maaseudun Tutkimus- ja Koulutuskeskus. Raportteja *changed to* 1796-0622 **1489**
1795-357X Inline (Finnish Edition) **1054**
1795-3588 Inline (English Edition) **1054**
1795-3596 Inline (Swedish Edition) **1054**
1795-360X Inline (German Edition) **1054**
1795-3693 *see* 1238-7169 **8779**
1795-3715 Forma & Furniture **4540**
1795-3766 Jyvaskylan Ammattikorkeakoulu. Raportteja **2879**
1795-3790 Kirjallisuudentutkimuksen Aikakauslehti Avain **5317**
1795-3863 Turun Yliopisto. Kulttuurien Tutkimuksen Laitoksen. Arkistot. Julkaisuja **4479**
1795-3898 Finland. Maa- ja Metsatalousministerio. Tietopalvelukeskus. Eurojyva **113**
1795-391X Osaava Kodinrakentaja **4548**
1795-3936 Tampereen Teknillinen Yliopisto. Digitaalisen Median Instituutti. Hypermedialaboratorio. Raportti *changed to* 1796-9859 **2439**
1795-4126 Kanssalainen **7149**
1795-4134 *see* 1795-4126 **7149**
1795-4215 Historia **4142**
1795-4282 *see* 0784-8196 **1046**
1795-4533 *see* 1455-6413 **4435**
1795-4568 C. C. **3838**
1795-4614 Kalkholm News **8649**
1795-4835 Tampereen Teknillinen Yliopisto. Ragnar Granit Instituutti. Raportti **751**
1795-4886 *see* 0784-9672 **1232**
1795-4932 *see* 0039-9922 **6750**
1795-4940 *see* 0355-4481 **6750**
1795-5165 Finland. Tilastokeskus. Suomen Virallinen Tilasto **8371**
1795-5211 Helsingin Yliopisto, Vasa Nation. Aarsbok **2983**
1795-5270 *see* 1796-5675 **7637**
1795-536X Finland. Tilastokeskus. Tiede, Teknologia ja Tietoyhteiskunta **7854**
1795-5564 Veneily.fi (Print) *changed to* 1797-3988 **8664**
1795-5610 Pohjois-Karjalan Maakuntaliitto. Julkaisu **3460**
1795-5742 Galilei **4453**
1795-5777 Tampereen Yliopisto. Kirjasto. Bulletiini **5050**
1795-5904 *see* 0789-0737 **3839**
1795-5920 Tampereen Teknillinen Yliopisto. Digitaali- ja Tietokonetekniikan Laitos. Tutkimusraportti **2474**
1795-5939 Tampereen Kaupunki. Yhdyskuntapalvelut Asemakaavoitus. Julkaisuja *changed to* 1797-321X **521**
1795-617X *see* 0784-9346 **4435**
1795-6420 In Look **2256**
1795-6641 Chydenius-Instituutin Selvityksiae **2837**
1795-6889 Human Technology **2323**
1795-6897 Finland. Sosiaali- ja Terveysalan Tutkimus- ja Kehittamiskeskus. Discussion Papers **8040**
1795-6900 Jyvaskylan Yliopisto. Bio- ja Ymparistotieteiden Laitos. Tiedonantoja **685**
1795-7079 Helsingin Yliopisto. Biotieteellinen Tiedekunta. Dissertationes Bioscientiarum Molecularium Universitatis Helsingiensis in Viikki **676**
1795-7222 F I L I S Rapport **5294**
1795-7230 *see* 1239-1638 **7437**
1795-7257 PhD Dissertations in Biology **697**
1795-729X Aabo Akademi. Department of Business Studies. Annual Report **1722**
1795-732X Finland. Tilastokeskus. Suomi Lukuina **8371**
1795-7389 Dissertationes Forestales **3687**
1795-746X *see* 1455-1233 **7132**
1795-7494 Acta Wasaensia. Kirjallisuuden- ja Kulttuurintutkimus **5249**
1795-7575 Suomen Pankki. Rahoitusmarkkinat. Tilastokatsaus **1269**
1795-7583 *see* 1795-7575 **1269**
1795-7672 Ilmavoimalainen **6424**
1795-7680 *see* 0788-0308 **4435**
1795-7745 Infotech Oulu. Annual Report **2423**
1795-7753 *see* 1795-7745 **2423**
1795-777X Euroopan Unionin Verolait **1922**
1795-7818 CrossCountry **8310**
1795-7834 Ikaalisten Kasi- ja Taideteollisuusoppilaitos. Julkaisu **495**
1795-7842 Finland. Huoltovarmuuskeskus. Julkaisu **1885**
1795-7850 -ing **3270**
1795-7877 Degree Student's Guide **2977**
1795-8016 Ananda **6982**
1795-8032 Kirahviposti **1600**
1795-8040 Kepa Newsletter **1600**
1795-8059 Finnish Institute of International Affairs. U P I Briefing Paper **7235**
1795-8083 G S 1 Info **6402**
1795-8113 *see* 0785-6016 **1232**
1795-8121 *see* 0785-9880 **1232**
1795-8202 *see* 1795-6897 **8040**
1795-8229 *see* 1795-7079 **676**
1795-8342 Lappeenrannan Teknillinen Yliopisto. Kauppatieteiden Kandidaatin ja Maisterin Tutkinnot. Opinto-Opas **2992**
1795-8628 Finland. Ministry of Foreign Affairs. Helsinki Process. Publication Series **1718**
1795-8822 Akavalainen **4589**
1795-8830 Hanasaari Agenda **7239**
1795-8857 *see* 1459-8035 **7360**
1795-8865 Techno Today **3004**
1795-8881 Finland. Tilastokeskus. Kansantalouden Tilinpito (Online) **1231**
1795-8903 Hot Wheels Magazine (Tampere) **2193**
1795-8938 E T - Ristikot **8170**
1795-9101 Agenda Magazine **7220**
1795-9128 Heeler Harrastajat **118**
1795-9284 Anna Kauneus *see* 0355-3035 **8851**
1795-9489 Dissertations in Interactive Technology **2470**
1795-9543 *see* 1239-8306 **2980**
1795-9551 *see* 1239-8314 **2980**
1795-9586 *see* 1459-6881 **2980**
1795-9799 Tieto&Trendit **8409**
1795-9837 Finnish Dance in Focus **2686**
1795-9861 Arvoasunta *see* 0782-6060 **1610**
1795-990X *see* 0355-3140 **6687**
1795-9977 Finnish Documentary Films **6501**
1796-010X Jyvaskylan Ammattikorkeakoulu. Puheenvuoroja **2879**
1796-0118 *see* 0788-544X **2638**
1796-0185 *see* 1238-3724 **2784**
1796-0363 i L E A P S. Newsletter **7864**
1796-0401 *see* 1796-0363 **7864**
1796-0479 Finland. Tilastokeskus. Suomen Virallinen Tilasto **8371**
1796-0495 Inline (Polish Edition) **1054**
1796-0614 Kasino A 4 **499**
1796-0622 Helsingin Yliopisto. Ruralia-Instituutti. Raportteja **1489**
1796-0630 *see* 1796-0622 **1489**
1796-0649 Helsingin Yliopisto. Ruralia-Instituutti. Julkaisuja **1489**
1796-0657 *see* 1796-0649 **1489**
1796-072X Finnish Short Films **6501**
1796-0738 Finnish Films **6501**
1796-0800 Merisotakoulu. Julkaisusarja. A, Tutkimuksia **6434**
1796-0878 *see* 0787-572X **4435**
1796-0940 Majakka **1366**
1796-0959 Ethnos-Tiedote **3616**
1796-0967 *see* 1796-0959 **3616**
1796-105X Jyvaskylan Yliopisto. Perhetutkimuskeskus. Julkaisu **8116**
1796-1076 Merisotakoulu. Julkaisusarja. B, Asiatietoja **6434**
1796-1211 Uudenmaan Insinoori Ins. **4604**
1796-1238 Finland. Maa- ja Metsatalousministerio. Tietopalvelukeskus. Maataloustilastotiedote **113**
1796-1246 *see* 0785-6172 **8524**
1796-1254 *see* 0788-1738 **1232**
1796-1394 Emergent Business Research Coalition. Research Reports **1815**
1796-1408 *see* 1796-1394 **1815**
1796-1475 Geofoorumi **2736**
1796-1483 Juoksu & Hiihto **8320**
1796-1599 *see* 0788-804X **6615**
1796-1637 *see* 1238-7312 **3468**
1796-1645 Finland. Ymparistoministerio. Ymparistohallinnon Ohjeita **7437**
1796-1653 *see* 1796-1645 **7437**
1796-1661 *see* 1239-1875 **3483**
1796-1688 *see* 0789-8789 **7543**
1796-1696 Finland. Ymparistoministerio. Raportteja **3486**
1796-170X *see* 1796-1696 **3486**
1796-1718 Suomen Ymparistokeskus. Raportteja **3491**
1796-1726 *see* 1796-1718 **3491**
1796-2021 Journal of Communications **2329**
1796-203X Journal of Computers **2428**
1796-2048 Journal of Multimedia **2330**
1796-2056 Journal of Networks **2500**
1796-217X Journal of Software **2593**
1796-2196 *see* 1457-084X **1232**
1796-220X *see* 0355-3191 **7832**
1796-2218 *see* 0355-3205 **4441**
1796-2226 *see* 0355-3213 **8415**
1796-2234 *see* 0355-3221 **5567**
1796-2242 *see* 0355-323X **7102**
1796-2250 *see* 0781-1306 **3838**
1796-2269 *see* 1455-2647 **1056**
1796-2285 Acta Wasaensia. Sosiaali- ja Terveyshallinto *changed to* 1796-9352 **8022**
1796-2420 Kasvatus ja Koti **2880**
1796-2439 Kotona **7597**
1796-2749 I B S Newsletter Russia **1241**
1796-2757 I B S Newsletter Baltic States **1241**
1796-2765 I B S Newsletter Central and Western Europe **1241**
1796-2986 COLLeGIUM **7955**
1796-3141 Kipuviesti **5658**
1796-315X *see* 1796-3141 **5658**
1796-3176 Humanistisen Tiedekunnan Jatko-Opiskelijan Opinto-Opas **2986**
1796-3206 Tampereen Teknillinen Yliopisto. Rakennetekniikan Laitos. Tutkimusraportti **1039**
1796-3257 *see* 1238-4623 **1046**
1796-329X Kaupunkilehti Ankkuri **3838**
1796-332X *see* 0789-2462 **1231**
1796-3338 Fine **603**
1796-3370 Plaza Koti **4562**
1796-3389 Energian Kulutus *changed to* 1797-4690 **3188**
1796-3516 *see* 0785-6288 **1232**
1796-3524 *see* 0784-820X **1231**
1796-3613 *see* 0784-817X **1232**
1796-3621 *see* 1236-9942 **1046**
1796-3656 Akseli **2938**
1796-3664 *see* 1796-3656 **2938**
1796-3737 *see* 0784-8218 **1231**
1796-3745 *see* 0786-0366 **8524**
1796-3753 Basso **6548**
1796-3907 *see* 0784-9613 **1231**
1796-4040 *see* 0785-613X **8524**
1796-4369 Finland. Elintarviketurvallisuusvirasto Evira. Julkaisu **7517**
1796-4636 *see* 1236-6641 **3584**
1796-4938 *see* 0784-7998 **1232**
1796-5152 Susel *changed to* 1796-7120 **2688**
1796-5195 *see* 0785-6245 **8524**
1796-539X Financial Stability **1345**
1796-5497 Ajankohtaista Kuluttajaoikeudesta **2634**
1796-5500 Current Issues on Consumer Law *see* 1796-5497 **2634**
1796-5551 S Q S **8130**
1796-5578 *see* 1796-539X **1345**
1796-5659 Finland. Kansaneläkelaitos. Kelan Tilastollinen Vuosikirja **4529**
1796-5667 *see* 1796-5659 **4529**
1796-5675 Diakonian Tutkimus **7637**
1796-590X Kotiristikko Extra **8184**
1796-6116 Farmasia **6841**
1796-6183 Finnish Yearbook of Population Research **7283**
1796-6191 *see* 1796-6183 **7283**
1796-6213 Sara **8882**
1796-6434 *see* 1459-0131 **1817**
1796-6507 Hifimaailma **8153**

ISSN

ISSN

ISSN

9812 1816-6148 ULRICH'S PERIODICALS

1816-6148 Corporate Law, Partnerships and Trusts 4864
1816-6253 I A V I Report 5816
1816-6261 *see* 1816-6253 5816
1816-6652 Aiyue 3960
1816-6822 Makerere Journal of Higher Education 2993
1816-711X Miromente 5334
1816-7446 Private Equity Asia 1161
1816-7454 *see* 1816-7446 1161
1816-7578 O E C D Education Statistics 2935
1816-7586 O E C D Agriculture Statistics 184
1816-7594 O E C D Banking Statistics 1256
1816-7616 O E C D Employment and Labour Market Statistics 1256
1816-7624 O E C D International Development Statistics (Online) 1256
1816-7632 E-beratungsjournal.net 2319
1816-7659 Marang 5330
1816-7667 Manglar 4464
1816-7713 Revista Peruana de Obstetricia y Enfermeria 6003
1816-7721 *see* 0864-4497 3631
1816-7748 Mindshift 7155
1816-7853 Journal of Research. Humanities *changed to* 2074-2061 7991
1816-7861 Visitor 8772
1816-7950 Water S A (Online) 8840
1816-7969 Water Wheel 8841
1816-7977 *see* 1816-7969 8841
1816-7985 Amanzi (Online Edition) 2792
1816-8124 O E C D Journal on Development 1602
1816-8396 African Natural History 651
1816-840X New Homes 4547
1816-8418 Bosvelder 3947
1816-8426 The Crest 3948
1816-8434 Market Forces 1778
1816-8442 Boat Owner Middle East 8272
1816-8523 *see* 1684-7075 6875
1816-8663 China Boating 8274
1816-8892 Ilanga le Theku 3948
1816-8957 Scientific Drilling 6791
1816-8965 One Small Seed 510
1816-8973 O E C D International Direct Investment Statistics (Online) 1256
1816-8981 O E C D International Migration Statistics 1256
1816-899X International Trade by Commodities Statistics 1244
1816-9007 Main Economic Indicators 1250
1816-9031 O E C D Economic Outlook: Statistics and Projections 1256
1816-904X O E C D Science, Technology and R & D Statistics 3233
1816-9058 O E C D Statistics on International Trade in Services 1257
1816-9066 O E C D Social Expenditure Statistics 1257
1816-9074 S T A N: O E C D Structural Analysis Statistics 1261
1816-9082 *see* 0496-7801 6538
1816-9112 Research Journal of Fisheries and Hydrobiology 3605
1816-9120 *see* 1816-9112 3605
1816-9139 Structural Statistics for Industry and Services (Online) *changed to* 1991-7899 1268
1816-9147 O E C D Telecommunications and Internet Statistics 2348
1816-9155 Agricultural Journal 84
1816-9260 Revista Paraguaya de Enfermeria 5980
1816-9279 *see* 1013-5294 6875
1816-9341 Kindred Spirits 4850
1816-949X Journal of Engineering & Applied Sciences (Faisalabad) 3204
1816-9503 International Journal of Soft Computing 2472
1816-9627 Africa Renewal 1435
1816-9783 P V Info 1298
1816-9821 Benchmark Repair 1974
1817-0196 Bantu 5065
1817-020X Heureka 7861
1817-0331 Movie & D V D 6507
1817-0358 Quart 7813
1817-0412 Wiener Veroeffentlichungen zur Musikgeschichte 6628
1817-0862 Postamble 4470
1817-0900 *see* 1812-3651 7697
1817-0919 *see* 1683-6162 3948
1817-0986 South Africa Writing 5375
1817-1044 Intern 27
1817-1060 Werbealmanach 37
1817-1079 *see* 1817-1060 37
1817-1087 Cash 1555
1817-1095 Cash Almanach 3629
1817-1109 *see* 1817-1095 3629
1817-115X Juniors 2257
1817-1168 Oesterreichische Textil Zeitung 8456
1817-1176 Oesterreichische Textil Zeitung Wohnen 8456
1817-1184 Bestseller 21
1817-1192 Traveller 8768
1817-1206 Hotel und G V - Praxis 4390
1817-1281 Hotel & Touristik 4390
1817-129X Das Touristik Telefonbuch 8764
1817-1303 La Revue Libanaise de l'Arbitrage Arabe et International *see* 1815-7165 4834
1817-1427 Car (Middle East Edition) 8571
1817-163X A V C J Weekly 1305
1817-1648 *see* 1817-163X 1305
1817-1656 M & A Asia 1366
1817-1664 *see* 1817-1656 1366
1817-1729 Z E I - E U - Turkey - Monitor 7275
1817-1737 Annals of Thoracic Medicine 5944
1817-1745 Journal of Pediatric Neurosciences 6155
1817-1931 South African Paddler 8283
1817-194X Recueil Africain des Decisions des Droits Humains 4851
1817-1958 African Outfitter 8301
1817-1966 Maverick 1147
1817-1974 BusinessBrief 1731
1817-2008 African Technology Development Forum Journal 1057
1817-2075 Revista Medica Vallejiana 5706
1817-2083 Zeitschrift fuer Stiftungswesen und Vermoegensverwalt 4906
1817-2091 A4 463
1817-2105 The Journal of Human Resources and Adult Learning 1868
1817-2172 Differentsial'nye Uravneniya i Protsessy Upravleniya 5483
1817-2245 Reviews in Conservation 2626
1817-2458 *see* 1561-4085 7028
1817-2520 Jet Asia-Pacific 63
1817-2709 Ebensolch 7560
1817-2717 The Zambian Marketer 1849
1817-3047 World Journal of Agricultural Sciences 170
1817-3055 World Journal of Medical Sciences 5731
1817-3098 World Journal of Zoology 968
1817-3179 Journal of Global Business Management 1766
1817-3195 *see* 1992-8645 2430
1817-3322 Journal of the Drylands 128
1817-3381 Journal of Fisheries International 3599
1817-3535 Juta's Tax Law Review 4708
1817-3721 Plant Tissue Culture and Biotechnology 813
1817-3853 L P Luxury Properties 7597
1817-4019 Wissenplus 3088
1817-4035 S P I E Professional 3218
1817-406X Botanical Studies 781
1817-4108 Manna 7661
1817-4167 Copyright Bulletin (Online) 4650
1817-4175 Boletin de Derecho de Autor (Online) *see* 1817-4167 4650
1817-4256 *see* 1816-0735 6024
1817-4264 *see* 1682-900X 7205
1817-4272 Time Out Dubai. Shopping 5084
1817-4280 Grazia 8866
1817-4337 Asian Journal of Traditional Medicines 5579
1817-4434 The Journal for Transdisciplinary Research in Southern Africa 8111
1817-4493 Positionen Architektur 453
1817-4507 *see* 1817-4493 453
1817-454X Horoshie Roditeli 2154
1817-4574 International Journal on Multicultural Societies 8110
1817-4604 Contemporary Issues and Ideas in Social Sciences 7956
1817-5082 *see* 1817-3047 170
1817-5090 Cost and Management 1286
1817-5104 *see* 1817-5090 1286
1817-5112 Design & Build 4356
1817-5325 Building Women 987
1817-5333 S A Jewellery News 4569
1817-5481 *see* 1069-2851 1383
1817-5562 The New Iraqi Journal of Medicine 5685
1817-5651 *see* 0042-1308 2083
1817-5694 Convergence (London) 4650
1817-5708 Competition Law International 4921
1817-5805 *see* 1812-9471 5548
1817-5813 African Agricultural Technology Foundation. Annual Report 79
1817-5996 *see* 1606-5581 6226
1817-6046 Continuing Medical Education Series 5600
1817-633X *see* 0261-152X 5013
1817-6356 Caoben Xinjiankang Lu/Herb & Health *changed to* 1992-6944 6644
1817-650X Al-Nashrat al-Ihbariyyat 1590
1817-6518 Istratigiyyat al-Hay'at al-'arabiyyat li-l-istithmar wa-al-Inma al-Zira'i li-l-A'wam *see* 1818-1619 1605
1817-6526 Al Haya'at al-'arabiyyat li-l-Istithmar wa-al-Inma al-Zira'i. Al-Taqrir al-Sanawi *see* 1817-6534 194
1817-6534 Arab Authority for Agricultural Investment and Development. Annual Report 194
1817-6585 Risk Management 6685
1817-7360 Sax Appeal 2300
1817-7417 African Journal of Business Ethics 1855
1817-7530 Scrinium 7706
1817-7565 *see* 1817-7530 7706
1817-762X Sociedad Paraguaya de Cardiologia. Revista 5799
1817-7638 *see* 1817-762X 5799
1817-7816 *see* 1813-7768 2263
1817-7824 *see* 1813-7768 2263
1817-7832 *see* 1813-7768 2263
1817-7840 *see* 1813-7768 2263
1817-7859 *see* 1813-7768 2263
1817-7867 *see* 1813-7768 2263
1817-7875 *see* 1813-7768 2263
1817-8391 Mosaico Cientifico 7883
1817-8987 Tvoe Zdorov'ye 8848
1817-9355 Greenprint 3435
1817-9770 Afring News 901
1818-0353 Science in School 3081
1818-0361 *see* 1818-0353 3081
1818-0876 Asian Journal of Pharmaceutical Sciences 6823
1818-1023 Revista Internacional de Psicologia 6182
1818-1139 International Journal of Computing and Information and Communication Technology Research 2425
1818-1228 Studies in Business and Economics 1180
1818-1295 Visnyk Morfolohii 5728
1818-1619 Strategy (Khartoum) 1605
1818-1627 Arabian Business. Yearbook 1060
1818-1686 *see* 1562-3009 231
1818-1783 Today's Trustee 1656
1818-2070 Wonderland 461
1818-2089 Men's Health Living 6285
1818-2097 PositionIT 3215
1818-2100 Elektron†
1818-2119 Vector (Muldersdrift) 3334
1818-2127 Energize 3158
1818-2364 Bogensport Journal 8162
1818-2380 M M S Mag 6469
1818-2704 *see* 1817-4280 8866
1818-2828 Qingshaonian Yixue ji Baojian Tongxun 6103
1818-2879 The Weekender 1193
1818-2909 Sankt-Peterburgskii Universitet. Vestnik. Seriya 11. Meditsina 5709
1818-295X Yunaya Ledi 2223
1818-3344 Pakistan Journal of Education 2895
1818-3565 Fountain Series in Education Studies 2858
1818-3689 Custom P C South Africa 2575
1818-3786 Gaming Equipment and Reviews 2477
1818-3794 Research Council of Zimbabwe. Symposium on Science and Technology. Proceedings 7902
1818-443X Innovate 3198
1818-4650 Tiyu Pindao *see* 1097-1998 8170
1818-4715 Landscape SA 3741
1818-4952 World Applied Sciences Journal 7930
1818-5193 Fynproe 603
1818-5401 African Cultures and Religion *changed to* Journal of African Cultures and Religion 8111
1818-5444 Neue Entwicklungen im Financial Planning 1371
1818-5487 Aquatic Invasions 933
1818-5800 The Social Sciences 8004
1818-6300 European Archives of Paediatric Dentistry 5843
1818-6556 I T A - Berichte 8425
1818-6661 7-Watch 8777
1818-6734 International Dentistry South Africa 5848
1818-6742 Nexo 3212
1818-6769 American-Eurasian Journal of Agricultural and Environmental Sciences 91
1818-6874 International Journal of African Renaissance Studies 4175
1818-6904 Stuff U Need! 8336
1818-7137 MeteoWorld 6391
1818-7145 MeteoMonde *see* 1818-7137 6391
1818-7153 *see* 1818-7137 6391
1818-7188 Umwelt und Bildung 8011
1818-7706 Entrepreneur 1960
1818-7781 *see* 1816-3211 6259
1818-779X *see* 1816-3319 5819
1818-7803 *see* 1816-949X 3204
1818-7854 Occident & Orient 409
1818-7927 Housemag
1818-815X Sandton Central Essential Directory 8754
1818-8745 *see* 1817-3721 813
1818-9059 Thoughts 7543
1818-9067 Gedagtes 7518
1818-9083 Dairy Mail Africa 263
1818-9091 S A Horseman 299
1818-9113 African Archer & Adventurer 8157
1818-9202 Liechtensteiner Vaterland 3905
1818-9253 Saltwater Girl Surf Magazine 8332
1818-930X Digital Africa 2416
1818-9342 Die Erdekruik 7640
1818-9628 Meatec Nachrichten 293
1818-975X Leading Brands 1829
1818-9814 Al Magallat al-'ilmiyyat li-l-Tanmiyat 1146
1818-9822 *see* 1818-9814 1146
1818-9849 Al Magallah al-'arabiyyah li-l-adab 4464
1818-9962 *see* 1995-0802 5509
1819-0324 Benchmark Tool 1974
1819-0618 Wirtschaft Regional 1525
1819-0626 *see* 1819-0618 1525
1819-1185 South African Bear 540
1819-1460 Clivia News 3727
1819-1495 Politravma 6071
1819-1509 E F - Z 4909
1819-1541 Asian Journal of Plant Pathology 777
1819-155X International Journal of Biological Chemistry 734
1819-169X GeoArabia Special Publication *see* 1025-6059 6771
1819-1819 I S S N Portal 626
1819-1878 Asian Journal of Animal Sciences 8793
1819-1886 Asian Journal of Earth Sciences 2702
1819-1894 Asian Journal of Agricultural Research 93
1819-1908 Research Journal of Veterinary Sciences 8806
1819-1924 Asian Journal of Marketing 1805
1819-1932 Research Journal of Business Management 1790
1819-1991 The Complete Guide to Bass Fishing Southern Africa 8310
1819-2041 South African Fitness Professionals 6997
1819-205X Mense 3949
1819-2408 Technicheskaya Akustika (Online) 7089
1819-2505 Fantastik Fur 2188
1819-2645 Ideas 4361
1819-2661 C J C P Issue Paper 4885
1819-2696 C I O 1414
1819-2718 *see* 1025-9589 5581
1819-2866 Qimam Sbaydarman 2209
1819-2971 Business Review 1730
1819-298X ZaZen 316
1819-334X Asian Journal of Information Management 2541
1819-3358 Asian Journal of Textile 8448
1819-3366 Current Research in Tuberculosis 6213
1819-3374 Kidney Research Journal 5896
1819-3382 Space Research Journal 71
1819-3390 Research Journal of Allergy 5765
1819-3404 Research Journal of Cardiology 5798
1819-3412 Research Journal of Environmental Sciences 3462
1819-3420 Research Journal of Environmental Toxicology 3501
1819-3439 Research Journal of Forestry 3700
1819-3455 Research Journal of Medicinal Plant 815
1819-3463 Research Journal of Physics 7037
1819-3471 Research Journal of Phytochemistry 744
1819-348X Research Journal of Radiology 6207
1819-3498 Research Journal of Soil Biology 700
1819-3552 Research Journal of Seed Science 250
1819-3560 Research Journal of Toxins 3501
1819-3579 Trends in Applied Sciences Research 7924
1819-3587 Trends in Medical Research 5724
1819-3595 International Journal of Plant Breeding and Genetics 794
1819-3609 Asian Journal of Poultry Science 279
1819-3889 FamZ 4910
1819-3994 RUFORUM Annual Report 152
1819-401X RUFORUM News 152
1819-4192 Issledovano v Rossii 7869
1819-4311 Journal of Software Engineering 2593
1819-4567 Guangtian Yixue Zazhi 5621
1819-4621 Marvel 2201

1819-4761 Hulk **2193**
1819-4966 International Journal of Computational and Applied Mathematics **5495**
1819-5164 Asian Journal of W T O & International Health Law and Policy **4917**
1819-5415 *see* 1816-1561 **150**
1819-544X *see* 1816-157X **7872**
1819-5458 *see* 1816-2746 **8805**
1819-5490 Bulletin for International Taxation **1913**
1819-5571 Majallat Markaz al-Dirasat al-Filastiniyyat **7251**
1819-5644 New Voices in Translation Studies **5155**
1819-5709 B I M C O Ice Handbook **8639**
1819-5717 *see* 0251-0952 **816**
1819-5741 Tax Magazine **1948**
1819-611X Money **1368**
1819-6357 *see* 1993-2820 **5661**
1819-6462 The Dialogue **7959**
1819-6489 Majallat al-Mansur **7881**
1819-6551 The State of Higher Education **3002**
1819-656X I A E N G International Journal of Computer Science **2420**
1819-6608 Journal of Engineering and Applied Sciences (Islamabad) **3204**
1819-6667 Teaching Times for Educators **2918**
1819-6675 JET Bulletin **2872**
1819-6713 Go! (Cape Town, 2006) **8713**
1819-6918 Wegbreek **8774**
1819-7094 *see* 1027-4510 **3396**
1819-7108 *see* 0742-0463 **2791**
1819-7124 Neurochemical Journal **6164**
1819-7132 *see* 1819-7124 **6164**
1819-7140 Russian Journal of Pacific Geology **2765**
1819-7159 *see* 1819-7140 **2765**
1819-754X Mires and Peat **689**
1819-7558 Submerge **8210**
1819-7655 *see* 1819-8775 **4886**
1819-7973 Gomal Journal of Medical Sciences **5620**
1819-8031 True Love Babe **8886**
1819-804X Artthrob **475**
1819-8430 Lanyang Yizhi **5660**
1819-8503 Off-Limits **2205**
1819-8538 World Journal for Tourism Development and Marketing **1848**
1819-8546 World Journal of Events and Sports Tourism **8776**
1819-8554 World Journal of Tourism and Hospitality Management **8776**
1819-8562 World Journal of Peace through Tourism **8776**
1819-8570 World Journal of Tourism, Leisure and Sports **8776**
1819-8589 World Journal of Business Management **1801**
1819-8597 World Journal of Public Policy **7194**
1819-8600 World Journal of Conflict Resolution **7274**
1819-8619 World Journal of International Relations **7274**
1819-8627 World Journal of Sciences and Educational Administration **3035**
1819-8635 World Journal of Community Development **8147**
1819-8643 World Journal of Management and Economics **1196**
1819-8651 World Journal of Sustainable Development **3475**
1819-866X World Journal of Public Administration and Management **7477**
1819-8678 Ethiopian Journal of Biological Sciences **671**
1819-8759 Parade **8295**
1819-8767 *see* 1819-8759 **8295**
1819-8775 Commentary on the Criminal Procedure Act **4886**
1819-9224 *see* 1819-656X **2420**
1820-0052 Bibliografija Srbije. Serijske Publikacije **617**
1820-0060 Bibliografija Srbije. Serijske Publikacije. Zvanicne Publikacije **617**
1820-0087 Bibliografija Srbije. Monografske Publikacije. Prevodi **617**
1820-0206 Scientific-Technical Review **3219**
1820-0710 Cosmopolitan (Belgrade) **8856**
1820-0737 Bilje i Zdravlje **8853**
1820-1202 *see* 0352-5252 **5833**
1820-1253 *see* 1450-9733 **4200**
1820-1776 *see* 1450-7994 **5675**
1820-2039 Udruzenje za Medunarodno Pravo Srbije i Crne Gore. Godisnjak **4943**
1820-2403 National Geographic Junior **4021**
1820-2802 Sport Specijal **8205**
1820-2969 Revija za Kriminologiju i Krivicno Pravo **2667**
1820-2977 Godisnjak Pozorista Srbije i Crne Gore **8471**
1820-3949 Pesticidi i Fitomedicina **247**
1820-4856 J A M A (Serbian Edition) *see* 0098-7484 **5642**
1820-4856 J A M A (Serbian Edition) *see* 1301-3491 **5643**
1820-4856 J A M A (Serbian Edition) *see* 1318-1092 **5642**
1820-4856 J A M A (Serbian Edition) *see* 1000-842X **5678**
1820-5054 Vocarstvo **258**
1820-5151 Maxim **6294**
1820-5682 *see* 1451-5342 **5160**
1820-6301 Serbian Journal of Sports Sciences **8200**
1820-7804 *see* 0353-7919 **8143**
1821-1291 Bulletin of Mathematical Analysis and Applications **5476**
1821-5017 HakiElimu. Annual Report **3024**
1821-5025 T E N / M E T Newsletter **2917**
1821-5068 HakiElimu. Working Paper Series **2862**
1821-5092 E R B Engineers News Brief **3187**
1821-5149 Mwanangu **2161**
1821-5335 The Foundation News **8041**
1821-5483 Changamoto **3961**
1821-5521 Wakili Bulletin **4810**
1821-5653 Tanzania Political Economy Series **1710**
1821-570X Habari Leo **3961**
1821-6404 Tanzania Journal of Health Research **5720**
1822-0347 Spectrum **3002**
1822-038X Computer Bild Lietuva **2411**
1822-1009 Lietuva Pristato **3905**
1822-1017 Litva Predstavlyaet **3906**
1822-1025 Lithuania Presents **3905**
1822-1904 Sostines Skelbimai **3906**
1822-3214 Princeses **2208**
1822-3788 Lietuvos Respublikos Mokejimu Balansas (Annual) **1365**
1822-427X The Baltic Journal of Road and Bridge Engineering **3260**
1822-4288 *see* 1822-427X **3260**
1822-430X Santalka **5171**
1822-4318 *see* 1822-430X **5171**
1822-5063 Lietuvos Bankas. Finansinio Stabilumo Apzvalga **1365**
1822-5071 *see* 1822-5063 **1365**
1822-511X Siauliai Mathematical Seminar **5536**
1822-5233 Bank of Lithuania. Financial Stability Review **1315**
1822-5241 *see* 1822-5233 **1315**
1822-6566 Greiti Ratai **2191**
1822-7805 *see* 1392-8600 **5200**
1822-7864 Problems of Education in the 21st Century **2900**
1823-2140 Medine & Health **5675**
1823-5530 Biomedical Imaging and Intervention Journal **6193**
1823-6138 Neurology Asia **6166**
1823-6243 International Journal of Asia - Pacific Studies **4457**
1823-7681 Al-Jazari International Journal of Civil Engineering **3273**
1823-8556 Journal of Sustainability Science and Management **3448**
1824-0100 Ittiopatologia **680**
1824-0119 Forest@ **3690**
1824-016X *see* 0037-8720 **581**
1824-0208 Bike Tour **8255**
1824-0232 In Cucina† **8963**
1824-0283 *see* 1724-6776 **6003**
1824-0348 Settimanale di Piu **3898**
1824-050X Bioarchitettura **435**
1824-0542 Civilta Arcaica dei Sabini nella Valle del Tevere **333**
1824-0550 Contributi alla Storia degli Studi Etruschi e Italici **333**
1824-0569 Corpus Inscriptionum Etruscarum **4136**
1824-0577 Latium Vetus **4151**
1824-0593 Musei e Collezioni d'Etruria **6530**
1824-0631 Thesaurus Linguae Etruscae **5187**
1824-0771 Nuova Informazione Bibliografica **632**
1824-078X Psicologia Clinica dello Sviluppo **7392**
1824-0852 Annali di Stomatologia **5835**
1824-0895 Il Quotidiano di Caserta **3898**
1824-0933 Orologi da Parete **4568**
1824-0941 *see* 1824-0895 **3898**
1824-095X *see* 1724-6121 **6923**
1824-0968 Le Guide di Campagna Amica Cibi & Natura **4359**
1824-0976 Le Guide di Campagna Amica Vacanze e Natura **8716**
1824-0984 Grandtour Toscana **8714**
1824-0992 Grandtour Sardegna **8714**
1824-100X Grandtour Dolomiti **8714**
1824-114X Ambiente Societa Territorio **3998**
1824-1204 Il Rosario di Padre Pio **7815**
1824-1247 Biblioteca di Filologia Romanza **5100**
1824-1255 Istituto di Scienze Amministrative e Sociali. Collana **7976**
1824-1298 Il Mio Prato **3743**
1824-1387 Biblioteca di Teologia Contemporanea **7627**
1824-1468 Monete Storiche da Collezione **6651**
1824-1484 Vita Notarile **4882**
1824-1492 Nuovi Quaderni di Vita Notarile *see* 1824-1484 **4882**
1824-1506 Vita Notarile Esperienze Giuridiche *see* 1824-1484 **4882**
1824-1530 Il Grande Jazz **6570**
1824-1603 Maxillo Ondontostomatologia **5855**
1824-1611 *see* 1824-1603 **5855**
1824-1670 Journal of Intercultural and Interdisciplinary Archaeology **401**
1824-1808 Collana Storica dell'Oltregiogo Ligure **4211**
1824-1816 Collana Storico - Archeologica della Liguria Occidentale **4211**
1824-1824 Scientific Nutrition Today (Online) **6669**
1824-1840 Bluemoon **5409**
1824-1859 Bluemoon. Le Collezioni *see* 1824-1840 **5409**
1824-1905 Urbanistica e Appalti **1042**
1824-1948 *see* 1724-6164 **5379**
1824-2030 Jekyll.comm *changed to* 1824-2049 **2330**
1824-2049 Journal of Science Communication **2330**
1824-212X Universita degli Studi di Salerno. Sezione Atti, Convegni, Miscellanee. Pubblicazioni **4479**
1824-2162 Rolling Stone Magazine **6613**
1824-2227 Il Mio Terrazzo† **8974**
1824-2235 Guida Ufficiale Monovolume† **8960**
1824-2359 Thalassa **2241**
1824-2367 Sanctorum **7816**
1824-2375 Gli Argomenti Umani **654**
1824-2421 Imago Shop & Fair **4543**
1824-243X Culture Antiche. Studi e Testi **2233**
1824-2448 Darwin **7849**
1824-2545 *see* 1827-6946 **4198**
1824-2588 Best Movie **6490**
1824-2707 Universita di Ferrara. Annali. Sezione: Museologia Scientifica e Naturalistica **6539**
1824-2715 Vinum **612**
1824-2723 Meridiani. Le Grandi Vie **8733**
1824-2731 Meridiani Montagne. Rifugi e Bivacchi **8322**
1824-274X Transcrime Reports **2670**
1824-2782 Formazione Permanente **6697**
1824-2804 Giardini e Paesaggio **3733**
1824-2820 Quaderni della Cineteca **6510**
1824-2898 Giochi e Programmi x il Mio Telefonino
1824-2979 The European Journal of Comparative Economics **1107**
1824-3010 Mediterranea. Ricerche Storiche **4244**
1824-3053 Biblion **2831**
1824-3061 *see* 1824-3053 **2831**
1824-307X Invertebrate Survival Journal **949**
1824-3096 *see* 0393-9383 **343**
1824-310X *see* 0393-9375 **341**
1824-3118 Contratti Collettivi di Lavoro **1673**
1824-3282 Indagine sulle Medie Imprese Industriali Italiane **1490**
1824-3290 *see* 1824-3282 **1490**
1824-3339 I Maestri dell'Arte Sarda **503**
1824-341X Macchine Alimentari **5455**
1824-3428 Tuning Generation **8608**
1824-3509 Newsletteravios *changed to* 1826-4662 **8131**
1824-3541 Ri - Vista. Ricerche per la Progettazione del Paesaggio. Quaderni **456**
1824-355X *see* 1724-6105 **5278**
1824-3568 *see* 1724-6148 **415**
1824-369X Studi Culturali **4476**
1824-372X Yatta!† **8999**
1824-3746 D H D **4384**
1824-3770 *see* 0394-5073 **6958**
1824-3886 Erasmus Law and Economics Review **4667**
1824-3932 CasAntica **437**
1824-3967 Textus **5387**
1824-3983 Horror Mania
1824-4025 Il Lazio Paese per Paese **8728**
1824-4130 L'Informatore Sportivo **8186**
1824-4173 Digital Music **6633**
1824-4181 Collana Matteo Ripa **547**
1824-4203 I Classici della Risata **5274**
1824-4483 D E P Deportate Esuli Profughe **8895**
1824-4491 Il Libro dei Codici† **8971**
1824-4556 Colloqui **4645**
1824-4564 Critica del Diritto (Naples) **4653**
1824-4572 Diritto e Cultura **4659**
1824-4602 *see* 1724-613X **5321**
1824-4696 Serramenti+Design **1055**
1824-4734 Quaderni sull'Investimento nel Capitale di Rischio **1646**
1824-4750 Quaderni di Teoria Sociale **7994**
1824-4777 Italian Journal of Vascular and Endovascular Surgery **6247**
1824-4785 The Quarterly Journal of Nuclear Medicine and Molecular Imaging **6205**
1824-484X L E A Letterature d'Europa e d'America (Online Edition) *see* 1824-4920 **5138**
1824-4920 L E A Letterature d'Europa e d'America (Print) **5138**
1824-4963 Filosofia e Teologia **6919**
1824-4971 Il Pensiero (Naples) **6938**
1824-498X Le Corti Calabresi **4651**
1824-4998 Le Corti Marchigiane **4651**
1824-5005 Le Corti Salernitane **4651**
1824-5013 Legalita e Giustizia **4721**
1824-5021 Le Radici & il Futuro **4471**
1824-5080 Istituto Italiano per gli Studi Filosofici. Saggi **6927**
1824-5188 Passigli Poesia **5429**
1824-5196 Rassegna Settimanale della Stampa Nazionale
1824-5285 Ipodworld Italia **2359**
1824-5293 GameStar Italia **2477**
1824-5439 *see* 1121-6840 **8494**
1824-5463 Advances in Transportation Studies **8489**
1824-5471 *see* 1120-415X **8505**
1824-548X I Veicoli: Profili Amministrativi **8610**
1824-5498 *see* 1824-548X **8610**
1824-5501 *see* 1120-4176 **8598**
1824-551X Il Trasporto e lo Smaltimento dei Rifiuti *changed to* 1828-597X **3513**
1824-5617 Le Revisioni dei Veicoli **8510**
1824-5625 *see* 1824-5617 **8510**
1824-5668 Accordo A T P e Norme Complementari sul Trasporto di Merci Deteriorabili **8666**
1824-5706 Maximum P C† **8973**
1824-5749 Cucina Light **4355**
1824-5870 Tu e il Tuo PC **2583**
1824-5889 I Maestri della Paura **5444**
1824-5897 Storia e Civilta **4268**
1824-5900 Gnosis **4890**
1824-5986 Filet Facile **6239**
1824-5994 Cucina e Tradizioni del Piemonte **4355**
1824-6095 Teknosport (Online) **8211**
1824-615X Tuning Bike **8269**
1824-6176 Acoustical Arts and Artifacts. Technology, Aesthetics, Communication **2311**
1824-6184 Arts and Artifacts in Movie Technology, Aesthetics, Communication **6490**
1824-6192 Eidola **487**
1824-6206 Musicalia **6594**
1824-6214 Marmora **405**
1824-6249 Paratesto **7570**
1824-6273 Resoconti di Letteratura Italiana **5360**
1824-629X Quaderni di Critica e Filologia Italiana **5164**
1824-6311 Raccontare la Poesia† **8984**
1824-632X I Racconti della Musica **6609**
1824-6338 Ricerche di Storia e Cultura
1824-6478 Papyrologica Florentina **5160**
1824-6486 Easy Shop **8859**
1824-6516 Il Pane e la Storia† **8980**
1824-6524 Personaggi in Primo Piano **3898**
1824-6559 La Scrittura e l'Interpretazione **7680**
1824-6621 2PN - Attualita Scientifica in Biologia della Riproduzione†
1824-6672 Statistica & Applicazioni **8403**
1824-6699 Invito all'Opera **8472**
1824-6710 Sintesi. Letteratura **5373**
1824-6729 Le Sirene **416**
1824-6745 *see* 0392-0224 **4458**
1824-6761 Storie d'Italia **5378**
1824-677X Studi di Storia e Storiografia† **8991**
1824-6796 Studi sul Petrarca **5379**
1824-6818 *see* 1122-5580 **5357**
1824-6966 Fieri **6919**
1824-7008 Giornale Italiano di Cardiologia Invasiva **5787**
1824-7016 Giornale Italiano di Cardiologia Invasiva. Supplemento *see* 1824-7008 **5787**
1824-7059 Archivi di Lecco e della Provincia **467**
1824-7075 Trieste Artecultura **4478**
1824-7121 Informacion Filosofica **6925**
1824-7180 *see* 1824-7199 **6596**
1824-7199 Musike **6596**
1824-7229 Tuttorario **8770**
1824-7237 Trieste A Z **8769**
1824-7245 Digital Japan Magazine
1824-727X Spolia **5376**
1824-7288 The Italian Journal of Pediatrics (Online) **6094**
1824-730X Prevenzione Odontostomatologica **5861**
1824-7326 *see* 1724-6156 **4325**
1824-7350 Music Compilation† **8975**
1824-7474 La Responsabilita Civile **4879**

ISSN

9816 1827-4870 ULRICH'S PERIODICALS

1827-4870 Istituto Accademico di Roma. Acta **4458**
1827-4889 *see* 1128-7594 **1965**
1827-4900 Eudossia **5292**
1827-4919 Torricelliana **7924**
1827-4927 Predella **512**
1827-4935 Automobile in Cifre (CD-ROM Edition) *see* 1827-4943
1827-4943 Autotrends
1827-4951 Anglistica Pisana **5254**
1827-5001 Left Avvenimenti **3897**
1827-5052 Guida al Pubblico Impiego Locale *changed to* 1827-5060 **1684**
1827-5060 Guida al Pubblico Impiego **1684**
1827-5087 Alter-Alter†
1827-5095 Voci **360**
1827-5133 Post Filosofie **6944**
1827-5184 Rivista del Cinematografo **6511**
1827-5249 Psicologia di Comunita **8127**
1827-5265 Exotic Files **8797**
1827-5354 Indici Mensili **1490**
1827-5362 Le Basi Razionali della Terapia
1827-5370 Giornale di Clinica Medica e Terapia
1827-5397 Studi Interdisciplinari sulla Famiglia **8141**
1827-5419 Il Corriere Vinicolo **602**
1827-5435 Enotria **603**
1827-5486 Accademie e Istituti Culturali
1827-5494 Agoge **371**
1827-5508 Rassegna dell'Avvocatura dello Stato **4765**
1827-5524 Collana Urbanistica **438**
1827-5567 Comparative and International Taxation **1917**
1827-5575 Dibattiti Storici in Parlamento **7130**
1827-5648 Recentissime **4766**
1827-577X Ortofrutta Italiana **245**
1827-5826 Polizia **2665**
1827-5834 Il Giornale di Filosofia **6921**
1827-5842 A e R **6105**
1827-5850 Play News **2480**
1827-5869 P S P Review **2480**
1827-5958 Il Mese di Modena **3897**
1827-5966 Il Mese di Reggio Emilia **3897**
1827-6091 Laboratorio sulle Varieta Romanze Antiche **5138**
1827-6105 Play Generation
1827-6148 *see* 0393-4578 **7029**
1827-6156 *see* 0017-0283 **7014**
1827-6164 *see* 1594-9974 **7036**
1827-6261 Off Road Capital *changed to* 1973-7807 **8561**
1827-6296 *see* 0394-9303 **7527**
1827-6318 *see* 1827-6326
1827-6326 Eventi Culturali
1827-6334 Istituto Italiano per l'Africa e l'Oriente. Reports and Memoirs **399**
1827-6350 Strumenti di Diritto Comparato **4789**
1827-6369 Strumenti per il Lavoro Psico - Sociale ed Educativo **2915**
1827-6377 Ville Venete **460**
1827-6393 Tra Storia e Cronaca **4478**
1827-6458 Annuari di Economia dell'Arte **466**
1827-6547 Of Arch **452**
1827-6555 Sphera Medical Journal **5717**
1827-6571 Trendy Girl **592**
1827-6598 Ascolta Sempre il Cuore Remi
1827-6601 Quaderni di Studi Ecumenici **7672**
1827-661X Guida Mutui **7592**
1827-6636 Universita di Catania. Facolta di Scienze Politiche. Pubblicazioni **7575**
1827-6652 Dipartimento di Scienze Giuridiche. Quaderni Brevi **4658**
1827-6660 International Review of Electrical Engineering **3321**
1827-6679 *see* 1827-6660 **3321**
1827-6717 SoloCase **7612**
1827-6741 Pensiero Giuridico e Politico. Nuova Serie **4757**
1827-675X *see* 0392-100X **6077**
1827-6784 Novecento Teologico **7666**
1827-6806 Giornale Italiano di Cardiologia **5787**
1827-6857 Collana di Diritto Pubblico **4860**
1827-6873 *see* 1827-1383 **7064**
1827-6881 *see* 1824-6699 **8472**
1827-6946 Annali di Storia di Firenze **4198**
1827-6954 Auto d'Epoca **8557**
1827-7004 La Barca per Tutti **8272**
1827-7047 Revue des Litteratures de l'Union Europeenne **5362**
1827-7055 Audio Video Foto Bild **2400**
1827-7071 Prospettive dell'Economia **1513**
1827-7144 *see* 1827-7152 **5991**
1827-7152 Il Ginecologo **5991**
1827-7349 Trittico Giuridico **4798**
1827-7357 Ricerche sulle Lingue di Frammentaria Attestazione **5169**
1827-7365 Rivista di Storia del Cristianesimo **7678**
1827-7373 La Previdenza Forense **4760**
1827-7438 Cucina (Milan)† **8947**
1827-7446 Cucina Dolci† **8947**
1827-7454 Golose in Cucina† **8960**
1827-7462 *see* 1827-7373 **4760**
1827-7489 Guida alla Novita Fiscale **1927**
1827-7527 Casino de la Vallee **8165**
1827-7535 Fior di Ricette **4358**
1827-7543 Collezione Kinder **2183**
1827-7578 Wild Life Serie Oro
1827-7594 Donnavventura Serie Oro
1827-7608 Esploriamo Serie Oro
1827-7632 World Heritage Serie Oro
1827-7659 La Cucina Serie Oro
1827-7667 Etnie Serie Oro
1827-7675 Studi sulla Cultura dell'Antico **419**
1827-7683 Circolo di Cultura Giuridica Nuova Giustizia. Quaderni **4642**
1827-7691 Dipartimento di Teoria dei Sistemi e delle Organizzazioni. Quaderni **7959**
1827-7713 *see* 0392-6672 **2748**
1827-7829 Photoshop Magazine **6980**
1827-7861 *see* 1121-8932 **2229**
1827-787X *see* 0001-9593 **5091**
1827-7888 *see* 0001-9046 **371**
1827-7942 *see* 0022-6955 **4708**
1827-7950 *see* 1593-0793 **4848**
1827-7977 *see* 0390-8240 **7784**
1827-7985 *see* 1122-1917 **5093**
1827-7993 *see* 1129-3764 **5095**
1827-8027 *see* 1128-2045 **5379**
1827-8035 *see* 0078-7760 **2999**
1827-8051 Chef d'Oro **4354**
1827-806X *see* 0392-6672 **2748**
1827-8086 Manu Sprint **2201**
1827-8094 *see* 0021-3071 **7507**
1827-8124 Direfarescrivere **5214**
1827-8183 La Gazzetta del Lunedi
1827-8213 *see* 0015-783X **4677**
1827-8221 *see* 0015-783X **4677**
1827-823X Eros **5409**
1827-8248 Fantaluna **5442**
1827-8256 D Cuore **5409**
1827-8361 European Diversity and Autonomy Papers **7134**
1827-837X La Guida ai Fuoristrada† **8960**
1827-8388 Universita di Palermo. Facolta di Economia. Annali
1827-8418 Cento per Cento Fuoristrada† **8940**
1827-8469 La Buona Cucina Golosa† **8938**
1827-8485 La Cucina Deliziosa† **8947**
1827-8582 Alimenti & Bevande **3626**
1827-8590 Nutrafoods **6664**
1827-8604 Golf Punk (Italian Edition) **8232**
1827-8655 *see* 1827-4927 **512**
1827-8698 Argomenti di Antiquariato **364**
1827-8701 Arredare la Casa (Milan) **4531**
1827-871X Bar Design **4532**
1827-8736 L'Ascensore Percorso Verticale e Orizzontale **4531**
1827-8779 La Femme Fatale
1827-8868 Web Journal on Cultural Patrimony **423**
1827-8930 *see* 1724-4625 **7166**
1827-8949 *see* 0012-978X **1676**
1827-8957 *see* 1825-6619 **5290**
1827-8965 *see* 1122-5300 **7164**
1827-8973 *see* 1826-5219 **4468**
1827-8981 Giornale Italiano di Cardiologia. Supplemento *see* 1827-6806 **5787**
1827-9244 Auto Annuario **8557**
1827-9279 Auto Dossier **8557**
1827-9589 L'Enciclopedia del Cavallo e del Cavaliere† **8971**
1827-9597 Le Guide Pratiche dei Nostri Amici Cavalli† **8960**
1827-9635 Acta Herpetologica **929**
1827-9643 *see* 1827-9635 **929**
1827-9716 Appalti e Contratti **4856**
1827-9724 *see* 0394-283X **4108**
1828-0005 Archeomedia **380**
1828-0226 Sanissimi **5709**
1828-0277 P S Mania 3.0 **2480**
1828-0315 *see* 1590-0304 **1115**
1828-0412 Collana di Psicologia della Religione **7634**
1828-0447 Internal and Emergency Medicine **5945**
1828-0595 Organs, Tissues and Cells **6255**
1828-0803 Psicoanalisi Corporea **6175**
1828-0811 AutoCapital Travel **8684**
1828-0889 Biblioteca di Studi Kantiani **6907**
1828-1036 Fiori & Decori **3756**
1828-1060 CER Magazine Italia **2038**
1828-1079 CER Punti Vendita Italia *changed to* 1828-1060 **2038**
1828-1087 CER Magazine International (French Edition) *see* 1828-1060 **2038**
1828-1095 CER Magazine International (Russian Edition) *see* 1828-1060 **2038**
1828-1109 CER Magazine International (English Edition) *see* 1828-1060 **2038**
1828-1117 CER Magazine International (German Edition) *see* 1828-1060 **2038**
1828-1141 Moto Design **8591**
1828-1273 Societa 24. Banca Dati **4881**
1828-146X Il Sistema Terra **2716**
1828-1478 Casa Felice **4535**
1828-1508 La Rivista di Bergamo **515**
1828-1524 Diabete, Obesita e Malattie Cardiovascolari
1828-1532 *see* 1828-1524
1828-1540 Studi Celtici **4476**
1828-1559 Naturalia Family Life **5078**
1828-1672 Domus d'Autore **4538**
1828-1761 Il Pesce Volante **6509**
1828-177X Musica e Letteratura **6593**
1828-1788 Iura Orientalia **4697**
1828-1818 Mediterranea. Ricerche Storiche. Quaderni *see* 1824-3010 **4244**
1828-1842 Newsletter di Psicologia Positiva **7388**
1828-1869 Decoupage Casa† **8949**
1828-1893 Star Music† **8990**
1828-1907 Soprintendenza Archeologica di Pompei. Studi **418**
1828-1923 Fashion Bijoux **4565**
1828-194X Agricoltura Istituzioni Mercati **191**
1828-1958 Attualita Lacaniana **7338**
1828-1974 Il Ruolo Terapeutico **7406**
1828-1982 Rivista di Statistica Ufficiale **8397**
1828-1990 Storia del Pensiero Economico. Nuova Serie **1549**
1828-2008 Storia in Lombardia **4268**
1828-2024 Innov@zione. P A **7446**
1828-2083 *see* 1828-2091 **8062**
1828-2091 Philanthropy Review **8062**
1828-2105 S T Journal of Research **3218**
1828-2121 Societa Friulana di Archeologia. Bollettino **416**
1828-2148 Seicento & Settecento **5369**
1828-2156 Studi sul Settecento e l'Ottocento **4476**
1828-2164 Early Modern and Modern Studies **487**
1828-2172 Casa Chic **4534**
1828-2199 Qui Magazine **3898**
1828-2237 Bicchieri d'Arte **364**
1828-2245 Karascio **6505**
1828-230X *see* 1824-3010 **4244**
1828-2326 Atlante Sintattico dell'Italia. Quaderni di Lavoro **5097**
1828-2334 Humanistica **4455**
1828-2377 Ignaziana **7800**
1828-2415 *see* 1724-9104 **450**
1828-2423 *see* 1128-9279 **7145**
1828-2431 *see* 0391-7495 **4233**
1828-2490 Il Quirinale **513**
1828-2504 *see* 1120-4540 **6543**
1828-2512 Amadeus Plus *see* 1120-4540 **6543**
1828-2563 *see* 1825-7712 **699**
1828-258X Veneto Paese per Paese **8771**
1828-2636 La Collana dei Piccoli **2183**
1828-2679 La Guida Photocamere Digitali† **8960**
1828-2830 Data Business†
1828-2857 Notiziario F I D A Inform *changed to* 1828-2865 **1751**
1828-2865 I C T Professional **1751**
1828-2873 Indicativo Presente **5308**
1828-2881 Italia Meravigliosa† **8967**
1828-2911 Clioh's Workshop **4135**
1828-292X Le Guide di Mondadori **2638**
1828-3004 Universita degli Studi di Sassari. Dipartimento di Storia. Collana **4165**
1828-3039 Archivi Reali di Ebla. Testi† **8931**
1828-311X Il Giusto Processo Civile **4832**
1828-3179 F O L D & R **393**
1828-3209 Il Mondo del Vino **607**
1828-3306 Collezionare Orologi Meccanici **4332**
1828-3330 Collezionare Soldatini d'Italia **4332**
1828-339X Autocar - Italia **8561**
1828-3454 Medioevo Plus **4244**
1828-3608 I Segreti dei Pescatori† **8987**
1828-3616 Camion Annual† **8939**
1828-3853 Marie Claire 2 Bellezza **589**
1828-3942 Scienza Riabilitativa **6116**
1828-4078 Buiatria **8794**
1828-4116 Business People **1074**
1828-4159 Agenda della Salute **6981**
1828-4205 Controllo di Gestione **1735**
1828-4213 *see* 1594-0810 **8805**
1828-423X Rivista Giuridica della Circolazione e dei Trasporti. Antologia (Year) **4776**
1828-4272 *see* 1824-7474 **4879**
1828-4302 Ce Fastu? **5105**
1828-4337 Multisport, Triathlete *changed to* 1828-4345 **8213**
1828-4345 Triathlete **8213**
1828-4353 Centro Studi di Psicologia e Letteratura. Giornale Storico **7344**
1828-4361 C D P. Notiziario **621**
1828-437X Antigone **2644**
1828-440X The European Journal of Trauma and Emergency Surgery† **8954**
1828-4418 Giurisdizione Amministrativa **4681**
1828-4434 Acer **3400**
1828-4450 Arketipo **432**
1828-4477 Geoinformatica **2722**
1828-4493 Fondazione Mariano Rumor. Annali **7136**
1828-4507 Guardia di Finanza. Archivio Storico. Museo Storico. Bollettino d'Archivio **2653**
1828-4515 Quaderni di Scultura Contemporanea **513**
1828-4523 La Razza Bruna **298**
1828-454X Acque Sotterranee **2792**
1828-4558 Universita degli Studi di Genova. Istituto Botanico Hanbury. Pubblicazioni **821**
1828-4566 Catalogo dei Periodici Italiani **622**
1828-4582 Nuova Secondaria **2892**
1828-4590 Tuttolibri Tempo Libero **7575**
1828-4639 La Guida Monaci del Sistema Lazio **8716**
1828-4647 L'Universita **2306**
1828-4655 I C S I M Newsletter **1120**
1828-4663 L'Uomo Nero **8484**
1828-4671 Francesco il Volto Secolare **7798**
1828-468X L'Italia dei Comuni **7494**
1828-4698 Diritto e Giurisprudenza Agraria, Alimentare e dell'Ambiente **105**
1828-4701 Agriturismi **8682**
1828-4728 Incontri di Finanza Aziendale **1352**
1828-4752 Catalogo Bolaffi della Grafica Italiana
1828-4760 Fondazione Cassa di Risparmio di Roma. Notiziario **1110**
1828-4779 Bologna dei Musei **6521**
1828-4809 L'Allevatore Trentino **261**
1828-4817 Il Pescatore Trentino **8328**
1828-4825 Il Cacciatore Trentino **8307**
1828-4841 Informazioni Parapsicologiche **6742**
1828-4876 Bibliographische Informationen zur Neueste Geschichte Italiens **4204**
1828-4892 Popolo e Liberta
1828-4914 Bollettino d'Informazione Agiscuola *see* 0017-0232 **2686**
1828-4965 Garante per la Protezione dei Dati Personali. Bollettino **7207**
1828-4973 Dei Delitti e delle Pene *changed to* 1590-5837 **2669**
1828-504X La Cucina Serie Argento
1828-5147 Studi Junghiani **7410**
1828-5155 Sintesi (Milan) **7183**
1828-5163 Quaderni di Tecnostruttura **1704**
1828-5171 Psicotech **7393**
1828-518X Istituzioni e Sviluppo Economico **1130**
1828-5198 Psicoterapia, Psicoterapie **6175**
1828-5317 Associazione Italiana Neurodisabili **6124**
1828-5368 *see* 1121-6530 **6951**
1828-5384 *see* Universita degli Studi di Sassari. Facolta di Lingue e Letterature Straniere. Annali **5190**
1828-5392 Golosita† **8960**
1828-5481 I S F O L Orienta **1686**
1828-5511 Carpfishing Magazine **8308**
1828-552X Corriere della Sera. Iniziative **3896**
1828-5538 Summa Animali da Compagnia **8807**
1828-5546 Summa Animali da Reddito **8807**
1828-5554 Rivista Amministrativa della Regione Veneto *see* 0035-5763 **7467**
1828-5562 Rivista Amministrativa della Regione Lombardia *see* 0035-5763 **7467**

1828-5570	Rivista Amministrativa della Regione Campania see 0035-5763 **7467**
1828-5589	Rivista Amministrativa della Regione Toscana see 0035-5763 **7467**
1828-583X	Il Punto (Pavia) **3898**
1828-5848	Testi e Commenti **2241**
1828-5856	Studi e Testi **4476**
1828-5864	Studi Ellenistici **2240**
1828-5872	Risorgimento. Idee e Realta **4259**
1828-5910	Studi Africanistici - Serie Ciado - Sudanese **4476**
1828-5929	Topologik.net **6958**
1828-597X	Il Trasporto e la Gestione dei Rifiuti **3513**
1828-5988	see 1828-597X **3513**
1828-5996	see 1828-597X **3513**
1828-6003	International Review on Computers and Software **2427**
1828-6011	see 1828-6003 **2427**
1828-6062	I Segreti del Mare **2818**
1828-6089	I Lavori di Carolina **6640**
1828-6097	I Lavori di Beatrice **6640**
1828-6100	Emozioni **4357**
1828-6119	Cronaca Oggi Magazine **3896**
1828-6186	Sonic **6617**
1828-6216	Il Reo e il Folle **2667**
1828-6224	see 1722-2206 **5673**
1828-6232	Nutritional Therapy & Metabolism **6667**
1828-6283	Istituto Superiore di Studi Medievali Cecco d'Ascoli. Atti e Memorie **4233**
1828-6518	Colori Martineghesi **8694**
1828-6526	PlayStation Magazine Ufficiale **2480**
1828-6534	Funghi & Tartufi **3644**
1828-6569	European Urology (Italian Edition) **6268**
1828-6577	Insight **5894**
1828-6593	The Journal of Urology (Italian Edition) **6270**
1828-6607	The Lancet Neurology (Italian Edition) **6158**
1828-6615	Tumori Femminili **6036**
1828-6682	I Quaderni di ADD **4344**
1828-6720	La Rivista di Venezia **8752**
1828-6763	Traces see 1128-9333 **7690**
1828-6771	Cosmopolis **4448**
1828-681X	Grand Tour Emozioni in Viaggio. Orizzonti **8714**
1828-6852	Letteratura e Dintorni **5321**
1828-6860	Lessici **4463**
1828-6879	Italiana. Per la Storia della Lingua Scritta in Italia **5131**
1828-6887	University of Venice. Department of Applied Mathematics. Working Papers **5545**
1828-6941	see 1828-5481 **1686**
1828-695X	Multidisciplinary Respiratory Medicine **6216**
1828-7131	see 0394-9370 **942**
1828-7158	La Stampa. CD-ROM see 1122-1763 **3898**
1828-7182	La Stampa. D V D see 1122-1763 **3898**
1828-7204	Vip **6516**
1828-731X	Lombardia Paese per Paese **8731**
1828-7379	Quaderni di Birdwatching **913**
1828-745X	Scrittori di Calabria **5368**
1828-7476	Colleziona le Prestigiose Decorazioni e Medaglie Militari **365**
1828-7484	Le Piu Belle Pipe da Collezione **4343**
1828-7492	Colleziona gli Autentici Vasi Cinesi **365**
1828-7506	Uova di Porcellana da Collezionare **540**
1828-7514	Colleziona le Bambole Romantiche di Porcellana **4332**
1828-7573	Collana di Teoria Letteraria di Critica e di Analisi Testuale **5107**
1828-7638	Corsi di Lingue. Il Francese **5108**
1828-7654	Adolescenza e Psicoanalisi (Print) **7331**
1828-7700	Forze Armate Italiane **4335**
1828-7743	Convivium Assisiense **7793**
1828-7778	Rescogitans **6947**
1828-7786	Quotidiano di Sicilia **3898**
1828-7824	see 1123-3990 **5359**
1828-7840	Internet Genius† **8966**
1828-7913	Case da Amare **437**
1828-793X	30 Buone Idee **4553**
1828-8081	La Ferrari Granturismo **8173**
1828-812X	Dissertatio. Series Romana **7795**
1828-8146	Dissertatio. Series Mediolanensis **7795**
1828-8243	Genti e Provincie d'Italia **8104**
1828-826X	R A P T Cahiers **5164**
1828-8278	Quaderni di Eutopia **412**
1828-8294	Anthropoi **325**
1828-8324	Biblioteca Morcelliana **4995**
1828-8375	Centro di Eccellenza **4920**
1828-8383	Collana di Studi di Storia dell'Arte **482**
1828-8413	Biblioteca. Cinema e Storia **6490**
1828-8421	Biblioteca. Letterature **5263**
1828-8472	Power Moto† **8982**
1828-8499	Pandere **511**
1828-8545	L N L Annual Report **7068**
1828-8553	see 1828-8545 **7068**
1828-8561	see 1828-8545 **7068**
1828-857X	Case di Campagna Raccolta **4535**
1828-8588	Chiesa Oggi Raccolta **437**
1828-8596	Il Camino Raccolta **4534**
1828-860X	Case di Montagna Raccolta **437**
1828-8618	99 Idee Casa Raccolta see 1125-1379 **462**
1828-8626	Casa Felice Raccolta **4535**
1828-8650	I Canti del Teatro Greco **8467**
1828-8669	Biblioteca di Studi Novecenteschi **5262**
1828-8677	Biblioteca di Quaderni Urbinati di Cultura Classica **2231**
1828-8685	Biblioteca di Pasiphae **384**
1828-8693	Biblioteca di Paratesto **7553**
1828-8707	Biblioteca di Materiali e Discussioni per l'Analisi dei Testi Classici **2231**
1828-8715	Biblioteca di Filosofia della Educazione **2831**
1828-8723	Biblioteca di Drammaturgia **8466**
1828-8731	Biblioteca della Rivista di Letteratura Italiana **5262**
1828-874X	Biblioteca degli Studi di Egittologia e Papirologia **4173**
1828-8758	Bibliotechina di Studi, Ricerche e Testi **5263**
1828-8766	Biblioteca Scandinava di Studi, Ricerche e Testi **5263**
1828-8774	Biblioteca di Eidola **478**
1828-8928	see 1828-8936 **6073**
1828-8936	Strategies in Trauma and Limb Reconstruction **6073**
1828-8944	Architettura & Citta **432**

1828-8987	Studi di Filologia Moderna **5178**
1828-8995	see 1828-8987 **5178**
1828-9029	I Quaderni del Mangiar Sano **6668**
1828-9037	Sicilia Imprenditoriale **1174**
1828-9231	see 1828-6771 **4448**
1828-9258	Golf e Tornei **8231**
1828-9266	Vele e Regate **8284**
1828-9274	Automata **7838**
1828-9282	Bormio Sport **8162**
1828-9290	Puglia Imperiale Magazine **8749**
1828-9355	Telebolero Mese see 1123-3516 **2396**
1828-9363	Rivista di Psicologia Clinica (Online Edition)†
1828-9371	see 1124-5425 **338**
1828-938X	Brividi Collection† **8937**
1828-9436	Tutto per il P C†
1828-9444	see 1824-7733 **4994**
1828-9460	Spinning Magazine **8335**
1828-9495	Biblioteca Storica Laterza **4204**
1828-9509	Insetti & Co. **947**
1828-9517	Universita degli Studi di Napoli. Dipartimento di Discipline Storiche. Quaderni **4165**
1828-9525	Rivista di Studi Danteschi. Quaderni see 1594-1000 **5433**
1828-9533	Da Libro a Libro **7559**
1828-955X	Universita degli Studi di Trento. Dipartimento di Sociologia e Ricerca Sociale. Quaderni **8145**
1828-9568	Costa Azzurra Agricola Forestale
1828-9592	Deliziose Ricette† **8949**
1828-9738	Giovani Genitori **5072**
1828-9754	Family D V D Games
1828-9797	Esploriamo Serie Plus
1828-9800	Etnie Serie Plus
1828-9827	Pilot Traveller Serie Plus
1828-9967	Costruisci il Rover Sojourner **4332**
1829-1163	Armenian Journal of Mathematics **5473**
1829-1171	Armenian Journal of Physics **7006**
1829-9539	Chip Foto-Video Digital **6979**
1830-0472	Gas and Electricity Market Statistics **3152**
1830-1029	Clean, Clever, Competitive **3411**
1830-2017	European Central Bank. Financial Stability Review **1339**
1830-2025	see 1830-2017 **1339**
1830-3609	E N I S A Quarterly **2513**
1830-4338	European Innovation†
1830-5865	European Central Bank. Payment and Securities Settlement Systems in the European Union and in the Acceding Countries changed to European Central Bank. Statistics on Payments, and Securities Trading, Clearing and Settlement **1339**
1830-7108	Eurofound News **7516**
1832-0031	Health Inequalities Monitoring Series† **8961**
1832-0066	Public Administration Today **7461**
1832-0090	Eddie Koiki Mabo Lecture **8099**
1832-0120	Southern Communicator **2339**
1832-0139	Muse **2994**
1832-0163	Filings **4566**
1832-018X	A S I C News (Online) **1609**
1832-0198	Holbrook Happenings **5073**
1832-0260	see 1442-696X **8026**
1832-0287	Research Paper **5703**
1832-0295	Australian Thoroughbred Record **8287**
1832-0309	Down Syndrome N S W. Newsletter **5607**
1832-0317	see 1832-0309 **5607**
1832-0333	Wills & Probate Bulletin **4814**
1832-0341	Omusubi (Email) **3556**
1832-035X	Zero Waste S A. Annual Report **3514**
1832-0368	Country Biz **1883**
1832-0384	C I S Classics **7111**
1832-0392	M T V Screen Australia†
1832-0406	Technology Park, Bentley Directory changed to Technology Park Tenant Directory **8442**
1832-0481	Synaptic Graffiti Collective **5384**
1832-0511	Capital F
1832-0554	Australian Defence Force Academy . Alumni Newsletter† **8933**
1832-0562	Trenchless Australasia **3285**
1832-0570	see 1446-2990 **4861**
1832-0589	See Yourself in Canberra **8755**
1832-0597	Bicycling Buyers' Guide **8254**
1832-0619	Society of Women Writers N S W Inc. Newsletter changed to Society of Woman Writers N S W. Images **4584**
1832-0635	Careers in Asia **6695**
1832-0643	The Journal of Migration and Refugee Issues **4850**
1832-0651	Shadowed Realms† **8988**
1832-066X	Assisted Reproductive Technology in Australia and New Zealand **5884**
1832-0686	Streets, Towns and Places Directory **5049**
1832-0708	Tarralla **5385**
1832-0732	VicRoads. Annual Report **8637**
1832-0740	Voces Hispanas
1832-0791	South Australia. Department of Trade and Economic Development. Annual Report **1582**
1832-0805	Integral Leadership Centre. Working Paper Series **1754**
1832-0813	Quodlibet (Online) changed to 1836-4845 **5242**
1832-0821	National Alternative Dispute Resolution Advisory Council. Annual Report **4738**
1832-083X	see 1832-0821 **4738**
1832-0848	Australia. Department of Parliamentary Services. Annual Report **7421**
1832-0899	Intheblack **1293**
1832-0910	AsiaRights Journal **7202**
1832-0929	Koori Business Network **1142**
1832-0937	Sustainable Grazing on Saline Lands Network News† **8991**
1832-0945	Building Price Index (Online) **1443**
1832-0953	Quarterly Essay **5235**
1832-0961	C P A Update **1283**
1832-097X	Y C W Action **7695**
1832-0988	New South Wales, Australia. Department of Environment and Conservation. Annual Report changed to 1835-3606 **7455**
1832-0996	Interface (Sydney)†† **8965**

1832-1011	International Journal of Science and Research **7868**
1832-1046	Discovering Sydney and Surrounds **8698**
1832-1054	Flourish Magazine W A **8863**
1832-1070	Australian Patent Applications Scoreboard (Year) **6745**
1832-1151	Journal of Internet Business **1137**
1832-116X	R + B Home† **8983**
1832-1224	Sumptuous **3665**
1832-1232	New South Wales, Department of Commerce. Annual Report **1431**
1832-1267	Australian Association of Consulting Archaeologists. Newsletter (Online) **382**
1832-1291	Australian Crime Commission. Annual Report **2644**
1832-1356	Australian Centre for International Agricultural Research. Annual Operational Plan **93**
1832-1364	Early Learnings† **8952**
1832-1372	Quilter's Ultimate Resource **4344**
1832-1429	Office of the Renewable Energy Regulator. Financial Annual Report **3143**
1832-1437	Venue **4552**
1832-1461	Football Budget **8228**
1832-1526	Australian Review of Public Affairs **7108**
1832-1542	Urban Animal **6816**
1832-1550	Office for the Ageing. Annual Report **8060**
1832-1585	New South Wales. Rental Bond Board. Annual Report **4420**
1832-1593	Fair Trading Administration Corporation, Building Insurers' Guarantee Corporation. Annual Reports **7436**
1832-1615	Premie Press **2166**
1832-1623	Antiques & Art in New South Wales **466**
1832-164X	Australia. Bureau of Statistics. Job Search Experience, Australia (Print) changed to Australia. Bureau of Statistics. Job Search Experience, Australia (Online) **6706**
1832-1666	Official Community Visitors. Annual Report **8060**
1832-1704	Australian Quarter Horse News **8287**
1832-1712	Law Enforcement (Controlled Operations) Act. Annual Report (Year) **2659**
1832-1739	M L M Australia & New Zealand **1830**
1832-1755	I P A A Byte **1121**
1832-1798	Association of Professional Engineers, Scientists and Managers. Collieries' Staff Division. Employment & Remuneration Survey Report **1665**
1832-1828	Sussex Inletter **3796**
1832-1844	Bamboo Bulletin **778**
1832-1852	see 1832-1844 **778**
1832-1909	National Blood Authority. Annual Report **5940**
1832-1925	UnitingCare Wesley News **8075**
1832-1968	Australia. Air Transport Statistics. Domestic Airline Activity (Major Australian Airlines) Monthly Status Report **8521**
1832-200X	Tasmanian Pen Craft **521**
1832-2018	Victorian Small Business Commissioner. Annual Report **1969**
1832-2034	Businesssales.com.au Magazine **1808**
1832-2042	Dairy Projects **263**
1832-2050	Studies in Learning, Evaluation, Innovation and Development **2916**
1832-2077	The International Journal of Environmental, Cultural, Economic and Social Sustainability **3442**
1832-2085	Basin Links changed to Lower Basin Links **2797**
1832-2107	Bob White Memorial Lecture **8090**
1832-2115	Longbreak **8321**
1832-2158	ACTive Archives **4987**
1832-2166	Service Tasmania Board. Annual Report **7468**
1832-2174	see 1324-5864 **1825**
1832-2271	What's New in Process Technology **3226**
1832-2298	Vive +† **8997**
1832-2301	In Aeternum **2287**
1832-231X	BIGonblue **8272**
1832-2328	Rhizome **3000**
1832-2336	Holiday Special **5306**
1832-2352	New South Wales in Focus (Print) changed to N S W State and Regional Indicators **7288**
1832-2360	Artary†
1832-2379	H M Info Newsletter **1010**
1832-2387	Building Blocks changed to 1834-8335 **8028**
1832-2395	KidZsay Magazine **2197**
1832-2409	Fundraising & Philanthropy Australasia **1746**
1832-2417	University of Melbourne. Department of Economics. Research Paper **1188**
1832-2425	Ensis Link†
1832-2433	Air Power Australia Analyses **6409**
1832-2468	Arthur Rylah Institute for Environmental Research. Annual Business Review **3404**
1832-2484	Abode Magazine **4531**
1832-2492	Furniture History Society Journal **4557**
1832-2506	Dykonoclast **4372**
1832-2514	Contemporary Issues **4448**
1832-2522	Provenance (Online) **5040**
1832-2530	N S W Women **8876**
1832-2549	Extend changed to 1832-8113 **4549**
1832-2557	Australian Country Music **6546**
1832-2565	Partnership for Aboriginal Care. Annual Report **8061**
1832-2573	Headlines **7140**
1832-262X	Tasmania's Financial Management Reform Strategy **1386**
1832-2662	Waste Streams changed to 1834-917X **3512**
1832-2697	Australia. Intergovernmental Committee on Surveying and Mapping. Biennial Report **3999**
1832-2700	New South Wales. Public Employment Office. Occasional Paper **1699**
1832-2719	Traveltalk Australia **8769**
1832-2735	Recollections (Hawthorn) **2903**
1832-2743	Bushfire Arson Bulletin **2645**
1832-2751	Learning and Teaching **3070**
1832-276X	International Journal of Practical Experiences in Professional Education **2870**
1832-2794	Investigate **7144**
1832-2824	Little Angel **2200**
1832-2840	Centre for Applied Finance. Working Paper Series† **8940**
1832-2859	Kogarahlife **7450**

1832-9179 Bite **5836**
1832-9187 Local Government Postal Elections Report **7451**
1832-9195 Smart Investor **1651**
1832-9241 Rural Lands Protection Boards. Annual Report **2626**
1832-925X Victorian Environmental Assessment Council. Annual Report **2718**
1832-9268 The Garden Guru **3731**
1832-9306 Australian A P E C Studies Centre. Issues Paper (Online) **1553**
1832-9373 The Advocate† **8928**
1832-9403 E S A A News (Online) **3127**
1832-9411 Western Australia. Office of the Public Sector Standards Commissioner. Annual Report **7477**
1832-9446 Dog and Cat Management Board of South Australia. Annual Report **6807**
1832-9462 Queensland. Department of Mines and Energy. Annual Report **3145**
1832-9470 A C M A Consumer Bulletin† **8927**
1832-9489 Australian Bureau of Agricultural and Resource Economics. Australian Fisheries Surveys Report **3612**
1832-9497 Australasian College of Road Safety. Journal **8490**
1832-9543 International Review of Business Research Papers **1129**
1832-9586 Carp Management Program. Annual Report **3588**
1832-9594 Riot† **8986**
1832-9624 Auditing Guidance Note†
1832-9667 Redcliffe City News **3796**
1832-9683 *see* 1557-3605 **4222**
1832-9691 Australian Hearing. Annual Report **6078**
1832-9705 Council on Australia Latin America Relations. Annual Report **7228**
1832-9713 Western Australia. Corruption and Crime Commission. Annual Report **4900**
1832-9748 Digital Photo ART
1832-9772 Tasmania. Anti-Discrimination Commission. Annual Report *changed to* Tasmania. Office of the Anti-Discrimination Commissioner. Annual Report **1710**
1832-9799 Northern and Far Western Regional Health Service. Annual Report†
1832-9802 Australian Capital Territory. Emergency Services Authority. Annual Report **7421**
1832-9810 Repatriation General Hospital. Annual Report **7538**
1832-9829 Aromatherapy Today **307**
1832-9837 Western Australia. Department of Environment. Annual Report *changed to* 1835-1131 **2631**
1832-9861 Advances in Contemporary Nursing **5950**
1832-987X FourFourTwo **8221**
1832-9888 From My Desk† **8958**
1832-9926 The Queensland Journal of Labour History **4194**
1832-9942 Australian Official Journal of Designs (Online) **6745**
1832-9950 Australian Official Journal of Patents (Online) **6745**
1832-9969 Australian Official Journal of Trade Marks (Online) **6745**
1832-9985 Leigh Creek Health Service. Annual Report **4105**
1833-0002 South Australia. Department of Health. Annual Report **7542**
1833-0010 Crystal Dragon Rumblings Newsletters **308**
1833-0029 Il Ficodindia **3533**
1833-0126 Our Lady's Rosary Makers of Australia. Annual Report **7811**
1833-0177 BreastScreen Victoria. Annual Report (Year) **5987**
1833-0185 Kokoda Papers **2227**
1833-0215 Security Solutions **2680**
1833-0258 Priorities in Progress Report **1512**
1833-0266 Life etc **5075**
1833-0282 Construction Worker **998**
1833-0290 Museum Victoria Science Reports **7884**
1833-0320 Cityscape **437**
1833-0347 Motor Vehicle Repair Industry Authority. Annual Report **8504**
1833-0355 Inside Out **4543**
1833-0398 Real Living (Sydney) **4562**
1833-0401 Nickelodeon†
1833-0428 Renmark Paringa District Hospital Board. Annual Report **4110**
1833-0436 The Cemetorian **3719**
1833-0460 *see* 0008-8420 **7791**
1833-0479 *see* 1836-4268 **1521**
1833-0509 A G S M Working Paper Series†
1833-0517 N S W Department of Primary Industries. Science and Research Division. Forest Resources Research. Research Papers **3697**
1833-0533 Interactive Media **6504**
1833-0541 Mini Foxie Newsletter **6811**
1833-055X Acute Myeloid Leukemia Research Today **5933**
1833-0576 A D H D Research Today **6117**
1833-0584 Cystic Fibrosis Research Today **6213**
1833-0592 Melanoma Research Today **5880**
1833-0606 Down Syndrome Research Today **6091**
1833-0614 Regional Programs Report **2715**
1833-0622 Fostering Our Future **8041**
1833-0673 International New Landscape **3739**
1833-0711 E - Permanence Bulletin† **8952**
1833-072X Port Augusta Hospital and Regional Health Services. Annual Report **4109**
1833-0738 *see* 1832-598X **8710**
1833-0754 National Relay Service Performance Report **2370**
1833-0762 Telecommunications Performance Reports *changed to* A C M A Communications Report **2310**
1833-0800 Fast Thinking **1745**
1833-0827 Rural Pharmacy Newsletter **6879**
1833-0886 Australian Horsewyse **8287**
1833-0916 Outback Utes Annual **3795**
1833-0924 Mallee Catchment Management Authority. Annual Report **8828**
1833-0932 A P I Review of Books **4986**
1833-0940 Coober Pedy Hospital and Health Services. Annual Report **4091**
1833-0959 Policy Bites **7460**
1833-0975 C + A **988**
1833-0991 Arthritis Series **6222**
1833-1025 Arid Areas Catchment Water Management Board. Annual Report **8818**
1833-1033 Country Arts. Annual Report **4448**
1833-1068 University of Queensland, Department of Economics. Discussion Papers **1189**
1833-1076 University of Queensland. East Asian Economic Research Group. Discussion Paper Series† **8996**
1833-1084 Namoi C M A Annual Report **3454**
1833-1122 Leaded **8589**
1833-1173 Monash University. Centre for Health Economics. Research Paper **1150**
1833-119X Rouge Magazine **5365**
1833-1238 Data Linkage Series **7513**
1833-1254 C E O Forum **1731**
1833-1270 La Trobe University. Annual Research Report (Online) **2920**
1833-1289 Bendigo Magazine **8686**
1833-1319 Top Management Remuneration Report **1876**
1833-1335 reCollections (Canberra) **6536**
1833-136X Hawke Research Institute. Postgraduate Working Paper Series (Online) **7968**
1833-1378 Jaguar **8586**
1833-1424 Central Northern Adelaide Health Service. Annual Report **7512**
1833-1440 Jmag **4978**
1833-1459 Security Challenges **6445**
1833-1467 Northern Territory Grants Commission. Annual Report **7457**
1833-1483 A C S S A Wrap **8850**
1833-1564 Australian Stamp Bulletin **6891**
1833-1599 Carter's Criminal Law of Queensland **4886**
1833-1602 InFinsia *changed to* 1834-4232 **1353**
1833-1637 Spice **4367**
1833-1661 P A C F A enews **6172**
1833-1734 Writing Edge Magazine **5087**
1833-1769 Roads and Traffic Authority of N S W. Research Report **8634**
1833-1793 Freerider M X Photo Annual *see* 1443-1998 **8259**
1833-1831 Coober Pedy Regional Times **3793**
1833-184X Bushfires and the Media **4572**
1833-1866 The International Journal of the Arts in Society **4457**
1833-1874 Design Principles and Practices **486**
1833-1882 The International Journal of Interdisciplinary Social Sciences **7974**
1833-1890 Primary Voice (Gippsland) **148**
1833-1904 Primary Voice (Glenelg Hopkins and Wimmera) **148**
1833-1912 Primary Voice (Mallee and North Central) **148**
1833-1920 Primary Voice (North East and Goulburn Broken) **148**
1833-1947 A S S H Studies in Sports History **8156**
1833-1963 Metropolitan Domiciliary Care. Annual Report **4107**
1833-1971 Educational Activities for Kids & Teens. Victoria *changed to* 1836-2826 **2849**
1833-1998 Crime Zine **5413**
1833-2005 Cogito **6910**
1833-203X Extension Farming Systems Journal **109**
1833-2048 *see* 1833-203X **109**
1833-2080 New South Wales. Department of Primary Industries. Annual Report **140**
1833-2102 Tango **5412**
1833-2110 Public Policy **7174**
1833-2129 S A G E S Working Papers in Development (Print) *changed to* 1834-5654 **354**
1833-2145 Scoop Traveller (Northern Territory & South Australia Edition) *changed to* 1834-2922 **8755**
1833-2145 Scoop Traveller (Northern Territory & South Australia Edition) *changed to* 1834-2914 **8755**
1833-2153 Living Sustainably **3451**
1833-2188 The Conservative† **8943**
1833-2293 Informed Voice **5761**
1833-2307 Pathways† **8980**
1833-2331 C S I R O Marine and Atmospheric Research Paper **3408**
1833-2404 Antarctic Climate and Ecosystems Cooperative Research Centre. Technical Report **6346**
1833-2412 Inside Tax **1929**
1833-2420 *see* 1833-2331 **3408**
1833-2439 Just Holdens Magazine **8587**
1833-2447 C S C I Islamic Issues Briefing Paper Series **7709**
1833-248X Fire Fatalities Report **3577**
1833-2498 Australia. Bureau of Statistics. Regional Population Growth. Australia **7301**
1833-2501 The Source **3467**
1833-2528 Spa Life **5083**
1833-2552 The Spirit Guide to Spellcraft **6744**
1833-2595 International Journal of Educational Integrity **2869**
1833-2609 Manual of Motorcycle Sport **8260**
1833-2757 Casino Magazine **5067**
1833-282X Monitoring for Marine Pests at Garden Point, Melville Island **3602**
1833-2838 Australian Archaeological Consultancy Monograph Series **382**
1833-2889 Residential Developer Magazine **7611**
1833-2919 The Australian and New Zealand Olive Industry Directory **219**
1833-3044 Australian National Security Magazine *changed to* 1835-7555 **2225**
1833-3060 Rural Social Work and Community Practice **8066**
1833-3125 The Mining Advocate **6472**
1833-3133 My Child **2161**
1833-315X Heart Wise Living *changed to* 1833-8798 **5627**
1833-3222 Zoo Weekly **6302**
1833-3230 Juvenile Justice Series **4954**
1833-3249 Old Bike Australasia **8265**
1833-3257 Xbox 360 **2482**
1833-329X Seymour Lecture in Biography **645**
1833-3303 W P R **1042**
1833-3338 10,000 Steps Working Paper Series **8019**
1833-3362 Inveresk Play Series **8472**
1833-3370 Agrifood Industry Skills Council. Annual Report **3625**
1833-3397 Shi Jie Guan Dao Gong Cheng Hui Gu *see* 1833-3303 **1042**
1833-3427 Horse Racing Australia Magazine **8292**
1833-3435 *see* 1833-3427 **8292**
1833-3508 Barossa Living **4000**
1833-3516 Diving and Hyperbaric Medicine **5606**
1833-3524 Choices **4073**
1833-3532 Farming Small Areas **112**
1833-3575 *see* 1833-3583 **5625**
1833-3583 Health Information Management Journal **5625**
1833-3613 Dunstan Papers **7960**
1833-3621 Honestly Woman **8867**
1833-363X Thinking Business† **8993**
1833-3648 Coast **5068**
1833-3656 George Research **7518**
1833-3672 Journal of Management & Organization **1767**
1833-3818 Asia Pacific Journal of Health Management **4088**
1833-3834 Best of Blitz **8161**
1833-3842 Transnational Policy Forum Report **7269**
1833-3850 International Journal of Business and Management **1755**
1833-3869 Small Business Stats **1967**
1833-4105 International Journal of Pedagogies and Learning **3065**
1833-4148 Fisheries Technical Publications Catalogue **3593**
1833-4156 Primary Industries Technical Publications Catalogue **148**
1833-4180 *see* 1039-0170 **6742**
1833-4202 Catholic Education Office. Annual Report **7788**
1833-4229 The Australian Constitutional Defender **7108**
1833-4237 C R C Salinity Bulletin **223**
1833-427X Somersault Gymnastics Magazine **8202**
1833-4318 Journal of Business Systems, Governance and Ethics **1764**
1833-4326 LexisNexis Concise Tax Legislation **1933**
1833-4369 Social Policy Research Paper **8133**
1833-4377 The Guardian **5218**
1833-4407 Fa C S I A Research News **8039**
1833-4415 Australia. Department of Families, Community Services and Indigenous Affairs. Occasional Paper **8026**
1833-4458 Tide **5388**
1833-4490 Surveillance Devices Act 2004 **4791**
1833-4504 Highschool Formal *changed to* 1834-5212 **2255**
1833-4512 Gay and Lesbian Issues and Psychology Review **4374**
1833-4520 A P E S M A / F A S T S Professional Scientist Remuneration Survey Report **6691**
1833-4539 Who's Who of Australian Women **648**
1833-4547 Marketing Navigator **1832**
1833-4563 C S I R O Land and Water Science Report **2793**
1833-4652 Canteen News **3019**
1833-4687 Australia. Department of Families, Community Services and Indigenous Affairs. Annual Report **8026**
1833-4733 Donna Hay Magazine **4356**
1833-4741 Macquarie Law Symposium **4726**
1833-4784 Fisheries R & D News *changed to* Fish **3591**
1833-4814 Landscape Architecture Australia **3741**
1833-4857 Village Communities of Australia **8076**
1833-4881 History Australia (Online) **4192**
1833-492X Architects Board of South Australia. Annual Report **428**
1833-4946 *see* 1833-1335 **6536**
1833-4954 Devil Facial Tumour Disease Newsletter **8796**
1833-4962 U F O Logist Magazine **6648**
1833-4989 *see* 1037-9851 **4157**
1833-5020 *see* 1834-2469 **1146**
1833-5047 Water Week **8841**
1833-508X The Blade **7110**
1833-5098 Food & Drink Business **3637**
1833-5136 Green Markets Brief†
1833-5152 Gas Week Brief (Email) *changed to* 1444-9064 **6770**
1833-5179 Travel Weekly (Australia) **8768**
1833-5187 Queensland Energy Brief **3145**
1833-5195 Electricity Week Brief†
1833-5209 Human Resources *changed to* Human Resources Leader **1865**
1833-5241 Houses Style: Kitchens + Bathrooms **4542**
1833-525X Victorian Catholic Schools Parent Body **7822**
1833-5292 Water Solutions (Print) *changed to* Water Solutions (Online) **8840**
1833-5306 Information and Cultural Exchange Inc. Annual Report **496**
1833-5314 The Little Black Book **6294**
1833-5322 Our Wedding (Illawarra Edition) **5560**
1833-5357 Drugspeak **7514**
1833-5365 Diabetes Management Journal **5888**
1833-5373 Melbourne 2030. Implementation Bulletin **8120**
1833-5403 Bookseller + Publisher **7555**
1833-5454 *see* 1833-5462 **2822**
1833-5462 A P Q N Annual Report **2822**
1833-5497 *see* 1833-5500 **955**
1833-5500 Marine Technical Report Series **955**
1833-5632 *see* 1833-5640 **148**
1833-5640 Primary Industries Technical Annual Report **148**
1833-5659 Psycho-social Update **7394**
1833-5667 Supreme Court History Program Yearbook (Year) **4852**
1833-5683 *see* 1324-6542 **8870**
1833-573X Broome Happenings **3793**
1833-5799 Junior Bookseller + Publisher **5022**
1833-5802 *see* 1322-5235 **3794**
1833-5810 *see* 1322-5243 **3796**
1833-5845 Tree Line **3705**
1833-5853 *see* 1833-5845 **3705**
1833-5861 C I P Newsletter **2225**
1833-5888 *see* 1833-5861 **2225**
1833-5896 State of the Beaches **3467**
1833-5950 S A R D I Impacts **153**
1833-5969 *see* 1833-5950 **153**
1833-5977 Gawler Community Information & Business Directory **8042**
1833-5985 Australian Master Human Resources Guide **1856**
1833-5993 Commercial Applications of Company Law **4860**
1833-6027 *see* 1447-8986 **5257**
1833-6043 Osteogenesis Imperfecta (Brittle Bones) Society of Australia. Newsletter **5691**
1833-6051 UpRoar **8250**
1833-606X The Australian Acreage & Property Review **7583**
1833-6094 Ymi Australia **3797**
1833-6108 *see* 1833-6094 **3797**
1833-6116 Tarmac Topics **72**
1833-6124 *see* 1833-6116 **72**

ISSN

1834-3287 Parrhesia **6938**
1834-3309 *see* 1834-3317 **1082**
1834-3317 Ceteris Paribus **1082**
1834-3406 Wugong Whispers **8842**
1834-3422 Graduate Opportunities in Accounting, Business, Finance **6698**
1834-3430 *see* 1834-3422 **6698**
1834-3449 Graduate Opportunities in Engineering & Information Technology **6698**
1834-3457 *see* 1834-3449 **6698**
1834-3465 Graduate Opportunities **6698**
1834-3481 Communities for Communities **3411**
1834-3511 Journal of Administration and Governance **7448**
1834-352X *see* 1834-3511 **7448**
1834-3546 Soybean **254**
1834-3554 ActKM Online Journal of Knowledge Management **1056**
1834-3570 W A Organic Life **3753**
1834-3627 Journal for the Renewal of Religion and Theology **7653**
1834-3635 Practice Reflexions **8062**
1834-3643 *see* 1834-3651 **3512**
1834-3651 The State of Waste and Recycling in Queensland **3512**
1834-366X D V I R C Quarterly **8036**
1834-3708 Queensland Mines and Quarries Safety Performance and Health Report **6477**
1834-3716 *see* 1834-3708 **6477**
1834-3775 Australasian Education Directory **2828**
1834-3805 PlayStation **2480**
1834-3856 Melbourne 2030 Email Update **1148**
1834-3902 Southern Argus **3796**
1834-3937 Sydney Alumni Magazine **2303**
1834-3961 Local Connections **3451**
1834-397X *see* 1834-3961 **3451**
1834-402X Aboriginal Studies Association. Collected Papers **3515**
1834-4070 The Wayfarer **5437**
1834-4089 *see* 1834-4070 **5437**
1834-4097 Rainbow-Jeparit Argus **3796**
1834-4100 Pyrenees Advocate **3796**
1834-4127 *see* 1834-4135 **6686**
1834-4135 SafetyLine Newsletter for Safety and Health Representatives **6686**
1834-4143 SafetyLine Newsletter for Small Business **6686**
1834-4151 SafetyLine Newsletter for O S H Professionals **6686**
1834-4208 Studies in Contemporary and Emergent Heritage **4163**
1834-4216 Our Languages are the Voice of the Land **5158**
1834-4224 T I M S S Australia Monograph **2917**
1834-4232 InFinance **1353**
1834-4259 Malacological Society of Australasia. Newsletter **954**
1834-4267 Compass Bearings **6644**
1834-4437 International Roundup News **1762**
1834-4453 *see* 0003-8121 **378**
1834-4461 *see* 0029-8077 **350**
1834-4488 Occasional A U R A Publication **409**
1834-4496 Street Rights N S W **8073**
1834-450X *see* 1834-4496 **8073**
1834-4542 Food News Bulletin **3640**
1834-4550 *see* 1834-4542 **3640**
1834-4593 Research **7611**
1834-4607 Torque **4379**
1834-4712 *see* 1834-3198 **2923**
1834-4720 The A R A Retailer **1055**
1834-478X Knowledge for Regional N R M Programme E-newsletter **3449**
1834-4798 Q F F Weekly Bulletin **149**
1834-4879 Australia. Auditing and Assurance Standards Board. Bulletin **1281**
1834-4887 *see* 1833-8550 **4066**
1834-4909 Journal of Pacific Rim Psychology **7377**
1834-4917 Prospective **7537**
1834-4933 Leading Minds **8118**
1834-4941 Women in Welfare Education (Online) **8078**
1834-4984 *see* 1834-4992 **4192**
1834-4992 Friends of Boroondara (Kew) Cemetery. Newsletter **4192**
1834-500X Pharmaceutical Reforms **6870**
1834-5026 Freelance Register **7561**
1834-5034 *see* 1834-5026 **7561**
1834-5069 Industrial Relations Newsletter **1688**
1834-5077 Pacific Outlook **1580**
1834-5107 Extreme Street **8580**
1834-5131 QHistory **2901**
1834-5190 Northern Voice **1700**
1834-5204 The Adventure Journal **8681**
1834-5212 Formal Australia **2255**
1834-5328 Australian F O I Law Journal **4624**
1834-5352 Indigenous Employment in Action **6698**
1834-5360 *see* 1834-5352 **6698**
1834-5409 N C C Occasional Series **1151**
1834-5433 Victorian Recreational Boating Safety Handbook **8284**
1834-5441 *see* 1834-5433 **8284**
1834-5484 Practice Brief **8062**
1834-5506 South Australian Football Budget **8246**
1834-5530 *see* 1321-103X **6611**
1834-5557 N S W Department of Primary Industries. Science and Research Division. Forests N S W. Research and Development Annual Report **3697**
1834-562X *see* 0045-0618 **5912**
1834-5654 S S E E Working Papers in Development (Online) **354**
1834-5662 Australian and New Zealand Property Journal **7583**
1834-5719 Fragrances of the World (Year) **594**
1834-5913 Cruise Weekly **8642**
1834-5921 The Beacon **6009**
1834-593X *see* 1834-5921 **6009**
1834-5948 The Inside Story *see* 1834-5921 **6009**
1834-5999 Education News **2848**
1834-6006 *see* 1834-5999 **2848**
1834-6049 Shima **355**
1834-6057 *see* 1834-6049 **355**
1834-6073 *see* 1327-8991 **4431**
1834-609X Chinese Southern Diaspora Studies **3527**
1834-6103 Thomson's Corporations Law Academic Alert† **8993**
1834-6308 *see* 1834-6316 **8476**
1834-6316 Prologue **8476**
1834-6472 Emporium **8861**
1834-6529 A P I National Newsletter **7581**
1834-6537 *see* 1834-6545 **6707**
1834-6545 Women in the Professions Survey Report **6707**
1834-6553 Snake Ranch News **963**
1834-6650 Victorian Population Bulletin **7295**
1834-6669 *see* 1834-6650 **7295**
1834-6766 Curtin University of Technology. School of Economics and Finance. Area of Research Excellence in Oil & Gas Management. Working Paper Series **6766**
1834-6774 SeaRead **3465**
1834-6782 *see* 1834-6774 **3465**
1834-7258 Journal of Catholic School Studies **2874**
1834-7320 National Trust Magazine **2620**
1834-7533 *see* 0812-3985 **2780**
1834-7541 *see* 1036-9872 **2625**
1834-7649 International Journal of Accounting and Information Management **1292**
1834-7819 *see* 0045-0421 **5835**
1834-7940 Artist Profile **473**
1834-8335 Brighter Futures **8028**
1834-8491 *see* 1440-0669 **4456**
1834-8602 Investor Weekly **1633**
1834-8610 *see* 1034-7674 **7532**
1834-8971 Asia Pacific Economic Papers **1552**
1834-9013 Script & Print **7573**
1834-917X Sustainability Matters **3512**
1834-9455 *see* 0817-8038 **1510**
1834-9706 Aged Care Action **5950**
1834-9714 Private & Confidential **5978**
1834-9854 Australia. Deptartment of Parliamentary Services. Parliamentary Library. Research Paper **7421**
1835-0151 Sydney Journal **4194**
1835-0186 Australian Indigenous Law Review **7202**
1835-0313 *see* 1834-8602 **1633**
1835-0321 Great Walks **8316**
1835-0402 Queensland. Department of Education, Training and the Arts. Annual Report **7464**
1835-0410 *see* 1835-0402 **7464**
1835-047X Fenner School of Environment & Society. Yearbook **3431**
1835-0550 Public Space **4763**
1835-1131 Western Australia. Department of Environment and Conservation. Annual Report **2631**
1835-114X *see* 1835-1131 **2631**
1835-1190 *see* 1832-4835 **6560**
1835-1336 Golfer Pacific.com.au **8233**
1835-1794 *see* 0156-1316 **397**
1835-2014 The International Journal of the Inclusive Museum **6526**
1835-2030 Journal of the World Universities Forum **2991**
1835-2340 Global Media Journal: Australian Edition **2321**
1835-2480 A P S Jobs **7418**
1835-2561 *see* 1035-6908 **1281**
1835-2693 Australian Journal of Crop Science **220**
1835-2707 *see* 1835-2693 **220**
1835-2766 UNESCO Observatory E-Journal Multi-Disciplinary Research in the Arts **4479**
1835-3606 New South Wales. Department of Environment and Climate Change. Annual Report **7455**
1835-3789 *see* 1833-3338 **8019**
1835-3800 Journal of Human Security **7147**
1835-3827 Arthur Rylah Institute for Environmental Research. Technical Report Series **3404**
1835-4270 *see* 0040-2486 **2341**
1835-4416 Eye of the Heart **7642**
1835-4432 The Global Studies Journal **7967**
1835-4440 *see* 1833-1467 **7457**
1835-4823 *see* 0312-4991 **4993**
1835-517X *see* 0313-5373 **2968**
1835-5218 Let's Find Out **3070**
1835-5412 International Journal of e-Business Management **1756**
1835-5617 Healthcare Infection **5814**
1835-5625 *see* 1835-5617 **5814**
1835-5862 Health Voices **4096**
1835-6060 Australasian Yachting **8271**
1835-6354 Australasian Journal of Construction Economics and Building **977**
1835-6419 *see* 1444-3058 **4192**
1835-663X Hospital & Agedcare **4099**
1835-6656 *see* 1329-9441 **505**
1835-6680 *see* 1445-2723 **8156**
1835-6923 Australasian Sporting Shooter **8304**
1835-7040 Essays in French Literature and Culture **5291**
1835-7091 Wildlife Queensland **2632**
1835-7105 *see* 1835-7091 **2632**
1835-7156 The International Journal of Climate Change: Impacts and Responses **3441**
1835-7555 Australian Security Magazine **2225**
1835-7652 Dictionary of Australian Artists Online **642**
1835-7814 For Keeps Creative Paper **535**
1835-789X Asset Management & Maintenance Journal **3182**
1835-7903 *see* 1835-789X **3182**
1835-8063 *see* 1325-8338 **4444**
1835-8330 N S W Public Health Bulletin. Supplement *see* 1034-7674 **7532**
1835-839X Victorian Journal of Home Economics **4369**
1835-8454 C B E R S Network **8029**
1835-8624 Pandora's Box **4755**
1835-8780 The International Journal of Emerging Technologies and Society **7867**
1835-8799 Place **7992**
1835-8810 *see* 1835-5862 **4096**
1835-9019 *see* 1833-248X **3577**
1835-9442 Creative Approaches to Research **7956**
1835-9469 *see* 1443-2447 **7286**
1835-9795 Ubiquitous Learning **3086**
1836-0246 *see* 1325-8362 **8026**
1836-0343 *see* 1038-2909 **6605**
1836-0394 Commonwealth Journal of Local Governance **7490**
1836-0416 Cultural Science **7957**
1836-0661 Plant Omics **811**
1836-084X *see* 1443-2471 **2788**
1836-0939 Animal Production Science **218**
1836-0947 Crop and Pasture Science **103**
1836-1110 Corporate Governance eJournal **4864**
1836-1129 Sports Law eJournal **4786**
1836-1447 Victorian Equal Opportunity & Human Rights Commission. Annual Report **7218**
1836-148X A Guide to the Australian Government **7443**
1836-1803 Australian and New Zealand Journal of European Studies **7222**
1836-263X *see* 1441-2799 **4905**
1836-2818 Educational Activities. Queensland **2849**
1836-2826 Educational Activities. Victoria **2849**
1836-2842 Educational Activities. N S W **2849**
1836-2966 Tourism Tasmania. Annual Report **8764**
1836-3083 Australia. Department of Innovation, Industry, Science and Research. Annual Report **1911**
1836-3644 *see* 1836-0661 **811**
1836-425X *see* 1832-4371 **1719**
1836-4268 T D Securities Melbourne Institute Monthly Inflation Gauge **1521**
1836-4845 Transnational Literature **5242**
1836-5787 *see* 1836-0939 **218**
1836-5795 *see* 1836-0947 **103**
1836-6147 The National Library Magazine **5034**
1836-6384 *see* 1832-6153 **4960**
1836-7399 *see* 1448-7527 **5581**
1836-7402 *see* 0310-0049 **934**
1836-7720 Australian Pilot **47**
1836-9022 International Journal of Social Security and Workers Compensation **1930**
1837-0659 N C V E R Monograph Series **2944**
1840-0132 Ljekarska Komora Zenicko-Dobojskog Kantona. Medicinski Glasnik **5662**
1840-0655 Sarajevo Journal of Mathematics **5533**
1840-0809 Herbologia **792**
1840-118X South East European Journal of Economics and Business (English Edition) **1177**
1840-1198 South East European Journal of Economics and Business (Bosnian Edition) *see* 1840-118X **1177**
1840-1848 Acta Medica Academica **5566**
1840-2291 HealthMED **5627**
1840-3719 Epiphany **7961**
1840-3956 *see* 0350-364X **5567**
1840-4529 International Journal of Collaborative Research on Internal Medicine & Public Health **7526**
18402445 *see* 1840-0132 **5662**
1841-0677 *see* 1223-4737 **3934**
1841-0715 European Association for Health Information and Libraries. Journal **5610**
1841-0987 Acta Endocrinologica **5883**
1841-1088 Studii si Certerari de Virusologie **5827**
1841-2416 Management and Marketing **1774**
1841-3781 Top Gear **8607**
1841-3943 *see* 1221-4167 **5930**
1841-4273 *see* 1582-8271 **7263**
1841-527X Computer Bild **2411**
1841-5288 Vacanta ta Perfecta **8771**
1841-5296 Lucru de Mana **6640**
1841-5512 R O M A I Journal **5527**
1841-6136 *see* 1584-708X **8869**
1841-7051 Transylvanian Review of Systematical and Ecological Research **3471**
1841-7655 *see* 1841-7663 **7706**
1841-7663 Romanian Patriarchate News Bulletin **7706**
1841-8325 Universitatea din Craiova. Analele. Seria: Filosofie **6958**
1841-8678 Economie Teoretica si Aplicata **1101**
1841-9836 International Journal of Computers, Communications and Control **2425**
1841-9844 *see* 1841-9836 **2425**
1842-0273 Familia Mea **8862**
1842-2799 Studia Universitatis "Babes-Bolyai". Dramatica **8479**
1842-3140 Elle Decoration **4539**
1842-3191 Economics, Management, and Financial Markets **1101**
1842-3582 Digest Journal of Nanomaterials and Biostructures **763**
1842-368X *see* 1221-9118 **6239**
1842-4090 Carpathian Journal of Earth and Environmental Sciences **2703**
1842-4309 *see* 0255-965X **806**
1842-4562 Journal of Applied Quantitative Methods **2428**
1842-5712 Cercetari Practice si Teoretice in Managementul Urban *changed to* 2065-3913 **4428**
1842-6298 *see* 1843-7265 **5540**
1842-6433 *see* 1224-5119 **709**
1842-6573 Optoelectronics and Advanced Materials Rapid Communications **3110**
1842-7340 Timisoara Journal of Economics **1183**
1842-8088 *see* 1453-1305 **2422**
1843-1046 Journal of Applied Computer Science *changed to* 2066-4273 **5500**
1843-3707 *see* 1582-9596 **3424**
1843-4401 *see* 1584-2851 **5477**
1843-5246 University of Agricultural Sciences and Veterinary Medicine Cluj-Napoca. Bulletin. Agriculture **165**
1843-5254 University of Agricultural Sciences and Veterinary Medicine Cluj-Napoca. Bulletin. Horticulture **165**
1843-5262 University of Agricultural Sciences and Veterinary Medicine Cluj-Napoca. Bulletin. Animal Science and Biotechnology **8810**
1843-5270 University of Agricultural Sciences and Veterinary Medicine Cluj-Napoca. Bulletin. Veterinary Medicine **8810**
1843-536X *see* 1843-5262 **8810**
1843-5378 *see* 1843-5270 **8810**
1843-5386 *see* 1843-5246 **165**
1843-5394 *see* 1843-5254 **165**
1843-5610 Journal of Identity and Migration Studies **7147**
1843-5637 Biharean Biologist **656**
1843-570X Agora International Journal of Juridical Sciences **4611**
1843-598X Studia Universitatis "Babes-Bolyai". Bioethica **6954**
1843-7265 Surveys in Mathematics and its Applications **5540**
1843-8105 Accounting and Management Information Systems *see* 1583-4387 **1285**

ISSN

ISSN

1866-489X Bonner Zentrum fuer Religion und Gesellschaft. Studien **7628**
1866-5039 Deutscher Waldbesitzer **3687**
1866-5055 Bibliotheca Academica. Reihe Soziologie **8090**
1866-5063 Bibliotheca Academica. Reihe Paedagogik **2831**
1866-5071 Bibliotheca Academica. Reihe Orientalistik **545**
1866-5233 *see* 0340-9341 **5111**
1866-5365 Wegweiser Journalismus **4585**
1866-5381 *see* 0003-8970 **5096**
1866-5438 Marke 41 **1830**
1866-5462 *see* 1439-8907 **7449**
1866-5608 Bankinformation **1317**
1866-5616 A D A C Ski-Guide **8301**
1866-5756 ProMed Komplementaer **5700**
1866-5861 Onkopipeline **6031**
1866-587X *see* 1866-5861 **6031**
1866-5888 Journal of Personnel Psychology **7378**
1866-6116 A D H D - Attention Deficit and Hyperactivity Disorders **6117**
1866-6140 Psychology Science Quarterly **7400**
1866-6272 *see* 1615-3502 **3726**
1866-6566 *see* 1006-9097 **6467**
1866-6647 *see* 1866-6116 **6117**
1866-6663 Rechnungswesen und Controlling *changed to* 1867-0091 **1299**
1866-6868 Aktueller E U - Foerderbrief fuer Betriebe, Berater und Behoerden **1058**
1866-6892 Journal of Infrared, Millimeter and Terahertz Waves **7078**
1866-6906 Journal of Infrared, Millimeter and Terahertz Waves (Online) *see* 1866-6892 **7078**
1866-7058 Werben und Verkaufen. Media **1848**
1866-7198 V M B G - Mitteilungen (Ausgabe B G M S) *changed to* 1866-7201 **1425**
1866-7201 V M B G - Mitteilungen (Ausgabe B G M) **1425**
1866-7414 *see* 0343-6993 **5513**
1866-7473 Trends in Classics **2241**
1866-7481 *see* 1866-7473 **2241**
1866-749X Public Transport **8509**
1866-7511 Arabian Journal of Geosciences **2725**
1866-7538 *see* 1866-7511 **2725**
1866-7651 Goettinger Forum fuer Altertumswissenschaft. Beihefte *see* 1437-9082 **4140**
1866-7724 Freeride **8259**
1866-7759 Life & Style Weekly **5075**
1866-7805 SpielRaeume der Antike **4162**
1866-7910 Food Engineering Reviews **3638**
1866-7929 *see* 1866-7910 **3638**
1866-802X Journal of Politics in Latin America **7249**
1866-8313 Language, Context and Cognition **5140**
1866-8429 Zeno **1044**
1866-8453 Steel Grips **6333**
1866-8658 Business Research **1075**
1866-8720 Die Internistische Welt Onkologie *changed to* 1869-0874 **5948**
1866-8836 *see* 1867-416X **6015**
1866-8887 *see* 1867-0717 **8495**
1866-8992 Radio-Kurier - Weltweit Hoeren **2362**
1866-9085 Spektrum Patholinguistik **5177**
1866-9123 Woche Heute **8889**
1866-9271 D I I R - Forum **1737**
1866-928X *see* 1866-9298 **3998**
1866-9298 Applied Geomatics **3998**
1866-9433 *see* 1866-9085 **5177**
1866-9557 Archaeological and Anthropological Sciences **375**
1866-9565 *see* 1866-9557 **375**
1866-9611 Die Schwester - Der Pfleger Plus **7541**
1866-9808 Language and Cognition **5139**
1866-9859 *see* 1866-9808 **5139**
1866-993X Der Verkehrsanwalt **4807**
1866-9956 Cognitive Computation **6133**
1866-9964 *see* 1866-9956 **6133**
1867-0083 E K - Experte Aktuell **1815**
1867-0091 Rechnungs-Wesen Kompakt **1299**
1867-0180 Soziale Passagen **8006**
1867-0199 *see* 1867-0180 **8006**
1867-0202 Business & Information Systems Engineering **1413**
1867-030X Millennium-Jahrbuch **4153**
1867-0318 *see* 1867-030X **4153**
1867-0326 Box.de *changed to* Box **4371**
1867-0334 Food and Environmental Virology **886**
1867-0342 *see* 1867-0334 **886**
1867-0466 Journal of Biorheology **754**
1867-0474 *see* 1867-0466 **754**
1867-0628 Kultura **7250**
1867-0644 Waldenser-Magazin **7693**
1867-0652 Integers (Print) **5494**
1867-0687 *see* 1708-8569 **6105**
1867-0717 European Transport Research Review **8495**
1867-0725 *see* 1226-9239 **797**
1867-0822 Kommunale Verwaltungssteuerung **7450**
1867-0903 *see* 0942-4040 **5111**
1867-0911 Journal fuer Kulturpflanzen **238**
1867-1004 Infamily **2402**
1867-1071 Japanese Journal of Radiology **6199**
1867-108X *see* 1867-1071 **6199**
1867-1233 *see* 1042-1726 **2949**
1867-1268 Julius Kuehn-Institut, Bundesforschungsinstitut fuer Kulturpflanzen. Mitteilungen **129**
1867-1284 Diana - Muj Kreativni Svet **4356**
1867-1381 Atmospheric Measurement Techniques **6347**
1867-139X Field Actions Science Reports **1595**
1867-1462 *see* 1913-2751 **765**
1867-1551 *see* 0066-6459 **4131**
1867-1594 Palaeobiodiversity and Palaeoenvironments **6727**
1867-1608 *see* 1867-1594 **6727**
1867-1616 Marine Biodiversity **2811**
1867-1624 *see* 1867-1616 **2811**
1867-1632 *see* 0178-7888 **3500**
1867-1691 Zeitschrift fuer Rezensionen zur Germanistischen Sprachwissenschaft **5199**
1867-1705 *see* 1867-1691 **5199**
1867-1748 Race and Social Problems **7994**
1867-1756 *see* 1867-1748 **7994**
1867-1764 Statistics in BioSciences **720**
1867-1772 *see* 1867-1764 **720**
1867-1977 Sport- und Praeventivmedizin **6233**
1867-1985 *see* 1867-1977 **6233**
1867-2086 Bioanalytical Reviews **724**
1867-2094 *see* 1867-2086 **724**
1867-2221 International Journal of Stomatology & Occlusion Medicine **5849**
1867-223X *see* 1867-2221 **5849**
1867-2280 *see* 0933-2480 **8363**
1867-2302 Evidence-Based Spine Surgery *changed to* Evidence-Based Spine-Care Surgery **6243**
1867-2310 *see* Evidence-Based Spine-Care Surgery **6243**
1867-2450 Biophysical Reviews **752**
1867-2469 *see* 1867-2450 **752**
1867-2477 Geoheritage **2736**
1867-2485 *see* 1867-2477 **2736**
1867-2493 H T M **6314**
1867-2590 Mechatronik **3209**
1867-2809 Masterrind **293**
1867-2949 Mathematical Programming Computation **5554**
1867-2957 *see* 1867-2949 **5554**
1867-3015 W I F I S Aktuell **7272**
1867-3147 Detecon Management Report **1416**
1867-3198 Relationes **7902**
1867-3236 The Review of Socionetwork Strategies **2352**
1867-3325 Berichte des Lehr- und Forschungsgebietes Geotechnik **3260**
1867-383X *see* 1432-847X **3424**
1867-416X Cellular Therapy and Transplantation **6015**
1867-4615 Dow Jones Einkaeufer im Markt **1814**
1867-4623 Dow Jones Montan Aktuell **1621**
1867-4704 Dow Jones Ostwirtschaftsreport **1477**
1867-4828 Journal of Internet Services and Applications **2563**
1867-4879 Dortmunder Beitraege zu Kommunikationsnetzen und -systemen **2319**
1867-495X Automotive Agenda **8564**
1867-5565 International Journal of Advanced Corporate Learning **2868**
1867-5700 Forschungsberichte Leistungselektronik und Steuerungen **3308**
1867-5964 Ventura **1191**
1867-5999 Archiv fuer Familiengeschichtsforschung **3759**
1867-6081 Zeitschrift fuer Komplementaermedizin **5734**
1867-6103 *see* 1867-6081 **5734**
1867-6294 Palaeodiversity **2761**
1867-6723 Das Jugendamt **4705**
1867-6812 *see* 0031-0220 **6728**
1867-6936 Annals of Solid and Structural Mechanics **3374**
1867-7185 *see* 1001-0521 **6330**
1867-7371 Mechatronik Mobil **3209**
1867-7940 Zeitschrift fuer Bilanzierung und Rechnungswesen **1304**
1867-8076 *see* 0945-7968 **3045**
1867-8254 D B B - Report **7432**
1867-8343 *see* 1614-3485 **1717**
1867-8521 *see* 1867-139X **1595**
1867-8548 *see* 1867-1381 **6347**
1867-8610 Atmospheric Measurement Techniques Discussions **6347**
1867-8882 *see* 0025-3863 **1834**
1867-8904 China Aktuell. Data Supplement (Print) *changed to* China Data Supplement **7115**
1867-9595 D U Z Europa Kompakt **2977**
1867-9854 Climb! **8309**
1868-0038 D I Y International **4437**
1868-0089 B B S R - Info **4404**
1868-0267 *see* 0023-9909 **5143**
1868-0356 Senckenberg Gesellschaft fuer Naturforschung. Abhandlungen **704**
1868-0437 *see* 0940-8711 **8810**
1868-0445 *see* 1860-3203 **8804**
1868-0860 Journal of Paper Conservation **499**
1868-0941 Texts in Computer Science **2439**
1868-1026 Journal of Current Chinese Affairs **7146**
1868-1034 Journal of Current Southeast Asian Affairs **7146**
1868-1069 *see* 0342-2380 **8208**
1868-1220 Pferde Heute *changed to* 1861-4205 **8294**
1868-1247 ProWald **3700**
1868-128X TechTarget Magazin **2516**
1868-131X Jahrbuch fuer Europaeische Ethnologie **3619**
1868-1581 Goettingen Journal of Intenational Law **4927**
1868-1883 Hormone Molecular Biology and Clinical Investigation **5894**
1868-1891 *see* 1868-1883 **5894**
1868-193X *see* 1868-1948 **8808**
1868-1948 Team Spiegel **8808**
1868-2278 Einkauf *changed to* 1867-0083 **1815**
1868-2502 C E A S Space Journal **50**
1868-2510 *see* 1868-2502 **50**
1868-3207 Implants **5847**
1868-4297 *see* 1868-4300 **5781**
1868-4300 Cardiovascular Intervention and Therapeutics **5781**
1868-4459 Diamant Hochleistungswerkzeuge **6461**
1868-4599 Kant Yearbook **6930**
1868-4874 *see* 1868-1026 **7146**
1868-4904 Central European Neurosurgery **6130**
1868-5021 BioMolecular Concepts **758**
1868-503X *see* 1868-5021 **758**
1868-6249 *see* 0947-0867 **661**
1868-6303 Bloomsbury Review of Applied Linguistics and Communication **5101**
1868-6311 *see* 1868-6303 **5101**
1868-632X Yearbook of Phraseology **5197**
1868-6338 *see* 1868-632X **5197**
1868-6346 Laboratory Phonology **5138**
1868-6354 *see* 1868-6346 **5138**
1868-6397 *see* 0511-9618 **823**
1868-6540 V F D B **3257**
1868-6958 Cancer Nanotechnology **6013**
1868-6966 *see* 1868-6958 **6013**
1868-6982 *see* Journal of Hepato - Biliary - Pancreatic Sciences **6248**
1868-7091 Rueckert-Studien **5365**
1868-7431 Wittgenstein Studien. Neue Folge **6961**
1868-7458 *see* 1868-7431 **6961**
1868-8268 Cerebrospinal Fluid **6130**
1868-8276 *see* 1868-8268 **6130**
1868-8497 Hormones and Cancer **5894**
1868-8500 *see* 1868-8497 **5894**
1868-8551 *see* 0946-7785 **5902**
1868-856X *see* 0947-0875 **6164**
1868-8810 *see* 1863-9984 **4699**
1868-8888 *see* 1436-3038 **7622**
1868-8934 Zeitschrift fuer die Welt der Tuerken **4483**
1868-9078 Zeitschrift fuer Orientarchaeologie **424**
1868-9191 *see* 0373-9767 **7833**
1868-937X *see* 0916-7005 **5499**
1868-9418 *see* 1431-5041 **5368**
1868-9426 Angermion **5254**
1868-9957 MONTAGEtechnik **3370**
1869-0327 A C I **5829**
1869-0874 Onkologische Welt **5948**
1870-0063 Andamios **7947**
1870-0160 Revista Salud Publica y Nutricion **7539**
1870-0195 *see* 1027-3956 **6879**
1870-0365 Contribuciones desde Coatepec **7956**
1870-0462 Tropical and Subtropical Agroecosystems **163**
1870-0713 CICIMAR Oceanides **2802**
1870-1191 Culturales **8097**
1870-199X Revista Odontologica Mexicana **5864**
1870-2333 Polis **7167**
1870-3267 Universidad Veracruzana. Revista Medica **5726**
1870-3429 Discuso Visual **534**
1870-3453 Revista Mexicana de Biodiversidad **2626**
1870-3569 Confines de Relacions Internacionales y Ciencia Politica **7118**
1870-4050 Signos Literarios **5372**
1870-4069 Research in Computing Science **2436**
1870-4492 Pensares y Quehaceres **6938**
1870-4573 Cancerologia **6015**
1870-4654 Anuario Mexicano de Derecho Internacional **4917**
1870-4662 Lampara de Diogenes **6931**
1870-4905 *see* 0011-1503 **6912**
1870-557X Daena **6913**
1870-5820 L E A A **5138**
1870-6525 Morfismos **5518**
1870-9095 Latin - American Journal of Physics Education **7024**
1871-000X Dier Tuin **6806**
1871-0034 Jaarboek KennisSamenleving **7447**
1871-0050 Centrum voor Kinderfilosofie. Nieuwsbrief **6910**
1871-0069 Perspectives in Bioanalysis **742**
1871-0093 Arresten Handelsrecht *changed to* 1877-2080 **4946**
1871-0107 Praktijkgids Zorg en Inkomen **4760**
1871-0115 Architecture - Technology - Culture **5256**
1871-0131 Asian Journal of Criminology **2644**
1871-014X *see* 1871-0131 **2644**
1871-0204 Handboek Financiele Verslaggeving. Jaarrekening **1289**
1871-0212 Index Vleeswetgeving *changed to* 1874-7736 **8997**
1871-0220 Richtlijnen voor de Jaarverslaggeving voor Kleine Rechtspersonen **1301**
1871-0239 Geneesmiddelen, Zwangerschap en Borstvoeding **6844**
1871-028X Wettelijke Onderzoekstaken Natuur en Milieu. Rapporten **3474**
1871-0298 WOt-Studies **3476**
1871-0301 Handbook of Computing and Statistics with Applications **5552**
1871-031X Religion and Human Rights **7674**
1871-0328 *see* 1871-031X **7674**
1871-0352 ProcesNieuws **7260**
1871-0360 Zwembadbranche.nl **461**
1871-0395 International Studies in Population **7285**
1871-0409 Studies in Global Justice **4941**
1871-0417 Principles of European Contract Law **4938**
1871-0425 Hardware.info Magazine **2539**
1871-0433 Monitoring Beheerskosten Algemene wet Bijzondere Ziektekosten† **8975**
1871-0468 Sdu Wettenverzameling. Arbeidsrecht **4781**
1871-0476 Magazijn
1871-0484 Script Oncologie *changed to* 1874-1827 **6030**
1871-0492 Bouwkennis Kwartaalrapport *changed to* Bouwkennis Marketingmagazine **983**
1871-0506 B.ND **4590**
1871-0522 WinxClub **2222**
1871-0549 Nieuw Commercieel Vastgoed in Nederland **1371**
1871-0557 Hypothekengids **1351**
1871-0581 Jaarboek Integrale Verzuimaanpak Casemanagement en Reintegratie *changed to* 1874-8678 **1684**
1871-059X De Arbokolom **1664**
1871-0603 Bodyguard **4371**
1871-0611 Bietenstatistiek **176**
1871-062X Monitor Gesubsidieerde Rechtsbijstand **4968**
1871-0638 Tekst en Toelichting Wet Werk en Bijstand (The Hague) **1710**
1871-0646 Dichters in de Prinsentuin **5420**
1871-0654 DELPHI. The Reservoir Characterization and Flow Simulation Project **2705**
1871-0670 R K D Bulletin **514**
1871-0697 Wellness Magazine **315**
1871-0700 Oog voor Welstand **4421**
1871-0719 Dialoog **5890**
1871-0727 ZOA Magazine **8079**
1871-0743 Agora Editie *changed to* 1871-0751 **6902**
1871-0751 Agora Reeks **6902**
1871-0794 Signaleringsrapport Hulpmiddelen **6116**
1871-0808 Scholenbouwprijs **456**
1871-0816 T N O Magazine. T N O Ruimte en Infrastructuur **3285**
1871-0824 T N O Magazine. T N O Industrie en Techniek **1905**
1871-0832 T N O Magazine. T N O Kwaliteit van Leven **7543**
1871-0840 T N O Magazine. T N O Defensie en Veiligheid **7471**
1871-0859 T N O Magazine. T N O Informatie- en Communicatietechnologie **2439**
1871-0875 Nieuwe Oogst (Noord Edition) **243**

ISSN

1872-4248 Vreemdelingenwet 2000 **4853**
1872-4264 6 Daagsen Statistieken **8270**
1872-4329 *see* 1931-9045 **2169**
1872-4353 *see* 1176-7529 **4460**
1872-4396 Silhouet **6185**
1872-4426 N B D BouwPraktijk *changed to* 1877-2684 **1025**
1872-4442 Quoto Jaarboek **8600**
1872-4450 Moderne Kaarten *changed to* 1872-4469 **4342**
1872-4469 Nederlandse Freecard Catalogus **4342**
1872-4477 Intercultural Theology and Study of Religions **7650**
1872-4485 Wegwijs in Arbeidsvoorwaarden **1714**
1872-4507 Donald Duck Extra **2186**
1872-4515 Infanterie **6424**
1872-4531 La Jurisprudence de l'O M C **4954**
1872-454X Booming Futsal **8224**
1872-4590 Goede Papieren **6524**
1872-4612 Werkgever Alert **1714**
1872-4639 Leadership **1772**
1872-4647 Arbeidsmarktrapportage Onderwijs *changed to* 1872-3381 **2892**
1872-4655 K R O Magazine **2384**
1872-468X Offices in Figures **7603**
1872-471X *see* European Journal of Jewish Studies **7721**
1872-4728 Mahkuzine **504**
1872-4744 Ajax Kick Off **8220**
1872-4760 HCC!link *changed to* 1876-1585 **2419**
1872-4779 MEEdelen *changed to* 1875-0516 **4067**
1872-4795 Archeon Journaal **2967**
1872-4809 RegiOpinie (Mid-Netherlands Edition) *changed to* De Status (Mid-Netherlands Edition) **1968**
1872-4817 RegiOpinie (Rhine Edition)† **8985**
1872-4825 RegiOpinie (Northwest Netherlands Edition)† **8985**
1872-4833 RegiOpinie (East Edition) *changed to* De Status (East Edition) **1968**
1872-4841 V O A Magazine **1800**
1872-485X PrO-Krant **6702**
1872-4868 Whisky Passion **612**
1872-4906 Arnulfus Post **7784**
1872-4922 iX *changed to* 1388-0276 **2415**
1872-4930 D R S Magazine **2841**
1872-4949 Bio Update **96**
1872-4957 Plafond & Wand **1029**
1872-4965 Ecomare Bericht **2609**
1872-4973 Forensic Science International: Genetics **5913**
1872-4981 Intelligent Decision Technologies **2450**
1872-5023 E U Market Survey. Cut Flowers and Foliage *changed to* The Cut Flowers and Foliage Market in the E U **3755**
1872-5031 Diabetes Informatieboek **5887**
1872-504X Basisboek Salarisadministratie BKL **1667**
1872-5058 Belasting Toegevoegde Waarde en Overdrachtsbelasting in de Vastgoedsector **1912**
1872-5066 F D Strategie *changed to* 1877-2374 **1744**
1872-5074 Bouwend Nederland Podium **983**
1872-5082 International Journal of the Platonic Tradition **6926**
1872-5090 Volkscultuur Magazine **3624**
1872-5104 De KrantvandeAarde **2616**
1872-5120 Journal of Pharmaceutical Innovation **6855**
1872-5147 Employment in the Netherlands **1679**
1872-5155 Global Economic History Series **1718**
1872-5163 Journal of Reformed Theology **7655**
1872-5171 International Journal of Public Theology **7650**
1872-518X PluZ **4053**
1872-5198 Werken in het Buitenland **1714**
1872-521X V L A K - Verslag **422**
1872-5228 Light **6992**
1872-5252 Sociale Cohesie in Nederland **8134**
1872-5260 Kroniek Sint Aegten **7659**
1872-5325 Systems and Synthetic Biology **751**
1872-5333 *see* 1872-5325 **751**
1872-535X Contactblad Spreken bij Uitvaarten **6911**
1872-5368 Wah Wah **6627**
1872-5384 Opel Klassiek **8597**
1872-5406 Start!-krant **7574**
1872-5414 BouwTotaal **983**
1872-5422 Villa Pardoes Magazine **8076**
1872-5457 African Diaspora **7945**
1872-5465 *see* 1872-5457 **7945**
1872-5473 *see* 1872-5082 **6926**
1872-5481 Brill Classics in Islam **7709**
1872-549X Glastuinbouwtechniek Magazine **2042**
1872-5503 Hematology Education **5937**
1872-552X Netherlands Journal of Psychology **7386**
1872-5546 Surf 'n Beach **8336**
1872-5554 A O P A Pilots & Planes **8533**
1872-5570 Het Ondernemersbelang Wageningen, Ede, Rhenen en Veenendaal **1783**
1872-5589 Toets **7543**
1872-5597 Mzine **8055**
1872-5600 Ambition Magazine **1725**
1872-5619 Hofjeskrant **445**
1872-5635 De Vagebond **5394**
1872-5643 Dedicon Bulletin **4081**
1872-5651 Tulpia **3569**
1872-5678 Baptisten.nl **7748**
1872-5686 Gribb Salarisadviseur **1684**
1872-5694 Gribb Belastingadviseur **1927**
1872-5708 4 W D & S U V Auto-Magazine **8613**
1872-5759 De Klepel **4237**
1872-5767 S P C L **3916**
1872-5775 Wraf! **6817**
1872-5783 Triv' **6301**
1872-5791 *see* 1005-2321 **2705**
1872-5805 New Carbon Materials (English Edition) (Online) **3251**
1872-5813 *see* 0253-2409 **3254**
1872-583X China Population, Resources and Environment **7279**
1872-5848 Facility and Finance Select† **8955**
1872-5856 De Handhavingskrant **7494**
1872-5872 F D Persoonlijk **1108**
1872-5880 ProRail Magazine **8622**
1872-5929 Magazine Materialenkennis
1872-5937 Het Ondernemersbelang Noord-Holland Noord **1782**
1872-5988 Handbuch der Orientalistik. 2. Abteilung. Indien, Ergaenzungsband **550**
1872-602X Stichting Bouwhistorie Nederland. Nieuwsbrief **1038**
1872-6038 Het Ondernemersbelang Rivierenland **1782**
1872-6046 Het Ondernemersbelang van Noord-Brabant **1783**
1872-6054 *see* 0168-8510 **7522**
1872-6062 *see* 0169-2046 **2617**
1872-6089 *see* 0304-3878 **1600**
1872-6097 *see* 0377-0273 **2785**
1872-6100 *see* 0019-3577 **5492**
1872-6119 *see* 0020-0190 **2537**
1872-6127 View2 **8462**
1872-6135 *see* 0024-3841 **5144**
1872-6143 *see* 0024-4937 **2752**
1872-6151 *see* 0025-3227 **2812**
1872-616X *see* 0031-0182 **6727**
1872-6178 *see* 0378-7788 **3130**
1872-6186 *see* 0377-8398 **6726**
1872-6194 *see* 0166-3615 **1415**
1872-6208 *see* 0167-4048 **2512**
1872-6216 *see* 0047-6374 **4051**
1872-6232 *see* 0378-3782 **5989**
1872-6240 *see* 0006-8993 **6128**
1872-6259 *see* 0016-7061 **232**
1872-6275 Tring! **8269**
1872-6283 *see* 0379-0738 **5913**
1872-6291 *see* 0020-0255 **2545**
1872-6305 *see* 1566-2535 **2467**
1872-6313 *see* 0929-1199 **1360**
1872-6321 *see* 0165-0173 **6128**
1872-633X *see* 0926-6690 **236**
1872-6356 *see* 0925-4773 **834**
1872-6364 *see* 0921-8181 **2744**
1872-6372 *see* 0378-4266 **1360**
1872-6399 Music Emotion **8154**
1872-6402 D V D Branden† **8948**
1872-6410 MotoPlus **8591**
1872-6461 Rijksdienst voor Archeologie, Cultuurlandschap en Monumenten. Nieuwsbrief **456**
1872-6488 Diva en Donna *changed to* Diva **3914**
1872-6496 Dossier V P B 2007† **8951**
1872-650X Liftbouw **3388**
1872-6518 En Toch **7796**
1872-6526 FEDActueel **3378**
1872-6534 A P **2643**
1872-6550 Navigator NL **8655**
1872-6569 MR Magazine **6701**
1872-6577 Bryologische + Lichenologische Werkgroep. Nieuwsbrief **782**
1872-6585 Vereniging van Vrienden van Museum Het Valkhof. Nieuwsbrief **6539**
1872-6607 InstallateursZaken **4121**
1872-6623 *see* 0304-3959 **6172**
1872-6631 Xcellent **1721**
1872-664X A V S Magazine **8286**
1872-6658 Glaucoommagazine **6043**
1872-6666 GaultMillau **4387**
1872-6674 O P C Nieuws **8507**
1872-6704 TooN/SpeZiaal *changed to* SpeZiaal **2914**
1872-6712 OK Operationeel **6254**
1872-6739 Muldersnijs **450**
1872-6763 *see* 0165-7836 **3592**
1872-6771 *see* 0166-218X **5483**
1872-678X *see* 0165-0270 **6155**
1872-6798 M B O Magazine **2944**
1872-6801 *see* 0165-0114 **5489**
1872-681X *see* 0012-365X **5483**
1872-6828 *see* 0012-8252 **2706**
1872-6836 *see* 0009-2541 **2703**
1872-6844 *see* 0920-1211 **6138**
1872-6852 *see* 0378-4290 **231**
1872-6860 *see* 0377-2217 **1742**
1872-6879 *see* 0377-0265 **6352**
1872-6887 *see* 0341-8162 **2728**
1872-6895 *see* 0304-4076 **1544**
1872-6909 *see* 0142-694X **440**
1872-6917 *see* 0013-7952 **3266**
1872-6925 *see* 0168-874X **3291**
1872-6933 *see* 0169-023X **2416**
1872-695X *see* 0169-555X **2743**
1872-6968 *see* 0303-8467 **6132**
1872-6976 *see* 0167-4943 **4041**
1872-6984 *see* 0926-2245 **5482**
1872-6992 *see* 0925-8574 **3417**
1872-700X *see* 0924-7947 **4041**
1872-7018 *see* 0920-5489 **2412**
1872-7026 *see* 0304-3800 **3481**
1872-7034 *see* 1470-160X **3417**
1872-7042 *see* 0378-1127 **3688**
1872-7050 *see* 1389-9341 **3689**
1872-7069 *see* 1389-1286 **2496**
1872-7077 *see* 1382-6689 **3497**
1872-7085 TVM.info *changed to* 1876-2301 **8994**
1872-7107 *see* 0168-1699 **215**
1872-7115 *see* 0167-739X **2520**
1872-7123 *see* 0165-1781 **6178**
1872-7131 *see* 0387-7604 **6127**
1872-7158 Center for Oceans Law and Policy **4969**
1872-7166 *see* 0378-4754 **2517**
1872-7182 *see* 0167-6393 **5177**
1872-7190 The China Legal Development Yearbook **546**
1872-7212 The China Environment Yearbook **3410**
1872-7220 The China Economy Yearbook **546**
1872-7239 The China Society Yearbook **546**
1872-7255 Academic Press Advanced Finance Series **1305**
1872-7263 Research in International Business **1581**
1872-7298 *see* 1567-133X **867**
1872-7301 Germany Real Estate Yearbook **7591**
1872-7336 *see* 0167-8191 **2468**
1872-7344 *see* 0167-8655 **2456**
1872-7352 *see* 0167-9473 **5551**
1872-7360 *see* 0169-1368 **2761**
1872-7379 *see* 0378-3839 **3263**
1872-7387 *see* 0141-9382 **2485**
1872-7395 *see* 0031-9201 **2787**
1872-7409 *see* 0950-7051 **2454**
1872-7433 *see* 0301-9268 **2762**
1872-7441 *see* 0165-232X **8418**
1872-745X *see* 0166-5316 **2435**
1872-7468 *see* 0167-6377 **7896**
1872-7484 *see* 1566-0702 **6125**
1872-7492 *see* 0168-1702 **897**
1872-7506 *see* 0925-4927 **6178**
1872-7514 *see* 0304-422X **5352**
1872-7522 *see* 0167-9260 **3319**
1872-7530 *see* 0378-7206 **2521**
1872-7549 *see* 0166-4328 **6126**
1872-7557 *see* 0165-1684 **2464**
1872-7565 *see* 0169-2607 **5829**
1872-7573 *see* 0378-8741 **6853**
1872-7581 *see* 0304-4203 **2712**
1872-759X *see* 0029-5493 **3355**
1872-7603 *see* 0165-0378 **5763**
1872-762X *see* 0040-6031 **2141**
1872-7638 *see* 0167-8442 **7063**
1872-7646 *see* 0167-9457 **5630**
1872-7654 *see* 0301-2115 **5990**
1872-7670 Nederlands Tijdschrift voor Allergie. Huisartseneditie **5764**
1872-7689 *see* 0167-2738 **7041**
1872-7697 *see* 0167-8760 **7365**
1872-7719 *see* 0167-4870 **1824**
1872-7727 *see* 0720-048X **6196**
1872-7735 Nieuwsbrief Oud Deventer **4248**
1872-7743 *see* 0167-6636 **3354**
1872-7751 dlk **5069**
1872-7786 *see* 0009-2797 **3495**
1872-7832 Cahiers Isabelle de Charriere **5268**
1872-7840 *see* 0166-5162 **2748**
1872-7859 M A S T. Maritime Studies **3451**
1872-7867 *see* 0165-9111 **4169**
1872-7875 Later Medieval Europe **4239**
1872-7883 *see* 0022-2313 **7078**
1872-7891 *see* 0926-5805 **2458**
1872-7905 *see* 0022-1759 **5762**
1872-7913 *see* 0924-8579 **887**
1872-7921 *see* 0004-3702 **2446**
1872-793X *see* 0921-8890 **2586**
1872-7948 Tijdschrift voor Veiligheid **2681**
1872-7956 *see* 0167-6911 **2464**
1872-7964 *see* 0167-6423 **2510**
1872-7972 *see* 0304-3940 **6169**
1872-7980 *see* 0304-3835 **6013**
1872-7999 *see* 0166-1280 **2068**
1872-8006 *see* 0304-4165 **723**
1872-8014 *see* 0022-2860 **2068**
1872-8022 *see* 0167-2789 **7031**
1872-8057 *see* 0303-7207 **5897**
1872-8081 *see* 0951-6433 **726**
1872-8103 East Central and Eastern Europe in the Middle Ages, 450-1450 **4216**
1872-8111 *see* 0168-0102 **6169**
1872-8138 *see* 0262-8856 **2487**
1872-8162 *see* 0896-8446 **2103**
1872-8197 *see* 0167-6105 **3387**
1872-8200 *see* 0169-2070 **1493**
1872-8219 *see* 0169-8141 **3201**
1872-8227 *see* 0168-8227 **5888**
1872-8235 *see* 0924-2716 **4014**
1872-8243 *see* 1386-5056 **5831**
1872-826X *see* 1569-8432 **4016**
1872-8278 *see* 1567-7249 **893**
1872-8286 *see* 0925-2312 **2455**
1872-8294 *see* 0169-409X **6819**
1872-8308 *see* 0376-6357 **6126**
1872-8316 *see* 0167-6253 **6169**
1872-8324 *see* 0303-2647 **662**
1872-8332 *see* 0169-5002 **6026**
1872-8340 *see* 0929-7820
1872-8359 *see* 0167-7012 **889**
1872-8367 *see* 0920-6876 **2280**
1872-8375 *see* 0165-4683 **2407**
1872-8383 *see* 0169-5347 **708**
1872-8405 *see* 0072-1026 **2737**
1872-8421 *see* 0165-5728 **6154**
1872-8456 *see* 1359-6462 **6331**
1872-8464 *see* 0165-5876 **6081**
1872-8480 *see* 0307-904X **5550**
1872-8561 *see* 0022-328X **2125**
1872-8685 Amsterdam. Gemeentelijke Archiefdienst. Verslagen der Bedrijven, Diensten en Commissies van Amsterdam†
1872-8820 Rechtspraak Financieel Recht **4959**
1872-8839 Rechtspraak Ondernemingsrecht **4959**
1872-8847 *see* 1872-8855 **839**
1872-8855 Arthropod - Plant Interactions **839**
1872-8863 Diplomatic Studies **7231**
1872-8952 *see* 1388-2457 **6132**
1872-9045 *see* 0168-1591 **933**
1872-9053 *see* 0169-1317 **2724**
1872-9061 *see* 0300-2977 **5947**
1872-9088 *see* 1367-5788 **2505**
1872-9096 *see* 0166-3542 **881**
1872-910X *see* 0003-682X **7086**
1872-9118 *see* 0306-2619 **3124**
1872-9126 *see* 0003-6870 **3181**
1872-9134 *see* 0883-2927 **2724**
1872-9142 *see* 0161-5890 **739**
1872-9177 *see* 1769-7255 **6272**
1872-9185 *see* 0964-7775 **6531**
1872-924X Flora Malesiana. Series 1: Seed Plants **788**
1872-9258 Ondernemerspanel M K B-Nederland - T N S N I P O **1720**
1872-9282 Script Neurologie **6184**
1872-9312 Artery Research **5872**

ISSN

1873-4081 *see* 1369-8001 **3108**
1873-409X Vroegop **460**
1873-4103 *see* 1369-7021 **2072**
1873-4111 *see* 0378-5122 **5998**
1873-412X *see* 0263-2241 **6403**
1873-4138 *see* 0309-1740 **3656**
1873-4154 Het Ondernemersbelang van Rijn en Gouwe *changed to* Het Ondernemersbelang Het Groene Hart **1782**
1873-4162 *see* 1344-6223 **5915**
1873-4170 *see* 0951-8339 **3388**
1873-4189 *see* 1044-5803 **6322**
1873-4197 *see* 0264-1275 **3352**
1873-4200 *see* 0301-4622 **752**
1873-4227 *see* 0025-5408 **2111**
1873-4235 *see* 0956-5663 **759**
1873-4243 *see* 1093-3263 **2108**
1873-4251 *see* 1570-162X **5812**
1873-426X *see* 0008-6215 **2120**
1873-4286 *see* 1381-6128 **6831**
1873-4294 *see* 1568-0266 **5603**
1873-4308 *see* 0920-5861 **3237**
1873-4316 *see* 1389-2010 **763**
1873-4324 *see* 0003-2670 **2097**
1873-4332 *see* 1083-3188 **6095**
1873-4359 *see* 0927-7757 **2134**
1873-4367 *see* 0927-7765 **2134**
1873-4375 *see* 0098-1354 **2108**
1873-4383 *see* 1085-6862 **5739**
1873-4391 *see* 0196-4399 **883**
1873-4405 *see* 0009-2509 **3239**
1873-4413 *see* 0035-1598 **6730**
1873-4421 *see* 0301-0104 **2133**
1873-443X *see* 1877-7821 **6012**
1873-4448 *see* 0009-2614 **2133**
1873-4456 *see* 0165-4608 **6012**
1873-4464 *see* 0011-9164 **8820**
1873-4472 *see* 0079-6611 **2816**
1873-4480 *see* 1098-3597 **4090**
1873-4499 *see* 0899-7071 **6193**
1873-4502 *see* 0886-3350 **6044**
1873-4510 *see* 0305-9006 **4424**
1873-4529 *see* 0952-8180 **5772**
1873-4537 *see* 0363-8111 **33**
1873-4545 *see* 1365-1609 **6466**
1873-4553 *see* 1040-6182 **2763**
1873-457X *see* 0277-3791 **2763**
1873-4588 *see* 0892-1997 **6082**
1873-4596 *see* 0891-5849 **673**
1873-460X *see* 1056-8727 **5895**
1873-4626 *see* 1091-255X **6248**
1873-4634 *see* 0263-7863 **1419**
1873-4669 *see* 0925-8388 **6319**
1873-4693 *see* 0278-4319 **4391**
1873-4707 *see* 0268-4012 **2547**
1873-4715 *see* 0920-4105 **6776**
1873-4723 *see* 1467-0895 **1292**
1873-4731 *see* 0888-613X **2450**
1873-474X *see* 0736-5748 **6146**
1873-4758 *see* 0955-3959 **2695**
1873-4766 *see* 0304-8853 **7020**
1873-4774 *see* 0924-0136 **3386**
1873-4782 *see* 0022-5096 **7060**
1873-4804 *see* 1875-6867 **6284**
1873-4812 *see* 0022-3093 **7021**
1873-4820 *see* 0022-3115 **7067**
1873-4839 *see* 1361-3111 **5966**
1873-4847 *see* 0955-2863 **6662**
1873-4855 *see* 0021-8928 **3349**
1873-4863 *see* 0168-1656 **767**
1873-4871 *see* 0738-0593 **2869**
1873-488X *see* 1056-8719 **3499**
1873-4898 *see* 1477-5131 **6270**
1873-491X *see* 0020-7489 **5962**
1873-4936 *see* 0921-5093 **3353**
1873-4944 *see* Materials Science and Engineering B: Advanced Functional Solid-state Materials **3353**
1873-4952 C C, Christenen in Contact† **8938**
1873-4960 Service Magazine **4398**
1873-4979 *see* 0167-577X **7025**
1873-4995 *see* 0168-3659 **6853**
1873-5002 *see* 0022-0248 **2111**
1873-5010 *see* 1569-1993 **5927**
1873-5037 Iconicity in Language and Literature **5126**
1873-5061 Stem Cell Research **878**
1873-507X *see* 0031-9384 **927**
1873-5088 *see* 0032-0633 **579**
1873-5096 *see* 0962-6298 **7168**
1873-510X Bulletin Pastorale Dienstverlening **7629**
1873-5118 *see* 0301-0082 **927**
1873-5126 *see* 1353-8020 **6173**
1873-5134 *see* 0738-3991 **7535**
1873-5142 *see* 0031-3203 **2456**
1873-5150 *see* 0887-8994 **6101**
1873-5169 *see* 0196-9781 **741**
1873-5177 *see* 0091-3057 **6872**
1873-5185 Zens
1873-5193 Physics and Chemistry of the Earth (Online) *see* 1474-7065 **2714**
1873-5215 *see* 0362-546X **3212**
1873-5223 *see* 1471-5953 **5971**
1873-524X *see* 0964-5691 **2814**
1873-5258 *see* 0029-8018 **2814**
1873-5274 *see* 0305-0483 **1782**
1873-5282 *see* 0030-4387 **7256**
1873-5290 *see* 0146-6380 **2128**
1873-5312 *see* 0306-3747 **7090**
1873-5320 *see* 1474-0346 **2445**
1873-5339 *see* 0965-9978 **3288**
1873-5347 *see* 0277-9536 **5715**
1873-5355 *see* 0362-3319 **8004**
1873-5371 *see* 0306-4573 **5016**
1873-538X *see* 0883-0355 **2869**
1873-5398 *see* 1081-602X **7969**
1873-5401 Infobulletin Gemeenschappelijk Landbouwbeleid *changed to* 1874-7396 **105**
1873-541X *see* 0191-6599 **6923**
1873-5428 *see* 0197-3975 **4411**
1873-5436 Milieu (Den Bosch) **3452**
1873-5452 *see* 0893-9659 **5472**
1873-5460 *see* 0168-9274 **5550**
1873-5487 *see* 0188-4409 **5577**
1873-5495 *see* 1467-8039 **839**
1873-5509 *see* 0040-1625 **8441**
1873-5517 *see* 1369-8478 **8517**
1873-5525 *see* 1096-7516 **2560**
1873-555X Jippo Zomerboek **2195**
1873-5568 *see* 0167-9317 **3108**
1873-5584 *see* 0169-4332 **6305**
1873-5592 *see* 1389-4501 **6831**
1873-5606 *see* 1359-4311 **7053**
1873-5614 *see* 0144-8609 **3584**
1873-5622 *see* 0044-8486 **3584**
1873-5630 Pingu† **8981**
1873-5649 *see* 0096-3003 **5472**
1873-5657 *see* 0306-9192 **198**
1873-5665 *see* 1044-0283 **1349**
1873-5673 *see* 1057-0810 **1345**
1873-5681 *see* 0263-2373 **1742**
1873-569X *see* 0923-1811 **5878**
1873-5703 *see* 0176-2680 **7134**
1873-5711 *see* 1050-6411 **754**
1873-572X *see* 0014-2921 **1107**
1873-5738 *see* 0304-3886 **3322**
1873-5746 *see* 0388-0001 **5141**
1873-5754 *see* 0264-8377 **4418**
1873-5762 De Gelderse Roos **3914**
1873-5770 *see* 0260-8774 **3650**
1873-5797 *see* 0167-9236 **1738**
1873-5800 *see* 0968-0160 **925**
1873-5819 Forum Magazine (Utrecht) **8102**
1873-5835 *see* 0145-2126 **5940**
1873-5843 *see* 0887-6177 **6123**
1873-5851 *see* 0075-9511 **2796**
1873-586X Fris Nieuws **603**
1873-5878 *see* 0197-4556 **7336**
1873-5886 Inside + Insight **1753**
1873-5894 *see* 0730-725X **6202**
1873-5916 *see* 1075-2935 **3051**
1873-5924 *see* 1058-3300 **1166**
1873-5940 *see* 1567-8326 **2508**
1873-5959 *see* 0167-6687 **4508**
1873-5967 *see* 1386-6532 **5819**
1873-5975 *see* 0167-6245 **2325**
1873-5983 *see* 0143-974X **3275**
1873-5991 *see* 0305-750X **1608**
1873-6009 *see* 0169-7722 **3488**
1873-6017 *see* 0954-349X **1549**
1873-6025 *see* 0950-5849 **2591**
1873-6041 *see* 0038-0121 **7468**
1873-605X *see* 1363-4127 **2514**
1873-6068 *see* 0007-6813 **1072**
1873-6076 *see* 0306-4379 **2521**
1873-6084 *see* 0264-2751 **7489**
1873-6092 Tijdschrift Antropologie en Ontwikkelingsstudies **358**
1873-6106 *see* 0921-8009 **3416**
1873-6114 *see* 1754-4548 **2514**
1873-6122 *see* 0264-9993 **1539**
1873-6130 *see* 1570-677X **7961**
1873-6149 *see* 0969-5931 **1126**
1873-6165 *see* 1383-7621 **2523**
1873-6173 *see* 1566-0141 **1337**
1873-6181 *see* 0140-9883 **3130**
1873-619X *see* 0955-2219 **2040**
1873-6203 *see* 0047-2352 **4892**
1873-622X *see* 0005-7967 **7340**
1873-6238 *see* 1146-609X **650**
1873-6246 *see* 0301-0511 **7340**
1873-6254 *see* 0001-706X **5808**
1873-6270 *see* 0370-1573 **7034**
1873-6289 *see* 0361-3682 **1278**
1873-6297 *see* 0001-6918 **7330**
1873-6300 *see* 0891-0618 **6150**
1873-6319 *see* 1366-0071 **5567**
1873-6327 *see* 0306-4603 **2690**
1873-6335 *see* 1359-1789 **7332**
1873-6343 *see* 0950-3293 **3641**
1873-6351 *see* 0278-6915 **3497**
1873-636X *see* 1572-5286 **5552**
1873-6378 *see* 0016-3287 **1487**
1873-6386 *see* 0160-2527 **4695**
1873-6394 *see* 0144-8188 **4696**
1873-6416 *see* 1462-9011 **3428**
1873-6424 *see* 0269-7491 **3486**
1873-6432 *see* 0195-9255 **3425**
1873-6440 *see* 1365-6937 **3367**
1873-6475 *see* 1246-7391 **5915**
1873-6483 *see* 0740-5472 **2696**
1873-6505 *see* 1478-4092 **1826**
1873-6513 *see* 0885-3924 **6155**
1873-6521 *see* 0965-2590 **3090**
1873-653X Egodocuments and History Series **7560**
1873-6564 Transnational Classic in International Law **4942**
1873-6580 Procedural Aspects of International Law Monograph Series **4938**
1873-6599 International Environmental Law **3441**
1873-6602 International Law and Development **4931**
1873-6629 International and Comparative Criminal Law Series **4891**
1873-6637 Moments **607**
1873-6645 F C Groningen Presentatiegids **8227**
1873-6653 W M O Magazine **4070**
1873-6661 Het Ondernemersbelang van Haarlemmermeerlanden **1783**
1873-667X Het Ondernemersbelang van Twente **1783**
1873-6688 Het Ondernemersbelang van Revuss **1783**
1873-6696 Handicap en Beleid. Nieuwsbrief *changed to* 1873-670X **4070**
1873-670X W M O Magazine. Nieuwsbrief **4070**
1873-6718 Het Ondernemersbelang van De Kempen **1783**
1873-6726 *see* 1364-8152 **3482**
1873-6734 *see* 0267-3649 **2512**
1873-6750 *see* 0160-4120 **3421**
1873-6769 *see* 0952-1976 **2448**
1873-6777 *see* 0301-4215 **3132**
1873-6785 *see* 0360-5442 **3130**
1873-6793 *see* 0957-4174 **2448**
1873-6807 *see* 1740-1445 **7341**
1873-6815 *see* 0531-5565 **4044**
1873-6823 *see* 0741-8329 **2690**
1873-684X *see* 0360-1323 **984**
1873-6866 *see* 1477-8424 **2506**
1873-6874 *see* 1040-6190 **3157**
1873-6882 *see* 0959-4388 **6134**
1873-6890 *see* 0261-3794 **7132**
1873-6904 *see* 0261-2194 **3242**
1873-6920 *see* 0967-067X **7117**
1873-6939 *see* 0967-0661 **3290**
1873-6947 *see* 1744-3881 **5956**
1873-6955 *see* 0278-4343 **2802**
1873-6963 *see* 0965-2299 **5804**
1873-6998 *see* 0955-5986 **4486**
1873-7005 *see* 0169-5983 **3361**
1873-7013 *see* 1351-4180 **2094**
1873-7021 *see* 0969-6210 **6722**
1873-703X *see* 0140-3664 **2533**
1873-7048 *see* 1364-5439 **6722**
1873-7056 *see* 1361-3723 **2512**
1873-7064 *see* 0028-3908 **6863**
1873-7072 *see* 0308-8146 **2061**
1873-7099 Het Ondernemersbelang van Drechtsteden **1783**
1873-7102 Het Ondernemersbelang van Haaglanden **1783**
1873-7110 Het Ondernemersbelang van Zeeland **1783**
1873-7129 *see* 0956-7135 **3638**
1873-7137 *see* 0268-005X **3639**
1873-7145 *see* 0963-9969 **3641**
1873-7153 *see* 0016-2361 **6769**
1873-7161 *see* 0140-6701 **6800**
1873-717X *see* 1464-2859 **3135**
1873-7188 *see* 0378-3820 **6769**
1873-7196 *see* 0920-3796 **3378**
1873-720X Sport Marketing Europe **1844**
1873-7218 *see* 0015-1882 **3244**
1873-7226 *see* 0379-7112 **3578**
1873-7234 *see* 1631-0721 **3372**
1873-7242 Het Ondernemersbelang van 't Gooi **1783**
1873-7269 Het Ondernemersbelang van De Graafschap-Liemers **1783**
1873-7277 *see* 0033-2984 **7397**
1873-7285 *see* 0997-7538 **7058**
1873-7293 *see* 0962-1849 **7335**
1873-7307 *see* 0098-8472 **786**
1873-7315 *see* 0013-7944 **3344**
1873-7323 *see* 0141-0296 **3266**
1873-7331 *see* 1161-0301 **229**
1873-734X *see* 1010-7940 **5786**
1873-7358 *see* 1471-0153 **7353**
1873-7366 Het Ondernemersbelang Noordwest Veluwe en Eemland **1782**
1873-7374 *see* 0165-1765 **1540**
1873-7382 *see* 0272-7757 **3020**
1873-7390 *see* 0997-7546 **7058**
1873-7412 Het Ondernemersbelang Westerkwartier **1783**
1873-7420 Het Ondernemersbelang van Leiden **1783**
1873-7439 Het Ondernemersbelang van Amsterdam **1783**
1873-7447 Smart **3664**
1873-7455 Zanders Magazine **1955**
1873-7463 The Study of Time. Supplements *see* 0170-9704 **582**
1873-7471 Het Ondernemersbelang van Waalboss **1783**
1873-7498 Het Ondernemersbelang van Utrecht **1783**
1873-7501 Het Ondernemersbelang van IJmond **1783**
1873-7528 *see* 0149-7634 **6169**
1873-7544 *see* 0306-4522 **6169**
1873-7552 *see* 0147-1767 **8109**
1873-7587 *see* 0198-9715 **3481**
1873-7617 Small-Scale Forestry **3703**
1873-7633 *see* 0266-352X **3290**
1873-7641 *see* 0301-4207 **3146**
1873-765X *see* 0305-0548 **2413**
1873-7668 *see* 0898-1221 **5552**
1873-7684 *see* 0097-8493 **2484**
1873-7692 *see* 0747-5632 **8151**
1873-7706 *see* 0885-2006 **2844**
1873-7714 *see* 0163-8343 **6143**
1873-7722 *see* 0160-7383 **8683**
1873-7730 *see* 0143-6228 **3998**
1873-7749 Web Semantics *see* 1570-8268 **2563**
1873-7757 *see* 0145-2134 **2147**
1873-7765 *see* 0190-7409 **2148**
1873-7781 *see* 1043-951X **1447**
1873-7803 *see* 0098-3004 **2721**
1873-7811 *see* 0272-7358 **7345**
1873-782X *see* 0360-1315 **2974**
1873-7838 *see* 0010-0277 **7346**
1873-7846 *see* 1567-4223 **2543**
1873-7854 *see* 1873-7617 **3703**
1873-7862 *see* 0924-977X **6140**
1873-7870 *see* 0149-7189 **7963**
1873-7889 *see* 1053-4822 **1864**
1873-7897 *see* 0887-6185 **7368**
1873-7900 *see* 0193-3973 **7369**
1873-7919 *see* 1471-7727 **1290**
1873-7927 *see* 1049-0078 **1494**
1873-7935 *see* 0160-2896 **7363**
1873-7943 *see* 0005-7916 **6149**
1873-801X *see* 0094-730X **7374**
1873-8028 *see* 0732-3123 **5505**

ISSN

1875-5798 *see* 1574-0099 **3436**
1875-5801 *see* 1574-0102 **1350**
1875-581X *see* 1574-0110 **8043**
1875-5828 *see* 1567-2050 **6134**
1875-5844 *see* 1567-2700 **5801**
1875-5879 *see* 1751-1577 **2548**
1875-5887 *see* 1871-174X **6728**
1875-5909 *see* 0270-4013 **3036**
1875-5941 *see* 0165-2176 **8813**
1875-595X *see* 0020-6539 **5848**
1875-5992 *see* 1871-5206 **6008**
1875-6018 *see* 1871-5214 **6821**
1875-6026 Vrouw **8888**
1875-6034 HEIMvizier **6525**
1875-6093 Daniel den Hoed Cancer News **6018**
1875-6115 *see* 1871-5222 **5894**
1875-6123 Human **6923**
1875-614X *see* 1871-5230 **6821**
1875-6166 *see* 1871-5249 **6130**
1875-6182 *see* 1871-5257 **5780**
1875-6190 *see* 1570-159X **6134**
1875-6212 *see* 1570-1611 **5785**
1875-6220 *see* 1570-1638 **6830**
1875-6247 *see* 1570-1646 **730**
1875-6255 *see* 1570-1786 **2126**
1875-6263 *see* 1028-4559 **6005**
1875-6271 *see* 1570-1794 **2122**
1875-628X *see* 1570-1808 **6858**
1875-6298 *see* 1570-193X **2127**
1875-6301 *see* 1573-3947 **6017**
1875-631X *see* 1573-3955 **5757**
1875-6336 *see* 1573-3963 **6091**
1875-6360 *see* 1573-3971 **6223**
1875-6379 *see* 0037-5411 **517**
1875-6387 *see* 1573-398X **6213**
1875-6409 *see* 1383-7079 **6583**
1875-6417 *see* 1573-3998 **5885**
1875-6433 *see* 1566-6573 **4934**
1875-6441 *see* 1573-4005 **6135**
1875-6468 *see* 1569-755X **1567**
1875-6484 *see* 1572-4638 **4871**
1875-6506 *see* 1573-4021 **5784**
1875-6530 *see* 1572-4999 **4867**
1875-6549 *see* 1574-3330 **4917**
1875-6557 *see* 1573-403X **5784**
1875-6565 *see* 0926-3837 **4009**
1875-6573 *see* 1386-3541 **6186**
1875-6581 *see* 1573-4048 **5989**
1875-659X *see* 0006-1913 **4169**
1875-6603 *see* 1573-4056 **6194**
1875-6638 *see* 1573-4064 **5673**
1875-6646 *see* 1573-4072 **2059**
1875-6654 *see* 0066-1554 **4179**
1875-6662 *see* 1573-4080 **6831**
1875-6670 *see* 0922-3444 **3914**
1875-6689 *see* 0045-7183 **5598**
1875-6697 *see* 1573-4099 **5830**
1875-6719 *see* 0165-7305 **5253**
1875-6727 *see* 1573-4110 **2099**
1875-6735 *see* 0165-9227 **6922**
1875-6743 *see* 0168-9878 **5273**
1875-6751 *see* 0169-894X **5268**
1875-676X *see* 1573-4129 **6831**
1875-6778 *see* 0171-1288 **6939**
1875-6786 *see* 1573-4137 **3186**
1875-6794 *see* 0165-0874 **7543**
1875-6808 *see* 0167-1685 **5867**
1875-6824 *see* 0167-238X **7353**
1875-6832 *see* 0167-9228 **4057**
1875-6840 *see* 0376-7442 **6104**
1875-6867 Journal of Men's Health **6284**
1875-6875 *see* 1386-1514 **5722**
1875-6913 *see* 1875-6921 **6831**
1875-6921 Current Pharmacogenomics and Personalized Medicine **6831**
1875-693X The Open Genomics Journal **877**
1875-7049 *see* 1389-2630 **5693**
1875-7065 *see* 1571-4136 **6096**
1875-7073 *see* 1574-1842 **2700**
1875-7081 *see* 1574-4280 **5601**
1875-709X *see* 0043-5414 **6961**
1875-7103 Krisis (Online) **6931**
1875-7111 *see* 0165-0076 **2666**
1875-712X *see* 1389-0069 **7109**
1875-7138 *see* 1574-3314 **8138**
1875-7170 Medecine et Longevite **5666**
1875-7235 *see* 0921-5077 **4094**
1875-7243 *see* 0303-8157 **6944**
1875-7251 *see* 0926-3977 **8134**
1875-726X *see* 0304-6257 **5253**
1875-7278 *see* 0921-2507 **5282**
1875-7286 *see* 1384-6930 **2342**
1875-7294 *see* 0921-5034 **5203**
1875-7316 *see* 0923-0483 **5353**
1875-7332 *see* 0923-411X **5280**
1875-7340 *see* 0923-9855 **5293**
1875-7375 *see* 0925-8620 **5297**
1875-7391 *see* 0927-1910 **5217**
1875-7405 *see* 0927-3131 **5366**
1875-7413 *see* 1389-4633 **4935**
1875-7421 *see* 0932-9714 **5331**
1875-743X *see* 1385-0393 **8473**
1875-7448 *see* 0169-7161 **8375**
1875-7456 *see* 0303-7339 **6188**
1875-7537 *see* 0193-2306 **1548**
1875-760X Entomologische Tabellen **846**
1875-7634 Atlantis Studies in Mathematics **5474**
1875-7642 Atlantis Studies in Mathematics for Engineering and Science **5474**
1875-7669 Atlantis Ambient and Pervasive Intelligence **2407**
1875-7685 O S B Today **6682**
1875-7839 Publicatiereeks Amsterdamse Monumenten **412**

1875-7855 *see* 0079-6123 **6174**
1875-7863 *see* 0079-6468 **2077**
1875-7871 *see* 0163-786X **8128**
1875-788X *see* 0166-526X **2099**
1875-7901 *see* 0167-7306 **740**
1875-791X *see* 0168-7069 **5824**
1875-7928 *see* 0196-1152 **8128**
1875-7936 *see* 0275-4959 **5703**
1875-7944 *see* 0277-2833 **8128**
1875-7952 *see* 0732-0671 **4987**
1875-7960 *see* 0735-004X **3036**
1875-7979 *see* 0739-8859 **8510**
1875-8002 Kamerkrant voor Ondernemend Oost-Nederland (Ed. Regio Twente) **1720**
1875-8029 *see* 1047-0042 **8128**
1875-8053 *see* 1057-6290 **8085**
1875-8088 *see* 1059-4337 **4790**
1875-810X *see* 1069-0964 **1804**
1875-8118 *see* 1388-3720 **4257**
1875-8126 *see* 1074-7540 **1724**
1875-8134 *see* 1566-0958 **6628**
1875-8142 *see* 1094-5334 **1165**
1875-8150 *see* 1568-1858 **7234**
1875-8177 *see* 1022-6583 **1588**
1875-8185 *see* 1572-3429 **6911**
1875-8193 *see* 1871-7551 **5813**
1875-8207 *see* 1354-3725 **4925**
1875-8215 *see* 0165-8476 **4810**
1875-8223 *see* 1384-6299 **7233**
1875-824X *see* 1572-3097 **1379**
1875-8258 *see* 1385-2140 **3404**
1875-8274 *see* 1387-2370 **4669**
1875-8290 *see* 1388-7084 **4871**
1875-8312 *see* 1569-5794 **5790**
1875-8320 *see* 0165-0750 **4921**
1875-8339 *see* 0927-3379 **8534**
1875-8347 *see* 0165-2826 **1572**
1875-8355 *see* 1572-3887 **743**
1875-8363 *see* 0928-2750 **1921**
1875-8371 *see* 0928-9801 **4925**
1875-838X *see* 0952-617X **4695**
1875-8398 *see* 0957-0411 **4917**
1875-8401 Tijdschrift voor Openbare Financien (Online) **1905**
1875-841X *see* 0959-6941 **4668**
1875-8436 *see* 1011-4548 **4944**
1875-8444 *see* 1019-2557 **4622**
1875-8452 *see* 0921-7126 **2444**
1875-8460 *see* 0025-8245 **5676**
1875-8479 *see* 0971-3573 **775**
1875-8517 Koken en Genieten **4362**
1875-8525 Web Designer **2568**
1875-8533 *see* 1570-5838 **7335**
1875-855X *see* 1905-7415 **5579**
1875-8568 *see* 0972-9860 **3404**
1875-8576 *see* 0921-7134 **5474**
1875-8584 *see* 0953-4180 **6126**
1875-8592 *see* 1574-0153 **6011**
1875-8606 *see* 1570-5870 **830**
1875-8614 *see* 1572-4778 **2107**
1875-8622 *see* 1386-0291 **5935**
1875-8630 *see* 0278-0240 **6018**
1875-8649 *see* 0167-8329 **5008**
1875-8657 *see* 1574-1826 **753**
1875-8665 Advanced Photoshop **6979**
1875-8681 *see* 0169-2968 **5552**
1875-869X *see* 1093-2607 **5758**
1875-8703 *see* 0167-2533 **1750**
1875-8711 *see* 0019-5251 **3738**
1875-8754 *see* 1570-1255 **5061**
1875-8762 *see* 1389-1995 **2545**
1875-8789 *see* 0167-5265 **2545**
1875-8797 T P E Digitaal **7187**
1875-8800 *see* 1383-5416 **3320**
1875-8819 *see* 1448-5869 **2451**
1875-8827 *see* 1327-2314 **2451**
1875-8835 *see* 1069-2509 **3291**
1875-8843 *see* 1872-4981 **2450**
1875-8851 *see* 0972-4907 **7243**
1875-886X *see* 1573-417X **7975**
1875-8886 *see* 1084-4678 **2558**
1875-8894 *see* 1874-5393 **6095**
1875-8908 *see* 1387-2877 **6149**
1875-8916 Jaarboek Multiculturele Samenleving in Ontwikkeling **7286**
1875-8924 *see* 0926-227X **2515**
1875-8932 *see* 0747-9662 **8382**
1875-8940 *see* 0926-6801 **2500**
1875-8959 *see* 1092-0617 **3205**
1875-8967 *see* 1064-1246 **5504**
1875-8975 *see* 1343-8875 **7060**
1875-8983 *see* 1472-7978 **5502**
1875-9025 *see* 1740-4460 **2429**
1875-9033 *see* 1872-3276 **5793**
1875-9041 *see* 1304-2580 **6095**
1875-905X *see* 1574-017X **2334**
1875-9068 *see* 1574-1699 **8388**
1875-9076 *see* 1574-1702 **2432**
1875-9092 *see* 1359-9364 **6682**
1875-9106 *see* 1873-894X **6001**
1875-9114 *see* 0277-0008 **6872**
1875-9149 *see* 0973-0516 **3146**
1875-9165 *see* 1382-6980 **3501**
1875-9173 *see* 1569-7371 **1791**
1875-919X *see* 1058-9244 **2597**
1875-9203 *see* 1070-9622 **7089**
1875-9211 *see* 0924-8625 **71**
1875-922X *see* 0712-4813 **745**
1875-9246 *see* 0940-5569 **7416**
1875-9254 *see* 1874-7655 **8379**
1875-9262 *see* 1567-2069 **7063**
1875-9270 *see* 1051-9815 **6688**
1875-9289 *see* 1570-1263 **2457**

1875-9297 *see* 0972-6721 **3148**
1875-9300 Radio Nieuws **2362**
1875-9327 The Open Fuel Cells Journal **3214**
1875-9335 The Open Nanomedicine Journal **5690**
1875-9343 The Ergonomics Open Journal **3366**
1875-9424 Tijdschrift voor Bloedtransfusie **5941**
1875-9483 Checklist Administratie **1284**
1875-9521 Entertainment Computing **2476**
1875-9572 Pediatrics and Neonatology **6102**
1875-9599 Amsterdamse Gouden Eeuw Reeks **4198**
1875-9637 Aeolian Research **3401**
1875-9734 Script Hematologie **5941**
1875-9742 British Journal of Medical and Surgical Urology **6266**
1875-9769 Schaun het Schaap **2211**
1875-9807 The Travaux Preparatoires of Multilateral Treaties **7269**
1875-984X *see* 1875-9858 **7238**
1875-9858 Global Responsibility to Protect **7238**
1875-9866 *see* 1383-4517 **939**
1876-0104 *see* 1613-7272 **4699**
1876-0155 Hockey.nl **8235**
1876-0171 Best Practices Zorg **1728**
1876-0228 New Technology-Based Firms in the New Millennium **1153**
1876-0341 Journal of Infection and Public Health **5820**
1876-0473 Z - E Actueel *see* 1873-9180 **1802**
1876-0481 North American Tax Handbook **1937**
1876-049X *see* 1876-0481 **1937**
1876-052X H E I M - Hengelo's Educatief Industrie-Museum *changed to* 1875-6034 **6525**
1876-0635 Wakker Nieuws **322**
1876-0678 Identity in the Information Society **2514**
1876-0740 Script Huisartsgeneeskunde **5711**
1876-0759 *see* 0167-3831 **4683**
1876-0791 In Logistiek **1752**
1876-0848 Handboekbinden **7562**
1876-1038 *see* 1574-8871 **5704**
1876-1070 Taiwan Institute of Chemical Engineers. Journal **3256**
1876-1275 Off the Record **6601**
1876-1364 Journal of Ambient Intelligence and Smart Environments **2452**
1876-1399 Clinical Simulation in Nursing **5955**
1876-1429 Recent Patents on Food, Nutrition & Agriculture **6757**
1876-1550 Waag Society Magazine **4585**
1876-1585 H C C Magazine **2419**
1876-1658 Water Quality, Exposure and Health **3493**
1876-1666 *see* 1876-1658 **3493**
1876-1674 Kamer van Koophandel Limburg. Kamerkrant *changed to* 1876-2980 **1719**
1876-1674 Kamer van Koophandel Limburg. Kamerkrant *changed to* 1876-3006 **1719**
1876-1704 H Z Discovery **7859**
1876-1739 Direct **3020**
1876-1747 I'dee **1820**
1876-178X Pruttelpot **8266**
1876-1798 Zie Zoo **969**
1876-1801 Control **2475**
1876-1895 Lichaamstaal **5661**
1876-1909 HanzeMag **2862**
1876-1917 Energiegids.nl **3129**
1876-1933 Constructions and Frames **5108**
1876-1941 *see* 1876-1933 **5108**
1876-195X Italie in Bedrijf **1762**
1876-1984 Waterstand **8841**
1876-1992 Gala† **8958**
1876-2018 Asian Journal of Psychiatry **6124**
1876-2034 Margreet DVD **8473**
1876-2050 Boekverkoper (Amsterdam) **7553**
1876-2085 Q5 Magazine **3030**
1876-2093 Bratz **2180**
1876-214X The Open Catalysis Journal **2104**
1876-2166 The Open Occupational Health & Safety Journal **7534**
1876-2182 K R O Extra **2384**
1876-2190 Monitor Arbeidsongevallen in de Bouw **6681**
1876-2255 Wetgeving Toezicht Financiele Markten **4814**
1876-2271 Nynade **5428**
1876-2301 Trib Magazine† **8994**
1876-231X Geo.brief **2735**
1876-2328 Sample of Dutch F A D N **206**
1876-2409 Zakboek Proces-Verbaal en Bewijsrecht **2672**
1876-2476 G L Compendium **7561**
1876-2611 Advies over het Macrobudget Huishoudelijke WMO-hulp (Year) **1279**
1876-2697 MedNet Jaarboek **5677**
1876-2700 *see* 1932-2798 **5188**
1876-2832 European Association of Zoos and Aquaria Conference. Proceedings **942**
1876-2840 Checklist Belastingen **1917**
1876-2859 Academic Pediatrics **6086**
1876-2883 Beneficial Microbes **882**
1876-2891 *see* 1876-2883 **882**
1876-2921 NotaBene **6600**
1876-293X Handboek Arbobesluit **1684**
1876-2980 Kamerkrant (Ed. Zuid-Limburg) **1719**
1876-3006 Kamerkrant (Ed. Noord- en Midden-Limburg) **1719**
1876-3073 Checklist Externe Verslaggeving **1284**
1876-3081 Handboek Arboregeling **1684**
1876-3111 Research on Chrysomelidae **857**
1876-312X *see* 1399-560X **849**
1876-3200 Dus **4593**
1876-3251 The Open Environmental Sciences **3458**
1876-326X Open Longevity Science **4053**
1876-3308 *see* 0094-3037 **4216**
1876-3316 *see* 0094-288X **4260**
1876-3324 *see* 1075-1262 **4266**
1876-3332 *see* 0094-4467 **4266**
1876-3367 Middle East Law and Governance **555**
1876-3375 *see* 1876-3367 **555**
1876-3499 Speelhuis Zomerboek **2214**
1876-3502 Dora Vakantie! **2186**
1876-3510 Het Zandkasteel Vakantie! **2224**
1876-3529 Aandachtsgroepenmonitor **1661**
1876-3537 Monitor Verslaafden en Daklozen Enschede **2660**

ISSN

9838 1876-3545 ULRICH'S PERIODICALS

1876-3545 Top I C T Werkgevers 2494
1876-3561 Oog 6535
1876-3618 Archaeopteryx Veterinaris 8793
1876-3766 Chidushim 7720
1876-3820 European Journal of Integrative Medicine 5611
1876-3863 The Open Pain Journal 6172
1876-3871 The Open Renewable Energy Journal 3144
1876-388X The Open Nuclear Medicine Journal 6205
1876-3901 The Open Cell Signaling Journal 835
1876-391X The Open Complementary Medicine Journal 313
1876-3928 The Open Systems Biology Journal 926
1876-3952 The Open Ceramic Science Journal 2044
1876-3960 The Open Nutraceuticals Journal 6667
1876-3979 The Open Environmental Pollution & Toxicology Journal 3458
1876-3987 The Open Polymer Science Journal 3251
1876-3995 The Open Translational Medicine Journal 5690
1876-4002 The Open Waste Management Journal 3510
1876-4010 The Open Cancer Immunology Journal 6031
1876-4029 Micro and Nanosystems 2454
1876-4037 *see* 1876-4029 2454
1876-4045 The Hague Journal on the Rule of Law 4684
1876-4053 *see* 1876-4045 4684
1876-407X *see* 1598-1037 2827
1876-4096 Studiebijbel Magazine 7684
1876-4150 Bank Wereld 1316
1876-4169 Theo Knippenberg's Bulkboekvandemaand 5387
1876-4177 Scheurkalender van de Globalisering 1582
1876-4185 Huidspecialist 589
1876-4193 Iguana Magazine 947
1876-4215 Fiscaal Recht (Year) 1925
1876-4223 Praktijkblad Preventie 6684
1876-424X Wet Marktordening Gezondheidszorg 7545
1876-4258 Drinks Slijtersvakblad 603
1876-4266 Vraagbaak Arbeidstijden Wegvervoer 1714
1876-4274 Praktijkboek Binnenvaart 8657
1876-4290 Jurisprudentie Telecommunicatierecht 2330
1876-4363 F Z 339
1876-4517 *see* 1876-4525 231
1876-4525 Food Security 231
1876-4533 Medicine Studies 5674
1876-4541 *see* 1876-4533 5674
1876-455X Supporters MagAZine 8248
1876-4584 Telecom Review 2341
1876-4606 Hengelo Toen & Nu 4226
1876-4622 Tijdschrift vor Lerarenopleiders 3005
1876-4630 Handboek Non-Profitorganisaties *changed to* 1876-4649 4095
1876-4630 Handboek Non-Profitorganisaties *changed to* 1876-4703 2956
1876-4630 Handboek Non-Profitorganisaties *changed to* 1876-469X 1423
1876-4649 Handboek Zorginstellingen 4095
1876-469X Handboek Woningscorporaties 1423
1876-4703 Handboek Onderwijsinstellingen 2956
1876-4746 *see* 0965-206X 5879
1876-486X Information Design Journal 2325
1876-4886 *see* 1876-0171 1728
1876-4983 The American College of Certified Wound Specialists. Journal 6055
1876-5025 The Open Biomaterials Journal 5690
1876-5033 The Open Corrosion Journal 6328
1876-5041 The Open Surgical Oncology Journal 6254
1876-505X The Open Electrochemistry Journal 2114
1876-5068 The Open Atherosclerosis & Thrombosis Journal 5796
1876-5092 The China Nonprofit Review 8033
1876-5149 *see* 1876-5092 8033
1876-5165 *see* 0147-1694 3528
1876-5173 The Open Hepatology Journal 5930
1876-5181 The Open Antimicrobial Agents Journal 894
1876-519X The Open Medical Education Journal 5690
1876-5203 The Open Textile Journal 8456
1876-5211 The Open Drug Resistance Journal 6865
1876-522X The Open Microcirculation & Microvascular Journal 5797
1876-5238 The Open Neuropsychopharmacology Journal 6171
1876-5246 The Open Diabetes Journal 5898
1876-5254 The Open Bone Journal 5898
1876-5262 The Open Hypertension Journal 5797
1876-5270 The Open Statistics & Probability Journal 5523
1876-5289 The Open Neuroendocrinology Journal 5898
1876-5297 The Open Neurosurgery Journal 6171
1876-5300 The Open Colloid Science Journal 2139
1876-5319 The Open Surface Science Journal 7029
1876-5327 The Open Spine Journal 6068
1876-5335 The Open Cardiovascular and Thoracic Surgery Journal 5796
1876-5343 The Open Plasma Physics Journal 7029
1876-5351 Open Heart Failure Journal 5796
1876-536X The Open Pacing, Electrophysiology & Therapy Journal 5797
1876-5386 The Open Cardiovascular Imaging Journal 6204
1876-5394 The Open Arthritis Journal 6225
1876-5424 The Open Emergency Medicine Journal 6068
1876-5513 Get In Shape 8845
1876-5580 Brill's Studies in the Indigenous Languages of the Americas 5101
1876-5610 *see* 1058-3947 7977
1876-5866 E T F R N News 669
1876-6102 Energy Procedia 3133
1876-6137 Bonsai Focus (American Edition) 3725
1876-6153 Studia Judaeoslavica 7730
1876-6188 Noodzaak (Alphen aan den Rijn) 2679
1876-6196 Procedia Chemistry 2077
1876-620X Wijzer 8612
1876-6358 Jaarbericht Bevolkingsonderzoek 7528
1876-6633 Brill's Annual of Afroasiatic Languages and Linguistics 5101
1876-7036 The World of Cavaliers (Years) 6817
1876-7117 Prinses Lillifee 2209
1876-7184 *see* 0334-2123 247
1876-7354 Surveys in Operations Research and Management Science 2438
1876-7702 Top I C T Werkgevers Nederland 2494
1876-7761 *see* 1543-5946 6819
1876-7826 Fifi en Haar Bloemenvriendjes 2188
1876-8156 Amsterdam Law Forum 4917
1876-8202 The Open Colorectal Cancer Journal 6031
1876-8229 Open Prostate Cancer Journal 6032
1876-8237 Open Obesity Journal 5948
1876-8253 The Open Signal Processing Journal 3327
1876-861X *see* 1934-5925 5792
1876-8830 Journal of Social Intervention: Theory and Practice 8115
1876-8903 C R V Magazine (Zuid-West Edition) 864
1876-8911 C R V Magazine (Oost Edition) 864
1876-892X C R V Magazine (Noord Edition) 864
1876-8946 The Open Autoimmunity Journal 5764
1876-9055 Studium 3003
1876-9098 Erasmus Journal for Philosophy and Economics 1105
1876-9217 E B Live 6563
1876-9586 Print Matters 7326
1876-9667 Regio Amsterdam in Beeld *changed to* 1876-9675 7287
1876-9675 Metropoolregio Amsterdam in Beeld 7287
1876-990X Silicon 2118
1876-9918 *see* 1876-990X 2118
18762077 *see* 0375-7587 2766
18762174 *see* 0024-0672 957
1877-0320 Revue Francaise d'Allergologie 5765
1877-038X iCreate 2422
1877-0428 Procedia - Social and Behavioral Sciences 7993
1877-0517 Revue de Chirurgie Orthopedique et Traumatologique 6072
1877-0533 Set-Valued and Variational Analysis 5535
1877-0541 *see* 1877-0533 5535
1877-0568 Orthopaedics & Traumatology: Surgery & Research 6069
1877-0657 Annals of Physical and Rehabilitation Medicine 6106
1877-0711 MagMa 1021
1877-0959 Tijdschrift voor Coaching 1798
1877-105X Cut! 6495
1877-1203 Revue des Maladies Respiratoires Actualites 6219
1877-1319 Health Outcomes Research in Medicine 5625
1877-1327 Orthopaedics and Trauma 6069
1877-1386 Foodies 4358
1877-1610 B G Magazine 1666
1877-1653 Holstein International Plus! 288
1877-1661 Holland Shipbuilding 8646
1877-1718 Separation Science and Technology (San Diego) 2105
1877-2080 Arresten Handelsrecht en Ondernemingsrecht 4946
1877-2226 PIT Pro Rege Nieuws 6441
1877-2374 F D Outlook 1744
1877-2684 N B D Magazine 1025
1877-296X Savvy 2437
1877-2978 Check 2553
1877-3095 International Review of Pragmatics 5203
1877-3109 *see* 1877-3095 5203
1877-3273 Atlantis Thinking Machines 2407
1877-3397 Tinkelbel† 8993
1877-3435 Current Opinion in Environmental Sustainability 3413
1877-3451 The Development of the Anglo-Saxon Language and Linguistic Universals 5111
1877-346X Task-Based Language Teaching 5185
1877-3478 Kamerkrant voor Ondernemend Gooi-, Eem- en Flevoland 1406
1877-3699 Aanbevelende Rassenlijst Akkerbouwgewassen 215
1877-3702 Aanbevelende Rassenlijst Voedergewassen 215
1877-3893 Trekker 214
1877-4563 Mediazine Koopgids. Platte T V's 2385
1877-4598 Mediazine Koopgids. Foto en Video 6971
1877-4601 Mediazine Koopgids. Huishoudelijk 4364
1877-4628 Mediazine Koopgids. Telecom en Navigatie 2333
1877-4636 Mediazine Koopgids. Notebooks 2431
1877-4644 Mediazine Koopgids. Wellness en Verzorging 7531
1877-4970 Compendia Rerum Iudaicarum Ad Novum Testamentum 7720
1877-5543 Publieke Werken 4424
1877-6248 Tokyo University of Foreign Studies 5188
1877-6531 Language Faculty and Beyond 5140
1877-6558 The H U G O Journal 5622
1877-6566 *see* 1877-6558 5622
1877-6884 Argumentation in Context 5096
1877-6930 *see* 1876-6633 5101
1877-7015 Journal of Archaeology in the Low Countries 400
1877-7023 *see* 1877-7015 400
1877-7031 Chinese Language and Discourse 5105
1877-7066 Scientific Instruments and Collections 4489
1877-7538 Superwijngids 610
1877-7821 Cancer Epidemiology 6012
1877-8216 Sociologie Magazine 8138
1877-8372 *see* 0078-6527 557
1877-8755 *see* 1138-7548 5654
1877-9492 Business 1070
1877-9751 Review of Cognitive Linguistics 5166
1877-976X *see* 1877-9751 5166
1878-0164 *see* 1746-0689 6062
1878-0318 *see* 1871-403X 5689
1878-0326 *see* 1872-4973 5913
1878-044X *see* 1748-0132 750
1878-0466 *see* 1574-0668 5792
1878-0806 *see* 1745-0454 6218
1878-0849 *see* 1769-7212 866
1878-089X *see* 1355-1841 5965
1878-0938 *see* 1553-8389 5781
1878-0946 *see* 1744-165X 6004
1878-125X *see* 1479-2354 5804
1878-1470 *see* 1568-9883 886
1878-1497 *see* 1475-1585 3067
1878-1551 *see* 1534-5807 832
1878-1632 *see* 1529-9430 6073
1878-1667 *see* 0147-9571 883
1878-1683 *see* 1473-0502 5941
1878-1888 *see* 0005-7894 7339
1878-3511 *see* 1201-9712 5818
1878-3562 *see* 1590-8658 5922
1878-3570 *see* 0002-8223 6654
1878-3619 *see* 0959-2989 747
1878-3627 *see* 0922-6028 6181
1878-3686 *see* 1535-6108 6011
1878-4046 *see* 1076-6332 6191
1878-4186 *see* 0969-2126 706
1878-4208 *see* 0960-8974 2112
1878-4240 *see* 0079-6816 7036
1878-4259 *see* 1062-9769 1163
1878-4275 *see* 0266-8920 3393
1878-4291 *see* 0968-4328 899
1878-4356 *see* 0957-1787 3333
1878-4364 *see* 0886-7798 3224
1878-4712 *see* 0957-9656 7566
1878-4755 Seeing and Perceiving 5555
1878-4763 *see* 1878-4755 5555
1878-5034 *see* 0006-355X 752
1878-5050 *see* 1567-5688 5778
1878-5174 *see* 0256-2928 2855
1878-5212 *see* 0891-2556 2727
1878-531X *see* 1016-9040 7356
1878-5395 *see* 0378-777X 3427
1878-5492 *see* 0966-3274 5766
1878-5514 *see* 1468-6996 3357
1878-5573 *see* 1090-9516 1574
1878-5638 *see* 0020-7462 3347
1878-5646 *see* 0042-6989 6053
1878-5786 *see* 1367-9120 2749
1878-5794 *see* 1366-5545 8517
1878-5832 *see* 1359-6446 6834
1878-5875 *see* 1357-2725 734
1878-5891 *see* 0378-5955 6080
1878-5905 *see* 0142-9612 5585
1878-5913 *see* 0959-3020 6230
1878-5921 *see* 0895-4356 5647
1878-6316 *see* 1052-2263 7381
1878-6324 *see* 1053-8127 6063
1878-643X *see* 1055-4181 4070
1878-6448 *see* 1053-8135 6168
1878-6464 *see* 0957-4271 925
1878-6642 *see* 0278-6125 3386
1878-6723 *see* 0923-1730 6785
1878-6731 *see* 0967-0653 2720
1878-674X *see* 1058-6628 3482
1878-6847 *see* 0924-6479 4509
1878-7398 *see* 1550-8579 5618
1878-7401 *see* 0928-7329 5720
1878-7460 *see* 1751-570X 2433
1878-7568 *see* 1742-7061 755
1878-7665 *see* 0334-5114
1878-8718 Gerardus 7799
1878-8815 E H B O Post 5607
1879-0038 Gene - C O M B I S *see* 0378-1119 764
1879-0046 *see* 0376-8716 2693
1879-0054 *see* 0739-7240 8796
1879-0070 *see* 0732-8893 884
1879-0089 *see* 0145-305X 5757
1879-0097 *see* 0109-5641 5840
1879-0127 *see* 0143-7496 7093
1879-0135 *see* 0020-7519 5818
1879-0178 *see* 0735-1933 3381
1879-0208 *see* 0964-8305 765
1879-0216 *see* 0966-9795 6316
1879-0240 *see* 0965-1748 849
1879-0267 *see* 0020-1383 6061
1879-0305 *see* 1359-6101 730
1879-0313 *see* 0011-393X 6832
1879-0356 *see* 1369-5266 785
1879-0364 *see* 1369-5274 884
1879-0372 *see* 0952-7915 5743
1879-0380 *see* 0959-437X 865
1879-0399 *see* 1359-0294 2134
1879-0402 *see* 1367-5931 730
1879-0410 *see* 0955-0674 831
1879-0429 *see* 0958-1669 762
1879-0445 *see* 0960-9822 667
1879-0461 *see* 1040-8428 6017
1879-0518 *see* 0010-7824 971
1879-0534 *see* 0010-4825 825
1879-0542 *see* 0165-2478 5760
1879-0550 *see* 0360-8352 3290
1879-0674 *see* 0034-4877 7037
1879-0682 *see* 0960-1481 3146
1879-0690 *see* 1364-0321 3146
1879-0712 *see* 0014-2999 6838
1879-0720 *see* 0928-0987 6838
1879-0739 *see* 0271-5317 6666
1879-0747 *see* 0045-7930 3290
1879-0771 *see* 0895-6111 5829
1879-0836 *see* 0951-8320 3217
1879-0844 *see* 1388-9842 5786
1879-0852 *see* 0959-8049 6019
1879-0860 *see* 1062-9408 1502
1879-0895 *see* 0969-806X 7071
1879-095X *see* 0098-7913 5047
1879-0992 *see* 0306-4565 754
1879-1085 *see* 0263-8223 3263
1879-1107 *see* 1096-4959 729
1879-1131 *see* 0738-081X 5873
1879-114X *see* 0149-2918 6829
1879-1158 *see* 0304-386X 6315
1879-1174 *see* 0963-8695 3355
1879-1204 *see* 0022-4898 8501
1879-1212 *see* 0022-474X 853
1879-1220 *see* 0960-0760 737
1879-1239 *see* 1053-5357 1546
1879-1247 *see* 0022-4375 6680
1879-1271 *see* 0268-0033 5804
1879-1298 *see* 0045-6535 3495
1879-1301 *see* 1074-5521 2056

1879-1336 *see* 1054-8807 **5781**
1879-1344 *see* 0144-8617 **2120**
1879-1352 *see* 0022-4073 **7079**
1879-1379 *see* 0022-3956 **6156**
1879-1409 *see* 0305-4179 **6057**
1879-1476 *see* 0385-8146 **6078**
1879-1484 *see* 0021-9150 **5778**
1879-1506 *see* 0003-9969 **934**
1879-1514 *see* 0166-445X **3493**
1879-1603 *see* 1061-9518 **1295**
1879-1611 *see* 0022-1910 **852**
1879-1638 *see* 1047-8310 **1419**
1879-1670 *see* 0264-3707 **2785**
1879-1700 *see* 0265-931X **3446**
1879-176X *see* 0300-5712 **5851**
1879-1824 *see* 1364-6826 **2784**
1879-1891 *see* 0002-9394 **6038**
1879-1913 *see* 0002-9149 **5776**
1879-193X *see* 0890-4065 **4048**
1879-1956 *see* 1464-343X **2749**
1879-1964 *see* 0021-8502 **6711**
1879-1999 *see* 0099-1333 **5020**
1879-2057 *see* 0001-4575 **7506**
1879-2081 *see* 0140-7007 **4122**
1879-2146 *see* 0020-7683 **7059**
1879-2154 *see* 0749-6419 **3348**
1879-2162 *see* 0020-7403 **3347**
1879-2189 *see* 0017-9310 **3382**
1879-2219 *see* 0966-6362 **5617**
1879-2227 *see* 0196-8904 **3130**
1879-2235 *see* 0011-2275 **7053**
1879-2243 *see* 0045-7949 **3290**
1879-226X *see* 0885-2014 **7347**
1879-2340 *see* 1361-9209 **8517**
1879-2359 *see* 0968-090X **8517**
1879-2367 *see* 0191-2615 **8517**
1879-2375 *see* 0965-8564 **8516**
1879-2383 *see* 0166-4972 **8443**
1879-2405 *see* 0038-1101 **3114**
1879-243X *see* 0277-5395 **8905**
1879-2448 *see* 0043-1354 **8838**
1879-2456 *see* 0956-053X **3513**
1879-2464 *see* 0301-679X **3398**
1879-2480 *see* 0742-051X **3084**
1879-2499 *see* 1369-8486 **706**
1879-2502 *see* 1355-2198 **7041**
1879-2510 *see* 0039-3681 **7920**
1879-2529 *see* 0191-491X **3083**
1879-2545 *see* 0030-3992 **7082**
1879-2553 *see* 0022-3697 **7022**
1879-2685 *see* 0010-4485 **3289**
1879-2693 *see* 0016-0032 **7013**
1879-2715 *see* 0042-207X **7045**
1879-2766 *see* 0038-1098 **7040**
1879-2782 *see* 0893-6080 **2455**
1879-291X *see* 0301-5629 **709**
1879-2944 *see* 0010-4655 **7050**
1879-3088 *see* 0962-8924 **837**
1879-310X *see* 0967-070X **8515**
1879-3150 *see* 0041-0101 **6883**
1879-3177 *see* 0887-2333 **3502**
1879-3193 *see* 0261-5177 **8763**
1879-3215 *see* 0040-9383 **5542**
1879-3223 *see* 0263-8231 **3397**
1879-324X *see* 0736-5853 **2342**
1879-3258 *see* 0308-5961 **2341**
1879-3274 *see* 0160-791X **8143**
1879-3282 *see* 0346-251X **3083**
1879-3320 *see* 0960-7404 **6035**
1879-3363 *see* 0025-326X **3488**
1879-338X *see* 0265-9646 **71**
1879-341X *see* 0267-7261 **2790**
1879-3428 *see* 0038-0717 **745**
1879-3452 *see* 0142-1123 **3346**
1879-3487 *see* 0360-3199 **3139**
1879-3509 *see* 0734-743X **3201**
1879-3517 *see* 0142-0615 **3321**
1879-3533 *see* 0301-9322 **3382**
1879-3541 *see* 0308-0161 **3383**
1879-355X *see* 0360-3016 **6199**
1879-3576 *see* 0375-6505 **2708**
1879-3584 *see* 0266-1144 **8451**
1879-3649 *see* 1537-1891 **6884**
1880-0041 Sansouken Today **7907**
1880-0270 Ningen Kagaku Kenkyuu **350**
1880-0408 *see* 0389-2441 **7056**
1880-0556 Nature Digest **7889**
1880-0572 Nihon Gaishou Shigakkai Zasshi **5857**
1880-0815 *see* 1348-9615 **5857**
1880-0823 *see* 1348-9623 **5853**
1880-0912 Toukyou Kaiyou Daigaku Kenkyuu Houkoku **3610**
1880-0920 *see* 1347-4367 **5607**
1880-1013 *see* 1342-6230 **2330**
1880-1293 *see* 0022-9717 **5657**
1880-1323 Nihon Hou Kagaku Gijutsu Gakkaishi **5916**
1880-1390 *see* 0027-0741 **556**
1880-1404 *see* 0916-717X **727**
1880-1447 Journal of Traditional Medicines **6856**
1880-151X *see* 1880-1528 **5714**
1880-1528 Shouwa Byouin Zasshi **5714**
1880-1579 Anti-Aging Medicine **5576**
1880-1587 Bird Research (Print Edition) **903**
1880-1595 Bird Research (Online Edition) **903**
1880-1765 *see* 0033-9008 **8624**
1880-1986 *see* 0371-0580 **8457**
1880-2028 Shokubutsu Kankyou Kougaku **156**
1880-2117 *see* 0912-4047 **961**
1880-2206 *see* 1347-3182 **6202**
1880-2230 Kokubungaku Kenkyuu Shiryoukan Kiyou. Bungaku Kenkyuu Hen **5318**
1880-2273 *see* 0918-1067 **856**
1880-229X Shounen Fisshu **3608**
1880-2338 *see* 0385-8839 **3396**
1880-2370 Hazama Kenkyu Nenpo (CD-ROM) **3268**
1880-2419 Mie Daigaku Kyouiku Gakubu Kenkyuu Kiyou **2886**
1880-2540 E E Times Japan **3187**
1880-2869 Renkei Iryou **4110**
1880-2877 *see* 1349-8975 **5686**
1880-3016 Journal of Developments in Sustanable Agriculture **127**
1880-3024 *see* 1880-3016 **127**
1880-3121 Nihon Frudo Pawa Shisutemu Gakkai Rombunshuu **3363**
1880-313X *see* 0388-6107 **5586**
1880-3415 Pesutoroji
1880-3431 Touhoku Gakuin Daigaku Keizaigaku Ronshuu **1183**
1880-344X *see* 1349-0222 **5793**
1880-3482 Business & Economic Review **1070**
1880-3555 *see* 1880-2028 **156**
1880-3717 Nihon Sempaku Kaiyou Kougakkai Rombunshuu **8655**
1880-3725 Kanrin **8649**
1880-3865 *see* 1349-0079 **5852**
1880-3873 *see* 1340-3478 **5791**
1880-3903 Fukushima University. Faculty of Human Development and Culture. Bulletin **340**
1880-3989 *see* 0388-1350 **3499**
1880-3997 *see* 0917-2394 **5860**
1880-4004 *see* 0285-0192 **7025**
1880-4012 *see* 1348-1509 **6990**
1880-4047 *see* 0386-9784 **5880**
1880-4233 *see* 1340-6868 **6009**
1880-4276 Journal of Arrhythmia **5791**
1880-4306 Toukyou Gakugei Daigaku Kiyou. Sougou Kyouiku Kagakukei **2920**
1880-4314 Toukyou Gakugei Daigaku Kiyou. Jimbun Shakai Kagakukei. 1 **4478**
1880-4322 Toukyou Gakugei Daigaku Kiyou. Jimbun Shakai Kagakukei. 2 **4478**
1880-4535 Denshi Jouhou Tsuushin Gakkai Rombunshi. D, Jouhou Shisutemu **2542**
1880-4683 *see* 0914-5508 **6254**
1880-4829 Chishitsu Osen Iryou Chishitsu Shakai Chishitsu Gakkaishi **3410**
1880-487X Journal of Rural Medicine **5654**
1880-4888 *see* 1880-487X **5654**
1880-4926 *see* 1343-4934 **5852**
1880-4977 Iyo Gazo Joho Gakkai Zasshi (Online) **6199**
1880-5116 Kyouritsu Yakka Daigaku Zasshi **6858**
1880-5469 *see* 1344-6835 **6008**
1880-5515 Kochi Journal of Mathematics **5507**
1880-5523 Chiiki Rihabiriteshon **8032**
1880-554X Environment Control in Biology **671**
1880-5779 *see* 1341-7568 **867**
1880-5884 N E C Technical Journal **8432**
1880-5906 Microvascular Reviews and Communications **5796**
1880-6015 Toyama Mathematical Journal **5542**
1880-6023 *see* 1883-4760 **3264**
1880-6031 *see* 1883-4779 **3361**
1880-604X *see* 1883-4787 **2732**
1880-6058 *see* 1883-4795 **3265**
1880-6066 *see* 1883-4809 **1003**
1880-6074 *see* 1883-4817 **1003**
1880-6082 *see* 1883-4825 **3414**
1880-6090 Doboku Gakkai Rombunshuu. A (CD-ROM) *changed to* 1883-4760 **3264**
1880-6104 Doboku Gakkai Rombunshuu. B (CD-ROM) *changed to* 1883-4779 **3361**
1880-6120 Doboku Gakkai Rombunshuu. C (CD-ROM) *changed to* 1883-4787 **2732**
1880-6120 Doboku Gakkai Rombunshuu. D (CD-ROM) *changed to* 1883-4795 **3265**
1880-6139 Doboku Gakkai Rombunshuu. E (CD-ROM) *changed to* 1883-4809 **1003**
1880-6147 Doboku Gakkai Rombunshuu. F (CD-ROM) *changed to* 1883-4817 **1003**
1880-6155 Doboku Gakkai Rombunshuu. G (CD-ROM) *changed to* 1883-4825 **3414**
1880-6465 *see* 0287-6256 **4002**
1880-649X Seizonken Kenkyuu *see* 1880-6503 **3469**
1880-6503 Sustainable Humanosphere **3469**
1880-6546 Journal of Physiological Sciences **924**
1880-6554 *see* 1348-4818 **6158**
1880-6562 *see* 1880-6546 **924**
1880-6589 Miyagi Daigaku Shokusangyou Gakubu Kiyou **137**
1880-6767 Yamanashi Kokusai Kenkyuu **7275**
1880-6775 Yamanashi Kenritsu Daigaku Ningen Fukushi Gakubu Kiyou **2927**
1880-6791 Journal of Physiological Anthropology **924**
1880-6805 *see* 1880-6791 **924**
1880-6821 Plasma and Fusion Research **7035**
1880-7208 Magune **7025**
1880-7283 Boira Kuren Yousetsu no Jitsu Ten **5450**
1880-7437 Gifuken Kasen Kankyou Kenkyuujo Kenkyuu Houkoku **3595**
1880-7577 *see* Mokuzai Gakkaishi (Japanese Edition) **3714**
1880-7852 *see* 0001-5202 **929**
1880-8026 *see* 0019-8366 **6678**
1880-8204 Nihon Shiruku Gakkaishi **8455**
1880-8247 Plankton & Benthos Research **2816**
1880-8824 Shoku to Midori no Kagaku **3750**
1880-9863 Journal of Biomechanical Science and Engineering **749**
1880-9952 *see* 1346-4280 **5939**
1881-0373 Aichi Shukutoku Daigaku Gendai Shakai Kenkyuuka Kenkyuu Houkoku **8086**
1881-0551 Sanshi Konchuu Baiotekku **858**
1881-0942 *see* 0385-5414 **2123**
1881-1361 *see* 0287-4547 **5840**
1881-1469 *see* 0021-8820 **5645**
1881-1566 Izumo Shiritsu Sougou Iryou Senta Nempou **4103**
1881-1639 *see* 0288-6200 **5687**
1881-1698 *see* 1880-8204 **8455**
1881-1736 *see* 0030-154X **695**
1881-1930 Rinshou Men'eki Arerugika **5765**
1881-2058 *see* 0037-105X **8438**
1881-2090 *see* 0023-5679 **5659**
1881-2236 *see* 1347-6416 **8802**
1881-2473 Journal of Disaster Research **2227**
1881-2732 *see* 0913-5006 **6834**
1881-3062 Journal of Power and Energy Systems **3386**
1881-3364 Asian Economy and Social Environment **1062**
1881-347X Kagaku Keisatsu Kenkyuujo Houkoku **2658**
1881-3585 Circulation Up-to-Date **5782**
1881-3674 Aioi Kisoken Review **4491**
1881-4263 Frontiers in Dry Eye **6042**
1881-4506 Chouompa Kensa Gijutsu **6193**
1881-4670 Gete Nenkan *changed to* 1863-2769 **5301**
1881-4794 *see* 1881-4808 **5831**
1881-4808 Japanese Journal of Applied I T Healthcare **5831**
1881-4883 *see* 0369-4305 **7069**
1881-5766 Nursing Business **5973**
1881-5936 Chromosome Botany **784**
1881-6096 Brain and Nerve **6127**
1881-6754 Plant Root **812**
1881-7122 *see* 1341-1357 **5905**
1881-7203 *see* 1347-7986 **5478**
1881-7629 International Journal of Automation Technology **2461**
1881-7718 *see* 0484-6710 **2917**
1881-7734 Nihon Iyou Shika Kiki Gakkaishi **5857**
1881-8285 *see* 1881-5936 **784**
1881-8706 *see* 1349-6913 **7907**
1881-9893 Nihon Kotsu, Kansetsu Kansenshou Gakkai Zasshi **6067**
1882-0018 Hitz Gihou **3195**
1882-0115 Nihon Sutoma Haisetsu Rihabiriteshon Gakkaishi **5929**
1882-0123 Journal of Environmental Dermatology and Cutaneous Allergology **5879**
1882-0476 *see* 0916-4804 **894**
1882-0549 Taiki Denki Gakkaishi **6396**
1882-0654 *see* 0009-918X **6183**
1882-0743 Ceramic Society of Japan. Journal **2039**
1882-0778 Applied Physics Express **7006**
1882-0786 *see* 1882-0778 **7006**
1882-0824 *see* 0485-1439 **5941**
1882-1006 *see* 0015-6426 **7542**
1882-1863 *see* 1345-9074 **6068**
1882-2576 Thermal Medicine **6035**
1882-2770 Suido no Chi **159**
1882-3351 Japanese Society for Horticultural Science. Journal **3739**
1882-3750 *see* 1882-2576 **6035**
1882-4110 *see* 0021-4930 **5823**
1882-4773 Nihon Shokuiku Gakkaishi **6664**
1882-4781 *see* 1340-2242 **6253**
1882-4889 S I C E Journal of Control, Measurement, and System Integration **2436**
1882-5567 Epilepsy & Seizure **6138**
1882-6482 *see* 0021-5082 **6994**
1882-6865 Asian Ethnology **329**
1882-6946 Kyouto Furitsu Daigaku Gakujutsu Houkoku. Seimei Kankyougaku **3449**
1882-7055 *see* 0288-3635 **2572**
1882-7616 Japanese Dental Science Review **5850**
1882-7756 Higashiajia Bunka Koushou Kenkyuu. Bessatsu **7969**
1882-9465 A M T C Letters **3335**
1883-0498 *see* 0023-2513 **5658**
1883-0854 *see* 0030-6622 **6082**
1883-0870 Seppyou Kenkyuu Taikai Kouen Youshishuu **3219**
1883-0889 *see* 1883-0870 **3219**
1883-1958 Journal of Prosthodontic Research **5853**
1883-2083 *see* 0021-5384 **5948**
1883-4760 Doboku Gakkai Rombunshuu. A (DVD-ROM) **3264**
1883-4779 Doboku Gakkai Rombunshuu. B (DVD-ROM) **3361**
1883-4787 Doboku Gakkai Rombunshuu. C (DVD-ROM) **2732**
1883-4795 Doboku Gakkai Rombunshuu. D (DVD-ROM) **3265**
1883-4809 Doboku Gakkai Rombunshuu. E (DVD-ROM) **1003**
1883-4817 Doboku Gakkai Rombunshuu. F (DVD-ROM) **1003**
1883-4825 Doboku Gakkai Rombunshuu. G (DVD-ROM) **3414**
1883-8014 *see* 1343-0130 **2548**
1883-8022 *see* 1881-7629 **2461**
1883-8030 *see* 1881-2473 **2227**
1883-8049 *see* 0915-3942 **2585**
1885-0391 Comercio 45† **8942**
1885-0642 Suelo Pelvico **6005**
1885-0685 Bibliodoc **4994**
1885-0723 Tantagora **5385**
1885-0812 Bratz **2180**
1885-1002 Full Metal Panic! **490**
1885-1169 Jugon! **8236**
1885-1398 *see* 1699-258X **6226**
1885-1541 U O C. Papers **8011**
1885-1630 Libros de Economia y Empresa **1144**
1885-2173 La Ley, Temas de Hoy **4723**
1885-2211 MarcoELE **2885**
1885-2483 Foro Pediatrico **6092**
1885-2491 *see* 1885-2483 **6092**
1885-2556 *see* 1138-901X **7642**
1885-2718 Revista de Historiografia **4158**
1885-2785 Papers Lextra **4755**
1885-3137 Revista Internacional de Ciencias del Deporte **8196**
1885-3617 S I B F **6950**
1885-4052 Optometria Informacion (Castilla y Leon Edition) **6049**
1885-4060 Optometria Information (Castilla-La Mancha, Extremadura y Madrid Edition) **6049**
1885-4133 Unica **2262**
1885-446X Ocnos **2893**
1885-4486 Revista Espanola de Inovacion, Calidad e Ingenieria del Software **2436**
1885-4516 *see* 1135-934X **3216**
1885-527X T O G **6116**
1885-5563 Acordes **6542**
1885-5571 Guitarrista **6571**
1885-5598 Barcos R C **4328**
1885-5687 Escritura e Imagen **6916**
1885-5709 Revista Catalana de Dret Public **4770**
1885-5857 *see* 1579-2242 **5799**
1885-589X Revista Internacional de Pensamiento Politico **7178**

ISSN

DIRECTORY 2010 1910-2399 9843

1903-0665 Danske Specialmedier 24
1903-0681 J P Master Magazine *see* 0109-1182 3834
1903-072X Kommunernes Oekonomi 7495
1903-0770 Foraeldre & Boern 2153
1903-0819 Nyt fra Bibliotek og Medier 5037
1903-0827 *see* 1903-0819 5037
1903-0894 Designbase 2040
1903-0916 Gladsaxe Lokalhistoriske Forening. Aarbog 4224
1903-0983 AgroForum 1425
1903-0991 *see* 1903-0983 1425
1903-1025 Beton 982
1903-1033 *see* 1903-1025 982
1903-1106 Refleksion (Muslimernes Faellesraad) 7715
1903-1165 *see* 0024-287X 1020
1903-1173 Faroe Business Report 1565
1903-1181 *see* 1903-1173 1565
1903-1300 Taxi 8512
1903-1432 *see* 0107-6981 4592
1903-1637 *see* 1902-1526 5603
1903-1726 *see* 0013-2896 7589
1903-1785 *see* 0904-1699 2322
1903-1807 *see* 0025-5521 5512
1903-1815 Idenyt, Vi med Hus og Have *changed to* 1903-184X 4543
1903-1823 Oekonomi og Miljoe 1505
1903-1831 *see* 1903-1823 1505
1903-184X Idenyt, Vi i Villa 4543
1903-2080 FokusEuropa 7235
1903-2099 Kreativ Strik 6639
1903-2153 Aeldre Sagen Nu 4038
1903-2161 Aeldre Sagen Nyt 4038
1903-2188 *see* 0109-792X 1105
1903-2331 *see* 1604-1267 268
1903-2439 Energinet.dk. Market Report 3307
1903-2447 *see* 1903-2439 3307
1903-2455 *see* 1901-0818 3307
1903-2471 *see* 0016-7223 4009
1903-2498 Orientering 8393
1903-2633 *see* 1903-2153 4038
1903-2684 Budgetoversigt 7489
1903-2692 *see* 1903-2684 7489
1903-2730 *see* 1901-6069 3674
1903-2811 *see* 1600-8529 5369
1903-2862 *see* 0900-0461 240
1903-2897 *see* 1903-2161 4038
1903-3125 D L Magasinet 4592
1903-3176 Fit Living 6985
1903-3338 Danish Golden Age Studies 4449
1903-3346 Texts from Golden Age Denmark 3834
1903-3370 Goal, Dansk Fodbold *see* 0909-8208 8230
1903-3478 High School Musical 2192
1903-3494 Vand i Tal 8843
1903-3508 *see* 1903-3494 8843
1903-380X *see* 1604-6781 4594
1903-3990 Aarets Bedste Bogarbejde 7550
1903-4075 Filmmagasinet Ekko 6500
1903-4083 *see* 1903-4075 6500
1903-4091 C B S Observer 1077
1903-4202 Foraarsudstillingen 490
1903-4350 Fiskehandleren 3594
1903-4555 Denmark. Danmarks Statistik. Nationalregnskab 1223
1903-4563 *see* 1903-4555 1223
1903-4644 Stern und Spielplatz 5377
1903-4652 *see* 1903-4091 1077
1903-4695 Autobranchen.info 8561
1903-4709 *see* 1903-4695 8561
1903-4725 Praemis 148
1903-475X Suggestopaedisk Forening. Nyhedsbrev 2916
1903-4911 Cultures 4449
1903-4954 Action Magazine 7219
1903-4997 Register til Aarsskriftet Witherloese 4257
1903-5047 Hjertestatistik 5747
1903-5063 *see* 1903-5047 5747
1903-5373 Blink 1807
1903-5632 Tidsskriftet den Frie Laererskole 2919
1903-5659 Aaret i Billeder 4195
1903-5829 F A U-Conference 1595
1903-5837 *see* 1903-5829 1595
1903-6361 *see* 1903-5373 1807
1903-6418 C S R 3408
1903-6523 Dansk Tidsskrift for Teologi og Kirke 7637
1903-6906 *see* 1903-0002 7389
1903-7104 T I B 1052
1903-7139 Uddannelsesbladet 2921
1903-7155 *see* 1903-7139 2921
1903-7457 Taenk, Penge 2641
1903-7627 Denmark. Civilstyrelsen. Lovtidende, C 4656
1903-7635 Denmark. Civilstyrelsen. Lovtidende, B 4656
1903-7643 Denmark. Civilstyrelsen. Lovtidende, A 4656
1903-766X Denmark. Civilstyrelsen. Ministerialtidende 4656
1903-7880 Ridehesten Junior 8298
1903-8372 Laesoe Museum. Museumsforeningen for Laesoe 6527
1903-8461 Helsejob 6988
1903-847X *see* 1903-8461 6988
1903-945X Kyperen 606
1904-0350 Erhvervspolitisk Fokus 264
1905-4637 *see* 0125-4685 6882
1905-7415 Asian Biomedicine 5579
1905-7873 Maejo International Journal of Science and Technology 7880
1905-9159 Silpakorn University. Science and Technology Journal 7916
1906-1714 EnvironmentAsia 4182
1908-7330 Kritike 6931
1909-0056 *see* 1657-7663 2519
1909-0366 Studiositas 2916
1909-0544 *see* 0122-0268 8806
1909-1710 ABC del Bebe 2142
1909-2474 Luna Azul 3451
1909-2822 *see* 0121-733X 860
1909-3128 Stetika 591
1909-4477 *see* 1657-5946 1479
1909-5384 Propiedades 7606
1909-6119 Resumen 4583
1909-7719 *see* 0121-6805 1130
1909-8758 *see* 0123-3475 770
1909-9711 *see* 0123-9155 7330
1910-0019 Quebec. Ministere de l'Agriculture, des Pecheries et de l'Alimentation. Direction Regionale de Quebec-Capitale-Nationale. Bilan des Regions 205
1910-0035 Immunization Initiatives 7524
1910-0043 Discover Southwest Alberta 8698
1910-0051 Privacy Commissioner of Canada. Annual Report to Parliament (Year) Report on the Personal Information Protection and Electronic Documents Act 4761
1910-006X Privacy Commissioner of Canada. Annual Report to Parliament (Year) Report on the Privacy Act 4761
1910-0116 Northwest Territories. Equal Pay Commissioner. Annual Report 1700
1910-0124 Alaska Yukon Travel Magazine 8682
1910-0132 Services Integres. Bulletin *changed to* 1715-9326 6090
1910-0140 C A A Magazine 8690
1910-0159 Realizations (Estrie) 150
1910-0167 C R N Canada News *changed to* 1910-0175 2511
1910-0175 C R N Canada 2511
1910-0183 Canada's Best Drives 8691
1910-0191 Activities Idea Booklet 3515
1910-0213 Canadian Association of Broadcasters. Annual Report 2314
1910-0221 Code de la Securite Routiere Analytique 4643
1910-0299 La Situation Zoosanitaire au Canada 300
1910-0302 Yukon Heritage Resources Board. Annual Report 3476
1910-0329 Aboriginal Business 3515
1910-0337 Hospital Mental Health Services in Canada 6145
1910-0345 Services de Sante Mentale en Milieu Hospitalier au Canada 7541
1910-0353 *see* 1704-5061 3531
1910-040X How to Cite Statistics Canada Products *see* 1910-0418 5003
1910-0418 Comment Citer les Produits de Statistique Canada 5003
1910-0426 *see* 1714-6119 4108
1910-0434 Programme des Services de Sante Non Assures. Rapport Annuel 7537
1910-0442 Public Service Human Resources Management Agency of Canada. Annual Report on Official Languages (Online) *changed to* Canada Public Service Agency. Annual Report on Official Languages (Online) 1857
1910-0450 Agence de Gestion des Ressources Humaines de la Fonction Publique du Canada. Rapport Annuel sur les Langues Officielles *changed to* Agence de la Fonction Publique du Canada. Rapport Annuel sur les Langues Officielles 1855
1910-0469 Info Parkinson 6146
1910-0477 Canadian Companion to 1040 Preparation and Planning 1915
1910-0515 Pulp and Paper Technical Association of Canada. Annual Meeting Preprints CD *see* 1494-7722 6738
1910-0523 Festival Presence Autochtone a Montreal *changed to* 1910-0531 3559
1910-0531 Presence Autochtone a Montreal (Year) 3559
1910-054X First Peoples' Festival *changed to* 1910-0558 3551
1910-0558 Montreal's First Peoples' Festival (Year) 3551
1910-0582 Western Canada Stallion Edition *changed to* 1914-0835 8300
1910-0590 Horoscope 566
1910-0604 Hamilton - Halton Homebuilder 1010
1910-0639 The Nigerian Monitor 3554
1910-0647 Leisure Time, Your Time 4980
1910-0663 Natural Gas Exports *see* 1910-0671 6768
1910-0671 Exportations de Gaz Naturel 6768
1910-068X Natural Gas Imports *see* 1910-0698 6773
1910-0698 Importations de Gaz Naturel 6773
1910-071X British Columbia Real Estate Law Developments 7584
1910-0728 *see* 0045-3056 1913
1910-0817 Canadian Insurance Law Reporter Newsletter 4639
1910-085X Chronicle on Cuba 3527
1910-0884 Dictionnaire Societas Criticus 7130
1910-0892 Director's Briefing 1739
1910-0914 Epicentre 2853
1910-0930 *see* 1181-7097 1915
1910-0949 Drug Expenditures in Canada *see* 1910-0957 6832
1910-0957 Depenses en Medicaments au Canada 6832
1910-0965 Friedberg's Focus on Futures 1625
1910-0973 Fondation Quebecoise des Maladies Mentales. Rapport d'Activites 6141
1910-0981 Canadian Employment Benefits and Pension Guide 4498
1910-1007 Canadian Government Debt 1915
1910-1023 Commercial Times 4861
1910-1031 Discharge Abstract Database Abstracting Manual 5744
1910-104X D A D Resource Intensity Weights and Expected Length of Stay 5743
1910-1058 Environmental Indicators 3425
1910-1112 O P / Position 7160
1910-1120 Health Canada Science Forum. Book of Abstracts 5624
1910-1139 Forum Scientifique de Sante Canada. Livre des Resumes *see* 1910-1120 5624
1910-1147 Policy Monitoring Program 6606
1910-1155 Programme de Suivi de la Politique, au Rythme de l'Industrie *see* 1910-1147 6606
1910-1163 Canadian Institutes of Health Research. Institute of Aging. Biennial Report 8092
1910-1171 Instituts de Recherche en Sante du Canada, Institut du Vieillissement. Rapport Biennal *see* 1910-1163 8092
1910-118X On-site 1028
1910-1198 The Air Travel Complaints Commissioner's Report *changed to* 1719-9352 8535
1910-1201 Tariffs 3148
1910-121X Tarifs *see* 1910-1201 3148
1910-1236 Western Living Travels 8774
1910-1244 Biological and Oceanographic Data from the Harmful Algae Monitoring Program Associated with Salmon Farm Sites on the West Coast of Canada 3587
1910-1252 La Vitrine. Bulletin 1713
1910-1260 Prime Minister's Awards for Excellence in Early Childhood Education, Exemplary Practice 2899
1910-1341 Atout Hasard 6124
1910-135X C P F N W T News 3524
1910-1392 An Open Book 510
1910-1406 Common Vision 4064
1910-1414 Society for International Hockey Research. Newsletter 8202
1910-1422 Notes Nouvelles 6600
1910-1481 Airdrie City View 3805
1910-152X C T C Tourism Intelligence Bulletin *see* 1910-1538 8751
1910-1538 Renseignements sur le Tourisme. Bulletin 8751
1910-1546 C T C Tourism Intelligence Bulletin. Executive Summary *see* 1910-1554 8751
1910-1554 Renseignements sur le Tourisme. Sommaire. Bulletin 8751
1910-1562 L S M B Newsletter 5659
1910-1570 Alberta Construction Safety Association Industries 7506
1910-1589 Canadian Securities Law News 1615
1910-1597 Guide to Health Authority Accountability Documents 7520
1910-1600 Ontario Accident Benefit Case Summaries 4517
1910-1619 Labour Notes 1694
1910-1627 *see* Canadian Real Estate Income Tax Guide 1915
1910-1635 *see* 1912-1806 1669
1910-1643 Canadian Employment Law Guide 4639
1910-1651 Canadian Health Facilities Law Guide *changed to* 1910-1686 4686
1910-1686 Health Law Matters 4686
1910-1694 *see* Canadian Employment Safety and Health Guide 6675
1910-1740 Historians Recount 4295
1910-1759 *see* 1709-156X 1915
1910-1767 *see* 0047-5971 1934
1910-1775 *see* Manitoba and Saskatchewan Tax Reporter 1934
1910-1783 *see* 0048-1866 1938
1910-1791 Canadian Income Tax Act, Regulations and Rulings 1915
1910-1805 Canadian Family Law Matters 4907
1910-1813 Corporate Brief 4863
1910-1821 Club des Ornithologues de l'Outaouais 905
1910-183X Il Etait une Fois l'Imaginaire de Paule Doyon 5421
1910-1856 Canadian Tax Objection and Appeal Procedures Newsletter *changed to* Federal Tax Practice News 1924
1910-1864 Estate Planner Newsletter 4902
1910-1872 G O L Public Report 7518
1910-1880 G E D. Rapport Public *see* 1910-1872 7518
1910-1899 T E Wealth Strategies 1654
1910-1902 The C I A C's Electronic Art Magazine *changed to* 1910-1929 480
1910-1929 The C I A C's Electronic Magazine 480
1910-1945 *see* 1717-8703 1099
1910-1953 Foreign Exchange Strategy. Quarterly Strategy Outlook 1566
1910-1961 Foreign Exchange Strategy. Weekly Bulletin 1566
1910-197X Friedberg's Commodity & Currency Comments (Online Edition) 1625
1910-1988 Antigonish and Eastern Shore 8683
1910-1996 Animal Health Laboratory User's Guide and Fee Schedule 8792
1910-2003 Hockey Now 8177
1910-202X C F N S News 3408
1910-2038 Deer & Elk Farmers' Digest Newsletter 104
1910-2046 Public Library Services Newsletter (Online) 5041
1910-2054 Services de Bibliotheques Publiques. Bulletin d'Information (Online Edition) 5047
1910-2062 Repertoire des Medecins de Famille Accoucheurs du Quebec 6002
1910-2070 Ars Medica 5578
1910-2089 Universite d'Ottawa, Centre de Recherche en Civilisation Canadienne-Francaise. Rapport Annuel 4316
1910-2097 *see* 1713-3610 7534
1910-2100 Dominion Tax Cases Newsletter 1920
1910-2135 *see* 1489-2294 5148
1910-2143 Food Safety in Canada *changed to* Food Safety & Quality 3641
1910-2178 Cheneliere - Didactique. Apprentissage 2939
1910-2186 Anokhi Vibe *changed to* 1710-4793 2251
1910-2194 Espace Poetique de Huguette Bertrand 5421
1910-2224 Aboriginal Review 3515
1910-2232 Jib 8277
1910-2240 Ecoweek.ca 3478
1910-2259 Broadcasting Policy Monitoring Reports (Online Edition) 2314
1910-2267 Surveillance de la Politique sur la Radiodiffusion. Rapport (Online Edition) *see* 1910-2259 2314
1910-2275 The Rider.com 8298
1910-2283 Support to Sector Associations Program, a 'Sound' Program *see* 1910-2291 6607
1910-2291 Programme d'Aide aux Associations Sectorielles, un Programme a l'Ecoute 6607
1910-2305 Administration and Enforcement of the Fish Habitat Protection and Pollution Prevention Provisions of the Fisheries Act. Annual Report to Parliament *changed to* 1910-2356 3604
1910-2321 Administration and Enforcement of the Fish Habitat Protection and Pollution Prevention Provisions of the Fisheries Act. Annual Report *changed to* 1910-2356 3604
1910-2356 On the Administration and Enforcement of the Fish Habitat Protection and Pollution Prevention Provisions of the Fisheries Act. Annual Report to Parliament 3604
1910-2364 Sur l'Administration et l'Application des Dispositions de la Loi sur les Peches Relatives a la Protection de l'Habitat du Poisson et a la Prevention de la Pollution. Rapport Annuel au Parlement *see* 1910-2356 3604
1910-2372 Skim 518
1910-2380 Violet Miranda, Girl Pirate 2219
1910-2399 The Crown 2976

ISSN

ISSN

DIRECTORY 2010 1930-3955 9849

1916-0194 *see* 1206-0143 **4478**
1916-0216 Journal of Otolaryngology - Head & Neck Surgery **6082**
1916-0348 Paideusis (Online) **2895**
1916-050X S F U Educational Review **2908**
1916-0518 Journal of Interventional Oncology **6024**
1916-0615 *see* 0315-5986 **2536**
1916-0666 *see* 0024-9033 **2885**
1916-0674 Mechanical Business **4123**
1916-100X Photo Solution Magazine **6973**
1916-2413 Revista Productos Naturales **314**
1916-257X International Journal of Therapeutic Massage & Bodywork **6990**
1916-2790 Botany **781**
1916-2804 *see* 1916-2790 **781**
1916-4645 Environnement Urbain **3430**
1916-4742 English Language Teaching **5115**
1916-4750 *see* 1916-4742 **5115**
1916-7075 *see* 0828-282X **5779**
1916-8128 Journal of Unschooling and Alternative Learning **2879**
1916-9639 Applied Physics Research **7006**
1916-9655 Asian Culture and History **543**
1916-9663 *see* 1916-9655 **543**
1916-9671 International Journal of Biology **679**
1916-968X *see* 1916-9671 **679**
1916-9698 International Journal of Chemistry **2065**
1916-9701 *see* 1916-9698 **2065**
1916-971X International Journal of Economics and Finance **1357**
1916-9728 *see* 1916-971X **1357**
1916-9736 Global Journal of Health Science **5620**
1916-9744 *see* 1916-9736 **5620**
1916-9752 Journal of Agricultural Science **126**
1916-9779 Journal of Geography and Geology **2750**
1916-9795 Journal of Mathematics Research **5506**
1916-9809 *see* 1916-9795 **5506**
1916-9833 Rotman International Journal of Pension Management **1874**
1916-9841 *see* 1916-9833 **1874**
19169787 *see* 1916-9779 **2750**
1917-4071 *see* 1707-9101 **5081**
1917-411X Qian **1646**
1918-1345 Aporia **5951**
1918-2104 Wi: Journal of Mobile Media **8014**
1918-2325 Business Intelligence Service **1073**
1918-5227 Exceptionality Education International (Online) **3040**
1918-5561 Pharmaceutical Reviews **6870**
1918-5901 Global Media Journal: Canadian Edition **2321**
1918-6371 *see* 0826-9831 **7690**
1918-8722 School of Doctoral Studies Journal **7907**
1918-8730 *see* 1918-8722 **7907**
1930-000X BPMEnterprise Insights **1069**
1930-0018 BookBrowse Recommends **620**
1930-0026 K B Journal **5316**
1930-0034 Red Shtick Magazine **5236**
1930-0042 *see* 1930-0034 **5236**
1930-0069 Epidemiologic Inquiry **7516**
1930-0077 Birds of North America Online **904**
1930-0085 The Sales Advisor **1842**
1930-0107 The Panthic Weekly **7740**
1930-0115 *see* 0022-5169 **4300**
1930-0131 Nordo News **67**
1930-014X Fast Capitalism **7135**
1930-0158 Journal of Behavioral and Applied Management **1763**
1930-0166 *see* 0895-6308 **1790**
1930-0174 *see* 0741-7594 **2223**
1930-0190 The Dreamers Edge **7352**
1930-0204 *see* 1064-6671 **6791**
1930-0212 *see* 1094-6470 **6791**
1930-0220 *see* 1086-055X **6791**
1930-0239 Crime and Suspense **5413**
1930-0271 A Place of Peace **314**
1930-0298 Management Sciences for Health. Occasional Papers **7531**
1930-0301 Mathematical Reflections **5514**
1930-031X Women in Journey **8890**
1930-0328 *see* 1930-0336 **751**
1930-0336 Synthesis Lectures on Biomedical Engineering **751**
1930-0360 Body Dialogue **6983**
1930-0379 Edification **7353**
1930-0387 Michael Gray C P A's Real Estate Tax Letter **1296**
1930-0395 I E E E Sensors. Proceedings **2421**
1930-0417 Online-C T O **2335**
1930-0425 Don't Remember This **7352**
1930-0433 Radiology Case Reports **6207**
1930-0441 Intelligence Insights **7363**
1930-045X Michigan War Studies Review **6434**
1930-0468 G A F F Magazine **8315**
1930-0476 Carroll Magazine **5067**
1930-0506 The Ester Republic **3975**
1930-0514 Et Cetera **5291**
1930-0522 *see* 1540-3149 **8974**
1930-0530 *see* 0270-5214 **7019**
1930-0549 *see* 1075-2382 **3535**
1930-0557 *see* 0272-3646 **2714**
1930-0573 *see* 1535-7414 **2691**
1930-0581 Mivhar ha-Peninim **3551**
1930-059X *see* 1930-0581 **3551**
1930-0603 L T U Web Design **2563**
1930-0611 *see* 1062-7243 **6601**
1930-062X Immigration Daily **4849**
1930-0646 Gas Leads for Suppliers of Products and Services to the World Gas Community **6770**
1930-0654 Gas Leads *see* 1930-0646 **6770**
1930-0662 Lalitamba **5319**
1930-0689 Kindness Speaks All Languages **6810**
1930-0697 *see* 1930-0689 **6810**
1930-0719 Tahoe Quarterly **5084**
1930-0743 NoExcusesgym.com **6994**
1930-0751 Marketing Comet **1963**
1930-076X *see* 1558-6235 **8180**
1930-0778 Leading Edge Living **6645**
1930-0794 Supply Chain Manufacturing & Logistics *changed to* E R I Journal
1930-0808 Chamber News (Tucson) **1399**
1930-0816 Your N C L B Advisor *changed to* 1551-2223 **2892**
1930-0824 Triathlon Life **8213**
1930-0832 The Rising Times **8066**
1930-0867 Travel Medicine Advisor **5724**
1930-093X Pitkin Review **5351**
1930-0948 *see* 1930-093X **5351**
1930-0964 Federal and Florida Evidence Rules **4672**
1930-0972 *see* 0002-9890 **5468**
1930-0980 *see* 0025-570X **5515**
1930-1006 Weekly Challenger **315**
1930-1014 Integrated Ocean Drilling Program. Proceedings *see* 1930-1022 **2807**
1930-1022 Integrated Ocean Drilling Program. Proceedings. Expedition Reports **2807**
1930-1030 *see* 1930-1049 **7703**
1930-1049 The Voice of Clear Light **7703**
1930-1057 *see* 0734-8177 **7328**
1930-1065 Public Printer's Annual Report *see* 0734-8177 **7328**
1930-1073 Financial Services and Insurance Industry Litigation **4674**
1930-1081 MuniWireless Magazine **2564**
1930-109X Private Grants Alert **8063**
1930-1103 Practical Summaries in Acute Care **6071**
1930-1111 *see* 0740-2570 **5712**
1930-1146 Restaurant Facility Business **4396**
1930-1162 *see* 1930-109X **8063**
1930-1189 Journal for the Study of Radicalism **7146**
1930-1197 *see* 1930-1189 **7146**
1930-1219 *see* 0147-1937 **5528**
1930-1251 Peace Corps. Performance and Accountability Report **7258**
1930-126X The Journal of Business Forecasting **1134**
1930-1278 Cross & Crescent **2280**
1930-1286 Cross & Crescent of Lambda Chi Alpha†
1930-1294 *see* 0317-0500 **5273**
1930-1316 Military Embedded Systems **6435**
1930-1324 Turning Point Christian Worldview Series **7691**
1930-1332 Tygodnik Kalifornijski **3569**
1930-1340 *see* 1930-1391 **1501**
1930-1359 Manufacturing Today **1778**
1930-1367 Tennesseana Editions **4314**
1930-1375 Journal of the Holy Roman Empire **4236**
1930-1383 The Fall Line Review **5295**
1930-1391 News. Real Earnings in (Year) **1501**
1930-1405 *see* 0192-6365 **3027**
1930-1421 *see* 1930-1359 **1778**
1930-1448 Fish and Wildlife Research Institute Technical Reports **673**
1930-1456 *see* 1075-8569 **7231**
1930-1464 Trends in Domestic Box Office **6515**
1930-1472 Syntheses in Ecology and Evolution **706**
1930-1480 Center for Global Studies Bulletin *changed to* 1558-8947 **7225**
1930-1502 Moon Handbooks: Nova Scotia **8738**
1930-1529 *see* 1548-6613 **2921**
1930-1537 Annals of International Business Studies **1552**
1930-1545 Sports Illustrated Presents World Champs *see* Sports Illustrated (Swimsuit Edition) **2261**
1930-1545 Sports Illustrated Presents World Champs *see* 0038-822X **8207**
1930-1553 *see* 1548-7709 **2351**
1930-157X Survey Report on Hospital and Health Care Professional, Nursing, and Allied Services Personnel Compensation **4112**
1930-1588 Mergent Public Utility & Transportation Manual **7453**
1930-1596 Annuities Answer Book **1610**
1930-160X Review of Optometry **6051**
1930-1618 Steinway & Sons Official Magazine **6619**
1930-1634 Florida Criminal and Traffic Court Rules of Procedure **4890**
1930-1642 H D T V Retailer **2382**
1930-1650 International Journal of Information Security and Privacy **2514**
1930-1669 *see* 1930-1650 **2514**
1930-1677 Weiss Ratings' Consumer Guide to Medicare Prescription Drug Coverage *changed to* 1934-4147 **4525**
1930-1685 Taste of Home's America's Family Recipes **4368**
1930-1693 L L Journal **5138**
1930-1723 *see* 0887-736X **2100**
1930-174X Niuyue Renwen Xuekan **5155**
1930-1766 The Outsourcing Revolution *changed to* 1935-8385 **4934**
1930-1774 Massachusetts Criminal Law and Motor Vehicle Handbook **4893**
1930-1782 Discipulado Cristiano **7754**
1930-1790 Exploring the Bible: Bible Studies for the Deaf **7757**
1930-1804 Dorsaneo's Texas Discovery **4660**
1930-1812 The Eighteenth Century Current Bibliography **624**
1930-1820 Sobriquet Magazine **5374**
1930-1855 S P E Production & Operations **6791**
1930-1863 *see* 1930-1855 **6791**
1930-1871 Categorical Course Syllabus **6193**
1930-1944 Critical Interventions **484**
1930-1979 Regional Economic Development **1432**
1930-1987 Making Connections **2885**
1930-2010 The Complete Do-it-Yourself Human Resources Department **6696**
1930-2029 O B D I I Drive Cycle Guide: Domestic & Import Cars, Light Trucks, Vans & SUVs **3213**
1930-2037 Chilton Asian Diagnostic Service **8574**
1930-2045 Texas Journal on Civil Liberties and Civil Rights **4843**
1930-2053 The New CartoPhilatelist **6897**
1930-2061 *see* 1548-6605 **4732**
1930-207X *see* 0889-2237 **1067**
1930-2088 *see* 1548-6648 **5655**
1930-2096 Leading Chain Tenants *see* 1551-2495 **1987**
1930-2118 *see* 1548-7695 **4933**
1930-2126 BioResources **6732**
1930-2134 Advances in Heart and Lung Transplantation **6235**
1930-2142 Remodel Spokane Magazine **4549**
1930-2207 The Indianapolis Recorder **3978**
1930-2215 N Y U Physician's Directory **5682**
1930-224X The Gallup Poll Briefing **7137**
1930-2258 The Maple News **242**
1930-2266 Event Marketer **1816**
1930-2282 Watching Baseball **8251**
1930-2290 Consultant (Louisville) **3632**
1930-2363 1040 Preparation and Planning Guide **1956**
1930-2371 West's Jury Verdicts. Maryland Reports **4813**
1930-2401 Ideas & Inspiration Series
1930-2436 Employers State Law Alert **1677**
1930-2444 C **3971**
1930-2452 Inviting Arkansas **5074**
1930-2460 Construction & Demolition Recycling **3505**
1930-2479 G I E Media's Snow **8315**
1930-2487 Natural Forces School Leadership Journal **2890**
1930-2495 West's Jury Verdicts. Oklahoma Reports **4813**
1930-2509 West's Jury Verdicts. Indiana Reports **4813**
1930-2517 West's Jury Verdicts. Georgia Reports **4813**
1930-2525 *see* 1930-2266 **1816**
1930-2541 Radiant **2260**
1930-255X The Boston Catholic Television Monthly **7786**
1930-2568 Florida Practice Series. Florida Estate Planning **4902**
1930-2592 Smash **8245**
1930-2606 I S S I G Review **1751**
1930-2614 Biomedical Business & Technology **5585**
1930-2622 Hideaways Life **8718**
1930-2630 Moon Handbooks: New Jersey **8738**
1930-2649 Rum & Reggae's Hawai'i **8753**
1930-2657 eDoula **5989**
1930-2681 Women's Diaries and Letters of the South **4318**
1930-269X Sourcingmag Insights **1794**
1930-2703 C F A Institute Conference Proceedings Quarterly **1614**
1930-2797 The Coastal Review **5106**
1930-2851 *see* 1534-0333 **7413**
1930-286X Vestnik **8013**
1930-2878 Cezanne's Carrot **5272**
1930-2886 Verb (Bethlehem) **4481**
1930-2894 *see* 1930-2886 **4481**
1930-2908 U S P Pharmacists' Pharmacopeia **6884**
1930-2916 *see* 1930-2908 **6884**
1930-2924 *see* 0195-7996 **6884**
1930-2932 U S P - N F *see* 0195-7996 **6884**
1930-2940 Language in India **5140**
1930-2967 Arizona Geriatrics Society Journal **4041**
1930-2975 Judgment and Decision Making **1138**
1930-2983 Structural Durability & Health Monitoring **3220**
1930-2991 *see* 1930-2983 **3220**
1930-3009 Journal of Global Initiatives **7979**
1930-3017 Socialism and Liberation **7183**
1930-3041 Virginia Practice Series. Probate Handbook **4906**
1930-305X Prior Art **4761**
1930-3068 Corporate Counsel Forum **4863**
1930-3076 Voyaging **8284**
1930-3092 The Best Political Cartoons of the Year **7109**
1930-3106 Navigating Trademark Practice Before the P T O **4739**
1930-3149 Sporting News Ultimate Baseball Scouting Guide **8247**
1930-3157 The 100 Best Trends†
1930-3165 Biography Today Business Leaders Series **641**
1930-3173 Moving & Relocation Directory **7600**
1930-3203 *see* 1041-794X **2339**
1930-3211 *see* 0882-4096 **8094**
1930-322X *see* 0277-3945 **5362**
1930-3246 Voices of the Civil War Series **4317**
1930-3262 Who's Who in Finance and Business **647**
1930-3270 A N A Journal **6648**
1930-3289 Answers (Hebron) **7622**
1930-3297 *see* 1930-3289 **7622**
1930-3300 Information Plus Reference Series. World Poverty **8046**
1930-3319 Information Plus Reference Series. Endangered Species **3439**
1930-3408 Missouri Practice Series. Landlord-Tenant Handbook **4735**
1930-3424 Death & Taxes **6561**
1930-3475 Thompson's Special Ed Advisor **3048**
1930-3483 Thompson's N C L B Advisor **3034**
1930-3491 Fodor's See It. New Zealand **8709**
1930-3505 Fodor's Walt Disney World, Universal Orlando & Central Florida *changed to* Fodor's Walt Disney World **8710**
1930-3513 Frommer's Barcelona **8710**
1930-3521 Insiders' Guide to Gettysburg **8722**
1930-353X Genealogy Guidebook *see* 1529-0298 **3766**
1930-3564 America's Hottest Colleges **2966**
1930-3572 Tools & Techniques of Employee Benefit and Retirement Planning **1711**
1930-3580 The Mailbox. Grades 2-3 Yearbook **2201**
1930-3599 A L M Experts. New England Directory **5564**
1930-3602 A L M Experts. National Medical Directory **5564**
1930-3610 New York State Grade 8 Intermediate Social Studies Test **2891**
1930-3645 Horn of Africa Journal of AIDS **5816**
1930-3653 *see* 0037-7724 **3082**
1930-3661 *see* Law - Technology **4845**
1930-367X *see* 0361-5669 **6691**
1930-370X New Spirit Journal **6646**
1930-3718 Asia-Pacific Harrier **8684**
1930-3742 Electric Sales and Revenue *changed to* 1930-3750 **3155**
1930-3750 U.S. Department of Energy. Energy Information Administration. Electric Sales, Revenue, and Average Price **3155**
1930-3777 Studies in Christian-Jewish Relations **7685**
1930-3807 *see* 0363-7425 **1723**
1930-3815 *see* 0001-8392 **7419**
1930-3831 *see* 0003-0724 **6544**
1930-384X *see* 1062-3442 **2802**
1930-3858 *see* 1552-9983 **5440**
1930-3874 Print Culture History in Modern America **4309**
1930-3912 Studies in American History **4163**
1930-3920 Studies in Photographic Arts **6977**
1930-3947 *see* 0199-1337 **6445**
1930-3955 *see* 0894-203X **5938**

ISSN

DIRECTORY 2010 1931-3500 9851

1930-8604 Iowa Practice Series. Methods of Practice **4697**
1930-8612 Hate Crimes Law **4685**
1930-8620 The A S T D Training & Performance Sourcebook **6691**
1930-8639 Leadership in Project Management Annual **1772**
1930-8647 Plunkett's Insurance Industry Almanac **2024**
1930-8655 Plunkett's Wireless, Wi-Fi, R F I D & Cellular Industry Almanac **2371**
1930-8671 *see* 1073-6719 **7132**
1930-868X *see* 1057-736X **8033**
1930-8698 *see* 1559-162X **6411**
1930-8701 Entertainment Law Review **4666**
1930-871X *see* 1930-8701 **4666**
1930-8728 *see* 1930-8736 **5832**
1930-8736 A D A Professional Product Review **5832**
1930-8787 Court Rules Pamphlet(s). Vermont Rules of Court, State and Federal **4652**
1930-8795 Anderson's Ohio Search Warrant Manual **4616**
1930-8809 Wisconsin's Forest Resources in (Year) **3707**
1930-8817 *see* 0893-4940 **7532**
1930-8833 E S S C I R C. Proceedings **3094**
1930-8841 I E E E International Integrated Reliability Workshop Final Report **2420**
1930-885X International Power Modulator Symposium and High-Voltage Workshop. Proceedings **3321**
1930-8868 I E E E International Symposium on V L S I Technology. Proceedings of Technical Papers **2465**
1930-8876 European Solid State Device Research Conference. Proceedings **7087**
1930-8892 *see* 1084-5453 **4138**
1930-8906 *see* 0887-9486 **3084**
1930-8914 *see* 1521-4842 **7597**
1930-8922 *see* 0002-371X **4612**
1930-8930 *see* 0009-0328 **2039**
1930-8957 *see* 0039-0895 **1752**
1930-8973 Annual Review of O C L C Research (Online Edition) **4989**
1930-8981 Soybean Genetics Newsletter (Online Edition) **878**
1930-899X Tax Management Interactive Forms for Windows **1948**
1930-9007 Journal of Scholarly and Scientific Perspectives **7980**
1930-9023 Michael Gray C P A's Tax & Business Insight **1935**
1930-9058 Developing Highly Qualified Paraeducators **3020**
1930-9074 Christian Apologetics Journal **7631**
1930-9082 *see* 1930-9074 **7631**
1930-9090 Wiley C P A Examination Review. Business Environment and Concepts **4883**
1930-9236 Fundraising Success Advisor **8041**
1930-9309 Outside Magazine's Urban Adventure: Seattle **8746**
1930-9325 *see* 1524-0754 **3044**
1930-9376 Crossroads (Macon) **3528**
1930-9384 The Treasures and Pleasures of Mexico **8769**
1930-9406 Bottle Rockets **5418**
1930-9422 Loyola Law and Technology Annual **8431**
1930-9430 *see* 1044-9469 **8537**
1930-9449 *see* 0048-7376 **2626**
1930-9457 *see* 0898-3097 **3537**
1930-9503 Industrial & Institutional Cleaning Chemicals **2065**
1930-952X Disposable Medical Supplies
1930-9546 Tech I Q **2525**
1930-9554 Court Rules Pamphlet(s). Arkansas Rules of Court, State **4652**
1930-9570 Anderson's Ohio Probate Practice and Procedure **4900**
1930-9589 Taunton Tool Guide **1052**
1930-9597 *see* 0364-6149 **6354**
1930-9619 Sada al-Watan **3562**
1930-9635 Jewelry Arts & Lapidary Journal *changed to* 1936-5942 **4568**
1930-9643 The Journal of Associated Graduates in Near Eastern Studies **3544**
1930-9651 The Morse Target **7253**
1930-9686 Boston Spirit **4371**
1930-9740 GeminiFocus **575**
1930-9791 Dining in, Dining Out in Northern Michigan **4384**
1930-9805 *see* 0015-2587 **3577**
1930-9813 *see* 0010-6151 **4648**
1930-9821 Discretionary Land Use Controls **7434**
1930-983X Texas Pharmacy Laws and Regulations **4795**
1930-9848 GreenSource **1010**
1930-9856 Bus Conversion Sources **3374**
1930-9864 The Best Test Preparation for the Advanced Placement Examinations. A P Physics B & C **7006**
1930-9880 Guide to College Majors **2983**
1930-9902 Florida Practice Series. Florida D U I Handbook **2652**
1930-9910 Washington (State) Department of Community, Trade, and Economic Development. Biennial Energy Report **3150**
1930-9988 The Kosciuszko Foundation. Annual Report **3546**
1930-9996 Kids Avenue **2197**
1931-0013 Ohio Business Law Journal **4878**
1931-0021 Women's Psychology **7415**
1931-0072 A Comprehensive List of Halal Food Products in U.S. and Canadian Supermarkets **7710**
1931-0080 Analysis & Explanation of California Taxes **1910**
1931-0102 Redbook: Bakery Production and Marketing **3675**
1931-0110 The New Look **2249**
1931-0129 American Handgunner Tactical Annual **6285**
1931-0137 International Conference On Mobile Systems, Applications And Services **2424**
1931-0145 S I G K D D Explorations **2436**
1931-0153 *see* 1931-0145 **2436**
1931-017X America's Top 101 Jobs For People Without a Four-Year Degree **6692**
1931-020X Warman's Baseball Card Field Guide† **8998**
1931-0226 Connecticut Fire Service Laws **4648**
1931-0234 *see* 0014-0767 **5291**
1931-0269 The International Journal of Business and Finance Research **1631**
1931-0277 Global Journal of Business Research **1114**
1931-0293 Journal of Humanistic Counseling, Education and Development **7375**
1931-0307 Cornsnake Morph Guide **939**
1931-0315 The Buyer's Guide to Cornsnake Morphs *changed to* 1931-0307 **939**
1931-0366 Garden Doctor **3731**
1931-0390 Birnbaum's Disney Cruise Line **8687**
1931-0420 Anderson's Ohio Criminal Practice and Procedure **4884**
1931-0447 Michie's Annotated Rules of New Mexico **4733**
1931-0471 Swadharma **7708**
1931-0528 The Back Stage Book of New American Short Plays **8466**
1931-0536 Annual S I G C S E Conference on Innovation and Technology in Computer Science Education. Proceedings **2406**
1931-0544 International Symposium on Code Generation and Optimization **2507**
1931-0560 Checklists and Illustrative Financial Statements for Depository and Lending Institutions **1285**
1931-0579 The Rough Guide to Barcelona **8753**
1931-0587 I E E E Intelligent Vehicles Symposium **8498**
1931-0641 Guanxi **1887**
1931-065X *see* 1931-0641 **1887**
1931-0668 *see* 0147-0590 **7176**
1931-0676 *see* 0039-7709 **5384**
1931-0684 *see* 0149-0737 **4580**
1931-0692 *see* 0018-6813 **4688**
1931-0706 *see* 0099-0280 **3551**
1931-0714 Robert Hsu's China Strategy **1581**
1931-0722 Kansas' Forest Resources in (Year) **3695**
1931-0730 Missouri's Forest Resources in (Year) **3697**
1931-0757 *see* 1931-0714 **1581**
1931-0781 Virginia Practice Series **4809**
1931-0811 Rogov's Guide to Israeli Wines **609**
1931-0862 Compensation Survey Report **1672**
1931-0889 8 Ways to Avoid Probate **4906**
1931-0897 Texas Legislative Guide **4795**
1931-0919 The Complete Guide to Human Resources and the Law **1858**
1931-0927 Guide to Homeland Security **4683**
1931-0935 Princeton Series in Geochemistry **2762**
1931-0943 Sources for Biblical and Theological Study **7682**
1931-0951 Sound & Vision H D T V Guide **2391**
1931-096X U S T A Mid-Atlantic Section Yearbook
1931-0978 African Studies **4172**
1931-1044 Michigan Probate Laws and Rules **4904**
1931-1087 Spouse and Child Support in New York **4914**
1931-1125 Audio Video *see* 1535-6132
1931-1125 Audio Video *see* 1946-8776 **5028**
1931-1125 Audio Video *see* 0363-0277 **5028**
1931-1133 A C M Workshop on Rapid Malcode. Proceedings **2405**
1931-1168 I E E E Workshop on Applications of Signal Processing to Audio and Acoustics **7087**
1931-1176 Health and Welfare Plans. Colorado & Wyoming **1685**
1931-1192 *see* 0161-7435 **5423**
1931-1206 Tilt **5389**
1931-1214 Nimrod International Journal **5341**
1931-1222 *see* 1559-1662 **2333**
1931-1303 I P G E-News **7323**
1931-1311 *see* 1061-7264 **2506**
1931-132X *see* 1048-9487 **4376**
1931-1346 *see* 0746-8342 **5478**
1931-1354 *see* 1050-6098 **4986**
1931-1362 *see* 0009-5982 **2972**
1931-1370 Breyer Animal Collector's Guide **4330**
1931-1400 International Journal of Management Studies **1759**
1931-1427 *see* 0748-2558 **8478**
1931-1443 Wild Fibers **8462**
1931-146X Managing Clinically Important Drug Interactions **6860**
1931-1486 Estate Planning Conference **4902**
1931-1494 Environmental Permitting and Permitting Litigation **3427**
1931-1508 Representing Asylum Seekers **4769**
1931-1516 *see* 1528-3542 **7354**
1931-1524 National Geographic Online *see* 0027-9358 **4020**
1931-1532 The Virtual Journal for Biomedical Optics **710**
1931-1559 *see* 0894-4105 **6168**
1931-1567 America's Top Jobs for People Without a Four-Year Degree *changed to* 1931-017X **6692**
1931-1575 Official Overstreet Comic Book Companion *see* 1551-403X **4342**
1931-1605 Trial Handbook for Tennessee Lawyers **4798**
1931-1621 Elegant Homes **4539**
1931-163X Multistate Guide to Regulation and Taxation of Nonprofits **1935**
1931-1664 Fundamentals of Federal Litigation **4678**
1931-1672 Northern Michigan Almanac **8742**
1931-1680 Survey of State Class Action Law **4791**
1931-1745 S I G W E B Newsletter†
1931-1761 Boxcar Poetry Review **5418**
1931-177X Asian Petrochemicalscan **6763**
1931-1788 *see* Platt's Oilgram Bunkerwire
1931-1796 Europe & Americas Petrochemical Scan **6768**
1931-180X Platts Asia-Pacific/Arab Gulf Marketscan (Online) **6789**
1931-1826 Fodor's Amsterdam's 25 Best **8704**
1931-1885 Chinawire **6766**
1931-1893 Clean Tankerwire **8641**
1931-1907 Crude Oil Market Wire **6766**
1931-1915 Intermediateswire **6774**
1931-1923 Latin American Wire **6777**
1931-1931 Dirty Tankerwire **8642**
1931-194X The Good Life, Central New York Magazine **5072**
1931-1974 Journal of Government Leasing **7596**
1931-1982 Metamorphoses (Ridgecrest) **5333**
1931-1990 Ohio Workers' Compensation Law **1701**
1931-2008 Ohio Workers' Compensation Law. Companion Laws and Rules **1701**
1931-2016 Immigration Law Conference **4690**
1931-2024 The Baseball Chronicle **8222**
1931-2075 Technology Law Forum **4793**
1931-2091 Counseling and Clinical Psychology Journal *changed to* 1931-5694 **7399**
1931-2105 N A S C A R NEXTEL Cup Series **8594**
1931-2156 *see* 1931-4906 **3412**
1931-2164 P E T Europe *changed to* 1937-1691 **6771**
1931-2172 Platt's Solventswire (Online) **6789**
1931-2180 P P Europe **6786**
1931-2199 Platt's Polymerscan (Online) **6789**
1931-2202 Platt's Olefinscan (Online) **6789**
1931-2210 North American Crude Wire **6781**
1931-2229 Platt's L P Gaswire (Online) **6789**
1931-2253 *see* 0959-6682 **6876**
1931-2261 *see* 1468-9871 **6843**
1931-227X *see* 1367-7543 **6174**
1931-2288 *see* 1362-5306 **6275**
1931-230X Northeast Regional Employment Law Institute. Annual **4748**
1931-2318 California Civil Courtroom Handbook and Desktop Reference **4828**
1931-2326 Police Misconduct **2664**
1931-2334 Toll's Pennsylvania Crimes Code Annotated **4899**
1931-2350 Alabama Criminal Trial Practice Forms **4883**
1931-2377 Oregon Legislation Highlights **4754**
1931-2385 International Conference on Quality of Service in Heterogeneous Wired/Wireless Networks. Proceedings **3320**
1931-2393 *see* 1538-6341 **6001**
1931-2407 First Aid for the N B D E Part 1 **5844**
1931-2423 Tort Law Journal of Ohio **4797**
1931-2431 Electronic News (Mahwah) **4575**
1931-244X *see* 1931-2431 **4575**
1931-2458 Communication Methods and Measures **2315**
1931-2466 *see* 1931-2458 **2315**
1931-2474 Arkansas Civil Procedure Laws **4827**
1931-2482 Contemporary Hematology **5935**
1931-2490 Asbestos Litigation in the 21st Century **4622**
1931-2504 U.S. Coast Guard No. 515. Rules and Regulations for Foreign Vessels Operating in the Navigable Waters of the United States. Volume #1, Navigation and Navigable Waters **4971**
1931-2512 U.S. Coast Guard No. 515. Rules and Regulations for Foreign Vessels Operating in the Navigable Waters of the United States. Volume 2, Shipping **4971**
1931-2539 Eolas **4217**
1931-2555 Studies in American Naturalism **5380**
1931-2563 West's Jury Verdicts. Ohio Reports **4967**
1931-2571 West's Jury Verdicts. Minnesota Reports **4967**
1931-2598 Fodor's See It. Costa Rica **8709**
1931-2628 The Rough Guide to Travel Survival **8753**
1931-2644 Survey of Dental Education. Volume 4, Curriculum **5867**
1931-2652 Survey of Dental Education. Volume 3. Faculty and Support Staff **5867**
1931-2660 Survey of Dental Education. Volume 2, Tuition, Admission, and Attrition **5867**
1931-2679 Survey of Dental Education. Volume 1, Academic Programs, Enrollment, and Graduates **5866**
1931-2695 Temporary Disability Insurance and Unemployment Insurance Laws of Rhode Island **4525**
1931-2725 Michigan Civil Procedure **4837**
1931-2741 Daniel's Georgia Criminal Trial Practice **4888**
1931-275X International Journal of Motorcycle Studies **8260**
1931-2768 Michael Gray C P A's Option Alert **1639**
1931-2776 Kansas City Voices **5317**
1931-2784 Nylon Guys (New York) **6296**
1931-2792 Seattle Metropolitan **3988**
1931-2822 U.S. Congressional Serial Set **7472**
1931-2830 United States Participation in the United Nations **7474**
1931-2849 U S A I D in Africa **1606**
1931-2857 *see* 0193-6603 **189**
1931-2865 Virgin Islands Blue Book **8772**
1931-2873 Vital Statistics of the United States **7550**
1931-2903 Situation & Outlook Report. Wheat Yearbook **253**
1931-2911 *see* Wood Products: International Trade and Foreign Markets **208**
1931-2938 Joint Center for Poverty Research. Working Paper Series **8048**
1931-2946 *see* 1531-5649 **7530**
1931-2954 *see* 1531-5673 **7531**
1931-2962 *see* 1933-0138 **7549**
1931-2970 Summary Health Statistics for U.S. Children **7549**
1931-2989 Federal Reserve Bank of Dallas. Economic Research Working Papers **1342**
1931-2997 University of Chicago. Center for Research in Security Prices. Working Paper Series **1389**
1931-3004 *see* 1931-2997 **1389**
1931-3012 A I P Conference Proceedings. Accelerators & Beams **7002**
1931-3020 A I P Conference Proceedings. Astronomy & Astrophysics **7002**
1931-3039 A I P Conference Proceedings. Atomic, Molecular & Statistical Physics **7002**
1931-3047 A I P Conference Proceedings. Materials Physics & Applications **7002**
1931-3055 A I P Conference Proceedings. Mathematical & Statistical Physics **5463**
1931-3063 A I P Conference Proceedings. Nuclear & High Energy Physics **7064**
1931-3071 A I P Conference Proceedings. Plasma Physics **7002**
1931-3098 Creative Quarterly **484**
1931-311X Journal of Global Business Issues **1136**
1931-3128 Cell Host & Microbe **883**
1931-3144 T L Infobits **3004**
1931-3152 International Multilingual Research Journal **5130**
1931-3160 *see* 1931-3152 **5130**
1931-3195 Journal of Applied Remote Sensing **7077**
1931-3209 *see* 1931-3268 **6226**
1931-3268 The Rheumatologist **6226**
1931-3322 *see* 1559-6311 **5675**
1931-3349 Pacific Northwest Fungi *changed to* 1937-786X **805**
1931-3357 Journal of Usability Studies **3206**
1931-3365 Online Journal of Analytic Combinatorics **5523**
1931-3381 The Stone Circle **5378**
1931-342X KotaPress Journal **5425**
1931-3438 Yeti **6629**
1931-3454 Flyer (Logan) **8040**
1931-3462 *see* 1931-3454 **8040**
1931-3470 Ranger Rick Educator's Guide *see* 0738-6656 **2210**
1931-3489 Heath Haussamen on New Mexico Politics **7140**
1931-3497 Money Fund Intelligence **1640**
1931-3500 Survey of State Tax Departments **1946**

ISSN

Link to your serials resources and content with ulrichsweb.com

DIRECTORY 2010 1932-2488 9853

1931-8235 Journal of World Christianity (Online) **7657**
1931-8243 *see* 1931-7867 **1253**
1931-8251 Dell Original Sudoku **4333**
1931-826X Surface Fabrication **4551**
1931-8278 Paper & Packaging **6736**
1931-8286 Ei8ht Magazine **2380**
1931-8294 Outdoors Magazine **8327**
1931-8308 Beauty Packaging **1807**
1931-8316 O'Dwyer's P R Report **31**
1931-8332 Mega Dream Homes International **7599**
1931-8340 Homicide Trends in the United States **2654**
1931-8359 *see* 1931-8340 **2654**
1931-8367 Symmetry **7042**
1931-8375 *see* 1931-8367 **7042**
1931-8405 *see* 0889-2229 **5809**
1931-8413 *see* 1935-472X **868**
1931-8421 *see* 1550-9087 **765**
1931-843X *see* 1540-9996 **8846**
1931-8448 *see* 1076-6294 **5679**
1931-8464 Energy Pipeline News **6768**
1931-8529 Guide to Specialists **7443**
1931-8545 National Municipal Policy and Resolutions†
1931-857X American Journal of Physiology: Renal Physiology **919**
1931-8588 Monitoring the Future: National Survey Results on Drug Use **2697**
1931-8596 *see* 1931-8588 **2697**
1931-860X U.S. Department of Transportation. Federal Railroad Administration. Office of Safety Analysis. Railroad Safety Statistics. Annual Report (Year) **8532**
1931-8618 *see* 1931-860X **8532**
1931-8626 U.S. Department of Labor. Bureau of Labor Statistics. News. Multifactor Productivity Trends **1272**
1931-8634 Rite *changed to* 1946-9586 **6604**
1931-8642 World History Connected **4167**
1931-8669 Monitoring the Future, National Results on Adolescent Drug Use. Overview of Key Findings **7532**
1931-8677 *see* 1931-8669 **7532**
1931-8693 Democracy (Washington, D.C.) **7129**
1931-8707 *see* 1931-8693 **7129**
1931-8715 *see* 1931-8723 **473**
1931-8723 Artists' Resource Guide **473**
1931-8731 K C Business **1139**
1931-874X Historical Dictionaries of Latin America Series **4296**
1931-8782 National Museum of Natural History. Arctic Studies Center. Newsletter **6534**
1931-8790 NewsM A C **408**
1931-8804 Operating & Financial Performance Profiles of 18-hole Golf Facilities in the U.S. **1157**
1931-8812 Peabody Museum of Archaeology and Ethnology. Monographs **411**
1931-8820 Resource Directory **8477**
1931-8839 The Savings Directory†
1931-8847 U N I M A - U S A Membership Directory **523**
1931-8855 Annual Firearms Manufacturing and Export Report **6410**
1931-8863 The Champion **3972**
1931-891X Bleech Magazine **2251**
1931-8928 *see* 0744-7523 **183**
1931-8936 Library Administration and Management Section. Journals **5026**
1931-8944 Edible Brooklyn **3634**
1931-8952 Working Papers in Linguistics (Online) **5196**
1931-9010 BioWorld Phase III Report **6826**
1931-9029 Written **5087**
1931-9037 Hospital Medicine Alert **4100**
1931-9045 Thymos **2169**
1931-907X International Journal of Business and Economics Perspectives **1127**
1931-9088 Flyway **5297**
1931-9096 Quail Forever **3461**
1931-9118 Money Fund Report **1640**
1931-9126 Boating Safety Circular **8273**
1931-9134 United States. Department of Veterans Affairs. Health Services Research and Development Service. Forum **6451**
1931-9142 *see* 1931-9134 **6451**
1931-9223 J C P: Biochemical Physics **7018**
1931-9231 Rough Stuff **515**
1931-9282 Signal Smoke **914**
1931-9320 Subcontracting Directory *see* 1931-9339 **1180**
1931-9339 Subcontracting Opportunities with D o D Major Prime Contractors **1180**
1931-9347 U.S. Federal Deposit Insurance Corp. Summary of Deposits (Online) *see* F D I C. Summary of Deposits. Bank & Thrift Branch Office Data Book. Northeast Region **1341**
1931-9347 U.S. Federal Deposit Insurance Corp. Summary of Deposits (Online) *see* F D I C. Summary of Deposits. Bank & Thrift Branch Office Data Book. National **1341**
1931-9347 U.S. Federal Deposit Insurance Corp. Summary of Deposits (Online) *see* F D I C. Summary of Deposits. Bank & Thrift Branch Office Data Book. Central Region **1340**
1931-9347 U.S. Federal Deposit Insurance Corp. Summary of Deposits (Online) *see* F D I C. Summary of Deposits. Bank & Thrift Branch Office Data Book. Southeast Region **1341**
1931-9347 U.S. Federal Deposit Insurance Corp. Summary of Deposits (Online) *see* F D I C. Summary of Deposits. Bank & Thrift Branch Office Data Book. Southwest Region **1341**
1931-9347 U.S. Federal Deposit Insurance Corp. Summary of Deposits (Online) *see* F D I C. Summary of Deposits. Bank & Thrift Branch Office Data Book. Midwest Region **1340**
1931-9355 *see* 1931-9126 **8273**
1931-9401 Applied Physics Reviews **7006**
1931-941X *see* 1555-4880 **8433**
1931-9428 Multilingual **2432**
1931-9436 Multihousing Professional **7601**
1931-9495 C P R & A E D **5590**
1931-9509 Standard First Aid, C P R and A E D **5717**
1931-9525 Synthesis Lectures on Power Electronics **3114**
1931-9533 *see* 1931-9525 **3114**
1931-9541 Near East Quarterly **7254**
1931-955X Log Home Design **1021**
1931-9568 Kentucky Journal of Manufacturing & Industry **1140**
1931-9584 LawyersU S A **4718**
1931-9592 Profiles in Healthcare Communications†
1931-9606 *see* 0741-5435 **2304**
1931-9622 Practical Guide to Estate Planning **4904**
1931-9630 The Sarasota, Sanibel Island & Naples Book **8754**
1931-9649 Lubavitch International Update **3548**
1931-9657 Semiconductor International SemiSource **3113**
1931-9665 Auditor's Risk Management Guide **1281**
1931-9673 PaperKuts†
1931-9703 Intellectual Property Licensing Today **4694**
1931-9711 The Green Bag Almanac & Reader (Year) **4682**
1931-972X Simply Perfect Italian *changed to* 1939-2273 **4361**
1931-9738 Manual for Police in the State of New York **2660**
1931-9746 Kentucky Wrongful Death Actions **4892**
1931-9754 Healthcare Trends & Forecasts **7523**
1931-9762 Minnesota Practice Series. Real Estate Law **7600**
1931-9770 Edwards' North Carolina Probate Handbook **4901**
1931-9789 Federal Motor Carrier Safety Regulations: Administrator Edition **8670**
1931-9819 Collector Car Price Guide **8575**
1931-986X Wisteria **5438**
1931-9894 Healthcare Marketing Advisor **4097**
1931-9908 Worth **1660**
1931-9916 Contemporary Esthetics *changed to* 1555-7979 **5848**
1931-9924 Chem.info **3237**
1931-9932 Stepping Up **4602**
1931-9959 Home Electronic Ideas **3101**
1931-9967 How to File for Divorce in Pennsylvania **4911**
1931-9975 Insurance and Financial Meetings Management **6280**
1931-9983 *see* 1547-9641 **2991**
1932-0108 Mistletoe Leaves **4304**
1932-0124 Beckett Anime & Manga *changed to* 1935-7818 **4330**
1932-0140 COMMON.Connect **2410**
1932-0159 Destination Wine Country - Santa Barbara **8697**
1932-0167 Genetic and Evolutionary Computation **868**
1932-0175 *see* 1932-0167 **868**
1932-0183 Basic Income Studies **1718**
1932-0191 Journal of Imagery Research in Sport and Physical Activity **7375**
1932-0205 Asian Journal of Comparative Law **4846**
1932-0213 Capitalism and Society **1537**
1932-0221 American Journal of Business Research **1725**
1932-023X The Pyrates Way **4344**
1932-0248 Journal of Hunger and Environmental Nutrition **6661**
1932-0256 *see* 1932-0248 **6661**
1932-0264 Fusion Authority Quarterly Update **2062**
1932-0280 *see* 1550-5340 **5378**
1932-0299 Sprouse Bros. CODE **2214**
1932-0329 Motor Trend Classic†
1932-0337 Fundamentals of Municipal Bond Law Seminar **4868**
1932-037X Yale Economic Review **1197**
1932-0388 Multifactor Productivity Trends *see* 1931-8626 **1272**
1932-0396 Northern Hemisphere Winter Summary **6392**
1932-040X Q U E R I Quarterly **7538**
1932-0418 Southern Hemisphere Winter Summary **6395**
1932-0426 Federal Reserve Bank of New York. Economic Policy Review **1486**
1932-0434 PolymerCafe **538**
1932-0442 Jottings (Greenville) **7737**
1932-0450 Clarion (Sacramento) **5002**
1932-0477 California Jury Instructions. Civil. C A C I Forms **4828**
1932-0485 California Jury Instructions - Criminal (C A L J I C) Forms **4885**
1932-0493 California Jury Instructions - Civil (B A J I) Forms **4828**
1932-0507 Ohio Education Laws **2893**
1932-0515 California Directory of Attorneys **4636**
1932-0523 Colorado Criminal and Motor Vehicle Law **4886**
1932-0531 Federal Criminal Practice. Seventh Circuit Handbook **4889**
1932-0582 Artscope (Quincy) **475**
1932-0590 Every Day with Rachael Ray **5070**
1932-0604 *see* 1932-0426 **1486**
1932-0612 Popular Culture and Politics in Asia Pacific **7172**
1932-0620 Journal of Addiction Medicine **2695**
1932-0663 Eurasian Population and Family History **7283**
1932-0795 Dexter: Ionia County Magazine **5069**
1932-0809 Liberty University Law Review **4723**
1932-0833 *see* 1932-0841 **1628**
1932-0841 Hidden Values Alert **1628**
1932-085X Workplace Injuries and Illnesses in (Year) **6691**
1932-0876 H S R & D Research Briefs **6423**
1932-0884 *see* 1932-085X **6691**
1932-0892 The Hurricane Review **5424**
1932-0906 Doubletruck Magazine **4574**
1932-0957 Moon Handbooks: Puerto Rico **8738**
1932-0965 Chem & Bio News **728**
1932-099X Ohio Construction and Code Journal **1028**
1932-1007 Traditional Rod & Kulture Illustrated **4349**
1932-1015 Dell Variety Word Search *changed to* 1944-429X **4333**
1932-1023 *see* 1932-0965 **728**
1932-1031 *see* 1932-104X **6764**
1932-104X Biofuels, Bioproducts and Biorefining **6764**
1932-1058 Biomicrofluidics **7006**
1932-1074 Current Diagnosis and Treatment in Neurology **6134**
1932-1082 Hunt Club Digest **8317**
1932-1112 Maine Curiosities **8732**
1932-1171 Every Woman **8845**
1932-1198 African Vibes **3516**
1932-1201 E D M O **3301**
1932-121X Synthesis Lectures on Speech and Audio Processing **5185**
1932-1228 Synthesis Lectures on Computer Science **2438**
1932-1236 Synthesis Lectures on Signal Processing **3221**
1932-1244 Synthesis Lectures on Communications **2339**
1932-1252 Synthesis Lectures on Computational Electromagnetics **3332**
1932-1260 Synthesis Lectures on Solid State Materials and Devices **3332**
1932-1279 Vehicle Search Law Deskbook **4807**
1932-1287 Batteries **1880**
1932-1295 Annual Intellectual Property Law Conference **6745**
1932-1309 The Sourcebook to Public Record Information **7469**
1932-1317 International Air Safety Seminar. Proceedings **60**
1932-1325 Knit Simple **6639**
1932-1333 N I A I D Funding News **5682**
1932-1341 Uniformed Services University of the Health Sciences Journal **6450**
1932-135X Hunting the Country **8318**
1932-1368 Professional Issues in Criminal Justice **4896**
1932-1376 *see* 1932-1368 **4896**
1932-1384 Virtual Instruments **6627**
1932-1406 Praeger Series on the Ancient World **4156**
1932-1422 *see* 1552-3136 **2525**
1932-1430 Uzuri **2262**
1932-1449 Asian Avenue Magazine **3520**
1932-1457 *see* 1932-1449 **3520**
1932-1465 International Review of Environmental and Resource Economics **1130**
1932-1473 *see* 1932-1465 **1130**
1932-1481 Journal of Neurodegeneration & Regeneration **6153**
1932-149X American Journal of Disaster Medicine **5572**
1932-1503 I E P Team Leader **3041**
1932-1511 Getting Started in Boats **8275**
1932-152X *see* 1932-1511 **8275**
1932-1562 Missouri D W I Handbook **4894**
1932-1570 Real Analysis Exchange. Summer Symposium Conference Reports *see* 0147-1937 **5528**
1932-1589 Florida Rules Of Civil Procedure **4831**
1932-1597 The A S T D State of the Industry Report *see* 1535-7740 **1876**
1932-1600 Shojo Beat **2213**
1932-1619 Natural Cures Newsletter **313**
1932-1627 Pegaso **5350**
1932-1635 The Washington State Genealogist **3787**
1932-1643 *see* 1932-1651 **7506**
1932-1651 Aging Trends **7506**
1932-1678 *see* 1932-121X **5185**
1932-1686 *see* 1932-1228 **2438**
1932-1694 *see* 1932-1236 **3221**
1932-1708 *see* 1932-1244 **2339**
1932-1716 *see* 1932-1252 **3332**
1932-1724 *see* 1932-1260 **3332**
1932-1732 Liberty Tree **7152**
1932-1740 Nolo's Quick LLC **1154**
1932-1767 A A A Living (Iowa Edition) **8679**
1932-1775 A A A Living (Illinois/N. Indiana Edition) **8679**
1932-1791 A A A Living (Minnesota Edition) **8679**
1932-1813 Cape May Magazine **8691**
1932-1821 Pittsburgh Tax Review **1939**
1932-183X American Law Reports, 6th **4615**
1932-1864 Statistical Analysis and Data Mining **8403**
1932-1872 *see* 1932-1864 **8403**
1932-1899 Interactive Citation Workbook for A L W D Citation Manual **4694**
1932-1902 International Wildland-Urban Interface Code **4696**
1932-1910 Directory of Law Reviews (Print)† **8950**
1932-1929 Officer's D U I Handbook **2662**
1932-1937 20 C F R 1910 O S H A General Industry Regulations Book **6689**
1932-1953 Pharma D D† **8980**
1932-1996 *see* 1932-1821 **1939**
1932-2003 *see* 1932-2011 **5289**
1932-2011 Electronic Literature Collection **5289**
1932-202X Journal of Advanced Academics **3042**
1932-2038 *see* 1932-2046 **4829**
1932-2046 The Connecticut Public Interest Law Journal **4829**
1932-2054 Global Business and Organizational Excellence **1748**
1932-2062 *see* 1932-2054 **1748**
1932-2070 Mountain Plains Journal of Business and Economics **1151**
1932-2089 North Carolina Juvenile Code: Practice and Procedure **4748**
1932-2100 Pennsylvania Super Lawyers **4757**
1932-2119 I E E E International Workshop on Source Code Analysis and Manipulation. Proceedings *changed to* 1942-5430 **2507**
1932-2127 International Topics **7246**
1932-2135 Asia-Pacific Journal of Chemical Engineering **3236**
1932-2143 *see* 1932-2135 **3236**
1932-216X 29 C F R 1926 O S H A Construction Industry Regulations **6689**
1932-2186 Limited Liability Entities **4875**
1932-2194 West's Colorado Civil Procedure Law **4844**
1932-2208 Pennsylvania Employment Law **1871**
1932-2216 National Fair Housing Advocate **4420**
1932-2224 *see* 1932-2216 **4420**
1932-2232 A C M Communications in Computer Algebra **5549**
1932-2240 *see* 1932-2232 **5549**
1932-2259 Journal of Cancer Survivorship **6024**
1932-2267 *see* 1932-2259 **6024**
1932-2275 Anesthesiology Clinics **5770**
1932-2291 *see* 1932-2704 **7506**
1932-2305 Philanthropy *changed to* 1932-2313 **8062**
1932-2313 Philanthropy World **8062**
1932-2321 Reliability: Theory & Applications **3217**
1932-2348 Cho Trin **7701**
1932-2356 U F R A Straight Tip **3581**
1932-2364 Annual Survey of International and Comparative Law **4917**
1932-2372 Dispatch *changed to* 1948-1217 **5285**
1932-2380 I E E E International Frequency Control Symposium & Exposition. Proceedings **3102**
1932-2399 Morningstar E T Fs 100 *changed to* Morningstar E T Fs 150 **1641**
1932-2402 Home Business Tax Deductions **1961**
1932-2410 Institutional Pharmacy Practice. Handbook **6849**
1932-2437 The Status of Women in the States **8903**
1932-2453 From the Cellar **603**
1932-2461 Carolina Uncorked **601**
1932-2488 Industrial Embedded Systems **2461**

ISSN

Link to your serials resources and content with ulrichsweb.com

1932-670X Environmental & Energy Law & Policy Journal **3134**
1932-6718 Hermit Kingdom Studies in Christianity and Judaism **7647**
1932-6726 Hermit Kingdom Studies in Identity and Society **8105**
1932-6742 West's Jury Verdicts. Nevada Reports **4967**
1932-6769 The R Ver's Friend **8675**
1932-6777 Who's Buying for Travel **8775**
1932-6785 Who's Buying Groceries **3667**
1932-6793 Who's Buying Entertainment **4984**
1932-6807 Who's Buying Information Products and Services **1848**
1932-6815 Who's Buying Apparel **2250**
1932-6823 Who's Buying at Restaurants and Carry-Outs **3667**
1932-6831 Fodor's See It. Prague **8709**
1932-6858 Expose (New London) **5294**
1932-6866 Southern Indiana Review **5375**
1932-6882 Draw! **487**
1932-6904 Back Issue **477**
1932-6912 The Jack Kirby Collector **498**
1932-6920 *see* 0090-2934 **6267**
1932-6947 Democracy and the News **4574**
1932-6963 The S R V Journal **8130**
1932-6971 U - The Union Magazine **5085**
1932-698X @ This Point **7623**
1932-6998 Righteous Nurse Magazine **5980**
1932-7005 *see* 1932-6254 **750**
1932-7013 Blueeyes Magazine **6964**
1932-7021 Healthcare Finance News **4097**
1932-703X A A Golf Magazine **8219**
1932-7048 Cities and the Environment **3410**
1932-7056 The Journal of Cuban Business Studies **1134**
1932-7129 Neonatology Today **6097**
1932-7137 *see* 1932-7129 **6097**
1932-7145 Research Foundation Literature Reviews **1647**
1932-7153 *see* 1931-3500 **1946**
1932-7161 Case in Point (Reno) **4641**
1932-7188 Advanced Issues & Practical Application of the (Year) Divorce Code Amendments† **8928**
1932-720X A I R A Journal **1055**
1932-7218 Litigation Watch. Welding Fume **4724**
1932-7226 Profiles of Texas **3122**
1932-7242 Christian Retail Trends Report **1810**
1932-7250 New Hampshire Juvenile and Family Law and Rules **4913**
1932-7269 Mid-Atlantic Executive Legal Adviser **4876**
1932-7293 Proxy Solicitor Comparison Report **1646**
1932-7315 Wild Bird News (Fairfield County Edition) *see* Wild Bird News **917**
1932-7323 New Jersey Curiosities **8741**
1932-7331 Kansas Curiosities **8727**
1932-734X Virginia Curiosities **8772**
1932-7358 Kentucky Curiosities **8727**
1932-7366 Indiana Curiosities **8721**
1932-7374 Palabra (Los Angeles) **5348**
1932-7382 Testify Sister Magazine **8885**
1932-7404 ViaMei **8772**
1932-7420 *see* 1550-4131 **829**
1932-7447 The Journal of Physical Chemistry Part C: Nanomaterials and Interfaces **2137**
1932-7455 *see* 1932-7447 **2137**
1932-748X I A B E Annual Conference. Proceedings (Online) **1120**
1932-7498 *see* 1932-748X **1120**
1932-7501 Journal of Cardiopulmonary Rehabilitation and Prevention **5792**
1932-751X *see* 1932-7501 **5792**
1932-7528 Journal for Learning through the Arts **2873**
1932-7587 Sensing and Instrumentation for Food Quality and Safety **3663**
1932-7595 Haruah: Breath of Heaven **7646**
1932-7609 *see* 1932-7595 **7646**
1932-7625 The L L I Review **2881**
1932-7633 *see* 1932-7625 **2881**
1932-7641 *see* 1932-765X **7848**
1932-765X Columbia Undergraduate Science Journal **7848**
1932-7692 Cosmetic Surgery Products **6240**
1932-7706 Smart Labels **1176**
1932-7714 Clean Room Consumables **1083**
1932-7722 Private Security Services **2679**
1932-7730 World Cement & Concrete Additives **1908**
1932-7749 Innovate (Boston) **1753**
1932-7757 Diagnostics & Imaging Week **5905**
1932-7765 BioWorld Week **662**
1932-779X C 16 Autostyle **8570**
1932-7803 B P M **5065**
1932-782X Chicago Lifestyle Magazine **5068**
1932-7846 I C C T E Journal **2865**
1932-7862 The Source (Schaumburg) **4111**
1932-7870 Moon Handbooks. Bermuda **8737**
1932-7889 International Journal of Terrorism and Political Hot Spots **7244**
1932-7897 Adobe illustrator Techniques **2483**
1932-7927 Respiratory Management **6218**
1932-796X Tiger Beat **2217**
1932-7978 *see* 1932-7986 **7104**
1932-7986 Albanian Journal of Politics **7104**
1932-8001 Gastroenterology Hepatology Annual Review **5925**
1932-8028 Business Torts **4859**
1932-8036 International Journal of Communication **8108**
1932-8044 Missbehave Magazine **8875**
1932-8052 V-Twin Annual **8270**
1932-8060 Global-e **7966**
1932-8079 Praeger Series on Contemporary Health and Living **5698**
1932-8087 Professional Case Management **5978**
1932-8095 *see* 1932-8087 **5978**
1932-8109 E H S Quarterly Review **7514**
1932-8117 The American (Washington, D.C.) **7104**
1932-8125 *see* 1932-8117 **7104**
1932-8133 The Guide to Experts in Animal Issues **319**
1932-8141 N O B C Ch E News Online **3251**
1932-8184 I E E E Systems Journal **2520**
1932-8206 N H Writer **7568**
1932-8214 Speech Strategy News **2339**
1932-8222 Greatest Uncommon Denominator Magazine **5302**
1932-8230 *see* 1932-8222 **5302**
1932-8249 Innovation (Albuquerque) **1889**
1932-8257 Journal of Life Sciences **683**
1932-829X Annual editions: Film **6489**
1932-8303 Total Landscape Care **3752**
1932-8311 Next Truck **8674**
1932-832X The Woodson Review **3572**
1932-8338 A S A L H's Annual Theme Magazine *changed to* 1932-832X **3572**
1932-8346 Foundations and Trends in Signal Processing **5552**
1932-8354 *see* 1932-8346 **5552**
1932-8362 Sportsfield Management **3751**
1932-8370 Foodservice Disposables **3643**
1932-8397 Biocides **3236**
1932-8400 Automotive Aftermarket in China **1806**
1932-8419 H V A C Equipment **4120**
1932-8427 Insulation (Cleveland) **1015**
1932-8435 Prefabricated Building Systems, Nonresidential **1029**
1932-8443 International Journal of Education Research **2869**
1932-8451 Developmental Neurobiology **921**
1932-846X *see* 1932-8451 **921**
1932-8478 Contemporary Aesthetics **6911**
1932-8486 The Anatomical Record **652**
1932-8494 *see* 1932-8486 **652**
1932-8524 The Auditor **1281**
1932-8540 I E E E - R I T A **2865**
1932-8575 Journal of Human Capital **1136**
1932-8591 Journal of the U S S J W P **8827**
1932-8605 Impressions Newsletter **5073**
1932-8621 Personality and Mental Health **6173**
1932-863X *see* 1932-8621 **6173**
1932-8648 The Global South **5218**
1932-8656 *see* 1932-8648 **5218**
1932-8664 *see* 1932-8575 **1136**
1932-8680 Polyphony H S **5353**
1932-8699 Let's Prepare for the Grade Eight Intermediate Social Studies Test *changed to* 1930-3610 **2891**
1932-8710 Current Nursing in Geriatric Care **4043**
1932-8729 Current Activities in Longterm Care **4043**
1932-8737 *see* 0160-9289 **5783**
1932-8745 *see* 0161-0457 **900**
1932-8788 Onsite Fitness **6994**
1932-8796 N B E R International Seminar on Macroeconomics **1720**
1932-880X AbqArts **4975**
1932-8818 International Journal for the History of Mathematics Education **5495**
1932-8826 *see* 1932-8818 **5495**
1932-8842 Fit Yoga **6985**
1932-8893 Your Health Now **5734**
1932-8907 Mealey's Litigation Report: Benzene **4836**
1932-8931 Ventanas **4552**
1932-894X *see* 1932-8931 **4552**
1932-8966 Registered Nurse **5979**
1932-8982 The Healthcare Ledger **5626**
1932-8990 Hotel Design **4389**
1932-9008 Inside Alternative Mortgages **7595**
1932-9024 Executive Counsel **1743**
1932-9032 *see* 0898-6630 **5893**
1932-9040 West's Jury Verdicts. Virginia Reports **4813**
1932-9059 Guide to Federal Pharmacy Law **4869**
1932-9067 West's Jury Verdicts. Washington Reports **4813**
1932-9075 E S R Review **1336**
1932-9083 *see* 1930-8132 **5335**
1932-9091 Hair's How **588**
1932-9105 Aggieland Illustrated Magazine **8220**
1932-9113 Sherman's Travel **8755**
1932-9121 Craft **532**
1932-9148 Journal of Tort Law **4704**
1932-9156 Journal of Business Valuation and Economic Loss Analysis **1134**
1932-9164 Mobile Display Report **3109**
1932-9237 Pet Style News **6813**
1932-9253 *see* 1932-9997 **6989**
1932-9261 Journal of Clinical Sport Psychology **7370**
1932-927X *see* 1932-9261 **7370**
1932-9288 Journal of Online Business **1420**
1932-9296 Taking Sides: Clashing Views on Latin American Issues **4314**
1932-9326 Lifted Magazine **7660**
1932-9334 Protective Packaging **6714**
1932-9342 Wheelchairs & Other Personal Mobility Devices **1194**
1932-9369 Information Security (Cleveland) **2677**
1932-9377 World Water Treatment Products **8842**
1932-9385 Wall Coverings **4552**
1932-9407 Glimpse (Providence)†
1932-9431 Media & Communications Report **2332**
1932-944X Victorian Life and Times **4277**
1932-9466 Applications and Applied Mathematics **5471**
1932-9474 Terrain.Org (Tucson) **2629**
1932-9482 Persistently Safe Schools. Proceedings **2897**
1932-9490 *see* 1932-9482 **2897**
1932-9504 *see* 1932-9482 **2897**
1932-9520 Current Cardiovascular Risk Reports **5784**
1932-9555 *see* 1932-4855 **5026**
1932-9563 *see* 1932-9520 **5784**
1932-958X *see* 1070-6488 **7825**
1932-9598 Le Fanu Studies **5414**
1932-9601 Gleanings (Buhler) **6639**
1932-961X PharmaVoice **6874**
1932-9628 The Santa Cruz Comic News **7181**
1932-9636 Workers' Comp. Illinois **1715**
1932-9644 *see* 1932-9636 **1715**
1932-9652 Workers' Comp. New York **1715**
1932-9660 *see* 1932-9652 **1715**
1932-9679 Workers' Comp. Ohio **1715**
1932-9687 *see* 1932-9679 **1715**
1932-9695 Workers' Comp. Pennsylvania **1715**
1932-9709 *see* 1932-9695 **1715**
1932-9717 Workers' Comp. Texas **1715**
1932-9725 *see* 1932-9717 **1715**
1932-9733 The School District Budget Report **3031**
1932-9741 *see* 1932-9733 **3031**
1932-975X Landlord Tenant. California **7598**
1932-9768 *see* 1932-975X **7598**
1932-9776 Landlord Tenant. New York **7598**
1932-9784 *see* 1932-9776 **7598**
1932-9792 Landlord Tenant. Ohio **7598**
1932-9806 *see* 1932-9792 **7598**
1932-9814 Landlord Tenant. Pennsylvania **7598**
1932-9822 *see* 1932-9814 **7598**
1932-9830 Computer Crime and Technology in Law Enforcement **2512**
1932-9849 *see* 1932-9830 **2512**
1932-9857 Workers' Comp. Florida **1715**
1932-9865 *see* 1932-9857 **1715**
1932-9881 U S C W C Journal on Wireless Communications **2343**
1932-9911 C O B R A Handbook **4497**
1932-992X *see* 1932-9911 **4497**
1932-9954 *see* 1932-7587 **3663**
1932-9962 M C Magazine **1021**
1932-9970 *see* 1932-9962 **1021**
1932-9997 International Journal of Aquatic Research and Education **6989**
1933-0022 *see* 1933-0030 **1222**
1933-0030 Consumer Price Index. Pacific Cities & U.S. Average **1222**
1933-0049 Interdisciplinary Journal of Human Rights Law **7210**
1933-0057 Confluence (Norman) **2974**
1933-0065 Early Modern Women **8895**
1933-0111 Lotus Leaves **503**
1933-0138 Summary Health Statistics for U.S. Adults **7549**
1933-0197 Geek Monthly **2381**
1933-0219 Mucosal Immunology **5764**
1933-0227 Spanglish Times **3565**
1933-0243 Accounting Policy & Practice Series **1278**
1933-0251 *see* 1060-8265 **6302**
1933-026X *see* 1537-6680 **8102**
1933-0278 *see* 1532-6306 **6284**
1933-0286 Landlord Tenant. Florida **7598**
1933-0294 *see* 1933-0286 **7598**
1933-0308 Landlord Tenant. Illinois **7598**
1933-0316 *see* 1933-0308 **7598**
1933-0324 Journal of Nature Science and Sustainable Technology **3140**
1933-0383 *see* 1933-0391 **5323**
1933-0391 Literafeelya Magazine **5323**
1933-0405 C S E R Review **7629**
1933-0421 *see* 1939-8565 **3204**
1933-0529 LexisNexis Antitrust Litigation News **4723**
1933-0553 LexisNexis Real Estate Report **7598**
1933-057X W f m **4527**
1933-0596 North Dakota Medicine **5688**
1933-060X Advisor Guide to Microsoft Visual FoxPro *changed to* Databased Advisor Magazine **2554**
1933-0618 MiBiz **1149**
1933-0626 North Carolina Conference Christian Advocate **7769**
1933-0634 Romantic Times Book Reviews **5412**
1933-0642 Krave Magazine **3546**
1933-0677 Clinical Oncology News **6016**
1933-0693 *see* 0022-3085 **6155**
1933-0707 Journal of Neurosurgery: Pediatrics **6155**
1933-0715 *see* 1933-0707 **6155**
1933-0723 Rome Directions **8753**
1933-0731 Ibiza & Formentera Directions **8720**
1933-074X Armenia and Karabagh **8684**
1933-0766 Frommer's Irreverent Guide to Walt Disney World **8711**
1933-0774 Costa Rica for Dummies **8695**
1933-0782 StyleCity Rome **8758**
1933-0790 Florence Directions **8703**
1933-0839 Frommer's Los Cabos & Baja **8711**
1933-0847 Scleroderma **5881**
1933-0855 *see* 1933-0847 **5881**
1933-0863 Kidney Cancer Journal **6026**
1933-0871 *see* 1933-0863 **6026**
1933-088X Advances in Pulmonary Hypertension **5775**
1933-0898 *see* 1933-088X **5775**
1933-0901 Profile (Washington, D C) **1787**
1933-091X *see* 1933-0901 **1787**
1933-0928 Fodor's Prague's 25 Best **8708**
1933-0936 Fodor's Munich's 25 Best **8707**
1933-0944 Fodor's Toronto's 25 Best **8709**
1933-0952 Fodor's Tokyo's 25 Best **8709**
1933-0960 Key to Rome **8727**
1933-0979 Critical Perspectives on Modern Culture **8096**
1933-0987 Critical Perspectives in Social Theory **7956**
1933-0995 $1,000,000aire Blueprints **1149**
1933-1010 Southern Genealogist's Exchange Society Quarterly **3783**
1933-1029 North Carolina Notary Law Primer **4748**
1933-1045 Berkeley Journal of Gender, Law & Justice **4629**
1933-1053 Cracking the A P Spanish Exam **2975**
1933-1061 Winter Bird Highlights **917**
1933-107X World Monuments Fund. Annual Report **461**
1933-1088 Maryland & the District of Columbia Laws Governing Business Entities **4875**
1933-1096 704 **5087**
1933-1126 Survey Report on Accounting & Finance Personnel Compensation **1709**
1933-1134 Natural Home **4364**
1933-1185 Journal of Ethics in Leadership **8113**
1933-1193 Urgent Care† **8996**
1933-1223 Pacific Islands Policy **7163**
1933-124X United States. Federal Library and Information Center Committee. Annual Report **5052**
1933-1258 Hate Crime Statistics (Online) **2674**
1933-1266 Neurology, Neurophysiology and Neuroscience (Online) **6166**
1933-1274 L L R **1691**
1933-1304 Executive Decision **1743**
1933-1312 I B M Systems Magazine (Mainframe Edition) **2520**
1933-1347 Committee on Pretrial Practice & Discovery **4947**

ISSN

1934-6859 *see* 1934-6840 **2870**
1934-6867 Online Journal of Rural and Urban Research
1934-6875 Journal of Educational Research & Policy Studies **2876**
1934-6883 *see* 1934-6875 **2876**
1934-6980 Sustainable Facility **3148**
1934-6999 Debt-Proof Living **2637**
1934-7030 Sunshine State T E S O L Journal **2916**
1934-7065 Shimmy Magazine **6299**
1934-709X Beauty / Truth **5417**
1934-7103 Strategic Financial Planning **4112**
1934-7111 Michigan Sociological Review **8121**
1934-712X The Last Gunfighter **5411**
1934-7138 Rough Justice **5365**
1934-7146 Alien Deception **5439**
1934-7154 Billibub Baddings and the Case of the Singing Sword **5440**
1934-7170 Issues in Aviation Law and Policy **4697**
1934-7189 Journal of Medical and Biological Sciences **5651**
1934-7197 Journal of Engineering, Computing & Architecture **3204**
1934-7200 Journal of Education & Human Development **2875**
1934-7219 Journal of Business and Public Affairs (St. Cloud) **1133**
1934-7227 Journal of Humanities & Social Sciences **4460**
1934-7235 Journal of Agricultural, Food, and Environmental Sciences **126**
1934-7243 *see* 0736-9387 **3036**
1934-7251 Milestones in Business History **1546**
1934-7294 *see* 1559-3096 **4582**
1934-7316 The Progressive Christian **7771**
1934-7332 Computer Technology and Application **2412**
1934-7340 *see* 1934-7332 **2412**
1934-7359 Journal of Civil Engineering and Architecture **3274**
1934-7367 *see* 1934-7359 **3274**
1934-7375 Journal of Chemistry and Chemical Engineering **2067**
1934-7383 *see* 1934-7375 **2067**
1934-7391 Journal of Life Sciences (Libertyville) **683**
1934-7405 *see* 1934-7391 **683**
1934-7413 ExtraOrdinary Technology **8422**
1934-7421 The Rampant Colt **4345**
1934-743X Fuel **1886**
1934-7448 The Watermark (Boston) **5397**
1934-7502 The Business of Caring **5953**
1934-7529 The Jewish Role in American Life **3543**
1934-7545 Industry In:Site **589**
1934-7553 Residential Design and Build **1033**
1934-7561 Y-te **5732**
1934-7588 New York Nurse **5971**
1934-7596 *see* 1934-7588 **5971**
1934-7626 Nu Delta Alpha. Journal **2687**
1934-7634 *see* 1934-7626 **2687**
1934-7642 Central Texas Pony Express Magazine **8289**
1934-7650 Intercultural Human Rights Law Review **4694**
1934-7677 Journal of Undergraduate Materials Research **3351**
1934-7715 *see* 1064-5578 **7414**
1934-7790 Bath Makeovers **4532**
1934-7804 Old Home Renovation **1028**
1934-7820 Gastrointestinal Cancer Research **6020**
1934-7847 Beverage Business Insights **599**
1934-7855 *see* 1063-4541 **5532**
1934-7863 *see* 0190-2717 **573**
1934-7871 *see* 0747-9239 **2789**
1934-788X *see* 1061-3862 **7055**
1934-7898 *see* 1060-992X **7082**
1934-7901 *see* 1068-7998 **69**
1934-791X *see* 0096-3925 **690**
1934-7928 *see* 0147-6874 **242**
1934-7936 *see* 0025-6544 **7061**
1934-7944 *see* 8756-6990 **3110**
1934-7979 Voz Latina **3571**
1934-7987 *see* 1934-7820 **6020**
1934-8002 *see* 1068-3755 **3396**
1934-8010 *see* 1068-3712 **3329**
1934-8029 *see* 0361-5219 **3255**
1934-8037 *see* 1068-3674 **153**
1934-8045 *see* 1066-5307 **5513**
1934-8061 *see* 0735-2727 **3112**
1934-807X *see* 1541-308X **7034**
1934-8088 *see* 1068-798X **5459**
1934-8096 *see* 1068-3739 **6394**
1934-810X *see* 1066-369X **5531**
1934-8118 *see* 0147-6882 **5046**
1934-8126 *see* 1055-1344 **5536**
1934-8134 CoffeeHouse Digest **4383**
1934-8142 Carolinas Commercial Properties **7586**
1934-8150 *see* 1551-7411 **6878**
1934-8169 Georgia Commercial Properties **7591**
1934-8177 Residential Concrete **1032**
1934-8193 In the Ring **8107**
1934-8207 *see* 1934-8193 **8107**
1934-8223 International Comparisons of Manufacturing Productivity and Unit Labor Cost Trends (Year) **1688**
1934-8231 Pharmaceutical Research and Manufacturers of America. Industry Profile **6870**
1934-824X *see* University of Wisconsin, Madison. Institute for Research on Poverty. Discussion Papers **8013**
1934-8274 On-E Magazine **6972**
1934-8282 Current Protocols in Pharmacology **6831**
1934-8290 *see* 1934-8282 **6831**
1934-8304 Onsite Water Treatment **3509**
1934-8312 *see* 1934-8304 **3509**
1934-8339 International Journal of Development Studies **1599**
1934-8347 Paddling Life **8280**
1934-8363 National Geographic Little Kids **2204**
1934-8371 *see* 0005-1055 **5202**
1934-838X *see* 1068-3356 **7024**
1934-8398 *see* 1068-364X **3241**
1934-8401 *see* 0884-5913 **577**
1934-841X *see* 0891-4168 **893**
1934-8428 *see* 0278-6419 **2527**
1934-8436 *see* 0145-8752 **2756**
1934-8444 *see* 0027-1322 **5519**
1934-8452 *see* 0027-1330 **7061**
1934-8460 *see* 0027-1349 **7026**
1934-8479 Water Efficiency **8837**
1934-8487 *see* 1934-8479 **8837**
1934-8495 International Energy Annual (Year) (Online Edition) **3138**
1934-8509 U.S. Department of Energy. Energy Information Administration. International Petroleum Monthly (Online) **6795**
1934-8592 Journal of Geophysical Research: Planets *see* 1934-8843 **2750**
1934-8592 Journal of Geophysical Research: Planets *see* 0148-0227 **2785**
1934-8606 Creative College Teaching Journal **3055**
1934-8630 Biointerphases **7841**
1934-8665 World Art Glass Quarterly **2046**
1934-8673 U.S. Merchandise Trade. FT920, Selected Highlights **1272**
1934-8681 Collision (Kirkland) **7513**
1934-8703 *see* 1058-0530 **5061**
1934-8711 Theology for Ministry **7777**
1934-8754 Kidney Disease Research Updates **6270**
1934-8762 Urologic Diseases Research Updates **6276**
1934-8770 Research Updates in Kidney and Urologic Health *changed to* 1934-8762 **6276**
1934-8770 Research Updates in Kidney and Urologic Health *changed to* 1934-8754 **6270**
1934-8800 *see* 0163-6383 **7362**
1934-8819 Hardware Retailing (Indianapolis) **4438**
1934-8827 Publio **5355**
1934-8835 International Journal of Organizational Analysis **1760**
1934-8843 Journal of Geophysical Research: Solid Earth **2750**
1934-8851 U.S. National Oceanic and Atmospheric Administration. Annual Climate Diagnostics and Prediction Workshop. Proceedings **6397**
1934-8908 The Hardy Review **5303**
1934-8916 *see* 1934-8908 **5303**
1934-8924 *see* 0748-8491 **2847**
1934-8932 Journal of Environmental Science and Engineering **3446**
1934-8940 *see* 1934-8932 **3446**
1934-8959 Journal of Materials Science and Engineering **3350**
1934-8967 *see* 1934-8959 **3350**
1934-8975 Journal of Energy and Power Engineering **3140**
1934-8983 *see* 1934-8975 **3140**
1934-9009 *see* 1096-2492 **8088**
1934-9017 Dapper **3974**
1934-9041 *see* 0016-9862 **3040**
1934-9076 Speaker (Tempe) **5176**
1934-922X Senior Softball News **8245**
1934-9238 Science Studies Weekly. Exploration **7911**
1934-9246 U S A Studies Weekly - 1865 to Present **4315**
1934-9319 Kansas Statistical Abstract (Online) **8384**
1934-9343 *see* 0023-0790 **7269**
1934-936X *see* 1063-455X **8827**
1934-9378 *see* 1068-3372 **7020**
1934-9386 *see* 1068-3666 **3385**
1934-9394 *see* 1052-6188 **5454**
1934-9408 *see* 1063-4576 **7023**
1934-9416 *see* 1068-3623 **5502**
1934-9424 *see* 0003-701X **3176**
1934-9432 *see* 1062-8738 **7038**
1934-9440 *see* 0095-4527 **865**
1934-9467 Poet Express **5430**
1934-9475 Hunter Jumper **8293**
1934-9491 Intellectual and Developmental Disabilities **3041**
1934-9521 T & E Magazine **8759**
1934-9548 *see* 1934-3884 **1367**
1934-9556 *see* 1934-9491 **3041**
1934-9602 Journal of Learning Management **2877**
1934-9610 *see* 1934-9602 **2877**
1934-9629 Berkeley Journal of Criminal Law **4629**
1934-9637 Journal of Spirituality in Mental Health **7381**
1934-9645 *see* 1934-9637 **7381**
1934-9653 *see* 1934-9629 **4629**
1934-967X Current G E R D Reports†
1934-9688 Projections (New York) **6510**
1934-9696 *see* 1934-9688 **6510**
1934-970X *see* 1067-8212 **6331**
1934-9718 Mealey's Insurance Regulatory Compliance Report **4514**
1934-9726 International Journal of Teacher Leadership **2871**
1934-9742 Jebsen Center for Counter-Terrorism Studies Research Briefing Series **7247**
1934-9750 World Spine Journal **6075**
1934-9769 TheStreet.com Ratings' Guide to Closed-End Mutual Funds *changed to* 1936-9840 **1655**
1934-9777 Kids on Wheels (Kids' Edition) **2158**
1934-9785 Play Therapy **6174**
1934-9793 Western Price Summary **3717**
1934-9807 Nature's Garden **3744**
1934-9831 Create Magazine (West Coast Edition) *see* 1935-0813 **23**
1934-984X Create Magazine. (Midwest Edition) *see* 1935-0813 **23**
1934-9858 Create Magazine. (Northeast Edition) *see* 1935-0813 **23**
1934-9866 Neuroaxis **6067**
1934-9882 Home Media Magazine **2401**
1934-9890 *see* 1934-9882 **2401**
1934-9904 Eating Napa & Sonoma **8699**
1934-9920 *see* 1934-9793 **3717**
1934-9939 Value (Plymouth) **1191**
1934-9947 *see* 1934-9939 **1191**
1934-9963 Stone Canoe **5378**
1934-9971 Journal of the Society for Chemical Industry **2069**
1934-998X Journal of Applied Chemistry†
1935-0007 A E L E Monthly Law Journal **4607**
1935-0015 Florida Super Lawyers **4676**
1935-0031 TheStreet.com Ratings' Guide to Common Stocks **1655**
1935-004X TheStreet.com Ratings' Guide to Bond and Money Market Mutual Funds **1655**
1935-0058 TheStreet.com Ratings' Guide to Banks and Thrifts **1386**
1935-0090 Applied Mathematics & Information Sciences **5472**
1935-0104 Menopause (Norwalk) **5998**
1935-0112 The Journal of Design & Management **498**
1935-0120 *see* 1935-0112 **498**
1935-0139 *see* 0474-4772 **2128**
1935-0163 Pluck! **5352**
1935-0171 Salvo (Chicago) **7741**
1935-018X *see* 1521-1525 **2112**
1935-0198 Outreach (Athens) **2997**
1935-0201 *see* 0193-5380 **4217**
1935-021X *see* 0093-8297 **5287**
1935-0228 *see* 0160-0923 **5304**
1935-0236 *see* 0034-4338 **5359**
1935-0244 *see* 0196-6286 **5399**
1935-0252 *see* 0010-6356 **5278**
1935-0260 *see* 0027-1314 **2073**
1935-0279 Trader Monthly†
1935-0309 Environmental Alert **3506**
1935-0317 Frommer's Amalfi Coast with Naples, Capri & Pompeii **8710**
1935-0325 General Structures **443**
1935-0333 Fodor's Venice's 25 Best **8710**
1935-0341 National Geographic Traveler. Canada **8740**
1935-035X General Structures. Questions & Answers **443**
1935-0368 Motley Fool Global Gains **1641**
1935-0384 Faith Grand Rapids **7797**
1935-0392 Ohio Outdoor News **8326**
1935-0414 J P G **6970**
1935-0422 Kinetic Art Words **500**
1935-0430 A V Woman **8850**
1935-0449 Total Texas Baseball **8249**
1935-0457 People Style Watch **2260**
1935-049X Database of Foodservice Technology **3633**
1935-052X Journal of Education Research **2875**
1935-0546 Standard Catalog of Baseball Cards **8209**
1935-0562 North American Coins & Prices **6652**
1935-0570 Sci D A C Review **2437**
1935-0589 *see* 1935-0570 **2437**
1935-0600 Privacy & Data Security Law Journal **2515**
1935-0619 The Rough Guide to First-Time Asia **8753**
1935-0627 An Unauthorized Guide to Fire-King Glasswares **2046**
1935-0635 Goldmine Records & Prices **4335**
1935-0643 The Journal for the Study of Sephardic and Mizrahi Jewry **7725**
1935-066X L T T R **502**
1935-0678 Remodel **455**
1935-0686 Looking Up **1021**
1935-0694 *see* 1935-0686 **1021**
1935-0716 California School Business **2834**
1935-0724 Slow Cooker Favorites **4367**
1935-0759 *see* 1933-1762 **7818**
1935-0767 *see* 1933-9275 **2631**
1935-0783 Jefferson Journal of Psychiatry (Online) **6149**
1935-0791 Ellipsis **5289**
1935-0805 Medical Product Outsourcing **1148**
1935-0813 Create Magazine (Southeast Edition) **23**
1935-0821 Create Magazine (Southwest Edition) *see* 1935-0813 **23**
1935-083X China Trade **1616**
1935-0848 Site Planning **457**
1935-0856 Old Fishing Lures & Tackle **8326**
1935-0880 Advanced Topics in Information Resources Management **1724**
1935-0929 I B M Systems Magazine (Open Systems Edition) **2520**
1935-0937 Access California Wine Country **8680**
1935-0945 The Best Test Preparation for the C L E P **4285**
1935-0961 Fashion Rocks **2255**
1935-097X Ha-Tanin **7721**
1935-0988 *see* 0967-0912 **6333**
1935-1011 *see* 0002-8312 **2825**
1935-102X E R Online *see* 0013-189X **2851**
1935-1038 *see* 0091-732X **2905**
1935-1046 *see* 0034-6543 **2905**
1935-1054 *see* 1076-9986 **2934**
1935-1062 *see* 0162-3737 **3021**
1935-1089 Retinal Cases & Brief Reports **6050**
1935-1097 I B M Systems Magazine (i5 Business Systems Edition) **2420**
1935-1100 EServer Magazine (Iseries Edition) *changed to* 1935-1097 **2420**
1935-1135 Oregon Curiosities **8745**
1935-1178 International Corporate Responsibility Series **1754**
1935-1216 Child Abuse and Domestic Violence **8032**
1935-1232 Clinical Schizophrenia & Related Psychoses **7345**
1935-1259 Sporting Woman Quarterly **8206**
1935-1275 *see* 0082-500X **2082**
1935-1291 Perspectives on Language and Literacy **3045**
1935-1305 Bayou **5260**
1935-1313 *see* 1934-2780 **3978**
1935-1429 You Name it Sports **8217**
1935-1437 Inside the Hospital C-Suite **1753**
1935-1445 E M S Product News **7514**
1935-1453 Report of the Tarlton Law Library **5043**
1935-147X Sales Insider **1903**
1935-1488 Good **3976**
1935-1496 S X S World **34**
1935-150X Home & Towne **5073**
1935-1518 *see* 1935-150X **5073**
1935-1526 Congress Quarterly **6240**
1935-1534 Journal of Computing and e-Systems **2523**
1935-1542 HmoobTeen **3538**
1935-1569 F G **5118**
1935-1577 Journal of Brief, Strategic & Systemic Therapies **7369**
1935-1585 Scotts Lawns & Landscapes **3750**
1935-1593 The Little Lutheran **7765**
1935-1607 Drumhead **6563**
1935-1615 UP Magazine **5243**
1935-1623 O N S Connect **6029**
1935-1631 Memorytrends Magazine *changed to* Craftrends (Online) **8946**
1935-164X Harvard Medical School Perspectives on Prostate Disease **6268**
1935-1658 Find It! (Des Moines) **2152**
1935-1666 Custom Storage **4536**

ISSN

ISSN

ISSN

1937-6278	China Economic Law Review†	
1937-6286	China Public Policy Review†	
1937-6294	China Agricultural Economics†	
1937-6308	China Tourism Journal†	
1937-6316	China Accounting Journal†	
1937-6324	China Management Empirical Research†	
1937-6332	China International Trade Research†	
1937-6340	China Media and Publishing†	
1937-6359	Blasting and Fragmentation 3236	
1937-6375	M C A T Workout 5662	
1937-6405	Western Shooting Horse 8300	
1937-6413	see 1937-6405 8300	
1937-6421	Scrip Drug Market Developments 5711	
1937-643X	see 1937-6421 5711	
1937-6448	International Review of Cell and Molecular Biology 833	
1937-6456	Journal of Scientific Conference Proceedings 7873	
1937-6464	see 1937-6456 7873	
1937-6472	Progress in Electromagnetics Research B 7052	
1937-6480	Progress in Electromagnetics Research Letters 7052	
1937-6510	Women and Minorities in Politics 7193	
1937-6529	Journal of Radio & Audio Media 2359	
1937-6537	see 1937-6529 2359	
1937-6545	The Nay Sprayer 3500	
1937-6561	Coastal Style 3727	
1937-657X	see 1937-6561 3727	
1937-6626	TheStreet.com Ratings' Guide to Life and Annuity Insurers 4525	
1937-6634	Report on Research Compliance 4769	
1937-6642	Medicare Part D Compliance News 4515	
1937-6650	Health Plan Week 4505	
1937-6669	The H C C A - A I S Medicaid Compliance News 4504	
1937-6677	Inside Consumer-Directed Care 4102	
1937-6685	Specialty Pharmacy News 6881	
1937-6693	see 1937-6650 4505	
1937-6707	see 1937-6669 4504	
1937-6715	see 1937-6677 4102	
1937-6723	see 1937-6685 6881	
1937-6731	see 1937-6642 4515	
1937-674X	see 1937-6634 4769	
1937-6774	Gases & Instrumentation 3244	
1937-6782	see 1937-6774 3244	
1937-6790	The Home Railway Journal 8618	
1937-6804	The Journal of a Musician 6580	
1937-6812	African Geographical Review 3997	
1937-6820	Journal of Financial and Economic Practice 1361	
1937-6839	The Journal of Business Management and Change 1764	
1937-6847	Eastview 2979	
1937-6855	The Learning Principal 3026	
1937-6863	The Learning System 3026	
1937-6871	Journal of Biomedical Science and Engineering 5646	
1937-688X	see 1937-6871 5646	
1937-6898	International Pharmaceutical Quality 6850	
1937-6901	see 1937-6898 6850	
1937-691X	Trips & Getaways 8769	
1937-6928	Learning Disabilities 3043	
1937-6936	see 1937-6928 3043	
1937-6944	Second Sight 4111	
1937-6952	Cardiovascular Business 5780	
1937-6960	see 1937-6952 5780	
1937-6979	C V B News 5779	
1937-6995	see 1556-9039 6854	
1937-7002	Bridges (Conway) 6908	
1937-7010	Virtual Mentor 5728	
1937-7029	Colorado Research in Linguistics (Online Edition) 5107	
1937-7037	Rune 5365	
1937-710X	see 1062-3264 5951	
1937-7126	Natural Food Network 3657	
1937-7134	Fender Bender (Midwest Edition) 1745	
1937-7142	Fender Bender (Northeast Edition) see 1937-7134 1745	
1937-7150	Fender Bender (South Edition) see 1937-7134 1745	
1937-7169	Fender Bender (Southeast Edition) see 1937-7134 1745	
1937-7177	Fender Bender (West Edition) see 1937-7134 1745	
1937-7185	Accent Gwinnett 5064	
1937-7193	see 1937-7185 5064	
1937-7207	The Hackett Money Flow Report 1116	
1937-7215	The Hackett Stock Report 1628	
1937-7223	Chittlin' Circuit 6555	
1937-7231	Mind Body & Soul 8875	
1937-724X	East Bay Business Times changed to 0890-0337 1432	
1937-7274	Great Lakes Boating 8276	
1937-7290	Primera Revista Latinoamericana de Libros 5234	
1937-7304	see 1937-7290 5234	
1937-7312	Sixty-Six 5435	
1937-7320	see 1076-6022 4107	
1937-7339	see 1076-5980 4089	
1937-7347	see 1052-4924 4106	
1937-7355	see 1087-8599 4096	
1937-7363	see 1542-2844 7543	
1937-7371	see 1098-0571 4089	
1937-738X	see 1937-2728 4089	
1937-7398	see 1089-4705 4089	
1937-7401	see 1535-0894 4089	
1937-741X	see 1523-7575 4097	
1937-7428	see 1521-4990 4109	
1937-7436	see 1528-7637 4089	
1937-7444	see 1537-0216 4089	
1937-7452	see 1527-0246 4088	
1937-7460	see 0733-2262 4092	
1937-7479	see 1543-7264 4095	
1937-7487	see 1545-7028 5954	
1937-7495	see 1934-189X 4090	
1937-7525	see 1933-3307 4109	
1937-7533	see 1939-5671 5959	
1937-7541	Oklahoma Edge 3984	
1937-755X	The Staff Educator 4111	
1937-7568	see 1937-755X 4111	
1937-7576	Physician Compensation & Recruitment 4109	
1937-7584	see 1937-7576 4109	
1937-7592	see 1931-9894 4097	
1937-7606	see 1085-3502 4114	

1937-7614	see 1559-3606 4101	
1937-7622	see 0888-3068 4100	
1937-7630	see 1090-1574 4090	
1937-7649	see 1530-6607 4089	
1937-7665	see 1535-7945 4087	
1937-7673	see 1535-847X 5982	
1937-7681	see 1554-3285 4106	
1937-769X	see 8756-4513 26	
1937-7703	see 1542-0914 4091	
1937-7711	see 1531-5681 4092	
1937-772X	see 1083-3641 4106	
1937-7738	see 1558-7312 4109	
1937-7746	A P C Payment Insider 4087	
1937-7754	see 1937-7746 4087	
1937-7762	see 1082-6718 4097	
1937-7789	Plastic Antinomy 512	
1937-7797	Healthcare Journal of Baton Rouge 5626	
1937-7800	see 1937-7797 5626	
1937-7835	Ocean Science Foundation. Journal 2815	
1937-7843	Clarkesworld Magazine 5441	
1937-7851	India Property Times 7595	
1937-786X	North American Fungi 805	
1937-7878	The High Hat 3977	
1937-7886	Latino 3547	
1937-7894	Tennis View 8249	
1937-7908	The Pennsylvania Review 5350	
1937-7924	International Journal of Global Sustainability 3442	
1937-7932	New Love Stories Magazine 5411	
1937-7975	Journal of Characterization and Development of Novel Materials 2067	
1937-7983	Journal of Information, Intelligence and Knowledge 2453	
1937-7991	Advances in Sustainable Petroleum Engineering Science 6761	
1937-8009	Quilts & Gifts to Give 6641	
1937-8106	The Irish in America 7801	
1937-8114	see 1941-3564 8207	
1937-8149	Standards for Diagnostic Imaging Services 6209	
1937-8157	see 0012-6616 6836	
1937-8165	The Internet Journal of Veterinary Medicine 8799	
1937-8173	The Internet Journal of Laserneedle Medicine 5640	
1937-8181	The Internet Journal of Laboratory Medicine 5906	
1937-819X	The Internet Journal of Head and Neck Surgery 6246	
1937-8203	The Internet Journal of Hand Surgery 6246	
1937-8211	The Internet Journal of Geriatrics and Gerontology 4048	
1937-822X	The Internet Journal of Endovascular Medicine 5790	
1937-8238	The Internet Journal of Dental Science 5849	
1937-8246	The Internet Journal of Bioengineering 749	
1937-8254	The Internet Journal of Minimally Invasive Spinal Technology 6246	
1937-8262	The Internet Journal of Nanotechnology 8428	
1937-8270	The Internet Journal of Spine Surgery 6246	
1937-8289	The Internet Journal of Microbiology 888	
1937-8297	The Internet Journal of Nutrition and Wellness 6661	
1937-8300	The Internet Journal of Medical Informatics 5640	
1937-8319	The Bump (Denver Edition) 8854	
1937-8327	see 0898-5952 3076	
1937-8335	Vapor Intrusion Report 3503	
1937-8343	Scarabs 858	
1937-8351	see 1937-8343 858	
1937-836X	Soil & Mulch Producer News 253	
1937-8386	see 0032-8413 7771	
1937-8424	Indiana Employment Law (Falls Church) 1687	
1937-8432	North Carolina Employment Law 1700	
1937-8475	Hidden Gems Pay Dirt 1628	
1937-8483	North Star Family Matters 4365	
1937-8491	see 1937-8483 4365	
1937-853X	see 1546-0002 6197	
1937-8548	see 1941-0549 6203	
1937-8556	see 1941-0549 6203	
1937-8564	Meeting Professional European Digest changed to 1947-4733 6282	
1937-8572	Karpa 8472	
1937-8602	see 1221-0803 2770	
1937-8629	Engineering Studies 3190	
1937-8645	see 1937-8653 5720	
1937-8653	TeleHealth World 5720	
1937-8688	Pan African Medical Journal 5693	
1937-8696	see 1936-2994 5624	
1937-870X	Women of the Year 1990-2006 648	
1937-8718	Progress in Electromagnetics Research C 7052	
1937-8726	Progress in Electromagnetics Research M 7052	
1937-8734	Soky Happenings 5083	
1937-8742	see 1937-8734 5083	
1937-8769	Medical Tourism 5672	
1937-8777	see 1937-8769 5672	
1937-8785	Smart Company 1176	
1937-8823	Revista Latinoamericana y del Caribe de la Asociacion de Sistemas de Informacion 2550	
1937-8831	see 1937-8823 2550	
1937-8874	Barron's A P World History 4132	
1937-8882	Townhall 7189	
1937-8890	Green Products and Technology changed to 1941-7470 1005	
1937-8904	Theological Librarianship 5050	
1937-8912	Semantics & Pragmatics 5173	
1937-8947	see 1941-4005 7383	
1937-8955	Journal of Interaction Recipes 2950	
1937-8963	Medical Connectivity 5667	
1937-8971	see 1937-8963 5667	
1937-898X	Epiphany Magazine 8861	
1937-9005	International Journal of Applied Accounting and Finance 1292	
1937-9013	International Journal of Decision Science and Information Technology 1756	
1937-9021	Pratt's Stats Update 1645	
1937-903X	Easy Family Food 4356	
1937-9056	Answers Research Journal 7622	
1937-9064	N C A A Champion 8189	
1937-9080	American Journal of Biomedical Sciences 5571	
1937-9099	see 1937-9064 8189	

1937-9145	see 1945-0877 7911	
1937-9196	On Korea 1156	
1937-9234	see 1932-8184 2520	
1937-9242	Middle Eastern Outlook 7253	
1937-9250	Potawatomi Trail of Death Association. Newsletter 3559	
1937-9269	Cigar Magazine (Whippany) 8486	
1937-9315	Military Logistics Forum (Rockville) 6437	
1937-9331	C U E S Staffing Manual for Credit Unions 1323	
1937-934X	Fundamentals of Engineering Supplied-Reference Handbook 3193	
1937-9358	Emerging Issues in Academic Library Cataloging & Technical Services 5008	
1937-9366	Simply Perfect Lighting changed to 1941-3459 4545	
1937-9374	L P-Gas Code Handbook 6776	
1937-9382	New York Canudo on Evidence Laws 4957	
1937-9390	International Journal of Information Systems for Crisis Response and Management 2522	
1937-9404	see 1937-9412 2426	
1937-9412	International Journal of Mobile Computing and Multimedia Communications 2426	
1937-9420	see 1937-9390 2522	
1937-9439	Duke Journal of Constitutional Law & Public Policy 7434	
1937-9447	Maui Revealed 8733	
1937-9463	Private Equity Partnership Terms & Conditions 1645	
1937-9471	Flame Retardants 3578	
1937-948X	World Commercial Refrigeration Equipment 4128	
1937-9498	see 1937-9439 7434	
1937-9501	The National Geographic Traveler. The Caribbean 8740	
1937-9609	A Visitor's Guide to Colonial & Revolutionary New England 8772	
1937-9633	The International Journal of E-Adoption 2559	
1937-9641	see 1937-9633 2559	
1937-965X	International Journal of Advanced Pervasive and Ubiquitous Computing 2424	
1937-9668	see 1937-965X 2424	
1937-9676	Industrial Valves 3379	
1937-9714	Equipo Minero 6461	
1937-9722	Somerset Workshop 540	
1937-9730	Sales of Natural Gas Liquids and Liquified Refinery Gases (Year) 6801	
1937-9803	Epiphany (New York) 5290	
1937-9811	see 1937-9803 5290	
1937-9854	CropLife. Iron 226	
1937-9862	Cornish Courier 3763	
1937-9870	Large Display Report 2384	
1937-9889	Lifetime for Women Considering Adoption 2159	
1937-9900	We Magazine for Women 8888	
1937-9935	see 1940-1655 7610	
1937-9951	Construction Claims Advisor 4649	
1937-996X	see 1937-9951 4649	
1937-9978	Wrightsville Beach Magazine 5087	
1937-9986	see 1937-9978 5087	
1938-0011	J U C M 6062	
1938-002X	see 1938-0011 6062	
1938-0100	Family Times Newsletter 1885	
1938-0127	B M I, Body, Mind, Inspiration 5920	
1938-016X	Texas Employment Law 1710	
1938-0178	see 1938-016X 1710	
1938-0194	International Journal of Web Portals 2560	
1938-0208	see 1938-0194 2560	
1938-0216	International Journal of Healthcare Delivery Reform Initiative 4102	
1938-0224	see 1938-0216 4102	
1938-0232	International Journal of Information Technology Project Management 2426	
1938-0240	see 1938-0232 2426	
1938-0259	International Journal of Grid and High Performance Computing 2425	
1938-0267	see 1938-0259 2425	
1938-0275	see 1022-0461 7266	
1938-0283	University of Pennsylvania. Journal of International Law 4944	
1938-0291	Redmond Developer News 2509	
1938-033X	see 1934-1334 7908	
1938-0399	American Journal of Play 2143	
1938-0402	see 1938-0399 2143	
1938-0445	Med-Tech Precision 4489	
1938-0453	Teacher-Scholar 2918	
1938-0461	see 1938-0453 2918	
1938-047X	Mujeres de espiritu see 1078-9650 7780	
1938-0569	Looking Back 5327	
1938-0585	Silencio 5372	
1938-0593	see 0892-1121 8555	
1938-0666	see 1526-8209 6016	
1938-0674	see 1533-0028 6016	
1938-0682	see 1558-7673 6016	
1938-0690	see 1525-7304 6016	
1938-0704	see 1931-6925 6016	
1938-0712	see 1557-9190 6016	
1938-0739	Four Corners Economic Quarterly 1886	
1938-0755	Econometer changed to 1938-0739 1886	
1938-0771	E-Drive e-Report 3376	
1938-078X	Battery Power Products & Technology e-Report 3296	
1938-0798	Equipment Protection e-Report 3307	
1938-0801	Instrument Design & Technology e-Report 4487	
1938-081X	L E D Journal e-Report 3323	
1938-0828	Magnetics Business & Technology e-Report 7025	
1938-0836	Materials Engineering News e-Report 3209	
1938-0844	Organic & Printed Electronics e-Report 3327	
1938-0852	Software Business Executive Report 2597	
1938-0860	Thermal News e-Report 3332	
1938-0879	Scientific & Engineering Software e-Report 2596	
1938-0887	Green Tech News e-Report 3136	
1938-0895	Domestic Violence Benchbook 4660	
1938-0909	see 1938-0895 4660	
1938-0917	International Journal of Digital Evidence 2655	
1938-0925	Journal of Economic Crime Management 4892	
1938-0976	The Columbia Science and Technology Law Review 4645	
1938-1050	Sustainable Land Development Today 1038	
1938-1077	Hispanic Enterprise 3537	

1938-114X Cascadia Scorecard **3409**
1938-1158 Biomedical Sciences Instrumentation (CD-ROM) **5586**
1938-1166 *see* 1082-801X **6843**
1938-1174 California Executive **1882**
1938-1212 Creating Together Journal **534**
1938-1247 Molecular and Cellular Pharmacology **6861**
1938-1255 S P Magazine **4366**
1938-128X So Be Fit **6997**
1938-1298 *see* 1938-128X **6997**
1938-1301 *see* 1542-8672 **4103**
1938-131X *see* 1553-7250 **4103**
1938-1328 *see* 0021-9584 **2067**
1938-1344 *see* 0190-6011 **6230**
1938-1352 *see* 0748-7711 **6065**
1938-1360 *see* 0045-8201 **1735**
1938-1379 *see* 0013-1261 **2847**
1938-1387 *see* 1042-346X **7078**
1938-1395 *see* 0149-9009 **6194**
1938-1409 *see* 1539-5367 **2850**
1938-1417 *see* 8750-7730 **2965**
1938-1425 *see* 0883-7694 **3352**
1938-1433 *see* 0048-105X **3143**
1938-1441 *see* 1050-9135 **5830**
1938-1484 *see* 1098-8130 **1649**
1938-1492 *see* 1098-8149 **1649**
1938-1506 *see* 0030-3607 **6602**
1938-1557 *see* 0748-5492 **7869**
1938-1573 *see* 0884-9382 **7254**
1938-1581 Women in Sport and Physical Activity Journal (Online) **8906**
1938-159X *see* 0010-9312 **3375**
1938-1603 *see* 0022-1864 **2876**
1938-1611 *see* 1059-7107 **2840**
1938-162X *see* 1062-6050 **6230**
1938-1638 *see* 1071-3778 **7796**
1938-1646 *see* 1532-5490 **6935**
1938-1670 Strategic Insights **6448**
1938-1689 Journal of Current Business Studies **1134**
1938-1697 Analytics **1725**
1938-1719 Exopolitics Journal **53**
1938-1727 Synthesis Lectures on Algorithms and Software in Engineering **2599**
1938-1735 *see* 1938-1727 **2599**
1938-1743 Synthesis Lectures on Mathematics and Statistics **8408**
1938-1751 *see* 1938-1743 **8408**
1938-176X Agriculture Business Week **1879**
1938-1778 *see* 1938-176X **1879**
1938-1786 Agriculture Week **86**
1938-1794 *see* 1938-1786 **86**
1938-1808 *see* 1938-1816 **1061**
1938-1816 Asia Business Newsweekly **1061**
1938-1824 Education Business Weekly **1884**
1938-1832 *see* 1938-1824 **1884**
1938-1840 Education Letter **2848**
1938-1859 *see* 1938-1840 **2848**
1938-1867 A Suitable Solution **1803**
1938-1875 Spiritual Living Digest **7683**
1938-1905 Awareness (Powder Springs) **2225**
1938-1913 *see* 1062-8061 **5973**
1938-1921 The Ministry of the Word **7663**
1938-193X *see* 1044-9493 **3492**
1938-1948 *see* 1087-3384 **3474**
1938-1956 Chimerism **666**
1938-1964 *see* 1938-1956 **666**
1938-1972 Dermato-Endocrinology **5874**
1938-1980 *see* 1938-1972 **5874**
1938-1999 G M Crops **232**
1938-2006 *see* 1938-1999 **232**
1938-2014 Islets **5895**
1938-2022 *see* 1938-2014 **5895**
1938-2030 Self Nonself **5766**
1938-2049 *see* 1938-2030 **5766**
1938-2057 *see* 0895-0695 **2789**
1938-2065 Visions of Research in Music Education **6627**
1938-2073 *see* 1940-1833 **2989**
1938-2081 I C O S A **1751**
1938-209X *see* 1938-2081 **1751**
1938-212X *see* 1842-3191 **1101**
1938-2154 Southeast Case Research Journal **1177**
1938-2162 Screem Magazine **5447**
1938-2197 Hawaii Pacific Journal of Social Work Practice **8044**
1938-2200 U C E **2262**
1938-2235 The Abingdon Children's Sermon Library **7619**
1938-2278 *see* 1938-5056 **6648**
1938-2340 *see* 0882-228X **4152**
1938-2359 *see* 0090-4481 **6100**
1938-2367 *see* 0147-7447 **6070**
1938-2375 *see* 1542-8877 **6254**
1938-2383 *see* 1539-4492 **5688**
1938-2391 *see* 1081-597X **6249**
1938-2405 *see* 0191-3913 **6045**
1938-2413 *see* 0279-3695 **5967**
1938-2421 *see* 0148-4834 **5966**
1938-243X *see* 0098-9134 **4049**
1938-2448 *see* 0891-0162 **5951**
1938-2456 *see* 0048-5713 **6176**
1938-2464 *see* 1940-4921 **4054**
1938-2472 *see* 0022-0124 **5964**
1938-2480 *see* 1538-8506 **6248**
1938-2529 *see* 1941-384X **8557**
1938-2545 Law & Ethics of Human Rights **7211**
1938-2596 Unconventional Natural Gas Report **6796**
1938-2618 Hawk & Whippoorwill **5423**
1938-2626 *see* 0897-3962 **5504**
1938-2650 *see* 0001-5547 **826**
1938-2669 *see* 1099-8012 **6820**
1938-2707 *see* 0009-9228 **6090**
1938-2715 *see* The American Journal of Hospice and Palliative Medicine **5572**
1938-2723 *see* 1076-0296 **5935**
1938-2731 *see* 1533-3175 **4040**
1938-274X *see* 1065-9129 **7169**
1938-2766 *see* 0885-1158 **5670**
1938-2790 Carolina Public Health **7512**
1938-2804 *see* 1938-2790 **7512**
1938-2812 *see* 0081-024X **817**
1938-2820 *see* 0279-4977 **450**
1938-2839 *see* 0020-6814 **2748**
1938-2847 *see* 0272-3638 **4430**
1938-2855 *see* 1060-586X **1512**
1938-2863 *see* 1538-7216 **4006**
1938-2871 *see* 1082-6742 **8800**
1938-288X *see* 0007-9367 **782**
1938-2898 *see* 1070-0048 **792**
1938-2901 *see* 0013-8746 **845**
1938-291X *see* 0022-0493 **851**
1938-2928 *see* 0022-2585 **852**
1938-2936 *see* 0046-225X **847**
1938-2944 *see* 1043-4534 **792**
1938-2952 *see* 1525-2647 **938**
1938-2960 *see* 1098-7096 **7875**
1938-2979 *see* 0006-9698 **936**
1938-2987 *see* 0027-4100 **956**
1938-2995 *see* 1073-7472 **5966**
1938-3061 *see* 1935-6137 **7582**
1938-307X *see* 1527-2311 **1947**
1938-3088 *see* 1537-1093 **4647**
1938-3096 *see* 1094-3528 **1280**
1938-310X *see* 1072-009X **7582**
1938-3118 *see* 1938-3185 **7602**
1938-3126 *see* 0736-0517 **7586**
1938-3134 *see* 0898-2961 **7602**
1938-3169 Commercial Property Management Insider **1734**
1938-3177 *see* 1938-3169 **1734**
1938-3185 New York Landlord vs. Tenant **7602**
1938-3207 *see* 0002-9165 **6655**
1938-3223 *see* 0040-4470 **5721**
1938-3231 *see* 1092-2598 **4677**
1938-324X Superstition Review **5383**
1938-3274 *see* 1062-3957 **1007**
1938-3282 *see* 0096-3402 **7224**
1938-3290 *see* 0895-8750 **7378**
1938-3304 *see* 1546-508X **4926**
1938-3312 *see* 0015-198X **1623**
1938-3320 *see* 0046-9777 **1323**
1938-3339 *see* 1543-1398 **1323**
1938-3347 *see* 1930-2703 **1614**
1938-3371 Information Week Online *see* 8750-6874 **2531**
1938-338X *see* 0197-3622 **5542**
1938-3398 *see* 0889-5392 **5481**
1938-3401 *see* 0035-4902 **815**
1938-3436 The Journal of Information Technology in Social Change **8114**
1938-3444 The Journal of Networks and Civil Society **8115**
1938-3460 Infection, Protection & Control **5817**
1938-3495 *see* 0199-350X **7164**
1938-3509 *see* 1050-4818 **2745**
1938-3517 *see* 0018-7259 **341**
1938-3525 *see* 0018-7259 **341**
1938-3533 *see* 0899-1855 **6111**
1938-3584 Cameroon Journal on Democracy and Human Rights **7113**
1938-3592 Reconfigurations **5433**
1938-3614 The Art of Luxury Living **5065**
1938-3630 Plum **6001**
1938-3657 *see* 1071-0922 **2490**
1938-369X *see* 0049-3155 **2340**
1938-3703 *see* 0021-8855 **7368**
1938-3711 *see* 0022-5002 **7381**
1938-3738 *see* 0015-749X **3689**
1938-3746 *see* 0022-1201 **3695**
1938-3754 *see* 0148-4419 **3703**
1938-3762 *see* 0742-6348 **3698**
1938-3770 *see* 0885-6095 **3707**
1938-3789 *see* 1070-485X **2786**
1938-3797 *see* 1086-8089 **6259**
1938-3800 *see* 0742-3225 **5613**
1938-3819 *see* 1091-0808 **5016**
1938-3835 *see* 1943-1929 **3646**
1938-3851 *see* 0362-4064 **6682**
1938-3886 *see* 1079-6533 **4103**
1938-3916 American Bar Association. Commission on Lawyer Assistance Programs. Highlights **4614**
1938-3924 *see* 1938-3916 **4614**
1938-3932 Wingman **6454**
1938-3940 Museum **6531**
1938-4041 H.A.S. Magazine **2256**
1938-405X *see* 1938-4041 **2256**
1938-4114 *see* 1937-1888 **2696**
1938-4122 Digital Humanities Quarterly **4485**
1938-4149 Amputee Golfer **8220**
1938-4157 Women's Skiing *see* 0037-6264 **8333**
1938-4165 Military Advanced Education **6435**
1938-419X Colloquium, Music, Worship, Arts **6558**
1938-4203 *see* 1938-419X **6558**
1938-4211 *see* 0002-7685 **652**
1938-422X *see* 0002-8444 **774**
1938-4238 *see* 0003-0031 **7834**
1938-4246 *see* 1523-0430 **7836**
1938-4254 *see* 0004-8038 **901**
1938-4300 I E E E / A C M International Conference on Automated Software Engineering **2590**
1938-4351 *see* 0005-2086 **8794**
1938-436X *see* 0007-196X **782**
1938-4378 *see* 0007-2745 **782**
1938-4386 *see* 0008-7475 **783**
1938-4394 *see* 0010-065X **842**
1938-4408 *see* 1934-0451 **842**
1938-4424 Find it! (Chicago)† **8956**
1938-4459 Inquest Gamer† **8964**
1938-4491 Warman's Depression Glass **369**
1938-4505 Leonard Maltin's Movie Crazy **6506**
1938-4513 R L G News **5042**
1938-4548 *see* 1547-3112 **2768**
1938-4556 Words Without Music **6629**
1938-4564 Encinitas (Encinitas, 2008) **3975**
1938-4572 Akron Intellecutal Property Journal **4612**
1938-4580 *see* 1938-4572 **4612**
1938-4785 The Paterson Literary Review **5233**
1938-4823 N Y U Alumni Magazine **2293**
1938-4831 Garden & Gun **5071**
1938-484X State B E A R F A C T S (Year) Alabama **1267**
1938-4866 The Rough Guide to Colorado **8753**
1938-4890 Illinois Staff Directory **7445**
1938-4904 Journal on Jewish Aging **4050**
1938-4920 Journal of Hospital Ethics **4104**
1938-4955 *see* 1938-4920 **4104**
1938-4963 Kids' Parties† **8969**
1938-4971 Bible Studies for Life: Lifematters **7626**
1938-4998 Journal of Workplace Rights **1691**
1938-5005 *see* 1938-4998 **1691**
1938-5048 Senior Directions Magazine **4055**
1938-5056 Tarot World Magazine **6648**
1938-5064 TsuInfo Alert **2771**
1938-5072 *see* 1938-5064 **2771**
1938-5099 *see* 0018-0831 **946**
1938-5102 *see* 0015-4040 **847**
1938-5110 *see* 0045-8511 **939**
1938-5129 *see* 0010-5422 **905**
1938-5137 *see* 0733-1347 **946**
1938-5153 Gulfstream Tropical Bonsai Journal **3735**
1938-5161 *see* 1938-5153 **3735**
1938-5196 A L S C Newsletter **5247**
1938-5285 New York City **8741**
1938-5293 *see* 0097-3157 **7831**
1938-5307 *see* 1092-6194 **805**
1938-5315 *see* 1051-1733 **959**
1938-5323 *see* 0883-1351 **6728**
1938-5331 *see* 0094-8373 **6728**
1938-534X Easy Holiday Cooking & Crafts **4356**
1938-5358 International Symposium on Electromagnetic Compatibility and Electromagnetic Ecology. Proceedings **7018**
1938-5366 Ocular Surgery News (India Edition) **6047**
1938-5374 Ocular Surgery News (China Edition) **6047**
1938-5390 *see* 1524-4695 **916**
1938-5404 *see* 0033-7587 **7072**
1938-5412 *see* 1528-7092 **818**
1938-5420 *see* 0022-8443 **7874**
1938-5439 *see* 1537-6176 **966**
1938-5447 *see* 1559-4491 **917**
1938-5455 *see* 0084-0173 **968**
1938-5552 Lectionary Preaching Workbook **7659**
1938-5560 Lectionary Worship Workbook **7659**
1938-5579 Preaching the Parables **7671**
1938-5595 N A L S Journal **2888**
1938-5617 *see* 1934-4430 **5475**
1938-565X Federal-State Court Directory (Year) **4951**
1938-5668 Babel und Bibel **4320**
1938-5676 Tredyffrin Easttown History Quarterly **4315**
1938-5684 Profiles of Connecticut and Rhode Island **3121**
1938-5714 Prime (Spokane) **5080**
1938-5749 Greenability **2613**
1938-5765 Journal of Medical Sciences Research **5652**
1938-5773 Literature in the Early American Republic **5326**
1938-5781 A M S Studies in American Literature†
1938-579X Clever! **5068**
1938-5803 G S N J Newsletter **3767**
1938-5811 State B E A R F A C T S (Year) Alaska **1267**
1938-582X Life Story **644**
1938-5838 QuizFest **2209**
1938-5862 E C S Transactions **3242**
1938-5870 Astro Girl **565**
1938-5897 Year in Soaps **2399**
1938-5927 Journal of Family and Consumer Sciences Education **4361**
1938-5951 Northeastern University Alumni Magazine **2294**
1938-5978 The New England Journal of Higher Education **2995**
1938-5986 The Bump (Atlanta Edition) **8844**
1938-6036 *see* 0021-4183 **5313**
1938-6052 Plumbing Business Owner†
1938-6060 Journal of e-Media Studies **2329**
1938-6095 Growing Up **8105**
1938-6109 Inside the Workshop **2867**
1938-6117 Bombin' Magazine **479**
1938-6125 Bodyboarder **8162**
1938-6133 *see* 0360-2370 **4476**
1938-6141 Cocktail Weekly†
1938-615X The Ilan Stavans' Library of Latino Civilization **3538**
1938-6168 Global Security Watch Series **7238**
1938-6176 Christian Science Quarterly. Bible Lessons (English Citation Edition) **7734**
1938-6184 Christian Science Quarterly. Bible Lessons (Study Edition) **7734**
1938-6206 Print Professional **7326**
1938-6214 *see* 1546-007X **5377**
1938-6222 Uniforms **2262**
1938-6230 Little Green **2200**
1938-6249 Global Internet Geography **2557**
1938-6257 E S L Grammar Intermediate & Advanced **5113**
1938-6265 E S L Writing Intermediate & Advanced **5113**
1938-629X The Royal Dispatch **6814**
1938-6303 Harbor Style **5072**
1938-6311 Today's Wound Clinic **6074**
1938-632X A C P Hospitalist **5563**
1938-6338 *see* 1938-632X **5563**
1938-6354 Northeast Boating **8279**
1938-6362 International Journal of Geotechnical Engineering **3201**
1938-6389 Journal of Library Metadata **2563**
1938-6400 Foot and Ankle Specialist **6060**
1938-6419 Sexualidades **4379**
1938-6427 Florida Probate Code and Related Provisions, with Commentary **4675**
1938-6435 Music Education Research International **6590**
1938-6443 Verdant Hills of Connecticut **5086**

ISSN

9866 1938-6451 ULRICH'S PERIODICALS

1938-6451 *see* First International Symposium on Empirical Software Engineering and Measurement. Proceedings **2590**
1938-6478 Water Environment Federation. Proceedings **3492**
1938-6486 The Westchester Review **5245**
1938-6532 Key West Magazine **5074**
1938-6540 *see* 1938-6532 **5074**
1938-6559 Zarin's Radiology Liability Alert **4818**
1938-6613 Senior Living Business **1793**
1938-6621 P P O Focus **6032**
1938-663X Professional Association for Cactus Development. Journal **814**
1938-6648 *see* 1938-663X **814**
1938-6656 Black History Bulletin **3522**
1938-6672 Macular Degeneration & Other Diseases of the Aging Eye **6046**
1938-6729 Investment Company Fact Book **1632**
1938-6737 *see* 1938-5862 **3242**
1938-680X Rocket (Agouro Hills) **515**
1938-6818 Manufactured Home Living **7599**
1938-6885 Slow Cooking **4367**
1938-6893 Easy Knit & Crochet Ideas **6638**
1938-6907 Remodeling & Makeovers **455**
1938-6915 Budget Decorating (New York) **4534**
1938-6923 Slice Magazine **5373**
1938-6931 Democracy Studies Weekly **7129**
1938-694X Biblical Research Bulletin **384**
1938-6958 *see* 0003-1186 **372**
1938-6974 Sport Management Education Journal **8204**
1938-6990 Gamut **6569**
1938-7008 *see* 1938-7717 **1600**
1938-7016 Journal of Coaching Education **8182**
1938-7024 Lessons in Conservation **2617**
1938-7032 Aviation Litigation Quarterly **8538**
1938-7040 *see* 1938-7032 **8538**
1938-7075 Common Interest Realty Associations Industry Developments **1285**
1938-7083 A L M Experts. Southeastern Directory **4608**
1938-7105 Barron's P S A T/ N M S Q T **2830**
1938-7156 LaTeen **2199**
1938-7172 Anesthesia Abstracts **5769**
1938-7202 Acupuncture and Oriental Medicine State Laws and Regulations **4609**
1938-7253 Grafemas **5301**
1938-7261 *see* 1938-727X **4063**
1938-727X Assistive Technology Outcomes and Benefits **4063**
1938-7296 *see* 1936-7619 **4694**
1938-7326 Energy Priorities Magazine **3133**
1938-7350 Initium **7142**
1938-7369 Weekend Homes **4369**
1938-7377 Lectionary Tales for the Pulpit **7659**
1938-7393 *see* 1542-9466 **1609**
1938-744X *see* 1935-7893 **7514**
1938-7458 *see* 1534-5084 **3036**
1938-7466 California G C S A E-magazine **3726**
1938-7490 *see* 1938-7504 **1386**
1938-7504 Total Securitization **1386**
1938-7547 Conjuring Arts Bulletin **4332**
1938-761X Additions†
1938-7628 Better Homes and Gardens Beautiful Baths **4533**
1938-7636 *see* 1938-6400 **6060**
1938-7644 European Fuel Price Service **6768**
1938-7679 International Building Code **1015**
1938-7687 Music and Politics **6589**
1938-7709 Midwest Journal for Educational Communications and Technology **2950**
1938-7717 Journal of Knowledge Globalization **1600**
1938-7725 Practical and Applied Psychology **7391**
1938-7733 The Bump (Phoenix Edition) **8844**
1938-7741 Journal of Transportation Security **8501**
1938-775X *see* 1938-7741 **8501**
1938-7768 *see* 1527-1560 **6025**
1938-7784 Massachusetts Rules of Criminal Court Handbook **4894**
1938-7806 ArchNet - I J A R **432**
1938-7814 Bible Studies for Life. Lifematters Leader Pack **7626**
1938-7830 A S H E / Lumina Fellows Series **2964**
1938-7849 Journal of Transport and Land Use **4417**
1938-7857 Journal of Information Technology Research **2429**
1938-7865 *see* 1938-7857 **2429**
1938-7873 A P French **5088**
1938-7938 Synergy (Washington D.C.) **5049**
1938-7946 *see* 1938-7830 **2964**
1938-7954 International Structural Health Monitoring **3273**
1938-7989 Statistics and its Interface **8406**
1938-7997 *see* 1938-7989 **8406**
1938-8004 National Geographic Extreme Explorer **4020**
1938-8012 *see* 1938-8004 **4020**
1938-8020 *see* 1041-8385 **4471**
1938-8063 *see* 1938-8071 **3070**
1938-8071 Literacy Research and Instruction **3070**
1938-808X *see* 1040-2446 **5564**
1938-8098 *see* 0013-1725 **2979**
1938-8101 *see* 0887-8730 **3004**
1938-8128 Journal of Evolutionary and Historical Sciences **873**
1938-8152 Nomenus Quarterly **509**
1938-8160 Journal of China Tourism Research **8725**
1938-8179 *see* 1938-8160 **8725**
1938-8209 Girlhood Studies **8104**
1938-8233 White Paper Series on Email Marketing **1848**
1938-8276 Who's Who in Black New York City **646**
1938-8292 Who's Who in Black Philadelphia **647**
1938-8306 The Church in History **7633**
1938-8322 *see* 1938-8209 **8104**
1938-8462 Trendy Africa **3568**
1938-8489 Common Patriot **4289**
1938-8497 *see* 1938-8489 **4289**
1938-8500 American Association for Nude Recreation. Bulletin **6981**
1938-8519 Lush for Life **5225**
1938-8527 Geek 411 **2285**
1938-8543 Not Born Yesterday **4052**
1938-8594 Investment Company Institute. Annual Report to Members **1632**
1938-8616 L'dor V'dor **3547**
1938-8640 Clinical Nutrition Insight **6656**
1938-8675 Rhode Island Catholic **7815**
1938-8845 Forward (Washington D.C.) **5010**
1938-8853 State B E A R F A C T S (Year) Arizona **1267**
1938-8861 State B E A R F A C T S (Year) Arkansas **1267**
1938-887X *see* 0889-8391 **7371**
1938-8888 Advanced Design & Manufacturing **3365**
1938-8896 Information Plus Reference Series. Alcohol, Tobacco, and Illicit Drugs **2695**
1938-890X Information Plus Reference Series. Crime, Prisons, and Jails **2655**
1938-8918 Paper Monument **511**
1938-8926 Journal of Diversity in Higher Education **2990**
1938-8934 *see* 1938-8926 **2990**
1938-8969 *see* 1941-7322 **831**
1938-8977 Action Transmittal **2142**
1938-8985 *see* 1938-8977 **2142**
1938-8993 *see* 1540-4153 **5960**
1938-9000 *see* 1559-4343 **6139**
1938-9019 *see* 1521-0987 **5954**
1938-9035 Professional Liability Litigation @lert **4762**
1938-9043 *see* 1938-9035 **4762**
1938-9051 Michigan Merit **1024**
1938-906X Salt Life Magazine **8199**
1938-9086 In Wheeling Magazine **5073**
1938-9094 The Journal of Borderland Studies **4017**
1938-9116 *see* 1538-5744 **6262**
1938-9132 Fabric Graphics **8450**
1938-9140 *see* 0897-6627 **3215**
1938-9159 *see* 1549-9928 **6882**
1938-9167 *see* 1055-0259 **3215**
1938-9191 Pediatrics (Chinese Edition) *see* 0210-5721 **6102**
1938-9191 Pediatrics (Chinese Edition) *see* 0031-4005 **6102**
1938-9221 Survey Report on Compensation Policies & Procedures **1875**
1938-9272 Malibu Magazine **5076**
1938-9302 Venus Zine **6626**
1938-9310 Aerospace & Defense Manufacturing *see* 0361-0853 **3209**
1938-9361 King Air **64**
1938-937X Distinctly Northwest **5069**
1938-9388 *see* 1938-937X **5069**
1938-9434 Survey Report on College & University Personnel Compensation **1875**
1938-9485 Studies in the History of Ethics **6955**
1938-9507 *see* 8756-9728 **1787**
1938-9515 M P R (Urologists Edition) **6859**
1938-9523 M P R (Pharmacists' Edition) **6859**
1938-9531 M P R (Long Term Care Edition) **6859**
1938-954X U S M L E Road Map: Emergency Medicine **5725**
1938-9558 Tuscan Style **4551**
1938-9574 Journal of Dermatology for Physician Assistants **5879**
1938-9582 *see* 1544-1059 **6845**
1938-9612 *see* 0038-8661 **254**
1938-9620 Bond (San Francisco) **5556**
1938-9639 Robb Report Watch Collector **4569**
1938-9655 Cornell Hospitality Quarterly **4384**
1938-9663 *see* 1938-9655 **4384**
1938-9671 Geriatric Cardiologist
1938-968X *see* 1938-9671
1938-9701 Derm Products **5874**
1938-971X Psychological Injury and Law **7396**
1938-9728 *see* 1938-971X **7396**
1938-9736 Topics in Companion Animal Medicine **8808**
1938-9744 *see* 1055-0925 **1135**
1938-9752 The Pragmatic Marketer **1837**
1938-9760 *see* 1938-9752 **1837**
1938-9787 Communications in Mathematical Analysis (Washington, DC) **5479**
1938-9795 Nature Matters **2621**
1938-9809 *see* 1556-763X **7965**
1938-9892 Summary Health Statistics for the U.S. Population **8407**
1938-9906 *see* 1938-9892 **8407**
1938-9914 *see* 1937-4968 **2163**
1938-9930 *see* 1939-442X **2669**
1938-9981 U.S. National Forest Campground Guide. Eastern Region **8339**
1938-999X Weissenberger's Ohio Civil Procedure (Year) Litigation Manual **4844**
1939-0017 The World Almanac Book of Records **3123**
1939-0025 *see* 0002-9432 **7333**
1939-0033 Girls and Corpses **6292**
1939-0041 Wiley Interdisciplinary Reviews. Nanomedicine and Nanobiotechnology **5731**
1939-005X *see* 1939-5094 **711**
1939-0068 *see* 1939-5108 **5556**
1939-0076 Texas Apartments **7613**
1939-0084 *see* 0735-7044 **7339**
1939-0092 *see* 1938-7350 **7142**
1939-0106 *see* 1099-9809 **8097**
1939-0114 *see* 1939-0122 **2338**
1939-0122 Security and Communication Networks **2338**
1939-0130 *see* 0194-4363 **4403**
1939-019X *see* 0008-4034 **3237**
1939-0203 The Ethics of American Foreign Policy **7232**
1939-0211 Journal of Dietary Supplements **6853**
1939-022X *see* 1939-0211 **6853**
1939-0246 Early Modern Culture **4138**
1939-0262 Survey Report on Compensation in the Commercial Real Estate Industry **7613**
1939-0289 *see* 1939-0297 **4052**
1939-0297 Older Americans (Year) **4052**
1939-0300 *see* 1546-3214 **61**
1939-0343 The Absinthe Literary Review **5248**
1939-036X La Petite Zine **5429**
1939-0378 Medieval Forum **5332**
1939-0416 Laboratory Accreditation Standards **5908**
1939-0424 Auto Physical Damage Basics **8559**
1939-0432 Variable Universal Life Basics **4526**
1939-0440 Multicultural Marketing in America **1835**
1939-0459 Journal of Natural Resources Policy Research **2616**
1939-0467 *see* 1939-0459 **2616**
1939-0513 *see* 1088-937X **4024**
1939-0548 Reflections (University Center) **2298**
1939-0564 Synthesis Lectures on Control and Mechatronics **3396**
1939-0572 *see* 1939-0564 **3396**
1939-0580 Communication on Contemporary Anthropology **333**
1939-0599 *see* 0012-1649 **7351**
1939-0602 *see* 1091-7527 **5613**
1939-0610 *see* 1093-4510 **7360**
1939-0629 *see* 1555-6824 **7365**
1939-0637 Journal of Nanoneuroscience **6153**
1939-0645 Novaya Kozha **5343**
1939-0653 *see* 1939-0637 **6153**
1939-0661 The Journal of African Traditional Studies **4176**
1939-0688 *see* 1939-0696
1939-0696 Mechanics in Chemistry & Biology†
1939-0726 *see* 0029-4527 **5521**
1939-0734 Known Leader **7658**
1939-0742 Known **7658**
1939-0750 Major League Soccer **8238**
1939-0777 The Cheap Bastard's Guide to San Francisco **8693**
1939-0807 Journal of Commutative Algebra **5501**
1939-0831 LifeWalk **7660**
1939-0947 North American Windpower **3178**
1939-0955 *see* 1939-0947 **3178**
1939-098X Cardiology Today **5780**
1939-1161 International Journal of Mobile Marketing **1822**
1939-117X Insurance Journal. West Edition **4507**
1939-1188 Insurance Journal. South Central Edition **4507**
1939-1196 Insurance Journal. East Edition **4507**
1939-120X Insurance Journal. Midwest Edition **4507**
1939-1218 Artists of the American Mosaic **473**
1939-1226 American Social and Political Movements **8087**
1939-1234 Bioenergy Research **3124**
1939-1242 *see* 1939-1234 **3124**
1939-1250 Journal of Agricultural Science and Technology **126**
1939-1269 *see* 1939-1250 **126**
1939-1285 *see* 0278-7393 **7373**
1939-1293 *see* 0893-3200 **7374**
1939-1307 *see* 1076-8998 **6680**
1939-1315 *see* 0022-3514 **7377**
1939-1323 *see* 0735-7028 **7392**
1939-1331 *see* 0736-9735 **7395**
1939-134X *see* 1040-3590 **7396**
1939-1374 I E E E Transactions on Services Computing **2421**
1939-1382 I E E E Transactions on Learning Technologies **2949**
1939-1390 I E E E Intelligent Transportation Systems Magazine **8498**
1939-1404 I E E E Journal of Selected Topics in Applied Earth Observations and Remote Sensing **3196**
1939-1412 I E E E Transactions on Haptics **2584**
1939-1439 S E G Compilations **2765**
1939-1447 Beer Northwest **599**
1939-1455 *see* 0033-2909 **7396**
1939-1463 *see* 1082-989X **7396**
1939-1471 *see* 0033-295X **7397**
1939-148X *see* 1541-1559 **7397**
1939-1498 *see* 0882-7974 **4053**
1939-1501 *see* 0893-164X **2698**
1939-151X *see* 1524-9220 **7399**
1939-1528 *see* 1076-8971 **7400**
1939-1536 *see* 0033-3204 **7401**
1939-1544 *see* 0090-5550 **7402**
1939-1552 *see* 1089-2680 **7403**
1939-1560 *see* 1045-3830 **7406**
1939-1579 Storage (Des Moines) **4550**
1939-1587 Holiday Baking (Des Moines) **4360**
1939-1595 Transaction Trends **1394**
1939-1609 *see* 1939-1595 **1394**
1939-1617 Firewise Newsletter **3578**
1939-1625 Wildfire News and Notes **3582**
1939-1633 The Graziadio Business Report **1115**
1939-165X *see* 0275-6382 **8812**
1939-1668 *see* 1071-7641 **4544**
1939-1676 *see* 0891-6640 **8801**
1939-1684 State B E A R F A C T S (Year) California **1267**
1939-1811 Historical Studies in the Natural Sciences **7862**
1939-182X *see* 1939-1811 **7862**
1939-1846 *see* 0021-843X **7368**
1939-1854 *see* 0021-9010 **7369**
1939-1862 *see* 1542-166X **6825**
1939-1870 *see* 0893-2522 **8257**
1939-1889 *see* 1527-5949 **2103**
1939-1900 *see* 0887-6703 **2105**
1939-1919 *see* 8750-7943 **8813**
1939-1927 Distinctly Oklahoma **5069**
1939-1935 *see* 1936-007X **7430**
1939-196X Importing into the United States **1569**
1939-1986 Secrecy News **7468**
1939-2001 *see* 1939-201X **2674**
1939-201X Justice Expenditure and Employment in the United States **2674**
1939-2044 *see* 0090-1830 **3601**
1939-2079 Princeton Report on Knowledge **4470**
1939-2087 *see* 0735-7036 **7371**
1939-2095 Clinical Scholars Review **5955**
1939-2109 *see* 1939-2095 **5955**
1939-2117 *see* 0022-006X **7371**
1939-2125 Desserts from America's Top Chefs **4356**
1939-2133 The Bump (Portland Edition) **8844**
1939-2141 Boomer **4041**
1939-215X *see* 1939-2141 **4041**
1939-2168 *see* 0022-0167 **7372**
1939-2176 *see* 0022-0663 **2875**
1939-2184 *see* 0097-7403 **7373**
1939-2192 *see* 1076-898X **7373**
1939-2206 African Security **7103**
1939-2214 *see* 1939-2206 **7103**
1939-2222 *see* 0096-3445 **7373**
1939-2230 Academy of Banking Studies Journal **1305**

Link to your serials resources and content with ulrichsweb.com

9868 1939-8565 ULRICH'S PERIODICALS

1939-8565 Journal of Applied Science & Engineering Technology **3204**
1939-8573 *see* 0038-0407 **2913**
1939-8581 *see* 0038-9765 **4787**
1939-859X *see* 0041-9494 **4803**
1939-8603 *see* 0043-3810 **4317**
1939-8611 *see* 0044-0094 **4817**
1939-862X *see* 0092-055X **8143**
1939-8638 *see* 0094-3061 **8095**
1939-8654 Journal of Medical Imaging and Radiation Sciences **6200**
1939-8662 *see* 1060-0043 **8830**
1939-8670 The American Dream Belongs to Everyone **4063**
1939-8689 United States Mint. Strategic Plan **1187**
1939-8697 *see* 0006-3185 **658**
1939-8891 *see* 1082-6998 **1631**
1939-8980 *see* 0003-486X **5471**
1939-8999 *see* 0190-2725 **8134**
1939-9006 *see* 0010-096X **3055**
1939-9022 *see* 0738-2480 **4713**
1939-9111 *see* 0012-7086 **4661**
1939-912X *see* 0009-8655 **2837**
1939-9138 *see* 0011-1619 **5280**
1939-9146 *see* 0009-1383 **2971**
1939-9154 *see* 0013-9157 **3420**
1939-9162 *see* 0362-9805 **7151**
1939-9170 *see* 0012-9658 **3417**
1939-9189 *see* 1939-7771 **1655**
1939-9197 Physician License & Practice Today **5696**
1939-9200 *see* 1939-9197 **5696**
1939-9227 Pest Management Professional **246**
1939-9235 *see* 0027-9358 **4020**
1939-926X *see* 0014-4940 **5294**
1939-9278 *see* 0018-5868 **4101**
1939-9340 *see* 0018-9235 **3313**
1939-9359 *see* 0018-9545 **3316**
1939-9367 *see* 0093-9994 **3315**
1939-9375 *see* 0093-3813 **7015**
1939-9383 Global Economy and Development Working Paper **1596**
1939-974X *see* 1077-4289 **6566**
1939-9774 *see* 1939-6589 **5219**
1939-9782 *see* 1062-2969 **6111**
1939-9790 *see* 0009-4455 **7226**
1939-9804 *see* 0019-4646 **7972**
1939-9855 Fodor's in Focus Bahamas **8706**
1939-9863 Fodor's in Focus Savannah & Charleston *changed to* 1943-0167 **8706**
1939-9863 Fodor's in Focus Savannah & Charleston *changed to* 1943-0116 **8706**
1939-9871 Fodor's in Focus Puerto Rico **8706**
1939-991X Munich & Bavaria **8739**
1939-9952 The Montana Magazine of History *changed to* 0026-9891 **4304**
1939-9987 *see* 0020-8817 **7245**
1940-0004 New Global Studies **8122**
1940-0012 Personal Development **7390**
1940-0020 Gorgias Studies in Philosophy and Theology **6922**
1940-0047 A P Italian Language and Culture **5088**
1940-008X Lange U S M L E Road Map: Genetics **5660**
1940-011X Serviam **7265**
1940-0144 A R I E L **7717**
1940-0233 The Costumer **2253**
1940-0241 *see* 1940-0233 **2253**
1940-025X Baquiana Revista Literaria **5260**
1940-0268 *see* 1940-025X **5260**
1940-0284 *see* 0971-3336 **7398**
1940-0292 *see* 0971-3557 **1765**
1940-0306 *see* 0971-5215 **8899**
1940-0314 *see* 0971-6858 **1766**
1940-0322 *see* 0971-7218 **7911**
1940-0330 *see* 1940-0349 **2830**
1940-0349 Best Study Series for G E D. Social Studies **2830**
1940-0357 *see* 1940-0365 **2830**
1940-0365 The Best Study Series for G E D. Language Arts, Reading **2830**
1940-0411 Rural Poverty at a Glance **8083**
1940-042X Rural America at a Glance **8150**
1940-0438 Rural Children at a Glance **2174**
1940-0446 Rural Hispanics at a Glance **7314**
1940-0454 The Colorado Connection **3411**
1940-0470 *see* 1940-0489 **3492**
1940-0489 The Volunteer Monitor **3492**
1940-0500 *see* 1940-0519 **2652**
1940-0519 Felony Defendants in Large Urban Counties **2652**
1940-0543 *see* 0741-692X **4951**
1940-0551 I.M. Cowgirl **8868**
1940-0616 *see* 1095-5674 **820**
1940-0624 Voir **525**
1940-0632 Addiction Science & Clinical Practice **2689**
1940-0640 *see* 1940-0632 **2689**
1940-0659 Wade Research Foundation Reports **7928**
1940-0675 *see* 0022-0671 **2875**
1940-0683 *see* 0022-0973 **3067**
1940-0691 Current Essentials of Pediatrics **6090**
1940-0705 *see* 1940-0713 **2830**
1940-0713 The Best Study Series for G E D. Science **2830**
1940-073X Rasenna **2239**
1940-0748 The International Directory of Experts and Expertise **643**
1940-0764 Journal of Transnational American Studies **7980**
1940-0810 Journal of Spanish Language Media **2330**
1940-0829 Tropical Conservation Science **821**
1940-0837 Landshaft **6931**
1940-0853 G R C Expert **2419**
1940-0861 Journal of Textile Bioengineering and Informatics
1940-087X Journal of Visualized Experiments **685**
1940-0888 *see* 0022-1309 **7374**
1940-0896 *see* 0022-1325 **873**
1940-090X U.S. Census Bureau. Nonemployer Statistics **1272**
1940-0977 *see* 0065-6801 **465**
1940-0985 Claims Advisor **4499**
1940-0993 *see* 1940-0985 **4499**
1940-1000 Arab-American Yearbook **6692**
1940-1019 *see* 0022-3980 **7378**
1940-1027 *see* 0022-2895 **7376**
1940-1043 Upgrade (Birmingham) **5085**
1940-106X H R Skills Trainer **4095**
1940-1086 Arab-American Affairs **3519**
1940-1132 Culture and Customs of North America **334**
1940-1140 Berkshire Business Quarterly **1066**
1940-1159 Rock and Pop Perspectives
1940-1167 *see* 1940-1159
1940-1175 *see* 0971-8524 **8898**
1940-1183 *see* 0022-4545 **7380**
1940-1191 *see* 0035-7529 **6478**
1940-123X Montana Farm Bureau Federation News Brief **137**
1940-1248 The Activity Director's Companion **4038**
1940-1256 Promo Marketing **1838**
1940-1280 Chronogram (Hudson Valley Edition) **3972**
1940-1302 *see* 0036-8121 **7908**
1940-1310 *see* 0043-1672 **6398**
1940-1329 M.D. Anderson Breast Medical Oncology **6026**
1940-1337 The Genealogical Inquirer **3767**
1940-1345 National Underwriter. Life & Health **4516**
1940-1353 National Underwriter. P & C **4516**
1940-1361 Small Winery **610**
1940-137X Industry. Sarasota **5074**
1940-1388 Industry. Tampa Bay **5074**
1940-1396 Industry. Orlando **5074**
1940-140X Industry. Palm Beach **5074**
1940-1418 Industry. Kansas City **5074**
1940-1426 *see* 0972-0634 **5649**
1940-1434 I E E E Computer Security Foundations Symposium. Proceedings **2513**
1940-1450 St Tikhon's Theological Journal **7706**
1940-1485 Journal of International Business Ethics **6928**
1940-1493 Journal of Building Performance Simulation **1018**
1940-1507 *see* 1940-1493 **1018**
1940-1515 Jewish Living **3543**
1940-1531 Boston University Studies in Philosophy and Religion **7628**
1940-154X College of St. Elizabeth Journal of the Behavioral Sciences **7348**
1940-1558 *see* 0972-1509 **1114**
1940-1566 *see* 1391-5614 **1518**
1940-1574 *see* 0003-3197 **5777**
1940-1582 *see* 0043-8200 **7274**
1940-1590 *see* 0092-7678 **7222**
1940-1604 Pulse Magazine **5081**
1940-1612 International Journal of Press / Politics **4577**
1940-1620 *see* 1940-1612 **4577**
1940-1639 Journal of College and Character **2989**
1940-1647 The Proclamation **3559**
1940-1655 Real Law Central **7610**
1940-1663 Technology Transfer Tactics **1845**
1940-1671 *see* 1940-1663 **1845**
1940-168X Arkansas Sports 360.com *see* 1053-6582 **1061**
1940-1698 International Journal of Veterinary Pathology
1940-1701 *see* 1940-1698
1940-171X Agricultural Genetics
1940-1728 *see* 1940-171X
1940-1736 Mitochondrial D N A **738**
1940-1744 *see* 1940-1736 **738**
1940-1779 Phytoproduction†
1940-1787 *see* 1940-1779
1940-1795 *see* 1532-0928 **5270**
1940-1833 Journal of Applied Global Research **2989**
1940-1841 *see* 1940-1833 **2989**
1940-185X Journal of International Business Management & Research **1767**
1940-1876 Intellectbase International Consortium. Conference Proceedings **2987**
1940-1884 *see* 1940-1876 **2987**
1940-1892 *see* 0095-8964 **3445**
1940-1906 *see* 0161-5440 **8149**
1940-1914 Conference Addresses of the Long Island Philosophical Society Online **6911**
1940-1922 The Lowbrow Reader **5328**
1940-1949 Standard & Poor's Current Statistics **1652**
1940-1973 Workplace Immigration Report **1716**
1940-1981 *see* 1940-1973 **1716**
1940-2007 P M Q's Pizza Magazine **3659**
1940-2031 Ink Filled Page **5309**
1940-204X I M A Educational Case Journal **1290**
1940-2058 Knit 1 **6639**
1940-2074 N L C H S Newsletter **3775**
1940-2112 Purple Sky **6608**
1940-2120 Narrow Gauge Annual **4342**
1940-2198 Open (Fargo) **5079**
1940-2260 New Jersey A S K Grade 4 Language Arts Literacy Test **2891**
1940-2309 *see* 0099-2453 **1240**
1940-2317 *see* Urban Studies Abstracts **4437**
1940-2325 *see* 0091-5521 **2974**
1940-2376 Black M B A Magazine **1068**
1940-2414 California Camping **8690**
1940-2422 Taking Sides: Clashing views in Human Sexuality **7411**
1940-2430 The Rough Guide to First-Time Africa **8753**
1940-2449 Nonprescription Drug Therapy **6864**
1940-2465 *see* 1066-8969 **6246**
1940-2473 *see* 0887-302X **2246**
1940-2481 *see* 1047-4862 **4058**
1940-249X The Bump (San Diego Edition) **8844**
1940-2503 Computational Thermal Sciences **7053**
1940-2511 C O B A Passages **1078**
1940-252X *see* 1940-2511 **1078**
1940-2538 C O B A Connections **2276**
1940-2546 *see* 1940-2538 **2276**
1940-2554 *see* 1940-2503 **7053**
1940-2600 Revenue Recognition Guide **1300**
1940-2708 The Rough Guide to Yellowstone and Grand Teton **8753**
1940-2716 Travel + Leisure Family **8767**
1940-2791 The Green Book (Newton) **588**
1940-2805 Lancaster General Hospital. Journal **5659**
1940-2813 *see* 1940-2805 **5659**
1940-2821 Himalayan Journal of Development and Democracy **4183**
1940-283X Liberal Democracy Nepal Bulletin **4185**
1940-2848 Change Waves **1082**
1940-2880 California Transportation News **8669**
1940-2899 S G I M Forum **5948**
1940-2902 *see* 1940-2899 **5948**
1940-2910 *see* 1940-0659 **7928**
1940-2937 In Part **7761**
1940-2945 *see* 1940-2937 **7761**
1940-2953 Current Reviews for PeriAnesthesia Nurses **5771**
1940-2988 Metrologist **6404**
1940-2996 *see* 1940-2988 **6404**
1940-3003 High Performing Buildings **1011**
1940-3011 Innate Immunity **678**
1940-302X *see* 1940-3011 **678**
1940-3046 *see* 0742-4248 **5275**
1940-3054 *see* 1940-3003 **1011**
1940-3089 Barron's A P Calculus **5475**
1940-3097 Mark Lipinski's Quilter's Home **6640**
1940-3100 *see* 1062-9351 **3085**
1940-3119 Barron's A P Calculus with CD-ROM **5475**
1940-3135 The Advent Truth **7620**
1940-3143 The Legal Description **7598**
1940-3151 *see* 1542-9423 **63**
1940-316X The W A H M magazine *changed to* 1943-930X **1969**
1940-3178 M C L A **8238**
1940-3186 Critical Issues in Justice and Politics **7127**
1940-3194 Entro **2187**
1940-3208 *see* 0744-8481 **6990**
1940-3216 *see* 0883-1157 **5364**
1940-3224 American Society for Chinese Scholars. Journal **4442**
1940-3259 The International Journal of Soil, Sediment and Water **237**
1940-3267 Making Sense of Psychology **7384**
1940-3283 Fodor's in Focus Jamaica **8706**
1940-3291 Fodor's Greek Islands **8706**
1940-3305 Fodor's in Focus Virgin Islands **8706**
1940-3313 Fodor's in Focus California Wine Country **8706**
1940-3321 Fodor's in Focus Martha's Vineyard and Nantucket **8706**
1940-3348 WebSphere Journal **2510**
1940-3356 *see* 0883-2323 **1136**
1940-3364 *see* 0895-769X **5248**
1940-3372 The Plant Genome **877**
1940-3380 Research Notes on Educational Effectiveness **2904**
1940-3399 Soundings **6618**
1940-3402 Cold Spring Harbor Protocols **666**
1940-3410 Momentum (New York) **6161**
1940-3429 StemBook **878**
1940-3437 African Journalism and Communication Monographs
1940-3445 International Journal of Defense Acquisition Management **2227**
1940-3461 *see* 0026-3141 **7252**
1940-347X Russia & Eurasia Economic Digest **1581**
1940-3488 *see* 1940-347X **1581**
1940-3496 *see* 1936-5209 **798**
1940-350X R E S P A News Monthly **4765**
1940-3593 I P L Newsletter **6751**
1940-3615 N R H S Bulletin **8621**
1940-3623 Black Memorabilia **4330**
1940-3631 Putnam County Genealogical Society Journal **3780**
1940-364X Fees, Utilization, and Other Key Metrics **1745**
1940-3674 The Triangle/Triad Construction News **1041**
1940-3682 The Charlotte Construction News **991**
1940-3704 New Hampshire Wedding Magazine **5560**
1940-3755 Alpine Living **5064**
1940-3763 'Mo **4376**
1940-3771 Fastpitch Forever **8228**
1940-3801 Winners Within Us **3993**
1940-3844 Profiles of California **3121**
1940-3860 Sand Addiction **8268**
1940-3879 Inside Archery **8318**
1940-3917 U.S. National Forest Campground Guide. Intermountain Region **8339**
1940-3925 The Best of America's Test Kitchen **4352**
1940-3968 P C Building Bible **2579**
1940-3976 *see* 1939-571X **2969**
1940-3992 Laminate Flooring **1047**
1940-4026 *see* 0896-4289 **7339**
1940-4034 *see* 1074-2484 **6852**
1940-4042 National Intelligence Journal **7254**
1940-4050 *see* 1077-2197 **8151**
1940-4093 Orthopaedic Knowledge Online **6069**
1940-4107 Support Net **5766**
1940-4115 *see* 1940-4107 **5766**
1940-4123 TheStreet.com Ratings' Guide to Health Insurers **4525**
1940-4131 Tennessee Journal of Law & Policy **4793**
1940-414X *see* 1937-0717 **6849**
1940-4158 Australian Journal of Learning Difficulties **3036**
1940-4166 *see* 1940-4158 **3036**
1940-4220 Prisonworld **2666**
1940-4239 The Boca Raton Observer **5066**
1940-4247 Lake Erie Living **5075**
1940-4255 The Molloy Literary Journal **5336**
1940-431X *see* 1072-8325 **3206**
1940-4328 *see* 1521-9429 **795**
1940-4336 *see* 1065-3090 **3385**
1940-4344 *see* 1521-9437 **794**
1940-4352 *see* 1543-1649 **3272**
1940-4360 *see* 1093-3611 **2135**
1940-4379 *see* 1050-6934 **6248**
1940-4387 *see* 1045-988X **3045**
1940-4395 *see* 1063-2913 **475**
1940-4417 California Weds **5557**
1940-4425 *see* 1940-4417 **5557**
1940-4433 The Bump (Orange County Edition) **8844**
1940-4441 Green Customer News **3435**
1940-445X Biographies of Disease **5585**
1940-4468 *see* 1933-9607 **6162**

DIRECTORY 2010 1940-9818 9869

1940-4476 R M L E Online: Research in Middle Level Education **2902**
1940-4484 The Hardball Times Baseball Annual **8235**
1940-4514 Frommer's Portable Turks & Caicos **8711**
1940-4557 Standards for Telehealth **5717**
1940-4565 Standards for Medical/Dental Centers **4111**
1940-4573 Standards for Clinical Respiratory Services **4111**
1940-4581 Standards for Home Medical Equipment **4111**
1940-459X *see* 0090-6514 **6956**
1940-4603 *see* 1074-6846 **7129**
1940-4638 Juniata Voices (Online) **2288**
1940-4646 Renal Business Today **6273**
1940-4654 Calabar Magazine **5067**
1940-4662 *see* 0885-3436 **8140**
1940-476X *see* 1940-4778 **2700**
1940-4778 U.S. Department of Justice. National Drug Intelligence Center. National Drug Threat Assessment **2700**
1940-4840 *see* 1940-4859 **4825**
1940-4859 United States Attorneys Annual Statistical Report **4825**
1940-4921 Research In Gerontological Nursing **4054**
1940-493X Breathing **6212**
1940-4948 Diabetessource **5889**
1940-4964 Journal of Educational Concepts **3067**
1940-4972 *see* 1940-4964 **3067**
1940-4980 Journal of Tax Credit Housing **1932**
1940-5006 *see* 1536-0555 **5378**
1940-5014 *see* 1545-3855 **7374**
1940-5049 *see* 1031-461X **4132**
1940-5057 *see* 0043-325X **4317**
1940-5065 *see* 1521-5385 **4189**
1940-5073 *see* 1558-4313 **8183**
1940-509X *see* 0149-7677 **2684**
1940-5103 *see* 1540-3084 **5406**
1940-5111 *see* 1556-8547 **6742**
1940-512X *see* 1058-7446 **8904**
1940-5138 *see* 1557-637X **341**
1940-5146 Moshiach Times **7727**
1940-5162 Global Refining & Fuels Report **6771**
1940-5170 *see* 1940-5162 **6771**
1940-5189 Oil and Gas Investor This Week **6783**
1940-5197 *see* 1940-5189 **6783**
1940-5200 *see* 1078-3458 **5648**
1940-5227 Commercial Refrigeration Equipment **4117**
1940-5235 World Dyes & Organic Pigments **2244**
1940-5243 Construction Chemicals **1045**
1940-5251 World Flat Glass **1587**
1940-526X Challenge (Rockville) **4077**
1940-5278 *see* 1547-3929 **5351**
1940-5294 *see* 1940-526X **4077**
1940-5308 Kitchen Cabinets and Countertops **1047**
1940-5316 Wood Flooring **1049**
1940-5340 *see* 0971-9458 **4152**
1940-5359 *see* 1940-2031 **5309**
1940-5367 *see* 1940-3143 **7598**
1940-5405 eMarketing and Commerce **1427**
1940-5464 Townsend Letter **315**
1940-5480 *see* 1067-151X **6055**
1940-5510 Developmental Disabilities Research Reviews **6136**
1940-5529 *see* 1940-5510 **6136**
1940-5537 Sehnsucht **5369**
1940-5553 Ethics (Chicago) **4501**
1940-5561 Medical Tests and Signs **4514**
1940-5588 *see* 1084-7138 **6085**
1940-5596 *see* 1089-2532 **5799**
1940-5618 *see* 1092-2849 **6772**
1940-5626 Journal of Advanced Practice Nursing **5964**
1940-5634 American Nursing Review **5951**
1940-5642 Chronicle of Nursing **5955**
1940-5650 New York City Tails **6812**
1940-5669 *see* 1940-5650 **6812**
1940-5677 L.A. Tails **6810**
1940-5685 *see* 1940-5677 **6810**
1940-5707 Practical Promulgation **7536**
1940-574X Uranium Intelligence Weekly **3175**
1940-5758 The Code4Lib Journal **5002**
1940-5766 Southern California Real Estate Magazine **7613**
1940-5774 Pennsylvania Borough News **7500**
1940-5782 Life Images **6970**
1940-5790 Americana **4283**
1940-5804 Praeger Series on Healing and Managing Injury and Disease **5698**
1940-5812 Turfnet **8249**
1940-5820 Advances in Computational Mechanics **5549**
1940-5839 *see* 1940-5820 **5549**
1940-5847 Conemporary Issues in Education Research **2839**
1940-5855 Bike Monkey Magazine **8255**
1940-5898 Spirit of the West **8758**
1940-5901 International Journal of Clinical and Experimental Medicine **5906**
1940-5952 *see* 0252-9203 **8004**
1940-5960 Nephrology Times **6272**
1940-5979 Review of Behavioral Finance **1379**
1940-5987 *see* 1940-5979 **1379**
1940-6010 *see* 1938-6206 **7326**
1940-6029 *see* 1064-3745 **689**
1940-6037 *see* 1543-1894 **5947**
1940-6045 *see* 0893-2336 **926**
1940-6053 *see* 1557-2153 **6861**
1940-6061 Methods in Biotechnology **768**
1940-607X *see* 1940-6061 **768**
1940-6088 Florida English **5297**
1940-6096 DriftyTips **2637**
1940-6126 The Raymond Carver Review **5358**
1940-6134 Barron's Regents Exams and Answers. Integrated Algebra **5475**
1940-6207 Cancer Prevention Research **6013**
1940-6215 *see* 1940-6207 **6013**
1940-6223 International Journal of Applied Research in Natural Products **310**
1940-624X Journal for the School of Professional Counseling **7367**
1940-6258 *see* 1940-624X **7367**
1940-6282 How to Probate an Estate in California **4903**
1940-6320 *see* 0887-3631 **4017**
1940-6339 *see* 0196-6219 **2038**
1940-6355 The Alternative Media Handbook **7551**
1940-6363 *see* 1940-6355 **7551**
1940-6371 European Communication†
1940-638X *see* 1940-6371
1940-6398 Journal of Securities & Futures Law **1636**
1940-6401 5 Ingredient Meals **4369**
1940-6444 Variance **4526**
1940-6452 *see* 1940-6444 **4526**
1940-6479 H M E Business **5622**
1940-6487 *see* 0031-7217 **2898**
1940-6495 Meat Goat Monthly News **293**
1940-6509 Greater Fort Wayne Business Weekly **1115**
1940-6533 Skyline Review **5239**
1940-6541 *see* 1940-6533 **5239**
1940-6592 *see* 1559-6397 **6010**
1940-6606 Key Employee **4511**
1940-6614 G A E Mag **490**
1940-6622 Peterson's Master A P U.S. Government & Politics **7165**
1940-6630 National Concrete & Masonry Estimator **1025**
1940-672X Rock Slate **6444**
1940-6800 *see* 0193-7804 **348**
1940-6886 U.S. National Forest Campground Guide. Pacific Southwestern Region, North Section **8339**
1940-6940 International Journal of Sport Policy **8180**
1940-6959 *see* 1940-6940 **8180**
1940-6967 Journal of Nursing **5965**
1940-6975 Nursing Today **5975**
1940-6983 Nursing Shortage Update **5975**
1940-6991 World News & Nursing Report **5984**
1940-7009 Intelligence Reports **5961**
1940-7025 Shroud **5447**
1940-7033 Biology (Hauppauge) **660**
1940-7041 Current Orthopaedic Practice **6058**
1940-705X Rural Education Policy and Practice. Journal **2908**
1940-7068 Journal of Nursing Practice **5966**
1940-7106 B W / B I Expert **2408**
1940-7122 Iowa Archaeological Society. Newsletter **399**
1940-7211 Survey Report on Hi-Tech Industry Personnel Compensation **2494**
1940-7238 Perspectives on Administration and Supervision **1785**
1940-7246 *see* 1940-7238 **1785**
1940-7270 Material Handling Equipment & Systems **3389**
1940-7289 Electronic chemicals **3095**
1940-7319 M.D. Anderson Clinical Perspectives. Lymphoma & Myeloma **6027**
1940-7475 Perspectives on Augmentative and Alternative Communication **5160**
1940-7483 *see* 1940-7475 **5160**
1940-7491 *see* 1940-7505 **5160**
1940-7505 Perspectives on Voice and Voice Disorders **5160**
1940-7513 Perspectives on Issues in Higher Education (Online) **3045**
1940-7521 Perspectives on Issues in Higher Education (Print) *changed to* 1940-7513 **3045**
1940-753X Perspectives on Communication Disorders and Sciences in Culturally and Linguistically Diverse Populations **5160**
1940-7548 *see* 1940-753X **5160**
1940-7556 Perspectives on Swallowing and Swallowing Disorders **6084**
1940-7564 *see* 1940-7556 **6084**
1940-7572 Perspectives on Speech Science and Orofacial Disorders **6084**
1940-7580 *see* 1940-7572 **6084**
1940-7599 Perspectives on Fluency and Fluency Disorders **5160**
1940-7602 *see* 1940-7599 **5160**
1940-7610 Music and the Moving Image **6508**
1940-7629 Prevention Portal **6032**
1940-7661 *see* 1940-767X **6084**
1940-767X Perspectives on Hearing and Hearing Disorders. Research and Diagnostics **6084**
1940-7688 Perspectives on Aural Rehabilitation and its Instrumentation **4076**
1940-7696 *see* 1940-7688 **4076**
1940-770X Perspectives on Hearing and Hearing Disorders in Childhood **2165**
1940-7718 *see* 1940-770X **2165**
1940-7734 Perspectives on Hearing Conservation and Occupational Audiology (Online) **4076**
1940-7742 Perspectives on Language Learning and Education **3045**
1940-7750 *see* 1940-7742 **3045**
1940-7769 Perspectives on Neurophysiology and Neurogenic Speech and Language Disorders (Print) *changed to* 1940-7777 **6173**
1940-7777 Perspectives on Neurophysiology and Neurogenic Speech and Language Disorders (Online) **6173**
1940-7785 Perspectives on Gerontology **4053**
1940-7793 *see* 1940-7785 **4053**
1940-7807 Perspectives on School-Based Issues **3076**
1940-7815 *see* 1940-7807 **3076**
1940-7874 *see* 0253-3952 **8002**
1940-7882 Journal About Women in Higher Education **8869**
1940-7890 *see* 1940-7882 **8869**
1940-7947 Early Modern Japan **4181**
1940-7955 *see* 1940-7947 **4181**
1940-7963 Journal of Policy Research in Tourism, Leisure and Events **8726**
1940-7971 *see* 1940-7963 **8726**
1940-798X The Hardball Times Season Preview **8235**
1940-7998 The Bill James Gold Mine **8223**
1940-8013 Clinica Cardiology **5782**
1940-8021 *see* 1940-8013 **5782**
1940-8048 Perspectives on History **4156**
1940-8064 University of Pennsylvania. Journal of Business and Employment Law *changed to* 1945-2934 **4882**
1940-8064 University of Pennsylvania Journal of Business and Employment Law† **8996**
1940-8072 Minnesota Employment Law **1697**
1940-8080 Colorado Employment Law **1671**
1940-8153 Natural Solutions **313**
1940-8161 Virginia Wine Lover **612**
1940-8218 *see* 1940-7106 **2408**
1940-8250 *see* 0279-5442 **5956**
1940-8269 W S A Today **7942**
1940-8277 The Rockport Guide **8752**
1940-8293 Voces de la Frontera **3571**
1940-8307 Compendium (Yardley) **8795**
1940-8315 *see* 1940-8307 **8795**
1940-8323 Bottomline (Neenah) **1667**
1940-834X Current Trends in Islamist Ideology **7710**
1940-8358 *see* 1940-834X **7710**
1940-8366 Fodor's in Focus Bermuda **8706**
1940-8374 *see* 1937-8629 **3190**
1940-8382 South Asian Magazine for Action and Reflection (Online Edition) **3565**
1940-8390 American Holistic Veterinary Medical Association. Journal **8791**
1940-8404 Burrill Personalized Medicine Report **5589**
1940-8412 *see* 0305-7267 **3083**
1940-8420 Heritage Management **340**
1940-8439 *see* 1940-8420 **340**
1940-8447 International Review of Qualitative Research **7975**
1940-8455 *see* 1940-8447 **7975**
1940-8463 Minneapolis Observer Quarterly **5077**
1940-8471 Oil and Gas Investor's A & D Watch **6783**
1940-848X *see* 1940-8471 **6783**
1940-8498 Greatest Geniuses of the 21st Century **643**
1940-8501 *see* 1940-8293 **3571**
1940-8536 Concrete Today **993**
1940-8544 Desert Dog News **6806**
1940-8579 '76 Pyro **3258**
1940-8587 Perspectives on Audiology **4075**
1940-8595 *see* 1940-8587 **4075**
1940-8609 Education Week's Digital Directions **2948**
1940-8617 *see* 1940-8609 **2948**
1940-865X *see* 0278-3193 **3079**
1940-8668 The Bill James Handbook **8223**
1940-8676 Journal of Fibre Bioengineering and Informatics **750**
1940-8684 Healthcare Imaging Update **4097**
1940-8692 I B M S BoneKEy **5805**
1940-8706 Discharge Planning Advisor **5605**
1940-8714 New Haven Review **508**
1940-8722 *see* 1940-8714 **508**
1940-8730 Lectionary Worship Aids **7659**
1940-8749 Preaching the Miracles **7671**
1940-8781 Climate Change Business Journal **3411**
1940-879X *see* 1940-8781 **3411**
1940-8803 Dansiki **3529**
1940-8838 Beds & Borders **3724**
1940-8846 Garden Structures **3731**
1940-8862 Media History Monographs **4579**
1940-8870 Certified Organic **224**
1940-8889 *see* 1940-8870 **224**
1940-8935 The Career Champion **6694**
1940-8943 Organic Directory (Santa Cruz) *changed to* 1942-4264 **244**
1940-8951 B W Chicago† **8934**
1940-896X *see* 1940-8951 **8934**
1940-8994 Milk **6587**
1940-9001 Mealey's Diet Drugs Report **4731**
1940-901X Disaster and Trauma Psychology **7352**
1940-9036 *see* 1940-9044 **5913**
1940-9044 Forensic Science Policy & Management **5913**
1940-9052 The International Journal of Jungian Studies **7365**
1940-9060 *see* 1940-9052 **7365**
1940-9079 *see* 1048-6380 **5344**
1940-9095 *see* 0008-6533 **7953**
1940-9109 Hometown Cooking (Des Moines) **4360**
1940-9125 Roundtable Viewpoints. Physical Anthropology **354**
1940-9133 *see* 0735-1690 **7395**
1940-9141 *see* 1555-1024 **7365**
1940-915X Interface (Forest Grove) **2558**
1940-9176 The Anderson Agency Report **4530**
1940-9206 *see* 1524-0657 **8142**
1940-9214 *see* 1528-9168 **7375**
1940-9222 *see* 1048-1885 **7395**
1940-9257 Modern Pharmaceutical Research **6861**
1940-9281 *see* 1933-3218 **2329**
1940-929X American Journal of Media Psychology **7333**
1940-9303 *see* 1940-929X **7333**
1940-9311 International Journal of Media & Foreign Affairs **7243**
1940-932X *see* 1940-9311 **7243**
1940-9338 Journal of Communication Studies **8112**
1940-9346 *see* 1940-9338 **8112**
1940-9354 Journal of Health & Mass Communication **8113**
1940-9362 *see* 1940-9354 **8113**
1940-9370 Journal of Media Law & Ethics **4703**
1940-9389 *see* 1940-9370 **4703**
1940-9397 Journal of Media Sociology **8114**
1940-9400 *see* 1940-9397 **8114**
1940-9419 Russian Journal of Communication **7264**
1940-9427 *see* 1940-9419 **7264**
1940-9435 Infection Control Source **5817**
1940-9443 Catalog Success Tactics & Tips *changed to* 1947-9425 **1804**
1940-9451 Historicity **4144**
1940-9494 Review of Higher Education and Self-Learning **3000**
1940-9508 *see* 1940-9494 **3000**
1940-9516 *see* 1940-9494 **3000**
1940-9524 International Journal of Accounting Information Science and Leadership **1292**
1940-9532 *see* 1940-9524 **1292**
1940-9540 *see* 1940-9524 **1292**
1940-9583 Entorno **441**
1940-9591 *see* 1940-9583 **441**
1940-9613 Everywhere **8702**
1940-9664 Prominent **3559**
1940-9788 Clinica Diagnostics **5903**
1940-980X *see* 1940-9788 **5903**
1940-9818 *see* 0736-6205 **759**

ISSN

1941-5311 *see* 1941-482X **1937**
1941-532X Review (Ann Arbor) **7501**
1941-5338 Direction **2265**
1941-5362 Keyhole (Nashville) **5222**
1941-5370 Local Table **3742**
1941-5389 Abundant Living (Searcy) **4038**
1941-5419 Fodor's Complete Guide to the National Parks of the West **8705**
1941-5451 Watercolor Artist **526**
1941-546X *see* 1941-5370 **3742**
1941-5494 *see* 1097-5349 **4679**
1941-5508 *see* 1941-563X **1133**
1941-5516 Journal of Daoist Studies **7737**
1941-5524 *see* 1941-5516 **7737**
1941-5532 Effective Education **2852**
1941-5540 *see* 1941-5532 **2852**
1941-5559 Craftrends (Print) *changed to* Craftrends (Online) **8946**
1941-5583 Culture, Society and Masculinities **6302**
1941-5591 *see* 1941-5583 **6302**
1941-5605 The Broome Review **5266**
1941-563X Journal of Behavioral Studies in Business **1133**
1941-5656 Patriots of the American Revolution **4308**
1941-5664 *see* 1941-5656 **4308**
1941-5672 Miller-McCune **7155**
1941-5680 *see* 1933-2866 **711**
1941-5699 No Fluff Just Stuff Anthology **2509**
1941-5745 Michigan Journal of Business **1149**
1941-5753 *see* 1941-5745 **1149**
1941-5788 Journal of Business & Technology Law **4872**
1941-5834 Woodworking Magazine **1053**
1941-5842 Ereview of Tourism Research **8701**
1941-5877 Briefings on the Joint Commission **4089**
1941-5885 *see* 1941-5877 **4089**
1941-5893 Journal of Vascular and Interventional Neurology **6157**
1941-5907 Motherwords **2161**
1941-5915 *see* 1941-5907 **2161**
1941-5923 The American Journal of Case Reports **5571**
1941-594X Fathers Perspective **6290**
1941-5958 *see* 1941-594X **6290**
1941-6008 Studies in Ethics, Law, and Technology **4790**
1941-6024 Prince George's Suite **5080**
1941-6059 In Buona Salute Magazine **3539**
1941-6067 *see* 1941-6520 **1723**
1941-6083 Self Improvement Magazine **6647**
1941-6156 C C B J Weekly News **3407**
1941-6164 Small Scale Digital Device Forensics Journal **2675**
1941-6172 Teach Kids! Essentials **7777**
1941-6199 Conflict and Trade in the Middle East **4320**
1941-6210 International Journal of Digital Crime and Forensics **5914**
1941-6229 *see* 1941-6210 **5914**
1941-6237 International Journal of Ambient Computing and Intelligence **2424**
1941-6245 *see* 1941-6237 **2424**
1941-6253 International Journal of Sociotechnology and Knowledge Development **8110**
1941-6261 *see* 1941-6253 **8110**
1941-627X International Journal of e-Services and Mobile Applications **2327**
1941-6288 *see* 1941-627X **2327**
1941-6296 International Journal of Decision Support System Technology **2451**
1941-630X *see* 1941-6296 **2451**
1941-6318 International Journal of Nanotechnology and Molecular Computation **7017**
1941-6326 *see* 1941-6318 **7017**
1941-6334 U N C Medical Bulletin **5725**
1941-6342 Journal of Intercollegiate Sport **8182**
1941-6350 Kiki **2197**
1941-6369 Bank Directory **1974**
1941-6393 Primal Parenting **2166**
1941-6431 Compensation in Consulting **1671**
1941-644X The Global Consulting Marketplace **1748**
1941-6466 Baker Institute Policy Report **7109**
1941-6490 The 45th **4369**
1941-6520 The Academy of Management Annals **1723**
1941-6539 M J S A Journal **4568**
1941-6555 Mob Candy **5077**
1941-6563 Alternative Investment Law Report **4613**
1941-6571 *see* 1941-6563 **4613**
1941-658X Journal of Cost Analysis and Parametrics **1294**
1941-6628 Journal of Gastrointestinal Cancer **5896**
1941-6636 *see* 1941-6628 **5896**
1941-6652 Texas Neuroscience Review **6187**
1941-6660 *see* 1941-6652 **6187**
1941-6679 *see* 1543-5962 **1767**
1941-6687 *see* 1543-5970 **2542**
1941-6695 Official N A I C Quarterly Statement Blank. Life **4517**
1941-6741 *see* 1530-5678 **5869**
1941-6768 C Q Global Researcher **7111**
1941-6857 Metromom's Direct Connect **8875**
1941-6881 After Culture **323**
1941-689X InterStat **8380**
1941-6903 Latino Suave **3547**
1941-6911 Journal of Atrial Fibrillation **5791**
1941-6938 Aisthesis **4441**
1941-6946 New York Penal Law and Related Provisions **4895**
1941-7012 Journal of Renewable and Sustainable Energy **3140**
1941-7020 American Journal of Engineering and Applied Sciences **3181**
1941-7039 *see* 1941-7020 **3181**
1941-7047 W W E Kids Magazine **2221**
1941-7063 Yea Alabama **8252**
1941-7071 Sea of Red **8245**
1941-7098 Successful Promotions **1845**
1941-7128 The Players Club†
1941-7144 Pennsylvania Patient Safety Advisory **7535**
1941-7160 Music Cataloging Bulletin (Online) **5033**
1941-7179 *see* Adunagow Magazine **3515**
1941-7187 Seniors Housing & Care Journal **4056**
1941-7195 Issues in Intercultural Communications **5130**
1941-7209 Issues in Political Discourse Analysis **7145**
1941-7225 *see* 0895-7061 **5776**
1941-7233 International Journal of Psychology: A Biopsychosocial Approach **7365**
1941-725X *see* 0742-7433 **8906**
1941-7284 Marine Tactical **6432**
1941-7292 *see* 1941-7284 **6432**
1941-7306 DesignIntelligence **440**
1941-7314 Cal Literature & Arts Magazine **5269**
1941-7322 Current Protocols in Stem Cell Biology **831**
1941-7330 *see* 1932-6157 **8345**
1941-7349 Business and Economic History On-line **1070**
1941-7357 Earth Jurisprudence Student Series **3415**
1941-7373 Virtualities **3009**
1941-7381 Sports Health **6233**
1941-739X Nursing (Year) Student Drug Handbook **6864**
1941-7403 *see* 1941-4110 **7515**
1941-7411 Terahertz Science & Technology **7923**
1941-7462 Family & Intimate Partner Violence Quarterly **8040**
1941-7470 EcoHome **1005**
1941-7497 *see* 0022-2909 **6580**
1941-7519 Opuscula Philolichenum **806**
1941-7527 *see* 1941-7519 **806**
1941-7535 HospitalCodeChek **4101**
1941-7543 CorrectCodeChek **4091**
1941-7551 *see* 1940-7041 **6058**
1941-7586 Project on Gobal Migration and Transnational Politics **7291**
1941-7594 *see* 1941-7586 **7291**
1941-7624 *see* 1942-2709 **7621**
1941-7632 *see* 1941-7640 **5782**
1941-7640 Circulation. Cardiovascular Interventions **5782**
1941-7659 Tropical Lepidoptera Research **860**
1941-7683 Southwestern Economic Review **1519**
1941-7691 *see* 1941-7683 **1519**
1941-7705 *see* 1941-7713 **5782**
1941-7713 Circulation. Cardiovascular Quality and Outcomes **5782**
1941-7721 Old-House Journal's New Old House **1028**
1941-7764 H I P A A Compliance Alert **4094**
1941-7772 ObGyn Coder's Pink Sheet **6000**
1941-7799 Interamerican Journal of Education for Democracy **2867**
1941-7837 Orthopedic Coder's Pink Sheet **6070**
1941-7845 Primary Care Coder's Pink Sheet **5699**
1941-7853 *see* 1941-7837 **6070**
1941-7861 A M S Studies in Music **6541**
1941-7934 Pedagogy and the Human Sciences **7389**
1941-7985 Social and Psychological Issues **7408**
1941-7993 Cardiology Coder's Pink Sheet **5779**
1941-8000 *see* 1941-7993 **5779**
1941-8027 Journal of Educational Technology Development and Exchange **8429**
1941-8035 *see* 1941-8027 **8429**
1941-8043 Journal of Collective Bargaining in the Academy **2989**
1941-806X Gastroenterology Coder's Pink Sheet **5924**
1941-8078 *see* 1941-806X **5924**
1941-8132 Keatinge and Conaway on Choice of Business Entity **1890**
1941-8167 Sacred Tribes Journal **7741**
1941-8205 Chesapeake Times **3972**
1941-823X The Awakening **6907**
1941-8248 Deduct It! **1959**
1941-8264 Lithosphere **2753**
1941-8299 Anesthesia & Pain Coder's Pink Sheet **5769**
1941-8302 *see* 1941-8299 **5769**
1941-8310 Health Sciences Review **5626**
1941-8329 *see* 1941-8310 **5626**
1941-8337 Journal of Public Health Leadership **7529**
1941-8345 *see* 1941-8337 **7529**
1941-8353 Craftstylish **533**
1941-837X *see* 1369-6998 **5651**
1941-8388 Architechural S S L **4553**
1941-8396 Discovery **1002**
1941-840X General Surgery Coder's Pink Sheet **6244**
1941-8418 International Journal of Prevention Practice and Research **5639**
1941-8426 *see* 1941-8418 **5639**
1941-8434 *see* 0741-6563 **5040**
1941-8442 Education Channel Partner **3020**
1941-8450 *see* 1522-5658 **7656**
1941-8477 Journal of Virtual Worlds Research **2330**
1941-8485 The Ranger's Guide to Yellowstone **8750**
1941-8493 Hemostasis Laboratory **5938**
1941-8531 Food & Beverage Packaging **6710**
1941-854X Confection & Snack Retailing **3673**
1941-8558 Art Ltd. **470**
1941-8574 *see* 1559-8543 **4049**
1941-8612 Urology Coder's Pink Sheet **6276**
1941-8620 Interventional Procedure Coder's Pink Sheet **5641**
1941-8639 The Counter Terrorist **2226**
1941-8647 International Journal of Mobile and Blended Learning **2949**
1941-8655 *see* 1941-8647 **2949**
1941-8663 International Journal of Interdisciplinary Telecommunications and Networking **2327**
1941-8671 *see* 1941-8663 **2327**
1941-868X International Journal of Information Systems and Social Change **2522**
1941-8698 *see* 1941-868X **2522**
1941-8701 Bonbon **2180**
1941-871X The History of the Holy Mar Ma'in **7648**
1941-8728 Grill It! **4359**
1941-8760 Journal of Global Change and Governance **7248**
1941-8787 Pediatric Coder's Pink Sheet **6100**
1941-8795 Ophthalmology Coder's Pink Sheet **6048**
1941-8809 Bicycle Quarterly **8254**
1941-8817 Today's Medical Developments **5722**
1941-8833 International Journal of Advanced Case Analysis in Health **5637**
1941-8841 *see* 1941-8833 **5637**
1941-885X Transplantation Updates **6261**
1941-8868 *see* 1941-885X **6261**
1941-8884 West Shore Magazine **5086**
1941-8930 The Journal of Eurasian Law **4933**
1941-8949 *see* 1941-8930 **4933**
1941-8957 Diagnosis Coding Pro for Home Health **4501**
1941-8965 Home Care Outcomes **4098**
1941-904X How We Live Magazine **4542**
1941-9058 MultiSpecialty Coding Pro **4515**
1941-9066 Current Cardiovascular Imaging Reports **5784**
1941-9074 *see* 1941-9066 **5784**
1941-9104 Vibe Vixen Presents Teen Dreamz† **8997**
1941-9120 Wild Apples **5399**
1941-9155 The Brides of Oklahoma **5557**
1941-9198 Loci **5509**
1941-9201 Private Payment Watch **4519**
1941-921X *see* 1941-9201 **4519**
1941-9228 R V Pro **8509**
1941-9236 Got Genealogy News **3769**
1941-9244 *see* 1941-9236 **3769**
1941-9260 *see* 0032-5481 **5698**
1941-9295 *see* 1067-2206 **5910**
1941-9309 Home Health Line's Private Duty Insider **4098**
1941-9333 The South Asian Times **3565**
1941-9341 *see* 1941-9333 **3565**
1941-9376 Atlantic Reports **8026**
1941-9430 The Journal of Physician Assistant Education **5654**
1941-9449 *see* 1941-9430 **5654**
1941-9457 Moonset **5336**
1941-9465 Black Clock **5263**
1941-9473 Performance Boats **8280**
1941-9481 P.R.N. **6866**
1941-949X Pasticcio Quartz **511**
1941-9511 *see* 0742-3330 **4475**
1941-9546 Ambulatory Surgery Coding & Reimbursement Insider **4087**
1941-9554 *see* 1941-9546 **4087**
1941-9562 New Wineskins **7809**
1941-9570 *see* 1941-9562 **7809**
1941-9600 C B A Retailers + Resources **7557**
1941-9619 Georgia Studies Weekly. My State **2859**
1941-9635 *see* 0091-9578 **7097**
1941-9651 Circulation. Cardiovascular Imaging **5782**
1941-9724 *see* 1084-7146 **4092**
1941-9732 Modern Republic **7155**
1941-9740 Texas Motions in Limine **4966**
1941-9759 Conscious Choice **3412**
1941-9775 California Search and Seizure **4885**
1941-9783 Global Urban Development Magazine **4411**
1941-9848 E U E C. Online Journal **3127**
1941-9864 Advances in Investment Analysis and Portfolio Management. New Series **1306**
1941-9872 G P W A Times **8174**
1941-9880 *see* 1941-9872 **8174**
1941-9899 Psychology of Sexualities **7399**
1941-9902 *see* 1941-9899 **7399**
1941-997X Pet Industry Directory and Buying Guide *see* 1935-6323 **6813**
1942-0013 Electronic Liquid Crystal Communications **2110**
1942-0021 Pass It On **4756**
1942-0064 New Mexico Business Magazine **1153**
1942-0080 *see* 1941-9651 **5782**
1942-0102 Scandals in American History **4312**
1942-0129 Traveling Sportsman† **8994**
1942-0137 New York State Grade 3 Elementary-Level Math Test **2891**
1942-0145 New York State Grade 3 Elementary-Level English Language Arts Test **2891**
1942-0161 *see* 1059-1729 **4689**
1942-0196 Louisiana Practice Series. Louisiana Construction Law **4725**
1942-020X New Jersey Attorney Discipline **4743**
1942-0218 Special Study for Corporate Counsel on Corporate Lobbying Activity **4881**
1942-0226 North Carolina Family Law Statutes **4913**
1942-0234 West's Code of Federal Regulations Annotated. Title 20, Employees' Benefits **1714**
1942-0242 West's Code of Federal Regulations Annotated. Title 42, Public Health **7545**
1942-0250 West's Code of Federal Regulations Annotated. Title 37, Patents, Trademarks, and Copyrights **6760**
1942-0269 Expert Witnesses in Civil Trials **4670**
1942-0277 Michigan Nonstandard Jury Instructions. Civil **4733**
1942-0285 Michigan Nonstandard Jury Instructions. Criminal **4894**
1942-0293 State Securities. Blue Sky Statutes Annotated **4881**
1942-0307 Practitioner's Manual of Patent Examining Procedure **4759**
1942-0315 West's 50 State Surveys: Family Law **4915**
1942-0323 Motions in Limine **4956**
1942-0331 Ohio Motions in Limine **4958**
1942-034X Federal Motions in Limine **4951**
1942-0358 North Carolina Motions in Limine **4958**
1942-0455 Educating Children with Exceptionalities **3039**
1942-0536 Success Magazine Ltd **1795**
1942-0560 Meet the Mets **8238**
1942-0579 America's Registry of Outstanding Professionals **1725**
1942-0587 Aspect **434**
1942-0595 Buckeye Battle Cry **8224**
1942-0609 Disfunkshion Magazine **2253**
1942-0617 Beliefs and Values **7624**
1942-0625 *see* 1942-0617 **7624**
1942-0633 Website Magazine **2569**
1942-0641 *see* 1942-0633 **2569**
1942-065X I E E E Women in Engineering Magazine **3196**
1942-0668 *see* 1942-065X **3196**
1942-0676 Journal of Social Entrepreneurship **1769**
1942-0684 *see* 1942-0676 **1769**
1942-0714 Tar Heel Tip-Off **8248**
1942-0730 Journal of Electromagnetic Analysis and Applications **7052**
1942-0749 *see* 1942-0730 **7052**
1942-0773 *see* 0256-0054 **4574**
1942-0846 The Battered Suitcase **5260**
1942-0862 mAbs **5763**
1942-0870 *see* 1942-0862 **5763**
1942-0889 Communicative & Integrative Biology **666**

1942-6704 see 1942-6712 2170
1942-6712 U C Davis Journal of Juvenile Law and Policy 2170
1942-6720 see 1075-2846 7238
1942-6739 see 1539-5693 4805
1942-6755 see 0085-8269 4815
1942-6763 see 1081-549X 8889
1942-6771 see 1942-678X 4807
1942-678X Vanderbilt Journal of Entertainment and Technology Law 4807
1942-6801 4 Health 5739
1942-681X see 1942-6801 5739
1942-6828 Policy & Practice 8062
1942-6836 Salute to Freedom 6444
1942-6852 Scene in S.A. 3988
1942-6860 The Writers Studio Journal 5401
1942-6879 Journal of Unconventional Parks, Tourism & Recreation Research 4979
1942-6917 Affordable Mansion 4531
1942-6968 Youth Connex 7696
1942-6976 Plateau (Richmond Hill) 6606
1942-7085 Small Plant News 3664
1942-7123 see Estimated Use of Water in the United States in (Year) 8823
1942-7158 see 1936-394X 1715
1942-7166 Coalition Chronicle 6416
1942-7182 Undergraduate Leadership Review 3006
1942-7190 Studies in the Fantastic 5382
1942-7239 Landslide 4712
1942-7255 University of Missouri Observatory. Publications 583
1942-7271 C P A Client Bulletin 1283
1942-7298 MacTribe 2577
1942-7387 Mealey's Litigation Report: Data and Identity Security 4731
1942-7395 Building the Everyday 436
1942-7417 The Shakespeare Papers 5434
1942-7425 Information Digest for the Skilled Nursing Industry 5961
1942-7433 see 1942-7425 5961
1942-7441 New Jersey Judicial Discipline 4957
1942-745X Nevada Business Law Desk Book 4876
1942-7468 Family Circle Quick & Easy Cooking 4357
1942-7476 Family Circle Annual Recipes 4357
1942-7514 F M L A Revealed 1681
1942-7522 see 0145-5613 6079
1942-7530 Quick Reference to Payroll Compliance 1299
1942-7557 International Cold Chain Directory 4121
1942-7573 Technology, Psychology, and Health 5720
1942-7581 Swiss International Arbitration Law Reports 4942
1942-759X see 1942-7581 4942
1942-7603 Drug Testing and Analysis 6836
1942-7611 see 1942-7603 6836
1942-7743 Preventing Sexual Violence 6103
1942-7751 Journal of Research on Leadership Education 3026
1942-776X F B C O Today
1942-7778 see 1942-776X
1942-7786 Human Geography 8106
1942-7794 The Investigative Sciences Journal 7868
1942-7808 see 1932-4510 2571
1942-7824 Moultrie County, Illinois Heritage Journal 3775
1942-7867 Transportation Letters 8516
1942-7875 see 1942-7867 8516
1942-7891 Population Health Management 5697
1942-7905 see 1942-7891 5697
1942-7999 Ultimate Italian 4368
1942-8006 Country French 4536
1942-8014 Cast Polymer Connection 7091
1942-8022 Justice Research and Policy (Online) 2658
1942-8154 The Mississippi Episcopalian 7768
1942-8162 International Journal of Business, Marketing, and Decision Sciences 1821
1942-8189 Journal of Global Intelligence & Policy 7248
1942-8197 see 1942-8189 7248
1942-8200 Anthropology Now 327
1942-8227 Game Changers 1626
1942-826X see 1062-6212 4803
1942-8286 see 1527-5787 4803
1942-8308 see 0008-7262 4641
1942-8324 see 0042-2363 4806
1942-8340 see 0191-9822 4814
1942-8375 see 1097-0800 4795
1942-8383 see 0043-0420 4810
1942-8391 see 0009-6881 4803
1942-8405 see 0041-9915 4805
1942-8421 The University of Chicago Publications in Anthropology. Social Anthropological Series 359
1942-8456 Tauber Institute for the Study of European Jewry Series 4272
1942-8464 Cracking the C A H S E E. Mathematics 5481
1942-8472 Cracking the C A H S E E. English-Language Arts 2840
1942-8480 Great Western Fiction†
1942-8502 see 1068-7955 4809
1942-8510 see 1527-0874 7267
1942-8529 see 0042-1448 4806
1942-8553 see 0733-401X 3471
1942-8561 see 1521-2823 4853
1942-857X see 0040-4411 4794
1942-8588 see 1942-9789 4795
1942-860X see 0564-6197 4795
1942-8618 see 1098-4577 4795
1942-8626 see 1047-8035 4702
1942-8634 see 1081-5449 4795
1942-8642 Best's Financial Suite. State/Line, P / C Lines, US 4495
1942-8650 see 1942-8669 4745
1942-8669 New York Real Property Law Handbook 4745
1942-8677 New York Pattern Jury Instructions Companion Handbook 4745
1942-8685 Louisiana Civil Jury Instruction Companion Handbook 4725
1942-8693 see 1943-9296 5444
1942-8790 The Armor & Cavalry Journal 6411
1942-8812 Public Health 7537
1942-8820 Appraisal Press 7582
1942-8839 see 1942-8820 7582
1942-8847 Conservation Footprints 2607
1942-8871 eNewsbytes, News Updates from Delaware N R C S 2610
1942-9002 Steel Market Update 6333
1942-9010 International Journal of Virtual Communities and Social Networking 2559
1942-9029 see 1942-9010 2559
1942-9037 see 1942-9045 2592
1942-9045 International Journal of Software Science and Computational Intelligence 2592
1942-907X Wiley Operations Management Series for Professionals 1801
1942-9088 Wiley Series in Survey Methodology 8414
1942-910X Math + Science Connection 2885
1942-9118 see 1942-910X 2885
1942-9126 Wissenschaftliche Abhandlungen 6628
1942-9169 see Environmental Justice Quarterly 3425
1942-9177 see 0892-5593 4803
1942-9185 see 1555-5070 4931
1942-9193 Gonzaga Journal of International Law 4927
1942-9207 see 0162-9174 4803
1942-9223 see 0271-9835 4804
1942-9231 see 0276-9948 4804
1942-9258 see 0083-4025 4804
1942-9266 see University of Louisville Law Review 4915
1942-9312 Transaction Series in Higher Education 3005
1942-9347 Ecopsychology 7353
1942-9371 Harvest (Portland) 7799
1942-938X Modern Scientific Evidence. Forensics 2660
1942-9436 I Heart Magazine 6969
1942-9444 Directory of the New Urbanism 441
1942-9452 Fire Investigator's Law Bulletin 2652
1942-9460 Powder Diffraction File. Hanawalt Seach Manual for Experimental Patterns. Inorganic Phases 2104
1942-9479 see 1934-2926 4404
1942-9487 Federal Circuit Historical Society. Journal 4951
1942-9525 Journal of Instruction-Level Parallelism 2429
1942-9533 Electronics and Communications in Japan 3096
1942-9541 see 1942-9533 3096
1942-9568 Singular 5083
1942-9592 Roundtable Viewpoints. Business Law 4880
1942-9665 International Journal of Social Health Information Management 7527
1942-9673 see 1942-9665 7527
1942-9681 Psychological Trauma 7397
1942-969X see 1942-9681 7397
1942-9711 see 0019-6673 4298
1942-972X Extreme Fighting Magazine 8172
1942-9762 Journal of Food Law & Policy 4701
1942-9770 see 1942-9762 4701
1942-9789 Texas Tech Administrative Law Journal 4795
1942-9819 see 0566-2389 4805
1942-9843 see 8756-7326 4797
1942-9851 see 0042-0190 4805
1942-986X see 1538-9979 4798
1942-9886 see 0042-2533 4807
1942-9894 see 0145-2908 4808
1942-9908 see 1047-6857 3471
1942-9924 Wyoming Law Review 4816
1942-9932 see 1942-9924 4816
1942-9940 see 1045-5183 3473
1942-9991 see 0043-1621 4811
1943-0000 see 1533-4686 4811
1943-0035 see 0195-7643 4814
1943-0043 see 0190-6593 4812
1943-0051 see 0270-272X 4814
1943-0094 Compass American Guides: Yellowstone & Grand Teton National Parks 8694
1943-0108 Fodor's in Focus Great Smoky Mountains National Park 8706
1943-0116 Fodor's in Focus Savannah 8706
1943-0132 Fodor's Family Boston with Kids 8705
1943-0140 Fodor's Family Washington, D.C. with Kids 8705
1943-0159 Fodor's Family San Francisco with Kids 8705
1943-0167 Fodor's in Focus Charleston 8706
1943-0205 Cases in Public Health Communication and Marketing 7512
1943-0213 Journal of Advanced Researches on Bioinformatics 826
1943-023X Journal of Advanced Researches on Dynamical and Control Systems 3384
1943-0248 Journal of Advanced Researches on Differential Equations 5500
1943-0256 F & B 197
1943-0264 Cold Spring Harbor Perspectives in Biology 666
1943-0272 Vocational Education & Training Abstracts 2937
1943-0280 see 1943-0272 2937
1943-0302 Unitarian Universalist Service. Service Committee News changed to 1943-0310 7741
1943-0310 Rights Now 7741
1943-0353 see 0306-9400 4717
1943-0361 see The I A L L T Journal of Language Learning Technologies 5125
1943-0396 Uniformed Services University of the Health Sciences. Report 5726
1943-040X U S U Newsletter 6450
1943-0442 The Daily Charge 6417
1943-0515 eNewsbytes, News Updates from Idaho N R C S 2610
1943-0582 I E E E Solid State Circuits Magazine 3102
1943-0590 see 1943-0582 3102
1943-0604 I E E E Transactions on Autonomous Mental Development 7361
1943-0612 see 1943-0604 7361
1943-0620 Journal of Optical Communications and Networking 7079
1943-0639 see 1943-0620 7079
1943-0647 see 1943-0655 7076
1943-0655 I E E E Photonics Journal 7076
1943-0663 I E E E Embedded Systems Letters 2471
1943-0671 see 1943-0663 2471
1943-068X I E E E Transactions on Computational Intelligence and A I in Games 2449
1943-0698 see 1943-068X 2449
1943-0701 Medical Innovation & Business 5669
1943-0744 International Journal of Agent Technologies and Systems 2450
1943-0752 see 1943-0744 2450
1943-0760 The Normal School 5342
1943-0779 Asian Politics and Policy 7222
1943-0787 see 1943-0779 7222
1943-0817 China Maritime Studies 6416
1943-0825 see 1943-0817 6416
1943-085X International Journal of Green Nanotechnology. Biomedicine 766
1943-0868 see 1943-085X 766
1943-0876 International Journal of Green Nanotechnology: Physics and Chemistry 7016
1943-0884 see 1943-0876 7016
1943-0892 International Journal of Green Nanotechnology 3347
1943-0906 see 1943-0892 3347
1943-0922 Journal of Radiology Case Reports 6201
1943-0930 see 0036-8423 7910
1943-0949 P R E P (Year) Self Assessment see 1943-0965 6098
1943-0965 P R E P, the Curriculum 6098
1943-0973 B S A / A M L Update 1310
1943-099X Executive for Christ 7642
1943-1007 see 1943-099X 7642
1943-1015 Spokane Metro Magazine 5083
1943-1023 Planos y Capacetes 3280
1943-1031 Indy Kids 2194
1943-104X Black Belt African American Genealogical and Historical Society. Journal 3522
1943-1082 Hawaii Rules of Evidence Manual 4685
1943-1090 see 1943-1082 4685
1943-1104 see 1091-9724 3475
1943-1120 see 0043-650X 4815
1943-1139 see 1943-1600 4815
1943-1147 see 0026-4148 6436
1943-1155 see 1058-5427 4794
1943-1163 see 1060-1007 4796
1943-118X see 1543-3234 4843
1943-121X see 0502-4110 2937
1943-1228 see 0041-056X 6759
1943-1252 Columbia Journal of East European Law changed to 1941-8930 4933
1943-1260 International Journal of Civil Society Law 4833
1943-1279 see 1558-9226 4935
1943-1287 see 1089-5450 4931
1943-1295 see 1527-8352 4932
1943-1309 Maximum Travel Per Diem Allowances for Foreign Areas (Email) 4730
1943-1317 see 1548-4076 4853
1943-1333 see 1933-5555 4814
1943-135X see 1065-8254 4853
1943-1449 Renewable Fuels Supply Americas 3254
1943-1457 Above the Fold 4986
1943-1465 Highlights High Five 2193
1943-1473 Think Journal 5388
1943-1481 Wichita Falls Literature & Art Review 5398
1943-152X Green Electronics Daily 3100
1943-1562 see 1941-1022 7399
1943-1600 Wisconsin Journal of Law, Gender & Society 4815
1943-1651 Paper Trends changed to 1946-0457 539
1943-1708 see 1068-9893 4799
1943-1716 U C L A Journal of Law and Technology 4799
1943-1724 see 0041-5650 4799
1943-1732 see 0197-4564 4799
1943-1767 Women, Minorities, and Persons with Disabilities in Science and Engineering (Online) 8147
1943-1775 Women, Minorities, and Persons with Disabilities in Science and Engineering (Print) changed to 1943-1767 8147
1943-1813 International Journal of Organizational Innovation 1760
1943-183X Modern Filmmakers 6507
1943-1848 Search (Washington DC) 7680
1943-1856 see 1943-1848 7680
1943-1864 One+ 6282
1943-1880 Stance 6953
1943-1899 see 1943-1880 6953
1943-1902 News China 3554
1943-1910 Auto Events Magazine 8558
1943-1929 Independent Provisioner 3646
1943-2119 Louisiana N R C S Conservation Update 2618
1943-2135 First State Update changed to 1942-8871 2610
1943-2143 First State E-bytes changed to 1942-8871 2610
1943-2151 see 0898-2511 2856
1943-2178 see 0266-6286 5246
1943-2186 see 1460-1176 3751
1943-2194 Administrative Professional Today 1724
1943-2208 The Jury Expert 4707
1943-2216 see 0007-8204 3060
1943-2348 see 0034-527X 3078
1943-2356 see 0098-6291 3004
1943-2402 see 0360-9170 3070
1943-2437 Journal of Heart Failure Nursing†
1943-2445 Rehabilitation Compensation Report 4110
1943-2461 Annals of Advances in Automotive Medicine 5575
1943-247X see 1943-2461 5575
1943-2496 see 1943-2437
1943-2534 Cancer Summaries & Commentaries 6014
1943-2550 Collaborative Anthropologies 333
1943-2569 Native South 6635
1943-2593 Briefings in Entrepreneurial Finance 1729
1943-2607 see 1943-2593 1729
1943-2615 Diabetic Living Everyday Cooking 4356
1943-2623 Fastcompany.com 1745
1943-2631 see 0016-6731 869
1943-264X see 0096-1191 6725
1943-2658 see 1083-1363 2785
1943-2666 see 1529-6466 6477
1943-2674 see 0016-7606 2738
1943-2682 see 0091-7613 2742
1943-2690 see 1052-5173 2734
1943-2704 see 1044-7946 6075
1943-2720 see 0889-5899 6070

ISSN

DIRECTORY 2010 1944-5431 9875

1943-832X Current Diagnosis & Treatment Nephrology & Hypertension **6266**
1943-8338 Journal of Family Life **8113**
1943-8400 M S A Link **7713**
1943-8419 Implementation of the National Coral Reef Action Strategy **3439**
1943-8435 European Fuel Price Service. Germany and Italy **6768**
1943-8443 European Fuel Price Service. United Kingdom **6768**
1943-8451 Survey Report on Compensation Policies & Practices in the Insurance Industry **1709**
1943-846X Survey Report on Hospital & Health Care Compensation Policies & Practices **1709**
1943-8494 Connecticut Criminal and Motor Vehicle Laws **4886**
1943-8508 Georgia Civil Discovery **4831**
1943-8524 Pennsylvania Worker's Compensation **4757**
1943-8532 C E O Q Magazine **1731**
1943-8540 *see* 1943-8532 **1731**
1943-8613 Global Studies: Europe **7238**
1943-8621 Music and Medicine **5681**
1943-863X *see* 1943-8621 **5681**
1943-8648 Interiors & Sources **4559**
1943-8656 Pilates Style Annual *see* 1549-6937 **6994**
1943-8672 Information Systems and eBusiness Spending **2537**
1943-9008 *see* 0566-0785 **4801**
1943-9296 Macabre Cadaver **5444**
1943-930X The Work-at-Home Parent Magazine **1969**
1943-9334 Pure and Applied Undergraduate Texts **5526**
1943-9342 Journal of Development Effectiveness **1600**
1943-9369 Bible in Technology **7625**
1943-9377 Biblical Intersections **7627**
1943-9385 American Music Review **6544**
1943-9393 *see* 1943-9385 **6544**
1943-9407 *see* 1943-9342 **1600**
1943-9490 P C A S Newsletter (Harrisonburg) **351**
1943-9598 Northwest Florida Heritage Magazine **4306**
1943-9601 Land Development **4418**
1943-961X The Journal of Medicine **5652**
1943-9628 *see* 1943-961X **5652**
1943-9636 American Aerospace Archive **46**
1943-9644 Walloomsack Review **4317**
1943-9652 The Comparative Humanities Review **4448**
1943-9660 *see* 0077-5630 **7838**
1943-9687 Watershed (Bloomsburg) **5397**
1943-9695 Tuckasegee Valley Historical Review **4315**
1943-9709 The Land Report **7597**
1943-9717 *see* 1943-9709 **7597**
1943-9725 Journal for Computing Teachers **2428**
1943-9733 J C S E Online *changed to* 1943-9725 **2428**
1943-9741 Focus on Global Resources **5010**
1943-975X Global Resources *changed to* 1943-9741 **5010**
1943-9784 *see* 1532-835X **2609**
1943-9792 Bikes & Gear **8255**
1943-9806 World at War **6454**
1943-9814 Human Sexualities **7361**
1943-9830 R C Buggy & Truggy **4344**
1943-9881 Radio Control Heli Pilot **4345**
1943-992X The New Anonymous **5339**
1943-9938 ASIANetwork Exchange **544**
1943-9946 *see* 1943-9938 **544**
1943-9954 *see* 0272-2011 **7947**
1943-9962 Journal of Transportation Safety & Security **8501**
1943-9970 *see* 1943-9962 **8501**
1944-0014 A E R A Gram **370**
1944-0022 *see* 1944-0014 **370**
1944-0049 Food Additives & Contaminants: Part A - Chemistry, Analysis, Control, Exposure & Risk Assessment **6842**
1944-0057 *see* 1944-0049 **6842**
1944-0065 Perspectives **7897**
1944-009X The Journal of Aging in Emerging Economies **4048**
1944-0103 Rx Complement **314**
1944-0146 *see* 0890-3352 **5386**
1944-0154 Field Notes **339**
1944-0162 *see* 1944-0154 **339**
1944-0170 Trail of the Coeur d'Alenes **8765**
1944-0189 Lady Jane's Miscellany **5425**
1944-0197 Today's Home Educator Magazine **3086**
1944-0200 Ask the Recruiter **1856**
1944-0219 *see* 1076-0180 **2994**
1944-0294 Minnesota Journal of International Law **1578**
1944-0359 *see* 0148-1045 **2332**
1944-0391 International Perspectives on Sexual and Reproductive Health **5994**
1944-0405 *see* 1944-0391 **5994**
1944-0413 Excelsior (Schoharie) **2941**
1944-0421 Journal of Prolotherapy **6224**
1944-043X *see* 1944-0421 **6224**
1944-0456 Political Handbook of the Americas **7168**
1944-0464 Journal of Strategic Security **2227**
1944-0472 *see* 1944-0464 **2227**
1944-0499 *see* 1943-0701 **5669**
1944-0510 Popular Photography **6975**
1944-0561 Washington Business Law **4883**
1944-057X Insurance Codes Annotated **4506**
1944-0634 InterReview **497**
1944-0685 BarPassers Bar Review. California Essay Workbook **4627**
1944-0693 Oklahoma Construction Law **4752**
1944-0707 Arizona Estate Planning and Probate Handbook **4901**
1944-0715 Maryland Motions in Limine **4955**
1944-0731 Fresh Americas **3678**
1944-074X Sommelier Journal **610**
1944-0804 Delmar Nurse's Drug Handbook **5957**
1944-0839 Coastal and Environmental Management **3411**
1944-0855 *see* 1944-0839 **3411**
1944-0863 Pond Biz Magazine *changed to* 1949-0585 **3748**
1944-0898 R C Crawler **4344**
1944-0901 Private Duty Salary & Benefits Report **1703**
1944-0928 *see* 0007-5108 **5267**
1944-0952 Naugatuck River Review **5338**
1944-0960 *see* 1944-0952 **5338**
1944-0987 *see* 1812-8602 **8518**
1944-1061 Partnerships **2997**
1944-1088 Journal of Alternative Perspectives in the Social Sciences **7977**
1944-1096 *see* 1944-1088 **7977**
1944-110X Shock Totem **5447**
1944-1118 California Motions in Limine **4947**
1944-1126 Funeral Home & Cemetery News **3719**
1944-1215 Island Sports Media **8181**
1944-138X United States. Federal Housing Finance Board. Office of Inspector General. Semiannual Report **7473**
1944-1401 Black Hills Faces **5066**
1944-1436 International Journal of Construction Project Management **1016**
1944-1819 Internet, Networks & Communications **2561**
1944-1827 *see* 1944-1819 **2561**
1944-1835 Journal of India **127**
1944-1843 *see* 1944-1835 **127**
1944-1851 Journal of Robotics & Machine Learning **2585**
1944-186X *see* 1944-1851 **2585**
1944-1878 Journal of Technology **128**
1944-1886 *see* 1944-1878 **128**
1944-1894 Journal of Technology & Science **2586**
1944-1908 *see* 1944-1894 **2586**
1944-1916 Journal of Transportation **8501**
1944-1924 *see* 1944-1916 **8501**
1944-1959 Barron's Regents Exams and Answers. Geometry **5475**
1944-1967 I S A C A Journal **2461**
1944-1975 *see* 1944-1967 **2461**
1944-1983 Kitchen & Bath Ideas Under $100 **4544**
1944-1991 D I A Global Forum **6832**
1944-2009 Needle Tips **5823**
1944-2017 *see* 1944-2009 **5823**
1944-2068 Essential Slow Cooker **4357**
1944-2084 Interest Rate Risk Exposure Report. Area: Assets $100 Million - $1 Billion **1355**
1944-2092 Interest Rate Risk Exposure Report. Area: OH **1355**
1944-2106 Interest Rate Risk Exposure Report. Area: Assets $1 Billion **1355**
1944-2114 Interest Rate Risk Exposure Report. Area: U.S. Total **1355**
1944-2122 Interest Rate Risk Exposure Report. Area: Northeast **1355**
1944-2130 Interest Rate Risk Exposure Report. Area: Midwest **1355**
1944-2149 Interest Rate Risk Exposure Report. Area: Assets Less Than One Hundred Million Dollars **1355**
1944-2157 Interest Rate Risk Exposure Report. Area: West **1355**
1944-2165 Interest Rate Risk Exposure Report. Area: F H L B 11th District **1355**
1944-219X *see* Head Start Bulletin **2862**
1944-222X Global Security Studies **2677**
1944-2238 *see* 1087-7398 **2196**
1944-2246 Entertainment & Travel **8701**
1944-2254 *see* 1944-2246 **8701**
1944-2262 Insurance Business Weekly **4506**
1944-2270 *see* 1944-2262 **4506**
1944-2289 Insurance Weekly News **4509**
1944-2297 *see* 1944-2289 **4509**
1944-2300 Internet Business Newsweekly **2560**
1944-2319 *see* 1944-2300 **2560**
1944-2327 Internet Weekly News **2562**
1944-2335 *see* 1944-2327 **2562**
1944-2343 Journal of Farming **127**
1944-2351 *see* 1944-2343 **127**
1944-236X Leisure & Travel Business **8728**
1944-2378 *see* 1944-236X **8728**
1944-2386 Leisure & Travel Week **8728**
1944-2394 *see* 1944-2386 **8728**
1944-2408 Marketing Business Weekly **1831**
1944-2416 *see* 1944-2408 **1831**
1944-2424 Marketing Weekly News **1834**
1944-2432 *see* 1944-2424 **1834**
1944-2440 Mathematics Week **5516**
1944-2459 *see* 1944-2440 **5516**
1944-2467 Mining & Minerals **6472**
1944-2475 *see* 1944-2467 **6472**
1944-2483 Nanotechnology Weekly **768**
1944-2491 *see* 1944-2483 **768**
1944-2505 Interest Rate Risk Exposure Report. Area: Southeast **1355**
1944-253X Network Weekly News **2502**
1944-2548 *see* 1944-253X **2502**
1944-2556 News of Science **2074**
1944-2564 *see* 1944-2556 **2074**
1944-2572 NewsRX Health **6863**
1944-2580 *see* 1944-2572 **6863**
1944-2599 NewsRx Health & Science **5686**
1944-2602 *see* 1944-2599 **5686**
1944-2610 NewsRx Science **7892**
1944-2629 *see* 1944-2610 **7892**
1944-2637 Pediatrics Week **6102**
1944-2645 *see* 1944-2637 **6102**
1944-2653 Physics Week **7034**
1944-2661 *see* 1944-2653 **7034**
1944-267X Politics & Government Business **1939**
1944-2688 *see* 1944-267X **1939**
1944-2696 Politics & Government Week **7170**
1944-270X *see* 1944-2696 **7170**
1944-2718 Psychology & Psychiatry Journal **7399**
1944-2726 *see* 1944-2718 **7399**
1944-2734 Technology News Focus **8442**
1944-2742 *see* 1944-2734 **8442**
1944-2750 Veterinary Research Week **8814**
1944-2769 *see* 1944-2750 **8814**
1944-2777 Veterinary Week **8814**
1944-2785 *see* 1944-2777 **8814**
1944-2807 *see* 1553-1813 **7023**
1944-2815 Journal of Ancient Egyptian Interconnections **400**
1944-2823 Screenwriter's & Playwright's Market **5368**
1944-284X Journal of Classroom Teaching & Learning **2874**
1944-2858 Poverty & Public Policy **8062**
1944-2866 Journal of Internet Policy **2563**
1944-2874 Journal of Business and Accounting **1294**
1944-2890 Ethnoarchaeology **393**
1944-2904 *see* 1944-2890 **393**
1944-2912 Fodor's Provence & the French Riviera **8708**
1944-2963 Inside the Fence **60**
1944-2998 Classroom Connections **2837**
1944-303X *see* 0364-5886 **7473**
1944-3064 National Advisory Dental and Craniofacial Research Council. Minutes of Meeting **5856**
1944-3188 I A E E Energy Forum **3137**
1944-3226 World Drywall & Building Plasters **1049**
1944-3234 Water Treatment in China **2096**
1944-3242 Bricks & Blocks **1044**
1944-3250 Plumbing Fixtures & Fittings in China **4128**
1944-3269 Estate Buyout and Options Program for Siblings
1944-3285 Journal of Biotech Research **767**
1944-3293 Pasticcio Zine *changed to* 1941-949X **511**
1944-3307 Epidemiologic Focus **5609**
1944-3323 Cargo Business News **8640**
1944-334X The Delaware Business Ledger **1090**
1944-3366 Viking Magazine for the Members of Sons of Norway **3571**
1944-3382 Kevin Zraly's American Wine Guide **606**
1944-3404 Hamodia Magazine *see* 1553-9490 **3536**
1944-3455 Public C I O **7462**
1944-3501 Academy for Jewish Religion. Journal *changed to* 1944-3528 **7721**
1944-3528 G'vanim (Riverdale) **7721**
1944-3536 *see* 1944-3528 **7721**
1944-3544 Barista Magazine **3628**
1944-3552 *see* 1944-3544 **3628**
1944-3560 Yallah Magazine **2688**
1944-3579 Specs **5376**
1944-3587 *see* 1083-933X **7489**
1944-3595 *see* 1086-1114 **7489**
1944-3609 *see* 1082-1929 **7489**
1944-3617 *see* 1080-4919 **7429**
1944-3625 *see* 1082-3182 **7429**
1944-3633 Big Game Tournament Guide *see* 0886-4411 **8280**
1944-3676 The Baltic International Yearbook of Cognition, Logic and Communication (Online) **6907**
1944-3706 Southwestern Law Review **4786**
1944-3757 Polki W Swiecie **8880**
1944-3773 *see* 1945-2675 **4876**
1944-3781 Paying for College Without Going Broke **2997**
1944-379X Cracking the S A T Literature Subject Test **2976**
1944-3803 Lome Magazine **4545**
1944-3811 Didi Magazine **2253**
1944-382X University of La Verne Law Review **4915**
1944-3854 Fetch!
1944-3862 H q **444**
1944-3870 Maple Street Press Phillies Annual **8238**
1944-3889 Maple Street Press Cardinals Annual **8238**
1944-3897 Maple Street Press Indians Annual **8238**
1944-3900 Association for Information Systems Transactions on Human-Computer Interaction **2446**
1944-3919 *see* 1944-3927 **8482**
1944-3927 Theatre, Dance and Performance Training **8482**
1944-3935 Hire Up! **1685**
1944-3943 Sew Simple **4367**
1944-3978 Culture Frame **4449**
1944-4001 Advances in Computational Motor Control **6120**
1944-401X A S E B L Journal **5248**
1944-4028 *see* 0739-6686 **5951**
1944-4036 *see* 0198-8794 **4040**
1944-4079 Risks, Hazards & Crisis in Public Policy **7467**
1944-4133 The Journal of Developmental Processes **7372**
1944-4141 *see* 1944-4133 **7372**
1944-4168 *see* 1938-3932 **6454**
1944-4176 Involve **5498**
1944-4184 *see* 1944-4176 **5498**
1944-4192 Worldwide Survey of L I M S Users **6689**
1944-4214 Dell's Best all Easy Crosswords **4333**
1944-4222 Dell's Best Easy Fast 'n' Fun Crosswords **4333**
1944-429X Dell Official Variety Word Search **4333**
1944-4303 Puzzler's Pocket Word Search **4344**
1944-4346 Live (San Francisco) **6528**
1944-4370 California Journal of Politics and Policy **7112**
1944-4389 G for Women **8230**
1944-4397 G **8230**
1944-446X Chinese Journal of Cancer **6015**
1944-4478 Higher Education F E R P A Bulletin **3024**
1944-4486 *see* 1944-4478 **3024**
1944-4516 I C U Director **4102**
1944-4524 *see* 1944-4516 **4102**
1944-4583 Intelligent Utility **3159**
1944-4591 Mercatus Policy Series: Policy Comment **7154**
1944-4605 *see* 1944-4591 **7154**
1944-4664 Cities go Green **2606**
1944-4672 *see* 1944-4664 **2606**
1944-4702 Moon Outdoors: Take a Hike Portland **8739**
1944-4710 The Best Teachers' Test Preparation for the F T C E: English 6-12 **3018**
1944-4842 A C T Comprehensive Program **2964**
1944-4885 International Journal of Business and Security
1944-4893 Indigenous Studies Journal **3539**
1944-4907 The Journal of Health Informatics and Information Management Research **5649**
1944-4915 Lawyer and Judicial Ethics **4718**
1944-4923 Tax Practice Plus (DVD) **1949**
1944-4931 *see* 0888-4064 **3048**
1944-494X Pinyon **5429**
1944-4958 Teen Graffiti **2216**
1944-4966 Saint Charles Business Magazine **1170**
1944-4974 Saint Charles Magazine **5082**
1944-4982 The Journal of Media Literacy **8114**
1944-4990 Adoption & Culture **8023**
1944-5008 Military Space & Missile Forum **6436**
1944-513X Utah Criminal and Traffic Code **4899**
1944-5180 Coalbed Methane Extra **6460**
1944-5199 U S C I S Monthly **7294**
1944-527X New York Motions in Limine **4958**
1944-5431 Waccamaw **5396**

ISSN

1945-2292 *see* 0018-2745 **4145**
1945-2306 *see* 0021-8251 **3066**
1945-2314 *see* 0021-8723 **4298**
1945-2322 *see* 0023-9186 **4713**
1945-2330 *see* 0197-1360 **465**
1945-2349 *see* 0734-4392 **6544**
1945-2365 *see* 0026-2285 **5517**
1945-2381 Vocare **7779**
1945-239X *see* 0021-9665 **2101**
1945-2403 *see* 0146-4760 **3498**
1945-2411 Planning for Retirement Needs **1644**
1945-242X Group Benefits **4504**
1945-2438 Fundamentals of Insurance Planning **4503**
1945-2462 McGill's Life Insurance **4514**
1945-2470 Qualified Retirement Plans (Bryn Mawr) **4905**
1945-2500 *see* 1945-1288 **5633**
1945-2535 *see* 0163-321X **3111**
1945-2543 *see* 0744-6616 **7318**
1945-2551 *see* 1540-2800 **3111**
1945-256X *see* 0043-1001 **3513**
1945-2578 *see* 1078-5892 **3510**
1945-2586 *see* 1943-7404 **5529**
1945-2608 *see* 0730-0743 **1272**
1945-2659 C J: Voices of Conservative/Masorti Judaism **7719**
1945-2675 New Appleman Insurance Law Practice Guide **4876**
1945-2691 *see* 0497-2325 **4793**
1945-2705 *see* 0002-7812 **2037**
1945-2764 All States Quickfinder Handbook **1910**
1945-2802 Bird's Eye Review **5417**
1945-2810 *see* 0888-0395 **5965**
1945-2829 Journal of Human Development and Capabilities **345**
1945-2837 *see* 1945-2829 **345**
1945-2934 University of Pennsylvania. Journal of Business Law **4882**
1945-2977 European Journal of Business Research **1107**
1945-2993 *see* 1052-4800 **2991**
1945-3027 The American Mineralogist (Online) **6456**
1945-3043 Currents in Teaching and Learning **3056**
1945-3051 *see* 0026-556X **5679**
1945-3140 The Gabriel **7798**
1945-3159 *see* 1945-3140 **7798**
1945-3256 Religion and Security Monograph Sieries **7674**
1945-3337 Pharmaceutical Outsourcing **6869**
1945-3345 *see* 1945-3337 **6869**
1945-3361 National Society of Allied Health. Journal **7533**
1945-337X *see* 1078-4497 **5614**
1945-3388 *see* 0198-7569 **5849**
1945-3396 *see* 1064-6655 **5853**
1945-340X *see* 1533-9211 **7580**
1945-3418 *see* 0197-6060 **1789**
1945-3469 Workplace Assistance & Benefits **1878**
1945-3515 *see* 1062-2357 **4584**
1945-3523 *see* 1099-7210 **7561**
1945-3531 *see* 1099-7229 **2334**
1945-3566 Guide to the Secondary Market **1628**
1945-3574 *see* 0894-959X **5904**
1945-3582 Marine Technology and S N A M E News **8652**
1945-3590 Linguistic Issues in Language Technology **5203**
1945-3604 *see* 1945-3590 **5203**
1945-3620 Ultimate Slow Cooker **4368**
1945-3639 Heritage Iron **211**
1945-3647 Kilter **500**
1945-3655 The Investment Professional **1633**
1945-3663 *see* 1945-3655 **1633**
1945-3698 *see* 1945-3647 **500**
1945-3744 Southeastern Teacher Education Journal **2914**
1945-3892 *see* 0164-7954 **850**
1945-3906 Glimpse **8104**
1945-4007 Aesthetic Surgery & Medicine **6235**
1945-4015 *see* 1945-4007 **6235**
1945-4066 The Tea Room **3666**
1945-4082 *see* 1939-6791 **3716**
1945-4171 Kentucky Motions in Limine **4834**
1945-4384 Urgent Communications **2364**
1945-4449 Securities Industry and Financial Markets Association. Fact Book **1650**
1945-4503 The Super Advisor **6687**
1945-4511 American Journal of Health Studies (Online) **6982**
1945-4570 Stem Cell **896**
1945-4589 Aging **5985**
1945-4600 Journal of Fair Trade Studies **1573**
1945-4635 Journal of Architectural Coatings **447**
1945-4694 Lloyd's Asbestos Litigation Reporter **4724**
1945-4708 O A S Chronicle†
1945-4732 *see* 1945-4570 **896**
1945-4783 The Shepherd's Voice **2213**
1945-4791 The Voice of Zion **7779**
1945-4805 Christmas in Zion **7751**
1945-4880 Hotel F & B **4389**
1945-4902 Southwest Wealth Management Business *changed to* Texas Wealth Management Business (Print) **8993**
1945-4953 *see* 0891-8929 **5884**
1945-4961 Water Environment Regulation Watch **3492**
1945-497X S I A M Journal on Financial Mathematics **5531**
1945-5011 *see* 0748-5336 **1226**
1945-5089 *see* 1059-6038 **1863**
1945-5186 Jung History **6930**
1945-5208 Bible Light Newsletter **7625**
1945-5216 Labor Life **1692**
1945-5240 Journal of Information Systems Technology and Planning **2523**
1945-5259 *see* 1945-5240 **2523**
1945-5267 *see* 1945-5240 **2523**
1945-5275 Journal of Knowledge & Human Resource Management **1868**
1945-5283 *see* 1945-5275 **1868**
1945-5291 *see* 1945-5275 **1868**
1945-5437 *see* 1935-2298 **8415**
1945-5445 Journal of Trance Research **7657**
1945-5453 *see* 0030-4948 **2128**
1945-5461 Large-Scale Railroading **4338**
1945-5488 American Journal of Economics and Business Administration **1059**
1945-5496 *see* 1945-5488 **1059**
1945-550X The Kitchen Collection By Professional Designers **4544**
1945-5534 *see* 0067-270X **4173**
1945-5569 A E R Journal **4078**
1945-5623 Management in Practice (Corpus Christi) **1776**
1945-5771 *see* 1528-4336 **5906**
1945-578X *see* 0002-7561 **1307**
1945-5828 Fido Friendly **8703**
1945-5852 *see* 0090-8657 **7827**
1945-5879 *see* 1046-7890 **5647**
1945-5887 U.S. National Forest Campground Guide. Pacific Southwest Region, South Section **8339**
1945-5917 The Business of Global Warming **1881**
1945-5925 *see* 1945-5917 **1881**
1945-600X Mergers & Acquisitions Business **1779**
1945-6018 *see* 1945-600X **1779**
1945-6026 Mergers & Acquisitions Week **1779**
1945-6034 *see* 1945-6026 **1779**
1945-6042 Corporate Governance Handbook **4864**
1945-6123 Journal of Registry Management **5748**
1945-6131 *see* 1945-6123 **5748**
1945-6204 *see* 1081-0226 **6051**
1945-6212 *see* 1523-8806 **4103**
1945-6239 *see* 1531-3999 **2970**
1945-6247 *see* 1551-2800 **3018**
1945-6263 *see* 1094-3757 **1861**
1945-628X Residence International **7611**
1945-6301 Hospitality Style **4388**
1945-6360 Healthcare Cost Containment **4097**
1945-6379 *see* 1945-6360 **4097**
1945-6387 *see* 1935-4711 **2662**
1945-6433 Business & Finance week **1322**
1945-6441 *see* 1945-6433 **1322**
1945-6514 Twin & Turbine and Light Jets **73**
1945-6522 New York Dispute Resolution Lawyer **4957**
1945-6530 *see* 1945-6522 **4957**
1945-6565 U S Residential Real Estate Market Report **7614**
1945-662X *see* 0363-6941 **5312**
1945-6638 Capital Tails **6805**
1945-6646 *see* 1945-6638 **6805**
1945-6654 Greater Philly Tails **6808**
1945-6662 *see* 1945-6654 **6808**
1945-6670 Indy Tails **6809**
1945-6689 *see* 1945-6670 **6809**
1945-6697 Jersey Tails **6810**
1945-6700 *see* 1945-6697 **6810**
1945-6719 Michigan Tails **6811**
1945-6727 *see* 1945-6719 **6811**
1945-6735 Ohio Valley Tails **6812**
1945-6743 *see* 1945-6735 **6812**
1945-6751 River City Tails **6814**
1945-676X *see* 1945-6751 **6814**
1945-6778 Rocky Mountain Tails **6814**
1945-6786 *see* 1945-6778 **6814**
1945-6794 Silicon Valley Tails **6815**
1945-6808 *see* 1945-6794 **6815**
1945-6816 Sonoran Tails **6815**
1945-6824 *see* 1945-6816 **6815**
1945-6832 St. Louie Tails **6815**
1945-6840 *see* 1945-6832 **6815**
1945-6905 Economics Week **1101**
1945-6913 *see* 1945-6905 **1101**
1945-6921 Energy & Ecology **1884**
1945-693X *see* 1945-6921 **1884**
1945-6948 Energy & Ecology Business **1884**
1945-6956 *see* 1945-6948 **1884**
1945-6964 Energy Business Journal **1885**
1945-6972 *see* 1945-6964 **1885**
1945-7014 *see* 0161-5297 **577**
1945-7049 *see* 1061-3749 **5966**
1945-7065 *see* 1542-6319 **661**
1945-7073 *see* 0886-6708 **8146**
1945-7081 *see* 1546-993X **310**
1945-709X *see* 1527-6619 **2980**
1945-7103 *see* 0003-3219 **5834**
1945-7111 *see* 0013-4651 **2113**
1945-7154 *see* 1525-1756 **2532**
1945-7170 *see* 0013-7227 **5891**
1945-7189 *see* 0163-769X **5891**
1945-7197 *see* 0021-972X **5895**
1945-7200 Alliance for Progress **8024**
1945-7219 *see* 1945-7200 **8024**
1945-7227 *see* 1536-2612 **2509**
1945-7235 Yoga Therapy in Practice *changed to* Yoga Therapy Today **7001**
1945-7243 *see* 0046-9580 **5635**
1945-7286 *see* 1541-6577 **5979**
1945-7294 *see* Yoga Therapy Today **7001**
1945-7316 Youth Media Reporter **8147**
1945-7324 *see* 1945-7316 **8147**
1945-7359 *see* 1087-3244 **6981**
1945-7367 *see* 1535-2064 **4102**
1945-7375 The Science Educator (Charlottesville) **3081**
1945-7391 *see* 1531-1082 **6074**
1945-7405 *see* 1945-7375 **3081**
1945-7413 *see* 0885-7156 **3215**
1945-7421 *see* 0091-0260 **1873**
1945-743X *see* 0022-040X **5502**
1945-7448 *see* 1945-7502 **5506**
1945-7502 Journal of Mathematics Education **5506**
1945-7529 The Volunteer Connection **3571**
1945-7596 *see* 0146-1079 **7627**
1945-760X Dermatology Nurses' Association. Journal **5957**
1945-7618 *see* 1945-760X **5957**
1945-7634 Engine Professional **5451**
1945-7650 *see* 1945-7634 **5451**
1945-7669 American Economic Journal. Microeconomics **1535**
1945-7677 American Journal of Traditional Chinese Veterinary Medicine **8791**
1945-7685 *see* 1945-7669 **1535**
1945-7693 *see* 1945-7677 **8791**
1945-7707 American Economic Journal. Macroeconomics **1717**
1945-7715 *see* 1945-7707 **1717**
1945-7723 The Standerd Wake Quarterly **8336**
1945-7731 American Economic Journal: Economic Policy **1059**
1945-774X *see* 1945-7731 **1059**
1945-7774 Journal of Financial Therapy†
1945-7782 American Economic Journal: Applied Economics **1059**
1945-7790 *see* 1945-7782 **1059**
1945-7804 Sports Unlimited **8208**
1945-7812 *see* 1945-7731 **1059**
1945-7820 *see* 1945-7804 **8208**
1945-7928 International Symposium on Biomedical Imaging. Proceedings **6199**
1945-7936 *see* 1945-7928 **6199**
1945-7944 *see* 1945-6565 **7614**
1945-7987 *see* 0898-4212 **4128**
1945-8029 *see* 1945-6565 **7614**
1945-8045 The Glass Bead **2042**
1945-8053 Mid Atlantic Real Estate Journal **7599**
1945-8096 The Straddler **5240**
1945-810X Northwest Coast **5078**
1945-8118 *see* 1945-810X **5078**
1945-8126 Stanislaus Historical Quarterly **4314**
1945-8134 *see* 0196-3570 **5400**
1945-8142 *see* 0047-7559 **5334**
1945-8193 Journal of Physics Research **7022**
1945-8207 *see* 1945-8193 **7022**
1945-8215 Mining & Minerals Business **6472**
1945-8223 *see* 1945-8215 **6472**
1945-8231 Nanotechnology Business Journal **7027**
1945-824X *see* 1945-8231 **7027**
1945-8258 Network Business Weekly **2501**
1945-8266 *see* 1945-8258 **2501**
1945-8274 Real Estate & Investment Business **7608**
1945-8282 *see* 1945-8274 **7608**
1945-8290 Real Estate & Investment Week **7608**
1945-8304 *see* 1945-8290 **7608**
1945-8312 Real Estate Business Journal **7608**
1945-8320 *see* 1945-8312 **7608**
1945-8339 Real Estate Weekly News **7610**
1945-8347 *see* 1945-8339 **7610**
1945-8355 Resource Week **1903**
1945-8363 *see* 1945-8355 **1903**
1945-8371 Robotics & Machine Learning **2586**
1945-838X *see* 1945-8371 **2586**
1945-8398 Technology Business Journal **1182**
1945-8401 *see* 1945-8398 **1182**
1945-841X Telecommunications Weekly **2341**
1945-8428 *see* 1945-841X **2341**
1945-8436 Transportation Business Journal **8516**
1945-8444 *see* 1945-8436 **8516**
1945-8452 *see* 1945-7928 **6199**
1945-8460 The Sierra Nevada Review **5372**
1945-8479 @anime! **466**
1945-8509 *see* 0029-5132 **5344**
1945-8517 *see* 0010-4124 **5277**
1945-8592 Huumanists News **7648**
1945-8622 *see* Institutional Real Estate Newsline **7596**
1945-8649 Stories for Children Magazine **2215**
1945-8657 S F C Newsletter for Writers **2211**
1945-8681 The Tufts Historical Review **4165**
1945-869X Information Technology Business **1123**
1945-8703 *see* 1945-869X **1123**
1945-8711 Journal of Engineering **3385**
1945-872X *see* 1945-8711 **3385**
1945-8738 Journal of Mathematics **5505**
1945-8746 *see* 1945-8738 **5505**
1945-8754 Telecommunications Business **2341**
1945-8762 *see* 1945-8754 **2341**
1945-8770 Every Landlord's Tax Deduction Guide **7590**
1945-8797 *see* 1943-829X **5416**
1945-8851 Library Leadership & Management **5028**
1945-886X *see* 1945-8851 **5028**
1945-8908 *see* 1939-6465 **5417**
1945-8924 American Journal of Rhinology & Allergy **6077**
1945-8932 *see* 1945-8924 **6077**
1945-8959 Journal of Cognitive Education and Psychology **3067**
1945-8967 Journal of New Communications Research **8115**
1945-8991 Tattoo Annual **591**
1945-9106 Bags, Pillows & Pincushions **6637**
1945-9114 Utility Sourcing Advisor **7475**
1945-9122 Subprime Institute **4791**
1945-9181 *see* 0974-2689 **5489**
1945-919X *see* 0973-4317 **5493**
1945-9203 *see* 0970-2466 **3177**
1945-9238 Walt Disney World with Kids **8773**
1945-9289 G E D en Espanol **2941**
1945-9297 SAT Subject Test: U.S. History **4312**
1945-9300 Creating True Wealth **6644**
1945-9327 Collate Art Magazine **482**
1945-9580 Ultimate Motorcycling **8269**
1945-9599 E H S Today **6676**
1945-9629 Lift & Crane Applications and Equipment **5454**
1945-9645 Journal of Coatings Technology and Research **6718**
1945-9653 Hospital Infection Control & Prevention **5816**
1945-9696 Converge Point **7752**
1945-970X Pretty Boy Magazine **5080**
1945-9718 *see* 0080-5459 **7798**
1945-9890 Spark (Washington) **582**
1945-9971 New Society (Cambridge) **7255**
1946-0023 Mississippi Homes & Gardens *see* 0747-1602 **3982**
1946-0058 Military Miniatures in Review **4340**
1946-0104 Reinsurance Law **4879**
1946-0155 Titanium **5868**
1946-0163 Journal of Artificial General Intelligence **2453**
1946-0171 Critical Policy Studies **7127**
1946-018X *see* 1946-0171 **7127**
1946-0198 Coal Combustion and Gasification Products **6766**
1946-0236 Conflict Resolution & Negotiation Journal **7227**
1946-0260 Zone 4 **3754**
1946-0279 *see* 1046-8390 **6731**

ISSN

1946-0295 Vermont's Local Banquet **3667**
1946-035X Pharmacy Technician's Letter **6874**
1946-0384 A P I C S **1722**
1946-0392 Audience Development **7552**
1946-0414 *see* 1946-035X **6874**
1946-0457 Simply Handmade **539**
1946-0511 Elder Mountain **4291**
1946-052X Asian Journal of Finance & Accounting **1280**
1946-0538 Alternative Spirituality and Religion Review **6643**
1946-0554 Deck, Patio & Pool **439**
1946-0562 SpokeWrite **5376**
1946-0570 Packingtown Review **5347**
1946-0589 Near Us Digest **5078**
1946-0597 Learning Communities Journal **2943**
1946-0600 *see* 1946-0597 **2943**
1946-0619 Tomorrow's Technology Transfer **2951**
1946-0627 B O W **5259**
1946-0635 Quilt It For Kids **6641**
1946-0651 Romantic Country **4549**
1946-0783 SurgiStrategies **4112**
1946-0805 EnlightenNext **7640**
1946-0813 P B S Hawaii **2387**
1946-0910 *see* 0012-3846 **7130**
1946-0929 *see* 1946-0937 **3772**
1946-0937 Keith & Kin **3772**
1946-0945 Advanced Studies in Oncology **6007**
1946-0953 *see* 1946-0945 **6007**
1946-0961 Developer **1002**
1946-097X Residential Developer *changed to* 1946-0961 **1002**
1946-1011 The Hybrid Vehicle and Alternative Fuel Report **8498**
1946-1038 Compass Points (Portland) **4064**
1946-1062 Selling Essentials **1793**
1946-1070 *see* 1946-1062 **1793**
1946-1097 *see* 1934-5429 **5662**
1946-1100 *see* 1077-5676 **4098**
1946-1135 Career Experts **6694**
1946-1143 Journal of Terrestrial Observation **684**
1946-1151 *see* 1946-1143 **684**
1946-116X The Water Report **8838**
1946-1178 *see* 1946-116X **8838**
1946-1186 C T B U H Journal **4406**
1946-1194 *see* 1946-1186 **4406**
1946-1208 The Arbitrator (Online) **8638**
1946-1224 Portland Spaces **3748**
1946-1267 E A to V A Insights **1093**
1946-1283 The Honey Land Review **5423**
1946-1305 Alliance for Children & Families Magazine **8024**
1946-1313 Compass (Raleigh) **8641**
1946-1321 *see* 1946-1305 **8024**
1946-1399 Japan Economic Currents (Print) *changed to* 1946-1402 **1131**
1946-1402 Japan Economic Currents (Online) **1131**
1946-1410 B D P A Today **8089**
1946-1429 *see* 1946-1410 **8089**
1946-1437 Brownbag **8091**
1946-1461 Thoi Bao USA **3568**
1946-1534 F I B E R **2247**
1946-1585 *see* 1063-990X **7458**
1946-1593 *see* 1941-9376 **8026**
1946-1607 *see* 1532-4400 **7186**
1946-1615 *see* 0276-3605 **6549**
1946-1623 *see* 1085-4274 **6789**
1946-164X Kirk's Current Veterinary Therapy **8802**
1946-1666 Dark Gothic Resurrected Magazine **5441**
1946-1690 Live Fit E-Zine **6992**
1946-1712 Flash fiction **5442**
1946-1739 Portland Tails **6814**
1946-1747 *see* 1946-1739 **6814**
1946-1755 Beantown Tails **6804**
1946-1763 *see* 1946-1755 **6804**
1946-1771 *see* 1059-2733 **7661**
1946-178X Weddings for a Living **5562**
1946-1836 Journal of Information Systems Applied Research **2523**
1946-1852 Libology Blog **5025**
1946-1860 A P A C News **2964**
1946-1879 A S A G E **6901**
1946-1895 *see* 1078-4535 **5956**
1946-1909 Journal of Chinese Herbal Medicine and Acupuncture **311**
1946-1917 Energy Parenting **2151**
1946-1925 Centaur's Yell **6278**
1946-1933 *see* 1946-1925 **6278**
1946-1968 *see* 1524-0436 **5725**
1946-1976 T Q **4792**
1946-200X Arkitip **467**
1946-2034 Harvard College Economics Review **1542**
1946-2042 *see* 1946-2034 **1542**
1946-2107 Georgia Philological Association. Journal **5122**
1946-214X A P Psychology **7330**
1946-2166 Argument & Computation **2407**
1946-2174 *see* 1946-2166 **2407**
1946-2182 R H N Magazine **6608**
1946-2204 Storyworlds **5378**
1946-2212 Gorgias Ottoman Travelers **4321**
1946-2220 Bibliotheca Nisibinensis **5100**
1946-2263 Floyd County Moonshine **5297**
1946-2271 Tempus **4164**
1946-2379 White Collar Crime **4900**
1946-2522 *see* 1939-7941 **3544**
1946-2530 Spencer's Compliance Guide for Health & Benefit Plans **1708**
1946-2603 Schedule of Proposed Action for the Wasatch-Cache National Forest **2626**
1946-2638 N S F Current **7885**
1946-2697 Daily Radio Newsline **104**
1946-2700 Housing & Community Developments **1351**
1946-2719 Advancements **1306**
1946-2727 Bank Talk **1316**
1946-2778 Solar Energy Technologies Program. Newsletter **3177**
1946-2875 Federal Home Loan Bank of Boston. Results **1341**
1946-293X *see* United States. Appalachian Regional Commission. Office of Inspector General. Semiannual Report **1187**
1946-2948 Weapons Journal *changed to* 1938-3932 **6454**
1946-2964 Schedule of Proposed Action for the Uinta National Forest **2626**
1946-3030 Current Diagnosis & Treatment: Gastroenterology, Hepatology, & Endoscopy **5921**
1946-3073 1,012 G M A T Practice Questions **3011**
1946-309X Fodor's in Focus Zion & Bryce Canyon National Parks **8706**
1946-312X Moon Handbooks: Michigan's Upper Peninsula **8738**
1946-3138 Journal of the Urban Environment *changed to* 1756-5723 **4416**
1946-3170 *see* 0163-755X **5328**
1946-3189 Compete **8167**
1946-3197 *see* 1946-3189 **8167**
1946-3200 The Year in A D H D **6190**
1946-3219 *see* 1946-3200 **6190**
1946-3227 S A E Vehicle Engineering **3218**
1946-3251 S P I E Reviews **7084**
1946-326X *see* 0021-3624 **1543**
1946-3278 Road Trip U S A: Pacific Coast Highway **8752**
1946-3286 Road Trip U S A: Route 66 **8752**
1946-3294 Community Revitalization Ideas **4408**
1946-3324 Global Business and Management Journal **1567**
1946-3332 *see* 1946-3324 **1567**
1946-3367 The Mailbox. Grade 1 Yearbook **3071**
1946-3375 Briefings in Palliative, Hospice, and Pain Medicine and Management **5588**
1946-3383 Long Island City **8731**
1946-3391 Roosevelt Island **8753**
1946-3405 Morningside Heights **8739**
1946-343X *see* 1526-5188 **8637**
1946-3472 Hotline (Washington) **7141**
1946-3480 Diner Journal **4384**
1946-3618 *see* 1526-9841 **4081**
1946-3634 U.S. Office of Private Sector Initiatives. Peace Corps. Partnership **8075**
1946-3715 Zambia Food Security Update *changed to* 2150-0746 **1608**
1946-3723 Malawi Food Security Update **1601**
1946-3804 Jacob's Well **7801**
1946-3812 The First Messenger **5893**
1946-3855 S A E International Journal of Aerospace **69**
1946-388X Escenario Magazine *changed to* 1946-3898 **8770**
1946-3898 Upscale Traveler **8770**
1946-3901 *see* 1946-3855 **69**
1946-391X S A E International Journal of Commercial Vehicles **8510**
1946-3928 *see* 1946-391X **8510**
1946-3936 S A E International Journal of Engines **8602**
1946-3944 *see* 1946-3936 **8602**
1946-3952 S A E International Journal of Fuels and Lubricants **6790**
1946-3960 *see* 1946-3952 **6790**
1946-3979 S A E International Journal of Materials & Manufacturing **3357**
1946-3987 *see* 1946-3979 **3357**
1946-3995 S A E International Journal of Passenger Cars - Mechanical Systems **3395**
1946-4002 *see* 1946-3995 **3395**
1946-4037 Migration Information Source **7287**
1946-4207 Bible Light on the News **7625**
1946-4274 *see* 0272-9172 **7025**
1946-4312 Lola **8872**
1946-4320 Wood Coin **5400**
1946-4401 Les Dames d' Escoffier International Quarterly **3633**
1946-4495 Bernard Sands Retail Performance Monitor **1807**
1946-4509 Statistical Report. Distilled Spirits **614**
1946-4525 Harris Poll (Online) **8149**
1946-4568 *see* ClimateWire **6349**
1946-4606 People & Strategy **1871**
1946-4614 S A E International Journal of Passenger Cars - Electronic and Electrical Systems **3329**
1946-4622 *see* 1946-4614 **3329**
1946-4657 The Masik **8278**
1946-4746 Sign Tech **35**
1946-4770 The Journal of Diving History **8182**
1946-4789 Knowledge, Technology and Policy **7981**
1946-4940 Journal of Capillary Electrophoresis and Microchip Technology† **8968**
1946-4967 E M S Magazine **6058**
1946-5041 National Council of Jewish Women. New York Section. Bulletin **8056**
1946-5165 Skirt! Magazine **8884**
1946-5203 Currents (Los Alamos) **7849**
1946-5211 Afrika Travel & Tourism Magazine **8681**
1946-5246 Hudson Heights **8720**
1946-5254 Methodist Review **7767**
1946-5262 Cerise Press **5272**
1946-5300 Black Business News **1068**
1946-5327 Journalism for Human Rights **7211**
1946-5335 *see* 1946-5327 **7211**
1946-5343 *see* 1948-6529 **4187**
1946-536X Sugar & Spice Magazine **8885**
1946-5378 *see* 1946-536X **8885**
1946-5416 Focus (Topeka) **1624**
1946-5424 Home to Hill **1351**
1946-5432 The Conference Board Review **1735**
1946-5440 Back Stage **8466**
1946-5548 The Uninsured in America ..., Estimates for the U.S. Civilian Noninstitutionalized Population Under Age 65 **4526**
1946-5580 1 MagDenver **5087**
1946-5599 *see* 1946-5580 **5087**
1946-5602 La femme desprit *see* 1078-9650 **7780**
1946-5610 *see* 1946-5629 **6640**
1946-5629 Modern Seamster **6640**
1946-5785 Atlantic Pacific Press **5258**
1946-5793 Many Good Turns **1051**
1946-5807 *see* 1946-5793 **1051**
1946-584X Journal of Studies on Alcohol and Drugs. Supplement **2696**
1946-5858 *see* 1946-584X **2696**
1946-5920 New Identity Magazine **7665**
1946-5939 *see* 1946-5920 **7665**
1946-5947 Valley Theatre Arts **8484**
1946-6161 Rick Steves' Budapest **8752**
1946-6188 Journal of Sino-Western Communications **7656**
1946-6226 A C M Transactions on Computing Education **2822**
1946-6234 Science Translational Medicine **5711**
1946-6242 *see* 1946-6234 **5711**
1946-6277 Art X X Magazine **8852**
1946-6285 Detroit Entertainers & Musicians News **6561**
1946-6293 *see* 1946-6285 **6561**
1946-6307 *see* 1944-5458 **5349**
1946-6315 Statistics in Biopharmaceutical Research **6881**
1946-6331 European Journal of Educational Studies **2855**
1946-6358 Entertaining **4357**
1946-6366 Bicycle Times **8254**
1946-6420 Zakar Magazine **8892**
1946-6439 *see* 1946-6420 **8892**
1946-6447 Disneyland Alumni Club and Historical Society Magazine **2265**
1946-6455 *see* 1946-6447 **2265**
1946-6463 *see* 1946-6447 **2265**
1946-6471 Vivacious† **8997**
1946-648X Unfinished **7691**
1946-6498 Telluride Magazine **8760**
1946-6501 *see* 1946-6498 **8760**
1946-6587 International Journal for Responsible Employment Practices and Principles **1689**
1946-6595 *see* 1946-6587 **1689**
1946-6609 *see* 0973-3159 **8652**
1946-6722 *see* Inside Smithsonian Research **7866**
1946-6765 *see* 0734-4414 **7192**
1946-6803 Ethiopia Food Security Update **1595**
1946-6811 *see* Midwest Art History Society. Newsletter
1946-6838 Ghana Studies Council. Newsletter **7966**
1946-6978 L E R A News **1691**
1946-6986 Daily Compilation of Presidential Documents **7128**
1946-701X iChina **3825**
1946-7028 *see* 1946-701X **3825**
1946-7060 *see* Cognitive Critique **7347**
1946-7079 Journal of Behavior Analysis in Health, Sports, Fitness and Medicine **7528**
1946-7087 *see* 0036-8733 **7912**
1946-7109 Penn G S E Perspectives on Urban Education **2897**
1946-7117 Truck & Bus Engineering **3224**
1946-7133 Cousteau Kids **2184**
1946-7141 A W W A Streamlines **8817**
1946-715X Public Employee Quarterly **1704**
1946-7230 Global Economist Review **1114**
1946-7249 R A A Review **5979**
1946-7257 The Pulse Magazine **5979**
1946-7338 Agile Product & Project Management Executive Report **2505**
1946-7532 *see* 1946-7540 **6608**
1946-7540 Psaltiki **6608**
1946-7567 World Future Review **7930**
1946-7605 Crosley Quarterly **8576**
1946-7613 Trap Shooting U S A **8338**
1946-7621 *see* 1946-7613 **8338**
1946-7648 Fusion Teaching Guide **7644**
1946-7656 Fusion (Nashville) **7644**
1946-7664 Mathematical and Computational Forestry & Natural Resource Sciences **3696**
1946-7729 S I G S P A T I A L Special **2436**
1946-7842 *see* 1529-9104 **4181**
1946-8032 Audemus **5258**
1946-8121 Cultivate **227**
1946-8156 Home Theater Design **2382**
1946-8180 Fancy Fowl U S A **286**
1946-8245 Buchanan Ingersoll & Rooney PC. Annual Report **4633**
1946-8253 *see* 1946-8245 **4633**
1946-8261 I A News **2865**
1946-827X S F S News **7264**
1946-8296 Periplous **8747**
1946-8350 *see* 1946-8261 **2865**
1946-8369 Higher Education Marketing Report **3024**
1946-844X U C R **2304**
1946-8466 U T E P Magazine **2305**
1946-8474 Security Technology Executive **2680**
1946-8482 BizTimes (Milwaukee) **1068**
1946-8490 Skip Shot **8201**
1946-8504 Watch & Jewelry Review **4570**
1946-8547 *see* 1946-8563 **491**
1946-8563 Gallinas **491**
1946-8717 Womuunweb W & R **7694**
1946-8776 Library Journal netConnect **5028**
1946-8784 Southern California Review **5375**
1946-8857 OnSite **1373**
1946-8873 Price Watch **1603**
1946-8881 West Africa Monthly Bulletin of Cereal Prices **208**
1946-8911 N C D B E-News **4083**
1946-892X Arizona Home & Design's Creative Designer **4531**
1946-8946 Islamic Perspective **7712**
1946-8989 African American History Month **7782**
1946-9020 Estate Law Update **4902**
1946-9039 Connecticut Genealogy News **3763**
1946-9152 Arizona Business Magazine **1849**
1946-9160 Experience A Z **8702**
1946-9179 Ranking Arizona **1965**
1946-9187 Arizona Home & Design **4531**
1946-9195 A Z R E **7581**
1946-9209 A Z R E Directory *changed to* People to Know (Phoenix) **7603**
1946-9225 *see* 1946-9233 **4456**
1946-9233 Insight (Nashua) **4456**
1946-9314 Job Choices in Business & Liberal Arts Students (Year) **6699**
1946-9365 *see* 1946-4967 **6058**
1946-9381 Bridges (San Diego) **2832**
1946-939X *see* 1946-9381 **2832**
1946-9403 The Messenger (Coxsackie) **537**
1946-9411 Advanced Underwriting Service (Erlanger) **1057**

ISSN

ISSN

1953-6623 Societe Francaise de Psychanalyse Adlerienne. Bulletin **7409**
1953-6674 Stiletto Homme **2261**
1953-6720 Ideo Mag† **8963**
1953-6828 C O D E R P A 59 **8029**
1953-6909 Vegetariens Magazine **6670**
1953-695X Nutritions & Endocrinologie **5898**
1953-7042 Le Foot Nancy-Metz **8228**
1953-7077 Systemes d'Informations Scientifiques pour la Mer **2818**
1953-7204 E J E Journal **2843**
1953-7441 Bordeaux Pays Gourmand
1953-745X Nice Pays Gourmand
1953-7514 Astrologie Magazine **565**
1953-7603 Lichen **7152**
1953-762X Contacts sans Frontiere **8095**
1953-7743 Question d'Education **2902**
1953-7751 Les Antennes **5064**
1953-7816 Procto Digest **5930**
1953-7840 Made in Alsace **5076**
1953-793X Reflets de la Physique **7037**
1953-7948 Entreprendre International **1960**
1953-8022 *see* 1246-7820 **5942**
1953-8030 *see* 0245-7466 **7510**
1953-8049 Terra Economica **1182**
1953-8111 *see* 0035-3337 **4939**
1953-812X *see* 0035-1326 **515**
1953-8197 Diotime l'Agora **6914**
1953-8316 Espace Kinshasa **7961**
1953-8359 *see* 0768-9179 **6871**
1953-8413 *see* 0395-451X **1729**
1953-8421 *see* 0753-5732 **1682**
1953-910X Medecine a Travers les Siecles **5666**
1953-9584 Droit et Societe. Serie Ethique **4661**
1953-9770 Therapies Naturelles **315**
1954-1031 Techniques de l'Ingenieur. Energies. La Lettre **3148**
1954-1074 Collectionneur & Chineur **4332**
1954-1228 Corps **333**
1954-1295 2512 **3932**
1954-1376 Chine Plus **1083**
1954-149X S O S Education. Le Bulletin *changed to* 1958-1904 **2908**
1954-1562 Rissala **7715**
1954-1600 Le Grand Betisier **4576**
1954-1732 Cuisine by Cyril Lignac **4355**
1954-1864 Projet Construction Maison **1030**
1954-1929 Fight Talk **8173**
1954-1988 Visite Pharma **6885**
1954-2062 Sante Famille Magazine **4084**
1954-2356 Passe-Murailles **2945**
1954-2399 Maison Revue. Sud†
1954-2534 Transfoplus **6739**
1954-2542 Amicus Curiae **7105**
1954-2577 Tout Tango **2688**
1954-2763 Cote Coiffure **587**
1954-2844 Internautes Micro **2560**
1954-2925 Grandir Autrement **2154**
1954-3018 Stardust Memories.com **6514**
1954-3093 *see* 1623-5770 **4209**
1954-3123 *see* 1958-1467 **1600**
1954-3131 *see* 1958-539X **1590**
1954-3204 Journal Africain d'Hepato-Gastroenterologie **5927**
1954-3212 *see* 1954-3204 **5927**
1954-3344 Collection Oeuvre Lyrique **6557**
1954-3387 Durabilis **3414**
1954-3395 *see* 0078-6608 **5860**
1954-3433 Migrations et Citoyennete en Europe **8121**
1954-345X *see* 1950-2184 **6031**
1954-3484 *see* 1955-544X **1902**
1954-3492 *see* 1955-5431 **1902**
1954-3522 E-S T A **3377**
1954-3603 *see* 1957-2417 **8241**
1954-3611 *see* 1954-9954 **8060**
1954-362X *see* 1955-9488 **1682**
1954-3646 *see* 1245-1436 **346**
1954-3670 Histoire@Politique **4227**
1954-3697 Association pour le Developpement de la Securite des Systemes d'Information. Le Journal **2511**
1954-3727 *see* 1956-2845 **4056**
1954-3786 *see* 1958-1815 **3535**
1954-3875 Futsal Spirit **8229**
1954-3891 Asociacion para le Fomento de los Estudios Historicos en Centroamerica. Boletin **4131**
1954-3921 *see* 1957-5912 **7208**
1954-393X *see* 1958-3249 **3524**
1954-4049 Barricata **7109**
1954-4235 Les Biographies.com. Les Organismes Syndicaux et Professionnels de la Presse **4572**
1954-4243 Les Biographies.com. Union Europeenne. La Commission Europeenne - Les Institutions Europeennes **640**
1954-4251 Les Biographies.com. L'Assemblee Nationale **640**
1954-426X Les Biographies.com. Agences et Societes de Publicite **640**
1954-4278 Les Biographies.com. Union Europeenne. Comite Economique et Social Europeen **640**
1954-4286 Les Biographies.com. Le Conseil d'Etat **640**
1954-4294 Les Biographies.com. Le Tribunal de Commerce de Paris **640**
1954-4308 Les Biographies.com. Les Presidents des Conseils Regionaux, les Presidents des Conseil Generaux **640**
1954-4316 Les Biographies.com. Le Conseil de Paris **640**
1954-4324 Les Biographies.com. Corps Diplomatique et Consulaire, Conseillers et Attaches Commerciaux et Financiers **640**
1954-4332 Les Biographies.com. Les Biographies de la Publicite **640**
1954-4340 Les Biographies.com. Le Conseil Economique et Social **640**
1954-4359 Les Biographies.com. Les Organismes Syndicaux et Professionnels de la Publicite **640**
1954-4367 Les Biographies.com. La Cour de Cassation **640**
1954-4383 Descriptifs pour la Maison Individuelle **1002**
1954-4391 Les Biographies.com. Ministere de l'Interieur et de l'Amenagement du Territoire **640**
1954-4529 Les Cahiers de l'Eveil **7343**
1954-4626 Securite et Conditions de Travail **1966**
1954-4758 D F O Mag **8226**
1954-4790 Pilloune† **8981**
1954-4820 Correspondances en Onco-Hematologie **6017**
1954-4863 Territoire en Movement **4031**
1954-491X Alternative Sante **5571**
1954-5010 Revue Francophone d'Odontologie Pediatrique **5864**
1954-507X Un Autre Regard **6125**
1954-5231 Paris Aeroports Magazine **8785**
1954-5797 Ordre des Veterinaires. Revue
1954-5800 Techniques de l'Ingenieur. Qualite et Securite au Laboratoire **3222**
1954-7269 *see* 0998-4313 **4923**
1954-8281 Ma Cuisine **4363**
1954-8893 Descubre **8697**
1954-9059 Envies Creatives **535**
1954-9067 Maison Revue. Special†
1954-9075 Revue de l'Habitat **7611**
1954-9083 Droit de Cites† **8951**
1954-9172 Lecture au Bout des Doigts **4082**
1954-9199 Better Life Magazine† **8935**
1954-9229 Geneva International Peace Research Institute. Cahiers **7237**
1954-944X Leo **8053**
1954-9709 Cote Bebe **2150**
1954-9849 Isiaca **4175**
1954-9865 Association d'Egyptologie Isis. Cahiers **4320**
1954-9954 Observatoire des Dispositifs de Prise en Charge et d'Accompagnement de la Maladie d'Alzheimer. La Lettre **8060**
1955-0081 System I News **2525**
1955-0103 Cent pour Cent Badminton **8224**
1955-012X Le Foot St-Etienne Magazine **8228**
1955-0146 Midi-Pyrenees Info **7497**
1955-0251 Small Caps Profits **1651**
1955-0413 L'Annee du Cyclisme **8253**
1955-0502 Banque de France. Recueil de la Reglementation Relative a l'Exercice des Activites Bancaires et Financieres **1319**
1955-057X Police Pro **4896**
1955-0588 Windows Vista **2600**
1955-0677 L P O Info Isere **909**
1955-0960 Paradis **5079**
1955-0979 Vivre Ma Maison (Edition Dordogne, Gironde, Lot-et-Garonne) **1042**
1955-1010 Plaisir(s) **4982**
1955-1029 Au Sud de l'Est **476**
1955-1177 Hopitaux Magazine **4099**
1955-1576 L'Oeil de Lynx **3457**
1955-1754 Echo de la Polonia **2265**
1955-1878 L'Homme Nouveau Magazine **7648**
1955-1932 A R I S T Signal **1878**
1955-1959 Syntheses Technologiques **1905**
1955-1983 Statistiques des Importations et Exportations Etrangeres de Vins et Spiritueux en (Year) **1583**
1955-205X *see* 1955-2068 **676**
1955-2068 H F S P Journal **676**
1955-2343 *see* 0035-1776 **6949**
1955-2351 *see* 1639-8319 **6177**
1955-2424 *see* 1272-9752 **4208**
1955-2432 *see* 0184-1068 **390**
1955-2440 *see* 1772-757X **5142**
1955-2505 *see* 1955-2513 **3379**
1955-2513 I J I D E M **3379**
1955-2564 *see* 0335-5322 **7945**
1955-2580 *see* 0003-5033 **7334**
1955-2629 Journal of Language Contact **5134**
1955-2637 Regulation & Gestion d'Actifs **1647**
1955-2645 Regulation & Asset Management **1647**
1955-270X *see* 0755-7256 **4137**
1955-2890 Rencontres **5166**
1955-4397 Les Cahiers Russie **4208**
1955-4621 Thanatologie **8143**
1955-5024 Liaisons Sociales Quotidien **1695**
1955-5199 Documents et Debats **1477**
1955-5237 F F C G E A. La Lettre **1960**
1955-5377 Decryptages **3127**
1955-5385 Fines **393**
1955-5431 Regards Technologiques **1902**
1955-544X Profils Sectoriels **1902**
1955-5474 Neosapiens
1955-5490 Risques et Responsabilites Territoriales *changed to* 1967-7529 **7496**
1955-5628 Les Mondes Antiques **4154**
1955-5911 Alimentation Nutrition **6654**
1955-592X Le Magazine des Livres **7567**
1955-6004 Ego, Moi, Mes Cheveux **587**
1955-6063 Images Spectacles Photo **6969**
1955-6276 Association Francaise des Interpretes en Langue des Signes. Le Journal **4072**
1955-6306 Mag'Hotel **8732**
1955-642X Finances Hospitalieres **4093**
1955-6497 Karbone **447**
1955-6519 Corail **2802**
1955-6527 B T P Materiaux **978**
1955-6888 Chiens & Chats Magazine **6806**
1955-6926 Toute l'Occasion Moto **8269**
1955-6969 L'Essentiel de l'Immobilier **7589**
1955-7027 Legislation Professionnelle. Produits Cosmetiques **4722**
1955-7167 Kaiserin **4375**
1955-7248 Dessilogique Diabolique *changed to* 1961-0823 **8949**
1955-7337 Confrontations Europe. La Revue **7118**
1955-7523 La Remuneration des Expatries **1873**
1955-7701 Association Francaise pour l'Archeologie du Verre. Bulletin **382**
1955-7841 Dimension Medicale **4092**
1955-8082 Proximites **7501**
1955-8104 Vins et Sante **6670**
1955-8198 Pretorien **4254**
1955-8783 Arche Itecture **428**
1955-8864 Woodcraft et Pourquoi Pas? **2271**
1955-8937 Correspondances International **334**
1955-8945 Le Cahier de l'International **1554**
1955-897X Monk **5445**
1955-9003 Metro Tramway Magazine **8504**
1955-9011 L'Officiel Galeries et Musees *changed to* 1955-902X **6535**
1955-9011 L'Officiel Galeries et Musees *changed to* 1957-0392 **6535**
1955-902X L'Officiel Galeries & Musees (Paris Edition) **6535**
1955-9135 Astro (Year)† **8931**
1955-9186 Orthophonies **5691**
1955-9232 Ingenierie, Conseil, Informatique **3270**
1955-9267 Le Moniteur du D A F **1150**
1955-9402 Cuisinez Comme un Chef **4355**
1955-9410 Le Jouet Enrage **3802**
1955-9488 France. Centre d'Etudes de l'Emploi. Info **1682**
1955-9631 Le Nouvel Entrepreneur **1964**
1955-9712 Ecologie & Bien-Etre **3417**
1955-9798 Les Cahiers de Sol et Civilisation **8092**
1955-9828 Chloro Fil **3727**
1956-0141 Archeologies de la France **379**
1956-0206 L'Univers Psychologique **7413**
1956-1059 *see* 1290-6115 **105**
1956-1881 *see* 1768-4099 **4841**
1956-189X *see* 1770-9377 **4880**
1956-1903 *see* 1772-6646 **4775**
1956-2241 Le Magazine Chiens et Chats *changed to* 1963-2436 **6806**
1956-2438 La Lettre de la Responsabilite Medicale **4723**
1956-2527 Matieres a Profits **1638**
1956-2551 La Vie Est Belle **3842**
1956-2594 Ophtalmologies **6047**
1956-2713 Lapinpin† **8970**
1956-2756 Bordeaux Aujourd'hui **600**
1956-2845 Seniors Vox **4056**
1956-2969 Industrie & Services **1889**
1956-2977 A C A M. La Lettre **1275**
1956-306X La Production Audiovisuelle Aidee en (Year) **2402**
1956-3132 Technic'Baie **1039**
1956-3280 Sportmag, Rhone-Alpes† **8990**
1956-3396 Artisanat Mag (Dordogne-Perigord) **1956**
1956-340X Territoire Originel **8760**
1956-3434 Tangente Education **5540**
1956-3442 Paris Region Magazine **1408**
1956-3477 Actes Pratiques et Strategie Patrimoniale **4900**
1956-3493 Le Foot Rennes-Nantes Magazine **8228**
1956-3639 Equestrio France
1956-3752 Vie Pratique Sante **8848**
1956-3833 Maquettes Militaires Magazine **4339**
1956-3841 Street Monsters **8268**
1956-5119 Planete Inde **351**
1956-5372 Bibliotheque Geopolitique **7109**
1956-5429 Echanges, Sante, Social. Collection **8038**
1956-5488 Sante Travail **7541**
1956-5542 Univers de la Danse **2688**
1956-5550 Groupe E I D O S. Collection **492**
1956-5569 Nommer les Langues **5155**
1956-6824 L'Harmattan Burkina Faso **7140**
1956-6956 Maladies Infectieuses **5822**
1956-6964 Maladies Chroniques et Traumatisme **5664**
1956-7030 Ecopolis **3128**
1956-7049 Generique(s) **2381**
1956-7081 Sciences Mag I D F
1956-7332 Francoscopie (Year) **8103**
1956-7383 Top Alerte **3842**
1956-7405 Te M A **207**
1956-7421 Association du Refuge des Tortues. La Gazette **318**
1956-7480 Les Nouvelles Patchwork et Creation Textile **6640**
1956-7502 Magazine Paris Premiere
1956-7545 L'Annuaire de la Peche de Loisir **8303**
1956-7553 Heritages Magazine **4903**
1956-7561 Accoucher† **8928**
1956-757X Revue de Droit des Transports **4774**
1956-7812 L'Arbre a Palabres **8088**
1956-7820 Revue Africaine **4473**
1956-7855 Geo Histoire **4140**
1956-807X *see* 1953-4612 **4676**
1956-8088 Lamy Patrimoine (CD-ROM Edition) *see* 1951-8498 **4903**
1956-8096 *see* 1773-4134 **7495**
1956-8150 *see* 0035-2640 **5706**
1956-8169 *see* 0989-2737 **5706**
1956-8231 *see* 1951-8404 **4712**
1956-824X *see* Lamy Emploi et Competences **1695**
1956-8274 *see* Lamy Droit du Sport **8185**
1956-8304 *see* 1953-4345 **1933**
1956-9009 Demographie Medicale Francaise *changed to* 1965-2372 **5580**
1956-9106 Process Alimentaire **268**
1956-9157 Aimer et Servir **7744**
1956-9327 Les Cahiers de la Librairie **7557**
1956-9599 Le Guide du Textile et de l'Habillement **2247**
1956-9629 Circuler Autrement **8493**
1956-9785 La Depeche A S V **8796**
1956-9793 Les Cahiers Pratiques de la Depeche **8795**
1956-9831 Le Moniteur des Pharmacies **6862**
1956-984X Cultures Sud **5281**
1956-9866 Revue de Medecine Manuelle-Osteopathie **5807**
1957-0031 Le P I A F **7161**
1957-0260 Arts & Gastronomie **4352**
1957-0341 La Nouvelle Revue de l'Adaptation et de la Scolarisation **3044**
1957-0392 L'Officiel Galeries & Musees (Ed. de Paris et Regions) **6535**
1957-066X Parole de Mamans **8879**
1957-0716 Association Francaise des Anthropologues. La Lettre **329**
1957-0953 La Pharmacie **6871**
1957-1046 Flash Sante
1957-1283 Dossiers du Canard Enchaine **5214**

9884 1957-1364 ULRICH'S PERIODICALS

1957-1364 Helicoptere Business Loisirs *changed to* 1957-1372 **58**
1957-1372 Helicoptere Magazine **58**
1957-1410 Livres en Vie **7566**
1957-1488 Animal Sante & Bien-Etre **6803**
1957-150X Blue Line **8782**
1957-1550 C M P Bois **3710**
1957-1615 France. Delegation Generale a la Langue Francaise et aux Langues de France. Bilan **5120**
1957-1674 Ink **7323**
1957-1755 Fight Inside **8173**
1957-1828 Label Pack **6711**
1957-195X J C I. Bail a Loyer *see* 0750-8328 **4706**
1957-1992 A D E M E & Vous **3123**
1957-200X Agenda Astrologique **564**
1957-2050 Pasteur Le Mag' **5824**
1957-2069 Le Figaro Reussir *see* 0184-9336 **3840**
1957-2069 Le Figaro Reussir *see* 0182-5852 **3840**
1957-2069 Le Figaro Reussir *see* 0015-0843 **5216**
1957-2069 Le Figaro Reussir *see* 0246-5205 **8872**
1957-2166 Cause Commune **4446**
1957-2190 Silence, ca Pousse **3750**
1957-228X Office et Culture **4548**
1957-231X Seculive Magazine† **8987**
1957-2360 Film(s) **6500**
1957-2409 Champs de Bataille. Thematique **6415**
1957-2417 L'Officiel du Badminton **8241**
1957-2492 Cyclotourisme Sante **6229**
1957-2557 Medecine des Maladies Metaboliques **5897**
1957-2778 Sun Residences **7613**
1957-2840 ZebrasO'Mag **6817**
1957-2891 Techniques de l'Ingenieur. Risques Industriels et Environnement. La Lettre **3371**
1957-2913 Poissons Fumes Seches & Sales **3605**
1957-2956 *see* 1954-3018 **6514**
1957-3146 Office National de la Chasse et de la Faune Sauvage. Rapport d'Activite
1957-3197 La Flandre des Irreguliers **8703**
1957-3219 Alpes Magazine Balades et Randonnees **8302**
1957-3251 Yaourts et Laits Fermentes *changed to* 1957-326X **269**
1957-326X Reference Probiotique **269**
1957-3286 Probiotics Reference *see* 1957-326X **269**
1957-3294 C E S A. Les Fiches *changed to* 1963-2150 **6442**
1957-3367 DocSciences **7851**
1957-3642 Oogolo Voyages **8745**
1957-3650 Terriciae Litterature **5386**
1957-3782 La Peche aux Leurres Mer & Ocean **8328**
1957-3928 Missionnaires Serviteurs des Pauvres du Tiers-Monde **7807**
1957-4045 European Alternative Investments Journal **1339**
1957-4061 M Comme Maison **4545**
1957-4193 T N T **6448**
1957-4207 Seminaire Magazine **1843**
1957-4215 Le Partenaire Humanitaire **8061**
1957-4223 Driven **8578**
1957-4290 MicroMineral Magazine **6470**
1957-4576 Cine Heros† **8941**
1957-4584 Le Foot Paris Magazine **8228**
1957-4614 Question Emploi **6703**
1957-4622 Cuisinons Sante† **8947**
1957-4762 Pourquoi Magazine **4470**
1957-4800 Bretagne Culture & Decouverte **8688**
1957-4819 Eurobjet Conso Magazine **25**
1957-4827 Eurobjet Pro Magazine **25**
1957-486X La Revue des Auxiliaires de Puericulture **2167**
1957-4886 Impact-Entreprises **1752**
1957-4959 Info en Sante **4102**
1957-5017 Le Quai d'en Face **7214**
1957-5041 L S A les Essentiels. Les Metiers de la Distribution **1829**
1957-5130 Cove-Atakpame **8096**
1957-5181 Model Magazine International **4341**
1957-519X La Lettre de Nitassinan **7211**
1957-522X Mixman **2203**
1957-5238 Diabete & Obesite **5886**
1957-5246 Histoire & Missions Chretiennes **7800**
1957-5262 S L A M. La Lettre **7572**
1957-5319 Paris-International Magazine **5079**
1957-5335 Foreign Policy (French Edition) **7235**
1957-5440 Traffic (Paris) **5085**
1957-5491 Desirs de Voyages **8697**
1957-5513 Corsica Magazine **8783**
1957-5580 E P N France **3094**
1957-5696 Passion Construction **1029**
1957-5750 Les Orientations de la Politique de l'Immigration **7459**
1957-5793 Action-Entreprise
1957-584X Navigation Douce **8740**
1957-5858 Annuaire de l'Hospitalisation **4087**
1957-5912 Haute Autorite de Lutte Contre les Discriminations et pour l'Egalite. Rapport Annuel **7208**
1957-5971 Historail **8618**
1957-6021 Priorite **8599**
1957-603X Statut et Gestion des Personnels Medicaux et Hospitaliers **4111**
1957-6099 Guide Pratique des Alternatives a l'Hospitalisation Traditionnelle **4683**
1957-6129 La Maitrise des Risques et la Securite Sanitaire au Quotidien dans un Etablissement de Sante **4106**
1957-6137 G F N P (English Edition) **7591**
1957-617X Cuisine & Jeux **4355**
1957-6234 Dracenie Point Mag **7434**
1957-6242 Guide Pratique de la Medecine du Travail **5621**
1957-6250 Guide de l'Acheteur Public **7493**
1957-6269 Gerer un Service d'Aide a Domicile **4094**
1957-6285 Protection de l'Enfance et de l'Adolescence **8063**
1957-6293 Petite Enfance. Guide Pratique de l'Accueil **2897**
1957-6307 Memento du Sport **7497**
1957-6315 Les Carnets de l'Animation **3054**
1957-6323 Guide Pratique du C L S H **4978**
1957-6358 Vitrines & Meubles Miniatures **4350**
1957-6455 Le Magazine du Piegeur & Petit Gibier **8321**
1957-6471 Memento de l'Action Culturelle **7452**
1957-648X Management et Gestion des Ressources Humaines **1869**
1957-6498 Sport et Responsabilite **8203**
1957-6501 Gestion du Personnel Territorial au Quotidien **7493**
1957-651X Direction et Gestion d'une Entreprise Culturelle **1739**
1957-6536 Guide Pratique des Centres de Vacances **4978**
1957-6552 Management de Projet. Methodes et Outils **1775**
1957-6579 Le Nouveau Guide Pratique du Responsable C D I **5037**
1957-6587 Les Biographies.com. Documentation Electorale **7423**
1957-6595 Guide Pratique du Tresorier C E **1749**
1957-6609 Amenagements et Developpements Durables **3722**
1957-6641 La Lettre de l'Arboriculture **3696**
1957-6668 F A L Mag **8101**
1957-6757 Feminin Decoration Sud **4539**
1957-682X Reussir sa Piscine & son Spa **1033**
1957-6935 Haberdar **3536**
1957-6986 The Sociovision International Observer **1844**
1957-701X *see* 0153-9345 **6729**
1957-7273 Histoire(s) de l'Amerique Latine **4295**
1957-7729 ArgoSpine News & Journal **6056**
1957-7737 *see* 1957-7729 **6056**
1957-7745 *see* 0982-1783 **4141**
1957-7753 *see* 1766-2842 **339**
1957-7761 Cahiers de Civilisation Espagnole **4208**
1957-777X *see* 1266-5304 **2743**
1957-7788 Metropoles **450**
1957-7796 Revue de la Regulation **1515**
1957-780X *see* 0761-2990 **5173**
1957-7842 *see* 0037-9174 **356**
1957-7850 *see* 0399-0346 **344**
1957-7958 *see* 0048-8593 **5364**
1957-7966 *see* 0032-4663 **7289**
1957-7982 *see* 0023-8368 **5142**
1957-9012 La Librairie des Humanites. Sentiers de la Liberte **4151**
1957-9136 Petit Voyage **8747**
1957-9241 Revolutic **6611**
1957-9403 Social en Pratiques **8069**
1957-9578 Defense, Strategie & Relations Internationales **7230**
1958-1017 Polyarthrite Infos **6225**
1958-1025 Carpe Challenge† **8940**
1958-1084 Realites en Nutrition **6668**
1958-1122 France Fiction **490**
1958-1254 R H Publiques† **8984**
1958-1327 Journal de l'Abolition **7211**
1958-136X Transversales Immobilieres **7614**
1958-1408 College de France. The Letter **4447**
1958-1440 Liberation. Next **5075**
1958-1467 Jumbo **1600**
1958-1718 OK Sante **6667**
1958-1815 Gazeta Paryska **3535**
1958-1904 S O S Education. La Lettre **2908**
1958-1947 100% Recettes **4369**
1958-1955 Viva Cuisine **4369**
1958-2099 *see* 0758-3389 **2045**
1958-2730 Statuts des Medecins Hospitaliers **4111**
1958-2994 Sociovision C O F R E M C A. La Lettre **1844**
1958-3184 Rein-Echos **5703**
1958-3249 Cafe Latino **3524**
1958-3273 L'Oriental
1958-3303 A N D A R Infos **6221**
1958-3346 Faire Face. I M C **4077**
1958-3370 Horizons Strategiques **7444**
1958-3494 Hommes Street Hommes **6292**
1958-3532 Atelier de Sociolinguistique. Carnets **8089**
1958-3621 Oeuvre d'Assistance aux Betes d'Abattoirs. Lettre **321**
1958-3672 Europe Federale **7233**
1958-3710 Mir **5334**
1958-3923 Institut National de la Recherche Agronomique. Magazine **122**
1958-4210 Contentieux des Refugies (Annual) **7204**
1958-4229 Contentieux des Refugies (Quarterly) **7204**
1958-4385 KineR **6112**
1958-4490 Revue Generale du Froid et du Conditionnement d'Air **4126**
1958-4512 Dictionnaire Permanent: Epargne et Produits Financiers **1335**
1958-5101 Reseau National des Sports de Nature. La Lettre **8330**
1958-5144 Peche & Innovations **3604**
1958-5152 *see* 1962-3402 **672**
1958-5268 *see* 1955-2890 **5166**
1958-5330 Decideur Public **5005**
1958-5373 *see* 0023-1576 **6112**
1958-5381 *see* 0767-0974 **5666**
1958-539X Agence Francaise de Developpement. Document de Travail **1590**
1958-5462 *see* 1767-8862 **4931**
1958-5470 *see* 0395-8582 **8638**
1958-5500 L'Espace Politique **7133**
1958-5535 *see* 1958-7856 **7181**
1958-5551 *see* 0018-6368 **8824**
1958-556X *see* 1147-9213 **3163**
1958-5578 *see* 0040-5957 **5721**
1958-5586 Dairy Science & Technology **884**
1958-5594 *see* 1958-5586 **884**
1958-5608 *see* 0765-0019 **7044**
1958-5632 *see* 0035-1601 **6611**
1958-5691 *see* 0035-2969 **8129**
1958-5713 Groupe de Recherche Archeologique sur le Haut Moyen Age. Cahiers **396**
1958-5748 *see* 0992-499X **2456**
1958-5764 *see* 0337-307X **8103**
1958-5780 *see* 1166-3081 **2453**
1958-5799 *see* 1169-7954 **3357**
1958-5802 *see* 1295-926X **4011**
1958-5829 *see* 1779-7179 **3357**
1958-587X Dossiers Solidarite et Sante (Online) **8082**
1958-5926 *see* 0047-4800 **5327**
1958-5934 *see* 0151-9107 **2050**
1958-7023 Boxe Magazine **8162**
1958-704X Les Grands Mysteres des Sciences Sacrees. Hors-Serie **6922**
1958-7074 Law Actuality Magazine **4713**
1958-7465 Private Equity Magazine. Guide du Financement par le Capital Investissement **1645**
1958-7627 Bull & Dogue News† **8938**
1958-7708 La Revue du Droit de la Distribution **4880**
1958-7813 Tradicioun **3623**
1958-7821 Interiors Deco **4543**
1958-7856 Savoir - Agir. La Revue **7181**
1958-7945 Dossier Japon **53**
1958-802X Le Guide des Methodes de Musique & Recueils Pedagogiques **6571**
1958-8143 Document Brut† **8951**
1958-8348 Excel Performance **2589**
1958-8429 Le Triporteur **3513**
1958-847X Revue Juridique de l'Economie Publique **1942**
1958-8496 Voix de S U D et d'Ailleurs **4605**
1958-8518 Special Cheval **8298**
1958-8542 Afriscope **3517**
1958-8585 Les Plumes de Libres d'Apprendre et d'Instruire Autrement **2898**
1958-8992 *see* 0032-342X **7260**
1958-9247 Groupe de Recherches Interdisciplinaires sur l'Histoire du Litteraire. Les Dossiers **5218**
1958-9301 Post-Soviet Armies Newsletter **7172**
1958-9395 *see* 0003-4347 **2312**
1958-9514 *see* 1244-5460 **5118**
1958-9549 *see* 0458-726X **5139**
1958-9719 Sante Environnement **7541**
1958-9743 Multitudes-Idees **7156**
1959-0040 Couleur Maison† **8944**
1959-0067 Coiffure Club **586**
1959-0091 La Gazette des Seniors
1959-0164 MondoSports **8239**
1959-0202 L'Epagneul Breton **6808**
1959-0318 I R B M News **765**
1959-0504 S'Enrichir Magazine **1382**
1959-0601 Bien Vieillir en Cote d'Or **8028**
1959-0857 Holiday's† **8962**
1959-0873 Lakoom Info **3547**
1959-0970 Special Chiens **6815**
1959-111X Profession Territoriale **7501**
1959-1195 Ligorodo **3548**
1959-1519 Maka **7881**
1959-1527 Rugby Selection† **8986**
1959-1578 Sante et Cafe **5709**
1959-1624 Style Papers **3842**
1959-173X Animal Attitude **6803**
1959-1764 Grande Galerie **6524**
1959-2108 Resonance Generale **5433**
1959-2302 L'Accueil du Jeune Enfant en (Year) **8053**
1959-2388 Croquer la Vie dans son Assiette **6657**
1959-2442 Idees 100% Broderie **6639**
1959-2590 Mat Environnement **1022**
1959-2841 Cheval Lusitanien Magazine **8289**
1959-285X Bouge ton Rhumatisme **6222**
1959-2957 Petit Tom Vert **3459**
1959-4135 Chien de Chasse Magazine **6806**
1959-4275 Guetteur de l'Aube **6645**
1959-4437 Animaux et Nature **933**
1959-4569 Guide Pratique des Medecines Traditionnelles Orientales **309**
1959-4593 A F I D E O. News **4071**
1959-4631 Invention Passion **6753**
1959-4658 Le Magazine du Cirque et de l'Illusion **8473**
1959-4690 B C **477**
1959-4720 O E **6972**
1959-4747 R P F **4125**
1959-4755 Barometre des T P E **1957**
1959-4763 Barometre des T P E. Grandes Lignes **1957**
1959-4836 Afrique Liberte **323**
1959-4860 Prepa Magazine **2998**
1959-4909 Madaplus **3549**
1959-5093 Anarchosyndicalisme **7106**
1959-5115 Finance Grandes Ecoles **1109**
1959-5123 Marketing Grandes Ecoles **1147**
1959-5190 Maison & Jardin **4546**
1959-531X Trajectoires **4478**
1959-5344 Centre International de Ressources et d'Innovation pour le Developpement Durable. Lettre **1592**
1959-5360 I D Magazine **7141**
1959-5379 L'Anjou Eco **1395**
1959-5387 Vedanta **7708**
1959-5409 Pratique Magazine **4366**
1959-5425 Nymphos Libertines **6296**
1959-5484 Femmes Mures Frustrees **6290**
1959-6057 La Lettre des Professionnels de l'Enfance **2159**
1959-6219 Le Monde de l'Enfance **2161**
1959-626X Le Courrier du Grand Paris **1401**
1959-6324 La Situation du Cancer en France en (Year) **6034**
1959-6375 Vivre Nice **4984**
1959-6421 No. Wine **608**
1959-6448 Placements Magazine **1644**
1959-6553 Les Statistiques Professionnelles Pharmacie (Year) **1904**
1959-6642 Exterieurs Design **3729**
1959-6766 Idees - Job **6698**
1959-6782 Securite Globale **7999**
1959-6960 Tout Savoir **4478**
1959-7010 L'Etudiant Autonome **2283**
1959-7061 Global Security Mag **2513**
1959-7118 Grand Voile Magazine **8276**
1959-7320 Legendes de Chats **6810**
1959-7398 Les Recres de TiJi **2210**
1959-7428 Cavaliere **8289**
1959-7568 R B M News **770**
1959-7606 Office Mag **1853**
1959-7630 Solutions Logiciels **1794**
1959-7649 Ma Maison A des Idees. Design **4545**
1959-7800 G Q (French Edition) **6291**
1959-7819 Tricot Magazine **6642**
1959-9161 L'Esplumeoir **5291**
1959-920X Les Baux Commerciaux **7583**

1970-9234 Notiziario di Radioprotezione dell'Esperto Qualificato **5857**
1970-9250 Inside Quality Design **446**
1970-9323 Piazza Grande
1970-9331 Mondo Baby **2161**
1970-9358 Inside Italia **3897**
1970-9366 *see* 1828-0447 **5945**
1970-9374 *see* 0544-7771 **4107**
1970-9390 La Grande Biblioteca della Psicologia **7359**
1970-9455 La Mia Casa (Formello)† **8974**
1970-9463 Progetto Casa† **8982**
1970-9498 *see* 1826-0373 **106**
1970-9501 *see* 1970-951X **560**
1970-951X Rivista di Studi Sudasiatici **560**
1970-9528 *see* 0394-6975 **965**
1970-9587 Quaderni del Menocchio **5356**
1970-9609 Guide ai Classici **5302**
1970-9617 Guide di Architettura **444**
1970-9676 Commercio Porte & Finestre **1049**
1970-9684 Italian Food Materials and Machinery **6711**
1970-9692 Opera Ipogea **2761**
1970-9722 *see* 1970-9730 **4090**
1970-9730 Codice dell'Ospedalita Privata **4090**
1970-9870 *see* 1970-9889 **459**
1970-9889 Tema **459**
1970-9927 Le Grandi Civilta **4140**
1971-0011 Concerto Grosso **6558**
1971-0062 Sismondiana **1549**
1971-0143 *see* 0394-2309 **7926**
1971-0224 Best Motoring **8569**
1971-0232 Auto Tuning **8561**
1971-0240 Tutto Tuning **8609**
1971-0259 Guida all'Acquisto dello Scooter **8259**
1971-0267 Hot Bikes **8259**
1971-0313 Testi e Discorsi **5187**
1971-0321 Tesori di Citta **522**
1971-033X Rivista di Criminologia, Vittimologia e Sicurezza **2679**
1971-0364 Psicoanalisi (Milan) **7392**
1971-0372 Grounding **675**
1971-0380 Rivista di Economia e Statistica del Territorio **1515**
1971-0399 Forum. Journal of International Association of Group Therapy **6141**
1971-0402 Egitto. Nuove Scoperte e Antichi Mestieri **4174**
1971-0410 L'Operatore Geriatrico **4053**
1971-0461 Ipnosi **7366**
1971-0534 Reti Medievali Monografie **4257**
1971-0542 La Repubblica Napoletana del 1799 **4257**
1971-0577 Ragione & Fede **6946**
1971-0593 Quaderni di Hesperides. Serie Manuali **5164**
1971-0607 Quaderni di Hesperides. Serie Testi **5356**
1971-0615 Quaderni di Hesperides. Serie Saggi **5356**
1971-0682 Hi.tech Dermo **5877**
1971-0690 Tabloid Radiologia **6209**
1971-0704 Quaderni di Diritto Penale Comparato, Internazionale ed Europeo **4897**
1971-0712 Rivista Internazionale di Filosofia del Diritto. Quaderni **4776**
1971-0720 Futuribili **8103**
1971-0755 Fertilitas Agrorum **787**
1971-1042 Q G **7571**
1971-1050 Istituto di Diritto Romano. Pubblicazioni **4833**
1971-1093 History of Education & Children's Literature **2864**
1971-1115 I Protagonisti della Cultura Giuridica Europea **4938**
1971-1131 *see* 1971-1093 **2864**
1971-1239 Sistema Letterario Italiano **5373**
1971-1255 Storia delle Dottrine Politiche. Saggi e Ricerche **7186**
1971-128X Casamia Cucina **4353**
1971-1352 The Language of Science **7878**
1971-1387 *see* 0391-9048 **6143**
1971-1395 *see* 1724-2908 **5845**
1971-1409 *see* 0392-128X **6020**
1971-1417 *see* 1127-395X **6175**
1971-1425 *see* 1121-4171 **5845**
1971-1433 *see* 0391-9013 **5991**
1971-1441 *see* 1824-0852 **5835**
1971-145X *see* 0391-9005 **6244**
1971-1530 Le Origini dell'Uomo **877**
1971-1557 Memoirs on Biodiversity **689**
1971-1603 Trasporto Commerciale **8518**
1971-1638 Barche a Vela **8272**
1971-1735 M M Maintenance and Facility Management **1897**
1971-1859 Rivista Storica dei Cappuccini di Napoli **7815**
1971-1867 Campania Serafica **7787**
1971-1883 Amico Cavallo **8287**
1971-1891 *see* 1724-8922 **6183**
1971-1905 Tecniche Chirurgiche in Ortopedia e Traumatologia **6073**
1971-1913 *see* 1971-1921 **7179**
1971-1921 Rivista Italiana di Conflittologia **7179**
1971-1956 Piemonte Cucina e Tradizioni **8747**
1971-2022 Archi Magazine **6545**
1971-2103 Stampe Botaniche dell' 800 **519**
1971-226X Manuali Universitari **7567**
1971-2294 Novecento Europeo **4250**
1971-2316 Problemi e Prospettive. Serie di Storia
1971-2375 Il Pensiero Politico (Rome) **7164**
1971-2456 Scuola di Alta Formazione. Quaderni **2945**
1971-2464 *see* 1971-2472 **458**
1971-2472 T A L E & A **458**
1971-2707 Dipingere & Decorare **4538**
1971-2715 I Nostri Amici Cavalli Collection *see* 1724-2959 **8295**
1971-2731 Pesca e Nautica **8328**
1971-2820 Institut Francais de Florence. Publications. 4e Serie. Essais Bibliographiques **627**
1971-2847 Universita di Bologna. Dipartimento di Paleografia e Medievistica. Dottorato.Quaderni
1971-2863 Firenze Made in Tuscany **3897**
1971-2871 Rocinante **6950**
1971-2987 Windows Vista Magazine Ufficiale **2600**
1971-3002 Complessita e Sostenibilita **438**
1971-3029 Universita degli Studi di Salerno. Dipartimento di Scienze Economiche e Statistiche. Working Papers **1187**
1971-3037 Universita degli Studi di Salerno. Dipartimento di Scienze Economiche e Statistiche. Ricerche **1187**
1971-3045 Universita degli Studi di Salerno. Dipartimento di Scienze Economiche e Statistiche. Quaderni **1187**
1971-310X Espanol24
1971-3177 Notiziario di Archeologia e Storia dell'Arte del Vicino Oriente Antico **409**
1971-3193 Roma e il Lazio **515**
1971-3266 *see* 1724-8914 **5804**
1971-3274 *see* 0393-5264 **6142**
1971-3282 Journal of Prenatal Medicine **5997**
1971-3290 *see* 1971-3282 **5997**
1971-3339 La Scrittura (Rome)†
1971-3363 Chip Foto Video Digitale
1971-3444 La Scrittura e la Storia. Scrittori Contemporanei **5368**
1971-3495 Journal of Ultrasound **6201**
1971-3509 Giornale Italiano di Ecografia *changed to* 1971-3495 **6201**
1971-3614 Your House in Italy **7616**
1971-369X Analecta Mercedaria **7783**
1971-3703 Bibliotheca Mercedaria **7786**
1971-3711 Psicologia dell'Educazione **2900**
1971-372X *see* 1826-008X **4047**
1971-3738 *see* 1129-0846 **6175**
1971-3746 *see* 0391-8904 **5602**
1971-3754 *see* 1125-632X **6023**
1971-3762 *see* 0391-8920 **5991**
1971-3770 *see* 0391-8912 **5875**
1971-3835 Biblioteca Mercedaria *changed to* 1971-3703 **7786**
1971-3843 Psoriasis **5862**
1971-3878 *see* 1971-6419 **1147**
1971-4009 The Neuroradiology Journal **6204**
1971-4017 Q A **205**
1971-4076 Controlli della Produttivita del Latte in Italia **262**
1971-4106 Il Bollettino **3407**
1971-419X Quaderni Romani† **8983**
1971-4289 Rivista Storica dell'Anarchismo. Quaderni **4159**
1971-4394 La Scuola Domenicale **7741**
1971-4424 L'Economia dell'Abruzzo Montano **1402**
1971-4483 Journal of Commodity Science, Technology and Quality **1430**
1971-4491 Ennebi **1105**
1971-4505 L'Economia delle Regioni Italiane **1479**
1971-4556 Piacenza Economica **1511**
1971-4580 Citta di Milano†
1971-4629 Italy. Istituto Nazionale di Statistica. Statistiche della Previdenza, della Sanita e dell'Assistenza Sociale† **8967**
1971-4653 Quaderni di Dermatologia **8805**
1971-467X Medicina Felina†
1971-4793 La Rivista di Pedagogia e Didattica **2908**
1971-4807 Il Parmigiano Reggiano **268**
1971-4815 Antropologia Museale **6519**
1971-4823 Studi e Ricerche di Geografia **4030**
1971-4831 *see* 1594-6770 **1639**
1971-4858 Quaderni di Filologia e Lingue Romanze **5164**
1971-4912 Patrimoni **1643**
1971-4920 L'Annuario dell'Investitore *see* 1594-6770 **1639**
1971-4963 Quaderni di Oriente Moderno *see* 0030-5472 **558**
1971-4998 La Giustizia Penale
1971-5005 Il Mondo Giudiziario **4956**
1971-5013 Amministrazione e Finanza **1307**
1971-503X Italy. Istituto Nazionale di Statistica. Statistiche dell'Attivita Edilizia (Year) **1047**
1971-5048 Italy. Istituto Nazionale di Statistica. Statistiche Opere Pubbliche (Year) **1047**
1971-5080 Statistiche Ambientali **3481**
1971-517X Osservatorio Economico della Provincia di Chieti **1505**
1971-5188 Produzione e Cultura **4470**
1971-5234 Import Export **1568**
1971-5242 Informazioni Nautiche **8646**
1971-5250 Avviso ai Naviganti **8639**
1971-5269 *see* 0406-6685 **2306**
1971-5285 Fondazione Italiana per il Notariato. Quaderni **4676**
1971-5293 Esperienze d'Impresa **1105**
1971-5307 Il Mosaico **4465**
1971-5315 Civica Scuola di Musica. Quaderni† **8941**
1971-5390 Comunicazioni e Studi **2317**
1971-5404 La Magistratura **4726**
1971-5412 Rivista di Archeologia, Storia, Costume **4259**
1971-5420 Annali della Pubblica Istruzione **3050**
1971-5439 I Mercoledi dell'Accademia **7882**
1971-5447 Hydrogeo *changed to* 1971-5455 **3402**
1971-5455 Ambiente Territorio **3402**
1971-5463 Rassegna dell'Imballaggio **6715**
1971-5471 L'Azione Mazziniana *see* 0031-482X **7164**
1971-551X Fitoterapia **788**
1971-5544 Catalogo dell'Arte Moderna Italiana
1971-5684 Studi Tanatologici **6954**
1971-5692 Studi Economico - Giuridici† **8991**
1971-5706 Ricerche Pedagogiche **2907**
1971-5714 C I R S E. Bollettino *changed to* 1972-6562 **2833**
1971-5730 A I S C A T Informazioni **8628**
1971-5781 Accademia delle Scienze di Torino. Atti. Classe di Scienze Fisiche, Matematiche e Naturali. Supplementi *see* 0001-4419 **7831**
1971-5811 Labirinti del Fantastico **5319**
1971-6052 Galilaeana **7857**
1971-6230 *see* 1971-6249 **4419**
1971-6249 Macrame (Florence) **4419**
1971-6419 Mathematical Methods in Economics and Finance **1147**
1971-6524 Trasporti & Cultura **8518**
1971-6591 Scuola & Amministrazione **3033**
1971-6605 Il Tacco d'Italia **3899**
1971-6745 I Segreti delle Piante Aromatiche **816**
1971-6796 *see* 1971-680X **7018**
1971-680X International Review of Physics **7018**
1971-6818 Cardiologia Ambulatoriale **5779**
1971-6885 Un Futuro per l'Uomo **7856**
1971-6966 Rivista di Diritto dei Trasporti **4776**
1971-6974 Diritto e Processo Amministrativo **4950**
1971-7105 Diritti Umani e Diritto Internazionale **4923**
1971-7172 Gli Speciali di Funghi e Tartufi **3664**
1971-7296 Tutor **6105**
1971-730X Giornale Italiano di Aritmologia e Cardiostimolazione **5787**
1971-7415 Q A (Torino) **7538**
1971-7431 P S P Magazine Ufficiale **2480**
1971-7458 iForest **3693**
1971-7644 Historica (Rome) **4143**
1971-7946 Achab (Milan) **322**
1971-7954 *see* 1971-7946 **322**
1971-7962 Focus Brain Trainer **3897**
1971-7989 Regione del Veneto. Bollettino Ufficiale **7465**
1971-7997 *see* 1971-7989 **7465**
1971-8160 Le Signore del Thriller **5415**
1971-8187 Orto Facile **3746**
1971-8225 *see* 1592-2898 **8118**
1971-8233 *see* 0040-3989 **5241**
1971-8241 Venezia Musica e Dintorni **6626**
1971-8322 Grazia Casa **4359**
1971-8330 *see* 1828-2148 **5369**
1971-8349 *see* 1828-1958 **7338**
1971-8357 *see* 1125-9116 **1956**
1971-8365 *see* 1972-7410 **645**
1971-8373 *see* 1828-194X **191**
1971-8403 *see* 0392-4939 **8136**
1971-8411 *see* 1828-5147 **7410**
1971-842X *see* 1827-5249 **8127**
1971-8438 *see* 1828-5171 **7393**
1971-8446 *see* 1121-1148 **8136**
1971-8454 *see* 1825-5442 **6183**
1971-8462 *see* 1827-0263 **4776**
1971-8470 *see* 0390-105X **1704**
1971-8489 *see* 1828-5163 **1704**
1971-8497 *see* 0390-1181 **8085**
1971-8500 *see* 1828-518X **1130**
1971-8519 *see* 0004-0177 **4403**
1971-8551 *see* 1971-7296 **6105**
1971-856X *see* 1971-730X **5787**
1971-8594 Road Bike Action Magazine **8267**
1971-8616 Cucina che Passione **4355**
1971-8632 Numero Beaute **590**
1971-8748 Di Piu T V Cucina **4356**
1971-8764 *see* 1825-8298 **5145**
1971-8772 *see* 1127-8951 **4135**
1971-8799 Q T Questotrentino **3898**
1971-8802 *see* 1971-8799 **3898**
1971-8853 Sociologica **8136**
1971-8888 MenteCorpo **6992**
1971-8993 Frattura e Integrita Strutturale **3345**
1971-9027 Scripta **5172**
1971-9035 Pirandelliana **5351**
1971-9043 Bollettino dell' Atlante Linguistico degli Antichi Volgari Italiani **5101**
1971-9051 Facta **2234**
1971-906X Letteratura e Letterature **5321**
1971-9078 Philologia Antiqua **2239**
1971-9086 Tipofilologia **5187**
1971-9094 Cucina Regionale di Mare **4355**
1971-9108 I Romanzi Passione
1971-9175 Literary **5323**
1971-9299 Ageing Lung **6211**
1971-9310 S U V Magazine **8603**
1971-9353 Uncinetto Facile Facile **6642**
1971-9450 *see* 1971-9558 **7358**
1971-9493 Balochistan Studies **5098**
1971-9515 *see* 0035-5615 **1380**
1971-9558 Giornale di Psicologia **7358**
1971-9612 Indagini e Prospettive **7141**
1971-968X Computer Week Giochi **2475**
1971-9736 Benessere in Cucina **4352**
1971-9817 *see* 1971-999X **7435**
1971-9949 Viaggiare in Italia **8772**
1971-999X Esproprionline **7435**
1972-0033 Centro Pio Rajna. Pubblicazioni. Sez.1. Studi e Saggi **7558**
1972-0041 Centro Pio Rajna. Pubblicazioni. Sez.1. Documenti **7558**
1972-005X Centro Pio Rajna. Pubblicazioni. Periodici **7558**
1972-0068 Quaderni di Filologia e Critica **5164**
1972-0084 Studi e Saggi **5378**
1972-0092 Vaghe Stelle dell'Orsa **5394**
1972-0122 La Rivista dei Combustibili e dell'Industria Chimica **6790**
1972-019X World Journal of Acupuncture - Moxibustion (Italian Edition) **315**
1972-0203 Biblioteca. Barataria Saggi **5262**
1972-0211 Biblioteca. Il Leone e l'Unicorno **5263**
1972-022X Biblioteca. Laocoonte **6907**
1972-0238 Biblioteca. Infanzia, Psicoanalisi e Istituzioni **6126**
1972-0246 Biblioteca. Le Mappe **8090**
1972-0262 Biblioteca. Lo Specchio di Psiche **6126**
1972-0270 Biblioteca. Mente e Societa **7340**
1972-0297 Biblioteca. Sociologia dei Media **8090**
1972-0300 Biblioteca. Studi sulla Modernizzazione e lo Sviluppo†
1972-0327 Profili. Arcadia†
1972-0335 Profili. Biografie†
1972-0386 Profili. Metropolis **8126**
1972-0459 I Diritti Economici **4659**
1972-0505 A E S T **1909**
1972-0513 Antologia **5255**
1972-0521 L'Arte del Diritto **4621**
1972-053X Atti e Pareri per l'Esame di Avvocato **4623**
1972-0548 La Biblioteca del Penalista **4885**
1972-0556 Biblioteca Giuridica **4629**
1972-0564 Breviaria Juris **4631**
1972-0572 Breviaria Juris. I Formulari Annotati **4631**
1972-0580 Collana di Diritto Amministrativo e Pratica Forense **4644**
1972-0599 Collana di Diritto dei Trasporti **4644**

ISSN

1980-6302 *see* 1516-2680 **1059**
1980-6523 *see* 0102-9460 **5864**
1980-654X Climatologia e Estudos da Paisagem **6349**
1980-6574 Motriz. Revista de Educacao Fisica **8188**
1980-6620 *see* 1516-2907 **2856**
1980-6906 Revista de Psicologia: Teoria e Pratica *see* 1516-3687 **7393**
1980-6973 *see* 0104-9224 **6343**
1980-7589 Contingentia **5108**
1980-7686 Acolhendo a Alfabetizacao nos Paises de Lingua Portuguesa **2823**
1980-7872 Ave Maria **7785**
1980-8194 *see* 1415-8566 **8005**
1980-8372 Revista Electronica de Estudos Hegelianos **6948**
1980-850X *see* 1516-7313 **2837**
1980-8623 *see* 0103-5371 **7392**
1980-8631 *see* 1414-5111 **7846**
1980-864X *see* 0101-4064 **3532**
1980-9697 *see* 1678-8222 **2897**
1980-9743 Soils and Rocks **3220**
1980-993X Revista Ambiente & Agua **3463**
1981-0296 Windows Vista **2600**
1981-0431 *see* 1516-4896 **2883**
1981-0482 *see* 1980-5594 **2845**
1981-0997 *see* 1981-1160 **81**
1981-1160 Agraria **81**
1981-1616 *see* 1413-666X **7361**
1981-1802 *see* 0102-7735 **2906**
1981-1829 *see* 1413-7054 **101**
1981-2787 Feng Shui **4540**
1981-3252 Curso de Memorizacao **7351**
1981-335X Emergencia Clinica **6059**
1981-3368 Mundo da Optica News **6046**
1981-3376 Producao Profissional Cine **6510**
1981-3821 Brazilian Political Science Review **7110**
1981-5115 Integracao Profissional **1015**
1981-5271 *see* 0100-5502 **5704**
1981-528X *see* 0102-695X **6878**
1981-5700 R A C Eletronica **1788**
1981-5794 *see* 0002-5216 **5092**
1981-5956 City & Time **437**
1981-6162 Revista Brasileira de Estudos Constitucionais **4852**
1981-6324 Brazilian Journal of Biomotricity **6229**
1981-6472 Interpersona **7366**
1981-7398 Revista de Direito do UniFOA **4771**
1981-7509 *see* 1981-7517 **6948**
1981-7517 Revista Conatus **6948**
1981-7746 *see* 1678-1007 **1711**
1981-8106 *see* 1517-9869 **2845**
1981-8386 Revista Eletronica do C E J U R **4772**
1981-8637 *see* 0103-6971 **5862**
1981-8920 Informacao & Informacao (Online) **5015**
1981-8963 U F P E. Revista de Enfermagem on Line **5983**
1981-9250 *see* 1518-4684 **2905**
1981-9854 *see* 1808-4079 **4572**
1982-0127 *see* 1808-513X **4773**
1982-0224 *see* 1679-6225 **958**
1982-0240 *see* 0102-8529 **7172**
1982-0445 *see* 1679-1851 **7997**
1982-0747 High School Musical **2192**
1982-1123 *see* 1519-0099 **2852**
1982-2073 Matrizes **2332**
1982-2928 Revista Philosophos **6949**
1982-4327 *see* 0103-863X **7389**
1982-4335 *see* 0103-507X **5704**
1982-4343 *see* 0104-8775 **4316**
1982-4351 *see* 0102-7786 **6394**
1982-4513 *see* 0103-1570 **4029**
1982-4688 *see* 0015-3826 **3688**
1982-4882 Estudos de Direito Cooperativo e Cidadania **4668**
1982-520X *see* Elektor **3097**
1982-5269 Revista Debates **7178**
1982-5412 Revista Discurso Juridico **4772**
1982-5676 Tropical Plant Pathology **821**
1982-5765 *see* 1414-4077 **2968**
1982-579X Hot Wheels **2193**
1982-5803 Polly Pocket **2208**
1982-5811 Barbie **2178**
1982-6206 International Journal of High Dilution Resarch **5639**
1982-6524 Espaco Amerindio **336**
1982-6621 *see* 0102-4698 **2845**
1982-7709 *see* 1807-300X **6334**
1982-8292 *see* 1982-4882 **4668**
1982-8756 *see* 1809-1040 **1167**
1982-9310 Contos de Princesas Barbie **2183**
19827849 *see* 1415-6555 **1790**
1983-0246 Brazilian Journal of Veterinary Pathology **8794**
1983-0572 EntomoBrasilis **844**
1983-196X *see* 0104-4249 **488**
1983-2052 *see* 1982-5676 **821**
1983-2109 *see* 0104-8694 **6945**
1983-2478 *see* 1809-8479 **7650**
1983-3482 Contextos Clinicos **7349**
1983-4500 Cadernos de Relacoes Internacionais **7112**
1983-4632 *see* 1519-0501 **5861**
1983-4675 Acta Scientiarum. Language and Culture **7945**
1983-4683 *see* 1983-4675 **7945**
1983-6635 R G O. Revista Gestao Organizacional **7994**
1983-7151 Turismo (Online) **8769**
1983-716X Revista Alcance (Online) **150**
1983-8727 Conhecimento em Construcao **3263**
1983-9928 Historia da Historiografia **4142**
1984-3356 Antiteses **4284**
1984-3917 Museologia e Patrimonio **6530**
1984-4670 Zoologia (Curitiba) **969**
1984-4689 *see* 1984-4670 **969**
1984-6428 Orbital **2075**
1984-6835 Revista Virtual de Quimica **2079**
1984-8250 B J P S Brazilian Journal of Pharmaceutical Sciences **6824**
1985-0735 International Journal of Natural Products and Pharmaceutical Sciences **6849**
1985-1553 International Journal of Computer Science and Security **2514**
1985-207X Malaysian Family Physician **5664**
1985-2304 International Journal of Image Processing **2487**
1985-2312 International Journal of Engineering **3201**
1985-2320 International Journal of Security **2426**
1985-2339 Signal Processing **2437**
1985-2347 International Journal of Biometrics and Informatics **679**
1985-2517 Journal of Financial Reporting and Accounting **1294**
1985-4668 International Food Research Journal **6660**
1988-0065 *see* 1988-0073 **7417**
1988-0073 Psicodoc **7417**
1988-0081 *see* 1698-4153 **7143**
1988-0847 Sortuz **4784**
1988-0928 Revista Internacional de Sostenibilidad, Tecnologia y Humanismo **7997**
1988-1274 *see* 1695-3576 **449**
1988-1630 Cuadernos Aranzadi de Jurisprudencia Tributaria **4653**
1988-2041 *see* 1579-1726 **8196**
1988-2041 *see* 1579-1726 **8196**
1988-2130 Surgam (Online) **2916**
1988-2327 *see* 1131-6993 **4212**
1988-2408 *see* 1131-5598 **472**
1988-2505 *see* 1137-4144 **3528**
1988-2580 *see* 1132-1660 **6723**
1988-2807 *see* 1139-1138 **5529**
1988-2955 *see* 0211-3589 **5164**
1988-2963 1611 **5200**
1988-303X *see* 0210-1963 **7948**
1988-3064 *see* 1137-3601 **2450**
1988-3072 *see* 1696-1641 **7539**
1988-3102 *see* 0210-4466 **5579**
1988-3110 *see* 0066-6742 **380**
1988-317X Revista Andaluza de Patologia Digestiva **5930**
1988-3188 *see* 0034-8341 **4311**
1988-320X *see* 0037-0894 **4325**
1988-3226 *see* 0465-2746 **1022**
1988-3234 *see* 0020-0883 **1014**
1988-3250 *see* 0367-0449 **2707**
1988-3269 *see* 1135-4712 **7649**
1988-4168 *see* 0436-029X **366**
1988-4214 *see* 0017-3495 **2123**
1988-4222 *see* 0034-8570 **6330**
1988-4230 *see* 0066-5061 **4199**
1988-4265 *see* 0018-215X **7647**
1988-4273 *see* 0210-5810 **7947**
1988-4281 *see* 0373-2568 **697**
1988-429X *see* 0034-9712 **8129**
1988-4621 *see* 0210-0614 **5043**
1988-4672 *see* 1138-4891 **1300**
1988-5202 Journal of Human Sport and Exercise **6230**
1988-5210 *see* 1888-1815 **8502**
1988-5237 Athena Occasional Papers *changed to* Athena Intelligence Journal **7222**
1988-5350 *see* 1888-1807 **3716**
1988-5393 Biblioteca de Linguistica† **8936**
1988-5482 *see* 1888-1823 **8491**
1988-5504 *see* 0005-1691 **8560**
1988-561X *see* 1699-8855 **5705**
1988-5806 *see* 1576-0952 **6879**
1988-5903 *see* 0210-5233 **8129**
1988-5911 Ikastorratza **2865**
1988-625X European Journal of ePractice **5009**
1988-6705 *see* 1887-8369 **314**
1988-6780 *see* 0212-5382 **5972**
1988-7116 Revista de Globalizacion, Competitividad y Gobernabilidad **1790**
1988-7272 Mucho Mas en ... Teia **8739**
1988-7302 Asociacion de Sociologia de la Educacion. Revista **8089**
1988-7310 Lorca Digital **3952**
1988-7329 Laborstat Huelva **1693**
1988-7337 Bits **2408**
1988-7345 Tesouro Informatizadoda Lingua Galela **5187**
1988-7353 Monografica Biblioteca de Humanidades. Teoria y Critica Literarias **5336**
1988-7396 Coleccion Informes y Estudios. Serie Relaciones Laborales **1670**
1988-740X A I D R O M. Actas **4607**
1988-7418 Andalucia es Salud **7507**
1988-7426 Cultura Museus **6523**
1988-7485 Guias para Ensenanzas Medias. Ciencias de la Naturaleza **7859**
1988-7493 Guias para Ensenanzas Medias. Tecnologia **8423**
1988-7507 Guias para Ensenanzas Medias. Etica **6922**
1988-7515 *see* 1888-3362 **5047**
1988-7523 Guias para Ensenanzas Medias. Lengua y Literatura **5302**
1988-7531 Guias para Ensenanzas Medias. Matematicas **5491**
1988-754X Guias para Ensenanzas Medias. Musica **6571**
1988-7558 Guias para Ensenanzas Medias. Educacion Plastica **535**
1988-7566 Guias para Ensenanzas Medias. Geografia e Historia **4013**
1988-7574 Canarias Arqueologica **386**
1988-7590 E-justice **4662**
1988-7604 Infoportalsocial.net **8046**
1988-7612 Inf@ncia **2155**
1988-7620 Institut Catala de les Dones. Butlleti **1354**
1988-7639 Butlleti de la Dependencia **8029**
1988-7663 Biblioteca Inform@ **4994**
1988-7671 Esfera **5115**
1988-768X Punica Fides **5163**
1988-7698 La Sombrereria **5239**
1988-7701 Espiral **2854**
1988-771X El Menor Digital **4580**
1988-7736 Documents de Treball **1739**
1988-7744 Monograficos de Arte 10 **506**
1988-7752 Guias para Ensenanzas Medias. Fisica y Quimica **2062**
1988-7760 Guias para Ensenanzas Medias. Biologia y Geologia **676**
1988-7779 Guias para Ensenanzas Medias. Educacion para la Ciudadania **7139**
1988-7787 Guias para Ensenanzas Medias. Interdisciplinar **4454**
1988-7795 Guias para Ensenanzas Medias. Educacion Fisica **8176**
1988-7809 Guias para Formacion Profesional **2861**
1988-7817 Veintiocho de Abril **1713**
1988-7825 Statistical Reports **8404**
1988-7833 Contribuciones a las Ciencias Sociales **7956**
1988-7841 Public Marketing Idea **1838**
1988-785X Coleccion Estudios Economicos **1083**
1988-7868 *see* 0212-4408 **4314**
1988-7876 Congreso Internacional de la Difusion del Espanol y su Cultura en Internet. Actas **5107**
1988-7884 Ciencia Cognitiva **7846**
1988-7892 Eridu **4182**
1988-7906 Siringa **2912**
1988-7914 C A L A S S **5590**
1988-7922 *see* 1131-8872 **2835**
1988-7930 Recursos de Fisica **7037**
1988-7949 International E-journal of Criminal Sciences **4891**
1988-7957 Biotechvana Informatics **761**
1988-7965 Artloft **474**
1988-7973 Etica de los Ciudadanos **6918**
1988-7981 *see* 1888-5357 **7257**
1988-799X *see* 1138-5952 **7854**
1988-8015 Estudios del Patrimonio Cultural **4218**
1988-8023 Divulgacion Cientifica, Innovacion e Investigacion Hispanica **7851**
1988-8031 Lebrija Digital **4579**
1988-804X Revista Doces **2906**
1988-8058 Criminoticias **4888**
1988-8074 Serie de Informes Tecnicos **5173**
1988-8082 *see* 1888-5535 **6841**
1988-8090 Universidad Pablo de Olavide. Centro de Sociologia y Politicas Locales. Documentos de Trabajo **8145**
1988-8104 *see* 1695-4785 **2833**
1988-8112 Recursos Didacticos e Investigacion **3078**
1988-8120 Futuro Africano **1488**
1988-8139 E D A C A R **5113**
1988-8147 Annals of Pharmacotherapy (Online Spanish Edition) **6820**
1988-8155 Info R U V I D **7865**
1988-8163 Cartografia-O en Galicia **4001**
1988-8198 Instituto de Posturologia y Podoposturologia. Revista **6229**
1988-8325 *see* 0569-9878 **5093**
1988-8333 *see* 0210-847X **7957**
1988-8384 *see* 0013-6662 **5114**
1988-8430 Tejuelo **5385**
1988-8457 *see* 0034-7981 **5167**
1988-8511 *see* 0004-0428 **467**
1988-8538 *see* 0210-9174 **5167**
1988-8546 *see* 0014-1496 **4005**
1988-8627 Logistica Profesional Digital *see* 1888-1815 **8502**
1988-8643 *see* 1887-1992 **2077**
1988-8651 Proyectos Quimicos Digital *see* 1887-1992 **2077**
1988-8686 TecniMadera Digital *see* 1888-1807 **3716**
1988-8694 Auto Revista Digital *see* 0005-1691 **8560**
1988-8740 *see* 1133-0953 **4037**
1988-8759 Autobuses & Autocares Digital *see* 1888-1823 **8491**
1988-8767 Fundacion de las Cajas de Ahorros Confederadas. Documentos de Trabajo **1112**
1988-8856 *see* 1888-4415 **6072**
1988-8910 Abel Martin **5248**
1988-8929 Todotransporte Digital *see* 0212-8357 **8513**
1988-8937 *see* 0212-8357 **8513**
1988-9011 Gestion Joven **1747**
1988-902X Estaciones de Servicio Digital *see* 1888-7864 **8579**
1988-9119 *see* 1888-7864 **8579**
1988-9259 *see* 1697-3119 **6323**
1988-9518 *see* 0214-3429 **5910**
1988-9542 *see* 1697-8021 **3676**
1988-9550 Aral Digital *see* 1697-8021 **3676**
1988-9569 Energias **3128**
1988-9577 C I C. Arquitectura Digital *see* 1576-1118 **989**
1988-9593 *see* 1576-1118 **989**
1988-9666 Asociacion de Historia Actual. Boletin **4131**
1988-9674 HostelService Digital† **8962**
1988-9984 *see* 0300-3787 **3109**
1988-9992 Automatica e Instrumentacion Digital *see* 0213-3113 **2458**
19882157 *see* 1131-6837 **1737**
1989-0176 *see* 0213-3113 **2458**
1989-0257 Revista de Formacion e Innovacion Educativa Universitaria **2906**
1989-0311 *see* 0472-8807 **3663**
1989-032X *see* 1695-0089 **3659**
1989-0346 *see* 1579-2390 **8595**
1989-0362 *see* 1579-2404 **8600**
1989-0389 *see* 1888-4008 **5705**
1989-0508 *see* 0210-3230 **380**
1989-0516 Nueva Ferreteria Digital *see* 0213-0823 **1054**
1989-0524 *see* 0213-0823 **1054**
1989-0540 *see* 0211-2264 **416**
1989-0613 *see* 0048-7694 **7178**
1989-063X *see* 1575-0361 **4228**
1989-0648 *see* 0211-5743 **4852**
1989-0656 *see* 0034-7639 **7466**
1989-0842 *see* 1130-2542 **6236**
1989-0931 Clasicos Madrilenos **5274**
1989-1490 *see* 0012-7361 **3187**
1989-1660 International Journal of Interactive Multimedia and Artificial Intelligence **2426**
1989-1725 Revista Internacional de la Pequena y Mediana Empresa **1966**
1989-2039 *see* 1698-532X **5361**
1989-2209 *see* 1888-8992 **7355**
1989-2217 Revista de Critica Literaria Marxista **7178**
1989-2284 *see* 0211-6995 **6271**
1989-2705 *see* 1889-1489 **8096**
1989-2829 Paginasenferurg.com **5977**
1989-3477 @tic **3051**

ISSN

DIRECTORY 2010 2041-3009 9893

1999-6675 Nox **6296**
1999-6683 Torque **8607**
1999-6918 *see* International Society for the Systems Sciences. Proceedings **7868**
1999-7086 J E M T A C **5946**
1999-7094 *see* 1999-7086 **5946**
1999-7639 South African Journal of Bioethics and Law **4785**
1999-7671 *see* 1994-3032 **6104**
1999-8228 Jus I T **4708**
1999-8856 Jiaoke Shu Yanjiu **2872**
1999-8864 *see* 1999-8856 **2872**
1999-9275 Paedagogische Akademie des Bundes in Oberoesterreich. Schriften **3075**
1999-9283 Centrum fuer Juedische Studien. Schriften **7719**
2000-0049 Driva Eget **1740**
2000-0073 Dentalmagazinet **5842**
2000-1967 *see* 0300-9734 **5727**
2000-2092 Mina Djurvaenner
2005-1085 *see* 1598-5245 **5748**
2005-1115 The International Journal of Korean Art and Archaeology **398**
2005-1603 Seobiseu-eob Saengsan Jisu (Online) **1262**
2005-1662 *see* 1228-8047 **1261**
2005-1743 Gi'gye Suju Tong'gye (Online) **1235**
2005-2162 Korea **7149**
2005-2472 *see* 1228-8071 **1236**
2005-2499 *see* 1228-8101 **8376**
2005-2863 *see* 1226-3192 **8384**
2005-2901 Journal of Acupuncture and Meridian Studies **311**
2005-307X Geomechanics and Engineering **3378**
2005-3894 *see* 1013-9087 **5871**
2005-4149 *see* 1598-9623 **6325**
2005-4602 *see* 1229-8557 **3348**
2005-5269 *see* 0075-6873 **7307**
2005-7172 *see* 1738-5261 **2815**
2005-8276 *see* 1975-9479 **239**
2006-7593 Edo Journal of Counselling **7353**
2007-0411 Cultura Cientifica y Tecnologica **7849**
2008-0255 *see* 1735-3327 **5841**
2008-0387 Journal of Medical Ethics and History of Medicine **5651**
2008-0468 Global Media Journal: Persian Edition **2322**
2008-1898 The Journal of Nonlinear Sciences and its Applications **5506**
2008-1901 *see* 2008-1898 **5506**
2008-2010 Journal of Ophthalmic & Vision Research **6045**
2008-2053 Journal of Injury and Violence Research **8050**
2008-2835 Avicenna Journal of Medical Biotechnology **756**
2008-322X *see* 2008-2010 **6045**
2008-3866 Iranian Journal of Basic Medical Sciences **5641**
2008-3874 *see* 2008-3866 **5641**
2008-4072 *see* 2008-2053 **8050**
2009-0005 Ireland. Central Statistics Office. Production in Building and Construction Index **1047**
2009-0021 *see* 1393-7197 **5514**
2009-003X *see* 0791-7945 **660**
2009-0048 *see* 0035-8991 **415**
2009-0056 *see* 0332-0758 **5290**
2009-0064 *see* 0790-1763 **2710**
2009-0072 *see* 0332-1460 **7246**
2009-0080 Ballyfermot Echo **3892**
2009-0188 Ireland. Central Statistics Office. Earnings and Labour Costs **1244**
2009-020X National Library of Ireland. Report of the Board **5034**
2009-0226 Plant & Machinery **5458**
2009-0234 All-Ireland Health Data Inventory. Part 1: Metadata for Key Data Sources **7506**
2009-0307 Business Munster **1074**
2009-0315 Ecopolitics Online Journal *changed to* 2041-806X **3482**
2009-0323 Cover Point **8226**
2009-0331 Localisation Research Centre. Annual Conference Proceedings **2352**
2009-0374 The Irish Journal of Gothic and Horror Studies **5443**
2009-0390 B Wedding Magazine **5556**
2009-0404 Car Buyers Guide (Leinster Edition) **8572**
2009-0412 Meath Post **3894**
2009-0420 Translocations **7294**
2009-0455 The Metropolitan Complex **505**
2009-0471 N R A Scheme Monographs **4247**
2009-048X Ireland. Central Statistics Office. Institutional Sector Accounts, Non-Financial **1245**
2009-051X Multi News Ireland **3894**
2009-0587 The Scaldy Detail **5367**
2009-0595 Wicklow News **3895**
2009-0714 B E A I Spectrum **747**
2009-0722 Camfest Magazine **7629**
2009-0757 Love and Marriage **5559**
2009-0781 The Video Journal of Psychiatry **6189**
2009-0846 Irish Cervical Screening Programme. Annual Report **5994**
2009-0854 Sustainability **3491**
2009-0870 Irish Theatre International **8472**
2009-0897 State **6619**
2009-1060 Call Out **7511**
2009-1079 Department of Social, Community and Family Affairs. Annual Report *changed to* 2009-1087 **8037**
2009-1087 Department of Social and Family Affairs. Annual Report **8037**
2009-1095 Roinn Gnothai Soisialacha agus Teaghlaigh. Tuairisc Bhliantuil *see* 2009-1087 **8037**
2009-1397 Historical Association of Ireland. Life and Times Series **643**
2011-0170 Cuadernos **1737**
2011-0324 CS **7957**
2011-0332 Ensayo Sobre Arte Contemporaneo en Colombia **487**
2011-043X English School **2853**
2011-0499 Bandas **2830**
2011-0529 Petrobras. Annual Report **6786**
2011-0588 Balance Social Internacional de Seguridad **8027**
2011-0626 International Journal of South American Archeology **398**
2011-0731 Academia y Virtualidad **2965**
2011-0790 Didactica Universitaria **2977**
2011-0839 *see* 0041-9095 **5727**
2011-1169 Boletin Palabrerio **2832**
2011-1304 Cepiensa **2835**
2011-1363 Asocars **3404**
2011-1428 Asoarabes **8287**
2011-1479 Base de Datos Kit Empresarial **1727**
2011-1525 Administracion Hoy **1723**
2011-1622 Encuentro de Avances en Psicologia, Gerontologia y Neurociencias **7354**
2011-1649 Agronomia al Dia **88**
2011-169X Estudios Masonicos **1007**
2011-1703 *see* 1692-8156 **4931**
2011-1711 *see* 0041-9060 **4966**
2011-1738 Cromos Telefonia **2318**
2011-1789 Blog **2553**
2011-1827 E-Revista **7852**
2011-2017 Boletin del Observatorio sobre Desarrollo Humano **7951**
2011-2246 Belleza **8853**
2011-2254 Decoracion **4537**
2011-2289 Buena Mesa **4353**
2011-2297 Crosscar **8576**
2011-2319 Colegios **2972**
2011-2335 Eventos Empresariales **1743**
2011-2483 Apuntes de Gobierno **7420**
2011-2505 Universidad del Valle. Escuela de Estudios Literarios. Cuadernos de Posgrado **5392**
2011-2548 Cartillas para Ninos y Ninas **2835**
2011-2610 A Domicilio **3830**
2011-2629 *see* 0121-3709 **3458**
2011-2637 Boletin Estadistico **2969**
2011-2750 Revista Virtual de Derecho Procesal **4773**
2011-2769 *see* 0123-2126 **3198**
2011-2785 Defensa Judicial **4655**
2011-2807 Boletines Tematicos **2832**
2011-2866 Universidad de Tolima. Boletin Estadistico **2937**
2011-2920 Agricultura Organica Agro, Vida y Sociedad **83**
2011-2939 Arado **92**
2011-3048 Deportes Quindio **8169**
2011-3188 Dearquitectura **439**
2011-3196 Energia y Desarrollo **3128**
2011-3277 Constructores de Paz **7635**
2011-3439 Agenda Fe y Alegria de Colombia **8086**
2011-3455 A N P I S S Informativo **8022**
2011-3501 Dialectica Libertadora **7959**
2011-3552 Desafios (Ibague) **5604**
2011-3617 Didaje **2842**
2011-365X Cuadernos del Habitat **4408**
2011-3684 Cuadernos de Gestion del Conocimiento **2840**
2011-3692 Cuadernos de Inteligencia Empresarial **1737**
2011-3714 Camandula **4637**
2011-3749 Contacto Vital **5600**
2011-3870 Boletin Informativo Gobernar **8028**
2011-3897 Desde la Rectoria **2977**
2011-3919 Colegio el Minuto de Dios. Anuario **2837**
2011-3986 Financial Quarter **1345**
2011-3994 *see* 2011-401X **2505**
2011-401X Clave 019-97 **2505**
2011-4044 Cali in Cifras **1079**
2011-4052 Bogota Despierta **3830**
2011-4079 Conuco **1086**
2011-4087 Boletin Tecnico Biodiversidad **2604**
2011-4109 Biocombustibles **3236**
2011-4168 Farandula **8862**
2011-4214 Contador Internacional **1285**
2011-4281 Cabecera **7952**
2011-4559 En Clave Joven La Revista **7961**
2011-4583 Demosophia **6913**
2011-4591 Humanitas **4455**
2011-4605 Cundinamarca. Corazon de Colombia **7432**
2011-4796 Actualidad Fiscal de Bogota **1909**
2011-5474 Revista Latinoamericana de Etnomatematica **5529**
2011-7965 *see* 0121-0793 **5632**
2013-0007 Novela Historica **5344**
2013-035X *see* 1133-6595 **7224**
2013-052X *see* 1134-7724 **5148**
2013-0864 Contextos **333**
2013-0953 Journal of Industrial Engineering and Management **3369**
2013-1453 *see* 0212-5056 **7466**
2013-1631 *see* 1888-5063 **2516**
2013-3413 *see* 1132-6107 **7229**
2013-407X Catalan Historical Review **4209**
2013-4088 *see* 2013-407X **4209**
2024-9950 France. Commission Centrale pour la Navigation du Rhin. Rapport Annuel **8644**
2027-1174 Magis **2884**
2030-1006 Journal of the Writing Research **5316**
2030-2363 GRAMM - R. **5123**
2031-0242 *see* 0890-2917 **5438**
2031-3098 In Monte Artium **6575**
2031-356X *see* 0772-084X **4173**
2031-4876 Corpus Christianorum. Series Apocryphorum **7793**
2031-5929 Annali di Scienze Religiose **7621**
2031-5937 Semitica et Classica **2240**
2035-0686 Journal of Plastic Dermatology **5879**
2035-2611 *see* 0006-6583 **2231**
2035-262X *see* 0042-5079 **5193**
2035-2638 *see* 0390-0142 **5280**
2035-2646 *see* 1122-259X **2238**
2035-276X *see* 0392-0887 **403**
2035-3065 *see* 1971-9086 **5187**
2035-3545 *see* 1128-7772 **7638**
2035-3561 *see* 1971-9078 **2239**
2035-3898 Giornale Italiano di Medicina Sessuale e Riproduttiva *changed to* 2035-3901 **5645**
2035-3901 Journal of Andrological Sciences **5645**
2035-4215 H P Trasporti Club **8631**
2035-4444 *see* 1826-0772 **442**
2035-4614 Household and Personal Care Today **6989**
2035-4738 *see* 2035-4614 **6989**
2035-5106 Musculoskeletal Surgery **6252**
2035-5114 *see* 2035-5106 **6252**
2035-5556 Genus (Online) **7283**
2035-7362 Doctor Virtualis **6914**
2035-8164 *see* 2035-8237 **6070**
2035-8237 Orthopedic Reviews **6070**
2035-8377 *see* 2035-8385 **6166**
2035-8385 Neurology International **6166**
2035-9411 Journal of Medicine and the Person **5652**
2035-973X Communicative Business **1734**
2035-9969 Journal of Endometriosis **5995**
2036-038X Biblioteca della Ricerca. Cultura Straniera **4444**
2036-041X Biblioteca della Ricerca. Linguistica **5100**
2036-2579 Heart International **5788**
2036-282X *see* 2035-9969 **5995**
2036-3176 Critical Ultrasound Journal **6194**
2036-3605 Rare Tumors **6033**
2036-3613 *see* 2036-3605 **6033**
2036-3877 *see* 2035-9411 **5652**
2036-7902 *see* 2036-3176 **6194**
2037-0245 Segno e Testo **7573**
2040-0500 Building Sustainable Design **4116**
2040-0705 African Journal of Economic and Management Studies **1724**
2040-0721 International Journal of Social Computing and Cyber-Physical Systems **2522**
2040-073X *see* 2040-0721 **2522**
2040-0756 Computing (London, 2008) **2415**
2040-106X International Journal of Multicriteria Decision Making **2452**
2040-1078 *see* 2040-106X **2452**
2040-1310 School Leadership **2909**
2040-1566 *see* 0015-203X **1230**
2040-1574 *see* 1465-1645 **7284**
2040-1582 *see* 0308-6666 **8389**
2040-1590 *see* 0307-4463 **7291**
2040-1604 *see* 1350-4401 **1273**
2040-1744 Journal of Developmental Origins of Health and Disease **5648**
2040-1752 *see* 2040-1744 **5648**
2040-2066 Antiviral Chemistry and Chemotherapy (Online) **723**
2040-2201 Insider **1354**
2040-2244 Journal of Water and Climate **6359**
2040-2252 International Journal of Experimental Design and Process Optimisation **3368**
2040-2260 *see* 2040-2252 **3368**
2040-2295 Journal of Healthcare Engineering **3385**
2040-2317 Journal of Structural Fire Engineering **3386**
2040-2473 Jane's Foreign Report *changed to* 2040-8315 **7247**
2040-252X Great Britain. Office for National Statistics. Mortality Statistics. Deaths Registered in (Year) **7307**
2040-3364 Nanoscale **2074**
2040-3372 *see* 2040-3364 **2074**
2040-3585 Journal of International Dispute Settlement **4933**
2040-3593 *see* 2040-3585 **4933**
2040-3607 International Journal of Mathematical Modelling and Numerical Optimisation **5496**
2040-3615 *see* 2040-3607 **5496**
2040-3968 People and Science **7897**
2040-4026 International Journal of Care Pathways **4509**
2040-4034 International Journal of Care Pathways (Online) *see* 2040-4026 **4509**
2040-4069 Assessment & Development Matters **1726**
2040-4247 International Journal of Sudan Research, Policy and Sustainable Development **7868**
2040-4255 *see* 2040-4247 **7868**
2040-4468 International Journal of Knowledge-Based Development **8109**
2040-4476 *see* 2040-4468 **8109**
2040-4549 International Journal of Physiotherapy and Life Physics **311**
2040-4557 *see* 2040-4549 **311**
2040-476X Airline Ground Services **8536**
2040-4867 *see* 0021-969X **7654**
2040-5111 The Journal of Interactional Research in Communication Disorders **5134**
2040-512X *see* 2040-5111 **5134**
2040-5162 Textile Month International **8460**
2040-5316 Sphere **8757**
2040-5340 U K Alcohol Alert **2700**
2040-5790 Applied Economic Perspectives and Policy **193**
2040-5804 *see* 2040-5790 **193**
2040-5847 Sport & E U Review **8203**
2040-5960 postmedieval **5353**
2040-5979 *see* 2040-5960 **5353**
2040-6207 Therapeutic Advances in Hematology **5941**
2040-6223 Therapeutic Advances in Chronic Disease **5721**
2040-7122 Journal of Research in Interactive Marketing **1826**
2040-7149 Equality, Diversity and Inclusion **8895**
2040-8005 Journal of Chinese Human Resources Management **1868**
2040-8021 Sustainability Accounting, Management and Policy Journal **1302**
2040-8056 Voluntary Sector Review **8014**
2040-8064 *see* 2040-8056 **8014**
2040-8072 *see* 0038-7134 **4266**
2040-8099 Journal of International Academic Research **1137**
2040-8102 Journal of Business Context **1134**
2040-8110 International Journal of Primary Research **1128**
2040-8315 Jane's Intelligence Weekly **7247**
2040-8633 *see* 1360-1431 **3067**
2040-8706 *see* 0082-2884 **4164**
2040-8730 Current Law Weekly (Online) **4653**
2040-8749 Nankai Business Review International **1780**
2040-8978 Journal of Optics (Print) **7079**
2041-0980 *see* 0309-8168 **1536**
2041-0999 *see* 1757-8949 **7692**
2041-1022 Modernist Cultures **8121**
2041-2487 companion **8795**
2041-2568 Journal of Global Responsibility **1766**
2041-2967 *see* 0957-6509 **3380**
2041-2975 *see* 0954-4054 **3380**
2041-2983 *see* 0954-4062 **3380**
2041-2991 *see* 0954-4070 **8585**
2041-3009 *see* 0954-4089 **3380**

ISSN

9894 2041-3017 ULRICH'S PERIODICALS

2041-3017 *see* 0954-4097 **8619**
2041-3025 *see* 0954-4100 **60**
2041-3033 *see* 0954-4119 **749**
2041-3041 *see* 0959-6518 **3380**
2041-305X *see* 1350-6501 **3381**
2041-3068 *see* 1464-4193 **3381**
2041-3076 *see* 1464-4207 **3381**
2041-3084 *see* 1475-0902 **8646**
2041-3092 *see* 1740-3499 **7016**
2041-3130 *see* 0309-3247 **3351**
2041-3149 *see* 1468-0874 **3382**
2041-3335 *see* 0212-6109 **1515**
2041-3831 Luxury Intelligence **1145**
2041-384X *see* 2041-3831 **1145**
2041-4056 Stand (Leeds) **5377**
2041-4196 International Journal of Protective Structures **3273**
2041-4889 Cell Death & Disease **829**
2041-5370 *see* 0076-0730 **2241**
2041-6962 *see* 0038-4283 **6953**
2041-7764 Journal of European Competition Law & Practice **4701**
2041-7802 Export & Freight **8495**
2041-7810 *see* 2041-7802 **8495**
2041-806X Advances in Ecopolitics **3482**
2041-868X International Journal of Economics and Accounting **1292**
2041-8698 *see* 2041-868X **1292**
2041-9430 *see* 0020-3203 **3713**
2060-0518 Fifi Viragoskertje *see* 1747-437X **2188**
2060-1662 Hannah Montana **2192**
2060-1670 Spider-Man **2214**
2060-1689 Verdak **2219**
2060-1786 DreamWorks Magazin **2187**
2060-1794 Power Rangers Magazin **2208**
2060-4033 Noddy **2205**
2060-4696 Camp Rock **2181**
2060-5102 Hot Wheels Magazin **2193**
2060-6036 Egmont Posztermagazin **2187**
2060-6249 Clinical and Experimental Medical Journal **5904**
2060-730X H2O **2192**
2060-8543 *see* 0546-8191 **244**
2060-9035 Tini Sztarok Titkai **2217**
2060-9469 International Quarterly of Sport Science **8181**
2060-968X *see* 2060-6249 **5904**
2065-1430 Acta Didactica Napocensia **2823**
2065-3891 *see* 1844-8062 **4802**
2065-3913 Theoretical and Empirical Researches in Urban Management **4428**
2065-3921 *see* 2065-3913 **4428**
2065-4855 Jurnalul Pediatrului **6095**
2065-7285 Public Reason **6945**
2065-7714 *see* 1841-5512 **5527**
2065-8958 *see* 2065-7285 **6945**
2066-3129 *see* 2066-4273 **5500**
2066-4273 Journal of Applied Computer Science & Mathematics **5500**
2066-8325 Oeconomics of Knowledge **1156**
2070-0083 *see* 1994-9057 **2824**
2070-0237 Journal of Scientific Research **7873**
2070-0245 *see* 2070-0237 **7873**
2070-0393 *see* 1024-8560 **4404**
2070-0466 P-Adic Numbers, Ultrametric Analysis, and Applications **5524**
2070-0474 *see* 2070-0466 **5524**
2070-0482 Mathematical Models and Computer Simulations **5554**
2070-0490 *see* 2070-0482 **5554**
2070-0504 Catalysis in Industry **3237**
2070-0555 *see* 2070-0504 **3237**
2070-1055 Kuaiji yu Caijin Yanjiu Qikan **1296**
2070-1802 Edition Sozialwissenschaften **7961**
2070-2027 Risafa Medical Digest **5707**
2070-2051 Protection of Metals and Physical Chemistry of Surfaces **6330**
2070-206X *see* 2070-2051 **6330**
2070-254X Pan Arab Journal of Oncology **6032**
2070-2620 Southern Forests **3703**
2070-2779 *see* 0759-1063 **8091**
2070-2825 *see* 1607-1069 **4447**
2070-3368 *see* 0556-3321 **807**
2070-3392 *see* 1020-041X
2070-3449 China Perspectives **7226**
2070-3740 World Academy of Science, Engineering and Technology. Proceedings **7929**
2070-3872 *see* 1306-973X **7974**
2070-4658 Journal of Islamic Economics, Banking and Finance **1362**
2070-4666 *see* 2070-4658 **1362**
2070-5948 Electronic Journal of Applied Statistical Analysis **8367**
2070-6065 F A O Fisheries and Aquaculture Circular **3591**
2070-626X *see* 1812-1004 **6581**
2070-6405 Studia Interdisciplinaria Aenipontana **5180**
2070-7185 International Council for the Exploration of the Sea. Annual Report **2808**
2070-7266 Tobacco Induced Diseases (Print) *changed to* 1617-9625 **8488**
2070-8157 Revista Boliviana de Derecho **4770**
2070-8335 *see* I F L A Serials and Other Continuing Resources Section. Newsletter **5014**
2070-8998 *see* 1813-8535 **3386**
2071-1050 Sustainability **3468**
2071-1255 *see* 1607-3894 **8800**
2071-6141 Tul'skii Gosudarstvennyi Universitet. Izvestiya. Gumanitarnye Nauki **8011**
2071-6168 Tul'skii Gosudarstvennyi Universitet. Izvestiya. Tekhnicheskie Nauki **7925**
2071-6176 Tul'skii Gosudarstvennyi Universitet. Izvestiya. Estestvennye Nauki **708**
2071-6184 Tul'skii Gosudarstvennyi Universitet. Izvestiya. Ekonomicheskie i Yuridicheskie Nauki **1185**
2071-6559 Journal of Asian Arts & Aesthetics **498**
2071-7113 International Journal of Meat Science **3648**
2071-7296 S i b A D I. Vestnik **8510**
2072-0041 Voronezhskii Gosudarstvennyi Arkhitekturno-Stroitel'nyi Universitet. Nauchnyi Vestnik. Stroitel'stvo i Arkhitektura **460**
2072-0815 C I S Iron and Steel Review **6307**
2072-0823 Eurasian Mining **6462**
2072-0904 *see* 1993-3541 **1130**
2072-4292 Remote Sensing **7037**
2072-5124 *see* 1995-3844 **1951**
2072-5310 *see* 1996-3459 **6483**
2072-6767 *see* 1019-9039 **7932**
2072-8506 Ethiopian Journal of Crop Science **229**
2072-974X Snub **2261**
2072-9758 Snob Al-Hasna Decor **4550**
2072-9766 Snub al-Hasna Tajmil **8884**
2072-9774 Al-Umm **8886**
2073-2740 Global Media Journal: African Edition **2321**
2073-5146 Ulum-e-Islamia **7716**
2073-5782 Positionen **7172**
2073-607X International Journal of Communication Networks and Information Security **2424**
2073-7122 Interdisciplinary Journal of Contemporary Research in Business **1125**
2074-1057 *see* 0732-183X **6024**
2074-2061 Pakistan Journal of Social Sciences (Multan) **7991**
2074-2827 International Journal of Open Problems in Complex Analysis **5497**
2075-1087 Gyroscopy and Navigation **2783**
2075-1109 *see* 2075-1087 **2783**
2075-1117 Russian Journal of Biological Invasions **702**
2075-1125 *see* 2075-1117 **702**
2075-1133 Inorganic Materials: Applied Research **2116**
2075-115X *see* 2075-1133 **2116**
2075-2245 *see* 1812-0857 **2424**
2075-5783 Basistexte zur Wirtschafts- und Sozialgeschichte **4203**
2075-6933 Khyber Behavioural Studies **7382**
2080-2145 *see* 1897-8649 **2453**
2090-0007 Journal of Transplantation **6250**
2090-0015 *see* 2090-0007 **6250**
2090-0112 Journal of Amino Acids **734**
2090-0163 Cardiovascular Psychiatry and Neurology **6130**
2090-0171 *see* 2090-0163 **6130**
2090-021X Journal of Nucleic Acids **736**
2090-0252 International Journal of Alzheimer's Disease **6146**
2090-052X International Journal of Evolutionary Biology **872**
2092-6456 *see* 1226-7708 **3641**
2094-0734 The International Journal of Educational and Psychological Assessment **2869**
2094-1420 The Internatioanl Journal of Research and Review **7974**
2100-000X *see* 0003-4088 **2792**
2100-0808 Education Therapeutique du Patient **6108**
2100-0816 *see* 2100-0808 **6108**
2100-9511 Neurologie.com **6166**
2100-9619 Correspondances en M H N D **5885**
2100-9864 *see* 1161-2770 **1105**
2101-0366 *see* 1270-6841 **2320**
2101-115X L'Esprit Voyageur **4005**
2101-1680 Le Guide de l'Eau **8824**
2101-8308 Vitaform' **6670**
2102-0663 Transform ! **7189**
2103-2874 Developpements **7352**
2103-3137 Cheval Arabe News **8289**
2150-0274 R C D A Newsletter **7673**
2150-0401 Pisgah Astronomical Research Institute. Annual Report **579**
2150-0711 Hawaii Vegetables **181**
2150-0738 Atumpan **4132**
2150-0746 Zambia Food Security Outlook **1608**
2150-0800 Ocean Style Magazine **4306**
2150-0819 Memoir, a Noun **5332**
2150-0835 The Money for Main Street Monitor **1150**
2150-0916 Real Estate Litigation **7609**
2150-0959 *see* 1552-9592 **8035**
2150-1041 Cancer Biology **920**
2150-105X *see* 2150-1041 **920**
2150-1092 *see* 0748-4364 **2933**
2150-1106 Changing Schools (Denver) **3054**
2150-1114 *see* 2150-1106 **3054**
2150-1149 *see* 1533-3159 **5773**
2150-1297 Journal of Asthma & Allergy Educators **5762**
2150-1300 *see* 2150-1297 **5762**
2150-1319 Journal of Primary Care & Community Health **5654**
2150-1335 Cardiac Cath Lab Director **5779**
2150-1351 World Journal for Pediatric and Congenital Heart Surgery **6262**
2150-1378 Counseling Outcome Research and Evaluation **7349**
2150-1386 *see* 2150-1378 **7349**
2150-1696 Managed Care First Report **4106**
2150-1882 *see* 1521-5237 **4517**
2150-1955 Northwest Sportsman **8325**
2150-1971 LifeExcellence Newsletter **7383**
2150-198X Futureclaw **6969**
2150-2064 *see* 1072-3145 **8533**
2150-2072 *see* 1081-4485 **8599**
2150-2080 *see* 1553-6211 **3393**
2150-2099 *see* 1547-9463 **7329**
2150-2196 Digital Magazines **7559**
2150-3125 Washington Literary Review (Online) **5437**
2150-3133 Get Money Magazine **6645**
2150-3141 MacCompanion **2594**
2150-3206 Virginia Policy Review **7192**
2150-3214 *see* 2150-3206 **7192**
2150-3265 Rural Education Review **2908**
2150-3273 Mayan Studies Journal **5150**
2150-332X Bishop McGuinness Catholic High School Alumni Association. Newsletter **2264**
2150-3346 *see* 2150-0819 **5332**
2150-3370 Early Intervention & School Special Interest Section Quarterly **3039**
2150-3478 Focus on Healthy Aging **4044**
2150-3486 Smith Lake Living **3988**
2150-3559 Journal of the New Comprehensive College **2991**
2150-3567 *see* 2150-3559 **2991**
2150-3583 *see* 1551-9295 **900**
2150-377X Energy and the Earth **6461**
2150-3818 Bloomberg Law Reports. Health Law **7510**
2150-3958 Russian-American Education Forum **2908**
2150-3966 Rossiisko-Amerikanskii Forum Obrazovaniia *see* 2150-3958 **2908**
2150-3974 Teaching American Literature **5385**
2150-3990 State Tax Essentials **1944**
2150-4008 *see* 0000-0019 **7571**
2150-4016 *see* 1934-2861 **57**
2150-4024 *see* 0025-0929 **1021**
2150-4091 Natural Science **7888**
2150-4105 *see* 2150-4091 **7888**
2150-4113 *see* 1079-0969 **7520**
2150-413X *see* 0364-3484 **8503**
2150-4539 *see* 1072-1797 **46**
2150-4628 Journal of Somaliland Studies **3545**
2150-4636 *see* 2150-4628 **3545**
2150-4644 *see* 1060-5126 **2659**
2150-4679 Eastern **2979**
2150-4911 Fleet Maintenance **8496**
2150-492X *see* 2150-4911 **8496**
2150-4954 Ribbons **5433**
2150-4970 Movement and Rhythm **2887**
2150-4997 Optimizing Process and Technology **1784**
2150-5004 Marie June InspireME **7384**
2150-5047 Indiana University. African Studies Program. Events **4175**
2150-5063 Academy for Economics and Economic Education. Proceedings **1056**
2150-508X Billing & O S S World **2366**
2150-5098 Academy for Studies in International Business. Proceedings **1056**
2150-5101 *see* 2150-508X **2366**
2150-511X Academy of Strategic Management. Proceedings **1723**
2150-5136 Academy for Studies in Business. Proceedings **1056**
2150-5160 Academy for Legal, Ethical and Regulatory Issues. Proceedings **4608**
2150-5187 Academy of Marketing Studies. Proceedings **1803**
2150-5233 Leaflet **5425**
2150-5462 Penn Bioethics Journal **6938**
2150-5470 *see* 2150-5462 **6938**
2150-556X *see* 0039-5854 **1709**
2150-5586 Style-Ology Magazine **2262**
2150-5780 The Inland Episcopalian **7761**
2150-5802 Ufahamu (Online) **3569**
2150-5845 See Jane Succeed **1793**
2150-5896 P D C **2434**
2150-590X *see* 2150-5896 **2434**
2150-5950 Scots' Charitable Society Wittins **2270**
2150-6167 Star City Sports **8209**
2150-6175 L **5075**
2150-6183 Zeromile **2310**
2150-6221 Agent's Sales Journal (National Edition) **4491**
2150-623X *see* 1064-8542 **5576**
2150-6264 *see* 0090-3159 **5988**
2150-6299 Career & Work Life Matters **6644**
2150-6345 *see* 8750-0507 **6090**
2150-640X *see* 0011-8737 **5841**
2150-6523 *see* 0196-6197 **5875**
2150-6566 *see* 0012-7337 **8796**
2150-6590 *see* 1552-5791 **4701**
2150-6639 Supersafemark Guia de Referencia Rapida las Mejores Practicas de Seguridad e Higiene en la Venta Directa de Alimentos al Consumidor **6687**
2150-668X *see* 1529-6407 **5041**
2150-6698 *see* 0099-0086 **5003**
2150-6701 *see* 0010-0870 **5002**
2150-6728 Dermatology Coding Alert **4501**
2150-6736 *see* 2150-6728 **4501**
2150-6760 *see* 1942-9665 **7527**
2150-6795 Clarion (Boston) **5274**
2150-6825 *see* 1942-8189 **7248**
2150-6876 Spectrumite **3565**
2150-6906 *see* 1940-1876 **2987**
2150-6930 *see* 1535-0118 **7449**
2150-7090 *see* 1079-6630 **4488**
2150-7120 *see* 1533-9300 **4106**
2150-7155 *see* 0025-7206 **5668**
2150-721X *see* 1558-9242 **5856**
2150-7333 *see* 0193-032X **6048**
2150-7376 *see* 1543-2521 **6870**
2150-7384 *see* 0093-9722 **6276**
2150-7449 Bible Teaching for Preteens. BTX. A Bible Teaching Experience for Preteens. Leader Pack **7626**
2150-7457 Bible Teaching for Preteens. BTX. A Bible Teaching Experience for Preteens. Teaching Pictures **7627**
2150-7643 *see* 2150-7651 **2170**
2150-7651 Toy Tips & Parenting Hints **2170**
2150-7694 *see* 1934-7553 **1033**
2175-2524 Magazine of Hispanic Genealogy **3774**
2175-344X *see* 0006-5943 **7341**
2175-3504 *see* 1413-2907 **7363**
2175-3539 *see* 1413-8557 **7392**
2175-3563 *see* 1413-8271 **7392**
2175-3571 *see* 1415-1138 **7394**
2175-3601 *see* 0486-641X **7403**
2306-2525 Family Planning International Assistance Newsletter†
2658-1205 The Green Disk
3002-1472 D M W Disk-Archiv **5744**
3403-3246 Der Landkreis (Hessian State Edition) *see* 0342-2259 **7451**
5617-1099 I S A Analysis Division Symposium. Proceedings (CD-ROM) **4487**
6209-9450 Enviro Report†
6394-2925 Brandschutz *see* 0011-4782 **439**
7141-410X L'Arca International **428**
7865-8717 *see* 0306-0322 **7577**
8750-0124 Supply Line **4348**
8750-0140 Variety Puzzles & Games
8750-0183 Earthwatch **7852**
8750-0434 Biometric Bulletin **8358**

Link to your serials resources and content with ulrichsweb.com

8750-0477 Art & Style International
8750-0507 Contemporary Pediatrics **6090**
8750-0515 Georgia Advance Sheets **4680**
8750-068X Film & Video News†
8750-0973 Connecticut Law Journal **4648**
8750-0981 Oakland Business Monthly†
8750-1082 U K Magazine
8750-1090 Herb Basket†
8750-1104 Shepard's Corporation Law Citations†
8750-1112 Shepard's Partnership Law Citations†
8750-1120 Shepard's Texas Case Names Citator **4964**
8750-1139 Shepard's Products Liability Citations†
8750-1155 Movers News **8673**
8750-1228 Better Health (Birmingham) **6983**
8750-1236 Condo Sales Report **7587**
8750-1287 Fishing Tackle Retailer **8313**
8750-1430 Valley Magazine (Granada Hills) **3991**
8750-1465 Camping Today **8308**
8750-1481 Antique Bottle and Glass Collector **362**
8750-1562 Union Advocate Newspaper **4604**
8750-1600 Signpost for Northwest Trails **8332**
8750-1627 Perfins Bulletin
8750-1708 Scanner King County Labor News **4602**
8750-1716 Cook's Crier†
8750-1724 Retail Market Report
8750-1732 Dusty Times **8258**
8750-1767 SuperTeen†
8750-1813 California Physician **5591**
8750-1937 Current Notes
8750-1953 Sighthound Review **6815**
8750-1961 Boston Jewish Times **7719**
8750-2011 Leaven (Schaumburg) **2159**
8750-2100 Mass High Tech **8431**
8750-2127 Limousin World **292**
8750-2135 New Perspectives†
8750-216X New England Monthly†
8750-2186 Dentistry Today **5842**
8750-2224 Prepress Bulletin *changed to* 1539-137X **7323**
8750-2313 Labor Paper (Peoria) **4597**
8750-233X Trapper & Predator Caller **8338**
8750-2348 Sandara **3562**
8750-2356 S R C Blue Book of 5-Trend Cycli-Graphs **1649**
8750-2410 Best Fares
8750-2453 Accessories **2245**
8750-2526 L S U Magazine **2289**
8750-2534 *see* 0745-9173 **7779**
8750-2585 A P M A News **6054**
8750-2623 West's California Reporter **4813**
8750-2712 Communication Age†
8750-2720 City Sun†
8750-2763 Attorneys Personnel Report†
8750-2836 Hospital Practice†
8750-295X Western World Avon Collectors Marketplace†
8750-3042 Horoscope Guide **566**
8750-3085 Ocular Surgery News (US Edition) **6254**
8750-3158 S B A N E Enterprise **1966**
8750-3255 American Theatre **8465**
8750-3298 Street Rodding Illustrated†
8750-3301 V W Trends†
8750-331X International Journal of Chinese Medicine†
8750-3379 Berks County Law Journal **4946**
8750-345X Kitchen & Bath Design News **4544**
8750-3530 Festival Quarterly†
8750-3549 Rhodesian Ridgeback Quarterly **6814**
8750-3557 Labrador Quarterly **6810**
8750-3603 Bowling Digest†
8750-3670 Business Travel News **8689**
8750-3697 Culpepper Letter†
8750-376X Inspector General Brief
8750-4022 Idaho Business Review **1121**
8750-4081 Indoor Garden†
8750-409X Yale Alumni Magazine **2310**
8750-4170 Spokane, A Great Place, The Magazine†
8750-4197 Jewish Chronicle (Yonkers) **7722**
8750-4219 The Puller **8194**
8750-4278 Phillies Report†
8750-4286 Retail News West
8750-4294 Southwest Journal of Business and Economics **1178**
8750-4308 El Centinela (Nampa)
8750-4367 Marvel Age†
8750-4375 Computer Living - New York
8750-4502 Investment Coin Review†
8750-4634 Southwest Hotel - Motel Review†
8750-474X Tennessee Granger
8750-4774 Heating, Air Conditioning & Plumbing Products†
8750-4790 Pharmacy News and Review **6873**
8750-4812 Convention Herald **7635**
8750-4898 Cat Fanciers' Almanac†
8750-5088 Tri-State Real Estate Journal†
8750-510X Real Estate Syndication Alert†
8750-5142 E F T Press Alert†
8750-5169 Caribbean Reporter†
8750-5266 Bridge **3296**
8750-5290 Observer (Nashville) **7727**
8750-5347 The Sinfonian **2301**
8750-5401 Movie Collector's World **2402**
8750-5428 Interamericana **2288**
8750-5452 Providence Visitor *changed to* 1938-8675 **7815**
8750-5487 Maltese Magazine **6811**
8750-5622 Focus Magazine (Hartford)
8750-5630 Record Horseman **8297**
8750-5649 Home & Away (Indianapolis Edition) **8719**
8750-5673 Premier Hog Producer
8750-5746 Kalamazoo College Quarterly **2289**
8750-5835 Talking Turkey†
8750-5975 Voice of the Southwest **7822**
8750-6033 El Paso Economic Review **1104**
8750-6041 Plumbing & Mechanical **4125**
8750-6106 Progressive Rentals **1787**
8750-6149 Finance and Commerce **1342**
8750-6238 Valley Catholic
8750-6580 Nation's Building News **1026**
8750-6629 Hunting Retriever **6809**
8750-6637 State Policy Reports
8750-6645 Iowa Commerce **1430**
8750-6653 Powder / Bulk Solids **3253**
8750-6718 Pacific Banker†
8750-6807 Florida Hotel & Motel Journal *changed to* 1556-1313 **4398**
8750-684X Gifted Children Monthly
8750-6866 Sickle & Sheaf **2270**
8750-6874 Information Week (US Edition) **2531**
8750-6890 San Diego Business Journal **1170**
8750-7242 Bop **2180**
8750-7269 The Pinto Horse **8296**
8750-7315 American Podiatric Medical Association. Journal **6055**
8750-734X Daily Commercial Recorder **1090**
8750-7366 Needle's Eye Worldwide **2249**
8750-7471 Antique Radio Classified **2356**
8750-7536 Shield & Diamond **2300**
8750-7544 Physician Assistant (Springhouse)†
8750-7587 Journal of Applied Physiology **923**
8750-7595 Countryside and Small Stock Journal **3973**
8750-7730 Academic Leader **2965**
8750-7757 Puget Sound Business Journal **1162**
8750-7765 Christian Mission
8750-7897 The Shepherd **300**
8750-7927 U S C Trojan Family **2305**
8750-7943 Veterinary Medicine **8813**
8750-801X Lottery & Gaming Review
8750-8028 Bridges (Reston) **3523**
8750-8044 New York State Jury Verdict Review & Analysis **4745**
8750-8052 Pennsylvania Jury Verdict Review & Analysis **4756**
8750-8060 New Jersey Jury Verdict Review & Analysis **4743**
8750-8133 W & J Magazine **2308**
8750-8281 Arizona Cattlelog **279**
8750-8397 Transportation Worldwide†
8750-846X Colorado Nurse **5955**
8750-8516 Masscitizen **3452**
8750-8613 Church Life **7751**
8750-8656 Orlando Business Journal **1157**
8750-880X Hispanic U S A Magazine
8750-8877 Crochet Fantasy **6638**
8750-8915 Flex **6986**
8750-8923 Nostalgia (Milwaukee)
8750-8990 Veterinary Technician **8814**
8750-9067 Telemarketer **1845**
8750-9075 Poland Today
8750-9148 Hokie Huddler†
8750-9210 Stone Review *changed to* Stone, Sand & Gravel Review **6480**
8750-9229 Roads & Bridges **3282**
8750-927X Business New York†
8750-9326 El Pregonero **7813**
8750-9334 Electronic Engineering Manager†
8750-9350 A A S Newsletter **567**
8750-9393 Pasta Journal **3659**
8750-9407 Physicians Financial News†
8750-9415 Symphony User's Journal†
8750-9431 Army Organizational Effectiveness Journal†
8750-944X C Y L A Quarterly **4635**
8750-9520 Greater Danbury Business Digest
8750-9563 Welcome Home†
8750-9652 Contemporary Longterm Care **4091**
8750-9687 A A P S News **5563**
8750-9741 Medigram **5675**
8750-9776 Afghan Hound Review **6802**
8750-9903 Local 3 Bakery Workers News **4598**
8750-9989 Red & Black (Middletown)†
8755-0032 Advances in Neural and Behavioral Development†
8755-0040 Current Topics in Human Intelligence†
8755-0059 Kansas Medicine†
8755-013X Exporters' Encyclopaedia† **8955**
8755-0229 Journal of Medical Practice Management **5652**
8755-0253 Professional Document Retrieval†
8755-027X Africa Commentary†
8755-0415 Cite **437**
8755-0431 Official Guide to Food Service and Hospitality Management Careers **6701**
8755-044X Official Guide to Flight Attendants Careers **6701**
8755-0458 Official Guide to Travel Agent & Travel Careers **6701**
8755-0466 Official Guide to Airline Careers **6701**
8755-0474 Oceans Policy Study Series†
8755-0504 Journal of Language for International Business **5134**
8755-0547 Sherbondy Beacon **3782**
8755-0555 Sound Management†
8755-058X Local Climatological Data. Paducah, Kentucky. Monthly Summary **6380**
8755-0628 Tax Management Real Estate Journal **7613**
8755-0709 Annual Report on Alaska's Mineral Resources **6305**
8755-075X Lamp (Chicago)†
8755-0954 Panorama (Pittsburgh, 1960) **2296**
8755-0962 Reference Books Bulletin **5042**
8755-0970 Topics in Ocular Pharmacology and Toxicology†
8755-1020 National Association of Document Examiners. Journal **2661**
8755-1039 Diagnostic Cytopathology **832**
8755-1128 Plan **453**
8755-1195 Optical Memory Report
8755-1209 Reviews of Geophysics **2788**
8755-1217 History of Geophysics Series **2783**
8755-1225 Journal of Pharmacy Technology **6856**
8755-1233 Update (Print)†
8755-125X Wyoming Lawyer **4816**
8755-1284 The Labor Page
8755-139X Libertarian Party News **7151**
8755-156X Frogpond **5422**
8755-1608 U S Real Estate Register **7614**
8755-1675 American Computer Law Digest
8755-1721 Johnson Journal†
8755-1748 Southern Genealogical Index†
8755-1756 German Connection **3768**
8755-1829 National Education Association. Handbook **2889**
8755-1969 Delaware Geological Survey. Special Publication **2730**
8755-1985 Journal of Protective Coatings & Linings **6718**
8755-2019 Center (Austin)†
8755-2035 Porticus **6536**
8755-2043 University of Virginia Medical Center. Claude Moore Health Sciences Library. Annual Report **5053**
8755-2094 Educational Media and Technology Yearbook **3059**
8755-2167 Waconda Roots and Branches **3787**
8755-2256 Southern Landscape & Turf **3751**
8755-2353 Dorchester County Genealogical Magazine **3764**
8755-2450 Women's Annual†
8755-2469 Idaho Wildlife†
8755-2574 Immigration Law Advisory
8755-2582 Corporate Artnews†
8755-2590 Research Roundup **3030**
8755-2655 The Cloth Doll **6637**
8755-2841 Utah Directory of Business and Industry **2033**
8755-2876 Washington Telecom Directory **2373**
8755-2914 The Columbia (Rhinebeck) **3762**
8755-2922 Learning Resources Directory for Healthcare Executives†
8755-2930 Earthquake Spectra **2780**
8755-3023 Golden Roots of the Mother Lode **3769**
8755-3112 Nautica
8755-3139 Stamp Dealer Forum†
8755-3163 American Fireworks News **3236**
8755-321X Successful Marketing to Senior Citizens†
8755-3228 Llewellyn's Astrological Guide to California†
8755-3252 Institute for Orgonomic Science. Annals **6146**
8755-3317 Futures Research Quarterly *changed to* 1946-7567 **7930**
8755-3325 Critica **3528**
8755-3449 Journal of Third World Studies **4150**
8755-3473 Collections (Newark) **5002**
8755-3546 Standard Methods for the Examination of Water and Wastewater **8832**
8755-3554 Standard Methods for the Examination of Dairy Products **269**
8755-3651 El Gato Tuerto
8755-366X L.C. Subject Headings Weekly Lists: A Working Cumulation†
8755-3716 Harvard Education Letter **2862**
8755-3724 InterMarket†
8755-3732 C A A S News **7585**
8755-3767 Wrestling Masters
8755-3805 Johannes Schwalm Historical Association. Journal†
8755-3848 P A D F News **1603**
8755-3856 Zoning News *changed to* 1548-0135 **4432**
8755-3910 Anais†
8755-3929 Show Horse†
8755-4054 Southern California Counties Public Schools. Survey
8755-4151 Mutual Fund Sourcebook†
8755-416X Legal Newsletters in Print (Year) **4823**
8755-4178 Journal of Feminist Studies in Religion **7655**
8755-4208 The Journal of Kentucky Studies **2876**
8755-4259 C I I T Activities **3494**
8755-4291 Mutual Fund Monitor
8755-4305 International Journal of Personal Property Appraising†
8755-4313 L C and You
8755-433X Executive Memorandum **7234**
8755-4348 Appraisers' Information Exchange (Print Edition)†
8755-4356 International Society of Appraisers. Membership Directory **2009**
8755-4372 Fireworks Business **1428**
8755-4380 T S R Hotline
8755-4461 American Lawyer Guide to Leading Law Firms†
8755-4550 Women and Language **5195**
8755-4593 Newsletter East Asian Art & Archaeology **508**
8755-4615 Computers and Composition **2469**
8755-4623 Nevada Hospitality **8190**
8755-464X Profiles (Solana Beach)†
8755-4658 What Color is Your Parachute? (Year) **6705**
8755-4682 Seiche **8831**
8755-4712 Supplement to Employment, Hours, and Earnings: States and Areas *see* Employment, Hours, and Earnings: States and Areas **8953**
8755-4747 Pathways (Maynardville) **4308**
8755-4755 Takeover Target Weekly Forecast†
8755-4836 United States Department of Transportation. Office of Inspector General. Semiannual Report to the Congress **8519**
8755-4917 Washington Report on Middle East Affairs **7273**
8755-4925 Mundus Arabicus **5337**
8755-4941 Alternative Agriculture News†
8755-500X A H A! Hispanic Arts News **462**
8755-5026 Adams Family Chronicle **3758**
8755-5034 Africa International†
8755-514X The Nebraska Review **5339**
8755-5298 I Know You Know
8755-5301 Lanthanide and Actinide Research†
8755-531X U.S. Geological Survey Bulletin **2771**
8755-5352 Lesbian Ethics
8755-5360 Studies in Social Welfare Policies and Programs† **8991**
8755-5379 E R I S A Newsletter **1676**
8755-5492 U.S. National Endowment for the Humanities. Annual Report **4479**
8755-5565 African Intelligence Digest†
8755-562X American Political Report†
8755-5670 Tau Beta Pi. Bulletin **3221**
8755-5689 Draw Magazine†
8755-5700 Next Magazine **4377**
8755-5727 C D Data Report†
8755-5735 Acquisition Mart
8755-5786 Micro Software Report (Library Edition)†
8755-5794 Micro Software Evaluations†
8755-5808 Vaba Eesti Sona **3570**
8755-5824 Electrum†
8755-5832 Boombah Herald†
8755-5964 International Trumpet Guild. Membership Directory **6577**
8755-6014 Palatine Patter **3778**
8755-6073 Hardin County Historical Quarterly **4294**
8755-6103 Casino Digest

Link to your serials resources and content with ulrichsweb.com

ISSN

Title Index

This section lists all current and ceased serials included in the directory. References from parallel, variant, former and related edition titles are included. The country of publication code and ISSN, if known, are provided. Page references in bold refer to the title's complete entry in the CLASSIFIED LIST OF SERIALS or in the Cessations section.

The triangle (▼) symbol indicates new and forthcoming titles begun in the past three years. The dagger (†) symbol denotes a ceased title. The bullet (•) symbol indicates that the title is available in one or more electronic formats, including online, CD-ROM or e-mail, either exclusively or in addition to printed formats. The arrow (➤) symbol indicates that a title is refereed or peer-reviewed by an editorial board.

DIRECTORY 2010 A C H S HANDBOOK 9901

A B C (POL) **3928**
A B C (ROM ISSN 1454-9778) **3932**
A B C *see* Approved Bioequivalency Codes **6822**
A B C *see* African Building Contractor **975**
A B C (Canarias Edition) (ESP ISSN 1699-8383) **3950**
A B C (Castilla y Leon Edition) (ESP ISSN 1698-5052) **3951**
• A B C (Comunidad Valencia Edition) (ESP ISSN 1698-5079) **3951**
• A B C (Cordoba Edition) (ESP ISSN 1698-5060) **3951**
A B C (Sevilla Edition) (ESP ISSN 1136-0208) **3951**
A B C (Toledo Edition) (ESP ISSN 1696-9111) **3951**
A B C Alergii (POL ISSN 1734-2392) **5752**
A B C & D *see* Architect, Builder, Contractor & Developer **976**
A B C Apteki (POL ISSN 1642-445X) **6817**
• A B C Belge pour le Commerce et l'Industrie (BEL ISSN 0775-6178) **1970**
A B C Blue Book: Canadian Daily Newspapers (Audit Bureau of Circulations) (USA) **37**
A B C Blue Book: Canadian Periodicals (Audit Bureau of Circulations) (USA) **7550**
A B C Blue Book: Canadian Weekly Newspapers (Audit Bureau of Circulations) (USA) **37**
A B C Blue Book: U S and Canadian Business Publications (Audit Bureau of Circulations) (USA) **7550**
A B C Blue Book: U S and Canadian Farm Publications (Audit Bureau of Circulations) (USA) **173**
A B C Blue Book: U S and Canadian Magazines (Audit Bureau of Circulations) (USA) **7550**
A B C Blue Book: U S Daily Newspapers (Audit Bureau of Circulations) (USA) **37**
A B C Blue Book: U S Weekly Newspapers (Audit Bureau of Circulations) (USA) **37**
A B C. Casopis Urgentne Medicine (SRB ISSN 1451-1053) **5563**
A B C Circulation Review (GBR) **4570**
A B C Collectors' Circle (USA) **4326**
• A B C Color (PRY ISSN 1605-5705) **3927**
A B C D *see* Arquivos Brasileiros de Cirurgia Digestiva **5920**
A B C D (Online Edition) *see* A B C D (Print) **3951**
A B C D (Print) (ESP ISSN 1699-8367) **3951**
A B C D E Focus (Association of B.C. Drama Educators) (CAN) **3049**
A B C D - Fairy Tales, Games and Lessons *see* A B V G D - Skazki, Igry i Uroki **2174**
A B C Delicious *see* Delicious **4356**
• A B C der Deutschen Wirtschaft - Quellenwerk fur Einkauf-Verkauf (DEU ISSN 0947-6148) **1970**
A B C Dialogue (Association of Bridal Consultants) (USA ISSN 1053-9107) **1956**
A B C Digital *see* A B C Color **3927**
• A B C Europ Production (DEU ISSN 0944-5641) **1551**
A B C Freight Guide (GBR ISSN 0308-9304) **8666**
A B C Gardening Australia (AUS ISSN 1325-1465) **3721**
A B C Hudong Yingyu *see* A B C Interactive English Magazine **5088**
A B C Interactive English Magazine/A B C Hudong Yingyu (TWN ISSN 1683-8548) **5088**
• A B C Luxembourgeois pour le Commerce et l'Industrie (BEL ISSN 0776-9954) **1970**
A B C Madrid *see* A B C **3950**
A B C Madrid *see* Abc.es **3951**
A B C Neurologies (Actualites Bibliographiques Commentees) (FRA ISSN 1767-5936) **6117**
A B C News Bulletin (Audit Bureau of Circulations) (USA) **18**
A B C News Index (USA ISSN 0891-8775) **2346**
A B C News Transcripts (USA ISSN 1089-0343) **4570**
A B C Newsletter *see* A B C's Between the Covers **8927**
• A B C Newsletter (America's Blood Centers) (USA ISSN 1092-0412) **5933**
• A B C of Evidence (AUS) **4606**
A B C of Magic Sets (DEU) **4326**
• A B C of Offers (AUS ISSN 1832-6544) **2963**
The A B C of Russian Business Law (RUS) **4853**
A B C Pinpin Dudu Huabao/A B C Spelling and Reading Pictorial (CHN ISSN 1006-1622) **2821**
A B C Przeziebienia (POL ISSN 1733-3040) **5807**
A B C Revista (PRY) **3927**
• A B C Soaps in Depth (USA ISSN 1525-7800) **2374**
A B C Spelling and Reading Pictorial *see* A B C Pinpin Dudu Huabao **2821**
A B C Today (Associated Builders & Contractors, Inc.) (USA ISSN 1062-3698) **974**
A B C Toledo *see* A B C (Toledo Edition) **3951**
A B C V H *see* Australian Bus & Commercial Vehicle Heritage **8490**
A B C Z (Associacao Brasileira dos Criadores de Zebu) (BRA ISSN 0101-1960) **276**
† A B C's Between the Covers (NLD ISSN 1871-6202) **8927**
• A B C's of Making Money Online (USA) **2552**
• A B C's of Net Marketing E-zine (USA) **2552**
A B D (BEL ISSN 1784-1976) **5883**
A B D *see* Aviation Buyers Directory **48**
A B D Asian-Pacific Book Development *see* Asian - Pacific Book Development **7552**
A B D O S - Mitteilungen (Arbeitsgemeinschaft der Bibliotheken und Dokumentationsstellen der Ost-, Ostmittel- und Suedosteurop) (DEU ISSN 1861-5473) **4985**
A B E L Journal *see* Adult Basic Education and Literacy Journal **2937**
A B E M. Revista (Associacao Brasileira de Educacao Musical) (BRA ISSN 1518-2630) **6541**
A B E N O. Revista (Associacao Brasileira de Ensino Odontologico) (BRA ISSN 1679-5954) **5832**
A B E S *see* Annotated Bibliography for English Studies **5406**
• A B Europe (GBR ISSN 1367-885X) **4975**
A B F *see* Australian Banking and Finance **1309**
A B F Journal (USA) **1305**
A B H B *see* Annual Bibliography of the History of the Printed Book and Library **7577**
A B H Bulletin (Association for the Bibliography of History) (USA ISSN 0892-4600) **4128**
A B H E Newsletter (The Association for Biblical Higher Education) (USA) **2963**
A B H L *see* Annual Bulletin of Historical Literature **4199**
A B I - Auftrag, Rechnung, Zahlung (Aktuelle Berichte und Informationen fuer Architekten und Ingenieure) (DEU) **426**
A B I - B C I S House Rebuilding Cost Index (Association for British Insurers - Building Cost Information Service) (GBR) **974**
• A B I - INFORM (American Business Information) (USA) **1199**
A B I Journal (American Bankruptcy Institute) (USA ISSN 1931-7522) **1305**
A B I - Risiken, Haftung, Schadenersatz (Aktuelle Berichte und Informationen fuer Architekten und Ingenieure) (DEU) **426**
A B I T - Buero Heute (DEU) **426**
A B I Technik (DEU ISSN 0720-6763) **4985**
A B I - Wirtschaft, Recht, Steuer (Aktuelle Berichte und Informationen fuer Architekten und Ingenieure) (DEU) **426**
A B K *see* Australasian Beekeeper **93**
A B L *see* American Biotechnology Laboratory **755**
A B L Monthly Bulletin (Association of Banks in Lebanon) (LBN) **1305**
† A B L O Nyt (Andelsbolighavernes Lands-Organisation) (DNK ISSN 1603-4546) **8927**
A B L R *see* Australian Business Law Review **4857**
A B M *see* Asian Business & Management **1726**
A B M *see* ARTbibliographies Modern **529**
A B M Metalurgia e Materiais (Associacao Brasileira de Metalurgia e Materiais) (BRA ISSN 0104-0898) **6303**
A B M S Medical Specialists Plus *see* A B M S Plus **5563**
• A B M S Plus (American Board of Medical Specialties) (USA) **5563**
A B N Correspondence (USA ISSN 0001-0545) **7101**
• ➤ A B N F Journal (Association of Black Nursing Faculty in Higher Education, Inc.) (USA ISSN 1046-7041) **5949**
• A B O (PRT ISSN 0874-2731) **5933**
A B O P. Revista (Associacao Brasileira de Orientadores Profissionais) (BRA ISSN 1414-8889) **6691**
A B P (Afrika, Asien - Brasilien - Portugal) (DEU ISSN 0947-1723) **5247**
A B P C on C D - R O M *see* American Book Prices Current **7577**
A B P Contact (Association Belge des Paralyses) (BEL ISSN 0777-4761) **4063**
A B P I News (Association of the British Pharmaceutical Industry) (GBR ISSN 0001-0561) **6817**
A B P Magazine (Algemeen Burgerlijk Pensioenfonds) (NLD ISSN 1572-1728) **4490**
A B P Ports Handbook (Associated British Port) (GBR ISSN 1358-1783) **8638**
A B P Position Papers (Algemeen Burgerlijk Pensioenfonds) (NLD) **1661**
A B P R *see* American Book Publishing Record **7551**
A B P Wereld (Algemeen Burgerlijk Pensioenfonds) (NLD ISSN 1569-3341) **3914**
A B P Working Papers (Algemeen Burgerlijk Pensioenfonds) (NLD) **1661**
• A B Q Correspondent (USA ISSN 1066-3878) **8415**
A B R *see* Australian Biblical Review **7624**
• A B R (Australian Book Review) (AUS ISSN 0155-2864) **5204**
A B R *see* Australian Bar Review **4623**
A B R A L I N. Revista (Associacao Brasileira de Linguistica) (BRA ISSN 1678-1805) **5088**
A B R A P L I P. Revista (Associacao Brasileira de Professores de Literatura Portuguesa) (BRA ISSN 1676-9929) **5247**
A B R E E S (Abstracts Russian and East European Series) (GBR) **1199**
A B R N *see* Automotive Body Repair News **8564**
A B S A M E Newsletter (Association for the Behavioral Sciences and Medical Education) (USA) **5563**
A B S E E S *see* American Bibliography of Slavic and East European Studies **4168**
A B S E L Conference Proceedings *see* Developments in Business Simulation & Experiential Exercises **2517**
A B S E L News & Views (Association for Business Simulation and Experiential Learning) (USA) **2517**
• A B S I (Abstracte in Bibliologie si Stiinta Informarii) (ROM ISSN 1220-3092) **5056**
A B T E C Koen Ronbunshu/A B T E C Proceedings (JPN) **3372**
A B T E C Proceedings *see* A B T E C Koen Ronbunshu **3372**
A.B. - The Samaritan News/Had'shot Ha-Shomronim (ISR ISSN 0333-7286) **3514**
A B U Technical Review (Asia - Pacific Broadcasting Union) (MYS ISSN 0126-6209) **2374**
A B V (Issue Number) *see* Art Bulletin of Victoria **6519**
A B V G D - Skazki, Igry i Uroki/A B C D - Fairy Tales, Games and Lessons (RUS) **2174**
A B Y C News *see* Reference Point (Annapolis) **8281**
A B Z (USA ISSN 1933-8317) **5415**
A Babord (CAN ISSN 1710-209X) **7101**
A Byte of Godley Counsel *see* Godly Counsel **7645**
A C A Bulletin (Association of Canadian Archivists) (CAN ISSN 0709-4604) **4985**
A C A I Q Magazine (Association des Courtiers et Agents Immobiliers du Quebec) (CAN ISSN 1198-8541) **7581**
• A C A L eNews (Australian Council For Adult Literacy) (AUS) **2937**
A C A M H Occasional Papers (Association for Child and Adolescent Mental Health) (GBR) **7330**
▼ A C A M. La Lettre (FRA ISSN 1956-2977) **1275**
A C A News (Alberta Council on Aging) (CAN ISSN 0826-497X) **4037**
A C A News (American Chiropractic Association) (USA) **5803**
A C A Newsletter *see* A C A Reflexions **2108**
A C A R M Newsletter *see* Association of Commonwealth Archivists and Records Managers Newsletter **4992**
A C A R T S O D Monograph Series (African Centre for Applied Research and Training in Social Development) (LBY) **1589**
A C A R T S O D Newsletter (African Centre for Applied Research and Training in Social Development) (LBY) **1589**
• A C A Reflexions (American Crystallographic Association) (USA ISSN 1933-2785) **2108**
A C A Review (Anglers' Conservation Association) (GBR ISSN 0044-8257) **3582**
A C A S Bulletin (Association of Concerned Africa Scholars) (USA ISSN 1051-0842) **4172**
A C A S I A (Association for Central Asian Studies) (USA ISSN 0897-8050) **4179**
A C & U *see* American Colleges & Universities **2953**
A C & Y H S News (Akron, Canton and Youngstown Railroad Historical Society) (USA ISSN 1076-6693) **8614**
A C Autocaravan (ITA) **8679**
• A C B F Newsletter (African Capacity Building Foundation) (ZWE ISSN 1684-6079) **1589**
A C B Infos (Association des Conservateurs de Bibliotheque) (FRA ISSN 1163-4979) **4985**
• A C B News (Association of Clinical Biochemists) (GBR ISSN 1461-0337) **721**
A C C A Docket *see* A C C Docket **4854**
• A C C A Focus - Australia Newsletter (GBR) **1275**
• A C C A Focus - Canada Newsletter (GBR) **1275**
• A C C A Focus - Malaysia Newsletter (GBR) **1275**
• A C C A Focus - Pakistan Newsletter (GBR) **1275**
• A C C A Focus - Singapore Newsletter (GBR) **1275**
• A C C A Focus - U S A Newsletter (GBR) **1275**
A C C A News (Air Conditioning Contractors of America) (USA) **4115**
A C C A Quality Contractor's Catalog of Materials, Products and Services (Air Conditioning Contractors of America) (USA) **4128**
• A C C A Research Report (Association of Chartered Certified Accountants) (GBR) **1275**
A C C A Research T & R. Occasional Research Paper (Association of Chartered Certified Accountants) (GBR) **1275**
A C C A Students' Newsletter *see* Student Accountant **1302**
A C C A Technician Bulletin *see* Student Accountant **1302**
A C C. Annual Report *see* Australian Crime Commission. Annual Report **2644**
A C C Area Sports Journal (USA) **8156**
A C C Basketball Handbook (Atlantic Coast Conference) (USA ISSN 0733-0448) **8220**
• A C C C eJournal (Online) (Australian Competition and Consumer Commission) (AUS) **4853**
A C C C International (Association of Canadian Community Colleges) (CAN ISSN 1192-1846) **1589**
A C C C Journal (Print) *see* A C C C eJournal (Online) **4853**
† • ➤ A C C Cardiosource Review Journal (American College of Cardiology) (USA ISSN 1556-8571) **8927**
A C C Current Journal Review *see* A C C Cardiosource Review Journal **8927**
A C C Docket (Association of Corporate Counsel) (USA ISSN 1546-4776) **4854**
• A C C E (Asociacion Cultural Castillo de Embid) (ESP ISSN 1699-8057) **7944**
A C C E L (American College of Cardiology Extended Learning) (USA ISSN 1520-5959) **5775**
A C C E O Matters (Association of Caravan & Camping Exempted Organisations) (GBR ISSN 1750-5984) **8301**
A C C Football Annual *see* Lindy's A C C Football Annual **8237**
A C C I S Newsletter (Advisory Committee for the Coordination of Information Systems) (CHE ISSN 0254-3133) **2519**
A C C J Directory (American Chamber of Commerce in Japan) (JPN) **1970**
A C C L A I M Bulletin (Associated Chinese Chambers of Commerce and Industry of Malaysia) (MYS) **1394**
A C C L L S Newsletter/A C C L L S Nuusbrief (Advancement Committee for Comparative Linguistics and Literary Studies) (ZAF) **5088**
A C C L L S Nuusbrief *see* A C C L L S Newsletter **5088**
A C C M *see* Advances in Chemoinformatics and Computational Methods **2049**
A C C N *see* Canadian Chemical News **2052**
A C C N Bulletin (Associated Court and Commercial Newspapers) (USA) **4570**
A C C O S C A Newsletter (African Confederation of Savings and Credit Cooperatives) (KEN) **1305**
• A C C Plus (Australian Case Citator) (AUS) **4606**
A C C Q *see* Australian Correspondence Chess Quarterly **8160**
A C C R A Cost of Living Index (Association for Applied Community Research) (USA ISSN 1070-9169) **1199**
A C C R A Research in Review (Association for Applied Community Research) (USA) **1394**
A C Current (Amarillo College) (USA) **2271**
A C D A Bulletin (USA) **4985**
• A C D C en Acao (Associacao dos Cirurgioes Dentistas de Campinas) (BRA ISSN 1678-1899) **5832**
A C D I Marches/C I D A Contracts (Agence Canadienne de Developpment International) (CAN ISSN 1709-853X) **1589**
A C D I - V O C A World Report (Agricultural Cooperative Development International, Volunteer in Overseas Cooperative Assistant) (USA) **1589**
A C D Tales (Atmospheric Chemistry Division) (USA ISSN 1949-4335) **2722**
A C E *see* Australian Chief Executive **1727**
➤ A C E (BEL ISSN 1783-3639) **1722**
A C E *see* Architecture, City and Environment **430**
A C E. Bulletin *see* Societe des Auteurs, Compositeurs, Editeurs pour la Gerance des Droits de Reproduction Mecanique. Bulletin **4784**
A C E Bulletin *see* Ask A C E **3017**
A C E C O M S News & Views (THA) **3258**
A C E Fitness Matters *see* A C E FitnessMatters **6980**
A C E FitnessMatters (American Council on Exercise) (USA ISSN 1082-0361) **6980**
A C E I D News (Asia-Pacific Centre of Educational Innovation for Development) (THA) **2821**
A C E International (GBR) **2374**
• L'A C E L F en Action (Association Canadienne d'Education de Langue Francaise) (CAN ISSN 1715-1198) **5088**
A C E Lenkrad (Auto Club Europa e.V.) (DEU ISSN 0943-3945) **8553**
A C E P News (American College of Emergency Physicians) (USA ISSN 1551-9171) **6054**
• A C E Papers (Auckland College of Education) (NZL ISSN 1174-748X) **2822**
A C E S Journal *see* Applied Computational Electromagnetics Society Journal **7051**
A C E S Newsletter *see* Applied Computational Electromagnetics Society Newsletter **7051**
➤ A C E T Journal of Computer Education and Research (Association for Computer Education in Texas) (USA ISSN 1547-3716) **2404**
A C F A Bulletin (American Cat Fanciers Association) (USA ISSN 0744-9631) **6802**
A C F A O M Newsletter *see* American College of Foot and Ankle Orthopedics and Medicine Newsletter **6055**
A C F Bulletin (American Checker Federation) (USA ISSN 1045-8034) **8156**
A C F D Forum (Association of Canadian Faculties of Dentistry) (CAN ISSN 0820-5949) **5832**
A C F Journal *see* A C I Year Book **6802**
A C G A Multilogue (American Community Gardening Association) (USA) **3721**
➤ A C G C Chemical Research Communications (Asian Coordinating Group for Chemistry) (AUS ISSN 1020-5586) **2096**
A C H A Action (American College Health Association) (USA ISSN 0002-7952) **6980**
A C H I M Magazine (USA) **7717**
A C H Newsletter (Association for Computers and the Humanities) (USA ISSN 0190-6631) **4485**
A C H P E R Active and Healthy Magazine (Australian Council for Health Physical Education and Recreation) (AUS ISSN 1328-7133) **6980**
A C H P E R Australia Healthy Lifestyles Journal (Australian Council for Health Physical Education and Recreation) (AUS ISSN 1445-8918) **2822**
A C H Participant Directory (USA ISSN 1063-1410) **1970**
A C H R News *see* Air Conditioning, Heating & Refrigeration News **4116**
A C H S *see* Australian Catholic Historical Society. Journal **7785**
A C H S Handbook *see* Association of College Honor Societies. Handbook **2273**

Title

9902 A C H: THE JOURNAL OF THE HISTORY OF CULTURE IN AUSTRALIA ULRICH'S PERIODICALS

• ➤ A C H: The Journal of the History of Culture in Australia (AUS) **4191**

▼ • ➤ A C I (Applied Clinical Informatics) (DEU ISSN 1869-0327) **5829**

A C I A R Monograph Series (Australian Centre for International Agricultural Research) (AUS ISSN 1031-8194) **77**

• A C I A R Newsletter (Australian Centre for International Agricultural Research) (AUS ISSN 0813-7234) **77**

• A C I A R Partners Magazine (Australian Centre for International Agricultural Research) (AUS ISSN 1031-1009) **77**

• A C I A R Proceedings (Australian Centre for International Agricultural Research) (AUS ISSN 1038-6920) **77**

A C I A R Technical Reports Series (Australian Centre for International Agricultural Research) (AUS ISSN 0816-7923) **77**

A C I A R Working Papers (Australian Centre for International Agricultural Research) (AUS ISSN 0819-7857) **77**

• A C I Digital (Agencia Catolica de Informaciones en America Latina Digital) (PER ISSN 1609-9885) **7781**

A C I International *see* Allergy and Clinical Immunology International **8929**

• A C I L Newsletter (American Council of Independent Laboratories) (USA) **5901**

A C I M Newsletter (American Committee on Italian Migration) (USA) **7276**

• A C I Manual of Concrete Practice (American Concrete Institute) (USA ISSN 0065-7875) **974**

• ➤ A C I Materials Journal (American Concrete Institute) (USA ISSN 0889-325X) **974**

A C I News (Automobile Club d'Italia) (ITA) **8553**

▼ • A C I P S S Newsletter (Austrian Center for Intelligence, Propaganda and Security Studies) (AUT ISSN 1993-4939) **7219**

A C I R R T Working Paper (Australian Centre for Industrial Relations Research and Teaching) (AUS ISSN 1327-5704) **1661**

A C I S Newsletter (American Conference for Irish Studies) (USA) **4195**

• ➤ A C I Structural Journal (American Concrete Institute) (USA ISSN 0889-3241) **974**

A C I Year Book (Australian Cat Federation) (AUS) **6802**

A C J S Employment Bulletin (Academy of Criminal Justice Sciences) (USA) **1855**

A C J S Program Book (Academy of Criminal Justice Sciences) (USA) **2964**

A C J S Today (Academy of Criminal Justice Sciences) (USA) **2643**

• A C L A I I R Newsletter (Advisory Council on Latin American and Iberian Information Resources) (GBR ISSN 0969-4625) **4985**

A C L I Life Insurers Fact Book *see* Life Insurers Fact Book **4513**

A C L I Oggi (Associazioni Cristiane Lavoratori Italiani) (ITA ISSN 1970-8343) **7101**

A C L R *see* American Criminal Law Review **2643**

A C L S Annual Report (American Council of Learned Societies) (USA ISSN 0065-7972) **4439**

A C L S Newsletter *see* American Council of Learned Societies. Newsletter **4442**

• A C L S Occasional Papers (American Council of Learned Societies) (USA ISSN 1041-536X) **4439**

• A C L U Cyber-Liberties Update (American Civil Liberties Union) (USA) **7201**

A C L U News (American Civil Liberties Union of Northern California) (USA) **7201**

A C M *see* Australian Country Music **6546**

A C M *see* Another Chicago Magazine **5255**

A C M A Annual Report (Years) *see* Australian Communications and Media Authority. Annual Report (Years) **2313**

• A C M A Communications Report (Australian Communications and Media Authority (A C M A)) (AUS) **2310**

† • A C M A Consumer Bulletin (Australian Communications and Media Authority (A C M A)) (AUS ISSN 1832-9470) **8927**

A C M A Newsletter (American Cutlery Manufacturers Association) (USA) **1878**

• A C M A Sphere (Australian Communications and Media Authority) (AUS ISSN 1832-8784) **2310**

A C M C Forum (Association of Canadian Medical Colleges) (CAN ISSN 0836-3463) **5563**

A C M Collected Algorithm Supplement (Association for Computing Machinery) (USA ISSN 0149-1989) **5549**

• A C M Communications in Computer Algebra (USA ISSN 1932-2232) **5549**

• ➤ A C M Computing Surveys (Association for Computing Machinery) (USA ISSN 0360-0300) **2405**

A C M Conference on Computer and Communications Security. Proceedings (USA ISSN 1543-7221) **2511**

• A C M Conference on Hypertext and Hypermedia. Proceedings (USA) **2504**

A C M Distinguished Dissertations (USA ISSN 0891-4265) **2405**

• A C M Electronic Guide to Computing Literature (Association for Computing Machinery) (USA ISSN 1089-5310) **2442**

• A C M / I E E E Design Automation Conference. Proceedings (USA ISSN 0738-100X) **2457**

• A C M / I E E E International Workshop on Timing Issues in the Specification and Synthesis of Digital Systems. Proceedings (Association for Computing Machinery / Institute of Electrical and Electronics Engineers) (USA) **2405**

• A C M / I E E E Joint Conference on Digital Libraries. Proceedings (USA ISSN 1552-5996) **4985**

A C M - I E E E Symposium on Volume Visualization (Association for Computing Machinery - Institute of Electrical and Electronics Engineers) (USA) **2482**

A C M Interactions *see* Interactions (New York) **2507**

• A C M International Symposium on Mobile Ad Hoc Networking and Computing. Proceeding (USA) **2405**

A C M International Workshop on Modeling, Analysis and Simulation of Wireless and Mobile Systems. Proceedings (Association for Computing Machinery) (USA ISSN 1547-0547) **2310**

• A C M International Workshop on Multimedia Databases. Proceedings (USA) **2528**

• A C M International Workshop on Wireless Mobile Applications and Services on W L A N Hotspots (USA) **2310**

• ➤ A C M Journal of Computer Documentation (Association of Computing Machinery) (USA ISSN 1527-6805) **2541**

▼ • ➤ A C M Journal of Data and Information Quality (Association for Computing Machinery) (USA) **2528**

▼ • ➤ A C M Journal on Computing and Cultural Heritage (Association for Computing Machinery) (USA ISSN 1556-4673) **2405**

▼ A C M Journal on Data and Information Quality (Association for Computing Machinery) (USA ISSN 1936-1955) **2528**

• A C M Journal on Emerging Technologies in Computing Systems (Association for Computing Machinery) (USA ISSN 1550-4832) **2569**

A C M M *see* Anti-Corrosion Methods and Materials **6305**

A C M M C 2 R *see* Mobile Computing and Communications Review **2333**

➤ A C M Monograph Series (Association for Computing Machinery) (USA ISSN 0572-4252) **2405**

• ➤ A C M Queue (USA ISSN 1542-7730) **2587**

A C M R Newsletter *see* A C M R Reports **6541**

➤ A C M R Reports (Association for Chinese Music Research) (USA) **6541**

A C M S I G A C C E S S Accessibility and Computing *see* Accessibility and Computing **4071**

A C M S I G A C T News *see* S I G A C T News **2464**

A C M S I G A R C H Computer Architecture News *see* S I G A R C H Computer Architecture News **2468**

A C M S I G Ada Annual International Conference. Proceedings *see* S I G Ada Annual International Conference. Proceedings **2596**

A C M S I G B E D Review *see* S I G B E D Review **2509**

A C M S I G C H I Bulletin *see* S I G C H I Bulletin **8151**

A C M S I G C S E Bulletin *see* S I G C S E Bulletin Inroads **2951**

A C M S I G D A Newsletter *see* S I G D A Newsletter (Online) **2464**

A C M S I G D O C Newsletter *see* S I G D O C Newsletter **2524**

A C M S I G I R Forum *see* S I G I R Forum **2550**

A C M S I G M E T R I C S Performance Evaluation Review *see* S I G M E T R I C S Performance Evaluation Review **2474**

A C M - S I G M I S - C P R Conference. Proceedings (Association for Computing Machinery - Special Interest Group on Management Information Systems - Com) (USA) **1661**

▼ • A C M S I G M M Records (Association for Machine Computing Special Interest Group Multimedia) (USA ISSN 1947-4598) **2405**

A C M S I G M O B I L E *see* Mobile Computing and Communications Review **2333**

A C M S I G M O D Record *see* S I G M O D Record **2532**

A C M S I G P L A N Conference on Programming Language Design and Implementation. Proceedings (Association for Computing Machinery) (USA ISSN 1531-7102) **2504**

• A C M / S I G P L A N Notices (Association for Computing Machinery / Special Interest Group on Programming Languages) (USA ISSN 1523-2867) **2504**

A C M S I G P L A N Symposium on Principles and Practice of Parallel Programming (Association for Computing Machinery) (USA ISSN 1542-0205) **2504**

• A C M / S I G P L A N Workshop on Partial Evaluation and Semantics-Based Program Manipulation. Proceedings (Association for Computing Machinery/Special Interest Group on Programming Languages) (USA) **2504**

A C M S I G S A M Bulletin *see* A C M Communications in Computer Algebra **5549**

A C M S I G S O F T International Symposium on the Foundations of Software (Association for Computing Machinery) (USA ISSN 1539-7521) **2504**

A C M S I G U C C S User Services Conference. Proceedings *see* S I G U C C S User Services Conference. Proceedings **2436**

• A C M S I GAda Ada Letters (Association for Computing Machinery Special Interest Group) (USA ISSN 1557-9476) **2504**

A C M SIGACT-SIGMOD-SIGART Symposium on Principles of Database Systems. Proceedings (Association for Computing Machinery) (USA ISSN 1055-6338) **2528**

A C M SIGACT-SIGMOD Symposium on Principles of Database Systems. Proceedings *see* A C M SIGACT-SIGMOD-SIGART Symposium on Principles of Database Systems. Proceedings **2528**

A C M SIGCOMM Internet Measurment Conference. Proceedings (Association for Computing Machinery) (USA) **2552**

A C M SIGGRAPH Eurographics Symposium on Computer Animation *see* A C M Special Interest Group in Computer Graphics / Eurographics Symposium on Computer Animation. Proceedings **2483**

A C M SIGGRAPH Symposium on Interactive 3D Graphics and Games. Proceedings (Association for Computing Machinery) (USA ISSN 1931-4027) **2483**

A C M SIGGRAPH Symposium on Interactive 3D Graphics. Proceedings *see* A C M SIGGRAPH Symposium on Interactive 3D Graphics and Games. Proceedings **2483**

A C M SIGPLAN Notices *see* A C M / S I G P L A N Notices **2504**

• A C M Special Interest Group in Computer Graphics / Eurographics Symposium on Computer Animation. Proceedings (Association for Computing Machinery) (USA ISSN 1548-4580) **2483**

A C M Symposium on Interactive 3D Graphics. Proceedings *see* A C M SIGGRAPH Symposium on Interactive 3D Graphics and Games. Proceedings **2483**

A C M Symposium on Operating Systems Principles. Proceedings. (Association for Computing Machinery) (USA ISSN 0736-6663) **2587**

A C M Symposium on Principles of Database Systems. Proceedings *see* A C M SIGACT-SIGMOD-SIGART Symposium on Principles of Database Systems. Proceedings **2528**

A C M Symposium on Principles of Programming Languages. Annual Conference Record (Association for Computing Machinery) (USA ISSN 0730-8566) **2457**

A C M Symposium on Principles of Programming Languages. Conference Record *see* A C M Symposium on Principles of Programming Languages. Annual Conference Record **2457**

A C M Symposium on Software Visualization. Proceedings *see* Software Visualization: A C M Symposium on Software Visualization. Proceedings **2598**

A C M Transactions on Accessibility *see* A C M Transactions on Accessible Computing **2405**

▼ • A C M Transactions on Accessible Computing (Association for Computing Machinery) (USA ISSN 1936-7228) **2405**

• A C M Transactions on Algorithms (USA ISSN 1549-6325) **5549**

• A C M Transactions on Applied Perception (Association for Computing Machinery, Inc.) (USA ISSN 1544-3558) **2405**

• A C M Transactions on Architecture and Code Optimization (Association for Computing Machinery) (USA ISSN 1544-3566) **2466**

• ➤ A C M Transactions on Asian Language Information Processing (Association for Computing Machinery, Inc.) (USA ISSN 1530-0226) **5202**

• ➤ A C M Transactions on Autonomous and Adaptive Systems (USA ISSN 1556-4665) **2519**

• ➤ A C M Transactions on Computational Logic (Association for Computing Machinery, Inc.) (USA ISSN 1529-3785) **2405**

▼ • ➤ A C M Transactions on Computational Theory (Association for Computing Machinery, Inc.) (USA ISSN 1942-3454) **5549**

• ➤ A C M Transactions on Computer - Human Interaction (Association for Computing Machinery) (USA ISSN 1073-0516) **2470**

• ➤ A C M Transactions on Computer Systems (Association for Computing Machinery) (USA ISSN 0734-2071) **2519**

• ➤ A C M Transactions on Computing Education (Association for Computing Education) (USA ISSN 1946-6226) **2822**

• ➤ A C M Transactions on Database Systems (Association for Computing Machinery) (USA ISSN 0362-5915) **2529**

• ➤ A C M Transactions on Embedded Computing Systems (USA ISSN 1539-9087) **2405**

• ➤ A C M Transactions on Graphics (Association for Computing Machinery) (USA ISSN 0730-0301) **2483**

• ➤ A C M Transactions on Information and System Security (USA ISSN 1094-9224) **2511**

A C M Transactions on Information Systems *see* A C M Transactions on Information Systems **1413**

• ➤ A C M Transactions on Information Systems (Association for Computing Machinery) (USA ISSN 1046-8188) **1413**

• ➤ A C M Transactions on Internet Technology (USA ISSN 1533-5399) **2552**

▼ • A C M Transactions on Knowledge Discovery from Data (Association for Computing Machinery) (USA ISSN 1556-4681) **2405**

• ➤ A C M Transactions on Mathematical Software (Association for Computing Machinery) (USA ISSN 0098-3500) **2587**

• ➤ A C M Transactions on Modeling and Computer Simulation (Association for Computing Machinery) (USA ISSN 1049-3301) **2405**

• ➤ A C M Transactions on Multimedia Computing Communications and Applications (Association for Computing Machinery) (USA ISSN 1551-6857) **2532**

• ➤ A C M Transactions on Programming Languages and Systems (Association for Computing Machinery) (USA ISSN 0164-0925) **2504**

▼ • A C M Transactions on Reconfigurable Technology and Systems (USA ISSN 1936-7406) **2519**

• A C M Transactions on Sensor Networks (USA ISSN 1550-4859) **2495**

• ➤ A C M Transactions on Software Engineering and Methodology (Association for Computing Machinery) (USA ISSN 1049-331X) **2587**

• A C M Transactions on Speech and Language Processing (Association for Computing Machinery) (USA ISSN 1550-4875) **2505**

• A C M Transactions on Storage (Association for Computing Machinery) (USA ISSN 1553-3077) **2519**

• ➤ A C M Transactions on the Web (Association for Computing Machinery) (USA ISSN 1559-1131) **2552**

• A C M Washington Update (Association for Computing Machinery) (USA) **2405**

A C M Workshop on Geographic Information Retrieval. Proceedings (Association for Computing Machinery) (USA ISSN 1933-7825) **2405**

A C M Workshop on Next-Generation Residential Broadband Challenges. Proceedings (Association for Computing Machinery) (USA ISSN 1559-419X) **2405**

A C M Workshop on Privacy in the Electronic Society. Proceedings (Association for Computing Machinery, Inc.) (USA) **4846**

A C M Workshop on Rapid Malcode. Proceedings (USA ISSN 1931-1133) **2405**

A C M Workshop on Security of Ad Hoc and Sensor Networks. Proceedings (Association for Computing Machinery) (USA ISSN 1559-4459) **2405**

A C M Workshop on Wireless Security. Proceedings (USA) **2310**

A C M Workshop on X M L Security. Proceedings (USA) **2505**

A C N E M Journal *see* Australasian College of Nutritional and Environmental Medicine. Journal **5580**

• A C Nielsen China Media Index (HKG) **2346**

A C Nielsen Media Directory *see* Media Directory **29**

A C O A Action News (American Committee on Africa) (USA ISSN 0743-8834) **7219**

• A C O G Clinical Review (American College of Obstetricians and Gynecologists) (USA ISSN 1085-6862) **5739**

A C O G Committee Opinions (American College of Obstetricians and Gynecologists) (USA ISSN 1074-861X) **5984**

A C O G Educational Bulletin (American College of Obstetricians and Gynecologists) (USA) **5984**

A C O G Patient Education (USA ISSN 1074-8601) **5984**

A C O G Practice Bulletin (American College of Obstetricians and Gynecologists) (USA ISSN 1099-3630) **5984**

A C O N A Outdoor Adventure (Adventure Club of North America) (USA ISSN 1521-0189) **8301**

A C O Newsletter (American College of Orgonomy) (USA) **6117**

• A C O R E New Energy Finance Briefing U S (American Council On Renewable Energy) (GBR ISSN 1750-8541) **3123**

A C O R E New Energy Finance Briefing United States *see* A C O R E New Energy Finance Briefing U S **3123**

➤ A C O R N (Australian Confederation of Operating Room Nurses) (AUS ISSN 1448-7535) **4086**

A C O R Newsletter (American Center of Oriental Research) (JOR) **370**

A C O S C A News (Africa Cooperative Savings and Credit Association) (KEN) **1305**

• A C O S News (American College of Osteopathic Surgeons) (USA ISSN 0001-0790) **6234**

• A C O S S Info (Australian Council of Social Service) (AUS ISSN 1442-486X) **8022**

A C O S S Papers *see* Australian Council of Social Service Papers **8026**

A C P *see* Applied Cardiopulmonary Pathophysiology **919**

A C P A (Asociacion Cubana de Produccion Animal) (CUB ISSN 0138-6247) **276**

A C P A C S Occasional Paper Series *see* The Australian Centre for Peace and Conflict Studies. Occasional Papers Series **7222**

A C P C Series (Area Child Protection Comittee) (GBR ISSN 1464-2212) **2142**

Link to your serials resources and content with ulrichsweb.com

Title

9904 **A E - ARBEITSRECHTLICHE ENTSCHEIDUNGEN** **ULRICH'S PERIODICALS**

A E - Arbeitsrechtliche Entscheidungen (DEU ISSN 1619-6600) **1661**
A E B *see* Annual Egyptological Bibliography **4169**
A E B *see* A S E A N Economic Bulletin **1055**
• A E Bladet (Arbejderbevaegelsens Erhvervsraad) (DNK ISSN 1902-3782) **4589**
A E C (Amicizia Ebraico-Cristiana) (ITA ISSN 1825-893X) **7619**
A E C B Staff Annual Report for (Year) on the Canadian Nuclear Power Industry *see* On the Safety Performance of the Canadian Nuclear Power Industry. Annual C N S C Staff Report for (Year) **3173**
A E C C (Asociacion Espanola Contra el Cancer) (ESP ISSN 1133-3871) **6007**
• A E C Finance News (USA) **1305**
† A & C International (Archi e Colonne) (ITA ISSN 1123-9255) **8927**
A E C L Report Series (Atomic Energy of Canada Ltd) (CAN ISSN 0067-0367) **3164**
A E C Magazine (GBR) **3288**
A E C Outsourcing Guide & Report *see* Food Processing **3640**
• A E: Canadian Aesthetics Journal - Revue Canadienne d'Esthetique (CAN) **6901**
A E D *see* Australasian Education Directory **2828**
A E D E M Bibliometrica (Asociacion Europea de Direccion y Economia de la Empresa) (ESP ISSN 1697-0217) **1722**
A E D O M Boletin *see* Boletin DM **4997**
A E D P *see* Australian Educational and Developmental Psychologist **7338**
A E E C: An International Journal *see* Applied Environmental Education and Communication **3403**
• A E E Energy Insight (Association of Energy Engineers) (USA) **3123**
A E F A. Association des Entraineurs Francais d'Athletisme (FRA ISSN 1623-944X) **8156**
A E G News (Association of Engineering Geologists - Texas) (USA ISSN 0899-5788) **2722**
A E H R *see* Australian Economic History Review **1536**
A E I *see* Australian Education Index (Online) **2930**
A E I *see* A E I T **3089**
A E I *see* Asia Electronics Industry **3295**
• A E I Newsletter (Asian Energy Institute) (IND) **3123**
A E I T (ITA ISSN 1825-828X) **3089**
A e J A M H *see* Australian e-Journal for the Advancement of Mental Health **6125**
A E J: Economic Policy *see* American Economic Journal: Economic Policy **1059**
A E J M C News (Association for Education in Journalism and Mass Communication) (USA ISSN 0747-8909) **4570**
A E J N E *see* The Australian Electronic Journal of Nursing Education **8933**
A E L *see* The Australian Educational Leader **3017**
A E L E Liability Reporter *see* Law Enforcement Liability Reporter **4834**
▼ A E L E Monthly Law Journal (Americans for Effective Law Enforcement) (USA ISSN 1935-0007) **4607**
• A E L F A. Boletin (Asociacion Espanola de Logopedia, Foniatria y Audiologia. Boletin) (ESP ISSN 1137-8174) **6076**
A E L J *see* Cardozo Arts & Entertainment Law Journal **4640**
A E Legal Newsletter (Architects and Engineers) (USA ISSN 0090-2411) **4607**
A E M *see* Ag Equipment Manufacturer **209**
A E M I Journal (Association of European Migration Institutions) (DNK ISSN 1729-3561) **7276**
A E M J *see* Marketing Tactics **1833**
A E N Infos *see* N E A News **3171**
A E N J *see* Australasian Emergency Nursing Journal **5952**
• A E N Journal (Aotearoa Ethnic Network) (NZL ISSN 1177-3472) **3514**
A E N. Rapport Annuel *see* O E C D Nuclear Energy Agency. Annual Report (Year) **3173**
A E - Nyt (Online Edition) *see* A E Bladet **4589**
A E P *see* Australian Economic Papers **1064**
A E P (Automotive Engineering Partners) (DEU ISSN 1435-6074) **8554**
A e P *see* Adolescenza e Psicoanalisi (Print) **7331**
A E P *see* Asian Economic Papers **1062**
A E P Appointments Broadsheet (Association of Educational Psychologists) (GBR) **6691**
A E P H Rapport *see* L M A P D Report **4067**
• A E P Online (USA) **2822**
A E Q *see* Academic Exchange Quarterly **3050**
A E R *see* Australian Education Review **2828**
• ➤ A E R (Australian Educational Researcher) (AUS ISSN 0311-6999) **2822**
A e R (ITA ISSN 1827-5842) **6105**
A E R *see* Arizona Education Review **2827**
• A E R A Gram (Ancient Egypt Research Associates, Inc.) (USA ISSN 1944-0014) **370**
▼ A E R Journal (USA ISSN 1945-5569) **4078**
A E R O Sun Times (Alternative Energy Resources Organization) (USA ISSN 1046-0993) **77**
A E R Report (Association for Education and Rehabilitation) (USA) **4078**
A E S (Advanced Energy Systems) (USA ISSN 1071-6947) **3335**
➤ A E S (Audio Engineering Society) (USA ISSN 1549-4950) **8151**
A E S Bug Club News (Amateur Entomologists' Society) (GBR) **2174**
A E S C Directory (Association of Energy Service Companies) (USA) **1970**
• A E S F Annual Technical Conference Proceedings (CD-ROM Edition) (American Electroplaters and Surface Finishers Society) (USA) **6303**
A E S F Annual Technical Conference Proceedings (Print Edition) *see* A E S F Annual Technical Conference Proceedings (CD-ROM Edition) **6303**
A E S I E A P Goldbook (Year) (Association of the Electricity Supply Industry of East Asia and the Western Pacific) (GBR ISSN 1365-9200) **7051**
A E S T (ITA ISSN 1972-0505) **1909**
A E - South Carolina Crop and Livestock Reporting Service (Agricultural Economics) (USA ISSN 0561-0095) **77**
A E T A Journal (Asian Education Teachers Association) (AUS ISSN 1832-6870) **2822**
• A E U News - Victoria (Australian Education Union, Victorian Branch) (AUS) **2822**
A E U S A Branch Journal (Australian Education Union, South Australian Branch) (AUS ISSN 1440-2971) **2822**
• ➤ A E Ue: International Journal of Electronics and Communication (Archiv fuer Elektronik und Uebertragungstechnik) (DEU ISSN 1434-8411) **2310**
• A E V E-News (Email) (Art Education Victoria) (AUS) **3049**
A & V Elettronica (ITA) **3089**
• A ERaadet. Beretning (Arbejderbevaegelsens Erhvervsraad) (DNK ISSN 1901-3728) **1661**
A F *see* Australian Forestry **3684**
A F A A Bulletin d'Information *see* A F A A Newsletter **77**
A F A A Newsletter/A F A A Bulletin d'Information (Association of Faculties of Agriculture in Africa) (MAR) **77**
A F A Bulletin *see* Autrey - Autry - Autery Bulletin **3759**
• A F A Danmark, Faeroeerne, Groenland, Dansk Vestindien Frimaerkekatalog (DNK ISSN 0901-7003) **6891**
A F A Danmark Fireblokke (DNK ISSN 0901-6996) **6891**
A F A Danmark Frimaerkekatalog *see* A F A Danmark, Faeroeerne, Groenland, Dansk Vestindien Frimaerkekatalog **6891**
A F A E (Association Francaise des Administrateurs de l'Education) (FRA ISSN 0222-674X) **3016**
A F A Journal (American Family Association) (USA) **7743**
A F A N Newsletter (Association for Astrological Networking) (USA ISSN 1049-6181) **564**
A F A Oesteuropa Frimaerkekatalog (DNK ISSN 0901-6643) **6891**
A F A R Annual Report (American Foundation for AIDS Research) (USA) **5807**
A F A Skandinavien Frimaerkekatalog (DNK ISSN 0901-6635) **6891**
A F A Specialkatalog (DNK ISSN 1395-0320) **6891**
A F A Vesteuropa Frimaerkekatalog (DNK ISSN 0901-702X) **6891**
The A F A Watchbird (American Federation of Aviculture) (USA ISSN 0199-543X) **900**
A F & P A Statistical Roundup (American Forest & Paper Association) (USA) **1803**
• A F B Directory of Services for Blind and Visually Impaired Persons in the United States and Canada (American Foundation for the Blind) (USA ISSN 1067-5833) **4079**
• A F B eNews (American Foundation for the Blind) (USA) **4079**
A F B Info (Arbeitsstelle Friedensforschung Bonn) (DEU ISSN 0930-8199) **7101**
• ➤ A F B M Journal (Australian Farm Business Management) (AUS ISSN 1449-5937) **190**
A F B News *see* A F B eNews **4079**
A F C News *see* Screen Australia News **6512**
A F C O M's Annual Survey of Data Processing Operations Salaries (Association for Computer Operations Management) (USA) **1199**
A F D A Forum (American Fish Decoy Association) (USA) **4326**
A F D R *see* African Development Review **1590**
▼ • A F E I Financial Newsletter (FRA ISSN 1961-7038) **1608**
A F E I Newsletter *see* A F E I Financial Newsletter **1608**
A F E Newsline (Association for Facilities Engineering) (USA ISSN 1088-7253) **3179**
• A F E R (KEN ISSN 0250-4650) **7781**
A F E S Z Magazin (Altalanos Fogyasztasi es Ertekesito Szovetkezetek) (HUN ISSN 1217-7040) **1421**
A F E T - Mitglieder - Rundbrief *see* Dialog Erziehungshilfe **3038**
A F E T Veroeffentlichungen (Arbeitsgemeinschaft fuer Erziehungshilfe) (DEU) **3035**
A F E T Wissenschaftliche Informationsschriften (Arbeitsgemeinschaft fuer Erziehungshilfe) (DEU ISSN 0932-8874) **3036**
A F F *see* Norinsho Koho **142**
• A F F Families Journal (Army Families Federation) (GBR) **5064**
• A F F H O Newsflash (Australasian Federation of Family History Organisations) (AUS) **3757**
A F F I Business Insights (American Frozen Food Institute) (USA) **3624**
A F F I Letter (American Frozen Food Institute) (USA) **3624**
A F G *see* American Fruit Grower **3722**
A F G Wirtschaft - Das Erfrischungsgetraenk (DEU) **597**
• A F H R C Factsheets (Atlantic Food and Horticulture Research Centre) (CAN) **77**
A F I A Safetygram (American Feed Industry Association) (USA) **276**
A F I Buying Directory (USA) **1970**
A F I D E O. News (FRA ISSN 1959-4593) **4071**
A F I P Atlas of Tumor Pathology (Armed Forces Institute of Pathology) (USA) **6007**
A F I P Letter (Armed Forces Institute of Pathology) (USA ISSN 0498-3564) **6191**
A F I S C Annual Report *see* Agrifood Industry Skills Council. Annual Report **3625**
A F J A Review *see* Asia's Fashion Jewellery & Accessories Review **4564**
The A F J M H Newsletter *see* In Touch (Moorestown) **3539**
A F L A Quarterly (Africa Legal Aid) (NLD ISSN 1384-282X) **7201**
A F L - C I O, American Federation of State, County & Municipal Employees Works *see* A F S C M E Works **4589**
A F L - C I O. Constitutional Convention. Proceedings (USA ISSN 0569-4515) **4589**
• A F L - C I O Now (American Federation of Labor - Congress of Industrial Organizations) (USA) **4589**
A F L Preview (Arena Football League) (USA) **8220**
A F L Record (Australian Football League) (AUS ISSN 1444-2973) **8220**
A F M *see* Advanced Functional Materials **2112**
A F M *see* American Football Monthly **8220**
A F M *see* Arizona Foothills Magazine **3969**
A F M A Update *see* Australian Fisheries Management Authority Update **3586**
A F N Echo *see* L' Echo de l'A P N **3531**
A F O *see* Archiv fuer Orientforschung **4320**
A f P (Archiv fuer Presserecht) (DEU ISSN 0949-2100) **4607**
A F P *see* American Family Physician **5571**
A F P C Council Review (American Foreign Policy Council) (USA ISSN 1941-4501) **7219**
A F P C Issue Paper (Agricultural and Food Policy Center) (USA) **77**
• A F P - Doc sur CD-ROM (Agence France-Presse) (FRA) **4570**
• A F P Exchange (Association for Financial Professionals) (USA ISSN 1528-4077) **1305**
A F P Family Practice Annual (American Family Physician) (USA ISSN 0198-7461) **5564**
A F P P Newsletter (Association for Perioperative Practice) (GBR) **5949**
• A F P Sciences (Agence France-Presse) (FRA) **5564**
• A F P Sciences sur CD-ROM (Agence France-Presse) (FRA) **7829**
A F R A Boletin Informativo (Asociacion Filatelica de la Republica Argentina) (ARG ISSN 0001-1193) **6891**
A F R A News (Association for Rural Advancement) (ZAF) **7201**
A F R A Special Reports (Association for Rural Advancement) (ZAF) **7201**
A F R Boss *see* Financial Review Boss **1109**
• A F R C Briefing (Australian Family Relationships Clearinghouse) (AUS ISSN 1834-2434) **8084**
A F R E (African Trade Review) (ESP ISSN 0001-1207) **1551**
† A F R I Liaison (Association Francaise de Robotique Industrielle) (FRA) **8927**
• A F R M A Chapters - Rules & Guidelines (American Fancy Rat and Mouse Association) (USA) **6802**
A F R Magazine *see* Australian Financial Review Magazine **1064**
A F R R *see* African Research Review **2824**
A F R Smart Investor *see* Smart Investor **1651**
A F S *see* Arbetsmiljoeverkets Foerfattningssamling **6673**
A F S C M E 93 News (American Federation of State, County and Municipal Employees) (USA ISSN 1946-9497) **4589**
A F S C M E Public Employee *see* A F S C M E Works **4589**
• A F S C M E Works (A F L - C I O, American Federation of State, County & Municipal Employees) (USA ISSN 1936-7562) **4589**
A F S M International *see* The Professional Journal **2493**
A F S Newsletter (American Filtration and Separations) (USA) **3234**
A F S Newsletter (Atlanta Freethought Society) (USA) **6901**
A F S S A. Cahiers *see* French Studies in Southern Africa **5298**
A F T *see* Algemeen Fiskaal Tijdschrift **1279**
A F T (Archivio Fotografico Toscano) (ITA ISSN 1120-205X) **6963**
A F T A Monitor (ASEAN Free Trade Area) (PHL) **1551**
• A F T A Monograph Series (USA ISSN 1556-1364) **7330**
A F T C Index (Year) *see* Australian Family Tree Connections **3759**
A F T E Journal (Association of Firearm and Tool Mark Examiners) (USA ISSN 1048-9959) **4883**
A F T Occasional Papers (Association for Family Therapy) (GBR ISSN 0264-1933) **6117**
A F T. Quaderni *see* A F T **6963**
A F T R A (American Federation of Television and Radio Artists) (USA ISSN 0044-7676) **2356**
A F T R S Annual Report *see* Australian Film, Television and Radio School. Annual Report **2356**
A F T R S Handbook *see* Australian Film, Television and Radio School Handbook **2356**
• A F V Modeller (Armored Fighting Vehicles) (GBR ISSN 1747-4183) **4326**
A F Z. Allgemeine Fleischer-Zeitung. OB (DEU ISSN 0942-8062) **3624**
A F Z. Allgemeine Fleischer-Zeitung. OBMS (DEU ISSN 0942-8070) **3624**
A F Z. Allgemeine Fleischer-Zeitung. OBS (DEU ISSN 0942-8046) **3624**
A F Z. Allgemeine Fleischer-Zeitung. OBSMW (DEU ISSN 0942-8054) **3625**
A F Z. Allgemeine Fleischer-Zeitung. OBSMWN (DEU ISSN 0942-8089) **3625**
• A F Z - Der Wald (Allgemeine Forst Zeitschrift) (DEU ISSN 1430-2713) **3682**
A F Z Journal (Allgemeine Fleischer Zeitung) (DEU ISSN 1615-9845) **3625**
A FalconGuide to Everglades National Park and the Surrounding Area (USA ISSN 1553-9598) **8680**
A FalconGuide to Saguaro National Park & the Santa Catalina Mountains Guide Book (USA ISSN 1555-4902) **8680**
A FalconGuide to the San Juan Islands (USA ISSN 1553-1112) **8680**
A G *see* The Australian Gemmologist **4564**
A G *see* Die Aktiengesellschaft **1879**
• A G (Atuagagdliutit - Groenlandsposten) (GRL ISSN 0904-2458) **3874**
A G A (Asociacion General de Agricultores) (GTM ISSN 0001-1274) **77**
A G A B (Association des Geologues Amateurs de Belgique) (BEL ISSN 1784-2417) **2722**
• A G A News (American Gastroenterological Association) (USA ISSN 1064-8097) **5919**
• A G A Perpectives (USA ISSN 1554-3366) **5919**
A G A Rate Service (American Gas Association) (USA) **6761**
A G A T E (Alberta Gifted and Talented Education) (CAN ISSN 0833-0603) **3036**
• A G / B I A Decisions Listing (Online) (USA) **7276**
• A G B Newsletter (Asymptotic Giant Branch) (FRA) **567**
• A G B U Magazine (USA) **3515**
A G Bulletin (National Association of Attorneys General) (USA ISSN 1081-0161) **4607**
A G C *see* Architectural Glass Concepts **429**
A G C News Service (Associated General Contractors of Houston) (USA) **974**
A G C - Ohio (Associated General Contractors of Ohio) (USA) **974**
A G D Impact (Academy of General Dentistry) (USA ISSN 0194-729X) **5832**
A G D N *see* Advances in Group Decision and Negotiation **8085**
A G D Quartal *see* A G D Viertel **462**
A G D Viertel (Allianz Deutscher Designer e.V.) (DEU ISSN 1864-7421) **462**
L'A G E F I Actifs (FRA ISSN 1627-4857) **1609**
• L'A G E F I Edition de 7h (FRA ISSN 1776-3193) **1305**
L'A G E F I Edition de Sept Heures *see* L' A G E F I Edition de 7h **1305**
L'A G E F I Hebdo (Agence Economique et Financiere) (FRA ISSN 1777-165X) **1305**
• A G E F I Luxembourg (Agence Economique et Financiere) (LUX ISSN 1561-8366) **1305**
A G E L E News (Association for Gender Equity Leadership in Education) (USA ISSN 1543-0006) **3016**
A G E S (Asociacion de Garajes y Estaciones de Servicio) (ARG) **8554**
A G H E. Brief Bibliography *see* Association for Gerontology in Higher Education. Brief Bibliography **4058**
A G H E Exchange (Association for Gerontology in Higher Education) (USA ISSN 0890-278X) **4037**
A G I (Aktuel Grafisk Information) (DNK ISSN 1603-1083) **7318**
A G I A Alimentation *see* Agra Alimentation **80**
A G I F Forumeer (American G I Forum) (USA) **3515**
A G I F O R S Proceedings *see* International Federation of Operational Research Societies. Airline Group. Proceedings **8546**
A G I M O Annual Report *see* Australian Government Information Management Office. Annual Report **8933**
A G I Norsk Grafisk Tidsskrift (NOR ISSN 0809-3334) **7318**
• A G I R (Association Generale des Insuffisants Renaux) (CAN ISSN 1180-4939) **6264**
• A G I Source Book for Geographic Information Systems (CD-ROM) (Association for Geographic Information) (GBR ISSN 1478-2707) **3996**
A G I Source Book for Geographic Information Systems (Print) *see* A G I Source Book for Geographic Information Systems (CD-ROM) **3996**
A G L *see* Agricultural Law (Springfield) **84**
A G L *see* Above Ground Level **2365**
A G M *see* Australian General Mining Year Book **6457**
A G M A Zine (American Guild of Musical Artists) (USA ISSN 0002-0990) **6541**
A G M - Magazin *see* Arbeitsgemeinschaft Malta. Rundbriefe **6891**

Title

9906 A I P CONFERENCE PROCEEDINGS. ATOMIC, MOLECULAR ULRICH'S PERIODICALS

• A I P Conference Proceedings. Atomic, Molecular & Statistical Physics (American Institute of Physics) (USA ISSN 1931-3039) **7002**
• A I P Conference Proceedings. Materials Physics & Applications (American Institute of Physics) (USA ISSN 1931-3047) **7002**
• A I P Conference Proceedings. Mathematical & Statistical Physics (American Institute of Physics) (USA ISSN 1931-3055) **5463**
• A I P Conference Proceedings. Nuclear & High Energy Physics (American Institute of Physics) (USA ISSN 1931-3063) **7064**
• A I P Conference Proceedings. Plasma Physics (American Institute of Physics) (USA ISSN 1931-3071) **7002**
• A I P Conference Proceedings Series (American Institute of Physics) (USA ISSN 0094-243X) **7002**
A I P Informacao (Associacao Industrial Portuguesa) (PRT ISSN 0870-287X) **1878**
A I P J *see* Australian Intellectual Property Journal **6745**
• A I P L A Bulletin (American Intellectual Property Law Association) (USA) **4607**
• A I P L A Quarterly Journal (American Intellectual Property Law Association) (USA ISSN 0883-6078) **4607**
A I P P I. Japanese Group. Journal (International Edition) *see* International Association for the Protection of Intellectual Property. Japanese Group. Journal (International Edition) **6753**
A I P P I. Japanese Group. Journal (Japanese Edition) *see* International Association for the Protection of Intellectual Property. Japanese Group. Journal (Japanese Edition) **6753**
A I P Translation Series (American Institute of Physics) (USA ISSN 1050-9062) **7002**
A I: Performance for the Planet (Arts International) (USA ISSN 1529-3777) **463**
A I Perspectives (Artificial Intelligence) (GBR) **2445**
• A I Q Noticias Online (Asociacion de Ingenieros Quimicos del Uruguay) (URY ISSN 1688-1788) **3234**
A I Quarterly *see* Architecture of Israel **431**
A I R *see* Australasian Investment Review **1552**
A I R (Australia/Israel Review) (AUS ISSN 1833-8631) **7201**
A I R *see* The Annals of Improbable Research **7835**
A I R A Journal (Association of Insolvency & Restructuring Advisors) (USA ISSN 1932-720X) **1055**
A I R I M P - Passenger (Air Reservations Interline Message Procedures) (CAN ISSN 0256-3290) **8533**
• A I R Mail (DEU) **8415**
A I R O E. Liaisons (Association pour l'Information et la Recherche sur les Orthographes et les Systemes d'Ecriture) (FRA ISSN 1770-5207) **5088**
The A I R Professional File (Association for Institutional Research) (USA ISSN 8756-6168) **2964**
A I Ri M News (Associazione Italiana per il Ritardo Mentale) (ITA ISSN 1970-6618) **6117**
A I S Alumni News *see* Australian Institute of Sport Alumni News **2968**
† A I S B J (Artificial Intelligence and Simulation of Behaviour Journal) (GBR ISSN 1476-3036) **8927**
A I S B Quarterly (Artificial Intelligence and Simulation of Behaviour) (GBR ISSN 0268-4179) **2445**
A I S C A T Informazioni (Associazione Italiana Societa Concessionarie Autostrade e Trafori) (ITA ISSN 1971-5730) **8628**
• A I S E Annual Convention Proceedings (Association of Iron and Steel Engineers) (USA) **6303**
A I S E Steel Technology *see* Iron & Steel Technology **6317**
A I S M *see* Institute of Statistical Mathematics. Annals **5494**
A I S Newsletter *see* Association for Integrative Studies Newsletter **2827**
A I S Newsletter (American Indian Society) (USA) **6634**
The A I S Report *see* The A I S Report on Blue Cross and Blue Shield Plans **4490**
• The A I S Report on Blue Cross and Blue Shield Plans (Atlantic Information Services) (USA ISSN 1542-4790) **4490**
A I S T Bulletin of Metrology *see* Sansouken Keiryou Hyoujun Houkoku **6406**
A I S T E C H *see* A I S Tech (Year) Conference Proceedings **6303**
A I S T Today (English Edition) (Advanced Industrial Science and Technology) (JPN ISSN 1346-602X) **7829**
A I S T Today (Nihongo-Ban) *see* Sansouken Today **7907**
A I S T Update (USA) **3179**
• A I S Tech (Year) Conference Proceedings (Association for Iron & Steel Technology) (USA ISSN 1551-6997) **6303**
A I S Transactions on Human-Computer Interaction *see* Association for Information Systems Transactions on Human-Computer Interaction **2446**
A I S V Annual Review *see* Association of Independent Schools of Victoria. Annual Review **2827**
A I T (Architektur, Innenarchitektur, Technischer Ausbau) (DEU ISSN 0173-8046) **426**
• A I T I M Boletin de Informacion Tecnica (Asociacion de Investigacion Tecnica de las Industrias de la Madera) (ESP ISSN 0044-9261) **3709**
• A I T Review (Asian Institute of Technology) (THA ISSN 0125-6505) **3179**
• A I U M Sound Waves (American Institute for Ultrasound in Medicine) (USA) **6191**
• A I Xpert (Advanced Interactive) (USA ISSN 1081-6283) **2445**
A I Z - Allgemeine Immobilien-Zeitung *see* A I Z - Das Immobilienmagazin **7581**
A I Z - Das Immobilienmagazin (DEU) **7581**
A in E *see* Accounting in Europe **1278**
A Is A (USA) **5204**
A J *see* Architects' Journal **429**
A J A Benchmark (American Judges Association) (USA) **4607**
A J A D D *see* American Journal of Alzheimer's Disease and Other Dementias **4040**
A J A N *see* The Australian Journal of Advanced Nursing **5952**
A J A R E *see* The Australian Journal of Agricultural and Resource Economics **194**
• ➤ A J A S (Australasian Journal of American Studies) (AUS ISSN 0705-7113) **4281**
A J A S *see* Asian - Australasian Journal of Animal Sciences **279**
A J B *see* Australian Journal of Physiotherapy **6107**
A J B R *see* African Journal of Biochemistry Research **722**
A J C *see* Australian Journal of Chemistry **2051**
A J C *see* Asian Journal of Communication **2312**
A J C D *see* Australian Journal of Career Development **6692**
A J C E *see* Australian Journal of Civil Engineering **3259**
A J C E B *see* Australasian Journal of Construction Economics and Building **977**
A J C E H *see* Australian Journal of Clinical and Experimental Hypnosis **5942**
† A J C Journal (American Jewish Committee) (USA ISSN 0899-2150) **8927**
A J C L *see* Australian Journal of Corporate Law **4857**
A J C L *see* American Journal of Criminal Law **2643**
A J C M *see* The American Journal of Chinese Medicine **5740**
A J D *see* Australasian Journal of Dermatology **5872**
A J D A *see* L' Actualite Juridique. Droit Administratif **4609**
A J D T *see* Australian Journal of Dairy Technology **261**
A J E *see* Australasian Journal of Ecotoxicology **3494**
A J E *see* African Journal of Ecology **651**
A J E *see* African Journal of Ecology Online **651**
A J E *see* American Journal of Education **2826**
A J E A M *see* African Journal of Environmental Assessment and Management **3493**
A J E C *see* Ancient Judaism and Early Christianity **7718**
A J E D P *see* Australian Journal of Educational and Developmental Psychology **2829**
A J E E *see* Australian Journal of Environmental Education **2603**
A J E E *see* Australasian Journal of Economics Education **2968**
A J E E E *see* Australian Journal of Electrical and Electronic Engineering **3296**
A J E M *see* Australasian Journal of Environmental Management **3405**
A J E R *see* Alberta Journal of Educational Research **2825**
A J E S *see* African Journal of Education Studies **2824**
A J E S *see* Adirondack Journal of Environmental Studies **3401**
A J E S T *see* African Journal of Environmental Science and Technology **3401**
A J E T *see* Australasian Journal of Educational Technology (Online) **3051**
A J E T *see* Africa Journal of Evangelical Theology **7744**
A J F L *see* Australian Journal of Family Law **4907**
A J F S *see* Australian Journal of French Studies **5259**
A J F S *see* African Journal of Food Science **6654**
A J G P *see* The American Journal of Geriatric Pharmacotherapy **6819**
A J H *see* American Journal of Hypertension **5776**
A J H G *see* American Journal of Human Genetics **862**
A J H P *see* American Journal of Health Promotion **6982**
A J H P *see* American Journal of Health-System Pharmacy **6819**
A J H R *see* Australian Journal of Human Rights **7203**
A J H S J *see* Australian Jewish Historical Society. Journal **3521**
A J I A *see* Australian Journal of International Affairs **7222**
A J I C *see* American Journal of Infection Control **5809**
A J I C L *see* African Journal of International and Comparative Law **4916**
A J I C L *see* Arizona Journal of International & Comparative Law **4917**
A J I C T *see* African Journal of Information and Communication Technology **2311**
A J I D D *see* American Journal on Intellectual and Developmental Disabilities **6122**
A J I L *see* American Journal of International Law **4916**
A J I S Online *see* Australasian Journal of Information Systems **2519**
A J I S S *see* American Journal of Islamic Social Sciences **7709**
A J I T *see* Asian Journal of Information Technology **2407**
A J J *see* American Journal of Jurisprudence **4614**
A J J S *see* Australian Journal of Jewish Studies **7718**
• A J L (Australian Journal of Liturgy) (AUS ISSN 1030-617X) **7619**
The A J L *see* The Australasian Journal of Logic **6906**
A J L D *see* Australian Journal of Learning Difficulties **3036**
A J L E *see* Australian Journal of Labour Economics **1666**
A J L J *see* Australian Judiciary Law Journal **4946**
A J L L *see* Australian Journal of Labour Law **4857**
A J L L *see* Australian Journal of Language and Literacy **3017**
A J L M *see* American Journal of Law & Medicine **4614**
A J L Newsletter (Association of Jewish Libraries) (USA ISSN 0747-6175) **4985**
A J L P *see* Australian Journal of Legal Philosophy **4624**
A J L S *see* African Journal of Legal Studies **4611**
A J M *see* Australian Journal of Mining **6457**
A J M *see* The Australian Journal of Mineralogy **6457**
A J M *see* Australian Journal of Management **1727**
A J M *see* Asian Journal of Marketing **1805**
A J M *see* The Asian Journal of Mathematics **5474**
A J M *see* M J S A Journal **4568**
A J M A A *see* The Australian Journal of Mathematical Analysis and Applications **5474**
A J M C *see* The American Journal of Managed Care **5572**
A J M D E *see* Australian Journal of Multi-Disciplinary Engineering **3182**
A J M E *see* Australian Journal of Mechanical Engineering **3374**
A J M H *see* Australian Journal of Medical Herbalism **307**
A J M R *see* African Journal of Microbiology Research **880**
A J M S *see* Australian Journal of Medical Science **5581**
A J M S R *see* Australasian Journal of Market & Social Research (Online) **1806**
A J M T *see* Australian Journal of Music Therapy **6546**
A J N *see* American Journal of Nursing **5951**
A J N - Mosby Nursing Boards Review for the N C L E X - R N Examination (American Journal of Nursing) (USA) **5949**
A J N R *see* American Journal of Neuroradiology **6192**
A J N R L P *see* The Australasian Journal of Natural Resources Law and Policy **2603**
A J O D O *see* American Journal of Orthodontics and Dentofacial Orthopedics **5834**
A J O V *see* Australian Journal on Volunteering **8026**
A J P *see* Australian Journal of Psychology **7338**
A J P *see* The American Journal of Pathology **5573**
A J P *see* American Journal of Physiology (Consolidated) **918**
A J P *see* American Journal of Psychiatry **6122**
A J P *see* The American Journal of Psychoanalysis **7333**
A J P *see* American Journal of Psychology **7333**
A J P A *see* Australian Journal of Public Administration **7421**
A J P A C *see* African Journal of Pure and Applied Chemistry **2049**
A J P C *see* Journal of Spirituality in Mental Health **7381**
A J P: Cell Physiology Online *see* American Journal of Physiology: Cell Physiology **918**
A J P E *see* American Journal of Pharmaceutical Education **6820**
A J P: Endocrinology and Metabolism Online *see* American Journal of Physiology: Endocrinology and Metabolism **918**
A J P: Gastrointestinal and Liver Physiology Online *see* American Journal of Physiology: Gastrointestinal and Liver Physiology **919**
A J P H *see* Australian Journal of Politics and History **7108**
A J P H *see* Australian Journal of Primary Health **5581**
A J P: Heart and Circulatory Physiology Online *see* American Journal of Physiology: Heart and Circulatory Physiology **919**
A J P: Lung Cellular and Molecular Physiology Online *see* American Journal of Physiology: Lung Cellular and Molecular Physiology **919**
A J P Online *see* American Journal of Physiology (Consolidated) **918**
A J P P *see* African Journal of Pharmacy and Pharmacology **6819**
A J P R S Reporter (American Jewish Public Relations Society) (USA) **18**
A J P: Regulatory, Integrative and Comparative Physiology Online *see* American Journal of Physiology: Regulatory, Integrative and Comparative Physiology **919**
A J P: Renal Physiology Online *see* American Journal of Physiology: Renal Physiology **919**
A J P S *see* Australian Journal of Political Science **7108**
A J P S *see* Asian Journal of Political Science **7107**
A J P S *see* African Journal of Plant Science **774**
A J P S *see* American Journal of Political Science **7105**
A J P S I R *see* African Journal of Political Science and International Relations **7103**
A J P T *see* Auditing **1280**
A J R *see* American Journal of Roentgenology **6192**
A J R *see* American Journalism Review **4571**
A J R C *see* The Australian Journal of Rehabilitation Counselling **3036**
A J R C C M *see* American Journal of Respiratory and Critical Care Medicine **6211**
A J R C M B *see* American Journal of Respiratory Cell and Molecular Biology **6211**
A J R H *see* Australian Journal of Rural Health **7509**
A J R NewsLink *see* American Journalism Review **4571**
A J R S *see* Australasian Journal of Regional Studies **1438**
A J S *see* American Journal of Science **2701**
A J S E *see* Australian Journal of Structural Engineering **3259**
A J S Informationen *see* Aktion Jugendschutz. Informationen **2143**
A J S Perspectives (USA ISSN 1529-6423) **7717**
• ➤ A J S Review (Association for Jewish Studies) (GBR ISSN 0364-0094) **7717**
A J Specification *see* Architect's Journal Specification **429**
A J T *see* American Journal of Transplantation **6235**
A J T M H *see* American Journal of Tropical Medicine and Hygiene **5810**
A J V S *see* Australasian Journal of Victorian Studies **4443**
A J W R *see* Australian Journal of Water Resources **8818**
A J W S *see* Asian Journal of Women's Studies **8893**
• A Jour (FIN ISSN 1457-7704) **2689**
A Journal of Jewish Medical Ethics and Halacha *see* Jewish Medical Ethics and Halacha **7723**
A K (CHE ISSN 1422-2426) **4370**
A K Aktuell (AUT) **1055**
A K C E International Journal of Graphs and Combinatorics (Arulmigu Kalasalingam College of Engineering) (IND ISSN 0972-8600) **5463**
A K C Family Dog (American Kennel Club) (USA ISSN 1559-5072) **6802**
• A K C Gazette (American Kennel Club) (USA ISSN 1086-0940) **6802**
A K D *see* Anadolu Kardiyoloji Dergisi **5776**
A K Holz *see* Holz **1050**
A K I Press (KGZ) **3903**
A K M Informationen (Autoren, Komponisten und Musikverleger) (AUT) **6744**
A K M - Studien (Arbeitsgruppe Kommunikationsforschung Muenchen) (DEU ISSN 0939-8074) **8084**
A K O O Employment Law Insider (Anderson Kill Olick LLP) (USA) **1661**
A K O O Policyholder Advisor (Anderson Kill Olick LLP) (USA) **4490**
A K P - Alternative Kommunalpolitik (DEU ISSN 0941-9225) **7418**
A K S B - Inform (Arbeitsgemeinschaft Katholisch-Sozialer Bildungswerke) (DEU ISSN 0937-8375) **2937**
A K S E Newsletter *see* Association for Korean Studies in Europe. Newsletter **4180**
A K T (Aktuelles Theater) (DEU) **8464**
A K V/St Joost. Academieboek (Akademie voor Kunst en Vormgeving) (NLD ISSN 1874-0065) **2822**
The A K W A Letter (USA) **6981**
The A-Ki-Ki (USA ISSN 0091-1607) **3757**
A L *see* Australian Administrative Law **7421**
A L *see* American Laboratory **2097**
A L *see* Journal of Electronic Resources Librarianship **5020**
A L *see* Administrative Law (Springfield) **4610**
A L A (ARG ISSN 0002-4090) **5415**
A L A Black Caucus Newsletter *see* Black Caucus of ALA Newsletter **4997**
• A L A Handbook of Organization (American Library Association) (USA ISSN 0084-6406) **4985**
A L A Magazine (USA) **40**
A L A N *see* Australian Lawyers Alliance News **4624**
A L A N *see* Archivos Latinoamericanos de Nutricion **6655**
• ➤ The A L A N Review (Assembly on Literature for Adolescents) (USA ISSN 0882-2840) **3049**
A L A News (Chicago) (American Lawyers Auxiliary) (USA) **4607**
A L A News (Lincolnshire) (Association of Legal Administrators) (USA ISSN 1045-1153) **4607**
A L A R M Course Syllabus (Advances in Labour and Risk Management) (CAN ISSN 1719-9182) **5985**
• A L A S B I M N Journal (Asociacion Latinoamericana de Sociedades de Biologia y Medicina Nuclear) (CHL ISSN 0717-4055) **6191**

Link to your serials resources and content with ulrichsweb.com

Title

9908 A M S STUDIES IN LIBRARY AND INFORMATION SCIENCE ULRICH'S PERIODICALS

A M S Studies in Library and Information Science (Abrahams Magazine Service) (USA ISSN 1040-5631) **4986**
A M S Studies in Modern Literature (Abrahams Magazine Service) (USA ISSN 0270-2983) **5247**
A M S Studies in Modern Society (Abrahams Magazine Service) (USA ISSN 0275-8407) **7505**
▼ A M S Studies in Music (USA ISSN 1941-7861) **6541**
A M S Studies in Nineteenth-Century Literature and Culture (Abrahams Magazine Service) (USA ISSN 1059-5406) **5247**
A M S Studies in Religious Tradition (Abrahams Magazine Service) (USA ISSN 1059-7255) **7619**
† A M S Studies in Social History (Abrahams Magazine Service) (USA ISSN 0270-6253) **8927**
A M S Studies in the Eighteenth Century (Abrahams Magazine Service) (USA ISSN 0196-6561) **5247**
A M S Studies in the Emblem (Abrahams Magazine Service) (USA ISSN 0892-4201) **3757**
A M S Studies in the Middle Ages (Abrahams Magazine Service) (USA ISSN 0270-6261) **4128**
A M S Studies in the Nineteenth Century (Abrahams Magazine Service) (USA ISSN 0196-657X) **5247**
A M S Studies in the Renaissance (Abrahams Magazine Service) (USA ISSN 0195-8011) **5247**
A M S Studies in the Seventeenth Century (Abrahams Magazine Service) (USA ISSN 0731-2342) **5248**
A M S Test Book (Auto Motor eae Sport) (GRC) **8554**
A m S - Tilvekst (Arkeologisk museum i Stavanger) (NOR ISSN 0803-5903) **370**
• A M S Update (American Meteorological Society) (USA) **6345**
A m S - Varia (Arkeologisk Museum i Stavanger) (NOR ISSN 0332-6306) **370**
A M Show Days (USA) **1803**
A M T *see* Australian Mathematics Teacher **3051**
A M T *see* Arzneimitteltherapie **6823**
A M T (Auto Modell und Technik) (DEU ISSN 0935-4212) **4326**
A M T *see* The Alternative Minimum Tax **1910**
• A M T (Aircraft Maintenance Technology) (USA ISSN 1072-3145) **8533**
A M T. Advanced Manufacturing Technology *see* A M T Electronics **3294**
▼ A M T C Letters (Advanced Microscopy and Theoretical Calculations) (JPN ISSN 1882-9465) **3335**
A M T Electronics (Advanced Manufacturing Technology) (IRL) **3294**
A M T Events (USA ISSN 0746-9217) **2822**
A M T Magazine *see* Australian Manufacturing Technology **6306**
A M T N Y S News (USA) **2822**
• A M T Newsletter (Aircraft Maintenance Technology) (USA) **8533**
† A M U (Annuario Italiano Macchine Utensili e Complementari) (ITA ISSN 0393-0483) **8927**
A.M. Update (USA) **3625**
• A M W A Freelance Directory (American Medical Writers Association) (USA ISSN 0194-004X) **5564**
A M W A Journal (American Medical Writers Association) (USA ISSN 1075-6361) **5564**
A M W U News (AUS) **4589**
• A M Z (Auto Motor Zubehoer) (DEU ISSN 0001-1983) **8554**
A M Z *see* Access to the Music Zone **6542**
A Magyar Allami Foldtani Intezet evi jelentese (HUN ISSN 0368-9751) **2722**
A mas T *see* A + T **425**
A Minima (ESP ISSN 1697-7777) **463**
A Mother's Gift (USA ISSN 1932-6211) **6654**
A-Muse (GBR ISSN 1755-6112) **3036**
A N *see* Anthropology Now **327**
• A N A B A D Boletin (Asociacion Espanola de Archiveros Bibliotecarios Museologos y Documentalistas) (ESP ISSN 0210-4164) **4986**
A N A C C *see* Australian National Avons Collectors Club. Newsletter **8933**
▼ • A N A C E M. Revista (Asociacion Nacional Cientifica de Estudiantes de Medicina de Chile) (CHL ISSN 0718-5308) **2822**
A N A C Eastern Nutrition Conference *see* Animal Nutrition Association of Canada. Eastern Nutrition Conference. Proceedings **278**
A N A Clinical Conferences (American Nurses Association) (USA ISSN 0093-0423) **5949**
A N A D: Working Together (National Association of Anorexia Nervosa and Associated Disorders) (USA) **7330**
➤ A N A E (Approche Neuropsychologique des Apprentissages chez l'Enfant) (FRA ISSN 0999-792X) **6118**
➤ A N A Journal (American Numismatic Association) (USA ISSN 1930-3270) **6648**
A N A P (Departamento de Exportacion) (CUB ISSN 0514-9797) **77**
A N A R E Journal *see* Aurora **3999**
† A N A R E Reports (Australian National Antarctic Research Expeditions) (AUS ISSN 1038-2135) **8927**
† A N A R E Research Notes (Australian National Antarctic Research Expeditions) (AUS ISSN 0729-6533) **8927**
A N A V Newsletter *see* Associazione Nazionale Autotrasporto Viaggiatori. Newsletter **8490**
A N B O - Vizier (NLD ISSN 1574-4841) **4038**
A N C I Rivista (Associazione Nazionale dei Comuni Italiani) (ITA ISSN 0393-3938) **7487**
A N C O L D Bulletin (Australian National Committee on Large Dams Inc.) (AUS ISSN 0045-0731) **3258**
A N D A R Infos (FRA ISSN 1958-3303) **6221**
A N D E (Associacao Nacional de Educacao) (BRA ISSN 0101-5028) **2822**
A N D I L. Annuario (Year) (Associazione Nazionale degli Industriali dei Laterizi) (ITA) **2037**
A N D I M A Retrospectiva (Associacao Nacional das Instituicoes do Mercado Aberto) (BRA) **1434**
A N D I News (Autism Network for Dietary Intervention) (USA) **6118**
A N E C (Asociacion Nacional de Enfermeras de Colombia) (COL ISSN 0120-1832) **5949**
A N E R A Newsletter (American Near East Refugee Aid) (USA ISSN 1066-3584) **7219**
• A N F I A Notiziario Statistico (Associazione Nazionale fra le Industrie Automobilistiche) (ITA ISSN 0001-2033) **8520**
A N G F A News (Australia New Guinea Fishes Association) (AUS) **3582**
A N G R A D Revista (Associacao Nacional dos Cursos de Graduacao em Administracao) (BRA ISSN 1518-5532) **1722**
A N H *see* Archives of Natural History **7836**
A N I G Publicacion (ESP) **4570**
A N I N C E *see* Asociacion Nacional de Investigadores de Incendios de Espana **3575**
A N J *see* Australian Nursing Journal **5952**
A N J E C Report (Association of New Jersey Environmental Commissions) (USA ISSN 1538-0742) **2601**
A N J E E Newsletter (Alliance for New Jersey Environmental Education) (USA) **3050**
A N J U P E C (Asociacion Nacional de Jubilados y Pensionados de Comunicaciones) (CUB) **8022**
A N L A Bulletin (Association of Newfoundland Labrador Archives) (CAN ISSN 0821-7157) **4986**
A N M C Annual Report *see* Australian Nursing and Midwifery Council. Annual Report **5952**
A N M C Newsletter *see* Australian Nursing and Midwifery Council. Newsletter (Online) **5952**
• A N Magazine (Artists Newsletter) (GBR) **463**
A N N *see* Aero - News Network **42**
A N N *see* A A F P News Now (Online) **5563**
A N P I Magazine (Dutch Edition) (Association Nationale pour la Protection contre l'Incendie et l'Intrusion) (BEL ISSN 1780-874X) **3575**
A N P I Magazine (French Edition) (Association Nationale pour la Protection contre l'Incendie et l'Intrusion) (BEL ISSN 0778-7383) **3575**
▼ A N P I S S Informativo (Asociacion Nacional de Pensionados por el Instituto del Seguro Social) (COL ISSN 2011-3455) **8022**
▼ ➤ A N P J (Association for Nurse Prescribing Journal) (GBR ISSN 1754-3185) **5949**
• ➤ A N Q: A Quarterly Journal of Short Articles, Notes and Reviews (USA ISSN 0895-769X) **5248**
• A N R E D (Anorexia Nervosa & Related Eating Disorders) (USA) **6118**
A N R I *see* Apparatura i Novosti Radiatsionnykh Izmerenii **7064**
A N R S. Information (Agence Nationale de Recherches sur le SIDA) (FRA ISSN 1158-2901) **5807**
A N S (Algemeen Nijmeegs Studentenblad) (NLD ISSN 1872-1958) **2271**
• A N S Bulletin (USA) **2356**
A N S Bulletin (American Name Society) (USA) **5088**
• A N S I Reporter (American National Standards Institute) (USA ISSN 0038-9676) **6400**
A N S Magazine *see* American Numismatic Society. Magazine **6648**
A N S Newsletter *see* American Numismatic Society. Magazine **6648**
• A N S O M (Army - Navy Store & Outdoor Merchandiser) (USA) **2245**
A N S S Currents (Anthropology and Sociology Section) (USA ISSN 0888-5559) **4986**
A N S T O - E *see* Australian Nuclear Science and Technology Organisation - E **3165**
A N S T O - M *see* Australian Nuclear Science and Technology Organisation - M **3165**
• A N S Topical Meeting Proceedings (USA) **3164**
A N T E *see* Abstracts in New Technologies and Engineering **8446**
A N T E C Conference Proceedings *see* Society of Plastics Engineers. Annual Technical Conference (Antec). Proceedings **7100**
• A N U Reporter (Australian National University) (AUS ISSN 0727-386X) **2271**
• A N U Reporter Online (Australian National University) (AUS ISSN 1326-2254) **2271**
A N V Reeks (Algemeen Nederlands Verbond) (NLD ISSN 1875-3329) **4195**
▼ A N W B Auto (Algemeene Nederlandsche Wielrijdersbond) (NLD ISSN 1874-5547) **8554**
A N W B Boot (Algemene Nederlandse Wielrijders Bond) (NLD) **8270**
A N W B Campinggids Nederland (Algemene Nederlandse Wielrijders Bond) (NLD ISSN 1871-9597) **8301**
A N W B Campinggids Nederland-Belgie-Luxemburg *see* A N W B Campinggids Nederland **8301**
† A N Z A A S Congress Papers (Australian and New Zealand Association for the Advancement of Science) (AUS ISSN 0312-8059) **8927**
A N Z A News (Australia - New Zealand Association) (CAN ISSN 0045-0170) **3793**
• A N Z C C A R T News (Online) (Australian and New Zealand Council for the Care of Animals in Research and Teaching Ltd.) (AUS) **316**
• ➤ The A N Z I A M Journal (Australian & New Zealand Industrial and Applied Mathematics) (GBR ISSN 1446-1811) **5463**
A N Z I D E C C *see* Australian and New Zealand Industry Defence Equipment and Capability Catalogue **6412**
A N Z I I F Journal *see* Australian and New Zealand Institute of Insurance and Finance. Journal **4493**
A N Z J F T *see* Australian and New Zealand Journal of Family Therapy **8089**
A N Z J L E *see* Australia & New Zealand Journal of Law & Education **4623**
A N Z J O G *see* The Australian and New Zealand Journal of Obstetrics and Gynecology **5986**
A N Z J S *see* Australian & New Zealand Journal of Statistics **8356**
• ➤ A N Z Journal of Surgery (Australia and New Zealand) (AUS ISSN 1445-1433) **6234**
A N Z Nuclear Medicine *see* Australian and New Zealand Nuclear Medicine **5581**
A N Z S C O *see* Australia. Bureau of Statistics. Australian and New Zealand Standard Classification of Occupations **6706**
• A N Z S I Newsletter (Australian and New Zealand Society of Indexers) (AUS ISSN 1832-3855) **1**
• A N Z S L A Commentator (Australian and New Zealand Sports Law Association) (AUS ISSN 1444-3244) **4608**
A-News *see* Avetra News **2829**
• A Noter Annotez (CAN ISSN 1719-9670) **2964**
A Notre Sante (CAN ISSN 1912-4864) **7505**
A Nous Cote d'Azur (FRA ISSN 1960-1131) **4975**
A Nous Marseille Aix-en-Provence (FRA ISSN 1960-1123) **4975**
A Nous Nice - Cannes - Antibes - Monaco *see* A Nous Cote d'Azur **4975**
A O (Actuele Onderwerpen) (NLD) **3914**
A O *see* Applied Optics **7074**
• ➤ A O A C International. Journal (Association of Analytical Communities) (USA ISSN 1060-3271) **2096**
• A O A eNews (Administration on Aging) (USA) **4038**
• A O A O Newsletter (USA) **5803**
• A O A Yearbook and Directory of Osteopathic Physicians (Online Edition) (American Osteopathic Association) (USA) **5803**
A O A Yearbook and Directory of Osteopathic Physicians (Print Edition) *see* A O A Yearbook and Directory of Osteopathic Physicians (Online Edition) **5803**
A O B *see* Annals of Botany **775**
▼ • A o B Plants (Annals of Botany) (GBR ISSN 1759-6653) **771**
A O Dialogue (Arbeitsgemeinschaft fuer Osteosynthesefragen) (CHE) **6054**
A O G *see* Asian Oil and Gas **6763**
A O G Mitteilungen (CHE) **6408**
A O G S Guide *see* Australia's Open Garden Scheme Guidebook **3724**
A O I *see* Annuario Ottico Italiano **1972**
A O I Business Viewpoint (Associated Oregon Industries) (USA ISSN 0892-1067) **1055**
A O J *see* Australian Orthodontic Journal **5835**
A O J *see* American Orthoptic Journal **6038**
A O J D *see* Australian Official Journal of Designs (Online) **6745**
A O J P *see* Australian Official Journal of Patents (Online) **6745**
A O J T M *see* Australian Official Journal of Trade Marks (Online) **6745**
A O J T Newsletter (Association of Orthodox Jewish Teachers) (USA ISSN 1075-4601) **2822**
Das A O L - Magazin (DEU) **2552**
A O M A R *see* Accounting Office Management & Administration Report **1278**
A O N Cityscope (GBR) **1434**
A O N T A S Newsheet (IRL) **2937**
A O P A *see* Australian Pilot **47**
• A O P A Flight Training (Aircraft Owners and Pilots Association) (USA) **41**
A O P A Letter (Aircraft Owners and Pilots Association) (DEU) **41**
A O P A Magazine *see* A O P A Pilot **41**
A O P A Netherlands Bulletin *see* A O P A Pilots & Planes **8533**
A O P A Pilot (Aircraft Owners and Pilots Association) (AUS) **41**
• A O P A Pilot (Aircraft Owners and Pilots Association) (USA ISSN 0001-2084) **41**
A O P A Pilots & Planes (NLD ISSN 1872-5554) **8533**
A O P A's Airport Directory (Aircraft Owners and Pilots Association) (USA) **41**
A O P Awards (Association of Photographers) (GBR) **6963**
• A O R N Journal (Association of Operating Room Nurses) (USA ISSN 0001-2092) **5949**
A O S A and S C S T *see* The Seed Technologist Newsletter **251**
A O S A - S C S T Seed Technologist News (Association of Official Seed Analysts - Society of Commercial Seed Technologists) (USA) **771**
A O S Awards Quarterly (American Orchid Society) (USA ISSN 0747-3109) **3721**
• Der A O Steuer-Berater (DEU ISSN 1617-2272) **1909**
A O T A Self Study Series (American Occupational Therapy Association) (USA ISSN 1059-1753) **6672**
A O T Journal *see* Australian Occupational Therapy Journal **6107**
A O T T *see* Acta Orthopaedica et Traumatologica Turcica **6054**
A P *see* Australian Printer **7318**
A P *see* Aslib Proceedings **4991**
▼ A P (NLD ISSN 1872-6534) **2643**
A P *see* Alternative Press **6543**
A P A *see* I F E PsychologIA **7361**
A P A A Newsletter (American Physicians Art Association) (USA) **463**
▼ • A P A C News (Academic Professional Advisory Committee) (USA ISSN 1946-1860) **2964**
A P A G Marketscan *see* Platts Asia-Pacific/Arab Gulf Marketscan (Online) **6789**
• A P A I S: Australian Public Affairs Information Service (Online) (AUS) **7478**
A P A Journal (Auto Parts and Accessories) (AUS) **8554**
A P A Journal *see* Asian Pacific American Journal **5257**
• A P A - Journal. Bau (Austria Presse Agentur) (AUT) **974**
• A P A - Journal. Bildung (Austria Presse Agentur) (AUT) **6691**
• A P A - Journal. Chemie (Austria Presse Agentur) (AUT) **3235**
• A P A - Journal. Economist (Austria Presse Agentur) (AUT) **1434**
• A P A - Journal. Economist - Konjunktur (Austria Presse Agentur) (AUT) **1434**
• A P A - Journal. Elektronik (Austria Presse Agentur) (AUT) **3089**
• A P A - Journal. Emerging Markets - Asien (Austria Presse Agentur) (AUT) **1434**
• A P A - Journal. Emerging Markets - Osteuropa (Austria Presse Agentur) (AUT) **1434**
• A P A - Journal. Energie (Austria Presse Agentur) (AUT) **3123**
• A P A - Journal. Europa (Austria Presse Agentur) (AUT) **1434**
• A P A - Journal. Forschung (Austria Presse Agentur) (AUT) **7829**
• A P A - Journal. Fuehrungskraefte-Buero (Austria Presse Agentur) (AUT) **1434**
• A P A - Journal. Gesundheit (Austria Presse Agentur) (AUT) **6981**
• A P A - Journal. Holz - Papier (Austria Presse Agentur) (AUT) **3710**
• A P A - Journal. Innovation (Austria Presse Agentur) (AUT) **8415**
• A P A - Journal. Maschinen (Austria Presse Agentur) (AUT) **3372**
• A P A - Journal. Medien (Austria Presse Agentur) (AUT) **2311**
• A P A - Journal. Motor (Austria Presse Agentur) (AUT) **3372**
• A P A - Journal. Motor - Mobilitaet (Austria Presse Agentur) (AUT) **8489**
• A P A - Journal. Oeffentliche Hand (Austria Presse Agentur) (AUT) **7418**
• A P A - Journal. Recycling (Austria Presse Agentur) (AUT) **3503**
• A P A - Journal. Telekom (Austria Presse Agentur) (AUT) **2311**
• A P A - Journal. Terminvorschau (Austria Presse Agentur) (AUT) **1434**
• A P A - Journal. Touristik (Austria Presse Agentur) (AUT) **8680**
• A P A - Journal. Umwelt (Austria Presse Agentur) (AUT) **3400**
A P A L A Newsletter *see* Asian - Pacific American Librarians Association Newsletter **4991**
A P A L J *see* Asian Pacific American Law Journal **4622**
A P A List (Apatinska Pivara) (SRB) **597**
A P A Member Bulletin *see* Arkansas Publisher Weekly **4571**
A P A Members Directory (Australian Publishers Association) (AUS) **7550**
A P A. Membership Register (USA ISSN 0737-1446) **639**
A P A News and Views (American Poultry Association) (USA) **276**
A P A Newsletters (American Philosophical Association) (USA ISSN 1067-9464) **6901**
A P A Newsletters on the Black Experience, Computer Use, Feminism, Law, Medicine, Teaching *see* A P A Newsletters **6901**
A P A Q *see* Adapted Physical Activity Quarterly **3036**
• A P A Research Psychology Funding Bulletin (American Psychological Association) (USA) **7330**
A P & Q *see* Australian Patchwork and Quilting **6637**
A P & T *see* Alimentary Pharmacology and Therapeutics **5920**
A P B A Rules for Stock Outboard, Modified Outboard, Pro Outboard, Outboard Performance Craft, J Class, Outboard Drag, and Performance Inflatable Racing (American Power Boat Association) (USA ISSN 1542-3735) **8270**
A P Bulletin *see* Food Connect **7517**

DIRECTORY 2010 A R D ONLINE 9909

A P C (AUS) **2406**
A P C *see* Australasian Plant Conservation **2603**
• A P C Answer Letter (USA ISSN 1535-7945) **4087**
• ➤ A P C D Journal (Associacao Paulista de Cirurgioes Dentistas) (BRA) **5832**
• A P C e-News (Association of Professional Chaplains) (USA) **7619**
A P C G *see* Association of Pacific Coast Geographers. Yearbook **4035**
A P C J *see* Asia Pacific Coatings Journal **6716**
A P C O M (Year) (Application of Computers and Operations Research in the Mineral Industry) (CAN) **6488**
• A P C Payment Insider (USA ISSN 1937-7746) **4087**
A P C R I Newsletter (Association for Prevention and Control of Rabies in India) (IND ISSN 0973-6115) **5564**
A P C T News Bulletin (American Postal Chess Tournaments) (USA) **8156**
A P D *see* Asia Pacific Digestive News **5920**
A P D E *see* Analysis & P D E **5470**
A P D R J *see* Asia Pacific Disability Rehabilitation Journal **8026**
A P D U Newsletter (Association of Public Data Users) (USA) **3288**
A P E (Advice to Publishers and Editors) (GBR ISSN 1368-2954) **7550**
A P E C (Analise e Perspectiva Economica) (BRA ISSN 0001-2181) **1435**
A P E C *see* I E E E Applied Power Electronics Conference and Exposition. Conference Proceedings **3101**
A P E F Newsletter (Association Provinciale des Enseignantes et Enseignants des Ecoles Fransaskoises) (CAN) **5088**
A P E L *see* Asian - Pacific Economic Literature **1200**
• A P E S M A / F A S T S Professional Scientist Remuneration Survey Report (Association of Professional Engineers, Scientists and Managers - Federation of Australian Scientific) (AUS ISSN 1833-4520) **6691**
• A P E S M A National e-News (Association of Professional Engineers, Scientists and Managers) (AUS) **1055**
A P E X (Association of Professional, Executive, Clerical and Computer Staff) (GBR) **4589**
A P E X - J *see* Asia - Pacific Exchange Journal **2967**
A P Ex - J *see* Asia - Pacific Exchange Journal **2967**
A P F *see* Ausbildung Pruefung Fortbildung (Baden-Wuerttemberg Edition) **7421**
A P F (Ausgabe Bayern) *see* Ausbildung Pruefung Fortbildung (Bayern Edition) **7421**
A P F (Ausgabe Berlin) *see* Ausbildung Pruefung Fortbildung (Berlin Edition) **7421**
A P F (Ausgabe Brandenburg) *see* Ausbildung Pruefung Fortbildung (Brandenburg Edition) **7421**
A P F (Ausgabe Sachsen-Anhalt) *see* Ausbildung Pruefung Fortbildung (Sachsen-Anhalt Edition) **7421**
A P F (Ausgabe Sachsen) *see* Ausbildung Pruefung Fortbildung (Sachsen Edition) **7421**
A P F (Ausgabe Thueringen) *see* Ausbildung Pruefung Fortbildung (Thueringen Edition) **7421**
A P F I C Report *see* Asia - Pacific Fishery Commission. Report **3586**
A P F News (Association of Professional Foresters) (GBR ISSN 1462-1746) **3682**
• A P F News (American Physicians Fellowship) (USA) **5564**
• A P F Reporter (Alicia Patterson Foundation) (USA ISSN 0193-4562) **4571**
A P French (Advance Placement) (USA ISSN 1938-7873) **5088**
A P H A Letter (American Printing History Association) (USA ISSN 0898-1078) **7318**
A P H A Newsletter *see* A P H A Letter **7318**
A P H A Z Reports *see* Aircraft Proximity Hazards Reports **8535**
• A P H News (USA) **4079**
† • A P H Technology Update (American Printing House) (USA) **8927**
A P H V Magazin (Allgemeiner Postwertzeichen Haendler Verband e.V.) (DEU) **6891**
A P I *see* Australian Property Investor **7583**
• A P I Account (Accountants for the Public Interest) (USA ISSN 0883-2102) **1275**
A P I Affiliate Newsbrief (Accountants for the Public Interest) (USA) **1275**
• A P I C S (American Production and Inventory Control Society) (USA ISSN 1946-0384) **1722**
A P I C S Conference Proceedings (USA) **1722**
A P I C S - The Performance Advantage *see* A P I C S **1722**
A.P.I.C. Series *see* A P I C Studies in Data Processing **2505**
A P I C Studies in Data Processing (Automatic Programming Information Centre) (USA ISSN 0067-2483) **2505**
A.P.I.C. Studies in Data Processing *see* A P I C Studies in Data Processing **2505**
A P I Lit *see* Ei EnCompassLit **6799**
• A P I National Newsletter (AUS ISSN 1834-6529) **7581**
A P I Newsbriefs (American Prepaid Legal Services Institute) (USA) **4608**
A P I Pat *see* Patents Abstracts **6801**
A P I Publication (American Petroleum Institute) (USA ISSN 0271-2253) **6761**
• A P I Review of Books (Australian Public Intellectual) (AUS ISSN 1833-0932) **4986**
▼ A P Italian Language and Culture (Advanced Placement) (USA ISSN 1940-0047) **5088**
A P J *see* Australian Police Journal **2644**
A P J C N *see* Asia Pacific Journal of Clinical Nutrition **6655**
A P J H M *see* Asia Pacific Journal of Health Management **4088**
A P J H R *see* Asia Pacific Journal of Human Resources **1856**
A P J M L *see* Asia Pacific Journal of Marketing and Logistics **1805**
A P J T R *see* Asia Pacific Journal of Tourism Research **8684**
A P K: Ekonomika, Upravlenie (Agro-Promyshlennyi Kompleks) (RUS ISSN 0235-2443) **190**
A P L (Year) *see* The International Conference On Array-Prog Language. Proceedings **2507**
A P L A Bulletin (Atlantic Provinces Library Association) (CAN ISSN 0001-2203) **4986**
A P L A R Journal of Rheumatology *see* International Journal of Rheumatic Diseases **6224**
A P L I C Communicator (Association for Population - Family Planning Library & Information Center International) (USA ISSN 0891-0847) **4986**
A P L I U T. Cahiers (Association des Professeurs de Langues des Instituts Universitaires de Technologie) (FRA ISSN 0248-9430) **2964**
A P L J *see* Australian Property Law Journal **4827**
A P L Journal (Array Programming Language) (DEU ISSN 1438-4531) **2457**
A P L Newsletter (Association of Professional Librarians) (MUS ISSN 1694-0210) **4986**
• A P L: Organic Electronics and Photonics (Applied Physics Letters) (USA ISSN 1941-420X) **7051**
• A P L Quote Quad (USA ISSN 0163-6006) **2574**
A P Latin: Vergil & Literature *see* The Best Test Prepartation for the A P Latin **2969**
A P Latin: Vergil Exam, Literature Exam *see* The Best Test Prepartation for the A P Latin **2969**
A P M A News (American Podiatric Medical Association) (USA ISSN 8750-2585) **6054**
A P M A Newsletter (American Paper Machinery Association) (USA) **5449**
A P M Bulletin (Air Power Museum) (USA ISSN 0048-2358) **362**
A P M C *see* Australian Primary Mathematics Classroom **2829**
A P M E *see* AsiaPacific MediaEducator **4572**
A P M E News (USA ISSN 0733-7795) **4571**
A P M E P. Bulletin (Association des Professeurs de Mathematiques de l'Enseignement Public) (FRA ISSN 0240-5709) **5463**
A P M I *see* Australian Property Market Indicators **4434**
A P M I S *see* Acta Pathologica Microbiologica et Immunologica Scandinavica **650**
• ➤ A P M I S Supplementum (Acta Pathologica, Microbiologica et Immunologica Scandinavica) (DNK ISSN 0903-465X) **648**
A P M Monograph Series (Antique Phonograph Monthly) (USA) **6541**
A P N *see* Anaesthesia Product News **5768**
A P N *see* Anestesia Pediatrica e Neonatale **5769**
A P N A News (American Psychiatric Nurses Association) (USA ISSN 1050-5237) **5950**
A P N Y Magazine (Advertising Photographers of New York) (USA) **6963**
A P O Annual Report (Asian Productivity Organization) (JPN ISSN 0066-846X) **1878**
A P O News (Asian Productivity Organization) (JPN ISSN 0044-9229) **1878**
A P O Productivity Journal (Asian Productivity Organization) (JPN ISSN 0919-0589) **1878**
A P P *see* Applied and Preventive Psychology **7335**
A P P *see* Atlantic Pacific Press **5258**
A P P A Digest (American Professional Practice Association) (USA) **1609**
A P P A Newsletter *see* Inside A P P A Newsletter **3025**
• A P P E A Annual Report (Australian Petroleum Production and Exploration Association) (AUS) **6761**
The A P P E A Journal (DVD) (Australian Petroleum Production and Exploration Association) (AUS) **6761**
The A P P E A Journal (Print) *see* The A P P E A Journal (DVD) **6761**
A P P Guide *see* Australian Prescription Products Guide **6824**
A P P I. Cahiers *see* Association pour la Promotion de la Protection des Invertebres. Cahiers **840**
• ➤ A P P L E S (Applied Language Studies) (FIN ISSN 1457-9863) **5088**
A P P P A H Newsletter (Association for Pre- & Perinatal Psychology and Health) (USA) **7330**
† A P P R (Asian Power Projects Review) (USA ISSN 1084-600X) **8927**
A P P R J *see* Asia Pacific Public Relations Journal **7107**
A P P V A Magazine *see* Australian Peacekeeper and Peacemaker **8026**
A P Physics B & C *see* The Best Test Preparation for the Advanced Placement Examinations. A P Physics B & C **7006**
A P Psychology (Advanced Placement) (USA ISSN 1934-6816) **7330**
A P Psychology (Advanced Placement) (USA ISSN 1946-214X) **7330**
A P Q *see* American Philosophical Quarterly **6903**
• A P Q N Annual Report (Asia - Pacific Quality Network) (AUS ISSN 1833-5462) **2822**
A P R *see* Algemene Practische Rechtverzameling **4613**
• A P R (Allgemeine Papier-Rundschau) (DEU ISSN 0002-5917) **6731**
† A P R (Accessory & Performance Retailer) (USA) **8927**
A P R A (Year) Membership Directory (Automotive Parts Rebuilders Association) (USA) **1970**
A P R A News (American Private Radio Association) (USA) **2356**
A P R E S Proceedings (American Peanut Research and Education Society) (USA ISSN 0197-8748) **215**
A P R I Journal (African Peace Research Institute) (NGA) **7219**
The A P R M Monitor (African Peer Review Mechanism) (CAN ISSN 1718-7818) **1551**
A P R O Directory (Airline Public Relations Organisation) (GBR) **8680**
A P R T Newsletter *see* International Association for Regression Research and Therapies. Newsletter **7363**
• A P S A Directory of Political Science Department Chairpersons (Online Edition) (American Political Science Association) (USA) **7101**
A P S A Directory of Political Science Faculty (Year) (American Political Science Association) (USA) **7101**
A P S A Survey of Political Science Departments (American Political Science Association) (USA ISSN 1087-3872) **7101**
A P S Bulletin (All Africa Press Service) (KEN) **7619**
• A P S Bulletin (American Pain Society) (USA ISSN 1057-1590) **5767**
• A P S C C Newsletter (Asia-Pacific Satellite Communications Council) (KOR ISSN 1226-8844) **2311**
• A P S C C Yearbook (Asia-Pacific Satellite Communications Council) (GBR ISSN 1748-7285) **2311**
A P S Conference on Antennas and Propagation for Wireless Communications. Proceedings (Antennas and Propagation Society) (USA) **2311**
A P S Diplomat Fate of the Arabian Peninsula *see* The Fate of the Arabian Peninsula **3135**
A P S Diplomat News Service *see* A P S News Service **3123**
A P S Diplomat Operations in Oil Diplomacy *see* Operations in Oil Diplomacy **7256**
A P S Diplomat Re-Drawing the Islamic Map *see* Re-Drawing the Islamic Map **7261**
• A P S Diplomat Recorder (Arab Press Service) (CYP) **7219**
A P S Diplomat Redrawing the Islamic Map (Arab Press Service) (CYP) **7101**
A P S Diplomat Strategic Balance in the Middle East *see* Strategic Balance in the Middle East **7266**
A P S E C *see* Asia Pacific Software Engineering Conference. Proceedings **2587**
A P S Employment Gazette *see* A P S Jobs **7418**
• A P S Jobs (Australian Public Service) (AUS ISSN 1835-2480) **7418**
A P S Monograph Series (American Phytopathological Society) (USA ISSN 1051-1113) **771**
• A P S News (American Physical Society) (USA ISSN 1058-8132) **7002**
• A P S News Service (Arab Press Service) (CYP) **3123**
• A P S Observer (Association for Psychological Science) (USA ISSN 1050-4672) **7330**
• A P S Oil Market Trends (CYP) **3123**
A P S R *see* American Political Science Review **7105**
A P S Review Downstream Trends *see* Downstream Trends **3127**
A P S Review Downstream Trends (Arab Press Service) (CYP) **6761**
• A P S Review Gas Market Trends (Arab Press Service) (CYP) **6761**
A P S Review Gas Market Trends *see* Gas Market Trends **3136**
• A P S Science (Advanced Photon Source) (USA ISSN 1931-5015) **7064**
• A P S Strategic Balance in the Middle East (CYP) **7219**
A P T *see* Advances in Psychiatric Treatment **6120**
A P T *see* Asia - Pacific Telecommunity Journal **2365**
A P T *see* Advanced Psychology Texts **7331**
A P T Aluminium News (DEU ISSN 1745-0330) **6303**
A P T B *see* Asia - Pacific Tax Bulletin **1910**
A P T Bulletin *see* Association for Preservation Technology International. Bulletin **434**
A P T Communique (Association for Preservation Technology) (USA ISSN 1062-6190) **2601**
• A P T I Bulletin (Association of Pharmaceutical Teachers of India) (IND ISSN 0973-1288) **6818**
† A P T International (DEU) **8927**
A P T News *see* A P T Aluminium News **6303**
A P T S Project Summaries (Advanced Public Transportation Systems) (USA) **8489**
• The A P T T Bulletin (Association of Part-Time Tutors) (GBR ISSN 1755-0971) **2822**
A P T Yearbook (Asia - Pacific Telecommunity) (GBR ISSN 1353-0356) **2365**
A P U *see* Administrative Professional Update **1724**
A P U Life (Azusa Pacific University) (USA ISSN 0895-5433) **2271**
A P U Press Alaskana Book Series (Alaska Pacific University Press) (USA) **4281**
• A P V M A Gazette (Australian Pesticides & Veterinary Medicines Authority) (AUS) **4854**
A P V News (Arbeitsgemeinschaft fuer Pharmazeutische Verfahrenstechnik) (DEU) **6818**
A P W A Newsletter (All Pakistan Women's Association) (PAK ISSN 0001-2262) **8022**
A P W A Reporter (American Public Works Association) (USA ISSN 0092-4873) **3258**
A P World History *see* Barron's A P World History **4132**
A Penny Saved (USA ISSN 1522-9688) **2634**
• A Place in the Sun (GBR) **7581**
A Plus Architecture (BEL) **426**
A Plus Architectuur *see* A Plus Architecture **426**
A+O Fonds Gemeenten. Jaarverslag (NLD) **1661**
A Pochemu?/But Why? (RUS ISSN 0868-7137) **2175**
A Practical Guide to Disputes Between Adjoining Landowners - Easements (USA) **7581**
A-Prior (BEL ISSN 1376-7135) **463**
A Propos *see* Candid Facts **5592**
• A Propos (FIN ISSN 1456-5080) **7829**
A Propos Culina (CHE) **7944**
A Propos de l'Eau *see* Water News **8837**
A Propos des Habitats Canadiens (CAN ISSN 1912-5348) **3400**
• A Proposito (PRI) **463**
A Q (ESP ISSN 1130-2046) **426**
A Q (Aromatherapy Quarterly) (GBR ISSN 0966-7164) **305**
A Q *see* Anthropological Quarterly **325**
A Q *see* Adoption Quarterly **8023**
• ➤ A Q (Balmain) (Australian Quarterly) (AUS ISSN 1443-3605) **7101**
A Q A (A) Psychology Review *see* Psychology Review **7400**
A Q C S Catalogue for Reference Materials and Intercomparison Exercises (AUT) **3164**
• A Q I S Bulletin (Australian Quarantine and Inspection Service) (AUS ISSN 1033-9280) **78**
A Q Online *see* Academic Questions **2965**
A Q S - Merkblaetter fuer die Wasser-, Abwasser- und Schlammuntersuchung (DEU) **8817**
A R *see* Amateur Radio **2356**
A R *see* Architectural Review Australia **430**
A R *see* The Architectural Review **430**
A R *see* Arhitektura, Raziskave **432**
A R *see* Adventist Review **7744**
A R *see* Arizona's Economy **7420**
A R A *see* Asian Review of Accounting **1280**
A R A *see* American Recovery Association. News and Views **1307**
A R A L *see* Australian Review of Applied Linguistics **5097**
• A R A Newsletter (American Romanian Academy of Arts and Sciences) (USA ISSN 1081-3985) **2964**
A R A Newsletter (Automotive Recyclers Association) (USA) **8554**
A R A Research Bulletin (Anti-Racist Action) (CAN) **7201**
▼ The A R A Retailer (Australian Retailers Association) (AUS ISSN 1834-4720) **1055**
A R A Z P A Blueprint (Australasian Regional Association of Zoological Parks and Aquaria) (AUS) **929**
A R Australia *see* Architectural Review Australia **430**
A R B M *see* Annuaire de la Recherche Bio-Medicale **8930**
A R C *see* Archaeological Review from Cambridge **376**
A R C Action (Atlanta Regional Commission) (USA) **4402**
A R C Arabic Journal (Arab Republic Community) (CAN ISSN 0700-9771) **3515**
A R C E Newsletter Samvadi (Archives and Research Centre for Ethnomusicology) (IND) **6541**
A R C H *see* Australian Architecture Database **462**
A R C H *see* Actuarial Research Clearinghouse **4491**
A R C News (USA ISSN 1064-6108) **4036**
A R C O Master the P C A T *see* Master the P C A T **6860**
A R C O P C A T *see* Master the P C A T **6860**
A R C P *see* The Georgetown Law Journal Annual Review of Criminal Procedure **4890**
A R C Publicaties (Archaeological Research & Consultancy) (NLD ISSN 1574-6879) **370**
A R C S Australia. Newsletter (Association of Regulatory & Clinical Scientists) (AUS ISSN 1448-5923) **7829**
• A R C Strategic Plan (Years) (Australian Research Council) (AUS ISSN 1832-4347) **2822**
A R D - Buffet (Arbeitsgemeinschaft der oeffentlich-rechtlichen Rundfunkanstalten der Bundesrepublik Deutschland) (DEU) **3843**
A R D - Jahrbuch (Arbeitsgemeinschaft der Oeffentlich-Rechtlichen Rundfunkanstalten der Bundesrepublik Deutschland) (DEU ISSN 0066-5746) **2356**
A R D Online *see* Annals of the Rheumatic Diseases **6221**

Title

▼ *new title* † *ceased* • *electronic media* ➤ *refereed*

DIRECTORY 2010 A T D F JOURNAL 9911

A S F A 2: Ocean Technology, Policy and Non-living Resources *see* Aquatic Sciences & Fisheries Abstracts. Part 2: Ocean Technology, Policy and Non-living Resources **8842**
A S F A 3: Aquatic Pollution and Environmental Quality *see* Aquatic Sciences & Fisheries Abstracts. Part 3: Aquatic Pollution and Environmental Quality **3477**
• A S F A Aquaculture Abstracts (Online) (Aquatic Sciences & Fisheries Abstracts) (USA ISSN 1555-6166) **3612**
• A S F A Marine Biotechnology Abstracts (Online) (USA ISSN 1555-6182) **712**
A S F M R A Journal *see* American Society of Farm Managers and Rural Appraisers. Journal **91**
A S G C *see* Australia. Bureau of Statistics. Australian Standard Geographical Classification (Online) **4035**
• A S G E Clinical Update (American Society for Gastrointestinal Endoscopy) (USA ISSN 1070-7212) **5919**
A S H A *see* A S H A Leader **4071**
• A S H A Leader (American Speech - Language - Hearing Association) (USA ISSN 1085-9586) **4071**
A S H E - E R I C Higher Education Report Series *see* A S H E Higher Education Report Series **2964**
A S H E - E R I C Higher Education Reports *see* A S H E Higher Education Report Series **2964**
• ➤ A S H E Higher Education Report Series (Association for the Study of Higher Education) (USA ISSN 1551-6970) **2964**
A S H E Lumina Fellows Series *see* A S H E / Lumina Fellows Series **2964**
▼ • A S H E / Lumina Fellows Series (Association for the Study of Higher Education) (USA ISSN 1938-7830) **2964**
A S H E / Lumina Policy Briefs and Critical Essays Series *see* A S H E / Lumina Fellows Series **2964**
A S H E Newsletter (Association for the Study of Higher Education) (USA) **2964**
A S H Image Bank *see* American Society of Hematology Image Bank **5933**
A S H Journal *see* Australian Stock Horse Journal **8287**
• ➤ A S H M Journal Club (Australian Society for HIV Medicine Inc.) (AUS) **5807**
A S H P Midyear Clinical Meeting Symposium Highlights (American Society of Health-System Pharmacists) (USA ISSN 1557-0606) **6818**
A S H P Newsletter (American Society of Health-System Pharmacists) (USA ISSN 0001-2483) **6818**
A S H Publication Series (Association of Studies on Himalayas) (IND) **541**
A S H R A E Guideline (American Society of Heating, Refrigerating and Air-Conditioning Engineers, Inc. (A S H R A E)) (USA ISSN 1049-894X) **4115**
A S H R A E Guidelines *see* A S H R A E Guideline **4115**
• The A S H R A E Handbook CD. Fundamentals (American Society of Heating, Refrigerating and Air-Conditioning Engineers, Inc. (A S H R A E)) (USA ISSN 1930-8043) **4115**
The A S H R A E Handbook CD. H V A C Applications *see* A S H R A E Handbook. Heating, Ventilating and Air-Conditioning Applications (S I Edition) **4115**
• The A S H R A E Handbook CD. H V A C Systems and Equipment (American Society of Heating, Refrigerating and Air-Conditioning Engineers, Inc. (A S H R A E)) (USA ISSN 1930-7713) **4115**
• The A S H R A E Handbook CD. Refrigeration (American Society of Heating, Refrigerating and Air-Conditioning Engineers, Inc. (A S H R A E)) (USA ISSN 1930-7187) **4115**
• A S H R A E Handbook. Fundamentals (Inch-Pound Edition) (American Society of Heating, Refrigerating and Air-Conditioning Engineers) (USA ISSN 1523-7222) **4115**
A S H R A E Handbook. Fundamentals (S I Edition) (American Society of Heating, Refrigerating and Air-Conditioning Engineers) (USA ISSN 1523-7230) **4115**
A S H R A E Handbook. H V A C Systems and Equipment *see* A S H R A E Handbook. Heating, Ventilating and Air-Conditioning Systems and Equipment (Inch-Pound Edition) **4115**
• A S H R A E Handbook. Heating, Ventilating and Air-Conditioning Applications (S I Edition) (American Society of Heating, Refrigerating and Air-Conditioning Engineers, Inc. (A S H R A E)) (USA ISSN 1078-6082) **4115**
• A S H R A E Handbook. Heating, Ventilating and Air-Conditioning Systems and Equipment (Inch-Pound Edition) (American Society of Heating, Refrigerating and Air-Conditioning Engineers, Inc. (A S H R A E)) (USA ISSN 1078-6066) **4115**
• A S H R A E Handbook. Heating, Ventilating and Air-Conditioning Systems and Equipment (S I Edition) (American Society of Heating, Refrigerating and Air-Conditioning Engineers, Inc. (A S H R A E)) (USA ISSN 1930-7705) **4115**
• A S H R A E Handbook. Refrigeration (I-P Edition) (American Society of Heating, Refrigerating and Air-Conditioning Engineers, Inc. (A S H R A E)) (USA ISSN 1930-7195) **4115**
A S H R A E Handbook. Refrigeration (S I Edition) *see* The A S H R A E Handbook CD. Refrigeration **4115**
A S H R A E Handbook. Refrigeration (S I Edition) *see* A S H R A E Handbook. Refrigeration (I-P Edition) **4115**
A S H R A E Handbook. Refrigeration (S I Edition) *see* A S H R A E Handbook. Refrigeration (I-P Edition) **4115**
A S H R A E. I A Q Applications (American Society of Heating, Refrigerating and Air-Conditioning Engineers/Indoor Air Quality) (USA ISSN 1527-4519) **4115**
• A S H R A E Insights (USA ISSN 0891-4249) **4115**
• ➤ A S H R A E Journal (American Society of Heating, Refrigerating and Air-Conditioning Engineers) (USA ISSN 0001-2491) **4115**
A S H R A E Seminar Recordings *see* A S H R A E Seminar Recordings DVD **4116**
• A S H R A E Seminar Recordings DVD (American Society of Heating, Refrigerating and Air-Conditioning Engineers, Inc. (A S H R A E)) (USA ISSN 1551-3319) **4116**
A S H R A E Standard (American Society of Heating, Refrigerating and Air-Conditioning Engineers) (USA ISSN 1041-2336) **4116**
A S H R A E Technical Data Bulletin (American Society of Heating, Refrigerating and Air-Conditioning Engineers) (USA ISSN 0884-0490) **3372**
• A S H R A E Transactions (American Society of Heating, Refrigerating and Air-Conditioning Engineers) (USA ISSN 0001-2505) **4116**
A S H S Membership Directory *see* HortScience **3738**
A S H S Newsletter (American Society for Horticultural Science) (USA ISSN 0882-8024) **3721**
A S H Smoking and Health Review (Action on Smoking & Health) (USA ISSN 1048-907X) **4608**
A S I *see* Agricultural Supply Industry **85**
A S I *see* Aviation Security International **8538**
A S I *see* Adhesives & Sealants Industry **3235**
• A S I C Gazette (CD-ROM) (Australian Securities and Investments Commission) (AUS ISSN 1445-6079) **4854**
• A S I C News (Online) (Australian Securities and Investments Commission) (AUS ISSN 1832-018X) **1609**
A S I C News (Print) *see* A S I C News (Online) **1609**
• A S I D I C Newsletter (Association of Information and Dissemination Centers) (USA ISSN 0887-9915) **4986**
A S I D Icon (American Society of Interior Designers) (USA) **4531**
A S I D Report *see* A S I D Icon **4531**
A S I F A Magazine (Association Internationale du Film d'Animation) (CAN) **6488**
A S I Journal (Architecture and Surveying Institute) (GBR ISSN 0956-4241) **426**
• A S I L Insights (American Society of International Law) (USA) **4915**
A S I L Newsletter (American Society of International Law) (USA ISSN 1049-7803) **4915**
A S I Posten (American Swedish Institute) (USA) **6518**
A S I S & T Handbook and Directory (American Society for Information Science & Technology) (USA ISSN 1550-2163) **4986**
A S I S Dynamics (American Society for Industrial Security) (USA ISSN 1098-1489) **1722**
A S I S. Quaderni di Lavoro *see* Atlante Sintattico dell'Italia. Quaderni di Lavoro **5097**
A S I S Security Industry Buyers Guide (American Society for Industrial Security) (USA) **1970**
A S It. Quaderni *see* Atlante Sintattico dell'Italia. Quaderni di Lavoro **5097**
• A S J (Kent Town) (Australian Shooters Journal) (AUS ISSN 1443-5713) **8301**
A S J A Newsletter (American Society of Journalists and Authors) (USA ISSN 1056-3849) **4571**
A S J C L *see* Asian Journal of Comparative Law **4846**
A S K Hollis (Associations, Sources, Knowledge) (GBR ISSN 1471-4256) **1970**
A S L *see* Australia's Surfing Life **8305**
A S L A Members Handbook (American Society of Landscape Architects) (USA ISSN 0192-5067) **426**
• A S L E F Journal (GBR) **8614**
A S L H Newsletter (American Society for Legal History) (USA) **4608**
A S L Newsletter (Australian Society for Limnology) (AUS ISSN 1037-2512) **2792**
A S L P Bulletin (Association of Special Libraries of the Philippines) (PHL ISSN 0001-2548) **4986**
A S M A *see* Aarhus Studies in Mediterranean Antiquity **2229**
A S M A News (American Society of Marine Artists) (USA ISSN 1936-7732) **463**
A S M A News (American Sports Medicine Association, Board of Certification) (USA) **8156**
A S M C Proceedings *see* I E E E - S E M I Advanced Semiconductor Manufacturing Conference and Workshop **3313**
A S M E Boiler and Pressure Vessel Code (American Society of Mechanical Engineers) (USA ISSN 0517-5321) **3372**
A S M E Boiler and Pressure Vessel Code. Section 7: Recommended Guidelines for the Care of Power Boilers (American Society of Mechanical Engineers) (USA ISSN 0272-3506) **3372**
A S M E - I E E E Joint Railroad Conference *see* I E E E - A S M E Joint Rail Conference. Proceedings **8618**
A S M E International International Solar Energy Conference. Proceedings *see* A S M E International Solar Energy Conference. Proceedings **3176**
A S M E International News *see* A S M E News **3372**
➤ A S M E International Solar Energy Conference. Proceedings (A S M E International) (USA ISSN 1546-8402) **3176**
• A S M E News (A S M E International) (USA ISSN 0279-9316) **3372**
A S M I C Newsletter (American Society of Military Insignia Collectors) (USA) **4326**
A S M Ink (Archeological Society of Maryland) (USA) **370**
A S M J *see* Australian Senior Mathematics Journal **3052**
A S M News (Washington) *see* Microbe **891**
A S M Z *see* Allgemeine Schweizerische Militaerzeitschrift **6410**
A S N E L Papers (Association for the Study of New Literatures in English) (NLD ISSN 1385-2981) **5248**
▼ • A S N Kidney News (American Society of Nephrology) (USA ISSN 1943-8044) **6264**
▼ • ➤ A S N Neuro (American Society for Neurochemistry) (GBR ISSN 1759-0914) **918**
A S O C *see* Australia. Bureau of Statistics. Australian Standard Offence Classification (Online) **2672**
• A S O R Bulletin (Australian Society for Operations Research Inc.) (AUS ISSN 0812-860X) **1722**
A S O R Newsletter *see* American Schools of Oriental Research. Newsletter **542**
• The A S P A Journal (American Society of Pension Actuaries) (USA ISSN 1544-9769) **4490**
A S P A Report (American Salvage Pool Association) (USA) **8554**
• A S P B News (American Society of Plant Biologists) (USA ISSN 1535-5489) **771**
A S P C A Action (American Society for the Prevention of Cruelty to Animals) (USA ISSN 1554-6624) **316**
A S P Catalog (Astronomical Society of the Pacific) (USA) **568**
• The A S P E Highlighter (Assistant Secretary for Planning and Evaluation) (USA ISSN 1930-6903) **7505**
A S P E Papers: Managing Primary Education Series (Association for the Study of Primary Education) (GBR ISSN 1367-5605) **2822**
A S P I F Newsletter (Association of Small Presses in Florida) (USA) **7550**
A S P I Technical Series (Appalachia - Science in the Public Interest) (USA) **3400**
• A S P Island (Application Service Provider) (USA) **2587**
A S P L O Newsletter (Administrators of Small Public Libraries of Ontario) (CAN) **4986**
A S P M N Pathways (American Society of Pain Management Nursing) (USA) **5950**
A S P R Newsletter (American Society for Psychical Research) (USA ISSN 0044-7919) **6740**
A S P T Newsletter *see* American Society of Plant Taxonomists Newsletter **775**
A.S. Pratt & Sons Anti-Money Laundering Update *see* B S A / A M L Update **1310**
A S Q *see* Administrative Science Quarterly **7419**
A S Q *see* Autism Spectrum Quarterly **6125**
A S Q Six Sigma Forum Magazine *see* Six Sigma Forum **1904**
A S R *see* Architectural Science Review **430**
A S R *see* The Adam Smith Review **5250**
A S R *see* American Sociological Review **8087**
A S R A Journal (Association for the Study of Reptilia and Amphibia) (GBR ISSN 0142-5145) **929**
A S R A Monographs (Association for the Study of Reptilia and Amphibia) (GBR ISSN 0261-992X) **929**
A S R - Anwalt/Anwaeltin im Sozialrecht (DEU ISSN 1438-3365) **4608**
A S R C Newsletter *see* American Studies Research Centre. Newsletter **4283**
A S R T Scanner (American Society of Radiologic Technologists) (USA ISSN 0161-3863) **6191**
A S S A H *see* Anglo-Saxon Studies in Archaeology and History **373**
A S S C Newsletter (Arkansas School Study Council) (USA) **3016**
A S S H Studies in Sports History (Australian Society for Sports History) (AUS ISSN 1833-1947) **8156**
• A S S I A (Applied Social Sciences Index & Abstracts) (USA) **8019**
A S T *see* Adsorption Science and Technology **3235**
A S T *see* Avtomatizatsiya i Sovremennye Tekhnologii **2459**
A S T A Congress Dailies (GBR) **6277**
A S T A Network (GBR) **8680**
A S T A Newsletter (American Seed Trade Association) (USA) **3721**
A S T C Dimensions (Association of Science-Technology Centers) (USA ISSN 1528-820X) **7829**
• A S T D Buyers Guide and Consultants Directory (American Society for Training & Development) (USA) **1855**
A S T D Learning Circuits *see* Learning Circuits **1869**
The A S T D State of the Industry Report *see* T+D **1876**
The A S T D Training & Performance Sourcebook (American Society for Training & Development) (USA ISSN 1930-8620) **6691**
A S T I R *see* Astir **3051**
• A S T I S Bibliography (CAN) **7935**
• A S T I S Occasional Publications (Arctic Science & Technology Information System) (CAN ISSN 0225-5170) **2718**
A S T M Geotechnical Testing Journal *see* Geotechnical Testing Journal **3268**
• ➤ A S T M International. Journal (American Society for Testing and Materials) (USA ISSN 1546-962X) **3179**
A S T M Journal of Testing and Evaluation *see* Journal of Testing and Evaluation **3351**
• ➤ A S T M Standards in Building Codes (American Society for Testing and Materials) (USA ISSN 0066-0523) **3335**
A S T R Newsletter (American Society for Theatre Research) (USA ISSN 0044-7927) **8464**
A S T R O Meeting Supplement *see* International Journal of Radiation: Oncology - Biology - Physics **6199**
A S U *see* American School & University **3017**
A S U Newsletter (Association of Simula Users) (FRA ISSN 1102-593X) **2505**
A S U People (Australian Services Union) (AUS) **4589**
A S U Protect *see* Arbeitsmedizin, Sozialmedizin, Umweltmedizin **7508**
A S U Protect *see* Arbeitsmedizin, Sozialmedizin, Umweltmedizin. Supplement **7508**
• A S U Research (Arizona State University) (USA ISSN 1093-1295) **2822**
• A S U Travel Guide (Airline Services Unlimited) (USA) **8680**
• A S V A B (Armed Services Vocational Aptitude Battery) (USA ISSN 1933-5679) **6408**
A S V A B *see* McGraw-Hill's A S V A B **6434**
A S V A B Basic Training for the A F Q T *see* McGraw-Hill's A S V A B Basic Training for the A F Q T **6434**
A S W *see* Administration in Social Work **8023**
A S W E A Journal for Social Work Education in Africa (Association for Social Work Education in Africa) (ETH) **8022**
A S W E C *see* Australian Software Engineering Conference. Proceedings **2588**
• A S X (USA) **8156**
• ➤ A St A - Advances in Statistical Analysis (DEU ISSN 1863-8171) **8343**
• A St A La Vista (DEU ISSN 1862-426X) **2271**
▼ • A St A - Wirtschafts- und Sozialstatistisches Archiv (DEU ISSN 1863-8155) **8343**
▼ A Suitable Solution (USA ISSN 1938-1867) **1803**
A T *see* Automatisierungstechnik **2458**
A T *see* Anthropology Today **327**
A T *see* Architecture Today **431**
A T *see* Architectural Technology **976**
A T *see* Avtomobil'nyi Transport **8568**
A T *see* Analysis in Theory and Applications **5470**
A T A A Journal *see* Australian Technical Analysts Association. Journal **1064**
A T A C (Asociacion de Tecnicos Azucareros de Cuba) (CUB ISSN 0138-7553) **215**
A T A Chronicle (American Translators Association) (USA ISSN 1078-6457) **5088**
A T A - I A T A Reservations Interline Message Procedures - Passenger *see* A I R I M P - Passenger **8533**
A T A Ingegneria Automotoristica *see* Ingegneria dell'Autoveicolo **8585**
A T A J L T R *see* A T A Journal of Legal Tax Research **1909**
A T A Journal (HKG ISSN 1015-8138) **8447**
• A T A Journal of Legal Tax Research (American Taxation Association) (USA ISSN 1543-866X) **1909**
A T A S Bulletin (Advance Technology Alert System) (USA ISSN 0257-5973) **8415**
A T A S Information Technology for Development (Advanced Technology Assesment System) (CHE ISSN 1020-4199) **1589**
➤ A T A Scholarly Monograph Series (American Translators Association) (NLD ISSN 0890-4111) **5088**
• A T. Actualidad Tecnologica (ESP ISSN 1132-9327) **8415**
A T - Arkitekttidningen *see* Arkitekten **433**
A T C N Clubblad *see* Airedale Magazine **6802**
A T C. Nouvelles *see* T A C News **8512**
A T C P (MEX) **6731**
A T C P Revista (Asociacion Mexicana de Tecnicos de las Industrias de la Celulosa y del Papel, A.C.) (MEX) **6732**
A T D *see* Motor Trader **8593**
A T D *see* Allen's Trademark Digest **4613**
A T D *see* Across the Disciplines **5089**
A T D F Journal *see* African Technology Development Forum Journal **1057**

Title

DIRECTORY 2010 ACADEMIE ROYALE DES SCIENCES D'OUTRE-MER. CLASSE DES 9915

Academia Boliviana de la Lengua. Anales (BOL) **5089**
● ➤ Academia Brasileira de Ciencias. Anais/Annals of the Brazilian Academy of Sciences (BRA ISSN 0001-3765) **7829**
Academia Brasileira de Ciencias Morais e Politicas. Revista (BRA ISSN 1413-9871) **6901**
Academia Brasileira de Direito Constitucional. Revista (BRA ISSN 1676-1480) **4846**
Academia Brasileira de Filologia. Revista (BRA ISSN 1676-1545) **5089**
● Academia Brasileira de Letras. Revista Brasileira (BRA ISSN 0103-7072) **4439**
Academia Brasileira de Literatura. Revista (BRA) **5248**
Academia. Bungaku, Gogaku Hen/Academia. Literature and Language (JPN ISSN 0389-8431) **5248**
Academia Campinense de Letras. Publicacoes (BRA ISSN 0065-0447) **5248**
Academia Canaria de Ciencias. Revista (ESP ISSN 1130-4723) **7829**
Academia Cearense de Letras. Revista (BRA ISSN 0102-8820) **5248**
➤ Academia Chilena de la Historia. Boletin (CHL ISSN 0716-5439) **4281**
Academia Chilena de Medicina. Boletin Anual (CHL ISSN 0716-2588) **5564**
● Academia Colombiana de Ciencias Exactas, Fisicas y Naturales. Revista (COL ISSN 0370-3908) **7829**
Academia das Ciencias de Lisboa. Classe de Letras. Memorias (PRT ISSN 0378-116X) **4439**
Academia de Ciencias de Cuba. Instituto de Oceanologia. Reporte de Investigacion (CUB ISSN 1010-450X) **2799**
Academia de Ciencias de la Republica Dominicana. Anuario (DOM ISSN 1023-9065) **7829**
Academia de Ciencias Exactas, Fisicas, Quimicas y Naturales de Zaragoza. Monografias (ESP ISSN 1132-6360) **7829**
Academia de Ciencias Exactas, Fisico-Quimicas y Naturales. Revista (ESP ISSN 0370-3207) **7829**
➤ Academia de Ciencias Fisicas Matematicas y Naturales. Boletin (VEN ISSN 0366-1652) **7829**
Academia de Ciencias Politicas y Sociales. Boletin (VEN ISSN 0798-1457) **7101**
Academia de Cultura Valenciana. Anales (ESP ISSN 1130-426X) **7945**
Academia de Educacion. Boletin (ARG ISSN 0327-0637) **2823**
Academia de Geografia e Historia de Guatemala. Anales (GTM ISSN 0252-337X) **3997**
Academia de Historia del Tachira. Boletin (VEN) **4281**
Academia de Stiinte a Republicii Moldova. Buletinul. Economie si Sociologie/Akademiya Nauk Respubliki Moldova. Izvestiya. Ekonomika i Sotsiologiya (MDA) **1435**
Academia de Stiinte a Republicii Moldova. Buletinul. Fizica si Tehnica (MDA) **7002**
➤ Academia de Stiinte a Republicii Moldova. Buletinul. Matematica/Akademiya Nauk Respubliki Moldova. Izvestiya. Matematika (MDA ISSN 1024-7696) **5463**
Academia de Stiinte a Republicii Moldova. Buletinul. Stiinte Biologice si Chimice/Akademiya Nauk Respubliki Moldova. Izvestiya. Biologicheskie i Khimicheskie Nauki (MDA ISSN 1019-5289) **649**
Academia de Stiinte a Republicii Moldova. Revista Filosofie si Drept/Akademiya Nauk Respubliki Moldova. Voprosy Filosofii i Prava (MDA) **6902**
Academia de Stiinte Agricole si Silvice. Buletin Informativ (ROM ISSN 1010-3589) **78**
Academia Diplomatica Boliviana. Revista Anual (BOL) **7219**
Academia Dominicana de la Historia. Publicaciones (DOM ISSN 0567-5871) **4281**
➤ Academia Economic Papers/Jingji Lunwen. Zhongyang Yanjiuyuan Jingji Yanjiusuo (TWN ISSN 1018-161X) **1056**
Academia Espanola, Madrid. Anejos del Boletin (ESP ISSN 0065-0455) **5248**
▼ Academia Galega do Audiovisual. Papeis (ESP ISSN 1888-1912) **3050**
Academia Guatemalteca de Estudios Genealogicos, Heraldicos e Historicos. Revista (GTM ISSN 0065-0463) **3757**
Academia Hondurena de la Lengua. Boletin (HND ISSN 0065-0471) **5089**
Academia. Humanities, Social Sciences *see* Academia. Jinbun, Shakai Kagaku Hen **4439**
Academia. Jinbun, Shakai Kagaku Hen/Academia. Humanities, Social Sciences (JPN ISSN 0389-8458) **4439**
Academia Latinitati Fovendae. Commentarii (ITA ISSN 1121-8991) **5089**
Academia. Literature and Language *see* Academia. Bungaku, Gogaku Hen **5248**
● Academia Luventicus Reportes/Luventicus Academy Reports (ARG ISSN 1667-5061) **6902**
Academia Matritense del Notariado. Anales (ESP ISSN 0210-3249) **4608**
† Academia Medica Pragensis. Bulletin (CZE ISSN 1801-0466) **8927**
Academia Mexicana de la Historia. Memorias (MEX ISSN 0188-7416) **4281**
Academia Nacional de Bellas Artes. Anuario (ARG) **463**
Academia Nacional de Ciencias. Boletin (ARG ISSN 0325-2051) **7829**
Academia Nacional de Ciencias Exactas, Fisicas y Naturales de Buenos Aires. Anales (ARG ISSN 0365-1185) **7829**
Academia Nacional de Ciencias Exactas, Fisicas y Naturales de Buenos Aires. Monografias (ARG ISSN 0327-5426) **7829**
Academia Nacional de Ciencias Exactas, Fisicas y Naturales de Buenos Aires. Noticias (ARG) **7829**
Academia Nacional de Ciencias. Miscelanea (ARG ISSN 0325-3406) **7830**
Academia Nacional de Ciencias Morales y Politicas. Anales (ARG) **7101**
Academia Nacional de Derecho y Ciencias Sociales de Cordoba. Anales (ARG ISSN 0325-5425) **4608**
Academia Nacional de Educacion. Boletin *see* Academia de Educacion. Boletin **2823**
▼ Academia Nacional de Farmacia y Bioquimica (ARG ISSN 1851-0612) **6818**
Academia Nacional de la Historia. Boletin (ARG ISSN 0325-0482) **4128**
Academia Nacional de la Historia. Boletin (VEN ISSN 0254-7325) **4281**
Academia Nacional de la Historia. Investigaciones y Ensayos (ARG ISSN 0539-242X) **4281**
Academia Nacional de Medicina. Anais (BRA ISSN 0104-4885) **5943**
Academia Nacional de Medicina. Boletin (ARG ISSN 0374-647X) **5564**
Academia Nacional de Medicina. Boletin de Informacion Clinica Terapeutica (MEX) **5564**
Academia. Natural Science and Physical Education *see* Akademia. Shizen Kagaku, Hoken Taiiku Hen **5467**
Academia Norteamericana de la Lengua Espanola. Boletin (USA ISSN 0884-0091) **5248**
Academia On Line *see* Academia **7550**
● ➤ Academia Paedagogica Nyiregyhaziensis. Acta Mathematica (HUN ISSN 0866-0182) **5464**
Academia Paulista de Letras. Revista (BRA ISSN 0001-3846) **5248**
Academia Pernambucana de Letras. Revista (BRA) **5248**
Academia Portuguesa da Historia. Anais (PRT) **4195**
Academia Romana. Sectia de Stiinte Istorice si Arheologie. Memoriile (ROM ISSN 0258-9133) **4195**
Academia Romana. Sectiilor Stiintifice. Memoriile. Seria IV *see* Academia Romana. Sectia de Stiinte Istorice si Arheologie. Memoriile **4195**
Academia Scientiarum et Artium Slovenica. Classis 2, Philologia et Litterae. Dissertationes *see* Slovenska Akademija Znanosti in Umetnosti. Razred za Filoloske in Literarne Vede. Razprave **5175**
Academia Scientiarum et Artium Slovenica. Classis 4: Historia Naturalis. Dissertationes *see* Slovenska Akademija Znanosti in Umetnosti. Razred za Naravoslovne Vede. Razprave **7917**
Academia Scientiarum Fennica. Yearbook *see* Suomalainen Tiedeakatemia. Vuosikirja **7921**
➤ Academia Sinica. Institute of Chemistry. Bulletin (TWN ISSN 0001-3927) **2048**
Academia Sinica. Institute of History and Philology. Bulletin (TWN ISSN 1012-4195) **4179**
Academia Sinica. Institute of Mathematics. Bulletin *see* Academia Sinica. Institute of Mathematics. Bulletin. New Series **5464**
➤ Academia Sinica. Institute of Mathematics. Bulletin. New Series/Chung Yang Yen Chiu Yuan. Shu Hsueh Yen Chiu So T'ung Pao (TWN) **5464**
➤ Academia Sinica. Institute of Modern History. Bulletin/Chung Yang Yen Chiu Yuan. Chin Tai Shih Yen Chiu So Ch'i K'an (TWN ISSN 1029-4740) **4128**
Academia Sinica. Institute of Physics. Annual Report/Chung Yang Yen Chiu Yuan Wu Li Hsueh Yen Chiu So Nien Pao (TWN ISSN 0304-5293) **7003**
▼ Academia y Virtualidad (COL ISSN 2011-0731) **2965**
Academiae Analecta. Klasse van de Kunsten (BEL) **463**
Academiae Analecta. Klasse van de Menswetenschappen (BEL) **4439**
Academiae Analecta. Klasse van de Natuurwetenschappen (BEL) **7830**
● ➤ Academiae Scientiarum Hungarica. Acta Zoologica (HUN ISSN 1217-8837) **929**
● Academic Abstracts CD-ROM (USA ISSN 1056-7496) **1**
Academic Association of Koreanology in Japan. Journal *see* Chosen Gakuho **3527**
Academic Clinical Practice (USA) **5564**
Academic Degrees and Graduate Education *see* Xuewei yu Yanjiusheng Jiaoyu **3011**
● ➤ Academic Emergency Medicine (USA ISSN 1069-6563) **6054**
● ➤ Academic Exchange Quarterly (USA ISSN 1096-1453) **3050**
● Academic File International News & Photo Syndication (GBR) **463**
† Academic Freedom (GBR ISSN 1369-8257) **8927**
Academic Jobs Digest (USA) **6691**
Academic Journal E S S H *see* European Studies in Sports History **8172**
Academic Journal of Guangdong College of Pharmacy *see* Guangdong Yaoxueyuan Xuebao **6845**
Academic Journal of Guangzhou Medical College *see* Guangzhou Yixueyuan Xuebao **5621**
Academic Journal of Jinyang *see* Jinyang Xuekan **7977**
Academic Journal of Kunming Medical College *see* Kunming Yixueyuan Xuebao **5659**
Academic Journal of P L A Postgraduate Medical School *see* Junyi Jinxiu Xueyuan Xuebao **5656**
Academic Journal of Second Military Medical University *see* Di-Er Jun-Yi Daxue Xuebao **5604**
Academic Journal of Xi'an Jiaotong University (English Edition) *see* Xi'an Jiatong University. Academic Journal **7931**
Academic Journal of Zhongzhou *see* Zhongzhou Xuekan **8019**
● Academic Leader (USA ISSN 8750-7730) **2965**
● ➤ Academic Leadership (Hernando) (USA ISSN 1533-7812) **2823**
Academic Leadership (Mesa) (USA ISSN 1086-1149) **2965**
Academic Library Book Review (USA ISSN 0894-993X) **7550**
Academic Life *see* Akademiska Dzive **3517**
Academic Matters (CAN ISSN 1719-010X) **2965**
● ➤ Academic Medicine (USA ISSN 1040-2446) **5564**
Academic Monthly *see* Xueshu Yuekan **8016**
Academic Newswire *see* Library Journal Academic Newswire **5028**
The Academic Nurse (USA ISSN 1062-0249) **5950**
● Academic Open Internet Journal (BGR ISSN 1311-4360) **7830**
● ➤ Academic Pediatrics (USA ISSN 1876-2859) **6086**
Academic Periodical Abstracts of China *see* Zhongguo Xueshu Qikan Wenzhai **18**
Academic Physician and Scientist (USA ISSN 1093-1139) **6691**
● Academic Practice Faculty Compensation and Production Survey (USA ISSN 1049-7072) **5565**
● Academic Practice Management Compensation Survey (USA ISSN 1076-1586) **5565**
Academic Press Advanced Finance Series (GBR ISSN 1872-7255) **1305**
➤ Academic Press Geology Series (USA ISSN 1050-8309) **2722**
➤ Academic Press Series in Cognition and Perception (USA) **7330**
Academic Press Series in Engineering (USA) **3179**
Academic Press Series in Magnetism (USA) **7003**
Academic Professional Advisory Committee News *see* A P A C News **2964**
● ➤ Academic Psychiatry (USA ISSN 1042-9670) **6118**
● ➤ Academic Questions (USA ISSN 0895-4852) **2965**
● ➤ Academic Radiology (NLD ISSN 1076-6332) **6191**
Academic Research *see* Xueshu Yanjiu **8016**
Academic Review *see* Design Management Journal **1738**
● Academic Search (USA) **1**
Academic Testing Materials: Market Analysis and Forecast *see* Academic Testing Materials: Market Analysis & Forecast (Year) **3050**
● Academic Testing Materials: Market Analysis & Forecast (Year) (USA) **3050**
Academic. Writing. *see* Across the Disciplines **5089**
● ➤ Academic.Writing (USA ISSN 1552-325X) **5248**
Academic Year Abroad (USA ISSN 1047-2576) **3011**
Academic Year - European University Institute *see* European University Institute. Academic Year **2855**
● Academica (BRA ISSN 1517-610X) **1722**
Academica (ROM ISSN 1220-5737) **4439**
Academie Arabe de Damas. Revue *see* Majma' al-Lughah al-Arabiyyah bi Dimashq. Majallah **5329**
Academie Bulgare des Sciences. Comptes Rendus *see* Bulgarska Akademiya na Naukite. Dokladi **7842**
L'Academie Canadienne de Psychiatrie de l'Enfant et de l'Adolescent. Journal *see* Canadian Academy of Child and Adolescent Psychiatry. Journal **6129**
Academie d'Agriculture de France. Comptes Rendus (FRA ISSN 0989-6988) **78**
Academie de Droit Europeen. Recueil des Cours *see* Academy of European Law. The Collected Courses **4916**
➤ Academie de Droit International de la Haye. Recueil des Cours/Hague Academy of International Law. Collected Courses (USA ISSN 0169-5436) **4916**
Academie de Nantes. Les Cahiers E P S (Education Physique et Sportive) (FRA ISSN 1281-3605) **6981**
Academie des Inscriptions et Belles-Lettres. Comptes-Rendus des Seances de l'Annee (Year) (FRA ISSN 0065-0536) **4128**
Academie des Inscriptions et Belles-Lettres. Etudes et Commentaires (FRA ISSN 0065-0544) **5089**
● Academie des Lettres et des Sciences Humaines. Presentations (CAN ISSN 0317-0179) **7945**
Academie des Sciences. Annuaire (FRA ISSN 0065-0552) **7830**
Academie des Sciences, Arts et Belles Lettres de Dijon. Memoires (FRA ISSN 0755-3617) **4440**
Academie des Sciences, Belles-Lettres et Arts de Savoie. Memoires (FRA ISSN 1157-075X) **4440**
● ➤ Academie des Sciences. Comptes Rendus. Biologies (FRA ISSN 1631-0691) **649**
● ➤ Academie des Sciences. Comptes Rendus. Chimie (FRA ISSN 1631-0748) **2048**
● ➤ Academie des Sciences. Comptes Rendus. Geoscience (FRA ISSN 1631-0713) **7830**
● ➤ Academie des Sciences. Comptes Rendus. Mathematique (FRA ISSN 1631-073X) **5464**
Academie des Sciences. Comptes Rendus Mathematiques/Academy of Science. Mathematical Reports (CAN ISSN 0706-1994) **5464**
● ➤ Academie des Sciences. Comptes Rendus. Mecanique (FRA ISSN 1631-0721) **3372**
● ➤ Academie des Sciences. Comptes Rendus. Palevol (FRA ISSN 1631-0683) **6722**
● ➤ Academie des Sciences. Comptes Rendus. Physique (FRA ISSN 1631-0705) **2132**
Academie des Sciences. Comptes Rendus. Series IIA. Earth and Planetary Science *see* Academie des Sciences. Comptes Rendus. Palevol **6722**
Academie des Sciences et Lettres de Montpellier. Bulletin Mensuel (FRA ISSN 1146-7282) **7830**
Academie des Sciences, Inscriptions, et Belles Lettres de Toulouse. Memoires (FRA ISSN 0369-1896) **4440**
Academie Francaise. Annuaire (FRA ISSN 1140-7344) **5248**
Academie Internationale de Pathologie. Division Francaise. Bulletin (FRA ISSN 0989-8921) **5565**
Academie Internationale des Arts et Collections. la Lettre (FRA ISSN 1770-4995) **463**
† ➤ Academie Internationale d'Histoire des Sciences. Collection des Travaux (NLD ISSN 1163-5657) **8928**
● ➤ Academie Lorraine de Sciences. Bulletin (FRA ISSN 1635-8597) **7830**
Academie Malgache. Bulletin d'Information et de Liaison (MDG ISSN 1021-0474) **7830**
Academie Malgache. Memoires (MDG ISSN 0374-9002) **7830**
Academie Nationale de Chirurgie Dentaire. Bulletin (FRA ISSN 0339-9710) **5833**
● ➤ Academie Nationale de Chirurgie. E-Memoires (FRA ISSN 1634-0647) **6234**
Academie Nationale de Medecine. Annuaire (FRA ISSN 1169-2014) **5565**
Academie Nationale de Medecine. Bulletin (FRA ISSN 0001-4079) **5565**
● Academie Nationale de Medecine. Lettre (FRA ISSN 1620-9931) **5565**
Academie Nationale de Metz. Memoires (FRA ISSN 1149-0349) **4440**
➤ Academie Polonaise des Sciences. Centre d'Archeologie Mediterraneenne. Etudes et Travaux (POL ISSN 0079-3566) **370**
➤ Academie Polonaise des Sciences. Centre d'Archeologie Mediterraneenne. Travaux/Polska Akademia Nauk. Zaklad Archeologii Srodziemnomorskiej. Prace (POL ISSN 0554-5927) **370**
Academie Royale d'Agriculture et de Sylviculture de Suede. Annales *see* Kungliga Skogs- och Lantbruksakademiens Tidskrift **131**
Academie Royale de Langue et de Litterature Francaises. Annuaires (BEL ISSN 0567-6584) **5089**
Academie Royale de Langue et de Litterature Francaises. Bulletin (BEL ISSN 0770-7061) **5089**
➤ Academie Royale de Marine de Belgique. Communications/Koninklijke Belgische Marine Academie. Mededelingen (BEL ISSN 0776-3468) **8638**
Academie Royale de Medecine de Belgique. Bulletin et Memoires (BEL ISSN 0377-8231) **5565**
Academie Royale des Sciences, des Lettres et des Beaux-Arts de Belgique. Annuaire (BEL ISSN 0373-0778) **4440**
Academie Royale des Sciences, des Lettres et des Beaux-Arts de Belgique. Classe des Beaux-Arts. Bulletin (BEL ISSN 0378-0716) **4440**
Academie Royale des Sciences, des Lettres et des Beaux-Arts de Belgique. Classe des Beaux-Arts. Memoires (BEL ISSN 0378-7923) **463**
Academie Royale des Sciences, des Lettres et des Beaux-Arts de Belgique. Classe des Lettres et des Sciences Morales et Politiques. Bulletin (BEL ISSN 0001-4133) **4440**
Academie Royale des Sciences, des Lettres et des Beaux-Arts de Belgique. Classe des Lettres et des Sciences Morales et Politiques. Memoires (BEL) **4440**
Academie Royale des Sciences, des Lettres et des Beaux-Arts de Belgique. Classe des Sciences. Bulletin (BEL ISSN 0001-4141) **7830**
Academie Royale des Sciences, des Lettres et des Beaux-Arts de Belgique. Classe des Sciences. Memoires (BEL ISSN 0365-0936) **7830**
Academie Royale des Sciences, des Lettres et des Beaux-Arts de Belgique. Index Biographique des Membres, Correspondants et Associes (BEL ISSN 0065-0609) **639**
Academie Royale des Sciences d'Outre-Mer. Bulletin des Seances/Koninklijke Academie voor Overzeese Wetenschappen. Mededelingen der Zittingen (BEL ISSN 0001-4176) **7830**
Academie Royale des Sciences d'Outre-Mer. Classe des Sciences Morales et Politiques. Memoires in 8/Koninklijke Academie voor Overzeese Wetenschappen. Klasse voor Morele en Politieke Wetenschappen. Verhandelingen in 8 (BEL ISSN 0776-2933) **4440**

Title

9916 ACADEMIE ROYALE DES SCIENCES D'OUTRE-MER. CLASSE DES ULRICH'S PERIODICALS

Academie Royale des Sciences d'Outre-Mer. Classe des Sciences Naturelles et Medicales. Collection in 4 (BEL ISSN 0379-1920) **7830**
Academie Royale des Sciences d'Outre-Mer. Classe des Sciences Naturelles et Medicales. Collection in 8/Koninklijke Academie voor Overzeese Wetenschappen. Klasse voor Natuur- en Geneeskundige Wetenschappen. Verzameling in 8 (BEL ISSN 0770-1896) **7830**
Academie Royale des Sciences d'Outre-Mer. Classe des Sciences Techniques. Collection in 4 (BEL ISSN 0373-7063) **7830**
Academie Royale des Sciences d'Outre-Mer. Classe des Sciences Techniques. Collection in 8/Koninklijke Academie voor Overzeese Wetenschappen. Klasse voor Technische Wetenschappen. Verzameling in 8 (BEL ISSN 0777-1525) **7830**
Academie Serbe des Sciences et des Arts. Classe des Sciences Historiques. Bulletin *see* Srpska Akademija Nauka i Umetnosti. Odeljenje Istorijskih Nauka. Glas **7920**
Academie Serbe des Sciences et des Arts. Classe des Sciences Historiques. Conferences Scientifiques *see* Srpska Akademija Nauka i Umetnosti. Odeljenje Istorijskih Nauka. Naucni Skupovi **7920**
• ➤ Academie Serbe des Sciences et des Arts. Classe des Sciences Mathematiques et Naturelles. Bulletin Sciences Mathematiques (SRB ISSN 0561-7332) **5464**
Academie Serbe des Sciences et des Arts. Classe des Sciences Mathematiques et Naturelles. Bulletin Sciences Naturelles (SRB ISSN 0352-5740) **7830**
Academie Serbe des Sciences et des Arts. Classe des Sciences Medicales. Bulletin (SRB ISSN 0584-9829) **5565**
Academie Serbe des Sciences et des Arts. Classe des Sciences Medicales. Monographies *see* Srpska Akademija Nauka i Umetnosti. Odeljenje Medicinskih Nauka. Posebna Izdanja **5717**
Academie Serbe des Sciences et des Arts. Classe des Sciences Sociales. Bulletin *see* Srpska Akademija Nauka i Umetnosti. Odeljenje Drustvenih Nauka. Glas **8007**
Academie Serbe des Sciences et des Arts. Classe des Sciences Sociales. Conferences Scientifiques *see* Srpska Akademija Nauka i Umetnosti. Odeljenje Drustvenih Nauka. Naucni Skupovi **8007**
Academie Serbe des Sciences et des Arts. Classe des Sciences Techniques.Bulletin (SRB ISSN 0374-0781) **8415**
Academie Serbe des Sciences et des Arts. Contributions Onomatologiques *see* Srpska Adamemija Nauka i Umetnosti. Onomatoloski Prilozi **8439**
Academie Serbe des Sciences et des Arts. Publications de la Bibliotheque S A S S A *see* Srpska Akademija Nauka i Umetnosti. Izdanja Biblioteke S A N U **5049**
Academie Serbe des Sciences et des Arts. Recueil de Chilandar *see* Srpska Akademija Nauka i Umetnosti. Hilandarski Zbornik **4267**
Academie Serbe des Sciences et des Arts. Recueil de l'Histoire de Bosnie et Herzegovine *see* Srpska Akademija Nauka i Umetnosti. Zbornik za Istoriju Bosne i Hercegovine **4267**
Academie Serbe des Sciences et des Arts. Recueil de Sentandreja *see* Srpska Akademija Nauka i Umetnosti. Sentandrejski Zbornik **4267**
Academie Serbe des Sciences et des Arts. Recueil de Vardar *see* Srpska Akademija Nauka i Umetnosti. Vardarski Zbornik **4267**
Academie Serbe des Sciences et des Arts. Recueil des Travaux sur les Serbes en Croatie *see* Srpska Akademija Nauka i Umetnosti. Zbornik o Srbima u Hrvatskoj **4267**
Academie Serbe des Sciences et des Arts. Recueil d'Etudes Orientales *see* Srpska Akademija Nauka i Umetnosti. Zbornik za Orijentalne Studije **561**
Academie Serbe des Sciences et des Arts. Section des Beaux-Arts et de la Musique. Bulletin *see* Srpska Akademija Nauka i Umetnosti. Odeljenje Likovne i Muzicke Umetnosti. Glas **6619**
Academie Veterinaire de France. Bulletin (FRA ISSN 0001-4192) **8790**
➤ De Academische Boekengids (NLD ISSN 1567-7842) **7550**
AcademiX (LBN ISSN 1816-3513) **6691**
The Academy (USA) **8156**
Academy Computing Times (USA) **2406**
• Academy Digest (SGP ISSN 0218-8406) **4608**
• Academy Exchange (GBR ISSN 1748-5533) **2965**
• Academy for Economics and Economic Education. Proceedings (USA ISSN 2150-5063) **1056**
➤ Academy for Evangelism in Theological Education. Journal (USA ISSN 0894-9034) **7619**
Academy for Jewish Religion. Journal *see* G'vanim (Riverdale) **7721**
• Academy for Legal, Ethical and Regulatory Issues. Proceedings (USA ISSN 2150-5160) **4608**
Academy for Studies in Business Law Journal *see* Journal of Legal, Ethical and Regulatory Issues **4703**
Academy for Studies in Business Law. Proceedings *see* Academy for Legal, Ethical and Regulatory Issues. Proceedings **4608**
Academy for Studies in Business Law. Proceedings *see* Academy of Marketing Studies. Proceedings **1803**
▼ • Academy for Studies in Business. Proceedings (USA ISSN 2150-5136) **1056**
• Academy for Studies in International Business. Proceedings (USA ISSN 2150-5098) **1056**
➤ Academy Forum (USA ISSN 0192-1088) **7330**
Academy Law Review (IND) **4608**
Academy Magazine (NLD ISSN 1871-9341) **5089**
Academy News (Colorado Springs) (USA ISSN 0739-7666) **5912**
Academy News (Milwaukee) (USA ISSN 1094-4745) **5752**
• ➤ Academy of Accounting and Financial Studies Journal (USA ISSN 1096-3685) **1276**
Academy of American Franciscan History. Documentary Series (USA ISSN 0065-0633) **7782**
Academy of American Franciscan History. Monograph Series (USA ISSN 0065-0641) **7782**
Academy of American Franciscan History. Propaganda Fide Series (USA ISSN 0065-065X) **7782**
Academy of American Poets. James Laughlin Award and Walt Whitman Award (USA) **5415**
• ➤ Academy of Banking Studies Journal (USA ISSN 1939-2230) **1305**
• ➤ Academy of Business and Economics. Journal (USA ISSN 1542-8710) **1551**
▼ • Academy of Business & Public Policy. Proceedings of the International Conference (USA ISSN 1948-2272) **1056**
Academy of Criminal Justice Sciences Employment Bulletin *see* A C J S Employment Bulletin **1855**
Academy of Criminal Justice Sciences Program Book *see* A C J S Program Book **2964**
Academy of Criminal Justice Sciences Today *see* A C J S Today **2643**
Academy of Dentistry for Persons with Disabilities. Bulletin (USA) **5833**
• ➤ Academy of Educational Leadership Journal (USA ISSN 1095-6328) **3050**
• Academy of Educational Leadership. Proceedings (USA ISSN 1948-3163) **2823**
• ➤ Academy of Entrepreneurship Journal (USA ISSN 1087-9595) **1722**
• Academy of Entrepreneurship. Proceedings (USA ISSN 1948-5638) **1722**
Academy of Equipment Command & Technology. Journal *see* Zhuangbei Zhihui Jishu Xueyuan Xuebao **5462**
Academy of European Law. The Collected Courses/Academie de Droit Europeen. Recueil des Cours (GBR) **4916**
Academy of Fellows Directory (CAN ISSN 1483-7242) **1609**
The Academy of Finland. Publications *see* Suomen Akatemia. Julkaisuja **7921**
Academy of General Dentistry Impact *see* A G D Impact **5832**
• Academy of Health Care Management Journal (USA ISSN 1559-7628) **4087**
Academy of Hospital Administration. Journal (IND ISSN 0970-9452) **1722**
• ➤ Academy of Information and Management Sciences Journal (USA ISSN 1524-7252) **2519**
Academy of International Business Newsletter *see* A I B Newsletter **1551**
Academy of Legal Studies in Business Newsletter *see* A L S B Newsletter **4854**
▼ • The Academy of Management Annals (USA ISSN 1941-6520) **1723**
• Academy of Management. Annual Meeting Proceedings (USA) **1723**
• ➤ Academy of Management Journal (USA ISSN 0001-4273) **1723**
• ➤ Academy of Management Learning and Education (USA ISSN 1537-260X) **1723**
• The Academy of Management News (USA ISSN 1557-5241) **1723**
• ➤ The Academy of Management Perspectives (USA ISSN 1558-9080) **1723**
• ➤ Academy of Management Review (USA ISSN 0363-7425) **1723**
Academy of Managerial Communications. Proceedings *see* Academy of Organizational Culture, Communications and Conflict. Proceedings **1723**
• ➤ Academy of Marketing Science. Journal (USA ISSN 0092-0703) **1803**
• ➤ Academy of Marketing Science Review (USA ISSN 1526-1794) **1803**
• ➤ Academy of Marketing Studies Journal (USA ISSN 1095-6298) **1803**
• Academy of Marketing Studies. Proceedings (USA ISSN 2150-5187) **1803**
Academy of Medical-Surgical Nurses News *see* A M S N News **5949**
• ➤ Academy of Medicine, Singapore. Annals (SGP ISSN 0304-4602) **5565**
Academy of Medicine, Toronto. Bulletin (CAN ISSN 0001-4311) **5565**
Academy of Meteorological Science. Annual Report *see* Zhongguo Qixiang Kexue Yanjiuyuan Nianbao **6400**
Academy of Military Medical Sciences. Bulletin *see* Junshi Yixue Kexueyuan Yuankan **5656**
Academy of Military Transportation. Journal *see* Junshi Jiaotong Xueyuan Xuebao **8501**
Academy of Natural Sciences of Philadelphia. Monographs (USA ISSN 0096-7750) **7831**
• ➤ Academy of Natural Sciences of Philadelphia. Proceedings (USA ISSN 0097-3157) **7831**
Academy of Natural Sciences of Philadelphia. Special Publications (USA ISSN 0097-3254) **7831**
• Academy of Organizational Culture, Communications and Conflict. Proceedings (USA ISSN 1948-3155) **1723**
➤ Academy of Rehabilitative Audiology. Journal (USA ISSN 0149-8886) **6076**
Academy of Religion and Psychical Research. Proceedings (USA) **6740**
Academy of Sanskrit Research. Journal *see* Tattvadipah **8009**
Academy of Science. Mathematical Reports *see* Academie des Sciences. Comptes Rendus Mathematiques **5464**
Academy of Sciences News *see* Shinjleh Uhaany Akademiyn Medee **7915**
Academy of Sciences of Georgia. Proceedings. Biological Series *see* Sakartvelos Metsnierebata Akademia. Matsne. Biologiis Seria **702**
• Academy of Sciences of the Czech Republic. Institute of Hydrobiolgy. Biology Centre. Annual Report (CZE ISSN 1210-9649) **2792**
Academy of Sciences of the Turkmenistan. Series of Biological Sciences. Proceedings *see* Turkmenistan Ylymlar Akademiasynyn Habarlary. Biologik Ylymlaryn Seriasy **708**
Academy of Strategic and Organizational Leadership. Proceedings *see* Academy of Strategic Management. Proceedings **1723**
• ➤ Academy of Strategic Management Journal (USA ISSN 1544-1458) **1723**
• Academy of Strategic Management. Proceedings (USA ISSN 2150-511X) **1723**
Academy of the Hebrew Language. Text & Studies *see* Aqadem **5095**
• Academy of the Social Sciences in Australia. Annual Report (AUS ISSN 1328-5947) **7945**
Academy of the Social Sciences in Australia. Dialogue (AUS ISSN 1441-8460) **7945**
• Academy of the Social Sciences in Australia. Occasional Paper Series (AUS ISSN 1323-7136) **7945**
Academy of Veterinary Homeopathy. Journal (USA ISSN 1550-2813) **8790**
Academy Players Directory (USA) **6488**
Acadia Bulletin (CAN ISSN 0044-5843) **2271**
Acadian Genealogy Exchange (USA ISSN 0199-9591) **3757**
Acadiana Catholic (USA ISSN 0888-0247) **7782**
Acadiana Profile (USA ISSN 0001-4397) **3968**
➤ Acadiensis (CAN ISSN 0044-5851) **4281**
Acamedia Research Monograph (GBR ISSN 0956-9057) **8085**
Acao Games (BRA ISSN 0104-1630) **2474**
Acapulco (Year) (USA ISSN 1055-5633) **8680**
Acari Bibliographia Acarologica (DEU ISSN 1618-8977) **649**
Acarina (RUS ISSN 0132-8077) **837**
Acarological Society of Japan. Journal *see* Nihon Dani Gakkaishi **856**
• Acarology Bulletin (GBR ISSN 1361-8091) **837**
Acasa Magazin (ROM ISSN 1454-4539) **3932**
Acata Medica Portugesa. Supplement *see* Acta Medica Portuguesa **5566**
Acatech Berichtet und Empfiehlt (DEU ISSN 1862-4200) **8415**
• Acatiimi (FIN ISSN 1455-1608) **2965**
• Acaua (BRA ISSN 1678-1996) **4129**
Accademia Clementina. Atti e Memorie (ITA ISSN 0394-7157) **4195**
† Accademia Creativa (ITA ISSN 1970-7215) **8928**
Accademia dei Concordi Rovigo. Collana di Musiche (ITA) **6542**
Accademia delle Scienze dell'Istituto di Bologna. Atti. Classi di Scienze Fisiche. Memorie (ITA ISSN 0515-2143) **7831**
Accademia delle Scienze dell'Istituto di Bologna. Atti. Classi di Scienze Fisiche. Rendiconti (ITA ISSN 0365-0057) **7831**
Accademia delle Scienze di Siena Detta de Fisiocritici. Atti (ITA ISSN 0390-7783) **5565**
Accademia delle Scienze di Torino. Atti. Classe di Scienze Fisiche, Matematiche e Naturali (ITA ISSN 0001-4419) **7831**
Accademia delle Scienze di Torino. Atti. Classe di Scienze Fisiche, Matematiche e Naturali. Supplementi *see* Accademia delle Scienze di Torino. Atti. Classe di Scienze Fisiche, Matematiche e Naturali **7831**
Accademia delle Scienze di Torino. Atti. Classe di Scienze Morali, Storiche e Filologiche (ITA ISSN 1122-1380) **4440**
Accademia delle Scienze di Torino. Memorie. Classe di Scienze Fisiche, Matematiche e Naturali (ITA ISSN 1120-1630) **7831**
Accademia delle Scienze di Torino. Memorie. Classe di Scienze Morali, Storiche e Filologiche (ITA ISSN 1120-1622) **4440**
Accademia delle Scienze di Torino. Quaderni (ITA ISSN 1125-0402) **7831**
Accademia delle Scienze Fisiche e Matematiche. Rendiconto (ITA ISSN 0370-3568) **7831**
Accademia di Archeologia Lettere e Belle Arti. Rendiconti (ITA ISSN 0393-2931) **4129**
Accademia di Storia dell'Arte Sanitaria. Atti e Memorie (ITA ISSN 0365-4109) **7506**
Accademia Etrusca di Cortona. Annuario (ITA ISSN 0065-0730) **4195**
Accademia Filarmonica Romana. Newsletter (ITA) **6542**
Accademia Italiana della Cucina. Rivista *see* Civilta della Tavola **3631**
Accademia Italiana di Scienze Forestali. Annali (ITA ISSN 0515-2178) **3682**
Accademia Ligure di Scienze e Lettere. Atti (ITA ISSN 1122-651X) **7831**
Accademia Nazionale dei Lincei. Atti dei Convegni Lincei (ITA ISSN 0391-805X) **4440**
• ➤ Accademia Nazionale dei Lincei. Atti. Matematica e Applicazioni. Rendiconti (CHE ISSN 1120-6330) **5464**
• Accademia Nazionale dei Lincei. Atti. Notizie degli Scavi di Antichita (ITA ISSN 0391-8157) **4440**
• ➤ Accademia Nazionale dei Lincei. Atti. Scienze Fisiche e Naturali. Rendiconti (ITA ISSN 1120-6349) **7831**
Accademia Nazionale dei Lincei. Atti. Scienze Morali, Storiche e Filologiche. Rendiconti (ITA ISSN 0391-8181) **4129**
Accademia Nazionale dei Lincei. Bollettino dei Classici *see* Bollettino dei Classici **2231**
Accademia Nazionale dei Lincei. Fondazione Leone Caetani (ITA ISSN 0391-8130) **7708**
Accademia Nazionale di San Luca. Annuario (ITA ISSN 0393-859X) **427**
† Accademia Nazionale di Santa Cecilia. Archivi di Etnomusicologia. Annuario (ITA) **8928**
Accademia Nazionale Italiana di Entomologia. Rendiconti (ITA ISSN 0065-0757) **837**
Accademia Nazionale Virgiliana di Scienze Lettere ed Arti. Atti e Memorie (ITA ISSN 1124-3783) **4195**
• ➤ Accademia Peloritana dei Pericolanti. Classe di Scienze Fisiche Matematiche e Naturali. Atti (ITA ISSN 0365-0359) **7831**
Accademia Peloritana dei Pericolanti. Classe di Scienze Medico - Biologiche. Atti (ITA ISSN 0365-0294) **7831**
Accademia Petrarca di Lettere, Arti e Scienza. Atti e Memorie (ITA ISSN 0393-2397) **4440**
Accademia Pontaniana. Atti (ITA ISSN 1121-9238) **4195**
Accademia Roveretana degli Agiati. Atti. Fasc. A: Classe di Scienze Umane, Lettere ed Arti (ITA ISSN 1122-6064) **4440**
Accademia Roveretana degli Agiati. Atti. Fasc. B: Classe di Scienze Matematiche, Fisiche e Naturali (ITA ISSN 1124-0350) **7831**
Accademia Roveretana degli Agiati. Memorie (ITA) **4440**
Accademia Roveretana degli Agiati. Pubblicazioni Diverse (ITA) **4440**
Accademia Toscana di Scienze e Lettere La Colombaria. Atti e Memorie (ITA ISSN 0392-0836) **7831**
Accademia Toscana di Scienze e Lettere La Colombaria. Studi (ITA ISSN 0065-0781) **7831**
Accademie e Biblioteche d'Italia (ITA ISSN 0001-4451) **4986**
Accao Socialista (PRT ISSN 0871-102X) **7101**
Accelerator (CAN ISSN 1193-7114) **7831**
Accelerator *see* XLR8R **3993**
Accelerator (USA) **362**
Accelerator Newsletter (USA ISSN 0001-4478) **2048**
Accelerators and Storage Rings Series *see* Physics and Technology of Particle and Photon Beams **7070**
† Accent (AUS ISSN 1033-9035) **8928**
➤ Accent (BEL) **5248**
• Accent (ESP ISSN 1698-7500) **463**
Accent (NLD ISSN 1875-1253) **2271**
Accent (SWE ISSN 0345-0406) **2689**
Accent (Birmingham) (USA ISSN 0162-1955) **7744**
Accent (Exeter) (USA) **4351**
• Accent Gwinnett (USA ISSN 1937-7185) **5064**
Accent on Tampa Bay Magazine (USA) **3968**
Accent West Amarillo (USA ISSN 0740-0365) **8680**
▼ Accents Danse (CAN ISSN 1913-8636) **2682**
Accents on Shakespeare (GBR) **5249**
Acceptable Identification and Classification of Goods and Services Manual (USA) **1056**
† Acceptance (AUS) **8928**
Acces Libre (FRA ISSN 1764-9943) **2587**
• Acceso. Revista Puertorriquena de Bibliotecologia y Documentacion (PRI ISSN 1536-1772) **4986**
• Access (CAN ISSN 1201-0472) **4987**
• ➤ Access (NZL ISSN 0111-8889) **2823**
† Access (Chicago, 1990) (USA ISSN 1057-4212) **8928**
• Access (Chicago) (USA ISSN 1050-0758) **5833**
Access (Franklin) (USA) **1305**
• Access (Morisset) (AUS) **306**
Access (Newark) (USA ISSN 1935-3502) **6518**
• Access (Online) (AUS ISSN 1449-8510) **4063**
Access (Rockville) (USA ISSN 1050-1878) **2570**
Access (Seattle) (USA ISSN 1056-4101) **463**
Access (Toorak) (AUS ISSN 0817-1351) **5565**
➤ Access (Vermont) (AUS ISSN 1030-0155) **4987**
Access (Washington) (USA) **6691**
Access All Areas (GBR ISSN 0960-6416) **6277**
Access and Privacy Directory (CAN ISSN 1486-3103) **7418**
• Access by Design (GBR ISSN 0959-1591) **4063**
Access California Wine Country (USA ISSN 1935-0937) **8680**
• Access Control & Security Systems (USA) **2676**
• Access Currents (USA) **4077**
Access Directv (USA ISSN 1935-4525) **2374**
• Access Economics Business Outlook (AUS) **1435**
• ➤ Access: History (AUS ISSN 1440-8449) **4129**

Title

Acta Crystallographica. Section B: Structural Science. Online see Acta Crystallographica. Section B: Structural Science **2109**
● ➤ Acta Crystallographica. Section C: Crystal Structure Communications (DNK ISSN 0108-2701) **2109**
● ➤ Acta Crystallographica. Section D: Biological Crystallography/Biological Crystallography (DNK ISSN 0907-4449) **2109**
● ➤ Acta Crystallographica. Section E: Structure Reports Online (DNK ISSN 1600-5368) **2109**
● Acta Crystallographica. Section F: Structural Biology and Crystallization Communications Online (DNK ISSN 1744-3091) **2109**
● ➤ Acta Cytologica (USA ISSN 0001-5547) **826**
Acta de l'Institut d'Anesthesiologie *see* Institut d'Anesthesiologie. Acta **8965**
Acta de Odontologia Pediatrica (DOM ISSN 0252-1032) **5833**
➤ Acta Demographica (CZE ISSN 0232-0479) **7276**
Acta Dendrobiologica (SVK ISSN 0231-5335) **3682**
● Acta Dental Internacional (ESP ISSN 1578-1259) **5833**
● ➤ Acta Dermatovenerologica Alpina, Pannonica et Adriatica (SVN ISSN 1318-4458) **5870**
● ➤ Acta Dermatovenerologica Croatica (HRV ISSN 1330-027X) **5870**
● ➤ Acta Diabetologica (ITA ISSN 0940-5429) **5883**
● Acta Didactica (NOR ISSN 1502-2013) **2823**
▼ ● Acta Didactica Napocensia (ROM ISSN 2065-1430) **2823**
▼ ● Acta Didaktica Norge (NOR ISSN 1504-9922) **2823**
Acta Ecclesiastica Sloveniae (SVN ISSN 0351-2789) **7620**
➤ Acta Ecologica (IND ISSN 0970-2881) **3400**
Acta Ecologica Sinica *see* Shengtai Xuebao **3466**
Acta Editologica *see* Bianji Xuebao **7552**
Acta Edulis Fungi *see* Shiyongjun Xuebao **817**
Acta Electronica Napocensis *see* Acta Electrotehnica **3294**
Acta Electronica Sinica *see* Dianzi Xuebao **3092**
● ➤ Acta Electrotehnica (ROM) **3294**
● ➤ Acta Endocrinologica/Revue Roumaine d'Endocrinologie (ROM ISSN 1841-0987) **5883**
● Acta Endoscopica (FRA ISSN 0240-642X) **5919**
Acta Endoscopica. Supplement (FRA ISSN 1242-1383) **5919**
Acta Energiae Solaris Sinica *see* Taiyang Neng Xuebao **3178**
Acta Entomologica Bulgarica (BGR ISSN 1310-5914) **837**
➤ Acta Entomologica Chilena (CHL ISSN 0716-5072) **837**
Acta Entomologica Musei Nationalis Pragae *see* Musei Nationalis Pragae. Acta Entomologica **855**
Acta Entomologica Serbica (SRB ISSN 0354-9410) **929**
➤ Acta Entomologica Silesiana (POL ISSN 1230-7777) **837**
Acta Entomologica Sinica *see* Kunchong Xuebao **853**
Acta Entomologica Slovenica (SVN ISSN 1318-1998) **837**
Acta Estrabologica (ESP ISSN 0210-4695) **6037**
➤ Acta et Commentationes Universitatis Tartuensis de Mathematica (EST ISSN 1406-2283) **5464**
● Acta Ethnographica Hungarica (HUN ISSN 1216-9803) **322**
Acta Ethnologica et Linguistica (AUT ISSN 0400-4019) **322**
● ➤ Acta Ethologica (DEU ISSN 0873-9749) **929**
● Acta Ethologica Online (DEU ISSN 1437-9546) **649**
Acta Facultatis Ecologiae, Zvolen (SVK ISSN 1336-300X) **3400**
Acta Facultatis Forestalis, Zvolen/Technical University in Zvolen. Faculty of Forestry. Collection of Scientific Works/Technicka Univerzita vo Zvolene. Lesnicka Fakulta. Zbornik Vedeckych Prac/Technischen Universitaet in Zvolen. Forstliche Fakultaet. Sammlung von Wissenschaftlichen Arbeiten/Universite Technique de Zvolen. Faculte des Forets. Collection des Travaux Scientifiques (SVK ISSN 0231-5785) **3682**
Acta Facultatis Medicae Fluminensis (HRV ISSN 0065-1206) **5565**
● ➤ Acta Facultatis Medicae Naissensis (SRB ISSN 0351-6083) **5566**
Acta Facultatis Medicae Universitatis Brunensis Masarykianae (CZE ISSN 0521-2561) **5566**
Acta Facultatis Politico-Juridicae Universitatis Scientiarum Budapestiensis de Rolando Eotvos Nominatae (HUN ISSN 0524-904X) **4608**
➤ Acta Facultatis Studiorum Humanitatis et Naturae Universitatis Presoviensis (SVK) **649**
Acta Farmaceutica Bonaerense *see* Latin American Journal of Pharmacy **6858**
● ➤ Acta Fisiatrica (BRA ISSN 0104-7795) **6054**
Acta Futura Fennica (FIN ISSN 0788-365X) **3838**
● ➤ Acta Fytotechnica et Zootechnica (SVK ISSN 1335-258X) **216**
● ➤ Acta Gastro-Enterologica Belgica (BEL ISSN 1784-3227) **5919**
Acta Gastro-Enterologica Belgica (Multilingual Edition) *see* Acta Gastro-Enterologica Belgica **5919**
● ➤ Acta Gastroenterologica Latinoamericana (ARG ISSN 0300-9033) **5919**
Acta Genealogica (SWE ISSN 1401-8462) **3757**
Acta Geodaetica et Cartographica Sinica *see* Cehui Xuebao **2778**
● Acta Geodaetica et Geophysica Hungarica (HUN ISSN 1217-8977) **2776**
➤ Acta Geodynamica et Geomaterialia (CZE ISSN 1214-9705) **2722**
Acta Geographica ac Geologica et Meteorologica Debrecina (HUN ISSN 0209-9004) **3997**
Acta Geographica Croatica (HRV ISSN 1330-0466) **3997**
Acta Geographica Lodziensia (POL ISSN 0065-1249) **3997**
Acta Geographica Lovaniensia (BEL ISSN 0065-1257) **3997**
Acta Geographica Sinica *see* Dili Xuebao **4004**
● Acta Geographica Slovenica (SVN ISSN 1581-6613) **3997**
Acta Geographica Slovenica (Online English Edition) *see* Acta Geographica Slovenica (Online Slovenian Edition) **3997**
Acta Geographica Slovenica (Online English Edition) *see* Acta Geographica Slovenica **3997**
● ➤ Acta Geographica Slovenica (Online Slovenian Edition) (SVN ISSN 1581-8314) **3997**
Acta Geographica Szegediensis (HUN ISSN 1217-6907) **3997**
➤ Acta Geologica (HRV ISSN 0448-0155) **2722**
Acta Geologica Hispanica *see* Geologica Acta **2737**
Acta Geologica Hungarica *see* Central European Geology **2728**
Acta Geologica Leopoldensia (BRA ISSN 0102-1249) **7832**
Acta Geologica Lilloana (ARG ISSN 0567-7513) **2722**
● Acta Geologica Polonica (POL ISSN 0001-5709) **2722**
Acta Geologica Sichuan *see* Sichuan Dizhi Xuebao **2767**
● ➤ Acta Geologica Sinica (AUS ISSN 1000-9515) **2723**
Acta Geologica Sinica *see* Dizhi Xuebao **2732**
➤ Acta Geologica Taiwanica (TWN ISSN 0065-1265) **2723**
➤ Acta Geologica Universitatis Comenianae (SVK ISSN 1335-2830) **2723**
● ➤ Acta Geophysica (POL ISSN 1895-6572) **2776**
Acta Geophysica Polonica *see* Acta Geophysica **2776**
Acta Geophysica Sinica *see* Diqiu Wuli Xuebao **2779**
Acta Geoscientia Sinica *see* Diqiu Xuebao **2731**
● Acta Geotechnica (DEU ISSN 1861-1125) **2776**
➤ Acta Geotechnica Slovenica (SVN ISSN 1854-0171) **2777**
● ➤ Acta Germanica (DEU ISSN 0065-1273) **5089**
Acta Germanica (HUN ISSN 1216-9455) **5089**
Acta Ginecologica (ESP ISSN 0001-5776) **5985**
Acta Graphica (HRV ISSN 0353-4707) **8415**
● ➤ Acta Haematologica (CHE ISSN 0001-5792) **5933**
➤ Acta Haematologica Polonica (POL ISSN 0001-5814) **5933**
Acta Hepatologica Japonica *see* Kanzo **5928**
Acta Herediana (PER ISSN 0567-753X) **3927**
● Acta Herpetologica (ITA ISSN 1827-9635) **929**
● ➤ Acta Histochemica (DEU ISSN 0065-1281) **721**
● Acta Histochemica et Cytochemica (Online) (JPN ISSN 1347-5800) **826**
● ➤ Acta Historiae Artis Slovenica (SVN ISSN 1408-0419) **463**
Acta Historiae Artium *see* Acta Historiae Artium Academiae Scientiarium Hungaricae **463**
● Acta Historiae Artium Academiae Scientiarium Hungaricae (HUN ISSN 0001-5830) **463**
Acta Historiae Rerum Naturalium nec non Technicarum. New Series (CZE ISSN 1211-958X) **4196**
Acta Historiae Scientiarum Baltica/Baltijas Zinatnu Vestures Apcerejumi (LVA) **7832**
● Acta Historica Astronomiae (DEU ISSN 1422-8521) **568**
Acta Historica et Archaeologica Mediaevalia (ESP ISSN 0212-2960) **371**
Acta Historica Leopoldina (DEU ISSN 0001-5857) **7832**
† Acta Historica Leopoldina. Supplement (DEU ISSN 0232-8615) **8928**
Acta Historica Neosoliensia (SVK ISSN 1336-9148) **4129**
Acta Historica Nova (HRV) **4196**
Acta Historica Scientiarum Naturalium et Medicinalium (DNK ISSN 0065-1311) **7832**
● ➤ Acta Historica Tallinnensia (EST ISSN 1406-2925) **4129**
Acta Historico-Oeconomica (HRV ISSN 1330-0024) **1535**
Acta Histriae (SVN ISSN 1318-0185) **4196**
➤ Acta Horti Botanici Bucurestiensis (ROM ISSN 1453-8830) **3721**
● Acta Horticulturae (BEL ISSN 0567-7572) **3721**
➤ Acta Horticulturae et Regiotecturae (SVK ISSN 1335-2563) **3721**
Acta Horticulturae Sinica *see* Yuanyi Xuebao **3754**
Acta Hospitalia (BEL ISSN 0044-6009) **4087**
Acta Humaniora (NOR ISSN 0806-3222) **4441**
Acta Humanistica et Scientifica Universitatis Sangio Kyotiensis. Natural Science Series *see* Kyoto Sangyo Daigaku Ronshu. Shizen Kagaku Keiretsu **7878**
Acta Hydrobiologica *see* Ecohydrology & Hydrobiology **2793**
Acta Hydrobiologica Sinica *see* Shuisheng Shengwu Xuebao **704**
Acta Hydrochimica et Hydrobiologica (Online Edition) *see* CLEAN - Soil, Air, Water (Online Edition) **8820**
Acta Hydrochimica et Hydrobiologica (Print Edition) *see* CLEAN - Soil, Air, Water (Print Edition) **8820**
● ➤ Acta hydrotechnica (SVN ISSN 0352-3551) **3360**
➤ Acta Hygienica, Epidemiologica et Microbiologica (CZE ISSN 0862-5956) **879**
➤ Acta Hyperborea (DNK ISSN 0904-2067) **371**
Acta I M E K O (International Measurement Confederation (IMEKO)) (HUN ISSN 0237-028X) **6400**
Acta Ibseniana (NOR ISSN 1503-2981) **5249**
● ➤ Acta Ichthyologica et Piscatoria (POL ISSN 0137-1592) **929**
● ➤ Acta Informatica (DEU ISSN 0001-5903) **2541**
● ➤ Acta Informatica Medica (BIH ISSN 0353-8109) **5829**
Acta Instituti Atheniensis Regni Sueciae *see* Svenska Institutet i Athen. Skrifter. Serie 8 **420**
Acta Instituti Atheniensis Regni Sueciae, 4 *see* Svenska Institutet i Athen. Skrifter. Serie 4 **2241**
Acta Instituti Romani Regni Sueciae *see* Svenska Institutet i Rom. Skrifter. Acta Series Prima. 4:o **420**
Acta Instituti Upsaliensis Jurisprudentiae Comparativae (SWE ISSN 0502-7497) **4608**
Acta Iranica (BEL ISSN 0378-4215) **541**
Acta Judaica Slovaca (SVK) **7717**
● Acta Juridica (ZAF ISSN 0065-1346) **4608**
● Acta Juridica Hungarica/Hungarian Journal of Legal Studies (HUN ISSN 1216-2574) **4609**
Acta Jutlandia. University Life Series *see* Acta Jutlandica. Universitetshistorisk Serie **3833**
Acta Jutlandica/Publications of the University of Aarhus (DNK ISSN 0065-1354) **3833**
Acta Jutlandica. Humanistisk Serie (DNK ISSN 0901-0556) **4441**
Acta Jutlandica. Naturvidenskabelig Serie (DNK ISSN 0105-6824) **7832**
Acta Jutlandica. Samfundsvidenskabelig Serie/Acta Jutlandica. Social Sciences Series (DNK ISSN 0106-0937) **7945**
Acta Jutlandica. Social Sciences Series *see* Acta Jutlandica. Samfundsvidenskabelig Serie **7945**
Acta Jutlandica. Teologisk Serie/Acta Jutlandica. Theology Series (DNK ISSN 0106-0945) **7620**
Acta Jutlandica. Theology Series *see* Acta Jutlandica. Teologisk Serie **7620**
Acta Jutlandica. Universitetshistorisk Serie/Acta Jutlandia. University Life Series (DNK ISSN 1600-3543) **3833**
● ➤ Acta Koreana (KOR ISSN 1520-7412) **541**
Acta Laboratorium Animalis Scientia Sinica *see* Zhongguo Shiyan Dongwu Xuebao **969**
Acta Laser Biology Sinica *see* Jiguang Shengwu Xuebao **734**
Acta Leprologica (CHE ISSN 0001-5938) **5808**
Acta Limnologica Brasiliensia (BRA ISSN 0102-6712) **2792**
● Acta Linguistica Hafniensia (GBR ISSN 0374-0463) **5089**
● Acta Linguistica Hungarica (HUN ISSN 1216-8076) **5090**
➤ Acta Linguistica Lithuanica (LTU ISSN 1648-4444) **5090**
● Acta Literaria (CHL ISSN 0716-0909) **5249**
Acta Magnetica (POL ISSN 0209-3316) **7003**
Acta Manilana, Series A: Natural and Applied Sciences (PHL ISSN 0065-1370) **7832**
● ➤ Acta Materialia (GBR ISSN 1359-6454) **6303**
● ➤ Acta Mathematica (NLD ISSN 0001-5962) **5464**
Acta Mathematica *see* Uniwersytet Jagiellonski. Zeszyty Naukowe. Acta Mathematica **5545**
Acta Mathematicae Applicatae Sinca *see* Yingyong Shuxue Xuebao **5547**
● ➤ Acta Mathematica Hungarica (HUN ISSN 0236-5294) **5464**
● ➤ Acta Mathematica Scientia (NLD ISSN 0252-9602) **5464**
● ➤ Acta Mathematica Sinica (DEU ISSN 1439-8516) **5464**
Acta Mathematica Universitatis Comenianae *see* Universitas Comeniana. Acta Mathematica **5544**
➤ Acta Mathematica Universitatis Ostraviensis (CZE ISSN 1214-8148) **5465**
➤ Acta Mathematica Vietnamica (VNM ISSN 0251-4184) **5465**
● ➤ Acta Mathematicae Applicatae Sinica/Chinese Journal of Applied Mathematics (DEU ISSN 0168-9673) **5465**
● ➤ Acta Mechanica (AUT ISSN 0001-5970) **3372**
Acta Mechanica Sinica *see* Lixue Xuebao **7060**
● ➤ Acta Mechanica Sinica (DEU ISSN 0567-7718) **7057**
● ➤ Acta Mechanica Solida Sinica (CHN ISSN 0894-9166) **7057**
Acta Mediaevalia (POL ISSN 0137-3064) **7782**
● Acta Medica (CUB ISSN 0864-3210) **5566**
Acta Medica *see* Acta Medica Hradec Kralove **5566**
● ➤ Acta Medica Academica (BIH ISSN 1840-1848) **5566**
Acta Medica Austriaca *see* Wiener Klinische Wochenschrift **5730**
† ➤ Acta Medica Auxologica (ITA ISSN 0001-6004) **8928**
➤ Acta Medica Bulgarica (BGR ISSN 0324-1750) **5901**
Acta Medica Catholica (BEL ISSN 0775-9053) **6902**
● Acta Medica Colombiana (COL ISSN 0120-2448) **5943**
● Acta Medica Costarricense (CRI ISSN 0001-6012) **5566**
Acta Medica Croatica (HRV ISSN 1330-0164) **5566**
Acta Medica de Sonora (MEX ISSN 1405-8960) **5566**
Acta Medica Dominicana (DOM ISSN 0379-4857) **5566**
Acta Medica Empirica *see* Erfahrungsheilkunde **5610**
Acta Medica et Biologica/Igaku Seibutsugaku Kenkyu Kiyo (JPN ISSN 0567-7734) **5566**
Acta Medica Grupo Angeles (MEX) **5566**
● ➤ Acta Medica Hradec Kralove (CZE) **5566**
● ➤ Acta Medica Iranica (IRN ISSN 0044-6025) **5566**
➤ Acta Medica Kinki University (JPN ISSN 0386-6092) **5566**
Acta Medica Lituanica (LTU ISSN 1392-0138) **5566**
● ➤ Acta Medica Medianae (SRB ISSN 0365-4478) **5566**
Acta Medica Mediterranea (ITA ISSN 0393-6384) **5808**
● ➤ Acta Medica Nagasakiensia (JPN ISSN 0001-6055) **5566**
● ➤ Acta Medica Okayama (JPN ISSN 0386-300X) **5566**
● Acta Medica Peruana (PER ISSN 1018-8800) **5566**
● Acta Medica Portuguesa (PRT ISSN 0870-399X) **5566**
Acta Medica Puno (PER ISSN 1812-9072) **5566**
Acta Medica Romana (ITA ISSN 0001-6098) **5566**
● ➤ Acta Medica Saliniana (BIH ISSN 0350-364X) **5567**
Acta Medica Semendrica (SRB ISSN 0354-2785) **5567**
† ➤ Acta Medica. Supplementum (CZE ISSN 1211-247X) **8928**
Acta Medicinal Sinica *see* Huaxia Yixue **5630**
● Acta Medico-Historica Adriatica (HRV ISSN 1334-4366) **5567**
Acta Mediterranea di Patologia Infettiva e Tropicale (ITA ISSN 0392-9515) **5808**
Acta Metallurgica Sinica *see* Jinshu Xuebao **6318**
● Acta Metallurgica Sinica (CHN ISSN 1006-7191) **6303**
● ➤ Acta Meteorologica Sinica (CHN ISSN 0894-0525) **6345**
Acta Metrologica Sinica *see* Jiliang Xuebao **6403**
Acta Mexicana de Ciencia y Tecnologia (MEX ISSN 0567-7785) **7832**
● ➤ Acta Microbiologica et Immunologica Hungarica (HUN ISSN 1217-8950) **880**
Acta Microbiologica Polonica *see* Polish Journal of Microbiology **895**
Acta Microbiologica Sinica *see* Weishengwu Xuebao **898**
Acta Micropalaeontologica Sinica *see* Weiti Gushengwu Xuebao **898**
Acta Mineralogica - Petrographica *see* Acta Universitatis Szegediensis. Acta Mineralogica - Petrographica **6456**
Acta Mineralogica Sinica *see* Kuangwu Xuebao **6468**
Acta Montana - Rada A (Geodynamics) *see* Acta Geodynamica et Geomaterialia **2722**
Acta Montana - Rada AB (Miscellanea) *see* Acta Research Report **2777**
Acta Montana - Rada B (Fuel, Carbon, Mineral Processing) *see* Acta Geodynamica et Geomaterialia **2722**
● ➤ Acta Montanistica Slovaca (SVK ISSN 1335-1788) **2723**
➤ Acta Morphologica et Anthropologica (BGR ISSN 1311-8773) **650**
Acta Mozartiana (DEU ISSN 0001-6233) **6542**
Acta Musealia *see* Muzeum Jihovychodni Moravy. Acta Musealia **4247**
Acta Musei Apulensis *see* Apulum **4199**
Acta Musei Macedonici Scientiarum Naturalium (MKD ISSN 0583-4988) **650**
➤ Acta Musei Moraviae. Scientiae Biologicae/Moravske Zemske Muzeum. Casopis. Vedy Biologicke (CZE ISSN 1211-8788) **650**
➤ Acta Musei Moraviae. Scientiae Geologicae/Moravske Zemske Muzeum. Casopis. Vedy Geologicke (CZE ISSN 1211-8796) **2723**
➤ Acta Musei Moraviae. Scientiae Sociales/Moravske Zemske Muzeum. Casopis. Vedy Spolecenske (CZE ISSN 0323-0570) **4196**
➤ Acta Musei Moraviae. Supplementum: Folia Ethnographica (CZE ISSN 0862-1209) **322**
Acta Musei Moraviae. Supplementum: Folia Mendeliana (CZE ISSN 0085-0748) **861**
Acta Musei Moraviae. Supplementum: Folia Numismatica (CZE ISSN 0862-1195) **6648**
Acta Musei Nationalis Pragae. Series A: Historia *see* Narodni Muzeum v Praze. Sbornik. Rada A: Historie **6533**
Acta Musei Nationalis Pragae. Series B: Historia Naturalis *see* Narodni Muzeum v Praze. Sbornik. Rada B: Prirodni Vedy **6533**
Acta Musei Nationalis Pragae. Series C: Historia Litterarum *see* Narodni Muzeum v Praze. Sbornik. Rada C: Literarni Historie **6533**

Title

9920 ACTA MUSICOLOGICA ULRICH'S PERIODICALS

• ➤ Acta Musicologica (CZE ISSN 1214-5955) **6542**
• ➤ Acta Musicologica (DEU ISSN 0001-6241) **6542**
Acta Musicologica Fennica (FIN ISSN 0587-2448) **6542**
➤ Acta Mycologica (POL ISSN 0001-625X) **772**
➤ Acta Myologica (ITA ISSN 1128-2460) **5775**
➤ Acta Neophilologica (POL ISSN 1509-1619) **5090**
Acta Neophilologica (SVN ISSN 0567-784X) **5090**
• ➤ Acta Neurobiologiae Experimentalis (POL ISSN 0065-1400) **6118**
• ➤ Acta Neurochirurgica (AUT ISSN 0001-6268) **6234**
➤ Acta Neurochirurgica. Supplementum (AUT ISSN 0065-1419) **6118**
➤ Acta Neurologica Belgica (BEL ISSN 0300-9009) **6118**
• Acta Neurologica Colombiana (COL ISSN 0120-8748) **6118**
• ➤ Acta Neurologica Scandinavica (DNK ISSN 0001-6314) **6118**
• ➤ Acta Neurologica Scandinavica. Supplementum (DNK ISSN 0065-1427) **6118**
Acta Neurologica Taiwanica (TWN ISSN 1028-768X) **6118**
• ➤ Acta Neuropathologica (DEU ISSN 0001-6322) **6118**
• ➤ Acta Neuropsychiatrica (DNK ISSN 0924-2708) **6118**
• ➤ Acta Neuropsychologica (POL ISSN 1730-7503) **6119**
• ➤ Acta Numerica (GBR ISSN 0962-4929) **5465**
Acta Numismatica (ESP ISSN 0211-8386) **6648**
Acta Nuntiaturae Gallicae (ITA ISSN 0065-1443) **7782**
Acta Nutrimenta Sinica *see* Yingyang Xuebao **6671**
Acta Obstetrica et Gynaecologica Japonica *see* Nihon Sanka Fujinka Gakkai Zasshi **6000**
• ➤ Acta Obstetricia et Gynecologica Scandinavica (GBR ISSN 0001-6349) **5985**
Acta Oceanografica del Pacifico (ECU ISSN 1010-4402) **2799**
Acta Oceanographica Taiwanica (TWN ISSN 0379-7481) **2799**
• ➤ Acta Oceanologica Sinica (CHN ISSN 0253-505X) **2799**
Acta Odonatologica *see* Tombo **860**
Acta Odontologica Latinoamericana (ARG ISSN 0326-4815) **5833**
• ➤ Acta Odontologica Scandinavica (GBR ISSN 0001-6357) **5833**
• Acta Odontologica Venezolana (VEN ISSN 0001-6365) **5833**
• ➤ Acta Oecologica (FRA ISSN 1146-609X) **650**
• Acta Oeconomica (HUN ISSN 0001-6373) **1056**
• ➤ Acta Oeconomica et Informatica (SVK ISSN 1335-2571) **191**
➤ Acta of Bioengineering and Biomechanics (POL ISSN 1509-409X) **746**
• ➤ Acta Oncologica (GBR ISSN 0284-186X) **6007**
Acta Oncologica Brasileira (BRA ISSN 0100-3127) **6007**
• Acta Oncologica. Supplement (SWE ISSN 1100-1704) **6007**
Acta Onomastica (CZE ISSN 1211-4413) **4196**
• ➤ Acta Ophthalmologica (DNK ISSN 1755-375X) **6037**
Acta Ophthalmologica Scandinavica *see* Acta Ophthalmologica **6037**
Acta Ophthalmologica Scandinavica. Supplementum *see* Acta Ophthalmologica. Supplementum **6037**
• ➤ Acta Ophthalmologica. Supplementum (DNK) **6037**
• Acta Ophthamologica (Online) (DNK ISSN 1755-3768) **6037**
Acta Ophthamologica Scandinavica (Online) *see* Acta Ophthamologica (Online) **6037**
Acta Optica Sinica *see* Guangxue Xuebao **7076**
Acta Ordinis Fratrum Minorum (ITA ISSN 0001-6411) **7782**
† Acta Ordinis Sancti Augustini (ITA ISSN 0001-642X) **8928**
Acta Organologica (DEU ISSN 0567-7874) **6542**
Acta Orientalia *see* Acta Orientalia Academiae Scientiarum Hungaricae **541**
• ➤ Acta Orientalia (NOR ISSN 0001-6438) **541**
• ➤ Acta Orientalia Academiae Scientiarum Hungaricae (HUN ISSN 0001-6446) **541**
➤ Acta Ornithoecologica (DEU ISSN 0233-2914) **901**
• ➤ Acta Ornithologica (POL ISSN 0001-6454) **901**
• Acta Orthopaedica (Online) (GBR ISSN 1745-3682) **6054**
• ➤ Acta Orthopaedica (Print) (GBR ISSN 1745-3674) **6054**
Acta Orthopaedica Belgica (BEL ISSN 1784-407X) **6054**
Acta Orthopaedica Belgica (Bilingual Edition) *see* Acta Orthopaedica Belgica **6054**
Acta Orthopaedica Belgica. Supplementum (BEL ISSN 0772-7623) **6054**
• ➤ Acta Orthopaedica et Traumatologica Turcica (TUR ISSN 1017-995X) **6054**
➤ Acta Orthopaedica Iugoslavica (SRB ISSN 0350-2309) **6054**
Acta Orthopaedica Scandinavica. Supplementum (Online Edition) *see* Acta Orthopaedica. Supplementum (Online Edition) **6054**
Acta Orthopaedica Scandinavica. Supplementum (Print Edition) *see* Acta Orthopaedica. Supplementum (Print Edition) **6054**
• Acta Orthopaedica. Supplementum (Online Edition) (SWE ISSN 1745-3704) **6054**
• Acta Orthopaedica. Supplementum (Print Edition) (SWE ISSN 1745-3690) **6054**
• Acta Ortopedica Brasileira (BRA ISSN 1413-7852) **6054**
• Acta Ortopedica Mexicana (MEX) **6054**
• ➤ Acta Oto-Laryngologica (GBR ISSN 0001-6489) **6076**
• Acta Oto-Laryngologica. Supplement (GBR ISSN 0365-5237) **6076**
Acta Oto-Rhino-Laryngologica Belgica *see* B - E N T **6078**
• Acta Otorhinolaryngologica Italica (ITA ISSN 0392-100X) **6077**
Acta Otorhinolaryngologica Italica. Supplement (ITA ISSN 0393-7976) **6077**
• ➤ Acta Otorrinolaringologica Espanola (ESP ISSN 0001-6519) **6077**
Acta Pacis Westphalicae (DEU ISSN 0065-146X) **4196**
➤ Acta Paedagogica Debrecina (HUN ISSN 0230-6476) **2823**
• ➤ Acta Paediatrica (GBR ISSN 0803-5253) **6086**
† Acta Paediatrica Latina (ITA ISSN 0365-5504) **8928**
Acta Paediatrica. Supplement *see* Acta Paediatrica **6086**
Acta Paediatrica Taiwanica *see* Pediatrics and Neonatology **6102**
➤ Acta Palaeobotanica (POL ISSN 0001-6594) **6722**
Acta Palaeobotanica. Supplementum *see* Acta Palaeobotanica **6722**
• ➤ Acta Palaeontologica Polonica (POL ISSN 0567-7920) **6722**
Acta Palaeontologica Sinica *see* Gushengwu Xuebao **6725**
• ➤ Acta Parasitologica (POL ISSN 1230-2821) **880**
Acta Parasitologica et Medica Entomologica Sinica *see* Jishengchong yu Yixue Kunchong Xuebao **851**
Acta Parasitologica Portuguesa (PRT ISSN 0872-5292) **880**
• ➤ Acta Pathologica Microbiologica et Immunologica Scandinavica (DNK ISSN 0903-4641) **650**
Acta Pathologica, Microbiologica et Immunologica Scandinavica Supplementum *see* A P M I S Supplementum **648**
• ➤ Acta Patristica et Byzantina (ZAF ISSN 1022-6486) **5090**
• Acta Paulista de Enfermagem (BRA ISSN 0103-2100) **5950**
• Acta Pediatrica Costarricense (CRI ISSN 1409-0090) **6087**
• Acta Pediatrica de Mexico (MEX ISSN 0186-2391) **6087**
• ➤ Acta Pediatrica Espanola (ESP ISSN 0001-6640) **6087**
Acta Pediatrica Mediterranea (ITA ISSN 0393-6392) **6087**
Acta Pediatrica Portuguesa (PRT ISSN 0873-9781) **6087**
Acta Pedologica Sinica *see* Turang Xuebao **2717**
➤ Acta Periodica Technologica (SRB ISSN 1450-7188) **8415**
Acta Petrolei Sinica *see* Shiyou Xuebao **6792**
Acta Petrolei Sinica. Petroleum Processing Section *see* Shiyou Xuebao. Shiyou Jiagong **6792**
Acta Petrologica et Mineralogica *see* Yanshi Kuangwuxue Zazhi **6798**
Acta Petrologica Mineralogica et Analytica *see* Yankuang Ceshi **2775**
Acta Petrologica Sinica *see* Yanshi Xuebao **2775**
• ➤ Acta Pharmaceutica (HRV ISSN 1330-0075) **6818**
• Acta Pharmaceutica Hungarica (HUN ISSN 0001-6659) **6818**
• ➤ Acta Pharmaceutica Sciencia (TUR ISSN 1307-2080) **6818**
Acta Pharmaceutica Sinica *see* Yaoxue Xuebao **6886**
Acta Pharmaceutica Turcica *see* Acta Pharmaceutica Sciencia **6818**
• Acta Pharmacologica Sinica (USA ISSN 1671-4083) **6818**
Acta Philologica Fennica *see* Arctos; Acta Philologica Fennica **2230**
• Acta Philosophica (ITA ISSN 1121-2179) **6902**
Acta Philosophica *see* Filozofski Vestnik **6920**
➤ Acta Philosophica Fennica (FIN ISSN 0355-1792) **6902**
Acta Philosophica Gothoburgensia (SWE ISSN 0283-2380) **6902**
• Acta Phlebologica (ITA ISSN 1593-232X) **5933**
Acta Phoniatrica Latina (ITA ISSN 0392-3088) **6235**
Acta Photographica (ITA ISSN 1724-9821) **6963**
Acta Photonica Sinica *see* Guangzi Xuebao **7076**
Acta Physica et Chimica Debrecina *see* Acta Physica et Chimica Debrecina **7003**
Acta Physica et Chimica Debrecina (HUN ISSN 0567-7947) **7003**
Acta Physica Hungarica. A. Heavy Ion Physics *see* European Physical Journal A. Hadrons and Nuclei **7065**
Acta Physica Hungarica. B. Quantum Electronics *see* European Physical Journal A. Hadrons and Nuclei **7065**
➤ Acta Physica Polonica. Series A: General Physics, Physics of Condensed Matter, Optics and Quantum Electronics, Atomic and Molecular Physics, Applied Physics (POL ISSN 0587-4246) **7003**
• ➤ Acta Physica Polonica. Series B: Elementary Particle Physics, Nuclear Physics, Statistical Physics, Theory of Relativity, Field Theory (POL ISSN 0587-4254) **7003**
Acta Physica Sinica *see* Wuli Xuebao **7046**
• ➤ Acta Physica Slovaca (SVK ISSN 0323-0465) **7003**
Acta Physica Universitatis Comenianae (SVK ISSN 0231-889X) **7003**
Acta Physico - Chimica Sinica *see* Wuli Huaxue Xuebao **2142**
† • Acta Physico - Chimica Sinica (NLD ISSN 1872-1508) **8928**
• ➤ Acta Physiologiae Plantarum (DEU ISSN 0137-5881) **773**
• Acta Physiologica (Online) (GBR ISSN 1748-1716) **918**
• ➤ Acta Physiologica (Print) (GBR ISSN 1748-1708) **918**
Acta Physiologica et Pharmacologica Bulgarica (BGR ISSN 0323-9950) **918**
• Acta Physiologica Hungarica (HUN ISSN 0231-424X) **918**
➤ Acta Physiologica Pharmacologica et Therapeutica Latinoamericana (ARG ISSN 0327-6309) **918**
† • Acta Physiologica Scandinavica. Supplementum (GBR ISSN 0302-2994) **8928**
Acta Physiologica Sinica *see* Shengli Xuebao **928**
Acta Phytoecologica Sinica *see* Zhiwu Shengtai Xuebao **824**
➤ Acta Phytogeographica Suecica (SWE ISSN 0084-5914) **773**
• Acta Phytopathologica et Entomologica Hungarica (HUN ISSN 0238-1249) **773**
Acta Phytopathologica Sinica *see* Zhiwu Bingli Xuebao **823**
Acta Phytophylacica Sinica *see* Zhiwu Baohu Xuebao **823**
Acta Phytotaxonomica et Geobotanica (JPN ISSN 1346-7565) **773**
• Acta Poetica (MEX ISSN 0185-3082) **5415**
• ➤ Acta Politica (GBR ISSN 0001-6810) **7101**
➤ Acta Poloniae Historica (POL ISSN 0001-6829) **4196**
➤ Acta Poloniae Pharmaceutica (POL ISSN 0001-6837) **6818**
Acta Poloniae Toxicologica *see* Acta Toxicologica **6818**
➤ Acta Polono-Ruthenica (POL ISSN 1427-549X) **5090**
Acta Polymerica Sinica *see* Gaofenzi Xuebao **2135**
• ➤ Acta Polytechnica (CZE ISSN 1210-2709) **3179**
Acta Polytechnica Scandinavica. C H. Chemical Technology Series (FIN ISSN 1239-0518) **2048**
Acta Polytechnica Scandinavica. E L. Electrical Engineering Series (FIN ISSN 0001-6845) **3294**
Acta Polytechnica Scandinavica. Industrial Management and Business Administration Series (FIN ISSN 1456-9426) **1723**
Acta Polytechnica Scandinavica. M A. Mathematics and Computing Series (FIN ISSN 1456-9418) **3288**
Acta Polytechnica Scandinavica. M E. Mechanical Engineering Series (FIN ISSN 0001-687X) **3372**
Acta Polytechnica Scandinavica. P H. Applied Physics Series (FIN ISSN 0355-2721) **7003**
Acta Praehistorica et Archaeologica (DEU ISSN 0341-1184) **371**
Acta Prataculturae Sinica *see* Caoye Xuebao **783**
• ➤ Acta Protozoologica (POL ISSN 0065-1583) **880**
➤ Acta Psiquiatrica y Psicologica de America Latina (ARG ISSN 0001-6896) **6119**
Acta Psychiatrica, Psychoterapeutica et Etologica Tavrica *see* Tavricheskii Zhurnal Psikhiatrii **6187**
• ➤ Acta Psychiatrica Scandinavica (GBR ISSN 0001-690X) **6119**
• ➤ Acta Psychiatrica Scandinavica. Supplementum (DNK ISSN 0065-1591) **6119**
• ➤ Acta Psychologica (NLD ISSN 0001-6918) **7330**
Acta Psychologica Fennica (FIN ISSN 0515-3115) **7330**
Acta Psychologica Sinica *see* Xinli Xuebao **7415**
• ➤ Acta Radiologica (GBR ISSN 0284-1851) **6192**
Acta Regiae Societatis Humaniorum Litterarum Lundensis (SWE ISSN 0347-5123) **371**
Acta Regiae Societatis Scientiarum et Litterarum Gothoburgensis. Biomedica (SWE ISSN 1101-8429) **650**
Acta Regiae Societatis Scientiarum et Litterarum Gothoburgensis. Botanica (SWE ISSN 0347-4917) **773**
Acta Regiae Societatis Scientiarum et Litterarum Gothoburgensis. Geophysica (SWE ISSN 0072-4815) **2777**
Acta Regiae Societatis Scientiarum et Litterarum Gothoburgensis. Humaniora (SWE ISSN 0072-4823) **4441**
Acta Regiae Societatis Scientiarum et Litterarum Gothoburgensis. Interdisciplinaria (SWE ISSN 0347-4925) **4441**
Acta Regiae Societatis Scientiarum et Litterarum Gothoburgensis. Zoologica (SWE ISSN 0072-4807) **929**
• ➤ Acta Regionalia et Environmentalica (SVK ISSN 1336-5452) **3400**
Acta Rei Cretariae Romanae Fautorum. Supplementa (CHE) **371**
• ➤ Acta Rerum Naturalium (CZE ISSN 1801-5972) **7832**
Acta Rerum Naturalium Musei Nationalis Slovenici Bratislava *see* Slovenske Narodne Muzeum. Zbornik. Prirodne Vedy **705**
➤ Acta Research Report (CZE) **2777**
Acta Reumatologica Portuguesa (PRT ISSN 0303-464X) **6221**
Acta Rhumatologica Belgica (BEL ISSN 0378-9497) **6221**
Acta Romanica (DEU ISSN 0939-8333) **5090**
Acta Romanorum Pontificum (VAT) **7782**
Acta Sagittariana (DEU ISSN 0001-6942) **6542**
Acta Scandinavica Juris Gentium *see* Nordic Journal of International Law **4936**
Acta Scholae Medicinalis Universitatis in Gifu *see* Gifu Daigaku Igakubu Kiyo **5619**
• ➤ Acta Scientarium. Animal Sciences (BRA ISSN 1806-2636) **8790**
Acta Scientia Sinica *see* Science in China. Series C: Life Sciences **703**
Acta Scientia Sinica *see* Science in China. Series B: Chemistry **2080**
▼ • ➤ Acta Scientiae (USA ISSN 1947-7929) **7832**
Acta Scientiae Circumstantiae *see* Huanjing Kexue Xuebao **3437**
• ➤ Acta Scientiae Veterinariae (BRA ISSN 1678-0345) **8790**
• Acta Scientiarum. Agronomy (BRA ISSN 1679-9275) **79**
• ➤ Acta Scientiarum. Biological Sciences (BRA ISSN 1679-9283) **650**
• ➤ Acta Scientiarum. Health Sciences (BRA ISSN 1679-9291) **5567**
Acta Scientiarum. Human and Social Sciences *see* Acta Scientiarum. Language and Culture **7945**
• ➤ Acta Scientiarum. Language and Culture (BRA ISSN 1983-4675) **7945**
Acta Scientiarum Naturalium *see* Hunan Shifan Daxue. Ziran Kexue Xuebao **7863**
Acta Scientiarum Naturalium Universitatis Nankaiensis (Natural Science Edition) *see* Nankai Daxue Xuebao **7886**
Acta Scientiarum Naturalium Universitatis Neimongol *see* Nei Menggu Daxue Xuebao (Ziran Kexue Ban) **7891**
Acta Scientiarum Naturalium Universitatis Pekinensis *see* Beijing Daxue Xuebao (Ziran Kexue Ban) **7839**
Acta Scientiarum Naturalium Universitatis Sunyatseni *see* Zhongshan Daxue Xuebao (Ziran Kexue Ban) **7935**
• ➤ Acta Scientiarum Polonorum. Administratio Locorum/Acta Scientiarum Polonorum. Gospodarka Przestrzenna (POL ISSN 1644-0749) **4402**
• Acta Scientiarum Polonorum. Agricultura (POL ISSN 1644-0625) **79**
• ➤ Acta Scientiarum Polonorum. Architectura (POL ISSN 1644-0633) **427**
• ➤ Acta Scientiarum Polonorum. Biologia (POL ISSN 1644-0641) **650**
• ➤ Acta Scientiarum Polonorum. Biotechnologia (POL ISSN 1644-065X) **755**
Acta Scientiarum Polonorum. Ekonomia *see* Acta Scientiarum Polonorum. Oeconomia **1056**
• ➤ Acta Scientiarum Polonorum. Formatio Circumiectus (POL ISSN 1644-0765) **3400**
• ➤ Acta Scientiarum Polonorum. Geodesia et Descriptio Terrarum/Acta Scientiarum Polonorum. Geodezja i Kartografia (POL ISSN 1644-0668) **3997**
Acta Scientiarum Polonorum. Geodezja i Kartografia *see* Acta Scientiarum Polonorum. Geodesia et Descriptio Terrarum **3997**
Acta Scientiarum Polonorum. Gospodarka Przestrzenna *see* Acta Scientiarum Polonorum. Administratio Locorum **4402**
• ➤ Acta Scientiarum Polonorum. Hortorum Cultus/Acta Scientiarum Polonorum. Ogrodnictwo (POL ISSN 1644-0692) **3721**
Acta Scientiarum Polonorum. Lesnictwo i Drzewnictwo *see* Acta Scientiarum Polonorum. Silvarum Colendarum Ratio et Industria Lignaria **3682**
• ➤ Acta Scientiarum Polonorum. Medicina Veterinaria/Acta Scientiarum Polonorum. Weterynaria (POL ISSN 1644-0676) **8790**
• ➤ Acta Scientiarum Polonorum. Oeconomia/Acta Scientiarum Polonorum. Ekonomia (POL ISSN 1644-0757) **1056**
Acta Scientiarum Polonorum. Ogrodnictwo *see* Acta Scientiarum Polonorum. Hortorum Cultus **3721**
• ➤ Acta Scientiarum Polonorum. Piscaria/Acta Scientiarum Polonorum. Rybactwo (POL ISSN 1644-0706) **3582**
Acta Scientiarum Polonorum. Rybactwo *see* Acta Scientiarum Polonorum. Piscaria **3582**
• ➤ Acta Scientiarum Polonorum. Silvarum Colendarum Ratio et Industria Lignaria/Acta Scientiarum Polonorum. Lesnictwo i Drzewnictwo (POL ISSN 1644-0722) **3682**
• ➤ Acta Scientiarum Polonorum. Technica Agraria (POL ISSN 1644-0684) **209**

• ➤ Acta Scientiarum Polonorum. Technologia Alimentaria/Acta Scientiarum Polonorum. Technologia Zywnosci i Zywienia (POL ISSN 1644-0730) **3625**
Acta Scientiarum Polonorum. Technologia Zywnosci i Zywienia *see* Acta Scientiarum Polonorum. Technologia Alimentaria **3625**
Acta Scientiarum Polonorum. Weterynaria *see* Acta Scientiarum Polonorum. Medicina Veterinaria **8790**
• Acta Scientiarum Polonorum. Zootechnica (POL ISSN 1644-0714) **277**
• ➤ Acta Scientiarum. Technology (BRA ISSN 1806-2563) **8415**
Acta Sedimentologica Sinica *see* Chenji Xuebao **2728**
Acta Seismologica Sinica *see* Dizhen Xuebao **2780**
• ➤ Acta Seismologica Sinica (CHN ISSN 1000-9116) **2777**
Acta Semiotica et Linguistica (BRA ISSN 0102-4264) **5090**
Acta Silesiaca *see* Slezsky Sbornik **8132**
Acta Sinica Quantum Optica *see* Liangzi Guangxue Xuebao **7025**
• Acta Slavica Iaponica (JPN ISSN 0288-3503) **3515**
➤ Acta Societatis Botanicorum Poloniae/Polish Journal of Botany (POL ISSN 0001-6977) **773**
Acta Societatis Fennicae Iuris Gentium. A (FIN ISSN 0788-4397) **4916**
Acta Societatis Fennicae Iuris Gentium. B (FIN ISSN 0787-0221) **4916**
Acta Societatis Fennicae Iuris Gentium. C (FIN ISSN 1235-2683) **4916**
Acta Societatis Historicae Ouluensis *see* Scripta Historica **4263**
• Acta Societatis Martensis (EST ISSN 1736-3918) **7202**
➤ Acta Societatis Zoologicae Bohemicae (CZE ISSN 1211-376X) **929**
• ➤ Acta Sociologica (GBR ISSN 0001-6993) **8085**
Acta Sociologica (MEX ISSN 0186-6028) **8085**
• ➤ Acta Stomatologica Croatica (HRV ISSN 0001-7019) **5833**
• ➤ Acta Stomatologica Naissi (SRB ISSN 0352-5252) **5833**
➤ Acta Stomatologica Naissi. Supplement (SRB ISSN 0354-7957) **5833**
Acta Structilia (ZAF ISSN 1023-0564) **427**
Acta Studentica (AUT) **4129**
➤ Acta Sueco-Polonica (SWE ISSN 1104-3431) **3515**
Acta Sueco-Polonica. Bokserie *see* Acta Sueco-Polonica **3515**
Acta Sumerologica (JPN ISSN 0387-8082) **5090**
➤ Acta Technica C S A V (Czech Science Advanced Views) (CZE ISSN 0001-7043) **3179**
➤ Acta Technologica Agriculturae (SVK ISSN 1335-2555) **79**
Acta Terramaris (VEN ISSN 0798-118X) **930**
Acta Theologica (NOR ISSN 1502-010X) **7620**
• ➤ Acta Theologica (ZAF ISSN 1015-8758) **7620**
• ➤ Acta Theriologica (POL ISSN 0001-7051) **930**
Acta Theriologica Sinica *see* Shoulei Xuebao **963**
Acta Toxicologica (POL ISSN 1731-6383) **6818**
• Acta Toxicologica Argentina (ARG ISSN 0327-9286) **3493**
• ➤ Acta Tropica (NLD ISSN 0001-706X) **5808**
Acta Tropica. Supplementum *see* Acta Tropica **5808**
▼ • ➤ Acta Turcica (TUR ISSN 1308-8351) **541**
Acta Turistica (HRV ISSN 0353-4316) **8680**
• ➤ Acta Universitaria (MEX ISSN 0188-6266) **7832**
Acta Universitatis Agriculturae et Silviculturae Mendelianae Brunensis/Mendelova Zemedelska a Lesnicka Univerzita v Brne. Sbornik (CZE ISSN 1211-8516) **79**
• Acta Universitatis Agriculturae Sueciae (SWE ISSN 1652-6880) **79**
Acta Universitatis Agriculturae Sueciae. Agraria *see* Acta Universitatis Agriculturae Sueciae **79**
Acta Universitatis Agriculturae Sueciae. Silvestria *see* Acta Universitatis Agriculturae Sueciae **79**
Acta Universitatis Agriculturae Sueciae. Veterinaria *see* Acta Universitatis Agriculturae Sueciae **79**
Acta Universitatis Apulensis. Mathematics - Informatics (ROM ISSN 1582-5329) **5465**
Acta Universitatis Carolinae. Biologica (CZE ISSN 0001-7124) **650**
➤ Acta Universitatis Carolinae. Environmentalica (CZE ISSN 0862-6529) **3400**
➤ Acta Universitatis Carolinae. Geographica (CZE ISSN 0300-5402) **3997**
Acta Universitatis Carolinae. Geologica (CZE ISSN 0001-7132) **2723**
Acta Universitatis Carolinae. Historia Universitatis Carolinas Pragensis (CZE ISSN 0323-0562) **4196**
➤ Acta Universitatis Carolinae. Kinanthropologica (CZE ISSN 1212-1428) **6228**
Acta Universitatis Carolinae. Mathematica et Physica (CZE ISSN 0001-7140) **5465**
Acta Universitatis Carolinae. Medica (CZE ISSN 0001-7116) **5567**
➤ Acta Universitatis Carolinae. Medica. Monographia (CZE ISSN 0567-8250) **5567**
Acta Universitatis Carolinae Oeconomica *see* A U C O Czech Economic Review **1056**
Acta Universitatis Carolinae Oeconomicacz Czech Economic Review *see* A U C O Czech Economic Review **1056**
Acta Universitatis Carolinae. Philosophica et Historica (CZE ISSN 0567-8293) **4196**
Acta Universitatis Carolinae: Philosophica et Historica. Studia Sociologica *see* Studia Sociologica **8141**
Acta Universitatis Danubius. Juridica *see* Universitas Danubius. Acta. Juridica **4802**
Acta Universitatis de Attila Jozsef Nominatae. Acta Biologica *see* Acta Biologica Szegediensis **649**
Acta Universitatis Debreceniensis. Series Historica (HUN ISSN 1786-9846) **4196**
Acta Universitatis Gothoburgensis (SWE ISSN 0346-7740) **4441**
Acta Universitatis Lappeenrantaensis (FIN ISSN 1456-4491) **3179**
Acta Universitatis Lodziensis: Folia Archaeologica (POL ISSN 0208-6034) **371**
Acta Universitatis Lodziensis: Folia Biochimica et Biophysica (POL ISSN 0208-614X) **721**
Acta Universitatis Lodziensis: Folia Botanica (POL ISSN 0208-6174) **773**
Acta Universitatis Lodziensis: Folia Chimica (POL ISSN 0208-6182) **2048**
Acta Universitatis Lodziensis: Folia Ethnologica (POL ISSN 0208-6042) **322**
Acta Universitatis Lodziensis: Folia Geographica (POL ISSN 0208-6123) **3997**
Acta Universitatis Lodziensis: Folia Historica (POL ISSN 0208-6050) **4129**
Acta Universitatis Lodziensis: Folia Iuridica (POL ISSN 0208-6069) **4609**
Acta Universitatis Lodziensis: Folia Librorum (POL ISSN 0860-7435) **4441**
Acta Universitatis Lodziensis: Folia Limnologica (POL ISSN 0208-6158) **2792**
Acta Universitatis Lodziensis: Folia Linguistica (POL ISSN 0208-6077) **5090**
Acta Universitatis Lodziensis: Folia Litteraria Anglica (POL ISSN 1427-9673) **5249**
Acta Universitatis Lodziensis: Folia Litteraria Germanica (POL ISSN 1427-9665) **5249**
Acta Universitatis Lodziensis: Folia Litteraria Polonica (POL ISSN 1505-9057) **5249**
Acta Universitatis Lodziensis: Folia Litteraria Romanica (POL ISSN 1505-9065) **5249**
Acta Universitatis Lodziensis: Folia Litteraria Rossica (POL ISSN 1427-9681) **5249**
Acta Universitatis Lodziensis: Folia Mathematica (POL ISSN 0208-6204) **5465**
Acta Universitatis Lodziensis: Folia Oeconomica (POL ISSN 0208-6018) **1056**
Acta Universitatis Lodziensis: Folia Paedagogica (POL ISSN 1427-9703) **2823**
Acta Universitatis Lodziensis: Folia Philosophica (POL ISSN 0208-6107) **6902**
Acta Universitatis Lodziensis: Folia Physiologica Cytologica et Genetica (POL ISSN 0860-3111) **773**
Acta Universitatis Lodziensis: Folia Psychologica (POL ISSN 1427-969X) **7330**
Acta Universitatis Lodziensis: Folia Scientiae Artium et Litterarum (POL ISSN 0860-7443) **8464**
Acta Universitatis Lodziensis: Folia Sociologica (POL ISSN 0208-600X) **8085**
Acta Universitatis Lodziensis: Folia Sozologica (POL ISSN 0208-6131) **2601**
Acta Universitatis Lodziensis: Folia Zoologica (POL ISSN 1230-0527) **930**
Acta Universitatis Lodziensis: Turyzm (POL ISSN 0860-1119) **8680**
Acta Universitatis Lundensis. Sectio 1. Theologica, Juridica, Humaniora (SWE ISSN 0459-9969) **7620**
Acta Universitatis Matthiae Belii. Natural Science Series. Series Mathematics (SVK) **5465**
Acta Universitatis Medicinalis Anhui *see* Anhui Yike Daxue Xuebao **5574**
Acta Universitatis Medicinalis Nanjing *see* Nanjing Yike Daxue Xuebao (Ziran Kexue Ban) **5682**
Acta Universitatis Medicinalis Nanjing (Social Science) *see* Nanjing Yike Daxue Xuebao (Shehui Kexue Ban) **7987**
Acta Universitatis Nicolai Copernici. Biologia (POL ISSN 0208-4449) **650**
Acta Universitatis Nicolai Copernici. Geografia (POL ISSN 0208-5291) **3997**
Acta Universitatis Nicolai Copernici. Humanities and Social Studies. English Studies/Acta Universitatis Nicolai Copernici. Nauki Humanistyczno-Spoleczne. Filologia Angielska (POL ISSN 0860-7265) **5090**
Acta Universitatis Nicolai Copernici. Nauki Humanistyczno-Spoleczne. Archeologia (POL ISSN 0137-6616) **371**
Acta Universitatis Nicolai Copernici. Nauki Humanistyczno-Spoleczne. Ekonomia (POL ISSN 0208-5305) **1056**
Acta Universitatis Nicolai Copernici. Nauki Humanistyczno-Spoleczne. Filologia Angielska *see* Acta Universitatis Nicolai Copernici. Humanities and Social Studies. English Studies **5090**
Acta Universitatis Nicolai Copernici. Nauki Humanistyczno-Spoleczne. Filologia Germanska (POL ISSN 0208-5259) **5090**
Acta Universitatis Nicolai Copernici. Nauki Humanistyczno-Spoleczne. Filologia Polska (POL ISSN 0208-5321) **5090**
Acta Universitatis Nicolai Copernici. Nauki Humanistyczno-Spoleczne. Pedagogika (POL ISSN 0208-5313) **2823**
Acta Universitatis Nicolai Copernici. Nauki Humanistyczno-Spoleczne. Socjologia Wychowania (POL ISSN 0208-5267) **2824**
Acta Universitatis Nicolai Copernici. Nauki Humanistyczno-Spoleczne. Studia Rosjoznawcze (POL ISSN 1232-8847) **5090**
Acta Universitatis Nicolai Copernici. Nauki Humanistyczno-Spoleczne. Zabytkoznawstwo i Konserwatorstwo (POL ISSN 0208-533X) **463**
➤ Acta Universitatis Nicolai Copernici. Prace Limnologiczne/Nicolaus Copernicus University. Limnological Papers (POL ISSN 0208-5348) **2792**
• Acta Universitatis Oeconomicae Helsingiensis. A/Helsingin Kauppakorkeakoulu. Julkaisusarja A. Vaitoskirjat (FIN ISSN 1237-556X) **1056**
Acta Universitatis Orebroensis (SWE ISSN 1653-4131) **2965**
• Acta Universitatis Ouluensis. Series A. Scientiae Rerum Naturalium (FIN ISSN 0355-3191) **7832**
• Acta Universitatis Ouluensis. Series B. Humaniora (FIN ISSN 0355-3205) **4441**
• Acta Universitatis Ouluensis. Series C. Technica (FIN ISSN 0355-3213) **8415**
• ➤ Acta Universitatis Ouluensis. Series D. Medica (FIN ISSN 0355-3221) **5567**
• Acta Universitatis Ouluensis. Series E. Scientiae Rerum Socialium (FIN ISSN 0355-323X) **7102**
• Acta Universitatis Ouluensis. Series F. Scripta Academica (FIN ISSN 0781-1306) **3838**
• Acta Universitatis Ouluensis. Series G. Oeconomica (FIN ISSN 1455-2647) **1056**
Acta Universitatis Palackianae Olomucensis Facultas Philosophica. Historica *see* Sbornik Praci Historickych **4261**
➤ Acta Universitatis Palackianae Olomucensis. Facultas Rerum Naturalium. Biologica (CZE ISSN 0231-8121) **650**
Acta Universitatis Palackianae Olomucensis. Facultas Rerum Naturalium. Chemica (CZE ISSN 0232-0061) **2048**
➤ Acta Universitatis Palackianae Olomucensis. Facultas Rerum Naturalium. Geographica (CZE ISSN 1212-2157) **3997**
➤ Acta Universitatis Palackianae Olomucensis. Facultas Rerum Naturalium. Geologica (CZE ISSN 1212-2025) **2723**
➤ Acta Universitatis Palackianae Olomucensis. Facultas Rerum Naturalium. Mathematica (CZE ISSN 0231-9721) **5465**
➤ Acta Universitatis Palackianae Olomucensis. Facultas Rerum Naturalium. Physica (CZE ISSN 0231-9772) **7003**
Acta Universitatis Palackianae Olomucensis Facultatis Medicae. Biomedical Papers *see* Palacky University in Olomouc. Medical Faculty. Biomedical Papers **5692**
• ➤ Acta Universitatis Palackianae Olomucensis. Gymnica (CZE ISSN 1212-1185) **5567**
Acta Universitatis Scodvensis (DEU ISSN 0948-3403) **5090**
Acta Universitatis Stockholmiensis (SWE ISSN 0346-6418) **4441**
Acta Universitatis Szagediensis. Opuscula Byzantina (HUN ISSN 0139-2751) **541**
Acta Universitatis Szegediensis. Acta Antiqua et Archaeologica (HUN ISSN 0567-7246) **2229**
Acta Universitatis Szegediensis: Acta Biologica *see* Acta Biologica Szegediensis **649**
Acta Universitatis Szegediensis: Acta Climatologica et Chorologica *see* Acta Climatologica **6345**
Acta Universitatis Szegediensis. Acta Hispanica (HUN ISSN 1416-7263) **5249**
Acta Universitatis Szegediensis. Acta Historiae Litterarum Hungaricarum (HUN ISSN 0586-3708) **5249**
Acta Universitatis Szegediensis. Acta Historica (HUN ISSN 0324-6965) **4196**
Acta Universitatis Szegediensis. Acta Iuridica et Politica (HUN ISSN 0563-0606) **4609**
Acta Universitatis Szegediensis. Acta Mineralogica - Petrographica (HUN ISSN 0365-8066) **6456**
Acta Universitatis Szegediensis. Acta Oeconomica (HUN ISSN 1219-6762) **1056**
Acta Universitatis Szegediensis. Acta Romanica (HUN ISSN 0567-8099) **5090**
➤ Acta Universitatis Szegediensis. Acta Scientiarum Mathematicarum (HUN ISSN 0001-6969) **5465**
Acta Universitatis Szegediensis. Dissertationes Slavicae. Sectio Linguistica (HUN ISSN 0237-9554) **5090**
Acta Universitatis Szegediensis. Papers in English and American Studies (HUN ISSN 0230-2780) **5090**
Acta Universitatis Szegediensis. Sectio Ethnographica et Linguistica/Neprajz es Nyelvtudomany (HUN ISSN 0209-9543) **5090**
Acta Universitatis Szegediensis. Sectio Linguistica *see* Nyelvtudomany **5157**
Acta Universitatis Tamperensis (FIN ISSN 1455-1616) **7832**
➤ Acta Universitatis Upsaliensis (SWE ISSN 0346-5462) **7832**
Acta Universitatis Wratislaviensis. Anglica Wratislaviensia (POL ISSN 0301-7966) **5090**
Acta Universitatis Wratislaviensis. Antiquitas (POL ISSN 0524-4463) **2229**
Acta Universitatis Wratislaviensis. Bibliotekoznawstwo (POL ISSN 0524-4471) **4987**
Acta Universitatis Wratislaviensis. Classica Wratislaviensia (POL ISSN 0578-4387) **2229**
Acta Universitatis Wratislaviensis. Ekonomia (POL) **1056**
Acta Universitatis Wratislaviensis. Ethnologica (POL) **323**
Acta Universitatis Wratislaviensis. Filozofia (POL) **6902**
Acta Universitatis Wratislaviensis. Germanica Wratislaviensia (POL ISSN 0435-5865) **5090**
Acta Universitatis Wratislaviensis. Historia (POL ISSN 0524-4498) **4129**
Acta Universitatis Wratislaviensis. Historia Sztuki (POL ISSN 0860-4746) **464**
Acta Universitatis Wratislaviensis. Literatura i Kultura Popularna (POL ISSN 0867-7441) **5249**
Acta Universitatis Wratislaviensis. Logika (POL) **6902**
Acta Universitatis Wratislaviensis. Neerlandica Wratislaviensia (POL ISSN 0860-0716) **5090**
Acta Universitatis Wratislaviensis. Niemcoznawstwo (POL ISSN 0239-6661) **4196**
Acta Universitatis Wratislaviensis. Politologia (POL ISSN 0867-7409) **7102**
Acta Universitatis Wratislaviensis. Prace Botaniczne (POL ISSN 0524-451X) **773**
Acta Universitatis Wratislaviensis. Prace Geologiczno - Mineralogiczne (POL ISSN 0525-4132) **2723**
Acta Universitatis Wratislaviensis. Prace Kulturoznawcze (POL ISSN 0860-6668) **4441**
Acta Universitatis Wratislaviensis. Prace Literackie (POL ISSN 0079-4767) **5249**
Acta Universitatis Wratislaviensis. Prace Pedagogiczne (POL ISSN 0137-1096) **2824**
Acta Universitatis Wratislaviensis. Prace Psychologiczne (POL ISSN 0137-110X) **7330**
Acta Universitatis Wratislaviensis. Prace Zoologiczne (POL ISSN 0554-9051) **930**
Acta Universitatis Wratislaviensis. Prawo (POL ISSN 0524-4544) **4609**
Acta Universitatis Wratislaviensis. Przeglad Prawa i Administracji (POL ISSN 0137-1134) **7418**
Acta Universitatis Wratislaviensis. Romanica Wratislaviensia (POL ISSN 0557-2665) **5091**
Acta Universitatis Wratislaviensis. Slavica Wratislaviensia (POL ISSN 0137-1150) **5091**
Acta Universitatis Wratislaviensis. Socjologia (POL) **8085**
Acta Universitatis Wratislaviensis. Studia Antropologiczne (POL ISSN 1425-8064) **323**
Acta Universitatis Wratislaviensis. Studia Archeologiczne (POL ISSN 0081-6302) **371**
Acta Universitatis Wratislaviensis. Studia Geograficzne (POL ISSN 0591-2776) **3997**
Acta Universitatis Wratislaviensis. Studia i Materialy z Dziejow Uniwersytetu Wroclawskiego (POL ISSN 0866-9279) **2965**
Acta Universitatis Wratislaviensis. Studia Linguistica (POL ISSN 0137-1169) **5091**
Acta Universitatis Wratislaviensis. Studia nad Faszyzmem i Zbrodniami Hitlerowskimi (POL ISSN 0137-1126) **4196**
Acta Universitatis Wratislaviensis. Wroclawskie Studia Wschodnie (POL ISSN 1429-4168) **4196**
Acta Urologica Japonica *see* Hinyokika Kiyo **6268**
➤ Acta Veterinaria (SRB ISSN 0567-8315) **8790**
• ➤ Acta Veterinaria Brno (CZE ISSN 0001-7213) **8790**
Acta Veterinaria et Zootechnica Sinica *see* Xumu Shouyi Xuebao **8815**
• ➤ Acta Veterinaria Hungarica (HUN ISSN 0236-6290) **8790**
• Acta Veterinaria Scandinavica (Online) (GBR ISSN 1751-0147) **8790**
† • ➤ Acta Veterinaria Scandinavica (Print) (DNK ISSN 0044-605X) **8928**
Acta Veterinaria Scandinavica. Supplementum (DNK ISSN 0065-1699) **8790**
➤ Acta Victoriana (CAN ISSN 0700-8406) **5249**
• ➤ Acta Virologica (SVK ISSN 0001-723X) **880**
• Acta Vulcanologica (ITA ISSN 1121-9114) **2777**
• Acta Vulnologica (ITA ISSN 1721-2596) **5919**
Acta Wasaensia (FIN ISSN 0355-2667) **1535**
Acta Wasaensia. Administrative Science/Acta Wasaensia. Hallintotiede (FIN ISSN 1235-7863) **7418**
Acta Wasaensia. Aluetiede/Acta Wasaensia. Regional Studies (FIN ISSN 1458-7866) **1305**
Acta Wasaensia. Business Administration (FIN ISSN 1235-7871) **1723**
Acta Wasaensia. Economics (FIN ISSN 1235-788X) **1056**
Acta. Wasaensia. Geography *see* Acta Wasaensia. Aluetiede **1305**
Acta Wasaensia. Hallintotiede *see* Acta Wasaensia. Administrative Science **7418**
Acta Wasaensia. Industrial Management (FIN ISSN 1456-3738) **1879**
Acta Wasaensia. Kielitiede/Acta Wasaensia. Philologie (FIN ISSN 1235-791X) **5091**
Acta Wasaensia. Kirjallisuuden- ja Kulttuurintutkimus/Acta Wasaensia. Literatur- und Kulturstudien, Germanistik (FIN ISSN 1795-7494) **5249**
Acta Wasaensia. Literatur- und Kulturstudien, Germanistik *see* Acta Wasaensia. Kirjallisuuden-ja Kulttuurintutkimus **5249**
Acta Wasaensia. Mathematics (FIN ISSN 1235-7928) **5465**
Acta Wasaensia. Philologie *see* Acta Wasaensia. Kielitiede **5091**
Acta Wasaensia. Raettsvetenskap (FIN ISSN 1457-7992) **4846**

Title

Acta Wasaensia. Regional Studies *see* Acta Wasaensia. Aluetiede **1305**
Acta Wasaensia. Sosiaali- ja Terveyshallinto *see* Acta Wasaensia. Sosiaali- ja Terveyshallintotiede **8022**
• Acta Wasaensia. Sosiaali- ja Terveyshallintotiede (FIN ISSN 1796-9352) **8022**
Acta Wasaensia. Statistics (FIN ISSN 1235-7936) **8343**
Acta Wexionensia (SWE ISSN 1404-4307) **7832**
• ➤ Acta Zoologica (GBR ISSN 0001-7272) **930**
Acta Zoologica Bulgarica (BGR ISSN 0324-0770) **930**
• ➤ Acta Zoologica Cracoviensia (POL ISSN 0065-1710) **930**
• ➤ Acta Zoologica Fennica (FIN ISSN 0001-7299) **930**
Acta Zoologica Lilloana (ARG ISSN 0065-1729) **930**
• ➤ Acta Zoologica Lituanica (LTU ISSN 1392-1657) **650**
• Acta Zoologica Mexicana (MEX ISSN 0065-1737) **930**
• ➤ Acta Zoologica Online (GBR ISSN 1463-6395) **930**
➤ Acta Zoologica Taiwanica/Dongwu Xuekan (TWN ISSN 1019-5858) **930**
Acta Zootaxonomica Sinica *see* Dongwu Fenlei Xuebao **940**
Actas Americanas (CHL) **4441**
Actas Cardiovasculares (ARG) **5775**
Actas Colombinas (CHL ISSN 0716-8098) **4281**
Actas de Derecho Industrial y Derecho de Autor (ESP ISSN 1139-3289) **4854**
Actas de Dermatologia y Dermatopatologia (MEX) **5870**
• Actas de Fisiologia (URY ISSN 0797-7883) **918**
• Actas de la Academia Luventicus/Luventicus Academy. Transactions (ARG ISSN 1666-7573) **7832**
Actas de Lengua y Literatura Mapuche (CHL ISSN 0716-6869) **5091**
Actas del Cabildo Colonial de Guayaquil (ECU) **4281**
• ➤ Actas Dermo-Sifiliograficas (ESP ISSN 0001-7310) **5871**
• ➤ Actas Espanolas de Psiquiatria (ESP ISSN 1139-9287) **6119**
Actas Espanolas de Psiquiatria. Monografias (ESP ISSN 1575-071X) **6119**
Actas - Jornadas Investigaciones en la Facultad de Ciencias Economicas y Estadistica *see* Facultad de Ciencias Economicas y Estadisticas. Actas de las Jornadas Anuales Investigaciones **8369**
Actas Pedagogicas (COL ISSN 0123-2088) **2824**
• Actas Urologicas Espanolas (ESP ISSN 0210-4806) **6264**
Acteens Accessories (USA) **7744**
Actes (FRA ISSN 0769-0266) **8489**
Actes de Colloques - IFREMER *see* Institut Francais de Recherche pour l'Exploitation de la Mer. Actes de Colloques **2807**
• ➤ Actes de la Recherche en Sciences Sociales (FRA ISSN 0335-5322) **7945**
• ➤ Les Actes de Lecture (FRA ISSN 0758-1475) **5249**
Actes de l'Histoire de l'Immigration (Online Edition) *see* Actes de l'Histoire de l'Immigration (Print Edition) **7276**
➤ Actes de l'Histoire de l'Immigration (Print Edition) (FRA ISSN 1630-7356) **7276**
• ➤ Actes des Colloques Insectes Sociaux (FRA ISSN 0257-0076) **837**
Actes du G A R S *see* Recherches sur le Francais Parle **5165**
Actes et Documents de la Premiere a la Septieme Session (1893-1951) *see* Conference de la Haye de Droit International Prive. Actes et Documents **4922**
Actes et Documents Relatifs a l'Organisation de la Cour - Cour Internationale de Justice *see* Cour Internationale de Justice. Actes et Documents **4922**
▼ Actes Pratiques et Strategie Patrimoniale (FRA ISSN 1956-3477) **4900**
Acteurs de la Societe (FRA ISSN 1950-0610) **8085**
Acteurs Publics (FRA ISSN 1765-2022) **7102**
Actexpress (CAN) **6277**
Acti - Espana (GBR ISSN 1476-1424) **3011**
Actif (CAN ISSN 0840-657X) **3805**
Actif's (FRA ISSN 1951-8285) **6654**
Actinomycetologica *see* Nihon Hosenkin Gakkaishi **894**
Action (Cincinnati) (USA) **8022**
• Action (Clearwater) (USA) **3050**
• Action (Elwood) (AUS) **317**
Action (New York, 1977) *see* Scholastic Action **3079**
Action (Ottawa)/Action - Bulletin du Comite National Canadien (CAN) **3400**
† • Action (Potts Point) (AUS) **8928**
Action (Sydney) (AUS) **3123**
Action Abroad *see* The Humanitarian **8045**
† Action Africa (GBR ISSN 1033-1913) **8928**
• Action Against Infection (CHE) **5808**
Action Agricole de Tarn et Garonne (FRA ISSN 0338-182X) **79**
Action Agricole de Touraine (FRA ISSN 0767-8711) **79**
Action Agricole Picarde (FRA ISSN 0750-862X) **79**
Action Alert (New York) (USA) **317**
Action Alert (San Francisco) (USA ISSN 1081-5120) **3400**
Action Alert (Washington, 1980) (USA ISSN 1053-4083) **4609**
Action Asia (HKG ISSN 1019-4630) **8680**
Action Asia (Singapore Edition) *see* Action Asia **8680**
• Action Auto Moto (FRA ISSN 1762-9314) **8555**
Action - Bulletin du Comite National Canadien *see* Action (Ottawa) **3400**
Action Canada - France (CAN ISSN 0318-7306) **1394**
Action Canada Magazine (CAN) **8156**
Action Commerciale (FRA ISSN 0752-5192) **1056**
Action Contre la Marche au Ralenti (CAN ISSN 1911-1746) **3400**
• ➤ Action, Criticism & Theory for Music Education (USA ISSN 1545-4517) **6542**
L'Action de l'Union Europeene en Matiere d'Environnement *see* European Union Activities on Environmental Matters **3431**
L'Action du Mercredi (CAN) **3805**
Action Era Vehicle (USA ISSN 0044-6092) **362**
Action Figure News & Toy Review *see* Lee's Toy Review **4060**
▼ • Action for Children and Youth Aotearoa Incorporated. Working Paper (NZL ISSN 1177-7656) **4906**
• Action for Libraries (USA ISSN 0363-0250) **4987**
L'Action Francaise 2000 (FRA) **7102**
Action Grecque Canadienne *see* Greek Canadian Action - Drassis **3535**
Action Hero (GBR) **2175**
Action Holidays (GBR ISSN 0962-1865) **8681**
• Action in Teacher Education (USA ISSN 0162-6620) **2824**
Action Juridique (Paris, 1978) (FRA ISSN 0181-2874) **4589**
Action Kit for Hospital Law (USA) **4609**
Action Kit for Hospital Trustees (USA) **4087**
• ➤ Action Learning (GBR ISSN 1476-7333) **2824**
• Action Learning News (GBR ISSN 1750-4384) **3011**
Action Line (Annapolis) (USA ISSN 0001-7442) **2965**
Action Line (Darien) *see* Act'ionLine **317**
Action Line (Sacramento) (USA ISSN 1524-105X) **2643**
Action-Line (Tallahassee) (USA) **4900**
• Action Magazine (DNK ISSN 1903-4954) **7219**
Action Magazine (USA ISSN 1949-3436) **4116**
Action Martial Arts (CAN) **6981**
• ➤ Action Nationale (CAN ISSN 0001-7469) **7102**
• Action Newsletter (GBR ISSN 0143-3253) **2311**
• Action Nouvelles (CAN ISSN 1482-0455) **2689**
Action Now!/A l'Action (CAN ISSN 1187-5305) **8850**
Action on Poverty Today (IRL ISSN 1649-3796) **8023**
Action on Smoking & Health Smoking and Health Review *see* A S H Smoking and Health Review **4608**
Action Parents (CAN ISSN 1712-7637) **2142**
• Action Plan. Implementation of Section 41 of the Official Languages Act (CAN ISSN 1713-5036) **2311**
• Action Plus (POL ISSN 1429-964X) **2474**
Action Poetique (FRA ISSN 0001-7477) **5415**
Action Poetique. Supplement *see* Action Poetique **5415**
Action Populaire (BEN ISSN 0044-6106) **7102**
▼ Action Publique/Public Action (BEL) **7418**
Action Pursuit Games (USA ISSN 0893-9489) **8156**
Action - Reflexion - Culture (BFA) **2824**
Action Report (USA) **7219**
• ➤ Action Research (GBR ISSN 1476-7503) **5567**
† • ➤ Action Research International (AUS ISSN 1445-6125) **8928**
Action Sociale (CHE ISSN 0001-7507) **7102**
Action Sociale *see* C A N A R E P Infos Retraites **1857**
Action Sociale et Sante (FRA ISSN 0335-136X) **1661**
Action T V (GBR ISSN 1752-6604) **2374**
• Action Transmittal (USA ISSN 1938-8977) **2142**
Action Universitaire (FRA ISSN 0065-177X) **2965**
L'Action Week-End (CAN) **3805**
Actiongram (USA) **79**
Act'ionLine (USA ISSN 1072-2068) **317**
Actionlines Magazine (USA) **7487**
Actions for Threatened People (DEU ISSN 0930-3251) **7202**
• Actions of the Board, its Staff, and the Federal Reserve Banks; Applications and Reports Received (USA) **1305**
Actions Sante (FRA ISSN 0298-5268) **5567**
Actions Sociales (FRA ISSN 1269-8377) **8023**
Activa *see* Activa Design Management **427**
Activa (PRT ISSN 0874-0453) **8850**
Activa Design Management (ITA ISSN 1591-4135) **427**
Activate (GBR ISSN 1367-207X) **3400**
Activate *see* Actv8 **2175**
Activate! (USA ISSN 1931-4736) **6542**
Activate (Print) *see* eCatalyst **24**
Activate For Animals (USA) **317**
Activate Quarterly *see* eCatalyst **24**
Active Adult (CAN ISSN 1483-569X) **4038**
• Active & Intelligent Pack News (GBR ISSN 1478-7059) **6708**
• ➤ Active and Passive Electronic Components (USA ISSN 0882-7516) **3294**
• ACTive Archives (AUS ISSN 1832-2158) **4987**
† Active Communities Update (NZL ISSN 1177-4169) **8928**
• Active Home (GBR ISSN 1746-9503) **3089**
• ➤ Active Learning in Higher Education (GBR ISSN 1469-7874) **2965**
Active Life (GBR ISSN 0965-8289) **4975**
• Active Living (CAN ISSN 1206-0941) **4063**
Active Living *see* Y Life **7000**
Active Living Kansas City *see* Y Life Kansas City **7000**
Active Living Nashville *see* Y Life Nashville **7000**
Active Magazine (GBR) **8843**
Active Single's Life (USA ISSN 1553-7730) **7942**
Active Sports and Bodywear (GBR ISSN 1752-0932) **2245**
• Active State (AUS ISSN 1445-2723) **8156**
Active Times *see* The Best Times **4041**
• Active Trader (USA ISSN 1542-9466) **1609**
Active Travel *see* Active Travel News **8253**
• Active Travel Cymru News (GBR ISSN 1751-6943) **8253**
• Active Travel News (GBR ISSN 1745-0438) **8253**
Active Voice (CAN ISSN 1182-3968) **7550**
Active Voice (USA ISSN 1074-2360) **7102**
† Active Woman Canada (CAN ISSN 1705-2688) **8928**
Activeto (FRA ISSN 1630-4101) **8790**
• Actividad de Fondos de Inversion (URY ISSN 1688-0706) **1609**
• Actividad Dietetica (ESP ISSN 1138-0322) **6654**
Actividad Minera (ARG ISSN 0326-6672) **6456**
The Activist (CAN ISSN 1201-7892) **7202**
• Activist (NLD ISSN 1871-5885) **8023**
➤ Activitas Nervosa Superior (CZE ISSN 1802-9698) **6119**
Activite Economique *see* Agir et Entreprendre **1057**
Activite, Emploi et Chomage (MAR ISSN 1113-9536) **8023**
Activite et Emploi dans le BTP *see* France. Ministere de l'Ecologie, de l'Energie, du Developpement Durable, et de l'Amenagement du Territoire. Activite et Emploi dans le B T P **4411**
Activite Humaine et l'Environnement *see* Canada. Statistics Canada. Human Activity and the Environment **3408**
Activite Immobiliere (FRA ISSN 0764-5066) **7581**
Activite Metallurgique au Canada. Fer et Acier de Premiere Fusion *see* Metallurgical Works in Canada, Primary Iron and Steel (Year) **6470**
Activiteitensektor *see* A S **8022**
• Activites (FRA ISSN 1765-2723) **7331**
Activites Bancaires Canadiennes *see* Canadian Bank Facts **1324**
Activites de la Semaine Quebecoise des Personnes Handicapees. Bilan *see* Semaine Quebecoise des Personnes Handicapees. Rapport d'Evaluation **4069**
Activites de la Semaine Quebecoise des Personnes Handicapees. Rapport *see* Semaine Quebecoise des Personnes Handicapees. Rapport d'Evaluation **4069**
Les Activites Fleurus (FRA ISSN 1275-5028) **530**
Activites Minieres au Cameroun (CMR ISSN 0575-7258) **6456**
ACTivities (USA) **2535**
• ➤ Activities, Adaptation & Aging (USA ISSN 0192-4788) **4038**
Activities - Chemical Industry Institute of Toxicology *see* C I I T Activities **3494**
Activities Directors' Quarterly for Alzheimer's & Other Dementia Patients (USA ISSN 1531-7277) **6119**
Activities Idea Booklet (CAN ISSN 1910-0191) **3515**
Activities Integrating Mathematics and Science Magazine *see* A I M S Magazine **2822**
Activities Integrating Mathematics & Science News *see* A I M S News **2822**
Activities of Irish Psychiatric Services (Year) (IRL ISSN 1393-7472) **6119**
Activities Report of the R & D Associates *see* Research & Development Associates for Military Food and Packaging Systems. Activities Report **6443**
ACTivity (USA ISSN 0001-7620) **2824**
▼ The Activity Director's Companion (USA ISSN 1940-1248) **4038**
Activity Director's Guide *see* Current Activities in Longterm Care **4043**
Activity Holidays Market Report *see* Key Note Market Assessment. Activity Holidays **8727**
Activnews (AUS ISSN 1030-7451) **8023**
• ➤ ActKM Online Journal of Knowledge Management (CAN ISSN 1834-3554) **1056**
Acto (ESP ISSN 1578-0910) **464**
Acton/Agua Dulce News (USA) **3515**
Actors Theatre (USA) **8464**
Acts & Facts (USA ISSN 1094-8562) **7620**
• Acts of New Brunswick (CAN ISSN 0704-464X) **4609**
Acts of the General Assembly of Prince Edward Island (CAN ISSN 0709-1419) **4609**
Acts of the General Assembly of the Province of Nova Scotia *see* Statutes of Nova Scotia **4788**
Acts of the Legislature of New Brunswick *see* Acts of New Brunswick **4609**
Acts of the Parliament of the Commonwealth of Australia (AUS ISSN 0727-6311) **7418**
Acts of Women of Power (USA) **8850**
L'Actu (FRA ISSN 1288-6939) **2175**
Actu Eco (NLD ISSN 0165-0246) **2824**
Actual (ESP) **8681**
Actual (MEX ISSN 0188-9192) **3907**
Actual (VEN ISSN 1315-8589) **5249**
Actual Bebe (ESP ISSN 1578-1232) **2142**
Actual Problems of Aviation and Aerospace Systems: Processes, Models, Experiment *see* Aktual'nye Problemy Aviatsionnykh i Aerokosmicheskikh Sistem: Protsessy, Modeli, Eksperiment **46**
Actual Problems of Electronics Instrument Engineering (USA) **3089**
• ➤ Actual Virtual (GBR ISSN 1752-5624) **5249**
Actualidad Administrativa (ARG ISSN 0325-724X) **7418**
Actualidad Administrativa (Quarterly Edition) (ESP ISSN 1139-8167) **4609**
Actualidad Administrativa (Weekly Edition) (ESP ISSN 1130-9946) **1661**
Actualidad Administrativa. Legislacion (ESP ISSN 1137-7631) **4846**
Actualidad Administrativa. Tribunales Superiores de Justicia (ESP ISSN 1133-2549) **4846**
Actualidad Aseguradora (ESP ISSN 0012-947X) **4491**
• Actualidad Aseguradora Internacional (Online Edition) (ESP ISSN 1699-3470) **4491**
Actualidad Aseguradora Internacional (Print Edition) *see* Actualidad Aseguradora Internacional (Online Edition) **4491**
Actualidad Bibliografica de Filosofia y Teologia (ESP ISSN 0211-4143) **7697**
Actualidad Civil (Quarterly Edition) (ESP ISSN 1139-8108) **4826**
Actualidad Civil (Weekly Edition) (ESP ISSN 0213-7100) **4826**
Actualidad Civil. Audiencias (ESP ISSN 1130-7382) **4826**
Actualidad Civil. Legislacion (ESP ISSN 1130-7390) **4826**
Actualidad Civil. Legislacion (Semi-annual Edition) (ESP ISSN 1139-8078) **4826**
Actualidad Civil. Registros (ESP ISSN 1133-2573) **4826**
• Actualidad Colombiana (COL) **4609**
• ➤ Actualidad Contable Faces (VEN ISSN 1316-8533) **1279**
• Actualidad Dermatologica (ESP ISSN 0210-279X) **5871**
Actualidad Docente (ESP ISSN 0210-2714) **2824**
• Actualidad Economica (ESP ISSN 0001-7655) **1435**
• Actualidad Economica en CD-ROM (USA) **1056**
• ➤ La Actualidad en Cirugia Oral y Maxilofacial (ESP ISSN 1576-0332) **6235**
Actualidad en Seguros y Fianzas (MEX) **4491**
Actualidad Farmaceutica (CHL ISSN 0716-9663) **6818**
▼ Actualidad Fiscal de Bogota (COL ISSN 2011-4796) **1909**
Actualidad Hostelera y Turistica (ESP) **4381**
• Actualidad Juridica Aranzadi (ESP ISSN 1132-0257) **4609**
Actualidad Juridica Uria & Menendez (ESP ISSN 1578-956X) **4609**
• Actualidad Laboral (Quarterly Edition) (ESP ISSN 1139-8396) **1661**
Actualidad Laboral (Weekly Edition) (ESP ISSN 0213-7097) **1661**
Actualidad Laboral. Legislacion, Convenios Colectivos (ESP ISSN 1133-2603) **1661**
Actualidad Pastoral (ARG ISSN 0587-4300) **7732**
• Actualidad Penal (ESP ISSN 0213-6562) **4883**
Actualidad Penal. Audiencias (ESP ISSN 1133-2522) **4883**
Actualidad Penal. Legislacion (ESP ISSN 1133-2514) **4883**
• Actualidad Tributaria (CRI ISSN 1409-4592) **1909**
➤ Actualidades Biologicas (COL ISSN 0304-3584) **650**
➤ Actualidades en Psicologia (CRI ISSN 0258-6444) **7331**
• Actualidades Ornitologicas (BRA ISSN 0104-2386) **901**
• Actualidades y Noticias del Aikido (CHL ISSN 0718-5669) **8156**
Actualitat Flequera de Catalunya (ESP) **3670**
Actualitates Interlingua i Norden (DNK ISSN 1395-2455) **5091**
• L'Actualite (CAN ISSN 0383-8714) **3805**
L'Actualite au Feminin *see* Women's News **8891**
➤ L'Actualite Chimique (FRA ISSN 0151-9093) **2048**
L'Actualite Chimique Canadienne *see* Canadian Chemical News **2052**
Actualite Comptable *see* Samsom Actualite Comptable **1301**
Actualite de la Formation Permanente (FRA ISSN 0397-331X) **2937**
Actualite de la Psychanalyse (FRA ISSN 1272-1573) **7331**
Actualite des Arts Plastiques (FRA ISSN 0293-9789) **464**
L'Actualite des Nations Unies (FRA ISSN 1772-8436) **7219**
Actualite des Religions *see* Le Monde des Religions **7808**
Actualite Diocesaine (CAN ISSN 0823-552X) **7782**
• Actualite Economique (CAN ISSN 0001-771X) **1056**
Actualite et Dossier en Sante Publique *see* A D S P **7505**
• Actualite et Droit International (FRA ISSN 1764-7185) **4916**
L'Actualite Juridique. Droit Administratif (FRA ISSN 0001-7728) **4609**

L'Actualite Juridique. Droit Immobilier (FRA ISSN 1286-0700) **4609**
• Actualite Juridique. Famille (FRA ISSN 1630-2206) **4906**
Actualite Juridique. Penal (FRA ISSN 1762-8407) **4883**
L'Actualite Langagiere/Language Update (CAN ISSN 1712-0063) **5091**
• L'Actualite Medicale (CAN ISSN 0229-9429) **5567**
▼ L'Actualite Municipale (CAN ISSN 1914-0665) **7487**
• L'Actualite Pharmaceutique (CAN ISSN 1195-2857) **6818**
L'Actualite Rhumatologique (FRA ISSN 0065-1818) **6221**
Actualite Semence *see* Seed Scoop **251**
Actualite Terminologique *see* L' Actualite Langagiere **5091**
Actualiteiten Sociaal Recht (NLD ISSN 1572-395X) **4609**
Actualites Bibliographiques Commentees Neurologies *see* A B C Neurologies **6117**
Actualites Bibliques (CAN ISSN 1184-7204) **7620**
† Actualites Commerce (FRA ISSN 1141-7102) **8928**
Actualites Communautaires (FRA ISSN 1011-923X) **4609**
Actualites de l'Audiovisuel a la Bibliotheque Nationale de France *see* Bibliotheque Nationale de France. Actualites de l'Audiovisuel **4996**
Actualites de Rohde et Schwarz *see* Neues von Rohde und Schwarz **2335**
Actualites du Droit (BEL ISSN 0778-1695) **4609**
• Actualites du Droit de l'Information (Online Edition) (FRA ISSN 1769-7190) **4946**
Actualites du Droit de l'Information (Print Edition) *see* Actualites du Droit de l'Information (Online Edition) **4946**
Actualites en Anesthesie Reanimation *see* A C T U A R **8927**
Actualites en Epidemiologie sur le VIH/Sida *see* HIV/AIDS Epi Updates **7524**
➤ Les Actualites en Gastroenterologie (FRA ISSN 1622-4191) **5919**
➤ Les Actualites en Hypertension et Prevention Cardiovasculaire (FRA ISSN 1621-7284) **5775**
Actualites en Kinesitherapie de Reanimation (FRA ISSN 1282-853X) **5768**
Actualites en Reanimation et Urgences (FRA ISSN 1297-4749) **5768**
• Actualites Ergotherapiques (CAN ISSN 1481-5923) **6106**
† Actualites & Environnement (FRA ISSN 1951-4247) **8928**
Actualites H L M (Habitations a Loyer Modere) (FRA) **4402**
Actualites Habitation (Ile-du-Prince-Edouard) *see* Actualites Habitation. Canada Atlantique **4402**
Actualites Habitation (Nouveau-Brunswick) *see* Actualites Habitation. Canada Atlantique **4402**
Actualites Habitation (Province de l'Ontario) *see* Actualites Habitation. Ontario **4402**
Actualites Habitation (Sherbrooke) *see* Actualites Habitation. Province de Quebec **4432**
Actualites Habitation (St. John's) *see* Actualites Habitation. Province de Quebec **4432**
Actualites Habitation (Terre-Neuve et Labrador) *see* Actualites Habitation. Canada Atlantique **4402**
Actualites Habitation (Trois-Rivieres) *see* Actualites Habitation. Province de Quebec **4432**
Actualites Habitation. Alberta *see* Actualites Habitation. Prairies **4402**
• Actualites Habitation. Canada Atlantique (CAN ISSN 1719-7066) **4402**
• Actualites Habitation. Charlottetown/Housing Now (CAN ISSN 1719-704X) **4402**
• Actualites Habitation. Colombie-Britannique/ Housing Now (British Columbia) (CAN ISSN 1719-7422) **4402**
• Actualites Habitation. Gatineau/Housing Now (Gatineau) (CAN ISSN 1719-752X) **4402**
• Actualites Habitation. Hamilton (CAN ISSN 1719-4245) **4402**
• Actualites Habitation. Kitchener/Housing Now (Kitchener) (CAN ISSN 1719-7457) **4402**
• Actualites Habitation. London (CAN ISSN 1719-511X) **4402**
Actualites Habitation. Manitoba *see* Actualites Habitation. Prairies **4402**
• Actualites Habitation. Nord de l'Ontario (CAN ISSN 1719-5136) **4402**
• Actualites Habitation. Ontario (CAN ISSN 1496-1121) **4402**
• Actualites Habitation. Oshawa (CAN ISSN 1910-3026) **4402**
• Actualites Habitation. Prairies (CAN ISSN 1910-3417) **4402**
• Actualites Habitation. Province de Quebec/Housing Now (Province of Quebec) (CAN ISSN 1719-8003) **4432**
• Actualites Habitation. Quebec/Housing Now (Quebec) (CAN ISSN 1719-7570) **4432**
• Actualites Habitation. Regina/Housing Now (Regina) (CAN ISSN 1719-802X) **4432**
• Actualites Habitation. Saguenay/Housing Now (Saguenay) (CAN ISSN 1719-7600) **4432**
• Actualites Habitation. Saint John, Moncton et Fredericton/Housing Now (Saint John, Moncton and Fredericton) (CAN ISSN 1719-7473) **4432**
Actualites Habitation. Saskatchewan *see* Actualites Habitation. Prairies **4402**
• Actualites Habitation. Saskatoon/Housing Now (Saskatoon) (CAN ISSN 1719-7643) **4432**
• Actualites Habitation. Windsor (CAN ISSN 1719-5152) **4402**
Actualites Industrielles Lorraines (FRA ISSN 0044-6165) **6303**
Actualites Justice *see* Justice Report **2658**
Actualites Medicales Internationales. Gastroenterologie *see* Les Actualites en Gastroenterologie **5919**
Actualites Nephrologiques Jean Hamburger (FRA ISSN 1168-1098) **6264**
Actualites Neurophysiologiques/Trends in Neurophysiology (FRA ISSN 0567-882X) **6119**
Actualites O F S *see* B F S Aktuell **7478**
• Actualites Odonto-Stomatologiques (FRA ISSN 0001-7817) **5833**
• Actualites Pharmaceutiques (FRA ISSN 0515-3700) **6818**
Actualites Pharmaceutiques Hospitalieres (FRA ISSN 1769-7344) **6818**
Actualites Professionnelles (CAN ISSN 1482-4590) **5950**
Actualites Reglementaires (FRA ISSN 0240-8236) **1551**
Actualites S D M (Services Documentaires Multimedia) (CAN ISSN 0842-1854) **4987**
Actualites Sociales Hebdomadaires (FRA ISSN 1145-8690) **8023**
Actualizacion de las Inversiones Azucareras (CUB) **1609**
Actualizacion Politica (ARG ISSN 0327-6058) **7102**
Actualizaciones en Anestesiologia y Reanimacion (ESP ISSN 1132-0095) **5768**
Actualizaciones en Cirugia Ortopedica y Traumatologia (ESP ISSN 1699-3543) **6055**
Actualizaciones en Enfermeria (COL ISSN 0123-5583) **5950**
Actuapress (English-Dutch Edition) (BEL ISSN 1376-6333) **5091**
Actuapress (English-French Edition) (BEL ISSN 1376-6325) **5091**
ACTUAR *see* A C T U A R **8927**
Actuarial Digest (USA) **4491**
Actuarial Research Clearinghouse (USA ISSN 0732-5428) **4491**
Actuarial Review (USA ISSN 1046-5081) **4491**
Actuarial Update (USA) **4491**
De Actuaris (NLD ISSN 0929-4562) **4491**
The Actuary (USA ISSN 0001-7825) **4491**
Actueel Recht voor P & O *see* Actueel Recht voor Personeel en Organisatie **4609**
Actueel Recht voor Personeel en Organisatie (NLD ISSN 1568-8380) **4609**
Actuel (FRA) **5204**
Actuel Marx (FRA ISSN 0994-4524) **7102**
Actuel Marx Intervenciones (CHL ISSN 0718-0179) **7102**
Actuele Onderwerpen *see* A O **3914**
Actuele Ontwikkeling van Bedrijfsresultaten en Inkomens (NLD ISSN 0929-7790) **173**
Actuele Themata uit de Psychomotorische Therapie (BEL ISSN 1386-8977) **6119**
Actum Luce (ITA ISSN 0391-9994) **4196**
• Actv8 (NZL ISSN 1177-1518) **2175**
Acuacuba (CUB ISSN 1608-0467) **3582**
Acuario Practico (ESP ISSN 1136-6427) **4326**
El Acuario Practico *see* Acuario Practico **4326**
Acuicultura (PAN) **3612**
Acuity Care Technology (USA ISSN 1551-6105) **5567**
Acumen (AUS ISSN 1449-308X) **1723**
Acumen Magazine (GBR ISSN 0964-0304) **5415**
Acupressure News (USA) **306**
• ➤ Acupuncture and Electro-Therapeutics Research (USA ISSN 0360-1293) **306**
Acupuncture & Moxibustion (FRA ISSN 1633-3454) **306**
Acupuncture and Oriental Medicine State Laws and Regulations (USA ISSN 1938-7202) **4609**
• ➤ Acupuncture in Medicine (GBR ISSN 0964-5284) **306**
Acupuncture Research *see* Zhenci Yanjiu **316**
Acupuncture Today (USA) **306**
Acura Style (CAN) **8555**
• ➤ Acustica United with Acta Acustica (DEU ISSN 1610-1928) **7086**
The Acuta Journal of Telecommunications in Higher Education (USA) **2365**
• ➤ Acute Cardiac Care (Online Edition) (GBR ISSN 1748-295X) **5775**
• ➤ Acute Cardiac Care (Print Edition) (GBR ISSN 1748-2941) **5775**
Acute Care Perspectives (USA ISSN 1551-9147) **6106**
➤ Acute Coronary Care (NLD ISSN 0884-6863) **5775**
Acute Coronary Care Updates *see* Acute Coronary Care **5775**
• ➤ Acute Coronary Syndromes (GBR ISSN 1369-5312) **5775**
Acute Coronary Syndromes Online *see* Acute Coronary Syndromes **5775**
➤ Acute Medicine (GBR ISSN 1747-4884) **5943**
• ➤ Acute Medicine (Online Edition) (GBR ISSN 1747-4892) **5943**
• Acute Myeloid Leukemia Research Today (AUS ISSN 1833-055X) **5933**
• ➤ Acute Pain (NLD ISSN 1366-0071) **5567**
Ad Agency Insider (USA) **19**
• Ad Astra (USA ISSN 1041-102X) **41**
Ad! Dict (BEL ISSN 1376-3156) **464**
Ad $ Summary (USA ISSN 0190-7166) **19**
Ad Familiares (SWE ISSN 1400-3899) **4441**
Ad Feminam (USA ISSN 1559-2634) **5249**
➤ Ad Fontes (DEU ISSN 0944-4580) **4196**
Ad Gentes (ITA ISSN 1826-0756) **7782**
Ad Hoc (AUS) **4609**
Ad Hoc (CAN) **5249**
Ad-hoc *see* Friday Weekly **2189**
Ad Hoc & Sensor Wireless Networks *see* Ad-Hoc & Sensor Wireless Networks **5465**
• ➤ Ad-Hoc & Sensor Wireless Networks (USA ISSN 1551-9899) **5465**
• ➤ Ad Hoc Networks (NLD ISSN 1570-8705) **2495**
Ad Ideas (USA) **19**
† Ad Interim (NLD ISSN 1871-8515) **8928**
Ad Kahn (USA) **3515**
Ad Labor (ITA) **5833**
Ad Litteram (FRA ISSN 1634-3832) **5249**
Ad Mag (IRL ISSN 1649-1432) **19**
Ad Mag (Clare and South Galway Edition) *see* The Irish View **4233**
Ad Marginem (DEU ISSN 0001-7965) **6542**
• Ad/Media's Agencies & Clients (NZL ISSN 0112-8876) **19**
• Ad News (AUS ISSN 0814-6942) **19**
Ad News (USA) **19**
Ad News Handbook (AUS ISSN 0816-3650) **19**
Ad News Point of Purchase Directory (AUS) **1804**
Ad News Promotional Products Directory (AUS ISSN 1329-1130) **1970**
Ad News the Annual (AUS ISSN 1832-3243) **19**
• Ad Notam (CZE ISSN 1211-0558) **4609**
➤ Ad Parnassum (ITA ISSN 1722-3954) **6542**
• Ad Quintum (ITA ISSN 1723-9524) **371**
Ad Rem (BEL ISSN 0774-613X) **8489**
Ad Rem (DEU ISSN 1619-6473) **2271**
Ad Sack (USA) **2634**
Ad - Tier Newsletter (USA) **19**
Ad-Viser (CAN) **79**
AD-Visie (NLD ISSN 1382-7162) **1661**
Ada (FRA ISSN 1774-5853) **8893**
• Ada IC News (USA ISSN 1064-1505) **2505**
ADA Magazine *see* A D A Magazine **426**
• Ada User Journal (PRT ISSN 1381-6551) **2505**
Adabiiot va San'yat (TJK) **5249**
• ADAD (USA) **2311**
Academie Gemeinnutziger Wissenschaften zu Erfurt. Mathematisch-Naturwissenschaftlichen Klasse. Sitzungsberichte (DEU ISSN 0940-2241) **7832**
Adalat (TKM) **3963**
Adalet Istatistikleri *see* Turkey. Turkiye Istatistik Kurumu. Adalet Istatistikleri **4825**
Adam (DEU ISSN 0949-3417) **4370**
Adam Black Video Directory of Adult Film (USA ISSN 1533-5992) **2399**
Adam Black Video Illustrated (USA ISSN 1533-5976) **6285**
Adam Erotomic (USA) **6285**
Adam Film World Guide (USA ISSN 1533-5984) **6488**
Adam Film World Guide. Directory of Adult Film & Video (USA ISSN 0743-6335) **6488**
Adam Gay Video Directory (USA) **2399**
Adam Gay Video Erotica (USA) **4370**
Adam Gay Video XXX Showcase (USA ISSN 1533-595X) **4370**
Adam Girls International Teenz (USA) **6285**
Adam Hilger Series on Sensors *see* Sensors Series **7084**
† Adam International Review (GBR ISSN 0001-8015) **8928**
Adam Magazine (USA) **6285**
➤ The Adam Smith Review (GBR ISSN 1743-5285) **5250**
Adam vs. Eve (USA) **5064**
➤ Adamantius (ITA ISSN 1126-6244) **5091**
Adamianis Uplebebi (GEO) **7202**
Adams Beer Handbook *see* Beer Handbook **598**
Adams County Trumpeter (USA) **4281**
Adams Cover Letter Almanac (USA) **6691**
† Adams Executive Recruiters Almanac (USA ISSN 1099-0216) **8928**
Adams Family Chronicle (USA ISSN 8755-5026) **3758**
† Adams Internet Job Search Almanac (USA) **8928**
• Adams Job Interview Almanac (USA) **6691**
Adams Jobs Almanac (USA ISSN 1072-592X) **6691**
Adams Resume Almanac (USA) **6691**
• ➤ Adansonia (FRA ISSN 1280-8571) **773**
Adansonia *see* Adansonia **773**
Adapt Japan: Employment Opportunities for You (JPN) **1661**
▼ • ➤ Adaptation (GBR ISSN 1755-0637) **5250**
Adaptations Theatrales (FRA ISSN 1952-5516) **8464**
• ➤ Adapted Physical Activity Quarterly (USA ISSN 0736-5829) **3036**
• ➤ Adaptive Behavior (GBR ISSN 1059-7123) **2445**
Adaptive Behaviour *see* Adaptive Behavior **2445**
• Adaptive Structures & Material Systems (USA ISSN 1522-2756) **41**
• Adarve (ESP ISSN 1885-9720) **5415**
➤ Adaxe (ESP ISSN 0213-4705) **3016**
• Adbrief (AUS ISSN 0311-2225) **19**
Adbrief Register: Agencies & Marketers (AUS ISSN 0819-6648) **19**
• Adbusters (CAN ISSN 0847-9097) **3400**
Adcebra (MEX) **1804**
Adclubber (USA) **19**
• AdCom Net (USA) **19**
Adcrafter (USA ISSN 0001-8066) **19**
Add-a-Line (NZL ISSN 1176-872X) **6542**
Addab Journal (SDN ISSN 0302-8844) **4441**
Addaline *see* Add-a-Line **6542**
ADDC *see* Association Departementale de Developpement Culturel (A D D C) **4976**
Addcon World (Year) (GBR) **3235**
Addenda to Television Factbook *see* Television and Cable Factbook **2396**
Addendum (Indianapolis) (USA ISSN 0884-514X) **4609**
Addict *see* Ad! Dict **464**
• ➤ Addiction (GBR ISSN 0965-2140) **2689**
• Addiction Abstracts (GBR ISSN 0968-7610) **2689**
• ➤ Addiction Biology (GBR ISSN 1355-6215) **2689**
• Addiction Professional (USA ISSN 1542-8435) **2689**
• ➤ Addiction Research and Theory (GBR ISSN 1606-6359) **2689**
• Addiction Science & Clinical Practice (USA ISSN 1940-0632) **2689**
• Addiction. Supplement (GBR ISSN 1359-6357) **2689**
• Addiction Today (GBR ISSN 1471-5511) **2689**
• Addiction Treatment Forum (USA) **2690**
• Addiction Treatment Research News (NZL ISSN 1177-8083) **2690**
Addictions (FRA ISSN 1762-1097) **2690**
• ➤ Addictive Behaviors (GBR ISSN 0306-4603) **2690**
• ➤ Addictive Disorders & Their Treatment (USA ISSN 1531-5754) **2690**
Adding Value *see* Institute of Chartered Accountants in England and Wales. Adding Value: For the General Practitioner Supporting Small Business **1291**
Addis Ababa Chamber of Commerce. Chamber News (ETH) **1394**
Addis Ababa University. College of Technology. Library Bulletin (ETH ISSN 0017-6680) **4987**
Addis Ababa University, Institute of Ethiopian Studies Bulletin *see* I E S Bulletin **4175**
• Addis Tribune (ETH ISSN 1028-5474) **3837**
Addis Zemen (ETH) **3837**
Addison Report (USA) **1609**
Additional Earnings and Union Membership Data *see* Union Membership and Earnings Data Book **4604**
Additions & Decks (USA ISSN 1547-5719) **975**
Additions and Decks *see* Additions & Decks **975**
• Additives for Polymers (GBR ISSN 0306-3747) **7090**
ADDitude (USA ISSN 1529-1014) **4063**
Address (IRL) **7581**
• Address List, Regional and Subregional Libraries for the Blind and Physically Handicapped (USA ISSN 0163-3805) **4079**
Addvantage Magazine (USA ISSN 0149-4082) **8220**
Adelaar (NLD ISSN 0001-8139) **2271**
Adelaide Advertiser *see* Advertiser (Adelaide) **3793**
Adelaide Botanic Garden. Journal (AUS ISSN 0313-4083) **773**
Adelaide Botanic Garden. Report For Year *see* Government of South Australia. Department for Environment and Heritage. Board of the Botanic Gardens and State Herbarium. Annual Report **791**
• Adelaide Cityscope (AUS) **7616**
• ➤ Adelaide Law Review (AUS ISSN 0065-1915) **4609**
• The Adelaide Review (AUS ISSN 0815-5992) **5204**
Adelaide to Outback G P Training Program. Newsletter *see* Regional Roundup **2903**
• Adelaide Update (AUS ISSN 1833-9972) **8023**
Adelaide's Child (AUS) **2143**
• El Adelantado de Segovia (ESP) **3951**
• Adelante (MEX) **3907**
Adeline *see* Add-a-Line **6542**
• Adelphi Lifecycle Solutions (GBR ISSN 1752-5713) **6818**
The Adelphi Papers *see* Adelphi Series **7219**
• ➤ Adelphi Series (GBR ISSN 1944-5571) **7219**
• Adelphia Law Journal (USA ISSN 8756-3630) **4609**
Adem (BEL ISSN 0001-8171) **6542**
Aden (FRA ISSN 1638-9867) **5250**
† Adequate Information Management in Europe. Working Papers (DEU) **8928**
Adesso (DEU ISSN 0947-2096) **8681**
† Adessonapoli (ITA) **8928**
Adevarul/Truth (ROM ISSN 1220-7489) **3932**
Adevarul (Bucharest) (ROM ISSN 1016-7587) **3932**
Adevarul Economic (ROM ISSN 1220-6156) **1057**
Adevarul Literar si Artistic (ROM ISSN 1220-9821) **5205**
Adfo Bureaubijlage Update *see* Adformatie Bureaubijlage **19**
Adfo Corporate Sponsoring Actueel *see* AdfoXtract **1804**
Adfo Direct *see* Adforesult **1804**
Adfo Direct Jaarboek *see* Branchebijlage **1807**
AdfoFlash *see* AdfoXtract **1804**
Adfomedianieuws (NLD ISSN 0926-7670) **1804**
Adforesult (NLD ISSN 1871-3149) **1804**
Adformatie (NLD ISSN 0165-0726) **19**
Adformatie Bureaubijlage (NLD ISSN 1389-1294) **19**
• AdfoXtract (NLD ISSN 1569-5344) **1804**
adfsdfsf *see* Assiut Journal of Environmental Studies. Overview Series **3405**
AdFundum (NLD ISSN 0929-6247) **597**
Adhaesion - Kleben & Dichten (DEU ISSN 1619-1919) **7090**

Title

9924 ADHESION AND ADHESIVES ULRICH'S PERIODICALS

Adhesion and Adhesives/Setchaku (JPN ISSN 0037-0495) 7090
† • Adhesion Communications (USA ISSN 1025-9287) 8928
Adhesion Society. Annual Meeting. Proceedings (USA ISSN 1086-9506) 3235
Adhesive and Sealant Council. Convention Proceedings (USA) 3235
Adhesive and Sealant Council. Newsletter (USA ISSN 1083-3919) 3235
Adhesive Dentistry see Setchaku Shigaku 5865
Adhesive Technology Yearbook (Year) (GBR) 3235
• Adhesives Abstracts (GBR ISSN 0891-7760) 2085
Adhesives and Sealants Directory see British Adhesives and Sealants Association. Handbooks 1977
• Adhesives & Sealants Industry (USA ISSN 1070-9592) 3235
Adhesives and Sealants Industry see Adhesives & Sealants Industry 3235
Adhesives D.A.T.A. Digest (USA ISSN 1041-2050) 3335
Adhikar (IND) 3878
Adhuna (BGD ISSN 0042-1057) 8023
Adhunik Rajasthan (IND) 3878
Al-Adhwaa' (BHR) 3799
• ➤ Adicciones (ESP ISSN 0214-4840) 2690
Adidas International (AUS) 8220
Adiestramiento (MEX) 4589
Adikushon to Kazoku/Japanese Journal of Addiction & Family (JPN ISSN 1344-4743) 2690
Adineh (IRN ISSN 1017-4095) 5250
Adipocytes (USA ISSN 1550-2082) 5567
▼ Adipositas (DEU ISSN 1865-1739) 6654
• Adipositasforeningen. Nyhedsbrev (DNK ISSN 1602-6780) 6654
Adirondac (USA ISSN 0001-8236) 8301
➤ Adirondack Journal of Environmental Studies (USA ISSN 1075-0436) 3401
Adirondack Life (USA ISSN 0001-8252) 8301
Adirondack Trail Improvement Society Newsletter (USA) 8301
Adivaram Anubhandham see Andhra Prabha 3879
Adivasi (IND) 323
Adjourn Magazine (USA) 8681
Adjudicator (USA) 7102
• The Adjunct Advocate (USA ISSN 1078-5264) 2965
Adjusters' Reference Guide (USA) 4491
Adjusting to Leaner Times see Centre for European Policy Studies. Macroeconomic Policy Group. Annual Report. Adjusting to Leaner Times 1081
† Adjuvant Therapy of Cancer (NLD ISSN 1040-5089) 8928
AdLaw Bulletin (USA) 4609
Adler (AUT ISSN 0001-8260) 3758
Der Adler (DEU ISSN 0001-8279) 41
Adler Museum Bulletin (ZAF ISSN 0379-6531) 5567
The Adler Star (USA ISSN 1932-4316) 568
• Adli Bilimler Dergisi/Turkish Journal of Forensic Sciences (TUR ISSN 1303-6793) 5912
• Adli Psikiyatri Dergisi/Journal of Forensic Psychiatry (TUR ISSN 1304-396X) 5912
• ➤ Adli Tip (TUR ISSN 1304-5040) 5912
• Adli Tip Bulteni/The Bulletin of Legal Medicine/Forensic Medicine Bulletin (TUR ISSN 1300-865X) 5912
† Adli Tip Dergisi (TUR ISSN 1018-5275) 8928
• Admap (GBR ISSN 0001-8295) 19
Admarine (GBR ISSN 0964-0932) 8271
• AdMedia (NZL ISSN 0112-6997) 19
AdMedia's Agencies & Clients see Ad/Media's Agencies & Clients 19
• Admin Review (AUS ISSN 0814-1231) 4610
Adminisrativno Pravosudie (BGR) 4946
Administracao do Porto de Lisboa. Relatorio e Contas (PRT) 8638
• Administracao On Line (BRA ISSN 1517-7912) 1723
Administracion (ARG ISSN 0325-0814) 1723
• Administracion & Ciudadania (Gallegan Edition) (ESP ISSN 1887-0287) 7418
• Administracion & Ciudadania (Spanish Edition) (ESP ISSN 1887-0279) 7418
Administracion de Andalucia (ESP ISSN 1130-376X) 7487
▼ Administracion Hoy (COL ISSN 2011-1525) 1723
Administracion Publica y Sociedad (ARG) 7418
Administracion y Desarrollo (COL ISSN 0120-3754) 7418
• Administracion y Economia UC (CHL ISSN 0716-7628) 1723
Administracion y Economica Universidad Catolica see Administracion y Economia UC 1723
• Administracion y Organizaciones (MEX ISSN 1665-014X) 1723
➤ Administratie si Management Public/Administration and Public Management Review (ROM ISSN 1583-9583) 1724
Administratief en Gerechtelijk Jaarboek voor Belgie see Annuaire Administratif et Judiciaire de Belgique 7420
Administration (FRA ISSN 0223-5439) 7418
Administration (IND) 5205
Administration (IRL ISSN 0001-8325) 7418
Administration see Uprava 1190
Administration and Development see Al- Idarah wal-Tanmiyah 7445
Administration and Enforcement of the Fish Habitat Protection and Pollution Prevention Provisions of the Fisheries Act. Annual Report see On the Administration and Enforcement of the Fish Habitat Protection and Pollution Prevention Provisions of the Fisheries Act. Annual Report to Parliament 3604
Administration and Enforcement of the Fish Habitat Protection and Pollution Prevention Provisions of the Fisheries Act. Annual Report to Parliament see On the Administration and Enforcement of the Fish Habitat Protection and Pollution Prevention Provisions of the Fisheries Act. Annual Report to Parliament 3604
Administration & Governance. Journal see Journal of Administration and Governance 7448
Administration & Management Special Interest Section Quarterly (USA ISSN 1093-720X) 6672
Administration and Policy in Mental Health see Administration and Policy in Mental Health and Mental Health Services Research 5567
• ➤ Administration and Policy in Mental Health and Mental Health Services Research (USA) 5567
Administration and Public Management Review see Administratie si Management Public 1724
• ➤ Administration & Society (USA ISSN 0095-3997) 7418
Administration de Pilotage des Grands Lacs. Rapport Annuel see Great Lakes Pilotage Authority. Annual Report (Online Edition) 8644
Administration des Directions Regionales de l'Industrie, de la Recherche et de l'Environnement. Annuaire (FRA ISSN 1169-6931) 3123
Administration du Pipe-line du Nord. Rapport Annuel see Northern Pipeline Agency. Annual Report 3143
• ➤ Administration in Social Work (USA ISSN 0364-3107) 8023
Administration of Elementary and Secondary School see Zhongxiaoxue Guanli 3035
Administration of Income Tax (CAN ISSN 1719-9395) 1909
• Administration of Justice Bulletin (USA) 4610
Administration of the Marine Mammal Protection Act of 1972 (United States, Fish and Wildlife Service) (USA ISSN 0194-1488) 2601
Administration of the Toxic Substances Control Act. Annual Report see Toxic Substances Control Act: Report to Congress for Fiscal Year 3501
Administration on Aging eNews see A O A eNews 4038
• Administration on Children, Youth and Families. Family and Youth Services Bureau. Report to Congress on the Youth Programs of the Family and Youth Services Bureau for Fiscal Years (Year) (USA ISSN 1942-4957) 7418
Administration Publique (BEL ISSN 0771-4084) 7418
Administration Publique au Quebec (CAN ISSN 1481-4420) 7419
Administration Publique du Canada see Canadian Public Administration 7429
Administrative Affairs in Bangladesh (BGD) 7419
Administrative and Local Government Law News (USA) 4846
Administrative and Office Support Survey (USA) 1661
Administrative & Regulatory Law News (USA ISSN 1544-1547) 4610
Administrative and Support Staff Compensation Survey (Year) (CAN) 6706
Administrative Angle see Updating School Board Policies 3035
Administrative Appeals Reports (AUS ISSN 0813-779X) 4610
Administrative Appeals Unit Reporter see A A U Reporter 4606
Administrative Assistants Association of the U.S. House of Representatives. Newsletter (USA) 7419
• Administrative Assistant's Update (CAN ISSN 1191-7881) 1855
Administrative Change (IND ISSN 0302-2986) 7419
Administrative Compensation Survey (USA) 1661
Administrative Court Digest (GBR ISSN 1473-4834) 4610
Administrative Eyecare (USA ISSN 1087-2809) 6037
Administrative Focus (USA ISSN 1056-1293) 3016
Administrative Law see Gilbert Law Summaries. Administrative Law 4681
Administrative Law (New York) (USA) 4610
• ➤ Administrative Law (Springfield) (USA) 4610
• Administrative Law Decisions (AUS ISSN 0726-5816) 4610
Administrative Law Letter (USA) 4610
Administrative Law Reports (CAN ISSN 0824-2615) 4610
Administrative Law Review see Xingzheng Faxue Yanjiu 7477
• ➤ Administrative Law Review (Chicago) (USA ISSN 0001-8368) 4610
➤ Administrative Law Review (Washington) (USA) 4610
• Administrative Notes (USA) 4987
• Administrative Office of the United States Courts. Statistics Division. Statistical Tables for the Federal Judiciary (Online) (USA) 4820
Administrative Ophthalmology see Administrative Eyecare 6037
Administrative Professional Today (USA ISSN 1943-2194) 1724
Administrative Professional Update (USA ISSN 1549-974X) 1724
Administrative Research Review see Magallat al-Buhuth al-Idariyyat 7452
Administrative Review Council. Annual Report (AUS ISSN 0155-025X) 4610
Administrative Rulemaking (USA) 4610
• ➤ Administrative Science Quarterly (USA ISSN 0001-8392) 7419
➤ Administrative Sciences Association of Canada. Annual Conference Proceedings (CAN) 1724
Administrative Sciences Association of Canada Bulletin see A S A C E-Bulletin 1855
Administrative Staff College of India Journal of Management see A S C I Journal of Management 1722
• ➤ Administrative Theory & Praxis (USA ISSN 1084-1806) 7419
Administratives Management (DEU ISSN 0720-6690) 1724
Administrativo e Constitucional see A & C 4845
Administrator (IDN ISSN 0304-6117) 3016
The Administrator (IND) 7419
Administrator, Steering Committee and Response Team Manual (USA) 3016
Administrators' Computer Letter (USA) 7485
Administrators of Small Public Libraries of Ontario Newsletter see A S P L O Newsletter 4986
Administrer (FRA ISSN 0767-9939) 7581
Admiralty Marine Science Publication (GBR ISSN 0436-4309) 8638
• Admiralty Notices to Mariners (GBR ISSN 1464-1607) 8638
Admiralty Notices to Mariners (Small Craft Edition) (GBR ISSN 1464-8032) 8638
• Admiralty Notices to Mariners. Annual Summary (GBR) 8638
Admission Requirements of U S and Canadian Dental Schools see Official Guide to Dental Schools 5858
Admissions Marketing Report see Higher Education Marketing Report 3024
• Adnan Menderes Universitesi Tip Fakultesi. Dergisi/Adnan Menderes University. Faculty of Medicine. Journal (TUR ISSN 1302-6755) 5567
Adnan Menderes University. Faculty of Medicine. Journal see Adnan Menderes Universitesi Tip Fakultesi. Dergisi 5567
AdNews see Advertising Club of New York. Newsletter 20
• Adnews On-line Daily (Online) (CAN ISSN 1719-5527) 19
Adnews On-line Daily (Print) see Adnews On-line Daily (Online) 19
Adobe illustrator Techniques (USA ISSN 1932-7897) 2483
Adobe Journal (USA) 427
• Adolescence (FRA ISSN 0751-7696) 6119
• ➤ Adolescence (USA ISSN 0001-8449) 2143
Adolescence and Education (USA ISSN 1538-2052) 2824
• Adolescence Education Newsletter (THA ISSN 1564-2984) 2824
• Adolescencia y Salud (CRI ISSN 1409-4185) 5567
† • ➤ Adolescent & Family Health (USA ISSN 1533-9890) 8928
Adolescent Cultures, School and Society (USA ISSN 1091-1464) 2143
Adolescent Literature see Wenxue Shaonian 5398
Adolescent Lives (USA) 2143
• ➤ Adolescent Medicine (Elk Grove) (USA ISSN 1934-4287) 6087
Adolescent Medicine (Philadelphia) see Adolescent Medicine (Elk Grove) 6087
Adolescent Medicine Clinics see Adolescent Medicine (Elk Grove) 6087
• ➤ Adolescent Psychiatry (USA ISSN 0065-2008) 6119
Adolescent Psychology see Annual Editions: Adolescent Psychology 7334
Adolescent Studies see Shaonian Ertong Yanjiu 2168
➤ Adolescenta (ROM) 2143
Adolescentology see Shishunkigaku 2168
Adolescenza e Psicoanalisi (Online) see Adolescenza e Psicoanalisi (Print) 7331
Adolescenza e Psicoanalisi (Print) (ITA ISSN 1828-7654) 7331
• Adonde? (PER ISSN 1609-8528) 3927
• Adong Ganho Haghoeji/Korean Academy of Child Health Nursing. Journal (KOR ISSN 1226-1815) 5950
Adoptalk (USA ISSN 0273-6497) 8023
Adoptees' Liberty Movement Association Searchlight see A L M A Searchlight 8022
Adoptie see Adoptietijdschrift 8023
Adoptietijdschrift (NLD ISSN 1388-3526) 8023
▼ Adoption & Culture (USA ISSN 1944-4990) 8023
• ➤ Adoption and Fostering (GBR ISSN 0308-5759) 8023
Adoption Applications in Scotland (GBR) 8023
Adoption Factbook (USA) 8023
Adoption Guide see Adoptive Families 2143
Adoption Helper see Family Helper 4909
Adoption Law and Practice (USA) 4906
• ➤ Adoption Quarterly (USA ISSN 1092-6755) 8023
Adoption Today (USA ISSN 1527-8522) 8023
Das Adoptionsdreieck (USA) 3758
Adoptive Families (USA ISSN 1076-1020) 2143
Adorable see Adorable au Summum 6285
Adorable au Summum (CAN ISSN 1719-5349) 6285
Adoranten (SWE ISSN 0349-8808) 371
• Adore Shop (USA) 2251
Adrenalin (London, 1997) (GBR ISSN 1369-8060) 6285
Adrenalin (London, 1999) (GBR) 8156
Adres voor het Boekenvak (BEL) 7551
Adresboek voor Biologen (NLD ISSN 0924-2872) 1970
Adressbuch des Sports (DEU) 8156
Adressbuch fuer den Deutschsprachigen Buchhandel (DEU ISSN 0065-2032) 7551
• Adressbuch fuer den Deutschsprachigen Buchhandel CD-ROM (DEU) 7551
• Adresseavisen (NOR ISSN 0805-3804) 3921
Adresseloese Forsendelser (DNK ISSN 1396-4828) 2353
Adrian (ITA ISSN 1723-1604) 4564
Adriatic Meteorology see Jadranska Meteorologija 6358
Adriatico (ITA ISSN 1826-8897) 1435
L'Adriatico (ITA ISSN 1970-0652) 8681
Adrichalut Yisraelit see Architecture of Israel 431
Adrift (USA ISSN 0736-4970) 5250
Adroddiad Blynyddol C G G C see W C V A Annual Report 8077
Adsmart (GBR ISSN 1463-0664) 3861
• ➤ Adsorption (USA ISSN 0929-5607) 3235
Adsorption News (JPN ISSN 0917-9917) 2048
• ➤ Adsorption Science and Technology (GBR ISSN 0263-6174) 3235
Adsum (CAN ISSN 0705-0992) 6408
ADTmag.com see Application Trends 2529
Adulescens (ITA ISSN 0766-0774) 5091
Adult Amateur Summer Music Workshop Directory see Music for the Love of It 6590
Adult and Community Learning Monograph Series see Journal of Adult Learning 2943
Adult and Youth Training (GBR ISSN 0960-6580) 1855
Adult Basic Education see Adult Basic Education and Literacy Journal 2937
• ➤ Adult Basic Education and Literacy Journal (USA ISSN 1934-2322) 2937
Adult Bible Lessons for the Deaf see Exploring the Bible: Bible Studies for the Deaf 7757
Adult Bible Studies (USA ISSN 0149-8347) 7744
Adult Bible Studies Student (USA) 7744
• Adult Bible Studies Teacher (USA ISSN 1059-9118) 7744
• Adult Christian Life (USA ISSN 0746-6919) 7744
• Adult, Community and Further Education Board. Annual Reports (AUS) 2937
• Adult Day Services Letter (USA) 4038
Adult Devotions see Devotions 7754
Adult Education see Chengren Jiaoyu Xuekan 2939
Adult Education see Aikuiskasvatus 2938
• Adult Education and Development (DEU ISSN 0342-7633) 2937
Adult Education College: An Grianan Programme (IRL) 2938
Adult Education Programme (GBR) 2938
• ➤ Adult Education Quarterly (USA ISSN 0741-7136) 2938
• The Adult Learner (IRL ISSN 0790-8040) 2938
• Adult Learning (USA ISSN 1045-1595) 2938
Adult Learning and Literacy - A L L Points Bulletin (USA) 2938
Adult Learning Yearbook (Year) (GBR ISSN 1472-5061) 2938
Adult Literacy and Employment in Wanganui (NZL ISSN 1176-9807) 2938
Adult Quarterly see Adult Christian Life 7744
• Adult Quarterly (USA) 7744
Adult Study Guide (USA) 7744
Adult Video News (USA ISSN 0883-7090) 2399
Adult Video News Online Magazine see A V N Online Magazine 2552
Adultita (ITA) 8085
• Adults Learning (GBR ISSN 0955-2308) 2938
• Adultspan Journal (USA ISSN 1524-6817) 7331
Adumatu (SAU ISSN 1319-8947) 371
▼ • Adunagow Magazine (USA) 3515
Adv. Mater. Sci. Eng. see Advances in Materials Science and Engineering 3335
• Advance (DEU) 3179
Advance (DNK ISSN 0109-1743) 7732
Advance (NZL ISSN 1176-7391) 2965
▼ Advance (USA) 4846
Advance (Richmond) (USA ISSN 0363-2733) 8023
Advance (Washington) (USA ISSN 0886-778X) 7219
Advance Annotation Service to Annotated Code of Maryland (USA ISSN 0747-7023) 4610
Advance Band Magazine (USA) 6542
• Advance Book Information (SGP) 7551
• Advance Consultancy News (TON) 2552
Advance Data from Vital and Health Statistics see U.S. Department of Health and Human Services. National Center for Health Statistics. Advance Data from Vital and Health Statistics 7549
• Advance for Administrators of the Laboratory (USA ISSN 1096-6277) 5901
• Advance for Audiologists (USA ISSN 1542-5134) 5567
• Advance for Directors in Rehabilitation (USA ISSN 1096-6269) 5568
• Advance for Health Information Executives (USA) 2532
• Advance for Health Information Professionals (USA ISSN 1061-3269) 5568
• Advance for Healthy Aging (USA) 5568

Title

Title

Title

DIRECTORY 2010 AGENCE DE DEVELOPPEMENT ET D'URBANISME DE L'AGGLOMERATION 9931

African Newsletter on Occupational Health and Safety - Online see African Newsletter on Occupational Health and Safety **6672**
African Notes (NGA ISSN 0002-0087) **3516**
African Occasional Papers Series (CAN ISSN 0832-8277) **323**
• ➤ African On-line International Journals (GBR ISSN 1750-8193) **5570**
African Online International Journals see African On-line International Journals **5570**
African Outfitter (ZAF ISSN 1817-1958) **8301**
African Peace Research Institute Journal see A P R I Journal **7219**
African Peer Review Mechanism Monitor see The A P R M Monitor **1551**
➤ African Performance Review (GBR ISSN 1753-5964) **8464**
African Philosophical Journal see Cahiers Philosophiques Africains **6909**
• African Philosophy (USA ISSN 1533-1067) **4172**
▼ • African Physical Reviews (ITA ISSN 1970-4097) **7004**
• ➤ African Plant Protection (ZAF ISSN 1023-3121) **774**
African Population Newsletter (Bilingual Edition) (ETH ISSN 0258-980X) **7276**
African Population Studies see Etude de la Population Africaine **7283**
African Primates (KEN ISSN 1026-2865) **2601**
African Printer (ZAF ISSN 1071-3263) **7318**
African Profiles U S A (USA ISSN 1092-9851) **3516**
African Publishers Networking Directory (Year) (GBR) **7551**
African Publishing Review/Revista das Edicoes Africanas/Revue de l'Edition Africaine (ZWE ISSN 1019-5823) **7551**
African Recorder (IND ISSN 0002-0133) **7103**
African Research and Documentation (GBR ISSN 0305-862X) **3516**
▼ • African Research Review (ETH ISSN 1994-9057) **2824**
African Review (TZA ISSN 0856-0056) **7103**
• African Review of Business and Technology (GBR ISSN 0954-6782) **8415**
African Review of Educational Sciences see Revue Africaine des Sciences de l'Education **2907**
African Review of Money (ITA ISSN 1124-3163) **1306**
African Review of Money Finance and Banking see African Review of Money **1306**
African Safaris (ZAF ISSN 1813-1360) **8681**
• African Safety Promotion (ZAF ISSN 1728-774X) **8024**
▼ • African Security (USA ISSN 1939-2206) **7103**
• African Security Review (ZAF ISSN 1024-6029) **6408**
African Small Mammal Newsletter (ZAF) **931**
African Soccer (GBR ISSN 0967-5477) **8220**
African Social Challenges see A C A R T S O D Monograph Series **1589**
➤ African Social Research (ZMB ISSN 0002-0168) **7945**
African Social Studies Series (NLD ISSN 1568-1203) **8086**
• ➤ African Sociological Review/Revue Africaine de Sociologie (SEN ISSN 1027-4332) **8086**
African Soils see Sols Africains **254**
African Sources for African History (NLD ISSN 1567-6951) **4172**
† African Special Bibliographic Series (USA ISSN 0749-2308) **8928**
▼ African Sports Network Journal (USA ISSN 1941-2754) **8157**
• ➤ African Studies (GBR ISSN 0002-0184) **323**
➤ African Studies (USA ISSN 1931-0978) **4172**
• African Studies (ZAF) **4168**
African Studies Association Annual Meeting Papers see A S A Annual Meeting Papers **3515**
African Studies Association News (Online) see A S A News (Online) **3515**
African Studies Center Newsletter (East Lansing) see A S C Newsletter (East Lansing) **3515**
African Studies Centre. Occasional Papers Series (GBR ISSN 1460-1648) **7945**
African Studies Centre. Working Papers (NLD ISSN 0924-3534) **4173**
African Studies Journal (GHA) **4173**
• ➤ African Studies Quarterly (USA ISSN 1093-2658) **7945**
• ➤ African Studies Review (USA ISSN 0002-0206) **3516**
African Studies Series (GBR ISSN 0065-406X) **4173**
African Study Monographs (JPN ISSN 0285-1601) **323**
African Study Monographs. Supplementary Issue (JPN ISSN 0286-9667) **323**
African Success (ZAF ISSN 1992-013X) **1057**
The African Sun Times (USA ISSN 1526-2200) **3789**
African Tax Systems see Africa - Taxation & Investment **1909**
• African Technology Development Forum Journal (ZMB ISSN 1817-2008) **1057**
▼ • African Theatre (USA ISSN 1941-4781) **8464**
African Thought and Perspectives see Pensee et Perspectives Africaines **7991**
African Times (USA) **3516**
African Trade Review see A F R E **1551**
African Trade Union News (TGO) **4589**
• African Urban and Regional Science Index (KEN ISSN 1018-2136) **7936**
African Urban Quarterly (KEN ISSN 0747-6108) **4402**
• African Vibes (USA ISSN 1932-1198) **3516**
African Violet Magazine (USA ISSN 0002-0265) **3721**
African Voices (USA ISSN 1530-0668) **5250**
African Voices see U S A I D in Africa **1606**
➤ African Wildlife (ZAF ISSN 0256-6273) **2601**
African Wildlife (Multilingual Edition) see African Wildlife **2601**
African Wildlife News (USA) **2601**
• African Wildlife Update (USA ISSN 1058-9805) **2601**
The African Woman Magazine (GHA) **8850**
African Women Leaders in Agriculture and the Environment Series see A W L A E Series **78**
African Writers' Handbook (GBR) **7551**
African Writers Series (USA ISSN 0065-4108) **5250**
➤ African Yearbook of International Law/Annuaire Africain de Droit International (NLD ISSN 1380-7412) **4916**
▼ African Yearbook on International Humanitarian Law (ZAF ISSN 1997-8391) **4916**
• ➤ African Zoology (ZAF ISSN 1562-7020) **931**
Africana (PRT ISSN 0871-2336) **7945**
• Africana (USA) **3516**
Africana Bulletin (POL ISSN 0002-029X) **7945**
Africana.com see Africana **3516**
Africana Gandensia (BEL ISSN 0776-7323) **323**
• Africana Libraries Newsletter (USA) **4987**
Africana Marburgensia (DEU ISSN 0002-0311) **4173**
Africana Society. Journal/Africana Vereniging. Joernaal (ZAF) **4173**
Africana Society. Yearbook/Africana Vereniging. Jaarboek (ZAF ISSN 0379-6574) **4173**
Africana Studia/International Journal of African Studies (PRT ISSN 0874-2375) **7946**
Africana Vereniging. Jaarboek see Africana Society. Yearbook **4173**
Africana Vereniging. Joernaal see Africana Society. Journal **4173**
Africans in Partnership Against Aids. Newsletter see Kibaru **3546**
• ➤ Africanus (ZAF ISSN 0304-615X) **7103**
• Africascan (SWE ISSN 1653-283X) **3789**
Afriche (ITA ISSN 1123-7775) **4173**
Africom (KEN) **2312**
Africultures (FRA ISSN 1276-2458) **4441**
• Afrik Etudiant (FRA ISSN 1766-6562) **3516**
Afrika, Asien - Brasilien - Portugal see A B P **5247**
Afrika Bulletin (CHE) **4571**
• ➤ Afrika Focus (BEL ISSN 0772-084X) **4173**
Afrika im Blickpunkt (Online Edition) see G I G A Focus. Afrika **7236**
Afrika Jahrbuch (DEU ISSN 0935-3534) **7103**
Afrika Matematica see Afrika Mathematica **5467**
Afrika Mathematica (FRA ISSN 1012-9405) **5467**
Afrika-Post (DEU ISSN 0002-0389) **3517**
• ➤ Afrika Spectrum (DEU ISSN 0002-0397) **7103**
Afrika-Studiecentrum Series (NLD ISSN 1570-9310) **4173**
Afrika Studien (DEU) **1057**
Afrika Studies see Cahiers Africains **4174**
Afrika Sued (DEU ISSN 0947-8353) **1590**
Afrika Travel and Tourism Magazine see Afrika Travel & Tourism Magazine **8681**
▼ Afrika Travel & Tourism Magazine (USA ISSN 1946-5211) **8681**
Afrika und Europa. Koloniale und Postkoloniale Begegnungen/Africa and Europe. Colonial and Postcolonial Encounters (DEU ISSN 1614-9904) **4173**
Afrika und Uebersee (DEU ISSN 0002-0427) **5091**
Afrika und Uebersee. Beiheft (DEU ISSN 0720-8189) **5091**
Afrika ya Kesho (KEN) **7620**
➤ Afrika Zamani (SEN) **1590**
Afrikan Truth Crusader (ZWE) **3789**
Die Afrikaner (ZAF ISSN 1994-9340) **7103**
Afrikaner Beesjoernaal (ZAF ISSN 0515-6203) **277**
Afrikanisch-Asiatische Studentenfoerderung. Jahrbuch (DEU) **3011**
Afrikanischer Heimatkalender (NAM ISSN 0400-714X) **7744**
• ➤ Afrikanistik Online (DEU ISSN 1860-7462) **4173**
Afrikanistische Arbeitspapiere see Annual Publication in African Linguistics **5094**
Afrikanskii Rynok/African Market (RUS) **1551**
Afring News (ZAF ISSN 1817-9770) **901**
Afriqiyah (FRA ISSN 1777-7364) **8782**
Afrique (FRA ISSN 1161-8051) **191**
Afrique 2000 (BEL ISSN 1017-0952) **7220**
Afrique Asie (FRA ISSN 1779-0042) **7103**
• Afrique Contemporaine (FRA ISSN 0002-0478) **7220**
L'Afrique dans Tous Ses Etats (FRA ISSN 1778-6193) **5205**
Afrique Economie (TUN) **1435**
▼ Afrique Enjeux (FRA ISSN 1960-2405) **3517**
Afrique et Developpement see Africa Development **1589**
• Afrique & Histoire (FRA ISSN 1764-1977) **4173**
Afrique et Philosophie (COD) **6902**
▼ Afrique Liberte (FRA ISSN 1959-4836) **323**
Afrique Magazine (FRA ISSN 0998-9307) **3839**
L'Afrique Politique (Revue) see Collection L'Afrique Politique **4174**
L'Afrique Politique. Collection see Collection L'Afrique Politique **4174**
Afrique Relance. Document d'Information see Africa Renewal **1435**
Afrique Tribune (CAN) **3789**
▼ • Les Afriques (FRA ISSN 1961-5523) **3517**
▼ Afriscope (FRA ISSN 1958-8542) **3517**
Afro-American Culture and Society Monograph Series (USA ISSN 0882-5297) **3517**
Afro-American Historical and Genealogical Society Historical Journal of the African American Experience in Arkansas see A A H G S Historical Journal of the African American Experience in Arkansas **3514**
Afro-American Historical and Genealogical Society. Journal (USA ISSN 0272-1937) **3758**
Afro-American Historical and Genealogical Society News see A A H G S News **3757**
• ➤ Afro-Americans in New York Life and History (USA ISSN 0364-2437) **3517**
Afro - Arave Revue (MLI) **3517**
Afro-Asia (BRA ISSN 0002-0591) **4441**
Afro-Asian Artists' Register see Equity African, Caribbean, Oriental & Asian Artists Register **1992**
Afro - Asian Book Council Newsletter see A A B C Newsletter **7550**
▼ • ➤ Afro-Asian Journal of Finance and Accounting (GBR ISSN 1751-6447) **1279**
Afro - Asian Journal of Nematology see International Journal of Nematology **948**
Afro-Asian Nematology Network (IND) **931**
† Afro-Asian Peoples' Conference. Proceedings (EGY ISSN 0065-4191) **8928**
Afro-Asian Rural Development Newsletter see A A R D O Newsletter **1589**
• ➤ Afro-Hispanic Review (USA ISSN 0278-8969) **3517**
Afro-Latin/American Research Association. Publication (USA ISSN 1093-5398) **3517**
The Afro News (CAN ISSN 1208-7777) **3517**
Afro Scholar Newsletter (USA ISSN 0894-0762) **3517**
Afro Times (USA) **3517**
AfroAmericanist (USA) **3517**
Afroasiatic Dialects (USA ISSN 0732-6416) **5091**
Afrodite (NOR ISSN 1504-5250) **8024**
▼ • ➤ Afroeuropa (ESP ISSN 1887-3456) **5091**
Afroscope (KEN) **7744**
Afryka, Azja, Ameryka Lacinska (POL ISSN 0208-8010) **3789**
Afscheid Nemen van een Overledene see Contactblad Spreken bij Uitvaarten **6911**
Afspaending, Psykomotorik (DNK ISSN 1902-3375) **6981**
Afspaendingspaedagogen see Afspaending, Psykomotorik **6981**
• Aftenposten (NOR ISSN 0804-3116) **3921**
▼ • After Culture (USA ISSN 1941-6881) **323**
After Dark (DEU) **3843**
After Five (USA) **4975**
After Hours (GBR) **4079**
After School (USA ISSN 1930-4986) **2824**
After the Battle (GBR ISSN 0306-154X) **6408**
• Afterall (GBR ISSN 1465-4253) **464**
• Afterimage (USA ISSN 0300-7472) **6963**
Afterloss (USA ISSN 1044-0534) **6120**
• Aftermarket Business (USA ISSN 0892-1121) **8555**
Aftermarket Canada (CAN ISSN 0828-6116) **8555**
Aftermarket Distribution (USA) **8555**
Aftermarket Insider (USA ISSN 1526-4475) **8555**
Aftermarket News (English Edition) see Aftermarket News (French Edition) **975**
Aftermarket News (French Edition) (FRA ISSN 1774-7295) **975**
Afternoon (JPN) **2175**
The Afternoon Despatch & Courier (IND) **3878**
• AfterNoon Magazine (USA) **464**
Afternoon on Sunday (IND) **3878**
Afternoon Season Zokan (JPN) **2175**
AfterTouch (USA) **6632**
• Aftonbladet (SWE ISSN 1103-9000) **3954**
Afurika Kenkyu see Journal of African Studies **4176**
Afvalgids (BEL) **3503**
Afvalwaterwetenschap (NLD ISSN 1569-2361) **3503**
Afya (KEN ISSN 0378-4851) **5570**
Afyon Kocatepe Universitesi Sosyal Bilimler Enstitusu Dergisi/Afyon Kocatepe University. Institute of Social Sciences. Journal (TUR ISSN 1302-2407) **7946**
Afyon Kocatepe University. Institute of Social Sciences. Journal see Afyon Kocatepe Universitesi Sosyal Bilimler Enstitusu Dergisi **7946**
Ag (GBR ISSN 1475-116X) **6963**
Ag Alert (USA ISSN 0161-5408) **80**
• The Ag Bioethics Forum (USA) **80**
Ag-Chem Age/Noyaku Jidai (JPN ISSN 0029-5426) **80**
Ag Chem New Compound Review (USA ISSN 1072-7361) **216**
Ag Equipment Intelligence (USA ISSN 1934-3272) **80**
Ag Equipment Manufacturer (USA ISSN 1558-9099) **209**
Ag Equipment Power (USA ISSN 1535-9409) **209**
Ag Executive (USA ISSN 1053-2692) **191**
Ag Executive's Farm and Ranch Tax Letter see Farm and Ranch Tax Letter **198**
Ag Facts (USA ISSN 1063-0120) **80**
Ag Focus (USA ISSN 0899-7535) **80**
Ag Industrial Materials & Products (USA) **80**
Ag Journal (Harlington) (USA) **80**
• Ag Journal (La Junta) (USA) **80**
• Ag Lender (USA ISSN 1532-8902) **1306**
Ag News see Agricultural News (LaFayette) **84**
Ag News (USA) **80**
Ag+ Photographic see Ag **6963**
Ag-Pilot International (USA ISSN 0740-1434) **44**
• Ag Professional (USA ISSN 1545-4541) **216**
AG Science Journal see Agricultural Science **84**
Ag Trader (NZL) **80**
Ag Waste Management (USA) **261**
• Ag Weekly (USA) **80**
Ag Youth Magazine (USA) **80**
Agada (USA ISSN 0740-2392) **5250**
Again (USA ISSN 0885-9795) **7703**
• Against All Reason (USA ISSN 1741-0754) **7332**
• Against Sleep and Nightmare (USA) **7103**
• ➤ Against the Current (USA ISSN 0739-4853) **7103**
Against the Grain (USA ISSN 1043-2094) **4987**
Agalma (ITA ISSN 1723-0284) **6902**
Agape Nieuws (NLD ISSN 1571-6635) **7620**
Agapit (UKR) **5570**
• Agassiz - Harrison Observer (CAN ISSN 1194-448X) **3805**
Agathos (ESP ISSN 1578-3103) **7506**
Agazen (ETH) **2601**
• ➤ AgBioforum (USA ISSN 1522-936X) **191**
AgBiotech Bulletin see Bio-Bulletin **96**
• AgBiotech News and Information (GBR ISSN 0954-9897) **712**
• AgBiotech Reporter (USA ISSN 1757-2029) **80**
AgBiotechNet see AgBiotech News and Information **712**
Agder - Flekkefjords Tidende (NOR) **3921**
Agder Naturmuseum. Aarbok (NOR ISSN 0808-9655) **7833**
Agderposten (NOR) **3921**
• The Age (AUS ISSN 0312-6307) **3793**
• ➤ Age (NLD) **4038**
• Age Agenda Bulletin (Online) (GBR) **4038**
• ➤ Age and Ageing (GBR ISSN 0002-0729) **4038**
Age & Nutrition see Age et Nutrition **6654**
Age and Sex Profile of Overseas Visitors to the U K (Year) (GBR) **8777**
Age Concern Information Bulletin (Print) see Age Agenda Bulletin (Online) **4038**
L'Age de Faire (FRA ISSN 1777-1323) **2602**
L'Age des Lumieres (FRA ISSN 1278-3862) **6902**
Age Discrimination (USA) **7202**
Age et Nutrition (FRA ISSN 1158-0259) **6654**
• Age.Info CD-ROM (GBR ISSN 1358-1376) **4058**
Age News (USA) **4038**
Age of Information Marketing see A I M **1803**
➤ Age of Johnson (USA ISSN 0884-5816) **5250**
The Age of Revolution and Romanticism: Interdisciplinary Studies (USA ISSN 1045-4497) **4196**
▼ The Age of Shakespeare (USA ISSN 1936-6388) **5250**
Age of Tomorrow (JPN ISSN 0002-0753) **3899**
Age Venture News (USA) **4038**
Aged Care Action (AUS ISSN 1834-9706) **5950**
Aged Society Journal see Korei Shakai Janaru **4050**
Ageha/Swallow-Tail (JPN) **651**
Ageing and Health (GBR ISSN 1364-9752) **4038**
• ➤ Ageing and Society (GBR ISSN 0144-686X) **4039**
• Ageing International (USA ISSN 0163-5158) **4039**
▼ Ageing Lung (ITA ISSN 1971-9299) **6211**
• Ageing Research Reviews (IRL ISSN 1568-1637) **4039**
Ageless (USA ISSN 1527-5310) **8850**
• AgeLine (USA) **4058**
Agence Canadienne de Developpement International. Rapport Annuel (CAN ISSN 1482-6526) **1590**
Agence Canadienne de Developpment International Marches see A C D I Marches **1589**
Agence Canadienne de Developpment International. Marches de Services et Lignes de Credit see A C D I Marches **1589**
Agence Canadienne des Medicaments et des Technologies de la Sante. Rapport Technologique (CAN ISSN 1914-4717) **5570**
Agence de Developpement de Reseaux Locaux de Services de Sante et de Services Sociaux de la Capitale Nationale. Rapport Annuel de Gestion (CAN ISSN 1719-8593) **8024**
Agence de Developpement de Reseaux Locaux de Services de Sante et de Services Sociaux de la Cote-Nord. Rapport Annuel (CAN ISSN 1719-8577) **7506**
Agence de Developpement de Reseaux Locaux de Services de Sante et de Services Sociaux de l'Outaouais (Quebec). Rapport Annuel des Plaintes see L' Application de la Procedure d'Examen des Plaintes en Matiere de Sante et de Services Sociaux et sur l'Amelioration de la Qualite des Services Dispenses dans le Reseau de la Sante et des Services Sociaux de l'Outaouais. Rapport Annuel **8025**
Agence de Developpement de Reseaux Locaux de Services de Sante et de Services Sociaux de l'Outaouais. Rapport Annuel (CAN ISSN 1718-0120) **7506**
Agence de Developpement de Reseaux Locaux de Services de Sante et de Services Sociaux de l'Outaouais. Rapport Annuel de Gestion see Agence de Developpement de Reseaux Locaux de Services de Sante et de Services Sociaux de l'Outaouais. Rapport Annuel **7506**
Agence de Developpement et d'Urbanisme de l'Agglomeration Strasbourgeoise see A D E U S **4402**

Title

Title

DIRECTORY 2010 AIRCRAFT PROXIMITY HAZARDS REPORTS 9935

• AIDS & Hepatitis Digest (Acquired Immune Deficiency Syndrome) (GBR ISSN 1473-012X) **5808**
• ➤ AIDS & Public Policy Journal (Acquired Immune Deficiency Syndrome) (USA ISSN 0887-3852) **5808**
Aids and Research Tools in Ancient Near Eastern Studies (USA ISSN 0732-6505) **4319**
Aids and Research Tools in Middle Eastern Studies (USA ISSN 0742-1109) **4319**
AIDS & T B Weekly Abstracts from Conference Proceedings (Tuberculosis) (USA ISSN 1074-2891) **5740**
AIDS-Bestrijding *see* S O A Aids Magazine **5765**
• AIDS Book Review Journal (USA ISSN 1068-4174) **5808**
AIDS Bulletin (ZAF ISSN 1019-8334) **5808**
• AIDS Clinical Care (USA ISSN 1043-1543) **5808**
AIDS Committee of Toronto. Annual Report *see* AIDS Committee of Toronto Report to Donors **8024**
• AIDS Committee of Toronto Report to Donors (CAN ISSN 1719-8208) **8024**
• ➤ AIDS Education and Prevention (Acquired Immune Deficiency Syndrome) (USA ISSN 0899-9546) **7506**
AIDS / HIV (Farmington Hills) *see* Information Plus Reference Series. AIDS / HIV **5818**
• AIDS in New York State (USA) **5809**
• AIDS Info (NOR ISSN 0801-6003) **7506**
† The AIDS Informer (GBR ISSN 1465-5470) **8929**
AIDS Infothek (CHE ISSN 1021-321X) **5809**
AIDS Law & Litigation Reporter (USA) **4611**
AIDS Legal Bibliography (Acquired Immune Deficiency Syndrome) (USA) **4820**
AIDS Literature & Law Review (USA ISSN 1083-8589) **5740**
AIDS Litigation Digest *see* Health Law Week **4686**
AIDS Organisations Worldwide *see* HIV & AIDS Services Worldwide **5815**
• ➤ AIDS Patient Care and S T Ds (USA ISSN 1087-2914) **5809**
• AIDS Policy and Law (Acquired Immune Deficiency Syndrome) (USA ISSN 0887-1493) **4612**
➤ AIDS Prevention and Mental Health (USA ISSN 1566-0761) **5809**
AIDS Reference Guide (USA) **5809**
AIDS Reference Manual (GBR) **5809**
• ➤ AIDS Research and Human Retroviruses (USA ISSN 0889-2229) **5809**
• ➤ AIDS Research and Therapy (GBR ISSN 1742-6405) **5752**
• AIDS Reviews (ESP ISSN 1139-6121) **5809**
AIDS Sourcebook (USA) **5809**
AIDS Therapies and Vaccines *see* AIDS Therapies & Vaccines **5809**
• AIDS Therapies & Vaccines (USA ISSN 1537-7695) **5809**
Aids to Library Administration Series *see* A T L A S **4986**
• AIDS Treatment Data Network Information Bulletin (USA) **5809**
• AIDS Treatment News (USA ISSN 1052-4207) **5809**
• AIDS Treatment Review (USA) **5809**
AIDS Treatment Update *see* HIV Treatment Update **5816**
• AIDS Vaccine Week (USA ISSN 1543-6918) **5809**
• AIDS Weekly (USA) **5809**
AIDS Weekly and Law *see* AIDS Weekly & Law **4612**
• AIDS Weekly & Law (USA ISSN 1553-3344) **4612**
† • AIDS Weekly Plus (USA) **8929**
† • ➤ AIDScience (USA ISSN 1546-279X) **8929**
• AIDSearch (USA) **5740**
AIDSida Info (USA) **4370**
AiF *see* Argumenty i Fakty **3934**
• Aigis (DNK ISSN 1901-6859) **5091**
Aiguillon *see* Hosteni **5219**
Aiheita (FIN ISSN 1236-9845) **8024**
Aiiku Tsushin/Letters of Human Growth (JPN) **2825**
Aikatan Gaveshana Patra/Aikatan Research Journal (IND) **8086**
Aikatan Research Journal *see* Aikatan Gaveshana Patra **8086**
Aiken no Tomo/Friends of Dog (JPN ISSN 1345-8841) **6802**
• Aikido Journal (JPN ISSN 1340-5624) **8157**
Aikido Today Magazine (USA ISSN 1060-9415) **8157**
➤ Aikuiskasvatus/Adult Education (FIN ISSN 0358-6197) **2938**
Aikya (IND) **3878**
• Ailem ve Ben (TUR) **4351**
† Ailes Magazine (FRA ISSN 1166-0422) **8929**
L'Ailleurs du Corps (FRA ISSN 1778-4972) **7332**
Ailleurs et Demain (FRA ISSN 0065-4787) **5250**
Aim (CAN ISSN 0382-4373) **8157**
Aim (IND) **7732**
▼ • Aim Homeschool Magazine (USA ISSN 1937-3953) **2825**
Aim Liturgy Resources (USA ISSN 1079-459X) **6542**
Aim Magazine (Chicago) (USA) **3517**
AIMA News *see* A I M A News **1722**
Aimer et Servir (FRA ISSN 1956-9157) **7744**
Aiming High Mexico (MEX) **3907**
L'Ain Agricole (FRA ISSN 0002-2136) **89**
Al-Ain Assahirah (OMN) **2643**
Ain Shams Dental Journal (EGY ISSN 1110-7642) **5833**
'Ain Shams. Hawliyyat Kulliyyat al-'Adab *see* Ain Shams University. Faculty of Arts. Annals **5250**
▼ Ain Shams Journal of Anesthesiology (EGY ISSN 1687-7934) **5768**
Ain Shams Medical Journal (EGY ISSN 0002-2144) **5570**
Ain Shams Science Bulletin/Al-Nasrat al-'Lmiyyat Lgami't 'In Sams (EGY ISSN 1110-0397) **7833**
Ain Shams University. Economic and Business Review/Al-Magallah al-'Ilmiyyah lil-Iqtisad wa-al-Tigarah (EGY ISSN 1110-1008) **1057**
Ain Shams University. Faculty of Arts. Annals/'Ain Shams. Hawliyyat Kulliyyat al-'Adab (EGY ISSN 1110-7227) **5250**
Ain Shams University. Faculty of Education. Journal. Education and Psychology/Magallat Kulliyyat al-Tarbiyyat. Tarbiyya Wa'ilm al-Nafs (EGY ISSN 1110-7626) **2825**
† Ain Shams University. Faculty of Education. Journal. Literary Section/Magallat Kolliyat al-Tarbiyat. Al-Qesm al-Adabi (EGY) **8929**
Ain Shams University. Faculty of Education. Journal. Scientific Section/Magallat Kulliyyat al-Tarbiyyat al-Qism al-'ilmi (EGY ISSN 1110-7634) **7833**
Ain Shams University. Scientific Bulletin of the Faculty of Engineering (EGY ISSN 1110-1385) **3180**
Aina (AZE) **3798**
• Les Aines au Canada (CAN ISSN 1912-2349) **8024**
Aines Generations (CHE) **4039**
Ainm (GBR ISSN 0953-461X) **5091**
Aioi Kisoken Review (JPN ISSN 1881-3674) **4491**
Aiolika Grammata (GRC ISSN 1010-4569) **5250**
Aiolos (SWE ISSN 1400-7770) **5250**
Aiqing Hunyin Jiating (Lengnuan Rensheng) (CHN) **4351**
Aiqing Hunyin Jiating (Shenghuo Jishi)/Love, Marriage and Family (CHN) **4351**
Aiqing Hunyin Jiating (Sifang Xinqing)/Love Marriage and Family (CHN ISSN 1003-0883) **4351**
Air Actualites (FRA ISSN 0002-2152) **6408**
• Air Affairs (ZAF) **4491**
The Air Almanac (USA ISSN 0400-8456) **44**
• Air & Business Travel News (GBR ISSN 0963-9993) **8534**
• ➤ Air & Space Law (NLD ISSN 0927-3379) **8534**
Air and Space Lawyer (USA ISSN 0747-7449) **4612**
• ➤ The Air & Space Power Journal (USA ISSN 1555-385X) **6408**
• Air & Space Power Journal bil-'Arabiya (USA ISSN 1555-3868) **6409**
• Air & Space Power Journal en Francais (USA ISSN 1931-728X) **6409**
• Air & Space Power Journal Espanol (USA ISSN 1555-3833) **6409**
▼ Air & Space Power Journal in Chinese (USA ISSN 1937-1373) **6409**
• Air & Space Power Journal in Portuguese (USA ISSN 1555-3825) **6409**
• Air & Space - Smithsonian (USA ISSN 0886-2257) **44**
• Air & Waste Management Association. Annual Meeting & Exhibition Proceedings (CD-ROM) (USA) **3401**
• ➤ Air & Waste Management Association. Journal (USA ISSN 1096-2247) **3503**
† • Air & Waste Management Association. Meeting Proceedings (USA ISSN 1052-6102) **8929**
Air-Britain Airline Fleets (GBR) **8534**
Air-Britain Digest (GBR ISSN 0950-7434) **44**
Air-Britain News (GBR ISSN 0950-7442) **44**
• Air Bulletin (USA) **44**
Air Cadet (GBR) **2175**
• Air Cargo Agents Association of India. News (IND) **8614**
Air Cargo Guide *see* Guia da Carga Aerea **8543**
Air Cargo News (USA) **8534**
• Air Cargo World (USA ISSN 0745-5100) **8534**
Air Cargo Yearbook (Year) (GBR ISSN 1476-2684) **8534**
Air Carrier Financial Statistics (USA ISSN 0002-2225) **8521**
Air Carrier Industry Schedule Service Traffic Statistics. Medium Regional Carriers (USA) **8521**
• Air Carrier Traffic at Canadian Airports (CAN ISSN 1483-2399) **8521**
• The Air Charter Guide (USA ISSN 0890-2925) **8534**
Air China/Zhongguo Guoji Hangkong Gongsi Jinei Zazhi (GBR ISSN 1003-3823) **8782**
Air Circle *see* Meishu Jie **505**
• Air Classics (USA ISSN 0002-2241) **44**
† Air Comprime (FRA ISSN 0002-225X) **8929**
• Air Conditioning & Heating Service & Repair - Domestic Cars, Light Trucks & Vans (USA) **8555**
• Air Conditioning & Heating Service & Repair - Imported Cars & Trucks (USA) **8555**
Air Conditioning & Refrigeration News (GBR ISSN 0266-6871) **4116**
Air-Conditioning & Refrigeration Wholesalers Counterline *see* A R W Counterline **4115**
Air Conditioning Contractors of America News *see* A C C A News **4115**
Air Conditioning Contractors of America Quality Contractor's Catalog of Materials, Products and Services *see* A C C A Quality Contractor's Catalog of Materials, Products and Services **4128**
• Air Conditioning, Heating & Refrigeration News (USA ISSN 0002-2276) **4116**
Air Conditioning Home and Commercial *see* Audel Air Conditioning Home and Commercial **4116**
• Air Currents (USA ISSN 0400-8510) **3482**
Air Daily (Online) (USA ISSN 1538-9332) **3482**
Air Defense Artillery Yearbook (USA) **6409**
Air Enthusiast (GBR ISSN 0143-5450) **44**
• Air & Cosmos (FRA ISSN 0983-1592) **44**
Air & Cosmos - Aviation Magazine International (FRA ISSN 1240-3113) **44**
Air Fan (FRA ISSN 0223-0038) **6409**
Air Finance Annual (Years) *see* Airfinance Annual **1306**
Air Finance Journal *see* Airfinance Journal **8535**
• The Air Force Civil Engineer (USA ISSN 1555-8991) **3259**
• Air Force Comptroller (USA ISSN 0002-2365) **6409**
Air Force Engineering University. Journal (Natural Science Edition) *see* Kongjun Gongcheng Daxue Xuebao (Ziran Kexue Ban) **7877**
Air Force Interchangeable and Substitution Report (USA) **6409**
• ➤ Air Force Journal of Logistics (USA ISSN 0270-403X) **6409**
• Air Force Law Review (USA ISSN 0094-8381) **4971**
Air Force List (GBR ISSN 0266-8610) **6409**
• Air Force Magazine (USA ISSN 0730-6784) **6409**
Air Force Report (USA ISSN 0273-4370) **6409**
• Air Force Times (U.S. Edition) (USA ISSN 0002-2403) **6409**
Air Force Times (Worldwide Edition) *see* Air Force Times (U.S. Edition) **6409**
Air France Madame (FRA ISSN 0980-7519) **8782**
Air France Magazine (FRA ISSN 1290-1563) **8682**
† Air France Rendez-vous (FRA ISSN 1288-1201) **8929**
Air Freight Directory (USA ISSN 0092-2870) **8534**
Air Freight Market Report *see* Key Note Market Report: Air Freight **8547**
Air Gazette *see* Gaceta Aerea **56**
Air Gunner (GBR ISSN 0266-4224) **8157**
Air in the Paragraph Line (USA) **3968**
• Air Information Review (BEL) **3123**
Air Intel Weekly *see* AirIntel Weekly **8536**
• Air International (GBR ISSN 0306-5634) **44**
Air Jobs Digest (USA ISSN 1056-5051) **44**
Air-Launched Weapons *see* Jane's Air-Launched Weapons **6426**
• The Air Letter (GBR) **44**
• Air Letter On-Line (GBR) **44**
Air Line Employee (USA ISSN 0002-2411) **4589**
Air Line Pilot (USA ISSN 0002-242X) **44**
Air Market News (USA) **44**
• ➤ Air Medical Journal (USA ISSN 1067-991X) **5570**
• Air Modeller (GBR ISSN 1747-177X) **4327**
• Air Navigation International (GBR ISSN 1360-4635) **44**
Air Navigation - The Order and the Regulations (GBR) **8534**
Air New Zealand *see* Kia Ora **8784**
Air New Zealand. Annual Report (NZL ISSN 0065-4817) **8534**
Air Pictorial International (GBR ISSN 0965-1896) **44**
Air Pilot *see* Australian Air Pilot **8538**
• The Air Pollution Consultant (USA ISSN 1058-6628) **3482**
Air Pollution International Conference (GBR ISSN 1365-5868) **3482**
Air Pollution Law (USA) **3482**
• Air Pollution Management (USA) **3482**
Air Pollution Modeling and its Applications *see* N A T O Challenges of Modern Society **7884**
• Air Pollution Monitoring and Sampling (USA) **3483**
Air Pollution Monitoring & Sampling *see* Air Pollution Monitoring and Sampling **3483**
Air Pollution Reviews (GBR ISSN 0219-9785) **3483**
• Air Power (IND) **44**
• ➤ Air Power Australia Analyses (AUS ISSN 1832-2433) **6409**
Air Power Australia Analysis *see* Air Power Australia Analyses **6409**
• ➤ Air Power History (USA ISSN 1044-016X) **44**
Air Power Museum Bulletin *see* A P M Bulletin **362**
• Air Power Review (GBR ISSN 1463-6298) **6409**
† Air Press (ITA) **8929**
Air Pulse (USA) **6409**
▼ • Air Quality, Atmosphere and Health (NLD ISSN 1873-9318) **3483**
Air Quality Bulletin (GBR ISSN 1751-150X) **3483**
Air Quality Data (USA ISSN 0093-8165) **3483**
Air Quality Data Management Software Report (USA ISSN 1084-9394) **3481**
Air Quality in Ontario (CAN ISSN 0840-9366) **3483**
Air Quality Indicator *see* Canadian Environmental Sustainability Indicators. Air Quality Indicator **3409**
Air Quality Management (GBR ISSN 1461-0027) **3483**
➤ Air Quality Monographs (NLD ISSN 1382-3078) **3483**
Air Reservations Interline Message Procedures Passenger *see* A I R I M P - Passenger **8533**
• Air Safety Week (Online) (USA) **44**
Air Service Rights in U S International Air Transport Agreements (USA) **8534**
Air Shows (USA ISSN 1097-3133) **45**
▼ • ➤ Air, Soil and Water Research (NZL ISSN 1178-6221) **3401**
• Air Sports International (CHE) **45**
Air Sports Mail (NLD ISSN 1574-2091) **45**
Air Taxi Guide *see* Guia do Taxi Aereo **8543**
Air Traffic Control (USA) **8534**
Air Traffic Control Association. Bulletin (USA ISSN 0400-1915) **8534**
Air Traffic Control Association. Fall Conference Proceedings (USA ISSN 0192-8740) **45**
Air Traffic Control Licensing (GBR) **8534**
➤ Air Traffic Control Quarterly (USA ISSN 1064-3818) **8534**
• Air Traffic Management (GBR ISSN 0969-6725) **8534**
Air Traffic Management Directory (GBR ISSN 1742-8378) **8534**
Air Traffic Management Yearbook (GBR ISSN 1364-2189) **8535**
Air Traffic Services Engineering Requirements (GBR) **8535**
Air Traffic Technology International (GBR ISSN 1366-7041) **8535**
Air Transport (GBR ISSN 1751-9098) **8535**
Air Transport (USA ISSN 0190-552X) **8535**
Air Transport & Business *see* Kongyun Shangwu **8547**
Air Transport Association of Canada. Annual Report (CAN ISSN 0065-485X) **8535**
Air Transport Facts & Figures *see* Air Transport **8535**
Air Transport Observer *see* Aviatransportnoe Obozrenie **8538**
• Air Transport World (USA ISSN 0002-2543) **45**
Air Travel Complaints Commissioner. Report (Online) *see* Air Travel Complaints Report (Online) **8535**
The Air Travel Complaints Commissioner's Report *see* Air Travel Complaints Report (Print) **8535**
• Air Travel Complaints Report (Online) (CAN ISSN 1719-9379) **8535**
• Air Travel Complaints Report (Print)/Rapport sur les Plaintes Relatives au Transport Aerien (CAN ISSN 1719-9352) **8535**
Air Travel Journal (USA) **8682**
Air Travel Survey (USA) **8521**
Air Ukraine (UKR) **8782**
• Air University Library Index to Military Periodicals (USA ISSN 0002-2586) **6455**
Air Zimbabwe Annual Report (ZWE) **8535**
Aira County Medical Association. Journal *see* Aira-gun Ishikai Igakkaishi **5570**
Aira-gun Ishikai Igakkaishi/Aira County Medical Association. Journal (JPN ISSN 0917-9267) **5570**
• Airbase (BEL) **3483**
Airborn (NZL ISSN 1170-9928) **8157**
Airborne (Tullamarine) (AUS ISSN 1030-0090) **4327**
Airborne Electronics Forecast *see* Market Intelligence Reports: Airborne Electronics Forecast **3108**
Airborne Retrofit and Modernization Forecast *see* Market Intelligence Reports: Airborne Retrofit and Modernization Forecast **65**
• Airbrush Action (USA ISSN 1040-8509) **464**
Airbrush Art & Action (DEU ISSN 1434-3223) **464**
Airbrush Art & Action (USA ISSN 1363-5565) **464**
Airbrush Total (DEU) **464**
• Airbrush Zeitung (Online Edition) (DEU) **464**
• Aircargo Asia - Pacific (AUS ISSN 1328-7192) **8535**
• Airclaims Space Intelligencer Newsletter (GBR) **45**
Aircraft *see* Samolyot **70**
Aircraft Accident Digest (CAN ISSN 0443-7926) **45**
Aircraft Accident Reports *see* U.S. National Transportation Safety Board. Aircraft Accident Reports **8552**
Aircraft & Aerospace Asia Pacific *see* Aviation Business Asia Pacific Magazine **48**
• Aircraft Economics (GBR ISSN 0966-7857) **8535**
Aircraft Economics Yearbook (GBR ISSN 1354-8085) **8535**
Aircraft Engineering *see* Koku Gijutsu **64**
• ➤ Aircraft Engineering and Aerospace Technology (GBR ISSN 1748-8842) **45**
Aircraft Finance (GBR) **8535**
Aircraft Illustrated (GBR ISSN 0002-2675) **45**
† Aircraft in Miniature Magazine (GBR) **8929**
Aircraft Incident Report (GBR ISSN 1367-5117) **8535**
Aircraft Interiors International (GBR ISSN 1463-8932) **45**
Aircraft Liens & Detention Rights (GBR) **8535**
Aircraft Maintenance & Engineering Directory (Year) (GBR ISSN 1369-1031) **8535**
Aircraft Maintenance International Yearbook (GBR ISSN 0961-6047) **8535**
Aircraft Maintenance Technology *see* A M T **8533**
Aircraft Maintenance Technology Newsletter *see* A M T Newsletter **8533**
Aircraft Movement Statistics. Monthly Report (CAN ISSN 1193-9087) **8521**
Aircraft Owner (USA) **8535**
Aircraft Owners and Pilots Association Flight Training *see* A O P A Flight Training **41**
Aircraft Owners and Pilots Association Letter *see* A O P A Letter **41**
Aircraft Owners and Pilots Association Pilot *see* A O P A Pilot **41**
Aircraft Owners and Pilots Association Pilot *see* A O P A Pilot **41**
Aircraft Owners and Pilots Association's Airport Directory *see* A O P A's Airport Directory **41**
Aircraft Proximity Hazards Reports (GBR ISSN 0960-9261) **8535**

Title

▼ *new title* † *ceased* • *electronic media* ➤ *refereed*

Akademiai Ilmhoi Cumhurii Tocikiston. Su'bai Ilmhoi Haetsinosi. Ahbori (TJK ISSN 1026-3047) **652**
Akademicky Bulletin *see* Akademie Ved Ceske Republiky. Akademicky Bulletin **7834**
Akademie (DEU ISSN 0944-582X) **6692**
● Akademie Aktuell (DEU ISSN 1436-753X) **3117**
Akademie der Wissenschaften in Goettingen. Sonderheft *see* Akademie der Wissenschaften zu Goettingen. Abhandlungen. Mathematisch-Physikalische Klasse. Dritte Folge **5467**
Akademie der Wissenschaften und der Literatur. Geistes- und Sozialwissenschaftliche Klasse. Abhandlungen (DEU ISSN 0002-2977) **4441**
Akademie der Wissenschaften und der Literatur, Mainz. Jahrbuch (DEU ISSN 0084-6104) **7833**
Akademie der Wissenschaften und der Literatur, Mainz. Klasse der Literatur. Abhandlungen (DEU ISSN 0002-2985) **5250**
Akademie der Wissenschaften und der Literatur, Mainz. Mathematisch - Naturwissenschaftliche Klasse. Abhandlungen (DEU ISSN 0002-2993) **7833**
Akademie der Wissenschaften und der Literatur, Mainz. Orientalische Kommission. Veroeffentlichungen (DEU ISSN 0568-4447) **542**
Akademie der Wissenschaften zu Goettingen. Abhandlungen. Mathematisch-Physikalische Klasse. Dritte Folge (DEU ISSN 0341-9843) **5467**
➤ Akademie der Wissenschaften zu Goettingen. Abhandlungen. Philologisch-Historische Klasse (DEU) **6903**
● ➤ Akademie der Wissenschaften zu Goettingen. Jahrbuch (DEU ISSN 0373-9767) **7833**
Akademie der Wissenschaften zu Goettingen. Nachrichten 1. Philologisch-Historische Klasse (DEU ISSN 0065-5287) **5091**
Akademie der Wissenschaften zu Goettingen. Nachrichten 2. Mathematisch-Physikalische Klasse (DEU ISSN 0065-5295) **5467**
Akademie-Forum (DEU ISSN 1860-4056) **2602**
Akademie Forum Masonicum Jahrbuch (DEU) **5205**
Akademie fuer Migration und Integration. Beitraege (DEU ISSN 1437-1200) **7276**
Akademie fuer Mozart-Forschung der Internationalen Stiftung Mozarteum Salzburg. Mozart-Jahrbuch (DEU ISSN 1861-9053) **6543**
Akademie fuer Natur- und Umweltschutz Baden-Wuerttemberg. Beitraege (DEU) **2602**
Akademie fuer Oeffentliches Gesundheitswesen. Berichte und Materialien (DEU ISSN 0930-1364) **7506**
Akademie fuer Oeffentliches Gesundheitswesen. Schriftenreihe (DEU ISSN 0172-2131) **7506**
Akademie Gemeinnuetziger Wissenschaften zu Erfurt. Geisteswissenschaftlichen Klasse. Sitzungsberichte (DEU ISSN 0940-2233) **7946**
Akademie Ved Ceske Republiky. Akademicky Bulletin (CZE ISSN 1210-9525) **7834**
Akademie voor Kunst en Vormgeving St Joost. Academieboek *see* A K V/St Joost. Academieboek **2822**
Akademiet for de Tekniske Videnskaber. Aarsberetning *see* Akademiet for de Tekniske Videnskaber. Aarsrapport **8415**
● Akademiet for de Tekniske Videnskaber. Aarsrapport (DNK ISSN 1901-8444) **8415**
Akademiet for de Tekniske Videnskaber. Nyt (Online) *see* A T V Nyt (Online) **8415**
Akademiet for de Tekniske Videnskaber Nyt (Online) *see* A T V Nyt (Online) **8415**
Akademija Nauka i Umjetnosti Bosne i Hercegovine. Centar za Balkanoloska Ispitivanja. Godisnjak (BIH ISSN 0350-0020) **4197**
Akademija Nauka i Umjetnosti Bosne i Hercegovine. Odeljenje Medicinskih Nauka. Centar za Medicinska Istrazivanja. Radovi *see* Acta Medica Academica **5566**
Akademija Nauka i Umjetnosti Bosne i Hercegovine. Odeljenje Medicinskih Nauka. Radovi *see* Acta Medica Academica **5566**
Akademija Nauka i Umjetnosti Bosne i Hercegovine. Odjeljenje Drustvenih Nauka. Djela (BIH) **4197**
Akademija Nauka i Umjetnosti Bosne i Hercegovine. Odjeljenje Drustvenih Nauka. Radovi (BIH ISSN 0350-0039) **7946**
Akademiker-Stellenmarkt.de (DEU) **6692**
Akademikern (SWE ISSN 1652-9898) **8024**
Akademische Blaetter (DEU ISSN 1612-9741) **5205**
Akademische Monatsblaetter (DEU ISSN 0002-3000) **7782**
Akademische Reden und Kolloquien (DEU ISSN 0178-2479) **2966**
Akademiska Dzive/Academic Life (USA ISSN 0516-3145) **3517**
Akademix (SWE ISSN 0283-0345) **2966**
Akademiya (UKR) **3963**
➤ Akademiya Agrarnykh Navuk Respubliki Belarusi. Vestsi (BLR ISSN 1029-6891) **89**
➤ Akademiya Medychnykh Nauk Ukrainy. Zhurnal (UKR) **5570**
Akademiya Nauk Armenii. Doklady *see* Hayastany Guitoutyunnery Azgayin Academia Zekuyts'ner **7860**
Akademiya Nauk Armenii. Izvestiya. Seriya Fizika *see* Hayastany Guitoutyunnery Azgayin Academia. Teghekagir. Fizika **7015**
Akademiya Nauk Armenii. Izvestiya. Seriya Matematika/Hayastani Gitutsunneri Azgain Academiay Teghekagir Matematika (ARM) **5467**
Akademiya Nauk Armenii. Izvestiya. Seriya Tekhnicheskikh Nauk/Hayastani Hanrapetutian Gitutsunneri Azgain Academiay Tekhnikakan Gitutsunnery Handes (ARM) **8415**
Akademiya Nauk C.S.S.R. Vostochno-Sibirskii Filial, Irkutsk. Institut Geokhimii. Geokhimicheskie Metody Poiskov, Metody Analiza (RUS) **2701**
Akademiya Nauk C.S.S.R. Vostochno-Sibirskii Filial, Irkutsk. Institut Geokhimii. Geokhimiya Endogennych Protsessov (RUS) **2701**
Akademiya Nauk Estonii. Izvestiya. Fizika, Matematika *see* Estonian Academy of Sciences. Proceedings. Physics. Mathematics **7011**
Akademiya Nauk Estonii. Izvestiya. Geologiya *see* Estonian Journal of Earth Sciences **2733**
Akademiya Nauk Estonii. Izvestiya. Khimiya *see* Estonian Academy of Sciences. Proceedings. Chemistry **2061**
Akademiya Nauk Gruzii. Izvestiya. Seriya Biologiceskaya *see* Sakartvelos Metsnierebata Akademia. Matsne. Biologiis Seria **702**
Akademiya Nauk Kazakhstana. Izvestiya. Seriya Filologicheskaya (KAZ) **5092**
Akademiya Nauk Respubliki Moldova. Izvestiya. Biologicheskie i Khimicheskie Nauki *see* Academia de Stiinte a Republicii Moldova. Buletinul. Stiinte Biologice si Chimice **649**
Akademiya Nauk Respubliki Moldova. Izvestiya. Ekonomika i Sotsiologiya *see* Academia de Stiinte a Republicii Moldova. Buletinul. Economie si Sociologie **1435**
Akademiya Nauk Respubliki Moldova. Izvestiya. Matematika *see* Academia de Stiinte a Republicii Moldova. Buletinul. Matematica **5463**
Akademiya Nauk Respubliki Moldova. Voprosy Filosofii i Prava *see* Academia de Stiinte a Republicii Moldova. Revista Filosofie si Drept **6902**
Akademiya Nauk Respubliki Uzbekistan. Doklady: Matematika, Tekhnicheskie Nauki, Estestvoznanie (UZB) **5467**
Akademiya Nauk Turkmenistana. Izvestiya. Seriya Fiziko-Tekhnicheskikh, Khimicheskikh i Geologicheskikh Nauk (TKM) **7004**
Akademiya Nauk Turkmenistana. Izvestiya. Seriya Obshchestvennykh Nauk (TKM) **7946**
Akademiya Nauk Ukrainy. Visnyk (UKR ISSN 1027-3239) **7834**
Akademiya Nauk Uzbekistana. Doklady. Matematika, Tekhnicheskie Nauki, Estestvoznanie (UZB ISSN 1019-8954) **7834**
Akademiya Nauk Vysshei Shkoly Rossii. Doklady (RUS ISSN 1727-2769) **7834**
Akademiya Nauk Vysshei Shkoly. Sibirskoe Otdelenie. Doklady *see* Akademiya Nauk Vysshei Shkoly Rossii. Doklady **7834**
Akademiya Promyshlennoi Ekologii. Izvestiya (RUS) **3401**
Akademiya Zdorov'ya (UKR) **5570**
● Akademos (VEN ISSN 1317-1798) **2825**
Akahige/Takko Town Hospital. Annual Report (JPN ISSN 0911-1549) **4087**
Akal Arqueologia (ESP ISSN 1699-9622) **371**
Akal Universitaria. Serie: Arqueologia *see* Akal Arqueologia **371**
Akali Patrika (IND) **3878**
Akaroa Mail (NZL ISSN 0002-3612) **3916**
Akasawa Botanical Laboratory. Phytotaxonomic Reports *see* Akasawa Shokubutsu Jikkenshitsu Shokubutsu Bunrui Kenkyu Hokoku **774**
Akasawa Shokubutsu Jikkenshitsu Shokubutsu Bunrui Kenkyu Hokoku/Akasawa Botanical Laboratory. Phytotaxonomic Reports (JPN) **774**
Akashi (IND ISSN 0002-3620) **2356**
Akava-Uutiset *see* Akavalainen **4589**
● Akavalainen (FIN ISSN 1795-8822) **4589**
Akavita (IND ISSN 0970-096X) **5416**
Akcent (POL ISSN 0208-6220) **5205**
Akcenty (POL) **7744**
● Akciger Arsivi/Archives of Pulmonary (TUR ISSN 1302-8715) **6211**
● Akciova Spolecnost a Jeji Rizeni (CZE ISSN 1801-8076) **4854**
Akershus Amtstidende (NOR) **3921**
Akershus - Romerikes Blad (NOR) **3921**
Akhalitaoba (GEO) **3843**
Akhand Anand (IND ISSN 0002-3639) **3878**
Al-Akhbar (EGY) **3835**
Akhbar A D N O C *see* A D N O C News **6761**
Akhbar al-A'alam al-Islami (SAU ISSN 1319-0725) **7708**
Akhbar al-Butrul was-Sina'a/Petroleum and Industry News (UAE) **6761**
Akhbar al-Hisab al-Ali al-Sharq al-Awsat *see* Computer News Middle East **2491**
Akhbar al-Usbo'/News of the Week (JOR) **3901**
Akhbar al-Usbu' (QAT) **3912**
Akhbar al-Yawm (EGY) **3835**
Akhbar B A P C O (BHR) **6761**
Akhbar-E-Mashriq (IND) **3878**
Akhbar El-Yom *see* Akhbar al-Yawm **3835**
Akher Sa'a (EGY ISSN 0002-3655) **3835**
Aki Yerushalayim (ISR ISSN 0793-1166) **3517**
Akikai Chile (Print) *see* Actualidades y Noticias del Aikido **8156**
Akila (SWE ISSN 1404-8434) **8302**
Akinita *see* O Phileleftheros **3832**
Akita Daigaku Kyoikugakubu Kenkyu Kiyo/Akita University. College of Education. Memoirs, Natural Science (JPN ISSN 1348-5296) **5467**
Akita Dog (USA) **6802**
Akita Eiyou Tanki Daigaku. Ronso/Akita Keizaihoka University. Collected Papers (JPN) **7834**
Akita Fruit-tree Experiment Station. Bulletin *see* Akita-ken Kaju Shikenjuo Kenkyuu Huokoku **89**
➤ Akita Igaku/Akita Journal of Medicine (JPN ISSN 0386-6106) **5570**
Akita Journal of Medicine *see* Akita Igaku **5570**
Akita Journal of Rural Medicine *see* Akitaken Noson Igakkai Zasshi **5570**
Akita Keizai Hoka Daigaku. Tanki Daigakubu. Ronso/Akita Keizai Hoka University. Junior College. Collected Papers *see* Akita Eiyou Tanki Daigaku. Ronso **7834**
Akita Keizaihoka University. Collected Papers *see* Akita Eiyou Tanki Daigaku. Ronso **7834**
Akita-ken Kaju Shikenjuo Kenkyuu Huokoku/Akita Fruit-tree Experiment Station. Bulletin (JPN ISSN 0385-3152) **89**
Akita Kenritsu Daigaku Tanki Daigakubu Kiyo/Akita Prefectural College of Agriculture. Bulletin (JPN ISSN 1346-1443) **89**
Akita-kenritsu Hakubutsukan Kenkyu Hokoku/Akita Prefectural Museum. Annual Report (JPN ISSN 0385-1354) **6518**
Akita Medical Journal *see* Akitaken Ishikai Zasshi **5570**
Akita Prefectural College of Agriculture. Bulletin *see* Akita Kenritsu Daigaku Tanki Dargakubu Kiyo **89**
Akita Prefectural Museum. Annual Report *see* Akita-kenritsu Hakubutsukan Kenkyu Hokoku **6518**
Akita Shizenshi Kenkyu (JPN ISSN 0285-0257) **7834**
Akita Society of Obstetrics and Gynecology. Journal *see* Nihon Sanka Fujinka Gakkai Akita Chihobu Kaishi **5999**
Akita University. College of Education. Memoirs, Natural Science *see* Akita Daigaku Kyoikugakubu Kenkyu Kiyo **5467**
Akita World (USA ISSN 0745-1296) **6802**
Akitaken Ishikai Zasshi/Akita Medical Journal (JPN ISSN 0286-7656) **5570**
Akitaken Noson Igakkai Zasshi/Akita Journal of Rural Medicine (JPN ISSN 0002-368X) **5570**
Akitu/Kyoto Entomological Society. Journal (JPN ISSN 0389-2751) **838**
Akiyoshi-dai Kagaku Hakubutsukan Hokoku (JPN ISSN 0065-5554) **6518**
Akkadica *see* Akkadica **371**
Akkadica (BEL ISSN 1378-5087) **371**
Akkadica Plus (BEL ISSN 0779-7842) **372**
Akkas Daily (IND) **3878**
Akker Magazine (NLD) **89**
Akkerbouw (Doetinchem) (NLD ISSN 0169-0116) **89**
Akkerbouw (The Hague) (NLD ISSN 0923-7143) **193**
Akkerbouw & Veeteelt (BEL ISSN 1373-2722) **89**
Akkoord (NLD ISSN 0929-3787) **6543**
Akkro Free *see* Akkro Magazine **8157**
Akkro Magazine (FRA ISSN 1774-4873) **8157**
● Akmallurksissmajul (CAN ISSN 1193-8706) **3517**
Ako (HRV ISSN 1331-5706) **4441**
Akora Soa (MDG) **975**
Akos - Enciclopedia Pratica di Medicina *see* Encyclopedie Medico-Chirurgicale. Traite de Medecine Akos **5609**
Akosutikku Emisshon Sogo Konfarensu Ronbunshu/National Conference on Acoustic Emission. Proceedings (JPN) **7086**
Akron (USA) **2272**
Akron, Canton and Youngstown Railroad Historical Society News *see* A C & Y H S News **8614**
Akron Dental Society. Bulletin (USA ISSN 0002-3701) **5833**
● Akron Family (USA) **2143**
▼ ● Akron Intellecutal Property Journal (USA ISSN 1938-4572) **4612**
Akron Jewish News (USA) **3517**
● Akron Law Review (USA ISSN 0002-371X) **4612**
● Akron Legal News (USA) **4612**
Akron Life & Leisure (USA ISSN 1542-4456) **3968**
Akron Rose Rambler (USA) **3721**
● Akron Tax Journal (USA ISSN 1044-4130) **1909**
● ➤ Akroterion (ZAF ISSN 0303-1896) **2229**
Aks (IND) **5251**
● Akseli (FIN ISSN 1796-3656) **2938**
Akseltrykmaalinger (DNK ISSN 0908-4037) **8629**
Akshara (IND ISSN 0973-6565) **5251**
Akt (NOR ISSN 0801-9975) **7744**
Akt-Nytt fraan Teaterfoerbundet (SWE) **8464**
Aktief (BEL ISSN 1373-8356) **5205**
Aktief *see* Lava **7150**
Aktiemarknaden *see* Kapitalmarknaden **1363**
Aktien-Analyze (DEU ISSN 0944-7598) **1609**
† Aktien & Co. (DEU ISSN 1618-7768) **8929**
Die Aktiengesellschaft (DEU ISSN 0002-3752) **1879**
Der Aktiensammler (DEU ISSN 1611-8006) **1436**
● Aktiespararen/Shareholder (SWE ISSN 0345-049X) **1609**
Aktines/Beam (GRC ISSN 1106-3076) **7620**
Die Aktion (Hamburg) (DEU ISSN 0516-334X) **5205**
Aktion Jugendschutz. Informationen/A J S Informationen (DEU ISSN 0720-3551) **2143**
Aktion Unabhaengiger Frauen *see* A U F **8850**
Der Aktionaer (DEU ISSN 1432-4911) **1609**
Der AktionaersReport (DEU) **1879**
Aktiv (CHE) **3710**
Aktiv (Hannover) (DEU ISSN 0949-622X) **6120**
Aktiv (Munich) (DEU ISSN 1860-4757) **6981**
Aktiv im Leben (DEU) **8850**
Aktiv im Ruhestand (DEU ISSN 1438-4841) **4039**
Aktiv Islam (DNK ISSN 0108-7290) **7708**
Aktiv Laufen (DEU) **8157**
● Aktiv Livsstil (Online Edition) (NOR) **8157**
Aktiv Livsstil (Print Edition) *see* Aktiv Livsstil (Online Edition) **8157**
Aktiv Radfahren (DEU ISSN 0940-4929) **8253**
Aktiv Sportmagazin (DEU) **8157**
Aktiv und Gesund (AUT) **7506**
Aktiv Wirtschaftszeitung (DEU) **1058**
Aktiva Skolfoeraeldrar (SWE ISSN 1401-8594) **2825**
● Aktive Kvinder (DNK ISSN 1398-0580) **8850**
▼ Aktivne (CZE ISSN 1803-3261) **6981**
Aktsent (UKR) **3963**
● ➤ Aktuality v Nefrologii (CZE ISSN 1210-955X) **6264**
● Aktualne.sk (SVK ISSN 1337-0219) **3946**
● Aktualne Vzorove Zmluvy a Pravne Podania (SVK ISSN 1336-8400) **4854**
● Aktualni Prakticky Pruvodce Cerpanim Financnich Postredku a Podpurne Pomoci z Programu Statni Podpory a Evropske Unie (CZE ISSN 1801-805X) **1956**
† Aktualni Prirucka se Vzory pro Stavebni Praxi (CZE ISSN 1801-7770) **8929**
● ➤ Aktual'ni Problemy Suchasnoi Medytsyny (UKR) **5834**
● Aktualni Vzorove Smlouvy pro Obchodni Styk (CZE ISSN 1801-8025) **1662**
Aktualnosci Techniki Rolniczej Express *see* A T R Express **209**
➤ Aktual'nye Problemy Aviatsionnykh i Aerokosmicheskikh Sistem: Protsessy, Modeli, Eksperiment/Actual Problems of Aviation and Aerospace Systems: Processes, Models, Experiment (RUS ISSN 1727-6853) **46**
Aktual'nye Problemy Evropy (RUS ISSN 0235-5620) **7220**
Aktual'nye Problemy Sovremennoi Nauki (RUS ISSN 1680-2721) **7834**
Der Aktuar (DEU ISSN 0948-7794) **4491**
Aktueel Primo (NLD) **3914**
Aktueel Sportief *see* Aktueel Primo **3914**
Aktuel (TUR ISSN 1300-8048) **3962**
† Aktuel Arkaeologi (DNK ISSN 1603-2861) **8929**
Aktuel Astronomi (DNK ISSN 0905-8958) **568**
● Aktuel Elektronik (DNK ISSN 0105-2373) **3295**
Aktuel Grafisk Information *see* A G I **7318**
Aktuel Grafisk Information Danmark *see* A G I **7318**
Aktuel Nordisk Odontologi (DNK ISSN 1902-3545) **5834**
Aktuel Sikkerhed (DNK ISSN 1396-1780) **2643**
Aktuell (GBR ISSN 0959-5740) **5092**
Aktuell Ekonomi (SWE ISSN 0345-0236) **1717**
Aktuell Forskning och Utveckling *see* Aktuell FoU **2966**
Aktuell FoU (Forskning och Utveckling) (SWE ISSN 1403-4182) **2966**
Aktuell Grafisk Information (SWE ISSN 0347-9846) **7318**
Aktuell Informiert (DEU ISSN 1435-8034) **8024**
Aktuell Josefs-Gesellschaft (DEU) **8024**
Aktuell Optik och Optometri *see* Optik **6049**
Aktuell Saekerhet (SWE ISSN 0282-7336) **1725**
Aktuell Sikkerhet (NOR ISSN 0808-6567) **2676**
Aktuella Byggen (SWE ISSN 1401-4149) **975**
Die Aktuelle (DEU ISSN 0946-6355) **3843**
Aktuelle Beitraege zur Angewandten Psychologie (DEU ISSN 0937-4973) **7332**
Aktuelle Beitraege zur Sozialwissenschaftlichen Forschung (DEU ISSN 0937-1761) **7946**
Aktuelle Berichte aus der Mikrosystemtechnik (DEU ISSN 1862-5711) **3365**
Aktuelle Berichte und Informationen fuer Architekten und Ingenieure Auftrag, Rechnung, Zahlung *see* A B I - Auftrag, Rechnung, Zahlung **426**
Aktuelle Berichte und Informationen fuer Architekten und Ingenieure Risiken, Haftung, Schadenersatz *see* A B I - Risiken, Haftung, Schadenersatz **426**
Aktuelle Berichte und Informationen fuer Architekten und Ingenieure Wirtschaft, Recht, Steuer *see* A B I - Wirtschaft, Recht, Steuer **426**
● ➤ Aktuelle Dermatologie (DEU ISSN 0340-2541) **5871**
● ➤ Aktuelle Ernaehrungsmedizin (DEU ISSN 0341-0501) **6654**
Aktuelle Fragen der Vermoegensanlagepraxis (DEU ISSN 0944-7741) **4492**
Aktuelle Fragen in der Versicherungswirtschaft *see* Leipziger Versicherungsseminare **4512**
Aktuelle Frauenforschung (DEU ISSN 0934-554X) **8893**
➤ Aktuelle Immunologie (DEU ISSN 0931-2579) **5752**
Aktuelle Informationen *see* D J B Z **4654**
Aktuelle Juristische Praxis (CHE ISSN 1660-3362) **4946**
● ➤ Aktuelle Neurologie (DEU ISSN 0302-4350) **6120**
➤ Aktuelle Onkologie (DEU ISSN 0174-2744) **6007**
Aktuelle Ostinformationen (DEU ISSN 0939-3099) **7103**
Die Aktuelle Preisraetsel Magazin (DEU) **8157**
● ➤ Aktuelle Rheumatologie (DEU ISSN 0341-051X) **6221**
Aktuelle Rheumatologie. Supplement *see* Aktuelle Rheumatologie **6221**
Aktuelle Steuer News (AUT ISSN 1563-3675) **1909**
Aktuelle Technik (CHE) **8416**
Aktuelle Traumatologie *see* Zeitschrift fuer Orthopaedie und Unfallchirurgie **6075**
● ➤ Aktuelle Urologie (DEU ISSN 0001-7868) **6264**

Title

DIRECTORY 2010 ALBERTA CHILDREN'S SERVICES ANNUAL REPORT 9939

Alabama, Louisiana & Mississippi *see* TourBook: Alabama, Louisiana, Mississippi **8761**
Alabama, Louisiana, Mississippi TourBook *see* TourBook: Alabama, Louisiana, Mississippi **8761**
Alabama Magazine (USA ISSN 1040-2349) **5205**
• Alabama Manufacturers Register (USA ISSN 1045-2664) **1971**
Alabama: Manufacturing *see* Harris Directory. Alabama Manufacturing **1999**
Alabama Municipal Data Book (USA ISSN 1072-7620) **7419**
Alabama Municipal Journal (USA ISSN 0002-4309) **7487**
Alabama Museum of Natural History. Bulletin (USA ISSN 0196-1039) **7834**
• Alabama Nurse (USA ISSN 0002-4317) **5950**
Alabama. Office of the Attorney General. Quarterly Report of the Attorney General (USA) **4612**
Alabama Press Association. Rate and Data Guide (USA) **4988**
Alabama Propane Gas News (USA) **6761**
Alabama Property Rights and Remedies (USA) **7581**
Alabama Public Library Service. Annual Report (USA) **4988**
Alabama Purchasor (USA ISSN 0002-4325) **1804**
Alabama Rate and Data *see* Alabama Press Association. Rate and Data Guide **4988**
• ➤ The Alabama Review (USA ISSN 0002-4341) **4282**
• The Alabama Roadbuilder (USA) **8629**
Alabama Rules of Criminal Procedure (USA) **4883**
Alabama School Directory *see* M D R's School Directory. Alabama **2958**
Alabama School Journal (USA ISSN 0002-435X) **2825**
• Alabama State Data Center Newsletter (USA) **7276**
Alabama Today (USA ISSN 0745-5771) **1394**
Alabama Tort Law (USA) **4826**
Alabama Vacation Guide (USA) **8682**
Alabama Weddings (USA) **5556**
Alabama Wildlife (USA ISSN 0894-8356) **2602**
Alabama's Health (USA ISSN 0145-6857) **7506**
Alabama's Treasured Forests (USA ISSN 0894-9654) **3683**
Alabama's Vital Events (USA ISSN 0095-3431) **8343**
The Alabamian (USA) **2272**
• Alabo Shijie/Journal of Arab World Studies (CHN ISSN 1004-5104) **5092**
Alabrent (ESP) **7318**
Aladdin's Window (USA ISSN 1070-6836) **6302**
• Aladin (FRA ISSN 0981-1389) **362**
Alafolie *see* Oui Magazine **8879**
Alahli Bank of Kuwait K.S.C. Annual Report and Balance Sheet (KWT) **1306**
Alai Tan (KGZ) **3903**
Al-Alam (GBR) **3912**
Alam al-Handasah/World of Engineering (UAE) **3180**
Alam al-Insa'at al-'Arabiyya ad-duwaliyyat *see* 'Alam al-insha'at al-'arabi **975**
• 'Alam al-insha'at al-'arabi/Alam al-Insa'at al-'Arabiyya ad-duwaliyyat (LBN ISSN 1990-3936) **975**
• 'Alam al-Miyah al-'arabi/Alam al-Miyah al-Arabi ad-Duwali (LBN ISSN 1990-3952) **8817**
Alam al-Miyah al-Arabi ad-Duwali *see* 'Alam al-Miyah al-'arabi **8817**
• 'Alam al-Sihhat al-'Arabi/Arab Health World (LBN ISSN 1990-3944) **7506**
• Al-Alam Al-Youm (EGY) **1058**
A'lam ar-riyadat *see* Aalam ar-Riyadah **8156**
† Alam Attijarat (USA ISSN 0002-4392) **8929**
Alam-e-Niswan/Pakistan Journal of Women's Studies (PAK ISSN 1024-1256) **8893**
Alam Tib al-Asnan *see* Arab Dental **5835**
Alamanaque Brasil (BRA) **3117**
Alamance Magazine (USA) **3969**
Alambique (ESP ISSN 1133-9837) **7834**
Alameda (USA) **5064**
Alameda-Contra Costa Medical Association. Bulletin (USA ISSN 0002-4414) **5570**
Alameda County Bar Association Bulletin (USA) **4612**
Alameda Magazine (USA) **3969**
▼ • Alamire Foundation. Journal (BEL) **6543**
Alamo Area Council of Governments Region *see* A A C O G Region **7486**
Alan Rogers Directory of Camping and Caravanning, All Year Round (GBR ISSN 0969-9708) **8682**
Alan Shawn Feinstein Insiders Report (USA) **1610**
Alan Shawn Feinstein's International Insiders Report *see* Alan Shawn Feinstein Insiders Report **1610**
Alara (FIN ISSN 1235-1970) **6192**
Alarm/Alarme/Allarme (CHE) **3575**
Alarm (USA ISSN 1555-8819) **6543**
Alarm Clock (USA) **6543**
Alarma (VEN) **7104**
Alarme *see* Alarm **3575**
Alarmes - Protection - Securite (FRA ISSN 0290-0106) **2676**
Alarming Cry (USA) **7745**
Alaska (DEU ISSN 1436-3100) **1590**
• Alaska (USA ISSN 0002-4562) **3969**
Alaska (American Edition) (USA ISSN 1935-7583) **8682**
Alaska Action (USA) **1394**
Alaska Adult Education (USA) **2938**
Alaska Agricultural Statistics (USA) **174**
Alaska Airlines Magazine (USA) **8782**
Alaska Almanac: Facts about Alaska (USA) **3117**
Alaska and the Yukon for Families *see* Going Places: Alaska and the Yukon for Families **8714**
The Alaska Angler (USA ISSN 1047-5176) **8302**
• Alaska Bar Rag (USA ISSN 0276-1025) **4612**
Alaska Basin Outlook Report (USA) **6400**
• Alaska Business Directory (USA ISSN 1048-7069) **1971**
• Alaska Business Monthly (USA ISSN 8756-4092) **1058**
Alaska Center for the Environment. Center News (USA) **2602**
• Alaska Court Rules, State and Federal (USA ISSN 1070-3519) **4946**
• Alaska Criminal and Traffic Law Manual (USA ISSN 1540-0921) **4883**
† • Alaska Criminal Law, Motor Vehicles and Related Statutes (USA) **8929**
Alaska Department of Fish and Game. Annual Perfomance Report of Survey Inventory Activities (USA) **3583**
Alaska. Department of Fish and Game. Completion Report (USA) **3583**
Alaska Department of Fish and Game. Division of Commercial Fisheries. Special Publication (USA) **3583**
Alaska Department of Fish and Game. Division of Wildlife Conservation. Annual Performance Report (USA) **3583**
Alaska Department of Fish and Game. Division of Wildlife Conservation. Federal Aid in Wildlife Restoration. Annual Monitoring Report (USA) **3583**
Alaska Department of Fish and Game. Division of Wildlife Conservation. Federal Aid in Wildlife Restoration. Annual Performance Report of Survey (USA) **3583**
Alaska Department of Fish and Game. Division of Wildlife Conservation. Federal Aid in Wildlife Restoration. Annual Research Performance Report (USA) **3583**
Alaska Department of Fish and Game. Division of Wildlife Conservation. Federal Aid in Wildlife Restoration. Research Progress Report (USA) **3583**
Alaska Department of Fish and Game. Division of Wildlife Conservation. Federal Aid in Wildlife Restoration. Survey-Inventory Management Report (USA) **3583**
Alaska Department of Fish and Game. Division of Wildlife Conservation. Federal Aid in Wildlife Restoration. Wildlife Technical Bulletin (USA) **3583**
Alaska Department of Fish and Game. Division of Wildlife Conservation. Final Report (USA) **3583**
Alaska Department of Fish and Game. Research Final Report, Survey-Inventory Activities (USA) **3583**
Alaska Department of Fish and Game. Research Progress Report, Survey-Inventory Activities (USA) **3583**
• Alaska Department of Fish and Game. Sport Fish Division's Newsletter (USA) **8302**
Alaska. Department of Fish and Game. Wildlife Notebook Series (USA) **2602**
Alaska. Department of Health and Social Services. Division of Alcoholism and Drug Abuse. Report (USA) **2690**
Alaska. Department of Revenue. Revenue Sources (USA) **1910**
Alaska. Department of Revenue. State Investment Portfolio (USA ISSN 0092-6736) **1610**
Alaska. Division of Geological and Geophysical Surveys. Administrative Reports (USA) **2723**
Alaska. Division of Geological and Geophysical Surveys. Alaska Territorial Department of Mines Reports (USA) **6456**
Alaska. Division of Geological and Geophysical Surveys. Alaska's Mineral Industry (USA ISSN 0741-5168) **2723**
Alaska. Division of Geological and Geophysical Surveys. Catalog of Alaskan Earthquakes (USA) **2777**
Alaska. Division of Geological and Geophysical Surveys. Geophysical Reports (USA) **2777**
Alaska. Division of Geological and Geophysical Surveys. Guidebook of Permafrost and Related Features of the Dalton Highway, Yukon River to Prudhoe Bay, Alaska. Volume 2 (USA) **2723**
Alaska. Division of Geological and Geophysical Surveys. Guidebook to Permafrost and Quaternary Geology along the Richardson and Glenn Highways between Fairbanks and Anchorage, Alaska (USA) **2723**
Alaska. Division of Geological and Geophysical Surveys. Guidebook to Permafrost and Related Features along the Elliott and Dalton Highways, Fox to Prudhoe Bay (USA) **2723**
Alaska. Division of Geological and Geophysical Surveys. Guidebook to Permafrost and Related Features at Prudhoe Bay (USA) **2723**
Alaska. Division of Geological and Geophysical Surveys. Guidebook to Permafrost and Related Features of the Colville River Delta, Alaska (USA) **2723**
Alaska. Division of Geological and Geophysical Surveys. Guidebook to Permafrost and Related Features of the Dalton Highway, Yukon River to Prudhoe Bay, Alaska. Volume 1 (USA) **2723**
Alaska. Division of Geological and Geophysical Surveys. Guidebook to Permafrost and Related Features of the Northern Yukon Territory and MacKenzie Delta, Alaska (USA) **2723**
Alaska. Division of Geological and Geophysical Surveys. Guidebooks (USA) **2724**
➤ Alaska. Division of Geological and Geophysical Surveys. Information Circular (USA ISSN 0065-5759) **2724**
Alaska. Division of Geological and Geophysical Surveys. Miscellaneous Papers (USA ISSN 0065-5783) **2724**
Alaska. Division of Geological and Geophysical Surveys. Preliminary Investigative Reports (USA) **2724**
➤ Alaska. Division of Geological and Geophysical Surveys. Professional Reports (USA ISSN 0737-6022) **2724**
Alaska. Division of Geological and Geophysical Surveys. Raw Data Files (USA) **2724**
Alaska. Division of Geological and Geophysical Surveys. Report of Investigations (USA) **2724**
Alaska. Division of Geological and Geophysical Surveys. Short Notes on Alaskan Geology (USA) **2724**
➤ Alaska. Division of Geological and Geophysical Surveys. Special Report (USA ISSN 0360-3881) **2724**
Alaska. Division of Geological and Geophysical Surveys. The Alaska Railroad between Anchorage and Fairbanks (USA) **2724**
Alaska. Division of Wildlife Conservation. Annual Report of Survey - Inventory Activities (USA ISSN 0362-6962) **2602**
Alaska Economic Report (USA ISSN 1072-8139) **1436**
• Alaska Economic Trends (USA ISSN 0160-3345) **1436**
Alaska Employment and Earnings Report (USA ISSN 1063-3782) **1199**
• Alaska Employment Law Letter (USA ISSN 1085-9144) **4612**
Alaska Farm Reporter (USA) **174**
Alaska Fisherman's Journal (USA ISSN 0164-8330) **3583**
• Alaska Fishery Research Bulletin (USA ISSN 1091-7306) **3583**
• Alaska Geographic (USA ISSN 0361-1353) **3997**
• Alaska Highway News (CAN ISSN 1483-975X) **3805**
➤ Alaska History (USA ISSN 0890-6149) **4282**
Alaska Horse Journal (USA) **8286**
• Alaska Housing Finance Corporation. Annual Report (USA ISSN 0272-4146) **4403**
• Alaska Housing Market Indicators (Online) (USA) **4403**
The Alaska Hunter (USA ISSN 1047-5184) **8302**
• Alaska Hunting Bulletin (USA) **8302**
Alaska Journal of Anthropology (USA ISSN 1544-9793) **323**
• Alaska Journal of Commerce (USA ISSN 1537-4947) **1425**
• Alaska Law Review (USA ISSN 0883-0568) **4612**
Alaska Legislative Digest (USA ISSN 1072-8058) **7104**
Alaska. Legislature. Budget and Audit Committee. Annual Report (USA ISSN 0095-3865) **7104**
Alaska Library Directory (USA ISSN 0146-1028) **4988**
Alaska Magazine *see* Alaska **3969**
• Alaska Manufacturers Directory (USA ISSN 1085-746X) **1971**
Alaska Medicine (USA ISSN 0002-4538) **5570**
Alaska Municipal League (USA) **7487**
Alaska Municipal Officials Directory (USA ISSN 0363-4167) **7487**
Alaska Native Business & Resource Directory (USA) **1971**
Alaska Native Language Center Research Papers (USA ISSN 0883-8526) **5092**
• Alaska Nurse (USA ISSN 0002-4546) **5950**
Alaska Pacific University Press Press Alaskana Book Series *see* A P U Press Alaskana Book Series **4281**
Alaska Park Science (USA ISSN 1545-4967) **7834**
• Alaska Population Overview (USA ISSN 1063-3790) **7276**
• Alaska Potato Stocks (USA ISSN 1948-6014) **90**
Alaska Quarterly Review (USA ISSN 0737-268X) **5251**
Alaska Region *see* Drilling Wire. Alaska Region Report **6767**
Alaska Reporter *see* West's Alaska Reporter **4812**
Alaska Review of Social and Economic Conditions (USA ISSN 0162-5403) **1436**
Alaska School Directory *see* M D R's School Directory. Alaska **2958**
Alaska Sea Grant Report (USA ISSN 0271-7069) **652**
• Alaska Snow Survey Report (USA) **8817**
• Alaska. State Council on the Arts. Communique (USA) **464**
Alaska State Council on the Arts. Communique (USA) **464**
Alaska Statutes. Advance Legislative Service (USA ISSN 0736-1157) **4612**
Alaska. Violent Crimes Compensation Board. Annual Report (USA ISSN 0095-3415) **2643**
• Alaska Wage Rates (Year) (USA ISSN 1063-3758) **1662**
Alaska Weekly Crop Weather (USA) **174**
• Alaska Wildlife News (USA) **2602**
Alaska Women (USA) **5205**
Alaska Yukon Community Travel Guide *see* Alaska Yukon Travel Magazine **8682**
Alaska Yukon Deutsches Reisemagazin *see* Alaska Yukon Travel Magazine **8682**
Alaska Yukon Travel Guide *see* Alaska Yukon Travel Magazine **8682**
Alaska Yukon Travel Magazine (CAN ISSN 1910-0124) **8682**
AlaskaMen U S A (USA ISSN 1041-4002) **7943**
Alaskan Malamute Club of America. Newsletter (USA ISSN 0199-1310) **6802**
Alateen Link-Up *see* Austra-Link **2692**
Alateen Talk (USA ISSN 1054-1411) **2175**
Alauda (FRA ISSN 0002-4619) **901**
▼ • ➤ Alavesia (ESP ISSN 1887-7419) **838**
• ALawI News (CAN) **4612**
Alazet (ESP ISSN 0214-7602) **5092**
Alba (ESP ISSN 0213-4896) **4129**
➤ Alba de America (USA ISSN 0888-3181) **5251**
Alba Pompeia (ITA ISSN 0394-9427) **372**
Alba Regia (HUN ISSN 0324-542X) **6518**
Albania: A General Briefing *see* Eastern Europe Newsletter - Briefing. Albania **7131**
Albanian Agriculture *see* Bujqesta Shqiptare **98**
• Albanian Daily News (ALB) **1436**
The Albanian Ethnography *see* Etnografia Shqiptare **338**
• ➤ Albanian Journal of Politics (USA ISSN 1932-7986) **7104**
Albanian Mail/Gazeta Shqiptare (GBR ISSN 1741-5500) **3517**
Albanische Forschungen (DEU ISSN 0568-8957) **4197**
Albanische Hefte (DEU ISSN 0930-1437) **3517**
Albanological Research: Folklore and Ethnology Series *see* Gjurmime Albanologjike: Folklor dhe Etnologji **3618**
Albanological Research: Historical Sciences Series *see* Gjurmime Albanologjike. Seria e Shkencave Historike **4140**
Albanologycal Researches: Philological Science Series *see* Gjurmime Albanologjike. Seria e Shkencave Filologjike **6921**
Albany (USA) **2272**
Albany Institute of History & Art. Annual Report (USA) **4282**
• Albany Law Journal of Science and Technology (USA ISSN 1059-4280) **4826**
• ➤ Albany Law Review (USA) **4612**
† Albany Law School. Annual Conference on Intellectual Property (USA) **8929**
Albatroz (DNK ISSN 1902-4665) **8271**
† Albatroz (FRA ISSN 0984-8983) **8929**
Albedo One (IRL) **5439**
• Albeiteria Argentina (ARG ISSN 1666-8227) **8790**
Albemarle (USA ISSN 1052-7974) **3969**
Alber Texte Philosophie (DEU) **6903**
Alber Thesen Philosophie (DEU) **6903**
Alberghi d'Italia (ITA) **4381**
Alberi e Territorio (ITA ISSN 1724-4021) **3683**
• Alberni Valley Times (CAN ISSN 0839-2706) **3805**
L'Albero delle Fiabe (ITA ISSN 1970-7363) **2175**
† Albert (FRA ISSN 1950-1765) **8929**
Albert Einstein Institution Monograph Series *see* Albert Einstein Institution. Monograph Series **7104**
Albert Einstein Institution. Monograph Series (USA ISSN 1052-1054) **7104**
Albert-Ludwigs-Universitaet Freiburg. Forschungsbericht (DEU ISSN 0720-8618) **3016**
Albert-Ludwigs-Universitaet Freiburg. Vorlesungsverzeichnis (DEU ISSN 0176-909X) **3016**
Albert Talks *see* Albertalks **2966**
Alberta Advanced Education. Annual Report (CAN ISSN 1715-3492) **2966**
Alberta Agriculture. Annual Report (CAN ISSN 0702-3030) **90**
Alberta Agriculture, Food and Rural Development. Crop Report (CAN ISSN 0707-8293) **218**
Alberta Agrologist (CAN) **90**
Alberta. Alberta Infrastructure and Transportation. Annual Report (CAN ISSN 1715-5029) **8489**
Alberta. Alberta Innovation and Science. Annual Report (CAN ISSN 1497-0732) **7419**
Alberta. Alberta Justice. Annual Report (CAN ISSN 1198-2020) **4612**
Alberta. Alberta Municipal Affairs. Annual Report (CAN ISSN 0701-6522) **7487**
Alberta. Alberta Treasury. Annual Report *see* Alberta Revenue Annual Report **1058**
Alberta Alcohol and Drug Abuse Commission. Annual Report (CAN ISSN 0840-7819) **2690**
• Alberta and Territories Tax Reporter (CAN ISSN 1719-9689) **1910**
Alberta Archaeological Review (CAN ISSN 0701-1776) **372**
Alberta Association of College Librarians. Newsletter (CAN ISSN 0829-4321) **4988**
• Alberta Associations Directory On-Line (CAN ISSN 1195-8332) **1971**
Alberta Beef (CAN ISSN 1187-0761) **277**
Alberta Biennial of Contemporary Art (CAN ISSN 1494-1023) **464**
• Alberta Business Directory (USA ISSN 1203-5149) **1971**
Alberta Cancer Board. Annual Report (CAN ISSN 0839-8135) **6007**
• Alberta Cancer Board. Business Plan (CAN ISSN 1703-6305) **1058**
Alberta Catholic Directory (CAN ISSN 0316-473X) **7782**
Alberta Children's Services Annual Report (CAN ISSN 1497-0457) **8024**

Title

9940 ALBERTA COAL INDUSTRY, ANNUAL STATISTICS ULRICH'S PERIODICALS

Alberta Coal Industry, Annual Statistics (CAN ISSN 0380-4321) 6484
Alberta College of Medical Diagnostic & Therapeutic Technologists. Annual Report (CAN ISSN 1719-9239) 5570
Alberta College of Pharmacists News see A C P News 6817
Alberta Community Development. Annual Report (CAN ISSN 1207-4977) 7946
Alberta Conservation Association. Annual Report (CAN ISSN 1912-6085) 3402
Alberta Construction Association Membership Roster and Buyers' Guide (CAN ISSN 0822-6237) 975
Alberta Construction Magazine (CAN ISSN 1499-6308) 975
Alberta Construction Safety Association Industries (CAN ISSN 1910-1570) 7506
Alberta Construction Service & Supply Directory (CAN ISSN 1498-6728) 1971
Alberta Corporation Manual (CAN ISSN 1912-0559) 4854
• Alberta Corporations Law Guide (CAN) 4612
Alberta Council on Aging News see A C A News 4037
Alberta Crop Report see Alberta Agriculture, Food and Rural Development. Crop Report 218
• Alberta Decisions. Civil and Criminal Cases (CAN ISSN 0319-7980) 4612
Alberta Decisions - Civil and Criminal Cases. Monthly Headnotes (CAN ISSN 1480-4565) 4613
Alberta Dental Association. Updater (CAN) 5834
Alberta Doctors' Digest (CAN ISSN 0833-8477) 5571
Alberta Drilling Progress Weekly Report (CAN) 6799
Alberta Economic Development Authority. Activity Report (CAN ISSN 1710-9299) 1058
• Alberta Economic Quick Facts (CAN ISSN 1718-1402) 1058
Alberta Education. Annual Report (CAN ISSN 1715-4391) 2825
Alberta Education. Annual Report and Annual Results Report see Alberta Education. Annual Report 2825
Alberta Education. Annual Report and Annual Results Report see Alberta Advanced Education. Annual Report 2966
Alberta Electric Industry, Annual Statistics (CAN ISSN 0706-1420) 3155
Alberta Energy and Utilities Board. Regulatory Highlights see Alberta Energy and Utilities Board. Year-end Review 3123
Alberta Energy and Utilities Board. Year-end Review (CAN ISSN 1912-8266) 3123
Alberta Energy Resource Industries. Monthly Statistics (CAN ISSN 0710-6874) 3150
Alberta Environment. Annual Report (CAN ISSN 1492-9910) 3402
Alberta Environment Department Highlights (CAN ISSN 1912-4384) 3402
Alberta. Environmental Appeals Board. Business Plan (CAN ISSN 1910-6289) 1058
Alberta, Evocations Rurales see Evocations Rurales 197
The Alberta Express (CAN ISSN 1714-6003) 90
Alberta Family Law (CAN) 4906
Alberta FarmLife (CAN) 209
• Alberta Finance Annual Report (CAN ISSN 1708-4075) 1058
• Alberta Finance Ministry. Activity Report (CAN ISSN 1700-2567) 1058
• Alberta Finance Ministry. Quarter Fiscal Update (CAN) 1306
Alberta Financial Services Corporation. Annual Report (CAN ISSN 1207-4195) 218
Alberta Fire News (CAN) 3575
Alberta Fishing Guide (CAN ISSN 0318-4943) 8302
Alberta Game Warden (CAN) 2602
Alberta Gaming. Annual Report (CAN ISSN 1492-9635) 7419
• Alberta Gaming Research Institute. Annual Report (CAN ISSN 1499-7436) 8157
Alberta Gardener see Alberta Gardener Living 3721
Alberta Gardener Living (CAN ISSN 1910-9431) 3721
Alberta Gazette (CAN ISSN 0002-4775) 3806
Alberta Geological Survey. Earth Science Reports (CAN) 2701
Alberta Geological Survey. Information Series (CAN) 8416
Alberta Geological Survey. Reports (CAN) 8416
Alberta Gifted and Talented Education see A G A T E 3036
Alberta Government Libraries' Newsletter (CAN ISSN 0707-0306) 4988
Alberta Hansard (CAN ISSN 0383-3623) 4613
Alberta Health and Wellness. Annual Report (CAN ISSN 1492-8884) 4087
Alberta Health and Wellness. Annual Report. Highlights (CAN ISSN 1912-6093) 7506
Alberta Health Care Insurance Plan. Statistical Supplement see Alberta Health and Wellness. Annual Report 4087
Alberta Health Records Association Record see A H R A Record 5564
• ➤ Alberta History (CAN ISSN 0316-1552) 4282
Alberta Hockey Now see Hockey Now 8177
▼ Alberta Home (CAN ISSN 1913-3111) 975
Alberta Home and School Councils' Association News for Parents on School Council see A H S C A News for Parents on School Council 3016

Alberta Home and School Councils' Association News for Parents on School Council see A H S C A News for Parents on School Council 3016

Alberta Home Economics Association Newsletter see Fusion 4359
Alberta Hospital Injury Admissions see National Trauma Registry Provincial Report. Alberta: Hospital Injury Admissions 4107
Alberta Industry and Resources ... Database (CAN ISSN 0838-8377) 1879
Alberta Infrastructure. Annual Report see Alberta. Alberta Infrastructure and Transportation. Annual Report 8489
Alberta Innovators (CAN ISSN 1910-331X) 3180
Alberta Insurance Directory (CAN ISSN 0712-9343) 4492
Alberta Italian Times (CAN ISSN 0845-9061) 3517
• ➤ Alberta Journal of Educational Research (CAN ISSN 0002-4805) 2825
Alberta Labour and Employment Legislation (CAN ISSN 1715-0019) 4854
Alberta Land Surveyors' Association News see A L S News 3258
• Alberta Law Reform Institute. Annual Report (CAN ISSN 0229-6276) 4613
• Alberta Law Reform Institute. Report (CAN ISSN 1209-0409) 4613
Alberta Law Reports (CAN ISSN 0703-3117) 4613
• ➤ Alberta Law Review (CAN ISSN 0002-4821) 4613
Alberta Learning. Annual Report see Alberta Education. Annual Report 2825
Alberta Learning. Annual Report see Alberta Advanced Education. Annual Report 2966
Alberta Legal Telephone Directory (CAN ISSN 0823-2350) 1971
Alberta Limitations Manual (CAN) 4613
Alberta Linear Property Assessment Manual. Appendix II see Alberta Linear Property Assessment Minister's Guidelines 1910
Alberta Linear Property Assessment Minister's Guidelines (CAN ISSN 1914-1319) 1910
Alberta Machinery & Equipment Assessment Manual. Appendix III see Alberta Machinery & Equipment Assessment Minister's Guidelines 1910
Alberta Machinery & Equipment Assessment Minister's Guidelines (CAN ISSN 1914-1718) 1910
Alberta. Ministry of Energy. Annual Report (CAN ISSN 1703-4574) 3123
Alberta. Ministry of Science, Research and Information Technology. Annual Report see Alberta. Alberta Innovation and Science. Annual Report 7419
Alberta. Ministry of Sustainable Resource Development. Annual Report (CAN ISSN 1703-8634) 7419
Alberta Museums Association. Awards Program (CAN ISSN 1719-377X) 6518
Alberta Museums Review (CAN ISSN 0380-3279) 6518
• Alberta, N.W.T. & Yukon Tax Reports (CAN) 1910
Alberta Native News (CAN ISSN 0829-4135) 3517
Alberta. Natural Resources Conservation Board. Year-in-review (CAN ISSN 1912-6417) 3402
Alberta Naturalist see Nature Alberta 2621
Alberta Oil (CAN ISSN 1912-5291) 6761
Alberta Oil & Gas Directory (CAN ISSN 0831-019X) 1971
Alberta Paleontological Society Bulletin (CAN ISSN 1497-2018) 6722
Alberta Poultry Research Centre. Technical Bulletin (CAN ISSN 1912-645X) 277
Alberta. Public Affairs Bureau. Catalogue - Alberta. Queen's Printer (CAN ISSN 1482-5864) 7478
• Alberta R N (Registered Nurses) (CAN ISSN 1481-9988) 5950
Alberta Railway Assessment Manual see Alberta Railway Property Assessment Minister's Guidelines 8614
Alberta Railway Assessment Minister's Guidelines see Alberta Railway Property Assessment Minister's Guidelines 8614
Alberta Railway Property Assessment Minister's Guidelines (CAN ISSN 1912-7286) 8614
• Alberta Reports (CAN ISSN 0703-3109) 4613
Alberta Reproductive Health, Pregnancies and Births (CAN ISSN 1712-0780) 5985
Alberta Reproductive Health, Pregnancy Outcomes see Alberta Reproductive Health, Pregnancies and Births 5985
• Alberta Research Council. Annual Report (CAN ISSN 0701-5151) 8416
Alberta Research Council. Bulletin (CAN ISSN 0383-5359) 2701
Alberta Research Council. Information Series see Alberta Geological Survey. Information Series 8416
• Alberta Revenue Annual Report (CAN ISSN 1708-4083) 1058
• Alberta Romance Writers' Association. Connections (CAN ISSN 1715-3719) 5251
Alberta Rules of Court Annotated (CAN ISSN 1189-8070) 4613
Alberta Rural Reminder see Rural Reminder 206
• Alberta Senior Annual Report (CAN ISSN 1703-7646) 4039
Alberta South Vacation Guide see Discover Southwest Alberta 8698
• Alberta Sweetgrass (CAN ISSN 1199-6773) 3517
The Alberta Thoroughbred (CAN) 8286
Alberta Tourism Quick Facts (CAN ISSN 1718-1429) 8682
Alberta Transportation. Annual Report (Year) see Alberta. Alberta Infrastructure and Transportation. Annual Report 8489
Alberta Venture (CAN ISSN 1207-2591) 1058
Alberta Views see Albertaviews 5205
• Alberta Vital Statistics Annual Review (CAN ISSN 1485-3809) 7296
Alberta Weekly Law Digest (CAN ISSN 0713-892X) 4613
• Alberta. Workers' Compensation Board. Annual Report (CAN ISSN 1489-4084) 1662
Albertalks (CAN ISSN 1910-9407) 2966
Alberta's Endangered Species Conservation Committee. Report (CAN ISSN 1912-3523) 652
Alberta's Energy Resources in Review (CAN ISSN 1205-8734) 2602
▼ Alberta's Horse Community Guide (CAN ISSN 1913-3537) 8286
Alberta's Reserve of Gas: Complete Listing (CAN ISSN 0229-8546) 6761
Albertaviews (CAN ISSN 1480-3151) 5205
• Albertiana (ITA ISSN 1126-9588) 6903
Albertiana (NLD ISSN 0169-4324) 6722
Albertine Rift Technical Reports (USA ISSN 1543-4109) 3583
Albertoa (BRA ISSN 0103-4944) 774
Albina (ROM ISSN 1220-7888) 3932
Albmag (DEU) 5064
Albo see Arubo 840
Albo Albo (POL ISSN 1230-0802) 7332
Albricias (USA) 2264
Albrightian (USA) 2272
Albron Footnote Nieuws see Foodnote Nieuws 25
Het Album (NLD) 6963
Album, Letras y Artes (ESP ISSN 1131-6411) 464
Album of Visualization (JPN ISSN 0919-4630) 7073
Album Page (USA) 6891
Album Slavnych Sportovcov (SVK) 8157
Albums de Croy (BEL ISSN 0774-3106) 4197
Albuquerque (Albuquerque) (USA ISSN 1936-4350) 3969
Albuquerque Archaeological Society Newsletter (USA ISSN 0002-4953) 372
Albuquerque Arts Magazine see AbqArts 4975
• Albuquerque Genealogical Society. Quarterly Newsletter (USA ISSN 1946-9969) 3758
Albury & District Historical Society. Bulletin (AUS ISSN 0813-6645) 4191
Alcabala (ESP ISSN 0214-6770) 1306
The Alcalde (USA) 2272
Alcances (CHL ISSN 0718-316X) 6903
Alcatel Telecommunications Review see Enriching Communications 2367
Alcazar de Sevilla. Apuntes (ESP ISSN 1578-0619) 372
• ➤ Alces (CAN ISSN 0835-5851) 931
• Alchemist (GBR ISSN 1369-7048) 2049
• Alchemist Review (USA ISSN 1948-0156) 5251
• ➤ Alcheringa (GBR ISSN 0311-5518) 6722
Alchimie (FRA ISSN 1778-6649) 7732
• Alcmeon (ARG ISSN 0327-3954) 6121
• ➤ Alcohol (New York) (USA ISSN 0741-8329) 2690
Alcohol Alert see U K Alcohol Alert 2700
• ➤ Alcohol and Alcoholism (GBR ISSN 0735-0414) 2690
Alcohol & Alcoholism. Supplement see Alcohol and Alcoholism 2690
Alcohol and Other Drugs see Alkohol & Narkotika 2691
• Alcohol Concern Annual Report (GBR) 2690
Alcohol Issues Insights (USA ISSN 1067-3105) 597
• Alcohol.org.nz (NZL ISSN 1175-2831) 2690
• ➤ Alcohol Research & Health (USA ISSN 1535-7414) 2691
• Alcohol Studies Bulletin (AUS ISSN 1445-4475) 2691
Alcoholic and Nonalcoholic Beverages see Who's Buying Alcoholic and Nonalcoholic Beverages 612
Alcoholic Beverage Control Law of New York see New York Alcoholic Beverage Control Law 608
• Alcoholic Beverage Control - State Capitals (USA) 4613
Alcoholic Beverage Executives' Newsletter (USA ISSN 0889-3519) 597
Alcoholis (GBR ISSN 1752-4725) 2691
• ➤ Alcoholism (HRV ISSN 0002-502X) 2691
Alcoholism & Drug Abuse Week see Alcoholism & Drug Abuse Weekly 2691
• Alcoholism & Drug Abuse Weekly (USA ISSN 1042-1394) 2691
• ➤ Alcoholism: Clinical and Experimental Research (USA ISSN 0145-6008) 2691
• Alcoholism. Supplement (HRV ISSN 1330-6170) 2691
• Alcoholism Treatment Quarterly (USA ISSN 0734-7324) 2691
Alcolholism see Alcoholis 2691
Alcologia (ITA ISSN 0394-9826) 2691
Alcon en Iberoamerica (Spanish Edition) (PAN ISSN 1990-598X) 6038
Alcon na Iberoamerica (Portuguese Edition) see Alcon en Iberoamerica (Spanish Edition) 6038
Alcool ou Sante see Addictions 2690
Alcores (ESP ISSN 1886-8770) 4197
Alcovit (LUX) 90
Alcoy; Fiesta de Moros y Cristianos (ESP ISSN 0065-6127) 3614
Alcuin Club Collections (GBR ISSN 0140-1238) 7745
Alcuza (ESP ISSN 1135-0253) 218
• ➤ Aldea Mundo (VEN ISSN 1316-6727) 7946
• Aldea Periodismo (CHL ISSN 0717-8816) 4571
Aldeas (CHL ISSN 0718-4751) 2143
Aldeburgh Studies in Music (GBR ISSN 0969-3548) 6543
Aldeezkaria (ESP) 4988
Alderlea Magazine (CAN) 3806
L'Aldila (ITA ISSN 1825-1536) 6903
The Aldine Press (USA) 615
Aldous Huxley Annual (DEU ISSN 1619-7267) 5251
Aldrich Entomology Club. Newsletter (USA ISSN 0065-6143) 838
Aldrichimica Acta (USA ISSN 0002-5100) 2119
Aldring og Eldre see Aldring og Livsloep 4040
Aldring og Livsloep (NOR ISSN 1503-0849) 4040
Aldrovandia (ITA ISSN 1825-2613) 931
Ale (SWE ISSN 0345-0708) 4197
† 'ale Hinnukh (ISR ISSN 0793-1344) 8929
'Ale Sefer see Ale Sefer 5056
Ale Sefer (ISR ISSN 0334-4754) 5056
Ale Street News (USA) 597
• Alea (BRA ISSN 1517-106X) 5092
Alea (ESP ISSN 1576-4494) 6903
• ➤ Alea (Rio de Janeiro) (BRA ISSN 1980-0436) 5467
➤ Alectoris (GIB ISSN 1352-8734) 901
• Alegatos (MEX ISSN 0187-5973) 7946
† Alei Esev (ISR) 8929
† Alei Merchavim (ISR) 8929
Al-Alem (ETH) 3837
Alemannia Studens (DEU ISSN 0940-8401) 4197
Alemannisch Dunkt Ues Guet (DEU ISSN 0722-0332) 5092
Alemannisches Institut. Veroeffentlichungen (DEU) 4197
Alemannisches Jahrbuch (DEU ISSN 0516-5644) 4197
The Alembic (USA) 5251
Aleph (COL ISSN 0120-0216) 5205
Aleph (HRV ISSN 1331-470X) 5251
• The Aleph (USA ISSN 1937-0474) 5251
• ALEPH: Historical Studies in Science and Judaism (USA ISSN 1565-1525) 7717
Alephzero (MEX) 7834
Aleppo Temple Shriners News (USA) 2264
Alergia see Revista Alergia Mexico 5765
• Alergia, Asma e Inmunologia Pediatricas (MEX ISSN 1405-1699) 5752
Alergia Astma Immunologia (POL ISSN 1427-3101) 5752
• ➤ Alergie (CZE ISSN 1212-3536) 5752
• Alergologia e Inmunologia Clinica (ESP ISSN 1575-734X) 5752
Alergologia e Inmunologia Clinica. Extraordinario see Alergologia e Inmunologia Clinica 5752
Alergologia, Immunologia/Allergology & Immunology (POL ISSN 1731-9404) 5752
Alero (GTM ISSN 0252-8711) 5251
Alert (DEU) 3843
Alert (NLD ISSN 0920-3168) 2225
Alert (Austin) (USA) 4968
• Alert (Ewing) (USA) 2691
• Alert (New York) (USA) 8024
• Alert (Renton) (USA ISSN 1069-0743) 6802
Alert (Rocky Hill) (USA) 1804
• Alert (Washington, 1995) (USA) 2552
Alert Diver (USA ISSN 1084-2985) 8157
Alerta Agrario (PER ISSN 1021-1810) 90
Alerta de Farmacovigilancia see Boletin Terapeutico Andaluz 6826
• Alerta Publicitaria (PER) 1804
Alerta Tarea see Tarea 2917
• Alertbox (USA ISSN 1548-5552) 2495
• Alertbox (Deutsche Ausgabe) (CHE) 2495
Alerte au S I D A Oceanie see Pacific AIDS Alert Bulletin 5824
Alerugika/Allergology see Rinshou Men'eki Arerugika 5765
Alestle (USA) 2272
Aletheia (BRA ISSN 1413-0394) 7332
Aletheia (CHE ISSN 0149-2004) 6903
Aletheia see Jie Di Xuekan 6927
Alexander Lectures (CAN ISSN 0065-616X) 5251
Alexander von Humboldt-Stiftung (DEU ISSN 0935-3828) 4441
Alexander von Humboldt-Stiftung. Jahresbericht (DEU ISSN 0342-6785) 4442
Alexander von Humboldt-Stiftung. Mitteilungen see Humboldt Kosmos 4456
Alexandra, Eildon, Marysville Standard (AUS) 3793
➤ Alexandria (USA) 6903
Alexandria Archaeology Volunteer News (USA ISSN 0894-2625) 372
Alexandria Dental Journal/Al-Magallat al-Iskandiriyyah li-Tibb al-Asnan (EGY ISSN 1110-015X) 5834
Alexandria Engineering Journal (EGY ISSN 1110-0168) 3180
Alexandria Faculty of Medicine Bulletin see University of Alexandria. Faculty of Medicine. Bulletin 5727
Alexandria. High Institute of Public Health. Bulletin (EGY ISSN 1110-0036) 7506
➤ Alexandria Journal of Agricultural Research (EGY ISSN 0044-7250) 90
➤ Alexandria: Journal of National & International Library & Information Issues (GBR ISSN 0955-7490) 4988

DIRECTORY 2010 ALL-STATER SPORTS 9941

Alexandria Journal of Pharmaceutical Sciences (EGY ISSN 1110-1792) **6819**
† The Alexandria Journal of the History of Medicine (GBR ISSN 1743-6745) **8929**
Alexandria Journal of Veterinary Sciences (EGY ISSN 1110-2047) **8790**
Alexandria Medical Journal (EGY ISSN 1110-0060) **5571**
➤ Alexandria Science Exchange (EGY ISSN 1110-0176) **7834**
Alexandria University. Faculty of Engineering. Bulletin *see* Alexandria Engineering Journal **3180**
➤ Alexandrie (POL ISSN 0138-0486) **372**
Alexandru Ioan Cuza University of Iasi. Scientific Annals. Economic Sciences Series *see* Universitatea "Al. I. Cuza" din Iasi. Analele Stiintifice. Sectiunea 3c: Stiinte Economice **1187**
Alexanor (FRA ISSN 0002-5208) **838**
• Alex's Paper Airplanes (GBR) **4327**
• ➤ Alfa (BRA ISSN 0002-5216) **5092**
• Alfa (ESP ISSN 1137-8360) **6903**
Alfa (ESP ISSN 1888-8925) **3180**
Alfa Friends & Family (USA ISSN 1522-0648) **90**
Alfa-Gamma (ECU) **1058**
➤ Al'fa i Omega (RUS ISSN 0203-3488) **7620**
ALFA-Nieuws (NLD ISSN 1571-3512) **2825**
Alfa Owner (USA ISSN 0364-930X) **8555**
• Alfa - Redi (PER ISSN 1681-5726) **4844**
Alfa Reeks (NLD) **5251**
Alfa Romeo Collection (ITA ISSN 1824-7717) **8555**
Alfavit (RUS) **3934**
Alfijir (NGA) **3920**
Alfil Dama (COL) **8157**
Alfinge (ESP ISSN 0213-1854) **5092**
Alfold (HUN ISSN 0401-3174) **5205**
Alforja (ESP ISSN 0210-3168) **3626**
Alfred Cauchie Reeks (BEL) **4129**
Alfred Hitchcock's Mystery Magazine (Palm O S & Windows C E Edition) *see* Alfred Hitchcock's Mystery Magazine (Print Edition) **5413**
Alfred Hitchcock's Mystery Magazine (Print Edition) (USA ISSN 0002-5224) **5413**
Alfred Wegener Institute Foundation for Polar and Marine Research. Report *see* Stiftung Alfred-Wegener-Institut fuer Polar- und Meeresforschung. Zweijahresbericht **706**
Alfreda's Recipe Series (USA ISSN 1098-3856) **4351**
The Alfred's Yachtsman (AUS ISSN 1034-6651) **8271**
Alfresco (NZL ISSN 1175-0162) **3721**
Alfreton Chad *see* Chad (Alfreton Edition) **3967**
Algae (KOR ISSN 1226-2617) **774**
▼ Algebra and Discrete Mathematics (SGP) **5467**
Algebra and Discrete Mathematics (UKR ISSN 1726-3255) **5467**
• ➤ Algebra and Logic (USA ISSN 0002-5232) **5467**
▼ • ➤ Algebra & Number Theory (USA ISSN 1937-0652) **5468**
• ➤ Algebra Colloquium (SGP ISSN 1005-3867) **5468**
Algebra i Analiz (RUS ISSN 0234-0852) **5468**
Algebra i Logika (RUS ISSN 0373-9252) **5468**
➤ Algebra, Logic and Applications (USA ISSN 1041-5394) **5468**
• Algebra Montpellier Announcements/Annonces de Montpellier en Algebre (FRA) **5468**
• ➤ Algebra Universalis (CHE ISSN 0002-5240) **5468**
• ➤ Algebraic & Geometric Topology (GBR ISSN 1472-2747) **5468**
Algebraic Methodology and Software Technology Series in Computing *see* A M A S T Series in Computing **2406**
• ➤ Algebras and Representation Theory (NLD ISSN 1386-923X) **5468**
➤ Algebras, Groups and Geometries (USA ISSN 0741-9937) **5468**
Algemeen Burgerlijk Pensioenfonds. Jaarverslag (NLD ISSN 0926-6224) **1662**
Algemeen Burgerlijk Pensioenfonds Magazine *see* A B P Magazine **4490**
Algemeen Burgerlijk Pensioenfonds Position Papers *see* A B P Position Papers **1661**
Algemeen Burgerlijk Pensioenfonds, Uitvoeringsinstelling Sociale Zekerheid voor Overheids- en Onderwijspersoneel. Nieuws *see* A B P Magazine **4490**
Algemeen Burgerlijk Pensioenfonds Wereld *see* A B P Wereld **3914**
Algemeen Burgerlijk Pensioenfonds Working Papers *see* A B P Working Papers **1661**
• Algemeen Dagblad (NLD) **3914**
Algemeen Doopsgezind Weekblad *see* Doopsgezind nl **7754**
Algemeen Fiskaal Tijdschrift (BEL ISSN 0772-6465) **1279**
Algemeen Jaarboek der Schone Kunsten *see* Jaarboek der Schone Kunsten **498**
Algemeen Maconniek Tijdschrift *see* Ken Uzelve **7658**
➤ Algemeen Nederlands Tijdschrift voor Wijsbegeerte (NLD ISSN 0002-5275) **6903**
Algemeen Nederlands Verbond Reeks *see* A N V Reeks **4195**
Algemeen Nijmeegs Studentenblad *see* A N S **2271**
Algemeen Politieblad van het Koninkrijk der Nederlanden *see* Blauw **4630**
Algemeen Verslag over de Werkzaamheden van de Europese Unie *see* General Report on the Activities of the European Union **3837**
Algemeene Nederlandsche Wierlrijdersbond Auto *see* A N W B Auto **8554**
Der Algemeiner Journal (USA) **7717**
Algemene Bijstandswet *see* Wet Werk en Bijstand (Doetinchem) **7477**
Algemene Fiscale, Administratieve en Sociale Verzekeringsaspecten (NLD ISSN 1871-2142) **1910**
Algemene Nederlandse Wielrijders Bond Boot *see* A N W B Boot **8270**
Algemene Nederlandse Wielrijders Bond Campinggids Nederland *see* A N W B Campinggids Nederland **8301**
Algemene Practische Rechtverzameling (BEL) **4613**
Algemene Vereeniging Radio Omroep Bode *see* A V R O-Bode **2374**
Algemene wet Bestuursrecht (NLD ISSN 1574-8995) **4846**
Algemene wet Bestuursrecht *see* Tekst en Toelichting Algemene wet Bestuursrecht **4793**
Algemene wet Bestuursrecht (Handboek Milieuvergunningen) (NLD ISSN 1572-3275) **3402**
Algemene Wet Bestuursrecht en Aanverwante Regelgeving (NLD ISSN 1387-7828) **4613**
Algeria *see* The P R S Group. Country Reports: Algeria **1505**
Algeria. Direction des Douanes. Bulletin Comparatif Trimestriel (DZA) **1910**
• Algeria Focus (GBR ISSN 1477-2442) **1436**
Algeria. Office National des Statistiques. Annuaire Statistique *see* Annuaire Statistique de l'Algerie **8345**
Algeria. Office National des Statistiques. Annuaire Statistique des Wilayate de l'Est (DZA ISSN 1111-7680) **8344**
Algeria. Office National des Statistiques. Annuaire Statistique des Wilayate de l'Ouest (DZA ISSN 1111-0368) **8344**
Algeria. Office National des Statistiques. Annuaire Statistique des Wilayate du Centre (DZA ISSN 1111-0376) **8344**
Algeria. Office National des Statistiques. Bulletin de Statistiques Courantes (DZA ISSN 1111-5696) **8344**
Algeria. Office National des Statistiques. Collections Statistiques (DZA ISSN 1111-0392) **8344**
Algeria. Office National des Statistiques. Donnees Statistiques (DZA ISSN 1111-5939) **8344**
Algeria. Office National des Statistiques. Indices des Prix a la Consommation (DZA) **1199**
Algeria. Office National des Statistiques. Informations Statistiques sur la Conjoncture (DZA ISSN 1111-7001) **8344**
Algeria. Office National des Statistiques. Statistiques (Revue Trimestrielle) (DZA ISSN 1111-0384) **8344**
Algeria. Office Nationale de la Geologie. Bulletin (DZA) **2724**
Algeria Petrochemicals and Chemicals Report *see* Algeria Petrochemicals Report **6762**
Algeria Petrochemicals Report (GBR ISSN 1749-2114) **6762**
Algerian Chemical Society. Journal *see* Societe Algerienne de Chimie. Journal **2080**
L'Algerie en Quelques Chiffres (DZA ISSN 1010-1284) **8344**
Algerie Litterature - Action (FRA ISSN 1270-9131) **5205**
† Algesie und Analgesie (BRD ISSN 0721-5193) **8929**
• ➤ Algological Studies (DEU ISSN 1864-1318) **652**
➤ Al'gologiya/Algology (UKR ISSN 0868-8540) **774**
Algology *see* Al'gologiya **774**
The Algonkian (USA) **5251**
Algonquian and Iroquoian Linguistics (CAN ISSN 0711-382X) **5092**
➤ Algonquian Conference. Papers (CAN ISSN 0831-5671) **323**
Algonquin Times (CAN) **2272**
• ➤ Algorithmic Operations Research (CAN ISSN 1718-3235) **5468**
• ➤ Algorithmica (USA ISSN 0178-4617) **2406**
▼ • Algorithms (CHE ISSN 1999-4893) **5468**
Algorithms and Combinatorics (USA ISSN 0937-5511) **5468**
Algorithms and Computation in Mathematics (DEU ISSN 1431-1550) **5468**
• Algorithms for Molecular Biology (GBR ISSN 1748-7188) **862**
Algorithms for Synthetic Aperture Radar Imagery (USA ISSN 1087-6146) **7073**
† Alhambra (ESP ISSN 0401-3689) **8929**
ALI-ABA Course of Study Materials *see* Financial Services and Insurance Industry Litigation **4674**
Alias (GBR ISSN 1740-3626) **2374**
Alibi (FIN ISSN 0357-542X) **4883**
L'Alibi du Colibri (FRA ISSN 1774-7309) **2175**
• Alice Blue (USA ISSN 1559-6567) **5251**
• Alice Magazine (USA ISSN 1529-7586) **8850**
Alice Reports (USA) **7104**
• Alice's Love Adventure to Wonderland (USA) **5408**
Alicia Johnson Memorial Lecture (AUS ISSN 1326-0197) **8850**
Alicia Patterson Foundation Reporter *see* A P F Reporter **4571**
Alieftika Nea/Fishing News (GRC ISSN 1106-4641) **3583**
• Alien Contact (Online Edition) (DEU ISSN 1611-5058) **5439**
Alien Contact (Print Edition) *see* Alien Contact (Online Edition) **5439**
• Alien Deception (USA ISSN 1934-7146) **5439**
Alien Encounters (GBR ISSN 1362-5098) **5439**
• Alien Hideout Weekly Ezine (USA) **46**
Aliens (Auckland) (NZL ISSN 1173-5988) **774**
• ➤ Alif (EGY ISSN 1110-8673) **5416**
Alif: Journal of Comparative Poetics *see* Alif **5416**
Aligarh Bulletin of Mathematics (IND ISSN 0304-9787) **5468**
Aligarh Journal of English Studies (IND ISSN 0258-0365) **5251**
Aligarh Journal of Oriental Studies (IND ISSN 0970-0994) **542**
Aligarh Journal of Statistics (IND ISSN 0971-0388) **8344**
L'Alighieri (ITA ISSN 0516-6551) **5416**
Alignment (CAN) **6055**
Alignment Tech-Talk (USA ISSN 1058-9082) **8555**
† Alim (ISR ISSN 0334-5084) **8929**
• Alimarket (ESP ISSN 1134-816X) **3626**
• Alimarket. Alimentacion no Perecedera (ESP ISSN 1134-8119) **3676**
• Alimarket. Alimentacion Perecedera (ESP ISSN 1134-8100) **3626**
• Alimarket. Bebidas (ESP ISSN 1134-8127) **597**
• Alimarket. Comerciales (ESP ISSN 1575-3646) **1804**
• Alimarket. Distribucion (ESP ISSN 1134-8135) **1804**
Alimarket. Distribucion Alimentaria *see* Alimarket. Distribucion **1804**
• Alimarket. Hosteleria (ESP ISSN 1138-7637) **4381**
• Alimarket. No Alimentacion (ESP ISSN 1139-6903) **6654**
Alimarket Revista (ESP ISSN 1134-8151) **3626**
➤ Alimenta (CHE ISSN 0002-5402) **3626**
Alimenta (CHE) **261**
Alimenta (FIN ISSN 1239-4602) **90**
Alimentacao (BRA ISSN 0100-9397) **3626**
• La Alimentacion en Espana (ESP ISSN 1136-1336) **6654**
La Alimentacion Latinoamericana (ARG ISSN 0325-3384) **3626**
Alimentacion, Nutricion y Salud (ESP ISSN 1136-4815) **6654**
Alimentar (PRT) **3626**
Alimentaria (ESP ISSN 0300-5755) **3626**
• ➤ Alimentary Pharmacology and Therapeutics (GBR ISSN 0269-2813) **5920**
• Alimentary Pharmacology and Therapeutics. Supplement (GBR ISSN 0953-0673) **5920**
L'Alimentation au Quebec (CAN ISSN 0002-5410) **3676**
• Alimentation et Precarite (FRA ISSN 1629-1212) **6654**
L'Alimentation Francaise *see* C A P S Infos **3676**
Alimentation Nutrition (FRA ISSN 1955-5911) **6654**
• Alimenti & Bevande (ITA ISSN 1827-8582) **3626**
Alimentos (CHL ISSN 0716-0968) **3626**
Alimentos Ciencia e Ingenieria (ECU ISSN 1390-2180) **3626**
Alimentos de Espana (ESP) **3626**
Alimentos e Bebidas America Latina (GBR ISSN 1752-0681) **3626**
➤ Alimentos e Nutricao (BRA ISSN 0103-4235) **6654**
Alimentos y Bebidas Latinoamerica (GBR ISSN 1752-0673) **3626**
Aliments du Pacifique Sud *see* South Pacific Foods **3664**
• Alimentum (USA) **5416**
Alinea (FRA ISSN 1267-3625) **7946**
Alingsaas Tidning - Elfsborgs Laens Tidning (SWE ISSN 1103-9019) **3954**
➤ Aliso (USA ISSN 0065-6275) **774**
Alithia (CYP) **3831**
• Alive (CAN ISSN 0228-586X) **6981**
Alive (IND ISSN 0971-0639) **5205**
Alive! (IRL) **7782**
Alive (NZL ISSN 1178-5403) **5064**
• @live (TWN) **3089**
Alive! (USA) **4040**
Alive (Milwaukee) (USA) **317**
Alive & W E L (Women's Electoral Lobby) (AUS) **8850**
Alive and Well Saint Patrick's Cathedral (USA) **7782**
ALIVE Magazine (AUS ISSN 1442-5572) **7745**
• Alive Now (USA ISSN 0891-8767) **7745**
• Alizes (FRA ISSN 1630-7445) **4282**
• Alizes (REU ISSN 1155-4363) **5092**
• La Aljaba (ARG ISSN 0328-6169) **8893**
Aljadid *see* Al Jadid **3541**
Aljamila *see* Al Jamila **8869**
➤ Alkalmazott Matematikai Lapok (HUN ISSN 0133-3399) **5468**
• Alkaloids: Chemical and Biological Perspectives (USA ISSN 0735-8210) **722**
• ➤ The Alkaloids: Chemistry and Biology (USA ISSN 1099-4831) **2119**
The Alkaloids: Chemistry and Pharmacology *see* The Alkaloids: Chemistry and Biology **2119**
• Alki (USA ISSN 8756-4173) **4988**
Alkmaarse Historische Reeks (NLD ISSN 0929-9750) **4197**
Alkohol-Industrie (DEU ISSN 0002-5496) **597**
Alkohol & Narkotika/Alcohol and Other Drugs (SWE ISSN 0345-0732) **2691**
Alkoholizm i Narkomania (POL ISSN 0867-4361) **2691**
• All About Baby & Child (USA) **2143**
• All About Beer (USA ISSN 0898-9001) **597**
All About Business in Hawaii (USA ISSN 1046-5480) **1436**
All about Cats (GBR ISSN 1352-285X) **6802**
All about Dogs (GBR ISSN 1361-8458) **6802**
All About Dogs in South Africa (ZAF ISSN 1683-4224) **6802**
All About Food and Cooking *see* Allt om Mat & Vin **3626**
• All About Jazz (USA) **6543**
All About Kids (USA) **2143**
All about Making Money (GBR ISSN 1366-2295) **1804**
All About Medicare (USA ISSN 1044-9426) **4492**
• All about Net Profits (USA) **1058**
All About Ports Cruise Guide (GBR ISSN 1474-1067) **8638**
• All About R O I (Retail/Catalog Online Integration) (USA ISSN 1947-9425) **1804**
All About Soap (GBR ISSN 1468-4047) **2374**
• All About Women Consumers (USA ISSN 1089-2435) **1804**
All Access (USA) **6489**
All Access Pass (CAN ISSN 0838-7796) **6543**
All Africa Conference of Churches Bulletin *see* A A C C Bulletin **7619**
All Africa Conference of Churches. Refugee Department. Progress Report (KEN) **7620**
All Africa Conference of Churches. Refugee Department. Project List (KEN) **7620**
All Africa Press Service Bulletin *see* A P S Bulletin **7619**
All American Aviation Association News (USA) **8538**
All Animals *see* AllAnimals **317**
• All Around Kentucky (USA ISSN 1082-1570) **90**
All Available Light (USA) **5416**
• All Brevard Magazine (USA) **8682**
• All Canada Weekly Summaries - National (CAN ISSN 0705-1360) **4613**
• All England Law Reports (GBR ISSN 0002-5569) **4946**
All England Law Reports. Annual Review (GBR ISSN 0265-766X) **4946**
All England Law Reports. Commercial Cases (GBR ISSN 1470-5303) **4946**
All England Law Reports. European Cases (GBR ISSN 1464-5599) **4946**
All England Legal Opinion (GBR ISSN 1474-7146) **4613**
All-European Human Rights Yearbook (DEU) **7202**
• All Hands (USA ISSN 0002-5577) **6410**
▼ All Horse (DNK ISSN 1902-7842) **8286**
All+ Hudong Yingyu *see* All+ Interactive English **5092**
All In (GBR) **5416**
All In (USA ISSN 1554-7167) **8157**
All In Magazine *see* All In **8157**
All-in Success (GBR ISSN 0953-9700) **2825**
All-India Anglo-Indian Association. Review (IND ISSN 0002-5585) **7220**
All India Appointment Gazette (IND) **3878**
All-India Conference of Linguists. Souvenir (IND) **5092**
All India Congress Committee. Congress Bulletin (IND) **7104**
All India Institute of Local Self Government. Quarterly Journal (IND ISSN 0024-5623) **7487**
All India Magic Circle Bulletin (IND) **4327**
All India Organisation of Employers Labour News *see* A I O E Labour News **1661**
• All India Reporter (IND ISSN 0002-5593) **4613**
All India Services Law Journal (IND) **4613**
All Indian Management Association News *see* A I M A News **1722**
All Inn Home Magazine (NLD) **7581**
All+ Interactive English/All+ Hudong Yingyu (TWN ISSN 1813-3452) **5092**
▼ All-Ireland Health Data Inventory. Part 1: Metadata for Key Data Sources (IRL ISSN 2009-0234) **7506**
All Ireland Journal of Nursing and Midwifery (IRL ISSN 1471-0854) **5951**
All Man (USA ISSN 1083-2459) **6285**
All-Music Guide *see* Allmusic **6543**
All New Tom & Jerry (GBR ISSN 1460-6410) **2175**
All Over the Globe *see* Vremya po Grinvichu **3902**
All Pakistan Legal Decisions (PAK ISSN 0030-9958) **4613**
• All Pakistan Textile Mills Association. Chairman's Review (Online) (PAK) **1879**
All Pakistan Textile Mills Association. Chairman's Review (Print) *see* All Pakistan Textile Mills Association. Chairman's Review (Online) **1879**
All Pakistan Women's Association Newsletter *see* A P W A Newsletter **8022**
All Pakistan Women's Association. Triennial Conference Report (PAK) **8850**
All Pro Weekly (USA) **8220**
All Reading Matters *see* Ooru Yomimono **5346**
All Roads Lead to Branson (USA) **8682**
All-Round Southeast Asia *see* Dongnanya Zongheng **7960**
• All South African Law Reports (ZAF ISSN 1025-6466) **4613**
All Sport & Leisure Monthly (GBR) **4975**
All State (USA) **2272**
All-Stater Sports (USA) **8157**

Title

All States Individual Income Tax Quickfinder Handbook see All States Quickfinder Handbook 1910
All States Quickfinder Handbook (USA ISSN 1945-2764) 1910
• All States Tax Guide (USA) 1910
All States Tax Guide Report Bulletin see All States Tax Guide 1910
All States Tax Handbook (Year) (USA ISSN 0148-9976) 1910
• All Terrain Adventures (USA) 8682
All-Terrain Vehicle (USA) 8302
All Terrain Vehicle see All-Terrain Vehicle 8302
All Terrain Vehicle 4-Wheel Action see A T V 4-Wheel Action 8554
All Terrain Vehicle Industry Magazine see A T V - Industry Magazine 8253
All Terrain Vehicle Magazine see A T V Magazine 8554
All Terrain Vehicle Rider see A T V Rider 8253
All Terrain Vehicle Sport see A T V Sport 8554
All-Terrain-Vehicle Trail Rider see A T V Trail Rider 8253
All Terrain Vehicle Trail Rider see A T V Trail Rider 8253
All Terrain Vehicles und Quad see A T V und Quad 8554
• All the Secrets (AUS) 2552
• All the Way (USA ISSN 1040-2055) 7104
All the World (GBR ISSN 0002-5623) 7745
† All Time Favorite Crochet (USA) 8929
All-Time Favorites: Slow Cooker (USA ISSN 1541-258X) 4351
All Vaerldens Kvinnor (SWE ISSN 1103-291X) 8850
All Woman (USA) 8850
All Yomimono (JPN) 5251
All You (USA ISSN 1550-6924) 8850
• Alla (SWE ISSN 1404-8868) 8024
Alla Bilar (SWE ISSN 1101-7546) 8555
Alla Bottega (ITA ISSN 0002-5631) 5251
Alla Ledare (SWE ISSN 1104-2060) 7745
Alla Tiders Boecker (SWE ISSN 1104-2974) 7551
I Allaghi (GRC) 3873
Allahabad Mathematical Society. Bulletin (IND ISSN 0971-0493) 5468
Allam- es Jogtudomany/Political Science and Jurisprudence (HUN ISSN 0002-564X) 4613
Allami Gazdasag/State Farming (HUN) 90
AllAnimals (USA) 317
Allarme see Alarm 3575
All'Art see Kunstzone 6583
Allas (SWE ISSN 1652-6333) 3954
Allattani Kozlemenyek/Zoological Proceedings (HUN ISSN 0002-5658) 931
Allattenyesztes es Takarmanyozas/Hungarian Journal of Animal Production (HUN ISSN 0230-1814) 277
Alle Bestel- en Vrachtauto's (NLD) 8490
Alle Bestelauto's see Alle Bestel- en Vrachtauto's 8490
Alle Hens (NLD ISSN 0002-5674) 6410
Alle Risico's (BEL ISSN 0772-4764) 4492
Alle Tiders Odsherred (DNK ISSN 0108-9846) 4197
Alle Volken (NLD) 7745
Alledaagse Dingen see Volkscultuur Magazine 3624
The Alledger (USA) 4613
Allees All Around (USA ISSN 0883-5926) 3758
Allegheny County Medical Society. Bulletin (USA ISSN 0098-3772) 5571
Allegheny Review (USA ISSN 0742-096X) 5251
† Allegra (DEU ISSN 0948-6488) 8929
Allegro (DEU ISSN 1436-8323) 5753
Allegro (USA ISSN 0002-5704) 4589
• ➤ Allelopathy Journal (IND ISSN 0971-4693) 774
➤ Allemagne d'Aujourd'hui (FRA ISSN 0002-5712) 5205
Allen and Overy Legal Practice (NLD ISSN 1568-1335) 4613
Allen Confidential (USA ISSN 1535-5837) 4403
Allen County Lines (USA ISSN 1067-7747) 3758
Allen County Reporter (USA) 4282
(Year) Allen D. Leman Swine Conference. Proceedings (USA) 8791
Allen Family Circle (USA ISSN 0885-3215) 3758
Allen Letter (USA ISSN 1525-2159) 1058
• Allen's Trademark Digest (USA ISSN 0899-191X) 4613
Allen's V A T News (Value Added Tax) (GBR ISSN 1353-3460) 1910
Allensbacher Almanach (DEU) 4197
Allensbacher Berichte (DEU ISSN 0176-9251) 7946
• Allensbacher Computer- und Telekommunikationsanalyse (DEU) 2312
Allensbacher Jahrbuch der Demoskopie (DEU ISSN 0175-9191) 8086
• Allensbacher Markt-Analyse und Werbetraeger-Analyse (DEU) 1804
Aller Simple (USA) 3517
Allergi i Praksis (NOR ISSN 0806-5462) 5753
Allergia (SWE ISSN 0002-5747) 5753
Allergic Disease and Therapy (USA ISSN 1053-1092) 5753
Allergie et Immunologie see European Annals of Allergy and Clinical Immunology 5758
Allergie Konkret (DEU) 5753
Allergies & Asthma Health Monitor see Health Monitor Allergies & Asthma 6214
Allergikus (DEU) 5753
➤ Allergo Journal (DEU ISSN 0941-8849) 5753
• Allergologen (NOR ISSN 0332-8295) 5753
Allergologia es Klinikai Immunologia (HUN ISSN 1418-2653) 5753
• ➤ Allergologia et Immunopathologia/International Journal for Clinical and Investigative Allergology and Clinical Immunology (ESP ISSN 0301-0546) 5753
➤ Allergologie (DEU ISSN 0344-5062) 5753
Allergology & Immunology see Arerugi, Men'eki 5754
Allergology & Immunology see Alergologia, Immunologia 5752
• ➤ Allergology International (JPN ISSN 1323-8930) 5753
• ➤ Allergy (GBR ISSN 0105-4538) 5753
Allergy (GBR) 5753
• Allergy & Asthma Advocate (Online) (USA) 5753
Allergy & Asthma Advocate (Print) see Allergy & Asthma Advocate (Online) 5753
Allergy and Asthma Health (USA ISSN 1529-4668) 5753
• ➤ Allergy and Asthma Proceedings (USA ISSN 1088-5412) 5753
Allergy & Asthma Today (USA ISSN 1543-0804) 5753
† • ➤ Allergy and Clinical Immunology International (USA ISSN 1097-1424) 8929
Allergy and Immunology Week see Allergy & Immunology Week 5753
• Allergy & Immunology Week (USA ISSN 1532-4532) 5753
• ➤ Allergy, Asthma, and Clinical Immunology (CAN ISSN 1710-1484) 5753
† • Allergy Coding Alert (USA ISSN 1536-8297) 8929
Allergy in Practice see Arerugi no Rinsho 5754
• ➤ Allergy. Supplement (GBR ISSN 0108-1675) 5754
Allers (NOR ISSN 0805-9713) 3921
Allers (SWE ISSN 0002-578X) 3954
Allers Kryss og Tvers (NOR) 4327
Allers Traedgaard (SWE ISSN 1403-252X) 3721
➤ Allertonia (USA ISSN 0735-8032) 774
Alles fuer die Frau (DEU ISSN 1862-0388) 8851
Alles ueber Wein (DEU ISSN 0175-8314) 3626
Allesoe, Broby, Naesby Lokalarkiv see Allesoe-Broby-Naesby Lokalarkiv. Aarsskrift 4197
Allesoe-Broby-Naesby Lokalarkiv. Aarsskrift (DNK ISSN 1902-794X) 4197
Allestire (ITA ISSN 1594-5332) 1058
Allevare. Il Canile Moderno (ITA ISSN 1825-3202) 6802
L'Allevatore see L' Allevatore Magazine 8791
L'Allevatore Magazine (ITA ISSN 1972-8034) 8791
L'Allevatore Trentino (ITA ISSN 1828-4809) 261
Allgaeuer Bauernblatt (DEU) 90
Allgaeuer Zeitung (DEU) 3843
• Der Allgemeinarzt (DEU ISSN 0172-7249) 5571
Allgemeine Baecker-Zeitung (DEU ISSN 0341-2490) 3670
Allgemeine Bauern Zeitung (AUT) 90
Allgemeine Bauzeitung (DEU ISSN 0002-5801) 975
† Allgemeine Bedingungen fuer die Kraftfahrtversicherung (DEU ISSN 0933-2081) 8929
Allgemeine Deutsche Imkerzeitung (DEU ISSN 0002-5828) 90
Allgemeine Deutsche Zeitung fuer Rumaenien (ROM ISSN 1221-7956) 3932
Allgemeine Fleischer Zeitung (DEU ISSN 0170-9828) 3626
Allgemeine Fleischer Zeitung Journal see A F Z Journal 3625
Allgemeine Forst- und Jagdzeitung (DEU ISSN 0002-5852) 3683
Allgemeine Forst Zeitschrift Der Wald see A F Z - Der Wald 3682
Allgemeine Geschichtforschende Gesellschaft der Schweiz. Bulletin see Schweizerische Gesellschaft fuer Geschichte. Bulletin 4160
• Allgemeine Homoeopathische Zeitung (DEU ISSN 1438-2563) 5803
Allgemeine Hotel- und Gaststaetten-Zeitung (DEU ISSN 0002-5895) 4381
Allgemeine Juedische Wochenzeitung see Juedische Allgemeine 3545
Allgemeine Papier-Rundschau see A P R 6731
Allgemeine Schweizerische Militaerzeitschrift (CHE ISSN 0002-5925) 6410
Allgemeine Sparkasse. Kurz Notiert (AUT) 1306
▼ • Allgemeine und Viszeralchirurgie Up2date (DEU ISSN 1611-6437) 6235
Allgemeine Vermessungs-Nachrichten (DEU ISSN 0002-5968) 3259
➤ Allgemeine Zeitschrift fuer Philosophie (DEU ISSN 0340-7969) 6903
Allgemeine Zeitung (DEU ISSN 0935-0063) 3843
Allgemeine Zeitung (NAM ISSN 1560-9421) 3913
Allgemeiner Caecilien-Verband. Schriftenreihe (DEU ISSN 0569-0609) 6543
Allgemeiner Deutscher Automobil-Club e.V. Auto Test Neuwagen see A D A C Auto Test Neuwagen 8553
Allgemeiner Deutscher Automobil-Club e.V. AutoAtlas Deutschland - Europa see A D A C AutoAtlas Deutschland - Europa 8679
Allgemeiner Deutscher Automobil-Club e.V. Camping-Caravaning-Fuehrer. Band 2: Deutschland, Nordeuropa see A D A C Camping-Caravaning-Fuehrer. Band 2: Deutschland, Nordeuropa 8301
Allgemeiner Deutscher Automobil-Club e.V. Camping-Caravaning-Fuehrer. Suedeuropa see A D A C Camping-Caravaning-Fuehrer. Suedeuropa 8301
Allgemeiner Deutscher Automobil-Club e.V. Freizeit Mobil see A D A C Freizeit Mobil 8301
Allgemeiner Deutscher Automobil-Club e.V. Handbuch: Reiserecht Entscheidungen see A D A C Handbuch: Reiserecht Entscheidungen 4607
Allgemeiner Deutscher Automobil-Club e.V. Handbuch: Schadenersatz bei Verletzung und Toetung see A D A C Handbuch: Schadenersatz bei Verletzung und Toetung 4607
Allgemeiner Deutscher Automobil-Club e.V. Handbuch: Schmerzensgeld-Betraege see A D A C Handbuch: Schmerzensgeld-Betraege 4915
Allgemeiner Deutscher Automobil-Club e.V. Handbuch: Unfall im Ausland - Schadensregulierung see A D A C Handbuch: Unfall im Ausland - Schadensregulierung 4607
Allgemeiner Deutscher Automobil-Club e.V. Handbuch: Unfall Ratgeber see A D A C Handbuch: Unfall Ratgeber 4607
Allgemeiner Deutscher Automobil-Club e.V. Motorradwelt see A D A C Motorradwelt 8252
Allgemeiner Deutscher Automobil-Club e.V. Motorwelt see A D A C Motorwelt 8554
Allgemeiner Deutscher Automobil-Club e.V. Reisemagazin see A D A C Reisemagazin 8680
Allgemeiner Deutscher Automobil-Club e.V. Reisemagazin Extra Ski see A D A C Reisemagazin Extra Ski 8680
Allgemeiner Deutscher Automobil-Club e.V. Signale see A D A C Signale 8554
Allgemeiner Deutscher Automobil-Club e.V. Ski and Snowboard see A D A C Ski and Snowboard 8301
Allgemeiner Deutscher Automobil-Club e.V. Ski-Guide see A D A C Ski-Guide 8301
Allgemeiner Deutscher Automobil-Club e.V. Special Gebrauchtwagen Test see A D A C Special Gebrauchtwagen Test 8554
Allgemeiner Hochschul-Anzeiger (DEU ISSN 0938-7250) 6692
Allgemeiner Postwertzeichen Haendler Verband e.V. Magazin see A P H V Magazin 6891
Allgemeiner Vliestoff-Report see A V R 8447
Allgemeines Statistisches Archiv see A St A - Advances in Statistical Analysis 8343
• ➤ Alliage (FRA ISSN 1144-5645) 7834
• Alliance (GBR ISSN 1359-4621) 4916
Alliance (Charleston) (USA) 2272
Alliance (English Edition) (CAN ISSN 0838-7990) 4589
Alliance (French Edition) see Alliance (English Edition) 4589
• Alliance (Wisconsin) (USA) 6121
L'Alliance Agricole (BEL) 90
• The Alliance Analyst (USA ISSN 1079-1191) 1725
Alliance Autochtone du Quebec (CAN) 6634
Alliance des Femmes de la Francophonie Canadienne. Rapport Annuel (CAN ISSN 1912-1482) 8851
† Alliance Environmental Law Newsletter (NLD ISSN 0928-1894) 8929
The Alliance for Children and Families. Directory of Member Agencies in the United States and Canada (USA) 8024
• Alliance for Children & Families Magazine (USA ISSN 1946-1305) 8024
Alliance for New Jersey Environmental Education Newsletter see A N J E E Newsletter 3050
Alliance for Peace in Rumania. Information Bulletin (ROM) 7220
▼ • Alliance for Progress (USA ISSN 1945-7200) 8024
Alliance Francaise de Canberra. Bulletin d'Information (AUS) 2825
Alliance Gazette (USA) 6518
Alliance Inter-Monasteres Bulletin see A I M. Bulletin 7781
Alliance Israelite Universelle en France. Cahiers (FRA ISSN 0002-6050) 7717
➤ Alliance Journal of Business Research (IND ISSN 0973-0850) 1725
Alliance Life (USA ISSN 1040-6794) 7745
Alliance News (GBR ISSN 0002-6085) 7104
Alliance of Information and Referral Systems. Journal see Information and Referral 8046
Alliance Pastorale. Bulletin (FRA) 277
Alliance pour une Europe des Consciences (FRA ISSN 1770-3670) 8086
Alliance Review (USA ISSN 0002-6093) 2825
Alliance Update see UPDATE (Reston) 6999
Alliancebladet see Evangelisk Alliance. Nyhedsbrev 7757
Alliances and Joint Ventures Worldwide (GBR) 3626
Allianz Deutscher Designer e.V. Viertel see A G D Viertel 462
Allianz In Zukunft Eins (DEU) 4492
Allied and Complementary Medicine Database see A M E D 316
Allied Artists of America. Exhibition Catalog (USA ISSN 0065-6410) 6519
Allied Arts Newsletter (USA) 465
Allied Dunbar Investment and Savings Handbook see Investment & Savings Handbook 1632
Allied Irish Bank Review (IRL ISSN 0332-320X) 1306
Allied Irish Banks Review see A I B Review 1305
The Allied Worker (CAN) 4589
Alligator Juniper (USA ISSN 1547-187X) 5251
† Allionia (ITA ISSN 0065-6429) 8929
Alliston Herald see Herald (Alliston) 3811
Allmaenna Avdelingens Publikationer see Yleisen Osaston Julkaisuja 4817
Allmaenna Raad see Naturvaardsverket. Handbok 3455
Allman Rapport om Europeiska Unionens Verksamhet see General Report on the Activities of the European Union 3837
Allmaxx (DEU) 5064
Allmende (DEU ISSN 0720-3098) 5416
• Allmountain (DEU) 8682
• Allmusic (USA) 6543
Allo 18 see Allo Dix-Huit 3575
Allo Dix-Huit (FRA ISSN 0983-3889) 3575
Allochtonen in Nederland see Jaarrapport Integratie 7211
Allografts in Bone Healing: Biology and Clinical Applications (SGP) 5571
Allons-Y (GBR ISSN 1356-1332) 3011
• ➤ Alloy Digest (USA ISSN 0002-614X) 6304
Alloy Girl see AlloyGirl 8851
Alloy Metals & Steel Report (GBR) 6304
AlloyGirl (USA) 8851
• Alloys Index (USA ISSN 0094-8233) 6338
Allpanchis (PER ISSN 0252-8835) 7946
Allpanchis Phuturinga see Allpanchis 7946
• Allskog (NOR ISSN 0809-9006) 3683
AllSports Magazine (USA) 8157
Allt om Digitalfoto see Kamera & Bild 6970
▼ Allt om Drycker (SWE ISSN 1654-1251) 4351
Allt om DVD see Allt om Film 6489
Allt om Eget Foeretag see Eget Foeretag 1740
Allt om Elektronik see Elektor 3097
Allt om Energi (SWE ISSN 1653-6916) 3123
▼ Allt om Film (SWE ISSN 1654-4994) 6489
Allt om Flugfiske (SWE ISSN 1650-6812) 8302
Allt om Handarbete (SWE ISSN 1653-8080) 4351
Allt om Historia (SWE ISSN 1653-3224) 4129
Allt om Hjaelpmedel (SWE ISSN 1103-8063) 4063
Allt om Hobby (SWE ISSN 0002-6190) 4327
Allt om Hotell & Resor (SWE ISSN 1653-6959) 8682
Allt om Husvagn & Camping (SWE ISSN 0346-9190) 8302
Allt om Klockor & Smycken (SWE ISSN 1653-7084) 4564
Allt om M C (MotorCyclar) (SWE ISSN 0345-0813) 8253
Allt om Mat & Vin/All About Food and Cooking (SWE ISSN 0002-6204) 3626
▼ Allt om Moebler (SWE ISSN 1654-1243) 4553
Allt om P C (SWE ISSN 1651-8837) 2406
Allt om Resor (SWE ISSN 1403-6967) 8682
Allt om Traedgaard (SWE ISSN 1103-6575) 3721
Allt om Vetenskap (SWE ISSN 1652-3318) 7834
Allt om Villor & Hus (SWE ISSN 1653-6703) 4553
Allt om Vin see Allt om Vin & Mat 4351
• Allt om Vin & Mat (SWE ISSN 1653-3925) 4351
▼ Alltag, Medien und Kultur (DEU ISSN 1864-4058) 8086
Alltag und Kultur (DEU) 4197
Alluminio e Architettura (ITA ISSN 1825-8972) 427
• Allure (ITA ISSN 1120-5415) 592
• Allure (USA ISSN 1054-7711) 8851
† Allure Club (ITA ISSN 1121-9580) 8929
• Allured's Cosmetics and Toiletries (USA ISSN 1530-1338) 592
Allyn Museum. Bulletin (USA ISSN 0097-3211) 931
Alm und Bergbauer (AUT) 90
• Alma (CHE ISSN 1422-5980) 2272
Alma Magazine (USA ISSN 1553-510X) 3969
• Alma Mater (CUB ISSN 0864-0572) 7104
• Alma Mater (PER ISSN 1021-9633) 2966
• Alma Mater (POL ISSN 1427-1176) 2966
Alma Mater (RUS) 2825
Almacenero (ARG ISSN 0516-7493) 3676
Almanac for Farmers and City Folk (USA ISSN 0739-6961) 3117
Almanac for Geodetic Engineers (PHL ISSN 0569-0838) 568
Almanac Investor see Almanac Investor Newsletter 1610
• Almanac Investor Newsletter (USA ISSN 1931-7956) 1610
• The Almanac of American Employers (USA ISSN 1088-3150) 1662
• Almanac of American Politics (USA ISSN 0362-076X) 7104
Almanac of Business and Industrial Financial Ratios (USA ISSN 0747-9107) 1307
Almanac of China's Commerce see Zhongguo Shangye Nianjian 1434
Almanac of China's Economy see Zhongguo Jingji Nianjian 1803
Almanac of China's Foreign Economic Relations and Trade (CHN) 1590
• Almanac of China's Paper Industry (CHN) 6732
• Almanac of Famous People (USA ISSN 1040-127X) 639
• The Almanac of Russian and Caspian Petroleum (USA ISSN 1930-4897) 6762
Almanac of Seapower (USA ISSN 0736-3559) 6410
The Almanac of the Canning, Freezing, Preserving Industries (USA ISSN 0887-4999) 3626
Almanac of the 50 States (USA ISSN 0887-0519) 8086
• Almanac of the Unelected (USA ISSN 1047-0999) 7104
Almanac of Think Tanks in Japan see Shinku Tanku Nenpo 7939

DIRECTORY 2010 ALTSCHUL SYMPOSIA SERIES 9943

The Almanac of Virginia Politics (USA ISSN 0276-9980) 7104
The Almanac of Virginia Politics. Supplement *see* The Almanac of Virginia Politics 7104
Almanacco (Year) *see* Far da Se Almanacco (Year) 4438
Almanacco Calcistico Svizzero (CHE) 8220
Almanacco. Caravan & Camper *see* Caravan e Camper 8692
• Almanacco della Scienza (ITA) 7834
Almanacco dello Specchio (ITA ISSN 0393-9871) 5416
Almanacco di Fotografare (ITA ISSN 0393-9758) 6963
Almanacco Navale (ITA ISSN 1590-9131) 8638
Almanacco Piemontese/Armanach Piemonteis (ITA) 3614
ALManach (DEU) 372
Almanach de l'Auto (CAN ISSN 0821-7505) 8555
Almanach des Banques au Liban (LBN) 1307
Almanach du Peuple (CAN ISSN 0065-650X) 3117
† Almanach fuer die Aerztliche Fortbildung (BRD ISSN 0065-6518) 8929
Almanach Reklamy (SVK) 20
Almanach Sadecki (POL ISSN 1232-5910) 5205
Almanach Sceny Polskiej (POL ISSN 0065-6526) 8465
Almanahul Femeia (ROM ISSN 1454-4040) 8851
Almanak fyrir Island (ISL ISSN 1022-8527) 568
Almanak voor Watertoerisme *see* Wateralmanak 8284
Al'manakh Teni Strannika (RUS) 5205
Al'manakh Ukrains'koho Narodnoho Soiuzu *see* Ukrainian National Association. Alamanac 3966
Almanako (GRC ISSN 1106-1391) 2175
• Almanaque Abril (BRA ISSN 0104-4788) 3117
Almanaque Colore Especial (BRA ISSN 1678-4278) 2176
Almanaque Colore Pre-Escolar Especial (BRA ISSN 1806-3934) 2176
Almanaque Disney (BRA ISSN 0104-3390) 2176
Almanaque Mega Vamos Brincar (BRA ISSN 1806-3896) 2176
Almanaque Mundial (ARG) 3117
• Almanaque Nautico (ESP ISSN 0210-735X) 568
Almanaque Puertorriqueno (Year) (PRI) 3117
Almanaque Vamos Brincar Baratinho (BRA ISSN 1415-644X) 2176
Almanaque Vamos Brincar com a Turma Especial (BRA ISSN 1806-387X) 2176
Almanaque Vamos Brincar e Colorir (BRA ISSN 1806-3861) 2176
Almanaque Vamos Brincar Especial (BRA ISSN 1676-8884) 2176
Almanaue Nautico ... para PC *see* Almanaque Nautico 568
Almas (MEX ISSN 0002-628X) 7620
Almazy Rossii Sakha. Vestnik (RUS) 1610
Der Almbauer (DEU ISSN 0002-6298) 90
• Almegatidningen (SWE ISSN 1654-8752) 1879
Almen Semiotik (DNK ISSN 0905-4545) 6903
Almennyttige Boligafdelingers Regnskaber (DNK ISSN 0908-6722) 4432
Almeria Economica (ESP) 1425
Alminar (ESP ISSN 1133-0163) 2825
Den Almindelige Beretning om de Europeiske Unions Virksomhed *see* General Report on the Activities of the European Union 3837
Almond Facts (USA ISSN 0886-4365) 3721
Almoraima (ESP ISSN 1133-5319) 838
Almost Free Cookbooks & Recipes Update (USA ISSN 0736-170X) 4351
Almshouse Association. Annual Report and Statement of Accounts (GBR) 8024
Almshouses Gazette (GBR) 8024
Alnavco Log (USA) 8157
Alo Hayati (USA) 3517
ALO Magazine *see* Alo Hayati 3517
Alodis (GBR) 1058
➤ Aloe (ZAF ISSN 0002-6301) 774
Aloisiana (ITA ISSN 1126-8476) 7782
Alokpaat (IND) 3878
Aloma (ESP ISSN 1138-3194) 7332
Alon Hanotea (ISR ISSN 0333-8886) 218
'Alon L'Morim L'Anglit *see* English Teachers' Journal (Israel) 8953
Along the Towpath (USA) 2602
Alp G M (Grandi Montagne) (ITA ISSN 1722-7828) 8302
ALP Newsletter *see* Association of Logic Programming. Newsletter 2505
Alp Speciali (ITA ISSN 1972-683X) 8302
Alp Wall *see* Alp Speciali 8302
Alpaca *see* Alpaca Hmmm 277
▼ • Alpaca Advantage (USA ISSN 1945-208X) 277
• Alpaca Hmmm (AUS ISSN 1834-1977) 277
Alpacas Australia (AUS ISSN 1328-8318) 277
➤ Alpe Adria Microbiology Journal (ITA ISSN 1121-9750) 880
Die Alpen/Alpes/Alpi (CHE ISSN 0002-6336) 8302
Alpen-Journal *see* Alpenadria 8682
• Alpena News (USA) 3969
Alpenadria (DEU) 8682
Alpenhorn (USA ISSN 0891-5555) 6802
Alpenlaendische Bienenzeitung (AUT ISSN 0002-6352) 90
Alpenverein Graz. Nachrichten (AUT) 8302
Alpenwelle (CHE ISSN 1661-6634) 3957
Alpes *see* Die Alpen 8302
Alpes Loisirs (FRA ISSN 1250-0089) 8682
Alpes Magazine (Toulouse) (FRA ISSN 1151-0854) 3997
Alpes Magazine Balades et Randonnees (FRA ISSN 1957-3219) 8302
ALPH *see* A L P H 5439
Alpha (AUS ISSN 1832-6838) 6285
Alpha (IND) 2312
• Alpha (NZL ISSN 0111-1957) 7834
† • Alpha (New York) (USA ISSN 1930-8434) 8929
• Alpha (Osorno) (CHL ISSN 0716-4254) 5251
Alpha (Year): Current Research in Literacy (DEU ISSN 1184-6836) 3016
Alpha (Year): Recherches en Alphabetisation *see* Alpha (Year): Current Research in Literacy 3016
Alpha Communications Monthly (IND) 2312
Alpha Control (AUS) 5439
Alpha Digest (IND) 3878
Alpha Guide (GRC ISSN 1108-7048) 4381
• Alpha Investor (NZL ISSN 1177-617X) 1610
Alpha Kappa Psi. Diary (USA) 2272
• Alpha-Lien (CAN ISSN 1705-7329) 2938
• Alpha Link (CAN ISSN 1705-9992) 2938
Alpha Magazine *see* Alpha (New York) 8929
➤ Alpha Omega (ITA ISSN 1126-8557) 7782
Alpha-Omega. Reihe A, Lexika, Indizes, Konkordanzen zur Klassischen Philologie (DEU ISSN 0175-8586) 5092
• Alpha Omegan (USA ISSN 0002-6417) 5834
Alpha Psi Omega: Playbill (USA) 8465
Alpha Tau Omega Palm *see* A T O Palm 2271
Alphabet *see* Azbuki 2829
Alphabets *see* Abgadiyat 5089
Alphanumeric Reports Publications Index (GBR ISSN 0964-3400) 615
Alpi *see* Die Alpen 8302
Le Alpi Venete (ITA ISSN 0002-6468) 8302
Alpijn (NLD ISSN 1382-2209) 3402
Alpin (DEU ISSN 0177-3542) 8302
Alpin jo, Mame! (ITA) 6410
Alpine Garden Club of British Columbia. Bulletin (CAN ISSN 0836-320X) 3721
Alpine Garden Society Guides *see* A G S Guides 3721
Alpine Garden Society Quarterly Newsletter (GBR) 3721
Alpine Gardener (GBR ISSN 1475-0449) 774
The Alpine Journal (GBR ISSN 0065-6569) 8302
▼ Alpine Living (USA ISSN 1940-3755) 5064
Alpine Magazine (NLD ISSN 1872-0803) 8555
• Alpinegolf.com (USA) 8220
Alpinisme & Randonnee (FRA ISSN 1254-714X) 8302
Alpinist *see* Gakujin 8315
Alpinist Magazine (USA ISSN 1540-725X) 8302
Alpino (ITA ISSN 0002-6492) 3896
Alpinwelt (DEU) 8302
• Alquibla (ESP ISSN 1134-5535) 2792
Alquimia (MEX ISSN 1405-7786) 6963
L'Alsace (FRA ISSN 0245-663X) 3997
L'Alsace. Decouvertes et Passions *see* L' Alsace 3997
L'Alsace. Hors Serie Balades *see* L' Alsace 3997
Alsatiques (FRA ISSN 1769-6224) 5092
ALSConnect *see* A L S Connect (Online) 4986
Alsfelder Allgemeine (DEU) 3843
Alsic *see* A L S I C 3049
• The Alsop Review (USA) 5439
Alstediana (DEU ISSN 0940-7243) 4197
Alster Magazin (DEU) 3843
Alstertal Magazin (DEU) 3843
Alsterverein Jahrbuch (DEU ISSN 1432-1661) 4197
• Alt for Damerne (DNK ISSN 0002-6506) 8851
• Alt-Health Watch (USA) 316
Alt om Baby *see* Gravid 5991
• Alt om Data (DNK ISSN 0109-2847) 2535
Alt om Fiske (NOR ISSN 0804-5887) 8302
Alt om Foto & Video (DNK ISSN 0908-3316) 6963
• Alt om Gymnastik (DNK ISSN 1604-8660) 8157
Alt om Haandarbeide (NOR ISSN 1503-4585) 4351
Alt om Haandarbejde Ingelise *see* Ingelise 4361
† Alt om Motorcykler (DNK ISSN 1395-6515) 8929
Alt Pick Magazine (USA ISSN 1930-5001) 6963
• Alt-Press Watch (USA) 2
Alt-Thueringen (DEU ISSN 0065-6585) 4197
Alt und Jung Metten (DEU ISSN 0949-8869) 7782
Alt- und Neu-Indische Studien (DEU ISSN 0170-3242) 4179
• Alta Direccion (ESP ISSN 0002-6549) 1725
Alta Direccion. Monografias (ESP) 1725
Alta Fidelidad *see* Alta Fidelidad en Audio y Video 8151
Alta Fidelidad en Audio y Video (ESP ISSN 1130-4855) 8151
Alta Gerencia (URY) 1804
• Alta Hoteleria Internacional (MEX) 4381
Alta Museum. Pamphlets *see* Alta Museum. Smaaskrifter 4197
Alta Museum. Schriftreihe *see* Alta Museum. Smaaskrifter 4197
Alta Museum. Smaaskrifter (NOR ISSN 0805-9128) 4197
† Alta Nizza (FRA ISSN 0240-902X) 8929
Alta Relojeria (ESP) 4564
† Alta Val Tanaro (ITA) 8929
Altagama Motor (ESP) 8555
Altaiskaya Pravda (RUS) 3934
Altalanos Fogyasztasi es Ertekesito Szovetkezetek Magazin *see* A F E S Z Magazin 1421
Altalanos Nyelveszeti Tanulmanyok (HUN ISSN 0569-1338) 5092
Altamira (ESP ISSN 0211-4003) 7487
Altamura (ITA ISSN 0569-1346) 6519
Altaposten (NOR) 3921
Altar Magazine (USA) 8086
Altarum. Center for Energy and Environmental Research. Report (USA) 3402
➤ Altbabylonische Briefe im Umschrift und Uebersetzung (NLD ISSN 0065-6593) 542
Altbayerische Heimatpost (DEU) 3843
Altdeutsche Textbibliothek (DEU ISSN 0342-6661) 5251
Alte Abenteuerliche Reiseberichte (DEU) 5251
Alte Musik Aktuell (DEU ISSN 0942-9034) 6543
Die Alte Stadt (DEU ISSN 0170-9364) 4403
Die Alten Sprachen im Unterricht (DEU ISSN 0179-387X) 2229
Alten- und Pflegeheime in Deutschland und Lieferantenverzeichnis (DEU) 4040
Altenburger Naturwissenschaftliche Forschungen (DEU ISSN 0232-5381) 652
Altenheim (DEU ISSN 0002-6573) 5951
Altenheim Adressbuch (DEU ISSN 0065-664X) 4040
Altenheim Einkaufsfuehrer (DEU) 4040
Altenpflege (DEU ISSN 0341-0455) 5951
Alter (BRA ISSN 0100-1655) 7332
▼ • ➤ Alter (FRA ISSN 1875-0672) 4063
Alter Ego (POL ISSN 1641-3490) 5205
➤ Alter Orient und Altes Testament (DEU ISSN 0931-4296) 4319
Altercatif (FRA ISSN 1764-2558) 3180
Altercation (USA ISSN 1937-2701) 6543
Altered Couture (USA ISSN 1941-2339) 2251
• Alteridades (MEX ISSN 0188-7017) 323
• Alterites (CAN ISSN 1205-8009) 323
Altermondes (FRA ISSN 1772-869X) 1590
Alternate Care Purchasing & Products (USA ISSN 1934-4228) 5571
• Alternate Music Press (USA ISSN 1524-6272) 6543
Alternate Roots Newsletter (USA) 8465
• ➤ Alternate Routes (CAN ISSN 0702-8865) 7946
Alternatibaz (FRA ISSN 1774-7414) 1422
➤ Alternation (ZAF ISSN 1023-1757) 5251
Al'ternativa (UKR) 7104
Alternativa 2000 (ESP) 7620
Alternativa Cultura (ARG) 5205
Alternativas. Serie: Espacio Pedagogico (ARG ISSN 0328-8064) 2825
Alternativas. Serie: Historia y Practicas Pedagogicas (ARG ISSN 0329-8485) 2825
† Alternativas Sur (ESP ISSN 1579-9867) 8929
➤ AlterNative (NZL ISSN 1177-1801) 3517
• The Alternative (Online) (AUS ISSN 1441-9106) 7620
• Alternative Alternative (GBR ISSN 0260-0552) 8148
Alternative America (USA) 2264
• ➤ Alternative & Complementary Therapies (USA ISSN 1076-2809) 306
Alternative - Appropriate Technologies in Agriculture (IND ISSN 0970-4671) 90
Alternative Aquaculture Network Newsletter (USA ISSN 8755-7894) 3583
Alternative Cinema Magazine (USA) 2400
• Alternative Currents (USA ISSN 1522-9823) 1307
Alternative Democratique (SEN ISSN 0850-0622) 7104
Alternative Dispute Resolution Bulletin *see* The A D R Bulletin 4826
Alternative Dispute Resolution Bulletin *see* The A D R Bulletin 4826
Alternative Dispute Resolution Currents *see* A D R Currents 8927
Alternative Dispute Resolution Forum *see* A D R Forum 4607
Alternative Dispute Resolution News *see* A D R News 4607
Alternative Dispute Resolution the Law *see* A D R & the Law 4854
Alternative Energy Resources Organization Sun Times *see* A E R O Sun Times 77
† Alternative Energy Retailer (USA ISSN 0273-8163) 8929
Alternative England and Wales (GBR) 3117
Alternative Fuel News *see* Clean Cities News 8575
Alternative Fuels in Trucking (USA) 3124
Alternative Fund Services Review *see* Hedge Fund Manager 1628
Alternative Healthcare Market Assessment *see* Key Note Market Assessment. Alternative Healthcare 5657
† Alternative/i (ITA ISSN 1594-5812) 8929
Alternative Insurance Capital (GBR ISSN 1369-9628) 4492
▼ • Alternative Investment Law Report (USA ISSN 1941-6563) 4613
• Alternative Investment Market (GBR ISSN 1752-4342) 1610
Alternative Investment Market Newsletter *see* A I M & P L U S Newsletter 1609
Alternative Investment Marketing Bulletin *see* A I M Bulletin 1609
• Alternative Investment News (USA ISSN 1544-7596) 1610
• ➤ Alternative Law Journal (AUS ISSN 1037-969X) 4613
• Alternative Libertaire (FRA ISSN 1157-8661) 7104
Alternative Lifestyles Directory (USA ISSN 1075-6906) 7943
▼ • The Alternative Media Handbook (GBR ISSN 1940-6355) 7551
• Alternative Medicine Alert (USA ISSN 1096-942X) 306
Alternative Medicine Magazine *see* Natural Solutions 313
• ➤ Alternative Medicine Review (USA ISSN 1089-5159) 306
Alternative Medicine Sourcebook (USA) 306
• The Alternative Minimum Tax (USA ISSN 1043-6960) 1910
Alternative Minimum Tax *see* The Alternative Minimum Tax 1910
The Alternative Pick Magazine *see* Alt Pick Magazine 6963
• Alternative Press (USA ISSN 1065-1667) 6543
• Alternative Press Index (USA ISSN 0002-662X) 4571
Alternative Publishers of Books in North America (USA ISSN 1094-4559) 615
Alternative Research Newsletter (USA) 5205
The Alternative Route (HKG) 2938
Alternative Sante (FRA ISSN 1954-491X) 5571
Alternative Sante l'Impatient *see* Alternative Sante 5571
▼ • ➤ Alternative Spirituality and Religion Review (USA ISSN 1946-0538) 6643
Alternative Teacher Certification (USA ISSN 1082-1759) 3016
• ➤ Alternative Therapies in Health and Medicine (USA ISSN 1078-6791) 306
• Alternative Therapies in Women's Health (USA ISSN 1522-3396) 306
Alternative Tibetaine (FRA ISSN 1953-1222) 7104
Alternative Times (GBR ISSN 0261-6033) 3124
Alternative Times (USA) 7104
Alternative Trading News (USA ISSN 0892-2950) 1590
• Alternative Transportation Fuels Today (USA) 8490
• Alternatives (TUR ISSN 1303-5525) 7220
• ➤ Alternatives (USA ISSN 0304-3754) 7220
Alternatives (Ingram) (USA ISSN 0893-5025) 5571
Alternatives (New York) *see* Alternatives to the High Cost of Litigation 4613
Alternatives Economiques (FRA ISSN 0247-3739) 1058
Alternatives Economiques. Hors-Serie *see* Alternatives Economiques 1058
Alternatives for the Health Conscious Individual *see* Alternatives (Ingram) 5571
• ➤ Alternatives Journal (CAN ISSN 1205-7398) 3402
Alternatives News Magazine (USA) 3969
Alternatives Sud (BEL ISSN 1026-2253) 5205
➤ Alternatives to Laboratory Animals (GBR ISSN 0261-1929) 5902
• Alternatives to the High Cost of Litigation (USA ISSN 1549-4373) 4613
• Alternatives to the Use of Live Vertebrates in Biomedical Research and Testing (USA) 747
Alternativt Nettverk *see* Visjon 315
• AlterNet (USA) 5205
• Alterra-Rapport/Alterra Report (NLD ISSN 1566-7197) 3402
Alterra Report *see* Alterra-Rapport 3402
• AlterTexto (MEX ISSN 1665-4862) 5251
➤ Altertumskunde des Vorderen Orients (DEU ISSN 0948-1737) 542
Altertumswissenschaften - Archaeologie (DEU ISSN 1863-4397) 4129
Altertumswissenschaftliche Texte und Studien (DEU ISSN 0175-8411) 5251
Altertumswissenschaftliches Kolloquium (DEU ISSN 1438-0552) 2229
Altes Handwerk (DEU) 3614
Alteuropaeische Forschungen (DEU) 372
• Altex (DEU ISSN 0946-7785) 5902
Altfraenkische Bilder (DEU ISSN 1862-7404) 4197
Altfraenkische Bilder und Wappenkalender *see* Altfraenkische Bilder 4197
• AltFuels Advisor (USA ISSN 1528-6746) 8555
Althaus Modernisieren (DEU ISSN 0943-061X) 975
Althingiskosningar/Elections to the Althing (ISL ISSN 1017-6667) 7198
Althistorische Studien der Universitaet Wuerzburg *see* Historische Studien der Universitaet Wuerzburg 4228
Althochdeutsches Woerterbuch (DEU) 5092
• ➤ Altitude (AUS ISSN 1444-1160) 8086
Altkatholische Kirchenzeitung (AUT ISSN 0002-6514) 7745
• Altlasten - Spektrum (DEU ISSN 0942-3818) 3503
Altman Weil Pensa Report to Legal Management *see* Report to Legal Management 1789
Altmark-Zeitung (DEU) 3843
Altmuehlseebericht (DEU ISSN 0948-4264) 901
• Alto Adige (ITA ISSN 1592-9663) 3896
Alto Peinado (MEX) 585
Altoettinger Liebfrauenbote (DEU ISSN 0341-2563) 7620
Alton Times & Mail (GBR) 3861
Altonaer Museum in Hamburg. Nordeutsches Landesmuseum. Jahrbuch (DEU ISSN 0440-1417) 6519
• ➤ Altorientalische Forschungen (DEU ISSN 0232-8461) 4319
Altos Estudios (BOL) 7104
† Altra (ITA) 8929
• Altreitalie (ITA ISSN 1120-0413) 7276
L'Altro Diritto, Centro di Documentazione su Carcere, Devianza e Marginalita (ITA ISSN 1827-0565) 4884
† Altro Polo (AUS ISSN 0727-0046) 8929
Altro Telescope (USA) 3969
Altroquando (ITA) 5251
Altschul Symposia Series (USA) 5571

Title

DIRECTORY 2010 AMERICAN ASSOCIATION OF VARIABLE STAR OBSERVERS ALERT 9945

American Academy of Arts and Sciences. Bulletin (USA ISSN 0002-712X) **4442**
• ➤ American Academy of Audiology. Journal (USA ISSN 1050-0545) **6077**
• ➤ American Academy of Business, Cambridge. Journal (USA ISSN 1540-1200) **1058**
American Academy of Cardiovascular Perfusion. Proceedings (USA ISSN 0894-1084) **5775**
• ➤ American Academy of Child and Adolescent Psychiatry. Journal (USA ISSN 0890-8567) **6121**
American Academy of Clinical Neurophysiology Bold Voices *see* A A C N Bold Voices **6117**
American Academy of Dermatology. Directory (USA ISSN 0278-9000) **5871**
• ➤ American Academy of Dermatology. Journal (USA ISSN 0190-9622) **5871**
American Academy of Family Physicians. Membership Directory of Members of Record (USA ISSN 0898-0551) **1971**
American Academy of Forensic Sciences. Academy News *see* Academy News (Colorado Springs) **5912**
American Academy of Gnathologic Orthopedics. Journal (USA ISSN 0886-1064) **5834**
• American Academy of Matrimonial Lawyers. Journal (USA ISSN 0882-6714) **4906**
American Academy of Medical Acupuncture Review *see* Medical Acupuncture **312**
American Academy of Medical Administrators Executive Online *see* A A M A Executive Online **5563**
American Academy of Ministry. Journal (USA ISSN 1084-1008) **7782**
• ➤ American Academy of Nurse Practitioners. Journal (USA ISSN 1041-2972) **5951**
American Academy of Orthopaedic Surgeons. Bulletin *see* A A O S Now **6054**
American Academy of Orthopaedic Surgeons. Committee on Instructional Courses. Instructional Course Lectures (USA ISSN 0065-6895) **6055**
American Academy of Orthopaedic Surgeons. Directory (USA ISSN 0516-8856) **6055**
• ➤ American Academy of Orthopaedic Surgeons. Journal (USA ISSN 1067-151X) **6055**
• American Academy of Orthopaedic Surgeons. Journal (Spanish Edition) (ESP ISSN 1579-2080) **6055**
American Academy of Osteopathy Journal *see* The A A O Journal **5803**
American Academy of Osteopathy Yearbook (USA ISSN 0732-703X) **5803**
American Academy of Otolaryngic Allergy News *see* A A O A News **5752**
American Academy of Otolaryngology - Head and Neck Surgery. Bulletin (USA ISSN 0731-8359) **6077**
• American Academy of Pediatrics. Committee on Infectious Diseases. Red Book (Year) (USA ISSN 1080-0131) **6087**
American Academy of Pediatrics Grand Rounds *see* A A P Grand Rounds **5739**
American Academy of Pediatrics. Journal. Indian Edition (IND) **6087**
American Academy of Pediatrics News *see* A A P News **6086**
American Academy of Physical Medicine & Rehabilitation. Study Guide *see* Archives of Physical Medicine and Rehabilitation **6106**
American Academy of Physician Assistants News *see* A A P A News **5563**
• ➤ American Academy of Political and Social Science. Annals (USA ISSN 0002-7162) **7104**
• American Academy of Psychiatry and the Law. Journal (USA ISSN 1093-6793) **6121**
• ➤ American Academy of Psychoanalysis and Dynamic Psychiatry. Journal (USA ISSN 1546-0371) **7332**
American Academy of Religion Academy Series *see* A A R Academy Series **7619**
American Academy of Religion. Annual Meeting (USA) **7620**
• ➤ American Academy of Religion. Journal (USA ISSN 0002-7189) **7620**
American Academy of Religion. Journal. Studies (USA) **7620**
• American Acreage (USA) **90**
• The American Acupuncturist (USA ISSN 1520-7714) **306**
▼ American Aerospace Archive (USA ISSN 1943-9636) **46**
• American Agent and Broker (USA ISSN 0002-7200) **4492**
American Aging Association. Journal *see* Age **4038**
American Agricultural Editors Association Byline *see* A A E A Byline **77**
• American Agriculturist (USA ISSN 0161-8237) **90**
American Aircraft & Airshow Magazine (USA ISSN 1541-0455) **46**
American Airgun Field Target Association. Newsletter (USA) **8157**
American Alliance for Theatre & Education Newsletter *see* A A T E Newsletter **8927**
American Alpine Journal (USA ISSN 0065-6925) **8302**
American Alpine News (USA ISSN 0147-9288) **8303**
• American Amateur Journalist (USA ISSN 1046-0470) **4571**
• American Angler (USA ISSN 1055-6737) **8303**
American Animal Hospital Association. Annual Meeting Scientific Proceedings (USA ISSN 0164-1999) **8791**
• ➤ American Animal Hospital Association. Journal (Online Edition) (USA ISSN 1547-3317) **8791**
American Animal Hospital Association. Journal (Print Edition) *see* American Animal Hospital Association. Journal (Online Edition) **8791**
• ➤ American Annals of the Deaf (USA ISSN 0002-726X) **4071**
American Anthropological Association. Abstracts of Meetings (USA ISSN 0160-1873) **324**
• American Anthropological Association. Archaeological Papers (USA ISSN 1551-823X) **372**
American Anthropological Association. Bulletin (USA ISSN 0002-7278) **324**
American Anthropological Association Guide (Year) *see* A A A Guide (Year) **322**
• ➤ American Anthropologist (USA ISSN 0002-7294) **324**
American Anti-Vivisection Society Magazine *see* The A V Magazine **316**
American Antiquarian Society. Almanac (USA ISSN 1098-7878) **4988**
➤ American Antiquarian Society. Proceedings (USA ISSN 0044-751X) **4988**
• ➤ American Antiquity (USA ISSN 0002-7316) **372**
American Apparel Manufacturers Association Committee Manual *see* A A M A Committee Manual **8927**
American Apparel Producers' Network News *see* A A P N News **2244**
American-Arab Anti-Discrimination Committee Times *see* A D C Times **3514**
American Arachnology (USA ISSN 0364-9504) **931**
American Arbitration Association Annual Report *see* A A A Annual Report **4606**
American Arbitration Association. Dispute Resolution Journal *see* Dispute Resolution Journal **1675**
➤ American Archaeology (USA ISSN 1093-8400) **372**
American Archeology (USA ISSN 0740-8358) **372**
American Architectural Manufacturers Association Industry Statistical Review and Forecast *see* A A M A Industry Statistical Review and Forecast **1044**
American Architectural Manufacturers Association Scope *see* A A M A Scope **974**
American Architectural Manufacturers Association Update *see* A A M A Update **974**
• ➤ American Archivist (USA ISSN 0360-9081) **4988**
• ➤ American Art (USA ISSN 1073-9300) **465**
American Art Collector (Berkeley) (USA ISSN 1556-6781) **465**
American Art Collector (Scottsdale) (USA ISSN 1547-7088) **465**
American Art Directory (USA ISSN 0065-6968) **465**
American Art Review (USA ISSN 0092-1327) **465**
American Art Therapy Association Newsletter *see* A A T A Newsletter **462**
• American Artist (USA ISSN 0002-7375) **465**
American Artist. Drawing (USA) **465**
• American Artist. Watercolor (USA ISSN 1053-3915) **465**
American Artist. Workshop (USA) **465**
American Arts Quarterly (USA ISSN 1540-9872) **465**
American Assembly. Report (USA ISSN 0569-2245) **7104**
American Association - Electronic Voice Phenomena Newsletter *see* A A - E V P Newsletter **6740**
American Association for Accreditation of Ambulatory Surgery Facilities Newsletter *see* A A A A S F Newsletter **6234**
American Association for Affirmative Action News *see* A A A A News **7201**
American Association for Artificial Intelligence (Year) *see* A A A I (Year) **2444**
➤ American Association for Cancer Research. Proceedings of the Annual Meeting (USA ISSN 0197-016X) **6007**
American Association for Career Education Bonus Briefs *see* A A C E Bonus Briefs **2937**
American Association for Career Education Careers Update *see* A A C E Careers Update **2937**
American Association for Career Education Distinguished Member Series on Career Education *see* A A C E Distinguished Member Series on Career Education **2937**
American Association for Crystal Growth Newsletter (USA ISSN 0896-1654) **2109**
American Association for Fuel Cells. Newsletter (USA) **3155**
American Association for History and Computing. Journal *see* Association for History and Computing. Journal **4171**
American Association for Laboratory Animal Science in Action *see* A A L A S in Action **8790**
• ➤ American Association for Laboratory Animal Science. Journal (USA ISSN 1559-6109) **5902**
American Association for Leisure & Recreation Reporter *see* A A L R Reporter **4975**
American Association for Nude Recreation. Bulletin (USA ISSN 1938-8500) **6981**
• ➤ American Association for Pediatric Ophthalmology and Strabismus. Journal (USA ISSN 1091-8531) **6038**
American Association for Public Opinion Research News *see* A A P O R News **8084**
American Association for Respiratory Care Times *see* A A R C Times **6211**
American Association for the Advancement of Science Annual Meeting *see* A A A S Annual Meeting **7935**
American Association for the Advancement of Science Handbook *see* A A A S Handbook **8927**
American Association for the Advancement of Science Report: Research and Development *see* A A A S Report: Research and Development **7829**
American Association for the Advancement of Slavic Studies Directory of Programs in Russian, Eurasian & East European Studies *see* A A A S S Directory of Programs in Russian, Eurasian & East European Studies **3514**
American Association for the History of Nursing. Bulletin (USA ISSN 0898-6622) **5951**
American Association of Bioanalysts Bulletin *see* A A B Bulletin **5901**
• American Association of Blood Banks. Membership Directory (Online Edition) (USA) **5571**
American Association of Blood Banks. Membership Directory (Print Edition) *see* American Association of Blood Banks. Membership Directory (Online Edition) **5571**
American Association of Blood Banks News (Online Edition) *see* A A B B News (Online Edition) **5563**
American Association of Blood Banks Weekly Report (Online Edition) *see* A A B B Weekly Report (Online Edition) **5563**
American Association of Bovine Practitioners Conference (USA ISSN 1079-9737) **8791**
American Association of Cereal Chemists. Monograph Series (USA ISSN 0065-7107) **3626**
American Association of Christian Schools. Directory (USA) **2953**
American Association of Colleges for Teacher Education. Briefs (USA ISSN 0731-602X) **2966**
American Association of Colleges for Teacher Education. Directory (USA ISSN 0516-9313) **2966**
American Association of Colleges of Pharmacy. (Year) Profile of Pharmacy Faculty (USA) **6819**
American Association of Colleges of Pharmacy News *see* A A C P News **6817**
American Association of Collegiate Registrars and Admissions Officers Data Dispenser *see* A A C R A O Data Dispenser **2963**
American Association of Cost Engineers International Transactions *see* A A C E International Transactions **3179**
American Association of Critical Care Nurses Advanced Critical Care *see* A A C N Advanced Critical Care **5563**
American Association of Dental Editors. Newsletter (USA) **4571**
• American Association of Dental Examiners. Board Bulletin (USA ISSN 0002-7421) **5834**
• American Association of Engineering Societies. Engineering Workforce Commission. Engineering and Technology Degrees (USA) **3181**
• American Association of Engineering Societies. Engineering Workforce Commission. Engineering and Technology Enrollments (Year) (USA ISSN 0278-8985) **3181**
American Association of Engineering Societies. Engineering Workforce Commission. Professional Income of Engineers (Year) (USA ISSN 0735-7850) **3181**
American Association of Engineering Societies. Engineering Workforce Commission. Salaries of Engineers in Education (Year) (USA) **3181**
➤ American Association of Equine Practitioners. Proceedings of the Annual Convention (USA ISSN 0065-7182) **8791**
American Association of Forensic Dentists. Journal (USA ISSN 0743-491X) **5834**
American Association of Gynecologic Laparoscopists. Journal *see* Journal of Minimally Invasive Gynecology **5995**
American Association of Handwriting Analysts Dialogue *see* A A H A Dialogue **7329**
American Association of Housing Educators. Proceedings (USA ISSN 0735-6765) **4403**
American Association of Individual Investors Journal *see* A A I I Journal **1608**
American Association of Insurance Services Viewpoint *see* A A I S Viewpoint **4490**
American Association of Law Libraries Directory and Handbook *see* A A L L Directory and Handbook **4606**
American Association of Law Libraries Publications Series *see* A A L L Publications Series **4606**
American Association of Law Libraries Spectrum *see* A A L L Spectrum **4985**
American Association of Meat Processors *see* AAMPLifier **276**
American Association of Motor Vehicle Administrators Bulletin *see* A A M V A Bulletin **8553**
American Association of Neurological Surgeons Neurosurgeon *see* A A N S Neurosurgeon **6117**
American Association of Neuroscience Nurses Synapse *see* A A N N Synapse **5949**
American Association of Nurse Anesthetists Journal *see* A A N A Journal **5949**
American Association of Nurserymen Today *see* A A N Today **77**
American Association of Nurserymen Update (USA) **90**
American Association of Nurserymen Who's Who in the Nursery Industry Member Directory (USA) **90**
• ➤ American Association of Occupational Health Nurses Journal (USA ISSN 0891-0162) **5951**
American Association of Occupational Health Nurses News *see* A A O H N News **5949**
American Association of Oral and Maxillofacial Surgeons Today *see* A A O M S Today **5832**
American Association of Petroleum Geologists Bulletin *see* A A P G Bulletin **6761**
American Association of Petroleum Geologists Continuing Education Course Note Series *see* A A P G Continuing Education Course Note Series **2722**
American Association of Petroleum Geologists Explorer *see* A A P G Explorer **6761**
American Association of Petroleum Geologists Memoir *see* A A P G Memoir **2722**
American Association of Petroleum Geologists Studies in Geology Series *see* A A P G Studies in Geology Series **6761**
American Association of Pharmaceutical Scientists Journal. Annual Meeting Abstracts *see* The A A P S Journal. Annual Meeting Abstracts **6888**
American Association of Pharmaceutical Scientists Newsmagazine *see* A A P S Newsmagazine **6817**
American Association of Pharmaceutical Scientists PharmSciTech *see* A A P S PharmSciTech **6817**
American Association of Port Authorities Seaports *see* A A P A Seaports **8638**
American Association of Port Authorities Seaports of the Americas *see* A A P A Seaports of the Americas **8638**
American Association of Railroad Superintendents Journal *see* A A R S Journal **8614**
American Association of Retired Persons Bulletin *see* A A R P Bulletin **4037**
American Association of Retired Persons. Public Policy Institute. Issue Brief (USA ISSN 1063-3189) **8024**
American Association of Retired Persons The Magazine *see* A A R P: The Magazine **5064**
American Association of School Administrators Journal of Scholarship & Practice *see* A A S A Journal of Scholarship & Practice **3016**
American Association of School Librarians Hotlinks *see* A A S L Hotlinks **4985**
American Association of State Highway and Transportation Officials Journal *see* A A S H T O Journal **8628**
American Association of State Highway and Transportation Officials Quarterly *see* A A S H T O Quarterly **3258**
American Association of State Highway and Transportation Officials Reference Book of Member Department Personnel and Committees *see* A A S H T O Reference Book of Member Department Personnel and Committees **8489**
➤ American Association of Stratigraphic Palynologists. Contributions Series (USA ISSN 0160-8843) **6723**
American Association of Stratigraphic Palynologists Foundation. Field Trip Guide (USA ISSN 0192-737X) **6723**
American Association of Stratigraphic Palynologists, Inc. Membership Directory (USA ISSN 0192-7280) **774**
• American Association of Stratigraphic Palynologists. Newsletter (USA ISSN 0192-7299) **2724**
American Association of Suicidology. Proceedings of the Annual Meeting (USA) **7332**
American Association of Teachers of Esperanto Quarterly Bulletin/Amerika Asocio de Instruistoj de Esperanto Kvaronjara Bulteno (USA ISSN 0002-7499) **3050**
American Association of Teachers of French National Bulletin *see* A A T F National Bulletin **5088**
American Association of Teachers of German Newsletter *see* A A T G Newsletter **5088**
American Association of Teachers of Italian Newsletter *see* A A T I Newsletter **5088**
American Association of Teachers of Italian Newsletter *see* A A T I Newsletter **2821**
American Association of Teachers of Slavic and East European Languages Newsletter *see* A A T S E E L Newsletter **5088**
American Association of Teachers of Turkic Languages Bulletin *see* A A T T Bulletin **5088**
American Association of Textile Chemists and Colorists. Buyer's Guide (USA) **8448**
American Association of Textile Chemists and Colorists. International Conference & Exhibition. Book of Papers (USA ISSN 0892-2713) **8448**
American Association of Textile Chemists and Colorists Review *see* A A T C C Review **8447**
American Association of Textile Chemists and Colorists. Symposia Papers (USA) **8448**
American Association of Textile Chemists and Colorists Technical Manual *see* A A T C C Technical Manual **8447**
• American Association of Textile Chemists and Colorists. Technical Manual (Year) (USA ISSN 0883-4539) **8448**
American Association of Tissue Banks Newsletter (USA ISSN 0270-2673) **5571**
American Association of University Women Outlook *see* A A U W Outlook **2963**
American Association of Variable Star Observers Alert Notice *see* A A V S O Alert Notice **567**

Title

▼ *new title* † *ceased* • *electronic media* ➤ *refereed*

9946 AMERICAN ASSOCIATION OF VARIABLE STAR OBSERVERS BULLETIN ULRICH'S PERIODICALS

American Association of Variable Star Observers Bulletin *see* A A V S O Bulletin **567**
American Association of Variable Star Observers Ephemerides *see* A A V S O Ephemerides **567**
American Association of Variable Star Observers Journal *see* A A V S O Journal **567**
American Association of Variable Star Observers Monographs and Monograph Supplements *see* A A V S O Monographs and Monograph Supplements **567**
American Association of Variable Star Observers Newsletter *see* A A V S O Newsletter **567**
American Association of Variable Star Observers Photoelectric Photometry Newsletter *see* A A V S O Photoelectric Photometry Newsletter **567**
American Association of Variable Star Observers Solar Bulletin *see* A A V S O Solar Bulletin **567**
American Association of Women Dentists. Chronicle (USA) **5834**
American Association of Women in Community and Junior Colleges Newsletter *see* A A W C J C Newsletter **2963**
• American Association of Zoo Veterinarians. Annual Conference Proceedings (USA) **8791**
American Association on Mental Retardation. Monographs (USA ISSN 0895-8009) **7332**
† American Association on Mental Retardation. News and Notes (USA ISSN 0895-8033) **8929**
† American Astrology (USA ISSN 0002-7529) **8929**
American Astronautical Society Astrodynamics Conference. Proceedings *see* A A S Astrodynamics Conference. Proceedings **40**
American Astronautical Society / Goddard Space Flight Center International Symposium on Spaceflight Dynamics *see* A A S / G S F C International Symposium on Spaceflight Dynamics **40**
American Astronautical Society History Series *see* A A S History Series **40**
American Astronautical Society Microfiche Series *see* A A S Microfiche Series **40**
American Astronautical Society. Proceedings of the Annual Meeting (USA ISSN 0516-9593) **46**
The American Astronomer (USA) **568**
American Astronomical Society. Bulletin (USA ISSN 0002-7537) **568**
American Astronomical Society Job Register *see* A A S Job Register **567**
American Astronomical Society Newsletter *see* A A S Newsletter **567**
• American Atheist (USA ISSN 0516-9623) **7732**
• American Atheist Newsletter (USA ISSN 1072-2548) **6903**
American Austin Bantam Club News (USA) **362**
American Automatic Control Council Newsletter *see* A A C C Newsletter **3288**
American Automobile Association Arizona Highroads *see* A A A Arizona Highroads **8679**
American Automobile Association Carolinas Go Magazine *see* A A A Carolinas Go Magazine **3968**
American Automobile Association Digest of Motor Laws *see* A A A Digest of Motor Laws **8553**
American Automobile Association. Florida Tourbook *see* Guide de la Route: La Floride **8716**
American Automobile Association Going Places (Buffalo) *see* A A A Going Places (Buffalo) **8679**
American Automobile Association Living (Iowa Edition) *see* A A A Living (Iowa Edition) **8679**
American Automobile Association Living (Wisconsin Edition) *see* A A A Living (Wisconsin Edition) **8679**
American Automobile Association. Maine, New Hampshire, Vermont TourBook *see* Guide de la Route: Le Maine, le New Hampshire, et le Vermont **8716**
American Automobile Association. Mid-Atlantic Tourbook *see* Guide de la Route: Le Centre de la Cote Atlantique **8716**
American Automobile Association. Quebec and the Atlantic Provinces Tourbook *see* Guide de la Route: Le Quebec et les Provinces de l'Atlantique **8716**
American Automobile Association Road Atlas Road Atlas *see* A A A Road Atlas **8553**
American Automobile Association Travel Topics *see* A A A Travel Topics **8679**
American Automobile Association Traveler (Allentown) *see* A A A Traveler (Allentown) **8553**
American Automobile Association Traveler (Florham Park) *see* A A A Traveler (Florham Park) **8679**
American Automobile Association World (Hamilton) *see* A A A World (Hamilton) **8553**
American Aviation Historical Society Journal *see* A A H S Journal **40**
• American Baby (USA ISSN 0044-7544) **2143**
American Baby. The First Year of Life (USA ISSN 1076-1756) **2143**
American Baha'i (USA ISSN 1062-1113) **7709**
• American Banker (USA ISSN 0002-7561) **1307**
• American Banker Index (USA ISSN 0893-2468) **1199**
American Bankers Association Bank Compliance *see* A B A Bank Compliance **1304**
American Bankers Association Bank Counsel Directory *see* A B A Bank Counsel Directory **4606**
American Bankers Association Bank Directors Briefing *see* A B A Bank Directors Briefing **1304**
American Bankers Association Banking Journal *see* A B A Banking Journal **1304**
American Bankers Association. Community Banker *see* Community Banker (Washington) **1328**
American Bankers Association, Compliance Division Compliance Sourcebook *see* A B A Compliance Sourcebook **1304**
American Bankers Association Consumer Banking Digest *see* A B A Consumer Banking Digest **1304**
American Bankers Association Key to Routing Numbers (USA ISSN 1064-5349) **1307**
American Bankers Association Trust Letter *see* A B A Trust Letter **1305**
• American Banker's Financial Modernization Report (USA ISSN 1524-0886) **1307**
American Bankruptcy Institute Journal *see* A B I Journal **1305**
• American Bankruptcy Institute Law Review (USA ISSN 1068-0861) **1307**
• ➤ American Bankruptcy Law Journal (USA ISSN 0027-9048) **4614**
American Bantam Association. Yearbook (USA ISSN 0065-745X) **277**
American Baptist Planning Calender: Resource and Staff Directory (USA) **7745**
➤ American Baptist Quarterly (USA ISSN 0745-3698) **7745**
American Baptists in Mission (USA) **7745**
American Bar Association. Access *see* Access (Chicago, 1990) **8928**
American Bar Association. Antitrust Law Section. Annual Meeting (USA ISSN 1551-6253) **4854**
American Bar Association. Bulletin to Bar Association Elder Law Sections and Committees (USA) **4040**
American Bar Association, Bureau of National Affairs / B N A Lawyers' Manual on Professional Conduct *see* A B A / B N A Lawyers' Manual on Professional Conduct **4606**
American Bar Association, Bureau of National Affairs / B N A Lawyers' Manual on Professional Conduct Current Reports *see* A B A / B N A Lawyers' Manual on Professional Conduct Current Reports **4606**
American Bar Association Child Law Practice *see* A B A Child Law Practice **2142**
• American Bar Association. Commission on Lawyer Assistance Programs. Highlights (USA ISSN 1938-3916) **4614**
American Bar Association Journal *see* A B A Journal **4606**
American Bar Association. Leadership Directory (USA ISSN 1538-7232) **4614**
American Bar Association. Office of Policy Administration. Summary and Reports (USA) **4614**
American Bar Association. Section of Public Utility, Communications and Transportation Law. Annual Report (USA ISSN 1064-0959) **4614**
American Bar Association. Section of Public Utility, Communications and Transportation Law. News *see* Infrastructure (Chicago) **4692**
American Bar Association. Section of Taxation. Newsletter (USA ISSN 0277-2361) **4614**
American Bar Association UNIX - Group Newsletter *see* A B A - UNIX - Group Newsletter **4844**
American Bar Association Washington Letter (Online Edition) *see* A B A Washington Letter (Online Edition) **4606**
The American Bar. Reference Handbook (USA) **4614**
American Bartenders' Association Newsletter *see* A B A Newsletter **597**
The American Beagler (USA ISSN 1539-7637) **6802**
American Bee Journal (USA ISSN 0002-7626) **90**
American Beekeeping Federation. Newsletter (USA ISSN 0014-9438) **91**
• ➤ American Behavioral Scientist (USA ISSN 0002-7642) **7946**
American Bell Association. Directory (USA ISSN 0093-1330) **4327**
The American Bench (USA ISSN 0160-2578) **4614**
➤ The American Benedictine Review (USA ISSN 0002-7650) **7782**
The American Benefactor (USA ISSN 1092-5414) **8024**
• American Bible Society Record (USA ISSN 0006-0801) **7621**
• American Bibliography of Slavic and East European Studies (USA ISSN 0094-3770) **4168**
American Bicyclist (USA ISSN 1095-7375) **8253**
• American Big Businesses Directory (USA ISSN 1069-8442) **1971**
† American Big Twin Dealer (USA) **8929**
• ➤ The American Biology Teacher (USA ISSN 0002-7685) **652**
• American Biotechnology Laboratory (USA ISSN 0749-3223) **755**
American Biotechnology Laboratory. Buyers' Guide *see* American Biotechnology Laboratory **755**
American Black Book Writers Association Journal *see* A B B W A Journal **7550**
• The American Blue Book of Funeral Directors (USA ISSN 0065-7565) **1971**
• ➤ American Board of Family Medicine. Journal (USA ISSN 1557-2625) **5571**
American Board of Family Medicine. Journal (Online Edition) *see* American Board of Family Medicine. Journal **5571**
American Board of Family Practice. Journal *see* American Board of Family Medicine. Journal **5571**
American Board of Medical Specialties. Annual Report & Reference Handbook (USA ISSN 0272-9741) **5571**
American Board of Medical Specialties Plus *see* A B M S Plus **5563**
American Board of Nuclear Medicine. Information Policies and Procedures (USA ISSN 1073-0214) **6192**
▼ • ➤ American Board of Sport Psychology. Journal (USA) **7332**
The American Book Center *see* A B C's Between the Covers **8927**
The American Book Center News *see* A B C's Between the Covers **8927**
• American Book Prices Current (USA ISSN 0091-9357) **7577**
American Book Prices Current. Four Year Index (USA) **7577**
• American Book Publishing Record (USA ISSN 0002-7707) **7551**
• American Book Review (USA ISSN 0149-9408) **5205**
American Book Trade Directory (USA ISSN 0065-759X) **7551**
American Book Trade Directory. Updating Service *see* American Book Trade Directory **7551**
American Booksellers Association, Inc. Book Buyer's Handbook (Year) *see* A B A Book Buyer's Handbook (Year) **7550**
American Bowler *see* U S Bowler **8250**
American Brahms Society. Newsletter (USA ISSN 8756-8357) **6543**
• American Brewer and Distiller (USA ISSN 1536-0792) **597**
American Brewer Magazine (USA) **597**
American Brewer Magazine & Distiller *see* American Brewer Magazine **597**
American Breweriana Journal (USA ISSN 0748-8343) **4327**
American Brittany (USA ISSN 0199-7297) **6803**
American Brussels Griffon Association. Bulletin (USA) **6803**
American Buddhist News (USA) **7700**
American Builder Magazine (USA) **975**
American Bullmastiff Association. Bulletin (USA) **6803**
• American Bungalow (USA ISSN 1055-0674) **427**
American Burn Association. Annual Meeting. Proceeding (USA ISSN 0361-7726) **6055**
American Business Clubs *see* A M B U C S **2264**
• The American Business Disk (USA ISSN 1062-5119) **1971**
American Business Information INFORM *see* A B I - INFORM **1199**
• ➤ American Business Law Journal (USA ISSN 0002-7766) **4854**
▼ American Business Woman (USA) **8851**
American Butterflies (USA ISSN 1087-450X) **838**
• American Cake Decorating (USA ISSN 1094-8732) **3670**
American Camellia Yearbook (USA ISSN 0065-762X) **3722**
American-Canadian Genealogist (USA) **3758**
American Canals (USA ISSN 0740-588X) **8638**
• American Cancer Society. Annual Report (Online) (USA ISSN 0190-5147) **6007**
American Cancer Society. Annual Report (Print) *see* American Cancer Society. Annual Report (Online) **6007**
• American Car World (GBR ISSN 0969-3726) **8490**
American Carbon Society. Biennial Conference on Carbon - Extended Abstracts and Program (USA ISSN 0160-7464) **3235**
American Careers (USA ISSN 1075-0355) **6692**
American Carnival Glass News (USA ISSN 0738-3290) **2037**
American Carriage Driver (USA ISSN 1930-5796) **8286**
American Casebook Series (USA ISSN 1555-8053) **4614**
American Cash Flow Journal (USA ISSN 1548-8845) **1307**
American Cat Fanciers Association Bulletin *see* A C F A Bulletin **6802**
American Catholic Identities (USA) **7782**
• ➤ American Catholic Philosophical Association. Proceedings (USA ISSN 0065-7638) **6903**
• ➤ American Catholic Philosophical Quarterly (USA ISSN 1051-3558) **6903**
American Catholic Society of Philadelphia. Records *see* American Catholic Studies **7782**
➤ American Catholic Studies (USA) **7782**
American Catholic Studies Newsletter (USA ISSN 1081-4019) **7783**
• American Cattlemen (USA) **277**
American CattleWoman (USA ISSN 1042-5233) **277**
American Cement Directory (USA ISSN 0065-7646) **975**
American Cemetery (USA ISSN 0002-7804) **3719**
American Center for the Study of Distance Education Research Monograph Series *see* A C S D E Research Monograph Series **2937**
American Center of Oriental Research Newsletter *see* A C O R Newsletter **370**
American Center of Oriental Research Publications (JOR ISSN 1815-2651) **372**
• American Ceramic Society. Bulletin (USA ISSN 0002-7812) **2037**
• ➤ American Ceramic Society. Journal (USA ISSN 0002-7820) **2037**
American Chamber of Commerce for Brazil. Annual Directory (BRA ISSN 0065-7662) **1394**
American Chamber of Commerce in Argentina. Directory (ARG) **1972**
American Chamber of Commerce in Austria. Austria in U S A *see* Amerikanische Handelskammer in Oesterreich. Austria in U S A **1395**
American Chamber of Commerce in Austria. East West Trade *see* Amerikanische Handelskammer in Oesterreich. East West Trade **1395**
American Chamber of Commerce in Austria. U.S. List *see* Amerikanische Handelskammmer in Oesterreich. U.S. List **1395**
American Chamber of Commerce in France. Directory (FRA ISSN 0065-7670) **1394**
American Chamber of Commerce in Germany. Membership Directory and Yearbook (USA ISSN 0172-9799) **1394**
American Chamber of Commerce in Italy. Newsletter (ITA) **1394**
American Chamber of Commerce in Italy. Yearbook (ITA ISSN 0569-3667) **1394**
American Chamber of Commerce in Japan Directory *see* A C C J Directory **1970**
• American Chamber of Commerce in Japan. Journal (JPN ISSN 0002-7847) **1395**
• American Chamber of Commerce in New Zealand. Newsletter (NZL) **1395**
American Chamber of Commerce in Thailand. Handbook Directory (THA) **1395**
• American Chamber of Commerce in Ukraine. Electronic Bi-weekly Bulletin (UKR) **1395**
American Chamber of Commerce in Ukraine. Membership Directory (UKR) **1972**
American Chamber of Commerce of the Philippines. Weekly Executive Update (PHL ISSN 0115-3188) **1395**
American Checker Federation Bulletin *see* A C F Bulletin **8156**
American Checkered Giant Rabbit Club. News Bulletin (USA) **6803**
• American Cheerleader (USA ISSN 1079-9885) **8158**
American Cheerleader All - Star Insider *see* American Cheerleader **8158**
American Cheerleader Caoch's Handbook *see* American Cheerleader **8158**
American Chemical Society Applied Materials and Interfaces *see* A C S Applied Materials and Interfaces **3234**
American Chemical Society Chemical Biology *see* A C S Chemical Biology **2047**
American Chemical Society Chemical Neuroscience *see* A C S Chemical Neuroscience **721**
• American Chemical Society. Directory of Graduate Research (USA ISSN 0193-5011) **2049**
American Chemical Society. Division of Fuel Chemistry. Preprints of Symposia (USA ISSN 1521-4648) **6762**
American Chemical Society. Division of Polymer Chemistry. Papers Presented at the Meeting *see* Polymer Preprints **2129**
• ➤ American Chemical Society. Journal (USA ISSN 0002-7863) **2049**
American Chemical Society Nano *see* A C S Nano **2047**
American Chemical Society. Petroleum Chemistry Division. Preprints (USA ISSN 0569-3799) **2119**
American Chemical Society Symposium Series *see* A C S Symposium Series **2047**
American Chemistry (CAN) **2049**
American Chesapeake Club. Bulletin (USA) **6803**
American Chianina Journal (USA ISSN 0198-8816) **91**
• American Chiropractic Association. Journal (USA ISSN 1081-7166) **5803**
American Chiropractic Association News *see* A C A News **5803**
• The American Chiropractor (USA ISSN 0194-6536) **5803**
American Choral Foundation. Research Memorandum Series (USA ISSN 0002-788X) **6543**
• American Choral Review (USA ISSN 0002-7898) **6543**
American Christmas Tree Journal (USA ISSN 0569-3845) **3722**
• American Cinematographer (USA ISSN 0002-7928) **6489**
• American City & County (USA ISSN 0149-337X) **7487**
The American Civil Defense Association Alert *see* T A C D A Alert **2228**
American Civil Liberties Union Cyber-Liberties Update *see* A C L U Cyber-Liberties Update **7201**
American Civil Liberties Union of Northern California News *see* A C L U News **7201**
American Classic Screen (USA ISSN 0195-8267) **6489**
American Classical League. Newsletter (USA ISSN 0196-2086) **2229**
American Classical Review (USA ISSN 0044-7633) **2229**
American Classical Studies (USA ISSN 0278-5943) **2229**
▼ American Clean Skies (USA ISSN 1948-1020) **3124**
• American Clinical and Climatological Association. Transactions (USA ISSN 0065-7778) **5571**
• American Coin-Op (USA ISSN 0092-2811) **2242**
American Coke and Coal Chemicals Institute. Newsletter (USA) **3235**

DIRECTORY 2010 THE AMERICAN FORECASTER NEWSLETTER 9947

American College Health Association Action see A C H A Action **6980**
American College of Angiology. Journal (USA ISSN 1548-761X) **5776**
➤ American College of Cardiology. Abstracts (USA) **5740**
American College of Cardiology Cardiosource Review Journal see A C C Cardiosource Review Journal **8927**
American College of Cardiology Extended Learning see A C C E L **5775**
• ➤ American College of Cardiology. Journal (USA ISSN 0735-1097) **5776**
• American College of Cardiology. Journal (Spanish Edition) (ESP ISSN 1133-4304) **5776**
American College of Cardiology Scientific Session News (USA) **5776**
▼ ➤ The American College of Certified Wound Specialists. Journal (USA ISSN 1876-4983) **6055**
➤ American College of Dentists. Journal (USA ISSN 0002-7979) **5834**
American College of Emergency Physicians News see A C E P News **6054**
American College of Foot and Ankle Orthopedics and Medicine Newsletter (USA) **6055**
American College of Healthcare Executives. Directory (USA) **4087**
• American College of International Physicians. Annual Program and Report (USA) **5571**
➤ American College of Laboratory Animal Medicine Series (USA) **5902**
American College of Medical Quality Focus (USA) **5571**
American College of Neuropsychiatrists. Journal (USA ISSN 0517-0613) **6121**
• ➤ American College of Nutrition. Journal (USA ISSN 0731-5724) **6654**
American College of Obstetricians and Gynecologists Clinical Review see A C O G Clinical Review **5739**
American College of Obstetricians and Gynecologists Committee Opinions see A C O G Committee Opinions **5984**
American College of Obstetricians and Gynecologists Educational Bulletin see A C O G Educational Bulletin **5984**
American College of Obstetricians and Gynecologists Practice Bulletin see A C O G Practice Bulletin **5984**
American College of Orgonomy Newsletter see A C O Newsletter **6117**
American College of Osteopathic Surgeons News see A C O S News **6234**
American College of Physician Medicine (Loose-leaf) see A C P Medicine (Loose-leaf) **5943**
American College of Physicians Hospitalist see A C P Hospitalist **5563**
American College of Physicians Internist see A C P Internist **5563**
American College of Physicians Medicine see A C P Medicine **5943**
American College of Preventive Medicine Headlines see A C P M Headlines **5564**
American College of Radiology Bulletin see A C R Bulletin **6191**
• American College of Radiology. Journal (USA ISSN 1546-1440) **6192**
American College of Sports Medicine. Certified News (USA ISSN 1056-9677) **6228**
American College of Sports Medicine's Health & Fitness Journal see A C S M's Health & Fitness Journal **6981**
American College of Surgeons. Bulletin (USA ISSN 0002-8045) **6235**
American College of Surgeons. Directory see American College of Surgeons. Yearbook **6235**
• ➤ American College of Surgeons. Journal (USA ISSN 1072-7515) **6235**
American College of Surgeons. Yearbook (USA ISSN 0094-1999) **6235**
American College of Trust and Estate Counsel Journal see A C T E C Journal **4900**
American College of Trust and Estate Counsel Newsletter see A C T E C Newsletter **4606**
American College Tests Comprehensive Program see A C T Comprehensive Program **2964**
American Colleges & Universities (USA) **2953**
American Committee on Africa Action News see A C O A Action News **7219**
American Committee on Italian Migration Newsletter see A C I M Newsletter **7276**
• ➤ American Communication Journal (USA ISSN 1532-5865) **8086**
• ➤ American Communist History (GBR ISSN 1474-3892) **4282**
American Community Colleges (USA ISSN 1079-7599) **2966**
American Community Gardening Association Multilogue see A C G A Multilogue **3721**
American Companies: Guide to Sources of Information/Americanische Handelsgesellschaften: Handbuch der Informationsquellen/Societes Americaines: Repertoire des Sources de Documentation (GBR) **1200**
American Comparative Literature Association. Bulletin (USA) **5252**
American Composers Alliance Bulletin (USA) **6543**
American Conchologist (USA ISSN 1072-2440) **931**
American Concrete Institute. Compilation (USA ISSN 0517-0745) **975**
American Concrete Institute Manual of Concrete Practice see A C I Manual of Concrete Practice **974**
American Concrete Institute Materials Journal see A C I Materials Journal **974**
American Concrete Institute. Publication SP (USA ISSN 0193-2527) **975**
American Concrete Institute Structural Journal see A C I Structural Journal **974**
American Concrete Paving Association. Newsletter (USA) **3259**
American Conference for Irish Studies Newsletter see A C I S Newsletter **4195**
American Congress of Physical Medicine & Rehabilitation. Education Issue see Archives of Physical Medicine and Rehabilitation **6106**
American Congress on Surveying and Mapping Bulletin see A C S M Bulletin **3996**
American Connemara (USA ISSN 1046-1361) **8286**
The American Conservative (USA ISSN 1540-966X) **7104**
American Construction Catalog (GBR) **975**
American Consulting Engineer (USA ISSN 1050-2203) **3181**
American Contractor (USA) **975**
• American Control Conference. Proceedings (USA ISSN 0743-1619) **3295**
American Cooner (USA ISSN 0002-807X) **8303**
American Cooperation Yearbook (USA ISSN 0065-793X) **1422**
• American Cop (USA ISSN 1557-2609) **2643**
American Copper Council. Newsletter (USA) **6305**
American Corporate Entertainment (USA) **3969**
American Corporate Identity (USA ISSN 1052-0236) **21**
American Correctional Association. The State of Corrections. Proceedings A C A Annual Conferences (USA ISSN 1081-8367) **2643**
American Council for Judaism. Issues (USA ISSN 0741-465X) **7717**
American Council for Judaism. Special Interest Report (USA ISSN 0740-8528) **7717**
American Council of Independent Laboratories Newsletter see A C I L Newsletter **5901**
American Council of Learned Societies Annual Report see A C L S Annual Report **4439**
• American Council of Learned Societies. Newsletter (USA ISSN 1041-5963) **4442**
American Council of Learned Societies Occasional Papers see A C L S Occasional Papers **4439**
American Council of Life Insurance. Medical Section. Proceedings of the Annual Meeting (USA ISSN 0148-4931) **4492**
American Council on Consumer Interests. Conference see Consumer Interests Annual **2636**
American Council on Education. Center for Adult Learning Update (USA) **6410**
American Council on Exercise FitnessMatters see A C E FitnessMatters **6980**
American Council on Pharmaceutical Education Annual Directory (Year) see Accredited Professional Programs of Colleges and Schools of Pharmacy **6818**
American Council On Renewable Energy New Energy Finance Briefing U S see A C O R E New Energy Finance Briefing U S **3123**
American Council on Science and Health Media Update see A C S H Media Update **7505**
• American Council on Science and Health. Special Reports (Online) (USA) **6981**
American Council on Science and Health. Special Reports (Print) see American Council on Science and Health. Special Reports (Online) **6981**
American Council on the Teaching of Foreign Languages Foreign Language Education Series see A C T F L Foreign Language Education Series **3049**
† American Country Collectibles (USA ISSN 1072-6268) **8929**
American Cowboy (USA ISSN 1079-3690) **5064**
• American Craft (USA ISSN 0194-8008) **531**
American Cranes and Transport (USA ISSN 1555-1830) **5449**
• ➤ American Criminal Law Review (USA ISSN 0164-0364) **2643**
American Critical Archives (GBR) **5252**
American Cryonics Society Digest see A C S Digest **5901**
American Crystallographic Association. Annual Reports (USA) **2109**
American Crystallographic Association. Monographs (USA ISSN 0514-8863) **2109**
American Crystallographic Association. Program & Abstracts (USA ISSN 0569-4221) **2085**
American Crystallographic Association Reflexions see A C A Reflexions **2108**
American Crystallographic Association. Transactions (USA ISSN 0065-8006) **2109**
American Cultures Series (USA) **324**
American Currents (USA ISSN 1070-7352) **931**
American Curves (CAN) **6285**
American Cutlery Manufacturers Association Newsletter see A C M A Newsletter **1878**
• American Cynic (USA ISSN 1527-1099) **5205**
American Dahlia Society. Bulletin (USA ISSN 0002-8150) **3722**
American Dance Circle (USA) **2682**
American Dance Guild Quarterly (USA) **2682**
American Dance Therapy Association. (No.) Annual Conference Proceedings (USA ISSN 0065-8022) **6106**
American Dance Therapy Association Newsletter (Online Edition) see A D T A Newsletter (Online Edition) **6105**
American Deafness & Rehabilitation Association (A D A R A) Update see A D A R A Update **4071**
• ➤ American Dental Association. Journal (USA ISSN 0002-8177) **5834**
• American Dental Association News (USA ISSN 0895-2930) **5834**
† • American Dental Directory (USA ISSN 0065-8073) **8929**
American Dermatoglyphics Association. Newsletter (USA) **324**
American Dexter Cattle Association. Bulletin (USA) **277**
American Dexter Cattle Association. Herd Book (USA ISSN 0065-8081) **277**
American Diabetes Association Abstract Book see A D A Abstract Book **5883**
American Diabetes Association. Resource Guide see Diabetes Forecast **5887**
American Diabetes Newsletter (USA) **5883**
➤ American Dialect Society. Centennial Series (NLD ISSN 0929-631X) **5092**
American Dialect Society. Newsletter (USA ISSN 0002-8193) **5092**
American Dietetic Association Courier see A D A Courier **6654**
• ➤ American Dietetic Association. Journal (USA ISSN 0002-8223) **6654**
American Dietetic Association Times see A D A Times **6654**
• American Diplomacy (USA ISSN 1094-8120) **7104**
The American Directory of Writer's Guidelines (USA ISSN 1555-7448) **7551**
American Dispatches (USA) **4571**
• American Doctoral Dissertations (USA ISSN 0065-809X) **2966**
American Dove Association Newsletter (USA) **6803**
American Dowser (USA ISSN 0093-089X) **8817**
• ➤ American Drama (USA ISSN 1061-0057) **8465**
• The American Dream Belongs to Everyone (USA ISSN 1939-8670) **4063**
• American Dream Homes (USA ISSN 1540-7683) **975**
American Driver (USA) **8555**
American Driver and Traffic Safety Education Association. Chronicle (USA) **8629**
American Drop-Shippers Directory (USA ISSN 0065-8103) **1805**
• American Drug Discovery (USA ISSN 1558-4461) **6819**
• American Drug Index (USA ISSN 0065-8111) **6888**
• American Drycleaner (USA ISSN 0002-8258) **2242**
American Eagle Latitudes South (USA ISSN 1083-690X) **8782**
American Economic Association. Papers and Proceedings of the Annual Meeting (USA ISSN 0065-812X) **1436**
American Economic Development Council. Council News (USA) **1436**
▼ • ➤ American Economic Journal: Applied Economics (USA ISSN 1945-7782) **1059**
▼ • American Economic Journal: Economic Policy (USA ISSN 1945-7731) **1059**
▼ • American Economic Journal. Macroeconomics (USA ISSN 1945-7707) **1717**
▼ • American Economic Journal. Microeconomics (USA ISSN 1945-7669) **1535**
• ➤ The American Economic Review (USA ISSN 0002-8282) **1436**
• ➤ American Economist (USA ISSN 0569-4345) **1436**
• American Editor (USA ISSN 1083-5210) **4571**
• ➤ American Educational History Journal (USA ISSN 1535-0584) **2825**
American Educational Research Association. Annual Meeting Program (USA ISSN 0163-9676) **2825**
• ➤ American Educational Research Journal (USA ISSN 0002-8312) **2825**
• American Educator (USA ISSN 0148-432X) **2825**
• American Electronics Association. Member Directory (Online) (USA) **3295**
American Electroplaters and Surface Finishers Society Annual Technical Conference Proceedings (CD-ROM Edition) see A E S F Annual Technical Conference Proceedings (CD-ROM Edition) **6303**
American Employer Digest (CAN) **6692**
American Enterprise see The American (Washington, D.C.) **7104**
American Enterprise Institute for Public Policy Research. Annual Report (USA ISSN 0748-626X) **7104**
➤ American Entomological Institute. Contributions (USA ISSN 0569-4450) **838**
• ➤ American Entomological Institute. Memoirs (USA ISSN 0065-8162) **838**
American Entomological Society. Memoirs (USA ISSN 0065-8170) **838**
➤ American Entomological Society. Transactions (USA ISSN 0002-8320) **838**
➤ American Entomologist (USA ISSN 1046-2821) **838**
American Era (USA ISSN 1059-9150) **4072**
• ➤ American Ethnologist (USA ISSN 0094-0496) **324**
• ➤ American-Eurasian Journal of Agricultural and Environmental Sciences (PAK ISSN 1818-6769) **91**
▼ • ➤ American - Eurasian Journal of Sustainable Agriculture (PAK ISSN 1995-0748) **91**
• American Executive Education Directory (Online) (NLD) **2966**
American Executive Education Directory (Print) see American Executive Education Directory (Online) **2966**
American Exploration and Travel (USA ISSN 0065-8219) **4282**
American Express Centurion Magazin see Centurion Magazin **5067**
American Express Departures Magazin see Departures Magazin **8697**
American Express Platinum Magazin see Platinum Magazin **5080**
The American Family (Farmington Hills) see Information Plus Reference Series. The American Family **8964**
American Family Association Journal see A F A Journal **7743**
• ➤ American Family Physician (USA ISSN 0002-838X) **5571**
American Family Physician Family Practice Annual see A F P Family Practice Annual **5564**
American Fancy Rat and Mouse Association Chapters - Rules & Guidelines see A F R M A Chapters - Rules & Guidelines **6802**
American Fancy Rat and Mouse Association Directory (USA) **6803**
American Fancy Rat and Mouse Association Show Regulations and Standards Book (USA) **6803**
American Farmer Series (USA) **5252**
American Farmland Trust (USA) **91**
American Farrier's Association Newsletter (USA) **8286**
American Farriers Journal (USA ISSN 0274-6565) **8286**
• American Fastener Journal (USA ISSN 1064-3834) **3373**
American Federation of Aviculture Watchbird see The A F A Watchbird **900**
American Federation of Labor - Congress of Industrial Organizations Now see A F L - C I O Now **4589**
American Federation of State, County and Municipal Employees 93 News see A F S C M E 93 News **4589**
American Federation of Television and Radio Artists see A F T R A **2356**
American Feed Industry Association. Annual and Semiannual Meetings of the Nutrition Council. Proceedings (USA ISSN 1057-6649) **278**
American Feed Industry Association. Production School Proceedings (USA) **278**
American Feed Industry Association Safetygram see A F I A Safetygram **276**
• American Feminist (USA ISSN 1532-6861) **7202**
American Fencing (USA ISSN 0002-8436) **8158**
• ➤ American Fern Journal (USA ISSN 0002-8444) **774**
American Ferret Report (USA ISSN 1068-9451) **6803**
▼ • American Fiction (USA ISSN 1937-6006) **5252**
American Field (USA ISSN 0002-8452) **8303**
American Film & Video Review (USA) **6489**
American Film Institute Monograph Series (USA) **6489**
American Filtration and Separations Newsletter see A F S Newsletter **3234**
American Financial Directory (USA ISSN 1047-9759) **1307**
American Firearms Industry (USA ISSN 0164-8136) **8158**
American Fireworks News (USA ISSN 8755-3163) **3236**
American Fish Decoy Association Forum see A F D A Forum **4326**
• American Fisheries Abstracts (USA) **3612**
American Fisheries Society. Membership Directory and Handbook (USA ISSN 0736-475X) **3583**
➤ American Fisheries Society Monograph (USA ISSN 0362-1715) **3583**
➤ American Fisheries Society. Special Publications (USA ISSN 0097-0638) **3583**
➤ American Fisheries Society. Symposium (USA ISSN 0892-2284) **3584**
• ➤ American Fisheries Society. Transactions (USA ISSN 0002-8487) **3584**
• American Fitness (USA ISSN 0893-5238) **6981**
American Flock Association Directory (USA) **1972**
• American Folk (USA) **3969**
American Folk Music and Musicians Series (USA) **6543**
American Folk Presents The Biscuits & Gravy Quarterly see The Biscuits & Gravy Quarterly **3615**
• American Folklore Society News (USA ISSN 1074-8857) **3614**
American Food and Ag Exporter Directory (USA ISSN 1065-3775) **193**
American Food and Ag Exporter Magazine (USA) **193**
• American Football Monthly (USA ISSN 1533-1180) **8220**
The American Forecaster Almanac (USA ISSN 0897-8964) **1436**
The American Forecaster Newsletter (USA ISSN 1087-4410) **1436**

Title

▼ *new title* † *ceased* • *electronic media* ➤ *refereed*

American Italian Historical Association. Newsletter (USA ISSN 0569-5961) **3518**
American Italian Historical Association. Proceedings (USA) **3518**
• American Jails (USA ISSN 1056-0319) **2643**
• American Jewish Archives Journal (Online Edition) (USA ISSN 1537-7989) **7717**
American Jewish Archives Journal (Print Edition) *see* American Jewish Archives Journal (Online Edition) **7717**
American Jewish Committee Journal *see* A J C Journal **8927**
• American Jewish Congress. Congress Monthly (USA ISSN 0887-0764) **7718**
• ➤ American Jewish History (USA ISSN 0164-0178) **7718**
American Jewish Life (USA) **3518**
American Jewish Public Relations Society Reporter *see* A J P R S Reporter **18**
American Jewish Spirit (USA) **3518**
American Jewish Times Outlook (USA ISSN 0002-9076) **7718**
American Jewish World (USA ISSN 0002-9084) **3518**
American Jewish Year Book (USA ISSN 0065-8987) **7718**
▼ • American Journal (Bridgewater) (USA ISSN 1934-1407) **4571**
American Journal for Nurse Practitioners (USA ISSN 1522-1431) **5951**
• American Journal of Agricultural and Biological Sciences (USA ISSN 1557-4989) **91**
• ➤ American Journal of Agricultural Economics (USA ISSN 0002-9092) **193**
American Journal of Alternative Agriculture (Online Edition) *see* Renewable Agriculture and Food Systems (Online) **150**
American Journal of Alternative Agriculture (Print Edition) *see* Renewable Agriculture and Food Systems (Print) **150**
American Journal of Alzheimer's Care and Research *see* American Journal of Alzheimer's Disease and Other Dementias **4040**
• ➤ American Journal of Alzheimer's Disease and Other Dementias (USA ISSN 1533-3175) **4040**
➤ American Journal of Ancient History (USA ISSN 0362-8914) **4129**
• ➤ American Journal of Animal and Veterinary Sciences (USA ISSN 1557-4555) **8791**
• American Journal of Anthropomorphics (USA ISSN 1071-8745) **465**
• ➤ American Journal of Applied Sciences (USA ISSN 1546-9239) **7834**
• ➤ American Journal of Archaeology (USA ISSN 0002-9114) **372**
American Journal of Art Therapy *see* Art Therapy **6106**
• American Journal of Audiology (USA ISSN 1059-0889) **4072**
American Journal of Bariatric Medicine *see* Bariatrician **5944**
• ➤ American Journal of Biochemistry and Biotechnology (USA ISSN 1553-3468) **722**
• ➤ The American Journal of Bioethics (USA ISSN 1526-5161) **862**
▼ • ➤ American Journal of Biomedical Sciences (USA ISSN 1937-9080) **5571**
• ➤ American Journal of Botany (USA ISSN 0002-9122) **774**
• ➤ American Journal of Business (USA ISSN 1935-519X) **1059**
▼ • ➤ American Journal of Business Education (USA ISSN 1942-2504) **1059**
▼ American Journal of Business Research (USA ISSN 1932-0221) **1725**
• ➤ The American Journal of Cardiology (USA ISSN 0002-9149) **5776**
• American Journal of Cardiovascular Drugs (NZL ISSN 1175-3277) **5776**
The American Journal of Case Reports (USA ISSN 1941-5923) **5571**
• ➤ The American Journal of Chinese Medicine (SGP ISSN 0192-415X) **5740**
➤ American Journal of Chinese Studies (USA ISSN 0742-5929) **542**
• ➤ American Journal of Clinical Dermatology (NZL ISSN 1175-0561) **5871**
• ➤ American Journal of Clinical Hypnosis (USA ISSN 0002-9157) **5942**
• American Journal of Clinical Medicine (USA ISSN 1559-5242) **5572**
• ➤ American Journal of Clinical Nutrition (USA ISSN 0002-9165) **6655**
• ➤ American Journal of Clinical Oncology (USA ISSN 0277-3732) **6007**
• ➤ American Journal of Clinical Pathology (USA ISSN 0002-9173) **5572**
• ➤ American Journal of Community Psychology (USA ISSN 0091-0562) **8086**
• ➤ American Journal of Comparative Law (USA ISSN 0002-919X) **4916**
American Journal of Contact Dermatitis *see* Dermatitis **5874**
➤ American Journal of Cosmetic Surgery (USA ISSN 0748-8068) **6235**
• ➤ American Journal of Criminal Justice (USA ISSN 1066-2316) **2643**
• American Journal of Criminal Law (USA ISSN 0092-2315) **2643**
• ➤ American Journal of Critical Care (USA ISSN 1062-3264) **5951**
• ➤ American Journal of Dance Therapy (USA ISSN 0146-3721) **2682**
• ➤ American Journal of Dentistry (USA ISSN 0894-8275) **5834**
• ➤ American Journal of Dermatopathology (USA ISSN 0193-1091) **5572**
• American Journal of Diabetes (USA ISSN 1547-9064) **5883**
➤ American Journal of Disaster Medicine (USA ISSN 1932-149X) **5572**
• ➤ American Journal of Distance Education (USA ISSN 0892-3647) **2938**
• ➤ American Journal of Drug and Alcohol Abuse (USA ISSN 0095-2990) **2691**
▼ • ➤ American Journal of Economics and Business Administration (USA ISSN 1945-5488) **1059**
• ➤ American Journal of Economics and Sociology (USA ISSN 0002-9246) **1059**
• ➤ American Journal of Education (USA ISSN 0195-6744) **2826**
• ➤ American Journal of Electroneurodiagnostic Technology (USA ISSN 1086-508X) **6121**
• ➤ American Journal of Emergency Medicine (USA ISSN 0735-6757) **6055**
▼ • American Journal of Engineering and Applied Sciences (USA ISSN 1941-7020) **3181**
• ➤ American Journal of Enology and Viticulture (USA ISSN 0002-9254) **597**
• ➤ American Journal of Environmental Sciences (USA ISSN 1553-345X) **3402**
• ➤ American Journal of Epidemiology (USA ISSN 0002-9262) **5572**
• ➤ American Journal of Evaluation (USA ISSN 1098-2140) **7946**
• ➤ American Journal of Family Law (USA ISSN 0891-6330) **4906**
• ➤ American Journal of Family Therapy (USA ISSN 0192-6187) **7333**
▼ • ➤ American Journal of Finance and Accounting (GBR ISSN 1752-7767) **1280**
• ➤ American Journal of Food Technology (USA ISSN 1557-4571) **3626**
• ➤ American Journal of Forensic Medicine and Pathology (USA ISSN 0195-7910) **5912**
➤ American Journal of Forensic Psychiatry (USA ISSN 0163-1942) **5912**
➤ American Journal of Forensic Psychology (USA ISSN 0733-1290) **7333**
American Journal of Gastroenterologia (Spanish Edition) (ESP) **5920**
• ➤ American Journal of Gastroenterology (USA ISSN 0002-9270) **5920**
• ➤ American Journal of Geriatric Cardiology (USA ISSN 1076-7460) **5776**
• ➤ The American Journal of Geriatric Pharmacotherapy (USA ISSN 1543-5946) **6819**
• ➤ American Journal of Geriatric Psychiatry (USA ISSN 1064-7481) **4040**
• ➤ American Journal of Health Behavior (USA ISSN 1087-3244) **6981**
• ➤ American Journal of Health Education (USA ISSN 1932-5037) **3050**
➤ American Journal of Health Promotion (USA ISSN 0890-1171) **6982**
• American Journal of Health Studies (Online) (USA ISSN 1945-4511) **6982**
† • ➤ American Journal of Health Studies (Print) (USA ISSN 1090-0500) **8929**
• ➤ American Journal of Health-System Pharmacy (USA ISSN 1079-2082) **6819**
• ➤ American Journal of Hematology (USA ISSN 0361-8609) **5933**
➤ The American Journal of Hematology/Oncology (USA ISSN 1939-6163) **6008**
• ➤ American Journal of Homeopathic Medicine (USA ISSN 1934-2454) **5803**
The American Journal of Hospice and Palliative Care *see* The American Journal of Hospice and Palliative Medicine **5572**
• ➤ The American Journal of Hospice and Palliative Medicine (USA) **5572**
• ➤ American Journal of Human Biology (USA ISSN 1042-0533) **652**
• ➤ American Journal of Human Genetics (USA ISSN 0002-9297) **862**
• ➤ American Journal of Hypertension (USA ISSN 0895-7061) **5776**
American Journal of Hypertension (Spanish Edition) (ESP ISSN 1139-5990) **5776**
• ➤ American Journal of Immunology (USA ISSN 1553-619X) **5754**
• ➤ American Journal of Industrial Medicine (USA ISSN 0271-3586) **6672**
American Journal of Industrial Medicine Supplement *see* American Journal of Industrial Medicine **6672**
• ➤ American Journal of Infection Control (USA ISSN 0196-6553) **5809**
• ➤ American Journal of Infectious Diseases (USA ISSN 1553-6203) **5809**
▼ American Journal of Information Technology (USA ISSN 1943-7498) **2406**
• ➤ American Journal of International Law (USA ISSN 0002-9300) **4916**
• ➤ American Journal of Islamic Social Sciences (USA ISSN 0887-7653) **7709**
• American Journal of Italian Studies (USA ISSN 1524-0770) **5252**
• American Journal of Jurisprudence (USA ISSN 0065-8995) **4614**
• ➤ American Journal of Kidney Diseases (USA ISSN 0272-6386) **6265**
• ➤ American Journal of Law & Medicine (USA ISSN 0098-8588) **4614**
† • ➤ American Journal of Legal History (USA ISSN 0002-9319) **8929**
▼ • ➤ American Journal of Lifestyle Medicine (USA ISSN 1559-8276) **5572**
• ➤ The American Journal of Managed Care (USA ISSN 1096-1860) **5572**
American Journal of Maternal Child Nursing *see* M C N: American Journal of Maternal Child Nursing **5969**
➤ American Journal of Mathematical and Management Sciences (USA ISSN 0196-6324) **5468**
• ➤ American Journal of Mathematics (USA ISSN 0002-9327) **5468**
▼ • ➤ American Journal of Media Psychology (USA ISSN 1940-929X) **7333**
▼ • American Journal of Mediation (USA ISSN 1947-9557) **4614**
American Journal of Medical Genetics *see* American Journal of Medical Genetics. Part B: Neuropsychiatric Genetics **862**
American Journal of Medical Genetics *see* American Journal of Medical Genetics. Part A **862**
• ➤ American Journal of Medical Genetics. Part A (USA ISSN 1552-4825) **862**
• American Journal of Medical Genetics. Part B: Neuropsychiatric Genetics (USA ISSN 1552-4841) **862**
• American Journal of Medical Genetics. Part C: Seminars in Medical Genetics (USA ISSN 1552-4868) **862**
• ➤ American Journal of Medical Quality (USA ISSN 1062-8606) **5572**
• ➤ The American Journal of Medicine (USA ISSN 0002-9343) **5572**
• The American Journal of Medicine. Supplement (USA ISSN 1548-2766) **5573**
▼ • ➤ American Journal of Men's Health (USA ISSN 1557-9883) **6283**
• ➤ American Journal of Nephrology (CHE ISSN 0250-8095) **6265**
• ➤ American Journal of Neuroradiology (USA ISSN 0195-6108) **6192**
American Journal of Numismatics (USA ISSN 1053-8356) **6648**
• ➤ American Journal of Nursing (USA ISSN 0002-936X) **5951**
American Journal of Nursing Mosby Nursing Boards Review for the N C L E X - R N Examination *see* A J N - Mosby Nursing Boards Review for the N C L E X - R N Examination **5949**
• ➤ American Journal of Obstetrics and Gynecology (USA ISSN 0002-9378) **5985**
• ➤ American Journal of Occupational Therapy (USA ISSN 0272-9490) **6672**
The American Journal of Oncology Review *see* The American Journal of Hematology/Oncology **6008**
• ➤ American Journal of Ophthalmology (USA ISSN 0002-9394) **6038**
• ➤ American Journal of Orthodontics and Dentofacial Orthopedics (USA ISSN 0889-5406) **5834**
• ➤ The American Journal of Orthopedics (USA ISSN 1078-4519) **6055**
• ➤ American Journal of Orthopsychiatry (USA ISSN 0002-9432) **7333**
• ➤ American Journal of Otolaryngology (USA ISSN 0196-0709) **6077**
➤ American Journal of Pain Management (USA ISSN 1059-1494) **5573**
American Journal of Pastoral Counseling *see* Journal of Spirituality in Mental Health **7381**
• ➤ The American Journal of Pathology (USA ISSN 0002-9440) **5573**
The American Journal of Pathology, Part B *see* The Journal of Molecular Diagnostics **5653**
• ➤ American Journal of Perinatology (USA ISSN 0735-1631) **5985**
• ➤ American Journal of Pharmaceutical Education (USA ISSN 0002-9459) **6820**
American Journal of Pharmacogenomics *see* Molecular Diagnosis and Therapy **5680**
• ➤ American Journal of Pharmacology and Toxicology (USA ISSN 1557-4962) **6820**
• ➤ American Journal of Philology (USA ISSN 0002-9475) **5092**
• ➤ American Journal of Physical Anthropology (USA ISSN 0002-9483) **324**
• ➤ American Journal of Physical Medicine and Rehabilitation (USA ISSN 0894-9115) **6106**
• ➤ American Journal of Physics (USA ISSN 0002-9505) **7004**
• ➤ American Journal of Physiology (Consolidated) (USA ISSN 0002-9513) **918**
• ➤ American Journal of Physiology: Cell Physiology (USA ISSN 0363-6143) **918**
• ➤ American Journal of Physiology: Endocrinology and Metabolism (USA ISSN 0193-1849) **918**
• ➤ American Journal of Physiology: Gastrointestinal and Liver Physiology (USA ISSN 0193-1857) **919**
• ➤ American Journal of Physiology: Heart and Circulatory Physiology (USA ISSN 0363-6135) **919**
• ➤ American Journal of Physiology: Lung Cellular and Molecular Physiology (USA ISSN 1040-0605) **919**
• ➤ American Journal of Physiology: Regulatory, Integrative and Comparative Physiology (USA ISSN 0363-6119) **919**
• ➤ American Journal of Physiology: Renal Physiology (USA ISSN 1931-857X) **919**
• ➤ American Journal of Plant Physiology (USA ISSN 1557-4539) **775**
▼ • American Journal of Play (USA ISSN 1938-0399) **2143**
• ➤ American Journal of Political Science (USA ISSN 0092-5853) **7105**
• ➤ American Journal of Potato Research (USA ISSN 1099-209X) **218**
• ➤ American Journal of Preventive Medicine (USA ISSN 0749-3797) **5573**
• ➤ American Journal of Primatology (USA ISSN 0275-2565) **931**
• American Journal of Psychiatric Rehabilitation (USA ISSN 1548-7768) **6121**
• ➤ American Journal of Psychiatry (USA ISSN 0002-953X) **6122**
The American Journal of Psychiatry (Spanish Edition) (ESP ISSN 1139-3475) **6122**
• ➤ The American Journal of Psychoanalysis (USA ISSN 0002-9548) **7333**
• ➤ American Journal of Psychology (USA ISSN 0002-9556) **7333**
• ➤ American Journal of Psychotherapy (USA ISSN 0002-9564) **6122**
• ➤ American Journal of Public Health (USA ISSN 0090-0036) **7507**
➤ American Journal of Recreation Therapy (USA ISSN 1539-4131) **6106**
• ➤ American Journal of Reproductive Immunology (DNK ISSN 1046-7408) **5754**
• American Journal of Reproductive Immunology Online (DNK ISSN 1600-0897) **5754**
• American Journal of Reproductive Immunology. Supplement (GBR ISSN 1745-0004) **5754**
• ➤ American Journal of Respiratory and Critical Care Medicine (USA ISSN 1073-449X) **6211**
• ➤ American Journal of Respiratory Cell and Molecular Biology (USA ISSN 1044-1549) **6211**
American Journal of Rhinology *see* American Journal of Rhinology & Allergy **6077**
• ➤ American Journal of Rhinology & Allergy (USA ISSN 1945-8924) **6077**
• ➤ American Journal of Roentgenology (USA ISSN 0361-803X) **6192**
American Journal of Roentgenology (Chinese Selected Articles Edition) (GBR ISSN 1748-7005) **6192**
• ➤ American Journal of Science (USA ISSN 0002-9599) **2701**
• ➤ The American Journal of Semiotics (USA ISSN 0277-7126) **4442**
• ➤ American Journal of Sexuality Education (USA ISSN 1554-6128) **6982**
• ➤ American Journal of Sociology (USA ISSN 0002-9602) **8087**
• The American Journal of Speech - Language Pathology (USA ISSN 1058-0360) **4072**
• ➤ American Journal of Sports Medicine (USA ISSN 0363-5465) **6228**
• ➤ The American Journal of Surgery (USA ISSN 0002-9610) **6235**
• ➤ American Journal of Surgical Pathology (USA ISSN 0147-5185) **5573**
American Journal of Surgical Pathology. Part B: Diagnostic Molecular Pathology *see* Diagnostic Molecular Pathology **5605**
• American Journal of Tax Policy (USA ISSN 0739-7569) **1910**
• ➤ American Journal of the Medical Sciences (USA ISSN 0002-9629) **5573**
• ➤ American Journal of Theology & Philosophy (USA ISSN 0194-3448) **7621**
• ➤ American Journal of Therapeutics (USA ISSN 1075-2765) **5573**
• ➤ American Journal of Traditional Chinese Veterinary Medicine (USA ISSN 1945-7677) **8791**
▼ • American Journal of Translational Research (USA ISSN 1943-8141) **5573**
• ➤ American Journal of Transplantation (GBR ISSN 1600-6135) **6235**
• ➤ American Journal of Transplantation (Online) (DNK ISSN 1600-6143) **6236**
American Journal of Transplantation. Supplement (Online) *see* American Journal of Transplantation. Supplement (Print) **6236**
• American Journal of Transplantation. Supplement (Print) (GBR ISSN 1601-2577) **6236**
The American Journal of Transportation (USA ISSN 1529-1820) **8490**
• American Journal of Trial Advocacy (USA ISSN 0160-0281) **4614**
• ➤ American Journal of Tropical Medicine and Hygiene (USA ISSN 0002-9637) **5810**
➤ American Journal of Undergraduate Research (USA ISSN 1536-4585) **7834**
➤ The American Journal of Urology Review (USA ISSN 1542-8745) **6265**
• ➤ American Journal of Veterinary Research (USA ISSN 0002-9645) **8791**
• ➤ American Journal on Addictions (GBR ISSN 1055-0496) **2691**
• ➤ American Journal on Intellectual and Developmental Disabilities (USA ISSN 1944-7515) **6122**

Title

9950 AMERICAN JOURNAL ON MENTAL RETARDATION (PRINT) ULRICH'S PERIODICALS

American Journal on Mental Retardation (Print) *see* American Journal on Intellectual and Developmental Disabilities **6122**
• ➤ American Journalism (USA ISSN 0882-1127) **4571**
• American Journalism Review (USA ISSN 1067-8654) **4571**
American Judges Association Benchmark *see* A J A Benchmark **4607**
American Kennel Club Awards (USA ISSN 0888-627X) **6803**
American Kennel Club Family Dog *see* A K C Family Dog **6802**
American Kennel Club Gazette *see* A K C Gazette **6802**
American Kennel Club Puppies (USA) **6803**
American Kennel Gazette *see* A K C Gazette **6802**
American Kidney Fund. Annual Report (USA) **6265**
American Killifish Association. Journal (USA ISSN 0002-967X) **3584**
• ➤ American Laboratory (USA ISSN 0044-7749) **2097**
American Laboratory News (USA ISSN 0893-8830) **2097**
American Laryngological Association. Transactions of the Annual Meeting (USA ISSN 0891-1940) **6077**
• American Laundry News (USA ISSN 1091-9201) **2242**
• ➤ American Law and Economics Review (GBR ISSN 1465-7252) **4614**
American Law Institute - American Bar Association Business Law Course Materials Journal *see* A L I - A B A Business Law Course Materials Journal **4607**
American Law Institute - American Bar Association Committee on Continuing Professional Education Review *see* A L I - A B A C L E Review **4607**
American Law Institute - American Bar Association Estate Planning Course Materials Journal *see* A L I - A B A Estate Planning Course Materials Journal **4607**
American Law Institute - American Bar Association Estate Planning Course Materials Journal *see* A L I - A B A Estate Planning Course Materials Journal **4900**
American Law Institute. Annual Meeting. Proceedings (USA ISSN 0065-9045) **4615**
American Law Institute. Annual Report (USA ISSN 0277-3872) **4615**
American Law Institute Reporter *see* The A L I Reporter **4607**
• American Law of Mining (USA) **6456**
American Law Reports, 5th *see* American Law Reports, 6th **4615**
American Law Reports, 6th (USA ISSN 1932-183X) **4615**
American Law Reports, ALR 6th, Annotations and Cases *see* American Law Reports, 6th **4615**
American Law Yearbook (USA ISSN 1521-0901) **4615**
American Lawn Bowls Association Bowls *see* A L B A Bowls **8220**
• The American Lawyer (USA ISSN 0162-3397) **4615**
American Lawyer Media Experts. Mid-Atlantic Directory *see* A L M Experts. Mid-Atlantic Directory **4607**
American Lawyer Media Experts. National Medical Directory *see* A L M Experts. National Medical Directory **5564**
American Lawyer Media Experts. New England Directory *see* A L M Experts. New England Directory **5564**
American Lawyer Media Experts. Southwestern Directory *see* A L M Experts. Southwestern Directory **4608**
American Lawyers Auxiliary News (Chicago) *see* A L A News (Chicago) **4607**
➤ American Leather Chemists Association. Journal (USA ISSN 0002-9726) **4972**
• American Legacy (USA ISSN 1086-7201) **3518**
American Legacy Magazine *see* American Legacy **3518**
• The American Legion (USA ISSN 0886-1234) **2264**
• American Legion Auxiliary. National News (USA ISSN 1062-4244) **2264**
American Legion Press Association News-Letter (USA ISSN 0002-9742) **4571**
American Leprosy Missions Annual Report (USA) **5810**
• American Letters & Commentary (USA ISSN 1049-7153) **5205**
American Liberal Religious Thought (USA ISSN 1080-5389) **7621**
• American Libraries (USA ISSN 0002-9769) **4988**
• American Libraries Direct (USA ISSN 1559-369X) **4988**
American Library Association. Annual Conference Program (USA) **4988**
American Library Association Handbook of Organization *see* A L A Handbook of Organization **4985**
American Library Association. Membership Directory (USA ISSN 1099-033X) **4988**
American Library Association Survey of Librarian Salaries *see* A L A Survey of Librarian Salaries **4985**
American Library Association Washington Office Newsline *see* A L A W O N **4985**
American Library Association, Washington Office Washington News *see* A L A Washington News **4985**
American Library Association's Guide to Best Reading *see* A L A's Guide to Best Reading **5056**
• American Library Directory (USA ISSN 0065-910X) **4988**
American Library Directory on Disc *see* American Library Directory **4988**
American Library Directory Online *see* American Library Directory **4988**
American Life & Traditions (USA) **5064**
American Life and Traditions *see* American Life & Traditions **5064**
• American Lift & Handlers (USA ISSN 1935-6781) **5449**
➤ American Liszt Society. Journal (USA ISSN 0147-4413) **6543**
American Liszt Society. Newsletter (USA ISSN 0749-341X) **6544**
• ➤ American Literary History (USA ISSN 0896-7148) **5252**
• ➤ American Literary Realism (USA ISSN 1540-3084) **5406**
American Literary Review (USA ISSN 1051-5062) **5416**
• American Literary Scholarship (USA ISSN 0065-9142) **5252**
American Literary Translators Association Newsletter *see* A L T A Newsletter **5088**
• ➤ American Literature (USA ISSN 0002-9831) **5252**
American Literature Section (USA) **5252**
American Literature Society of Japan. Journal (JPN ISSN 1348-1681) **5252**
American Littoral Society. Special Publications (USA ISSN 0065-9150) **2602**
American Living Press (USA) **465**
American Logistics Association Worldwide Directory and Fact Book *see* A L A Worldwide Directory and Fact Book **6408**
American Longwall Magazine *see* Coal USA **6460**
American Lutherie (USA ISSN 1041-7176) **6544**
American M G B Association Octagon *see* A M G B A Octagon **8554**
• American Machinist (USA ISSN 1041-7958) **1879**
American Magazine (USA) **3969**
➤ American Malacological Bulletin (USA ISSN 0740-2783) **931**
American Malacological Society News *see* A M S News **929**
American Management Association Management Briefings *see* A M A Management Briefings **1722**
American Management Association. Seminar Program (USA ISSN 0065-9193) **1725**
American Management Association Survey Reports *see* A M A Survey Reports **1722**
• American Manufacturers Directory (USA ISSN 1061-219X) **1972**
• American Maritime Cases (USA ISSN 0160-6786) **4969**
American Maritime Officer (USA ISSN 0002-9882) **4589**
American Market (IND) **1552**
American Marketing Association Educators' Proceedings (CD-ROM) *see* A M A Educators' Proceedings (CD-ROM) **1803**
American Marketing Association Winter Educators' Conference. Proceedings *see* A M A Winter Educators' Conference. Proceedings **1803**
American Markets Newsletter (USA) **4571**
• The American Matchcover Collectors Club (Online Edition) (USA) **4327**
American Mathematical Association of Two-Year Colleges Review *see* A M A T Y C Review **5463**
• ➤ American Mathematical Monthly (USA ISSN 0002-9890) **5468**
American Mathematical Society. Abstracts of Papers Presented (USA ISSN 0192-5857) **5548**
• ➤ American Mathematical Society. Bulletin. New Series (USA ISSN 0273-0979) **5469**
➤ American Mathematical Society. C B M S Regional Conference Series in Mathematics (Conference Board of the Mathematical Sciences) (USA ISSN 0160-7642) **5469**
➤ American Mathematical Society. Colloquium Publications (USA ISSN 0065-9258) **5469**
American Mathematical Society. Electronic Research Announcements *see* Electronic Research Announcements in Mathematical Sciences **5486**
American Mathematical Society. Graduate Studies in Mathematics (USA ISSN 1065-7339) **5469**
• ➤ American Mathematical Society. Journal (USA ISSN 0894-0347) **5469**
American Mathematical Society, Mathematical Association of America, and the Society for Industrial and Applied Mathematics. Combined Membership List (USA ISSN 0569-6461) **5469**
➤ American Mathematical Society. Memoirs (USA ISSN 0065-9266) **5469**
• ➤ American Mathematical Society. Notices (USA ISSN 0002-9920) **5469**
• ➤ American Mathematical Society. Proceedings (USA ISSN 0002-9939) **5469**
➤ American Mathematical Society. Proceedings of Symposia in Applied Mathematics (USA ISSN 0160-7634) **5469**
➤ American Mathematical Society. Proceedings of Symposia in Pure Mathematics (USA ISSN 0082-0717) **5469**
American Mathematical Society Studies in Advanced Mathematics *see* A M S - I P Studies in Advanced Mathematics **5463**
• ➤ American Mathematical Society. Transactions (USA ISSN 0002-9947) **5469**
American Mathematical Society. Translations (USA ISSN 0065-9290) **5469**
American Meat Institute Newsletter *see* A M I Newsletter **3625**
American Medical Association. Council on Ethical and Judicial Affairs. Code of Medical Ethics. Current Opinions with Annotations (USA ISSN 1540-2916) **5573**
• American Medical Association. Graduate Medical Education Directory (Year) (USA ISSN 1079-0519) **2953**
• ➤ American Medical Athletic Association. Journal (USA) **6228**
American Medical Directors Association Advocacy in Action *see* A M D A Advocacy in Action **5564**
• ➤ American Medical Directors Association. Journal (USA ISSN 1525-8610) **4087**
American Medical Directors Association Reports *see* A M D A Reports **4038**
American Medical Informatics Association Annual Symposium. Proceedings *see* A M I A Annual Symposium. Proceedings **5829**
• ➤ American Medical Informatics Association. Journal (USA ISSN 1067-5027) **5829**
American Medical Informatics Association Proceedings *see* A M I A Annual Symposium. Proceedings **5829**
• American Medical News (USA ISSN 0001-1843) **5573**
American Medical Writers Association Freelance Directory *see* A M W A Freelance Directory **5564**
American Medical Writers Association Journal *see* A M W A Journal **5564**
• American Men and Women of Science (USA ISSN 0000-1287) **639**
American Men & Women of Science *see* American Men and Women of Science **639**
• American Merchant Marine Conference. Proceedings (USA ISSN 0364-7374) **8638**
American Merchant Marine Library Association. Annual Report (USA) **4988**
• American Metal Market (USA ISSN 0002-9998) **1805**
• American Metal Market - Weekly (USA) **1805**
• ➤ American Meteorological Society. Bulletin (USA ISSN 0003-0007) **6346**
➤ American Meteorological Society. Historical Monograph Series (USA) **6346**
• ➤ American Meteorological Society. Meteorological Monographs (USA ISSN 0065-9401) **6346**
American Meteorological Society Update *see* A M S Update **6345**
• ➤ American Midland Naturalist (USA ISSN 0003-0031) **7834**
• The American Mineralogist (Online) (USA ISSN 1945-3027) **6456**
• ➤ The American Mineralogist (Print) (USA ISSN 0003-004X) **6456**
American Mines Handbook *see* Canadian and American Mines Handbook **6459**
American Miniature Schnauzer Club Newsletter *see* A M S C O P E Newsletter **6802**
▼ American Missionaries in the Ottoman Empire (USA ISSN 1936-1769) **4319**
American Missionary Fellowship News *see* A M F News **7619**
American Modeler (USA ISSN 1061-9399) **4327**
American Monastic Newsletter (USA) **7783**
American Monographs in American Studies *see* Amsterdam Monographs in American Studies **4442**
American Montessori Consulting Newsletter *see* A M C Newsletter **2822**
• ➤ American Mosquito Control Association. Journal (USA ISSN 8756-971X) **838**
American Mosquito Control Association. Journal. Supplement *see* American Mosquito Control Association. Journal **838**
American Mosquito Control Association Newsletter *see* A M C A Newsletter **837**
American Mother (USA) **2143**
American Motor Carrier Directory: North American Edition (USA ISSN 0897-0807) **8666**
American Motorcycle Dealer (GBR ISSN 1465-7627) **8253**
American Motorcyclist (USA ISSN 0277-9358) **8253**
American Motorcyclist Association Supercross Souvenir Yearbook *see* A M A Supercross Souvenir Yearbook **8252**
American Movie Classics Magazine (USA) **6489**
American Moving and Storage Association Scale Directory *see* A M S A Scale Directory **1970**
• ➤ American Museum Novitates (USA ISSN 0003-0082) **931**
American Museum of Natural History. Annual Report (USA) **6519**
➤ American Museum of Natural History. Anthropological Papers (USA ISSN 0065-9452) **324**
American Museum of Natural History. Biennial Report (USA) **6519**
• ➤ American Museum of Natural History. Bulletin (USA ISSN 0003-0090) **931**
• ➤ American Music (USA ISSN 0734-4392) **6544**
American Music Press Magazine *see* A M P Magazine **6541**
➤ American Music Research Center Journal (USA ISSN 1058-3572) **6544**
• American Music Review (USA ISSN 1943-9385) **6544**
• American Music Teacher (USA ISSN 0003-0112) **6544**
• ➤ American Musical Instrument Society. Journal (USA ISSN 0362-3300) **6544**
American Musical Instrument Society. Newsletter (USA ISSN 0160-2365) **6544**
American Musicological Society. Annual Meeting. Abstracts of Papers Read *see* Abstracts of Papers Read at the Annual Meeting of the American Musicological Society **6631**
American Musicological Society. Bulletin *see* American Musicological Society. Journal **6544**
American Musicological Society. Directory (USA ISSN 1099-6796) **6544**
• ➤ American Musicological Society. Journal (USA ISSN 0003-0139) **6544**
American Musicological Society. L G B T Q Study Group. Newsletter (Lesbian, Gay, Bisexual, Transgender, Queer) (USA ISSN 1556-0406) **4370**
American Musicological Society Newsletter *see* AMS Newsletter **6545**
The American Muslim (Alexandria) (USA ISSN 1545-3820) **7709**
The American Muslim Resource Directory (USA ISSN 1078-8808) **7709**
American Name Society Bulletin *see* A N S Bulletin **5088**
• American Naprapathic Association. Journal (USA) **306**
• American National Standards Institute. Catalog of American Standards (USA) **6401**
American National Standards Institute Reporter *see* A N S I Reporter **6400**
• ➤ The American Naturalist (USA ISSN 0003-0147) **652**
American Nature Writing (Year) (USA ISSN 1072-4273) **5252**
American Near East Refugee Aid Newsletter *see* A N E R A Newsletter **7219**
• American Neuromodulation Society. Newsletter (USA) **6122**
American News - San Bernardino (USA) **3518**
• American Newspeak (USA) **3969**
• ➤ American Nineteenth Century History (GBR ISSN 1466-4658) **4282**
American Notary (USA ISSN 0044-7773) **4615**
The American Novel (GBR) **5252**
American Nuclear Society. Annual Meeting Proceedings (USA) **3164**
• ➤ American Nuclear Society. Transactions (USA ISSN 0003-018X) **3164**
American Nudist Research Library Newsletter (USA) **6982**
American Numismatic Association Journal *see* A N A Journal **6648**
American Numismatic Society. Annual Report (USA ISSN 0569-6720) **6648**
• American Numismatic Society. Magazine (USA) **6648**
• The American Nurse (USA ISSN 0098-1486) **5951**
• ➤ American Nurse Today (USA ISSN 1930-5583) **5951**
• American Nurseryman (USA ISSN 0003-0198) **3722**
American Nurses Association Clinical Conferences *see* A N A Clinical Conferences **5949**
▼ • American Nursing Review (USA ISSN 1940-5634) **5951**
American Nursing Student (USA ISSN 1536-3929) **5951**
➤ American Nutraceutical Association. Journal (USA ISSN 1521-4524) **6655**
American O R T Annual Report (Organization for Rehabilitation through Training) (USA) **3011**
American O R T News (USA) **3518**
American Occupational Therapy Association. Annual Report (USA ISSN 0145-8922) **6672**
American Occupational Therapy Association Self Study Series *see* A O T A Self Study Series **6672**
American Oil & Gas Reporter (USA ISSN 0145-9198) **6762**
American Oil Chemists' Society. Journal *see* J A O C S **2124**
• American Ophthalmological Society. Transactions (USA ISSN 0065-9533) **6038**
• American Optician (USA) **6038**
American Optometric Association News (USA ISSN 0094-9620) **6038**
American Orchid Society Awards Quarterly *see* A O S Awards Quarterly **3721**
The American Organist Magazine (USA ISSN 0164-3150) **6544**
American Organization for Rehabilitation Through Training Bulletin *see* O R T Bulletin **3556**
American Oriental Series (USA ISSN 0065-9541) **542**
• ➤ American Oriental Society. Journal (USA ISSN 0003-0279) **542**
• ➤ American Orthoptic Journal (USA ISSN 0065-955X) **6038**

Link to your serials resources and content with ulrichsweb.com

DIRECTORY 2010 AMERICAN SOCIETY FOR ARTIFICIAL INTERNAL ORGANS. ABSTRACTS 9951

American Osteopathic Association Yearbook and Directory of Osteopathic Physicians (Online Edition) see A O A Yearbook and Directory of Osteopathic Physicians (Online Edition) 5803
➤ American Otological Society. Transactions (USA ISSN 0096-6851) 6077
American Outlook (USA ISSN 1099-8896) 7105
American Oxonian (USA ISSN 0003-0295) 5205
American Pain Society Bulletin see A P S Bulletin 5767
American Painting Contractor (USA ISSN 0003-0325) 6716
American Paleontologist (USA ISSN 1066-8772) 6723
American Paper Machinery Association Newsletter see A P M A Newsletter 5449
• American Parkinson Disease Association. Newsletter (USA) 8025
American Patchwork and Quilting see American Patchwork & Quilting 6636
American Patchwork & Quilting (USA ISSN 1066-758X) 6636
American Peanut Research and Education Society Proceedings see A P R E S Proceedings 215
American Penstemon Society Bulletin (USA ISSN 0065-9584) 3722
American Peony Society. Bulletin (USA) 3722
American Period Furniture (USA ISSN 1542-0299) 4553
• ➤ American Periodicals (USA ISSN 1054-7479) 5252
• American Petroleum Institute. Division of Statistics. Weekly Statistical Bulletin (USA) 6799
• American Petroleum Institute. Monthly Completion Report (USA) 6799
American Petroleum Institute. Monthly Statistical Report (USA) 6799
American Petroleum Institute Publication see A P I Publication 6761
† • American Petroleum Institute. Quarterly Completion Report (USA ISSN 1045-4020) 8929
American Petroleum Institute. Thesaurus (USA ISSN 0193-5151) 6799
American Petroleum Institute. Weekly Statistical Bulletin and Monthly Statistical Report see American Petroleum Institute. Division of Statistics. Weekly Statistical Bulletin 6799
American Pharmaceutical Outsourcing see Pharmaceutical Outsourcing 6869
• American Pharmaceutical Review (USA ISSN 1099-8012) 6820
• ➤ American Pharmacists Association. Journal (USA ISSN 1544-3191) 6820
American Pheasant and Waterfowl Society Magazine (USA ISSN 0892-6387) 901
American Philatelic Congress. Congress Book (USA ISSN 0271-390X) 6891
American Philatelist (USA ISSN 0003-0473) 6891
American Philological Association. Newsletter (USA ISSN 0569-6941) 5252
American Philological Association. Special Publications (USA ISSN 0065-9703) 5092
• ➤ American Philological Association. Transactions (USA ISSN 0360-5949) 2229
American Philosophical Association Newsletters see A P A Newsletters 6901
• American Philosophical Association. Proceedings and Addresses (USA ISSN 0065-972X) 6903
• ➤ American Philosophical Quarterly (USA ISSN 0003-0481) 6903
➤ American Philosophical Society. Memoirs (USA ISSN 0065-9738) 4442
• American Philosophical Society. Proceedings (USA ISSN 0003-049X) 4442
• ➤ American Philosophical Society. Transactions (USA ISSN 0065-9746) 4442
American Philosophical Society. Yearbook (USA ISSN 0065-9762) 4442
• American Photo (USA ISSN 1046-8986) 6963
American Photography (New York, N.Y. 1985) (USA ISSN 0898-1124) 6963
American Physical Society. Bulletin see A P S News 7002
• American Physical Society. Bulletin (USA ISSN 0003-0503) 7005
American Physical Society. Membership Directory (USA ISSN 1088-0348) 7005
American Physical Society News see A P S News 7002
American Physical Therapy Association, Health Policy & Administration Section Resource see H P A Resource 4095
American Physical Therapy Association. Sports Physical Therapy Section. Newsletter (USA) 6228
American Physicians Art Association Newsletter see A P A A Newsletter 463
American Physicians Fellowship News see A P F News 5564
American Physiological Society Methods in Physiology Series see Methods in Physiology Series 925
American Phytopathological Society Monograph Series see A P S Monograph Series 771
• ➤ American Planning Association. Journal (USA ISSN 0194-4363) 4403
• ➤ American Podiatric Medical Association. Journal (USA ISSN 8750-7315) 6055
American Podiatric Medical Association News see A P M A News 6054
American Podiatric Medical Writers Association. Newsletter (USA) 4571
American Poet (USA) 5416
• American Poetry Review (USA ISSN 0360-3709) 5416
American Police Beat (USA ISSN 1082-653X) 2643
American Political Parties and Election Series (USA) 7105
American Political Science Association Directory of Political Science Department Chairpersons (Online Edition) see A P S A Directory of Political Science Department Chairpersons (Online Edition) 7101
American Political Science Association Directory of Political Science Faculty (Year) see A P S A Directory of Political Science Faculty (Year) 7101
American Political Science Association Survey of Political Science Departments see A P S A Survey of Political Science Departments 7101
• ➤ American Political Science Review (GBR ISSN 0003-0554) 7105
• ➤ American Politics Research (USA ISSN 1532-673X) 7105
American Polygraph Association Newsletter see The Truth 2670
American Polypay Sheep News (USA) 278
• ➤ American Pomological Society. Journal (USA ISSN 1527-3741) 3722
American Popular Culture (USA ISSN 0193-6859) 4282
American Postal Chess Tournaments News Bulletin see A P C T News Bulletin 8156
The American Postal Worker (USA ISSN 0044-7811) 2353
American Poultry Association News and Views see A P A News and Views 276
American Power Boat Association. A P B A Reference Book (USA) 8271
American Power Boat Association Rules for Stock Outboard, Modified Outboard, Pro Outboard, Outboard Performance Craft, J Class, Outboard Drag, and Performance Inflatable Racing see A P B A Rules for Stock Outboard, Modified Outboard, Pro Outboard, Outboard Performance Craft, J Class, Outboard Drag, and Performance Inflatable Racing 8270
American Prepaid Legal Services Institute Newsbriefs see A P I Newsbriefs 4608
American Pride Country Home Plans (USA ISSN 1553-2801) 4351
American Pride Home Plans see American Pride Country Home Plans 4351
• American Printer (USA ISSN 0744-6616) 7318
American Printing History Association Letter see A P H A Letter 7318
American Printing House for the Blind. Department of Educational and Technical Research. Report of Research and Development Activities (USA) 4079
American Printing House Technology Update see A P H Technology Update 8927
American Private Radio Association News see A P R A News 2356
American Production and Inventory Control Society see A P I C S 1722
➤ The American Professional Constructor (USA ISSN 0146-7557) 975
American Professional Practice Association Digest see A P P A Digest 1609
American Profile (USA) 3969
• The American Prospect (USA ISSN 1049-7285) 7105
• American Psychiatric Association. Annual Meeting (USA) 6122
American Psychiatric Association. Task Force Reports (USA ISSN 1048-4159) 6122
• ➤ American Psychiatric Nurses Association. Journal (USA ISSN 1078-3903) 5951
American Psychiatric Nurses Association News see A P N A News 5950
The American Psychoanalyst (USA ISSN 1052-7958) 7333
• ➤ American Psychoanalytic Association. Journal (USA ISSN 0003-0651) 7333
➤ American Psychoanalytic Association. Journal. Monograph (USA ISSN 0065-9843) 7333
➤ American Psychoanalytic Association. Workshop Series (USA) 7333
American Psychological Association. Directory (USA ISSN 0196-6545) 639
American Psychological Association Research Psychology Funding Bulletin see A P A Research Psychology Funding Bulletin 7330
• ➤ American Psychologist (USA ISSN 0003-066X) 7333
American Psychopathological Association. Proceedings of the Annual Meeting (USA ISSN 0091-7389) 6122
➤ American Psychopathological Association Series (USA) 6122
• ➤ American Psychotherapy Association. Annals (USA ISSN 1535-4075) 6122
American Public Gardens Association. Newsletter (USA) 3722
American Public Gas Association. Public Gas News (USA) 6762
American Public Health Association. Annual Meeting. Abstracts (USA ISSN 1524-0835) 7507
American Public Health Association. Annual Meeting and Exposition. Final Program (USA ISSN 1524-0827) 7507
• American Public Warehouse Register (USA ISSN 1546-2595) 8490
American Public Welfare Association. W - Memo (USA ISSN 0163-8300) 8025
American Public Works Association Reporter see A P W A Reporter 3258
The American Quarter Horse Journal (USA ISSN 1538-3490) 8286
• ➤ American Quarterly (USA ISSN 0003-0678) 4442
American Quaternary Association. Conference. Program and Abstracts (USA ISSN 0741-059X) 2719
American Quilter (USA ISSN 8756-6591) 6636
American Racing Pigeon News (USA ISSN 0003-0686) 8158
American Radio (USA ISSN 0738-8675) 2346
American Radio Relay League Antenna Book see The A R R L Antenna Book 2356
American Radio Relay League Countries List see A R R L - D X X C Countries List 2356
American Radio Relay League Digital Communications Conference see A R R L Digital Communications Conference 2356
American Radio Relay League Handbook for Radio Amateurs see A R R L Handbook for Radio Amateurs 2356
American Radio Relay League, Inc.'s F C C Rule Book see The A A R L's F C C Rule Book 2356
American Radio Relay League License Manual Series see A R R L License Manual Series 2356
American Radio Relay League National Educational Workshop Proceedings see A R R L National Educational Workshop Proceedings 2356
American Radio Relay League Net Directory see The A R R L Net Directory 2356
American Radio Relay League Periodicals CD-ROM see (Year) A R R L Periodicals CD-ROM 2356
American Radio Relay League Repeater Directory see The A R R L Repeater Directory 2356
• American Railway Engineering and Maintenance-of-Way Association. Annual Conference. Proceedings (USA ISSN 1542-9253) 8614
American Rambouillet Sheep Breeders Association. Newsletter (USA) 278
American Rationalist (USA ISSN 0003-0708) 6903
• American Reading Forum. Yearbook (Online Edition) (USA) 2826
American Reading Forum. Yearbook (Print Edition) see American Reading Forum. Yearbook (Online Edition) 2826
American Real Estate Society Newsletter see A R E S Newsletter 7581
American Reconstruction (USA ISSN 1932-281X) 976
• American Record Guide (USA ISSN 0003-0716) 6544
• American Recorder (USA ISSN 0003-0724) 6544
• American Recorder Society Members' Library (USA) 6544
American Recorder Society Newsletter (USA) 6544
American Recovery Association. News and Views (USA) 1307
American Recycler (USA) 3503
American Recycling Market (USA ISSN 1067-9057) 3503
American Red Angus (USA ISSN 0886-4357) 278
• American Red Cross. Annual Report (USA ISSN 0894-5454) 8025
American Reference Books Annual (USA ISSN 0065-9959) 7551
• American Renaissance (USA ISSN 1086-9905) 3518
American Research Center in Egypt. Journal (USA ISSN 0065-9991) 372
➤ American Research Center in Egypt. Reports (USA ISSN 0732-6432) 372
American Revenuer (USA ISSN 0163-1608) 6891
➤ American Review (JPN ISSN 0387-2815) 4282
American Review (USA) 465
• ➤ American Review of Canadian Studies (USA ISSN 0272-2011) 7947
• American Review of International Arbitration (USA ISSN 1050-4109) 4916
• ➤ American Review of Political Economy (USA ISSN 1551-1383) 1535
➤ American Review of Politics (USA) 7105
• ➤ American Review of Public Administration (USA ISSN 0275-0740) 7419
➤ American Rhododendron Society. Journal (USA ISSN 0745-7839) 3722
• American Rider (USA ISSN 1072-4893) 8253
• American Rifleman (USA ISSN 0003-083X) 8158
American Rivers (USA) 2602
• American Road (USA ISSN 1542-4316) 4282
American Road & Transportation Builders Association Transportation Officials and Engineers Directory, State and Federal Transportation Agency Personnel see A R T B A Transportation Officials and Engineers Directory, State and Federal Transportation Agency Personnel 8629
• American Roads (USA) 8682
American Rodder (USA ISSN 1041-3138) 8555
American Rodder. Annual Buyer's Guide see American Rodder 8555
➤ American Romanian Academy of Arts and Sciences. Journal (USA ISSN 0896-1018) 465
American Romanian Academy of Arts and Sciences Newsletter see A R A Newsletter 2964
American Rose (USA ISSN 1078-5833) 3722
American Rose Rambler (USA) 3722
• American Runner (USA ISSN 1091-482X) 8303
▼ American Rural Education Journal (USA ISSN 1948-9455) 2826
American Russian Institute for Enrichment of Life see A R I E L 7717
The American Saddlebred (USA ISSN 0746-6153) 8286
American Sailing (USA) 8271
American Sailing Association Affiliate and Instructor News see A S A Affiliate and Instructor News 8270
American Sailor (USA ISSN 0279-9553) 8271
American Salaries and Wages Survey (USA ISSN 1055-7628) 1200
• American Salesman (USA ISSN 0003-0902) 1805
• American Salon (USA ISSN 0741-5737) 585
American Saluki Association. Newsletter (USA) 6803
American Salvage Pool Association Report see A S P A Report 8554
American Samoa Consumer Price Index (ASM) 8344
American Samoa Government. Comprehensive Annual Financial Report (ASM) 1910
American Samoa Population (Year) (ASM) 7296
American Samoa Statistical Yearbook (Year) (ASM) 8344
American Savings Directory (USA) 1307
The American Scannergram (USA) 2356
American Scene (Washington) (USA) 2272
American Schleswig - Holstein Heritage Society Newsletter (USA ISSN 1045-9960) 4197
• ➤ American Scholar (USA ISSN 0003-0937) 5206
American School & Hospital Facility (USA) 3016
American School and Hospital Maintenance see American School & Hospital Facility 3016
• American School & University (USA ISSN 0003-0945) 3017
• American School Board Journal (USA ISSN 0003-0953) 3017
American School of Classical Studies at Athens. Annual Report (GRC ISSN 0360-6651) 372
American School of Classical Studies at Athens. Newsletter (GRC ISSN 1105-2554) 372
➤ American School of Prehistoric Research. Bulletins (USA ISSN 0066-0027) 372
American School of Prehistoric Research Monograph Series (NLD ISSN 1543-0529) 372
• American Schools of Oriental Research. Annual (USA ISSN 0066-0035) 4319
• ➤ American Schools of Oriental Research. Bulletin (USA ISSN 0003-097X) 542
• American Schools of Oriental Research. Newsletter (USA ISSN 0361-6029) 542
• American Scientist (USA ISSN 0003-0996) 7835
The American Scottish Gazette (USA) 3518
American Seafood Institute. Report (USA ISSN 1050-0839) 3584
• ➤ American Secondary Education (USA ISSN 0003-1003) 3017
American Seed Trade Association Newsletter see A S T A Newsletter 3721
American Sephardi (USA ISSN 0003-102X) 7718
American Serbian see American Srbobran 3518
American Series of Foreign Penal Codes (USA ISSN 0066-0051) 4884
The American Sex Scene: Guide to Bordellos (USA) 6285
• American Sexuality (USA) 8087
American Shetland Pony Club. Journal (USA) 8286
American Shetland Sheepdog Association. Bulletin Board (USA) 6803
American Ship Review see Professional Mariner 8657
• American Shipper (USA ISSN 1074-8350) 8638
American Shoemaking see Shoemaking International 7942
American Shoemaking Directory see American Shoemaking Directory of Shoe Manufacturers 7940
American Shoemaking Directory of Shoe Manufacturers (USA ISSN 0146-6437) 7940
• American Shooting Magazine (USA) 8303
American Shore and Beach Preservation Association. Newsletter (USA ISSN 0517-4856) 3402
American Short Fiction (USA ISSN 1051-4813) 5252
American Showcase Illustration see Showcase Illustration 517
American Small Businesses Association Today see A S B A Today 1956
American Small Farm (USA ISSN 1543-1487) 91
American Small Farm Magazine see American Small Farm 91
• American Snowmobiler (USA ISSN 1078-6414) 8303
▼ American Social and Political Movements (USA ISSN 1939-1226) 8087
American Social Experience (USA) 4282
American Society for Adolescent Psychiatry. Annals see Adolescent Psychiatry 6119
American Society for Adolescent Psychiatry. Newsletter (USA) 6122
American Society for Aesthetics Graduate Ejournal see A S A G E 6901
American Society for Aesthetics Newsletter see A S A Newsletter 463
American Society for Artificial Internal Organs. Abstracts, Annual Meeting (USA) 5943

Title

▼ new title † ceased • electronic media ➤ refereed

9952 AMERICAN SOCIETY FOR ARTIFICIAL INTERNAL ORGANS JOURNAL ULRICH'S PERIODICALS

American Society for Artificial Internal Organs Journal see A S A I O Journal 5564
American Society for Biochemistry and Molecular Biology Today see A S B M B Today 721
American Society for Cell Biology Newsletter see A S C B Newsletter 826
▼ • ➤ American Society for Chinese Scholars. Journal (USA ISSN 1940-3224) 4442
American Society for Church Growth. Journal (USA ISSN 1091-2711) 7621
American Society for Clinical Laboratory Science Today see A S C L S Today 5901
• American Society for Composites Technical Conference. Proceedings (USA ISSN 1084-7243) 3336
American Society for Conservation Archaeology Report (USA ISSN 0748-5107) 372
American Society for Dental Aesthetics Today see A S D A Today 5833
American Society for Eighteenth-Century Studies News Circular see A S E C S News Circular 4128
• American Society for Engineering Education. Annual Conference Proceedings (USA ISSN 0190-1052) 3181
American Society for Engineering Education Prism see A S E E Prism 3179
American Society for Gastrointestinal Endoscopy Clinical Update see A S G E Clinical Update 5919
• ➤ American Society for Horticultural Science. Journal (USA ISSN 0003-1062) 3722
American Society for Horticultural Science Newsletter see A S H S Newsletter 3721
• American Society for Hospital Materials Management. Conference Proceedings (USA) 4087
American Society for Industrial Security Dynamics see A S I S Dynamics 1722
American Society for Industrial Security Security Industry Buyers Guide see A S I S Security Industry Buyers Guide 1970
American Society for Information Science and Technology. Annual Meeting Proceedings see American Society for Information Science & Technology. Annual Meeting Proceedings 4988
• American Society for Information Science & Technology. Annual Meeting Proceedings (USA) 4988
• American Society for Information Science and Technology. Bulletin (USA ISSN 1550-8366) 4989
American Society for Information Science & Technology Handbook and Directory see A S I S & T Handbook and Directory 4986
• ➤ American Society for Information Science and Technology. Journal (USA ISSN 1532-2882) 4989
American Society for Legal History Newsletter see A S L H Newsletter 4608
• ➤ American Society for Mass Spectrometry. Journal (USA ISSN 1044-0305) 7073
• American Society for Microbiology. Abstracts of the General Meeting (USA ISSN 1060-2011) 712
American Society for Netherlands Philately. Newsletter (USA) 6891
American Society for Neurochemistry Neuro see A S N Neuro 918
American Society for Neurochemistry. Transactions (USA ISSN 0066-0132) 6122
American Society for Ophthalmology and Optometry. Archives see Sociedad Americana de Oftalmologia y Optometria. Archivos 6051
American Society for Philatelic Pages and Panels. Page & Panel Journal (USA ISSN 1055-8616) 6891
American Society for Photogrammetry and Remote Sensing. Technical Papers from the Annual Meeting (USA) 3998
➤ American Society for Psychical Research. Journal (USA ISSN 0003-1070) 6741
American Society for Psychical Research Newsletter see A S P R Newsletter 6740
American Society for Public Administration. Section on International and Comparative Administration. Occasional Papers (USA) 7419
• American Society for Quality Control. World Conference on Quality and Improvement Proceedings (CD-ROM) (USA) 6401
American Society for Quality Control. World Conference on Quality and Improvement Proceedings (Print Edition) see American Society for Quality Control. World Conference on Quality and Improvement Proceedings (CD-ROM) 6401
• American Society for Quality. Proceedings (USA) 6401
• American Society for Reproductive Medicine. Abstract Search (USA) 5985
• ➤ American Society for Surgery of the Hand. Journal (USA ISSN 1531-0914) 6236
American Society for Testing and Materials Geotechnical Testing Journal see Geotechnical Testing Journal 3268
American Society for Testing and Materials International. Journal see A S T M International. Journal 3179
American Society for Testing and Materials Standards in Building Codes see A S T M Standards in Building Codes 3335
American Society for the Advancement of Anesthesia in Dentistry. Proceedings (USA ISSN 0164-1700) 5834
American Society for the Prevention of Cruelty to Animals Action see A S P C A Action 316
American Society for Theatre Research Newsletter see A S T R Newsletter 8464
American Society for Training & Development Buyers Guide and Consultants Directory see A S T D Buyers Guide and Consultants Directory 1855
American Society for Training & Development Training & Performance Sourcebook see The A S T D Training & Performance Sourcebook 6691
American Society of Addiction Medicine News see A S A M News 2689
American Society of Agricultural and Biological Engineers Annual Meeting Papers see A S A B E. Annual Meeting Papers 78
American Society of Agricultural and Biological Engineers Distinguished Lecture Series: Tractor Design see A S A E Distinguished Lecture Series: Tractor Design 3372
American Society of Agricultural and Biological Engineers Member Roster see A S A E Member Roster 78
American Society of Agricultural and Biological Engineers Standards see A S A B E Standards 215
• ➤ American Society of Agricultural and Biological Engineers. Transactions (USA) 91
American Society of Agronomy. Annual Meetings Abstracts (CD-ROM) (USA) 174
American Society of Agronomy Special Publication see A S A Special Publication 78
American Society of Anesthesiologists Annual Meeting Abstracts see A S A Annual Meeting Abstracts 5767
American Society of Anesthesiologists Newsletter (USA ISSN 0270-5877) 5768
American Society of Anesthesiologists Refresher Courses in Anesthesiology see A S A Refresher Courses in Anesthesiology 5767
American Society of Animal Science. Abstracts (USA ISSN 0198-9863) 8791
American Society of Animal Science. Triennial Symposium. Proceedings (USA) 278
American Society of Animal Science. Western Section Meeting. Proceedings (USA) 278
• American Society of Appraisers. Newsline (USA) 7581
American Society of Appraisers Professional see A S A Professional 7581
American Society of Artists Artisan see A S A Artisan 463
American Society of Association Executives Associate Member Update see A S A E Associate Member Update 1722
American Society of Bariatric Physicians. News (USA) 5943
American Society of Bookplate Collectors and Designers. Year Book (USA ISSN 0275-1569) 4327
➤ American Society of Brewing Chemists. Journal (USA ISSN 0361-0470) 597
American Society of Brewing Chemists Newsletter see A S B C Newsletter 597
American Society of Business and Behavioral Sciences E-Journal see A S B B S E-Journal 1055
American Society of Business Publication Editors Editor's Notes see A S B P E Editor's Notes 4571
American Society of Christian Ethics. Selected Papers. Annual Meeting see Society of Christian Ethics. Journal 7682
American Society of Civil Engineers News see A S C E News 3258
American Society of Civil Engineers. Official Register (USA ISSN 0402-1142) 3259
• ➤ American Society of Civil Engineers. Proceedings (USA) 3259
American Society of Civil Engineers Salary Survey (Online Edition) see A S C E Salary Survey (Online Edition) 3258
American Society of Civil Engineers. Transactions (USA ISSN 0066-0604) 3228
American Society of Clinical Oncology Annual Meeting Proceedings see A S C O Annual Meeting Proceedings 6007
American Society of Clinical Oncology News and Forum see A S C O News and Forum 6007
American Society of Composers, Authors and Publishers Biographical Dictionary see A S C A P Biographical Dictionary 6541
American Society of Composers, Authors and Publishers Symphonic Catalog see A S C A P Symphonic Catalog 6541
American Society of Consultant Pharmacists Update see A S C P Update 6818
American Society of Consulting Planners Directory see A S C P Directory 4402
American Society of Corporate Secretaries. Los Angeles Chapter. Newsletter (USA ISSN 0894-0622) 1725
• ➤ American Society of Echocardiography. Journal (USA ISSN 0894-7317) 5776
American Society of Electroneurodiagnostic Technologists Newsletter see A S E T Newsletter 6118
American Society of Exercise Physiologists Newsletter see A S E P Newsletter 918
American Society of Extra-Corporeal Technology Today see A M S E C T Today 5564
• ➤ American Society of Farm Managers and Rural Appraisers. Journal (USA ISSN 0003-116X) 91
American Society of Farm Managers and Rural Appraisers News see F M R A News 197
American Society of Health-System Pharmacists Midyear Clinical Meeting Symposium Highlights see A S H P Midyear Clinical Meeting Symposium Highlights 6818
American Society of Health-System Pharmacists Newsletter see A S H P Newsletter 6818
American Society of Heating, Refrigerating and Air-Conditioning Engineers Handbook see A S H R A E Handbook. Heating, Ventilating and Air-Conditioning Systems and Equipment (S I Edition) 4115
American Society of Heating, Refrigerating and Air-Conditioning Engineers Handbook. Fundamentals (Inch-Pound Edition) see A S H R A E Handbook. Fundamentals (Inch-Pound Edition) 4115
American Society of Heating, Refrigerating and Air-Conditioning Engineers Handbook. Fundamentals (S I Edition) see A S H R A E Handbook. Fundamentals (S I Edition) 4115
American Society of Heating, Refrigerating and Air-Conditioning Engineers, Inc. (A S H R A E) Guideline see A S H R A E Guideline 4115
American Society of Heating, Refrigerating and Air-Conditioning Engineers, Inc. (A S H R A E) Handbook CD. Fundamentals see The A S H R A E Handbook CD. Fundamentals 4115
American Society of Heating, Refrigerating and Air-Conditioning Engineers, Inc. (A S H R A E) Handbook CD. H V A C Systems and Equipment see The A S H R A E Handbook CD. H V A C Systems and Equipment 4115
American Society of Heating, Refrigerating and Air-Conditioning Engineers, Inc. (A S H R A E) Handbook CD. Refrigeration see The A S H R A E Handbook CD. Refrigeration 4115
American Society of Heating, Refrigerating and Air-Conditioning Engineers, Inc. (A S H R A E) Handbook. Heating, Ventilating and Air-Conditioning Applications (S I Edition) see A S H R A E Handbook. Heating, Ventilating and Air-Conditioning Applications (S I Edition) 4115
American Society of Heating, Refrigerating and Air-Conditioning Engineers, Inc. (A S H R A E) Handbook. Heating, Ventilating and Air-Conditioning Systems and Equipment (Inch-Pound Edition) see A S H R A E Handbook. Heating, Ventilating and Air-Conditioning Systems and Equipment (Inch-Pound Edition) 4115
American Society of Heating, Refrigerating and Air-Conditioning Engineers, Inc. (A S H R A E) Handbook. Heating, Ventilating and Air-Conditioning Systems and Equipment (S I Edition) see A S H R A E Handbook. Heating, Ventilating and Air-Conditioning Systems and Equipment (S I Edition) 4115
American Society of Heating, Refrigerating and Air-Conditioning Engineers, Inc. (A S H R A E) Handbook. Refrigeration (I-P Edition) see A S H R A E Handbook. Refrigeration (I-P Edition) 4115
American Society of Heating, Refrigerating and Air-Conditioning Engineers, Inc. (A S H R A E) Seminar Recordings DVD see A S H R A E Seminar Recordings DVD 4116
American Society of Heating, Refrigerating and Air-Conditioning Engineers/Indoor Air Quality I A Q Applications see A S H R A E. I A Q Applications 4115
American Society of Heating, Refrigerating and Air-Conditioning Engineers Journal see A S H R A E Journal 4115
American Society of Heating, Refrigerating and Air-Conditioning Engineers Standard see A S H R A E Standard 4116
American Society of Heating, Refrigerating and Air-Conditioning Engineers Technical Data Bulletin see A S H R A E Technical Data Bulletin 3372
American Society of Heating, Refrigerating and Air-Conditioning Engineers Transactions see A S H R A E Transactions 4116
• American Society of Hematology Image Bank (USA ISSN 1559-7237) 5933
▼ • ➤ American Society of Hypertension. Journal (USA ISSN 1933-1711) 5573
➤ American Society of Hypertension. Symposia Highlights (USA) 5776
American Society of Hypertension. Symposium Series see American Society of Hypertension. Symposia Highlights 5776
American Society of Ichthyologists and Herpetologists. Special Publication (USA ISSN 0748-0539) 931
American Society of Interior Designers Icon see A S I D Icon 4531
American Society of International Law Insights see A S I L Insights 4915
American Society of International Law Newsletter see A S I L Newsletter 4915
American Society of International Law. Occasional Papers see Studies in Transnational Legal Policy 4941
• American Society of International Law. Proceedings of the Annual Meeting (USA ISSN 0272-5037) 4916
American Society of Journalists and Authors Newsletter see A S J A Newsletter 4571
American Society of Landscape Architects Members Handbook see A S L A Members Handbook 426
American Society of Legislative Clerks and Secretaries. Journal (USA ISSN 1084-5437) 7420
➤ American Society of Mammalogists. Special Publications (USA ISSN 0569-8219) 932
American Society of Marine Artists News see A S M A News 463
• American Society of Mechanical Engineers. Advanced Energy Systems Division. Newsletter (USA) 3373
American Society of Mechanical Engineers. Aerospace Division. Newsletter see Adaptive Structures & Material Systems 41
American Society of Mechanical Engineers. Aerospace Division. Publication AD (USA ISSN 0733-4230) 46
➤ American Society of Mechanical Engineers. Applied Mechanics Division. A M D Symposia Series (USA ISSN 0160-8835) 3336
• American Society of Mechanical Engineers. Applied Mechanics Division. Newsletter (USA) 3373
• American Society of Mechanical Engineers. Bioengineering Division. Newsletter (USA) 747
American Society of Mechanical Engineers Boiler and Pressure Vessel Code see A S M E Boiler and Pressure Vessel Code 3372
American Society of Mechanical Engineers Boiler and Pressure Vessel Code. Section 7: Recommended Guidelines for the Care of Power Boilers see A S M E Boiler and Pressure Vessel Code. Section 7: Recommended Guidelines for the Care of Power Boilers 3372
• American Society of Mechanical Engineers. Computers & Information in Engineering Division. Newsletter (USA) 3288
• American Society of Mechanical Engineers. Design Engineering Division. Newsletter (USA) 3181
• American Society of Mechanical Engineers. Dynamic Systems and Control Division. Newsletter (USA) 3373
• American Society of Mechanical Engineers. Electronic & Photonic Packaging Division. Newsletter (USA) 3295
• American Society of Mechanical Engineers. Environmental Engineering Division. Newsletter (USA) 3403
• American Society of Mechanical Engineers. Fluid Power Systems & Technology Division. Newsletter (USA) 3360
• American Society of Mechanical Engineers. Fluids Engineering Division. Newsletter (USA) 3360
• American Society of Mechanical Engineers. Fuels & Combustion Technologies Division. Newsletter (USA) 3373
• American Society of Mechanical Engineers. Heat Transfer Division. Newsletter (USA) 3336
• ➤ American Society of Mechanical Engineers. Heat Transfer Division. Publication HTD (USA ISSN 0272-5673) 3336
• American Society of Mechanical Engineers. Information Storage & Processing Systems Division. Newsletter (USA) 3373
• American Society of Mechanical Engineers. Internal Combustion Engine Division. Newsletter (USA) 3373
American Society of Mechanical Engineers. Internal Combustion Engine Division. Proceedings of the Spring Technical Conference (USA ISSN 1529-6598) 3373
• American Society of Mechanical Engineers. Management Division. Newsletter (USA) 3336
• American Society of Mechanical Engineers. Manufacturing Engineering Division. Newsletter (USA) 3373
• American Society of Mechanical Engineers. Materials Division. Newsletter (USA) 3336
• American Society of Mechanical Engineers. Materials Handling Engineering Division. Newsletter (USA) 3336
American Society of Mechanical Engineers. Mixed Waste Committee. Newsletter see Mixed Messages 3509
• American Society of Mechanical Engineers. Noise Control and Acoustics Division. Newsletter (USA) 3373
• American Society of Mechanical Engineers. Nondestructive Evaluation Engineering Division. Newsletter (USA) 3373
• American Society of Mechanical Engineers. Nuclear Engineering Division. Newsletter (USA) 3373
American Society of Mechanical Engineers. Paper (USA ISSN 0402-1215) 3336
American Society of Mechanical Engineers. Petroleum Division. Newsletter see EnergyUpdate 3377
• American Society of Mechanical Engineers. Pipeline Systems Division. Newsletter (USA) 3373
• American Society of Mechanical Engineers. Plant Engineering & Maintenance Division. Newsletter (USA) 3373

Link to your serials resources and content with ulrichsweb.com

Title

9954 AMERICAN UNIVERSITY STUDIES. SERIES 26. THEATER ARTS ULRICH'S PERIODICALS

American University Studies. Series 26. Theater Arts (USA ISSN 0899-9880) **8465**
American University Studies. Series 27. Feminist Studies (USA ISSN 1042-5985) **8893**
American University Studies. Series 3. Comparative Literature (USA ISSN 0724-1445) **5253**
American University Studies. Series 4. English Language and Literature (USA ISSN 0741-0700) **5253**
American University Studies. Series 5. Philosophy (USA ISSN 0739-6392) **6903**
American University Studies. Series 6. Foreign Language Instruction (USA ISSN 0739-6406) **5093**
American University Studies. Series 7. Theology and Religion (USA ISSN 0740-0446) **7621**
➤ American University Studies. Series 8. Psychology (USA ISSN 0740-0454) **7333**
American University Studies. Series 9. History (USA ISSN 0740-0462) **4129**
American Urological Association News *see* A U A News **6264**
• American Vegetable Grower (USA ISSN 0741-9848) **218**
• American Venture (USA ISSN 1093-0116) **1610**
• American Veteran (USA) **6410**
American Veterans Committee Bulletin *see* A V C Bulletin **6408**
American Veterinary Medical Association Directory and Resource Manual *see* A V M A Directory and Resource Manual **8790**
• ➤ American Veterinary Medical Association. Journal (USA ISSN 0003-1488) **8791**
➤ American Viola Society. Journal (USA ISSN 0898-5987) **6544**
American Volleyball Coaches Association. Power Tips *see* Volleyball Ace Power Tips **8251**
The American Wanderer (USA ISSN 0748-7444) **6982**
American Waste Digest (USA) **3504**
• American Water Resources Association. Journal (USA ISSN 1093-474X) **8817**
American Water Resources Association. Monographs (USA ISSN 0894-847X) **8817**
American Water Resources Association Technical Publication Series (USA ISSN 1070-6763) **8817**
American Water Works Association Distribution System Symposium. Proceedings *see* A W W A Distribution System Symposium. Proceedings **8817**
American Water Works Association. E-Journal *see* American Water Works Association. Journal **8817**
• ➤ American Water Works Association. Journal (USA ISSN 0003-150X) **8817**
American Water Works Association Mainstream *see* A W W A Mainstream **8927**
American Water Works Association Streamlines *see* A W W A Streamlines **8817**
American Water Works Association Streamlines *see* A W W A Streamlines **8817**
American Waterways Operators Letter *see* A W O Letter **8638**
• American Way (USA ISSN 0003-1518) **8782**
American Weather Observer (USA ISSN 8755-9552) **6346**
American Welding Society Annual Meeting. Abstracts of Papers (USA) **6338**
American Whitewater (USA ISSN 0300-7626) **8271**
American Wholesale Marketers Association Buying Guide & Annual Membership Directory *see* A W M A Buying Guide & Annual Membership Directory **1970**
• American Wholesalers and Distributors Directory (USA ISSN 1061-2114) **1972**
American Wind Energy Association Wind Energy Weekly *see* A W E A Wind Energy Weekly **3178**
American Window Cleaner (USA ISSN 1047-9090) **6692**
American Windsurfer (USA ISSN 1092-6909) **8303**
American Wine Guide *see* Kevin Zraly's American Wine Guide **606**
• American Wine on the Web (USA) **597**
American Wine Society Bulletin (USA ISSN 0149-6778) **597**
American Wine Society Journal (USA ISSN 0364-698X) **597**
American Wine Society Manual (USA ISSN 0149-676X) **597**
American Wine Society News (USA ISSN 1543-205X) **597**
The American Woman (Year) (USA) **8906**
American Woman Road & Travel (USA) **8303**
American Women's Society of Certified Public Accountants Newsletter *see* A W S C P A Newsletter **1275**
American Wood-Preservers' Association. Book of Standards (USA) **3710**
American Wood-Preservers' Association Newsline (USA) **3710**
American Wood-Preservers' Association. Proceedings (USA ISSN 0066-1198) **3710**
American Woodturner (USA ISSN 0895-9005) **1049**
• American Woodworker (USA ISSN 1077-7997) **4437**
American Writers Classics (USA ISSN 1541-4507) **5253**
American Writers Review (USA ISSN 1087-9269) **4571**
American Writing (USA ISSN 1049-815X) **5253**
• American Yacht Review (USA ISSN 1546-4806) **8271**
American Zoo and Aquarium Association. Proceedings (USA) **932**
American Zoo and Aquarium Association. Regional Conference Proceedings (USA ISSN 1088-0402) **932**
• American@ (ESP ISSN 1695-7814) **5253**
• Americana (HUN ISSN 1787-4637) **5253**
▼ Americana (USA ISSN 1940-5790) **4283**
• ➤ Americana (Hollywood) (USA ISSN 1553-8931) **8087**
Americana Annual (USA ISSN 0196-0180) **3118**
• Americana Exchange Monthly (USA) **7551**
Americana Eystettensia. Serie A, Actas *see* Americana Eystettensia. Serie A, Kongressakten **4283**
Americana Eystettensia. Serie A, Kongressakten/Americana Eystettensia. Serie A, Actas (DEU ISSN 1611-1079) **4283**
Americana Philatelic News (USA) **6891**
Americanische Handelsgesellschaften: Handbuch der Informationsquellen *see* American Companies: Guide to Sources of Information **1200**
Americans Before Columbus (USA ISSN 0066-121X) **4283**
Americans for Democratic Action News and Notes *see* A D A News and Notes **7101**
Americans for Democratic Action Today *see* A D A Today **7417**
Americans for Effective Law Enforcement Monthly Law Journal *see* A E L E Monthly Law Journal **4607**
• Americans for the Arts. Monographs (USA) **466**
Americans for the Universality of UNESCO Newsletter (USA) **3011**
Americans Traveling Abroad: What You Should Know before You Go (USA ISSN 1070-3365) **8682**
Americans with Disabilities Act (USA) **4615**
Americans with Disabilities Act Compliance Guide *see* A D A Compliance Guide **8022**
Americans with Disabilities Act Compliance Manual for Employers *see* A D A Compliance Manual for Employers **4589**
• Americans with Disabilities Act: Employee Rights and Employer Obligations (USA) **4063**
Americans with Disabilities Act FastSearch *see* A D A FastSearch **4063**
Americans with Disabilities Act Manual *see* B N A's Americans with Disabilities Act Manual. Newsletter **4968**
• Americans with Disabilities Act: Public Accommodations and Commercial Facilities (USA) **4063**
Americans with Disabilities Act Technical Assistance Manual: Title I (USA) **8025**
Americans with Disabilities Act Technical Assistance Manual: Title II (USA) **8025**
Americans with Disabilities Act Technical Assistance Manual: Title III (USA) **8025**
• Americans with Disabilities Cases (USA ISSN 1076-2531) **4615**
Americans with Disabilities Practice and Compliance Manual (USA) **4615**
• ➤ The Americas (USA ISSN 0003-1615) **4283**
• Americas (English Edition) (USA ISSN 0379-0940) **4442**
Americas (Spanish Edition) *see* Americas (English Edition) **4442**
America's 1st Freedom (USA ISSN 1530-8448) **5206**
• The Americas Art Directory/Directorio de Arte de las Americas (USA ISSN 1554-9135) **466**
• Americas Automotives Insight (GBR ISSN 1750-7723) **8555**
• America's Best Colleges (USA ISSN 1042-8267) **2953**
• America's Best Graduate Schools (USA ISSN 1939-3652) **2953**
† America's Best-Selling Home Plans (USA) **8929**
America's Best Value Colleges (USA ISSN 1551-7322) **2953**
America's Blood Centers Newsletter *see* A B C Newsletter **5933**
America's Blues Alley (GBR) **8682**
• America's Byways Bulletin (USA ISSN 1942-3691) **8629**
America's Car Care Business (USA ISSN 1534-9241) **8555**
• America's Civil War (USA ISSN 1046-2899) **4283**
America's Community Bankers. Regulatory Report (USA) **1307**
America's Corporate Families (USA ISSN 0890-6645) **1879**
America's Corporate Families and International Affiliates (USA ISSN 0740-4018) **1972**
America's Corporate Finance Directory (USA ISSN 1080-1227) **1972**
• Las Americas Crime Review (USA) **4917**
America's Driving Force (USA ISSN 1091-9384) **8668**
• America's Families and Living Arrangements (USA) **7296**
➤ America's Family Support Magazine (USA ISSN 1527-7488) **8025**
America's Favorite Inns, B & Bs & Small Hotels: New England (USA) **4381**
America's Favorite Inns, B & Bs & Small Hotels: Rocky Mountains & the Southwest (USA) **4381**
America's Favorite Inns, B & Bs & Small Hotels: The Middle Atlantic (USA ISSN 1098-2191) **4381**
America's Favorite Inns, B and Bs and Small Hotels: The Middle Atlantic *see* America's Favorite Inns, B & Bs & Small Hotels: The Middle Atlantic **4381**
America's Favorite Inns, B & Bs & Small Hotels: The Midwest (USA) **4381**
America's Favorite Inns, B & Bs & Small Hotels: The South (USA ISSN 1098-2108) **4381**
America's Favorite Inns, B & Bs & Small Hotels: The West Coast (USA ISSN 1098-2205) **4381**
America's Favorite Inns, B and Bs and Small Hotels: The West Coast *see* America's Favorite Inns, B & Bs & Small Hotels: The West Coast **4381**
America's Favorite Inns, B and Bs and Small Hotels: U S A and Canada *see* America's Favorite Inns, B & Bs & Small Hotels: U S A & Canada (Year) **4381**
America's Favorite Inns, B & Bs & Small Hotels: U S A & Canada (Year) (USA) **4381**
America's Finest Companies (USA ISSN 1057-5642) **1972**
America's First Freedom *see* America's 1st Freedom **5206**
America's First Freedom (USA) **8158**
America's Flyways (USA) **8538**
• Americas Food and Drink Insight (GBR ISSN 1750-7626) **1879**
• America's Future (USA ISSN 0003-1593) **7105**
America's Health Insurance Plans Coverage *see* A H I P Coverage **4490**
• America's Horniest People (USA) **6285**
America's Horse (USA ISSN 1522-8983) **8287**
America's Hottest Colleges (USA ISSN 1930-3564) **2966**
America's Intercultural Magazine *see* A I M **5204**
▼ The Americas Journal of Plant Science and Biotechnology (GBR ISSN 1752-3877) **775**
Americas Market & MediaFact (GBR ISSN 1364-0267) **8345**
America's Most Wanted to Buy (USA) **4327**
America's National Parks for Dummies *see* National Parks of the American West For Dummies **8740**
America's Network *see* FierceTelecom **2367**
• Americas Oil and Gas Insight (GBR ISSN 1750-7529) **6762**
• Americas Pharma & Healthcare Insight (GBR ISSN 1750-757X) **6820**
America's Pharmacist (USA ISSN 1093-5401) **6820**
• Americas Plural (GBR ISSN 1745-249X) **5253**
America's Premier Community Newspapers (USA) **1972**
Americas Quarterly (USA ISSN 1936-797X) **7220**
America's Registry of Outstanding Professionals (USA ISSN 1942-0579) **1725**
• Americas Review (GBR ISSN 1351-4571) **1436**
America's Spirit (USA ISSN 0886-1196) **8025**
• Americas Telecommunications Insight (GBR ISSN 1750-7677) **2312**
America's Top 101 Jobs for College Graduates (USA) **6692**
America's Top 101 Jobs For People Without a Four-Year Degree (USA ISSN 1931-017X) **6692**
America's Top 70 Food Groups (GBR) **3626**
America's Top Doctors (USA ISSN 1559-5153) **5573**
America's Top Doctors for Cancer (USA ISSN 1934-2233) **6008**
America's Top Jobs for College Graduates *see* America's Top 101 Jobs for College Graduates **6692**
America's Top Jobs for People Without a Four-Year Degree *see* America's Top 101 Jobs For People Without a Four-Year Degree **6692**
America's Top Jobs for People Without College Degrees *see* America's Top 101 Jobs For People Without a Four-Year Degree **6692**
America's Top-Rated Cities: A Statistical Handbbook (Year). Volume 1 - Southern Region (USA ISSN 1082-7102) **4432**
America's Top-Rated Cities: A Statistical Handbook (Year). Volume 2 - Western Region (USA ISSN 1082-7110) **4432**
America's Top-Rated Cities: A Statistical Handbook (Year). Volume 3 - Central Region (USA ISSN 1082-7129) **4432**
America's Top-Rated Cities: A Statistical Handbook (Year). Volume 4 - Eastern Region (USA ISSN 1082-7137) **4432**
America's Top-Rated Cities. Vol. IV, Northeastern Region *see* America's Top-Rated Cities: A Statistical Handbook (Year). Volume 4 - Eastern Region **4432**
• America's Top-Rated Smaller Cities (Years) (USA ISSN 1094-4893) **4432**
Americas Update (CAN ISSN 1195-7166) **7220**
AmeriForce Reserve & National Guard Magazine *see* Reserve & National Guard Magazine **6443**
• AmeriHost Inn & Suites. (Year) Directory of Hotels (USA) **4382**
Amerika *see* AmericA **8682**
Amerika Asocio de Instruistoj de Esperanto Kvaronjara Bulteno *see* American Association of Teachers of Esperanto Quarterly Bulletin **3050**
Amerika Gakkai Kaiho/American Studies Newsletter (JPN ISSN 0916-9237) **4283**
Amerika - Nahost - Europa (DEU) **7220**
Amerika Woche (USA ISSN 0745-6557) **3518**
➤ Amerikai Magyar Levelestar/Hungarian Archives of America (USA ISSN 1054-4607) **4197**
Amerikai Magyar Szo/Hungarian Word (USA ISSN 0194-7990) **3518**
Amerikan Uutiset *see* Pohjois Amerikan Uutiset **3558**
• Amerikanische Handelskammer in Oesterreich. Austria in U S A/American Chamber of Commerce in Austria. Austria in U S A (AUT) **1395**
• Amerikanische Handelskammer in Oesterreich. East West Trade/American Chamber of Commerce in Austria. East West Trade (AUT) **1395**
Amerikanische Handelskammer in Oesterreich. Newsletter (AUT) **1395**
• Amerikanische Handelskammmer in Oesterreich. U.S. List/American Chamber of Commerce in Austria. U.S. List (AUT) **1395**
Amerikanische Tochtergesellschaften Deutscher Unternehmen *see* American Subsidiaries of German Firms **1395**
Amerikanische Unternehmen in Deutschland *see* U S Firms in Germany **2032**
➤ Amerikastudien/American Studies (DEU ISSN 0340-2827) **4283**
• Amerindia (FRA ISSN 0221-8852) **5093**
Amerindia (URY) **324**
Amerique Francaise/French America (CAN ISSN 0381-5889) **4283**
• Amerique Latine (FRA ISSN 0246-2745) **3839**
Amerique - Pays Iberiques (FRA ISSN 1275-2592) **3840**
Ameriques (FRA ISSN 1951-3631) **5253**
• ➤ AmeriQuests (USA ISSN 1553-4316) **4442**
Ameriska Domovina/American Home (USA ISSN 0164-680X) **3518**
Ameristica (MEX) **7947**
Amerisure Safety News (USA) **7507**
• Amernick Market Report (USA ISSN 1088-0194) **1610**
Ameron News (USA) **8416**
Ameryka/America - Ukrainian Catholic Weekly (USA ISSN 0279-6201) **7783**
Ametrias (MEX) **5253**
▼ Amgola Business Forecast Report Annual (GBR ISSN 1753-6855) **1059**
Amgueddfeydd ac Orielau Cenedlaethol Cymru. Adroddiad Blynyddol *see* National Museums & Galleries of Wales. Annual Report **6534**
Amherst (USA) **2272**
Amherst Daily News (CAN) **3806**
• The Amherst Student (USA) **2272**
Amherster Kolloquien zur Deutschen Literatur (DEU ISSN 0946-9362) **5253**
Ami de la Nature *see* Naturfreund **8740**
L'Ami des Jardins et de la Maison (FRA ISSN 1277-7765) **3723**
Ami du Peuple/Volksfreund (FRA ISSN 0003-1704) **3840**
L'Ami Hebdo *see* Ami du Peuple **3840**
• Amica (DEU ISSN 0949-9210) **8851**
Amica (ITA ISSN 1120-432X) **8851**
Amica (JPN ISSN 0288-4402) **838**
Amica Accessorio *see* Amica **8851**
Amici (USA) **4989**
Amici di Brugg. Rivista di Odontoiatria (ITA ISSN 0393-4780) **5834**
Amici di Casa (ITA ISSN 1591-0628) **6803**
Amici di Terra Santa (ISR) **7783**
† Amici Miei (ITA ISSN 0394-5987) **8929**
Amicizia Ebraico-Cristiana *see* A E C **7619**
Amicizia.Studenti Esteri (ITA ISSN 1124-4275) **2826**
Amico (DEU) **6286**
▼ Amico Cavallo (ITA ISSN 1971-1883) **8287**
† Amico Cavallo (Rome) (ITA ISSN 1121-4139) **8929**
• L'Amico del Popolo (ITA) **3896**
Amico dell'Arte Cristiana (ITA ISSN 0003-1747) **466**
• Amicus Curiae (FRA ISSN 1954-2542) **7105**
Amicus Curiae (GBR ISSN 1461-2097) **4946**
Amicus Health World (GBR ISSN 1747-0889) **5573**
† Amicus Union News (GBR) **8929**
Amiga (BRA ISSN 0003-1755) **8851**
• Amiga Magazin (DEU) **2574**
The Amiga One (GBR) **2474**
Amiga Plus - Powered by AmigaOS (DEU) **2474**
• Amiga Report Magazine (USA) **2574**
Amigo del Hogar (DOM) **7783**
Amigos de Jesus (USA) **7783**
Amigos de los Museos (ESP ISSN 1887-6498) **6519**
Amigos de los Museos de Osuna. Cuadernos (ESP ISSN 1697-1019) **6519**
Amigos Volando (USA) **8782**
Amina (FRA ISSN 0244-0008) **8851**
• ➤ Amino Acids (AUT ISSN 0939-4451) **722**
Amino Acids and Biotic Resources *see* Anjisuan He Shengwu Ziyuan **2050**
Amino Acids, Peptides and Proteins (GBR ISSN 1361-5904) **722**
Amir Kabir *see* Amirkabir **7835**
Amiraze Shinpojumu/Proceedings of the Symposium on Amylase (JPN ISSN 0385-213X) **751**
Amirkabir (IRN ISSN 1015-0951) **7835**
Amis d'Andre Gide. Bulletin (FRA ISSN 0044-8133) **5253**
Les Amis de Curnonsky (FRA) **4382**
Les Amis de George Sand (FRA ISSN 0244-2906) **5253**
Les Amis de Jean-Giraudoux. Bulletin *see* Bulletin Jean Giraudoux **5267**
Amis de l'Oeuvre et la Pensee de Georges Migot. Bulletin d'Information (FRA ISSN 0154-7283) **6544**
Amis de Milosz *see* Association Les Amis de Milosz. Cahiers **5258**

Title

● The Anatomy of Workers' Compensation Medical Costs and Utilization in California (USA ISSN 1557-1475) **1662**
● The Anatomy of Workers' Compensation Medical Costs and Utilization in Florida (USA ISSN 1557-1491) **1662**
● The Anatomy of Workers' Compensation Medical Costs and Utilization in Louisiana (USA ISSN 1557-1513) **1662**
● The Anatomy of Workers' Compensation Medical Costs and Utilization in Massachusetts (USA ISSN 1557-153X) **1662**
● The Anatomy of Workers' Compensation Medical Costs and Utilization in North Carolina (USA ISSN 1557-1556) **1662**
● The Anatomy of Workers' Compensation Medical Costs and Utilization in Pennsylvania (USA ISSN 1557-1572) **1662**
● The Anatomy of Workers' Compensation Medical Costs and Utilization in Tennessee (USA ISSN 1557-1610) **1662**
● The Anatomy of Workers' Compensation Medical Costs and Utilization in Texas (USA ISSN 1557-1599) **1663**
● The Anatomy of Workers' Compensation Medical Costs and Utilization in Wisconsin (USA ISSN 1557-1637) **1663**
Anatomy Research *see* Jiepouxue Yanjiu **923**
Anba al-Jami'ah/Jordan University News (JOR) **2966**
Anbiss (DEU) **5834**
Anblick (AUT ISSN 0003-2824) **8303**
AnbudsJournalen (SWE) **1805**
● Ancaster News (CAN ISSN 1205-3430) **3806**
Ance Vesela (CZE) **5206**
Ancestor (AUS ISSN 0044-8222) **3758**
Ancestor Hunt (USA ISSN 0736-9115) **3758**
➤ Ancestoring (USA ISSN 0272-0426) **3758**
Ancestors - Descendants of Futral - Clifford, Watkins - Wood (USA ISSN 1046-7378) **3758**
Ancestors West (USA ISSN 0734-4988) **3758**
The Ancestral Searcher (AUS ISSN 0313-251X) **3758**
Ancestry (USA ISSN 1527-8581) **3758**
Ancestry Magazine (USA ISSN 1075-475X) **3758**
L'Ancetre (CAN ISSN 0316-0513) **3758**
Anchi Eijingu Igaku *see* Anti-Aging Medicine **5576**
† Anchor (AUS) **8930**
The Anchor (USA) **7783**
Anchor Handling Tugs and Supply Vessels of the World (GBR) **8638**
Anchor News (USA) **8638**
Anchor Point Magazine (USA ISSN 0895-366X) **7334**
Anchor Studies (GBR) **8025**
Anchora (USA) **2264**
Anchorage Philatelist (USA) **6891**
Anciens des Forces Francaises en Allemagne et en Autriche. Ceux (FRA ISSN 1243-3306) **6410**
Anciens Pays et Assemblees d'Etats (BEL ISSN 0066-1589) **7106**
➤ Ancient America (USA ISSN 1531-2097) **4283**
Ancient American (USA ISSN 1077-1646) **373**
Ancient and Medieval Philosophy. Series 1, Publications of De Wulf-Mansion Centre (BEL) **6904**
Ancient and Medieval Philosophy. Series 2, Henrici de Gandavo Opera Omnia (BEL) **6904**
Ancient Ceylon (LKA ISSN 0258-9257) **373**
● ➤ Ancient Civilizations from Scythia to Siberia (NLD ISSN 0929-077X) **4179**
Ancient Coins in North American Collections (USA ISSN 0271-4019) **6649**
Ancient Egypt Research Associates, Inc. Gram *see* A E R A Gram **370**
Ancient Greek Cities Report (GRC) **4403**
➤ Ancient History (AUS ISSN 1032-3686) **4130**
● ➤ Ancient History Bulletin/Revista de Historia Antigua/Revue d'Histoire Ancienne/Rivista di Storia Antica/Zeitschrift fur alte Geschichte (CAN ISSN 0835-3638) **4130**
➤ Ancient Judaism and Early Christianity (NLD ISSN 1871-6636) **7718**
Ancient Magic and Divination (NLD ISSN 1566-7952) **6741**
Ancient Mediterranean and Medieval Texts and Contexts (NLD ISSN 1871-188X) **6904**
Ancient Mediterranean and Medieval Texts and Contexts. Medieval Philosophy, Mathematics and Science (NLD ISSN 1543-9941) **4198**
Ancient Mediterranean and Medieval Texts and Contexts. Studies in Philo of Alexandria and Mediterranean Antiquity *see* Studies in Philo of Alexandria **6955**
● ➤ Ancient Mesoamerica (GBR ISSN 0956-5361) **4283**
Ancient Monuments Society Transactions (GBR ISSN 0951-001X) **427**
● ➤ Ancient Narrative (NLD ISSN 1568-3532) **5254**
Ancient Narrative. Supplementum (NLD ISSN 1574-5066) **5254**
➤ Ancient Near East Studies Supplements (BEL) **373**
➤ Ancient Near Eastern Society. Journal (USA ISSN 0897-6074) **542**
● ➤ Ancient Near Eastern Studies (BEL ISSN 1378-4641) **373**
➤ Ancient Near Eastern Texts and Studies (USA) **4319**
Ancient Nepal (NPL) **542**
● ➤ Ancient Philosophy (USA ISSN 0740-2007) **6904**
Ancient Science of Life (IND ISSN 0257-7941) **306**
● Ancient Society (BEL ISSN 0066-1619) **2230**
Ancient States in the Territory of the U.S.S.R. *see* Drevneishie Gosudarstva Vostocnoi Evropy **391**
● ➤ Ancient T L (GBR ISSN 0735-1348) **373**
The Ancient Times (USA ISSN 0091-7176) **6545**
● Ancient West & East (BEL ISSN 1783-8363) **2230**
➤ Ancient World (USA ISSN 0160-9645) **4130**
● ➤ Ancilla Iuris (CHE ISSN 1661-8610) **4615**
Anclajes (ARG ISSN 0329-3807) **5093**
Ancorae. Steunpunten voor Studie en Onderwijs (BEL) **4442**
And Baby (USA ISSN 1542-1627) **4370**
And It's Going to Get Better! *see* Og Bedre Skal Det Bli! **8060**
The And Review (USA ISSN 1043-6413) **5416**
Anda (DEU ISSN 1433-6146) **2682**
† Anda (FRA ISSN 1166-3235) **8930**
Andalucia Costa del Sol (ESP ISSN 1136-6524) **5064**
● Andalucia Educativa (ESP ISSN 1139-5044) **2826**
Andalucia en la Historia (ESP ISSN 1695-1956) **4198**
▼ ● Andalucia es Salud (ESP ISSN 1988-7418) **7507**
Andalucia Handbook (GBR ISSN 1363-7517) **8683**
Al-Andalus-Magreb (ESP ISSN 1133-8571) **542**
Andaman Science Association. Journal (IND ISSN 0970-4183) **7835**
▼ Andamento (GBR ISSN 1752-5578) **466**
➤ Andamios (MEX ISSN 1870-0063) **7947**
▼ Andante (ARG ISSN 1851-362X) **8490**
● El Andar (Online Edition) (USA) **3518**
El Andar (Print Edition) *see* El Andar (Online Edition) **3518**
● El Andar Worldwide (USA) **3518**
Andares *see* La Republica (Online) **3928**
Andares *see* Andares **3927**
● Andares (PER ISSN 1605-332X) **3927**
● ➤ Andean Geology (CHL ISSN 0718-7106) **2724**
➤ Andean Past (USA ISSN 1055-8756) **373**
● Andean Report (PER ISSN 0251-2491) **1436**
Andelsbladet *see* Foodculture **1423**
Andelsbolighavernes Lands-Organisation Nyt *see* A B L O Nyt **8927**
Ander Nieuws (NLD ISSN 1385-7304) **7221**
● anderbo.com (USA) **5206**
Andere Tijden (NLD ISSN 1572-493X) **4198**
Anderman: The Law of Unfair Dismissal (GBR) **4615**
● Andersenian a (DNK ISSN 0084-6465) **5254**
The Anderson Agency Report (USA ISSN 1940-9176) **4530**
Anderson Kill Olick LLP Employment Law Insider *see* A K O O Employment Law Insider **1661**
Anderson Kill Olick LLP Policyholder Advisor *see* A K O O Policyholder Advisor **4490**
Anderson's (Year) Ohio Traffic Law Handbook *see* Ohio Traffic Law Handbook **8507**
● Anderson's Estate Planning Forms and Clauses (USA) **4900**
Anderson's Ohio Annotated Commercial Law Handbook (USA ISSN 1559-8748) **4615**
Anderson's Ohio Annotated Workers' Compensation Law Handbook (Years) (USA ISSN 1935-8555) **1663**
Anderson's (Year) Ohio Bankruptcy Handbook (USA) **4854**
Anderson's (Year) Ohio Business Entities Handbook (USA) **4854**
Anderson's Ohio Case Locator (USA ISSN 1059-518X) **4615**
● Anderson's Ohio Civil Practice with Forms (USA) **4826**
Anderson's Ohio Civil Procedure *see* Weissenberger's Ohio Civil Procedure (Year) Litigation Manual **4844**
† Anderson's (Year) Ohio Commercial Law Handbook (USA) **8930**
Anderson's Ohio Criminal Code Handbook (Year) (USA) **4884**
● Anderson's Ohio Criminal Law Handbook (Year) (USA) **4884**
Anderson's Ohio Criminal Practice and Procedure (USA ISSN 1931-0420) **4884**
Anderson's Ohio E P A Laws and Regulations *see* Anderson's Ohio E P A on CD-ROM **3493**
● Anderson's Ohio E P A on CD-ROM (Environmental Protection Agency) (USA) **3493**
Anderson's Ohio Employment Law Handbook (USA ISSN 1933-1401) **1663**
Anderson's Ohio Family Law (USA ISSN 1557-6396) **4906**
● Anderson's Ohio Forms on Disc (USA ISSN 1930-823X) **4615**
Anderson's (Year) Ohio Insurance Law Handbook (USA ISSN 1554-2866) **4492**
† ● Anderson's Ohio Law on Disc (USA ISSN 1534-4746) **8930**
Anderson's Ohio Probate Law Handbook (USA ISSN 1550-2236) **4900**
Anderson's Ohio Probate Practice & Procedure *see* Anderson's Ohio Probate Practice and Procedure **4900**
● Anderson's Ohio Probate Practice and Procedure (USA ISSN 1930-9570) **4900**
Anderson's Ohio Real Estate Law Handbook (USA ISSN 1554-7876) **7581**
Anderson's Ohio Residential Real Estate Manual *see* Ohio Residential Real Estate Manual **7603**
Anderson's Ohio School Law Guide (USA) **3017**
Anderson's Ohio Search Warrant Manual (USA ISSN 1930-8795) **4616**
Anderson's Ohio Securities Law and Practice (USA) **4854**
Anderson's Ohio Securities Law & Practice *see* Anderson's Ohio Securities Law and Practice **4854**
Anderson's Ohio Securities Law Handbook (USA) **1307**
Anderson's Rules Governing the Courts of Ohio (USA) **4946**
Andersson Elffers Felix. Jaarboek (NLD ISSN 1871-7683) **1422**
Andersson Elffers Felix. Verslag *see* Andersson Elffers Felix. Jaarboek **1422**
● Andes (ARG ISSN 0327-1676) **324**
● Los Andes (ARG ISSN 1514-9404) **3790**
Andes (POL ISSN 1428-1384) **373**
Andesha (TJK) **466**
Andhra Agricultural Journal (IND ISSN 0003-2956) **91**
Andhra Bhoomi (IND) **3878**
Andhra Bhoomi Sachitra Vara Patrika (IND) **3879**
Andhra Historical Research Society. Journal (IND) **4179**
Andhra Jyoti (IND) **3879**
Andhra Jyoti Sachitra Vara Patrika (IND) **3879**
● Andhra Prabha (IND) **3879**
Andhra Prabha Illustrated Weekly (IND) **3879**
Andhra Pradesh (IND ISSN 0570-0655) **4179**
Andhra Pradesh, India. Department of Archaeology and Museums. Annual Report (IND) **373**
Andhra Pradesh, India. Department of Archaeology and Museums. Archaeological Series (IND) **373**
Andhra Pradesh, India. Department of Archaeology and Museums. Archaeological Series: A.P. Journal of Archaeology (IND) **373**
Andhra Pradesh, India. Department of Archaeology and Museums. Epigraphy Series (IND) **373**
Andhra Pradesh, India. Department of Archaeology and Museums. Museum Series (IND) **6649**
Andhra Pradesh Productivity Council. Target (IND ISSN 0003-2964) **91**
Andhra Pradesh Small Scale Industrial Development Corporation. Annual Report (IND ISSN 0376-804X) **1956**
Andhra Pradesh State Financial Corporation. Report and Accounts (IND) **1910**
Andhra Pradesh State Trading Corporation Limited. Annual Report (IND ISSN 0376-5512) **1805**
Andhra University Memoirs in Oceanography (IND ISSN 0066-1686) **2800**
Andima Retrospectiva *see* A N D I M A Retrospectiva **1434**
Andina On Line *see* El Peruano **3928**
Andoeyposten (NOR) **3921**
➤ Andon (NLD ISSN 0168-2997) **466**
& (USA) **3969**
➤ Andragoske Studije (SRB ISSN 0354-5415) **2938**
Andral (BGR ISSN 1311-266X) **3518**
● Andre Gayot's Tastes (USA ISSN 1062-0184) **5064**
Der Andreaner (DEU) **3017**
Andrei (RUS ISSN 0868-8915) **6286**
Andres Bello Biblioteca. Coleccion (CHL) **5254**
● The Andrew Harper Collection (USA) **8683**
● Andrew Harper's Hideaway Report (USA ISSN 0884-7622) **8683**
Andrew M. Freeman Zine *see* A M F E-Zine **2587**
Andrew Marshall's Audio Ideas Guide *see* Audio Ideas Guide **3089**
Andrew W. Mellon Foundation. Report (USA ISSN 0066-1694) **4442**
Andrews Disability Litigation Reporter *see* Andrews Litigation Reporter: Disability **4855**
Andrews E-Business Law Bulletin *see* Andrews Litigation Reporter: E-Business Law Bulletin **8930**
Andrews Expert and Scientific Evidence Ligitation Reporter *see* Andrews Litigation Reporter: Expert & Scientific Evidence **4946**
Andrews Expert & Scientific Evidence Litigation Reporter *see* Andrews Litigation Reporter: Expert & Scientific Evidence **4946**
● Andrews Health and Life Insurance Litigation Reporter (USA ISSN 1095-2101) **4616**
Andrews Insurance Coverage Litigation Report *see* Andrews Litigation Reporter: Insurance Coverage **4492**
● Andrews Latex Allergy Litigation Reporter (USA ISSN 1095-208X) **4616**
● Andrews Litigation Reporter: Antitrust (USA ISSN 1554-4060) **4854**
● Andrews Litigation Reporter: Asbestos (USA ISSN 1556-9985) **4616**
● Andrews Litigation Reporter: Automotive (USA ISSN 1557-0452) **4616**
● Andrews Litigation Reporter: Aviation (USA ISSN 1556-9977) **4616**
● Andrews Litigation Reporter: Bank & Lender Liability (USA ISSN 1557-0010) **4616**
Andrews Litigation Reporter: Bank and Lender Liability *see* Andrews Litigation Reporter: Bank & Lender Liability **4616**
● Andrews Litigation Reporter: Bankruptcy (USA ISSN 1556-9969) **1307**
● Andrews Litigation Reporter: Class Action (USA ISSN 1556-9950) **4616**
● Andrews Litigation Reporter: Computer & Internet (USA ISSN 1557-0169) **2490**
Andrews Litigation Reporter: Construction Defect and Mold *see* Andrews Litigation Reporter: Construction Defect & Mold **4616**
● Andrews Litigation Reporter: Construction Defect & Mold (USA ISSN 1555-5933) **4616**
Andrews Litigation Reporter: Corporate Officers and Directors Liability *see* Andrews Litigation Reporter: Corporate Officers & Directors Liability **4854**
● Andrews Litigation Reporter: Corporate Officers & Directors Liability (USA ISSN 1557-1009) **4854**
● Andrews Litigation Reporter: Delaware Corporate (USA ISSN 1557-0525) **4855**
● Andrews Litigation Reporter: Delaware Corporation Law Update (USA ISSN 1557-0487) **4855**
● Andrews Litigation Reporter: Derivatives (USA ISSN 1556-8830) **4616**
Andrews Litigation Reporter: Disability (USA ISSN 1557-0509) **4855**
Andrews Litigation Reporter: Drug Recall (USA ISSN 1555-8916) **4616**
† Andrews Litigation Reporter: E-Business Law Bulletin (USA ISSN 1555-5941) **8930**
● Andrews Litigation Reporter: Employment (USA ISSN 1557-0517) **4616**
● Andrews Litigation Reporter: Entertainment Industry (USA ISSN 1557-0029) **4616**
● Andrews Litigation Reporter: Environmental (USA ISSN 1551-4269) **4616**
Andrews Litigation Reporter: Expert and Scientific Evidence *see* Andrews Litigation Reporter: Expert & Scientific Evidence **4946**
Andrews Litigation Reporter: Expert & Scientific Evidence (USA ISSN 1548-8683) **4946**
Andrews Litigation Reporter: Food Health and Safety *see* Andrews Litigation Reporter: Food Health & Safety **7507**
Andrews Litigation Reporter: Food Health & Safety (USA ISSN 1553-0906) **7507**
Andrews Litigation Reporter: Franchise and Distribution *see* Andrews Litigation Reporter: Franchise & Distribution **4855**
Andrews Litigation Reporter: Franchise & Distribution (USA ISSN 1557-0150) **4855**
● Andrews Litigation Reporter: Government Contract (USA ISSN 1553-6718) **4884**
● Andrews Litigation Reporter: Gun Industry (USA ISSN 1555-5739) **4616**
● Andrews Litigation Reporter: Health Care Fraud (USA ISSN 1553-670X) **4616**
● Andrews Litigation Reporter: Health Law (USA ISSN 1557-0002) **4826**
● Andrews Litigation Reporter: Infectious Disease (USA ISSN 1553-7110) **4616**
Andrews Litigation Reporter: Insurance Bad Faith (USA ISSN 1557-0460) **4855**
Andrews Litigation Reporter: Insurance Coverage (USA ISSN 1557-024X) **4492**
● Andrews Litigation Reporter: Intellectual Property (USA ISSN 1554-4052) **1552**
● Andrews Litigation Reporter: Medical Devices (USA ISSN 1557-0185) **5574**
Andrews Litigation Reporter: Mergers and Acquisitions *see* Andrews Litigation Reporter: Mergers & Acquisitions **4855**
● Andrews Litigation Reporter: Mergers & Acquisitions (USA ISSN 1557-0495) **4855**
● Andrews Litigation Reporter: Nursing Home (USA ISSN 1556-9993) **5951**
Andrews Litigation Reporter: Patent (USA ISSN 1551-773X) **4855**
● Andrews Litigation Reporter: Pharmaceutical (USA ISSN 1553-6696) **4826**
Andrews Litigation Reporter: Privacy (USA ISSN 1555-5720) **4846**
Andrews Litigation Reporter: Products Liability *see* Products Liability (Wayne) **4762**
● Andrews Litigation Reporter: Professional Liability (USA ISSN 1555-595X) **4617**
Andrews Litigation Reporter: Securities Litigation and Regulation *see* Andrews Litigation Reporter: Securities Litigation & Regulation **4617**
Andrews Litigation Reporter: Securities Litigation & Regulation (USA ISSN 1557-0533) **4617**
● Andrews Litigation Reporter: Sexual Harassment (USA ISSN 1557-0258) **4827**
● Andrews Litigation Reporter: Software Law Bulletin (USA ISSN 1557-0479) **2587**
● Andrews Litigation Reporter: Telecommunications Industry (USA ISSN 1555-8908) **2312**
Andrew's Litigation Reporter: Tire Defect (USA ISSN 1554-978X) **4617**
● Andrew's Litigation Reporter: Tobacco Industry (USA ISSN 1555-4406) **4617**
Andrews Litigation Reporter. Toxic Chemicals *see* Andrews Litigation Reporter: Toxic Torts **4617**
● Andrews Litigation Reporter: Toxic Torts (USA ISSN 1557-0037) **4617**
● Andrews Litigation Reporter: Utilities Industry (USA ISSN 1555-5747) **4617**
● Andrews Litigation Reporter: White-Collar Crime (USA ISSN 1557-0045) **2643**
● Andrews Managed Care Litigation Reporter (USA ISSN 1095-2098) **4617**
Andrews Medical Devices Litigation Reporter *see* Andrews Litigation Reporter: Medical Devices **5574**
Andrews Pension Fund Litigation Reporter *see* Pension Fund Litigation Reporter **8980**
Andrews Telecommunications Industry Litigation Reporter *see* Andrews Litigation Reporter: Telecommunications Industry **2312**

Title

9958 ANDREWS UNIVERSITY SEMINARY STUDIES ULRICH'S PERIODICALS

➤ Andrews University Seminary Studies (USA ISSN 0003-2980) **7621**
Andriaka Chronika (GRC ISSN 1105-0144) **4130**
Andriaka Meletemata (GRC) **7835**
Andrias (DEU ISSN 0721-6513) **775**
Andriot *see* Guide to U S Government Publications **7480**
▼ • Androgyny (GBR ISSN 1752-8879) **2251**
• ➤ Andrologia (DEU ISSN 0303-4569) **5574**
• Andrologie (FRA ISSN 1166-2654) **5574**
Andrology Update (USA ISSN 1934-3809) **5574**
Andromeda (BGR ISSN 1310-3571) **568**
• Andromeda Spaceways Inflight Magazine (AUS ISSN 1446-781X) **5439**
Andvari (ISL ISSN 0258-3771) **4198**
Andy Awards Creative Book (USA) **21**
Andy's Front Hall (USA) **6545**
Andy's Front Hall. Buyer's Guide *see* Andy's Front Hall **6545**
L'Ane d'Or (FRA ISSN 1158-9035) **4442**
Anejos de Analecta Malacitana (ESP ISSN 0211-9358) **5093**
Anejos de Archivo Espanol de Arqueologia (ESP ISSN 0561-3663) **373**
➤ Anejos de Dieciocho (USA) **4198**
➤ L'Anello che Non Tiene (USA ISSN 0899-5273) **5254**
➤ Anestesia en Mexico (MEX ISSN 1405-0056) **5769**
• Anestesia Pediatrica e Neonatale (ITA ISSN 1723-0330) **5769**
Anestesia - Rianimazione *see* Encyclopedie Medico-Chirurgicale. Anestesia - Rianimazione **5771**
L'Anestesista *see* Il Nuovo Anestesista Rianimatore **5772**
➤ Anestezi Dergisi (TUR ISSN 1300-0578) **5769**
➤ Anesteziologie a Intenzivni Medicina/ Anaesthesiology and Intensive Medicine (CZE ISSN 1214-2158) **5769**
Anesteziologie a Neodkladna Pece *see* Anesteziologie a Intenzivni Medicina **5769**
Anesteziologiia i Intensivno Lechenie (BGR ISSN 1310-4284) **5769**
Anesteziologiya i Reanimatologiya/Anesthesiology and Intensive Care (RUS ISSN 0201-7563) **5769**
Anestezjologia i Intensywna Terapia (POL ISSN 0209-1712) **5769**
▼ • Anesthesia Abstracts (USA ISSN 1938-7172) **5769**
• ➤ Anesthesia and Analgesia (USA ISSN 0003-2999) **5769**
• ➤ Anesthesia & Analgesia (Spanish Edition) (ESP ISSN 1138-1868) **5769**
• Anesthesia & Pain Coder's Pink Sheet (USA ISSN 1941-8299) **5769**
• Anesthesia & Pain Management Coding Alert (USA ISSN 1535-590X) **4492**
Anesthesia and Pain Management Coding Alert *see* Anesthesia & Pain Management Coding Alert **4492**
Anesthesia and Resuscitation *see* Masui to Sosei **5772**
• Anesthesia News (CAN) **5769**
Anesthesia Patient Safety Foundation. Newsletter (USA) **5769**
• ➤ Anesthesia Progress (USA ISSN 0003-3006) **5834**
Anesthesia Today (USA ISSN 1043-0555) **5769**
Anesthesie et Reanimation d'Aujourd'hui (FRA ISSN 0993-7994) **5769**
Anesthesie - Reanimation *see* Encyclopedie Medico-Chirurgicale. Anesthesie - Reanimation **5771**
• ➤ Anesthesiology (USA ISSN 0003-3022) **5769**
Anesthesiology (Section 24 EMBASE) *see* Excerpta Medica. Section 24: Anesthesiology **5745**
Anesthesiology and Intensive Care *see* Anesteziologiya i Reanimatologiya **5769**
• Anesthesiology Clinics (USA ISSN 1932-2275) **5770**
Anesthesiology Clinics of North America *see* Anesthesiology Clinics **5770**
• Anesthesiology News (USA ISSN 0747-4679) **5770**
▼ • ➤ Anesthesiology Research and Practice (USA ISSN 1687-6962) **5770**
Anew *see* Brava Magazine **8844**
• Anex Bulletin (AUS ISSN 1447-7483) **7507**
Anexartitos/Independent (CYP) **3831**
• Anfang (SWE ISSN 1404-4218) **4571**
Anfora (ARG) **5254**
Ang Tagamasid (PHL ISSN 0115-5032) **6346**
Angarskaya Pravda (RUS) **3934**
Ange Gardien (FRA ISSN 0751-6460) **7621**
Angeiologie (FRA ISSN 0003-3049) **5777**
Angel Advisor (USA ISSN 1532-3552) **1610**
• Angel de la Guarda (NIC ISSN 1607-1425) **8025**
• Angel de Puebla (MEX ISSN 1606-7347) **3907**
Angela Thirkell Society. Journal (GBR ISSN 0963-2581) **5254**
Angelaeget (SWE) **2143**
• ➤ Angelaki (GBR ISSN 0969-725X) **4443**
• Angeleno (USA) **3969**
➤ Angelicum (VAT ISSN 1123-5772) **7783**
† Angelo di Fuoco (ITA ISSN 1722-5884) **8930**
Angels on Earth (USA ISSN 1082-3107) **7621**
The Angelus (USA ISSN 1073-5003) **7783**
AngelWoche (DEU ISSN 0179-843X) **8303**
• Anger Management - Controlling the Volcano Within (USA) **7334**
▼ • Angermion (DEU ISSN 1868-9426) **5254**
Angewandte Arbeitswissenschaft (DEU ISSN 0341-0900) **1663**
Angewandte Carabidologie (DEU ISSN 1437-0867) **838**
Angewandte Carabidologie. Supplement *see* Angewandte Carabidologie **838**
• ➤ Angewandte Chemie (DEU ISSN 0044-8249) **2050**
• ➤ Angewandte Chemie (International Edition) (DEU ISSN 1433-7851) **2050**
Angewandte Ethik (DEU) **6904**
Angewandte Festkoerperphysik (DEU ISSN 1616-3427) **7005**
Angewandte Linguistik aus Interdisziplinaerer Sicht (DEU ISSN 1861-8421) **5093**
Angewandte Medienforschung (DEU) **2312**
▼ • Angewandte Schmerztherapie und Palliativmedizin (DEU ISSN 1866-1424) **5770**
Angewandte Sozialforschung (AUT ISSN 0587-5234) **8087**
Angewandte Sprach- und Uebersetzungswissenschaft (DEU ISSN 1619-6406) **5093**
Angewandte Sprachwissenschaft (DEU ISSN 1435-4365) **5093**
Angewandte Statistik und Oekonometrie (DEU ISSN 0720-8227) **1535**
Angewandte Versicherungsmathematik (DEU ISSN 0178-8116) **4492**
• ➤ Angiogenesis (NLD ISSN 0969-6970) **6008**
• Angiogenesis Weekly (USA ISSN 1531-6416) **6820**
• Angiologia (ESP ISSN 0003-3170) **5777**
Angiologiya i Sosudistaya Khirurgiya/Angiology and Vascular Surgery (RUS ISSN 1027-6661) **6236**
• ➤ Angiology (USA ISSN 0003-3197) **5777**
Angiology (Spanish Edition) *see* Angiology **5777**
Angiology and Vascular Surgery *see* Angiologiya i Sosudistaya Khirurgiya **6236**
Angiology Frontier (JPN ISSN 1347-6874) **5777**
Angiosperm Taxonomy (IND) **775**
Anglais de Specialite *see* ASp **5096**
Angle (JPN) **3899**
• ➤ Angle Orthodontist (USA ISSN 0003-3219) **5834**
• Angler News (AUS) **3584**
Anglers' Conservation Association Review *see* A C A Review **3582**
Anglers Guide to Ireland (IRL) **8683**
Angler's Mail (GBR ISSN 0003-3243) **8303**
➤ Angles on the English-Speaking World (DNK ISSN 0903-1723) **5093**
Anglesey Antiquarian Society Transactions (GBR ISSN 0306-5790) **373**
Anglesey Visitor (GBR ISSN 1754-1824) **8683**
• Anglia (DEU ISSN 0340-5222) **5093**
Anglia Auto Trader (GBR ISSN 0958-2495) **8556**
Anglia Builder (GBR) **976**
• Anglia Business (GBR) **1059**
Anglia Farmer and Contractor (GBR) **91**
Anglia Industry & Business *see* Anglia Business **1059**
Anglia Property Guide (GBR ISSN 1473-3986) **7582**
• Anglian Water. Annual Report and Account (GBR) **8818**
Anglica Germanica: Series 2 (GBR) **5094**
• Anglican (CAN ISSN 0517-7731) **7745**
Anglican Advance (USA ISSN 1059-6763) **7745**
• ➤ Anglican and Episcopal History (USA ISSN 0896-8039) **7745**
Anglican Church Directory (CAN ISSN 1193-9737) **7745**
Anglican Church of Australia. Diocese of Grafton. Year Book (AUS ISSN 1833-7899) **7745**
Anglican Church of Canada. General Synod. Journal (CAN ISSN 0826-3205) **7745**
Anglican Digest (USA ISSN 0003-3278) **7745**
Anglican Encounter (AUS ISSN 1032-9234) **7745**
The Anglican Gazette (AUS) **7745**
• The Anglican Guardian (Online) (AUS) **7745**
Anglican Historical Society (Diocese of Sydney). Journal (AUS ISSN 1443-5993) **7745**
• Anglican Journal/Journal Anglican (CAN ISSN 0847-978X) **7745**
Anglican Messenger (AUS) **7746**
• The Anglican Peacemaker (GBR ISSN 1474-4902) **7746**
• ➤ Anglican Theological Review (USA ISSN 0003-3286) **7746**
Anglicans for Renewal (GBR) **7746**
Angliiskii Yazyk (RUS) **5094**
Angliiskii Yazyk dlya Detei (RUS) **5094**
• Angling Europe (GBR) **8271**
Angling Guide (GBR ISSN 0956-5477) **8303**
The Angling Report (USA ISSN 1045-3539) **8303**
Angling Times (GBR ISSN 0003-3308) **8303**
Anglistentag (DEU) **5094**
Anglistica (DNK ISSN 0066-1805) **5254**
Anglistica Pisana (ITA ISSN 1827-4951) **5254**
Anglistik (DEU ISSN 0947-0034) **5254**
Anglistik und Englischunterricht. Neue Folge (DEU) **5094**
Anglistische Forschungen (DEU ISSN 0179-1389) **5254**
Anglistische Studien (DEU ISSN 0570-0930) **5254**
Anglistische und Amerikanistische Texte und Studien (DEU ISSN 0179-9207) **5254**
† Anglo-American Forum (DEU ISSN 0170-8163) **8930**
Anglo-American Studies *see* Anglo-Amerikanische Studien **5254**
Anglo-Amerikanische Studien/Anglo-American Studies (DEU ISSN 0177-6959) **5254**
Anglo-Australian Observatory. Annual Report (AUS ISSN 1443-8550) **568**
Anglo-Australian Observatory Newsletter *see* A A O Newsletter **567**
The Anglo-Boer War Philatelist (GBR ISSN 0269-9249) **6891**
• ➤ Anglo-Catalan Society. Occasional Publications (GBR ISSN 0144-5863) **4198**
The Anglo-Celt (IRL ISSN 1649-0290) **3892**
Anglo-Celtic Roots (CAN ISSN 1201-3072) **3758**
• ➤ Anglo-Israel Archaeological Society. Bulletin (GBR ISSN 0266-2442) **373**
Anglo-Mauritius Assurance Society Limited. Annual Report (MUS ISSN 1694-0431) **1307**
Anglo-Nordic Times International (GBR ISSN 1350-4819) **1552**
Anglo-Norman Studies (GBR ISSN 0954-9927) **4198**
Anglo-Norman Text Society. Annual Texts Series (GBR ISSN 0066-183X) **5254**
➤ Anglo-Norman Text Society. Occasional Publications Series (GBR) **4198**
Anglo Nytt (SWE ISSN 1653-9117) **8287**
Anglo-Portuguese News (PRT) **3518**
Anglo-Russian Affinities (GBR ISSN 1354-3709) **7221**
• Anglo-Saxon England (GBR ISSN 0263-6751) **4198**
Anglo-Saxon Studies in Archaeology and History (GBR ISSN 0264-5254) **373**
• Anglo-Spanish Quarterly Review (GBR ISSN 0003-3383) **7221**
Anglo-Spanish Trade Directory/Directorio Comercial Hispano Britanico (GBR) **1395**
Anglofile (USA) **6489**
• ➤ Anglogermanica Online (ESP ISSN 1695-6168) **5094**
➤ Anglophonia (FRA ISSN 1278-3331) **5254**
Angola. Direccao dos Servicos de Estatistica. Anuario Estatistico (AGO ISSN 0066-5193) **8345**
Angola. Direccao dos Servicos de Estatistica. Boletim Mensal (AGO ISSN 0003-3413) **8345**
Angola. Direccao dos Servicos de Estatistica. Estatistica dos Veiculos Motorisados (AGO) **8521**
Angola. Direccao dos Servicos de Estatistica. Estatisticas do Comercio Externo (AGO ISSN 0066-1848) **1200**
Angola. Direccao dos Servicos de Estatistica. Informacoes Estatisticas (AGO) **8345**
Angola. Direccao Provincial dos Servicos de Geologia e Minas. Boletim (AGO ISSN 0003-3456) **2724**
Angola. Instituto Nacional de Estatistica. Unidade de Analise Demografica. Boletim Demografico (AGO) **7276**
Angola. Ministerio da Saude. Departamento de Estatistica. Relatorio Estatistico (AGO) **7276**
• Angola Monitor (GBR) **7221**
Angola Peace Monitor *see* Angola Monitor **7221**
• The Angolan Mission Observer (USA) **3790**
Angolite (USA ISSN 0402-4249) **2643**
Angora Goat & Mohair Journal/Angorabok- en Sybokhaarblad (ZAF ISSN 0003-3464) **278**
Angora Goat Exchange (USA) **278**
Angorabok- en Sybokhaarblad *see* Angora Goat & Mohair Journal **278**
• Angry Monkey (USA) **5206**
Angry Thoreauan (USA) **5206**
Angus (USA) **278**
Angus Beef Bulletin (USA ISSN 1524-8488) **278**
• Angus Council. Housing Plan (GBR) **4403**
Angus Herd Book of New Zealand (NZL ISSN 0300-3345) **278**
• Angus Journal (USA ISSN 0194-9543) **278**
Angus Topics (USA ISSN 0402-4265) **278**
Anhoerig (SWE ISSN 0280-512X) **2692**
Anhui Agricultural College. Journal *see* Anhui Nongxueyuan Xuebao **91**
Anhui Agricultural Science *see* Anhui Nongye Kexue **91**
Anhui Agricultural University. Journal *see* Anhui Nongye Daxue Xuebao **7835**
Anhui Agricultural University. Journal (Social Sciences Edition) *see* Anhui Nongye Daxue Xuebao (Shehui Kexue Ban) **7947**
Anhui Almanac *see* Anhui Nianjian **3118**
Anhui Business Daily *see* Anhui Shangbao **1059**
Anhui Caikuai/Anhui Finance & Accounting (CHN ISSN 1003-8248) **1280**
Anhui Chemical Industry *see* Anhui Huagong **3236**
Anhui Communications News *see* Anhui Jiaotongbao **8490**
Anhui Dangshi Yanjiu *see* Dangshi Zonglan **7128**
• Anhui Daxue Xuebao (Zhexue Shehui Kexue Ban)/Anhui University. Journal (Philosophy and Social Sciences) (CHN ISSN 1001-5019) **7947**
• Anhui Daxue Xuebao (Ziran Kexue Ban)/Anhui University. Journal (Natural Science Edition) (CHN ISSN 1000-2162) **7835**
Anhui Education *see* Anhui Jiaoyu **2826**
Anhui Fazhibao/Anhui Legal System (CHN) **4617**
Anhui Finance & Accounting *see* Anhui Caikuai **1280**
Anhui Fire Protection *see* Anhui Xiaofang **8930**
• Anhui Gongye Daxue Xuebao (Shehui Kexue Ban)/Anhui University of Technology. Journal (Social Sciences Edition) (CHN ISSN 1671-9247) **7947**
• Anhui Guangbo Dianshi Daxue Xuebao/Anhui Radio & TV University. Journal (CHN ISSN 1008-6021) **2375**
Anhui Health Vocational & Technical College. Journal *see* Anhui Weisheng Zhiye Jishu Xueyuan Xuebao **5574**
• Anhui Huabao/Anhui Pictorial (CHN ISSN 1007-0141) **3822**
• Anhui Huagong/Anhui Chemical Industry (CHN ISSN 1008-553X) **3236**
Anhui Institute of Architecture Industry. Journal *see* Anhui Jianzhu Gongye Xueyuan Xuebao (Ziran Kexue Ban) **7835**
Anhui Institute of Education. Journal (Philosophy and Social Science Edition) *see* Anhui Jiaoyu Xueyuan Xuebao (Shehui Kexue Ban) **2826**
Anhui Institute of Mechanical and Electrical Engineering. Journal *see* Anhui Jidian Xueyuan Xuebao **3373**
• Anhui Jianzhu Gongye Xueyuan Xuebao (Ziran Kexue Ban)/Anhui Institute of Architecture Industry. Journal (CHN ISSN 1006-4540) **7835**
Anhui Jiaotongbao/Anhui Communications News (CHN) **8490**
Anhui Jiaoyu/Anhui Education (CHN ISSN 1005-6149) **2826**
• Anhui Jiaoyu Xueyuan Xuebao (Shehui Kexue Ban)/Anhui Institute of Education. Journal (Philosophy and Social Science Edition) (CHN ISSN 1001-5116) **2826**
• Anhui Jidian Xueyuan Xuebao/Anhui Institute of Mechanical and Electrical Engineering. Journal (CHN ISSN 1007-5240) **3373**
Anhui Journal of Preventive Medicine *see* Anhui Yufang Yixue Zazhi **5574**
Anhui Keji/Anhui Science & Technology (CHN ISSN 1007-7855) **7835**
Anhui Keji yu Qiye/Anhui Technology and Enterprises (CHN ISSN 1007-3981) **8416**
Anhui Legal System *see* Anhui Fazhibao **4617**
• Anhui Ligong Daxue Xuebao/Anhui University of Science and Technology. Journal (Natural Science) (CHN ISSN 1672-1098) **7835**
Anhui Medical Sciences *see* Anhui Yixue **5574**
Anhui Nianjian/Anhui Almanac (CHN ISSN 1004-5252) **3118**
Anhui Nongcun Tongxun (CHN ISSN 1003-966X) **91**
• Anhui Nongxueyuan Xuebao/Anhui Agricultural College. Journal (CHN ISSN 1000-2197) **91**
• Anhui Nongye Daxue Xuebao/Anhui Agricultural University. Journal (CHN ISSN 1672-352X) **7835**
• Anhui Nongye Daxue Xuebao (Shehui Kexue Ban)/Anhui Agricultural University. Journal (Social Sciences Edition) (CHN ISSN 1009-2463) **7947**
• Anhui Nongye Kexue/Anhui Agricultural Science (CHN ISSN 0517-6611) **91**
Anhui Normal University. Journal *see* Anhui Shida Xuebao **7835**
Anhui Normal University. Journal (Philosophy and Social Sciences Edition) *see* Anhui Shida Xuebao (Zhe She Ban) **7947**
Anhui Pictorial *see* Anhui Huabao **3822**
Anhui Radio & TV University. Journal *see* Anhui Guangbo Dianshi Daxue Xuebao **2375**
Anhui Ribao/Ahjui Daily (CHN) **3822**
Anhui Ribao (Hedinben) *see* Anhui Ribao **3822**
Anhui Science & Technology *see* Anhui Keji **7835**
• Anhui Shangbao/Anhui Business Daily (CHN) **1059**
• Anhui Shida Xuebao/Anhui Normal University. Journal (CHN ISSN 1001-2443) **7835**
• Anhui Shida Xuebao (Zhe She Ban)/Anhui Normal University. Journal (Philosophy and Social Sciences Edition) (CHN ISSN 1001-2435) **7947**
• Anhui Shixue/Historiography Research in Anhui (CHN ISSN 1005-605X) **4179**
† Anhui Shuiwu (CHN ISSN 1005-6181) **8930**
Anhui Technology and Enterprises *see* Anhui Keji yu Qiye **8416**
Anhui Traditional Chinese Medical College. Journal *see* Anhui Zhongyi Xueyuan Xuebao **5574**
Anhui University. Journal (Natural Science Edition) *see* Anhui Daxue Xuebao (Ziran Kexue Ban) **7835**
Anhui University. Journal (Philosophy and Social Sciences) *see* Anhui Daxue Xuebao (Zhexue Shehui Kexue Ban) **7947**
Anhui University of Science and Technology. Journal (Natural Science) *see* Anhui Ligong Daxue Xuebao **7835**
Anhui University of Technology. Journal (Natural Science Edition) *see* Anhui Gongye Daxue Xuebao (Ziran Kexue Ban) **6304**
Anhui University of Technology. Journal (Social Sciences Edition) *see* Anhui Gongye Daxue Xuebao (Shehui Kexue Ban) **7947**
• Anhui Weisheng Zhiye Jishu Xueyuan Xuebao/Anhui Health Vocational & Technical College. Journal (CHN ISSN 1671-8054) **5574**
† Anhui Xiaofang/Anhui Fire Protection (CHN ISSN 1003-756X) **8930**
Anhui Xin Xi (CHN) **8465**
• Anhui Yike Daxue Xuebao/Acta Universitatis Medicinalis Anhui (CHN ISSN 1000-1492) **5574**
• Anhui Yixue/Anhui Medical Sciences (CHN ISSN 1000-0399) **5574**
Anhui Yufang Yixue Zazhi/Anhui Journal of Preventive Medicine (CHN ISSN 1007-1040) **5574**

DIRECTORY 2010 ANNALES DE DROIT AERIEN ET SPATIAL 9959

• Anhui Zhengbao/Journal of the Anhui (CHN ISSN 1009-0746) **7420**
• Anhui Zhongyi Xueyuan Xuebao/Anhui Traditional Chinese Medical College. Journal (CHN ISSN 1000-2219) **5574**
➤ Ani (PHL ISSN 0116-4791) **5255**
Anichti Orizontes - Angheliaforos (GRC) **7783**
• ➤ Anil Aggrawal's Internet Journal of Forensic Medicine and Toxicology (IND ISSN 0972-8074) **5912**
Anima (FRA ISSN 0180-1430) **2272**
Anima (ITA ISSN 1126-0661) **7334**
Anima Mundi (ITA ISSN 1594-9745) **4443**
Animagi (SWE ISSN 1651-694X) **6489**
Animais e Cia (BRA ISSN 1413-5507) **6803**
▼ • ➤ Animal (GBR ISSN 1751-7311) **932**
Animal Action (GBR ISSN 1354-7437) **317**
Animal Activist Alert (USA ISSN 1045-9979) **317**
Animal and Animal Products Outlook *see* Agri-Food Perspectives **81**
Animal Anti-Cruelty League. Chairman's Report (ZAF ISSN 0379-654X) **317**
▼ Animal Attitude (FRA ISSN 1959-173X) **6803**
• Animal Behavior Abstracts (USA ISSN 0301-8695) **712**
• ➤ Animal Behaviour (GBR ISSN 0003-3472) **932**
• ➤ Animal Biodiversity and Conservation (ESP ISSN 1578-665X) **932**
• ➤ Animal Biology (NLD ISSN 1570-7555) **932**
Animal Biotechnology (Online Edition) *see* Animal Biotechnology (Print Edition) **755**
• ➤ Animal Biotechnology (Print Edition) (USA ISSN 1049-5398) **755**
• Animal Breeding Abstracts (GBR ISSN 0003-3499) **174**
Animal Cell Technology (NLD) **827**
• Animal Cells and Systems (KOR ISSN 1976-8354) **932**
• ➤ Animal Cognition (DEU ISSN 1435-9448) **7334**
Animal Concern. Annual Report (GBR) **317**
• Animal Concern News (GBR) **317**
Animal Concern News Update (GBR) **317**
• ➤ Animal Conservation (GBR ISSN 1367-9430) **2602**
Animal Damage Control *see* Animal Damage Management **218**
Animal Damage Management (USA) **218**
Animal Defence League of Canada. Bulletin (CAN ISSN 1204-6639) **317**
Animal Defender & Campaigner (GBR ISSN 1748-5452) **317**
Animal Distribution (FRA ISSN 0246-1854) **6803**
Animal Experimentation. Improvements and Alternatives *see* Alternatives to Laboratory Animals **5902**
Animal Fair (USA ISSN 1525-3309) **6803**
• ➤ Animal Feed Science and Technology (NLD ISSN 0377-8401) **270**
➤ Animal Feeding and Nutrition (USA) **8792**
Animal Feedstuffs *see* Key Note Market Report: Animal Feedstuffs **273**
Animal Feedstuffs Market Report *see* Key Note Market Report: Animal Feedstuffs **273**
Animal Finders' Guide (USA) **278**
Animal Genetic Resources Information/Boletin de Informacion Sobre Recursos Geneticos Animales/Bulletin d'Information sur les Resources Genetiques Animales (FRA ISSN 1014-2339) **862**
• ➤ Animal Genetics (GBR ISSN 0268-9146) **862**
Animal Guardian (USA ISSN 1061-4141) **317**
Animal Health (GBR ISSN 0266-8629) **278**
• Animal Health (Online Edition) (USA) **278**
Animal Health (Print Edition) *see* Animal Health (Online Edition) **278**
Animal Health Advisory Leaflet (NCL ISSN 1019-8458) **8792**
• Animal Health Board. Annual Research Report (NZL ISSN 1177-6986) **8792**
• Animal Health in Australia (AUS ISSN 1322-7084) **8792**
• Animal Health in Denmark (DNK ISSN 1902-5599) **278**
Animal Health Laboratory User's Guide and Fee Schedule (CAN ISSN 1910-1996) **8792**
Animal Health. Proceedings (PAK ISSN 1728-9521) **8792**
Animal Health Research Centre. Annual Report (UGA) **8792**
• ➤ Animal Health Research Reviews (GBR ISSN 1466-2523) **8792**
• Animal Health Sciences Newsletter (AUS ISSN 1832-567X) **8792**
• Animal Health Surveillance Quarterly Reports (AUS ISSN 1445-9701) **317**
Animal Health Technician Dental Newsletter *see* Journal of Veterinary Dentistry **8801**
• Animal Health Trust. Annual Review (GBR) **8792**
Animal Hebdo *see* Magazine Animal **6811**
Animal Husbandry *see* Chikusan no Kenkyu **284**
Animal Husbandry. Proceedings (PAK ISSN 1728-9505) **317**
Animal Industry Foundation Newsletter *see* A I F Newsletter **276**
Animal Issues *see* Animal Issues Digest **317**
➤ Animal Issues Digest (USA) **317**
➤ Animal Keepers' Forum (USA ISSN 0164-9531) **932**
• Animal Lab News (USA ISSN 1552-5694) **8792**
• Animal Law (USA ISSN 1088-8802) **317**
Animal Law Conference (USA ISSN 1942-2857) **317**
Animal Law Review *see* Animal Law **317**
Animal Law Seminar *see* Animal Law Conference **317**
• Animal Legal Report (USA ISSN 1933-2807) **317**
• Animal Liberation Philosophy and Policy Journal (USA ISSN 1933-8325) **317**
Animal Life (GBR ISSN 0964-4628) **317**
• Animal Life (USA) **318**
Animal Life of Denmark *see* Danmarks Dyreliv **8948**
Animal Medical Center CenterScope *see* A M C CenterScope **6802**
Animal Natural History Series (USA) **7835**
• Animal Nutrition and Feed Technology (IND ISSN 0972-2963) **318**
Animal Nutrition Association of Canada. Eastern Nutrition Conference. Proceedings (CAN ISSN 1497-2727) **278**
Animal People (USA ISSN 1071-0035) **318**
• Animal Pharm (GBR ISSN 0262-2238) **8792**
Animal Production and Health Newsletter (AUT ISSN 1011-2529) **6192**
• ➤ Animal Production in Australia (CD-ROM) (AUS) **278**
• ➤ Animal Production Research Advances (NGA ISSN 0794-4721) **278**
• ➤ Animal Production Science (AUS ISSN 1836-0939) **218**
• ➤ Animal Reproduction (BRA ISSN 1806-9614) **932**
• ➤ Animal Reproduction Science (NLD ISSN 0378-4320) **278**
Animal Reproduction Techniques/Hanshoku Gijutsu (JPN ISSN 0017-7520) **278**
Animal Research *see* Animal **932**
Animal Rights (Farmington Hills) *see* Information Plus Reference Series. Animal Rights **320**
▼ Animal Sante & Bien-Etre (FRA ISSN 1957-1488) **6803**
Animal Science *see* Animal **932**
• ➤ Animal Science Journal (AUS ISSN 1344-3941) **278**
• ➤ Animal Science Papers and Reports (POL ISSN 0860-4037) **278**
Animal Sheltering (USA) **318**
Animal Sospechoso (ESP ISSN 1695-3924) **5416**
Animal Talk *see* Animaltalk **318**
Animal Talk (ZAF) **6803**
• Animal Technology and Welfare (GBR ISSN 1742-0385) **8792**
Animal Transportation Association. International Conference. Proceedings (USA ISSN 1054-0288) **8490**
• ➤ Animal Welfare (GBR ISSN 0962-7286) **318**
• Animal Welfare Information Center Bulletin (USA ISSN 1522-7553) **318**
Animal Welfare Information Center Resource Series *see* A W I C Resource Series **316**
Animal Welfare Institute Quarterly *see* A W I Quarterly **317**
Animal Wellness Magazine (CAN ISSN 1710-1190) **6803**
Animaldom (USA ISSN 0003-360X) **6803**
Animalerie (FRA ISSN 0296-6700) **6803**
Animalia (ESP ISSN 0214-3151) **6803**
Animalia (ITA ISSN 0391-7746) **932**
• AnimaLife (USA) **318**
AnimalNews (USA) **6803**
• Animals' Advocate (USA) **318**
Animals and You (GBR) **2176**
Animals and Zoos *see* Dobutsu to Dobutsuen **940**
Animals' Defender *see* Animal Defender & Campaigner **317**
Animals Exotic and Small *see* Rare Breeds Journal **6814**
Animal's Eye Research *see* Hikaku Ganka Kenkyu **6043**
Animals International (GBR ISSN 0254-3923) **318**
• Animals Today (AUS ISSN 1320-2464) **318**
Animals' Voice (CAN ISSN 0700-8392) **318**
Animaltalk (CAN ISSN 1192-4861) **318**
Animaltown News (USA) **6803**
Animan (CHE) **3998**
The Animated Stories From the Bible (GBR ISSN 1747-101X) **7621**
• ➤ Animation (GBR ISSN 1746-8477) **6489**
Animation & Education *see* Animation et Education **2826**
• Animation Blast (USA) **5206**
Animation Directory *see* Imagine Animation Directory **6503**
Animation et Education (FRA ISSN 0395-0840) **2826**
Animation Invaders (BRA ISSN 1808-9356) **466**
• Animation Journal (USA ISSN 1061-0308) **6489**
• Animation Magazine (USA ISSN 1041-617X) **466**
Animation U K (Quarterly edition) *see* Imagine **6503**
Animation UK *see* Imagine Animation Directory **6503**
Animations *see* Animations in Print **8465**
• Animations in Print (GBR ISSN 1754-3053) **8465**
➤ Animatrix (USA ISSN 1069-2088) **6489**
▼ Animaux et Nature (FRA ISSN 1959-4437) **933**
Animaux Magazine (FRA ISSN 0986-3354) **318**
Animazione Sociale (ITA ISSN 0392-5870) **8087**
• @nime! (USA ISSN 1945-8479) **466**
Anime Do (BRA ISSN 1516-9960) **466**
Anime-do *see* Anime Do **466**
Anime News Network *see* Protoculture Addicts **513**
Anime Play (USA) **4327**
Animedia (JPN) **466**
AnimeFantastique (USA ISSN 1521-7205) **6489**
Animer (FRA ISSN 1252-3224) **1436**
• Animerica (USA ISSN 1067-0831) **466**
Animerica Extra (USA ISSN 1533-1822) **466**
Animo (NLD ISSN 0003-3669) **2272**
• ➤ Animus (CAN ISSN 1209-0689) **6904**
▼ Ani's Green Pages (CAN ISSN 1913-4304) **3403**
Anishinabek News (CAN ISSN 1182-3178) **3518**
• ➤ Anistoriton (GRC ISSN 1108-4081) **4130**
Anitekkusu/Laboratory Animal Technology and Science (JPN ISSN 0915-3667) **5902**
Anja (SVN ISSN 1580-1446) **8851**
• Anjisuan He Shengwu Ziyuan/Amino Acids and Biotic Resources (CHN ISSN 1006-8376) **2050**
Anjoman-i Riyazi-i Iran. Bulitan-i *see* Iranian Mathematical Society. Bulletin **5498**
Anjou Agricole (FRA) **91**
L'Anjou Eco (FRA ISSN 1959-5379) **1395**
Anjou Economique *see* L' Anjou Eco **1395**
† ➤ Anka (FRA ISSN 0992-0285) **8930**
Anka Review/Turkey's Economic and Financial Weekly (TUR ISSN 1301-2002) **1059**
• Ankang Shi-Zhuan Xuebao/Ankang Teachers College. Journal (CHN ISSN 1009-024X) **2826**
Ankang Teachers College. Journal *see* Ankang Shi-Zhuan Xuebao **2826**
• Ankara Medical School. Journal (TUR ISSN 1300-5464) **5574**
Ankara Universitesi. Dil ve Tarih-Cografya Fakultesi Dergisi (TUR ISSN 0378-2905) **4319**
Ankara Universitesi. Eczacilik Fakultesi. Dergisi/Ankara University. Faculty of Pharmacy. Journal (TUR ISSN 1015-3918) **6820**
• Ankara Universitesi. Siyasal Bilgiler Fakultesi Dergisi (TUR ISSN 0378-2921) **7106**
• ➤ Ankara Universitesi. Tip Fakultesi. Mecmuasi/University of Ankara. Faculty of Medicine. Journal (TUR ISSN 0365-8104) **5574**
Ankara Universitesi. Tip Fakultesi. Mecmuasi. Supplementum *see* Ankara Universitesi. Tip Fakultesi. Mecmuasi **5574**
Ankara Universitesi Veteriner Fakultesi Dergisi/University of Ankara. Faculty of Veterinary Medicine. Journal (TUR ISSN 1300-0861) **8792**
• Ankara University. Faculty of Educational Sciences. Journal (TUR ISSN 1301-3718) **2826**
Ankara University. Faculty of Pharmacy. Journal *see* Ankara Universitesi. Eczacilik Fakultesi. Dergisi **6820**
• Ankem Dergisi/Journal of Ankem (TUR ISSN 1301-3114) **5943**
Anker Magazin (DEU) **8303**
• Ankulegi (ESP ISSN 1138-347X) **324**
Ankyou Nyusu *see* Boira Kuren Yousetsu no Jitsu Ten **5450**
Ankyra (GRC ISSN 1109-1681) **4130**
Anlaeg Brutto (DNK ISSN 0904-3616) **976**
Anlaeg Netto (DNK ISSN 0904-3594) **976**
• Anlaegsplan (Year) for El- Gastransmission i Danmark (DNK ISSN 1902-1186) **3295**
Anlaegsplan (Year) for Eltransmission i Danmark *see* Anlaegsplan (Year) for El- Gastransmission i Danmark **3295**
Anlaegsplan (Year) for Transmissionssystemet *see* Anlaegsplan (Year) for El- Gastransmission i Danmark **3295**
Anlagefonds *see* Finanz und Wirtschaft **1624**
Anlagen- und Betriebssicherheit (DEU ISSN 1610-2835) **6672**
Anlegg & Transport (NOR ISSN 0800-6504) **3181**
Anleggsmaskinen (NOR ISSN 0003-3715) **976**
AnMal Electronica *see* Analecta Malacitana **5093**
Ann Arbor Business Review (USA ISSN 1932-2712) **1059**
Ann Arbor Magazine (USA ISSN 1542-782X) **3969**
Ann Arbor Observer (USA ISSN 0192-5717) **3969**
The Ann Craft Trust Bulletin (GBR) **8025**
† Anna (CZE) **8930**
Anna (DEU ISSN 0937-3527) **8851**
Anna (FIN ISSN 0355-3035) **8851**
Anna (FRA ISSN 0243-3672) **6636**
Anna (POL) **8851**
Anna (RUS ISSN 1560-5507) **6636**
Anna (UKR) **6636**
Anna (English Edition) (ITA) **8851**
Anna (Italian Edition) (ITA ISSN 1120-4346) **8851**
Anna Ajourstickerei (DEU) **6636**
Anna Fensterbilder (DEU) **6636**
Anna Filethaekeln (DEU) **6636**
Anna Hardanger (DEU ISSN 0948-9061) **6636**
Anna Kauneus *see* Anna **8851**
Anna Kreuzstich (DEU ISSN 1614-9955) **6636**
Anna Ostern (DEU) **6636**
Anna Patchwork (DEU) **6637**
Anna Spitzenhaekeln (DEU ISSN 1430-2535) **6637**
Anna Weihnachten (DEU) **6637**
Anna Window Color (DEU) **531**
Annabelle (CHE ISSN 1421-5829) **8851**
Annabel's (GBR) **5064**
Annaeus (ESP ISSN 1699-7301) **4198**
Annalen der Meteorologie. Neue Folge (DEU ISSN 0072-4122) **6346**
• ➤ Annalen der Physik (DEU ISSN 0003-3804) **7005**
Annalen des Historischen Vereins fuer den Niederrhein insbesondere das alte Erzbistum Koeln *see* Historischen Vereins fuer den Niederrhein. Annalen **4228**
Annalen des Naturhistorischen Museums in Wien. Serie A *see* Naturhistorisches Museum in Wien. Annalen. Serie A, Mineralogie und Petrographie, Geologie und Palaeontologie, Anthropologie und Praehistorie **7889**
➤ Annales (Paris) (FRA ISSN 0395-2649) **8087**
Annales Academiae Cracoviensis. Studia Zoologica (POL ISSN 1644-1893) **933**
Annales Academiae Medicae Bialostocensis *see* Advances in Medical Sciences **5568**
Annales Academiae Medicae Gedanensis (POL ISSN 0303-4135) **5574**
Annales Academiae Medicae Silesiensis (POL ISSN 0208-5607) **5574**
Annales Academiae Medicae Stetinensis *see* Pomorska Akademia Medyczna w Szczecinie. Roczniki **5697**
➤ Annales Academiae Medicae Stetinensis. Suplement (POL ISSN 1427-4930) **5574**
Annales Academiae Paedagogicae Cracoviensis. Studia ad Bibliothecarum Scientiam Pertinentia (POL ISSN 1643-6539) **4989**
Annales Academiae Paedagogicae Cracoviensis. Studia ad Calculum Probabilitatis Eiusque Didacticam Pertinentia (POL ISSN 1644-1869) **5470**
Annales Academiae Paedagogicae Cracoviensis. Studia ad Educationem Defensoriam Pertinentia (POL ISSN 1734-9133) **2225**
Annales Academiae Paedagogicae Cracoviensis. Studia ad Institutionem et Educationem Pertinentia (POL ISSN 1895-751X) **2826**
Annales Academiae Paedagogicae Cracoviensis. Studia de Arte et Educatione (POL ISSN 1895-5118) **466**
Annales Academiae Paedagogicae Cracoviensis. Studia Historica (POL ISSN 1643-6547) **4130**
Annales Academiae Paedagogicae Cracoviensis. Studia Historicolitteraria (POL ISSN 1644-1885) **5255**
Annales Academiae Paedagogicae Cracoviensis. Studia Linguistica (POL ISSN 1644-1877) **5094**
Annales Academiae Paedagogicae Cracoviensis. Studia Logopaedica (POL ISSN 1896-1215) **3036**
Annales Academiae Paedagogicae Cracoviensis. Studia Mathematica (POL ISSN 1643-6555) **5470**
Annales Academiae Paedagogicae Cracoviensis. Studia Philosophica (POL ISSN 1644-793X) **6904**
Annales Academiae Paedagogicae Cracoviensis. Studia Politologica (POL ISSN 1644-7921) **7106**
Annales Academiae Paedagogicae Cracoviensis. Studia Psychologica (POL ISSN 1732-1085) **7334**
Annales Academiae Paedagogicae Cracoviensis. Studia Romanica (POL ISSN 1643-6520) **5094**
Annales Academiae Paedagogicae Cracoviensis. Studia Technica (POL ISSN 1896-1223) **8416**
Annales Academiae Regiae Scientiarum Upsaliensis (SWE ISSN 0504-0736) **7835**
Annales Academiae Scientiarum Fennicae. Chemica (FIN ISSN 1239-6311) **2050**
➤ Annales Academiae Scientiarum Fennicae. Geologica-Geographica (FIN ISSN 1239-632X) **2724**
• ➤ Annales Academiae Scientiarum Fennicae. Mathematica (FIN ISSN 1239-629X) **5470**
• Annales Academiae Scientiarum Fennicae. Mathematica Dissertationes (FIN ISSN 1239-6303) **5470**
➤ Annales Academiae Scientiarum Fennicae. Series Humaniora (FIN ISSN 1239-6982) **4443**
• Annales Aequatoria (BEL ISSN 0254-4296) **324**
Annales Africaines (SEN) **4617**
➤ Annales Benjamin Constant (CHE ISSN 0263-7383) **4443**
• ➤ Annales Botanici Fennici (FIN ISSN 0003-3847) **775**
Annales Canadiennes d'Histoire *see* Canadian Journal of History **4134**
Annales Chirurgiae et Gynaecologiae Fenniae. Supplementum *see* Annales Chirurgiae et Gynaecologiae. Supplementum **6236**
Annales Chirurgiae et Gynaecologiae. Supplementum (FIN ISSN 0355-9874) **6236**
Annales Collegii Medici Universitatis Iagiellonicae Cracoviensis (POL ISSN 1232-9371) **5740**
Annales de Biochimie Clinique du Quebec *see* Annales de Biologie Clinique du Quebec **5902**
• ➤ Annales de Biologie Clinique (FRA ISSN 0003-3898) **653**
Annales de Biologie Clinique du Quebec (CAN ISSN 1705-6322) **5902**
Annales de Bourgogne (FRA ISSN 0003-3901) **4198**
† Annales de Bretagne et des Pays de l'Ouest (FRA ISSN 0399-0826) **8930**
• ➤ Annales de Cardiologie et d'Angeiologie (FRA ISSN 0003-3928) **5777**
• ➤ Annales de Chimie, Science des Materiaux (FRA ISSN 0151-9107) **2050**
Annales de Chirurgie *see* Journal de Chirurgie **6247**
• Annales de Chirurgie Plastique Esthetique (FRA ISSN 0294-1260) **6236**
Annales de Chirurgie Plastique et Esthetique *see* Annales de Chirurgie Plastique Esthetique **6236**
• ➤ Annales de Chirurgie Vasculaire (FRA ISSN 0299-2213) **6236**
• Annales de Demographie Historique (FRA ISSN 0066-2062) **7276**
Annales de Demographie Historique D H *see* Annales de Demographie Historique **7276**
• ➤ Annales de Dermatologie et de Venereologie (FRA ISSN 0151-9638) **5871**
Annales de Droit Aerien et Spatial *see* Annals of Air and Space Law **46**

▼ *new title* † *ceased* • *electronic media* ➤ *refereed*

Title

9960 ANNALES DE DROIT DE LOUVAIN ULRICH'S PERIODICALS

➤ Annales de Droit de Louvain (BEL ISSN 0770-6472) **4917**
Annales de Genetique *see* European Journal of Medical Genetics **866**
• Annales de Geographie (FRA ISSN 0003-4010) **3998**
Annales de Geomorphologie *see* Zeitschrift fuer Geomorphologie **2776**
▼ • ➤ Annales de Gerontologie (FRA ISSN 1968-0805) **4040**
➤ Annales de la Recherche Forestiere au Maroc (MAR ISSN 0483-8009) **3683**
Annales de la Voirie (FRA ISSN 1151-5430) **4617**
➤ Annales de l'I S U P (FRA ISSN 1626-1607) **5548**
• ➤ Annales de Limnologie (FRA ISSN 0003-4088) **2792**
Annales de l'Institut Fourier *see* Institut Fourier. Annales **5493**
† Annales de Medecine et de Chirurgie (FRA ISSN 0398-7701) **8930**
• ➤ Annales de Medecine Veterinaire (Online Edition) (BEL ISSN 1781-3875) **8792**
Annales de Medecine Veterinaire (Print Edition) *see* Annales de Medecine Veterinaire (Online Edition) **8792**
Annales de Normandie (FRA ISSN 0003-4134) **4198**
Annales de Normandie. Cahiers *see* Annales de Normandie **4198**
• ➤ Annales de Paleontologie (FRA ISSN 0753-3969) **6723**
• ➤ Annales de Pathologie (FRA ISSN 0242-6498) **653**
Annales de Physique *see* European Physical Journal H **7011**
Annales de Readaptation et de Medecine Physique *see* Annals of Physical and Rehabilitation Medicine **6106**
Annales de Toxicologie Analytique *see* Toxicologie Analytique. Annales **2106**
• ➤ Annales d'Endocrinologie (FRA ISSN 0003-4266) **5883**
➤ Annales des Falsifications de l'Expertise Chimique et Toxicologique (FRA ISSN 0242-6110) **3493**
Annales des Mines et de la Geologie (TUN ISSN 0365-4397) **2724**
➤ Annales des Sciences Mathematiques du Quebec (CAN ISSN 0707-9109) **5470**
• ➤ Annales des Telecommunications/Annals of Telecommunications (FRA ISSN 0003-4347) **2312**
Annales des Travaux Publics de Belgique/Tijdschrift der Openbare Werken van Belgie (BEL ISSN 0373-0891) **3259**
Annales d'Esthetique *see* Chronika Aisthetikes **6910**
Annales d'Ethiopie (ETH ISSN 0066-2127) **373**
Annales d'Histoire Caledonienne (FRA ISSN 1774-5373) **4191**
Annales d'Histoire de l'Art Canadien *see* The Journal of Canadian Art History **498**
Annales d'Histoire Sociale et Economiques *see* Roczniki Dziejow Spolecznych i Gospodarczych **4259**
• Annales d'Oto-Laryngologie et de Chirurgie Cervico Faciale (FRA ISSN 0003-438X) **6077**
Annales du Batiment et des Travaux Publics (FRA ISSN 1270-9840) **976**
† Annales du Levant (FRA ISSN 0980-5842) **8930**
Annales du Midi (FRA ISSN 0003-4398) **373**
Annales du Museum du Havre (FRA ISSN 0335-5160) **6519**
† Annales du Tabac. Section 1 (FRA ISSN 0399-0206) **8930**
† Annales du Tabac. Section 2 (FRA ISSN 0399-0354) **8930**
† • ➤ Annales d'Urologie (FRA ISSN 0003-4401) **8930**
Annales Forestales/Anali za Sumarstvo (HRV ISSN 1330-2728) **3683**
• ➤ Annales Francaises d'Anesthesie et de Reanimation (FRA ISSN 0750-7658) **5770**
Annales Francaises de Microtechniques et de Chronometrie (FRA ISSN 0294-1228) **3374**
Annales Geologiques de la Peninsule Balkanique *see* Geoloski Anali Balkanskoga Poluostrva **2742**
Annales Geologiques des Pays Helleniques (GRC ISSN 1105-0004) **2724**
• ➤ Annales Geophysicae (DEU ISSN 0992-7689) **2777**
• ➤ Annales Henri Poincare (CHE ISSN 1424-0637) **7005**
Annales Hindemith *see* Hindemith - Jahrbuch **6573**
Annales Historico-Naturales Musei Nationalis Hungarici *see* Musei Nationalis Hungarici. Annales Historico-Naturales **7883**
• Annales Historiques de la Revolution Francaise (FRA ISSN 0003-4436) **4198**
Annales Hydrographiques (FRA ISSN 0373-3629) **8638**
Annales Internationales de Criminologie/Anales Internacionales de Criminologia/International Annals of Criminology (FRA ISSN 0003-4452) **2643**
• Annales Islamologiques (EGY ISSN 0570-1716) **7709**
Annales Jean-Jacques Rousseau (CHE ISSN 0259-6563) **5255**
Annales Mathematicae Silesianae *see* Uniwersytet Slaski w Katowicach. Prace Naukowe. Annales Mathematicae Silesianae **5545**
Annales Mathematiques Blaise Pascal (FRA ISSN 1259-1734) **5470**
Annales Medicales de Lorraine (FRA ISSN 1622-2350) **5574**
Annales Medicinae Militaris Fenniae *see* Sotilaslaaketieteellinen Aikakauslehti **5716**
• ➤ Annales Medico-Psychologiques (FRA ISSN 0003-4487) **7334**
Annales Medico-Psychologiques, Revue Psychiatrique *see* Annales Medico-Psychologiques **7334**
Annales Monegasques (MCO ISSN 0257-960X) **4198**
Annales Musei Archaeologici Posnaniensis *see* Fontes Archaeologici Posnanienses **393**
Annales Musei Goulandris (GRC ISSN 0302-1033) **6519**
• Annales Nestle (English Edition) (CHE ISSN 0517-8606) **5574**
• Annales Nestle (French Edition) (CHE ISSN 0250-9644) **5575**
• Annales Nestle (German Edition) (CHE ISSN 0250-9652) **5575**
Annales Nestle (Spanish Edition) *see* Annales Nestle (French Edition) **5575**
Annales Nestle (Spanish Edition) *see* Annales Nestle (German Edition) **5575**
Annales Nestle (Spanish Edition) *see* Annales Nestle (English Edition) **5574**
Annales Paderewski (CHE) **6545**
Annales Pharmaceutiques Belges (BEL ISSN 0365-5474) **6820**
• Annales Pharmaceutiques Francaises (FRA ISSN 0003-4509) **6820**
• ➤ Annales Polonici Mathematici (POL ISSN 0066-2216) **5470**
Annales Psychologici *see* Masarykova Univerzita. Filozoficka Fakulta. Sbornik Praci. P: Rada Psychologicka **8973**
Annales Publiees par la Faculte des Lettres de Toulouse. Pallas *see* Pallas **2238**
Annales Scientiarum Stetinenses, Nauki Morskie *see* Szczecinskie Roczniki Naukowe, Nauki Morskie **2818**
Annales Scientiarum Stetinenses, Nauki Przyrodnicze i Rolnicze *see* Szczecinskie Roczniki Naukowe, Nauki Przyrodnicze i Rolnicze **819**
Annales Scientiarum Stetinenses, Nauki Spoleczne *see* Szczecinskie Roczniki Naukowe, Nauki Spoleczne **8009**
• ➤ Annales Scientifiques de l'Ecole Normale Superieure (FRA ISSN 0012-9593) **5470**
Annales Silesiae (POL ISSN 0066-2224) **4198**
Annales Societatis Geologorum Poloniae *see* Societatis Geologorum Poloniae. Annales **2767**
Annales Societatis Mathematicae Polonae. Series 1: Commentationes Mathematicae - Prace Matematyczne (POL ISSN 0373-8299) **5470**
Annales Societatis Scientiarum Faeroensis. Supplementum (FRO ISSN 0365-6772) **3837**
Annales Suisses de Musicologie *see* Schweizer Jahrbuch fuer Musikwissenschaft **6615**
Annales Techniques *see* Technika Chronika **7922**
• Annales Theologici (ITA ISSN 0394-8226) **7783**
➤ Annales Universitatis Mariae Curie-Sklodowska. Sectio A. Mathematica (POL ISSN 0365-1029) **5470**
Annales Universitatis Mariae Curie-Sklodowska. Sectio AA. Chemia (POL ISSN 0137-6853) **2050**
➤ Annales Universitatis Mariae Curie-Sklodowska. Sectio AAA. Physica (POL ISSN 0137-6861) **7005**
Annales Universitatis Mariae Curie-Sklodowska. Sectio AI. Informatica (POL ISSN 1732-1360) **2406**
➤ Annales Universitatis Mariae Curie-Sklodowska. Sectio B. Geographia, Geologia, Mineralogia et Petrographia (POL ISSN 0137-1983) **3998**
➤ Annales Universitatis Mariae Curie-Sklodowska. Sectio C. Biologia (POL ISSN 0066-2232) **653**
• ➤ Annales Universitatis Mariae Curie-Sklodowska. Sectio D. Medicina (POL ISSN 0066-2240) **5575**
➤ Annales Universitatis Mariae Curie-Sklodowska. Sectio DD. Medicina Veterinaria (POL ISSN 0301-7737) **8792**
➤ Annales Universitatis Mariae Curie-Sklodowska. Sectio DDD. Pharmacia (POL ISSN 0867-0609) **6820**
➤ Annales Universitatis Mariae Curie-Sklodowska. Sectio E. Agricultura (POL ISSN 0365-1118) **91**
➤ Annales Universitatis Mariae Curie-Sklodowska. Sectio EE. Zootechnika (POL ISSN 0239-4243) **8792**
➤ Annales Universitatis Mariae Curie-Sklodowska. Sectio EEE. Horticultura (POL ISSN 1233-2127) **3723**
➤ Annales Universitatis Mariae Curie-Sklodowska. Sectio F. Historia (POL ISSN 0239-4251) **4130**
➤ Annales Universitatis Mariae Curie-Sklodowska. Sectio FF. Philologiae (POL ISSN 0239-426X) **5094**
➤ Annales Universitatis Mariae Curie-Sklodowska. Sectio G. Ius (POL ISSN 0458-4317) **4617**
➤ Annales Universitatis Mariae Curie-Sklodowska. Sectio H. Oeconomia (POL ISSN 0459-9586) **1059**
➤ Annales Universitatis Mariae Curie-Sklodowska. Sectio I. Philosophia - Sociologia (POL ISSN 0137-2025) **6904**
➤ Annales Universitatis Mariae Curie-Sklodowska. Sectio J. Paedagogia - Psychologia (POL ISSN 0867-2040) **2826**
➤ Annales Universitatis Mariae Curie-Sklodowska. Sectio K. Politologia (POL ISSN 1428-9512) **7106**
➤ Annales Universitatis Mariae Curie-Sklodowska. Sectio L. Artes (POL ISSN 1732-1352) **466**
Annales Universitatis Saraviensis. Rechts- und Wirtschaftswissenschaftliche Abteilung. Schriftenreihe (DEU ISSN 0563-1475) **4617**
Annales Universitatis Saraviensis. Reihe Philosophische Fakultaet (DEU ISSN 0563-1483) **6904**
Annales Universitatis Saraviensis. Series Mathematicae (DEU ISSN 0933-8268) **5470**
Annales Universitatis Turkuensis *see* Turun Yliopisto. Julkaisuja. Sarja A. II. Biologica - Geographica - Geologica **708**
Annales Universitatis Turkuensis *see* Turun Yliopisto. Julkaisuja. Sarja B. Humaniora **4478**
Annales Universitatis Turkuensis *see* Turun Yliopisto. Julkaisuja. Sarja C. Scripta Lingua Fennica Edita **4479**
Annales Universitatis Turkuensis *see* Turun Yliopisto. Julkaisuja. Sarja A. I. Astronomica - Chemica - Physica - Mathematica **7925**
Annales Universitatis Turkuensis *see* Turun Yliopisto. Julkaisuja. Sarja D. Medica - Odontologica **5725**
• ➤ Annales Zoologici (POL ISSN 0003-4541) **933**
• ➤ Annales Zoologici Fennici (FIN ISSN 0003-455X) **933**
Annali Alfieriani (ITA ISSN 1972-9073) **5255**
Annali Aretini (ITA ISSN 1126-232X) **4198**
Annali Benacensi (ITA ISSN 1724-0565) **373**
Annali del Barocco in Sicilia (ITA ISSN 1125-9205) **427**
Annali del Dipartimento di Filosofia *see* Universita degli Sudi di Firenze. Dipartimento di Filosofia. Annali **6958**
Annali del Dipartimento di Storia delle Arti e dello Spettacolo, Universita di Firenze *see* Arte Musica Spettacolo **5257**
Annali dell' Istruzione *see* Annali della Pubblica Istruzione **3050**
Annali della Carita (ITA ISSN 0003-4568) **8025**
Annali della Facolta di Agraria *see* Universita Cattolica del Sacro Cuore. Facolta di Agraria. Annali **165**
Annali della Facolta di Medicina Veterinaria di Pisa *see* Universita degli Studi di Pisa. Facolta di Medicina Veterinaria di Pisa. Annali **8809**
Annali della Fondazione Luigi Einaudi *see* Fondazione Luigi Einaudi. Annali **7964**
Annali della Pubblica Istruzione (ITA ISSN 1971-5420) **3050**
• Annali della Sanita Pubblica (ITA ISSN 0021-3071) **7507**
Annali dell'Istruzione. Quaderni (ITA ISSN 1826-8609) **3050**
Annali di Archeologia e Storia Antica (ITA ISSN 1127-7130) **373**
Annali di Botanica (ITA ISSN 0365-0812) **775**
Annali di Ca' Foscari *see* Ca' Foscari. Annali **5103**
Annali di Chimica (Print) *see* ChemSusChem (Print) **2058**
Annali di Geofisica *see* Annals of Geophysics **2777**
• Annali di Igiene, Medicina Preventiva e di Comunita (ITA ISSN 1120-9135) **7507**
• ➤ Annali di Matematica Pura ed Applicata (DEU ISSN 0373-3114) **5470**
Annali di Neurologia e Psichiatria. Psichiatria (ITA ISSN 1827-4439) **6122**
† Annali di Ostetricia, Ginecologia e Medicina Perinatale (ITA ISSN 0300-0087) **8930**
† ➤ Annali di Ottalmologia e Clinica Oculistica (ITA ISSN 0003-4665) **8930**
† Annali di Ricerche e Studi di Geografia (ITA ISSN 0392-8713) **8930**
▼ • Annali di Scienze Religiose (BEL ISSN 2031-5929) **7621**
• Annali di Sociologia (Trent)/Soziologisches Jahrbuch (DEU ISSN 0394-2120) **8087**
• Annali di Stomatologia (ITA ISSN 1824-0852) **5835**
Annali di Storia dell'Esegesi (ITA ISSN 1120-4001) **7783**
• Annali di Storia di Firenze (ITA ISSN 1827-6946) **4198**
• Annali di Storia Moderna e Contemporanea (ITA ISSN 1124-0296) **4130**
➤ Annali d'Italianistica (USA ISSN 0741-7527) **5255**
• Annali Italiani (Online Edition) (ITA ISSN 1825-179X) **4199**
Annali Italiani (Print Edition) *see* Annali Italiani (Online Edition) **4199**
➤ Annali Italiani di Chirurgia (ITA ISSN 0003-469X) **6236**
† Annali Italiani di Dermatologia Allergologica Clinica e Sperimentale (ITA ISSN 1592-6826) **8930**
Annali Italiani di Medicina Interna *see* Internal and Emergency Medicine **5945**
Annali Italiani di Medicina Interna. Supplement *see* Internal and Emergency Medicine **5945**
† Annali Queriniani (ITA ISSN 1970-5980) **8930**
Annals d'Oftalmologia (ESP ISSN 1133-7737) **6038**
Annals for Aesthetics *see* Chronika Aisthetikes **6910**
• ➤ Annals of Actuarial Science (GBR ISSN 1748-4995) **4492**
• Annals of Advances in Automotive Medicine (USA ISSN 1943-2461) **5575**
• Annals of African Medicine (NGA ISSN 1596-3519) **5575**
➤ Annals of Agrarian Science (GEO ISSN 1512-1887) **91**
Annals of Agri Bio Research (IND ISSN 0971-9660) **91**
• Annals of Agricultural and Environmental Medicine (POL ISSN 1232-1966) **3403**
Annals of Agricultural Research (IND ISSN 0970-3179) **91**
Annals of Agricultural Science/Hawliyat al-'lum al-Zira'iyyat (EGY ISSN 0570-1783) **91**
Annals of Agricultural Science, Moshtohor/Hawliyyaat al-'ulum al-Zira'iyyat bi-Mustuhur (EGY ISSN 1110-0419) **91**
Annals of Agricultural Sciences. Series E. Plant Protection (POL ISSN 1505-7216) **218**
• ➤ Annals of Air and Space Law/Annales de Droit Aerien et Spatial (CAN ISSN 0701-158X) **46**
• ➤ Annals of Allergy, Asthma, & Immunology (USA ISSN 1081-1206) **5754**
• ➤ Annals of Anatomy (DEU ISSN 0940-9602) **5575**
Annals of Animal Science (POL ISSN 1642-3402) **318**
• ➤ Annals of Applied Biology (GBR ISSN 0003-4746) **653**
• ➤ Annals of Applied Probability (USA ISSN 1050-5164) **5470**
▼ • ➤ Annals of Applied Statistics (USA ISSN 1932-6157) **8345**
➤ Annals of Arid Zone (IND ISSN 0570-1791) **218**
Annals of Balloon History and Museology (USA ISSN 1062-6174) **46**
Annals of Bangladesh Agriculture (BGD ISSN 1025-482X) **92**
• ➤ Annals of Behavioral Medicine (USA ISSN 0883-6612) **5575**
➤ Annals of Behavioral Science and Medical Education (USA ISSN 1075-1211) **2826**
• Annals of Bioethics (GBR ISSN 1567-2468) **6904**
Annals of Biology (IND ISSN 0970-0153) **653**
• ➤ Annals of Biomedical Engineering (USA ISSN 0090-6964) **5575**
➤ Annals of Borno (NGA ISSN 0189-2207) **4173**
• ➤ Annals of Botany (GBR ISSN 0305-7364) **775**
Annals of Botany Plants *see* A o B Plants **771**
Annals of Botany. Supplement *see* Annals of Botany **775**
• Annals of Cancer Research and Therapy (USA ISSN 1344-6835) **6008**
• ➤ Annals of Cardiac Anaesthesia (IND ISSN 0971-9784) **5777**
Annals of Carnegie Museum *see* Carnegie Museum of Natural History. Annals **7844**
Annals of Cases on Information Technology *see* Journals of Cases on Information Technology **1770**
• ➤ Annals of Clinical Biochemistry (GBR ISSN 0004-5632) **722**
• ➤ Annals of Clinical Microbiology and Antimicrobials (GBR ISSN 1476-0711) **881**
• ➤ Annals of Clinical Psychiatry (GBR ISSN 1040-1237) **6123**
• ➤ Annals of Combinatorics (CHE ISSN 0218-0006) **5470**
Annals of Contemporary Diagnostic Pathology (HKG ISSN 0219-0753) **5575**
• ➤ Annals of D A A A M & Proceedings (Danube Adria Association for Automation and Manufacturing) (AUT ISSN 1726-9679) **3365**
Annals of Dendrology *see* Polskie Towarzystwo Botaniczne. Sekcja Dendrologiczna. Rocznik Dendrologiczny **813**
• Annals of Dentistry (MYS) **5835**
Annals of Dentistry *see* New York Academy of Dentistry. Annals **5856**
• Annals of Dermatology (KOR ISSN 1013-9087) **5871**
Annals of Dermatology and Venereology *see* Vestnik Dermatologii i Venerologii **5882**
• Annals of Diagnostic Pathology (USA ISSN 1092-9134) **5575**
• Annals of Differential Equations/Weifen Fangcheng Niankan (CHN ISSN 1002-0942) **5471**
• Annals of Disaster Medicine (TWN ISSN 1684-0291) **5575**
• ➤ Annals of Discrete Mathematics (NLD ISSN 0167-5060) **5471**
• ➤ Annals of Dyslexia (USA ISSN 0736-9387) **3036**
Annals of Earth (USA ISSN 1070-9983) **3403**
Annals of Economic Studies *see* Kagawa Daigaku Keizai Gakubu Kenkyu Nenpo **1139**
Annals of Economics and Business (Kobe) *see* Kobe University. Research Institute for Economics and Business Administration. Annals of Economics and Business **1140**
• ➤ Annals of Emergency Medicine (USA ISSN 0196-0644) **6055**
Annals of Entomology (IND ISSN 0970-3721) **838**
▼ • ➤ Annals of Environmental Science (USA ISSN 1939-2621) **3403**
• ➤ Annals of Epidemiology (USA ISSN 1047-2797) **7507**
• ➤ Annals of Family Medicine (USA ISSN 1544-1709) **5575**
• Annals of Finance (DEU ISSN 1614-2446) **1307**
• ➤ Annals of Forest Science (FRA ISSN 1286-4560) **3683**
Annals of Forest Science Online *see* Annals of Forest Science **3683**

DIRECTORY 2010 ANNUAIRE DE L'HOSPITALISATION 9961

Annals of Forestry (IND ISSN 0971-4022) 3683
• ➤ Annals of Gastroenterology (GRC ISSN 1108-7471) 5920
• Annals of Genealogical Research (USA ISSN 1555-9904) 3758
Annals of General Hospital Psychiatry *see* Annals of General Psychiatry 6123
• ➤ Annals of General Psychiatry (GBR ISSN 1744-859X) 6123
Annals of Geomorphology *see* Zeitschrift fuer Geomorphologie 2776
Annals of Geophysics/Annali di Geofisica (ITA ISSN 1593-5213) 2777
• ➤ Annals of Glaciology (GBR ISSN 0260-3055) 2724
• ➤ Annals of Global Analysis and Geometry (NLD ISSN 0232-704X) 5471
• ➤ Annals of Health Law (USA ISSN 1075-2994) 4617
• ➤ Annals of Hematology (DEU ISSN 0939-5555) 5933
Annals of Hematology. Supplement *see* Annals of Hematology 5933
• Annals of Hepatology (MEX ISSN 1665-2681) 5933
• ➤ Annals of Human Biology (GBR ISSN 0301-4460) 653
• ➤ Annals of Human Genetics (GBR ISSN 0003-4800) 862
• ➤ The Annals of Improbable Research (USA ISSN 1079-5146) 7835
• ➤ Annals of Internal Medicine (USA ISSN 0003-4819) 5943
Annals of Internal Medicine. Supplement *see* Annals of Internal Medicine 5943
➤ Annals of International Business Studies (RUS ISSN 1930-1537) 1552
➤ The Annals of Iowa (USA ISSN 0003-4827) 4283
Annals of Latin American Studies *see* Raten Amerika Kenkyu Nenpo 4309
Annals of Library and Information Studies (IND ISSN 0972-5423) 4989
• ➤ Annals of Long-Term Care (USA ISSN 1524-7929) 4040
• ➤ Annals of Mathematics (USA ISSN 0003-486X) 5471
• ➤ Annals of Mathematics and Artificial Intelligence (NLD ISSN 1012-2443) 2445
Annals of Mathematics Studies (USA ISSN 0066-2313) 5471
The Annals of Medical Entomology (IND ISSN 0971-135X) 5575
The Annals of Medical Entomology Newsletter (IND) 5575
• ➤ Annals of Medical Sciences (TUR ISSN 1300-0683) 5575
• ➤ Annals of Medicine (SWE ISSN 0785-3890) 5902
➤ Annals of Microbiology (ITA ISSN 1590-4261) 722
• ➤ Annals of Neurology (USA ISSN 0364-5134) 6123
➤ Annals of Nigerian Medicine (NGA ISSN 0331-3131) 5575
• ➤ Annals of Noninvasive Electrocardiology (USA ISSN 1082-720X) 5777
• ➤ Annals of Nuclear Energy (GBR ISSN 0306-4549) 3164
• Annals of Nuclear Medicine (JPN ISSN 0914-7187) 6192
• ➤ Annals of Nutrition and Metabolism (CHE ISSN 0250-6807) 6655
• ➤ Annals of Occupational Hygiene (GBR ISSN 0003-4878) 6672
• ➤ Annals of Oncology (GBR ISSN 0923-7534) 6008
Annals of Oncology (Spanish Edition) (ESP ISSN 1132-0109) 6008
Annals of Oncology. Supplement *see* Annals of Oncology 6008
• ➤ Annals of Operations Research (USA ISSN 0254-5330) 2406
Annals of Ophthalmology *see* Vestnik Oftal'mologii 6052
• ➤ Annals of Ophthalmology (USA ISSN 1530-4086) 6038
Annals of Oriental Research (IND) 542
• ➤ Annals of Otology, Rhinology and Laryngology (USA ISSN 0003-4894) 6077
Annals of Otology, Rhinology & Laryngology. Supplement *see* Annals of Otology, Rhinology and Laryngology 6077
Annals of Otorhinolaryngology *see* Vestnik Otorinolaringologii 6086
▼ • Annals of Pediatric Cardiology (IND ISSN 0974-2069) 5777
• ➤ The Annals of Pharmacotherapy (USA ISSN 1060-0280) 6820
▼ • Annals of Pharmacotherapy (Online Spanish Edition) (ESP ISSN 1988-8147) 6820
• Annals of Pharmacotherapy (Spanish Edition) (ESP ISSN 1133-178X) 6820
• ➤ Annals of Physical and Rehabilitation Medicine (FRA ISSN 1877-0657) 6106
• ➤ Annals of Physics (USA ISSN 0003-4916) 7005
• Annals of Plant Protection Sciences (IND ISSN 0971-3573) 775
• ➤ Annals of Plastic Surgery (USA ISSN 0148-7043) 6236
• ➤ Annals of Probability (USA ISSN 0091-1798) 5471
• ➤ Annals of Public and Cooperative Economics (GBR ISSN 1370-4788) 1422
• ➤ Annals of Pure and Applied Logic (NLD ISSN 0168-0072) 5471
• ➤ The Annals of Regional Science (DEU ISSN 0570-1864) 1060
Annals of Roentgenology and Radiology *see* Vestnik Rentgenologii i Radiologii 6210
The Annals of Saint Anne de Beaupre (CAN) 7621
• ➤ Annals of Saudi Medicine (SAU ISSN 0256-4947) 5576
• ➤ Annals of Science (GBR ISSN 0003-3790) 7835
▼ • Annals of Solid and Structural Mechanics (DEU ISSN 1867-6936) 3374
• ➤ Annals of Statistics (USA ISSN 0090-5364) 8345
• ➤ Annals of Surgery (USA ISSN 0003-4932) 6236
Annals of Surgical Hepatology *see* Annaly Khirurgicheskoi Gepatologii 6237
• ➤ Annals of Surgical Innovation and Research (GBR ISSN 1750-1164) 6236
• ➤ Annals of Surgical Oncology (USA ISSN 1068-9265) 6236
Annals of Telecommunications *see* Annales des Telecommunications 2312
Annals of the American Psychotherapy Association *see* American Psychotherapy Association. Annals 6122
Annals of the Antiquities Service of Egypt *see* Service des Antiquites de l'Egypte. Annales 8988
Annals of the Arts and Social Sciences *see* Hawliyyat Kulliyyat al-Adab 4454
Annals of the Association of American Geographers *see* Association of American Geographers. Annals 3999
Annals of the Brazilian Academy of Sciences *see* Academia Brasileira de Ciencias. Anais 7829
Annals of the College of Medicine, Mosul *see* Mosul University. College of Medicine. Annals 5681
➤ Annals of the Eastern Cape Museums (ZAF ISSN 1562-5273) 7835
Annals of the I C R P *see* International Commission on Radiological Protection. Annals 6198
Annals of the International Society of Dynamic Games *see* International Society of Dynamic Games. Annals 2478
Annals of the Lothian Foundation *see* Lothian Foundation. Annals 4241
Annals of the Naprstek Museum *see* Naprstek Museum. Annals 349
Annals of the New York Academy of Sciences *see* New York Academy of Sciences. Annals 7892
Annals of the Pomeranian Medical University *see* Pomorska Akademia Medyczna w Szczecinie. Roczniki 5697
• ➤ Annals of the Rheumatic Diseases (GBR ISSN 0003-4967) 6221
Annals of the South African Museum *see* African Natural History 651
Annals of Theology *see* Roczniki Teologiczne 7815
Annals of Thoracic and Cardiovascular Surgery (JPN ISSN 1341-1098) 6237
• Annals of Thoracic Medicine (IND ISSN 1817-1737) 5944
• ➤ The Annals of Thoracic Surgery (USA ISSN 0003-4975) 6237
Annals of Tourism Resarch en Espanol (ESP ISSN 1575-443X) 8683
• ➤ Annals of Tourism Research (GBR ISSN 0160-7383) 8683
Annals of Traditional Chinese Medicine (SGP ISSN 1793-0138) 5576
Annals of Transplantation (POL ISSN 1425-9524) 6237
• ➤ Annals of Tropical Medicine & Parasitology (GBR ISSN 0003-4983) 5810
• Annals of Tropical Medicine and Public Health (IND ISSN 1755-6783) 5576
• ➤ Annals of Tropical Paediatrics (GBR ISSN 0272-4936) 6087
➤ Annals of Tropical Research (PHL ISSN 0116-0710) 92
• ➤ Annals of Vascular Surgery (USA ISSN 0890-5096) 6237
➤ Annals of Wyoming (USA) 4283
Annals of Zoology (IND ISSN 0003-5009) 933
Annaly Khirurgicheskoi Gepatologii/Annals of Surgical Hepatology (RUS) 6237
Annaly Khirurgii (RUS ISSN 1560-9502) 6237
▼ ➤ Annamalai Journal of Management (IND ISSN 0974-0406) 1725
Annandale Campus Peashooter (USA) 2272
• Annapolis Online Forum (USA) 3969
Anne (EST ISSN 1406-1112) 8851
▼ L'Annee (Year) en 500 questions (FRA ISSN 1962-9389) 3840
L'Annee Balzacienne (FRA ISSN 0084-6473) 5255
L'Annee Canonique (FRA ISSN 0570-1953) 4855
L'Annee de l'Action Sociale (Year) (FRA ISSN 1772-3701) 8025
L'Annee du Cinema (FRA ISSN 0180-3492) 6489
L'Annee du Cyclisme (FRA ISSN 1955-0413) 8253
L'Annee du Football (FRA) 8220
L'Annee du Maghreb (FRA ISSN 1952-8108) 7947
L'Annee du Rugby (FRA ISSN 0990-1760) 8220
L'Annee du Tennis (FRA ISSN 0242-4878) 8220
L'Annee Epigraphique (FRA ISSN 0066-2348) 2230
L'Annee Francophone Internationale (CAN ISSN 1188-9160) 5094
L'Annee Hippique (NLD ISSN 0168-3608) 8287
L'Annee Immobiliere *see* Business Immo. Annuaire 7585
• L'Annee Philologique (FRA ISSN 0184-6949) 2242
Annee Politique Africaine (SEN ISSN 0066-2364) 7106
L'Annee Politique, Economique et Sociale (FRA ISSN 1286-3920) 7106
Annee Politique Suisse/Schweizerische Politik (CHE ISSN 0066-2372) 7106
• ➤ L'Annee Psychologique (FRA ISSN 0003-5033) 7334
Annee Sociale - Institut de Sociologie *see* Universite Libre de Bruxelles. Institut de Sociologie. Annee Sociale 8145
L'Annee Sociologique (FRA ISSN 0066-2399) 8088
Annee Sportive U.S.M.T. (FRA ISSN 1162-0900) 8158
L'Annee Technologique (FRA ISSN 0994-7663) 8446
Annemarie Wildeisen's Kochen *see* Kochen 4362
• Annex Guardian (CAN) 3806
Annexes to the Convention on Civil Aviation *see* International Civil Aviation Organization. Annexes to the Convention on Civil Aviation 8545
Annie's Hooked on Crochet! (USA ISSN 1936-4946) 6637
† Annie's Plastic Canvas (USA ISSN 1556-8113) 8930
• Un Anno di Bruna (ITA) 174
Anno Domini (DEU ISSN 1430-8711) 4199
Anno Domini Jahrbuch (DEU ISSN 1437-3270) 4199
Het Anno Vakantieboek (NLD ISSN 1873-9423) 3051
Annonce (CZE ISSN 1211-4871) 21
Annonce (DEU) 21
Annonces (FRA ISSN 0982-9822) 21
Annonces Camping-Car *see* L' Argus du Camping-Car 8931
Les Annonces de l'Industrie (BEL ISSN 0003-505X) 1879
Les Annonces de l'Optique (FRA ISSN 1766-9766) 6038
Annonces de Montpellier en Algebre *see* Algebra Montpellier Announcements 5468
Annonces de Montpellier en Algebre - Algebra Montpellier Announcements *see* A M A 5463
Annonsblad till Tidskrift foer Landtmaen *see* A T L 78
• Annonsoeren (SWE ISSN 1653-1973) 21
Annotated Alberta Franchises Act (CAN ISSN 1480-7084) 4855
The (Year) Annotated Bankruptcy and Insolvency Act (CAN ISSN 1197-8503) 4617
Annotated Bibliographies of Serials: A Subject Approach (USA ISSN 0748-5190) 615
Annotated Bibliography for English Studies *see* Annotated Bibliography for English Studies 5406
• Annotated Bibliography for English Studies (GBR ISSN 1385-1020) 5406
Annotated Bibliography of Literature on Cooperative Movements in South-East Asia (IND) 615
Annotated Books Received *see* Translation Review 5188
Annotated British Columbia Assessment Act (CAN ISSN 1206-4831) 7582
Annotated British Columbia Business Corporations Act (CAN) 4855
Annotated British Columbia Company Act *see* Annotated British Columbia Business Corporations Act 4855
Annotated British Columbia Human Rights Code (CAN ISSN 1480-3445) 7202
Annotated British Columbia Labour Relations Code (CAN) 4617
Annotated British Columbia Legal Profession Act (CAN ISSN 1480-7092) 4617
Annotated British Columbia Mineral Tenure Act (CAN ISSN 1480-4549) 4946
Annotated British Columbia Motor Vehicle Act (CAN) 8629
Annotated British Columbia Occupiers Liability Act (CAN) 7582
Annotated British Columbia Residential Tenancy Act (CAN ISSN 1480-1248) 4403
Annotated Canada Labour Code (CAN ISSN 1202-0206) 4617
Annotated Canada Pension Plan and Old Age Security Act (CAN) 4617
Annotated Checklists of Fishes (USA ISSN 1545-150X) 3584
The (Year) Annotated Copyright Act (CAN ISSN 1196-7528) 6745
▼ The Annotated Digest of the International Criminal Court (NLD ISSN 1874-7957) 4884
Annotated Divorce Act (CAN ISSN 1189-8119) 8088
Annotated Employment Insurance Statutes (CAN ISSN 1209-6563) 4617
Annotated Estates Practice (Year) (CAN ISSN 1910-3719) 4900
Annotated Federal Income Tax Act F I T A (CAN ISSN 1708-332X) 1910
The Annotated Firearms Act and Related Legislation (CAN ISSN 1489-7555) 4617
Annotated Guide to Current National Bibliographies (DEU) 5056
The Annotated Immigration Act of Canada *see* The Annotated Immigration and Refugee Protection Act of Canada 4846
The Annotated Immigration and Refugee Protection Act of Canada (CAN ISSN 1709-2051) 4846
Annotated Index to Indian Social Science Journals (IND) 5056
Annotated Indian Act *see* Annotated Indian Act and Aboriginal Constitutional Provisions 6634
Annotated Indian Act and Aboriginal Constitutional Provisions (CAN ISSN 1486-9926) 6634
Annotated Ontario Business Corporations Act (CAN ISSN 1189-8100) 4855
The Annotated Ontario Personal Property Security Act (Year) (CAN ISSN 1196-7277) 4617
Annotated Ontario Provincial Offences Act (CAN ISSN 1204-3613) 4618
Annotated Ontario Securities Legislation (CAN ISSN 1487-4296) 4618
Annotated Reference Tools in Music Series (USA ISSN 1062-4058) 6545
• Annotated Statue & Code Series. McKinney's Consolidated Laws of New York Annotated (USA) 4618
Annotated Statute & Code Series (USA) 4618
• Annotated Statute & Code Series. Massachusetts General Laws Annotated (USA) 4618
• Annotated Statute & Code Series. New Jersey Statutes Annotated (USA) 4618
• Annotated Statute & Code Series. Oklahoma Statutes Annotated (USA) 4618
Annotated Statute & Code Series. Revised Code of Washington Annotated (USA) 4618
† Annotated Tax Cases (GBR ISSN 0141-6766) 8930
Annotated Tremeear's Criminal Code (CAN ISSN 1184-0293) 4884
• Annotated Youth Criminal Justice Act (CAN) 4618
• Annotation (USA ISSN 0160-8460) 4283
Annotationes Zoologicae et Botanicae (SVK ISSN 0570-202X) 933
Annotations (Year) (USA) 4571
Annotations to the New Zealand Statutes *see* Butterworths Annotations to the New Zealand Statutes 4634
Annotazioni Numismatiche (ITA ISSN 1121-7464) 6649
Announced... (USA ISSN 1051-287X) 6545
Announces Judiciaires et Legales (FRA ISSN 0242-6366) 4618
• Annoyed (USA) 5206
Annrinya (IND ISSN 0003-5203) 5206
➤ Annua Nuntia Lovaniensia (BEL) 7783
Annuaire - A N D E S E *see* Annuaire des Docteurs en Sciences Economiques 1060
Annuaire Administratif et Judiciaire de Belgique/Administratief en Gerechtelijk Jaarboek voor Belgie (BEL ISSN 0066-2461) 7420
Annuaire Africain de Droit International *see* African Yearbook of International Law 4916
Annuaire Canadien de Droit International *see* Canadian Yearbook of International Law 4920
Annuaire Canadien des Orchestres et Ensembles Musicaux *see* Orchestras Canada. Membership Directory 6602
• Annuaire Cooperatives Francaises (FRA) 1425
Annuaire de Droit Maritime et Oceanique (FRA ISSN 1259-4962) 4969
Annuaire de Jurisprudence et de Doctrine du Quebec (CAN ISSN 1180-9434) 4618
Annuaire de la Boulangerie et de la Boulangerie-Patisserie (FRA ISSN 1774-7554) 3670
† Annuaire de la Bureautique, Informatique, Materiel et Mobilier de Bureau, Mecanographie (FRA ISSN 0998-6723) 8930
Annuaire de la Chaussure et des Cuirs *see* France Cuirs 4973
† Annuaire de la Construction et de la Reparation Navales (FRA ISSN 0396-0269) 8930
Annuaire de la France Protestante *see* Federation Protestante de France. Annuaire 7758
Annuaire de la Gestion Financiere *see* Association Francaise de la Gestion Financiere. Annuaire 1611
Annuaire de la Marine Marchande (FRA ISSN 1257-6360) 8638
Annuaire de la Meunerie Francaise (FRA ISSN 0295-7868) 270
Annuaire de la Musique, de l'Image et du Son (FRA ISSN 1296-705X) 6545
▼ L'Annuaire de la Peche de Loisir (FRA ISSN 1956-7545) 8303
Annuaire de la Presse, de la Publicite et de la Communication (FRA ISSN 0992-6437) 4571
† Annuaire de la Recherche Bio-Medicale (FRA ISSN 1157-4135) 8930
Annuaire de l'Afrique du Nord *see* L' Annee du Maghreb 7947
† Annuaire de l'Armement a la Peche (FRA ISSN 0066-2623) 8930
† Annuaire de l'Eclairage (FRA ISSN 0066-264X) 8930
Annuaire de l'Eglise Catholique a Madagascar *see* Eglise Catholique a Madagascar 7796
Annuaire de l'Eglise Catholique au Zaire (COD) 7783
Annuaire de l'Exportation du Danemark *see* Trade Directory for Denmark 8994
Annuaire de l'Hospitalisation (FRA ISSN 1957-5858) 4087

Title

▼ *new title* † *ceased* • *electronic media* ➤ *refereed*

▼ *new title*   † *ceased*   ● *electronic media*   ➤ *refereed*

Title

▼ *new title*　† *ceased*　● *electronic media*　➤ *refereed*

Title

The Anomalist (Online Edition) (USA) **6741**
Anon Nine (USA) **5255**
Anonyma Alkoholister. Bulletinen (SWE ISSN 0281-577X) **2692**
Anoplate News (USA) **6305**
Anorak (GBR ISSN 1752-878X) **2176**
Anorexia Nervosa & Related Eating Disorders *see* A N R E D **6118**
Another (GBR) **2251**
▼ Another Book (USA ISSN 1947-2692) **5255**
➤ Another Chicago Magazine (USA ISSN 0272-4359) **5255**
Another Comforter Series (USA) **7621**
• Another Day in Paradise (MEX ISSN 1606-8122) **3908**
• Another Magazine (GBR ISSN 1355-5901) **3861**
Another Man (GBR ISSN 1746-7713) **6286**
• Another Perspective (USA) **5206**
• Anotherealm (USA ISSN 1524-7120) **5439**
• ➤ Anpere (SWE ISSN 1653-6355) **325**
• Anquan/Safety (CHN ISSN 1002-3631) **7508**
Anquan lishihui huiyi biaoti suoyin, Lianheguo *see* United Nations. Security Council. Index to Proceedings **7201**
• Anquan yu Huanjing Gongcheng/Safety and Environmental Engineering (CHN ISSN 1671-1556) **3403**
• Anquan yu Huanjing Xuebao/Journal of Safety and Environment (CHN ISSN 1009-6094) **3403**
• Anquan yu Jiankang/Safety & Health (CHN ISSN 1671-4636) **7508**
Die Anregung (Nettetal) (DEU ISSN 0003-519X) **7621**
Anritsu Technical Bulletin/Anritsu Tekunikaru (JPN ISSN 0003-5211) **3295**
Anritsu Technical Review (JPN ISSN 0914-7195) **3295**
Anritsu Tekunikaru *see* Anritsu Technical Bulletin **3295**
Anruf (DEU) **7621**
Ansaetze (DEU ISSN 0721-2291) **7621**
Anschauliche Wissenschaft (DEU ISSN 1437-9376) **6904**
Der Anschnitt (DEU ISSN 0003-5238) **6456**
• Anschriften fuer die Aussenwirtschaft (DEU ISSN 0937-2423) **1552**
Anser (SWE ISSN 0347-9595) **901**
Anser. Supplement (SWE ISSN 0347-9609) **901**
Anshan Keji Daxue Xuebao/Anshan University of Science and Technology. Journal *see* Liaoning Keji Daxue Xuebao **6320**
• Anshu Keji/Eucalypt Science & Technology (CHN ISSN 1674-3172) **776**
• Anshun Shifan Gaodeng Zhuanke Xuexiao Xuebao/Anshun Teachers College. Journal (CHN ISSN 1672-3694) **2826**
Anshun Teachers College. Journal *see* Anshun Shifan Gaodeng Zhuanke Xuexiao Xuebao **2826**
• Ansible (GBR ISSN 0265-9816) **5439**
• Ansiedad y Estres/Anxiety and Stress (ESP ISSN 1134-7937) **6123**
Anstoesse (DEU ISSN 0003-5270) **7622**
Anstoesse zur Friedensarbeit (DEU ISSN 0937-7476) **8088**
Anstoss (DEU ISSN 1434-1352) **8158**
Ansuda Magazine (USA) **5255**
The Ansul (CAN ISSN 1704-7900) **2272**
• AnsurNews Site Promotion Newsletter (USA) **2552**
Ansvarskommitten. Skriftserie (SWE ISSN 1653-5502) **8025**
Answer Book, Income Tax Law for Accountants, Income Tax Law for Tax Agents (AUS ISSN 1440-0286) **1910**
• Answers (Hebron) (USA ISSN 1930-3289) **7622**
• Answers (La Habra) (USA) **2552**
• Answers (Richmond) (USA) **4040**
▼ • ➤ Answers Research Journal (USA ISSN 1937-9056) **7622**
Answers to Your Top 25 Questions *see* Human Resources: Answers to Your Top 25 Questions **1864**
AnswerStat (USA) **5576**
Ant *see* Ari **839**
Antaeus (HUN ISSN 0238-0218) **374**
Antal Modtagere (DNK) **2353**
Antarctic (NZL ISSN 0003-5327) **3998**
• Antarctic and Southern Ocean Law and Policy Occasional Papers (AUS ISSN 1034-361X) **4917**
Antarctic Climate and Ecosystems Cooperative Research Centre. Technical Report (AUS ISSN 1833-2404) **6346**
Antarctic Meteorite Newsletter (USA ISSN 0270-7179) **568**
Antarctic Meteorite Research *see* Polar Science **2715**
Antarctic Meteorological Data (JPN) **6346**
Antarctic Record *see* Nankyoku Shiryo **4020**
Antarctic Research Book Series (USA) **2777**
• ➤ Antarctic Science (GBR ISSN 0954-1020) **653**
• Antarctica New Zealand. Annual Report (NZL ISSN 1174-3948) **7420**
The Antarctica Project (USA) **2602**
Antartida (ARG ISSN 0302-5691) **3998**
Antecedentes Parlamentarios (ARG ISSN 1666-714X) **4618**
• Antecedentes Regionales (CHL) **1308**
Antelope Specialist Group Gnusletter *see* Gnusletter **2612**
Antelope Valley Journal (USA) **4618**
Antelope Valley Woman *see* A V Woman **8850**
Antena (SVN ISSN 0003-536X) **5206**
Antena de Profesionales, de Radio y Television (ESP) **2375**
† Antena de Telecomunicacion (ESP) **8930**
Antena Krzyku (POL ISSN 1509-4308) **6545**
Antenna (GBR ISSN 0140-1890) **838**
† L'Antenna (ITA ISSN 0392-470X) **8930**
Antenna (RUS) **2375**
• Antenna (UKR) **3963**
▼ • Antenna (USA ISSN 1936-8852) **2176**
Antenna - Eletronica Popular (BRA ISSN 0101-9112) **2375**
Antenna Measurement Techniques Association. Annual Meeting and Symposium Proceedings (USA) **2312**
• Antenna Measurement Techniques Association. Newsletter (USA) **2312**
• Antenna Survey Tower File (USA) **2346**
Antenna Systems and Technology *see* Antenna Systems & Technology **3089**
• Antenna Systems & Technology (USA ISSN 1099-2553) **3089**
Antennas and Propagation (USA ISSN 0272-4693) **3295**
Antennas and Propagation Society Conference on Antennas and Propagation for Wireless Communications. Proceedings *see* A P S Conference on Antennas and Propagation for Wireless Communications. Proceedings **2311**
• Antennas Series (GBR) **2312**
Antenne (DEU) **6410**
• L'Antenne (FRA ISSN 0395-8582) **8638**
Antenne Aktuell (DEU) **2826**
Antenne Francaise de Sinologie a Hong Kong. Bulletin Mensuel *see* Perspectives Chinoises **7259**
Les Antennes (FRA ISSN 1953-7751) **5064**
Antenny (RUS ISSN 0320-9601) **2375**
Antepasados (USA ISSN 0044-8362) **4283**
• ➤ AntePodium (NZL ISSN 1173-5716) **7106**
Antepost *see* Betting Monthly **8161**
Anterem (ITA ISSN 0393-1838) **5255**
Anthem (USA) **6545**
Anthem (Nashville) (USA) **6545**
• Anthem (St. Petersburg) (USA) **5255**
Antheon (USA) **5255**
Antholoica Annua (ITA ISSN 0074-0160) **4130**
• Anthology (USA ISSN 1559-3703) **3051**
Anthology of Korean Studies (KOR) **3519**
Anthology of Medicine *see* Weichuang Yixue **5751**
Anthology of New England Writers (USA ISSN 1053-8615) **5416**
The Anthonian (USA ISSN 1060-0345) **7783**
Anthony and Berryman's Magistrates' Court Guide (GBR ISSN 0262-3234) **4946**
Anthony Burgess Centre Series (FRA ISSN 1775-1462) **5255**
Anthos (CHE ISSN 0003-5424) **427**
• Anthro-At-Large (USA ISSN 1558-7347) **325**
• AnthroGlobe Journal (CAN ISSN 1481-3440) **325**
➤ Anthropo-logiques (BEL) **5094**
• ➤ Anthropoetics (USA ISSN 1083-7264) **325**
Anthropoi (ITA ISSN 1828-8294) **325**
➤ Anthropologiai Kozlemenyek (HUN ISSN 0003-5440) **325**
• ➤ Anthropologica (CAN ISSN 0003-5459) **325**
Anthropologica (ESP ISSN 0301-6587) **325**
➤ Anthropologica (PER ISSN 0254-9212) **325**
Anthropologica del Departamento de Ciencias Sociales *see* Anthropologica **325**
➤ Anthropologica et Praehistorica (BEL ISSN 1377-5723) **325**
• Anthropological Abstracts: Cultural - Social Anthropology from Austria, Germany, Switzerland (DEU) **361**
• ➤ Anthropological Forum (AUS ISSN 0066-4677) **325**
• Anthropological Index Online (GBR) **361**
• ➤ Anthropological Index to Current Periodicals in the Museum of Mankind Library (GBR) **361**
• Anthropological Journal of European Cultures (GBR ISSN 1755-2923) **325**
• ➤ Anthropological Linguistics (USA ISSN 0003-5483) **5094**
• Anthropological Literature (USA ISSN 0190-3373) **361**
• ➤ Anthropological Notebooks (SVN ISSN 1408-032X) **325**
Anthropological Papers of the University of Alaska *see* University of Alaska. Anthropological Papers **359**
• ➤ Anthropological Quarterly (USA ISSN 0003-5491) **325**
Anthropological Reports *see* Jinruigaku Shuho **344**
• ➤ Anthropological Review (POL ISSN 1898-6773) **325**
• ➤ Anthropological Science (JPN ISSN 0918-7960) **326**
• Anthropological Science. Japanese Series (JPN ISSN 1344-3992) **326**
Anthropological Society of Nippon. Division of Kinesiology. Newsletter *see* Nippon Jinrui Gakkai Kineshioroji Bunkakai Nyusureta **350**
Anthropological Society of Oxford. Journal (GBR ISSN 0044-8370) **326**
Anthropological Society of Oxford. Occasional Papers Series (GBR) **326**
• ➤ Anthropological Theory (GBR ISSN 1463-4996) **326**
Anthropological Yearbook of European Cultures *see* Anthropological Journal of European Cultures **325**
➤ Anthropologie/Anthropology (CZE ISSN 0323-1119) **326**
Anthropologie (DEU ISSN 0066-4685) **326**
• ➤ L'Anthropologie (FRA ISSN 0003-5521) **326**
Anthropologie Critique (FRA ISSN 1292-4474) **326**
Anthropologie du Monde Occidental (FRA ISSN 1275-2886) **326**
Anthropologie et Prehistoire *see* Anthropologica et Praehistorica **325**
• ➤ Anthropologie et Societes (CAN ISSN 0702-8997) **326**
Anthropologie Sociale *see* Social Anthropology **355**
Anthropologie Visuelle (FRA ISSN 0993-4871) **326**
Anthropologika (GRC ISSN 0253-5092) **374**
Anthropologische Gesellschaft in Wien. Mitteilungen (AUT ISSN 0373-5656) **326**
Anthropologische Gesellschaft, Vienna. Mitteilungen (AUT ISSN 0066-4693) **326**
• ➤ Anthropologischer Anzeiger (DEU ISSN 0003-5548) **361**
• ➤ The Anthropologist (IND ISSN 0972-0073) **326**
L'Anthropologue Africain *see* The African Anthropologist **323**
Anthropology *see* Anthropologie **326**
Anthropology *see* Annual Editions: Anthropology **325**
• ➤ Anthropology and Archeology of Eurasia (USA ISSN 1061-1959) **326**
• ➤ Anthropology & Education Quarterly (USA ISSN 0161-7761) **326**
• Anthropology and Humanism (USA ISSN 1559-9167) **326**
• ➤ Anthropology & Medicine (GBR ISSN 1364-8470) **327**
Anthropology and Sociology *see* American University Studies. Series 11. Anthropology and Sociology **7947**
Anthropology and Sociology Section Currents *see* A N S S Currents **4986**
• ➤ Anthropology in Action (GBR ISSN 0967-201X) **327**
• Anthropology Matters Journal (GBR ISSN 1758-6453) **327**
• Anthropology News (USA ISSN 1541-6151) **327**
▼ • ➤ Anthropology Now (USA ISSN 1942-8200) **327**
• ➤ Anthropology of Consciousness (USA ISSN 1053-4202) **327**
The Anthropology of East Europe Review (USA ISSN 1054-4720) **327**
• ➤ Anthropology of Food (FRA ISSN 1609-9168) **3627**
Anthropology of Food and Nutrition (USA) **3627**
• ➤ Anthropology of the Middle East (GBR ISSN 1746-0719) **327**
• Anthropology of Work Review (USA ISSN 0883-024X) **327**
Anthropology Research Association. Research Bulletin (IND) **327**
• ➤ Anthropology Southern Africa/Suid-Afrikaanse Tydskrif vir Etnologie (ZAF) **327**
• Anthropology Today (GBR ISSN 0268-540X) **327**
Anthropos (ARG ISSN 0326-145X) **327**
➤ Anthropos (CHE ISSN 0257-9774) **327**
Anthropos (CZE ISSN 0003-5572) **6723**
Anthropos (ITA ISSN 0390-1289) **327**
Anthropos (POL) **327**
Anthropos (SVN ISSN 0587-5161) **7335**
Anthropos (VEN ISSN 0254-1629) **327**
➤ Anthropos: Yearbook in Anthropology (GRC ISSN 1105-2155) **328**
Anthropotes (VAT ISSN 1120-2874) **328**
Anthropozoologica (FRA ISSN 0761-3032) **933**
Anthropozoologica Numero Special (FRA ISSN 0994-7213) **933**
Anthroquest (USA ISSN 0749-1751) **328**
• ➤ Anthrozoos (GBR ISSN 0892-7936) **933**
• ➤ Anthurium (USA ISSN 1547-7150) **3519**
• ➤ Anti (GRC) **7106**
Anti-Aging & Cosmetic Surgery Magazine: Men's Guide (AUS ISSN 1442-8083) **585**
Anti-Aging Medicine/Anchi Eijingu Igaku (JPN ISSN 1880-1579) **5576**
Anti-Aging Medizin (DEU) **5576**
Anti-Bolshevik Bloc of Nations Correspondence *see* A B N Correspondence **7101**
Anti-Cancer Agents *see* Anti-Cancer Agents in Medicinal Chemistry **6008**
• ➤ Anti-Cancer Agents in Medicinal Chemistry (NLD ISSN 1871-5206) **6008**
Anti-Cancer Drug Design *see* Oncology Research **6031**
• ➤ Anti-Cancer Drugs (USA ISSN 0959-4973) **6008**
• ➤ Anti-Corrosion Methods and Materials (GBR ISSN 0003-5599) **6305**
Anti Corruption *see* Anti-Corruption **4884**
▼ Anti-Corruption (GBR ISSN 1754-4874) **4884**
Anti-Defamation League on the Frontline *see* A D L on the Frontline **7201**
Anti-Fascist Forum *see* Antifa Forum **7106**
Anti-Infection Pharmacy *see* Kangganran Yaoxue **6857**
• ➤ Anti-Infective Agents in Medicinal Chemistry (NLD ISSN 1871-5214) **6821**
Anti-Infectives Today (NZL ISSN 1174-5924) **6821**
• Anti-Infectives Week (USA ISSN 1543-6896) **5810**
Anti-Inflammatory & Anti-Allergy Agents *see* Anti-Inflammatory & Anti-Allergy Agents in Medicinal Chemistry **6821**
• ➤ Anti-Inflammatory & Anti-Allergy Agents in Medicinal Chemistry (NLD ISSN 1871-5230) **6821**
Anti-Money Laundering Alert *see* B S A / A M L Update **1310**
Anti-Money Laundering Compliance Alert *see* A M L Compliance Alert **1305**
• Anti Money Laundering Guide (GBR) **2644**
Anti-Money Laundering Update *see* B S A / A M L Update **1310**
Anti-Racist Action Research Bulletin *see* A R A Research Bulletin **7201**
• Anti-Semitism Worldwide (USA ISSN 0793-1840) **7202**
• Anti-Slavery Reporter (GBR ISSN 1362-0258) **7202**
Anti-Submarine Warfare Forecast *see* Market Intelligence Reports: Anti-Submarine Warfare Forecast **6432**
• ➤ Antibiotics and Chemotherapy (CHE ISSN 0066-4758) **6821**
Antibiotics and Chemotherapy *see* Kagaku Ryoho no Ryoiki **5947**
Antibiotics and Chemotherapy *see* Antibiotiki i Khimioterapiya **6821**
Antibiotics Chemotherapy (GBR ISSN 1366-5146) **5576**
Antibiotiki i Khimioterapiya/Antibiotics and Chemotherapy (RUS ISSN 0235-2990) **6821**
• Antibiotiques (FRA ISSN 1294-5501) **6821**
Anticancer *see* Kang'ai **6025**
➤ Anticancer Research (GRC ISSN 0250-7005) **6008**
➤ Antichthon (AUS ISSN 0066-4774) **2230**
Anticipatia (ROM ISSN 1220-8620) **5439**
• Antieau on Local Government Law (USA) **7488**
Antiek & Curiosa (BEL) **362**
Antiek & Verzamelkrant (NLD ISSN 1568-8968) **4327**
Antietam Review (USA ISSN 1078-0580) **5255**
Antifa (DEU ISSN 0863-2936) **7106**
Antifa Forum (CAN) **7106**
• Antifurto (ITA ISSN 0391-6227) **2644**
Antigona (ARG ISSN 1515-8438) **8088**
Antigone (ITA ISSN 1828-437X) **2644**
Antigonish and Eastern Shore (CAN ISSN 1910-1988) **8683**
• ➤ The Antigonish Review (CAN ISSN 0003-5661) **5255**
Antigrama (ESP ISSN 0213-1498) **466**
Antigua Commercial Bank. Annual Report (ATG) **1308**
Antiguedad y Cristianismo (ESP ISSN 0214-7165) **7622**
Antiguo Oriente (ARG ISSN 1667-9202) **542**
Antik & Auktion (SWE ISSN 0282-8200) **362**
Antik & Auktion (DNK ISSN 1397-8799) **362**
• Antik Tanulmanyok/Studies in Antiquity (HUN ISSN 0003-567X) **2230**
Antikboersen *see* Antikvaerlden **362**
† Die Antike (DEU ISSN 0174-8246) **8930**
➤ Antike Kunst (CHE ISSN 0003-5688) **374**
Antike Kunst. Beihefte (CHE ISSN 0066-4782) **374**
Antike Naturwissenschaft und Ihre Rezeption (DEU ISSN 0942-0398) **7836**
• Antike und Abendland (DEU ISSN 0003-5696) **2230**
Antike Welt (DEU ISSN 0003-570X) **374**
Antikvaerlden (SWE ISSN 1653-7629) **362**
Antikvariatet (SWE ISSN 0283-1333) **4989**
Antilia (ESP ISSN 1136-2049) **653**
Antilla (MTQ ISSN 0757-3960) **3995**
Antilliaanse Nieuwsbrief (NLD ISSN 0003-5718) **3916**
▼ • ➤ AntiMatters (IND ISSN 0973-8606) **4443**
• ➤ Antimicrobial Agents and Chemotherapy (USA ISSN 0066-4804) **881**
Antimovski Han (BGR) **466**
• Antincendio (ITA ISSN 0393-7089) **3575**
† Antinquinamento (ITA ISSN 1123-3370) **8930**
Antioch New England Notes (USA) **2966**
• Antioch Review (USA ISSN 0003-5769) **5206**
Antioquia. Secretaria de Educacion y Cultura. Revista Cultura (COL) **5255**
• ➤ Antioxidants & Redox Signaling (USA ISSN 1523-0864) **5576**
Antiphon (USA ISSN 1543-9925) **7784**
• ➤ Antipoda (COL ISSN 1900-5407) **328**
➤ Antipodas (AUS ISSN 0113-2415) **5094**
• ➤ Antipode (GBR ISSN 0066-4812) **3998**
• Antipodean S F (Science Fiction) (AUS ISSN 1442-0686) **5439**
Antipodes (AUS ISSN 1032-3368) **5255**
• ➤ Antipodes (USA ISSN 0893-5580) **5255**
Antiquarian (USA) **4283**
Antiquarian Book Review *see* Rare Book Review **7572**
Antiquarian Booksellers' Association of America Newsletter *see* The A B A A Newsletter **7550**
Antiquarian Horology (GBR ISSN 0003-5785) **4564**
† Antiquarian, Specialty and Used Book Sellers (USA ISSN 1522-2985) **8930**
Antiquariato (ITA ISSN 1124-8335) **362**
• ➤ The Antiquaries Journal (GBR ISSN 0003-5815) **374**
Antique Airplane Association News (USA ISSN 0003-5823) **46**
Antique & Classic (AUS) **8556**
Antique & Collectables *see* Antiques & Collectibles Journal **8930**
† Antique & Collectibles Showcase (CAN ISSN 1708-6469) **8930**

DIRECTORY 2010 ANUARIO ESTADISTICO DE BAJA CALIFORNIA 9967

Antique Angler (USA ISSN 0744-3749) **8304**
Antique Appraisal Association of America. Newsletter (USA) **362**
Antique Automobile (USA ISSN 0003-5831) **362**
Antique Bottle and Glass Collector (USA ISSN 8750-1481) **362**
Antique Car Times (USA ISSN 0164-7237) **362**
Antique Collecting (GBR ISSN 0003-584X) **362**
Antique Comb Collector (USA ISSN 0892-7162) **362**
Antique Dealer & Collectors Guide *see* Antique Collecting **362**
Antique Doll Collector (USA ISSN 1096-8474) **363**
Antique Interiors International (GBR ISSN 1366-9923) **363**
Antique Journal *see* Antiques & Collectibles Journal **8930**
† Antique Journal for the Northwest (USA) **8930**
• Antique Map Price Record (Macintosh) (USA ISSN 1541-4795) **3998**
• Antique Map Price Record (MS/Windows) (USA ISSN 1540-3904) **3998**
Antique Outboard Motor Club Newsletter (USA) **363**
Antique Outboarder (USA ISSN 0003-5904) **8271**
Antique Phonograph Monthly Monograph Series *see* A P M Monograph Series **6541**
Antique Power (USA ISSN 1042-7392) **209**
Antique Radio Classified (USA ISSN 8750-7471) **2356**
Antique Shop Guide *see* AntiqueWeek **363**
Antique Showcase *see* Antique & Collectibles Showcase **8930**
Antique Stove Association Quarterly (USA) **363**
Antique Stove Association. Yearbook (USA) **363**
Antique Toy World (USA ISSN 0742-0420) **4327**
The Antique Trade Calendar (GBR) **363**
• Antique Trader (USA) **363**
Antique Trader Books Antiques and Collectibles Price Guide *see* Antique Trader Books Antiques & Collectibles Price Guide **363**
Antique Trader Books Antiques & Collectibles Price Guide (USA ISSN 1083-8430) **363**
Antique Trader Vintage Magazines Price Guide (USA ISSN 1932-5746) **363**
Antique Truck Registry (USA) **8668**
Antique Week *see* AntiqueWeek **363**
Antique Wireless Association Journal *see* The A W A Journal **4326**
Antiques (New York) *see* The Magazine Antiques **367**
• Antiques and Art Around Florida (USA) **363**
Antiques & Art in New South Wales (AUS ISSN 1832-1623) **466**
Antiques & Art Independent (Online Edition) *see* Antiquesnews **363**
Antiques & Art Independent (Print Edition) *see* Antiquesnews **363**
Antiques & Auction News (USA) **363**
Antiques & Collectables Magazine *see* What's It Worth? **369**
† Antiques & Collectibles Journal (USA) **8930**
Antiques & Collectibles Magazine (USA ISSN 0274-6085) **363**
• Antiques and Collectibles Newsletter (USA ISSN 1520-4464) **363**
• Antiques & Collecting Magazine (USA ISSN 1084-0818) **363**
• Antiques & Fine Art (USA ISSN 1535-5500) **363**
Antiques & Fine Art Dealers and Auctioneers *see* Business Ratio. Antiques and Fine Art Dealers and Auctioneers **364**
Antiques & Period Properties *see* Ireland's Antiques and Period Properties **366**
• Antiques Bulletin (USA) **363**
• Antiques Diary (GBR ISSN 1476-9913) **363**
Antiques Fairs Guide (GBR ISSN 1351-5047) **363**
Antiques Folio *see* Antiquesnews **363**
Antiques Info Magazine (GBR ISSN 1365-585X) **363**
Antiques Lifestyle (GBR) **363**
Antiques Magazine (GBR ISSN 1464-9438) **363**
Antiques Roadshow Insider (USA ISSN 1544-2659) **363**
• Antiques Trade Gazette (GBR ISSN 0306-1051) **363**
• Antiquesnews (GBR) **363**
• AntiqueWeek (USA ISSN 0888-5451) **363**
AntiqueWeek - Central Edition (USA) **364**
AntiqueWeek - Eastern Edition (USA) **364**
Antiquitaeten-Zeitung (DEU) **364**
Antiquitas. Reihe 1. Abhandlungen zur Alten Geschichte (DEU ISSN 0066-4839) **4130**
Antiquitas. Reihe 2. Abhandlungen aus dem Gebiete der Vor- und Fruehgeschichte (DEU ISSN 0066-4847) **4130**
Antiquitas. Reihe 3. Abhandlungen zur Vor- und Fruehgeschichte, zur Klassischen und Provinzial-Roemischen Archaeologie und zur Geschichte des Altertums (DEU ISSN 0066-4855) **4130**
Antiquitas. Reihe 4. Beitraege zur Historia-Augusta-Forschung (DEU ISSN 0066-4863) **4130**
Antiquitas. Reihe 4, Serie 2. Bibliographien (DEU ISSN 0931-0797) **4130**
Antiquitas. Reihe 4, Serie 3. Kommentare (DEU ISSN 1433-5700) **4130**
Antiquitates (DEU ISSN 1435-7445) **374**
• ➤ L'Antiquite Classique (BEL ISSN 0770-2817) **2230**
• Antiquite Tardive (BEL ISSN 1250-7334) **374**
Antiquite Vivante *see* Ziva Antika **5405**
Antiquites Africaines (FRA ISSN 0066-4871) **4173**
Antiquites - Info (FRA ISSN 1164-2483) **364**
Antiquites Nationales (FRA ISSN 0997-0576) **328**
• ➤ Antiquity (GBR ISSN 0003-598X) **374**
Antiquity Papers (GBR ISSN 1754-9809) **374**
• Antirasisten (NOR ISSN 1501-6048) **8088**
• Antisemitism World Report (Year) (GBR ISSN 1350-0996) **7202**
Antisense and Nucleic Acid Drug Development *see* Oligonucleotides **877**
The Antiseptic (IND ISSN 0003-5998) **6237**
Antishyster (USA) **4618**
Antiskios (USA) **5206**
▼ • Antiteses (BRA ISSN 1984-3356) **4284**
• Antitetradia tis Ekpaedefsis (GRC) **2826**
➤ Antithesis (AUS ISSN 1030-3839) **5206**
Antithetical Couplet - Folk Stories about Antithetical Couplet *see* Duilian - Minjian Duilian Gushi **5286**
Antitrust Adviser (USA) **4855**
Antitrust and American Business Abroad (USA) **4855**
Antitrust & Commerce Report (USA) **4855**
• Antitrust & Trade Regulation Daily (USA ISSN 1526-520X) **1879**
Antitrust and Trade Regulation Report *see* Antitrust & Trade Regulation Report **4855**
• Antitrust & Trade Regulation Report (USA ISSN 0003-6021) **4855**
Antitrust & Unfair Competition Law *see* Antitrust and Unfair Competition Law **4619**
• ➤ Antitrust and Unfair Competition Law (USA) **4619**
• Antitrust Bulletin (USA ISSN 0003-603X) **4855**
• Antitrust Counseling and Litigation Techniques (USA) **4855**
The Antitrust Counselor (USA ISSN 1080-2843) **4856**
Antitrust Deskbook (USA) **4856**
Antitrust Developments in Europe *see* Cleary Gottlieb Antitrust Developments in Europe **4643**
• Antitrust Freedom of Information Log (USA ISSN 0891-8546) **1552**
• Antitrust Law and Economics Review (USA ISSN 0003-6048) **4856**
Antitrust Law Handbook (USA ISSN 0738-5919) **4856**
• ➤ Antitrust Law Journal (USA ISSN 0003-6056) **4856**
Antitrust Law Sourcebook for the United States and Europe (USA) **4856**
• Antitrust Laws and Trade Regulation (USA) **4856**
• Antitrust Laws and Trade Regulation: Desk Edition (USA) **4856**
Antitrust Laws and Trade Regulation Newsletter (USA) **4619**
• Antitrust Magazine (USA ISSN 0162-7996) **4856**
• Antitrust Report (USA ISSN 1057-8919) **4619**
Antitrust Report (New York) (USA ISSN 1045-9650) **4856**
The Antitrust Review of the Americas (GBR ISSN 1468-7054) **4856**
• ➤ Antiviral Chemistry and Chemotherapy (Online) (GBR ISSN 2040-2066) **723**
† • ➤ Antiviral Chemistry and Chemotherapy (Print) (GBR ISSN 0956-3202) **8930**
• ➤ Antiviral Research (NLD ISSN 0166-3542) **881**
• ➤ Antiviral Therapy (GBR ISSN 1359-6535) **5810**
Antologia (ARG) **5255**
Antologia (ITA ISSN 1972-0513) **5255**
Antologia di Belle Arti (ITA ISSN 0394-0136) **466**
Antologia Poetica de Esteban Echevarria *see* Antologia Poetica del Partido de Esteban Echeverria **5416**
Antologia Poetica del Partido de Esteban Echeverria (ARG) **5416**
Antologia Vieusseux (ITA ISSN 1124-3678) **5206**
Antonianum (ITA ISSN 0003-6064) **7784**
• ➤ Antonie van Leeuwenhoek (NLD ISSN 0003-6072) **756**
Antonius (DEU) **7784**
Antrieb (DEU ISSN 0003-6080) **8638**
Antriebspraxis (DEU ISSN 1860-5230) **3365**
• Antriebstechnik (DEU ISSN 0722-8546) **3374**
Antriebstechnik, Maschinenelemente und -baugruppen, Getriebe *see* Informationsdienst F I Z Technik. Antriebstechnik, Maschinenelemente und -baugruppen, Getriebe **3230**
• Antropo (ESP ISSN 1578-2603) **328**
➤ Antropologi (DNK ISSN 0906-3021) **328**
Antropologi i Finland *see* Suomen Antropologi **357**
Antropologia (BOL) **328**
Antropologia (MEX ISSN 0188-3437) **328**
Antropologia Andina (PER) **328**
† Antropologia Contemporanea (ITA ISSN 0392-9035) **8930**
Antropologia Museale (ITA ISSN 1971-4815) **6519**
➤ Antropologia Portuguesa (PRT ISSN 0870-0990) **328**
Antropologia y Paleoecologia Humana (ESP ISSN 0210-959X) **328**
Antropologia y Tecnica (MEX ISSN 0186-9787) **328**
Antropologica (VEN ISSN 0003-6110) **328**
Antropologicas (MEX ISSN 1029-0931) **328**
• Antropologicas (PRT ISSN 0873-819X) **328**
Antropologicheskii Forum *see* Antropologicheskij Forum **328**
Antropologicheskij Forum (RUS ISSN 1815-8870) **328**
• Antropologies (ESP ISSN 0213-7720) **328**
• Antropologos Iberoamericanos en Red (ESP ISSN 1695-9752) **4199**
Antroposana (NLD ISSN 1574-8723) **307**
Anturi (FIN ISSN 0782-7849) **2967**
Antwerp Maritime Law Reports *see* Jurisprudence du Port d'Anvers **4970**
Antwerp Papers in Linguistics (BEL ISSN 0776-3859) **5094**
Antwerpse Studies over Nederlandse Literatuurgeschiedenis (BEL) **5255**
Anty Magazine (JOR) **3901**
Antyfon (POL ISSN 1505-4454) **7703**
Anuari de Filologia. Seccio A, Filologia Anglesa i Alemana (ESP ISSN 1131-6861) **5094**
Anuari de Filologia. Seccio B, Estudis Arabs (ESP ISSN 1131-687X) **5094**
Anuari de Filologia. Seccio C, Llengua i Literatura Catalanes (ESP ISSN 1131-6888) **5094**
Anuari de Filologia. Seccio D, Studia Graeca et Latina (ESP ISSN 1131-6896) **5094**
Anuari de Filologia. Seccio E, Estudis Hebreus i Arameus (ESP ISSN 1131-8597) **5095**
Anuari de Filologia. Seccio F, Estudios de Lengua y Literatura Espanola (ESP ISSN 1131-690X) **5095**
Anuari de Filologia. Seccio G, Filologia Romanica (ESP ISSN 1131-6918) **5095**
Anuari de Psicologia de la Societat Valenciana de Psicologia *see* Societat Valenciana de Psicologia. Anuari de Psicologia **7409**
• Anuari Estadistic de Catalunya (ESP ISSN 1130-166X) **8345**
Anuari Ornitologic de les Balears (ESP ISSN 1137-831X) **901**
Anuari Xarxa de Biblioteques Populars (ESP ISSN 1133-8490) **4989**
Anuario Aerospacial Brasileiro/Brazilian Aerospace Yearbook (BRA ISSN 0103-5002) **46**
• Anuario Alimentacion, Equipos y Tecnologia (ESP ISSN 1136-0429) **3627**
Anuario Americanista Europeo (FRA ISSN 1767-3623) **4284**
Anuario Antropologico (BRA ISSN 0102-4302) **328**
Anuario Asia - Pacifico (ESP ISSN 1699-8111) **7221**
Anuario Automatica e Instrumentacion (ESP) **2457**
Anuario Automotor (BRA) **8556**
Anuario Avicola & Suinicola (BRA) **279**
Anuario Bibliografico Cervantino (ESP ISSN 1578-3642) **5406**
Anuario Bibliografico Colombiano (COL ISSN 0570-393X) **615**
Anuario Bibliografico Costarricense (CRI ISSN 0066-5010) **615**
Anuario Bibliografico Ecuatoriano (ECU ISSN 0252-8649) **615**
Anuario Bibliografico Uruguayo (URY ISSN 0304-8861) **615**
Anuario Brasileiro da Industria Grafica (BRA ISSN 1414-2791) **7318**
Anuario Brasileiro do Plastico (BRA) **7090**
• Anuario Brigantino (ESP ISSN 1130-7625) **7488**
Anuario Bursatil (MEX ISSN 0188-3860) **1200**
Anuario Climatologico (PRT ISSN 0870-2950) **6346**
Anuario Colombiano de Historia Social y de la Cultura (COL ISSN 0120-2456) **7947**
Anuario da Facultade de Dereito da Universidade da Coruna *see* Universidade da Coruna. Facultade de Dereito. Anuario **4802**
Anuario das Industrias (BRA ISSN 0100-9745) **1972**
Anuario de Cuentas Nacionales (CHL ISSN 0717-3660) **1308**
Anuario de Derecho Administrativo (URY ISSN 0797-0463) **7420**
Anuario de Derecho Civil (ESP ISSN 0210-301X) **4827**
Anuario de Derecho Civil Uruguayo (URY ISSN 0797-0773) **4619**
Anuario de Derecho Concursal (ESP ISSN 1698-997X) **4619**
Anuario de Derecho Eclesiastico del Estado (ESP ISSN 0213-8123) **4619**
Anuario de Derecho Europeo (ESP ISSN 1579-1750) **4917**
Anuario de Derecho Internacional *see* Anuario Espanol de Derecho Internacional **4917**
Anuario de Derecho Maritimo (ESP ISSN 0211-8432) **4969**
Anuario de Derecho Penal y Ciencias Penales (ESP ISSN 0210-3001) **4884**
Anuario de Derecho Tributario (URY ISSN 0797-7050) **4917**
Anuario de Derechos Humanos (ESP ISSN 0212-0364) **7202**
Anuario de Drogueria y Perfumeria (ESP ISSN 1137-9030) **592**
Anuario de Estadisticas del Trabajo *see* Year Book of Labour Statistics **1275**
Anuario de Estadisticas Estatales (MEX) **8345**
Anuario de Estadisticas Laborales y de Asuntos Sociales (ESP ISSN 1137-1676) **1200**
• Anuario de Estudios Americanos (ESP ISSN 0210-5810) **7947**
• Anuario de Estudios Centroamericanos (CRI ISSN 0377-7316) **7947**
Anuario de Estudios Cooperativos/Kooperatiba Ikaskuntzen Urtekaria (ESP ISSN 1130-8966) **7947**
Anuario de Estudios de Turismo (ARG ISSN 1666-504X) **8683**
➤ Anuario de Estudios Indigenas (MEX) **328**
Anuario de Estudios Literarios Galegos (ESP ISSN 1133-4533) **5255**
• Anuario de Estudios Medievales (ESP ISSN 0066-5061) **4199**
Anuario de Esuko-Folklore (ESP ISSN 0210-7732) **328**
Anuario de Filosofia del Derecho (ESP ISSN 0518-0872) **4619**
Anuario de Gaita (ESP ISSN 1136-2642) **6545**
• Anuario de Historia de la Iglesia (ESP ISSN 1133-0104) **7622**
Anuario de Historia del Derecho Espanol (ESP ISSN 0304-4319) **4619**
➤ Anuario de Historia Regional y de las Fronteras (COL ISSN 0122-2066) **4284**
Anuario de Importacion - Exportacion del Uruguay (URY ISSN 0797-8243) **1200**
• Anuario de Informatica (BRA) **2490**
Anuario de Inovacoes em Comunicacoes e Artes (BRA ISSN 0103-9652) **466**
Anuario de Investigacion en Literatura Infantil y Juvenil (ESP ISSN 1578-6072) **5255**
Anuario de Investigaciones - Facultad de Psicologia. Universidad de Buenos Aires *see* Universidad de Buenos Aires. Facultad de Psicologia. Anuario de Investigaciones **7413**
Anuario de Jornalismo (BRA ISSN 1519-2407) **1663**
• Anuario de Justicia Alternativa: Derecho Arbitral (ESP ISSN 1578-3162) **4619**
Anuario de Justicia de Menores (ESP ISSN 1579-4784) **4619**
Anuario de la Aviacion Comercial Espanola (ESP) **8538**
Anuario de la Distribucion *see* Anuario Distribucion **1972**
Anuario de la Economia Argentina/Argentine Economy Annual (ARG) **1060**
Anuario de la Exportacion de Dinamarca *see* Trade Directory for Denmark **8994**
Anuario de la Historia de la Iglesia en Chile (CHL ISSN 0716-1662) **7622**
Anuario de la Iglesia (ESP) **7784**
Anuario de la Inmigracion en Espana *see* La Inmigracion en Espana **7285**
Anuario de la Mineria de Chile (CHL ISSN 0066-5096) **6456**
• Anuario de las Comarcas de Aragon (ESP ISSN 1699-5341) **1060**
➤ Anuario de Letras (MEX ISSN 0185-1373) **5255**
Anuario de Letras Modernas (MEX ISSN 0186-0526) **5255**
Anuario de Linguistica Hispanica (ESP ISSN 0213-053X) **5095**
• ➤ Anuario de Literatura (BRA ISSN 1414-5235) **5255**
Anuario de los Hechos (ESP ISSN 1135-6103) **3951**
Anuario de Migraciones (ESP ISSN 1134-5837) **7296**
Anuario de Nacimientos (PER) **7296**
Anuario de Pedagogia (ESP ISSN 1575-6386) **2826**
Anuario de Poesia (MEX) **5416**
• Anuario de Principales Sociedades Espanolas (ESP ISSN 1579-833X) **1972**
Anuario de Productos Forestales *see* Yearbook of Forest Products **3718**
• ➤ Anuario de Psicologia (ESP ISSN 0066-5126) **7335**
• Anuario de Psicologia Clinica y de la Salud (ESP ISSN 1699-6410) **7335**
• Anuario de Psicologia Juridica (ESP ISSN 1133-0740) **7335**
Anuario de Voleibol (BRA) **8220**
Anuario del Comercio Exterior de Venezuela (VEN ISSN 1013-3771) **1200**
Anuario del Departamento de Historia y Teoria del Arte (ESP ISSN 1130-5517) **466**
• Anuario del Empaque (COL ISSN 0121-7968) **1972**
Anuario del Instituto Ignacio de Loyola (ESP ISSN 1135-8513) **7784**
Anuario del Sector de la Informatica y Telecomunicaciones *see* Quien es Quien en Informatica y Telecomunicaciones **2493**
Anuario del Seminario Permanente Sobre Derechos Humanos (ESP ISSN 1135-7118) **7202**
Anuario Delta Larousse (BRA) **3118**
• Anuario Distribucion (ESP ISSN 1137-3164) **1972**
Anuario Ecuatoriano de Derecho Internacional (ECU ISSN 0570-4251) **4917**
• Anuario Espanol de Derecho Internacional (ESP) **4917**
Anuario Espanol de Derecho Internacional Privado (ESP ISSN 1578-3138) **4917**
Anuario Espanol de la Automocion (ESP ISSN 1130-5983) **8556**
• Anuario Espanol de la Seguridad (ESP) **2676**
Anuario Espanol de Mantenimiento y Limpieza (ESP ISSN 1576-3013) **2242**
Anuario Espanol de Seguros (ESP ISSN 0211-125X) **4492**
Anuario Espanol del Vidrio Hueco *see* Revista del Vidrio Hueco **2045**
Anuario Espanol del Vidrio Plano *see* Revista del Vidrio Plano **2045**
Anuario Estadistico Centroamericano de Comercio Exterior (GTM ISSN 0570-426X) **1200**
Anuario Estadistico da Defensa Nacional (PRT ISSN 0011-765X) **6410**
Anuario Estadistico da Industria Automobilistica Brasileira (BRA ISSN 1517-1663) **8556**
• Anuario Estadistico de America Latina y el Caribe/Statistical Yearbook for Latin America and the Caribbean (CHL ISSN 1014-0697) **8345**
• Anuario Estadistico de Andalucia (ESP ISSN 1135-9846) **7296**
Anuario Estadistico de Baja California (MEX ISSN 0188-8609) **8345**

Title

9968 ANUARIO ESTADISTICO DE BAJA CALIFORNIA SUR ULRICH'S PERIODICALS

Anuario Estadistico de Baja California Sur (MEX ISSN 0188-8595) **8345**
Anuario Estadistico de Comercio Exterior de los Estados Unidos Mexicanos (MEX) **1200**
Anuario Estadistico de Cuba (CUB ISSN 0574-6132) **8345**
Anuario Estadistico de Durango (MEX ISSN 0188-8641) **8345**
Anuario Estadistico de Existencias, Faena y Exportacion (URY ISSN 0797-5716) **3669**
• Anuario Estadistico de Extranjeria (ESP ISSN 1133-9934) **7296**
• Anuario Estadistico de la Banca en Espana (ESP ISSN 1578-942X) **1308**
Anuario Estadistico de la Comunidad de Madrid *see* Comunidad de Madrid. Anuario Estadistico **8364**
Anuario Estadistico de la Siderurgia y Mineria de Hierro en America Latina (CHL) **6338**
Anuario Estadistico de los Estados Unidos Mexicanos (MEX ISSN 0185-7126) **8345**
Anuario Estadistico de Macau *see* Governo da Regiao Administrativa Especial de Macau. Direccao dos Servicos de Estatistica e Censos. Anuario Estatistico **8374**
Anuario Estadistico de Nayarit (MEX ISSN 0188-848X) **8345**
• Anuario Estadistico de Pesca (MEX) **3612**
Anuario Estadistico de Sonora (MEX ISSN 0188-8633) **8346**
Anuario Estadistico de Tlaxcala (MEX ISSN 0187-4756) **8346**
Anuario Estadistico de Zacatecas (MEX ISSN 0187-4748) **8346**
Anuario Estadistico del Area Metropolitana de L'Horta (ESP) **8346**
Anuario Estadistico del Area Metropolitana de Valencia *see* Anuario Estadistico del Area Metropolitana de L'Horta **8346**
Anuario Estadistico del Distrito Federal (MEX ISSN 0188-8544) **8346**
Anuario Estadistico del Estado de Aguascalientes (MEX ISSN 0188-8676) **8346**
Anuario Estadistico del Estado de Campeche (MEX ISSN 0188-8587) **8346**
Anuario Estadistico del Estado de Chiapas (MEX ISSN 0188-8552) **8346**
Anuario Estadistico del Estado de Chihuahua (MEX ISSN 0188-8668) **8346**
Anuario Estadistico del Estado de Coahuila (MEX ISSN 0188-8560) **8346**
Anuario Estadistico del Estado de Colima (MEX ISSN 0188-8579) **8346**
Anuario Estadistico del Estado de Guanajuato (MEX ISSN 0188-8536) **8346**
Anuario Estadistico del Estado de Guerrero (MEX ISSN 0188-865X) **8346**
Anuario Estadistico del Estado de Hidalgo (MEX ISSN 0188-8625) **8346**
Anuario Estadistico del Estado de Jalisco (MEX ISSN 0188-8528) **8346**
Anuario Estadistico del Estado de Mexico (MEX ISSN 0188-851X) **8346**
Anuario Estadistico del Estado de Morelos (MEX ISSN 0188-8498) **8346**
Anuario Estadistico del Estado de Nuevo Leon (MEX ISSN 0188-8471) **8346**
Anuario Estadistico del Estado de Oaxaca (MEX ISSN 0188-8463) **8346**
Anuario Estadistico del Estado de Puebla (MEX ISSN 0188-8684) **8346**
Anuario Estadistico del Estado de Queretaro (MEX ISSN 0188-8455) **8346**
Anuario Estadistico del Estado de Quintana Roo (MEX ISSN 0188-8617) **8346**
Anuario Estadistico del Estado de San Luis Potosi (MEX ISSN 0188-8447) **8346**
Anuario Estadistico del Estado de Sinaloa (MEX ISSN 0188-8439) **8346**
Anuario Estadistico del Estado de Tabasco (MEX ISSN 0188-8420) **8346**
Anuario Estadistico del Estado de Tamaulipas (MEX ISSN 0188-8412) **8346**
Anuario Estadistico del Estado de Veracruz (MEX ISSN 0187-4764) **8346**
Anuario Estadistico del Estado de Yucatan (MEX ISSN 0188-8404) **8346**
Anuario Estadistico del Paraguay (PRY ISSN 0252-8932) **8346**
Anuario Estadistico del Sector Agroalimentario C.A.P.V. *see* Nekazal Elikagai Sektorearen Estatistika Urtekaria E.A.E. **184**
Anuario Estadistico del Transporte Aereo Espana - (Year) (ESP ISSN 0213-0009) **8521**
Anuario Estadistico - Direccion Nacional de Estadisticas, Ministerio de Salud Publica *see* Cuba. Ministerio de Salud Publica. Direccion Nacional de Estadisticas. Anuario Estadistico **5743**
Anuario Estadistico Pesquero (ARG) **3612**
Anuario Estadistico - Seguros y Prevision Social (SLV) **4529**
Anuario Estatistico da Bahia (BRA ISSN 0102-0676) **8346**
Anuario Estatistico da Cidade do Rio de Janeiro (BRA) **8346**
Anuario Estatistico de Mocambique *see* Mozambique Statistical Yearbook **8389**
Anuario Estatistico de Portugal (PRT ISSN 0871-8741) **8346**
• Anuario Estatistico do Brasil/Statistical Yearbook of Brazil (BRA ISSN 0100-1299) **8347**
Anuario Estatistico do Estado de Sao Paulo (BRA ISSN 0100-8730) **8347**
Anuario Estatistico do Estado do Para (BRA ISSN 0103-5274) **8347**
• Anuario Estatistico dos Transportes (BRA ISSN 0102-4671) **8490**
† Anuario Etnologico de Andalucia (ESP) **8930**
Anuario Evolucion (ESP ISSN 1133-5947) **1717**
Anuario F.H.I. Argentina: Frutas y Hortalizas Industrializadas y Frescas/F.H.I. Annual: Fresh and Industrialized Fruits and Vegetables (ARG ISSN 0066-5207) **218**
Anuario Filosofia, Psicologia y Sociologia (ESP ISSN 1139-8132) **6904**
• ➤ Anuario Filosofico (ESP ISSN 0066-5215) **6904**
Anuario Geografico del Peru (PER ISSN 0066-5223) **4284**
Anuario Hipico (ESP) **8287**
• Anuario Hispano/Hispanic Yearbook (USA ISSN 1067-330X) **6692**
Anuario Hortofruticola Espanol (ESP ISSN 0210-637X) **193**
Anuario Iberoamericano (ESP ISSN 1139-7225) **3118**
Anuario Iberoamericano (ESP ISSN 0570-4324) **7947**
Anuario Iberoamericano de Derecho Notarial (ESP ISSN 1695-2189) **4619**
Anuario Iberoamericano de Justicia Constitucional (ESP ISSN 1138-4824) **4846**
Anuario Indigenista/Indianist Yearbook (MEX ISSN 0304-2596) **328**
Anuario Industrial de la Provincia (ESP) **1395**
• Anuario Ininco (VEN ISSN 0798-2992) **8088**
Anuario Interamericano de Derechos Humanos/Inter-American Yearbook on Human Rights (NLD ISSN 0920-7775) **4917**
Anuario Interinstitucional. Quem e Quem na Uniao Europeia? *see* Interinstitutional Directory. Who's Who in the European Union? **643**
Anuario Interinstitucional. Quien es Quien en la Union Europea *see* Interinstitutional Directory. Who's Who in the European Union? **643**
• Anuario Internacional C I D O B (Centre d'Informacio i Documentacio Internacionals a Barcelona) (ESP ISSN 1133-2743) **7221**
• Anuario Juridico (MEX ISSN 0185-3295) **4619**
• Anuario Juridico de La Rioja (ESP ISSN 1135-7096) **4619**
Anuario Juridico Escurialense *see* Anuario Juridico y Economico Escurialense **4619**
Anuario Juridico y Economico Escurialense (ESP ISSN 1133-3677) **4619**
Anuario L L Estudios Linguisticos (Literatura Linguistica) (CUB) **5095**
Anuario L L Estudios Literarios (Literatura Linguistica) (CUB) **5255**
Anuario Latinoamericano de Educacion Quimica (ARG ISSN 0328-087X) **2050**
Anuario Lope de Vega (ESP ISSN 1136-5773) **5095**
Anuario Manutencion y Almacenaje (ESP) **5449**
Anuario Medieval (USA ISSN 1044-8594) **4199**
• Anuario Mexicano de Derecho Internacional (MEX ISSN 1870-4654) **4917**
Anuario Mexicano de Historia del Derecho (MEX ISSN 0188-0837) **4619**
Anuario Mineral Brasileiro (BRA ISSN 0100-9303) **6456**
• Anuario Musical (ESP ISSN 0211-3538) **6545**
Anuario Politico de America Latina (MEX) **7106**
Anuario Profesional del Medio Ambiente (ESP ISSN 1133-2875) **3403**
• Anuario Social de Espana (ESP ISSN 1577-5380) **7296**
Anuario Social y Politico de America Latina y el Caribe (VEN ISSN 1316-7162) **7948**
Anuario Urtekaria (ESP) **8253**
Anuarul Arhivei de Folclor (ROM ISSN 1220-3661) **3614**
Anuarul Institutului Geologic al Romaneiei *see* Institutul Geologic al Romaniei. Anuarul **2747**
Anuarul Muzeului National de Istorie a Romaniei (ROM) **6519**
Anuarul Statistic al Romaniei/Statistical Yearbook of Romania (ROM ISSN 1220-3246) **8347**
Anuncios (ESP ISSN 0214-4905) **21**
Anunt de la A la Z (ROM ISSN 1221-5805) **21**
Anustup (IND) **5206**
Anuvad/Translation (IND ISSN 0003-6218) **5095**
Anvesak (IND ISSN 0378-4568) **1060**
Anvil (GBR ISSN 0969-7373) **7746**
Anvil Magazine (USA ISSN 1059-2997) **6305**
The Anvil's Ring (USA ISSN 0889-177X) **531**
• Anwalt- und Notarverzeichnis (DEU ISSN 0944-212X) **1972**
AnwaltDirekt C D (DEU ISSN 1614-8118) **4619**
AnwaltInfo Mietrecht (DEU ISSN 1611-7719) **7582**
Anwalts-Report (DEU ISSN 1433-4453) **4619**
Anwaltsblatt (DEU ISSN 0171-7227) **4619**
Anwaltsgebuehren Spezial (DEU) **4619**
† Anwaltspraxis Wirtschaftsrecht (DEU ISSN 1613-0006) **8930**
Anwaltsrevue / Revue de l'Avocat/Revue de l'Avocat (CHE ISSN 1422-5778) **4619**
• Al-Anwar (LBN ISSN 1563-8499) **3905**
Anwar-E-Qaum (IND) **3879**
anwbAuto *see* A N W B Auto **8554**
anwbBoot *see* A N W B Boot **8270**
Anxiety and Stress *see* Ansiedad y Estres **6123**
Anxiety Disorders Alliance Newsletter *see* A D A Newsletter **6117**
Anxiety Disorders Association of America Hot Sheet *see* A D A A Hot Sheet **7330**
• ➤ Anxiety, Stress and Coping (GBR ISSN 1061-5806) **7335**
Any Amsbaugh Ancestors? (USA ISSN 1081-2288) **3758**
• Any Swing Goes (USA ISSN 1524-6728) **6545**
Any Time Now (CAN) **7106**
A+Cs (HUN ISSN 0003-6242) **8638**
Anyagmozgatasi es Csomagolasi Szakirodalmi Tajekoztato/Abstract Journal for Materials Handling and Packaging (HUN ISSN 0230-5348) **8521**
Anyang Daxue Xuebao/Anyang University. Journal *see* Anyang Gongxueyuan Xuebao **8416**
• Anyang Gongxueyuan Xuebao/Anyang Institute of Technology. Journal (CHN ISSN 1673-2928) **8416**
Anyang Institute of Technology. Journal *see* Anyang Gongxueyuan Xuebao **8416**
• Anyang Shifan Xueyuan Xuebao/Anyang Teachers College. Journal (CHN ISSN 1671-5330) **5255**
Anyang Teachers College. Journal *see* Anyang Shifan Xueyuan Xuebao **5255**
• Anyatha (IND) **5255**
AnyBody (DEU) **5065**
• L'Anysetiers (FRA ISSN 1249-6960) **2264**
• Anything That Moves (USA) **4371**
ANytt *see* AfghanistanNytt **4179**
anyway (DEU) **8683**
Anzac Test *see* Australia v New Zealand **8221**
Anzeigen Beobachter Moebel (DEU) **4553**
Anzeiger (AUT) **7551**
Anzeiger (CHE) **3957**
➤ Anzeiger des Germanischen Nationalmuseums (DEU ISSN 1430-5496) **4199**
Anzeiger des Vereins Thueringer Ornithologen (DEU ISSN 0940-4708) **901**
Anzeiger fuer die Altertumswissenschaft (AUT ISSN 0003-6293) **2230**
Anzeiger fuer die Seelsorge (DEU ISSN 0721-1937) **7784**
Anzeiger fuer Schaedlingskunde *see* Journal of Pest Science **852**
Anzeiger fuer Slavische Philologie (AUT ISSN 0066-5282) **5095**
Anzen Eisei no Hiroba/Safety and Health (JPN ISSN 0911-0011) **6672**
Anzen Kogaku/Japan Society for Safety Engineering. Journal (JPN ISSN 0570-4480) **3181**
Anzen no Hiroba *see* Anzen Eisei no Hiroba **6672**
• El Anzuelo (English Edition) (GBR) **3403**
• El Anzuelo (French Edition) (GBR) **3403**
A+O Fonds Rijk. Nieuwsbrief (NLD ISSN 1872-0250) **1663**
A+O Magazine (Arbeidsmarkt- en Opleidingsfonds) (NLD ISSN 1574-3241) **1663**
AoA eNews *see* A O A eNews **4038**
AOA. Revista (Asociacion de Oficinas de Arquitectos) (CHL ISSN 0718-3186) **427**
Das AOL-Magazin *see* Das A O L - Magazin **2552**
Aomen Minhang Xuekan/Institute of Macao Civil Aviation. Journal (MAC ISSN 1814-8662) **47**
Aomori Akenohoshi Junior College Research Bulletin *see* Aomori Akenohoshi Tanki Daigaku Kenkyu Kiyo **7836**
Aomori Akenohoshi Tanki Daigaku Kenkyu Kiyo/Aomori Akenohoshi Junior College Research Bulletin (JPN ISSN 1346-1311) **7836**
Aomori Apple Experiment Station. Annual Report *see* Gyomu Nenpo - Aomori-ken Ringo Shikenjo **117**
Aomori City Hospital. Medical Journal *see* Aomori Shimin Byoin Ishi **5576**
Aomori-ken Ishikaiho/Aomori Medical Association. Journal (JPN ISSN 0914-6873) **5576**
Aomori-ken Noson Igakkai Zasshi/Aomori Society of Rural Medicine. Journal (JPN ISSN 0916-0450) **5576**
Aomori-ken Noson Igaku Kenkyukaishi *see* Aomori-ken Noson Igakkai Zasshi **5576**
Aomori Kenritsu Byoin Nenpo/Aomori Prefectural Hospitals. Annual Reports (JPN) **4088**
Aomori Kenritsu Chuo Byoin Ishi/Aomori Prefectural Central Hospital. Medical Journal (JPN ISSN 0387-0138) **4088**
Aomori Medical Association. Journal *see* Aomori-ken Ishikaiho **5576**
Aomori Municipal Hospital Establishment Association. Journal *see* Aomoriken Jichitai Igakkaishi **5576**
Aomori Nogyo (JPN ISSN 0003-6331) **92**
Aomori Prefectural Central Hospital. Medical Journal *see* Aomori Kenritsu Chuo Byoin Ishi **4088**
Aomori Prefectural Hospitals. Annual Reports *see* Aomori Kenritsu Byoin Nenpo **4088**
Aomori Prefecture. Monthly Report of Meteorology *see* Aomoriken Kisho Geppo **6346**
Aomori Rosai Byoin Ishi/Aomori Rosai Medical Journal (JPN ISSN 0918-1369) **5576**
Aomori Rosai Medical Journal *see* Aomori Rosai Byoin Ishi **5576**
Aomori Shimin Byoin Ishi/Aomori City Hospital. Medical Journal (JPN ISSN 0914-7500) **5576**
Aomori Society of Obstetricians and Gynecologists. Journal *see* Aomoriken Rinsho Sanfujinka Ikaishi **5986**
Aomori Society of Rural Medicine. Journal *see* Aomori-ken Noson Igakkai Zasshi **5576**
Aomori Society of Sports Medicine. Journal *see* Aomoriken Supotsu Igaku Kenkyukaishi **6228**
Aomoriken Biological Society. Journal *see* Aomoriken Seibutsu Gakkaishi **653**
Aomoriken Jichitai Igakkaishi/Aomori Municipal Hospital Establishment Association. Journal (JPN ISSN 0913-4581) **5576**
Aomoriken Kisho Geppo/Aomori Prefecture. Monthly Report of Meteorology (JPN ISSN 0029-7399) **6346**
Aomoriken Rinsho Sanfujinka Ikaishi/Aomori Society of Obstetricians and Gynecologists. Journal (JPN ISSN 0913-8307) **5986**
Aomoriken Sagyo Ryoho Kenkyu/Bulletin of Aomori Occupational Therapy (JPN ISSN 0918-1431) **6106**
Aomoriken Seibutsu Gakkaishi/Aomoriken Biological Society. Journal (JPN ISSN 0286-4444) **653**
Aomoriken Supotsu Igaku Kenkyukaishi/Aomori Society of Sports Medicine. Journal (JPN ISSN 0918-0257) **6228**
Aontacht Cumann Riartha Aitreabhthoiri News *see* A C R A News **3892**
• Aoraki Librarians (Online) (NZL ISSN 1176-5356) **4989**
• Aoraki Polytechnic. Annual Report (NZL ISSN 1171-8722) **3017**
Aorta (SWE ISSN 1402-7984) **5255**
Aotearoa Ethnic Network Journal *see* A E N Journal **3514**
• Aotearoa New Zealand International Development Studies Network. Proceedings of the Biennial Conference (NZL ISSN 1176-550X) **1590**
• Aotearoa New Zealand Social Work Review (NZL ISSN 1178-5527) **8025**
Aouzou (LBY) **4443**
Aoyama Journal of Social Sciences/Aoyama Shakai Kagaku Kiyo (JPN ISSN 0286-3901) **7948**
Aoyama Shakai Kagaku Kiyo *see* Aoyama Journal of Social Sciences **7948**
Aozhou Caihongying/Australian Winner (AUS ISSN 1832-3456) **1552**
Aozhou Yanjiu/Taiwanese Journal of Australian Studies (TWN ISSN 1816-3114) **7221**
APA Journal *see* A P A Journal **8554**
† • Apache Week (GBR) **8930**
Apaja (FIN ISSN 1238-9587) **3584**
Apalachee Quarterly *see* Apalachee Review **5256**
• Apalachee Review (USA) **5256**
Aparato Locomotor *see* Encyclopedie Medico-Chirurgicale. Aparato Locomotor **6223**
Apartment Age (USA ISSN 0192-0030) **4403**
• Apartment Building Management Insider (USA ISSN 1935-6137) **7582**
• Apartment Finance Today (USA ISSN 1097-4059) **7582**
Apartment Gazetteer (Europe) (GBR) **8683**
Apartment Management Magazine (USA) **4403**
Apartment Management Magazine (Los Angeles Edition) *see* Apartment Management Magazine **4403**
Apartment Management Magazine (Orange County Edition) *see* Apartment Management Magazine **4403**
Apartment Management Newsletter (USA ISSN 0744-9143) **7582**
Apartment Moves (USA) **7582**
Apartment News (USA) **7582**
Apartment Owner (USA ISSN 0191-8826) **7582**
The Apartment Professional *see* Multihousing Professional **7601**
Apartment Professionals' Resources & Services Guide *see* Multihousing Professional **7601**
Apatinska Pivara List *see* A P A List **597**
• Ape Culture (USA) **2375**
Ape del Conca (ITA) **3896**
➤ Apeiron (Kelowna) (CAN ISSN 0003-6390) **6904**
• ➤ Apeiron (Montreal) (CAN ISSN 0843-6061) **568**
Apendice al Indice Progresivo de Jurisprudencia *see* Indice Progresivo de Jurisprudencia **4823**
Apendice al Indice Progresivo de Jurisprudencia *see* Repertorio de Jurisprudencia. Indices Auxiliares **4825**
Apendice al Indice Progresivo de Jurisprudencia *see* Repertorio de Jurisprudencia **4768**
Apendice al Indice Progresivo de Legislacion (ESP ISSN 1139-0395) **4820**
Apercu de la Securite Sociale en Belgique *see* Beknopt Overzicht van de Sociale Zekerheid in Belgie **7422**
Apercu de la Statistique Federale Allemande *see* Survey of German Federal Statistics **8408**
Aperio (CZE ISSN 1214-7389) **2143**
Aperitif (SWE ISSN 0283-3387) **4382**
Apertura (ARG ISSN 0328-6401) **7106**
Apertura (MEX ISSN 1665-6180) **2826**
• Aperturas Psicoanaliticas (ESP ISSN 1699-4825) **7335**
• Aperture (USA ISSN 0003-6420) **6964**
Apex (USA) **8304**
Apex (Leeds) (GBR ISSN 1460-1729) **5835**
Apex (Lexington) (USA ISSN 1553-7269) **5439**
Apex Digest *see* Apex (Lexington) **5439**
Apex Science Fiction & Horror Digest *see* Apex (Lexington) **5439**
Apex to Zenith (USA) **8304**
• ➤ Aphasiology (GBR ISSN 0268-7038) **6123**
• Aphelion (USA) **5439**
Aphra (GBR) **8851**
• Apiacta (ITA ISSN 0003-6455) **92**
O Apicultor (PRT ISSN 0873-2981) **92**
Apiculture *see* Pchelovodstvo **146**
Apiculture of China *see* Zhongguo Yangfeng **173**
• ➤ Apidologie (FRA ISSN 0044-8435) **839**

Title

DIRECTORY 2010 ARBEIDETS RETT 9971

• ➤ Aquaculture Nutrition (GBR ISSN 1353-5773) **3585**
Aquaculture Outlook (USA) **3585**
• ➤ Aquaculture Research (GBR ISSN 1355-557X) **3585**
Aquaculture Research. Supplement *see* Aquaculture Research **3585**
• AquaKE Government Documents Library (USA) **3585**
Aqual Life *see* Gekkan Akua Raifu **2804**
Aqualine *see* Aqualine Abstracts **8842**
• Aqualine Abstracts (USA ISSN 0263-5534) **8842**
Aqualines (GBR) **6106**
Aquamonde (FRA ISSN 1771-4621) **933**
• Aquanaut (USA ISSN 0264-259X) **6762**
Aquanews (NOR ISSN 1504-5528) **3585**
AquaNoticias (CHL) **3585**
Aquaphyte (USA ISSN 0893-7702) **776**
Aquapress International (AUT) **8818**
Aquarama (Dutch Edition) (BEL ISSN 1784-648X) **3360**
Aquarama (French Edition) (BEL ISSN 1784-6498) **3360**
Aquarama Magazine (SGP) **6803**
Aquarian Arrow (GBR ISSN 0141-0121) **6741**
The Aquarian Weekly (USA ISSN 1067-5108) **6545**
Aquarien-Praxis (DEU) **3585**
Aquarien - Terrarien - Information (AUT ISSN 1021-2221) **3586**
Aquaristik (DEU ISSN 1863-1282) **3586**
Aquaristik - Fachmagazin (DEU ISSN 1437-4854) **3586**
Het Aquarium (NLD ISSN 0003-729X) **933**
L'Aquarium a la Maison (FRA ISSN 1278-060X) **6803**
Aquarium and Terrarium Animals *see* Seibutsu Shiiku Kenkyukai Kaishi **703**
• Aquarium Fish International (USA ISSN 1942-5678) **6803**
Aquarium Fish Magazine *see* Aquarium Fish International **6803**
Aquarium Live (DEU ISSN 1432-413X) **6803**
† Aquarium Magazine (FRA ISSN 0769-6361) **8930**
Aquarium U S A (USA ISSN 1069-1871) **6803**
Aquariumwereld (BEL ISSN 1372-6501) **6803**
Aquarius (GBR ISSN 0003-7303) **5416**
Aquarius (PER ISSN 0251-0499) **3586**
Aquas Vivas (ARG) **3790**
Aquatec (ARG ISSN 0327-7755) **2792**
Aquatechnic International (GBR ISSN 0261-5355) **8818**
Aquaterra *see* Aqua Terra **8818**
• AquaTIC (ESP ISSN 1578-4541) **3586**
▼ • ➤ Aquatic Biology (DEU ISSN 1864-7782) **654**
• Aquatic Biology, Aquaculture & Fisheries Resources (ZAF ISSN 1083-883X) **713**
• ➤ Aquatic Botany (NLD ISSN 0304-3770) **776**
• ➤ Aquatic Conservation (GBR ISSN 1052-7613) **2602**
• ➤ Aquatic Ecology (NLD ISSN 1386-2588) **654**
• ➤ Aquatic Ecosystem Health & Management (USA ISSN 1463-4988) **776**
• Aquatic Environment Monitoring Report (GBR ISSN 0142-2499) **3403**
• Aquatic Environment Protection (GBR ISSN 0953-4466) **3403**
The Aquatic Gardener (USA ISSN 1073-6999) **3723**
• ➤ Aquatic Geochemistry (NLD ISSN 1380-6165) **2701**
• ➤ Aquatic Insects (GBR ISSN 0165-0424) **839**
• Aquatic Invaders (USA ISSN 1535-6868) **933**
• ➤ Aquatic Invasions (RUS ISSN 1818-5487) **933**
• ➤ Aquatic Living Resources (FRA ISSN 0990-7440) **3586**
• ➤ Aquatic Mammals (USA ISSN 0167-5427) **933**
• ➤ Aquatic Microbial Ecology (DEU ISSN 0948-3055) **881**
Aquatic Plant News (USA ISSN 1046-9397) **776**
➤ Aquatic Plant Studies (NLD ISSN 0921-8572) **776**
Aquatic Pollution and Environmental Quality *see* Aquatic Sciences & Fisheries Abstracts. Part 3: Aquatic Pollution and Environmental Quality **3477**
Aquatic Resource Management for Local Communities News *see* A L C O M News **3582**
Aquatic Resource Management for Local Communities Reports *see* A L C O M Reports **3582**
• ➤ Aquatic Sciences (CHE ISSN 1015-1621) **2792**
Aquatic Sciences & Fisheries Abstracts Aquaculture Abstracts (Online) *see* A S F A Aquaculture Abstracts (Online) **3612**
• Aquatic Sciences & Fisheries Abstracts. Part 1: Biological Sciences and Living Resources (USA ISSN 0140-5373) **2634**
• Aquatic Sciences & Fisheries Abstracts. Part 2: Ocean Technology, Policy and Non-living Resources (USA ISSN 0140-5381) **8842**
• Aquatic Sciences & Fisheries Abstracts. Part 3: Aquatic Pollution and Environmental Quality (USA ISSN 1045-6031) **3477**
Aquatic Therapy Journal (USA ISSN 1534-5459) **6106**
Aquatic Toxicity Workshop. Proceedings of the Annual (CAN ISSN 1716-5989) **3483**
• ➤ Aquatic Toxicology (NLD ISSN 0166-445X) **3493**
• Aquatics International (USA ISSN 1058-7039) **8158**
Aquatics International Directory (USA ISSN 1553-3441) **1972**
• Aquaworld Magazine (ITA) **3586**
Aqueduct 2000 (USA) **8818**
• Aquent Magazine (USA) **1956**
Aqui (BOL ISSN 1013-5081) **3802**
Aqui (PRY ISSN 0044-8524) **8088**
Aqui (URY ISSN 0066-5606) **5256**
Aqui L L E G O (National Latino -a Lesbian, Gay, Bisexual & Transgender Organization) (USA) **4371**
Aqui Milwaukee (USA) **6545**
Aqui y Ahora (HND) **8683**
• Aquichan (COL ISSN 1657-5997) **7948**
Aquila (GBR ISSN 0965-4003) **2176**
Aquila Legionis (ESP ISSN 1578-1518) **4130**
Aquilegia (USA) **776**
➤ Aquilo. Serie Botanica (FIN ISSN 0570-5169) **776**
Aquilo. Serie Zoologica (FIN ISSN 0570-5177) **933**
L'Aquilon (CAN ISSN 0834-1443) **3806**
Aquinas (VAT ISSN 0003-7362) **6904**
➤ Aquinas Journal (LKA) **7784**
Aquinas Lecture Series (USA ISSN 0066-5614) **6905**
Aquincumi Zsebkonyvek (HUN ISSN 1787-8624) **328**
Aquinian (CAN) **2272**
Aquiri (BRA) **4443**
Aquitaine Ocean (FRA ISSN 1261-6818) **2800**
Aquitania (FRA ISSN 0758-9670) **4199**
Aquitania. Supplement *see* Aquitania **4199**
Ar Gwyr *see* Cahiers Bretons **7952**
Ara (HUN ISSN 1587-2084) **8851**
Al-Arab (SAU) **4319**
Arab Agriculture (GBR ISSN 0265-556X) **194**
Arab Agriculture Yearbook/Al-Zira'ah al-Arabiyyah (BHR) **92**
Al-Arab al-Yawm (JOR) **3901**
• Arab-American Affairs (USA ISSN 1940-1086) **3519**
Arab American Almanac (USA ISSN 0742-9576) **3519**
Arab-American Almanac *see* Arab-American Affairs **3519**
Arab - American Business (USA) **3519**
Arab American News *see* Sada al-Watan **3562**
▼ • Arab-American Yearbook (USA ISSN 1940-1000) **6692**
† Arab and Islamic Law Series (NLD ISSN 1574-3446) **8930**
Arab - Asian Affairs (GBR ISSN 0196-3538) **7221**
Arab Authority for Agricultural Investment and Development. Annual Report (SDN ISSN 1817-6534) **194**
Arab Aviation Review (GBR) **47**
Arab Bank for Economic Development in Africa. Annual Report (SDN) **1308**
Arab Bank for Economic Development in Africa. Quarterly Review (SDN) **1308**
Arab Banking and Finance (BHR) **1308**
• Arab - British Business (GBR ISSN 0958-8116) **1060**
• Arab - British Trade (GBR ISSN 1351-0495) **1395**
Arab Buyers' Guide to British Industry (GBR ISSN 0958-2339) **1972**
Arab Competitiveness Report *see* At Taqrir at-Tanafusiyyat al-'arabiyyat **1521**
Arab Construction World *see* 'Alam al-insha'at al-'arabi **975**
Arab Construction World International *see* 'Alam al-insha'at al-'arabi **975**
Arab Defence and Aerospace Business (DEU) **6410**
Arab Defense Journal *see* Al- Difa' al-Arabi **6419**
Arab Dental/Alam Tib al-Asnan (DEU) **5835**
Arab Directory/Dalil el Arab (CAN ISSN 0706-7917) **3519**
Arab Film and Television Center News (LBN ISSN 0003-7397) **6489**
Arab Fund for Economic and Social Development. Annual Report (KWT ISSN 0304-6729) **1590**
Arab Future *see* Al- Mustaqbal al-Arabi **7986**
Arab Guide (CAN ISSN 1483-1252) **3519**
➤ Arab Gulf Journal of Scientific Research (SAU ISSN 1015-4442) **7836**
Arab Health International *see* 'Alam al-Sihhat al-'Arabi **7506**
Arab Health World *see* 'Alam al-Sihhat al-'Arabi **7506**
Arab Health World *see* 'Alam al-Sihhat al-'Arabi **7506**
Arab Historical Review for Ottoman Studies (TUN ISSN 0330-8081) **4319**
Arab Horse Stud Book (GBR ISSN 1746-3386) **8287**
• Arab Human Development Report (Year) (USA ISSN 1992-7622) **8088**
Arab Industry Review (BHR) **1879**
▼ • Arab Insight (USA ISSN 1936-8984) **7221**
• Arab Institute for Training & Research in Statistics. Statistical Bulletin (JOR) **8347**
The Arab Journal for Arts *see* Al Magallah al-'arabiyyah li-l-adab **4464**
Arab Journal for Librarianship & Information Science *see* Arab Journal of Library and Information Science **4989**
Arab Journal for the Humanities *see* Al- Majallat al-Arabiyyat lil-Uloom al-Insaniyyat **4464**
➤ Arab Journal of Administrative Sciences (KWT ISSN 1029-855X) **1725**
• ➤ Arab Journal of Biotechnology (EGY ISSN 1110-6875) **756**
The Arab Journal of Laboratory Medicine/Al-Magalat al-'Arabiyyat lil-Tib al-Mahbari (EGY ISSN 1110-1822) **5902**
Arab Journal of Language Studies/Al-Majallah al-'Arabiyyah lil-Dirasat al-Lughawiyyah (SDN) **5095**
Arab Journal of Library and Information Science (SAU) **4989**
Arab Journal of Mathematical Sciences (SAU ISSN 1319-5166) **5473**
Arab Journal of Nuclear Sciences and Applications/Al-Magallat al-'Arabiyyat lil-'Ulum al-Nawawiyyat Wa-Tatbiqatiha (EGY ISSN 1110-0451) **3164**
Arab Journal of Plant Protection (LBN ISSN 0255-982X) **776**
The Arab Journal of Psychiatry *see* Al Magallah Al-'arabiyyah Li-l-tibb Al-nafsi **6159**
• ➤ Arab Law Quarterly (NLD ISSN 0268-0556) **4619**
Arab League Educational, Scientific, and Cultural Organization. Information Newsletter (TUN) **2827**
• ➤ Arab Media & Society (EGY ISSN 1687-7721) **2312**
Arab Medical Bulletin (SDN ISSN 0254-9492) **5577**
Arab Medico (DEU ISSN 0723-5100) **5577**
Arab Mining Journal (JOR ISSN 0250-9881) **6456**
• Arab News (SAU ISSN 0254-833X) **3912**
Arab News International (CAN ISSN 0839-4547) **3519**
• Arab Oil & Gas Directory (FRA ISSN 0304-8551) **6762**
Arab Oil & Gas Magazine (Monthly) (FRA ISSN 0378-7184) **6762**
Arab Oil Review (LBY ISSN 0003-7435) **6762**
Arab Palestinian Resistance (SYR) **3960**
Arab Petroleum (LBY ISSN 0003-7443) **6762**
Arab Postal Union. Review *see* Ittihad al-Baridi al-Arabi **2354**
Arab Press Service Diplomat Recorder *see* A P S Diplomat Recorder **7219**
Arab Press Service Diplomat Redrawing the Islamic Map *see* A P S Diplomat Redrawing the Islamic Map **7101**
Arab Press Service News Service *see* A P S News Service **3123**
Arab Press Service Review Downstream Trends *see* A P S Review Downstream Trends **6761**
Arab Press Service Review Gas Market Trends *see* A P S Review Gas Market Trends **6761**
• Arab Reform Bulletin (USA ISSN 1942-5805) **7107**
Arab Republic Community Arabic Journal *see* A R C Arabic Journal **3515**
Arab Roads (EGY ISSN 1110-046X) **8629**
▼ ➤ Arab Statistical Sciences Journal (JOR) **8347**
Arab Studies *see* Dirasat Arabiyat **7130**
➤ Arab Studies Journal (USA ISSN 1083-4753) **542**
Arab - Swiss Chamber of Commerce and Industry. Annual Directory (CHE) **1395**
Arab - Swiss Co-operation (CHE) **1395**
• Arab Times (KWT) **3903**
Arab Trade Directory (GBR) **1972**
Arab Traveller *see* Al- Musafir al-Arabi **8739**
Arab Universities Journal of Agricultural Sciences/Magallat Itihad Al-Gami'at Al-'Arabiyyat Lil-Dirasat Wa-Al-Buhut Al-Zira'iyyat (EGY ISSN 1110-2675) **92**
Arab Water World *see* 'Alam al-Miyah al-'arabi **8817**
Arab Water World International *see* 'Alam al-Miyah al-'arabi **8817**
Arab World (KEN) **7221**
The Arab World (LBN) **7221**
Arab World Agribusiness/Al-Zira'ah fi-l-Alam al-Arabi (BHR) **92**
Arab World and Islamic Resources and School Services's Middle East Resources *see* A W A I R's Middle East Resources **7944**
➤ Arab World Geographer (CAN ISSN 1480-6800) **3999**
Arabella (GBR ISSN 1747-1494) **3519**
ArabellaSheraton (DEU) **8782**
Araber Journal *see* Araber Weltweit **8287**
Araber Weltweit (DEU ISSN 1614-192X) **8287**
Arabesk (NOR ISSN 0809-0807) **6545**
• Arabesques (FRA ISSN 1269-0589) **4989**
Al-Arabi (KWT ISSN 0258-3941) **3903**
• Al 'arabi as-Saghir (KWT ISSN 1811-8275) **3903**
Arabia Past & Present Series (GBR) **4319**
• ➤ Arabian Archaeology and Epigraphy (DNK ISSN 0905-7196) **374**
• Arabian Archaeology and Epigraphy Online (DNK ISSN 1600-0471) **374**
Arabian Business (UAE ISSN 1475-9837) **1060**
Arabian Business. Yearbook (UAE ISSN 1818-1627) **1060**
Arabian Gulf Information (BHR) **4989**
Arabian Gulf Research Review (UAE) **4319**
Arabian Horse Country (USA) **8287**
Arabian Horse Express (AUS ISSN 1445-9191) **8287**
Arabian Horse Express (USA ISSN 0194-6803) **8287**
Arabian Horse Magazine *see* Modern Arabian Horse **8294**
The Arabian Horse Newspaper (USA ISSN 1545-6706) **8287**
Arabian Horse Times (USA ISSN 0279-8425) **8287**
• Arabian Horse World (USA ISSN 0003-7494) **8287**
➤ Arabian Journal for Science and Engineering (SAU ISSN 0377-9211) **3181**
• Arabian Journal for Science and Engineering. Section B: Engineering (SAU ISSN 1319-8025) **3181**
▼ • ➤ Arabian Journal of Geosciences (DEU ISSN 1866-7511) **2725**
Arabian Studs & Stallions (AUS) **8287**
• Arabic Sciences and Philosophy (GBR ISSN 0957-4239) **4131**
• ➤ Arabica (NLD ISSN 0570-5398) **542**
• The Arabidopsis Book (USA ISSN 1543-8120) **776**
Arabies (FRA ISSN 0983-1509) **3921**
• Arabies Trends (FRA ISSN 1288-2828) **3912**
Arabische Studien (DEU ISSN 1860-5117) **542**
Arabische Volbloedpaarden Stamboek Magazine *see* A V S Magazine **8286**
Arabisches Aerzteblatt (DEU) **5577**
Arabism *see* Al- Urubah **3912**
➤ The Arabist (HUN ISSN 0239-1619) **5095**
Arabistische Texte und Studien (DEU ISSN 0931-0789) **5256**
➤ Al-Arabiyya (USA ISSN 0889-8731) **5200**
Arable Monitoring Report *see* Horticulture and Arable Monitoring Report **200**
Arabusiness International (CAN ISSN 0830-8888) **1060**
Arachne (USA) **5416**
† • Arachnion (ITA ISSN 1123-9328) **8930**
Arachnologische Mitteilungen (DEU ISSN 1018-4171) **839**
Arachnologische Mitteilungen. Sonderband (DEU ISSN 1420-1445) **839**
Aracnet *see* Sociedad Entomologica Aragonesa. Boletin **859**
➤ Aracnologia (URY ISSN 0254-5578) **933**
▼ Arado (COL ISSN 2011-2939) **92**
Arafmi News (AUS) **6123**
• Aragil News (ARM) **3792**
• Aragon en la Edad Media (ESP ISSN 0213-2486) **4131**
Aragon Turistico y Monumental (ESP) **8683**
Aragonese Anthropology *see* Temas de Antropologia Aragonesa **358**
Aragonia (ESP ISSN 1579-7511) **6519**
Aragonia Sacra (ESP ISSN 0213-7631) **4131**
• Aral (ESP ISSN 1697-8021) **3676**
Aral Digital *see* Aral **3676**
Aral Direkt (DEU) **6762**
Araldo della Christian Science *see* The Herald of Christian Science **8962**
Araldo della Christian Science *see* Le Heraut de la Christian Science **7736**
† Araldo di S. Antonio (ITA ISSN 0003-7559) **8930**
• ➤ ARAM Periodical (BEL ISSN 0959-4213) **4319**
• Aramaic Studies (NLD ISSN 1477-8351) **7622**
Aranzadi Civil (Biweekly Edition) *see* Aranzadi Civil (Qarterly Edition) **4827**
Aranzadi Civil (Qarterly Edition) (ESP ISSN 1139-0638) **4827**
Aranzadi Civil. Cuadernos *see* Aranzadi Civil (Qarterly Edition) **4827**
Aranzadi Civil. Indices Auxiliares *see* Aranzadi Civil (Qarterly Edition) **4827**
Aranzadi Social (ESP ISSN 1131-5369) **4620**
Aranzadi Social (Quarterly Edition) (ESP ISSN 1139-031X) **4620**
Aranzadi Social. Cuadernos *see* Aranzadi Social **4620**
Aranzadi Social. Cuadernos *see* Aranzadi Social. Indices Auxiliares **4620**
Aranzadi Social. Cuadernos *see* Estudio Sistematico de la Jurisprudencia Recaida en Unificacion de Doctrina **4668**
Aranzadi Social. Indices Auxiliares (ESP ISSN 1139-0611) **4620**
Aranzadiana (ESP ISSN 1132-2292) **7836**
Ararajuba (BRA ISSN 0103-5657) **901**
Ararat (USA ISSN 0003-7583) **5256**
Arasaradi Journal of Theological Reflection (IND) **7784**
Arasiyal Tharasu (IND) **7107**
Arastirma Sonuclari Toplantisi (TUR ISSN 1017-7663) **374**
• Araucaria (ESP ISSN 1575-6823) **7948**
Araucaria C&T (Araucaria Ciencia e Tecnologia) (BRA ISSN 1676-501X) **8416**
Arauto da Ciencia Crista *see* Le Heraut de la Christian Science **7736**
Arauto da Ciencia Crista *see* The Herald of Christian Science **8962**
O Arauto do Vendedor (BRA) **1805**
Aravot (ARM) **3792**
Arba Sicula (USA ISSN 0271-0730) **3519**
Arbeid & Beloning *see* Wettenpocket Arbeid en Beloning **1715**
Arbeid Anders *see* Personeel en Recht **1703**
Arbeid en Zorg in C A O's *see* Arbeid en Zorg in Collectieve Arbeidsovereenkomsten **1663**
Arbeid en Zorg in Collectieve Arbeidsovereenkomsten (NLD ISSN 1872-1931) **1663**
Arbeid in Zorg en Welzijn (NLD ISSN 1872-1192) **6672**
Arbeid in Zorg en Welzijn (Utrecht) (NLD ISSN 1872-3535) **6672**
• Arbeid og Helse (NOR ISSN 0806-3648) **6672**
• Arbeid og Velferd (NOR ISSN 1504-8217) **1663**
Arbeiderhistorie (NOR ISSN 0801-7778) **1663**
Arbeidervern (NOR ISSN 0332-7124) **6672**
Arbeidets Rett (NOR) **3921**

Title

DIRECTORY 2010 ARKANSAS AMATEUR 9977

Argos (ARG ISSN 0325-4194) **2230**
Argos (FRA ISSN 0995-2187) **2827**
Argos (ITA ISSN 1125-1115) **6804**
• Argos (MEX ISSN 1562-4072) **5256**
Argos (NLD ISSN 0923-3970) **8793**
• ➤ Argos (VEN ISSN 0254-1637) **7948**
Argos Annual (ITA ISSN 1129-1761) **6804**
Argos Spine News *see* ArgoSpine News & Journal **6056**
† Argos Trend (ITA ISSN 1125-1123) **8931**
• ArgoSpine News & Journal (FRA ISSN 1957-7729) **6056**
Argosy (CAN ISSN 0044-8818) **2272**
Argosy (USA) **5409**
Argosy (Taylor) (USA) **5256**
Das Argument (DEU ISSN 0004-1157) **7948**
▼ • Argument & Computation (GBR ISSN 1946-2166) **2407**
➤ Argumenta Oeconomica Cracoviensia (POL ISSN 1642-168X) **1061**
• ➤ Argumentation (NLD ISSN 0920-427X) **6905**
• ➤ Argumentation & Advocacy (USA ISSN 1051-1431) **5096**
▼ Argumentation in Context (NLD ISSN 1877-6884) **5096**
Argumente (Berlin) (DEU ISSN 0939-0650) **92**
Argumente (Cologne) (DEU) **1061**
Argumente. Situationsbericht (DEU ISSN 0939-0235) **93**
Argumente und Fakten der Medizin (DEU ISSN 0939-8570) **5577**
Argumente zu Marktwirtschaft und Politik (DEU) **1437**
Argumento (BRA) **7948**
• Argumentos (ARG ISSN 1666-8979) **8088**
• Argumentos (MEX ISSN 0187-5795) **8088**
Argumentos de Razon Tecnica (ESP ISSN 1139-3327) **6905**
Arguments of the Philosophers (GBR) **6905**
• ➤ Argumentum (HUN ISSN 1787-3606) **5096**
• Argumenty i Fakty (RUS ISSN 0204-0476) **3934**
Argumenty i Fakty *see* A I F K A **2175**
Argumenty i Fakty Detskaya Entsiklopediya *see* A i F. Detskaya Entsiklopediya **2175**
Argumenty i Fakty Dochki-Materi *see* A i F. Dochki-Materi **8850**
Argumenty i Fakty Dolgozhitel' *see* A I F. Dolgozhitel' **4037**
Argumenty i Fakty IKS-pilot dlya Devochek *see* A i F. IKS-pilot dlya Devochek **2175**
Argumenty i Fakty IKS-pilot dlya Mal'chikov *see* A i F. IKS-pilot dlya Mal'chikov **2175**
Argumenty i Fakty Kazakhstan *see* A i F Kazakhstan **3902**
Argumenty i Fakty Kot i Pes *see* A i F. Kot i Pes **6802**
Argumenty i Fakty Lyubov' *see* A i F. Lyubov' **6285**
Argumenty i Fakty Moskva *see* A i F. Moskva **3934**
Argumenty i Fakty Na Dache *see* A i F. Na Dache **3934**
Argumenty i Fakty na Enisee *see* A i F na Enisee **3934**
Argumenty i Fakty Peterburg *see* A i F. Peterburg **3934**
Argumenty i Fakty Rabota-Ekspress *see* A i F. Rabota-Ekspress **1661**
Argumenty i Fakty Semeinyi Sovet *see* A i F. Semeinyi Sovet **2142**
Argumenty i Fakty Superzvezdy *see* A i F. Superzvezdy **3934**
Argumenty i Fakty Tvoi Kurs *see* A i F. Tvoi Kurs **2175**
Argumenty i Fakty Udmurtii *see* A i F Udmurtii **3934**
• Argumenty i Fakty v Belorusii (BLR) **3800**
Argumenty i Fakty Ya Khochu Vse Uznat'! *see* A I F. Ya Khochu Vse Uznat'! **2175**
Argumenty i Fakty Zdorov'e *see* A i F. Zdorov'e **6981**
Argus (HUN ISSN 1586-5363) **2511**
Argus *see* EyeNet **6042**
• The Argus (ZAF ISSN 1017-6128) **3947**
• Argus (Bloomington) (USA ISSN 0004-1181) **2273**
Argus (Dalaroe) (SWE ISSN 0284-3242) **6519**
Argus (Dutch Edition) (BEL) **4059**
Argus (French Edition) (BEL) **4059**
• Argus (Montreal) (CAN ISSN 0315-9930) **4990**
The Argus (Thunder Bay) (CAN ISSN 0004-1165) **2273**
• Argus Area (SWE ISSN 1401-9779) **5417**
▼ Argus China Petroleum (USA) **6762**
L'Argus de la Legislation Libanaise (LBN ISSN 0570-8915) **4620**
Argus de la Miniature (FRA ISSN 0182-0230) **4327**
L'Argus de L'Assurance (FRA ISSN 1626-4428) **4493**
L'Argus de l'Automobile et des Locomotions (FRA ISSN 0751-5545) **8556**
L'Argus de l'Economie Libanaise (LBN) **1061**
L'Argus des Commerces (FRA) **1061**
Argus des Metaux (FRA ISSN 0220-3332) **6305**
L'Argus du Bateau (FRA ISSN 1638-6272) **8271**
† Argus du Bateau et de Tout le Materiel Nautique (FRA ISSN 0395-1804) **8931**
† L'Argus du Camping-Car (FRA ISSN 1779-2533) **8931**
Argus du Livre de Collection (FRA ISSN 1266-7080) **5406**
Argus F S U Energy *see* F S U Energy **3135**
• Argus Freight (GBR ISSN 1751-309X) **8639**
Argus Freight Report *see* Argus Freight **8639**
• Argus Fundamentals (GBR ISSN 0957-039X) **6762**
• Argus Gas Connections (GBR ISSN 1460-695X) **6762**
• Argus Global Markets (GBR ISSN 1368-7433) **6762**
Argus L P G World *see* L P G World **6776**
Argus LatAm Energy *see* LatAm Energy **3141**
Argus Magazine (USA ISSN 0746-7788) **3969**
Argus Neftepanorama *see* Neftepanorama **6780**
• Argus Russian Coal (GBR ISSN 1753-0857) **3124**
Argus Russian Fuel Oil (GBR) **6762**
▼ • Argus U S Carbon (USA ISSN 1942-387X) **3404**
The Argus Weekender (IRL ISSN 1393-8401) **3892**
Argus Weekly Staff Report (USA) **1610**
Argyll Colony Plus (USA ISSN 1067-8638) **3759**
Arh & Art Borsa (BGR ISSN 0861-4008) **432**
Arhaiologike Efemeris (GRC ISSN 1105-0950) **380**
Arheia Ellenikes Iatrikes/Archives of Hellenic Medicine (GRC ISSN 1105-3992) **5577**
• Arheografski Prilozi/Archeographic Supplements (SRB ISSN 0351-2819) **4200**
Arheologia Moldovei/Archeologie de la Moldavie (ROM ISSN 0066-7358) **4200**
Arheologija un Etnografija (LVA ISSN 0320-9415) **380**
Arheologiya, Etnografiya i Antropologiya Evrazii (RUS ISSN 1563-0102) **380**
Arheoloski Muzej u Zagrebu. Vjesnik (HRV ISSN 0350-7165) **380**
Arheoloski Radovi i Rasprave (HRV ISSN 0570-8958) **380**
➤ Arheoloski Vestnik/Acta Archaeologica (SVN ISSN 0570-8966) **380**
Arhitectura (ROM ISSN 0300-5356) **432**
➤ Arhitektura (HRV ISSN 0350-3666) **432**
Arhitektura i Urbanizam (SRB ISSN 0354-6055) **432**
• Arhitektura, Raziskave/Architecture, Research (SVN ISSN 1580-5573) **432**
• Arhiv (SRB ISSN 1450-9733) **4200**
• Arhiv za Farmaciju (SRB ISSN 0004-1963) **6822**
• ➤ Arhiv za Higijenu Rada i Toksikologiju/Archives of Industrial Hygiene and Toxicology (HRV ISSN 0004-1254) **3494**
Arhiva Genealogica (ROM ISSN 1222-5630) **3759**
Arhivele Olteniei (ROM ISSN 1015-9118) **4131**
Arhivi (SVN ISSN 0351-2835) **4991**
➤ Arhivski Vjesnik/Bulletin d'Archives (HRV ISSN 0570-9008) **4200**
Ari/Ant (JPN ISSN 1344-8501) **839**
• ➤ Ari (TUR ISSN 1301-8256) **2725**
Ariadna (ESP ISSN 1130-8141) **3951**
Ariadne (DEU ISSN 0178-1073) **8851**
• Ariadne (Print) (GBR ISSN 1361-3197) **4991**
Ariadne at Home (NLD ISSN 1569-6626) **4531**
Ariadne Wonen *see* Ariadne at Home **4531**
Arian (ESP ISSN 1576-4400) **8159**
• Ariana Afghan Magazine (USA) **3519**
Ariane (PRT ISSN 0870-1253) **5256**
• Ariba B2B Update (USA) **2552**
Ariba Magazine (USA) **2552**
Arid Areas Catchment Water Management Board. Annual Report (AUS ISSN 1833-1025) **8818**
Arid Land Geography *see* Ganhanqu Dili **4007**
• ➤ Arid Land Research and Management (USA ISSN 1532-4982) **219**
Arid Lands Newsletter (Abridged Print Edition) (USA ISSN 0277-9455) **2602**
• Arid Lands Newsletter (Online) (USA ISSN 1092-5481) **2603**
Arid Zone Research *see* Ganhanqu Yanjiu **6353**
Ariel *see* A R I E L **5248**
Ariel (GBR ISSN 0004-1335) **2375**
Ariel (ITA ISSN 1125-3967) **8465**
➤ Ariel (PAK ISSN 0254-3028) **5256**
• Ariel (SWE ISSN 1104-196X) **3954**
† Ariel (English Edition) (ISR ISSN 0004-1343) **8931**
Arielu (EST ISSN 1406-1252) **1061**
• ➤ Aries (NLD ISSN 1567-9896) **6643**
➤ Aries Book Series (NLD ISSN 1871-1405) **6643**
• Ariete (CHL ISSN 0718-5138) **5417**
Aril Society International Newsletter (USA) **3723**
Aril Society International Yearbook (USA) **3723**
Arion (DEU ISSN 0938-0248) **5256**
• Arion (RUS ISSN 1562-8515) **5206**
• Arion (USA ISSN 0095-5809) **2230**
Aripaev (EST ISSN 1406-2585) **3836**
Arise (UGA) **8852**
Arise Magazine (USA ISSN 1534-2174) **3519**
Arise Shine (NZL ISSN 1176-810X) **7623**
Aristas (ARG ISSN 1667-4944) **4131**
➤ Aristote (BEL) **6905**
Aristoteleion Panepistemion Thessalonikes. Philosophike Schole. Epistomonike Ereterida - Periodos Beta: Teuchos Thematos Philologias (GRC ISSN 1106-4838) **4200**
Aristoteleion Panepistemion Thessalonikes. Philosophike Schole. Ereterida - Periodos Beta: Tmema Gallikes Glossas kai Philologias (GRC ISSN 1106-0247) **4201**
Aristoteles (GRC ISSN 1105-9419) **4201**
Aristoteles Semitico-Latinus (NLD ISSN 0927-4103) **6905**
• Aristotelian Society. Proceedings (Hardback Edition) (GBR) **6905**
• Aristotelian Society. Proceedings (Online) (GBR ISSN 1467-9264) **6905**
• Aristotelian Society. Proceedings (Paper Back Edition) (GBR ISSN 0066-7374) **6905**
• ➤ Aristotelian Society. Proceedings. Supplementary Volume (GBR ISSN 0309-7013) **6906**
The Arithmetic Teacher *see* Xiaoxue Shuxue Jiaoshi **5547**
Arizona (USA) **8220**
Arizona A A A Highroads (USA) **8683**
Arizona Agent (USA) **4493**
• Arizona Agri-Weekly (USA ISSN 1948-6049) **93**
Arizona Agricultural Experiment Station. Bulletin A (USA ISSN 0518-5416) **93**
Arizona Agriculture (USA ISSN 1557-1831) **93**
Arizona: All-Industries *see* Harris Directory. Arizona All-Industries **1999**
Arizona Alumnus (USA ISSN 0004-1394) **2273**
Arizona & the Grand Canyon (USA ISSN 1559-6230) **8683**
➤ Arizona Anthropologist (USA ISSN 1062-1601) **329**
Arizona Appeal Reports (USA) **4620**
➤ Arizona Archaeologist (USA) **380**
Arizona Artists Guild Newsletter (USA) **6519**
• Arizona Attorney (USA ISSN 1040-4090) **4620**
Arizona Beverage Analyst (USA ISSN 0164-6281) **597**
• Arizona Beverage Guide (USA ISSN 0746-1151) **597**
• Arizona Business Credit Directory (USA) **1972**
• Arizona Business Directory (USA ISSN 1046-3011) **1973**
• Arizona Business Gazette (USA ISSN 0273-6950) **1061**
Arizona Business Magazine (USA ISSN 1946-9152) **1849**
Arizona Capitol Times (USA ISSN 0744-7477) **7420**
Arizona Catalog (USA) **279**
Arizona Cattlelog (USA ISSN 8750-8281) **279**
Arizona Coast (USA) **8683**
Arizona Commercial Real Estate *see* A Z R E **7581**
• Arizona Commission on the Arts. Report to the Governor (Year) (USA ISSN 0098-7387) **467**
Arizona Construction Reports (USA) **976**
Arizona Courtroom Evidence Manual Reporter (USA) **4946**
• Arizona Criminal and Traffic Law Manual (USA ISSN 1546-8607) **4884**
• Arizona Criminal Code, Transportation and Related Statutes (USA) **4884**
Arizona Curiosities (USA ISSN 1545-6633) **8683**
Arizona Daily Wildcat (USA) **2273**
Arizona Department of Economic Security Activities Report *see* D E S Activities Report **7432**
Arizona. Department of Education. Superintendent of Public Instruction. Annual Report (USA ISSN 0095-5310) **3017**
• Arizona. Department of Law. Office of the Attorney General. Opinions of the Attorney General (USA) **4620**
Arizona Economic Indicators (Tucson) (USA) **1061**
Arizona Economic Profile (USA) **1437**
Arizona Economic Trends (USA) **1061**
Arizona Education Association Advocate *see* A E A Advocate **2822**
• Arizona Education Laws and Rules Annotated (USA ISSN 1546-8682) **4621**
• Arizona Education Review (USA ISSN 1555-5895) **2827**
The Arizona Employer (USA ISSN 1559-5862) **1665**
• Arizona Employment Law Letter (USA ISSN 1075-9611) **4621**
➤ Arizona English Bulletin (USA ISSN 0004-1483) **5096**
▼ Arizona Estate Planning and Probate Handbook (USA ISSN 1944-0707) **4901**
Arizona Facts (USA ISSN 1043-1659) **3118**
▼ Arizona Family Law Rules Handbook (USA ISSN 1944-8538) **4907**
Arizona Farm Bureau News *see* Arizona Agriculture **93**
Arizona Food Industry Journal (USA) **3627**
Arizona Foothills *see* Arizona Foothills Magazine **3969**
• Arizona Foothills Magazine (USA ISSN 1548-4351) **3969**
Arizona Garden (USA) **3723**
➤ Arizona Geological Society Digest (USA ISSN 0066-7412) **2725**
Arizona Geological Survey. Oil, Gas & Helium Production (USA ISSN 0570-9520) **6762**
Arizona Geological Survey. Open-File Report (USA) **6763**
Arizona Geology (USA ISSN 1045-4802) **2725**
• ➤ Arizona Geriatrics Society Journal (USA ISSN 1930-2967) **4041**
Arizona Gourmet (USA) **3627**
Arizona Health (USA) **7508**
• Arizona Highways (USA ISSN 0004-1521) **8683**
Arizona Historical Society. Historical Monographs (USA) **4284**
Arizona Historical Society. Museum Monograph Series (USA) **4284**
Arizona Home & Design (USA ISSN 1946-9187) **4531**
Arizona Home and Design *see* Arizona Home & Design **4531**
Arizona Home & Design's Creative Designer (USA ISSN 1946-892X) **4531**
Arizona Horse Connection (USA) **8287**
Arizona Hunter and Angler (USA ISSN 0888-840X) **8304**
• Arizona Industrial Directory (USA ISSN 1071-3514) **1973**
Arizona Informant (USA ISSN 1095-2861) **3519**
• Arizona Jazz (USA) **6545**
Arizona Jewish Post (USA ISSN 1053-5616) **7718**
• ➤ Arizona Journal of Hispanic Cultural Studies (USA ISSN 1096-2492) **8088**
• ➤ Arizona Journal of International & Comparative Law (USA ISSN 0743-6963) **4917**
Arizona Journal of Pharmacy (USA ISSN 1949-0941) **6822**
Arizona Land and People (USA ISSN 0744-5474) **93**
• ➤ Arizona Law Review (USA ISSN 0004-153X) **4621**
• Arizona Legislative Report (USA) **4846**
Arizona Legislative Service (USA ISSN 0094-4246) **4621**
Arizona Library Association Newsletter *see* A Z L A Newsletter **4986**
Arizona Lifestyle's Creative Designer *see* Arizona Home & Design's Creative Designer **4531**
• Arizona Manufacturers Directory (USA ISSN 1525-4070) **1973**
Arizona: Manufacturing *see* Harris Directory. Arizona Manufacturing **1999**
Arizona Medical Association. Legislative Report (USA) **5577**
Arizona Medicine *see* Az Medicine **5582**
Arizona Monthly (USA) **3969**
Arizona Music News (USA ISSN 0518-6129) **6545**
Arizona Networking News (USA) **6643**
• Arizona-Nevada Academy of Science. Journal (USA ISSN 0193-8509) **7837**
Arizona-Nevada Academy of Science. Journal. Proceedings Supplement (USA ISSN 0895-4860) **7837**
Arizona, New Mexico TourBook *see* TourBook: Arizona, New Mexico **8761**
Arizona Notary Law Primer (USA ISSN 1555-8797) **4621**
• Arizona Nurse (USA ISSN 0004-1599) **5952**
• Arizona Parenting (USA) **2143**
Arizona Pharmacist *see* Arizona Journal of Pharmacy **6822**
• Arizona Philatelist (USA) **6891**
Arizona Practice Series. Trial Handbook for Arizona Lawyers (USA ISSN 1930-4862) **4827**
• ➤ Arizona Quarterly (USA ISSN 0004-1610) **5207**
Arizona Radiation Regulatory Agency. Annual Report (USA ISSN 0736-492X) **3164**
Arizona Radiation Review (USA) **3164**
Arizona Real Estate *see* A Z R E **7581**
▼ Arizona Real Estate Law (USA ISSN 1944-8546) **7582**
Arizona Realtor Digest (USA ISSN 0199-9206) **7582**
Arizona Revised Statutes (USA ISSN 1043-6200) **4621**
Arizona Rules of Court Annotated (USA) **4621**
Arizona School Directory *see* M D R's School Directory. Arizona **2958**
Arizona-Sonora Desert Museum Studies in Natural History (USA ISSN 1559-2618) **934**
Arizona State Board of Nursing. Newsletter (USA) **5952**
• ➤ Arizona State Law Journal (USA ISSN 0164-4297) **4621**
Arizona State University Anthropological Research Papers (USA ISSN 0271-0641) **329**
Arizona State University. Center for Business Research. Population Estimates and Projections (USA) **7296**
Arizona State University. Center for Latin American Studies. Monographs (USA) **4284**
Arizona State University. Center for Latin American Studies. Special Studies (USA) **4284**
Arizona State University Law Forum (USA ISSN 0742-0226) **4621**
Arizona State University Research *see* A S U Research **2822**
Arizona Statistical Abstract (USA ISSN 1045-4195) **1200**
Arizona Trends (USA ISSN 0742-034X) **5065**
• Arizona Weddings (USA) **5556**
Arizona Wildlife Views (USA ISSN 0882-5572) **2603**
Arizona Women's Voice (USA) **8852**
Arizona Working Papers in Second Language Acquisition and Teaching (USA) **5096**
• Arizona's Economy (USA ISSN 1557-4601) **7420**
Arizona's Workforce (USA) **1665**
The Ark (GBR ISSN 0004-167X) **318**
Ark (Colorado Springs) (USA) **6804**
The Ark (Faversham) (GBR ISSN 0306-8870) **2603**
Ark.byg *see* Danske ark byg **439**
• Ark Online (USA) **318**
Arka-Tech (USA ISSN 0004-1882) **2273**
Arkada (POL ISSN 1427-2431) **5207**
Arkadia (POL ISSN 1508-0447) **5207**
† Arkaeologiske Udgravninger i Danmark (DNK ISSN 0901-0815) **8931**
➤ Arkansas Academy of Science. Journal (USA) **7837**
Arkansas Academy of Science. Proceedings *see* Arkansas Academy of Science. Journal **7837**
Arkansas. Agricultural Experiment Station. Research Bulletin *see* Arkansas. Agricultural Experiment Station. Research Report **219**
• Arkansas. Agricultural Experiment Station. Research Report (USA) **219**
• Arkansas. Agricultural Experiment Station. Research Series (USA ISSN 1051-3140) **219**
Arkansas. Agricultural Experiment Station. Special Reports *see* Arkansas. Agricultural Experiment Station. Research Report **219**
Arkansas: All-Industries *see* Harris Directory. Arkansas All-Industries **1999**
Arkansas Amateur (USA ISSN 0518-6617) **380**

Title

9978 ARKANSAS ANIMAL SCIENCE DEPARTMENT REPORT ULRICH'S PERIODICALS

• Arkansas Animal Science Department Report (USA ISSN 1941-1677) **279**
Arkansas Archeological Society. Field Notes (USA ISSN 0015-0711) **380**
Arkansas Archeological Survey. Publications on Archeology. Popular Series (USA ISSN 0587-3533) **380**
Arkansas Archeological Survey. Publications on Archeology. Research Reports (USA ISSN 0277-6308) **380**
Arkansas Archeological Survey. Publications on Archeology. Research Series (USA ISSN 0882-5491) **380**
Arkansas Archeological Survey. Publications on Archeology. Technical Papers (USA) **380**
Arkansas Archeologist (USA ISSN 0004-1718) **380**
• Arkansas Banker (USA ISSN 0004-1726) **1308**
Arkansas Bar Association. Legislative Newsletter (USA) **4621**
Arkansas Bar Association. News Bulletin (USA ISSN 0198-702X) **4621**
• ➤ Arkansas Business and Economic Review (USA ISSN 0004-1742) **1061**
• Arkansas Business Directory (USA ISSN 1048-7190) **1973**
• Arkansas Business Journal (USA ISSN 1053-6582) **1061**
Arkansas Case Names Citator *see* Shepard's Arkansas Case Names Citator **4783**
Arkansas Catholic (USA ISSN 1057-8439) **7784**
Arkansas Cattle Business (USA ISSN 0004-1750) **279**
Arkansas Cities & Counties Graphic Performance Analysis (USA ISSN 1935-5459) **7478**
Arkansas Cities and Counties Graphic Performance Analysis *see* Arkansas Cities & Counties Graphic Performance Analysis **7478**
Arkansas Civil Procedure Laws (USA ISSN 1931-2474) **4827**
• Arkansas Corn and Grain Sorghum Performance Tests (USA ISSN 1941-1650) **270**
Arkansas Corn Performance Tests for (Year) *see* Arkansas Corn and Grain Sorghum Performance Tests **270**
Arkansas Corporations, Partnerships and Associations Law Annotated (USA) **4856**
Arkansas Cotton Variety and Strains Tests *see* Arkansas Cotton Variety Tests **219**
• Arkansas Cotton Variety Tests (USA ISSN 1941-1529) **219**
Arkansas Country Dancer (USA) **2682**
Arkansas Court Rules Annotated (USA ISSN 0898-879X) **4621**
Arkansas Covered Employment and Earnings (USA) **1665**
• Arkansas Criminal and Traffic Law Manual (USA ISSN 1545-4983) **4884**
Arkansas Criminal And Traffic Manual *see* Arkansas Criminal and Traffic Law Manual **4884**
• Arkansas Criminal, Transportation & Related Statutes (USA) **4884**
• Arkansas Daily Legislative Digest (USA) **4846**
Arkansas Dentistry (USA ISSN 1056-4764) **5835**
• Arkansas Directory of Manufacturers (USA) **1973**
Arkansas Educational Research and Policy Studies Journal *see* Journal of Educational Research & Policy Studies **2876**
Arkansas Educator (USA ISSN 0161-7753) **2827**
• Arkansas Employment Law Letter (USA ISSN 1083-9674) **4621**
Arkansas. Employment Security Department. Annual Report (USA) **6692**
Arkansas. Employment Security Department. Statistical Review (USA) **1200**
Arkansas Episcopalian (USA ISSN 0890-5258) **7746**
Arkansas Family Historian (USA ISSN 0571-0472) **3759**
• Arkansas Family Physician (USA) **5577**
Arkansas. Geological Commission. Bulletin (USA) **2725**
Arkansas. Geological Commission. Information Circulars (USA) **2725**
Arkansas. Geological Commission. Miscellaneous Publications (USA) **2725**
Arkansas. Geological Commission. Water Resources Circulars (USA ISSN 0571-0278) **8818**
Arkansas Grain Sorghum Performance Tests (Year) *see* Arkansas Corn and Grain Sorghum Performance Tests **270**
Arkansas Grocers and Retail Merchants News (USA) **3676**
Arkansas Highways (USA ISSN 0403-1792) **8629**
• ➤ Arkansas Historical Quarterly (USA ISSN 0004-1823) **4284**
Arkansas Homes & Lifestyles (USA) **3969**
• Arkansas Hospitals (USA) **4088**
Arkansas, Kansas, Missouri, Oklahoma TourBook *see* TourBook: Arkansas, Kansas, Missouri, Oklahoma **8761**
• Arkansas Law Notes (USA ISSN 1052-293X) **4621**
• ➤ Arkansas Law Review (USA ISSN 0004-1831) **4621**
• Arkansas Lawyer (USA ISSN 0571-0502) **4621**
Arkansas Legionnaire (USA) **2264**
• Arkansas Libraries (USA ISSN 0004-184X) **4991**
• Arkansas Manufacturers Register (USA ISSN 1082-0264) **1973**
Arkansas: Manufacturing *see* Harris Directory. Arkansas Manufacturing **1999**
➤ Arkansas Medical Society. Journal (USA ISSN 0004-1858) **5577**
Arkansas Model Jury Instructions - Criminal (USA) **4884**
• Arkansas Motor Vehicle and Traffic Laws and State Highway Commission Regulations (USA) **8490**
Arkansas Nursing News (USA ISSN 1539-8528) **5952**
Arkansas Oil and Gas Statistical Bulletin (USA ISSN 0004-1874) **6799**
Arkansas Outdoors (USA ISSN 0884-9145) **2603**
Arkansas Preservation Digest (USA ISSN 1529-3750) **4284**
Arkansas Press Association Directory (USA) **4571**
Arkansas Propane Gas News (USA) **6763**
Arkansas Publisher (USA) **4571**
Arkansas Publisher Weekly (USA) **4571**
• Arkansas Register (USA) **4621**
• ➤ Arkansas Review (USA) **5207**
Arkansas School Directory *see* M D R's School Directory. Arkansas **2958**
Arkansas School Study Council Newsletter *see* A S S C Newsletter **3016**
Arkansas Soil Fertility Studies *see* Wayne E. Sabbe Arkansas Soil Fertility Studies **258**
• Arkansas Soybean Performance Tests (USA ISSN 1941-1634) **219**
Arkansas Sports 360.com *see* Arkansas Business Journal **1061**
Arkansas Sportsman (USA ISSN 0744-4184) **8304**
Arkansas State Board of Nursing Update *see* A S B N Update **5950**
Arkansas State Directory (USA) **7420**
Arkansas Tech University. Department of History. Occasional Papers (USA) **4284**
Arkansas Travel and Tourism Report (USA) **8684**
The Arkansas Traveler (USA) **2273**
Arkansas Trial Lawyers Association Advocate (Little Rock) *see* A T L A Advocate (Little Rock) **4608**
Arkansas Trial Lawyers Association Docket *see* A T L A Docket **4608**
Arkansas Trial Lawyers Association. Legislative Bulletin (USA) **4621**
• Arkansas Trucking Report (USA) **8668**
▼ • Arkansas Turfgrass Studies (USA ISSN 1941-188X) **3723**
Arkansas United Methodist (USA ISSN 1080-2819) **7746**
Arkansas Vital Statistics (USA ISSN 0364-0728) **7296**
Arkansas Wildlife (USA ISSN 1063-0953) **2603**
Arken (DNK ISSN 0107-363X) **7623**
Arken Bulletin (DNK ISSN 1602-9402) **467**
† Arken-Tryk (DNK ISSN 0107-4520) **8931**
Arkeo Junior (FRA ISSN 1256-7809) **2176**
Arkeoikuska (ESP ISSN 0213-8921) **380**
Arkeologisk museum i Stavanger Rapport *see* A m S - Rapport **370**
Arkeologisk Museum i Stavanger Skrifter *see* A m S - Skrifter **370**
Arkeologisk Museum i Stavanger Smaatrykk *see* A m S - Smaatrykk **370**
Arkeologisk museum i Stavanger Tilvekst *see* A m S - Tilvekst **370**
Arkeologisk Museum i Stavanger Varia *see* A m S - Varia **370**
▼ Arkeologiska Rapporter (SWE ISSN 1654-4927) **380**
Arkeologiska Skrifter *see* Gotarc. Serie C, Arkeologiska Skrifter **395**
▼ Arkeologiske Rapporter (NOR ISSN 1504-6869) **380**
Arkeometri Sonuclari Toplantisi (TUR ISSN 1017-7671) **380**
▼ • ➤ The Arkeotek Journal (FRA ISSN 1961-9863) **380**
Arketipo (ITA ISSN 1828-4450) **432**
Arketypo (ESP ISSN 1886-4767) **432**
Arkfile (GBR) **934**
• Arkfokus (DNK ISSN 1604-8164) **432**
Arkheograficheskii Ezhegodnik (RUS) **4131**
Arkheologicheskie Vesti (RUS) **381**
Arkheologiia (BGR ISSN 0324-1203) **381**
Arkheologiya i Etnografiya Udmurtii (RUS ISSN 0320-9431) **381**
Arkheolohichnyi Litopys Livoberezhnoi Ukrainy (UKR) **381**
Arkheolohiya (UKR ISSN 0235-3490) **381**
Arkhimedes (FIN ISSN 0004-1920) **5473**
Arkhitektura (BGR ISSN 0324-1254) **432**
Arkhitektura i Prestizh (UKR) **432**
Arkhitektura i Stroitel'stvo (BLR) **432**
Arkhitektura i Stroitel'stvo Rossii (RUS ISSN 0235-7259) **433**
Arkhitektura, Teoriya, Istoriya/Architecture, Theory, History (BGR) **433**
Arkhiv Patologii/Archives of Pathology (RUS ISSN 0004-1955) **5578**
➤ Arkhiven Pregled/Archival Review (BGR ISSN 0204-8132) **4991**
Arkhivite Govoryat (BGR) **4201**
• Arkhivy Ukrainy (UKR ISSN 0320-9466) **4201**
Arkib Negara Malaysia. Laporan Tahunan *see* National Archives of Malaysia. Annual Report **4186**
• ➤ Arkitekten (DNK ISSN 0004-198X) **433**
• Arkitekten (SWE ISSN 0347-058X) **433**
Arkitekten (Stockholm, 2002) (SWE) **433**
Arkitekthoegskolen. Aarbok *see* Oslo School of Architecture and Design. A H O **452**
Arkitektnytt *see* Arkkitehtiuutiset **433**
Arkitektnytt (NOR ISSN 0004-1998) **433**
Arkitektur (SWE ISSN 0004-2021) **433**
➤ Arkitektur DK (DNK ISSN 0004-2013) **433**
Arkitektur N (NOR ISSN 1504-7628) **433**
Arkitektur- og Designhoegskolen i Oslo. Aarbok *see* Oslo School of Architecture and Design. A H O **452**
Arkitektur- og Designhoegskolen i Oslo. AHO-Skrift (NOR ISSN 0332-8317) **433**
Arkitektur Verktaekni Skipulag *see* A V S **426**
Arkitip (USA ISSN 1946-200X) **467**
Arkiv (DNK ISSN 0004-203X) **4131**
• ➤ Arkiv foer Matematik (NLD ISSN 0004-2080) **5473**
Arkiv foer Nordisk Filologi/Archives for Scandinavian Philology (SWE ISSN 0066-7668) **5096**
Arkiv foer Svenska Oesterbotten (FIN ISSN 0358-7061) **4201**
➤ Arkiv for Studier i Arbetarroerelsens Historia (SWE ISSN 0345-0333) **4590**
Arkiv, Samhaelle och Forskning (SWE ISSN 0349-0505) **4991**
Arkkitehti/Finnish Architectural Review/Finsk Arkitekturtidskrift (FIN ISSN 0783-3660) **433**
Arkkitehtiuutiset/Arkitektnytt (FIN ISSN 0044-8915) **433**
Arkkitehtuurikilpailuja/Architectural Competitions in Finland (FIN ISSN 0066-7676) **433**
Arkkitehtuurin Tutkimuksia (FIN ISSN 1797-3511) **433**
Arkleton Research Papers (GBR ISSN 1472-3824) **8088**
Arko Catalogus Bouwwereld (NLD) **976**
† ➤ Arkos (ITA) **8931**
Arktisen Keskus. Tiedotteita/Arctic Centre. Reports (FIN ISSN 1235-0583) **7837**
Arkzin (HRV ISSN 1330-4011) **3831**
• Arlequins (ITA) **6545**
Arlington Catholic Herald (USA ISSN 0361-3712) **7784**
Arlington Historical Magazine (USA ISSN 0066-7684) **4284**
▼ Arlington National Cemetery (USA ISSN 1949-064X) **8684**
Arlis / A N Z News (Arts Libraries Society - Australia and New Zealand) (AUS ISSN 0157-4043) **4991**
ARLIS Annual Directory (GBR ISSN 1469-4298) **4991**
ARLIS News-sheet (GBR ISSN 0308-809X) **4991**
Arlo Guthrie's Rolling Blunder Review *see* Rolling Blunder Review **6613**
Armada Compendium (CHE ISSN 1560-4616) **6410**
• Armada International (CHE ISSN 0252-9793) **47**
➤ Armamentaria (NLD ISSN 0168-1672) **6410**
Armaments and Technology *see* Defense & Security **6418**
Armanach Piemonteis *see* Almanacco Piemontese **3614**
Armarium Trevirense (DEU ISSN 1613-8198) **4201**
Armas (ESP) **6410**
Armas e Trofeus (PRT) **3759**
Armas y Municiones (ESP) **8159**
Armband Uhren (DEU ISSN 1431-3677) **4564**
Armbanduhren Katalog (DEU) **4564**
The ArmBender (USA ISSN 1043-3120) **8159**
• The Armchair Astronomer (USA ISSN 1529-1294) **569**
Armchair General (USA ISSN 1546-055X) **639**
• ➤ Armed Forces and Society (USA ISSN 0095-327X) **6410**
• Armed Forces Comptroller (USA ISSN 0004-2188) **6410**
Armed Forces Institute of Pathology Atlas of Tumor Pathology *see* A F I P Atlas of Tumor Pathology **6007**
Armed Forces Institute of Pathology Letter *see* A F I P Letter **6191**
• Armed Forces Journal (USA ISSN 1559-162X) **6411**
Armed Forces Libraries Roundtable of A L A Newsletter (USA) **4991**
Armed Forces Medical Journal *see* Medical Journal Armed Forces India **5669**
Armed Forces Radiobiology Research Institute. Contract Reports (USA) **6411**
Armed Forces Radiobiology Research Institute. Scientific Reports (USA) **6411**
Armed Forces Radiobiology Research Institute. Special Publications (USA) **6411**
Armed Forces Radiobiology Research Institute. Technical Reports (USA) **6411**
Armed Services Vocational Aptitude Battery *see* A S V A B **6408**
Armed Services Vocational Aptitude Battery Basic Training for the Armed Forces Qualifying Test *see* McGraw-Hill's A S V A B Basic Training for the A F Q T **6434**
L'Armee du Canada. Journal *see* The Canadian Army Journal **6415**
Armee du Peuple (BFA) **6411**
Armee et Defense (FRA ISSN 1621-4544) **6411**
Armee-Logistik (CHE ISSN 1423-7008) **6411**
• Armees d'Aujourd'hui (FRA ISSN 0338-3520) **6411**
Armeiskii Sbornik (RUS) **6411**
Armemuseum. Meddelande (SWE ISSN 0349-1048) **6519**
ArMen (FRA ISSN 0297-8644) **3999**
Armenia and Karabagh (USA ISSN 1933-074X) **8684**
The Armenian Church (USA ISSN 1075-7066) **7703**
➤ Armenian Forum (USA ISSN 1091-4714) **8089**
• Armenian International Magazine (USA ISSN 1050-3471) **3519**
▼ • ➤ Armenian Journal of Mathematics (ARM ISSN 1829-1163) **5473**
▼ • ➤ Armenian Journal of Physics (ARM ISSN 1829-1171) **7006**
Armenian Journal of Public Policy (USA ISSN 1550-1450) **4201**
Armenian Medical Journal *see* Hayastani Bzhshkagitutyun **5905**
Armenian Mirror - Spectator (USA ISSN 0004-234X) **3519**
Armenian Missionary Association of America News *see* A M A A News **7703**
Armenian Numismatic Journal (USA ISSN 0884-0180) **6649**
Armenian Observer (USA ISSN 0044-894X) **3519**
Armenian Relief Society Hai Sird *see* A R S Hai Sird **8022**
• Armenian Reporter (USA) **3519**
The Armenian Reporter International *see* Armenian Reporter **3519**
➤ Armenian Review (USA ISSN 0004-2366) **5207**
Armenian Texts and Studies (BEL) **4201**
Armenian Weekly (USA ISSN 0004-2374) **3519**
Armenytt *see* Insats & Foersvar **6425**
▼ • Armer & Bein (NOR ISSN 1504-789X) **4077**
Armes de Chasse (FRA ISSN 1627-3184) **8304**
Armex (NLD ISSN 0922-2979) **6411**
Armi da Caccia (ITA ISSN 1970-0776) **8304**
• Armi e Tiro (ITA ISSN 1122-6560) **8304**
Armi Magazine (ITA ISSN 1125-551X) **8304**
Armidale and District Historical Society. Journal and Proceedings (AUS ISSN 0084-6732) **4191**
Armiger's News (USA ISSN 1084-4015) **3759**
Armiya Ukrainy (UKR) **6411**
Armonia (MEX ISSN 0188-8854) **6546**
Armonia di Voci (ITA ISSN 0391-5425) **6546**
• Armor (FRA ISSN 0044-8966) **3840**
• Armor (USA ISSN 0004-2420) **6411**
▼ The Armor & Cavalry Journal (USA ISSN 1942-8790) **6411**
Armored Fighting Vehicles Modeller *see* A F V Modeller **4326**
Armorial Francais (BEL) **3759**
Armour on Valuation (GBR) **1308**
The Armour Research Society. Journal (USA ISSN 1557-1297) **364**
Armourer (GBR ISSN 1363-1004) **6411**
• ➤ Arms & Armour (GBR ISSN 1741-6124) **6411**
Arms and Armour Society Journal (GBR ISSN 0004-2439) **364**
Arms Collecting (USA ISSN 0380-982X) **364**
Arms Control Impact Statements (USA ISSN 0195-4741) **7221**
• The Arms Control Reporter (USA ISSN 0886-3490) **7221**
• Arms Control Today (USA ISSN 0196-125X) **4917**
Arms Control Verification Studies (CAN ISSN 0828-3664) **7221**
Arms Sales Monitor (USA ISSN 1542-9792) **6411**
Armstrong Bulletin Board (USA) **3759**
Armstrong News (USA ISSN 0265-2269) **3519**
Armstrong Oil Directories: Louisiana, Texas Gulf Coast, East Texas, Arkansas and Mississippi Edition (USA ISSN 0273-4931) **6763**
Armstrong Oil Directories: Mini Briefcase Edition (USA) **6763**
Armstrong Oil Directories: Rocky Mountain - Central United States Edition (USA ISSN 0273-5229) **6763**
Armstrong Oil Directories: Texas and Southeastern New Mexico Edition (USA ISSN 0277-2280) **6763**
• Army (AUS ISSN 0729-5685) **6411**
Army *see* Camouflage **2181**
• Army (USA ISSN 0004-2455) **6411**
• Army A L & T (Acquisition, Logistics and Technology) (USA ISSN 1529-8507) **6411**
The Army Air Corps Journal (GBR ISSN 0307-0069) **6411**
Army Aviation (USA ISSN 0004-248X) **6411**
• Army Chaplaincy (USA ISSN 1542-8907) **6411**
• Army Communicator (USA ISSN 0362-5745) **6412**
Army Doctrine and Training Bulletin *see* The Canadian Army Journal **6415**
Army Families Federation Families Journal *see* A F F Families Journal **5064**
Army Flier (USA) **6412**
Army History (USA ISSN 1546-5330) **6412**
• The Army Lawyer (USA ISSN 0364-1287) **4971**
Army List (GBR ISSN 0965-9544) **6412**
Army List. Supplement (GBR ISSN 0965-9552) **6412**
Army Literature and Arts *see* Van Nghe Quan Doi **5394**
• Army Logistician (USA ISSN 0004-2528) **6412**
† Army Magazine (AUS ISSN 1034-3695) **8931**
Army Master Data File: Army Retrieval Microform Systems and Interc (USA) **6412**
Army Motors (USA ISSN 0195-5632) **4327**
Army - Navy Store & Outdoor Merchandiser *see* A N S O M **2245**
Army Navy Store and Outdoor Merchandiser *see* A N S O M **2245**
Army News *see* N Z Army News **6437**
† Army Quarterly and Defence Journal (GBR ISSN 0004-2552) **8931**
Army R D & A (Research, Development and Acquisition) (USA) **6412**
• Army Reserve Magazine (USA ISSN 0004-2579) **6412**

Title

Title

9982 ASIA AFRICA INTELLIGENCE WIRE ULRICH'S PERIODICALS

• Asia Africa Intelligence Wire (JPN) **3899**
Asia and Middle East Food Trade (DEU) **3627**
Asia and Pacific Bibliography (THA) **4169**
• Asia & Pacific Review (GBR ISSN 1351-458X) **1437**
Asia and South Pacific Design Automation Conference. Proceedings (USA) **2457**
Asia Bridge mit Asien-Contact (DEU) **1437**
Asia Business Law Review (SGP ISSN 0218-3986) **4622**
Asia Business Law Series (NLD ISSN 1871-6113) **4856**
▼ • Asia Business Newsweekly (USA ISSN 1938-1816) **1061**
• Asia Computer Weekly (SGP ISSN 0129-5896) **2407**
• Asia Cover (GBR ISSN 1366-0276) **4493**
Asia Doko-Nenpo *see* Yearbook of Asian Affairs **1197**
Asia Education Teachers' Journal *see* A E T A Journal **2822**
Asia Electronics Industry (JPN ISSN 1342-422X) **3295**
Asia Environmental Business Journal (USA) **3404**
Asia Environmental Review (GBR ISSN 1360-1644) **3404**
Asia F A B (GBR ISSN 0968-672X) **219**
Asia Foundation. Annual Report (USA) **4180**
Asia Gas Report (GBR) **3124**
A'sia Gyoyug Yeon'gu/Asian Journal of Education (KOR ISSN 1229-9448) **2827**
Asia HORECA (HKG) **1973**
Asia Hotel, Restaurant and Catering *see* Asia HORECA **1973**
• Asia Image (SGP ISSN 0219-6158) **2356**
• Asia In Focus (USA ISSN 1934-385X) **7107**
• Asia Inc (SGP ISSN 1019-2239) **1061**
Asia Info *see* N Z A I Bulletin **556**
➤ Asia Institute. Bulletin (USA ISSN 0890-4464) **543**
• Asia Insurance Review (SGP ISSN 0218-2696) **4493**
• Asia Intelligence Wire (GBR) **1061**
• Asia Journal of Theology (SGP ISSN 0218-0812) **7623**
Asia Labour Monitor *see* Asian Labour Update **1665**
Asia Law *see* AsiaLaw **4856**
Asia Letter (HKG ISSN 0004-4466) **1437**
➤ Asia Life Sciences (PHL ISSN 0117-3375) **654**
➤ Asia Major (USA ISSN 0004-4482) **543**
Asia Market Review (JPN) **1061**
Asia Marketing Data and Statistics (GBR) **1200**
The Asia Miner (AUS ISSN 1832-7966) **6456**
Asia Minor Studien (DEU ISSN 1430-0680) **4320**
Asia Money *see* AsiaMoney **1308**
Asia Monitor. China & North Asia *see* Asia Monitor. China & North East Asia **1437**
• Asia Monitor. China & North East Asia (GBR ISSN 1474-5615) **1437**
Asia Monitor. Indian Subcontinent *see* Asia Monitor. South Asia **1437**
• Asia Monitor. South Asia (GBR ISSN 1479-5744) **1437**
• Asia Monitor. South East Asia (GBR ISSN 1470-7810) **1437**
Asia Monthly *see* Ajia Mansuri **1057**
ASIA Network Exchange *see* ASIANetwork Exchange **544**
• Asia New Zealand Foundation. Outlook (NZL ISSN 1177-0031) **7222**
• Asia New Zealand Foundation. Review (Online) (NZL ISSN 1177-9586) **7222**
• Asia News (ITA ISSN 1125-3576) **7784**
The Asia Pacific Advocate (USA) **7202**
Asia-Pacific Agency Directory (HKG) **1973**
Asia - Pacific Agribusiness Report (HKG) **194**
The (Year) Asia Pacific Antitrust & Trade Review *see* The Asia Pacific Antitrust Review **4856**
The Asia Pacific Antitrust Review (GBR ISSN 1743-7989) **4856**
▼ The Asia-Pacific Arbitration Review (GBR ISSN 1753-917X) **4917**
Asia - Pacific Aviation and Engineering Journal (SGP ISSN 0129-1289) **47**
Asia - Pacific Baker (GBR ISSN 1461-3050) **3671**
Asia Pacific Biotech Directory (Year) (SGP) **756**
Asia - Pacific Biotech News *see* Asia Pacific Biotech News (English Edition) **756**
• ➤ Asia Pacific Biotech News (English Edition) (SGP ISSN 0219-0303) **756**
• Asia-Pacific Boating (HKG) **8271**
Asia - Pacific Broadcasting (SGP) **2375**
Asia - Pacific Broadcasting Union Technical Review *see* A B U Technical Review **2374**
• Asia Pacific Bulletin (CAN) **1061**
• ➤ Asia Pacific Business Review (GBR ISSN 1360-2381) **1061**
Asia - Pacific Business Series (SGP ISSN 1793-3137) **1061**
Asia-Pacific Centre of Educational Innovation for Development News *see* A C E I D News **2821**
• Asia Pacific Channels (AUS ISSN 1328-2115) **2682**
Asia-Pacific Co-op Research Conferences (IND) **1422**
• Asia Pacific Coatings Journal (GBR ISSN 1468-1412) **6716**
• Asia Pacific Consensus Forcasts (GBR ISSN 1351-0967) **1437**
† Asia - Pacific Constitutional Yearbook (AUS ISSN 1323-0425) **8931**
Asia - Pacific Cultural Centre for UNESCO. Organization and Activities (JPN) **543**
• Asia - Pacific Defence Reporter (USA ISSN 1446-6880) **6412**
• Asia - Pacific Defense Forum (USA) **6412**
Asia - Pacific Dental News (HKG) **5835**
Asia - Pacific Development Journal (THA ISSN 1020-1246) **1437**
• Asia Pacific Digestive News (AUS ISSN 1445-0232) **5920**
Asia-Pacific Digital Directory *see* Media **29**
➤ Asia Pacific Disability Rehabilitation Journal (IND) **8026**
Asia Pacific Disability Rehabilitation Journal. Selected Readings Series (IND) **8026**
Asia Pacific Duty-Free (GBR) **1552**
Asia Pacific Economic Outlook (AUS) **1062**
• ➤ Asia Pacific Economic Papers (AUS ISSN 1834-8971) **1552**
• Asia Pacific Education Review (NLD ISSN 1598-1037) **2827**
• Asia - Pacific Exchange Journal (USA ISSN 1077-114X) **2967**
• Asia Pacific Executive Education Directory (Online Edition) (NLD) **1725**
Asia Pacific Executive Education Directory (Print Edition) *see* Asia Pacific Executive Education Directory (Online Edition) **1725**
• ➤ Asia Pacific Family Medicine (Online) (GBR ISSN 1447-056X) **5579**
• ➤ Asia Pacific Family Medicine (Print) (SGP ISSN 1444-1683) **5579**
• ➤ Asia - Pacific Financial Markets (USA ISSN 1387-2834) **1392**
Asia - Pacific Fishery Commission. Report (THA) **3586**
Asia - Pacific Focus *see* Tax Planning International **1949**
Asia - Pacific Focus *see* Tax Management International Forum **1948**
• Asia Pacific Food Industry (SGP ISSN 0218-2734) **3627**
• Asia Pacific Forum (USA) **4180**
• ➤ Asia - Pacific Forum on Science Learning and Teaching (HKG ISSN 1609-4913) **2827**
Asia Pacific Foundation of Canada. Annual Report (CAN ISSN 1912-7715) **1062**
Asia Pacific Foundation of Canada. Annual Review *see* Asia Pacific Foundation of Canada. Annual Report **1062**
• Asia Pacific Foundation of Canada. APSummit Series (CAN) **1062**
• Asia Pacific Foundation of Canada. Event Reports (CAN) **1062**
• Asia Pacific Foundation of Canada. Impact Reports (CAN) **1062**
• Asia Pacific Foundation of Canada. RoundTable Workshop Reports (CAN) **1062**
• Asia Pacific Foundation of Canada. Surveys (CAN) **1062**
Asia-Pacific Harrier (USA ISSN 1930-3718) **8684**
Asia - Pacific I.T. Times (SGP ISSN 0218-2599) **2519**
Asia - Pacific in Figures (THA ISSN 1014-3750) **8347**
• Asia-Pacific Insight (AUS ISSN 1833-6507) **543**
Asia-Pacific Insurance (GBR ISSN 1468-1870) **4493**
Asia - Pacific Issues (USA ISSN 1522-0966) **7948**
Asia Pacific J H R *see* Asia Pacific Journal of Human Resources **1856**
➤ Asia - Pacific Journal of Accounting & Economics (HKG ISSN 1608-1625) **1280**
• ➤ The Asia Pacific Journal of Anthropology (AUS ISSN 1444-2213) **329**
▼ • ➤ Asia-Pacific Journal of Business Administration (GBR ISSN 1757-4323) **1725**
• ➤ Asia-Pacific Journal of Chemical Engineering (GBR ISSN 1932-2135) **3236**
▼ • Asia Pacific Journal of Climate Change (SGP ISSN 1793-6187) **3404**
• ➤ Asia Pacific Journal of Clinical Nutrition (AUS ISSN 0964-7058) **6655**
• ➤ Asia Pacific Journal of Clinical Oncology (GBR ISSN 1743-7555) **6009**
Asia-Pacific Journal of Clinical Oncology *see* Asia Pacific Journal of Clinical Oncology **6009**
➤ Asia Pacific Journal of Economics & Business (AUS ISSN 1326-8481) **1062**
• ➤ Asia Pacific Journal of Education (GBR ISSN 0218-8791) **2827**
• ➤ Asia Pacific Journal of Environmental Law (AUS ISSN 1385-2140) **3404**
▼ • ➤ Asia Pacific Journal of Finance and Banking Research (USA ISSN 1933-3390) **1308**
➤ Asia Pacific Journal of Health Management (AUS ISSN 1833-3818) **4088**
• ➤ Asia Pacific Journal of Human Resources (GBR ISSN 1038-4111) **1856**
Asia Pacific Journal of Language in Education (HKG ISSN 1029-0680) **5096**
• Asia Pacific Journal of Life Sciences (USA) **543**
• Asia Pacific Journal of Management (USA ISSN 0217-4561) **1725**
• ➤ Asia Pacific Journal of Marketing and Logistics (GBR ISSN 1355-5855) **1805**
➤ Asia - Pacific Journal of Molecular Biology & Biotechnology (MYS ISSN 0128-7451) **756**
▼ ➤ The Asia-Pacific Journal of Oncology & Hematology (GBR ISSN 1759-6637) **6009**
The Asia-Pacific Journal of Oncology and Hematology *see* The Asia-Pacific Journal of Oncology & Hematology **6009**
• ➤ Asia Pacific Journal of Operational Research (SGP ISSN 0217-5959) **2407**
➤ Asia - Pacific Journal of Ophthalmology (SGP ISSN 0129-1653) **6038**
➤ Asia Pacific Journal of Pharmacology (SGP ISSN 0217-9687) **6823**
• Asia-Pacific Journal of Public Health (USA ISSN 1010-5395) **7508**
Asia - Pacific Journal of Rural Development (BGD ISSN 1018-5291) **194**
➤ Asia Pacific Journal of Social Work (SGP ISSN 0218-5385) **8026**
Asia - Pacific Journal of Taxation (HKG ISSN 1027-5592) **1910**
• ➤ Asia - Pacific Journal of Teacher Education (AUS ISSN 1359-866X) **3051**
Asia Pacific Journal of Teacher Education *see* Asia - Pacific Journal of Teacher Education **3051**
• ➤ Asia Pacific Journal of Tourism Research (GBR ISSN 1094-1665) **8684**
• Asia Pacific Journal of Transport (AUS ISSN 1322-1337) **8490**
Asia Pacific Journal on Environment and Development (BGD) **3404**
• ➤ Asia - Pacific Journal on Human Rights and the Law (NLD ISSN 1388-1906) **7202**
• ➤ Asia Pacific Law Review (HKG ISSN 1019-2557) **4622**
• The Asia Pacific Legal 500 (GBR) **4622**
➤ Asia Pacific Management Review (TWN ISSN 1029-3132) **1725**
Asia Pacific Market & MediaFact (GBR ISSN 0968-2171) **8347**
Asia - Pacific Markets (USA) **1552**
Asia Pacific Media Educator *see* AsiaPacific MediaEducator **4572**
• Asia Pacific Metalworking Equipment News (SGP ISSN 0129-5519) **5449**
• Asia Pacific Microwave Conference. Proceedings (USA) **3295**
Asia - Pacific Military Balance (MYS) **7222**
Asia-Pacific Ministers Conferences (SGP) **1422**
Asia-Pacific P R Directory *see* Media **29**
• Asia Pacific Packaging (AUS) **6708**
Asia Pacific Papermaker *see* P I M A's Asia Pacific Papermaker **6735**
Asia Pacific Personal Care (GBR) **585**
Asia-Pacific Perspectives: Japan+ (JPN) **3899**
• Asia - Pacific Population & Policy (USA ISSN 0891-6683) **7277**
• ➤ Asia - Pacific Population Journal (THA ISSN 0259-238X) **7277**
• ➤ Asia - Pacific Population Research Abstracts (USA ISSN 1083-0294) **7296**
➤ Asia - Pacific Population Research Reports (USA ISSN 1079-0284) **7277**
▼ • ➤ Asia-Pacific Psychiatry (AUS ISSN 1758-5864) **6124**
• ➤ Asia Pacific Public Relations Journal (AUS ISSN 1440-4389) **7107**
Asia - Pacific Quality Network Annual Report *see* A P Q N Annual Report **2822**
• Asia Pacific Rail (GBR ISSN 1367-3017) **8614**
Asia-Pacific Regional Co-operative Forums (SGP) **1422**
Asia Pacific Review *see* Asia - Pacific Review **7222**
• ➤ Asia - Pacific Review (GBR ISSN 1343-9006) **7222**
Asia - Pacific Review of Business *see* International Journal of Business and Management **1755**
Asia-Pacific Satellite Communications Council Newsletter *see* A P S C C Newsletter **2311**
Asia-Pacific Satellite Communications Council Yearbook *see* A P S C C Yearbook **2311**
Asia-Pacific Satellite Communications Council Yearbook *see* A P S C C Yearbook **2311**
Asia - Pacific Satellite Yearbook (Year) (GBR ISSN 1460-6194) **2375**
• Asia Pacific School of Economics and Management Working Papers. East Asia (AUS ISSN 1442-0589) **1591**
• Asia Pacific School of Economics and Management Working Papers. South Pacific (AUS ISSN 1441-9858) **1591**
• Asia Pacific School of Economics and Management Working Papers. Southeast Asia (AUS ISSN 1442-0228) **1591**
Asia-Pacific Scouting (PHL) **2264**
Asia Pacific Shipping *see* Ships and Shipping **8661**
➤ Asia-Pacific Social Science Review (PHL ISSN 0119-8386) **7948**
• Asia Pacific Software Engineering Conference. Proceedings (USA ISSN 1530-1362) **2587**
• Asia - Pacific Tax Bulletin (NLD ISSN 1385-3082) **1910**
• Asia-Pacific - Taxation & Investment Database (NLD) **1911**
Asia Pacific Tech Monitor (IND ISSN 0256-9957) **8416**
Asia-Pacific Telecom *see* Asia - Pacific Telecom Newsletter **2365**
• Asia - Pacific Telecom Newsletter (USA ISSN 1097-8283) **2365**
Asia - Pacific Telecommunity Journal (GBR) **2365**
Asia - Pacific Telecommunity Yearbook *see* A P T Yearbook **2365**
Asia Pacific Traveltalk *see* Traveltalk Asia Pacific **8768**
Asia-Pacific Tropical Homes (THA) **434**
Asia-Pacific Viewpoint *see* Asia Pacific Viewpoint **1591**
• ➤ Asia Pacific Viewpoint (AUS ISSN 1360-7456) **1591**
Asia Pacific Weekly Financial News Summary (GBR) **1062**
• Asia Policy (USA ISSN 1559-0968) **7222**
• Asia Policy Calendar (USA ISSN 1543-1177) **7222**
• Asia Policy Weekly (USA ISSN 1543-1185) **7222**
• Asia Recovery Report (Year) (PHL) **1438**
Asia Rights Journal *see* AsiaRights Journal **7202**
Asia Risk (GBR ISSN 1464-1011) **1308**
The Asia Society. Annual Report (USA ISSN 0098-1214) **4180**
• Asia Spa (HKG) **585**
Asia Spa Men *see* Asia Spa **585**
Asia Steel (GBR ISSN 1362-3621) **6305**
• Asia. Telecoms, Mobile and Broadband in Hong Kong and Macau (Year) (AUS) **2312**
Asia Times/Yazhou Shidai (AUS ISSN 1833-9638) **3519**
• Asia Times (HKG) **7107**
Asia Times *see* A Chau Thoi Bao Newspaper **3514**
• Asia Today International (AUS ISSN 1445-4300) **1062**
Asia Trademart News (TWN ISSN 1609-1566) **1062**
Asia Travel News (PAK) **8684**
Asia Urbs Magazine (BEL ISSN 1725-1370) **1591**
Asia Weekly Economic Alert *see* Asia Weekly Financial Alert **1438**
• Asia Weekly Financial Alert (GBR ISSN 1475-5203) **1438**
• AsiaCom (GBR ISSN 1084-0710) **2312**
AsiaFAB. Asia Fertiliser and Agrochemicals Bulletin *see* Asia F A B **219**
AsiaHedge (GBR ISSN 1473-3161) **1610**
• Asiainfo Daily China News (GBR) **1062**
• Asiaint Economic Intelligence Review (GBR ISSN 1479-7844) **1062**
AsiaInt Political & Strategic Review *see* AsiaInt South Asia Review **8931**
† • AsiaInt South Asia Review (GBR ISSN 1756-7114) **8931**
• Asiaint Special Reports (GBR ISSN 1743-5463) **1062**
• Asiaint Weekly Alert (GBR ISSN 1479-7828) **1062**
• Asiaint's China Watch Monthly Review (GBR ISSN 1749-8724) **1062**
• Asiaint's China Watch Quarterly Forecasts (GBR ISSN 1750-354X) **1062**
• Asiaint's China Watch Weekly Briefing (GBR ISSN 1750-0729) **1062**
• AsiaLaw (HKG ISSN 1022-0267) **4856**
• AsiaMoney (HKG) **1308**
• Asian Affairs (GBR ISSN 0306-8374) **543**
• Asian Affairs (HKG ISSN 1029-1903) **7107**
Asian Affairs (New York) *see* Asian Affairs: An American Review **7222**
• ➤ Asian Affairs: An American Review (USA ISSN 0092-7678) **7222**
• Asian Affairs Online (HKG ISSN 1607-0631) **7107**
Asian, African, and Middle Eastern Section of the Association of College and Research Libraries. Newsletter (USA ISSN 1548-4343) **4991**
Asian - African Journal of Economics and Econometrics (IND ISSN 0972-3986) **1062**
Asian Agri-History (IND ISSN 0971-7730) **93**
Asian Air Transport (TWN ISSN 1021-3740) **8538**
Asian Airlines & Aerospace (MYS) **8538**
Asian Almanac (SGP ISSN 0004-4520) **7198**
Asian America (USA) **3520**
Asian American and Pacific Islander Nexus (USA) **3520**
Asian American Golf Magazine *see* A A Golf Magazine **8219**
Asian American Hotel Owners Association Hospitality *see* A A H O A Hospitality **4380**
Asian American Hotel Owners Association Lodging Business *see* A A H O A Lodging Business **4380**
Asian American Journalists Association Newsletter *see* A A J A Newsletter **4570**
• ➤ Asian American Law Journal (USA ISSN 1939-8417) **4917**
• Asian American Movement Ezine (USA) **3520**
• ➤ Asian American Policy Review (USA ISSN 1062-1830) **3520**
• Asian-American Yearbook (USA ISSN 1551-0867) **6692**
Asian Americans Pacific Islanders Nexus *see* A A P I Nexus **3514**
Asian and African Studies (SVK ISSN 1335-1257) **543**
Asian and Australasian Companies (GBR ISSN 1352-3198) **1200**
▼ The Asian and Australasian Journal of Plant Science and Biotechnology (GBR ISSN 1752-3818) **777**
Asian and Pacific Coconut Community. Bibliography Series (IDN) **175**
Asian and Pacific Coconut Community. Technical Meetings. Proceedings (IDN) **219**
Asian and Pacific Council. Food and Fertilizer Technology Center. Extension - Technical Bulletin (TWN) **93**
Asian and Pacific Development Centre Newsletter (MYS ISSN 0127-3337) **1438**
Asian and Pacific Economic Review *see* Ya-tai Jingji **1197**
Asian and Pacific Island Community Directory (USA) **3520**
Asian and Pacific Labour (SGP) **4590**
➤ Asian and Pacific Migration Journal (PHL ISSN 0117-1968) **7277**

DIRECTORY 2010 ASIAN STUDIES REVIEW 9983

Asian and Pacific Women's Resource and Action Series (MYS) **8852**
➤ Asian Anthropology (HKG ISSN 1683-478X) **329**
Asian Aquaculture (PHL ISSN 0115-4974) **3586**
Asian Architect & Contractor (HKG) **434**
Asian Art News (HKG ISSN 1023-5884) **476**
• Asian Arts (USA) **476**
• ➤ Asian - Australasian Journal of Animal Sciences (KOR ISSN 1011-2367) **279**
Asian Auto Abstracts (JPN) **8521**
• Asian Avenue Magazine (USA ISSN 1932-1449) **3520**
• Asian Aviation (SGP ISSN 0129-9972) **47**
Asian Babes (GBR ISSN 1364-6214) **6286**
Asian Banker Journal (SGP) **1308**
• Asian Banker Monitor (SGP) **1308**
Asian Banking & Finance (SGP) **1308**
Asian Beacon (MYS ISSN 0044-9180) **7732**
• Asian Biomedicine (THA ISSN 1905-7415) **5579**
Asian Biotechnology and Development Review (IND ISSN 0972-7566) **756**
Asian Books Newsletter (IND ISSN 0004-4547) **616**
Asian Brand News (HKG ISSN 1561-7343) **1805**
Asian Bride (GBR ISSN 1473-4141) **3520**
Asian Building & Construction (SGP) **976**
• ➤ Asian Business & Management (GBR ISSN 1472-4782) **1726**
Asian Business and Management *see* Asian Business & Management **1726**
• Asian Cardiovascular & Thoracic Annals (GBR ISSN 0218-4923) **5778**
• ➤ Asian Case Research Journal (SGP ISSN 0218-9275) **1062**
Asian Ceramics (GBR ISSN 1476-1467) **2037**
Asian Ceramics and Glass *see* Asian Ceramics **2037**
Asian Chemistry Letters (IND ISSN 0971-9822) **2050**
Asian Church Today (IND) **7623**
➤ Asian Cinema (GBR ISSN 1744-8719) **6490**
Asian Cinema Journal (USA ISSN 1059-440X) **6490**
• Asian Classics Input Program (USA) **7700**
Asian Commercial Aviation (MYS) **8538**
† Asian Commercial Law Review (GBR ISSN 1360-8223) **8931**
➤ Asian Communication Research (KOR ISSN 1738-2084) **2312**
• Asian Communications (GBR ISSN 0952-7516) **2365**
Asian Communications (SGP) **2312**
Asian Community Times (USA) **3520**
• Asian Conference on Diarrhoeal Diseases and Nutrition (BGD) **5579**
Asian Coordinating Group for Chemistry Chemical Research Communications *see* A C G C Chemical Research Communications **2096**
Asian Counsel (HKG ISSN 1729-3405) **4622**
Asian Cult Cinema (USA) **6490**
Asian Cultural Studies (JPN ISSN 0454-2150) **4180**
▼ • ➤ Asian Culture and History (CAN ISSN 1916-9655) **543**
Asian Database Online Community Electronic Newsletter *see* AsianDOC Electronic Newsletter **544**
Asian Defence and Diplomacy (MYS ISSN 1394-178X) **6412**
• Asian Defence Journal (MYS ISSN 0126-6403) **6412**
• Asian Development Bank. Annual Report (PHL ISSN 0116-1164) **1308**
Asian Development Bank. Board of Governors. Summary of Proceedings. (PHL ISSN 0066-8389) **1591**
Asian Development Bank Business Opportunities *see* A D B Business Opportunities **1055**
Asian Development Bank. Economic Staff Paper (Number) (PHL) **1308**
Asian Development Bank. Key Indicators of Developing Asian and Pacific Countries (PHL ISSN 0116-3000) **1308**
Asian Development Bank Review *see* A D B Review **1589**
Asian Development Bank. Statistical Report Series (PHL ISSN 0116-2799) **1200**
• Asian Development Outlook (PHL ISSN 0117-0481) **1062**
• ➤ Asian Development Review (PHL ISSN 0116-1105) **1591**
Asian Diver (SGP ISSN 0218-3064) **8304**
• Asian E-Banker (SGP) **1309**
• ➤ Asian E F L Journal (English as a Foreign Language) (VGB ISSN 1738-1460) **5096**
Asian Economic and Social Review (IND ISSN 0970-6305) **7948**
• ➤ Asian Economic Journal (AUS ISSN 1351-3958) **1535**
• Asian Economic Papers (USA ISSN 1535-3516) **1062**
• ➤ Asian Economic Policy Review (AUS ISSN 1832-8105) **1438**
• Asian Economic Review (IND ISSN 0004-4555) **1062**
➤ Asian Economies/Ajia Keizai (JPN ISSN 0002-2942) **1591**
Asian Economy and Social Environment (JPN ISSN 1881-3364) **1062**
Asian Education Teachers Association Journal *see* A E T A Journal **2822**
• Asian Electronics Engineer (PHL ISSN 1010-8327) **3295**
Asian Energy Institute Newsletter *see* A E I Newsletter **3123**
• Asian Energy News (THA ISSN 0858-4419) **3124**
Asian Energy Yearbook (GBR ISSN 1461-555X) **3124**
Asian Enterprise (USA ISSN 1521-2939) **1956**
Asian Environmental Technology (GBR ISSN 1363-7134) **3404**
• ➤ Asian Ethnicity (GBR ISSN 1463-1369) **3520**
• ➤ Asian Ethnology (JPN ISSN 1882-6865) **329**
▼ • Asian-European Journal of Mathematics (SGP ISSN 1793-5571) **5473**
Asian Fisheries Science (MYS ISSN 0116-6514) **934**
Asian Fisheries Society. Indian Branch. Special Publication (IND) **3586**
Asian Fisheries Society. Special Publication (PHL ISSN 0117-2778) **3586**
The Asian Foodbookery (USA) **4352**
Asian Fortune (USA ISSN 1074-8822) **3520**
• Asian Furniture News (HKG) **4553**
Asian Furniture News Online *see* Asian Furniture News **4553**
➤ Asian Geographer (HKG ISSN 1022-5706) **3999**
Asian Geographic (SGP) **2603**
Asian Golfer (HKG ISSN 1024-4565) **8221**
Asian Gourmet *see* Dongfang Meishi **4385**
Asian Hospital & Healthcare Management (GBR) **4088**
Asian Hotel & Catering Times (HKG) **4382**
Asian Identities *see* Kavita Asia **5425**
Asian Information - Science - Life *see* Asia Pacific Journal of Life Sciences **543**
• Asian Infrastructure (GBR ISSN 1742-9943) **8490**
Asian Infrastructure Monthly *see* Asian Infrastructure **8490**
Asian Institute of Technology. A I T Annual Report (THA) **3017**
Asian Institute of Technology. Abstracts on Management of Technology and International Business (THA ISSN 0857-9253) **8446**
Asian Institute of Technology. Annual Research and Activities Report (THA) **8416**
Asian Institute of Technology. Environmental Systems Information Center. Occasional Publications (THA) **3404**
Asian Institute of Technology. H S D Conference - Seminar Proceedings (THA) **8089**
Asian Institute of Technology. H S D Monographs (THA) **8089**
Asian Institute of Technology. H S D Research Papers and Reports (THA) **7948**
Asian Institute of Technology. H S D Working Papers (THA) **4403**
Asian Institute of Technology. M O T I C Monographs (THA) **1200**
Asian Institute of Technology Review *see* A I T Review **3179**
Asian Institute of Technology. School of Advanced Technologies. Catalogue (THA) **8416**
• Asian International Arbitration Journal (NLD ISSN 1574-3330) **4917**
Asian Journal of Aesthetic Dentistry (SGP ISSN 0218-3781) **5835**
• Asian Journal of Agricultural Research (USA ISSN 1819-1894) **93**
▼ • ➤ Asian Journal of Algebra (PAK ISSN 1994-540X) **5474**
• Asian Journal of Andrology (USA ISSN 1008-682X) **5579**
• Asian Journal of Animal and Veterinary Advances (USA ISSN 1683-9919) **8793**
• Asian Journal of Animal Sciences (USA ISSN 1819-1878) **8793**
• ➤ Asian Journal of Biochemistry (USA ISSN 1815-9923) **723**
Asian Journal of Cardiovascular Nursing (IND) **5778**
• Asian Journal of Cell Biology (USA ISSN 1814-0068) **654**
• ➤ Asian Journal of Chemistry (IND ISSN 0970-7077) **2051**
Asian Journal of Civil Engineering (IRN) **3259**
Asian Journal of Clinical Cardiology (IND) **5778**
• ➤ Asian Journal of Clinical Nutrition (PAK ISSN 1992-1470) **6655**
• ➤ Asian Journal of Communication (GBR ISSN 0129-2986) **2312**
• Asian Journal of Comparative Law (USA ISSN 1932-0205) **4846**
• ➤ Asian Journal of Control (USA ISSN 1561-8625) **2519**
Asian Journal of Counselling/Yazhou Fudao Xuebao (HKG ISSN 1560-8255) **7337**
• ➤ Asian Journal of Criminology (NLD ISSN 1871-0131) **2644**
▼ • ➤ Asian Journal of Crop Science (PAK ISSN 1994-7879) **219**
Asian Journal of Drug Metabolism and Pharmacokinetics *see* Asian Journal of Pharmacodynamics and Pharmacokinetics **6823**
• Asian Journal of Earth Sciences (USA ISSN 1819-1886) **2702**
Asian Journal of Ecotoxicolog *see* Shengtai Duli Xuebao **3466**
Asian Journal of Education *see* A'sia Gyoyug Yeon'gu **2827**
▼ • ➤ Asian Journal of Endoscopic Surgery (GBR ISSN 1758-5902) **6237**
Asian Journal of English Language Teaching (HKG ISSN 1026-2652) **5096**
▼ • ➤ Asian Journal of Epidemiology (PAK ISSN 1992-1462) **5579**
Asian Journal of European Studies (IND ISSN 0378-7516) **4201**
▼ • ➤ Asian Journal of Finance & Accounting (USA ISSN 1946-052X) **1280**
Asian Journal of Finance and Accounting *see* Asian Journal of Finance & Accounting **1280**
Asian Journal of Geoinformatics (THA ISSN 1513-6728) **2725**
• Asian Journal of Information Management (USA ISSN 1819-334X) **2541**
• Asian Journal of Information Technology (PAK ISSN 1682-3915) **2407**
• Asian Journal of Latin American Studies (KOR) **3520**
• ➤ Asian Journal of Management Cases (IND ISSN 0972-8201) **1726**
➤ Asian Journal of Marketing (SGP ISSN 0218-6101) **1805**
• Asian Journal of Marketing (USA ISSN 1819-1924) **1805**
• ➤ The Asian Journal of Mathematics (USA ISSN 1093-6106) **5474**
▼ • ➤ Asian Journal of Mathematics & Statistics (PAK ISSN 1994-5418) **5474**
Asian Journal of Microbiology, Biotechnology and Environmental Science (IND ISSN 0972-3005) **882**
• Asian Journal of Mining (AUS ISSN 1321-0408) **6457**
➤ Asian Journal of Nursing Studies (HKG ISSN 1022-2464) **5952**
• Asian Journal of Occupational Therapy (JPN ISSN 1347-3476) **6106**
Asian Journal of Ophthalmology (HKG ISSN 1560-2133) **6038**
Asian Journal of Oral and Maxillofacial Surgery (HKG ISSN 0915-6992) **5835**
• Asian Journal of Pentecostal Studies (PHL ISSN 0118-8534) **7732**
▼ • Asian Journal of Pharmaceutical and Clinical Research (IND ISSN 0974-2441) **6823**
➤ Asian Journal of Pharmaceutical Sciences (HKG ISSN 1818-0876) **6823**
• ➤ Asian Journal of Pharmaceutics (IND ISSN 0973-8398) **6823**
Asian Journal of Pharmacodynamics and Pharmacokinetics (HKG) **6823**
Asian Journal of Philosophy (TWN) **6906**
Asian Journal of Physics (IND ISSN 0971-3093) **7006**
• Asian Journal of Plant Pathology (USA ISSN 1819-1541) **777**
➤ Asian Journal of Plant Science (IND ISSN 0971-2402) **777**
• ➤ Asian Journal of Plant Sciences (PAK ISSN 1682-3974) **777**
• ➤ Asian Journal of Political Science (GBR ISSN 0218-5377) **7107**
• Asian Journal of Poultry Science (USA ISSN 1819-3609) **279**
▼ ➤ Asian Journal of Psychiatry (NLD ISSN 1876-2018) **6124**
Asian Journal of Psychology and Education (IND ISSN 0971-2909) **2827**
Asian Journal of Quality (KOR ISSN 1598-2688) **1880**
• ➤ Asian Journal of Scientific Research (PAK ISSN 1992-1454) **7837**
Asian Journal of Social Pharmacy (HKG) **6823**
• ➤ Asian Journal of Social Psychology (AUS ISSN 1367-2223) **7337**
• ➤ Asian Journal of Social Science (NLD ISSN 1568-4849) **7948**
• Asian Journal of Spectroscopy (IND ISSN 0971-9237) **7074**
• Asian Journal of Textile (USA ISSN 1819-3358) **8448**
➤ Asian Journal of Traditional Medicines (HKG ISSN 1817-4337) **5579**
• ➤ Asian Journal of Transfusion Science (IND ISSN 0973-6247) **5933**
Asian Journal of W T O & International Health Law and Policy (World Trade Organization) (TWN ISSN 1819-5164) **4917**
• Asian Journal of Water, Environment and Pollution (NLD ISSN 0972-9860) **3404**
• ➤ Asian Journal of Women's Studies (KOR ISSN 1225-9276) **8893**
Asian Labour Update (HKG ISSN 0258-0268) **1665**
Asian Legal Briefing *see* Asian Counsel **4622**
† Asian Legal Journals Index (GBR ISSN 1560-2494) **8931**
Asian Literary Market Review (IND ISSN 0254-6183) **7552**
Asian Long-Term Outlook (USA ISSN 1541-6135) **1552**
Asian Magazine *see* New Zealand A M **3554**
Asian Management Review (IND) **1726**
• ➤ The Asian Manager (PHL ISSN 0116-7790) **1726**
• Asian Manufacturers Journal (HKG ISSN 1015-504X) **1880**
➤ Asian Marine Biology (HKG ISSN 1011-4041) **654**
Asian Mass Communications Bulletin (SGP ISSN 0129-2056) **8089**
Asian Medical News *see* Medical Tribune **5672**
• Asian Medicine (NLD ISSN 1573-420X) **5579**
Asian Migrant (PHL ISSN 1013-8064) **7277**
• Asian Migration News (PHL) **7277**
Asian Mobile News (SGP) **2365**
Asian Mould & Die (HKG) **1973**
• ➤ Asian Music (USA ISSN 0044-9202) **6546**
Asian News Sheet (CHE ISSN 0518-8881) **4493**
▼ • ➤ Asian Nursing Research (KOR ISSN 1976-1317) **5952**
Asian Oceanian Journal of Radiology (IND ISSN 0972-2688) **6192**
Asian Oil and Gas (USA ISSN 1026-6461) **6763**
• Asian Outlook (CAN) **1062**
Asian Pacific American Journal (USA ISSN 1067-778X) **5257**
➤ Asian Pacific American Law Journal (USA) **4622**
Asian - Pacific American Librarians Association Newsletter (USA ISSN 1040-8517) **4991**
Asian Pacific American Political Almanac (USA) **3520**
Asian - Pacific Book Development (JPN ISSN 0916-7838) **7552**
Asian-Pacific Business Review (IND ISSN 0973-2470) **1726**
Asian Pacific Congress of Cardiology. Symposia (JPN ISSN 0587-5471) **5778**
Asian Pacific Culture Quarterly (TWN) **543**
Asian Pacific Economic Literature *see* Asian - Pacific Economic Literature **1200**
• Asian - Pacific Economic Literature (AUS ISSN 0818-9935) **1200**
Asian Pacific Economic Times *see* Yatai Jingji Shibao **1197**
Asian - Pacific Environment (MYS ISSN 0127-7170) **3404**
➤ Asian Pacific Journal of Allergy & Immunology (THA ISSN 0125-877X) **5754**
• Asian Pacific Journal of Cancer Prevention (THA ISSN 1513-7368) **6009**
Asian Pacific Journal of Public Administration/Ya Tai gong gong xing zheng xue (HKG) **7421**
Asian Pacific Law & Policy Journal *see* Asian-Pacific Law & Policy Journal **4622**
• ➤ Asian-Pacific Law & Policy Journal (USA ISSN 1541-244X) **4622**
• Asian - Pacific Newsletter on Occupational Health and Safety (FIN ISSN 1237-0843) **6673**
Asian-Pacific Population Programme News *see* Population Headliners **7290**
• Asian Pages (USA ISSN 1526-8675) **543**
• ➤ Asian Perspective (KOR ISSN 0258-9184) **7107**
• ➤ Asian Perspectives (USA ISSN 0066-8435) **381**
• Asian Petrochemicalscan (USA ISSN 1931-177X) **6763**
• ➤ Asian Philosophy (GBR ISSN 0955-2367) **6906**
Asian Plastics News (SGP ISSN 0966-1867) **7090**
• Asian Political News (USA) **7107**
▼ • ➤ Asian Politics and Policy (USA ISSN 1943-0779) **7222**
• ➤ Asian Population Studies (GBR ISSN 1744-1730) **7277**
Asian Power (GBR ISSN 1353-4602) **3295**
Asian Power (SGP) **3124**
Asian Power Projects Review *see* A P P R **8927**
Asian Productivity Organization Annual Report *see* A P O Annual Report **1878**
Asian Productivity Organization News *see* A P O News **1878**
Asian Productivity Organization Productivity Journal *see* A P O Productivity Journal **1878**
➤ Asian Profile (CAN ISSN 0304-8675) **543**
Asian Recorder (IND ISSN 0004-4644) **3879**
Asian Regional Organisation of the International Textile Garment and Leather Workers' Federation News *see* T W A R O News **8458**
• The Asian Reporter (USA ISSN 1094-9453) **3520**
Asian Research Trends (JPN ISSN 0917-1479) **543**
Asian Resources Room. Bulletin *see* Ajia Jouhoushitsu Tsuuhou **4988**
• ➤ Asian Review of Accounting (GBR ISSN 1321-7348) **1280**
• Asian Review of Business and Technology (GBR ISSN 0956-3784) **8416**
• ➤ Asian Security (GBR ISSN 1479-9855) **2676**
Asian Security & Safety Journal (HKG ISSN 0259-059X) **2676**
• ➤ Asian Social Science (CAN ISSN 1911-2017) **7949**
Asian Social Science Bibliography with Annotations and Abstracts (IND ISSN 0066-8478) **8019**
Asian Social Science Series *see* Social Sciences in Asia **560**
▼ • Asian Social Work and Policy Review (AUS ISSN 1753-1403) **7949**
▼ Asian Society for International Relations and Public Affairs. Journal (USA ISSN 1944-6640) **8026**
Asian Sources Electronics *see* Global Sources Electronics **3100**
Asian Sources Security Products (HKG) **2676**
Asian Sources Timepieces *see* Global Sources Fashion Accessories **2256**
Asian Sources Timepieces *see* Global Sources Gifts & Home Products **4060**
▼ • Asian Spine Journal (KOR ISSN 1976-1902) **6056**
Asian Studies (PHL ISSN 0004-4679) **543**
Asian Studies Association of Australia. Conference Papers (AUS ISSN 0156-0182) **543**
• Asian Studies Institute. Translation Paper (NZL ISSN 1174-7676) **5096**
Asian Studies Newsletter (USA ISSN 0362-4811) **543**
• ➤ Asian Studies Review (AUS ISSN 1035-7823) **4180**

Title

▼ *new title* † *ceased* • *electronic media* ➤ *refereed*

• The Asian Studies W W W Monitor (World Wide Web) (AUS ISSN 1329-9778) **564**
Asian Sunews (USA) **1395**
• ➤ Asian Survey (USA ISSN 0004-4687) **7107**
Asian Symposium on Information Display. Proceedings (USA) **7074**
• Asian Test Symposium. Proceedings (USA ISSN 1081-7735) **2539**
• Asian Textile Business (JPN ISSN 1346-3276) **8448**
Asian Textile Journal (IND ISSN 0971-3425) **8448**
Asian Textile Record (JPN) **8448**
• Asian Textile Weekly (JPN ISSN 1346-3284) **8448**
• ➤ Asian Theatre Journal (USA ISSN 0742-5457) **8466**
Asian Thought and Culture (USA ISSN 0893-6870) **544**
Asian Times (GBR ISSN 0264-8490) **3520**
• Asian Trader (GBR ISSN 0961-7132) **1973**
Asian Tribune (CAN ISSN 0707-3380) **3520**
Asian Vegetable Research and Development Center Report *see* A V R D C Report **78**
Asian Vegetable Research and Development Center. Technical Bulletin (TWN ISSN 1010-142X) **93**
The Asian Venture Capital Journal *see* A V C J Weekly **1305**
Asian Venture Capital Journal Weekly *see* A V C J Weekly **1305**
• The Asian Wall Street Journal (HKG ISSN 0377-9920) **1309**
Asian Water (MYS) **3404**
Asian Wedding *see* Asian Bride **3520**
• Asian Wisconzine (USA) **3520**
Asian Woman & Bride *see* Asian Bride **3520**
• ➤ Asian Women (KOR ISSN 1225-925X) **8894**
➤ Asian Yearbook of International Law (NLD ISSN 0928-432X) **4917**
Asiana (GBR) **8852**
Asiana Wedding (GBR ISSN 1742-237X) **5556**
• AsianDOC Electronic Newsletter (USA ISSN 1098-9145) **544**
• ASIANetwork Exchange (USA ISSN 1943-9938) **544**
AsianGeographic *see* Asian Geographic **2603**
• AsianInvestor (GBR) **1610**
• The Asianists' Asia (FRA ISSN 1298-0358) **544**
Asians on Wheels (USA) **3520**
• AsianWeek (USA ISSN 0195-2056) **3520**
➤ AsiaPacific MediaEducator (AUS ISSN 1326-365X) **4572**
• AsiaPulse News (AUS) **1062**
• AsiaRights Journal (AUS ISSN 1832-0910) **7202**
Asia's 10000 Largest Companies *see* Asia's 10,000 Largest Companies (Year) **1309**
• Asia's 10,000 Largest Companies (Year) (GBR) **1309**
Asia's 10,000 Largest Companies on CD-ROM *see* Asia's 10,000 Largest Companies (Year) **1309**
Asia's 7,500 Largest Companies *see* Asia's 10,000 Largest Companies (Year) **1309**
Asia's Best Local Gourmet Restaurants (SGP) **4382**
• Asia's Fashion Jewellery & Accessories Review (HKG) **4564**
Asias Millioner (NOR ISSN 1504-5560) **7746**
Asia's Ten Thousand Largest Companies *see* Asia's 10,000 Largest Companies (Year) **1309**
Asia's Top 60 Food Groups (GBR) **3627**
Asiatic Herpetological Research (USA ISSN 1051-3825) **934**
Asiatic Society. Annual Report (IND ISSN 0403-4457) **3879**
Asiatic Society, Calcutta. Journal (IND ISSN 0571-3161) **544**
Asiatic Society, Calcutta. Monograph Series (IND) **544**
Asiatic Society, Calcutta. Seminar Series (IND) **544**
Asiatic Society. Journal (IND ISSN 0368-3303) **544**
Asiatic Society of Bangladesh. Annual General Meeting: Report of the General Secretary (BGD) **544**
Asiatic Society of Bangladesh. Journal: Humanities (BGD ISSN 1015-6836) **4443**
Asiatic Society of Bangladesh. Journal: Science (BGD ISSN 1016-6947) **7837**
➤ Asiatic Society of Bombay. Journal (IND ISSN 0004-4709) **544**
Asiatic Society of Japan. Transactions. 4th Series (JPN ISSN 0913-4271) **544**
Asiatische Forschungen (DEU ISSN 0571-320X) **544**
➤ Asiatische Studien/Etudes Asiatiques (CHE ISSN 0004-4717) **544**
Asiatiske Skrifter (DNK ISSN 1397-1158) **544**
• Asiaview (AUS ISSN 1037-6534) **3926**
Aside World (USA) **8287**
Asie et Monde Insulindien (BEL ISSN 1147-5161) **5096**
Asie Orientale (FRA ISSN 1298-8723) **4180**
➤ Asien (DEU ISSN 0721-5231) **544**
Asien-Pazifik *see* Asien-Pazifik. Wirtschaftshandbuch **1438**
Asien-Pazifik. Wirtschaftshandbuch (DEU) **1438**
Asien- und Afrika- Studien der Humboldt Universitaet zu Berlin (DEU) **544**
Asien und Pazifik (DEU ISSN 1437-3688) **544**
• Asilomar Conference on Signals, Systems and Computers. Conference Record (USA ISSN 1058-6393) **2519**
• Asimmetrie (ITA ISSN 1827-1383) **7064**
Asimov's Science Fiction (Palm O S & Windows C E Edition) *see* Asimov's Science Fiction (Print Edition) **5440**
• Asimov's Science Fiction (Print Edition) (USA ISSN 1065-2698) **5440**
Asimow, Bonfield and Levin's - State and Federal Administrative Law (USA) **4622**
Asimptoticheskie Metody v Teorii Sistem (RUS ISSN 0320-0914) **5474**
Asinto (ESP ISSN 0571-3226) **976**
Ask! (USA ISSN 0731-2350) **1726**
• Ask (USA ISSN 1535-4105) **2176**
• Ask A C E (Advisory Centre for Education) (GBR ISSN 1754-7202) **3017**
▼ Ask Deanna! (USA ISSN 1947-427X) **7337**
Ask Deanna! The Magazine *see* Ask Deanna! **7337**
• Ask Harley (USA ISSN 1547-6006) **3969**
ASK Hollis *see* A S K Hollis **1970**
• Ask the Book Sistah (USA ISSN 1557-6523) **7552**
• Ask The Computer Lady (USA) **2407**
▼ • Ask the Recruiter (USA ISSN 1944-0200) **1856**
Asker og Baerums Budstikke (NOR) **3921**
Asklepii (UKR) **5579**
ASko (POL ISSN 1231-6857) **6804**
Askoeyvaeringen (NOR) **3921**
Askov Hoejskole og Efterskole. Aarsskrift (DNK ISSN 1604-7761) **2938**
• Aslan (Online) (DNK ISSN 1901-6646) **7623**
Aslan (Print) *see* Aslan (Online) **7623**
Aslib Annual Report (GBR ISSN 0957-0470) **4991**
Aslib Guide to Copyright (GBR ISSN 1353-1530) **4622**
• ➤ Aslib Proceedings (GBR ISSN 0001-253X) **4991**
Al Asmant al-'Alamiyyat *see* Cement International **990**
Asmara Chamber of Commerce. Trade and Development Bulletin (ERI) **1395**
Asme Humanitas Bulletin (DEU) **8026**
• Asmoz Ta Jakitez (ESP ISSN 1132-7952) **329**
Asmoz Ta Jakitez (French Edition) (ESP ISSN 1254-2199) **329**
Asmoz Ta Jakitez (Spanish Edition) (ESP ISSN 1133-9861) **329**
▼ Asoarabes (COL ISSN 2011-1428) **8287**
Asobancaria Semana Economica (COL ISSN 0122-6657) **1438**
Asocars (Asociacion de Corporaciones Autonomas Regionales y de Desarrollo Sostenible) (COL ISSN 2011-1363) **3404**
Asociacin Profesional Gallega de Terapeutas Ocupacionales. Revista de Terapia Ocupacional *see* T O G **6116**
Asociacion (URY) **2143**
• Asociacion Andaluza de Bibliotecarios. Boletin (ESP ISSN 0213-6333) **4991**
Asociacion Argentina Criadores de Cerdos. Revista (ARG ISSN 0004-4741) **279**
Asociacion Argentina de Actores. Memoria y Balance (ARG) **4590**
• Asociacion Argentina de Astronomia. Boletin (Online) (ARG) **569**
Asociacion Argentina de Geologos Economistas. Revista (ARG ISSN 0327-7054) **2725**
Asociacion Argentina de los Quimicos y Tecnicos de la Industria del Cuero. Revista (ARG ISSN 0518-9152) **4972**
Asociacion Argentina de Mineralogia, Petrologia y Sedimentologia. Revista (ARG ISSN 0325-0253) **2702**
• Asociacion Argentina de Odontologia para Ninos. Boletin (ARG ISSN 0518-9160) **5835**
Asociacion Argentina de Ortopedia Funcional de los Maxilares. Revista (ARG ISSN 0326-5404) **6056**
Asociacion Argentina de Ortopedia y Traumatologia. Revista (ARG ISSN 1515-1786) **6056**
Asociacion Argentina de Sedimentologia. Revista *see* Latin American Journal of Sedimentology and Basin Analysis **2752**
Asociacion Argentina para el Estudio del Climaterio. Revista (ARG ISSN 1666-0056) **5986**
• Asociacion Chilena de Astronomia y Astronautica. Boletin (CHL ISSN 0716-2049) **569**
Asociacion Chilena de Proteccion de la Familia. Boletin (CHL ISSN 0716-2057) **4088**
Asociacion Chilena de Seguridad. Boletin Cientifico *see* Ciencia & Trabajo **6675**
Asociacion Civil Argentina de Auditoria Odontologica. Revista (ARG ISSN 1667-1090) **5835**
Asociacion Colombiana de Bibliotecologos y Documentalistas Revista *see* A S C O L B I Revista **4986**
Asociacion Colombiana de Ciencias Biologicas. Revista (COL ISSN 0120-4173) **654**
Asociacion Colombiana de Exportadores de Flores. Revista (COL ISSN 0121-1455) **3755**
Asociacion Colombiana de Tecnicos de la Industria de la Pulpa, Papel y Carton. Revista (COL ISSN 0122-9052) **6732**
Asociacion Costarricense de Bibliotecarios. Boletin (CRI ISSN 0004-4784) **4991**
Asociacion Cubana de Produccion Animal *see* A C P A **276**
Asociacion Cultural Castillo de Embid *see* A C C E **7944**
Asociacion de Autocontrol de la Publicidad (ESP ISSN 1137-1153) **21**
Asociacion de Bibliotecarios de Instituciones de Ensenanza Superior e Investigacion. Archivos (MEX) **4991**
Asociacion de Bibliotecarios de Instituciones de Ensenanza Superior e Investigacion. Boletin (MEX ISSN 0185-0377) **4991**
Asociacion de Diplomados y Alumnos de Biblioteconomia y Documentacion. Cuadernos (ESP ISSN 1139-112X) **4991**
Asociacion de Directores de Escena de Espana Teatro *see* A D E - Teatro **8464**
Asociacion de Economistas Argentinos. Coleccion Instituto Superior (ARG) **1063**
Asociacion de Ensenantes con Gitanos. Boletin (ESP ISSN 1130-5118) **2827**
Asociacion de Ensenantes con Gitanos. Centro de Documentacion. Boletin *see* Asociacion de Ensenantes con Gitanos. Boletin **2827**
Asociacion de Escribanos del Uruguay. Revista (URY ISSN 0376-5024) **4622**
Asociacion de Ex-Alumnos de la Escuela Nacional de Bibliotecarios. Boletin (ARG ISSN 0004-4806) **4992**
Asociacion de Fabricantes de Celulosa y Papel Noticias *see* AFCP Noticias **6732**
Asociacion de Ferreterias, Pinturerias y Bazares de la Republica Argentina. Revista (ARG ISSN 0328-6460) **1053**
Asociacion de Garajes y Estaciones de Servicio *see* A G E S **8554**
Asociacion de Geografos Espanoles. Boletin (ESP ISSN 0212-9426) **3999**
Asociacion de Hispanistas de las Americas. Publicaciones. Coleccion Monografias (USA ISSN 0277-6782) **5417**
Asociacion de Historia Actual. Boletin (ESP ISSN 1988-9666) **4131**
Asociacion de Ingenieros Quimicos del Uruguay Noticias Online *see* A I Q Noticias Online **3234**
Asociacion de Investigacion Tecnica de las Industrias de la Madera Boletin de Informacion Tecnica *see* A I T I M Boletin de Informacion Tecnica **3709**
Asociacion de Investigacion Tecnologia de Equipos Mineros. Boletin (ESP) **6457**
Asociacion de Licenciados en Informatica Base Informatica *see* A L I Base Informatica **2405**
Asociacion de Licenciados y Doctores Espanoles en los Estados Unidos Cuadernos *see* A L D E E U. Cuadernos **2264**
Asociacion de Oficinas de Arquitectos Revista *see* AOA. Revista **427**
Asociacion de Quimica y Farmacia del Uruguay. Revista (URY ISSN 0797-9150) **6823**
▼ • Asociacion de Sociologia de la Educacion. Revista (ESP ISSN 1988-7302) **8089**
Asociacion de Tecnicos Azucareros de Cuba *see* A T A C **215**
Asociacion del Congreso Panamericano de Ferrocarriles. Boletin (ARG) **8614**
Asociacion Demografica Costarricense. Memoria (CRI) **7277**
Asociacion Escuela Argentina de Psicoterapia para Graduados. Revista (ARG ISSN 0326-0704) **6124**
Asociacion Espanola Contra el Cancer *see* A E C C **6007**
Asociacion Espanola Contra el Cancer. Memoria (ESP) **6009**
Asociacion Espanola de A T S en Urologia. Revista (ESP ISSN 0210-9476) **6265**
Asociacion Espanola de Amigos de la Arqueologia. Boletin (ESP ISSN 0210-4741) **381**
Asociacion Espanola de Archiveros Bibliotecarios Museologos y Documentalistas Boletin *see* A N A B A D Boletin **4986**
† Asociacion Espanola de Ensayos Non-Destructivos. Boletin Informativo (ESP ISSN 1888-9271) **8931**
➤ Asociacion Espanola de Entomologia. Boletin (ESP ISSN 0210-8984) **840**
Asociacion Espanola de Especialistas en Medicina del Trabajo. Revista (ESP ISSN 1132-6255) **6673**
Asociacion Espanola de Logopedia, Foniatria y Audiologia. Boletin Boletin *see* A E L F A. Boletin **6076**
Asociacion Espanola de Neuropsiquiatria. Boletin (ESP ISSN 0210-8194) **6124**
• Asociacion Espanola de Neuropsiquiatria. Revista (ESP ISSN 0211-5735) **6124**
Asociacion Espanola de Orientalistas. Boletin (ESP ISSN 0571-3692) **544**
• ➤ Asociacion Espanola de Reumatologia. Seminarios (ESP ISSN 1577-3566) **6222**
Asociacion Espanola de Tecnicos de Cerveza y Malta. Anuario (ESP) **597**
Asociacion Espanola de Tecnicos de Maquinaria para la Construccion, Obras Publicas y Mineria *see* A T E M C O P **3258**
Asociacion Europea de Direccion y Economia de la Empresa Bibliometrica *see* A E D E M Bibliometrica **1722**
Asociacion Filatelica de la Republica Argentina Boletin Informativo *see* A F R A Boletin Informativo **6891**
Asociacion Forestal Argentina. Revista (ARG ISSN 0328-3372) **3684**
Asociacion Franco-Mexicana de Ingenieros y Tecnicos. Boletin (MEX ISSN 0004-4814) **3182**
Asociacion General de Agricultores *see* A G A **77**
Asociacion Geologica Argentina. Boletin Informativo (ARG ISSN 0328-2724) **2725**
• ➤ Asociacion Geologica Argentina. Revista (ARG ISSN 0004-4822) **2725**
• Asociacion Herpetologica Espanola. Boletin (ESP ISSN 1130-6939) **934**
• Asociacion Hotelera de Colombia. Boletin Informativo (COL) **4382**
Asociacion Iberoamericana de Centros de Investigacion y Estudio de Telecomunicaciones Revista de Telecomunicaciones *see* A H C I E T Revista de Telecomunicaciones **2311**
Asociacion Iberoamericana de Derecho Romano Actas *see* A I D R O M. Actas **4607**
Asociacion Implantodontologica Argentina. Revista (ARG ISSN 0327-8581) **5835**
Asociacion Interamericana de Bibliotecarios, Documentalistas y Especialistas en Informacion Agricola. Boletin Informativo (CRI) **4992**
Asociacion Interamericana de Bibliotecarios, Documentalistas y Especialistas en Informacion Agricola. Boletin Tecnico (CRI) **93**
Asociacion Interamericana de Bibliotecarios y Documentalistas Agricolas. Revista (CRI ISSN 0250-3190) **4992**
• Asociacion Jueces para la Democracia. Boletin Informativo (ESP) **4622**
Asociacion Latinoamericana de Diabetes. Revista (ARG ISSN 0327-9154) **5884**
Asociacion Latinoamericana de Escuelas de Bibliotecologia y Ciencias de la Informacion Boletin Informativo *see* A L E B C I Boletin Informativo **4986**
Asociacion Latinoamericana de Produccion Animal. Memoria (VEN) **279**
Asociacion Latinoamericana de Sociedades de Biologia y Medicina Nuclear Journal *see* A L A S B I M N Journal **6191**
• ➤ Asociacion Matematica Venezolana. Boletin/Venezuelan Mathematical Association. Bulletin (VEN ISSN 1315-4125) **5474**
• Asociacion Medica Argentina. Boletin (ARG ISSN 1666-2687) **5579**
Asociacion Medica Argentina de Anticoncepcion. Revista (ARG ISSN 1669-2411) **971**
• Asociacion Medica Argentina. Revista (ARG ISSN 0004-4830) **5579**
Asociacion Medica de Bahia Blanca. Revista (ARG ISSN 1515-8659) **5579**
Asociacion Medica de Puerto Rico. Boletin (PRI ISSN 0004-4849) **5579**
Asociacion Meteorologica Espanola. Boletin (ESP ISSN 1696-764X) **6346**
Asociacion Mexicana de Bibliotecarios, A.C. Noticiero *see* A M B A C Noticiero **4986**
• Asociacion Mexicana de Medicina Critica y Terapia Intensiva. Revista (MEX ISSN 0187-8433) **5944**
Asociacion Mexicana de Medicos Veterinarios Especialistas en Pequenas Especies. Revista Revista *see* A M M V E P E. Revista **8790**
Asociacion Mexicana de Tecnicos de las Industrias de la Celulosa y del Papel, A.C. Revista *see* A T C P Revista **6732**
Asociacion Nacional Cientifica de Estudiantes de Medicina de Chile Revista *see* A N A C E M. Revista **2822**
Asociacion Nacional de Enfermeras de Colombia *see* A N E C **5949**
Asociacion Nacional de Industriales. Revista Bimestral (COL ISSN 0120-9515) **1880**
Asociacion Nacional de Instituciones Financieras. Carta Financiera (COL) **1438**
▼ ➤ Asociacion Nacional de Investigadores de Incendios de Espana (ESP ISSN 1888-623X) **3575**
Asociacion Nacional de Jubilados y Pensionados de Comunicaciones *see* A N J U P E C **8022**
Asociacion Nacional de Pensionados por el Instituto del Seguro Social Informativo *see* A N P I S S Informativo **8022**
• Asociacion Nacional de Porcinocultura Cientifica (A N A P O R C). Revista (ESP) **279**
Asociacion Nacional de Promotores Constructores de Edificios Urbanos. Annual Report (ESP) **4403**
Asociacion Nacional de Promotores Constructores de Edificios Urbanos. Promocion (ESP) **4404**
Asociacion Nacional del Cafe. Departamento de Asuntos Agricolas. Informe Anual (GTM ISSN 0066-8567) **597**
➤ Asociacion Odontologica Argentina. Revista (ARG ISSN 0004-4881) **5835**
Asociacion Paleontologica Argentina. Publicaciones Especiales (ARG ISSN 0328-347X) **6723**
Asociacion para El Desarrollo de la Direccion. Revista (ESP ISSN 1886-1709) **1063**
▼ Asociacion para el Desarrollo de la Ingenieria de la Organizacion. Boletin (ESP ISSN 1888-3184) **3182**
• Asociacion para le Fomento de los Estudios Historicos en Centroamerica. Boletin (FRA ISSN 1954-3891) **4131**
• Asociacion Primatologica Espanola. Boletin (ESP ISSN 1577-2802) **934**
Asociacion Proyecto Hombre. Memoria (ESP ISSN 1136-8861) **2692**
• ➤ Asociacion Quimica Argentina. Anales (ARG ISSN 0365-0375) **2051**
• Asociacion Quimica Espanola de la Industria del Cuero. Boletin Tecnico (ESP ISSN 0365-5873) **4972**
Asociacion Rural del Uruguay. Revista (URY ISSN 0044-9326) **93**
Asociacion Salvadorena de Industriales Directorio de Asociados (SLV) **1973**
Asociacion Venezolana de Archiveros. Boletin Informativo (VEN) **4992**

Title

9986 ASSOCIATION AMICALE DES ANCIENS COMBATTANTS DU 8E REGIMENT ULRICH'S PERIODICALS

Association Amicale des Anciens Combattants du 8e Regiment de Cuirassiers. Bulletin Trimestriel (FRA ISSN 1774-9719) **2264**
Association & Meeting Director (CAN ISSN 1498-6094) **1726**
Association Belge de Documentation. Cahiers de la Documentation/Belgische Vereniging voor Documentatie. Bladen voor de Documentatie (BEL ISSN 0007-9804) **4992**
Association Belge de Radioprotection. Annales *see* Belgische Vereniging voor Stralingsbescherming. Annalen **7509**
Association Belge des Paralyses Contact *see* A B P Contact **4063**
Association Belge des Professeurs de Francais. Bulletin *see* Francais 2000 **5120**
Association Belge des Technologues de Laboratoire. Revue/Belgische Vereniging van Laboratorium Technologen. Tijdschrift (BEL ISSN 0770-1578) **2051**
Association Belge du Diabete *see* A B D **5883**
Association Belge pour l'Etude, l'Essai et l'Emploi des Materiaux. Proces Verbal de l'Assemblee Generale Ordinaire (BEL ISSN 0066-8818) **3341**
Association Belge pour l'Etude, l'Essai et l'Emploi des Materiaux. Publication A.B.E.M (BEL ISSN 0066-8796) **3341**
Association Canadienne de la Police Professionnelle Express *see* Express **2652**
Association Canadienne de Linguistique Appliquee. Revue *see* Canadian Journal of Applied Linguistics **5104**
Association Canadienne de Volley-ball. Regle de Jeu *see* Canadian Volleyball Association. Rule Book **8224**
Association Canadienne d'Education. Bulletin (CAN ISSN 0004-5306) **2827**
Association Canadienne d'Education de Langue Francaise en Action *see* L' A C E L F en Action **5088**
Association Canadienne des Eaux Potables et Usees. Bulletin *see* Canadian Water and Wastewater Association. Bulletin **8819**
Association Canadienne des Enseignants(es) des Sourds(es) et des Malentendants(es). Revue *see* C A E D H H Journal **4072**
Association Canadienne des Etudes Africaines. Bulletin *see* Canadian Association of African Studies. Newsletter **2971**
Association Canadienne des Pates et Papiers. Statistiques Mensuelles sur le Papier Journal *see* Canadian Pulp and Paper Association. Monthly Newsprint Statistics **6732**
Association Canadienne des Policiers. Express *see* Express **2652**
Association Canadienne des Radiodiffuseurs. Rapport Annuel *see* Canadian Association of Broadcasters. Annual Report **2314**
Association Canadienne des Radiologistes. Journal *see* Canadian Association of Radiologists Journal **6193**
Association Canadienne Droit et Societe. Bulletin *see* Canadian Law and Society Association. Bulletin **4639**
Association Canadienne - Francaise pour l'Avancement des Sciences. Annales (CAN ISSN 0066-8842) **7837**
Association Canadienne - Francaise pour l'Avancement des Sciences. Cahiers Scientifiques (CAN) **7837**
Association Canadienne pour la Sante Mentale. Rapport Annuel *see* Canadian Mental Health Association. Annual Report **7344**
Association Contact (USA ISSN 1054-352X) **2827**
▼ Association Conventions & Facilities (USA) **6277**
Association d'Amitie Franco-Vietnamienne. Bulletin d'Information et de Documentation *see* Perspective France Vietnam **8125**
Association d'Art des Universites du Canada. Journal *see* Universities Art Association of Canada. Journal **523**
Association de Geographes Francais. Bulletin (FRA ISSN 0004-5322) **3999**
Association de la Construction de Montreal et du Quebec. Bulletin (CAN ISSN 0833-8388) **977**
Association de la Recherche Theatrale au Canada. Bulletin de Liaison *see* Association for Canadian Theatre Research. Newsletter **8466**
Association d'Egyptologie Isis. Cahiers (FRA ISSN 1954-9865) **4320**
Association Dentaire Canadienne. Journal *see* Canadian Dental Association. Journal **5837**
Association Departementale de Developpement Culturel (A D D C) (FRA ISSN 1779-6431) **4976**
Association des Amis d'Alfred de Vigny. Bulletin (FRA ISSN 0066-8893) **5257**
† Association des Amis de la Bibliotheque de France. Reseaux (FRA ISSN 1142-2815) **8931**
† Association des Amis de Pierre Teilhard de Chardin. Bulletin (FRA ISSN 0066-8907) **8931**
Association des Amis de Rabelais et de la Deviniere. Bulletin (FRA ISSN 0571-5350) **5257**
Association des Anciens du 8e Cuirassiers *see* Association Amicale des Anciens Combattants du 8e Regiment de Cuirassiers. Bulletin Trimestriel **2264**
Association des Anciens Eleves de l'Ecole d'Ingenieurs de Geneve. Bulletin Technique (CHE) **3182**
Association des Architectes Paysagistes du Quebec. Repertoire *see* Association des Architectes Paysagistes du Quebec. Repertoire Annuel **3723**
Association des Architectes Paysagistes du Quebec. Repertoire Annuel (CAN ISSN 1718-1194) **3723**
Association des Archivistes du Quebec. Rapport Annuel (CAN ISSN 1719-4504) **4992**
Association des Auteurs Realisateurs du Sud Est'A A R S E *see* L'A A R S E **6506**
Association des Banques du Liban. Rapport Annuel *see* Association des Banques du Liban. Rapport du Conseil **1438**
Association des Banques du Liban. Rapport du Conseil (LBN) **1438**
Association des Bibliothecaires Francais. Groupe Centre. Bulletin d'Information *see* Association des Bibliothecaires Francais. Groupe Centre. Le Journal **4992**
Association des Bibliothecaires Francais. Groupe Centre. Le Journal (FRA ISSN 1761-9718) **4992**
Association des Bibliotheques Chretiennes de France. Bulletin de Liaison (FRA ISSN 1773-2565) **4992**
Association des Bibliotheques de la Sante du Canada. Journal *see* Canadian Health Libraries Association. Journal **5000**
• Association des Bibliotheques de Recherche du Canada. Rapport Annuel (CAN ISSN 1912-1113) **4992**
Association des Cadres des Colleges du Quebec. Le Journal *see* L' Entrecadre **2980**
Association des Colleges Prives du Quebec. Annuaire *see* Repertoire des Colleges Prives du Quebec **2904**
Association des Conservateurs de Bibliotheque. Annuaire (FRA) **4992**
Association des Conservateurs de Bibliotheque Infos *see* A C B Infos **4985**
Association des Constructeurs de Routes et Grands Travaux du Quebec Informe ses Membres *see* L' A C R G T Q Informe ses Membres **974**
Association des Courtiers et Agents Immobiliers du Quebec Magazine *see* A C A I Q Magazine **7581**
Association des Diplomes de l'Ecole de Bibliothecaires Documentalistes. Bulletin d'Information *see* Bibdoc **4994**
Association des Enseignantes et des Enseignants Francophones du Nouveau-Brunswick. Nouvelles (CAN ISSN 1197-7523) **2827**
Association des Entreprises Electriques Suisses. Bulletin *see* Electrosuisse, S E V, Verband fur Elektro-, Energie- und Informationstechnik. Bulletin **3305**
Association des Garderies Privees du Quebec. Programme de Formation Continue (CAN ISSN 1715-5746) **2938**
Association des Geologues Amateurs de Belgique *see* A G A B **2722**
Association des Geologues du Bassin de Paris. Bulletin d'Information (FRA ISSN 0374-1346) **2725**
Association des Ingenieurs Electriciens Sortis de l'Institut Electrotechnique Montefiore. Bulletin Scientifique *see* Association des Ingenieurs Electriciens Sortis de l'Institut Montefiore. Bulletin Scientifique **3296**
Association des Ingenieurs Electriciens Sortis de l'Institut Montefiore. Bulletin Scientifique (BEL ISSN 1376-4160) **3296**
Association des Ingenieurs et Anciens Eleves de l'Ecole Superieure d'Ingenieurs et Techniciens pour l'Agriculture. Annuaire (FRA) **219**
Association des Journalistes Agricoles. Annuaire (FRA) **93**
Association des Medecins de Langue Francaise du Canada Bulletin *see* A M L F C Bulletin **5564**
† Association des Medecins de Langue Francaise. Revue (FRA ISSN 0571-5415) **8931**
Association des Morphologistes. Bulletin *see* Morphologie **5680**
Association des Naturalistes de la Vallee du Loing et du Massif de Fontainebleau. Bulletin (FRA ISSN 0296-3086) **777**
Association des Naturalistes des Yvelines. Bulletin (FRA ISSN 1167-9786) **7837**
Association des Naturalistes du Mali. Bulletin (MLI) **7837**
Association des Professeurs de Languages des Instituts Universitaires de Technologie Cahiers *see* A P L I U T. Cahiers **2964**
Association des Professeurs de Mathematiques de l'Enseignement Public Bulletin *see* A P M E P. Bulletin **5463**
Association des Sedimentologistes Francais (FRA ISSN 0990-3925) **2725**
Association des Traducteurs et Interpretes de l'Ontario. InformATIO/Association of Translators and Interpreters of Ontario. InformATIO (CAN ISSN 0381-5781) **5097**
Association des Traducteurs et Interpretes de l'Ontario. Repertoire/Association of Translators and Interpreters of Ontario. Directory (CAN ISSN 0066-9016) **5097**
Association des Urologues du Canada. Journal *see* Canadian Urological Association. Journal **6266**
▼ Association du Refuge des Tortues. La Gazette (FRA ISSN 1956-7421) **318**
Association Educator (USA) **1726**
Association Entomologique d'Evreux. Bulletin de Liaison (FRA ISSN 1168-3597) **840**
• Association Euro-Africaine pour l'Anthropologie du Changement Social et du Developpement. Bulletin (Online) (FRA ISSN 1950-6929) **8089**
• Association Euro-Africaine pour l'Anthropologie du Changement Social et du Developpement. Bulletin (Print) (DEU) **329**
Association Europeenne de Libre-echange. Rapport Annuel (CHE ISSN 0258-0756) **1552**
Association Europeenne des Femmes pour la Recherche Theologique. Annuaire *see* European Society of Women in Theological Research. Journal **7641**
• Association Executive (USA) **1726**
Association for Academic Minority Physicians. Journal (USA ISSN 1048-9886) **5580**
Association for Applied Community Research Cost of Living Index *see* A C C R A Cost of Living Index **1199**
Association for Applied Community Research Research in Review *see* A C C R A Research in Review **1394**
• Association for Applied Psychophysiology and Biofeedback. Proceedings of the Annual Meeting (USA) **7337**
• Association for Asian Studies. Abstracts of the Annual Meeting (USA) **544**
Association for Asian Studies. Abstracts of the Annual Meeting (Print) *see* Association for Asian Studies. Abstracts of the Annual Meeting **544**
Association for Asian Studies. Monographs (USA ISSN 0066-9059) **4180**
Association for Asian Studies. Monographs, Occasional Papers and Reference Series (USA) **4180**
Association for Astrological Networking Newsletter *see* A F A N Newsletter **564**
Association for Behavior Analysis Newsletter (Kalamazoo) *see* A B A Newsletter (Kalamazoo) **7330**
The Association for Biblical Higher Education Newsletter *see* A B H E Newsletter **2963**
Association for British Insurers - Building Cost Information Service House Rebuilding Cost Index *see* A B I - B C I S House Rebuilding Cost Index **974**
Association for Business Simulation and Experiential Learning News & Views *see* A B S E L News & Views **2517**
Association for Canadian Studies. Canadian Issues *see* Canadian Issues **4446**
• Association for Canadian Theatre Research. Newsletter/Association de la Recherche Theatrale au Canada. Bulletin de Liaison (CAN ISSN 1193-7564) **8466**
Association for Career and Technical Education. Techniques *see* Techniques **2918**
Association for Central Asian Studies *see* A C A S I A **4179**
Association for Child and Adolescent Mental Health Occasional Papers *see* A C A M H Occasional Papers **7330**
Association for Child Psychoanalysis. Newsletter (USA ISSN 1077-0305) **2144**
Association for Child Psychology and Psychiatry. Occasional Papers *see* A C A M H Occasional Papers **7330**
Association for Chinese Music Research Reports *see* A C M R Reports **6541**
• Association for Communication Administration. Journal (USA) **1726**
• Association for Computational Linguistics. Annual Meeting Conference Proceedings (USA ISSN 0736-587X) **5202**
Association for Computer Education in Texas Journal of Computer Education and Research *see* A C E T Journal of Computer Education and Research **2404**
Association for Computer Operations Management's Annual Survey of Data Processing Operations Salaries *see* A F C O M's Annual Survey of Data Processing Operations Salaries **1199**
Association for Computers and the Humanities Newsletter *see* A C H Newsletter **4485**
Association for Computing Education Transactions on Computing Education *see* A C M Transactions on Computing Education **2822**
Association for Computing Machinery. Annual Report (Year) (USA) **2533**
Association for Computing Machinery Collected Algorithm Supplement *see* A C M Collected Algorithm Supplement **5549**
• ➤ Association for Computing Machinery. Communications (USA ISSN 0001-0782) **2533**
Association for Computing Machinery. Computer Service (USA) **2539**
Association for Computing Machinery Computing Surveys *see* A C M Computing Surveys **2405**
Association for Computing Machinery. Conference on Computer and Communications Security. Proceedings *see* A C M Conference on Computer and Communications Security. Proceedings **2511**
• Association for Computing Machinery. Conference Proceedings (USA) **2539**
Association for Computing Machinery Electronic Guide to Computing Literature *see* A C M Electronic Guide to Computing Literature **2442**
Association for Computing Machinery, Inc. Transactions on Applied Perception *see* A C M Transactions on Applied Perception **2405**
Association for Computing Machinery, Inc. Transactions on Asian Language Information Processing *see* A C M Transactions on Asian Language Information Processing **5202**
Association for Computing Machinery, Inc. Transactions on Computational Logic *see* A C M Transactions on Computational Logic **2405**
Association for Computing Machinery, Inc. Transactions on Computational Theory *see* A C M Transactions on Computational Theory **5549**
Association for Computing Machinery, Inc. Workshop on Privacy in the Electronic Society. Proceedings *see* A C M Workshop on Privacy in the Electronic Society. Proceedings **4846**
Association for Computing Machinery / Institute of Electrical and Electronics Engineers Design Automation Conference. Proceedings *see* A C M / I E E E Design Automation Conference. Proceedings **2457**
Association for Computing Machinery / Institute of Electrical and Electronics Engineers / I E E E International Workshop on Timing Issues in the Specification and Synthesis of Digital Systems. Proceedings *see* A C M / I E E E International Workshop on Timing Issues in the Specification and Synthesis of Digital Systems. Proceedings **2405**
Association for Computing Machinery / Institute of Electrical and Electronics Engineers Joint Conference on Digital Libraries. Proceedings *see* A C M / I E E E Joint Conference on Digital Libraries. Proceedings **4985**
Association for Computing Machinery - Institute of Electrical and Electronics Engineers Symposium on Volume Visualization *see* A C M - I E E E Symposium on Volume Visualization **2482**
Association for Computing Machinery International Workshop on Modeling, Analysis and Simulation of Wireless and Mobile Systems. Proceedings *see* A C M International Workshop on Modeling, Analysis and Simulation of Wireless and Mobile Systems. Proceedings **2310**
• ➤ Association for Computing Machinery. Journal (USA ISSN 0004-5411) **2407**
Association for Computing Machinery Journal of Data and Information Quality *see* A C M Journal of Data and Information Quality **2528**
Association for Computing Machinery Journal on Computing and Cultural Heritage *see* A C M Journal on Computing and Cultural Heritage **2405**
Association for Computing Machinery Journal on Data and Information Quality *see* A C M Journal on Data and Information Quality **2528**
Association for Computing Machinery Journal on Emerging Technologies in Computing Systems *see* A C M Journal on Emerging Technologies in Computing Systems **2569**
Association for Computing Machinery Monograph Series *see* A C M Monograph Series **2405**
• Association for Computing Machinery New Zealand. Bulletin (NZL ISSN 1176-9998) **2407**
Association for Computing Machinery S I G P L A N Conference on Programming Language Design and Implementation. Proceedings *see* A C M S I G P L A N Conference on Programming Language Design and Implementation. Proceedings **2504**
Association for Computing Machinery S I G P L A N Symposium on Principles and Practice of Parallel Programming *see* A C M S I G P L A N Symposium on Principles and Practice of Parallel Programming **2504**
Association for Computing Machinery S I G S O F T International Symposium on the Foundations of Software *see* A C M S I G S O F T International Symposium on the Foundations of Software **2504**
Association for Computing Machinery SIGACT-SIGMOD-SIGART Symposium on Principles of Database Systems. Proceedings *see* A C M SIGACT-SIGMOD-SIGART Symposium on Principles of Database Systems. Proceedings **2528**
Association for Computing Machinery SIGCOMM Internet Measurment Conference. Proceedings *see* A C M SIGCOMM Internet Measurment Conference. Proceedings **2552**
Association for Computing Machinery SIGGRAPH Symposium on Interactive 3D Graphics and Games. Proceedings *see* A C M SIGGRAPH Symposium on Interactive 3D Graphics and Games. Proceedings **2483**
Association for Computing Machinery. Special Interest Group for Management Information Systems. Conference Proceedings (USA) **2529**
Association for Computing Machinery Special Interest Group GAda Ada Letters *see* A C M S I GAda Ada Letters **2504**
Association for Computing Machinery Special Interest Group in Computer Graphics / Eurographics Symposium on Computer Animation. Proceedings *see* A C M Special Interest Group in Computer Graphics / Eurographics Symposium on Computer Animation. Proceedings **2483**
Association for Computing Machinery Special Interest Group in Computer Graphics Symposium on Interactive 3D Graphics and Games. Proceedings *see* A C M SIGGRAPH Symposium on Interactive 3D Graphics and Games. Proceedings **2483**

Association for Computing Machinery - Special Interest Group on Management Information Systems - Com Conference. Proceedings *see* A C M - S I G M I S - C P R Conference. Proceedings **1661**

Association for Computing Machinery. Special Interest Group on Management of Data. International Conference Proceedings (USA ISSN 0730-8078) **2529**

Association for Computing Machinery / Special Interest Group on Programming Languages / S I G P L A N Notices *see* A C M / S I G P L A N Notices **2504**

Association for Computing Machinery/Special Interest Group on Programming Languages / S I G P L A N Workshop on Partial Evaluation and Semantics-Based Program Manipulation. Proceedings *see* A C M / S I G P L A N Workshop on Partial Evaluation and Semantics-Based Program Manipulation. Proceedings **2504**

Association for Computing Machinery Symposium on Operating Systems Principles. Proceedings. *see* A C M Symposium on Operating Systems Principles. Proceedings. **2587**

Association for Computing Machinery Symposium on Principles of Programming Languages. Annual Conference Record *see* A C M Symposium on Principles of Programming Languages. Annual Conference Record **2457**

Association for Computing Machinery Transactions on Accessible Computing *see* A C M Transactions on Accessible Computing **2405**

Association for Computing Machinery Transactions on Architecture and Code Optimization *see* A C M Transactions on Architecture and Code Optimization **2466**

Association for Computing Machinery Transactions on Computer - Human Interaction *see* A C M Transactions on Computer - Human Interaction **2470**

Association for Computing Machinery Transactions on Computer Systems *see* A C M Transactions on Computer Systems **2519**

Association for Computing Machinery Transactions on Database Systems *see* A C M Transactions on Database Systems **2529**

Association for Computing Machinery Transactions on Graphics *see* A C M Transactions on Graphics **2483**

Association for Computing Machinery Transactions on Information Systems *see* A C M Transactions on Information Systems **1413**

Association for Computing Machinery Transactions on Knowledge Discovery from Data *see* A C M Transactions on Knowledge Discovery from Data **2405**

Association for Computing Machinery Transactions on Mathematical Software *see* A C M Transactions on Mathematical Software **2587**

Association for Computing Machinery Transactions on Modeling and Computer Simulation *see* A C M Transactions on Modeling and Computer Simulation **2405**

Association for Computing Machinery Transactions on Multimedia Computing Communications and Applications *see* A C M Transactions on Multimedia Computing Communications and Applications **2532**

Association for Computing Machinery Transactions on Programming Languages and Systems *see* A C M Transactions on Programming Languages and Systems **2504**

Association for Computing Machinery Transactions on Sensor Networks *see* A C M Transactions on Sensor Networks **2495**

Association for Computing Machinery Transactions on Software Engineering and Methodology *see* A C M Transactions on Software Engineering and Methodology **2587**

Association for Computing Machinery Transactions on Speech and Language Processing *see* A C M Transactions on Speech and Language Processing **2505**

Association for Computing Machinery Transactions on Storage *see* A C M Transactions on Storage **2519**

Association for Computing Machinery Transactions on the Web *see* A C M Transactions on the Web **2552**

Association for Computing Machinery Washington Update *see* A C M Washington Update **2405**

Association for Computing Machinery Workshop on Geographic Information Retrieval. Proceedings *see* A C M Workshop on Geographic Information Retrieval. Proceedings **2405**

Association for Computing Machinery Workshop on Next-Generation Residential Broadband Challenges. Proceedings *see* A C M Workshop on Next-Generation Residential Broadband Challenges. Proceedings **2405**

Association for Computing Machinery Workshop on Security of Ad Hoc and Sensor Networks. Proceedings *see* A C M Workshop on Security of Ad Hoc and Sensor Networks. Proceedings **2405**

Association for Computuing Machinery Transactions on Asian Language Information Processing *see* A C M Transactions on Asian Language Information Processing **5202**

Association for Continuing Higher Education. Proceedings (USA) **2967**

• Association for Death Education & Counseling. Forum Newsletter (USA ISSN 1091-4846) **7337**

• Association for Diplomatic Studies and Training. Newsletter (USA ISSN 1944-8732) **7222**

Association for Education and Rehabilitation Report *see* A E R Report **4078**

Association for Education in Journalism and Mass Communication News *see* A E J M C News **4570**

Association for Environmental Archaeology. Symposia Series (GBR) **381**

Association for Facilities Engineering Newsline *see* A F E Newsline **3179**

Association for Family Therapy Occasional Papers *see* A F T Occasional Papers **6117**

Association for Financial Professionals Exchange *see* A F P Exchange **1305**

Association for Gender Equity Leadership in Education News *see* A G E L E News **3016**

Association for Geographic Information Source Book for Geographic Information Systems (CD-ROM) *see* A G I Source Book for Geographic Information Systems (CD-ROM) **3996**

Association for Geological Collaboration in Japan. Bulletin *see* Chidanken Senpo **2728**

Association for Gerontology in Higher Education. Brief Bibliography (USA ISSN 1045-0157) **4058**

Association for Gerontology in Higher Education Exchange *see* A G H E Exchange **4037**

Association for Gravestone Studies Quarterly *see* A G S Quarterly **462**

Association for Healthcare Accreditation Professionals Insider *see* A H A P Insider **4086**

Association for Healthcare Accreditation Professionals Staff Challenge *see* A H A P Staff Challenge **4086**

Association for Healthcare Philanthropy Journal *see* A H P Journal **8022**

• Association for Heritage Interpretation. Interpretation Journal (GBR) **8089**

• ➤ Association for History and Computing. Journal (USA ISSN 1937-5905) **4171**

Association for Humanistic Psychology Perspective *see* A H P Perspective **7330**

Association for Improvements in Maternity Services Journal *see* A I M S Journal **5985**

• Association for Information Systems. Communications (USA ISSN 1529-3181) **2542**

▼ • ➤ Association for Information Systems Transactions on Human-Computer Interaction (USA ISSN 1944-3900) **2446**

Association for Institutional Research Professional File *see* The A I R Professional File **2964**

Association for Integrative Studies Newsletter (USA ISSN 1081-647X) **2827**

Association for International Broadcasting Global Broadcasting Sourcebook *see* A I B Global Broadcasting Sourcebook **2311**

Association for Investment Management and Research. Membership Directory (USA ISSN 1056-6074) **1611**

Association for Investment Management and Research. Seminar Proceedings (USA) **1309**

Association for Iron and Steel Technology - Materials Science and Technology (USA) **3341**

Association for Iron & Steel Technology Tech (Year) Conference Proceedings *see* A I S Tech (Year) Conference Proceedings **6303**

Association for Jewish Studies Review *see* A J S Review **7717**

Association for Kansai Patent Information Center News *see* Kansai Tokkyu Joho Senta Shinkokai Nyusu **6753**

• Association for Korean Studies in Europe. Newsletter (GBR ISSN 0141-1101) **4180**

• ➤ The Association for Laboratory Automation. Journal (USA ISSN 1535-5535) **2584**

Association for Language Learning. Newsletter (GBR) **5097**

Association for Learning Technology Journal *see* A L T - J **2964**

Association for Library and Information Science Education. Membership Directory (USA ISSN 1557-0738) **4992**

Association for Library Collections and Technical Services Acquisition Guidelines Series *see* A L C T S Acquisition Guidelines Series **4985**

Association for Library Collections & Technical Services Collection and Development Guides *see* A L C T S Collection and Development Guides **4985**

Association for Library Collections and Technical Services Network News *see* A L C T S Network News **5060**

Association for Library Collections and Technical Services Newsletter Online *see* A L C T S Newsletter Online **4985**

Association for Library Collections & Technical Services Papers on Library Technical Services and Collections *see* A L C T S Papers on Library Technical Services and Collections **4985**

Association for Library Service to Children Connect (Online) *see* A L S Connect (Online) **4986**

Association for Machine Computing Special Interest Group Multimedia Records *see* A C M S I G M M Records **2405**

Association for Manitoba Archives. Communique Newsletter (CAN ISSN 1193-9958) **4992**

Association for Microwave Power in Europe for Research and Education Newsletter (Online) *see* A M P E R E Newsletter (Online) **7053**

• Association for Music and Imagery. Journal (USA ISSN 1098-8009) **6546**

Association for Nurse Prescribing Journal *see* A N P J **5949**

Association for Perioperative Practice Newsletter *see* A F P P Newsletter **5949**

Association for Play Therapy. Newsletter *see* Play Therapy **6174**

Association for Population - Family Planning Library & Information Center International Communicator *see* A P L I C Communicator **4986**

Association for Pre- & Perinatal Psychology and Health Newsletter *see* A P P P A H Newsletter **7330**

Association for Preservation Technology Communique *see* A P T Communique **2601**

• ➤ Association for Preservation Technology International. Bulletin (USA ISSN 0848-8525) **434**

Association for Prevention and Control of Rabies in India Newsletter *see* A P C R I Newsletter **5564**

Association for Professional Education for Ministry. Report of the Biennial Meeting (USA) **2967**

Association for Psychoanalytic Medicine. Bulletin (USA ISSN 0004-542X) **7337**

Association for Psychological Science Observer *see* A P S Observer **7330**

• Association for Quality and Participation. Annual Conference and Resource Mart Transactions (Online) (USA) **1726**

Association for Quality and Participation. Annual Conference and Resource Mart Transactions (Print) *see* Association for Quality and Participation. Annual Conference and Resource Mart Transactions (Online) **1726**

Association for Rapid Method and Automation in Microbiology. Journal *see* Rinsho Biseibutsu Jinsoku Shindan Kenkyukaishi **896**

Association for Recorded Sound Collections, Inc. Newsletter *see* A R S C Newsletter **8151**

Association for Recorded Sound Collections Journal *see* A R S C Journal **8151**

Association for Research in the Voluntary and Community Sector Bulletin (Online) *see* A R V A C Bulletin (Online) **8022**

Association for Research in Vision and Ophthalmology Annual Meeting Abstract Search and Program Planner *see* A R V O Annual Meeting Abstract Search and Program Planner **6037**

• ➤ Association for Research on Mothering. Journal (CAN ISSN 1488-0989) **8089**

Association for Research on Nonprofit Organizations and Voluntary Action Abstracts *see* A R N O V A Abstracts **8079**

Association for Research on Nonprofit Organizations and Voluntary Action News *see* A R N O V A News **8022**

Association for Rural Advancement News *see* A F R A News **7201**

Association for Rural Advancement Special Reports *see* A F R A Special Reports **7201**

Association for Scottish Literary Studies. Annual Volumes (GBR) **5257**

The Association for Scottish Literary Studies. Occasional Paper (GBR ISSN 0305-8611) **5257**

Association for Social Anthropology in Oceania. Monograph Series (USA ISSN 0066-9172) **329**

Association for Social Anthropology in Oceania. Newsletter (USA ISSN 1095-3000) **329**

Association for Social Work Education in Africa Journal for Social Work Education in Africa *see* A S W E A Journal for Social Work Education in Africa **8022**

† Association for Supervision and Curriculum Development. Annual Conference (USA ISSN 0272-5282) **8931**

• Association for Supervision and Curriculum Development. Executive Directors Annual Report (USA) **3051**

Association for Technology in Music Instruction International Newsletter *see* A T M I International Newsletter **6632**

Association for Technology in Music Instruction Technology Directory *see* A T M I Technology Directory **6632**

Association for the Advancement of Automotive Medicine. Annual Proceedings *see* Annals of Advances in Automotive Medicine **5575**

Association for the Advancement of Automotive Medicine. Conference Proceedings *see* Annals of Advances in Automotive Medicine **5575**

Association for the Advancement of Automotive Medicine. Proceedings *see* Annals of Advances in Automotive Medicine **5575**

Association for the Advancement of Computing in Education Journal *see* A A C E Journal **2947**

Association for the Advancement of Medical Instrumentation News *see* A A M I News **4486**

Association for the Behavioral Sciences and Medical Education Newsletter *see* A B S A M E Newsletter **5563**

Association for the Bibliography of History Bulletin *see* A B H Bulletin **4128**

Association for the Development of a Better Environment Gold Canyon Ledger *see* A.D.O.B.E. Gold Canyon Ledger **5064**

Association for the Development of Religious Information Services Newsletter *see* A D R I S Newsletter **7619**

Association for the Help of Retarded Children Chronicle *see* A H R C Chronicle **6117**

➤ Association for the Interdisciplinary Study of the Arts. Journal (USA ISSN 1083-6586) **476**

Association for the Port and Harbour Engineering Promotion. Proceedings of the Meeting *see* Kowan Gijutsu Shinkokai. Koenkai Koen Gaiyo **3277**

Association for the Social Scientific Study of Jewry. Newsletter (USA) **3520**

• Association for the Sociology of Religion. News and Announcements (USA) **8089**

• ➤ Association for the Study of Australian Literature. Journal (AUS ISSN 1447-8986) **5257**

Association for the Study of Ethical Behavior in Literature Journal *see* A S E B L Journal **5248**

Association for the Study of Flow Measurements of Japan. Journal *see* Nagare no Keisoku **6404**

Association for the Study of Higher Education Higher Education Report Series *see* A S H E Higher Education Report Series **2964**

Association for the Study of Higher Education / Lumina Fellows Series *see* A S H E / Lumina Fellows Series **2964**

Association for the Study of Higher Education Newsletter *see* A S H E Newsletter **2964**

Association for the Study of New Literatures in English Papers *see* A S N E L Papers **5248**

Association for the Study of Play Newsletter (USA) **7337**

Association for the Study of Primary Education Papers: Managing Primary Education Series *see* A S P E Papers: Managing Primary Education Series **2822**

Association for the Study of Reptilia and Amphibia Journal *see* A S R A Journal **929**

Association for the Study of Reptilia and Amphibia Monographs *see* A S R A Monographs **929**

Association for the Study of the World Refugee Problem Bulletin *see* A W R Bulletin **7219**

Association for the Teaching of English to Speakers of Other Languages Aotearoa New Zealand. Journal *see* T E S O L A N Z Journal **5185**

Association for the Teaching of the Social Sciences Newsletter *see* A T S S Newsletter **3050**

Association for University and College Counselling Journal *see* A U C C Journal **7330**

• Association for Vascular Access. Journal (USA ISSN 1552-8855) **5778**

• Association for Veterinary Informatics Newsletter (USA) **8793**

Association for Women in Mathematics. Newsletter (USA ISSN 1058-6466) **8852**

Association for Women in Science Magazine *see* A W I S Magazine **8850**

Association for Worksite Health Promotion Action *see* A W H P Action **6981**

• Association Francaise contre les Myopathies. Newsletter (FRA ISSN 1772-9874) **5580**

Association Francaise de la Gestion Financiere. Annuaire (FRA ISSN 1627-9433) **1611**

Association Francaise de Lutte Antirhumatismale. Journal *see* Bouge ton Rhumatisme **6222**

Association Francaise de Robotique Industrielle Liaison *see* A F R I Liaison **8927**

Association Francaise de Topographie. Annuaire *see* X Y Z **4034**

Association Francaise des Administrateurs de l'Education *see* A F A E **3016**

Association Francaise des Amis des Chemins de Fer. Revue (FRA ISSN 0760-548X) **8614**

▼ Association Francaise des Anthropologues. La Lettre (FRA ISSN 1957-0716) **329**

Association Francaise des Ingenieurs et Cadres du Caoutchouc et des Plastiques. Annuaire (FRA) **7824**

Association Francaise des Interpretes en Langue des Signes. Le Journal (FRA ISSN 1955-6276) **4072**

Association Francaise des Techniciens du Petrole. Annuaire (FRA ISSN 1144-486X) **6763**

Association Francaise pour l'Archeologie du Verre. Bulletin (FRA ISSN 1955-7701) **382**

Association Francaise pour l'Etude du Sol. Lettre (FRA ISSN 0295-1347) **219**

Association Francis Jammes. Bulletin (FRA ISSN 0766-2610) **5257**

Association Francophone pour le Savoir. Decouvrir (CAN ISSN 1498-5845) **7837**

Association Generale des Conservateurs de Musees et Collections Publiques de France. Annuaire (FRA) **6520**

Association Generale des Insuffisants Renaux *see* A G I R **6264**

Association Geologique Auboise. Bulletin Annuel (FRA ISSN 0249-0102) **2725**

Association George Onslow. Bulletin (FRA ISSN 1266-7870) **6546**

Association Guillaume Bude. Bulletin (FRA ISSN 0004-5527) **5097**

Association Historique Internationale de l'Ocean Indien. Bulletin de Liaison et d'Information (REU) **4131**

Association Hoteliere du Valais. Bulletin d'Information (CHE) **4382**

Association Huntington *see* A H F Huntington France **6117**

Association Huntington France Huntington France *see* A H F Huntington France **6117**

Association Impact (USA ISSN 1931-4388) **6692**

Association Internationale de Bibliophilie. Nouvelles (FRA ISSN 0220-388X) **7552**

Title

9988 ASSOCIATION INTERNATIONALE DE CYBERNETIQUE. CONGRES ULRICH'S PERIODICALS

Association Internationale de Cybernetique. Congres International de Cybernetique. Actes *see* International Congress for Cybernetics. Proceedings **2527**
Association Internationale de Geodesie. Commission des Marees Terrestres. Marees Terrestres Bulletin d'Information (BEL ISSN 0542-6766) **2778**
Association Internationale de Linguistique Appliquee Applied Linguistics Series *see* A I L A Applied Linguistics Series **5088**
Association Internationale de Linguistique Appliquee News *see* A I L A News **5088**
Association Internationale de Linguistique Appliquee Review *see* A I L A Review **5088**
Association Internationale de Navigation. Bulletin *see* On Course **8656**
Association Internationale de Signalisation Maritime. Bulletin/I A L A Bulletin (FRA ISSN 0373-9090) **8639**
Association Internationale des Journalistes Philateliques. Bulletin *see* International Association of Philatelic Journalists. Bulletin **6896**
Association Internationale des Numismates Professionnels. Publication (BEL) **6649**
➤ Association Internationale d'Etudes du Sud-Est Europeen. Bulletin (ROM ISSN 0004-5551) **4201**
Association Internationale d'Etudes Patristiques. Bulletin d'Information et de Liaison (BEL ISSN 0587-1999) **7623**
Association Internationale du Film d'Animation Magazine *see* A S I F A Magazine **6488**
Association Internationale pour l'Histoire du Verre. Annales des Congres (NLD ISSN 0589-2546) **2037**
Association Jean-Jacques Rousseau. Bulletin (CHE ISSN 1423-1018) **5258**
Association Lacanienne Internationale. Cahiers (FRA ISSN 1775-6871) **7337**
Association Lavalloise de Parents pour le Bien-Etre Mental. Bulletin *see* Oxygene Familles et Sante Mentale **6172**
† Association Le Faubourg. Banque de Projets (FRA ISSN 1775-2892) **8931**
• Association Leadership (USA ISSN 1086-8291) **6277**
Association Les Amis de Milosz. Cahiers (FRA ISSN 0003-181X) **5258**
Association Les Amis de Saint Jacques. Bulletin (FRA ISSN 1774-5268) **7623**
Association Linguistique des Provinces Atlantiques. Congres Annuel. Actes *see* Atlantic Provinces Linguistic Association. Annual Meeting. Papers **5097**
Association Management *see* Association Now **1726**
Association Manager *see* Membership Today **1779**
Association Matters *see* Think **3005**
Association Medicale Canadienne. Journal *see* C M A J **5590**
• Association Meetings (USA ISSN 1042-3141) **6278**
Association Meetings International (GBR ISSN 0958-0271) **6278**
Association National de Defense contre l'Arthrite Rhumatoide Infos *see* A N D A R Infos **6221**
Association Nationale de la Recherche Technique. Lettre Europeenne (FRA ISSN 1770-9547) **8416**
Association Nationale de Medecine du Travail et d'Ergonomie du Personnel des Hopitaux. Bulletin d'Information (FRA ISSN 1952-9929) **5580**
† Association Nationale des Communautes Educatives. Bulletin Mensuel d'Informations (FRA ISSN 0245-5668) **8931**
Association Nationale d'Etude et de Lutte contre les Fleaux Atmospheriques. Rapport de Campagne (FRA ISSN 0242-4002) **6346**
Association Nationale Hector Berlioz. Bulletin de Liaison (FRA ISSN 0243-3559) **6546**
Association Nationale pour la Protection contre l'Incendie et l'Intrusion Magazine (Dutch Edition) *see* A N P I Magazine (Dutch Edition) **3575**
Association Nationale pour la Protection contre l'Incendie et l'Intrusion Magazine (French Edition) *see* A N P I Magazine (French Edition) **3575**
Association News *see* Association Impact **6692**
Association News! (Fort Collins) (USA) **7508**
Association News (Los Angeles) (USA) **1726**
• Association Now (USA ISSN 1557-7562) **1726**
Association of Academic Health Centers. Directory (USA ISSN 1093-8222) **5580**
Association of Administrative Law Judges Newsletter (USA) **4622**
Association of Advanced Rabbinical and Talmudic Schools. Accreditation Commission. Handbook (USA) **2967**
Association of African Universities. Annual Report (GHA) **2967**
Association of African Universities. Bibliography on Higher Education in Africa (GHA) **2930**
Association of African Universities. C O R E V I P Proceedings (Conference of Rectors, Vice-Chancellors and Presidents) (GHA) **2967**
Association of African Universities. Guide to Higher Education in Africa (GHA) **2967**
Association of African Universities Newsletter *see* A A U Newsletter **2963**
Association of African Universities. Report of the General Conference (GHA) **2967**
Association of American Feed Control Officials. Official Publication (USA) **270**
• ➤ Association of American Geographers. Annals (USA ISSN 0004-5608) **3999**
Association of American Geographers. Annual Meeting Abstracts (USA ISSN 0197-1700) **3999**
Association of American Geographers Newsletter *see* A A G Newsletter **3996**
Association of American Indian Physicians Newsletter (USA) **5580**
Association of American Law Schools Directory of Law Teachers *see* A A L S Directory of Law Teachers **4606**
Association of American Law Schools. Newsletter (USA ISSN 0519-1025) **4622**
Association of American Law Schools. Proceedings (USA ISSN 0066-9407) **4622**
Association of American Medical Colleges Curriculum Directory (Online Edition) *see* A A M C Curriculum Directory (Online Edition) **3049**
Association of American Medical Colleges Medical Reporter *see* A A M C Medical Reporter **5563**
Association of American Medical Colleges. Proceedings of the Annual Conference. Research in Medical Education (USA ISSN 0892-2543) **5580**
Association of American Military Uniforms Collectors Footlocker *see* A A M U C Footlocker **4326**
Association of American Pesticide Control Officials. Official Publication (USA ISSN 0066-9431) **219**
Association of American Physicians & Surgeons, Inc. News *see* A A P S News **5563**
Association of American Plant Food Control Officials. Official Publication (USA ISSN 0094-8764) **219**
Association of American Publishers. Annual Report (USA ISSN 0276-5349) **7552**
Association of American Publishers. Monthly Report (USA ISSN 0748-8173) **7552**
Association of American University Presses Book and Jacket Show *see* A A U P Book and Jacket Show **7550**
Association of American University Presses Directory (USA ISSN 0739-3024) **7552**
Association of Analytical Communities International. Journal *see* A O A C International. Journal **2096**
➤ Association of Ancient Historians. Publications (USA ISSN 1059-7840) **4201**
➤ Association of Arab Universities for Basic And Applied Sciences. Journal (BHR ISSN 1815-3852) **7837**
• Association of Art Historians. Bulletin (GBR ISSN 0307-9163) **476**
Association of Asia Pacific Physical Societies Bulletin *see* A A P P S Bulletin **7002**
Association of Asphalt Paving Technologists. Journal (USA) **3259**
➤ Association of Australasian Palaeontologists. Memoirs (AUS ISSN 0810-8889) **6723**
• Association of Avian Veterinarians. Proceedings (USA) **8793**
Association of B.C. Drama Educators Focus *see* A B C D E Focus **3049**
Association of Banks in Lebanon Monthly Bulletin *see* A B L Monthly Bulletin **1305**
Association of Behavioral Health Management Newsletter (USA) **7508**
Association of Black Nursing Faculty in Higher Education, Inc. Journal *see* A B N F Journal **5949**
Association of Bridal Consultants Dialogue *see* A B C Dialogue **1956**
Association of British Columbia Forest Professionals. Annual Report (CAN ISSN 1716-7205) **3684**
Association of British Columbia Foresters. Forum *see* Forum (Vancouver) **3691**
Association of British Columbia Professional Foresters. Annual Report *see* Association of British Columbia Forest Professionals. Annual Report **3684**
Association of British Theological and Philosophical Libraries. Bulletin (GBR ISSN 0305-781X) **4992**
Association of Burial Authorities Information *see* A B A Information **3719**
Association of California Water Agencies News *see* A C W A News **8817**
Association of Canadian Archivists Bulletin *see* A C A Bulletin **4985**
Association of Canadian Archivists. Membership Directory (CAN ISSN 0841-288X) **4992**
Association of Canadian Community Colleges International *see* A C C C International **1589**
Association of Canadian Ergonomists. Communique (CAN ISSN 1491-7971) **6673**
Association of Canadian Faculties of Dentistry Forum *see* A C F D Forum **5832**
Association of Canadian Map Libraries and Archives. Bulletin (CAN ISSN 0840-9331) **3999**
Association of Canadian Medical Colleges Forum *see* A C M C Forum **5563**
Association of Caravan & Camping Exempted Organisations Matters *see* A C C E O Matters **8301**
Association of Caribbean Studies. Abstracts (USA) **4169**
Association of Caribbean University Research and Institutional Libraries. Carta Informativa de A C U R I L/A C U R I L Newsletter (PRI) **4992**
Association of Chartered Certified Accountants Research Report *see* A C C A Research Report **1275**
Association of Chartered Certified Accountants Research T & R. Occasional Research Paper *see* A C C A Research T & R. Occasional Research Paper **1275**
Association of Chartered Physiotherapists in Women's Health. Journal (GBR ISSN 1367-7845) **6106**
Association of Childrens Welfare Agencies News *see* A C W A News **8022**
Association of Chinese Scientists and Engineers Newsletter *see* A C S E Newsletter **3179**
Association of Christians in Higher Education. Forum (GBR ISSN 0952-6889) **2967**
Association of Clinical Biochemists News *see* A C B News **721**
Association of Clinical Biochemists of India. News Bulletin (IND) **723**
Association of College and Research Libraries, College Libraries Section Newsletter *see* C L S Newsletter **4999**
• Association of College and Research Libraries. Law and Political Science Section News (USA ISSN 0885-7342) **4622**
Association of College and Research Libraries Publications in Librarianship *see* A C R L Publications in Librarianship **4985**
Association of College and Research Libraries, Rare Books and Manuscripts Section Newsletter *see* R B M S Newsletter **5041**
Association of College and Research Libraries. Slavic and Eastern European Section Newsletter (USA ISSN 0897-6465) **4992**
Association of College and Research Libraries. Western European Specialists Section Newsletter *see* Association of College and Research Libraries. Western European Studies Section Newsletter **4992**
• Association of College and Research Libraries. Western European Studies Section Newsletter (USA) **4992**
Association of College and University Telecommunications Administrators Journal of Telecommunications in Higher Education *see* A C U T A Journal of Telecommunications in Higher Education **2964**
Association of College and University Telecommunications Administrators News *see* A C U T A News **2310**
Association of College Honor Societies. Handbook (USA) **2273**
Association of College Unions - International. Bulletin (USA ISSN 0004-5659) **2967**
• Association of College Unions - International. Directory & Catalog (USA) **2967**
Association of College Unions - International. Union Wire (USA ISSN 0004-5667) **2967**
Association of Collegiate Schools of Architecture, Inc. Faculty Directory *see* A C S A Faculty Directory **426**
Association of Collegiate Schools of Architecture. Proceedings of the Annual Meeting (USA ISSN 0194-410X) **434**
• Association of Commonwealth Archivists and Records Managers Newsletter (GBR ISSN 0258-2163) **4992**
Association of Commonwealth Universities. Annual Report of the Council Together with the Accounts of the Association (GBR ISSN 0307-2274) **2967**
Association of Commonwealth Universities Bulletin *see* A C U Bulletin **2930**
Association of Commonwealth Universities. Who's Who (Year) (GBR) **2968**
Association of Computing Machinery Journal of Computer Documentation *see* A C M Journal of Computer Documentation **2541**
Association of Concerned Africa Scholars Bulletin *see* A C A S Bulletin **4172**
Association of Consulting Engineers. International Work Entrusted to Members (Year) (GBR) **3259**
Association of Corporate Counsel Docket *see* A C C Docket **4854**
Association of Departments of English Bulletin *see* A D E Bulletin **2964**
Association of Departments of Foreign Languages Bulletin *see* A D F L Bulletin **2964**
Association of District Councils Review *see* A D C Review **7486**
Association of Drilled Shaft Contractors Membership Directory *see* A D S C Membership Directory **1970**
Association of Drilled Shaft Contractors Products and Services Guide *see* A D S C Products and Services Guide **974**
Association of Drilled Shaft Contractors Technical Library Catalog *see* A D S C Technical Library Catalog **974**
Association of Economic Geographers. Annals (JPN ISSN 0004-5683) **1063**
Association of Educational Psychologists Appointments Broadsheet *see* A E P Appointments Broadsheet **6691**
Association of Energy Engineers Energy Insight *see* A E E Energy Insight **3123**
Association of Energy Service Companies Directory *see* A E S C Directory **1970**
Association of Engineering Geologists. Special Publications (USA) **2725**
Association of Engineering Geologists - Texas News *see* A E G News **2722**
Association of Engineers, India. Journal (IND ISSN 0044-9598) **3182**
Association of Engineers, Kerala P.W.D. News Letter (IND) **3182**
Association of European Migration Institutions Journal *see* A E M I Journal **7276**
Association of Exploration Geophysicists. Journal (IND ISSN 0257-1412) **2778**
Association of Faculties of Agriculture in Africa Newsletter *see* A F A A Newsletter **77**
Association of Faculties of Pharmacy of Canada. Proceedings (CAN ISSN 0066-9555) **6823**
Association of Firearm and Tool Mark Examiners Journal *see* A F T E Journal **4883**
• ➤ Association of Food and Drug Officials. Journal (Online Edition) (USA) **3627**
Association of Food and Drug Officials. Journal (Print Edition) *see* Association of Food and Drug Officials. Journal (Online Edition) **3627**
Association of Football Statisticians. Annual (GBR ISSN 0263-0354) **8221**
Association of Gay and Lesbian Psychiatrists. Newsletter (USA) **4371**
Association of Genetic Technologists Cytogenetics Laboratory Technical Manual *see* The A G T Cytogenetics Laboratory Technical Manual **861**
Association of Genetic Technologists International Membership Directory *see* The A G T International Membership Directory **5901**
Association of Genetic Technologists. Journal (USA ISSN 1523-7834) **863**
Association of Gospel Rescue Missions Membership Directory & Resource Guide (USA) **8026**
Association of Hispanic Arts Hispanic Arts News *see* A H A! Hispanic Arts News **462**
Association of Home Appliance Manufacturers Major Appliance Factory Shipment Report *see* A H A M Major Appliance Factory Shipment Report **4553**
Association of Home Appliance Manufacturers Major Appliance Industry Fact Book (Year) *see* A H A M Major Appliance Industry Fact Book (Year) **4553**
• Association of Home Appliance Manufacturers. Trends and Forecasts (USA) **1880**
Association of Illustrators. Journal (GBR ISSN 1474-1679) **476**
Association of Independent Commercial Producers Membership Directory *see* A I C P Membership Directory **1970**
• Association of Independent Museums Bulletin (GBR ISSN 0142-887X) **6520**
Association of Independent Schools of Victoria. Annual Report *see* Association of Independent Schools of Victoria. Annual Review **2827**
• Association of Independent Schools of Victoria. Annual Review (AUS) **2827**
Association of Indian Muslims *see* A I M **7708**
Association of Industry Manufacturers Representatives News *see* A I M - R News **1878**
Association of Information and Dissemination Centers Newsletter *see* A S I D I C Newsletter **4986**
• Association of Information Systems. Journal (USA ISSN 1536-9323) **2542**
Association of Insolvency & Restructuring Advisors Journal *see* A I R A Journal **1055**
Association of Insolvency & Restructuring Advisors Newsletter (USA) **1280**
Association of Internal Management Consultants (A I M C) Newsletter *see* A I M C Newsletter **1722**
Association of International Meeting Planners. Newsletter (USA) **6278**
Association of Iron and Steel Engineers Annual Convention Proceedings *see* A I S E Annual Convention Proceedings **6303**
Association of Japanese Cavers. Journal *see* Dojin **6724**
Association of Japanese Geographers. Special Publication (JPN ISSN 0066-958X) **3999**
Association of Jesuit Colleges and Universities and Jesuit Secondary Education Association Directory (USA ISSN 1053-8941) **2968**
Association of Jewish Libraries Newsletter *see* A J L Newsletter **4985**
• Association of Jewish Libraries. Proceedings of the Annual Convention (Online Edition) (USA) **4992**
Association of Jewish Libraries. Proceedings of the Annual Convention (Print Edition) *see* Association of Jewish Libraries. Proceedings of the Annual Convention (Online Edition) **4992**
Association of Jewish Sponsored Camps. Camp Directory (USA) **8304**
Association of Law Libraries of Upstate New York. Newsletter (USA ISSN 0197-4815) **4622**
Association of Legal Administrators News (Lincolnshire) *see* A L A News (Lincolnshire) **4607**
Association of Legal Writing Directors. Journal (USA ISSN 1550-0950) **4622**
Association of Libertarian Feminists News. Newsletter *see* A L F News. Newsletter **7101**
Association of Life Insurance Medicine of Japan. Journal *see* Nihon Hoken Igakkai Shi **5686**
Association of Literary Scholars and Critics Newsletter *see* A L S C Newsletter **5247**
• Association of Logic Programming. Newsletter (USA) **2505**
Association of London Government London Government Directory (Year) *see* A L G London Government Directory (Year) **7487**

DIRECTORY 2010 ASSOCIATIONS SECTORIELLES PARITAIRES, LESIONS PROFESSIONNELLES 9989

Association of London Government Transport and Environment Committee Annual Report (Year) see A L G Transport and Environment Committee Annual Report (Year) **7487**

➤ Association of Lunar and Planetary Observers. Journal (USA ISSN 0039-2502) **569**

Association of M B As Address Book (GBR) **1726**

Association of Major City Building Officials Directory of Building Codes and Regulations see A M C B O Directory of Building Codes and Regulations **7487**

Association of Major City Building Officials Newsletter see A M C B O Newsletter **7487**

Association of Manitoba Museums. Newsletter (CAN ISSN 0849-5858) **6520**

The Association of Marian Helpers Bulletin see Marian Helper **7806**

Association of Marine Laboratories of the Caribbean. Newsletter (PRI) **2800**

Association of Marine Laboratories of the Caribbean. Proceedings (PRI) **2800**

Association of Mechanical Technology. News see Kikai Gijutsu Kyokai Nyusu **3387**

Association of Medical Illustrators News see A M I News **5564**

Association of Midwest Museums News Brief see A M M News Brief **6518**

Association of Moving Image Archivists Newsletter see A M I A Newsletter **4986**

Association of Muslim Social Scientists Bulletin see The A M S S Bulletin **7708**

➤ Association of Neurophysiological Scientists. Journal (GBR ISSN 1757-8973) **920**

Association of New Jersey Environmental Commissions Report see A N J E C Report **2601**

Association of Newfoundland Labrador Archives Bulletin see A N L A Bulletin **4986**

• ➤ Association of Nurses in AIDS Care. Journal (USA ISSN 1055-3290) **5810**

Association of Nurses in Substance Abuse. Journal Bulletin (GBR ISSN 1467-5625) **5952**

Association of Obedience Clubs and Judges. Newsletter (USA) **6804**

Association of Official Seed Analysts - Society of Commercial Seed Technologists Seed Technologist News see A O S A - S C S T Seed Technologist News **771**

Association of Official Seed Certifying Agencies. Report of Acres Applied for Certification by Seed Certifying Agencies (USA) **219**

Association of Ontario Land Surveyors. Annual Report (CAN ISSN 0700-5989) **3259**

Association of Open University Graduates. Journal (GBR ISSN 0964-4229) **2968**

Association of Operating Room Nurses Journal see A O R N Journal **5949**

Association of Operative Millers. Bulletin (USA) **270**

Association of Orthodox Jewish Teachers Newsletter see A O J T Newsletter **2822**

• Association of Pacific Coast Geographers. Yearbook (USA ISSN 0066-9628) **4035**

➤ Association of Paediatric Chartered Physiotherapists. Journal (GBR ISSN 1368-7360) **6106**

Association of Part-Time Tutors Bulletin see The A P T T Bulletin **2822**

Association of Pharmaceutical Teachers of India Bulletin see A P T I Bulletin **6818**

Association of Photographers Awards see A O P Awards **6963**

• ➤ Association of Physicians of India. Journal (IND ISSN 0004-5772) **5580**

Association of Political and Social Sciences. Journal see Kokka Gakkai Zasshi **7149**

Association of Professional Chaplains News see A P C e-News **7619**

Association of Professional Engineers of Trinidad and Tobago. Journal (TTO ISSN 1010-7924) **3182**

Association of Professional Engineers, Scientists and Managers. Collieries' Staff Division. Employment & Remuneration Survey Report (AUS ISSN 1832-1798) **1665**

Association of Professional Engineers, Scientists and Managers - Federation of Australian Scientific / F A S T S Professional Scientist Remuneration Survey Report see A P E S M A / F A S T S Professional Scientist Remuneration Survey Report **6691**

Association of Professional Engineers, Scientists and Managers National e-News see A P E S M A National e-News **1055**

Association of Professional, Executive, Clerical and Computer Staff see A P E X **4589**

Association of Professional Foresters News see A P F News **3682**

Association of Professional Genealogists Quarterly (USA ISSN 1056-6732) **3759**

Association of Professional Librarians Newsletter see A P L Newsletter **4986**

Association of Public Data Users Newsletter see A P D U Newsletter **3288**

Association of Railroad Editors. Proof (USA) **8614**

Association of Registered Interior Designers of Ontario Newsletter see A R I D O Newsletter **4531**

Association of Registered Nurses of Newfoundland and Labrador Access see A R N N L Access **5950**

Association of Regulatory & Clinical Scientists Australia. Newsletter see A R C S Australia. Newsletter **7829**

Association of Rehabilitation Nurses Network see A R N Network **5950**

Association of Research Libraries see A R L **4986**

Association of Research Libraries Academic Law Library Statistics see A R L Academic Law Library Statistics **5056**

Association of Research Libraries Annual Salary Survey see A R L Annual Salary Survey **6691**

Association of Research Libraries Preservation Statistics see A R L Preservation Statistics **5056**

Association of Research Libraries Proceedings of the Meetings see A R L Proceedings of the Meetings **4986**

Association of Research Libraries Statistics see A R L Statistics **5056**

Association of Retail Travel Agents Agent see A R T A Agent **8680**

➤ Association of Russian - American Scholars in the U S A. Transactions/Zapiski (USA ISSN 0066-9717) **3520**

Association of School Business Officials Accents (Email Edition) see A S B O Accents (Email Edition) **3016**

Association of Science-Technology Centers Dimensions see A S T C Dimensions **7829**

Association of Senior Anthropologists. Occasional Papers (USA) **329**

Association of Simula Users Newsletter see A S U Newsletter **2505**

Association of Small Presses in Florida Newsletter see A S P I F Newsletter **7550**

Association of Social Anthropologists Research Methods in Social Anthropology see A S A Research Methods in Social Anthropology **322**

Association of South East Asian Nations Economic Info View see A S E A N Economic Info View **1589**

Association of South East Asian Nations Journal on Hospitality and Tourism see A S E A N Journal on Hospitality and Tourism **8680**

Association of Southeast Asian Institutions of Higher Learning. Handbook: Southeast Asian Institutions of Higher Learning (THA ISSN 0066-9687) **2968**

Association of Southeast Asian Institutions of Higher Learning. Newsletter (THA ISSN 0572-4325) **2968**

Association of Southeast Asian Institutions of Higher Learning Seminar Reports see A S A I H L Seminar Reports **2964**

Association of Southeast Asian Nations Briefing see A S E A N Briefing **1435**

Association of Southeast Asian Nations Insurance Directory see A S E A N Insurance Directory **1970**

Association of Southeast Asian Studies in the United Kingdom News see A S E A S U K. News **3515**

Association of Southern African Indexers and Bibliographers. Newsletter (ZAF) **4992**

Association of Southern African Indexers and Bibliographers. Publications (ZAF) **4992**

Association of Special Libraries of the Philippines Bulletin see A S L P Bulletin **4986**

Association of State Dam Safety Officials Newsletter see A S D S O Newsletter **3258**

Association of State Drinking Water Administrators Update see A S D W A Update **8817**

Association of Steel Distributors. News and Views (USA) **6305**

Association of Studies on Himalayas Publication Series see A S H Publication Series **541**

• Association of Surgeons of East Africa. Newsletter (ZMB) **6237**

Association of Synthetic Crystal Science and Technology. Abstracts of the Special Meeting see Jinko Kessho Kogakkai Tokubetsu Koenkai Koen Yoshishu **2094**

Association of Talent Agents. Newsletter (USA) **8466**

Association of Teacher Educators Newsletter (USA ISSN 0001-2718) **2828**

Association of Teachers and Lecturers Report see A T L Report **2823**

Association of Teachers of Japanese. Journal see Japanese Language and Literature **5131**

• Association of Teachers of Japanese. Newsletter (USA ISSN 0894-6728) **5097**

Association of Teachers of Russian. Newsletter (GBR ISSN 0306-7432) **5097**

Association of Teachers of Technical Writing Bulletin see A T T W Bulletin **3050**

Association of the Bar of the City of New York. Legislative Bulletin (USA) **4622**

• Association of the Bar of the City of New York. Record (USA ISSN 0004-5837) **4622**

The Association of the British Pharmaceutical Industry. Annual Review (GBR ISSN 1460-034X) **6823**

Association of the British Pharmaceutical Industry News see A B P I News **6817**

Association of the Electricity Supply Industry of East Asia and the Western Pacific Goldbook (Year) see A E S I E A P Goldbook (Year) **7051**

• Association of Theological Schools in the United States and Canada. Bulletin (USA ISSN 0362-1472) **7623**

Association of Translators and Interpreters of Ontario. Directory see Association des Traducteurs et Interpretes de l'Ontario. Repertoire **5097**

Association of Translators and Interpreters of Ontario. InformATIO see Association des Traducteurs et Interpretes de l'Ontario. InformATIO **5097**

Association of Universities and Colleges in Canada. Research File (CAN ISSN 1201-639X) **2968**

Association of University Programs in Health Administration Exchange see A U P H A Exchange **4087**

Association of University Summer Sessions. Summary of Reports (USA ISSN 0066-975X) **2968**

Association of University Teachers Look see A U T Look **2964**

Association of Urban Authorities. Annual Bulletin (MUS ISSN 0304-6451) **7488**

Association of Visual Language Interpreters of Canada News (Online) see The A V L I C News (Online) **5088**

Association of Water Transportation Accounting Officers Annual Report see A W T A O Annual Report **1275**

Association of Water Transportation Accounting Officers Bulletin see A W T A O Bulletin **1275**

Association of Wild Plant in Kurashiki. Journal see Kibi no Kusabana **3740**

Association of Wine Suppliers. Bankruptcy Update (USA) **598**

Association of Women's Clubs. News (ZWE) **8852**

Association Paritaire pour la Sante et la Securite du Travail du Secteur Administration Provinciale see Associations Sectorielles Paritaires, Lesions Professionnelles, Statistiques. Tome 5. Association Paritaire pour la Sante et la Securite du Travail du Secteur Administration Provinciale **6690**

Association Paritaire pour la Sante et la Securite du Travail du Secteur de la Construction see Associations Sectorielles Paritaires, Lesions Professionnelles, Statistiques. Tome 9. Association Paritaire pour la Sante et la Securite du Travail du Secteur de la Construction **6690**

Association Paritaire pour la Sante et la Securite du Travail du Secteur de la Fabrication de Produits en Metal et de Produits Electriques see Associations Sectorielles Paritaires, Lesions Professionnelles, Statistiques. Tome 7. Association Paritaire pour la Sante et la Securite du Travail du Secteur de la Fabrication de Produits en Metal et de Produits Electriques **6690**

Association Paritaire pour la Sante et la Securite du Travail du Secteur de l'Habillement see Associations Sectorielles Paritaires, Lesions Professionnelles, Statistiques. Tome 13. Association Paritaire pour la Sante et la Securite du Travail du Secteur de l'Habillement **6690**

Association Paritaire pour la Sante et la Securite du Travail du Secteur de l'Imprimerie et Activites Connexes see Associations Sectorielles Paritaires, Lesions Professionnelles, Statistiques. Tome 4. Association Paritaire pour la Sante et la Securite du Travail du Secteur de l'Imprimerie et Activites Connexes **6690**

Association Paritaire pour la Sante et la Securite du Travail du Secteur des Affaires Municipales see Associations Sectorielles Paritaires, Lesions Professionnelles, Statistiques. Tome 12. Association Paritaire pour la Sante et la Securite du Travail du Secteur des Affaires Municipales **6690**

Association Paritaire pour la Sante et la Securite du Travail du Secteur des Services Automobiles see Associations Sectorielles Paritaires, Lesions Professionnelles, Statistiques. Tome 8. Association Paritaire pour la Sante et la Securite du Travail du Secteur des Services Automobiles **6690**

Association Paritaire pour la Sante et la Securite du Travail du Secteur Fabrication d'Equipement de Transport et de Machines see Associations Sectorielles Paritaires, Lesions Professionnelles, Statistiques. Tome 6. Association Paritaire pour la Sante et la Securite du Travail du Secteur Fabrication d'Equipement de Transport et de Machines **6690**

Association Paritaire pour la Sante et la Securite du Travail du Secteur Transport et Entreposage see Associations Sectorielles Paritaires, Lesions Professionnelles, Statistiques. Tome 3. Association Paritaire pour la Sante et la Securite du Travail du Secteur Transport et Entreposage **6690**

➤ Association pour la Promotion de la Protection des Invertebres. Cahiers (FRA ISSN 1262-3350) **840**

Association pour la Promotion de la Recherche Archeologique en Alsace. Cahiers (FRA ISSN 0987-2205) **382**

Association pour la Restauration du Fort d'Uxegney et de la Place d'Epinal see L' Arfupeen **6410**

Association pour l'Autobiographie et le Patrimoine Autobiographique. Cahiers (FRA ISSN 1779-3556) **5258**

Association pour l'Avancement des Sciences et des Techniques de la Documentation Nouvelles see ASTED. Nouvelles **4992**

Association pour l'Avancement des Sciences et des Techniques de la Documentation. Rapport Annuel (CAN ISSN 0316-0955) **4992**

Association pour le Developpement de la Recherche en Economie et en Statistique Annales d'Economie et de Statistique see A D R E S. Annales d'Economie et de Statistique **1055**

▼ • Association pour le Developpement de la Securite des Systemes d'Information. Le Journal (FRA ISSN 1954-3697) **2511**

Association pour le Developpement de l'Education en Afrique Lettre see A D E A. Lettre **8927**

Association pour le Developpement International de l'Observatoire de Nice. Bulletin (FRA ISSN 0249-7522) **569**

† Association pour l'Etude des Problemes d'Outre Mer. Documentation-Developpement (FRA ISSN 0153-3657) **8931**

Association pour l'Information et la Recherche sur les Orthographes et les Systemes d'Ecriture Liaisons see A I R O E. Liaisons **5088**

Association Provinciale des Enseignantes et Enseignants des Ecoles Fransaskoises Newsletter see A P E F Newsletter **5088**

Association Publishing (USA) **7552**

Association Quebecoise d'Etablissements de Sante et de Services Sociaux. Repertoire des Etablissements Membres (CAN ISSN 1910-6661) **8026**

Association Quebecoise du Cheval Canadien. Journal (CAN) **8287**

Association Roussillonnaise d'Entomologie. Revue (FRA ISSN 1288-5509) **840**

Association Scientifique Europeenne pour l'Eau et la Sante. Cahiers (FRA ISSN 1027-4820) **2792**

Association Senegalaise pour l'Etude du Quaternaire Africain. Bulletin de Liaison (SEN) **7108**

Association Source (USA ISSN 1066-8691) **1063**

Association Suisse de l'Arbitrage Bulletin see A S A Bulletin **4915**

Association Suisse des Actuaires. Bulletin see Schweizerische Aktuarvereinigung. Mitteilungen **4522**

† Association Technique de l'Importation Charbonniere. Annual Report (FRA) **8931**

† Association Technique de l'Importation Charbonniere. Monthly Statistics (FRA) **8931**

Association Technique de l'Industrie Papetiere see A T I P **6732**

Association Technique des Pates et Papiers du Canada. Congres Annuel. Pretires A see Pulp and Paper Technical Association of Canada. Annual Meeting. Preprints A **6738**

Association Technique des Pates et Papiers du Canada. Congres Annuel. Pretires B see Pulp and Paper Technical Association of Canada. Annual Meeting. Preprints B **6738**

Association Technique des Pates et Papiers du Canada. Listes see Pulp & Paper Technical Association of Canada. Indices **6740**

Association Technique Maritime et Aeronautique Bulletin (FRA ISSN 0066-9814) **8639**

Association to Advance Collegiate Schools of Business eNewsline see A A C S B eNewsline **2963**

• Associations Canada (CAN ISSN 1186-9798) **1973**

Associations Forum News (AUS ISSN 1449-9614) **1726**

Associations Quebec (CAN ISSN 1188-4274) **3118**

Associations Sectorielles Paritaires, Lesions Professionnelles, Statistiques. Tome 1. Association Paritaire pour la Sante et la Securite du Travail du Secteur Affaires Sociales (CAN ISSN 1910-7366) **6689**

Associations Sectorielles Paritaires, Lesions Professionnelles, Statistiques. Tome 11. Association Paritaire pour la Sante et la Securite du Travail du Secteur Minier (CAN ISSN 1910-7315) **6689**

Associations Sectorielles Paritaires, Lesions Professionnelles, Statistiques. Tome 12. Association Paritaire pour la Sante et la Securite du Travail du Secteur des Affaires Municipales (CAN ISSN 1910-7323) **6690**

Associations Sectorielles Paritaires, Lesions Professionnelles, Statistiques. Tome 13. Association Paritaire pour la Sante et la Securite du Travail du Secteur de l'Habillement (CAN ISSN 1910-734X) **6690**

Associations Sectorielles Paritaires, Lesions Professionnelles, Statistiques. Tome 2. Preventex - Association Paritaire du Textile (CAN ISSN 1910-7374) **6690**

Associations Sectorielles Paritaires, Lesions Professionnelles, Statistiques. Tome 3. Association Paritaire pour la Sante et la Securite du Travail du Secteur Transport et Entreposage (CAN ISSN 1910-7382) **6690**

Associations Sectorielles Paritaires, Lesions Professionnelles, Statistiques. Tome 4. Association Paritaire pour la Sante et la Securite du Travail du Secteur de l'Imprimerie et Activites Connexes (CAN ISSN 1910-7390) **6690**

Associations Sectorielles Paritaires, Lesions Professionnelles, Statistiques. Tome 5. Association Paritaire pour la Sante et la Securite du Travail du Secteur Administration Provinciale (CAN ISSN 1910-7404) **6690**

Title

Associations Sectorielles Paritaires, Lesions Professionnelles, Statistiques. Tome 6. Association Paritaire pour la Sante et la Securite du Travail du Secteur Fabrication d'Equipement de Transport et de Machines (CAN ISSN 1910-7277) **6690**
Associations Sectorielles Paritaires, Lesions Professionnelles, Statistiques. Tome 7. Association Paritaire pour la Sante et la Securite du Travail du Secteur de la Fabrication de Produits en Metal et de Produits Electriques (CAN ISSN 1910-7285) **6690**
Associations Sectorielles Paritaires, Lesions Professionnelles, Statistiques. Tome 8. Association Paritaire pour la Sante et la Securite du Travail du Secteur des Services Automobiles (CAN ISSN 1910-7293) **6690**
Associations Sectorielles Paritaires, Lesions Professionnelles, Statistiques. Tome 9. Association Paritaire pour la Sante et la Securite du Travail du Secteur de la Construction (CAN ISSN 1910-7307) **6690**
Associations, Sources, Knowledge Hollis *see* A S K Hollis **1970**
Associations Transnationales *see* Transnational Associations **7268**
Associations U S A (USA ISSN 1934-452X) **4992**
• Associations Yellow Book (USA ISSN 1054-4070) **1973**
• Associative Economics Monthly (GBR ISSN 1750-9025) **1536**
Associazione Biologica Italo-Giapponese Bollettino *see* Nichii Seibutsugaku Kyokai Kaiho **694**
Associazione Europea Studi Tributari *see* A E S T **1909**
Associazione Ginecologi Universitari Italiani News *see* A G U I News **5984**
• Associazione Italiana Biblioteche. Bollettino (ITA ISSN 1121-1490) **4992**
Associazione Italiana Biblioteche Notizie *see* A I B Notizie **4985**
Associazione Italiana di Cartografia Bollettino *see* A I C Bollettino **4014**
Associazione Italiana Ingegneria del Traffico e dei Trasporti. Newsletter (ITA) **8629**
Associazione Italiana Laringectomizzati. Atti (del) Convegno Nazionale (ITA ISSN 0066-9865) **6078**
• Associazione Italiana Neurodisabili (ITA ISSN 1828-5317) **6124**
Associazione Italiana per il Ritardo Mentale Ri M News *see* A I Ri M News **6117**
Associazione Italiana per la Documentazione Avanzata Informazioni *see* A I D A Informazioni **4985**
• Associazione Italiana per la Ricerca Industriale. Notizie (ITA) **3365**
Associazione Italiana Societa Concessionarie Autostrade e Trafori Informazioni *see* A I S C A T Informazioni **8628**
Associazione Italiana Studi di Musicoterapia. Bollettino (ITA) **7337**
Associazione Italiana Veterinari per Piccoli Animali. Bollettino (ITA ISSN 0004-5977) **8793**
† Associazione Laica (ITA) **8931**
Associazione Malacologica Internazionale. Notiziario (ITA) **934**
Associazione Nazionale Autotrasporto Viaggiatori. Newsletter (ITA) **8490**
Associazione Nazionale degli Industriali dei Laterizi. Annuario *see* A N D I L. Annuario (Year) **2037**
Associazione Nazionale degli Industriali dei Laterizi Annuario (Year) *see* A N D I L. Annuario (Year) **2037**
Associazione Nazionale dei Comuni Italiani Rivista *see* A N C I Rivista **7487**
Associazione Nazionale fra le Industrie Automobilistiche Notiziario Statistico *see* A N F I A Notiziario Statistico **8520**
† Associazione Nobilitazione Tessile. Notiziario (ITA) **8931**
Associazione Pedagogica Italiana. Bollettino (ITA) **2828**
Associazione per Imola Storico Artistica. Atti (ITA ISSN 0403-7790) **382**
Associazione per lo Studio e il Controllo della Contaminazione Ambientale News *see* A S C C A News **3482**
Associazione Romana di Entomologia. Bollettino (ITA ISSN 0004-6000) **840**
Associazione Svizzera per l'Arbitrato. Bulletin *see* A S A Bulletin **4915**
Associazioni Cristiane Lavoratori Italiani Oggi *see* A C L I Oggi **7101**
Assotsyatsiya Radio. Vestnik (RUS) **2356**
Assotsyatsiya Rossiiskikh Bankov. Vestnik (RUS) **1309**
Assoziation Schweizer Aerztegesellschaften fuer Akupunktur und Chinesische Medizin Newsletter fuer Akupunktur *see* A S A - Newsletter fuer Akupunktur **305**
Assuit University. Faculty of Science. Bulletin: A. Physics *see* Assiut University Journal of Physics **7006**
Assuit University. Faculty of Science. Bulletin. Section D. Botany *see* Assiut University Journal of Botany **777**
Assur (USA ISSN 0145-6334) **4320**
Assurance des Particuliers (FRA) **4493**
Assurances *see* Assurances et Gestion des Risques **4493**
• Assurances et Gestion des Risques (CAN ISSN 1705-7299) **4493**
• Assurandoer Kredsen (DNK ISSN 1902-9519) **4493**
Assurandoer Nyt *see* Assurandoer Kredsen **4493**
Assurantie Agenda (NLD) **4493**
Assurantie Beurs Nota (NLD) **4493**
Assurantie Magazine (NLD ISSN 0167-3882) **4493**
Assurantie Zakboek Actueel *see* A Z - Actueel **4490**
Assurantie Zakboerk Nieuwsbrief *see* A Z - Actueel **4490**
Assure Social (FRA ISSN 0587-3746) **8089**
➤ The Assyrian Observer (GBR ISSN 0144-7122) **3520**
Assyrian Star (USA ISSN 0004-6051) **3520**
Assyriological Studies (USA ISSN 0066-9903) **5097**
AStA La Vista *see* A St A La Vista **2271**
† Aste Giudiziarie (ITA ISSN 0004-606X) **8931**
AsteCasa (ITA ISSN 1722-0637) **7583**
ASTED. Nouvelles (Association pour l'Avancement des Sciences et des Techniques de la Documentation) (CAN ISSN 0316-0963) **4992**
➤ Aster (FRA ISSN 0297-9373) **2828**
• ➤ Asterion (FRA ISSN 1762-6110) **6906**
Asterisco (PER) **476**
• ➤ Asterisk (DNK ISSN 1601-5754) **2828**
➤ Asterisque (FRA ISSN 0303-1179) **5474**
Asthma *see* Zensoku **6221**
Asthma and Allergy *see* Astma ta Alerhiya **6212**
• Asthma and Respiratory News (NZL ISSN 1175-4141) **6211**
• Asthma Foundation of New South Wales. Annual Report (AUS) **6211**
Asthma Frontier (JPN ISSN 1347-4650) **6211**
• Asthma Matters (AUS ISSN 1442-7583) **6211**
Asthma Society of Canada Quarterly Newsletter (CAN) **5754**
• Asthma Update Newsletter (AUS) **5754**
• El Astillero (ESP ISSN 1699-4310) **6412**
• ➤ Astin Bulletin (BEL ISSN 0515-0361) **4493**
Astir (IRL ISSN 0790-6560) **3051**
• Astma-Allergi Bladet (DNK ISSN 0900-4262) **5754**
Astma i Allergiya *see* Astma ta Alerhiya **6212**
• ➤ Astma ta Alerhiya/Asthma and Allergy/Astma i Allergiya (UKR) **6212**
• AstmaAllergi (NOR ISSN 0801-3799) **5754**
AStN *see* Aktuelle Steuer News **1909**
Astolfo (ITA ISSN 1122-7095) **5258**
Aston Martin Quaterly *see* A M Quaterly **8554**
➤ Aston University. Public Services Management Research Centre. Working Paper (GBR) **1063**
Astonishing Spiderman (GBR ISSN 1360-5178) **2176**
• The Astounding B Monster (USA) **6490**
Astra (HRV ISSN 1332-3474) **564**
Astra (ITA ISSN 0392-226X) **565**
Astra (ROM ISSN 1221-8286) **5207**
Astra Nova (FIN ISSN 1238-1837) **8852**
Astrado (FRA ISSN 0004-6116) **5258**
Astragalo (ESP ISSN 1134-3672) **434**
Astrakhanskaya Nedelya (RUS) **3934**
Astrakhanskie Izvestiya (RUS) **3934**
Astrakhanskie Vedomosti (RUS) **3934**
Astral (DEU ISSN 1434-0658) **565**
Astralog (USA) **8490**
Astrapi (FRA ISSN 0220-1186) **2176**
Astrella (ITA ISSN 1129-0277) **565**
Astres (FRA) **565**
Astro (DEU) **565**
Astro *see* Telescopium **582**
† Astro (Year) (FRA ISSN 1955-9135) **8931**
Astro Agents *see* Power Agent **567**
Astro Analytics Newsletter (USA) **565**
Astro Girl (USA ISSN 1938-5870) **565**
• Astro! Go (USA) **565**
The Astro-Investor (USA) **1611**
Astro Magazin (HRV ISSN 1331-2308) **565**
Astro Magazin Posebno Izd (HRV ISSN 1331-3185) **565**
Astro Revue (FRA ISSN 1631-8102) **565**
Astro Vodic (HRV ISSN 1331-4408) **565**
• ➤ Astrobiology (USA ISSN 1531-1074) **654**
Astrodynamics (Year) *see* A A S Astrodynamics Conference. Proceedings **40**
Astrofax (USA) **6891**
Astrofizika (ARM ISSN 0571-7132) **569**
Astrogirl *see* Astro Girl **565**
† Astrolab (FRA ISSN 0398-074X) **8932**
• Astrolabio (ARG ISSN 1668-7515) **8089**
• Astrolabio (ESP ISSN 1699-7549) **6906**
Astrolabos (GRC ISSN 1106-2878) **5474**
Astrolei (ITA ISSN 1129-0269) **5207**
† Astrolettre (FRA ISSN 0764-2997) **8932**
Astrolog (CHE ISSN 0257-9235) **565**
Astrolog (RUS) **565**
The Astrological Journal (GBR ISSN 0144-6754) **565**
➤ The Astrological Magazine (IND ISSN 0004-6140) **565**
Astrologie Heute (CHE) **565**
Astrologie Magazine (FRA ISSN 1953-7514) **565**
Astrologiya (RUS) **565**
Astrologos (GRC ISSN 1108-8060) **565**
Astrology and Psychic News (USA) **565**
• Astrology Quarterly (GBR ISSN 1464-0589) **565**
• AstroMind (USA) **565**
Astronautyka (POL ISSN 0004-623X) **47**
Astronnews (NLD ISSN 1871-6644) **569**
• ➤ The Astronomer (GBR ISSN 0950-138X) **569**
• Astronomi (NOR ISSN 0802-7587) **569**
† Astronomia (ESP ISSN 1699-7751) **8932**
• L'Astronomia (Milan) (ITA ISSN 1129-7662) **569**
The Astronomical Almanac (USA ISSN 0737-6421) **569**
• ➤ Astronomical and Astrophysical Transactions (IND ISSN 1055-6796) **569**
Astronomical Circular *see* Tenmon Kaiho **582**
Astronomical Ephemeris of Geocentric Places of Planets (IND ISSN 0066-9970) **569**
Astronomical Herald *see* Tenmon Geppo **582**
Astronomical Institute of the Academy of Sciences of the Czech Republic. Publications (CZE ISSN 1211-9105) **569**
• ➤ The Astronomical Journal (USA ISSN 0004-6256) **569**
Astronomical Notes *see* Astronomische Nachrichten **570**
Astronomical Observatory on Skalnate Pleso. Contributions (SVK ISSN 0862-920X) **569**
Astronomical Phenomena (USA ISSN 0083-2421) **569**
• ➤ Astronomical Society of Australia. Publications (Online) (AUS ISSN 1448-6083) **569**
• ➤ Astronomical Society of India. Bulletin (IND ISSN 0304-9523) **569**
Astronomical Society of New York. Newsletter (USA) **569**
➤ Astronomical Society of Southern Africa. Monthly Notes (ZAF ISSN 0024-8266) **570**
Astronomical Society of the Pacific Catalog *see* A S P Catalog **568**
Astronomical Society of the Pacific. Conference Proceedings (USA ISSN 1050-3390) **6278**
• ➤ Astronomical Society of the Pacific. Publications (USA ISSN 0004-6280) **570**
Astronomical Society of Victoria. Astronomical Yearbook (AUS ISSN 0067-0006) **570**
Astronomical Yearbook *see* Astronomicheskii Ezhegodnik **570**
Astronomicheski Kalendar (BGR ISSN 0861-1270) **570**
Astronomicheskii Ezhegodnik/Astronomical Yearbook (RUS ISSN 0373-3343) **570**
• Astronomicheskii Vestnik (RUS ISSN 0320-930X) **570**
• Astronomicheskii Zhurnal (RUS ISSN 0004-6299) **570**
Astronomie (DEU ISSN 1616-0894) **570**
L'Astronomie (FRA ISSN 0004-6302) **570**
Astronomie Heute *see* Sterne und Weltraum **582**
Astronomie Passion (FRA ISSN 1283-3339) **570**
Astronomie Quebec (CAN ISSN 1183-5362) **570**
Astronomie und Raumfahrt im Unterricht (DEU ISSN 1437-8639) **570**
Astronomische Gesellschaft. Mitteilungen (DEU ISSN 0374-1958) **570**
Astronomische Gesellschaft. Short Contributions (DEU) **570**
Astronomische Grundlagen fuer den Kalender (DEU ISSN 0067-0014) **570**
• ➤ Astronomische Nachrichten/Astronomical Notes (DEU ISSN 0004-6337) **570**
• Astronomy (USA ISSN 0091-6358) **570**
Astronomy (Year) (AUS) **570**
• ➤ Astronomy & Astrophysics (FRA ISSN 0004-6361) **570**
• ➤ The Astronomy and Astrophysics Review (DEU ISSN 0935-4956) **571**
• ➤ Astronomy & Geophysics (GBR ISSN 1366-8781) **571**
Astronomy & Space (IRL ISSN 0791-8062) **571**
Astronomy and Space (London) *see* Astronomy & Space **571**
• Astronomy Education Review (USA ISSN 1539-1515) **571**
• Astronomy in Latin America (MEX) **571**
• ➤ Astronomy Letters (RUS ISSN 1063-7737) **571**
• Astronomy Now (GBR ISSN 0951-9726) **571**
Astronomy Presents Explore The Universe (USA ISSN 1089-4926) **571**
• ➤ Astronomy Reports (RUS ISSN 1063-7729) **571**
Astronomy through Practical Investigation (USA) **571**
• ➤ Astroparticle Physics (NLD ISSN 0927-6505) **571**
• ➤ Astrophysical Bulletin (RUS ISSN 1990-3413) **571**
• ➤ The Astrophysical Journal (USA ISSN 0004-637X) **571**
• ➤ The Astrophysical Journal Letters (USA) **571**
• ➤ The Astrophysical Journal Supplement Series (USA ISSN 0067-0049) **572**
• The Astrophysicist's Tango Partner Speaks (USA ISSN 1523-5386) **5417**
• ➤ Astrophysics (USA ISSN 0571-7256) **572**
• ➤ Astrophysics and Space Science (NLD ISSN 0004-640X) **572**
➤ Astrophysics and Space Science Library (NLD ISSN 0067-0057) **572**
• ➤ Astrophysics and Space Sciences Transactions (Online) (DEU ISSN 1810-6536) **572**
• ➤ Astrophysics and Space Sciences Transactions (Print) (DEU ISSN 1810-6528) **572**
• Astropoetica (USA ISSN 1559-6052) **5417**
• ➤ Astropolitics (GBR ISSN 1477-7622) **572**
• Astrosolutions (USA ISSN 1529-1278) **565**
Astrotalk Bulletin (USA) **565**
Astrowoche (DEU) **565**
Astruim (NLD ISSN 1384-7546) **572**
Astrum (ESP ISSN 0210-4105) **572**
Astuces et Conseils Batiment (BEL ISSN 1373-3001) **1726**
Astuces et Conseils Commercant (BEL ISSN 1373-9204) **1425**
Astuces et Conseils Impots (BEL ISSN 1371-192X) **1911**
Astuces & Conseils (BEL ISSN 1370-1487) **1726**
Astuces & Conseils Horeca (BEL ISSN 1371-1911) **4382**
Astuces & Conseils Immobilier (BEL ISSN 1372-6420) **7583**
Astuces & Conseils Internet (BEL ISSN 1371-1938) **2552**
Astuces & Conseils Personnel (BEL ISSN 1373-4741) **1856**
Asturias (ESP) **1425**
Asturiensia Medievalia (ESP ISSN 0301-889X) **4131**
Astute Investor (USA ISSN 0736-7643) **1611**
Asu ja Rakenna (FIN ISSN 1237-0703) **3405**
Asu no Tomo/Friend of Tomorrow (JPN) **4041**
Asu o Kizuku/Construction Tomorrow (JPN) **3259**
Asukii-.P C/ASCII .P C (JPN) **2407**
Asunto (VEN) **8089**
• Asuntos Indigenas (DNK ISSN 1024-3275) **329**
Aswan Science and Technology Bulletin/Nasrat Aswan lil-A!lum wa al-Tiknulugyyaa (EGY ISSN 1110-0184) **7837**
Al-Aswaq (SAU ISSN 1319-3449) **1063**
Aswaq al-Khalij (QAT) **1063**
Asyl (CHE) **4918**
• Asymmetric Information (NZL ISSN 1177-634X) **1063**
• ➤ Asymptotic Analysis (NLD ISSN 0921-7134) **5474**
Asymptotic Giant Branch Newsletter *see* A G B Newsletter **567**
Asynchronous Transfer Mode Financial Self-Service Executive Summary *see* A T M & Financial Self-Service Executive Summary **1305**
Asynchronous Transfer Mode World *see* A T M World **2495**
At 16 or 17 in One's Life *see* Rensheng Shiliuqi **2210**
• At a Glance (CAN ISSN 1719-5535) **5580**
At Anime *see* @anime! **466**
At-Bashy Janaliktary (KGZ) **3903**
At Cooper Union (USA ISSN 0004-6434) **2273**
At Ease (USA ISSN 0190-4280) **7623**
• @Eco.News (GBR ISSN 1368-9371) **3405**
At Home & Overseas *see* Hainei yu Haiwai **3824**
• At-Home Dad (USA ISSN 1081-5767) **6286**
At Home in Arkansas (USA) **4531**
At Home in Memphis (USA) **4531**
At Home with Chris Madden (USA) **4532**
At Home with Donald A Gardner (USA ISSN 1553-6807) **4553**
At Home with Jennifer (USA) **4352**
At Home with Our Faith (USA) **7785**
At Issue (USA) **4622**
At L A C M A (USA ISSN 1555-8185) **476**
At Large (USA) **2144**
@Law (USA ISSN 1089-7216) **4622**
† • @ M C H (Ministry for Culture and Heritage) (NZL ISSN 1177-0430) **8932**
• @ Philia (CAN) **8089**
At Play (USA ISSN 1544-3027) **5258**
• At Random (USA ISSN 1062-0036) **7552**
At-Taqrir al-'Alam 'an al-Ajdiyat *see* World Food Report **3668**
At-Taqrir - Al-Gamiyyat al-Umumiyyat ad-Dawarat. Al-Lagnat al-Fanmiyyat *see* International Civil Aviation Organization. Assembly. Report of the Technical Commission **60**
At-Taqrir as-Sanawi. Bank al-Kuwayt al-Markazi (KWT ISSN 1029-4589) **1309**
At-Taqrir as-Sanawi - S A M A *see* Saudi Arabian Monetary Agency. Annual Report **1942**
At-Taqrir - Munazzamant at-Tayaran al Madani ad-Duwali. Al-Gammiyat al-Umumiyyat ad-Dawarat. Al-Lagnat al-Idarriyyat *see* International Civil Aviation Organization. Assembly. Report and Minutes of the Administrative Commission **8545**
At-Taqrir - Munazzamat at-Tayaran al-Madani ad-Duwali. Al-Gamiyyat al-Umumiyyat ad-Dawarat. Al-Lagnat at-Tanfidyyat *see* International Civil Aviation Organization. Assembly. Reports and Minutes of the Executive Committee **8545**
At-Taqrir - Munazzamat at-Tayaran al-Madani ad-Duwali. Al-Qararat at-Taqrir al Wataiq. Al-Gamiyyat al-Umumiyyat *see* International Civil Aviation Organization. Assembly. Minutes of the Plenary Meetings **8545**
At-Taqrir - Munazzamat at-Tayaran al-Umumiyyat ad-Dawrat. Al Langnat al-Qanumiyyat *see* International Civil Aviation Organization. Assembly. Report and Minutes of the Legal Commission **8545**
At the Beat *see* Na Boevom Postu **6437**
➤ At the Interface/Probing the Boundaries (NLD ISSN 1570-7113) **4443**
At the L A T A Level (USA) **2365**
At the Lake (USA) **3969**
At the Museum *see* At L A C M A **476**
• At the Park (USA ISSN 1048-9118) **4976**
• @ This Point (USA ISSN 1932-698X) **7623**
At Your Library *see* What's New @ St. Catharines Public Library **5055**
Ata-Zhurt (KGZ) **3903**
Ataka (RUS) **5207**
Atakpame *see* Cove-Atakpame **8096**
Atalanta (DEU ISSN 0171-0079) **840**
Atalanta (ITA) **5258**

Title

9992 ATLAS POETICA ULRICH'S PERIODICALS

▼ • Atlas Poetica (USA ISSN 1939-6465) **5417**
Atlas Polskich Strojow Ludowych (POL ISSN 0067-0316) **329**
Atlas Rozmieszczenia Geograficznego Mchow w Polsce/Atlas of the Geographical Distribution of Mosses in Poland (POL) **777**
Atlas Rozmieszczenia Geograficznego Porostow w Polsce/Atlas of the Geographical Distribution of Lichens in Poland (POL) **777**
Atlasblue.mag (FRA ISSN 1771-0146) **8782**
Atlatl *see* Arizona Anthropologist **329**
Atleticamente (ITA ISSN 1825-9944) **8159**
• Atleticastudi (ITA ISSN 0390-6671) **8159**
Atletico de Madrid (ESP ISSN 1133-8946) **8159**
Atletismo Espanol (ESP) **8304**
Atma Jaya Research Centre. Annual Report (IDN) **2828**
Atma Jaya Research Centre. Education Development Research Report/Pusat Penelitian Atma Jaya. Studi Tentang Pengembangan Pendidikan (IDN) **2828**
Atma Jaya Research Centre. International Contract Labour (IDN) **1665**
Atma Jaya Research Centre. Library Bulletin (IDN ISSN 0126-1630) **4993**
Atma Jaya Research Centre. Newsletter (IDN ISSN 0126-1584) **2968**
Atma Jaya Research Centre. Socio-Medical Research Report/Pusat Penelitian Atma Jaya. Penelitian Tentang Kebutuhan Kesehatan Masyarakat dan Sistem Peleyanan Kesehatan di Kecamatan Penjaringan (IDN) **5580**
Atma Jaya Research Centre. Socio-Religious Research Report/Pusat Penelitian Atma Jaya. Laporan Penelitian Keagamaan (IDN) **7623**
• ➤ Atmosfera (MEX ISSN 0187-6236) **6346**
• Atmosfera (RUS ISSN 1681-3529) **5065**
• Atmosphere (AUS ISSN 1325-0299) **6346**
Atmosphere (Miami Beach) (USA) **8782**
• ➤ Atmosphere - Ocean (CAN ISSN 0705-5900) **6347**
Atmospheres (FRA ISSN 1273-1579) **8852**
• Atmospheric and Oceanic Optics (RUS ISSN 1024-8560) **4404**
➤ Atmospheric and Oceanographic Sciences Library (NLD ISSN 1383-8601) **2702**
• ➤ Atmospheric Chemistry and Physics (DEU ISSN 1680-7316) **6347**
• ➤ Atmospheric Chemistry and Physics Discussions (DEU ISSN 1680-7367) **6347**
Atmospheric Chemistry Division Tales *see* A C D Tales **2722**
• ➤ Atmospheric Environment (GBR ISSN 1352-2310) **3483**
• ➤ Atmospheric Measurement Techniques (DEU ISSN 1867-1381) **6347**
▼ • ➤ Atmospheric Measurement Techniques Discussions (DEU ISSN 1867-8610) **6347**
• ➤ Atmospheric Research (NLD ISSN 0169-8095) **6347**
• ➤ Atmospheric Science Letters (GBR ISSN 1530-261X) **6347**
Atmospheric Sciences *see* Daqi Kexue **6351**
Atoka (NGA ISSN 0004-7007) **5258**
• Atoll Research Bulletin (USA ISSN 0077-5630) **7838**
Atom (GBR ISSN 0004-7015) **3164**
Atom (RUS) **7064**
Atom Indonesia (IDN ISSN 0126-1568) **3164**
Atom Mind (USA ISSN 0004-704X) **5207**
Atomic and Plasma-Material Interaction Data for Fusion (AUT ISSN 1018-5577) **7064**
Atomic Collision Research in Japan. Progress Report (JPN) **7065**
• ➤ Atomic Data and Nuclear Data Tables (USA ISSN 0092-640X) **7065**
• ➤ Atomic Energy (USA ISSN 1063-4258) **3164**
Atomic Energy Authority of Sri Lanka. Bulletin *see* Nuclear News **3172**
Atomic Energy Commission. Journal *see* Genshiryoku Iinkai Geppo **3167**
Atomic Energy News *see* Genshiryoku Nyusu **3167**
Atomic Energy of Canada Limited. Low Level Radioactive Waste Management Office. Annual Report (CAN ISSN 1910-4278) **3164**
Atomic Energy of Canada Ltd Report Series *see* A E C L Report Series **3164**
Atomic Energy Pocketbook (JPN) **3164**
Atomic Energy Research Report of National Laboratories *see* Kokuritsu Kikan Genshiryoku Shiken Kenkyu Seika Hokokusho **3170**
Atomic Energy Society of Japan. Abstracts of Spring Meeting *see* Nihon Genshiryoku Gakkai. Haruno Nenkai Yoshishu **3153**
Atomic Energy Society of Japan. Fall Meeting *see* Fall Meeting of the Atomic Energy Society of Japan **3167**
Atomic Energy Society of Japan. Journal *see* Atomos **3165**
Atomic Energy Society of Japan. Proceedings of Fall Meeting *see* Nihon Genshiryoku Gakkai. Akino Taikai Yokoshu **3153**
Atomic M P C *see* Atomic Maximum Power Computing **2574**
Atomic Maximum Power Computing (AUS ISSN 1444-8998) **2574**
Atomic Ranch (USA ISSN 1547-3902) **4532**
➤ Atomic Spectroscopy (USA ISSN 0195-5373) **2098**
Atomica (USA ISSN 1541-6569) **3970**
• Atomix (MEX) **2474**
• ➤ Atomization and Sprays (USA ISSN 1044-5110) **3236**
ATOMKI Annual Report (HUN ISSN 0231-3596) **7065**
• Atomnaya Energiya (RUS ISSN 0004-7163) **3165**
Atomnaya Tekhnika za Rubezhom/Nuclear Engineering Abroad (RUS ISSN 0320-9326) **3165**
➤ Atomos/Atomic Energy Society of Japan. Journal (JPN) **3165**
AtomoSigma *see* Atomos **3165**
• ➤ Atoms for Peace (GBR ISSN 1741-640X) **3165**
• Atoms in Japan (JPN ISSN 0403-9319) **3165**
Atomu Fukushima (JPN ISSN 0386-1430) **3165**
Atomwirtschaft Internationale Zeitschrift fuer Kernenergie *see* A T W - Internationale Zeitschrift fuer Kernenergie **3164**
Atopia: Philosophy, Political Theory, Aesthetics (USA) **6906**
Atout Carre (FRA ISSN 1635-5253) **531**
Atout Chat (FRA ISSN 0769-6027) **6804**
Atout Chien (FRA ISSN 0298-2919) **6804**
Atout Hasard (CAN ISSN 1910-1341) **6124**
Atout Micro (CAN ISSN 0835-6661) **2407**
• L'Atout Reussite (FRA ISSN 1773-1240) **2407**
Atout Timbres (FRA ISSN 1277-2054) **6891**
Atque (ITA ISSN 1120-9364) **6906**
Atraves (BRA) **5258**
Atril (PER ISSN 1990-9497) **2828**
Atrio (ESP ISSN 0214-8293) **476**
Atrium (CHE ISSN 1423-7377) **4532**
Atrium (HUN ISSN 1219-0101) **434**
Atrium Construction (FRA ISSN 1636-3434) **434**
Atrium Special Baeder *see* Baeder **4554**
Atrium Special Garten *see* Garten **3732**
Atrium Special Kuechen *see* Kuechen **4560**
Atrium Special Waerme *see* Waerme **4127**
The Atrocity (USA ISSN 1061-7000) **5207**
• Atropos (GBR ISSN 1478-8128) **840**
• Atsuryoku Gijutsu/Journal of High Pressure Institute of Japan (JPN ISSN 0387-0154) **3182**
Att Adoptera (SWE ISSN 0347-6324) **8026**
Att Undervisa (SWE ISSN 0345-0384) **3036**
Attaalim/Revue Attaalim (MRT) **2828**
▼ Attachment (GBR ISSN 1753-5980) **7337**
• ➤ Attachment and Human Development (GBR ISSN 1461-6734) **7337**
• Attachment Connection (USA) **5449**
• Attacks on the Press (USA ISSN 1078-3334) **4572**
• Attainment Business Startups Journal (USA ISSN 1092-3012) **1063**
Attakapas Gazette (USA ISSN 0571-8236) **4285**
Attendance Centre News (GBR ISSN 0143-8387) **2644**
• Attenderingsbulletin Bibliotheek Staring-gebouw: Land, Bodem, Water (NLD) **3477**
➤ Attending to Early Modern Women (USA) **8894**
Attention! (USA ISSN 1551-0980) **6125**
➤ Attention and Performance (USA ISSN 1047-0387) **7337**
Attention Deficit Hyperactivity Disorder *see* A D H D Report **6117**
Attention Deficit Hyperactivity Disorder Report *see* A D H D Report **6117**
Attention-Deficit Hyperactivity Disorder Research Today *see* A D H D Research Today **6117**
Attention Magazine *see* Attention! **6125**
• ➤ Attention, Perception & Psychophysics (USA ISSN 1943-3921) **7337**
Atti dei Convegni di Studi Etruschi ed Italici *see* Atti di Convegni di Studi Etruschi ed Italici **382**
Atti di Convegni di Studi Etruschi ed Italici (ITA ISSN 1970-5409) **382**
Atti e Pareri per l'Esame di Avvocato (ITA ISSN 1972-053X) **4623**
➤ Atti Ticinensi di Scienze della Terra (ITA ISSN 0394-0691) **2702**
▼ • @tic (ESP ISSN 1989-3477) **3051**
Attic (USA ISSN 1931-5368) **5258**
Attiosjuan Axelsson *see* 87: an Axelsson **5247**
Attitude (BEL ISSN 0775-4221) **5065**
Attitude (GBR ISSN 1353-1875) **4371**
• Attitude: The Dancers' Magazine (USA ISSN 0882-3472) **2682**
Attitudes (FRA ISSN 1952-0077) **5207**
Attitudes and Arabesques (USA ISSN 0889-8847) **2688**
† Attivita Dopolavoristiche (ITA) **8932**
Attivita Produttive (ITA) **1880**
Attorney *see* Pravnik **4760**
• Attorney - C P A (USA ISSN 0571-8279) **4856**
Attorney Discipline *see* New Jersey Attorney Discipline **4743**
Attorney Fee Awards (USA) **4623**
Attorney General / Board of Immigration Appeals Decisions Listing *see* A G / B I A Decisions Listing (Online) **7276**
Attorney Jobs: National and Federal Legal Employment Report (USA) **6692**
Attorneys and Agents Registered to Practice before the U.S. Patent and Trademark Office (USA ISSN 0361-3844) **6745**
• Attorneys' Dictionary of Medicine (USA) **4623**
Attorney's Dictionary of Patent Claims (USA) **6745**
• Attorney's Fees in Florida (USA) **4623**
• Attorney's Handbook of Accounting, Auditing and Financial Reporting (USA) **4856**
• Attorney's Medical Advisor / Atlas (USA) **5580**
• Attorney's Medical Deskbook (USA) **5580**
Attorney's Report (USA) **1280**
• Attorneys' Textbook of Medicine (USA) **4623**
• L'Attracteur (CAN ISSN 1207-0203) **7006**
• Attractions Management (GBR ISSN 1479-9154) **4976**
† Attraverso il Mondo (ITA ISSN 0394-414X) **8932**
Attualita Grafologica (ITA ISSN 0394-3747) **7337**
Attualita in Senologia (ITA ISSN 1121-936X) **6009**
Attualita Italia - Australia (ITA) **1396**
• Attualita Lacaniana (ITA ISSN 1828-1958) **7338**
Atuagagdliutit *see* A G **3874**
Atuagagdliutit - Groenlandsposten *see* A G **3874**
• Atumpan (USA ISSN 2150-0738) **4132**
Atunes y Peces Picudos en el Oceano Pacifico Oriental *see* Tunas and Billfishes in the Eastern Pacific Ocean **3610**
ATV & Quad *see* A T V und Quad **8554**
ATV-Industry Magazine *see* A T V - Industry Magazine **8253**
ATV Sport *see* A T V Sport **8554**
Atwood Ancestors (USA) **3759**
• AU-A Weekly Updates Including Master Index on CD-ROM (AUS) **6745**
Au Coeur de l'Afrique (BDI ISSN 0563-4245) **7623**
Au Courant (English Edition) (CAN ISSN 1915-0229) **6520**
Au Courant (French Edition) (CAN ISSN 1915-0237) **6520**
Au-dela du Risque *see* Beyond Risk **4496**
Au Fil de l'Hers (FRA ISSN 1774-7422) **8818**
Au Fil des Evenements (CAN ISSN 0225-1965) **2828**
• Au Magazine (USA) **1063**
Au Pays de Matane (CAN ISSN 0836-3102) **4285**
Au Pied du Mur (FRA ISSN 1765-7601) **434**
• Au S H R M News (AUS ISSN 1834-2078) **1726**
Au Sud de l'Est (FRA ISSN 1955-1029) **476**
Auberges de Jeunesse en Amerique du Nord *see* Hostelling North America: The Official Guide to Hostels in Canada and the United States of America **8719**
Auburn Magazine (USA ISSN 1077-8640) **2273**
• Auburn Plainsman (USA ISSN 1071-1279) **2273**
Auburn University. Agricultural Experiment Station. Circular (USA ISSN 0097-3505) **93**
Auburn University. Environmental Institute. Annual Report (USA) **8818**
Auburn University, Environmental Institute Newsletter *see* A U E I Newsletter **8817**
Auckland City Harbour News (NZL ISSN 1170-0041) **3916**
Auckland City's State of the Environment Report *see* Our Changing Environment **3458**
Auckland College of Education. Calendar *see* University of Auckland. Calendar **3008**
Auckland College of Education Papers *see* A C E Papers **2822**
• Auckland District Crime Statistics (NZL ISSN 1178-1556) **2672**
➤ Auckland Museum. Records (NZL) **6520**
Auckland Tourist Times (NZL) **8684**
• Auckland University Law Review (NZL ISSN 0067-0510) **4623**
Auckland University Press Studies in Cultural and Social History *see* A U P Studies in Cultural and Social History **8085**
➤ Auckland War Memorial Museum. Bulletin (NZL) **6520**
Aucklander (North Edition) *see* The Aucklander North Shore **3916**
Aucklander (Shore Edition) *see* The Aucklander North Shore **3916**
Aucklander (South Edition) *see* The Aucklander Manukau City **3916**
▼ The Aucklander Manukau City (NZL) **3916**
The Aucklander North Shore (NZL) **3916**
▼ Auckland's Great Restaurant Guide (NZL ISSN 1177-6838) **4382**
AuClock (DNK ISSN 1604-9659) **4564**
Auction Block (USA) **1611**
Auction Bulletin (USA) **1805**
• Auction Bytes - Update (USA ISSN 1528-6703) **4327**
Auction Price Guide (USA) **1805**
The Auctioneer (USA ISSN 0004-7465) **1805**
Audace *see* Adorable au Summum **6285**
AudArena Stadium International Guide & Facility Buyers Guide (USA) **8466**
Audel Air Conditioning Home and Commercial (USA ISSN 1930-8515) **4116**
Audel Carpenter's and Builder's Layout, Foundation, and Framing (USA ISSN 1932-6521) **1049**
Audel Carpenter's and Builder's Math, Plans, and Specifications (USA ISSN 1932-6505) **1049**
Audel Carpenter's and Builder's Millwork, Power Tools, and Painting (USA ISSN 1932-6513) **1049**
Audel Carpenter's and Builder's Tools, Steel Squares & Joinery (USA ISSN 1930-8507) **1049**
Audel Pumps & Hydraulics *see* Pumps & Hydraulics **3364**
▼ Audemus (USA ISSN 1946-8032) **5258**
† Auden Studies (GBR ISSN 1366-056X) **8932**
Audenshaw Papers (GBR ISSN 0004-7481) **7623**
Audi Driver (GBR ISSN 1369-4340) **8556**
Audi Magazin (CZE ISSN 1211-9857) **8556**
Audi Magazin (DEU) **8556**
Audi Magazine (NLD ISSN 1871-7918) **8556**
Audi Scene Live (DEU ISSN 1610-9899) **8556**
Audi Tuning (DEU) **8556**
• Audience (Online Edition) (USA) **6490**
• Audience Development (USA ISSN 1946-0392) **7552**
• Aud!max (DEU ISSN 1439-233X) **2273**
Aud!max Reifepruefung (DEU) **6692**
• Audio (DEU ISSN 0171-4147) **7086**
Audio (POL ISSN 1425-171X) **3089**
• Audio (Year) (Scottsdale) (USA ISSN 0883-8437) **8152**
Audio Arts Magazine (Audio Cassette Edition) *see* Audio Arts Magazine (CD-ROM Edition) **5258**
• Audio Arts Magazine (CD-ROM Edition) (GBR) **5258**
Audio Arts Magazine (Print Edition) *see* Audio Arts Magazine (CD-ROM Edition) **5258**
Audio Car (ESP) **8152**
Audio Critic (USA ISSN 0146-4701) **8152**
➤ Audio-Digest Anesthesiology (USA ISSN 0271-1265) **5770**
• ➤ Audio-Digest Emergency Medicine (USA ISSN 0748-8947) **6056**
➤ Audio-Digest Family Practice (USA ISSN 0271-1362) **5580**
➤ Audio-Digest Gastroenterology (USA ISSN 0892-9386) **5920**
➤ Audio-Digest General Surgery (USA ISSN 1047-6954) **6237**
➤ Audio-Digest Internal Medicine (USA ISSN 0271-1303) **5944**
➤ Audio-Digest Obstetrics - Gynecology (USA ISSN 0271-129X) **5986**
➤ Audio-Digest Ophthalmology (USA ISSN 0271-1281) **6038**
• ➤ Audio-Digest Orthopaedics (USA ISSN 0271-132X) **6056**
• ➤ Audio-Digest Otolaryngology - Head and Neck Surgery (USA) **6078**
➤ Audio-Digest Pediatrics (USA ISSN 0271-1346) **6088**
➤ Audio-Digest Psychiatry (USA ISSN 0271-1311) **6125**
➤ Audio-Digest Urology (USA ISSN 0271-1338) **6265**
Audio Engineering Society *see* A E S **8151**
Audio Engineering Society. Journal *see* A E S **8151**
• Audio Estate Planner (USA) **4901**
Audio Ideas Guide (CAN ISSN 0833-9198) **3089**
• Audio Journal of Oncology (USA ISSN 1350-9667) **6009**
• Audio Media (GBR ISSN 0960-7471) **8152**
Audio Pro *see* M I Pro **6586**
• Audio Programmers' Database (CAN ISSN 1481-8515) **6546**
Audio Review *see* Audioreview **8152**
Audio Technology *see* M J Musen to Jikken **8154**
Audio Video (NOR) **8152**
Audio Video *see* Library Journal netConnect **5028**
Audio Video *see* Library Journal **5028**
† Audio Video Echos (FRA ISSN 1253-5559) **8932**
Audio Video Foto Bild (DEU ISSN 1613-3161) **2400**
Audio Video Foto Bild (ITA ISSN 1827-7055) **2400**
Audio Video Front *see* Gekkan Ebui Furonto **8153**
Audio Video Live *see* A V Live **2311**
Audio Video Max *see* A V Max **6541**
Audio Video Prestige (FRA ISSN 1766-4098) **8152**
Audio-Visual Advisor *see* A-V Advisor **2374**
Audio Visual Directory (GBR ISSN 0956-2931) **2312**
Audio-Visual Education *see* Shichokaku Kyoiku **2912**
Audio-Visual Education in Japan *see* A V E in Japan **3050**
Audio Visual Haandbogen *see* A V Haandbogen **18**
Audio Visual Magazine *see* A V Magazine **2374**
Audio Visual Presentations Handbook *see* A V Presentations Handbook **3050**
Audio-Visual Preservation Trust of Canada. Annual Report *see* A V Preservation Trust of Canada. Annual Report **6488**
Audio Visual Retailing Market Assessment *see* Key Note Market Report: Household Appliances (Brown Goods) **3107**
Audio Visual Retailing Market Assessment *see* Key Note Market Assessment. Audio Visual Retailing **3107**
Audio Visual Symposium on Dynamics *see* Dainamikkusu ni Kansaru Odio Bijuaru Shinpojiumu **8948**
Audio-Visual Teaching of Foreign Languages *see* Waiyu Dianhua Jiaoxue **3087**
Audio-Visual World *see* Yinxiang Shijie **6629**
Audio Visuell Views *see* A V Views **2374**
Audio Yearbook *see* Home Cinema & Hi-Fi Living **8153**
• Audiocarstereo (ITA ISSN 1123-2692) **8152**
Audiocraft (USA) **8152**
AudioFile (USA ISSN 1063-0244) **5258**
Audioguida Car (ITA ISSN 1592-3770) **8152**
Audioguida Hi-Fi (ITA ISSN 1592-3819) **8152**
▼ Audiologia Practica (ESP ISSN 1887-8679) **6078**
Audiological Acoustics *see* Zeitschrift fuer Audiologie **7090**
• ➤ Audiological Medicine (GBR ISSN 1651-386X) **6078**
• Audiology/Shinavayi / Shinasi (IRN ISSN 1735-1936) **6078**
Audiology and Neuro-Otology *see* Audiology and Neurotology **6078**
• ➤ Audiology and Neurotology (CHE) **6078**
• Audiology Today (USA ISSN 1535-2609) **6078**
† Audionews (ITA) **8932**
• Audiophile (DEU) **8152**
Audioreview (ITA) **8152**
Audiotex Directory & Buyer's Guide (USA ISSN 1042-6329) **2365**
Audiotex News *see* Infotech Industry News **2368**
• Audiotex Update (USA ISSN 1045-5795) **2349**

Title

Title

9996 AUSTRALIA. BUREAU OF STATISTICS. CENSUS OF POPULATION ULRICH'S PERIODICALS

• Australia. Bureau of Statistics. Census of Population and Housing: Census Guide (AUS) **7297**

• Australia. Bureau of Statistics. Census of Population and Housing: Classification Counts, Australia (AUS) **7297**

Australia. Bureau of Statistics. Census of Population and Housing: Collection District and Statistical Local Area Reference Maps, Australia (AUS) **7297**

• Australia. Bureau of Statistics. Census of Population and Housing: Community Profiles, Australia (Online) (AUS) **7297**

Australia. Bureau of Statistics. Census of Population and Housing: Community Profiles, Australia (Print) *see* Australia. Bureau of Statistics. Census of Population and Housing: Community Profiles, Australia (Online) **7297**

Australia. Bureau of Statistics. Census of Population and Housing: Customized Tables, Australia (AUS) **7298**

Australia. Bureau of Statistics. Census of Population and Housing: Digital Boundaries, Australia (AUS) **7298**

• Australia. Bureau of Statistics. Census of Population and Housing: Expanded Community Profile (AUS) **7298**

• Australia. Bureau of Statistics. Census of Population and Housing: Household Sample File (AUS) **7298**

• Australia. Bureau of Statistics. Census of Population and Housing: Indigenous Profile (AUS) **7298**

Australia. Bureau of Statistics. Census of Population and Housing: Nature and Content *see* Australia. Bureau of Statistics. Census of Population and Housing: Nature and Content (Online) **7298**

• Australia. Bureau of Statistics. Census of Population and Housing: Nature and Content (Online) (AUS) **7298**

• Australia. Bureau of Statistics. Census of Population and Housing: Occasional Paper - Counting the Homeless (Online) (AUS) **8080**

• Australia. Bureau of Statistics. Census of Population and Housing: Place of Enumeration Profile (AUS) **7298**

• Australia. Bureau of Statistics. Census of Population and Housing: Population Growth and Distribution, Australia (Online) (AUS) **7298**

Australia. Bureau of Statistics. Census of Population and Housing: Population Growth and Distribution, Australia (Print) *see* Australia. Bureau of Statistics. Census of Population and Housing: Population Growth and Distribution, Australia (Online) **7298**

• Australia. Bureau of Statistics. Census of Population and Housing: Selected Characteristics for Urban Centres and Localities, New South Wales and Australian Capital Territory (Online) (AUS) **7298**

• Australia. Bureau of Statistics. Census of Population and Housing: Selected Characteristics for Urban Centres, Australia (Online) (AUS) **7298**

Australia. Bureau of Statistics. Census of Population and Housing: Selected Characteristics for Urban Centres, Australia (Print) *see* Australia. Bureau of Statistics. Census of Population and Housing: Selected Characteristics for Urban Centres, Australia (Online) **7298**

• Australia. Bureau of Statistics. Census of Population and Housing: Selected Education and Labour Force Characteristics, Australia (Online) (AUS) **7298**

Australia. Bureau of Statistics. Census of Population and Housing: Selected Education and Labour Force Characteristics, Australia (Print) *see* Australia. Bureau of Statistics. Census of Population and Housing: Selected Education and Labour Force Characteristics, Australia (Online) **7298**

• Australia. Bureau of Statistics. Census of Population and Housing: Selected Education and Labour Force Characteristics for Statistical Local Areas, Australian Capital Territory (Online) (AUS) **7298**

• Australia. Bureau of Statistics. Census of Population and Housing: Selected Social and Housing Characteristics, Australia (Online) (AUS) **7298**

Australia. Bureau of Statistics. Census of Population and Housing: Selected Social and Housing Characteristics, Australia (Print) *see* Australia. Bureau of Statistics. Census of Population and Housing: Selected Social and Housing Characteristics, Australia (Online) **7298**

• Australia. Bureau of Statistics. Census of Population and Housing: Selected Social and Housing Characteristics for Statistical Local Areas, Australian Capital Territory (Online) (AUS) **7298**

• Australia. Bureau of Statistics. Census of Population and Housing: Socio-Economic Indexes for Areas, Australia (AUS) **7298**

† Australia. Bureau of Statistics. Census of Population and Housing: Socio-Economic Indexes for Areas, Australian Capital Territory (AUS) **8932**

Australia. Bureau of Statistics. Census of Population and Housing: Thematic Profile Service, Australia (AUS) **7298**

• Australia. Bureau of Statistics. Census of Population and Housing: Time Series Profile (AUS) **7298**

• Australia. Bureau of Statistics. Census of Population and Housing: Working Population Profile (AUS) **7298**

Australia. Bureau of Statistics. Census: Selected Social and Housing Characteristics for Statistical Local Areas, Victoria *see* Australia. Bureau of Statistics. Victorian Office. Census of Population and Housing: Selected Social and Housing Characteristics for Statistical Local Areas, Victoria (Online) **7302**

Australia. Bureau of Statistics. Child Care, Australia (Online) (AUS) **2173**

Australia. Bureau of Statistics. Children, Australia: A Social Report *see* Australia. Bureau of Statistics. Children, Australia: A Social Report (Online) **2173**

• Australia. Bureau of Statistics. Children, Australia: A Social Report (Online) (AUS) **2173**

• Australia. Bureau of Statistics. Children's Health Screening (Online) (AUS) **5740**

• Australia. Bureau of Statistics. Children's Immunisation, Australia (Online) (AUS) **5740**

• Australia. Bureau of Statistics. Children's Participation in Cultural and Leisure Activities, Australia (Online) (AUS) **4984**

• Australia. Bureau of Statistics. Chiropractic and Osteopathic Services, Australia (Online) (AUS) **5740**

• Australia. Bureau of Statistics. Cleaning Services Industry, Australia (Online) (AUS) **4370**

• Australia. Bureau of Statistics. Clubs, Pubs, Taverns and Bars, Australia (Online) (AUS) **4401**

• Australia. Bureau of Statistics. Collection District Comparability Listing, Australia (AUS) **7298**

Australia. Bureau of Statistics. Colonial Microfiche Series - Colonial Statistics (AUS) **4169**

• Australia. Bureau of Statistics. Commercial Art Galleries, Australia (Online) (AUS) **6541**

Australia. Bureau of Statistics. Community Attitudes to Crime and Policing, Australia (AUS) **2672**

• Australia. Bureau of Statistics. Community Services, Australia (Online) (AUS) **8080**

Australia. Bureau of Statistics. Community Services, Australia (Print) *see* Australia. Bureau of Statistics. Community Services, Australia (Online) **8080**

• Australia. Bureau of Statistics. Community Services, Australia, Preliminary (Online) (AUS) **8080**

Australia. Bureau of Statistics. Community Services, Australia, Preliminary (Print) *see* Australia. Bureau of Statistics. Community Services, Australia, Preliminary (Online) **8080**

• Australia. Bureau of Statistics. Complete Set of Social Atlases (AUS) **7298**

• Australia. Bureau of Statistics. Computing Services Industry, Australia (AUS) **2442**

Australia. Bureau of Statistics. Concepts, Sources and Methods for Australia's Water and Greenhouse Gas Emissions Accounts (AUS) **3151**

† Australia. Bureau of Statistics. Constant Price Estimates of Manufacturing Production, Australia (AUS ISSN 1034-4748) **8932**

• Australia. Bureau of Statistics. Construction Activity: Chain Volume Measures, Australia (Online) (AUS) **4433**

• Australia. Bureau of Statistics. Construction Work Done, Australia, Preliminary (Online) (AUS) **4433**

• Australia. Bureau of Statistics. Consultant Engineering Services, Australia (Online) (AUS) **3228**

Australia. Bureau of Statistics. Consultant Engineering Services, Australia (Print) *see* Australia. Bureau of Statistics. Consultant Engineering Services, Australia (Online) **3228**

• Australia. Bureau of Statistics. Consumer Price Index, Australia (Online) (AUS) **1203**

• Australia. Bureau of Statistics. Consumer Price Index: Concordance with Household Expenditure Classification, Australia (Online) (AUS) **1203**

Australia. Bureau of Statistics. Consumer Price Index: Concordance with Household Expenditure Classification, Australia (Print) *see* Australia. Bureau of Statistics. Consumer Price Index: Concordance with Household Expenditure Classification, Australia (Online) **1203**

• Australia. Bureau of Statistics. Consumer Price Index Standard Data Report: Capital Cities Index Numbers by Expenditure Class (AUS) **1203**

• Australia. Bureau of Statistics. Corrective Services, Australia (Online) (AUS) **4820**

• Australia. Bureau of Statistics. Crime and Safety, Australia (Online) (AUS) **2672**

Australia. Bureau of Statistics. Crime and Safety, Australia (Print) *see* Australia. Bureau of Statistics. Crime and Safety, Australia (Online) **2672**

• Australia. Bureau of Statistics. Criminal Courts, Australia (Online) (AUS) **4821**

Australia. Bureau of Statistics. Criminal Courts, Australia (Print) *see* Australia. Bureau of Statistics. Criminal Courts, Australia (Online) **4821**

• Australia. Bureau of Statistics. Cultural Funding by Government, Australia (Online) (AUS) **529**

Australia. Bureau of Statistics. Cultural Industries, Australia, Preliminary (AUS) **1203**

Australia. Bureau of Statistics. Deaths, Australia (Online) (AUS) **7298**

• Australia. Bureau of Statistics. Deaths Due to Diseases and Cancers of the Respiratory System, Australia (Online) (AUS) **5740**

Australia. Bureau of Statistics. Deaths Due to Diseases and Cancers of the Respiratory System, Australia (Print) *see* Australia. Bureau of Statistics. Deaths Due to Diseases and Cancers of the Respiratory System, Australia (Online) **5740**

• Australia. Bureau of Statistics. Demographic Variables (AUS) **7298**

† • Australia. Bureau of Statistics. Demography, Australian Capital Territory (Online) (AUS) **8932**

• Australia. Bureau of Statistics. Dental Services, Australia (Online) (AUS) **5740**

Australia. Bureau of Statistics. Detailed Industry Performance, Incorporating Business Income Tax Data, Australia (AUS) **1203**

• Australia. Bureau of Statistics. Directory of Agricultural and Rural Statistics (Online) (AUS) **175**

Australia. Bureau of Statistics. Directory of Capital Expenditure Data Sources and Related Statistics (AUS) **1203**

• Australia. Bureau of Statistics. Directory of Census Statistics (Online) (AUS) **7298**

• Australia. Bureau of Statistics. Directory of Child and Family Statistics (Online) (AUS) **7299**

Australia. Bureau of Statistics. Directory of Construction Statistics (AUS) **1044**

• Australia. Bureau of Statistics. Directory of Culture and Leisure Statistics - Web Site Version (AUS) **8217**

• Australia. Bureau of Statistics. Directory of Electricity, Gas, Water and Sewerage Statistics (Online) (AUS) **3155**

• Australia. Bureau of Statistics. Directory of Energy Statistics (Online) (AUS) **3151**

Australia. Bureau of Statistics. Directory of Housing Related Statistics (AUS ISSN 1032-0865) **4433**

• Australia. Bureau of Statistics. Directory of Industrial Relations Statistics (Online) (AUS) **1203**

• Australia. Bureau of Statistics. Directory of Labour Market and Social Survey Data (Online) (AUS) **1203**

• Australia. Bureau of Statistics. Directory of Mining Statistics (Online) (AUS) **6484**

• Australia. Bureau of Statistics. Directory of Superannuation Related Statistics (AUS) **1203**

• Australia. Bureau of Statistics. Directory of Tourism Statistics (Online) (AUS) **8777**

• Australia. Bureau of Statistics. Directory of Transport Statistics (Online) (AUS) **8521**

† • Australia. Bureau of Statistics. Directory of Transport Statistics (Print) (AUS) **8932**

• Australia. Bureau of Statistics. Disability, Ageing and Carers, Australia: Disability and Long-term Health Conditions (Online) (AUS) **8080**

Australia. Bureau of Statistics. Disability, Ageing and Carers, Australia: Disability and Long-term Health Conditions (Print) *see* Australia. Bureau of Statistics. Disability, Ageing and Carers, Australia: Disability and Long-term Health Conditions (Online) **8080**

• Australia. Bureau of Statistics. Disability, Ageing and Carers, Australia: Hearing Impairment (Online) (AUS) **8080**

Australia. Bureau of Statistics. Disability, Ageing and Carers, Australia: Hearing Impairment (Print) *see* Australia. Bureau of Statistics. Disability, Ageing and Carers, Australia: Hearing Impairment (Online) **8080**

• Australia. Bureau of Statistics. Disability, Ageing and Carers, Australia: Summary of Findings (Online) (AUS) **8080**

Australia. Bureau of Statistics. Disability, Ageing and Carers, Australia: Summary of Findings (Print) *see* Australia. Bureau of Statistics. Disability, Ageing and Carers, Australia: Summary of Findings (Online) **8080**

• Australia. Bureau of Statistics. Disability, Ageing and Carers, Australia: Visual Impairment (Online) (AUS) **8080**

Australia. Bureau of Statistics. Disability, Ageing and Carers, Australia: Visual Impairment (Print) *see* Australia. Bureau of Statistics. Disability, Ageing and Carers, Australia: Visual Impairment (Online) **8080**

• Australia. Bureau of Statistics. Disability, Ageing and Carers, Summary Tables, Australian Capital Territory (Online) (AUS) **8080**

Australia. Bureau of Statistics. Disability, Ageing and Carers, Summary Tables, Australian Capital Territory (Print) *see* Australia. Bureau of Statistics. Disability, Ageing and Carers, Summary Tables, Australian Capital Territory (Online) **8080**

• Australia. Bureau of Statistics. Disability, Ageing and Carers: User Guide, Australia (Online) (AUS) **8080**

Australia. Bureau of Statistics. Disability, Ageing and Carers: User Guide, Australia (Print) *see* Australia. Bureau of Statistics. Disability, Ageing and Carers: User Guide, Australia (Online) **8080**

• Australia. Bureau of Statistics. Disability and Disabling Conditions (Online) (AUS) **8080**

Australia. Bureau of Statistics. Disability and Disabling Conditions (Print) *see* Australia. Bureau of Statistics. Disability and Disabling Conditions (Online) **8080**

• Australia. Bureau of Statistics. Education and Training Experience, Australia (Online) (AUS) **1203**

Australia. Bureau of Statistics. Education and Training Experience, Australia (Print) *see* Australia. Bureau of Statistics. Education and Training Experience, Australia (Online) **1203**

• Australia. Bureau of Statistics. Education and Training Indicators, Australia (Online) (AUS) **2930**

Australia. Bureau of Statistics. Education and Training Indicators, Australia (Print) *see* Australia. Bureau of Statistics. Education and Training Indicators, Australia (Online) **2930**

• Australia. Bureau of Statistics. Education and Work, Australia (Online) (AUS) **6706**

• Australia. Bureau of Statistics. Electricity, Gas, Water and Waste Services, Australia (Online) (AUS) **3151**

• Australia. Bureau of Statistics. Employee Earnings and Hours, Australia (Online) (AUS) **1203**

• Australia. Bureau of Statistics. Employee Earnings and Hours, Australia, Preliminary (Online) (AUS) **1203**

Australia. Bureau of Statistics. Employee Earnings and Hours, States and Australia - Data Service (AUS) **1203**

• Australia. Bureau of Statistics. Employee Earnings, Benefits and Trade Union Membership, Australia (Online) (AUS) **1203**

• Australia. Bureau of Statistics. Employer Training Expenditure and Practices, Australia (Online) (AUS) **1203**

Australia. Bureau of Statistics. Employer Training Expenditure and Practices, Australia (Print) *see* Australia. Bureau of Statistics. Employer Training Expenditure and Practices, Australia (Online) **1203**

Australia. Bureau of Statistics. Employment Arrangements and Superannuation, Australia (Print) *see* Australia. Bureau of Statistics. Employment Arrangements, Retirement and Superannuation, Australia **1203**

• Australia. Bureau of Statistics. Employment Arrangements, Retirement and Superannuation, Australia (AUS) **1203**

• Australia. Bureau of Statistics. Employment in Culture, Australia (Online) (AUS) **1203**

• Australia. Bureau of Statistics. Employment in Selected Sport and Recreation Occupations, Australia (Online) (AUS) **1203**

• Australia. Bureau of Statistics. Employment in Sport and Recreation, Australia (Online) (AUS) **8218**

• Australia. Bureau of Statistics. Employment Services, Australia (Online) (AUS) **1203**

• Australia. Bureau of Statistics. Engineering Construction Activity, Australia (Online) (AUS) **1044**

• Australia. Bureau of Statistics. Environment Expenditure, Local Government, Australia (Online) (AUS) **3477**

Australia. Bureau of Statistics. Environment Expenditure, Local Government, Australia (Print) *see* Australia. Bureau of Statistics. Environment Expenditure, Local Government, Australia (Online) **3477**

† Australia. Bureau of Statistics. Environment Protection Expenditure, Australia (AUS) **8932**

• Australia. Bureau of Statistics. Environment Protection, Mining and Manufacturing Industries, Australia (Online) (AUS) **3477**

Australia. Bureau of Statistics. Environment Protection, Mining and Manufacturing Industries, Australia (Print) *see* Australia. Bureau of Statistics. Environment Protection, Mining and Manufacturing Industries, Australia (Online) **3477**

† • Australia. Bureau of Statistics. Environmental Issues: People's Views and Practices (Online) (AUS) **8932**

Australia. Bureau of Statistics. Environmental Issues: People's Views and Practices (Print) *see* Australia. Bureau of Statistics. Environmental Issues: People's Views and Practices (Online) **8932**

Australia. Bureau of Statistics. Experimental Estimates and Projections of Indigenous Australians (AUS) **7299**

• Australia. Bureau of Statistics. Experimental Estimates, Australian Industry, a State Perspective (Online) (AUS) **1203**

• Australia. Bureau of Statistics. Experimental Estimates of the Aboriginal and Torres Strait Islander Population (Online) (AUS) **7299**

Australia. Bureau of Statistics. Experimental Estimates of the Aboriginal and Torres Strait Islander Population (Print) *see* Australia. Bureau of Statistics. Experimental Estimates of the Aboriginal and Torres Strait Islander Population (Online) **7299**

• Australia. Bureau of Statistics. Experimental Estimates, Regional Small Business Statistics, Australia (Online) (AUS) **1204**

Title

• Australia. Bureau of Statistics. Information Paper: Quality of Australian Balance of Payments Statistics (Online) (AUS) **1206**
Australia. Bureau of Statistics. Information Paper: Questionnaires in the Labour Force (AUS) **1206**
• Australia. Bureau of Statistics. Information Paper: Regional Labour Force Statistics (Online) (AUS) **1206**
• Australia. Bureau of Statistics. Information Paper: Review of the Import Price Index and Export Price Index, Australia (Online) (AUS) **1206**
• Australia. Bureau of Statistics. Information Paper: Seasonal Influences on Retail Trade (Online) (AUS) **1206**
• Australia. Bureau of Statistics. Information Paper: Upgraded Australian National Accounts (Online) (AUS) **1206**
Australia. Bureau of Statistics. Information Paper: Upgraded Australian National Accounts (Print) *see* Australia. Bureau of Statistics. Information Paper: Upgraded Australian National Accounts (Online) **1206**
• Australia. Bureau of Statistics. Information Paper: Upgraded Australian National Accounts: Financial Accounts (Online) (AUS) **1206**
Australia. Bureau of Statistics. Information Paper: Upgraded Australian National Accounts: Financial Accounts (Print) *see* Australia. Bureau of Statistics. Information Paper: Upgraded Australian National Accounts: Financial Accounts (Online) **1206**
Australia. Bureau of Statistics. Information Paper: Upgraded Balance of Payments and International Investment Position Statistics (Online) (AUS) **1206**
Australia. Bureau of Statistics. Information Paper: Use of Business Income Tax Data for Regional Small Business Statistics — Experimental Estimates, Selected Regions, Australia *see* Australia. Bureau of Statistics. Experimental Estimates, Regional Small Business Statistics, Australia (Online) **1204**
• Australia. Bureau of Statistics. Information Paper: Use of Individual Income Tax Data for Regional Statistics (Online) (AUS) **1206**
Australia. Bureau of Statistics. Information Paper: Use of Individual Income Tax Data for Regional Statistics (Print) *see* Australia. Bureau of Statistics. Information Paper: Use of Individual Income Tax Data for Regional Statistics (Online) **1206**
Australia. Bureau of Statistics. Information Paper: Using the A S G C Remoteness Structure to Analyse Characteristics of Wage and Salary Earners of Australia (AUS) **1206**
• Australia. Bureau of Statistics. Information Technology, Australia, Preliminary (Online) (AUS) **2442**
Australia. Bureau of Statistics. Injuries, Australia (AUS) **5740**
• Australia. Bureau of Statistics. Innovation in Manufacturing, Australia (Online) (AUS) **1206**
• Australia. Bureau of Statistics. Innovation in Mining, Australia (Online) (AUS) **6484**
• Australia. Bureau of Statistics. Innovation in Selected Industries, Australia (Online) (AUS) **1206**
Australia. Bureau of Statistics. International Health - How Australia Compares (AUS) **8080**
Australia. Bureau of Statistics. International Investment Position. Australia: Australian Securities Held by Nominees on Behalf of Non-residents (AUS) **1206**
• Australia. Bureau of Statistics. International Investment Position, Australia: Supplementary Country Statistics (Online) (AUS) **1206**
† Australia. Bureau of Statistics. International Merchandise Exports, Australia - Electronic Delivery (AUS) **8932**
• Australia. Bureau of Statistics. International Merchandise Imports, Australia (Online) (AUS) **1206**
† Australia. Bureau of Statistics. International Merchandise Trade, Australia (AUS ISSN 1321-3512) **8932**
• Australia. Bureau of Statistics. International Merchandise Trade, Australia: Concepts, Sources and Methods (Online) (AUS) **1207**
Australia. Bureau of Statistics. International Merchandise Trade, Australia: Concepts, Sources and Methods (Print) *see* Australia. Bureau of Statistics. International Merchandise Trade, Australia: Concepts, Sources and Methods (Online) **1207**
Australia. Bureau of Statistics. International Trade, Australia - Information Consultancy Ad Hoc Service (AUS) **1207**
• Australia. Bureau of Statistics. International Trade in Goods and Services, Australia (Online) (AUS) **1207**
Australia. Bureau of Statistics. International Trade in Goods and Services, Australia (Print) *see* Australia. Bureau of Statistics. International Trade in Goods and Services, Australia (Online) **1207**
• Australia. Bureau of Statistics. International Trade in Goods and Services, Australia: Monthly Forward Seasonal Factors (Online) (AUS) **1207**
Australia. Bureau of Statistics. International Trade in Goods and Services, Monthly Forward Seasonal Factors Service, Australia (AUS) **1207**
• Australia. Bureau of Statistics. International Trade Price Indexes, Australia (Online) (AUS) **1207**
• Australia. Bureau of Statistics. Internet Activity, Australia (Online) (AUS) **2442**
• Australia. Bureau of Statistics. Involvement in Organised Sport and Physical Activity, Australia (Online) (AUS) **1207**
Australia. Bureau of Statistics. Involvement in Organised Sport and Physical Activity, Australia (Print) *see* Australia. Bureau of Statistics. Involvement in Organised Sport and Physical Activity, Australia (Online) **1207**
• Australia. Bureau of Statistics. Involvement in Organized Sport and Physical Activity, Australia (Online) (AUS) **8218**
• Australia. Bureau of Statistics. Job Search Experience, Australia (Online) (AUS) **6706**
Australia. Bureau of Statistics. Job Search Experience, Australia (Print) *see* Australia. Bureau of Statistics. Job Search Experience, Australia (Online) **6706**
† • Australia. Bureau of Statistics. Job Vacancies, Australia (Online) (AUS) **8932**
• Australia. Bureau of Statistics. Labour Costs, Australia (Online) (AUS) **1207**
• Australia. Bureau of Statistics. Labour Force, Australia (Online) (AUS) **1207**
† Australia. Bureau of Statistics. Labour Force, Australia, Preliminary (AUS ISSN 1031-038X) **8932**
Australia. Bureau of Statistics. Labour Force, Australia - Preliminary Data on Floppy Disk *see* Australia. Bureau of Statistics. Labour Force, Australia, Preliminary **8932**
Australia. Bureau of Statistics. Labour Force, Australia - Seasonal Factors (AUS ISSN 1443-0045) **1207**
† Australia. Bureau of Statistics. Labour Force, Australia - Standard Tables on Microfiche (AUS) **8932**
• Australia. Bureau of Statistics. Labour Force Experience, Australia (Online) (AUS) **1207**
• Australia. Bureau of Statistics. Labour Force Projections, Australia (Online) (AUS) **1207**
• Australia. Bureau of Statistics. Labour Force, Selected Summary Tables, Australia (Online) (AUS) **1207**
Australia. Bureau of Statistics. Labour Force, Selected Summary Tables, Australia (Print) *see* Australia. Bureau of Statistics. Labour Force, Selected Summary Tables, Australia (Online) **1207**
• Australia. Bureau of Statistics. Labour Force Status and Other Characteristics of Families, Australia (Online) (AUS) **1207**
• Australia. Bureau of Statistics. Labour Force Status and Other Characteristics of Migrants, Australia (Online) (AUS) **1207**
• Australia. Bureau of Statistics. Labour Force Survey Standard Errors (Online) (AUS) **1207**
Australia. Bureau of Statistics. Labour Force Survey Standard Errors (Print) *see* Australia. Bureau of Statistics. Labour Force Survey Standard Errors (Online) **1207**
• Australia. Bureau of Statistics. Labour Mobility, Australia (Online) (AUS) **1207**
• Australia. Bureau of Statistics. Labour Price Index: Concepts, Sources and Methods (AUS) **1207**
• Australia. Bureau of Statistics. Labour Statistics: Concepts, Sources and Methods (Online) (AUS) **1207**
• Australia. Bureau of Statistics. Labour Statistics in Brief, Australia (Online) (AUS) **1207**
Australia. Bureau of Statistics. Legal and Accounting Services, Australia *see* Australia. Bureau of Statistics. Accounting Services, Australia **1201**
• Australia. Bureau of Statistics. Legal Practices, Australia (Online) (AUS) **4821**
• Australia. Bureau of Statistics. Lending Finance, Australia (Online) (AUS) **1208**
Australia. Bureau of Statistics. Libraries, Australia (AUS) **5057**
• Australia. Bureau of Statistics. Livestock and Meat, Australia (Online) (AUS) **175**
• Australia. Bureau of Statistics. Livestock Products, Australia (Online) (AUS) **175**
• Australia. Bureau of Statistics. Locations of Work, Australia (Online) (AUS) **1208**
Australia. Bureau of Statistics. Locations of Work, Australia (Print) *see* Australia. Bureau of Statistics. Locations of Work, Australia (Online) **1208**
Australia. Bureau of Statistics. Managed Funds, Australia (Online) (AUS) **1208**
† Australia. Bureau of Statistics. Manufacturing, Australia (AUS ISSN 1329-4741) **8932**
• Australia. Bureau of Statistics. Manufacturing Industry, Australia (Online) (AUS) **1208**
• Australia. Bureau of Statistics. Manufacturing Industry, Australia, Preliminary (Online) (AUS) **1208**
• Australia. Bureau of Statistics. Manufacturing Production, Australia (Online) (AUS) **1208**
• Australia. Bureau of Statistics. Market Research Services, Australia (Online) (AUS) **1208**
• Australia. Bureau of Statistics. Measuring Australia's Economy (Online) (AUS ISSN 1449-1710) **1208**
• Australia. Bureau of Statistics. Measuring Australia's Progress (Online) (AUS) **1208**
• Australia. Bureau of Statistics. Measuring Wellbeing: Frameworks for Australian Social Statistics (Online) (AUS) **8148**
Australia. Bureau of Statistics. Medical Labour Force (AUS) **5740**
• Australia. Bureau of Statistics. Mental Health and Wellbeing: Profile of Adults, Australia (Online) (AUS) **8080**
• Australia. Bureau of Statistics. Migration, Australia (Online) (AUS) **7299**
Australia. Bureau of Statistics. Migration, Australia (Print) *see* Australia. Bureau of Statistics. Migration, Australia (Online) **7299**
• Australia. Bureau of Statistics. Mineral Account, Australia (Online) (AUS) **2719**
Australia. Bureau of Statistics. Mineral Account, Australia (Print) *see* Australia. Bureau of Statistics. Mineral Account, Australia (Online) **2719**
• Australia. Bureau of Statistics. Mineral and Petroleum Exploration, Australia (Online) (AUS) **6484**
• Australia. Bureau of Statistics. Mining Operations Australia (Online) (AUS) **6485**
Australia. Bureau of Statistics. Modellers' Database (AUS) **1208**
• Australia. Bureau of Statistics. Motion Picture Exhibition, Australia (Online) (AUS) **6517**
Australia. Bureau of Statistics. Motion Picture Exhibition, Australia (Print) *see* Australia. Bureau of Statistics. Motion Picture Exhibition, Australia (Online) **6517**
• Australia. Bureau of Statistics. Motor Vehicle Census, Australia (Online) (AUS) **8521**
• Australia. Bureau of Statistics. Motor Vehicle Hire Industry, Australia (Online) (AUS) **8521**
Australia. Bureau of Statistics. Motor Vehicle Hire Industry, Australia (Print) *see* Australia. Bureau of Statistics. Motor Vehicle Hire Industry, Australia (Online) **8521**
• Australia. Bureau of Statistics. Multiple Jobholding, Australia (Online) (AUS) **1208**
Australia. Bureau of Statistics. Multiple Jobholding, Australia (Print) *see* Australia. Bureau of Statistics. Multiple Jobholding, Australia (Online) **1208**
• Australia. Bureau of Statistics. Museums, Australia (Online) (AUS) **6541**
† Australia. Bureau of Statistics. N I F - 10S Model Data Base Manual (National Income Forecasting) (AUS ISSN 1031-2641) **8932**
Australia. Bureau of Statistics. N M V R Data on SuperTABLE *see* Australia. Bureau of Statistics. New Motor Vehicle Registration, Australia, Motorcycles Data on SuperTABLE (Online) **8218**
• Australia. Bureau of Statistics. National Aboriginal and Torres Strait Islander Social Survey (AUS) **7299**
Australia. Bureau of Statistics. National Aboriginal and Torres Strait Islander Survey: Unit Record File (Diskette) *see* Australia. Bureau of Statistics. National Aboriginal and Torres Strait Islander Survey: Unit Record File (Online) **7299**
• Australia. Bureau of Statistics. National Aboriginal and Torres Strait Islander Survey: Unit Record File (Online) (AUS) **7299**
• Australia. Bureau of Statistics. National Health Survey: Aboriginal and Torres Strait Islander Results, Australia (Online) (AUS) **7299**
Australia. Bureau of Statistics. National Health Survey: Aboriginal and Torres Strait Islander Results, Australia (Online) *see* Australia. Bureau of Statistics. National Health Survey: Aboriginal and Torres Strait Islander Results, Australia (Online) **7299**
• Australia. Bureau of Statistics. National Health Survey: Asthma and Other Respiratory Conditions, Australia (Online) (AUS) **5740**
Australia. Bureau of Statistics. National Health Survey: Asthma and Other Respiratory Conditions, Australia (Print) *see* Australia. Bureau of Statistics. National Health Survey: Asthma and Other Respiratory Conditions, Australia (Online) **5740**
• Australia. Bureau of Statistics. National Health Survey: Cancer Screening, Australia (Online) (AUS) **5740**
Australia. Bureau of Statistics. National Health Survey: Cancer Screening, Australia (Print) *see* Australia. Bureau of Statistics. National Health Survey: Cancer Screening, Australia (Online) **5740**
• Australia. Bureau of Statistics. National Health Survey: Cardiovascular and Related Conditions, Australia (Online) (AUS) **5740**
Australia. Bureau of Statistics. National Health Survey: Cardiovascular and Related Conditions, Australia (Print) *see* Australia. Bureau of Statistics. National Health Survey: Cardiovascular and Related Conditions, Australia (Online) **5740**
• Australia. Bureau of Statistics. National Health Survey: Diabetes, Australia (Online) (AUS) **5740**
Australia. Bureau of Statistics. National Health Survey: Diabetes, Australia (Print) *see* Australia. Bureau of Statistics. National Health Survey: Diabetes, Australia (Online) **5740**
• Australia. Bureau of Statistics. National Health Survey: Health Risk Factors, Australia (Online) (AUS) **7547**
• Australia. Bureau of Statistics. National Health Survey: Injuries, Australia (Online) (AUS) **7547**
† • Australia. Bureau of Statistics. National Health Survey: Injuries, Australia (Print) (AUS) **8932**
• Australia. Bureau of Statistics. National Health Survey: Private Health Insurance, Australia (Online) (AUS) **4529**
Australia. Bureau of Statistics. National Health Survey: Private Health Insurance, Australia (Print) *see* Australia. Bureau of Statistics. National Health Survey: Private Health Insurance, Australia (Online) **4529**
• Australia. Bureau of Statistics. National Health Survey: SF36 Population Norms, Australia (Online) (AUS) **7299**
Australia. Bureau of Statistics. National Health Survey: SF36 Population Norms, Australia (Print) *see* Australia. Bureau of Statistics. National Health Survey: SF36 Population Norms, Australia (Online) **7299**
• Australia. Bureau of Statistics. National Health Survey: Summary of Results (Online) (AUS) **7547**
† • Australia. Bureau of Statistics. National Health Survey: Summary of Results (Print) (AUS) **8932**
• Australia. Bureau of Statistics. National Health Survey: Use of Medications, Australia (Online) (AUS) **5740**
Australia. Bureau of Statistics. National Health Survey: Use of Medications, Australia (Print) *see* Australia. Bureau of Statistics. National Health Survey: Use of Medications, Australia (Online) **5740**
† • Australia. Bureau of Statistics. National Localities Index, Australia (Online Edition) (AUS) **8932**
• Australia. Bureau of Statistics. National Nutrition Survey: Foods Eaten, Australia (Online) (AUS) **6671**
Australia. Bureau of Statistics. National Nutrition Survey: Foods Eaten, Australia (Print) *see* Australia. Bureau of Statistics. National Nutrition Survey: Foods Eaten, Australia (Online) **6671**
• Australia. Bureau of Statistics. National Nutrition Survey: Nutrient Intakes and Physical Measurements, Australia (Online) (AUS) **6671**
Australia. Bureau of Statistics. National Nutrition Survey: Nutrient Intakes and Physical Measurements, Australia (Print) *see* Australia. Bureau of Statistics. National Nutrition Survey: Nutrient Intakes and Physical Measurements, Australia (Online) **6671**
• Australia. Bureau of Statistics. National Survey of Mental Health and Wellbeing: User's Guide (Online) (AUS) **8080**
• Australia. Bureau of Statistics. Natural Resource Accounting - Australian Energy Accounts (Online) (AUS) **3151**
Australia. Bureau of Statistics. Natural Resource Accounting - Australian Energy Accounts (Print) *see* Australia. Bureau of Statistics. Natural Resource Accounting - Australian Energy Accounts (Online) **3151**
• Australia. Bureau of Statistics. New Motor Vehicle Registration, Australia, Motorcycles Data on SuperTABLE (Online) (AUS) **8218**
Australia. Bureau of Statistics. New Motor Vehicle Registration, Australia, Motorcycles Data on SuperTABLE (Print) *see* Australia. Bureau of Statistics. New Motor Vehicle Registration, Australia, Motorcycles Data on SuperTABLE (Online) **8218**
• Australia. Bureau of Statistics. New South Wales Office. Australian Housing Survey: New South Wales - Data Report (Online) (AUS) **7299**
Australia. Bureau of Statistics. New South Wales Office. Australian Housing Survey: New South Wales - Data Report on Hardcopy *see* Australia. Bureau of Statistics. New South Wales Office. Australian Housing Survey: New South Wales - Data Report (Online) **7299**
• Australia. Bureau of Statistics. New South Wales Office. Census of Population and Housing: Aboriginal and Torres Strait Islander People, New South Wales (Online) (AUS) **7299**
Australia. Bureau of Statistics. New South Wales Office. Census of Population and Housing: Aboriginal and Torres Strait Islander People, New South Wales (Print) *see* Australia. Bureau of Statistics. New South Wales Office. Census of Population and Housing: Aboriginal and Torres Strait Islander People, New South Wales (Online) **7299**
† • Australia. Bureau of Statistics. New South Wales Office. Census of Population and Housing: CDATA2001, New South Wales - Full GIS (AUS) **8932**
† Australia. Bureau of Statistics. New South Wales Office. Census of Population and Housing: CDATA2001 - Quickbuild, New South Wales (AUS) **8932**
• Australia. Bureau of Statistics. New South Wales Office. Census of Population and Housing: Census Basics, New South Wales (AUS) **7299**
• Australia. Bureau of Statistics. New South Wales Office. Census of Population and Housing: Selected Characteristics for Urban Centres and Localities, New South Wales and Australian Capital Territory (Online) (AUS) **7299**

Australia. Bureau of Statistics. New South Wales Office. Census of Population and Housing: Selected Characteristics for Urban Centres and Localities, New South Wales and Australian Capital Territory (Print) see Australia. Bureau of Statistics. New South Wales Office. Census of Population and Housing: Selected Characteristics for Urban Centres and Localities, New South Wales and Australian Capital Territory (Online) **7299**

• Australia. Bureau of Statistics. New South Wales Office. Census of Population and Housing: Selected Education and Labour Force Characteristics for Statistical Local Areas, New South Wales and Jervis Bay (Online) (AUS) **7300**

Australia. Bureau of Statistics. New South Wales Office. Census of Population and Housing: Selected Education and Labour Force Characteristics for Statistical Local Areas, New South Wales and Jervis Bay (Print) see Australia. Bureau of Statistics. New South Wales Office. Census of Population and Housing: Selected Education and Labour Force Characteristics for Statistical Local Areas, New South Wales and Jervis Bay (Online) **7300**

† • Australia. Bureau of Statistics. New South Wales Office. Census of Population and Housing: Selected Social and Housing Characteristics for Statistical Local Areas, New South Wales and Jervis Bay (AUS) **8932**

† • Australia. Bureau of Statistics. New South Wales Office. Census of Population and Housing: Socio-Economic Indexes for Areas, New South Wales (AUS) **8932**

• Australia. Bureau of Statistics. New South Wales Office. Child Care, New South Wales, Data Report (Online) (AUS) **8081**

Australia. Bureau of Statistics. New South Wales Office. Child Care, New South Wales, Data Report Hardcopy *see* Australia. Bureau of Statistics. New South Wales Office. Child Care, New South Wales, Data Report (Online) **8081**

• Australia. Bureau of Statistics. New South Wales Office. Crime and Safety, New South Wales (Online) (AUS) **4821**

† • Australia. Bureau of Statistics. New South Wales Office. Demography, New South Wales (Online) (AUS) **8932**

Australia. Bureau of Statistics. New South Wales Office. Demography, New South Wales (Print) *see* Australia. Bureau of Statistics. New South Wales Office. Demography, New South Wales (Online) **8932**

• Australia. Bureau of Statistics. New South Wales Office. Disability, Ageing and Carers, Summary Tables, New South Wales (Online) (AUS) **8081**

Australia. Bureau of Statistics. New South Wales Office. Disability, Ageing and Carers, Summary Tables, New South Wales (Print) *see* Australia. Bureau of Statistics. New South Wales Office. Disability, Ageing and Carers, Summary Tables, New South Wales (Online) **8081**

• Australia. Bureau of Statistics. New South Wales Office. Disability, New South Wales (Online) (AUS) **8081**

• Australia. Bureau of Statistics. New South Wales Office. Government Financial Estimates, New South Wales, Electronic Delivery (AUS) **1208**

• Australia. Bureau of Statistics. New South Wales Office. Home Security Precautions, New South Wales (Online) (AUS) **2672**

Australia. Bureau of Statistics. New South Wales Office. Home Security Precautions, New South Wales (Print) *see* Australia. Bureau of Statistics. New South Wales Office. Home Security Precautions, New South Wales (Online) **2672**

• Australia. Bureau of Statistics. New South Wales Office. Manufacturing Industry, New South Wales and Australian Capital Territory (Online) (AUS) **1208**

• Australia. Bureau of Statistics. New South Wales Office. Mental Health and Wellbeing: Profile of Adults, New South Wales, Data Report (AUS) **8081**

• Australia. Bureau of Statistics. New South Wales Office. New South Wales at a Glance (Online) (AUS) **7300**

Australia. Bureau of Statistics. New South Wales Office. New South Wales' Young People (AUS) **7617**

• Australia. Bureau of Statistics. New South Wales Office. Older People, New South Wales (Online) (AUS) **8081**

Australia. Bureau of Statistics. New South Wales Office. Older People, New South Wales (Print) *see* Australia. Bureau of Statistics. New South Wales Office. Older People, New South Wales (Online) **8081**

† • Australia. Bureau of Statistics. New South Wales Office. Population by Age and Sex, New South Wales - Electronic Delivery (AUS) **8932**

Australia. Bureau of Statistics. New South Wales Office. Retailing in New South Wales *see* Australia. Bureau of Statistics. New South Wales Office. Retailing in New South Wales (Online) **1208**

• Australia. Bureau of Statistics. New South Wales Office. Retailing in New South Wales (Online) (AUS) **1208**

• Australia. Bureau of Statistics. New South Wales Office. Sydney. A Social Atlas (AUS) **7300**

• Australia. Bureau of Statistics. New South Wales Office. Tourist Accommodation, Small Area Data, New South Wales (Online) (AUS) **4401**

• Australia. Bureau of Statistics. Northern Territory Office. Census of Population and Housing: Aboriginal and Torres Strait Islander People, Northern Territory (Online) (AUS) **7300**

Australia. Bureau of Statistics. Northern Territory Office. Census of Population and Housing: Aboriginal and Torres Strait Islander People, Northern Territory (Print) *see* Australia. Bureau of Statistics. Northern Territory Office. Census of Population and Housing: Aboriginal and Torres Strait Islander People, Northern Territory (Online) **7300**

† • Australia. Bureau of Statistics. Northern Territory Office. Census of Population and Housing: CDATA2001, Northern Territory - Full GIS (AUS) **8932**

† • Australia. Bureau of Statistics. Northern Territory Office. Census of Population and Housing: CDATA2001 - Quickbuild, Northern Territory (AUS) **8932**

• Australia. Bureau of Statistics. Northern Territory Office. Census of Population and Housing: Census Basics, Northern Territory (AUS) **7300**

† • Australia. Bureau of Statistics. Northern Territory Office. Census of Population and Housing: Population Summary, Northern Territory (Online) (AUS) **8932**

Australia. Bureau of Statistics. Northern Territory Office. Census of Population and Housing: Population Summary, Northern Territory (Print) *see* Australia. Bureau of Statistics. Northern Territory Office. Census of Population and Housing: Population Summary, Northern Territory (Online) **8932**

• Australia. Bureau of Statistics. Northern Territory Office. Census of Population and Housing: Selected Characteristics for Urban Centres and Localities, Northern Territory (Online) (AUS) **7300**

Australia. Bureau of Statistics. Northern Territory Office. Census of Population and Housing: Selected Characteristics for Urban Centres and Localities, Northern Territory (Print) *see* Australia. Bureau of Statistics. Northern Territory Office. Census of Population and Housing: Selected Characteristics for Urban Centres and Localities, Northern Territory (Online) **7300**

• Australia. Bureau of Statistics. Northern Territory Office. Census of Population and Housing: Selected Education and Labour Force Characteristics for Statistical Local Areas, Northern Territory (Online) (AUS) **7300**

Australia. Bureau of Statistics. Northern Territory Office. Census of Population and Housing: Selected Education and Labour Force Characteristics for Statistical Local Areas, Northern Territory (Print) see Australia. Bureau of Statistics. Northern Territory Office. Census of Population and Housing: Selected Education and Labour Force Characteristics for Statistical Local Areas, Northern Territory (Online) **7300**

• Australia. Bureau of Statistics. Northern Territory Office. Census of Population and Housing: Selected Social and Housing Characteristics for Statistical Local Areas, Northern Territory (Online) (AUS) **7300**

• Australia. Bureau of Statistics. Northern Territory Office. Census of Population and Housing: Socio-Economic Indexes for Areas, Northern Territory (AUS) **7300**

• Australia. Bureau of Statistics. Northern Territory Office. Darwin and Palmerston. A Social Atlas (AUS) **7300**

† • Australia. Bureau of Statistics. Northern Territory Office. Demography, Northern Territory (Online) (AUS) **8932**

• Australia. Bureau of Statistics. Northern Territory Office. Disability, Ageing and Carers, Summary Tables, Northern Territory (Online) (AUS) **8081**

Australia. Bureau of Statistics. Northern Territory Office. Disability, Ageing and Carers, Summary Tables, Northern Territory (Print) *see* Australia. Bureau of Statistics. Northern Territory Office. Disability, Ageing and Carers, Summary Tables, Northern Territory (Online) **8081**

• Australia. Bureau of Statistics. Northern Territory Office. Government Financial Estimates, Northern Territory, Electronic Delivery (AUS) **1208**

• Australia. Bureau of Statistics. Northern Territory Office. National Health Survey: Darwin-Palmerston and Alice Springs (Online) (AUS) **7547**

Australia. Bureau of Statistics. Northern Territory Office. National Health Survey: Darwin-Palmerston and Alice Springs (Print) *see* Australia. Bureau of Statistics. Northern Territory Office. National Health Survey: Darwin-Palmerston and Alice Springs (Online) **7547**

• Australia. Bureau of Statistics. Northern Territory Office. Northern Territory at a Glance (Online) (AUS) **8352**

Australia. Bureau of Statistics. Northern Territory Office. Northern Territory at a Glance (Print) *see* Australia. Bureau of Statistics. Northern Territory Office. Northern Territory at a Glance (Online) **8352**

• Australia. Bureau of Statistics. Northern Territory Office. Northern Territory's Young People (Online) (AUS) **7617**

Australia. Bureau of Statistics. Northern Territory Office. Northern Territory's Young People (Print) *see* Australia. Bureau of Statistics. Northern Territory Office. Northern Territory's Young People (Online) **7617**

• Australia. Bureau of Statistics. Northern Territory Office. Population Projections, Northern Territory (Online) (AUS) **7300**

Australia. Bureau of Statistics. Northern Territory Office. Population Projections, Northern Territory (Print) *see* Australia. Bureau of Statistics. Northern Territory Office. Population Projections, Northern Territory (Online) **7300**

• Australia. Bureau of Statistics. Northern Territory Office. Regional Statistics, Northern Territory (Online) (AUS) **7300**

• Australia. Bureau of Statistics. Northern Territory Office. Tourist Accommodation, Small Area Data, Northern Territory (Online) (AUS) **4401**

• Australia. Bureau of Statistics. Occasional Paper: A Risk Index Approach to Unemployment - An Application Using the Survey of Employment and Unemployment Patterns (Online) (AUS) **1208**

Australia. Bureau of Statistics. Occasional Paper: A Risk Index Approach to Unemployment - An Application Using the Survey of Employment and Unemployment Patterns (Print) *see* Australia. Bureau of Statistics. Occasional Paper: A Risk Index Approach to Unemployment - An Application Using the Survey of Employment and Unemployment Patterns (Online) **1208**

• Australia. Bureau of Statistics. Occasional Paper: Australian Business Register - A Snapshot (Online) (AUS) **1208**

Australia. Bureau of Statistics. Occasional Paper: Australian Business Register - A Snapshot (Print) *see* Australia. Bureau of Statistics. Occasional Paper: Australian Business Register - A Snapshot (Online) **1208**

• Australia. Bureau of Statistics. Occasional Paper: Cigarette Smoking among Indigenous Australians (Online) (AUS) **7001**

Australia. Bureau of Statistics. Occasional Paper: Cigarette Smoking among Indigenous Australians (Print) *see* Australia. Bureau of Statistics. Occasional Paper: Cigarette Smoking among Indigenous Australians (Online) **7001**

Australia. Bureau of Statistics. Occasional Paper: Dynamics of Earned Income - An Application Using the S E U P *see* Australia. Bureau of Statistics. Occasional Paper: Dynamics of Earned Income - An Application Using the Survey of Employment and Unemployment Patterns (Online) **1209**

• Australia. Bureau of Statistics. Occasional Paper: Dynamics of Earned Income - An Application Using the Survey of Employment and Unemployment Patterns (Online) (AUS) **1209**

• Australia. Bureau of Statistics. Occasional Paper: Hospital Statistics, Aboriginal and Torres Strait Islander Australians (Online) (AUS) **4113**

Australia. Bureau of Statistics. Occasional Paper: Hospital Statistics, Aboriginal and Torres Strait Islander Australians (Print) *see* Australia. Bureau of Statistics. Occasional Paper: Hospital Statistics, Aboriginal and Torres Strait Islander Australians (Online) **4113**

Australia. Bureau of Statistics. Occasional Paper: Indigenous Languages, Australia (AUS) **5200**

Australia. Bureau of Statistics. Occasional Paper: Innovation, Productivity and Profitability of Australian Manufacturers (AUS) **2442**

• Australia. Bureau of Statistics. Occasional Paper: Job Quality and Churning of the Pool of the Unemployed (Online) (AUS) **1209**

Australia. Bureau of Statistics. Occasional Paper: Job Quality and Churning of the Pool of the Unemployed (Print) *see* Australia. Bureau of Statistics. Occasional Paper: Job Quality and Churning of the Pool of the Unemployed (Online) **1209**

• Australia. Bureau of Statistics. Occasional Paper: Labour Force Characteristics of Aboriginal and Torres Strait Islander Australians (Online) (AUS) **1209**

• Australia. Bureau of Statistics. Occasional Paper: Labour Market Dynamics in Australia - An Application Using the Survey of Employment and Unemployment Patterns (Online) (AUS) **1209**

• Australia. Bureau of Statistics. Occasional Paper: Labour Market Outcomes of Low Paid Adult Workers (Online) (AUS) **1209**

• Australia. Bureau of Statistics. Occasional Paper: Labour Market Programs, Unemployment and Employment Hazards (Online) (AUS) **1209**

Australia. Bureau of Statistics. Occasional Paper: Labour Market Programs, Unemployment and Employment Hazards (Print) *see* Australia. Bureau of Statistics. Occasional Paper: Labour Market Programs, Unemployment and Employment Hazards (Online) **1209**

• Australia. Bureau of Statistics. Occasional Paper: Mortality of Indigenous Australians (Online) (AUS) **7617**

Australia. Bureau of Statistics. Occasional Paper: Mortality of Indigenous Australians (Print) *see* Australia. Bureau of Statistics. Occasional Paper: Mortality of Indigenous Australians (Online) **7617**

• Australia. Bureau of Statistics. Occasional Paper: Overweight and Obesity, Indigenous Australians (Online) (AUS) **7001**

Australia. Bureau of Statistics. Occasional Paper: Overweight and Obesity, Indigenous Australians (Print) *see* Australia. Bureau of Statistics. Occasional Paper: Overweight and Obesity, Indigenous Australians (Online) **7001**

• Australia. Bureau of Statistics. Occasional Paper: Population Issues, Indigenous Australians (Online) (AUS) **7300**

Australia. Bureau of Statistics. Occasional Paper: Population Issues, Indigenous Australians (Print) *see* Australia. Bureau of Statistics. Occasional Paper: Population Issues, Indigenous Australians (Online) **7300**

† Australia. Bureau of Statistics. Occasional Paper: Recent Changes in Unpaid Work (AUS) **8932**

• Australia. Bureau of Statistics. Occasional Paper: Self-Assessed Health Status, Indigenous Australians (Online) (AUS) **7001**

Australia. Bureau of Statistics. Occasional Paper: Self-Assessed Health Status, Indigenous Australians (Print) *see* Australia. Bureau of Statistics. Occasional Paper: Self-Assessed Health Status, Indigenous Australians (Online) **7001**

Australia. Bureau of Statistics. Occasional Paper: The Dynamics of Welfare Receipt and Labour Market Status (AUS) **1209**

• Australia. Bureau of Statistics. Older People, Australia: A Social Report (Online) (AUS) **8081**

• Australia. Bureau of Statistics. Optometry and Optical Dispensing Services, Australia (Online) (AUS) **5741**

Australia. Bureau of Statistics. Optometry and Optical Dispensing Services, Australia (Print) *see* Australia. Bureau of Statistics. Optometry and Optical Dispensing Services, Australia (Online) **5741**

• Australia. Bureau of Statistics. Origin of Guests, Australia (Online) (AUS) **8777**

• Australia. Bureau of Statistics. Overseas Arrivals and Departures, Australia (Monthly) (Online) (AUS) **7300**

• Australia. Bureau of Statistics. Performing Arts, Australia (Online) (AUS) **8485**

Australia. Bureau of Statistics. Performing Arts Industry, Australia (Print) *see* Australia. Bureau of Statistics. Performing Arts, Australia (Online) **8485**

• Australia. Bureau of Statistics. Persons Not in the Labour Force, Australia (Online) (AUS) **1209**

• Australia. Bureau of Statistics. Physiotherapy Services, Australia (Online) (AUS) **5741**

• Australia. Bureau of Statistics. Population by Age and Sex, Australian States and Territories (Online) (AUS) **7300**

• Australia. Bureau of Statistics. Population Characteristics, Aboriginal and Torres Strait Islander Australians (Online) (AUS) **7300**

Australia. Bureau of Statistics. Population Characteristics, Aboriginal and Torres Strait Islander Australians (Print) *see* Australia. Bureau of Statistics. Population Characteristics, Aboriginal and Torres Strait Islander Australians (Online) **7300**

• Australia. Bureau of Statistics. Population Distribution, Aboriginal and Torres Strait Islander Australians (Online) (AUS) **7300**

Australia. Bureau of Statistics. Population Distribution, Aboriginal and Torres Strait Islander Australians (Print) *see* Australia. Bureau of Statistics. Population Distribution, Aboriginal and Torres Strait Islander Australians (Online) **7300**

Australia. Bureau of Statistics. Population Distribution, Australia (AUS) **7300**

• Australia. Bureau of Statistics. Population Projections, Australia (Online) (AUS) **7300**

Australia. Bureau of Statistics. Postal Area to Statistical Local Area Concordance, Australia (AUS) **2346**

• Australia. Bureau of Statistics. Principal Agricultural Commodities, Australia, Preliminary (Online) (AUS) **175**

• Australia. Bureau of Statistics. Private Hospitals, Australia (Online) (AUS) **4113**

• Australia. Bureau of Statistics. Private Medical Practices, Australia (Online) (AUS) **5741**

Australia. Bureau of Statistics. Private Medical Practices, Australia (Print) *see* Australia. Bureau of Statistics. Private Medical Practices, Australia (Online) **5741**

• Australia. Bureau of Statistics. Private Medical Practitioners, Australia (Online) (AUS) **5741**

Australia. Bureau of Statistics. Private Medical Practitioners, Australia (Print) *see* Australia. Bureau of Statistics. Private Medical Practitioners, Australia (Online) **5741**

• Australia. Bureau of Statistics. Private New Capital Expenditure and Expected Expenditure, Australia (Online) (AUS) **1209**

• Australia. Bureau of Statistics. Private Sector Construction Industry, Australia (Online) (AUS) **1044**

10000 AUSTRALIA. BUREAU OF STATISTICS. PRIVATE SECTOR CONSTRUCTION ULRICH'S PERIODICALS

• Australia. Bureau of Statistics. Private Sector Construction Industry, Australia, Preliminary (AUS) **1044**

• Australia. Bureau of Statistics. Producer Price Indexes, Australia (Online) (AUS) **1209**

• Australia. Bureau of Statistics. Public Libraries, Australia (Online) (AUS) **6541**

Australia. Bureau of Statistics. Public Libraries, Australia (Print) *see* Australia. Bureau of Statistics. Public Libraries, Australia (Online) **6541**

• Australia. Bureau of Statistics. Queensland Office. Brisbane. A Social Atlas (AUS) **7300**

Australia. Bureau of Statistics. Queensland Office. Cattle Breeds, Queensland (AUS) **175**

• Australia. Bureau of Statistics. Queensland Office. Census of Population and Housing: Aboriginal and Torres Strait Islander People, Queensland (Online) (AUS) **7300**

Australia. Bureau of Statistics. Queensland Office. Census of Population and Housing: Aboriginal and Torres Strait Islander People, Queensland (Print) *see* Australia. Bureau of Statistics. Queensland Office. Census of Population and Housing: Aboriginal and Torres Strait Islander People, Queensland (Online) **7300**

• Australia. Bureau of Statistics. Queensland Office. Census of Population and Housing: CDATA2001, Queensland - Full GIS (AUS) **7301**

• Australia. Bureau of Statistics. Queensland Office. Census of Population and Housing: CDATA2001 - Quickbuild, Queensland (AUS) **7301**

• Australia. Bureau of Statistics. Queensland Office. Census of Population and Housing: Census Basics, Queensland (AUS) **7301**

• Australia. Bureau of Statistics. Queensland Office. Census of Population and Housing: Selected Characteristics for Urban Centres and Localities, Queensland (Online) (AUS) **7301**

Australia. Bureau of Statistics. Queensland Office. Census of Population and Housing: Selected Characteristics for Urban Centres and Localities, Queensland (Print) *see* Australia. Bureau of Statistics. Queensland Office. Census of Population and Housing: Selected Characteristics for Urban Centres and Localities, Queensland (Online) **7301**

• Australia. Bureau of Statistics. Queensland Office. Census of Population and Housing: Selected Education and Labour Force Characteristics for Statistical Local Areas, Queensland (Online) (AUS) **7301**

Australia. Bureau of Statistics. Queensland Office. Census of Population and Housing: Selected Education and Labour Force Characteristics for Statistical Local Areas, Queensland (Print) *see* Australia. Bureau of Statistics. Queensland Office. Census of Population and Housing: Selected Education and Labour Force Characteristics for Statistical Local Areas, Queensland (Online) **7301**

• Australia. Bureau of Statistics. Queensland Office. Census of Population and Housing: Selected Social and Housing Characteristics for Statistical Local Areas, Queensland (Online) (AUS) **7301**

Australia. Bureau of Statistics. Queensland Office. Census of Population and Housing: Selected Social and Housing Characteristics for Statistical Local Areas, Queensland (Print) *see* Australia. Bureau of Statistics. Queensland Office. Census of Population and Housing: Selected Social and Housing Characteristics for Statistical Local Areas, Queensland (Online) **7301**

• Australia. Bureau of Statistics. Queensland Office. Census of Population and Housing: Socio-Economic Indexes for Areas, Queensland (AUS) **7301**

† Australia. Bureau of Statistics. Queensland Office. Demography, Queensland (Online) (AUS) **8933**

Australia. Bureau of Statistics. Queensland Office. Demography, Queensland (Print) *see* Australia. Bureau of Statistics. Queensland Office. Demography, Queensland (Online) **8933**

• Australia. Bureau of Statistics. Queensland Office. Disability, Ageing and Carers, Summary Tables, Queensland (Online) (AUS) **8081**

† Australia. Bureau of Statistics. Queensland Office. Estimated Resident Population: Components of Change, Queensland (AUS ISSN 1031-6264) **8933**

Australia. Bureau of Statistics. Queensland Office. Estimated Resident Population, Queensland (AUS) **7301**

Australia. Bureau of Statistics. Queensland Office. Fertility Trends in Queensland (AUS) **7301**

• Australia. Bureau of Statistics. Queensland Office. Government Financial Estimates, Queensland (Online) (AUS) **1209**

Australia. Bureau of Statistics. Queensland Office. Government Financial Estimates, Queensland (Print) *see* Australia. Bureau of Statistics. Queensland Office. Government Financial Estimates, Queensland (Online) **1209**

Australia. Bureau of Statistics. Queensland Office. Household Expenditure Survey, Queensland (AUS) **4370**

• Australia. Bureau of Statistics. Queensland Office. Manufacturing Industry, Queensland (Online) (AUS) **1209**

Australia. Bureau of Statistics. Queensland Office. Manufacturing Industry, Queensland (Print) *see* Australia. Bureau of Statistics. Queensland Office. Manufacturing Industry, Queensland (Online) **1209**

• Australia. Bureau of Statistics. Queensland Office. Mental Health and Wellbeing: Profile of Adults, Queensland, Data Report (Online) (AUS) **8081**

Australia. Bureau of Statistics. Queensland Office. Migration, Queensland (AUS) **7301**

• Australia. Bureau of Statistics. Queensland Office. National Aboriginal and Torres Strait Islander Survey: Queensland (Online) (AUS) **7301**

• Australia. Bureau of Statistics. Queensland Office. Persons Aged Fifty Years and Over, Queensland (Online) (AUS) **8081**

• Australia. Bureau of Statistics. Queensland Office. Population Mobility, Queensland (Online) (AUS) **7301**

• Australia. Bureau of Statistics. Queensland Office. Queensland at a Glance (Online) (AUS) **8353**

Australia. Bureau of Statistics. Queensland Office. Queensland at a Glance (Print) *see* Australia. Bureau of Statistics. Queensland Office. Queensland at a Glance (Online) **8353**

• Australia. Bureau of Statistics. Queensland Office. Queensland's Young People (Online) (AUS) **7617**

Australia. Bureau of Statistics. Queensland Office. Queensland's Young People (Print) *see* Australia. Bureau of Statistics. Queensland Office. Queensland's Young People (Online) **7617**

Australia. Bureau of Statistics. Queensland Office. Recent Population and Housing Trends in Queensland (AUS ISSN 1036-5001) **7301**

† • Australia. Bureau of Statistics. Queensland Office. Regional Statistics, Queensland (Online) (AUS) **8933**

Australia. Bureau of Statistics. Queensland Office. Regional Statistics, Queensland (Print) *see* Australia. Bureau of Statistics. Queensland Office. Regional Statistics, Queensland (Online) **8933**

Australia. Bureau of Statistics. Queensland Office. Retail Industry: Small Area Statistics, Queensland (AUS) **1209**

• Australia. Bureau of Statistics. Queensland Office. Safety in the Home, Queensland (Online) (AUS) **6671**

Australia. Bureau of Statistics. Queensland Office. Safety in the Home, Queensland (Print) *see* Australia. Bureau of Statistics. Queensland Office. Safety in the Home, Queensland (Online) **6671**

• Australia. Bureau of Statistics. Queensland Office. Tourist Accommodation, Small Area Data, Queensland (Online) (AUS) **4401**

Australia. Bureau of Statistics. Queensland Office. Tourist Accommodation, Small Area Data, Queensland (Print) *see* Australia. Bureau of Statistics. Queensland Office. Tourist Accommodation, Small Area Data, Queensland (Online) **4401**

• Australia. Bureau of Statistics. Queensland Office. Working Hours of Wage and Salary Earners, Queensland (AUS) **1209**

• Australia. Bureau of Statistics. Real Estate Services, Australia (Online) (AUS) **7617**

• Australia. Bureau of Statistics. Regional Population Growth, Australia (AUS ISSN 1833-2498) **7301**

† Australia. Bureau of Statistics. Register of Commonwealth Statistical Collections (AUS ISSN 0818-3856) **8933**

• Australia. Bureau of Statistics. Renters in Australia (Online) (AUS) **7617**

Australia. Bureau of Statistics. Renters in Australia (Print) *see* Australia. Bureau of Statistics. Renters in Australia (Online) **7617**

† Australia. Bureau of Statistics. Research and Experimental Development, All Sector Summary (Inter-Year Survey), Australia (AUS ISSN 0819-9876) **8933**

• Australia. Bureau of Statistics. Research and Experimental Development, All Sector Summary, Australia (Online) (AUS) **8353**

† Australia. Bureau of Statistics. Research and Experimental Development, Business Enterprises, Australia, Preliminary (AUS ISSN 0159-1584) **8933**

• Australia. Bureau of Statistics. Research and Experimental Development, Businesses, Australia (Online) (AUS) **1209**

• Australia. Bureau of Statistics. Research and Experimental Development, Government and Private Non-Profit Organisations, Australia (Online) (AUS) **1209**

Australia. Bureau of Statistics. Research and Experimental Development, Higher Education Organisations, Australia (Online) (AUS) **2930**

• Australia. Bureau of Statistics. Retail and Wholesale Industries, Australia (Online) (AUS) **1209**

Australia. Bureau of Statistics. Retail and Wholesale Industries, Australia (Print) *see* Australia. Bureau of Statistics. Retail and Wholesale Industries, Australia (Online) **1209**

• Australia. Bureau of Statistics. Retail and Wholesale Industries, Australia: Commodities (Online) (AUS) **1209**

Australia. Bureau of Statistics. Retail and Wholesale Industries, Australia: Commodities (Print) *see* Australia. Bureau of Statistics. Retail and Wholesale Industries, Australia: Commodities (Online) **1209**

• Australia. Bureau of Statistics. Retail Industry, State and Territory Summary (Online) (AUS) **1209**

Australia. Bureau of Statistics. Retail Industry, State and Territory Summary (Print) *see* Australia. Bureau of Statistics. Retail Industry, State and Territory Summary (Online) **1209**

• Australia. Bureau of Statistics. Retail Trade, Australia (Online) (AUS) **1209**

† Australia. Bureau of Statistics. Retail Trade, Australia: Commodity Details (AUS ISSN 1031-8046) **8933**

Australia. Bureau of Statistics. Retail Trade Special Data Service: Customised Reports - Data Report (Online) (AUS) **1210**

† Australia. Bureau of Statistics. Retail Trade Special Data Services: Performance Reports - Data Report (AUS) **8933**

† Australia. Bureau of Statistics. Retail Trade Special Data Services: Self Comparison Reports - Data Report (AUS) **8933**

Australia. Bureau of Statistics. Retailing in Australia (AUS) **1210**

• Australia. Bureau of Statistics. Retirement and Retirement Intentions, Australia (Online) (AUS) **1210**

• Australia. Bureau of Statistics. Retrenchment and Redundancy, Australia (Online) (AUS) **1210**

• Australia. Bureau of Statistics. Sales of Australian Wine and Brandy by Winemakers (Online) (AUS) **614**

† • Australia. Bureau of Statistics. Sales of New Motor Vehicles, Electronic Delivery (AUS) **8933**

• Australia. Bureau of Statistics. Salinity on Australian Farms (Online) (AUS) **3477**

Australia. Bureau of Statistics. Salinity on Australian Farms (Print) *see* Australia. Bureau of Statistics. Salinity on Australian Farms (Online) **3477**

• Australia. Bureau of Statistics. Schools, Australia (Online) (AUS) **2930**

• Australia. Bureau of Statistics. Security Services, Australia (Online) (AUS) **2673**

• Australia. Bureau of Statistics. Selected Amusement and Leisure Industries, Australia (Online) (AUS) **8218**

Australia. Bureau of Statistics. Selected Amusement and Leisure Industries, Australia (Print) *see* Australia. Bureau of Statistics. Selected Amusement and Leisure Industries, Australia (Online) **8218**

• Australia. Bureau of Statistics. Selected Business Services, Australia (Online) (AUS) **1210**

Australia. Bureau of Statistics. Selected Business Services, Australia (Print) *see* Australia. Bureau of Statistics. Selected Business Services, Australia (Online) **1210**

• Australia. Bureau of Statistics. Selected Museums, Australia (Online) (AUS) **6541**

† Australia. Bureau of Statistics. Siena Group Papers: Families at the End of the 20th Century - Vol 1 (AUS) **8933**

† Australia. Bureau of Statistics. Siena Group Papers: Family Statistics Country Papers - Vol 2 (AUS) **8933**

† Australia. Bureau of Statistics. Siena Group Papers: Future Directions for the Siena Group - Vol 3 (AUS) **8933**

• Australia. Bureau of Statistics. Small Business in Australia (Online) (AUS) **1210**

† Australia. Bureau of Statistics. Social Indicators, Australia (AUS) **8933**

• Australia. Bureau of Statistics. Sound Recording Studios, Australia (Online) (AUS) **7047**

• Australia. Bureau of Statistics. South Australian Office. Adelaide. A Social Atlas (AUS) **7301**

• Australia. Bureau of Statistics. South Australian Office. Australian Housing Survey: South Australia (AUS) **4434**

Australia. Bureau of Statistics. South Australian Office. Australian Housing Survey: South Australia - Data Report on Hardcopy *see* Australia. Bureau of Statistics. South Australian Office. Australian Housing Survey: South Australia **4434**

• Australia. Bureau of Statistics. South Australian Office. Census of Population and Housing: Aboriginal and Torres Strait Islander People, South Australia (Online) (AUS) **7301**

Australia. Bureau of Statistics. South Australian Office. Census of Population and Housing: Aboriginal and Torres Strait Islander People, South Australia (Print) *see* Australia. Bureau of Statistics. South Australian Office. Census of Population and Housing: Aboriginal and Torres Strait Islander People, South Australia (Online) **7301**

• Australia. Bureau of Statistics. South Australian Office. Census of Population and Housing: CDATA2001, South Australia - Full GIS (AUS) **7301**

• Australia. Bureau of Statistics. South Australian Office. Census of Population and Housing: Census Basics, South Australia (AUS) **7301**

• Australia. Bureau of Statistics. South Australian Office. Census of Population and Housing: Selected Characteristics for Urban Centres and Localities, South Australia (Online) (AUS) **7301**

• Australia. Bureau of Statistics. South Australian Office. Census of Population and Housing: Selected Education and Labour Force Characteristics for Statistical Local Areas, South Australia (Online) (AUS) **7301**

• Australia. Bureau of Statistics. South Australian Office. Census of Population and Housing: Selected Social and Housing Characteristics for Statistical Local Areas, South Australia (Online) (AUS) **7301**

† • Australia. Bureau of Statistics. South Australian Office. Census of Population and Housing: Socio-Economic Indexes for Areas, South Australia (AUS) **8933**

• Australia. Bureau of Statistics. South Australian Office. Crime and Safety, South Australia (Online) (AUS) **2673**

• Australia. Bureau of Statistics. South Australian Office. Disability, Ageing and Carers, Summary Tables, South Australia (Online) (AUS) **8081**

Australia. Bureau of Statistics. South Australian Office. Disability, Ageing and Carers, Summary Tables, South Australia (Print) *see* Australia. Bureau of Statistics. South Australian Office. Disability, Ageing and Carers, Summary Tables, South Australia (Online) **8081**

• Australia. Bureau of Statistics. South Australian Office. Government Financial Estimates, South Australia, Electronic Delivery (AUS) **1210**

• Australia. Bureau of Statistics. South Australian Office. Manufacturing Industry, South Australia (Online) (AUS) **1210**

Australia. Bureau of Statistics. South Australian Office. Manufacturing Industry, South Australia (Print) *see* Australia. Bureau of Statistics. South Australian Office. Manufacturing Industry, South Australia (Online) **1210**

• Australia. Bureau of Statistics. South Australian Office. Mental Health and Wellbeing: Profile of Adults, South Australia, Data Report (Online) (AUS) **8081**

Australia. Bureau of Statistics. South Australian Office. Mental Health and Wellbeing: Profile of Adults, South Australia, Data Report (Print) *see* Australia. Bureau of Statistics. South Australian Office. Mental Health and Wellbeing: Profile of Adults, South Australia, Data Report (Online) **8081**

• Australia. Bureau of Statistics. South Australian Office. Regional Statistics, South Australia (Online) (AUS) **8354**

Australia. Bureau of Statistics. South Australian Office. Regional Statistics, South Australia (Print) *see* Australia. Bureau of Statistics. South Australian Office. Regional Statistics, South Australia (Online) **8354**

• Australia. Bureau of Statistics. South Australian Office. Sales of Goods and Services by Businesses Involved in Water Related Activity in South Australia (Online) (AUS) **1210**

Australia. Bureau of Statistics. South Australian Office. Sales of Goods and Services by Businesses Involved in Water Related Activity in South Australia (Print) *see* Australia. Bureau of Statistics. South Australian Office. Sales of Goods and Services by Businesses Involved in Water Related Activity in South Australia (Online) **1210**

Australia. Bureau of Statistics. South Australian Office. South Australia at a Glance (AUS ISSN 0814-0871) **8354**

• Australia. Bureau of Statistics. South Australian Office. South Australia's Young People (Online) (AUS) **7617**

Australia. Bureau of Statistics. South Australian Office. South Australia's Young People (Print) *see* Australia. Bureau of Statistics. South Australian Office. South Australia's Young People (Online) **7617**

• Australia. Bureau of Statistics. South Australian Office. Tourist Accommodation, Small Area Data, South Australia (Online) (AUS) **8777**

• Australia. Bureau of Statistics. South Australian Office. Travel to Work and Place of Education, Adelaide Statistical Division (Online) (AUS) **8521**

Australia. Bureau of Statistics. South Australian Office. Travel to Work and Place of Education, Adelaide Statistical Division (Print) *see* Australia. Bureau of Statistics. South Australian Office. Travel to Work and Place of Education, Adelaide Statistical Division (Online) **8521**

Australia. Bureau of Statistics. Sport and Recreation: A Statistical Overview, Australia *see* Australia. Bureau of Statistics. Sports and Physical Recreation: A Statistical Overview, Australia **8218**

• Australia. Bureau of Statistics. Sport and Recreation Funding by Government, Australia (Online) (AUS) **8218**

Australia. Bureau of Statistics. Sport and Recreation Funding by Government, Australia (Print) *see* Australia. Bureau of Statistics. Sport and Recreation Funding by Government, Australia (Online) **8218**

• Australia. Bureau of Statistics. Sport, Recreation and Gambling Industries, Australia, Preliminary (Online) (AUS) **8218**

- Australia. Bureau of Statistics. Victorian Office. Victoria in Future: Overview. The Victorian Government's Population Projections (Online) (AUS) 7303
† • Australia. Bureau of Statistics. Victorian Office. Victoria in Future - The Victorian Government's Population Projections for the State's Local Government Areas (AUS) 8933
Australia. Bureau of Statistics. Victorian Office. Victoria in Time - (Year) Census Statistics for Victoria's New Local Government Areas (AUS) 7303
† • Australia. Bureau of Statistics. Victorian Office. Victorian Year Book (AUS ISSN 0067-1223) 8933
- Australia. Bureau of Statistics. Victorian Office. Victoria's Young People (AUS) 7617
- Australia. Bureau of Statistics. Video Hire Industry, Australia (Online) (AUS) 1211
Australia. Bureau of Statistics. Video Hire Industry, Australia (Print) see Australia. Bureau of Statistics. Video Hire Industry, Australia (Online) 1211
- Australia. Bureau of Statistics. Video Hire Outlets, Australia (Online) (AUS) 2346
- Australia. Bureau of Statistics. Voluntary Work, Australia (Online) (AUS) 8081
Australia. Bureau of Statistics. Voluntary Work, Australia (Print) see Australia. Bureau of Statistics. Voluntary Work, Australia (Online) 8081
- Australia. Bureau of Statistics. Voluntary Work, Australia, Preliminary (Online) (AUS) 8081
Australia. Bureau of Statistics. Voluntary Work, Australia, Preliminary (Print) see Australia. Bureau of Statistics. Voluntary Work, Australia, Preliminary (Online) 8081
† • Australia. Bureau of Statistics. Wage and Salary Earners, Public Sector, Australia (Online) (AUS) 8933
- Australia. Bureau of Statistics. Waste Management Services, Australia (Online) (AUS) 3477
Australia. Bureau of Statistics. Waste Management Services, Australia (Print) see Australia. Bureau of Statistics. Waste Management Services, Australia (Online) 3477
- Australia. Bureau of Statistics. Water Account, Australia (Online) (AUS) 8843
† Australia. Bureau of Statistics. Western Australian Office. Census of Population and Housing: Aboriginal and Torres Strait Islander People, Western Australia (AUS) 8933
† • Australia. Bureau of Statistics. Western Australian Office. Census of Population and Housing: CDATA2001, Western Australia - Full GIS (AUS) 8933
- Australia. Bureau of Statistics. Western Australian Office. Census of Population and Housing: Census Basics, Western Australia (AUS) 7303
- Australia. Bureau of Statistics. Western Australian Office. Census of Population and Housing: Selected Characteristics for Urban Centres and Localities, Western Australia, Cocos (Keeling) and Christmas Islands (Online) (AUS) 7303
Australia. Bureau of Statistics. Western Australian Office. Census of Population and Housing: Selected Characteristics for Urban Centres and Localities, Western Australia, Cocos (Keeling) and Christmas Islands (Print) see Australia. Bureau of Statistics. Western Australian Office. Census of Population and Housing: Selected Characteristics for Urban Centres and Localities, Western Australia, Cocos (Keeling) and Christmas Islands (Online) 7303
- Australia. Bureau of Statistics. Western Australian Office. Census of Population and Housing: Selected Education and Labour Force Characteristics for Statistical Local Areas, Western Australia, Cocos (Keeling) and Christmas Islands (Online) (AUS) 7303
Australia. Bureau of Statistics. Western Australian Office. Census of Population and Housing: Selected Education and Labour Force Characteristics for Statistical Local Areas, Western Australia, Cocos (Keeling) and Christmas Islands (Print) see Australia. Bureau of Statistics. Western Australian Office. Census of Population and Housing: Selected Education and Labour Force Characteristics for Statistical Local Areas, Western Australia, Cocos (Keeling) and Christmas Islands (Online) 7303
- Australia. Bureau of Statistics. Western Australian Office. Census of Population and Housing: Selected Social and Housing Characteristics for Statistical Local Areas, Western Australia, Cocos (Keeling) and Christmas Islands (Online) (AUS) 7303
Australia. Bureau of Statistics. Western Australian Office. Census of Population and Housing: Selected Social and Housing Characteristics for Statistical Local Areas, Western Australia, Cocos (Keeling) and Christmas Islands (Print) see Australia. Bureau of Statistics. Western Australian Office. Census of Population and Housing: Selected Social and Housing Characteristics for Statistical Local Areas, Western Australia, Cocos (Keeling) and Christmas Islands (Online) 7303

- Australia. Bureau of Statistics. Western Australian Office. Census of Population and Housing: Selected Social and Housing Characteristics for Suburbs and Postal Areas, Western Australia (Online) (AUS) 7303
Australia. Bureau of Statistics. Western Australian Office. Census of Population and Housing: Selected Social and Housing Characteristics for Suburbs and Postal Areas, Western Australia (Print) see Australia. Bureau of Statistics. Western Australian Office. Census of Population and Housing: Selected Social and Housing Characteristics for Suburbs and Postal Areas, Western Australia (Online) 7303
† • Australia. Bureau of Statistics. Western Australian Office. Census of Population and Housing: Socio-Economic Indexes for Areas, Western Australia (AUS) 8933
- Australia. Bureau of Statistics. Western Australian Office. Crime and Safety, Western Australia (Online) (AUS) 2673
† Australia. Bureau of Statistics. Western Australian Office. Demography, Western Australia (AUS ISSN 1036-2665) 8933
† Australia. Bureau of Statistics. Western Australian Office. Estimated Stocks of Dwellings, Western Australia (AUS ISSN 1445-3789) 8933
- Australia. Bureau of Statistics. Western Australian Office. Government Financial Estimates, Western Australia, Electronic Delivery (AUS) 1211
- Australia. Bureau of Statistics. Western Australian Office. Manufacturing Industry, Western Australia (Online) (AUS) 1211
Australia. Bureau of Statistics. Western Australian Office. Manufacturing Industry, Western Australia (Print) see Australia. Bureau of Statistics. Western Australian Office. Manufacturing Industry, Western Australia (Online) 1211
- Australia. Bureau of Statistics. Western Australian Office. Mental Health and Wellbeing of Adults, Western Australia: Confidentialised Unit Record File on CD-ROM (AUS) 8081
- Australia. Bureau of Statistics. Western Australian Office. Perth. A Social Atlas (AUS) 7303
- Australia. Bureau of Statistics. Western Australian Office. StatSearch, A Reference Guide to Western Australian Statistics (Online) (AUS) 7303
Australia. Bureau of Statistics. Western Australian Office. StatSearch, A Reference Guide to Western Australian Statistics (Print) see Australia. Bureau of Statistics. Western Australian Office. StatSearch, A Reference Guide to Western Australian Statistics (Online) 7303
Australia. Bureau of Statistics. Western Australian Office. Western Australia at a Glance see Australia. Bureau of Statistics. Western Australian Office. Western Australia at a Glance (Online) 8355
- Australia. Bureau of Statistics. Western Australian Office. Western Australia at a Glance (Online) (AUS) 8355
- Australia. Bureau of Statistics. Western Australian Office. Western Australian Statistical Indicators (Online) (AUS) 8355
- Australia. Bureau of Statistics. Western Australian Office. Western Australian Statistical Indicators (Print) see Australia. Bureau of Statistics. Western Australian Office. Western Australian Statistical Indicators (Online) 8355
- Australia. Bureau of Statistics. Western Australian Office. Western Australia's Aboriginal People (Online) (AUS) 8355
Australia. Bureau of Statistics. Western Australian Office. Western Australia's Aboriginal People (Print) see Australia. Bureau of Statistics. Western Australian Office. Western Australia's Aboriginal People (Online) 8355
- Australia. Bureau of Statistics. Western Australian Office. Western Australia's Seniors (AUS) 7303
- Australia. Bureau of Statistics. Western Australian Office. Western Australia's Young People (AUS) 7617
- Australia. Bureau of Statistics. Work in Selected Culture and Leisure Activities, Australia (Online) (AUS) 1211
Australia. Bureau of Statistics. Work in Selected Culture and Leisure Activities, Australia (Print) see Australia. Bureau of Statistics. Work in Selected Culture and Leisure Activities, Australia (Online) 1211
- Australia. Bureau of Statistics. Work-Related Injuries, Australia (Online) (AUS) 1666
Australia. Bureau of Statistics. Work-Related Injuries, Australia (Print) see Australia. Bureau of Statistics. Work-Related Injuries, Australia (Online) 1666
- Australia. Bureau of Statistics. Working Papers in Econometrics and Applied Statistics (Online) (AUS) 1211
- Australia. Bureau of Statistics. Working Time Arrangements, Australia (Online) (AUS) 1211
Australia. Bureau of Statistics. Working Time Arrangements, Australia (Print) see Australia. Bureau of Statistics. Working Time Arrangements, Australia (Online) 1211
† • Australia. Bureau of Statistics. Year 2000 Problem, Australia (AUS) 8933
† • Australia. Bureau of Statistics. Year 2000 Problem, Australia, Preliminary (AUS) 8933

- Australia. Bureau of Statistics. Year Book Australia (AUS ISSN 0810-8633) 8356
- Australia. Bureau of Statistics. Youth, Australia: A Social Report (Online) (AUS) 2173
Australia. Bureau of Statistics. Youth, Australia: A Social Report (Print) see Australia. Bureau of Statistics. Youth, Australia: A Social Report (Online) 2173
- Australia. Bureau of Statistics. Zoos, Parks and Gardens Industry, Australia (Online) (AUS) 4984
Australia. Bureau of Statistics. Zoos, Parks and Gardens Industry, Australia (Print) see Australia. Bureau of Statistics. Zoos, Parks and Gardens Industry, Australia (Online) 4984
Australia. Bureau of Tourism Research. Occasional Papers see Tourism Research Australia. Occasional paper 8781
Australia Camera Craft Photographer's Handbook see CAMERA Photographer's Handbook 6965
- Australia China Connections (AUS) 1063
- Australia. Commonwealth Competitive Neutrality Complaints Office. Investigations (Online) (AUS) 1063
- Australia Country Monitor (USA) 1438
- Australia Defence & Security Report (GBR ISSN 1749-1266) 6412
- Australia. Department of Agriculture, Fisheries and Forestry. Annual Report (AUS ISSN 1443-0452) 1438
- Australia. Department of Employment and Workplace Relations. Annual Report (AUS ISSN 1447-5758) 1666
- Australia. Department of Families, Community Services and Indigenous Affairs. Annual Report (AUS ISSN 1833-4687) 8026
Australia. Department of Families, Community Services and Indigenous Affairs. Occasional Paper (AUS ISSN 1833-4415) 8026
Australia. Department of Families, Community Services and Indigenous Affairs. Research News see Fa C S I A Research News 8039
- Australia. Department of Families, Community Services and Indigenous Affairs. Statistical Paper (AUS ISSN 1832-7451) 7303
Australia. Department of Family and Community Services. Annual Report see Australia. Department of Families, Community Services and Indigenous Affairs. Annual Report 8026
Australia. Department of Family and Community Services. Occasional Paper Series see Australia. Department of Families, Community Services and Indigenous Affairs. Occasional Paper 8026
Australia. Department of Family and Community Services. Policy Research Paper see Social Policy Research Paper 8133
- Australia. Department of Foreign Affairs and Trade. Annual Report (AUS ISSN 1032-2019) 1591
Australia. Department of Foreign Affairs and Trade. Select Documents on International Affairs (AUS ISSN 0519-5950) 7222
- Australia. Department of Health and Ageing. Annual Report (AUS ISSN 1447-8722) 7421
Australia. Department of Health & Ageing. Chief Medical Officer's Report (AUS) 7508
Australia. Department of Health & Ageing. Occasional Papers New Series (AUS) 7508
Australia. Department of Industry, Science and Resources. Annual Report see Australia. Department of Innovation, Industry, Science and Research. Annual Report 1911
Australia. Department of Innovation, Industry, Science and Research. Annual Report (AUS ISSN 1836-3083) 1911
- Australia. Department of Parliamentary Services. Annual Report (AUS ISSN 1832-0848) 7421
Australia. Department of Parliamentary Sevices. Information and Research Services. Current Issues Brief see Australia. Deptartment of Parliamentary Services. Parliamentary Library. Research Paper 7421
Australia. Department of Planning and Development. Annual Report see Australia. Office of Housing. Summary of Housing Assistance Programs 7421
Australia. Department of Primary Industries and Energy. Cotton Market News (AUS) 219
Australia. Department of Primary Industries and Energy. Raw Cotton Marketing Advisory Committee. Annual Report (AUS) 219
Australia. Department of Primary Industry and Fisheries. Fishery Report (AUS ISSN 0158-2224) 3586
Australia. Department of the Environment. Annual Report (AUS ISSN 1441-9335) 3405
Australia. Department of the Parliamentary Library. Information and Research Services. Current Issues Brief see Australia. Deptartment of Parliamentary Services. Parliamentary Library. Research Paper 7421
- Australia. Department of the Treasury. Advisory Panel on the Marketing of Infant Formula. Annual Report (AUS) 7508
- Australia. Department of the Treasury. Annual Report (AUS ISSN 0728-9405) 1438
- Australia. Department of the Treasury. Budget (AUS ISSN 0810-5677) 1438
- Australia. Department of the Treasury. Economic Round-Up (AUS ISSN 1031-8968) 1211

Australia. Department of the Treasury. Economic Roundup see Australia. Department of the Treasury. Economic Round-Up 1211
Australia. Department of the Treasury. Foreign Investment Review Board. Annual Report see Australia. Department of the Treasury. Foreign Investment Review Board. Report 1611
- Australia. Department of the Treasury. Foreign Investment Review Board. Report (AUS ISSN 0155-0802) 1611
- Australia. Department of the Treasury. Mid - Year Economic and Fiscal Outlook (AUS) 1211
† • Australia. Department of the Treasury. National Fiscal Outlook (AUS) 8933
- Australia. Department of the Treasury. Pre-election Economic and Fiscal Outlook (AUS) 1211
- Australia. Department of the Treasury. Tax Expenditures Statement (AUS ISSN 1031-4121) 1911
† • Australia. Department of the Treasury. Treasury Economic Papers (AUS) 8933
- Australia. Department of the Treasury. Treasury Research Papers (AUS ISSN 1323-9546) 1438
Australia. Deptartment of Parliamentary Services. Parliamentary Library. Research Brief see Australia. Deptartment of Parliamentary Services. Parliamentary Library. Research Paper 7421
Australia. Deptartment of Parliamentary Services. Parliamentary Library. Research Note see Australia. Deptartment of Parliamentary Services. Parliamentary Library. Research Paper 7421
▼ • Australia. Deptartment of Parliamentary Services. Parliamentary Library. Research Paper (AUS ISSN 1834-9854) 7421
- Australia.edu (AUS ISSN 1443-4628) 2828
Australia Freight Transport Report (GBR ISSN 1752-5233) 8490
Australia. Geoscience Australia. Mineral Resource Report (AUS) 6457
Australia Highlife Downs Living see Highlife Downs Living 3794
- Australia in Antarctica (AUS ISSN 1833-9891) 7838
Australia in Britain (GBR) 1396
Australia-India Council. Annual Report (AUS ISSN 1321-1080) 7222
Australia Indonesia Arts Alliance. Journal see Inspirasi 496
▼ • The Australia Insurance Report (GBR ISSN 1752-7945) 4493
Australia. Intergovernmental Committee on Surveying and Mapping. Biennial Report (AUS ISSN 1832-2697) 3999
Australia, Israel and Jewish Affairs Council. The Review see A I R 7201
Australia/Israel Review see A I R 7201
Australia Law Reform Commission Report Series see A L R C Report Series 4608
Australia New Guinea Fishes Association News see A N G F A News 3582
Australia - New Zealand Association News see A N Z A News 3793
- Australia. Office of Housing. Summary of Housing Assistance Programs (AUS) 7421
Australia Petrochemicals Report (GBR ISSN 1749-2130) 6763
- Australia. Productivity Commission. Annual Report (AUS) 1438
- Australia. Productivity Commission. Commission Research Papers (AUS) 1063
Australia. Productivity Commission. Commissioned Studies see Australia. Productivity Commission. Research Report 1439
- Australia. Productivity Commission. Conference Proceedings (AUS) 1439
- Australia. Productivity Commission. Inquiry Reports. Draft Report (AUS) 1439
- Australia. Productivity Commission. Inquiry Reports. Final Report (AUS) 1439
- Australia. Productivity Commission. P C Update (AUS ISSN 1443-6671) 1439
- Australia. Productivity Commission. Research Report (AUS) 1439
- Australia. Productivity Commission. Staff Research Papers (AUS) 1439
- Australia. Productivity Commission. Submissions (AUS) 1063
Australia. Rehabilitation and Compensation of Commonwealth Employees. Commission for the Safety. Annual Report see Australia. Safety, Rehabilitation and Compensation Commission. Annual Report 8026
- Australia. Safety, Rehabilitation and Compensation Commission. Annual Report (AUS ISSN 1442-696X) 8026
- Australia. Steering Committee for the Review of Government Service Provision. Report on Government Services (AUS) 1063
Australia v New Zealand (AUS ISSN 1832-5076) 8221
Australia Verses New Zealand see Australia v New Zealand 8221
- The Australian (AUS ISSN 1038-8761) 3793
- Australian 4 W D Action (AUS) 8159
Australian 4 W D Buyers Guide (AUS ISSN 1832-7575) 8556
Australian 4 Wheel Drive see Australian 4 W D Action 8159
Australian 4WD Monthly see Australian 4 W D Action 8159

DIRECTORY 2010 AUSTRALIAN CONSERVATION FOUNDATION. ANNUAL REPORT 10003

Australian 4WD Monthly Action *see* Australian 4 W D Action **8159**
• Australian A P E C Studies Centre. Issues Paper (Online) (Asia-Pacific Economic Cooperation) (AUS ISSN 1832-9306) **1553**
Australian A P E C Studies Centre. Issues Paper (Print) *see* Australian A P E C Studies Centre. Issues Paper (Online) **1553**
Australian A T V Action (All Terrain Vehicle) (AUS) **8253**
• ➤ Australian Aboriginal Studies (AUS ISSN 0729-4352) **330**
• ➤ Australian Academic & Research Libraries (AUS ISSN 0004-8623) **4993**
Australian Academic and Research Libraries *see* Australian Academic & Research Libraries **4993**
• Australian Academy of Science. Annual Report (AUS ISSN 1448-2037) **7838**
Australian Academy of Science. National Committee for the History and Philosophy of Science. Annual Lecture (AUS) **7838**
• Australian Academy of Science. Newsletter (AUS ISSN 1031-9204) **7838**
Australian Academy of Technological Sciences and Engineering Focus *see* A T S E Focus **8415**
Australian Academy of the Humanities. Lecture Series (No.) (AUS ISSN 1320-243X) **4443**
Australian Academy of the Humanities. Occasional Papers (AUS ISSN 1443-7678) **4444**
Australian Academy of the Humanities. Proceedings (AUS ISSN 0067-1592) **4444**
• ➤ Australian Accounting Review (AUS ISSN 1035-6908) **1281**
• Australian Accounting Standards Board. Accounting Standards (AUS ISSN 1036-4803) **4856**
Australian Accounting Standards Board. Discussion Paper (AUS) **1281**
Australian Accounting Standards Board. Urgent Issues Group. Abstract *see* Urgent Issues Group Interpretation **1303**
• Australian Acoustical Society. Annual Conference (AUS ISSN 1446-0998) **7086**
The Australian Acreage & Property Review (AUS ISSN 1833-606X) **7583**
• Australian Administrative Law (AUS ISSN 0816-3030) **7421**
Australian Administrative Law Journal (AUS ISSN 1321-4489) **4856**
Australian Adventure Angler (AUS) **8304**
• Australian Adverse Drug Reactions Bulletin (AUS ISSN 0812-3837) **6823**
Australian Agroforestry (AUS) **3684**
Australian Air Pilot (AUS ISSN 0727-338X) **8538**
Australian Al-Anon Highlights *see* Austra-Link **2692**
Australian Alpaca Central Coast & Hunter Region Alpaca Hmmm *see* Alpaca Hmmm **277**
† Australian Amiga Review (AUS) **8933**
Australian and New Zealand Academy of Management. Journal *see* Journal of Management & Organization **1767**
• Australian & New Zealand Apparel (NZL ISSN 1176-337X) **8448**
Australian and New Zealand Association for the Advancement of Science Congress Papers *see* A N Z A A S Congress Papers **8927**
• Australian and New Zealand Citator to UK Reports (AUS ISSN 1321-1269) **4821**
• ➤ Australian and New Zealand Continence Journal (AUS ISSN 1448-0131) **6265**
Australian and New Zealand Council for the Care of Animals in Research and Teaching Ltd. News (Online) *see* A N Z C C A R T News (Online) **316**
Australian & New Zealand Defence Business Directory of Suppliers (AUS ISSN 1446-0564) **1973**
Australian & New Zealand Grapegrower & Winemaker (AUS ISSN 1446-8212) **219**
Australian and New Zealand Grapegrower and Winemaker *see* Australian & New Zealand Grapegrower & Winemaker **219**
Australian & New Zealand Handgun (AUS ISSN 1448-3939) **8159**
Australian and New Zealand Handgun *see* Australian & New Zealand Handgun **8159**
Australian & New Zealand Industrial and Applied Mathematics Journal *see* The A N Z I A M Journal **5463**
Australian & New Zealand industrial and Applied Mathematics Journal. Electronic Supplement *see* The A N Z I A M Journal **5463**
• Australian and New Zealand Industry Defence Equipment and Capability Catalogue (AUS ISSN 1039-1738) **6412**
• Australian and New Zealand Institute of Insurance and Finance. Journal (AUS ISSN 1444-8505) **4493**
➤ Australian and New Zealand Journal of Art (AUS ISSN 1443-4318) **477**
• ➤ Australian and New Zealand Journal of Audiology (AUS ISSN 1443-4873) **4072**
• ➤ Australian and New Zealand Journal of Criminology (AUS ISSN 0004-8658) **2644**
▼ ➤ Australian and New Zealand Journal of European Studies (AUS ISSN 1836-1803) **7222**
• ➤ Australian and New Zealand Journal of Family Therapy (AUS ISSN 0814-723X) **8089**
• ➤ The Australian and New Zealand Journal of Obstetrics and Gynecology (AUS ISSN 0004-8666) **5986**
• ➤ Australian & New Zealand Journal of Psychiatry (GBR ISSN 0004-8674) **6125**
• ➤ Australian and New Zealand Journal of Public Health (AUS ISSN 1326-0200) **7508**
• ➤ Australian & New Zealand Journal of Statistics (AUS ISSN 1369-1473) **8356**
• Australian and New Zealand Map Society. Newsletter (AUS) **3999**
• ➤ Australian and New Zealand Maritime Law Journal (AUS ISSN 1834-0881) **4969**
Australian and New Zealand Nuclear Medicine (AUS ISSN 1324-1435) **5581**
The Australian and New Zealand Olive Industry Directory (AUS ISSN 1833-2919) **219**
Australian & New Zealand Olivegrower & Processor/Australian and New Zealand Olivegrower and Processor (AUS) **93**
Australian and New Zealand Olivegrower and Processor *see* Australian & New Zealand Olivegrower & Processor **93**
▼ Australian and New Zealand Property Journal (AUS ISSN 1834-5662) **7583**
Australian and New Zealand Skiing (AUS) **8304**
Australian and New Zealand Snowboarding (AUS) **8159**
Australian and New Zealand Society of Indexers Newsletter *see* A N Z S I Newsletter **1**
Australian and New Zealand Sports Law Association Commentator *see* A N Z S L A Commentator **4608**
Australian and New Zealand Sports Law Journal (AUS ISSN 1833-8852) **4623**
• Australian and New Zealand Student Services Association. Journal (AUS ISSN 1320-2480) **2828**
Australian and New Zealand Studies in German Language and Literature (CHE ISSN 0171-6867) **5258**
Australian and New Zealand Wine Industry Directory (AUS ISSN 1033-7954) **598**
Australian and New Zealand Wine Industry Journal (AUS ISSN 0819-2421) **598**
• Australian and Security Cooperation in the Asia Pacific Newsletter (AUS ISSN 1327-0125) **2676**
• Australian Anthill (AUS ISSN 1448-7330) **1064**
Australian Anthropological Society Newsletter *see* A A S Newsletter **322**
Australian Arabian Horse News (AUS ISSN 0727-4092) **8287**
• ➤ Australian Archaeological Consultancy Monograph Series (AUS ISSN 1833-2838) **382**
• ➤ Australian Archaeology (AUS ISSN 0312-2417) **382**
• Australian Architecture Database (AUS) **462**
Australian Army Journal (AUS ISSN 1448-2843) **6412**
Australian Army Rowell Profession of Arms Seminar Series (AUS ISSN 1832-3286) **6412**
Australian Army Transport Journal *see* Par Oneri **6441**
• Australian Art Auction Records (AUS ISSN 0819-923X) **477**
➤ Australian Art Education (AUS ISSN 1032-1942) **477**
† Australian Art Museums and Public Galleries Directory (AUS) **8933**
Australian Artist (AUS ISSN 0813-8095) **477**
Australian Asphalt Pavement Association International Flexible Pavements Conference. Conference Proceedings *see* A A P A International Flexible Pavements Conference. Conference Proceedings **3258**
Australian Association for Infant Mental Health Inc Newsletter *see* A A I M H I Newsletter **6117**
Australian Association of Clinical Biochemists. Newsletter (AUS) **723**
• Australian Association of Consulting Archaeologists. Newsletter (Online) (AUS ISSN 1832-1267) **382**
• Australian Association of Jewish Studies. Newsletter (Online) (AUS) **7718**
Australian Association of Jewish Studies. Newsletter (Print) *see* Australian Association of Jewish Studies. Newsletter (Online) **7718**
➤ Australian Association of Massage Therapists. Journal (AUS ISSN 1448-997X) **6107**
Australian Association of Occupational Therapists. Journal *see* Australian Occupational Therapy Journal **6107**
Australian Author (AUS ISSN 0045-026X) **7552**
Australian Auto Action (AUS ISSN 1320-2073) **8159**
Australian Aviary Life (AUS ISSN 1832-3405) **902**
• Australian Aviation (AUS ISSN 0813-0876) **47**
Australian Aviation Annual (AUS) **47**
Australian Aviation Yearbook *see* Australian Aviation Annual **47**
• Australian Baking Business (AUS) **3671**
• Australian Ballet News (AUS ISSN 0818-6022) **2682**
Australian Banking & Finance *see* Australian Banking and Finance **1309**
• Australian Banking and Finance (AUS ISSN 1325-1228) **1309**
Australian Banking Statistics *see* Monthly Banking Statistics **1368**
• Australian Bar Review (AUS ISSN 0814-8589) **4623**
Australian Beacon (AUS ISSN 1022-3347) **7624**
Australian Beader Magazine (AUS ISSN 1832-5815) **4564**
Australian Bear Creations (AUS) **531**
Australian Bee Journal (AUS ISSN 0045-0294) **93**
Australian Beef Improvement News *see* Beef Improvement News **280**
Australian Benefits Review (AUS ISSN 1325-6858) **1856**
• ➤ Australian Biblical Review (AUS ISSN 0045-0308) **7624**
† ➤ Australian Biologist (AUS ISSN 1030-6234) **8933**
Australian Biotechnology News (Online) (AUS) **756**
Australian Biotechnology News (Print) *see* Australian Biotechnology News (Online) **756**
Australian Bird Watcher *see* Australian Field Ornithology **902**
Australian Birdkeeper Magazine (AUS ISSN 1030-8954) **6804**
Australian Birds (AUS ISSN 0311-8150) **902**
Australian Book Review *see* A B R **5204**
† Australian Books in Print (AUS ISSN 0067-172X) **8933**
Australian Bookseller and Publisher *see* Bookseller + Publisher **7555**
Australian Bridal Directory (AUS ISSN 1449-8278) **8852**
Australian Bridge (AUS ISSN 0814-3889) **8159**
Australian Broker (AUS ISSN 1449-7743) **7583**
• Australian Bulletin of Labour (AUS ISSN 0311-6336) **1666**
• Australian Bureau of Agricultural and Resource Economics. Australian Commodities (AUS ISSN 1321-7844) **194**
• Australian Bureau of Agricultural and Resource Economics. Australian Commodity Statistics (AUS ISSN 1325-8109) **1211**
• Australian Bureau of Agricultural and Resource Economics. Australian Crop Report (Online) (AUS ISSN 1444-5468) **194**
• Australian Bureau of Agricultural and Resource Economics. Australian Fisheries Statistics (Year) (Online) (AUS) **3612**
• Australian Bureau of Agricultural and Resource Economics. Australian Fisheries Surveys Report (AUS ISSN 1832-9489) **3612**
• Australian Bureau of Agricultural and Resource Economics. Australian Forest and Wood Products Statistics (AUS ISSN 1449-1850) **3708**
• Australian Bureau of Agricultural and Resource Economics. Australian Mineral Statistics (AUS ISSN 1447-1159) **6485**
Australian Bureau of Agricultural and Resource Economics Farm Surveys Report (Year) (Online) *see* A B A R E Farm Surveys Report (Year) (Online) **190**
Australian Bureau of Agricultural and Resource Economics Research Reports *see* A B A R E Research Reports **1055**
• Australian Bureau of Statistics. Directory of Child & Family Statistics (Online) (AUS) **2173**
Australian Bus & Commercial Vehicle Heritage (AUS ISSN 1449-1613) **8490**
• Australian Business Law Review (AUS ISSN 0310-1053) **4857**
Australian Business News *see* Business Connect Magazine **1881**
• Australian Business Volunteers. Annual Report (Online) (AUS ISSN 1834-2116) **1591**
Australian C P A *see* Intheblack **1293**
Australian Camera, Photo, Video, Digital *see* Camera **6965**
Australian Campdrafting Magazine (AUS ISSN 1834-0091) **8287**
Australian-Canadian Studies *see* Australasian Canadian Studies **329**
Australian Canegrower (AUS ISSN 0157-3039) **220**
Australian Capital Territory Attorney-General's Department. Annual Report (AUS ISSN 1325-2453) **2635**
Australian Capital Territory Australian Football League Programme *see* A C T A F L Programme **8927**
Australian Capital Territory. Department of Justice and Community Services. Annual Report *see* Australian Capital Territory. Emergency Services Authority. Annual Report **7421**
• Australian Capital Territory. Emergency Services Authority. Annual Report (AUS ISSN 1832-9802) **7421**
Australian Case Citator on CD-ROM *see* A C C Plus **4606**
Australian Case Citator Plus *see* A C C Plus **4606**
Australian Cat Federation Year Book *see* A C I Year Book **6802**
• Australian Catholic Historical Society. Journal (AUS ISSN 0084-7259) **7785**
• Australian Cattle & Sheep Industry Overview (AUS) **279**
Australian Caver *see* Caves Australia **2728**
➤ Australian Centre for Egyptology. Bulletin (AUS ISSN 1035-7254) **382**
Australian Centre for Industrial Relations Research and Teaching Working Paper *see* A C I R R T Working Paper **1661**
• Australian Centre for International Agricultural Research. Annual Operational Plan (AUS ISSN 1832-1356) **93**
• Australian Centre for International Agricultural Research. Annual Report (AUS ISSN 0810-8315) **93**
Australian Centre for International Agricultural Research Monograph Series *see* A C I A R Monograph Series **77**
Australian Centre for International Agricultural Research Newsletter *see* A C I A R Newsletter **77**
Australian Centre for International Agricultural Research Partners Magazine *see* A C I A R Partners Magazine **77**
Australian Centre for International Agricultural Research Proceedings *see* A C I A R Proceedings **77**
Australian Centre for International Agricultural Research Technical Reports Series *see* A C I A R Technical Reports Series **77**
Australian Centre for International Agricultural Research Working Papers *see* A C I A R Working Papers **77**
• ➤ The Australian Centre for Peace and Conflict Studies. Occasional Papers Series (AUS ISSN 1833-9603) **7222**
Australian Ceramics & Pottery *see* Australian Ceramics Glasswork & Pottery **2037**
Australian Ceramics Glasswork & Pottery (AUS) **2037**
Australian Ceramics - In Touch (AUS) **531**
Australian Chess Forum (AUS ISSN 1442-7745) **8159**
† Australian Chess Magazine (AUS ISSN 0159-4958) **8933**
Australian Chief Executive (AUS ISSN 1446-6708) **1727**
• Australian Children's Rights News (AUS ISSN 1320-7091) **7202**
• The Australian Chiropractor (AUS) **5803**
• Australian Christian (Online) (AUS) **7624**
Australian Christian (Print) *see* Australian Christian (Online) **7624**
Australian Christian Woman (AUS) **7624**
• Australian Churches of Christ Historical Society. Digest (AUS ISSN 1324-9436) **7624**
Australian Citrus News (AUS ISSN 0004-8283) **3723**
• Australian Classic Car (AUS ISSN 1329-4660) **8556**
Australian Classic Car Yearbook & Desk Diary *see* Australian Classic Car **8556**
† Australian Clay Journal & Ceramic News (AUS ISSN 1035-4611) **8933**
• Australian Clay Target Shooting News (AUS ISSN 1321-3903) **8160**
• Australian Coal Year Book (AUS ISSN 0814-446X) **6457**
• Australian Coast & Country (AUS ISSN 1442-6730) **8684**
Australian College of Education. New South Wales Branch Newsletter (AUS ISSN 0813-3085) **2828**
Australian College of Education. New South Wales Chapter Newsletter *see* Australian College of Education. New South Wales Branch Newsletter **2828**
• Australian College of Health Service Executive. Annual Report (AUS ISSN 1320-3843) **4088**
Australian College of Health Service Executives. Monograph Series (AUS ISSN 1039-3986) **4088**
Australian Commodities *see* Australian Bureau of Agricultural and Resource Economics. Australian Commodities **194**
Australian Commodity Statistics *see* Australian Bureau of Agricultural and Resource Economics. Australian Commodity Statistics **1211**
Australian Communications and Media Authority (A C M A) Communications Report *see* A C M A Communications Report **2310**
Australian Communications and Media Authority (A C M A) Consumer Bulletin *see* A C M A Consumer Bulletin **8927**
• Australian Communications and Media Authority. Annual Report (Years) (AUS ISSN 1834-0776) **2313**
Australian Communications and Media Authority Sphere *see* A C M A Sphere **2310**
Australian Communications Authority. Annual Report *see* Australian Communications and Media Authority. Annual Report (Years) **2313**
Australian Communications Authority. Telecommunications Performance Report *see* A C M A Communications Report **2310**
• Australian Company Law Cases (Year) (AUS) **4857**
Australian Competition and Consumer Commission eJournal (Online) *see* A C C C eJournal (Online) **4853**
• Australian Computer Architechture Conference. Proceedings (USA ISSN 1530-0927) **2466**
Australian Computer Science Communications (USA ISSN 0157-3055) **2407**
Australian Computer Society Inc., New South Wales Branch N S W ENews *see* A C S N S W ENews **2405**
Australian Concrete Construction (AUS ISSN 1034-7860) **977**
Australian Confederation of Operating Room Nurses *see* A C O R N **4086**
Australian Conference on Nuclear and Complementary Techniques of Analysis. Proceedings (AUS) **2098**
Australian Conference on Nuclear Techniques of Analysis. Proceedings *see* Australian Conference on Nuclear and Complementary Techniques of Analysis. Proceedings **2098**
Australian Conservation Foundation. A C T Update *see* Habitat Australia **2613**
Australian Conservation Foundation. Annual Report (AUS ISSN 0587-5846) **2603**

Title

10004 THE AUSTRALIAN CONSTITUTIONAL DEFENDER ULRICH'S PERIODICALS

The Australian Constitutional Defender (AUS ISSN 1833-4229) **7108**
• Australian Consumer Credit Law (AUS) **4623**
• Australian Convenience Store News (AUS) **8556**
Australian Copyright Council. Practical Guides and Discussion Papers (AUS) **6745**
• Australian Corporation Law - A S I C Releases (AUS) **4623**
• Australian Corporation Law - Legislation (AUS) **4857**
• Australian Corporation Law - Principles and Practice (AUS) **4857**
• Australian Corporation Practice (AUS) **4857**
• Australian Corporations and Securities Reports (AUS ISSN 1033-7466) **4857**
Australian Corporations Law Journal (AUS ISSN 1321-747X) **4857**
Australian Correspondence Chess Quarterly (AUS ISSN 0819-7806) **8160**
• Australian Cotton Cooperative Research Centre. Annual Report (AUS ISSN 1446-6503) **220**
Australian Cotton Outlook (AUS ISSN 1443-9778) **220**
• The Australian Cottongrower (AUS ISSN 0159-1290) **220**
Australian Cottongrower. Cotton Yearbook (AUS) **220**
Australian Council For Adult Literacy eNews *see* A C A L eNews **2937**
• Australian Council for Educational Research. Annual Report (Online) (AUS) **2828**
Australian Council for Educational Research. Annual Report (Print) *see* Australian Council for Educational Research. Annual Report (Online) **2828**
• Australian Council for Educational Research. Research Monograph (AUS ISSN 1442-1364) **2828**
Australian Council for Health Physical Education and Recreation Active and Healthy Magazine *see* A C H P E R Active and Healthy Magazine **6980**
Australian Council for Health Physical Education and Recreation Australia Healthy Lifestyles Journal *see* A C H P E R Australia Healthy Lifestyles Journal **2822**
Australian Council of Social Service Info *see* A C O S S Info **8022**
➤ Australian Council of Social Service Papers (AUS ISSN 1326-7124) **8026**
Australian Council of State School Organisations, Inc. Policy Document (Year) *see* A C S S O Policy Document (Year) **3016**
Australian Country Collections (AUS ISSN 1323-9708) **4553**
• Australian Country Craft and Decorating (AUS ISSN 1037-2369) **4532**
Australian Country Music (AUS ISSN 1832-2557) **6546**
Australian Country Music Newsletter (AUS) **6546**
Australian Country Style (AUS ISSN 1033-6060) **5065**
Australian Country Threads (AUS) **6637**
• Australian Creative (AUS ISSN 1324-1613) **21**
Australian Cricket Tour Guide (AUS) **8221**
• Australian Crime Commission. Annual Report (AUS ISSN 1832-1291) **2644**
• ➤ Australian Crime Prosecution Law Journal (AUS ISSN 1321-4500) **4885**
• Australian Criminal Reports (AUS ISSN 0159-6667) **2644**
• Australian Criminal Trial Directions (AUS) **4885**
• ➤ Australian Critical Care (USA ISSN 1036-7314) **5952**
Australian Current Law Legislation (AUS ISSN 1036-0425) **4821**
• Australian Current Law Reporter (AUS ISSN 1036-0417) **4821**
Australian Cyclist (AUS ISSN 1034-3016) **8253**
Australian Dairy Corporation Report *see* A D C Report **261**
Australian Dairy Farmer (AUS ISSN 0814-4494) **261**
Australian Dairy Foods (AUS ISSN 0157-7964) **261**
• Australian Dairy Industry In Focus (AUS ISSN 1448-9392) **261**
Australian Decorative Painting (AUS) **4328**
Australian Deer Farming (AUS ISSN 1034-6171) **280**
• Australian Defamation Law and Practice (AUS) **4827**
• Australian Defence Business Review (AUS ISSN 1329-9980) **6412**
† Australian Defence Force Academy . Alumni Newsletter (AUS ISSN 1832-0554) **8933**
• ➤ Australian Defence Force Journal (AUS ISSN 1320-2545) **6413**
Australian Defence Intelligencer (AUS ISSN 1032-1063) **6413**
Australian Defence Magazine *see* A D M **6408**
Australian Defence News (AUS) **6413**
† Australian Defence Report (AUS ISSN 1034-6023) **8933**
Australian Defense Force Health *see* A D F Health **5564**
Australian Dental Association Inc. - Western Australian Branch W A Newsletter *see* A D A W A Newsletter **5832**
Australian Dental Association. News Bulletin (AUS ISSN 0810-7440) **5835**
• ➤ Australian Dental Journal (GBR ISSN 0045-0421) **5835**
• Australian Department of Health & Aged Care. Budget Papers (AUS) **7508**
• Australian Department of Health & Aged Care. Corporate Plan (AUS) **7508**
† • Australian Department of Health & Aged Care. Health Financing Series Occasional Papers (AUS) **8933**
Australian Developer *see* International Developer **2424**
• Australian Dictionary of Biography (Online) (AUS ISSN 1833-7538) **639**
• Australian Dictionary of Biography (Print) (AUS) **640**
• Australian Digest (AUS ISSN 0067-1843) **4623**
• Australian Directory of Academics (AUS ISSN 1038-6432) **2968**
• Australian Directory of Professors (AUS ISSN 1449-4914) **2968**
Australian Dispute Resolution Journal *see* Australasian Dispute Resolution Journal **4623**
• Australian Doctor (AUS ISSN 1039-7116) **5581**
Australian Dolls, Bears, and Collectables (AUS) **4328**
Australian Drama Education Magazine (AUS ISSN 1323-8086) **2828**
• ➤ Australian e-Journal for the Advancement of Mental Health (AUS ISSN 1446-7984) **6125**
Australian Early Childhood Association. Victorian Branch. Newsletter (AUS) **2828**
• ➤ Australian Early Medieval Association. Journal (AUS ISSN 1449-9320) **4191**
• ➤ Australian Economic History Review (AUS ISSN 0004-8992) **1536**
• ➤ Australian Economic Papers (AUS ISSN 0004-900X) **1064**
Australian Economic Policy (AUS) **1439**
• ➤ The Australian Economic Review (AUS ISSN 0004-9018) **1064**
The Australian Economy (AUS ISSN 0812-2261) **1439**
Australian Education Directory *see* Australasian Education Directory **2828**
• Australian Education Index (Online) (AUS) **2930**
• Australian Education Review (AUS ISSN 0311-6875) **2828**
Australian Education Union, South Australian Branch Branch Journal *see* A E U S A Branch Journal **2822**
Australian Education Union, Victorian Branch News - Victoria *see* A E U News - Victoria **2822**
➤ Australian Educational and Developmental Psychologist (AUS ISSN 0816-5122) **7338**
• ➤ Australian Educational Computing (AUS ISSN 0816-9020) **2948**
• The Australian Educational Leader (AUS ISSN 1832-8245) **3017**
Australian Educational Researcher *see* A E R **2822**
Australian Educator (AUS ISSN 1328-6021) **2828**
• ➤ Australian Ejournal of Theology (AUS ISSN 1448-6326) **7785**
† • ➤ The Australian Electronic Journal of Nursing Education (AUS ISSN 1322-8676) **8933**
• Australian Electronics Directory (AUS ISSN 0159-2947) **3089**
Australian Embroidery and Cross Stitch (AUS ISSN 1446-2958) **6637**
Australian Employment Law Journal (AUS ISSN 1321-5957) **1666**
• Australian Encyclopedia of Forms and Precedents (AUS) **4624**
• ➤ Australian Endodontic Journal (AUS ISSN 1329-1947) **5835**
† Australian Energy News (Melbourne) (AUS) **8933**
Australian Engineering Directory (AUS ISSN 0159-2955) **3182**
Australian Entomological Society. Miscellaneous Publications (AUS ISSN 0374-5147) **840**
➤ Australian Entomologist (AUS ISSN 1320-6133) **840**
Australian Environment Review (AUS ISSN 1035-137X) **2603**
Australian Environmental Law News *see* National Environmental Law Review **4738**
• ➤ Australian Equine Veterinarian (AUS ISSN 1032-6626) **8793**
▼ Australian F O I Law Journal (Freedom of Information) (AUS ISSN 1834-5328) **4624**
• Australian Fabian News (AUS ISSN 1448-210X) **7108**
• The Australian Family (AUS ISSN 0811-3661) **2144**
Australian Family Court Legislation (AUS) **4907**
Australian Family Law Journal (AUS ISSN 1321-5949) **4907**
• Australian Family Law Service (AUS) **4907**
• Australian Family Law State Legislation (AUS) **4907**
• Australian Family Lawyer (AUS ISSN 0817-6531) **4907**
• ➤ Australian Family Physician (AUS ISSN 0300-8495) **5581**
Australian Family Relationships Clearinghouse Briefing *see* A F R C Briefing **8084**
Australian Family Tree Connections (AUS ISSN 1320-4823) **3759**
Australian Farm Business Management Journal *see* A F B M Journal **190**
Australian Farm Journal (AUS ISSN 1036-6474) **93**
➤ The Australian Feminist Law Journal (AUS ISSN 1320-0968) **8894**
• ➤ Australian Feminist Studies (AUS ISSN 0816-4649) **8894**
➤ Australian Field Ornithology (AUS ISSN 1448-0107) **902**
The Australian Filipina Woman's Magazine (AUS ISSN 1834-0962) **3521**
Australian Film Commission News *see* Screen Australia News **6512**
• Australian Film Institute Newsletter (Email) (AUS) **6490**
• Australian Film, Television and Radio School. Annual Report (AUS ISSN 0819-2316) **2356**
• Australian Film, Television and Radio School Handbook (AUS ISSN 1035-1019) **2356**
• Australian Financial Review (AUS ISSN 0404-2018) **1309**
Australian Financial Review Archive CD *see* Australian Financial Review **1309**
Australian Financial Review Magazine (AUS ISSN 1328-3774) **1064**
Australian Financial Review Quarterly on CD-ROM *see* Australian Financial Review **1309**
• Australian Fisheries Management Authority. Annual Report (AUS ISSN 1039-3099) **3586**
• Australian Fisheries Management Authority. Corporate Plan (AUS ISSN 1440-2173) **3586**
• Australian Fisheries Management Authority Update (AUS ISSN 1449-7697) **3586**
Australian Fluoridation News (AUS ISSN 1445-2847) **8818**
Australian Flying (AUS ISSN 0004-9123) **47**
➤ Australian Folklore (AUS ISSN 0819-0852) **3615**
Australian Folklore. Bulletin *see* Australian Folklore **3615**
Australian Folklore. Newsletter *see* Australian Folklore **3615**
• Australian Food Shop (AUS) **3627**
Australian Football League Record *see* A F L Record **8220**
• Australian Forest Grower (AUS ISSN 0156-448X) **3684**
• ➤ Australian Forestry (AUS ISSN 0004-9158) **3684**
FourFourTwo (AUS ISSN 1832-987X) **8221**
The Australian Fundraising Magazine (AUS ISSN 1449-4116) **1309**
• Australian Gambling Statistics (Online) (AUS ISSN 1833-6337) **8218**
† Australian GamePro (AUS ISSN 1448-8825) **8933**
Australian Garden History (AUS ISSN 1033-3673) **3723**
➤ Australian Garden History. Studies (AUS ISSN 1448-3858) **3723**
Australian Gas Association. Directory *see* The Australian Gas Industry Directory **6763**
Australian Gas Association. Research Paper (AUS ISSN 1324-6283) **6763**
The Australian Gas Industry Directory (AUS ISSN 0727-3541) **6763**
The Australian Gemmologist (AUS ISSN 0004-9174) **4564**
• Australian General Mining Year Book (AUS ISSN 1034-6953) **6457**
• ➤ Australian Geographer (AUS ISSN 0004-9182) **3999**
• Australian Geographic (AUS ISSN 0816-1658) **4000**
Australian Geographical Studies *see* Geographical Research **4011**
Australian Geological Survey Organisation. Bulletin (AUS ISSN 1039-2645) **2702**
• The Australian Geologist (AUS ISSN 0312-4711) **2726**
Australian Geomechanics Journal (AUS ISSN 0818-9110) **6457**
Australian Gift Guide Magazine *see* Australian Giftguide **4059**
Australian Giftguide (AUS ISSN 0312-5327) **4059**
† Australian Gliding Yearbook (AUS ISSN 0084-7364) **8933**
Australian Goat World (AUS ISSN 0045-0472) **280**
Australian Gold, Gem and Treasure Magazine (AUS ISSN 0817-654X) **6457**
• Australian Golf Digest (AUS ISSN 1324-7476) **8221**
Australian Good Taste (AUS ISSN 1327-7650) **5065**
• Australian Gourmet Traveller (AUS ISSN 1034-9006) **8684**
• Australian Gourmet Traveller Wine (AUS ISSN 1446-9510) **598**
Australian Government Department of Health and Ageing, Therapeutic Goods Administration News *see* T G A News **6882**
† Australian Government Information Management Office. Annual Report (AUS ISSN 1832-3731) **8933**
Australian Government Solicitor. Annual Report (AUS ISSN 1444-6154) **4624**
Australian Graduate School of Entrepreneurship Research Report Series (AUS ISSN 1448-7128) **1064**
Australian Guitar Magazine (AUS ISSN 1329-7686) **6546**
• Australian Hardware Journal (AUS ISSN 0004-9255) **1053**
The Australian Health Consumer *see* Health Voices **4096**
• ➤ Australian Health Review (AUS ISSN 0156-5788) **4088**
Australian Healthy Food Guide (AUS ISSN 1832-875X) **3627**
• Australian Hearing. Annual Report (AUS ISSN 1832-9691) **6078**
Australian Hereford Quarterly *see* Hereford Advantage (Northern Edition) **288**
Australian Hi-Fi and Home Theatre Technology (AUS ISSN 1442-1259) **8152**
Australian Hi-Fi Annual *see* Home Cinema & Hi-Fi Living **8153**
• ➤ Australian Historical Studies (AUS ISSN 1031-461X) **4132**
• Australian HIV Surveillance Report (AUS ISSN 1035-221X) **5810**
The Australian Holstein Journal (AUS ISSN 1328-6196) **261**
• Australian Home Beautiful (AUS ISSN 0004-928X) **5065**
Australian Homespun (AUS ISSN 1443-4792) **4352**
• Australian Horsewyse (AUS ISSN 1833-0886) **8287**
Australian Horticulture (AUS ISSN 0726-2256) **3723**
Australian Hot Talk (AUS ISSN 0818-3589) **6286**
Australian Hotelier (AUS ISSN 0814-9348) **4382**
• Australian House & Garden (AUS ISSN 0004-931X) **4532**
• ➤ Australian Humanities Review (AUS ISSN 1325-8338) **4444**
• Australian Immigration Law (AUS) **4846**
Australian InCar Entertainment (AUS ISSN 1035-8323) **8152**
• ➤ Australian Indigenous Health Bulletin (AUS ISSN 1445-7253) **7509**
Australian Indigenous Law Reporter *see* Australian Indigenous Law Review **7202**
• ➤ Australian Indigenous Law Review (AUS ISSN 1835-0186) **7202**
Australian Infection Control *see* Healthcare Infection **5814**
† Australian Innovation Magazine (AUS ISSN 1444-5026) **8933**
Australian Insolvency Journal (AUS ISSN 1441-189X) **1309**
Australian Insolvency Law Journal (AUS ISSN 1321-618X) **4827**
➤ Australian Institute for the Conservation of Cultural Material. Bulletin (AUS ISSN 1034-4233) **477**
Australian Institute for the Conservation of Cultural Material National Newsletter *see* A I C C M National Newsletter **4439**
Australian Institute of Administrative Law Forum *see* A I A L Forum **4607**
Australian Institute of Administrative Law National Lecture Series on Administrative Law *see* A I A L National Lecture Series on Administrative Law **4607**
Australian Institute of Agricultural Science Occasional Publication *see* A I A S Occasional Publication **77**
• Australian Institute of Criminology. Annual Report (AUS ISSN 0311-449X) **2644**
Australian Institute of Criminology Newsletter *see* A I C Newsletter **2643**
• Australian Institute of Family Studies. Annual Report (AUS ISSN 0819-2588) **7277**
Australian Institute of Family Studies, Australian Centre for the Study of Sexual Assault Wrap *see* A C S S A Wrap **8850**
• Australian Institute of Family Studies. National Child Protection Clearing House. Research Brief (AUS ISSN 1833-7074) **2144**
• Australian Institute of Family Studies. Research Paper (AUS ISSN 1446-9863) **7277**
• ➤ Australian Institute of Geoscientists. Journal (AUS ISSN 1443-1017) **2702**
• Australian Institute of Marine Science. Annual Report (AUS ISSN 1037-3314) **2800**
Australian Institute of Marine Science Report *see* A I M S Report **2799**
Australian Institute of Marine Science Report *see* A I M S Report **2799**
• Australian Institute of Marine Science. Research Plan (AUS ISSN 1327-7286) **2800**
Australian Institute of Petroleum. Annual Report (AUS ISSN 0314-3171) **6763**
• Australian Institute of Sport Alumni News (AUS ISSN 1448-3475) **2968**
• ➤ Australian Intellectual Property Journal (AUS ISSN 1038-1635) **6745**
Australian International Airshow (AUS ISSN 1832-7036) **47**
➤ Australian International Law Journal (AUS ISSN 1325-5029) **4918**
Australian International U F O Flying Saucer Research (AUS ISSN 0156-742X) **47**
Australian Ironman (AUS ISSN 1322-8307) **6982**
• The Australian Jaguar Driver (AUS) **8556**
Australian Jeweller *see* Jeweller **4567**
• Australian Jewish Historical Society. Journal (AUS ISSN 0819-0615) **3521**
Australian Jewish Historical Society. Journal and Proceedings *see* Australian Jewish Historical Society. Journal **3521**
• Australian Jewish Historical Society. Newsletter (AUS ISSN 0816-7141) **7718**
• The Australian Jewish News (AUS ISSN 1325-5975) **3521**
Australian Jewish News (Sydney Edition) (AUS ISSN 1325-5967) **3521**
• Australian Jobs (AUS ISSN 1832-7230) **1666**
Australian Joint Conference on Artificial Intelligence. Proceedings (GBR) **2446**
➤ Australian Journal of Acupuncture and Chinese Medicine (AUS ISSN 1833-9735) **307**
• Australian Journal of Administrative Law (AUS ISSN 1320-7105) **4846**

Australian O H S File *see* Australian Occupational Health & Safety File **6673**

● Australian Occupational Health & Safety File (AUS ISSN 1328-9071) **6673**

† ● Australian Occupational Health & Safety Yearbook (AUS ISSN 1329-430X) **8933**

● ➤ Australian Occupational Therapy Journal (AUS ISSN 0045-0766) **6107**

● Australian Official Journal of Designs (Online) (AUS ISSN 1832-9942) **6745**

Australian Official Journal of Designs (Print) *see* Australian Official Journal of Designs (Online) **6745**

● Australian Official Journal of Patents (Online) (AUS ISSN 1832-9950) **6745**

Australian Official Journal of Patents (Print) *see* Australian Official Journal of Patents (Online) **6745**

● Australian Official Journal of Trade Marks (Online) (AUS ISSN 1832-9969) **6745**

Australian Official Journal of Trade Marks (Print) *see* Australian Official Journal of Trade Marks (Online) **6745**

Australian Open Official Tournament Magazine (AUS ISSN 1321-4217) **8221**

Australian Optometry (AUS ISSN 0726-5018) **6039**

Australian Orchid Review (AUS ISSN 0045-0782) **3724**

Australian Orienteer (AUS ISSN 0818-6510) **8304**

● ➤ Australian Orthodontic Journal (AUS ISSN 0587-3908) **5835**

➤ Australian Orthoptic Journal (AUS ISSN 0814-0936) **6039**

Australian Outlook (GBR ISSN 0301-5785) **3793**

Australian P C Authority (AUS ISSN 1329-2978) **2574**

● Australian P C User (AUS ISSN 1322-3712) **2574**

● Australian P C World (Online) (AUS) **2407**

† ● Australian P C World (Print) (AUS ISSN 0813-1384) **8933**

● Australian P W C Magazine (Australian Personal Watercraft Magazine) (AUS) **8271**

Australian Paper Crafts (AUS ISSN 1449-7018) **6732**

Australian Parapsychological Review *see* Australian Journal of Parapsychology **6741**

Australian Parliamentary Law Journal (AUS ISSN 1321-5930) **4846**

Australian Patchwork and Quilting (AUS ISSN 1322-1159) **6637**

● Australian Patent Abstracts on CD-ROM (AUS) **6760**

Australian Patent Applications Scoreboard (Year) (AUS ISSN 1832-1070) **6745**

● Australian Peacekeeper and Peacemaker (AUS ISSN 1832-6390) **8026**

Australian Peacekeeper and Peacemaker Veterans' Association Inc. *see* Australian Peacekeeper and Peacemaker **8026**

Australian Penthouse (AUS ISSN 0158-0655) **6286**

Australian Performance Horse (AUS ISSN 1446-5132) **8287**

● Australian Personal Computer (AUS ISSN 0725-4415) **2574**

Australian Pesticides & Veterinary Medicines Authority Gazette *see* A P V M A Gazette **4854**

Australian Petroleum Cooperative Research Centre. Annual Report (AUS ISSN 1327-8312) **6763**

Australian Petroleum Production and Exploration Association Annual Report *see* A P P E A Annual Report **6761**

Australian Petroleum Production and Exploration Association Journal (DVD) *see* The A P P E A Journal (DVD) **6761**

Australian Pharmacist (AUS ISSN 0728-4632) **6823**

Australian Photography (AUS ISSN 0004-9964) **6964**

● Australian Physiological Society. Proceedings (AUS) **920**

● Australian Pilot (AUS ISSN 1836-7720) **47**

● The Australian Pipeliner (AUS ISSN 0310-1258) **3260**

● ➤ Australian Planner (AUS ISSN 0729-3682) **4404**

● Australian Plants (AUS ISSN 0005-0008) **777**

Australian Playwrights (NLD ISSN 0921-2531) **5259**

Australian Plumbing Cost Guide (AUS ISSN 1834-0245) **977**

● Australian Plumbing Industry (AUS ISSN 0817-6337) **4116**

Australian Police Journal (AUS ISSN 0005-0024) **2644**

Australian Poll Dorset Journal (AUS) **280**

The Australian Pork Newspaper (AUS) **280**

● Australian Poultry Science Symposium (Year). Proceedings (AUS ISSN 1034-6260) **280**

Australian Powerboat (AUS ISSN 0313-766X) **8271**

● Australian Presbyterian (AUS ISSN 1445-7962) **7746**

● ➤ Australian Prescriber (AUS ISSN 0312-8008) **6823**

● Australian Prescription Products Guide (AUS ISSN 1321-9758) **6824**

Australian Prescription Products Guide *see* Australian Prescription Products Guide **6824**

● Australian Press Council News (AUS ISSN 1033-470X) **4572**

● Australian Primary Mathematics Classroom (AUS ISSN 1326-0286) **2829**

● Australian Printer (AUS ISSN 1328-2573) **7318**

Australian Private Doctor (AUS ISSN 0817-3834) **5581**

Australian Project Manager *see* Project Manager **1787**

Australian Proofing Buyer's Guide *see* Australian Printer **7318**

● Australian Property Investor (AUS ISSN 1329-2447) **7583**

Australian Property Journal *see* Australian and New Zealand Property Journal **7583**

● Australian Property Law Journal (AUS ISSN 1038-5959) **4827**

Australian Property Market Indicators (AUS ISSN 1447-6614) **4434**

● Australian Prospect (AUS ISSN 1834-2736) **7108**

● Australian Prudential Regulation Authority. Annual Report (AUS ISSN 1442-7885) **4493**

● Australian Prudential Regulation Authority. Half Yearly Financial Bulletin on Life Insurance (Online) (AUS) **4493**

● ➤ Australian Psychologist (GBR ISSN 0005-0067) **7338**

Australian Public Intellectual Review of Books *see* A P I Review of Books **4986**

● Australian Public Policy Program Working Paper (AUS ISSN 1832-424X) **7422**

Australian Public Service Jobs *see* A P S Jobs **7418**

Australian Publishers Association Members Directory *see* A P A Members Directory **7550**

Australian Purebred Pig Herd Book (AUS) **280**

Australian Quarantine and Inspection Service Bulletin *see* A Q I S Bulletin **78**

Australian Quarter Horse News (AUS ISSN 1832-1704) **8287**

Australian Quarterly (Balmain) *see* A Q (Balmain) **7101**

● Australian Rail Tram & Bus Worker (AUS) **4590**

Australian Railway Enthusiast (AUS ISSN 1030-021X) **8615**

Australian Railway Historical Society. Queensland Division. Bulletin. Supplement *see* Sunshine Express **8625**

Australian Railway History (AUS ISSN 1449-6291) **8615**

Australian Railways Union. National Office News (AUS) **4590**

● Australian Rationalist (AUS ISSN 1036-8191) **6906**

Australian Recalls and Cancellations Bulletin (AUS) **7509**

● ➤ Australian Religion Studies Review (GBR ISSN 1031-2943) **7624**

Australian Research Council Strategic Plan (Years) *see* A R C Strategic Plan (Years) **2822**

● ➤ Australian Research in Early Childhood Education (AUS ISSN 1320-6648) **2829**

Australian Reseller News *see* A R N **2510**

Australian Resources and Energy Law Journal (AUS ISSN 1447-9710) **6457**

Australian Retail Tobacconist (AUS ISSN 0727-078X) **8485**

Australian Retailer *see* The A R A Retailer **1055**

Australian Retailer Magazine *see* The Australian Retailer Magazine **1806**

The Australian Retailer Magazine (AUS ISSN 1448-9015) **1806**

Australian Retailers Association Retailer *see* The A R A Retailer **1055**

Australian Retired Persons Association News *see* A R P A News **4038**

● ➤ Australian Review of Applied Linguistics (AUS ISSN 0155-0640) **5097**

Australian Review of Applied Linguistics. Series 5 *see* Australian Review of Applied Linguistics **5097**

● ➤ Australian Review of Public Affairs (AUS ISSN 1832-1526) **7108**

† Australian Road and Track (AUS ISSN 1036-3254) **8933**

Australian Road Research Board. Briefing *see* A R R B Transport Research. Briefing **8629**

Australian Road Research Board. Proceedings (CD-ROM Edition) *see* A R R B Transport Research. Proceedings (CD-ROM Edition) **8629**

Australian Rugby News and Review *see* Australian Rugby Review **8221**

Australian Rugby Review (AUS ISSN 1326-4303) **8221**

Australian Rural Science Annual (AUS ISSN 0819-2995) **93**

Australian Safeguards and Non-Proliferation Office. Annual Report (AUS ISSN 1442-7699) **2225**

● Australian Sailing (AUS ISSN 0726-5646) **8271**

● Australian Science Fiction Bullsheet (AUS ISSN 1445-4319) **5440**

† Australian Scout (AUS ISSN 0815-4627) **8933**

Australian Screen Education *see* Screen Education **3081**

Australian Screen Education *see* Screen Education **3081**

● Australian Sea Freight (AUS) **8522**

Australian Sea Heritage (AUS ISSN 0813-0523) **6520**

† Australian SeaChange (AUS ISSN 1832-7273) **8933**

● Australian Seafood Industry Directory (Year) (AUS ISSN 1324-2385) **3587**

Australian Securities and Investments Commission Gazette (CD-ROM) *see* A S I C Gazette (CD-ROM) **4854**

Australian Securities and Investments Commission News (Online) *see* A S I C News (Online) **1609**

Australian Security Intelligence Organization. Annual Report to Parliament (AUS ISSN 0815-4562) **7222**

Australian Security Magazine (AUS ISSN 1835-7555) **2225**

● ➤ Australian Senior Mathematics Journal (AUS ISSN 0819-4564) **3052**

Australian Services Union People *see* A S U People **4589**

Australian Shooter (AUS ISSN 1442-7354) **8304**

Australian Shooters Journal (Kent Town) *see* A S J (Kent Town) **8301**

● ➤ Australian Slavonic and East European Studies (AUS ISSN 0818-8149) **4444**

Australian Smart Home Ideas (AUS) **5065**

Australian Snowboarder Magazine (AUS ISSN 1321-5914) **8304**

➤ Australian Social Monitor (AUS ISSN 1440-4842) **7949**

Australian Social Policy (Canberra) (AUS ISSN 1442-6331) **8027**

➤ Australian Social Work (AUS ISSN 0312-407X) **8027**

Australian Society and Events *see* Australian Society & Events **5065**

Australian Society & Events (AUS ISSN 1832-3847) **5065**

Australian Society for Antimicrobials Newsletters *see* A S A Newsletters **879**

Australian Society for HIV Medicine Inc. Journal Club *see* A S H M Journal Club **5807**

Australian Society for Limnology Newsletter *see* A S L Newsletter **2792**

Australian Society for Limnology. Special Publication (AUS ISSN 0156-8426) **2792**

Australian Society for Operations Research Inc. Bulletin *see* A S O R Bulletin **1722**

Australian Society for Sports History. Journal *see* Sporting Traditions **8206**

Australian Society for Sports History Studies in Sports History *see* A S S H Studies in Sports History **8156**

Australian Society of Anaesthetists Ltd. News *see* A S A News **5767**

Australian Society of Anaesthetists. Newsletter *see* A S A News **5767**

● Australian Society of Archivists. Bulletin (AUS ISSN 0312-4991) **4993**

● Australian Society of Archivists. New South Wales Branch. Newsletter (AUS) **4993**

● Australian Society of Archivists. Queensland Branch. Newsletter (AUS ISSN 1444-1551) **4993**

Australian Society of Authors Ltd. Newsletter *see* A S A Newsletter **7550**

Australian Society of Certified Practising Accountants. Annual Report (Print) *see* C P A Annual Report **1283**

● Australian Society of Exploration Geophysicists. Extended Abstracts (AUS) **2719**

Australian Society of Indexers. Newsletter *see* A N Z S I Newsletter **1**

Australian Society of Indexers Newsletter Online *see* A N Z S I Newsletter **1**

● Australian Society of Soil Science. Profile (AUS ISSN 1328-2883) **220**

➤ Australian Society of Sugar Cane Technologists. Proceedings (AUS ISSN 0726-0822) **3627**

● Australian Software Engineering Conference. Proceedings (USA ISSN 1530-0803) **2588**

† Australian Sommelier (AUS ISSN 1832-5726) **8933**

● Australian Sports Anti-Doping Authority. Annual Report (AUS ISSN 1833-8976) **7509**

Australian Sports Drug Agency. Annual Report *see* Australian Sports Anti-Doping Authority. Annual Report **7509**

● Australian Sports Foundation. Newsletter (AUS ISSN 1448-3467) **8160**

● Australian Stamp Bulletin (AUS ISSN 1833-1564) **6891**

Australian Stamp Duties Bulletin *see* Australian Stamp Duties Law **1911**

● Australian Stamp Duties Law (AUS) **1911**

● Australian Stamp Explorer (AUS) **6892**

Australian Stitches (AUS ISSN 1322-5464) **6637**

Australian Stock Horse Journal (AUS ISSN 0817-8550) **8287**

➤ Australian Stream Management Conference. Proceedings (AUS ISSN 1441-8053) **2792**

➤ Australian Studies (GBR ISSN 0954-0954) **4191**

† Australian Studies in Health Service Administration (AUS ISSN 0067-2165) **8933**

† ● ➤ Australian Studies in Journalism (AUS ISSN 1038-6130) **8934**

● Australian Style (Macquarie) (AUS ISSN 1320-0941) **5097**

Australian Sugar Industry Handbook (AUS ISSN 1327-9289) **220**

Australian Sugar Year Book (AUS ISSN 0817-3176) **3627**

† Australian Surf Lifesaver (AUS ISSN 1321-2036) **8934**

Australian Surfrider (AUS ISSN 1832-2956) **8304**

Australian Surveyors Congress. Technical Papers (AUS ISSN 1327-0753) **4000**

● ➤ Australian Systematic Botany (AUS ISSN 1030-1887) **777**

➤ Australian T A F E Teacher (Technical and Further Education) (AUS ISSN 0815-3701) **3052**

Australian T3 (AUS ISSN 1445-2901) **8416**

● Australian Table (AUS ISSN 1442-5807) **3627**

Australian Target Rifle (AUS ISSN 1832-3944) **8305**

Australian Tattoo (AUS) **477**

● ➤ Australian Tax Forum (AUS ISSN 0812-695X) **1911**

● Australian Tax Handbook (AUS ISSN 1325-7935) **1911**

Australian Tax Legislation (AUS ISSN 1325-7927) **1911**

● ➤ Australian Tax Review (AUS ISSN 0311-094X) **1911**

● ➤ Australian Taxation Law Journal (AUS ISSN 1321-7488) **1911**

Australian Technical Analysts Association. Journal (AUS ISSN 1832-3693) **1064**

Australian Telecom (AUS) **2313**

Australian Telecom Directory *see* Australian Telecom **2313**

● Australian Tenancy Practice and Precedents (AUS) **4624**

Australian Tennis Magazine (AUS ISSN 1321-0262) **8221**

Australian Terrier Club of America Newsletter *see* Talkabout **6815**

Australian Thoroughbred Record (AUS ISSN 1832-0295) **8287**

Australian Tourist Commission. Annual Report *see* Tourism Australia. Annual Report **8763**

● ➤ Australian Traditional-Medicine Society. Journal (AUS ISSN 1326-3390) **307**

Australian Trail & Track Monthly (AUS) **8254**

● Australian Treaty Series (AUS ISSN 1036-3467) **4918**

Australian Triathlete (AUS ISSN 1320-5773) **8160**

Australian Tyre Dealer (AUS ISSN 1447-3127) **8556**

The Australian U F O Bulletin (AUS) **47**

● ➤ Australian Universities Quality Agency. Occasional Publications (AUS ISSN 1446-4268) **2968**

● ➤ Australian Universities' Review (AUS ISSN 0818-8068) **2968**

● Australian Uranium Association. Newsletter (AUS ISSN 0728-2400) **6457**

● ➤ Australian Veterinary Association. Annual Report (AUS ISSN 1320-9582) **8793**

● ➤ Australian Veterinary Journal (GBR ISSN 0005-0423) **8793**

➤ Australian Veterinary Practitioner (AUS ISSN 0310-138X) **8793**

Australian Vice-Chancellors' Committee Directory Postgraduate (Online) *see* A V C C Directory Postgraduate (Online) **2964**

† Australian Videocamera and Desktop Video (AUS ISSN 1327-0338) **8934**

Australian Videography & Camcorder Review (AUS) **2400**

Australian Vignerons (AUS) **220**

Australian Vital Magazine (AUS ISSN 1446-5000) **6982**

● Australian Viticulture (AUS ISSN 1329-0436) **598**

➤ Australian Voice (AUS ISSN 1325-1317) **6546**

Australian Water Resources Council. Water Resources Series (AUS ISSN 0811-5397) **8818**

Australian Wildlife Magazine (AUS) **2603**

Australian Wine Research Institute. Technical Review (AUS ISSN 0816-0805) **598**

Australian Winner *see* Aozhou Caihongying **1552**

The Australian Wish (AUS) **5065**

● Australian Women's Health (AUS) **8844**

● The Australian Women's Weekly (AUS ISSN 0005-0458) **8852**

Australian Women's Weekly (NZL ISSN 1174-2755) **8852**

Australian Wood Review (AUS ISSN 1039-9925) **3710**

● Australian Woodworker (AUS ISSN 0818-0261) **1049**

Australian Woodworker Source Book *see* Australian Woodworker **1049**

● Australian Wool Compendium (AUS) **8448**

Australian Wool Exchange Wool Statistics Yearbook *see* A W E X Wool Statistics Yearbook **8463**

Australian Wool Market Review *see* Wool Market Review **8462**

● Australian Wool Production Forecast Report (AUS) **8448**

Australian Wool Statistics *see* A W E X Wool Statistics Yearbook **8463**

● The Australian Worker (Sydney) (AUS ISSN 1324-4094) **4590**

Australian Workshop Manager (AUS) **1806**

Australian Writer (AUS ISSN 1327-340X) **7552**

● The Australian Writer's Marketplace (AUS ISSN 1448-5699) **1973**

† Australian Writers Series (GBR) **8934**

Australian Yachting *see* Australasian Yachting **8271**

● ➤ Australian Yearbook of International Law (AUS ISSN 0084-7658) **4918**

Australian Yoga Life (AUS ISSN 1446-1056) **6643**

➤ Australian Zoologist (AUS ISSN 0067-2238) **935**

The Australian's Review of Books *see* The Australian **3793**

Australia's Economic Statistics (AUS ISSN 1035-6142) **1211**

Australia's Longwalls (AUS ISSN 1327-6115) **6458**

Australia's Mining Monthly (AUS ISSN 1328-8032) **6458**

Australia's Open Garden Scheme Guidebook (AUS ISSN 1326-7981) **3724**

† Australia's Overseas Aid Program (AUS) **8934**

Title

10008 AUTO SPECIAL ULRICH'S PERIODICALS

† Auto Special (ITA) **8934**
Auto - Strassenverkehr (DEU ISSN 0863-3940) **8629**
Auto Sukces (POL ISSN 1230-8536) **8560**
Auto Super Market (ITA ISSN 1124-9978) **8560**
Auto Swiat (POL ISSN 1234-0294) **8560**
Auto Swiat Katalog (POL ISSN 1427-3535) **8560**
Auto Tankstelle Garage (AUT) **8560**
Auto Tecnica *see* Autotecnica **8567**
Auto Test (ARG ISSN 1514-0016) **8560**
Auto Test Libro de Pruebas (ARG ISSN 0329-3327) **8560**
Auto Testes (PRT) **8560**
Auto Tests (DEU) **8560**
Auto Testy (POL ISSN 1509-6874) **8560**
Auto Time *see* Cheshidai **8573**
Auto Tip Extra (CZE ISSN 1214-6323) **8560**
Auto Touring (AUT ISSN 0001-2688) **8560**
Auto Trader (IRL) **8560**
Auto Trader (NZL) **8560**
Auto Trader (USA) **8560**
Auto Trader Interactive *see* South African Auto Trader **8604**
Auto Travel *see* Dazhong Qiche (Qiche Luxing) **8577**
• Auto Travel in the U.S. (USA ISSN 1548-3223) **8560**
Auto Trim and Restyling News *see* Auto Trim & Restyling News **8560**
• Auto Trim & Restyling News (USA ISSN 1049-9601) **8560**
Auto Triti (GRC ISSN 1108-779X) **8560**
Auto Triti 4 x 4 & S U V Test Book (GRC) **8561**
Auto Triti Aggelies (GRC ISSN 1108-7684) **8561**
Auto Triti Best Value for Money (GRC) **8561**
Auto Triti Epaggelmatika (GRC) **8561**
Auto Triti Epaggelmatika Test Book (GRC) **8561**
Auto Triti Ikanopiisi Katochou (GRC) **8561**
Auto Triti Test Book (GRC ISSN 1108-7803) **8561**
Auto Triti Top Cars *see* Top Cars **8607**
Auto Triti Touring (GRC ISSN 1108-7811) **8561**
Auto Triti Voreia Ellada (GRC) **8561**
Auto Tuning (ITA ISSN 1971-0232) **8561**
Auto und Reise (DEU ISSN 0045-1010) **8684**
Auto und Wirtschaft (AUT) **8561**
Auto Vending (GBR) **1806**
Auto Verte (FRA ISSN 0222-3996) **8561**
Auto Week *see* Xing Bao **8612**
• Auto Weekly (USA) **1064**
Auto Welt (DEU ISSN 0944-5005) **8561**
Auto Woman (IRL ISSN 1393-7634) **8561**
Auto World Magazine (USA) **8561**
Auto-X and Grassroots Motorsports *see* Grassroots Motorsports **8583**
Auto Zeitung (DEU ISSN 0171-8452) **8561**
Auto Zubehoer Markt: Autofahrerhandbuch (DEU) **8561**
Auto Zubehoer Markt: Die Sonderseiten (DEU ISSN 0939-7329) **8561**
Auto Zubehoer Markt: Freie Werkstatt (DEU ISSN 1436-0543) **8561**
Auto Zubehoer Markt: Teilehandel (DEU) **8561**
Auto Zurnal (SVK ISSN 1336-7900) **8561**
Auto7 (CZE ISSN 1214-6781) **8561**
• AutoAsia (GBR ISSN 1360-9416) **8561**
• AutoAsia Data (GBR ISSN 1462-4095) **8561**
Autobranchen *see* Autobranchen.info **8561**
• Autobranchen.info (DNK ISSN 1903-4695) **8561**
Autobus (ITA ISSN 1825-6716) **8490**
Autobuses & Autocares Digital *see* Autobuses y Autocares **8491**
• Autobuses y Autocares (ESP ISSN 1888-1823) **8491**
Autobuskroniek (NLD ISSN 1384-0436) **8491**
AutoCAD Magazin (DEU ISSN 0934-1749) **2588**
Autocad Magazine (ESP) **3288**
AutoCAD User (CAN ISSN 1198-0869) **2588**
Autocapital S U V (Sport Utility Vehicle) (ITA ISSN 1973-7807) **8561**
AutoCapital Travel (ITA ISSN 1828-0811) **8684**
Autocar *see* Autocar **8561**
Autocar (CZE ISSN 1803-2273) **8561**
• Autocar (GBR ISSN 1355-8293) **8561**
Autocar - Italia (ITA ISSN 1828-339X) **8561**
Autocasion Cataluna (ESP ISSN 1699-1990) **8561**
Autocatalogo (ARG ISSN 0329-3335) **8561**
Autocatalogo (ESP) **8561**
Autoccasion (BEL ISSN 0778-3574) **8562**
• Autocentre (UKR ISSN 1605-5330) **8562**
AutoClassic (DEU) **8562**
Autoclub (ARG ISSN 0005-0946) **8562**
AutoConnect (Dutch Edition) (NLD ISSN 1574-1087) **2313**
Autocourse (GBR ISSN 0067-2432) **8160**
Autocourse Cart Official Yearbook (GBR) **8160**
Autodefinidos (ESP ISSN 1139-8922) **8160**
Autodefinidos Boom (ARG ISSN 1850-3489) **4328**
Autodefinidos Express (ARG ISSN 1514-8513) **4328**
Autodefinidos Extreme (ARG ISSN 1850-2970) **4328**
Autodefinidos Fantasticos (ARG ISSN 1514-4232) **4328**
Autodefinidos Gold (ARG ISSN 1514-8505) **4328**
Autodefinidos Mania (ARG ISSN 1850-3470) **4328**
Autodefinidos Pocket (ARG ISSN 1514-6022) **4328**
Autodefinidos Pocket. Extra (ARG ISSN 1515-0348) **4328**
Autodefinidos Premier (ARG ISSN 1850-2989) **4328**
Autodefinidos Quick (ARG ISSN 1515-0321) **4328**
† Autodesk News (CZE ISSN 1212-3501) **8934**
Autodesk Noticias (ESP) **2588**
Autodeterminacion (BOL ISSN 1029-4341) **7108**
Autodoprava *see* Autodoprava v Praxi **4624**
• Autodoprava v Praxi (CZE ISSN 1802-3436) **4624**
Autoengineer Australasia (AUS ISSN 1444-8599) **8562**
• Autoesporte (BRA ISSN 1413-9308) **8562**
AutoExpert (CZE ISSN 1211-2380) **8562**
• AutoExpert (POL ISSN 1234-480X) **3374**
• Autoextremist.com (USA) **8562**
AutoFace Ink (USA ISSN 1154-5720) **6546**
Autofachmann (DEU) **8562**
Autofacts *see* Autofile New and Used Annual **8934**
Autofil (NOR ISSN 1503-318X) **8562**
Autofil Aarbok 4x4guiden *see* 4x4guiden **8614**
Autofile (NZL ISSN 0112-3475) **8562**
AutoFile *see* AutoWeek Strategic Buyer's Guide **8567**
† Autofile New and Used Annual (NZL) **8934**
† Autofile Quarterly Report (NZL) **8934**
Autoflotte (DEU ISSN 0948-6682) **8562**
▼ Das AutoGas Journal (DEU ISSN 1865-8644) **8562**
• De Autogids (BEL ISSN 0773-3380) **8562**
AutoGlass (USA ISSN 1047-2061) **2037**
Autograph Catalogue (USA ISSN 1941-062X) **4328**
Autograph Collector (USA ISSN 1071-3425) **4328**
Autograph Research (USA ISSN 1069-6008) **4328**
† AutoGraphics (USA ISSN 1523-6277) **8934**
Autoguide (IND) **8562**
Autohaus (DEU ISSN 0005-0989) **8562**
Autohit (CZE ISSN 1212-8791) **8562**
Autohit Special (CZE) **8562**
Autohof Guide (DEU) **8684**
Autohof Guide L K W (DEU) **8685**
Autohof Guide LKW *see* Autohof Guide L K W **8685**
Autohoje Catalogo (PRT) **8562**
Autoillen Euroopassa (FIN ISSN 1796-7031) **8685**
• Autoimmune Drug Focus (GBR ISSN 1746-1243) **5755**
• ➤ Autoimmunity (GBR ISSN 0891-6934) **5755**
• Autoimmunity Reviews (USA ISSN 1568-9972) **5755**
• AutoInc. (USA ISSN 1047-5559) **8562**
Autoindustria (MEX) **8562**
† • Autoindustry (GBR ISSN 1469-204X) **8934**
Autojournalist (AUT) **4572**
Autokampioen (NLD ISSN 0005-0997) **8562**
Autokatalog *see* Auto Pruvodce **8560**
Autokaufmann (DEU ISSN 0174-6863) **8562**
Autokompas (NLD ISSN 1385-6669) **8562**
Autokompas Skoop *see* Skoop **8988**
Autokosten und Steuern Aktuell (DEU ISSN 0937-3381) **8562**
Autolla Ulkomaille *see* Autoillen Euroopassa **8685**
➤ Automa (CZE ISSN 1210-9592) **5449**
Automacao (BRA ISSN 1415-2134) **1880**
AutoMais (PRT ISSN 0872-3400) **8685**
The Automarket (USA) **8562**
Automasjon *see* Amnytt Magazine **2457**
Automat (ITA ISSN 0005-1012) **2457**
Automata (ITA ISSN 1828-9274) **7838**
The Automated Agency Report *see* The Anderson Agency Report **4530**
Automated Builder (USA ISSN 0899-5540) **977**
Automated Builder Annual Buyers' Guide (USA) **977**
➤ Automated Reasoning Series (NLD ISSN 0927-1023) **2446**
• ➤ Automated Software Engineering (USA ISSN 0928-8910) **2446**
Automated Teller Machine Debit News *see* A T M & Debit News **1305**
Automated Vending Technologies Magazine *see* A V T Magazine **1956**
Automaten-Markt (DEU ISSN 0005-1039) **1806**
• ➤ Automatic Control and Computer Sciences (USA ISSN 0146-4116) **2457**
Automatic Data Collection News *see* A D C News **2457**
• ➤ Automatic Documentation and Mathematical Linguistics (USA ISSN 0005-1055) **5202**
Automatic Machining (USA ISSN 0005-1071) **5449**
• Automatic Merchandiser (USA ISSN 1061-1797) **1806**
Automatic Meter Reading Association News *see* A M R A News **2535**
Automatic Musical Instrument Collectors' Association News Bulletin *see* The A M I C A News Bulletin **6541**
Automatic Programming Information Centre Studies in Data Processing *see* A P I C Studies in Data Processing **2505**
Automatic Testing Conference *see* I E E E Autotestcon **3311**
• ➤ Automatica (GBR ISSN 0005-1098) **2458**
• Automatica e Instrumentacion (ESP ISSN 0213-3113) **2458**
Automatica e Instrumentacion. Anuario *see* Automatica e Instrumentacion **2458**
Automatica e Instrumentacion Digital *see* Automatica e Instrumentacion **2458**
Automatica & Robotica (ESP) **2458**
Automatie (NLD ISSN 0005-1128) **2458**
• Automatik & Proces (DNK ISSN 1902-0228) **2458**
Automatik, Teknisk Udvikling *see* Automatik & Proces **2458**
Automatika (HRV ISSN 0005-1144) **2458**
Automation *see* Automatizace **2458**
Automation (DEU ISSN 1612-6475) **2458**
Automation *see* Automatizalas **3374**
Automation (SWE ISSN 0345-1011) **3374**
Automation *see* Otomasyon **1157**
Automation and Drives Kompendium *see* A & D Kompendium **2457**
Automation and Drives Lexikon *see* A & D Lexikon **2457**
Automation and Drives Newsletter *see* A & D Newsletter **2457**
Automation and Drives Software Guide *see* A & D Software Guide **2457**
Automation & Information Engineering *see* Zidonghua yu Xinxi Gongcheng **2465**
Automation & Instrumentation *see* Zidonghua yu Yiqi Yibiao **2465**
Automation & Qualitaet (DEU ISSN 1437-5435) **2458**
• ➤ Automation and Remote Control (RUS ISSN 0005-1179) **2458**
Automation Computers Applied Mathematics (ROM ISSN 1221-437X) **2458**
Automation, Computing. Computers & Measurement Abstracts *see* Automatizalasi, Szamitastechnikai es Merestechnikai Szakirodalmi Tajekoztato **7047**
• ➤ Automation in Construction (NLD ISSN 0926-5805) **2458**
Automation in Petro-Chemical Industry *see* Shiyou Huagong Zidonghua **6792**
Automation in Water Resources and Hydrology *see* Shuili Shuiwen Zidonghua **8832**
Automation of Electric Power Systems *see* Dianli Xitong Zidonghua **3156**
Automation World (USA ISSN 1553-1244) **2458**
Automationspraxis (DEU ISSN 1863-401X) **3365**
Automatisering *see* Automatisering & Industridata **2458**
• Automatisering Gids (NLD ISSN 0165-4683) **2407**
Automatisering & Industridata (NOR ISSN 1504-6184) **2458**
• ➤ Automatisierungstechnik (DEU ISSN 0178-2312) **2458**
➤ Automatisierungstechnische Praxis (DEU ISSN 0178-2320) **4486**
Automatisierungstechnische Praxis International (DEU ISSN 1613-2319) **4486**
➤ Automatizace/Automation (CZE ISSN 0005-125X) **2458**
Automatizacion (ESP) **2458**
Automatizalas/Automation (HUN ISSN 0133-1620) **3374**
Automatizalasi, Szamitastechnikai es Merestechnikai Szakirodalmi Tajekoztato/Automation, Computing. Computers & Measurement Abstracts (HUN ISSN 0231-0643) **7047**
Automatome (USA ISSN 1065-1772) **4844**
➤ Automatyka (POL ISSN 1429-3447) **2458**
Automazione e Strumentazione (ITA ISSN 0005-1284) **2459**
Automazione Industriale (ITA) **3374**
• Automazione Integrata (ITA ISSN 0393-3911) **2459**
Automazione Oggi (ITA ISSN 0392-8829) **2459**
Automercado (ESP) **8562**
Automobiel *see* Het Automobiel **364**
Het Automobiel (NLD ISSN 1572-2392) **364**
Automobiel Klassiek en Exclusief *see* Het Automobiel **364**
Automobiel Management (NLD ISSN 0929-1083) **8562**
Automobil (ROM ISSN 1582-5248) **8563**
• Automobil (SWE ISSN 0280-1981) **8563**
Automobil (ZAF ISSN 0304-8721) **8563**
Automobil-Club de Schweiz Zurich *see* A C S Zurich **8553**
Automobil-Club Verkehr Profil *see* A C V Profil **8553**
Automobil-Elektronik (DEU ISSN 0939-5326) **8563**
Automobil Entwicklung (DEU ISSN 1435-0408) **8563**
Automobil-Industrie (DEU ISSN 0005-1306) **8563**
Automobil Jahrbuch (DEU ISSN 1614-3418) **8563**
Automobil Produktion (DEU ISSN 0934-0394) **8563**
Automobil - Revue *see* Revue Automobile **8510**
Automobil Revue (CZE ISSN 1211-9555) **8563**
Automobil Test *see* Auto Tests **8560**
Automobil Tests Cabrios (DEU) **8563**
Automobile *see* L' AutoMobile **8563**
L'AutoMobile (CAN ISSN 1711-7526) **8563**
The Automobile (GBR ISSN 0955-1328) **8563**
Automobile (ITA ISSN 0005-1349) **8563**
Automobile *see* Collectible Automobile **8575**
• Automobile (USA) **8563**
Automobile Abstracts (Online Edition) (GBR ISSN 1743-260X) **8522**
Automobile Abstracts (Print Edition) *see* Automobile Abstracts (Online Edition) **8522**
Automobile Association Bed and Breakfast *see* A A Bed and Breakfast **8679**
Automobile Association Bed & Breakfast Guide (Year) *see* A A Bed & Breakfast Guide (Year) **8679**
Automobile Association Hotels, Lodges, Guest Houses, Bed & Breakfasts *see* A A Hotels, Lodges, Guest Houses, Bed & Breakfasts **8679**
Automobile Association Members Handbook (GBR) **8685**
Automobile Association Members Handbook. Ireland *see* A A Members Handbook. Ireland **8553**
Automobile Association Motoring *see* A A Motoring **8553**
Automobile Association of Zimbabwe Magazine *see* A A Magazine **8553**
Automobile Association of Zimbabwe. Members' Handbook (ZWE) **8563**
Automobile Association Self-Catering Getaways *see* A A Self-Catering Getaways **8679**
Automobile Blue Book Used Car Valuations (USA) **8563**
Automobile Club d'Italia News *see* A C I News **8553**
Automobile Dealers & The Law (USA) **8563**
Automobile Design Liability (USA) **4624**
Automobile Engineering *see* Jidosha Kogaku **8587**
L'Automobile - Formule 1 (FRA) **8160**
• Automobile in Cifre (Year)/Motor Industry in Figures (Year) (ITA) **8522**
Automobile Industry Almanac *see* Plunkett's Automobile Industry Almanac **8598**
Automobile Industry China (CHN) **8563**
The Automobile Industry: Domestic & Foreign Auto Manufacturers (USA) **8563**
The Automobile Industry - Toyota and Japan (JPN) **8563**
Automobile Insurance Losses, Collision Coverages, Variations by Make and Series (USA ISSN 0093-0466) **4494**
L'Automobile - Les Essais (FRA) **8563**
L'Automobile - Les Occasions (FRA) **8563**
† Automobile Luxus und Leben (DEU ISSN 1611-7085) **8934**
L'Automobile Magazine (FRA ISSN 0982-9156) **8563**
L'Automobile Magazine Diesel (FRA) **8563**
L'Automobile Magazine Hors-Serie - Toutes les Voitures du Monde (Year) (FRA) **8563**
Automobile Magazine's Field Guide to Sport-Utility Vehicles, Pickups, & Vans *see* Automobile **8563**
Automobile Magazine's Guide to Buying & Leasing *see* Automobile **8563**
▼ Automobile Magazine's Ultimate New Car Guide (USA) **8563**
Automobile Management International (DEU) **8563**
▼ • L'Automobile Passion (FRA ISSN 1961-4047) **8563**
Automobile Quarterly (USA ISSN 0005-1438) **8563**
Automobile Revue. Classique & Sport (FRA ISSN 1778-1760) **8563**
Automobile Revue. Diesel (FRA ISSN 1777-6295) **8563**
Automobile Revue. Special 4 x 4 (FRA ISSN 1778-8129) **8160**
Automobile Revue. Special Quatre Fois Quatre *see* Automobile Revue. Special 4 x 4 **8160**
Automobile Science & Technology *see* Qiche Keji **8600**
Automobile Story (FRA ISSN 1960-2286) **8564**
Automobile Technology *see* Qiche Jishu **8600**
Automobile, Tractor, Scooter Report (IND) **209**
Automobile Year (CHE ISSN 0084-7674) **8564**
Automobiler (USA) **8564**
Automobiles and Highways in Finland (Year). Statistics *see* Auto Ja Tie **8522**
Automobiles Classiques (FRA ISSN 0759-6065) **8564**
Automobiles G P L Magazine *see* Automobiles Gaz de Petrole Liquefie Magazine **8934**
† Automobiles Gaz de Petrole Liquefie Magazine (FRA ISSN 1292-0371) **8934**
Automobilia (FRA ISSN 1270-217X) **8564**
• Automobilismo (ITA ISSN 0394-0128) **8564**
• Automobilismo d'Epoca (ITA ISSN 1723-4549) **8564**
Automobiltechnische Zeitschrift *see* A T Z **8554**
Automobiltechnische Zeitschrift Autotechnology *see* A T Z Autotechnology **8554**
Automobiltechnische Zeitschrift Elektronik *see* A T Z Elektronik **8554**
Automobiltechnische Zeitschrift Produktion *see* A T Z Produktion **8555**
AutomobilWirtschaft (DEU ISSN 1616-654X) **8564**
• Automobilwoche (DEU ISSN 1619-0327) **8564**
Automobile Technology & Material *see* Qiche Gongyi yu Cailiao **8600**
Automocion y Transporte 3 *see* Transporte 3 **8517**
Automonat (DEU ISSN 1862-3883) **8564**
• Automotive Aftermarket in China (USA ISSN 1932-8400) **1806**
Automotive Aftermarket Products Expo Today *see* A A P E X Today **6277**
Automotive Aftermarket Training Guide *see* ImportCar **8585**
Automotive Aftermarket World Buyers' Guide (GBR ISSN 1467-906X) **8564**
▼ Automotive Agenda (DEU ISSN 1867-495X) **8564**
• Automotive & Aerospace Test Report (USA) **3296**
• Automotive Body Repair News (USA ISSN 0192-0995) **8564**
The Automotive Booster of California (USA ISSN 0191-6459) **8564**
• Automotive Components Analyst (GBR ISSN 1354-117X) **8564**
• Automotive Components Manufacturers (GBR) **8564**
Automotive Contact (USA) **8564**
Automotive Contact Directory. Indiana (USA) **8564**
Automotive Cooling Journal (USA ISSN 0005-1497) **8564**
Automotive Dealers Digest (USA) **8564**
Automotive Design and Production *see* Automotive Design & Production **8564**
• Automotive Design & Production (USA ISSN 1536-8823) **8564**
• Automotive Electonics (GBR ISSN 1749-1819) **8564**
• Automotive, Electrical & Air Conditioning News (AUS) **8564**
Automotive Emerging Markets (GBR ISSN 1460-552X) **8564**
Automotive Engineer (AUS) **8564**

Link to your serials resources and content with ulrichsweb.com

DIRECTORY 2010 AVERAGE DAILY TRAFFIC VOLUMES WITH VEHICLE CLASSIFICATION 10009

• Automotive Engineer (GBR ISSN 0307-6490) **8564**
Automotive Engineering *see* Qiche Gongcheng **8600**
Automotive Engineering International *see* Guoji Qiche Gongcheng **8583**
• Automotive Engineering International (USA ISSN 1543-849X) **8565**
Automotive Engineering International - en Espanol *see* Automotive Engineering International **8565**
Automotive Engineering Partners *see* A E P **8554**
• Automotive Environment Analyst (GBR ISSN 1357-4922) **8565**
Automotive Executive *see* N A D A's Automotive Executive **8594**
Automotive Exports (TUR ISSN 1301-4633) **1553**
Automotive Fine Art (USA) **477**
† • Automotive Finishing (USA) **8934**
• Automotive Fleet (USA ISSN 0005-1519) **8565**
Automotive Fuel Economy Program. Annual Report to the Congress (USA ISSN 0146-5236) **6763**
Automotive History Review (USA ISSN 1056-2729) **8565**
• Automotive Industries (USA ISSN 1099-4130) **8565**
Automotive Industry *see* Otomotiv Endustrisi **8597**
The Automotive Industry: A Look at Dealership, Repair Services and Auto Parts Retailers (USA) **8565**
• Automotive Industry Data Newsletter (GBR ISSN 0951-158X) **8565**
Automotive Industry Matters. Newsletter *see* A I M Newsletter **8554**
Automotive Industry Matters Newsletter *see* A I M Newsletter **8554**
Automotive Industry of India - Facts & Figures (IND) **8565**
• Automotive Intelligence News (USA) **8565**
• Automotive Interior (GBR ISSN 1747-7301) **8565**
• Automotive Logistics (GBR ISSN 1471-6003) **8491**
Automotive Management *see* A M **8554**
Automotive Management Information Systems Council Newsletter (USA) **1849**
• Automotive Manufacturing Solutions (GBR ISSN 1471-6038) **8565**
Automotive Market Report (USA ISSN 0733-2084) **8565**
Automotive Marketer Annual Buyer's Guide *see* Jobber News Annual Marketing Guide **8587**
Automotive Materials (DEU ISSN 1613-9321) **8565**
• Automotive News (USA ISSN 0005-1551) **8565**
• Automotive News Europe (Online) (GBR) **8565**
† • Automotive News Europe (Print) (GBR) **8934**
Automotive News. Market Data Book *see* Automotive News **8565**
Automotive News of the Pacific Northwest (USA ISSN 0005-156X) **8565**
Automotive Parts & Technology *see* Canadian Technician **8571**
Automotive Parts Rebuilders Association (Year) Membership Directory *see* A P R A (Year) Membership Directory **1970**
Automotive Polymers (GBR) **7091**
Automotive Recyclers Association. Membership Directory and Buyer's Guide (USA) **1974**
Automotive Recyclers Association Newsletter *see* A R A Newsletter **8554**
Automotive Recycling (USA ISSN 1058-9376) **8565**
• Automotive Service Data Book (CAN ISSN 0068-9629) **8565**
Automotive Services *see* Key Note Market Report: Automotive Services **8588**
• Automotive Sourcing (GBR ISSN 1354-4306) **8565**
Automotive Supply (FRA ISSN 1622-860X) **8566**
Automotive Test Report *see* Automotive & Aerospace Test Report **3296**
Automotive Testing Technology International (GBR ISSN 1751-0341) **3374**
• Automotive Thermal (GBR ISSN 1747-7298) **8566**
Automotive Trade (CAN ISSN 1706-8568) **1211**
• Automotive Week (USA ISSN 0889-3918) **8566**
Automotive Week / The Greensheet *see* Automotive Week **8566**
Automotive World (GBR ISSN 1470-6660) **8566**
Automoto (TUR) **8566**
• Automotor (PRT ISSN 0871-6153) **8566**
Automovel Club de Portugal. Revista *see* Revista A C P **8601**
Automovil (ESP) **8566**
Automovil de Venezuela (VEN ISSN 0005-1616) **8566**
Automovil Panamericano (MEX) **8566**
Automovilismo en Espana (ESP ISSN 0005-1632) **8566**
Automundo Deportivo (MEX) **8160**
Autonews International (ZAF) **8566**
AutoNewsFast Newsletter *see* Auto News Fast Newsletter **8559**
• ➤ Autonomic & Autacoid Pharmacology (GBR ISSN 1474-8665) **6824**
• ➤ Autonomic & Autacoid Pharmacology Online (GBR ISSN 1474-8673) **6824**
➤ Autonomic Nervous System (USA ISSN 1047-5125) **920**
• ➤ Autonomic Neuroscience: Basic and Clinical (NLD ISSN 1566-0702) **6125**
† Autonomie e Diritto (ITA) **8934**
• Autonomie Locali e Servizi Sociali (ITA ISSN 0392-2278) **8027**
Autonomies (Catalan Edition) *see* Revista Catalana de Dret Public **4770**
Autonomies (Spanish Edition) *see* Revista Catalana de Dret Public **4770**
• Autonomous Agents and Multi-Agent Systems (USA ISSN 1387-2532) **2447**
• ➤ Autonomous Robots (USA ISSN 0929-5593) **2584**
Autopart (ZAF) **8566**
Autoparts *see* Key Note Market Report: Autoparts **8588**
• The Autoparts Report (USA ISSN 1045-1978) **8566**
• ➤ Autophagy (USA ISSN 1554-8627) **655**
Autopiac (HUN ISSN 0239-0426) **8566**
Autopinion (CAN ISSN 0836-1630) **8566**
• Autopista (ESP ISSN 0567-2392) **8566**
Autopista Formula 1 (ESP) **8566**
Autopista Pruebas (ESP) **8566**
† AutoPodium (NLD) **8934**
Autopoesis (BRA ISSN 1678-345X) **7949**
Autopro (ITA ISSN 1129-3330) **8566**
AutoProfi (CZE ISSN 1210-7441) **8566**
Autorama (ITA ISSN 0005-1683) **8566**
Autoren, Komponisten und Musikverleger Informationen *see* A K M Informationen **6744**
† Los Autores (ESP ISSN 1699-468X) **8934**
Autores (PRT) **8466**
Autores Africanos (BRA) **5259**
• Autorev (AUS) **8566**
AutoReview *see* AvtoRevyu **8568**
• Autorevue (AUT ISSN 0005-0830) **8491**
AutoRevue (LUX) **8566**
• AutoRevue.cz (CZE ISSN 1214-1895) **8566**
Autorevuu (EST ISSN 0868-4405) **8566**
† • Autoridades de la Biblioteca Nacional de Espana en CD-ROM (ESP ISSN 1136-8217) **8934**
Autorita Garante della Concorrenza e del Mercato. Bollettino (ITA ISSN 1121-2861) **4857**
Autorita Garante della Concorrenza e del Mercato. Bollettino Settimanale *see* Autorita Garante della Concorrenza e del Mercato. Bollettino **4857**
Autorite de Controle des Assurances et des Mutuelles. La Lettre *see* A C A M. La Lettre **1275**
• L'Autorite des Marches Financiers. Bulletin (CAN ISSN 1710-4149) **1309**
Autorite des Marches Financiers. Revue *see* Autorite des Marches Financiers. Revue Mensuelle **1611**
• Autorite des Marches Financiers. Revue Mensuelle (FRA ISSN 1767-848X) **1611**
Autoruote 4 x 4 *see* A 4. Autoruote 4 x 4 **8553**
Autos bis 5,000 Euros (DEU) **8566**
Autos de Epoca (ARG ISSN 0329-3319) **8566**
Autos Report for Grece *see* Greece Autos Report **8583**
• Autos Y Mas (USA) **8566**
Autosalon (CZE ISSN 1212-7264) **8566**
AutoService Quarterly (CAN ISSN 1480-347X) **8566**
Autoservicios, Supermercados & Almaceneros (ARG) **3676**
AutoShow (TUR) **8566**
Autospark (IND ISSN 0005-0695) **8566**
Autosport (DNK ISSN 0908-7648) **8160**
• Autosport (GBR ISSN 0269-946X) **8567**
† Autosport (ITA) **8934**
• AutoSport (PRT ISSN 0870-1857) **8567**
Autosport es Formula (HUN ISSN 1785-9484) **8160**
Autosprint (ITA ISSN 0005-1748) **8160**
Autostrada (ROM) **8567**
Autostyle *see* Zuojia **8613**
AutoSuccess (USA ISSN 1931-4272) **1806**
AutoSuperMarket *see* Auto Super Market **8560**
▼ Autot (FIN ISSN 1797-3082) **2177**
Autotec (ESP ISSN 1134-2080) **8567**
Autotech (ESP) **8567**
AutoTechnology *see* A T Z Autotechnology **8554**
Autotecnica (ITA ISSN 1121-3450) **8567**
AutoTip (CZE ISSN 1210-1087) **8567**
Autotrader Green (USA) **8567**
Autotrends *see* Che Wang **8573**
Autotuning (DEU ISSN 1435-4454) **8567**
Autotuning Autohifi *see* A T Magazin **8554**
Autotuning. Samurai (DEU ISSN 1614-7235) **8567**
Autotuning. Tuningfakes (DEU ISSN 1860-8442) **8567**
Autoverde 4 x 4 (ESP) **8567**
Der Autovermieter (DEU ISSN 0931-2366) **8567**
Autovia (ESP) **8567**
Autovisie (NLD ISSN 0005-0873) **8567**
Die Autowaesche (DEU) **8567**
• AutoWeek (BEL ISSN 1381-7973) **8567**
• AutoWeek (USA ISSN 0192-9674) **8567**
AutoWeek Complete Buyer's Guide *see* AutoWeek Strategic Buyer's Guide **8567**
AutoWeek Online *see* AutoWeek **8567**
AutoWeek Racing Fan Guide (USA) **8567**
AutoWeek Strategic Buyer's Guide (USA) **8567**
Autowoman *see* Auto Woman **8561**
Autozaken (NLD ISSN 1871-9821) **8567**
Autozeitschrift Mot *see* Mot **8975**
L'Autre Forum (CAN ISSN 1718-2506) **2829**
L'Autre Paris (FRA ISSN 1950-4624) **7108**
Un Autre Regard (FRA ISSN 1954-507X) **6125**
Autre Sud (FRA ISSN 1286-7160) **5417**
Autrement - C E R I *see* Mondes et Nations **7986**
Autrement - CERI *see* Mondes et Nations **7986**
Autrement dit (FRA ISSN 1243-6003) **7949**
Autrement Junior. Serie Histoire (FRA ISSN 1630-0246) **2177**
Autrement Junior. Serie Societe (FRA ISSN 1625-8851) **2177**
Autrement. Serie France *see* Collection France **4211**
Autrement. Serie Morales *see* Morales **6935**
Autrement. Serie Mutations *see* Collection Mutations **7955**
• Autrepart (FRA ISSN 1278-3986) **7949**
Autrey - Autry - Autery Bulletin (USA ISSN 0892-0303) **3759**
Autumn Combinable Crop Pocket Book (GBR) **220**
Autumn Farm Revenue and Production Report *see* Meat and Wool Boards' Economic Service. Autumn Farm Revenue and Production Report **203**
Autumn Home (IRL ISSN 1393-0710) **4532**
• Autumn Report (SVN ISSN 1318-3842) **1717**
Auvergne Agricole (FRA ISSN 0988-9256) **93**
Auvergne Economique (FRA ISSN 0045-1142) **1439**
Aux Ecoutes (CHE ISSN 0254-9921) **4072**
Aux Sources des Conflits (FRA ISSN 1778-3445) **4132**
Aux Trouvailles (CHE) **3957**
L'Auxiliaire Veterinaire (FRA ISSN 1769-0072) **8793**
Auxiliary to the American Osteopathic Association Accents *see* A A O A Accents **5803**
Auxology: Advances in the Study of Human Growth and Development (GBR ISSN 1467-4653) **8089**
AV - Magasinet (SWE) **2574**
AV Marketplace *see* A V Market Place **1970**
Ava (ARG ISSN 1515-2413) **330**
AvaCient (MEX) **7838**
Avain *see* Kirjallisuudentutkimuksen Aikakauslehti Avain **5317**
• Avain Suomen Metsateollisuuteen (FIN ISSN 1238-4135) **3684**
Avakash (IND) **3879**
• Aval Vikatan (IND) **8852**
Avalanche Review (USA ISSN 1528-6487) **2702**
• Avaliacao (BRA ISSN 1414-4077) **2968**
Avallaunius (GBR ISSN 0955-3584) **5259**
Avalon Hill General (USA ISSN 0888-1081) **8160**
Avance (NIC) **7108**
Avance Agricola (CHL ISSN 0717-6732) **93**
Avance de Informacion Economica. Balanza Comercial (MEX ISSN 0187-4942) **1211**
Avance de Informacion Economica. Empleo (MEX ISSN 0187-4969) **1211**
Avance de Informacion Economica. Encuesta sobre Establecimientos Comerciales. Ciudades de: Mexico, Guadalajara y Monterrey (MEX) **1211**
Avance de Informacion Economica. Indicadores de la Actividad Industrial (MEX) **1211**
Avance de Informacion Economica. Indicadores del Sector Manufacturero (MEX ISSN 0187-4977) **1211**
Avance de Informacion Economica. Industria de la Construccion (MEX ISSN 0187-4950) **1044**
Avance de Informacion Economica. Industria Maquiladora de Exportacion (MEX ISSN 0187-5019) **1211**
Avance de Informacion Economica. Industria Minerometalurgica (MEX ISSN 0187-5027) **6485**
Avance de Informacion Economica. Producto Interno Bruto Trimestral (MEX) **1211**
Avance Magazine (USA ISSN 0737-0490) **3521**
Avance Normativo Fiscal (ESP ISSN 1134-9255) **1911**
Avance Normativo Laboral y Seguridad Social (ESP ISSN 1136-0283) **4624**
Avance Regional (MEX) **3908**
Avance y Perspectiva (MEX ISSN 0185-1411) **7838**
Avancees & Perspectives Scientifiques (FRA ISSN 1960-2375) **94**
• Avances de la Ciencia y la Tecnologia (ECU ISSN 1390-3012) **7838**
Avances en Alfalfa. Ensayos Territoriales (ARG ISSN 1515-4602) **220**
† Avances en Alimentacion y Mejora Animal (ESP ISSN 0005-1896) **8934**
Avances en Analisis por Tecnicas de Rayos X (ARG ISSN 1515-1565) **7006**
Avances en Biotecnologia Moderna *see* Advances in Modern Biotechnology **755**
Avances en Ciencias Veterinarias (CHL ISSN 0716-260X) **8793**
• Avances en Diabetologia (ESP ISSN 1134-3230) **5884**
Avances en Enfermeria (COL ISSN 0121-4500) **5952**
▼ Avances en Higiene Bucodental (ESP ISSN 1888-4032) **5836**
• Avances en Investigacion Agropecuaria (MEX ISSN 0188-7890) **94**
Avances en Medicina (COL ISSN 0124-2180) **5581**
• Avances en Odontoestomatologia (ESP ISSN 0213-1285) **5836**
• Avances en Periodoncia e Implantologia Oral (ESP ISSN 1699-6585) **5836**
• Avances en Produccion Animal (CHL ISSN 0378-4509) **280**
Avances en Psicologia (PER ISSN 1812-9536) **7338**
Avances en Psicologia Clinica Latinoamericana *see* Avances en Psicologia Latinoamericana **7338**
• Avances en Psicologia Latinoamericana (COL ISSN 1794-4724) **7338**
• Avances en Quimica (VEN ISSN 1856-5301) **2051**
• Avances en Recursos Hidraulicos (COL ISSN 0121-5701) **3360**
• ➤ Avances en Sistemas e Informatica (COL ISSN 1657-7663) **2519**
Avances en Traumatologia, Cirugia, Rehabilitacion, Medicina Preventiva y Deportiva (ESP ISSN 0214-4077) **6237**
Avances Informativos. Administrativo (ESP ISSN 1575-2879) **4624**
Avances Informativos. Civil (ESP ISSN 1575-3026) **4827**
Avances Informativos. Especial (ESP ISSN 1135-4356) **4624**
Avances Informativos. Laboral (ESP ISSN 1132-9769) **1666**
Avances Informativos. Mercantil (ESP ISSN 1577-4511) **4624**
Avances Informativos. Penal (ESP ISSN 1575-2895) **4885**
Avances Informativos. Tributario (ESP ISSN 1132-9785) **1911**
• Avances Medicos de Cuba (CUB ISSN 1025-6539) **5581**
Avant-Garde & Modernism Studies (USA) **5259**
• Avant Garde Critical Studies (NLD ISSN 1387-3008) **5259**
Avant Garden (CHE ISSN 1661-8408) **3724**
The Avant Gardener (USA ISSN 0005-1926) **3724**
Avant Guide. Chicago (USA ISSN 1559-8861) **8685**
L'Avant-Scene. Cinema (FRA ISSN 0045-1150) **6490**
L'Avant-Scene du Theatre *see* L' Avant-Scene. Theatre **8466**
L'Avant-Scene. Opera (FRA ISSN 0295-1371) **6546**
L'Avant-Scene. Theatre (FRA ISSN 0045-1169) **8466**
Avantage Recherche (CAN ISSN 1718-5777) **2968**
• Avantages (CAN ISSN 1196-8915) **1666**
Avantages (FRA ISSN 0992-9967) **8852**
Avantaje (ROM ISSN 1224-4376) **8852**
† • ➤ Avante (CAN ISSN 1201-6144) **8934**
Avante (MEX) **7108**
Avante (PRT ISSN 0870-1865) **7108**
AvantGarde (NLD ISSN 0926-910X) **3914**
Avantgarde Design Koeln *see* Avantgarde Design Selection Koeln **4532**
Avantgarde Design Selection Koeln (ITA ISSN 1720-7991) **4532**
AvantgardeMEN (NLD ISSN 1872-2849) **6286**
Avanti (DEU) **8852**
Avanti Magazine (USA ISSN 0889-6267) **8567**
Avanzada (MEX) **3908**
• Avanzada Cientifica (CUB ISSN 1029-3450) **7838**
Avard Magazine (IRN ISSN 1021-6316) **8160**
Avariinost' v Elekroenergetike (RUS) **3155**
Avaruusluotain/Rymdsonden (FIN ISSN 0356-021X) **47**
Avaruusutiset *see* Euroopan Tiede ja Teknologia **53**
Avatar Journal (USA) **6643**
Avatares (MEX ISSN 1665-1103) **6906**
AvBR *see* Huig **445**
Avdet (UKR) **3963**
Ave. *see* Avenue **5065**
The Ave (USA ISSN 1544-3434) **3521**
• Ave Maria (BRA ISSN 1980-7872) **7785**
• Ave Maria Law Review (USA ISSN 1541-4221) **4624**
Avebury Series in Philosophy (GBR ISSN 0955-9582) **6906**
Avec Mes Dix Doigts (FRA ISSN 1778-6592) **2177**
L'Avenc (ESP ISSN 0210-0150) **4202**
Avene (LVA ISSN 1407-9283) **2177**
Avengers United (GBR ISSN 1474-1571) **2177**
• Avenir Agricole (Laval) (FRA ISSN 1261-5102) **94**
Avenir Agricole de l'Ardeche (FRA ISSN 0998-0210) **94**
Avenir Agricole et Rural de la Haute Marne (FRA ISSN 1148-3121) **94**
Avenir Agricole et Viticole Aquitain (FRA ISSN 0300-2942) **220**
Avenir de l'Est (CAN) **3806**
Avenir du Luxembourg (Arlon Regional Edition) *see* Vers l'Avenir **3802**
L'Avenir Ensemble (FRA ISSN 1775-2760) **7488**
• La Aventura de la Historia (ESP ISSN 1579-427X) **4132**
• Aventuras na Historia (BRA) **4132**
Les Aventures de Bibounet et Patagloum (FRA ISSN 1773-5920) **2177**
Les Aventures de la Connaissance (FRA ISSN 1950-0297) **4444**
Aventures et Passions (FRA ISSN 1272-2731) **5409**
Avenue (CAN ISSN 1497-9195) **5065**
Avenue (DEU) **8567**
Avenue (GBR ISSN 0950-7167) **2273**
Avenue (USA ISSN 0279-1226) **3970**
• Avenue - Innovationsletter (DEU ISSN 1862-4677) **21**
▼ Avenue Report (USA ISSN 1939-2893) **2251**
Avenuel *see* E'bi nyu'el **8859**
• Avenues to Marketing Success (USA ISSN 1555-7030) **1806**
† • Average Annual Pay by State and Industry (USA ISSN 1934-0974) **8934**
† Average Annual Pay Levels in Metropolitan Areas (Year) (USA) **8934**
Average Calendar Day Allowable Report (USA) **6763**
Average Daily Traffic Volumes on Interstate, Arterial and Primary Routes *see* Average Daily Traffic Volumes with Vehicle Classification Data on Interstate, Arterial and Primary Routes **8522**
Average Daily Traffic Volumes with Vehicle Classification Data on Interstate, Arterial and Primary Routes (USA) **8522**

Title

10010 AVERAGE DAILY WAGES OF WORKERS ENGAGED IN GOVERNMENT ULRICH'S PERIODICALS

Average Daily Wages of Workers Engaged in Government Building and Construction Projects *see* Hong Kong Special Administrative Region of China. Census and Statistics Department. Average Daily Wages of Workers Engaged in Government Building and Construction Projects **1237**
Average Prices of British Academic Books (GBR ISSN 0142-4955) **4993**
Average Prices Received by Farmers for Farm Produce *see* U.S. Department of Agriculture. National Agricultural Statistics Service. Agricultural Prices **187**
• Average Retail Prices of Goods and Services by Rural Areas (ETH) **1211**
• Average Retail Prices of Goods and Services by Urban Center (ETH) **8356**
Average Wholesale Prices of Selected Building Materials *see* Hong Kong Special Administrative Region of China. Census and Statistics Department. Average Wholesale Prices of Selected Building Materials **1046**
Averill's Uniform Probate Code in a Nutshell *see* Uniform Probate Code **4906**
➤ Averroes Latinus (BEL) **6906**
Avertissements Agricole. Champagne-Ardenne. Pommes de Terre (FRA ISSN 1774-5381) **94**
Avery Cardoza's Player (USA ISSN 1547-2426) **8160**
• Avery Index to Architectural Periodicals (USA ISSN 1085-2875) **462**
The Avery Review (USA ISSN 1931-4752) **3521**
Aves (BEL ISSN 0005-1993) **902**
Aves Contact *see* Natagora **910**
Aves del Arca (URY ISSN 0067-2637) **5259**
Avesta Tidning (SWE ISSN 1103-9051) **3954**
• Avetra News (AUS) **2829**
Avfall och Miljoe (SWE ISSN 1654-5087) **3504**
• Avfall Sverige Utveckling. Rapport (SWE ISSN 1654-5303) **3504**
• Avfallnorge (NOR ISSN 1890-0720) **3504**
Avfallsnytt (SWE ISSN 1401-1840) **3504**
Avia Mini (GBR) **4328**
Aviacao em Revista/Aviation Magazine (BRA ISSN 0102-4876) **47**
Aviacija *see* Aviation **48**
Aviacion (PER ISSN 0005-2078) **6413**
Aviacion General y Deportiva (ESP ISSN 1575-1112) **8160**
Aviacion y Turismo (ESP ISSN 0211-2361) **8685**
• Aviakosmicheskaya i Ekologicheskaya Meditsina/Aerospace and Environmental Medicine (RUS ISSN 0233-528X) **5581**
Aviakosmicheskaya Tekhnika i Tekhnologiya (RUS) **48**
Aviakosmicheskoe Priborostroenie (RUS) **48**
Aviamaster (RUS) **48**
Avian and Poultry Biology Reviews *see* Avian Biology Research **935**
• ➤ Avian Biology Research (GBR ISSN 1758-1559) **935**
• Avian Conservation and Ecology/Ecologie et Conservation des Oiseaux (CAN ISSN 1712-6568) **935**
• ➤ Avian Diseases (USA ISSN 0005-2086) **8794**
• Avian Diseases Digest (USA ISSN 1933-5334) **902**
Avian Ecology and Behaviour (RUS ISSN 1561-9958) **655**
Avian Ecology and Behaviour Supplement *see* Avian Ecology and Behaviour **655**
• ➤ Avian Pathology (GBR ISSN 0307-9457) **8794**
➤ Avian Science (CHE ISSN 1424-8743) **902**
Aviapanorama (RUS ISSN 1726-6173) **48**
Aviary Life *see* Australian Aviary Life **902**
➤ Aviation (LTU ISSN 1648-7788) **48**
Aviation Accident Law & Practice (USA) **48**
Aviation Accident Law and Practice *see* Aviation Accident Law & Practice **48**
Aviation and Air Transport Abstracts *see* Repulesi Szakirodalmi Tajekoztato **8529**
• Aviation and Environment News (USA) **3405**
Aviation and Safety Magazine (ZAF ISSN 1814-5485) **48**
Aviation & Space Journal (IND ISSN 0970-3578) **8538**
† Aviation & Space Law Reports (GBR ISSN 1352-4003) **8934**
• Aviation Business Asia Pacific Magazine (AUS) **48**
Aviation Business Journal (USA) **8538**
Aviation Business Magazine *see* Aviation Business Asia Pacific Magazine **48**
Aviation Buyers Directory (USA ISSN 0001-0502) **48**
Aviation Canada (Ottawa) (CAN ISSN 1496-7863) **48**
Aviation Civile (FRA ISSN 1248-9980) **8538**
Aviation Consultation Papers *see* Great Britain. Department of the Environment, Transport and the Regions. Aviation Consultation Papers **8543**
The Aviation Consumer (USA ISSN 0147-9911) **48**
• Aviation Daily (USA ISSN 0193-4597) **8538**
Aviation Daily Japan *see* Nikkan Koku Tsushin **1154**
Aviation Education News (USA) **8538**
Aviation Engineering and Maintenance *see* Hangkong Weiziu yu Gongcheng **58**
Aviation & Pilote (FRA ISSN 1252-6096) **8538**
Aviation Facilities Energy Association. Annual Report (USA) **48**
Aviation Facilities Energy Association. Energy Consumption Analysis Report (USA) **48**
† Aviation Francaise Magazine (FRA ISSN 1951-9583) **8934**
Aviation Heritage (AUS ISSN 0815-4392) **48**
Aviation Historical Society of New Zealand. Journal (NZL ISSN 0110-5493) **48**
• Aviation History (USA ISSN 1076-8858) **48**
• Aviation Illustrated Magazine (Online) (USA) **48**
Aviation in Canada (CAN) **48**
Aviation Industry Barometer *see* Barometre du Transport Aerien **49**
• Aviation Intelligence (GBR ISSN 1751-9381) **8538**
Aviation International (FRA ISSN 1770-9229) **48**
• Aviation International News (USA ISSN 0887-9877) **8538**
• Aviation Law Reporter (USA) **8538**
Aviation Law Reports *see* Aviation Law Reporter **8538**
• Aviation Litigation Quarterly (USA ISSN 1938-7032) **8538**
Aviation Magazine *see* Aviacao em Revista **47**
• Aviation Maintenance (USA ISSN 1090-221X) **48**
Aviation Maintenance Alerts (USA) **48**
Aviation Maintenance & Engineering *see* Hangkong Weixiu yu Gongcheng **57**
Aviation Maintenance Foundation International Industry News *see* A M F I Industry News **40**
Aviation Maintenance Foundation International. Industry Report (USA) **48**
Aviation Master File (USA) **2346**
Aviation Mechanics Bulletin *see* AeroSafety World **8533**
Aviation Medicine (NZL) **5581**
Aviation Modeller International (GBR ISSN 1360-5526) **4328**
Aviation Monthly (USA ISSN 0145-1014) **48**
Aviation News *see* New Zealand Aviation News **8549**
Aviation News Weekly *see* Hangkong Zhoukan **8961**
Aviation Precision Manufacturing Technology *see* Hangkong Jingmi Zhizao Jishu **57**
Aviation Regulatory Digest Service (USA) **8538**
Aviation Regulatory Watch Group Reports (CAN) **8538**
Aviation Review (CAN ISSN 1184-0366) **48**
Aviation Safety (USA ISSN 0277-1764) **48**
Aviation Safety Letter (Online Edition) *see* Aviation Safety Letter (Print Edition) **48**
• Aviation Safety Letter (Print Edition) (CAN ISSN 0709-8103) **48**
Aviation Safety Maintainer *see* Aviation Safety Letter (Print Edition) **48**
Aviation Safety Reflexions *see* Transportation Safety Reflexions. Air **8517**
Aviation Safety Vortex *see* Aviation Safety Letter (Print Edition) **48**
Aviation Safety World *see* AeroSafety World **8533**
• Aviation Security International (GBR ISSN 1352-0148) **8538**
• ➤ Aviation, Space, and Environmental Medicine (USA ISSN 0095-6562) **5581**
• Aviation Strategy (GBR ISSN 1463-9254) **8538**
Aviation Telephone Directory. Eastern, Western, Southwestern and North Central States (USA ISSN 1075-1378) **8538**
Aviation Telephone Directory. Western & Northcentral States (USA ISSN 1075-136X) **8538**
• Aviation Trader (AUS ISSN 1322-8242) **48**
Aviation Tradescan (USA ISSN 0899-1928) **76**
• Aviation Week & Space Technology (USA ISSN 0005-2175) **49**
Aviation Week and Space Technology *see* Aviation Week & Space Technology **49**
• Aviation Week's Homeland Security & Defense (USA ISSN 1545-486X) **49**
Aviation Week's Netdefense *see* NetDefense **6439**
Aviation Week's NetDefense *see* NetDefense **6439**
Aviation Week's World Aerospace Database *see* World Aerospace Database **75**
Aviation Who's Who in Japan *see* Koku Uchu Jinmeiroku **2010**
AviationCareer.net (USA) **49**
• The Aviator (ZAF) **49**
Aviator's Guide (USA) **8685**
Aviators Hot Line (USA ISSN 0195-0347) **49**
Aviators Journal *see* America's Flyways **8538**
Aviatransportnoe Obozrenie/Air Transport Observer (RUS) **8538**
Aviatsionnaya i Raketnaya Tekhnika (RUS ISSN 0202-2745) **49**
Aviatsionnaya Promyshlennost' (RUS ISSN 0869-530X) **49**
Aviatsionnaya Technology *see* Russian Aeronautics **69**
Aviatsiya i Vremya (UKR) **49**
▼ • ➤ Avicenna Journal of Medical Biotechnology (IRN ISSN 2008-2835) **756**
➤ Avicenna Latinus (BEL) **6906**
Avicennia (ESP ISSN 1134-1785) **655**
Avicennia Suplemento *see* Avicennia **655**
Avicultura Colombiana (COL) **280**
• Avicultura Industrial (BRA ISSN 0009-0905) **280**
Avicultura. Konijnenfokker *see* Kleindier Magazine Avicultura - Fokkersbelangen **291**
Avicultura Profesional (USA ISSN 0736-2056) **280**
Avicultura Professional (NLD) **280**
➤ Avicultural Journal (CAN ISSN 0317-5650) **902**
Avicultural Magazine (GBR ISSN 0005-2256) **902**
• AVideoZine (USA ISSN 1525-8998) **5417**
Avifaunistischer Informationsdienst Bayern (DEU ISSN 1430-8819) **902**
Avimo Info (BEL ISSN 0776-2461) **2829**
† Avioflap (ITA ISSN 1124-5433) **8934**
• Avion Online Newspaper (USA) **49**
Avion Revue (ESP) **8538**
• Avionics Magazine (USA ISSN 1085-9284) **49**
Avionics Maintenance Conference. Booklet (USA) **49**
Avionics Maintenance Conference. Conference Program (USA) **49**
Avionics Maintenance Conference. Conference Report (USA) **49**
Avionics News Magazine (USA ISSN 0567-2899) **49**
Avions (FRA ISSN 1243-8650) **8539**
Aviron (FRA ISSN 0988-1956) **8271**
Avis 81 (DNK ISSN 0109-0135) **3037**
Avis aux Navigateurs (Edition de l'Est) *see* Avis aux Navigateurs. Publication (Edition de l'Est) **8639**
Avis aux Navigateurs. Edition de l'Est *see* Avis aux Navigateurs. Publication (Edition de l'Est) **8639**
• Avis aux Navigateurs. Publication (Edition de l'Est) (CAN ISSN 1719-7694) **8639**
Avis de la Commission de la Concurrence et de la Commission Technique des Ententes et des Positions Dominantes *see* Avis et Decisions du Conseil de la Concurrence **1309**
Avis d'Invasion *see* Pest Alert **246**
Avis et Decisions du Conseil de la Concurrence (FRA ISSN 1283-8691) **1309**
Avis Traveler (USA) **8685**
Avisaarbogen (year) (DNK ISSN 0109-9272) **4132**
Aviserat *see* S N D S Magazine **4583**
Aviso (CAN ISSN 0830-0011) **3017**
• Aviso (NOR ISSN 0809-9111) **3405**
Aviso (UKR) **3963**
Aviso (USA ISSN 0739-7747) **6520**
Aviso (Ottawa) (CAN ISSN 1207-5647) **4088**
Aviso-avto (UKR) **8567**
Avisos a los Navegantes de Hidrovia Paraguay-Parana (ARG ISSN 1514-8262) **2800**
Avisos de Flandes (BEL) **4202**
Avispa (ARG) **7108**
• Aviva: Women's World Wide Web (GBR) **8852**
Avizite (LVA) **3904**
Avizo (UKR) **3964**
Avls-Information (DNK ISSN 0907-0567) **280**
† Avls- og Aarbog for Langhaaret Hoensehund (DNK ISSN 0905-7080) **8934**
† The Avmark Aviation Economist (GBR ISSN 0961-2513) **8934**
Avmedia *see* Australasian Society of Aerospace Medicine. Journal **5581**
Avocado *see* Avokado **4352**
➤ Avocetta (ITA ISSN 0404-4266) **902**
'Avoda Ur'waha Uvittu-ah L'ummi *see* Labour and Social Affairs and National Insurance **8970**
Avokado (ZAF ISSN 1991-0436) **4352**
Avon Bird Report (GBR ISSN 0956-5744) **902**
Avon Contact (GBR) **592**
Avos'-Ka (RUS) **2177**
Avosetta Series (NLD ISSN 1572-0012) **3405**
Avotakka (FIN ISSN 0355-2950) **4553**
• Avotaynu (USA ISSN 0882-6501) **7718**
Avriani (GRC) **3874**
Avrora (RUS ISSN 0320-6858) **5259**
Avrupa (GBR ISSN 1749-1886) **3521**
• AvStop Magazine Online (USA) **49**
AVTO (RUS) **8567**
Avto-Ekspress/Auto-Express (MDA) **8567**
• Avto Fokus (SVN ISSN 1580-1195) **8567**
Avto Foto Prodazha (UKR) **8567**
Avto Magazin (SVN ISSN 0352-5368) **8567**
Avto Magazin. Moto Katalog (SVN) **8254**
Avto Stil' (RUS ISSN 1682-2390) **8567**
Avto-Yunior (RUS) **8567**
AvtoGid (RUS) **8567**
Avtomaticheskaya Svarka (UKR ISSN 0005-111X) **6342**
Avtomatika i Informatika (BGR ISSN 0861-7562) **2459**
➤ Avtomatika i Telemekhanika (RUS ISSN 0005-2310) **2459**
➤ Avtomatika i Vychislitel'naya Tekhnika (LVA ISSN 0132-4160) **2459**
Avtomatika, Svyaz', Informatika (RUS) **2459**
Avtomatizatsiya i Sovremennye Tekhnologii (RUS ISSN 0869-4931) **2459**
Avtomatizatsiya, Telemekhanizatsiya i Svyaz' v Neftyanoi Promyshlennosti (RUS ISSN 0132-2222) **6763**
Avtomatizatsiya v Promyshlennosti (RUS) **5462**
• ➤ Avtometriya (RUS ISSN 0320-7102) **7074**
Avtomir (RUS ISSN 1560-5396) **8568**
Avtomir (UKR) **8567**
Avtomir. Avtokatalog (RUS ISSN 1607-9663) **8568**
Avtomir. Avtokatalog (UKR) **8568**
Avtomobil' (UKR) **8568**
Avtomobili *see* What Car? **8612**
Avtomobili (RUS ISSN 1811-0037) **8568**
Avtomobil'naya Promyshlennost' (RUS ISSN 0005-2337) **8568**
Avtomobil'nye Dorogi (RUS ISSN 0005-2353) **3260**
Avtomobil'nyi Transport (RUS ISSN 0005-2345) **8568**
Avtopanorama (RUS) **8568**
Avtoperevozchik (RUS ISSN 1608-8174) **8491**
Avtopilot (RUS) **8568**
Avtoprofi (UKR) **8568**
AvtoRevyu/AutoReview (RUS) **8568**
Avtoshlyakhovyk Ukrainy (UKR ISSN 0365-8392) **8629**
Avtoshop (RUS) **8568**
Avtostroenie za Rubezhom (RUS ISSN 1684-7725) **8568**
Avtotrio (RUS ISSN 1683-2841) **8568**
Avtovisnyk-lyudyna, doroga, avtomobil' (UKR) **8568**
• Avui (ESP) **3951**
Avvenimenti *see* Left Avvenimenti **3897**
• Avvenire (ITA ISSN 1120-6020) **3896**
• L'Avvenire Agricolo (ITA ISSN 0005-2361) **94**
† L'Avvenire Medico (ITA ISSN 0392-6877) **8934**
• Avventure nel Mondo (ITA) **8685**
• Avvisatore Marittimo (ITA) **8639**
Avviso ai Naviganti (ITA ISSN 1971-5250) **8639**
• AVWeb (USA) **49**
Avyabiznes (UKR) **49**
Awaji Ishikai Nyusu/Awaji Medical Association News (JPN) **5581**
Awaji Medical Association News *see* Awaji Ishikai Nyusu **5581**
Awake! (USA ISSN 0005-237X) **7733**
Awakened India *see* Prabuddha Bharata **7708**
The Awakening (USA ISSN 1941-823X) **6907**
Awal (FRA ISSN 0764-7573) **7709**
Awana Ideas (USA) **7746**
Awanyu (USA ISSN 0749-1816) **382**
• Award Magazine (CAN ISSN 1202-5925) **977**
Awards and Engraving Magazine *see* A & E Magazine **462**
Awards & Engravings Magazine *see* A & E Magazine **462**
Awards Digest (IND ISSN 0973-0427) **1666**
• Awards, Honors and Prizes (USA ISSN 0196-6316) **3118**
Awards Quarterly *see* A O S Awards Quarterly **3721**
Aware (USA ISSN 0162-6833) **7746**
➤ Awareness (AUS ISSN 1448-7837) **3504**
▼ • Awareness (Powder Springs) (USA ISSN 1938-1905) **2225**
• Awareness Magazine (USA) **307**
Awasis Journal (CAN ISSN 0823-9231) **6634**
Awasis Newsletter (CAN) **6634**
Away from It All (GBR) **8685**
Awaz (IND) **3879**
Awaz-E-Mulk (IND) **3879**
'Awdat Subirman (KWT ISSN 1991-4555) **2177**
Awdurdod Datblygu Cymru. Adroddiad Blynyddol *see* Welsh Development Agency. Annual Report **1607**
Awe (USA ISSN 1540-9759) **7746**
Awishkara (IND ISSN 0970-6607) **7838**
Awmag *see* Aquaworld Magazine **3586**
Aworerin (NGA ISSN 0331-426X) **2829**
Awraq (ESP ISSN 0214-834X) **4202**
• 'Awraq 'Amal Markaz Badil Lil-Niqash (PSE ISSN 1995-9818) **7203**
AXA Konzern Magazin (DEU) **4494**
Axbridge Archaeological and Local History Society. Journal (GBR ISSN 0260-4671) **4202**
Axcess (USA ISSN 1072-5032) **6546**
• Axcess Magazine (USA) **3970**
Axe Factory (USA ISSN 1525-3937) **5259**
Axel Johnson AB. Annual Report (Year) (SWE) **3627**
Axelle (BEL ISSN 1373-3028) **8852**
Axioma (ARG ISSN 1515-744X) **5475**
• Axiomathes (Online) (NLD ISSN 1572-8390) **6907**
Axios (BLZ ISSN 0278-551X) **7703**
† Axis (GBR ISSN 1467-9086) **8934**
Axis (JPN ISSN 0285-8223) **4532**
Axis Mundi (SVK ISSN 1337-0626) **7624**
Axon *see* Canadian Journal of Neuroscience Nursing **5954**
Axplock (SWE ISSN 0282-1575) **5259**
• ➤ Ayaangwaamizin (CAN ISSN 1206-8683) **3521**
Ayandeh (IRN ISSN 1017-4109) **544**
Ayeneh-e Pazhoohesh/Mirat al-Tahqiq/Mirror of Research (IRN ISSN 1023-7992) **7709**
• Ayer (ESP ISSN 1134-2277) **4202**
Ayeres (ESP ISSN 1130-5126) **4202**
Ayil Turmushu (KGZ) **3903**
Ayin l'Tzion (USA) **3521**
Ayinah-i Pizhuhish *see* Ayeneh-e Pazhoohesh **7709**
Ayk Aktiv (DEU) **585**
Aylesford Carmelite Newsletter (USA) **7785**
Aylik Dis Ticaret Ozeti *see* Turkey. Turkiye Istatistik Kurumu. Aylik Dis Ticaret Ozeti **8994**
Aylik Istatistik Bulteni - Istatistik Enstitusu *see* Turkey. Devlet Istatistik Enstitusu. Aylik Istatistik Bulteni **8994**
• Aylik Istatistiki Bilgiler Bulteni/Monthly Statistical Bulletin (TUR) **8568**
Ayn Rand Studies (USA) **5259**
Ayojon (NZL ISSN 1177-0988) **3521**
Ayr News (CAN ISSN 0834-5813) **3806**
Ayrshire Cattle Society's Journal (GBR ISSN 0005-2442) **261**
Ayrshire Dairyman (GBR) **261**
Ayrshire Digest (USA ISSN 0005-2450) **261**
The Ayrshire Journal (GBR) **261**
† Ayrshire Monographs (GBR) **8934**
• Ayrshire Notes (GBR ISSN 1474-3531) **382**
• Ayub Medical College. Journal (PAK ISSN 1025-9589) **5581**
Ayuda a la Iglesia Necesitada. Boletin *see* Mirror **7807**
Ayuda a la Iglesia Necesitada. Boletin *see* Echo der Liebe **7796**
• Ayudando a los Estudiantes a Aprender (Escuela Intermedia) (USA ISSN 1526-9310) **2829**
• Ayudando a los Estudiantes a Aprender (Escuela Secundaria) (USA ISSN 1526-9329) **2829**
• Ayudando a los Ninos a Aprender (Escuela Primaria) (USA ISSN 1526-9302) **2829**
• Ayudando a los Ninos a Aprender (Preparacion para la Escuela) (USA ISSN 1526-9299) **2829**
Ayuruveda Kenkyu/Studies on Ayurveda in Japan (JPN ISSN 0914-8248) **307**
Ayuruveda Tsushin/Research Society for Ayurveda in Japan. News (JPN ISSN 0914-1367) **307**

Title

10012 B B I A MEMBERSHIP AND PRODUCT INFORMATION GUIDE ULRICH'S PERIODICALS

B B I A Membership and Product Information Guide (Billiard and Bowling Institute of America) (USA) **1974**
B B I A Newsline (Billiard and Bowling Institute of America) (USA) **8221**
The B B I Newsletter *see* Biomedical Business & Technology **5585**
B B Jahresbericht (Branchenbrief) (DEU) **4059**
B B K - Betrieb und Rechnungswesen (Buchfuehrung, Bilanz, Kostenrechnung) (DEU) **4625**
B B L *see* Baurechtliche Blaetter **981**
B B M I R *see* Blue Book Marketing Information Reports **7318**
B B Q *see* Berkshire Business Quarterly **1066**
B B Q *see* Black Business Quarterly **1068**
▼ B B Q World Magazine (USA ISSN 1947-668X) **4382**
B B R (DEU ISSN 1611-1478) **8818**
B B R *see* Back Brain Recluse **5440**
B B R - Wasser, Kanal- und Rohrleitungsbau *see* B B R **8818**
B B S *see* Behavioral and Brain Sciences **7339**
B B S A Buyers Guide of Blinds & Shutters *see* Blinds and Shutters Buyers Guide **1975**
B B S A Directory of Blinds & Shutters *see* Blinds and Shutters Buyers Guide **1975**
B B S I (Beauty & Barber Supply Institute) (USA) **585**
B B S Magazine (Bulletin Board Systems) (USA) **2552**
B B S R C Business (Biotechnology and Biological Sciences Research Council) (GBR ISSN 1354-3393) **756**
B B S R C Science Brief (Biotechnology and Biological Sciences Research Council) (GBR ISSN 1359-6586) **756**
B B S R - Info (Bundesinstitut fuer Bau-, Stadt- und Raumforschung) (DEU ISSN 1868-0089) **4404**
B B U Info-Dienst (Bundesverband Buergerinitiativen Umweltschutz) (DEU) **3405**
• B B W (Online Edition) (Big Beautiful Woman) (USA) **2251**
B B W (Print Edition) *see* B B W (Online Edition) **2251**
B B W Magazin (Beamtenbund Baden-Wuerttemberg) (DEU ISSN 1437-9856) **7488**
B C *see* Building Connection **985**
▼ B C (FRA ISSN 1959-4690) **477**
• B C (Business Confidential) (GBR ISSN 1752-0819) **1064**
B C A *see* Building Code of Australia **985**
• B C A Break (Billiard Congress of America) (USA) **8221**
B C A Bulletin (British Cement Association) (GBR ISSN 0953-1688) **977**
B C A Directory of Registered Contractors (Year) (Building and Construction Authority) (SGP) **1974**
B C A M T Newsletter (B.C. Association of Mathematics Teachers) (CAN ISSN 0836-4818) **3052**
B C A News (Business Committee for the Arts) (USA ISSN 0005-2841) **1064**
B C A T A Journal for Art Teachers (B.C. Art Teachers' Association) (CAN ISSN 0710-0744) **3052**
B C A T M L Newsletter (B.C. Association of Teachers of Modern Languages) (CAN ISSN 0229-0235) **3052**
B C Alternate Education Association Newsletter (CAN ISSN 1182-1019) **3052**
B C & T News (Bakery, Confectionery and Tobacco) (USA ISSN 0163-447X) **4590**
B.C. Archer (CAN ISSN 0226-7691) **8160**
B.C. Art Teachers' Association Journal for Art Teachers *see* B C A T A Journal for Art Teachers **3052**
B.C. Association of Mathematics Teachers Newsletter *see* B C A M T Newsletter **3052**
B.C. Association of Teachers of Modern Languages Newsletter *see* B C A T M L Newsletter **3052**
B C Baseball *see* Play Ball! **8242**
B C Birding (CAN ISSN 1206-1611) **902**
B C Bookworld (CAN ISSN 0847-7728) **5259**
B.C. Broker (CAN ISSN 0841-7660) **4494**
• B C Business (CAN ISSN 0829-481X) **1064**
B C C Evening Reporter (Bronx Community College) (USA) **2273**
B C Catholic (CAN ISSN 0007-0483) **7785**
B C Christian News (CAN) **7624**
B C Coach's Perspective (CAN ISSN 1209-6245) **8160**
B C Counsellor (CAN ISSN 0225-5693) **3052**
B C Crime Prevention Pages, Directory of Services (CAN ISSN 1719-8321) **2644**
B C D *see* Bass Club Digest **8305**
B C D S Newsletter *see* Bergen County Dental Society. Newsletter **5836**
B C Dairy Directory *see* B C Dairy Directory & Farm Handbook **1974**
B C Dairy Directory and Farm Handbook *see* B C Dairy Directory & Farm Handbook **1974**
B C Dairy Directory & Farm Handbook (CAN ISSN 1912-1210) **1974**
B C Deaf News (British Columbia) (CAN) **4072**
B C E A Reporter (Bergen County Education Association) (USA) **2829**
† B C E. Boletin de Derecho de las Comunidades Europeas (ESP ISSN 0213-6945) **8934**
B C Fellowship Baptist (CAN ISSN 0833-4587) **7746**
B C Fishing Directory & Atlas (British Columbia) (CAN) **8305**
B C Fuchsia and Begonia Society. Monthly Newsletter (CAN) **3724**
B C G A Code of Practice *see* British Compressed Gases Association. Code of Practice **3366**
B C Gazette. Part 1 (CAN) **4625**
B C Historical News *see* British Columbia Historical News **4286**
B C Hospitality Industry Membership Directory (British Columbia) (CAN ISSN 1719-7236) **4382**
B C I *see* Business Community Intelligence **1071**
B C I *see* Bird Conservation International **902**
B C I L L *see* Institut de Linguistique de Louvain. Bibliotheque des Cahiers **5127**
B C I S Guide to House Rebuilding Costs (Building Cost Information Service) (GBR ISSN 1350-9500) **977**
B C I S Quarterly Review of Building Prices (Building Cost Information Service) (GBR ISSN 0260-6216) **977**
B C I T Annual Report (British Columbia Institute of Technology) (CAN) **8416**
B C I T Update (British Columbia Institute of Technology) (CAN) **8416**
B C Innovation Council. Annual Service Plan Report (CAN ISSN 1911-0553) **8416**
• B C Journal of Ecosystems and Management (CAN ISSN 1488-4666) **3684**
B C L *see* Building and Construction Law Journal **984**
B C L A Reporter (British Columbia Library Association) (CAN ISSN 1207-1846) **4993**
B C L R *see* Boston College Law Review **4631**
B C Labour Directory (CAN ISSN 0715-2574) **1666**
B C M *see* The British Catalogue of Music **6551**
B C M E *see* Building Construction Materials & Equipment **985**
• B C Magazine (HKG) **3875**
B C Massage Practitioner (CAN ISSN 1195-3292) **6107**
B C Mine Rescue Manual (CAN) **6458**
B C Monitor *see* Black Congressional Monitor **7110**
B.C. Monthly *see* British Columbia Monthly **5418**
B.C. Mountaineering Club Newsletter *see* British Columbia Mountaineering Club Newsletter **8307**
B C Municipal Red Book *see* Municipal Redbook (British Columbia) **7498**
B.C. Music Educator (CAN ISSN 0705-9019) **6547**
B C N *see* British Church Newspaper **7749**
B C N (Board Converting News) (USA ISSN 1752-167X) **6708**
B.C. Naturalist *see* B C Nature **7838**
B C Nature (CAN ISSN 1912-3280) **7838**
B C News (Boise Cascade Corporation) (USA) **6732**
B C O Q Directory (Baptist Convention of Ontario and Quebec) (CAN) **7746**
B.C. Orchardist *see* British Columbia Orchardist **3726**
B C Outdoors *see* B C Outdoors Sport Fishing and Outdoor Adventure **8305**
B C Outdoors *see* B C Outdoors Hunting and Shooting **8305**
B C Outdoors Hunting and Shooting (CAN ISSN 1496-7642) **8305**
B C Outdoors Sport Fishing and Outdoor Adventure (CAN ISSN 1496-7634) **8305**
B C P *see* Behavioural and Cognitive Psychotherapy **7340**
B C P T *see* Basic & Clinical Pharmacology & Toxicology **6824**
B C Pharmacy (CAN ISSN 1203-214X) **6824**
B C R A Cave Studies Series (British Cave Research Association) (GBR) **2726**
B C R Group of Companies. Annual Report *see* British Columbia Railway Company Annual Report **8615**
• B.C. Real Estate Association. Bulletin (Online Edition) (CAN) **7583**
B C S *see* Buddhist - Christian Studies **7700**
B C S C Service Plan *see* British Columbia Securities Commission. Service Plan **1614**
B C S P (Bollettino del Centro Camuno di Studi Preistorici) (ITA ISSN 1594-7084) **383**
B C S P Newsletter (Board of Certified Safety Professionals) (USA) **6673**
B C School Sports Report (CAN) **8221**
• B C Seniors' Guide (British Columbia) (CAN ISSN 1910-6955) **8027**
• ➤ B C Studies (CAN ISSN 0005-2949) **7949**
B C T C - C A M R A S O - Focus (British Carpet Technical Centre, Cleaning & Maintenance Research & Services Organization) (GBR) **8448**
B C T G M News (Bakery, Confectionery & Tobacco Workers) (USA) **3671**
B C T V *see* Bibliography on Cable Television **2346**
B C T V Monthly *see* The Boston Catholic Television Monthly **7786**
B C Timber Sales. Annual Service Plan Report (British Columbia) (CAN ISSN 1715-4308) **3710**
B C U N Briefing *see* U N A - U S A Policy Brief. Occational Papers **7269**
B C - Verified Beef Production Program Newsletter (British Columbia) (CAN ISSN 1914-0770) **280**
B C Voice (CAN ISSN 0045-3080) **8852**
B C Well Tape (CAN) **6799**
B C Wine Trails (CAN ISSN 1188-1348) **598**
▼ B C's Horse Community Guide (CAN ISSN 1913-3545) **8287**
B D *see* Behavioral Disorders **3037**
B D B *see* A B A Bank Directors Briefing **1304**
B D B - Argumente (Bundesverband der Berufsbetreuer/-innen) (DEU) **6692**
B D B - Aspekte (Bundesverband der Berufsbetreuer/-innen) (DEU ISSN 1611-0404) **6692**
B D B - Direkt (Bund Deutscher Baumeister) (DEU) **434**
B D - Baumaschinendienst (DEU ISSN 0171-8908) **977**
† B.D. Body Book (ITA ISSN 1124-8971) **8934**
B D + C *see* Building Design + Construction **985**
B D C I Aid Information Digest (Book Development Council International) (GBR ISSN 1465-6132) **7552**
B D D *see* Bekhol Derakhekha Da'ehu **7719**
B D E F - Jahrbuch (Bund Deutscher Eisenbahn-Freunde) (DEU) **8615**
B D E W - Wasserstatistik (Bundesverband der Energie- und Wasserwirtschaft) (DEU) **8843**
B D Ex Aussenwirtschaftsinformationen (Bundesverband des Deutschen Exporthandels) (DEU) **1553**
B D F Aktuell (Bund Deutscher Forstleute) (DEU ISSN 0945-6538) **3684**
• B D F Magazine (Baltic Development Forum) (DNK ISSN 1902-6080) **1064**
B D H Kurier (Bund Deutscher Hirnbeschaedigter) (DEU ISSN 0343-1614) **5582**
B D I *see* Bridge d'Italia **8163**
B D I Aktuell (Berufsverband Deutscher Internisten) (DEU) **5944**
B D I Alemania Suministra *see* B D I Deutschland Liefert **1553**
B D I C Journal (Bund Deutscher Ingenieur Corporationen) (DEU) **2264**
• B D I Deutschland Liefert/B D I Alemania Suministra/B D I Germany Supplies/B D I L'Allemagne Fournit (Bundesverband der Deutschen Industrie) (DEU ISSN 0415-7508) **1553**
B D I Germany Supplies *see* B D I Deutschland Liefert **1553**
B D I Handbuch der Forschungs- und Innovationsfoerderung (Bundesverband der Deutschen Industrie) (DEU ISSN 0937-2385) **1064**
B D I L'Allemagne Fournit *see* B D I Deutschland Liefert **1553**
B D I Z - E D I Konkret (Bundesverband der Implantologisch Taetigen Zahnaerzte in Europa - European Association of Dental Imp) (DEU) **5836**
B D J Online *see* British Dental Journal **5836**
B D K J Journal (Bund der Deutschen Katholischen Jugend) (DEU ISSN 0948-0188) **7785**
B D K Mitteilungen (Bund Deutscher Kunsterzieher) (DEU ISSN 0005-2981) **3052**
B d L *see* Biblioteca della Liberta **7109**
B D M V Info (Bundesvereinigung Deutscher Musikverbaende) (DEU ISSN 1610-1529) **6547**
B D Magazine *see* Building Design **436**
▼ • B D P A Today (Black Data Processing Associates) (USA ISSN 1946-1410) **8089**
B D S (USA ISSN 1072-1061) **8254**
B D V I - Forum (Bund der Oeffentlich Bestellten Vermessungsingenieure e.V.) (DEU ISSN 0342-6165) **3260**
B d V Nachrichten (Bund der Vertriebenen) (DEU) **7109**
B D V T Journal (Berufsverband der Verkaufsfoerderer und Trainer e.V.) (DEU) **1727**
• B D Week (Broker - Dealer) (USA) **1611**
B D Z Magazin (Bund der Deutschen Zollbeamten) (DEU ISSN 1437-9864) **1911**
B dot Open *see* B.Open **8090**
B E *see* The Building Economist **985**
B E *see* Business Economics **1071**
B E A I Spectrum (Biomedical / Clinical Engineering Association of Ireland) (IRL ISSN 2009-0714) **747**
• B E A R S (Brown Electronic Article Review Service) (USA) **7109**
B E B R Monographs (USA) **1439**
B E D Series (USA ISSN 1521-4613) **747**
B.E. - Delegation Regionale de Cooperation dans le Cone Sud et le Bresil *see* Delegation Regionale de Cooperation dans le Cone Sud et le Bresil. Bulletin Eletronique **7850**
B E E *see* Bulletin on Energy Efficiency **3125**
B E E - j *see* Bioscience Education Electronic Journal **661**
B E F A R. Publication (Bibliotheque des Ecoles Francaises d'Athenes et de Rome) (FRA) **383**
B E H *see* Bulletin Epidemiologique Hebdomadaire **7510**
B E I - Informaciones *see* European Investment Bank. Information **1622**
A B E I. Journal *see* Associacao Brasileira de Estudos Irlandeses. Journal **5257**
• The B E Journal in Theoretical Economics (Berkeley Electronic Press) (USA ISSN 1935-1704) **1536**
▼ • The B.E. Journal of Economic Analysis & Policy (USA ISSN 1935-1682) **1536**
▼ • The B.E. Journal of Macroeconomics (USA ISSN 1935-1690) **1717**
• The B E Journals in Economic Analysis & Policy (Berkeley Electronic Press) (USA ISSN 1555-0494) **1536**
• The B E Journals in Macroeconomics (Berkeley Electronic Press) (USA ISSN 1555-0486) **1718**
The B E Journals in Theoretical Economics *see* The B E Journal in Theoretical Economics **1536**
➤ B E L L (BEL ISSN 1376-2958) **5098**
B E L L E Newsletter (Biological Effects of Low Level Exposures) (USA ISSN 1092-4736) **3494**
B E M A Bulletin (Bristol and Western Engineering Manufacturers Association) (GBR ISSN 0005-304X) **3182**
B E M A C News *see* Brisbane Ethnic Music & Arts Centre News **479**
B E M A Engineering Directory (Bristol and Western Engineering Manufacturers Association) (GBR ISSN 0067-5709) **3182**
B E M Specifier (ZAF) **977**
• B E N (Botanical Electronic News) (CAN ISSN 1188-603X) **778**
B E N E R Digest Update (Biological Effects of Nonionizing Electromagnetic Radiation) (USA ISSN 1056-9138) **752**
B - E N T (Belgian Ear Nose Throat) (BEL ISSN 1781-782X) **6078**
B E P *see* Boletin Estadistico del Petroleo **6764**
B E Q *see* Business Ethics Quarterly **6909**
B E R *see* Business & Economic Review **1070**
B E R J *see* British Educational Research Journal **2832**
B E R L Forecasts (Business & Economic Research Ltd.) (NZL ISSN 1170-4861) **1439**
B E Radio *see* Radio **2362**
B E S Symposium Series *see* British Ecological Society. Symposium **3407**
B E S T (Best European Studies on Time) (IRL ISSN 1017-4877) **8089**
• B.E.S.T. (Biuletyn Efektywnie Studiujacych Talentow) (POL ISSN 1509-9849) **2273**
B.E.S.T. Plus *see* B.E.S.T. **2273**
• B E T A (Bulletin of Experimental Treatment for AIDS) (USA ISSN 1058-708X) **5810**
B E W *see* Burma Economic Watch **1070**
B & G (NLD ISSN 0166-8528) **1911**
• B en M (Beleid en Maatschappij) (NLD ISSN 1389-0069) **7109**
B en U *see* Bouw en Uitvoering voor Rijk, Provincie en Gemeente **4405**
A B F *see* Arab Banking and Finance **1308**
B F B *see* Bibliotheksforum Bayern **4996**
B F B Bericht (Biologisches Forschungsinstitut Burgenland) (AUT ISSN 0257-3105) **655**
B F Bladet *see* Butikslederen **1422**
† B F Bulletin (Business & Finance) (USA ISSN 1048-5376) **8934**
B F D (Boletin de la Facultad de Derecho) (ESP ISSN 1133-1259) **4625**
B F G P *see* Briefings in Functional Genomics & Proteomics **864**
B F H I News (Baby-Friendly Hospital Initiative) (USA) **8027**
B F H - N V (Bundesfinanzhof - Nicht Veroeffentlichten) (DEU ISSN 0179-0498) **7422**
B F H - P R (Bundesfinanzhof - Praxis) (DEU ISSN 1431-3928) **1911**
B F I Film Handbook (Year) (British Film Institute) (GBR ISSN 1748-0736) **6490**
B F J *see* British Food Journal **3628**
B F L *see* Building for Leisure **985**
B F M (Black Filmmaker) (GBR ISSN 1465-2242) **6490**
B F N Informerar (Bokfoereningsnaemnden) (SWE ISSN 1103-5765) **1281**
B F P - Betriebsfuhrpark *see* B F P - Fuhrpark und Management **1727**
B F P - Fuhrpark und Management (DEU ISSN 1610-563X) **1727**
B F P P *see* Knowledge and Management of Aquatic Ecosystems **2616**
B F P P - Bulletin Francais de la Peche et de la Protection des Milieux Aquatiques (Online) *see* Knowledge and Management of Aquatic Ecosystems **2616**
B F S Aktuell/Actualites O F S (Bundesamt fuer Statistik) (CHE) **7478**
B f S - Berichte (Bundesamt fuer Strahlenschutz) (DEU ISSN 0937-4426) **3165**
B f S - E T (Bundesamt fuer Strahlenschutz - Entsorgung und Transport) (DEU ISSN 0949-2216) **3165**
B f S - I A R (Bundesamt fuer Strahlenschutz - Atmosphaerische Radioaktivitaet) (DEU) **3165**
B f S - K T (Bundesamt fuer Strahlenschutz - Kerntechnische Sicherheit) (DEU ISSN 0949-3204) **3165**
B f S - S H Berichte (Bundesamt fuer Strahlenschutz) (DEU ISSN 1616-7333) **3165**
B f S - S T (Bundesamt fuer Strahlenschutz - Strahlenschutz) (DEU ISSN 0949-3212) **3165**
B f S - Schriften (Bundesamt fuer Strahlenschutz) (DEU ISSN 0937-4469) **3165**
• B F u P - Betriebswirtschaftliche Forschung und Praxis (DEU ISSN 0340-5370) **1727**
B F W *see* British Football Week **8224**
† B F Z - Info (Berufsfoerderungszentrum Essen e.V.) (DEU) **8934**
• Die B G (DEU ISSN 0723-7561) **4494**
B G B I - Index (AUT) **4821**
B G C World *see* Converge Point **7752**
† • B G H - C D (Bundesgerichtshof) (DEU ISSN 1865-2107) **8934**
• B G H - Report (Bundesgerichtshof) (DEU ISSN 1616-9743) **4827**
B G I *see* Bibliographie Geographique Internationale (Paris, 1996) **4035**

Title

• ➤ B M C Genetics (BioMed Central) (GBR ISSN 1471-2156) **863**
• ➤ B M C Genomics (BioMed Central) (GBR ISSN 1471-2164) **863**
• ➤ B M C Geriatrics (BioMed Central) (GBR ISSN 1471-2318) **4041**
• ➤ B M C Health Services Research (BioMed Central) (GBR ISSN 1472-6963) **5582**
• ➤ B M C Immunology (BioMed Central) (GBR ISSN 1471-2172) **5755**
• ➤ B M C Infectious Diseases (BioMed Central) (GBR ISSN 1471-2334) **5810**
• ➤ B M C International Health and Human Rights (BioMed Central) (GBR ISSN 1472-698X) **7509**
• ➤ B M C Medical Education (BioMed Central) (GBR ISSN 1472-6920) **5582**
• ➤ B M C Medical Ethics (BioMed Central) (GBR ISSN 1472-6939) **5582**
• ➤ B M C Medical Genetics (BioMed Central) (GBR ISSN 1471-2350) **863**
▼ • B M C Medical Genomics (BioMed Central) (GBR ISSN 1755-8794) **863**
• ➤ B M C Medical Imaging (BioMed Central) (GBR ISSN 1471-2342) **6193**
• ➤ B M C Medical Informatics and Decision Making (BioMed Central) (GBR ISSN 1472-6947) **5829**
• ➤ B M C Medical Physics (BioMed Central) (GBR ISSN 1756-6649) **6193**
• ➤ B M C Medical Research Methodology (BioMed Central) (GBR ISSN 1471-2288) **5582**
• ➤ B M C Medicine (BioMed Central) (GBR ISSN 1741-7015) **5582**
• ➤ B M C Microbiology (BioMed Central) (GBR ISSN 1471-2180) **882**
• ➤ B M C Molecular Biology (BioMed Central) (GBR ISSN 1471-2199) **655**
• ➤ B M C Musculoskeletal Disorders (BioMed Central) (GBR ISSN 1471-2474) **6056**
• ➤ B M C Nephrology (BioMed Central) (GBR ISSN 1471-2369) **6265**
• ➤ B M C Neurology (BioMed Central) (GBR ISSN 1471-2377) **6125**
• ➤ B M C Neuroscience (BioMed Central) (GBR ISSN 1471-2202) **920**
B M C News (Baptist Medical Centers) (USA) **4088**
B M C Nuclear Medicine *see* B M C Medical Physics **6193**
• ➤ B M C Nursing (BioMed Central) (GBR ISSN 1472-6955) **5952**
• ➤ B M C Ophthalmology (BioMed Central) (GBR ISSN 1471-2415) **6039**
• ➤ B M C Oral Health (BioMed Central) (GBR ISSN 1472-6831) **5836**
• ➤ B M C Palliative Care (BioMed Central) (GBR ISSN 1472-684X) **5582**
• ➤ B M C Pediatrics (BioMed Central) (GBR ISSN 1471-2431) **6088**
• ➤ B M C Pharmacology (BioMed Central) (GBR ISSN 1471-2210) **6824**
• ➤ B M C Physiology (BioMed Central) (GBR ISSN 1472-6793) **920**
• ➤ B M C Plant Biology (BioMed Central) (GBR ISSN 1471-2229) **778**
• ➤ B M C Pregnancy and Childbirth (BioMed Central) (GBR ISSN 1471-2393) **5986**
▼ • ➤ B M C Proceedings (BioMed Central Ltd.) (GBR ISSN 1753-6561) **7838**
• ➤ B M C Psychiatry (BioMed Central) (GBR ISSN 1471-244X) **6126**
• ➤ B M C Public Health (BioMed Central) (GBR ISSN 1471-2458) **7509**
• ➤ B M C Pulmonary Medicine (BioMed Central) (GBR ISSN 1471-2466) **6212**
▼ • B M C Research Notes (BioMed Central) (GBR ISSN 1756-0500) **655**
• ➤ B M C Structural Biology (BioMed Central) (GBR ISSN 1472-6807) **655**
• ➤ B M C Surgery (BioMed Central) (GBR ISSN 1471-2482) **6237**
▼ • ➤ B M C Systems Biology (BioMed Central) (GBR ISSN 1752-0509) **655**
• ➤ B M C Urology (BioMed Central) (GBR ISSN 1471-2490) **6265**
• ➤ B M C Veterinary Research (GBR ISSN 1746-6148) **8794**
• ➤ B M C Women's Health (BioMed Central Ltd.) (GBR ISSN 1472-6874) **8844**
• B M E S Bulletin (Biomedical Engineering Society) (USA) **5582**
B M G N *see* Bijdragen en Mededelingen Betreffende de Geschiedenis der Nederlanden **4205**
B M I *see* Bulk Materials International **1881**
▼ • B M I, Body, Mind, Inspiration (USA ISSN 1938-0127) **5920**
B M I Building Maintenance Price Book (Building Maintenance Information) (GBR) **978**
B M I: Music World (Broadcast Music Inc.) (USA ISSN 1042-6736) **6547**
B.M.J. *see* Bangladesh Medical Journal **5583**
• ➤ B M J (British Medical Journal) (GBR ISSN 0959-535X) **5582**
B M J (Chinese Edition) *see* Yingguo Yixue Zazhi (Chinese Edition) **5733**
• ➤ B M J (Clinical Research Edition) (British Medical Journal) (GBR ISSN 0959-8138) **5582**
B M J (Compact Edition) *see* B M J **5582**
B M J (Compact Edition) *see* B M J (Online) **5583**
B M J (Greek Edition) *see* B M J **5582**
B M J (Hungarian Edition) *see* B M J **5582**
B M J (International Edition) *see* B M J **5582**
B M J (Middle East Edition) *see* B M J **5582**
B M J (Nigerian Edition) *see* B M J **5582**
• ➤ B M J (Online) (British Medical Journal) (GBR ISSN 1756-1833) **5583**
B M J (Portuguese Edition) *see* B M J **5582**
B M J (Practice Observed Edition) *see* B M J - General Practice Edition **5583**
B M J (Romanian Edition) *see* B M J **5582**
B M J (South Asia Edition) *see* Selections from B M J (South Asia Edition) **5711**
B M J (West African Edition) *see* B M J **5582**
• B M J Career Focus (Online) (GBR ISSN 1742-6774) **6692**
▼ • ➤ B M J Case Reports (British Medical Journal) (GBR ISSN 1757-790X) **5583**
B M J Clinical Evidence *see* Clinical Evidence (Online) **5596**
B M J.com *see* B M J (Online) **5583**
• ➤ B M J - General Practice Edition (British Medical Journal) (GBR ISSN 0959-8154) **5583**
B M J International Edition *see* B M J **5582**
B M L Quarterly Update *see* Quarterly Update **7571**
B M Magazine (British Museum Society) (GBR ISSN 0965-8297) **6521**
B M P Forecasts (Building Material Producers) (GBR ISSN 0144-9060) **978**
B M P Information (Building Material Producers) (GBR ISSN 0144-9052) **978**
B M P Monthly Statistical Bulletin (Building Material Producers) (GBR ISSN 0144-9036) **1044**
B M P State of Trade (Building Material Producers) (GBR) **978**
• B M R A Rubber and Polyurethane Directory (British Rubber Manufacturers' Association Ltd.) (GBR ISSN 0955-8772) **7824**
† B M R - Correspondenz (Bayerischer Musikrat e.V.) (DEU) **8934**
B M R J *see* Black Music Research Journal **6549**
B M S *see* Bulletin de Methodologie Sociologique **8091**
B M S T *see* France. Ministere de l'Emploi et de la Solidarite. Bulletin Mensuel des Statistiques du Travail **8958**
• B M T Abstracts (British Maritime Technology Ltd.) (GBR ISSN 0268-9650) **8522**
B M T News (British Maritime Technology) (GBR) **8639**
B M T Newsletter *see* Blood & Marrow Transplant Newsletter **5903**
B M W (HKG) **8568**
B M W Car (Bayerische Motoren Werke) (GBR ISSN 1353-7954) **8568**
B M W E Journal (Brotherhood of Maintenance of Way Employes) (USA ISSN 1049-3921) **4590**
B M W Magazin (Bayerische Motoren Werke AG) (DEU ISSN 0946-8390) **8568**
• B M W Magazine (Bayerische Motoren Werke) (AUS ISSN 1444-402X) **8568**
B M W Motorraeder (Bayerische Motoren Werke) (DEU) **8254**
B M W - O N (Bayerische Motoren Werke - Owners News) (USA ISSN 1080-5729) **8254**
B M W Scene Live (Bayerische Motor Werken) (DEU ISSN 1610-9902) **8568**
B M W Tuning (Bayerische Motor Werken) (DEU) **8568**
B M X Action (USA) **8254**
• B M X Plus (Bicycle Motocross) (USA ISSN 0195-0320) **8254**
B M Xpress (Bicycle Motorcross) (AUS) **8254**
B M Z - Materialien (Bundesministerium fuer Wirtschaftliche Zusammenarbeit und Entwicklung) (DEU) **1591**
➤ B Ma (USA ISSN 1078-0955) **5259**
B N *see* Blues News **6550**
B N *see* Bianco & Nero **6490**
B N A/A C C A Compliance Manual: Prevention of Corporate Liability *see* Prevention of Corporate Liability: Current Report **4879**
B N A / A C C A Compliance Manual: Prevention of Corporate Liability (Bureau of National Affairs, American Corporate Counsel Association) (USA) **4857**
B N A C Communicator (Bureau of National Affairs) (USA ISSN 1051-208X) **1064**
B N A Labor Relations Reporter *see* Labor Relations Reporter **1693**
B N A Labor Relations Reporter. Wage and Hour Cases *see* Labor Relations Reporter. Wage and Hour Cases **1693**
• B N A Policy and Practice Series (Bureau of National Affairs) (USA ISSN 0005-3228) **1856**
• B N A Policy and Practice Series. Fair Employment Practices (Bureau of National Affairs) (USA ISSN 0149-2683) **1666**
B N A Portraits (British North America) (CAN ISSN 1203-4657) **6892**
B N A Topics (British North America) (CAN ISSN 0045-3129) **6892**
B N A's Americans with Disabilities Act Manual (Bureau of National Affairs) (USA) **4968**
• B N A's Americans with Disabilities Act Manual. Newsletter (Bureau of National Affairs) (USA ISSN 1063-3111) **4968**
• B N A's Banking Report (Online) (Bureau of National Affairs) (USA ISSN 1522-5984) **1310**
• B N A's Banking Report (Print) (Bureau of National Affairs) (USA ISSN 0891-0634) **1310**
• B N A's Corporate Counsel Weekly (Bureau of National Affairs) (USA ISSN 0886-0475) **1727**
• B N A's Directory of State & Federal Courts, Judges, and Clerks (Bureau of National Affairs) (USA ISSN 1078-5582) **4625**
B N A's Disabilities Law Library on CD *see* Americans with Disabilities Cases **4615**
• B N A's Eastern Europe Reporter (Bureau of National Affairs) (USA ISSN 1058-7365) **1439**
† • B N A's Employee Benefits Library on CD (Bureau of National Affairs) (USA ISSN 1094-7809) **8934**
B N A's Employee Benefits Library on DVD *see* B N A's Employee Benefits Library on CD **8934**
B N A's Employee Benefits Library on DVD *see* Benefits & Compensation Management Update **1667**
• B N A's Employment Discrimination Report (Bureau of National Affairs) (USA ISSN 1072-1967) **1856**
† B N A's Environment & Safety Compliance Calendar (Bureau of National Affairs) (USA) **8934**
B N A's Environment and Safety Compliance Calendar *see* B N A's Environment & Safety Compliance Calendar **8934**
• B N A's Environmental Compliance Bulletin (Bureau of National Affairs) (USA ISSN 1073-5798) **4625**
• B N A's Environmental Due Diligence Guide (Bureau of National Affairs) (USA ISSN 1931-6615) **4625**
• B N A's Federal Environment & Safety Regulatory Monitoring Report (Bureau of National Affairs) (USA ISSN 1524-7716) **3405**
B N A's Federal Environment and Safety Regulatory Monitoring Report *see* B N A's Federal Environment & Safety Regulatory Monitoring Report **3405**
• B N A's Health Care Daily Report (Bureau of National Affairs) (USA ISSN 1091-4021) **4088**
• B N A's Health Care Fraud Report (Bureau of National Affairs) (USA ISSN 1092-1079) **4088**
• B N A's Health Care Policy Report (Bureau of National Affairs) (USA ISSN 1068-1213) **7509**
B N A's Health Law & Business Library on CD *see* Health Law & Business Library **4096**
• B N A's Health Law & Business Series (Bureau of National Affairs) (USA ISSN 1087-7185) **4088**
• B N A's Health Law Reporter (Online) (Bureau of National Affairs) (USA ISSN 1521-5350) **4625**
• B N A's Health Law Reporter (Print) (Bureau of National Affairs) (USA ISSN 1064-2137) **4625**
B N A's Human Resources Library on Compact Disk *see* Human Resources Library **1865**
• B N A's Intellectual Property Library on C D (Bureau of National Affairs) (USA ISSN 1095-5615) **6746**
▼ • B N A's Introduction to Environmental Law Series (Bureau of National Affairs) (USA ISSN 1936-8429) **3405**
B N A's Labor & Employment Law Library on CD *see* Labor and Employment Law Library **5024**
• B N A's Medicare Report (Bureau of National Affairs) (USA ISSN 1049-7986) **5583**
• B N A's Patent, Trademark & Copyright Journal (Bureau of National Affairs) (USA ISSN 0148-7965) **6746**
B N A's Patent, Trademark and Copyright Journal *see* B N A's Patent, Trademark & Copyright Journal **6746**
B N A's Safety Library on C D *see* Safety Library **6686**
• B N A's SafetyNet (Bureau of National Affairs) (USA ISSN 1091-2894) **6674**
• B N A's State Environment & Safety Regulatory Monitoring Report (Bureau of National Affairs) (USA ISSN 1522-4228) **3405**
B N A's State Environment and Safety Regulatory Monitoring Report *see* B N A's State Environment & Safety Regulatory Monitoring Report **3405**
• B N A's State H I P A A and Privacy Monitoring Report (Bureau of National Affairs, Health Insurance and Portability and Accountability Act) (USA ISSN 1545-4444) **4494**
B N B. Beslissingen in Belastingzaken. Nederlandse Belastingrechtspraak *see* Beslissingen in Belastingzaken **1912**
• B N B on CD-ROM (British National Bibliography) (GBR ISSN 0968-3097) **616**
B N - Betriebswirtschaftliche Nachrichten fuer die Landwirtschaft (DEU ISSN 0179-5066) **194**
B N D E S Annual Report (Banco Nacional do Desenvolvimento Economico. e Social) (BRA) **1310**
B N D E S Economic Bulletin (Banco Nacional do Desenvolvimento Economico e Social) (BRA) **1439**
B N D E S International Bulletin/B N D E S Sinopse Internacional (Banco Nacional do Desenvolvimento Economico e Social) (BRA) **1440**
B N D E S News/Banco Nacional do Desenvolvimento Economico. Plan of Action (BRA) **1440**
B N D E S Relatorio Anual (Banco Nacional do Desenvolvimento Economico e Social) (BRA) **1440**
B N D E S Sinopse Internacional *see* B N D E S International Bulletin **1440**
B N E *see* Broadcast Engineering News **2376**
B N F Annual Conference Proceedings (British Nutrition Foundation) (GBR) **6655**
B N F Briefing Papers (British Nutrition Foundation) (GBR ISSN 1350-6854) **6655**
B N F L News (British Nuclear Fuels plc) (GBR) **3165**
B N F Task Force Reports (British Nutrition Foundation) (GBR) **6655**
B N I F Nuclear Business. Directory (British Nuclear Industry Forum) (GBR) **3182**
B N J *see* British Numismatic Journal **6649**
B N L Basic Statistics on the Italian Economy (Banca Nazionale del Lavoro) (ITA) **1212**
B N N A *see* Bibliography of Native North Americans **3574**
B.ND (NLD ISSN 1871-0506) **4590**
• B# Newsletter (USA) **6547**
B O A C *see* France. Ministere de l'Economie, des Finances et du Budget. Bulletin Officiel de l'Administration Centrale **7438**
• B O A T - U S Magazine (Boat Owners Association of the United States) (USA ISSN 1090-1272) **8271**
Le B O. Bulletin Officiel de l'Education Nationale (FRA ISSN 1254-7131) **3017**
B O C A Bulletin (Building Officials and Code Administrators) (USA) **978**
B O C A National Energy Conservation Code (Building Officials and Code Administrators) (USA ISSN 1055-6168) **3124**
B O C A National Property Maintenance Code (Building Officials and Code Administrators) (USA ISSN 1055-6192) **978**
B O C A Research Report (Building Officials and Code Administrators) (USA) **7488**
B O C News (Bristol Ornithological Club) (GBR) **902**
• B O F I T Discussion Papers (Online Edition) (Bank of Finland - Institute for Economies in Transition) (FIN ISSN 1456-5889) **1440**
• B O F I T Online (Bank of Finland Institute for Economies in Transition) (FIN ISSN 1456-811X) **1440**
• B O F I T Weekly (Bank of Finland Institute for Economies in Transition) (FIN) **1440**
▼ • B o F Online (Bank of Finland) (FIN ISSN 1796-9123) **1310**
B O J *see* Briefings on the Joint Commission **4089**
B O M A Experience Exchange Report (Building Owners and Managers Association International) (USA ISSN 0738-2170) **7583**
B O M A International Convention Directory (Building Owners and Managers Association International) (USA) **6278**
B O M A.org (Building Owners and Managers Association) (USA) **978**
B O M C Reading Room *see* Book-Of-The-Month Club News **7554**
B O P A *see* Principado de Asturias. Boletin Oficial **4761**
B O P I Brevets d'Invention - Certificats Complimentaires de Protection - Topographies (Bulletin Officiel de la Propriete Industrielle) (FRA) **6746**
B O P I Dessins & Modeles (Bulletin Officiel de la Propriete Industrielle) (FRA ISSN 0223-3398) **3365**
B O P I Marques de Fabrique, de Commerce ou de Service (Bulletin Officiel de la Propriete Industrielle) (FRA ISSN 0223-3401) **6746**
B O P I Statistiques de la Propriete Industrielle (Bulletin Officiel de la Propriete Industrielle) (FRA) **6746**
B O R *see* Biology of Reproduction **660**
B O R M E *see* Spain. Registro Mercantil. Boletin Oficial **1178**
• The B.O.S.S. Report (USA) **8160**
B O T S A *see* Bulletin for Old Testament Studies in Africa (Online Edition) **7629**
B O U Checklist (British Ornithologists' Union) (GBR ISSN 0962-0877) **902**
▼ B O W (Big Open World) (USA ISSN 1946-0627) **5259**
• B O Z P & P O Aktualne (Bezpecnost a Ochrana Zdravi pri Praci a Pozarni Ochrana) (CZE ISSN 1801-3724) **6674**
B og B (ISL ISSN 1670-5971) **8090**
▼ • B.Open (IRL ISSN 1649-9859) **8090**
B P *see* Business Pulse **1668**
B P *see* British Politics **7110**
B P A *see* British Poultry Abstracts **176**
B P A International. Annual Report (USA) **21**
B P Bulletin (Building Professionals) (AUS ISSN 1832-3820) **978**
B P I *see* Building Price Index (Online) **1443**
B P I *see* Bookman's Price Index **7555**
B P I A. Business Products Industry Report (USA ISSN 1078-5809) **1849**
A B P I. Annual Review *see* The Association of the British Pharmaceutical Industry. Annual Review **6823**
B P I Geschaeftsbericht (Bundesverband der Pharmazeutischen Industrie e.V.) (DEU) **6824**
B P I News (British Photographic Industry News) (GBR ISSN 1364-7784) **6964**
B P I Newsletter (Business and Professional People for the Public Interest) (USA) **3405**
B P I Statistical Handbook (British Phonographic Industry) (GBR ISSN 0968-008X) **6631**
B P J M Aktuell (Bundespruefstelle fuer Jugendgefaehrdende Medien) (DEU) **2144**
B P J S Aktuell *see* B P J M Aktuell **2144**
B P M *see* British Postgraduate Musicology (Online) **6552**

10016 BABRAHAM INSTITUTE. REPORT ULRICH'S PERIODICALS

• Babraham Institute. Report (GBR ISSN 1354-8425) **920**
Babraham Publications (GBR ISSN 1363-9773) **724**
Babson Bulletin (USA) **2273**
Baby *see* Diana Baby **8950**
▼ Baby (ROM) **2144**
Baby *see* Southern Baby **4367**
Baby *see* Martha Stewart Baby **8972**
Baby and Child Care Quick Reference Encyclopedia (CAN ISSN 1193-3313) **8852**
Baby & Children's Products *see* Global Sources Baby & Children's Products **1818**
Baby & Junior (DEU ISSN 0005-3554) **2245**
Baby & You *see* Pregnancy, Baby & You **8880**
Baby Boomer Collectibles (USA) **4328**
Baby Boomer News (USA) **5065**
Baby Born (DEU) **2177**
Baby Center (USA ISSN 1557-5403) **4352**
Baby Couture (USA) **2144**
• Baby Doe's Obsessed (USA) **3970**
Baby Foods Market Assessment *see* Key Note Market Assessment. Baby Foods **3652**
Baby-Friendly Hospital Initiative News *see* B F H I News **8027**
Baby, Hobby, Leketoey (NOR ISSN 1503-1810) **4059**
Baby Magazine Infant Care Guide (USA) **6088**
Baby Post (DEU ISSN 0724-1119) **2144**
Baby Products *see* Key Note Market Assessment. Baby Products **2157**
Baby Shop (USA) **4059**
• Baby Talk (USA ISSN 1529-5389) **2144**
Baby und Co. (DEU) **2144**
Baby und die Ersten Lebensjahre *see* Baby und Familie **8852**
Baby und Familie (DEU ISSN 1861-0552) **8852**
Baby Unser Glueck (DEU ISSN 1619-4349) **2144**
Baby Wereld (NLD ISSN 1388-9389) **2144**
Babybug (USA ISSN 1077-1131) **2177**
Babycare and Pregnancy (GBR ISSN 1465-170X) **2144**
Babycare Book (AUS ISSN 1326-1665) **6088**
babydallas (USA) **2144**
Babygids (NLD) **2144**
BabyLife *see* ParentLife **7770**
Babylon (DEU ISSN 0931-6418) **7718**
Babylon 5: The Offical Magazine (GBR ISSN 1368-7018) **5440**
Babylonia (CHE ISSN 1420-0007) **5098**
Babys Erstes Jahr *see* Ratgeber fuer Babys Erste Monate **2166**
Babys Erstes Jahr (DEU) **2144**
Babys Lernen Schlafen (DEU) **2144**
Babys und Kinder Richtig Foerdern (DEU) **2144**
BabySteps (USA) **2144**
BabyStuf (NLD ISSN 1871-8469) **2144**
• babysue (USA ISSN 1076-8890) **5417**
Babytalk *see* Baby Talk **2144**
Le Bac en Tete. Geographie (FRA ISSN 1288-863X) **2829**
Le Bac en Tete. Histoire (FRA ISSN 1288-8621) **2830**
Le Bac en Tete. Mathematiques (FRA ISSN 1295-1927) **2830**
Le Bac en Tete. Physique-Chimie (FRA ISSN 1622-5740) **2830**
Le Bac en Tete. Sciences de la Vie et de la Terre (FRA ISSN 1631-994X) **2830**
Le Bac en Tete. Sciences Economiques et Sociales (FRA ISSN 1297-9066) **2830**
Baca/Read (IDN ISSN 0125-9008) **4993**
Baccara (DEU ISSN 0949-5886) **5409**
† Bacchus (ITA) **8934**
➤ Bach (USA ISSN 0005-3600) **6547**
Bach-Jahrbuch (DEU ISSN 0084-7682) **6547**
• ➤ Bach Perspectives (USA ISSN 1072-1924) **6547**
Bach Tanulmanyok (HUN ISSN 1216-9005) **6547**
Le Bachelier (FRA ISSN 1621-1227) **7338**
Bachelor to Groom *see* B II G **2251**
▼ The Back Bay Review (USA ISSN 1936-0878) **5259**
Back Brain Recluse (GBR ISSN 0269-9990) **5440**
Back Business (DEU) **3671**
Back Forty (USA ISSN 1049-3972) **2603**
Back Home in Kentucky (USA ISSN 0199-6290) **3970**
Back Home - The Newsletter of the Nonresident Lawyers Division (USA) **4625**
Back in the Bronx (USA) **3970**
• Back Issue (USA ISSN 1932-6904) **477**
• The Back Letter (USA ISSN 0894-7376) **6056**
† Back Office Focus (GBR ISSN 1354-8247) **8934**
Back Paddock (AUS) **94**
Back Pain and Osteoporosis (USA ISSN 1549-6252) **6056**
▼ • Back Stage (USA ISSN 1946-5440) **8466**
The Back Stage Book of New American Short Plays (USA ISSN 1931-0528) **8466**
Back Stage East *see* Back Stage **8466**
Back Stage/Shoot *see* Shoot **35**
Back Stage West *see* Back Stage **8466**
Back Street Heroes (GBR ISSN 0267-9841) **8568**
Back - Talk Magazine (USA) **4371**
➤ Back to Godhead (USA ISSN 0005-3643) **7707**
• Back to Work (CAN ISSN 1206-6826) **6674**
Backbone Magazine (CAN ISSN 1498-086X) **1065**
Backbone Technologies (TWN) **1806**
Backcountry (USA ISSN 1083-5350) **8305**
• Backdirt (USA) **383**
Backen fuer Weihnachten (DEU) **4352**
Backen im Fruehling (DEU) **4352**
Backen im Herbst (DEU) **4352**
Backen im Sommer (DEU) **4352**
Backen Leichtgemacht (DEU ISSN 0948-5201) **3671**
Backen Nach Grossmutters Art (DEU) **4352**
Backflow Prevention Reference Manual (USA ISSN 1936-685X) **4116**
• Background Notes (USA ISSN 1942-3195) **4000**
Background Notes Series *see* Background Notes **4000**
Background of World News *see* Dubao Cankao **3824**
Background Reports (LBN) **7223**
• Backgrounder (CAN ISSN 1499-7983) **7422**
Backgrounder (Washington, DC) (USA ISSN 1061-3889) **7278**
BackHome (USA ISSN 1051-323X) **4352**
Backjournal (DEU ISSN 0940-0362) **3671**
The Backletter *see* The Back Letter **6056**
• Backpacker (USA ISSN 0277-867X) **8305**
• Backpacker Essentials (AUS ISSN 1328-6749) **8685**
Backpackers *see* Meridian Travel **8733**
Backpacking.com *see* Backpacking Light **8305**
• Backpacking Light (USA ISSN 1550-4417) **8305**
Backpacking Newsletter (USA) **8305**
Backroads (USA) **8254**
• Backspin (DEU) **6547**
Backspin (IRL ISSN 1393-9122) **8221**
Backspin Manitoba's Golf Newspaper (CAN) **8221**
Backstage (BRA ISSN 1414-6398) **6547**
BackStage (DEU) **3844**
Backstreets (USA ISSN 0746-990X) **6547**
Backtechnik Europe (DEU) **3671**
Backtechnik International *see* Backtechnik Europe **3671**
• BackTrack (GBR ISSN 0955-5382) **8615**
Backtracker (USA ISSN 0094-6915) **3759**
Backwards City Review (USA ISSN 1559-5080) **5259**
Backwash (USA) **3970**
• Backwoods Home Magazine (USA ISSN 1050-9712) **3970**
Backwoodsman (USA) **4285**
Backyard Bird News (USA ISSN 1098-0229) **902**
• Backyard Flyer (USA ISSN 1542-2135) **4328**
Backyard Living (USA ISSN 1550-9990) **3724**
• Backyard Nature Notes (USA) **3724**
Backyard Solutions (USA) **3724**
• Backyard Wildlife Habitat (USA) **2603**
Bacon Busters (AUS ISSN 1441-4368) **8305**
Baconiana (GBR ISSN 0961-2173) **5208**
Bacon's Internet Media Directory (USA ISSN 1533-4317) **2552**
• Bacon's Media Calendar Directory (USA ISSN 1089-098X) **1974**
Bacon's New York Publicity Outlets (USA ISSN 1525-464X) **21**
Bacon's Newspaper - Magazine Directory (USA) **1974**
Bacon's Radio - T V - Cable Directory (USA) **2375**
➤ Bacteriologia, Virusologia, Parazitologia, Epidemiologia (ROM ISSN 1220-3696) **882**
Bacus (GBR) **2273**
Das Bad (Stuttgart) (DEU) **4532**
Bad Aachen (DEU) **3844**
Bad Abbacher Kur- und Geschaeftsanzeiger (DEU) **8685**
Bad Attitude (USA ISSN 0896-9531) **4371**
Bad Faith Law Report (USA ISSN 8756-5374) **4494**
• Bad Golfer (USA) **8221**
Bad Heute und Morgen *see* Il Bagno Oggi e Domani **4532**
Bad Iburger Gespraeche zum Kommunalrecht (DEU) **4625**
Bad Idea (GBR ISSN 1751-9152) **5259**
Bad Kissingen Journal (DEU) **3844**
Bad Lauterberg Journal (DEU) **3844**
Bad Mergentheimer Kur-Zeitung (DEU) **3844**
Bad Nauheim Journal (DEU) **3844**
Bad- & Koekguiden (SWE ISSN 1653-7122) **4554**
Bad Pool Sauna (DEU) **4554**
Bad Salzuflen (DEU ISSN 1616-279X) **4202**
Bad Sassendorf Journal (DEU) **3844**
Bad Seed (USA ISSN 1059-8235) **8090**
• Bad Subjects (USA) **7109**
Bad Toelz Aktuell (DEU ISSN 1434-6672) **8685**
Bad & Kueche (DEU ISSN 1614-8320) **5065**
Das Bad und Wellness (DEU) **4554**
Bad Wiessee Aktuell (DEU) **8685**
➤ Bad Wiesseer Tagungen des Collegium Carolinum (DEU) **4202**
Bada *see* Birder **662**
Ba'da *see* Hangug Haeyang Haghoe Ji - Bada **2805**
Badaboom Gramophone (USA) **3970**
Badan Meteorologi dan Geofisika. Laporan Evaluasi Hujan dan Perkiraan Hujan (IDN ISSN 0126-0561) **6347**
➤ Badania Fizjograficzne nad Polska Zachodnia. Seria A. Geografia Fizyczna (POL ISSN 0067-2807) **4000**
➤ Badania Fizjograficzne nad Polska Zachodnia. Seria B. Botanika (POL ISSN 0067-2815) **778**
➤ Badania Fizjograficzne nad Polska Zachodnia. Seria C. Zoologia (POL ISSN 0137-6683) **935**
Baden-Baden Aktuell (DEU) **3844**
Baden-Wuerttemberg in Wort und Zahl (DEU ISSN 0721-1821) **8356**
Baden-Wuerttemberg. Ministerium fuer Ernaehrung und Laendlichen Raum. Forschungsreport (DEU) **2603**
Baden-Wuerttemberg. Statistisches Landesamt. Statistisch-Prognostischer Bericht (DEU ISSN 0724-3790) **7478**
Baden-Wuerttemberg. Statistisches Landesamt. Statistische Berichte (DEU) **7479**
Baden-Wuerttemberg. Statistisches Landesamt. Veroeffentlichungsverzeichnis (DEU) **8356**
Baden-Wuerttemberg Woche *see* B W - Woche **7422**
Baden-Wuerttembergische Biographien (DEU) **640**
Baden - Wuerttembergische Verwaltungspraxis (DEU ISSN 0340-3505) **7422**
Badenweiler Journal (DEU) **3844**
Badger Builder *see* Wisconsin Badger Builder **1043**
Badger Common'tater (USA ISSN 0271-5864) **220**
• Badger Herald (USA ISSN 0045-1304) **2273**
Badger Legionnaire (USA ISSN 0005-3767) **6413**
Badger Postal History (USA) **6892**
Badger Sportsman (USA ISSN 0005-3775) **8305**
Badia Greca di Grottaferrata. Bollettino (ITA ISSN 0005-3783) **7785**
Badil Resource Center for Palestinian Residency & Refugee Rights. Working Papers (PSE ISSN 1728-1660) **7203**
• Badische Bauern Zeitung (DEU ISSN 0936-4838) **94**
Badische Biographien Neue Folge (DEU) **4202**
Badische Heimat (DEU ISSN 0930-7001) **4202**
Badische Neueste Nachrichten (DEU) **3844**
Badische Saengerzeitung (DEU ISSN 1612-0345) **6547**
Badische Turnzeitung (DEU ISSN 0721-2828) **8160**
Der Badische Winzer (DEU ISSN 0172-0937) **598**
Badische Zeitung (DEU) **3844**
Badischer Landesverein fuer Naturkunde und Naturschutz, Freiburg. Mitteilungen. Neue Folge (DEU ISSN 0067-2858) **655**
Badisches Staatstheater Karlsruhe. Spielplan (DEU) **8466**
Badisches Staatstheater Karlsruhe. Theaterspiegel (DEU) **8466**
Badisches Tagblatt (DEU) **3844**
Badje Info (BEL ISSN 1784-3405) **8027**
Badkamer Studio (NLD ISSN 1570-7296) **4554**
Badminton (GBR ISSN 1355-5057) **8160**
Badminton Association of England. Annual Handbook (GBR ISSN 0262-1940) **8160**
Badminton Beat (AUS) **8160**
Badminton Canada (CAN ISSN 0711-124X) **8221**
Badminton Magazine (JPN) **8161**
Badminton Sport (DEU ISSN 0943-6014) **8161**
• Badopinion (USA) **5208**
Baecker und Konditor (CHE) **3671**
Baecker-Werk (DEU) **3671**
Baecker-Zeitung (DEU ISSN 0342-9911) **3671**
Baeckerblume (DEU) **3844**
Der Baeckermeister (DEU ISSN 0171-7502) **3671**
Baeder (CHE) **4554**
Baederland Bayerischische Rhoen Erleben (DEU) **8685**
BaederWelt (DEU ISSN 1438-2768) **4532**
Baejarposturinn (ISL ISSN 1670-5823) **3877**
Baejarposturinn (Dalvik) *see* Baejarposturinn **3877**
Baejarposturinn-Troellaskagatidendi *see* Baejarposturinn **3877**
Baeko Magazin (DEU ISSN 0939-5571) **3671**
Baelder (GBR ISSN 1355-1876) **6643**
Baender, Bleche, Rohre (DEU ISSN 0005-3848) **6306**
Der Baer von Berlin (DEU ISSN 0522-0033) **4202**
• Baeredygtige Byer & Bygninger (DNK ISSN 1901-4422) **3405**
Baerenreiter Studienbuecher Musik (DEU) **6547**
Baerner Channe (CHE) **4382**
Baer's Agricultural Almanac & Gardener's Guide *see* Agricultural Almanac **83**
Baer's Garden Newsletter (USA) **3724**
Baessler Archiv (DEU ISSN 0005-3856) **330**
Det Baesta/Reader's Digest (SWE ISSN 1100-4843) **3954**
Baetica (ESP ISSN 0212-5099) **477**
Baff (DEU) **8027**
The Baffler (USA ISSN 1059-9789) **5208**
† E Bafion (ITA) **8934**
Bag-o-Fun Magazine *see* Fun to Learn - Bag-o-Fun Magazine **2189**
Bag om E U-Sagerne *see* Europaeisk Politik **4924**
Bagalil Haelyon *see* Al Hatzafon **3895**
Bagdala (SRB ISSN 0005-3880) **5208**
Bagel Digest (CAN) **5259**
Baghdader Forschungen (DEU ISSN 0939-0022) **383**
Baghdader Mitteilungen *see* Zeitschrift fuer Orientarchaeologie **424**
• ➤ Bagimililik Dergisi/Journal of Dependence (TUR ISSN 1302-5570) **2692**
• Bagno Design (ITA ISSN 1723-5227) **4532**
Bagno e Accessori (ITA ISSN 0392-2723) **978**
Bagno e Accessori International *see* Bagno e Accessori **978**
† Bagno & Cucina (ITA ISSN 1591-7193) **8934**
Bagno e Cucina. Architettura e Interior Design *see* Bagno & Cucina **8934**
Il Bagno Oggi e Domani/Bad Heute und Morgen/Bain Aujourd'hui et Demain/Bathroom Today and Tomorrow (ITA ISSN 0392-2715) **4532**
The Bagpipe (USA ISSN 1088-4122) **280**
• Bagpipes (DEU) **3844**
▼ Bags, Pillows & Pincushions (USA ISSN 1945-9106) **6637**
Bague Exterieure Bague Interieure *see* Aftermarket News (French Edition) **975**
➤ Baha'i Studies (CAN ISSN 0708-5052) **7624**
• ➤ Baha'i Studies Review (GBR ISSN 1354-8697) **7709**
➤ Baha'i Vizier (NLD ISSN 1381-8872) **7733**
Baha'i World (ISR ISSN 0045-1320) **7709**
Bahamas (Year) Including Turks & Caicos (USA ISSN 1055-5625) **8685**
Bahamas. Chamber of Commerce. Annual Directory (BHS) **1396**
Bahamas Dateline (USA ISSN 0749-5714) **1611**
Bahamas Financial Digest & Business Today (BHS) **1611**
Bahamas Handbook and Businessman's Annual (BHS ISSN 0067-2912) **1440**
➤ Bahamas Historical Society. Journal (BHS ISSN 1025-9236) **4285**
• The Bahamas in Figures (BHS) **8356**
Bahamas Investor (BHS) **1611**
➤ Bahamas Journal of Science (BHS ISSN 1022-2189) **7838**
Bahamas. Ministry of Education and Culture. Annual Report (BHS) **2830**
Bahamas. Ministry of Transport. Port and Marine Department. Annual Report (BHS) **8639**
Bahamas. Ministry of Works and Utilities. Annual Report (BHS) **3260**
Bahamian Review (BHS ISSN 0005-397X) **1440**
Bahana (BRN ISSN 0005-3988) **5259**
Bahia Analise & Dados (BRA ISSN 0103-8117) **1212**
Bahia, Brazil (State). Secretaria das Minas e Energia. Boletim Estatistico Mensal de Energia Eletrica (BRA) **3151**
Bahir Dar Journal of Education *see* Ethiopian Journal of Technology, Education and Sustainable Development **8421**
Al-Bahith as-Sageer/Young Researcher (SDN) **7839**
• Bahiyah Woman Magazine (USA) **3521**
Das Bahn-Adressbuch (DEU ISSN 1860-143X) **8615**
Bahn-Extra (DEU ISSN 0937-7174) **8615**
Bahn-Report (DEU ISSN 0178-4528) **8615**
Bahnhofblatt (CHE) **8615**
Bahnsport Aktuell (DEU ISSN 0724-7192) **8254**
Al-Bahrain (BHR) **4320**
Bahrain al-Yaum *see* Bahrain Today Magazine **4320**
• Bahrain Autos Report (GBR ISSN 1748-9776) **8568**
Bahrain Bibliography (BHR) **616**
Bahrain Chamber of Commerce and Industry. Commerce Review/Al-Haya al-Tijariya (BHR) **1396**
Bahrain. Educational Documentation Library. Acquisitions List (BHR) **2930**
Bahrain. Educational Documentation Library. Bibliographic Lists (BHR) **2930**
• Bahrain Freight Transport Report (GBR ISSN 1752-7872) **1880**
Bahrain Information Technology Report *see* Business Monitor International. Information Technology Country Reports **2491**
▼ • Bahrain Infrastructure Report (GBR ISSN 1752-7821) **1065**
• Bahrain Medical Bulletin (BHR ISSN 1012-8298) **5583**
• ➤ Bahrain Medical Society. Journal (BHR ISSN 1015-6321) **5583**
Bahrain. Ministry of Information. Official Gazette/Bahrain. Wizarat al-Isti'lamat. Al-Jaridah al-Rasmiyah (BHR) **7422**
Bahrain. Monetary Agency. Annual Report (BHR) **1912**
Bahrain. Monetary Agency. Quarterly Statistical Bulletin (BHR) **1212**
Bahrain Today Magazine/Bahrain al-Yaum (BHR) **4320**
Bahrain. Wizarat al-Isti'lamat. Al-Jaridah al-Rasmiyah *see* Bahrain. Ministry of Information. Official Gazette **7422**
Baie - James (CAN ISSN 1719-8895) **8685**
Baie - James, Nord-du-Quebec *see* Baie - James **8685**
Baigal (RUS ISSN 0320-7455) **3934**
Baihua Zhou (CHN ISSN 1006-1444) **5259**
Baihuayuan/Hundred Flower Garden:The World of Short Stories (CHN ISSN 1003-7810) **5259**
Baijia Zuowen Zhidao (CHN ISSN 1001-4039) **5098**
• Baike Zhishi/Encyclopedic Knowledge (CHN ISSN 1002-9567) **7839**
Bailiu (MNG ISSN 1007-4600) **5260**
Bailliere's Best Practice & Research. Clinical Anaesthesiology *see* Best Practice & Research: Clinical Anaesthesiology **5770**
Bailliere's Best Practice & Research. Clinical Endocrinology & Metabolism *see* Best Practice & Research: Clinical Endocrinology & Metabolism **5884**
Bailliere's Best Practice & Research. Clinical Gastroenterology *see* Best Practice & Research: Clinical Gastroenterology **5920**
Bailliere's Best Practice & Research. Clinical Haematology *see* Best Practice & Research: Clinical Haematology **5934**
Bailliere's Best Practice & Research. Clinical Obstetrics and Gynaecology *see* Best Practice & Research: Clinical Obstetrics & Gynaecology **5986**
Bailliere's Best Practice & Research. Clinical Rheumatology *see* Best Practice & Research: Clinical Rheumatology **6222**
Bailliere's Midwives' Dictionary (GBR) **5986**

DIRECTORY 2010 BAMAH (GIVATAYIM) 10017

Bailliere's Nurses' Dictionary (GBR) **5952**
Bailrigg Memoranda (GBR ISSN 0969-6040) **7223**
Bailrigg Papers on International Security (GBR ISSN 0969-6032) **7223**
Baily's Hunting Directory (GBR ISSN 0067-2947) **1974**
Bain Aujourd'hui et Demain *see* Il Bagno Oggi e Domani **4532**
• Bainianchao/Hundred Year Tide (CHN ISSN 1007-4295) **4180**
Baio Indasutori *see* Bio Industry **757**
Baio Tekunoroji Janaru (JPN ISSN 1349-7448) **655**
Baioenjiniaringu Kouenkai Kouen Ronbunshuu/Japanese Society of Mechanical Engineers. Bioengineering Division Conference. Proceedings (JPN) **747**
Baioenjiniaringu Shinpojumu Ronbunshuu/Bioengineering Symposium. Proceedings (JPN) **747**
Baiofidobakku Kenkyu/Japanese Journal of Biofeedback Research (JPN ISSN 0386-1856) **7338**
• Baiofiria Rihabiriteshon Kenkyuu/Biophilia Rehabilitation Journal (JPN ISSN 1347-5568) **6107**
Baiomateriaru/Japanese Society for Biomaterials. Journal (JPN ISSN 1347-7080) **655**
Baiomedikaru Bunseki Kagaku Shimpojiumu Kouen Youshishuu/Symposium on Biomedical-Analytical Sciences (JPN ISSN 1347-2364) **2098**
• Baiomekanizumu/Biomechanisms (JPN ISSN 1348-7116) **752**
• Baiomekanizumu Gakkaishi/Society of Biomechanisms. Journal (JPN ISSN 0285-0885) **752**
Baiomekanizumu Gakujutsu Koenkai Yokoshu/Society of Biomechanisms. Proceedings of the Annual Meeting (JPN) **752**
Baiosaiensu to Indasutori/Bioscience and Industry (JPN ISSN 0914-8981) **757**
Baiotekunoroji Joho/Biotechnology Information (JPN) **757**
Baiotekunoroji Rebyu/Biotechnology Review (JPN) **757**
Baiotorendo/Biotrends (JPN ISSN 0915-4531) **656**
• Baiqiuen Junyi Xueyuan Xuebao/Belhune Military Medical College. Journal (CHN ISSN 1672-2876) **5583**
Baiqiuen Yike Daxue Xuebao/Bethune Medical University. Journal *see* Jilin Daxue Xuebao (Yixue Ban) **5644**
• Bairnsdale Advertiser (AUS ISSN 1440-5342) **5208**
Baisha Journal of GeoHistory *see* Baisha Lishi Dili Xuebao **4000**
Baisha Lishi Dili Xuebao/Baisha Journal of GeoHistory (TWN ISSN 1991-1475) **4000**
Baisho Igaku/Journal of Compensation Medicine (JPN ISSN 0910-5816) **5583**
Al-Bait (LBY) **3905**
Bait al-Imarat/Emirates Home (UAE) **4554**
Bait Fisherman (USA) **8305**
Baiu and Typhoon Prediction *see* Baiu to Taifu no Yoso **6347**
Baiu to Taifu no Yoso/Baiu and Typhoon Prediction (JPN) **6347**
Baixing/Common People (CHN ISSN 1009-8062) **3822**
Baixing Shenghuo (CHN ISSN 1673-7784) **3822**
Baixuebing/Journal of Leukemia *see* Baixuebing. Linbabing **5934**
• Baixuebing. Linbabing/Journal of Leukemia & Lymphopathy (CHN ISSN 1009-9921) **5934**
• ➤ Baiyi Keji (CHN ISSN 1001-1285) **220**
Baja Life (USA) **8685**
Baja Traveler (Chula Vista) (USA ISSN 1941-3076) **8685**
† Bajecna Nedele (CZE ISSN 1214-9624) **8934**
Bajecna Zena (SVK ISSN 1336-5614) **8852**
Bajecne Recepty (CZE ISSN 1213-0435) **4352**
Bajinobastanske Novine (SRB ISSN 0354-5296) **3944**
Bajo Aragon. Prehistoria (ESP ISSN 0210-6132) **383**
Bajo El Sol (USA) **3521**
Bakarski Zbornik (HRV ISSN 1330-7355) **4202**
Bake & Take (GBR ISSN 1475-4363) **3671**
• Baker and Joynt's Clinical Neurology on CD-ROM (USA) **6126**
• Baker Boulanger (USA) **3627**
Baker Double Taxation Conventions *see* Double Taxation Conventions **1920**
• Baker Institute Faculty Studies (USA) **7422**
Baker Institute Policy Report (USA ISSN 1941-6466) **7109**
• The Baker Institute Report (USA) **7422**
• Baker Institute Studies (USA) **7422**
Baker Institute Study *see* Baker Institute Policy Report **7109**
• Baker Institute Working Papers (USA) **7422**
Baker Street Journal (USA ISSN 0005-4070) **5413**
Baker Valley News (USA ISSN 0746-9888) **3970**
Bakeries *see* Business Ratio. Bakeries **3672**
Baker's Clinical Neurology on CD-ROM *see* Baker and Joynt's Clinical Neurology on CD-ROM **6126**
The Baker's Companion Magazine (USA ISSN 1933-5121) **4352**
Baker's Handbook of Ohio School Law (USA) **3017**
Bakers Journal (CAN ISSN 0005-4097) **3671**
Bakers' Review *see* Bake & Take **3671**
Bakers Way (USA) **3671**
Bakersfield News Observer (USA) **3521**
Bakery, Confectionery and Tobacco News *see* B C & T News **4590**
Bakery, Confectionery & Tobacco Workers News *see* B C T G M News **3671**
• Bakery-Net (USA) **3671**
• Bakery Newsletter (E-mail) (USA) **3671**
Bakery World (IRL ISSN 0790-2239) **3671**
Bakgrund (SWE ISSN 1101-5268) **7065**
Bakhus (BGR) **598**
Baki (AZE) **3798**
Baking and Snack *see* Baking & Snack **3671**
• Baking & Snack (USA ISSN 1092-0447) **3671**
• Baking & Snack International (USA ISSN 1555-5976) **3628**
Baking and Snack International *see* Baking & Snack International **3628**
• Baking Buyer (USA ISSN 1056-6007) **3671**
Baking Buyer Yearbook *see* Baking Buyer **3671**
Baking in Russia *see* Khlebopechenie Rossii **3674**
Baking Industry Directory *see* British Baker Directory **3672**
• Baking Management (USA ISSN 1096-1577) **3671**
Baking, Snack Directory and Buyers Guide *see* Baking, Snack Directory & Buyers Guide **270**
Baking, Snack Directory & Buyers Guide (USA ISSN 1549-8158) **270**
Bakinskii Rabochii (AZE ISSN 0233-3112) **3798**
• Bakirkoy Tip Dergisi/Medical Journal of Bakirkoy (TUR ISSN 1305-9327) **5583**
Bakkerswereld (NLD ISSN 0026-5934) **3671**
Bakkie and Recreational Vehicle *see* Bakkie and Truck Action **8669**
Bakkie and Truck Action (ZAF ISSN 1991-6450) **8669**
Baksteen (NLD ISSN 0925-5923) **978**
Baku *see* Baki **3798**
Baku Sun (AZE) **3798**
• Baku Today (AZE) **3798**
Bal Bharati (IND ISSN 0005-4194) **2177**
De Bal. Futsal *see* De Bal. Junioren/Senioren **8221**
De Bal. Junioren/Senioren (NLD ISSN 1574-2830) **8221**
De Bal. Pupillen (NLD ISSN 1574-2849) **8221**
De Bal. Scheidsrechters (NLD ISSN 1574-2857) **8221**
De Bal. Trainers/Coaches (NLD ISSN 1574-2865) **8161**
De Bal. Vrouwen/Meisjes *see* De Bal. Junioren/Senioren **8221**
Bala Jyoti (IND) **3879**
Al-Balaagh (ZAF) **7709**
Balades *see* Alpes Loisirs **8682**
Balades et Randonnees *see* Alpes Magazine Balades et Randonnees **8302**
Balades Nature (FRA ISSN 1291-9896) **8685**
Le Baladeur (CAN ISSN 1180-0127) **4063**
Baladiah Ras al-Khaimah/Ras al-Khaimah Municipality (UAE) **7488**
Balagan (DEU ISSN 0949-4855) **8466**
Balai Penelitian Perusahaan Perkebunan Gula. Proceedings Pertemuan Teknis (IDN ISSN 0216-0021) **220**
Balair - C T A Yellow Wings (CHE) **8782**
Balance (FJI ISSN 1605-2048) **8852**
Balance (GBR ISSN 0005-4216) **5884**
• Balance (Alexandria) (USA ISSN 1094-6195) **4041**
Balance (Branford) (USA) **6907**
• Balance (Philadelphia) (USA) **8305**
Balance Activist (USA ISSN 1083-3498) **7278**
Balance High School Athlete (USA) **8161**
Balance of Payments Monthly *see* Bank of Japan. Balance of Payments Monthly **1912**
Balance of Payments of Barbados *see* Central Bank of Barbados. Balance of Payments **1220**
Balance of Payments of Jamaica (JAM ISSN 0259-6776) **1553**
Balance of Payments of the Republic of Lithuania *see* Lietuvos Respublikos Mokejimu Balansas **1365**
Balance of Payments of the Republic of Lithuania (Annual) *see* Lietuvos Respublikos Mokejimu Balansas (Annual) **1365**
Balance of Payments of Trinidad and Tobago (TTO ISSN 0067-3005) **1212**
Balance of Payments Quarterly, Republic of China *see* Zhonghua Minguo Guoji Shouzhi Pinghengbiao Jibao **1392**
Balance of Payments Statistics of Hong Kong *see* Hong Kong Special Administrative Region of China. Census and Statistics Department. Balance of Payments Statistics of Hong Kong **1237**
Balance of Payments Statistics of Hong Kong (Cumulative Edition) *see* Hong Kong Special Administrative Region of China. Census and Statistics Department. Balance of Payments Statistics of Hong Kong (Cumulative Edition) **1237**
Balance Preliminar de las Economias de America Latina y el Caribe (Year) (CHL ISSN 1014-7810) **1440**
Balance Sheet Analysis of Joint Stock Companies (PAK) **1212**
Balance Sheets (GRC ISSN 1105-2511) **1212**
Balance Social Internacional de Seguridad (COL ISSN 2011-0588) **8027**
Balance Suisse des Paiements *see* Zahlungsbilanz der Schweiz **1955**
Balance Touristique de la Suisse *see* Fremdenverkehrsbilanz der Schweiz **8779**
▼ • Balanced Nutrition Index/Indice de Nutricion Equilibrada (NZL ISSN 1177-8849) **6655**
Balanced Reading Instruction (USA ISSN 1074-4266) **3052**
• Balanced Scorecard Report (USA ISSN 1526-145X) **1065**
Balances y Estadisticas de la Banca en Espana (ESP) **1310**
Balancing Act (USA) **1310**
• The Balancing Act e-Newsletter (USA ISSN 1934-3116) **7338**
• Balancing the Act (AUS ISSN 1441-4872) **7203**
• Balanco Energetico Nacional (BRA ISSN 0101-6636) **3151**
Balanco Financeiro (BRA ISSN 0100-767X) **1611**
Balancos de Aprovisionamento (PRT ISSN 0870-4422) **8356**
Balans (BEL ISSN 0772-4853) **1281**
Balans (NLD ISSN 0005-4259) **2645**
Balans (SWE ISSN 0346-8208) **1281**
Balans (Amsterdam) (NLD ISSN 1384-0487) **1281**
Balans Belang *see* Balans Magazine **3037**
Balans Magazine (NLD ISSN 1872-0560) **3037**
Balanza de Pagos de Espana *see* Balanza de Pagos de Espana y Posicion de Inversion Internacional de Espana **1912**
• Balanza de Pagos de Espana y Posicion de Inversion Internacional de Espana (ESP ISSN 1698-2487) **1912**
Balarama (IND) **2177**
Balarama Amar Chithrakatha (IND) **2177**
• ➤ Balayi (AUS ISSN 1444-2094) **5260**
➤ Balcan Medical Union. Archives (ROM) **5583**
Balcanica (SRB ISSN 0350-7653) **4202**
Balde Branco (BRA ISSN 0005-4275) **261**
Baldrige Award Winning Quality (USA ISSN 1082-8028) **1727**
Baldwin's Ohio Legislative Service (USA ISSN 0092-0959) **4625**
Baldwin's Ohio Revised Code Annotated (USA) **4625**
Baldwin's Ohio School Law Journal (USA ISSN 1055-0100) **4626**
Baleares Magazine (ESP ISSN 1134-1149) **8685**
La Balestra (ITA ISSN 1825-3326) **4202**
Balet (RUS ISSN 0869-5199) **2682**
Balhans (IND) **2177**
Balinghad (PHL) **2273**
• Balint-Journal (DEU ISSN 1439-5142) **6126**
Baliraja (IND) **94**
Baljivan (IND ISSN 0005-4291) **2177**
Balkan Geophysical Society. Journal (GRC ISSN 1302-1672) **2778**
Balkan Industrial Review (BGR) **1880**
• ➤ Balkan Journal of Geometry and Its Applications (ROM ISSN 1224-2780) **5475**
• Balkan Journal of Medical Genetics (MKD ISSN 1311-0160) **863**
Balkan Journal of Stomatology (GRC ISSN 1107-1141) **5836**
Balkan-Kommission. Schriften (AUT ISSN 1012-571X) **4202**
Balkan Media (BGR) **5260**
Balkan Physics Letters (GRC ISSN 1301-8329) **7006**
➤ Balkan Studies (GRC ISSN 0005-4313) **4202**
Balkan Studies (USA ISSN 1068-3836) **5260**
➤ Balkan Tribological Association. Journal (BGR ISSN 1310-4772) **7057**
Balkan Union of Oncology. Journal (GRC ISSN 1107-0625) **6009**
Balkanika Symmeikta (GRC ISSN 1105-0136) **4202**
Balkanistic Forum (BGR ISSN 1310-3970) **4202**
➤ Balkanistica (USA ISSN 0360-2206) **4202**
Balkanologische Veroeffentlichungen *see* Freie Universitaet Berlin. Osteuropa-Institut. Balkanologische Veroeffentlichungen **5120**
Balkans Stamp Catalogue (GBR ISSN 0142-9779) **6892**
Balkanskie Issledovaniya (RUS) **4202**
• Balkon (HUN ISSN 1216-8890) **477**
Ball Beginnings (USA ISSN 8756-7237) **3759**
Ball Magazine (USA) **5208**
• Ball State Daily News (USA) **2273**
• Ballantine and Sterling: California Corporation Laws (USA) **4857**
Ballast Quarterly Review (USA ISSN 1093-5789) **5208**
➤ Ballena Press Anthropological Papers (USA) **330**
Ballerup Historical Society *see* Byhornet **4208**
Ballet (JPN) **2682**
Ballet 2000 (FRA ISSN 1166-5025) **2682**
• Ballet Alert Online (USA) **2682**
Ballet-Hoo (CAN ISSN 0045-1347) **2682**
Ballet News *see* Australian Ballet News **2682**
• Ballet Review (USA ISSN 0522-0653) **2682**
Ballettanz (DEU ISSN 1612-6890) **2682**
Balletto Oggi (ITA ISSN 1123-7813) **2682**
Ballista (GBR ISSN 1750-6646) **5440**
Ballonsport Magazin (DEU) **8305**
Balloon (JPN) **2145**
Balloon Life (USA ISSN 0887-6061) **8161**
Ballooning (USA ISSN 0194-6854) **49**
Balloons & Parties (USA) **531**
• Ballot Access News (USA ISSN 1043-6898) **7203**
The Ballroom Dancer's Rag (USA ISSN 1057-4042) **2682**
Ballroom Dancing Times *see* Dance Today! **2685**
Ballroom Rockstar (USA) **4371**
Balls Weekly *see* Qiubao **8243**
Ballyfermot Echo (IRL ISSN 2009-0080) **3892**
Ballymena Guardian (GBR) **3861**
• Balnea (ESP ISSN 1887-1933) **307**
Balneario d'Hotels (ESP ISSN 1888-2986) **8161**
Balnearios (MEX) **8161**
Balneologia Polska/Polish Balneology (POL ISSN 0005-4402) **6107**
Balneological Society of Japan. Journal *see* Onsen Kagaku **2760**
Balochistan Studies (ITA ISSN 1971-9493) **5098**
Balon (BGR ISSN 1310-4314) **3962**
Balon (MEX ISSN 0005-4410) **8222**
Balsa de la Medusa (ESP ISSN 0214-9982) **477**
Balshanut Ivrit/Hebrew Linguistics (ISR ISSN 0792-3252) **5202**
• Baltic 21 Newsletter (SWE ISSN 1691-001X) **8090**
• Baltic 21 Series (SWE ISSN 1029-7790) **8090**
Baltic and International Maritime Council Bulletin *see* B I M C O Bulletin **8639**
Baltic and International Maritime Council Ice Handbook *see* B I M C O Ice Handbook **8639**
Baltic Astronomy (LTU ISSN 1392-0049) **572**
Baltic Business District *see* The Baltic Times **3904**
Baltic Business News (EST) **1065**
Baltic Chronology (USA) **7223**
Baltic Defence Review *see* Baltic Security and Defence Review **2225**
Baltic Development Forum Magazine *see* B D F Magazine **1064**
Baltic Development Forum Magazine *see* B D F Magazine **1064**
Baltic Development Forum. Report *see* B D F Magazine **1064**
Baltic Dialogue *see* Baltic Sea Dialogue **2939**
➤ Baltic Forestry (LTU ISSN 1392-1355) **3684**
The Baltic Guide (EST) **3836**
Baltic Horizons (EST ISSN 1736-1834) **7223**
Baltic I T Review (LVA) **4993**
Baltic Information Technology Review *see* Baltic I T Review **4993**
• The Baltic International Yearbook of Cognition, Logic and Communication (Online) (USA ISSN 1944-3676) **6907**
The Baltic International Yearbook of Cognition, Logic and Communication (Print) *see* The Baltic International Yearbook of Cognition, Logic and Communication (Online) **6907**
Baltic Journal of Coleopterology (LVA ISSN 1407-8619) **840**
➤ Baltic Journal of Economics (LVA ISSN 1406-099X) **1065**
• ➤ Baltic Journal of Management (GBR ISSN 1746-5265) **1727**
➤ Baltic Journal of Psychology/Baltijas Psihologijas Zurnals (LVA ISSN 1407-768X) **7338**
• The Baltic Journal of Road and Bridge Engineering (LTU ISSN 1822-427X) **3260**
Baltic Marine Biologists. Publication (SWE ISSN 0282-8839) **656**
Baltic News *see* Baltic Business News **1065**
The Baltic Review (EST ISSN 1021-8149) **1065**
• Baltic Sea Dialogue (SWE ISSN 1403-3194) **2939**
Baltic Sea Environment Proceedings (FIN ISSN 0357-2994) **3405**
• Baltic Security and Defence Review (EST ISSN 1736-3772) **2225**
Baltic Security and Defence Review (Online Edition) *see* Baltic Security and Defence Review **2225**
Baltic Studies Newsletter *see* Baltic Studies Newsletter (Online Edition) **4202**
Baltic Studies Newsletter (Online Edition) (USA) **4202**
• The Baltic Times (LVA ISSN 1407-2300) **3904**
Baltic Twenty One Newsletter *see* Baltic 21 Newsletter **8090**
Baltic Twenty One Series *see* Baltic 21 Series **8090**
• ➤ Baltica (LTU ISSN 0067-3064) **2726**
Baltijas Psihologijas Zurnals *see* Baltic Journal of Psychology **7338**
Baltijas Zinatnu Vestures Apcerejumi *see* Acta Historiae Scientiarum Baltica **7832**
Baltimore Afro-American Newspaper (USA) **3521**
• Baltimore Alternative (USA ISSN 1080-8930) **4371**
Baltimore Bride (USA) **5556**
• Baltimore Business Journal (USA ISSN 0747-1823) **1065**
▼ Baltimore County Suburban Life (USA ISSN 1942-471X) **3970**
Baltimore Engineer (USA ISSN 0005-4496) **3182**
• Baltimore Gay Paper (USA ISSN 1065-3821) **4371**
• Baltimore Jewish Times (USA ISSN 0005-450X) **7718**
Baltimore Magazine (USA ISSN 0005-4453) **5065**
Baltimore Opera Magazine (USA) **6547**
Baltimore Quick Guide *see* Where GuestBook. Baltimore **8787**
➤ The Baltimore Review (USA ISSN 1092-5716) **5260**
Baltimore SmartCEO (Chief Executive Officer) (USA) **1727**
† Baltimore Studies in Nationalism and Internationalism (GBR ISSN 1360-9335) **8934**
• Baltimore's Child (USA ISSN 1520-7374) **2145**
Baltische Briefe (DEU ISSN 0005-4526) **7109**
Baltische Studien (DEU ISSN 0067-3099) **4203**
Baltistica (LTU ISSN 0132-6503) **5098**
Balto Alternative *see* Baltimore Alternative **4371**
Baltos Lankos (LTU ISSN 1392-0189) **5260**
Baluarte (ESP ISSN 1135-7983) **3521**
➤ Balungan (USA ISSN 0885-7113) **6547**
† Bama'aleh (ISR) **8934**
Bamah (Givatayim) (ISR) **6009**

▼ *new title* † *ceased* • *electronic media* ➤ *refereed*

Title

10018 BAMAH (JERUSALEM) ULRICH'S PERIODICALS

Bamah (Jerusalem) (ISR ISSN 0045-138X) **8466**
Bamberger Theologische Studien (DEU ISSN 0948-177X) **7624**
Bambi (FRA ISSN 0996-5777) **2177**
Bambin (FRA ISSN 1950-9650) **2177**
Bambini (ITA ISSN 0393-4209) **2145**
Bambini Collezioni *see* Collezioni Bambini **2252**
Bambini in Europa (ITA ISSN 1593-1986) **2145**
† Bambino (FRA ISSN 1636-4651) **8934**
Bambino (ITA) **7940**
† Bambino-Baby (DEU) **8934**
Bamboo (USA ISSN 1554-8295) **778**
• Bamboo Bulletin (AUS ISSN 1832-1844) **778**
Bamboo Girl (USA) **8852**
Bamboo Journal (JPN ISSN 0289-2111) **778**
• Bamboo Ridge (USA ISSN 0733-0308) **5260**
Bamboo Science & Culture (USA ISSN 1535-7635) **778**
Bamboos of Sabah (MYS ISSN 0128-6471) **3684**
Bamla Ekademi Gabeshana Patrika (BGD) **5260**
Bamladesa Pasu Bijnana Samayiki *see* Bangladesh Journal of Animal Science **280**
Bampton Lectures in America (USA ISSN 0067-3129) **7624**
Bamse (NOR ISSN 0807-3287) **2177**
Bamse (SWE ISSN 0345-1267) **2177**
Ban Ni Tongxing/Companion (CHN ISSN 1009-4261) **8629**
† Ban y Coc (ESP ISSN 1576-1444) **8934**
• ➤ Banach Center Publications (POL ISSN 0137-6934) **5475**
▼ • ➤ Banach Journal of Mathematical Analysis (IRN ISSN 1735-8787) **5475**
Banadesa *see* Guatemala. Banco Nacional de Desarrollo Agricola. Memoria **199**
Banal Probe (USA) **5260**
† Banana Book (ITA ISSN 1124-2825) **8934**
Banana Bulletin (AUS) **220**
Banana Split (DNK ISSN 0906-6489) **5260**
Banaras Hindu University. Journal of Scientific Research (IND ISSN 0447-9483) **7839**
Banaras Metallurgist (IND ISSN 0366-1210) **6306**
Banasthali Patrika (IND ISSN 0970-4825) **5260**
Banaten Zeitung *see* Allgemeine Deutsche Zeitung fuer Rumaenien **3932**
➤ Banber Hayastani Arkhivneri/Vestnik Arkhivov Armenii (ARM ISSN 0321-0340) **4203**
Banbridge Chronicle (GBR) **3861**
Banbury Reports (USA ISSN 0198-0068) **656**
Banbury Reports Series *see* Banbury Reports **656**
Banca & Finanzas (ESP ISSN 1135-0652) **1310**
• Banca Borsa e Titoli di Credito (ITA ISSN 0390-9522) **1310**
Banca Centrale Europea. Bollettino Mensile (DEU ISSN 1561-0276) **1310**
Banca Centrale Europea. Rapporto Annuale *see* European Central Bank. Annual Report **1339**
Banca dei Regolamenti Internazionali. Relazione Annuale *see* Bank for International Settlements. Annual Report **1313**
Banca d'Italia. Assemblea Generale Ordinaria dei Partecipanti (ITA ISSN 0391-4712) **1310**
Banca d'Italia. Bollettino di Vigilanza (ITA) **1310**
• Banca d'Italia. Bollettino Economico (ITA ISSN 0393-2400) **1440**
Banca d'Italia. Economic Bulletin *see* Banca d'Italia. Bollettino Economico **1440**
• Banca d'Italia. Il Bollettino Statistico. (ITA) **1310**
Banca d'Italia. Il Quadro di Sintesi del Bollettino Statistico (ITA) **1212**
• Banca d'Italia. Newsletter (ITA) **1310**
Banca d'Italia. Ordinary General Meetings of Shareholders *see* Banca d'Italia. Assemblea Generale Ordinaria dei Partecipanti **1310**
Banca d'Italia. Temi di Discussione (ITA) **1310**
Banca Espanola (ESP ISSN 0210-1688) **1310**
Banca Europea per gli Investimenti. Informazioni *see* European Investment Bank. Information **1622**
• Banca Impresa Societa (ITA ISSN 1120-9453) **1310**
Banca Nazionale del Lavoro Basic Statistics on the Italian Economy *see* B N L Basic Statistics on the Italian Economy **1212**
Banca Nazionale del Lavoro. Quaderni di Ricerca (ITA) **1310**
• Banca Nazionale del Lavoro. Quarterly Review (ITA ISSN 0005-4607) **1310**
Banca Nazionale Svizzera. Rapporto di Gestione *see* Schweizerische Nationalbank. Geschaeftsbericht **1382**
Banca y Comercio (MEX ISSN 0005-4615) **1310**
Banca y Finanzas (COL ISSN 0120-7040) **1310**
BancaFinanza (ITA) **1310**
• Bancamatica (ITA ISSN 0393-7062) **1310**
Bancaria (ITA ISSN 0005-4623) **1310**
Bancassurance Report (GBR) **4494**
Banche e Banchieri (ITA ISSN 0390-1378) **1311**
• Bancni Vestnik/Banking Newsletter (SVN ISSN 0005-4631) **1311**
Banco Agrario del Peru. Memoria (PER) **194**
• Banco Central de Bolivia. Boletin del Sector Externo (BOL) **1212**
• Banco Central de Bolivia. Boletin Estadistico (BOL ISSN 0522-0939) **1212**
• Banco Central de Bolivia. Boletin Mensual (BOL) **1212**
➤ Banco Central de Bolivia. Fundacion Cultural. Revista (BOL) **4444**
• Banco Central de Bolivia. Memoria (BOL ISSN 1023-361X) **1212**
Banco Central de Bolivia. Revista de Analisis (BOL) **1311**
Banco Central de Chile. Annual Report (CHL ISSN 0716-2901) **1311**
Banco Central de Chile. Boletin Mensual (CHL ISSN 0716-2367) **1311**
Banco Central de Chile. Documento de Trabajo (CHL) **1065**
Banco Central de Chile. Memoria Anual (CHL ISSN 0716-2448) **1311**
Banco Central de Chile. Serie de Estudios Economicos (CHL ISSN 0716-2502) **1065**
Banco Central de Honduras. Departamento de Estudios Economicos. Boletin Estadistico Mensual (HND ISSN 1012-9510) **1212**
Banco Central de Honduras. Informe Economico (HND) **1440**
Banco Central de Honduras. Memoria (Year) (HND) **1440**
Banco Central de la Republica Argentina. Boletin Estadistico (ARG ISSN 0005-4674) **1212**
• Banco Central de la Republica de Argentina. Serie Estudios (ARG ISSN 1850-2695) **1311**
Banco Central de la Republica Dominicana. Boletin Trimestral (DOM) **1311**
Banco Central de la Republica Dominicana. Memoria (DOM) **1311**
Banco Central de la Republica Dominicana. Principales Indicadores Economicos (DOM) **1311**
Banco Central de Reserva de El Salvador. Boletin Economico (SLV) **1311**
Banco Central de Reserva de El Salvador. Memoria de Labores (SLV) **1311**
Banco Central de Reserva de El Salvador. Revista Trimestral (SLV) **1311**
Banco Central de Reserva del Peru. Boletin (PER ISSN 0005-4712) **1311**
Banco Central de Reserva del Peru. Memoria (PER) **1311**
Banco Central de Venezuela. Anuario de Balanza de Pagos (VEN ISSN 0798-295X) **1212**
Banco Central de Venezuela. Anuario de Cuentas Nacionales (VEN) **1212**
Banco Central de Venezuela. Anuario de Estadisticas Internacionales (VEN) **1212**
Banco Central de Venezuela. Anuario de Estadisticas: Precios y Mercado Laboral (VEN ISSN 1316-0664) **1212**
Banco Central de Venezuela. Anuario de Estadisticas: Sector Financiero (VEN) **1212**
Banco Central de Venezuela. Boletin de Indicadores Semanales (VEN) **1212**
Banco Central de Venezuela. Boletin Mensual (VEN ISSN 0252-8991) **1212**
Banco Central de Venezuela. Informe Economico (VEN ISSN 0067-3250) **1440**
Banco Central de Venezuela. Informe Semestral (VEN ISSN 1316-0680) **1311**
Banco Central de Venezuela. Revista (VEN ISSN 0005-4720) **1311**
Banco Central del Ecuador. Balanza de Pagos (ECU) **1212**
Banco Central del Ecuador. Boletin (ECU ISSN 0005-4739) **1311**
Banco Central del Ecuador. Cuentas Nacionales Anuales (ECU) **1440**
Banco Central del Ecuador. Informacion Estadistica Mensual (ECU) **1212**
Banco Central del Paraguay. Boletin Estadistico (PRY ISSN 0408-330X) **1311**
Banco Central del Paraguay. Gerencia de Estudios Economicos. Estadisticas Economicas (PRY) **1212**
Banco Central del Paraguay. Memoria (PRY ISSN 0067-3285) **1311**
• Banco Central del Uruguay. Boletin Estadistico (URY ISSN 0797-0684) **1212**
Banco Central del Uruguay. Cuentas Nacionales (URY) **1440**
Banco Central del Uruguay. Departamento de Estadisticas Economicas. Boletin Estadistico (URY) **1212**
Banco Central del Uruguay. Departamento de Estadisticas Economicas. Producto e Ingreso Nacionales (URY) **1718**
Banco Central del Uruguay. Resena de la Actividad Economico-Financiera (URY) **1311**
Banco Central del Uruguay. Seleccion de Temas (URY) **1440**
Banco Central do Brasil. Boletim (BRA ISSN 0101-4668) **1311**
Banco Central do Brasil. Relatorio Anual *see* Banco Central do Brasil. Boletim **1311**
• Banco Central Europeo. Boletin Mensual (DEU ISSN 1561-0268) **1311**
Banco Central Europeo. Informe Anual *see* European Central Bank. Annual Report **1339**
Banco Central Europeu. Boletin Mensal (DEU ISSN 1561-0284) **1311**
Banco Central Europeu. Relatorio Anual *see* European Central Bank. Annual Report **1339**
Banco Centroamericano de Integracion Economica. Memoria Anual (HND) **1311**
† Banco de Bilbao. Agenda Financiera (ESP ISSN 1135-8289) **8934**
† Banco de Bilbao. Economic Report (ESP ISSN 0522-1307) **8934**
Banco de Bilbao. Informacion Semanal de Valores (ESP ISSN 0213-2648) **1611**
Banco de Bilbao. Informe - Memoria (ESP) **1311**
† Banco de Bilbao - Vizcaya . Informe Economico (ESP ISSN 0214-2724) **8934**
Banco de Datos de Becas y Cursos (ESP) **3011**
Banco de Desenvolvimento do Parana. Information on Parana *see* Information on Parana **1491**
• Banco de Espana. Boletin Economico (ESP ISSN 0210-3737) **1440**
• Banco de Espana. Boletin Estadistico (Online) (ESP ISSN 1579-8631) **1311**
† • Banco de Espana. Boletin Estadistico (Print) (ESP ISSN 0005-4798) **8934**
• Banco de Espana. Documento de Trabajo (ESP ISSN 0213-2710) **1311**
• Banco de Espana. Economic Bulletin (ESP ISSN 1130-4987) **1440**
• Banco de Espana. Estudios de Historia Economica (ESP ISSN 0213-2702) **1536**
• Banco de Espana. Estudios Economicos (ESP ISSN 0213-2699) **1440**
• Banco de Espana. Informe Anual (ESP ISSN 0067-3315) **1311**
• Banco de Espana. Notas Estadisticas (ESP ISSN 1699-3985) **1312**
Banco de Guatemala. Boletin Estadistico (GTM ISSN 0005-481X) **1312**
Banco de Guatemala. Estudio Economico y Memoria de Labores (GTM) **1312**
• Banco de Guatemala. Notas Monetarias (GTM) **1312**
Banco de la Republica. Biblioteca Luis Angel Arango. Boletin Cultural y Bibliografico (COL ISSN 0006-6184) **616**
Banco de la Republica. Revista (COL ISSN 0005-4828) **1312**
Banco de Mexico. Indicadores del Sector Externo (MEX) **1212**
Banco de Mexico. Indicadores Economicos (MEX) **1440**
Banco de Mexico. Indice de Precios (MEX) **1212**
• Banco de Mexico. Informe Anual (MEX ISSN 0185-1098) **1312**
Banco de Mexico. Serie Documentos de Investigacion (MEX) **1312**
Banco de Pagos Internacionales. Informe Anual *see* Bank for International Settlements. Annual Report **1313**
Banco de Portugal. Boletim Economico (PRT ISSN 0872-9794) **1440**
Banco de Portugal. Estatistica e Estudos Economicos (PRT) **1212**
Banco de Portugal. Relatorio do Conselho de Administracao *see* Banco de Portugal. Report of the Directors and Economic and Financial Survey **1312**
• Banco de Portugal. Report of the Directors and Economic and Financial Survey (PRT ISSN 0870-0060) **1312**
Banco de Venezuela. Informe Semestral (VEN) **1312**
Banco do Brasil. Annual Report (BRA ISSN 0101-0646) **1312**
Banco do Estado de Pernambuco. BANDEPE Relatorio (BRA) **1312**
Banco do Nordeste do Brasil. Serie Estudos Economicos e Sociais (BRA) **1440**
Banco Gubernamental de Fomento para Puerto Rico Informe Anual *see* Government Development Bank for Puerto Rico. Annual Report **1350**
Banco Hipotecario del Uruguay. Boletin Estadistico (URY) **1212**
Banco Interamericano de Desarollo. Informe Anual *see* Inter-American Development Bank. Annual Report **1355**
Banco Interamericano de Desarollo. Junta Directiva. Anales de la Reunion *see* Inter-American Development Bank. Board of Governors. Proceedings of the Meeting **1355**
Banco Minero de Bolivia. Memoria (BOL) **1312**
Banco Nacional de Comercio Exterior, Mexico. Annual Report (MEX) **1312**
Banco Nacional de Comercio Exterior, Mexico. Informe Anual (MEX ISSN 0188-2783) **1312**
Banco Nacional de Desarrollo Agricola. Memoria Anual (HND) **1312**
Banco Nacional de Fomento. Boletin (ECU) **1312**
Banco Nacional de Fomento. Informe de Labores (ECU) **1440**
Banco Nacional de Panama. Informacion Economica y Financiera de la Republica de Panama (PAN) **1912**
Banco Nacional de Panama. Informe del Gerente General (PAN) **1312**
Banco Nacional de Panama. Memoria Anual (PAN) **1312**
Banco Nacional do Desenvolvimento Economico. e Social Annual Report *see* B N D E S Annual Report **1310**
Banco Nacional do Desenvolvimento Economico e Social Economic Bulletin *see* B N D E S Economic Bulletin **1439**
Banco Nacional do Desenvolvimento Economico e Social International Bulletin *see* B N D E S International Bulletin **1440**
Banco Nacional do Desenvolvimento Economico e Social Relatorio Anual *see* B N D E S Relatorio Anual **1440**
Banco Nacional do Desenvolvimento Economico. Plan of Action *see* B N D E S News **1440**
Banco Regional de Desenvolvimento do Extremo Sul. Annual Report (BRA) **1440**
Bancos Centrales de los Paises del Acuerdo de Cartagena. Boletin Estadistico (COL) **1312**
Bancos y Bancarios de Colombia (COL ISSN 0120-5226) **1312**
Bancroftiana (USA ISSN 0067-3412) **4993**
Bancs d'Essai du Tourisme (FRA ISSN 0764-3578) **8685**
Das Band (DEU ISSN 0170-902X) **3037**
Band Journal (JPN ISSN 0005-4933) **6547**
Band Music Guide (USA ISSN 0084-7704) **6547**
Band- und Flechtindustrie *see* Melliand Textilberichte **8455**
† Banda Aparte (ESP ISSN 1138-1981) **8934**
Bandalag Haskolamanna Tidindi *see* B H M Tidindi **4590**
• Bandao Chenbao (CHN) **3822**
• Bandao Dushi Bao/Peninsular Metropolitan News (CHN) **3822**
• Bandao Xin Shenghuo/SoLife Magazine (CHN ISSN 1672-7754) **3822**
• Bandaoti Guangdian/Semiconductor Optoelectronics (CHN ISSN 1001-5868) **7051**
• Bandaoti Jishu/Semiconductor Technology (CHN ISSN 1003-353X) **3296**
• ➤ Bandaoti Xuebao/Chinese Journal of Semiconductors (CHN ISSN 0253-4177) **3089**
▼ Bandas (COL ISSN 2011-0499) **2830**
Banderas (ESP ISSN 0213-0955) **3759**
Bandersnatch (CAN) **2273**
Bandersnatch (GBR ISSN 0306-8404) **5260**
Bandiera Rossa (ITA ISSN 1122-519X) **7109**
† • Bandolier (GBR ISSN 1353-9906) **8934**
▼ • Bandolier Journal (GBR) **5583**
• Bandwagon (USA ISSN 0005-4968) **8466**
Bandwidth Intelligence Alert *see* Dow Jones Bandwidth Intelligence Alert **2497**
Bandworld (USA ISSN 0887-9036) **6547**
Bane/Spring (JPN ISSN 0914-4994) **3374**
• Bane Ronbunshu/Japan Spring Manufacturers Association (JPN ISSN 0385-6917) **3374**
• Banedanmark. Aarsrapport (DNK ISSN 1604-309X) **8615**
Baner Kernewek *see* Cornish Banner **3528**
Banestyrelsen. Aarsrapport *see* Banedanmark. Aarsrapport **8615**
Banff Centre. Report to the Community (CAN ISSN 1914-0711) **477**
Bang *see* Verve (Toronto) **2219**
Bang (SWE) **8894**
Bang Board (USA) **4328**
Bang Jin Mei Duo (CHN) **3615**
Bang Magazine (TZA ISSN 0856-9975) **3522**
Bang on the Door Little Girls *see* Little Girls (London) **2200**
➤ Bangalore Theological Forum (IND ISSN 0253-9365) **7624**
Bangbang (CAN ISSN 1718-3529) **6547**
• Bangbu Yixueyuan Xuebao/Acta Academiae Medicinae Bengbu (CHN ISSN 1000-2200) **5583**
Banger. Verlage - Vertretungen - Auslieferungen (Year) *see* Verlage - Vertretungen - Auslieferungen (Year) **638**
Banger. Zeitschriften - Loseblattwerke - Jahrbuecher (Year) *see* Zeitschriften - Loseblattwerke - Jahrbuecher (Year) **639**
Bangiya Sahityakosha/Sahityik Barsapanjee (IND) **616**
• Bangko Sentral ng Pilipinas. Annual Report (PHL ISSN 1655-5112) **1312**
• Bangko Sentral ng Pilipinas. Inflation Report (PHL ISSN 1655-5104) **1065**
• Bangko Sentral ng Pilipinas. Monthly Selected Philippine Economic Indicators (PHL) **1440**
Bangko Sentral Review (PHL) **1312**
Bangkok Bank. Monthly Review (THA ISSN 0125-0302) **1312**
• Bangkok Post (THA ISSN 0125-0337) **3961**
• Bangkok Post Student Weekly (THA) **2177**
Bangkok Shipowners and Agents Association (Year) Thailand Shipping Handbook *see* B S A A (Year) Thailand Shipping Handbook **8639**
Bangkok Weekly (THA) **3961**
Bangla Academy Journal (BGD) **5260**
Bangladesh (BGD) **3799**
➤ Bangladesh Academy of Sciences. Journal (BGD ISSN 0378-8121) **7839**
Bangladesh Agricultural Sciences Abstracts (BGD) **175**
Bangladesh Arthanaitika Jarip (BGD) **1065**
Bangladesh Bank. Annual Report (BGD) **1312**
Bangladesh Bank. Bulletin (BGD ISSN 0304-9345) **1440**
Bangladesh Bank. Statistics Department. Annual Balance of Payments (BGD) **1212**
Bangladesh Bank. Statistics Department. Annual Import Payments (BGD) **1212**
Bangladesh Bank. Statistics Department. Balance of Payments (BGD) **1212**
Bangladesh Bank. Statistics Department. Quarterly Scheduled Banks Statistics (BGD) **1212**
Bangladesh Chemical Society. Journal (BGD ISSN 1022-016X) **2051**
Bangladesh Development Studies (BGD ISSN 0304-095X) **1440**
Bangladesh Directory and Year Book (IND) **1974**
• ➤ Bangladesh e-Journal of Sociology (BGD) **8090**
Bangladesh. Education Directorate. Report on Pilot Project on Adult Education (BGD ISSN 0070-8135) **2939**
Bangladesh Education in Statistics (Year) (BGD) **2930**
Bangladesh Environmental Newsletter (BGD) **3405**
Bangladesh Forest Industries Development Corporation. Annual Report (BGD) **3710**
• Bangladesh Gazette (BGD) **7422**

▼ *new title*   † *ceased*   ● *electronic media*   ➤ *refereed*

Title

Title

Title

10026 BEHAVIOUR AND INFORMATION TECHNOLOGY ULRICH'S PERIODICALS

● ➤ Behaviour and Information Technology (GBR ISSN 0144-929X) **7340**
● ➤ Behaviour Change (AUS ISSN 0813-4839) **7340**
● ➤ Behaviour Research and Therapy (GBR ISSN 0005-7967) **7340**
Behaviour Research and Therapy Series in Clinical Psychology *see* B R A T Series in Clinical Psychology **7338**
● ➤ Behavioural and Cognitive Psychotherapy (GBR ISSN 1352-4658) **7340**
● ➤ Behavioural Brain Research (NLD ISSN 0166-4328) **6126**
● ➤ Behavioural Neurology (NLD ISSN 0953-4180) **6126**
● ➤ Behavioural Pharmacology (USA ISSN 0955-8810) **6825**
● ➤ Behavioural Processes (NLD ISSN 0376-6357) **6126**
Behavioural Psychotherapist (GBR ISSN 0953-7074) **7340**
Behavioural Scientist (IND) **7340**
Beheer en Onderhoud (NLD ISSN 0165-2540) **7583**
Beheerkosten Openbare Ruimte *see* C R O W et cetera **3261**
▼ ● ➤ Behemoth (DEU ISSN 1866-2447) **7109**
● Behind the Headlines (CAN ISSN 0005-7983) **7223**
● Behind the Orange Curtain (USA) **6548**
Behind the Scenes *see* Paraskino **3832**
Behindertenhilfe Durch Erziehung, Unterricht und Therapie (DEU ISSN 0171-9718) **3037**
Behindertenpaedagogik (DEU ISSN 0341-7301) **3037**
Behindertenpaedagogik in Bayern *see* Sonderpaedagogik in Bayern **3046**
Behindertenrecht (DEU ISSN 0341-3888) **4064**
● Behinderung und Dritte Welt (DEU ISSN 1430-5895) **3037**
Behoerden Spiegel (DEU ISSN 1437-8337) **7488**
Behoerden und Organisationen der Land- Forst- und Ernaehrungswirtschaft *see* Behoerden und Organisationen Ernaehrungswirtschaft und Landwirtschaft **95**
Behoerden und Organisationen Ernaehrungswirtschaft und Landwirtschaft (DEU ISSN 1861-8480) **95**
Behold *see* Jumu **7657**
Behold (Inver Grove Heights) (USA ISSN 1555-6344) **478**
The Behrend Beacon (USA ISSN 1071-9288) **2274**
Behrend Collegian *see* The Behrend Beacon **2274**
BEI. Cahiers *see* Banque Europeenne d'Investissement. Cahiers **1320**
Bei Uns in Hamburg (DEU ISSN 1618-047X) **6693**
Beida Ban Xin Yidai Duiwai Hanyu Jiaocai. Jichu Jiaocheng Xilie (CHN ISSN 1673-4475) **5098**
Beida Ban Xin Yidai Duiwai Hanyu Jiaocai. Kouyu Jiaocheng Xilie (CHN ISSN 1673-4467) **5098**
Beida Ban Xin Yidai Duiwai Hanyu Jiaocai. Shangwu Hanyu Jiaocheng Xilie (CHN ISSN 1673-3940) **5098**
Beida Ban Xin Yidai Duiwai Hanyu Jiaocai. Shiyong Hanyu Jiaocheng Xilie (CHN ISSN 1673-4483) **5098**
Beidaban Xin - Beida Ban Xin Yidai Duiwai Hanyu Jiaocai. Jichu Jiaocheng Xilie *see* Beida Ban Xin Yidai Duiwai Hanyu Jiaocai. Jichu Jiaocheng Xilie **5098**
Beidahuang Nongye *see* Xiandaihua Nongye **171**
Beidahuang Nonji *see* Xiandaihua Nongye **171**
Die Beiden Tuerme (DEU) **7624**
† Beiersdorf Journal (DEU) **8935**
● Beifang Chenbao (CHN) **3822**
▼ Beifang Faxue/Northern Legal Science (CHN ISSN 1673-8330) **4628**
● Beifang Gongye Daxue Xuebao/North China University of Technology. Journal (CHN ISSN 1001-5477) **7839**
● Beifang Guoshu/Northern Fruits (CHN ISSN 1001-5698) **221**
Beifang Huanjing/Northern Environment (CHN) **3406**
Beifang Jiaotong Daxue Xuebao (Shehui Kexue Ban) *see* Beijing Jiaotong Daxue Xuebao (Shehui Kexue Ban) **7950**
Beifang Jiaotong Daxue Xuebao/North Communications University. Journal *see* Beijing Jiaotong Daxue Xuebao (Ziran Kexue Ban) **7839**
● Beifang Jingmao/Northern Economy and Trade (CHN ISSN 1005-913X) **1066**
● Beifang Luncong/Northern Forum (CHN ISSN 1000-3541) **4444**
Beifang Qiyi/Northern Chess *see* Qiyi **8194**
● Beifang Shibao/Northern Times (CHN) **3822**
● Beifang Shuidao/North Rice (CHN ISSN 1673-6737) **270**
● Beifang Wenwu/Northern Cultural Relics (CHN ISSN 1001-0483) **383**
● Beifang Wenxue/Northern Literature (CHN ISSN 0476-031X) **5261**
● Beifang Yinyue/Northern Music (CHN ISSN 1002-767X) **6548**
● ➤ Beifang Yuanyi/Northern Horticulture (CHN ISSN 1001-0009) **3724**
Beifang Zuojia/Northern Writers (CHN ISSN 1674-1420) **5261**
Beifangren/Northman (CHN ISSN 1006-2548) **3822**
Beihefte der Bonner Jahrbuecher (DEU ISSN 0067-4893) **383**
† Beihefte fuer den Mathematischen Unterricht (DEU ISSN 0522-6090) **8935**
† Beihefte fuer den Physikalischen Unterricht (BRD ISSN 0408-7917) **8935**
Beihefte zu Editio (DEU ISSN 0939-5946) **5261**
Beihefte zu Kredit und Kapital (DEU ISSN 0720-6801) **1321**
Beihefte zum Archiv fuer Kulturgeschichte (DEU ISSN 0570-6742) **4132**
Beihefte zum Euphorion (DEU ISSN 0531-2167) **5261**
Beihefte zum Language and Culture Atlas of Ashkenazic Jewry (DEU ISSN 1860-174X) **5261**
Beihefte zur Iberoromania (DEU ISSN 0177-199X) **5098**
Beihefte zur Mediaevistik (DEU ISSN 1617-657X) **4203**
Beihefte Zur Sydowia (AUT ISSN 1016-0019) **778**
Beihefte zur Wiener Zeitschrift fuer die Kunde des Morgenlandes (AUT ISSN 0259-0654) **544**
Beihefte zur Zeitschrift fuer Romanische Philologie *see* Zeitschrift fuer Romanische Philologie. Beihefte **5199**
Beihua Daxue Xuebao (Shehui Kexue Ban)/Jilin Teachers College. Journal (CHN ISSN 1009-5101) **7949**
● Beihua Daxue Xuebao (Ziran Kexue Ban)/Beihua University. Journal (Natural Science Edition) (CHN ISSN 1009-4822) **7839**
Beihua University. Journal (Natural Science Edition) *see* Beihua Daxue Xuebao (Ziran Kexue Ban) **7839**
Beiji Guang/Northern Lights (CHN) **5261**
Beijiguang/Northern Lights (CHN ISSN 1002-8137) **5261**
Beijing Accounting *see* Beijing Caikuai **1281**
Beijing Adult Education *see* Beijing Chengren Jiaoyu **8935**
Beijing Agricultural Science *see* Beijing Nongye Kexue **95**
Beijing Agriculture *see* Beijing Nongye **95**
Beijing Archives *see* Beijing Dang'an **4994**
Beijing Biomedical Engineering *see* Beijing Shengwu Yixue Gongcheng **5584**
Beijing C D C Newsletter *see* Beijing Jikong Zhongxinbao **5584**
Beijing Caikuai/Beijing Accounting (CHN) **1281**
● Beijing Caimao Zhiye Xueyuan Xuebao/Beijing Vocational College of Finance and Commerce. Journal (CHN ISSN 1674-2923) **1066**
● Beijing Chenbao/Beijing Morning Post (CHN) **3822**
† ● Beijing Chengren Jiaoyu/Beijing Adult Education (CHN ISSN 1002-414X) **8935**
Beijing Children's Weekly *see* Beijing Shaonianbao **2178**
Beijing Cultural Relics and Museums *see* Beijing Wenbo **6521**
Beijing Daily *see* Beijing Ribao **3822**
Beijing Dance Academy. Journal *see* Beijing Wudao Xueyuan Xuebao **2682**
● Beijing Dang'an/Beijing Archives (CHN ISSN 1002-1051) **4994**
● Beijing Daxue Jiaoyu Pinglun/Peking University Education Review (CHN ISSN 1671-9468) **2830**
● ➤ Beijing Daxue Xuebao (Yixue Ban)/Peking University. Journal (Health Sciences) (CHN ISSN 1671-167X) **5584**
● Beijing Daxue Xuebao (Zhexue Shehui Kexue Ban)/Beijing University. Journal (Philosophy and Social Science Edition) (CHN ISSN 1000-5919) **4444**
● Beijing Daxue Xuebao (Ziran Kexue Ban)/Acta Scientiarum Naturalium Universitatis Pekinensis/Beijing University. Journal (Natural Science Edition) (CHN ISSN 0479-8023) **7839**
Beijing Daxue Zhongguo Yuyan Wenxue Jiaocai Xilie (CHN ISSN 1673-7008) **5098**
● Beijing Di-er Waiguoyu Xueyuan Xuebao/Beijing International Studies University. Journal (CHN ISSN 1003-6539) **7223**
● Beijing Dianying Xueyuan Xuebao/Beijing Film Academy. Journal (CHN ISSN 1002-6142) **6490**
● Beijing Dizhi/Beijing Geology (CHN ISSN 1007-1903) **2726**
Beijing Document *see* Beijing Jishi **3822**
Beijing Economic Information News *see* Beijing Jingji Bao **1442**
Beijing Education *see* Beijing Jiaoyu **2830**
Beijing Evening News *see* Beijing Wanbao **3822**
Beijing Fangdichan/Beijing Real Estate (CHN) **7583**
† ● Beijing Fangzhi/Beijing Textile (CHN ISSN 1002-3348) **8935**
Beijing Film Academy. Journal *see* Beijing Dianying Xueyuan Xuebao **6490**
Beijing Film Studio Pictorial *see* Beiying Huabao **6490**
Beijing Forestry Management Staff College. Journal *see* Beijing Linye Guanli Ganbu Xueyuan Xuebao **3684**
Beijing Forestry University. Journal *see* Beijing Linye Daxue Xuebao **7840**
Beijing Forestry University. Journal (Social Sciencs) *see* Beijing Linye Daxue Xuebao (Shehui Kexue Ban) **7950**
Beijing Fuzhuang Fangzhi *see* Shishang Beijing **2261**
● Beijing Fuzhuang Xueyuan Xuebao (Ziran Kexue Ban)/Beijing Institute of Clothing Technology. Journal (CHN ISSN 1001-0564) **7839**
Beijing Gangtie Jishu Daxue Xuebao *see* Beijing University of Iron and Steel Technology. Journal **6306**
Beijing Geology *see* Beijing Dizhi **2726**
Beijing Golf Club News (JPN) **8223**
Beijing Gongren/Beijing Workers *see* Gonghui Bolan **4595**
● Beijing Gongshang/Beijing Industry and Commerce (CHN ISSN 1671-9557) **1066**
● Beijing Gongshang Daxue Xuebao (Shehui Kexue Ban)/Beijing Technology and Business University. Jorunal (Social Science Edition) (CHN ISSN 1009-6116) **7949**
● Beijing Gongshang Daxue Xuebao (Ziran Kexue Ban)/Beijing Technology and Business University. Journal (Natural Science Edition) (CHN ISSN 1671-1513) **1066**
Beijing Gongshang Guanli/Beijing Industrial and Commercial Management *see* Beijing Gongshang **1066**
● Beijing Gongye Daxue Xuebao/Beijing University of Technology. Journal (CHN ISSN 0254-0037) **7839**
● Beijing Gongye Daxue Xuebao (Shehui Kexue Ban)/Beijing University of Technology. Journal (Social Sciences Edition) (CHN ISSN 1671-0398) **7949**
Beijing Guancha/Beijing Observation (CHN ISSN 1008-1208) **7109**
● ➤ Beijing Hangkong Hangtian Daxue Xuebao/Beijing University of Aeronautics and Astronautics. Journal (CHN ISSN 1001-5965) **49**
● Beijing Hangkong Hangtian Daxue Xuebao (Shehui Kexue Ban)/Beijing University of Aeronautics and Astronautics. Journal (Social Sciences Edition) (CHN ISSN 1008-2204) **7949**
Beijing Huagong Daxue Xuebao *see* Beijing Huagong Daxue Xuebao (Ziran Kexue Ban) **7839**
● Beijing Huagong Daxue Xuebao (Shehui Kexue Ban)/Beijing University of Chemical Technology. Journal (Social Sciences Edition) (CHN ISSN 1671-6639) **7949**
● Beijing Huagong Daxue Xuebao (Ziran Kexue Ban)/Beijing University of Chemical Technology. Journal (Natural Science Edition) (CHN ISSN 1671-4628) **7839**
Beijing Industry and Commerce *see* Beijing Gongshang **1066**
Beijing Informa *see* Beijing Review **3822**
Beijing Information (CHN ISSN 0251-3137) **3822**
Beijing Institute of Civil Engineering and Architecture. Journal *see* Beijing Jianzhu Gongcheng Xueyuan Xuebao **3260**
Beijing Institute of Clothing Technology. Journal *see* Beijing Fuzhuang Xueyuan Xuebao (Ziran Kexue Ban) **7839**
Beijing Institute of Education. Journal *see* Beijing Jiaoyu Xueyuan Xuebao **2830**
Beijing Institute of Graphic Communication. Journal *see* Beijing Yinshua Xueyuan Xuebao **7318**
Beijing Institute of Machinery. Journal *see* Beijing Jijie Gongye Xueyuan Xuebao (Zonghe Ban) **5449**
Beijing Institute of Petro-chemical Technology. Journal *see* Beijing Shiyou Huagong Xueyuan Xuebao **3236**
● Beijing Institute of Technology. Journal (CHN ISSN 1004-0579) **7839**
Beijing Institute of Technology. Journal (Social Sciences Edition) *see* Beijing Ligong Daxue Xuebao (Shehui Kexue Ban) **7950**
Beijing International Studies University. Journal *see* Beijing Di-er Waiguoyu Xueyuan Xuebao **7223**
● Beijing Jianzhu Gongcheng Xueyuan Xuebao/Beijing Institute of Civil Engineering and Architecture. Journal (CHN ISSN 1004-6011) **3260**
● Beijing Jiaotong Daxue Xuebao (Shehui Kexue Ban)/Beijing Jiaotong University. Journal (Social Sciences Edition) (CHN ISSN 1672-8106) **7950**
● Beijing Jiaotong Daxue Xuebao (Ziran Kexue Ban)/Beijing Jiaotong University. Journal (Natural Science Edition) (CHN ISSN 1673-0291) **7839**
Beijing Jiaotong University. Journal (Natural Science Edition) *see* Beijing Jiaotong Daxue Xuebao (Ziran Kexue Ban) **7839**
Beijing Jiaotong University. Journal (Social Sciences Edition) *see* Beijing Jiaotong Daxue Xuebao (Shehui Kexue Ban) **7950**
● Beijing Jiaoyu/Beijing Education (CHN ISSN 1000-7997) **2830**
● Beijing Jiaoyu Xueyuan Xuebao/Beijing Institute of Education. Journal (CHN ISSN 1008-228X) **2830**
● Beijing Jijie Gongye Xueyuan Xuebao (Zonghe Ban)/Beijing Institute of Machinery. Journal (CHN ISSN 1008-1658) **5449**
● Beijing Jikong Zhongxinbao/Beijing C D C Newsletter (CHN) **5584**
Beijing Jingji Bao/Beijing Economic Information News (CHN) **1442**
Beijing Jishi/Beijing Document (CHN ISSN 1005-9075) **3822**
Beijing Journal of Stomatology *see* Beijing Kouqiang Yixue **5836**
Beijing Journal of Traditional Chinese Medicine *see* Beijing Zhongyi **307**
● Beijing Keji Daxue Xuebao (CHN ISSN 1001-053X) **6458**
● Beijing Keji Daxue Xuebao (Shehui Kexue Ban)/University of Science and Technology Beijing. Journal (Social Sciences Edition) (CHN ISSN 1008-2689) **7950**
● Beijing Kejie Bao/Beijing Science Technology Report (CHN) **7840**
● Beijing Kouqiang Yixue/Beijing Journal of Stomatology (CHN ISSN 1006-673X) **5836**
● Beijing Lianhe Daxue Xuebao (Renwen Shehui Kexue Ban)/Beijing Union University. Journal (Humanities and Social Sciences Edition) (CHN ISSN 1672-4917) **4444**
● Beijing Lianhe Daxue Xuebao (Ziran Kexue Ban) (CHN ISSN 1005-0310) **7840**
● Beijing Ligong Daxue Xuebao (CHN ISSN 1001-0645) **7840**
● Beijing Ligong Daxue Xuebao (Shehui Kexue Ban)/Beijing Institute of Technology. Journal (Social Sciences Edition) (CHN ISSN 1009-3370) **7950**
● Beijing Linye Daxue Xuebao/Beijing Forestry University. Journal (CHN ISSN 1000-1522) **7840**
● Beijing Linye Daxue Xuebao (Shehui Kexue Ban)/Beijing Forestry University. Journal (Social Sciencs) (CHN ISSN 1671-6116) **7950**
Beijing Linye Guanli Ganbu Xueyuan Xuebao/Beijing Forestry Management Staff College. Journal (CHN ISSN 1671-7589) **3684**
Beijing Literature *see* Beijing Wenxue **5261**
Beijing Medical Journal *see* Beijing Yixue **5584**
Beijing Modern Business Daily *see* Beijing Xiandai Shangbao **1066**
Beijing Morning Post *see* Beijing Chenbao **3822**
● Beijing Nongye/Beijing Agriculture (CHN ISSN 1000-6966) **95**
● Beijing Nongye Kexue/Beijing Agricultural Science (CHN ISSN 1001-8344) **95**
Beijing Normal University. Journal (Natural Science Edition) *see* Beijing Shifan Daxue Xuebao (Ziran Kexue Ban) **7840**
Beijing Normal University. Journal (Social Science Edition) *see* Beijing Shifan Daxue Xuebao (Shehui Kexue Ban) **7950**
Beijing Observation *see* Beijing Guancha **7109**
Beijing Polytechnic University. Journal *see* Beijing Gongye Daxue Xuebao **7839**
Beijing Qingnian Bao/Beijing Youth News (CHN) **2178**
● Beijing Qingnian Zhengzhi Xueyuan Xuebao/Beijing Youth Politics College. Journal (CHN ISSN 1008-4002) **7109**
● Beijing Qingnian Zhoukan/Beijing Youth Weekly (CHN) **2178**
Beijing Real Estate *see* Beijing Fangdichan **7583**
● Beijing Review (CHN ISSN 1000-9140) **3822**
● Beijing Ribao/Beijing Daily (CHN) **3822**
Beijing Ribao Hedingben *see* Beijing Ribao **3822**
Beijing Rundschau *see* Beijing Review **3822**
Beijing Sci Tech Report *see* Beijing Kejie Bao **7840**
Beijing Science Technology Report *see* Beijing Kejie Bao **7840**
● Beijing Shaonianbao/Beijing Children's Weekly (CHN) **2178**
Beijing Shehui Bao (CHN) **3822**
● Beijing Shehui Kexue/Beijing Social Sciences (CHN ISSN 1002-3054) **7950**
● Beijing Shengwu Yixue Gongcheng/Beijing Biomedical Engineering (CHN ISSN 1002-3208) **5584**
● Beijing Shi Renmin Zhengfu Gongbao/People's Government of Beijing Municipality. Gazette (CHN ISSN 1009-2862) **7422**
● Beijing Shifan Daxue Xuebao (Shehui Kexue Ban)/Beijing Normal University. Journal (Social Science Edition) (CHN ISSN 1002-0209) **7950**
● Beijing Shifan Daxue Xuebao (Ziran Kexue Ban)/Beijing Normal University. Journal (Natural Science Edition) (CHN ISSN 0476-0301) **7840**
● Beijing Shiyou Huagong Xueyuan Xuebao/Beijing Institute of Petro-chemical Technology. Journal (CHN ISSN 1008-2565) **3236**
Beijing Shuili/Beijing Water Resources *see* Beijing Shuiwu **8818**
● Beijing Shuiwu/Beijing Water (CHN ISSN 1673-4637) **8818**
Beijing Social Sciences *see* Beijing Shehui Kexue **7950**
Beijing Spring (USA ISSN 1074-469X) **7203**
Beijing Statistical Yearbook *see* Beijing Tongji Nianjian **7278**
Beijing Suburbs Daily *see* Jingjiao Ribao **3825**
Beijing Technology and Business University. Jorunal (Social Science Edition) *see* Beijing Gongshang Daxue Xuebao (Shehui Kexue Ban) **7949**
Beijing Technology and Business University. Journal (Natural Science Edition) *see* Beijing Gongshang Daxue Xuebao (Ziran Kexue Ban) **1066**
Beijing Textile *see* Beijing Fangzhi **8935**
● Beijing This Month (CHN) **1066**
● Beijing Tiyu Daxue Xuebao/Beijing University of Physical Education. Journal (CHN ISSN 1007-3612) **6982**
● Beijing Today (CHN) **3822**
Beijing Tongji Nianjian/Beijing Statistical Yearbook (CHN) **7278**
Beijing Union University. Journal (Humanities and Social Sciences Edition) *see* Beijing Lianhe Daxue Xuebao (Renwen Shehui Kexue Ban) **4444**
Beijing University. Journal (Health Sciences) *see* Beijing Daxue Xuebao (Yixue Ban) **5584**
Beijing University. Journal (Natural Science Edition) *see* Beijing Daxue Xuebao (Ziran Kexue Ban) **7839**

Title

10028 BEITRAEGE ZUR VERHALTENSFORSCHUNG ULRICH'S PERIODICALS

Beitraege zur Verhaltensforschung (DEU ISSN 0522-7194) **1066**
Beitraege zur Volkskultur in Nordwestdeutschland (DEU ISSN 0724-4096) **4204**
Beitraege zur Volkskunde in Baden-Wuerttemberg (DEU ISSN 0931-007X) **4204**
Beitraege zur Volkskunde und Hausforschung *see* Westfaelisches Freilichtmuseum Detmold. Schriften **360**
Beitraege zur Westfaelischen Familienforschung (DEU ISSN 0067-5261) **3760**
Beitraege zur Wirtschafts und Sozialgeschichte (DEU ISSN 0723-5453) **4204**
Beitraege zur Wirtschaftsgeographie Regensburg (DEU ISSN 1437-6113) **4000**
➤ Beitraege zur Wirtschaftspolitik (CHE ISSN 0522-7216) **1536**
Beitraege zur Wissenschaft vom Alten und Neuen Testament (DEU) **7624**
Beitraege zur Zeitgeschichte Oberoesterreichs (AUT) **4204**
➤ Beitraege zur Zikadenkunde (DEU ISSN 1434-2065) **840**
† Beitraege zur Zuechtungsforschung (DEU ISSN 0948-5538) **8935**
Beiying Huabao/Beijing Film Studio Pictorial (CHN ISSN 1005-183X) **6490**
Beiyue Feng/Selected Popular Literature (CHN ISSN 1006-0197) **5261**
• Bekaempelsesmiddelforskning fra Miljoestyrelsen (DNK ISSN 1395-5403) **221**
• Bekes Megyei Hirlap (HUN ISSN 1215-1068) **3876**
Bekes Megyei Hirlap. Vasarnap Reggel *see* Bekes Megyei Hirlap **3876**
Bekesi Elet (HUN ISSN 0522-7232) **4204**
Bekhol Derakhekha Da'ehu (ISR ISSN 0793-3894) **7719**
• Die Bekleidungs- und Waesche-Industrie und Ihre Helfer/Clothing and Lingerie Industries and Their Suppliers (DEU) **2245**
Bekleidungstechnik, Management, Wirtschaft *see* Informationsdienst F I Z Technik. Bekleidungstechnik, Management, Wirtschaft **8463**
• Beknopt Overzicht van de Sociale Zekerheid in Belgie/Survey of Social Security in Belgium (BEL ISSN 1375-4424) **7422**
• Le Bel Age (CAN ISSN 0835-8702) **4041**
Het Belang van Limburg (BEL) **3801**
Belangenbehartiging. Nieuws en ons Dienstenaanbod *see* B.ND **4590**
Belarra (ESP ISSN 1132-2179) **778**
Belarus' (BLR ISSN 0320-7544) **3800**
Belarus and Business *see* Delo (Minsk) **1090**
• Belarus Defence & Security Report (GBR ISSN 1749-1274) **6413**
Belarus in the World *see* Belarus' v Mire **3800**
Belarus. Ministerstvo Inostrannykh Del. Vestnik (BLR) **3800**
Belarus News *see* Interfax. Belarus News **8965**
Belarus Science Development *see* Razvitiye Nauki Belarusi **7901**
Belarus' v Mire/Belarus in the World (BLR) **3800**
Belarus. Vysheishy Gaspadarchy Sud. Vesnik (BLR) **4946**
Belarusian Historical Review *see* Belaruski Histarychny Ahliad **4204**
The Belarusian Linguistics *see* Belaruskaya Lingvistyka **5099**
Belarusian Review (USA ISSN 1064-7716) **1066**
The Belarusian Studies *see* Belarusistyka **4444**
Belarusistyka/The Belarusian Studies (BLR) **4444**
Belaruskaya Lingvistyka/The Belarusian Linguistics (BLR ISSN 0320-7552) **5099**
➤ Belaruskaya Litaratura (BLR ISSN 0134-9686) **5261**
Belaruskaya Maladzezhnaya (BLR) **3800**
➤ Belaruskaya Mova (BLR ISSN 1010-3996) **5099**
Belaruski Histarychny Ahliad/Belarusian Historical Review (BLR ISSN 1392-902X) **4204**
Belasting- en Premieheffingen, Uitkeringen en Minimumloon (Year) (NLD ISSN 1574-583X) **1667**
Belasting Toegevoegde Waarde Brief *see* B T W Brief **1911**
Belasting Toegevoegde Waarde Bulletin *see* B T W Bulletin **1912**
Belasting Toegevoegde Waarde en Overdrachtsbelasting in de Vastgoedsector (NLD ISSN 1872-5058) **1912**
Belasting Toegevoegde Waarde Jurisprudentie van het Hof van Justitie van de Europese Gemeenschappen *see* B T W-Jurisprudentie van het Hof van Justitie van de Europese Gemeenschappen **1912**
De Belastingadviseur *see* Gribb Belastingadviseur **1927**
Belastingbeleid Successie en Rechtsverkeer *see* Pocket Belastingbeleid Successie en Rechtsverkeer **1939**
Belastingbiblioteek *see* Tax Library **1948**
Belastingblad (NLD ISSN 0167-4293) **1912**
Belastingbrief (NLD ISSN 1569-6766) **1912**
Belastingmagazine (NLD) **1912**
Belastingrecht voor Ondernemers (NLD ISSN 1874-219X) **1912**
Belastingrecht voor Particulieren (NLD ISSN 1874-2084) **1912**
Belastingzaken (NLD ISSN 0922-2316) **1912**
Belaya Koldun'ya (UKR) **4444**
Belcher Bulletin (USA) **3760**
Beleggen met van Lanschot *see* Private Investments **1645**
Beleggers Belangen *see* Financieel Economisch Weekblad Beleggers Belangen **1346**
Beleggers Belangen Internet *see* Financieel Economisch Weekblad Beleggers Belangen **1346**
Beleggingsontleders Tydskrif *see* Investment Analysts Journal **1632**
Beleidsberichten *see* Ampersand **7420**
Beleidswetenschap (NLD ISSN 0921-1934) **7422**
▼ Beletra Almanako (USA ISSN 1937-3325) **5261**
• Belfagor (ITA ISSN 0005-8351) **5208**
Belfast Gazette (IRL ISSN 0951-0370) **3861**
• Belfast In Your Pocket (IRL ISSN 1747-0021) **8686**
• The Belfast News Letter (IRL ISSN 0307-5923) **3892**
Belfast Studies in Language, Culture and Politics (GBR) **5099**
• Belfast Telegraph (GBR ISSN 0307-5664) **3861**
Belgeo *see* Revue Belge de Geographie **4027**
Belgian Ear Nose Throat *see* B - E N T **6078**
Belgian Francophone Library (USA ISSN 1074-6757) **5261**
• ➤ Belgian Journal of Botany (BEL ISSN 0778-4031) **779**
Belgian Journal of English Language and Literatures *see* B E L L **5098**
➤ Belgian Journal of Entomology (BEL ISSN 1374-5514) **841**
Belgian Journal of Geography *see* Revue Belge de Geographie **4027**
• ➤ Belgian Journal of Linguistics (NLD ISSN 0774-5141) **5099**
➤ Belgian Journal of Zoology (BEL ISSN 0777-6276) **935**
• Belgian Laces (USA ISSN 1046-0462) **3522**
Belgian Mathematical Society - Simon Stevin. Bulletin (BEL ISSN 1370-1444) **5475**
Belgian Motor Sport (Dutch Edition) (BEL ISSN 1784-2999) **8161**
Belgian Motor Sport (French Edition) (BEL ISSN 1784-2980) **8161**
Belgian Review of International Law *see* Revue Belge de Droit International **4939**
The Belgian Sheepdog (USA ISSN 1077-9841) **6804**
The Belgian Sheepdog Newsletter *see* The Belgian Sheepdog **6804**
Belgian Social Security Journal *see* Revue Belge de Securite Sociale **7466**
Belgian Social Security Journal *see* De Belgisch Tijdschrift voor Sociale Zekerheid **7422**
▼ Belgien im Fokus (DEU ISSN 1862-796X) **4204**
Belgiophile (USA) **6892**
Het Belgisch A G F Adresboek (Aardappelen - Groenten - Fruit) (NLD) **194**
Belgisch Centrum voor Landelijke Geschiedenis. Publikaties *see* Centre Belge d'Histoire Rurale. Publications **4209**
Belgisch Staatsblad *see* Moniteur Belge **4736**
Belgisch Tijdschrift voor Geneeskunde *see* Tijdschrift voor Geneeskunde **5722**
Belgisch Tijdschrift voor Geografie *see* Revue Belge de Geographie **4027**
Belgisch Tijdschrift voor Internationaal Recht *see* Revue Belge de Droit International **4939**
Belgisch Tijdschrift voor Militaire Geschiedenis *see* Revue Belge d'Histoire Militaire **6443**
Belgisch Tijdschrift voor Muziekwetenschap *see* Revue Belge de Musicologie **6611**
Belgisch Tijdschrift voor Nieuwste Geschiedenis *see* Revue Belge d'Histoire Contemporaine **4159**
Belgisch Tijdschrift voor Oudheidkunde en Kunstgeshiedenis *see* Revue Belge d'Archeologie et d'Histoire de l'Art **515**
De Belgisch Tijdschrift voor Sociale Zekerheid/Belgian Social Security Journal (BEL ISSN 0775-0234) **7422**
Belgisch Tijdschrift voor Tandheelkunde *see* Revue Belge de Medecine Dentaire **5864**
Belgisch Ziekenhuis *see* Hospitals.be **4101**
Belgische Beenhouwerij *see* La Boucherie Belge **3628**
Belgische Bibliografie *see* Bibliographie de Belgique **618**
Belgische Cementnijverheid *see* Industrie Cimentiere Belge **1014**
Belgische Vereniging van Laboratorium Technologen. Tijdschrift *see* Association Belge des Technologues de Laboratoire. Revue **2051**
Belgische Vereniging voor Documentatie. Bladen voor de Documentatie *see* Association Belge de Documentation. Cahiers de la Documentation **4992**
Belgische Vereniging voor Stralingsbescherming. Annalen/Association Belge de Radioprotection. Annales (BEL ISSN 0250-5010) **7509**
Belgische Verminkte *see* Invalide Belge **6425**
Belgische Visser *see* Pecheur Belge **3604**
Belgishe Geologische Dienst. Verhandeling *see* Geological Survey of Belgium. Memoirs **2740**
Belgishe Zeitschrift fuer Geographie *see* Revue Belge de Geographie **4027**
Belgium. Administration des Affaires Maritimes et de la Navigation. Rapport Annuel sur l'Evolution de la Flotte de Peche (BEL) **8639**
Belgium. Agriculture Research Center. Department of Plant Genetics and Breeding. Report *see* Dep. Plantengenetica en-Veredeling. Activiteitenverslag **3728**
Belgium. Centrum voor Bevolkings- en Gezinsstudien. Progress Report (BEL) **7278**
Belgium. Communaute Francaise de Belgique. Institut National de Statistique. Annuaire Statistique (BEL ISSN 0779-4312) **1214**
Belgium. Conseil Superieur des Classes Moyennes. Rapport Annuel (BEL ISSN 0067-5393) **1957**
Belgium. Cour de Cassation. Bulletin des Arrets (BEL) **4628**
Belgium. Department Zeevisserij. Mededelingen (BEL) **3587**
Belgium. Federaal Ministerie van Sociale Zaken, Volksgezondheid en Leefmilieu. Algemeen Verslag over de Sociale Zekerheid (BEL ISSN 1374-8254) **7422**
• Belgium. Federaal Ministerie van Sociale Zaken, Volksgezondheid en Leefmilieu. Hanidgids/Guide of the Disabled Person (BEL ISSN 1371-4074) **4064**
Belgium. Federaal Ministerie van Sociale Zaken, Volksgezondheid en Leefmilieu. Statistisch Jaarboek van de Sociale Zekerheid/Statistics Social Security Yearbook (BEL ISSN 0772-3962) **4529**
Belgium. Federaal Ministerie van Sociale Zaken, Volksgezondheid en Leefmilieu. Tegemoetkomingen aan Gehandicapten/Benefits for the Disabled (BEL ISSN 1375-4386) **4064**
• Belgium. Fonds voor Wetenschappelijk Onderzoek - Vlaanderen. Jaarverslag (Online Edition) (BEL) **7840**
Belgium. Fonds voor Wetenschappelijk Onderzoek - Vlaanderen. Jaarverslag (Print Edition) *see* Belgium. Fonds voor Wetenschappelijk Onderzoek - Vlaanderen. Jaarverslag (Online Edition) **7840**
Belgium. Fonds voor Wetenschappelijk Onderzoek - Vlaanderen. Lijst der Kredietgenieters (BEL) **7840**
Belgium. Geological Survey of Belgium. Professional Papers (BEL ISSN 0378-0902) **2726**
Belgium. Hoge Raad voor de Middenstand. Jaarverslag (BEL) **7423**
Belgium. Institut National d'Assurance Maladie Invalidite. I N A M I Bulletin d'Information (BEL ISSN 0046-9726) **4494**
Belgium. Institut National d'Assurances Sociales pour Travailleurs Independants. Rapport Annuel (BEL) **4494**
Belgium. Institut National d'Assurances Sociales pour Travailleurs Independants. Statistique des Enfants Beneficiaires d'Allocations Familiales/Belgium. Rijksinstituut voor de Sociale Verzekeringen der Zelfstandigen. Statistiek van de Kinderen die Recht Geven op Kinderbijslag (BEL) **4529**
Belgium. Institut National d'Assurances Sociales pour Travailleurs Independants. Statistiques des Beneficiaires de Prestations de Retraite et de Survie/Belgium. Rijksinstituut voor de Sociale Verzekeringen der Zelfstandigen. Statistiek van de Personen die een Rust- en Overlevingsprestatie Genieten (BEL) **4529**
Belgium. Institut National d'Assurances Sociales pour Travailleurs Independants. Statistiques des Personnes Assujetties au Statut Social des Travailleurs Independants/Belgium. Rijksinstituut voor de Sociale Verzekeringen der Zelfstandigen. Statistiek van de Personen die onder de Toepassing Vallen van het Sociaal Statuut van de Zelfstandigen (BEL) **4529**
Belgium. Institut National de Statistique. Accidents de la Circulation sur la Voie Publique avec Tues et Blesses *see* Belgium. Institut National de Statistique. Sante. Accidents de la Circulation sur la Voie Publique avec Tues et Blesses en (Annee) **8522**
Belgium. Institut National de Statistique. Agriculture. Statistiques Agricoles (BEL ISSN 1379-4752) **175**
Belgium. Institut National de Statistique. Annuaire de Statistiques Regionales (BEL ISSN 0770-0369) **1214**
Belgium. Institut National de Statistique. Bulletin de Statistique (BEL ISSN 0045-1703) **1214**
Belgium. Institut National de Statistique. Catalogue des Produits et Services (BEL) **8357**
Belgium. Institut National de Statistique. Communique Hebdomadaire (BEL ISSN 0772-6341) **1214**
Belgium. Institut National de Statistique. Demographie Mathematique. Tables de Mortalite (BEL ISSN 1379-4051) **7303**
Belgium. Institut National de Statistique. Emploi et Chomage. Enquete sur les Forces de Travail (Year) (BEL ISSN 1379-3845) **1214**
Belgium. Institut National de Statistique. Enquete sur les Budgets des Menages (BEL) **1214**
Belgium. Institut National de Statistique. Enquete sur les Forces de Travail *see* Belgium. Institut National de Statistique. Emploi et Chomage. Enquete sur les Forces de Travail (Year) **1214**
Belgium. Institut National de Statistique. Etudes Statistiques (BEL ISSN 0069-8075) **8357**
Belgium. Institut National de Statistique. Industrie et Construction (BEL ISSN 1377-137X) **1214**
Belgium. Institut National de Statistique. Industrie et Construction. Construction et Logement (BEL ISSN 1379-2938) **4434**
Belgium. Institut National de Statistique. Media. Nombre de Licences d'Appareils de Radio sur Vehicule et de Television (BEL ISSN 1379-4027) **1214**
Belgium. Institut National de Statistique. Nombre de Licences d'Appareils de Radio sur Vehicule et de Television au 31 Decembre *see* Belgium. Institut National de Statistique. Media. Nombre de Licences d'Appareils de Radio sur Vehicule et de Television **1214**
Belgium. Institut National de Statistique. Nouvelles Economiques (BEL ISSN 1371-6271) **1214**
Belgium. Institut National de Statistique. Parc de Vehicules a Moteur *see* Belgium. Institut National de Statistique. Statistiques du Transport. Parc des Vehicules a Moteur au (Year) **8522**
Belgium. Institut National de Statistique. Perspectives de Population (BEL) **7303**
Belgium. Institut National de Statistique. Sante. Accidents de la Circulation sur la Voie Publique avec Tues et Blesses en (Annee) (BEL ISSN 1378-1227) **8522**
Belgium. Institut National de Statistique. Sante. Causes de Deces (BEL ISSN 1379-4078) **7303**
Belgium. Institut National de Statistique. Statistique du Tourisme et de l'Hotellerie (BEL ISSN 0067-5547) **8778**
Belgium. Institut National de Statistique. Statistique du Trafic International des Ports (U E B L) (BEL ISSN 0772-7739) **8522**
Belgium. Institut National de Statistique. Statistiques Agricoles *see* Belgium. Institut National de Statistique. Agriculture. Statistiques Agricoles **175**
Belgium. Institut National de Statistique. Statistiques Demographiques *see* Belgium. Institut National de Statistique. Demographie Mathematique. Tables de Mortalite **7303**
Belgium. Institut National de Statistique. Statistiques des Causes de Deces *see* Belgium. Institut National de Statistique. Sante. Causes de Deces **7303**
Belgium. Institut National de Statistique. Statistiques du Transport. Parc des Vehicules a Moteur au (Year) (BEL ISSN 1379-3780) **8522**
Belgium. Institut National de Statistique. Statistiques Industrielles *see* Belgium. Institut National de Statistique. Industrie et Construction **1214**
Belgium. Institut National de Statistique. Statistiques Sociales (BEL ISSN 0067-5563) **8081**
Belgium. Institut National de Statistique. Statistiques sur les Medias et l'Audiovisuel. Nombre de Licences d'Appareils de Radio sur Vehicule et de Television *see* Belgium. Institut National de Statistique. Media. Nombre de Licences d'Appareils de Radio sur Vehicule et de Television **1214**
Belgium. Institut National de Statistique. Transport. Navigation Interieure (BEL ISSN 1379-3888) **8522**
Belgium. Institut National de Statistique. Transport. Vehicules a Moteur Neufs et d'Occasion Mis en Circulation en (Annee) (BEL ISSN 1377-4271) **8522**
Belgium. La Poste. Rapport d'Activite (BEL) **2353**
Belgium. Ministere de l'Education, de la Recherche et de la Formation. Annuaire Statistique (BEL) **2930**
Belgium. Ministere de l'Education, de la Recherche et de la Formation. Tableau de Bord de l'Enseignement (BEL) **2830**
Belgium. Ministere de l'Education Nationale. Revue (BEL) **2830**
Belgium. Ministere des Affaires Sociales de la Sante Publique et de l'Environnement. Administration des Soins de Sante. Annuaire Statistique des Hopitaux/Belgium. Ministerie van Volksgezondheid en Leefmilieu. Bestuur voor de Verzorgingsinstellingen. Statistisch Jaarboek van de Ziekenhuizen (BEL) **7547**
Belgium. Ministere des Finances. Administration des Contributions. Bulletin des Contributions (BEL ISSN 0005-853X) **1912**
Belgium. Ministere des Finances. Bulletin de Documentation *see* Belgium. Ministerie van Financien. Documentatieblad **1912**
Belgium. Ministere Federal des Affaires Sociales de la Sante Publique et de l'Environnement. Allocations aux Handicapes *see* Belgium. Federaal Ministerie van Sociale Zaken, Volksgezondheid en Leefmilieu. Tegemoetkomingen aan Gehandicapten **4064**
Belgium. Ministere Federal des Affaires Sociales de la Sante Publique et de l'Environnement. Annuaire Statistique de Securite Sociale/Statistics Social Security Yearbook (BEL) **4529**
Belgium. Ministere Federal des Affaires Sociales, de la Sante Publique et de l'Environnement. Rapport General sur la Securite Sociale (BEL ISSN 1374-8262) **4495**
Belgium. Ministerie van Financien. Documentatieblad/Belgium. Ministere des Finances. Bulletin de Documentation (BEL ISSN 0779-8601) **1912**
Belgium. Ministerie van Financien. Hoofdbestuur der Directe Belastingen. Bulletin der Belastingen *see* Belgium. Ministere des Finances. Administration des Contributions. Bulletin des Contributions **1912**

DIRECTORY 2010 BENEDICTIJNS TIJDSCHRIFT 10029

Belgium. Ministerie van Volksgezondheid en Leefmilieu. Bestuur voor de Verzorgingsinstellingen. Statistisch Jaarboek van de Ziekenhuizen see Belgium. Ministere des Affaires Sociales de la Sante Publique et de l'Environnement. Administration des Soins de Sante. Annuaire Statistique des Hopitaux **7547**
Belgium. Nationaal Instituut voor de Statistiek. Aantal Vergunningen voor Autoradio's en Televisietoestellen see Belgium. Nationaal Instituut voor de Statistiek. Media. Aantal Vergunningen voor Autoradio's en Televisietoestellen **1214**
Belgium. Nationaal Instituut voor de Statistiek. Binnenscheepvaart see Belgium. Nationaal Instituut voor de Statistiek. Vervoer. Binnenscheepvaart (Jaar) **8522**
Belgium. Nationaal Instituut voor de Statistiek. Catalogus van de Produkten en Diensten (BEL) **8357**
Belgium. Nationaal Instituut voor de Statistiek. Economische Nieuws (BEL ISSN 1371-7111) **1214**
Belgium. Nationaal Instituut voor de Statistiek. Gezondheid. Doodsoorzaken (BEL ISSN 1379-406X) **7303**
Belgium. Nationaal Instituut voor de Statistiek. Gezondheid. Verkeersongevallen op de Openbare Weg met Doden en Gewonden in (Year) (BEL ISSN 1378-1219) **7547**
Belgium. Nationaal Instituut voor de Statistiek. Industrie en Bouwnijverheid (BEL ISSN 1377-1361) **1214**
Belgium. Nationaal Instituut voor de Statistiek. Industrie en Bouwnijverheid. Bouwnijverheid en Huisvesting (BEL ISSN 1379-2946) **4434**
Belgium. Nationaal Instituut voor de Statistiek. Industriele Statistieken see Belgium. Nationaal Instituut voor de Statistiek. Industrie en Bouwnijverheid **1214**
Belgium. Nationaal Instituut voor de Statistiek. Landbouw. Landbouwstatistieken (BEL ISSN 1379-4744) **176**
Belgium. Nationaal Instituut voor de Statistiek. Landbouwstatistieken see Belgium. Nationaal Instituut voor de Statistiek. Landbouw. Landbouwstatistieken **176**
Belgium. Nationaal Instituut voor de Statistiek. Mathematische Demografie. Sterftetafels (BEL ISSN 1379-4043) **7278**
Belgium. Nationaal Instituut voor de Statistiek. Media. Aantal Vergunningen voor Autoradio's en Televisietoestellen (BEL ISSN 1379-4035) **1214**
Belgium. Nationaal Instituut voor de Statistiek. Motorvoertuigenpark see Belgium. Nationaal Instituut voor de Statistiek. Vervoerstatistieken. Motorvoertuigenpark op (Year) **8522**
Belgium. Nationaal Instituut voor de Statistiek. Nieuwe to het Verkeer Toegelaten Motorvoergtuigen see Belgium. Nationaal Instituut voor de Statistiek. Vervoer. In het Verkeer Gebrachte Nieuwe en Tweedehands Motorvoertuigen in (Year) **8522**
Belgium. Nationaal Instituut voor de Statistiek. Regionaal Statistisch Jaarboek (BEL ISSN 0770-772X) **1214**
Belgium. Nationaal Instituut voor de Statistiek. Sociale Statistieken (BEL ISSN 0771-7881) **8081**
Belgium. Nationaal Instituut voor de Statistiek. Sociale Statistieken. Enquete naar de Arbeidskrachten see Belgium. Nationaal Instituut voor de Statistiek. Werkgelegenheid en Werkloosheid. Enquete naar de Arbeidskrachten (Year) **1214**
Belgium. Nationaal Instituut voor de Statistiek. Sociale Statistieken: Enquete naar de Beroepsbevolking see Belgium. Nationaal Instituut voor de Statistiek. Werkgelegenheid en Werkloosheid. Enquete naar de Arbeidskrachten (Year) **1214**
Belgium. Nationaal Instituut voor de Statistiek. Statistiek over de Internationale Trafiek (B.L.E.U.) in de Havens (BEL ISSN 0772-800X) **8522**
Belgium. Nationaal Instituut voor de Statistiek. Statistiek van Doodsoorzaken see Belgium. Nationaal Instituut voor de Statistiek. Gezondheid. Doodsoorzaken **7303**
Belgium. Nationaal Instituut voor de Statistiek. Statistiek van het Toerisme en het Hotelwezen (BEL ISSN 0773-3097) **8778**
Belgium. Nationaal Instituut voor de Statistiek. Statistieken over communicatiemedia. Aantal Vergunningen voor Autoradio's en Televisietoestellen see Belgium. Nationaal Instituut voor de Statistiek. Media. Aantal Vergunningen voor Autoradio's en Televisietoestellen **1214**
Belgium. Nationaal Instituut voor de Statistiek. Statistisch Tijdschrift (BEL ISSN 0778-8789) **1214**
Belgium. Nationaal Instituut voor de Statistiek. Statistisch Zakjaarboek (BEL ISSN 1370-1754) **1214**
Belgium. Nationaal Instituut voor de Statistiek. Statistische Studien (BEL ISSN 0772-1838) **8358**
Belgium. Nationaal Instituut voor de Statistiek. Verkeersongevallen op de Openbare Weg met Doden of Gewonden see Belgium. Nationaal Instituut voor de Statistiek. Gezondheid. Verkeersongevallen op de Openbare Weg met Doden en Gewonden in (Year) **7547**
Belgium. Nationaal Instituut voor de Statistiek. Vervoer. Binnenscheepvaart (Jaar) (BEL ISSN 1379-387X) **8522**
Belgium. Nationaal Instituut voor de Statistiek. Vervoer. In het Verkeer Gebrachte Nieuwe en Tweedehands Motorvoertuigen in (Year) (BEL ISSN 1377-4263) **8522**
Belgium. Nationaal Instituut voor de Statistiek. Vervoerstatistieken. Motorvoertuigenpark op (Year) (BEL ISSN 1379-3772) **8522**
Belgium. Nationaal Instituut voor de Statistiek. Weekbericht (BEL ISSN 0771-0410) **1214**
Belgium. Nationaal Instituut voor de Statistiek. Werkgelegenheid en Werkloosheid. Enquete naar de Arbeidskrachten (Year) (BEL ISSN 1379-3853) **1214**
† Belgium. Nederlands Interuniversitair Demografisch Instituut. Bevolking en Gezin (BEL ISSN 0772-764X) **8935**
Belgium. Office National de l'Emploi. Bulletin Mensuel (BEL) **1667**
Belgium. Office National de l'Emploi. Communique Mensuel (BEL ISSN 1375-7881) **1667**
Belgium. Office National de l'Emploi. Etudes Economiques et Sociales (BEL) **1667**
Belgium Petrochemicals Report (GBR ISSN 1749-2157) **6763**
Belgium Real Estate Yearbook (NLD ISSN 1871-5591) **7583**
Belgium. Rijksdienst voor Arbeidsvoorziening. Jaarverslag see Belgium. Office National de l'Emploi. Etudes Economiques et Sociales **1667**
Belgium. Rijksdienst voor Arbeidsvoorziening. Maandelijks Mededeling see Belgium. Office National de l'Emploi. Communique Mensuel **1667**
Belgium. Rijksinstituut voor de Sociale Verzekeringen der Zelfstandigen. Jaarverslag (BEL) **4495**
Belgium. Rijksinstituut voor de Sociale Verzekeringen der Zelfstandigen. Statistiek van de Kinderen die Recht Geven op Kinderbijslag see Belgium. Institut National d'Assurances Sociales pour Travailleurs Independants. Statistique des Enfants Beneficiaires d'Allocations Familiales **4529**
Belgium. Rijksinstituut voor de Sociale Verzekeringen der Zelfstandigen. Statistiek van de Personen die een Rust- en Overlevingsprestatie Genieten see Belgium. Institut National d'Assurances Sociales pour Travailleurs Independants. Statistiques des Beneficiaires de Prestations de Retraite et de Survie **4529**
Belgium. Rijksinstituut voor de Sociale Verzekeringen der Zelfstandigen. Statistiek van de Personen die onder de Toepassing Vallen van het Sociaal Statuut van de Zelfstandigen see Belgium. Institut National d'Assurances Sociales pour Travailleurs Independants. Statistiques des Personnes Assujetties au Statut Social des Travailleurs Independants **4529**
Belgium. Rijksinstituut voor Ziekte- en Invaliditeitsverzekering. R I Z I V Informatieblad see Belgium. Institut National d'Assurance Maladie Invalidite. I N A M I Bulletin d'Information **4494**
Belgium. Station de Recherches Forestieres et Hydrobiologiques. Travaux. Serie D. Hydrobiologie (BEL) **724**
• Belgium Today (USA) **8686**
Belgo Bijoux (BEL ISSN 0773-2325) **4564**
Belgo-Luxembourg Chamber of Commerce in Great Britain. Journal (GBR ISSN 1357-6879) **1396**
Belgorodskaya Pravda (RUS) **3934**
Belgrade Stock Exchange Annual Report see Beogradske Berze. Godisnji Izvestaj **1612**
Belgrade Stock Exchange Bulletin see Beogradska Berza. Bilten **1612**
Belhune Military Medical College. Journal see Baiqiuen Junyi Xueyuan Xuebao **5583**
▼ • Beliefs and Values (USA ISSN 1942-0617) **7624**
The Believer (USA ISSN 1543-6101) **5208**
Belize. Central Statistical Office. Abstract of Statistics (BLZ) **7303**
Belize Collector (USA) **6892**
Belize. Department of Agriculture. Annual Report and Summary of Statistics (BLZ) **95**
• Belize First Magazine (USA ISSN 1521-2815) **8686**
(Year) Belize Labour Force Indicators (BLZ) **1214**
Belize National Census Report (BLZ) **7303**
Belize National Population Report (BLZ) **7303**
Belize Social Indicators Report (BLZ) **8019**
Belize Times (BLZ) **7109**
Belize Today (BLZ) **3995**
Belizean Studies (BLZ ISSN 0250-6831) **4285**
Bell see Canadian Brown Swiss and Braunvieh Association Newsletter **262**
The Bell (USA) **7340**
Bell Canada Papers Series (CAN) **1536**
Bell Chimes (USA ISSN 1041-231X) **3760**
• ➤ Bell Labs Technical Journal (USA ISSN 1089-7089) **2365**
Bell Labs Technology (USA ISSN 1094-3323) **2366**
Bell of Freedom see Die Freiheitsglocke **7207**
Bell T V Magazine see Show Magazine **2390**
Bell Tower (USA ISSN 0092-8666) **4330**
Bella (DEU ISSN 0935-6207) **8853**
Bella (GBR ISSN 0953-0983) **8853**
† Bella (ITA ISSN 1970-6898) **8935**
• Bella (USA) **8853**
▼ La Bella Bride (USA) **5556**
Bella Cookbook see Cookbook **4354**
• The Bellaire Buzz (USA) **3970**
Bellas Artes (ESP ISSN 1695-761X) **478**
• Belle (AUS ISSN 0310-1452) **4533**
Belle Armoire (USA ISSN 1533-8835) **4564**
Belle Armoire Jewelry (USA ISSN 1941-2312) **4564**
La Belle France (USA) **4382**
Belle-Sante see Belle Sante **307**
Belle Sante (FRA ISSN 1249-2868) **307**
Belle-Sante. Hors Serie (FRA ISSN 1951-1434) **307**
Belle W. Baruch Library in Marine Science (USA ISSN 0361-4360) **2800**
Les Belles Histoires (FRA ISSN 1770-4758) **2178**
Les Belles Histoires de Pomme d'Api see Les Belles Histoires **2178**
Bell'Europa (ITA ISSN 1124-8408) **8686**
• Bellevue (DEU ISSN 0938-8893) **7583**
† Bellevue Guide Marbella, Costa del Sol (DEU ISSN 1439-2046) **8935**
Bellevue Literary Review (USA ISSN 1537-5048) **5208**
▼ Belleza (COL ISSN 2011-2246) **8853**
• Bellingham Review (USA ISSN 0734-2934) **5261**
• Bellissima (USA) **586**
Bell'Italia (ITA ISSN 0394-7203) **8686**
Bell'Italia (USA ISSN 1543-0014) **8686**
Bell'Italia. Le Guide. Guida della Montagna see Guida della Montagna **8316**
Bellmansstudier (SWE ISSN 0405-3923) **5261**
Bello (USA) **5066**
Bellowing Ark (USA ISSN 0887-4115) **5261**
BellSouth Classic Spectator Handbook (USA) **8223**
Belly (GBR ISSN 1463-9122) **6286**
▼ Belly Dance (USA ISSN 1941-3998) **2683**
Belmonda Letero (DEU) **7709**
Belmont Vision (USA) **2274**
Beloit College Magazine (USA) **2274**
Beloit Fiction Journal (USA ISSN 0883-9131) **5261**
• ➤ Beloit Poetry Journal (USA ISSN 0005-8661) **5417**
➤ Beloit Poetry Journal. Chapbook (USA ISSN 0067-5695) **5417**
Beloning en Belasting (NLD ISSN 0925-4544) **1912**
Belorussian Business Newspaper see Belorusskaya Delovaya Gazeta **1066**
Belorussian State University. Proceedings. Series 1. Physics, Mathematics, Computer Science see Belorusskii Gosudarstvennyi Universitet. Vestnik. Seriya 1. Fizika, Matematika, Informatika **5475**
Belorussian State University. Proceedings. Series 2. Chemistry, Biology, Geography see Belorusskii Gosudarstvennyi Universitet. Vestnik. Seriya 2. Khimiya, Biologiya, Geografiya **2051**
Belorussian State University. Proceedings. Series 3. History, Philosophy, Psychology, Sociology, Politology, Economics, Law see Belorusskii Gosudarstvennyi Universitet. Vestnik. Seriya 3. Istoriya, Filosofiya, Psikhologiya, Sotsiologiya, Politologiya, Ekonomika, Pravo **7950**
Belorussian State University. Proceedings. Series 4. Philology, Journalism, Pedagogy see Belorusskii Gosudarstvennyi Universitet. Vestnik. Seriya 4. Filologiya, Zhurnalistika, Pedagogika **4444**
• Belorusskaya Delovaya Gazeta/Belorussian Business Newspaper (BLR) **1066**
Belorusskii Gosudarstvennyi Universitet. Vestnik. Gystoriya, Filasofiya, Palitologiya, Sotsiologiya, Ekonomika, Pravo (BLR) **4444**
➤ Belorusskii Gosudarstvennyi Universitet. Vestnik. Seriya 1. Fizika, Matematika, Informatika/Belorussian State University. Proceedings. Series 1. Physics, Mathematics, Computer Science (BLR ISSN 1561-834X) **5475**
➤ Belorusskii Gosudarstvennyi Universitet. Vestnik. Seriya 2. Khimiya, Biologiya, Geografiya/Belorussian State University. Proceedings. Series 2. Chemistry, Biology, Geography (BLR) **2051**
Belorusskii Gosudarstvennyi Universitet. Vestnik. Seriya 3. Gystoriya, Filasofiya, Palitalogiya, Sotsiyalogiya, Ekonomika, Prava see Belorusskii Gosudarstvennyi Universitet. Vestnik. Seriya 3. Istoriya, Filosofiya, Psikhologiya, Sotsiologiya, Politologiya, Ekonomika, Pravo **7950**
Belorusskii Gosudarstvennyi Universitet. Vestnik. Seriya 3. Istoriya, Filosofiya, Psikhologiya, Sotsiologiya, Politologiya, Ekonomika, Pravo/Belorussian State University. Proceedings. Series 3. History, Philosophy, Psychology, Sociology, Politology, Economics, Law (BLR) **7950**
➤ Belorusskii Gosudarstvennyi Universitet. Vestnik. Seriya 4. Filologiya, Zhurnalistika, Pedagogika/Belorussian State University. Proceedings. Series 4. Philology, Journalism, Pedagogy (BLR) **4444**
Belorusskii Gosudarstvennyi Universitet. Vestnik. Seriya 4. Filologiya, Zhurnalistika, Pedagogika, Psikhologiya see Belorusskii Gosudarstvennyi Universitet. Vestnik. Seriya 4. Filologiya, Zhurnalistika, Pedagogika **4444**
Belorusskii Rynok (BLR) **1066**
• ➤ Belphegor (CAN ISSN 1499-7185) **5261**
Belser Kunst Quartal see Kunstquartal **6527**
Belt Line (USA) **2245**
The Belt Pulley (USA ISSN 1060-0833) **4330**
• The Beltane Papers (USA ISSN 1074-3634) **8853**
Bel'ton see B:ton **983**
Belton Magazine see B:ton **983**
➤ Beltsville Symposia in Agricultural Research (NLD ISSN 0160-3612) **95**
Beltwide Cotton Conferences. Proceedings (USA ISSN 1059-2644) **221**
Belugyi Szemle (HUN ISSN 1218-8956) **7423**
Bem see Bem on Line **5440**
Bem Lingua Portuguesa (PRT) **5099**
• Bem on Line (AND) **5440**
To Bema tou Asklepiou see To Vima tou Asklipiou **5728**
† • Bembix (DEU ISSN 0946-6193) **8935**
Bemdez (FRA ISSN 1772-2543) **7203**
▼ Ben 10 (GBR ISSN 1758-9495) **2178**
Ben-Gurion University Now see B G U Now **2273**
• The Ben Jonson Journal (GBR ISSN 1079-3453) **5261**
Benakeio Futopathologico Institouto. chorika see Institut Phytopathologique Benaki. Annales. Nouvelle Serie **122**
Benbella and Lulu (NGA) **478**
• Bench & Bar (USA ISSN 1521-6497) **4628**
• Bench & Bar of Minnesota (USA ISSN 0276-1505) **4628**
• Benchmark (USA) **4628**
Benchmark (Glasgow) (GBR ISSN 0951-6859) **3183**
Benchmark Auto (TWN ISSN 1990-7672) **1974**
Benchmark Information for Key Stage (GBR) **3052**
• Benchmark Magazine (USA) **5475**
Benchmark of I T Spending (Year) (Information Technology) (GBR ISSN 1751-5327) **1880**
• Benchmark of Salaries and Employment Trends in I T. Business Report (Year) (Information Technology) (GBR ISSN 1745-8129) **6693**
• Benchmark of Salaries and Employment Trends in I T. Reseach Report (Year) (Information Technology) (GBR ISSN 1745-8110) **6693**
Benchmark Repair (TWN ISSN 1816-9821) **1974**
Benchmark Report for Manufacturers' Shipments, Inventories, and Orders see Current Industrial Reports. M3-3, Benchmark Report for Manufacturers' Shipments, Inventories, and Orders **1223**
Benchmark Tool (TWN ISSN 1819-0324) **1974**
Benchmark Tool News Update see Benchmark Tool **1974**
• Benchmarking (DNK ISSN 1902-4258) **4128**
• ➤ Benchmarking (GBR ISSN 1463-5771) **1727**
• Benchmarking H R (AUS ISSN 1321-6287) **1856**
Benchmarking In Practice (USA) **1066**
Benchmarking Sci-Tech Development see Keji Fazhan Biaogan **7875**
• Benchmarks (USA ISSN 1066-0380) **2408**
Benchmarks (Manhasset) see C R N **2510**
Benchmarks (Year) (Brisbane Office Buildings Edition) see Benchmarks (Year) (Sydney Office Buildings Edition) **7617**
Benchmarks (Year) (Canberra Office Buildings Edition) see Benchmarks (Year) (Sydney Office Buildings Edition) **7617**
Benchmarks (Year) (Melbourne Office Buildings Edition) see Benchmarks (Year) (Sydney Office Buildings Edition) **7617**
Benchmarks (Year) (New South Wales Shopping Centers Edition) (AUS) **7617**
Benchmarks (Year) (Perth Office Buildings Edition) see Benchmarks (Year) (Sydney Office Buildings Edition) **7617**
Benchmarks (Year) (Queensland Shopping Centers Edition) see Benchmarks (Year) (New South Wales Shopping Centers Edition) **7617**
Benchmarks (Year) (Sydney Office Buildings Edition) (AUS) **7617**
Benchmarks (Year) (Victoria Shopping Centers Edition) see Benchmarks (Year) (New South Wales Shopping Centers Edition) **7617**
Benchmarks (Year) (Western Australia Shopping Centers Edition) see Benchmarks (Year) (New South Wales Shopping Centers Edition) **7617**
Bend of the River (USA ISSN 1063-9241) **4285**
Bendel State Gazette (NGA) **7109**
Bendel State. Ministry of Information, Social Development and Sports. Estimate (NGA) **8027**
Bender's California Labor and Employment Bulletin see Bender's California Labor & Employment Bulletin **1667**
Bender's California Labor & Employment Bulletin (USA ISSN 1550-7610) **1667**
Bender's Dictionary of 1040 Deductions (USA ISSN 0270-5206) **4628**
• Bender's Federal Practice Forms (USA) **4628**
Bender's Federal Practice Manual (USA) **4628**
• Bender's Forms for the Civil Practice (USA) **4827**
• Bender's Forms for the Consolidated Laws of New York (USA) **4628**
• Bender's Forms of Discovery (USA) **4628**
• Bender's Forms of Pleading (USA) **4628**
Bender's Immigration and Nationality Act Service (USA) **7278**
Bender's Immigration Regulations Service (USA) **7278**
Bender's New York Evidence (USA) **4629**
Bendigo Advertiser (AUS) **3793**
Bendigo Magazine (AUS ISSN 1833-1289) **8686**
Bene (USA) **3522**
• Benedict on Admiralty (USA) **4969**
Benedict Tiger Newspaper (USA) **2274**
Benedictijns Tijdschrift (NLD ISSN 0005-8734) **7785**

Title

DIRECTORY 2010 BESCHICHTEN, BESCHICHTUNGSANLAGEN, OBERFLAECHENBEHANDLUNG 10031

Berita Ilmu Pengetahuan dan Teknologi (IDN ISSN 0125-9156) **7840**
• Berita M M A/Malaysian Medical Association Newsletter (MYS ISSN 0126-7140) **5584**
Berita Minggu (SGP) **3945**
Berita Negara (IDN) **3891**
Berita - Pusat Penelitian Perkebunan Gula Indonesia/Indonesian Sugar Research Center. News (IDN ISSN 0852-0321) **221**
Berita Selulosa (IDN ISSN 0005-9145) **3684**
Berita Shell (SGP ISSN 0005-9153) **6764**
Berkala Ilmu Kedokteran/Journal of the Medical Sciences (IDN ISSN 0126-1312) **5584**
Berkeley Business Law Journal (USA ISSN 1548-7067) **4857**
▼ Berkeley Dutch Studies (DEU ISSN 1865-8555) **5099**
Berkeley Electronic Press Journal in Theoretical Economics *see* The B E Journal in Theoretical Economics **1536**
Berkeley Electronic Press Journals in Economic Analysis & Policy *see* The B E Journals in Economic Analysis & Policy **1536**
Berkeley Electronic Press Journals in Macroeconomics *see* The B E Journals in Macroeconomics **1718**
Berkeley Insights in Linguistics and Semiotics (USA ISSN 0893-6935) **5099**
• Berkeley Journal of African-American Law & Policy (USA ISSN 1943-4278) **4629**
• Berkeley Journal of Criminal Law (USA ISSN 1934-9629) **4629**
• ➤ Berkeley Journal of Employment and Labor Law (USA ISSN 1067-7666) **1667**
• ➤ Berkeley Journal of Gender, Law & Justice (USA ISSN 1933-1045) **4629**
• ➤ Berkeley Journal of International Law (USA ISSN 1085-5718) **4918**
▼ Berkeley Journal of Middle Eastern and Islamic Law (USA ISSN 1941-4951) **4629**
Berkeley Journal of Sociology (USA ISSN 0067-5830) **8090**
• ➤ Berkeley La Raza Law Journal (USA ISSN 1544-9882) **4629**
• Berkeley Language Center Newsletter (USA ISSN 1941-3890) **5099**
• Berkeley Law and Economics Working Papers (Online Edition) (USA) **4629**
• Berkeley Law and Economics Working Papers (Print Edition) (USA) **4629**
Berkeley Linguistics Society. Proceedings of the Annual Meeting (USA ISSN 0363-2946) **5099**
Berkeley Monthly (USA ISSN 0191-7080) **5208**
Berkeley Papers in History of Science (USA ISSN 0145-0379) **7936**
➤ Berkeley Planning Journal (USA ISSN 1047-5192) **4404**
➤ The Berkeley Review of Books (USA) **7552**
Berkeley Roundtable on the International Economy Working Papers *see* B R I E Working Papers **1553**
• ➤ Berkeley Technology Law Journal (USA ISSN 1086-3818) **4629**
Berkeley Tri-City Post (USA) **3522**
Berklee Today (USA ISSN 1052-3839) **6549**
Berks, Bucks and Oxon Farmer (GBR ISSN 0954-9609) **95**
Berks Business to Business *see* Berks Business2Business **1728**
• Berks Business2Business (USA) **1728**
Berks County Genealogical Society. Journal (USA ISSN 1091-322X) **3760**
Berks County Law Journal (USA ISSN 8750-3379) **4946**
Berks County Living (USA ISSN 1528-9877) **5066**
Berks County Newcomer (USA ISSN 1542-9334) **5066**
Berkshire & Chilterns Life (GBR ISSN 1752-6930) **3861**
➤ Berkshire Archaeological Journal (GBR ISSN 0309-3093) **383**
▼ Berkshire Business Quarterly (USA ISSN 1940-1140) **1066**
Berkshire Home Style *see* Berkshire HomeStyle **5066**
Berkshire HomeStyle (USA) **5066**
Berkshire Living (USA ISSN 1553-5118) **5066**
Berkshire Living Magazine *see* Berkshire Living **5066**
Berkshire News, Chester White Journal, Poland China Advantage, Spotted News (USA ISSN 1087-643X) **280**
Berkshire News/Chester White Journal/Poland Chinaadvantage/Spotted News *see* Breeders Digest **281**
The Berkshire Savant (USA ISSN 1556-2468) **8686**
Berlage Cahiers (NLD) **435**
▼ Berlin (USA ISSN 1937-0407) **8686**
Berlin Berlitz Travel Guide *see* Berlitz Berlin Pocket Guide **8686**
• Berlin - Brandenburger Naturmagazin (DEU) **2604**
Berlin - Brandenburgische Handwerk (DEU ISSN 0939-4443) **1396**
Berlin - Brandenburgisches Sonntagsblatt Die Kirche (DEU) **7748**
† Berlin Forschung (DEU) **8935**
Berlin in Geschichte und Gegenwart (DEU ISSN 0175-8446) **4204**
Berlin Medical (DEU ISSN 1614-0990) **5584**
• Berlin Online (DEU) **3844**
Berlin Programm (DEU ISSN 0005-9250) **8686**
Berlin. Senatsverwaltung fuer Frauen, Jugend und Familie. Statistischer Dienst (DEU) **8081**
Berlin Studies on Southeast Asia *see* Berliner Suedostasien-Studien **545**
Berlin von Hinten (DEU) **4371**
Berliner Abhandlungen zum Presserecht (DEU ISSN 0409-1949) **4629**
Berliner Aerzte (DEU ISSN 0939-5784) **5584**
Berliner Aerzteblatt (DEU ISSN 0172-8490) **5584**
Berliner Anwaltsblatt (DEU ISSN 0930-3065) **4629**
Berliner Arbeiten zur Bibliothekswissenschaft (DEU ISSN 1439-6688) **4994**
Berliner Arbeiten zur Erziehungs- und Kulturwissenschaft (DEU ISSN 1616-8860) **330**
Berliner Archaeologische Forschungen (DEU ISSN 1611-3551) **383**
Berliner Ausgaben (DEU ISSN 0930-7583) **7840**
† Berliner Bank. Boersenbrief (DEU ISSN 0172-0236) **8935**
Berliner Behoerden Spiegel (DEU ISSN 1437-8353) **7488**
Berliner Beitraege zur Amerikanistik (DEU ISSN 0948-941X) **4285**
➤ Berliner Beitraege zur Archaeometrie (DEU ISSN 0344-5089) **383**
Berliner Beitraege zur Editionswissenschaft (DEU) **5262**
Berliner Beitraege zur Neueren Deutschen Literaturgeschichte (DEU ISSN 0721-2984) **5262**
Berliner Blaetter (DEU ISSN 1434-0542) **3615**
Berliner Debatte Initial (DEU ISSN 0863-4564) **5208**
• Berliner Dialog (DEU ISSN 0948-0390) **7625**
Berliner Flughaefen (DEU) **8539**
Berliner Gartenfreund (DEU ISSN 0174-3589) **3724**
Berliner Geographische Studien (DEU ISSN 0341-8537) **4000**
† Berliner Geowissenschaftliche Abhandlungen. Reihe A, Geologie und Palaeontologie (DEU ISSN 0172-8784) **8935**
† Berliner Geowissenschaftliche Abhandlungen. Reihe B, Geophysik (DEU ISSN 0722-687X) **8935**
† Berliner Geowissenschaftliche Abhandlungen. Reihe C, Kartographie (DEU ISSN 0722-6888) **8935**
Berliner Gesellschaft fuer Anthropologie, Ethnologie und Urgeschichte. Mitteilungen (DEU ISSN 0178-7896) **330**
Berliner Historische Studien (DEU ISSN 0720-6941) **4132**
Berliner Hochschulschriften zum Gewerblichen Rechtsschutz und Urheberrecht (DEU ISSN 0170-883X) **4857**
Berliner Islamstudien (DEU ISSN 0174-2477) **7709**
• ➤ Berliner Journal fuer Soziologie (DEU ISSN 0863-1808) **8090**
Berliner Juristische Abhandlungen (DEU ISSN 0523-0209) **4629**
Berliner Juristische Universitaetsschriften - Grundlagen des Rechts (DEU) **4629**
Berliner Juristische Universitaetsschriften - Oeffentliches Recht (DEU) **4629**
Berliner Juristische Universitaetsschriften - Strafrecht (DEU) **4629**
Berliner Juristische Universitaetsschriften - Zivilrecht (DEU) **4629**
Berliner Kommentar zum Grundgesetz (DEU) **4629**
Berliner Kommentar zum Insolvenzrecht *see* Insolvenzrecht **4871**
Berliner Kulturanalysen (DEU ISSN 1863-4346) **7950**
Berliner Kurier (DEU ISSN 1437-3475) **3844**
Berliner Kurier am Sonntag (DEU) **3844**
Berliner Lehrerinnen Zeitung *see* B L Z **3017**
Berliner Merkur (DEU ISSN 0863-2952) **1066**
Berliner Morgenpost (DEU ISSN 0949-5126) **3844**
Berliner Naturschutzblaetter *see* Naturschutzblaetter **693**
Berliner Numismatische Forschungen (DEU ISSN 0233-0148) **6649**
Berliner Ornithologischer Bericht (DEU ISSN 0941-1828) **902**
Berliner Osteuropa Info (DEU ISSN 0945-4721) **7109**
Berliner Palaeobiologische Abhandlungen (DEU ISSN 1612-0361) **6723**
Berliner Philharmoniker (DEU) **6549**
Berliner Rechtsvorschriften (DEU) **4827**
Berliner Reihe (DEU ISSN 0943-9609) **4495**
Berliner Schriften zur Agrar- und Umweltsoekonomik (DEU) **194**
Berliner Schriften zur Anwendungsorientierten Bankbetriebslehre (DEU ISSN 1610-4935) **1321**
Berliner Schriften zur Museumskunde (DEU) **6521**
Berliner Schriftenreihe zum Steuer- und Wirtschaftsrecht (DEU ISSN 1619-8093) **1912**
Berliner Slawistische Arbeiten (DEU ISSN 1430-192X) **5099**
Berliner Sprachwissenschaftliche Studien (DEU) **5099**
Berliner Statistik. Statistische Monatsschrift (DEU ISSN 1437-4196) **7479**
Berliner Suedostasien-Studien/Berlin Studies on Southeast Asia (DEU ISSN 1619-7593) **545**
Berliner Theaterwissenschaft (DEU) **8466**
Berliner Theologische Zeitschrift (DEU ISSN 0724-6137) **7748**
Berliner Tierfreund (DEU ISSN 0936-3815) **318**
Berliner Tierpark-Buch (DEU ISSN 0067-6098) **936**
Der Berliner Tischlermeister (DEU) **1049**
Berliner Turfantexte (BEL ISSN 0138-4228) **545**
Berliner Type (DEU) **21**
• ➤ Berliner und Muenchener Tieraerztliche Wochenschrift (DEU ISSN 0005-9366) **8794**
Berliner Verkehrsblaetter (DEU ISSN 0722-9399) **8491**
Die Berliner Wirtschaft (DEU ISSN 0405-5756) **1396**
Berliner Wissenschaftliche Gesellschaft. Jahrbuch (DEU ISSN 0171-3302) **7840**
Berliner Woche (DEU) **3845**
Berliner Zeitung (DEU ISSN 0947-174X) **3845**
Berliner Zeitung am Sonntag *see* B Z am Sonntag **3844**
Berlinfoerderungsgesetz (DEU ISSN 0933-4343) **7488**
Berlingske Nyhedsmagasin (DNK ISSN 1604-2603) **1066**
• Berlingske Tidende (DNK ISSN 0106-4223) **3833**
Berlingske Tidendes Nyhedsmagasin *see* Berlingske Nyhedsmagasin **1066**
Berlinische Reminiszenzen (DEU ISSN 0067-611X) **4204**
Berlins Universelles Studentenmagazin *see* B U S **2273**
Berlinskaya Gazeta (DEU) **3845**
Berlitz Australia Pocket Guide (USA) **8686**
Berlitz Berlin Pocket Guide (USA) **8686**
Berlitz California Pocket Guide (USA) **8686**
Berlitz Canada Pocket Guide (USA) **8686**
Berlitz Costa Rica Pocket Guide (USA ISSN 1527-8824) **8686**
Berlitz France *see* Berlitz France Pocket Guide **8686**
Berlitz France Pocket Guide (USA ISSN 1528-2937) **8686**
Berlitz Greek Islands of the Aegean Pocket Guide (USA ISSN 1527-8751) **8686**
Berlitz Hawaii Pocket Guide (USA ISSN 1528-2988) **8686**
Berlitz Ireland Pocket Guide (USA) **8686**
Berlitz Italy Pocket Guide (USA) **8686**
Berlitz London *see* Berlitz London Pocket Guide **8686**
Berlitz London Pocket Guide (USA ISSN 1528-493X) **8686**
Berlitz Mexico Pocket Guide (USA) **8686**
Berlitz Munich Pocket Guide (USA ISSN 1527-8794) **8686**
Berlitz New York Pocket Guide (USA ISSN 1528-4956) **8687**
Berlitz Portugal Pocket Guide (USA ISSN 1528-459X) **8687**
Berlitz San Francisco Pocket Guide (USA) **8687**
Berlitz Southern Caribbean *see* Berlitz Southern Caribbean Pocket Guide **8687**
Berlitz Southern Caribbean Pocket Guide (USA ISSN 1528-7831) **8687**
Berlitz Spain Pocket Guide (USA ISSN 1528-4913) **8687**
Berlitz Turkey Pocket Guide (USA ISSN 1528-4921) **8687**
Berliz California *see* Berlitz California Pocket Guide **8686**
Bermuda (BMU) **8687**
Bermuda (Year) (USA ISSN 1055-5684) **8687**
Bermuda Biological Station for Research. Annual Report (BMU) **3406**
Bermuda. Biological Station for Research. Special Publications (BMU) **3406**
Bermuda. Department of Agriculture and Fisheries. Monthly Bulletin (BMU) **95**
Bermuda. Department of Agriculture and Fisheries. Report for the Year (BMU) **95**
➤ Bermuda Journal of Archaeology and Maritime History (BMU ISSN 1013-431X) **383**
Bermuda Monetary Authority. Reports & Accounts (BMU) **1321**
Bermuda National Bibliography (BMU ISSN 0255-0067) **616**
Bermuda Post (USA ISSN 1046-2813) **6892**
• The Bermuda Sun (BMU) **3802**
The Bermudian (BMU ISSN 0005-9382) **3802**
Bermudian Business (BMU) **1066**
Bern Events/Semaine a Berne/This Week in Berne (CHE ISSN 1661-3856) **8687**
Bern Porter International (USA) **5262**
Bern Universitaet. Seminar fuer Klassische Archaeologie. Hefte (CHE ISSN 0259-7764) **383**
Bern Universitaet. Seminar fuer Klassische Archeologie. Beiheft (CHE ISSN 1422-3694) **383**
• Bernard & Audre Rapoport Foundation. Annual Report (USA ISSN 1933-4915) **8027**
• Bernard Sands Retail Performance Monitor (USA ISSN 1946-4495) **1807**
Bernards and Babani Press Radio & Electronics & Computer Books (GBR) **2357**
Berner Baer (CHE ISSN 1661-4623) **3957**
Berner Beitraege zur Nationaloekonomie (CHE ISSN 0067-6128) **1066**
Berner Boersenverein. Jahresbericht (CHE) **1612**
• Berner Briefmarken-Zeitung/Journal Philatelique de Berne (CHE ISSN 0005-9404) **6892**
Berner Hauseigentuemer (CHE) **7583**
Berner Kunstmitteilungen (CHE ISSN 1010-559X) **478**
Berner Veroeffentlichungen zur Musikforschung (CHE ISSN 1661-4283) **6549**
Berner Wald (CHE) **3684**
Berner Zeitschrift fuer Geschichte und Heimatkunde (CHE ISSN 0005-9420) **4204**
† ➤ Bernhard-Harms-Vorlesungen (DEU) **8935**
Bernice Pauahi Bishop Museum, Honolulu. Special Publications (USA ISSN 0067-6179) **7840**
Bernische Staatspersonal Zeitung (CHE) **7488**
• ➤ Bernoulli (NLD ISSN 1350-7265) **5475**
Bernoulli Aerodynamics International (GBR ISSN 1751-2670) **8569**
• Bernoulli News (NLD ISSN 1360-6727) **5475**
• Bernstein on Stock (USA) **1066**
▼ • Beroep: Docent (NLD ISSN 1875-2004) **2830**
Beroepsfederatie der Voortbrengers en Verdelers van Elektriciteit in Belgie. Jaarverslag (BEL ISSN 0773-1442) **3155**
Beroepsfederatie der Voortbrengers en Verdelers van Elektriciteit in Belgie. Statistisch Jaarboek (Year) *see* Beroepsfederatie van de Elektriciteitssector in Belgie. Statistisch Jaarboek (Year) **3151**
Beroepsfederatie van de Elektriciteitssector in Belgie. Statistisch Jaarboek (Year) (BEL) **3151**
Beroepsleven *see* Vie Professionnelle **3676**
Beroepsonderwijs en Volwasseneneducatie Almanak *see* B V E-Almanak **2939**
Berry Production Guide for Commercial Growers *see* British Columbia. Ministry of Agriculture Fisheries and Food. Berry Production Guide for Commercial Growers **222**
Berry Yearbook and Buyer's Guide (GBR ISSN 1747-6674) **221**
Bert Dohmen's Wellington Letter (USA) **1612**
† • Bert Sugar's Fight Game (USA ISSN 0732-5630) **8935**
† Bertelsmann Briefe (DEU ISSN 0005-9455) **8935**
Bertelsmann Lexikothek Plus (DEU) **7840**
The Bertrand Russell Research Centre Newsletter (USA) **6907**
Bertrand Russell Society Quarterly (USA ISSN 1547-0334) **6907**
Bertrand Vacances (FRA ISSN 1246-225X) **7583**
Beruf und Gesinnung (AUT ISSN 0005-9471) **2830**
Berufliche Rehabilitation (DEU ISSN 0931-8895) **6693**
Berufs- und Karriere-Planer. I T und E-Business (DEU) **6693**
Berufs- und Karriere-Planer. Technik (DEU) **6693**
Berufs- und Karriere-Planer. Wirtschaft (DEU) **6693**
• Berufs- und Wirtschaftspaedagogik Online (DEU ISSN 1618-8543) **1066**
Berufsakademie Baden-Wuerttemberg. Fachrichtung Versicherung. Veroeffentlichungen (DEU ISSN 1619-8883) **4495**
Berufsakademie Mannheim. Fachrichtung Versicherung. Veroeffentlichungen (DEU ISSN 0722-656X) **4495**
Berufsausbildung Jugendarbeitslosigkeit (DEU) **8027**
Die Berufsbildende Schule (DEU ISSN 0005-951X) **2939**
Berufsbilder (CHE) **6693**
Berufsbildung (DEU ISSN 0005-9536) **2830**
Berufsbildung im Oeffentlichen Dienst (DEU ISSN 0933-4505) **6693**
Berufsbildung in Wissenschaft und Praxis (DEU ISSN 0341-4515) **6693**
Berufsbildungsbericht (DEU ISSN 0344-578X) **7840**
Berufsbildungsbrief (DEU) **1396**
Berufsbildungsgesetz (DEU) **4858**
Berufsfoerderungszentrum Essen e.V. Info *see* B F Z - Info **8934**
Berufsgenossenschaft fuer Gesundheitsdienst und Wohlfahrtspflege Jahresbericht *see* B G W Jahresbericht **6674**
Berufsgenossenschaft fuer Gesundheitsdienst und Wohlfahrtspflege. Mitteilungen (DEU ISSN 1435-8492) **4495**
Berufsgenossenschaftliches Institut fuer Arbeitssicherheit Handbuch *see* B G I A Handbuch **6674**
Berufskraftfahrer Zeitung (DEU ISSN 0949-1740) **8669**
Berufskrankheitenverordnung (DEU ISSN 0933-4289) **6674**
Berufsplanung fuer den I T Nachwuchs (DEU) **6693**
Berufsplanung fuer den Management Nachwuchs (DEU) **6693**
Berufsplanung fuer Ingenieure (DEU) **6693**
Berufsstart Technik (DEU) **6693**
Berufsstart Wirtschaft (DEU) **6693**
Berufsverband der Verkaufsfoerderer und Trainer e.V. Journal *see* B D V T Journal **1727**
Berufsverband Deutscher Internisten Aktuell *see* B D I Aktuell **5944**
Berufsverband Deutscher Rheumatologen. Mitteilungen (DEU ISSN 0340-0719) **6222**
Berufswahl und Ausbildung (CHE) **6693**
Berwick Advertiser (GBR) **3861**
➤ Berytus Archeological Studies (LBN ISSN 0067-6195) **383**
Berza (Belgrade) (SRB ISSN 0354-1975) **1612**
Berzsenyi Daniel Megyei Konyvtar. Evkonyve (HUN ISSN 0563-0819) **4994**
Beschaeftigung in Europa *see* Employment in Europe **1678**
Beschaffung Aktuell (DEU ISSN 0341-4507) **1807**
Beschaffung Special (DEU) **1807**
Beschaffungs-Markt (DEU) **1807**
Beschaffungsdienst Galabau (DEU ISSN 0943-4275) **3724**
Beschaffungsmanagement (CHE) **1807**
Beschichten, Beschichtungsanlagen, Oberflaechenbehandlung *see* Informationsdienst F I Z Technik. Beschichten, Beschichtungsanlagen, Oberflaechenbehandlung **3230**

Title

Title

10034 BEZOPASNOST' INFORMATSIONNYKH TEKHNOLOGII ULRICH'S PERIODICALS

Bezopasnost' Informatsionnykh Tekhnologii (RUS) **8417**
➤ Bezopasnost' Truda v Promyshlennosti/Labour Safety in Industry (RUS ISSN 0409-2961) **6674**
Bezpecna Pocitacova Sit (CZE ISSN 1801-8033) **2511**
• Bezpecna Praca (SVK ISSN 0322-8347) **6674**
Bezpecnost a Hygiena Prace/Safety and Hygiene of Work (CZE ISSN 0006-0453) **6674**
Bezpecnost a Ochrana Zdravi pri Praci a Pozarni Ochrana Aktualne *see* B O Z P & P O Aktualne **6674**
Bezpieczenstwo Jadrowe i Ochrona Radiologiczna (POL ISSN 0867-4752) **7509**
➤ Bezpieczenstwo Pracy (POL ISSN 0137-7043) **6674**
Bezpieczna Zywnosc (POL ISSN 1426-7918) **7509**
BFuP *see* B F u P - Betriebswirtschaftliche Forschung und Praxis **1727**
BG News *see* B G News **2273**
BgNS Transactions *see* B A D. Dokladi **3165**
Bhabha Atomic Research Centre. Nuclear Physics Division. Annual Report (IND) **7065**
Bhagawan Mahaveer International Management Review (IND) **1728**
Bhagirath (IND ISSN 0006-0461) **8818**
➤ Bhandarkar Oriental Research Institute. Annals (IND ISSN 0378-1143) **545**
Bharat Desh Hamara (IND) **3879**
• Bharat Dharsha (NZL) **5262**
Bharat Heavy Electricals Ltd. Journal *see* B H E L Journal **3296**
Bharat Janani (IND) **3879**
Bharat Times (CAN ISSN 1715-717X) **3806**
Bharatha Darshana (IND ISSN 0006-0496) **6907**
Bharati Te Videshi Sahita (IND ISSN 0006-050X) **5262**
Bharatiya Aadhunik Shiksha *see* Journal of Indian Education **2876**
Bharatiya Purabhilekha Patrika *see* Studies in Indian Epigraphy **5182**
Bharatiya Samajik Chintan (IND) **7950**
Bharatiya Sthalanama Patrika *see* Studies in Indian Place Names **5182**
Bharatiya Sugar (IND ISSN 0970-6240) **221**
Bharatjan (IND) **3879**
Bharatya Vidya (IND ISSN 0378-1984) **7733**
Bhartiya Krishi Anusandhan Patrika (IND ISSN 0303-3821) **936**
Bhashaposhini (IND) **5208**
Bhau Vishnu Ashetar Vedic Research Series (IND) **7707**
• Bhavan Australia (AUS) **7707**
Bhavan's Journal (IND ISSN 0006-0518) **5262**
Bhavan's News Australia *see* Bhavan Australia **7707**
Bhoomi Daily (IND) **3879**
Bhor (IND) **3879**
Bhratach Albanach *see* The Scottish Banner **3563**
Bhugola Samayiki (BGD) **4000**
Bhushan's World Trade Enquiries (IND ISSN 0006-0542) **1553**
BI Journal *see* Business Integration Journal **1073**
Bi-Lifestyles (USA) **6287**
• BI.research (DEU ISSN 1863-8775) **7840**
Bia *see* B I A **434**
Biaf/Israel Aviation and Space Magazine (ISR ISSN 0302-8194) **49**
Bialostockie Archiwum Jezykowe (POL ISSN 1641-6961) **5099**
Bialostockie Towarzystwo Naukowe. Prace (POL ISSN 0067-6470) **4204**
Bialy Orzel (Florida Edition) (USA ISSN 1556-2395) **3522**
Bialy Orzel (New England Edition) *see* Bialy Orzel (Florida Edition) **3522**
Bianca (DEU ISSN 0949-5835) **5409**
Bianca (HUN ISSN 0866-0867) **5409**
† Bianca Arztroman (DEU ISSN 1439-9512) **8935**
Bianca Exklusiv (DEU ISSN 0949-5851) **5409**
Bianca Hochzeitsband *see* Julia Hochzeitsband **5410**
Bianco & Nero (ITA ISSN 0394-008X) **6490**
Bianco Nero (ITA) **281**
I Biancospini (ITA ISSN 1970-6324) **4444**
• ➤ Bianji Xuebao/Acta Editologica (CHN ISSN 1001-4314) **7552**
• Bianji Xuekan/Editors Bimonthly (CHN ISSN 1007-3884) **7552**
• Bianji zhi You/Editors' Friend (CHN ISSN 1003-6687) **7552**
• Bianjiang Jingji yu Wenhua/The Border Economy and Culture (CHN ISSN 1672-5409) **1067**
• Bianjiang Wenxue/Frontier Literature (CHN ISSN 1007-4155) **5262**
Bianliu Jishu yu Dianli Qianyin/Converter Technology & Electric Traction (CHN ISSN 1671-8410) **7051**
• ➤ Bianyaqi/Transformer (CHN ISSN 1001-8425) **3296**
• Biaoji Mianyi Fenxi yu Linchuang/Labeled Immunoassays and Clinical Medicine (CHN ISSN 1006-1703) **5755**
• Biaomian Gongcheng Zixun/Information of Surface Engineering (CHN ISSN 1672-3732) **3183**
Biaoti suoyin dahui huiyi jilu, Lianheguo *see* United Nations. General Assembly. Index to Proceedings **7201**
Biarozka (BLR ISSN 0320-7579) **4444**
▼ • Biawak (USA ISSN 1936-296X) **936**
Biba (FRA ISSN 0221-7996) **2251**
La Bibbia dei Codici (ITA ISSN 1826-5529) **2474**
Bibbia e Oriente (ITA ISSN 0006-0585) **7625**
Bibdoc (FRA ISSN 1777-8190) **4994**
Bibel Aktuell (CHE ISSN 1660-2641) **7625**
Bibel Heute (DEU ISSN 0006-0593) **7785**
Bibel im Jahr (DEU) **7625**
Bibel og Historie (DNK ISSN 0900-6915) **7625**
Bibel und Gemeinde (DEU ISSN 0006-0615) **7748**
Bibel und Kirche (DEU ISSN 0006-0623) **7785**
Bibel und Liturgie (AUT ISSN 0006-064X) **7625**
Bibellektionen (USA) **7625**
Bibellese Plan (DEU) **7785**
Bibellesebuch Mittendrin (DEU ISSN 1611-8367) **7748**
Bibelreport (DEU ISSN 0933-9949) **7625**
Bibesco (PRI ISSN 1544-9785) **4994**
Bibi (USA) **5556**
Bibi Blocksberg (DEU) **2179**
Bibi Magazine (USA) **3522**
Bibi und Tina (DEU) **2179**
Bibiliotheque Centrale Commission Europeenne. Rapport d'activite *see* Central Library European Commission. Activity Report **5001**
† • Bibione Vacanze (ITA) **8935**
Bible Advocate (USA ISSN 0746-0104) **7625**
• ➤ The Bible and Critical Theory (AUS ISSN 1832-3391) **7625**
Bible and Spade (USA ISSN 1079-6959) **383**
La Bible Aujourd'hui *see* Bibel Aktuell **7625**
Bible Discovery (USA ISSN 0899-7055) **7748**
Bible Exploration Material and Annual Project (GBR) **7625**
Bible Express (USA ISSN 1068-2775) **7748**
Bible Friend (USA ISSN 0006-0739) **7625**
The Bible in Ancient Christianity (NLD ISSN 1542-1295) **7625**
Bible-in-Life Friends (USA ISSN 0278-0259) **7625**
▼ Bible in Technology (USA ISSN 1943-9369) **7625**
The Bible in the World (GBR ISSN 0409-3151) **7625**
Bible Lands (GBR ISSN 0006-0763) **7748**
Bible Lessons *see* Bibellektionen **7625**
Bible Light Newsletter (USA ISSN 1945-5208) **7625**
Bible Light on the News (USA ISSN 1946-4207) **7625**
• Bible Magazine Internet Edition (CAN) **7625**
Bible Researcher (SWE ISSN 0347-2787) **7625**
Bible Standard (USA ISSN 1556-8555) **7625**
Bible Standard and Herald of Christ's Kingdom *see* Bible Standard **7625**
Bible Studies for Life: Access Leader Guide *see* Access Leader Guide **7619**
Bible Studies for Life: Access Leader Pack *see* Access Leader Pack **7620**
Bible Studies for Life: Advanced Bible Study Commentary *see* Advanced Bible Study. Commentary **7744**
Bible Studies for Life: Advanced Bible Study Commentary *see* Bible Studies for Life: Holman Christian Standard Bible Advanced Bible Study Commentary **7625**
Bible Studies for Life: Holman Christian Standard Bible Advanced Bible Study Commentary (USA ISSN 1557-4334) **7625**
Bible Studies for Life: Leader Quicksource (USA ISSN 1557-4350) **7748**
Bible Studies for Life: Life Answers Leader Guide *see* Bible Studies for Life: Lifematters **7626**
Bible Studies for Life: Life Focus All Youth Learner Guide Holman C S B (Christian Standard Bible) (USA ISSN 1557-4725) **7625**
Bible Studies for Life: Life Focus All Youth Learner Guide K J V (King James Version) (USA ISSN 1557-4717) **7625**
Bible Studies for Life: Life Lessons Learner Guide (USA ISSN 1557-4741) **7625**
Bible Studies for Life: Life/LifeF X Younger and Older Youth Leader Guide (USA ISSN 1557-5020) **7748**
Bible Studies for Life: Life Truths Leader Guide (USA ISSN 1557-475X) **7625**
Bible Studies for Life: Life Ventures Leader Guide (USA ISSN 1557-492X) **7748**
Bible Studies for Life. Life Ventures Leader Pack *see* Bible Studies for Life: LifeFX Older Youth Leader Pack **7626**
Bible Studies for Life: Life Ventures Learner Guide (USA ISSN 1557-4776) **7748**
Bible Studies for Life: Life Words K J V Leader Guide (King James Version) (USA ISSN 1557-4954) **7625**
Bible Studies for Life: Life Words K J V Leader Pack (King James Version) (USA ISSN 1557-4148) **7625**
Bible Studies for Life: Life2 Younger Youth Leader Pack (USA ISSN 1557-3850) **7625**
Bible Studies for Life: LifeFX Older Youth Leader Pack (USA ISSN 1557-3842) **7626**
Bible Studies for Life: LifeFX Older Youth Learner (USA ISSN 1557-4938) **7626**
Bible Studies for Life: Lifematters (USA ISSN 1938-4971) **7626**
▼ Bible Studies for Life. Lifematters Leader Pack (USA ISSN 1938-7814) **7626**
Bible Studies for Life: Lifewords K J V Learner Guide Large Print *see* Life Words: K J V Leader Guide (Large Print Edition) **7764**
▼ Bible Study (USA ISSN 1945-0923) **7748**
Bible Study Magazine *see* Bible Study **7748**
Bible Study Monthly (GBR) **7626**
Bible Teacher and Leader (USA) **7626**
Bible Teaching for 1's & 2's. Leader Guide *see* Bible Teaching for Kids: 1s & 2s Leader Guide **7626**
Bible Teaching for 1's & 2's. Leader Pack *see* Bible Teaching for Kids: 1s & 2s Leader Pack **7626**
Bible Teaching for 3's-Pre-K. Leader Guide *see* Bible Teaching for Kids: 3s-Pre-K. Leader Guide **7626**
Bible Teaching for Babies. Leader Pack *see* Bible Teaching for Kids: Babies Leader Pack **7626**
Bible Teaching for Kids: (Broadly) Grades 1-3 & 4-6 Leader Pack *see* Bible Teaching for Kids: Grades 1-3 & 4-6 Leader Pack **7626**
Bible Teaching for Kids: 1s and 2s Leader Guide *see* Bible Teaching for Kids: 1s & 2s Leader Guide **7626**
Bible Teaching for Kids: 1s & 2s Leader Guide (USA ISSN 1559-2146) **7626**
Bible Teaching for Kids: 1s and 2s Leader Pack *see* Bible Teaching for Kids: 1s & 2s Leader Pack **7626**
Bible Teaching for Kids: 1s & 2s Leader Pack (USA ISSN 1559-2014) **7626**
Bible Teaching for Kids: 1st and 2nd Graders Leader Guide *see* Bible Teaching for Kids: 1st & 2nd Graders Leader Guide **7626**
Bible Teaching for Kids: 1st & 2nd Graders Leader Guide (USA ISSN 1557-4393) **7626**
Bible Teaching for Kids: 1st and 2nd Graders Leader Pack *see* Bible Teaching for Kids: 1st & 2nd Graders Leader Pack **7626**
Bible Teaching for Kids: 1st & 2nd Graders Leader Pack (USA ISSN 1557-3893) **7626**
Bible Teaching for Kids: 1st and 2nd Graders. Teaching Pictures (USA ISSN 1558-8270) **7626**
Bible Teaching for Kids: 3rd and 4th Graders' Leader Guide (USA ISSN 1557-4377) **7626**
Bible Teaching for Kids: 3rd and 4th Graders. Leader Pack (USA ISSN 1557-3915) **7626**
Bible Teaching for Kids: 3rd and 4th Graders' Learner Guide (USA ISSN 1557-4318) **7626**
Bible Teaching for Kids: 3rd & 4th Graders Teaching Pictures (USA ISSN 1558-8289) **7626**
Bible Teaching for Kids: 3rd avd 4th Graders Teaching Pictures *see* Bible Teaching for Kids: 3rd & 4th Graders Teaching Pictures **7626**
Bible Teaching for Kids: 3s-Pre-K. Leader Guide (USA ISSN 1559-2154) **7626**
• Bible Teaching for Kids: 3s-PreK Music & More Enhanced CD (Kindergarten) (USA ISSN 1557-4032) **7748**
Bible Teaching for Kids. B T X. A Bible Teaching Experience for Preteens. Leader Guide (USA ISSN 1936-8747) **7626**
Bible Teaching for Kids. B T X. A Bible Teaching Experience for Preteens. Leader Pack *see* Bible Teaching for Preteens. BTX. A Bible Teaching Experience for Preteens. Leader Pack **7626**
Bible Teaching for Kids. B T X. A Bible Teaching Experience for Preteens. Learner Guide (USA ISSN 1936-8410) **7626**
Bible Teaching for Kids: B T X Preteen Leader Guide *see* Bible Teaching for Kids. B T X. A Bible Teaching Experience for Preteens. Leader Guide **7626**
Bible Teaching for Kids: B T X Preteen Learner Guide *see* Bible Teaching for Kids. B T X. A Bible Teaching Experience for Preteens. Learner Guide **7626**
Bible Teaching for Kids: Babies, 1s and 2s Music and More Enhanced CD *see* Bible Teaching for Kids: Babies, 1s & 2s Music & More Enhanced CD **7748**
• Bible Teaching for Kids: Babies, 1s & 2s Music & More Enhanced CD (USA ISSN 1557-4040) **7748**
Bible Teaching for Kids: Babies Leader Pack (USA ISSN 1559-1999) **7626**
Bible Teaching for Kids: BTX. Teaching Pictures. A Bible Teaching Experience for Preteens *see* Bible Teaching for Preteens. BTX. A Bible Teaching Experience for Preteens. Teaching Pictures **7627**
Bible Teaching for Kids: First & Second Graders Leader Guide *see* Bible Teaching for Kids: 1st & 2nd Graders Leader Guide **7626**
Bible Teaching for Kids: First & Second Graders Leader Pack *see* Bible Teaching for Kids: 1st & 2nd Graders Leader Pack **7626**
Bible Teaching for Kids: First and Second Graders. Teaching Pictures *see* Bible Teaching for Kids: 1st and 2nd Graders. Teaching Pictures **7626**
Bible Teaching for Kids: Grades 1-3 & 4-6 Leader Guide (USA ISSN 1557-444X) **7626**
Bible Teaching for Kids: Grades 1-3 & 4-6 Leader Pack (USA ISSN 1557-3931) **7626**
Bible Teaching for Kids: Grades One-Three & Four-Six Leader Guide *see* Bible Teaching for Kids: Grades 1-3 & 4-6 Leader Guide **7626**
Bible Teaching for Kids: Grades One-Three & Four-Six Leader Pack *see* Bible Teaching for Kids: Grades 1-3 & 4-6 Leader Pack **7626**
Bible Teaching for Kids: Kindergarten Connection Learner Guide (USA ISSN 1557-4490) **7626**
Bible Teaching for Kids: Kindergarten Leader Pack (USA ISSN 1559-2022) **7626**
Bible Teaching for Kids: Kindergarten Music and More Enhanced CD *see* Bible Teaching for Kids: Kindergarten Music & More Enhanced CD **7748**
• Bible Teaching for Kids: Kindergarten Music & More Enhanced CD (USA ISSN 1557-4059) **7748**
Bible Teaching for Kids: Ones & Twoes Leader Guide *see* Bible Teaching for Kids: 1s & 2s Leader Guide **7626**
Bible Teaching for Kids: Ones & Twoes Leader Pack *see* Bible Teaching for Kids: 1s & 2s Leader Pack **7626**
Bible Teaching for Kids: Preteen Leader Guide *see* Bible Teaching for Kids. B T X. A Bible Teaching Experience for Preteens. Leader Guide **7626**
Bible Teaching for Kids: Preteen Learner Guide *see* Bible Teaching for Kids. B T X. A Bible Teaching Experience for Preteens. Learner Guide **7626**
Bible Teaching for Kids: Preteens. Leader Pack *see* Bible Teaching for Preteens. BTX. A Bible Teaching Experience for Preteens. Leader Pack **7626**
Bible Teaching for Kids: Preteens. Teaching Pictures *see* Bible Teaching for Preteens. BTX. A Bible Teaching Experience for Preteens. Teaching Pictures **7627**
▼ Bible Teaching for Kids: Special Buddies Grades 1-6. Leader Guide (USA ISSN 1935-6242) **7626**
▼ Bible Teaching for Kids: Special Buddies Grades 1-6. Learner Guide (USA ISSN 1935-6250) **7626**
Bible Teaching for Kids: Special Buddies Grades One-Six. Leader Guide *see* Bible Teaching for Kids: Special Buddies Grades 1-6. Leader Guide **7626**
Bible Teaching for Kids: Special Buddies Grades One-Six. Learner Guide *see* Bible Teaching for Kids: Special Buddies Grades 1-6. Learner Guide **7626**
Bible Teaching for Kids: Third and Fourth Graders' Leader Guide *see* Bible Teaching for Kids: 3rd and 4th Graders' Leader Guide **7626**
Bible Teaching for Kids. Third and Fourth Graders. Leader Pack *see* Bible Teaching for Kids: 3rd and 4th Graders. Leader Pack **7626**
Bible Teaching for Kids: Third and Fourth Graders' Learner Guide *see* Bible Teaching for Kids: 3rd and 4th Graders' Learner Guide **7626**
Bible Teaching for Kids: Third & Fourth Graders Teaching Pictures *see* Bible Teaching for Kids: 3rd & 4th Graders Teaching Pictures **7626**
Bible Teaching for Kids: Three's-PreK Leader Guide *see* Bible Teaching for Kids: 3s-Pre-K. Leader Guide **7626**
Bible Teaching for Kids: Threes-PreK Music & More Enhanced CD *see* Bible Teaching for Kids: 3s-PreK Music & More Enhanced CD **7748**
Bible Teaching for Kindergarten. Leader Guide *see* Family Bible Study: Bible Teaching for Kindergarten **7758**
Bible Teaching for Kindergarten. Leader Pack *see* Bible Teaching for Kids: Kindergarten Leader Pack **7626**
Bible Teaching for Preteens. BTX. A Bible Teaching Experience for Preteens. Leader Pack (USA ISSN 2150-7449) **7626**
Bible Teaching for Preteens. BTX. A Bible Teaching Experience for Preteens. Teaching Pictures (USA ISSN 2150-7457) **7627**
The Bible Today (USA ISSN 0006-0836) **7627**
Bible Translation Update (USA) **7627**
➤ Bible Translator. Practical Papers (GBR ISSN 0260-0943) **5099**
➤ Bible Translator. Technical Papers (GBR ISSN 0260-0935) **5099**
Biblebhashyam (IND ISSN 0970-2288) **7785**
Bibles for the World Report (USA) **7627**
Biblia (FRA ISSN 1630-4977) **7627**
Biblia (JPN ISSN 0006-0860) **5057**
Biblia Coptica (DEU) **7703**
Biblia - Gente (BRA) **7786**
† Biblia y Fe (ESP ISSN 0210-5209) **8935**
• Bibliana (DNK ISSN 1399-1361) **7627**
• Biblica (ITA ISSN 0006-0887) **7786**
Biblica et Orientalia (ITA) **7786**
• Biblical Archaeology Review (USA ISSN 0098-9444) **383**
Biblical Encyclopedia (NLD ISSN 1874-3927) **7627**
• The Biblical Evangelist (USA ISSN 0740-7998) **7748**
• Biblical Illustrator (USA ISSN 0195-1351) **7748**
• ➤ Biblical Interpretation (NLD ISSN 0927-2569) **7627**
➤ Biblical Interpretation Series (NLD ISSN 0928-0731) **7627**
▼ Biblical Intersections (USA ISSN 1943-9377) **7627**
Biblical Missions (USA ISSN 0006-0909) **7748**
Biblical Preaching Journal (USA ISSN 1043-5522) **7627**
Biblical Recorder (USA ISSN 0279-8182) **7748**
➤ Biblical Research (USA ISSN 0067-6535) **7627**
▼ Biblical Research Bulletin (USA ISSN 1938-694X) **384**
Biblical Scholarship in North America (USA ISSN 0277-0474) **7627**
Biblical Studies Bulletin (GBR ISSN 1365-6090) **7748**
Biblical Theology (IRL ISSN 0006-0917) **7627**
• ➤ Biblical Theology Bulletin (GBR ISSN 0146-1079) **7627**
Biblicum (SWE ISSN 0345-1453) **7627**
Biblija Danas (HRV ISSN 1331-5757) **7627**
Biblijske Lekcije (SRB) **7748**
Biblio 17 (DEU ISSN 1434-6397) **5262**
• Biblio 3W (ESP ISSN 1138-9796) **8019**
Biblio Country Reports *see* Biblio International (Online) **616**
• Biblio Europe (Online) (BEL) **4994**
Biblio Europe (Print) *see* Biblio Europe (Online) **4994**
Biblio-Flash (Online) (BEL) **616**
Biblio-Flash (Print) *see* Biblio-Flash (Online) **616**
• Biblio International (Online) (BEL) **616**

Biblio International (Print) *see* Biblio International (Online) **616**
Biblio Siebzehn *see* Biblio 17 **5262**
• Biblio Tech Review (GBR ISSN 1463-7146) **5060**
• Bibliodoc (ESP ISSN 1885-0685) **4994**
• BiblioFile (USA ISSN 0743-7935) **4994**
• La Bibliofilia (ITA ISSN 0006-0941) **7553**
Bibliografi Nasional Indonesia/Indonesian National Bibliography (IDN ISSN 0523-1639) **616**
† Bibliografi over Europaeiske Kunstneres Ex Libris/Europaeische Ex Libris/European Book Plates/Ex Libris d'Europe (DNK) **8935**
Bibliografia Analityczna Bibliotekoznawstwa i Informacji Naukowej (POL ISSN 0033-233X) **5057**
• Bibliografia Bibliografii Polskich/Bibliography of Polish Bibliographies (POL ISSN 0860-6579) **616**
Bibliografia Bibliotecologica Argentina (ARG ISSN 0067-656X) **5057**
• Bibliografia Brasileira de Odontologia (CD-ROM Edition) (BRA) **5741**
• Bibliografia Brasileira de Odontologia (Online Edition) (BRA) **5741**
Bibliografia Chilena (CHL ISSN 0716-176X) **616**
Bibliografia Cubana (CUB ISSN 0067-6705) **616**
Bibliografia de la Literatura Hispanica (ESP) **5406**
Bibliografia de Politica Industrial (BRA ISSN 0103-2038) **1214**
Bibliografia Dieciochista (ESP ISSN 1132-0427) **5406**
Bibliografia do Idoso (BRA) **4058**
† Bibliografia e Storia della Critica (ITA) **8936**
† Bibliografia e Storie del Libro e della Stampa. Monumenta (ITA ISSN 1970-5891) **8936**
† Bibliografia Espanola. Cartografia (ESP ISSN 1133-9519) **8936**
• Bibliografia Espanola de Revistas Cientificas de Ciencia y Tecnologia (ESP ISSN 1575-0183) **7936**
• Bibliografia Espanola de Revistas Cientificas de Ciencias Sociales y Humanidades/Spanish Bibliography of Scientific Journals in Social Sciences and Humanities (ESP ISSN 1575-0175) **8020**
Bibliografia Espanola. Monografias (ESP ISSN 1133-858X) **616**
† Bibliografia Espanola. Monografias. Indices Acumulativos (ESP ISSN 1133-8563) **8936**
† Bibliografia Espanola. Musica Impresa (ESP) **8936**
† Bibliografia Espanola. Publicaciones Periodicas (ESP ISSN 1134-6620) **8936**
† Bibliografia Filosofica Italiana (ITA ISSN 0409-3372) **8936**
Bibliografia Forestal de Venezuela (VEN) **3708**
• Bibliografia Generale della Lingua e della Letteratura Italiana (ITA ISSN 1122-2220) **616**
• Bibliografia Geografii Polskiej/Bibliography of Polish Geography (POL ISSN 0523-1787) **4035**
Bibliografia Geologica si Geofizica a Romaniei/Geological and Geophysical Bibliography of Romania (ROM ISSN 1221-4779) **2719**
Bibliografia Geologiczna Polski (POL ISSN 0373-1987) **2719**
Bibliografia Giuridica Svizzera *see* Schweizerische Rechtsbibliographie **4825**
Bibliografia Historica de Espana e Hispanoamerica *see* Indice Historico Espanol **4170**
Bibliografia Historii Polskiej (POL ISSN 0067-6721) **4169**
Bibliografia Internacional de Ciencias Historicas *see* International Bibliography of Historical Sciences **4170**
† Bibliografia Italiana di Storia della Scienza (ITA ISSN 1721-5757) **8936**
Bibliografia Kombetare e Librit qe Botohet ne Republiken e Shqiperise (ALB) **616**
Bibliografia Kombetare e Republikes se Shqiperise. Artikujt e Periodikut Shqiptar (ALB) **616**
• Bibliografia Latinoamericana (MEX ISSN 0185-2884) **617**
Bibliografia Mexicana (MEX ISSN 0006-1069) **617**
Bibliografia Missionaria (ITA ISSN 0394-9869) **7697**
† • Bibliografia Nacional Espanola (ESP ISSN 1136-9698) **8936**
• Bibliografia Nacional Portuguesa em CD-ROM (USA) **617**
Bibliografia Nationala Romana. Articole din Publicatii Periodice. Cultura (ROM ISSN 1454-7430) **617**
Bibliografia Nationala Romana. Carti. Albume. Harti (ROM ISSN 1221-9126) **617**
Bibliografia Nationala Romana. Documenta Romaniae (ROM ISSN 1583-3194) **617**
Bibliografia Nationala Romana. Note Muzicale. Discuri. Casete (ROM ISSN 1221-9134) **617**
Bibliografia Nationala Romana. Publicatii Seriale (ROM ISSN 1221-180X) **617**
Bibliografia Nationala Romana. Romanica *see* Bibliografia Nationala Romana. Documenta Romaniae **617**
Bibliografia Nationala Romana. Teze de Doctorat (ROM ISSN 1223-7485) **617**
Bibliografia Nazionale Italiana. Catalogo Alfabetico Annuale (ITA ISSN 1123-6205) **617**
• Bibliografia Nazionale Italiana. Monografie (ITA ISSN 1125-0879) **7577**
Bibliografia Pomorza Zachodniego. Pismiennictwo Polskie/Bibliography of West Pomerania. Polish Literature (POL ISSN 0409-3453) **5406**
Bibliografia Pomorza Zachodniego. Pismiennictwo Zagraniczne/Bibliography of West Pomerania. Foreign Literature (POL ISSN 0138-0702) **617**
• Bibliografia Publikacji Pracownikow Naukowych Akademii Ekonomicznej w Krakowie (Online Edition) (POL) **1214**
Bibliografia Publikacji Pracownikow Naukowych Akademii Ekonomicznej w Krakowie (Print Edition) *see* Bibliografia Publikacji Pracownikow Naukowych Akademii Ekonomicznej w Krakowie (Online Edition) **1214**
Bibliografia Seleccionada de Especies Forestal *see* Bibliografia Seleccionada de Especies y Topicos Forestales **3708**
Bibliografia Seleccionada de Especies y Topicos Forestales (VEN ISSN 0798-1937) **3708**
Bibliografia Slaska (POL ISSN 0523-1930) **617**
Bibliografia sobre la Economia Mexicana. Libros (MEX ISSN 0188-6673) **1214**
Bibliografia Storica Nazionale (ITA ISSN 0085-2317) **617**
Bibliografia Tematica sobre Judaismo Argentino (ARG) **7697**
• Bibliografia Venezolana (VEN ISSN 0798-0086) **4994**
• Bibliografia Wydawnictw Ciaglych/Bibliography of Polish Serials (POL ISSN 0239-4421) **617**
Bibliografia Wydawnictw Ciaglych Nowych, Zawieszonych i Zmieniajacych Tytul (POL ISSN 0239-5606) **617**
Bibliografia y Antologia Critica de las Vanguardias en el Mundo Iberico (DEU) **5406**
• Bibliografia Zawartosci Czasopism (POL ISSN 0006-1093) **617**
Bibliografias de Historia de Espana (ESP ISSN 1133-7001) **4169**
Bibliografica Folclorica (BRA ISSN 0104-060X) **3624**
Bibliografie Botaniczne/Botanical Bibliographies (POL ISSN 0860-4509) **713**
Bibliografie Ceske Lingvistiky/Bibliography of Czech Linguistics (CZE ISSN 0862-1462) **5200**
Bibliografie Ceske Onomastiky (CZE) **5200**
• Bibliografie Nederlandse Sociale Wetenschappen (Online Edition) (NLD) **8148**
Bibliografie Nederlandse Sociale Wetenschappen (Print Edition) *see* Bibliografie Nederlandse Sociale Wetenschappen (Online Edition) **8148**
Bibliografie van het Belgisch Sociaal Recht/Bibliographie du Droit Social Belge (BEL) **4821**
Bibliografija Jugoslavije. Knjige, Brosure i Muzikalije *see* Bibliografija Srbije. Monografske Publikacije **617**
Bibliografija Jugoslavije. Serijske Publikacije *see* Bibliografija Srbije. Serijske Publikacije **617**
Bibliografija Knjiga u Vojvodini (SRB ISSN 0354-6551) **617**
Bibliografija Nazzjonalita Malta *see* Malta National Bibliography **631**
Bibliografija Prevoda u S R J *see* Bibliografija Srbije. Monografske Publikacije. Prevodi **617**
Bibliografija Recenzija iz Domacih Listova i Casopisa (SRB ISSN 0351-6016) **617**
• Bibliografija Srbije. Monografske Publikacije (SRB ISSN 1451-5091) **617**
• Bibliografija Srbije. Monografske Publikacije. Prevodi/Bibliography of Serbia. Monographic Publications. Translations (SRB ISSN 1820-0087) **617**
• Bibliografija Srbije. Serijske Publikacije (SRB ISSN 1820-0052) **617**
• Bibliografija Srbije. Serijske Publikacije. Zvanicne Publikacije (SRB ISSN 1820-0060) **617**
Bibliografija Zvanicnih Publikacija S R J. Knjige, Serijske Publikacije *see* Bibliografija Srbije. Serijske Publikacije. Zvanicne Publikacije **617**
Bibliografijos Zinios. Knygos/Bibliographical News. Books (LTU ISSN 1392-1738) **617**
Bibliografijos Zinios. Lituanika/Bibliographical News. Lituanica (LTU ISSN 1392-1762) **618**
Bibliografijos Zinios. Serialiniai Leidiniai/ Bibliographical News. Serials (LTU ISSN 1392-1754) **618**
Bibliografijos Zinios. Straipsniai/Bibliographical News. Articles (LTU ISSN 1392-1746) **618**
Bibliografika *see* Vivliographika **5054**
Bibliografisch Repertorium van de Wijsbegeerte *see* Repertoire Bibliographique de la Philosophie **6963**
Bibliografisch Repertorium van de Wijsbegeerte *see* Revue Philosophique de Louvain **6949**
• Bibliografiya (RUS ISSN 0869-6020) **618**
Bibliografiya Izdanii Akademii Nauk *see* Rossiiskaya Akademiya Nauk. Bibliografiya Izdanii **634**
Bibliografiya Rossiiskoi Bibliografii (RUS ISSN 0204-3386) **618**
Bibliografski Vjesnik/Bibliographic Tribune (MNE ISSN 0409-3739) **4994**
Bibliographia Africana (IND ISSN 0006-1190) **618**
Bibliographia Asiatica (IND ISSN 0006-1212) **564**
Bibliographia Belgica (BEL ISSN 0409-3747) **618**
Bibliographia Cartographica (DEU ISSN 0340-0409) **4035**
Bibliographia de Interlingua (NLD ISSN 0920-7104) **5200**
Bibliographia Franciscana (ITA ISSN 1723-3585) **7698**
Bibliographia Historiae Rerum Rusticarum Internationalis/International Bibliography of Agricultural History (HUN) **176**
Bibliographia Humboldtiana (DEU ISSN 0933-131X) **4484**
Bibliographia Internationalis Spiritualitatis (VAT ISSN 0084-7836) **6962**
Bibliographia Medica Cechoslovaca (Print Edition) *see* BiblioMedica (CD-ROM Edition) **5741**
Bibliographia Mesostigmatologica *see* Acari Bibliographia Acarologica **649**
Bibliographia Oribatologica *see* Acari Bibliographia Acarologica **649**
Bibliographia Phytosociologica Syntaxonomica (DEU) **713**
Bibliographia Scientiae Naturalis Helvetica (CHE ISSN 0067-6829) **7936**
• Bibliographic Index (USA ISSN 0006-1255) **618**
Bibliographic Index Plus *see* Bibliographic Index **618**
Bibliographic Notebooks for Organometallic Chemistry *see* Cahiers Bibliographiques de Chimie Organometallique **2093**
Bibliographic Society of America. List of Members (USA ISSN 0737-0458) **618**
Bibliographic Tribune *see* Bibliografski Vjesnik **4994**
Bibliographica Carmelitana *see* Collectanea Bibliographica Carmelitana **7698**
Bibliographica et Fundamenta Romanica (DEU) **5099**
Bibliographica Judaica (USA ISSN 0067-6853) **7698**
Bibliographica Romanica *see* Bibliographica et Fundamenta Romanica **5099**
Bibliographical News. Articles *see* Bibliografijos Zinios. Straipsniai **618**
Bibliographical News. Books *see* Bibliografijos Zinios. Knygos **617**
Bibliographical News. Lituanica *see* Bibliografijos Zinios. Lituanika **618**
Bibliographical News. Serials *see* Bibliografijos Zinios. Serialiniai Leidiniai **618**
• ➤ Bibliographical Society of America. Papers (USA ISSN 0006-128X) **7553**
Bibliographical Society of Australia and New Zealand. Bulletin *see* Script & Print **7573**
• Bibliographical Society of Canada. Bulletin (CAN ISSN 0709-3756) **618**
• ➤ Bibliographical Society of Canada. Papers/Societe Bibliographique du Canada. Cahiers (CAN ISSN 0067-6896) **618**
Bibliographical Units of the Literary Museum *see* Petofi Irodalmi Muzeum Bibliografiai Fuzetei **633**
• Bibliographicas (ARG) **618**
Bibliographie Analytique de l'Afrique Antique (FRA) **4169**
Bibliographie Annuelle de l'Histoire de France (FRA ISSN 0067-6918) **4169**
Bibliographie Annuelle de Madagascar (MDG ISSN 0067-6926) **618**
Bibliographie Annuelle des Lettres Romandes (CHE ISSN 1012-1331) **618**
Bibliographie Annuelle du Moyen Age Tardif (BEL ISSN 0778-9777) **4169**
Bibliographie Courante de la Litterature Luxembourgeoise (LUX ISSN 1016-328X) **618**
• Bibliographie de Belgique/Belgische Bibliografie (BEL ISSN 0006-1336) **618**
Bibliographie de la C I I D. Irrigation, Drainage et Maitrise des Crues *see* Bibliography on Irrigation, Drainage, River Training and Flood Control **8843**
Bibliographie de la Cote d'Ivoire (CIV ISSN 0084-7860) **618**
Bibliographie de la Cour Internationale de Justice *see* Cour Internationale de Justice. Bibliographie **4821**
Bibliographie de la Litterature Francaise *see* Revue d'Histoire Litteraire de la France **5362**
• Bibliographie de la Philosophie/Bibliography of Philosophy (FRA ISSN 0006-1352) **6962**
Bibliographie de l'Afrique Sud-Saharienne (BEL ISSN 0773-3933) **8020**
Bibliographie de l'Algerie/Al-Bibliyugrafya al-Djazairiyah (DZA ISSN 0523-2392) **618**
Bibliographie de l'Histoire Bernoise *see* Bibliographie der Berner Geschichte **4169**
Bibliographie de l'Histoire Suisse *see* Bibliographie der Schweizergeschichte **618**
Bibliographie der Antiquariats-, Auktions- und Kunstkataloge (DEU) **529**
Bibliographie der Berner Geschichte/Bibliographie de l'Histoire Bernoise (CHE ISSN 0250-5665) **4169**
† Bibliographie der Buch- und Bibliotheksgeschichte (DEU ISSN 0723-3590) **8936**
Bibliographie der Deutschen Rechtsbibliographien (DEU) **4821**
• Bibliographie der Deutschen Sprach- und Literaturwissenschaft (DEU ISSN 0341-9363) **5406**
Bibliographie der Deutschsprachigen Frauenliteratur (DEU ISSN 0949-0124) **618**
Bibliographie der Franzoesischen Literaturwissenschaft (DEU ISSN 0523-2465) **5406**
Bibliographie der Schweizergeschichte/Bibliographie de l'Histoire Suisse (CHE ISSN 0378-4584) **618**
Bibliographie der Wirtschaftspresse (DEU ISSN 0006-1417) **1215**
Bibliographie der Wirtschaftswissenschaften (DEU ISSN 0340-6121) **618**
Bibliographie d'Histoire de l'Art *see* B H A Bibliography of the History of Art **529**
Bibliographie d'Histoire Luxembourgeoise (LUX ISSN 0067-7043) **4169**
Bibliographie du Droit Social Belge *see* Bibliografie van het Belgisch Sociaal Recht **4821**
Bibliographie du Quebec (CAN ISSN 0006-1441) **618**
Bibliographie du Senegal (SEN ISSN 0378-9942) **618**
Bibliographie Egyptologique Annuelle *see* Annual Egyptological Bibliography **4169**
Bibliographie en Langue Francaise d'Histoire du Droit de 987 a 1940 (FRA ISSN 0067-6985) **4821**
Bibliographie Europeenne des Travaux sur l'ex-URSS et l'Europe de l'Est *see* European Bibliography of Slavic and East European Slavonic Studies **4170**
• Bibliographie Geographique Internationale (Paris, 1996)/International Geographical Bibliography (FRA ISSN 1274-9249) **4035**
Bibliographie Geschichte der Technik (DEU ISSN 0323-4355) **8446**
† Bibliographie Informatik, Didaktik und Elementare Computeranwendungen fuer Schule, Hochschule und Weiterbildung (DEU ISSN 0935-8757) **8936**
Bibliographie Internationale de l'Humanisme et de la Renaissance (CHE ISSN 0067-7000) **4484**
Bibliographie Internationale de Science Politique *see* International Bibliography of Political Science **7200**
Bibliographie Internationale de Sciences Economiques *see* International Bibliography of the Social Sciences. Economics **1243**
Bibliographie Internationale de Sociologie *see* International Bibliography of the Social Sciences. Sociology **8149**
Bibliographie Internationale des Imprimes, Manuscrits et Enregistrements Musicaux *see* International Bibliography of Printed Music, Music Manuscripts and Recordings **6631**
Bibliographie Internationale des Sciences Historiques *see* International Bibliography of Historical Sciences **4170**
Bibliographie Internationale des Sciences Sociales *see* International Bibliography of the Social Sciences **8020**
Bibliographie Internationale d'Ethnologie *see* Internationale Volkskundliche Bibliographie **3624**
Bibliographie Internationale d'Histoire Militaire (NLD ISSN 0250-4308) **6413**
Bibliographie Juridique Suisse *see* Schweizerische Rechtsbibliographie **4825**
Bibliographie Juristischer Festschriften und Festschriftenbeitraege (DEU ISSN 0931-7686) **4821**
Bibliographie Linguistique *see* Linguistic Bibliography **5201**
Bibliographie Linguistischer Literatur/Bibliography of Linguistic Literature (DEU ISSN 0172-3960) **5406**
Bibliographie Luxembourgeoise (LUX ISSN 0253-1631) **618**
Bibliographie Moderner Fremdsprachenunterricht (DEU ISSN 0342-5576) **5100**
Bibliographie Nationale Francaise. Atlas, Cartes et Plans (Print Edition) *see* Bibliographie Nationale Francaise. Cartographie (Online Edition) **4035**
• Bibliographie Nationale Francaise. Cartographie (Online Edition) (FRA ISSN 1776-2634) **4035**
• Bibliographie Nationale Francaise. Livres (Online Edition) (FRA ISSN 1626-0104) **7577**
Bibliographie Nationale Francaise. Livres (Print Edition) *see* Bibliographie Nationale Francaise. Livres (Online Edition) **7577**
† • Bibliographie Nationale Francaise. Livres, Publications en Serie et Documents Electroniques (FRA ISSN 1626-0082) **8936**
• Bibliographie Nationale Francaise. Musique (Online Edition) (FRA ISSN 1765-288X) **6631**
Bibliographie Nationale Francaise. Musique (Print Edition) *see* Bibliographie Nationale Francaise. Musique (Online Edition) **6631**
• Bibliographie Nationale Francaise. Publications en Serie (FRA ISSN 1626-0112) **618**
Bibliographie Nationale Francaise. Publications en Serie (Print) *see* Bibliographie Nationale Francaise. Publications en Serie **618**
Bibliographie Papyrologique (BEL) **425**
• Bibliographie Prospective (FRA ISSN 0291-123X) **619**
Bibliographie Psychologischer Literatur aus den Deutschsprachigen Laendern (DEU ISSN 1436-2104) **7416**
Bibliographie zur Deutschsprachigen Schweizerliteratur (CHE ISSN 1420-3677) **5406**
Bibliographie zur Geschichte der Deutschen Arbeiterbewegung (DEU ISSN 0343-4117) **1215**
Bibliographie zur Geschichte Oberoesterreichs (AUT) **4204**
Bibliographie zur Geschichte und Kultur des Weines (DEU ISSN 1612-278X) **599**
Bibliographie zur Symbolik, Ikonographie und Mythologie (DEU ISSN 0067-706X) **361**
Bibliographie zur Zeitgeschichte (DEU ISSN 0523-2759) **4132**
† Bibliographien zur Deutschen Literatur des Mittelalters (DEU ISSN 0523-2767) **8936**
Bibliographien zur Geschichte des Parlamentarismus und der Politischen Parteien (DEU ISSN 0523-2775) **7198**
Bibliographien zur Geschichte und Landeskunde Ostmitteleuropas (DEU ISSN 0177-3631) **619**
Bibliographien zur Literatur- und Mediengeschichte (DEU ISSN 0940-8886) **5406**
Bibliographien zur Philosophie (DEU ISSN 0173-1831) **6907**

Title

▼ *new title* † *ceased* • *electronic media* ➤ *refereed*

Biblioteka Matematyczna (POL ISSN 0519-8356) **5475**
Biblioteka Matica Srpska. Godisnjak (SRB ISSN 0351-3580) **4995**
Biblioteka Matice Srpske. Bilten Prinovljenih Knjiga na Stranim Jezicima (SRB ISSN 0354-7655) **619**
Biblioteka Mechaniki Stosowanej (POL ISSN 0067-7701) **3342**
Biblioteka Narodowa. Biuletyn Informacyjny (POL ISSN 0006-3983) **4995**
• ➤ Biblioteka Narodowa. Rocznik/National Library Year-Book (POL ISSN 0083-7261) **4995**
Biblioteka Normatyvnykh Aktiv Ministerstv i Vidomstv Ukrainy (UKR) **4630**
Biblioteka Olsztynska *see* Osrodek Badan Naukowych im. Wojciecha Ketrzynskiego. Biblioteka Olsztynska **4251**
Biblioteka Pediatry (POL ISSN 0303-7827) **6089**
Biblioteka Polonijna/Polonia Library (POL ISSN 0138-094X) **7109**
Biblioteka Psychiatrii Polskiej (POL ISSN 1425-0640) **6126**
➤ Biblioteka Tradycji Literackich/Literary Tradition Collection (POL ISSN 1428-6998) **5263**
Biblioteka v Shkole (RUS) **4995**
Biblioteka w Szkole (POL ISSN 0867-5600) **4995**
Biblioteka Zakoni (BGR) **4846**
Bibliotekar/The Librarian (SRB ISSN 0006-1816) **4995**
Bibliotekarsamfundet Meddelar (Print) *see* Biblioteksbladet **4995**
➤ Bibliotekarstvo/Librarianship (BIH ISSN 0006-1832) **4995**
• Bibliotekarz (POL ISSN 0208-4333) **4995**
Bibliotekarz Zachodniopomorski/Librarian of West Pomerania (POL ISSN 0406-1578) **4995**
Bibliotekovedenie (RUS ISSN 0869-608X) **4995**
Bibliotekovedenie, Bibliografiya i Informatika (RUS) **4995**
Bibliotekovedenie i Bibliografiya za Rubezhom (RUS ISSN 0320-7838) **4995**
Biblioteksarbejde *see* Dansk Biblioteksforskning **5005**
Biblioteksbladet/Library Journal (SWE ISSN 1651-5447) **4995**
Bibliotekshistorie (DNK ISSN 0109-923X) **4996**
• Bibliotekspressen (DNK ISSN 1395-0401) **4996**
• Biblioteksskole Nyt (DNK ISSN 1395-9018) **4996**
• Biblioteksstyrelsen. Biblioteksaarbog (DNK ISSN 1601-6017) **4996**
Biblioteksvejviser/Guide to Danish Libraries (DNK ISSN 0420-1108) **4996**
Bibliotheca Academica. Reihe Kunst und Altertumswissenschaft (DEU ISSN 1612-6777) **478**
Bibliotheca Academica. Reihe Orientalistik (DEU ISSN 1866-5071) **545**
Bibliotheca Academica. Reihe Paedagogik (DEU ISSN 1866-5063) **2831**
Bibliotheca Academica. Reihe Soziologie (DEU ISSN 1866-5055) **8090**
Bibliotheca Aegyptiaca (BEL ISSN 0067-7817) **384**
Bibliotheca Afroasiatica (USA ISSN 0742-1117) **5100**
• Bibliotheca Alexandrina. Annual Report (Year) (EGY) **4996**
• Bibliotheca Alexandrina. Rapport Annuel (Year) (EGY) **4996**
Bibliotheca Archaeologica (ITA) **384**
† Bibliotheca Arnamagnaeana (DNK ISSN 0067-7841) **8936**
† Bibliotheca Arnamagnaeana. Supplementum (DNK ISSN 0067-785X) **8936**
Bibliotheca Ascetico-Mystica (ITA) **7698**
Bibliotheca Bibliographica Aureliana (DEU ISSN 0067-7884) **619**
Bibliotheca Bibliographica Neerlandica (NLD ISSN 1570-2162) **619**
Bibliotheca Bibliographica Neerlandica. Series Major (NLD ISSN 1574-2598) **619**
Bibliotheca Bodmeriana. Catalogues (CHE ISSN 1423-6559) **4169**
Bibliotheca Bodmeriana. Papyri (CHE ISSN 1423-6567) **4169**
Bibliotheca Bodmeriana. Textes (CHE ISSN 1423-6540) **4169**
Bibliotheca Botanica (DEU ISSN 0067-7892) **779**
Bibliotheca Diatomologica (DEU ISSN 1436-7270) **779**
➤ Bibliotheca Dissidentium (DEU ISSN 0931-3346) **619**
Bibliotheca Ephemeridum Theologicarum Lovaniensium (BEL) **7627**
Bibliotheca Franciscana Ascetica Medii Aevi (ITA) **7786**
Bibliotheca Germanica (DEU ISSN 0067-7477) **5100**
Bibliotheca Germanica. Series Nova (DEU ISSN 0939-544X) **5263**
Bibliotheca Helvetica Romana (CHE ISSN 0067-7965) **2231**
Bibliotheca Herpetologica (SWE ISSN 1653-3798) **936**
➤ Bibliotheca Hertziana. Roemisches Jahrbuch (DEU ISSN 0940-7855) **478**
Bibliotheca Hispano-Lusa (AUT ISSN 1019-1119) **5263**
Bibliotheca Historica (FIN ISSN 1238-3503) **4204**
Bibliotheca Historica Romaniae. Monographies (ROM ISSN 0067-799X) **4204**
Bibliotheca Historica Romaniae. Studies (ROM ISSN 0067-7981) **4205**
Bibliotheca Historico-Ecclesiastica Lundensis (SWE ISSN 0346-5438) **7748**
Bibliotheca Humanistica & Reformatorica (NLD ISSN 1567-8385) **7627**
Bibliotheca Humanistica Mexicana (MEX) **2231**
Bibliotheca Hungarica Antiqua (HUN ISSN 0067-8007) **7553**
Bibliotheca Ibero-Americana (DEU ISSN 0067-8015) **7199**
Bibliotheca Indonesica (NLD ISSN 0067-8023) **330**
Bibliotheca Instituti Historici Societatis Iesu (ITA) **7786**
Bibliotheca Iuridica Latina Mexicana (MEX) **4630**
Bibliotheca Latina Medii et Recentioris Aevi (POL ISSN 0067-8031) **2231**
Bibliotheca Latinitatis Novae (NLD ISSN 1873-1155) **2231**
Bibliotheca Lexicologiae Medii Aevi *see* Bibliography of Mediaeval Latin Lexicology **5200**
Bibliotheca Lichenologica (DEU ISSN 1436-1698) **779**
Bibliotheca Mercedaria (ITA ISSN 1971-3703) **7786**
Bibliotheca Mesopotamica (USA ISSN 0732-6440) **4320**
Bibliotheca Mycologica (DEU ISSN 0067-8066) **779**
▼ Bibliotheca Nisibinensis (USA ISSN 1946-2220) **5100**
Bibliotheca Nostratica (USA ISSN 0342-4871) **5100**
Bibliotheca Oeconomica (ROM ISSN 0067-8082) **1067**
• ➤ Bibliotheca Orientalis (NLD ISSN 0006-1913) **4169**
Bibliotheca Orientalis Hungarica (HUN ISSN 0067-8104) **545**
Bibliotheca Phycologica (DEU ISSN 0067-8112) **779**
Bibliotheca Psychiatrica *see* Key Issues in Mental Health **6157**
Bibliotheca Romanica (DEU ISSN 0067-7515) **5100**
• ➤ Bibliotheca Sacra (USA ISSN 0006-1921) **7748**
Bibliotheca Scriptorum Graecorum et Romanorum Mexicana (MEX) **2231**
Bibliotheca Scrptorum Latinorum (ITA ISSN 1970-772X) **2231**
Bibliotheca Seraphico-Capuccina. Sectio Historica (ITA ISSN 0067-8163) **7786**
Bibliotheca Victorina (BEL) **4205**
Bibliotheca Weidmanniana (DEU ISSN 0940-2136) **5263**
The Bibliotheck (GBR ISSN 0006-193X) **619**
Bibliotheek (NLD ISSN 1573-9597) **4996**
• ➤ Bibliotheek- & Archiefgids (BEL ISSN 0772-7003) **4996**
• Bibliotheek voor Hedendaagse Dokumentatie. Bulletin (BEL ISSN 0250-9725) **5060**
BibliotheekBlad *see* Bibliotheek **4996**
Bibliotheekspecial (NLD ISSN 1574-244X) **4996**
Bibliothek Compact (DEU) **4996**
Bibliothek der Erinnerung (DEU) **4205**
➤ Bibliothek der Griechischen Literatur (DEU ISSN 0340-7853) **2231**
Bibliothek der Klassischen Altertumswissenschaften. Neue Folge (DEU ISSN 0067-8201) **4133**
Bibliothek des Buchwesens (B B) (DEU ISSN 0340-8051) **4996**
Bibliothek des Deutschen Historischen Instituts in Rom (DEU ISSN 0070-4156) **4205**
Bibliothek des Literarischen Vereins in Stuttgart *see* Literarischer Verein in Stuttgart. Bibliothek **5323**
• Bibliothek Forschung und Praxis (DEU ISSN 0341-4183) **4996**
Bibliothek fuer Zeitgeschichte, Stuttgart. Schriften (DEU ISSN 0081-900X) **4133**
Bibliothek Information Technologie Online *see* B I T Online **5060**
Bibliothek Romanischer Sprachlehrwerke (DEU ISSN 0932-495X) **5100**
Bibliothek Seltener Texte (DEU) **619**
➤ Bibliothek und Wissenschaft (DEU ISSN 0067-8236) **4996**
BiblioTheke (DEU ISSN 1864-1725) **4996**
Bibliotheke tes en Athenais Archaiologikes Hetaireias/Archaeological Society at Athens Library (GRC ISSN 1105-7785) **384**
Bibliotheken der Bundesrepublik Deutschland. Datierte Handschriften (DEU ISSN 0175-6796) **4996**
Bibliotheks-Kalender *see* Bibliothek Compact **4996**
Bibliotheksarbeit (DEU ISSN 0945-4632) **4996**
• Bibliotheksdienst (DEU ISSN 0006-1972) **4996**
Bibliotheksforum Bayern (DEU ISSN 0340-000X) **4996**
Bibliothekspraxis (DEU ISSN 0300-287X) **4996**
• Bibliotheque Africaine. Liste des Acquisitions (BEL ISSN 0774-8353) **619**
Bibliotheque Allemande (FRA ISSN 1248-4695) **5263**
Bibliotheque Anglo-Saxonne (FRA ISSN 1248-6485) **5263**
Bibliotheque Augustinienne (BEL ISSN 0996-4657) **7627**
Bibliotheque Bresilienne (FRA ISSN 0291-493X) **4445**
Bibliotheque Copte de Nag Hammadi. Section Concordances *see* Bibliotheque Copte de Nag Hammadi. Section Textes **7627**
Bibliotheque Copte de Nag Hammadi. Section Etudes *see* Bibliotheque Copte de Nag Hammadi. Section Textes **7627**
➤ Bibliotheque Copte de Nag Hammadi. Section Textes (BEL ISSN 0824-9555) **7627**
Bibliotheque de Culture Religieuse (FRA ISSN 1771-9518) **7628**
Bibliotheque de Grammaire et Linguistiques (FRA ISSN 1278-3889) **5100**
Bibliotheque de la Famille (FRA ISSN 1251-6791) **5584**
Bibliotheque de la Mer (FRA ISSN 0067-8260) **8218**
Bibliotheque de la Revue d'Histoire Ecclesiastique (BEL ISSN 0067-8279) **7786**
➤ Bibliotheque de la S E L A F (BEL ISSN 0249-7050) **5100**
Bibliotheque de l'Autre. Collection Trauma (FRA ISSN 1951-3550) **6056**
Bibliotheque de l'Ecole des Chartes (CHE ISSN 0373-6237) **4133**
Bibliotheque de l'Ecole des Hautes Etudes. Quatrieme Section, Sciences Historiques et Philologiques (FRA ISSN 0768-3847) **4133**
➤ Bibliotheque de l'Ecole des Hautes Etudes Sciences Religieuses (BEL) **7628**
Bibliotheque de l'Evolution de l'Humanite (FRA ISSN 1255-1287) **4133**
Bibliotheque de l'Information Grammaticale (BEL ISSN 0767-0869) **5100**
Bibliotheque de Litterature Generale et Comparee (FRA ISSN 1262-2850) **5263**
Bibliotheque de Litterature Moderne (FRA ISSN 1159-0726) **5263**
† Bibliotheque de Travail (FRA ISSN 0005-335X) **8936**
† Bibliotheque de Travail 2eme Degre (FRA ISSN 0005-3414) **8936**
† Bibliotheque de Travail Junior (FRA ISSN 0005-3120) **8936**
Bibliotheque Departementale de Pret. La Lettre d'Information (FRA ISSN 1774-9816) **4996**
Bibliotheque des C I L L *see* Institut de Linguistique de Louvain. Bibliotheque des Cahiers **5127**
Bibliotheque des Ecoles Francaises d'Athenes et de Rome Publication *see* B E F A R. Publication **383**
• Bibliotheque des Nations Unies. Bibliographie Mensuelle (USA ISSN 1020-6558) **620**
Bibliotheque d'Etude - Institut Francais d'Archeologie Orientale *see* Institut Francais d'Archeologie Orientale du Caire. Bibliotheque d'Etude **397**
Bibliotheque d'Etudes Balkaniques (FRA ISSN 0067-8325) **5100**
Bibliotheque d'Etudes Comparatives *see* Komparatistische Bibliothek **7981**
Bibliotheque d'Etudes Coptes (EGY ISSN 1110-0001) **7703**
Bibliotheque d'Histoire Antillaise (GLP) **4285**
Bibliotheque d'Humanisme et Renaissance (CHE ISSN 0006-1999) **4205**
Bibliotheque du C N A M (Conservatoire National des Arts et Metiers) (FRA ISSN 0765-0639) **3374**
Bibliotheque du Quinzieme Siecle *see* Bibliotheque du XVe Siecle **5263**
Bibliotheque du XVe Siecle (FRA ISSN 0768-1674) **5263**
Bibliotheque Ecossaise (FRA ISSN 1284-6872) **4445**
Bibliotheque Francaise et Romane. Serie A: Manuels et Etudes Linguistiques (FRA ISSN 0067-8341) **5100**
Bibliotheque Francaise et Romane. Serie B: Editions Critiques de Textes (FRA ISSN 0067-835X) **5263**
Bibliotheque Francaise et Romane. Serie C: Etudes Litteraires (FRA ISSN 0067-8368) **5263**
Bibliotheque Francaise et Romane. Serie D: Initiation, Textes et Documents (FRA ISSN 0067-8376) **5263**
Bibliotheque Francaise et Romane. Serie E: Langue et Litterature Francaises au Canada (FRA ISSN 0067-8384) **5100**
Bibliotheque Franco Simone (FRA ISSN 0252-8282) **4205**
Bibliotheque Generale *see* Institut Francais d'Archeologie Orientale du Caire. Bibliotheque Generale **397**
▼ Bibliotheque Geopolitique (FRA ISSN 1956-5372) **7109**
Bibliotheque Hispanique (FRA ISSN 1264-3238) **4445**
Bibliotheque Historique (FRA ISSN 0520-0601) **4133**
Bibliotheque Historique et Litteraire *see* Collection Bibliotheque Historique et Litteraire **4135**
Bibliotheque Iranienne (BEL) **545**
Bibliotheque Italienne (FRA ISSN 1264-5834) **4445**
Bibliotheque Japonaise (FRA ISSN 0293-0684) **545**
Bibliotheque Jungienne (FRA ISSN 1257-9149) **7340**
Bibliotheque Maktaba (FRA ISSN 1760-379X) **4445**
Bibliotheque Nationale. Bibliographie Nationale (COD) **620**
Bibliotheque Nationale. Bulletin *see* National Library of Canada. Bulletin **5034**
• Bibliotheque Nationale de France. Actualites de l'Audiovisuel (FRA ISSN 1778-4123) **4996**
Bibliotheque Nationale de France. Autorites Collectivites (FRA ISSN 0989-635X) **620**
Bibliotheque Nationale de France. Autorites Personnes Physiques (FRA ISSN 1140-5570) **620**
Bibliotheque Nationale de France. Autorites Titres Uniformes (FRA ISSN 1140-5589) **620**
Bibliotheque Nationale de France. Revue (FRA ISSN 1254-7700) **4996**
• Bibliotheque Nationale du Canada. Bulletin (Online) (CAN ISSN 1492-4684) **4996**
Bibliotheque Nationale du Quebec. Rapport Annuel (CAN ISSN 1181-6449) **4996**
Bibliotheque Nationale Suisse. Rapport Annuel *see* Schweizerische Landesbibliothek. Jahresbericht (Bern, 2001) **5046**
Bibliotheque Nationale Suisse. Rapport Annuel (Bern, 1988) *see* Schweizerische Landesbibliothek. Jahresbericht (Bern, 2001) **5046**
Bibliotheque Nordique (FRA ISSN 1625-9297) **4445**
➤ Bibliotheque Philosophique de Louvain (BEL ISSN 0067-8430) **6907**
Bibliotheque Portugaise (FRA ISSN 0757-9276) **4445**
Bibliotheque Royal Albert 1er. Bulletin Trimestriel d'Information (BEL ISSN 0770-4372) **4996**
Bibliotheque Royale Albert 1er. Publications Annoncees/Koninklijke Bibliotheek Albert I. Aangekondigde Publikaties (BEL ISSN 0772-3776) **4997**
Bibliotheque Royale Albert 1er. Rapport Annuel *see* Koninklijke Bibliotheek Albert I. Jaarverslag **5023**
Bibliotheque Stendhalienne et Romantique (FRA ISSN 1294-0658) **5263**
Bibliotheque(s) (FRA) **7553**
Bibliotheques de Droit (FRA ISSN 1952-2657) **4630**
Bibliotheques de Droit Canadiennes *see* Canadian Law Libraries **5000**
Les Bibliotheques de France a l'Etranger. Bulletin (FRA ISSN 1267-6918) **4997**
• ➤ Bibliotheques de France. Bulletin (FRA ISSN 0006-2006) **4997**
Bibliotheques et Centres de Documents (CAN ISSN 1481-4439) **4997**
Bibliotheques et Musees (CHE ISSN 1011-8268) **4205**
Bibliotheques Publiques du Canada. *see* Public Libraries **5040**
Bibliotheques Suisses *see* Schweizerische Bibliotheken **5046**
• ➤ Bibliotime (ITA ISSN 1128-3564) **4997**
• Biblis (SWE ISSN 1403-3313) **7553**
Biblisch-Theologische Studien (DEU ISSN 0930-4800) **7628**
Biblische Beitraege (CHE ISSN 0582-1673) **7628**
Biblische Notizen (AUT ISSN 0178-2967) **7628**
Biblische Untersuchungen (DEU ISSN 0523-5154) **7628**
Biblische Zeitschrift (DEU ISSN 0006-2014) **7628**
Biblos (AUT ISSN 0006-2022) **4997**
Biblos *see* Biburosu (Online) **4997**
Biblos (PRT ISSN 0870-4112) **5263**
• Biburosu (Online)/Biblos (JPN ISSN 1344-8412) **4997**
Bicchieri d'Arte (ITA ISSN 1828-2237) **364**
Bicentenario: Revista de Historia de Chile y America (CHL ISSN 0717-7747) **4285**
Bichon Frise Reporter (USA ISSN 0199-8315) **6804**
Bicicatalogo a Fondo (ESP) **8254**
La Bicicletta (ITA ISSN 1123-9212) **8254**
Bicisport (ITA ISSN 1593-9812) **8254**
Bicitech (Year) (ESP) **8254**
Bicitech a Fondo (ESP) **8254**
Bicycle/Auto/Motor Asia *see* B A M Asia **8491**
Bicycle - Auto - Motor Asia *see* B A M Asia **8491**
Bicycle Handbook (CAN) **8254**
Bicycle Motocross Plus *see* B M X Plus **8254**
Bicycle Motorcross Xpress *see* B M Xpress **8254**
• Bicycle Paper (USA ISSN 0742-8308) **8254**
Bicycle Quarterly (USA ISSN 1941-8809) **8254**
• Bicycle Retailer and Industry News (USA ISSN 1069-8493) **8254**
▼ Bicycle Times (USA ISSN 1946-6366) **8254**
Bicycle Trade and Industry *see* B T I **8254**
Bicycle U S A Almanac *see* League of American Bicyclists Magazine **8260**
BicycleBusiness (GBR ISSN 1476-1505) **8254**
• Bicycling (USA ISSN 0006-2073) **8254**
Bicycling Australia (AUS ISSN 1034-8085) **8254**
Bicycling Buyers' Guide (AUS ISSN 1832-0597) **8254**
• Bid Information Newsletter (USA) **982**
Bid Magazine (USA) **1067**
Biddulph Chronicle (GBR ISSN 0964-7295) **3862**
Bide-A-Wee News (USA) **6804**
Bidebarrieta (ESP ISSN 1137-4888) **5100**
Bidoc Dossier (NLD ISSN 1574-860X) **4173**
Bidoun (USA ISSN 1551-4048) **478**
Bidrag till Kaennedom av Finlands Natur och Folk (FIN ISSN 0067-8481) **7950**
Bidrag till Kungliga Musikaliska Akademiens Historia (SWE ISSN 1404-1863) **6549**
† Bieb (NLD ISSN 1567-8962) **8936**
Bielarus (USA ISSN 0006-209X) **3522**
Bielaruskaya Dumka (USA) **3522**
Bielaruski Holas/Byelorussian Voice/Voix Bielarusienne (CAN ISSN 0837-0648) **3522**
Bielefelder (DEU) **3845**
Bielefelder Katalog - Jazz (DEU ISSN 0171-9505) **6549**
Bielefelder Katalog - Klassik (DEU ISSN 0721-7153) **6549**
Bielefelder Schriften zur Wirtschaftswissenschaftlichen Praxis (DEU) **1067**
Bielefelder Studien zur Entwicklungssoziologie (DEU ISSN 0171-7537) **8090**
Bielefelder Universitaetszeitung *see* H1 **2286**
† Bien dans Ma Vie (FRA) **8936**

Title

10038 BIEN DIRE ULRICH'S PERIODICALS

Bien Dire (FRA ISSN 1277-2690) **5100**
➤ Bien Dire et Bien Aprandre (FRA ISSN 0220-665X) **4205**
Bien-Etre (DZA ISSN 1112-5152) **6983**
Bien Grandir (CAN ISSN 1718-7346) **8090**
Bien Vieillir en Cote d'Or (FRA ISSN 1959-0601) **8028**
Die Biene (DEU ISSN 0006-212X) **96**
Die Biene Maja (DEU) **2179**
Das Bienenmuetterchen (DEU) **96**
Bienenpflege (DEU) **96**
Bienenvater (AUT ISSN 0006-2146) **96**
Bienenwelt (AUT ISSN 0006-2154) **96**
Bienes Culturales (ESP ISSN 1695-9698) **4445**
Biennale Nationale de Ceramique *see* Biennale Nationale de Sculpture Contemporaine **478**
Biennale Nationale de Sculpture Contemporaine (CAN ISSN 1716-284X) **478**
Biennial A P S A Conferences. Proceedings *see* Manipulating Pig Production **293**
Biennial Exhibition of Contemporary American Painting (USA ISSN 8756-4777) **478**
Biennial Report for the Department of Industrial Relations *see* California. Department of Industrial Relations. Biennial Report **1668**
▼ Biennial Review of Counseling Psychology (USA ISSN 1941-4250) **7340**
Biennial Waste Processing Conference. Proceedings (USA ISSN 1092-4515) **3504**
Biennial Workshop on Color Aerial Photography and Videography in the Plant Sciences and Related Fields (USA ISSN 1064-1149) **6964**
Bienvenidos a Miami (USA ISSN 0192-4249) **8782**
Bier Scheurkalender (NLD ISSN 1569-7681) **599**
Het Bierblad (NLD ISSN 1383-309X) **599**
Biercult (DEU) **5066**
Der Biergrosshandel - Der Getraenkegrosshandel (DEU) **600**
• Bierzo 7 (ESP) **3951**
Bietenstatistiek (NLD ISSN 1871-0611) **176**
Bietplanter *see* Le Betteravier **221**
De Bietplanter *see* Le Betteravier **221**
La Bievre (FRA ISSN 0223-7741) **902**
Biezunskie Zeszyty Historyczne (POL) **4205**
Bifidobacteria and Microflora *see* Bioscience and Microflora **661**
Bifocal *see* B I F O C A L **4625**
• Bifroest School of Business. Research Paper Series/Vidskiptahaskolinn Bifroest. Rannsoknarskyrsla (ISL ISSN 1670-0058) **1067**
• ➤ Bifurcaciones (CHL ISSN 0718-1132) **8090**
Big (GBR ISSN 0959-3217) **6549**
Big (USA ISSN 1553-0116) **6964**
Big 12 Basketball Handbook (USA) **8223**
• Big 6 eNewsletter (USA ISSN 1534-3049) **3052**
• Big AI Recruiting Newsletter (USA) **1667**
Big Almanaque Vamos Brincar Especial (BRA ISSN 1676-8183) **2179**
Big & Black (GBR ISSN 1366-9176) **6287**
Big Apple Blues (USA) **6549**
Big Apple Parent (USA) **2145**
Big Apple Users Digest *see* B A U D **2575**
Big Beans (USA) **3970**
Big Bear Magazine (USA) **4370**
Big Beat of the 50's (AUS) **6549**
Big Beautiful Woman (Online Edition) *see* B B W (Online Edition) **2251**
Big Beautiful Woman Magazine *see* B B W (Online Edition) **2251**
Big Bike (FRA ISSN 1638-4083) **8254**
The Big Blackpool Guide (GBR) **4976**
▼ The Big Blue (USA ISSN 1936-0150) **5066**
Big Blue Book (GBR ISSN 1472-7641) **982**
Big Boat (AUS) **8272**
Big Book of House Plans (USA ISSN 1930-6466) **435**
• The Big Book of Library Grant Money (USA ISSN 1086-0568) **4997**
Big Book of Photography (USA ISSN 1079-6746) **6964**
The Big Bopper *see* Bop **2180**
† Big Bremen (DEU) **8936**
• Big Bridge (USA) **5417**
Big Brother (USA ISSN 1073-1504) **8306**
Big Builder (USA ISSN 1550-2929) **982**
• Big Business for Not-So-Big Hospitals (USA ISSN 1933-3943) **4088**
Big Butt (USA ISSN 1083-2467) **6287**
The Big Cheese (GBR ISSN 1365-358X) **6287**
Big Comic (JPN) **3899**
Big Comic Original (JPN) **3899**
Big Comic Spirits (JPN) **3899**
Big Comic Superior (JPN) **3899**
Big Daddy (GBR ISSN 1469-316X) **6549**
• Big Dreams (CAN ISSN 1198-8819) **1957**
Big East Basketball Handbook (USA) **8223**
Big Game Tournament Guide *see* Power and Motoryacht **8280**
Big Grey Wolf Pictorial *see* Dahuilang Huabao **2184**
Big Grower *see* G P N **3756**
Big Horn County News (USA) **3522**
Big Interview (SVK ISSN 1336-894X) **3946**
Big Is Beautiful (NLD ISSN 1574-2911) **5066**
• Big Island Visitor (USA) **8687**
The Big Issue (AUS ISSN 1326-639X) **8090**
Big Issue (GBR ISSN 0967-5000) **3862**
Big Issue Cape Town (ZAF ISSN 1608-0378) **3947**
Big Issue Namibia (NAM ISSN 1684-2642) **3913**
Big League (AUS ISSN 0311-175X) **8223**
Big Little Times (USA) **7553**
Big Magazine *see* Big **6964**
▼ Big Man Magazine (USA ISSN 1944-6667) **6287**
Big Muddy (USA ISSN 1532-9860) **5263**
Big Official U C A S Guide to University and College Entrance (Universities and Colleges Admissions Service) (GBR ISSN 1366-8242) **2969**
† Big Oldenburg (DEU) **8936**
Big Ones International (GBR ISSN 1367-8116) **6287**
Big Open World *see* B O W **5259**
The Big Picture (USA) **7553**
• Big Picture (Cincinnati) (USA ISSN 1082-9660) **21**
Big Picture. Buyer's Guide *see* Big Picture (Cincinnati) **21**
• Big Picture On ... (GBR ISSN 1745-7777) **5584**
Big Picture On Series *see* Big Picture On ... **5584**
Big Print (GBR) **4079**
Big Print Codebreakers (GBR ISSN 1470-2754) **4330**
Big Red Barbour Compendium *see* Barbour Compendium **4532**
The Big Red Book (GBR ISSN 1751-6323) **1974**
† Big Reel (USA ISSN 0744-723X) **8936**
• Big Rig Owner (USA) **8669**
Big Scream (USA) **5263**
Big Screen (ZAF ISSN 1023-8247) **6490**
Big Shot (USA) **6549**
The Big Show Journal (USA) **8161**
Big Sky Journal (USA ISSN 1094-4680) **3970**
• Big Sky Libraries (USA) **4997**
• Big Spender (GBR ISSN 1749-1029) **2635**
Big Spender Shopping Magazine *see* Big Spender **2635**
• The Big Takeover (USA) **6549**
Big Ten *see* Athlon's Big Ten Football **8221**
Big Ten Basketball Handbook (USA) **8223**
Big Ten Conference Official Football Guide (USA) **8223**
(Year) Big Ten Records Book (USA) **8223**
Big Time *see* BigTime **6549**
• Big Twin (USA ISSN 1084-3183) **8254**
† Big Twin Dealer (USA) **8936**
Big Value Codebreakers *see* Take a Break's Big Value Codebreakers **4348**
Big View *see* Dashiye **7958**
Bigaku (JPN ISSN 0520-0962) **6907**
Bigaku Geijutsugaku Kenkyu (JPN ISSN 1342-6095) **4445**
Bigger, Faster, Stronger (USA ISSN 0889-5988) **8223**
BIGonblue (AUS ISSN 1832-231X) **8272**
BigShot (USA) **6549**
• BigSkyMac Ezine (USA) **2575**
BigTime (USA) **6549**
BigTwin (SWE) **8255**
Bigyo Munhwa Yeongu/Cross-Cultural Studies (KOR ISSN 1226-0568) **330**
Bihar Industries (IND ISSN 0006-2219) **1957**
▼ • Biharean Biologist (ROM ISSN 1843-5637) **656**
Bihari Naplo (ROM ISSN 1222-6734) **3932**
Bihoreanul (ROM ISSN 1582-2885) **3932**
BIIG *see* B II G **2251**
Biij *see* Biomedical Imaging and Intervention Journal **6193**
Bij de Les (NLD ISSN 1871-8728) **2969**
Bijbel en Wetenschap *see* Ellips **7640**
Bijblad (NLD) **6746**
Bijblad bij de Industriele Eigendom *see* Bijblad **6746**
• Bijblijven (Houten) (NLD ISSN 0168-9428) **5585**
• ➤ Bijdragen (BEL ISSN 0006-2278) **6907**
➤ Bijdragen en Mededelingen Betreffende de Geschiedenis der Nederlanden (NLD ISSN 0165-0505) **4205**
Bijdragen tot de Dierkunde *see* Contributions to Zoology **939**
Bijdragen tot de Eigentijdse Geschiedenis *see* Cahiers d'Histoire du Temps Present **4208**
➤ Bijdragen tot de Geschiedenis (BEL ISSN 0006-2286) **4133**
Bijdragen tot de Geschiedenis van Deinze en de Leiestreek (BEL ISSN 1373-640X) **4133**
➤ Bijdragen tot de Taal-, Land- en Volkenkunde/Journal of the Humanities and Social Sciences of Southeast Asia and Oceania (NLD ISSN 0006-2294) **330**
Bijen *see* Bijenhouden **96**
Bijenhouden (NLD) **96**
• Bijiao Jiaoyu Yanjiu/Comparative Education Review (CHN ISSN 1003-7667) **2831**
• Bijiaofa Yanjiu/Journal of Comparative Law (CHN ISSN 1004-8561) **4630**
Bijie Shifan Gaodeng Zhuanke Xuexiao Xuebao/Bijie Teachers College. Journal *see* Bijie Xueyuan Xuebao **2831**
Bijie University. Journal *see* Bijie Xueyuan Xuebao **2831**
• Bijie Xueyuan Xuebao/Bijie University. Journal (CHN) **2831**
Bijinesu Rebyu *see* Business Review **1075**
Bijlage Facility Management Magazine *see* Facility Management Magazine Jaarboek **1744**
Bijnor Times (IND) **3879**
Le Bijoutier (FRA ISSN 0766-6934) **4564**
Le Bijoutier International *see* Le Bijoutier **4564**
Bijstand (NLD) **8028**
Bijutsu Kenkyu/Journal of Art Studies (JPN ISSN 0021-9088) **478**
Bijutsu Shi *see* Journal of Art History **498**
Bijutsu Techo (JPN ISSN 0287-2218) **478**
Bijutsushigaku (JPN ISSN 0387-2688) **478**
Bijzijn (NLD ISSN 1871-7268) **5953**
Bijzijn. Thuiszorg (NLD ISSN 1871-7292) **5953**
Bijzijn. Ziekenhuizen (NLD ISSN 1871-7276) **5585**
Bikaan (SWE) **3954**
Bikalpa Chikitsa Sambad (IND) **307**
Bike (DEU ISSN 0936-7624) **8255**
Bike (FRA ISSN 1638-7724) **8255**
Bike (GBR ISSN 0140-4547) **8255**
Bike a Fondo (ESP ISSN 1576-429X) **8255**
Bike Action (BRA ISSN 1518-3963) **8255**
Bike & Business (DEU ISSN 1611-3438) **8255**
▼ Bike and Quad Mart (ZAF ISSN 1995-1353) **8255**
Bike Builder's Handbook for Harley-Davidson and V-Twin Owners (USA ISSN 1932-2747) **8255**
Bike Culture East Magazine *see* BikeCulture Magazine **8255**
Bike Europe (NLD ISSN 1387-1366) **8255**
Bike Guia do Comprador (PRT) **8255**
• Bike It Project Review (GBR ISSN 1755-3415) **8255**
Bike League News *see* BikeLeague News **8306**
Bike Magazine (PRT) **8255**
• Bike Magazine (USA ISSN 1072-4869) **8255**
▼ Bike Monkey Magazine (USA ISSN 1940-5855) **8255**
Bike S.A. (ZAF ISSN 0378-9128) **8255**
Bike Special Freeride *see* Freeride **8259**
Bike Sport News (DEU ISSN 1437-9767) **8255**
Bike Talk (ZAF ISSN 1992-092X) **8255**
Bike Tour (ITA ISSN 1824-0208) **8255**
† Bike-, Tour-, Trekkingbike-Markt (DEU) **8936**
• Bike Trader (GBR ISSN 1362-5640) **8255**
Bike Workshop (DEU ISSN 0946-1698) **8255**
BikeCulture Magazine (USA ISSN 1933-222X) **8255**
• BikeLeague News (USA) **8306**
Biker (GBR ISSN 1460-308X) **8255**
Biker (USA ISSN 1058-7926) **8255**
• Biker Boerse (DEU) **8255**
Biker Business Directory *see* Ozbike **8266**
Biker's Motorrad Katalog (DEU) **8255**
Bikers News (DEU ISSN 1614-9157) **8255**
▼ Bikes & Gear (USA ISSN 1943-9792) **8255**
Bikini (NLD ISSN 1573-6091) **8161**
Bikmaus (PNG ISSN 0255-7231) **5263**
Bikoret Ufarshanut/Criticism and Interpretation (ISR ISSN 0084-9456) **5263**
• Bikwil (AUS ISSN 1328-7842) **5263**
• Bil (NOR ISSN 0800-5850) **8569**
Bil Magasinet (DNK ISSN 0906-5474) **8569**
Bil-Revyen (DNK ISSN 0107-0924) **8569**
Bil', Znebolyuvannya i Intensyvna Terapiya (UKR) **5770**
Bilabladid Billinn (ISL ISSN 1025-255X) **8569**
Al-Bilad (SAU ISSN 1319-0245) **3944**
Biladi (UAE) **3966**
Bilan *see* Ordre des Comptables Agrees du Quebec. Bilan **1298**
• Bilan (CHE ISSN 0772-4861) **1442**
• Bilan Annuel d'Emploi - Quebec en Monteregie (CAN ISSN 1719-5616) **1667**
Bilan des Activites (Annee) et Plan d'Activites (Annee) de l'Association pour la Sante Publique du Quebec *see* Plan des Activites Generales. Bilan (Annee) **7535**
Bilan des Relations du Travail au Quebec (CAN ISSN 1712-9702) **1667**
Bilan Rapport (NLD ISSN 1572-3194) **384**
Bilans, Echanges, Projects (ITA ISSN 1826-8226) **7950**
Bilans Energetiques des Pays de l'O C D E (Organisation de Cooperation et de Developpement Economiques) *see* Energy Balances of O E C D Countries **3130**
Bilans Hebdomadaires (FRA ISSN 0755-2238) **1067**
Bilans Politiques Economiques et Sociaux Hebdomadaires *see* Bilans Hebdomadaires **1067**
• Bilanz (CHE ISSN 1022-3487) **1442**
Bilanz-, Pruefungs und Steuerwesen (DEU ISSN 1862-0922) **1913**
Bilanz- und Buchhaltung (DEU ISSN 0930-0597) **1281**
Bilanzbuchhalter und Controller *see* Zeitschrift fuer Bilanzierung und Rechnungswesen **1304**
Bilanzierung Plus (DEU ISSN 1612-1546) **1281**
Bilanzierungs-Richtlinien Special (DEU ISSN 1612-524X) **1913**
Bilar & Sport (ISL ISSN 1670-5378) **8161**
Bilarbogen (DNK ISSN 1603-8347) **8569**
Bilateral (PRT) **1396**
Bilboersen (SWE ISSN 1650-5913) **8569**
Bilbransjen - Bilteknisk Fagblad (NOR ISSN 0006-2367) **8569**
Bild (DEU ISSN 0949-5096) **3845**
Bild am Sonntag (DEU ISSN 0341-4906) **3845**
Bild der Frau (DEU ISSN 0949-6874) **8853**
Bild der Frau Gut Kochen & Backen (DEU ISSN 1436-6479) **4353**
Bild der Frau Schlank & Fit (DEU) **8844**
Bild der Wissenschaft (DEU ISSN 0006-2375) **7841**
• Bild i Skolan (SWE ISSN 0349-2117) **478**
Bild & Bubbla/Picture and Caption (SWE ISSN 0347-7096) **478**
Bild und Funk (DEU) **3845**
Bild und Funk Spezial Raetsel (DEU) **8161**
Bilderkennung und -verarbeitung *see* Informationsdienst F I Z Technik. Bilderkennung und -verarbeitung **2443**
➤ Bildhaan (USA ISSN 1528-6258) **4173**
Bildkonstnaeren (SWE ISSN 0348-0615) **478**
Bildteknik *see* Kart & Bildteknik **4018**
Bilduma (ESP ISSN 0214-624X) **4997**
Bildung Aktuell (DEU ISSN 0341-4922) **3018**
Bildung fuer Nachhaltige Entwicklung (DEU ISSN 1614-9971) **3037**
Bildung im Zahlenspiegel (DEU ISSN 0938-1104) **2930**
Bildung in Umbruchsgesellschaften (DEU ISSN 1619-9561) **8090**
Bildung+ Leben (DEU) **2145**
Bildung+ Lernen 1 bis 4 (DEU) **2145**
Bildung+ Medien (DEU) **2145**
Bildung+ Reisen (DEU) **2145**
Bildung+ Science (DEU) **2145**
Bildung Real (DEU ISSN 0343-4583) **3018**
Bildung und Beratung Agrar *see* B & B Agrar **6655**
➤ Bildung und Erziehung (DEU ISSN 0006-2456) **2831**
Bildung und Wissenschaft (Bonn) (DEU ISSN 0172-0171) **2831**
Bildung und Wissenschaft (Ludwigsburg) (DEU ISSN 0944-937X) **2831**
Bildungs- und Kulturgeschichtliche Beitraege fuer Berlin und Brandenburg (DEU) **4205**
Bildungsarbeit in der Zweitsprache Deutsch *see* Deutsch als Zweitsprache **2940**
Bildungsbrief (DEU ISSN 0935-8269) **6693**
• Bildungsforschung (DEU ISSN 1860-8213) **2831**
Die Bildungsmesse im Lehrerzimmer (DEU) **3052**
Bildungspraxis (DEU ISSN 0945-5469) **3052**
➤ Bildwelten des Wissens (DEU ISSN 1611-2512) **478**
Bildwoche (DEU ISSN 0949-4499) **3845**
• ➤ Bilgi Dunyasi/Information World (TUR ISSN 1302-3217) **4997**
• Bilgisayarli Tomografi Bulteni/Bulletin of Computed Tomography (TUR ISSN 1300-6487) **6193**
• ➤ Bilig (TUR ISSN 1301-0549) **7950**
Bilim *see* Ke Xue **7875**
Bilim *see* Spektrum der Wissenschaft **7919**
Bilim *see* Investigacion y Ciencia **7868**
Bilim *see* Pour la Science **7899**
Bilim *see* Tudomany **7925**
Bilim *see* Le Scienze **7913**
Bilim *see* Nikkei Saiensu **7893**
Bilim *see* Majallat al-Ulum **7881**
Bilim *see* Swiat Nauki **7921**
Bilim *see* Scientific American **7912**
Bilim Bulagy (KGZ) **3903**
Bilingual Dictionary of Criminal Justice (English - Spanish) (USA) **4885**
Bilingual Dictionary of Domestic Relation (English - Spanish) (USA) **4907**
Bilingual Dictionary of Immigration Terms (English/Spanish) (USA) **7278**
• The Bilingual Family Newsletter (GBR ISSN 0952-4096) **5100**
Bilingual Handbook for Public Safety Professionals (USA) **7509**
† Bilingual Magazine (NZL ISSN 1176-9270) **8936**
• ➤ Bilingual Research Journal (USA ISSN 1523-5882) **2831**
• ➤ Bilingual Review/Revista Bilingue (USA ISSN 0094-5366) **2831**
Bilingual Services Directory (USA) **1974**
Bilingual Student Post (TWN) **3960**
• ➤ Bilingualism (GBR ISSN 1366-7289) **5100**
Bilismen i Sverige (SWE ISSN 0282-0536) **8569**
Biljart Totaal (NLD ISSN 1381-3595) **8223**
Bilje i Zdravlje (SRB ISSN 1820-0737) **8853**
Biljni Lekar (SRB ISSN 0354-6160) **779**
Bill Gary's Price Perceptions (USA ISSN 1529-6199) **1612**
▼ The Bill James Gold Mine (USA ISSN 1940-7998) **8223**
The Bill James Handbook (USA ISSN 1940-8668) **8223**
Bill Nelson Newsletter (USA ISSN 0894-4911) **4330**
The Bill of Rights Handbook (ZAF) **4630**
• Bill of Rights in Action (USA ISSN 0160-7731) **7203**
• Bill Shipp's Georgia (USA ISSN 0894-9697) **7423**
Bill Status Sheet (USA ISSN 1077-4807) **7423**
• Bill Strong's Mississippi Photography Travel Culture (USA) **6964**
Billboard (Chambersburg) (USA) **2274**
• Billboard (New York) (USA ISSN 0006-2510) **6549**
• Billboard Bulletin (USA) **6549**
Billboard.com *see* Billboard (New York) **6549**
† Billboard History of Rock 'n Roll (USA) **8936**
Billboard International Disc - Tape Directory (USA) **1974**
Billboard International Latin Music Buyer's Guide (USA ISSN 1074-746X) **6549**
• Billboard International Talent and Touring Directory (Year) (USA ISSN 0732-0124) **6549**
Billboard Musician's Guide to Touring and Promotion *see* The Musician's Guide to Touring and Promotion **6594**
Billboard Radio Monitor *see* R & R **8983**
Billboard Record Retailing Directory (USA ISSN 1098-3791) **1974**
Billboard's International Buyer's Guide (Year) (USA ISSN 1098-3732) **6549**
Billboard's Year-End Awards Issue (USA) **6549**
Billed-bladet *see* Billedbladet **3833**
• Billedbladet (DNK ISSN 0006-2537) **3833**
Billeder *see* Aaret i Billeder **4195**
Billedkunst (DNK ISSN 0908-0465) **478**
• Billedkunstneren (DNK ISSN 1902-3618) **478**
Billedkunstneren (NOR ISSN 0332-723X) **478**
Billedpaedagogisk Tidsskrift (DNK ISSN 0908-6293) **478**
• Billet du Bilingue (FRA ISSN 1951-6061) **2831**
Billi Blue *see* Boerneavisen **3833**

Link to your serials resources and content with ulrichsweb.com

DIRECTORY 2010 LES BIOGRAPHIES.COM. LES BIOGRAPHIES DE LA PUBLICITE 10039

Billiard and Bowling Institute of America Membership and Product Information Guide see B B I A Membership and Product Information Guide 1974
Billiard and Bowling Institute of America Newsline see B B I A Newsline 8221
Billiard Congress of America Break see B C A Break 8221
• Billiards Digest (USA ISSN 0164-761X) 8223
Billiards Digest Interactive see Billiards Digest 8223
Billiards: The (Year) Official B C A Rules & Records Book (USA ISSN 1047-2444) 8223
• Billibub Baddings and the Case of the Singing Sword (USA ISSN 1934-7154) 5440
Billie Jo Williams International Fan Club (USA) 6549
Billiger-Telefonieren (DEU) 2366
• Billiken (ARG ISSN 0006-2553) 2179
• Billing Alert For Long-Term Care (USA ISSN 1527-0246) 4088
Billing & Customer Care Review (GBR ISSN 1467-2782) 1281
• Billing & O S S World (Operational Support Systems) (USA ISSN 2150-508X) 2366
Billing and Settlement Plans Data Interchange Specifications Handbook see B S P Data Interchange Specifications Handbook 1310
Billing Plus see O S S / B S S Analyst 2387
Billing Systems Review see Billing & Customer Care Review 1281
Billing World and O S S Today see Billing & O S S World 2366
Billins Agency Law see Agency Law 4854
Billionaire (USA) 4976
Billlet see The Telegraph 8663
• Billwatch (USA) 7203
Billy (NOR ISSN 1504-1182) 2179
Billy's Best Bottles (CAN) 600
Bilmagasinet see Bil Magasinet 8569
Bilmarkedet Plus see Bil Magasinet 8569
Bilsport (SWE ISSN 0347-2035) 8569
Bilsport Retro Cars (SWE ISSN 1652-5949) 364
Bilten Beogradske Berze see Beogradska Berza. Bilten 1612
Bilten Fonda za Naucna Istrazivanja za ... God see Fond za Naucna Istrazivanja. Bilten 4452
Bilten Pravne Sluzbe J N A (SRB ISSN 0006-2731) 4630
Bilten - Sluzbena Objasnjenja i Strucna Misljenja za Primenu Finansijskih Propisa (SRB ISSN 0354-3242) 1321
Bilten Sudske Prakse Vrhovnog Suda Srbije see Vrhovni Sud Srbije. Bilten Sudske Prakse 4810
Bilten za Hmelj, Sirak i Lekovito Bilje/Hops, Sorghums and Medicinal Herbs Bulletin (SRB ISSN 0351-9430) 779
➤ Bilten za Transfuziologiju (SRB ISSN 0354-4494) 5934
Biltmore Magazine (USA) 8782
Biltoki see Documentos de Trabajo Biltoki 8367
• Bilwaerlden (SWE ISSN 1654-0905) 8569
† Bilyeu by You (USA ISSN 1071-2356) 8936
Bilyeu by You Surname Booklet see Bilyeu by You 8936
Bimarihaye Guiahi see Iranian Journal of Plant Pathology 795
Bimbi e Bebe (ITA ISSN 1827-3149) 2245
Bimbisani e Belli (ITA ISSN 1124-1748) 2145
Bimbo (DEU ISSN 0342-8095) 2604
BIME. Bibliografia Musical Espanola (ESP ISSN 1138-0861) 6631
Bimmer (USA ISSN 1097-7465) 8569
Bimonthly Review of Law Books (USA ISSN 1048-8936) 4630
Bina Insaat Istatistikleri see Turkey. Turkiye Istatistik Kurumu. Bina Insaat Istatistikleri 8994
Binario (PRT ISSN 0006-2804) 435
▼ • Binary Bites (USA ISSN 1945-1598) 2552
Binary Web Design Newsletter see Binary Bites 2552
Bindereport (DEU ISSN 0342-3573) 7553
Binders' Guild Newsletter (USA ISSN 1075-1327) 7553
Bindu (SWE ISSN 1104-1722) 6643
Binfen/Colorfulness (CHN) 3615
Bingara Advocate (AUS) 3793
• Bingchuan Dongtu/Journal of Glaciology and Geocryology (CHN ISSN 1000-0240) 2778
• Bingdu Xuebao/Chinese Journal of Virology (CHN ISSN 1000-8721) 5585
• Binggong Xuebao (CHN ISSN 1000-1093) 6413
• ➤ Binggong Zidonghua/Ordnance Industry Automation (CHN ISSN 1006-1576) 6413
Binghamton Medieval and Early Modern Studies (BEL) 4205
Binghamton University Magazine (USA ISSN 1936-7066) 2274
Bingo (FRA ISSN 0005-6499) 3789
Bingo (NLD) 4330
• Bingo Bugle (USA) 8161
Bingo Caller News (CAN) 8161
• Bingqi Cailiao Kexue yu Gongcheng/Ordnance Material Science and Engineering (CHN ISSN 1004-244X) 6413
• Bingqi Zhishi/Ordnance Knowledge (CHN ISSN 1000-4912) 6413
Bingtuan Gong-yun (CHN ISSN 1006-5474) 3823
• Bingxue Yundong/China Winter Sports (CHN ISSN 1002-3488) 8306
Bini Sueif University Medical Journal see Beni Sueif University Medical Journal 5584
Binley's Guide to the New N H S see Binley's N H S Guide 4088
Binley's N H S Guide (National Health Service) (GBR ISSN 1742-7916) 4088
Binnen see Booming Futsal 8224
Die Binnengewaesser (DEU ISSN 0067-8643) 2793
Binnenlands Bestuur (NLD ISSN 0167-1146) 7423
Binnenschiffahrt (DEU ISSN 0939-1916) 8491
BinnensteBuiten (NLD) 7423
De Binnenwaard (NLD ISSN 1871-4501) 4205
• ➤ Binocular Vision & Strabismus Quarterly (USA ISSN 1088-6281) 6039
• Binsted's Bottling Directory (Year) (GBR) 1974
Binsted's Directory of Food Trade Marks and Brand Names (GBR ISSN 0067-8651) 3628
Binzhou Medical College. Journal see Binzhou Yixueyuan Xuebao 5585
• Binzhou Yixueyuan Xuebao/Binzhou Medical College. Journal (CHN ISSN 1001-9510) 5585
➤ Bio (BRA ISSN 0103-5134) 3260
Bio Actualites see Bio Aktuell 96
Bio Aktuell/Bio Actualites (CHE) 96
Bio Bencha see Baio Tekunoroji Janaru 655
Bio Bibliografia Boliviana (BOL) 620
† Bio-Bibliographies in Afro-American and African Studies (USA ISSN 0882-7044) 8936
† Bio-Bibliographies in American Literature (USA ISSN 0742-695X) 8936
† Bio-Bibliographies in Art and Architecture (USA ISSN 1055-6826) 8936
† Bio-Bibliographies in Economics (USA ISSN 1063-3197) 8936
† Bio-Bibliographies in Law and Political Science (USA ISSN 0882-7052) 8936
† Bio-Bibliographies in Music (USA ISSN 0742-6968) 8936
† Bio-Bibliographies in Sociology (USA ISSN 0893-8504) 8936
Bio-Bibliographies in the Performing Arts (USA ISSN 0892-5550) 8485
† Bio-Bibliographies in World Literature (USA ISSN 0894-2323) 8936
• Bio-Bulletin (CAN ISSN 1912-2063) 96
The Bio-Cleanup Report (USA ISSN 1086-1424) 3406
• Bio-Diplomacy and International Cooperation (GRC) 3406
• Bio-Etik i Praksis (DNK ISSN 1603-8444) 6907
• Bio - I T World (USA ISSN 1538-5728) 757
Bio Industry/Baio Indasutori (JPN ISSN 0910-6545) 757
Bio-IT World see Bio - I T World 757
Bio-IT World Japan (JPN) 824
• Bio Lineaires (FRA ISSN 1963-2169) 6656
Bio Magazin (DEU ISSN 0949-4642) 6983
➤ Bio-Math/Biomathematics (FRA ISSN 1027-6521) 5476
• ➤ Bio-Medical Materials and Engineering (NLD ISSN 0959-2989) 747
Bio-Medical Reviews (BGR ISSN 1310-392X) 827
Bio Nachrichten (DEU ISSN 0178-4765) 221
Bio-News see BioNyt 661
Bio News see Bionews 3406
Bio News (USA) 757
▼ • Bio-Optics World (USA) 757
Bio-Pharma Partnering see Scrip's Bio-Pharma Partnering 770
Bio-Prospects see Bio-Bulletin 96
➤ Bio-Research (NGA) 757
Bio Research International (USA ISSN 1939-4470) 757
Bio-Science Law Review (GBR ISSN 1365-8867) 4858
➤ Bio-Science Research Bulletin (IND ISSN 0970-0889) 656
• Bio-Syllabus (GRC) 3406
Bio-tech Breakthrough Stock Report (CAN ISSN 1712-7165) 1612
Bio Tech International (BEL) 757
• Bio Tribune Magazine (FRA ISSN 1772-9416) 656
Bio- und Gentechnik (DEU ISSN 1437-1634) 863
Bio Update (NLD ISSN 1872-4949) 96
• ➤ Bioacoustics (GBR ISSN 0952-4622) 936
• Bioagro (VEN ISSN 1316-3361) 96
▼ • ➤ Bioanalytical Reviews (AUT ISSN 1867-2086) 724
BioArchaeologica (DEU ISSN 1611-356X) 384
▼ • ➤ Bioarchaeology of the Near East (POL ISSN 1898-9403) 384
▼ • ➤ Bioarchitecture (USA ISSN 1949-0992) 827
Bioarchitettura (ITA ISSN 1824-050X) 435
• BioArray News (USA ISSN 1534-9926) 757
Biobibliographies et Exposes (BEL) 5200
Biocasa (ITA) 4533
• ➤ Biocatalysis and Biotransformation (GBR ISSN 1024-2422) 757
• ➤ Biocell (ARG ISSN 0327-9545) 827
Biocenosis (CRI ISSN 0250-6963) 2604
• BioCentury Extra (USA) 1067
BioCentury Part 2 see BioCentury Part II 1067
• BioCentury Part II (USA) 1067
BioCentury Quarterly Stock Reports (USA) 1612
• BioCentury: The Bernstein Report on BioBusiness (USA ISSN 1097-7201) 1067
• ➤ Biochemia Medica (HRV ISSN 1330-0962) 724
• ➤ Biochemical and Biophysical Research Communications (USA ISSN 0006-291X) 724
Biochemical and Cellular Archives (IND ISSN 0972-5075) 724
• ➤ Biochemical Engineering Journal (NLD ISSN 1369-703X) 724
• ➤ Biochemical Genetics (USA ISSN 0006-2928) 863
• ➤ Biochemical Journal (GBR ISSN 0264-6021) 724
Biochemical Journal Reviews (GBR ISSN 1356-739X) 724
• ➤ Biochemical Pharmacology (USA ISSN 0006-2952) 6825
Biochemical Reviews (IND ISSN 0365-9429) 724
• ➤ Biochemical Society Symposia (GBR ISSN 0067-8694) 724
• ➤ Biochemical Society Transactions (GBR ISSN 0300-5127) 725
• ➤ Biochemical Systematics and Ecology (GBR ISSN 0305-1978) 725
Biochemicals and Reagents for Life Science Research (USA) 725
• ➤ Biochemist (GBR ISSN 0954-982X) 725
• ➤ Biochemistry (USA ISSN 0006-2960) 725
• ➤ Biochemistry (Moscow) (RUS ISSN 0006-2979) 725
▼ • Biochemistry (Moscow). Supplement Series A: Membrane and Cell Biology (RUS ISSN 1990-7478) 725
• Biochemistry (Moscow). Supplement Series B: Biomedical Chemistry (RUS ISSN 1990-7508) 725
• Biochemistry and Biophysics Citation Index (USA) 713
• ➤ Biochemistry and Cell Biology/Biochimie et Biologie Cellulaire (CAN ISSN 0829-8211) 725
• ➤ Biochemistry and Molecular Biology Education (USA ISSN 1470-8175) 725
• ➤ Biochemistry & Molecular Biology of Fishes (NLD ISSN 1873-0140) 936
Biochemistry and Molecular Biology Reports see B M B Reports 724
▼ • ➤ Biochemistry Insight (NZL ISSN 1178-6264) 726
➤ Biochemistry of the Elements (USA ISSN 0887-6495) 726
Biochimica and Biophysica Acta Molecular and Cell Biology of Lipids see B B A - Molecular and Cell Biology of Lipids 723
Biochimica Clinica (ITA ISSN 0393-0564) 726
• ➤ Biochimica et Biophysica Acta (NLD ISSN 0006-3002) 726
Biochimica et Biophysica Acta Bioenergetics see B B A - Bioenergetics 778
Biochimica et Biophysica Acta Biomembranes see B B A - Biomembranes 827
• ➤ Biochimica et Biophysica Acta. Gene Regulatory Mechanisms (NLD ISSN 1874-9399) 864
• ➤ Biochimie (FRA ISSN 0300-9084) 726
Biochimie et Biologie Cellulaire see Biochemistry and Cell Biology 725
▼ • ➤ BioChip Journal (KOR ISSN 1976-0280) 757
▼ • Biochip Research (CHN) 757
Biocides (USA ISSN 1932-8397) 3236
• Biociencias (BRA ISSN 0104-3455) 656
▼ Biocombustibles (COL ISSN 2011-4109) 3236
BioCommerce Data's Business Profile Series. Volume 1: The U S Biotechnology Directory (GBR) 757
BioCommerce Data's Business Profile Series. Volume 2. The European Biotechnology Directory (GBR) 757
BioCommerce Data's Business Profile Series. Volume 3: The International Biotechnology Directory (GBR) 757
• BioCommerce Data's Business Profile Series. Volume 4: The U K Biotechnology Directory (GBR) 757
➤ Biocomputing (Year) (SGP) 824
• ➤ Bioconjugate Chemistry (USA ISSN 1043-1802) 726
Bioconnection (USA) 757
• ➤ BioControl (NLD ISSN 1386-6141) 841
• ➤ Biocontrol (PER ISSN 1026-2911) 882
• Biocontrol News and Information (GBR ISSN 0143-1404) 176
Biocontrol Science (JPN ISSN 1342-4815) 656
• ➤ Biocontrol Science and Technology (GBR ISSN 0958-3157) 221
Biocosme Mesogeen (FRA ISSN 0762-6428) 4205
Biocybernetics and Biomedical Engineering (POL ISSN 0208-5216) 747
• BioCycle (USA ISSN 0276-5055) 3504
▼ • ➤ BioData Mining (GBR ISSN 1756-0381) 824
• The Biodefence Funding Report (USA) 757
The Biodefense Funding Report (USA ISSN 1552-5856) 757
Biodefense Quarterly see Biosecurity Bulletin 7509
• ➤ Biodegradation (NLD ISSN 0923-9820) 3504
• ➤ Biodemography and Social Biology (USA ISSN 1948-5565) 864
• Biodiesel Magazine (USA ISSN 1935-7621) 6764
▼ Biodiesel Smarter (USA ISSN 1948-2116) 3236
BiodieselSMARTER see Biodiesel Smarter 3236
• Biodiversidad (ESP ISSN 0797-888X) 2604
➤ Biodiversidad & Conservacion Integral (VEN ISSN 1690-4753) 3406
➤ Biodiversity (CAN ISSN 1488-8386) 3406
• ➤ Biodiversity and Conservation (NLD ISSN 0960-3115) 2604
• ➤ Biodiversity Informatics (USA ISSN 1546-9735) 656
• Biodiversity News (GBR ISSN 1360-1164) 656
• ➤ BioDrugs (NZL ISSN 1173-8804) 6825
BioDynamics (USA ISSN 0006-2863) 221
Biodynamisk Ödling (SWE ISSN 1654-6555) 96
Biodynamisk Tidskrift see Biodynamisk Odling 96
• ➤ Bioelectrochemistry (NLD ISSN 1567-5394) 726
➤ Bioelectrochemistry: Principles and Practice (CHE ISSN 1422-4208) 726
• ➤ Bioelectromagnetics (USA ISSN 0197-8462) 752
• Bioelectromagnetics Newsletter (USA) 752
Bioelectromagnetics Society Newsletter see Bioelectromagnetics Newsletter 752
Bioenergi see Tidskriften Bioenergi 3223
• Bioenergi Magasinet (DNK ISSN 1902-7907) 3236
Bioenergimagasinet see Bioenergi Magasinet 3236
▼ • Bioenergy Business (GBR ISSN 1753-7576) 6764
▼ • Bioenergy Research (USA ISSN 1939-1234) 3124
▼ Bioengineered Bugs (USA) 841
• BioEngineering Abstracts (Online) (USA ISSN 1555-6271) 713
Bioengineering Symposium. Proceedings see Baioenjiniaringu Shinpojumu Ronbunshuu 747
• Bioentrepreneur (GBR ISSN 1542-6572) 757
• ➤ BioEssays (GBR ISSN 0265-9247) 657
Bioethica Forum see Bioethica Forum 6907
▼ • ➤ Bioethica Forum (CHE ISSN 1662-6001) 6907
• ➤ Bioethics (GBR ISSN 0269-9702) 6907
Bioethics Bulletin (USA ISSN 1063-3596) 4630
➤ Bioethics Forum (USA ISSN 1065-7274) 4445
Bioethics Literature Review (USA ISSN 0886-8913) 5741
Bioethics Outlook (AUS ISSN 1037-6410) 6908
• Bioethics Research Notes (AUS ISSN 1033-6206) 6908
• Bioethics Thesaurus (Online Edition) (USA ISSN 1936-5462) 5741
Bioetica (ITA ISSN 1122-2344) 657
Bioetica e Valori (ITA ISSN 1827-2606) 6908
• BioExecutive International (USA ISSN 1558-6464) 758
▼ • ➤ Biofabrication (GBR ISSN 1758-5082) 747
• ➤ BioFactors (USA ISSN 0951-6433) 726
• Biofeedback (Cincinnati) (USA ISSN 1060-2488) 657
• Biofeedback (Wheat Ridge) (USA ISSN 1081-5937) 7340
† • Biofilms (GBR ISSN 1479-0505) 8936
➤ Biofizika (RUS ISSN 0006-3029) 752
▼ • Biofokus-Rapport (NOR ISSN 1504-6370) 657
BioFood (English Edition) see BioFood (French Edition) 864
BioFood (French Edition) (FRA ISSN 1951-2856) 864
BioFormosa (TWN ISSN 1684-0925) 657
• Bioforsk Fokus (NOR ISSN 0809-8662) 96
• Bioforsk Tema (NOR ISSN 0809-8654) 96
Bioforum (DEU ISSN 0940-0079) 657
• Bioforum Europe (DEU ISSN 1611-597X) 657
BIOforum France (DEU ISSN 1619-7682) 657
Bioforum International see Bioforum Europe 657
BIOforum Zellbiologie (DEU) 827
• ➤ Biofouling (GBR ISSN 0892-7014) 3494
• Biofuels Abstracts (GBR) 3151
▼ • ➤ Biofuels, Bioproducts and Biorefining (GBR ISSN 1932-104X) 6764
▼ • Biofuels Brazil (GBR ISSN 1756-4883) 6764
▼ • Biofuels Business (USA) 6764
▼ Biofuels International (GBR ISSN 1754-2170) 6764
BioFuels Journal (USA) 6764
▼ Biofuels Technology (GBR ISSN 1757-6407) 3124
• ➤ Biogenic Amines (SVK ISSN 0168-8561) 726
• ➤ Biogeochemistry (NLD ISSN 0168-2563) 726
Biogeographical Society of Japan. Bulletin see Nihon Seibutsu Chiri Gakkai Kaiho 694
• ➤ Biogeosciences (DEU ISSN 1726-4170) 657
• ➤ Biogeosciences Discussions (DEU ISSN 1810-6277) 657
• ➤ Biogerontology (NLD ISSN 1389-5729) 4041
Biografias Hoy/Biography Today in Spanish (USA) 640
Biograficke Studie (SVK ISSN 0067-8724) 640
Biografie see P.M. Biografie 645
Biograph (DEU) 6490
Biographical Literature see Zhuanji Wenxue 5405
• Les Biographies.com. Agences et Societes de Publicite (FRA ISSN 1954-426X) 640
• Les Biographies.com. Corps Diplomatique et Consulaire, Conseillers et Attaches Commerciaux et Financiers (FRA ISSN 1954-4324) 640
Les Biographies.com. Documentation Electorale (FRA ISSN 1957-6587) 7423
• Les Biographies.com. La Cour de Cassation (FRA ISSN 1954-4367) 640
• Les Biographies.com. L'Assemblee Nationale (FRA ISSN 1954-4251) 640
• Les Biographies.com. Le Conseil de Paris (FRA ISSN 1954-4316) 640
• Les Biographies.com. Le Conseil d'Etat (FRA ISSN 1954-4286) 640
• Les Biographies.com. Le Conseil Economique et Social (FRA ISSN 1954-4340) 640
• Les Biographies.com. Le Tribunal de Commerce de Paris (FRA ISSN 1954-4294) 640
• Les Biographies.com. Les Biographies de la Publicite (FRA ISSN 1954-4332) 640

Title

Title

• Blue Jean (TUR ISSN 1300-5855) 6550
Blue Jean Magazine (USA ISSN 1086-3893) 8853
The Blue Journal see Taxation in Australia 1950
Blue Lake Information Guide (CAN ISSN 1710-3215) 8688
Blue Light Magazine see Blue Light National Magazine 2145
Blue Light National Magazine (AUS) 2145
Blue Lights (USA) 2375
▼ Blue Line (FRA ISSN 1957-150X) 8782
Blue Line Magazine (CAN ISSN 0847-8538) 2645
Blue Mesa Review (USA ISSN 1042-2951) 5264
• The Blue Moon Review (USA) 5264
The Blue Mountains Gazette (AUS) 3793
Blue Note Magazine (ITA ISSN 1124-5263) 6550
• ➤ The Blue Notebook (GBR ISSN 1751-1712) 5264
The Blue Pages (GBR) 7423
• Blue Print (DEU ISSN 0944-467X) 7223
• Blue Print (GBR ISSN 1366-6665) 49
Blue Raider Nation (USA) 8162
Blue Ribbon: College Football Yearbook (USA) 8223
Blue Ribbon Home Plans (USA ISSN 1936-7279) 435
Blue Ridge Country (USA ISSN 1041-3456) 3970
• Blue Ridge Highlander (USA) 8688
Blue Ridge, Including the Shenandoah Valley see Insiders' Guide to Virginia's Blue Ridge, Including the Shenandoah Valley 8723
• The Blue Seal Tech News (USA) 8569
Blue Shield see Landun 4712
Blue Skies (GBR ISSN 1754-3479) 4997
• Blue Skies Report (NZL ISSN 1177-3952) 8028
Blue Sky (USA) 8569
• Blue Sky Bulletin (MNG) 1591
• Blue Sky Law Reporter (USA) 4630
Blue Sky Practice For Public and Private Direct Participation Offerings (USA) 1612
Blue Sky Statutes Annotated see State Securities. Blue Sky Statutes Annotated 4881
• The Blue Star List (USA) 1612
Blue Suede News (USA ISSN 1075-6647) 6550
▼ Blue Tattoo (GBR ISSN 1753-6707) 5264
Blue Travel (DEU) 8688
Blue Unicorn (USA ISSN 0197-7016) 5418
Blue Violin (USA ISSN 1087-1500) 5418
The Blue Water Bulletin (AUS ISSN 1449-8537) 8272
Blue Water Sailing (USA ISSN 1091-1979) 8272
Blue Wings (FIN ISSN 0358-7703) 8782
Bluebell News (GBR ISSN 0520-3015) 4330
The Bluebird (USA ISSN 1050-0715) 2604
• Blueeyes Magazine (USA ISSN 1932-7013) 6964
Bluefieldian (USA) 2274
Bluegrass Automotive Report (USA) 8569
Bluegrass - Buehne (DEU ISSN 0936-2479) 6550
Bluegrass Canada Magazine (CAN ISSN 1180-761X) 6550
Bluegrass Horseman (USA ISSN 1068-8676) 8288
Bluegrass Music News (USA ISSN 0006-5129) 6550
• Bluegrass Unlimited (USA ISSN 0006-5137) 6550
The Bluejacket (USA) 6413
Blueline (GRC) 7223
Blueline (College Station) (USA) 2702
Blueline (Potsdam) (USA ISSN 0198-9901) 5264
Bluemont Muse (USA) 6550
Bluemoon (ITA ISSN 1824-1840) 5409
Bluemoon. Le Collezioni see Bluemoon 5409
Bluenose Rambler (CAN) 5264
Blueprint (Chelmsford) (GBR ISSN 0268-4926) 435
Blueprint (Durham) see Chronicle (Durham) 2277
† Blueprint (New York, 2006) (USA ISSN 1932-6378) 8937
• Blueprint (Washington, D.C.) (USA ISSN 1527-439X) 7110
Blueprint (Winfrith) (GBR) 2645
Blueprint Broadside (GBR ISSN 1744-750X) 435
Blueprint for Social Justice (USA ISSN 0895-5786) 7203
Blueprint Home Plans (IRL) 435
Blueprint Series (GBR) 3406
Blueprints (USA ISSN 0742-0552) 435
Blueprints for Economic Development (USA ISSN 1080-8604) 4404
Blues & Rhythm (GBR) 6550
• Blues & Soul (GBR ISSN 0959-6550) 6550
Blues at the Foundation (USA) 6550
The Blues Audience (USA) 6550
† Blues Buster (USA ISSN 1535-8364) 8937
Blue's Country Magazine (AUS ISSN 1448-8841) 1068
Blues Directory see Living Blues Blues Directory 6585
• Blues in Britain (GBR ISSN 1475-9721) 6550
Blues News (DEU ISSN 0948-5643) 6550
Blues News (FIN ISSN 0784-7726) 6550
• Blues Revue (USA ISSN 1091-7543) 6550
• Blues To-Do's Monthly (USA) 6550
† Blues Unlimited (GBR ISSN 0006-5153) 8937
• Bluesheets (USA) 4997
• Bluetooth World (GBR ISSN 1472-7188) 2313
BlueWater Boats & Sportsfishing (AUS ISSN 1449-6321) 8306
Bluff (USA) 8162
▼ Bluff (ZAF ISSN 1997-0552) 8162
Die Blume (DEU ISSN 1619-4969) 600
• ➤ Blumea (NLD ISSN 0006-5196) 779
➤ Blumea. Supplement (NLD ISSN 0373-4293) 780
† Blumen Worldwide (DEU ISSN 1439-9962) 8937
➤ Blumenau em Cadernos (BRA ISSN 0006-5218) 4285
Blumenwelt (DEU ISSN 1616-7759) 3755
Blum's Farmers & Planters Almanac (USA ISSN 0894-1386) 3971
Blunt (AUS) 6550
Bluprint Magazine (CAN ISSN 1703-8618) 2274
Blur (USA) 3971
▼ Blush (CAN) 2145
Blush! (GBR) 2179
Blushing Brides of Columbus (USA) 5556
Blutalkohol (DEU ISSN 0006-5250) 2692
Bluzki, Spodnie, Spodnice see Burda Special. Bluzki, Spodnie, Spodnice 2252
Blvd Man (NLD ISSN 1875-1725) 6287
Blyttia (NOR ISSN 0006-5269) 780
bmj.com see B M J (Online) 5583
BMW ON see B M W - O N 8254
BMXpress see B M Xpress 8254
The B'nai B'rith I J M see B'nai B'rith Magazine 7719
B'nai B'rith Magazine (USA ISSN 1549-4799) 7719
B'nai B'rith Messenger (USA ISSN 0006-5277) 7719
• Bo/Sports Events (CHN ISSN 1005-9024) 8162
Bo/Evenement Sportif (HKG) 8162
• Bo (NOR ISSN 0332-7582) 4404
• Bo Bedre (DNK ISSN 0006-5285) 4533
Bo Bygg og Bolig (NOR ISSN 0803-7485) 4533
• Boa Forma (BRA ISSN 0104-1533) 6983
Boa Mesa (PRT) 4353
Boa Semente (PRT) 2179
Boai/Faraternity (CHN ISSN 1007-8428) 6983
Boar Hunter (USA) 8306
The Board (USA ISSN 1947-3656) 3018
Board and Administrator: Association Edition (USA ISSN 1047-3718) 1728
• Board & Administrator. For Administrators Only (USA ISSN 1525-7878) 1728
Board and Administrator: Government Edition (USA ISSN 1058-7640) 1728
Board and Administrator: School Edition (USA ISSN 0894-816X) 1728
• The Board Builder (AUS ISSN 1832-438X) 1728
Board Converting News see B C N 6708
Board Converting News International (GBR) 6708
Board Earnings in FT-SE 100 Companies (GBR) 1442
• Board Leadership (USA ISSN 1061-4249) 1728
Board Manufacture & Processing (GBR ISSN 0306-4123) 3710
• Board Market Digest (GBR ISSN 1358-0701) 6708
Board Member (USA ISSN 1058-5419) 1729
• Board News (AUS ISSN 1832-8350) 3587
Board of Certified Safety Professionals Directory and International Registry of Certified Safety Professionals see C S P Directory and International Registry of Certified Safety Professionals 6675
Board of Certified Safety Professionals Newsletter see B C S P Newsletter 6673
Board of Directors Report (USA) 1729
• Board of Immigration Appeals. Interim Decisions (Online) (USA) 4846
Board of International Affairs of the Royal College of Psychiatrists. Bulletin see International Psychiatry 6147
Board of Registered Nursing Report see B R N Report 5952
Board of Trade of Thailand. Trade Directory (THA) 1976
• Board of Vocational Education and Training. Annual Report (AUS ISSN 1329-6868) 2831
The Boardgamer (USA) 8162
Boarding Schools & Colleges (GBR ISSN 0951-872X) 2954
The BoardRoom (GBR ISSN 1753-9226) 1729
Boardroom (GBR) 1068
Boardroom (ZAF ISSN 0378-9144) 1850
Boardroom Briefing (USA ISSN 1934-4422) 1729
• Boards (CAN ISSN 1488-6286) 2313
• Boards (GBR ISSN 0950-7337) 8272
† Boardstein (DEU) 8937
Boardtest Magazine (USA) 8306
Boat & Marine Accessories Mart International see Boat Mart International 4330
• Boat & Motor Dealer (USA ISSN 0006-5366) 8272
Boat Angler (GBR ISSN 0958-3602) 8306
Boat Broker (USA) 8272
Boat Guide (CAN ISSN 0826-2802) 8272
Boat International (GBR ISSN 0264-9136) 8272
Boat Mart International (GBR ISSN 0956-6589) 4330
Boat Modeler see Radio Control Boat Modeler 4344
Boat Owner Middle East (UAE ISSN 1816-8442) 8272
Boat Owners Association of the United States Magazine see B O A T - U S Magazine 8271
Boatbuilder (USA ISSN 0886-0254) 8272
Boatbuilder's International Directory (USA) 8272
Boaters Digest (USA ISSN 1530-065X) 8273
• Boating (USA ISSN 0006-5374) 8273
Boating Almanac, Volume 1: Massachusetts, Maine, New Hampshire (USA ISSN 0067-9356) 8273
Boating Almanac, Volume 2: Long Island, Connecticut, Rhode Island, Southern Massachusetts (USA) 8273
Boating Almanac, Volume 3: New Jersey, Delaware Bay, Hudson River, Lake Champlain, Erie Canal (USA) 8273
Boating Almanac, Volume 4: Chesapeake Bay, Delaware, Maryland, District of Columbia, Virginia (USA) 8273
Boating Business (AUS ISSN 1834-142X) 8273
Boating Business (CAN ISSN 0702-7524) 8273
Boating Business (GBR ISSN 0260-9452) 8273
• The Boating Directory (GBR ISSN 1466-2426) 8273
Boating East Cruising & Vacation Guide (CAN) 8688
• Boating Industry (USA ISSN 1543-4400) 8273
Boating Industry Canada (CAN) 8640
Boating Industry Marine Buyers' Guide (USA) 1976
• Boating Life (USA ISSN 1092-8219) 8273
Boating New Zealand (NZL ISSN 0113-0838) 8273
Boating News see Baatnytt 8272
Boating Registration Statistics (USA ISSN 0163-7207) 8218
• Boating Safety Circular (USA ISSN 1931-9126) 8273
Boating Statistics (USA) 8218
• Boating World (USA ISSN 1059-5155) 8273
Boats & Harbors (USA ISSN 0739-2257) 8273
Boats & Yachts for Sale (GBR ISSN 1467-579X) 8273
• BoatSafe and BoatSafeKids (USA) 8273
BoatUS Magazine see B O A T - U S Magazine 8271
Boatworks (USA) 8640
Boatworks for the Hands-On Sailor see Boatworks 8640
Boazodoallu-aaddasat see Reindriftsnytt 298
Boazodoallu-oddasat see Reindriftsnytt 298
bob (KOR ISSN 1739-2845) 4533
Bob see Bok og Bibliotek 4997
The Bob (USA) 6550
Bob Brinker's Marketimer (USA) 1612
Bob de Bouwer (NLD ISSN 1569-6006) 2179
Bob de Bouwer Activeiten Special (NLD ISSN 1872-1281) 2179
Bob de Bouwer Verhalen Special (NLD ISSN 1871-6709) 2179
Bob der Baumeister (DEU) 2179
Bob Ellsberg's Hunter & Fisherman's Planning Yearbook (USA) 8306
Bob the Builder (GBR ISSN 1466-1012) 2179
Bob the Builder (HRV ISSN 1334-8043) 2179
Bob Watkins Sports 24 Magazine (USA) 8162
• Bob White Memorial Lecture (AUS ISSN 1832-2107) 8090
Bobasu Janaru/Japan Bobath Association. Journal (JPN ISSN 0915-8634) 8028
• Bobbitt's Manufactured Structures Newsletter (USA ISSN 1524-9859) 982
Bobby (DEU) 2179
Boberg's Law of Persons and the Family (ZAF) 4907
Bobil & Caravan (NOR ISSN 1500-3051) 8306
Bobo (IDN) 2179
Bobo (NLD ISSN 0165-1196) 2179
Bobo (ROM ISSN 1583-6495) 2179
Bobo Vakantieboek (NLD ISSN 1574-4914) 2179
Bob's B B see Bop 2180
▼ • Boca (USA ISSN 1935-9071) 5101
Boca Design and Architectural Review see Boca Design & Architectural Review 4533
Boca Design & Architectural Review (USA) 4533
Boca Dog Magazine see BocaDog Magazine 6804
Boca Life (USA) 5066
Boca Raton Historical Society, Inc. Newsletter see B R H S Newsletter 4285
Boca Raton Magazine (USA ISSN 0740-2856) 3971
The Boca Raton Observer (USA ISSN 1940-4239) 5066
BocaDog Magazine (USA ISSN 1558-593X) 6804
Bocagiana (PRT ISSN 0523-7904) 936
Bochum Publications in Evolutionary Cultural Semiotics (DEU ISSN 1439-4073) 5264
Bochum Studies in International Adult Education (DEU ISSN 1617-3287) 2939
Bochumer Altertumswissenschaftliches Colloquium (DEU) 4133
Bochumer Arbeiten zur Musikwissenschaft (DEU) 6550
† Bochumer Arbeiten zur Sprach- und Literaturwissenschaft (NLD ISSN 0523-7971) 8937
Bochumer Beitraege zur Semiotik (DEU ISSN 1437-3335) 5264
Bochumer Chinareihe (DEU ISSN 1436-0845) 545
Bochumer Forschungen zur Rechtsgeschichte (DEU ISSN 1862-9474) 4630
Bochumer Fruehneuzeitstudien (DEU ISSN 0940-063X) 4133
Bochumer Geographische Arbeiten (DEU ISSN 0523-798X) 4000
Bochumer Germanistik (DEU ISSN 1616-0460) 5264
Bochumer Italien-Studien (DEU ISSN 1437-5443) 5264
➤ Bochumer Jahrbuch zur Ostasienforschung (DEU ISSN 0170-0006) 545
Bochumer Medizinische Schriften (DEU) 5588
• ➤ Bochumer Philosophisches Jahrbuch fuer Antike und Mittelalter (NLD ISSN 1384-6663) 6908
Bochumer Schriften zur Entwicklungsforschung und Entwicklungspolitik (DEU ISSN 0572-6654) 7224
Bochumer Studien zur Philosophie (NLD ISSN 1384-668X) 6908
Bochumer Volkswirtschaftslehre (DEU ISSN 1617-4062) 7488
Bochumer Zeitpunkte (DEU ISSN 0940-5453) 4205
Bock (DEU) 8255
Bocken (SWE ISSN 0347-299X) 6413
• El Bocon (PER ISSN 1605-3001) 8223
Bod-ljongs Zhib-vjug see Xizang Yanjiu 563
Bodaus (FIN ISSN 0788-9917) 6983
† Bode (NLD ISSN 1573-479X) 8937
Bode van het Heil in Christus see Bode 8937
Bodem (NLD ISSN 0925-1650) 3406
Boden, Wand, Decke (DEU ISSN 0006-5463) 4533
Bodendenkmalpflege in Mecklenburg-Vorpommern (DEU ISSN 0947-3998) 6521
➤ Die Bodenkultur (AUT ISSN 0006-5471) 96
Bodenkunde see Stiinta Solului 2769
Bodenkundliche Gesellschaft der Schweiz. Bulletin (CHE ISSN 1420-6773) 222
Bodenkundliche Gesellschaft der Schweiz Dokumente see B G S Dokumente 220
Bodenschutz (DEU ISSN 0935-2171) 2604
• Bodenschutz Zeitschrift (DEU ISSN 1432-170X) 2604
Bodensee Hefte (CHE ISSN 0006-548X) 4000
Bodensee Magazin (DEU ISSN 0178-4692) 8688
Bodhi (USA ISSN 1533-8053) 7700
• Bodhi Leaves (LKA ISSN 0520-3325) 7700
Bodine Motorgram (USA ISSN 0006-5498) 5449
➤ Bodleian Library Record (GBR ISSN 0067-9488) 4997
Bodrum Haberleri see Bodrum News 3962
• Bodrum News/Bodrum Haberleri (TUR ISSN 1303-5649) 3962
Body (DEU) 6238
Body (GBR ISSN 0006-5501) 8569
Body & Beauty Care (IND) 586
• ➤ Body & Society (GBR ISSN 1357-034X) 7951
Body + Soul see The Australian 3793
Body and Soul see Body + Soul 6643
Body & Soul see Body + Soul 6643
Body Beautiful see Weight Watchers Magazine 7000
• Body Beautiful (USA) 6983
Body Cast (CAN ISSN 1205-562X) 6056
Body, Commodity, Text (USA) 8090
Body Dialogue (USA ISSN 1930-0360) 6983
Body en Mind see Body + Mind. Woman 6983
Body Engineering (USA) 8569
• ➤ Body Image (NLD ISSN 1740-1445) 7341
The Body, in Theory (USA) 5264
Body Language (GBR ISSN 1475-665X) 6238
Body Language (USA) 8570
Body Life (DEU ISSN 1437-286X) 6983
Body Life (HUN ISSN 1586-2720) 586
Body Life (POL ISSN 1641-0106) 586
Body, Mind & Spirit Magazine see inPUT (Tauranga) 8964
Body + Mind. Woman (NLD ISSN 1871-3270) 6983
• Body Modification Ezine (CAN) 6643
• ➤ Body, Movement and Dance in Psychotherapy (GBR ISSN 1743-2979) 2683
• Body Politic (GBR) 6287
• Body Positive (USA ISSN 1048-4396) 5810
Body Shop Business see BodyShop Business 8570
• Body + Soul (USA ISSN 1539-0004) 6643
• Body, Space & Technology (GBR ISSN 1470-9120) 479
Bodyboard Magazine (FRA ISSN 1764-5549) 8306
▼ Bodyboarder (USA ISSN 1938-6125) 8162
Bodyguard (NLD ISSN 1871-0603) 4371
▼ Bodyguards & Bouncers (GBR ISSN 1754-7024) 2645
† Bodymagazine (NLD ISSN 1569-7436) 8937
Bodymedia (DEU) 6983
Bodyshop see L' AutoMobile 8563
• Bodyshop (English Edition) (CAN ISSN 0045-2319) 8570
• BodyShop Business (USA ISSN 0730-7241) 8570
• Bodyshop Buyer's Guide (GBR) 1976
Bodyshop Expo (USA) 8570
Bodyshop Magazine (GBR ISSN 1465-9514) 8570
Bodyshop Management Briefings (GBR) 8570
Bodystyle (DEU) 2251
BodyTalk (French Edition) see Equilibre 5610
Bodywear Directions (GBR ISSN 1464-9667) 2245
Boecker, Bilder och Saant (SWE ISSN 1100-780X) 2180
Boecksteiner Montana (AUT) 6458
Boei Daigakko Kiyo Rikogaku-hen see National Defense Academy. Memoirs. Mathematics, Physics, Chemistry and Engineering 7886
Boei Daigakko Kyokan Kenkyu Yoroku/National Defense Academy. Digest of Researches by Faculty Members (JPN ISSN 0523-8080) 6455
Boei Daigakko Rikogaku Kenkyu Hokoku/National Defense Academy. Scientific and Engineering Reports (JPN ISSN 0385-7301) 3183
Boei Gijutsu Janaru/Defense Technology Journal (JPN ISSN 0919-8555) 6413
Boei Ika Daigakko Shingaku Katei Kenkyu Kiyo/National Defense Medical College. Bulletin of Liberal Arts and Sciences (JPN ISSN 0386-8133) 4445
Boei Ika Daigakko Zasshi/National Defense Medical College. Journal (JPN ISSN 0385-1796) 5588
Boek (NLD ISSN 1574-2199) 7553
Het Boek (Antwerpen) see Quaerendo 7571
Boek.Bedrijf - V B V B (Vereniging ter Bevordering van het Vlaamse Boekwezen) (BEL ISSN 1377-8714) 7553
Boekblad see Boekblad Magazine 7553
• Boekblad Magazine (NLD ISSN 1568-2897) 7553
BoekBoek (NLD ISSN 1574-2458) 7553
▼ Boekenkrant (NLD ISSN 1875-2608) 5264
Boekenpost (NLD ISSN 0928-4230) 7553
De Boekenwereld (NLD ISSN 0168-8391) 7553
Boekhistorische Reeks (NLD ISSN 1382-3426) 5264
Boekidee see Leesgoed 2882
Boekie Boekie (NLD ISSN 0926-3985) 2180

Title

Boletin de Opinion *see* Economia y Sociedad **1479**
• Boletin de Ovinos (CHL ISSN 0718-0403) **281**
• ➤ Boletin de Pediatria (ESP ISSN 0214-2597) **6089**
Boletin de Pediatria de Asturias, Cantabria, Castilla y Leon *see* Boletin de Pediatria **6089**
• Boletin de Plantas Medicinales y Aromaticas (CHL ISSN 0718-0357) **780**
Boletin de Poblacion Activa, Comunidad de Madrid *see* Comunidad de Madrid. Boletin de Poblacion Activa (Diskette) **7279**
Boletin de Poblacion de las Naciones Unidas *see* Population Bulletin of the United Nations **7289**
Boletin de Politica Informatica (MEX ISSN 0186-0461) **7110**
Boletin de Prensa (COL) **97**
Boletin de Promecafe (GTM ISSN 1010-1527) **222**
Boletin de Psicologia (ESP ISSN 0212-8179) **7341**
Boletin de Resumenes de Patentes *see* Boletin Oficial de la Propiedad Industrial. 4: Resumenes de Patentes **6746**
Boletin de Seguros (ECU) **4496**
Boletin de Servicios Agricolas *see* F A O Agricultural Services Bulletin **197**
Boletin de Tratamientos Experimentales Contra el SIDA *see* B E T A **5810**
Boletin de Vias (COL ISSN 0120-2251) **8629**
Boletin del Centro de Documentacion en Ocio (A D O Z) (Aisiazko Dokumentazio Zentruaren) (ESP ISSN 1134-6019) **7951**
Boletin del Espanol *see* Embajada de Espana. Londres. Consejeria de Educacion y Ciencia. Boletin **3012**
Boletin del F M I *see* International Monetary Fund Survey **1244**
El Boletin del I C A E *see* I C A E Bulletin **2942**
Boletin del INEN *see* Instituto Nacional de Enfermedades Neoplasticas. Boletin **6022**
Boletin del Instituto de Investigaciones Bibliograficas *see* Universidad Nacional Autonoma de Mexico. Instituto de Investigaciones Bibliograficas. Boletin **638**
Boletin del Instituto Municipal de la Historia *see* Lopez de Gamiz **4151**
Boletin del Instituto Nacional de Salud *see* Instituto Nacional de Salud. Boletin **5636**
Boletin del Instituto Oceanografico de Venezuela *see* Instituto Oceanografico de Venezuela. Boletin **2807**
▼ Boletin del Observatorio sobre Desarrollo Humano (COL ISSN 2011-2017) **7951**
Boletin del Real Patronato. Cuaderno de Documentacion (ESP ISSN 1134-9123) **4064**
Boletin del Registro de Variedades (ESP) **222**
Boletin del Seminario de Estudios para la Descolonizacion de Mexico *see* Chicomoztoc **4288**
Boletin DM (Documentacion Musical) (ESP ISSN 1888-4814) **4997**
Boletin Eclesiastico de Filipinas (PHL ISSN 0116-1830) **7786**
Boletin Economico de Andalucia (ESP ISSN 0212-6621) **1442**
Boletin Economico de la Construccion (ESP ISSN 0210-1947) **1442**
Boletin Electoral Latinoamericano (CRI ISSN 1020-0940) **7110**
Boletin Epidemiologico (MEX ISSN 0366-1709) **7510**
Boletin Epidemiologico (USA ISSN 0255-6669) **7510**
Boletin Epidemiologico Fronterizo *see* Border Epidemiological Bulletin **7510**
Boletin Epidemiologico Periodico (ARG ISSN 1851-4014) **7510**
• Boletin Epidemiologico Semanal (CUB ISSN 1028-5083) **7510**
• Boletin Epidemiologico Semanal (ESP ISSN 1135-6286) **7510**
▼ Boletin Estadistico (COL ISSN 2011-2637) **2969**
Boletin Estadistico de Pesca *see* Bulletin of Fishery Statistics **8938**
Boletin Estadistico de Trafico Aereo Internacional (ECU) **8523**
Boletin Estadistico del Petroleo (ESP) **6764**
Boletin Estadistico Pesquero (URY ISSN 0797-194X) **3587**
Boletin Europeo de la Universidad de La Rioja *see* Universidad de La Rioja. Boletin Europeo **4943**
Boletin F A O de Estadisticas *see* F A O Bulletin of Statistics **179**
Boletin F A O, Fertilizantes y Nutricion Vegetal *see* F A O Fertilizer and Plant Nutrition Bulletin **197**
Boletin FAL *see* Facilitacion del Comercio y el Trasnporte en America Latina y el Caribe. Boletin **1428**
Boletin Fiscal (ESP ISSN 1136-0275) **1913**
➤ Boletin Galego de Literatura (ESP ISSN 0214-9117) **5265**
Boletin Genetico (ARG ISSN 0067-9720) **864**
Boletin Geologico (COL ISSN 0120-1425) **2726**
Boletin Geologico y Minero (ESP ISSN 0366-0176) **2726**
Boletin Geologico y Minero. Publicaciones Especiales (ESP) **2726**
Boletin Glaciologico Aragones (ESP ISSN 1695-7989) **2778**
Boletin Hidrologico (CRI ISSN 0067-9747) **2793**
Boletin Historico del Ejercito (URY) **4133**
Boletin Horticola (ARG ISSN 0328-719X) **3725**
Boletin I C E Economico *see* I C E Economico. Boletin **1429**
Boletin I I E *see* Instituto de Investigaciones Electricas. Boletin **3319**
Boletin I N S *see* Instituto Nacional de Salud. Boletin **5636**
Boletin I R A M *see* I R A M. Boletin **6402**
Boletin Indicadores Sectoriales de Competitividad y Productividad (ECU ISSN 1390-2067) **1321**
Boletin Indigenista Venezolano (VEN ISSN 0523-9133) **331**
Boletin Industrial (MEX ISSN 0187-7321) **1880**
• Boletin Informativo (ARG) **1068**
• Boletin Informativo (MEX) **6238**
Boletin Informativo de Accion Educativa *see* Accion Educativa. Boletin Informativo **2823**
Boletin Informativo de Arquitectos Tecnicos y Aparejadores *see* B I A **434**
Boletin Informativo de la Nacion Taina (USA) **3523**
Boletin Informativo de la Profesion de Arquitectos *see* Arquitectos **433**
• Boletin Informativo de la Seguridad Social. Gestion Economica (ESP ISSN 1576-026X) **4496**
Boletin Informativo de la Vigilancia Atmosferica *see* B I V A **6347**
Boletin Informativo de Legislacion Fiscal *see* Boletin de Legislacion, Tecnica Contable **4858**
Boletin Informativo de Lenguas (ESP ISSN 1132-7545) **5265**
Boletin Informativo de Telecomunicacion *see* B I T **2570**
Boletin Informativo Electronico Mensual *see* Instituto Geologico Minero y Metalurgico. Boletin. Serie D. Estudios Regionales **6466**
Boletin Informativo - Facultad de Ciencias Fisicas y Matematicas *see* Universidad de Chile. Facultad de Ciencias Fisicas y Matematicas. Boletin Informativo **5543**
▼ Boletin Informativo Gobernar (COL ISSN 2011-3870) **8028**
Boletin Informativo - Oficina de Cooperacion Internacional *see* Oficina de Cooperacion Internacional. Boletin Informativo **7256**
Boletin Informativo - S E F H *see* Sociedad Espanola de Farmacia Hospitalaria. Boletin Informativo **6881**
Boletin Informativo Semanal de Seguros (ESP) **4496**
Boletin Informativo sobre Desarrollo Social *see* Social Development Newsletter **8133**
Boletin Informativo Techint (ARG ISSN 0497-0292) **7951**
Boletin Informativo U D T *see* U D T Newsletter **5051**
Boletin Interamericano de Contabilidad/Interamerican Bulletin (USA) **1281**
Boletin Internacional de Bibliografia Sobre Educacion *see* International Bulletin of Bibliography on Education **2934**
Boletin Internacional de Ciencias del Mar *see* I M S Newsletter **2806**
Boletin Internacional de Lenguas y Culturas Amerindias (ESP ISSN 1138-154X) **331**
Boletin Internacional de Oportunidades (COL) **1396**
Boletin Juridico Militar (MEX ISSN 0006-6419) **4971**
Boletin Juridico y Financiero (COL ISSN 0121-0629) **1321**
Boletin La Pintura Prehispanica en Mexico (MEX ISSN 1405-4817) **384**
• Boletin Latinoamericano y del Caribe de Plantas Medicinales y Aromaticas (CHL ISSN 0717-7917) **780**
Boletin Medico de I P P F *see* I P P F Medical Bulletin **972**
• Boletin Medico Familiar (MEX) **5588**
Boletin Mensal de Estadistica (PRT ISSN 0032-5082) **8358**
† • Boletin Mensual de Coyuntura (ESP ISSN 1138-221X) **8937**
Boletin Mensual de Estadisticas del Sistema Financiero (HND) **1215**
Boletin Mensual de Fondos de Inversion *see* Actividad de Fondos de Inversion **1609**
Boletin Mercado de Suelo Urbano en el Gran Cocepcion *see* Mercado de Suelo **449**
Boletin Mercadologico I L A F A (CHL) **6306**
• Boletin Mexicano de Derecho Comparado (MEX ISSN 0041-8633) **4631**
Boletin Mexicano de Historia y Filosofia de la Medicina (MEX) **5588**
Boletin Micologico (CHL ISSN 0716-114X) **780**
† Boletin Millares Carlo (ESP ISSN 0211-2140) **8937**
Boletin Oficial da Provincia de Pontevedra *see* Provincia de Pontevedra. Boletin Oficial **7501**
Boletin Oficial de la Asociacion Gallega de Salud Mental *see* Siso Saude **6185**
• Boletin Oficial de la Propiedad Industrial. 1: Marcas y Otros Signos Distintivos (ESP ISSN 0211-0121) **6746**
• Boletin Oficial de la Propiedad Industrial. 2: Patentes y Modelos de Utilidad (ESP ISSN 0211-0105) **6746**
• Boletin Oficial de la Propiedad Industrial. 3: Modelos y Dibujos Industriales y Artisticos (ESP ISSN 0211-013X) **6746**
• Boletin Oficial de la Propiedad Industrial. 4: Resumenes de Patentes (ESP ISSN 1136-3312) **6746**
† Boletin Oficial de las Cortes Espanolas (ESP) **8937**
† Boletin Oficial de Navarra/Nafarroako Aldizkari (ESP ISSN 1130-5894) **8937**
Boletin Oficial del Parlamento de Navarra (ESP) **7423**
Boletin Oficial del Registro Mercantil *see* Spain. Registro Mercantil. Boletin Oficial **1178**
• Boletin Olivicola (CHL ISSN 0718-0330) **281**
▼ Boletin Palabrerio (COL ISSN 2011-1169) **2832**
• Boletin Posgrados (BOL) **7951**
• Boletin RADIAL (Boletin Red de Investigacion y Accion para el Desarrollo Local) (BOL) **8028**
• Boletin REDESMA (Boletin Red de Desarollo Sostenible y Medio Ambiente) (BOL ISSN 1609-6509) **3407**
• Boletin Reforme (VEN) **7423**
Boletin S A O *see* Sociedad Antioquena de Ornitologia. Boletin **914**
Boletin S I N I C Y T *see* Sistema Nacional de Informacion Cientifica y Tecnologia. Boletin **7917**
Boletin Semanal *see* Weekly Bulletin **3877**
Boletin Semanal *see* Wochenschau **3877**
▼ Boletin Tecnico Biodiversidad (COL ISSN 2011-4087) **2604**
Boletin Tecnico de Ergonomia (CHL ISSN 0718-4700) **3342**
Boletin Tecnico Instituto de Materiales y Modelos Estructurales *see* I M M E Boletin Tecnico **3269**
Boletin Tecnico Pulpa y Papel (CUB ISSN 0138-8940) **6732**
Boletin Teologico (PER) **7628**
Boletin Terapeutico Andaluz (ESP ISSN 0212-9450) **6826**
• Boletin UMC (Boletin Unidad de Medicion de la Calidad Educativa) (PER ISSN 1682-4849) **2832**
Boletin UNEBI *see* U N E B I Boletin **3015**
Boletin Unico de Licitaciones y Concurso (COL) **1068**
Boletin Uruguayo de Sociologia (URY ISSN 0006-6508) **8090**
Boletin Verde (ESP ISSN 0213-8980) **281**
▼ Boletin Veterinario (CHL ISSN 0718-5502) **8794**
▼ Boletines Tematicos (COL ISSN 2011-2807) **2832**
• ➤ Boli yu Tangci/Glass & Enamel (CHN ISSN 1000-2871) **2038**
Bolig, Hytte og Fritid *see* Boligfakta **982**
Bolig i Utlandet (NOR ISSN 0809-6562) **8688**
Bolig Liv *see* Boligliv **4353**
Bolig Magasinet (DNK ISSN 1399-8072) **4533**
• Boligen (DNK ISSN 0108-2590) **4405**
Boligetc.no (NOR ISSN 0809-6465) **982**
• Boligfakta (NOR ISSN 1504-4483) **982**
• Boligliv (DNK ISSN 1603-9610) **4353**
• Bolina (ITA ISSN 1121-3108) **8273**
Bolivar (COL) **4496**
Bolivia (DEU ISSN 0945-201X) **5209**
Bolivia. Camara de Diputados. Estadisticas Socio-economicas (BOL) **8358**
• Bolivia.com (BOL ISSN 1609-6916) **3802**
Bolivia Directorio de Exportadores *see* Bolivia Export Directory **1976**
Bolivia en Cifras (BOL ISSN 0302-5217) **8358**
Bolivia Export Directory/Bolivia Directorio de Exportadores (BOL) **1976**
Bolivia: Guia Eclesiastica (BOL) **7786**
Bolivia Handbook (GBR ISSN 1368-4264) **8688**
Bolivia. Instituto Nacional de Estadistica. Anuario de Comercio Exterior (BOL) **1215**
Bolivia. Instituto Nacional de Estadistica. Anuario de Estadisticas Industriales (BOL) **1215**
Bolivia. Instituto Nacional de Estadistica. Estadisticas Regionales Departamentales (BOL) **7303**
Bolivia. Instituto Nacional de Estadistica. Indice de Precios al Consumidor (BOL) **1215**
Bolivia. Servicio Nacional de Geologia y Mineria. Boletin (BOL ISSN 1023-7674) **2702**
• Bolivian Research Review (BOL) **4286**
Bolivian Studies *see* Bolivian Studies Journal **4286**
Bolivian Studies Journal (USA) **4286**
• Bolivian Times (BOL ISSN 1563-8219) **3802**
• Bolivia@Press (BOL ISSN 1609-6703) **3802**
• BoliviHoy.com (BOL ISSN 1609-6908) **3802**
Bolletino A I B *see* Associazione Italiana Biblioteche. Bollettino **4992**
• Bollettario (ITA ISSN 1723-9761) **5265**
Il Bollettino (ITA ISSN 1971-4106) **3407**
• ➤ Bollettino '900 (ITA ISSN 1126-7003) **5265**
• Bollettino '900 Online (ITA ISSN 1124-1578) **5265**
Bollettino Archivio Pace Diritti Umani *see* Pace, Diritti dell'Uomo, Diritti dei Popoli **7213**
† Bollettino Chimico Farmaceutico (ITA ISSN 0006-6648) **8937**
Bollettino d'Arte (ITA ISSN 0394-4573) **479**
Bollettino d'Arte. Supplemento (ITA ISSN 0394-4611) **479**
Bollettino dei Classici (ITA ISSN 0392-842X) **2231**
Bollettino dei Classici. Supplemento *see* Bollettino dei Classici **2231**
Bollettino dei Medici Svizzeri *see* Schweizerische Aerztezeitung **5710**
Bollettino dei Musei e degli Istituti Biologici dell'Universita di Genova *see* Universita degli Studi di Genova. Musei e Istituti Biologici. Bollettino **709**
Bollettino del Centro Camuno di Studi Preistorici *see* B C S P **383**
• Bollettino del Lavoro e dei Tributi (ITA ISSN 0394-6592) **4631**
▼ • Bollettino dell' Atlante Linguistico degli Antichi Volgari Italiani (ITA ISSN 1971-9043) **5101**
Bollettino della Societa Ticinese di Scienze Naturali *see* Societa Ticinese di Scienze Naturali. Bollettino **7917**
Bollettino dell'Atlante Linguistico Italiano (ITA ISSN 1122-1836) **5101**
Bollettino dell'Atlante Linguistico Mediterraneo (ITA ISSN 0067-9879) **5101**
Bollettino dell'Unione Europea *see* European Commission. European Union. Bulletin **7233**
Bollettino di Archeologia (ITA ISSN 1120-2742) **384**
† Bollettino di Farmacosorveglianza (ITA ISSN 1120-8678) **8937**
Bollettino di Geodesia e Scienze Affini (ITA ISSN 0006-6710) **2702**
Bollettino di Geofisica Teorica ed Applicata (ITA ISSN 0006-6729) **2778**
Bollettino di Italianistica (ITA ISSN 0168-7298) **5201**
• Bollettino di Legislazione Tecnica (ITA ISSN 0392-3789) **983**
Bollettino di Libri Antichi e Moderni di Varia Cultura Esauriti e Rari (ITA ISSN 0006-6745) **620**
Bollettino di Microbiologia ed Indagini di Laboratorio News (ITA ISSN 1590-5705) **882**
Bollettino di Numismatica (ITA ISSN 0392-971X) **6649**
➤ Bollettino di Psicologia Applicata (ITA ISSN 0006-6761) **7341**
Bollettino di S. Nicola (ITA ISSN 0404-9462) **7786**
• Bollettino di Storia delle Scienze Matematiche (ITA ISSN 0392-4432) **5476**
• Bollettino di Studi Latini (ITA ISSN 0006-6583) **2231**
• Bollettino di Studi Sartriani (ITA ISSN 1970-7983) **6908**
➤ Bollettino di Zoologia Agraria e di Bachicoltura (ITA ISSN 0366-2403) **936**
Bollettino d'Informazione Agiscuola *see* Giornale dello Spettacolo **2686**
† Bollettino d'Oculistica (ITA ISSN 0006-677X) **8937**
Bollettino Economico *see* Qui Economia **1409**
Bollettino Linguistico Campano (ITA ISSN 1722-0262) **5101**
Bollettino Malacologico *see* Societa Italiana di Malacologia. Bollettino Malacologico **963**
• Bollettino per le Farmacodipendenze e l'Alcoolismo/Bulletin on Drug Addiction and Alcoholism (ITA ISSN 0392-3126) **2692**
† Bollettino Petrolifero (ITA) **8937**
• Il Bollettino Salesiano (ITA ISSN 0391-5867) **7786**
• Bollettino Sistematico di Filosofia Politica (ITA ISSN 1591-4305) **7110**
Bollettino Storico-Bibliografico Subalpino (ITA ISSN 0391-6715) **4205**
Bollettino Storico della Basilicata (ITA ISSN 0394-1841) **7786**
Bollettino Storico della Citta di Foligno (ITA ISSN 0391-4550) **4205**
Bollettino Storico per la Provincia di Novara (ITA ISSN 0392-1107) **4205**
Bollettino Storico Piacentino (ITA ISSN 0006-6591) **4205**
Bollettino Storico Pisano (ITA ISSN 0391-1780) **4205**
Bollettino Svizzero di Micologia *see* Schweizerische Zeitschrift fuer Pilzkunde **816**
Bollettino Svizzero di Mineralogia e Petrografia *see* Schweizerische Mineralogische und Petrographische Mitteilungen **6479**
Bollingen Series (USA) **6908**
Bollywood (GBR ISSN 1477-691X) **6491**
Bollywood News (MUS ISSN 1694-0261) **6491**
Bol'nitsa (RUS) **5588**
Bologna dei Musei (ITA ISSN 1828-4779) **6521**
Bolovsrol/Education (MNG) **2832**
Bolsa (ARG ISSN 0325-4984) **1396**
Bolsa de Barcelona. Informe Anual (ESP ISSN 1132-3337) **1613**
Bolsa de Cereales. Numero Estadistico (ARG ISSN 0084-7968) **97**
Bolsa de Comercio de Mendoza. Centro de Informaciones. Boletin (ARG) **1396**
Bolsa de Comercio de Rosario. Informativo Semanal (ARG) **1613**
Bolsa de Comercio de Rosario. Revista (ARG ISSN 0006-6931) **1396**
Bolsa de Valores de Caracas. Anuario Estadistico (VEN) **1613**
Bolsa de Valores de Caracas. Boletin de Operaciones (VEN) **1613**
Bolsa de Valores de Caracas. Boletin Mensual (VEN) **1613**
Bolsa de Valores de Caracas. Diario (VEN) **1613**
• Bolsa de Valores de Lima. Boletin Diario (PER ISSN 1682-430X) **1613**
Bolsa de Valores de Lima. Memoria (PER) **1613**
• Bolsa de Valores de Lisboa. Boletim de Cotacoes (PRT) **1613**
Bolsa de Valores de Montevideo. Boletin Mensual (URY ISSN 0797-5198) **1613**
Bolsa de Valores de Montevideo. Estudio Estadisticos. Boletin Trimestral (URY) **1613**
Bolsa de Valores de Montevideo. Estudios Estadisticos (URY) **1321**
Bolsa de Valores de Quito. Boletin de Operaciones (ECU) **1215**
Bolsa de Valores de Quito. Informes y Memoria Anual (ECU) **1613**
Bolsa de Valores do Rio de Janeiro. Resumo Anual (BRA ISSN 0557-0506) **1613**
Bolsa Mexicana de Valores. Anuario Financiero (Year) (MEX ISSN 0188-3879) **1215**

10048 BOLSA MEXICANA DE VALORES. BOLETIN BURSATIL CAPITALES ULRICH'S PERIODICALS

Bolsa Mexicana de Valores. Boletin Bursatil Capitales/Mexican Stock Exchange. Capital Market Bulletin (MEX) **1613**
Bolsa Mexicana de Valores. Boletin Bursatil Dinero y Metales/Mexican Stock Exchange. Money & Metal Market Bulletin (MEX) **1613**
Bolsa Mexicana de Valores. Indicadores Financieros/Mexican Stock Exchange. Financial Facts and Figures (MEX ISSN 0188-3925) **1215**
Bolsa Mexicana de Valores. Informacion Financiera Anual sobre Asambleas/Mexican Stock Exchange. General Stockholders' Meetings Information (MEX) **1613**
Bolsa Mexicana de Valores. Informacion Financiera Mensual/Mexican Stock Exchange. Monthly Financial Information (MEX) **1613**
Bolsa Mexicana de Valores. Programa Extraordinario de Divulgacion de Informacion Financiera (MEX) **1613**
Bolsa Mexicana de Valores. Resumen Bursatil/Mexican Stock Exchange. Statistics Summary (MEX ISSN 1405-230X) **1215**
Bolsa. Suplemento (ARG ISSN 0325-4992) **1396**
Bolsa. Suplemento Semanal (ARG ISSN 0325-500X) **1396**
• Il Bolscevico (ITA ISSN 0392-3886) **7110**
Bolsilibros (URY ISSN 0067-9909) **5265**
Bolskan (ESP ISSN 0214-4999) **384**
Boltan-e-Pizhuhishi/Research Bulletin (IRN) **4445**
Bolton Journal (GBR) **3862**
Bolton Landing Conference. Proceedings (USA) **3183**
Bolzen (DEU) **8224**
Boma Lathu (MWI) **1442**
BOMA.org *see* B O M A.org **978**
Bomb (JPN) **2180**
• Bomb (USA ISSN 0743-3204) **479**
Bombala Times (AUS ISSN 1832-3782) **3793**
Bombay (IND) **3879**
Bombay Art Society's Art Journal (IND) **479**
Bombay Chartered Accountant Journal (IND) **1281**
Bombay Hospital Journal (IND ISSN 0524-0182) **5588**
Bombay Law Reporter (IND) **4631**
Bombay Market (IND ISSN 0006-6974) **1443**
• ➤ Bombay Natural History Society. Journal (IND ISSN 0006-6982) **7841**
Bombay Samachar Daily (IND) **3879**
Bombay Samachar Dipotsavi Ank (IND) **3879**
Bombay Samachar Weekly (IND) **3879**
Bombay Technologist (IND ISSN 0067-9925) **2051**
Bombay Textile Research Association Scan *see* B T R A Scan **8448**
▼ Bombers Broadside (USA ISSN 1942-2377) **8224**
▼ Bombin' Magazine (USA ISSN 1938-6117) **479**
Bombing Incidents *see* U.S. Federal Bureau of Investigation. (Year) Bombing Incidents **2670**
Bombus (DEU ISSN 0724-4223) **841**
† Bomdia Lusitano (FRA) **8937**
Bomen (NLD ISSN 1871-5982) **97**
Bomennieuws (NLD ISSN 0166-784X) **3725**
Bomenwerk (NLD ISSN 1574-4469) **435**
Bomond (USA ISSN 1934-4376) **5066**
Bomp (USA) **6550**
• Bon (SWE ISSN 1650-7711) **2251**
Bon a Savoir (CHE ISSN 1424-6635) **4353**
• Bon Appetit (USA ISSN 0006-6990) **4353**
• Le Bon Choix (CAN ISSN 1496-3779) **620**
Bon Cultivateur de l'Est (FRA) **97**
Bon Magazine *see* Bon **2251**
Bon Verre, Bonne Table *see* Food & Drink **603**
• Bon Vivant (MEX ISSN 1405-8111) **5066**
† Bon Week (FRA ISSN 1951-9486) **8937**
Bona (English Edition) (ZAF ISSN 0302-7244) **3947**
Bona (Sotho Edition) *see* Bona (English Edition) **3947**
Bona (Xhosa Edition) *see* Bona (English Edition) **3947**
Bona (Zulu Edition) *see* Bona (English Edition) **3947**
Bona Espero (ZAF ISSN 0006-7024) **5101**
Bona Gent (ESP ISSN 0214-0543) **4064**
The Bona Venture (USA) **2274**
Bonaire Nights (CAN) **8688**
Bonanza (JPN ISSN 0385-0501) **6458**
Bonbon (USA ISSN 1941-8701) **2180**
De Bond (BEL) **3801**
Bond (USA ISSN 0279-9111) **7749**
▼ Bond (San Francisco) (USA ISSN 1938-9620) **5556**
• The Bond Buyer (USA ISSN 0732-0469) **1613**
• The Bond Buyer's Municipal Marketplace (USA ISSN 1053-8658) **1976**
• Bond Dispute Resolution Newsletter (AUS) **4631**
Bond Guide *see* Standard & Poor's Bond Guide **1652**
• ➤ Bond Law Review (AUS ISSN 1033-4505) **4631**
Bond Market: Analysis and Outlook (USA) **1613**
Bond Negotiating International Software Licence and Data Transfer Agreements *see* Negotiating International Software Licence and Data Transfer Agreements **5063**
Bond Portfolio by Quality and Industry Classification (USA) **4496**
• Bond Teller (USA) **1913**
Bond van Ambtenaren bij met Rechtsmacht Beklede en Daaraan Verbonden Instellingen in Nederland Nova *see* B A R I Nova **4946**
Bond van Christelijke Gereformeerde Vrouwenverenigingen. Contact (NLD ISSN 0169-958X) **7749**
Bond van Personeel P T T Nederland *see* B V P P **2353**
• Bondage (USA) **5418**
Bonde og Smaabruker (NOR ISSN 0801-7662) **222**
Bondebladet (NOR ISSN 0332-8414) **97**
Bondevennen (NOR ISSN 0800-2126) **97**
Bondgenoten Magazine *see* Dus **4593**
The Bondholder (GBR ISSN 0961-8171) **1613**
Bondings (USA) **7786**
Bond's Franchise Guide (USA ISSN 1089-8794) **1613**
The Bone (JPN ISSN 0914-7047) **6056**
• ➤ Bone (USA ISSN 8756-3282) **6056**
Bone & Flesh (USA ISSN 1040-9130) **5418**
Bone & Joint *see* Lippincott's Bone and Joint Newsletter **6066**
• ➤ Bone Marrow Transplantation (GBR ISSN 0268-3369) **5903**
• Bone Marrow Transplantation. Supplement (GBR ISSN 0951-3078) **5903**
Bone Zone *see* BONEZone **6057**
• ➤ The Bonefolder (USA ISSN 1555-6565) **4997**
BoneKEy - Osteovision *see* I B M S BoneKEy **5805**
▼ Boneshaker (USA ISSN 1942-5597) **8255**
BONEZone (USA) **6057**
• Bonfire (GBR) **5418**
Bong Crier (LBR) **3789**
Bonger Reeks (NLD) **2645**
Bongeszo *see* Heves Megyei Hirlap **3876**
Bongo (DEU ISSN 0174-4038) **936**
† Bonheur (FRA ISSN 1271-545X) **8937**
Bonhomie (USA) **2274**
Bonifaciana (ITA ISSN 1826-1973) **4205**
Bonifatiusblatt (DEU ISSN 0006-7113) **7786**
Bonifatiusbote (DEU ISSN 0935-8897) **7786**
Bonita (USA ISSN 1555-9920) **3523**
Bonita Magazine *see* Bonita **3523**
Bonjour! (BEL ISSN 0773-0306) **2180**
Bonjour (GBR ISSN 0006-7121) **5101**
Bonjour! (GBR) **8688**
▼ Bonjour Brighton (GBR ISSN 1754-7199) **3967**
Bonjour Dimanche *see* La Revue **3816**
Bonjour Noel *see* Dauphin **2185**
Bonjour Vacances *see* Dauphin **2185**
Bonn Catalogue *see* Bonner Katalog **6631**
Bonn International Center for Conversion Brief *see* B I C C Brief **7223**
Bonn International Center for Conversion Bulletin *see* B I C C Bulletin **7223**
Bonn International Center for Conversion. Jahresbericht (DEU) **7224**
Bonn International Center for Conversion Paper *see* B I C C Paper **7223**
Bonn International Center for Conversion Report *see* B I C C Report **7223**
Bonne Fans (NLD ISSN 1872-1249) **6521**
Bonne Nouvelle (CAN ISSN 0225-0233) **7786**
Bonne Soiree *see* Cote Femme **8944**
Bonner Amerikanistische Studien (DEU ISSN 0176-6546) **7951**
Bonner Beitraege zur Kirchengeschichte (DEU) **7786**
Bonner Beitraege zur Kunstwissenschaft (DEU ISSN 0068-0036) **479**
Bonner General-Anzeiger *see* General-Anzeiger **3849**
Bonner Geographische Abhandlungen (DEU ISSN 0373-0468) **4000**
Bonner Geschichtsblaetter (DEU ISSN 0068-0052) **4206**
Bonner Historische Forschungen (DEU) **4206**
† Bonner Illustrierte (DEU ISSN 0949-0078) **8937**
Bonner Jahrbuecher (DEU ISSN 0938-9334) **4206**
Bonner Japanforschungen (DEU ISSN 0947-417X) **545**
• Bonner Katalog/Bonn Catalogue (DEU) **6631**
Bonner Kleine Reihe zur Alltagskultur (DEU ISSN 1436-1582) **4206**
Bonner Mathematische Schriften (DEU ISSN 0524-045X) **5476**
Bonner Meteorologische Abhandlungen (DEU ISSN 0006-7156) **6347**
† • Bonner Monatszahlen (DEU) **8937**
Bonner Romanistische Arbeiten (DEU ISSN 0170-821X) **5101**
Bonner Sammlung von Aegyptiaca (DEU ISSN 0947-1200) **545**
Bonner Schriften zur Politik und Zeitgeschichte (DEU ISSN 0935-1191) **4206**
Bonner Studien zur Frauengeschichte (DEU ISSN 0939-4532) **8894**
Bonner Studien zur Laendlichen Entwicklung in der Dritten Welt (DEU ISSN 0721-815X) **8090**
Bonner Umwelt Zeitung (DEU) **3407**
Bonner Zentrum fuer Religion und Gesellschaft. Studien (DEU ISSN 1866-489X) **7628**
➤ Bonner Zoologische Beitraege (DEU ISSN 0006-7172) **936**
Bonner Zoologische Monographien (DEU ISSN 0302-671X) **936**
• Bonneville Power Administration. Annual Report (USA ISSN 0898-3917) **3125**
Bonneville Racing News (USA) **8162**
Bonnier PC-Tidningen (SWE ISSN 1652-3407) **2408**
Bonniers Litteraera Magasin *see* Bonniers Litteraera Magasin **5209**
Bonniers Litteraera Magasin (SWE ISSN 0005-3198) **5209**
Bonny Moor Hen (GBR ISSN 0142-7660) **4206**
• Bonplandia (ARG ISSN 0524-0476) **780**
• Bons Fluidos (BRA ISSN 1414-5472) **5066**
Bons Fluidos em Casa (BRA ISSN 1516-8816) **5066**
Bonsai *see* Bonsai Focus (American Edition) **3725**
Bonsai & News (ITA ISSN 1120-706X) **3725**
Bonsai & Stone Appreciation Magazine (USA ISSN 1936-2129) **3725**
Bonsai Autoctono (ESP ISSN 1138-3518) **3725**
Bonsai Bulletin (USA ISSN 0006-7180) **3725**
Bonsai Canada. Yearbook (CAN) **3725**
Bonsai Europe (English Edition) *see* Bonsai Focus (American Edition) **3725**
Bonsai Europe (Netherlands Edition) *see* Bonsai Focus (Netherlands Edition) **3725**
▼ Bonsai Focus (American Edition) (NLD ISSN 1876-6137) **3725**
Bonsai Focus (Netherlands Edition) (NLD ISSN 1874-6896) **3725**
Bonsai Journal (USA ISSN 0149-9726) **3725**
Bonsai Magazine *see* Bonsai & Stone Appreciation Magazine **3725**
Bonsai - Priroda a Clovek *see* Bonsaje a Japonske Zahrady **3725**
▼ Bonsai Times (NZL ISSN 1177-7761) **3725**
Bonsai Today *see* Bonsai Focus (American Edition) **3725**
Bonsaje a Japonske Zahrady (CZE ISSN 1801-1683) **3725**
Bonus (DEU) **1422**
Bonus Education Guide *see* Nature & Health **313**
Bonytt/Design for Living (NOR ISSN 0800-1936) **4533**
Boobook (AUS ISSN 1442-4622) **904**
Boobs (GBR ISSN 1368-8022) **6287**
Boodschappen (NLD ISSN 1574-759X) **4353**
The Book *see* The Infospectrum Directory **8646**
The Book (USA ISSN 0740-8439) **7554**
• The Book (USA ISSN 1069-0514) **5450**
Book Alert (USA ISSN 0733-3005) **7554**
Book and Library *see* Konyv es Konyvtar **5023**
Book and Magazine Collector (GBR ISSN 0952-8601) **7554**
Book and Serial Industry Communications News *see* B A S I C News **4993**
The Book Arts Classified (USA) **7554**
• Book Arts Newsletter (GBR ISSN 1754-9078) **479**
† Book Boss (ITA) **8937**
Book Browse Previews *see* BookBrowse Previews **7554**
Book Browse Recommends *see* BookBrowse Recommends **620**
• Book Business (USA ISSN 1558-9889) **7554**
Book Club of California. Quarterly News-Letter (USA ISSN 0006-7202) **7554**
Book Collector (GBR ISSN 0006-7237) **7554**
Book Dealers World (USA ISSN 1098-8521) **7554**
Book-delen Dossier (NLD ISSN 1871-4242) **7554**
Book Development Council International Aid Information Digest *see* B D C I Aid Information Digest **7552**
Book Exchange (GBR ISSN 0006-7245) **7554**
• ➤ Book History (USA ISSN 1098-7371) **7554**
Book Industry Study Group. Research Report *see* Book Industry Trends **7554**
Book Industry Trends (USA ISSN 0160-970X) **7554**
The Book L A (USA) **6491**
• Book Links (USA ISSN 1055-4742) **2146**
Book Lovers (USA ISSN 1091-5540) **7554**
Book / Mark (USA ISSN 1081-3209) **4997**
Book Marketing Update (USA ISSN 0891-8813) **7554**
Book Marks (USA ISSN 0197-0437) **4997**
Book News (USA) **7554**
Book of Abstracts *see* Symposium on Horticulture in Europe. Book of Abstracts **186**
Book of Bantams (USA ISSN 0068-0117) **281**
Book of Baseball Records (USA) **8224**
The Book of Leads & Lists *see* Ingram's **1123**
Book of Lists (CAN ISSN 1719-3591) **1807**
The Book of Lists (PRI) **1976**
Book of Lists (ROM ISSN 1454-2773) **1068**
Book of Lists *see* The Business Review **1075**
Book of Lists (Budapest) *see* Budapest Book of Lists (Year) **1069**
(Year) Book of Modules (IRL) **2969**
• Book-Of-The-Month Club News (USA ISSN 0006-730X) **7554**
• The Book of the States (USA ISSN 0068-0125) **7110**
• Book Page (USA) **7554**
Book Peddler *see* Pakn Treger **7727**
Book Publishers *see* Business Ratio. Book Publishers **7556**
Book Publishers and Exclusive Agents. Data Tables *see* Book Publishers. Data Tables **7577**
• Book Publishers. Data Tables (CAN ISSN 1911-317X) **7577**
Book Publishing *see* Key Note Market Report: Book Publishing **7564**
• Book Publishing Report (USA ISSN 1086-1319) **7554**
• Book Publishing Resource Guide (USA) **7554**
The Book Reader (USA) **7554**
The Book Report *see* Library Media Connection **5028**
Book Retailing On the Internet Market Assessment *see* Key Note Market Assessment. Book Retailing on the Internet **7564**
Book Review *see* Los Angeles Times Book Review **7566**
• Book Review Digest (USA ISSN 0006-7326) **5209**
Book Review Digest Plus *see* Book Review Digest **5209**
• Book Review Index (USA ISSN 0524-0581) **7577**
Book Review Index: Africa (IND) **8020**
• Book Review Index: Annual Cumulation (USA) **7577**
Book Review Supplement *see* Canadian Military History **6415**
Book Reviews *see* Shupin **5047**
Book Science *see* Knygotyra **5023**
Book Series in the Best of Asia Food Guide: Series on Asia's Best Local Gourmet Restaurants *see* Asia's Best Local Gourmet Restaurants **4382**
▼ Book Series on Complex Metal Alloys (SGP) **6306**
Book Source Magazine (USA ISSN 1553-2690) **7554**
Book Source Monthly *see* Book Source Magazine **7554**
The Book Trade in Canada (CAN ISSN 1484-9313) **7554**
Book Trust. Annual Report and Financial Statements (GBR) **7554**
Book Trusted News (GBR ISSN 1748-6467) **2180**
• ➤ Bookbird (USA ISSN 0006-7377) **2180**
• BookBrowse Previews (USA ISSN 1937-5921) **7554**
• BookBrowse Recommends (USA ISSN 1930-0018) **620**
Bookdealer (GBR ISSN 1369-6572) **7554**
• The Bookdragon Review (USA ISSN 1527-0157) **5209**
• BookEnds (GBR) **7554**
Bookends (Kutztown) (USA ISSN 0893-6471) **4998**
Bookends (Youngstown) (USA) **4998**
• Bookforum (USA ISSN 1098-3376) **5209**
Bookforum - Artforum *see* Bookforum **5209**
Booking (DEU) **1976**
Bookkeeper's Tax Letter (USA) **1281**
Booklife *see* P W Booklife **7569**
• Booklist (USA ISSN 0006-7385) **7554**
Booklover *see* Bogvennen **7553**
BookLovers *see* Book Lovers **7554**
Bookman (BGD) **7555**
Bookman's Guide to Americana (USA ISSN 0068-0133) **7555**
Bookman's Price Index (USA ISSN 0068-0141) **7555**
Bookmark (GBR ISSN 0260-0315) **5265**
Bookmark (Moscow) (USA ISSN 0735-0295) **4998**
Bookmarks (USA ISSN 1546-0657) **7555**
• Bookmobiles and Outreach Services (USA ISSN 1529-4749) **4998**
Booknotes (NZL ISSN 1176-8851) **7555**
† Bookplate International (GBR ISSN 1353-8128) **8937**
Bookplate Journal (GBR ISSN 0264-3693) **7555**
Bookplate Society Newsletter (GBR ISSN 0309-7935) **7555**
Bookplates in the News *see* Ex Libris Chronicle **4334**
Books (GBR ISSN 0952-987X) **7555**
Books (NGA ISSN 0794-8603) **7555**
Books about Singapore (SGP ISSN 0068-0176) **8778**
Books and Culture *see* Books & Culture **5265**
• Books & Culture (USA ISSN 1082-8931) **5265**
Books and Essays/Tosho (JPN) **7555**
Books and History *see* Knihy a Dejiny **7565**
Books and Libraries at the University of Kansas (USA ISSN 0006-7458) **4998**
Books and Periodicals Online *see* Books and Periodicals ONLINE: Law, Business and News **620**
Books and Periodicals Online *see* Directory of Periodicals ONLINE: Medical and Pharmaceutical **5744**
Books and Periodicals Online *see* Directory of Periodicals ONLINE: Humanities and Religion **4484**
Books & Periodicals Online *see* Directory of Periodicals ONLINE: Science and Technology **7936**
• Books and Periodicals ONLINE: Law, Business and News (USA) **620**
Books & Serials Navigator *see* Kikan Shoshi Nabi **628**
† Books Are Everything (USA) **8937**
Books at Brown (USA ISSN 0147-0787) **620**
Books Bohemian (USA) **5265**
Books C J K *see* U.S. Library of Congress. Books C J K **637**
Books for College Libraries *see* Resources for College Libraries **3000**
Books for Everybody (CAN) **7555**
• Books for Growing Minds (USA) **2180**
Books for Keeps (GBR ISSN 0143-909X) **7555**
Books for the Teen Age (USA ISSN 0068-0192) **5057**
• ➤ Books from Finland (FIN ISSN 0006-7490) **7577**
Books from Korea (KOR) **7577**
Books from Pakistan (PAK ISSN 0068-0206) **620**
Books in Bosnia and Herzegovina (BIH ISSN 0352-1044) **7555**
† • Books in Canada (CAN ISSN 0045-2564) **8937**
Books in English (GBR ISSN 0045-2572) **620**
Books in Homes Newsletter *see* Read About It! **7572**
Books in Library and Information Science Series (USA) **5057**
• Books in Print (USA ISSN 0068-0214) **620**
• Books in Print on Disc (USA) **620**
Books in Print on Disc, Canadian Edition *see* Books in Print on Disc **620**

Link to your serials resources and content with ulrichsweb.com

Books in Print Plus (Canadian Edition) *see* Canadian Books in Print on Disc **622**
● Books in Print Supplement (USA ISSN 0000-0310) **620**
● Books in Print with Book Reviews on Disc (USA ISSN 1542-7218) **620**
Books in Print with Book Reviews on Disc, Canadian Edition *see* Books in Print with Book Reviews on Disc **620**
Books in Soils Plants and the Environment Series (USA) **222**
Books in Spanish/Libros en Espanol (USA ISSN 1531-6750) **4071**
Books in the Media (GBR ISSN 0961-2203) **7555**
Books Ireland (IRL ISSN 0376-6039) **7555**
Books of the Literary Museum *see* Petofi Irodalmi Muzeum Konyvei **5350**
Books of the Southwest (Online Edition) (USA) **7577**
Books of the Southwest (Print Edition) *see* Books of the Southwest (Online Edition) **7577**
● Books on Canada (CAN) **7555**
● Books on Japan (JPN ISSN 1347-7684) **620**
Books on Screen *see* Simon's Weekly Tax Intelligence **1943**
Books on Tape *see* Books Out Loud **620**
● Books Out Loud (USA ISSN 0000-1805) **620**
● Books Out-of-Print Online (USA) **620**
BooksandPeriodicals.com *see* Directory of Periodicals ONLINE: Science and Technology **7936**
BooksandPeriodicals.com *see* Directory of Periodicals ONLINE: Humanities and Religion **4484**
BooksandPeriodicals.com *see* Directory of Periodicals ONLINE: Medical and Pharmaceutical **5744**
BooksandPeriodicals.com *see* Books and Periodicals ONLINE: Law, Business and News **620**
● The Bookseller (GBR ISSN 0006-7539) **7555**
Bookseller (PAK ISSN 0006-7547) **7555**
Bookseller (USA) **7555**
● Bookseller + Publisher (AUS ISSN 1833-5403) **7555**
Bookseller + Publisher Magazine's Weekly Book Newsletter *see* Weekly Book Newsletter **8998**
Booksellers Association. Directory of Members (Year) (GBR ISSN 0952-1666) **7555**
Bookselling *see* Bookselling Essentials **7555**
Bookselling Essentials (GBR ISSN 1745-3798) **7555**
Bookselling Market Report *see* Key Note Market Report: Bookselling **7564**
● Bookselling This Week (USA) **7555**
Bookshop (ITA ISSN 1972-8565) **7555**
● Booksinprint.com (USA) **621**
Booksinprint.com: Professional *see* Booksinprint.com **621**
Booksinprint.com with Book Reviews *see* Books in Print with Book Reviews on Disc **620**
● books@ocg.at (AUT) **2408**
● Booksonline (GBR) **7555**
BooksPlus (GBR ISSN 1025-4854) **97**
Booktech, the Magazine *see* Book Business **7554**
● The Bookwatch (Online) (USA) **621**
● BookWire (USA ISSN 0000-1759) **7556**
Bookwoman (USA ISSN 0163-1128) **7556**
Boom! (USA) **3971**
Boomblad (NLD ISSN 0924-0101) **97**
▼ ● Boomer (USA ISSN 1939-2141) **4041**
● The Boomer (Online) (CAN) **5066**
● Boomer Advisor (USA) **4042**
● Boomer Market Advisor (USA ISSN 1551-9287) **1807**
Boomerang! (USA ISSN 1052-1682) **2180**
Boomerphile (USA ISSN 1071-5479) **5209**
Booming Futsal (NLD ISSN 1872-454X) **8224**
De Boomkwekerij (Doetinchem) (NLD ISSN 0923-2443) **3725**
Boon-Studies (BEL) **5265**
Boone County Historical Society. Newsletter (USA ISSN 1099-5617) **4286**
BOORnieuws (Bureau Oudheidhkundig Onderzoek van Gemeentewerken Rotterdam) (NLD ISSN 1874-0561) **384**
Boosey and Hawkes Newsletter (USA ISSN 0006-7598) **6550**
Booster (USA) **6413**
Booster & B W's *see* Scoot'n Scoot **8268**
● Boot Cove Economic Forecast (USA) **1443**
Boot Journaal (NLD ISSN 1570-6346) **8273**
Bootblack (USA ISSN 1040-7405) **641**
Boote (DEU ISSN 0006-7636) **8273**
Boote Exclusiv (DEU ISSN 0935-2961) **8273**
Bootleg (USA) **5066**
Boots Boerse (DEU ISSN 0949-4065) **8273**
Boots Health & Beauty (GBR) **8854**
Bootsmarkt (DEU ISSN 0947-7772) **8273**
● Bootstrappin' Entrepreneur (USA ISSN 1063-3561) **1957**
Bootwirtschaft Aktuell (DEU ISSN 0935-395X) **8273**
Bop (USA ISSN 8750-7242) **2180**
Bophuthatswana Broadcasting Corporation. Annual Report (ZAF) **2375**
● ➤ Bopuxue Zazhi/Chinese Journal of Magnetic Resonance (CHN ISSN 1000-4556) **7074**
Bor- es Cipotechnika, -Piac/Leather and Shoe Technique, - Market (HUN ISSN 1219-8706) **4972**
➤ B'Or Ha-Torah (ISR ISSN 0333-6298) **7719**
Boraas Tidning (SWE) **3955**
BoRaett (SWE ISSN 0283-0558) **4405**
● Borax Pioneer (USA) **2051**

Bor'ba s Gazom v Ugol'nykh Shakhtakh (RUS) **6458**
Borclar - Ticaret ve Banka Hukuku Bibliyografyasi (TUR) **4821**
Bord Iascaigh Mhara. Annual Report and Accounts (IRL ISSN 0068-0265) **3587**
Bord Iascaigh Mhara User Friendly Guides *see* B I M User Friendly Guides **1880**
▼ Bordeaux Aujourd'hui (FRA ISSN 1956-2756) **600**
Bordeaux Madame (FRA ISSN 1638-7740) **8854**
Border Agricultural Show Prize List (ZAF) **281**
● Border Connections (USA) **1591**
Border Control of I P Rights (Intellectual Property) (GBR) **6746**
● Border Crossings (CAN ISSN 0831-2559) **479**
Border Directory *see* Braby's Border Directory and Surrounding Areas **1976**
The Border Economy and Culture *see* Bianjiang Jingji yu Wenhua **1067**
Border Epidemiological Bulletin/Boletin Epidemiologico Fronterizo (USA ISSN 1086-4520) **7510**
Border Leicester Flock Book (GBR) **281**
Border Post (ZWE) **6892**
➤ Border States (USA ISSN 0092-4571) **4286**
● Border Watch (AUS ISSN 1329-5195) **4572**
Border X-ings (USA) **6551**
Borderlands (Austin) (USA ISSN 1065-0342) **5418**
Borderlands (Clarkston) (USA) **5440**
● ➤ Borderlands E - Journal (AUS ISSN 1447-0810) **4445**
Borderline (FRA ISSN 1778-1604) **5440**
Borderlines (Minneapolis) (USA) **7110**
Borderterrierbladet (SWE ISSN 1100-0716) **6804**
● Bordon (ESP ISSN 0210-5934) **7341**
Bordon Times & Mail (GBR) **3862**
† Bordtennisguiden (DNK ISSN 1604-7591) **8937**
Borduurblad (NLD ISSN 1574-7034) **6637**
Bore Da (GBR ISSN 0006-7709) **2180**
● ➤ Boreal Environment Research (FIN ISSN 1239-6095) **3483**
● Boreal Environment Research. Monographs (FIN ISSN 1239-1875) **3483**
Boreales (FRA ISSN 0395-3998) **4206**
Borealis (USA) **780**
Boreas (DEU ISSN 0344-810X) **384**
● ➤ Boreas (DNK ISSN 0300-9483) **2726**
Boreas (Uppsala) (SWE ISSN 0346-6442) **4320**
Boreas. Beiheft (DEU ISSN 0722-768X) **384**
➤ Borec (SVN ISSN 0006-7725) **4206**
Borehole Water (ZAF ISSN 1011-128X) **8819**
Boretti Magazine (NLD ISSN 1875-2667) **4554**
Borgaabladet (FIN ISSN 0358-6294) **3838**
Borgward - Owners' Club. Newsletter (USA ISSN 1556-0953) **364**
Borgyogyaszati es Venerologiai Szemle (HUN ISSN 0006-7768) **5872**
Borisovskie Novosti (BLR) **3800**
Bormio Sport (ITA ISSN 1828-9282) **8162**
Born to Shop: Hong Kong *see* Suzy Gershman's Born to Shop: Hong Kong, Shanghai & Beijing **8759**
Born to Shop: Hong Kong, Shanghai & Beijing *see* Suzy Gershman's Born to Shop: Hong Kong, Shanghai & Beijing **8759**
Born to Shop: Paris *see* Suzy Gershman's Born to Shop: Paris **8759**
● Borneo Bulletin (BRN ISSN 1563-9320) **3804**
Borneo Nature Series (MYS) **3685**
● Borneo Research Bulletin (USA ISSN 0006-7806) **331**
Borneo Research Council Monograph Series (USA) **331**
Borneo Research Council Proceedings Series (USA) **331**
● Borneo Review (MYS ISSN 0128-7397) **1068**
Bornholms Museum, Bornholms Kunstmuseum (DNK ISSN 1398-9073) **6521**
● Bornholms Tidende (DNK) **3833**
Bornholmske Samlinger (DNK ISSN 0084-7976) **4206**
Borno Museum Society. Newsletter (NGA ISSN 1115-0335) **6521**
Borough News *see* Pennsylvania Borough News **7500**
Borough of Twickenham Local History Society. Papers (GBR ISSN 0084-7984) **4206**
● ➤ Borrowers and Lenders (USA ISSN 1554-6985) **5265**
Borsodi Szemle (HUN ISSN 0520-626X) **4206**
Borthwick Institute of Historical Research. Borthwick Papers (GBR ISSN 0524-0913) **4206**
Borthwick Lists and Indexes (GBR ISSN 1361-3014) **4206**
Borthwick Studies in History (GBR ISSN 1361-3006) **4206**
Borthwick Texts and Calendars *see* Borthwick Texts and Studies **4206**
Borthwick Texts and Studies (GBR ISSN 1748-9474) **4206**
Borussen-Echo (AUT ISSN 0006-7865) **2274**
Borussia (POL ISSN 0867-6402) **4206**
Borysten (UKR) **5209**
Borzoi *see* Borzoi-Ringen **6804**
Borzoi Connection Magazine (USA) **6804**
Borzoi-Ringen (SWE ISSN 1653-5618) **6804**
Bos en Hout Berichten *see* Bosberichten **97**
Bosai/Disaster Prevention (JPN ISSN 0006-7873) **7510**
Bosai Kagaku Gijutsu Kenkyujo Kenkyu Hokoku (JPN ISSN 0916-6564) **2702**

Bosai Kagaku Gijutsu Kenkyujo Kenkyu Shiryo/National Research Institute for Earth Science and Disaster Prevention. Technical Note (JPN ISSN 0917-057X) **2702**
Bosai Kagaku Gijutsu Kenkyujo Nenpo/National Research Institute for Earth Science and Disaster Prevention. Annual Report (JPN ISSN 0918-6441) **2702**
Bosberichten (NLD ISSN 1574-6046) **97**
Bosbouw *see* Vakblad Natuur Bos Landschap **3707**
Bosch-Zuender (DEU) **1880**
● Bosei Eisei/Japanese Journal of Maternal Health (JPN ISSN 0388-1512) **8844**
Duh Bosne *see* The Spirit of Bosnia **3566**
● Bosnia & Herzegovina Defence & Security Report (GBR ISSN 1749-1282) **6414**
Bosnian Journal of Basic Medical Sciences (BIH ISSN 1512-8601) **5588**
Bosom Friend *see* Zhiyin **8892**
● Bosque (CHL ISSN 0304-8799) **3685**
Bosrevue (BEL ISSN 1378-5990) **3685**
Boss *see* Financial Review Boss **1109**
Boss (DEU ISSN 0938-1511) **1850**
● Boss (RUS) **1068**
● Boss Business News Poland (POL ISSN 1641-5574) **1068**
Boss Gospodarka (POL ISSN 1641-5566) **194**
Boss Magazine (USA) **983**
Boss Rolnictwo (POL ISSN 1641-5701) **97**
Boss Users Group Magazine *see* B U G Magazine **6632**
Bosschap. Nieuwsbrief *see* Bomen **97**
Bostadsraettsfoereningstidningen *see* BoRaett **4405**
Boston (Year) (USA ISSN 1056-4357) **8688**
Boston Airport Journal (USA) **5066**
▼ Boston & Cambridge Official Visitors Guide (USA) **8688**
Boston and Cambridge Official Visitors Guide *see* Boston & Cambridge Official Visitors Guide **8688**
Boston & Maine Bulletin *see* B & M Bulletin **8615**
Boston & Maine Railroad Historical Society. Newsletter (USA) **8615**
Boston Area Colloquium in Ancient Philosophy. Proceedings (NLD ISSN 1059-986X) **6908**
Boston Audio Society Speaker *see* B A S Speaker **8152**
● Boston Bar Journal (USA ISSN 0524-1111) **4631**
Boston Baseball (USA ISSN 1075-8542) **8224**
Boston Blues News (USA) **6551**
● The Boston Book Review (USA ISSN 1072-8317) **7556**
Boston Bruins Official Yearbook (USA) **8162**
● The Boston Business Journal (USA ISSN 0746-4975) **1068**
The Boston Catholic Television Monthly (USA ISSN 1930-255X) **7786**
Boston Celtics Yearbook (USA ISSN 0361-6894) **8224**
Boston City Record (USA ISSN 0006-7946) **7488**
● Boston College Environmental Affairs Law Review (USA ISSN 0190-7034) **3407**
● Boston College International and Comparative Law Review (USA ISSN 0277-5778) **4918**
● Boston College Law Review (USA ISSN 0161-6587) **4631**
● Boston College Magazine (USA ISSN 0885-2049) **2275**
● Boston College Third World Law Journal (USA ISSN 0276-3583) **4918**
Boston Common (USA) **3971**
† ● Boston ComputerUser (USA ISSN 1533-5674) **8937**
● Boston Consumers' Checkbook (USA ISSN 1542-3522) **2635**
Boston Early Music News (USA) **6551**
● The Boston Globe Index (USA ISSN 0893-2727) **4586**
● Boston Globe Magazine (USA) **3971**
● Boston Home (USA ISSN 1942-1451) **4353**
Boston I T Security Review (POL ISSN 1896-5032) **2511**
● The Boston Irish Reporter (USA ISSN 1061-5091) **3523**
Boston IT Security Review *see* Boston I T Security Review **2511**
Boston Jewish Times (USA ISSN 8750-1961) **7719**
Boston JobBank *see* The Boston JobBank **8937**
† The Boston JobBank (USA ISSN 1098-9757) **8937**
Boston Law Tribune (USA) **4631**
● Boston Magazine (USA ISSN 0006-7989) **3971**
Boston Magazine's Concierge (USA ISSN 1541-8111) **3971**
Boston Magazine's Elegant Wedding (USA ISSN 1099-2898) **5556**
Boston Magazine's Home *see* Boston Home **4353**
Boston Magazine's Home & Garden *see* Boston Home **4353**
Boston Marathon (USA) **8162**
Boston Office Buildings (USA) **7584**
● The Boston Parents' Paper (USA ISSN 1059-1710) **2146**
Boston Quarterly (USA ISSN 0892-9742) **6804**
● Boston Review (USA ISSN 0734-2306) **5209**
Boston Russian Bulletin (USA) **3523**
Boston Seaport Journal (USA) **1069**
Boston Seniority (USA) **4042**
Boston Society of Architects. ChapterLetter (USA) **435**
Boston Spirit (USA ISSN 1930-9686) **4371**
● Boston Stock Exchange Guide (USA) **1613**

➤ Boston Studies in Applied Economics (NLD) **1536**
➤ Boston Studies in the Philosophy of Science (NLD ISSN 0068-0346) **7841**
Boston Symphony Orchestra Program (USA) **6551**
● Boston Theological Institute. Bulletin (USA ISSN 1538-6597) **7628**
Boston University Conference on Language Development. Proceedings (USA ISSN 1080-692X) **5101**
● Boston University International Law Journal (USA ISSN 0737-8947) **4918**
Boston University Journal of Science and Technology Law *see* The Journal of Science & Technology Law **4704**
● ➤ Boston University Law Review (USA ISSN 0006-8047) **4631**
Boston University Public Interest Law Journal *see* Public Interest Law Journal **4763**
Boston University Studies in Philosophy and Religion (USA ISSN 1940-1531) **7628**
Boston with Kids *see* Fodor's Family Boston with Kids **8705**
Bostonia (USA ISSN 1067-2834) **3971**
Boston's Weekly Dig (USA) **5067**
Bostonterriern (SWE ISSN 0346-9344) **6804**
Bosui Janaru/Bosui Journal (JPN ISSN 0289-3894) **3260**
Bosui Journal *see* Bosui Janaru **3260**
Bosvelder (ZAF ISSN 1816-8418) **3947**
● Botanic Gardens Micropropagation News (GBR ISSN 0962-7448) **780**
The Botanica (IND ISSN 0045-2629) **780**
● ➤ Botanica Complutensis (ESP ISSN 0214-4565) **780**
Botanica Gothoburgensia (SWE ISSN 0068-0370) **780**
● ➤ Botanica Helvetica (CHE ISSN 0253-1453) **780**
● Botanica Lithuanica (LTU ISSN 1392-1665) **780**
➤ Botanica Macaronesica (ESP ISSN 0211-7150) **780**
● ➤ Botanica Marina (DEU ISSN 0006-8055) **780**
Botanical Bibliographies *see* Bibliografie Botaniczne **713**
Botanical Bulletin *see* Zhiwuxue Tongbao **824**
Botanical Cornwall (GBR ISSN 1364-4335) **780**
Botanical Descriptions of Cereal Varieties (GBR) **270**
Botanical Electronic News *see* B E N **778**
➤ Botanical Guidebooks (POL) **780**
Botanical Journal of Iran *see* Rostaniha **815**
The Botanical Journal of Scotland *see* Plant Ecology and Diversity **811**
Botanical Journal of the Linnean Society *see* Linnean Society. Botanical Journal **800**
Botanical Pathways (AUS ISSN 1444-3961) **307**
● Botanical Pesticides Abstracts (GBR) **3477**
Botanical Proceedings *see* Botanikai Kozlemenyek **781**
➤ Botanical Research Institute of Texas. Journal (USA ISSN 1934-5259) **781**
● ➤ The Botanical Review (USA ISSN 0006-8101) **781**
Botanical Society. Journal *see* Shokubutsu no Tomo **817**
Botanical Society of Edinburgh News *see* B S E News **778**
Botanical Society of Japan. Proceedings of the Annual Meeting *see* Nihon Shokubutsu Gakkai Taikai Kenkyu Happyo Kiroku **805**
Botanical Society of Nagano. Bulletin *see* Naganoken Shokubutsu Kenkyukaishi **803**
Botanical Society of Shizuoka. Bulletin *see* Shizuoka Shokubutsu Kenkyu Kaishi **817**
Botanical Society of the British Isles Abstracts *see* B S B I Abstracts **713**
Botanical Society of the British Isles News *see* B S B I News **778**
Botanical Society of Yamanashi. Bulletin *see* Yamanashi Shokubutsu Kenkyu **823**
● ➤ Botanical Studies (TWN ISSN 1817-406X) **781**
Botanical Survey of India. Bulletin (IND ISSN 0006-8128) **781**
Botanical Survey of India. Occasional Publications (IND) **781**
➤ Botanicheskii Zhurnal (RUS ISSN 0006-8136) **781**
The Botanics (GBR ISSN 0956-3237) **781**
† Botanicus Brief (DEU ISSN 0938-1759) **8937**
Botanik und Naturschutz in Hessen (DEU ISSN 0931-1904) **781**
➤ Botanika - Steciana (POL ISSN 1896-1908) **781**
Botanikai Kozlemenyek/Botanical Proceedings (HUN ISSN 0006-8144) **781**
Botanique Lorraine (FRA ISSN 0981-3519) **781**
● ➤ Botanische Jahrbuecher fuer Systematik, Pflanzengeschichte und Pflanzengeographie (DEU ISSN 0006-8152) **781**
Botanische Tuinen Utrecht (NLD ISSN 1871-4137) **781**
Botanischer Verein von Berlin und Brandenburg. Verhandlungen (DEU ISSN 0945-4292) **781**
Botaniska Notiser (Lund, 2001) (SWE ISSN 1650-3767) **3407**
● ➤ Botany/Journal Canadien de Botanique (CAN ISSN 1916-2790) **781**
Botany (JPN ISSN 0287-9794) **781**
Botany of Fukuoka *see* Fukuoka no Shokubutsu **790**
Botany of Saga *see* Saga no Shokubutsu **816**
Der Bote (CAN ISSN 0006-8209) **7733**

Title

Der Bote *see* Radeberger Gruppe Informiert **3661**
Der Bote aus dem Wehrgeschichtlichen Museum (DEU) **6414**
Bote fuer Tirol (AUT ISSN 0006-8225) **7488**
Both Sides Now (USA ISSN 0006-8233) **6644**
➤ Bothalia (ZAF ISSN 0006-8241) **781**
Botilda (SWE ISSN 1404-157X) **8894**
Botschaft Heute (DEU ISSN 0176-8573) **7628**
• BotSpot (USA) **2553**
Botswana (ZAF) **1069**
Botswana Advertiser (BWA) **22**
Botswana Agricultural Statistics *see* Botswana. Ministry of Agriculture. Agricultural Statistics **176**
Botswana. Annual Statements of Accounts (BWA ISSN 0068-0451) **1913**
Botswana Business Directory (ZAF) **1976**
Botswana Business Month Magazine (BWA) **1069**
Botswana Business News (BWA) **1069**
• Botswana. Central Statistics Office. Agriculture Statistics (BWA) **176**
• Botswana. Central Statistics Office. Consumer Price Statistics (BWA) **1215**
• Botswana. Central Statistics Office. Demographic and Health Survey (BWA) **1215**
• Botswana. Central Statistics Office. Education Statistics (BWA) **2931**
• Botswana. Central Statistics Office. Environment Statistics (BWA) **3477**
• Botswana. Central Statistics Office. External Trade Statistics (BWA ISSN 1013-5707) **1215**
• Botswana. Central Statistics Office. Health Statistics Report (BWA ISSN 1013-5723) **5741**
• Botswana. Central Statistics Office. Household Income and Expenditure Survey (BWA) **1215**
• Botswana. Central Statistics Office. Industrial Statistics (BWA) **1215**
• Botswana. Central Statistics Office. Labour Force Survey (BWA) **1215**
• Botswana. Central Statistics Office. Labour Statistics (BWA) **1215**
• Botswana. Central Statistics Office. Population and Housing Census (BWA) **7304**
• Botswana. Central Statistics Office. Statistical Bulletin (BWA ISSN 1013-5693) **1215**
• Botswana. Central Statistics Office. Tourist Statistics (BWA ISSN 1013-5715) **8778**
• Botswana. Central Statistics Office. Transport Statistics (BWA ISSN 1013-5731) **8491**
Botswana. Commissioner of the Police. Annual Report (BWA ISSN 0068-046X) **2645**
Botswana. Department of Income Tax. Annual Report (BWA) **1913**
Botswana. Department of Mines. Air Pollution Control. Annual Report (BWA) **3483**
Botswana Development Corporation. Annual Report (BWA) **1613**
Botswana Development Corporation. Newsletter (BWA) **1613**
Botswana Gazette (BWA) **3803**
Botswana. Geological Survey Department. Annotated Bibliography and Index of the Geology of Botswana (BWA ISSN 1011-9906) **2719**
Botswana. Geological Survey Department. Annual Reports (BWA ISSN 0524-1502) **2726**
Botswana. Geological Survey Department. Bulletins (BWA ISSN 0522-5612) **2726**
Botswana. Geological Survey Department. District Memoirs (BWA ISSN 0379-119X) **2726**
Botswana. Geological Survey Department. Mineral Resources Reports (BWA) **2726**
Botswana. Geological Survey Department. Records of the Geological Survey (BWA ISSN 0522-5620) **2727**
Botswana Guardian (BWA) **3803**
Botswana Handbook (BWA ISSN 0301-9020) **3803**
Botswana in Pictures (BWA) **3803**
Botswana International Trade Fair. Annual Exhibitors' Catalogue (BWA) **6278**
• Botswana Journal of Technology (BWA ISSN 1019-1593) **8417**
• The Botswana Law Reports (ZAF ISSN 1561-1582) **4631**
Botswana Manufacturing Directory (BWA) **1976**
Botswana Media Directory (BWA) **2313**
Botswana. Ministry of Agriculture. Agricultural Statistics (BWA ISSN 1013-574X) **176**
Botswana. Ministry of Agriculture. Annual Report (BWA ISSN 0068-0478) **97**
Botswana. Ministry of Agriculture. Division of Arable Crops Research. Annual Report (BWA) **222**
Botswana. Ministry of Agriculture. Division of Co-Operative Development. Annual Report (Year) (BWA) **1422**
Botswana. Ministry of Agriculture. Farm Management Survey Results (BWA) **195**
Botswana. Ministry of Agriculture. Livestock Management Survey Results (BWA) **281**
Botswana. National Archives. Report on the National Archives and Records Services (BWA) **4998**
Botswana. National Library Service. Report (BWA) **4998**
Botswana Notes and Records (BWA ISSN 0525-5090) **4173**
Botswana Society. Symposium Proceedings (BWA) **4173**
Botswana Trade Directory (BWA) **1976**
Bottin Administratif (FRA ISSN 1147-1999) **7423**
Bottin Communes *see* Bottin des Communes et de l'Intercommunalite **7488**
† Bottin de la Finance (FRA ISSN 1161-9430) **8937**
• Bottin des Communes et de l'Intercommunalite (FRA ISSN 1762-0589) **7488**
Bottin des Communications du Quebec (CAN ISSN 1203-6463) **2313**
Bottin des Services et d'Expertise-Conseil (CAN ISSN 1480-1574) **1069**
Bottin des Universites (year) *see* Universities Telephone Directory (Year) **3008**
Bottin du Pouvoir a Quebec *see* Guide du Pouvoir au Quebec **7443**
Bottin Entreprises (Paris, 2000) (FRA ISSN 1627-9158) **1069**
Le Bottin Gourmand. Le Guide de la Cuisine Etrangere a Paris (FRA ISSN 1777-6325) **4382**
Le Bottin Gourmand. Le Guide des Bistrots a Paris (FRA ISSN 1777-0319) **4382**
Bottin International du Quebec (CAN ISSN 1198-0249) **2366**
• Bottin Mondain (FRA ISSN 1268-7057) **641**
Bottin Touristique du Quebec (CAN ISSN 1198-1903) **8688**
Bottle Rockets (USA ISSN 1930-9406) **5418**
Bottle Shipwright (USA) **4330**
Bottled Water Market Assessment *see* Key Note Market Assessment. Bottled Water **606**
Bottled Water Reporter (USA) **600**
BottledWaterWorld (GBR) **600**
Bottom Line (BMU) **1069**
• The Bottom Line (CAN ISSN 0831-5477) **1069**
• ➤ The Bottom Line (GBR ISSN 0888-045X) **4998**
Bottom Line (San Francisco) (USA) **4631**
• ➤ The Bottom Line (Springfield) (USA) **4631**
Bottom Line / Health (USA ISSN 1092-0129) **6983**
Bottom Line Health *see* Bottom Line / Health **6983**
Bottom Line / Natural Healing (USA ISSN 1559-4718) **307**
The Bottom Line on Alcohol in Society *see* Monday Morning Report **2697**
Bottom Line Personal *see* Bottom Line, Personal **2635**
Bottom Line, Personal (USA ISSN 0274-4805) **2635**
Bottom Line Publications (USA) **5247**
Bottom Line Retirement *see* Bottom Line / Retirement **4042**
Bottom Line / Retirement (USA ISSN 1558-4844) **4042**
Bottom Line / Tomorrow *see* Bottom Line / Retirement **4042**
▼ Bottom Line Women's Health (USA ISSN 1941-1995) **8844**
Bottom Line Year Book *see* Bottom Line - Year Book **2635**
Bottom Line - Year Book (USA) **2635**
Bottomline *see* Signs **6616**
• The Bottomline (USA ISSN 0279-1889) **1281**
▼ Bottomline (Neenah) (USA ISSN 1940-8323) **1667**
Bottomline Benefits & Compensation *see* Bottomline (Neenah) **1667**
• BottomLine H R (Human Resources) (USA ISSN 1930-5575) **1857**
▼ • ➤ The Botulinum Journal (GBR ISSN 1754-7318) **6826**
Boucher - Charcutier *see* Metzger und Wurster **3656**
La Boucherie Belge (BEL) **3628**
Boucherie Francaise (FRA ISSN 0006-8284) **3628**
Boudoir & Autres (FRA ISSN 1951-1655) **5418**
Bouge ton Rhumatisme (FRA ISSN 1959-285X) **6222**
Bouillabaisse (USA) **5209**
La Boulangerie Francaise (FRA ISSN 0758-4164) **3672**
Boulay 300: World Auction Report (GBR) **479**
• The Boulder County Business Report (USA ISSN 1528-6320) **1425**
Boulder Weekly (USA) **5067**
The Boulders Magazine (USA) **4382**
Boulevard (CAN ISSN 1196-6807) **2635**
• Boulevard (USA ISSN 0885-9337) **5265**
Boulevard Man *see* Blvd Man **6287**
Boulisme (FRA ISSN 1950-943X) **8224**
La Boulite (FRA ISSN 0991-532X) **3615**
† Boulogne Informations (FRA ISSN 0988-9590) **8937**
Boumi Temple News (USA ISSN 0006-8306) **2264**
† Bounce (DEU) **8937**
Bound & Lettered (USA ISSN 1552-3160) **479**
• ➤ Boundary 2 (USA ISSN 0190-3659) **5265**
The Boundary Communicator (CAN ISSN 1911-0375) **3806**
➤ Boundary Element Communications (GBR ISSN 1462-2068) **3183**
➤ Boundary Elements (GBR ISSN 1462-6047) **3183**
• Boundary Law In Pennsylvania (USA ISSN 1931-5333) **4631**
• ➤ Boundary-Layer Meteorology (NLD ISSN 0006-8314) **6347**
Boundary Maps Complementary to Tables for Tertiary Planning Units and Constituency Areas see Hong Kong Special Administrative Region of China. Census and Statistics Department. Hong Kong (Year) Population By-Census. Boundary Maps Complementary to Tables for Tertiary Planning Units and Constituency Areas **7308**
• ➤ Boundary Value Problems (USA ISSN 1687-2762) **5476**
Boundary Waters Journal (USA ISSN 0899-2681) **2604**
• The Boundless Realm (USA) **5440**
Bounty Baby Book (GBR) **2146**
The Bounty Babycare Guide (GBR) **2146**
The Bounty Babycare Guide (IRL) **2146**
Bounty Guide to Fatherhood (GBR) **2146**
Bounty Hospital Information Guides (GBR) **4089**
The Bounty Pregnancy Guide (GBR) **5987**
The Bounty Pregnancy Guide (IRL) **5987**
Bounty Toddler Guide (GBR) **2146**
Bounty Young Family Guide (GBR) **2146**
Bouquet (ESP ISSN 0211-1071) **600**
Bouquet of Women (ZAF ISSN 1994-5337) **8854**
Les Bouquins Fusion (FRA ISSN 1773-8954) **7841**
Bourbonnais Rural (FRA ISSN 1257-144X) **97**
Bourgogne Aujourd'hui (FRA ISSN 1260-1063) **600**
Bourgogne Magazine *see* Voyages Patrimoines et Art de Vivre en Bourgogne **4034**
Bourgogne Magazine. Hors Serie Balades *see* Voyages Patrimoines et Art de Vivre en Bourgogne **4034**
Bourgogne Magazine. Hors Serie Gourmand *see* Voyages Patrimoines et Art de Vivre en Bourgogne **4034**
Bourland - Bulletin (USA ISSN 1075-2420) **3760**
Bourne Society Bulletin (GBR) **4206**
Bourne Society Local History Records (GBR ISSN 0520-6790) **4206**
Bournemouth University. School of Conservation Sciences. Occasional Paper (GBR ISSN 1362-6094) **2604**
Bournemouth University. School of Conservation Sciences. Research Reports (GBR) **2604**
† Bourse de Paris. Actions (FRA ISSN 1168-3155) **8937**
• Bout de Papier (CAN ISSN 0833-9864) **1591**
† La Bouteille a la Mer (FRA ISSN 0339-3801) **8937**
Boutique (POL ISSN 1733-1951) **8854**
The Boutonneur (GBR ISSN 1368-4175) **4330**
Bouw *see* Architectuur N L **976**
Bouw en Uitvoering voor Rijk, Provincie en Gemeente (NLD ISSN 0921-1667) **4405**
Bouw Intelligentie Quotient *see* BouwIQ **983**
Bouwbesluit in de Praktijk *see* Bouwregels in de Praktijk **983**
De Bouwbrief (NLD ISSN 1380-4545) **6551**
Bouwen aan de Nieuwe Aarde (NLD ISSN 0006-8349) **7786**
Bouwen met Staal (NLD ISSN 0166-6363) **983**
Bouwend Nederland Podium (NLD ISSN 1872-5074) **983**
BouwIQ (NLD ISSN 1871-9635) **983**
Bouwkennis Kwartaalrapport *see* Bouwkennis Marketingmagazine **983**
Bouwkennis Marketingmagazine (NLD) **983**
Bouwkosten (NLD ISSN 0165-2648) **983**
Bouwkracht (NLD) **983**
Bouwkrant Hanzelijn (NLD ISSN 1574-0625) **8615**
Bouwkroniek (BEL ISSN 1376-3490) **983**
Bouwkundige Richtlijnen bij het Ontwerpen van een Brandveilig Gebouw (BEL ISSN 1782-1185) **4496**
BouwMachines (NLD ISSN 0006-8373) **983**
Bouwmanagement en Technisch Beheer (NLD ISSN 0925-6466) **983**
Bouwmarkt (Doetinchem) (NLD ISSN 0166-641X) **983**
BouwNieuws *see* Nederlands Normalisatie-instituut BouwNieuws **1026**
Bouwondernemer (NLD ISSN 0006-8381) **4405**
Bouwpensioen (NLD ISSN 1871-9465) **4496**
Bouwplannen. A: Groningen, Friesland, Drenthe (NLD ISSN 1385-5972) **983**
Bouwplannen. B: Overijssel, Gelderland, Utrecht, Flevoland (NLD ISSN 1385-5980) **983**
Bouwplannen. C: Noord-Holland en Zuid-Holland (NLD ISSN 1385-5999) **983**
Bouwplannen. D: Noord-Brabant, Limburg, Zeeland (NLD ISSN 1385-948X) **983**
• Bouwrecht (NLD ISSN 0165-1528) **983**
Bouwrecht Monografieen (NLD ISSN 1574-1915) **983**
• Bouwregels in de Praktijk (NLD ISSN 1872-2245) **983**
BouwTotaal (NLD ISSN 1872-5414) **983**
• BouwWereld (NLD ISSN 0026-5942) **983**
Bovag Krant *see* De BovagKrant **8570**
De BovagKrant (NLD ISSN 1380-5320) **8570**
Boverkets Foerfattningssamling (SWE ISSN 1100-0856) **983**
• Bovilogisk (DNK ISSN 0906-009X) **261**
➤ Bovine Practitioner (USA ISSN 0524-1685) **8794**
Bovine Veterinarian (USA) **6656**
Bovins Limousins (FRA ISSN 0985-150X) **281**
• Bovis (ESP ISSN 1130-4804) **8794**
Bow and Arrow Hunting (USA ISSN 0894-7856) **8306**
Bow & Swing (USA ISSN 0274-6034) **2683**
The Bow Group. Policy Papers (GBR) **7110**
Bow Valley College. Calendar *see* Course Guide **2975**
Bow Valley College. Career Catalogue *see* Course Guide **2975**
Bow Valley This Week (CAN ISSN 1182-9893) **2375**
• Bowdoin (USA ISSN 0895-2604) **2275**
Bowdoin College. Museum of Art. Occasional Papers (USA ISSN 0084-7992) **6521**
Bowen Independent (AUS ISSN 1832-892X) **3793**
▼ Bowhunt America (USA ISSN 1947-3745) **8306**
• Bowhunter (USA ISSN 0273-7434) **8306**
• Bowhunting (USA ISSN 1049-9768) **8306**
Bowhunting New Zealand Magazine (NZL ISSN 1177-0511) **8306**
Bowhunting NZ Magazine *see* Bowhunting New Zealand Magazine **8306**
• Bowhunting World (USA ISSN 1043-5492) **8306**
Bowker Annual *see* Library and Book Trade Almanac (Year) **5026**
Bowker Annual Library and Book Trade Almanac *see* Library and Book Trade Almanac (Year) **5026**
The Bowker Annual Library and Book Trade Almanac (Year) *see* Library and Book Trade Almanac (Year) **5026**
Bowker Annual of Library & Book Trade Information *see* Library and Book Trade Almanac (Year) **5026**
† The Bowker Buyer's Guide (USA ISSN 0000-1775) **8937**
† Bowker Library Bulletin (USA) **8937**
Bowker - Whitaker Global Books in Print on Disc *see* Bowker's Global Books in Print on Disc **621**
• Bowker's British Books in Print (USA) **621**
• Bowker's Complete Video Directory (USA ISSN 1051-290X) **2400**
• Bowker's Global Books in Print (USA) **621**
• Bowker's Global Books in Print on Disc (USA) **621**
Bowker's Guide to Characters in Fiction (USA ISSN 1553-2062) **5406**
Bowker's Law Books and Serials in Print *see* Law Books and Serials in Print **4823**
† Bowker's News Media Directory (USA ISSN 0000-1783) **8937**
Bowker's Spanishbooksinprint.com *see* Booksinprint.com **621**
Bowlaren Magazinet (SWE ISSN 1101-3273) **8224**
Bowlers Journal International (USA ISSN 1095-0435) **8162**
Bowlers' World (GBR ISSN 0962-8096) **8224**
Bowles Notes (USA ISSN 1550-7661) **5265**
Bowling and Billiard Buyers Guide (USA ISSN 0068-0559) **8224**
Bowling Buyers Guide *see* Bowling and Billiard Buyers Guide **8224**
Bowling Center Management (USA) **1729**
Bowling Green News *see* B G News **2273**
Bowling News (USA) **8224**
† Bowling Open (ITA) **8937**
Bowls Alive *see* Bowls N S W Magazine **8224**
Bowls International (GBR ISSN 0262-6942) **8224**
Bowls N S W Magazine (AUS) **8224**
Bowman's Accounting Report *see* Inside Public Accounting **1290**
• Bowne Digest for Corporate & Securities Lawyers (USA ISSN 0896-906X) **4821**
• Bowne Review for C F Os and Investment Bankers (Online Edition) (USA) **1321**
Bowne Review for C F Os and Investment Bankers (Print Edition) *see* Bowne Review for C F Os and Investment Bankers (Online Edition) **1321**
Bowser Directory of Small Stocks (USA ISSN 1053-0908) **1613**
Bowser Report (USA ISSN 0738-7288) **1613**
The Bowyer's Journal (USA ISSN 1555-9521) **532**
Box (DEU) **4371**
Box *see* Box International Trade **4554**
Box (USA ISSN 1089-9685) **8162**
Box & Carton Blue Book *see* Davison's Box & Carton Blue Book **6709**
Box.de *see* Box **4371**
Box International Trade (ITA ISSN 1127-8935) **4554**
Box y Lucha (MEX ISSN 0006-8470) **8162**
• Boxcar Poetry Review (USA ISSN 1931-1761) **5418**
Boxe Magazine (FRA ISSN 1958-7023) **8162**
Boxer Review (USA ISSN 1067-8875) **6804**
Boxerbladet (SWE ISSN 0345-1690) **6804**
Boxing (Year) (USA ISSN 1042-5292) **8162**
Boxing Almanac and Book of Facts (USA ISSN 1084-9610) **8162**
Boxing and Football Illustrated (GHA) **8162**
Boxing Digest (USA ISSN 1531-4677) **8162**
Boxing Magazine (JPN) **8162**
Boxing Monthly (GBR ISSN 0956-098X) **8163**
Boxing News (GBR ISSN 0006-8519) **8163**
The Boxing Record Book (USA) **8163**
Boxing U S A (USA) **8163**
Boxoffice (ITA) **6491**
• Boxoffice (USA ISSN 0006-8527) **6491**
Boxsport (DEU ISSN 0948-2520) **8163**
Boxwood Bulletin (USA ISSN 0006-8535) **3725**
Boxwood Buyer's Guide (USA) **3725**
Boxwood Handbook (USA) **3725**
Boy Oh Boy (DEU) **4371**
• Boyce Thompson Institute for Plant Research. Annual Report (USA) **781**
Boyce's Service Station Manual (AUS) **8570**
Boycott Law Bulletin (USA ISSN 0162-1726) **4919**
Boyer Roots (USA) **3760**
▼ Boyne Berries (IRL ISSN 1649-9271) **5265**
Boyne Health & Beauty *see* Boyne Style & Beauty **586**
Boyne Style & Beauty (IRL ISSN 1649-928X) **586**
Boys and Girls *see* Shaonan Shaonu **5371**
Boys & Girls Clubs of America Bulletin *see* Connections (Atlanta) **2149**
Boys' Brigade. Annual Report (GBR ISSN 0068-0605) **2180**
Boys Brigade Gazette (GBR ISSN 0006-8578) **2180**
• Boys in Schools Bulletin (Online) (AUS) **2832**
• Boys' Life (USA ISSN 0006-8608) **2180**
• Boys' Quest (USA ISSN 1078-9006) **2180**
Boys Rush (JPN) **2146**
• Boys Town Journal (USA) **8028**
Boys Toys (GBR ISSN 1461-6939) **6287**
† Boz (GBR ISSN 1357-4612) **8937**
Bozarth Beacon (USA ISSN 1045-862X) **3760**
Bozje Okolje (SVN ISSN 1318-9328) **7786**

Link to your serials resources and content with ulrichsweb.com

10052 BRAZIL DEVELOPMENT SERIES ULRICH'S PERIODICALS

Brazil Development Series/Series Desenvolvimento Brasileiro (BRA) **1880**
• Brazil Focus (GBR ISSN 1477-2450) **1443**
Brazil Freight Transport Report (GBR ISSN 1752-5241) **8491**
Brazil. Fundacao Instituto Brasileiro de Geografia e Estadistica. Estatisticas do Registro Civil (BRA ISSN 0101-2207) **7304**
Brazil Handbook (GBR ISSN 1363-7401) **8688**
Brazil in Figures *see* Brasil em Numeros **8358**
• Brazil Insurance Report (GBR ISSN 1750-5615) **4496**
Brazil. Ministerio de Educacao. Departamento de Educacao Fisica e Desportos. Caderno Cultural (BRA) **3053**
Brazil. Ministerio de Educacao. Faculdade de Ciencias Agrarias do Para. Informe Tecnico (BRA ISSN 0100-9974) **97**
Brazil. Museu do Indio. Boletim. Documentacao (BRA ISSN 0101-0484) **331**
Brazil Petrochemicals Report (GBR ISSN 1749-2165) **6764**
Brazil Quarterly Forecast Report *see* Brazil Business Forecast Report **1443**
Brazil. Servico de Estatistica da Educacao e Cultura. Sinopse Estatistica da Educacao Pre-Escolar (BRA) **2931**
Brazil. Servico de Estatistica da Educacao e Cultura. Sinopse Estatistica do Ensino Superior (BRA) **2931**
Brazil. Servico de Estatistica da Educacao. Sinopse Estatistica do Ensino Regular de 1o Grau (BRA) **2931**
Brazil. Servico Nacional de Aprendizagem Comercial. Boletim Tecnico (BRA ISSN 0102-549X) **2832**
Brazil. Servico Social do Comercio. Administracao Regional no Estado de Sao Paulo. Relatorio Anual (BRA) **8028**
Brazil. Servico Social do Comercio. Anuario Estatistico (BRA) **7479**
Brazil. Superintendencia do Desenvolvimento do Nordeste. Relatorio Anual (BRA) **1443**
Brazil. Superintendencia do Desenvolvimento do Nordeste. S U D E N E Plano de Acao (BRA) **4405**
Brazil. Supremo Tribunal Federal. Indices de Legislacao Federal (BRA) **4631**
Brazil. Supremo Tribunal Federal. Relatorio dos Trabalhos Realizados (BRA) **4631**
Brazil. Tribunal Regional do Trabalho. Tercera Regiao. Revista (BRA ISSN 0076-8855) **4631**
• Brazil Watch (USA ISSN 0897-3067) **1443**
Brazil Watch Fax Bulletin (USA) **1443**
• The Brazilian (BRA) **3803**
• ➤ Brazilian Administration Review (BRA ISSN 1807-7692) **1729**
Brazilian Aerospace Yearbook *see* Anuario Aerospacial Brasileiro **46**
Brazilian American Chamber of Commerce News Bulletin (USA ISSN 0300-7464) **1396**
• ➤ Brazilian Archives of Biology and Technology (BRA ISSN 1516-8913) **762**
Brazilian Art Research Yearbook (BRA ISSN 0103-9636) **479**
The Brazilian Book Magazine (BRA ISSN 0104-1150) **5247**
• ➤ Brazilian Chemical Society. Journal (BRA ISSN 0103-5053) **2051**
Brazilian Communication Research Yearbook (BRA ISSN 0103-9318) **2313**
• ➤ Brazilian Computer Society. Journal (GBR ISSN 0104-6500) **2408**
• ➤ Brazilian Dental Journal (BRA ISSN 0103-6440) **5836**
Brazilian Dentral Sciencie *see* Ciencia Odontologica Brasileira **5838**
Brazilian Energy Statistics *see* Estatistica Brasileira de Energia **3152**
Brazilian Export Market (BRA) **1553**
Brazilian Geographic Journal *see* Revista Brasileira de Geografia **4026**
Brazilian Journal of Agricultural Research *see* Pesquisa Agropecuaria Brasileira **146**
Brazilian Journal of Animal Science *see* Revista Brasileira de Zootecnia **8806**
Brazilian Journal of Applied Economics *see* Revista de Economia Aplicada **1167**
• Brazilian Journal of Aquatic Science and Technology/Revista Brasileira de Ciencia e Tecnologia Aquatica (BRA ISSN 1808-7035) **2793**
• Brazilian Journal of Biology (BRA ISSN 1519-6984) **663**
▼ • Brazilian Journal of Biomotricity (BRA ISSN 1981-6324) **6229**
Brazilian Journal of Biosciences *see* Revista Brasileira de Biociencias **700**
Brazilian Journal of Botany *see* Revista Brasileira de Botanica **815**
Brazilian Journal of Cardiovascular Surgery *see* Revista Brasileira de Cirurgia Cardiovascular **5798**
• Brazilian Journal of Chemical Engineering (BRA ISSN 0104-6632) **3236**
Brazilian Journal of Cognitive Therapies *see* Revista Brasileira de Terapias Cognitivas **6181**
➤ Brazilian Journal of Food Technology (BRA ISSN 1516-7275) **3628**
Brazilian Journal of Geophysics *see* Revista Brasileira de Geofisica **2788**
Brazilian Journal of Health Surveillance *see* Revista Brasileira de Vigilancia Sanitaria **7539**
• ➤ The Brazilian Journal of Infectious Diseases (BRA ISSN 1413-8670) **5810**
Brazilian Journal of Maize and Sorghum *see* Revista Brasileira de Milho e Sorgo **275**
Brazilian Journal of Materials Science and Engineering (BRA ISSN 1415-7004) **3342**
• ➤ Brazilian Journal of Medical and Biological Research (BRA ISSN 0100-879X) **5588**
Brazilian Journal of Medicinal Plants *see* Revista Brasileira de Plantas Medicinais **815**
• ➤ Brazilian Journal of Microbiology (BRA ISSN 1517-8382) **882**
Brazilian Journal of Morphological Sciences *see* Revista Brasileira de Ciencias Morfologicas **927**
Brazilian Journal of Mother and Child Health *see* Revista Brasileira de Saude Materno Infantil **2167**
Brazilian Journal of Oceanography (BRA ISSN 1679-8759) **2800**
• ➤ Brazilian Journal of Oral Sciences (BRA ISSN 1677-3217) **5836**
Brazilian Journal of Orthopaedics *see* Revista Brasileira de Ortopedia **6072**
• ➤ Brazilian Journal of Physics (BRA ISSN 0103-9733) **7007**
• ➤ Brazilian Journal of Plant Physiology (BRA ISSN 1677-0420) **782**
Brazilian Journal of Political Economy *see* Revista de Economia Politica **7178**
• Brazilian Journal of Population Studies (BRA ISSN 1415-0158) **7278**
Brazilian Journal of Poultry Science *see* Revista Brasileira de Ciencia Avicola **298**
Brazilian Journal of Probability and Statistics (BRA) **5476**
Brazilian Journal of Psychiatry *see* Jornal Brasileiro de Psiquiatria **6149**
Brazilian Journal of Rheumatology *see* Revista Brasileira de Reumatologia **6226**
Brazilian Journal of School Health *see* Revista Brasileira de Saude Escolar **7538**
Brazilian Journal of Sports Medicine *see* Revista Brasileira de Medicina do Esporte **6232**
Brazilian Journal of Urology *see* International Brazilian Journal of Urology **6269**
Brazilian Journal of Vacuum Applications *see* Revista Brasileira de Aplicacoes de Vacuo **3394**
Brazilian Journal of Veterinary and Animal Sciences *see* Arquivo Brasileiro de Medicina Veterinaria e Zootecnia **8793**
Brazilian Journal of Veterinary Parasitology *see* Revista Brasileira de Parasitologia Veterinaria **8806**
▼ Brazilian Journal of Veterinary Pathology (BRA ISSN 1983-0246) **8794**
Brazilian Journal of Veterinary Research *see* Pesquisa Veterinaria Brasileira **8804**
• ➤ Brazilian Journal of Veterinary Research and Animal Science (BRA ISSN 1413-9596) **8794**
• Brazilian Journalism Research (BRA ISSN 1808-4079) **4572**
The Brazilian Management Review *see* R A E **1788**
Brazilian Mathematical Society. Bulletin, New Series *see* Sociedade Brasileira de Matematica. Boletim, Nova Serie **5536**
• Brazilian Meat Monitor (GBR ISSN 1750-2411) **281**
• Brazilian Oral Research (BRA ISSN 1806-8324) **5836**
▼ • Brazilian Political Science Review (BRA ISSN 1981-3821) **7110**
Brazilian Research in Pediatric Dentistry and Integrated Clinic *see* Pesquisa Brasileira em Odontopediatria e Clinica Integrada **5861**
Brazilian Review of Econometrics (BRA) **1536**
Brazilian Review of Open and Distance Learning *see* Revista Brasileira de Aprendizagem Aberta a Distancia **2905**
Brazilian Seed Journal *see* Revista Brasileira de Sementes **250**
• Brazilian Society of Mechanical Sciences and Engineering. Journal (BRA ISSN 1678-5878) **3374**
Brazilian Statistical Journal *see* Revista Brasileira de Estatistica **8396**
• Brazilian Symposium on Computer Graphics and Image Processing. Proceedings (USA ISSN 1530-1834) **2483**
Brazilian Symposium on Integrated Circuit Design (USA) **2539**
• Brazilian Symposium on Neural Networks. Proceedings (USA ISSN 1522-4899) **2447**
• The Brazilianist (CAN ISSN 1480-8161) **1553**
• Brazzil (Online) (USA) **3523**
Bread & Bakery Products Market Report *see* Key Note Market Report: Bread & Bakery Products **3674**
Bread & Butter Bulletin *see* B B Bulletin **5065**
Bread & Cakes (SWE ISSN 0284-9488) **3672**
Bread Caterers' Directory *see* Pan Directorio de Proveedores **3675**
Bread for the World Newsletter (USA ISSN 1045-1005) **8028**
The Bread of Life (CAN ISSN 0821-168X) **7786**
Bread Pudding Recipe Exchange (USA ISSN 1093-2925) **4353**
Bread Pudding Update (USA ISSN 1042-7139) **4353**
Break (USA) **8688**
Break Away *see* Breakaway **2180**
Break Bulk (USA ISSN 1948-9951) **8640**
Break-In (NZL ISSN 0006-9523) **2357**
• Break o' Day (AUS ISSN 1833-9123) **8224**
Breakaway (USA ISSN 1048-2881) **2180**
Breakaway: A Focus on Small Business (USA) **1069**
Breakfast All Day *see* B A D **5259**
Breakfast Cereals Market Report *see* Key Note Market Report: Breakfast Cereals **3652**
Breaking Ball (IRL ISSN 1649-0673) **8224**
Breaking Our Silence (GBR ISSN 0955-7652) **1667**
Breaking the Siege (USA) **7224**
• Breaking the Silence (USA) **5811**
Breakout Series (GBR) **2832**
Breakthrough (IND ISSN 0974-2433) **7841**
Breakthrough (San Francisco) (USA ISSN 1073-2519) **7110**
Breakthrough News (USA ISSN 1080-3009) **7224**
Breakthru (GBR ISSN 1368-2938) **6551**
• ➤ The Breast (GBR ISSN 0960-9776) **5987**
• ➤ Breast Cancer (JPN ISSN 1340-6868) **6009**
▼ • ➤ Breast Cancer (NZL ISSN 1178-2234) **6009**
Breast Cancer Action Source (USA ISSN 1933-2408) **8844**
• ➤ Breast Cancer Online (GBR ISSN 1470-9031) **6010**
• ➤ Breast Cancer Research (Online Edition) (GBR ISSN 1465-542X) **6010**
• ➤ Breast Cancer Research and Treatment (USA ISSN 0167-6806) **6010**
• Breast Cancer Research Review (NZL) **6010**
Breast Cancer Weekly (USA ISSN 1535-2749) **6010**
• ➤ Breast Care (CHE ISSN 1661-3791) **5987**
• ➤ Breast Disease (NLD ISSN 0888-6008) **5987**
Breast Disease Series (NLD) **5987**
• Breast Diseases: A Year Book Quarterly (USA ISSN 1043-321X) **5987**
• ➤ The Breast Journal (USA ISSN 1075-122X) **5987**
• Breast News (AUS ISSN 1324-7077) **6010**
Breastfeeding Abstracts (USA ISSN 0896-4572) **5741**
• ➤ Breastfeeding Medicine (USA ISSN 1556-8253) **920**
➤ Breastfeeding Review (AUS ISSN 0729-2759) **6656**
• BreastScreen Victoria. Annual Report (Year) (AUS ISSN 1833-0177) **5987**
Breath Exercise *see* Yangsheng Yuekan **7000**
Breath of God (USA ISSN 1930-5923) **7628**
Breath Series (USA) **6644**
➤ Breathe (GBR ISSN 1810-6838) **6212**
Breathe (Birmingham) (USA) **6212**
Breathe (New York) (USA) **6644**
Breathe Well (USA) **6212**
▼ Breathing (USA ISSN 1940-493X) **6212**
• Breathline (USA ISSN 0896-4882) **5770**
Brecha (URY ISSN 0797-5333) **3993**
Brechas (MEX) **4445**
Brecht Yearbook (USA ISSN 0734-8665) **5265**
Breda Business *see* West-Brabant Business **1721**
Bredband skaber Naerhet (NOR ISSN 1890-209X) **2495**
Brede Scholen in Nederland (NLD ISSN 1872-339X) **2832**
• A Breed Apart (USA ISSN 1084-0621) **6805**
Breeder Special (DEU) **6805**
Breeders Digest (USA) **281**
Breeders Journal (USA) **281**
Breeding Bird Survey (GBR ISSN 1368-9932) **904**
Breeding Research *see* Ikushugaku Kenkyu **677**
• ➤ Breeding Science (JPN ISSN 1344-7610) **97**
Breeze (Harrisonburg) (USA) **2275**
The Breeze (Mathiston) (USA) **2275**
Bref (FRA ISSN 0759-6898) **6491**
Bref Rhone - Alpes (FRA ISSN 0006-9566) **1443**
Bref til Storkaupmanna (ISL) **1976**
Brefskaktidindi (ISL) **8163**
Breifne (IRL ISSN 0068-0877) **4206**
Breithaupt *see* Sammlung von Entscheidungen aus dem Sozialrecht **8067**
• Brejk (SVK ISSN 1336-1457) **6287**
Bremen Magazin (DEU) **3845**
Bremer (DEU) **3845**
Bremer Aerztejournal (DEU ISSN 1432-2978) **5588**
Bremer Archaeologische Blaetter (DEU ISSN 0068-0907) **384**
Bremer Ausschuss fuer Wirtschaftsforschung Monatsbericht *see* B A W - Monatsbericht **8934**
Bremer Beitraege zur Geographie und Raumplanung (DEU ISSN 0720-9738) **4000**
Bremer Beitraege zur Literatur- und Ideengeschichte (DEU ISSN 0941-1488) **5265**
Bremer Jahrbuch fuer Musikkultur (DEU ISSN 0948-0285) **6551**
Bremer Kirchenzeitung (DEU ISSN 0949-2577) **7749**
Bremer Landwirtschaftliche Rundschau (DEU) **97**
Bremer Lehrerzeitung *see* B L Z **3052**
Bremer Nachrichten (DEU) **3845**
• Bremer Schulblatt (DEU ISSN 0006-9582) **3018**
Bremer Soziologische Texte (DEU ISSN 0935-6045) **7951**
Bremer Turnvereinigung von 1877 e.V. Spiegel *see* B T V Spiegel **8160**
Bremer Umschau (DEU) **3845**
Bremische Hausbesitzerzeitung (DEU) **7584**
Bremisches Jahrbuch (DEU ISSN 0341-9622) **4206**
Brenesia (CRI ISSN 0304-3711) **7841**
† Brenner-Studien (AUT ISSN 1021-5972) **8937**
Brenner-Texte (AUT) **4445**
Brennessel (DEU) **6908**
Brennpunkt (DEU ISSN 0932-7231) **6964**
Brennpunkt Energie *see* Innovation und Energie **3138**
• Brennpunkt Familie (AUT) **2180**
Brennpunkt Gemeinde (DEU ISSN 0944-4734) **7749**
† Brennpunkt Gesundheit (DEU ISSN 1619-8956) **8937**
Brennpunkt Lateinamerika (Print Edition) *see* G I G A Focus. Lateinamerika (Print Edition) **7236**
Brennpunkt Seelsorge (DEU ISSN 0171-5666) **7628**
Brennpunkte der Sportwissenschaft (DEU ISSN 0932-8823) **8163**
Brennpunkte des Arbeitsrechts (Year) (DEU) **1667**
Brennpunkte des Sozialrechts (Year) (DEU) **4827**
Brennstoffspiegel und Mineraloelrundschau (DEU ISSN 1864-8924) **6764**
Brennstoffzellen Magazin (DEU ISSN 1618-6478) **3125**
Brentano Studien (DEU ISSN 0935-7009) **6908**
Brentwood Gazette (GBR) **3862**
Brepols Binghamton Series *see* Binghamton Medieval and Early Modern Studies **4205**
Brepols Essays in European Culture (BEL ISSN 1780-5910) **4206**
Brepols Publishers Newsletter (BEL) **7556**
Bres (NLD ISSN 0165-7798) **5209**
Breslauer Kreis- und Stadtblatt (DEU) **3845**
Brestskii Kur'er (BLR) **3800**
La Bretagne Agricole (FRA ISSN 1774-7589) **97**
▼ Bretagne Culture & Decouverte (FRA ISSN 1957-4800) **8688**
Bretagne Economique (FRA ISSN 0153-6028) **1396**
Bretagne Magazine (FRA) **4000**
Bretagne Reelle (FRA ISSN 0006-9647) **7110**
Brethren Evangelist (USA ISSN 0747-4288) **7749**
Brethren in Christ History and Life (USA ISSN 1071-4200) **7628**
Brethren Journal (USA ISSN 0006-9655) **7628**
• Brethren Life and Thought (USA ISSN 0006-9663) **7749**
Brethren Peace Fellowship Newsletter (USA) **7628**
Bretons a Travers le Monde (FRA ISSN 1950-0491) **4206**
Bretons: Societe, Culture, Musique (FRA ISSN 1775-8246) **3840**
† Brett (DEU) **8937**
• Brettnews (USA) **5209**
Brev (SWE ISSN 0347-3546) **5266**
Brevard Business News (USA ISSN 0889-5104) **1069**
Brevard Users Group Newsletter *see* B U G Newsletter **2575**
Brevduvesport (SWE ISSN 0280-7769) **6805**
Breve Indland (DNK ISSN 0908-7796) **2353**
• Breves (FRA ISSN 0248-4625) **5209**
Breviaria Juris (ITA ISSN 1972-0564) **4631**
Breviaria Juris. I Formulari Annotati (ITA ISSN 1972-0572) **4631**
Breviarul Agentilor Economici din Judetul Brasov (ROM ISSN 1454-6558) **1396**
Breviora (USA ISSN 0006-9698) **936**
• Brevity (USA) **5266**
Brew-Info (GBR) **600**
• Brew-Net (USA) **5266**
Brew Your Own (USA ISSN 1081-826X) **600**
The Brewer & Distiller *see* The Brewer & Distiller International **600**
• The Brewer & Distiller International (GBR ISSN 1753-2086) **600**
The Brewer International *see* The Brewer & Distiller International **600**
Breweries & the Beer Market *see* Key Note Market Report: Breweries & the Beer Market **606**
Brewers *see* Business Ratio. Brewers **601**
Brewers Almanac (USA) **600**
Brewers and Licensed Retailers Association Statistical Handbook *see* B L R A Statistical Handbook **614**
Brewers Digest (USA ISSN 0006-971X) **600**
Brewers Digest. Annual Buyers' Guide *see* Brewers Digest **600**
• Brewers' Guardian (GBR ISSN 0006-9728) **600**
Brewers Guild Directory (GBR ISSN 0309-7625) **601**
The Brewery Manual (GBR) **601**
Brewery Manual & Who's Who in British Brewing & Scotch Whisky Distilling Industries *see* The Brewery Manual **601**
Brewing and Beverage Industry China (DEU) **601**
Brewing and Beverage Industry Espanol (DEU ISSN 1439-5452) **601**
Brewing and Beverage Industry International (DEU ISSN 0949-8877) **601**
Brewing & Distilling International *see* The Brewer & Distiller International **600**
Brewing and Malting Barley Research Institute. Annual Report (CAN ISSN 0068-094X) **601**
Brewing Society of Japan. Journal *see* Nippon Jozo Kyokaishi **608**
• Brews & News (USA ISSN 1941-5001) **601**
Breyer Animal Collector's Guide (USA ISSN 1931-1370) **4330**
The Briar Cliff Review (USA ISSN 1550-0926) **5266**
• Briarpatch (CAN ISSN 0703-8968) **7110**
Brick (CAN ISSN 0382-8565) **5209**
• Brick Bulletin (GBR ISSN 0307-9325) **983**
Brick in Architecture (USA ISSN 0743-0043) **983**
• Brick Journal (USA ISSN 1941-2347) **4059**
Brick - Tile *see* Zhuanwa **2047**
• Bricker's International Directory (USA ISSN 1078-2257) **1729**
The Bricklayer (CAN) **2275**
Bricks & Blocks (USA ISSN 1944-3242) **1044**

Title

10054 BRITISH AND IRISH STUDIES IN GERMAN LANGUAGE AND LITERATURE ULRICH'S PERIODICALS

British and Irish Studies in German Language and Literature *see* Britische und Irische Studien zur Deutschen Sprache und Literatur **5101**
British Antarctic Survey. Annual Report (GBR ISSN 0141-3325) **7841**
British Antarctic Survey. Scientific Reports (GBR ISSN 0068-1261) **7842**
British Antique Dealers' Association. Annual Handbook (GBR) **364**
British Antique Dealers' Association Journal *see* B A D A Journal **364**
British Antique Dealers' Association Yearbook *see* British Antique Dealers' Association. Annual Handbook **364**
British Approval Service for Electrical Equipment in Flammable Atmospheres List *see* B A S E E F A List **3296**
➤ British Arachnological Society. Bulletin (GBR ISSN 0524-4994) **936**
British Arachnological Society. Newsletter (GBR ISSN 0959-2261) **937**
British Archaeological Association. Conference Transactions (GBR ISSN 0144-0179) **384**
• ➤ British Archaeological Association. Journal (GBR ISSN 0068-1288) **384**
British Archaeological Reports British Series *see* B A R. British Series **382**
British Archaeological Reports International Series *see* B A R. International Series **382**
British Archaeology (GBR ISSN 1357-4442) **385**
British Army Review (GBR ISSN 0952-4134) **6414**
• ➤ The British Art Journal (GBR ISSN 1467-2006) **479**
British Artists (USA) **479**
British Association for Adoption & Fostering Discussion Series *see* B A A F Discussion Series **8027**
British Association for Adoption & Fostering News *see* B A A F News **8027**
British Association for Adoption & Fostering Practice Series *see* B A A F Practice Series **8027**
British Association for Adoption & Fostering Research Series *see* B A A F Research Series **8027**
British Association for Canadian Studies. Newsletter (GBR ISSN 1351-5667) **7951**
British Association for the Advancement of Science. Final Programme for the Annual Meeting (GBR ISSN 0263-1148) **7842**
British Association of Dermatologists News *see* B A D News **5872**
British Association of Dermatologists. Newsletter *see* B A D News **5872**
British Association of Friends of Museums Journal *see* B A F M Journal **6520**
British Association of Picture Libraries and Agencies Directory *see* B A P L A Directory **6964**
• ➤ British Association of Psychotherapists. Journal (GBR ISSN 0954-0350) **7341**
British Association of Public Safety Communication Officers Journal *see* The B A P C O Journal **2313**
British Association of Social Workers. Annual Report *see* British Association of Social Workers. Annual Report and Financial Statements **8028**
British Association of Social Workers. Annual Report and Financial Statements (GBR) **8028**
• British Association of Teachers of the Deaf. Magazine (GBR ISSN 1366-0799) **4072**
British Astronomical Association. Circular (GBR ISSN 0264-4185) **572**
➤ British Astronomical Association. Handbook (GBR ISSN 0068-130X) **572**
• ➤ British Astronomical Association. Journal (GBR ISSN 0007-0297) **572**
British Astronomical Association. Variable Star Section Circular (GBR ISSN 0267-9272) **572**
British Baker (GBR ISSN 0007-0300) **3672**
British Baker Directory (GBR ISSN 1750-127X) **3672**
British Balls (AUS ISSN 1833-8844) **5067**
• The British Bandsman (GBR ISSN 0007-0319) **6551**
British Bee Journal (GBR ISSN 0007-0327) **97**
• British Bio-Energy News (GBR ISSN 1743-7431) **3125**
• ➤ British Birds (GBR ISSN 0007-0335) **904**
British Books in Print *see* Bowker's British Books in Print **621**
British Brick Society. Information (GBR ISSN 0960-7870) **983**
British Broadcasting Corporation (B B C) Vegetarian Good Food *see* B B C Vegetarian Good Food **4352**
British Broadcasting Corporation Al-Mushahid *see* B B C Al-Mushahid **2357**
British Broadcasting Corporation Gardeners' World Magazine *see* B B C Gardeners' World Magazine **3724**
British Broadcasting Corporation Good Food *see* B B C Good Food **4352**
British Broadcasting Corporation Homes and Antiques *see* B B C Homes and Antiques **364**
British Broadcasting Corporation Music Magazine *see* B B C Music Magazine **6547**
British Broadcasting Corporation Music Magazine (North American Edition) *see* B B C Music Magazine (North American Edition) **6547**
British Broadcasting Corporation Music Magazine. Opera a Celebration *see* B B C Music Magazine. Opera a Celebration **6547**
British Broadcasting Corporation Music Magazine. Symphony Special *see* B B C Music Magazine. Symphony Special **6547**
British Broadcasting Corporation News Online *see* B B C News Online **3861**
British Broadcasting Corporation on Air *see* B B C on Air **2357**
British Broadcasting Corporation SMart *see* B B C SMart **2177**
British Broadcasting Corporation Top Gear *see* B B C Top Gear **8568**
British Bulletin of Publications on Latin America, the Caribbean, Portugal and Spain (GBR ISSN 0268-2400) **621**
British Business Group Calling *see* B B G Calling **1064**
British Cactus & Succulent Journal *see* Cactus World **782**
British Car (USA ISSN 1052-0929) **8570**
British Caribbean Philatelic Journal (USA ISSN 0045-2890) **6892**
British Carpet Technical Centre, Cleaning & Maintenance Research & Services Organization Focus *see* B C T C - C A M R A S O - Focus **8448**
British Cartographic Society Annual Symposium and Map Curators' Group Workshop. Proceedings (GBR) **4000**
• The British Catalogue of Music (USA ISSN 0068-1407) **6551**
British Cattle Breeders Club. Annual Conference Papers (GBR) **281**
British Cave Research Association Cave Studies Series *see* B C R A Cave Studies Series **2726**
The British Caver (GBR) **2793**
British Cement Association Bulletin *see* B C A Bulletin **977**
British Cement Association. Interim Technical Note (GBR) **983**
† British Ceramic Proceedings (GBR ISSN 0268-4373) **8937**
British Ceramic Research. Special Publications (GBR ISSN 0144-2147) **2038**
British Ceramic Transactions (Print Edition) *see* Advances in Applied Ceramics (Print) **2047**
British Chamber of Commerce. Monthly Information Service (THA) **1397**
† British Chamber of Commerce of Turkey. Trade Journal (TUR ISSN 0007-0416) **8937**
British Chess Magazine (GBR ISSN 0007-0440) **8163**
• British Chevening Scholarships Programme. Annual Report (GBR) **3012**
British Church Newspaper (GBR) **7749**
British Cichlid Association. Information Pamphlet (GBR ISSN 1367-7586) **3587**
The British Clothing Industry Yearbook (GBR ISSN 0141-1470) **2245**
British Codes of Advertising and Sales Promotion *see* The C A P Code **22**
British Columbia. Agricultural Land Commission. Annual Service Plan Report (CAN ISSN 1705-9348) **7423**
British Columbia Alliance Concerned with Early Pregnancy and Parenthood. Newsletter (CAN ISSN 1184-1478) **971**
British Columbia Annual Criminal Practice (CAN ISSN 1206-9833) **4885**
British Columbia Annual Practice (CAN ISSN 0836-0391) **4632**
• British Columbia Appeal Cases (CAN ISSN 1189-6302) **4632**
British Columbia Approved Accommodation Guide (CAN ISSN 1709-5751) **4382**
British Columbia Archer *see* B.C. Archer **8160**
British Columbia Assessment Authority. Annual Performance Report and a Report of the Creation of the Assessment Roll (CAN ISSN 1495-8864) **7423**
British Columbia Assessment Authority. Performance Plan *see* British Columbia Assessment Authority. Service Plan **1913**
British Columbia Assessment Authority. Service Plan (CAN ISSN 1710-1980) **1913**
British Columbia Assessment Authority. Strategic Plan *see* British Columbia Assessment Authority. Service Plan **1913**
British Columbia Birding *see* B C Birding **902**
British Columbia Board of Parole. Annual Report (CAN ISSN 0710-7412) **7423**
British Columbia Buildings Corporation. Annual Report (CAN ISSN 0702-0511) **4405**
British Columbia Business *see* B C Business **1064**
• British Columbia Business Directory (USA ISSN 1203-5165) **1977**
British Columbia Cancer Research Centre. Annual Report (CAN ISSN 1185-1031) **6010**
British Columbia Catholic *see* B C Catholic **7785**
British Columbia. Children's Commission. Annual Report *see* Child and Youth Officer for British Columbia. Annual Report **7430**
British Columbia Collective Bargaining Review and Outlook (CAN ISSN 0829-8319) **4591**
British Columbia Commercial Catch Statistics: By Species, Gear, Month and Area (CAN) **3612**
British Columbia Corporation Manual (CAN) **4858**
• British Columbia Corporations Law Guide (CAN) **4858**
• British Columbia Court Forms (CAN) **4632**
British Columbia Court Rules Citator (CAN ISSN 1205-8092) **4947**
British Columbia Deaf News *see* B C Deaf News **4072**
• British Columbia Decisions - Civil Cases (CAN ISSN 0824-717X) **4827**
British Columbia Decisions - Civil Cases. Table of Cases Reported (CAN ISSN 1205-8076) **4827**
British Columbia Decisions - Civil Cases. Weekly Headnotes (CAN ISSN 1206-4513) **4827**
British Columbia Decisions - Criminal Cases (CAN ISSN 1205-8106) **4885**
British Columbia Decisions - Criminal Cases. Monthly Headnotes (CAN ISSN 1481-6857) **4885**
British Columbia Decisions - Criminal Cases. Table of Cases Reported (CAN ISSN 1205-8084) **4885**
• British Columbia Decisions - Insurance Law Cases (CAN ISSN 0824-720X) **4632**
• British Columbia Decisions - Labour Arbitration (CAN ISSN 0824-7218) **4591**
British Columbia Decisions - Labour Arbitration: Cumulative Index (CAN) **1668**
• British Columbia Decisions - Municipal Law Cases (CAN ISSN 0824-7188) **4632**
British Columbia Decisions - Statute Citator (CAN ISSN 0715-4798) **4947**
British Columbia. Department of Mines and Petroleum Resources. Bulletin (CAN ISSN 0068-144X) **2727**
British Columbia Designated Heritage Sites Registry (CAN ISSN 0843-6959) **4286**
British Columbia. Division of Vital Statistics Agency. Quarterly Digest (CAN ISSN 1188-1437) **7547**
British Columbia Energy Supply and Requirements Forecast Update (CAN ISSN 0832-820X) **3125**
British Columbia. Environmental Appeal Board. Annual Report (CAN ISSN 1188-021X) **3407**
British Columbia Family Law (CAN ISSN 0824-7781) **4907**
British Columbia Family Practice Manual (CAN ISSN 1719-4393) **4907**
• British Columbia Financial and Economic Review (Online Edition) (CAN) **1215**
British Columbia Financial and Economic Review (Print Edition) *see* British Columbia Financial and Economic Review (Online Edition) **1215**
British Columbia First Nations Forestry Program. Newsletter *see* The Bridge **3685**
British Columbia Fishing Directory & Atlas *see* B C Fishing Directory & Atlas **8305**
• British Columbia. Forest Appeals Commission. Annual Report (CAN ISSN 1205-7606) **3685**
• The British Columbia Gazette, Part I (CAN ISSN 0007-0505) **4632**
The British Columbia Gazette. Part II: Regulations (CAN ISSN 0824-7986) **4632**
British Columbia Genealogist (CAN ISSN 0315-3835) **3760**
• British Columbia Government Publications Monthly Checklist (Online Edition) (CAN) **4998**
British Columbia Government Publications Monthly Checklist (Print Edition) *see* British Columbia Government Publications Monthly Checklist (Online Edition) **4998**
• ➤ British Columbia Historical News (CAN ISSN 1195-8294) **4286**
British Columbia Hospital Injury Admissions *see* National Trauma Registry Provincial Report. British Columbia: Hospital Injury Admissions **4107**
British Columbia Hospitality Industry Membership Directory *see* B C Hospitality Industry Membership Directory **4382**
British Columbia. Housing Management Commission. Annual Report (CAN ISSN 0225-509X) **4405**
British Columbia. Human Rights Commission. Annual Report (CAN) **7203**
British Columbia Hydro. Corporate Review (CAN ISSN 1201-9984) **8819**
British Columbia Hydro. Triple Bottom Line Report (CAN ISSN 1488-710X) **8819**
British Columbia. Industry Training Authority. Service Plan (CAN ISSN 1712-8137) **6693**
British Columbia Institute of Technology Annual Report *see* B C I T Annual Report **8416**
British Columbia Institute of Technology Update *see* B C I T Update **8416**
British Columbia Insurance Directory (CAN ISSN 0068-1598) **4496**
British Columbia. Job Protection Commission. Annual Report (CAN ISSN 1192-1099) **1668**
British Columbia. Labour Relations Board. Annual Report (CAN ISSN 1205-0245) **1668**
British Columbia Labour Relations Board Decisions - Cumulative Index (CAN) **1668**
• British Columbia Labour Relations Board Decisions - Digest (CAN ISSN 0715-5808) **1668**
British Columbia. Land Reserve Commission. Annual Report *see* British Columbia. Agricultural Land Commission. Annual Service Plan Report **7423**
British Columbia Law Institute. Annual Report (CAN) **4632**
British Columbia Law Institute. Reports (CAN) **4632**
British Columbia Law Reports (CAN ISSN 0703-3060) **4632**
British Columbia Legal Telephone Directory (CAN ISSN 0521-0585) **1977**
British Columbia. Legislative Assembly. Debates (Hansard Daily) (CAN ISSN 0825-6187) **7423**
British Columbia. Legislative Assembly. Debates (Hansard Paperbound) (CAN) **7424**
British Columbia. Legislative Assembly. Debates (Hansard Sessional Edition)/Journal des Debats (CAN ISSN 0825-6179) **7424**
British Columbia. Legislative Assembly. Journals (CAN ISSN 0706-0629) **7424**
British Columbia. Legislative Assembly. Select Standing Committee on Aboriginal Affairs. Report of Proceedings (Hansard) (CAN ISSN 1499-4143) **3523**
British Columbia. Legislative Assembly. Select Standing Committee on Education. Report of Proceedings (Hansard) (CAN ISSN 1499-4208) **2832**
British Columbia. Legislative Assembly. Select Standing Committee on Finance and Government Services. Report of Proceedings (Hansard) (CAN ISSN 1499-416X) **1913**
British Columbia. Legislative Assembly. Select Standing Committee on Health. Report of Proceedings (Hansard) (CAN ISSN 1499-4224) **7510**
British Columbia. Legislative Assembly. Special Committee on Sustainable Aquaculture. Report of Proceedings (Hansard) (CAN ISSN 1718-1054) **3587**
British Columbia. Legislative Assembly. Third Reading Bills (CAN ISSN 1185-3026) **7424**
British Columbia Library Association Reporter *see* B C L A Reporter **4993**
British Columbia Liquor Distribution Branch. Financial Statements (CAN ISSN 0709-4531) **7424**
British Columbia Lottery Corporation. Annual Report (CAN ISSN 0837-6859) **7424**
• British Columbia Magazine (CAN ISSN 1709-4623) **8688**
British Columbia Major Projects Inventory (CAN) **1321**
British Columbia Manufacturer's Directory (CAN ISSN 0704-6278) **1425**
British Columbia Market Share of United States Imports *see* Exports **1228**
• ➤ British Columbia Medical Journal (CAN ISSN 0007-0556) **5588**
British Columbia Mineral Exploration Review (CAN ISSN 0846-0051) **6458**
British Columbia. Ministry of Agriculture and Food. Annual Statistics (Year) (CAN) **176**
British Columbia. Ministry of Agriculture Fisheries and Food. Berry Production Guide for Commercial Growers (CAN ISSN 1190-8475) **222**
British Columbia. Ministry of Agriculture Fisheries and Food D.A.T.E. Program Report (CAN ISSN 0706-9308) **97**
British Columbia. Ministry of Agriculture Fisheries and Food. Field Crop Production Guide to Weed, Disease, Insect, Bird and Rodent Control (CAN ISSN 0228-8117) **98**
British Columbia. Ministry of Agriculture Fisheries and Food. Floriculture Production Guide for Commercial Growers (CAN ISSN 1198-2217) **222**
British Columbia. Ministry of Agriculture Fisheries and Food. Greenhouse Vegetable Production Guide for Commercial Growers (CAN ISSN 1192-9197) **222**
British Columbia. Ministry of Agriculture Fisheries and Food. Management Guide for Grapes (CAN ISSN 1198-001X) **223**
British Columbia. Ministry of Agriculture Fisheries and Food. Mushroom Production Guide (CAN ISSN 0706-4292) **3725**
British Columbia. Ministry of Agriculture Fisheries and Food. Nursery Crop Production Guide for Commercial Growers (CAN ISSN 1181-9820) **3725**
British Columbia. Ministry of Agriculture Fisheries and Food. Tree Fruit Production Guide for Interior Districts (CAN ISSN 0705-470X) **223**
British Columbia. Ministry of Agriculture Fisheries and Food. Vegetable Production Guide (CAN ISSN 0318-3661) **223**
British Columbia. Ministry of Attorney General. Annual Performance Report (CAN ISSN 1499-0210) **7424**
British Columbia. Ministry of Education. Annual Service Plan Report (CAN ISSN 1705-9097) **3018**
British Columbia. Ministry of Energy and Mines. Annual Report *see* British Columbia. Ministry of Energy and Mines. Annual Service Plan Report **7424**
British Columbia. Ministry of Energy and Mines. Annual Service Plan Report (CAN ISSN 1705-9275) **7424**
British Columbia. Ministry of Energy, Mines and Petroleum Resources. Mineral Resources Division. Summary of Operations (CAN ISSN 0825-6896) **6485**
British Columbia. Ministry of Environment, Lands and Parks. Annual Report *see* British Columbia. Ministry of Water, Land and Air Protection. Annual Service Plan Report **2604**
British Columbia. Ministry of Environment, Lands and Parks. Fisheries Branch. Fisheries Management Report (CAN ISSN 0705-5390) **3587**
British Columbia. Ministry of Environment, Lands and Parks. Fisheries Branch. Fisheries Technical Circular (CAN ISSN 0229-1150) **3587**

▼ new title   † ceased   ● electronic media   ➤ refereed

10056 BRITISH JOURNAL OF HEALTH PSYCHOLOGY ULRICH'S PERIODICALS

• ➤ British Journal of Health Psychology (GBR ISSN 1359-107X) **7342**
▼ • ➤ British Journal of Healthcare Assistants (GBR ISSN 1753-1586) **5953**
• British Journal of Healthcare Computing & Information Management (Online) (GBR) **5829**
British Journal of Healthcare Computing & Information Management (Print) *see* British Journal of Healthcare Computing & Information Management (Online) **5829**
➤ British Journal of Healthcare Management (GBR ISSN 1358-0574) **5588**
British Journal of Home Healthcare (GBR ISSN 1749-6055) **4089**
British Journal of Homecare (GBR ISSN 1462-1665) **8028**
British Journal of Hospital Medicine (Edicion Espanola) *see* British Journal of Hospital Medicine (London, 2005) **5588**
• ➤ British Journal of Hospital Medicine (London, 2005) (GBR ISSN 1750-8460) **5588**
• ➤ British Journal of Industrial Relations (GBR ISSN 0007-1080) **1668**
British Journal of Infection Control *see* Journal of Infection Prevention **5820**
The British Journal of Leadership in Public Services *see* The International Journal of Leadership in Public Service **7447**
• ➤ British Journal of Learning Disabilities (GBR ISSN 1354-4187) **6128**
• ➤ British Journal of Management (GBR ISSN 1045-3172) **1729**
• ➤ British Journal of Mathematical and Statistical Psychology (GBR ISSN 0007-1102) **7342**
▼ • ➤ British Journal of Medical and Surgical Urology (GBR ISSN 1875-9742) **6266**
▼ • ➤ British Journal of Medical Practitioners (GBR ISSN 1757-8515) **5589**
• ➤ British Journal of Middle Eastern Studies (GBR ISSN 1353-0194) **4320**
• British Journal of Midwifery (GBR ISSN 0969-4900) **5987**
• ➤ British Journal of Music Education (GBR ISSN 0265-0517) **6551**
British Journal of Music Therapy (GBR ISSN 1359-4575) **6107**
• ➤ British Journal of Neuroscience Nursing (GBR ISSN 1747-0307) **6128**
• ➤ British Journal of Neurosurgery (GBR ISSN 0268-8697) **6238**
• ➤ British Journal of Nursing (GBR ISSN 0966-0461) **5953**
• ➤ The British Journal of Nutrition (GBR ISSN 0007-1145) **6656**
• British Journal of Obstetrics & Gynaecology. Supplement (GBR ISSN 0140-7686) **5987**
• ➤ British Journal of Occupational Therapy (GBR ISSN 0308-0226) **5589**
The British Journal of Occupational Training (GBR ISSN 1479-2613) **2832**
• ➤ British Journal of Ophthalmology (GBR ISSN 0007-1161) **6039**
• ➤ British Journal of Oral and Maxillofacial Surgery (GBR ISSN 0266-4356) **6238**
• ➤ British Journal of Pharmacology (GBR ISSN 0007-1188) **6826**
British Journal of Pharmacology. Proceedings Supplement *see* British Journal of Pharmacology **6826**
• British Journal of Photography (GBR ISSN 0007-1196) **6965**
British Journal of Photography. Big Book (GBR ISSN 1465-2951) **6965**
• ➤ British Journal of Phytotherapy (GBR ISSN 0959-6879) **307**
British Journal of Plastic Surgery (Online Edition) *see* Journal of Plastic, Reconstructive & Aesthetic Surgery (Online Edition) **6249**
British Journal of Plastic Surgery (Print Edition) *see* Journal of Plastic, Reconstructive & Aesthetic Surgery (Print Edition) **6249**
British Journal of Play Therapy (GBR ISSN 1744-1145) **7342**
➤ British Journal of Podiatry (GBR ISSN 1460-7328) **6057**
• ➤ British Journal of Political Science (GBR ISSN 0007-1234) **7110**
• ➤ The British Journal of Politics and International Relations (GBR ISSN 1369-1481) **7110**
• ➤ The British Journal of Primary Care Nursing - Cardiovascular Disease, Diabetes and Kidney Care (GBR ISSN 1741-430X) **5953**
• The British Journal of Primary Care Nursing. Respiratory Diseases and Allergy (GBR ISSN 1752-4385) **5953**
• ➤ British Journal of Psychiatry (GBR ISSN 0007-1250) **6128**
British Journal of Psychiatry. Supplement *see* British Journal of Psychiatry **6128**
• ➤ British Journal of Psychology (GBR ISSN 0007-1269) **7342**
• ➤ British Journal of Psychotherapy (GBR ISSN 0265-9883) **6128**
• ➤ British Journal of Radiology (GBR ISSN 0007-1285) **6193**
• ➤ British Journal of Religious Education (GBR ISSN 0141-6200) **7628**
British Journal of Renal Medicine (GBR ISSN 1365-5604) **6266**
• ➤ British Journal of Social Psychology (GBR ISSN 0144-6665) **7342**
• ➤ The British Journal of Social Work (GBR ISSN 0045-3102) **8028**
• ➤ British Journal of Sociology (GBR ISSN 0007-1315) **8091**
• ➤ British Journal of Sociology of Education (GBR ISSN 0142-5692) **2832**
• British Journal of Special Education (GBR ISSN 0952-3383) **3037**
• ➤ British Journal of Sports Medicine (GBR ISSN 0306-3674) **6229**
• ➤ British Journal of Surgery (GBR ISSN 0007-1323) **6238**
British Journal of Surgery. Supplement *see* British Journal of Surgery **6238**
British Journal of Therapy & Rehabilitation *see* International Journal of Therapy and Rehabilitation **6110**
British Journal of Urology International (Online) *see* B J U International (Online) **6265**
British Journal of Urology International (Print) *see* B J U International (Print) **6265**
• British Journal of Visual Impairment (GBR ISSN 0264-6196) **4080**
• British Journalism Review (GBR ISSN 0956-4748) **4572**
British Journals of Radiology Supplement *see* B J R Supplement **6193**
British Landscapes Through Maps (GBR ISSN 0524-6385) **4001**
• British Library. Annual Report (Year) (GBR ISSN 0305-7887) **4998**
British Library. Document Supply Centre. Current Serials Received (Year) (GBR ISSN 0959-4914) **621**
British Library. Document Supply Centre. Document Supply News (GBR ISSN 0952-892X) **4998**
• British Library. Document Supply Centre. Index of Conference Proceedings (GBR ISSN 0959-4906) **6283**
British Library. Name Authority List (GBR ISSN 0265-8887) **5057**
British Library. National Bibliographic Service. Occasional Publications (GBR) **4998**
British Library of Political and Economic Science. Annual Report (GBR ISSN 0140-7023) **5057**
British Library. Research and Development Department. Research Lecture (GBR) **4998**
British Library Research Lecture *see* British Library. Research and Development Department. Research Lecture **4998**
British Library Research Series (DEU) **4998**
The British Library Studies in the History of the Book (GBR) **7556**
British Lichen Society Bulletin (GBR ISSN 0300-4562) **782**
British Life (GBR ISSN 1743-1514) **5067**
British Limbless Ex-Servicemen's Association *see* B L E S M A G **8027**
▼ British Livestock (GBR ISSN 1754-0968) **281**
British Machine Tools and Equipment (GBR ISSN 0141-0490) **3374**
British Marine Industries Federation Yearbook (GBR) **8640**
British Maritime Technology Ltd. Abstracts *see* B M T Abstracts **8522**
British Maritime Technology News *see* B M T News **8639**
British Masonry Society. Proceedings (GBR ISSN 0950-9615) **983**
British Masonry Society. Special Publication (GBR ISSN 1460-6909) **983**
British Medical Association News *see* B M A News **5582**
• ➤ British Medical Bulletin (GBR ISSN 0007-1420) **5589**
British Medical Journal *see* B M J **5582**
British Medical Journal (Clinical Research Edition) *see* B M J (Clinical Research Edition) **5582**
British Medical Journal (Dutch Edition) (NLD) **5589**
British Medical Journal (Online) *see* B M J (Online) **5583**
British Medical Journal Case Reports *see* B M J Case Reports **5583**
British Medical Journal General Practice Edition *see* B M J - General Practice Edition **5583**
British Menopause Society. Journal *see* Menopause International **5998**
British Micro Software News (GBR ISSN 0264-1283) **2588**
British Mining (GBR ISSN 0308-2199) **6459**
British Model Soldier Society. Bulletin (GBR ISSN 0306-7947) **4330**
British Mosquito Bulletin *see* European Mosquito Bulletin **229**
British Mouthpiece (GBR ISSN 0007-1463) **6552**
British Museum. Occasional Paper (No.) *see* British Museum. Research Publications **6521**
• ➤ British Museum. Research Publications (GBR) **6521**
British Museum Society Magazine *see* B M Magazine **6521**
British Museum Yearbook (GBR ISSN 0950-6357) **4998**
British Music (GBR ISSN 0958-5664) **6552**
British Music Education Yearbook (Year) (GBR ISSN 1758-3667) **6552**
British Music Society News (GBR ISSN 1462-9860) **6552**
British Mycological Society. Symposium Series (GBR ISSN 0275-0287) **782**
➤ British Myriapod and Isopod Group. Bulletin (GBR ISSN 1475-1739) **937**
• British National Bibliography (GBR ISSN 0007-1544) **621**
British National Bibliography on CD-ROM *see* B N B on CD-ROM **616**
• British National Formulary (GBR ISSN 0260-535X) **6826**
• British National Formulary for Children (GBR ISSN 1747-5503) **6826**
British Naturism (GBR ISSN 0264-0406) **6983**
British North America Portraits *see* B N A Portraits **6892**
British North America Topics *see* B N A Topics **6892**
British-North American Committee Publications (GBR) **1069**
British-North American Research Association. Occasional Papers (GBR) **1069**
British Nuclear Fuels plc News *see* B N F L News **3165**
British Nuclear Industry Forum Nuclear Business. Directory *see* B N I F Nuclear Business. Directory **3182**
• British Numismatic Journal (GBR ISSN 0143-8956) **6649**
• British Nursing Index (GBR ISSN 1366-5588) **5741**
British Nutrition Foundation Annual Conference Proceedings *see* B N F Annual Conference Proceedings **6655**
British Nutrition Foundation Briefing Papers *see* B N F Briefing Papers **6655**
British Nutrition Foundation Task Force Reports *see* B N F Task Force Reports **6655**
• British Occupational Hygiene Society. Technical Guide Series (GBR ISSN 0266-6936) **6674**
British Olympic Association Diary (GBR) **8163**
The British on Holiday (Year) (GBR) **8778**
British Origami (GBR ISSN 1745-3410) **532**
British Ornithologists' Club. Bulletin (GBR ISSN 0007-1595) **904**
† British Ornithologists' Club. Occasional Publications (GBR ISSN 1363-2965) **8937**
British Ornithologists' Union Checklist *see* B O U Checklist **902**
British Orthoptic Journal *see* British and Irish Orthoptic Journal **6039**
British Pelargonium & Geranium Society. Yearbook (GBR) **3726**
British Performing Arts Yearbook (GBR ISSN 0951-5208) **8467**
British Petroleum Statistical Review of World Energy Statistical Review of World Energy (Year) *see* B P Statistical Review of World Energy (Year) **6799**
• British Pharmacopoeia (GBR ISSN 1354-6643) **6826**
British Pharmacopoeia and British Pharmacopoeia (Veterinary) *see* British Pharmacopoeia **6826**
British Philatelic Bulletin (GBR ISSN 0953-8119) **6892**
British Philatelic Federation. Congress Handbook (GBR) **6892**
British Phonographic Industry Statistical Handbook *see* B P I Statistical Handbook **6631**
British Photographic Industry News News *see* B P I News **6964**
• British Plastics and Rubber Magazine (GBR ISSN 0307-6164) **7091**
British Plastics Federation. Analysis of the Bulk Polymer Market (GBR) **7091**
British Plastics Federation. Business Trends Survey (GBR ISSN 0143-5493) **7091**
British Plastics Federation. Composites Congress. Papers (GBR) **7091**
British Plastics Federation. Rotational Moulders Conference. Papers (GBR) **7091**
British Polio Fellowship. Bulletin (GBR ISSN 0007-1633) **6129**
• ➤ British Politics (GBR ISSN 1746-918X) **7110**
British Popular Cinema (GBR) **6491**
• ➤ British Postgraduate Musicology (Online) (GBR) **6552**
British Postmark Bulletin (GBR ISSN 0955-923X) **6892**
British Postmark Society. Journal (GBR ISSN 1753-0717) **6892**
British Postmark Society. Quarterly Bulletin *see* British Postmark Society. Journal **6892**
British Potato Council. News (GBR) **223**
• British Poultry Abstracts (GBR ISSN 1746-6202) **176**
• ➤ British Poultry Science (GBR ISSN 0007-1668) **281**
British Professional Photographers Association *see* B P P A **6964**
British Promotional Merchandise Association News *see* B P M A News **1806**
British Psychological Society. Annual Report (GBR ISSN 0309-7773) **7342**
British Psychological Society. Counselling Psychology Section. Review (GBR ISSN 0269-6975) **7342**
British Psychological Society. Division of Forensic Psychology. Occasional Papers *see* Issues in Forensic Psychology **7367**
• British Psychological Society. Proceedings (GBR ISSN 1350-472X) **7342**
British Psychological Society. Psychotherapy Section. Newsletter *see* Psychotherapy Section Review **7401**
British Pteridological Society. Bulletin (GBR ISSN 0301-9195) **782**
British Public Opinion (GBR ISSN 0265-6175) **7951**
British Puppet and Model Theatre Guild. Newsletter (GBR) **8467**
British Qualifications (GBR ISSN 0141-5972) **2832**
British Rabbit Council Year Book (GBR ISSN 0068-2411) **282**
British Racing Statistics (Years) (GBR) **8288**
British Railway Modelling (GBR ISSN 0968-0764) **4331**
British Railways Illustrated (GBR ISSN 0961-8244) **8615**
• British Rate and Data (GBR ISSN 0263-3515) **621**
British Rate and Data Direct *see* B R A D Direct **1806**
British Rate and Data Media Ownership Directory *see* B R A D Media Ownership Directory **1974**
British Rate and Data Recruitment Media *see* B R A D Recruitment Media **21**
British Regional Heart Study Newsletter *see* B R H S Newsletter **5583**
• British Review of New Zealand Studies (GBR ISSN 0951-6204) **4191**
The British Rifleman (GBR ISSN 1360-0419) **8163**
(Year) British Rowing Almanack. A R A Yearbook (GBR) **8273**
British Rubber Manufacturers' Association Ltd. Rubber and Polyurethane Directory *see* B M R A Rubber and Polyurethane Directory **7824**
British Safety Council Guides (GBR) **6674**
➤ British School at Athens. Annual (GBR ISSN 0068-2454) **385**
British School at Athens Newsletter *see* B S A Newsletter **383**
British School at Athens. Studies Series (GBR) **385**
British School at Athens. Supplementary Volume (GBR ISSN 1464-0813) **385**
➤ British School at Rome. Archaeological Monographs (GBR) **385**
➤ British School at Rome. Papers (GBR ISSN 0068-2462) **385**
British School of Archaeology at Athens. Studies Series *see* British School at Athens. Studies Series **385**
British School of Archaeology at Athens. Supplementary Volume *see* British School at Athens. Supplementary Volume **385**
• British Simuliid Group. Bulletin (GBR ISSN 1363-3376) **841**
British Social Attitudes (GBR ISSN 0267-6869) **7951**
British Social Attitudes Survey Series *see* British Social Attitudes **7951**
† British Society for Cell Biology. Symposia (GBR) **8937**
† British Society for Developmental Biology. Symposia (GBR) **8937**
British Society for Middle Eastern Studies *see* B R I S M E S **4320**
British Society for Music Therapy. Bulletin *see* Music Therapy Now **6592**
British Society for Parasitology. Symposia (GBR ISSN 0068-2497) **882**
• ➤ British Society for Phenomenology. Journal (GBR ISSN 0007-1773) **6908**
British Society for Plant Growth Regulation. Monographs (GBR ISSN 1351-6566) **223**
• ➤ British Society for the History of Mathematics. Bulletin (GBR ISSN 1749-8430) **5476**
• British Society for the History of Science. List of Theses (GBR) **7842**
British Society for the History of Science Monographs *see* B S H S Monographs **7838**
➤ British Society for the History of Science. Monographs (GBR) **7842**
British Society for the History of Science Newsletter *see* B S H S Newsletter **7838**
• British Society of Animal Science Newsletter (GBR) **937**
British Society of Animal Science. Occasional Publication (GBR ISSN 0263-967X) **282**
• British Society of Animal Science. Proceedings (GBR ISSN 1752-7562) **937**
British Society of Scientific Glassblowers. Journal (GBR) **2038**
British Standards Institution. Annual Reports and Accounts *see* British Standards Institution. Annual Review & Summary Financial Statements **6401**
British Standards Institution. Annual Review & Summary Financial Statements (GBR) **6401**
British Standards Institution. Catalogue *see* B S I Catalogue **1065**
British Standards Institution Catalogue *see* B S I Catalogue **1065**
British Standards Institution. Update Standards (GBR ISSN 1367-2134) **6747**
British Steel. Annual Report and Accounts (GBR) **6306**
British Studies in Applied Linguistics (GBR ISSN 0951-1482) **5101**
• British Studies Now (GBR) **5266**
British Style (GBR ISSN 0963-9438) **2245**
British Sugar Beet Review (GBR ISSN 0007-1854) **223**
• ➤ British Tarantula Society. Journal (GBR ISSN 0962-449X) **841**
• British Tax Cases (GBR ISSN 0266-1004) **1913**
• British Tax Review (GBR ISSN 0007-1870) **1913**
British Telecommunications Communications Technology *see* B T Communications Technology **2313**
British Telecommunications Technology Journal *see* B T Technology Journal **2313**

DIRECTORY 2010 DE BRUIDSETALAGE 10057

British Telecommunications Today see B T Today **2365**
• British Theatre Directory (GBR ISSN 0306-4107) **8467**
British Tourist Authority. Annual Report (GBR ISSN 0953-3540) **8688**
British Toy & Hobby Association Buyers Guide see B T H A Buyers Guide **4059**
• British Toys & Hobbies Briefing (GBR ISSN 1360-8436) **4059**
British Trades Alphabet Publications Directions Series see B T A Directions Series **3052**
British Trades Alphabet Publications Studycards see B T A Studycards **3052**
British Trust for Ornithology. Annual Report (GBR ISSN 0068-2675) **904**
British Trust for Ornithology News see B T O News **902**
British Trust for Ornithology Research Report see B T O Research Report **902**
British Unidentified Flying Object Research Association Bulletin see B U F O R A Bulletin **49**
British Value Added Tax Cases (GBR ISSN 0266-1020) **1913**
British Virgin Islands. Statistics Office. Balance of Payments (VGB) **1215**
British Virgin Islands. Statistics Office. National Income and Expenditure (VGB) **1215**
• British Virgin Islands Welcome Tourist Guide (VGB) **8688**
British Vogue see Vogue (British Edition) **2263**
• British Waterways Board. Annual Report and Accounts (GBR) **8640**
British West Indies Study Circle Bulletin see B W I Study Circle Bulletin **6892**
The British White Bulletin (AUS ISSN 1322-8064) **282**
British Wildlife (GBR ISSN 0958-0956) **937**
British Wind Energy Association. Proceedings (GBR) **3178**
British Wire Journal see Wire Industry **6336**
British Women Pilots Association Newsletter see B W P A Newsletter **49**
British Wood Preserving and Damp-Proofing Association Convention Proceedings see B W P D A Convention Proceedings **3710**
British Woodworking (GBR ISSN 1755-0157) **1049**
British Writers Classics (USA ISSN 1541-8995) **5266**
• British Year Book of International Law (GBR ISSN 0068-2691) **4919**
Briton's Index: Financial Institutions (GBR ISSN 0968-2716) **1977**
Briton's Index: Investment Research Analysts (GBR ISSN 0968-2708) **1977**
• ➤ Brittonia (USA ISSN 0007-196X) **782**
† Brividi Collection (ITA ISSN 1828-938X) **8937**
Brnenskw Univerzity. Sbornik Praci Fakulty Socialnich Studii. Socialni Studia see Socialni Studia **8135**
Brno Studies in English see Masarykova Univerzita. Filozoficka Fakulta. Sbornik Praci. S: Rada Anglisticka **5150**
• Brntwd Magazine (USA) **3971**
Broad Times see Wangkuan Shidai **8998**
• Broadband (Cramlington) (GBR ISSN 1751-0791) **2375**
Broadband Access Report (USA ISSN 1542-569X) **2553**
• Broadband Advertising (USA ISSN 1539-3690) **22**
Broadband Asia (GBR) **2375**
• Broadband Business Forecast (Online Edition) (USA) **2495**
Broadband Cable Financial Databook (USA ISSN 1536-8491) **2375**
• Broadband Daily (USA) **2349**
Broadband Fixed Wireless see Wireless Broadband **2373**
Broadband House (USA) **2553**
Broadband International ISDN Yellow Pages see I S D N Yellow Pages **2325**
Broadband Markets see Converging Media **2317**
Broadband Media see Converging Media **2317**
Broadband Properties (USA ISSN 1539-8803) **2375**
• Broadband Technology (USA ISSN 1530-1532) **2376**
Broadband Wireless Data Review (USA ISSN 1544-2756) **2533**
Broadband World (GBR ISSN 1740-4495) **2533**
Broadband World (USA ISSN 1529-1391) **2495**
• Broadcast (GBR ISSN 0040-2788) **2376**
Broadcast & Broadband Asia Pacific (SGP) **2376**
Broadcast and Production see Broadcast & Production. Italian Edition **2376**
† Broadcast and Production. Brasil Edition (USA) **8937**
Broadcast & Production. Chinese Edition (USA ISSN 1024-8390) **2376**
Broadcast and Production. Chinese Edition see Broadcast & Production. Chinese Edition **2376**
Broadcast and Production. French Edition (USA) **2376**
Broadcast & Production. Italian Edition (USA) **2376**
• Broadcast Archive (USA) **2357**
• Broadcast Engineering (USA ISSN 0007-1994) **2376**
• Broadcast Engineering (World Edition) (USA) **2376**
• Broadcast Engineering News (AUS ISSN 0155-3720) **2376**
Broadcast Hardware International (GBR ISSN 0269-493X) **2357**
Broadcast Hardware's U K Network (GBR ISSN 0953-7627) **2357**
Broadcast Investor: Deals and Finance see Broadcast Investor: Deals & Finance **1614**
• Broadcast Investor: Deals & Finance (USA ISSN 1548-3053) **1614**
Broadcast Magazine (NLD ISSN 1380-9237) **2376**
Broadcast Music Inc. Music World see B M I: Music World **6547**
• Broadcast Regulation (USA) **2376**
Broadcast Stats see B - Stats **8934**
Broadcast Technology (JPN ISSN 1345-4099) **2313**
• Broadcast Times (GBR) **4080**
• Broadcast Week (CAN) **2376**
Broadcast Yearbook and Diary (GBR) **2376**
• Broadcastaway (AUS) **2376**
• Broadcaster (CAN ISSN 0008-3038) **2376**
Broadcaster (LKA) **2376**
Broadcaster Directory (CAN) **2376**
• Broadcasting & Cable (USA ISSN 1068-6827) **2376**
Broadcasting and Cable see Broadcasting & Cable **2376**
• Broadcasting & Cable T V Fax (USA) **2376**
Broadcasting & Cable Yearbook (USA ISSN 0000-1511) **2376**
Broadcasting & Cable's Digital Television (USA ISSN 1099-7679) **2377**
† • Broadcasting & Cable's Television International (USA) **8937**
• Broadcasting and Telecommunications (CAN ISSN 1497-0422) **2346**
Broadcasting and Television see B & T **21**
• Broadcasting and the Law (USA ISSN 0161-5823) **2377**
Broadcasting Board of Governors. Annual Report (USA) **2377**
Broadcasting Equipment and Technology (JPN) **2313**
Broadcasting News see World Media. Broadcasting News **2365**
• Broadcasting Policy Monitoring Reports (Online Edition) (CAN ISSN 1910-2259) **2314**
• Broadcasting Policy Monitoring Reports (Print Edition) (CAN ISSN 1714-6569) **2314**
Broadcasting: Televidenie i Radioveshchanie (RUS) **2377**
Broadman Comments; International Sunday School Lessons (USA ISSN 0068-2721) **7628**
The Broadsheet see James Joyce Broadsheet **5312**
Broadside (Bend) (USA) **2275**
• Broadside (Fairfax) (USA) **2275**
Broadside (New York, 1940) (USA ISSN 0068-2748) **8467**
Broadside (Washington) (USA) **7111**
Broadsides (USA) **2605**
Broadsword (AUS ISSN 1326-4311) **6644**
▼ Broadway Magazine (USA) **8467**
▼ Brocante (FRA ISSN 1962-2198) **364**
▼ Brocante & Renovation (FRA) **364**
• ➤ Brocar (ESP ISSN 1885-8309) **4206**
Brocar. Cuadernos de Investigacion Historica see Brocar **4206**
➤ Brock Education (CAN ISSN 1183-1189) **2969**
• The Brock Press (CAN ISSN 1483-4561) **2275**
Brock Report (USA) **195**
• ➤ The Brock Review (Online) (CAN ISSN 1188-9071) **4445**
Broderskap (SWE ISSN 0007-2141) **7111**
Brodogradnja/Shipbuilding (HRV ISSN 0007-215X) **8640**
Broed (SWE ISSN 1100-0996) **3672**
Broedvogelmonitoring in het Nederlandse Waddengebied see Broedvogels in Nederland **904**
Broedvogels in Nederland (NLD ISSN 1874-169X) **904**
Broeker Bijdragen (NLD ISSN 1875-3876) **4207**
• Broen (DNK ISSN 1602-0502) **2181**
• Broen (NOR ISSN 0804-9297) **7786**
Broennoeysundsavis (NOR) **3921**
The Broken Fiddle (GBR) **5266**
• Broken Pencil (CAN ISSN 1201-8996) **5209**
Broken Spoke (CAN ISSN 0045-3226) **8570**
▼ The Broker (NLD ISSN 1874-2033) **1592**
Broker (USA ISSN 1527-7046) **1321**
• Broker Dealer (USA ISSN 1547-3627) **1614**
Broker Dealer Compliance Report see Broker/Dealer Compliance Report (Online) **1614**
• Broker/Dealer Compliance Report (Online) (USA ISSN 1527-2672) **1614**
Broker-Dealer Regulation (USA ISSN 0271-3535) **4632**
Broker - Dealer Week see B D Week **1611**
Broker Magazine (USA ISSN 1540-0824) **1614**
Broker News (USA) **4496**
• Broker World (USA ISSN 0273-6551) **4496**
• Brokerage Performance Report (USA ISSN 1935-1720) **7585**
Brokers and Dealers in Securities (USA ISSN 1550-3380) **1282**
Broker's Licensing Course Manual (CAN ISSN 1715-9636) **7585**
Brokers' Monthly and Insurance Adviser see Insurance Brokers' Monthly **4506**
➤ Brolga (AUS ISSN 1322-7645) **2683**
➤ Bromatologia i Chemia Toksykologiczna (POL ISSN 0365-9445) **6826**
Bromberg (DEU ISSN 0171-1644) **3845**
Bromberg and Lowenfels on Securities Fraud and Commodities Fraud (USA) **1614**
Brome County Historical Society. Publication (CAN ISSN 0381-6206) **4286**
Bromeliad (NZL ISSN 1177-0554) **3726**
➤ Bromeliad Society. Journal (USA ISSN 0090-8738) **782**
Bromeliad Society of New Zealand. Bulletin see Bromeliad **3726**
Die Bromelie (DEU ISSN 0724-0155) **782**
Bromley & Beckenham Times (GBR ISSN 0968-5774) **3862**
• Bromley News Shopper (GBR ISSN 1754-5293) **2635**
Bronca (ARG) **2181**
Bronekollektsiya (RUS) **6414**
Bronekollektsiya. Prilozhenie k Zhurnalu Modelist-Konstruktor (RUS) **6414**
Bronnen en Studies see Katholiek Documentatie Centrum. Bronnen en Studies **5022**
Bronnen voor de Studie van Afro-Surinaamse Samenlevingen see Bronnen voor de Studie van Suriname **4286**
Bronnen voor de Studie van Suriname (NLD) **4286**
Bronte Society Gazette (GBR ISSN 1355-5960) **5266**
• ➤ Bronte Studies (GBR ISSN 1474-8932) **5266**
Bronx Biannual (USA ISSN 1932-6394) **5266**
Bronx Community College Evening Reporter see B C C Evening Reporter **2273**
Bronx County Historical Society Journal (USA ISSN 0007-2249) **4286**
Bronx Realtor News (USA) **7585**
The Bronx Report (USA) **7489**
Bronze Swagman Book of Bush Verse (AUS ISSN 0310-2467) **5418**
Brood & Banket (BEL ISSN 1371-2632) **3672**
† Brood- en Banketzaken (NLD ISSN 1871-4803) **8937**
The Brookdale University Hospital and Medical Center Healthscope (USA) **4089**
Brookers Company and Securities Law Handbook (NZL ISSN 1177-8288) **4858**
Brookers Contract and Commercial Law Handbook (NZL ISSN 1177-827X) **4858**
▼ Brookers Medical Law Handbook (NZL ISSN 1178-5012) **4632**
▼ Brookers Pharmacy Law Handbook (NZL ISSN 1178-7899) **4858**
Brooker's Resource Management Gazette see YourEnvironment **4817**
Brookfield Bandarlog (USA ISSN 0068-2780) **937**
Brookgreen Journal (USA ISSN 0884-8815) **3726**
Brookhaven Bulletin (USA) **3165**
Brookhaven Courier (USA) **2275**
Brookhaven Highlights (USA ISSN 0092-1548) **3165**
Brookhaven Lecture Series (USA) **3165**
Brookhaven National Laboratory. Report (USA) **3165**
➤ Brookhaven Symposia in Biology (USA ISSN 0068-2799) **663**
Brookings Dialogues in Public Policy see Dialogues in Public Policy **7433**
• The Brookings Institution. Policy Brief (USA ISSN 1934-1156) **7424**
• ➤ Brookings Papers on Economic Activity (USA ISSN 0007-2303) **1536**
• ➤ Brookings Papers on Education Policy (Year) (USA ISSN 1096-2719) **3018**
Brookings Studies in Foreign Policy (USA) **7224**
• Brookings Trade Forum (USA ISSN 1520-5479) **1553**
• Brookings-Wharton Papers on Financial Services (USA ISSN 1098-3651) **1321**
• Brookings-Wharton Papers on Urban Affairs (Year) (USA ISSN 1528-7084) **8091**
Brooklands Society Gazette (GBR) **8491**
Brooklyn see BKLYN **3970**
Brooklyn! (USA) **5067**
Brooklyn Academy of Music Magazine see B A Magazine **6546**
Brooklyn Arts and Culture Association Arts Calendar see B A C A Arts Calendar **6520**
Brooklyn Barrister (USA ISSN 0007-232X) **4632**
Brooklyn Botanic Garden: 21st Century Gardening Series (USA) **3726**
Brooklyn Business Journal (USA) **1069**
Brooklyn Heights Press (USA ISSN 0007-2346) **3971**
Brooklyn Historical Society Newsletter (USA) **4286**
Brooklyn Home Journal (USA) **4353**
Brooklyn Journal of Arts & Urban Affairs (USA) **479**
• The Brooklyn Journal of Corporate, Financial and Commercial Law (USA ISSN 1934-2497) **4858**
• ➤ Brooklyn Journal of International Law (USA ISSN 0740-4824) **4919**
• ➤ Brooklyn Law Review (USA ISSN 0007-2362) **4632**
Brooklyn Law School LawNotes see B L S LawNotes **4625**
Brooklyn Parent (USA) **2146**
Brooklyn Record (USA) **3760**
➤ Brooklyn Review (USA ISSN 1942-4612) **5418**
• Brookside Columns (USA) **4286**
Broom, Brush & Mop (USA ISSN 0890-2933) **1069**
Broome Advertiser see Broome Happenings **3793**
Broome County Historical Society Newsletter (USA) **4286**
Broome County Public Library. Annual Report (USA) **4998**
Broome Happenings (AUS ISSN 1833-573X) **3793**
▼ The Broome Review (USA ISSN 1941-5605) **5266**
Brossapress (DEU ISSN 0178-4412) **6716**
Brot & Spiele (DEU) **6552**
Brot & Backwaren (DEU ISSN 0172-8180) **3672**
Broteria (PRT ISSN 0870-7618) **4445**
Broteria Genetica (PRT ISSN 0870-7235) **864**
Brotherhood Action see Building Better Lives **8029**
• Brotherhood Comment (AUS ISSN 1320-8632) **8028**
Brotherhood News see Building Better Lives **8029**
Brotherhood of Maintenance of Way Employes Journal see B M W E Journal **4590**
Bro'town Annual (NZL ISSN 1177-6439) **2377**
Brots de Collcerola (ESP) **2264**
Brottning (SWE ISSN 0345-1186) **8163**
• Brottsfoerebyggande Raadets Tidskrift Apropaa (SWE ISSN 0283-3352) **2645**
Brottsforebyggande Raadet. B R AA-Report (SWE ISSN 1101-2331) **2645**
Het Brouwersblad (BEL ISSN 1371-2438) **601**
Broward Design & Architectural Review (USA) **4534**
Broward Design and Architectural Review see Broward Design & Architectural Review **4534**
• Brown Alumni Magazine (USA ISSN 1520-863X) **2275**
Brown Bag see Brownbag **8091**
Brown Center Report on American Education (USA ISSN 1934-4635) **2832**
Brown Chart see The Brown Chart. Provincial Results **4496**
The Brown Chart. Provincial Results (CAN ISSN 0585-3680) **4496**
• The Brown Daily Herald (USA) **2275**
Brown Electronic Article Review Service see B E A R S **7109**
Brown Family Helper (USA) **3760**
Brown Gold (USA ISSN 0007-2494) **7628**
• Brown Journal of World Affairs (USA ISSN 1080-0786) **3971**
Brown Lines (USA) **479**
Brown Swiss Bulletin (USA ISSN 0007-2516) **262**
Brown Thrasher Books (USA) **4286**
• Brown University Child and Adolescent Behavior Letter (USA ISSN 1058-1073) **2146**
• Brown University Child & Adolescent Psychopharmacology Update (USA ISSN 1527-8395) **6089**
• Brown University Digest of Addiction Theory & Application (USA ISSN 1040-6328) **2692**
• The Brown University Geriatric Psychopharmacology Update (USA ISSN 1529-2584) **4042**
Brown University. Program in Judaic Studies. Annual Report (USA ISSN 1072-8198) **7719**
The Brown University Psychopharmacology Update see Psychopharmacology Update **6877**
The Brown University S T D Update (USA ISSN 0898-8323) **5589**
• Brownbag (USA ISSN 1946-1437) **8091**
Brownbag Press (USA ISSN 1060-2313) **5418**
Brownfield News see Brownfield Renewal **3483**
Brownfield News & Regional Report see Brownfield Renewal **3483**
Brownfield News & Sustainable Development see Brownfield Renewal **3483**
• Brownfield Renewal (USA ISSN 1947-5594) **3483**
Brownfield Renewal Magazine see Brownfield Renewal **3483**
Brownie (GBR ISSN 0007-2524) **2146**
• Browning Briefing (GBR ISSN 1474-2098) **3484**
• Browning Newsletter (USA ISSN 0896-3045) **6348**
Browning Society Notes (GBR ISSN 0950-6349) **5418**
Brown's Nautical Almanac (GBR ISSN 0068-290X) **8273**
The Brownstoner (USA) **7585**
Browse (CAN) **282**
La Broye (CHE ISSN 1660-4199) **3957**
Bruce County Historical Society. Year Book (CAN ISSN 0084-8115) **4286**
Bruce County Museum Newsletter (CAN) **4286**
Bruce Gould on Commodities (USA) **1614**
• Bruce Hopkins' Nonprofit Counsel (USA ISSN 1542-8419) **4632**
Bruce Trail News (CAN ISSN 0383-9249) **8307**
Bruce Von Stiers Reviews see B V S Reviews **2588**
Brucka (ZAF ISSN 0259-0115) **3947**
Brud Nevez (FRA ISSN 0399-7014) **5266**
➤ Brudstykker fra Blicheregnen (DNK ISSN 0908-7737) **4207**
Die Bruecke (AUT) **5209**
Bruecke (DEU) **8448**
Bruecke-Archiv (DEU ISSN 0300-2039) **480**
Brueder Grimm Gedenken (DEU ISSN 0177-834X) **5266**
Brueder-Grimm-Gesellschaft. Jahrbuch (DEU ISSN 0941-1879) **5266**
Brueder-Grimm-Gesellschaft. Schriften (DEU ISSN 0177-8366) **5266**
Bruehler Schriften zum Familienrecht (DEU) **4907**
• Bruel & Kjaer Technical Review (DNK ISSN 0007-2621) **7087**
Bruenner Beitraege zur Germanistik und Nordistik see Masarykova Univerzita. Filozoficka Fakulta. Sbornik Praci. R: Rada Germanisticka **5150**
Brugklas Enzo (NLD ISSN 1873-880X) **2832**
Brugsch Handelsblad (BEL ISSN 1375-9523) **3801**
• Bruid & Bruidegom (NLD ISSN 0926-8812) **5557**
▼ Bruidegom (NLD ISSN 1875-2217) **5557**
▼ Bruidsblinkers (NLD ISSN 1874-6950) **5557**
De Bruidsetalage (NLD) **5557**

Title

▼ *new title* † *ceased* • *electronic media* ➤ *refereed*

10058 BRUISER REVIEW ULRICH'S PERIODICALS

▼ Bruiser Review (USA) **5209**
➤ Brujula (USA ISSN 1542-5045) **4445**
La Brujula (Comodoro Rivadavia) (ARG ISSN 0328-0918) **2969**
La Brujula de Papel (ESP ISSN 1578-701X) **2833**
Brukshunden (SWE ISSN 0345-1771) **6805**
Brulures (FRA ISSN 1621-224X) **6238**
• Brum Beat (Online) (GBR) **6552**
Brumes Blondes (NLD ISSN 1874-0219) **5266**
Brunei Darussalam Newsletter (BRN) **2314**
Brunei Museum Journal (BRN ISSN 0068-2918) **6521**
Brunei Museum Journal. Monograph (BRN) **6521**
Brunei Museum. Special Publication/Muzium Brunei. Penerbitan Khas (BRN ISSN 0084-8131) **6521**
Brunel University. Department of Economics and Finance. Discussion Paper (GBR ISSN 1466-5182) **1069**
Brunel University. Department of Government. Working Papers (GBR) **7424**
Brunel University. Vice-Chancellor's Report to Court (Year) (GBR ISSN 1368-2164) **2969**
• Bruniana & Campanelliana (ITA ISSN 1125-3819) **6908**
▼ • Brunswick County Today (USA ISSN 1949-0267) **4286**
• Brunswickan (CAN ISSN 0007-2699) **2275**
Brusewitz Nordisk Papperskalender *see* Nordic Paper & Pulp Makers' Directory **6735**
† Brush (Newtown) (AUS ISSN 1449-6267) **8937**
Brushstrokes (GBR ISSN 1360-0923) **545**
Brushware (USA ISSN 0007-2710) **1053**
Brussels Exchanges. Monthly Statistics (BEL) **1614**
Brutarian (USA) **480**
† Brutium (ITA ISSN 0392-3894) **8937**
Brutus (JPN) **5067**
Bryan County Heritage Association Quarterly (USA) **3760**
Bryanskaya Pravda (RUS) **3935**
Bryanskie Izvestiya (RUS) **3935**
Bryanskii Rabochii (RUS) **3935**
• Bryanskoe Vremya (RUS) **3935**
Bryant Literary Review (USA ISSN 1526-9426) **5209**
† Brydning/Wrestling (DNK ISSN 0903-5524) **8937**
Bryggan (SWE ISSN 0345-178X) **7278**
Bryllup uden Besvaer *see* Woman Wedding **8998**
Bryn Mawr Alumnae Bulletin (USA) **2275**
• ➤ Bryn Mawr Classical Review (USA ISSN 1063-2948) **2231**
Bryn Mawr - Haverford College News (USA) **2275**
• ➤ The Bryn Mawr Review of Comparative Literature (USA ISSN 1523-5734) **5266**
➤ Bryobrothera (FIN ISSN 1235-3949) **782**
Bryological Research *see* Sentairui Kenkyu **816**
Bryologische + Lichenologische Werkgroep. Nieuwsbrief (NLD ISSN 1872-6577) **782**
Bryologische en Lichenologische Werkgroep Rapporten *see* B L W G Rapporten **778**
• ➤ Bryologist (USA ISSN 0007-2745) **782**
➤ Bryonora (CZE ISSN 0862-8904) **782**
Bryophytorum Bibliotheca (DEU ISSN 0258-3348) **782**
Bryozoa (Year) (USA ISSN 0108-0326) **937**
Bryzgi Shampanskogo (RUS) **5266**
• B'Tnua (USA) **7111**
B:ton (NLD ISSN 1874-4915) **983**
BTW en Overdrachtsbelasting in de Vastgoedsector *see* Belasting Toegevoegde Waarde en Overdrachtsbelasting in de Vastgoedsector **1912**
Buana Minggu (IDN) **3891**
▼ • ➤ Bubble Science, Engineering and Technology (GBR ISSN 1758-8960) **762**
Bubblegum Girls (CAN) **6287**
Bucarest Matin (ROM ISSN 1453-5092) **3932**
▼ • Bucerius Law Journal (DEU ISSN 1864-371X) **4633**
Das Buch - Buecherpick (CHE) **7556**
Buch-Journal *see* Buchjournal **5266**
Buch Select (DEU) **7556**
Buch und Co (AUT ISSN 1028-771X) **7579**
Buchanan Banner (USA) **3523**
• Buchanan Ingersoll & Rooney PC. Annual Report (USA ISSN 1946-8245) **4633**
Bucharest Business Week (ROM ISSN 1453-5572) **1069**
Bucharest In Your Pocket (ROM ISSN 1454-5276) **8688**
Bucharest Nightlife (ROM ISSN 1454-3184) **4976**
Buchen, Bilanzieren und Steuern Sparen von A-Z (DEU) **1282**
Bucher und Zeitschriften Italiens *see* Libri e Riviste d'Italia **7566**
Buchfinken (NLD) **5266**
Buchforschung (AUT ISSN 1562-9279) **7556**
Buchfuehrung, Bilanz, Kostenrechnung *see* B B K - Betrieb und Rechnungswesen **4625**
Buchfuehrung, Bilanz, Kostenrechnung Betrieb und Rechnungswesen *see* B B K - Betrieb und Rechnungswesen **4625**
Buchhaendler Heute (DEU ISSN 0007-2796) **7556**
Buchjournal (DEU ISSN 0178-7241) **5266**
Buchkalender Elbetal, Mittelgebirge (DEU ISSN 0177-0330) **3524**
Buchkalender Erzgebirge, Saazerland (DEU ISSN 0178-0301) **3524**
Buchkalender fuer Sudeten-Schlesien und Nordmahren (DEU ISSN 0177-3089) **3524**
Buchkultur (AUT ISSN 1026-082X) **5209**
Buchmarkt (DEU ISSN 0524-8426) **7556**
Buchprofile (DEU) **7556**
Buchreihe der Anglia (DEU ISSN 0340-5435) **5101**
Buchreihe der Zeitschrift fuer Celtische Philologie *see* Zeitschrift fuer Celtische Philologie. Buchreihe **5198**
Buchreihe Land-Berichte (DEU ISSN 1861-6968) **7951**
Buchreport Express (DEU ISSN 1615-0732) **7556**
Buchreport Magazin (DEU ISSN 1615-0724) **5266**
The Buchtelite (USA) **2275**
Buchwissenschaftliche Beitraege aus dem Deutschen Bucharchiv Muenchen (DEU ISSN 0724-7001) **7556**
Buchwissenschaftliche Forschungen (DEU ISSN 1616-3613) **7556**
Buci Maci (HUN ISSN 0866-2452) **2181**
Bucina (USA ISSN 1089-375X) **6552**
• El Bucio (ESP ISSN 1695-4785) **2833**
Buckaroo Scene (USA ISSN 1546-282X) **8163**
Buckeye Bark & Bunk Newsletter (USA) **3407**
▼ Buckeye Battle Cry (USA ISSN 1942-0595) **8224**
• Buckeye Farm News (USA ISSN 0007-2834) **98**
Buckeye Pietenpol Association Newsletter (USA ISSN 1059-3977) **50**
Buckeye Review (USA ISSN 0045-3285) **3524**
Buckeye Sports Bulletin (USA ISSN 0883-6833) **8163**
Buckeye Trailblazer (USA) **8307**
▼ Buckhead Home & Life Magazine (USA ISSN 1941-5079) **5067**
Buckhead Life (USA) **4382**
Buckle & (USA) **5418**
• Buckley on the Companies Acts (GBR) **4633**
Buckmasters GunHunter Magazine (USA ISSN 1936-8018) **8307**
• Buckmasters Whitetail (USA ISSN 0895-481X) **8307**
Bucknell Engineer (USA) **3183**
Bucknell World (USA ISSN 1044-7563) **2275**
The Bucknellian (USA) **2275**
Bucks (USA ISSN 1543-7779) **3971**
Bucks Advertiser (GBR ISSN 0144-784X) **3862**
Bucks County Genealogical Society. Newsletter (USA ISSN 1047-2770) **3760**
Bucks County Historical Society. Journal (USA ISSN 1541-986X) **3760**
▼ Bucks County House & Home (USA) **4534**
Bucks County Law Reporter (USA ISSN 0407-5501) **4633**
Bucks County Planning Commission. Planning Progress (USA) **4405**
Bucks County Writer (USA ISSN 1537-3231) **5266**
Bucks Free Press (GBR ISSN 0963-2336) **3862**
Bucks Free Press Midweek (GBR) **3862**
Buckskin Bulletin (USA ISSN 0045-3307) **4286**
Buckskinner (USA) **4286**
Bucuresti Pages for Residents & Visitors (ROM ISSN 1454-119X) **8688**
Bucuresti - What, Where, When (ROM ISSN 1222-5703) **8689**
Bud' Zdorov! (RUS) **6983**
Budapest *see* Rick Steves' Budapest **8752**
Budapest Book of Lists (Year) (HUN ISSN 1219-1841) **1069**
• Budapest Business Journal (HUN ISSN 1216-7304) **1069**
Budapest Business Journal's Who's Who in Finance/Ki Kicsoda a Penzugyi Eletben (HUN ISSN 1418-8937) **1321**
Budapest Business Journal's Who's Who in Hungarian Telecom/Ki Kicsoda a Magyar Tavkozlesben (HUN ISSN 1419-2063) **2314**
Budapest In Your Pocket (HUN ISSN 1585-1907) **8689**
Budapest Oriental Reprints, Series A (HUN ISSN 0139-4614) **545**
Budapest Statisztikai Evkonyve (HUN ISSN 0521-4882) **8359**
Budapest Statisztikai Zsebkonyve (HUN ISSN 0438-2242) **8359**
• The Budapest Sun (HUN ISSN 1217-0771) **3876**
Budapest University of Economic Sciences and Public Administration. Journal *see* Tarsadalom es Gazdasag **8992**
Budapest University of Economic Sciences and Public Administration. Journal *see* Society and Economy **1176**
• Budapest Week (HUN ISSN 1215-0959) **3524**
Budapester Studien zur Literaturwissenschaft (DEU ISSN 1617-903X) **5266**
Budapesti Nevelo (HUN ISSN 0133-2228) **2833**
Budapesti Statisztikai Tajekoztato (HUN ISSN 0133-2449) **8359**
Budbaeraren *see* E F S Missionstidning Budbaeraren **7755**
Budbaereren (NOR ISSN 0807-6375) **7749**
Budda (RUS) **7700**
Paul Budde's Information Superhighways Newsletter *see* Telecoms and Broadband Business Newsletter **2341**
Paul Budde's Telecommunications Business Newsletter *see* Telecoms and Broadband Business Newsletter **2341**
Paul Budde's Telecoms and Broadband Business Newsletter *see* Telecoms and Broadband Business Newsletter **2341**
Buddha World (USA) **7700**
Buddhadharma (CAN ISSN 1499-9927) **7700**
• BuddhaZine (AUS) **7700**
Buddhism Today (USA ISSN 1933-3609) **7700**
Buddhisms (USA) **7700**
• ➤ Buddhist - Christian Studies (USA ISSN 0882-0945) **7700**
Buddhist Culture *see* Fojiao Wenhua **7701**
Buddhist Humanism in Action *see* Soka **7702**
Buddhist Literature (USA ISSN 1090-056X) **5266**
• Buddhist Publication Society Newsletter (LKA) **7700**
Buddhist Studies (IND ISSN 0970-9754) **7700**
• ➤ Buddhist Studies Review (GBR ISSN 0265-2897) **7700**
Buddhist Tradition Series (IND) **7700**
Buddhistische Monatsblaetter (DEU) **7700**
Buddhistisk Forum (DNK ISSN 1395-0746) **7700**
The Budgerigar (GBR) **904**
Budgerigar World (GBR) **6805**
Budget (CYP) **1913**
The Budget (USA ISSN 0090-242X) **7733**
The Budget and Economic Outlook (USA ISSN 1932-3964) **1443**
• Budget & Tax News (USA) **1913**
Budget and Tax News *see* Budget & Tax News **1913**
Budget and the Region (USA ISSN 0896-3584) **7424**
Budget Control *see* Vade Mecum: Begrotingscontrole (Year) **7475**
Budget Decorating (New York) (USA ISSN 1938-6915) **4534**
Budget Decorating Ideas *see* Budget Decorating (New York) **4534**
Budget des Depenses. Partie I et II. Plan de Depenses du Gouvernement et Budget Principal des Depenses/Estimates. Part I and II. The Government Expenditure Plan and the Main Estimates (CAN ISSN 1910-8486) **7424**
Budget des Depenses. Partie III. Rapport sur les Plans et les Priorites *see* Assisted Human Reproduction Agency of Canada. Estimates. Part III. Report on Plans and Priorities **1911**
Budget Documents *see* Tasmania. Department of Treasury and Finance. Budget Papers **1946**
Budget en Recht *see* Budget et Droits **2635**
Budget Estimates for the United States Department of Agriculture (USA ISSN 0499-0803) **7424**
Budget et Droits (BEL ISSN 0772-9383) **2635**
Budget Guide to Washington, D.C. *see* Let's Go: Washington, D.C. (Year) **8730**
Budget Hebdo (BEL ISSN 0773-0748) **2635**
Budget Homes (USA) **983**
Budget-in-brief *see* United States. Department of Energy. Office of Energy Efficiency and Renewable Energy. Budget in Brief **3149**
Budget of the Government of Pakistan. Demands for Grants and Appropriations (PAK) **1913**
• The Budget of the United States Government (USA ISSN 0163-2000) **1443**
• Budget of the United States Government. Historical Tables (USA) **7424**
Budget Papers *see* Tasmania. Department of Treasury and Finance. Budget Papers **1946**
• Budget Sense (USA) **7424**
• Budget Speech (CAN ISSN 1202-6379) **7425**
Budget Speech by Minister for Finance and Planning *see* Kenya. Ministry of Finance and Planning. Budget Speech by Minister for Finance and Planning **7450**
Budget Summary and Annual Performance Plan *see* U.S. Department of Agriculture. Budget Summary and Annual Performance Plan **164**
Budget Travel *see* Arthur Frommer's Budget Travel **8684**
Budget Week *see* Budget Hebdo **2635**
Budget Wise Home Plans (USA) **4534**
• Budgetoversigt (DNK ISSN 1903-2684) **7489**
Budgets de Cultures *see* Budgets de Grandes Cultures **195**
Budgets de Grandes Cultures (CAN ISSN 1719-8585) **195**
Budgets - Municipal and Special Provincial Administrations and Villages *see* Turkey. Turkiye Istatistik Kurumu. Butceler - Belediyeler, Il Ozel Idarler ve Koyler (Year) **7485**
Budismo (BRA ISSN 1808-0332) **7700**
Budivnytstvo Ukrainy (UKR ISSN 1027-3255) **984**
Budkavlen (FIN ISSN 0302-2447) **3615**
Bud'mo Zdorovi (UKR) **4976**
Budo, Karate (DEU ISSN 1435-4683) **8163**
Der Budoka (DEU ISSN 0948-4124) **8163**
El Budoka (ESP ISSN 0214-9060) **8163**
Budowa Geologiczna Polski (POL) **2727**
Budownictwo Gornicze i Tunelowe (POL ISSN 1234-5342) **6459**
Budownictwo Okretowe (POL ISSN 1732-078X) **8640**
Budownictwo Okretowe i Gospodarka Morska *see* Budownictwo Okretowe **8640**
Budownictwo, Technologie, Architektura (POL ISSN 1644-745X) **984**
▼ Budstikken (DNK ISSN 1902-1445) **5101**
Budstikken (NOR ISSN 1504-3363) **6414**
Budstikken (USA ISSN 0749-0747) **3615**
Budstikken (Haerens Sambands Kameratforening) *see* Budstikken **6414**
Budujemy Dom (POL ISSN 1507-2789) **984**
Buecher (DEU ISSN 1860-8191) **7556**
Buecher aus Oesterreich (AUT) **7556**
Buechergilde-Magazin (DEU) **7556**
Buecherkarren (DEU) **5209**
Buechermenschen (DEU) **7556**
Buecherschau (AUT ISSN 0007-3040) **4998**
Buechmania Magazine (NLD ISSN 1574-3152) **5266**
Buechner-Studien (DEU ISSN 1619-425X) **5266**
Buechner Studien *see* Buechner-Studien **5266**
Der Buechsenmacher - Messer und Schere (DEU ISSN 0007-3067) **4331**
Buedinger Aerztepost (DEU ISSN 1616-6159) **5589**
Buedinger Forschungen (DEU) **4207**
† Buehler. Nachrichten (CHE ISSN 0176-926X) **8937**
Buehne (AUT ISSN 0007-3075) **8467**
Buehnen Magazin (DEU ISSN 1616-363X) **984**
Buehnengenossenschaft (DEU ISSN 0007-3083) **8467**
Buehnentechnische Rundschau (DEU ISSN 0007-3091) **8467**
BuemplitzWoche (CHE ISSN 1420-049X) **3958**
Buen Viaje! (MEX) **8689**
El Buen Vivir Magazine (COL) **3830**
▼ Buena Mesa (COL ISSN 2011-2289) **4353**
Buena Salud *see* Buena Vida **5067**
Buena Suerte (USA) **3524**
Buena Vida (PRI ISSN 1081-9703) **5067**
• Buena Vista Today (USA) **2275**
Buenas Ideas (ARG ISSN 1669-791X) **8854**
Buenas y Nuevas (ARG ISSN 1666-6704) **762**
Buendner Monatsblatt (CHE ISSN 1011-6885) **4207**
Buendner Sport Information (CHE) **8163**
Buendner Wald (CHE ISSN 1422-8084) **3685**
• Buenhogar (USA ISSN 0186-422X) **4353**
Buenos Aires. Archivo Historico. Publicaciones (ARG ISSN 0524-9864) **4286**
Buenos Aires. Camara de Comercio. Informativo Mensual (ARG) **1397**
Buenos Aires Herald (ARG ISSN 1666-1044) **3791**
Der Buerger im Staat (DEU ISSN 0007-3121) **7111**
Buerger in Sozialen Schwierigkeiten *see* B I S S **3844**
• Buergerrechte & Polizei (DEU ISSN 0932-5409) **2645**
Das Buero (Berlin) (DEU) **1850**
Das Buero (Marburg) (DEU) **4080**
Buero und Service Report (DEU) **1850**
Die Bueroberufe (DEU ISSN 1619-2583) **6693**
Der Bueromaschinen- und Buerobedarfshandel (DEU) **1850**
BueroSpezial *see* Das Buero (Berlin) **1850**
Buffalo (CAN ISSN 0045-334X) **2146**
Buffalo and Erie County Public Library Bulletin (USA ISSN 0020-966X) **4998**
Buffalo Business Journal (USA ISSN 0882-2859) **1069**
Buffalo Co, Wis Lore (USA ISSN 1939-8506) **4286**
Buffalo Criminal Law Review *see* New Criminal Law Review **4894**
Buffalo Criterion (USA) **3524**
• Buffalo Environmental Law Journal (USA ISSN 1066-8837) **4633**
Buffalo Fine Print News (USA) **3524**
• Buffalo Human Rights Law Review (USA ISSN 1098-3643) **4633**
Buffalo Human Rights Law Review *see* Buffalo Human Rights Law Review **4633**
Buffalo Intellectual Property Law Journal (USA ISSN 1539-9036) **4633**
Buffalo Jewish Review (USA) **7719**
Buffalo Journal (THA ISSN 0857-1554) **282**
• Buffalo Law Journal (USA ISSN 0197-4955) **4633**
• ➤ Buffalo Law Review (USA ISSN 0023-9356) **4633**
Buffalo Niagara Partnership Membership Directory (USA) **1977**
• The Buffalo Public Interest Law Journal (USA) **4633**
Buffalo Society of Natural Sciences. Occasional Papers (USA) **7842**
Buffalo Spree (USA ISSN 0300-7499) **3971**
† • Buffalo Women's Law Journal (USA ISSN 1523-5491) **8937**
Buffe (SWE) **3628**
▼ Buffed (DEU) **2475**
Buffy The Vampire Slayer (U.K. Edition) (GBR ISSN 1467-680X) **2377**
Buffy The Vampire Slayer (U.S. Edition) (USA) **2377**
• Bug (HRV ISSN 1330-0318) **2408**
Bug Report (USA) **2575**
Bugeye Times (USA ISSN 0882-651X) **6521**
Bugle (Missoula) (USA ISSN 0889-6445) **2605**
• BugNet (USA) **2575**
† Bugs Bunny (TUR ISSN 1301-031X) **8937**
• Bugun (TUR ISSN 1301-5869) **3962**
Buhardilla (PRY ISSN 1017-2777) **6644**
• Buho Rojo (PER ISSN 1609-9818) **3927**
Buhuth (SDN ISSN 0304-2561) **7951**
Buhuth al-Naza'ir Wa-al-Ish'a' *see* Isotope and Radiation Research **6199**
Buiatria (ITA ISSN 1828-4078) **8794**
The Buick Bugle (USA ISSN 0194-8415) **364**
Buick Open Tournament Program (USA) **8224**
build (DEU) **435**
▼ Build a Model Solar System (GBR ISSN 1754-8268) **572**
Build Aid Building and Pricing Guide *see* Resource Quantities and Pricing Guide **1033**
Build & Design Professional (GBR ISSN 0958-7438) **984**
Build Home (Victoria) (AUS ISSN 1444-8718) **4534**
Build It (GBR ISSN 0958-2681) **984**
Build Magazine (NZL ISSN 0110-4381) **984**
Build the Red Baron's Fighter Plane (GBR ISSN 1479-6643) **4331**
Builder (Columbus) (USA ISSN 0007-3261) **4496**
Builder (Scottdale) (USA ISSN 0745-1687) **7628**
The Builder (Washington, D.C.) (USA) **4591**
• Builder (Washington) (USA ISSN 0744-1193) **984**
Builder and Developer (USA) **984**
Builder & Remodeler (USA ISSN 1079-2910) **984**
Builder Architect (USA) **984**

Bulletin E T see Europaeische Gesellschaft fuer Katholische Theologie. Bulletin **7797**

Bulletin Economique see Chambre de Commerce et d'Industrie de Rouen. Bulletin Economique **1399**

Bulletin Economique et Fiscal du Burkina Faso (BFA) **1397**

● Bulletin Epidemiologique Hebdomadaire (FRA ISSN 0245-7466) **7510**

Bulletin Eucarpia (HUN ISSN 1010-6251) **782**

Bulletin Europeen (ITA ISSN 0407-8438) **7111**

Bulletin Europeen des Brevets see Europaeisches Patentblatt (Print) **8954**

Bulletin Europeen d'Etudes Europeennes sur le Temps see B E S T **8089**

Bulletin Europeen du Moniteur (FRA ISSN 1148-5531) **987**

† Bulletin Europeen et International (FRA ISSN 1264-9120) **8938**

Bulletin Evangelique d'Information et de Presse (GAB) **7629**

Bulletin F A O de Statistiques see F A O Bulletin of Statistics **179**

Bulletin F A O d'Engrais et Nutrition Vegetale see F A O Fertilizer and Plant Nutrition Bulletin **197**

Bulletin Fiscal (FRA ISSN 0242-5912) **1913**

Bulletin Flash (CAN ISSN 1715-6688) **1215**

Bulletin Flash (CAN ISSN 1912-6875) **6799**

Bulletin Flash. Investissements Prives et Publics, Quebec et ses Regions. Perspectives (Year) (CAN ISSN 1911-1452) **1614**

➤ Bulletin for Biblical Research (USA ISSN 1065-223X) **7629**

Bulletin for International Fiscal Documentation see Bulletin for International Taxation **1913**

● Bulletin for International Taxation (NLD ISSN 1819-5490) **1913**

● ➤ Bulletin for Old Testament Studies in Africa (Online Edition) (NOR ISSN 1502-0827) **7629**

Bulletin for the Conveyancer see Conveyancer and Property Lawyer **7587**

Bulletin for the History of Arts see Muveszettorteneti Ertesito **507**

Bulletin for the History of Chemistry (USA ISSN 1053-4385) **2052**

Bulletin Franco-Hellenique (FRA ISSN 1775-8122) **3524**

Bulletin from Johnny Cake Hill (USA ISSN 0474-084X) **4286**

Bulletin fuer Angewandte Geologie/Bulletin pour la Geologie Appliquee (CHE ISSN 1420-6846) **6764**

Bulletin fuer Europaeische Zeitstudien see B E S T **8089**

Bulletin Fulbrighter see Fulbrighter News **2981**

Bulletin G C I D see Greek Commission on Irrigation and Drainage. Bulletin **8824**

Bulletin - Genealogical Society of Old Tryon County see Genealogical Society of Old Tryon County. Bulletin **3768**

Bulletin Hebdomadaire see Wochenschau **3877**

Bulletin Hebdomadaire see Weekly Bulletin **3877**

Bulletin Hispanique (FRA ISSN 0007-4640) **4207**

Bulletin Historique et Scientifique de l'Auvergne (FRA ISSN 1153-2599) **4207**

Bulletin I F S see Inventar der Fundmuenzen der Schweiz. Bulletin **1359**

Bulletin I R P see Institut de Recherches Psychologiques. Bulletin **7363**

Bulletin in the Noahide Laws (AUS ISSN 1832-6498) **7719**

Bulletin Infermier du Cancer (FRA ISSN 1628-2205) **6010**

Bulletin Infoaction (CAN ISSN 1203-0996) **7425**

Bulletin Interimaire see Les Aines au Canada **8024**

Bulletin International de Bibliographie sur l'Education see International Bulletin of Bibliography on Education **2934**

Bulletin International des Douanes see International Customs Journal **1930**

Bulletin International des Sciences de la Mer see I M S Newsletter **2806**

Bulletin International d'Informations - Droit et Pharmacie see Droit & Pharmacie Actualites **6833**

Bulletin Jean Giraudoux (FRA ISSN 1962-5952) **5267**

● Bulletin Joly Bourse (FRA ISSN 1638-9468) **1614**

● Bulletin Joly Societes (FRA ISSN 1285-0888) **4858**

Bulletin Jugend und Literatur (DEU ISSN 0045-351X) **4998**

Le Bulletin Juridique du Praticien Hospitalier (FRA ISSN 1625-4104) **5589**

Bulletin K N O B see Koninklijke Nederlandse Oudheidkundige Bond. Bulletin **403**

Bulletin - Kamer van Koophandel en Nijverheid van Antwerpen see Kamer van Koophandel en Nijverheid van Antwerpen. Bulletin **1406**

Bulletin Koperasi see Edisi Chusus Bulletin Koperasi **1482**

Bulletin L A R F (COL) **1322**

Bulletin Legislatif Belge (BEL ISSN 0304-3665) **4633**

Bulletin Lemanique de Go (CHE ISSN 1661-5158) **8164**

Bulletin. Les Aines au Canada see Les Aines au Canada **8024**

Bulletin Luxembourgeois sur les Questions Sociales see Luxembourg. Inspection Generale de la Securite Sociale. Bulletin Luxembourgeois sur les Questions Sociales **4513**

Bulletin Marcel-Proust (FRA ISSN 1249-674X) **5267**

Bulletin Medicale de l'I P P F see I P P F Medical Bulletin **972**

Bulletin Medisch Onderwijs see Tijdschrift voor Medisch Onderwijs **3005**

Bulletin Mensuel de Theodore Champion (FRA ISSN 1167-4024) **6892**

Bulletin Mensuel d'Information sur le Logement see Housing Information Monthly **4413**

Bulletin Mensuel: Observations Climatologiques - Maandbulletin: Klimatologische Waarnemingen see Institut Royal Meteorologique de Belgique. Bulletin Mensuel: Observations Climatologiques **6357**

Bulletin Mensuel: Observations Geophysiques - Maandbulletin: Geofysische Waarnemingen see Institut Royal Meteorologique de Belgique. Bulletin Mensuel: Observations Geophysiques **2783**

Bulletin Mensuel: Observations Ionospheriques et du Rayonnement Cosmique - Maandbulletin van de Ionosfeer en de Kosmische Straling see Institut Royal Meteorologique de Belgique. Bulletin Mensuel: Observations Ionospheriques et du Rayonnement Cosmique **6357**

Bulletin Monumental (FRA ISSN 0007-473X) **385**

Bulletin Municipal Officiel de la Ville de Paris, Bulletin Departemental Officiel du Departement de Paris see Paris. Bulletin Municipal Officiel - Bulletin Departemental Officiel **7459**

Bulletin Muzea Romske Kultury see Muzeum Romske Kultury. Bulletin **4247**

Bulletin National du Service Canadien des Forets see Service Canadien des Forets. Point de Vue **3702**

Bulletin - New York State Archaeological Association (1987) see New York State Archaeological Association. Bulletin **408**

Bulletin O E P P see E P P O Bulletin **228**

Bulletin of Abstracts: Non-Destructive Testing see Literaturschau: Zerstoerungsfreie Pruefung **8971**

Bulletin of Agricultural Research in Botswana (BWA ISSN 0256-7512) **98**

Bulletin of Agricultural Science and Technology see Nongye Keji Tongxun **141**

Bulletin of Agriculture Prices (IND) **98**

Bulletin of Aichi Institute of Technology. Part A see Aichi Kogyo Daigaku Kenkyu Hokoku. A Kyoyo Kankei Ronbunshu **3180**

Bulletin of Aichi Institute of Technology. Part B see Aichi Kogyo Daigaku Kenkyu Hokoku. B Senmon Kankei Ronbunshu **3180**

➤ Bulletin of American Odonatology (USA ISSN 1061-3781) **841**

Bulletin of Anesthesia History (USA ISSN 1522-8649) **5770**

Bulletin of Animal Health and Production in Africa/Bulletin des Sante et Production Animales en Afrique (KEN ISSN 0378-9721) **282**

● Bulletin of Aomori Occupational Therapy see Aomoriken Sagyo Ryoho Kenkyu **6106**

● Bulletin of Applied Computing and Information Technology (NZL ISSN 1176-4120) **2408**

Bulletin of Asia-Pacific Studies see Ajia Taiheiyou Ronsou **4179**

Bulletin of Atmospheric Radioactivity see Taiki Hoshano Kansoku Seiseki **6396**

Bulletin of Biblical Studies see Deltion Biblikon Meleton **7637**

Bulletin of Biological Sciences (USA ISSN 1554-7647) **663**

Bulletin of Biological Technology see Shengwu Jishu Tongbao **770**

Bulletin of Biology see Shengwuxue Tongbao **704**

Bulletin of Botanical Research see Zhiwu Yanjiu **824**

● ➤ Bulletin of Chemical Recation Engineering & Catalysis (IDN ISSN 1978-2993) **2052**

Bulletin of Chinese Cancer see Zhongguo Zhongliu **6037**

Bulletin of Chinese Language Teaching see Yuwen Jiaoxue Tongxun **5197**

Bulletin of Clinical Psychopharmacology see Klinik Psikofarmakoloji Bulteni **6157**

Bulletin of Comparative Labour Relations (NLD ISSN 0770-3724) **1668**

Bulletin of Computed Tomography see Bilgisayarli Tomografi Bulteni **6193**

Bulletin of Computer and Information Engineering see Zixun Gongcheng Xuebao **2551**

Bulletin of Data and Information on the Matsushiro Earthquake Swarm see Matsushiro Gunpatsu Jishin Shiryo Hokoku **2786**

Bulletin of Dental Education (USA ISSN 0007-4837) **5837**

Bulletin of Earth Sciences (IND) **2703**

● ➤ Bulletin of Earthquake Engineering (NLD ISSN 1570-761X) **2778**

● ➤ Bulletin of Economic Research (GBR ISSN 0307-3378) **1070**

● Bulletin of Education and Research (PAK ISSN 0555-7747) **2833**

Bulletin of Educational Psychology see Jiaoyu Xinli Xuebao **2873**

Bulletin of Educational Research (TWN) **2969**

➤ Bulletin of Electrochemistry (IND ISSN 0256-1654) **2112**

● ➤ Bulletin of Engineering Geology and the Environment (DEU ISSN 1435-9529) **3261**

➤ Bulletin of Entomological Research (GBR ISSN 0007-4853) **841**

➤ Bulletin of Environmental Contamination and Toxicology (USA ISSN 0007-4861) **3494**

● ➤ Bulletin of Experimental Biology and Medicine (USA ISSN 0007-4888) **663**

Bulletin of Experimental Treatment for AIDS see B E T A **5810**

† Bulletin of Fishery Statistics/Boletin Estadistico de Pesca/Bulletin Statistique des Peches (ITA ISSN 1014-1189) **8938**

Bulletin of Food Research see Journal of Food and Nutrition Research **6661**

➤ Bulletin of Francophone Africa (GBR ISSN 0966-1018) **3789**

Bulletin of G T S J see Gas Turbine Society of Japan. Bulletin **3378**

Bulletin of Geography (POL ISSN 1732-4254) **4001**

● ➤ Bulletin of Geosciences/Cesky Geologicky Ustav. Vestnik (CZE ISSN 1214-1119) **2727**

➤ Bulletin of Glaciological Research (JPN ISSN 1345-3807) **2778**

● The Bulletin of Good Practice in Popular Education (AUS ISSN 1325-233X) **2833**

Bulletin of Grain Technology (IND ISSN 0007-4896) **98**

Bulletin of Health Sciences Kobe (JPN ISSN 1346-8707) **5589**

Bulletin of Higher Educational Institutions and C I S Energy Agencies. Energy see Izvestiya Vysshikh Uchebnykh Zavedenii i Energeticheskikh Ob'yedinenii S N G. Energetika **3140**

Bulletin of Higher Educational Institutions. North Caucasus Region.Series of Social Sciences see Izvestiya Vysshikh Uchebnykh Zavedenii. Severo-Kavkazskii Region. Seriya Obshchestvennye Nauki **7976**

● Bulletin of Hispanic Studies (Online Edition, Liverpool, 2002) (GBR ISSN 1478-3398) **5267**

● Bulletin of Hispanic Studies (Print Edition. Liverpool, 2002) (GBR ISSN 1475-3839) **5267**

Bulletin of Indian Society for History of Mathematics see Ganita Bharati **5489**

● ➤ Bulletin of Indonesian Economic Studies (AUS ISSN 0007-4918) **1443**

➤ Bulletin of Informatics and Cybernetics (JPN ISSN 0286-522X) **5476**

Bulletin of Information on Computing in Anthropology see B I C A **330**

Bulletin of Insectology (ITA ISSN 1721-8861) **841**

Bulletin of Inventions and Summary of Patent Specifications (GBR ISSN 0261-023X) **6747**

Bulletin of Iranian Studies see University of Teheran. Faculty of Letters and Humanities. Bulletin of Iranian Studies **4326**

➤ Bulletin of Judaeo-Greek Studies (GBR ISSN 0954-1179) **7719**

Bulletin of Labour Statistics (CHE ISSN 0007-4950) **1215**

● Bulletin of Latin American Research (GBR ISSN 0261-3050) **7951**

Bulletin of Legal Developments (GBR ISSN 0007-4969) **4633**

The Bulletin of Legal Medicine see Adli Tip Bulteni **5912**

Bulletin of Long Range Weather Forecasting of Tohoku District see Tohoku Chiho Choki Yoho Sokuho **6396**

Bulletin of Magnetic Resonance (USA ISSN 0163-559X) **7007**

● ➤ Bulletin of Marine Science (USA ISSN 0007-4977) **2801**

● ➤ Bulletin of Materials Science (IND ISSN 0250-4707) **3342**

▼ ● Bulletin of Mathematical Analysis and Applications (KOS ISSN 1821-1291) **5476**

● ➤ Bulletin of Mathematical Biology (USA ISSN 0092-8240) **663**

† ● Bulletin of Medical Ethics (GBR ISSN 0962-9564) **8938**

Bulletin of Medico-Ethno-Botanical Research (IND ISSN 0253-6889) **307**

Bulletin of Medieval Canon Law. New Series (USA ISSN 0146-2989) **4633**

Bulletin of Microbiology see Mikrobiyoloji Bulteni **892**

Bulletin of Mineralogy, Petrology and Geochemistry see Kuangwu Yanshi Diqiu Huaxue Tongbao **2752**

† Bulletin of Molecular Biology and Medicine (ITA ISSN 0391-481X) **8938**

Bulletin of Northern Ireland Law (GBR ISSN 0260-6550) **4633**

➤ Bulletin of Pharmaceutical Sciences/Nashrat al-'lum al-Saydaliyyat Gami't Asiut (EGY ISSN 1110-0052) **6827**

Bulletin of Physical Education (GBR ISSN 0007-5043) **3053**

▼ Bulletin of Political Economy (IND ISSN 0973-5747) **1592**

Bulletin of Portuguese-Japanese Studies (PRT ISSN 0874-8438) **4180**

Bulletin of Pure and Applied Mathematics (IND ISSN 0973-5933) **5476**

➤ Bulletin of Pure & Applied Sciences. Section A: Zoology (IND ISSN 0970-0765) **937**

➤ Bulletin of Pure & Applied Sciences. Section B: Botany (IND ISSN 0970-4612) **782**

➤ Bulletin of Pure & Applied Sciences. Section C: Chemistry (IND ISSN 0970-4620) **2052**

➤ Bulletin of Pure & Applied Sciences. Section D: Physics (IND ISSN 0970-6569) **7007**

➤ Bulletin of Pure & Applied Sciences. Section E: Mathematics (IND ISSN 0970-6577) **5476**

➤ Bulletin of Pure & Applied Sciences. Section F: Geology (IND ISSN 0970-4639) **2727**

Bulletin of Science and Technology see Keji Tongbao **7875**

➤ Bulletin of Science, Technology & Society (USA ISSN 0270-4676) **7842**

Bulletin of Scientific and Technological Achievements see Kexue Jishu Yanjiu Chengguo Gongbao **8969**

Bulletin of Soil and Water Conservation see Shuitu Baochi Tongbao **252**

● ➤ Bulletin of Spanish Studies (GBR ISSN 1475-3820) **5267**

Bulletin of Statistics see South Africa. Statistics South Africa. Bulletin of Statistics **8400**

Bulletin of Surveying and Mapping see Cehui Tongbao **4002**

● The Bulletin of Symbolic Logic (USA ISSN 1079-8986) **5476**

Bulletin of T I C M I see Tbilisi International Center of Mathematics and Informatics. Bulletin **5540**

Bulletin of Tall Timbers Research (USA ISSN 1066-6168) **3685**

Bulletin of the Agricultural Meteorology of Tohoku District see Tohoku no Nogyo Kisho **6396**

Bulletin of the American Society of Papyrologists. Supplements (USA ISSN 0191-8710) **385**

Bulletin of the Ancient Orient Museum see Kodai Oriento Hakubutsukan Kiyo **402**

Bulletin of the Asia Institute see Asia Institute. Bulletin **543**

The Bulletin of the Astronomical Society of South Australia see The Bulletin **572**

● ➤ Bulletin of the Atomic Scientists (USA ISSN 0096-3402) **7224**

➤ Bulletin of the Cantigueiros (USA ISSN 0898-8463) **7629**

● Bulletin of the Center for Children's Books see Center for Children's Books. Bulletin **2147**

Bulletin of the Chemists and Technologists of Macedonia see Macedonian Journal of Chemistry and Chemical Engineering **2072**

● ➤ Bulletin of the Comediantes (USA ISSN 0007-5108) **5267**

Bulletin of the Computational Statistics of Japan see Keisanki Tokeigaku **8384**

Bulletin of the Crimean Astrophysical Observatory see Crimean Astrophysical Observatory. Bulletin **573**

Bulletin of the Dipterists Forum see Dipterists Forum. Bulletin. **843**

Bulletin of the European Communities and Supplements (LUX ISSN 0068-4120) **1443**

Bulletin of the European Union see European Commission. European Union. Bulletin **7233**

Bulletin of the Higher Educational Institutions. North Caucases Region. Series of Technical Sciences see Izvestiya Vysshikh Uchebnykh Zavedenii. Severo-Kavkazskii Region. Seriya Tekhnicheskie Nauki **8428**

● ➤ Bulletin of the History of Medicine (USA ISSN 0007-5140) **5589**

Bulletin of the I C T M see International Council for Traditional Music. Bulletin **6576**

Bulletin of the Information Technology Division Te (Online Edition) see B/I Te (Online Edition) **4993**

Bulletin of the Institute of Space and Aeronautical Science. University of Tokyo A see Uchu Kagaku Kenkyujo Hokoku **583**

Bulletin of the Institute of Space and Aeronautical Science. University of Tokyo B see Uchu Kagaku Kenkyujo Hokoku. Tokushu **583**

Bulletin of the Kate Sharpley Library see K S L **7149**

Bulletin of the Menninger Clinic see Menninger Clinic. Bulletin **6159**

Bulletin of the National Archaeological Museum see Museo Arqueologico Nacional. Boletin **407**

Bulletin of the National Association of Student Anthropologists see National Association of Student Anthropologists. Bulletin **349**

Bulletin of the National Braille Association, Inc. see National Braille Association. Bulletin **4083**

Bulletin of the Philadelphia Herpetological Society see Philadelphia Herpetological Society. Bulletin **960**

Bulletin of the Russian Academy of Sciences. Division of Chemical Sciences see Russian Chemical Bulletin **2079**

Bulletin of the Russian Grand Priory of Malta, Sovereign Order of Saint John of Jerusalem Knights Hospitaller see Russian Grand Priory of Malta. Bulletin **2269**

Bulletin of the School of Oriental and African Studies see University of London. School of Oriental and African Studies. Bulletin **4480**

Bulletin of the Section of Logic see University of Lodz. Department of Logic. Bulletin of the Section of Logic **5545**

Bulletin of the Seismological Laboratory (Reno) see University of Nevada. Seismological Laboratory. Bulletin **2791**

Bulletin of the Seismological Society of America see Seismological Society of America. Bulletin **2789**

Bulletin of the Siberian Medicine see Byulleten' Sibirskoi Meditsiny **5589**

Bulletin of the Sinological Society of Japan see Nippon Chugoku Gakkaiho **4187**

Bulletin of the Stefan University see Stefan University. Bulletin **7920**

Bulletin of the United States Fish Commission see Fishery Bulletin **3593**

10062 BULLETIN OF THE UNIVERSITY OF BOTSWANA, HIGHER EDUCATION ULRICH'S PERIODICALS

Bulletin of the University of Botswana, Higher Education Development Unit *see* The H E D U Bulletin **2983**
Bulletin of the Veterinary Institute in Pulawy *see* Veterinary Institute, Pulawy. Bulletin **8812**
Bulletin of the W H O *see* World Health Organization. Bulletin **5731**
Bulletin of the Yamagata University (Natural Science) *see* Yamagata Daigaku Kiyo (Shizen Kagaku) **711**
Bulletin of the Yamaguchi Medical School *see* Yamaguchi University. School of Medicine. Bulletin **5733**
Bulletin of Tibetology (IND ISSN 0525-1516) **4180**
• Bulletin of Tropical Medicine and International Health (GBR ISSN 1356-0832) **5811**
• ➤ Bulletin of Volcanology (DEU ISSN 0258-8900) **2778**
Bulletin of Women and Gender Studies *see* Funu yu Xingbie Yanjiu Tongxun **8897**
Bulletin of Yale University *see* Yale University. Bulletin **3011**
Bulletin of Zimbabwean Law (ZWE) **4633**
➤ Bulletin of Zoological Nomenclature (GBR ISSN 0007-5167) **937**
Bulletin Officiel de la Comptabilite Publique (FRA ISSN 0984-9114) **1282**
† Le Bulletin Officiel de la Concurrence, de la Consommation et de la Repression des Fraudes (FRA ISSN 0298-511X) **8938**
Bulletin Officiel de la Propriete Industrielle Brevets d'Invention - Certificats Complimentaires de Protection - Topographies *see* B O P I Brevets d'Invention - Certificats Complimentaires de Protection - Topographies **6746**
Bulletin Officiel de la Propriete Industrielle Dessins & Modeles *see* B O P I Dessins & Modeles **3365**
Bulletin Officiel de la Propriete Industrielle Marques de Fabrique, de Commerce ou de Service *see* B O P I Marques de Fabrique, de Commerce ou de Service **6746**
Bulletin Officiel de la Propriete Industrielle Statistiques de la Propriete Industrielle *see* B O P I Statistiques de la Propriete Industrielle **6746**
† • Bulletin Officiel des Competitions Equestres et des Epreuves d'Elevage (FRA ISSN 1274-5626) **8938**
Bulletin Officiel des Douanes (FRA ISSN 0427-2129) **1913**
Bulletin Officiel des Impots (FRA ISSN 0982-801X) **1913**
† Le Bulletin Officiel du Ministere de la Justice (FRA ISSN 0750-0416) **8938**
Bulletin Officiel du Ministere de la Mer (1988) *see* France. Ministere de la Mer. Bulletin Officiel **8644**
Bulletin Officiel du Travail et de l'Emploi (FRA) **1729**
Bulletin on Ageing *see* Bulletin on Social Integration Policies **4042**
Bulletin on Consumption of Non-Ferrous Metals Copper, Lead & Zinc (IND) **6306**
Bulletin on Current Research in Soviet and East European Law (CAN) **4633**
Bulletin on Drug Addiction and Alcoholism *see* Bollettino per le Farmacodipendenze e l'Alcoolismo **2692**
• Bulletin on Energy Efficiency (IND) **3125**
• The Bulletin on Long-Term Care Law (USA ISSN 1093-6939) **4042**
Bulletin on Social Integration Policies (USA) **4042**
Bulletin on Vital Statistics in the E S C W A Region/Nasrat al-Ihsa'at al Hayawiyyat f Mintaqat al-Lagnat al-Iqtisadiyyat wa-al-Igtima'iyyat li-Garbi Asiya (LBN ISSN 1020-7368) **7304**
Bulletin Ornithologique (CAN ISSN 0007-5256) **904**
Bulletin Pastorale Dienstverlening (NLD ISSN 1873-510X) **7629**
Bulletin - Peabody Museum of Natural History *see* Peabody Museum of Natural History. Bulletin **7897**
Bulletin Physiology and Pathology of Respiration *see* Bulleten' Fiziologii i Patologii Dykhania **5589**
Bulletin Potravinarskeho Vyskumu *see* Journal of Food and Nutrition Research **6661**
Bulletin pour la Geologie Appliquee *see* Bulletin fuer Angewandte Geologie **6764**
Bulletin Quotidien (FRA ISSN 0766-5849) **7111**
Bulletin Quotidien du Temps - Dagelijks Weerbulletin *see* Institut Royal Meteorologique de Belgique. Bulletin Quotidien du Temps **6357**
Bulletin Quotidien Europe *see* Europe. Bulletin Quotidien **7233**
• Bulletin R B C (CAN) **1322**
Bulletin R O Totaal (Ruimtelijke Ordening) (NLD ISSN 1574-9428) **4405**
• Bulletin Rapide de Droit des Affaires (FRA ISSN 0395-451X) **1729**
Bulletin Regional d'Informations Universitaires *see* Centre Regional de Documentation Pedagogique de Toulouse. Annales **2835**
Bulletin Romand d'Entomologie *see* Entomo Helvetica **844**
Bulletin - Royal Tropical Institute *see* Royal Tropical Institute. Bulletin **354**
Bulletin S C M O *see* C M O S Bulletin **6348**
Bulletin S E V - A E S ((Verband Schweizerischer Elektrizitatsunternehmen - Association des Entreprises Electriques suisses)) *see* Electrosuisse, S E V, Verband fur Elektro-, Energie- und Informationstechnik. Bulletin **3305**
Bulletin S E V - V S E *see* Electrosuisse, S E V, Verband fur Elektro-, Energie- und Informationstechnik. Bulletin **3305**
Bulletin - S E V, Verband fur Elektro-, Energie- und Informationstechnik *see* Electrosuisse, S E V, Verband fur Elektro-, Energie- und Informationstechnik. Bulletin **3305**
Bulletin S Q S P *see* Societe Quebecoise de Science Politique. Bulletin **7184**
Bulletin S V S *see* G S T Bulletin **8797**
Bulletin Scientific of Feed Industry *see* Biuletyn Naukowy Przemyslu Paszowego **270**
Bulletin Scientifique de Bourgogne (FRA ISSN 0373-2061) **7842**
Bulletin Scientifique de l'Association des Ingenieurs Sortis de l'Institut d'Electricite Montefiore *see* Association des Ingenieurs Electriciens Sortis de l'Institut Montefiore. Bulletin Scientifique **3296**
Bulletin Signaletique de Documentation Generale *see* Port Autonome du Havre. Bulletin Analytique de Documentation Generale **8981**
Bulletin Social (FRA ISSN 0242-5874) **1668**
Bulletin St. Fonds voor Beeldende Kunsten, Vormgeving & Bouwkunst (NLD) **4445**
Bulletin Statistique des Peches *see* Bulletin of Fishery Statistics **8938**
Bulletin Statistique Regional. Abitibi-Temiscamingue (CAN ISSN 1712-1930) **7479**
Bulletin Statistique Regional. Bas-Saint-Laurent (CAN ISSN 1712-1949) **7479**
Bulletin Statistique Regional. Capitale-Nationale (CAN ISSN 1712-1957) **7479**
Bulletin Statistique Regional. Centre-du-Quebec (CAN ISSN 1712-1965) **7479**
Bulletin Statistique Regional. Chaudiere-Appalaches (CAN ISSN 1712-1973) **7479**
Bulletin Statistique Regional. Cote-Nord (CAN ISSN 1712-1981) **7479**
Bulletin Statistique Regional. Estrie (CAN ISSN 1712-199X) **7479**
Bulletin Statistique Regional. Gaspesie-Iles-de-la-Madeleine (CAN ISSN 1712-2007) **7479**
Bulletin Statistique Regional. Lanaudiere (CAN ISSN 1712-2015) **7479**
Bulletin Statistique Regional. Laurentides (CAN ISSN 1712-2023) **7479**
Bulletin Statistique Regional. Laval (CAN ISSN 1712-2031) **7479**
Bulletin Statistique Regional. Mauricie (CAN ISSN 1712-204X) **7479**
Bulletin Statistique Regional. Monteregie (CAN ISSN 1712-2058) **7479**
Bulletin Statistique Regional. Montreal (CAN ISSN 1712-2066) **7479**
Bulletin Statistique Regional. Nord-du-Quebec (CAN ISSN 1712-2074) **7479**
Bulletin Statistique Regional. Outaouais (CAN ISSN 1712-2082) **7479**
Bulletin Statistique Regional. Saguenay-Lac-Saint-Jean (CAN ISSN 1712-2090) **7479**
Bulletin Subterranea Britannica (GBR ISSN 0307-1650) **385**
Bulletin Suisse de Linguistique Appliquee (CHE ISSN 1023-2044) **5102**
Bulletin Suisse de Mineralogie et Petrographie *see* Schweizerische Mineralogische und Petrographische Mitteilungen **6479**
Bulletin Suisse de Mycologie *see* Schweizerische Zeitschrift fuer Pilzkunde **816**
Bulletin sur la Politique de Securite Suisse *see* Bulletin zur Schweizerischen Sicherheitspolitik **7224**
Bulletin sur les Relations du Travail (CAN ISSN 0704-0865) **1668**
Bulletin Technique *see* Fachhefte Bulletin Technique **7320**
• Bulletin Technique Apicole (FRA ISSN 0335-3710) **98**
Bulletin Technique de l'A.T.G. *see* Association des Anciens Eleves de l'Ecole d'Ingenieurs de Geneve. Bulletin Technique **3182**
• Bulletin to Management (USA ISSN 0525-2156) **1857**
Bulletin Trimestriel: Observations d'Ozone - Driemaandelijks Bulletin: Ozon Waarnemingen *see* Institut Royal Meteorologique de Belgique. Bulletin Trimestriel: Observations d'Ozone **6357**
Bulletin Trimestriel sur la Consommation *see* Consumer Quarterly **1811**
Bulletin Union des Professeurs Physique Chimie *see* Le B U P Physique Chimie **7838**
Bulletin Usuel des Lois et Arretes (BEL ISSN 0773-7467) **4633**
Bulletin van de Europese Unie *see* European Commission. European Union. Bulletin **7233**
Bulletin van de Generale Bank *see* Generale Bank. Bulletin **1349**
Bulletin van het Rijksmuseum *see* Rijksmuseum. Bulletin **515**
Bulletin voor Industriebeleid (NLD ISSN 1871-3955) **7425**
Bulletin Voyages (CAN ISSN 0706-215X) **8689**
Bulletin Werk en Dagbesteding (NLD ISSN 1871-8205) **8029**
Bulletin Wijnandsrade (NLD ISSN 1574-2245) **4207**
† • The Bulletin with Newsweek (AUS ISSN 1440-7485) **8938**
Bulletin - Yale University Art Gallery *see* Yale University Art Gallery Bulletin **6540**
Bulletin zur Schweizerischen Sicherheitspolitik (CHE ISSN 1024-0608) **7224**
Bulletinen for Den Europaeiske Union *see* European Commission. European Union. Bulletin **7233**
Bulletins des Reglements Salariaux *see* Wage Settlements Bulletin **1714**
➤ Bulletins of American Paleontology (USA ISSN 0007-5779) **6723**
† • Bulletpoint (GBR ISSN 1350-3197) **8938**
• Bullettino delle Scienze Mediche (ITA ISSN 0007-5787) **5589**
Bullettino di Paletnologia Italiana (ITA ISSN 1827-4781) **331**
➤ Bullettino Storico Empolese (ITA ISSN 0007-5795) **4207**
Bullettino Storico Pistoiese (ITA ISSN 0007-5809) **4207**
Bullfight (USA) **5209**
Bullpen (USA) **8224**
The Bullrush (USA) **3760**
Bulwark (GBR ISSN 0045-3536) **7749**
Bulwark (USA ISSN 0741-5788) **4827**
Bumerang (RUS) **2181**
• Bumerangen (SWE ISSN 1100-0961) **6414**
Bummi (DEU ISSN 0323-8954) **2181**
Bummmei/Civilizations (JPN ISSN 1347-6424) **331**
• The Bump (Atlanta Edition) (USA ISSN 1938-5986) **8844**
• The Bump (Dallas Edition) (USA ISSN 1937-528X) **8844**
The Bump (Denver Edition) (USA ISSN 1937-8319) **8854**
• The Bump (Houston) (USA) **8844**
• The Bump (Los Angeles Edition) (USA ISSN 1939-7925) **8844**
• The Bump (New York City Edition) (USA ISSN 1939-3253) **8844**
• The Bump (Orange County Edition) (USA ISSN 1940-4433) **8844**
• The Bump (Phoenix Edition) (USA ISSN 1938-7733) **8844**
• The Bump (Portland Edition) (USA ISSN 1939-2133) **8844**
• The Bump (San Diego Edition) (USA ISSN 1940-249X) **8844**
• The Bump (Seattle Edition) (USA ISSN 1941-3823) **8844**
Bumper Top Wordsearch Special (GBR ISSN 1361-5432) **4331**
Bunben to Masui/Journal of Obstetrics and Anesthesia (JPN ISSN 0387-2653) **5987**
Bunchgrass Historian (USA) **4133**
Der Bund (CHE ISSN 1421-1769) **3958**
Bund der Deutschen Katholischen Jugend Journal *see* B D K J Journal **7785**
Bund der Deutschen Zollbeamten Magazin *see* B D Z Magazin **1911**
Bund der Oeffentlich Bestellten Vermessungsingenieure e.V. Forum *see* B D V I - Forum **3260**
Bund der Technischen Beamten, Angestellten und Arbeiter Magazin *see* B T B Magazin **8416**
Bund der Vertriebenen Nachrichten *see* B d V Nachrichten **7109**
Bund Deutscher Baumeister Direkt *see* B D B - Direkt **434**
Bund Deutscher Eisenbahn-Freunde Jahrbuch *see* B D E F - Jahrbuch **8615**
Bund Deutscher Forstleute Aktuell *see* B D F Aktuell **3684**
Bund Deutscher Hirnbeschaedigter Kurier *see* B D H Kurier **5582**
Bund Deutscher Ingenieur Corporationen Journal *see* B D I C Journal **2264**
Bund Deutscher Kunsterzieher Mitteilungen *see* B D K Mitteilungen **3052**
Bund fuer Umwelt und Naturschutz Deutschland Magazin *see* B U N D Magazin **2603**
Bund Katholischer Unternehmer Journal *see* B K U - Journal **7785**
Bund Transparent und Aktuell (DEU) **5209**
Bund und Beruf (DEU ISSN 0932-8904) **6414**
Bundel Bouwregelgeving *see* Tekstuitgave Bouwrecht **4793**
Bundes-Angestelltentarif Taschenbuch fuer den Oeffentlichen Dienst *see* B A T: Taschenbuch fuer den Oeffentlichen Dienst **7422**
Bundes-Apotheken-Register (DEU ISSN 0521-7598) **6827**
• Bundesakademie fuer Oeffentliche Verwaltung. Akademiebrief (Online) (DEU) **4634**
Bundesakademie fuer Oeffentliche Verwaltung. Akademiebrief (Print) *see* Bundesakademie fuer Oeffentliche Verwaltung. Akademiebrief (Online) **4634**
Bundesamt fuer Bauwesen und Raumordnung. Arbeitspapiere (DEU ISSN 1434-9582) **4405**
Bundesamt fuer Bauwesen und Raumordnung. Berichte (DEU ISSN 1436-0055) **4405**
Bundesamt fuer Bauwesen und Raumordnung. Research News (DEU ISSN 1437-5850) **4405**
Bundesamt fuer Seeschifffahrt und Hydrographie. Jahresbericht (DEU ISSN 0938-8559) **2801**
Bundesamt fuer Sera und Impfstoffe. Paul-Ehrlich-Institut. Arbeiten (DEU ISSN 0936-8671) **5589**
Bundesamt fuer Statistik Aktuell *see* B F S Aktuell **7478**
Bundesamt fuer Statistik. Info (CHE) **7479**
Bundesamt fuer Strahlenschutz - Atmosphaerische Radioaktivitaet *see* B f S - I A R **3165**
Bundesamt fuer Strahlenschutz Berichte *see* B f S - Berichte **3165**
Bundesamt fuer Strahlenschutz Berichte *see* B f S - S H Berichte **3165**
Bundesamt fuer Strahlenschutz - Entsorgung und Transport *see* B f S - E T **3165**
Bundesamt fuer Strahlenschutz - Kerntechnische Sicherheit *see* B f S - K T **3165**
Bundesamt fuer Strahlenschutz Schriften *see* B f S - Schriften **3165**
Bundesamt fuer Strahlenschutz - Strahlenschutz *see* B f S - S T **3165**
Bundesamt fuer Verbraucherschutz und Lebensmittelsicherheit Reporte *see* B V L - Reporte **7509**
Bundesamt fuer Veterinaerwesen. Mitteilungen (CHE) **8795**
Bundesanstalt fuer Alpenlaendische Landwirtschaft. Bericht (AUT ISSN 1026-6267) **98**
Bundesanstalt fuer Alpenlaendische Landwirtschaft Gumpenstein Veroeffentlichungen *see* B A L Veroeffentlichungen **94**
Bundesanstalt fuer Arbeitsschutz und Arbeitsmedizin Aktuell *see* B A U A: Aktuell **6673**
Bundesanstalt fuer Arbeitsschutz und Arbeitsmedizin. Schriftenreihe Forschung (DEU ISSN 1433-2086) **6674**
Bundesanstalt fuer Arbeitsschutz und Arbeitsmedizin. Schriftenreihe Forschungsanwendung (DEU) **6674**
Bundesanstalt fuer Arbeitsschutz und Arbeitsmedizin. Schriftenreihe Gefaehrliche Arbeitsstoffe (DEU) **6674**
Bundesanstalt fuer Arbeitsschutz und Arbeitsmedizin. Schriftenreihe Literaturdokumentation (DEU ISSN 1433-2116) **6674**
Bundesanstalt fuer Arbeitsschutz und Arbeitsmedizin. Schriftenreihe Regelwerke (DEU) **6674**
Bundesanstalt fuer Arbeitsschutz und Arbeitsmedizin. Schriftenreihe Sonderschriften (DEU) **6674**
Bundesanstalt fuer Arbeitsschutz und Arbeitsmedizin. Schriftenreihe Tagungsbericht (DEU) **6674**
Bundesanstalt fuer Finanzdienstleistungsaufsicht. Veroeffentlichungen (DEU ISSN 1611-5716) **4496**
Bundesanstalt fuer Materialforschung- und Pruefung. Amts- und Mitteilungsblatt (DEU) **3342**
Bundesanstalt fuer Materialforschung und -pruefung Dissertationsreihe *see* B A M Dissertationsreihe **3341**
Bundesanstalt fuer Materialforschung und -pruefung. Forschungsbericht (DEU ISSN 0938-5533) **3342**
Bundesanzeiger (DEU ISSN 0344-7634) **4827**
Bundesarbeitsblatt (DEU ISSN 0007-5868) **1668**
Bundesarbeitsgemeinschaft Saar fuer Philatelie und Postgeschichte. Mitteilungsblatt (DEU) **6892**
Bundesarbeitsgemeinschaft Selbsthilfe. Jahresspiegel (DEU) **3037**
Bundesbaublatt (DEU ISSN 0007-5884) **4405**
Die Bundesbeauftragten fuer die Unterlagen des Staatssicherheitsdienstes der ehemaligen Deutschen Demokratischen Republik. Analysen und Dokumente (DEU) **4207**
Bundesbericht Forschung und Innovation *see* Bundesministerium fuer Bildung und Forschung. Bundesbericht Forschung und Innovation **7425**
Bundesdatenschutzgesetz (DEU ISSN 0933-4033) **2511**
Bundeselterngeld- und Elternzeitgesetz (DEU) **4907**
Bundesfinanzhof - Nicht Veroeffentlichten *see* B F H - N V **7422**
Bundesfinanzhof - Praxis *see* B F H - P R **1911**
Bundesforschungsanstalt fuer Fischerei. Jahresbericht (DEU ISSN 0721-9768) **3587**
Bundesforschungsanstalt fuer Fischerei. Schriften (DEU ISSN 0438-4547) **3587**
Bundesforschungsanstalt fuer Forst- und Holzwirtschaft. Mitteilungen (DEU ISSN 0368-8798) **3710**
Bundesgerichtshof *see* B G H - C D **8934**
Bundesgerichtshof Report *see* B G H - Report **4827**
Bundesgesetzblatt fuer die Republik Oesterreich (AUT) **4846**
Bundesgesetzblatt. Teil 1 (DEU ISSN 0341-1095) **4827**
Bundesgesetzblatt. Teil 2 (DEU ISSN 0341-1109) **4828**
• ➤ Bundesgesundheitsblatt - Gesundheitsforschung - Gesundheitsschutz (DEU ISSN 1436-9990) **7510**
Bundesinstitut fuer Bau-, Stadt- und Raumforschung Info *see* B B S R - Info **4404**
Bundesinstitut fuer Berufsbildung Report *see* B I B B Report **6692**
Bundesinstitut fuer Bevoelkerungsforschung Mitteilungen *see* B I B Mitteilungen **7277**
Bundesinstitut fuer Gesundheitlichen Verbraucherschutz und Veterinaermedizin Schriften *see* B g V V-Schriften **7509**
➤ Bundesinstitut fuer Kultur und Geschichte der Deutschen im Oestlichen Europa. Berichte und Forschungen (DEU) **4207**
Bundesinstitut fuer Ostdeutsche Kultur und Geschichte. Berichte und Forschungen *see* Bundesinstitut fuer Kultur und Geschichte der Deutschen im Oestlichen Europa. Berichte und Forschungen **4207**
• Bundesinstitut fuer Sportwissenschaft. Sportwissenschaftliche Forschungsprojekte (DEU) **8164**
Bundesliga (Year) (DEU ISSN 0949-2194) **8224**
Bundesliga-Magazin (CHE) **8224**

Title

▼ *new title*   † *ceased*   ● *electronic media*   ➤ *refereed*

DIRECTORY 2010 BYPLAN 10067

Business Valuation Alert Newsletter *see* Business Valuation Guide **1076**
• Business Valuation by Industry Review Series (USA ISSN 1091-5508) **1977**
Business Valuation Guide (USA) **1076**
Business Valuation Review (USA ISSN 0897-1781) **1322**
Business Valuation Wire *see* B V Wire **1065**
Business Venezuela (VEN ISSN 0045-3641) **1397**
Business Venezuela's Corporate Handbook (VEN) **1614**
• Business View (Hewlett-Packard) (USA) **1614**
▼ • The Business Vo I P Report (Voice Internet Provider) (USA) **2553**
Business Voice (GBR ISSN 1468-9162) **1076**
Business Watch Magazine *see* Shangwu Zhoukan **1173**
Business Week (POL ISSN 1642-6770) **1076**
Business Week. Asian Edition (USA) **1076**
Business Week Chicago *see* B W Chicago **8934**
Business Week Global *see* Business Week International **1076**
Business Week. Industrial Edition *see* BusinessWeek **1077**
Business Week International (USA ISSN 0739-8409) **1076**
Business Week Polska *see* Business Week **1076**
Business Week Small Biz (USA ISSN 1556-1232) **1958**
Business Week SmallBiz *see* Business Week Small Biz **1958**
Business Weekly *see* Delova Sedmitsa **1287**
Business Weekly (GHA) **1445**
• Business Weekly/Shang Yeh Chou K'an (TWN ISSN 1021-9536) **1076**
Business Weekly (Lagos) (NGA) **1076**
• Business West Midlands (GBR ISSN 0958-7942) **1076**
† • The Business Who's Who Australian Products and Tradenames Guide (AUS ISSN 1031-1343) **8938**
• The Business Who's Who of Australia (AUS ISSN 0068-4503) **1977**
• Business Wire (USA) **1076**
Business without Borders (USA) **4859**
• Business Woman Magazine (USA ISSN 1530-6267) **8854**
• The Business Woman's Advantage Newsletter (USA) **1958**
Business World *see* Jingji Shijie **1132**
• Business World (CZE ISSN 1213-1709) **1414**
Business World (GBR) **1076**
• Business World (IND ISSN 0970-8197) **1076**
• Business World (PHL ISSN 0116-3930) **1881**
• Business World Top 1000 Corporations in the Philippines (PHL ISSN 0118-5241) **1977**
• Business Writers Bonus (USA) **5267**
The Business Writer's Handbook (USA ISSN 1933-5687) **5267**
Business X L (GBR ISSN 1756-9788) **1730**
Business XL *see* Business X L **1730**
▼ Business Youth Link (ZAF ISSN 1995-199X) **1731**
BusinessAge (GBR ISSN 0966-0313) **1077**
BusinessBrief (ZAF ISSN 1817-1974) **1731**
• Businessdate (Online) (AUS) **1731**
Businessdate (Print) *see* Businessdate (Online) **1731**
Businesses & Assets (GBR) **1808**
• BusinessForum China (DEU) **1077**
Businesslink *see* Business Link **1554**
Businessman (BGD) **1554**
Businessman's Directory, The Republic of China (TWN) **1977**
BusinessMatters (GBR ISSN 0965-9455) **1731**
BusinessPeople (AUT) **1445**
Businesssales.com.au Magazine (AUS ISSN 1832-2034) **1808**
BusinessTech *see* Business Tech **2553**
BusinessUSA *see* The U S Business Directory **2032**
• BusinessWeek (USA ISSN 0007-7135) **1077**
BusinessWeek Online *see* BusinessWeek **1077**
• BusinessWest (USA ISSN 1049-9822) **1077**
Businessworld *see* Business World **1414**
BusinessWorld *see* Business World **1881**
• Buskap (NOR ISSN 0807-5069) **282**
Buskontakt (DEU) **8689**
Busline (USA) **8492**
Busmagazin (DEU ISSN 0942-346X) **8492**
• BusMart (USA) **8492**
Busoldtimer Kalender (CHE) **8492**
Busplaner (DEU) **8690**
Busqueda (BOL) **7951**
Busqueda (URY ISSN 0797-2008) **1445**
BusRide *see* Bus Ride **8492**
Bussei Kenkyu/Material Science Study (JPN ISSN 0525-2997) **7007**
Busseiken Dayori/Institute for Solid State Physics. News (JPN ISSN 0385-9843) **7007**
Busshitsu Zairyou Kenkyuu Kikou Fushoku Deta Shito *see* N I M S Corrosion Data Sheets **6327**
Busshitsu Zairyou Kenkyuu Kikou Hirou Deta Shito *see* N I M S Fatigue Data Sheet **6327**
Busshitsu Zairyou Kenkyuu Kikou Uchuu Kanren Zairyou Kyoudo Deta Shito *see* N I M S Space Use Materials Strength Data Sheet **6327**
Bussi Baer *see* Rolf Kaukas Bussi Baer **2908**
Bussums Historisch Tijdschrift (NLD ISSN 1871-2266) **4207**
Bust (USA ISSN 1089-4713) **8854**
Bustard Studies (GBR ISSN 0254-0878) **2605**
BusTech (USA) **8492**
Buster (GBR) **2181**
Busty Beauties (USA) **6287**
• Busy Freelancer (USA ISSN 1538-8107) **4572**
• Busy Marketing Tips (USA ISSN 1536-4097) **1808**
Busy Practitioner (GBR ISSN 1478-4718) **1913**
Busy Time (GBR ISSN 1743-5323) **2181**
But Viet News (USA) **3524**
But Why? *see* A Pochemu? **2175**
Butane - Propane News (USA ISSN 0007-7259) **6764**
Butceler - Belediyeler, Il Ozel Idarler ve Koyler *see* Turkey. Turkiye Istatistik Kurumu. Butceler - Belediyeler, Il Ozel Idarler ve Koyler (Year) **7485**
Butcher Block (USA ISSN 0890-9466) **3761**
The Butcher Shop (USA ISSN 1550-1442) **5267**
• Buteyko Newsletter (NZL) **5755**
Butikslederen (DNK ISSN 1901-6581) **1422**
Butler (ZAF ISSN 1995-6002) **4353**
Butler and Merkin's Reinsurance Law *see* Reinsurance Law **4520**
Butler Collegian (USA) **2275**
Butler Group Review (GBR ISSN 1478-0461) **1414**
Butler Magazine (USA) **2275**
Butler Society. Journal (IRL ISSN 0572-5828) **3761**
Butlleti CATcert/Boletin CATcert (ESP ISSN 1699-3373) **2408**
▼ • Butlleti de la Dependencia (ESP ISSN 1988-7639) **8029**
Butlleti d'Informacio Agraria (ESP) **223**
Butlleti Groc (ESP ISSN 0214-1930) **6827**
Butlleti Groc (Catalan Edition) (ESP ISSN 0214-1922) **6827**
Butlleti Invesbreu *see* Invesbreu Criminologia **4891**
Butonia (DEU ISSN 0341-521X) **2245**
Butonia - Modisches Dekor *see* Butonia **2245**
Al-Butrul wal-Sina'a fi Abu Dhabi/Petroleum and Industry in Abu Dhabi (UAE) **6799**
Butsuri/Physics (JPN ISSN 0029-0181) **7007**
➤ Butsuri Kyoiku/Physics Education Society of Japan. Journal (JPN ISSN 0385-6992) **7007**
Butsuri Tansa/Geophysical Exploration (JPN ISSN 0912-7984) **2778**
Butsuri Tansa Chosa Kenkyu Ichiran/Geophysical Activity in Japan (JPN) **2778**
Butsuri Tansa Gakkai Gakujutsu Koenkai Koen Ronbunshu/Society of Exploration Geophysicists of Japan. Conference. Proceedings (JPN) **2778**
➤ Butsurigakushi/Journal for the History of Physics (JPN ISSN 0912-4446) **7007**
Butt (NLD) **4371**
Butterflies (JPN ISSN 0919-0988) **841**
Butterflies of Ontario & Summaries of Lepidoptera Encountered in Ontario *see* Ontario Lepidoptera **856**
➤ Butterfly (GBR) **841**
Butterfly Conservation News *see* Butterfly **841**
Butterfly Gardener (USA ISSN 1541-9746) **841**
Butterfly Net (USA) **532**
Butterworths Accountants' Legal Service (GBR) **1282**
Butterworths Annotated Legislation Service (GBR) **4634**
Butterworths Annotations to the New Zealand Statutes (NZL) **4634**
Butterworths Best Value Manual *see* Tottel's Best Value Manual **4797**
Butterworths Booktrade News (GBR) **7556**
Butterworths Budget Tax Tables (GBR ISSN 0525-3063) **1913**
Butterworths Business Service (NZL) **4859**
Butterworths Civil Court Practice *see* The Civil Court Practice **4828**
Butterworths Civil Court Precedents (GBR) **4828**
Butterworths Class Action Defence Quarterly *see* Class Action Defence Quarterly **4643**
• Butterworths Company Law Cases (GBR ISSN 0267-145X) **4859**
Butterworths Company Law Handbook (Year) (GBR) **4859**
• Butterworths Company Law Service (GBR) **4859**
Butterworths Competition Law (GBR) **4859**
Butterworths Compulsory Purchase and Compensation Service *see* Tottel's Compulsory Purchase and Compensation Service **4797**
Butterworths Conveyancing Bulletin (NZL ISSN 0113-115X) **4634**
Butterworths Core Text Series (GBR) **4634**
Butterworths Costs Service (GBR) **4634**
• Butterworths Current Law (NZL ISSN 0110-070X) **4634**
Butterworths Custom Duties Handbook (Year) (GBR) **4919**
Butterworths Disciplinary and Regulatory Tribunals (GBR) **4828**
• Butterworths District Court Reports (NZL ISSN 0113-714X) **4634**
• Butterworths District Courts Practice - Civil (NZL) **4828**
• Butterworths E C Brief (GBR ISSN 0955-8888) **1445**
• Butterworths Employment Law Bulletin (NZL ISSN 0969-1669) **4859**
Butterworths European Law Service. Company Law (GBR ISSN 0967-3520) **4859**
Butterworths Family Law Journal *see* New Zealand Family Law Journal **4913**
• Butterworths Family Law Service (GBR) **4907**
Butterworths Family Law Service *see* LexisNexis Family Law Service **4912**
Butterworths Food Law (GBR) **7510**
Butterworths Insurance Law Handbook (GBR) **4497**
† Butterworths International Medical Reviews: Hematology (GBR ISSN 0260-0129) **8938**
• Butterworths Journal of International Banking and Financial Law (GBR ISSN 0269-2694) **4634**
• Butterworths Law Directory (GBR) **4634**
Butterworths Law in Context Series (GBR) **4634**
Butterworths Law of Food & Drugs (GBR) **4634**
Butterworths Legal Services Directory (GBR) **4634**
Butterworths Legal Updater (GBR ISSN 1471-9606) **4947**
Butterworths Legislation Service. Monthly Bulletin (ZAF) **4634**
Butterworths Local Authority Companies and Partnerships *see* Tottel's Local Authority Companies and Partnerships **7504**
Butterworths Local Government Law *see* Tottel's Local Government Law **7504**
Butterworths Local Government Reports (GBR ISSN 1474-8657) **4634**
Butterworths Merger Control Review (GBR ISSN 0964-7805) **4919**
Butterworths Money Laundering Law (GBR) **2645**
Butterworths Older Client Law Service *see* Tottel's Older Client Law Service **4915**
• Butterworths Ontario Motor Vehicle Insurance Practice Manual (CAN) **4497**
Butterworths Orange Tax Handbook (GBR ISSN 0141-1500) **1914**
Butterworths P F I Manual (GBR) **1322**
Butterworths Planning Law Handbook (GBR) **4634**
• Butterworths Planning Law Service (GBR) **4634**
Butterworths Police and Criminal Evidence Act Cases (GBR) **4885**
Butterworths Property Law Service (GBR) **4634**
Butterworths Regional Levies Report (ZAF) **4634**
Butterworths Road Traffic Service (GBR) **4635**
Butterworths Solicitors Accounts and Financial Management (GBR) **1282**
Butterworths Tax Alert (ZAF) **1914**
• Butterworths Trading and Consumer Law (GBR) **4635**
Butterworths V A T Gram (Value Added Tax) (ZAF) **1914**
Butterworths Welfare Law *see* Tottel's Welfare Law **4797**
Butterworths Workers' Compensation in Ontario Service (CAN) **4497**
Butterworths Yellow Tax Handbook (GBR ISSN 0141-3856) **1914**
▼ Button Magazine (USA ISSN 1947-6159) **6552**
Buvisindi *see* Icelandic Agricultural Sciences **119**
Buxbaumiella (NLD ISSN 0166-5405) **782**
Buy a Boat (GBR) **8273**
Buy a Business (NZL ISSN 1177-0260) **7585**
Buy & Sell (IRL ISSN 0791-5446) **1977**
Buy & Sell (Munster Edition) *see* Buy & Sell **1977**
Buy Books Where, Sell Books Where (USA ISSN 0732-6599) **7556**
Buy from India (IND ISSN 0304-968X) **1977**
Buy It *see* Caterer & Hotelkeeper **4383**
Buy-Side Technology (GBR ISSN 1753-6952) **1414**
Buy Wholesale by Mail (USA ISSN 1520-6181) **1808**
Buyer (GBR ISSN 0142-6796) **1554**
Buyers and Services Guide for Local Governments (Year) *see* Colorado Municipal and County Directory and Desk Reference (Year) **7490**
Buyers Gallery of Fine Boats *see* DuPont Registry: A Buyer's Gallery of Fine Boats **8275**
The Buyer's Guide *see* The Buyer's Guide to Respiratory Care Products **6212**
† Buyers' Guide (ITA ISSN 0007-7380) **8938**
Buyer's Guide (USA ISSN 1539-624X) **8570**
Buyer's Guide *see* Natural Products Industry Insider **6664**
Buyers Guide & Resource Directory *see* Appliance Design Buyers Guide **1972**
Buyer's Guide for the Sugar and Allied Industries (Year) (GBR) **3629**
Buyer's Guide of Tokyo (Year) (JPN) **2635**
The Buyer's Guide to Cornsnake Morphs *see* Cornsnake Morph Guide **939**
Buyer's Guide to D S P Processors (Digital Signal Processing) (USA) **2466**
Buyers' Guide to Outdoor Advertising (USA ISSN 0095-5531) **22**
• The Buyer's Guide to Respiratory Care Products (GBR ISSN 1995-5111) **6212**
Buyers Guide to U.S. Cotton (USA) **223**
Buyers of Men's and Boys' Apparel (USA ISSN 1556-4630) **1977**
Buyers of Women's and Children's Apparel (USA ISSN 1556-4622) **2245**
Buying and Selling in Europe (FRA) **1808**
Buying Business Travel (GBR) **8690**
† Buying Cameras (GBR ISSN 0961-0863) **8938**
• Buying Strategy Forecast (USA ISSN 1082-0035) **1809**
• Buyouts (USA ISSN 1040-0990) **1614**
Buyouts Yearbook (USA) **1614**
• Buyside (USA ISSN 1543-5563) **1614**
Buzetski Zbornik (HRV ISSN 0350-6088) **385**
Buzz (Rochester) (USA ISSN 1063-3383) **1809**
Buzz Daly's Players Guide to Las Vegas Sports Books (Year) - Football Edition (USA) **8164**
• Buzz Words (USA) **7510**
BuzzBytes (USA) **2539**
• Buzzine (USA) **6552**
• ➤ BWe (Basic Writing e-Journal) (USA) **5267**
BWP@ *see* Berufs- und Wirtschaftspaedagogik Online **1066**
By Design (USA) **4059**
By og Byg - Aarsberetning (DNK) **987**
By og Byg Anvisning (DNK ISSN 1600-8057) **987**
• By og Byg Dokumentation (DNK ISSN 1600-8022) **987**
• By og Byg Resultater (DNK ISSN 1600-8030) **987**
By og Bygd (NOR ISSN 0084-8212) **4207**
By og Land (DNK ISSN 1399-7696) **4405**
• By-the-Sea (USA) **8274**
By the Way (JPN ISSN 0917-7566) **7224**
By the Way (USA) **8029**
Byahornet (SWE ISSN 1101-6868) **5267**
Byarozka (BLR ISSN 0007-7429) **2181**
• Byavisa (NOR ISSN 0809-6511) **3921**
Bycatch Action Plan *see* Torres Strait Prawn Fishery Bycatch Action Plan **3610**
Bydgoskie Towarzystwo Naukowe. Wydzial Nauk Humanistycznych. Prace. Seria B (Jezyk i Literatura) (POL ISSN 0068-4570) **5102**
Bydgoskie Towarzystwo Naukowe. Wydzial Nauk Humanistycznych. Prace. Seria C (Historia i Archeologia) (POL ISSN 0068-4589) **4207**
Bydgoskie Towarzystwo Naukowe. Wydzial Nauk Humanistycznych. Prace. Seria D (Sztuka) (POL ISSN 0067-947X) **480**
Bydgoskie Towarzystwo Naukowe. Wydzial Nauk Technicznych. Prace. Seria Z (Prace Zbiorowe) (POL ISSN 0068-4597) **8417**
Bydleni (CZE ISSN 0232-0347) **4534**
Bydleni, Stavby, Reality (CZE ISSN 1801-7533) **987**
Bydlime s Kvetinami (CZE) **3726**
Byelorussian Books *see* Knigi Belarusi **628**
Byelorussian Voice *see* Bielaruski Holas **3522**
• Byens Naeringsliv (NOR ISSN 0809-6503) **1958**
Byers Election Law (USA) **4635**
Byg-Tek (DNK) **987**
Bygd och Natur (Skriftserie) (SWE ISSN 1101-4571) **4207**
Bygd och Natur (Tidskrift) (SWE ISSN 0345-7982) **2605**
Bygdanytt (NOR) **3921**
Bygdeposten (NOR) **3922**
Bygdeserien (FIN ISSN 0357-6574) **436**
Bygdeungdommen (NOR ISSN 0333-1997) **2181**
Bygdo (NOR ISSN 1504-1700) **3922**
Bygg och Jaernhandeln *see* Jaern, Bygg, Faerg **1823**
Bygg & Teknik (SWE ISSN 0281-658X) **987**
• Byggaktuelt (NOR ISSN 0800-7713) **987**
Byggare Bob Magasin (SWE ISSN 1650-7819) **2181**
Byggaren (SWE) **988**
Bygge og Bo (NOR) **4405**
Bygge- og Boligpolitiske Oversigt (DNK ISSN 0107-119X) **4405**
Byggeforskningsinstitut - Aarsberetning *see* By og Byg - Aarsberetning **987**
Byggeindustrien/Danish Building Industry (DNK ISSN 0007-750X) **988**
Byggeindustrien (NOR ISSN 0332-7086) **988**
Byggekunst *see* Arkitektur N **433**
Byggenytt (NOR ISSN 0333-3477) **988**
Byggeplads Danmark (DNK ISSN 0904-3241) **436**
Byggeri (DNK ISSN 1397-7997) **988**
Byggeri, Informationsteknologi, Produktivitet, Samarbejde Nyt *see* Bips **982**
• Byggeriet (DNK ISSN 0906-1037) **988**
• Byggeteknik (DNK ISSN 1602-6187) **988**
• Byggfagbladet (NOR ISSN 1504-4696) **4591**
Byggfakta Projektnytt (SWE ISSN 1101-8437) **988**
ByggGlas (SWE ISSN 0280-7076) **2038**
Byggherren (NOR ISSN 0332-6152) **988**
Byggindustrin (SWE ISSN 1104-5981) **988**
Byggmesteren (NOR ISSN 0332-7221) **988**
• Byggnadsarbetaren (SWE ISSN 0007-7569) **1049**
Byggnadskultur (SWE ISSN 0348-6885) **436**
Byggnadsstyrelsens Informationer (SWE) **4405**
Byggreferat (SWE ISSN 0345-1941) **1045**
▼ • Byggvaerlden (SWE ISSN 1654-9260) **988**
Bygningsdele (DNK ISSN 0108-0229) **988**
Bygningskulturens Dag (DNK ISSN 1603-5267) **436**
Bygningsstatiske Meddelelser (DNK ISSN 0106-3715) **988**
† Bygone Kent (GBR ISSN 0262-5342) **8938**
Byhistorisk Samling og Arkiv i Hoje-Taastrup Kommune. Aarskrift (DNK ISSN 0907-8789) **4207**
Byhistoriske Skrifter *see* University of Southern Denmark Studies in History and Social Sciences **4275**
➤ Byhornet/Ballerup Historical Society (DNK ISSN 0105-6433) **4208**
ByLine (USA ISSN 0744-4249) **4572**
Byminner (NOR ISSN 0007-7631) **4208**
• Byogen Biseibutsu Kenshutsu Joho Geppo/Infectious Agents Surveillance Report (JPN ISSN 0915-5813) **5811**
Byoin/Hospital (JPN ISSN 0385-2377) **4089**
➤ Byoin, Chiiki Seishin Igaku/Japanese Journal of Hospital and Community Psychiatry (JPN ISSN 0910-4798) **6129**
Byoin Kanri/Hospital Administration (JPN ISSN 0386-9571) **4089**
Byoin Setsubi/Hospital Equipment (JPN ISSN 0007-764X) **4089**
Byoin Yakugaku/Japanese Journal of Hospital Pharmacy *see* Iryo Yakugaku **6851**
Byoin Yoran/Japanese Hospital Directory (JPN ISSN 0408-0904) **4089**
Byotai Seiri (Tokyo)/Journal of Pathological Physiology (JPN ISSN 0387-9666) **920**
Byoux Etcetera (NLD ISSN 1871-7861) **2252**
Bypass (GBR) **621**
Byplan (DNK ISSN 0007-7658) **4405**

Title

10068 BYPLAN NYT ULRICH'S PERIODICALS

• Byplan Nyt (DNK ISSN 1602-9038) **4405**
Byplannyt *see* Byplan Nyt **4405**
• Byraaboken (SWE ISSN 1650-7924) **22**
Byron Journal (GBR ISSN 0301-7257) **5418**
Byt Magazin (CZE ISSN 1213-9580) **4534**
• Byte (BGR) **2408**
Byte (Russian Edition) (RUS) **2408**
† • Byte.com (USA) **8938**
Byte Espana (ESP ISSN 1135-0407) **2408**
• A Byte of Godly Counsel (USA) **1077**
Byte Tuerkiye (TUR ISSN 1300-6711) **2570**
• Bytes of Science (USA) **7842**
• Bytova Vystavba (CZE) **1045**
Byty a Nemovitosti *see* E-mail Noviny Byty a Nemovitosti **7589**
Byuleten' Ekolohichnoho Stanu Zony Vidchuzhennya (UKR) **2605**
Byuleten' Zakonodavstva i Yurydychnoi Praktyky Ukrainy (UKR) **4635**
➤ Byulleten' Eksperimental'noi Biologii i Meditsiny (RUS ISSN 0365-9615) **663**
Byulleten' Fondovogo Rynka Predpriyatii Tek (RUS) **1077**
Byulleten' Inostrannoi Kommercheskoi Informatsii (RUS ISSN 0320-4529) **1554**
Byulleten' Mezhdunarodnykh Dogovorov (RUS ISSN 0869-6705) **4919**
Byulleten' Mezhdunarodnykh Dogovorov, Soglashenii i Otdel'nykh Zakonodatel'nykh Aktov Respubliki Kazakhstan (KAZ) **7111**
Byulleten' Mezhdunarodnykh Nauchnykh S'ezdov, Konferentsii, Kongressov, Vystavok (RUS ISSN 0202-5442) **6283**
Byulleten' Ministerstva Obshchego i Professional'nogo Obrazovaniya Rossiiskoi Federatsii (RUS) **7111**
Byulleten' Normativnykh Aktov Federal'nykh Organov Ispolnitel'noi Vlasti (RUS) **4635**
Byulleten' Normativnykh Aktov Federal'nykh Organovispolnitel'noi Vlasti (KAZ) **7111**
Byulleten' po Narkoticheskim Sredstvam *see* United Nations. Bulletin on Narcotics **2700**
Byulleten' Pravovoi i Kommercheskoi Informatsii po Nedropol'zovaniyu (RUS) **4635**
Byulleten' Registratsii N I R i O K R. Seriya 1. Obshchestvennye Nauki v Tselom. Filosofiya. Sotsiologiya. Politika. Politicheskie Nauki. Psikhologiya. Religiya. Ateizm (RUS ISSN 0235-0254) **3118**
Byulleten' Registratsii N I R i O K R. Seriya 10. Geodeziya. Kartografiya. Geofizika. Geologiya. Geografiya. (RUS ISSN 0201-4610) **3118**
Byulleten' Registratsii N I R i O K R. Seriya 11. Naukovedenie. Informatika. Patentnoe Delo. Izobretatel'stvo. Ratsionalizatorstvo (RUS ISSN 0201-4521) **3118**
Byulleten' Registratsii N I R i O K R. Seriya 12. Pishchevaya Promyshlennost' (RUS ISSN 0201-453X) **3118**
Byulleten' Registratsii N I R i O K R. Seriya 13. Lesnaya i Derevoobrabatyvayushchaya Promyshlennost' (RUS ISSN 0201-4335) **3118**
Byulleten' Registratsii N I R i O K R. Seriya 14. Stroitel'stvo. Arkhitektura (RUS ISSN 0136-0981) **3118**
Byulleten' Registratsii N I R i O K R. Seriya 15. Transport (RUS ISSN 0132-3148) **3118**
Byulleten' Registratsii N I R i O K R. Seriya 16. Fizika. Mekhanika. Astronomiya. Issledovanie Kosmicheskogo Prostranstva (RUS ISSN 0132-7208) **3118**
Byulleten' Registratsii N I R i O K R. Seriya 17. Khimiya. Khimicheskaya Tekhnologiya. Khimicheskaya Promyshlennost' (RUS ISSN 0132-4152) **3118**
Byulleten' Registratsii N I R i O K R. Seriya 18. Demografiya. Ekonomika. Ekonomicheskie Nauki. Vneshnya Torgovlya. Organizatsii (RUS ISSN 0132-4586) **3118**
Byulleten' Registratsii N I R i O K R. Seriya 19. Elektronika. Radiotekhnika. Svyaz' (RUS ISSN 0132-294X) **3118**
Byulleten' Registratsii N I R i O K R. Seriya 2. Istoriya. Istoricheskie Nauki. Gosudarstvo i Pravo. Yuridicheskie Nauki. Voennoe Delo (RUS ISSN 0234-7709) **3118**
Byulleten' Registratsii N I R i O K R. Seriya 20. Energetika. Elektrotekhnika. Yadernaya Tekhnika (RUS ISSN 0132-3318) **3118**
Byulleten' Registratsii N I R i O K R. Seriya 21. Okhrana Okruzhayushchei Sredy. Ekologiya Cheloveka (RUS ISSN 0132-2958) **3118**
Byulleten' Registratsii N I R i O K R. Seriya 22. Matematika. Kibernetika. Avtomatika i Telemekhanika. Vychislitel'naya Tekhnika (RUS ISSN 0132-8026) **3118**
Byulleten' Registratsii N I R i O K R. Seriya 23. Priborostroenie. Poligrafiya. Reprografiya. Fotokinotekhnika. Standartizatsiya (RUS ISSN 0132-8042) **3118**
Byulleten' Registratsii N I R i O K R. Seriya 24. Gornoe Delo (RUS ISSN 0132-8034) **3118**
Byulleten' Registratsii N I R i O K R. Seriya 25. Sel'skoe i Lesnoe Khozyaistvo (RUS ISSN 0132-957X) **3118**
Byulleten' Registratsii N I R i O K R. Seriya 26. Rybnoe Khozyaistvo. Vodnoe Khozyaistvo. Melioratsiya (RUS ISSN 0132-9596) **3119**
Byulleten' Registratsii N I R i O K R. Seriya 27. Obshchie i Kompleksnye Problemy Tekhnich Eskikh i Prikladnykh Nauk i Otrasleinar (RUS ISSN 0132-9588) **3119**
Byulleten' Registratsii N I R i O K R. Seriya 3. Kul'tura. Narodnoe Obrazovanie. Pedagogika. Fizicheskaya Kul'tura i Sport (RUS ISSN 0206-3743) **3119**
Byulleten' Registratsii N I R i O K R. Seriya 4. Yazykoznanie. Literatura. Literaturovedenie. Narodnoe Poeticheskoe Tvorchestvo (RUS ISSN 0206-1325) **3119**
Byulleten' Registratsii N I R i O K R. Seriya 5. Biologiya. Biotekhnologiya (RUS ISSN 0206-1333) **3119**
Byulleten' Registratsii N I R i O K R. Seriya 6. Legkaya Promyshlennost'. Vnutrenniaya Torgovlya. Turistsko-Ekskusionnoe Obsluzhivanie. Zhilishchno-Kommunal'noe Kho (RUS) **3119**
Byulleten' Registratsii N I R i O K R. Seriya 7a. Otraslevoe Mashinostroenie (RUS ISSN 0206-3875) **3119**
Byulleten' Registratsii N I R i O K R. Seriya 7b. Tekhnologiya Mashinostroeniya (RUS ISSN 0206-3859) **3119**
Byulleten' Registratsii N I R i O K R. Seriya 8. Meditsina i Zdravookhranenie. Okhrana Truda (RUS ISSN 0204-3734) **3119**
Byulleten' Registratsii N I R i O K R. Seriya 9. Metallurgiya (RUS ISSN 0204-3726) **3119**
• ➤ Byulleten' Sibirskoi Meditsiny/Bulletin of the Siberian Medicine (RUS) **5589**
Byulleten' Stroitel'noi Tekhniki (RUS ISSN 0007-7690) **988**
Byulleten' Transportnoi Informatsii (RUS) **8492**
Byulleten' V M O *see* W M O Bulletin **6397**
Byways (Fairfax) (USA) **8690**
➤ Byzantina Australiensia (AUS ISSN 0725-3079) **4208**
Byzantina et Neograeca Vindobonensia (AUT ISSN 1816-3874) **4133**
• ➤ Byzantina Symmeikta (GRC ISSN 1791-4884) **2231**
Byzantina Vindobonensia *see* Byzantina et Neograeca Vindobonensia **4133**
• ➤ Byzantine and Modern Greek Studies (GBR ISSN 0307-0131) **4208**
Byzantine and Neohellenic Studies (GBR ISSN 1661-1187) **5267**
Byzantine Studies/Etudes Byzantines (USA ISSN 0095-4608) **4445**
Byzantinische Forschungen (ESP ISSN 0167-5346) **4208**
• Byzantinische Zeitschrift (DEU ISSN 0007-7704) **545**
Byzantinische Zeitschrift. Supplementum Bibliographicum *see* Byzantinische Zeitschrift **545**
➤ Byzantinoslavica (CZE ISSN 0007-7712) **545**
Byzantion (BEL ISSN 0378-2506) **545**
• Byzantion Nea Hellas (CHL ISSN 0716-2138) **4445**
• C (CAN ISSN 1480-5472) **480**
C (NLD ISSN 1874-5083) **1731**
C! (NOR ISSN 1503-8122) **3922**
C (USA ISSN 1930-2444) **3971**
C 16 Autostyle (USA ISSN 1932-779X) **8570**
C 21st Society *see* Twenty - First Century Society **8011**
• C 3 (DNK ISSN 1901-7561) **1077**
C 3 (Chronic Comorbidity in C N S Medicine) (USA) **6129**
C 3 I *see* Market Intelligence Reports: Command, Control, Communications & Intelligence Forecast **6432**
C 4 I S R (USA ISSN 1941-1286) **6414**
C A *see* Contemporary Architecture **438**
C + A (Cement Concrete & Aggregates) (AUS ISSN 1833-0975) **988**
C A *see* Confessio Augustana **7752**
C A *see* Current Archaeology **389**
• ➤ C A (USA ISSN 0007-9235) **6010**
C A A B U Briefings (Council for the Advancement of Arab-British Understanding) (GBR) **7224**
C A A C Inflight Magazine *see* Zhongguo Minhang **8789**
C A A Document *see* Great Britain. Civil Aviation Authority. Document **8542**
C A A I P *see* Civil Aircraft Airworthiness Information and Procedures **8539**
• C A A Magazine (Canadian Automobile Association) (CAN ISSN 1910-0140) **8690**
C A A N *see* Computer-Assisted Anthropology News **333**
C A A News *see* Computer-Assisted Anthropology News **333**
• C A A News (New York, Online) (College Art Association) (USA ISSN 1942-4892) **480**
C A A News (New York, Print) *see* C A A News (New York, Online) **480**
• C A A News (Sacramento, Online) (California Apartment Association) (USA) **7585**
C A A Newsletter (USA) **4999**
C A A Papers *see* Great Britain. Civil Aviation Authority. Papers **8543**
C A A R Communicator (Canadian Association of Agri-Retailers) (CAN) **98**
• C A A Reviews (College Art Association) (USA ISSN 1543-950X) **480**
C A A S Monograph Series *see* Afro-American Culture and Society Monograph Series **3517**
C A A S News (Computer-Assisted Appraisal Section) (USA ISSN 8755-3732) **7585**
C A A S Report (Center for African American Studies) (USA ISSN 1051-4589) **3524**
• The C A A S Research Report (Center for African American Studies) (USA ISSN 1540-1065) **7203**
C A A S Special Publication Series (Center for African American Studies) (USA ISSN 0882-5300) **3524**
C A A S Urban Policy Series (Center for African American Studies) (USA ISSN 1086-7945) **3524**
C A A Scientific Papers (Center for American Archeology) (USA) **385**
C A A Specifications (Civil Aviation Authority) (GBR) **8539**
C A A T Newsletter (Campaign Against Arms Trade) (GBR ISSN 0142-7113) **7224**
C A A Update (Chinese for Affirmative Action) (USA) **3524**
• C A B Abstracts (GBR) **176**
C A B Air Carrier Traffic Statistics (Civil Aeronautics Board) (USA ISSN 0731-3411) **8523**
C A B C D *see* C A B Abstracts **176**
• C A B E Journal (Connecticut Association of Boards of Education, Inc.) (USA ISSN 1092-1818) **3018**
C A B N *see* Cognitive, Affective, & Behavioral Neuroscience **7346**
C A B News (Canadian Association of Broadcasters) (CAN ISSN 1719-9867) **2314**
C A B News (Citizens Advice Bureaux) (GBR) **4635**
† C A B Newsletter (Conservazione negli Archivi e nelle Biblioteche) (ITA ISSN 1593-151X) **8938**
C A B S *see* Chemical Abstracts - Biochemistry Sections **714**
C A C Advisory (Citizens Advisory Council) (USA) **3407**
C A C D Journal (California Association for Counseling and Development) (USA ISSN 1052-3103) **7342**
C A C J Forum *see* Forum (North Hollywood) **4890**
C A C Newsletter (Chapter Activities Committee) (USA) **6892**
C A C P / A C C P Newsletter *see* C A C P Bulletin **2645**
C A C P Bulletin (Canadian Association of Chiefs of Police) (CAN ISSN 1719-6310) **2645**
C A C S A Broadsheet *see* Contemporary Art Centre of South Australia. Broadsheet **483**
C A C S Forum (Chemical Analysis Center Saitama University) (JPN) **2099**
• C A C T Advances (USA) **2038**
C A C y F (Circulo Argentino de Ciencia Ficcion y Fantasia) (ARG) **5440**
C.A. Ciudad/Arquitectura (CHL ISSN 0716-3622) **436**
C A D *see* Computer-Aided Design **3289**
C A D and Automation *see* C A D yu Zidonghua **3289**
C A D & Automation (Computer-Aided Design) (TWN) **2459**
C A D - C A M (Computer Aided Design - Computer Aided Manufacturing) (DEU ISSN 0723-1164) **3288**
• C A D - C A M (GBR ISSN 0963-5750) **3288**
C A D - C A M & Computer Graphics (GRC ISSN 1106-0077) **3288**
C A D / C A M / C A E Observer (Computer Aided Design / Computer Aided Manufacturing / Computer Aided Engineering) (LVA ISSN 1407-7183) **3288**
C A D - C A M - G I S World Annual (BGR) **3288**
C A D - C A M Report (Computer-Aided Design - Computer-Aided Manufacturing) (DEU ISSN 0930-7117) **3288**
• C A D / C A M Update (Computer-Aided Design / Computer-Aided Manufacturing) (USA) **3288**
• C A D Chat (Online Edition) (Canadian Association of the Deaf) (CAN ISSN 1199-0538) **6078**
C A D Chat (Print Edition) *see* C A D Chat (Online Edition) **6078**
C A D D. Computer Aided Draughting and Design *see* M C A D **3388**
† C A D D E T Analysis Series (Centre for the Analysis and Dissemination of Demonstrated Energy Technologies) (NLD ISSN 0925-0085) **8938**
C A D D M *see* Computer Aided Drafting, Design and Manufacturing **2483**
C A D Dealer (Computer-Aided Design) (GBR ISSN 1465-9743) **3288**
C A D Des (Computer-Aided Design) (GBR) **2588**
C A D - Info (Computer-Aided Design) (DEU) **3288**
C A D Magazine (FRA ISSN 1634-541X) **3288**
C A D Magazine (NLD ISSN 1386-1689) **2483**
C A D News (Computer Aided Design) (DEU) **3289**
C A D Plus (Computer Aided Design) (DEU ISSN 1436-3348) **3289**
C A D S *see* Committee on Class Actions & Derivative Suits **4646**
C A D - Schaltungsentwurf *see* Informationsdienst F I Z Technik. C A D - Schaltungsentwurf **3116**
C A D Update (Computer-Aided Design) (IRL) **3289**
C A D User (Computer-Aided Design) (GBR ISSN 0959-6259) **3289**
C A D User South East Asia (AUS ISSN 1323-0069) **3289**
C A D yu Zidonghua/C A D and Automation (TWN ISSN 1022-291X) **3289**
C A Design (Computer-Aided Design) (BRA ISSN 1413-2672) **3289**
C A E A L *see* Critical Approaches to Ethnic American Literature **5280**
➤ C A E D H H Journal/Association Canadienne des Enseignants(es) des Sourds(es) et des Malententendants(es). Revue (Canadian Association of Educators of the Deaf and Hard of Hearing) (CAN ISSN 1205-9765) **4072**
C A E Information Bulletin *see* Info Direct **3197**
C A E L Forum and News (Council for Adult and Experiential Learning) (USA ISSN 1528-6606) **2939**
C A E N Z Infodirect *see* Info Direct **3197**
C A E Newsletter (Chinese Academy of Engineering) (CHN) **3183**
• C A E P R News (Centre for Aboriginal Economic Policy Research) (AUS ISSN 1449-681X) **1077**
• C A E P R Working Paper (Australian National University, Centre for Aboriginal Economic Policy Research) (AUS ISSN 1442-3871) **3524**
• C A E R Working Paper (Centre for Applied Economic Research) (AUS ISSN 1329-1270) **1077**
C A E S A R Newsletter (Center of Advanced European Studies and Research) (DEU) **8417**
C A E T Journal *see* The Link **5928**
C A F I P Bulletin (Canadian Association for Israel Philately) (CAN) **6892**
C A F M System & Strategies (Year) (USA) **2529**
C A F O D Magazine (Catholic Fund for Overseas Development) (GBR) **7787**
C A F O D Report (Catholic Fund for Overseas Development) (GBR) **7787**
C A F P News (Colorado Academy of Family Physicians) (USA) **5590**
• C A F R A D Web News Letter (Centre Africain de Formation et de Recherche Administratives pour le Developpement) (MAR) **7425**
C A F R A News (Caribbean Association for Feminist Research and Action) (TTO ISSN 1016-9741) **8894**
C A F S Quarterly (University of Minnesota, Center for Advanced Feminist Studies) (USA) **8894**
C A F Working Papers *see* Centre for Analytical Finance. Working Papers Series **1326**
C A G L *see* Commentaria in Aristotelem Graeca **2233**
• C A G Newsletter (Canadian Association of Geographers) (CAN) **4001**
C A H P E R D Journal *see* Physical & Health Education Journal **7002**
C A H P E R D Journal/Times (California Association for Health, Physical Education, Recreation and Dance) (USA ISSN 0273-6896) **8164**
➤ C A H S Journal (Canadian Aviation Historical Society) (CAN ISSN 1207-1978) **50**
C A I C H A (Camara Argentina de la Industria de Chacinados y Afines) (ARG ISSN 0325-9331) **3629**
C A I D *see* Computer Abstracts **2442**
C A I Informa (Centro Argentino de Ingenieros) (ARG ISSN 0325-7525) **3183**
C A I P E Bulletin (Centre for the Advancement of Interprofessional Education) (GBR ISSN 1350-9160) **8029**
C A I's Journal of Community Association Law *see* The Journal of Community Association Law **4417**
C A J *see* Cambridge Archaeological Journal **386**
C A J Proceedings of Cement & Concrete *see* Semento, Konkurito Ronbunshu **1035**
C A L A S S (Congreso Asociacion Latina para el Analisis de los Sistemas de Salud) (ESP ISSN 1988-7914) **5590**
C A L C R I M *see* Judicial Council of California. Criminal Jury Instructions **4892**
➤ C A L I C O Journal (Computer Assisted Language Instruction Consortium) (USA ISSN 0742-7778) **2468**
C A L I C O. Monograph Series (Computer Assisted Language Instruction Consortium) (USA) **2969**
C A L I P S O *see* Conference Addresses of the Long Island Philosophical Society Online **6911**
C A L J I C Forms *see* California Jury Instructions - Criminal (C A L J I C) Forms **4885**
C A L L *see* Computer Assisted Language Learning **2468**
C A L L Bulletin (Chicago Association of Law Libraries) (USA) **4999**
C.A.L. - N-X-211 Collectors Society. Newsletter (USA) **50**
C A M *see* Chinese Annals of Mathematics. Series B **5478**
C A M (Complementary and Alternative Medicine) (GBR ISSN 1475-9403) **307**
C A M *see* Cambridge Alumni Magazine **2276**
C A M A C *see* Accreditation Manual for Ambulatory Care **4087**
C A M A C Bulletin (Computer Applications to Measurement and Control) (CHE ISSN 0374-2822) **2459**
C A M A C O L. Asamblea Nacional. Documento (Camara Colombiana de la Construccion) (COL) **988**
C A M A C O L Valle. Revista (Camara Colombiana de la Construccion) (COL ISSN 0122-3801) **3261**
C A M B H C *see* Comprehensive Accreditation Manual for Behavioral Health Care **8035**
C A M Directory (Complementary and Alternative Medicine) (GBR ISSN 1479-1218) **307**
• C A M E L (Central Asian Media Electronic Bulletin) (KGZ) **2314**
C A M E S *see* Computer Assisted Mechanics and Engineering Sciences **3375**

C A M E S E Compendium of Canadian Mining Suppliers (Canadian Association of Mining Equipment and Services for Export) (CAN ISSN 1485-8401) **4486**
C A M H *see* Child and Adolescent Mental Health **7344**
C A M H *see* Comprehensive Accreditation Manual for Hospitals **4091**
C A M H C *see* Comprehensive Accreditation Manual for Home Care **4091**
• C A M L Review/Revue de l'A C B M (Canadian Association of Music Libraries) (CAN ISSN 1496-9963) **6552**
C A M L T C *see* Comprehensive Accreditation Manual for Long Term Care **4091**
C A M M A C Toronto Region Newsletter (Canadian Amateur Musicians - Musiciens Amateurs du Canada) (CAN) **6552**
C A M M A News (Print) *see* C A A News (Sacramento, Online) **7585**
C A M Magazine (Construction Association of Michigan) (USA ISSN 0883-7880) **988**
C A M P Newsletter (Center for Advanced Material Processing) (USA) **3342**
• C A M S Magazine (Confederation of Australian Motor Sport) (AUS ISSN 1446-3911) **8164**
C A M S Manual of Motor Sport (Confederation of Australian Motor Sport) (AUS ISSN 1033-0526) **8164**
• C A Magazine (Chartered Accountant) (CAN ISSN 0317-6878) **1282**
• C A Magazine (Chartered Accountant) (GBR ISSN 1352-9021) **1282**
C A N A F E. Rapport Annuel *see* F I N T R A C Annual Report **1108**
C A N A, Inc. (Online Edition) *see* C A N A News **5953**
• C A N A News (California Association of Nurse Anesthetists) (USA) **5953**
C A N A R E P Infos Retraites (Caisse Nationale de Retraites Complementaires de l'Enseignement Prive) (FRA ISSN 1775-7894) **1857**
C A N B Gazette (Council of Archives of New Brunswick) (CAN) **4999**
• C A N F News (Cuban American National Foundation) (USA) **7203**
• C A N N T Journal (Canadian Association of Nephrology Nurses and Technologists) (CAN ISSN 1498-5136) **5953**
C A N S Digest of Social Legislation *see* Citizens Advice Notes Service **4642**
C A N S Digest on CD *see* Citizens Advice Notes Service **4642**
C A P *see* Companion Animal Practice **8795**
• C A P & Design (Computer Assisted Publishing) (SWE ISSN 1104-1099) **7579**
• The C A P Code (Committee on Advertising Practice Ltd.) (GBR ISSN 1479-8093) **22**
C A P E B infos (Marseille) (Confederation de l'Artisanat et des Petites Entreprises du Batiment) (FRA ISSN 1283-6516) **988**
• C A P E Outlook (Council for American Private Education) (USA ISSN 0271-1451) **2833**
C A P E S - Agregation. Anglais (Certificat d'Aptitude au Professorat de l'Enseignement du Second Degre) (FRA ISSN 1761-2918) **2969**
C A P E S - Agregation. Espagnol (Certificat d'Aptitude au Professorat de l'Enseignement du Second Degre) (FRA ISSN 1761-2942) **2969**
C A P E S - Agregation. Lettres (Certificat d'Aptitude au Professorat de l'Enseignement du Second Degre) (FRA ISSN 1761-2926) **2969**
C A P E S - Agregation. Mathematiques (Certificat d'Aptitude au Professorat de l'Enseignement du Second Degre) (FRA ISSN 1275-5176) **2969**
C A P E S - Agregation. Philosophie (Certificat d'Aptitude au Professorat de l'Enseignement du Second Degre) (FRA ISSN 1761-2934) **2969**
• C A P I C Review (Conferencia Economica Permanente de Investigacion Contable) (CHL ISSN 0718-4654) **1282**
C A P Journal (Canadian Association of Principals Journal) (CAN ISSN 1183-1995) **2833**
C A P Journal *see* Communicating Astronomy with the Public Journal **573**
C A P Legislation Quarterly (Common Agricultural Policy) (GBR ISSN 0953-5586) **98**
C A P Monitor (Common Agricultural Policy) (GBR ISSN 0142-5633) **98**
C A P P Brief (Council of Academic & Professional Publishers) (GBR ISSN 1466-0601) **7557**
C A P R A *see* Cave Archaeology & Palaeontology Research Archive **386**
C A P S Infos (Commerces Alimentaires Proximite Services) (FRA ISSN 1291-0732) **3676**
C A P S Report Newsletter (Christian Association for Psychological Studies, Inc.) (USA) **7629**
C A P S T Journal (Chinese Association of Professionals in Science and Technology) (USA ISSN 1545-7672) **3524**
C A P Sule (Levittown) (Children of Aging Parents) (USA ISSN 1076-4623) **4042**
• C A P Today (College of American Pathologists) (USA ISSN 0891-1525) **5590**
C A Quarterly (Creditanstalt-Bankverein) (AUT) **1445**
C A R *see* China Automotive Review **8574**
C A R *see* Class Action Reporter **4643**
C A R A Catholic Ministry Formation Directory (Center for Applied Research in the Apostolate) (USA ISSN 1092-9770) **7787**
C A R A F Books (Caribbean and African Literature Translated from French) (USA) **5267**
C A R A P H I N News (Caribbean Animal and Plant Health Information Network) (TTO ISSN 1018-1210) **98**
The C A R A Report (Center for Applied Research in the Apostolate) (USA ISSN 1089-5183) **7629**
C A R E C Surveillance Report *see* Communicable Diseases Feedback Report Surveillance Report **5811**
C A R F (Campaign Against Racism & Fascism) (GBR ISSN 0966-1050) **7111**
C A R I N G (USA ISSN 1551-9104) **5953**
C A R J *see* Canadian Association of Radiologists Journal **6193**
• C A R L Newsletter (Online) (California Academic and Research Librarians) (USA) **4999**
C A R L Newsletter (Print) *see* C A R L Newsletter (Online) **4999**
C A R N *see* Corporate Annual Report Newsletter **483**
C.A.R.N.E.S. *see* Computer Aided Research in Near Eastern Studies **4171**
• C A R P Fifty Plus (Canadian Association of Retired Persons) (CAN ISSN 1701-3674) **4042**
C A R - P G a Newsletter (Committee for the Advancement of Role-Playing Games) (USA ISSN 1071-7129) **8164**
C A R P News Fifty Plus *see* C A R P Fifty Plus **4042**
C A R R Review *see* Risk and Regulation **1168**
C A R T S Proceedings *see* Capacitor and Resistor Technology Symposium. Proceedings **3090**
C A R / U W O *see* Collectieve Arbeidsvoorwaarden voor de Sectie Gemeenten / Uitwerkingsovereenkomst **1670**
C A S *see* Critical Asian Studies **7228**
C A S *see* Comparative American Studies **7956**
C A S *see* British Institute of Learning Disabilities. Current Awareness Service **2931**
C A S *see* Construction Analysis System **994**
• C A S A Nyt (Center for Alternativ Samfundsanalyse) (DNK ISSN 0905-7218) **8091**
C A S B A A (Asia-Pacific Television) Directory *see* Media **29**
C A S B O Journal of School Business Management *see* California School Business **2834**
C A S C O N Proceedings (Center for Advanced Studies Conference) (CAN ISSN 1705-7345) **2408**
C A S Cade (GBR ISSN 1361-5882) **6089**
C A S E *see* International Workshop on Software Technology and Engineering Practice. Proceedings **2593**
C A S E A - A C E A S Newsletter (Canadian Association for Studies in Educational Administration) (CAN) **3018**
The C A S E International Journal of Educational Advancement *see* International Journal of Educational Advancement **2869**
The C A S E International Journal of Educational Advancement (Online) *see* International Journal of Educational Advancement (Online) **2869**
➤ C A S Journal (Catgut Acoustical Society) (USA ISSN 1053-7694) **6552**
C A S M E Newsletter (Centre for the Advancement of Science and Mathematics Education) (ZAF) **7842**
• C A S - Nyt (Statens Serum Institut, Centrale Afdeling for Sygehushygiejne) (DNK ISSN 0901-067X) **4089**
C A S S I *see* Chemical Abstracts Service Source Index **2093**
C A S S Journal of Law *see* Faxue Yanjiu **4671**
C A S S L Newspaper (Chartered Accountant Students' Society of London) (GBR) **1282**
C A S S Proceedings *see* Corporate Aviation Safety Seminar. Proceedings **52**
C A S Source Index Cumulative *see* Chemical Abstracts Service Source Index **2093**
C A S T M E Journal (Commonwealth Association of Science Technology & Math Educators) (GBR ISSN 0264-3138) **7842**
• C A S W Bulletin (Canadian Association of Social Workers) (CAN ISSN 1488-0296) **8029**
➤ C A S Y S (Computing Anticipatory Systems) (BEL ISSN 1373-5411) **2542**
• C A Selects (USA) **2085**
• ➤ C A Selects. Activated Carbon (USA ISSN 1045-8514) **2085**
• C A Selects. Adsorption (USA ISSN 1045-8506) **2085**
• C A Selects. Alkoxylated Oleochemicals (USA ISSN 1051-3884) **6888**
• C A Selects. Alkylation & Catalysts (USA ISSN 0895-5964) **2085**
• C A Selects. Allergy and Antiallergic Agents (USA ISSN 1047-8191) **5741**
• C A Selects. Alzheimer's Disease & Related Memory Dysfunctions (USA ISSN 1047-8183) **5741**
• C A Selects. Analytical Electrochemistry (USA ISSN 0160-8959) **2085**
• C A Selects. Anti-Inflammatory Agents and Arthritis (USA ISSN 0148-2394) **5741**
• C A Selects. Antibacterial Agents (USA ISSN 1045-8522) **2085**
• C A Selects. Antifungal & Antimycotic Agents (USA ISSN 1047-8167) **714**
• C A Selects. Antioxidants (USA ISSN 0275-7028) **2085**
• C A Selects. Artificial Sweeteners (USA ISSN 0890-1813) **3669**
• C A Selects. Atherosclerosis & Heart Disease (USA ISSN 0148-2378) **5741**
• C A Selects. Atomic Spectroscopy (USA ISSN 0195-4911) **7047**
• C A Selects. Beta-Lactam Antibiotics (USA ISSN 0148-2459) **6888**
• C A Selects. Biogenic Amines & the Nervous System (USA ISSN 0162-7716) **5741**
• C A Selects. Bismuth Chemistry (USA ISSN 1061-5342) **2085**
• C A Selects. Block & Graft Polymers (USA ISSN 0734-8851) **2085**
• C A Selects. Blood Coagulation (USA ISSN 0162-7732) **5742**
• C A Selects. Ceramic Materials (Journals) (USA ISSN 0895-5948) **2047**
• C A Selects. Ceramic Materials (Patents) (USA ISSN 0885-0100) **2047**
• C A Selects. Chelating Agents (USA ISSN 0734-8797) **2086**
• C A Selects. Chemical Engineering Operations (USA ISSN 1040-712X) **2086**
• C A Selects. Chemical Instrumentation (USA ISSN 0195-4938) **4490**
• C A Selects. Chemical Processing Apparatus (USA ISSN 0195-4946) **3237**
• C A Selects. Chemical Vapor Deposition (USA ISSN 0885-0119) **2086**
• C A Selects. Coal Science and Process Chemistry (USA ISSN 0146-4426) **2086**
• C A Selects. Coatings, Inks, & Related Products (USA ISSN 0275-7036) **6722**
• C A Selects. Colloids (Applied Aspects) (USA ISSN 0160-8967) **2086**
• C A Selects. Colloids (Macromolecular Aspects) (USA ISSN 0190-9444) **2086**
• C A Selects. Colloids (Physicochemical Aspects) (USA ISSN 0160-8975) **2086**
• C A Selects. Color Science (USA ISSN 0885-0127) **2086**
• C A Selects. Colorants and Dyes (USA ISSN 0734-8789) **2244**
• C A Selects. Composite Materials (Polymeric) (USA ISSN 1040-7154) **2086**
• C A Selects. Computers in Chemistry (USA ISSN 0160-9025) **2086**
• C A Selects. Conductive Polymers (USA ISSN 0885-0135) **2086**
• C A Selects. Corrosion (USA ISSN 0146-4434) **2086**
• C A Selects. Corrosion - Inhibiting Coatings (USA ISSN 0749-7296) **6722**
• C A Selects. Cosmetic Chemicals (USA ISSN 0275-7044) **592**
• C A Selects. Crosslinking Reactions (USA ISSN 0740-0721) **2086**
• C A Selects. Crystal Growth (USA ISSN 0162-7740) **2086**
• C A Selects. Detergents, Soaps, & Surfactants (USA ISSN 1524-5780) **2086**
• C A Selects. Distillation Technology (USA ISSN 0275-7052) **2086**
• C A Selects. Drilling Muds (USA ISSN 0749-730X) **6799**
• C A Selects. Drug Analysis Biological Fluids & Tissues (USA ISSN 1045-8530) **6888**
• C A Selects. Drug & Cosmetic Toxicity (USA ISSN 0162-7775) **6889**
• C A Selects. Elastomers (USA ISSN 1045-8557) **2086**
• C A Selects. Electrically Conductive Organics (USA ISSN 0885-0143) **2086**
• C A Selects. Electrochemical Organic Synthesis (USA ISSN 0734-8770) **2086**
• C A Selects. Electrochemical Reactions (USA ISSN 0146-4442) **2087**
• C A Selects. Electrodeposition (USA ISSN 0162-7783) **2087**
• C A Selects. Electron & Auger Spectroscopy (USA ISSN 0146-4450) **7047**
• C A Selects. Electron Spin Resonance (Chemical Aspects) (USA ISSN 0146-4469) **2087**
• C A Selects. Electronic Chemicals & Materials (USA ISSN 0885-0151) **2087**
• C A Selects. Emulsifiers and Demulsifiers (USA ISSN 0734-8754) **2087**
• C A Selects. Emulsion Polymerization (USA ISSN 0195-4970) **2087**
• C A Selects. Epoxy Resins (USA ISSN 0275-7060) **2087**
• C A Selects. Fats & Oils (USA ISSN 0275-7079) **2087**
• C A Selects. Fermentation Chemicals (USA ISSN 0740-0713) **2087**
• C A Selects. Fiber - Reinforced Plastics (USA ISSN 0734-869X) **7100**
• C A Selects. Flammability (USA ISSN 0162-7805) **2087**
• C A Selects. Fluidized Solids Technology (USA ISSN 0195-4989) **2087**
• C A Selects. Fluoropolymers (USA ISSN 0895-5921) **2087**
• C A Selects. Food & Feed Analysis (USA ISSN 0895-5913) **3669**
• C A Selects. Food, Drugs, & Cosmetics - Legislative & Regulatory Aspects (USA ISSN 1051-3914) **3669**
• C A Selects. Food Toxicity (USA ISSN 0162-7813) **2087**
• C A Selects. Formulation Chemistry (USA ISSN 0890-1880) **2087**
• C A Selects. Free Radicals (Biochemical Aspects) (USA ISSN 0895-5905) **714**
• C A Selects. Free Radicals (Organic Aspects) (USA ISSN 0895-5972) **2087**
• C A Selects. Fuel & Lubricant Additives (USA ISSN 0195-4997) **2087**
• C A Selects. Fungicides (USA ISSN 1524-5799) **176**
• C A Selects. Gaseous Waste Treatment (USA ISSN 0160-9076) **2087**
• C A Selects. Heat-Resistant and Ablative Polymers (USA ISSN 0162-7821) **2087**
• C A Selects. Herbicides (USA ISSN 1524-5802) **176**
• C A Selects. Hot-Melt Adhesives (USA ISSN 0895-5891) **2087**
• C A Selects. Infrared Spectroscopy (Organic Aspects) (USA ISSN 0190-9428) **2087**
• C A Selects. Infrared Spectroscopy (Physicochemical Aspects) (USA ISSN 0190-9436) **7047**
• C A Selects. Initiation of Polymerization (USA ISSN 0734-8843) **2088**
• C A Selects. Inorganic Analytical Chemistry (USA ISSN 0275-7087) **2088**
• C A Selects. Inorganic & Organometallic Reaction Mechanisms (USA ISSN 0195-5012) **2088**
• C A Selects. Inorganic Chemicals & Reactions (USA ISSN 0275-7095) **2088**
• C A Selects. Insecticides (USA ISSN 1524-5810) **176**
• C A Selects. Ion Chromatography (USA ISSN 0890-1899) **2088**
• C A Selects. Ion-Containing Polymers (USA ISSN 0195-5020) **2088**
• C A Selects. Ion Exchange (USA ISSN 0146-4493) **2088**
• C A Selects. Laser Applications (USA ISSN 0195-5039) **2088**
• C A Selects. Laser - Induced Chemical Reactions (USA ISSN 0885-0178) **2088**
• C A Selects. Liquid Crystals (USA ISSN 0148-2351) **2088**
• C A Selects. Lubricants, Greases, & Lubrication (USA ISSN 0734-8738) **2088**
• C A Selects. Membrane Separation (USA ISSN 1040-7197) **2088**
• C A Selects. Memory & Recording Devices & Materials (USA ISSN 0890-1821) **2088**
• C A Selects. Metallo Enzymes & Metallo Coenzymes (USA ISSN 0160-9114) **2088**
• C A Selects. Molecular Modeling (Biochemical Aspects) (USA ISSN 1059-2784) **2088**
• C A Selects. Natural Product Synthesis (USA ISSN 0740-0691) **2088**
• C A Selects. New Antibiotics (USA ISSN 0895-5875) **6889**
• C A Selects. New Books in Chemistry (USA ISSN 0148-2416) **2088**
• C A Selects. New Plastics (USA ISSN 0734-8673) **7100**
• C A Selects. Nonlinear Optical Materials (USA ISSN 0895-5867) **7047**
• C A Selects. Novel Natural Products (USA ISSN 0734-872X) **2088**
• C A Selects. Novel Pesticides & Herbicides (USA ISSN 0749-7318) **3229**
• C A Selects. Novel Polymers from Patents (USA ISSN 0734-8819) **6760**
• C A Selects. Novel Sulfur Heterocycles (USA ISSN 0275-7109) **2088**
• C A Selects. Occupational Exposure & Hazards (USA ISSN 1047-8124) **6690**
• C A Selects. Oleochemicals Containing Nitrogen (USA ISSN 1052-1976) **2089**
C A Selects on the Web *see* C A Selects **2085**
• C A Selects. Optical and Photosensitive Materials (USA ISSN 0195-5063) **7048**
• C A Selects. Optimization of Organic Reactions (USA ISSN 0195-5071) **2089**
• C A Selects. Organic Analytical Chemistry (USA ISSN 0275-7117) **2089**
• C A Selects. Organic Optical Materials (USA ISSN 0885-0186) **2089**
• C A Selects. Organic Reaction Mechanisms (USA ISSN 0162-7848) **2089**
• C A Selects. Organic Stereochemistry (USA ISSN 0195-508X) **2089**
• C A Selects. Organo-Transition Metal Complexes (USA ISSN 0160-9130) **2089**
• C A Selects. Organofluorine Chemistry (USA ISSN 0160-905X) **2089**
• C A Selects. Organometallics in Organic Synthesis (USA ISSN 0895-5859) **2089**
• C A Selects. Organophosphorus Chemistry (USA ISSN 0162-783X) **2089**
• C A Selects. Organosulfur Chemistry (Journals) (USA ISSN 1040-7189) **2089**
• C A Selects. Organotin Chemistry (USA ISSN 0195-5101) **2089**
• C A Selects. Osteoporosis & Related Bone Loss (USA ISSN 1047-8132) **5742**
• C A Selects. Oxidation Catalysts (USA ISSN 1040-7170) **2089**
• C A Selects. Oxide Superconductors (USA ISSN 1040-7219) **2089**
• C A Selects. Paint Additives (USA ISSN 0734-8762) **6722**
• C A Selects. Paper Additives (USA ISSN 0734-8711) **6740**
• C A Selects. Paper & Thin-Layer Chromatography (USA ISSN 0146-4515) **2089**

Title

• C A Selects. Paper Chemistry (USA ISSN 1040-7200) **2089**
• C A Selects. Pesticide Analysis (USA ISSN 1047-8140) **223**
• C A Selects. Pharmaceutical Chemistry (Journals) (USA ISSN 0890-1910) **6889**
• C A Selects. Pharmaceutical Chemistry (Patents) (USA ISSN 0890-1929) **6889**
• C A Selects. Phase Transfer Catalysis (USA ISSN 0885-0194) **2089**
• C A Selects. Photobiochemistry (USA ISSN 0148-2335) **2089**
• C A Selects. Photocatalysts (USA ISSN 1051-3949) **2089**
• C A Selects. Photochemical Organic Synthesis (USA ISSN 0885-0208) **2090**
• C A Selects. Photoresists (USA ISSN 0885-0216) **2090**
• C A Selects. Photosensitive Polymers (USA ISSN 0749-7326) **2090**
• C A Selects. Plastic Films (USA ISSN 0195-511X) **7100**
• C A Selects. Plastics Additives (USA ISSN 0734-8681) **7100**
• C A Selects. Plastics Fabrication & Uses (USA ISSN 0275-7125) **7100**
• C A Selects. Plastics Manufacture & Processing (USA ISSN 0275-7133) **7100**
• C A Selects. Platinum and Palladium Chemistry (USA ISSN 0890-1937) **2090**
• C A Selects Plus. Adhesives (USA ISSN 1083-2726) **2090**
• C A Selects Plus. Amino Acids, Peptides and Proteins (USA ISSN 1083-2750) **714**
• C A Selects Plus. Antitumor Agents (USA ISSN 1083-2661) **5742**
• C A Selects Plus. Asymmetric Synthesis & Induction (USA ISSN 1084-2306) **2090**
• C A Selects Plus. Batteries & Fuel Cells (USA ISSN 1083-267X) **2090**
• C A Selects Plus. Carbohydrates (Chemical Aspects) (USA ISSN 1084-2314) **2090**
• C A Selects Plus. Carbon & Heteroatom N M R (USA ISSN 1083-2793) **2090**
• C A Selects Plus. Carcinogens, Mutagens & Teratogens (USA ISSN 1084-2322) **5742**
• C A Selects Plus. Catalysis (Applied & Physical Aspects) (USA ISSN 1083-2777) **2090**
• C A Selects Plus. Catalysis (Organic Reactions) (USA ISSN 1083-2785) **2090**
• C A Selects Plus. Chemical Hazards, Health & Safety (USA ISSN 1083-2769) **6690**
• C A Selects Plus. Controlled Release Technology (USA ISSN 1084-2330) **2090**
• C A Selects Plus. Drug Delivery Systems & Dosage Forms (USA ISSN 1084-2349) **6889**
• C A Selects Plus. Electrophoresis (USA ISSN 1084-0036) **2090**
• C A Selects Plus. Environmental Pollution (USA ISSN 1084-0044) **3477**
• C A Selects Plus. Enzyme Applications (USA ISSN 1084-2357) **2090**
• C A Selects Plus. Flavors & Fragrances (USA ISSN 1083-2688) **592**
• C A Selects Plus. Forensic Chemistry (USA ISSN 1084-2365) **2090**
• C A Selects Plus. Gas Chromatography (USA ISSN 1083-2734) **2090**
• C A Selects Plus. Gel Permeation Chromatography (USA ISSN 1084-290X) **2090**
• C A Selects Plus. High Performance Liquid Chromatography (USA ISSN 1083-2815) **2090**
• C A Selects Plus. Liquid Waste Treatment (USA ISSN 1084-2381) **2090**
• C A Selects Plus. Mass Spectrometry (USA ISSN 1083-2742) **2091**
• C A Selects Plus. Organosilicon Chemistry (USA ISSN 1083-2653) **2091**
• C A Selects Plus. Pharmaceutical Analysis (USA ISSN 1084-239X) **6889**
• C A Selects Plus. Photochemistry (USA ISSN 1083-270X) **2091**
• C A Selects Plus. Pollution Monitoring (USA ISSN 1084-0079) **3477**
• C A Selects Plus. Polyurethanes (USA ISSN 1083-2696) **2091**
• C A Selects Plus. Recovery & Recycling of Wastes (USA ISSN 1084-0087) **2091**
• C A Selects Plus. Solid & Radioactive Waste Treatment (USA ISSN 1084-0095) **2091**
• C A Selects Plus. Ultrafiltration (USA ISSN 1084-0117) **2091**
• C A Selects Plus. Water Treatment (USA ISSN 1084-0109) **2091**
• C A Selects Plus. Zeolites (USA ISSN 1083-2718) **2091**
• C A Selects. Polyacrylates (Journals) (USA ISSN 0890-1945) **2091**
• C A Selects. Polyacrylates (Patents) (USA ISSN 1045-8549) **2091**
• C A Selects. Polyesters (USA ISSN 0734-8703) **2091**
• C A Selects. Polyimides (USA ISSN 0895-5840) **2091**
• C A Selects. Polymer Blends (USA ISSN 0734-8827) **2091**
• C A Selects. Polymer Degradation (USA ISSN 0734-8835) **2091**
• C A Selects. Polymer Morphology (USA ISSN 0195-5128) **2091**
• C A Selects. Polymerization Kinetics & Process Control (USA ISSN 0885-0224) **2091**
• C A Selects. Porphyrins (USA ISSN 0195-5136) **2091**
• C A Selects. Prostaglandins (USA ISSN 0148-2343) **2091**
• C A Selects. Proton Magnetic Resonance (USA ISSN 0190-941X) **2092**
• C A Selects. Psychobiochemistry (USA ISSN 0362-9848) **714**
• C A Selects. Quaternary Ammonium Compounds (USA ISSN 0890-1953) **2092**
• C A Selects. Radiation Chemistry (USA ISSN 0146-4523) **2092**
• C A Selects. Radiation Curing (USA ISSN 0749-7342) **2092**
• C A Selects. Raman Spectroscopy (USA ISSN 0148-2432) **2092**
• C A Selects. Selenium & Tellurium Chemistry (USA ISSN 0749-7350) **6338**
• C A Selects. Silicas & Silicates (USA ISSN 0890-1961) **2092**
• C A Selects. Siloxanes & Silicones (USA ISSN 0895-5832) **2092**
• C A Selects. Silver Chemistry (USA ISSN 0148-2440) **6338**
• C A Selects. Solar Energy (USA ISSN 0148-236X) **3151**
• C A Selects. Solid State N M R (Nuclear Magnetic Resonance) (USA ISSN 0895-5824) **2092**
• C A Selects. Solvent Extraction (USA ISSN 0146-4531) **2092**
• C A Selects. Spectrochemical Analysis (USA ISSN 0885-0232) **2092**
• C A Selects. Steroids (Biochemical Aspects) (USA ISSN 0160-9173) **714**
• C A Selects. Steroids (Chemical Aspects) (USA ISSN 0160-9181) **2092**
• C A Selects. Structure - Activity Relationships (USA ISSN 0895-5816) **2092**
• C A Selects. Surface Analysis (USA ISSN 0195-5152) **2092**
• C A Selects. Surface Chemistry (Physicochemical Aspects) (USA ISSN 0146-454X) **2092**
• C A Selects. Synfuels (USA ISSN 0195-5160) **2092**
• C A Selects. Synthetic High Polymers (USA ISSN 0275-7168) **2092**
• C A Selects. Synthetic Macrocyclic Compounds (USA ISSN 0195-5179) **2092**
• C A Selects. Thermal Analysis (USA ISSN 0195-5187) **2092**
• C A Selects. Thermochemistry (USA ISSN 0162-7864) **2092**
• C A Selects. Trace Element Analysis (USA ISSN 0160-919X) **2093**
• C A Selects. Water - Based Coatings (USA ISSN 0749-7369) **6722**
• C A Selects. X-Ray Analysis & Spectroscopy (USA ISSN 0162-7872) **7048**
C A T *see* Civil Aviation Training **8539**
C A T (Car & Accessory Trader) (GBR) **8570**
C A T E *see* Cities and the Environment **3410**
➤ C A T M O G (Concepts and Techniques in Modern Geography) (GBR ISSN 0306-6142) **4001**
The C A T O Handbook for Congress *see* C A T O Handbook on Policy **7111**
C A T O Handbook on Policy (USA ISSN 1936-038X) **7111**
C A T O Supreme Court Review *see* Cato Supreme Court Review **4947**
C A T S *see* Corporate Air Travel Survey **8540**
C A Techniek *see* Machinebouw **2462**
C A U C E Bulletin (CAN) **2939**
C A U S Color Forecasts (Color Association of the United States) (USA) **2245**
C A U S Effect (Color Association of the United States) (USA) **2246**
C A U S News *see* C A U S Effect **2246**
• C A U T Bulletin/A C P P U Bulletin (Canadian Association of University Teachers) (CAN ISSN 0834-9614) **2969**
C A U T Legal Advisory (Canadian Association of University Teachers) (CAN ISSN 1718-4371) **4635**
C A U T Legal Review/Revue de Droit de l'A C P P U/Revue de Droit de l'Association Canadienne des Professeures et Professeurs d'Universite (Canadian Association of University Teachers) (CAN ISSN 1718-4401) **4635**
C A V *see* Chemie-Anlagen und Verfahren **3240**
• C A V A L Annual Report (AUS ISSN 0157-4752) **4999**
• C A V A L Newsletter (AUS ISSN 0155-7025) **4999**
C A V - C P P Top Products (Chemie-Anlagen und Verfahren - Chemical Plants and Processing) (DEU) **3237**
C A W P News and Notes (Center for the American Woman and Politics) (USA ISSN 1060-3670) **8894**
C & C: Creativity and Cognition Conference. Proceedings (USA) **2408**
C & C R *see* Chronology and Catastrophism Review **6910**
C & D R *see* Construction & Demolition Recycling **3505**
C and D Recycler Equipment & Services Buyers' Guide *see* C & D Recycler Equipment & Services Buyers' Guide **3504**
C & D Recycler Equipment & Services Buyers' Guide (USA) **3504**
C & I T *see* Conference and Incentive Travel **8694**
C & R L *see* College & Research Libraries **5002**
C & R L *see* College & Research Libraries News **5003**
C & S C *see* Classic & Sports Car **8574**
C & T *see* Allured's Cosmetics and Toiletries **592**
C B *see* Collection Building **5002**
C B A A News (Christian Bookselling Association of Australia Inc.) (AUS) **7557**
C B A Annual Report (Council for British Archaeology) (GBR ISSN 0589-9028) **385**
C B A B *see* Crop Breeding and Applied Biotechnology **762**
C B A B *see* Commercial, Banking & Bankruptcy Law **4646**
C B A Fanfare (CAN ISSN 1487-9123) **6552**
C B A Legal Directory *see* Cincinnati Bar Association. Report **4642**
C B A Market Place *see* C B A Retailers + Resources **7557**
C B A Marketplace *see* C B A Retailers + Resources **7557**
C B A Newsletter (Continental Basketball Association) (USA) **8224**
C B A Newsnotes (Congressional Black Associates) (USA) **7425**
• C B A Record (Chicago Bar Association) (USA ISSN 0892-1822) **4635**
C B A Research Reports (Council for British Archaeology) (GBR ISSN 0589-9036) **385**
C B A Retailers + Resources (Christian Booksellers Association) (USA ISSN 1941-9600) **7557**
C B & E *see* California Builder & Engineer **989**
C B B *see* Cell Biochemistry and Biophysics **829**
C B C A Business *see* Canadian Business and Current Affairs Business **1219**
C B C A Complete *see* Canadian Business and Current Affairs Complete **1219**
C B C A Current Events *see* Canadian Business and Current Affairs Current Events **1219**
C B C A Education *see* Canadian Business and Current Affairs Education **2931**
C B C A Fulltext Business *see* Canadian Business and Current Affairs Business **1219**
C B C A Fulltext Education *see* Canadian Business and Current Affairs Education **2931**
C B C A Fulltext Reference *see* Canadian Business and Current Affairs Reference **5**
C B C A NEWS (Children's Book Council of Australia) (AUS) **7557**
C B C A Reference *see* Canadian Business and Current Affairs Reference **5**
C B C Classical Record Reference Book (Canadian Broadcasting Corporation) (CAN ISSN 0711-9828) **6552**
C B C Features (Children's Book Council, Inc.) (USA) **7557**
C B C Gijutsu Hokokukai/C B C Technical Information (Chubu - Nippon Broadcasting Co.) (JPN ISSN 0288-9323) **2377**
• C B C / Radio Canada Annual Report (CAN ISSN 1912-239X) **2314**
C B C - T V News in Review (CAN ISSN 1185-2321) **2377**
C B C Technical Information *see* C B C Gijutsu Hokokukai **2377**
• C B C Web-Mag (Comic Books Collectors) (USA) **480**
• C B D News (Convention on Biological Diversity) (CAN ISSN 1020-9018) **663**
C B D Weekly Release (Commerce Business Daily) (USA) **7425**
C B E Environmental Review (Citizens for a Better Environment) (USA ISSN 0886-8298) **2605**
• ➤ C B E Life Sciences Education (Cell Biology Education) (USA ISSN 1931-7913) **828**
C B E R S Ex-press *see* C B E R S Network **8029**
• C B E R S Network (Christian Brothers Ex-Residents and Students) (AUS ISSN 1835-8454) **8029**
C B G *see* Classic Bike Guide **8256**
C B H S Newsletter (Children's Books History Society) (GBR) **7557**
C B I A C Newsletter *see* Chemical and Biological Defense Information Analysis Center. Newsletter **3237**
C B I A News (USA ISSN 0199-686X) **1445**
C B I Annual Report (Confederation of British Industry) (GBR ISSN 0268-2273) **1077**
C B I Distributive Trades Survey (Confederation of British Industry) (GBR) **1809**
C B I Economic and Business Outlook (Confederation of British Industry) (GBR ISSN 1471-342X) **1445**
C B I. Human Resources Report (Confederation of British Industry) (GBR ISSN 1362-4482) **1668**
C B I Informerar (Cement- och Betong Institutet) (SWE ISSN 0282-6283) **988**
C B I Journal *see* Chem-Bio Informatics Journal **2107**
C B I Magazine *see* Club Business International **1958**
C B I Monthly Industrial Trends Survey (Confederation of British Industry) (GBR) **1077**
C B I Nytt (Cement- och Betonginstitutet) (SWE ISSN 0349-2060) **988**
• C B I P Newsletter (Central Board of Irrigation and Power) (IND) **8819**
C B I - Pannel Kerr Forster - S M E Trends Report (Confederation of British Industry) (GBR) **1958**
C B I - PriceWaterhouseCoopers Financial Services Survey (Confederation of British Industry) (GBR) **1077**
C B I Quarterly Industrial Trends Survey (Confederation of British Industry) (GBR ISSN 1752-7333) **1077**
C B I Rapporter - Reports (Cement- och Betong Institutet) (SWE ISSN 0346-8240) **988**
C B-Kurier (DEU) **2357**
C B L Journal *see* Cyberbanking & Law **1334**
C B L R *see* Columbia Business Law Review **4645**
C B M (Computer Business Magazine) (NLD ISSN 1388-218X) **2491**
C B M C Insider (USA) **1077**
C B M Freundesbrief (Christoffel-Blindenmission e.V.) (DEU ISSN 1615-1054) **8029**
C B M News (Certified Ballast Manufacturers) (USA ISSN 0007-7941) **3296**
C B M R Digest (Center for Black Music Research) (USA ISSN 1043-1241) **6552**
C B M R Monographs (Center for Black Music Research) (USA ISSN 1042-8836) **6552**
C B M S *see* I E E E Symposium on Computer - Based Medical Systems. Proceedings **5831**
➤ C B M S - N S F Regional Conference Series in Applied Mathematics (Conference Board of the Mathematical Sciences - National Science Foundation) (USA ISSN 0163-9439) **5476**
• C B News Communication (FRA ISSN 1623-4480) **1077**
C B O E Market Statistics (Chicago Board Options Exchange) (USA ISSN 0146-731X) **1614**
C B Q *see* Communication Booknotes Quarterly **2347**
C B Q M S *see* Catholic Bible Quarterly Monograph Series **7630**
C B R *see* Computer Business Review **2491**
C B R *see* Currents in Biblical Research **7636**
C B R Annual Report (BEL) **988**
C B R Construction Business Review (USA ISSN 1059-406X) **988**
C B R L Bulletin *see* Council for British Research in the Levant. Bulletin **388**
C B R Magazine (Classic Bike Rider) (USA ISSN 1536-4925) **8256**
C B R N Research and Technology Initiative. Annual Report *see* C R T I Annual Report **6414**
The C B Radio Story (Citizens Band) (USA) **2357**
C B S *see* Cardinal Bea Studies **7787**
C B S A Capsules (Copper & Brass Servicenter Association) (USA) **6307**
C B S G News (Conservation Breeding Specialist Group) (CHE) **2605**
† C B S Newsletter (Centraalbureau voor Schimmelcultures) (NLD ISSN 0169-6289) **8938**
C B S O Music Stand *see* MusicStand **6595**
• C B S Observer (Copenhagen Business School) (DNK ISSN 1903-4091) **1077**
• C B S Soaps in Depth (USA ISSN 1533-967X) **2377**
C B T - Computer Based Training (DEU ISSN 0942-7430) **2468**
C B U *see* China Automotive Review **8574**
C B W *see* Coach & Bus Week **8493**
▼ C B W Magazine (IND ISSN 0974-0619) **3237**
C++ Builder Developer's Journal (USA) **2505**
C C *see* Cabling Connection **2314**
C. C. (FIN ISSN 1795-4568) **3838**
• C C A Advocate (Community College Association) (USA) **2969**
C C: A & H *see* Current Contents: Arts & Humanities **4484**
C C: A B & E S *see* Current Contents: Agriculture, Biology & Environmental Sciences **178**
C C A B Circulate (Canadian Circulations Audit Board, Inc.) (CAN) **22**
C C A C Review (California College of Arts and Crafts) (USA ISSN 0045-3919) **2275**
C C A H T E *see* Canadian Creative Arts in Health, Training and Education **5591**
➤ C C - A I (Communication & Cognition - Artificial Intelligence) (BEL ISSN 0773-4182) **5202**
C C A I Monthly News Letter (Coal Consumers Association of India) (IND ISSN 0376-7787) **6459**
C C A M *see* Clavis Commentariorum Antiquitatis et Medii Aevi **2233**
• ➤ C C A M L R Science (Commission for the Conservation of Antarctic Marine Living Resources) (AUS ISSN 1023-4063) **2801**
C C A News (Consumer Credit Association) (GBR) **1322**
C C A News (Christian Conference of Asia) (THA ISSN 0129-9891) **7629**
C C A R Journal (Central Conference of American Rabbis) (USA ISSN 1058-8760) **7719**
C C A S Newsletter (Council of Colleges of Arts & Sciences) (USA) **2969**
C C: Agriculture, Biology & Environmental Sciences *see* Current Contents: Agriculture, Biology & Environmental Sciences **178**
C C & I (Control de Calidad & Inspeccion) (URY) **3587**
C C: Arts & Humanities *see* Current Contents: Arts & Humanities **4484**
• C C B D Newsletter (Council for Children with Behavioral Disorders) (USA) **3037**
▼ • C C B J Weekly News (Climate Change Business Journal) (USA ISSN 1941-6156) **3407**
C C Blaetter (DEU) **2264**
C C C *see* College Composition and Communication **3055**
C C C C Bulletin (Canadian Council of Christian Charities) (CAN ISSN 0838-6803) **8029**

Title

C E I see Clinical and Experimental Immunology 5756
• ➤ C E I C. Papeles (Centro de Estudios sobre la Identidad Colectiva) (ESP ISSN 1695-6494) 8091
▼ C E I M I G R A. Anuario (Centro de Estudios para la Integracion Social y Formacion de Inmigrantes) (ESP ISSN 1888-3044) 7278
C E I M Revista (Confederacion Empresarial de Madrid) (ESP) 480
• C E I - P E A Alert (Center for Education Innovation - Public Education Association) (USA) 2833
C E I Update (Competitive Enterprise Institute) (USA ISSN 1086-3036) 1077
C E International (Ceramica Edilizia) (ITA ISSN 1970-3392) 988
C E J. Revista (Centro de Estudios Judiciarios) (BRA ISSN 1414-008X) 4635
C E Journal see The Journal of Conscious Evolution 7371
C E Kensetsu Gyoukai/Civil Engineering Construction (Civil Engineering) (JPN ISSN 1349-2799) 3261
C E L A A N (Centre Etudes Litteratures Arts Afrique Nord) (USA ISSN 1547-1942) 5268
➤ C E L E A Journal (CHN) 5102
• C E L E Journal (Center for English Language Education) (JPN ISSN 1345-4854) 5102
C E L L S see California Educational Linkages in the Life Sciences 664
C E L S S Gakkaishi see C E L S S Journal 663
C E L S S Journal/C E L S S Gakkaishi (Japan Society for Controlled Ecological and Life Support Systems) (JPN ISSN 0915-4353) 663
C E L S S News (Japan Society for Controlled Ecological and Life Support Systems) (JPN ISSN 0917-4869) 663
C E L U L R see Communications Environmental & Land Use Law Report 2367
• C E M A Bulletin (Online) (Conveyor Equipment Manufacturers Association) (USA) 5450
C E M A Bulletin (Print) see C E M A Bulletin (Online) 5450
C E M A Consumer Electronics (Cores European Market Analysis) (GBR) 3090
C E M A G R E F. Gestion des Milieux Aquatiques. Etudes (Centre National de Machinisme Agricole du Genie Rural des Eaux et des Forets) (FRA ISSN 1272-4661) 210
C E M A G R E F. Groupement de Bordeaux. Etude (Centre National de Machinisme Agricole du Genie Rural des Eaux et des Forets) (FRA ISSN 0992-4302) 210
➤ C E M A M Reports (Centre pour l'Etude du Monde Arabe Moderne) (LBN) 545
C E M A Personal Computers and Peripherals (Cores European Market Analysis) (GBR) 2575
C E M A R E Miscellaneous Publications (University of Portsmouth, Centre for the Economics and Management of Aquatic Resources) (GBR) 3587
C E M A R E Reports (University of Portsmouth, Centre for the Economics and Management of Aquatic Resources) (GBR) 3587
C E M A Telecommunications (Cores European Market Analysis) (GBR) 2366
C E M L A Boletin Bimensual see Centro de Estudios Monetarios Latinoamericanos. Boletin Bimensual 1326
C E M O T I see Cahiers d'Etudes sur la Mediterranee Orientale et le Monde Turco-Iranien 7112
▼ C E M U S. Skriftserie (Centrum foer Miljoe- och Utvecklingsstudier) (SWE ISSN 1654-8744) 7951
C E Magazine see The Air Force Civil Engineer 3259
• C E Markt (Consumer Electronics) (DEU ISSN 1435-1145) 3090
• C E N D A (Centro Nacional de Derecho de Autor) (CUB ISSN 1607-6087) 7557
• C E N D O T E C Dossier (Centro Franco-Brasileiro de Documentacao Tecnica e Cientifica Dossier) (BRA ISSN 1518-8744) 8417
C E N S I S Note e Commenti (Centro Studi Investimenti Sociali) (ITA ISSN 1128-9163) 8091
C E N T R A Health Magazine (USA) 4089
C E N Y C Environmental Bulletin (Council on the Environment of New York City) (USA) 3407
C E News (USA ISSN 1051-9629) 3261
C E O (Chief Executive Officer) (GBR) 1731
• C E O (POL ISSN 1734-9478) 1414
C E O & C I O (CHN) 1077
C E O Brief see Chief Executive Magazine 1733
C E O Forum (Chief Executive Officer) (AUS ISSN 1833-1254) 1731
C E O Intelligence Quotient Magazine see C E O Q Magazine 1731
C E O M Annual Report see Catholic Education Office. Annual Report 7788
▼ • C E O Q Magazine (Chief Executive Officer Quarterly) (USA ISSN 1943-8532) 1731
C E O Refresher see The CEO Refresher 1732
• The C E O Report (USA) 1323
• C E O Traveler (USA ISSN 1529-4617) 8690
• ➤ C E Optometry (Continuing Education) (GBR ISSN 1367-899X) 6039
C E P see Comparative European Politics 7227
C E P see Chemical Engineering Progress 3239
C E P A. Annual Report (Canadian Environmental Protection Act) (CAN ISSN 1488-8556) 3407
C E P A L Cuadernos (Comision Economica para America Latina y el Caribe) (CHL ISSN 0252-2195) 1422
• C E P A L Review (Comision Economica para America Latina y el Caribe) (CHL ISSN 0251-2920) 1445
C E P A L Studies and Reports see Estudios e Informes de la C E P A L 1595
• C E P A O S Review (Centro de Estudos e Pesquisas Armando de Oliveira Souza) (BRA ISSN 1533-6476) 2833
C E P I I Lettre (Centre d'Etudes Prospectives et d'Informations Internationales) (FRA ISSN 0243-1947) 1445
C E P Journal/Journal S C E P (Communications, Energy and Paperworkers Union of Canada) (CAN) 6732
C E P M L P Conference Proceedings (Centre for Energy, Petroleum and Mineral Law and Policy) (GBR) 3408
• C E P M L P Internet Journal (Centre for Energy, Petroleum and Mineral Law and Policy) (GBR) 2703
• C E P News (Regional Co-ordinating Unit) (JAM) 3504
C E P R E M A P. Collection (Centre pour la Recherche Economique et ses Applications) (FRA ISSN 1951-7637) 1536
C E P Report (Council on Economic Priorities) (USA ISSN 0196-9021) 1445
C E P Reports and C E P Books (Council on Economic Priorities) (USA) 2635
C E P Research Report (Council on Economic Priorities) (USA ISSN 0898-4328) 2635
C E P S Financial Markets Unit Research Report see Centre for European Policy Studies. Financial Markets Unit. Research Report 1326
C E P S Papers (Centre for European Policy Studies) (BEL ISSN 0962-3876) 7224
C E P S Research Reports (Centre for European Policy Studies) (BEL) 1077
C E P S Task Force Reports see Centre for European Policy Studies. Task Force Reports 1616
C E P S Working Documents (Centre for European Policy Studies) (BEL) 7224
C E P Technical Report (Regional Co-ordinating Unit) (JAM) 3504
• C E Pro (Custom Electronics) (USA ISSN 1521-3307) 3090
▼ C E Pro Showroom (Custom Electronics) (USA ISSN 1945-0397) 3090
C E R see Central Europe Review 5210
C E R see Comparative Education Review 2838
C E R A see Concurrent Engineering: Research and Applications 2470
C E R A European Power Watch see European Power Watch 3134
C E R A News (Citizens Equal Rights Alliance) (USA) 6634
C E R C Instruction Reports see U.S. Coastal Engineering Research Center. Instruction Reports 2819
C E R C Miscellaneous Papers Series see Coastal Engineering Research Center. Miscellaneous Report 2802
C E R C Technical Reports see U.S. Coastal Engineering Research Center. Technical Reports 2819
The C E R Cular (U.S. Coastal Engineering Research Center) (USA) 2801
C E R E G E. Centre de Recherche en Gestion (Centre Europeen de Recherche et d'Enseignement des Geosciences de l' Environnement) (FRA ISSN 0994-7205) 1731
• ➤ C E R G E - E I Working Paper Series (Center for Economic Research and Graduate Education - Economics Institute) (CZE ISSN 1211-3298) 1078
C E R M see Civil Engineering Research Magazine 8941
• ➤ C E R N Courier (GBR ISSN 0304-288X) 7065
C E R N - H E R A Reports (CHE ISSN 0366-5690) 7065
C E R N Reports (CHE ISSN 0007-8328) 7065
C E R N School of Computing. Proceedings (CHE ISSN 0304-2898) 7939
C E R N School of Physics. Proceedings (CHE ISSN 0531-4283) 7065
C E S see Comparative Economic Studies 1537
† C E S A. Bulletin/Societe Canadienne d'Etudes Ethniques. Bulletin (CAN) 8938
C E S A. Les Fiches see Question' Air 6442
C E S Daily News (USA) 6278
C E S E T. Atti degli Incontri di Studio see C E S E T. Incontro di Studio 195
• C E S E T. Incontro di Studio (Centro di Studi di Estimo e di Economia Territoriale) (ITA ISSN 1826-2481) 195
• C E S - I F O Bulletin (Center for Economic Studies) (DEU) 1078
C E S - I F O - D I C E Report see D I C E Report 1089
• C E S - I F O Economic Studies (Center for Economic Studies - Ifo Institute for Economic Research) (GBR ISSN 1610-241X) 1078
• C E S - I F O Forum (Center for Economic Studies) (DEU ISSN 1615-245X) 1078
C E S - I F O Research Reports (DEU ISSN 1612-880X) 1078
• C E S - I F O Working Papers (Center for Economic Studies) (DEU) 1078
C E S - I F O World Economic Survey (DEU ISSN 1613-6012) 1078
C E S Odontologia (Institut de Ciencias de la Salud) (COL ISSN 0120-971X) 5837
C E S P see Ceramic Engineering and Science Proceedings 2038
C E S Prospectus (Cleveland Engineering Society) (USA ISSN 1077-6192) 3183
➤ C E S U M A R. Revista (Centro Universitario de Maringa) (BRA ISSN 1516-2664) 7951
C E T see Chemical Engineering and Technology 3238
C E T 500 see Consultant Engineers and Technologies 500 1981
C E T China Educational Technology see Zhongguo Dianhua Jiaoyu 2928
C E T I M E News/'Asda' al-Markiz at-Yaqni li-Assina'at al-Mikanikiyat Wa'al-Kahruba'iyat (Centre Technique des Industries Mecaniques et Electriques) (TUN ISSN 1737-7048) 3296
• C E T I M Informations (Centre Technique des Industries Mecaniques) (FRA ISSN 0399-0001) 7057
• C E T. Revista de Ciencias Exactas e Ingenieria (Ciencias Exactas y Tecnologia) (ARG ISSN 1668-8910) 7842
C E Tips see First Glimpse 3099
➤ C E U Privatization Reports (Privatization Project) (HUN) 1536
C E W Express see Canada Employment Weekly 1669
C F A A see The Canadian Fire Alarm Association 3576
• C F A Digest (Chartered Financial Analyst) (USA ISSN 0046-9777) 1323
• C F A Institute Conference Proceedings Quarterly (Chartered Financial Analyst) (USA ISSN 1930-2703) 1614
• C F A Magazine (Chartered Financial Analyst) (USA ISSN 1543-1398) 1323
C F A News (Washington) (Consumer Federation of America) (USA ISSN 0732-8281) 2635
• C F A Newsletter (Commonwealth Forestry Association) (GBR ISSN 1750-6417) 3685
C F A Q see Chapman Family Association Quarterly 3762
C - F A R Newsletter (Citizens for Foreign Aid Reform Inc.) (CAN ISSN 0826-4228) 1592
C F & F S see Contemporary French and Francophone Studies 5278
C F & Y's Foodservice Information Systems Report (Computers, Foodservice & You) (USA ISSN 1523-8644) 2535
C F Apartment Reporter (Clayton-Fillmore, Ltd.) (USA) 7585
C F B Cold Lake Courier (Canadian Forces Base) (CAN ISSN 0045-8872) 6414
C F B Comox Totem Times (Canadian Forces Base Comox) (CAN) 6414
C F B T see Child & Family Behavior Therapy 7344
C F-Blad see Cystisk Fibrose 5603
C F C A Actualites see Coop de France Infos 102
C F D see Contemporary Film Directors 6494
† C F D T en Direct (Confederation Francaise Democratique du Travail) (FRA ISSN 1270-1343) 8938
C F D T Magazine (Confederation Francaise Democratique du Travail) (FRA ISSN 0395-5621) 7951
C F D T. Revue see Confederation Francaise Democratique du Travail. Revue 4592
C F D Wakushoppu Seika Hokokushu (JPN) 3375
C F E Newsletter (Canadian Film Editors) (CAN ISSN 1719-9883) 6491
• C F I A's Biotechnology Highlights Report (Canadian Food Inspection Agency) (CAN ISSN 1711-0114) 762
C F I Focus (FRA ISSN 1769-292X) 2357
C F I International Directory (GBR) 2246
The C F Industrial Reporter (USA) 7585
C F J see Contract Flooring Journal 4535
C F - Journal Diabetes Aktuell fuer die Praxis (Conzema Fortbildungs) (DEU ISSN 1611-2520) 5884
C F - Journal fuer die Aerztliche Praxis see C F - Journal Diabetes Aktuell fuer die Praxis 5884
• C F K- Kortrapport (Centrum foer Konsumentvetenskap) (SWE ISSN 1653-8021) 1809
C F M A see Classiques Francais du Moyen Age 5274
C F M A Building Profits (Construction Financial Management Association) (USA ISSN 1078-2435) 988
• C F N S News (Calgary Field Naturalists' Society) (CAN ISSN 1910-202X) 3408
C F Nieuws see Nederlandse Cystic Fibrosis Stichting. C F Nieuws 6216
• C F O (Chief Financial Officer) (AUS ISSN 1325-9407) 1078
C F O (Chief Financial Officer) (POL ISSN 1732-5617) 1078
• C F O (Chief Financial Officer) (USA ISSN 8756-7113) 1078
C F O & Controller Alert (Chief Financial Officer) (USA ISSN 1081-9525) 1282
C F O and Controller Alert see C F O & Controller Alert 1282
• C F O Asia (Chief Financial Officer) (HKG ISSN 1560-3539) 1731
C F O China (HKG ISSN 1683-9986) 1078
• C F O Europe (Chief Financial Officer) (GBR ISSN 1462-5601) 1731
C F O Magazine see Chief Financial Officer 1733
C.F.P. Chaud - Froid - Plomberie (FRA ISSN 0750-1552) 4117
C F R see Carpet & Flooring Review 4554
C F R see Code of Federal Regulations 4643
† ➤ C F S (Courier Forschungsinstitut Senckenberg) (DEU ISSN 0341-4116) 8938
C F S see Child & Family Social Work 8032
C F S A Newsletter (Casket & Funeral Supply Association of America) (USA) 3719
C F S R (Centre for Study and Research) (GBR ISSN 1753-1381) 8091
C F U W. Women in Action see Women In Action 8890
C G see Computers & Graphics 2484
C G see Corporate Governance (Bradford) 1736
C G see Clinical Gerontologist 4043
C G A C. Revista (Centro Galego de Arte Contemporanea) (ESP ISSN 1576-8082) 480
C G A - Canada Research Foundation. Study Papers (Certified General Accountants) (CAN) 1282
• C G A Magazine (Certified General Accountants Association of Canada) (CAN ISSN 0318-742X) 1282
† C G A's News Report (FRA ISSN 1774-5004) 8938
• C G B Technical Report (Center for Genomics and Bioinformatics) (USA ISSN 1933-1916) 663
C G C E Administracion see Administracion 1723
C G. Car Graphic see Car Graphic 8572
• C G E R - Report (JPN ISSN 1341-4356) 3408
C. G. Jung Vereniging Nederland, Interdisciplinaire Vereniging voor Analytische Psychologie. Jaarboek (NLD ISSN 1872-1710) 7342
• C G L Reporter (Comprehensive - General Liability) (USA ISSN 0748-951X) 4497
C G Magazine (TWN ISSN 1609-0004) 2483
The C G S Bulletin (California Geographical Society) (USA) 4001
• C G S Journal of Research (Commonwealth Governor's School) (USA ISSN 1557-8313) 2833
C G S M Enterprise see Cornell Enterprise 1735
C G S News (California Genealogical Society) (USA ISSN 1058-5133) 3761
C G T Capital Losses (Capital Gains Tax) (GBR) 1614
C G T. Transports. Alpes du Nord (Confederation Generale du Travail) (FRA ISSN 1774-4644) 4591
C G W see Computer Graphics World 2484
C H A C Info/Info A C C S (Catholic Health Association of Canada) (CAN ISSN 0822-8426) 4089
C H A C Newsletter see Canadian Hungarian Artists' Collective Newsletter 481
C H A I Lights (Concern for Helping Animals in Israel) (USA) 318
C H E C K (Continuous Home Evaluation of Clinical Knowledge) (AUS ISSN 0812-9630) 5590
C H E C Points (Commonwealth Human Ecology Council) (GBR ISSN 0142-1972) 3408
• C H E P A in Review (Centre for Health Economics and Policy Analysis) (CAN ISSN 1912-1431) 7510
C H E R see Continuing Higher Education Review 2974
C H F see Community Health Funding Report 7431
• C H F Newsbriefs (Cooperative Housing Foundation) (CAN ISSN 1046-8196) 4405
C H I Dispatch (Confederate Historical Institute) (USA) 4286
C H I L D Newsletter (Children's Healthcare Is a Legal Duty) (USA) 2146
C H I N, the Year in Perspective see Canadian Heritage Information Network, the Year in Perspective 4134
C H I - P A C C Update (Children's Hospice International) (USA) 6089
C H I U Z see Chemie in Unserer Zeit 2055
C H L Annual Equipment Guide and C H L Monthly Equipment Guide (Contractors Hot Line) (USA) 7557
C H L Equipment Guide (Contractors Hot Line) (USA) 988
C H - Lit (CHE ISSN 1422-6111) 5268
C H P A Executive Newsletter (Consumer Healthcare Products Association) (USA) 6827
C H P Packer International (Cosmetics, Healthcare, Pharmaceuticals) (GBR ISSN 1465-2986) 6708
• C H P Packer International Directory (Year) (Cosmetics, Healthcare, Pharmaceuticals) (GBR) 6708
C H R see Canadian Historical Review 4134
C H R P National Knowledge Exam. Study Guide (Canadian Human Resources Press) (CAN ISSN 1912-0206) 6693
C H R R Revised Consolidated Index see Revised Consolidated Index 4939
C H S (USA) 4286
• C H S Demography/Statistique du Logement au Canada: Demographie (Canadian Housing Statistics) (CAN ISSN 1912-7049) 4434
C H S Newsletter (Construction History Society) (GBR ISSN 0951-9203) 988

• C H S Rental Market Survey/Statistique du Logement au Canada: Enquete sur le Marche Locatif (Canadian Housing Statistics) (CAN ISSN 1912-7057) **7617**
• C H S Residential Building Activity/Statistique du Logement au Canada: Construction Residentielle (Canadian Housing Statistics) (CAN ISSN 1912-7065) **1216**
C H U N *see* Chinesisch - Unterricht **5106**
C H U S Newsletter (Chinese Historians in the United States, Inc.) (USA) **545**
• ➤ C H Working Papers (Centre for Computing in Humanities) (CAN ISSN 1205-5743) **4485**
C I *see* Construction Innovation **996**
C I *see* Critical Inquiry **5212**
C I *see* Concrete International **993**
C I *see* Caspian Investor **1882**
C I *see* Intelligence Insights **7363**
C I A *see* Concrete in Australia **993**
C I A C Sintesis Informativa (Centro Informativo para las Americas y el Caribe) (CUB ISSN 0864-2478) **7111**
The C I A C's Electronic Art Magazine *see* The C I A C's Electronic Magazine **480**
• The C I A C's Electronic Magazine (CAN ISSN 1910-1929) **480**
C I A J Annual Report (Communications Industry Association of Japan) (JPN) **2314**
C I A J Journal *see* Tsushin Kogyo **2373**
• C I A M Flyer (FRA) **50**
C I A O Magazine (CAN) **3524**
C I A T en Perspectiva (Centro Internacional de Agricultura Tropical) (COL) **98**
C I A T in Perspective (Distribucion de Publicaciones) (COL) **98**
C I B C Observations *see* Commentaires de la C I B C **1328**
• C I B Daily Maritime Newsletter (Congressional Information Bureau, Inc.) (USA ISSN 1062-6506) **8640**
C I B Daily Maritime Newsletter Index (Congressional Information Bureau, Inc.) (USA) **8640**
C I B News (Chartered Institute of Bankers) (GBR ISSN 1360-4678) **1323**
C I B News (Communications in Business) (GBR) **4572**
• C I B S E Journal (Chartered Institution of Building Services Engineers) (GBR ISSN 1759-846X) **989**
C I C *see* Cuadernos de Informacion y Comunicacion **2318**
C I C A E Bulletin d'Information (Confederation Internationale des Cinemas d'Art et d'Essai) (FRA ISSN 0256-1336) **6491**
C I C A Handbook (Canadian Institute of Chartered Accountants) (CAN ISSN 0068-8983) **1283**
C I C A Public Sector Accounting Handbook (Canadian Institute of Chartered Accountants) (CAN ISSN 1910-751X) **1283**
C I C. Arquitectura Digital *see* C I C. Centro Informativo de la Construction **989**
C I C. Boletin Informativo (CUB) **2833**
• C I C Cascade (Construction Industry Council) (GBR) **989**
• C I C. Centro Informativo de la Construction (ESP ISSN 1576-1118) **989**
• C I C E R O. Policy Note (Center for International Climate and Environmental Research) (NOR ISSN 0804-4511) **6348**
• C I C E R O. Report (Center for International Climate and Environmental Research) (NOR ISSN 0804-4562) **6348**
• C I C E R O. Working Paper (Center for International Climate and Environmental Research) (NOR ISSN 0804-452X) **6348**
C I C J *see* Current Issues in Criminal Justice **2650**
C I C Productos (Centro Informativo de la Construccion) (ESP) **989**
C I C R *see* Captive Insurance Company Reports **4498**
C I C S D *see* Contemporary Issues in Communication Science & Disorders **6079**
• C I C S J Bulletin (Chemical Information and Computer Sciences) (JPN ISSN 0913-3747) **2052**
C I D *see* Clinical Infectious Diseases **5811**
C I D (Cuba Independiente y Democratica) (USA) **7111**
C I D A C *see* International Journal of Computer Integrated Design and Construction **1016**
C I D A Contracts *see* A C D I Marches **1589**
C I D A E (Direccion General de Aviacion Civil, Centro de Investigacion y Difusion Aeronautico Espacial) (URY ISSN 0797-0072) **50**
C I D E P I N T. Anales *see* Centro de Investigacion y Desarrollo en Tecnologia de Pinturas. Anales **6716**
C I D: Electronica y Procesamiento de Datos (CUB) **3090**
C I D L News *see* Nouvelles de l'I C B N **5037**
C I D L News *see* Nouvelles de l'I C B N **5037**
• C I D O B d'Afers Internationals (Centre d'Informacio i Documentacio Internacionals a Barcelona) (ESP ISSN 1133-6595) **7224**
C I D X Messenger (Canadian International DX Radio Club) (CAN ISSN 0045-3706) **2357**
C I Directory (Cosmetics International) (GBR) **593**
C I E *see* Computers & Industrial Engineering **3290**
C I E *see* Current Issues in Education **2840**
C I E F L Bulletin (Central Institute of English and Foreign Languages) (IND ISSN 0970-8340) **5102**
C I E L *see* Journal of Interdisciplinary Literary Studies **5315**
C I E M *see* Current Issues in Electronic Modeling **3091**
C I E M A T. Informes de Difusion de Proyectos (Centro de Investigaciones Energeticas, Medioambientales y Tecnologicas. Informes de Difusion de Proy) (ESP ISSN 1138-7041) **3125**
C I E M A T. Informes Tecnicos (Centro de Investigaciones Energeticas, Medioambientales y Tecnologicas) (ESP ISSN 1135-9420) **3166**
C I E N *see* Canadian Industrial Equipment News **5450**
▼ • C I E N S Rapport (Centre for Interdisciplinary Environmental and Social Research) (NOR ISSN 1890-4572) **3484**
C I E - News (Commission Internationale de l'Eclairage, Central Bureau) (AUT) **3296**
C I E Newsletter (Chinese Institute of Engineers) (TWN) **3183**
C I E. Publication (Commission Internationale de l'Eclairage, Central Bureau) (AUT ISSN 1011-6567) **3296**
C I E R E C Travaux *see* Centre Interdisciplinaire d'Etude et de Recherche sur l'Expression Contemporaine. Travaux **4446**
C I E S Food Business News (Comite International des Entreprises a Succursales) (FRA ISSN 1266-2550) **3629**
C I E S M Workshop Monographs (Commission Internationale pour l'Exploitation Scientifique de la Mer Mediterranee) (MCO ISSN 1726-5886) **2801**
C I E S M Workshop Series *see* C I E S M Workshop Monographs **2801**
C I F A Occasional Paper/C P C A Document Occasionnel (Food and Agriculture Organization of the United Nations (F A O), Committee for Inland Fisheries of) (ITA ISSN 1014-2452) **3587**
C I F A Technical Papers (Committee for Inland Fisheries of Africa) (ITA ISSN 0379-5616) **3588**
C I F E J Info (Centre International du Film pour l'Enfance et la Jeunesse) (CAN ISSN 1719-9891) **6491**
C I F N E T. Annual Report (Central Institute of Fisheries, Nautical & Engineering Training) (IND) **3375**
C I F N E T. Bulletin (Central Institute of Fisheries, Nautical & Engineering Training) (IND) **3375**
C I F T. Annual Report (Central Institute of Fisheries Technology) (IND ISSN 0972-0677) **3588**
• C I G A D Briefing Notes (Centre for Indigenous Governance and Development) (NZL ISSN 1176-9971) **8091**
• C I G A D Working Paper Series (Centre for Indigenous Governance and Development) (NZL ISSN 1176-9025) **8091**
C I H I Directions (Canadian Institute for Health Information) (CAN ISSN 1201-0383) **7510**
C I H M E C H (Centro de Investigaciones Humanisticas de Mesoamerica y el Estado de Chiapas) (MEX ISSN 0187-652X) **385**
• C I H R Institute of Infection and Immunity. Annual Report/Institut des Maladies Infectieuses et Immunitaires des I R S C. Rapport Annuel (Canadian Institutes of Health Research) (CAN ISSN 1717-2888) **5811**
• C I H R Institute of Infection and Immunity. Annual Report (Canadian Institutes of Health Research) (CAN ISSN 1910-8346) **5811**
C I H R/Rx & D Progress Report *see* Welcome to the C I H R - Rx & D Progress Report (Year) **6885**
C I I D Informa *see* I D R C Reports **1597**
C I I G Bulletin (Construction Industry Information Group) (GBR) **989**
C I I Journal (The Chartered Insurance Institute) (GBR ISSN 0957-4883) **4497**
C I I L Adult Literacy Series (Central Institute of Indian Languages) (IND) **2939**
C I I L - Apni Boli Series (Central Institute of Indian Languages) (IND) **5102**
C I I L Bilingual Education Series (Central Institute of Indian Languages) (IND) **5102**
C I I L Bilingual Hindi Series (Central Institute of Indian Languages) (IND) **5102**
C I I L Border and Tribal Languages. Adult Literacy Series (Central Institute of Indian Languages) (IND) **2939**
C I I L Common Vocabulary Series (Central Institute of Indian Languages) (IND) **5102**
C I I L Conferences and Seminars Series (Central Institute of Indian Languages) (IND) **5102**
C I I L Current Inquiries in Indian Languages (Central Institute of Indian Languages) (IND) **5102**
C I I L Doctoral Dissertation Series (Central Institute of Indian Languages) (IND) **5102**
C I I L Documentation Series (Central Institute of Indian Languages) (IND) **5102**
C I I L Folklore Series (Central Institute of Indian Languages) (IND) **3615**
C I I L Grammar Series (Central Institute of Indian Languages) (IND) **5102**
C I I L Intensive Course Series (Central Institute of Indian Languages) (IND) **5102**
C I I L Occasional Bulletin Series (Central Institute of Indian Languages) (IND) **5102**
C I I L Occasional Monograph Series (Central Institute of Indian Languages) (IND) **5102**
C I I L Phonetic Reader Series (Central Institute of Indian Languages) (IND) **5102**
C I I L Pictorial Glossary Series (Central Institute of Indian Languages) (IND) **5102**
C I I L Reading Series (Central Institute of Indian Languages) (IND) **5102**
C I I L Second Language Textbook Series (Central Institute of Indian Languages) (IND) **5102**
C I I L Sociolinguistics Series (Central Institute of Indian Languages) (IND) **5102**
C I I M Management Review (Cyprus International Institute of Management (C I I M)) (CYP) **1731**
C I I T Activities (Chemical Industry Institute of Toxicology) (USA ISSN 8755-4259) **3494**
C I J *see* Couture International Jeweler **4565**
C I L *see* Computers in Libraries **2570**
• C I L E A. Bollettino (Consorzio Interuniversitario Lombardo per l'Elaborazione Automatica) (ITA ISSN 1120-2440) **2408**
C I L E C T News (Centre International de Liaison des Ecoles de Cinema et de Television) (BEL) **2377**
C I L E Studies (Center for International Legal Education) (USA ISSN 1555-2365) **4919**
• C I L I P in Yorkshire & Humberside (Chartered Institute of Library and Information Professionals) (GBR ISSN 1740-7621) **4999**
C I L I P - M m I T News (Chartered Institute of Library and Information Professionals - Multimedia Information and Technology) (GBR) **5060**
C I L I P Yearbook (Year) (Chartered Institute of Library and Information Professionals) (GBR ISSN 1746-9929) **4999**
C I L J *see* Connecticut Insurance Law Journal **4648**
C I L L *see* Institut de Linguistique de Louvain. Cahiers **5127**
C I L T *see* Amsterdam Studies in the Theory and History of Linguistic Science. Series 4: Current Issues in Linguistic Theory **5093**
C I L T World (Chartered Institute of Logistics and Transport) (GBR) **8492**
C I M *see* Convention & Incentive Marketing **6279**
C I M *see* Canadian Industrial Machinery **5450**
C I M A C Recommendations (Conseil International des Machines a Combustion) (DEU) **3375**
• C I M A Insight (GBR ISSN 1748-7900) **1283**
➤ C I M A Questions and Suggested Answers (Chartered Institute of Management Accountants) (GBR) **1283**
C I M - Arbeitsmaterialien (Centrum fuer Internationale Migration und Entwicklung) (DEU ISSN 0722-9232) **8091**
• C I M B A G E. Cuadernos (Centro de Investigacion en Metodologia Borrosa Aplicada a la Gestion y Economia. Cuadernos) (ARG ISSN 1666-5112) **1731**
C I M Bulletin *see* C I M Magazine **6459**
C I M Buyers Guide *see* Cabling Installation and Maintenance **2378**
C I M C I M Newsletter (Comite International des Musees et Collections d'Instruments de Musique) (FRA) **6521**
C I M C I M Publications (Comite International des Musees et Collections d'Instruments de Musique) (FRA ISSN 1019-9977) **6522**
C I M - Conference and Incentive Management (DEU ISSN 1437-2878) **1731**
C I M Construction Journal (Construction Industries of Massachusetts, Inc.) (USA ISSN 0192-4435) **3261**
C I M Directory (Canadian Institute of Mining, Metallurgy and Petroleum) (CAN ISSN 0068-9009) **6459**
• C I M E L (Ciencia e Investigacion Medica Estudiantil Latinoamericana) (PER ISSN 1680-8398) **5590**
C I M - M C E *see* Clinical and Investigative Medicine (Print) **8941**
C I M M Y T Economics Working Paper (Centro International de Mejoramiento de Maiz y Trigo) (MEX) **270**
• C I M Magazine (Canadian Institute of Mining, Metallurgy and Petroleum) (CAN ISSN 1718-4177) **6459**
C I M Notes (Cleveland Institute of Music) (USA ISSN 0007-845X) **6552**
• C I M O S A News (Computer Integrated Manufacturing Open Systems Architecture) (DEU ISSN 1618-1638) **3183**
C I M Reporter (Canadian Institute of Mining, Metallurgy and Petroleum) (CAN ISSN 0701-0710) **6459**
C I N A (Canadian Intravenous Nurses Association) (CAN ISSN 1205-5611) **5953**
C I N A H L *see* Cumulative Index to Nursing & Allied Health Literature **5743**
C I N A H L News (Cumulative Index to Nursing & Allied Health Literature) (USA) **4999**
C I N A H L Subject Heading List (Cumulative Index to Nursing and Allied Health Literature) (USA ISSN 1522-1156) **5953**
• C I N: Computers, Informatics, Nursing (USA ISSN 1538-2931) **5829**
• C I N D A (AUT ISSN 1011-2545) **7048**
C I N D E Journal (Canadian Institute for Non-Destructive Evaluation) (CAN ISSN 1700-2729) **3342**
• C I N F E-news (Chemical Information) (USA ISSN 1559-7342) **2052**
C I N N Report (Chicago Institute of Neurosurgery and Neuroresearch) (USA ISSN 1068-9230) **6129**
C I N T E L. Revista (Centro de Investigacion de las Telecomunicaciones) (COL ISSN 0121-9685) **2314**
C I N T E R F O R Estudios y Monografias (Centro Interamericano de Investigacion y Documentacion Sobre Formacion Profesional) (URY ISSN 0577-2931) **2833**
C I N T R A F O R News (Center for International Trade in Forest Products) (USA) **3710**
• C I O (Chief Information Officer) (AUS ISSN 1328-4045) **1414**
C I O (Chief Information Officer) (BGR) **1414**
† C I O (DNK ISSN 1901-8398) **8938**
C I O (Chief Information Officer) (NLD ISSN 1570-9183) **2408**
C I O (Chief Information Officer) (POL ISSN 1733-6651) **1414**
C I O (Chief Information Officer) (RUS ISSN 1819-2696) **1414**
C I O *see* Direktor Informatsionnoi Sluzhby **1739**
• C I O (Chief Information Officer) (USA ISSN 0894-9301) **1414**
C I O (France) (Chief Information Officer) (FRA ISSN 1636-0575) **1414**
C I O Africa (Chief Information Officer) (ZAF ISSN 1812-3201) **1731**
C I O Agenda (Chief Information Officer) (GBR) **1414**
• C I O Asia (Chief Information Officer) (SGP) **1414**
C I O Business Standard Norway *see* C I O Computerworld **1414**
• C I O Canada (Chief Information Officer) (CAN ISSN 1195-6097) **1414**
• C I O Computerworld (NOR ISSN 1504-064X) **1414**
C I O D Aggiornamenti *see* Aggiornamenti C I O **6055**
• C I O Germany (Chief Information Officer) (DEU ISSN 1618-3487) **1414**
• C I O Governments' Review (Chief Information Officer) (CAN ISSN 1703-0072) **7485**
C I O India (Chief Information Officer) (IND) **1414**
C I O Insight *see* Xinxi Fanglue **1421**
• C I O Insight (Chief Information Officer) (USA ISSN 1535-0096) **1414**
C I O Italia (Chief Information Officer) (ITA ISSN 1826-459X) **1414**
• C I O Japan (Chief Information Officer) (JPN) **1415**
• C I O Korea (Chief Information Officer) (KOR) **1415**
C I O L A Directory (Careers Information Officers in Local Authorities) (GBR ISSN 0268-5450) **6694**
• C I O New Zealand (Chief Information Officer) (NZL ISSN 1174-992X) **1415**
C I O Plus *see* C I O **1414**
• C I O Sweden (Chief Information Officer) (SWE ISSN 1651-3118) **2553**
C I O Taiwan (Chief Information Officer) (TWN) **1415**
C I O Technology International *see* C I O Agenda **1414**
• C I O Today (USA ISSN 1557-2315) **1415**
C I O Today Magazine *see* C I O Today **1415**
C I P *see* Biblioteca Nationala a Romaniei. Bibliografia Cartilor in Curs de Aparitie **619**
C I P A (Chartered Institute of Patent Agents) (GBR ISSN 0306-0314) **6747**
C I P A E. Estudios (Comite de Iglesias para Ayudas de Emergencia) (PRY) **7203**
C I P A R S *see* Canadian Integrated Program for Antimicrobial Resistance Surveillance **5811**
† C I P. Anuario (Centro de Investigacion para la Paz) (ESP ISSN 1139-5222) **8938**
• C I P D Employment Law for People Managers (Chartered Institute of Personnel and Development) (GBR ISSN 1740-0252) **1668**
• C I P D Policies and Proceedures for People Managers (Chartered Institute of Personnel and Development) (GBR ISSN 1743-0402) **1857**
C I P E T Bulletin (Central Institute of Plastics Engineering & Technology) (IND ISSN 0972-6578) **7091**
C I P F A Fire and Rescue Service Statistics (Chartered Institute of Public Finance and Accountancy) (GBR ISSN 1745-9184) **3582**
• C I P Newsletter (Critical Infrastructure Protection) (AUS ISSN 1833-5861) **2225**
C I P Newsletter *see* C I P Report **4859**
• C I P Report (Center of Intellectual Property) (DEU ISSN 1864-2586) **4859**
C I P Working Paper Series *see* University of Manchester. The Centre for International Politics. Working Paper Series **7272**
C I R *see* China Industrial Reporter **5450**
C I R A Bulletin (Centre International de Recherches sur l'Anarchisme) (CHE) **7111**
C I R A Bulletin *see* Journal of Iranian Research and Analysis **7147**
C I R A S News (Center for Industrial Research and Service) (USA) **8417**
C I R C M E Lecture Series (Callaway International Resource Centre) (AUS ISSN 1321-196X) **6552**
C I R C M E Series *see* C I R C M E Lecture Series **6552**

Title

Title

C R C Handbook of Chemistry and Physics on CD-ROM *see* C R C Handbook of Chemistry and Physics **2052**
C R C Handbook Series in Nutrition and Food (USA ISSN 0192-6241) **6656**
• C R C P D Newsbrief (Online) (Conference of Radiation Control Program Directors) (USA) **3494**
C R C P D Newsbrief (Print) *see* C R C P D Newsbrief (Online) **3494**
• C R C Salinity Bulletin (Cooperative Research Centre) (AUS ISSN 1833-4237) **223**
C R D *see* Chronic Respiratory Disease **6212**
C R D I Explore *see* I D R C Reports **1597**
C R Delta Magazine (Regio Oost Edition) *see* C R V Magazine (Oost Edition) **864**
C R Delta Magazine (Regio Zuid-West Edition) *see* C R V Magazine (Zuid-West Edition) **864**
C R Delta Magazine (Region Noord Edition) *see* C R V Magazine (Noord Edition) **864**
C R E A M Quaderni (ITA ISSN 1970-867X) **331**
C R E A M Report (Centre for Research in Environmental Appraisal and Management) (GBR ISSN 1461-6548) **3408**
• C R E M O C. Cahiers (FRA ISSN 1634-4774) **4208**
C R E S R Lecture Series (Sheffield Hallam University, Centre for Regional Economic and Social Research) (GBR) **1445**
C R E S R Planning and Property Series (Sheffield Hallam University, Centre for Regional Economic and Social Research) (GBR) **1445**
C R E S R Research Paper (Sheffield Hallam University, Centre for Regional Economic and Social Research) (GBR) **1445**
C R E S R Social Policy Paper (Sheffield Hallam University, Centre for Regional Economic and Social Research) (GBR) **8029**
C R E S R Supertram Impact Series (Sheffield Hallam University, Centre for Regional Economic and Social Research) (GBR) **1445**
C R E S Report *see* Center for the Reproduction of Endangered Species. Report **938**
• C R E S T Newz (Creativity in Science and Technology) (NZL ISSN 1177-7923) **7843**
C R F S F S *see* Comprehensive Reviews in Food Science and Food Safety **3632**
C R H C S News (Commonwealth Regional Health Community Secretariat) (TZA ISSN 0856-4043) **7511**
C R I *see* China Review International **3823**
C R I A R L Newsletter (Consortium of Rhode Island Academic and Research Libraries) (USA ISSN 0882-6846) **4999**
C R I A W Newsletter *see* Canadian Research Institute for the Advancement of Women. Newsletter **8854**
C R I Abstracts *see* N C B Abstracts **1048**
C R I Annual Report (PNG ISSN 1680-1156) **3629**
C R I Current Contents *see* N C B Current Contents **1048**
C R I D E Cahiers (Centre de Recherches Interdisciplinaires pour le Developpement de l'Education) (COD) **2833**
C R I E P I. Abiko Research Laboratory. Report (English Edition) *see* Central Research Institute of Electric Power Industry. Abiko Research Laboratory. Report (English Edition) **3155**
C R I E P I. All Laboratories. Report (English Edition) *see* Central Research Institute of Electric Power Industry. All Laboratories. Report (English Edition) **3155**
C R I E P I. Komae Research Laboratory. Report (English Edition) *see* Central Research Institute of Electric Power Industry. Komae Research Laboratory. Report (English Edition) **3155**
C R I E P I Report. Electric Engineering Laboratory (Central Research Institute of Electric Power Industry) (JPN) **3297**
C R I E P I Report. Energy & Environment Laboratory (Central Research Institute of Electric Power Industry) (JPN) **3155**
C R I E P I. Socio-Economic Research Center. Report (English Edition) *see* Central Research Institute of Electric Power Industry. Socio-Economic Research Center. Technical Reports (English Edition) **8093**
C R I E R Newsletter (USA) **4286**
C R I E R Nuovi Quaderni (Centro di Ricerca sull'Italia nell'Europa Romantica) (ITA ISSN 1826-4328) **5268**
▼ C R I I R A D. Dossiers Clefs (Commission de Recherche et d'Information Independantes sur la Radioactivite) (FRA ISSN 1961-4144) **7065**
C R I L J *see* Centre de Recherche et d'Information sur la Litterature pour la Jeunesse **5271**
• C R I N (Cahiers de Recherche des Instituts Neerlandais de Langue et Litterature Francaise) (NLD ISSN 0169-894X) **5268**
C R I Occasional Papers (Centre for the Study of Regulated Industries) (GBR) **7425**
C R I P E L *see* Institut de Papyrologie et d'Egyptologie de Lille. Cahiers de Recherche **4175**
C R I Proceedings Series (Centre for the Study of Regulated Industries) (GBR ISSN 1362-9948) **7425**
C R I Regulatory Briefs (Centre for the Study of Regulated Industries) (GBR) **4635**
• C R I S P: Biomedical Research Information on CD-ROM (USA) **748**
C R I S P P *see* Critical Review of International Social and Political Philosophy **7229**
C R J Reporter (United Church of Christ, Commission for Racial Justice) (USA ISSN 0732-720X) **3524**
C R K *see* Care Home Management: Records & Procedures **8030**
C R L A Newsletter (College Reading and Learning Association) (USA) **2970**
C R L H. Cahiers Annuels (Centre des Recherches Litteraires et Historiques) (REU ISSN 0299-0628) **331**
C R L J *see* George Mason University. Civil Rights Law Journal **4831**
C R L News (Communications Research Laboratory) *see* N I C T News **2334**
C R L - Salmonella Interlaboratory Comparison Study on Typing of Salmonella spp. (Communautair Referentie Laboratorium) (NLD ISSN 1874-5865) **5590**
C R M *see* Cahiers de Recherches Medievales **4208**
C R M *see* Canadian Recycling Market **3504**
C R M *see* C R M Magazine **1731**
• C R M (Washington) (Cultural Resources Management) (USA ISSN 1068-4999) **385**
C R M A *see* Consumer Reports Money Adviser **2637**
• C R M Buyer (Customer Relations Management) (USA) **1078**
• C R M eWeekly (Customer Relationship Management) (USA) **1731**
• C R M Expert (Customer Relationship Management) (USA ISSN 1558-304X) **1078**
C R M - Handbuch Reisemedizin (Centrum fuer Reisemedizin) (DEU) **5590**
C R M - Handbuch zur Reisemedizinischen Beratung *see* C R M - Handbuch Reisemedizin **5590**
• C R M Magazine (USA ISSN 1529-8728) **1731**
C R M Monograph Series (Centre de Recherches Mathematiques) (USA ISSN 1065-8599) **5476**
C R M Profi (Customer Relationship Management) (DEU ISSN 1610-1065) **1731**
C R Money Adviser *see* Consumer Reports Money Adviser **2637**
C R N *see* C R N Australia **2510**
• C R N (USA ISSN 1539-7343) **2510**
C R N A News (USA) **5954**
C R N Australia (Computer Resellers News) (AUS ISSN 1447-6290) **2510**
• C R N Canada (Computer Reseller News) (CAN ISSN 1910-0175) **2511**
C R N Canada News *see* C R N Canada **2511**
C R N India (Computer Reseller News) (IND) **2511**
C R N News and Briefs Newsletter *see* Renalink **6274**
▼ • C R N Tech (USA ISSN 1935-5211) **2409**
C R O (USA ISSN 1933-5903) **1078**
• ➤ C R O M O H S (Cyber Review of Modern Historiography) (ITA ISSN 1123-7023) **4133**
C R O M T E C Working Paper Series (Centre for Research on Organisations, Management and Technical Change) (GBR) **1731**
C R O P Newsletter (NOR) **1445**
C R O W et cetera (Centrum voor Regelgeving en Onderzoek in de Grond-, Water- en Wegenbouw en de Verkeerstechniek) (NLD ISSN 1872-0129) **3261**
C R P C Info (Capital Region Planning Commission) (USA) **7425**
C R R *see* Corporate Reputation Review **1736**
C R R E L Report (Cold Regions Research and Engineering Laboratory) (USA ISSN 0501-5782) **3183**
C R R I Road Abstracts (Central Road Research Institute) (IND ISSN 0045-6055) **3229**
C R S H Guide des Detenteurs du Subventions *see* S S H R C Grant Holder's Guide **3031**
C R S J *see* Washington and Lee Journal of Civil Rights and Social Justice **4844**
C R S P Annual Report (Centre for Research in Social Policy) (GBR ISSN 0969-8914) **8091**
C R S S S de Quebec. Rapport Annuel *see* Agence de Developpement de Reseaux Locaux de Services de Sante et de Services Sociaux de la Capitale Nationale. Rapport Annuel de Gestion **8024**
C R Series *see* Monash University Accident Research Centre. Consultants' Reports Series **8632**
C R T *see* Conversations in Religion and Theology **7635**
▼ • C R T C 3-year Work Plan (Online Edition) (Canadian Radio-Television and Telecommunications Commission) (CAN ISSN 1719-8380) **2314**
▼ • C R T C 3-year Work Plan (Print Edition)/C R T C Plan de Travail Triennal (Canadian Radio-Television and Telecommunications Commission) (CAN ISSN 1716-4982) **2314**
• C R T C Accomplishments (Canadian Radio-Television and Telecommunications Commission) (CAN ISSN 1716-4990) **2314**
C R T C Action Plan. Implementation of Section 41 of the Official Languages Act *see* Action Plan. Implementation of Section 41 of the Official Languages Act **2311**
C R T C Plan de Travail Triennal *see* C R T C 3-year Work Plan (Print Edition) **2314**
C R T C Plan de Travail Triennal *see* C R T C 3-year Work Plan (Online Edition) **2314**
C R T C Telecom Decisions, Public Notices and News Releases *see* Decisions, Avis Publics, Circulaires et Communiques en Matiere de Telecommunications **2318**
C R T C Telecommunications Monitoring Report (Canadian Radio-Television and Telecommunications Commission) (CAN ISSN 1910-4154) **2314**
C R T I Annual Report/L' I R T C. Rapport Annuel (Chemical, Biological, Radiological, and Nuclear Research and Technology Initiative) (CAN ISSN 1912-0974) **6414**
• C R T I Summer Symposium. Proceedings of the (Year)/Symposium d'Ete de l'I R T C. Programme (Chemical, Biological, Radiological, and Nuclear (C B R N) Research and Technology Initiative) (CAN ISSN 1912-192X) **7843**
C R U International Metals Databook (GBR) **6459**
C R U International Steel Databook & Atlas (GBR) **6307**
C R U Metal Monitor Annual (GBR) **6307**
• C R U Monitor. Alumina (Commodities Research Unit) (GBR ISSN 1356-6628) **1881**
• C R U Monitor. Aluminium (Commodities Research Unit) (GBR ISSN 1356-6598) **1881**
• C R U Monitor. Bulk Ferroalloys (Commodities Research Unit) (GBR ISSN 1356-6717) **1881**
• C R U Monitor. Copper (Commodities Research Unit) (GBR ISSN 1356-6547) **1881**
• C R U Monitor. Copper Raw Materials: Concentrates, Blister and Scrap (Commodities Research Unit) (GBR ISSN 1476-668X) **1881**
• C R U Monitor. Copper Studies (Commodities Research Unit) (GBR ISSN 1356-6563) **1881**
• C R U Monitor. Flat Rolled Aluminium Products (Commodities Research Unit) (GBR ISSN 1356-6601) **1881**
• C R U Monitor. Lead and Zinc Concentrates (Commodities Research Unit) (GBR ISSN 1356-6652) **1881**
• C R U Monitor. Nickel, Chrome, Molybdenum (Commodities Research Unit) (GBR ISSN 1356-6709) **1881**
• C R U Monitor. Steel (Commodities Research Unit) (GBR ISSN 1356-6660) **1881**
• C R U Monitor. Steelmaking Raw Materials (Commodities Research Unit) (GBR ISSN 1356-6687) **1882**
• C R U Monitor. Tin (Commodities Research Unit) (GBR ISSN 1356-6725) **1882**
• C R U Monitor. Zinc (Commodities Research Unit) (GBR ISSN 1356-6644) **1882**
C R V Magazine (Noord Edition) (Cooperatie Rundveeverbetering) (NLD ISSN 1876-892X) **864**
C R V Magazine (Oost Edition) (Cooperatie Rundveeverbetering) (NLD ISSN 1876-8911) **864**
C R V Magazine (Zuid-West Edition) (Cooperatie Rundveeverbetering) (NLD ISSN 1876-8903) **864**
• C-Resonance (USA) **5440**
C S *see* Christian Single **7751**
C S *see* Colored Stone **4565**
C S *see* Cognitive Science (Hauppauge) **7347**
C S *see* Changing Schools (Denver) **3054**
C S *see* Chicago Social **3972**
C S 4 F N *see* Computer Science for Fun **2412**
C S A *see* Chain Store Age **1809**
C S A *see* The Customer Service Advantage **1812**
C S A. Agricultural & Environmental Biotechnology Abstracts *see* Agricultural & Environmental Biotechnology Abstracts (Online) **173**
C S A C. Monographs *see* Centre for Social Anthropology and Computing. Monographs **332**
• C S A Civil Engineering Abstracts (Cambridge Scientific Abstracts) (USA) **3229**
• C S A Human Population & Natural Resource Management (USA) **7304**
C S A J News *see* Nihon Shikisai Gakkai Nyuzu **7081**
C S A Journal (Czechoslovak Society of America) (USA ISSN 0195-9050) **3524**
C S A Journal (Denver) (Certified Senior Advisors) (USA ISSN 1542-9199) **4042**
• C S A Mechanical & Transportation Engineering Abstracts (Cambridge Scientific Abstracts) (USA) **3229**
• C S A Neurosciences Abstracts (Online) (Cambridge Scientific Abstracts) (USA ISSN 1555-4503) **5742**
C S A News (USA ISSN 1529-9163) **223**
C S A News (Brooklyn) (Council of Supervisors and Administrators of the City of New York) (USA) **3018**
C S A News (Earleville) (Costume Society of America) (USA) **2252**
• C S A Newsletter (Center of the Study of Architecture) (USA ISSN 1095-4872) **436**
C S A Newsletter *see* Communal Studies Association. Newsletter **4136**
• C S A Oncogenes and Growth Factors Abstracts (USA ISSN 1555-4538) **5742**
C S A P Prevention Monograph (Center for Substance Abuse Prevention) (USA) **2692**
• C S A Political Science & Government (Cambridge Scientific Abstracts) (USA ISSN 1542-9040) **7479**
C S A R S. Rapport Annuel *see* S I R C Annual Report **7264**
C S A S Bulletin *see* Central States Anthropology Society. Bulletin **332**
† • C S A Sentinel (Control Self-Assessment) (USA) **8938**
• C S A Sustainability Science Abstracts (Cambridge Scientific Abstracts) (USA) **3477**
• C S A Worldwide Political Science Abstracts (Cambridge Scientific Abstracts) (USA) **7199**
C S & D & C B *see* Journal of Consumer Satisfaction, Dissatisfaction and Complaining Behavior **1824**
• C S Arts (Chrysalis Seed) (NZL ISSN 1177-4592) **480**
C S B. Conference Proceedings (Computational Systems Bioinformatics) (GBR ISSN 1752-7791) **2409**
C S B S Examiner (Conference of State Bank Supervisors) (USA) **1323**
• C S Bladet (DNK ISSN 0902-3488) **6414**
C S C China Steel Technical Report - Zhonggang Jibao *see* China Steel Technical Report **6308**
C S C - Educ (Confederation des Syndicats Chretiens - Education) (BEL ISSN 1784-1240) **4591**
C S C I Islamic Issues Briefing Paper Series (Centre for the Study of Contemporary Islam) (AUS ISSN 1833-2447) **7709**
C S C News (Canadian Society of Cinematographers) (CAN ISSN 1202-5879) **6491**
C S C Newsletter (Community of the Sisters of the Church) (GBR ISSN 0007-9073) **7749**
C S C P A Newsletter *see* Connecticut C P A **1285**
C S C S Journal (GBR) **2833**
C S C W *see* Computer Supported Cooperative Work **2412**
C S C Working Papers *see* Centro Studi Confindustria. Working Papers **1616**
C S D A *see* Computational Statistics & Data Analysis **5551**
C S D G Working Paper *see* The Conflict, Security & Development Group. Working Papers **6416**
C S D Perspectives (University of Westminster, Centre for the Study of Democracy) (GBR) **7224**
C S - D R M S (Commonwealth Secretariat - Debt Recording Management System) (GBR) **1592**
C S D S Working Papers (University of KwaZulu-Natal, Centre for Social and Development Studies) (ZAF) **7952**
C S E *see* College Store Executive **1811**
C S E *see* Consulting - Specifying Engineer **3185**
C S E A Annual Report (California Society of Enrolled Agents) (USA) **1914**
C S E International Lecture (GBR) **3183**
C S E R G E G E C Working Paper *see* Centre for Social and Economic Research on the Global Environment. Working Paper. Global Environment Change **3409**
C S E R G E Working Paper P A *see* Centre for Social and Economic Research on the Global Environment. Working Paper. Policy Analysis **1081**
C S E R G E Working Paper W M *see* Centre for Social and Economic Research on the Global Environment. Working Paper. Waste Management **3504**
C S E R I A C Gateway *see* Human Systems I A C Gateway **6678**
C S E R Review (Committee for the Scientific Examination of Religion) (USA ISSN 1933-0405) **7629**
C S E T Multiple Subjects *see* The Best Teachers' Test Preparation for the C S E T Multiple Subjects **2831**
C S G Directory II *see* C S G State Directory. Directory II, Legislative Leadership, Committees & Staff **7112**
C S G Report Series (Computer Systems Group) (GBR) **2409**
• C S G State Directory. Directory I. Elective Officials (Council of State Governments) (USA ISSN 1521-7272) **7425**
• C S G State Directory. Directory II, Legislative Leadership, Committees & Staff (Council of State Governments) (USA ISSN 1536-4666) **7112**
• C S G State Directory. Directory III, Administrative Officials (Council of State Governments) (USA ISSN 1521-7264) **7425**
C S G State Directory I *see* C S G State Directory. Directory I. Elective Officials **7425**
C S G State Directory III *see* C S G State Directory. Directory III, Administrative Officials **7425**
C S H Protocols *see* Cold Spring Harbor Protocols **666**
C S I Communications (Computer Society of India) (IND ISSN 0970-647X) **2409**
C S I - F B I Computer Crime and Security Survey (Computer Security Institute - Federal Bureau of Investigation) (USA ISSN 1553-5983) **2511**
The C S I Handbook (Corporate Social Investment) (ZAF ISSN 1680-0095) **1615**
C S I Journal (IND) **2409**
• C S I NewsBrief (Construction Specifications Institute) (USA) **989**
C S I R Annual Report - Technology Impact (Council for Scientific and Industrial Research) (ZAF) **7843**
C S I R Building Technology. Complete List of Publications (Council for Scientific and Industrial Research) (ZAF) **1045**

Title

C S I R Handbook (Council for Scientific and Industrial Research) (GHA) **7843**
• C S I R O Annual Report (Commonwealth Scientific and Industrial Research Organization) (AUS ISSN 1030-4215) **8417**
• C S I R O Atmospheric Research Technical Paper (Commonwealth Scientific and Industrial Research Organization) (AUS ISSN 1445-6982) **6348**
C S I R O. Division of Livestock Industries. Divisional Information Sheets *see* Commonwealth Scientific and Industrial Research Organisation. Division of Livestock Industries. Divisional Information Sheets **921**
• C S I R O Entomology. Report of Research (Commonwealth Scientific and Industrial Research Organisation) (AUS ISSN 1443-8577) **841**
• ➤ C S I R O Land and Water Science Report (AUS ISSN 1833-4563) **2793**
C S I R O Land and Water. Technical Report *see* C S I R O Land and Water Science Report **2793**
• C S I R O Marine and Atmospheric Research Paper (Commonwealth Scientific and Industrial Research Organization) (AUS ISSN 1833-2331) **3408**
C S I R O. Marine Laboratories. Report *see* Commonwealth Scientific and Industrial Research Organization. Marine Laboratories. Report (Online) **2802**
C S I R Special Reports *see* South Africa. Division of Roads and Transport Technology. P A D Series **8635**
C S I S Reports (Center for Strategic and International Studies) (USA) **7224**
• C S I Weekly (USA) **989**
C S - Journal (DEU) **6553**
C S L *see* Corporation, Securities & Business Law **4865**
• C S L A Journal (California School Library Association) (USA) **4999**
C S L Bulletin (New York C.S. Lewis Society) (USA ISSN 0883-9980) **5268**
• C S L Connection (USA) **4999**
C S M *see* Campus Safety Magazine **3018**
C S M A Executive Newswatch (Chemical Specialties Manufacturers Association) (USA) **2052**
C S M C R I Newsletter (Central Salt and Marine Chemicals Research Institute) (IND ISSN 0971-8605) **2801**
† C S M Informatie (NLD ISSN 0165-9375) **8938**
C S N *see* Customer Service Newsletter **1737**
C S N *see* Convenience Store News **3677**
C S N *see* Construction Site News **998**
C S N *see* Comic Shop News **5211**
C S O (Chief Security Officer) (FRA ISSN 1765-1336) **2511**
C S O (Chief Security Officer) (POL ISSN 1734-946X) **2512**
• C S O (Chief Security Officer) (USA ISSN 1540-904X) **2512**
C.S.O. Statistical Bulletins (Central Statistical Office) (TTO) **8359**
C S P *see* Critical Social Policy **8036**
C S P *see* Contemporary Security Policy **7228**
• C S P (Convenience Store Petroleum) (USA ISSN 1077-5536) **3676**
• C S P Directory and International Registry of Certified Safety Professionals (Board of Certified Safety Professionals) (USA) **6675**
C S P Independent (Convenience Store Petroleum) (USA) **3676**
C S P R A Newsletter (California State Park Rangers Association) (USA ISSN 0887-9176) **2605**
C.S.P. World News (CAN ISSN 0702-7958) **5418**
• C S R (Corporate Social Responsibility) (DNK ISSN 1903-6418) **3408**
• The C S R Advisor (Customer Service Representative) (USA ISSN 1044-9884) **4497**
C S R & T I (Mysore) (IND) **8449**
• ➤ C S R C Research Report (Chicano Studies Research Center) (USA) **3524**
C S S C D *see* Computer Software and Services CD-ROM **2588**
C S S D *see* Campus Safety & Student Development **3018**
• C S S E (Cultural Studies of Science Education) (NLD ISSN 1871-1502) **3053**
C S S E Journal *see* International Journal of Computer Systems Science and Engineering **2522**
C S S H *see* Comparative Studies in Society and History **8095**
• C S S H E Professional File (Canadian Society for the Study of Higher Education) (CAN ISSN 0836-7973) **2970**
Le C S S Magazine/C S S Zeitung (Chretienne Sociale Suisse) (CHE) **4497**
C S S P Congressional Sourcebook (Council of Scientific Society Presidents) (USA) **7425**
• C S S P News (Council of Scientific Society Presidents) (USA) **2833**
La C S S Q Vous Informe (Coalition Sida des Sourds du Quebec) (CAN ISSN 1719-8828) **5811**
C S S R *see* Centre for Social Science Research Working Papers **7953**
C S S R Bulletin (Council of Societies for the Study of Religion) (USA ISSN 1060-1635) **7629**
C S S R Working Papers *see* Centre for Social Science Research Working Papers **7953**
C S S Zeitung *see* Le C S S Magazine **4497**
• C S T A Voice (Computer Science Teachers Association) (USA ISSN 1555-2128) **2409**
C S T D *see* Contemporary Stone & Tile Design **999**
A C S Transformations *see* Transformations (Atlanta) **4485**
C S U - E P S A. Proceedings *see* Dianli Xitong Jiqi Zidong Huaxue Bao **7850**
• C S U Handbook (Charles Sturt University) (AUS ISSN 1832-3278) **2970**
• C S W P Gazette (Committee on the Status of Women in Physics) (USA ISSN 0897-3539) **7007**
C-Sharp (NLD ISSN 1875-2624) **3914**
C-Store (NZL) **3676**
C-Store (ZAF) **3676**
C-Store Self-Service Executive Summary (Convenience Store) (USA) **3676**
C / Stores on Campus *see* On-Campus Hospitality **2295**
C T *see* C'T **2415**
C T *see* Christianity Today **7632**
C T *see* Communications Technology **2379**
C T *see* Circuitree Magazine **3090**
C T *see* CompressorTech Two **5450**
C T *see* Corporate Taxation **1918**
C T A *see* Zhongguo Fangzhi ji Chengyi **8463**
C T A *see* Clinical Trials Advisor **5598**
C T A B D A Newsletter (Connecticut American Ballroom Dance Association) (USA) **2683**
C T A Output (Corporate Transfer Agents Association) (USA) **1615**
C T A P Publication (Community Transportation Assistance Project) (USA) **8492**
C T & F *see* Ciencia Tecnologia y Futuro **6766**
C T & L *see* Caribbean Travel + Life **8692**
† C T B A Info (Centre Technique du Bois et de l'Ameublement) (FRA ISSN 0984-2438) **8939**
C T B S S P Research Results Digests (Commercial Truck and Bus Safety Synthesis Program) (USA) **8669**
C T B S S P Synthesis Reports/Synthesis Reports (Commercial Truck and Bus Safety Synthesis Program) (USA ISSN 1544-6808) **8669**
▼ • C T B U H Journal (Council on Tall Buildings and Urban Habitat) (USA ISSN 1946-1186) **4406**
C T C Cycling Yearbook (Cyclists Touring Club) (GBR) **8256**
C T C News (China Telecommunication Construction) (HKG ISSN 1024-5847) **2314**
† C T C Newsletter (Competitive Tendering and Contracting Research) (AUS ISSN 1325-6114) **8939**
C T C Tourism Intelligence Bulletin *see* Renseignements sur le Tourisme. Bulletin **8751**
C T C Tourism Intelligence Bulletin. Executive Summary *see* Renseignements sur le Tourisme. Sommaire. Bulletin **8751**
• C T D News (Cumulative Trauma Disorder) (USA ISSN 1062-6743) **6675**
• C T Digest (Cardiothoracic) (USA) **5779**
C T E R *see* Career and Technical Education Research **2834**
C T Europe *see* Construction Today Europe **998**
C T Genealogy News *see* Connecticut Genealogy News **3763**
C T I Centre for Nursing and Midwifery. Newsletter (GBR ISSN 1361-021X) **5954**
C T I Journal (Cooling Tower Institute) (USA ISSN 0273-3250) **6765**
C T I News (Houston) (Cooling Tower Institute) (USA) **6765**
C T I P Working Paper Series *see* Syracuse University. Center for Technology and Information Policy. Working Papers **8440**
C T I T Workshop Proceedings Series (Centre for Telematics and Information Technology) (NLD ISSN 1574-0846) **2409**
C T J *see* Christian Teachers Journal **2836**
C T L R *see* Computer and Telecommunications Law Review **4648**
† C T M News (Commercio Tessuti Moda) (ITA) **8939**
C T M S Directory & Buyers' Guide (Cosmetics Toiletries Manufacturers Suppliers) (GBR ISSN 1369-9490) **593**
C T N (Confectioner, Tobacconist, Newsagent) (GBR ISSN 0955-2758) **3672**
• C T N Magazine (USA) **4072**
The C T N S Bulletin (The Center for Theology and the Natural Sciences) (USA ISSN 0889-8243) **7629**
C T O. Computer Trade Only *see* P C Retail **2493**
C T O Magazine (Chief Technology Officer) (USA) **2491**
C T P A News (California Travel Parks Association, Inc.) (USA) **8690**
• C T P D C. Working Paper Series (Counselling Training Personal Development Consulting) (GBR ISSN 1747-4973) **7342**
C T R *see* Canadian Theatre Review **8467**
C T R *see* Contemporary Theatre Review **8468**
C T R *see* Computer Technology Review **2412**
C T R J *see* Clothing & Textiles Research Journal **2246**
C T S *see* Cultural Text Studies **8097**
C T S *see* Clinical and Translational Science **5596**
C T S Working Papers (Centre for Transport Studies) (GBR ISSN 1747-6232) **3261**
C T Singles Connection (Connecticut) (USA) **7943**
C.T.T.S. Annual (College of Textile Technology, Serampore) (IND ISSN 0084-8859) **8449**
C T U M S (Canadian Tobacco Use Monitoring Survey) (CAN ISSN 1492-1448) **8485**
C T W Newsletter *see* Composting Toilet World Newsletter **3505**
• ➤ C Theory (CAN ISSN 1190-9153) **7112**
C U *see* Cirugia del Uruguay **6239**
• C U 360 Newsletter (Credit Union) (USA) **1323**
C U A Magazine (Catholic University of America) (USA) **2276**
C U Amiga (Commodore User) (GBR ISSN 0963-0090) **2575**
C U B Communicator (Concerned United Birthparents, Inc.) (USA ISSN 0749-8799) **8091**
C U B Communicator. Adoption Newsletter (Concerned United Birthparents, Inc.) (USA) **8091**
C U D E M Working Paper Series (Centre for Urban Development and Environmental Management) (GBR ISSN 0956-9316) **4406**
C U E S Colloquium *see* University of Cape Town. Committee for Undergraduate Education in Science. Colloquium Series **7927**
C U E S - F Y I *see* C U E S - For Your Information **1323**
C U E S - For Your Information (Credit Union Executives Society) (USA ISSN 1087-108X) **1323**
C U E S Staffing Manual for Credit Unions (Credit Union Executives Society) (USA ISSN 1937-9331) **1323**
C U I S (Credit Union Information Service) (USA) **1323**
C U L *see* College & Undergraduate Libraries **5003**
• C U P A - H R eNews (College and University Personnel Association - Human Resources) (USA) **3018**
• C U P A - H R Journal (USA) **2970**
C U P A - H R News *see* C U P A - H R eNews **3018**
C U P A - Journal *see* C U P A - H R Journal **2970**
C U P A News *see* C U P A - H R eNews **3018**
C U P R Report *see* Center for Urban Policy Research Report **1081**
C U R D E S. Cahiers *see* Centre Universitaire de Recherche pour le Developpement Economique et Social. Cahiers **1592**
C U R D S Discussion Paper *see* Centre for Urban and Regional Development Studies. Discussion Paper **4406**
• C U R I H A M. Cuadernos (Centro Universitario Rosario de Investigaciones Hidroambientales. Cuadernos) (ARG ISSN 1514-2906) **2793**
C U S Bulletin (Centre for Urban Studies) (BGD) **4406**
C U S E C Journal (Central United States Earthquake Consortium) (USA) **2778**
C U S J *see* Columbia Undergraduate Science Journal **7848**
C U S L J *see* Canada - United States Law Journal **4919**
C U T A Forum A C T U (Canadian Urban Transit Association) (CAN ISSN 1183-2282) **8629**
C U T G Proceedings (Conference of University Teachers of German) (GBR ISSN 1424-0408) **5103**
C U Three Hundred and Sixty Newsletter *see* C U 360 Newsletter **1323**
▼ • C V B News (Cardiovascular Business) (USA ISSN 1937-6979) **5779**
C V B Rapporten (Centrum voor Beleidsstatistiek) (NLD ISSN 1572-3267) **7112**
C V C (Chauffage, Ventilation, Conditionnement d'Air) (FRA ISSN 1774-5071) **4117**
C V C Report (Creative Video Consulting, Inc.) (USA) **2400**
C V D *see* Chemical Vapor Deposition **2109**
C V D *see* C A Selects. Chemical Vapor Deposition **2086**
• ➤ C V D Prevention and Control (Cardiovascular Diseases) (NLD ISSN 1875-4570) **5779**
C V Guide *see* The Commercial Vehicle Guide **1980**
C V - Koers (Christen Vandaag) (NLD ISSN 1566-9084) **7629**
C V M Quarterly (College of Veterinary Medicine) (USA) **8795**
C V News (Curriculum Vitae) (BEL ISSN 0778-1032) **22**
• C V Photo (CAN ISSN 1196-9261) **6965**
C V R *see* Cardiovascular Research **5781**
C V R *see* Crime Victims Report **2649**
C-Ville Weekly (USA) **6491**
C W *see* Catholic Weekly **7791**
C W *see* Australian Christian Woman **7624**
C W *see* Circuit World **8418**
C W *see* Children's World **2182**
A C W *see* America's Civil War **4283**
• ➤ C W 3 Journal (GBR ISSN 1744-9618) **5268**
C W A News (Buffalo Grove) (Construction Writers Association) (USA) **989**
C W A News (Washington) (Communications Workers of America) (USA ISSN 0007-9227) **4591**
C W A Sector News (Communications Workers of America) (USA) **4591**
C W B *see* Custom Woodworking Business **1050**
C W B (Slaithwaite) (Childrenswear Buyer) (GBR) **2246**
• C W Canales (Computer World) (VEN) **2491**
C W G E A Newsletter (Cooperative Whole Grain Education Association) (USA) **3672**
C W I Herald (Christian Witness to Israel) (GBR ISSN 0308-5252) **7733**
➤ C W I Monographs (NLD ISSN 0169-4669) **5550**
C W I Newsletter (Clearinghouse on Women's Issues) (USA) **8854**
C W I Publications (Centrum voor Wiskunde en Informatica) (NLD) **5550**
C W I Reports. M A S Report Series: Modelling, Analysis and Simulation *see* Modelling, Analysis and Simulation **5554**
C W I S *see* Campus Wide Information Systems **2495**
C W I Syllabi (Centrum voor Wiskunde en Informatica) (NLD) **5550**
† C W I Tracts (Centrum voor Wiskunde en Informatica) (NLD) **8939**
C W Newsletter *see* Connect Wyoming **4064**
C W R *see* The Catholic World Report **7791**
C W R M *see* Communications in Waste and Resource Management **3505**
C W R Membership Newsletter (Center for Women and Religion) (USA) **8894**
C W R U Magazine *see* Case Magazine **2277**
C W S Migratory Birds Regulatory Reports (Canadian Wildlife Service) (CAN ISSN 1497-0139) **3408**
C W U Directory - Handbook (Church Women United) (USA) **7749**
C W U Voice (Postal Edition) *see* Voice (Postal Edition) **4605**
C W U Voice (Telecoms & Financial Services Edition) *see* Voice (Telecoms & Financial Services Edition) **4605**
C W Weekly *see* CenterWatch Weekly **5903**
C X (AUS ISSN 1448-2010) **8152**
C X O *see* C E O **1414**
C X O Canada *see* CxO **2496**
C Y A P forum (Canada's Year of Asia Pacific) (CAN ISSN 1484-9844) **1731**
C Y E *see* Children, Youth and Environments **2148**
C Y F *see* Children and Youth Funding Report **2148**
C Y H (Celebrate Young Heritage) (USA) **3971**
C Y L A Quarterly (California Young Lawyers Association) (USA ISSN 8750-944X) **4635**
C y L Moda Intima (Corseteria y Lenceria) (ESP) **2246**
C Y R I C Annual Report (Cyclotron Radioisotope Center) (JPN) **6193**
C Y R I C News/C Y R I C Nyusu (Cyclotron Radioisotope Center) (JPN ISSN 0916-3751) **3166**
C Y R I C Nyusu *see* C Y R I C News **3166**
C Y S *see* Child & Youth Services **8032**
• C y T A Journal of Food (Ciencia y Tecnologia Alimentaria) (GBR ISSN 1947-6337) **3629**
C Z I Register and Buyer's Guide *see* Confederation of Zimbabwe Industries. Register & Buyers Guide **1981**
C Z I Zimbabwe Export Directory *see* Zimbabwe Export Directory **2036**
C Z S O Monthly Statistics (Czech Statistical Office) (CZE) **8359**
• Copyright News (AUS ISSN 1833-9913) **6747**
C16 Autostyle *see* C 16 Autostyle **8570**
C2W *see* Chemisch2Weekblad **2056**
C2W Life Sciences *see* Life Sciences **2071**
C3 *see* C 3 **6129**
C3i (USA) **8164**
• C6necessaiRe (FRA ISSN 1951-6134) **7112**
Ca Dao Magazine *see* Tap Chi Ca Dao **3567**
• Ca' Foscari. Annali (ITA ISSN 1125-3762) **5103**
Ca M'Interesse (FRA ISSN 0243-1335) **3840**
Ca se Passe Comme Ca (FRA ISSN 1280-8008) **2181**
Ca Sexprime (CAN ISSN 1712-5782) **6983**
Ca Va (GBR ISSN 0007-9243) **5103**
Cab Driver (GBR) **8570**
CAB International. Abstract Journal (GBR) **3708**
Cab Nightflight (DEU) **6553**
• CAB Reviews: Perspectives in Agriculture, Veterinary Science, Nutrition and Natural Resources (GBR) **99**
Cabala (VEN) **6644**
▼ Cabecera (COL ISSN 2011-4281) **7952**
• Cabela's Outfitter Journal (USA ISSN 1931-6259) **8307**
• Cabell's Directory of Publishing Opportunities in Accounting (USA) **1216**
• Cabell's Directory of Publishing Opportunities in Economics and Finance (USA) **1216**
• Cabell's Directory of Publishing Opportunities in Educational Curriculum and Methods (USA) **2931**
• Cabell's Directory of Publishing Opportunities in Educational Psychology and Administration (USA) **2931**
• Cabell's Directory of Publishing Opportunities in Management (USA) **1216**
• Cabell's Directory of Publishing Opportunities in Marketing (USA) **1216**
• Cabell's Directory of Publishing Opportunities in Psychology (USA) **7417**
Cabin Crew Safety *see* AeroSafety World **8533**
Cabin Life *see* Cabin Life, Cabin Living **5067**
Cabin Life, Cabin Living (USA ISSN 1540-3785) **5067**
Cabinet (USA ISSN 1531-1430) **480**
• Cabinet Maker (GBR ISSN 0964-4199) **4554**
• CabinetMaker (USA ISSN 1048-0196) **4554**

DIRECTORY 2010 CAHIERS DE LA PHOTOGRAPHIE 10079

Cabins and Cottages *see* Getaway Cabins & Cottages **8959**
Cabirion: Gay Books Bulletin (USA ISSN 1043-383X) **4371**
Cable (GBR ISSN 0045-3714) **3297**
The Cable (USA) **2276**
Cable Addenda to Television Factbook *see* Television and Cable Factbook **2396**
• Cable and Satellite Europe (GBR ISSN 0265-6973) **2377**
Cable & Satellite International (GBR ISSN 1467-5935) **2377**
Cable & Satellite T V Market Report *see* Key Note Market Report: Cable & Satellite T V **2384**
• Cable and Satellite Yearbook (Year) (GBR ISSN 0956-6872) **2377**
Cable & Station Coverage Atlas *see* Cable & TV Station Coverage Atlas (Year) **2377**
• Cable & TV Station Coverage Atlas (Year) (USA) **2377**
Cable Connection (USA ISSN 0744-8570) **2377**
Cable Connection Magazine *see* Cable Connection **2377**
Cable Connection Monthly *see* Cable Connection **2377**
• Cable Digital News (USA) **2377**
• Cable in the Classroom (USA ISSN 1931-4418) **3053**
Cable Network Start-Up Strategies and Business Models *see* Cable Network Start-Up Strategies & Business Models **2377**
Cable Network Start-Up Strategies & Business Models (USA ISSN 1539-5324) **2377**
• Cable Optics (USA ISSN 1051-1938) **2314**
Cable Optics Monthly Newsletter *see* Cable Optics **2314**
Cable Optics Newsletter *see* Cable Optics **2314**
• Cable Program Investor (Online) (USA) **2378**
Cable Program Investor (Print) *see* Cable Program Investor (Online) **2378**
• Cable Semanal (ARG) **7843**
Cable T V Advertising Statistics (USA ISSN 1935-6072) **2346**
Cable T V Facts (USA) **22**
Cable T V Investor. Deals & Finance (USA ISSN 1545-6579) **1615**
† • Cable T V Law Reporter (USA ISSN 0749-7652) **8939**
• Cable T V Regulation (USA) **2378**
Cable Talk (GBR ISSN 1365-3288) **3297**
Cable Telephony *see* Future of Cable Telephony **2368**
Cable Television & Other Non-Broadcast Media (USA) **2378**
Cablecaster *see* Mediacaster **2385**
Cablecaster Directory *see* Mediacaster Directory **2385**
• Cablefax (USA ISSN 1069-6644) **2378**
CableTalk (ZAF) **2533**
Cabling Business Magazine (USA ISSN 1060-3050) **2366**
• Cabling Connection (AUS ISSN 1447-9915) **2314**
• Cabling Installation and Maintenance (USA ISSN 1073-3108) **2378**
Cabling Installation & Maintenance *see* Cabling Installation and Maintenance **2378**
Cabling Networking Systems (CAN ISSN 1711-7666) **2366**
Cabling Systems *see* Cabling Networking Systems **2366**
Cabling World *see* Electrical Times **3304**
• ➤ Cabo (ZAF ISSN 0379-4830) **4174**
Los Cabos (USA) **8690**
Cabot Market Letter (USA ISSN 0733-8554) **1615**
CaboVisao Magazine (PRT) **2378**
Cabrio und Sportcoupe (DEU) **8570**
† Caccia e Cani (ITA ISSN 1123-413X) **8939**
Caccia e Tiro (ITA) **8307**
Il Cacciatore Italiano (ITA) **8307**
Il Cacciatore Trentino (ITA ISSN 1828-4825) **8307**
Cache Citizen (USA) **3971**
Cachet (USA) **3971**
➤ Cactaceas y Suculentas Mexicanas (MEX ISSN 0526-717X) **782**
• Cactus (USA) **2409**
• Cactus and Succulent Journal (USA ISSN 0007-9367) **782**
Cactus World (GBR ISSN 1751-1429) **782**
Cactussen en Vetplanten (BEL ISSN 0774-4706) **783**
CAD-CAM *see* C A D - C A M **3288**
CAD/CAM/CAE Observer *see* C A D / C A M / C A E Observer **3288**
Cadalyst *see* CADalyst **3289**
• CADalyst (USA ISSN 0820-5450) **3289**
Cadastro Industrial do Para (BRA) **1882**
• Cadcamnet (USA) **2409**
CadDesk *see* A E C Magazine **3288**
Caddesk A E C *see* A E C Magazine **3288**
Caddoan Archeology (USA ISSN 1522-0427) **385**
Cadence (Redwood) (USA ISSN 0162-6973) **6553**
Cadence All-Years Index (CAN) **6631**
Cadenza (CAN ISSN 0703-8380) **6553**
Cadenza (USA ISSN 0007-9405) **6553**
Caderno C R H (Centro de Recursos Humanos) (BRA ISSN 0103-4979) **7952**
Caderno Catarinense de Ensino de Fisica (BRA ISSN 0102-3594) **7007**
Caderno Cientifico do Maestrado e Doutorado em Direito (BRA ISSN 1414-2937) **4635**
Caderno de Direito *see* Caderno Cientifico do Maestrado e Doutorado em Direito **4635**
Caderno de Geografia (BRA ISSN 0103-8427) **4001**
• Caderno de Gestao & Regionalidade (BRA ISSN 1809-1644) **1731**
• Caderno de Pesquisa. Serie Biologia (BRA ISSN 1677-5600) **663**
Caderno de Pesquisas Tributarias (BRA) **4635**
• Caderno Virtual de Turismo (BRA ISSN 1677-6976) **8690**
Cadernos B A D *see* Cadernos de Biblioteconomia, Arquivistica e Documentacao **4999**
Cadernos Cedes *see* C E D E S Cadernos **2833**
Cadernos da Area de Ciencias Bioloxicas. Inventarios (ESP ISSN 0214-848X) **663**
Cadernos da F A C E C A *see* Pontificia Universidade Catolica de Campinas. Faculdade de Ciencias Economicas Contabeis e Administrativas. Cadernos **1547**
Cadernos da F C E C A *see* Pontificia Universidade Catolica de Campinas. Faculdade de Ciencias Economicas Contabeis e Administrativas. Cadernos **1547**
Cadernos de Anglistica (PRT) **5268**
Cadernos de Antropologia e Imagem (BRA ISSN 0104-9658) **331**
Cadernos de Arqueologia (PRT ISSN 0870-6425) **385**
Cadernos de Arquitetura e Urbanismo (BRA ISSN 1413-2095) **436**
Cadernos de Atencion Primaria (ESP ISSN 1134-3583) **5590**
Cadernos de Biblioteconomia, Arquivistica e Documentacao (PRT ISSN 0007-9421) **4999**
Cadernos de Campo (BRA ISSN 0104-5679) **331**
• Cadernos de Ciencia e Tecnologia (BRA ISSN 0104-1096) **7843**
Cadernos de Ciencias Sociais (BRA ISSN 0104-0782) **7952**
Cadernos de Ciencias Sociais (PRT ISSN 0871-0945) **7952**
Cadernos de Consulta Psicologica (PRT ISSN 0871-7516) **7343**
➤ Cadernos de Direito Natural (BRA) **4635**
Cadernos de Direito Tributario e Financas Publicas (BRA) **4635**
➤ Cadernos de Divulgacao Cultural (BRA ISSN 0102-8227) **5590**
Cadernos de Economia *see* Jornal de Santa Catarina **3804**
Cadernos de Educacao (BRA ISSN 0104-1371) **2833**
Cadernos de Educacao Especial (BRA ISSN 0103-0000) **3037**
➤ Cadernos de Estudos Linguisticos (BRA ISSN 0102-5767) **5103**
Cadernos de Estudos Sociais (BRA ISSN 0102-4248) **7952**
Cadernos de Folclore (BRA ISSN 0575-0075) **3615**
Cadernos de Geociencias (BRA ISSN 0103-1597) **2703**
Cadernos de Historia *see* Cadernos de Historia da Educacao **4286**
Cadernos de Historia (BRA ISSN 1679-5636) **4133**
Cadernos de Historia da Educacao (BRA ISSN 1807-3859) **4286**
Cadernos de Historia e Filosofia da Ciencia (BRA ISSN 0101-3424) **7843**
Cadernos de Lingua (ESP ISSN 1130-5924) **5103**
Cadernos de Linguistica e Teoria da Literatura (BRA ISSN 0101-3548) **5103**
• ➤ Cadernos de Pesquisa (BRA ISSN 0100-1574) **2833**
Cadernos de Pesquisa (Caxias do Sul) (BRA ISSN 1516-0440) **7952**
Cadernos de Pos-Graduacao em Administracao de Empresas (BRA ISSN 1518-7322) **1732**
➤ Cadernos de Pos-Graduacao em Comunicacao e Letras (BRA ISSN 1518-9058) **5268**
➤ Cadernos de Pos-Graduacao em Direito Politico e Economico (BRA ISSN 1678-2127) **4635**
➤ Cadernos de Pos-Graduacao em Disturbios do Desenvolvimento (BRA ISSN 1519-0307) **6129**
➤ Cadernos de Pos-Graduacao em Educacao, Arte e Historia da Cultura (BRA ISSN 1519-776X) **4446**
➤ Cadernos de Pos-Graduacao em Engenharia Eletrica (BRA ISSN 1518-904X) **3297**
Cadernos de Pos - Graduacao em Letras (BRA ISSN 1679-1541) **5268**
➤ Cadernos de Pos-Graduacao en Arquitetura e Urbanismo (BRA ISSN 1676-6679) **436**
Cadernos de Psicanalise (BRA ISSN 0103-4251) **7343**
Cadernos de Psicolxia *see* Colexio Oficial de Psicologos de Galicia. Cadernos de Psicolxia **7347**
• Cadernos de Psicopedagogia (BRA ISSN 1676-1049) **2834**
▼ • Cadernos de Relacoes Internacionais (BRA ISSN 1983-4500) **7112**
• ➤ Cadernos de Saude Publica/Reports in Public Health (BRA ISSN 0102-311X) **7511**
Cadernos de Seguro (BRA ISSN 0101-5818) **4497**
Cadernos de Sociologia *see* Sociologias **8136**
Cadernos de Sociologia e Politica (BRA ISSN 1809-1814) **8091**
Cadernos de Traducao (BRA ISSN 1414-526X) **5103**
Cadernos do Area de Ciencias Agrarias (ESP ISSN 0214-8161) **99**
Cadernos do I.C.H. *see* Instituto de Ciencias Humanas. Cadernos **7973**
• Cadernos do Noroeste (PRT ISSN 0870-9874) **7952**
Cadernos do Patrimonio Cultural (BRA) **7952**
Cadernos do Povo (PRT ISSN 0870-9939) **5268**
Cadernos do Terceiro Mundo (BRA ISSN 0101-7993) **7112**
Cadernos ESP *see* E S P Cadernos **7515**
Cadernos Lava e Oficina *see* Lavra & Oficina **4463**
Cadernos Museologicos (BRA) **6522**
Cadernos P U C (Pontificia Universidade Catolica) (BRA ISSN 0102-2040) **1445**
• Cadernos Pagu (BRA ISSN 0104-8333) **8091**
Cadernos Pedagogicos (BRA) **2834**
Cadernos Rioarte (BRA ISSN 0102-6518) **8091**
Cadet Quest Magazine (USA) **7749**
Cadillac Cicatrix (USA ISSN 1934-2969) **5268**
• Cadiznoticias.com (ESP ISSN 1699-2067) **3951**
• Cadmo (ITA ISSN 1122-5165) **2834**
Cadogan Chess and Bridge Books (GBR) **8164**
Cadre (CAN) **2276**
Cadres C F D T (FRA ISSN 0398-3145) **4591**
▼ Cadres et Societe (FRA ISSN 1960-2316) **1732**
Caducee (CAN ISSN 0226-3467) **2276**
• Caeculus (BEL ISSN 1782-4907) **385**
Caelum (ZAF) **6348**
Caen Parler? (FRA ISSN 1774-9409) **2970**
• Caert-Thresoor (NLD ISSN 0167-4994) **4001**
Caes e Gatos (BRA ISSN 0103-278X) **6805**
Caesar Newsletter *see* C A E S A R Newsletter **8417**
➤ Caesaraugusta (ESP ISSN 0007-9502) **385**
Caesars Player (USA) **8164**
Cafard Libere (SEN ISSN 0850-8267) **5209**
Cafe (NZL ISSN 1174-1473) **4383**
• Cafe (SWE ISSN 1101-2021) **3955**
Cafe Annual (NZL ISSN 1177-1240) **4383**
Cafe Annual with Michael Guy's Eating Out *see* Cafe Annual **4383**
Cafe Bistro (CHE) **4383**
• Cafe Compendium (Online) (USA) **5210**
Cafe Compendium (Print) *see* Cafe Compendium (Online) **5210**
Cafe Eighties Magazine (USA ISSN 1089-5728) **6553**
Cafe Europa (GBR ISSN 1752-8429) **601**
• The Cafe Irreal (USA ISSN 1931-6763) **5268**
▼ • Cafe Latino (FRA ISSN 1958-3249) **3524**
• Cafe Magazine (GBR ISSN 1360-6875) **2553**
Cafe Psycho (FRA ISSN 1779-8450) **7343**
Cafe Racer (FRA ISSN 1273-6600) **8256**
† Cafe Racer (ITA ISSN 1127-1329) **8939**
Cafe Racer. Hors Serie *see* Cafe Racer **8256**
The Cafe Review (USA ISSN 1069-7179) **5268**
Cafe Revue (Dutch Edition) (BEL ISSN 0778-645X) **4383**
Cafe Revue (French Edition) (BEL ISSN 0778-3477) **4383**
Cafe Solo (USA) **5418**
Cafe - Sweets (JPN) **3672**
Cafejournal *see* Oesterreichisches Cafe Journal **4395**
Cafetal/Coffee Review (GTM) **3629**
Cafeteria (USA) **5418**
Cafetier, Restaurateur Parisien (FRA) **4383**
Caffaro Group. Annual Report. (ITA) **3237**
Caffaro Group. Environmental Report (ITA) **3237**
Il Caffe (CHE ISSN 1662-2332) **3958**
Il Caffe Illustrato (ITA ISSN 1592-7652) **5268**
Caffe Michelangiolo (ITA ISSN 1826-2546) **4446**
➤ Cag University Journal of Social Sciences (TUR ISSN 1304-8392) **1078**
† • Cagdas Cerrahi Dergisi/Journal of Current Surgery (TUR ISSN 1016-5118) **8939**
Cage & Aviary Birds (GBR ISSN 0007-9561) **904**
• Le Cahier de l'Agriculture Raisonnee (FRA ISSN 1962-5081) **99**
▼ Le Cahier de l'International (FRA ISSN 1955-8945) **1554**
Cahier du Designer (FRA ISSN 1639-6081) **2483**
Cahier du G I P R I *see* Geneva International Peace Research Institute. Cahiers **7237**
† Cahier Eveil (FRA ISSN 1776-3231) **8939**
Le Cahier Fermier (FRA ISSN 1953-0579) **262**
Cahier I & L Kennisbanken *see* I & L Kennisbanken **1819**
Cahier Marce (FRA ISSN 1952-241X) **6129**
Cahier Statistique Maritime (FRA) **8523**
Cahier Technique Automobile (FRA ISSN 1950-6643) **8570**
Cahiers (C I M A G L) *see* Universite de Copenhague. Institut du Moyen-Age Grec et Latin. Cahiers **4275**
• Les Cahiers A L H I M (Amerique Latine Histoire et Memoire) (FRA ISSN 1628-6731) **3524**
Cahiers Africains/Afrika Studies (BEL ISSN 1021-9994) **4174**
Cahiers Africains d'Administration Publique (MAR) **7425**
Cahiers Africains de Recherche en Education (FRA ISSN 1634-331X) **2834**
Cahiers Agricultures *see* Cahiers d'Etudes et de Recherches Francophones. Agricultures **99**
Cahiers Albert Schweitzer (FRA ISSN 0153-6087) **6909**
Les Cahiers Alexandre Dumas (FRA ISSN 0761-8034) **5268**
Cahiers Alsaciens d'Archeologie d'Art et d'Histoire (FRA ISSN 0575-0385) **386**
Cahiers Andre Gide (FRA ISSN 0068-4937) **5268**
Cahiers Balkaniques (FRA ISSN 0290-7402) **5103**
Les Cahiers Bernard Brunhes (FRA ISSN 1953-0498) **1445**
Cahiers Bibliographiques de Chimie Organometallique/Bibliographic Notebooks for Organometallic Chemistry (FRA ISSN 0756-5968) **2093**
Cahiers - Bijdragen *see* Cahiers d'Histoire du Temps Present **4208**
Cahiers Bio-Wetenschappen en Maatschappij (NLD ISSN 0921-3457) **663**
Les Cahiers Bouddhiques (FRA ISSN 1777-926X) **7700**
Cahiers Bourbonnais (FRA ISSN 0007-9618) **5268**
Cahiers Bretons/Ar Gwyr (FRA ISSN 0068-4953) **7952**
Cahiers Bruxellois (BEL ISSN 0007-9626) **4208**
Cahiers Charles V (FRA ISSN 0184-1025) **5103**
• ➤ Cahiers Chronos (NLD ISSN 1384-5357) **5103**
Cahiers Claude Simon (FRA ISSN 1774-9425) **5268**
Cahiers Colette (FRA ISSN 0291-2120) **5268**
† Cahiers Confrontation (FRA ISSN 0222-5956) **8939**
• ➤ Cahiers Critiques de Therapie Familiale et de Pratiques de Reseaux (BEL ISSN 1372-8202) **7343**
Les Cahiers d'Action Familiale (FRA ISSN 0299-3511) **8091**
Cahiers d'Anthropologie Sociale (FRA ISSN 1951-5030) **331**
Cahiers d'Archeologie Aveyronnaise (FRA ISSN 1166-0732) **386**
Cahiers d'Asie Centrale (FRA ISSN 1270-9247) **7952**
• ➤ Cahiers de Biologie Marine (FRA ISSN 0007-9723) **664**
Cahiers de Biotherapie (FRA ISSN 0301-1178) **5590**
Cahiers de Cantercel (FRA ISSN 1628-5735) **436**
• Cahiers de Chaillot (FRA ISSN 1017-7574) **7225**
▼ • Cahiers de Civilisation Espagnole (FRA ISSN 1957-7761) **4208**
Cahiers de Civilisation Medievale (FRA ISSN 0007-9731) **4133**
Cahiers de Civilisation Medievale. Bibliographie (FRA ISSN 0240-8678) **4133**
Cahiers de Cooperation Medicale *see* Quaderni di Cooperazione Sanitaria **5825**
Les Cahiers de Critique Communiste (FRA ISSN 1761-8630) **7112**
Cahiers de Defense Sociale (ITA ISSN 0223-582X) **2645**
† Les Cahiers de Direct (FRA ISSN 0180-9881) **8939**
• Les Cahiers de Droit (CAN ISSN 0007-974X) **4636**
Les Cahiers de Droit de la Sante du Sud-Est (FRA ISSN 1774-9832) **7511**
Cahiers de Droit de l'Entreprise (FRA ISSN 1779-0778) **4859**
➤ Cahiers de Droit Europeen (BEL ISSN 0007-9758) **4919**
Cahiers de Droit Fiscal International (NLD ISSN 0168-0455) **4919**
Cahiers de Fanjeaux (FRA ISSN 0575-061X) **4208**
Cahiers de Geographie de la Sante/Journal of Geography of Health (FRA) **5591**
• Cahiers de Geographie du Quebec (CAN ISSN 0007-9766) **4001**
Les Cahiers de Global Chance (FRA ISSN 1270-377X) **3125**
Cahiers de Grammaire (FRA ISSN 0242-1593) **5103**
Cahiers de Karnak (FRA) **386**
Les Cahiers de l' I P D/P A I D Reports (Institut Panafricain pour le Developpement) (CMR) **1592**
➤ Cahiers de la Bibliotheque Copte (BEL) **7704**
Cahiers de la Ceramique, du Verre et des Arts du Feu *see* Sevres **539**
Cahiers de la Ceramique Egyptienne (EGY ISSN 0259-7381) **386**
Les Cahiers de la Cinematheque (FRA ISSN 0764-8499) **6491**
Cahiers de la Cinematheque. Collection *see* Les Cahiers de la Cinematheque **6491**
Cahiers de la D A F I *see* Delegation Archeologique Francaise en Iran. Cahiers **389**
Cahiers de la Documentation *see* Association Belge de Documentation. Cahiers de la Documentation **4992**
Cahiers de la Femme *see* Canadian Woman Studies **8894**
Les Cahiers de la Fonction Publique et de l' Administration (FRA ISSN 0753-4418) **7489**
Les Cahiers de la Fonderie (BEL ISSN 0775-2202) **4208**
† Cahiers de la Formation (FRA ISSN 1167-1114) **8939**
Les Cahiers de la Guitare (FRA ISSN 0294-6939) **6553**
• Les Cahiers de la Librairie (FRA ISSN 1956-9327) **7557**
Les Cahiers de la Mediation (FRA ISSN 1292-6930) **8091**
Cahiers de la Mediterranee (FRA ISSN 0395-9317) **4208**
Cahiers de la Memoire (FRA ISSN 0248-3203) **4208**
Les Cahiers de la Nature (FRA ISSN 1628-4771) **307**
Les Cahiers de la Nouvelle *see* Journal of the Short Story in English **5316**
Cahiers de la Petanque (FRA ISSN 1773-4207) **8164**
† Cahiers de la Photographie (FRA ISSN 0294-4081) **8939**

Title

Title

10082 CALIFORNIA COUNTRY ULRICH'S PERIODICALS

California Country (USA ISSN 0743-0868) **7489**
California County Projections (Year) (USA ISSN 1050-303X) **1217**
California Courier (USA ISSN 0008-0950) **3524**
California Courtroom Evidence (USA ISSN 1936-8143) **4947**
• California Criminal Defense Practice (USA) **4885**
• California Criminal Defense Practice Reporter (USA ISSN 0731-8820) **4885**
California Criminal Law Case Finder (USA) **4885**
California Criminal Law Reporter (USA ISSN 0898-3623) **4885**
• California Criminal Law Review (USA) **4636**
California Crop - Weather *see* California. Agricultural Statistics Service. Crop Weather Report **176**
California Dairy Information Bulletin (USA ISSN 0892-4406) **176**
California Damages: Law and Proof (USA) **4636**
• ➤ California Dental Association. Journal (USA ISSN 1043-2256) **5837**
California. Department of Consumer Affairs. Annual Report (USA) **2635**
California. Department of Fish and Game. Fish Bulletin (USA ISSN 0096-0985) **3588**
California. Department of Industrial Relations. Biennial Report (USA) **1668**
California. Department of the Youth Authority. Affirmative Action Statistics (USA ISSN 0362-4110) **1668**
California Department of Transportation. Journal (USA) **8570**
California. Department of Water Resources. Bulletin (USA ISSN 0084-8263) **8819**
California Department of Water Resources News *see* D W R News **8820**
• California Deposition and Discovery Practice (USA) **4828**
California Desktop Codes. California Employment Laws (USA) **4636**
California Directory of Attorneys (USA ISSN 1932-0515) **4636**
California District Attorneys Association. Case Digest (USA ISSN 0890-8400) **2646**
California Diving News (USA ISSN 1084-3264) **8164**
California. Division of Mines and Geology. Special Report (USA ISSN 0527-0014) **2727**
California. Division of Oil, Gas and Geothermal Resources. Annual Report of the State Oil and Gas Supervisor (USA ISSN 0362-1243) **6765**
California Economic Growth (Year) (USA ISSN 1053-7252) **1217**
California Economic Indicators (USA ISSN 0364-2895) **1445**
California Educational Linkages in the Life Sciences (USA) **664**
California Educator (USA ISSN 1091-6148) **2970**
California Employer (USA ISSN 0098-1435) **1668**
California Employer Advisor (USA ISSN 1058-4293) **1668**
• California Employers' Guide to Employee Handbooks and Personnel Policy Manuals (USA) **1668**
• California Employment Law (USA) **1668**
▼ • California Employment Law (Falls Church) (USA ISSN 1934-1644) **1669**
• California Employment Law Letter (Year) (USA ISSN 1531-6599) **4636**
California Employment Law Monthly *see* VerdictSearch Employment Law **1713**
California Employment Law Reporter *see* Bender's California Labor & Employment Bulletin **1667**
California. Energy Commission. Biennial Fuels Report (USA) **3125**
California. Energy Commission. Biennial Report (USA ISSN 0270-8930) **3125**
California. Energy Commission. Quarterly Oil Report (USA) **6765**
California Energy Markets (USA ISSN 1044-2022) **3125**
California Engineer (USA ISSN 0008-1027) **3184**
California English (USA ISSN 0279-1161) **3053**
The California Enrolled Agent (USA) **1914**
• California Environmental Law and Land Use Practice (USA) **3408**
• California Environmental Law Reporter (USA ISSN 1061-365X) **3408**
California Environmental Laws (USA) **3408**
California Escrow Association News *see* C E A News **7585**
California Evidentiary Foundations (USA) **4947**
• California Executive (USA ISSN 1938-1174) **1882**
California Explorer (USA ISSN 0164-8748) **8307**
The California Eye (USA ISSN 0279-0246) **7112**
California Facts (USA ISSN 0883-6264) **3119**
• California Family Law First Alert (USA ISSN 1087-6197) **4907**
➤ California Family Law Monthly (USA ISSN 0882-7842) **4907**
• California Family Law: Practice and Procedure (USA) **4907**
California Family Law Report (USA ISSN 0164-7040) **4907**
• California Family Law Trial Guide (USA) **4907**
➤ California Family Physician (USA ISSN 0410-2894) **5591**
California Family Tax Planning (USA) **1914**
• California Farmer (USA ISSN 0008-1051) **99**
California Fiction (USA) **5269**
California Fire Service (USA ISSN 1048-5074) **3576**
California Fire Service Directory (USA) **3576**
California Fish and Game (USA ISSN 0008-1078) **937**
California Fish and Game Code. Supplement (USA) **2605**
California Fly Fisher (USA ISSN 1071-5673) **8307**
California Forestry and Forest Products (USA ISSN 0008-1094) **3710**
California Forestry Note (USA ISSN 0889-0102) **3685**
• California Forms of Jury Instruction (USA) **4636**
• California Forms of Pleading and Practice (USA) **4828**
• California G C S A E-magazine (Golf Course Superintendents Association) (USA ISSN 1938-7466) **3726**
California Game & Fish (USA ISSN 1056-0122) **8307**
California Garden (USA ISSN 0008-1116) **3726**
California Gardener (USA ISSN 1930-580X) **3726**
California Genealogical Society News *see* C G S News **3761**
➤ The California Geographer (USA ISSN 0575-5700) **4001**
California Geographical Society Bulletin *see* The C G S Bulletin **4001**
California Government & Politics Annual (USA ISSN 0084-8271) **7112**
California Grange News (USA ISSN 0008-1124) **99**
California Grocer (USA) **3676**
• California Healthfax (USA) **4090**
California Historian (USA ISSN 0575-5751) **4287**
• ➤ California History (San Francisco) (USA ISSN 0162-2897) **4287**
California Hockey & Skating (USA) **8164**
• California Home and Design (USA ISSN 1545-7915) **436**
California Horseman's Directory (USA) **8288**
California Horseman's News *see* Horseman's News **8293**
California Horticultural Society. Newsletter (USA) **3726**
The California Hotel & Motel Association Advantage (USA) **4383**
California Hungarians Weekly *see* Californiai Magyarsag **3525**
California in Perspective (USA ISSN 1065-5344) **4434**
➤ California Insect Survey. Bulletin (USA ISSN 0068-5631) **842**
• California Institute of Technology. Division of the Humanities and Social Sciences. Social Science Working Paper (USA ISSN 1933-7051) **7952**
California Insurance Disputes (USA) **4497**
• California Insurance Law & Litigation Alert (USA ISSN 1552-5139) **4497**
California Insurance Law and Litigation Alert *see* California Insurance Law & Litigation Alert **4497**
• California Insurance Law and Practice (USA) **4636**
California Insurance Law and Regulation Reporter (USA ISSN 1047-6466) **4497**
California Insurance Law Handbook (USA) **4497**
• California Intellectual Property Laws (USA) **6747**
• California International Law Section Newsletter (USA) **4919**
California International Practitioner (USA ISSN 1075-6049) **4919**
California Job Journal (USA ISSN 0892-6395) **6694**
California Journal of Health - System Pharmacy (USA ISSN 1097-6337) **6827**
• ➤ California Journal of Oriental Medicine (USA ISSN 1090-1965) **307**
▼ • ➤ California Journal of Politics and Policy (USA ISSN 1944-4370) **7112**
California Journal of Science Education (USA ISSN 1531-2488) **7843**
California Journal Roster & Government Guide *see* Roster & Government Guide **7180**
• California Jury Instructions - Civil (B A J I) Forms (Book of Approved Jury Instructions) (USA ISSN 1932-0493) **4828**
• California Jury Instructions. Civil. C A C I Forms (California Jury Instructions) (USA ISSN 1932-0477) **4828**
California Jury Instructions. Criminal *see* Judicial Council of California. Criminal Jury Instructions **4892**
California Jury Instructions - Criminal (C A L J I C) Forms (California Criminal Jury Instructions) (USA ISSN 1932-0485) **4885**
California Jury Instructions - Criminal Forms *see* California Jury Instructions - Criminal (C A L J I C) Forms **4885**
California Labor and Employment Alert Newsletter (USA) **1669**
California Labor & Employment Law Quarterly (USA) **4636**
• California Labor Market Bulletin (USA) **1445**
California Labor News (USA ISSN 1094-8724) **4591**
• California Land Use Law and Policy Reporter (USA ISSN 1058-8205) **7585**
California Landscaping (USA ISSN 1092-9630) **3726**
• California Law of Employee Injuries and Workers' Compensation (USA) **4636**
• ➤ California Law Review (USA ISSN 0008-1221) **4636**
California. Law Revision Commission. Reports, Recommendations and Studies (USA) **4637**
• California Lawyer (USA ISSN 0279-4063) **4637**
California Lawyers *see* California Directory of Attorneys **4636**
• California Legal Forms: Transaction Guide (USA) **4637**
➤ California Legal History (USA ISSN 1930-4943) **4947**
California Legionnaire (USA) **6414**
California Lettuce Research Board. Annual Report (USA) **195**
California Libraries (USA ISSN 1056-1528) **5000**
California Library Directory (USA ISSN 0740-7688) **5000**
California Library Statistics (USA ISSN 0741-031X) **5057**
California Linguistic Newsletter *see* California Linguistic Notes **5104**
California Linguistic Notes (USA) **5104**
California Macadamia Society. Yearbook (USA ISSN 0068-5720) **223**
• ➤ California Management Review (USA ISSN 0008-1256) **1732**
California Manufacturers Annual Register *see* California Manufacturers Register **1978**
• California Manufacturers Register (USA ISSN 0068-5739) **1978**
California: Manufacturing *see* Harris Directory. California Manufacturing **1999**
California Mechanics' Lien Law and Construction Industry Practice (USA) **989**
California Monthly (USA ISSN 0008-1302) **2276**
▼ California Motions in Limine (USA ISSN 1944-1118) **4947**
California Municipal Bond Advisor (USA ISSN 0749-2375) **1615**
California Music Educators Association Magazine *see* C M E A Magazine **6553**
California Native Plant Society. Bulletin (USA) **783**
California Native Plant Society Inventory of Rare and Endangered Vascular Plants of California *see* C N P S Inventory of Rare and Endangered Vascular Plants of California **782**
California Native Plant Society. Special Publication (USA ISSN 0190-8723) **783**
California Natural History Guides (USA ISSN 0068-5755) **664**
California Neighborhoods (USA ISSN 1084-2217) **4406**
California Notary Law Primer (USA ISSN 1096-9985) **4637**
• The California Numismatist (USA) **6649**
California Nurse *see* Registered Nurse **5979**
† • California Nuts (USA ISSN 1538-201X) **8939**
California Odd Fellow and Rebekah (USA) **2264**
California Official Reports *see* California Official Reports on DVD **4637**
• California Official Reports on DVD (USA ISSN 1937-6103) **4637**
California Optometry (USA ISSN 0273-804X) **6039**
California Orange County *see* Harris Directory. California Orange County **1999**
California Ornamental Crops Report (USA ISSN 0744-2653) **99**
• California P A T H Database (Partners for Advanced Transit and Highways) (USA) **8523**
California Paralegal's Checklist Guide (USA) **4637**
California Paralegal's Guide (USA) **4637**
California Parklands (USA) **2605**
• California Parks & Recreation (USA ISSN 0733-5326) **4976**
California Payroll Compliance Report (USA ISSN 1529-2282) **1669**
• California Penal and Vehicle Code (USA) **4885**
• California Penal Code Handbook (USA) **4637**
California Personnel & Guidance Association. Monographs (USA) **6694**
California Pharmacist (USA ISSN 0739-0483) **6827**
California Physician (USA ISSN 8750-1813) **5591**
• California Planning and Development Report (USA ISSN 0891-382X) **7425**
• California Plant Pest and Disease Report (Online) (USA ISSN 1947-0657) **842**
• California Points and Authorities (USA) **4637**
California Political Week (USA ISSN 0195-6175) **7112**
• California Probate Practice (USA) **4901**
California Probate Procedure (USA) **4901**
• California Products Liability Actions (USA) **4637**
The California Psychologist (USA ISSN 0890-0302) **7343**
California Public Employee Relations *see* C P E R **1668**
• California Public Employees' Retirement Law (USA) **1669**
• California Public School Directory (USA ISSN 0068-5771) **2954**
California Public Sector *see* California Staff Directory **7425**
• California Public Sector Labor Relations (USA) **1669**
California Publisher (USA ISSN 0008-1434) **4573**
California R V & Camping Guide (USA) **8690**
➤ California Reader (USA ISSN 0892-6964) **3053**
• California Real Estate (USA ISSN 0008-1450) **7585**
California Real Estate Journal (USA ISSN 1085-5750) **7586**
• California Real Estate Law and Practice (USA) **7586**
• California Real Estate Reporter (USA ISSN 1046-3844) **7586**
• California Real Property Journal (USA ISSN 1052-2921) **7586**
California Recreational Lakes and Rivers (USA) **8690**
California Riding Magazine (USA) **8288**
California San Diego County *see* Harris Directory. California San Diego County **1999**
California School Business (USA ISSN 1935-0716) **2834**
California School Directory *see* M D R's School Directory. California **2958**
• California School Law Digest (USA ISSN 0094-2057) **3018**
California School Library Association Journal *see* C S L A Journal **4999**
➤ California School Psychologist (USA ISSN 1087-3414) **7343**
California Schools (USA ISSN 1081-8936) **2834**
California Science Teachers Association Newspaper *see* California Educational Linkages in the Life Sciences **664**
California Sea Grant College Program. Report Series (USA) **2801**
California Search and Seizure (USA ISSN 1941-9775) **4885**
California Series in Public Anthropology (USA) **332**
California Series on Social Choice & Political Economy (USA ISSN 1051-032X) **7112**
California Society of Enrolled Agents Annual Report *see* C S E A Annual Report **1914**
California Song (USA ISSN 1537-2286) **6553**
California Southern Baptist (USA ISSN 0008-1558) **7749**
• California Special Education Alert (USA ISSN 1082-4448) **3053**
California Sports Car (USA ISSN 0747-0223) **8570**
California Sports Profiles Magazine (Los Angeles) (USA) **8164**
California Staats-Zeitung (USA ISSN 0890-1473) **3524**
California Staff Directory (USA ISSN 1934-5011) **7425**
• California State Association of Counties Legislative Bulletin (USA) **7489**
California. State Barbering and Cosmetology Program. Rules and Regulations (USA) **586**
California. State Board of Equalization. Annual Report (USA ISSN 0068-5801) **1914**
• California State Contracts Register (USA) **1079**
California State Genealogical Alliance (USA ISSN 1933-6993) **3761**
California State Library Foundation Bulletin (USA ISSN 0741-0344) **5000**
California State Library Newsletter (USA ISSN 0276-6973) **5000**
California State Park Rangers Association Newsletter *see* C S P R A Newsletter **2605**
California State Plan for Rehabilitation Facilities (USA) **8029**
California State Publications (USA ISSN 0008-1574) **622**
• California State Teachers' Retirement System. Comprehensive Annual Financial Report (USA) **1669**
• ➤ California State University, Stanislaus Journal of Research (USA ISSN 1099-5811) **2970**
California Statesman (USA) **7113**
California Statesman's Foreign Policy Review (USA) **7113**
California Statesman's Legislative Survey (USA) **7113**
California Statistical Abstracts (USA ISSN 0575-6200) **1324**
California Strawberry Report (USA ISSN 0194-8504) **99**
➤ California Studies in 19th Century Music (USA) **6553**
California Studies in Critical Human Geography (USA) **8092**
California Studies in Food and Culture (USA) **7952**
California Studies in German and European Romanticism and in the Age of Goethe (USA ISSN 1067-0025) **5269**
California Studies in Nineteenth Century Music *see* California Studies in 19th Century Music **6553**
California Studies in Public Anthropology *see* California Series in Public Anthropology **332**
➤ California Studies in the History of Art (USA ISSN 0068-5909) **480**
➤ California Studies in the History of Science (USA) **7843**
California Stylist & Salon (USA) **586**
The California Supreme Court Historical Society. Yearbook *see* California Legal History **4947**
California Supreme Court Service (USA ISSN 0164-3339) **4637**
California Surveyor (USA) **4001**
California Tax Analysis (Print Edition) *see* California and New York Tax Analysis (Online Edition) **1914**
California Tax Handbook (Year) (USA) **1914**
California Tax Lawyer (USA) **1914**
California Teacher (USA ISSN 0410-3556) **2834**
California Tech (USA ISSN 0008-1582) **2276**
• California Technology (USA) **8417**
California Technology Stock Letter (USA ISSN 8756-2154) **1615**
California Teen (USA) **2181**
California Territorial Quarterly (USA) **4287**
California Therapist *see* The Therapist **7412**
California Thoroughbred (USA ISSN 1092-7328) **8288**
• California Today (USA ISSN 0739-8042) **3408**
California Tomato Grower (USA ISSN 0527-3277) **223**
California Tort Reporter (USA ISSN 0744-6756) **4637**

• California Torts (USA) 4828
California Tour & Travel (USA) 8690
California Track & Running News (USA) 8307
California Transportation News (USA ISSN 1940-2880) 8669
California Travel Parks Association, Inc. News see C T P A News 8690
• California Trial Guide (USA) 4828
California Trucking Association. Newsletter see Caltrux 8669
• California Trust Practice (USA) 4901
California Trusts and Estates Quarterly (USA) 4901
California Turkish Times see U S A Turkish Times 3569
California Uninsured Motorist Law (USA) 4497
California Veckoblad (USA ISSN 0882-2719) 3524
California Vegetable Journal (USA) 99
California Verdict Search Newsletter (USA) 4947
California Veteran (USA ISSN 1069-8477) 6414
➤ California Veterinarian (USA ISSN 0008-1612) 8795
California Visitors Review (USA) 8690
California Water Code (USA) 3408
• California Water Environment Association. E-Bulletin (Online) (USA) 8819
California Water Law and Policy (USA) 8819
• California Water Law & Policy Reporter (USA ISSN 1053-4938) 4637
California Water Resources Center. Contribution (USA ISSN 0575-4941) 8819
California. Water Resources Center. Report (USA) 2793
▼ • California Weds (USA ISSN 1940-4417) 5557
California Weed Science Society. Annual Conference Proceedings (USA) 223
• California Weekly Explorer (USA ISSN 0197-7547) 2181
• California Western International Law Journal (USA ISSN 0886-3210) 4919
• California Western Law Review (USA ISSN 0008-1639) 4637
• California Wild (USA ISSN 1094-365X) 7843
• California Wills and Trusts: Text (USA) 4901
California Wine Winners (USA ISSN 0883-4423) 601
California Wool Growers Newsletter (USA) 282
California Workers' Comp Alert (USA ISSN 1548-9647) 1669
• California Workers' Comp Law Bulletin (USA ISSN 1546-5314) 1669
California Workers' Compensation Claims and Benefits (USA) 4497
California Workers' Compensation Claims & Benefits. Supplement see California Workers' Compensation Claims and Benefits 4497
California Workers' Compensation Handbook (USA ISSN 1083-3315) 4497
California Workers' Compensation Reporter (USA ISSN 0363-129X) 1669
California Young Lawyers Association Quarterly see C Y L A Quarterly 4635
Californiai Magyarsag/California Hungarians Weekly (USA ISSN 0744-8600) 3525
• ➤ Californian Journal of Health Promotion (USA ISSN 1545-8725) 6983
California's best bed and breakfasts see California's Best Bed & Breakfasts 8690
California's Best Bed & Breakfasts (USA ISSN 1094-110X) 8690
California's First Lifestyle Magazine see C 3971
California's Legislature (USA ISSN 0091-5548) 7425
• Calimed (MEX) 5591
Caliologists' Series (GBR ISSN 0959-8952) 905
Caliope (USA ISSN 1084-1490) 5418
Caliper (CAN ISSN 0045-4001) 4077
• Calitatea Vietii (ROM ISSN 1018-0389) 8092
Call (IND ISSN 0008-1728) 7113
Call (LKA ISSN 0045-401X) 5210
Call (TWN ISSN 1562-1227) 2366
➤ Call (USA ISSN 1546-6388) 5418
The Call (USA) 7719
• Call - A.P.P.L.E. (Online) (Apple Pugetsound Program Library Exchange) (USA) 2575
• Call & Post (USA) 3525
Call and Post (City Edition) see Call and Post (Cleveland Edition) 3525
Call and Post (Cleveland Edition) (USA ISSN 0045-4036) 3525
Call and Post (Columbus Edition) (USA) 3525
Call Center & C R M Marktfuehrer (DEU) 1809
Call Center Magazine see C C M. Customer Contact Magazine 1809
Call Center Magazine see Customer Management Insight (Print) 8947
• Call Center Profi (DEU ISSN 1433-0199) 1809
• Call Centre and Customer Service Renumeration Review (AUS ISSN 1442-424X) 1857
Call Centre Europe (GBR ISSN 1357-4868) 2314
• Call Centre Focus (GBR ISSN 1353-5439) 2366
• Call Centre Magazine (AUS) 2366
Call Centres Market Assessment see Key Note Market Assessment. Call Centres 2369
• ➤ Call-Ej Online (AUS ISSN 1442-438X) 3053
• Call Magazin (DEU) 2314
Call Number (USA ISSN 0008-1744) 5000
The Call of Islam see Nida'ul Islam 7715
Call of the Loon (CAN ISSN 1194-2258) 2605
▼ Call Out (IRL ISSN 2009-1060) 7511
Call-Sheet see CallSheet! 2378
• Call Sheet (USA ISSN 1948-1241) 2378
• A Call to Cud (USA) 262
Call to Earth see Environmental Philosophy 3427
Call to Prayer (USA) 7629
Call to the Truth see Da'wat al-Haqq 7710
Call to Unity (USA ISSN 1545-7311) 7629
➤ Call to Worship (USA ISSN 1534-8318) 7749
Callahan's Credit Union Directory (USA ISSN 0888-8671) 1079
Callahan's Credit Union Report (USA ISSN 1522-0745) 1324
• ➤ Callaloo (USA ISSN 0161-2492) 5269
• Callaway Golf (USA ISSN 1559-5552) 8224
Callaway International Resource Centre Lecture Series see C I R C M E Lecture Series 6552
Callboard (San Francisco) see Theatre Bay Area 8482
Callcenter (SWE) 1809
• Calle B (CUB ISSN 1682-2463) 7952
Called Bond Service (USA) 1615
The Caller (USA ISSN 1074-9209) 2605
Calligrapher (GBR) 4331
Calligraphic Art Weely see Shufa Bao 517
Calligraphy and Painting see Shu yu Hua 517
Calligraphy Appreciation see Shufa Shangping 517
Calligraphy World see Shufa Shijie 517
Calling (NLD ISSN 1574-2806) 2366
Calling Card (CAN) 4331
• Calliope (Peru) (USA ISSN 1050-7086) 4134
Calliostoma (BRA ISSN 1415-2827) 937
Callmann on Unfair Competition, Trademarks and Monopolies (USA) 6747
CallSeeker see R S G B Yearbook (Year) 2362
CallSheet! (NLD ISSN 1387-1986) 2378
CALMScience see Conservation Science Western Australia 2607
Calore e Tecnologia see International Journal of Heat and Technology 7055
Calorie Control Commentary (USA ISSN 1049-1791) 6656
Calorimetry and Thermal Analysis see Netsu Sokutei 7056
Caloundra Weekly (AUS) 3793
Calpeek see California Political Week 7112
CalPERS Watch see Cal P E R S Watch 1615
• ➤ CALPHAD (GBR ISSN 0364-5916) 2107
Calquarium (CAN ISSN 0045-4052) 6805
Caltaxletter (USA) 1914
Caltrux (USA ISSN 1040-2705) 8669
Calunderwriter see California Broker 1958
Calvert County Genealogy Newsletter (USA ISSN 0895-8939) 3761
Calvin Coolidge Memorial Foundation Newsletter (USA) 4287
• ➤ Calvin Theological Journal (USA ISSN 0008-1795) 7749
Calypso (ITA ISSN 1826-8900) 3408
Calypso Log (USA ISSN 8756-6354) 3408
Calyx (USA ISSN 0147-1627) 5269
Cam see Cambridge Alumni Magazine 2276
CAMAC Bulletin see C A M A C Bulletin 2459
CamaCol News (USA) 1397
Camaleon see El Siglo 3927
▼ Camandula (COL ISSN 2011-3714) 4637
La Camara (ESP ISSN 1130-832X) 1397
Camara Argentina de la Industria de Chacinados y Afines see C A I C H A 3629
Camara Argentina de la Industria del Aluminio y Metales Afines. Revista (ARG ISSN 0328-2007) 6307
Camara Argentina del Libro. Boletin Bibliografico Bimestral (ARG ISSN 0327-9189) 622
Camara Chilena de la Construccion. Documento de Trabajo (CHL ISSN 0718-3232) 3261
Camara Chileno - Alemana de Comercio e Industria. Annual Report (CHL) 1397
Camara Chileno - Suiza de Comercio. Boletin Nuevo (CHL) 1397
Camara Colombiana de la Construccion Asamblea Nacional. Documento see C A M A C O L. Asamblea Nacional. Documento 988
Camara Colombiana de la Construccion. Revista (COL ISSN 0120-5102) 989
Camara Colombiana de la Construccion Valle. Revista see C A M A C O L Valle. Revista 3261
Camara de Comercio Americana. Boletim (PRT) 1397
Camara de Comercio Americana. Directorio see Camara de Comercio Americana. Boletim 1397
Camara de Comercio Argentino-Britanica. Bulletin (ARG) 1397
Camara de Comercio de Bogota. Boletin (COL ISSN 0008-185X) 1397
Camara de Comercio de Bogota. Revista (COL ISSN 0120-4289) 1397
Camara de Comercio de Bogota. Servicio Informativo (COL) 1397
Camara de Comercio de Caracas. Boletin/Caracas Chamber of Commerce. Bulletin (VEN) 1397
Camara de Comercio de Costa Rica. Magazine (CRI) 1397
Camara de Comercio de Nicaragua. Boletin Comercial (NIC) 1397
Camara de Comercio de Quito. Boletin de Informacion Comercial (ECU) 1397
Camara de Comercio e Industria Boliviano - Alemana. Bulletin Bolivia - Germany (BOL) 1397
Camara de Comercio Hispano-Sueca de Madrid. Info (ESP) 1398
Camara de Comercio, Industria y Agricultura Venezolano-Italiano (VEN) 1398
Camara de Comercio, Industria y Produccion de la Republica Argentina. Boletin Informativo (ARG) 1398
Camara de Comercio Paraguayo - Alemana (PRY) 1398
Camara de Comercio Suiza-Argentina. Bulletin (ARG) 1398
Camara de Comercio Uruguay - U S A. Revista (URY) 1398
Camara de Comercio Uruguayo - Britanica. Boletin Informativo (URY) 1079
Camara de Industria y Comercio Argentino-Alemana. Boletin/Deutsch-Argentinische Industrie- und Handelskammer. Mitteilungen (ARG ISSN 0008-2112) 1398
Camara de Industriales de Caracas. Noti (VEN) 1079
▼ Camara Lenta (ESP ISSN 1886-9858) 6491
Camara Madrid (ESP) 1882
Camara Nacional de Comercio de Chile. Boletin de Informes Comerciales (CHL) 1398
Camara Nacional de Comercio de Chile. Informativo (CHL) 1398
Camara Nacional de Comercio. Informe Anual (URY ISSN 0797-5686) 1398
Camara Nacional de Comercio. Publicaciones (URY) 1398
Camara Nacional de Comercio. Revista (URY ISSN 0797-2989) 1398
Camara Nacional de la Industria de Transformacion. Boletin Informativo (MEX) 1882
Camara Oficial de Comercio e Industria de Alava. Boletin Informativo (ESP) 1398
† Camara Oficial de Comercio, Industria y Navegacion de Barcelona. Boletin/Cambra Oficial de Comerc, Industria i Navegacio de Barcelona. Butlleti (ESP ISSN 0008-1930) 8939
Camara Oficial de Comercio, Industria y Navegacion de Santa Cruz de Tenerife. Boletin Informativo (ESP ISSN 0558-5201) 1398
Camara Panamena de la Construccion. Lista de Precios de Materiales de Construccion (PAN) 989
Camara Venezolano-Britanica de Comercio e Industria. Anuario (VEN) 1398
Camaro Performers (USA ISSN 1944-8589) 8571
Camauto (CAN ISSN 1912-3132) 8571
Camauto Plus see Camauto 8571
Camauto Plus (Edition Annuel) see Camauto 8571
Cambiamento Sociale in Europa (ITA) 8092
Cambio (NIC) 3920
Cambio (URY) 3993
Cambio 16 (ESP ISSN 0211-285X) 5210
Cambio l'Automobile see Cambio Panoramauto 8571
Cambio Panoramauto (ITA) 8571
Cambio y Desarrollo (PER) 7113
Cambio y Progreso (COL ISSN 0120-6338) 8360
• Cambios (ARG) 7113
Cambios y Continuidades (ARG ISSN 1851-3301) 7952
Cambodia Times (KHM) 3805
• Cambra de la Propietat Urbana de Barcelona. Butlleti (ESP) 7586
Cambra Oficial de Comerc, Industria i Navegacio de Barcelona. Butlleti see Camara Oficial de Comercio, Industria y Navegacion de Barcelona. Boletin 8939
Cambrensis (GBR ISSN 0959-5589) 5269
• Cambria (GBR ISSN 1366-0675) 3862
Cambria: A Welsh Geographical Review (GBR ISSN 0306-9796) 4001
• Cambrian Law Review (GBR ISSN 0084-8328) 4637
Cambrian Medieval Celtic Studies (GBR ISSN 1353-0089) 4208
Cambrian News (GBR) 3862
Cambridge Aerospace Series (GBR) 50
Cambridge African Monographs (GBR) 4174
† Cambridge Air Surveys (GBR ISSN 0068-659X) 8939
Cambridge Alumni Magazine (GBR) 2276
Cambridge Anthropology (GBR ISSN 0305-7674) 332
➤ Cambridge Antiquarian Society. Proceedings (GBR ISSN 0309-3603) 4208
Cambridge Applied Linguistics (GBR) 5104
Cambridge Approaches to Linguistics (GBR) 5104
• ➤ Cambridge Archaeological Journal (GBR ISSN 0959-7743) 386
Cambridge Asia - Pacific Studies (GBR) 546
▼ Cambridge Astrobiology (GBR) 572
Cambridge Astrophysics Series (GBR ISSN 0950-141X) 572
Cambridge Bibliographical Society. Transactions (GBR ISSN 0068-6611) 5000
Cambridge Bibliographical Society. Transactions. Monograph Supplements (GBR ISSN 0575-6782) 5000
Cambridge Biotechnology Research Series. Agricultural & Environmental Biotechnology Abstracts see Agricultural & Environmental Biotechnology Abstracts (Online) 173
The Cambridge Classical Journal (GBR ISSN 1750-2705) 2231
Cambridge Classical Studies (GBR) 2231
Cambridge Classical Texts and Commentaries (GBR ISSN 0068-6638) 2232
Cambridge Companions to Literature (GBR) 5269
† Cambridge Computer Science Texts (GBR ISSN 0266-3236) 8939
• Cambridge Crier (GBR ISSN 1754-6680) 3967
Cambridge Edition (NZL ISSN 1170-0092) 3916
† The Cambridge Edition of the Works of Jane Austin (GBR ISSN 1754-2022) 8939
Cambridge Environmental Chemistry Series (GBR ISSN 1359-0243) 2052
Cambridge Expeditions Journal (GBR ISSN 0575-6790) 8690
Cambridge Film Classics (GBR) 6491
Cambridge Geographical Studies (GBR ISSN 0068-6654) 4001
Cambridge Greek and Latin Classics (GBR) 5269
Cambridge Group for the History of Population and Social Structure. Working Paper Series (GBR) 7278
Cambridge Guide to Literature in English (GBR) 5000
† Cambridge History of Arabic Literature (GBR) 8939
The Cambridge History of China (GBR) 4180
Cambridge Insider (GBR ISSN 1368-0234) 3862
† Cambridge International Documents Series (GBR ISSN 1362-7627) 8939
Cambridge International Series on Parallel Computation (GBR ISSN 1362-7635) 2409
• ➤ Cambridge Journal of Economics (GBR ISSN 0309-166X) 1079
• ➤ Cambridge Journal of Education (GBR ISSN 0305-764X) 2970
▼ • ➤ Cambridge Journal of Regions, Economy and Society (GBR ISSN 1752-1378) 7113
Cambridge Language Surveys (GBR) 5104
Cambridge Latin American Studies (GBR ISSN 0068-6689) 4287
• The Cambridge Law Journal (GBR ISSN 0008-1973) 4637
➤ Cambridge Lecture Notes in Physics (GBR) 7007
Cambridge Market Intelligence Technology Watch, Data Warehousing see C M I Technology Watch, Data Warehousing 2529
† Cambridge Medical Reviews. Neurology and Psychiatry (GBR ISSN 1350-1461) 8939
• Cambridge Medicine (GBR ISSN 0952-1119) 5591
Cambridge Microbiology Abstracts Series: Section B. Bacteriology see Microbiology Abstracts: Section B. Bacteriology 717
† Cambridge Middle East Library (GBR ISSN 0961-1398) 8939
Cambridge Middle East Studies (GBR) 546
Cambridge Military Histories (GBR ISSN 1754-758X) 4134
Cambridge Monographs on Applied and Computational Mathematics (GBR) 5477
Cambridge Monographs on Mathematical Physics (GBR ISSN 0269-8242) 7007
Cambridge Monographs on Mechanics (GBR) 7057
Cambridge Monographs on Particle Physics, Nuclear Physics and Cosmology (GBR ISSN 0965-6200) 7065
Cambridge Monographs on Plasma Physics (GBR) 7007
† Cambridge Nonlinear Science Series (GBR ISSN 0963-7141) 8939
Cambridge Opera Handbooks (GBR) 6553
• ➤ Cambridge Opera Journal (GBR ISSN 0954-5867) 6553
Cambridge Paleobiology Series (GBR) 6723
Cambridge Philological Society. Proceedings. Supplement (GBR ISSN 0068-6743) 2232
• ➤ Cambridge Philosophical Society. Mathematical Proceedings (GBR ISSN 0305-0041) 5477
Cambridge Planetary Science Series (GBR ISSN 0265-3044) 573
• ➤ The Cambridge Quarterly (GBR ISSN 0008-199X) 5269
• ➤ Cambridge Quarterly of Healthcare Ethics (GBR ISSN 0963-1801) 5591
• ➤ Cambridge Review of International Affairs (GBR ISSN 0955-7571) 7225
Cambridge Scientific Abstracts Civil Engineering Abstracts see C S A Civil Engineering Abstracts 3229
Cambridge Scientific Abstracts Mechanical & Transportation Engineering Abstracts see C S A Mechanical & Transportation Engineering Abstracts 3229
Cambridge Scientific Abstracts Neurosciences Abstracts (Online) see C S A Neurosciences Abstracts (Online) 5742
Cambridge Scientific Abstracts Political Science & Government see C S A Political Science & Government 7479
Cambridge Scientific Abstracts Sustainability Science Abstracts see C S A Sustainability Science Abstracts 3477
Cambridge Scientific Abstracts Worldwide Political Science Abstracts see C S A Worldwide Political Science Abstracts 7199
Cambridge Series on Human-Computer Interaction (GBR ISSN 0961-3099) 2409
Cambridge Solid State Science Series (GBR ISSN 0964-6752) 7007
† Cambridge South Asian Studies (GBR ISSN 0575-6863) 8939
Cambridge Student Law Review (GBR) 4637
Cambridge Studies in Advanced Mathematics (GBR ISSN 0950-6330) 5477
Cambridge Studies in African and Caribbean Literature (GBR ISSN 0962-0427) 5269
Cambridge Studies in American Literature and Culture (GBR) 5269
Cambridge Studies in American Theatre and Drama (GBR) 8467
➤ Cambridge Studies in Anglo-Saxon England (GBR ISSN 1747-311X) 4208

Title

Camping Life *see* Woodall's Camping Life Magazine **8342**
Camping Magazine (GBR ISSN 1350-1453) **8308**
• Camping Magazine (USA ISSN 0740-4131) **2146**
Camping & Fritid (SWE ISSN 1651-1611) **4976**
• Camping & Fritid (DNK ISSN 0907-4856) **8308**
Camping Revue (AUT) **8308**
Camping-Revue (CHE ISSN 1422-5786) **8308**
Camping Today (USA ISSN 8750-1465) **8308**
Campitur (ESP ISSN 1132-0389) **8308**
† Campo (ESP ISSN 0212-2146) **8939**
El Campo (MEX ISSN 0008-2473) **99**
➤ Campo Abierto (ESP ISSN 0213-9529) **3053**
Campo de Agramante (ESP ISSN 1578-2433) **5270**
Campo Grande (PRT) **5210**
Campo Libre (GBR) **3525**
▼ ➤ Campo Libre (USA ISSN 1948-5107) **3525**
Campo y Mecanica (USA ISSN 0211-4704) **99**
• Campos (BRA ISSN 1519-5538) **332**
• Campos (DEU ISSN 1615-3502) **3726**
Camps Familiaux *see* Les Centres de Vacances Familiales **8309**
Campus (DEU ISSN 0945-0041) **7843**
The Campus (USA) **2276**
Campus (Lennoxville) (CAN ISSN 0008-2481) **2276**
▼ • Campus 3 (DEU ISSN 1864-7006) **2954**
Campus Activities (USA) **2276**
Campus Activities Programming (USA ISSN 0746-2328) **2970**
Campus Camera (USA) **2276**
Campus Canada (CAN ISSN 0829-3309) **2276**
Campus Carrier (USA) **2276**
Campus Circle (USA) **6553**
• Campus de San Marcos (PER ISSN 1682-3001) **2970**
Campus Dining Today (USA) **3629**
Campus Drei *see* Campus 3 **2954**
• Campus Ekonomi (SWE ISSN 1401-5382) **2970**
• Campus Events Professional (USA ISSN 1547-0989) **2276**
† Campus Facility Maintenance (USA ISSN 1556-2999) **8939**
• Campus - Free College Degrees (USA ISSN 1043-2086) **2970**
Campus Jurist (SWE) **2970**
Campus Law Enforcement Journal (USA ISSN 0739-0394) **2646**
Campus Leader (PHL ISSN 0008-252X) **2834**
• Campus Legal Advisor (USA ISSN 1531-3999) **2970**
Campus Life *see* Ignite Your Faith **2194**
Campus Life's Ignite your Faith *see* Ignite Your Faith **2194**
Campus Link (IND) **7629**
Campus Magazine (USA ISSN 1084-693X) **2970**
Campus Maior (ITA ISSN 1825-1714) **4209**
Campus Marketplace (USA ISSN 1050-4621) **1809**
Campus Marketplace Bulletin *see* Campus Marketplace **1809**
Campus Report (GBR) **2970**
• Campus Report (USA ISSN 0890-4618) **2971**
• Campus Review (AUS) **2971**
Campus Review (LBR) **5210**
Campus Safety and Student Development *see* Campus Safety & Student Development **3018**
Campus Safety & Student Development (USA ISSN 1541-7662) **3018**
Campus Safety Journal (USA) **7511**
• Campus Safety Magazine (USA) **3018**
• Campus Security (USA) **3018**
• Campus Security Report (Horsham) (USA ISSN 1551-2800) **3018**
Campus Stellae (FRA ISSN 1167-6817) **4209**
• Campus Technology (USA ISSN 1553-7544) **3019**
• Campus Teknik (SWE ISSN 1401-5196) **2971**
• Campus Times (La Verne) (USA) **2276**
Campus Times (Rochester) (USA) **2276**
Campus U K (United Kingdom) (GBR) **2971**
Campus Voice *see* The Voice (Bloomsburg) **2308**
• Campus Web (ITA ISSN 1594-672X) **2276**
Campus Weekly (USA) **2276**
• ➤ Campus Wide Information Systems (GBR ISSN 1065-0741) **2495**
CampusAnzeiger (DEU) **2954**
• Campuskrant (BEL ISSN 0779-0821) **2276**
Campuskrant (Alumni Edition) *see* Campuskrant **2276**
CampusLife (DEU) **2276**
Camrose Booster (CAN ISSN 0710-4103) **3807**
• CAMsoc Update (Computer Aided Ministry Society) (USA) **2409**
The Can Makers Report *see* European Can Makers Report **603**
Can News (USA) **7629**
Can Shipments *see* Annual Can Shipments Report **6708**
Can Shipments Report (USA) **6708**
Can Shipments Report (Annual Edition) *see* Can Shipments Report **6708**
† La Cana de Flamenco (ESP ISSN 1135-2779) **8939**
Canada (Year) (USA ISSN 0884-1039) **8691**
Canada, a Portrait (CAN ISSN 0840-6014) **8360**
Canada A-Z (CAN ISSN 0824-4766) **1978**
• Canada. Agriculture and Agri-Food Canada. Performance Report (CAN ISSN 1483-6742) **7426**
• Canada. Agriculture & Agri-Food Canada. Policy Branch. Bi-Weekly Bulletin (CAN ISSN 1207-621X) **99**
Canada. Agriculture Canada. Hatchery Review (CAN ISSN 1182-638X) **282**
Canada. Agriculture Canada. Livestock Market Review (CAN ISSN 0068-7324) **282**
Canada Air Pilot (CAN ISSN 1910-3972) **50**
Canada. Alberta Seniors Annual Report *see* Alberta Senior Annual Report **4039**
• Canada Among Nations (CAN ISSN 0832-0683) **7225**
Canada & Arab World (CAN ISSN 0706-7909) **3525**
Canada and International Relations (CAN ISSN 0847-0510) **1554**
Canada and the United States Annual Joint Report *see* Canada-Etats-Unis. Rapport Annuel Conjoint **4001**
• Canada Asia Commentary (CAN ISSN 1481-0425) **1079**
• Canada Asia Review (CAN ISSN 1206-4017) **1079**
Canada Autos Report (GBR ISSN 1748-9806) **8571**
Canada. Bureau de l'Integrite de la Fonction Publique. Rapport Annuel au Parlement *see* Canada. Public Service Integrity Office. Annual Report to Parliament **7427**
Canada. Bureau du Conseiller Senatorial en Ethique. Rapport Annuel *see* Canada. Office of the Senate Ethics Officer. Annual Report **7427**
• Canada Business Service Centres. Annual Report/Centres de Services aux Entreprises du Canada. Rapport Annuel (CAN ISSN 1497-6609) **7426**
Canada Cahiers (NLD ISSN 1875-0583) **332**
Canada Camps (CAN ISSN 1911-5040) **8308**
• Canada. Canadian Forces Grievance Board. Annual Report/Canada. Comite des Griefs des Forces Canadiennes. Rapport Annuel (CAN ISSN 1498-9972) **4971**
• Canada. Canadian Heritage. Annual Report on the Operation of the Canadian Multiculturalism Act (CAN ISSN 1200-2569) **7426**
Canada. Canadian Heritage. Official Languages Annual Report/Canada. Patrimoine Canadien. Rapport Annuel Langues Officielles (CAN ISSN 1196-7323) **7426**
• Canada. Canadian Heritage. Performance Report (CAN ISSN 1483-9377) **7426**
Canada. Canadian International Trade Tribunal. Annual Report (CAN ISSN 0846-5991) **1554**
Canada. Canadian International Trade Tribunal. Bulletin/Canada. Tribunal Canadien du Commerce Exterieur. Bulletin (CAN ISSN 0843-6509) **1554**
Canada. Canadian Studies and Special Projects Directorate. Information and Application Guide *see* Canadian Studies Program Applicants' Guide **4287**
Canada. Centre des Statistiques de l'Aviation. Bulletin de Service *see* Canada. Statistics Canada. Aviation Statistics Centre. Service Bulletin **8523**
Canada. Chambre des Communes. Comite Permanent de la Defense Nationale. Proces-verbal *see* Canada. House of Commons. Standing Committee on National Defence. Minutes of Proceedings **6415**
Canada. Chambre des Communes. Comite Permanent de la Justice, des Droits de la Personne, de la Securite Publique et de la Protection Civile. Proces-Verbal *see* Canada. Chambre des Communes. Comite Permanent de la Justice et des Droits de la Personne. Proces-Verbal **4637**
Canada. Chambre des Communes. Comite Permanent de la Justice et des Droits de la Personne. Proces-Verbal *see* Canada. Chambre des Communes. Comite Permanent de la Justice et des Droits de la Personne. Proces-Verbal **4637**
Canada. Chambre des Communes. Comite Permanent de la Justice et des Droits de la Personne. Proces-Verbal (CAN ISSN 1912-5089) **4637**
Canada. Chambre des Communes. Comite Permanent de la Securite Publique et Nationale. Proces-verbal *see* Canada. Parliament. House of Commons. Standing Committee on Public Safety and National Security. Minutes of Proceedings **2676**
Canada. Chambre des Communes. Comite Permanent de l'Industrie, des Ressources Naturelles, des Sciences et de la Technologie. Proces-verbal *see* Canada. Chambre des Communes. Comite Permanent des Ressources Naturelles. Proces-verbal (French Print Edition) **2703**
Canada. Chambre des Communes. Comite Permanent de l'Industrie, des Ressources Naturelles, des Sciences et de la Technologie. Proces-verbal (French Online Edition) *see* Canada. Chambre des Communes. Comite Permanent des Ressources Naturelles. Proces-verbal (French Online Edition) **2703**
Canada. Chambre des Communes. Comite Permanent des Affaires des Anciens Combattants. Proces-verbal *see* Canada. House of Commons. Standing Committee on Veterans Affairs. Minutes of Proceedings **8029**
• Canada. Chambre des Communes. Comite Permanent des Ressources Naturelles. Proces-verbal (French Online Edition) (CAN) **2703**
• Canada. Chambre des Communes. Comite Permanent des Ressources Naturelles. Proces-verbal (French Print Edition) (CAN ISSN 1912-5402) **2703**
Canada. Chambre des Communes. Sous-comite de la Securite sur la Colline du Parlement. Proces-verbal *see* Canada. House of Commons. Subcommittee on Parliament Hill Security. Minutes of Proceedings **2676**
Canada. Chief Electoral Officer. Report (CAN ISSN 0700-1568) **7113**
• Canada. Chief of the Defence Staff. Annual Report (CAN ISSN 1495-3722) **6414**
Canada. Citizenship and Immigration Canada. Annual Immigration Plan *see* Planning Now for Canada's Future **7289**
• Canada. Citizenship and Immigration Canada. Performance Report (CAN ISSN 1483-6858) **7426**
Canada. Civil Aviation Tribunal. Annual Report/Canada. Tribunal de l'Aviation Civile. Rapport Annuel (CAN ISSN 0837-7065) **4971**
Canada. Civil Aviation Tribunal. Performance Report *see* Transportation Appeal Tribunal of Canada. Performance Report **8516**
Canada. Comite des Griefs des Forces Canadiennes. Rapport Annuel *see* Canada. Canadian Forces Grievance Board. Annual Report **4971**
Canada. Commission des Plaintes du Public contre la G R C. Rapport Annuel *see* Canada. Commission for Public Complaints Against the R C M P. Annual Report **7426**
Canada. Commission d'Examen des Plaintes Concernant la Police Militaire. Rapport Annuel *see* Canada. Military Police Complaints Commission. Annual Report **2646**
• Canada. Commission for Public Complaints Against the R C M P. Annual Report (Royal Canadian Mounted Police) (CAN ISSN 1700-5353) **7426**
Canada. Commission Geologique. Bulletin d'Information *see* Canada. Geological Survey. Information Circular **2719**
Canada. Commissioner of Official Languages. Annual Report (CAN ISSN 0382-1161) **7426**
• Canada Communicable Disease Report (CAN ISSN 1188-4169) **7511**
Canada. Communications Security Establishment Commissioner. Annual Report/Commissaire du Centre de la Securite des Telecommunications. Rapport Annuel (CAN ISSN 1206-7490) **6414**
Canada Conseil du Tresor. Budget des Depenses. Partie I: Plan de Depenses du Gouvernement et Points Saillants par Portefeuille *see* Canada. Treasury Board Secretariat. Estimates. Part I: Government Expenditure Plan and Highlights by Ministry **7428**
Canada. Conseil du Tresor. Detail des Depenses de Programmes: Profil des Depenses des Ministeres *see* Canada. Treasury Board. Program Expenditure Detail: A Profile of Departmental Spending **7428**
Canada. Conseil du Tresor. Partie II: Budget des Depenses Principal *see* Canada. Treasury Board Secretariat. Estimates. Part II: Estimates **7428**
Canada. Conseil du Tresor. Rapport sur l'Execution de la Loi sur la Pension du Service Publique *see* Canada. Treasury Board. Report on the Administration of the Public Service Superannuation Act **4846**
Canada. Conseil National des Produits Agricoles. Revue Annuelle *see* Canada. National Farm Products Council. Year in Review **195**
• Canada Corporations Law Reporter (CAN) **4860**
Canada. Correctional Investigator. Annual Report (CAN ISSN 0383-4379) **2646**
Canada Council for the Arts. Canadian Musical Diversity Program. Annual Report (CAN ISSN 1910-6963) **6553**
Canada Country Monitor (USA) **1445**
Canada Criminal Sentencing Digest/Abrege de Jurisprudence en Determination de la Peine (CAN ISSN 1719-2781) **4885**
Canada. Defence Research and Development Branch. Annual Report *see* Defence R & D Canada. Annual Report **6418**
Canada Department of Energy, Mines and Resources. Publications of the Earth Physics Branch (CAN ISSN 0373-4838) **3125**
Canada. Department of Finance. Annual Financial Report of the Government of Canada (CAN ISSN 1200-3557) **1914**
Canada. Department of Finance. Budget (CD-ROM Edition) *see* Canada. Department of Finance. Budget (Online Edition) **1914**
• Canada. Department of Finance. Budget (Online Edition) (CAN ISSN 1719-7740) **1914**
Canada. Department of Finance. Budget Plan (CAN ISSN 1189-8895) **1324**
• Canada. Department of Finance. Debt Management Report (CAN ISSN 1484-4591) **1914**
• Canada. Department of Finance. Economic and Fiscal Update (CAN ISSN 1706-3035) **1914**
Canada. Department of Finance. Economic Statement and Budget Update *see* Canada. Department of Finance. Economic and Fiscal Update **1914**
Canada. Department of Finance. Economic Update *see* Canada. Department of Finance. Economic and Fiscal Update **1914**
• Canada. Department of Finance. Fiscal Reference Tables (CAN ISSN 1208-4484) **1217**
Canada. Department of Finance. Government of Canada Tax Expenditures *see* Canada. Department of Finance. Tax Expenditures and Evaluations **1914**
• Canada. Department of Finance. Performance Report (CAN ISSN 1483-6866) **7426**
• Canada. Department of Finance. Report on the Management of Canada's Official International Reserves (CAN ISSN 1713-5567) **1324**
• Canada. Department of Finance. Report on the Management of Canada's Official International Reserves (CAN ISSN 1912-1075) **1324**
• Canada. Department of Finance. Tax Expenditures and Evaluations (CAN ISSN 1495-6489) **1914**
Canada. Department of Fisheries and Oceans. Administration and Enforcement of the Fish Habitat Protection and Pollution Prevention Provisions of the Fisheries Act. Annual Report (CAN ISSN 1701-0128) **4969**
• Canada. Department of Fisheries and Oceans. Atlantic Seal Hunt Management Plan/Peches et Oceans Canada. Plan de Gestion de Chasse au Phoque de l'Atlantic (CAN ISSN 1493-7581) **3588**
Canada. Department of Fisheries and Oceans. Economic and Commercial Analysis Report (CAN ISSN 0843-5626) **3588**
Canada. Department of Fisheries and Oceans. Fisheries Development Act. Annual Report (CAN) **3588**
Canada. Department of Fisheries and Oceans. General Education Series (CAN ISSN 0835-7005) **3588**
Canada. Department of Fisheries and Oceans. Pacific Region. Annual Summary of British Columbia Catch Statistics (CAN ISSN 0833-4064) **3612**
• Canada. Department of Fisheries and Oceans. Performance Report (CAN ISSN 1483-6696) **7426**
• Canada. Department of Foreign Affairs and International Trade. Performance Report (CAN ISSN 1483-8540) **7426**
Canada. Department of Indian Affairs and Northern Development. Alberta Region. Year in Review *see* Canada. Indian and Northern Affairs Canada. Alberta Region Year in Review **7426**
Canada. Department of Industry, Trade and Commerce. Trade News: Food and Agriculture *see* CanadExport (English Edition) **1554**
Canada. Department of Insurance. Report. Co-Operative Credit Associations (CAN ISSN 0068-7383) **4497**
Canada. Department of Insurance. Report. Small Loans Companies and Money-Lenders (CAN ISSN 0068-7413) **4497**
Canada. Department of Insurance. Report. Trust and Loan Companies (CAN ISSN 0068-7391) **4497**
• Canada. Department of Justice. Performance Report (CAN ISSN 1483-7781) **7426**
Canada. Department of National Defence. Defence (Year) (CAN ISSN 0383-4638) **6414**
Canada. Department of National Defence. Directorate of History. Monograph Series (CAN) **6415**
• Canada. Department of National Defence. Performance Report (CAN ISSN 1483-7102) **7426**
Canada. Department of National Defense. Report on Plans and Priorities (CAN ISSN 1498-3796) **6415**
Canada. Department of National Revenue. Excise News (CAN ISSN 0708-9031) **1915**
Canada. Department of National Revenue. Report: Customs, Excise and Taxation (CAN) **1915**
Canada. Department of Tourism and Small Business. Annual Report *see* Canada. Department of Tourism. Annual Report **8691**
Canada. Department of Tourism. Annual Report (CAN ISSN 0837-4171) **8691**
Canada Deposit Insurance Corporation. Annual Report/Societe d'Assurance-Depots du Canada. Rapport Annuel (CAN ISSN 0382-1498) **4497**
• Canada. Earth Sciences Sector. Annual Review (CAN ISSN 1709-5727) **2703**
Canada EarthSaver (CAN ISSN 1483-4618) **7511**
Canada. Employment and Immigration Canada. Annual Report to Parliament, Immigration Plan *see* Planning Now for Canada's Future **7289**
• Canada Employment Weekly (CAN ISSN 1198-2381) **1669**
• Canada. Environment Canada. Conservation and Protection Service. Annual Summary: National Air Pollution Surveillance (CAN ISSN 0381-2995) **3408**
• Canada. Environment Canada. Performance Report (CAN ISSN 1483-6793) **7426**
Canada-Etats-Unis. Rapport Annuel Conjoint/Canada and the United States Annual Joint Report (USA ISSN 0732-7412) **4001**
Canada. Expert Committee on Pesticide Use in Agriculture. Pesticide Research Report *see* Pest Management Research Report **246**
Canada Fashion *see* Fashion **2254**
• Canada. Federal Court of Canada. Statutes and Regulations Canada. Statutes and Regulations Alberta (CAN) **4638**

Title

Title

10088 CANADA. STATISTICS CANADA. LABOUR FORCE INFORMATION ULRICH'S PERIODICALS

Canada. Statistics Canada. Labour Force Information/Canada. Statistique Canada. Information Population Active (CAN ISSN 0708-3157) **1218**

Canada. Statistics Canada. Manufacturing Industries of Canada. National and Provincial Areas/Canada. Statistique Canada. Industries Manufacturieres du Canada: Provinces de l'Atlantique (CAN ISSN 0382-4144) **1079**

Canada. Statistics Canada. Market Research Handbook/Canada. Statistique Canada. Manuel Statistique pour Etudes de Marche (CAN ISSN 0590-9325) **1218**

• Canada. Statistics Canada. Marriages (Online Edition) (CAN ISSN 1712-6452) **7304**

Canada. Statistics Canada. Mental Health Statistics (CAN ISSN 1195-4027) **8029**

Canada. Statistics Canada. Metal Mines (Online Edition) *see* Canada. Statistics Canada. Metal Ore Mining **6485**

Canada. Statistics Canada. Metal Mines (Print Edition) *see* Canada. Statistics Canada. Metal Ore Mining **6485**

• Canada. Statistics Canada. Metal Ore Mining/Canada. Statistique Canada. Extraction de Minerais Metalliques (CAN ISSN 1708-6299) **6485**

Canada. Statistics Canada. Mineral Wool Including Fibrous Glass Insulation/Canada. Statistique Canada. Laine Minerale y compris les Isolants en Fibre de Verre (CAN ISSN 0229-6098) **1045**

Canada. Statistics Canada. Minority and Second Language Education, Elementary and Secondary Levels/Canada. Statistique Canada. Langue de la Minorite et Langue Seconde dans l'Enseignement, Niveaux Elementaire et Secondaire (CAN ISSN 0706-3717) **5201**

Canada. Statistics Canada. Mortality, Summary List of Causes *see* Canada. Statistics Canada. Mortality, Summary List of Causes. Shelf Tables **7304**

Canada. Statistics Canada. Mortality, Summary List of Causes. Shelf Tables (CAN) **7304**

Canada. Statistics Canada. National Income and Expenditure Accounts, Quarterly Estimates/Canada. Statistique Canada. Comptes Economiques et Financiers Nationaux, Estimations Trimestrielles (CAN ISSN 1488-576X) **1218**

Canada. Statistics Canada. National Tourism Indicators. Historical Estimates (CAN ISSN 1207-3016) **8778**

• Canada. Statistics Canada. National Tourism Indicators. Quarterly Estimates/Canada. Statistique Canada. Indicateurs Nationaux du Tourisme. Estimations Trimestrielles (CAN ISSN 1205-8467) **8778**

• Canada. Statistics Canada. New Motor Vehicle Sales (CAN ISSN 0705-5595) **8523**

• Canada. Statistics Canada. Oil and Gas Extraction (CAN ISSN 1481-4218) **6799**

• Canada. Statistics Canada. Oil and Gas Extraction (CAN ISSN 1703-4930) **6799**

Canada. Statistics Canada. Oil Pipe Line Transport (CAN ISSN 0380-4615) **6799**

• Canada. Statistics Canada. Oils and Fats/Canada. Statistique Canada. Huiles et Corps Gras (CAN ISSN 0527-5911) **3669**

Canada. Statistics Canada. Other Manufacturing Industries/Canada. Statistique Canada. Autres Industries Manufacturieres (CAN ISSN 0835-0191) **1218**

Canada. Statistics Canada. Pack of Processed Carrots (CAN ISSN 1180-596X) **3629**

Canada. Statistics Canada. Pack of Processed Corn (CAN ISSN 1180-5935) **3629**

Canada. Statistics Canada. Pack of Selected Processed Fruits, Excl. Apples (CAN ISSN 1180-5919) **3629**

• Canada. Statistics Canada. Passenger Bus and Urban Transit Statistics/Canada. Statistique Canda. Statistique du Transport des Voyageurs par Autobus et du Transport Urbain (CAN ISSN 0383-5766) **8523**

Canada. Statistics Canada. Pension Plans in Canada/Canada. Statistics Canada. Regimes de Pension au Canada (CAN ISSN 0701-5488) **4529**

• Canada. Statistics Canada. Pipeline Transportation of Crude Oil and Refined Petroleum Products (Online Edition) (CAN ISSN 1488-7754) **1218**

Canada. Statistics Canada. Police Personnel and Expenditures in Canada (Online Edition) *see* Canada. Statistics Canada. Police Resources in Canada (Online Edition) **2673**

• Canada. Statistics Canada. Police Resources in Canada (Online Edition) (CAN ISSN 1488-867X) **2673**

Canada. Statistics Canada. Postcensal Annual Estimates of Population by Marital Status, Age, Sex and Components of Growth for Canada, Provinces and Territories (CAN ISSN 0827-9624) **7304**

• Canada. Statistics Canada. Primary Iron and Steel/Canada. Statistique Canada. Fer et Acier Primaire (CAN ISSN 0380-7851) **6338**

• Canada. Statistics Canada. Primary Metal Industries (Online) (CAN ISSN 1701-2031) **6307**

• Canada. Statistics Canada. Printing, Publishing and Allied Industries/Canada. Statistique Canada. Imprimerie, Edition et Industries Connexes (CAN ISSN 0575-9412) **7578**

• Canada. Statistics Canada. Private and Public Investment in Canada. Intentions/Canada. Statistique Canada. Investissements Prives et Publics au Canada. Perspective (CAN ISSN 0823-065X) **1218**

• Canada. Statistics Canada. Private and Public Investment in Canada. Revised Intentions/Canada. Statistique Canada. Investissements Prives et Publics au Canada, Perspective Revisee (CAN ISSN 0823-0668) **1218**

• Canada. Statistics Canada. Production and Disposition of Tobacco Products/Canada. Statistique Canda. Production et Disposition des Produits du Tabac (CAN ISSN 0708-336X) **8489**

• Canada. Statistics Canada. Production and Value of Honey and Maple (Online Edition) (CAN ISSN 1481-6229) **177**

• Canada. Statistics Canada. Production of Poultry and Eggs/Canada. Statistique Canada. Production de Volaille et Oeufs (CAN ISSN 0068-7189) **177**

• Canada. Statistics Canada. Productivity Growth in Canada (CAN ISSN 1492-8612) **1218**

• Canada. Statistics Canada. Products Shipped by Canadian Manufacturers/Canada. Statistique Canada. Produits Livres par les Fabricants Canadiens (CAN ISSN 0575-9455) **1218**

• Canada. Statistics Canada. Provincial Economic Accounts. Annual Estimates, Tables and Analytical Document/Canada. Statistique Canada. Comptes Economiques Provinciaux Estimations Annuelles (CAN ISSN 1494-6815) **1218**

Canada. Statistics Canada. Public Sector Employment and Wages and Salaries *see* Canada. Statistics Canada. Public Sector Statistics **1218**

Canada. Statistics Canada. Public Sector Finance *see* Canada. Statistics Canada. Public Sector Statistics **1218**

• Canada. Statistics Canada. Public Sector Statistics (CAN ISSN 1494-5797) **1218**

Canada. Statistics Canada. Public Sector Statistics. Supplement *see* Canada. Statistics Canada. Public Sector Statistics **1218**

Canada. Statistics Canada. Quarries and Sand Pits/Canada. Statistique Canada. Carrieres (CAN ISSN 0226-4617) **6459**

• Canada. Statistics Canada. Quarterly Demographic Estimates (CAN ISSN 1911-0928) **7278**

• Canada. Statistics Canada. Quarterly Demographic Statistics (CAN ISSN 0835-4057) **7304**

Canada. Statistics Canada. Quarterly Estimates of Trusteed Pension Funds/Canada. Statistique Canada. Estimations Trimestrielles sur les Regimes de Pensions en Fiducie (CAN ISSN 0700-205X) **1218**

Canada. Statistics Canada. Quarterly Report on Energy Supply - Demand in Canada/Canada. Statistique Canada. Bulletin Trimestriel, Disponibilite et Ecoulement d'Energie au Canada (CAN ISSN 0702-0465) **3151**

• Canada. Statistics Canada. Radio and Television Broadcasting/Canada. Statistique Canada. Radiodiffusion et Television (CAN ISSN 0575-9560) **2347**

• Canada. Statistics Canada. Rail in Canada (CAN ISSN 1209-1316) **8523**

Canada. Statistics Canada. Railway Carloadings/Canada. Statistique Canada. Chargements Ferroviaires (CAN ISSN 0380-6308) **8523**

Canada. Statistics Canada. Refined Petroleum and Coal Products Industries/Canada. Statistique Canada. Industries des Produits Raffines du Petrole et du Charbon (CAN ISSN 0835-0175) **6799**

Canada. Statistics Canada. Regimes de Pension au Canada *see* Canada. Statistics Canada. Pension Plans in Canada **4529**

• Canada. Statistics Canada. Report on the Demographic Situation in Canada (CAN ISSN 0715-9293) **7278**

Canada. Statistics Canada. Restaurant, Caterer and Tavern Statistics/Canada. Statistique Canada. Statistiques des Restaurants, Traiteurs et Tavernes (CAN ISSN 0226-2320) **4401**

• Canada. Statistics Canada. Retail Chain and Department Stores/Canada. Statistique Canada. Magasins de Detail a Succursales et les Grandes Magasins (CAN ISSN 0227-017X) **1218**

• Canada. Statistics Canada. Retail Trade/Canada. Statistique Canada. Commerce de Detail (CAN ISSN 0380-6146) **1218**

Canada. Statistics Canada. Road Motor Vehicles, Fuel Sales/Canada. Statistique Canada. Vehicules Automobiles, Ventes de Carburants (CAN ISSN 0703-654X) **8523**

• Canada. Statistics Canada. Road Motor Vehicles, Registrations/Canada. Statistique Canada. Vehicules Automobiles, Immatriculations (CAN ISSN 0706-067X) **8523**

• Canada. Statistics Canada. Rubber and Plastic Products Industries (Online)/Canada. Statistique Canada. Industries des Produits en Caoutchouc et en Matiere Plastique (CAN ISSN 1481-9724) **7827**

Canada. Statistics Canada. Service Industries in the Canadian Input - Output Accounts: Current Prices, Sources of Data and Methods of Estimation/Canada. Statistique Canada. Industries de Services dans les Comptes d'Entrees - Sorties du Canada: En Prix Courants, Sources de Donnees et Methodes d'Estimation (CAN ISSN 1188-6293) **1218**

Canada. Statistics Canada. Services Price Indexes (CAN ISSN 1488-0261) **1219**

• Canada. Statistics Canada. Shipping in Canada/Canada. Statistiques Canada. Transport Maritime au Canada (CAN ISSN 0835-5533) **8523**

• Canada. Statistics Canada. Small Business Profiles (CAN ISSN 0835-2623) **1219**

Canada. Statistics Canada. Small Business Profiles, Alberta (CAN ISSN 0835-2801) **1219**

Canada. Statistics Canada. Small Business Profiles, British Columbia (CAN ISSN 0835-2828) **1219**

Canada. Statistics Canada. Small Business Profiles, Manitoba (CAN ISSN 0835-2763) **1219**

Canada. Statistics Canada. Small Business Profiles, New Brunswick (CAN ISSN 0835-2704) **1219**

Canada. Statistics Canada. Small Business Profiles, Newfoundland (CAN ISSN 0835-264X) **1219**

Canada. Statistics Canada. Small Business Profiles, Northwest Territories (CAN ISSN 0835-2860) **1219**

Canada. Statistics Canada. Small Business Profiles, Nova Scotia (CAN ISSN 0835-2682) **1219**

Canada. Statistics Canada. Small Business Profiles, Ontario (CAN ISSN 0835-2747) **1219**

Canada. Statistics Canada. Small Business Profiles, Prince Edward Island (CAN ISSN 0835-2666) **1219**

Canada. Statistics Canada. Small Business Profiles, Quebec (CAN ISSN 0835-2720) **1219**

Canada. Statistics Canada. Small Business Profiles, Saskatchewan (CAN ISSN 0835-278X) **1219**

Canada. Statistics Canada. Small Business Profiles, Yukon (CAN ISSN 0835-2844) **1219**

Canada. Statistics Canada. Software Development and Computer Service Industry/Canada. Statistique Canada. Industrie de la Production de Logiciels et des Services Informatiques (CAN ISSN 1181-9847) **2442**

• Canada. Statistics Canada. Spending Patterns in Canada (CAN ISSN 1488-3406) **1219**

• Canada. Statistics Canada. Statistiques sur le Secteur Public (CAN ISSN 1709-4585) **1219**

Canada. Statistics Canada. Surface and Marine Transport/Canada. Statistique Canada. Transports Terrestre et Maritime (CAN ISSN 0828-2897) **8523**

Canada. Statistics Canada. System of National Accounts, Canada's International Investment Position/Canada. Statistique Canada. Bilan des Investissements Internationaux du Canada (CAN) **1219**

• Canada. Statistics Canada. Telephone Statistics/Canada. Statistique Canada. Statistique du Telephone (CAN ISSN 0707-9753) **2347**

• Canada. Statistics Canada. Textile Products Industries/Canada. Statistique Canada. Industrie de Produits Textiles (CAN ISSN 0319-891X) **8463**

• Canada. Statistics Canada. The Daily (CAN ISSN 0827-0465) **8362**

• Canada. Statistics Canada. Travel-log (CAN ISSN 0713-2840) **8778**

Canada. Statistics Canada. Trusteed Pension Funds - Financial Statistics/Canada. Statistique Canada. Caisses de Retraite en Fiducie, Statistiques Financieres (CAN ISSN 0835-4634) **1219**

Canada. Statistics Canada. Unemployment Insurance Statistics. Annual Supplement/Canada. Statistique Canada. Statistiques sur l'Assurance-Chomage. Supplement Annuel (CAN ISSN 0828-3176) **4529**

Canada. Statistics Canada. Vending Machine Operators/Canada. Statistique Canada. Exploitants de Distributeurs Automatiques (CAN ISSN 0527-6411) **5462**

Canada. Statistics Canada. Vital Statistics Compendium (CAN) **7304**

• Canada. Statistics Canada. Wholesale Trade/Canada. Statistique Canada. Commerce de Gros (CAN ISSN 0380-7894) **1219**

Canada. Statistics Canada. Women's Labour Bureau. Women in the Labour Force (CAN) **1669**

• Canada. Statistics Canada. Youth Court Data Tables (Online Edition) (CAN ISSN 1488-4887) **2673**

Canada. Statistics Canada. Youth Court Data Tables (Print Edition) *see* Canada. Statistics Canada. Youth Court Data Tables (Online Edition) **2673**

Canada. Statistique Canada. Autres Industries Manufacturieres *see* Canada. Statistics Canada. Other Manufacturing Industries **1218**

Canada. Statistique Canada. Balance des Paiements Internationaux du Canada *see* Canada. Statistics Canada. Canada's Balance of International Payments **1217**

Canada. Statistique Canada. Bilan des Investissements Internationaux du Canada *see* Canada. Statistics Canada. System of National Accounts, Canada's International Investment Position **1219**

Canada. Statistique Canada. Bulletin Trimestriel, Disponibilite et Ecoulement d'Energie au Canada *see* Canada. Statistics Canada. Quarterly Report on Energy Supply - Demand in Canada **3151**

Canada. Statistique Canada. Caisses de Retraite en Fiducie, Statistiques Financieres *see* Canada. Statistics Canada. Trusteed Pension Funds - Financial Statistics **1219**

Canada. Statistique Canada. Carrieres *see* Canada. Statistics Canada. Quarries and Sand Pits **6459**

• Canada. Statistique Canada. Causes de Deces (CAN ISSN 1708-1459) **7304**

Canada. Statistique Canada. Chargements Ferroviaires *see* Canada. Statistics Canada. Railway Carloadings **8523**

Canada. Statistique Canada. Commerce de Detail *see* Canada. Statistics Canada. Retail Trade **1218**

Canada. Statistique Canada. Commerce de Gros *see* Canada. Statistics Canada. Wholesale Trade **1219**

Canada. Statistique Canada. Commerce International de Services du Canada *see* Canada. Statistics Canada. Canada's International Trade in Services **1554**

Canada. Statistique Canada. Comptes Economiques et Financiers Nationaux, Estimations Trimestrielles *see* Canada. Statistics Canada. National Income and Expenditure Accounts, Quarterly Estimates **1218**

Canada. Statistique Canada. Comptes Economiques Provinciaux Estimations Annuelles *see* Canada. Statistics Canada. Provincial Economic Accounts. Annual Estimates, Tables and Analytical Document **1218**

Canada. Statistique Canada. Depenses sur les Reparations et Renovations Effectuees par les Proprietaires de Logement au Canada *see* Canada. Statistics Canada. Homeowner Repair and Renovation Expenditure **1045**

Canada. Statistique Canada. Division des Statistiques sur la Sante. Deces *see* Canada. Statistics Canada. Health Division. Deaths **8361**

Canada. Statistique Canada. Emploi, Gains et Duree du Travail *see* Canada. Statistics Canada. Employment, Earnings and Hours **1217**

Canada. Statistique Canada. Enquete sur les Voyages des Canadiens. Voyages Interieurs *see* Canada. Statistics Canada. Canadian Travel Survey. Domestic Travel **8778**

Canada. Statistique Canada. Equipement Menager *see* Canada. Statistics Canada. Household Facilities and Equipment **4370**

Canada. Statistique Canada. Establissements du Patrimoine *see* Canada. Statistics Canada. Heritage Institutions **6541**

• Canada. Statistique Canada. Estimations Demographiques Trimestrielles (CAN ISSN 1911-0936) **8362**

Canada. Statistique Canada. Estimations Trimestrielles sur les Regimes de Pensions en Fiducie *see* Canada. Statistics Canada. Quarterly Estimates of Trusteed Pension Funds **1218**

Canada. Statistique Canada. Exploitants de Distributeurs Automatiques *see* Canada. Statistics Canada. Vending Machine Operators **5462**

Canada. Statistique Canada. Exportations, Commerce de Marchandises *see* Canada. Statistics Canada. Exports, Merchandise Trade **1217**

Canada. Statistique Canada. Exportations par Marchandises *see* Canada. Statistics Canada. Exports by Commodity **1217**

Canada. Statistique Canada. Extraction de Minerais Metalliques *see* Canada. Statistics Canada. Metal Ore Mining **6485**

Canada. Statistique Canada. Fer et Acier Primaire *see* Canada. Statistics Canada. Primary Iron and Steel **6338**

Canada. Statistique Canada. Flux et Stocks de Capital Fixe *see* Canada. Statistics Canada. Fixed Capital Flows and Stocks **7479**

Canada. Statistique Canada. Guide Statistique sur l'Energie *see* Canada. Statistics Canada. Energy Statistics Handbook **3125**

Canada. Statistique Canada. Huiles et Corps Gras *see* Canada. Statistics Canada. Oils and Fats **3669**

Canada. Statistique Canada. Importations, Commerce de Marchandises *see* Canada. Statistics Canada. Imports, Merchandise Trade **1217**

Canada. Statistique Canada. Imprimerie, Edition et Industries Connexes *see* Canada. Statistics Canada. Printing, Publishing and Allied Industries **7578**

Canada. Statistique Canada. Indicateurs Nationaux du Tourisme. Estimations Trimestrielles *see* Canada. Statistics Canada. National Tourism Indicators. Quarterly Estimates **8778**

Title

Canadian Association for Studies in Educational Administration Newsletter see C A S E A - A C E A S Newsletter 3018

Canadian Association of African Studies. Newsletter/Association Canadienne des Etudes Africaines. Bulletin (CAN ISSN 0228-8397) 2971

Canadian Association of Agri-Retailers Communicator see C A A R Communicator 98

Canadian Association of Broadcasters. Annual Report/Association Canadienne des Radiodiffuseurs. Rapport Annuel (CAN ISSN 1910-0213) 2314

Canadian Association of Broadcasters News see C A B News 2314

Canadian Association of Broadcasters News see C A B News 2314

Canadian Association of Chiefs of Police Annual Review (CAN ISSN 1910-7900) 2646

Canadian Association of Chiefs of Police Bulletin see C A C P Bulletin 2645

Canadian Association of Chiefs of Police. Directory & Buyer's Guide see Canadian Association of Chiefs of Police. Membership Directory 2646

Canadian Association of Chiefs of Police. Membership Directory (CAN ISSN 1707-6374) 2646

Canadian Association of Educators of the Deaf and Hard of Hearing Journal see C A E D H H Journal 4072

Canadian Association of Exposition Managers. Communique (CAN) 6278

Canadian Association of Geographers. Directory (CAN ISSN 0707-3844) 4001

Canadian Association of Geographers Newsletter see C A G Newsletter 4001

Canadian Association of Mining Equipment and Services for Export Compendium of Canadian Mining Suppliers see C A M E S E Compendium of Canadian Mining Suppliers 4486

Canadian Association of Music Libraries, Archives and Documentation Centres. Newsletter see C A M L Review 6552

Canadian Association of Music Libraries, Archives, and Documentation Centres. Review see C A M L Review 6552

Canadian Association of Music Libraries Review see C A M L Review 6552

Canadian Association of Nephrology Nurses and Technologists Journal see C A N N T Journal 5953

Canadian Association of Pathologists. Newsletter (CAN ISSN 0703-8372) 5591

Canadian Association of Principals Journal Journal see C A P Journal 2833

● Canadian Association of Radiologists. Forum (CAN ISSN 1203-9209) 6193

● ➤ Canadian Association of Radiologists Journal/Association Canadienne des Radiologistes. Journal (CAN ISSN 0846-5371) 6193

Canadian Association of Retired Persons Fifty Plus see C A R P Fifty Plus 4042

Canadian Association of Slavists Newsletter (CAN ISSN 0381-6133) 4446

Canadian Association of Social Workers Bulletin see C A S W Bulletin 8029

Canadian Association of Special Libraries and Information Services. National Salary Survey (CAN) 5057

Canadian Association of the Deaf Chat (Online Edition) see C A D Chat (Online Edition) 6078

Canadian Association of University Teachers Bulletin see C A U T Bulletin 2969

Canadian Association of University Teachers Legal Advisory see C A U T Legal Advisory 4635

Canadian Association of University Teachers Legal Review see C A U T Legal Review 4635

Canadian Authors Association National Newsline (CAN ISSN 0833-8558) 5270

● Canadian Auto Dealer (CAN ISSN 1715-8737) 8571

Canadian Automobile Agreement (USA ISSN 0162-587X) 4920

Canadian Automobile Association. Annual Report (CAN ISSN 0707-624X) 8571

Canadian Automobile Association Magazine see C A A Magazine 8690

Canadian Automobile Association. Statement of Policy (CAN ISSN 0702-2441) 8571

Canadian Automotive Fleet (CAN ISSN 0828-2161) 8571

Canadian Automotive Fleet. Fact Book see Canadian Automotive Fleet 8571

Canadian Autoworld (CAN ISSN 1192-2745) 8571

Canadian Aviation Historical Society Journal see C A H S Journal 50

Canadian Ayrshire Review (CAN ISSN 0008-2961) 282

Canadian Bank Facts (CAN ISSN 1486-4983) 1324

Canadian Bank Notes (CAN) 6649

● Canadian Banker (Online Edition) (CAN) 1324

● Canadian Banker (Print Edition) (CAN ISSN 0822-6830) 1324

Canadian Bankruptcy Reports (4th Series) (CAN ISSN 0068-8347) 1324

● Canadian Baptist (CAN ISSN 0008-2988) 7749

Canadian Bar Association. Annual Report of Proceedings (CAN ISSN 0318-4935) 4638

Canadian Bar National see National (Ottawa, 1974) 4738

● Canadian Bar Review (CAN ISSN 0008-3003) 4638

Canadian Beekeeping (CAN ISSN 0576-4688) 99

Canadian Benefits Administration Manual (CAN) 4498

● Canadian Benefits & Compensation Reporter (USA ISSN 1552-4744) 4638

Canadian Biker (CAN ISSN 1196-7218) 8256

● Canadian Bioethics Report (CAN ISSN 1488-2426) 6909

Canadian Bioproducts and Bioprocessing see Canadian BioProducts & BioProcessing 195

● Canadian BioProducts & BioProcessing (CAN ISSN 1910-3069) 195

Canadian Bioproducts from Renewable Resources see Canadian BioProducts & BioProcessing 195

➤ Canadian Biosystems Engineering/Le Genie des Biosystemes au Canada (CAN ISSN 1492-9058) 210

● Canadian Biotech News (CAN ISSN 1188-455X) 762

● Canadian Biotech Research (CAN) 762

● Canadian Biotechnology (CAN ISSN 1700-8492) 1978

● Canadian Biotechnology Advisory Committee. Annual Report (CAN ISSN 1497-8741) 762

Canadian Biotechnology Directory, Industry and Suppliers Guide see Canadian Biotechnology 1978

● Canadian Black Book. Vehicle Information Guide (USA ISSN 1493-1990) 1978

Canadian Book of Charities (CAN ISSN 0226-0409) 8030

Canadian Book Review Annual (CAN ISSN 0383-770X) 7557

Canadian Bookbinders & Book Artists Guild Newsletter (CAN ISSN 0822-9538) 7557

● Canadian Books in Print on Disc (USA) 622

Canadian Bookseller (CAN ISSN 0225-2392) 7557

Canadian Botanical Association. Bulletin (CAN ISSN 0008-3046) 783

Canadian Broadcasting Corporation. Annual Report see C B C / Radio Canada Annual Report 2314

Canadian Broadcasting Corporation Classical Record Reference Book see C B C Classical Record Reference Book 6552

● Canadian Brown Swiss and Braunvieh Association Newsletter/Cloche (CAN) 262

Canadian Bulletin of Medical History see Bulletin Canadien d'Histoire de la Medecine 5589

Canadian Bureau for International Education. Annual Report. (CAN ISSN 1191-9124) 3012

● Canadian Business (CAN ISSN 0008-3100) 1079

● Canadian Business and Current Affairs Business (USA ISSN 1484-6497) 1219

● Canadian Business and Current Affairs Complete (USA) 1219

● Canadian Business and Current Affairs Current Events (USA) 1219

● Canadian Business and Current Affairs Education (USA ISSN 1481-7586) 2931

● Canadian Business and Current Affairs Reference (USA ISSN 1484-6489) 5

● Canadian Business Conditions/Conjoncture Canadienne (CAN ISSN 0383-9893) 1079

● Canadian Business Economics (CAN ISSN 0705-8330) 1079

Canadian Business Franchise (CAN ISSN 1497-7125) 1079

Canadian Business Franchise Handbook (CAN ISSN 1486-584X) 1079

● Canadian Business Law Journal (CAN ISSN 0319-3322) 4860

Canadian Business Life (CAN ISSN 0829-1349) 1079

Canadian Business Management Manual (CAN) 1958

● Canadian Business Patterns. Revenue Ranges/Structure des Industries Canadiennes. Tranches de Revenu (CAN ISSN 1912-208X) 1079

Canadian C.S. Lewis Journal (CAN ISSN 0711-2173) 5270

Canadian Cable Television Association. Communique (CAN ISSN 1193-5898) 2378

Canadian Camera see Canadian Camera Magazine 6965

Canadian Camera Magazine (CAN ISSN 1702-062X) 6965

● Canadian Cancer Statistics (CAN ISSN 0835-2976) 5742

Canadian Canon Law Society. Newsletter (CAN ISSN 0703-1963) 7787

Canadian Capital Projects (CAN ISSN 0828-0622) 1426

Canadian Case Citations see Canadian Current Law and Canadian Case Citations 4638

Canadian Cases on Employment Law (3rd Series) (CAN) 4638

Canadian Cases on the Law of Insurance (3rd Series) (CAN ISSN 0824-2585) 4638

Canadian Cases on the Law of Torts (CAN ISSN 0701-1733) 4638

Canadian Catholic Historical Association. Bulletin (CAN ISSN 1182-9214) 7787

Canadian Cattle Buyer (CAN ISSN 0843-9613) 282

Canadian Caver (CAN ISSN 0833-0948) 2727

Canadian Centre for Management Development. Performance Report see Canada School of Public Service. Performance Report 7428

● Canadian Centre for Occupational Health and Safety. Performance Report (CAN ISSN 1483-9849) 7428

● Canadian Centre on Substance Abuse. Action News (CAN ISSN 1207-9030) 2692

Canadian Ceramics (CAN ISSN 1486-0945) 2038

● Canadian Champion (CAN ISSN 0834-6925) 3807

Canadian Charter of Rights Annotated (CAN) 4638

Canadian Charter of Rights Decisions see Charter of Rights Decisions 4641

Canadian Chemical Directory (CAN) 1978

● Canadian Chemical News/L' Actualite Chimique Canadienne (CAN ISSN 0823-5228) 2052

Canadian Chemical, Pharmaceutical and Product Directory (CAN ISSN 0068-8452) 1978

Canadian Chess Chat (CAN ISSN 0045-4540) 8164

The Canadian Child and Adolescent Psychiatry Review see Canadian Academy of Child and Adolescent Psychiatry. Journal 6129

Canadian Child Day Care Federation. Interaction (CAN ISSN 0835-5819) 8030

➤ Canadian Children (CAN ISSN 0833-7519) 2834

Canadian Children's Book News (CAN ISSN 1705-7809) 7557

Canadian Children's Literature see C C L 7557

● ➤ Canadian Chiropractic Association. Journal (CAN ISSN 0008-3194) 5803

Canadian Chiropractor (CAN ISSN 1488-6952) 5803

● ➤ Canadian Church Historical Society Journal (CAN ISSN 0008-3208) 7749

Canadian Circulation of U S Magazines (USA ISSN 1186-2955) 38

Canadian Circulations Audit Board, Inc. Circulate see C C A B Circulate 22

Canadian Circumpolar Institute. Northern Reference Series (CAN ISSN 1192-5620) 4287

Canadian Citizen see Cittadino Canadese 3527

Canadian Civil Aircraft Register (CD-ROM Edition) (CAN ISSN 1487-5381) 50

● Canadian Civil Aviation (CAN ISSN 0826-6026) 8523

Canadian Civil Engineer/Ingenieur Civil Canadien (CAN ISSN 0825-7515) 3261

Canadian Climate Summary (CAN ISSN 1207-8514) 6348

● Canadian Co-Operative Association. Annual Report (CAN ISSN 0849-7818) 1422

Canadian Co-operative Wool Growers Magazine (CAN ISSN 0829-075X) 282

Canadian Coast Guard. List of Lights, Buoys and Fog Signals: Atlantic Coast (CAN ISSN 0590-9384) 8640

Canadian Coast Guard. List of Lights, Buoys and Fog Signals: Newfoundland (CAN ISSN 0382-1072) 8640

Canadian Coin News (CAN ISSN 0702-3162) 6649

Canadian Coins (CAN ISSN 1716-0782) 6649

Canadian College & University Food Service Association Newsletter see C C U F S A Newsletter 3629

▼ Canadian College Guide (CAN ISSN 1914-0746) 2971

● Canadian Commerce & Industry (CAN ISSN 1713-7632) 1426

● Canadian Commercial Corporation. Annual Report (CAN ISSN 0382-2281) 7428

● Canadian Commercial Law Guide (CAN) 4860

Canadian Commercial Real Estate Manual (CAN) 7586

Canadian Commission for Unesco. Annual Report of the Secretary-General (CAN ISSN 1705-8724) 4920

Canadian Commission for UNESCO. Occasional Paper (CAN ISSN 0317-5693) 7225

Canadian Commission for UNESCO. Secretary General's Letter/Commission Canadienne pour l'UNESCO. Lettre du Secretaire General (CAN) 2834

Canadian Communications Network Letter see Networkletter 2370

● Canadian Communications Reports (CAN ISSN 0316-3083) 2378

Canadian Companion to 1040 Preparation and Planning (CAN ISSN 1910-0477) 1915

Canadian Companion to 1040 Preparation and Planning Guide see Canadian Companion to 1040 Preparation and Planning 1915

Canadian Companion to One-thousand and Forty Preparation see Canadian Companion to 1040 Preparation and Planning 1915

Canadian Competition Law (CAN) 4860

Canadian Competition Record (CAN ISSN 1195-8081) 4638

Canadian Conference of Catholic Bishops. National Bulletin on Liturgy (CAN) 7787

Canadian Conference on Computer and Robot Vision. Conference Proceedings/Compte Rendu (CAN) 2496

● Canadian Conference on Electrical and Computer Engineering (USA) 2470

The Canadian Connection (CAN ISSN 1195-0064) 6892

Canadian Conservation Institute Technical Bulletins see C C I Technical Bulletins 6521

Canadian Construction Labour and Employment Law (CAN) 4828

● Canadian Consulting Engineer (CAN ISSN 0008-3267) 3184

● Canadian Contractor (CAN ISSN 1498-8941) 990

Canadian Contractor Report of Hydrography and Ocean Sciences (CAN ISSN 0711-6748) 2801

Canadian Coordinating Office for Health Technology Assessment. Technology Report see Canadian Agency for Drugs and Technologies in Health. Technology Report 5591

Canadian Copper/Cuivre Canadien (CAN ISSN 0008-3291) 6308

Canadian Corporate R & D Directory (CAN) 8417

● Canadian Corporate Secretary's Guide (CAN ISSN 0838-9888) 1732

● Canadian Council for Donation and Transplantation. Annual Report (CAN ISSN 1719-9212) 5591

Canadian Council for the Arts. Annual Report/Conseil des Arts du Canada. Rapport Annuel (CAN ISSN 1490-3563) 481

Canadian Council of Christian Charities Bulletin see C C C C Bulletin 8029

Canadian Council of Teachers of English Language Arts see Canadian Council of Teachers of English Language Arts. News Update 3053

● Canadian Council of Teachers of English Language Arts. News Update (CAN ISSN 1707-3960) 3053

Canadian Council of Teachers of English. Newsletter (CAN ISSN 0705-386X) 3053

Canadian Council on International Law. Proceedings of the Annual Conference (CAN ISSN 0317-9087) 4920

Canadian Council on Social Development. Annual Report - Rapport Annuel (CAN ISSN 0068-8584) 8030

Canadian Council on Social Development. Board of Governors/Bureau des Gouverneurs (CAN ISSN 1719-5330) 8030

Canadian Council on Social Development. Board of Governors and Executive Committee see Canadian Council on Social Development. Board of Governors 8030

Canadian Courier see Corriere Canadese 3528

Canadian Cowboy Country (CAN ISSN 1701-1132) 5067

● Canadian Creative Arts in Health, Training and Education (CAN ISSN 1911-9755) 5591

Canadian Creative Home (CAN) 4534

The Canadian Credit and Collection Guide (CAN) 1615

Canadian Crime Statistics (CAN ISSN 0824-0337) 4821

● Canadian Criminal Cases (CAN ISSN 0008-3348) 4885

Canadian Criminal Evidence (CAN) 4885

Canadian Criminal Justice Association. Bulletin see Justice Report 2658

● Canadian Criminal Law Review/Revue Canadienne de Droit Penal (CAN ISSN 1203-8660) 4885

Canadian Curling Association. Fact Book (CAN ISSN 1493-9339) 8164

Canadian Current Law and Canadian Case Citations (CAN) 4638

Canadian Current Law Case Digests/Sommaires de la Jurisprudence (CAN ISSN 1205-4585) 4639

● Canadian Current Tax (CAN ISSN 0317-6495) 1915

Canadian Cycling News see Pedal 8266

● Canadian Cyclist (CAN ISSN 1180-1352) 8256

Canadian Dairy Commission. Annual Report (CAN ISSN 0382-3229) 262

Canadian Data Report of Fisheries and Aquatic Sciences (CAN ISSN 0706-6465) 664

Canadian Data Report of Hydrography and Ocean Sciences (CAN ISSN 0711-6721) 2801

Canadian Defence Almanac see Canadian Defence and Security Directory 6415

Canadian Defence & Security Almanac see Canadian Defence and Security Directory 6415

Canadian Defence & Security Directory see Canadian Defence and Security Directory 6415

Canadian Defence and Security Directory (CAN ISSN 1910-7021) 6415

Canadian Dental Assistants Association. Journal (CAN ISSN 1199-1666) 5837

● ➤ Canadian Dental Association. Journal/Association Dentaire Canadienne. Journal (CAN ISSN 0709-8936) 5837

● Canadian Dental Directory (CAN ISSN 1203-2832) 1978

Canadian Dermatology Report (CAN ISSN 1911-0618) 5872

Canadian Development Report (CAN ISSN 1206-2308) 1554

Canadian Diamonds (CAN ISSN 1719-9638) 6459

Canadian Diamonds and Jewellery see Canadian Diamonds 6459

● Canadian Dimension (CAN ISSN 0008-3402) 7113

● Canadian Directory of Health Care Conferences/Repertoire Canadien des Conferences de Soins de Sante (CAN ISSN 1193-6452) 6278

Canadian Directory of Search Firms (CAN ISSN 1209-6539) 1857

● Canadian Directory of Shopping Centres (CAN ISSN 0822-7799) 1809

● Canadian Directory of Top Computer Executives (USA) 2409

● Canadian Directory to Foundations and Grants (CAN ISSN 1490-764X) 8030

Canadian Donor's Guide (Year)/Guide des Donateurs Canadiens (CAN) 8030

Title

10092 CANADIAN INSTITUTE OF CHARTERED ACCOUNTANTS. UNIFORM ULRICH'S PERIODICALS

Canadian Institute of Chartered Accountants. Uniform Final Examination Report (CAN ISSN 0713-357X) **1284**
Canadian Institute of Fisheries Technology. Annual Report (CAN) **3629**
Canadian Institute of Mining and Metallurgy. Special Volume (CAN ISSN 0826-6166) **1882**
Canadian Institute of Mining, Metallurgy and Petroleum Directory *see* C I M Directory **6459**
Canadian Institute of Mining, Metallurgy and Petroleum Magazine *see* C I M Magazine **6459**
Canadian Institute of Mining, Metallurgy and Petroleum Reporter *see* C I M Reporter **6459**
Canadian Institute of Strategic Studies Bulletin *see* C I S S Bulletin **7224**
• Canadian Institutes of Health Research. Annual Report/Instituts de Recherche en Sante du Canada. Rapport Annuel (CAN ISSN 1702-2363) **5591**
• Canadian Institutes of Health Research. Institute of Aging. Annual Report of Activities (CAN ISSN 1706-3086) **8092**
• Canadian Institutes of Health Research. Institute of Aging. Biennial Report (CAN ISSN 1910-1163) **8092**
Canadian Institutes of Health Research Institute of Infection and Immunity. Annual Report *see* C I H R Institute of Infection and Immunity. Annual Report **5811**
Canadian Institutes of Health Research Institute of Infection and Immunity. Annual Report *see* C I H R Institute of Infection and Immunity. Annual Report **5811**
• Canadian Institutes of Health Research. Performance Report (CAN ISSN 1701-073X) **7428**
• Canadian Insurance (CAN ISSN 0008-3879) **4498**
Canadian Insurance. Annual Statistical Issue (CAN ISSN 0068-9025) **4529**
Canadian Insurance Claims Directory (CAN ISSN 0318-0352) **4498**
Canadian Insurance Law Bulletin Service (CAN ISSN 0068-9033) **4498**
• Canadian Insurance Law Reporter (CAN ISSN 0588-6562) **4639**
• Canadian Insurance Law Reporter Newsletter (CAN ISSN 1910-0817) **4639**
Canadian Integrated Program for Antimicrobial Resistance Surveillance (CAN ISSN 1910-4286) **5811**
• Canadian Intellectual Property Review (CAN ISSN 0825-7256) **6747**
Canadian Intelligence Service (CAN ISSN 0576-5501) **1445**
• Canadian Intergovernmental Conference Secretariat. Performance Report (CAN ISSN 1483-9482) **7428**
• Canadian Intergovernmental Conference Secretariat. Report to Governments/Rapport aux Gouvernements (CAN ISSN 0846-7986) **7428**
• Canadian Interiors (CAN ISSN 0008-3887) **4534**
Canadian International Development Agency. Development Information Program. Guidelines for Submitting Proposals *see* Canadian International Development Agency. Mass Media Initiative. Development Information Program. Guidelines for Submitting Proposals **1592**
Canadian International Development Agency. Mass Media Initiative. Development Information Program. Guidelines for Submitting Proposals (CAN ISSN 1707-7168) **1592**
Canadian International Development Agency, Multilateral Programs Branch. Branch Performance Report/Rapport sur le Rendement (CAN ISSN 1910-3603) **8030**
• Canadian International Development Agency. Performance Report (CAN ISSN 1483-9687) **1592**
Canadian International DX Radio Club Messenger *see* C I D X Messenger **2357**
Canadian International Lawyer (CAN ISSN 1911-1355) **4920**
• Canadian International Merchandise Trade/Le Commerce International de Marchandise du Canada (CAN ISSN 1198-7391) **1220**
Canadian International Trade Directory (CAN ISSN 1180-0828) **1978**
• Canadian International Trade Tribunal. Performance Report (CAN ISSN 1483-7315) **7428**
Canadian Internationalist (CAN ISSN 1484-8678) **3012**
Canadian Intravenous Nurses Association *see* C I N A **5953**
Canadian Investment Journal (CAN ISSN 1709-2108) **1615**
• Canadian Investment Review (CAN ISSN 0840-6863) **1615**
Canadian Iris Society. Newsletter (CAN ISSN 0715-3775) **3726**
• ➤ Canadian Issues/Themes Canadiens (CAN ISSN 0318-8442) **4446**
Canadian Jersey Breeder (CAN ISSN 0008-3909) **283**
Canadian Jersey Herd Record (CAN ISSN 0382-6406) **283**
• Canadian Jeweller (CAN ISSN 0008-3917) **4564**
Canadian Jewellery & Giftware Directory (CAN ISSN 0068-9041) **1978**
Canadian Jewish Archives (New Series) (CAN ISSN 0576-5528) **7719**
▼ • Canadian Jewish Congress Newsletter (CAN) **7719**
• Canadian Jewish News (CAN ISSN 0008-3941) **7719**
➤ Canadian Jewish Studies/Etudes Juives Canadiennes (CAN ISSN 1198-3493) **3525**
• ➤ Canadian Journal for the Study of Adult Education/Revue Canadienne pour l'Etude de l'Education des Adultes (CAN ISSN 0835-4944) **2939**
• ➤ Canadian Journal for Traditional Music/Revue de Musique Folklorique Canadienne (CAN ISSN 1485-4422) **6554**
• Canadian Journal for Women in Coaching Online (CAN ISSN 1496-1539) **8164**
• ➤ Canadian Journal of Aboriginal Community-Based HIV/AIDS Research (CAN ISSN 1912-0958) **8092**
• ➤ The Canadian Journal of Adlerian Psychology (CAN ISSN 1481-1715) **7343**
• Canadian Journal of Administrative Law and Practice (CAN ISSN 0835-6742) **4639**
• ➤ Canadian Journal of Administrative Sciences/Revue Canadienne des Sciences de l'Administration (GBR ISSN 0825-0383) **1080**
• ➤ Canadian Journal of African Studies/Revue Canadienne des Etudes Africaines (CAN ISSN 0008-3968) **7952**
• ➤ Canadian Journal of Agricultural Economics/Revue Canadienne d'Economie Rurale (USA ISSN 0008-3976) **195**
Canadian Journal of Allergy and Clinical Immunology *see* Allergy, Asthma, and Clinical Immunology **5753**
• ➤ Canadian Journal of Anaesthesia/Journal Canadien d'Anesthesie (USA ISSN 0832-610X) **5770**
➤ Canadian Journal of Analytical Sciences and Spectroscopy (CAN ISSN 1205-6685) **7074**
• ➤ Canadian Journal of Animal Science (CAN ISSN 0008-3984) **283**
➤ Canadian Journal of Applied Linguistics/Revue Canadienne de Linguistique Appliquee (CAN ISSN 1481-868X) **5104**
Canadian Journal of Applied Physiology *see* Applied Physiology, Nutrition and Metabolism **6228**
• ➤ Canadian Journal of Archaeology/Journal Canadien d'Archeologie (CAN ISSN 0705-2006) **386**
• ➤ Canadian Journal of Arthropod Identification (CAN ISSN 1911-2173) **937**
• ➤ Canadian Journal of Behavioural Science/Revue Canadienne des Sciences du Comportement (CAN ISSN 0008-400X) **7343**
Canadian Journal of Botany *see* Botany **781**
• ➤ Canadian Journal of Buddhist Studies (CAN ISSN 1710-825X) **7700**
• ➤ Canadian Journal of Cardiology (CAN ISSN 0828-282X) **5779**
➤ Canadian Journal of Cardiovascular Nursing (CAN ISSN 0843-6096) **5954**
• ➤ Canadian Journal of Chemical Engineering (USA ISSN 0008-4034) **3237**
• ➤ Canadian Journal of Chemistry/Journal Canadien de Chimie (CAN ISSN 0008-4042) **2052**
• ➤ Canadian Journal of Civil Engineering/Revue Canadienne de Genie Civil (CAN ISSN 0315-1468) **3261**
† Canadian Journal of Clinical Medicine (CAN ISSN 1481-028X) **8939**
• Canadian Journal of Clinical Pharmacology/Journal Canadien de Pharmacologie Clinique (CAN ISSN 1198-581X) **6827**
• ➤ Canadian Journal of Communication (CAN ISSN 0705-3657) **8092**
• Canadian Journal of Community Mental Health (Online)/Revue Canadienne de Sante Mentale Communautaire (CAN) **7343**
Canadian Journal of Community Mental Health (Print) *see* Canadian Journal of Community Mental Health (Online) **7343**
Canadian Journal of Contemporary Literary Stuff (CAN ISSN 1206-8314) **5210**
• Canadian Journal of Continuing Medical Education (CAN ISSN 0843-994X) **5591**
➤ Canadian Journal of Counselling/Revue Canadienne de Counseling (CAN ISSN 0828-3893) **7343**
• ➤ Canadian Journal of Criminology and Criminal Justice/Revue Canadienne de Criminologie a Justice Penale (CAN ISSN 1707-7753) **2646**
• Canadian Journal of Dental Hygiene (CAN ISSN 1712-171X) **5837**
• ➤ Canadian Journal of Development Studies/Revue Canadienne d'Etudes du Developpement (CAN ISSN 0225-5189) **7952**
• ➤ Canadian Journal of Diabetes (CAN ISSN 1499-2671) **5884**
Canadian Journal of Diabetes Care *see* Canadian Journal of Diabetes **5884**
• Canadian Journal of Diagnosis (CAN ISSN 0839-1866) **5592**
• ➤ Canadian Journal of Dietetic Practice and Research/Revue Canadienne de la Practique et de la Recherche en Dietetique (CAN ISSN 1486-3847) **6656**
• ➤ Canadian Journal of Earth Sciences/Journal Canadien des Sciences de la Terre (CAN ISSN 0008-4077) **2703**
• ➤ Canadian Journal of Economics/Revue Canadienne d'Economie (USA ISSN 0008-4085) **1080**
• ➤ Canadian Journal of Education/Revue Canadienne de l'Education (CAN ISSN 0380-2361) **3019**
• ➤ Canadian Journal of Educational Administration and Policy (CAN ISSN 1207-7798) **3019**
Canadian Journal of Educational Communication *see* Canadian Journal of Learning and Technology **3054**
• ➤ Canadian Journal of Electrical and Computer Engineering (CAN ISSN 0840-8688) **2470**
• ➤ Canadian Journal of Emergency Medicine/Journal Canadien de la Medicine d'urgence (CAN ISSN 1488-1543) **6057**
Canadian Journal of Environmental Education (CAN ISSN 1205-5352) **3409**
• ➤ Canadian Journal of Experimental Psychology/Revue Canadienne de Psychologie Experimentale (CAN ISSN 1196-1961) **7343**
• Canadian Journal of Family Law/Revue Canadienne de Droit Familial (CAN ISSN 0704-1225) **4639**
• ➤ Canadian Journal of Film Studies/Revue Canadienne d'Etudes Cinematographiques (CAN ISSN 0847-5911) **6492**
• ➤ Canadian Journal of Fisheries and Aquatic Sciences/Journal Canadien des Sciences Halieutiques et Aquatiques (CAN ISSN 0706-652X) **3588**
• ➤ Canadian Journal of Forest Research/Revue Canadienne de la Recherche Forestiere (CAN ISSN 0045-5067) **3685**
• ➤ Canadian Journal of Gastroenterology (CAN ISSN 0835-7900) **5921**
• ➤ Canadian Journal of Geriatrics (CAN ISSN 1718-1879) **4042**
Canadian Journal of Herbalism (CAN ISSN 0848-9629) **308**
• ➤ Canadian Journal of Higher Education/Revue Canadienne d'Enseignement Superieur (CAN ISSN 0316-1218) **2971**
• ➤ Canadian Journal of History/Annales Canadiennes d'Histoire (CAN ISSN 0008-4107) **4134**
• ➤ Canadian Journal of Hospital Pharmacy (CAN ISSN 0008-4123) **6827**
• ➤ Canadian Journal of Human Sexuality (CAN ISSN 1188-4517) **7343**
▼ • ➤ Canadian Journal of Hypnosis/Revue Canadienne d'Hypnose (CAN ISSN 1913-4150) **7343**
Canadian Journal of Infectious Diseases *see* Canadian Journal of Infectious Diseases & Medical Microbiology **5811**
• ➤ Canadian Journal of Infectious Diseases & Medical Microbiology/Journal Canadien des Maladies Infectieuses (CAN ISSN 1712-9532) **5811**
Canadian Journal of Infertility Awareness *see* Creating Families **5885**
• ➤ Canadian Journal of Information and Library Science/Revue Canadienne des Sciences de l'Information et des Bibliotheconomie (CAN ISSN 1195-096X) **5000**
• Canadian Journal of Insurance Law (CAN ISSN 0822-109X) **4498**
➤ The Canadian Journal of Irish Studies (CAN ISSN 0703-1459) **4446**
▼ Canadian Journal of Kinesiology (CAN ISSN 1914-721X) **308**
• ➤ Canadian Journal of Latin American and Caribbean Studies/Revue Canadienne des Etudes Latino-Americaines et Caraibes (CAN ISSN 0826-3663) **4287**
• ➤ Canadian Journal of Law and Jurisprudence (CAN ISSN 0841-8209) **4639**
• ➤ Canadian Journal of Law and Society (CAN ISSN 0829-3201) **4639**
• Canadian Journal of Law and Technology (CAN ISSN 1702-9228) **4639**
• ➤ Canadian Journal of Learning and Technology/La Revue Canadienne de l'Apprentissage et de la Technologie (CAN ISSN 1499-6677) **3054**
• Canadian Journal of Life Insurance (CAN) **4498**
• ➤ Canadian Journal of Linguistics/Revue Canadienne de Linguistique (CAN ISSN 0008-4131) **5104**
➤ Canadian Journal of Marketing Research (CAN ISSN 0829-4836) **1809**
• ➤ Canadian Journal of Mathematics/Journal Canadien de Mathematiques (CAN ISSN 0008-414X) **5477**
Canadian Journal of Medical Laboratory Science (CAN ISSN 1207-5833) **5903**
Canadian Journal of Medical Radiation Technology *see* Journal of Medical Imaging and Radiation Sciences **6200**
• ➤ Canadian Journal of Microbiology/Journal Canadien de Microbiologie (CAN ISSN 0008-4166) **882**
• ➤ Canadian Journal of Midwifery Research and Practice (CAN ISSN 1703-2121) **5988**
➤ Canadian Journal of Music Therapy/Revue Canadienne de Musicotherapie (CAN ISSN 1199-1054) **6554**
• ➤ Canadian Journal of Native Education (CAN ISSN 0710-1481) **2834**
• ➤ Canadian Journal of Native Studies (CAN ISSN 0715-3244) **3525**
➤ Canadian Journal of Netherlandic Studies/Revue Canadienne d'Etudes Neerlandaises (CAN ISSN 0225-0500) **5270**
• ➤ Canadian Journal of Neurological Sciences/Le Journal Canadien des Sciences Neurologiques (CAN ISSN 0317-1671) **6129**
➤ Canadian Journal of Neuroscience Nursing (CAN ISSN 1913-7176) **5954**
Canadian Journal of Nursing Leadership *see* Nursing Leadership **5974**
• ➤ The Canadian Journal of Nursing Research/Revue Canadienne de Recherche en Sciences Infirmieres (CAN ISSN 0844-5621) **5954**
• ➤ Canadian Journal of Occupational Therapy/Revue Canadienne d'Ergotherapie (CAN ISSN 0008-4174) **6107**
• ➤ Canadian Journal of Ophthalmology/Journal Canadien d'Ophtalmologie (CAN ISSN 0008-4182) **6039**
Canadian Journal of Pediatrics *see* Paediatrics and Child Health **6098**
• ➤ Canadian Journal of Philosophy (CAN ISSN 0045-5091) **6909**
• Canadian Journal of Philosophy. Supplementary Volume Series (CAN ISSN 0229-7051) **6909**
• ➤ Canadian Journal of Physics/Journal Canadien de Physique (CAN ISSN 0008-4204) **7007**
• ➤ Canadian Journal of Physiology and Pharmacology/Journal Canadien de Physiologie et Pharmacologie (CAN ISSN 0008-4212) **920**
• ➤ Canadian Journal of Plant Pathology (CAN ISSN 0706-0661) **783**
• ➤ Canadian Journal of Plant Science (CAN ISSN 0008-4220) **783**
• Canadian Journal of Plastic Surgery (CAN ISSN 1195-2199) **6238**
• ➤ Canadian Journal of Political Science/Revue Canadienne de Science Politique (GBR ISSN 0008-4239) **7113**
• ➤ Canadian Journal of Program Evaluation/La Revue Canadienne d'Evaluation de Programme (CAN ISSN 0834-1516) **7428**
• ➤ The Canadian Journal of Psychiatry/Revue Canadienne de Psychiatrie (CAN ISSN 0706-7437) **6129**
➤ Canadian Journal of Psychoanalysis/Revue Canadienne de Psychanalyse (CAN ISSN 1195-3330) **6129**
• ➤ Canadian Journal of Public Health/Revue Canadienne de Sante Publique (CAN ISSN 0008-4263) **7511**
▼ ➤ Canadian Journal of Pure and Applied Sciences (CAN ISSN 1715-9997) **7844**
Canadian Journal of Quantuum Economics (CAN ISSN 1705-3498) **7952**
• ➤ Canadian Journal of Regional Science/Revue Canadienne des Sciences Regionales (CAN ISSN 0705-4580) **1536**
• Canadian Journal of Remote Sensing (CD-ROM)/Journal Canadien de Teledetection (CAN ISSN 1712-798X) **50**
Canadian Journal of Remote Sensing (Print) *see* Canadian Journal of Remote Sensing (CD-ROM) **50**
Canadian Journal of Research in Music Education *see* Canadian Music Educator **6554**
• ➤ Canadian Journal of Respiratory Therapy/Revue Canadienne de la Therapie Respiratoire (CAN ISSN 1205-9838) **6212**
• ➤ The Canadian Journal of Rural Medicine/Journal Canadien de la Medecine Rurale (CAN ISSN 1203-7796) **5592**
• Canadian Journal of School Psychology (USA ISSN 0829-5735) **2834**
• ➤ Canadian Journal of Science, Mathematics and Technology Education/Revue Canadienne de l'Enseignement des Sciences, des Mathematiques et des Technologies (USA ISSN 1492-6156) **7844**
▼ Canadian Journal of Social Research (CAN) **7952**
• ➤ Canadian Journal of Sociology (Online) (CAN ISSN 1710-1123) **8092**
• ➤ Canadian Journal of Soil Science (CAN ISSN 0008-4271) **223**
➤ Canadian Journal of Speech-Language Pathology and Audiology/Revue d'Orthophonie et d'Audiologie (CAN ISSN 1913-200X) **3037**
• ➤ Canadian Journal of Statistics/Revue Canadienne de Statistique (USA ISSN 0319-5724) **8362**
• ➤ Canadian Journal of Surgery/Journal Canadien de Chirurgie (CAN ISSN 0008-428X) **6238**
• ➤ Canadian Journal of Urban Research/Revue Canadienne de Recherche Urbaine (CAN ISSN 1188-3774) **4406**
➤ Canadian Journal of Urology (CAN ISSN 1195-9479) **6266**
• ➤ Canadian Journal of Veterinary Research/Revue Canadienne de Recherche Veterinaire (CAN ISSN 0830-9000) **8795**
• ➤ Canadian Journal of Women and the Law/Revue Femmes et Droit (CAN ISSN 0832-8781) **4639**
• ➤ Canadian Journal of Zoology/Journal Canadien de Zoologie (CAN ISSN 0008-4301) **937**
• ➤ Canadian Journal on Aging/Revue Canadienne du Vieillissement (GBR ISSN 0714-9808) **4042**
• Canadian Judicial Council. Annual Report (CAN ISSN 0842-6694) **4947**

Title

Cape Times (ZAF ISSN 1016-3948) **3948**
Cape Verde. Ministry of Foreign Affairs. Boletim Informativo (CPV) **3789**
The Cape Verdean News (USA) **3525**
▼ Cape Wedding Guide (ZAF ISSN 1993-9647) **5557**
Cape Yorker (AUS ISSN 1832-2964) **8691**
Capell's Circulation Report, Inc. (USA ISSN 0736-9077) **7557**
Caper Times (CAN) **2276**
Capex Scoreboard (GBR ISSN 1465-1629) **1882**
• Capilano College. Annual Review (CAN) **2971**
• Capilano Courier (CAN) **2276**
Capilano Review (CAN ISSN 0315-3754) **5270**
Capital *see* Kapital **1139**
Capital (DEU ISSN 0008-5847) **1080**
† Capital (ESP) **8939**
Capital (FRA ISSN 1162-6704) **1080**
Capital (ITA ISSN 0392-3320) **1080**
• Capital (ROM ISSN 1221-3152) **1080**
• Capital (TUR ISSN 1300-5960) **1080**
• The Capital (Rhinebeck) (USA ISSN 0885-4718) **3761**
• Capital and Class (GBR ISSN 0309-8168) **1536**
Capital and Repair Expenditures, Manufacturing Sub-industries, Intentions *see* Canada. Statistics Canada. Capital and Repair Expenditures, Manufacturing Sub-Industries, Intentions **1217**
• Capital Changes Reports (USA ISSN 0008-5855) **1916**
• The Capital Chemist (Online) (USA) **2052**
Capital Chinese News (CAN ISSN 0711-6705) **3525**
Capital Comments (USA) **3710**
Capital Contruction News *see* Shoudu Jianshe Bao **1035**
• Capital Current (CAN) **3807**
Capital D (USA ISSN 1541-874X) **4073**
Capital de la Poesia (ARG) **5419**
† Capital Defense Journal (USA) **8939**
Capital District Business Review *see* The Business Review **1075**
The Capital Expenditure (NZL) **1284**
• Capital Eye (USA ISSN 1089-4500) **7114**
Capital Flyer (USA) **6415**
Capital for Shipping (GBR ISSN 0957-8668) **8640**
Capital Gains Tax Capital Losses *see* C G T Capital Losses **1614**
Capital Gains Tax Service (GBR ISSN 1466-5530) **1916**
Capital Gains Tax Service. Monthly Supplement *see* Capital Gains Tax Service **1916**
Capital Gains Tax Service. Stubbs Securities Taxation (GBR ISSN 1743-0836) **1916**
• Capital Growth Interactive (USA ISSN 1093-5630) **1615**
Capital-Health Magazine (DEU) **6983**
• Capital Humano (ESP ISSN 1130-8117) **1858**
Capital Ideas (Chicago) (USA ISSN 1934-0060) **1080**
Capital Institute of Physical Education. Journal *see* Shoudu Tiyu Xueyuan Xuebao **6996**
Capital Journal of Public Health *see* Shoudu Gonggong Weisheng **7542**
Capital La Vie (GBR) **3862**
The Capital Letter (NZL ISSN 0110-5655) **7429**
• Capital Librarian (USA ISSN 1942-3225) **5000**
• Capital Magazine (CAN) **2553**
The Capital Market *see* Ziben Shichang **1198**
• Capital Market (IND ISSN 0971-7048) **1324**
Capital Market Strategies (GBR) **1324**
Capital Markets *see* International Who's Who of Capital Markets Lawyers **4871**
• Capital Markets Eurasia (RUS ISSN 1562-9163) **1615**
• Capital Markets Law Journal (GBR ISSN 1750-7219) **1615**
Capital Markets Report (RUS) **1080**
Capital Medicine *see* Shoudu Yiyao **5714**
Capital Normal University. Journal (Natural Science Edition) *see* Shoudu Shifan Daxue Xuebao (Ziran Kexue Ban) **7916**
Capital Normal University. Journal (Social Science Edition) *see* Shoudu Shifan Daxue Xuebao (Shehui Kexue Ban) **8001**
Capital Nursing (USA) **5954**
Capital of Yan *see* Yan Du **8017**
Capital Outlook (USA) **3525**
Capital Press (USA ISSN 0740-3704) **100**
▼ Capital Prive Magazine (FRA ISSN 1961-0114) **1732**
Capital Punishment (Farmington Hills) *see* Information Plus Reference Series. Capital Punishment **2655**
• Capital Punishment (Year) (USA ISSN 0191-3220) **2673**
Capital Region Business Journal (USA) **1080**
Capital Region Planning Commission Info *see* C R P C Info **7425**
Capital Region U S A Holiday Guide (GBR ISSN 1366-6223) **8691**
• Capital Sante (CAN ISSN 1487-752X) **6983**
Capital Ship (GBR ISSN 1359-1088) **8274**
• Capital Source (USA ISSN 0898-6916) **7114**
Capital Style (CAN ISSN 1206-8667) **4287**
• Capital Tails (USA ISSN 1945-6638) **6805**
• Capital University Law Review (USA ISSN 0198-9693) **2646**
Capital University of Economics and Business. Journal *see* Shoudu Jingji Maoyi Daxue Xuebao **1174**
Capital University of Medical Sciences. Journal *see* Shoudu Yike Daxue Xuebao **5714**
• Capital Xtra (CAN ISSN 1195-6127) **4372**
Capitala (ROM ISSN 1582-0386) **3932**
Capitale-Nationale. Bulletin Regional (CAN ISSN 1912-6603) **1669**
Capitalia (ITA ISSN 1824-9132) **1324**
• ➤ Capitalism and Society (USA ISSN 1932-0213) **1537**
• Capitalism Magazine (BHS) **7114**
• ➤ Capitalism, Nature, Socialism (GBR ISSN 1045-5752) **7114**
• Capitation Rates and Data (USA ISSN 1090-1574) **4090**
▼ The Capitol (USA) **7429**
Capitol File (USA) **3971**
Capitol Government Reports Weekly (USA) **7114**
Capitol Line-Up (USA) **283**
Capitol Report *see* Hawver's Capitol Report **7443**
Capitol Report *see* Saint Paul Legal Ledger - Capitol Report **4880**
• Capitol Update (USA ISSN 0889-4841) **7429**
Capitol Weekly (USA ISSN 1049-1767) **6694**
Capitoline (USA) **1398**
• ➤ Capitulo Criminologico (VEN ISSN 0798-9598) **2646**
Caplletra (ESP ISSN 0214-8188) **5104**
I Capolavori (ITA ISSN 1721-8322) **6637**
I Capolavori del Punto Croce *see* I Capolavori **6637**
I Capolavori della Musica Classica (ITA ISSN 1970-5166) **6554**
I Capolavori di Arte Femminile *see* I Lavori di Carolina **6640**
Caponier (USA) **4287**
• Capper's (USA ISSN 0892-1148) **3971**
Capri (DEU ISSN 1431-8024) **4372**
• Capri Review (ITA) **8691**
• Capricho (BRA ISSN 0008-5944) **5409**
Caprinae News (CHE) **2606**
Caps and Flints (AUS ISSN 0045-5695) **4331**
Capsa (ESP ISSN 1576-5954) **2232**
† Capsicum & Eggplant Newsletter (ITA ISSN 1122-5548) **8939**
• The Capstone (Towson) (USA) **4064**
The Capstone (Washington, DC) (USA ISSN 1062-6778) **2276**
• Capsula Eburnea (ITA ISSN 1970-5492) **5592**
Capsule *see* Kapuseru **6857**
Capsule (NZL ISSN 1173-3624) **3525**
Capsule (Levittown) *see* C A P Sule (Levittown) **4042**
Capsule Report (USA) **990**
Capsules *see* Around the South (Online Edition) **8089**
Capsules (USA) **5592**
Captain's Log (GBR ISSN 1473-8767) **8274**
The Captain's Log (USA ISSN 1541-7131) **8539**
• Caption Center News (USA) **2378**
Captivate (NZL ISSN 1177-0783) **8030**
Captive & A R T Review *see* Captive Review **4498**
• Captive Insurance Company Reports (USA ISSN 1056-8158) **4498**
Captive Insurance Company Review (GBR ISSN 0262-7701) **4498**
Captive Review (GBR ISSN 1757-1251) **4498**
Capture (AUS ISSN 1445-6486) **6965**
Capture Section Reports (NCL) **3588**
Capturing Intelligence (NLD ISSN 1574-9576) **2447**
Car (GBR ISSN 0008-5987) **8571**
Car (ZAF ISSN 0008-5995) **8571**
▼ Car (Middle East Edition) (UAE ISSN 1817-1427) **8571**
Car Action Buyer's Guide *see* Radio Control Car Action Buyer's Guide **4345**
• Car Ad (GBR ISSN 1368-7123) **8571**
Car & Accessory Trader *see* C A T **8570**
Car & Bus Magazine (Edition Francaise) *see* Car & Bus Magazine (Nederlandse Editie) **8692**
Car & Bus Magazine (Nederlandse Editie) (BEL ISSN 1370-589X) **8692**
Car & Car (ITA ISSN 1827-076X) **8571**
Car and Driver *see* Mingchezhi **8590**
Car & Driver *see* Car and Driver **8571**
• Car and Driver (ESP) **8571**
Car and Driver/Ren che Zhi (HKG ISSN 1017-3323) **8571**
• Car and Driver (USA ISSN 0008-6002) **8571**
Car and Driver Buying Guide (USA) **8571**
Car and Driver Truck Buyers Guide (USA) **8669**
Car and Driver Ultimate Road Test Comparisons (USA ISSN 1546-4687) **8571**
Car & HiFi (DEU ISSN 0940-9157) **8571**
Car & HiFi Club (DEU) **8571**
Car and Locomotive Cyclopedia (USA) **8615**
Car & Locomotive Yearbook *see* Progressive Railroading's Car & Locomotive Yearbook & Buyers' Guide **8622**
• Car & Money News (USA) **1615**
Car & Motor (CHN ISSN 1009-0231) **8571**
Car & Travel Monthly (USA ISSN 1080-2290) **8572**
Car Auction (GBR ISSN 0955-3703) **8572**
Car Audio & Electronics (USA ISSN 0898-3720) **8152**
Car Audio and Electronics *see* Car Audio & Electronics **8152**
Car Busters (CZE) **8572**
Car Buyer (GBR ISSN 0308-9460) **8572**
Car Buyers Guide (IRL ISSN 1649-0592) **8572**
▼ Car Buyers Guide (Leinster Edition) (IRL ISSN 2009-0404) **8572**
Car Buyers Guide (North Leinster Edition) *see* Car Buyers Guide (Leinster Edition) **8572**
Car Buyers Guide (South Leinster Edition) *see* Car Buyers Guide (Leinster Edition) **8572**
Car Buyers Guide. Irish New Car Guide (IRL ISSN 1649-038X) **8572**
• Car Collector (USA ISSN 1094-3579) **8572**
• The Car Connection (USA) **8572**
• Car Craft (USA ISSN 0008-6010) **8572**
Car Dealer Insider (USA ISSN 1052-407X) **8572**
Car Dealer Insider (Rockville) (USA) **8572**
Car Design (ITA ISSN 1722-6546) **8572**
† Car Design & Technology (GBR ISSN 0961-9372) **8939**
• Car Design News (USA ISSN 1546-3117) **8572**
Car Emotion (ITA ISSN 1825-5183) **8572**
Car Free Cities Magazine (BEL) **4406**
Car Graphic (JPN ISSN 0915-1702) **8572**
Car HiFi (GBR ISSN 0953-0924) **8572**
Car Market Guide *see* Qiche Daogou **8600**
Car Mechanics (GBR ISSN 0008-6037) **8572**
Car Modeler Annuals *see* Scale Auto Contest Cars **4346**
Car Owners *see* Chezhu zhi You **8573**
Car Parts and Accessories Mart (GBR ISSN 1466-9781) **8572**
Car Road (JPN) **8572**
▼ The Car Room Magazine (USA ISSN 1949-3274) **8572**
• Car Stereo (Year) (USA ISSN 1046-3852) **8152**
Car Styling (JPN) **8572**
Car Top (JPN) **8572**
Car Toy Collectibles (USA ISSN 1524-3176) **4331**
Car Turkiye (TUR) **8572**
Cara (IRL ISSN 0008-6088) **8782**
Il Carabiniere (ITA ISSN 0008-610X) **7429**
• El Carabobeno (VEN) **3994**
Caracas Chamber of Commerce. Bulletin *see* Camara de Comercio de Caracas. Boletin **1397**
Caracola (ESP ISSN 0214-2872) **2181**
Caracola. Extra *see* Caracola **2181**
Caractere (FRA ISSN 0247-039X) **7319**
Caracteres (FRA ISSN 0008-6134) **5419**
Caracteristiques Culturelles et Linguistiques du Quebec (CAN ISSN 1911-6128) **5104**
Caramelo (BRA ISSN 0104-0251) **4406**
Carangos Especiais (BRA ISSN 1679-3560) **8572**
• Caras (ARG ISSN 0328-4301) **3791**
• Caras (BRA ISSN 0104-396X) **3803**
Caras (CHL) **8854**
Caras (PRT ISSN 0874-047X) **3931**
Caras Decoracao (PRT ISSN 0874-0488) **4534**
Carauto *see* Autocar **8561**
Caravan (CAN ISSN 0835-2003) **7787**
Caravan (DEU ISSN 0930-0309) **8308**
Caravan (GBR ISSN 1475-9004) **8692**
Caravan (Umm al-Quwain) *see* Al- Qafilah (Umm al-Quwain) **3621**
Caravan and Camping Guide - Britain & Ireland (Year) (GBR) **8308**
Caravan & Chalet Parks Guide (GBR ISSN 0269-8730) **8692**
Caravan & Motorhome (AUS) **8692**
Caravan and Outdoor Life (ZAF ISSN 0379-4636) **8692**
Caravan Bladet (SWE ISSN 0008-6169) **8308**
Caravan Camper Granturismo *see* Caravan e Camper **8692**
• The Caravan Club Magazine (GBR ISSN 1369-5088) **8308**
• Caravan e Camper (ITA ISSN 1121-7227) **8692**
Caravan Industry and Park Operator (GBR ISSN 1359-1223) **8692**
Caravan Industry Supplies & Services Directory (GBR) **8308**
Caravan Life *see* Which Caravan **8775**
Caravan, Motorcaravan & Camping Mart (GBR ISSN 0956-6562) **8308**
Caravan Parks News (AUS) **8493**
Caravan Trader (AUS ISSN 1449-633X) **8572**
Caravan World (AUS) **8692**
Caravane Magazine *see* Le Monde du Plein Air **8322**
Le Caravanier *see* Camping et Caravaning **8307**
Caravaning (DEU ISSN 0008-6185) **8493**
Caravaning (ESP) **4976**
Caravaning & Camping (ESP) **8692**
Caravans and Campervans Guide *see* Caravans & Campervans Guide **8493**
Caravans & Campervans Guide (AUS) **8493**
Caravelle (FRA ISSN 1147-6753) **4446**
CarbHealth Magazine (USA ISSN 1544-497X) **6656**
• Carbohydrate Chemistry (GBR) **2120**
• ➤ Carbohydrate Polymers (GBR ISSN 0144-8617) **2120**
• ➤ Carbohydrate Research (GBR ISSN 0008-6215) **2120**
• ➤ Carbon (GBR ISSN 0008-6223) **2121**
• Carbon 14 (USA) **481**
▼ • Carbon and Climate Law Review (DEU ISSN 1864-9904) **3484**
• Carbon Balance and Management (GBR ISSN 1750-0680) **6348**
▼ Carbon Business (GBR ISSN 1754-503X) **3495**
Carbon Dioxide and Climate (USA) **6348**
• Carbon Dioxide Emissions from Fuel Combustion (FRA ISSN 1562-7314) **3484**
Carbon Dioxide Information Analysis Center Communications *see* C D I A C Communications **6348**
Carbon Economy Monthly *see* Tan Jingji Yuekan **1181**
Carbon-Graphite Composite Material Study (USA ISSN 0731-1869) **2115**
▼ • Carbon Science and Technology (IND ISSN 0974-0546) **2121**
• Carbon Week (AUS ISSN 1448-8213) **3126**
• ➤ Carbonates and Evaporites (USA ISSN 0891-2556) **2727**
• Carbone Informazioni (ITA) **6459**
Carbonomics (GBR ISSN 1355-1590) **3409**
Carbonomics Countries (GBR) **3409**
Carbons *see* Tanso **2082**
Carburol (ESP ISSN 1130-8907) **8572**
Le Carcan (MLI ISSN 1607-2650) **3907**
CarCare *see* Popular Mechanics CarCare **8599**
• ➤ Carcinogenesis (GBR ISSN 0143-3334) **6015**
Carcinogenesis, Teratogenesis and Mutagenesis *see* Aibian, Jibian, Tubian **3401**
Carcinogenesis, Teratogenesis and Mutagenesis *see* Yanbian - Jibian - Tubian **6036**
Card Collector (DEU) **4331**
Card Collector Extra (DEU) **4331**
Card Collectors News (GBR ISSN 1472-4596) **4331**
Card-Forum (DEU ISSN 1437-2207) **1392**
Card-Forum International (DEU) **1392**
• Card Industry Directory (USA ISSN 1051-6778) **1324**
Card Making & Papercraft (GBR) **532**
Card Manufacturing (USA) **7091**
Card Master (DEU) **2181**
Card News *see* Electronic Payments Week **1393**
Card Player (USA ISSN 1089-2044) **8164**
Card Player College (USA) **8164**
Card Player Europe (USA ISSN 1747-0447) **8164**
Card Source One *see* Card Industry Directory **1324**
Card Talk (USA ISSN 1076-6081) **23**
• Card Technology Today (GBR ISSN 0965-2590) **3090**
Card Times (GBR ISSN 0956-5124) **4331**
Card Trade (USA ISSN 1081-2121) **4331**
Card World (GBR ISSN 0954-8564) **1324**
Card World User Guide (GBR ISSN 0967-8026) **1324**
CardDirectory (USA) **1324**
▼ • Cardiac Cath Lab Director (USA ISSN 2150-1335) **5779**
Cardiac Electrophysiology Review *see* Journal of Interventional Cardiac Electrophysiology **5793**
▼ Cardiac Intervention Today (USA) **5779**
Cardiac Practice (JPN ISSN 0915-874X) **5779**
Cardiac Surgery (USA ISSN 1072-9798) **6238**
➤ Cardiac Surgery Today (GBR ISSN 1478-2170) **5779**
Cardiff Business School. Discussion Paper Series in Financial and Banking Economics (GBR ISSN 0966-6656) **1324**
Cardiff Business School. Discussion Papers in Economics (GBR ISSN 1461-9318) **1080**
Cardiff Business School Working Paper Series (GBR) **1080**
• Cardiff Business School. Working Papers in Accounting and Finance (GBR ISSN 1750-6638) **1284**
• Cardiff Economics Working Papers (GBR ISSN 1749-6101) **1080**
• Cardiff Human Resource Management Working Papers (GBR ISSN 1753-1837) **1858**
• Cardiff Logistics and Operations Management Working Papers (GBR ISSN 1753-1829) **1732**
• Cardiff Marketing and Strategy Working Papers (GBR ISSN 1753-1632) **1732**
Cardinal (USA ISSN 0162-8186) **905**
Cardinal Bea Studies (PHL) **7787**
Cardinale *see* Cardiologie Cardinale **5779**
Cardinals Annual *see* Maple Street Press Cardinals Annual **8238**
Cardio Magazin (SVK ISSN 1337-0537) **5779**
Cardio News (DEU ISSN 1437-1073) **5779**
Cardio-Pulmonary Resuscitation & Automated External Defibrillation *see* C P R & A E D **5590**
Cardioangiology *see* Junkankika **5794**
Cardiologen Vademecum (NLD ISSN 1386-5315) **5779**
➤ Cardiologia Ambulatoriale (ITA ISSN 1971-6818) **5779**
• Cardiologia Hungarica (HUN ISSN 0133-5596) **5779**
Cardiologia Practica (ESP ISSN 1132-7359) **5779**
Cardiologie Cardinale (FRA ISSN 1960-1646) **5779**
Cardiologie Pratique (FRA ISSN 0766-3633) **5779**
Cardiologie Pratique. Supplement (FRA ISSN 1240-3318) **5779**
• Il Cardiologo (ITA ISSN 1592-842X) **5779**
Le Cardiologue (FRA ISSN 0769-0819) **5779**
• ➤ Cardiology (CHE ISSN 0008-6312) **5779**
† Cardiology (DEU ISSN 0947-0522) **8939**
▼ • The Cardiology (PAK ISSN 1811-8194) **5779**
Cardiology *see* Kardiologiya **5794**
Cardiology *see* Kardiologija **5794**
Cardiology *see* Kardiologia **5794**
Cardiology (Bethesda) (USA) **5779**
• Cardiology Clinics (USA ISSN 0733-8651) **5779**
• Cardiology Coder's Pink Sheet (USA ISSN 1941-7993) **5779**
• Cardiology Coding Alert (USA ISSN 1522-7472) **4498**
Cardiology Health Monitor (USA ISSN 1067-9332) **5779**
• Cardiology in Review (USA ISSN 1061-5377) **5780**
• ➤ Cardiology in the Young (GBR ISSN 1047-9511) **5780**
Cardiology Journal (POL ISSN 1897-5593) **5780**
Cardiology News (GBR ISSN 1368-8979) **5780**
• Cardiology News (USA ISSN 1544-8800) **5780**
Cardiology News (Australian Edition) (AUS ISSN 1832-6722) **5780**

Title

DIRECTORY 2010 CELLULAR PHYSIOLOGY AND BIOCHEMISTRY 10101

Catholics in Coalition for Justice and Peace National Newsletter (AUS) 7225
Catholiques en France (FRA ISSN 1771-0405) 7791
Catia Solutions (USA ISSN 1093-6629) 2409
Catnap (GBR ISSN 1357-8944) 6130
Catnip (USA ISSN 1069-6687) 6805
Cato Institute. Briefing Papers (USA ISSN 1061-7280) 7114
• ➤ The Cato Journal (USA ISSN 0273-3072) 7114
• Cato Policy Report (USA ISSN 0743-605X) 1422
The Cato Project on Social Security Choice (USA) 1916
Cato Supreme Court Review (USA ISSN 1936-0398) 4947
• El Catoblepas (ESP ISSN 1579-3974) 6910
Cats (JPN ISSN 1348-6667) 6805
• Cats & Kittens (USA ISSN 1079-8285) 6805
† Cats Magazine (Irvine) (USA ISSN 1548-6419) 8940
Cat's Pause (USA) 8165
Cats U S A (USA ISSN 1071-3999) 6805
Cattle *see* Nauta 294
Cattle *see* U.S. Department of Agriculture. National Agricultural Statistics Service. Cattle (Online) 187
Cattle Business in Mississippi (USA ISSN 0897-2737) 283
• Cattle Buyers Weekly (USA ISSN 1083-8392) 283
Cattle Country Magazine (AUS ISSN 1832-6935) 283
Cattle Guard (USA ISSN 0411-289X) 283
• Cattle Health Report (USA) 283
Cattle Practice (GBR ISSN 0969-1251) 283
The Cattleman *see* The New Zealand Angus Cattleman 294
• Cattleman (USA ISSN 0008-8552) 283
Cattleman of the Year (ZWE) 283
Cattlemen (CAN ISSN 0008-3143) 283
• Catt's Claws (USA) 7203
CatWatch *see* Cat Watch 6805
Caucasian Entomological Bulletin *see* Kavkazskii Entomologicheskii Bulleten' 853
Caucasian Journal of European Affairs *see* Caucasian Review of International Affairs 7114
Caucasian Regional Studies (GEO ISSN 1027-8540) 7114
• ➤ Caucasian Review of International Affairs (DEU ISSN 1865-6773) 7114
Caucasian Studies *see* Kaukasienstudien 4237
• Caucasus Business Forecast Report (GBR ISSN 1750-2144) 1081
• Caucasus Energy Monthly (GBR) 6765
Cauce (ESP ISSN 0212-0410) 5105
• Cauce 2000 (ESP ISSN 0212-761X) 3262
† Cauces (FRA ISSN 1626-1437) 8940
Cauces de Intercomunicacion (ESP ISSN 1135-0814) 7630
Cauchotecnia (ARG) 7824
➤ Cauda Pavonis (USA ISSN 1059-8308) 5271
Cauldron (USA) 2277
The Cauldron (USA) 2277
• Cauriensia (ESP ISSN 1886-4945) 7791
Causas y Azares (ARG) 8092
▼ Cause Commune (FRA ISSN 1957-2166) 4446
Cause di Morte (ITA ISSN 1121-0958) 7304
Causes Communes (FRA ISSN 1262-1218) 7225
Causes de Deces *see* Canada. Statistique Canada. Causes de Deces 7304
Causes en Appel au Quebec *see* Quebec Appeal Cases 4764
Causes of Action (USA) 4641
Causes of Death *see* Canada. Statistics Canada. Causes of Death (Ottawa, 1997) (Online Edition) 7304
Caustic (IND ISSN 0008-8579) 2053
Caustic Truths! (CAN) 6554
Caux Information (CHE) 7225
† Cavalcade of Acts & Attractions (USA ISSN 1521-1290) 8940
• The Cavalier Daily (USA ISSN 0008-8609) 2277
Cavalier King Charles Spaniel Club, U S A. Bulletin (USA) 6806
Cavaliere (FRA ISSN 1959-7428) 8289
Cavalli e Cavalieri (ITA ISSN 1121-3809) 8289
Cavallino Magazine (USA ISSN 0889-2504) 8573
• Cavallo (DEU ISSN 1430-9270) 8289
Cavallo Magazine (ITA ISSN 1590-413X) 319
Cavalos de Raca *see* Cavalos de Raca e Esporte 8289
Cavalos de Raca e Esporte (BRA) 8289
The Cavalry Journal (USA ISSN 1074-0252) 4288
➤ Cave and Karst Science (GBR ISSN 1356-191X) 2728
Cave Archaeology & Palaeontology Research Archive (GBR ISSN 1467-8837) 386
Cave e Costruzioni *see* Quarry and Construction 1031
Cave Geology (USA ISSN 0749-8969) 2728
▼ Cave Wall (USA ISSN 1937-2507) 5419
Caveat Emptor Consumers Bulletin (USA ISSN 0743-989X) 2635
Caveat Lector (USA ISSN 1084-6050) 5419
• La Caverna de Platon (ESP ISSN 1577-0567) 6910
Caves and Caverns (USA) 8692
Caves & Caving (GBR ISSN 0142-1832) 2728
Caves Australia (AUS ISSN 1449-2601) 2728
Caves of China (GBR ISSN 1744-9537) 2728
Cawaii (JPN) 8855
Cawaii!/Ka Wa Yi! Shaonu Liuxing Zhi (Zhongwen Ban) (TWN ISSN 1608-6600) 8855
• ➤ Cayapa (VEN ISSN 1317-5734) 8092
Cayman Executive (CYM) 1081
Cayman Financial Review (CYM) 1081
▼ Cayman Funds (GBR ISSN 1754-6060) 1616
Cayman Islands Annual Report and Official Handbook (CYM) 7429
Cayman Islands Chamber of Commerce Directory (CYM) 1398
Cayman Islands Chamber of Commerce Newsletter (CYM) 1398
Cayman Islands. Economics & Statistics Office. Compendium of Statistics (CYM) 8362
Cayman Islands. Education Department. Report of the Chief Education Officer (CYM ISSN 0303-8777) 2835
Cayman Islands Gazette (CYM) 4641
Cayman Islands Law Reports (GBR ISSN 0269-977X) 4641
Cayman Islands. Legislative Assembly. Minutes (CYM ISSN 0300-4740) 7114
Cayman Islands Monetary Authority. Annual Report (CYM) 1916
Cayman Islands Yearbook and Business Directory (CYM) 1979
Cayman Life (CYM) 3821
Cayman Observer (CYM) 3821
• Caymera Shop (ITA ISSN 1970-1098) 1809
Cayo (USA) 5271
Caza Feder (ESP) 8309
Caza Fotografica (ESP) 7844
Caza Mayor (ESP) 8309
Caza Ocasion (ESP) 8309
Caza y Pesca Nautica (VEN) 8309
Cazar Mas (ESP) 8309
CB-Kurier *see* C B-Kurier 2357
Cbeebies (POL ISSN 1689-8788) 2181
CBI - Coopers and Lybrand Deloitte Financial Services Survey *see* C B I - PriceWaterhouseCoopers Financial Services Survey 1077
CBI Nytt *see* C B I Nytt 988
• C++Builder Developer's Journal (Online Edition) (USA) 2505
CCNMatthews CCE Directory *see* C C N Matthews C C E Directory 22
• CD-Action (POL ISSN 1426-2916) 2475
CD Hotlist *see* C D Hotlist 4999
C@D-Info *see* C A D - Info 3288
Cd Notaberichten & Bronnen *see* C D Notaberichten en Bronnen 4635
CD-ROM Blue Book (Year) *see* Vanderbilt Rubber Handbook 7827
CD-ROM de Ejecutivos *see* Directorio de Empresas - Directorio de Proveedores - Directorio por Colonias - Directorio de Empresarios 1984
CD-ROM de Funcionarios *see* Directorio de Funcionarios 1984
• CD-ROM der Auslandszoelle (DEU) 1555
† • CD-ROM Electre (FRA ISSN 1626-0163) 8940
CD-ROM Facil (BRA ISSN 1517-3585) 2575
CD-ROM Magazine (GBR ISSN 1355-0659) 2588
CD-ROM Online (USA) 2588
• CD-ROM Review Magazine (USA) 2588
• CD-ROM Sportwissenschaft (DEU ISSN 0941-6633) 8218
Cd V N W *see* C D Verzameling Nederlandse Wetgeving 7425
CDA.nl (Christen Democratisch Appel) (NLD ISSN 1871-6733) 7114
cd:uk (GBR) 2181
CDW-G Ed Tech *see* Ed Tech 2948
CDW-G Ed Tech - Higher Education *see* Ed Tech Focus on Higher Education 2948
Ce B I T News (GBR) 2491
Ce Fastu? (ITA ISSN 1828-4302) 5105
Ce Que Je Crois (FRA ISSN 0768-231X) 5271
Ce que Mon Enfant Apprend a l'Ecole, Manuel a l'Intention des Parents. Cinquieme Annee *see* Curriculum Handbook for Parents. Grade 5 3056
Ce que Mon Enfant Apprend a l'Ecole, Manuel a l'Intention des Parents. Deuxieme Annee *see* Curriculum Handbook for Parents. Grade 2 3056
Ce que Mon Enfant Apprend a l'Ecole, Manuel a l'Intention des Parents. Huitieme Annee *see* Curriculum Handbook for Parents. Grade 8 3056
Ce que Mon Enfant Apprend a l'Ecole, Manuel a l'Intention des Parents. Neuvieme Annee *see* Curriculum Handbook for Parents. Grade 9 3056
Ce que Mon Enfant Apprend a l'Ecole, Manuel a l'Intention des Parents. Premiere Annee *see* Curriculum Handbook for Parents. Grade 1 3056
Ce que Mon Enfant Apprend a l'Ecole, Manuel a l'Intention des Parents. Quatrieme Annee *see* Curriculum Handbook for Parents. Grade 4 3056
Ce que Mon Enfant Apprend a l'Ecole, Manuel a l'Intention des Parents. Septieme Annee *see* Curriculum Handbook for Parents. Grade 7 3056
Ce que Mon Enfant Apprend a l'Ecole, Manuel a l'Intention des Parents. Sixieme Annee *see* Curriculum Handbook for Parents. Grade 6 3056
Ce que Mon Enfant Apprend a l'Ecole, Manuel a l'Intention des Parents. Troisieme Annee *see* Curriculum Handbook for Parents. Grade 3 3056
Ce Qu'il Faut Savoir des Nations Unies *see* Everyone's United Nations 8955
CEAMAGazine *see* C E A MAGazine 5267
• Cebem.com (Centro Boliviano de Estudios Multidisciplinarios) (BOL) 7953
Cebu (MEX) 283
Cecidologia Internationale (IND ISSN 0008-8676) 842
Cecidology (GBR ISSN 0268-2907) 783
Cecil Business Ledger (USA) 1081
Cedar Digest (USA) 2277
Cedar Hill Review (USA) 5271
Cedar Living (USA) 5067
Cedars-Sinai Compass *see* Cedars - Sinai Compass 4090
Cedars - Sinai Compass (USA) 4090
Cedarville Torch (USA ISSN 1093-4618) 7750
CeDEx Discussion Paper Series (Centre for Decision Research and Experimental Economics) (GBR ISSN 1749-3293) 1081
• ➤ Cedille (ESP ISSN 1699-4949) 5105
Cedula Gieldy Warszawskiej (POL ISSN 1231-9511) 1616
Il Cefalopodo (ITA ISSN 1128-7918) 7344
Cefiro (USA ISSN 1534-228X) 5271
• Cehui Gongcheng/Engineering of Surveying and Mapping (CHN ISSN 1006-7949) 4002
• ➤ Cehui Kexue/Science of Surveying and Mapping (CHN ISSN 1009-2307) 4002
• Cehui Kexue Jishu Xuebao/Zhengzhou Institute of Surveying and Mapping. Journal (CHN ISSN 1673-6338) 4002
† • Cehui Ruankexue Yanjiu/Research on Soft Science of Surveying and Mapping (CHN ISSN 1006-9712) 8940
• Cehui Tongbao/Bulletin of Surveying and Mapping (CHN ISSN 0494-0911) 4002
Cehui Wenzhai (Cehuixue)/Abstracts of Surveying and Mapping (CHN ISSN 1006-0642) 4035
• Cehui Xinxi yu Gongcheng/W T U S M Bulletin of Science and Technology (CHN ISSN 1007-3817) 4002
• Cehui Xuebao/Acta Geodaetica et Cartographica Sinica (CHN ISSN 1001-1595) 2778
• Cehui yu Kongjian Dili Xinxi/Geomatics & Spatial Information Technology (CHN ISSN 1672-5867) 4002
➤ Ceiba (HND ISSN 0008-8692) 100
Ceiba (PRI ISSN 0885-9906) 5271
• Ceiberweiber (AUT ISSN 1606-7932) 8855
CEIM Revista *see* C E I M Revista 480
Cejil Inryu Haghoeji/Korean Journal of Physical Anthropology (KOR ISSN 1225-150X) 332
• Cejing Jishu/Well Logging Technology (CHN ISSN 1004-1338) 6765
• Cekong Jishu/Measurement & Control Technology (CHN ISSN 1000-8829) 51
Celan-Jahrbuch (DEU ISSN 0933-4106) 5271
Celastrina (JPN ISSN 0388-6492) 842
The Celator (USA ISSN 1048-0986) 6649
Celeb Confidential (USA ISSN 1083-2645) 6287
Celeb Staff (USA) 5067
Celebrare Cantando (ITA) 6554
Celebrate (CAN ISSN 0843-2538) 7791
Celebrate (USA ISSN 0899-7063) 7750
• Celebrate Life (Stafford) (USA) 971
Celebrate Young Heritage *see* C Y H 3971
• Celebrated Living (USA ISSN 1553-8516) 5067
• Celebrating Australians (AUS ISSN 1832-4428) 641
Celebration *see* Beautiful Communities 3724
Celebration (Baltimore) (USA ISSN 0883-9174) 5419
Celebration (Kansas City) (USA ISSN 0094-2421) 7791
Celebrator Beer News (USA ISSN 1086-2587) 601
Celebremos / Let Us Celebrate (USA ISSN 1098-9994) 7791
Celebrer (FRA ISSN 0240-4656) 7791
Celebriamo (ITA ISSN 0008-8706) 6554
Celebrity (CHE ISSN 1661-1799) 6492
† Celebrity (NLD ISSN 1569-9587) 8940
Celebrity Birthday Directory (USA) 6492
Celebrity Birthday Guide (USA) 6492
Celebrity Bulletin (GBR ISSN 0045-6020) 641
Celebrity Cuts Hairstyles & Trends (USA ISSN 1533-8797) 586
Celebrity Directory (USA) 6492
Celebrity Dish (USA) 4354
Celebrity Hairstyles (USA ISSN 1058-305X) 586
Celebrity Hairstyles Presents: Bridal Star Hairstyles (USA) 586
Celebrity Hairstyles Presents: Teen Star Hairstyles (USA) 586
Celebrity Locator (USA) 6492
Celebrity Skin (USA ISSN 1075-0819) 6287
Celebrity Sleuth (USA) 6287
▼ • Celebrity Studies (GBR ISSN 1939-2397) 8092
Celebrity Style (USA ISSN 1464-5939) 5067
Celebrity Style: Soap Stars at Home (USA) 586
Celebrity Website and E-mail Directory (USA ISSN 1524-8704) 6492
Celebrity Worldwide Teen Hairstyles & Trends *see* Teen Hairstyles & Trends 591
➤ Celehis (ARG ISSN 0328-5766) 5271
• ➤ Celestial Mechanics and Dynamical Astronomy (NLD ISSN 0923-2958) 573
• ➤ Celestinesca (ESP ISSN 0147-3085) 5271
Celiac News (CAN ISSN 0833-1464) 5873
La Celibataire (FRA ISSN 1292-2048) 8093
Celibataires (CAN) 5067
Cell *see* Gekkan Saibo 832
• ➤ Cell (USA ISSN 0092-8674) 828
Cell Adhesion and Communication (Online Edition) *see* Cell Communication & Adhesion (Online Edition) 664
Cell Adhesion and Communication (Print Edition) *see* Cell Communication & Adhesion (Print Edition) 664
▼ • Cell Adhesion and Migration (USA ISSN 1933-6918) 828
• ➤ Cell & Chromosome (GBR ISSN 1475-9268) 828
➤ Cell and Chromosome Research Journal (IND ISSN 0254-2935) 828
• Cell and Molecular Responses to Stress (NLD ISSN 1568-1254) 727
• ➤ Cell and Tissue Banking (NLD ISSN 1389-9333) 828
• Cell and Tissue Biology (RUS ISSN 1990-519X) 828
• ➤ Cell and Tissue Research (DEU ISSN 0302-766X) 829
• ➤ Cell Biochemistry and Biophysics (USA ISSN 1085-9195) 829
• ➤ Cell Biochemistry & Function (GBR ISSN 0263-6484) 728
Cell Biology *see* Saibo Seibutsu 836
• ➤ Cell Biology and Toxicology (NLD ISSN 0742-2091) 3495
Cell Biology Education *see* C B E Life Sciences Education 828
Cell Biology Education Life Sciences Education *see* C B E Life Sciences Education 828
• ➤ Cell Biology International (GBR ISSN 1065-6995) 829
• ➤ Cell Calcium (GBR ISSN 0143-4160) 829
• Cell Communication & Adhesion (Online Edition) (USA ISSN 1543-5180) 664
• ➤ Cell Communication & Adhesion (Print Edition) (GBR ISSN 1541-9061) 664
• ➤ Cell Communication and Signaling (GBR ISSN 1478-811X) 665
• ➤ Cell Cycle (USA ISSN 1538-4101) 829
• ➤ Cell Death & Differentiation (GBR ISSN 1350-9047) 829
▼ • ➤ Cell Death & Disease (GBR ISSN 2041-4889) 829
• Cell Division (GBR ISSN 1747-1028) 829
▼ • ➤ Cell Host & Microbe (USA ISSN 1931-3128) 883
Cell Medicine (USA ISSN 1558-481X) 829
• ➤ Cell Metabolism (USA ISSN 1550-4131) 829
• ➤ Cell Motility and the Cytoskeleton (USA ISSN 0886-1544) 829
• ➤ Cell Proliferation (GBR ISSN 0960-7722) 830
• ➤ Cell Research/Xibao Yanjiu (GBR ISSN 1001-0602) 665
• Cell Signalling Biology (GBR ISSN 1749-7787) 665
▼ • ➤ Cell Stem Cell (USA ISSN 1934-5909) 665
• ➤ Cell Stress & Chaperones (NLD ISSN 1355-8145) 5592
• ➤ Cell Structure and Function (JPN ISSN 0386-7196) 830
Cell Technology *see* Saibo Kogaku 770
Cell Technology, Special Issue *see* Saibo Kogaku, Bessatsu 770
Cell Therapy News *see* Fuel Cell Technology News 7014
• ➤ Cell Transplantation (USA ISSN 0963-6897) 830
Cellar Notes (USA) 601
Celler Beitraege zur Landes- und Kulturgeschichte (DEU ISSN 1616-2986) 4209
Celler Blickpunkt (DEU) 3845
Celler Chronik (DEU ISSN 0177-719X) 4209
Celler Scene (DEU) 3845
Cellesche Zeitung (DEU) 3845
Cellexpo Awards Magazine (ZAF) 2314
▼ Cellfhelp (ZAF ISSN 1994-3741) 2366
Cellier (CAN ISSN 1911-2238) 601
• ➤ Cells, Tissues, Organs (CHE ISSN 1422-6405) 5593
• Cellscience Reviews (USA ISSN 1742-8130) 665
▼ • Cellular and Molecular Bioengineering (USA ISSN 1865-5025) 748
• ➤ Cellular and Molecular Biology (FRA ISSN 0145-5680) 665
• ➤ Cellular & Molecular Biology Letters (POL ISSN 1425-8153) 665
➤ Cellular & Molecular Immunology (CHN ISSN 1672-7681) 5755
• ➤ Cellular and Molecular Life Sciences (CHE ISSN 1420-682X) 665
• ➤ Cellular & Molecular Neurobiology (USA ISSN 0272-4340) 6130
• ➤ Cellular Immunology (USA ISSN 0008-8749) 5755
• Cellular Integration (USA ISSN 1086-7716) 2366
Cellular Marketing *see* Cellular Integration 2366
• ➤ Cellular Microbiology (GBR ISSN 1462-5814) 830
• ➤ Cellular Microbiology Online (GBR ISSN 1462-5822) 830
• ➤ Cellular Oncology (NLD ISSN 1570-5870) 830
Cellular Origin and Life in Extreme Habitats *see* Cellular Origin, Life in Extreme Habitats and Astrobiology 783
Cellular Origin, Life in Extreme Habitats and Astrobiologuy (NLD ISSN 1871-661X) 783
• ➤ Cellular Physiology and Biochemistry (CHE ISSN 1015-8987) 830

Title

Title

10104 CENTRAL INSTITUTE OF INDIAN LANGUAGES DOCTORAL DISSERTATION ULRICH'S PERIODICALS

Central Institute of Indian Languages Doctoral Dissertation Series *see* C I I L Doctoral Dissertation Series **5102**
Central Institute of Indian Languages Documentation Series *see* C I I L Documentation Series **5102**
Central Institute of Indian Languages Folklore Series *see* C I I L Folklore Series **3615**
Central Institute of Indian Languages Grammar Series *see* C I I L Grammar Series **5102**
Central Institute of Indian Languages Intensive Course Series *see* C I I L Intensive Course Series **5102**
Central Institute of Indian Languages Occasional Bulletin Series *see* C I I L Occasional Bulletin Series **5102**
Central Institute of Indian Languages Occasional Monograph Series *see* C I I L Occasional Monograph Series **5102**
Central Institute of Indian Languages Phonetic Reader Series *see* C I I L Phonetic Reader Series **5102**
Central Institute of Indian Languages Pictorial Glossary Series *see* C I I L Pictorial Glossary Series **5102**
Central Institute of Indian Languages Reading Series *see* C I I L Reading Series **5102**
Central Institute of Indian Languages Second Language Textbook Series *see* C I I L Second Language Textbook Series **5102**
Central Institute of Indian Languages Sociolinguistics Series *see* C I I L Sociolinguistics Series **5102**
Central Institute of Plastics Engineering & Technology Bulletin *see* C I P E T Bulletin **7091**
Central Intelligence Agency. Monographs (USA) **7225**
Central Intelligence Agency. Monographs. All Communist Countries Reports (USA) **7225**
Central Intelligence Agency. Monographs. All Countries Reports (USA) **7225**
Central Intelligence Agency. Monographs. All International Countries Reports (USA) **7226**
Central Intelligence Agency. Monographs. China Reports (USA) **7226**
Central Intelligence Agency. Monographs. Commonwealth of Independent States Report (USA) **7226**
Central Intelligence Agency. Monographs. Maps Only (USA) **7226**
▼ Central Iowa Boomer (USA) **3971**
Central Japan Association of Orthopaedic and Traumatic Surgery. Abstracts *see* Chubu Nippon Seikei Geka Saigai Geka Gakkai Shoroku **5742**
Central Japan Journal of Orthopaedic Surgery & Traumatology *see* Chubu Nippon Seikei Geka Saigai Geka Gakkai Zasshi **6057**
Central Jersey Family *see* New Jersey Family (Mountainside) **2162**
Central Kentucky Researcher (USA ISSN 0095-1439) **3761**
Central L H I N Annual Report (Local Health Integration Network) (CAN ISSN 1911-3374) **7512**
Central Leader (NZL ISSN 1170-0130) **3916**
Central Library European Commission. Activity Report (BEL ISSN 1681-0678) **5001**
Central London Salary Survey (GBR) **1670**
Central Luzon State University Scientific Journal *see* C L S U Scientific Journal **99**
Central Marine Fisheries Research Institute. Annual Report (IND ISSN 0972-2378) **3589**
Central Marine Fisheries Research Institute Bulletin *see* C M F R I Bulletin **3588**
Central Marine Fisheries Research Institute Newsletter *see* C M F R I Newsletter **3588**
Central Marine Fisheries Research Institute Special Publication *see* C M F R I Special Publication **3588**
Central Marine Fisheries Research Institute. Special Publication (IND) **3589**
Central Marine Fisheries Research Institute. Technical and Extension Series (IND ISSN 0254-380X) **938**
The Central Mediterranean Naturalist (MLT ISSN 1560-8417) **842**
Central Michigan Life (USA ISSN 0008-9451) **2277**
Central Mindanao University Journal of Science *see* C M U Journal of Science **99**
Central Mine Planning & Design Institute. Current Awareness Service (IND) **6485**
Central Mine Planning & Design Institute. Manuals (IND) **6459**
Central Mining Research Institute Annual Report *see* C M R I Annual Report **6459**
Central Mining Research Institute Newsletter *see* C M R I Newsletter **6459**
Central Mississippi Planning and Development District. Annual Report (USA) **4406**
Central Nervous System Agents *see* Central Nervous System Agents in Medicinal Chemistry **6130**
• Central Nervous System Agents in Medicinal Chemistry (NLD ISSN 1871-5249) **6130**
Central Nervous System Disorders Today *see* C N S Disorders Today **6129**
Central Nervous System Drug News *see* C N S Drug News **6827**
Central Nervous System Drugs *see* C N S Drugs **6827**
Central Nervous System Neurological Disorders *see* C N S & Neurological Disorders **6129**
Central Nervous System News *see* C N S News **6129**
• Central New York Business Journal (USA ISSN 1050-3005) **1446**
• Central Northern Adelaide Health Service. Annual Report (AUS ISSN 1833-1424) **7512**
Central Nova Business News (CAN) **1398**
• Central Oregon Labor Trends (USA) **1670**
• Central Oregon Rancher (USA) **210**
Central PA (USA ISSN 1096-701X) **2378**
Central Park Conservancy (USA) **2606**
• Central Penn Business Journal (USA ISSN 1058-3599) **1081**
Central Penn Parent (USA) **2147**
Central Pennsylvania *see* Central PA **2378**
Central Plains Medical Journal *see* Zhongyuan Yikan **5739**
Central Plantation Crops Research Institute. Annual Report (IND ISSN 0374-7115) **100**
Central Plantation Crops Research Institute. Newsletter (IND) **100**
Central Plantation Crops Research Institute. Research Highlights (IND) **100**
Central Queensland News (AUS) **3793**
Central Railway Chronicle (USA ISSN 0008-9532) **8616**
• Central Research Institute for Construction Technology. Newsletter (JPN) **3262**
Central Research Institute for Jute and Allied Fibres. Annual Report (IND ISSN 0973-0044) **8449**
Central Research Institute of Electric Power Industry. Abiko Research Laboratory. Report (English Edition) (JPN) **3155**
Central Research Institute of Electric Power Industry. All Laboratories. Report (English Edition) (JPN) **3155**
Central Research Institute of Electric Power Industry. Komae Research Laboratory. Report (English Edition) (JPN) **3155**
Central Research Institute of Electric Power Industry. News *see* Denryoku Chuo Kenkyujo Nyusu **3299**
Central Research Institute of Electric Power Industry. Quarterly Abstracts (JPN ISSN 0912-1307) **3297**
Central Research Institute of Electric Power Industry Report. Electric Engineering Laboratory *see* C R I E P I Report. Electric Engineering Laboratory **3297**
Central Research Institute of Electric Power Industry Report. Energy & Environment Laboratory *see* C R I E P I Report. Energy & Environment Laboratory **3155**
• Central Research Institute of Electric Power Industry. Socio-Economic Research Center. Technical Reports (English Edition) (JPN) **8093**
Central Review *see* Chuo Koron **3900**
Central Riverina Landcare Network Newsletter (AUS ISSN 1833-6728) **3409**
Central Road Research Institute, New Delhi. Road Research Paper (IND ISSN 0069-1690) **8630**
Central Road Research Institute Road Abstracts *see* C R R I Road Abstracts **3229**
Central Salt and Marine Chemicals Research Institute Newsletter *see* C S M C R I Newsletter **2801**
Central Scientific - Ethical Committee of Denmark. Report *see* Centrale Videnskabsetiske Komite. Aarsberetning **6910**
Central Scotland Chamber of Commerce Bulletin (GBR) **1398**
Central Scotland Salary Survey (GBR) **1670**
Central Sericultural Research and Training Institute. Annual Report (IND ISSN 0304-6818) **100**
Central South Forestry University. Journal *see* Zhongnan Linxueyuan Xuebao **3708**
Central South Pharmacy *see* Zhongnan Yaoxue **6888**
Central South University. Journal (Medical Sciences) *see* Zhongnan Daxue Xuebao (Yixue Ban) **5738**
Central South University. Journal (Science and Technology) *see* Zhongnan Daxue Xuebao (Ziran Kexue Ban) **6484**
Central South University. Journal (Social Science) *see* Zhongnan Daxue Xuebao (Shehui Kexue Ban) **8019**
Central-South University of Finance and Economics. Journal *see* Zhongnan Caijing Daxue Xuebao **1551**
• ➤ Central South University of Technology. Journal (CHN ISSN 1005-9784) **6460**
Central Southern Farmer (GBR) **100**
• Central States Anthropology Society. Bulletin (USA) **332**
➤ Central States Archaeological Journal (USA ISSN 0008-9559) **386**
➤ Central States Conference on the Teaching of Foreign Languages. Education Series (USA) **5105**
Central Statistical Office. Concise Statistical Year Book of Poland (POL ISSN 0554-436X) **8362**
Central Statistical Office Statistical Bulletins *see* C.S.O. Statistical Bulletins **8359**
Central Texas Pony Express Magazine (USA ISSN 1934-7642) **8289**
Central Tobacco Research Institute and its Regional Research Stations. Annual Report (IND) **8485**
Central United States Earthquake Consortium Journal *see* C U S E C Journal **2778**
Central University for Nationalities. Journal (Natural Sciences Edition) *see* Zhongyang Minzu Daxue Xuebao (Ziran Kexue Ban) **7935**
Central University for Nationalities. Journal (Philosophy and Social Sciences Edition) *see* Zhongyang Minzu Daxue Xuebao (Zhexue Shehui Kexue Ban) **8019**
Central University of Finance & Economics. Journal *see* Zhongyang Caizheng Jinrong Xueyuan Xuebao **1198**
Central Valley Homes & Lifestyles Magazine (USA ISSN 1544-337X) **5067**
Central Virginia Heritage (USA ISSN 1043-4895) **3761**
Central Wisconsin Resorter (USA) **8692**
Centrala Kongresu Ukraintsiv Kanadi. Bilten' (CAN ISSN 1196-3522) **3526**
➤ Centralblatt fuer das Gesamte Forstwesen (AUT ISSN 0008-9583) **3686**
Centrale Bank van Aruba. Quarterly Bulletin (ANT ISSN 0920-9905) **1326**
Centrale de l'Enseignement du Quebec. Nouvelles (CAN ISSN 0710-5568) **2835**
• Det Centrale Handicapraad. Aarsberetning (DNK ISSN 1395-4660) **8031**
Centrale Landsdienaren Organisatie Bulletin *see* C L O Bulletin **4591**
• Centrale Videnskabsetiske Komite. Aarsberetning/Central Scientific - Ethical Committee of Denmark. Report (DNK ISSN 1395-5470) **6910**
Centralfoerbundet foer Alkohol- och Narkotikaupplysning. Rapport (SWE ISSN 1400-5360) **2692**
Centralian Advocate (AUS ISSN 1447-1647) **3793**
Centraliens (FRA ISSN 1156-7104) **8417**
• Centralight (USA) **2277**
Centralite (PHL) **2277**
• Centralities (USA ISSN 1529-4684) **3761**
Centralne Laboratorium Technologii Przetworstwa i Przechowalnictwa Zboz w Warszawie. Biuletyn *see* Przeglad Zbozowo - Mlynarski **275**
• Centralny Katalog Zagranicznych Wydawnictw Ciaglych w Bibliotekach Polskich (POL ISSN 0239-8931) **622**
Centralorganisationen Soefart *see* C O Soefart **4591**
Centralstation (DEU) **3845**
Centre Africain de Formation et de Recherche Administratives pour le Developpement Web News Letter *see* C A F R A D Web News Letter **7425**
Centre Aixois de Recherches Anglaises. Actes du Colloque (FRA ISSN 0240-8864) **5271**
Centre Belge d'Histoire Rurale. Publications/Belgisch Centrum voor Landelijke Geschiedenis. Publikaties (BEL ISSN 0076-1192) **4209**
Centre Canadien de Recherches Policieres. Rapport Technique (CAN ISSN 1912-4252) **2646**
➤ Centre County Heritage (USA ISSN 0577-1099) **4288**
Centre Court (NLD ISSN 1574-2148) **8225**
➤ Centre Culturel Calouste Gulbenkian. Actes des Colloques (FRA) **4446**
Centre Culturel Francais de Yaounde. Programme Saison (CMR) **481**
Centre Culturel Francophone de Vancouver. Bulletin (CAN ISSN 1912-0478) **5105**
Centre d'Action Benevole de Quebec. Rapport Annuel (CAN ISSN 1910-6475) **8031**
Centre de Cooperation pour les Recherches Scientifiques Relatives au Tabac *see* C O R E S T A **8489**
Centre de Coservation et d'Etude des Collections. Cahiers Scientifiques (FRA ISSN 1627-3516) **7844**
Centre de Documentation de Politique de la Science. Nouvelles Acquisitions *see* Dokumentationsstelle fuer Wissenschaftspolitik. Neuanschaffungen **7937**
Centre de Documentation et d'Etudes Sociales. La Lettre - Toulouse *see* Anarchosyndicalisme **7106**
Centre de Documentation sur l'Education des Adultes et la Condition Feminine. Rapport Annuel (CAN ISSN 1910-975X) **8895**
† Centre de Genealogie et d'Histoire des Iles d'Amerique. Cahiers (FRA ISSN 0751-3860) **8940**
Centre de Genealogie Protestante. Cahiers (FRA ISSN 0753-4639) **7750**
Centre de la Famille Valcartier. Rapport Annuel (CAN ISSN 1912-1490) **8031**
Centre de la Famille Valcartier. Rapport d'Activites *see* Centre de la Famille Valcartier. Rapport Annuel **8031**
Centre de l'Astronomie et des Sciences Spatiales. Observations Solaires (ROM) **573**
Centre de Liaison d'Etude d'Information et de Recherche sur les Problemes des Personnes Agees Documents. Cahier *see* C L E I R P P A. Documents. Cahier **4042**
Centre de Musique Baroque de Versailles. Anthologies (FRA ISSN 1762-7907) **6555**
Centre de Musique Baroque de Versailles. Publications A (FRA ISSN 1285-2880) **6555**
Centre de Musique Baroque de Versailles. Publications B (FRA ISSN 1285-5979) **6555**
Centre de Prevision de l'Expansion. Tableau de Bord (FRA ISSN 1156-8380) **1446**
Centre de Readaptation Constance-Lethbridge. Rapport Annuel d'Activites/Constance-Lethbridge Rehabilitation Centre. Annual Activity Report (CAN ISSN 1718-0228) **7512**
Centre de Recherche d'Histoire et Civilisation de Byzance. Travaux et Memoires (FRA ISSN 0577-1471) **4209**
Centre de Recherche en Civilisation Canadienne-Francaise *see* C R C C F **8091**
▼ • Centre de Recherche et d'Etudes Catalanes. Revue (FRA ISSN 1961-9340) **8093**
Centre de Recherche et d'Information sur la Litterature pour la Jeunesse (FRA ISSN 0989-7828) **5271**
Centre de Recherche et d'Intervention sur la Reussite Scolaire. Bulletin (CAN ISSN 1204-2943) **3054**
Centre de Recherche et d'Intervention sur la Reussite Scolaire. Etudes et Recherches (CAN ISSN 1491-2252) **2835**
Centre de Recherche sur l'Europe et le Monde Contemporain. Cahiers *see* C R E M O C. Cahiers **4208**
Centre de Recherches Archeologiques. Monographie (Centre de Recherches Archeologiques) (FRA ISSN 1147-5358) **386**
Centre de Recherches du Service de Sante des Armees. Travaux Scientifiques *see* Travaux Scientifiques des Chercheurs du Service de Sante des Armees **4112**
† Centre de Recherches et d'Etudes sur Paris et l'Ile-de-France. Cahiers (FRA ISSN 0760-6079) **8940**
Centre de Recherches Interdisciplinaires pour le Developpement de l'Education Cahiers *see* C R I D E Cahiers **2833**
Centre de Recherches Mathematiques Monograph Series *see* C R M Monograph Series **5476**
Centre de Recherches pour le Developpement International. Rapport Annuel *see* International Development Research Centre. Annual Report **1126**
Centre de Recherches Semiologiques. Travaux (CHE ISSN 1013-8765) **6910**
Centre de Sante et de Services Sociaux de Cote-des-Neiges, Metro et Parc-Extension. Rapport Annuel d'Activites (CAN ISSN 1719-3915) **7512**
Centre de Sante et de Services Sociaux de la Petite Patrie et Villeray. Rapport Annuel d'Activites (CAN ISSN 1719-5780) **7512**
Centre de Sante et de Services Sociaux de la Pointe-de-l'Isle. Rapport Annuel d'Activites *see* Centre de Sante et de Services Sociaux de la Pointe-de-l'Isle. Rapport Annuel de Gestion **7512**
Centre de Sante et de Services Sociaux de la Pointe-de-l'Isle. Rapport Annuel de Gestion (CAN ISSN 1912-4066) **7512**
Centre de Sante et de Services Sociaux de Lac-Saint-Jean-Est. Rapport Annuel de Gestion (CAN ISSN 1912-4120) **7512**
Centre de Sante et de Services Sociaux de l'Ouest-de-l'Ile. Annual Report (CAN ISSN 1719-6434) **7512**
Centre de Sante et de Services Sociaux de l'Ouest-de-l'Ile. Rapport Annuel *see* Centre de Sante et de Services Sociaux de l'Ouest-de-l'Ile. Annual Report **7512**
Centre d'Enseignement Superieur de Brazzaville. Annales (COG) **2971**
Centre des Recherches Litteraires et Historiques Cahiers Annuels *see* C R L H. Cahiers Annuels **331**
Centre d'Estudes Financieres. Newsletter (BEL ISSN 0772-7798) **1326**
Centre d'Estudis de la Natura del Barcelones-Nord. Butlleti (ESP ISSN 0213-3598) **7844**
Centre d'Etude et de Developpement des Energies Renouvelables (FRA ISSN 1951-1418) **3126**
Centre d'Etude et de Recherche de Droit International et de Relations Internationales/Centre for Studies and Research in International Law and International Relations (NLD ISSN 1875-1091) **4920**
➤ Centre d'Etudes de l'Asie de l'Est. Cahiers (CAN ISSN 0839-4555) **546**
Centre d'Etudes de Recherche Economique et Social Revue Economique et Sociale *see* C E D R E S. Revue Economique et Sociale **195**
Centre d'Etudes et de Recherches Amazigh. Publications (FRA ISSN 0297-9977) **5271**
† Centre d'Etudes et de Recherches Economiques et Sociales de Picardie. Cahiers (FRA ISSN 1774-0444) **8940**
Centre d'Etudes et de Recherches Litteraires et Scientifiques de Mende. Bulletin (FRA ISSN 0335-038X) **4209**
Centre d'Etudes Ethnologiques Bandundu. Publications (COD) **332**
Centre d'Etudes Ethnologiques. Publications. Serie 2: Memoires et Monographies (COD) **332**
Centre d'Etudes Ethnologiques. Publications. Serie 3: Travaux Linguistiques (COD) **5105**
• Centre d'Etudes Medievales d'Auxerre. Bulletin (FRA ISSN 1623-5770) **4209**
Centre d'Etudes Politiques, Economiques et Sociales. Documents (BEL ISSN 0771-0097) **7226**
Centre d'Etudes Prospectives et d'Informations Internationales Lettre *see* C E P I I Lettre **1445**
Centre d'Etudes Superieures de la Renaissance de Tours *see* Le Savoir de Mantice **4261**
† Centre d'Etudes Techniques Maritime et Fluviales. Revue Technique (FRA ISSN 1624-7396) **8940**

Link to your serials resources and content with ulrichsweb.com

DIRECTORY 2010 CENTRE NATIONALE DE LA RECHERCHE SCIENTIFIQUE ETHNOLOGIE 10105

Centre d'Histoire et d'Art de la Thudinie. Publications (BEL) **4209**
Centre d'Informacio i Documentacio Internacionals a Barcelona *see* C I D O B **7229**
Centre d'Informacio i Documentacio Internacionals a Barcelona'Afers Internationals *see* C I D O B d'Afers Internationals **7224**
Centre d'Information des Utilisateurs de Progiciels. Catalogue (FRA ISSN 0985-0791) **1415**
Centre d'Information et de Documentation Scientifique et Technique. Archives du Centre National de Recherches Oceanographiques (MDG) **2801**
Centre d'Information et de Documentation Scientifique et Technique. Recherches pour le Developpement. Serie Sciences de l'Homme et de la Societe (MDG) **4446**
Centre d'Information et de Documentation Scientifique et Technique. Recherches pour le Developpement. Serie Sciences Technologiques (MDG) **8417**
Centre d'Information et de Ressources sur les Drogues et les Dependances 37 *see* C I R D D 37 **2692**
Centre Economique Magazine (FRA) **1398**
Centre Etudes Litteratures Arts Afrique Nord *see* C E L A A N **5268**
Centre Europeen de Geodynamique et de Seismologie. Cahiers (LUX ISSN 1026-1907) **2703**
• Centre Europeen de Recherche en Economie Financiere et Gestion des Entreprises. Cahier de Recherche (FRA ISSN 1960-2782) **1326**
Centre Europeen de Recherche et d'Enseignement des Geosciences de l' Environnement Centre de Recherche en Gestion *see* C E R E G E. Centre de Recherche en Gestion **1731**
• Centre Europeen d'Etudes Bourguignonnes (XIVe-XVIe S.). Publications (BEL ISSN 1016-4286) **4210**
Centre for Aboriginal Economic Policy Research News *see* C A E P R News **1077**
Centre for Addiction and Mental Health. Annual Report to the Community (CAN ISSN 1711-9677) **2692**
Centre for Advanced Studies of African Society. Notes and Records (ZAF ISSN 1560-3393) **5105**
Centre for Advanced Studies of African Society. Occasional Paper (ZAF ISSN 1560-3385) **5105**
Centre for Agricultural Strategy Series (GBR) **100**
• Centre for Analytical Finance. Working Papers Series (DNK ISSN 1398-6163) **1326**
Centre for Applied Economic Research Working Paper *see* C A E R Working Paper **1077**
† • Centre for Applied Finance. Working Paper Series (AUS ISSN 1832-2840) **8940**
• Centre for Asia-Pacific Studies News (GBR) **546**
➤ Centre for Business Law. Transactions (ZAF) **4860**
Centre for Children & Families in the Justice System. A Year in Review *see* Centre for Children & Families in the Justice System. Annual Report **4641**
Centre for Children & Families in the Justice System. Annual Report *see* Centre for Children & Families in the Justice System. Annual Report **4641**
Centre for Children & Families in the Justice System. Annual Report (CAN ISSN 1912-7960) **4641**
Centre for Computing in Humanities Working Papers *see* C H Working Papers **4485**
Centre for Conflict Resolution. Annual Report (ZAF) **8093**
Centre for Constitutional Analysis Centre for Constitutional Analysis *see* H S R C Centre for Constitutional Analysis **4684**
Centre for Development and Enterprise Focus *see* C D E Focus **1592**
Centre for Development and Enterprise In Depth (ZAF ISSN 1815-2937) **1537**
Centre for Development and Population Activities Network *see* C E D P A Network **8854**
Centre for Discrete Mathematics and Theoretical Computer Science Research Report Series *see* C D M T C S Research Report Series **5476**
• Centre for Economic Policy Research. Bulletin (GBR ISSN 0265-7996) **1537**
• Centre for Economic Policy Research. Discussion Papers (GBR ISSN 0265-8003) **1537**
• Centre for Economic Policy Research. Policy Papers (GBR) **1537**
• ➤ Centre for Education in the Built Environment. Transactions (GBR ISSN 1745-0322) **437**
Centre for Energy, Petroleum and Mineral Law and Policy Conference Proceedings *see* C E P M L P Conference Proceedings **3408**
Centre for Energy, Petroleum and Mineral Law and Policy Internet Journal *see* C E P M L P Internet Journal **2703**
Centre for Entomological Studies. Memoirs (TUR ISSN 1015-8227) **842**
• Centre for Entomological Studies. Miscellaneous Papers (TUR ISSN 1015-8235) **842**
Centre for Environmental History Policy Short Report *see* C E H P Short Report **3407**
Centre for Equality Research in Business. Research Paper (GBR ISSN 1363-9536) **2971**
• Centre for European Policy Studies. Financial Markets Unit. Research Report (BEL) **1326**
• Centre for European Policy Studies. Macroeconomic Policy Group. Annual Report. Adjusting to Leaner Times (BEL) **1081**
Centre for European Policy Studies. Newsletter (BEL) **7226**
Centre for European Policy Studies Papers *see* C E P S Papers **7224**
Centre for European Policy Studies Research Reports *see* C E P S Research Reports **1077**
Centre for European Policy Studies. Task Force Reports (BEL) **1616**
Centre for European Policy Studies Working Documents *see* C E P S Working Documents **7224**
Centre for European Studies. Working Papers *see* University of Durham. Centre for European Studies. Working Papers **8012**
Centre for Fisheries Economics. Report *see* Norges Handelhoegskole. Senter for Fiskerioekonomi. Rapport **3603**
Centre for Health Economics and Policy Analysis in Review *see* C H E P A in Review **7510**
• Centre for Housing Research Aotearoa New Zealand. Research Bulletin (NZL ISSN 1177-1593) **4406**
Centre for Housing Research. Discussion Paper (GBR ISSN 0952-2603) **4406**
Centre for Independent Studies. Classics *see* C I S Classics **7111**
Centre for Independent Studies Classics *see* C I S Classics **7111**
Centre for Independent Studies. Occasional Papers (AUS ISSN 0155-7386) **1537**
Centre for Independent Studies Policy Monographs *see* C I S Policy Monographs **7111**
Centre for Indigenous Governance and Development Briefing Notes *see* C I G A D Briefing Notes **8091**
Centre for Indigenous Governance and Development Working Paper Series *see* C I G A D Working Paper Series **8091**
Centre for Information Studies Research Reports *see* C I S Research Reports **4999**
Centre for Interdisciplinary Environmental and Social Research Rapport *see* C I E N S Rapport **3484**
Centre for International and Security Studies Monographs *see* C I S S Monographs **7224**
Centre for International and Security Studies Working Papers *see* C I S S Working Papers **7224**
Centre for Irish-German Studies. Yearbook *see* Zentrum fuer Deutsch-Irische Studien. Jahrbuch **5199**
The Centre for Islamic Studies and The Centre for the Study of Interreligious Relations. Newsletter (GBR) **7709**
Centre for Justice and Crime Prevention Issue Paper *see* C J C P Issue Paper **4885**
Centre for Justice and Crime Prevention. Research Bulletin (ZAF ISSN 1998-8001) **2646**
† Centre for Labour Market and Social Research. Working Papers (DNK ISSN 0908-8962) **8940**
• Centre for Labour Market Research. Discussion Paper Series (AUS ISSN 1329-2676) **1670**
• Centre for Law and Genetics. Occasional Paper (AUS ISSN 1445-2766) **4641**
• Centre for Legal Education. Newsletter (AUS ISSN 1038-3964) **2971**
Centre for Longitudinal Studies Briefings *see* C L S Briefings **8091**
Centre for Medicines Research, Research & Development International (Year) Pharmaceutical R & D Factbook *see* C M R International (Year) Pharmaceutical R & D Factbook **6827**
➤ Centre for Medicines Research Workshop (NLD) **6828**
Centre for Monetary and Financial Economics. Discussion Papers (GBR ISSN 1472-362X) **1326**
Centre for Policy on Ageing. Reports (GBR ISSN 1369-1872) **4042**
Centre for Public Service Management. Research Report (GBR) **7429**
• Centre for Research in Economic Development and International Trade. Research Paper (GBR ISSN 1366-1531) **1081**
Centre for Research in Algebra and Number Theory (CAN) **5477**
Centre for Research in Environmental Appraisal and Management Report *see* C R E A M Report **3408**
Centre for Research in Social Policy Annual Report *see* C R S P Annual Report **8091**
Centre for Research in Social Policy. Working Papers Series (GBR ISSN 1350-9101) **8093**
Centre for Research on European Urban Environments. Occasional Papers (GBR) **4406**
• Centre for Research on Introduced Marine Pests. Technical Report (Online) (AUS) **2801**
Centre for Research on Organisations, Management and Technical Change Working Paper Series *see* C R O M T E C Working Paper Series **1731**
† Centre for Research on the Cultural and Biological Diversity of Andean Rainforests. Technical Report (DNK ISSN 1396-5581) **8940**
Centre for Social and Economic Research on the Global Environment. Working Paper. Global Environment Change (GBR ISSN 0967-8875) **3409**
Centre for Social and Economic Research on the Global Environment. Working Paper. Policy Analysis (GBR ISSN 1466-0261) **1081**
Centre for Social and Economic Research on the Global Environment. Working Paper. Waste Management (GBR ISSN 1466-0253) **3504**
Centre for Social Anthropology and Computing. Monographs (GBR ISSN 1461-7706) **332**
• Centre for Social Science Research Working Papers (AUS ISSN 1833-6493) **7953**
Centre for South-East Asian Studies. Bibliography and Literature Series (GBR ISSN 0269-1760) **546**
Centre for South-East Asian Studies. Occasional Papers (GBR ISSN 0269-1779) **4181**
† Centre for South Pacific Studies. Newsletter (AUS ISSN 1030-245X) **8940**
Centre for Sports Science and History. Serial Holdings (GBR) **2931**
Centre for Studies and Research in International Law and International Relations *see* Centre d'Etude et de Recherche de Droit International et de Relations Internationales **4920**
• Centre for Studies in Australian Music. Review (AUS ISSN 1443-9018) **6555**
Centre for Studies in Religion and Society *see* Centre for Studies in Religion & Society **7630**
Centre for Studies in Religion & Society (CAN ISSN 1911-5474) **7630**
Centre for Study and Research *see* C F S R **8091**
Centre for Telematics and Information Technology Workshop Proceedings Series *see* C T I T Workshop Proceedings Series **2409**
Centre for the Advancement of Interprofessional Education Bulletin *see* C A I P E Bulletin **8029**
Centre for the Advancement of Science and Mathematics Education Newsletter *see* C A S M E Newsletter **7842**
Centre for the Analysis and Dissemination of Demonstrated Energy Technologies Analysis Series *see* C A D D E T Analysis Series **8938**
Centre for the Analysis of Nursing & Professional Practice. Research Commentaries Series (GBR) **5955**
• Centre for the Study of African Economies. Working Paper Series (GBR) **1081**
Centre for the Study of Contemporary Islam Islamic Issues Briefing Paper Series *see* C S C I Islamic Issues Briefing Paper Series **7709**
• Centre for the Study of Globalisation and Regionalisation. Working Paper Series (GBR) **1081**
Centre for the Study of Islam and Christian Muslim Relations. Newsletter *see* The Centre for Islamic Studies and The Centre for the Study of Interreligious Relations. Newsletter **7709**
Centre for the Study of Regulated Industries Occasional Papers *see* C R I Occasional Papers **7425**
Centre for the Study of Regulated Industries Proceedings Series *see* C R I Proceedings Series **7425**
Centre for the Study of Regulated Industries Regulatory Briefs *see* C R I Regulatory Briefs **4635**
Centre for Transport Studies Working Papers *see* C T S Working Papers **3261**
Centre for Transport Studies. Working Papers *see* C T S Working Papers **3261**
Centre for Urban and Community Studies. Bibliographic Series (CAN ISSN 0316-4691) **4406**
Centre for Urban and Community Studies. Major Report Series (CAN ISSN 0319-4620) **4406**
Centre for Urban and Community Studies. Research Papers (CAN ISSN 0316-0068) **4406**
Centre for Urban and Regional Development Studies. Discussion Paper (GBR ISSN 1462-5164) **4406**
Centre for Urban and Regional Research. Working Paper (GBR) **4406**
Centre for Urban Development and Environmental Management Working Paper Series *see* C U D E M Working Paper Series **4406**
Centre for Urban Studies Bulletin *see* C U S Bulletin **4406**
Centre Francais de Droit Compare (FRA ISSN 1779-7713) **4641**
Centre Genealogique de Loire-Atlantique. Revue (FRA) **3761**
Centre Genealogique de l'Ouest. Revue Trimestrielle *see* Centre Genealogique de Loire-Atlantique. Revue **3761**
Centre Genevois d'Anthropologie. Bulletin (CHE ISSN 1015-468X) **332**
Centre Gustave Glotz. Cahiers (FRA ISSN 1016-9008) **4134**
• Centre I N F F O. Fiches Pratiques (FRA ISSN 1951-431X) **2939**
Centre I N F F O. Guides Techniques (FRA ISSN 0242-259X) **1858**
Centre Interdisciplinaire d'Etude et de Recherche sur l'Expression Contemporaine. Travaux (FRA ISSN 0335-8402) **4446**
Centre International de Documentation Occitane. Bibliotheque. Catalogue (FRA) **5105**
Centre International de Documentation Occitane. Serie Bibliographique (FRA ISSN 0756-3442) **622**
Centre International de Documentation Occitane. Serie Etudes (FRA ISSN 0398-3765) **4210**
Centre International de Liaison des Ecoles de Cinema et de Television News *see* C I L E C T News **2377**
• Centre International de Myriapodologie. Bulletin (FRA ISSN 1161-2398) **665**
Centre International de Recherches sur l'Anarchisme Bulletin *see* C I R A Bulletin **7111**
Centre International de Rencontres Mathematiques. Publications (FRA ISSN 1561-2082) **7557**
▼ • Centre International de Ressources et d'Innovation pour le Developpement Durable. Lettre (FRA ISSN 1959-5344) **1592**
Centre International d'Etude des Textiles Anciens. Bulletin (FRA ISSN 1016-8982) **8449**
Centre International d'Etudes Platoniciennes et Aristoteliciennes. Serie Recherches (GRC ISSN 1015-2563) **6910**
Centre International du Film pour l'Enfance et la Jeunesse Info *see* C I F E J Info **6491**
Centre International du Film pour l'Enfance et la Jeunesse Info *see* C I F E J Info **6491**
Centre International pour la Formation et les Echanges Geologiques. Publication Occasionnelle/International Center for Training and Exchanges in the Geosciences. Occasional Publication (FRA ISSN 0769-0541) **2728**
Centre Interprofessionnel Technique d'Etudes de la Pollution Atmospherique. Etudes Documentaires (FRA ISSN 0152-5778) **3484**
Centre Interuniversitaire de Recherche sur la Renaissance Italienne (FRA ISSN 0768-1305) **5271**
Centre Interuniversitaire d'Histoire Contemporaine. Cahiers/Interuniversitair Centrum voor Hedendaagse Geschiedenis. Mededelingen (BEL ISSN 0577-179X) **4210**
Centre Jean Berard. Cahiers (ITA ISSN 1122-3278) **386**
Centre Le Jeannois. Rapport Annuel *see* Centre de Sante et de Services Sociaux de Lac-Saint-Jean-Est. Rapport Annuel de Gestion **7512**
Centre Local de Services Communautaires Cote-des-Neiges. Rapport annuel d'Activites *see* Centre de Sante et de Services Sociaux de Cote-des-Neiges, Metro et Parc-Extension. Rapport Annuel d'Activites **7512**
Centre Magazine *see* Hardware & Home Centre Magazine **1054**
Centre Metal.lurgic (ESP) **6308**
Centre National d'Archeologie et d'Histoire du Livre. Publications (NLD ISSN 0069-1984) **7558**
† Centre National d'Art et de Culture Georges Pompidou. Magazine (FRA ISSN 0996-4274) **8940**
Centre National de Documentation Pedagogique. Textes et Documents pour la Classe. (FRA ISSN 0395-6601) **2835**
Centre National de la Cinematographie Dossier *see* C N C. Dossier **6491**
Centre National de la Cinematographie Info (English Edition) *see* C N C Info (English Edition) **6491**
Centre National de la Recherche Scientifique. Colloques Internationaux (FRA ISSN 0366-7634) **7844**
Centre National de la Recherche Scientifique. Cristal (FRA ISSN 1777-9251) **7844**
Centre National de la Recherche Scientifique. Les Medailles d'Or (FRA ISSN 1777-0378) **7844**
Centre National de la Recherche Scientifique. Monographies d'Econometrie (FRA ISSN 0981-5066) **1081**
Centre National de Machinisme Agricole du Genie Rural des Eaux et des Forets Gestion des Milieux Aquatiques. Etudes *see* C E M A G R E F. Gestion des Milieux Aquatiques. Etudes **210**
Centre National de Machinisme Agricole du Genie Rural des Eaux et des Forets Groupement de Bordeaux. Etude *see* C E M A G R E F. Groupement de Bordeaux. Etude **210**
Centre National de Recherches Appliques au Developpement Rural. Departement de Recherches Agronomiques. Rapport Annuel (MDG) **100**
Centre National de Recherches Appliques au Developpement Rural. Departement de Recherches Agronomiques. Rapport d'Activite (MDG) **100**
Centre National de Recherches Oceanographiques. Document (MDG ISSN 0252-189X) **2801**
Centre National d'Etudes Spatiales Magazine *see* C N E S Magazine **50**
Centre National d'Etudes Spatiales. Rapport d'Activite (FRA ISSN 1269-6161) **51**
Centre National d'Information sur la Violence dans la Famile, Sante Canada. Liste des Publications *see* National Clearinghouse on Family Violence. Publications **8083**
Centre Nationale de la Recherche Scientifique *see* C N R S Droit **4635**
Centre Nationale de la Recherche Scientifique Anthropologie *see* C N R S Anthropologie **331**
Centre Nationale de la Recherche Scientifique Communication *see* C N R S Communication **2314**
Centre Nationale de la Recherche Scientifique Dictionnaires *see* C N R S Dictionnaires **4999**
Centre Nationale de la Recherche Scientifique Economie *see* C N R S Economie **1445**
Centre Nationale de la Recherche Scientifique Ethnologie *see* C N R S Ethnologie **331**

Title

10106 CENTRE NATIONALE DE LA RECHERCHE SCIENTIFIQUE HISTOIRE ULRICH'S PERIODICALS

Centre Nationale de la Recherche Scientifique Histoire *see* C N R S Histoire **4133**
Centre Nationale de la Recherche Scientifique Langage *see* C N R S Langage **5102**
Centre Nationale de la Recherche Scientifique Litterature *see* C N R S Litterature **5268**
Centre Nationale de la Recherche Scientifique Philosophie *see* C N R S Philosophie **6909**
Centre Nationale de la Recherche Scientifique Sociologie *see* C N R S Sociologie **8091**
Centre News *see* Energy Information Centre. CentreNews **1483**
Centre of Arabic Documentation. Research Bulletin (NGA ISSN 0331-5177) **5105**
† • Centre of the City (CAN ISSN 1719-9328) **8940**
➤ Centre on Governance (CAN ISSN 1487-3052) **7429**
• Centre on Regulation and Competition. Working Papers (GBR) **7115**
Centre Points (CAN ISSN 1719-9697) **5955**
Centre pour la Recherche Economique et ses Applications Collection *see* C E P R E M A P. Collection **1536**
Centre pour l'Etude du Monde Arabe Moderne Reports *see* C E M A M Reports **545**
Centre Protestant d'Etudes de Geneve. Bulletin (CHE ISSN 1015-1141) **7750**
Centre Protestant d'Etudes et de Documentation. Libresens (FRA ISSN 1157-7452) **7698**
† Centre Rankings (GBR ISSN 0958-7322) **8940**
Centre Regional de Documentation Pedagogique de Toulouse. Annales (FRA ISSN 0069-2069) **2835**
Centre Regional de Promotion du Livre en Afrique. Bulletin d'Information *see* Regional Centre for Book Promotion in Africa. Bulletin of Information **7572**
Centre Regional de Sante et de Services Sociaux de la Baie - James. Rapport sur l'Application de la Procedure d'Examen des Plaintes et l'Amelioration de la Qualite des Services (CAN ISSN 1719-3672) **8031**
• Centre Regional de Services aux Bibliotheques Publiques de l'Outaouais. Rapport Annuel (CAN ISSN 1719-8232) **5001**
Centre Regional d'Information et de Prevention du S I D A. Lettre d'Information (FRA ISSN 1242-1693) **5811**
Centre Regional d'Information et de Prevention du S I D A. Revue de Presse (FRA ISSN 1250-6958) **5811**
Centre Rosalie-Cadron-Jette. Bulletin (CAN ISSN 1718-7567) **7791**
Centre Technique des Industries Mecaniques et Electriques News *see* C E T I M E News **3296**
Centre Technique des Industries Mecaniques Informations *see* C E T I M Informations **7057**
Centre Technique du Bois et de l'Ameublement Info *see* C T B A Info **8939**
Centre Technique du Papier. Feuillets Bibliographiques (FRA ISSN 1280-5572) **6732**
Centre Universitaire de Recherche pour le Developpement Economique et Social. Cahiers (BDI) **1592**
CentrePiece (GBR ISSN 1362-3761) **1537**
Centrepiece (USA) **2277**
Centrepieces (GBR) **8855**
Centrepoint (GBR ISSN 0577-1935) **7115**
Centres, Bureaux & Research Institutes (GBR ISSN 1365-4322) **1979**
Centres d'Appels *see* Relation Client Magazine **1839**
Centres de Services aux Entreprises du Canada. Rapport Annuel *see* Canada Business Service Centres. Annual Report **7426**
Les Centres de Vacances Familiales (CAN ISSN 1911-9437) **8309**
Centres d'Excellence pour la Sante des Femmes. Bulletin de Recherche *see* Centres of Excellence for Women's Health. Research Bulletin **7512**
Centres for Health Research Annual Review *see* Princess Alexandra Hospital. Centres for Health Research. Annual Research Report **5700**
• Centres of Excellence for Women's Health. Research Bulletin (CAN ISSN 1496-3612) **7512**
• ➤ Centro (USA ISSN 1538-6279) **4446**
Centro Argentino de Ingenieros Informa *see* C A I Informa **3183**
• ➤ Centro Brasileiro de Analise e Planejamento. Novos Estudos (BRA ISSN 0101-3300) **7953**
Centro Calouste Gulbenkian. Archivos (FRA ISSN 0590-966X) **5407**
Centro Camuno di Studi Preistorici. Archivi (ITA) **386**
Centro Camuno di Studi Preistorici. Studi Camuni (ITA) **386**
Centro Camuno di Studi Preistorici. Symposia (ITA) **481**
Centro Control Contaminacion del Pacifico Boletin Cientifico *see* C C C P. Boletin Cientifico **3484**
• Centro Cultural Pablo de la Torriente Brau. Memoria (CUB ISSN 1684-2413) **481**
† Centro de Albacete. Anales (ESP ISSN 0211-5247) **8940**
Centro de Bibliotecologia, Archivologia e Informacion. Anuario (MEX) **5001**
Centro de Biodiversidad y Ambiente. Museo de Zoologia. Publicacion Especial (ECU) **665**
Centro de Biologia da Reproducao. Boletim (BRA ISSN 0101-9783) **665**
• Centro de Ciencias Agrarias. Anuario (BRA ISSN 1518-7586) **100**
Centro de Ciencias da Economia e Informatica. Revista (BRA ISSN 1415-2061) **2542**
Centro de Documentacion y Estudios. Informativo Campesino (PRY ISSN 1017-6047) **7279**
Centro de Documentacion y Estudios. Informativo Laboral (PRY ISSN 1017-6055) **1670**
Centro de Documentacion y Estudios. Informativo Mujer (PRY ISSN 1017-6063) **8855**
Centro de Documentacion y Estudios Josemaria Escriva de Balaguer. Cuadernos (ESP ISSN 1139-5346) **7630**
Centro de Ecologia Aplicada del Neuquen. Informe Tecnico (ARG) **665**
Centro de Edafologia y Biologia Aplicada del Segura. Monografias (ESP) **100**
Centro de Ensino e Pesquisas Arqueologicas. Revista Revista *see* CEPA. Revista **387**
Centro de Especializacao em Fonoaudiologia Clinica Revista *see* C E F A C Revista **6078**
Centro de Estadisticas Nacionales y Comercio Internacional del Uruguay. Costo de la Vida (URY) **8362**
Centro de Estudios Avanzados de Puerto Rico y el Caribe. Revista (PRI) **4288**
➤ Centro de Estudios Avanzados. Estudios (ARG ISSN 0328-185X) **7953**
Centro de Estudios Clasicos. Serie Didactica (MEX) **2232**
Centro de Estudios de la Realidad Puertorriquena. Cuadernos (PRI) **7115**
• Centro de Estudios del Maestrazgo. Boletin de Divulgacion Cultural (ESP ISSN 0212-3975) **2835**
Centro de Estudios del Sistema Alimentario. Cuadernos Cuadernos *see* C E A G R O. Cuadernos **98**
Centro de Estudios Genealogicos de Cordoba. Boletin (ARG ISSN 0327-7941) **3761**
Centro de Estudios Historicos Profesor Carlos S.A. Anuario (ARG ISSN 1666-6836) **4134**
Centro de Estudios Humanitarios *see* C E D H U **4635**
Centro de Estudios Internacionales. Boletin (NIC) **4447**
Centro de Estudios Judiciarios Revista *see* C E J. Revista **4635**
Centro de Estudios Martianos. Anuario (CUB ISSN 0864-1358) **4288**
• Centro de Estudios Monetarios Latinoamericanos. Boletin Bimensual (MEX ISSN 0186-7229) **1326**
• Centro de Estudios Monetarios Latinoamericanos. Ensayos (MEX ISSN 0577-2451) **1326**
Centro de Estudios Orientales. Anuario (MEX ISSN 0066-8249) **4181**
Centro de Estudios para la Integracion Social y Formacion de Inmigrantes Anuario *see* C E I M I G R A. Anuario **7278**
Centro de Estudios Publicos. Documento de Trabajo (CHL ISSN 0716-1123) **1446**
• Centro de Estudios sobre Bibliotecologia. Boletin Informativo Electronico (ARG ISSN 1667-6351) **5001**
Centro de Estudios sobre la Identidad Colectiva Papeles *see* C E I C. Papeles **8091**
Centro de Estudios Superiores de Mexico y Centroamerica. Anuario (MEX) **332**
Centro de Estudios Urbanos y Regionales. Boletin (ARG ISSN 0326-8470) **8093**
Centro de Estudios Urbanos y Regionales. Cuadernos (ARG ISSN 0326-1417) **8093**
Centro de Estudios Urbanos y Regionales. Informes de Investigacion (ARG) **8093**
Centro de Estudios y Asesoramiento Metalurgico Revista de Economia Industrial *see* C E A M - Revista de Economia Industrial **1077**
Centro de Estudios y Documentacion Latinoamericanos Latin America Studies *see* C E D L A Latin America Studies **7951**
Centro de Estudos de Educacao e Sociedade Cadernos *see* C E D E S Cadernos **2833**
Centro de Estudos e Acao Social Cadernos *see* C E A S Cadernos **8091**
Centro de Estudos e Pesquisas Armando de Oliveira Souza Review *see* C E P A O S Review **2833**
Centro de Estudos e Pesquisas Economicas. Estudos Estudos *see* CEPE. Estudos **1446**
Centro de Estudos Latino Americanos. Boletim (BRA) **8031**
Centro de Estudos Portugueses. Boletim (BRA ISSN 0101-7934) **4447**
Centro de Estudos Regionais. Boletim Cultural (PRT) **332**
Centro de Fisica da Atmosfera de Lisboa. Boletim (PRT ISSN 0870-4716) **2779**
Centro de Informacion Documental de Archivos. Boletin de Informacion (ESP ISSN 0210-9492) **5001**
Centro de Informacion y Gestion Tecnologica. Avances (CUB ISSN 1562-3297) **7844**
Centro de Informaciones y Estudios del Uruguay. Serie Documentos de Trabajo (URY) **7953**
Centro de Informaciones y Estudios del Uruguay. Serie Estudios (URY) **7953**
Centro de Informaciones y Estudios del Uruguay. Serie Informes (URY) **7953**
Centro de Innovacion y Servicios Madeira *see* C I S Madeira **3710**
Centro de Investigacion de las Telecomunicaciones Revista *see* C I N T E L. Revista **2314**
Centro de Investigacion en Metodologia Borrosa Aplicada a la Gestion y Economia. Cuadernos Cuadernos *see* C I M B A G E. Cuadernos **1731**
Centro de Investigacion en Zonas Aridas y Semiaridas. Revista (ARG ISSN 1515-0453) **100**
Centro de Investigacion para la Paz Anuario *see* C I P. Anuario **8938**
Centro de Investigacion y Accion Social. Revista (ARG ISSN 0325-1306) **7953**
Centro de Investigacion y Control de la Calidad (ESP ISSN 0214-6320) **1882**
Centro de Investigacion y Desarrollo en Tecnologia de Pinturas. Anales (ARG ISSN 0325-4186) **6716**
Centro de Investigacion y Desarrollo Tecnico. Revista Electronica *see* R E C I D T **8436**
Centro de Investigacion y Promocion del Campesinado. Cuadernos de Investigacion (BOL) **1446**
Centro de Investigaciones Agricolas de Tamaulipas. Informe Anual de Labores (MEX ISSN 0084-8697) **100**
➤ Centro de Investigaciones Biologicas. Memoria Cientifica (ESP) **665**
Centro de Investigaciones Energeticas, Medioambientales y Tecnologicas. Informes de Difusion de Proy Informes de Difusion de Proyectos *see* C I E M A T. Informes de Difusion de Proyectos **3125**
Centro de Investigaciones Energeticas, Medioambientales y Tecnologicas Informes Tecnicos *see* C I E M A T. Informes Tecnicos **3166**
Centro de Investigaciones, Facultad de Filosofia y Humanidades. Publicacion (ARG ISSN 1515-1859) **4447**
➤ Centro de Investigaciones Historicas y Esteticas. Boletin (VEN ISSN 0506-600X) **437**
Centro de Investigaciones Humanisticas de Mesoamerica y el Estado de Chiapas *see* C I H M E C H **385**
Centro de Investigaciones Penales y Criminologicas. Revista *see* Revista C E N I P E C **2667**
Centro de Investigaciones Socio Historicas. Cuadernos (ARG ISSN 1514-0113) **4134**
Centro de Letras e Ciencias Humanas (BRA ISSN 0102-6968) **4447**
Centro de Logica, Epistemiologia prints *see* C L E e-prints **6909**
Centro de Memoria Regional. Caderno (BRA ISSN 0104-2262) **333**
Centro de Navegacion. Handbook. River Plate Handbook for Shipowners and Agents (ARG) **8641**
Centro de Pesquisa Agroflorestal da Amazonia Oriental. Boletim de Pesquisa (BRA) **100**
Centro de Pesquisa Agropecuaria do Tropico Semi-Arido. Documentos *see* Embrapa Semi-Arido. Documentos **228**
Centro de Pesquisa e Extensao Pesqueira do Nordeste. Boletim Tecnico-Cientifico (BRA ISSN 0104-6411) **938**
• ➤ Centro de Pesquisa e Processamento de Alimentos. Boletim (BRA ISSN 0102-0323) **3630**
Centro de Pesquisas Biomedicas Gonzaga da Gama Filho. Revista Cientifica (BRA ISSN 1415-8280) **5593**
Centro de Pesquisas do Cacau. Boletim Tecnico (BRA ISSN 0100-0845) **100**
Centro de Pesquisas do Cacau. Informe de Pesquisas (BRA ISSN 0102-4256) **100**
• Centro de Profesores de Albacete. Programas (ESP ISSN 1131-8872) **2835**
• Centro Dermatologico Pascua. Revista (MEX ISSN 1405-1710) **5873**
Centro di Cultura e Storia Amalfitana. Rassegna (ITA) **4447**
Centro di Eccellenza (ITA ISSN 1828-8375) **4920**
Centro di Ricerca sull'Italia nell'Europa Romantica Nuovi Quaderni *see* C R I E R Nuovi Quaderni **5268**
Centro di Ricerche Etno-Antropologiche Milano *see* C R E A M Quaderni **331**
Centro di Ricerche Informatiche per i Beni Culturali. Bollettino d'Informazioni (ITA) **5001**
Centro di Ricerche Informatiche per i Beni Culturali. Quaderni (ITA) **5001**
Centro di Ricerche Storiche, Rovigno. Atti (HRV ISSN 0352-1427) **4210**
Centro di Ricerche Storiche, Rovigno. Collana degli Atti (HRV ISSN 0353-3301) **4210**
Centro di Ricerche Storiche, Rovigno. Documenti (HRV ISSN 0352-9312) **4210**
Centro di Ricerche Storiche, Rovigno. Etnia (HRV ISSN 0353-3271) **4210**
Centro di Ricerche Storiche, Rovigno. Fonti (HRV) **4210**
Centro di Ricerche Storiche, Rovigno. La Ricerca (HRV) **4210**
Centro di Ricerche Storiche, Rovigno. Monografie (HRV ISSN 0353-328X) **4210**
Centro di Ricerche Storiche, Rovigno. Quaderni (HRV ISSN 0350-6746) **4210**
Centro di Ricerche Storiche, Rovigno. Ricerche Sociali (HRV ISSN 0353-474X) **4210**
Centro di Studi di Estimo e di Economia Territoriale Incontro di Studio *see* C E S E T. Incontro di Studio **195**
Centro di Studi Filologici e Linguistici Siciliani. Bollettino (ITA ISSN 0577-277X) **5105**
Centro di Studi Vichiani. Bollettino (ITA ISSN 0392-7334) **6910**
Centro Estudiantes de Derecho. Revista Juridica (URY ISSN 0797-6011) **4641**
Centro Franco-Brasileiro de Documentacao Tecnica e Cientifica Dossier Dossier *see* C E N D O T E C Dossier **8417**
Centro Galego de Arte Contemporanea Revista *see* C G A C. Revista **480**
Centro Informativo de la Construccion Productos *see* C I C Productos **989**
Centro Informativo para las Americas y el Caribe Sintesis Informativa *see* C I A C Sintesis Informativa **7111**
Centro Informazione Vivisezionista Internazionale Scientifica International Foundation Report *see* C I V I S: International Foundation Report **318**
Centro Interamericano de Artesanias y Artes Populares. Centro de Documentacion. Boletin (ECU ISSN 1011-9531) **541**
Centro Interamericano de Investigacion y Documentacion Sobre Formacion Profesional Estudios y Monografias *see* C I N T E R F O R Estudios y Monografias **2833**
Centro Interamericano de Investigacion y Documentacion sobre Formacion Profesional. Informes (URY) **3054**
Centro Interamericano de Investigacion y Documentacion sobre Formacion Profesional. Oficina Tecnica. Papeles (URY) **2835**
Centro Interamericano de Investigacion y Documentacion Sobre Formacion Profesional Revista C I N T E R F O R *see* F P Revista C I N T E R F O R **5009**
Centro Interamericano de Investigacion y Documentacion sobre Formacion Profesional. Serie Bibliografica (URY) **2931**
Centro Interdisciplinario de Ciencias Marinas Oceanidades Oceanides *see* CICIMAR Oceanides **2802**
Centro Interdisciplinario de Estudios Culturales. Boletin de la Fundacion (ARG) **3761**
Centro Interdisciplinario de Estudios sobre el Desarrollo. Investigaciones (URY) **1592**
Centro Internacional de Agricultura Tropical en Perspectiva *see* C I A T en Perspectiva **98**
Centro Internacional de Investigacion e Informacion sobre la Economia Publica, Social y Cooperativa Espana *see* C I R I E C Espana **1445**
Centro International de Mejoramiento de Maiz y Trigo Economics Working Paper *see* C I M M Y T Economics Working Paper **270**
• Centro Internazionale di Ricerca sui Periodici Musicali. Newsletter (ITA) **6555**
• Centro Internazionale di Studi di Architettura Andrea Palladio. Annali di Architettura (ITA ISSN 1124-7169) **437**
Centro Internazionale Radio - Medico Research *see* C I R M Research **5590**
Centro Italiano di Studi sull'Alto Medioevo. Biblioteca (ITA) **4210**
Centro Italiano di Studi sull'Alto Medioevo. Quaderni (ITA) **4210**
Centro Italiano di Studi sull'Alto Medioevo.Settimane di Studio (ITA ISSN 0528-5666) **4210**
Centro Italiano per la Ricerca Storico - Educativa *see* C I R S E. Nuovo Bollettino **2833**
Centro Latinoamericano de Demografia. Boletin Demografico (CHL ISSN 0378-5386) **7279**
Centro Latinoamericano de Demografia. Notas de Poblacion (CHL ISSN 0303-1829) **7279**
Centro Latinoamericano de Demografia. Serie A/Latin American Demographic Centre. Serie A (CHL ISSN 0503-3934) **7279**
Centro Latinoamericano de Demografia. Serie C/Latin American Demographic Centre. Serie C (CHL ISSN 0503-3942) **7279**
Centro Latinoamericano de Demografia. Serie D/Latin American Demographic Centre. Serie D (CHL ISSN 0503-3950) **7279**
Centro Latinoamericano de Demografia. Serie E/Latin American Demographic Centre. Serie E (CHL) **7279**
Centro Latinoamericano de Demografia. Serie OI: Publicaciones Conjuntas con Instituciones Nacionales de Paises de America Latina (CHL) **7279**
Centro Latinoamericano de Economia Humana. Cuadernos (URY ISSN 0797-6062) **7953**
Centro Latinoamericano de Estudios en Informatica Electronic Journal Electronic Journal *see* C L E I Electronic Journal **4999**
Centro Linceo Interdisciplinare Beniamino Segre. Contributi (ITA ISSN 0394-0705) **7844**
Centro Micologico Friulano. Bollettino (ITA) **783**
Centro Nacional de Derecho de Autor *see* C E N D A **7557**
Centro Nacional de Informacion - Direccion General del Derecho de Autor Informa *see* C N I D A Informa **7557**
Centro Nacional de Investigaciones Metalurgicas. Memoria (ESP) **6308**
Centro Nacional de Pesquisa de Gado de Leite. Relatorio Tecnico (BRA ISSN 0100-7904) **262**
Centro Nacional de Pesquisa de Peixes Tropicais. Boletim Tecnico *see* Centro Nacional de Pesquisa e Gestao de Recursos Pesqueiros Continentais. Boletim Tecnico **3589**
Centro Nacional de Pesquisa e Gestao de Recursos Pesqueiros Continentais. Boletim Tecnico (BRA) **3589**

Title

10108 CESKA A SLOVENSKA GASTROENTEROLOGIE A HEPATOLOGIE ULRICH'S PERIODICALS

➤ Ceska a Slovenska Gastroenterologie a Hepatologie/Czech and Slovak Gastroenterology and Hepatology (CZE ISSN 1213-323X) **5921**
• ➤ Ceska a Slovenska Neurologie a Neurochirurgie (CZE ISSN 1210-7859) **6131**
➤ Ceska a Slovenska Oftalmologie/Czech and Slovak Ophtalmology (CZE ISSN 1211-9059) **6039**
➤ Ceska a Slovenska Psychiatrie/Czech and Slovak Psychiatry (CZE ISSN 1212-0383) **6131**
Ceska Akademie Ved. Archeologicky Ustav. Spisy/Czech Academy of Sciences. Archeological Institute. Letters (CZE) **387**
Ceska Akademie Ved. Archeologicky Ustav. Studie (CZE ISSN 1211-1457) **387**
Ceska Akademie Ved. Psychologicky Ustav. Bulletin (CZE ISSN 1211-216X) **7344**
Ceska Archeologicka Spolecnost. Zpravy/Czech Archaeological Society. News (CZE ISSN 1211-992X) **387**
Ceska Geologicka Spolecnost. Casopis *see* Journal of Geosciences **2750**
➤ Ceska Gynekologie/Czech Gynaecology (CZE ISSN 1210-7832) **5988**
➤ Ceska Literatura/Czech Literature (CZE ISSN 0009-0468) **5272**
Ceska Narodni Bibliografie. Clanky, State v Ceskem Tisku (Diskette Edition) *see* Ceska Narodni Bibliografie. Clanky v Novinach a Casopisech (CD-ROM Edition) **8940**
† • Ceska Narodni Bibliografie. Clanky v Novinach a Casopisech (CD-ROM Edition) (CZE) **8940**
† • Ceska Narodni Bibliografie. Grafika (CD-ROM Edition) (CZE) **8940**
Ceska Narodni Bibliografie. Grafika (Print Edition) *see* Ceska Narodni Bibliografie. Grafika (CD-ROM Edition) **8940**
† • Ceska Narodni Bibliografie. Hudebniny (CD-ROM Edition) (CZE) **8940**
Ceska Narodni Bibliografie. Hudebniny (Print Edition) *see* Ceska Narodni Bibliografie. Hudebniny (CD-ROM Edition) **8940**
† • Ceska Narodni Bibliografie. Knihy (CD-ROM Edition) (CZE) **8940**
Ceska Narodni Bibliografie. Knihy (Print Edition) *see* Ceska Narodni Bibliografie. Knihy (CD-ROM Edition) **8940**
† • Ceska Narodni Bibliografie. Zahranicni Bohemika (CD-ROM Edition) (CZE) **8940**
Ceska Narodni Bibliografie. Zahranicni Bohemika (Print Edition) *see* Ceska Narodni Bibliografie. Zahranicni Bohemika (CD-ROM Edition) **8940**
† • Ceska Narodni Bibliografie. Zvukove Dokumenty (CD-ROM Edition) (CZE) **8940**
Ceska Narodni Bibliografie. Zvukove Dokumenty (Print Edition) *see* Ceska Narodni Bibliografie. Zvukove Dokumenty (CD-ROM Edition) **8940**
• Ceska Parazitologicka Spolecnost. Zpravy/Czech Parasitology Society. Reports (CZE ISSN 1211-7897) **665**
➤ Ceska Radiologie (CZE ISSN 1210-7883) **6193**
➤ Ceska Revmatologie/Czech Rheumatology (CZE ISSN 1210-7905) **6222**
† • Ceska Skola (CZE ISSN 1213-6018) **8940**
➤ Ceska Stomatologie a Prakticke Zubni Lekarstvi/Czech Stomatology and Practical Dentistry (CZE ISSN 1213-0613) **5837**
Ceska Urologie (CZE ISSN 1211-8729) **6266**
• Ceska Zemedelska a Potravinarska Bibliografie (CZE) **178**
Ceske Loznice (CZE ISSN 1212-4052) **6287**
Ceske Panicky (CZE) **6287**
• ➤ Ceske Pracovni Lekarstvi/Czech Journal of Occupational Medicine (CZE ISSN 1212-6721) **5593**
Cesko Dnes *see* Chehiya Segodnya **3526**
➤ Cesko-Slovenska Dermatologie/Czecho-Slovak Dermatology (CZE ISSN 0009-0514) **5873**
➤ Cesko-Slovenska Patologie a Soudni Lekarstvi/Czecho-Slovak Pathology and Forensic Medicine (CZE ISSN 1210-7875) **5593**
➤ Cesko-Slovenska Pediatrie/Czecho-Slovak Pediatrics (CZE ISSN 0069-2328) **6089**
Ceskomoravske Veletrhy *see* Euroveletrhy **6279**
Ceskopis (CZE ISSN 1801-7258) **8692**
• ➤ Ceskoslovenska Fyziologie/Czechoslovak Physiology (CZE ISSN 1210-6313) **920**
Ceskoslovenska Pediatrie *see* Cesko-Slovenska Pediatrie **6089**
➤ Ceskoslovenska Psychologie/Czechoslovak Psychology (CZE ISSN 0009-062X) **7344**
Ceskoslovenska Spolecnost Mikrobiologicka. Bulletin (CZE ISSN 0009-0646) **883**
Ceskoslovensky Casopis pro Fyziku (CZE ISSN 0009-0700) **7008**
Cesky Autosalon *see* Autosalon **8566**
Cesky Casopis Historicky/Czech Historical Review (CZE ISSN 0862-6111) **4210**
Cesky Geologicky Ustav. Vestnik *see* Bulletin of Geosciences **2727**
Cesky Instalater (CZE ISSN 1210-695X) **3184**
➤ Cesky Jazyk a Literatura (CZE ISSN 0009-0786) **2835**
Cesky Kras (CZE ISSN 1211-1643) **4002**
➤ Cesky Lid/Czech People (CZE ISSN 0009-0794) **333**
† Cesky Spotr Ebitel (CZE) **8940**
Cesky Statisticky Urad. Aktuality (CZE ISSN 1214-1461) **8362**
Cesky Statisticky Urad. Energetika/Czech Statistical Office. Energy (CZE) **3126**
Cesky Statisticky Urad. Statisticka Rocenka Ceske Republiky/Czech Statistical Office. Statistical Yearbook (CZE ISSN 1211-4812) **1220**
Cesky Statisticky Urad. Ukazatele Socialniho a Hospodarskeho Vyvoje Ceske Republiky *see* Czech Statistical Office. Indicators of Social and Economic Development in the Czech Republic **1223**
Cesky Statisticky Urad. Zpravodaj (CZE ISSN 1210-6550) **8362**
▼ • CeskyKutil.cz (CZE ISSN 1802-4270) **4437**
➤ Cespedesia (COL ISSN 0121-0866) **783**
• Cessna Owner Magazine (USA ISSN 0745-3523) **51**
C'est a Vous (FRA ISSN 1779-8973) **1082**
• C'Est Facile! (ITA ISSN 0996-4967) **5105**
C'Est la Vie Aussi (FRA ISSN 1765-7210) **2147**
† C'Est Ma Vie (FRA ISSN 1779-207X) **8940**
C'Est pour Quand (CAN ISSN 0705-3215) **2147**
C'Est Quoi? (FRA ISSN 1297-8604) **4447**
Ceste i Mostovi/Roads and Bridges (HRV ISSN 0411-6380) **3262**
CET500 *see* Consultant Engineers and Technologies 500 **1981**
• Ceteris Paribus (AUS ISSN 1834-3317) **1082**
• Ceteris Paribus (PRI) **1082**
Cetoniidarum Generum Lexicon (BEL) **842**
Cetoniidarum Specierum Lexicon (BEL ISSN 1376-7402) **842**
Cetoniimania *see* Cetoniidarum Specierum Lexicon **842**
Ceux des A F F A A *see* Anciens des Forces Francaises en Allemagne et en Autriche. Ceux **6410**
Ceviribilim Uygulamalari/Journal of Translation Studies (TUR ISSN 1301-4145) **5105**
Ceylon Bird Club Notes (LKA ISSN 1019-8121) **905**
Ceylon Bird Club Notes. Special Publications Series (LKA) **905**
Ceylon Chamber of Commerce. Annual Review of Business and Trade (Year) (LKA) **1398**
Ceylon Chamber of Commerce. Register of Members (LKA) **1398**
Ceylon Churchman (LKA ISSN 1391-7064) **7750**
Ceylon Commerce (LKA) **1426**
Ceylon Dental Journal *see* Sri Lanka Dental Journal **5866**
Ceylon Geographer (LKA ISSN 0378-2514) **4002**
Ceylon Institute of Scientific & Industrial Research. Annual Report (LKA) **7845**
Ceylon Institute of Scientific & Industrial Research. News Bulletin (LKA) **7845**
➤ Ceylon Journal of Medical Science (LKA ISSN 0011-2232) **5593**
➤ Ceylon Journal of Science. Biological Sciences (LKA ISSN 0069-2379) **665**
Ceylon Journal of Science. Physical Sciences (LKA ISSN 1391-1465) **7845**
• ➤ Ceylon Medical Journal (LKA ISSN 0009-0875) **5593**
Ceylon Rationalist Ambassador (LKA ISSN 0577-4772) **6910**
Ceylon Shipping Corporation. Annual Report & Statement of Accounts (LKA) **8641**
Ceylon Tourist Board. Annual Statistical Report (LKA) **8778**
Ceylon Tourist Board. Monthly Bulletin on the Performance of the Tourism Sector (LKA) **8778**
• Cezanne's Carrot (USA ISSN 1930-2878) **5272**
CFNS News (Print) *see* C F N S News **3408**
CH-D Wirtschaft (CHE ISSN 1420-0953) **1555**
† CH4 Energia Gas (ITA ISSN 1972-6376) **8940**
Cha Bolan/Tea Times (CHN ISSN 1004-9223) **3630**
• C=Hacking (USA) **2512**
ChaCom (GBR ISSN 0266-4127) **1398**
Chacra y Campo Moderno (ARG ISSN 0325-7932) **100**
Chad (Alfreton Edition) (GBR ISSN 1751-1615) **3967**
Chad (Ashfield Edition) *see* Chad (Alfreton Edition) **3967**
Chad (Mansfield Edition) *see* Chad (Alfreton Edition) **3967**
Chad (Sherwood & Rainworth Edition) *see* Chad (Alfreton Edition) **3967**
Chad (Shirebrook & Bolsover Edition) *see* Chad (Alfreton Edition) **3967**
Chad (Woodhouse & Warsop Edition) *see* Chad (Alfreton Edition) **3967**
Chad Alfreton *see* Chad (Alfreton Edition) **3967**
Chad. Bulletin Mensuel de Statistiques (TCD) **1221**
• Chad Food Security Update (USA) **1592**
Chad Monthly Food Security Update *see* Chad Food Security Update **1592**
Chadburn (USA) **4288**
Chaeryo Madang *see* Jae'lyo Ma'dang **6318**
The Chaffin Journal (USA ISSN 1547-4879) **5272**
Chai Magazine (KEN) **3630**
• Chaidamu Kaifa Yanjiu/Studies of Developing Chaidamu (CHN ISSN 1005-6718) **7953**
• Chaillot Papers (FRA ISSN 1017-7566) **7226**
Chain (USA ISSN 1076-0520) **5272**
The Chain (Online) (AUS) **2606**
• Chain Drug Review (USA ISSN 0164-9914) **1732**
• Chain Leader (USA ISSN 1528-4999) **4383**
• Chain Reaction (AUS ISSN 0312-1372) **3410**
• Chain Reaction (USA) **7845**
• Chain Store Age (USA ISSN 1087-0601) **1809**
• Chain Store Age Executive Fax (USA ISSN 1079-6428) **1082**
Chain Store Guide Database of Foodservice Technology *see* Database of Foodservice Technology **3633**
Chaine/Keten (BEL) **319**
Chaine des Rotisseurs (GBR) **4383**
Chaire de Recherche du Canada en Mondialisation, Citoyennete et Democratie. Bulletin (CAN ISSN 1718-8148) **7226**
Chaire Glaverbel d'Etudes Europeennes. Actes (BEL ISSN 1377-476X) **7226**
• Chairman of the Joint Chiefs of Staff Strategy Essay Competition Essays (USA) **6415**
• Chairside (USA) **5837**
• Chaiyouji/Diesel Engine (CHN ISSN 1001-4357) **3375**
• Chaiyouji Sheji yu Zhizao/Design & Manufacture of Diesel Engine (CHN ISSN 1671-0614) **3375**
Chakra (BGD) **8031**
➤ Chakra (SWE ISSN 1652-0203) **7630**
Chalcedon Report (USA ISSN 1053-9018) **7630**
• Chalcogenide Letters (ROM ISSN 1584-8663) **7008**
ChaletDeco (ESP ISSN 1575-8281) **4535**
Chalice (USA) **3761**
Chalk Talk *see* Enterprise Matters **1885**
• Challenge (AUS ISSN 0311-0486) **2835**
• ➤ Challenge/Etgar (ISR ISSN 0792-4143) **7226**
• ➤ The Challenge (PAK ISSN 0528-7944) **6212**
• ➤ Challenge (Armonk) (USA ISSN 0577-5132) **1082**
• ➤ Challenge (Atlanta) (USA ISSN 1077-193X) **3526**
➤ The Challenge (Banning) (USA) **6015**
Challenge (Convent Station) (USA ISSN 0277-1675) **4372**
Challenge (London, 1960) (GBR ISSN 0009-1006) **2182**
Challenge (New York) (USA ISSN 0009-1049) **7115**
• Challenge (Rockville) (USA ISSN 1940-526X) **4077**
Challenge (Sandbach) (GBR ISSN 0009-1014) **7791**
• Challenge Europe (BEL) **1446**
Challenger (Buffalo) (USA ISSN 1040-8886) **3526**
Challenger (Petaluma) (USA ISSN 1084-2144) **7750**
• Challenges (FRA ISSN 0751-4417) **1082**
Challenges Haute-Marne (FRA ISSN 1148-9634) **1426**
Challenges in Language and Literacy (USA) **5105**
Challenges of Modern Society *see* N A T O Challenges of Modern Society **7884**
• Challenging Destiny (CAN ISSN 1719-9727) **5440**
Challenging Destiny (Print Edition) *see* Challenging Destiny **5440**
Chalmers Tekniska Hoegskola. Department of Materials Science and Engineering. Diploma Work *see* Chalmers Tekniska Hoegskola. Institutionen foer Material- och Tellverkningsteknik. Examensarbete **8418**
• Chalmers Tekniska Hoegskola. Doktorsavhandlingar (SWE ISSN 0366-8746) **8418**
Chalmers Tekniska Hoegskola. Doktorsavhandlingar. Ny Serie/Technical University of Chalmer. Doctoral Thesis. New Series (SWE ISSN 0346-718X) **3184**
Chalmers Tekniska Hoegskola. Forskargrupp Geologi. Publ. B *see* Chalmers University of Technology. Department of Civil and Environmental Engineering. Lic **991**
Chalmers Tekniska Hoegskola. Forskargrupp Geoteknik. Publ. A *see* Chalmers University of Technology. Department of Civil and Environmental Engineering. Lic **991**
Chalmers Tekniska Hoegskola. Institutionen foer Byggnadsfysik. Publikation *see* Chalmers Tekniska Hoegskola. Institutionen foer Byggnadsteknologi, Byggnadsfysik. Publikation **991**
Chalmers Tekniska Hoegskola. Institutionen foer Byggnadsteknologi, Byggnadsfysik. Publikation *see* Chalmers University of Technology. Department of Civil and Environmental Engineering. Lic **991**
• Chalmers Tekniska Hoegskola. Institutionen foer Byggnadsteknologi, Byggnadsfysik. Publikation (SWE) **991**
Chalmers Tekniska Hoegskola. Institutionen foer Material- och Tellverkningsteknik. Examensarbete/Chalmers University of Technology. Department of Materials and Manufacturing Technology. Master's Thesis (SWE ISSN 1652-8913) **8418**
Chalmers Tekniska Hoegskola. Institutionen foer Vatten Miljoe Transport. Doktorsavhandlingar och Licentiatuppsatser (SWE ISSN 1650-4143) **3360**
Chalmers Tekniska Hoegskola. Institutionen foer Vattenbyggnad. Report. Series A *see* Chalmers Tekniska Hoegskola. Institutionen foer Vatten Miljoe Transport. Doktorsavhandlingar och Licentiatuppsatser **3360**
Chalmers Tekniska Hoegskola. Vatten Miljoe Transport. Rapport (SWE ISSN 1404-966X) **8819**
Chalmers Tekniska Hoegskole. Institutionen foer Vattenbyggnad. Report. Series B *see* Chalmers Tekniska Hoegskola. Vatten Miljoe Transport. Rapport **8819**
Chalmers University of Technology and Goeteborg University. Department of Computer Science and Engineering. Technical Report. L (SWE ISSN 1652-876X) **2539**
Chalmers University of Technology. Department of Building Technology, Building Materials. Publication *see* Chalmers University of Technology. Department of Civil and Environmental Engineering. Lic **991**
Chalmers University of Technology. Department of Civil and Environmental Engineering. Lic (SWE ISSN 1652-9146) **991**
Chalmers University of Technology. Department of Materials and Manufacturing Technology. Master's Thesis *see* Chalmers Tekniska Hoegskola. Institutionen foer Material- och Tellverkningsteknik. Examensarbete **8418**
Chalmers University of Technology. Department of Sanitary Engineering. Dissertation *see* Chalmers Tekniska Hoegskola. Institutionen foer Vatten Miljoe Transport. Doktorsavhandlingar och Licentiatuppsatser **3360**
Chalmers University of Technology. School of Computer Science and Engineering.Technical report. L *see* Chalmers University of Technology and Goeteborg University. Department of Computer Science and Engineering. Technical Report. L **2539**
Chamber (GBR ISSN 1470-3955) **1398**
Chamber Connect (USA) **1398**
Chamber Executive (USA ISSN 0884-8114) **1398**
Chamber Executive Network (USA ISSN 1070-2342) **1398**
Chamber Insider (USA ISSN 1053-2811) **1398**
• Chamber Jobwatch (USA) **1399**
Chamber Journal (USA ISSN 0897-7917) **1399**
The Chamber L.I.N.C. (Legislative Information Network Community Development) (USA) **1399**
Chamber Music (USA ISSN 1071-1791) **6555**
Chamber Music America Matters *see* C M A Matters **6552**
Chamber Music Directory (USA) **6555**
Chamber News *see* Thai - Chinese Chamber of Commerce. News **1410**
Chamber News (USA) **1399**
Chamber News *see* Business Focus **1397**
Chamber News (Tucson) (USA ISSN 1930-0808) **1399**
Chamber of Commerce *see* ChaCom **1398**
Chamber of Commerce and Industry in West Java. Member List/Kamar Dagang dan Industri di Jawa Barat. Daftar Anggota (IDN) **1399**
Chamber of Commerce and Industry. Trade Journal (PAK) **1399**
Chamber of Commerce of the U S A in Uruguay. Newsletter (URY) **1399**
Chamber of Mines Journal (ZWE ISSN 0009-1162) **6460**
Chamber of Mines' Newsletter (ZAF) **6460**
Chamber of Mines of South Africa. Annual Report (ZAF ISSN 0379-4520) **6460**
• Chamber Online (CAN) **1399**
Chamber Patrika (NPL) **1399**
Chamber Review (USA) **1399**
The Chamber Today (USA ISSN 0279-0785) **1399**
Chamber Update (USA) **1399**
Chamber Vision *see* Chamber Connect **1398**
• The Chamber Voice (USA) **1399**
Chamberlain Chain (USA ISSN 1041-6579) **3762**
Chamberletter (USA) **1399**
Chambers Helping Chambers (USA ISSN 0736-2390) **3762**
Chamber's Trade Directory (PAK) **1979**
ChamberWay Germany-Midwest (USA) **1399**
Chambre de Commerce, d'Agriculture, d'Elevage, d'Industrie et des Mines de la Republique Islamique de Mauritanie. Bulletin (MRT) **1399**
Chambre de Commerce, d'Agriculture, d'Industrie et d'Artisanat du Niger. Weekly Bulletin (NER) **1399**
Chambre de Commerce, d'Agriculture, d'Industrie et des Mines du Gabon. Bulletin (GAB ISSN 0045-6276) **1399**
Chambre de Commerce, d'Agriculture et d'Industrie. Informations Economiques (TCD) **1399**
Chambre de Commerce de Brazzaville. Bulletin Mensuel (COG) **1399**
Chambre de Commerce de Tunis. Bulletin (TUN) **1399**
Chambre de Commerce, d'Industrie et d'Agriculture de Litturi. Bulletin (COD) **1399**
Chambre de Commerce, d'Industrie et d'Agriculture du Kisai. Bulletin (COD) **1399**
Chambre de Commerce, d'Industrie et d'Artisanat du Burkina Faso. Annuaire des Entreprises (BFA) **1399**
Chambre de Commerce, d'Industrie et d'Artisanat. Repertoire National des Entreprises (BFA) **1399**
Chambre de Commerce, d'Industrie et des Mines du Cameroun. Bulletin d'Information (CMR ISSN 0008-2198) **1399**
Chambre de Commerce, d'Industrie et des Mines du Cameroun. Compte-Rendu d'Activites (CMR) **1399**
Chambre de Commerce, d'Industrie et des Mines du Cameroun. Import Export (CMR) **1399**
Chambre de Commerce, d'Industrie et des Mines du Cameroun. Rapport Annuel (CMR ISSN 0069-2530) **6460**
Chambre de Commerce du Quebec. Rapport d'Activites *see* Federation des Chambres de Commerce du Quebec. Rapport Annuel **1402**
C C I. Infos Pratiques (FRA ISSN 1288-7080) **1399**
Chambre de Commerce et d'Industrie d'Anvers. Bulletin (BEL) **1399**

Title

▼ *new title*   † *ceased*   ● *electronic media*   ➤ *refereed*

Title

Title

DIRECTORY 2010 CHINESE HEPATOLOGY 10117

China Quarterly Forecast Report see The China Business Forecast Report 1447
China Railway Science see Zhongguo Tiedao Kexue 8628
China Railway Society. Journal see Tiedao Xuebao 8626
China Real Estate see Zhongguo Fangdichan 7616
China Real Estate News see Zhongguo Fangdichan Bao 7616
China Reflexology Journal see Shuangzu yu Baojian 6073
China Reform News see Zhongguo Gaige Bao 7198
China Religion see Zhongguo Zongjiao 7697
• ➤ China Report (IND ISSN 0009-4455) 7226
• China Report (USA ISSN 1543-9356) 1555
China Resources Comprehensive Utilization see Zhongguo Ziyuan Zonghe Liyong 6337
China Review (GBR ISSN 1359-5091) 3823
China Review see The China Review 3823
• ➤ The China Review (HKG ISSN 1680-2012) 3823
• China Review International (USA ISSN 1069-5834) 3823
China Revista Ilustrada (CHN ISSN 1000-9280) 3823
China Rice see Zhongguo Daomi 276
➤ China Rights Forum (USA ISSN 1068-4166) 7204
China Rubber see Zhongguo Xiangjiao 7100
China Rubber Industry see Xiangjiao Gongye 7827
China Rubber / Plastics Technology & Equipment see Xiangsu Jishu yu Zhuangbei 7100
China Rural Finance see Zhongguo Nongcun Jinrong 1392
China Rural Survey see Zhongguo Nongcun Guancha 209
China - Science & Scholarship (DEU ISSN 1616-1556) 546
China Science & Technology Resources Review see Zhongguo Keji Ziyuan Daokan 5056
China Securities see Zhongguo Zhengquan Bao 1660
• China Security (USA ISSN 1935-5564) 2225
China Seed Industry see Zhongguo Zhongye 260
China Ship News see Zhongguo Chuanbo Bao 8666
China Shipping Gazette see Zhongguo Hangwu Zhoukan 8666
China Shiprepair see Zhongguo Xiuchuan 8666
China Soccer see Zhongguo Zuqiu Bao 8252
China Social News see Zhongguo Shehui Bao 8019
China Society for Scientific and Technical Information. Journal see Qingbao Xuebao 5041
China Society Periodical see Zhongguo Shehui Daokan 8019
▼ The China Society Yearbook (NLD ISSN 1872-7239) 546
China Soft Science see Zhongguo Ruankexue 7934
China Southern Airlines First Class Magazine see Yunzhong Wanglai 8789
China Special Native Products see Zhongguo Techan Bao 1909
• China Sports/Zhongguo Tiyu (CHN ISSN 0577-8948) 8166
China Spring (USA ISSN 0735-8237) 7204
• China Staff (HKG) 1858
China Stamp Catalogue (GBR ISSN 0142-9892) 6893
China State Finance see Zhongguo Caizheng 1955
China Statistical Abstract (USA ISSN 1050-351X) 8363
China Statistical Yearbook (HKG ISSN 1052-9225) 8363
China Statistical Yearbook on Science and Technology see Zhongguo Keji Tongji Nianjian 7939
China Statistics see Zhongguo Tongji 8414
China Statistics Series (USA ISSN 1040-7979) 8363
➤ China Steel Technical Report/Chung Kang Chi Pao (TWN ISSN 1015-6070) 6308
China Studies (NLD ISSN 1570-1344) 4181
China Study Journal (GBR ISSN 0956-4314) 7631
China Study Project Journal see China Study Journal 7631
China Surface Engineering see Zhongguo Biaomian Gongcheng 3228
China Surfactant, Detergent & Cosmetics see Riyong Huaxue Gongye 2244
China Tax Review (HKG) 1917
China Taxation see Zhongguo Shuiwu 1955
• China - Taxation & Investment (NLD) 1917
China Taxation News see Zhongguo Shuiwu Bao 1955
China Telecom see China Telecom Newsletter 2315
• China Telecom Newsletter (USA ISSN 1078-2214) 2315
China Telecommunication Construction News see C T C News 2314
China Telecommunications Construction/Zhongguo Dianxin Jianshe (HKG ISSN 1017-5199) 2366
• China Telecommunications Report (GBR ISSN 1748-4472) 2315
China Terminology see Zhongguo Keji Shuyu 5199
China Textile see Zhongguo Fangzhi 8463
China Textile & Apparel see Zhongguo Fangzhi ji Chengyi 8463
China Textile & Garment Directory (GBR) 1980
China Textile Institute. Journal see Fangzhi Zhongxin Qikan 8450
China Textile Leader see Fangzhi Daobao 8450
• China Textile University. Journal (CHN ISSN 1000-1484) 8449
China Textiles News see Zhongguo Fangzhi Bao 8463
China Three Gorges University. Journal (Humanities & Social Sciences) see Sanxia Daxue Xuebao (Renwen Shehui Kexue Ban) 4474
China Three Gorges University. Journal (Natural Sciences) see Sanxia Daxue Xuebao (Ziran Kexue Ban) 7907
China Tibetology (English Edition) see Zhongguo Zangxue 564
China Tibetology (Tibetan Edition) see Krung-govi Bod-rig-pa 554
China Times see Zhonggo Shibao 3960
China Today see Jinri Zhongguo 3826
China Top Brands see Zhongguo Mingpai 1849
China Tourism see Zhongguo Luyou Zazhi 8777
China Tourism (HKG ISSN 1025-577X) 8693
China Tourism News see Zhongguo Luyou Bao 8777
China Tourism Report (GBR ISSN 1747-8855) 8693
China Tourism Research see Journal of China Tourism Research 8725
China Trade (USA ISSN 1935-083X) 1616
• China Trade Law and Practice (GBR ISSN 1741-9921) 4920
China Trade Link (CHN) 1555
China Trade News see Zhongguo Maoyi Bao 1588
China Trade Report (HKG ISSN 0009-448X) 1555
China Trader Newsletter (USA) 6893
China Tribune/Chung-kuo Lun T'an (TWN) 3960
China Tropical Medicine see Zhongguo Redai Yixue 5736
China TV Guide see Zhongguo Dianshi Bao 2399
• ➤ China University of Geosciences. Journal (CHN ISSN 1002-0705) 2704
China University of Geosciences. Journal (Social Sciences Edition) see Zhongguo Dizhi Daxue Xuebao (Shehui Kexue Ban) 8018
China University of Mining and Technology. Journal see Zhongguo Kuangye Daxue Xuebao 6484
China University of Mining & Technology. Journal (Social Sciences) see Zhongguo Kuangye Daxue Xuebao (Shehui Kexue Ban) 8018
China University of Petroleum. Journal (Natural Science Edition) see Zhongguo Shiyou Daxue Xuebao (Ziran Kexue Ban) 6798
China University of Political Science and Law. Journal see Zhengfa Luntan 4819
China University Teaching see Zhongguo Daxue Jiaoxue 3011
China Urban Finance see Zhongguo Chengshi Jinrong 1198
• China - USA Business Review/Meizhong Jingji Pinglun (USA ISSN 1555-7901) 1555
† • China Watch (USA ISSN 1093-5126) 8941
China Watch Monthly Review see Asiaint's China Watch Monthly Review 1062
China Watch Quarterly Forecasts see Asiaint's China Watch Quarterly Forecasts 1062
China Watch Weekly Briefing see Asiaint's China Watch Weekly Briefing 1062
China Water & Wastewater see Zhongguo Geshui Paishui 3287
China Water Resources News see Zhongguo Shuili Bao 8842
• China Welding (CHN ISSN 1004-5341) 6342
China Welding Institution. Transactions see Hanjie Xuebao 6342
China Well and Rock Salt see Zhongguo Jingkuangyan 6484
China West Normal University. Journal (Natural Science Edition) see Xihua Shifan Xueyuan Xuebao (Ziran Kexue Ban) 7931
China Winter Sports see Bingxue Yundong 8306
China Wireless Communications (HKG ISSN 1025-7004) 2366
China Women's News see Zhongguo Funu Bao 8892
China Women's University. Journal see Zhonghua Nuzi Xueyuan Xuebao 8906
China Wool Facts & Figures (AUS ISSN 1449-1192) 1083
China Youngster News see Zhongguo Shaonian Bao 2224
China Youth see Zhongguo Qingnian 2224
China Youth Study see Zhongguo Qingnian Yanjiu 2173
ChinaContact/Chuang Zhi Guozhong (DEU ISSN 1439-2194) 1555
Chinaero (CHN) 51
Chinafrica (CHN ISSN 1003-0298) 3823
Chinamac Journal/Jixie Zhizao (HKG ISSN 1021-1314) 5450
• ChinaOnline (USA) 1447
China's Customs Statistics (HKG ISSN 0258-3046) 1221
China's Ethnic Groups see Zhongguo Minzu 3573
China's Exports (CHN) 1555
China's External Trade Indices Monthly see Zhongguo Duiwai Maoyi Zhishu 1588
China's Food News see Zhongguo Shipin Bao 3668
• China's Foreign Trade (CHN ISSN 0009-4498) 1555
China's Fruit Trees see Zhongguo Guoshu 172
China's Naturopathy see Zhongguo Minjian Liaofa 316
China's Reform see Zhongguo Gaige 1198
China's Refractories (CHN ISSN 1004-4493) 6308
China's Scholars Abroad see Shenzhou Xueren 3002
China's Talents see Zhonghua Yingcai 3830
China's Tibet see Zhongguo Xizang 3830
China's Top 200 (HKG) 1083
China's Top Two-Hundred see China's Top 200 1083
China's Township Enterprises News see Zhongguo Xiangzhen Qiye 1969
• Chinascope (USA ISSN 1551-9589) 7226
• Chinawire (USA ISSN 1931-1885) 6766
Chinchilla Post (DEU ISSN 0341-5414) 938
Chincoteague Beachcomber (USA) 8693
• La Chine (CHN ISSN 1000-9272) 3823
La Chine au Present see Jinri Zhongguo 3826
• La Chine Libre (USA ISSN 0255-9854) 3527
Chine Plus (FRA ISSN 1954-1376) 1083
Chinese (Taiwan) Yearbook of International Law and Affairs (TWN) 4920
Chinese A V C J see Yazhou Chuangye Touzi Qikan (Zhongwen Ban) 1660
• Chinese Academic Journals Full-Text Database. Agriculture (CHN) 101
• Chinese Academic Journals Full-Text Database. Economics, Politics & Laws (CHN ISSN 1007-807X) 7954
• Chinese Academic Journals Full-Text Database. Education & Social Sciences (CHN) 2836
• Chinese Academic Journals Full-Text Database. Electronic Technology & Information Science (CHN ISSN 1008-6293) 5001
• Chinese Academic Journals Full-Text Database. Literature, History & Philosophy (CHN ISSN 1007-8061) 4447
• Chinese Academic Journals Full-Text Database. Medicine & Hygiene (CHN) 5594
• Chinese Academic Journals Full-Text Database. Science & Engineering, Series A (CHN ISSN 1007-8010) 7845
• Chinese Academic Journals Full-Text Database. Science & Engineering, Series B (CHN ISSN 1007-8029) 7845
• Chinese Academic Journals Full-Text Database. Science & Engineering, Series C (CHN ISSN 1007-8037) 7845
Chinese Academy of Engineering. Annual Report (CHN) 3184
Chinese Academy of Engineering Newsletter see C A E Newsletter 3183
Chinese Academy of Engineering. Yearbook (CHN) 3184
Chinese Academy of Sciences. Bulletin see Zhongguo Kexueyuan Yuankan 7934
Chinese Academy of Sciences. Bulletin (CHN ISSN 1003-3572) 7845
▼ Chinese Academy of Sciences. Frontiers of Research (SGP ISSN 1793-5733) 7845
Chinese Academy of Social Sciences. Graduate School. Journal see Zhongguo Shehui Kexueyuan Yanjiu Shengyuan Xuebao 8019
The Chinese Academy of Social Sciences Yearbooks: Economy see The China Economy Yearbook 546
The Chinese Academy of Social Sciences Yearbooks: Environment see The China Environment Yearbook 3410
The Chinese Academy of Social Sciences Yearbooks: Legal Development see The China Legal Development Yearbook 546
The Chinese Academy of Social Sciences Yearbooks: Society see The China Society Yearbook 546
Chinese Acupuncture & Moxibustion see Zhongguo Zhenjiu 316
Chinese Agricultural Abstracts - Agricultural Engineering see Zhongguo Nongye Wenzhai - Nongye Gongcheng 190
• ➤ Chinese America, History and Perspectives (USA ISSN 1051-7642) 3527
• Chinese American Forum (USA ISSN 0895-4690) 3527
Chinese and Foreign Fairy Tales Pictorial see Zhongwai Tonghua Huakan 2224
Chinese and Foreign Literature see Zhongwai Wenxue 5405
Chinese and Foreign Military Films and T V Programme see Zhongwai Junshi Yingshi 6517
Chinese and Foreign Stories see Zhongwai Gushi 5405
Chinese and International Philosophy of Medicine see International Journal of Chinese & Comparative Philosophy 5637
Chinese and Oriental Studies see Shukan Toyogaku 560
Chinese & Overseas T V Monthly see Zhongwai Dianshi Yuekan 9000
Chinese Annals of Mathematics. Series A see Shuxue Niankan (A Ji) 5535
• ➤ Chinese Annals of Mathematics. Series B (DEU ISSN 0252-9599) 5478
Chinese Antituberculosis Association. Bulletin see Zhongguo Fanglao Tongxun 6221
Chinese Architecture/Zhongguo Jianzhu (CHN) 437
Chinese Archives of Otolaryngology Head and Neck Surgery see Zhongguo Er-Bi-Yanhou-Tou-Jing Waike 6086
Chinese Archives of Traditional Chinese Medicine see Zhonghua Zhongyiyao Xuekan 5738
Chinese Art see Zhongguo Yishu 528
Chinese Association of Professionals in Science and Technology Journal see C A P S T Journal 3524
• ➤ Chinese Astronomy and Astrophysics (GBR ISSN 0275-1062) 573
Chinese Battery Industry see Dianchi Gongye 3156
Chinese Biodiversity see Shengwu Duoyangxing 704
Chinese Biological Abstracts see Zhongguo Shengwuxue Wenzhai 720
Chinese Breath Exercise see Zhonghua Yangsheng Baojian 7001
Chinese Bulletin of Life Sciences see Shengming Kexue 704
Chinese Business Journal (USA) 1447
• Chinese Business Review (USA ISSN 1537-1506) 1555
Chinese Business View see Huashangbao 1119
Chinese Cadres Tribune see Zhongguo Dangzheng Ganbu Luntan 7198
Chinese Calligraphy see Shufa 517
Chinese Calligraphy see Zhongguo Shufa 528
Chinese - Canadian Magazine (CAN ISSN 0837-3280) 3527
Chinese Ceramic Society. Journal see Guisuanyan Xuebao 2116
Chinese Ceramics see Zhongguo Taoci 2047
Chinese Cereals and Oils Association. Journal see Zhongguo Liangyou Xuebao 276
Chinese Character Culture see Hanzi Wenhua 4454
• ➤ Chinese Chemical Letters (GBR ISSN 1001-8417) 2058
➤ Chinese Chemical Society. Journal (TWN ISSN 0009-4536) 2058
Chinese Chess Studies see Xiangqi Yanjiu 8217
Chinese Children's Pictorial see Zhongguo Ertong Huabao 2173
Chinese Clinical Oncology see Linchuang Zhongliuxue Zazhi 6026
Chinese Colloid and Interface Society. Journal see Jiemian Kexue Huizhi 3248
Chinese Commodity Economics see Zhongguo Wuzi Jingji 1198
Chinese Community Doctors see Zhongguo Shequ Yishi 5736
Chinese Condiment see Zhongguo Tiaoweipin 3668
Chinese Consulting Engineers see Zhongguo Gongcheng Zixun 3228
• Chinese Control Conference (USA ISSN 1934-1768) 3297
Chinese Cookery see Zhongguo Pengren 4369
Chinese Criminal Science see Zhongguo Xingshifa Zazhi 2672
Chinese Critical Care Medicine see Zhongguo Weizhongbing Jijiu Yixue 5736
Chinese Cultural World see Huaren Wenhua Shijie 3825
Chinese Culture Association, Magazine (USA) 3527
Chinese Culture Quarterly see Jiuzhou Xuelin 4459
Chinese Culture Research see Zhongguo Wenhua Yanjiu 4483
Chinese Dental Journal (TWN) 5837
Chinese Economic Association Proceedings (AUS) 1592
Chinese Economic Information see Zhongguo Jingji Xinxi 1198
Chinese Economic Monthly (HKG) 1083
Chinese Economic Review/Chung-kuo Ching Chi P'ing Lun (TWN) 1083
• ➤ The Chinese Economy (USA ISSN 1097-1475) 1083
• ➤ Chinese Education and Society (USA ISSN 1061-1932) 2836
Chinese Education Daily see Zhongguo Jiaoyu Bao 2928
Chinese Electron Microscopy Society. Journal see Dianzi Xianwei Xuebao 7010
Chinese Electrotechnical Society. Transactions see Diangong Jishu Xuebao 3300
Chinese Entrepreneur see Zhongguo Qiyejia 1969
† ➤ Chinese Environmental Science (CHN ISSN 1003-1189) 8941
Chinese Fastener & Wire (TWN) 1053
Chinese Film Market (CHN) 6492
Chinese Fisheries see Zhongguo Shuichan 3612
Chinese Fisheries Abstracts see Zhongguo Shuichan Wenzhai 3614
Chinese Fisheries Abstracts (Chinese Edition) (CHN) 3613
Chinese Fishery Abstracts (English Edition) (CHN) 3613
Chinese Flowers - Potted Landscape see Zhongguo Huahui Penjing 3754
Chinese Folk Culture (CHN) 5273
Chinese for Affirmative Action Update see C A A Update 3524
Chinese Foreign Affairs see Zhongguo Waijiao 7276
Chinese Forestry Science and Technology (CHN ISSN 1671-492X) 3686
Chinese Forestry Selected Abstracts see Chinese Forestry Science and Technology 3686
Chinese Four Treasures of the Study see Zhongguo Wenfang Sibao 1855
Chinese General Practice see Zhongguo Quanke Yixue 5736
• ➤ Chinese Geographical Science/Zhongguo Dili Kexue (CHN ISSN 1002-0063) 2729
Chinese Geophysical Scoiety. Journal see Applied Geophysics 2777
• ➤ The Chinese - German Journal of Clinical Oncology (DEU ISSN 1610-1979) 5594
Chinese Green Times see Zhongguo Luse Shibao 3476
Chinese Health Care see Zhongguo Baojian 7546
Chinese Health Resources see Zhongguo Weisheng Ziyuan 7547
Chinese Heart Journal see Xinzang Zazhi 5802
Chinese Hepatology see Ganzang 5924

▼ new title † ceased • electronic media ➤ refereed

Title

Chinese High Technology Letters *see* Gaojishu Tongxun **8422**
Chinese Historians *see* The Chinese Historical Review **546**
Chinese Historians in the United States, Inc. Newsletter *see* C H U S Newsletter **545**
The Chinese Historical Review (USA ISSN 1547-402X) **546**
Chinese Historical Society of America. Bulletin (USA ISSN 0577-9065) **3527**
Chinese Hospital Management *see* Zhongguo Yiyuan Guanli **4113**
Chinese Hospitals *see* Zhongguo Yiyuan **4113**
Chinese Imaging Journal of Integrated Traditional and Western Medicine *see* Zhongguo Zhong-xiyi Jiehe Yingxiangxue Zazhi **5737**
Chinese Industry & Commerce News *see* Zhongguo Gongshang Bao **1434**
Chinese Information Processing *see* Zhongwen Xinxi **5056**
Chinese Inorganic Analytical Chemistry Abstracts *see* Zhongguo Wuji Fenxi Huaxue Wenzhai **2096**
Chinese Institute of Chemical Engineers. Journal *see* Taiwan Institute of Chemical Engineers. Journal **3256**
Chinese Institute of Civil and Hydraulic Engineering. Journal *see* Zhongguo Tumu Shuili Gongcheng Xuekan **3288**
Chinese Institute of Engineers. Journal *see* Zhongguo Gongcheng Xuekan **3228**
Chinese Institute of Engineers Newsletter *see* C I E Newsletter **3183**
Chinese Institute of Engineers. Transactions. Series E *see* International Journal of Electrical Engineering **3320**
Chinese Institute of Food Science and Technology. Journal *see* Zhongguo Shipin Xuebao **3668**
Chinese Institute of Industrial Engineers. Journal *see* Gongye Gongcheng Xuekan **3367**
Chinese Internal Combustion Engine Engineering *see* Neiranji Gongcheng **3355**
Chinese International Times *see* Zhongguo Yinjin Shibao **9000**
Chinese, Japanese, Korean Library of Congress. Books C J K *see* U.S. Library of Congress. Books C J K **637**
Chinese Journal for Health of Women in Childbirth *see* Zhongguo Shengyu Jiankang Zazhi **973**
• ➤ Chinese Journal of Acoustics (CHN ISSN 0217-9776) **7087**
Chinese Journal of Acoustics *see* Shengxue Xuebao **7089**
➤ Chinese Journal of Administration (TWN ISSN 0009-4579) **7430**
• Chinese Journal of Aeronautics (CHN ISSN 1000-9361) **51**
Chinese Journal of Aerospace Medicine *see* Zhonghua Hangkong Hangtian Yixue Zazhi **5738**
Chinese Journal of Aesthetic and Plastic Surgery *see* Zhongguo Meirong Zhengxing Waike Zazhi **6263**
Chinese Journal of Aesthetic Medicine *see* Zhongguo Meirong Yixue **5736**
• Chinese Journal of Agricultural Biotechnology (GBR ISSN 1479-2362) **101**
Chinese Journal of Agrometeorology *see* Zhongguo Nongye Qixiang **6400**
Chinese Journal of AIDS & STD *see* Zhongguo Aizibing Xingbing **5828**
Chinese Journal of Allergy & Clinical Immunology *see* Zhonghua Linchuang Mianyi he Biantai Fanying Zazhi **5767**
Chinese Journal of Analysis Laboratory *see* Fenxi Shiyanshi **7012**
Chinese Journal of Analytical Chemistry *see* Fenxi Huaxue **2100**
Chinese Journal of Anatomy *see* Jiepouxue Zazhi **680**
Chinese Journal of Andrology *see* Zhongguo Nankexue Zazhi **6285**
Chinese Journal of Anesthesiology *see* Zhonghua Mazuixue Zazhi **5775**
Chinese Journal of Animal Quarantine *see* Zhongguo Dongwu Jianyi **8815**
Chinese Journal of Animal Science *see* Zhongguo Xumu Zazhi **305**
Chinese Journal of Antibiotics *see* Zhongguo Kangshengsu Zazhi **6887**
Chinese Journal of Applied & Environmental Biology *see* Yingyong Yu Huanjing Shengwu Xuebao **711**
Chinese Journal of Applied Chemistry *see* Yingyong Huaxue **2084**
Chinese Journal of Applied Ecology *see* Yingyong Shengtai Xuebao **3476**
Chinese Journal of Applied Mathematics *see* Acta Mathematicae Applicatae Sinica **5465**
Chinese Journal of Applied Physiology *see* Zhongguo Yingyong Shenglixue Zazhi **929**
Chinese Journal of Applied Probability and Statistics *see* Yingyong Gailu Tongji **5547**
Chinese Journal of Arteriosclerosis *see* Zhongguo Dongmai Yinghua Zazhi **5735**
Chinese Journal of Astronomy and Astrophysics *see* Research in Astronomy and Astrophysics **580**
Chinese Journal of Atmospheric Science *see* Daiqi Kexue **6351**
• ➤ Chinese Journal of Atmospheric Sciences (USA ISSN 0891-3862) **6349**
Chinese Journal of Bases and Clinics in General Surgery *see* Zhongguo Pu-wai Jichu yu Linchuang Zazhi **6263**
Chinese Journal of Biochemistry and Molecular Biology *see* Zhongguo Shengwu Huaxue yu Fenzi Shengwu Xuebao **746**
Chinese Journal of Biological Control *see* Zhongguo Shengwu Fangzhi **712**
Chinese Journal of Biologicals *see* Zhongguo Shengwuzhipinxue Zazhi **712**
• Chinese Journal of Biomedical Engineering (CHN ISSN 1004-0552) **748**
➤ Chinese Journal of Bioprocess Engineering (CHN ISSN 1672-3678) **762**
Chinese Journal of Biotechnology *see* Shengwu Gongcheng Xuebao **770**
Chinese Journal of Blood Purification *see* Zhongguo Xueye Jinghua **5942**
Chinese Journal of Bone and Joint Injury *see* Zhongguo Gu yu Guanjie Sunshang Zazhi **6075**
Chinese Journal of Burns *see* Zhonghua Shaoshang Zazhi **5883**
Chinese Journal of Burns, Wounds & Surface Ulcers *see* Zhongguo Shaoshang Chuangshang Zazhi **6076**
Chinese Journal of Cancer *see* Aizheng **6007**
• Chinese Journal of Cancer (USA ISSN 1944-446X) **6015**
Chinese Journal of Cancer Biotherapy *see* Zhongguo Zhongliu Shengwu Zhiliao Zazhi **6037**
Chinese Journal of Cancer Prevention and Treatment *see* Zhonghua Zhongliu Fangzhi Zazhi **6037**
• ➤ Chinese Journal of Cancer Research/Zhongguo Aizheng Yanjiu (CHN ISSN 1000-9604) **6015**
Chinese Journal of Cardiac Pacing and Electrophysiology *see* Zhongguo Xinzang Qibo yu Xindian Shengli Zazhi **5802**
Chinese Journal of Cardiology *see* Zhonghua Xin-Xueguanbing Zazhi **5802**
Chinese Journal of Cardiovascular Rehabilition Medicine *see* Xinxueguan Kangfu Yixue Zazhi **5802**
Chinese Journal of Cardiovascular Review *see* Zhongguo Xinxueguanbing Yanjiu **5802**
Chinese Journal of Cerebrovascular Diseases *see* Zhongguo Naoxueguanbing Zazhi **5802**
Chinese Journal of Chemical Education *see* Huaxue Jiaoyu **2063**
• ➤ Chinese Journal of Chemical Engineering (CHN ISSN 1004-9541) **3241**
• Chinese Journal of Chemical Physics (GBR ISSN 1674-0068) **7008**
• ➤ Chinese Journal of Chemistry (CHN ISSN 1001-604X) **2058**
Chinese Journal of Child Health Care *see* Zhongguo Ertong Baojian Zazhi **6105**
Chinese Journal of Chromatography *see* Sepu **7084**
• Chinese Journal of Clinic and Hygiene (USA ISSN 1540-7632) **5594**
Chinese Journal of Clinical Anatomy *see* Zhongguo Linchuang Jiepouxue Zazhi **928**
Chinese Journal of Clinical Gastroenterology *see* Linchuang Xiaohuabing Zazhi **5928**
Chinese Journal of Clinical Hepatology *see* Linchuang Gandanbing Zazhi **5928**
Chinese Journal of Clinical Medicine *see* Zhongguo Linchuang Yixue **5736**
Chinese Journal of Clinical Neurosciences *see* Zhongguo Linchuang Shenjing Kexue **6191**
Chinese Journal of Clinical Nutrition *see* Zhongguo Linchuang Yingyang Zazhi **6671**
Chinese Journal of Clinical Obstetrics and Gynecology *see* Zhongguo Fuchanke Linchuang Zazhi **6006**
• Chinese Journal of Clinical Oncology (CHN ISSN 1672-7118) **6015**
The Chinese Journal of Clinical Pharmacology *see* Zhongguo Linchuang Yaolixue Zazhi **6887**
Chinese Journal of Clinical Pharmacology and Therapeutics *see* Zhongguo Linchuang Yaolixue yu Zhiliaoxue **6887**
Chinese Journal of Clinical Pharmacy *see* Zhongguo Linchuang Yaoxue Zazhi **6887**
Chinese Journal of Clinical Psychology *see* Zhongguo Linchuang Xinlixue Zazhi **6191**
Chinese Journal of Coal Industry Medicine *see* Zhongguo Meitan Gongye Yixue Zazhi **5736**
• ➤ Chinese Journal of Coffee Research (USA ISSN 1095-2799) **3631**
Chinese Journal of Coffee Research for Southerners *see* Chinese Journal of Coffee Research **3631**
Chinese Journal of Colo-Proctology *see* Zhongguo Gangchangbing Zazhi **5932**
▼ • ➤ Chinese Journal of Communication (GBR ISSN 1754-4750) **2315**
Chinese Journal of Computational Mechanics *see* Jisuan Lixue Xuebao **2428**
Chinese Journal of Computational Physics *see* Jisuan Wuli **7019**
Chinese Journal of Computers *see* Jisuanji Xuebao **2468**
Chinese Journal of Conservative Dentistry *see* Yati Yasui Yazhoubingxue Zazhi **5869**
➤ Chinese Journal of Contemporary Mathematics (USA ISSN 0898-5111) **5478**
Chinese Journal of Contemporary Pediatrics *see* Zhongguo Dangdai Erke Zazhi **6105**
Chinese Journal of Control of Endemic Diseases *see* Zhongguo Difangbing Fangzhi Zazhi **5735**
Chinese Journal of Critical Care Medicine *see* Zhongguo Jijiu Yixue **5736**
Chinese Journal of Current Advances in General Surgery *see* Zhongguo Xiandai Putong Waike Jinzhan **6263**
Chinese Journal of Current Clinical Medicine *see* Zhonghua Xiandai Linchuang Yixue Zazhi **5738**
Chinese Journal of Dental Materials and Devices *see* Kouqiang Cailiao Qixie Zazhi **5854**
The Chinese Journal of Dental Research (GBR ISSN 1462-6446) **5837**
Chinese Journal of Dentistry *see* Chunghua Yaihsueh Tsachih **5837**
Chinese Journal of Dermatology *see* Zhonghua Pifuke Zazhi **5883**
Chinese Journal of Dermatovenereology *see* Zhongguo Pifu Xingbingxue Zazhi **5883**
Chinese Journal of Dermatovenerology of Integrated Traditional and Western Medicine *see* Zhongguo Zhongxiyi Jiehe Pifu Xingbingxue Zazhi **5883**
Chinese Journal of Diabetes *see* Zhongguo Tangniaobing Zazhi **5901**
Chinese Journal of Difficult and Complicated Cases *see* Yinanbing Zazhi **5733**
Chinese Journal of Digestion *see* Zhonghua Xiaohua Zazhi **5933**
Chinese Journal of Digestive Diseases *see* Journal of Digestive Diseases (Print) **5927**
Chinese Journal of Digestive Diseases Online *see* Journal of Digestive Diseases (Online) **5927**
Chinese Journal of Digestive Endoscopy *see* Zhonghua Xiaohua Neijing Zazhi **5901**
Chinese Journal of Digestive Surgery *see* Zhonghua Xiaohua Waike Zazhi **5933**
Chinese Journal of Disease Control & Prevention *see* Zhonghua Jibing Kongzhi Zazhi **5829**
Chinese Journal of Disinfection Science *see* Zhongguo Xiaoduxue Zazhi **5737**
Chinese Journal of Drug Abuse Prevention and Treatment *see* Zhongguo Yaowu Lanyong Fangzhi Zazhi **2700**
Chinese Journal of Drug Application and Monitoring *see* Zhongguo Yaowu Yingyong yu Jiance **6887**
Chinese Journal of Drug Dependence *see* Zhongguo Yaowu Yilaixing Zazhi **2700**
Chinese Journal of Eco-Agriculture *see* Zhongguo Shengtai Nongye Xuebao **173**
Chinese Journal of Ecology *see* Shengtaixue Zazhi **3466**
Chinese Journal of Electron Devices *see* Dianzi Qijian **3092**
• Chinese Journal of Electronics (CHN ISSN 1022-4653) **3090**
Chinese Journal of Emergency Medicine *see* Zhonghua Jizhen Yixue Zazhi **6076**
Chinese Journal of Endemiology *see* Zhongguo Difangbingxue Zazhi **5736**
Chinese Journal of Endocrinology and Metabolism *see* Zhonghua Neifenmi Daixie Zazhi **5901**
Chinese Journal of Engineering Mathematics *see* Gongcheng Shuxue Xuebao **3194**
Chinese Journal of Entomology/Zhonghua Kunchong (TWN ISSN 0258-462X) **842**
Chinese Journal of Entomology. Special Publication *see* Chinese Journal of Entomology **842**
Chinese Journal of Environmental Science *see* Huanjing Kexue **3437**
Chinese Journal of Epidemiology *see* Zhonghua Liuxingbingxue Zazhi **5738**
Chinese Journal of Ergonomics *see* Renlei Gongxiaoxue **927**
Chinese Journal of Ethnomedicine and Ethnopharmacy *see* Zhongguo Minzu Yiyao Zazhi **5736**
Chinese Journal of European Studies *see* Ouzhou Yanjiu **7990**
Chinese Journal of Evidence-Based Medicine *see* Zhongguo Xunzheng Yixue Zazhi **5737**
Chinese Journal of Experimental and Clinical Virology *see* Zhonghua Shiyan he Linchuang Bingduxue Zazhi **5829**
Chinese Journal of Experimental Traditional Medical Formulae *see* Zhongguo Shiyan Fangjixue Zazhi **6887**
• Chinese Journal of Explosives & Propellants (CHN ISSN 1007-7812) **3241**
Chinese Journal of Family Planning *see* Zhongguo Jihua Zhengyuxue Zazhi **973**
Chinese Journal of Forensic Medicine *see* Zhongguo Fayixue Zazhi **5917**
Chinese Journal of Forensic Sciences *see* Zhongguo Sifa Jianding **5917**
Chinese Journal of Gastroenterology *see* Weichangbingxue **5932**
Chinese Journal of Gastroenterology *see* Taiwan Xiaohua Xiyi Xuehui Zazhi **5931**
Chinese Journal of Gastroenterology and Hepatology *see* Weichangbingxue he Ganbingxue Zazhi **5932**
Chinese Journal of Gastrointestinal Surgery *see* Zhonghua Wei-chang Waike Zazhi **6264**
Chinese Journal of General Practitioners *see* Zhonghua Quanke Yishi Zazhi **5738**
Chinese Journal of General Surgery *see* Zhongguo Putong Waike Zazhi **6263**
Chinese Journal of General Surgery *see* Zhonghua Putong Waike Zazhi **5738**
• ➤ Chinese Journal of Geochemistry (CHN ISSN 1000-9426) **2729**
Chinese Journal of Geophysics *see* Diqiu Wuli Xuebao **2779**
• ➤ Chinese Journal of Geophysics (Online Edition) (CHN) **2779**
Chinese Journal of Geotechnical Engineering *see* Yantu Gongcheng Xuebao **3287**
Chinese Journal of Geriatric Dentistry *see* Zhonghua Laonian Kouqiang Yixue Zazhi **5870**
Chinese Journal of Geriatric Heart Bratn and Vessel Diseases *see* Zhonghua Laonian Xin-Nao-Xueguanbing Zazhi **5802**
Chinese Journal of Geriatrics *see* Zhonghua Laonian Yixue Zazhi **4058**
Chinese Journal of Gerontology *see* Zhongguo Laonianxue Zazhi **4058**
Chinese Journal of Grassland *see* Zhongguo Caodi Xuebao **260**
Chinese Journal of Hand Surgery *see* Zhonghua Shouwaike Zazhi **6264**
Chinese Journal of Health Care and Medicine *see* Zhonghua Baojian Yixue Zazhi **5738**
Chinese Journal of Health Laboratory Technology *see* Zhongguo Weisheng Jianyan **5912**
Chinese Journal of Health Statistics *see* Zhongguo Weisheng Tongji **7002**
Chinese Journal of Hematology *see* Zhonghua Xueyexue Zazhi **5942**
Chinese Journal of Hepatobiliary Surgery *see* Zhonghua Gandan Waike Zazhi **6263**
Chinese Journal of Hepatology *see* Zhonghua Ganzangbing Zazhi **5949**
Chinese Journal of High Pressure Physics *see* Gaoya Wuli Xuebao **7059**
Chinese Journal of Hospital Administration *see* Zhonghua Yiyuan Guanli Zazhi **4113**
Chinese Journal of Hospital Pharmacy *see* Zhongguo Yiyuan Yaoxue Zazhi **6888**
Chinese Journal of Hypertension *see* Gaoxueya Zazhi **5787**
Chinese Journal of Immunology *see* Zhongguo Mianyixue Zazhi **5767**
Chinese Journal of Industrial Hygiene and Occupational Diseases *see* Zhonghua Laodong Weisheng Zhiyebing Zazhi **6689**
Chinese Journal of Industrial Medicine *see* Zhongguo Gongye Yixue Zazhi **6689**
Chinese Journal of Infection and Chemotherapy *see* Zhongguo Ganran Kongzhi Zazhi **5829**
Chinese Journal of Infectious Diseases *see* Zhonghua Chuanranbing Zazhi **5738**
Chinese Journal of Information on Traditional Chinese Medicine *see* Zhongguo Zhongyiyao Xinxi Zazhi **5738**
Chinese Journal of Inorganic Chemistry *see* Wuji Huaxue Xuebao **2119**
• ➤ Chinese Journal of Integrated Medicine (CHN ISSN 1672-0415) **5594**
Chinese Journal of Integrated Traditional and Western Medicine *see* Zhongguo Zhong-Xiyi Jiehe Zazhi **5737**
Chinese Journal of Integrated Traditional and Western Medicine on Digestion *see* Zhongguo Zhong-Xiyi Jiehe Xiaohua Zazhi **5932**
Chinese Journal of Integrated Traditional and Western Medicine on Liver Disease *see* Zhongxiyi Jiehe Ganbing Zazhi **5901**
Chinese Journal of Integrated Traditional and Western Nephrology *see* Zhongguo Zhong-Xiyi Jiehe Shenbing Zazhi **5737**
Chinese Journal of Integrated Traditional Chinese and Western in Intensive and Critical Care *see* Zhongguo Zhong-Xiyi Jiehe Jijiu Zazhi **5737**
Chinese Journal of Internal Medicine *see* Zhonghua Neike Zazhi **5949**
• ➤ Chinese Journal of International Law (GBR ISSN 1540-1650) **4920**
• ➤ Chinese Journal of International Politics (GBR ISSN 1750-8916) **7226**
Chinese Journal of Interventional Imaging and Therapy *see* Zhongguo Jieru Yingxiang yu Zhiliaoxue **6210**
Chinese Journal of Laboratory Medicine *see* Zhonghua Jianyan Yixue Zazhi **5912**
Chinese Journal of Laser Medicine & Surgery *see* Zhongguo Jiguang Yixue Zazhi **5736**
Chinese Journal of Lasers *see* Zhongguo Jiguang **7085**
Chinese Journal of Lasers *see* Chinese Optics Letters **7074**
• Chinese Journal of Library and Information Science (CHN) **5001**
Chinese Journal of Liquid Crystal and Displays *see* Yejing yu Xianshi **7085**
Chinese Journal of Low Temperature Physics *see* Diwen Wuli Xuebao **7054**
Chinese Journal of Luminescence *see* Faguang Xuebao **7075**
Chinese Journal of Lung Cancer *see* Zhongguo Feiyan Zazhi **6221**
Chinese Journal of Magnetic Resonance *see* Bopuxue Zazhi **7074**
Chinese Journal of Management *see* Guanli Xuebao **1749**
Chinese Journal of Management Science *see* Zhongguo Guanli Kexue **1803**
Chinese Journal of Marine Drugs *see* Zhongguo Haiyang Yaowu Zazhi **6887**
Chinese Journal of Materials Research *see* Cailiao Yanjiu Xuebao **6307**
Chinese Journal of Materials Science *see* Cailiao Kexue **6307**
• ➤ Chinese Journal of Mechanical Engineering (CHN ISSN 1000-9345) **3375**

▼ new title   † ceased   ● electronic media   ➤ refereed

Title

DIRECTORY 2010 CHRISTIAN EAR 10121

Chocolaterie (French Edition) (BEL ISSN 1783-8525) **3673**
Chocolaterie & Confiserie (Dutch Edition) *see* Chocolaterie (French Edition) **3673**
Chocolaterie et Confiserie (French Edition) *see* Chocolaterie (French Edition) **3673**
Chocolatier *see* Dessert Professional **3673**
Choconut Foundation Newsletter (USA) **8309**
➤ Chocs (FRA ISSN 1157-741X) **3166**
Choctaw Community News (USA) **3527**
Chodendo Energi Chozo Kenkyukai/Superconducting Magnetic Energy Storage (JPN) **7065**
Chodendo Energi Chozo Kenkyukai Kenkyu Hokokusho/Research Association of Superconducting Magnetic Energy Storage. Research Report (JPN) **7065**
Chodendo Kagaku Kenkyu Senta Hokoku/Research Institute of Superconductivity. Annual Report (JPN ISSN 1340-3818) **7065**
Choi Nenpo/Yearbook of Tidal Records (JPN) **2801**
• Choice (AUS ISSN 0009-496X) **2635**
• Choice! (AUS ISSN 1832-6536) **2836**
Choice (GBR ISSN 0262-2270) **4043**
Choice *see* Epilogi **1338**
Choice *see* Xuanze **2642**
• ➤ Choice (USA ISSN 0009-4978) **7558**
Choice (USA) **1858**
Choice (Chula Vista) (USA) **6015**
• Choice Computer (AUS) **2575**
Choice Health Reader (AUS ISSN 1324-8065) **6983**
Choice Magazine Listening (USA) **4080**
Choice Models for Buyers Behavior *see* Research in Marketing **1840**
• Choice Reviews on Cards (USA) **7558**
Choice Reviews Online *see* ChoiceReviews.online **7558**
• ChoiceReviews.online (USA ISSN 1523-8253) **7558**
Choices (AUS ISSN 1833-3524) **4073**
• Choices (CAN ISSN 0711-0677) **7115**
• Choices (DEU) **6492**
• Choices (Ames) (USA ISSN 0886-5558) **195**
• Choices (London) (BEL ISSN 1027-7412) **7279**
• Choices: A Core Collection for Young Reluctant Readers (USA ISSN 0735-6358) **2182**
• Choices for Young Readers. Library-Teacher Professional Edition (USA ISSN 1089-8018) **2149**
• Choices for Young Readers. Parent-Home Edition (USA ISSN 1089-8026) **2149**
Choices Magazine (USA) **3972**
• Choir & Organ (GBR ISSN 0968-7262) **6555**
Choisir (CHE ISSN 0009-4994) **7631**
• Choix (CAN ISSN 0711-0685) **7115**
Choju Kagaku Shinko Zaidan. Nyuzureta (JPN) **4043**
Choju Kankei Tokei/Annual Statistics of Birds and Animals (JPN) **714**
Chokehold (USA) **8166**
Choken Field/Study of Butterfly (JPN ISSN 0913-8323) **842**
† Chokolade og Konfekture (DNK ISSN 1601-863X) **8941**
Chole-Doc (FRA ISSN 1639-2558) **6656**
Chomusik (UKR) **6555**
• Chonai Saikingaku Zasshi/Journal of Intestinal Microbiology (JPN ISSN 1343-0882) **784**
Chongbo Kwahak Hoechi/Korea Information Science Society Review (KOR ISSN 1015-9908) **2542**
Chonghap Mulka Chongbo/Monthly Commodity Price News Service (KOR) **1327**
Chongi ui Segye/Korean Institute of Electrical Engineers. Proceedings (KOR ISSN 1598-4613) **3297**
Chongqing Daxue Xuebao *see* Chongqing Daxue Xuebao (Ziran Kexue Ban) **7846**
• Chongqing Daxue Xuebao (Shehui Kexue Ban)/Chongqing University. Journal (Social Sciences Edition) (CHN ISSN 1008-5831) **7954**
• Chongqing Daxue Xuebao (Ziran Kexue Ban)/Chongqing University. Journal (Natural Science Edition) (CHN) **7846**
Chongqing Environmental Sciences *see* Chongqing Huanjing Kexue **3410**
• Chongqing Gongshang Daxue Xuebao (Shehui Kexue Ban)/Chongqing Technology and Business University. Journal (Social Sciences Edition) (CHN ISSN 1672-0598) **7954**
• Chongqing Gongshang Daxue Xuebao (Ziran Kexue Ban)/Chongqing Technology and Business University. Journal (Natural Sciences Edition) (CHN ISSN 1672-058X) **7846**
• Chongqing Gongxueyuan Xuebao (Ziran Kexue Ban)/Chongqing Institute of Technology. Journal (Natural Science Edition) (CHN ISSN 1671-0924) **7846**
• Chongqing Guangbo Dianshi Daxue Xuebao/Chongqing R T V University. Journal (CHN ISSN 1008-6382) **2357**
• ➤ Chongqing Huanjing Kexue/Chongqing Environmental Sciences (CHN ISSN 1001-2141) **3410**
Chongqing Institute of Posts and Telecommunications. Journal (Natural Science Edition) *see* Chongqing Youdian Daxue Xuebao (Ziran Kexue Ban) **7846**
Chongqing Institute of Technology. Journal (Natural Science Edition) *see* Chongqing Gongxueyuan Xuebao (Ziran Kexue Ban) **7846**
• Chongqing Jianzhu (CHN ISSN 1671-9107) **437**
• Chongqing Jianzhu Daxue Xuebao/Chongqing Jianzhu University. Journal (CHN ISSN 1006-7329) **437**
• Chongqing Jianzhu Daxue Xuebao (Shehui Kexue Ban) (CHN) **7954**
Chongqing Jianzhu University. Journal *see* Chongqing Jianzhu Daxue Xuebao **437**
• Chongqing Jiaotong Daxue Xuebao (Shehui Kexue Ban)/Chongqing Jiaotong University. Journal (Social Sciences Edition) (CHN ISSN 1674-0297) **7115**
• Chongqing Jiaotong Daxue Xuebao (Ziran Kexue Ban)/Chongqing Jiaotong University. Journal (Natural Sciences) (CHN ISSN 1674-0696) **8493**
Chongqing Jiaotong University. Journal (Natural Sciences) *see* Chongqing Jiaotong Daxue Xuebao (Ziran Kexue Ban) **8493**
Chongqing Jiaotong University. Journal (Social Sciences Edition) *see* Chongqing Jiaotong Daxue Xuebao (Shehui Kexue Ban) **7115**
Chongqing Jiaotong Xueyuan Xuebao (Shehui Kexue Ban) *see* Chongqing Jiaotong Daxue Xuebao (Shehui Kexue Ban) **7115**
Chongqing Keji/Chongqing Science and Technology (CHN) **7846**
• Chongqing Keji Xueyuan Xuebao (Shehui Kexue Ban)/Chongqing University of Science and Technology. Journal (Social Sciences Edition) (CHN ISSN 1673-1999) **7954**
• Chongqing Keji Xueyuan Xuebao (Ziran Kexue Ban)/Chongqing University of Science and Technology. Journal (Natural Science Edition) (CHN ISSN 1673-1980) **7846**
Chongqing Medical Journal *see* Chongqing Yixue **5594**
Chongqing Medical University. Journal *see* Chongqing Yike Daxue Xuebao **5594**
Chongqing Nianjian/Chongqing Yearbook (CHN ISSN 1004-8383) **7430**
Chongqing Normal University. Journal (Natural Science Edition) *see* Chongqing Shifan Daxue Xuebao (Ziran Kexue Ban) **7846**
Chongqing Normal University. Journal (Social Sciences Edition) *see* Chongqing Shifan Daxue Xuebao (Zhexue Shehui Kexue Ban) **7954**
Chongqing R T V University. Journal *see* Chongqing Guangbo Dianshi Daxue Xuebao **2357**
• Chongqing Sanxia Xueyuan Xuebao/Chongqing Three Gorges University. Journal (CHN ISSN 1009-8135) **7954**
Chongqing Science and Technology *see* Chongqing Keji **7846**
• Chongqing Shifan Daxue Xuebao (Zhexue Shehui Kexue Ban)/Chongqing Normal University. Journal (Social Sciences Edition) (CHN ISSN 1673-0429) **7954**
• Chongqing Shifan Daxue Xuebao (Ziran Kexue Ban)/Chongqing Normal University. Journal (Natural Science Edition) (CHN ISSN 1672-6693) **7846**
Chongqing Shifan Xueyuan Xuebao (Zhexue Shehui Kexue Ban) *see* Chongqing Shifan Daxue Xuebao (Zhexue Shehui Kexue Ban) **7954**
Chongqing Shifan Xueyuan Xuebao (Ziran Kexue Ban)/Chongqing Teachers College. Journal (Natural Science Edition) *see* Chongqing Shifan Daxue Xuebao (Ziran Kexue Ban) **7846**
Chongqing Shiyou Gaodeng Zhuanke Xuexiao Xuebao/Chongqing Petroleum College. Journal *see* Chongqing Keji Xueyuan Xuebao (Ziran Kexue Ban) **7846**
Chongqing Technology and Business University. Journal (Natural Sciences Edition) *see* Chongqing Gongshang Daxue Xuebao (Ziran Kexue Ban) **7846**
Chongqing Technology and Business University. Journal (Social Sciences Edition) *see* Chongqing Gongshang Daxue Xuebao (Shehui Kexue Ban) **7954**
Chongqing Three Gorges University. Journal *see* Chongqing Sanxia Xueyuan Xuebao **7954**
➤ Chongqing University. Journal (CHN ISSN 1671-8224) **7954**
Chongqing University. Journal (Natural Science Edition) *see* Chongqing Daxue Xuebao (Ziran Kexue Ban) **7846**
Chongqing University. Journal (Social Sciences Edition) *see* Chongqing Daxue Xuebao (Shehui Kexue Ban) **7954**
Chongqing University of Arts and Sciences. Journal *see* Chongqing Wenli Xueyuan Xuebao (Ziran Kexue Ban) **7846**
Chongqing University of Arts and Sciences. Journal (Social Science Edition) *see* Chongqing Wenli Xueyuan Xuebao (Shehui Kexue Ban) **7954**
Chongqing University of Posts and Telecommunications. Journal (Social Science Edition) *see* Chongqing Youdian Daxue Xuebao (Shehui Kexue Ban) **7954**
Chongqing University of Science and Technology. Journal (Natural Science Edition) *see* Chongqing Keji Xueyuan Xuebao (Ziran Kexue Ban) **7846**
Chongqing University of Science and Technology. Journal (Social Sciences Edition) *see* Chongqing Keji Xueyuan Xuebao (Shehui Kexue Ban) **7954**
• Chongqing Wenli Xueyuan Xuebao (Shehui Kexue Ban)/Chongqing University of Arts and Sciences. Journal (Social Science Edition) (CHN ISSN 1673-8004) **7954**
Chongqing Wenli Xueyuan Xuebao (Ziran Kexue Ban)/Chongqing University of Arts and Sciences. Journal (CHN ISSN 1673-8012) **7846**
Chongqing Yearbook *see* Chongqing Nianjian **7430**
• Chongqing Yike Daxue Xuebao/Chongqing Medical University. Journal (CHN ISSN 0253-3626) **5594**
• Chongqing Yixue/Chongqing Medical Journal (CHN ISSN 1671-8348) **5594**
Chongqing Yiyao *see* Chongqing Yixue **5594**
Chongqing Youdian Daxue Xuebao (Shehui Kexue Ban)/Chongqing University of Posts and Telecommunications. Journal (Social Science Edition) (CHN ISSN 1673-8268) **7954**
• Chongqing Youdian Daxue Xuebao (Ziran Kexue Ban)/Chongqing Institute of Posts and Telecommunications. Journal (Natural Science Edition) (CHN) **7846**
Chongqing Youdian Xueyuan Xuebao (Zike Ban) *see* Chongqing Youdian Daxue Xuebao (Ziran Kexue Ban) **7846**
Chongqing Youdian Xueyuan Xuebao (Ziran Kexue Ban) *see* Chongqing Youdian Daxue Xuebao (Ziran Kexue Ban) **7846**
• Chongqing yu Shijie/The World & Chongqing (CHN ISSN 1007-7111) **3823**
Chongwu Shijie - Goumi/Petl Lfe - Dog (CHN) **6806**
Chongwu Shijie - Maomi (CHN) **6806**
• Chongyongnyon (Online) (KOR) **1447**
Chongyongnyon (Print) *see* Chongyongnyon (Online) **1447**
Chono Gengogaku Kenkyu *see* Kominikeisyon Syoigaigaku **6082**
Choonpa Techno/Ultrasonic Technology (JPN ISSN 0916-2410) **7087**
• Choosing a Credit Card (USA) **1327**
Choosing Your Degree Course & University (GBR) **2971**
➤ Chopin Studies (POL ISSN 0239-8567) **6555**
• Chopsticks New York (USA) **3527**
ChopTalk (USA ISSN 1555-1547) **8225**
Chor Aktuell (AUT) **6555**
Choral Director (USA) **6555**
• ➤ Choral Journal (USA ISSN 0009-5028) **6555**
▼ • ➤ The Choral Scholar (USA ISSN 1948-3058) **6555**
Chord Magazine (USA) **6555**
• Choregia (GRC ISSN 1791-4027) **1733**
Choregraphie (ITA ISSN 1125-6230) **2683**
Choreographers Theatre Newsletter *see* C C T Newsletter **2683**
Choreola (ITA ISSN 1121-3027) **2683**
Choreologica (GBR ISSN 1746-5737) **2683**
Choriner Forschungen (DEU ISSN 1436-0489) **7791**
The Chorister (USA ISSN 1948-4976) **6556**
Chorleywood Digest (GBR ISSN 0263-2632) **3631**
Chormagazin (AUT) **6556**
Chornomors'ki Novyny (UKR) **3964**
• ➤ Choroby Serca i Naczyn (POL ISSN 1733-2346) **5782**
Choros (SWE ISSN 0347-8521) **4002**
ChorPfalz (DEU ISSN 1614-2861) **6556**
Der Chorsaenger (DEU ISSN 0172-2255) **6556**
• Chortler (CAN) **5210**
Chorui Hyoshiki Chosa Hokokusho/Bird Migration Research Center. Report (JPN) **905**
Chorus (CAN ISSN 0821-1108) **6556**
Chorus (FRA ISSN 1241-7076) **6556**
Choseki Kansoku/Tidal Observations (JPN) **2801**
Chosekihyo 1. Nihon Oyobi Fukin/Tide Tables 1. Japan and Its Vicinities (JPN ISSN 0910-0458) **2801**
Chosekihyo 2. Taiheiyo Oyobi Indoyo/Tide Tables 2. Pacific and Indian Oceans (JPN ISSN 0910-0466) **2802**
Chosen Gakuho/Academic Association of Koreanology in Japan. Journal (JPN ISSN 0577-9766) **3527**
Chosen Gakujutsu Tsuho/Korean Scientific Information (JPN ISSN 0577-9774) **8446**
Chosen Shogakkai Gakujutsu Ronbunshu/Korean Scholarship Association in Japan. Science Report (JPN ISSN 0287-802X) **5478**
Chosen Words (USA ISSN 1559-4165) **3527**
Chosetsu Koho Niigata/Niigata Investigation and Design Office. News (JPN ISSN 0386-7471) **3360**
• Choson Ilbo/The Korea Daily News (KOR) **3902**
Choson Munhak/Korean Literature (PRK) **5273**
Choson Yesul/Korean Arts (PRK) **481**
Chosun Daily (New York) *see* Choson Ilbo **3902**
Chosun Daily (New York) *see* Korea Daily **3546**
• Chosun Hotel Webzine (KOR) **8782**
Chot Mai Het Thang Phaet *see* Medical Association of Thailand. Journal **5667**
Chouette (BEL ISSN 0774-9740) **5106**
➤ Chouompa Igaku (JPN ISSN 1346-1176) **6193**
Chouompa Kensa Gijutsu/Japanese Journal of Medical Ultrasound Technology (JPN ISSN 1881-4506) **6193**
Choutha Sansar (IND) **3880**
Chovatel (CZE ISSN 0323-1534) **284**
Chow Bydla (POL ISSN 0137-611X) **284**
➤ Chowanna (POL ISSN 0137-706X) **2836**
The Chowhound's Guide to the New York Tristate Area (USA ISSN 1930-5192) **4383**
Chr. Michelsen Institute Brief *see* C M I Brief **7224**
• Chr. Michelsen Institute. Report (NOR ISSN 0805-505X) **7954**
• Chr. Michelsen Institute. Working Paper (NOR ISSN 0804-3639) **7954**
• ➤ Chreods (GBR ISSN 1350-6781) **2836**
Chresis (CHE ISSN 1662-0801) **7631**
Chretienne Sociale Suisse Magazine *see* Le C S S Magazine **4497**
Chretiens de l'Est (FRA ISSN 0252-2578) **7791**
Chretiens et Societes Seizieme-Vingtieme Siecles *see* Chretiens et Societes XVIe-XXe Siecles **8093**
Chretiens et Societes XVIe-XXe Siecles (FRA ISSN 1257-127X) **8093**
Chrimatistirio (GRC) **1447**
Chris (DEU ISSN 1615-1062) **2182**
Chris and Tilde Stuart's Guide to Southern African Game & Nature Reserves (ZAF) **8693**
Chris Dickman's Corel Draw Journal (CAN ISSN 1190-8874) **2483**
Chrischona Magazin *see* Chrischona Panorama **7750**
Chrischona Panorama (CHE) **7750**
Chrism (GBR ISSN 0964-0886) **7631**
• Chrismon (DEU ISSN 1619-6384) **3845**
Christ au Monde *see* Cristo al Mondo **7794**
Christ. Community. Music. *see* C C M Magazine **8938**
Christ. Community. Music. Magazine *see* C C M Magazine **8938**
Christ for the Nations (USA ISSN 0889-8901) **7631**
Christ in der Gegenwart (DEU ISSN 0170-5148) **7792**
Christ in der Gegenwart im Bild (DEU ISSN 1432-4164) **7792**
Christ in Our Home (USA ISSN 0412-2968) **7750**
Christ-Online (DEU) **7750**
Christ to the World *see* Cristo al Mondo **7794**
The Christadelphian (GBR ISSN 0009-5117) **7631**
Christchurch Art Gallery. Bulletin (NZL ISSN 1176-0540) **482**
Christchurch City Council. Annual Financial Statement *see* Christchurch City Council. Annual Report **7489**
• Christchurch City Council. Annual Report (NZL ISSN 1171-3224) **7489**
Christchurch Family Times (NZL ISSN 1176-7944) **2149**
† Christchurch Mail (NZL ISSN 1170-1277) **8941**
The Christchurch Star *see* Star **3919**
Christelijk Pedagogisch Studiecentrum Nieuwsbrief *see* C P S Nieuwsbrief **2833**
De Christen *see* Baptisten.nl **7748**
Christen Democratisch Appel *see* CDA.nl **7114**
Christen Democratische Verkenningen (NLD ISSN 0167-9155) **7116**
Christen Heute (DEU ISSN 0930-5718) **7792**
Christen Vandaag Koers *see* C V - Koers **7629**
Die Christengemeinschaft (DEU ISSN 0009-5184) **7631**
Christenlehre - Religionsunterricht - Praxis *see* Praxis Gemeindepaedagogik **7771**
• Gordon J. Christensen Clinicians Report (USA) **5595**
▼ • Gordon J. Christensen Dental Hygiene Clinicians Report (USA) **5837**
Christentum und Islam *see* Judentum - Christentum - Islam **7657**
Christiaan de Wet Annale (ZAF ISSN 0379-4695) **4174**
Christian Advertising Forum (USA ISSN 0744-4370) **23**
Christian Aid News (GBR ISSN 0263-4023) **7750**
• Christian Apologetics Journal (USA ISSN 1930-9074) **7631**
Christian Association for Psychological Studies, Inc. Report Newsletter *see* C A P S Report Newsletter **7629**
The Christian Baptist (USA ISSN 0746-0171) **7750**
• ➤ Christian Bioethics (GBR ISSN 1380-3603) **5595**
▼ Christian Book Reader (USA) **5273**
Christian Booksellers Association Retailers + Resources *see* C B A Retailers + Resources **7557**
Christian Bookselling Association of Australia Inc. News *see* C B A A News **7557**
Christian Bride (USA ISSN 1532-9569) **5558**
Christian Brothers Ex-Residents and Students Network *see* C B E R S Network **8029**
Christian Camp and Conference Journal *see* Insite (Colorado Springs) **8319**
• The Christian Century (USA ISSN 0009-5281) **7631**
Christian Challenge (USA ISSN 0890-6793) **7750**
Christian Chiropractor (USA) **5804**
Christian Chiropractors Association Journal (USA) **5804**
The Christian Chronicle (USA) **7631**
Christian Civic League Record (USA) **7631**
The Christian Communicator (USA) **7631**
• Christian Computing Magazine (USA ISSN 1063-7672) **2575**
Christian Conference of Asia News *see* C C A News **7629**
Christian Conquest (USA ISSN 0892-9300) **7631**
The Christian Contender (Crockett) (USA) **7631**
Christian Council on Ageing. Occasional Paper (GBR) **7631**
Christian Counseling Today (USA ISSN 1076-9668) **7631**
Christian Courier (CAN ISSN 1192-3415) **7750**
Christian Crusade (USA ISSN 0195-265X) **7631**
Christian Democrat International Info *see* C D - Info **7111**
• Christian Ear (USA ISSN 1931-7107) **7631**

Title

• Chuanmei Guancha/Newsletter (CHN ISSN 1672-3406) **4573**
Chuanqi Gushi/Legend Story (CHN ISSN 1003-5664) **5273**
Chuanqi Wenxue Xuankan/Selected Legendary Literature (CHN ISSN 1003-2738) **5273**
Chuanranbing Xinxi/Infectious Disease Information (CHN ISSN 1007-8134) **5811**
Chuanshan Journal *see* Chuanshan Xuekan **4447**
• Chuanshan Xuekan/Chuanshan Journal (CHN ISSN 1004-7387) **4447**
• Chuban Cankao/Publishing Reference: New Readings (CHN ISSN 1006-5784) **7558**
• ➤ Chuban Faxing Yanjiu/Publishing Research (CHN ISSN 1001-9316) **7558**
Chuban Gongzuo/Publishing Work (CHN ISSN 1009-1645) **7558**
Chuban Guangjiao/A Vast View on Publishing (CHN ISSN 1006-7000) **7558**
Chuban Shiliao/Historical Material on Publishing (CHN) **7558**
• Chuban yu Guanli Yanjiu/Journal of Publishing and Management (TWN ISSN 1814-8859) **7558**
• Chuban yu Yinshua/Publishing & Printing (CHN ISSN 1007-1938) **7558**
Chubanren/China Publishers (CHN ISSN 1673-0119) **7559**
Chubu Byoin Igaku Zasshi/Okinawa Chubu Hospital. Bulletin *see* Okinawa Kenritsu Chubu Byoin Zasshi **5689**
Chubu Daigaku Kogakubu Kiyo *see* Chubu University. College of Engineering. Memoirs **3184**
Chubu Denryoku K.K. Kenkyu Shiryo/Chubu Electric Power Company. Memoirs (JPN ISSN 0387-0057) **3297**
Chubu Denryoku Shinbun/Chubu Electric Power News (JPN) **3297**
Chubu Electric Power Company. Memoirs *see* Chubu Denryoku K.K. Kenkyu Shiryo **3297**
Chubu Electric Power News *see* Chubu Denryoku Shinbun **3297**
Chubu Electronics Center Information *see* C E C Information **3090**
Chubu Geka Gakkai Sokaigo/Chubu Surgical Society. Proceedings of Annual Meeting (JPN) **6239**
Chubu - Nippon Broadcasting Co. Gijutsu Hokokukai *see* C B C Gijutsu Hokokukai **2377**
Chubu Nippon Seikei Geka Saigai Geka Gakkai Shoroku/Central Japan Association of Orthopaedic and Traumatic Surgery. Abstracts (JPN) **5742**
• Chubu Nippon Seikei Geka Saigai Geka Gakkai Zasshi/Central Japan Journal of Orthopaedic Surgery & Traumatology (JPN ISSN 0008-9443) **6057**
Chubu Rheumatism Association. Journal *see* Chubu Ryumachi **6223**
Chubu Ryumachi/Chubu Rheumatism Association. Journal (JPN ISSN 0916-6033) **6223**
Chubu Spider Study Group. Report *see* Kumo **853**
Chubu Surgical Society. Proceedings of Annual Meeting *see* Chubu Geka Gakkai Sokaigo **6239**
Chubu University. College of Business Administration and Information Science. Journal (JPN ISSN 0910-8874) **1083**
Chubu University. College of Engineering. Memoirs/Chubu Daigaku Kogakubu Kiyo (JPN ISSN 0910-8629) **3184**
Chubu University. College of International Studies. Journal (JPN ISSN 0910-8882) **1592**
• Chubu Weekly (JPN) **3900**
Chudeng Jiaoyu Xuebao/Journal of Basic Education (HKG ISSN 1025-1944) **2836**
Chudesa i Priklyucheniya (RUS ISSN 0868-8931) **5441**
Chudoku Kenkyu/Japanese Journal of Toxicology (JPN ISSN 0914-3777) **3495**
Chufeng Folk Literature of Hunan *see* Chu Feng **3615**
Chugoku Bungakuho/Journal of Chinese Literature (JPN ISSN 0578-0934) **3527**
Chugoku Chiho Denryoku Kisho Gaiho/Chugoku District. Report of the Power and Weather (JPN) **6349**
Chugoku District. Report of the Power and Weather *see* Chugoku Chiho Denryoku Kisho Gaiho **6349**
Chugoku Gaho (CHN ISSN 1000-9337) **3823**
Chugoku-Shikoku Orthopaedic Association. Journal *see* Chugoku Shikoku Seikei Geka Gakkai Zasshi **6057**
• Chugoku Shikoku Seikei Geka Gakkai Zasshi/Chugoku-Shikoku Orthopaedic Association. Journal (JPN ISSN 0915-2695) **6057**
Chugoku Soshikibetsu Jinmeibo *see* China Directory (Year) **7430**
Chui Rinsho/Clinical Journal of Traditional Chinese Medicine (JPN ISSN 0389-4843) **308**
Chuidiao (CHN ISSN 1009-7910) **8309**
• Chuki Keizai Yosoku/Five-Year Economic Forecast (JPN ISSN 0287-8119) **1447**
Chukou Shangpin Baozhuang/Export Commodities Packaging (CHN ISSN 1672-4380) **6709**
Chukung (TWN ISSN 1011-6761) **6308**
Chulalongkorn Medical Journal *see* Asian Biomedicine **5579**
Chulalongkorn University. Natural History Journal/Warasan Thammachat Witthaya haeng Chulalongkorn Mahawitthayalai (THA ISSN 1513-9700) **4135**
Ch'ulpan Moonwha/Korean Publishing Journal (KOR ISSN 1227-1985) **7559**
• Chumir Ethics Forum (CAN ISSN 1914-7600) **7116**
CHUN *see* Chinesisch - Unterricht **5106**
Ch'un Ch'iu *see* The Observation Post **509**
† Chun Feng/Spring Breeze (CHN ISSN 1001-621X) **8941**
Chunbish (TJK) **3961**
Chuncheng Evening News *see* Chuncheng Wanbao **3823**
Chuncheng Wanbao/Chuncheng Evening News (CHN) **3823**
• Chuncui Shuxue yu Yingyong Shuxue/Pure and Applied Mathematics (CHN ISSN 1008-5513) **5478**
Chung Cheng Institute of Technology. Journal *see* Chung Cheng Ling Hsueh Pao **8418**
Chung Cheng Ling Hsueh Pao/Chung Cheng Institute of Technology. Journal (TWN ISSN 0255-6030) **8418**
Chung Chi Bulletin (HKG ISSN 0009-6261) **2277**
Chung Hua Chu Wu Pao Hu Hsueh Hui Hui Kan *see* Zhiwu Baohuxuehui Huikan **260**
Chung Hua Min Kuo Chi Ch'i yu Tien Kung Ch'i Ts'ai Nien Chien *see* Taiwan, Republic of China. Machinery and Electrical Apparatus Industry Yearbook **3114**
Chung Hua Min Kuo T'ai-wan Sheng She Hui Shih Yeh T'ung Chi *see* Social Affairs Statistics of Taiwan **8084**
Chung-Hua Nei K'o Tsa Chih *see* Zhonghua Neike Zazhi **5949**
Chung Hua Nung Hsueh Hui Pao *see* Zhonghua Nongxue Huibao **173**
Chung-Hua Yen K'o Tsa Chih *see* Zhonghua Yanke Zazhi **6053**
Chung-Hwa Buddhist Studies *see* Zhonghua Foxue Yanjiu **7703**
Chung Kang Chi Pao *see* China Steel Technical Report **6308**
Chung Kung Yen Chiu/Studies on Chinese Communism (TWN ISSN 1015-9355) **7116**
Chung-Kuo Chi Hsueh Kung Ch'eng Hsueh Pao/Chinese Society of Mechanical Engineers. Journal (TWN ISSN 0257-9731) **3342**
Chung-kuo Ching Chi Chou Kan *see* Economic News Weekly: Business Taiwan **1100**
Chung-kuo Ching Chi P'ing Lun *see* Chinese Economic Review **1083**
Chung-kuo Fo Chiao (TWN) **7701**
Chung-kuo Lun T'an *see* China Tribune **3960**
Chung-kuo Sheng Li Hsueh Tsa Chih *see* Chinese Journal of Physiology **921**
Chung-kuo Yen Ch'ang Wen i Yen Chiu Hui Lun Chi *see* Chinoperl Papers **546**
Chung-kuo Yuwen/Chinese Language Monthly (TWN ISSN 1017-2300) **5106**
Chung-Mei Yueh-K'an *see* West & East **7273**
Chung Shan Hsueh Shu Wen Hua Ch'i K'an *see* Sun Yat-sen Cultural Foundation Bulletin **8008**
• Chung-sso Yon'gu/Sino-Soviet Affairs (KOR ISSN 1012-3563) **7116**
Chung T'ai Wan I Hsueh K'e Hsueh Tsa Chih *see* Zhong-Taiwan Yixue Kexue Zazhi **5735**
➤ Chung-Wai Literary Monthly (TWN ISSN 0303-0849) **5274**
Chung Yang Yen Chiu Yuan. Chin Tai Shih Yen Chiu So Ch'i K'an *see* Academia Sinica. Institute of Modern History. Bulletin **4128**
Chung Yang Yen Chiu Yuan. Shu Hsueh Yen Chiu So T'ung Pao *see* Academia Sinica. Institute of Mathematics. Bulletin. New Series **5464**
Chung Yang Yen Chiu Yuan Wu Li Hsueh Yen Chiu So Nien Pao *see* Academia Sinica. Institute of Physics. Annual Report **7003**
Chungang Journal of Medicine *see* Junnan Nuidaiji **5656**
Chungang Uidae Chi *see* Junnan Nuidaiji **5656**
• Chungara (Arica) (CHL ISSN 0717-7356) **387**
Chunghua Yaihsueh Tsachih/Chinese Journal of Dentistry (TWN) **5837**
Chungkuo Chiaotien *see* Zhongguo Jiaodian **3573**
Chunklet (USA) **6556**
Chunqiu (CHN ISSN 1672-5794) **7116**
Chuo Daigaku. Daigakuin Kenkyu Nenpo/Chuo University. Bulletin of Graduate Studies (JPN ISSN 0288-8750) **3229**
• Chuo Daigaku Rikogaku Kenkyujo Nenpo/Chuo University. Institute of Science and Engineering. Annual Report (JPN ISSN 1341-7304) **7846**
• Chuo Daigaku Rikogaku Kenkyujo Ronbunshu/Journal of the Institute of Science and Engineering, Chuo University (JPN ISSN 1343-0068) **7846**
Chuo Koron/Central Review (JPN ISSN 0529-6838) **3900**
Chuo Law Review/Hogaku Shinpo (JPN ISSN 0009-6296) **4642**
Chuo University. Bulletin of Graduate Studies *see* Chuo Daigaku. Daigakuin Kenkyu Nenpo **3229**
Chuo University. Institute of Science and Engineering. Annual Report *see* Chuo Daigaku Rikogaku Kenkyujo Nenpo **7846**
Chuquisaca Hoy (BOL) **7954**
Church (USA ISSN 0883-5667) **7792**
Church Advocate (USA ISSN 0009-630X) **7734**
Church & Society (USA ISSN 0037-7805) **7751**
Church & State (IRL ISSN 0332-3625) **7116**
• Church & State (USA ISSN 0009-6334) **7633**
Church and Synagogue Libraries *see* Congregational Libraries Today **5003**
Church & Worship Technology (USA ISSN 1531-8206) **7633**
Church Army. Annual Report (GBR) **7751**
Church Army. Share It (GBR) **7751**
The Church Bookstore *see* Christian Retailing **7558**
Church Business *see* Church Solutions **1733**
Church Business. Products & Technology (CAN ISSN 1198-1156) **7633**
Church Educator (USA ISSN 0164-5625) **2836**
Church Executive (USA) **1733**
Church Finance Today (USA) **7633**
Church Guardian (Print) *see* The Anglican Guardian (Online) **7745**
Church Herald (USA ISSN 0009-6393) **7751**
• ➤ Church Heritage (AUS ISSN 0156-224X) **7751**
• ➤ Church History (GBR ISSN 0009-6407) **7633**
• ➤ Church History and Religious Culture (NLD ISSN 1871-241X) **7633**
The Church in History (USA ISSN 1938-8306) **7633**
Church Lads' and Church Girls' Brigade. Annual Report (GBR ISSN 0045-2831) **7751**
Church Law and Tax Report *see* Church Law & Tax Report **7633**
• Church Law & Tax Report (USA) **7633**
Church Libraries (USA) **5002**
Church Life (USA ISSN 8750-8613) **7751**
Church Messenger (Brooklyn) *see* Holas Carkvy **7704**
The Church Messenger (Johnstown)/Cerkovnyj Vistnik (USA ISSN 0734-0036) **7704**
Church Missionary Society Checkpoint *see* C M S Checkpoint **7749**
Church Music Quarterly (GBR ISSN 0307-6334) **6556**
• The Church Music Report (USA) **6556**
Church Newsletter *see* Kirkebladet **7763**
• The Church Observer (GBR ISSN 0009-6482) **7751**
Church of England. General Synod. Report of Proceedings (GBR ISSN 0307-7225) **7751**
• Church of England Newspaper (GBR ISSN 0964-816X) **7751**
Church of England Yearbook (GBR ISSN 0069-3987) **7751**
Church of God Evangel (USA ISSN 0745-6778) **7751**
Church of God Missions (USA ISSN 0009-6504) **7751**
The Church of Ireland Gazette (GBR ISSN 0009-6512) **7751**
Church of Light Quarterly (USA ISSN 0009-6520) **6644**
Church of Scotland Braille Magazine (GBR) **4080**
Church of Scotland. Yearbook (GBR ISSN 0069-3995) **7751**
The Church Pianist (USA ISSN 0890-9032) **6556**
Church Pocket Book and Diary (GBR) **7633**
Church Production Magazine (USA) **7633**
➤ Church Pulpit Year Book (Year) (GBR ISSN 0069-4002) **7633**
Church Solutions (USA) **1733**
Church Times (GBR ISSN 0009-658X) **7751**
Church Treasurer Alert *see* Church Finance Today **7633**
Church Women United Directory - Handbook *see* C W U Directory - Handbook **7749**
Church World (USA ISSN 0009-6601) **7633**
• ChurchArt Pro (USA) **7751**
Churches Purchasing Scheme (GBR) **1083**
Churchill Handbook *see* Finest Hour **4139**
➤ Churchman (GBR ISSN 0009-661X) **7751**
Churchscape (GBR ISSN 0262-4966) **437**
Churchwoman (USA ISSN 0009-6598) **7752**
Chusho Kigyo *see* Gekkan Chusho-Kigyo **1961**
Chutanzo, Netsushori/Casting, Forging & Heat Treatments (JPN ISSN 0387-0502) **6308**
Chutes & Mississagi, Information Guide (CAN ISSN 1715-2186) **8693**
• Chutti Vikatan (IND) **2182**
Chuxiong Normal University. Journal *see* Chuxiong Shifan Xueyuan Xuebao **7955**
• Chuxiong Shifan Xueyuan Xuebao/Chuxiong Normal University. Journal (CHN ISSN 1671-7406) **7955**
Chuzhdestranni Periodichni Izdaniia v Bulgaria (BGR ISSN 1310-9146) **7936**
Chuzhdestranni Periodichni Izdaniia v Po-golemite Nauchni Biblioteki *see* Chuzhdestranni Periodichni Izdaniia v Bulgaria **7936**
Chuzhdoyezikovo Obuchenie (BGR ISSN 0205-1834) **5106**
Chuzhongsheng Bidu/Required Reading for Junior Middle Schools Students (CHN ISSN 1005-6130) **2836**
Chuzhongsheng Shuxue Xuexi *see* Chuzhongsheng Shuxue Xuexi (Chu Yi Ban) **2836**
Chuzhongsheng Shuxue Xuexi *see* Chuzhongsheng Shuxue Xuexi (Chusan Ban) **2836**
Chuzhongsheng Shuxue Xuexi (Chu Yi Ban) (CHN) **2836**
Chuzhongsheng Shuxue Xuexi (Chuer Ban) (CHN) **5478**
Chuzhongsheng Shuxue Xuexi (Chusan Ban) (CHN) **2836**
Chuzhongsheng Xuexi Zhidao/Study Guide to Junior Middle School Students (CHN ISSN 1002-820X) **2837**
Chuzhou Shi-Zhuan Xuebao *see* Chuzhou Xueyuan Xuebao **7955**
Chuzhou Xueyuan Xuebao (CHN ISSN 1673-1794) **7955**
➤ Chuzo Kogaku/Japan Foundry Engineering Society. Journal (JPN ISSN 1342-0429) **6308**
Chvilka pre Teba (SVK) **8855**
▼ Chvilka pro Relax (CZE) **4976**
Chvilka pro Tebe (CZE ISSN 1211-4324) **8855**
Chwarae dros Gymru *see* Play for Wales **2165**
Chwila dla Ciebie (POL ISSN 1234-3129) **8855**
Chwila na 100 Panoramicznych (POL ISSN 1643-1588) **8166**
Chwila na Sto Panoramicznych *see* Chwila na 100 Panoramicznych **8166**
• Chydenius-Instituutin Selvityksiae (FIN ISSN 1795-6641) **2837**
Chydenius-Instituutti. Julkaisuja *see* Jyvaskylan Yliopisto. Chydenius-Instituutti. Tutkimuksia **1139**
• Chynetti (FIN ISSN 1457-5345) **2972**
Chyrvonaya Zmena (BLR) **3800**
Ci-Net European Construction Forecast (GBR) **991**
▼ • Ci Simu (FRA ISSN 1962-4913) **3840**
Ciak (ITA ISSN 1121-1784) **6492**
Ciao (CAN ISSN 0382-8557) **3527**
Ciao! (NLD ISSN 1574-7360) **3914**
Ciao Amici (ITA ISSN 1591-3082) **2182**
• Ciao Italia (ITA ISSN 0997-0290) **5106**
Ciao Italia! (ITA) **5106**
• Ciber Revista EnfermeriadeUrgencias.com (ESP ISSN 1579-5527) **5955**
• Ciberdiario de Nicaragua (NIC) **3821**
• Ciberlegenda (BRA ISSN 1519-0617) **2315**
• ➤ Ciberletras (USA ISSN 1523-1720) **5274**
• Ciberp@is (Ciberpais) (ESP ISSN 1139-1847) **3951**
Cibles (FRA ISSN 0009-6679) **4331**
Cicada *see* Nihon Semi no Kai Kaiho **856**
Cicada (Bakersfield) (USA ISSN 0891-2386) **5419**
• Cicada (Peru) (USA ISSN 1097-4008) **2182**
Cicero (BEL ISSN 0772-8220) **7319**
Cicero (DEU) **5210**
Cicero (HRV ISSN 1331-7075) **3831**
Cicero (Dutch Edition) *see* Cicero **7319**
Cicerone *see* Klima **6359**
Ciceroniana (ITA ISSN 0009-6687) **5274**
The Cichlid Yearbook (GBR) **3589**
Cichlidae (GBR ISSN 1367-7578) **3589**
The Cichlids Yearbook (USA) **3589**
• ➤ CICIMAR Oceanides (Centro Interdisciplinario de Ciencias Marinas Oceanidades) (MEX ISSN 1870-0713) **2802**
• Ciclismo (ITA ISSN 1123-9107) **8256**
Ciclismo a Fondo (ESP ISSN 0213-4179) **8256**
Ciclo Evolutivo e Disabilita/Life Span and Disability (ITA ISSN 1721-0151) **6131**
• ➤ Ciclos (ARG ISSN 0327-4063) **4288**
Ciclos (ESP ISSN 1137-9960) **3410**
Cicloturismo (ITA ISSN 1593-9820) **8256**
Cicloturismo a Fondo (ESP) **8256**
Ciconia (FRA ISSN 0335-5721) **905**
Ciconia (SRB ISSN 0354-2181) **905**
• ➤ El Cid (USA ISSN 1082-5894) **5274**
• Cidades - Comunidades e Territorios (PRT ISSN 1645-0639) **4407**
Cider Press Review (USA ISSN 1527-1862) **5419**
• Ciel et Espace (FRA ISSN 0373-9139) **573**
➤ Ciel et Terre (BEL ISSN 0009-6709) **573**
Cien Dias (COL ISSN 0121-3385) **7955**
Ciencia (CUB) **7846**
Ciencia (DOM) **7846**
Ciencia (ECU ISSN 1390-1117) **7846**
Ciencia (MEX ISSN 1405-6550) **7846**
• Ciencia Abierta (CHL ISSN 0717-8948) **7846**
Ciencia. Academia Mexicana de Ciencias *see* Ciencia **7846**
➤ Ciencia Agronomica (BRA ISSN 0045-6888) **101**
Ciencia Agropecuaria (PAN ISSN 0258-6452) **101**
• Ciencia al Dia Internacional (CHL ISSN 0717-3849) **7846**
• ➤ Ciencia & Educacao (BRA ISSN 1516-7313) **2837**
• ➤ Ciencia & Trabajo (CHL ISSN 0718-0306) **6675**
Ciencia & Tropico (BRA ISSN 0304-2685) **7955**
• Ciencia Animal Brasileira (BRA ISSN 1518-2797) **284**
Ciencia Biologica: Biologia Molecular e Celular (PRT ISSN 0378-875X) **728**
Ciencia Biologica: Ecologia e Sistematica (PRT ISSN 0870-1695) **938**
Ciencia Biologica: Ecology and Systematics *see* Ciencia Biologica: Ecologia e Sistematica **938**
Ciencia Biologica: Molecular and Cellular Biology *see* Ciencia Biologica: Biologia Molecular e Celular **728**
▼ • Ciencia Cognitiva (ESP ISSN 1988-7884) **7846**
• Ciencia da Informacao (BRA ISSN 0100-1965) **5002**
• ➤ Ciencia del Suelo/Argentine Society of Soil Science. Journal (ARG ISSN 0326-3169) **224**
• ➤ Ciencia, Docencia y Tecnologia (ARG ISSN 0327-5566) **7846**
• Ciencia e Agrotecnologia (BRA ISSN 1413-7054) **101**
Ciencia e Ambiente (BRA ISSN 1676-4188) **3410**
• ➤ Ciencia e Cultura (BRA ISSN 0009-6725) **7846**
Ciencia & Engenharia (BRA ISSN 0103-944X) **7846**
• Ciencia & Ensino (BRA ISSN 1414-5111) **7846**

Title

• Circulo de Linguistica Aplicada a la Comunicacion (ESP ISSN 1576-4737) **5106**
Circulo Odontologico de Cordoba. Revista (ARG ISSN 0045-6942) **5838**
Circulo Poetico (USA) **5419**
Circumference (USA) **2265**
• Circumference: Poetry in Translation (USA) **5419**
▼ • Circumpolar Health Supplements (FIN ISSN 1797-2361) **5595**
Circumpolar Journal see Circumpolar Studies **4002**
Circumpolar Studies (NLD ISSN 1574-0374) **4002**
Circumvesuviana (NLD ISSN 1873-0531) **2232**
• ➤ Circunstancia (ESP ISSN 1696-1277) **7955**
Circus Directory of the British Isles see King Pole Circus Magazine **8472**
Circus Fanfare (USA ISSN 1056-1463) **8468**
Circus Magazine see Circus-Zeitung **8468**
Circus Report (USA ISSN 0889-5996) **8468**
Circus-Zeitung/Circus Magazine (DEU ISSN 0941-2867) **8468**
➤ Cirencester Excavations (GBR) **387**
Cirkeln (SWE ISSN 1652-1595) **2837**
• Cirkulation (SWE ISSN 1103-2855) **8820**
Cirplan (GBR ISSN 0950-8732) **7752**
Cirque dans l'Univers (FRA ISSN 1140-6178) **8468**
Cirque Magazine see Le Magazine du Cirque et de l'Illusion **8473**
• Cirugest Archivos de Cirugia General y Digestiva (ESP ISSN 1576-2025) **6239**
• Cirugia del Uruguay (URY ISSN 0009-7381) **6239**
• Cirugia Espanola (ESP ISSN 0009-739X) **6239**
• Cirugia Mayor Ambulatoria (ESP ISSN 1137-0882) **6239**
Cirugia Pediatrica (ESP ISSN 0214-1221) **6239**
• Cirugia Plastica (MEX ISSN 1405-0625) **6239**
• Cirugia Plastica Ibero Latinoamericana (ESP ISSN 0376-7892) **6239**
Cirugia Plastica Uruguaya (URY ISSN 0797-4884) **6239**
• Cirugia y Cirujanos (MEX ISSN 0009-7411) **6239**
• Cirujano General (Online Edition) (MEX) **5595**
Cirujano General (Print Edition) see Cirujano General (Online Edition) **5595**
CIS-Madera see C I S Madeira **3710**
Cisco Certified Internetwork Experts Central see C C I E Central **2553**
Cishan/Charity (CHN ISSN 1008-0376) **8033**
• Cishu Yanjiu/Journal of Lexicographical Studies (CHN ISSN 1000-6125) **5106**
CIStemic see C I Stemic **2408**
Cistercian History Abstracts see Bulletin d'Histoire Cistercienne **7698**
• ➤ Cistercian Studies Quarterly (USA ISSN 1062-6549) **7633**
Cistercium (ESP ISSN 0210-3990) **7633**
Citadel (IND) **3880**
Citadel see Fortetsya **3964**
Citadel Film Series (USA) **6494**
Citadelle (FRA ISSN 1775-6723) **4135**
Citas Latinoamericanas en Ciencias Sociales y Humanidades see C L A S E **8020**
Citation Jet see C J **8539**
• Citations for Serial Literature (USA ISSN 1061-7434) **5057**
Cite (FRA ISSN 0756-3205) **7116**
Cite (USA ISSN 8755-0415) **437**
Cite Europeenne see European Policy **7436**
➤ Citeaux (BEL ISSN 0009-7497) **7792**
Citeaux. Collection Studia et Documenta (BEL) **7792**
Citeaux. Collection Textes et Documents (BEL) **7792**
Cites (FRA ISSN 1299-5495) **6910**
• Cites & Insights. Crawford at Large (USA ISSN 1534-0937) **5002**
Cites News - Plantes see Cites News - Plants **784**
Cites News - Plants (GBR) **784**
Cites Nouvelles/City News (CAN) **3807**
Cites Unies/Ciudades Unidas/United Cities (FRA ISSN 0529-8016) **7227**
Cites Unies Informations (FRA ISSN 1015-0455) **7489**
Cithara (USA ISSN 0009-7527) **7633**
Citi Vision (ZAF) **3948**
The Citi World Official Agency Guide (GBR ISSN 1756-5367) **1327**
• ➤ Cities (GBR ISSN 0264-2751) **7489**
Cities and Ports see Villes et Ports **1586**
▼ • ➤ Cities and the Environment (USA ISSN 1932-7048) **3410**
Cities and Villages (USA ISSN 0009-7535) **4407**
▼ • Cities go Green (USA ISSN 1944-4664) **2606**
▼ • Cities in the 21st Century (USA ISSN 1948-2000) **4407**
Cities in the Twenty-First Century see Cities in the 21st Century **4407**
• Cities of the United States (USA ISSN 0899-6075) **4002**
• Cities of the World (USA ISSN 0889-2741) **4002**
CitiLife (GBR) **3862**
• Citius Altius Fortius (ROM ISSN 1582-8131) **8166**
• The Citizen (GBR) **7204**
The Citizen (SGP ISSN 0217-0779) **3945**
• The Citizen (ZAF ISSN 1016-3956) **3948**
Citizen (Colorado Springs) (USA ISSN 1084-6832) **7955**
Citizen Action (IND) **8093**
• Citizen Airman (USA ISSN 0887-9680) **51**
Citizen Alert Newsletter (USA) **3410**
† Citizen K (ESP) **8941**
Citizen K International (GBR ISSN 1366-8285) **5068**
Citizen Participation (USA ISSN 1055-7814) **7489**
Citizens Advice Bureaux News see C A B News **4635**
• Citizens Advice Notes Service (GBR ISSN 1362-7015) **4642**
Citizens Advisory Council Advisory see C A C Advisory **3407**
Citizens Band Radio Story see The C B Radio Story **2357**
Citizens' Business (USA ISSN 0009-756X) **7489**
• Citizens Centre Report (CAN ISSN 1707-0090) **3807**
The Citizens' Companion (USA ISSN 1075-9344) **4135**
Citizens Equal Rights Alliance News see C E R A News **6634**
Citizens for a Better Environment Environmental Review see C B E Environmental Review **2605**
Citizens for Excellence in Education Presidents Report see C E E Presidents Report **7749**
Citizens for Foreign Aid Reform Inc. Newsletter see C - F A R Newsletter **1592**
Citizens for Participation in Political Action Newsletter see C P P A X Newsletter **7224**
Citizens for Safe Cycling Newsletter (CAN ISSN 1183-7543) **8256**
Citizen's Income Newsletter (GBR ISSN 1464-7354) **1670**
Citizens Informer (USA ISSN 0887-3186) **7116**
Citizens' Nuclear Information Center News see Genshiryoku Shiryo Johoshitsu Tsushin **3168**
Citizen's Report on Brownfields (USA) **3410**
Citizen's Report on the Military and the Environment (USA) **6416**
Citizens Union Foundation. Occasional Paper Series (USA) **7489**
Citizens Union Reports (USA) **4591**
Citizen's Weekly see Shichang Zhoukan **1173**
• Citizenship and Immigration Manuals (CAN ISSN 1495-2114) **7279**
• Citizenship News (GBR ISSN 1748-8923) **7116**
➤ Citizenship, Social and Economics Education (GBR ISSN 1478-8047) **2837**
• ➤ Citizenship Studies (GBR ISSN 1362-1025) **7116**
Citoyen Canadien see Cittadino Canadese **3527**
Citrabikshana/Chitra-Bikshan (IND) **6494**
Citroen (USA) **8574**
Citrouille (FRA ISSN 1167-301X) **5274**
Citrus and Vegetable see Citrus & Vegetable **225**
• Citrus & Vegetable (USA ISSN 0009-7586) **225**
Citrus Engineering Conference. Transactions (USA ISSN 0412-6300) **225**
Citrus Fruits see U.S. Department of Agriculture. National Agricultural Statistics Service. Citrus Fruits **187**
Citrus Industry Magazine (USA ISSN 0009-7594) **3631**
• Citrus News (USA) **225**
Una Citta (ITA ISSN 1128-7799) **3896**
† Citta (Latina) (ITA) **8941**
Citta Bella/Duhui Jiaren (SGP ISSN 0218-6527) **8855**
Le Citta della Calabria (ITA) **8693**
Citta di Vita (ITA ISSN 0009-7632) **7633**
Citta d'Utopia (ITA) **7116**
† La Citta Nuova (Naples) (ITA ISSN 0393-6449) **8941**
• Citta Nuova (Rome) (ITA ISSN 0391-7681) **3896**
Citta Unite. Lettera see United Towns News. Newsletter **7504**
Cittadini e Societa dell'Informazione see Garante per la Protezione dei Dati Personali. Bollettino **7207**
• Il Cittadino (ITA ISSN 1970-0873) **7116**
Cittadino Canadese/Canadian Citizen/Citoyen Canadien (CAN ISSN 0009-7667) **3527**
• City (AUT) **3797**
City see Chengshi **4406**
City (DEU) **3845**
• City (GBR ISSN 1360-4813) **4407**
City (New York) (USA ISSN 1536-9633) **5068**
• ➤ City & Community (USA ISSN 1535-6841) **8033**
City & Country Club Life (USA ISSN 0897-4926) **3972**
City & Shore Magazine (USA) **3972**
• ➤ City & Society (USA ISSN 0893-0465) **333**
▼ • City & Time (BRA ISSN 1981-5956) **437**
City & Town (USA ISSN 0193-8371) **7489**
City Arts (USA) **3972**
▼ City Arts - Eastside (USA) **3972**
▼ City Arts - Seattle (USA) **3972**
City at the Center (USA ISSN 1947-2242) **2277**
City AZ (USA) **3972**
† City Beautiful (NZL ISSN 0009-7705) **8941**
• City Centre Mirror (CAN) **3807**
City Club Gadfly (USA) **7489**
City Commercial - Residential Codes (USA) **4407**
City - County Magazine see Alamance Magazine **3969**
City Crime Rankings (USA ISSN 1081-6453) **2673**
City Cycle Motorcycle Newsmagazine see C C Motorcycle Newsmagazine **8256**
City Cyclist (USA) **8256**
City Development see Chengshi Fazhan **4406**
City Development, Regional Development and Environmental Pollution Index see Toshi Kaihatsu Chiiki Kaihatsu Kankyo Kogai Kankei Indekkusu **3491**
† City Employment (Online) (USA) **8941**
City Faszinationen (DEU ISSN 1610-0328) **8693**
City Fiscal Conditions in (Year) (USA ISSN 1936-0088) **7489**
† • City Government Finances (USA ISSN 0082-9439) **8941**
City Guide Stadtfuehrer (DEU) **4383**
City Hall (USA) **7489**
City Health see CityHealth **6984**
City In see Chengse **3823**
City Journal (CAN ISSN 1912-2276) **3807**
City Journal (NLD ISSN 1574-8782) **7489**
• The City Journal (USA ISSN 1060-8540) **4407**
• City Law (USA ISSN 1083-3528) **4642**
• City Legacy (USA) **4288**
City Life Porirua News see Citylife Porirua News **3916**
• City Limits (Online) (USA) **7955**
City Limits (Print) see City Limits (Online) **7955**
▼ • City Limits Investigates (USA ISSN 1937-4127) **7955**
City Line News (USA) **1447**
The City Magazine (GBR ISSN 1369-1260) **1327**
CITY Magazine see City (New York) **5068**
City Magazine see Kentucky City Magazine **7495**
• City Mayors (GBR ISSN 1740-3952) **7116**
City News see Cites Nouvelles **3807**
City News (DEU) **5068**
• City News Oldenburg (DEU) **3846**
City Novel see Dushi Xiaoshuo **5286**
City of Birmingham Symphony Orchestra. Main Season Brochure (GBR) **6556**
City of Birmingham Symphony Orchestra. Summer Season Brochure (GBR) **6556**
City of Chicago Building Code (USA) **991**
City of Helsinki Urban Facts. Quarterly see Helsingin Kaupungin Tietokeskuksen Neljannesvuosijulkaisu. Kvartti **7444**
City of Helsinki Urban Facts. Statistics see Helsingin Kaupungin Tietokeskus. Tilastoja **7481**
City of London and Docklands Independent (GBR ISSN 1471-2881) **3862**
City of London Directory & Livery Companies Guide (GBR ISSN 0142-5072) **1980**
City of New York Council Digest (USA) **4642**
City of Stockholm. Annual Financial Report (Year) (SWE) **7489**
City of Vancouver Archives (CAN ISSN 1910-4596) **5002**
• The City Pages (USA ISSN 0744-0456) **3972**
City Palate (CAN) **3631**
City Paper see City Paper - The Baltic States **8693**
• City Paper - The Baltic States (EST ISSN 1406-2208) **8693**
City Pictorial see Cheng Shi Huabao **3823**
City Planning Review see Chengshi Guihua **4407**
City Planning Review see Toshi Keikaku **4428**
City Post (NGA ISSN 1596-7689) **3920**
City Press (ZAF ISSN 1016-3964) **3948**
City Primeval (USA ISSN 1083-4842) **5274**
City Products and Services Guide (USA) **1882**
City Profiles U S A (USA ISSN 1082-9938) **8693**
City Rant (USA) **5274**
City Record (USA) **7489**
• City Regs (USA) **4642**
• The City Review (USA) **3972**
City Runner (JPN) **8309**
City Scan (IND) **3880**
City Scan (Bismarck) (USA ISSN 1094-5784) **7490**
City Scene see CityScene **3972**
City Sierran (USA) **3411**
† City-Smart: Calgary (USA) **8941**
City-Smart Guidebook: Calgary see City-Smart: Calgary **8941**
City-Smart Guidebook: San Antonio see City-Smart: San Antonio **8941**
† City-Smart: Portland (USA ISSN 1530-8375) **8941**
† City-Smart: San Antonio (USA) **8941**
City Sports Magazine (Los Angeles Edition) see City Sports Monthly **8166**
City Sports Magazine (Metro Edition) see City Sports Monthly **8166**
• City Sports Monthly (USA ISSN 0191-8400) **8166**
City Sports Northwest Magazine see City Sports Monthly **8166**
City Sun see Chengshi Xinbao **3823**
City Terrace Comet (USA) **3527**
City to Cities (GBR ISSN 1355-1620) **8783**
City Trees (USA) **3686**
City Tribune (IRL ISSN 0791-1815) **3892**
City University Business School. Department of Banking & Finance. Finance Working Paper (GBR) **1327**
City University. Computer Science Technical Reports (GBR ISSN 1364-4009) **2410**
City Vision see Commerce (Winston-Salem) **1400**
† City Weekend (NZL ISSN 1172-4390) **8941**
City Woman see Ottawa City Woman **8847**
City-Zeitung (DEU) **3846**
Cityfile (GBR ISSN 1362-3672) **1327**
Cityguide U S A Magazine (USA) **8693**
CityHealth (CAN ISSN 1914-7856) **6984**
Cityin see Chengse **3823**
Cityland (USA ISSN 1551-711X) **4642**
Citylife see Citylife Porirua News **3916**
CityLife (North Edition) see CityLife Independent Herald **3916**
CityLife (West & North Edition) see CityLife Independent Herald **3916**
CityLife (West Edition) see CityLife Independent Herald **3916**
▼ CityLife Independent Herald (NZL) **3916**
• Citylife Porirua News (NZL) **3916**
CityManager (AUT) **3797**
Citypack Prague see Fodor's Prague's 25 Best **8708**
† CityPartner (DEU ISSN 1614-0389) **8941**
CitySCAN see City Scan (Bismarck) **7490**
• Cityscape (AUS ISSN 1833-0320) **437**
Cityscape (Des Moines) (USA ISSN 1088-5951) **4407**
• Cityscape (Washington, D.C.) (USA ISSN 1936-007X) **7430**
• CityScene (USA) **3972**
Cityside (CAN) **2277**
CitySlicker Entertainment Magazine (USA ISSN 1544-3736) **6556**
CitySports see City Sports Monthly **8166**
CitySports (USA) **8166**
CityTempo Magazine (USA) **4535**
Cityview (USA) **3972**
Ciuchcia (POL ISSN 1231-1677) **2182**
La Ciudad (ARG) **3791**
La Ciudad de Dios (ESP ISSN 0009-7756) **7792**
Ciudad de Melilla. Boletin Oficial (ESP ISSN 1135-4011) **4642**
Ciudad Invisible (CHL ISSN 0718-3348) **7279**
Ciudad Nueva Internacional (ESP) **3951**
➤ Ciudad y Territorio: Estudios Territoriales (ESP ISSN 1133-4762) **7430**
• Ciudadano de Dos Mundos (CHL ISSN 0718-1221) **5274**
Ciudades (ESP ISSN 1133-6579) **4407**
➤ Ciudades (MEX ISSN 0187-8611) **7490**
Ciudades Romanas de Hispania (ITA ISSN 1972-2389) **437**
Ciudades Unidas see Cites Unies **7227**
Ciudades Unidas. Informativo see United Towns News. Newsletter **7504**
Ciutat (ESP ISSN 1132-3094) **7955**
† La Civetta (ITA) **8941**
Civic Affairs (IND ISSN 0009-7772) **7490**
Civic Focus (GBR) **3411**
Civic Public Works (CAN ISSN 0829-772X) **7430**
Civic Trust Awards (GBR) **2606**
† • Civica Scuola di Musica. Quaderni (ITA ISSN 1971-5315) **8941**
Civiele Techniek (NLD ISSN 0925-7128) **3262**
Civil (SWE ISSN 1102-0180) **2225**
Civil Actions Against State Government: Its Divisions, Agencies, and Offices (USA) **4828**
Civil Actions Against the United States: Its Agencies, Officers, and Employees (USA) **4828**
Civil Aeronautics Board Air Carrier Traffic Statistics see C A B Air Carrier Traffic Statistics **8523**
Civil Air Patrol News (USA ISSN 0009-7810) **2225**
Civil Aircraft Accident Reports (HKG) **8539**
Civil Aircraft Airworthiness Information and Procedures (GBR) **8539**
Civil Aircraft Forecast see Market Intelligence Reports: Civil Aircraft Forecast **65**
Civil and Commercial Laws see Minshang Faxue **4734**
Civil and Environmental Engineering (USA) **3184**
Civil & Military Law Journal (IND ISSN 0045-7043) **4971**
Civil and Military Review (IND) **6416**
• Civil and Structural Engineering Series (GBR) **3262**
Civil Aviation see Luftfart **8527**
Civil Aviation see Al- Tairan al-Madani **72**
Civil Aviation Administration of China. Journal see Zhongguo Minhang Bao **8777**
• Civil Aviation Authority of New Zealand. Annual Report (NZL ISSN 1177-6072) **7430**
Civil Aviation Authority of New Zealand. Review see Vector **74**
• Civil Aviation Authority of New Zealand. Statement of Intent (NZL ISSN 1177-9411) **8539**
Civil Aviation Authority Specifications see C A A Specifications **8539**
Civil Aviation Economics and Technology see Zhongguo Minyong Hangkong **76**
Civil Aviation in Pakistan: Half-Yearly Newsletter (PAK) **51**
Civil Aviation Management see Minhang Guanli **8548**
Civil Aviation News (GBR) **8539**
Civil Aviation Statistics of the World (Year) (CAN) **8524**
Civil Aviation Training (GBR ISSN 0960-9024) **8539**
Civil Aviation University of China. Journal see Zhongguo Minhang Daxue Xuebao **76**
Civil Censorship Study Group Bulletin (GBR) **6893**
Civil Code of Quebec & Code of Civil Procedure see Code Civil du Quebec & Code de Procedure Civile **4829**
The Civil Court Practice (GBR) **4828**
Civil Defence Board. Strategic Plan (IRL ISSN 1649-7678) **2225**
Civil Document Processing Manual (CAN) **4828**
Civil Engineer (IND) **3262**
Civil Engineer see The Air Force Civil Engineer **3259**
Civil Engineering see Doboku Gijutsu **3265**
Civil Engineering see Ingenieria Civil **3270**
Civil Engineering see Inzinierske Stavby **3273**
• Civil Engineering/Siviele Ingenieurswese (ZAF ISSN 1021-2000) **3262**
• ➤ Civil Engineering (Reston) (USA ISSN 0885-7024) **3262**
The Civil Engineering and Building Contractor (ZAF) **3262**
• Civil Engineering and Environmental Systems (GBR ISSN 1028-6608) **3262**
Civil Engineering & Hydraulic Engineering Abstracts see Melyepitesi es Vizepitesi Szakirodalmi Tajekoztato **3232**
Civil Engineering Construction see C E Kensetsu Gyoukai **3261**

Civil Engineering Education (USA ISSN 0884-1926) **3262**
▼ • ➤ Civil Engineering Innovation/Tumu Gongcheng Chuangxin (GBR ISSN 1755-0890) **3262**
Civil Engineering, J S C E (JPN) **3262**
Civil Engineering Journal *see* Doboku Gijutsu Shiryo **3265**
Civil Engineering Kensetsu Gyoukai *see* C E Kensetsu Gyoukai **3261**
Civil Engineering News *see* C E News **3261**
Civil Engineering Newsletter (SGP ISSN 0219-3760) **3262**
➤ Civil Engineering Practice (USA ISSN 0886-9685) **3262**
Civil Engineering Research Institute. Monthly Report *see* Hokkaidou Kaihatsu Doboku Kenkyuujo Geppou **3269**
Civil Engineering Research Institute. Report *see* Kaihatsu Doboku Kenkyujo Hokoku **3277**
† Civil Engineering Research Magazine (EGY ISSN 1110-0990) **8941**
Civil Engineering Series (USA ISSN 0195-3664) **3263**
➤ Civil Engineering Surveyor (GBR ISSN 0266-139X) **3263**
Civil Engineering Technology (GBR ISSN 0264-9942) **3263**
† Civil Engineering Working Papers (AUS ISSN 0156-2126) **8941**
† Civil Evidence Trial Manual for Texas Lawyers (USA) **8941**
• Civil False Claims and Qui Tam Actions (USA) **4499**
Civil Jury Instruction Companion Handbook *see* Louisiana Civil Jury Instruction Companion Handbook **4725**
Civil Justice Digest (USA) **4828**
• Civil Justice Quarterly (GBR ISSN 0261-9261) **4828**
Civil Law (USA) **4828**
Civil Law Cases (PAK) **4828**
Civil Libertarian *see* L G L C Newsletter **5319**
Civil Liberties Alert (USA) **6278**
Civil Liberties Reporter (USA ISSN 0009-7934) **4828**
• ➤ Civil Liberty (AUS ISSN 1326-8333) **7204**
Civil Liberty Agenda (GBR ISSN 1358-4030) **7204**
Civil Litigation (GBR ISSN 1352-4496) **4828**
Civil Litigation Reporter (USA ISSN 0199-0802) **4829**
Civil Litigation Update, Annual *see* Annual Civil Litigation Update **4827**
Civil Penalty Case Digest Service (USA) **4829**
Civil Practice Law and Rules Handbook of New York *see* Gould's New York Civil Practice Law & Rules Handbook **4832**
Civil Practice Law Reports (GBR ISSN 1465-7414) **4829**
Civil Procedure *see* B A R - B R I Bar Review. Civil Procedure **4827**
• Civil Procedure (ZAF ISSN 1814-0564) **4947**
• Civil Procedure (Year) (GBR) **4829**
• Civil Procedure A.C.T. (AUS) **4829**
• Civil Procedure in Europe (NLD ISSN 1873-0477) **4642**
Civil Procedure News (GBR ISSN 1470-2525) **4947**
• Civil Procedure Queensland (AUS) **4947**
Civil Procedure Reports (GBR ISSN 1745-9613) **4829**
Civil Procedure Sibergramme *see* Civil Procedure **4947**
• Civil Procedure South Australia (AUS) **4829**
• Civil Procedure Victoria (AUS) **4829**
• Civil Procedure Western Australia (AUS) **4829**
Civil Protection (GBR ISSN 0961-2564) **2225**
Civil R I C O (Racketeer Influenced and Corrupt Organizations) (USA) **4642**
Civil R I C O Litigation Reporter (USA) **4829**
• Civil R I C O Report (USA ISSN 0884-0032) **4829**
• Civil Rights Actions (USA) **7204**
Civil Rights and Civil Liberties Litigation: The Law of Section 1983 (USA) **4829**
• Civil Rights Journal (USA) **7204**
Civil Rights Litigation and Attorney Fees Annual Handbook *see* Civil Rights Litigation and Attorney Fees Handbook **4829**
Civil Rights Litigation and Attorney Fees Handbook (USA) **4829**
Civil Rights Monitor (USA ISSN 1063-9454) **4829**
Civil Rights Research Review (USA ISSN 0732-5738) **7204**
Civil Rules (CAN ISSN 1719-489X) **4829**
Civil Servant *see* Dimosios Ypallilos **7433**
Civil Servant in the Defence Forces *see* Foersvarstjaenstemannen **1682**
Civil Service Law of New York *see* N Y Civil Service Law **4838**
Civil Service Law of the State of New York *see* N Y Civil Service Law **4838**
Civil Service News (MUS) **7430**
Civil Service News (USA) **7430**
Civil Service Pensioner (GBR ISSN 1360-3132) **4043**
Civil Service Reporter (PHL ISSN 0300-3620) **7430**
Civil Service Rewards (GBR ISSN 1477-6200) **1670**
Civil Service Statistics *see* Great Britain. H M Treasury. Civil Service Statistics **7480**
• Civil Service Year Book (GBR ISSN 0302-329X) **7430**
Civil War *see* America's Civil War **4283**
• Civil War Book Review (Online) (USA) **4288**
Civil War Book Review (Print) *see* Civil War Book Review (Online) **4288**
• ➤ Civil War History (USA ISSN 0009-8078) **4288**
Civil War News (USA ISSN 1053-1181) **4288**
Civil War Round Table Digest (USA ISSN 0009-8086) **4288**
Civil War Sites (USA ISSN 1541-8979) **8693**
Civil War Sites in the Southern States *see* Insiders' Guide to Civil War Sites in the Southern States **8964**
• Civil War Times (USA ISSN 1546-9980) **4288**
• ➤ Civil Wars (GBR ISSN 1369-8249) **7227**
Civilekonomen (SWE ISSN 1400-0997) **1733**
Civilian-Based Defense (USA) **6416**
Civilian Career Guide (USA ISSN 1042-7848) **6695**
Civilian Congress (USA) **4643**
• Civilian Job News (USA) **6695**
Civilian Manpower Statistics (USA ISSN 0882-8857) **1221**
• Civilica. Encyclopedia of Civil Engineering (IRN ISSN 1735-5540) **3263**
Civilingenjoeren *see* Ingenjoeren **3198**
Civilisation Medievale (FRA ISSN 1281-704X) **4210**
Civilisations (BEL ISSN 0009-8140) **8093**
Civilisations de l'Europe Mediane (FRA) **8094**
Civilisations et Societes (FRA ISSN 0069-4290) **4210**
Civilization of the American Indian (USA ISSN 0069-4304) **6634**
Civilizations *see* Bummmei **331**
Civiloekonomen *see* C 3 **1077**
Civilta Arcaica dei Sabini nella Valle del Tevere (ITA ISSN 1824-0542) **333**
• Civilta Cattolica (ITA ISSN 0009-8167) **7792**
† Civilta del Bere (ITA ISSN 0390-1572) **8941**
Civilta del Mediterraneo (ITA ISSN 1120-9860) **7955**
Civilta della Tavola (ITA) **3631**
Civilta Italiana. Nuova Serie (ITA ISSN 1827-0271) **4447**
• Civilta Musicale (ITA ISSN 1593-1277) **6556**
Civilta Veneziana. Dizionari Dialettali e Studi Linguistici (ITA ISSN 0069-4339) **5106**
Civilta Veneziana. Fonti e Testi. Serie Prima: Fonti e Testi per la Storia dell'Arte Veneta (ITA ISSN 0069-4355) **482**
Civilta Veneziana. Fonti e Testi. Serie Terza (ITA ISSN 0069-4347) **4211**
Civilta Veneziana. Quaderni (ITA) **5106**
Civilta Veneziana. Saggi (ITA ISSN 0069-4371) **4211**
Civilta Veneziana. Studi (ITA ISSN 0069-438X) **4211**
Civique (FRA ISSN 1275-7705) **7490**
Civis Mundi (NLD ISSN 0030-3283) **7116**
Civitan Magazine (USA ISSN 0194-5785) **2265**
• Civitas (BRA ISSN 1519-6089) **7955**
Civitas (CHE ISSN 1021-5980) **5211**
Civitas (ITA ISSN 0009-8191) **7116**
Civitas (SWE ISSN 1652-5728) **7116**
• Civitas. Revista Espanola de Derecho del Trabajo (ESP ISSN 0212-6095) **4860**
• Civitas. Revista Espanola de Derecho Deportivo (ESP ISSN 1132-9688) **4643**
• Civitas. Revista Espanola de Derecho Financiero (ESP ISSN 0210-8453) **4860**
Civvy Street (GBR ISSN 1746-8426) **6416**
Ciy Sledder (USA) **8309**
Cizi Jazyky (CZE ISSN 1210-0811) **2837**
CKM *see* C K M **6287**
Clackamas Literary Review (USA ISSN 1088-3665) **5211**
• ➤ Cladistics (GBR ISSN 0748-3007) **666**
The Claflin Review (USA ISSN 0895-5182) **5106**
Claim Statements (USA ISSN 1939-6775) **4499**
• Claims (USA ISSN 0895-7991) **4499**
▼ • Claims Advisor (USA ISSN 1940-0985) **4499**
Claims to the Possession of Land: Law and Practice (GBR) **4860**
Clairlieu: Tijdschrift Gewijd aan de Geschiedenis der Kruisheren (BEL ISSN 0774-7241) **7633**
Clan Guthrie News (USA) **3762**
Clan MacDonald Annual (CAN) **2277**
Clan MacLeod Society U S A. Newsletter (USA) **3762**
Clan MacNeil Association of America. Galley (USA ISSN 0163-9951) **3762**
Clan McLaren Society, U S A. Quarterly (USA ISSN 0009-8213) **3762**
Clan Ross News (USA) **3527**
Clapper (USA ISSN 1054-5824) **6556**
Clara (DEU) **8855**
• Clara (ESP ISSN 1132-3213) **8855**
Clara (FRA ISSN 0981-1850) **8855**
Clara (MEX) **8855**
Clara. Especial Belleza *see* Clara **8855**
Clara Venus (USA ISSN 1553-7285) **5274**
• The Clare Champion (IRL ISSN 1393-8843) **3892**
The Claremont Review (CAN ISSN 1188-5068) **5419**
Claremont Review of Books (USA ISSN 1554-0839) **5211**
Clarendon Lectures in English (GBR) **5274**
Clarendon Lectures in English Literature *see* Clarendon Lectures in English **5274**
Clarendon Library of Logic and Philosophy (USA) **6910**
• Claret & Blue (GBR ISSN 0946-8862) **8225**
Claretianum (ITA ISSN 0578-4182) **7792**
Claridad (ESP ISSN 0213-2931) **4591**
Claridad (PRI ISSN 0279-313X) **3931**
Claridad (URY ISSN 0009-823X) **3994**
Clarim (MAC) **7792**
O Clarim (PRT ISSN 0874-4963) **2182**
Clarin (ARG ISSN 1514-965X) **3791**
Clarin (ESP ISSN 1136-1182) **5274**
El Clarin de la Busca (USA) **622**
Clarin Economico (ARG ISSN 0009-8256) **1447**
Clarin Internacional (ARG ISSN 0327-4705) **3791**
➤ The Clarinet (USA ISSN 0361-5553) **6556**
Clarinet and Saxophone (GBR ISSN 0260-390X) **6556**
Clarington This Week (CAN) **3807**
Clarino (DEU ISSN 0937-5864) **6556**
The Clarion (GBR) **5106**
• Clarion (Boston) (USA ISSN 2150-6795) **5274**
Clarion (Sacramento) (USA ISSN 1932-0450) **5002**
Clarion Alumni News (USA) **2277**
Clarion Herald (USA) **7792**
Clarion Science Fiction and Fantasy Writers' Workshop Newsletter (USA) **5441**
➤ Claritas (BRA ISSN 1414-5243) **5106**
Clarity (IND) **7116**
Clark Clarion (USA ISSN 0883-2692) **3762**
Clark County Historical Society. Newsletter (USA) **4289**
Clark County History (USA ISSN 0090-449X) **4289**
• Clark on Surveying and Boundaries (USA) **4643**
Clark Reports (USA) **991**
Clarke College Courier (USA) **2278**
Clarke Hall & Morrison on Children (GBR) **4643**
Clarke's Canada Industrial Relations Board (CAN) **1670**
• Clarkesworld Magazine (USA ISSN 1937-7843) **5441**
• Clarknews (USA) **2278**
Clark's Bank Deposits & Payments Monthly *see* Clark's Bank Deposits and Payments Monthly **1327**
• Clark's Bank Deposits and Payments Monthly (USA ISSN 1063-2220) **1327**
Clark's Flea Market U S A (USA) **365**
Clark's Secured Lending Web Report *see* Mortgage Lending Expert **1369**
Clark's Secured Transactions Monthly (USA ISSN 1063-5289) **1327**
The Clarkson Integrator (USA) **3972**
Clarkson Register CD *see* Offshore Vessel Register **8656**
Clarkson Register CD *see* The Chemical Tanker Register **8641**
Clarkson Register CD *see* The Reefer Register **8658**
Clarkson Register CD *see* The Tanker Register **8663**
Clarkson Register CD *see* The Gas Carrier Register **8644**
Clarkson Register CD *see* The Bulk Carrier Register **8640**
• Claro (ARG ISSN 1514-6146) **3791**
Claro. Escuro (PRT ISSN 0871-3715) **482**
Clarte (SWE ISSN 0345-2085) **7116**
▼ Clartes Grandes Signatures (FRA ISSN 1963-2207) **4447**
• Clash Magazine (GBR ISSN 1743-0801) **6556**
Clasica Audio (ESP) **6556**
Clasicos Colombianos (COL ISSN 0069-4444) **5274**
Clasicos de la Arqueologia de Huelva (ESP ISSN 1133-2085) **387**
Clasicos de Ocasion (ESP) **8574**
Clasicos del Pensamiento Politico (ESP ISSN 1699-0528) **7116**
Clasicos Madrilenos (ESP ISSN 1989-0931) **5274**
Clasicos Medievales (ESP) **2232**
• Clasificacion de Instrumentos de Oferta Publica (CHL) **1327**
Clasificacion Mexicana de Ocupaciones (MEX) **6706**
CLASS (GBR) **601**
Class (ITA ISSN 1594-6754) **1858**
Class Action (CAN ISSN 1718-9489) **2837**
▼ Class Action Attorney Fee Digest (USA ISSN 1936-3370) **4643**
Class Action Defence Quarterly (CAN ISSN 1911-2270) **4643**
• Class Action Law Monitor (USA ISSN 1535-9573) **4643**
• Class Action Litigation Report (USA ISSN 1529-0115) **4643**
• Class Action Reporter (USA ISSN 1525-2272) **4643**
• Class Action Reports (USA ISSN 0746-7168) **4643**
Class Actions & Derivative Suits *see* Committee on Class Actions & Derivative Suits **4646**
Class Actions in Canada (CAN ISSN 1206-2375) **4829**
Class Actions Law & Practice (CAN) **4829**
Class N K Magazine (JPN ISSN 1341-0091) **2802**
Class N K Technical Bulletin (JPN) **7847**
Classe (FRA ISSN 1143-2802) **3019**
Classense (ITA ISSN 1825-7100) **623**
Classic American (GBR ISSN 0957-2406) **365**
The Classic and Antique Bicycle Exchange (USA) **4332**
Classic & Sports Car (GBR ISSN 0263-3183) **8574**
Classic & Sports Car Owner's Bible *see* Classic & Sports Car **8574**
Classic and Vintage Commercials (GBR ISSN 1362-9484) **8574**
Classic Arms and Militaria (GBR) **6416**
Classic Bike (GBR ISSN 0142-890X) **8256**
Classic Bike Guide (GBR ISSN 0959-7123) **8256**
Classic Bike Rider Magazine *see* C B R Magazine **8256**
• Classic Boat (GBR ISSN 0950-3315) **4332**
Classic Boating (USA ISSN 1070-9290) **8274**
Classic Bus (GBR ISSN 0966-8438) **8493**
Classic Car Mart (GBR ISSN 1351-1203) **8574**
Classic Car Weekly (GBR ISSN 0959-9738) **365**
Classic Cars (GBR ISSN 1365-9537) **8574**
Classic Cars for Sale (GBR ISSN 1468-9235) **8574**
▼ • Classic Country Life (USA ISSN 1935-8202) **5068**
Classic Dirt Bike Magazine (GBR ISSN 1752-6558) **8256**
Classic Dirtbike *see* Classic Dirt Bike Magazine **8256**
Classic Driver (NZL ISSN 1176-2993) **8574**
• Classic Driver (Online) (DEU ISSN 1611-5082) **8574**
Classic F M Magazine (GBR ISSN 1356-2592) **6556**
Classic Ford (GBR ISSN 1367-8809) **8575**
Classic Homestyles (CAN ISSN 1181-7925) **4407**
† Classic House Plans (USA) **8941**
Classic Images (USA ISSN 0275-8423) **6494**
• The Classic Insider Newsletter (USA) **2553**
Classic Literature Knowledge *see* Gudian Wenxue Zhishi **5302**
Classic Living *see* Decor Living **4537**
Classic Military Vehicle (GBR ISSN 1473-7779) **6416**
Classic Motor Magasin (SWE ISSN 1400-5506) **8575**
Classic MotorCycle (GBR ISSN 0263-0850) **8256**
Classic Motorcycle Mechanics (GBR ISSN 0959-0900) **8256**
Classic of Food *see* Shijing **3663**
➤ Classic Papers and Current Comments (USA) **6015**
Classic Pillsbury Cookbooks *see* Pillsbury Classic Cookbooks **4365**
Classic Plant & Machinery (GBR ISSN 1478-0054) **5450**
Classic Racer (GBR ISSN 0266-8106) **8256**
† Classic Railways (GBR ISSN 1464-0317) **8941**
Classic Ranges (USA) **4332**
Classic Record Collector (GBR ISSN 1472-5797) **6557**
➤ Classic Reprint Series (GBR ISSN 1354-361X) **5274**
Classic Rock (GBR ISSN 1464-7834) **6557**
Classic Saison (DEU) **8575**
Classic Stitches (GBR ISSN 1352-9730) **6637**
▼ Classic Style Magazine (USA) **2252**
• Classic Toy Trains (USA ISSN 0895-0997) **4332**
Classic Tractor (GBR ISSN 1472-9695) **210**
• Classic Trains (USA ISSN 1527-0718) **8616**
Classic Trucks (USA ISSN 1097-7988) **8575**
Classic Trucks & Vans (GBR ISSN 1740-0945) **4332**
Classic Van and Pick-up (GBR ISSN 1472-1821) **8669**
Classic Wings (NZL ISSN 1175-9690) **51**
Classica (FRA ISSN 1287-4329) **6557**
Classica (PRT ISSN 0870-0141) **2232**
• ➤ Classica et Mediaevalia (DNK ISSN 0106-5815) **2232**
Classica et Neolatina (DEU ISSN 1436-9478) **2232**
Classica Monacensia (DEU ISSN 0941-4274) **5274**
Classical and Byzantine Monographs (ESP ISSN 1381-2955) **2232**
Classical and Medieval Literature Criticism (USA ISSN 0896-0011) **5274**
Classical and Medieval Numismatic Society. Journal (CAN ISSN 1497-6498) **6649**
• ➤ Classical and Modern Literature (USA ISSN 0197-2227) **5274**
• ➤ Classical and Quantum Gravity (GBR ISSN 0264-9381) **7008**
• ➤ Classical Antiquity (USA ISSN 0278-6656) **2232**
Classical Association of New England. Annual Bulletin (USA) **2232**
Classical Association of the Pacific Northwest. Bulletin (USA) **2232**
† Classical Association. Proceedings (GBR ISSN 0069-4460) **8941**
• ➤ Classical Bulletin (USA ISSN 0009-8337) **2232**
• The Classical Catalogue (GBR ISSN 0961-5237) **6557**
Classical Fighting Arts (USA ISSN 1547-416X) **8166**
Classical Guitar (GBR ISSN 0950-429X) **6557**
• ➤ Classical Journal (USA ISSN 0009-8353) **2232**
• Classical London (GBR) **6557**
Classical Music (GBR ISSN 0961-2696) **6557**
Classical Music Guide to Festivals (GBR) **6557**
Classical Music Guide to Summer Schools and Music Courses *see* Guide to Summer Schools (Year) **6571**
Classical Numismatic Review (USA ISSN 1064-1181) **6650**
Classical Outlook (USA ISSN 0009-8361) **2232**
• ➤ Classical Philology (USA ISSN 0009-837X) **2232**
• ➤ Classical Quarterly (GBR ISSN 0009-8388) **2232**
▼ • Classical Receptions Journal (GBR ISSN 1759-5134) **2233**
• ➤ Classical Review (GBR ISSN 0009-840X) **2233**
Classical Russia (USA ISSN 1070-9711) **5274**
• Classical Singer (USA ISSN 1534-276X) **6557**
• ➤ Classical World (USA ISSN 0009-8418) **2233**
I Classici dei Classici (ITA ISSN 1970-0458) **5274**
I Classici del Fantasy (ITA ISSN 1724-9953) **5441**
I Classici della Risata (ITA ISSN 1824-4203) **5274**
Classici Italiani Minori (ITA) **5274**
➤ The Classicist (USA ISSN 1076-2922) **437**
Classics *see* Classics Monthly **8575**

Title

DIRECTORY 2010 CLUB RYTHM' AND BLUES 10129

• ➤ Clinical Neuropharmacology (USA ISSN 0362-5664) 6829
Clinical Neurophysiology see Neurophysiologie Clinique 6167
• ➤ Clinical Neurophysiology (IRL ISSN 1388-2457) 6132
➤ Clinical Neurophysiology. Supplement (NLD ISSN 1567-424X) 6132
Clinical Neuropsychiatry (ITA ISSN 1724-4935) 6132
The Clinical Neuropsychologist see Neuropsychology, Development and Cognition. Section D: The Clinical Neuropsychologist 7387
• ➤ Clinical Neuroradiology (DEU) 6194
† • Clinical Neuroscience Research (NLD ISSN 1566-2772) 8941
Clinical Neuroscience Research. Supplement see Clinical Neuroscience Research 8941
Clinical Neurosurgery (USA ISSN 0069-4827) 6132
• ➤ Clinical Nuclear Medicine (USA ISSN 0363-9762) 6194
• ➤ Clinical Nurse Specialist (USA ISSN 0887-6274) 5955
• ➤ Clinical Nursing Research (USA ISSN 1054-7738) 5955
• ➤ Clinical Nutrition (NLD ISSN 0261-5614) 6656
• Clinical Nutrition Insight (USA ISSN 1938-8640) 6656
• ➤ Clinical Obstetrics and Gynecology (USA ISSN 0009-9201) 5988
• ➤ Clinical Oncology (GBR ISSN 0936-6555) 6016
• Clinical Oncology Alert (USA ISSN 0886-7186) 6016
• Clinical Oncology News (USA ISSN 1933-0677) 6016
• Clinical Oncology Week (USA ISSN 1543-6799) 6016
▼ • ➤ Clinical Ophthalmology (Online) (GBR ISSN 1177-5483) 6040
† • Clinical Ophthalmology (Print) (NZL ISSN 1177-5467) 8941
Clinical Opinions (GBR ISSN 1749-1991) 5597
• ➤ Clinical Oral Implants Research (DNK ISSN 0905-7161) 5838
Clinical Oral Implants Research. Supplement see Clinical Oral Implants Research 5838
• ➤ Clinical Oral Investigations (DEU ISSN 1432-6981) 5838
Clinical Orthopaedic Surgery see Rinsho Seikei Geka 6072
• ➤ Clinical Orthopaedics and Related Research (USA ISSN 0009-921X) 6057
• ➤ Clinical Otolaryngology (GBR ISSN 1749-4478) 6078
▼ • Clinical Ovarian Cancer and Other Gynecologic Malignancies (USA ISSN 1941-4390) 5988
• Clinical Pediatric Emergency Medicine (USA ISSN 1522-8401) 6090
• Clinical Pediatric Endocrinology (JPN ISSN 0918-5739) 6090
• ➤ Clinical Pediatrics (USA ISSN 0009-9228) 6090
Clinical Perspectives in Gastroenterology see Clinical Gastroenterology and Hepatology 5921
Clinical Perspectives in Obstetrics and Gynecology (USA ISSN 0178-0328) 5988
Clinical Perspectives on Lysosomal Storage Disorders (USA ISSN 1540-3025) 5597
• Clinical Pharmacist (GBR ISSN 1758-9061) 6829
• ➤ Clinical Pharmacokinetics (NZL ISSN 0312-5963) 6829
Clinical Pharmacology see Yakuri to Rinsho 6886
• ➤ Clinical Pharmacology and Therapeutics (USA ISSN 0009-9236) 6829
Clinical Pharmacology Research see International Journal of Clinical Pharmacology Research 6849
Clinical Pharmacology Series (USA ISSN 0892-001X) 6829
Clinical Pharmacology and Therapy see Klinicheskaya Farmakologiya i Terapiya 6857
Clinical Pharmacy Symposium see Iryou Yakugaku Foramu Kouen Youshishuu 6851
Clinical Photodynamics (GBR ISSN 1474-015X) 5873
Clinical Photodynamics in Dermatology see Clinical Photodynamics 5873
• ➤ Clinical Physiology and Functional Imaging (GBR ISSN 1475-0961) 5597
Clinical Physiology of Circulation see Klinicheskaya Fiziologiya Krovoobrashcheniya 5795
Clinical Practice see Kurinikaru Purakutisu 5659
• ➤ Clinical Practice and Epidemiology in Mental Health (GBR ISSN 1745-0179) 7345
• Clinical Practice Guidelines (USA ISSN 1066-677X) 5597
Clinical Practice Recommendations (Year) (USA) 5885
Clinical Privilege Update see Credentialing Resource Center Connection 4091
Clinical Privileging Advisor see Credentialing Resource Center Connection 4091
Clinical Prostate Cancer see Clinical Genitourinary Cancer 6016
• Clinical Proteomics (USA ISSN 1542-6416) 729
Clinical Psychiatry see Seishin Igaku 6184
• Clinical Psychiatry News (USA ISSN 0270-6644) 6132
• ➤ Clinical Psychologist (GBR ISSN 1328-4207) 7345
• The Clinical Psychologist (USA ISSN 0009-9244) 7345
➤ Clinical Psychology (GBR ISSN 1473-8279) 7345
• ➤ Clinical Psychology (USA ISSN 0969-5893) 7345
Clinical Psychology & People with Learning Disabilities (GBR ISSN 1746-6008) 7345
• ➤ Clinical Psychology & Psychotherapy (GBR ISSN 1063-3995) 7345
• ➤ Clinical Psychology Review (GBR ISSN 0272-7358) 7345
Clinical Psychology Training Research & Development (GBR ISSN 1479-2524) 7345
• Clinical Pulmonary Medicine (USA ISSN 1068-0640) 6213
• ➤ Clinical Radiology (GBR ISSN 0009-9260) 6194
Clinical Radiology see Rinsho Hoshasen 6207
† • ➤ Clinical Radiology Extra (NLD ISSN 1477-6804) 8941
Clinical Radiology. Supplement see Clinical Radiology 6194
• ➤ Clinical Rehabilitation (GBR ISSN 0269-2155) 6107
• Clinical Reseach Manual (GBR ISSN 1355-4808) 5597
• Clinical Research & Contract Manufacturing (CAN ISSN 1912-0125) 1083
• ➤ Clinical Research and Regulatory Affairs (GBR ISSN 1060-1333) 6829
• ➤ Clinical Research in Cardiology (DEU ISSN 1861-0684) 5783
Clinical Research in Cardiology. Supplementum see Der Kardiologe 5794
• Clinical Research Resources Directory (USA) 5742
▼ • ➤ The Clinical Respiratory Journal (DNK ISSN 1752-6981) 6213
• ➤ Clinical Reviews in Allergy & Immunology (USA ISSN 1080-0549) 5756
• ➤ Clinical Reviews in Bone and Mineral Metabolism (USA ISSN 1534-8644) 6016
• ➤ Clinical Rheumatology (GBR ISSN 0770-3198) 6223
Clinical Rheumatology and Related Research see Rinshou Ryuumachi 6227
• Clinical Risk (GBR ISSN 1356-2622) 5597
▼ • ➤ Clinical Schizophrenia & Related Psychoses (USA ISSN 1935-1232) 7345
▼ • ➤ Clinical Scholars Review (USA ISSN 1939-2095) 5955
• ➤ Clinical Science (GBR ISSN 0143-5221) 5597
Clinical Science. Supplement see Clinical Science 5597
Clinical Series see N S L H A Clinical Series 6083
The Clinical Services Journal (GBR ISSN 1478-5641) 4090
• ➤ Clinical Simulation in Nursing (USA ISSN 1876-1399) 5955
Clinical Simulation in Nursing Education see Clinical Simulation in Nursing 5955
• ➤ Clinical Social Work Journal (USA ISSN 0091-1674) 8034
➤ Clinical Sociology (USA ISSN 1566-7847) 7955
Clinical Strategies: A K F Newsletter for Nephrology Professionals (USA) 6266
Clinical Study see Kurinikaru Sutadi 5968
• ➤ The Clinical Supervisor (USA ISSN 0732-5223) 8034
➤ Clinical Surveys in Endocrinology (USA ISSN 1050-3374) 5885
▼ Clinical Talk (GBR ISSN 1756-7793) 5597
• The Clinical Teacher (GBR ISSN 1743-4971) 5597
• ➤ Clinical Techniques in Equine Practice (USA ISSN 1534-7516) 8795
Clinical Techniques in Small Animal Practice see Topics in Companion Animal Medicine 8808
• ➤ Clinical Therapeutics (USA ISSN 0149-2918) 6829
• ➤ Clinical Toxicology (USA ISSN 1556-3650) 6829
• ➤ Clinical Transplantation (DNK ISSN 0902-0063) 6240
Clinical Transplantation. Supplement see Clinical Transplantation 6240
Clinical Transplants (USA ISSN 0890-9016) 6240
• ➤ Clinical Trials (GBR ISSN 1740-7745) 5904
• Clinical Trials Administrator (USA ISSN 1544-8460) 5904
• Clinical Trials Advisor (USA ISSN 1089-957X) 5598
Clinical Trials Monitor see Clinical Investigator News 6829
• Clinical Trials News (USA) 6016
• Clinical Trials Week (USA ISSN 1543-6772) 5904
• Clinical Update (AUS ISSN 1328-9454) 6016
• Clinical Updates in Infectious Diseases (USA) 5811
➤ Clinical Updates in Women's Health Care (USA ISSN 1536-3619) 8845
▼ Clinically - Oriented Biomedical Engineering (SGP) 5598
Clinicas de Anestesiologia de Norteamerica (ESP) 5770
• Clinic@s de Medicina Critica (CHL ISSN 0717-9863) 5598
Clinica's Device and Diagnostic Daily see Clinica 5595
Clinicas Pediatricas de Norteamerica (ESP ISSN 0186-159X) 6090
Clinicas Urologicas de la Complutense see Universidad Complutense. Clinicas Urologicas 6275
Clinician/Kurinishian (JPN ISSN 0387-1541) 5598
Clinician & Community (USA) 5598
Clinician in Management see The International Journal of Clinical Leadership 5638
† • Clinician News (USA ISSN 1077-9914) 8941
• Clinician Reviews (USA ISSN 1052-0627) 5598
▼ Clinician's Digest (USA ISSN 1935-9365) 5955
Clinician's Manual on Hypertension and Concomitant Hyperlipidaemia (GBR ISSN 0964-5969) 5742
• Clinician's Research Digest (USA ISSN 8756-3207) 7417
Clinician's Toolbox (USA) 7345
• Clinicien (CAN ISSN 0832-9184) 5598
• ➤ Clinics (BRA ISSN 1807-5932) 5598
• ➤ Clinics in Chest Medicine (USA ISSN 0272-5231) 6213
• ➤ Clinics in Colon & Rectal Surgery (USA ISSN 1531-0043) 6240
• ➤ Clinics in Dermatology (USA ISSN 0738-081X) 5873
Clinics in Developmental Medicine (GBR ISSN 0069-4835) 6090
• ➤ Clinics in Geriatric Medicine (USA ISSN 0749-0690) 4043
• ➤ Clinics in Laboratory Medicine (USA ISSN 0272-2712) 5904
• Clinics in Liver Disease (USA ISSN 1089-3261) 5921
• ➤ Clinics in Mother and Child Health (CMR ISSN 1812-5840) 5988
• Clinics in Occupational and Environmental Medicine (USA ISSN 1526-0046) 5598
• ➤ Clinics in Perinatology (USA ISSN 0095-5108) 5988
Clinics in Perinatology: Continuing Medical Education Supplement see Clinics in Perinatology 5988
• ➤ Clinics in Plastic Surgery (USA ISSN 0094-1298) 6240
Clinics in Podiatric Medicine and Surgery see Clinics in Podiatric Medicine and Surgery of North America 6057
• Clinics in Podiatric Medicine and Surgery of North America (USA ISSN 1559-6486) 6057
• ➤ Clinics in Sports Medicine (USA ISSN 0278-5919) 6229
Clinics of Lung Cancer: Epidemiology, Detection, Diagnoses, Treatments see Mook: Haigan no Rinsho 6028
CliniCum (AUT) 4090
CliniCum Akut (AUT) 4090
Clinicum Psy (AUT) 6132
• ClinicUS (Urgences Sante) (CAN ISSN 1499-4313) 7513
Clinique du Transfert (FRA ISSN 1770-7749) 6132
Clinique du Travail (FRA ISSN 1952-210X) 7345
• La Clinique Lacanienne (FRA ISSN 1288-6629) 6132
Clinique Psychanalitique et Psycho-Pathologie (FRA ISSN 1281-6124) 7346
• Cliniques Mediterraneennes (FRA ISSN 0762-7491) 6132
Clink (NLD) 1083
Clinton - Essex - Franklin Library System Trailblazer see C E F Trailblazer 4999
Clinton Historical Society. Newsletter (USA ISSN 0197-2871) 4289
Clinton St. (USA) 5274
• Clio (DEU ISSN 0933-0747) 8845
• Clio (DOM ISSN 0009-9376) 4135
• ➤ Clio (FRA ISSN 1252-7017) 8895
Clio (ITA ISSN 0391-6731) 4135
Clio (MEX) 4289
• Clio (PRT ISSN 0870-4104) 4211
• ➤ Clio (Ft. Wayne) (USA ISSN 0884-2043) 4135
• Clio (Madrid, 1998) (ESP ISSN 1139-6237) 4135
• Clio (Madrid, 2001) (ESP ISSN 1579-3532) 4135
Clio Bibliography Series (USA) 4169
• Clio Medica (NLD ISSN 0045-7183) 5598
Clioh's Workshop (ITA ISSN 1828-2911) 4135
▼ • ➤ Cliometrica (DEU ISSN 1863-2505) 1537
Clio's Psyche (USA ISSN 1080-2622) 7346
The Clipper (CHE ISSN 1012-9707) 3631
Clips (DEU ISSN 1863-2629) 586
Le Clique (USA) 4372
Clitheroe Advertiser & Times (GBR) 3863
Clitopile Pruineux (FRA ISSN 1774-2994) 482
Clivia (DEU) 586
Clivia News (ZAF ISSN 1819-1460) 3727
Cloche see Canadian Brown Swiss and Braunvieh Association Newsletter 262
ClockDial (USA) 601
Clocks (GBR ISSN 0968-2384) 4565
Clocktower (USA ISSN 0009-9430) 2278
• Clocktower Fiction (USA) 5441
Cloelia (USA ISSN 1543-8414) 8895
Clogher Record (IRL ISSN 0412-8079) 4211
Clon (COL ISSN 1692-6323) 5598
• Clon: Cyberzine de Arte y Cultura (MEX) 482
Clondalkin Echo (IRL ISSN 1649-962X) 3892
† • Clone (FRA) 8941
• ➤ Cloning and Stem Cells (USA ISSN 1536-2302) 864
• Close Quarter Combat (USA) 8166
Close Shave (USA) 6287
Close Up (DEU ISSN 1433-7673) 6494
• Close-up (USA) 6965
Close-up Hypnosis (CAN ISSN 1715-8486) 5942
Close-Up Magazine (SWE ISSN 1103-3568) 6557
Close Up Magazine (USA ISSN 0896-372X) 6557
Closed Circuit Television Market Report see Key Note Market Report: Closed Circuit T V 2384
Closed-End Fund Sourcebook (USA ISSN 1067-6279) 1616
• Closed-Head Injury (USA) 5598
Closeout News (USA) 1811
Closer (FRA ISSN 1774-7201) 8856
Closer (GBR ISSN 1478-078X) 8856
• Closer to God (GBR ISSN 1362-914X) 7752
Closer Walk (USA) 7634
• Closets (USA ISSN 1550-8536) 4535
CloseUp (USA) 2278
• Closing the Gap (USA ISSN 0886-1935) 3038
The Cloth Doll (USA ISSN 8755-2655) 6637
Cloth Paper Scissors (USA ISSN 1551-8175) 532
Clothing see New Mexico State University. Cooperative Extension Service. Guide C 4365
• Clothing & Footwear Industry (GBR ISSN 1741-1726) 2246
Clothing and Lingerie Industries and Their Suppliers see Die Bekleidungs- und Waesche-Industrie und Ihre Helfer 2245
• Clothing and Textile Arts Index (USA ISSN 0887-2937) 2250
• Clothing & Textiles Research Journal (USA ISSN 0887-302X) 2246
Clothing for Less Newsletter (USA ISSN 1053-6507) 2636
Clothing Manufacturers see Key Note Market Report. Clothing Manufacturing 2248
Clothing Manufacturers see Business Ratio. Clothing Manufacturers 2245
Clothing Manufacturers Association of the U S A. Members News Bulletin (USA) 2246
Clothing Retailers see Business Ratio. Clothing Retailers 2245
Clothing Retailing Marketing Report see Key Note Market Report: Clothing Retailing 2248
Clothing Technology Magazine see Konfeksiyon Teknik 2248
Clotilde's Sewing Savvy (USA ISSN 1548-6931) 6637
Cloud 9 Classics Yearbook see Cloud Nine Classics Yearbook 8575
• Cloud-Cuckoo-Land/Wolkenkuckucksheim - Cloud-Cuckoo-Land - Vozdushnyi zamok (DEU ISSN 1434-0984) 437
Cloud Family Journal (USA ISSN 0883-0940) 3762
Cloud Nine Classics Yearbook (GBR ISSN 1751-1313) 8575
• Clovek (CZE ISSN 1801-8785) 7116
• Clovek a Spolocnost (SVK ISSN 1335-3608) 8094
• Clover Information Index (GBR ISSN 0140-1939) 7578
Cloverdale Reporter News (CAN ISSN 1719-5888) 3807
Cloverdale Reporter Newsmagazine see Cloverdale Reporter News 3807
Cloverview (USA) 8418
Club (GBR ISSN 0307-4382) 5106
The Club (HKG) 8539
Club (POL) 8693
Club 3 (ITA ISSN 1124-1373) 4043
Club Alpino Italiano. La Rivista see La Rivista 8330
Club Business International (USA ISSN 1043-9692) 1958
Club Business Update see Fitness Update 8173
Club Business Update. Instructor see Fitness Update 8173
Club Business Update. Manager see Fitness Update 8173
Club Conchylia. Informationen (DEU ISSN 0931-797X) 938
Club Confidential (USA ISSN 1072-8066) 6288
Club Cricket Conference Official Yearbook (GBR) 8225
Club D A L I. Bulletin (Dessin Automatique des Lignes Isobathes) (FRA ISSN 1274-6991) 2793
Club de Gourmets (ESP ISSN 0210-170X) 4383
Club de Reflexion des Cabinets et Groupes d'Hepato-Gastroenterologie. Lettre (FRA ISSN 1261-7458) 5921
Club de Tango (ARG ISSN 0328-0403) 2683
• Club des Ornithologues de l'Outaouais (CAN ISSN 1910-1821) 905
Club Director (USA ISSN 1050-8600) 2265
▼ Club Donny (NLD) 5274
Club Extra - Geld und Mehr (DEU) 1327
Club Filatelico de Caracas. Gaceta Mensual (VEN) 6893
Club FreeTime (USA) 3973
Club Goldenrod (USA) 4372
Club-Illustrierte (DEU) 2265
Club Industry see Club Industry's Fitness Business Pro 6984
• Club Industry's Fitness Business Pro (USA ISSN 1552-5503) 6984
Club International (GBR ISSN 0955-1816) 6288
Club International (USA ISSN 0747-0819) 6288
• Club Journal (GBR ISSN 0268-0378) 2265
Club Knorr a la Carte Journal (CAN) 4354
† Club Magazin (DEU ISSN 0933-7075) 8941
Club Magazine (USA ISSN 0747-0827) 6288
• Club Management (USA ISSN 0009-9589) 2265
Club Management in Australia (AUS ISSN 0045-7205) 1733
• Club Marine (AUS ISSN 0817-8585) 5068
Club Mirror (GBR ISSN 0045-7213) 2265
• Club Network (AUS) 6984
Club News (GBR) 4977
Club Nintendo (ARG) 2475
Club On (GBR ISSN 1365-0092) 5068
Club Rythm' and Blues (FRA ISSN 1775-0113) 6557

Title

● ➤ CodeBreakers - Journal (DEU) **2410**
Codery on Solicitors (GBR) **4643**
Codes and Abbreviations for the Use of the International Telecommunications Services (CHE) **2367**
Codes & Standards (USA ISSN 0889-3616) **4407**
Codes et Lois. Traites de l'Europe Occidentale et Textes d'Application (FRA ISSN 0750-8468) **4643**
Codes Larcier (BEL ISSN 0010-0188) **4644**
Codes Larcier. Complements (BEL ISSN 0773-3569) **4644**
● CoDesign (GBR ISSN 1571-0882) **437**
Codeung Suhag Gyo'yug/Education of Primary School Mathematics (KOR ISSN 1226-6914) **5478**
● Codewords (NZL ISSN 1176-8290) **992**
Codex Alimentarius (English Edition) (ITA ISSN 0259-2916) **3631**
Codex Alimentarius (French Edition) *see* Codex Alimentarius (English Edition) **3631**
Codex Alimentarius (Spanish Edition) *see* Codex Alimentarius (English Edition) **3631**
Codex Aquilarensis (ESP ISSN 0214-896X) **4135**
Codex Arbeidsrecht (BEL ISSN 1781-8818) **1670**
Codex Diplomaticus *see* Diplomaticki Zbornik **4214**
Codex Economie (BEL ISSN 1784-5378) **4860**
Codex Filatelica (USA ISSN 0896-3533) **6893**
Codex Inlichtingen (BEL ISSN 1784-8148) **4920**
Codex Milieurecht (BEL ISSN 1374-8459) **3411**
Codex O C M W - Wetgeving (BEL ISSN 1782-1908) **8034**
Codex Openbare Hulpverlening. Hulpdiensten (BEL ISSN 1782-1207) **7430**
Codex Openbare Hulpverlening. Interventie (BEL ISSN 1782-1215) **7430**
Codex Openbare Hulpverlening. Preventie (BEL ISSN 1782-1193) **7430**
Codex Publiek Recht (BEL ISSN 0778-0680) **7430**
Codex Sociale Zekerheid (BEL ISSN 1783-8835) **8034**
Codex van de Architect (BEL ISSN 1782-2173) **438**
CodeXXI (ESP ISSN 1576-1746) **6557**
Codice (ESP ISSN 0213-6236) **7634**
● Il Codice della Strada (ITA ISSN 1121-6840) **8494**
● Codice dell'Ospedalita Privata (ITA ISSN 1970-9730) **4090**
Codices (CD-ROM Edition) *see* Bulletin de Jurisprudence Constitutionnelle **4846**
Codices (Online Edition) *see* Bulletin de Jurisprudence Constitutionnelle **4846**
Codices Arabici Antiqui (DEU ISSN 0340-6393) **547**
Codices Manuscripti (AUT ISSN 0379-3621) **5002**
† Codices Manuscripti Bibliothecae Universitatis Leidensis (NLD ISSN 0169-8672) **8941**
Codices Mirabiles (ITA ISSN 1970-3937) **7559**
● Codicillus (ZAF ISSN 0010-020X) **4644**
Codification Administrative de la Loi et des Reglements sur les Normes du Travail et de la Loi sur la Fete Nationale Incluant le Guide de la Gestion des Ressources Humaines (CAN ISSN 1910-9563) **1858**
● Codification of Statements on Auditing Standards (USA ISSN 0147-0469) **1285**
Codigos: Cuadernos de Comunicacion (MEX) **7955**
Coding Clinic for ICD-9-CM (USA ISSN 0742-9800) **4091**
▼ ● Coding Educator (USA ISSN 1949-5498) **5598**
● Coe-mmunety (USA) **2972**
Coe Review (USA) **5275**
➤ The Coelacanth (ZAF ISSN 0530-0231) **4174**
Le Coeur de l'Europe *see* Im Herzen Europas **5220**
† Coeur et Sante (FRA ISSN 0335-5306) **8941**
▼ Coexistence (USA) **6288**
Coffee & Cocoa International (GBR ISSN 0262-5938) **3631**
Coffee & Sandwich Shops Market Assessment *see* Key Note Market Assessment. Coffee and Sandwich Shops **4392**
Coffee Annual (USA) **3631**
Coffee Board of Kenya. Annual Report, Balance Sheet and Accounts (KEN) **3631**
Coffee Business (DEU) **4383**
Coffee County Historical Society Quarterly (USA) **4289**
Coffee Culture (NZL ISSN 1176-9696) **3631**
▼ ● Coffee Culture Handbook (NZL ISSN 1178-0126) **3631**
Coffee Industry Newsletter (PNG) **3631**
Coffee Intelligence (USA) **3631**
Coffee International Directory (GBR ISSN 0264-5378) **3631**
Coffee Mazdoor Sahakari (IND ISSN 0010-0250) **3631**
The Coffee Reporter (USA) **3631**
Coffee Research Institute. Annual Report. Coffee Research Station (ZWE) **225**
Coffee Research on Disc *see* Chinese Journal of Coffee Research **3631**
Coffee Review *see* Cafetal **3629**
Coffee Shop *see* Coffee Business **4383**
Coffee-Shop Politics *see* Politik Kedai Kopi **3985**
● The Coffee Shop Times (USA) **5211**
● Coffee Statistics (CD-ROM) (GBR ISSN 1755-5620) **1882**
● Coffee Working Papers (Centre of Full Employment and Equity) (AUS ISSN 1833-6949) **6695**
CoffeeHouse Digest (USA ISSN 1934-8134) **4383**
Coffeeshop *see* Coffee Business **4383**
Coffey Cousins' Clearinghouse (USA ISSN 0749-758X) **3762**
The Coffin Corner (USA) **8225**
Y Cofiadur (GBR) **7752**
Cogeneration and Competitive Power Journal *see* Cogeneration and Distributed Generation Journal **3126**
● Cogeneration and Distributed Generation Journal (USA ISSN 1545-3669) **3126**
● Cogeneration and On-Site Power Production (USA ISSN 1469-0349) **3155**
Cogent Comments (USA) **1616**
Coggins, Wilkinson and Leshy's Federal Public Land and Resources Law (USA) **7430**
Cogiscope (NLD ISSN 1871-1065) **4920**
Cogitations on Law and Government (USA ISSN 0741-9333) **4644**
➤ Cogito (AUS ISSN 1833-2005) **6910**
Cogito (DEU) **3846**
Cognitie, Creier, Comportament/Cognition, Brain, Behavior (ROM ISSN 1224-8398) **7346**
Cognitio (DEU ISSN 1434-6710) **5106**
● ➤ Cognition (NLD ISSN 0010-0277) **7346**
Cognition and Brain Sciences Unit. Annual Report (GBR ISSN 1467-5919) **6132**
Cognition and Dementia (JPN ISSN 1346-8685) **6132**
● ➤ Cognition and Emotion (GBR ISSN 0269-9931) **7346**
● ➤ Cognition and Instruction (USA ISSN 0737-0008) **7346**
➤ Cognition and Language (USA) **5106**
Cognition, Brain, Behavior *see* Cognitie, Creier, Comportament **7346**
● ➤ Cognition, Technology and Work (GBR ISSN 1435-5558) **7346**
● ➤ Cognitiva (ESP ISSN 0214-3550) **7346**
● ➤ Cognitive, Affective, & Behavioral Neuroscience (USA ISSN 1530-7026) **7346**
● ➤ Cognitive and Behavioral Neurology (USA ISSN 1543-3633) **6132**
● ➤ Cognitive and Behavioral Practice (USA ISSN 1077-7229) **7346**
▼ ● ➤ The Cognitive Behaviour Therapist (GBR ISSN 1754-470X) **7346**
Cognitive Behaviour Therapy *see* Behaviour Research and Therapy **7340**
● ➤ Cognitive Behaviour Therapy/Nordisk Tidskrift foer Beteendeterapi (GBR ISSN 1650-6073) **7346**
The Cognitive Behavioural Social Work Review (GBR ISSN 1466-3651) **8034**
Cognitive Brain Research *see* Brain Research **6128**
▼ ● ➤ Cognitive Computation (USA ISSN 1866-9956) **6133**
● ➤ Cognitive Critique (USA) **7347**
● ➤ Cognitive Development (GBR ISSN 0885-2014) **7347**
● ➤ Cognitive Linguistics (DEU ISSN 0936-5907) **5106**
● Cognitive Linguistics Bibliography (DEU ISSN 1861-048X) **5106**
Cognitive Linguistics in Practice (NLD ISSN 1388-6231) **5106**
Cognitive Linguistics Research (DEU ISSN 1861-4132) **5106**
▼ ● ➤ Cognitive Neurodynamics (NLD ISSN 1871-4080) **921**
● ➤ Cognitive Neuropsychiatry (GBR ISSN 1354-6805) **7347**
● ➤ Cognitive Neuropsychology (GBR ISSN 0264-3294) **6133**
Cognitive Neuropsychology Reviews (GBR ISSN 1368-3284) **7347**
Cognitive Neuroscience Society *see* Journal of Cognitive Neuroscience **6151**
● ➤ Cognitive Processing (DEU ISSN 1612-4782) **7347**
● ➤ Cognitive Psychology (USA ISSN 0010-0285) **7347**
Cognitive Science (NLD) **7347**
● ➤ Cognitive Science (USA ISSN 0364-0213) **7347**
● Cognitive Science (Hauppauge) (USA ISSN 1556-8237) **7347**
● Cognitive Science Quarterly (FRA ISSN 1466-6553) **7347**
Cognitive Science Research Papers (GBR ISSN 1368-9223) **7347**
➤ Cognitive Science Series: Technical Monographs and Edited Collections (USA) **7347**
Cognitive Science Society. Annual Conference. Proceedings (USA ISSN 1069-7977) **7347**
Cognitive Sciences *see* Cognitive Science (Hauppauge) **7347**
▼ ● Cognitive Semiotics (CHE ISSN 1662-1425) **5106**
Cognitive Strategy Concepts (DEU ISSN 1437-7128) **1733**
Cognitive Studies *see* Ninchi Kagaku **6171**
Cognitive Studies Research Paper (GBR ISSN 1350-3162) **7347**
Cognitive Systems (NLD ISSN 0256-663X) **7347**
● Cognitive Systems Research (Online) (USA ISSN 1389-0417) **2447**
● ➤ Cognitive Systems Research (Print) (USA) **2447**
➤ Cognitive Technology (USA ISSN 1091-8388) **7347**
● ➤ Cognitive Therapy and Research (USA ISSN 0147-5916) **7347**
Cognitivismo Clinico (ITA ISSN 1724-4927) **6133**
Cognotes (USA ISSN 0738-4319) **5002**
Cohabitation Law & Precedents (GBR) **7586**
Cohen Center for Modern Jewish Studies Centerpieces *see* C M J S Centerpieces **7719**
● ➤ Cohesion and Structure (NLD ISSN 0922-7725) **7008**
Cohesion Fund. Annual Report (Year) (LUX ISSN 1680-2187) **1083**
Coiffeur et Coiffures *see* Kapper en Kapsels **589**
Coiffure (NLD ISSN 0165-3679) **586**
▼ Coiffure Club (FRA ISSN 1959-0067) **586**
Coiffure et Styles (FRA ISSN 1161-899X) **586**
Coiffure Looks *see* Looks **589**
Coiffure Professionnelle (ESP ISSN 0214-5790) **586**
Coil Winding International & Electrical Insulation Magazine (GBR) **3297**
COILetter *see* C O I Letter **4497**
Coimisium um Rialail Cumarsaide. Tuarascail Bhliantuil *see* Ireland. Commission for Communications Regulation. Annual Report **2328**
Le Coin de Table (FRA) **5419**
Coin Dealer Newsletter (USA ISSN 1062-8169) **6650**
Coin Hoards (GBR ISSN 0140-1149) **6650**
Coin Laundry Association Guidelines *see* C L A Guidelines **8449**
Coin Monthly (GBR) **6650**
Coin News (GBR ISSN 0958-1391) **6650**
Coin-Op News Europe (IRL ISSN 1649-3060) **8167**
Coin Previewer (USA) **6650**
Coin Prices (USA ISSN 0010-0412) **6650**
Coin Slot *see* Coin Slot International **1811**
● Coin Slot International (GBR ISSN 1357-7441) **1811**
Coin Values *see* Coin World's Coin Values **6650**
● Coin World (USA ISSN 0010-0447) **6650**
Coin World Annual Price Guide (USA) **6650**
● Coin World's Coin Values (USA ISSN 1545-5319) **6650**
Coin World's Paper Money Values (USA ISSN 1556-0317) **6650**
Coin Yearbook (GBR ISSN 0307-6571) **6650**
● Coinage (USA ISSN 0010-0455) **6650**
COINage Magazine's Quarter Collector (Year) (USA) **6650**
Coinage of the Americas Conference. Proceedings (USA ISSN 8756-6265) **6650**
The COINfidential Report (USA) **6650**
● CoinLink.com (USA) **6650**
● Coins (USA ISSN 0010-0471) **6650**
Coins & Paper Money *see* Warman's Coins & Paper Money **6653**
Coins & Prices *see* North American Coins & Prices **6652**
Coinslot International *see* Coin Slot International **1811**
Coir (IND ISSN 0530-0495) **8449**
● ➤ Coke and Chemistry (USA ISSN 1068-364X) **3241**
Coke Oven Managers' Association. Year Book (GBR ISSN 0069-4991) **6460**
Cokefish (USA) **5419**
Col - lecio Formacio (ESP ISSN 1885-7493) **6696**
● Col.legi Oficial de Bibliotecaris-Documentalistes de Catalunya. Document (ESP ISSN 0213-4772) **5002**
Col-legi Oficial de Psicolegs de Catalunya. Revista (ESP ISSN 1887-9039) **7347**
● Colabor@ (BRA ISSN 1519-8529) **2837**
Colas y Lolas (ARG ISSN 1850-1451) **565**
● Colborne Chronicle (CAN ISSN 0834-6127) **3807**
● Colby Magazine (USA) **2278**
➤ Colby Quarterly (USA ISSN 1050-5873) **5275**
Colchester Archaeological Report (GBR ISSN 0264-6013) **387**
Colchester Express (GBR ISSN 0966-2294) **3863**
Colchester Inside Business *see* Inside Business. Colchester **1124**
Colciencias. Carta (COL ISSN 0120-5986) **7847**
Cold-Drill (USA ISSN 0084-8816) **5275**
Cold Facts (USA ISSN 1085-5262) **7053**
Cold Finished Steel Bar Institute. Monthly Import Analysis (USA) **6309**
Cold Fusion Developer's Journal *see* ColdFusion Developer's Journal **2588**
● Cold Fusion Times (USA ISSN 1072-2874) **3166**
Cold Mountain Review (USA ISSN 1547-5972) **5275**
Cold Regions Research and Engineering Laboratory Report *see* C R R E L Report **3183**
● ➤ Cold Regions Science and Technology (NLD ISSN 0165-232X) **8418**
Cold Spring Harbor Laboratory. Abstracts of Papers Presented at Meetings (USA ISSN 0084-8824) **714**
Cold Spring Harbor Laboratory. Abstracts of Papers Presented at the Meeting on Proteolysis & Biological Control (USA) **714**
Cold Spring Harbor Laboratory. Annual Report (USA) **666**
● ➤ Cold Spring Harbor Laboratory. Symposia on Quantitative Biology (USA ISSN 0091-7451) **666**
Cold Spring Harbor Monograph Series (USA ISSN 0270-1847) **666**
▼ ● Cold Spring Harbor Perspectives in Biology (USA ISSN 1943-0264) **666**
● Cold Spring Harbor Protocols (USA ISSN 1940-3402) **666**
Cold Storage & Distribution Federation. Directory (GBR) **4117**
Cold Storage Report (USA) **3631**
● ➤ Cold War History (GBR ISSN 1468-2745) **4135**
● Cold War International History Project Bulletin (USA ISSN 1071-9652) **4135**
● ColdFusion Developer's Journal (USA ISSN 1523-9101) **2588**
● Cole Papers (USA ISSN 1062-6727) **8418**
Colecao Biblioteca de Trabalhos Artesanais (BRA ISSN 1808-6314) **532**
Colecao das Leis da Republica Federativa do Brasil (BRA ISSN 0103-3646) **4644**
Colecao Guia de Racas (BRA ISSN 1808-5504) **6806**
Colecao Ideia Util (BRA ISSN 1808-608X) **532**
Colecao Maos que Criam (BRA ISSN 1808-4958) **532**
Colecao Pegue e Faca (BRA ISSN 1808-4966) **532**
Colecao Pintura em Tecido (BRA ISSN 1808-6098) **532**
Colecao Receitas Dia a Dia (BRA ISSN 1808-5547) **4354**
Coleccao Arquivos (PRT) **4211**
Coleccao Arquivos de Folclore (BRA) **3616**
Coleccao Caminhos Brasileiros (BRA) **7116**
Coleccao de Estudos Juridicos (BRA ISSN 0530-0657) **4947**
Coleccao Ensaio (PRT) **5275**
Coleccao Escritores Brasileiros (BRA) **5275**
Coleccao Forma (PRT) **5419**
Coleccao Horizonte Universitario (PRT) **7116**
Coleccao Jornalismo Catarinense (BRA) **4573**
Coleccao Literatura (PRT) **5275**
Coleccao N'gola (AGO) **4174**
Coleccao Pesquisa (BRA) **3616**
Coleccao: Poesia (Lisbon) (PRT) **5419**
Coleccao Poesia (Porto) (PRT) **5419**
Coleccao Questoes da Nossa Epoca (BRA) **5211**
Coleccao Rodolfo Garcia (BRA) **623**
Coleccao Teatro (BRA) **8468**
Coleccao Temas Brasileiros (BRA) **4289**
Coleccao Tendencias (BRA) **7116**
Coleccion (ARG ISSN 0328-7998) **7117**
Coleccion 500 Anos Despues (MEX) **4447**
Coleccion Abierta (ESP) **2972**
Coleccion "Aniversarios Culturales" (VEN ISSN 0069-5033) **641**
➤ Coleccion Antropologia e Historia (SLV ISSN 0256-7202) **333**
Coleccion Arte, Teoria y Critica (ARG ISSN 1515-906X) **482**
● Coleccion Barandiaran (ESP) **333**
Coleccion Bibliografia (ESP) **623**
Coleccion Bibliografica Cientifica Ecuatoriana (ECU) **7936**
Coleccion Biblioteca Soriana (ESP ISSN 0577-2486) **7955**
Coleccion C H I *see* Coleccion Ciencias, Humanidades e Ingenieria **7847**
Coleccion Canonica (ESP ISSN 0069-505X) **7634**
Coleccion Catalogos Documentales (ESP) **5002**
Coleccion Ciencias Biologicas (ESP) **666**
➤ Coleccion Ciencias, Humanidades e Ingenieria (ESP) **7847**
Coleccion Ciencias Medicas de Bolsillo (ESP) **5598**
Coleccion Correspondencia Diplomatica de los Nuncios en Espana (ESP) **4211**
Coleccion Cuadernos de Trabajo Social (ESP) **8034**
Coleccion Cultura Viva (ESP) **7955**
Coleccion de Bolsillo (ESP) **5275**
Coleccion de Economia (ESP) **1537**
Coleccion de Economia y Politica (ARG ISSN 1851-6459) **1083**
Coleccion de Estudios de Derecho Penal (COL) **4886**
Coleccion de Etnografia Luis Cortes Vazquez (ESP) **333**
Coleccion de Flamenco (ESP ISSN 1699-4477) **3616**
Coleccion de Recomendaciones y Manuales Tecnicos (ESP) **3263**
➤ Coleccion Debate (SLV) **7117**
Coleccion Direccion de Empresas y Organizaciones (ESP) **1733**
† Coleccion Directores de Cine (ESP) **8941**
Coleccion Editorial Universitaria (GTM) **2704**
▼ ● Coleccion Estudios Economicos (ESP ISSN 1988-785X) **1083**
Coleccion Estudios Latinoamericanos (ARG) **5275**
Coleccion Estudios Politicos (DOM) **7117**
Coleccion Ethos (ESP) **6557**
Coleccion F A O, Alimentacion y Nutricion *see* F A O Food and Nutrition Series **6658**
Coleccion F A O, Desarrollo Estadistico *see* F A O Statistical Development Series **8369**
Coleccion F A O, Fomento de Tierras Aguas *see* F A O Land and Water Development Series **109**
Coleccion Fe e Historia (CHL) **7955**
Coleccion Filosofica (ESP ISSN 0069-5076) **6910**
Coleccion "Foros y Seminarios." Serie Foros (VEN ISSN 0069-5084) **4289**
Coleccion "Foros y Seminarios." Serie Seminarios (VEN ISSN 0069-5092) **4289**
† Coleccion Garrigues & Andersen (ESP ISSN 1699-4469) **8941**
Coleccion Historia (ESP ISSN 1698-8124) **4211**
Coleccion Historia (PRY) **4289**
Coleccion Historia de la Educacion en Zamora (ESP) **2837**
Coleccion Historia de la Iglesia (ESP) **7792**
Coleccion Historia. Serie Investigacion (ESP ISSN 1698-8132) **4211**
Coleccion Historica (ESP ISSN 0069-5106) **4211**
Coleccion "Humanismo y Ciencia" (VEN ISSN 0069-5114) **4447**

Title

10134 COLLEGE OF AMERICAN PATHOLOGISTS TODAY ULRICH'S PERIODICALS

College of American Pathologists Today *see* C A P Today **5590**
College of Business Administration Business Review *see* U E Business Review **1799**
College of Business Administration Connections *see* C O B A Connections **2276**
College of Business Administration Passages *see* C O B A Passages **1078**
College of Engineering, Trivandrum. Magazine (IND) **3184**
College of Estate Management. Research Report (GBR ISSN 1367-126X) **2278**
College of Europe Studies/Cahiers du College d'Europe (BEL ISSN 1780-9665) **7227**
College of Insurance. Academic Bulletin (USA) **4499**
College of Islamic and Arabic Studies. Journal *see* Magallat Kulliyyat al-Dirasa al-Islamiyyat wa-al-Arabiyyat **5149**
The College of Law. Crash Course Lecture (GBR ISSN 0309-2771) **4644**
The College of Law. Lectures (GBR ISSN 0309-3166) **4644**
• The College of Law Practice Papers (AUS ISSN 1444-2957) **4644**
College of Law Practice Papers (Qld. and Vic. Ed.) *see* The College of Law Queensland Practice Papers **4644**
The College of Law Practice Papers NSW. Volume 4 (AUS) **4908**
The College of Law Practice Papers. Volume 1 *see* The College of Law Queensland Practice Papers. Volume 1 **4644**
The College of Law Practice Papers. Volume 2 *see* The College of Law Queensland Practice Papers. Volume 2 **4901**
The College of Law Practice Papers. Volume 3 *see* The College of Law Queensland Practice Papers. Volume 3 **4860**
The College of Law Queensland Practice Papers (AUS ISSN 1832-696X) **4644**
The College of Law Queensland Practice Papers. Volume 1 (AUS) **4644**
The College of Law Queensland Practice Papers. Volume 2 (AUS) **4901**
The College of Law Queensland Practice Papers. Volume 3 (AUS) **4860**
College of Medical Radiation Technologists and Therapists of Alberta. Journal *see* The Viewbox **6210**
College of Nurses of Ontario. Membership Statistics Report (CAN ISSN 1719-4318) **5955**
College of Physicians and Surgeons of Alberta. Medical Directory (CAN ISSN 0702-7826) **5599**
College of Physicians and Surgeons of British Columbia. Annual Report (CAN) **5599**
College of Physicians and Surgeons of British Columbia. Medical Directory (CAN ISSN 0069-5726) **5599**
• ➤ College of Physicians and Surgeons Pakistan. Journal (PAK ISSN 1022-386X) **5599**
College of Psychologists of Ontario. Bulletin (CAN) **7348**
College of Radiologists of Australasia. Journal *see* Journal of Medical Imaging and Radiation Oncology **6200**
College of St. Scholastica Times Magazine (USA) **2278**
▼ • College of St. Elizabeth Journal of the Behavioral Sciences (USA ISSN 1940-154X) **7348**
College of Surgeons Hong Kong. Annals *see* Surgical Practice **6260**
College of Teachers. Newsletter (GBR) **2837**
College of Textile Technology, Serampore Annual *see* C.T.T.S. Annual **8449**
• ➤ College of the Bahamas Research Journal (BHS ISSN 1607-1069) **4447**
College of Veterinarians of Ontario. Update (CAN) **8795**
College of Veterinary Medicine Quarterly *see* C V M Quarterly **8795**
College of William and Mary. William and Mary School of Law. Tax Conference (USA) **1917**
• College Outlook (Fall Edition) (USA) **6696**
College Outlook (Spring Edition) *see* College Outlook (Fall Edition) **6696**
College Pension Plan. (Year) Annual Report Summary *see* College Pension Plan. Report to Members **1671**
College Pension Plan Annual Report (CAN ISSN 1198-2330) **1617**
College Pension Plan. Pension News (CAN ISSN 1912-399X) **1670**
College Pension Plan. Report to Members (CAN ISSN 1912-3825) **1671**
College Physics *see* Daxue Wuli **7010**
• College Planning and Management (USA ISSN 1523-0910) **2973**
College Press. Annual Lecture Series (NGA) **7227**
• College Press Service (USA ISSN 0010-1125) **2973**
• College Preview (USA ISSN 1050-7159) **2973**
• College Publishing Market Forecast (Year) (USA ISSN 1933-2025) **1447**
• ➤ The College Quarterly (Online Edition) (CAN) **2973**
College Reading and Learning Association Newsletter *see* C R L A Newsletter **2970**
College Reading Association. Monographs (USA) **5003**
College Reporter (USA) **2278**
➤ College Research (GBR ISSN 1367-5664) **2973**
College Services (USA ISSN 1540-8434) **2973**
• College Source (USA) **2973**
College Sports Information Directors of America Digest *see* C O S I D A Digest **8164**
College Spotlight (USA ISSN 1525-4313) **2954**
• The College Store (USA) **1811**
College Store Executive (USA ISSN 0010-1141) **1811**
• ➤ College Student Affairs Journal (Online Edition) (USA ISSN 0888-210X) **2278**
College Student Affairs Journal (Print Edition) *see* College Student Affairs Journal (Online Edition) **2278**
College Student and the Courts (USA ISSN 0145-1472) **2973**
• ➤ College Student Journal (USA ISSN 0146-3934) **2973**
College Student's Guide to Merit and Other No-Need Funding (USA ISSN 1099-9086) **2973**
• ➤ College Teaching (USA ISSN 8756-7555) **2973**
➤ College Theology Society. Annual Publication (USA ISSN 1074-9403) **7793**
College Times *see* Daxue Shidai **2281**
The College Times (IRL ISSN 1649-0495) **2278**
College Transfer Guide (USA ISSN 0747-8836) **2954**
College - University Foodservice Who's Who (USA) **3631**
College View (USA ISSN 1539-2155) **5599**
College Voice (Staten Island) (USA) **2278**
▼ College voor Zorgverzekeringen. Zorgcijfers (NLD ISSN 1875-0508) **7513**
College Webguide Steamtunnels Internet Magazine (USA) **3973**
• CollegeFreshman (USA) **2278**
▼ Collegepreneur (USA ISSN 1941-3556) **1958**
Colleges for Students with Learning Disabilities or A D D (USA ISSN 1525-3813) **2954**
Colleges of Medicine of South Africa. Transactions (ZAF ISSN 0375-3220) **5599**
Colleges with a Conscience (USA ISSN 1932-5843) **2973**
Collegi Oficial de Metges de la Provincia de Girona. Butlleti de Illustre (ESP ISSN 1577-5593) **5599**
The Collegian (GBR ISSN 0305-1064) **2278**
• ➤ Collegian (NLD ISSN 1322-7696) **5955**
The Collegian *see* The Behrend Beacon **2274**
The Collegian *see* The Independent Collegian **2287**
Collegian (Brookings) (USA) **2278**
Collegian (Elyria) (USA ISSN 0010-1206) **2278**
The Collegian (Fayette) (USA) **2278**
The Collegian (Fresno) (USA) **2278**
Collegian (Richmond) (USA) **2278**
Collegian (Toledo) (USA) **2278**
Collegian (Tulsa) (USA) **2278**
Collegiate+ *see* Collegiate+ **7634**
Collegiate+ (USA ISSN 1557-4474) **7634**
Collegiate Baseball (USA ISSN 0530-9751) **8225**
Collegiate Plus *see* Collegiate+ **7634**
• Collegiate Times (USA) **2278**
Collegiate Trends (USA ISSN 1065-0296) **1811**
Collegii Medici Antverpiensis. Annales *see* Koninklijke Geneeskundige Kring van Antwerpen. Colmed Info **5658**
• Collegio (USA ISSN 0010-1249) **2278**
Collegium (BEL) **7227**
• ➤ COLLeGIUM (FIN ISSN 1796-2986) **7955**
Collegium (UKR) **2939**
➤ Collegium Antropologicum (HRV ISSN 0350-6134) **333**
Collegium Biologicum (ROM ISSN 1454-2021) **666**
➤ Collegium Carolinum. Veroeffentlichungen (DEU ISSN 0530-9794) **4211**
Collegium Hermeneuticum (DEU) **6911**
Collegium Medievale (NOR ISSN 0801-9282) **4135**
Collegium Medievale. Supplement *see* Collegium Medievale **4135**
➤ Collegium Musicum: Yale University (USA ISSN 0147-0108) **6558**
Collegium Philosophicum (DEU) **6911**
Das Collegmagazin Zahnarzt *see* Zahnarzt Wirtschaft Praxis **5870**
Colleziona gli Autentici Vasi Cinesi (ITA ISSN 1828-7492) **365**
Colleziona i Grandi Capolavori in Miniatura (ITA ISSN 1724-2215) **365**
Colleziona le Bambole Romantiche di Porcellana (ITA ISSN 1828-7514) **4332**
Colleziona le Prestigiose Decorazioni e Medaglie Militari (ITA ISSN 1828-7476) **365**
Collezionare Orologi Meccanici (ITA ISSN 1828-3306) **4332**
Collezionare Orologi Vintage (ITA ISSN 1970-0539) **4565**
Collezionare Soldatini d'Italia (ITA ISSN 1828-3330) **4332**
† Collezione di Cucina Creativa (ITA ISSN 1125-6826) **8942**
Collezione di Monografie Preistoriche e Archeologiche (ITA ISSN 0530-9867) **387**
Collezione di Psicologia (ITA ISSN 1970-7533) **7348**
Collezione Harmony *see* Harmony Collezione **5410**
Collezione Kinder (ITA ISSN 1827-7543) **2183**
Collezioni 0 - 3 Baby (ITA ISSN 1124-299X) **2252**
Collezioni Accessori (ITA ISSN 1120-1991) **2252**
Collezioni Bambini (ITA ISSN 1120-1983) **2252**
Collezioni Beachwear (ITA) **2252**
Collezioni Donna (ITA ISSN 1120-1975) **2252**
Collezioni e Musei Archeologici del Veneto (ITA ISSN 0392-0879) **387**
Collezioni Haute Couture (ITA) **2252**
Collezioni Sport & Street (ITA ISSN 1124-2949) **2252**
Collezioni Sposa (ITA ISSN 1126-473X) **5558**
Collezioni Uomo (ITA ISSN 1120-2033) **2253**
Collezioni Zero - Tre Baby *see* Collezioni 0 - 3 Baby **2252**
Il Collezionista. Francobolli (ITA ISSN 1123-5985) **6893**
Collie Club of America. Bulletin (USA) **6806**
Collier Bankruptcy Cases (USA ISSN 0099-1848) **1327**
• Collier Bankruptcy Compensation Guide (USA) **1327**
• Collier Bankruptcy Manual (USA) **1327**
• Collier Bankruptcy Practice Guide (USA) **1327**
• Collier Business Workout Guide (USA) **4860**
• Collier Family Law and Bankruptcy Code (USA) **4908**
• Collier Forms Manual (USA) **4644**
• Collier Handbook for Creditors' Committees (USA ISSN 1044-0917) **1327**
• Collier Lending Institutions and the Bankruptcy Code (USA) **1327**
• Collier on Bankruptcy (USA) **1327**
• Collier on Bankruptcy Taxation (USA) **4860**
• Collier Real Estate Transactions and the Bankruptcy Code (USA) **1328**
Collin Chronicles (USA ISSN 1060-0949) **3762**
• ➤ Collingwood and British Idealism Studies (GBR ISSN 1744-9413) **6911**
• Collingwood Connection (CAN ISSN 1182-9095) **3807**
Collingwood Studies *see* Collingwood and British Idealism Studies **6911**
• The Collins Center Update (USA ISSN 1947-0924) **6416**
Collision (USA ISSN 0739-7437) **8575**
Collision (Kirkland) (USA ISSN 1934-8681) **7513**
Collision Estimating & Reference Guide *see* Mitchell Collision Estimating & Reference Guide. Medium Duty Trucks & Commercial Vehicles **8591**
Collision Parts Journal (USA ISSN 1526-8934) **8575**
Collision Quarterly (CAN ISSN 1483-0256) **8575**
Collision Repair Product News (USA ISSN 1554-6543) **8575**
• ➤ Colloid and Polymer Science (DEU ISSN 0303-402X) **2122**
Colloid Journal of the Russian Academy of Sciences *see* Russian Academy of Sciences. Colloid Journal **2140**
• ➤ Colloids and Surfaces A: Physicochemical and Engineering Aspects (NLD ISSN 0927-7757) **2134**
• ➤ Colloids and Surfaces B: Biointerfaces (NLD ISSN 0927-7765) **2134**
Colloque Regional sur la Production Laitiere (CAN ISSN 1719-6043) **262**
Colloque Scientifique International sur le Cafe (CHE ISSN 1029-3701) **225**
Colloques, Congres et Conferences sur la Renaissance (FRA ISSN 1243-0587) **4211**
➤ Colloques d'Histoire des Connaissances Zoologiques (BEL ISSN 0777-2491) **938**
Colloques Langues'O (FRA ISSN 0248-5095) **547**
Colloques Phytosociologiques (DEU ISSN 1430-0540) **784**
Colloqui (ITA ISSN 1824-4556) **4645**
Colloqui (USA ISSN 1069-2606) **4407**
Colloqui sulla Repubblica (ITA ISSN 1970-3945) **7117**
➤ Colloquia (ROM) **4211**
Colloquia Academica. Geisteswissenschaften (DEU ISSN 0949-8788) **7847**
Colloquia Academica. Naturwissenschaften (DEU ISSN 0949-8133) **7847**
Colloquia Communia (POL ISSN 0239-6815) **6911**
• Colloquia Germanica (DEU ISSN 0010-1338) **5107**
• Colloquia Maruliana (HRV ISSN 1332-3431) **4447**
➤ Colloquia Mathematica Societatis Janos Bolyai (NLD ISSN 0139-3383) **5478**
Colloquia Pontica (NLD ISSN 1389-8477) **387**
Colloquia Tulliana. Atti *see* Ciceroniana **5274**
➤ Colloquium (AUS ISSN 0588-3237) **7634**
Colloquium (BRA ISSN 1413-7313) **7847**
Colloquium (CAN ISSN 1198-3930) **3185**
Colloquium Geographicum (DEU ISSN 0588-3253) **4003**
Colloquium Helveticum (CHE ISSN 0179-3780) **5276**
• ➤ Colloquium Mathematicum (POL ISSN 0010-1354) **5479**
• Colloquium, Music, Worship, Arts (USA ISSN 1938-419X) **6558**
➤ Colloquium on the History of Landscape Architecture. Papers (USA) **438**
Colloquium on the Law of Outer Space. Proceedings (USA ISSN 0069-5831) **51**
Colloquium Philosophicum (ITA ISSN 1126-9170) **6911**
• Colloquy (Milford) (USA) **1811**
• ➤ Colloquy (Online) (AUS) **5276**
• Colloquy (Pittsburg) (USA) **7634**
† • ➤ Colloquy (Print) (AUS ISSN 1325-9490) **8942**
Collor (BRA) **7955**
Colne Times (GBR) **3863**
• ➤ Colo-Proctology (DEU ISSN 0174-2442) **5921**
• Colofao (BRA ISSN 1518-9791) **5276**
Cologne Convention *see* Koelner Kongress Report **6281**
Colombia *see* The P R S Group. Country Reports: Colombia **1506**
• Colombia Autos Report (GBR ISSN 1748-9849) **8575**
• Colombia Business Forecast Report (GBR ISSN 1745-0519) **1447**
➤ Colombia: Ciencia y Tecnologia (COL ISSN 0120-5595) **7847**
Colombia. Corporacion Nacional de Turismo. Boletin Informativo C E N T U R (Corporacion Nacional de Turismo, Centro de Informacion Turistica) (COL) **8694**
Colombia. Corporacion Nacional de Turismo. Cronica Turistica (COL) **8694**
• Colombia Defence & Security Report (GBR ISSN 1749-1347) **6416**
Colombia. Departamento Administrativo Nacional de Estadistica. Anuario de Comercio Exterior (COL ISSN 0120-6419) **1555**
Colombia. Departamento Administrativo Nacional de Estadistica. Anuario de Industria Manufacturera (COL) **1221**
Colombia. Departamento Administrativo Nacional de Estadistica. Anuario Demografico (COL) **7305**
Colombia. Departamento Administrativo Nacional de Estadistica. Boletin de Estadistica (COL ISSN 0120-6281) **8364**
Colombia. Departamento Administrativo Nacional de Estadistica. Division Politico-Administrativa (COL) **7480**
Colombia. Departamento Administrativo Nacional de Estadistica. Estadisticas Historicas (COL) **8364**
Colombia Estadistica (COL ISSN 0120-6443) **8364**
Colombia Exporta (COL ISSN 0120-727X) **1555**
Colombia Forestal (COL ISSN 0120-0739) **3686**
Colombia Freight Transport Report (GBR ISSN 1752-5764) **8494**
Colombia Handbook (GBR ISSN 1369-1414) **8694**
• ➤ Colombia Internacional (COL ISSN 0121-5612) **7117**
• ➤ Colombia Medica (Online Edition) (COL ISSN 1657-9534) **5599**
Colombia. Ministerio de Hacienda y Credito Publico. Proyecto de Presupuesto General de la Nacion (COL) **1917**
Colombia. Ministerio de Trabajo y Seguridad Social. Carta Informativa (COL) **1671**
Colombia. Ministerio de Trabajo y Seguridad Social. Memoria al Congreso Nacional (COL) **1671**
Colombia. Observatorio Astronomico Nacional. Anuario (COL ISSN 0120-2758) **573**
Colombia. Observatorio Astronomico Nacional. Publicaciones (COL ISSN 0067-9518) **573**
Colombia Petrochemicals Report (GBR ISSN 1749-2211) **6766**
Colombia Quarterly Forecast Report *see* Colombia Business Forecast Report **1447**
Colombia Rotaria (COL) **2265**
Colombia. Superintendencia Bancaria. Informacion Estadistica por Ciudades (COL) **1221**
Colombia. Superintendencia Bancaria. Informe de Labores (COL) **1328**
Colombia. Superintendencia Bancaria. Revista (COL ISSN 0120-4017) **1328**
Colombia. Superintendencia Bancaria. Seguros y Capitalizacion (COL) **1084**
Colombian - American Business Annual Directory (COL) **1400**
Colombian Economic Journal (COL ISSN 1692-3065) **1084**
Colombian Economy (COL) **1718**
Colombiana de Control de Malezas y Fisiologia Vegetal Noticias *see* C O M A L F I. Noticias **223**
• El Colombiano (COL) **3830**
Le Colombien (CAN ISSN 0384-0298) **2265**
Colombo Plan Bureau. The Colombo Plan Council Report (LKA) **1592**
Colombo Plan for Co-operative Economic and Social Development in Asia and the Pacific. Consultative Committee. Proceedings and Conclusions (LKA) **1592**
Colombo Plan for Co-operative Economic and Social Development in Asia and the Pacific. Development Perspectives. Country Issues Papers by Member Governments to the Consultative Committee (LKA) **1592**
Colombo Plan Newsletter (LKA ISSN 0010-1419) **1592**
La Colombophilie Belge (BEL ISSN 0773-1825) **8309**
▼ • Colon & Rectum (FRA ISSN 1951-6371) **5599**
Colong Bulletin (AUS ISSN 1325-3336) **2606**
Colonia Romanica (DEU ISSN 0930-8555) **333**
Colonial Courier (USA ISSN 0010-1435) **3762**
➤ Colonial Latin American Historical Review (USA ISSN 1063-5769) **4289**
• ➤ Colonial Latin American Review (GBR ISSN 1060-9164) **4289**
† Colonial Mexico Handbook (USA ISSN 1095-8878) **8942**
† Colonial News (NLD ISSN 1389-5699) **8942**
Colonial Newsletter *see* C N L **6649**
Colonial Rottweiler Club Newsletter (USA) **6806**
Colonial Society of Massachusetts. Publications (USA) **4289**
Colonial Williamsburg (USA ISSN 1064-2501) **4289**
Colonial Williamsburg Archaeological Series (USA ISSN 0069-5971) **387**
Colonial Williamsburg Historic Trades (USA ISSN 0897-7216) **532**
Colonie Hi-Liter (USA) **3973**

Link to your serials resources and content with ulrichsweb.com

DIRECTORY 2010 COMBUSTION AND FLAME 10135

• Colonnade (USA) 2278
Colonnades (USA) 5211
Coloproctology see Colo-Proctology 5921
Coloquio: Letras (PRT ISSN 0010-1451) 5276
• Coloquios de Paleontologia (ESP ISSN 1132-1660) 6723
Color (JPN) 7074
Color (USA) 532
▼ Color and Aroma (USA) 601
Color Association of the United States Color Forecasts see C A U S Color Forecasts 2245
Color Association of the United States Effect see C A U S Effect 2246
Color Business Report (USA ISSN 1055-3339) 2483
• Color Foto (DEU ISSN 0343-3102) 6965
Color News (USA) 586
• ➤ Color Research and Application (USA ISSN 0361-2317) 3241
† Color Schemes (USA ISSN 1936-2765) 8942
Color Science Association of Japan. Journal see Nihon Shikisai Gakkaishi 7081
• Color Slides Newsletter (USA) 2588
Color Wheel (USA ISSN 1053-1831) 5419
▼ Color with Confidence (USA ISSN 1943-3034) 4535
Colorado Academy of Family Physicians News see C A F P News 5590
Colorado Agribusiness Roundup (USA ISSN 0732-7226) 196
Colorado Archaeological Society Memoir Series (USA) 387
Colorado Architect see American Institute of Architects. Colorado Architect 427
Colorado Association for Chicano Research Review (USA) 3527
Colorado Association of Libraries. Newsletter (USA ISSN 1939-3733) 5003
Colorado Avid Golfer (USA ISSN 1548-4335) 8225
Colorado Beverage Analyst (USA ISSN 0010-1516) 601
Colorado Birds (USA) 905
Colorado biz see ColoradoBiz 1447
Colorado Book Guide (USA) 7559
• Colorado Business Credit Directory (USA) 1980
• Colorado Business Directory (USA ISSN 1048-7204) 1980
Colorado Business Organization Forms (USA) 4860
Colorado Business Resource Directory (USA) 1400
The Colorado Catholic Herald (USA) 7793
Colorado Cities and Counties Graphic Performance Analysis see Colorado Cities & Counties Graphic Performance Analysis 7480
Colorado Cities & Counties Graphic Performance Analysis (USA ISSN 1935-5777) 7480
Colorado City Retail Sales by Standard Industrial Classification (USA ISSN 0732-071X) 1426
Colorado Collections (USA ISSN 0892-077X) 3762
Colorado College Bulletin (USA) 2278
Colorado College Studies (USA ISSN 0588-4934) 2973
Colorado: Compass American Guides see Compass American Guides: Colorado 8694
The Colorado Connection (USA ISSN 1940-0454) 3411
• Colorado Construction (USA ISSN 1546-9964) 992
Colorado Corporate Forms see Colorado Business Organization Forms 4860
Colorado Council of Genealogical Societies. Newsletter (USA) 3762
Colorado Country Life (USA ISSN 1090-2503) 3156
Colorado Courts (USA ISSN 0731-7964) 4947
Colorado Criminal and Motor Vehicle Law (USA ISSN 1932-0523) 4886
• Colorado Criminal Correction Vehicles and Related Statutes (USA) 8575
Colorado Daily (USA) 2278
➤ Colorado Dental Association. Journal (USA ISSN 0010-1559) 5838
• Colorado Directory of Camping, Cabins, Lodges, Country B & B's, Fun Things to Do (USA) 8694
Colorado. Division of Wildlife. Division Report (USA ISSN 0276-0231) 3411
Colorado. Division of Wildlife. Special Report (USA ISSN 0084-8875) 2606
Colorado. Division of Wildlife. Technical Publication (USA ISSN 0084-8883) 2606
Colorado. Division of Wildlife. Terrestrial and Aquatic Wildlife Research. Research Review (USA ISSN 1055-4238) 3589
• Colorado Domestic Relations Forms (USA) 4908
Colorado Editor (USA ISSN 0010-1567) 4573
• Colorado Education & Library Directory (USA) 5003
Colorado Education Association. Journal (USA ISSN 0279-3326) 2837
▼ • Colorado Employment Law (USA ISSN 1940-8080) 1671
• Colorado Employment Law Letter (USA ISSN 1059-504X) 4645
• Colorado Engineer Magazine (USA ISSN 0010-1583) 3185
• Colorado Environmental Compliance Update (USA ISSN 1072-057X) 4645
• Colorado Episcopalian (USA ISSN 0883-6728) 7752
• Colorado Estate Planning, Will Drafting and Estate Administration Forms (USA) 4901
Colorado Evidence Courtroom Manual (USA ISSN 1084-5747) 4947
▼ Colorado Explorer Magazine (USA) 8309
Colorado Express (USA ISSN 0146-9991) 8694
Colorado Expression (USA ISSN 1070-5066) 3973
Colorado Genealogical Chronicles (USA ISSN 0892-0788) 3762
Colorado Genealogist (USA ISSN 0010-1613) 3762
Colorado. General Support Services. Division of Accounts & Control. Comprehensive Annual Financial Report (USA) 7430
Colorado Geological Survey. Bulletin (USA ISSN 0375-6157) 2729
Colorado Geological Survey. Information Series (USA ISSN 0271-0285) 2729
Colorado Geological Survey. Special Publication (USA ISSN 0099-6459) 2729
Colorado Golf Magazine (USA ISSN 1099-7776) 8225
• Colorado Guide to Smoke-Free Dining (Online) (USA) 4383
Colorado Health & Welfare Plans see Health and Welfare Plans. Colorado & Wyoming 1685
Colorado Heritage (USA ISSN 0272-9377) 4289
Colorado High Technology Directory (USA ISSN 0883-8208) 8418
➤ Colorado History (USA ISSN 1091-7438) 4289
Colorado History Now (USA ISSN 1093-7595) 4289
Colorado Holiday Planner (GBR ISSN 1365-5094) 8694
Colorado Homes & Lifestyles (USA ISSN 0272-6904) 4535
Colorado Job Finder (USA) 7430
† The Colorado JobBank (USA) 8942
• Colorado Journal of International Environmental Law and Policy (USA ISSN 1050-0391) 4920
Colorado Labor Advocate (USA ISSN 0190-8235) 4592
Colorado Labor Force Review (USA) 1671
Colorado Language Arts Society. Currents (USA) 5107
➤ Colorado Language Arts Society. Statement (USA ISSN 1085-2549) 3055
Colorado Laws Enacted Affecting Municipal Governments (USA) 7490
• The Colorado Lawyer (USA ISSN 0363-7867) 4645
Colorado Legionnaire (USA) 6416
• Colorado Libraries (USA ISSN 0147-9733) 5003
• Colorado Manufacturers Directory (USA ISSN 1524-9999) 1980
Colorado: Manufacturing see Harris Directory. Colorado Manufacturing 1999
➤ Colorado Medicine (USA ISSN 0199-7343) 5599
▼ Colorado Meetings + Events (USA) 6278
Colorado Municipal and County Directory and Desk Reference (Year) (USA) 7490
Colorado Municipalities (USA ISSN 0010-1664) 7490
The Colorado Notary Law Primer (USA ISSN 1542-3557) 4645
Colorado Nurse (USA ISSN 8750-846X) 5955
Colorado Official State Vacation Guide (USA) 8694
Colorado Outdoors (USA ISSN 0010-1699) 8309
• Colorado Parent Magazine (USA ISSN 1937-1020) 2149
Colorado Pharmacists Society Journal (USA) 6829
Colorado Prospector (USA ISSN 0010-1702) 4289
• Colorado Real Estate Forms (USA) 7586
Colorado Real Estate Journal (USA ISSN 1060-4383) 7586
Colorado Realtor (USA) 7586
Colorado Realtor News see Colorado Realtor 7586
Colorado Register (USA) 7430
Colorado Reports see West's Jury Verdicts. Colorado Reports 4813
• ➤ Colorado Research in Linguistics (Online Edition) (USA ISSN 1937-7029) 5107
Colorado Research in Linguistics (Print Edition) see Colorado Research in Linguistics (Online Edition) 5107
• Colorado Review (USA ISSN 1046-3348) 5276
➤ Colorado Review of Hispanic Studies (USA ISSN 1545-2905) 3527
Colorado School Directory see M D R's School Directory. Colorado 2958
Colorado School of Mines Quarterly Review (USA ISSN 1536-6766) 1447
Colorado Ski Industry (USA) 1447
• Colorado Springs Business Journal (USA ISSN 1062-810X) 1084
The Colorado Springs Independent (USA) 5068
Colorado State and County Retail Sales by Standard Industrial Classification (USA ISSN 0732-1015) 1084
Colorado State University. Cooperative Extension Service. Bulletin (USA ISSN 0886-5132) 102
Colorado Super Lawyers (USA ISSN 1933-1827) 4645
• Colorado Technology (USA) 8418
Colorado, Utah TourBook see TourBook: Colorado, Utah 8762
Colorado Western (CZE ISSN 1213-032X) 5409
Colorado Wildlife (USA ISSN 0164-3193) 2606
• Colorado-Wyoming Academy of Sciences. Journal (USA ISSN 0096-2279) 7848
• ColoradoBiz (USA ISSN 1523-6366) 1447
• ➤ Coloration Technology (GBR ISSN 1472-3581) 2242
Colore Atividade Brincar (BRA ISSN 1414-4336) 2183
Colore Contos de Fadas para Ler e Colorir see Contos de Fadas Colore para Ler e Colorir 2183
Colore Contos do Folclore para Ler e Colorir see Contos do Folclore Colore para Ler e Colorir 2183
Colore e Hobby (ITA) 4535
Colore para Colorir (BRA ISSN 1807-8613) 2183
Colore Pre-Escolar (BRA ISSN 1676-8892) 2183
▼ Colorectal Cancer (USA ISSN 1947-8178) 6016
• ➤ Colorectal Disease (GBR ISSN 1462-8910) 5921
• ➤ Colorectal Disease Online (GBR ISSN 1463-1318) 5921
• Colorectal Oncology Research Review (NZL ISSN 1178-6094) 6016
• Colored Stone (USA ISSN 1046-462X) 4565
† Colorful Kitchens (USA ISSN 1936-2617) 8942
Colorfull Magazine (NLD ISSN 1871-2908) 3914
Colorfulness see Binfen 3615
Colori Martineghesi (ITA ISSN 1828-6518) 8694
• ColorLines (USA ISSN 1098-3503) 7117
Colors see De Farver 6717
Colors Catalunya see Couleurs Catalogne 4003
Colosoul (AUS ISSN 1832-4193) 2183
Colour (London) (GBR) 6965
Colour Hanjie (GBR ISSN 1749-334X) 4332
• Colour Index (GBR) 8449
Colour Index: Additions & Amendments (GBR) 8463
▼ Colour Magazin (SVK ISSN 1337-6209) 5068
Colour Society. Journal (IND ISSN 0588-5094) 6716
† Colour Tattoo (ITA ISSN 1129-1745) 8942
Colour Tsunami see Colour Hanjie 4332
Colourage (IND ISSN 0010-1826) 2243
Colourage Annual (IND ISSN 0588-5108) 2243
Colourama (GBR ISSN 1351-1696) 308
Colouring Activities & Fun (GBR ISSN 1746-7330) 4332
Colposcopia (ARG ISSN 0328-3968) 6266
Cols Bleus (FRA ISSN 0010-1834) 6416
Colstonian (GBR ISSN 0010-1842) 2837
† Coltivatore Ennese (ITA) 8942
† Coltivatore Reggiano (ITA) 8942
Il Coltivatore Cuneese (ITA) 102
Colton Clarion (USA ISSN 0896-9590) 3762
Colture Protette (ITA ISSN 0390-0444) 3727
Columban Mission (USA ISSN 0095-4438) 7793
• Columbia (New Haven) (USA ISSN 0010-1869) 7793
➤ Columbia (New York, 1977) (USA ISSN 1059-8189) 5211
Columbia (New York) (USA ISSN 0162-3893) 2278
The Columbia (Rhinebeck) (USA ISSN 8755-2914) 3762
Columbia (Tacoma) (USA ISSN 0892-3094) 4289
The Columbia Basin Farmer (USA ISSN 0010-1877) 102
Columbia Black News (USA) 3527
• Columbia Business Law Review (USA ISSN 0898-0721) 4645
• Columbia College Today (USA ISSN 0572-7820) 2278
Columbia Critical Guides (USA ISSN 1559-3002) 5276
• Columbia Daily Spectator (USA ISSN 0010-1893) 2278
• ➤ Columbia Earthscape (USA) 2704
Columbia East Asian Review (USA) 7117
Columbia Film View (USA) 6494
• Columbia Human Rights Law Review (USA ISSN 0090-7944) 4645
• Columbia Journal of American Studies (USA ISSN 1541-1419) 4289
• Columbia Journal of Asian Law (USA ISSN 1094-8449) 4645
Columbia Journal of East European Law see The Journal of Eurasian Law 4933
Columbia Journal of East European Law (USA) 4645
• Columbia Journal of Environmental Law (USA ISSN 0098-4582) 4645
• ➤ The Columbia Journal of European Law (USA ISSN 1076-6715) 4921
• Columbia Journal of Gender and the Law (USA ISSN 1062-6220) 4645
• Columbia Journal of Historiography (USA ISSN 1548-4793) 4136
• ➤ Columbia Journal of Law and Social Problems (USA ISSN 0010-1923) 4645
• Columbia Journal of Law & the Arts (USA ISSN 1544-4848) 482
• ➤ Columbia Journal of Transnational Law (USA ISSN 0010-1931) 4921
• Columbia Journalism Review (USA ISSN 0010-194X) 4573
Columbia Law Report (USA) 4645
• ➤ Columbia Law Review (USA ISSN 0010-1958) 4645
Columbia Law School News (USA) 2278
Columbia Library Columns (USA ISSN 0010-1966) 5003
Columbia London Law Series (GBR) 4645
Columbia Metropolitan (USA) 3973
Columbia Poetry Review (USA ISSN 1930-4900) 5419
➤ Columbia Review (USA ISSN 0010-1982) 5276
Columbia River Water Management Report (USA ISSN 0360-6864) 8820
• The Columbia Science and Technology Law Review (USA ISSN 1938-0976) 4645
Columbia Seminar on Art in Society (USA) 482
Columbia Series in Science and Religion (USA ISSN 1559-1409) 7848
Columbia Studies in Economics (USA ISSN 0069-6331) 1084
➤ Columbia Studies in the Classical Tradition (NLD ISSN 0166-1302) 2233
• ➤ Columbia Undergraduate Science Journal (USA ISSN 1932-765X) 7848
Columbia Union Visitor see Visitor 7693
Columbia University. American Language Program. Bulletin (USA) 5107
Columbia University. East Asian Institute. Studies (USA) 547
Columbia University Graduate School of Business. Dissertations Series (USA) 1084
Columbia University. Harriman Institute. Studies (USA) 4211
Columbia University. Institute on East Central Europe. East Central European Studies (USA) 4211
Columbia University-Presbyterian Hospital. School of Nursing Alumni Association. Alumni Magazine (USA ISSN 0898-4093) 5955
Columbia University Record (USA ISSN 0747-4504) 2279
Columbian (Columbus) (USA) 6893
Columbian (Indianapolis) (USA ISSN 1059-132X) 2265
Columbiana (USA ISSN 0893-276X) 2606
Columbo Newsletter (USA) 2378
Columbus (NLD ISSN 1871-1316) 4003
Columbus Bride (USA) 5558
• Columbus Business First (USA ISSN 0748-6146) 1084
Columbus C.E.O. (USA ISSN 1085-911X) 1734
• Columbus City Scene (USA) 5068
Columbus Cruise and Port Review (GBR) 8694
• Columbus Electronic Literary Magazine (USA) 5276
Columbus Link (GBR) 8694
Columbus Monthly (USA) 3973
Columbus Times (USA) 3527
Column (Elmira) (USA) 6522
The Column (Memphis) (USA) 6522
Columna (NOR ISSN 1504-1484) 5804
Columns (CAN) 438
Columns see HarrisMartin Columns. Silica 4684
Columns (USA) 2279
The Columns (Fairmont) (USA ISSN 0010-2091) 2279
Columns (Madison) (USA ISSN 0196-1306) 4289
Columns (Minneapolis) (USA) 4499
Columns (Seattle) (USA ISSN 1047-8604) 2279
• Com! (DEU ISSN 1612-7358) 2553
Com - A N D see Computer Audit News and Developments 1285
COM-and see Computer Audit News and Developments 1285
• Com Ciencia (BRA ISSN 1519-7654) 4573
• com-online.de (DEU) 2553
Com - S A C see Computer Security, Auditing and Controls 2512
† com.unique (DEU) 8942
La Comarca (URY) 1084
Comatose Rose Magazine (CAN ISSN 1705-9844) 5441
Combat (GBR) 8167
Combat (PAK ISSN 0010-2121) 7117
• ➤ COMBAT (USA ISSN 1542-1546) 5211
Combat Aircraft (GBR ISSN 1367-8418) 51
Combat & Survival Magazine (GBR ISSN 0955-9841) 6416
• The Combat Edge (USA ISSN 1063-8970) 51
• Combat Handguns (USA ISSN 1043-7584) 8167
Combat pour la Paix, la Paix en Mouvement see Planete Paix 7165
Combat Poverty Agency. Poverty and Policy Discussion Paper (IRL) 8034
Combat Poverty Agency. Resource Series see Action on Poverty Today 8023
Combat Sports (USA) 8167
Combat Studies Institute. U.S. Army Command and General Staff College. Research Survey (USA ISSN 0887-235X) 6416
Combat SyndicalisteToulouse see Anarchosyndicalisme 7106
• El Combatiente (PER ISSN 1680-0001) 6416
• Combats Magazine (FRA ISSN 1777-585X) 7955
Combinations (USA ISSN 0145-899X) 6965
• ➤ Combinatorial Chemistry (NLD ISSN 1464-3383) 2058
• ➤ Combinatorial Chemistry & High Throughput Screening (NLD ISSN 1386-2073) 2059
Combinatorial Chemistry and Molecular Diversity. Annual Reports (NLD ISSN 1384-2811) 2059
Combinatorial Optimization (NLD ISSN 1388-3011) 5551
• ➤ Combinatorica (DEU ISSN 0209-9683) 5479
• ➤ Combinatorics, Probability & Computing (GBR ISSN 0963-5483) 5551
• The Combined Chemical Dictionary on CD-ROM (GBR ISSN 1367-1952) 2059
Combined Federal/State Disclosure and Election Directory (USA ISSN 1936-0029) 7117
Combined Independents Holdings Directory (GBR) 1555
† Combinedsimulation (DNK ISSN 0106-357X) 8942
Comboni Missions (USA ISSN 0279-3652) 7793
Combustibles, Carburants, Chauffage (FRA ISSN 1778-1701) 3126
Combustibles et Carburants see Combustibles, Carburants, Chauffage 3126
➤ Combustion (FRA ISSN 1028-2599) 7053
• ➤ Combustion and Flame (USA ISSN 0010-2180) 3185

Title

▼ new title † ceased • electronic media ➤ refereed

10136 COMBUSTION, EXPLOSION AND SHOCK WAVES ULRICH'S PERIODICALS

Combustion, Explosion and Shock Waves *see* Fizika Goreniya i Vzryva **7054**
• ➤ Combustion, Explosion and Shock Waves (USA ISSN 0010-5082) **3241**
• Combustion Institute (British Section). Newsletter (GBR) **3241**
• ➤ Combustion Institute. Proceedings (USA ISSN 1540-7489) **2134**
Combustion Institute. Western States Section. Papers (USA ISSN 0010-2199) **3242**
• Combustion Research Facility. News (USA ISSN 1548-4300) **2134**
• ➤ Combustion Science and Technology (USA ISSN 0010-2202) **2134**
Combustion Science and Technology Book Series (USA ISSN 0883-5519) **2134**
• ➤ Combustion Theory and Modelling (GBR ISSN 1364-7830) **7053**
Comcare Australia. Annual Report *see* Australia. Safety, Rehabilitation and Compensation Commission. Annual Report **8026**
COMDA Key *see* C O M D A Key **1850**
Comdisco. Annual Report (USA) **1415**
Come *see* Charisma **7750**
Come - All - Ye (USA ISSN 0736-6132) **3616**
Come & Eat! (USA) **4354**
Come and See (CAN ISSN 0316-3040) **7634**
† Come Fare (ITA ISSN 1591-0237) **8942**
• Come Gardening (GBR ISSN 0952-9306) **3727**
Come Gardening. Supplement (GBR ISSN 0952-9314) **4080**
Come Learn Beginners (GBR ISSN 0950-7191) **7634**
Come Learn Juniors (GBR ISSN 0950-7213) **7634**
Come Learn Primaries (GBR ISSN 0950-7205) **7634**
Come Ristrutturare la Casa (ITA ISSN 1127-1922) **992**
Come Stai (ITA ISSN 1124-1705) **6984**
Come to Honduras (HND) **8694**
• Comechingonia (ARG ISSN 0326-7911) **388**
Comechingonia Virtual *see* Comechingonia **388**
CO'MED (DEU ISSN 0949-2402) **308**
Comedia (NLD ISSN 1380-9679) **2378**
Comedia Performance (USA ISSN 1553-6505) **8468**
Comedie Romantique (FRA ISSN 1775-1314) **5276**
Comedy Magazine (USA) **5211**
Comedy World *see* Xiju Shijie **8484**
Comenius-Jahrbuch (DEU ISSN 0945-313X) **4211**
Comentarios Economicos de Actualidad (BOL ISSN 1017-8856) **1084**
Comentarios Reales (PER) **2973**
Comentarios sobre la Situacion Economica (CHL ISSN 0716-4025) **1447**
Comer Bien (ESP ISSN 1698-5109) **4354**
Comer Bien Cada Dia *see* Comer Bien **4354**
Comer y Beber (ESP ISSN 1885-690X) **4354**
El Comercial (ARG) **1084**
Comerciantul *see* Jurnal Bihorean **3933**
Comercio (CRI) **1400**
• Comercio (ECU) **3835**
• El Comercio (ESP) **3951**
Comercio (HND ISSN 0010-2245) **1400**
Comercio (MEX) **1556**
• Comercio (PER ISSN 0010-2253) **1426**
† Comercio 45 (ESP ISSN 1885-0391) **8942**
Comercio da Franca (BRA) **3803**
Comercio de Gaia (PRT) **1426**
El Comercio Digital.com *see* El Comercio **3951**
Comercio e Industria de la Madera (ESP ISSN 1131-8694) **3710**
Comercio Ecuatoriano (ECU ISSN 0010-2296) **1400**
• Comercio Exterior (MEX ISSN 0185-0601) **1556**
Comercio Exterior *see* Vneshnaya Torgovlya **1586**
Comercio Exterior Argentino y Entrerriano (ARG ISSN 0329-5796) **1556**
† • Comercio Exterior de la Comunidad de Madrid (ESP ISSN 1139-6318) **8942**
† Comercio Exterior de la Comunidad Valenciana (ESP ISSN 1138-6428) **8942**
Comercio Exterior de Mexico. Informacion Preliminar (MEX ISSN 0186-0496) **1221**
Comercio Extracomunitario (PRT ISSN 0873-092X) **1221**
Comercio Hispano Britanico (GBR ISSN 0010-2326) **1400**
Comercio Industria *see* Camara Madrid **1882**
Comercio, Industria, Servicos (PRT) **1400**
Comercio y Distribucion (ESP) **1400**
Comercio y Produccion (DOM ISSN 0010-2342) **1400**
Comercio y Produccion (PER ISSN 0008-1892) **1400**
Comercio y Produccion (PRI ISSN 0010-2350) **1400**
Comertul Exterior al Romaniei/Foreign Trade of Romania (ROM ISSN 1223-5636) **1221**
Comes with a Smile (GBR) **6558**
Comestible (ESP) **3631**
Comet (AUS ISSN 0158-4243) **2837**
Comet (USA ISSN 1529-9058) **5211**
La Cometa (USA ISSN 1393-063X) **5107**
Cometbus (USA) **5276**
Comfort Engineering (GBR) **4117**
Comic Art (USA ISSN 1542-7447) **482**
The Comic Bible (USA) **5211**
Comic Bon Bon (JPN) **2183**
Comic Books Collectors Web-Mag *see* C B C Web-Mag **480**
Comic News (USA) **8468**
Comic Shop News (USA) **5211**
Comicos (CUB) **3831**
† Comics & Games Retailer (USA ISSN 1534-4606) **8942**
Comics and Games Retailer *see* Comics & Games Retailer **8942**
• Comics Buyer's Guide (USA ISSN 0745-4570) **4332**
Comics Journal (USA ISSN 0194-7869) **482**
Comics Values Monthly (USA ISSN 0887-8943) **482**
Comida y Familia (USA) **4354**
Coming Attractions (CAN ISSN 0828-802X) **5276**
Coming Attractions (USA) **2400**
Coming Clean (ZAF) **2243**
Coming Next (FRA ISSN 1631-9761) **2506**
• Coming Soon Magazine (USA) **2475**
Coming to Order (USA) **2588**
Comision Administradora del Rio Uruguay. Publicacion (URY ISSN 0797-4116) **8820**
Comision de Integracion Electrica Regional. Boletin (URY ISSN 0379-850X) **3156**
Comision de Integracion Electrica Regional. Revista (URY ISSN 0797-7565) **3156**
Comision de las Comunidades Europeas. Documentos *see* Commission of the European Communities. Documents **7227**
Comision de las Naciones Unidas para el Derecho Mercantil Internacional. Anuario (AUT ISSN 0251-4273) **4921**
Comision de las Nationes Unidas para el Derecho Mercantil Internacional. Informe sobre la Labor Realizada en su Periodo de Sesiones (AUT ISSN 0251-9143) **4921**
Comision Economica para America Latina y el Caribe Cuadernos *see* C E P A L Cuadernos **1422**
Comision Economica para America Latina y el Caribe Review *see* C E P A L Review **1445**
Comision Economica para America Latina y el Caribe. Serie Desarrollo Productivo (CHL ISSN 1020-5179) **1592**
Comision Economica para America Latina y el Caribe. Serie Financiamiento del Desarrollo (CHL) **1592**
Comision Economica para America Latina y el Caribe. Serie INFOPLAN (CHL ISSN 0259-0107) **1592**
Comision Economica para America Latina y el Caribe. Serie Reformas de Politica Publica (CHL) **1448**
Comision Estatal de Derechos Humanos, Nuevo Leon. Revista (MEX) **7204**
Comision Interamericana del Atun Tropical. Boletin *see* Inter-American Tropical Tuna Commission. Bulletin **3598**
Comision Interamericana del Atun Tropical. Informe Anual *see* Inter-American Tropical Tuna Commission. Annual Report **3598**
Comision Interamericana del Atun Tropical. Informe Trimestral *see* Inter-American Tropical Tuna Commission. Quarterly Report **3598**
Comision Internacional para la Conservacion del Atun Atlantico. Boletin Estadistico *see* International Commission for the Conservation of Atlantic Tunas. Statistical Bulletin **3613**
Comision Nacional de Arbitraje Medico Revista *see* C O N A M E D. Revista **5590**
Comision Oceanografica Intergubernamental. Coleccion Tecnica *see* Intergovernmental Oceanographic Commission. Technical Series **2808**
Comision para la Conservacion de los Recursos Vivos Marinos Antarticos. Informe de la Reunion del Comite Cientifico *see* Commission for the Conservation of Antarctic Marine Living Resources. Report of the Meeting of the Scientific Committee **2802**
Comision Sectorial para el Mercosur. Boletin (URY) **1592**
Comissao de las Comunidades Europeias. Documentos *see* Commission of the European Communities. Documents **7227**
Comissao Goiana de Folclore. Boletim (BRA) **3616**
† Comitato dei Geografi Italiani. Commissione per la Geografia Storica delle Sedi Umane in Italia. (Pubblicazioni No.) (ITA) **8942**
• ➤ Comitatus (USA ISSN 0069-6412) **5276**
➤ Comite Consultatif National d'Ethique pour les Sciences de la Vie et de la Sante. Les Cahiers (FRA ISSN 1260-8599) **6911**
† Comite Consultatif pour la Masse et les Grandeurs Apparentees/Consultative Committee for Mass and Related Quantities (FRA ISSN 1016-3778) **8942**
Comite de Accion Interamericana de Colombia. Boletin (COL) **7117**
Comite de Iglesias para Ayudas de Emergencia. Cuadernos (PRY) **7204**
Comite de Iglesias para Ayudas de Emergencia Estudios *see* C I P A E. Estudios **7203**
Comite de Iglesias para Ayudas de Emergencia. Notas Trimestrales (PRY) **7204**
Comite de Mise en Oeuvre de l'Entente sur la Revendication Territoriale Globale des Gwich'in. Rapport Annuel *see* Implementation Committee on the Implementation of the Gwich'in Comprehensive Land Claim Agreement. Annual Report **4691**
Comite d'Entreprise et la Formation Professionnelle *see* Le C E et la Formation Professionnelle **1857**
Comite Departemental des Retraites et Personnes Agees 59 *see* C O D E R P A 59 **8029**
Comite Departemental des Retraites et Personnes Agees. Bulletin *see* Bien Vieillir en Cote d'Or **8028**
Comite des Peches Continentales pour l'Afrique. Document Occasionnel *see* C I F A Occasional Paper **3587**
Comite Ejecutivo de la Pobreza en la Argentina. Estudios (ARG) **8034**
• Comite Electrotecnico Cubano. Boletin Trimestral (CUB ISSN 1609-0233) **3297**
Comite Espanol de la Detergencia. Comunicaciones de las Jornadas (ESP ISSN 0212-7466) **3242**
Comite Francais de Cartographie. Bulletin *see* Le Monde des Cartes **4019**
Comite Interafricain d'Etudes Hydrauliques *see* Interafrican Committee for Hydraulic Studies. Liaison Bulletin **8826**
Comite International de Cooperation dans les Recherches Nationales en Demographie. Actes des Seminaires (FRA) **7279**
Comite International de Dachau. Bulletin (BEL ISSN 0572-9327) **4211**
Comite International de la Croix Rouge. Rapport Annuel *see* International Committee of the Red Cross. Annual Report **8047**
Comite International de l'A I S S pour la Prevention des Risques Professionnels dus a l'Electricite. Bulletin *see* Internationale Sektion der I V S S fuer die Verhuetung von Arbeitsunfaellen und Berufskrankheiten durch Elektrizitaet. Bulletin **8966**
Comite International des Entreprises a Succursales Food Business News *see* C I E S Food Business News **3629**
Comite International des Musees et Collections d'Instruments de Musique Newsletter *see* C I M C I M Newsletter **6521**
Comite International des Musees et Collections d'Instruments de Musique Publications *see* C I M C I M Publications **6522**
† Comite International des Poids et Mesures. Comite Consultatif de l'Acoustique, des Ultrasons et des Vibrations/Consultative Committee for Acoustics, Ultrasound and Vibration (FRA ISSN 1606-3759) **8942**
† Comite International des Poids et Mesures. Comite Consultatif de Photometrie et Radiometrie. (Rapport et Annexes)/Consultative Committee for Photometry and Radiometry (FRA ISSN 0253-2166) **8942**
† Comite International des Poids et Mesures. Comite Consultatif de Thermometrie. Rapports et Annexes/Consultative Committee for Thermometry (FRA ISSN 0069-6463) **8942**
† Comite International des Poids et Mesures. Comite Consultatif d'Electricite et Magnetisme. (Rapport et Annexes)/Consultative Committee for Electricity and Magnetism (FRA ISSN 1608-4055) **8942**
† Comite International des Poids et Mesures. Comite Consultatif des Longueurs (Rapport et Annexes)/Consultative Committee for Length (FRA ISSN 1684-8845) **8942**
† Comite International des Poids et Mesures. Comite Consultatif des Rayonnements Ionisants (Rapport et Annexes)/Consultative Committee for Ionizing Radiation (FRA ISSN 1608-4047) **8942**
† Comite International des Poids et Mesures. Comite Consultatif des Unites (Rapport et Annexes)/Consultative Committee for Units (FRA ISSN 0373-3181) **8942**
† Comite International des Poids et Mesures. Comite Consultatif pour la Quantite de Matiere. (Rapport et Annexes)/Consultative Committee for Amount of Substance (FRA ISSN 1025-0034) **8942**
Comite International des Poids et Mesures. Proces-Verbaux des Seances (FRA ISSN 0370-2596) **6401**
Comite International des Poids et Mesures. Systeme International d'Unites/The International System of Units (FRA) **6401**
Comite International du Vocabulaire des Institutions et de la Communication Intellectuelles au Moyen *see* C I V I C I M A **4208**
Comite Maritime International Yearbooks & News Letters *see* C M I Yearbooks & News Letters **8640**
Comite Nationale d'Action pour la Securite et l'Hygiene dans la Construction Info *see* C N A C Info **6675**
Comite Scientifique pour la Conservation de la Faune et la Flore Marines de l'Antarctique. Rapport de la Reunion du Comite Scientifique *see* Commission for the Conservation of Antarctic Marine Living Resources. Report of the Meeting of the Scientific Committee **2802**
Comite Solidarite Philippines. Bulletin (FRA) **7204**
Comixene (DEU ISSN 0948-4523) **482**
• COMLINE: Biotechnology and Medical Industry of Japan (JPN) **5599**
• COMLINE: Chemical Industry of Japan (JPN) **3242**
• COMLINE: Computer Industry of Japan (JPN) **2491**
• COMLINE: Industrial Automation Industry of Japan (JPN) **1084**
• COMLINE: Telecommunications Industry of Japan (JPN) **2315**
• COMLINE: Transportation Industry of Japan (JPN) **1084**
Comma *see* Klink **8969**
Command (USA ISSN 0010-2474) **6416**
Command.com (BRA ISSN 1676-3688) **2575**
Command, Control, Communication, and Intelligence *see* C3i **8164**
Commandant's Bulletin *see* Coast Guard **6416**
Commando (GBR ISSN 0262-2629) **5409**
Comme un Pro! (FRA ISSN 1272-2502) **992**
▼ • Commedia dell'Arte (ITA ISSN 1974-1294) **8468**
Comment (CAN ISSN 0382-7038) **4499**
• Comment (GBR ISSN 1462-0227) **5211**
Comment (NLD ISSN 1574-9827) **23**
• Comment Citer les Produits de Statistique Canada (CAN ISSN 1910-0418) **5003**
Comment S I P P E' Rendre? (Services Integres en Perinatalite et pour la Petite Enfance) (CAN ISSN 1715-9326) **6090**
Commentaar Milieurecht (BEL ISSN 1374-805X) **3411**
Commentaar Vreemdelingenwet 2000 *see* Vreemdelingenwet 2000 **4853**
Commentaire (FRA ISSN 0180-8214) **5211**
Commentaires (CAN ISSN 0382-7046) **4499**
Commentaires de la C I B C (Canadian Imperial Bank of Commerce) (CAN) **1328**
Commentaires des Principales Decisions du Tribunal Administratif de la Reunion (REU) **7430**
Commentari d'Arte (ITA ISSN 1974-6385) **482**
▼ Commentaria (NLD ISSN 1874-8236) **7634**
Commentaria in Aristotelem Graeca (DEU) **2233**
Commentaries on Law & Economics: Yearbook (USA) **7430**
Commentarii *see* Academia Latinitati Fovendae. Commentarii **5089**
• ➤ Commentarii Mathematici Helvetici (CHE ISSN 0010-2571) **5479**
➤ Commentarii Mathematici Universitatis Sancti Pauli/Rikkyo Daigaku Sugaku Zasshi (JPN ISSN 0010-258X) **5479**
• Commentary (SGP ISSN 0084-8956) **5211**
• Commentary (USA ISSN 0010-2601) **7720**
Commentary on Northern Ireland Crime Statistics (GBR ISSN 0958-8973) **2647**
• Commentary on the Companies Act (ZAF ISSN 1991-4628) **4860**
• Commentary on the Criminal Procedure Act (ZAF ISSN 1819-8775) **4886**
A Commentary on the United Nations Convention on the Rights of the Child (NLD ISSN 1574-8626) **7204**
Commentationes Humanarum Litterarum (FIN ISSN 0069-6587) **4448**
• ➤ Commentationes Mathematicae Universitatis Carolinae (CZE ISSN 0010-2628) **5479**
Commentationes Physico-Mathematicae et Chemico-Medicae (FIN ISSN 0788-5717) **7008**
Commentationes Scientiarum Socialium (FIN ISSN 0355-256X) **7955**
Commentator (USA ISSN 0010-2652) **2279**
Commentator *see* Securities Arbitration Commentator **1650**
Comments & Criticisms (USA ISSN 0267-9469) **7348**
Comments on Argentine Trade (ARG ISSN 0010-2660) **1400**
• ➤ Comments on Inorganic Chemistry (USA ISSN 0260-3594) **2115**
Le Commercant (CHE) **1426**
Commerce (CAN ISSN 0380-9811) **1426**
Commerce (NPL) **1426**
Commerce *see* Thuong Mai **1433**
Commerce *see* Associated Chambers of Commerce of Zimbabwe. Commerce **1396**
Commerce (Baton Rouge) (USA) **1400**
Commerce (Winston-Salem) (USA) **1400**
Commerce & Industry Magazine *see* Canadian Commerce & Industry **1426**
Commerce and Mass Culture (USA) **2315**
Commerce Business Daily Weekly Release *see* C B D Weekly Release **7425**
Commerce Business Directories. Black Country (GBR ISSN 1368-6100) **1980**
Commerce Business Directories. Milton Keynes (GBR ISSN 0957-1051) **1980**
Commerce Business Directories. Northampton (GBR ISSN 0966-0550) **1980**
Commerce Business Directories. Oxford (GBR ISSN 0963-1356) **1980**
Commerce Business Directories. Peterborough and District (GBR) **1980**
Commerce Business Directories. Reading and District (GBR) **1980**
Commerce Business Directories. Redditch and Bromsgrole (GBR) **1980**
Commerce Business Directories. Telford and District (GBR) **1980**
Commerce Business Directories. Watford & Hemel Hempstead (GBR ISSN 0967-1501) **1980**
Commerce Clearing House Code and Regulations *see* C C H Code and Regulations **4635**
Commerce Clearing House Federal Tax Weekly Newsletter *see* C C H Federal Tax Weekly Newsletter **1914**
Commerce Clearing House Financial and Estate Planning *see* C C H Financial and Estate Planning **1322**
Commerce Clearing House Financial Planning *see* C C H Financial Planning **1322**
Commerce Comet (USA) **3527**
• Commerce Comments (CAN ISSN 1197-4192) **1400**
Commerce du Levant (LBN ISSN 0010-2814) **1426**
Commerce et Industrie de l'Indre (FRA ISSN 0996-1860) **1400**

Link to your serials resources and content with ulrichsweb.com

Commerce et Perspectives (FRA) **1084**
Commerce Exterieur see Vneshnaya Torgovlya **1586**
Commerce Exterieur de la Grece/Exoterikon Emporion tes Ellados (GRC ISSN 0071-738X) **1221**
Commerce Exterieur des Produits de la Mer see Commerce Exterieur des Produits de la Mer et de l'Aquaculture **3589**
Commerce Exterieur des Produits de la Mer et de l'Aquaculture (FRA ISSN 1293-7746) **3589**
† Commerce Exterieur des Regions Provence, Cote d'Azur et Corse (FRA) **8942**
Commerce Exterieur et Intra-Union Europeenne. Annuaire Statistique see External and Intra-European Union Trade. Statistical Yearbook **1228**
Commerce Exterieur et Intra-Union Europenne. Statistiques Mensuelles see External and Intra-European Union Trade. Monthly Statistics **1228**
Commerce Exterieur: Nomenclature des Pays see Aussnhandel. Warenverzeichnis **1552**
• Commerce Extra (USA) **1084**
Commerce Folio (USA) **1328**
Commerce Franco-Suisse (CHE ISSN 0010-2830) **1400**
Commerce in Germany (DEU ISSN 0010-2857) **1084**
• Commerce International (FRA ISSN 1622-2016) **1400**
Le Commerce International de Marchandise du Canada see Canadian International Merchandise Trade **1220**
Commerce Mag (FRA ISSN 1282-5212) **1958**
Commerce News see Edmonton Chamber of Commerce. Commerce News **1402**
Commerce U S A (GBR ISSN 0962-5267) **1556**
Commerce - Zimbabwe (ZWE) **1400**
Commerces Alimentaires Proximite Services Infos see C A P S Infos **3676**
The Commercial (OMN) **1084**
• Commercial Aircraft (USA) **51**
• Commercial and Consumer Warranties (USA) **4645**
Commercial and Debtor - Creditor Law (USA ISSN 1045-4705) **4860**
Commercial and Federal Litigation Section see Commercial and Federal Litigation Section Newsletter **4645**
• Commercial and Federal Litigation Section Newsletter (USA ISSN 1933-8570) **4645**
• The Commercial and Financial Accountant (ZAF) **1811**
Commercial and Industrial Directory of Panama see Directorio Comercial e Industrial de Panama **1984**
Commercial & Industrial Guide (SGP) **1980**
Commercial and Trading Economics see Maoyi Jingji **1431**
Commercial Applications of Company Law (AUS ISSN 1833-5993) **4860**
Commercial Arbitration Law and Practice (AUS) **4860**
Commercial Arbitration Law & Practice see Commercial Arbitration Law and Practice **4860**
Commercial Architecture (JPN) **438**
Commercial Architecture see Shoten Kenchiku **457**
Commercial Auto Coverage (USA ISSN 1939-6767) **4499**
• Commercial Auto Insurance (USA) **4499**
▼ Commercial Aviation Online (GBR) **8539**
Commercial Aviation Report (Print) see Commercial Aviation Online **8539**
Commercial Aviation Value Report (Print) see Commercial Aviation Online **8539**
Commercial Bank of Ethiopia. Annual Report (ETH ISSN 0588-6694) **1328**
Commercial Bank of Ethiopia. Market Report (ETH ISSN 0045-7574) **1328**
Commercial Bank of Ethiopia. Trade Directory (ETH) **1980**
Commercial Bank of Greece. Annual Report by the Chairman of the Board of Directors (GRC ISSN 0424-9402) **1328**
Commercial Bank of Greece. Economic Bulletin see Emporike Trapeza tes Ellados. Oikonomiko Deltio **1483**
Commercial Bank of Greece. Economic Review/Emporike Trapeza tes Ellados. Oikonomike Epitheorese (GRC ISSN 1106-6571) **1328**
Commercial Bank of Kuwait. Annual Report (KWT) **1328**
Commercial, Banking and Bankruptcy Law see Commercial, Banking & Bankruptcy Law **4646**
• ➤ Commercial, Banking & Bankruptcy Law (USA) **4646**
The Commercial Banking Regulatory Handbook (USA ISSN 1090-2538) **1328**
Commercial Bankruptcy Litigation (USA) **4860**
Commercial Banks in Bulgaria (BGR ISSN 1311-4824) **1328**
Commercial Builder (USA ISSN 1070-4728) **992**
Commercial Building Products (USA ISSN 1558-8440) **992**
• Commercial Carrier Journal (USA ISSN 1533-7502) **8669**
Commercial Communications (GBR) **2315**
▼ • Commercial Contracts (GBR ISSN 1753-9803) **4861**
Commercial Courier (MLT ISSN 0010-2938) **1400**
• Commercial Crime International (GBR ISSN 1012-2710) **2647**
• Commercial Damages (USA) **4646**
• Commercial Damages Reporter (USA) **4646**
• Commercial Dealer (USA ISSN 1540-7047) **3727**
Commercial Design Trends (NZL) **438**
Commercial Diving see Vodolaznoe Delo **8215**
Commercial Dynamics in Financial Services Market Assessment see Key Note Market Assessment. Commercial Dynamics in Financial Services **1363**
Commercial Environmental Law & Liability (GBR) **3411**
Commercial Fertilizers Report (USA) **178**
• Commercial Finance Guide (USA) **1328**
Commercial Fisheries News (USA ISSN 0273-6713) **3589**
• The Commercial Greenhouse Grower (GBR ISSN 1355-4301) **3727**
Commercial Herald (IND ISSN 0010-3012) **1426**
Commercial Horticulture (NZL ISSN 0113-6976) **3755**
Commercial Horticulture & Garden Centres see Business Ratio. Commercial Horticulture & Garden Centres **3726**
Commercial Inc. (USA ISSN 1061-138X) **7586**
• Commercial Insolvency Reporter (CAN ISSN 0832-7688) **4861**
Commercial Insurance see Commercial International/Commercial Insurance **4499**
Commercial Insurance For Small Business Market Assessment see Key Note Market Assessment. Commercial Insurance For Small Business **4511**
Commercial Interiors of Ireland (IRL ISSN 1649-1645) **438**
Commercial International/Commercial Insurance (GBR ISSN 1752-7236) **4499**
• Commercial Investment Real Estate (USA ISSN 1524-3249) **7586**
Commercial Journal (IND ISSN 0010-3039) **1426**
Commercial Law Adviser (USA ISSN 1930-8477) **4861**
Commercial Law and Practice (GBR ISSN 1353-3568) **4861**
Commercial Law & Practice (USA ISSN 0548-734X) **4829**
Commercial Law and Practice see Commercial Law & Practice **4829**
Commercial Law and Practice Course Handbook Series see Commercial Law & Practice **4829**
• Commercial Law and Practice Guide (USA) **4646**
• Commercial Law Bulletin (USA ISSN 0888-8000) **4646**
Commercial Law Handbook (USA) **4861**
• Commercial Law Journal (AUS ISSN 1833-9506) **4861**
• Commercial Law Journal (GBR ISSN 1464-7486) **4646**
➤ Commercial Law Practitioner (IRL ISSN 0791-895X) **4861**
• Commercial Law Quarterly (AUS ISSN 0819-4262) **4861**
Commercial Law Report (USA ISSN 1046-4751) **4646**
Commercial Laws of Europe (GBR ISSN 0141-7258) **4646**
• Commercial Laws of the World (USA) **4921**
Commercial Lawyer see Client Report **4860**
• Commercial Lease Law Insider (USA ISSN 0736-0517) **7586**
Commercial Leases (GBR ISSN 0951-9556) **4861**
• Commercial Leasing Law and Strategy (USA ISSN 0898-5634) **7587**
Commercial Leasing Update see Square Foot Magazine **7613**
Commercial, Legal & Scientific Information Group News (Online) see C L S I G News (Online) **4999**
• Commercial Lending Litigation News (USA) **1328**
• Commercial Lending Review (USA ISSN 0886-8204) **1328**
• Commercial Liability Insurance (USA) **4499**
Commercial Liability Law Review (GBR ISSN 1469-0144) **4499**
Commercial Litigation (GBR ISSN 1355-1779) **4861**
Commercial Litigation see Litigation. An International Who's Who of Commercial Litigators **4724**
Commercial Litigation (GBR) **4646**
The Commercial Litigation Journal (GBR ISSN 1747-5317) **4861**
Commercial Loan Documentation Guide (USA) **1328**
Commercial Marine Fishery see Ammattikalastus Merialueella Vuonna **3584**
• Commercial Mortgage Alert (USA ISSN 1520-3697) **7587**
Commercial Mortgage Backed Securities World see C M B S World **1323**
Commercial Mortgage Commitments (USA) **4499**
Commercial Mortgage Insight (USA ISSN 1095-0729) **7587**
• Commercial Motor (GBR ISSN 0010-3063) **8669**
• Commercial News U S A (USA ISSN 0161-9772) **1556**
• Commercial Notes (AUS ISSN 1443-9549) **4861**
Commercial Off-the-Shelf Journal see C O T S Journal **6414**
Commercial Opportunities in Cardiovascular Diagnosis see Diagnostics Intelligence **6833**
Commercial Opportunities in Pharmacogenomics see Diagnostics Intelligence **6833**
Commercial Photo (JPN) **6966**
Commercial Property (Bristol) (GBR ISSN 1473-0367) **4861**
Commercial Property Coverage (USA ISSN 1939-7755) **4499**
• Commercial Property Development Precedents (GBR) **7587**
Commercial Property Gazette (AUS ISSN 1449-1559) **1734**
Commercial Property Guide. East Midlands see Insider Commercial Property Guides. Midlands **7595**
Commercial Property Guide. Midlands see Insider Commercial Property Guides. Midlands **7595**
Commercial Property Guide. North West (GBR) **7587**
▼ Commercial Property Guide. Wales & South West (GBR ISSN 1755-3997) **7587**
Commercial Property Guide. West Midlands see Insider Commercial Property Guides. Midlands **7595**
Commercial Property Guide. Yorkshire & Humber see Yorkshire & Humber Commercial Property Guide **7616**
• Commercial Property Insurance (USA) **4499**
• Commercial Property Management Insider (USA ISSN 1938-3169) **1734**
Commercial Property Monthly (GBR) **7587**
• Commercial Property News (USA ISSN 1043-1675) **7587**
Commercial Radio Market Report see Key Note Market Report: Commercial Radio **2359**
• Commercial Realty Review (USA ISSN 1073-0370) **7587**
• The Commercial Record (Boston) (USA) **1328**
Commercial Recorder see Fort Worth Commercial Recorder **1428**
• Commercial Refrigeration Equipment (USA ISSN 1940-5227) **4117**
Commercial Research Editorial Department see Shangye Yanjiu **1173**
Commercial Review (USA ISSN 0010-3101) **271**
Commercial Review see Thuongmai **1584**
Commercial Review of Senshu University see Senshu Syogaku Ronshu **1172**
Commercial Square Foot Building Costs (USA) **992**
Commercial Studies and Research see Al Dirasat wa-al-Buhuth al-Tigariyyat **1092**
Commercial T V Market Report see Key Note Market Report: Free-to-Air T V **2384**
• Commercial Times (CAN ISSN 1910-1023) **4861**
Commercial Trader (ZAF ISSN 1812-271X) **8669**
Commercial Trailer Blue Book (USA ISSN 1058-3076) **8669**
Commercial Transactions Checklists (GBR) **1734**
Commercial Transport (ZAF) **8669**
Commercial Truck and Bus Safety Synthesis Program Research Results Digests see C T B S S P Research Results Digests **8669**
Commercial Truck and Bus Safety Synthesis Program Synthesis Reports see C T B S S P Synthesis Reports **8669**
• Commercial Update (ZAF) **4861**
Commercial Vehicle Data Digest (ZAF ISSN 1019-0899) **8669**
Commercial Vehicle Dealers' Guide (ZAF) **8670**
• The Commercial Vehicle Guide (GBR) **1980**
Commercial Vehicle Workshop (GBR ISSN 1757-577X) **8575**
Commercial Vehicles Market Report see Key Note Market Report: Commercial Vehicles **8588**
• Commercial Vehicles Monthly Digest (GBR ISSN 1755-1374) **8575**
Commercial Vessel Yearbook (AUS ISSN 1030-0759) **3589**
Commercial World Guide see Shangjie Daokan **1173**
➤ Commercialize (USA) **1811**
CommercialProperty see Irish Examiner **3893**
Il Commercio con l'Estero dei Prodotti Agroalimentari (ITA ISSN 1722-5728) **196**
Il Commercio Edile see Macchine Edili **1021**
• Il Commercio Edile (ITA ISSN 1594-8161) **992**
Il Commercio Edile. Macchine e Attrezzature see Macchine Edili **1021**
Il Commercio Edile. Materiali e Tecnologie see Il Commercio Edile **992**
Commercio Elettrico (ITA ISSN 0392-3479) **3297**
• Commercio Idrotermosanitario (ITA ISSN 1592-7458) **4117**
Commercio Internazionale (ITA ISSN 1126-1617) **1556**
• Commercio Porte & Finestre (ITA ISSN 1970-9676) **1049**
Commercio Tessuti Moda News see C T M News **8939**
Il Commercio Veronese (ITA) **1084**
Commercium (IND ISSN 0010-3160) **1426**
Commerical Banking Positions see Survey Report on Financial Institutions Compensation. Commercial Banking Positions **1709**
Commersant Weekly (USA) **1448**
Commerzbank Journal (DEU ISSN 1433-6081) **1328**
Commissaire a l'Information et a la Protection de la Vie Privee - Ontario. Rapport Annuel see Information and Privacy Commissioner - Ontario. Annual Report **4833**
Le Commissaire aux Comptes et le Passage aux I F R S (FRA ISSN 1773-4266) **4646**Commissaire de la Concurrence pour l'Exercice se Terminant le 31 Mars (Annee) sur l'Application et l'Administration des Lois Suivantes, Loi sur la Concurrence, Loi sur l'Emballage et l'Etiquetage des Produits de Consommation, Loi sur le Poinconnage des Metaux Precieux, Loi sur l'Etiquetage des Textiles see Commissioner of Competition (Year) on the Enforcement and Administration of the Competition Act, Consumer Packaging and Labelling Act, Precious Metals Marking Act, Textile Labelling Act. Annual Report **1084**
Commissaire du Centre de la Securite des Telecommunications. Rapport Annuel see Canada. Communications Security Establishment Commissioner. Annual Report **6414**
Commissariat a la Protection de la vie Privee du Canada. Rapport annuel au Parlement (Annee) Rapport Concernant la Loi sur la Protection des Renseignements Personnels see Privacy Commissioner of Canada. Annual Report to Parliament (Year) Report on the Privacy Act **4761**
Commissariat a la Protection de la vie Privee du Canada. Rapport annuel au Parlement (Annee) Rapport Concernant la Loi sur la Protection des Renseignements Personnels et les Documents Electroniques see Privacy Commissioner of Canada. Annual Report to Parliament (Year) Report on the Personal Information Protection and Electronic Documents Act **4761**
Commissariat a l'Energie Atomique Annual Report (Year) see C E A Annual Report (Year) **7842**
Commissariat a l'Energie Atomique Saclay. Le Journal see C E A Saclay. Le Journal **8938**
Commissariat a l'Energie Atomique Technologies see C E A Technologies **7065**
Commissie van de Europese Gemeenschappen. Dokumenten see Commission of the European Communities. Documents **7227**
Commission (USA ISSN 0010-3179) **7752**
Commission Belge de Bibliographie et de Bibliologie. Bulletin (BEL) **623**
Commission Canadienne de Surete Nucleaire. Raport sur le Rendement see Canadian Nuclear Safety Commission. Performance Report **7428**
Commission Canadienne des Grains. Rapport sur le Rendement see Canadian Grain Commission. Performance Report **271**
Commission Canadienne du Tourisme. Communique see Tourisme (Online) **8764**
Commission Canadienne du Tourisme. Sommaire du Plan d'Entreprise see Canadian Tourism Commission. Corporate Plan Summary **8691**
Commission Canadienne pour l'UNESCO. Lettre du Secretaire General see Canadian Commission for UNESCO. Secretary General's Letter **2834**
Commission Consultative de l'Enseignement Prive. Rapport Annuel (CAN ISSN 0317-7327) **2837**
Commission d'Acces aux Documents administratifs. Rapport d'Activite (FRA ISSN 1952-9759) **7430**
Commission de Developpement Economique Regional Restigouche. Rapport Annuel see Entreprise Restigouche. Agence de Developpement Regional. Rapport Annuel **1427**
Commission de la Fonction Publique du Canada. Rapport Annuel (En ligne) see Public Service Commission of Canada. Annual Report (Online) **7463**
• Commission de la Fonction Publique du Canada. Rapport Annuel. Points Saillants (CAN ISSN 1912-0729) **6696**
Commission de Pacifique Sud. Document Technique see South Pacific Commission. Technical Paper **8439**
Commission de Pacifique Sud. Fiche Technique see Pest Advisory Leaflet **246**
Commission de Pacifique Sud. Manuel see South Pacific Commission. Handbook **1605**
Commission de Pacifique Sud. Rapport Annuel see South Pacific Commission. Annual Report **7266**
Commission de Pacifique Sud. Rapport de Conference see South Pacific Commission. Report of Meetings **1519**
Commission de Recherche et d'Information Independantes sur la Radioactivite Dossiers Clefs see C R I I R A D. Dossiers Clefs **7065**
Commission des Communautes Europeennes. Documents see Commission of the European Communities. Documents **7227**
Commission des Droits de la Personne des Territoires du Nord-Ouest. Rapport Annuel see Northwest Territories Human Rights Commission. Annual Report **4839**
Commission des Droits de la Personne et des Droits de la Jeunesse. Rapport Annuel, Quebec see Commission des Droits de la Personne et des Droits de la Jeunesse. Rapport d'Activites et de Gestion, Quebec **7204**
Commission des Droits de la Personne et des Droits de la Jeunesse. Rapport d'Activites et de Gestion, Quebec (CAN ISSN 1706-9297) **7204**
Commission des Nations Unies pour le Droit Commercial International. Annuaire (AUT ISSN 0251-4257) **4921**
Commission des Nations Unies pour le Droit Commercial International. Rapport des Travaux de sa Session (AUT ISSN 0251-9151) **4921**
Commission des Valeurs Mobilieres du Quebec. Bulletin Hebdomadaire see L' Autorite des Marches Financiers. Bulletin **1309**
Commission du Droit d'Auteur Canada. Rapport Annuel see Copyright Board of Canada. Annual Report **4862**

Title

Title

Title

10142 COMPENSATION REVIEW BOARD. OPINIONS ULRICH'S PERIODICALS

Compensation Review Board. Opinions *see* Connecticut. Workers' Compensation Commission. Compensation Review Board. Opinions (Online) **4500**
• Compensation Survey Report (USA ISSN 1931-0862) **1672**
Compete! (GBR) **8418**
• Compete (USA ISSN 1946-3189) **8167**
➤ Competence/Hopital Suisse/Ospedale Svizzero (CHE ISSN 1424-2168) **4091**
• Competency & Emotional Intelligence Benchmarking (GBR ISSN 1469-3348) **1858**
Competency & Emotional Intelligence Benchmarking (Online Edition) *see* Competency & Emotional Intelligence Benchmarking **1858**
• Competency & Emotional Intelligence Monthly (Online Edition) (GBR ISSN 1469-3313) **1858**
• Competency & Emotional Intelligence Quarterly (GBR ISSN 1469-333X) **1858**
Competency & Emotional Intelligence Quarterly Online *see* Competency & Emotional Intelligence Quarterly **1858**
Competency Management Advisor *see* The Staff Educator **4111**
Competia Online Magazine (CAN) **1734**
Competition (GBR ISSN 1368-3136) **4647**
Competition (Harrisburg) (USA) **4332**
Competition (San Francisco) (USA) **4647**
• ➤ Competition & Change (GBR ISSN 1024-5294) **1085**
• Competition and Consumer Law Journal (AUS ISSN 1039-5598) **4862**
• Competition and Regulation in Network Industries (BEL ISSN 1783-5917) **4862**
Competition Forum (USA ISSN 1545-2581) **1085**
• Competition Handbook (GBR ISSN 1749-3234) **4647**
Competition Hotline *see* Competitions (Louisville) **438**
Competition in Health Insurance (USA ISSN 1930-7284) **4499**
Competition Law Handbook *see* Competition Handbook **4647**
• Competition Law in the European Communities (GBR ISSN 0141-769X) **4921**
Competition Law in Western Europe and the U S A (NLD) **4921**
Competition Law Insight (GBR ISSN 1478-5188) **4921**
• Competition Law International (GBR ISSN 1817-5708) **4921**
Competition Law Journal (GBR ISSN 1476-9085) **4647**
Competition Law Monitor (GBR ISSN 1474-6174) **4647**
Competition Law of the European Community (USA) **1556**
Competition Law Reports (ZAF ISSN 1727-3366) **4862**
Competition Law Service (CAN) **4862**
Competition Leader (IND) **1085**
• Competition Manual. E C Competition Law (European Community) (GBR ISSN 1754-8616) **4862**
• Competition Manual. U K Competition Law (GBR ISSN 1754-8594) **4862**
Competition Master (IND) **3055**
Competition Policy (CHE) **1556**
• ➤ Competition Policy International (USA ISSN 1554-0189) **4647**
• Competition Policy Newsletter (BEL ISSN 1025-2266) **1085**
Competition Refresher (IND ISSN 0971-8753) **1085**
Competition Success Review (IND) **1085**
• Competition Tribunal of Canada. Performance Report (CAN ISSN 1483-7544) **7431**
Competitions (Louisville) (USA ISSN 1058-6539) **438**
Competitions and Financial Opportunities for Artists (AUS ISSN 1322-3267) **483**
Competitions Bulletin (GBR ISSN 1750-5895) **5277**
The Competitive Advantage (USA ISSN 0886-1994) **1811**
Competitive Colleges *see* Peterson's Competitive Colleges (Year) **2961**
Competitive Edge (USA) **8167**
Competitive Enterprise Institute Update *see* C E I Update **1077**
Competitive Intelligence *see* Intelligence Insights **7363**
• Competitive Intelligence Magazine (USA ISSN 1521-5881) **1734**
Competitive Intelligence Resources (USA ISSN 1538-6953) **2442**
Competitive Tendering and Contracting Research Newsletter *see* C T C Newsletter **8939**
The (Year) Competitiveness Report on Argentina: Financials Returns, Labor Productivity and International Gaps (USA) **1085**
The (Year) Competitiveness Report on Beauport, Canada: Financials Returns, Labor Productivity, Benchmarks and International Gaps (USA) **1617**
The (Year) Competitiveness Report on Bolton, Canada: Financials Returns, Labor Productivity, Benchmarks and International Gaps (USA) **1617**
The (Year) Competitiveness Report on Brampton, Canada: Financials Returns, Labor Productivity, Benchmarks and International Gaps (USA) **1617**
The (Year) Competitiveness Report on Brantford, Canada: Financial Returns, Labor Productivity, Benchmarks and International Gaps (USA) **1617**
The (Year) Competitiveness Report on Brazil: Financials Returns, Labor Productivity and International Gaps (USA) **1085**
The (Year) Competitiveness Report on Calgary, Canada: Financial Returns, Labor Productivity, Benchmarks and International Gaps (USA) **1617**
The (Year) Competitiveness Report on Canada: Financials Returns, Labor Productivity and International Gaps (USA) **1085**
The (Year) Competitiveness Report on Charlottetown, Canada: Financial Returns, Labor Productivity, Benchmarks and International Gaps (USA) **1617**
The (Year) Competitiveness Report on Chile: Financials Returns, Labor Productivity and International Gaps (USA) **1085**
The (Year) Competitiveness Report on Colombia: Financials Returns, Labor Productivity and International Gaps (USA) **1085**
The (Year) Competitiveness Report on Don Mills, Canada: Financial Returns, Labor Productivity, Benchmarks and International Gaps (USA) **1617**
The (Year) Competitiveness Report on Dorval, Canada: Financial Returns, Labor Productivity, Benchmarks and International Gaps (USA) **1617**
The (Year) Competitiveness Report on Edmonton, Canada: Financial Returns, Labor Productivity, Benchmarks and International Gaps (USA) **1617**
The (Year) Competitiveness Report on Etobicoke, Canada: Financial Returns, Labor Productivity, Benchmarks and International Gaps (USA) **1617**
The (Year) Competitiveness Report on Granby, Canada: Financial Returns, Labor Productivity, Benchmarks and International Gaps (USA) **1617**
The (Year) Competitiveness Report on Guelph, Canada: Financial Returns, Labor Productivity, Benchmarks and International Gaps (USA) **1617**
The (Year) Competitiveness Report on Haley, Canada: Financial Returns, Labor Productivity, Benchmarks and International Gaps (USA) **1617**
The (Year) Competitiveness Report on Halifax, Canada: Financial Returns, Labor Productivity, Benchmarks and International Gaps (USA) **1617**
The (Year) Competitiveness Report on Kanata, Canada: Financial Returns, Labor Productivity, Benchmarks and International Gaps (USA) **1617**
The (Year) Competitiveness Report on Kelowna, Canada: Financial Returns, Labor Productivity, Benchmarks and International Gaps (USA) **1617**
The (Year) Competitiveness Report on Kingsey Falls, Canada: Financial Returns, Labor Productivity, Benchmarks and International Gaps (USA) **1618**
The (Year) Competitiveness Report on Kitchener, Canada: Financial Returns, Labor Productivity, Benchmarks and International Gaps (USA) **1618**
The (Year) Competitiveness Report on Latin America: Financials Returns, Labor Productivity and International Gaps (USA) **1085**
The (Year) Competitiveness Report on Laval, Canada: Financial Returns, Labor Productivity, Benchmarks and International Gaps (USA) **1618**
The (Year) Competitiveness Report on Lethbridge, Canada: Financial Returns, Labor Productivity, Benchmarks and International Gaps (USA) **1618**
The (Year) Competitiveness Report on Levis, Canada: Financial Returns, Labor Productivity, Benchmarks and International Gaps (USA) **1618**
The (Year) Competitiveness Report on Longueuil, Canada: Financial Returns, Labor Productivity, Benchmarks and International Gaps (USA) **1618**
The (Year) Competitiveness Report on Lunenburg, Canada: Financial Returns, Labor Productivity, Benchmarks and International Gaps (USA) **1618**
The (Year) Competitiveness Report on Markham, Canada: Financial Returns, Labor Productivity, Benchmarks and International Gaps (USA) **1618**
The (Year) Competitiveness Report on Mexico: Financials Returns, Labor Productivity and International Gaps (USA) **1085**
The (Year) Competitiveness Report on Mississauga, Canada: Financial Returns, Labor Productivity, Benchmarks and International Gaps (USA) **1618**
The (Year) Competitiveness Report on Montreal, Canada: Financial Returns, Labor Productivity, Benchmarks and International Gaps (USA) **1618**
The (Year) Competitiveness Report on Mount Royal, Canada: Financial Returns, Labor Productivity, Benchmarks and International Gaps (USA) **1618**
The (Year) Competitiveness Report on Nepean, Canada: Financial Returns, Labor Productivity, Benchmarks and International Gaps (USA) **1618**
The (Year) Competitiveness Report on Peru: Financials Returns, Labor Productivity and International Gaps (USA) **1085**
The (Year) Competitiveness Report on Quebec City, Canada: Financial Returns, Labor Productivity, Benchmarks and International Gaps (USA) **1618**
The (Year) Competitiveness Report on Regina, Canada: Financial Returns, Labor Productivity, Benchmarks and International Gaps (USA) **1618**
The (Year) Competitiveness Report on Saint-Damien Regina, Canada: Financial Returns, Labor Productivity, Benchmarks and International Gaps (USA) **1618**
The (Year) Competitiveness Report on Saint-Leonard, Canada: Financial Returns, Labor Productivity, Benchmarks and International Gaps (USA) **1618**
The (Year) Competitiveness Report on Sainte-Marie-de-Beauce, Canada: Financial Returns, Labor Productivity, Benchmarks and International Gaps (USA) **1618**
The (Year) Competitiveness Report on Saskatoon, Canada: Financial Returns, Labor Productivity, Benchmarks and International Gaps (USA) **1618**
The (Year) Competitiveness Report on Sherbrooke, Canada: Financial Returns, Labor Productivity, Benchmarks and International Gaps (USA) **1618**
The (Year) Competitiveness Report on Stellarton, Canada: Financial Returns, Labor Productivity, Benchmarks and International Gaps (USA) **1618**
The (Year) Competitiveness Report on Thornhill, Canada: Financial Returns, Labor Productivity, Benchmarks and International Gaps (USA) **1618**
The (Year) Competitiveness Report on Venezuela: Financials Returns, Labor Productivity and International Gaps (USA) **1085**
The (Year) Competitiveness Report on Ville de Saint-Georges, Canada: Financial Returns, Labor Productivity, Benchmarks and International Gaps (USA) **1618**
The (Year) Competitiveness Report on Westmount, Canada: Financial Returns, Labor Productivity, Benchmarks and International Gaps (USA) **1618**
The (Year) Competitiveness Report on Willowdale, Canada: Financial Returns, Labor Productivity, Benchmarks and International Gaps (USA) **1618**
The (Year) Competitiveness Report on Winnipeg, Canada: Financial Returns, Labor Productivity, Benchmarks and International Gaps (USA) **1618**
• ➤ Competitiveness Review (GBR ISSN 1059-5422) **1556**
Competitor (USA) **8167**
Competitors Companion (GBR) **8167**
Competitors Update (GBR) **8167**
Compeuro. Proceedings (USA) **2410**
Compilaciones Tematicas (CUB) **3831**
Compilation of Bar Exam Questions and Answers *see* Compilation of Bar Examination Questions & Answers **4647**
Compilation of Bar Examination Questions & Answers (USA) **4647**
Compilation of State and Federal Privacy Laws (USA ISSN 0882-9136) **4647**
Compilation of the Social Security Laws *see* U.S. Social Security Administration. Compilation of the Social Security Laws **4526**
Compilations *see* S E G Compilations **2765**
Compiler (USA ISSN 1059-6569) **2647**
† Complan Handbook (AUS ISSN 0314-0164) **8942**
Compleat Golfer (ZAF ISSN 1015-8014) **8225**
• The Compleat Mother (USA ISSN 0829-8564) **5988**
Complejidad, Ciencia y Estetica *see* Complexus **7513**
Complementaer-Medizin *see* CO'MED **308**
Los Complementarios (ESP ISSN 1131-6438) **5211**
Complementary and Alternative Medicine *see* C A M **307**
Complementary and Alternative Medicine (USA ISSN 1549-084X) **308**
Complementary and Alternative Medicine Directory *see* C A M Directory **307**
Complementary Care Journal (GBR ISSN 1360-418X) **8095**
• ➤ Complementary Health Practice Review (USA ISSN 1533-2101) **308**
Complementary Medicine *see* Journal of Complementary Medicine **5648**
Complementary Science (USA) **7848**
• ➤ Complementary Therapies in Clinical Practice (GBR ISSN 1744-3881) **5956**
• Complementary Therapies in Medicine (GBR ISSN 0965-2299) **5804**
Complementary Therapies in Nursing & Midwifery *see* Complementary Therapies in Clinical Practice **5956**
Complements au Nouveau Traite de Chimie Minerale (FRA ISSN 0338-9839) **2059**
▼ • Complessita e Sostenibilita (ITA ISSN 1971-3002) **438**
The Complete Baseball Record Book (USA ISSN 0885-9183) **8225**
Complete Book of Business Schools *see* Best Business Schools **2954**
• Complete Book of Colleges (USA ISSN 1088-8594) **2974**
Complete Catalog of Bibliographic Products and Services *see* U.S. Library of Congress. Product Catalog **637**
Complete Catalog of Plays (USA ISSN 1547-7460) **8468**
Complete Catalog of Plays and Musicals *see* Complete Catalog of Plays **8468**
Complete Coffee Coverage (USA) **3632**
• Complete Commodity Futures Directory (USA) **1981**
The Complete Database Catalog *see* Dialog zzzzh DataStar Database Catalog **5006**
• Complete Directory for People with Chronic Illness (USA ISSN 1080-7659) **5599**
• Complete Directory for People with Disabilities (USA ISSN 1063-0023) **4064**
• The Complete Directory of Large Print Books and Serials (USA ISSN 0000-1120) **4071**
The Complete Do-it-Yourself Human Resources Department (USA ISSN 1930-2010) **6696**
• Complete Entrepreneur (USA) **1958**
Complete Federal Tax Forms *see* R I A Complete Federal Tax Forms **1941**
The Complete Fly Fisherman (ZAF) **8310**
The Complete Gift Basket Industry Reference Directory (USA ISSN 1089-2664) **1958**
Complete Global Service Data for Orthopaedic Surgery (USA ISSN 1559-5315) **6058**
The Complete Guide to Bass Fishing Southern Africa (ZAF ISSN 1819-1991) **8310**
Complete Guide to Credit and Collection Law (USA ISSN 1931-4639) **4647**
The Complete Guide to Environmental Law (USA) **3412**
Complete Guide to Federal and State Garnishment (USA ISSN 1931-4612) **4647**
The Complete Guide to Hazardous Materials Enforcement and Liability: California (USA) **3505**
The Complete Guide to Human Resources and the Law (USA ISSN 1931-0919) **1858**
Complete Guide to Kayak Touring (USA ISSN 1527-4381) **8274**
The Complete Guide to Mechanic's and Materialman's Lien Laws of Texas (USA) **4647**
Complete Guide to the Ambulatory Care Survey Process *see* Accreditation Process Guide for Ambulatory Care **4087**
Complete Guide to the Behavioral Health Care Survey Process *see* Accreditation Process Guide for Behavioral Health Care **4087**
Complete Guide to the Laboratory Survey Process *see* Accreditation Process Guide for Laboratories **5901**
Complete Handbook of Pro Football (USA ISSN 0361-2988) **8225**
Complete Internal Revenue Code *see* Internal Revenue Code **1930**
The Complete Investor (USA ISSN 1546-0134) **1618**
• The Complete Legal Research System on CD-ROM (AUS) **4647**
• The Complete Marquis Who's Who on CD-ROM (USA) **641**
Complete Melbourne Wedding Guide (AUS ISSN 1039-4680) **5558**
The Complete Organ (USA ISSN 1089-3733) **6558**
The Complete Pet Travel Guide (NZL ISSN 1177-3766) **6806**
† Complete Retirement Planner (AUS ISSN 1442-0422) **8942**
Complete Wedding Sydney (AUS ISSN 1441-8576) **5558**
Complete Woman (USA ISSN 0278-0534) **8856**
Complete Works of G.B. Pergolesi (USA) **6558**
Complex (NOR ISSN 0806-1912) **4647**
▼ • ➤ Complex Analysis and Operator Theory (CHE ISSN 1661-8254) **5480**
Complex Control Systems (BGR ISSN 1310-8255) **2519**
Complex Magazine (USA ISSN 1538-6848) **5068**
➤ Complex Systems (USA ISSN 0891-2513) **5551**
Complex Systems and Complexity Science *see* Fuza Xitong yu Fuzaxing Kexue **7856**
▼ Complex Systems and Interdisciplinary Science (SGP ISSN 1793-4540) **7848**
Complex Use of National Resources *see* Kompleksnoe Ispol'zovanie Mineral'nogo Syr'ya **6468**
• ➤ Complex Variables and Elliptic Equations (GBR ISSN 1747-6933) **5480**
• ➤ Complexity (USA ISSN 1076-2787) **5480**
➤ Complexity and Chaos in Nursing (USA ISSN 1088-7911) **5956**
• Complexity Digest (USA) **7848**
• ➤ Complexity in Human Systems (USA ISSN 1084-2837) **7348**
• ➤ ComPlexUs (CHE ISSN 1424-8492) **666**
Complexus (CHL ISSN 0718-1515) **7513**
Compliance Alert (USA) **1328**

Link to your serials resources and content with ulrichsweb.com

Title

Comunicazione Digitale *see* Comunicazione e Innovazione Digitale **2317**
Comunicazione e Innovazione Digitale (ITA ISSN 1972-2370) **2317**
Comunicazione e Spettacolo (ITA ISSN 1825-3423) **2317**
• Comunicazione Filosofica (ITA ISSN 1128-9082) **6911**
• Comunicazione Politica (ITA ISSN 1594-6061) **2317**
† Comunicazioni (ITA ISSN 1970-0253) **8943**
Comunicazioni e Studi (ITA ISSN 1971-5390) **2317**
• Comunicazioni Sociali (ITA ISSN 0392-8667) **8095**
Comunidad (SWE ISSN 0283-2925) **7118**
La Comunidad *see* La Opinion **3556**
Comunidad 2000 (ESP) **7793**
• Comunidad de Madrid. Anuario Estadistico (ESP ISSN 1139-6407) **8364**
Comunidad de Madrid. Boletin de Poblacion Activa (Diskette) (ESP ISSN 1579-5187) **7279**
• La Comunidad de Madrid en Cifras (ESP ISSN 1139-8434) **8364**
Comunidad Educativa (ESP ISSN 0212-2650) **2838**
Comunidad Europea *see* Union Europea Aranzadi **4801**
Comunidad Informatica (MEX ISSN 0185-8114) **2443**
Comunidades (ARG) **7720**
Comunidades y Culturas Peruanas (PER ISSN 1022-1514) **333**
Comunife (PER ISSN 1810-6994) **2317**
• Comunismo (ITA ISSN 0393-6740) **7118**
Comunita Ebraica di Milano. Bollettino (ITA) **3528**
La Comunita Internazionale (ITA ISSN 0010-5066) **7227**
† Comunita Islamica (ITA) **8943**
† Comunitat Valenciana Agraria (ESP ISSN 1138-2775) **8943**
Con Brio (USA) **6558**
Con - Ciencia Social (ESP ISSN 1697-3127) **2838**
† Con Dados de Niebla (ESP ISSN 0214-6681) **8943**
• Con Ene (ESP ISSN 1137-4144) **3528**
Con Fundamento (ARG) **4080**
Con - Science (PHL) **8419**
Con-Temporal (USA) **5413**
Con-text (ZAF ISSN 1015-647X) **5277**
Con-tratto (ITA ISSN 1121-8444) **6911**
• Con.web (USA ISSN 1060-8907) **2607**
Conacex Informa (MEX) **1556**
Conan (BRA ISSN 0104-2157) **2183**
Conan o Barbaro *see* Conan **2183**
Conarquitectura (ESP ISSN 1578-0201) **438**
Concast Standard News (CHE ISSN 1423-1697) **6309**
Concatenation (GBR) **5441**
Concatenator (CAN ISSN 1206-520X) **5061**
Concealed Carry Magazine (USA ISSN 1550-7866) **2647**
Conceive Magazine (Florida) (USA ISSN 1550-8900) **971**
• Concentric/Tongxinyuan (TWN ISSN 1729-6897) **5277**
Concentus Musicus (DEU) **6558**
Concepcion Arenal (ESP ISSN 0212-2022) **4448**
Concept (GBR ISSN 1359-1983) **2839**
• Concept (USA ISSN 1553-0159) **4535**
Conception Maison (FRA ISSN 1950-9049) **4535**
Conceptions Southwest (USA ISSN 1048-8790) **483**
Conceptos Boletin (ARG ISSN 0327-7860) **8095**
Conceptos de Matematica (ARG ISSN 0010-5147) **5481**
Concepts and Techniques in Modern Geography *see* C A T M O G **4001**
† • ➤ Concepts and Transformation (NLD ISSN 1384-6639) **8943**
Concepts in Action (USA) **1085**
Concepts in Communication Informatics and Librarianship (IND) **5003**
Concepts in Magnetic Resonance *see* Concepts in Magnetic Resonance. Part B: Magnetic Resonance Engineering **6194**
Concepts in Magnetic Resonance *see* Concepts in Magnetic Resonance. Part A **6194**
• Concepts in Magnetic Resonance. Part A (USA ISSN 1546-6086) **6194**
Concepts in Magnetic Resonance. Part A (Online) *see* Concepts in Magnetic Resonance. Part A **6194**
• ➤ Concepts in Magnetic Resonance. Part B: Magnetic Resonance Engineering (USA ISSN 1552-5031) **6194**
Concepts in Magnetic Resonance. Part B: Magnetic Resonance Engineering (Online) *see* Concepts in Magnetic Resonance. Part B: Magnetic Resonance Engineering **6194**
Concepts in Modern Optics *see* Nonlinear Optics, Quantum Optics **7081**
Concepts in Sedimentology and Paleontology (USA ISSN 1059-8618) **2729**
Concepts in Social Thought Series (USA) **7118**
• Conceptual Advances in Brain Research (GBR ISSN 1029-2136) **6133**
Conceptus (DEU ISSN 0010-5155) **6911**
Conceptus - Studien (AUT ISSN 0259-0670) **6911**
Conceria (ITA) **4973**
Concern (CAN) **5956**
Concern for Helping Animals in Israel Lights *see* C H A I Lights **318**
• Concern News (USA) **8035**
Concerned Educators Allied for a Safe Environment News *see* C E A S E News **2605**
Concerned Singles Newsletter (USA) **7943**
Concerned United Birthparents, Inc. Communicator *see* C U B Communicator **8091**
Concerned United Birthparents, Inc. Communicator. Adoption Newsletter *see* C U B Communicator. Adoption Newsletter **8091**
ConcerNews *see* Concern News **8035**
Concerns (CAN ISSN 0045-799X) **2692**
➤ Concerns (New York) (USA ISSN 1068-204X) **8895**
Concert Artists Guild. Guide to Competitions (USA ISSN 1551-2266) **6558**
Concertacion (GTM) **7118**
Concertino (DEU ISSN 1611-4698) **6558**
Concerto (DEU ISSN 0177-5944) **6558**
Concerto Grosso (ITA ISSN 1971-0011) **6558**
Concession Profession (USA) **3632**
Concessionary Fares (GBR ISSN 1367-6059) **8494**
Concessionworks (USA) **3632**
Concetto (GBR ISSN 0140-315X) **2279**
• The Conch Republic Coconut Telegraph (USA ISSN 1948-1411) **3973**
† • ➤ La Conchiglia/The Shell (ITA ISSN 0394-0152) **8943**
➤ Concho River Review (USA ISSN 1048-9568) **5277**
The Conchological Newsletter *see* Mollusc World **955**
Conchological Society Special Publication (GBR ISSN 0144-9826) **667**
Conciencia Nacional (ARG) **7118**
Conciencia Social *see* Con - Ciencia Social **2838**
Concierge Preferred - Chicago (USA) **8694**
Concierge Preferred - St. Louis (USA) **8694**
Conciliation Quarterly (USA) **7734**
Concilium (DEU ISSN 0588-9804) **7634**
† Concilium (FRA ISSN 1140-7654) **8943**
➤ Concilium (GBR ISSN 0010-5236) **7634**
Concilium (ITA ISSN 1125-7164) **7634**
Concilium (Brazilian Edition) (BRA ISSN 1414-7327) **7634**
• ➤ Concilium Medii Aevi (DEU ISSN 1437-904X) **4136**
• The Concise A A C R 2 (Anglo-American Cataloging Rules) (USA) **5003**
• Concise B2B Aerospace (GBR ISSN 1475-6609) **51**
▼ Concise Delight (USA ISSN 1947-6051) **5419**
Concise International Chemical Assessment Documents (CHE ISSN 1020-6167) **2059**
A Concise Overview (USA) **1958**
Concise Statistical Year Book of Poland *see* Central Statistical Office. Concise Statistical Year Book of Poland **8362**
Concise Statistical Yearbook of Greece (GRC ISSN 0069-8245) **8364**
• ConclusionsOnline (USA) **1329**
Concord (GBR ISSN 1466-2280) **2279**
• Concord (Chicago) (USA ISSN 0741-9872) **7752**
Concord Business (USA) **1085**
The Concord Review (USA ISSN 0895-0539) **4136**
• ➤ Concord Saunterer (USA ISSN 1068-5359) **5277**
Concordia *see* K A S - Taidetta **6527**
Concordia (USA) **2279**
Concordia Alumni News *see* Concordia **2279**
Concordia Historical Institute Quarterly (USA ISSN 0010-5260) **7752**
• ➤ Concordia Journal (USA ISSN 0145-7233) **7634**
• ➤ Concordia Theological Quarterly (USA ISSN 0038-8610) **7635**
Concordia Torch (USA ISSN 0010-5287) **4499**
Concordian (CAN ISSN 1483-0078) **2279**
Concorsi (ITA ISSN 1724-5524) **2839**
Concours des Prix Essor. Document de Mise en Candidature *see* Le Concours des Prix Essor. Document d'Information et Fiche de Presentation **2839**
Le Concours des Prix Essor. Document d'Information et Fiche de Presentation (CAN ISSN 1912-8770) **2839**
• Concours Medical (FRA ISSN 0010-5309) **5600**
Concourse (GBR) **2279**
Concrete (NZL ISSN 1174-8540) **992**
Concrete *see* Jobsite. Tools & Materials for the Professional Concrete Surface Prep/Repair/Coatings Professional **1018**
Concrete/Beton (ZAF ISSN 0379-9824) **3185**
• Concrete (London) (GBR ISSN 0010-5317) **992**
Concrete & Masonry Construction Products (USA ISSN 1538-9219) **992**
Concrete Concepts *see* Concrete Contractor **993**
• Concrete Construction (USA ISSN 1533-7316) **992**
Concrete Construction and Architecture (IND ISSN 0010-5341) **993**
• Concrete Contractor (USA ISSN 1935-1887) **993**
Concrete Engineering (GBR ISSN 1475-9438) **993**
Concrete Engineering International *see* Concrete Engineering **993**
Concrete Homes (USA) **1049**
Concrete in Australia (AUS ISSN 1440-656X) **993**
Concrete Industry Bulletin (USA ISSN 0010-535X) **993**
• ➤ Concrete International (USA ISSN 0162-4075) **993**
Concrete Journal *see* Konkurito Kogaku **1019**
• Concrete Library International (CD-ROM)/Konkurito Raiburari Intanashonaru (JPN) **3263**
Concrete Library International (Print) *see* Concrete Library International (CD-ROM) **3263**
Concrete Masonry Designs (USA) **993**
Concrete Masonry News *see* C M News **989**
Concrete Monthly (USA) **993**
Concrete Openings (USA ISSN 1093-6483) **993**
Concrete Pipe Industry Statistics (USA ISSN 0360-2877) **3229**
Concrete Pipe News (USA ISSN 0045-8015) **993**
Concrete Plant International (DEU ISSN 1437-9023) **993**
• The Concrete Producer (USA ISSN 1528-0187) **993**
• Concrete Products (USA ISSN 0010-5368) **993**
Concrete Pumping (USA) **993**
Concrete Quarterly (GBR ISSN 0010-5376) **993**
Concrete Repair Bulletin (USA ISSN 1055-2936) **993**
Concrete Research and Technology *see* Konkurito Kogaku Ronbunshu **3277**
Concrete Research Magazine *see* Magazine of Concrete Research **1021**
Concrete Society Technical Report (GBR ISSN 0305-1986) **993**
• Concrete Technology Today (SGP) **993**
• Concrete Technology Today (USA) **993**
Concrete Today (USA ISSN 1940-8536) **993**
Concrete Wave (CAN ISSN 1708-3338) **8167**
Concrete Wolf (USA) **5420**
Concurrence, Consommation, Repression des Fraudes *see* Le Bulletin Officiel de la Concurrence, de la Consommation et de la Repression des Fraudes **8938**
Concurrences (FRA ISSN 1773-9578) **4862**
• ➤ Concurrency and Computation: Practice & Experience (GBR ISSN 1532-0626) **2506**
• ➤ Concurrent Engineering: Research and Applications (GBR ISSN 1063-293X) **2470**
➤ Concurrent Systems Engineering Series (NLD ISSN 1383-7575) **2470**
Concussion (USA) **8167**
† Conde Nast Portfolio (USA ISSN 1936-0916) **8943**
• Conde Nast Traveler (USA ISSN 0893-9683) **8694**
Conde Nast Traveler Gold (ITA ISSN 1127-8927) **8694**
Conde Nast Traveller (GBR ISSN 1368-597X) **8694**
Conde Nast's Traveler *see* Conde Nast Traveler **8694**
• ➤ Condensed Matter Physics (UKR ISSN 1607-324X) **7009**
➤ Condensed Matter Theories (USA ISSN 0893-861X) **7009**
Conditio Judaica (DEU ISSN 0941-5866) **5277**
Condition (DEU ISSN 0946-3003) **8167**
Condition Aktuell *see* Condition **8167**
Condition Feminine Canada. Perspectives *see* Status of Women Canada. Perspectives **8884**
• Condition Monitor (GBR ISSN 0268-8050) **3185**
Condition Monitoring and Diagnostic Engineering Management International. Proceedings *see* C O M A D E M International. Proceedings **8417**
• The Condition of Education (USA ISSN 0098-4752) **2931**
Condition Red Quarterly (USA) **7118**
Conditions and Scopes of Action in Development Policy *see* Handlungsbedingungen und Handlungsspielraeume fuer Entwicklungspolitik **7968**
Les Conditions de Detention en France (FRA ISSN 1777-3288) **2647**
Conditions de Travail et Securite *see* Securite et Conditions de Travail **1966**
Conditions d'Homologation et Procedures d'Exploitation des Aerodromes (FRA ISSN 1775-9226) **51**
Conditions of Democracy (SWE ISSN 1653-5561) **7118**
Condizionamento dell'Aria *see* C D A **4117**
Condo Life Magazine (CAN) **7587**
Condo Sales Report (USA ISSN 8750-1236) **7587**
Condobusiness (CAN ISSN 1489-8381) **4408**
• ➤ The Condor (USA ISSN 0010-5422) **905**
• Condor Call (USA) **2607**
Condor Magazin *see* Thomas Cook **8761**
Condorito (ARG ISSN 0328-8331) **2183**
Conduct of Civil Litigation in British Columbia (CAN) **4648**
• Conductas Adictivas (ESP ISSN 1578-8601) **6830**
Conducting Due Diligence *see* Conducting Due Diligence in M & A and Securities Offerings **4862**
Conducting Due Diligence in M & A and Securities Offerings (Merge & Acquisitions) (USA ISSN 1941-5052) **4862**
The Conductor (GBR) **6558**
Conductors Guild. Journal (USA ISSN 0734-1032) **6558**
Conductors' Guild Membership Directory (USA ISSN 1051-8649) **6558**
Conduit (GBR ISSN 0144-8439) **4212**
Conduit (USA ISSN 1073-6182) **5277**
Conduite de Projet (FRA ISSN 1773-4398) **1734**
• Conecta/Conecta: Bulletin of News in the History of Science and Technology (ESP ISSN 1576-4826) **7848**
Conecta: Bulletin of News in the History of Science and Technology *see* Conecta **7848**
Conectate *see* Panama America **3927**
• CONECtronica (ESP ISSN 1136-7539) **3185**
▼ Conemporary Issues in Education Research (USA ISSN 1940-5847) **2839**
Conexion (URY) **1592**
• Conexion Abierta (ARG ISSN 1666-2156) **2974**
▼ • Conexion Pediatrica (ARG ISSN 1851-5037) **6090**
▼ Conexion Salud (ARG ISSN 1851-3379) **5600**
• Conexoes (BRA ISSN 1516-4381) **8167**
Conexus (CAN ISSN 1718-1852) **1400**
Conexus Arts Centre. Annual Report (CAN ISSN 1912-8231) **483**
Confeccion Industrial (ESP ISSN 0211-3708) **2246**
Confection *see* Kennedy's Confection **3674**
• Confection & Snack Retailing (USA ISSN 1941-854X) **3673**
Confectionary Market Report Plus *see* Key Note Plus Market Report. Confectionery **3674**
Confectioner *see* Confection & Snack Retailing **3673**
Confectioner Buyers Guide *see* Confection & Snack Retailing **3673**
Confectioner, Tobacconist, Newsagent *see* C T N **3672**
Confectionery Industry Bulletin *see* Food Industry Updates. Confectionery **3673**
Confectionery Manufacture *see* Konditerskoe Proizvodstvo **3674**
➤ Confectionery Production (GBR ISSN 0010-5473) **3673**
Confederacao Brasileira de Futebol. Relatorio (BRA) **8167**
Confederacao Nacional do Comercio. Assessoria Juridica. Boletim Informativo (BRA) **1426**
Confederacao Nacional do Comercio. Conselho Tecnico Consultivo. Carta Mensal (BRA ISSN 0101-4315) **1426**
Confederacion de Empresarios de Castellon (ESP) **1426**
Confederacion de Organizaciones Turisticas de la America Latina *see* C O T A L **8690**
Confederacion Empresarial de Madrid Revista *see* C E I M Revista **480**
Confederacion Espanola de Cajas de Ahorros. Coyuntura Economica (ESP ISSN 0210-0738) **1448**
Confederacion International de Organizaciones Sindicales Libres. Informa Anual Sobre las Violaciones de los Derechos Sindicales *see* International Confederation of Free Trade Unions. Annual Survey of Violations of Trade Union Rights **4596**
Confederacion Latinoamericana de Asociaciones Cristianas de Jovenes. Carta (URY) **7635**
Confederacion Latinoamericana de Asociaciones Cristianas de Jovenes. Confederacion (URY) **7635**
Confederacion Latinoamericana de Asociaciones Cristianas de Jovenes. Contacto (URY) **7635**
Confederate Historical Institute Dispatch *see* C H I Dispatch **4286**
• Confederate Veteran (USA ISSN 0890-2216) **4289**
Confederated Umatilla Journal (USA) **6634**
Confederation de l'Artisanat et des Petites Entreprises du Batiment infos (Marseille) *see* C A P E B infos (Marseille) **988**
† Confederation des Industries Ceramiques de France. Annuaire (FRA ISSN 1265-616X) **8943**
Confederation des Syndicats Chretiens - Education Educ *see* C S C - Educ **4591**
• Confederation Francaise de l'Industrie des Papiers, Cartons et Celluloses. Rapport Annuel (FRA) **6740**
Confederation Francaise Democratique du Travail en Direct *see* C F D T en Direct **8938**
Confederation Francaise Democratique du Travail Magazine *see* C F D T Magazine **7951**
Confederation Francaise Democratique du Travail. Revue (FRA ISSN 1280-8180) **4592**
Confederation Generale du Travail Transports. Alpes du Nord *see* C G T. Transports. Alpes du Nord **4591**
Confederation Internationale des Cinemas d'Art et d'Essai Bulletin d'Information *see* C I C A E Bulletin d'Information **6491**
La Confederation Internationale des Syndicats Libres. Rapport Annuel des Violations des Droits Syndicaux *see* International Confederation of Free Trade Unions. Annual Survey of Violations of Trade Union Rights **4596**
Confederation Mondiale des Activites Subaquatiques Bulletin d'Information *see* C M A S Bulletin d'Information **2801**
Confederation of Australian Motor Sport Magazine *see* C A M S Magazine **8164**
Confederation of Australian Motor Sport Manual of Motor Sport *see* C A M S Manual of Motor Sport **8164**
Confederation of British Industry Annual Report *see* C B I Annual Report **1077**
Confederation of British Industry Distributive Trades Survey *see* C B I Distributive Trades Survey **1809**
Confederation of British Industry Economic and Business Outlook *see* C B I Economic and Business Outlook **1445**
Confederation of British Industry Human Resources Report *see* C B I. Human Resources Report **1668**
Confederation of British Industry Monthly Industrial Trends Survey *see* C B I Monthly Industrial Trends Survey **1077**
Confederation of British Industry Pannel Kerr Forster - S M E Trends Report *see* C B I - Pannel Kerr Forster - S M E Trends Report **1958**

Title

10148 CONGRESO ASOCIACION LATINA PARA EL ANALISIS DE LOS ULRICH'S PERIODICALS

Congreso Asociacion Latina para el Analisis de los Sistemas de Salud *see* C A L A S S **5590**
• Congreso Chileno de Sismologia e Ingenieria Antisismica (CHL ISSN 0718-2678) **2779**
• Congreso de la Republica del Peru (PER ISSN 1609-9788) **7431**
Congreso Dr. Antonio A.R. Monteiro. Acta (ARG ISSN 0327-9170) **5481**
Congreso Europeo de Medicina del Deporte. Resumen de Comunicaciones (ESP) **6229**
Congreso Geologico Argentino. Actas (ARG ISSN 0325-2620) **2730**
• Congreso Internacional de la Difusion del Espanol y su Cultura en Internet. Actas (ESP ISSN 1988-7876) **5107**
Congreso Internacional de Vivienda Popular (COL) **7956**
• Congreso Judio Latinoamericano. Boletin Informativo O J I (ARG ISSN 1023-0629) **3528**
Congreso Mexicano de Control de Calidad. Annual Proceedings (MEX) **6401**
Congreso Nacional de Femede. Libro de Actas (ESP) **6229**
Congresos (ESP ISSN 1697-0632) **5277**
Congresos Convenciones e Incentivos (ESP ISSN 0214-8056) **6279**
Congresos de Estudios Vascos (ESP) **333**
Congress (USA) **7431**
Congress and Foreign Policy (USA ISSN 0099-1295) **7228**
• Congress and the Nation (USA ISSN 1047-1324) **7118**
• ➤ Congress & the Presidency (USA ISSN 0734-3469) **7118**
• Congress Daily (USA) **7118**
Congress F A T I P E C (FRA ISSN 0430-2222) **6716**
Congress for Recreation and Parks. Symposium for Leisure Research. Abstracts (USA) **8218**
Congress in Park and Recreation Administration. Programme (GBR) **6279**
Congress in Park and Recreation Administration. Reports (GBR) **8310**
† • Congress in Print (USA ISSN 0193-4627) **8943**
Congress Marches Ahead (IND ISSN 0376-5776) **7118**
Congress Monthly *see* American Jewish Congress. Congress Monthly **7718**
Congress News (LKA ISSN 0045-6217) **4592**
Congress of Heterocyclic Chemistry. Book of Abstracts/Fukusokan Kagaku Toronkai Koen Yoshishu (JPN) **2094**
Congress of Local and Regional Authorities of Europe. AdoptedTexts (FRA) **7431**
Congress of Local and Regional Authorities of Europe. Official Reports of Debates (FRA) **7431**
Congress of Neurological Surgeons. Proceedings *see* Clinical Neurosurgery **6132**
Congress of Racial Equality Magazine *see* C O R E Magazine **7203**
Congress on Irrigation and Drainage. Transactions *see* International Commission on Irrigation and Drainage. Congress Reports **8826**
Congress on Research in Dance Membership Directory Membership Directory *see* C O R D Membership Directory **2683**
Congress on Research in Dance Newsletter *see* C O R D Newsletter **2683**
• Congress Quarterly (USA ISSN 1935-1526) **6240**
• Congressional Activities (USA ISSN 0733-0200) **7431**
Congressional Black Associates Newsnotes *see* C B A Newsnotes **7425**
• Congressional Digest (USA ISSN 0010-5899) **7118**
Congressional Directory *see* U.S. Congress. Congressional Directory **7190**
Congressional District Atlas (DVD) *see* Congressional District Atlas (Print) **7431**
Congressional District Atlas (Print) (USA) **7431**
Congressional Index (USA ISSN 0162-1203) **4821**
Congressional Information Bureau, Inc. Daily Maritime Newsletter *see* C I B Daily Maritime Newsletter **8640**
Congressional Information Bureau, Inc. Daily Maritime Newsletter Index *see* C I B Daily Maritime Newsletter Index **8640**
Congressional Information Service Annual *see* C I S Annual **4635**
Congressional Information Service, Inc. Index to Publications of the United States Congress *see* C I S Index to Publications of the United States Congress **7479**
Congressional Information Service, Inc. Legislative Histories Annual *see* C I S Legislative Histories Annual **4635**
Congressional Masterfile 2 *see* C I S Index to Publications of the United States Congress **7479**
• Congressional Member Organizations and Caucuses (USA ISSN 1068-6339) **7118**
• Congressional News Briefing (USA) **7118**
Congressional Pictorial Directory (USA ISSN 0589-3151) **7431**
Congressional Quarterly Almanac *see* C Q Almanac **7111**
Congressional Quarterly Global Researcher *see* C Q Global Researcher **7111**
Congressional Quarterly Guide to Current American Government *see* C Q Guide to Current American Government **8938**
Congressional Quarterly Researcher *see* C Q Researcher **7111**
Congressional Quarterly Researcher Bound Volume *see* C Q Researcher Bound Volume **7112**
Congressional Quarterly Today *see* C Q Today **7112**
Congressional Quarterly Weekly *see* C Q Weekly **7112**
Congressional Quarterly's Media Contact Directory *see* Media Contact Directory **2332**
Congressional Quarterly's Politics in America *see* C Q's Politics in America **7112**
Congressional Quarterly's State Fact Finder *see* State Fact Finder **7470**
• Congressional Record (USA ISSN 0363-7239) **7118**
Congressional Record Index (USA ISSN 0364-7544) **7431**
• Congressional Record Scanner (USA) **7199**
Congressional Report: Science, Energy & Environment (USA ISSN 0887-1914) **7431**
• Congressional Research Report (USA) **623**
• Congressional Research Service Index (USA) **4648**
• Congressional Research Service. Selected Reports (USA) **7118**
• Congressional Roll Call (Year) (USA ISSN 0191-1473) **7119**
• Congressional Staff Directory (USA ISSN 0589-3178) **7119**
➤ Congressional Studies Series (USA) **7119**
† The Congressional Yearbook (USA ISSN 1079-8129) **8943**
• Congressional Yellow Book (USA ISSN 0191-1422) **7431**
Congresso Brasileiro de Economia e Sociologia Rural. Anais (BRA ISSN 0102-2253) **196**
Congresso Brasileiro de Entomologia. Resumos *see* Embrapa Soja. Congresso Brasileiro de Entomologia. Resumos **843**
Congresso Brasileiro de Zoologia e Congresso Latino-Americano de Zoologia. Resumos (BRA) **938**
Congresso Internazionale di Studi sull'Alto Medioevo. Atti (ITA ISSN 0393-1056) **4212**
Congresso Internazionale di Studi Verdiani. Atti/International Congress of Verdi Studies. Proceedings (ITA) **6558**
Congresso Nazionale di Entomologia. Atti (ITA) **843**
➤ Congressus Numerantium (CAN ISSN 0384-9864) **5481**
▼ Conhecimento em Construcao (BRA ISSN 1983-8727) **3263**
Coniectanea Biblica. New Testament Series (SWE ISSN 0069-8946) **7635**
Coniectanea Biblica. Old Testament Series (SWE ISSN 0069-8954) **7635**
➤ Conifer Quarterly (USA) **3686**
Conimbriga (PRT ISSN 0084-9189) **388**
Coniunctio (SWE ISSN 1650-2302) **7348**
Conjonction (HTI ISSN 0304-5757) **3874**
Conjoncture/Al-Alam al-Iqtisadiy (TUN) **1448**
Conjoncture Canadienne *see* Canadian Business Conditions **1079**
La Conjoncture Canadienne *see* Canadian Business Conditions **1079**
Conjoncture Economique des Regions du Quebec en (Year) (CAN) **1883**
Conjoncture: Evolutions et Perspectives (MAR ISSN 1113-9048) **8364**
Conjonctures (CAN ISSN 0827-5548) **7956**
† Conjugaison (FRA ISSN 1951-2708) **8943**
• Conjunctions (USA ISSN 0278-2324) **5277**
• Conjunctions: The Web Forum for Innovative Writing (USA) **5277**
Conjunto (CUB ISSN 0010-5937) **8468**
Conjuntura & Planejamento (BRA ISSN 1413-1536) **1448**
• Conjuntura Economica (BRA ISSN 0010-5945) **1448**
Conjuring Arts Bulletin (USA ISSN 1938-7547) **4332**
Conmocion (USA) **4372**
• CONN - O S H A Quarterly (Email) (Connecticut Department of Labor, Division of Occupational Safety and Health) (USA) **6675**
Connacht Sentinel (IRL) **3892**
Connacht Tribune (IRL ISSN 0791-1807) **3892**
La Connaissance de... (FRA ISSN 1760-3870) **784**
Connaissance de Barres (FRA ISSN 1774-5470) **5278**
Connaissance de la Chasse (FRA ISSN 0396-5678) **8310**
• Connaissance de l'Emploi (FRA ISSN 1767-3356) **6696**
Connaissance de l'Eure (FRA ISSN 1142-5067) **4136**
Connaissance des Arts (FRA ISSN 0293-9274) **483**
Connaissance des Arts. Numero Hors - Serie *see* Connaissance des Arts **483**
➤ Connaissance des Invertebres (FRA ISSN 1287-3683) **843**
Connaissance des Peres de l'Eglise (FRA ISSN 0752-5346) **7635**
† Connaissance des Religions (FRA ISSN 0296-1288) **8943**
Connaissance du Francais *see* Enseigner le Francais **5115**
† Connaissance du Pays d'Oc (FRA ISSN 0336-9455) **8943**
Connaissance du Rail (FRA ISSN 1638-3281) **8616**
Connaissances de la Diversite *see* Connaissances de l'Education **2839**
Connaissances de l'Education (FRA ISSN 1275-1022) **2839**
Connaught Telegraph (IRL ISSN 1649-0088) **3892**
Connect (AUS ISSN 0158-4995) **2839**
Connect *see* Community Connect **8034**
• Connect! (CZE ISSN 1211-3085) **2317**
Connect (DEU ISSN 0944-6141) **2349**
Connect (ESP) **2367**
• Connect (FRA ISSN 0250-4499) **3412**
Connect *see* Tijdschrift voor Marketing **1846**
Connect (PRT) **2367**
• Connect (ROM ISSN 1582-7895) **2317**
• Connect (SVN ISSN 1580-450X) **2317**
Connect (USA ISSN 1532-8872) **483**
• Connect (Brattleboro) (USA ISSN 1041-682X) **3055**
Connect (Cambridge) (GBR) **6342**
† Connect (Christchurch) (NZL ISSN 1171-1426) **8943**
Connect (London) (GBR ISSN 1367-2495) **2317**
• Connect (Lympstone) (GBR ISSN 1749-5725) **3967**
Connect (Silver Spring) (USA) **938**
Connect Catalogo (ESP) **2367**
Connect! Mir Svyazi (RUS ISSN 1563-1958) **2317**
▼ Connect Professional (DEU) **2349**
• Connect Wyoming (USA) **4064**
Connect Youth International. Annual Report (GBR) **3012**
Connect Youth International. News (GBR) **3012**
Connected (NZL ISSN 1177-5599) **2183**
Connected Home (USA) **2415**
Connected Home Australia (AUS) **993**
Connected Home Solutions *see* Connected Home Australia **993**
† Connected Newsletter (USA ISSN 1554-4583) **8943**
• Connected Traveler (USA) **8695**
Connectez-moi! (FRA ISSN 1951-7270) **2553**
Connecticut *see* Fun with the Family in Connecticut **8711**
Connecticut Academy of Arts and Sciences. Memoirs (USA ISSN 0069-8970) **7848**
➤ Connecticut Academy of Arts and Sciences. Transactions (USA ISSN 0069-8989) **4448**
Connecticut. Agricultural Experiment Station, New Haven. Bulletin (USA ISSN 0097-0905) **843**
Connecticut: All-Industries *see* Harris Directory. Connecticut All-Industries **1999**
Connecticut American Ballroom Dance Association Newsletter *see* C T A B D A Newsletter **2683**
Connecticut Ancestry (USA ISSN 0197-2103) **3762**
Connecticut Appellate Reports (USA) **4648**
Connecticut Association of Boards of Education, Inc. Journal *see* C A B E Journal **3018**
Connecticut Banking (USA) **1329**
• Connecticut Bar Journal (USA ISSN 0010-6070) **4648**
Connecticut Beverage Journal (USA ISSN 0191-8818) **602**
• Connecticut Business Directory (USA ISSN 1048-7212) **1981**
Connecticut C P A (Certified Public Accountant) (USA ISSN 1934-3906) **1285**
Connecticut Chess Magazine (USA ISSN 1079-0500) **8167**
Connecticut Cities & Counties Graphic Performance Analysis (USA ISSN 1935-5769) **7480**
Connecticut Cities and Counties Graphic Performance Analysis *see* Connecticut Cities & Counties Graphic Performance Analysis **7480**
Connecticut. Commission on the Deaf and Hearing-Impaired. Annual Report (USA) **4073**
Connecticut Construction Highlights of the Week (USA) **993**
Connecticut Corporation Statutes and Forms (USA) **4862**
Connecticut Cottages & Gardens (USA) **3727**
• Connecticut. Council on Environmental Quality. Annual Report (USA ISSN 0095-4624) **3412**
Connecticut Criminal and Motor Vehicle Laws (USA ISSN 1943-8494) **4886**
• Connecticut Criminal Law (USA) **4886**
Connecticut Department of Labor, Division of Occupational Safety and Health - O S H A Quarterly (Email) *see* CONN - O S H A Quarterly (Email) **6675**
The Connecticut Economy (USA) **1426**
Connecticut Education Association Advisor *see* C E A Advisor **2833**
• Connecticut Employment Law Letter (USA ISSN 1064-4903) **4648**
Connecticut Engineer (USA) **3185**
Connecticut English Journal (USA ISSN 0893-0376) **5107**
Connecticut Facts - Rhode Island Facts (USA ISSN 1050-4613) **3119**
Connecticut Family Law Citations (USA) **4908**
• Connecticut Fire Service Laws (USA ISSN 1931-0226) **4648**
Connecticut Fireside (USA ISSN 0300-8258) **3973**
Connecticut Fireside and Review of Books *see* Connecticut Fireside **3973**
▼ Connecticut Foodie (USA ISSN 1936-6299) **4354**
• Connecticut Genealogy News (USA ISSN 1946-9039) **3763**
Connecticut Geologic and Natural History Bulletins (USA) **2730**
Connecticut Golf (USA ISSN 1523-6420) **8167**
Connecticut Government (USA ISSN 0010-6119) **7432**
Connecticut Greenhouse Newsletter *see* Yankee Grower **259**
• Connecticut History (USA ISSN 0884-7177) **4289**
• The Connecticut Hospice Newsletter (USA) **6984**
Connecticut Housing Production and Permit Authorized Construction (USA) **4408**
• ➤ Connecticut Insurance Law Journal (USA ISSN 1081-9436) **4648**
• Connecticut Insurance Law Review (USA ISSN 0742-924X) **4500**
† • The Connecticut JobBank (USA ISSN 1521-8724) **8943**
• ➤ Connecticut Journal of International Law (USA ISSN 0897-1218) **4922**
Connecticut. Judicial Branch. Biennial Report (USA) **4648**
Connecticut Law Enforcement Handbook (USA) **2647**
Connecticut Law Journal (USA ISSN 8750-0973) **4648**
The Connecticut Law Reporter (USA) **4948**
The Connecticut Law Reporter, Bound Series (USA) **4948**
• Connecticut Law Review (USA ISSN 0010-6151) **4648**
• Connecticut Law Tribune (USA ISSN 0198-0289) **4649**
Connecticut Lawyer (USA ISSN 1057-2384) **4649**
Connecticut Libraries (USA ISSN 0010-616X) **5003**
• Connecticut Magazine (USA ISSN 0889-7670) **3973**
• Connecticut Manufacturers Register (USA ISSN 1091-9600) **1981**
Connecticut: Manufacturing *see* Harris Directory. Connecticut Manufacturing **1999**
Connecticut Maple Leaf (USA ISSN 1081-6275) **3763**
Connecticut Market Data (USA ISSN 0573-665X) **1811**
Connecticut, Massachusetts, Rhode Island TourBook *see* TourBook: Connecticut, Massachusetts, Rhode Island **8762**
Connecticut Master Transportation Plan (USA ISSN 0069-9039) **8494**
• ➤ Connecticut Medicine (USA ISSN 0010-6178) **5600**
▼ Connecticut Motions in Limine (USA ISSN 1944-8511) **4948**
• Connecticut Motor Vehicle Laws (USA) **8575**
• Connecticut Nursing News (USA ISSN 0278-4092) **5956**
Connecticut Nutmegger (USA ISSN 0045-8120) **3763**
Connecticut, Off the Beaten Path *see* Off the Beaten Path: Connecticut **8743**
Connecticut. Office of State Treasurer. Annual Report for the Fiscal Year (USA) **1917**
Connecticut Opinions *see* Connecticut Law Tribune **4649**
Connecticut Pharmacist *see* Pharmacy Journal of New England **6873**
➤ Connecticut Poetry Review (USA ISSN 0277-7770) **5420**
• The Connecticut Public Interest Law Journal (USA ISSN 1932-2046) **4829**
Connecticut Real Estate Journal (USA) **7587**
• The Connecticut Realtor (USA) **7587**
Connecticut Reports (USA) **4649**
Connecticut - Rhode Island Telephone Tickler for Insurance Men & Women (USA) **4500**
• Connecticut River Environment (USA) **2607**
Connecticut River Review (USA ISSN 0897-0998) **5420**
Connecticut School Directory *see* M D R's School Directory. Connecticut **2958**
Connecticut Singles Connection *see* C T Singles Connection **7943**
Connecticut Society of Genealogists. Newsletter *see* Connecticut Genealogy News **3763**
Connecticut State Dental Association. Journal (USA ISSN 0010-6232) **5838**
Connecticut Super Lawyers (USA ISSN 1933-4982) **4649**
➤ Connecticut Supplement (USA) **4649**
Connecticut Town & City (USA) **7490**
Connecticut Traveler (USA ISSN 0746-8636) **8695**
• Connecticut Trial Evidence Notebook (USA) **4948**
• Connecticut Vacation Guide (USA) **8695**
Connecticut Walk Book (USA ISSN 0092-5764) **8310**
• ➤ Connecticut Warbler (USA ISSN 1077-0283) **905**
Connecticut Weekly Agricultural Report (USA ISSN 1059-8723) **102**
Connecticut West (USA) **8695**
Connecticut Wildlife (USA ISSN 1087-7525) **2607**
Connecticut Woodlands (USA ISSN 0010-6259) **3686**
• Connecticut. Workers' Compensation Commission. Compensation Review Board. Opinions (Online) (USA) **4500**
De Connectie (NLD ISSN 1871-3807) **2447**
Connecting (GRC ISSN 1108-7641) **2367**
Connecting *see* Pathways (Atlanta) **7770**
Connecting Drinks Yearbook (GBR ISSN 0961-7922) **602**
• Connecting Industry.com / Automation (GBR ISSN 1472-1244) **2584**
Connecting: Solo Travel News (CAN ISSN 1194-8841) **8695**
Connectingdrinks Yearbook *see* Connecting Drinks Yearbook **602**

▼ *new title*   † *ceased*   ● *electronic media*   ➤ *refereed*

Title

DIRECTORY 2010 CONSUMER POLICY REVIEW 10151

Construction News Weekly Covering Pittsburgh, Pennsylvania and Vicinity *see* F.W. Dodge Construction News Weekly Covering Pittsburgh, Pennsylvania and Vicinity **1004**
• Construction News Weekly, Covering Rhode Island, Eastern Connecticut and Bristol County Massachusetts (USA ISSN 1089-4829) **997**
Construction News Weekly Covering Richmond, Virginia and Vicinity *see* F.W. Dodge Construction News Weekly Covering Richmond, Virginia and Vicinity **1004**
• Construction News Weekly, Covering Roanoke, Virginia and Vicinity (USA ISSN 1095-1016) **997**
Construction News Weekly Covering Rochester, New York and Vicinity *see* F.W. Dodge Construction News Weekly Covering Rochester, New York and Vicinity **1004**
• Construction News Weekly, Covering Shreveport & Vicinity (USA ISSN 1086-6175) **997**
Construction News Weekly, Covering Shreveport and Vicinity *see* Construction News Weekly, Covering Shreveport & Vicinity **997**
Construction News Weekly Covering Southern Indiana *see* F.W. Dodge Construction News Weekly Covering Southern Indiana **1004**
• Construction News Weekly, Covering Southern Mississippi (USA ISSN 1086-6124) **997**
Construction News Weekly Covering Southern New Jersey and Delaware *see* F.W. Dodge Construction News Weekly Covering Southern New Jersey and Delaware **1004**
• Construction News Weekly, Covering Southern Wisconsin (USA ISSN 1085-1852) **997**
Construction News Weekly Covering St. Louis, Missouri and Vicinity *see* F.W. Dodge Construction News Weekly Covering St. Louis, Missouri and Vicinity **1004**
• Construction News Weekly Covering State of Kansas Excluding Kansas City (USA ISSN 1550-8684) **997**
Construction News Weekly Covering Syracuse, New York & Vicinity *see* F.W. Dodge Construction News Weekly Covering Syracuse, New York & Vicinity **1004**
Construction News Weekly, Covering the Bronx, Manhattan and Staten Island *see* Construction News Weekly, Covering the Bronx, Manhattan, & Staten Island **997**
• Construction News Weekly, Covering the Bronx, Manhattan, & Staten Island (USA ISSN 1085-8210) **997**
Construction News Weekly Covering the Hudson Valley, New York *see* F.W. Dodge Construction News Weekly Covering the Hudson Valley, New York **1004**
Construction News Weekly Covering the North Shore, Massachusetts *see* F.W. Dodge Construction News Weekly Covering the North Shore, Massachusetts **1004**
• Construction News Weekly, Covering the Rio Grande Valley (USA ISSN 1086-6221) **998**
Construction News Weekly Covering the South Shore, Massachusetts *see* F.W. Dodge Construction News Weekly Covering the South Shore, Massachusetts **1004**
• Construction News Weekly Covering the State of Alabama (USA ISSN 1551-0107) **998**
• Construction News Weekly Covering the State of Arkansas (USA ISSN 1550-8994) **998**
• Construction News Weekly Covering the State of Georgia (USA ISSN 1551-0115) **998**
• Construction News Weekly Covering the State of Iowa (USA ISSN 1550-8986) **998**
Construction News Weekly Covering the State of Kansas, Excluding Kansas City *see* Construction News Weekly Covering State of Kansas Excluding Kansas City **997**
Construction News Weekly Covering the State of Maine *see* F.W. Dodge Construction News Weekly Covering the State of Maine **1004**
• Construction News Weekly, Covering the State of Mississippi (USA ISSN 1086-6140) **998**
• Construction News Weekly Covering the State of Nebraska (USA ISSN 1550-0861) **998**
Construction News Weekly Covering the State of New Hampshire *see* F.W. Dodge Construction News Weekly Covering the State of New Hampshire **1004**
• Construction News Weekly, Covering the State of Vermont (USA ISSN 1095-0915) **998**
Construction News Weekly Covering the State of West Virginia *see* F.W. Dodge Construction News Weekly Covering the State of West Virginia **1004**
Construction News Weekly Covering Washington D.C. *see* F.W. Dodge Construction News Weekly Covering Washington D.C. **1004**
Construction News Weekly Covering West Central Florida *see* F.W. Dodge Construction News Weekly Covering West Central Florida **1004**
Construction News Weekly Covering Western Massachusetts *see* F.W. Dodge Construction News Weekly Covering Western Massachusetts **1004**
• Construction News Weekly, Covering Western Missouri (USA ISSN 1086-6248) **998**
Construction News Weekly Covering Western North Carolina *see* F.W. Dodge Construction News Weekly Covering Western North Carolina **1004**
• Construction News Weekly Covering Western Oklahoma (USA ISSN 1086-6108) **998**
Construction Newsletter *see* Tottel's Construction Newsletter **1041**
Construction North (GBR) **998**
Construction of Oil and Gas Wells on Dry Land and Offshore *see* Stroitel'stvo Neftyanykh i Gazovykh Skvazhin na Sushe i na More **6793**
The Construction Plant - Hire Association Bulletin (GBR) **998**
Construction Products (London) (GBR ISSN 1745-5855) **998**
Construction Products Trade Surveys *see* Construction Industry Trade Surveys **996**
• Construction Project Controls (USA ISSN 1522-3930) **998**
Construction Project Listing (SGP) **998**
Construction Purchasing *see* Green Construction Purchasing **1010**
Construction Regulatory Update *see* Keller's Construction Regulatory Update **1019**
Construction Reports. C40, Housing Authorized in Individual Permit-Issuing Places *see* Housing Units Authorized by Building Permits (Online) **4414**
• Construction Review (USA ISSN 0010-6917) **1045**
• Construction Risk Management (USA) **998**
Construction Safety *see* Jianzhu Anquan **1017**
Construction Site News (USA ISSN 1542-2828) **998**
Construction Specifications Institute NewsBrief *see* C S I NewsBrief **989**
The Construction Specifier (USA ISSN 0010-6925) **998**
• Construction Spending (USA) **1045**
Construction Supervisor (AUS) **998**
Construction Supervisor's Safety Bulletin (USA ISSN 1554-1878) **6675**
▼ Construction Supply (USA) **998**
• Construction Survey (USA) **998**
Construction Technology *see* Shigong Jishu **457**
• Construction Today (USA ISSN 1559-2650) **998**
Construction Today Europe (GBR) **998**
Construction Tomorrow *see* Asu o Kizuku **3259**
• Construction Worker (AUS ISSN 1833-0282) **998**
Construction Workers *see* Jianzhu Gongren **1017**
Construction World *see* Insaat Dunyasi **1014**
Construction World (ZAF ISSN 1607-9612) **998**
Construction Writers Association News (Buffalo Grove) *see* C W A News (Buffalo Grove) **989**
➤ Constructional Approaches to Language (NLD ISSN 1573-594X) **5108**
Constructional Steelwork Manufacturers *see* Business Ratio. Constructional Steelwork Manufacturers **987**
• Constructioneer (USA ISSN 0010-6968) **1049**
Constructioneer. Buyer's Guide (USA) **998**
Constructioneer Directory *see* Constructioneer. Buyer's Guide **998**
• ➤ Constructions (DEU ISSN 1860-2010) **5108**
▼ • ➤ Constructions and Frames (NLD ISSN 1876-1933) **5108**
Constructions Equipements pour les Loisirs (FRA ISSN 0010-6976) **998**
Constructiva (ESP ISSN 1578-5483) **438**
• ➤ Constructive Approximation (USA ISSN 0176-4276) **5481**
Constructive People *see* Des Gens Constructifs **3193**
Constructiviana (DEU ISSN 1619-9219) **6911**
Constructivism in the Human Sciences (USA ISSN 1520-2984) **7348**
Constructor (ARG ISSN 0010-7018) **998**
• Constructor (USA ISSN 0162-6191) **999**
Constructor Quarterly (GBR) **4332**
▼ Constructores de Paz (COL ISSN 2011-3277) **7635**
Constructs Series (USA) **5278**
Constructura (BRA) **5108**
Construdata (PRT) **999**
• Construinter (ESP) **999**
Construire (CAN ISSN 0833-0239) **999**
Construire (CHE ISSN 0010-7034) **999**
Construire (MAR ISSN 0851-0210) **999**
Construire en Acier *see* Bauen in Stahl **435**
Construire Ensemble (BFA) **102**
Construire l'Afrique (SEN) **1086**
Construire les Alternatives (FRA ISSN 1775-7290) **7119**
Construire sa Maison (FRA ISSN 0293-8634) **999**
Consudel (NLD ISSN 0010-7042) **3673**
Consular Requirements *see* Lloyd's Loading List **8650**
Consulente Immobiliare (ITA ISSN 0010-7050) **7587**
• Consulenza (ITA ISSN 1972-8425) **1086**
• Consulenza Lavoro (ITA) **4862**
Consult (AUS) **5600**
† Consult (DEU) **8943**
Consultant *see* SteuerConsultant **1945**
Consultant *see* Konsul'tant **1932**
Consultant (Columbia) (USA ISSN 0010-7085) **3686**
• ➤ Consultant (Greenwich) (USA ISSN 0010-7069) **5600**
Consultant (Louisville) (USA ISSN 1930-2290) **3632**
Consultant Engineers 500 *see* Consultant Engineers and Technologies 500 **1981**
• Consultant Engineers and Technologies 500 (GBR) **1981**
• ➤ Consultant for Pediatricians (USA ISSN 1545-8539) **6090**
• ➤ The Consultant Pharmacist (USA ISSN 0888-5109) **6830**
Consultants Advisory (GBR ISSN 1468-8441) **1735**
• Consultants & Consulting Organizations Directory (USA ISSN 0196-1292) **1735**
Consultants and Consulting Organizations Directory *see* Consultants & Consulting Organizations Directory **1735**
• Consultants News (USA ISSN 0045-8201) **1735**
Consultative Committee for Acoustics, Ultrasound and Vibration *see* Comite International des Poids et Mesures. Comite Consultatif de l'Acoustique, des Ultrasons et des Vibrations **8942**
Consultative Committee for Amount of Substance *see* Comite International des Poids et Mesures. Comite Consultatif pour la Quantite de Matiere. (Rapport et Annexes) **8942**
Consultative Committee for Electricity and Magnetism *see* Comite International des Poids et Mesures. Comite Consultatif d'Electricite et Magnetisme. (Rapport et Annexes) **8942**
Consultative Committee for Ionizing Radiation *see* Comite International des Poids et Mesures. Comite Consultatif des Rayonnements Ionisants (Rapport et Annexes) **8942**
Consultative Committee for Length *see* Comite International des Poids et Mesures. Comite Consultatif des Longueurs (Rapport et Annexes) **8942**
Consultative Committee for Mass and Related Quantities *see* Comite Consultatif pour la Masse et les Grandeurs Apparentees **8942**
Consultative Committee for Photometry and Radiometry *see* Comite International des Poids et Mesures. Comite Consultatif de Photometrie et Radiometrie. (Rapport et Annexes) **8942**
Consultative Committee for Thermometry *see* Comite International des Poids et Mesures. Comite Consultatif de Thermometrie. Rapports et Annexes **8942**
Consultative Committee for Units *see* Comite International des Poids et Mesures. Comite Consultatif des Unites (Rapport et Annexes) **8942**
Consulting Alert (USA ISSN 1534-0562) **1735**
† Consulting Engineer (GBR ISSN 1366-5189) **8943**
Consulting Engineer Africa *see* Government Digest **7493**
Consulting Engineers of British Columbia. Directory of Member Firms and Fields of Practice (CAN ISSN 1191-7857) **3185**
Consulting Industry Almanac *see* Plunkett's Consulting Industry Almanac **2024**
Consulting Intelligence *see* Consulting Tips Newsletter **1086**
• Consulting Magazine (USA ISSN 1525-4321) **1735**
Consulting Medical Laboratories. Bulletin (JOR ISSN 0254-7147) **5600**
Consulting Opportunities Journal (USA ISSN 0273-4613) **1735**
• ➤ Consulting Psychology Journal (USA ISSN 1065-9293) **7348**
Consulting Rates and Business Practices. Annual Survey (USA) **6696**
Consulting Services (USA ISSN 1064-2811) **2059**
• Consulting - Specifying Engineer (USA ISSN 0892-5046) **3185**
Consulting Success *see* Consulting Success Online **23**
• Consulting Success Online (USA) **23**
Consulting Tips Newsletter (USA) **1086**
• ➤ Consulting to Management (USA ISSN 1530-0153) **1735**
• El Consultor de los Ayuntamientos y de los Juzgados (ESP ISSN 0210-2161) **7490**
• Consultor Practico Laboral y Seguridad Social (CHL ISSN 0718-2643) **1673**
• Consultor Practico Tributario (CHL ISSN 0718-2651) **1917**
Consultorio Inmobiliario (ESP ISSN 1576-8252) **4901**
consum (CHE) **5068**
• Consumable Online (USA) **6558**
Consumatori (ITA) **2636**
Consumenten Geldgids *see* ConsumentenGeldgids **1329**
Consumenten Reisgids *see* De Reisgids **8751**
ConsumentenGeld *see* ConsumentenGeldgids **1329**
ConsumentenGeldgids (NLD ISSN 1569-3333) **1329**
Consumentengids (NLD ISSN 0165-6775) **2636**
The Consumer *see* O Katanalotis **2640**
Consumer (NZL ISSN 0110-5949) **2636**
• The Consumer Action Handbook (USA ISSN 1932-3980) **2636**
Consumer Affairs Council. Annual Report (AUS) **2636**
• Consumer Alert Comments (USA ISSN 0740-4964) **2636**
Consumer Asia (Year) (GBR) **1811**
The Consumer Banking Regulatory Handbook (USA ISSN 1090-2546) **1329**
• Consumer Bankruptcy News (USA ISSN 1058-3963) **4649**
Consumer Bulletin *see* A C M A Consumer Bulletin **8927**
Consumer China (Year) (GBR ISSN 1358-2437) **1811**
Consumer Choice (IRL ISSN 0790-486X) **2636**
• Consumer Comments (USA ISSN 0735-7362) **2636**
• Consumer Confidence Survey (USA ISSN 1046-1876) **1811**
• Consumer Connections (USA ISSN 1090-7033) **5600**
Consumer Credit (GBR ISSN 0966-6370) **1329**
Consumer Credit & Truth in Lending Compliance Report *see* Pratt's Consumer Credit and Truth in Lending Compliance Report **4760**
Consumer Credit Association News *see* C C A News **1322**
• Consumer Credit Delinquency Bulletin (USA ISSN 1058-8841) **1329**
• Consumer Credit Guide (USA) **4649**
Consumer Credit Insurance Association Newsletter *see* C C I A Newsletter **4497**
Consumer Credit: Law Transactions and Forms (USA) **1329**
Consumer Dimensions (USA ISSN 1536-6502) **2636**
Consumer-Directed Health Care (USA ISSN 1933-4117) **4091**
• Consumer Driven Healthcare (USA ISSN 1542-0914) **4091**
Consumer Drug Reference (USA ISSN 1543-754X) **6830**
• Consumer E-News Alert (USA) **1426**
Consumer Eastern Europe (Year) (GBR ISSN 0967-3601) **1811**
Consumer Economics *see* Xiaofei Jingji **1196**
Consumer Electronic Tips *see* First Glimpse **3099**
Consumer Electronics Daily *see* Warren's Consumer Electronics Daily **8445**
• Consumer Electronics Daily (USA) **3091**
The Consumer Electronics Industry: An Overview (USA) **3091**
Consumer Electronics Markt *see* C E Markt **3090**
Consumer Electronics Review *see* Dianqi Pingjie **3092**
Consumer Electronics Trade *see* C E & Trade **3090**
Consumer Electronics Vision (USA ISSN 1093-5231) **3091**
Consumer Expenditure Survey (USA ISSN 1935-9950) **1448**
† Consumer Expenditure Survey: Quarterly Data from the Interview Survey (USA) **8943**
• Consumer Expenditures in (Year) (USA) **1448**
Consumer Federation of America News (Washington) *see* C F A News (Washington) **2635**
Consumer Finance Bulletin (USA) **1329**
• Consumer Finance Law Quarterly Report (USA ISSN 0883-4555) **4649**
† Consumer Gardening (NZL ISSN 1175-8376) **8943**
• Consumer Goods Europe (GBR ISSN 1464-102X) **1811**
• Consumer Goods Industry Remuneration Review (AUS ISSN 1325-6785) **1859**
Consumer Goods Intelligence (GBR) **1883**
• Consumer Goods Technology (USA ISSN 1530-8421) **1735**
Consumer Goods U K (GBR ISSN 1464-1852) **1811**
• Consumer Guide Magazine (USA ISSN 0097-8337) **8576**
Consumer Guide to Homeowners Insurance *see* TheStreet.com Ratings' Consumer Guide to Homeowners Insurance **4525**
Consumer Guide to Long-term Care Insurance *see* TheStreet.com Ratings' Consumer Guide to Long-term Care Insurance **4525**
Consumer Guide to Medicare Prescription Drug Coverage *see* TheStreet.com Ratings' Consumer Guide to Medicare Prescription Drug Coverage **4525**
Consumer Guide to Medicare Supplement Insurance *see* TheStreet.com Ratings' Consumer Guide to Medicare Supplement Insurance **4525**
Consumer Guide to Term Life Insurance *see* TheStreet.com Ratings' Consumer Guide to Term Life Insurance **4525**
Consumer Guide to Variable Annuities *see* TheStreet.com Ratings' Consumer Guide to Variable Annuities **1655**
Consumer Guide's Best Buys Online (USA) **2636**
Consumer Healthcare Products Association Executive Newsletter *see* C H P A Executive Newsletter **6827**
Consumer Info News (USA) **2636**
• Consumer Information Catalog (USA) **623**
• Consumer Information Series (USA) **2400**
• Consumer Interests Annual (USA ISSN 1548-8705) **2636**
Consumer International (GBR ISSN 1359-0960) **1811**
Consumer Internet Usage Market Report *see* Key Note Market Report: Consumer Internet Usage **1893**
Consumer Latin America (Year) (GBR ISSN 1359-0979) **1811**
† Consumer Law Journal (GBR ISSN 0967-1978) **8943**
Consumer Law Review *see* Loyola Consumer Law Review **4726**
Consumer Law Today - The Fair Trading Monitor (GBR ISSN 0140-8518) **4649**
Consumer Lending News (USA ISSN 1077-0445) **1329**
Consumer Magazine Advertising Source *see* S R D S Consumer Magazine Advertising Source **39**
Consumer Magazines Market Reprot *see* Key Note Market Report: Consumer Magazines **1893**
Consumer Middle East (Year) (GBR) **1811**
• Consumer News and Reviews (Online) (USA) **2636**
Consumer Pharmacist (USA ISSN 0738-0615) **6830**
† • Consumer Policy Review (GBR ISSN 0961-1134) **8943**

Title

▼ *new title* † *ceased* • *electronic media* ➤ *refereed*

10152 CONSUMER PRICE INDEX ULRICH'S PERIODICALS

Consumer Price Index *see* Hong Kong Special Administrative Region of China. Census and Statistics Department. Consumer Price Index **1237**
• Consumer Price Index (Victoria) (CAN ISSN 0846-4871) **1222**
Consumer Price Index Bureau of Labor Statistics. C P I Detailed Report (Online) *see* U.S. Bureau of Labor Statistics. C P I Detailed Report (Online) **1522**
Consumer Price Index Bureau of Labor Statistics. C P I Detailed Report (Print) *see* U.S. Bureau of Labor Statistics. C P I Detailed Report (Print) **8995**
Consumer Price Index Detailed Report *see* U.S. Bureau of Labor Statistics. C P I Detailed Report (Print) **8995**
Consumer Price Index Detailed Report *see* U.S. Bureau of Labor Statistics. C P I Detailed Report (Online) **1522**
Consumer Price Index in Urban Areas of Iran (IRN) **1718**
Consumer Price Index Monthly *see* So'bija Mulga **1263**
Consumer Price Index of Belize (BLZ) **1222**
• Consumer Price Index. Pacific Cities & U.S. Average (USA ISSN 1933-0030) **1222**
• Consumer Price Indices of Ethiopia at Country, Rural and Urban Levels (ETH) **1222**
• Consumer Product Safety Commission Monitor (USA) **2636**
• Consumer Product Safety Guide (USA ISSN 0162-119X) **2636**
Consumer Product Safety Review *see* The Safety Review **2641**
Consumer Products Buyer (USA ISSN 1559-5161) **1811**
Consumer Products Employers *see* Vault Guide to the Top Consumer Products Employers **1713**
Consumer Protection, Antitrust & Unfair Business Practices Newsletter (USA) **2636**
• Consumer Protection Report (USA ISSN 0362-157X) **2636**
Consumer Psychology of Tourism, Hospitality and Leisure (GBR) **7349**
Consumer Purchases and Price Trends of Textiles (IND ISSN 0970-9800) **8449**
• Consumer Quarterly (CAN ISSN 1206-9744) **1811**
• Consumer Reports (USA ISSN 0010-7174) **2636**
Consumer Reports Best and Worst New Cars *see* Consumer Reports Best & Worst New Cars **2636**
Consumer Reports Best & Worst New Cars (USA ISSN 1556-2158) **2636**
Consumer Reports Best Buys for Your Home (USA ISSN 1528-4743) **2636**
Consumer Reports Brides Guide (USA ISSN 1538-8581) **2636**
• Consumer Reports Buying Guide (USA ISSN 1555-2357) **2636**
Consumer Reports Cars: Best & Worst New Cars *see* Consumer Reports Best & Worst New Cars **2636**
Consumer Reports Cars. New Car Ratings & Reviews (USA ISSN 1935-4002) **8576**
Consumer Reports Cars: Ratings & Pricing Guide (USA) **2636**
Consumer Reports Cars: Ratings and Pricing Guide *see* Consumer Reports Cars: Ratings & Pricing Guide **2636**
Consumer Reports Consumer Drug Reference *see* Consumer Drug Reference **6830**
• Consumer Reports for Kids Online (USA) **2183**
Consumer Reports Guide to Online Shopping (USA ISSN 1530-647X) **2637**
▼ Consumer Reports Health: Best Buy Drugs for Less (USA ISSN 1944-6357) **6830**
Consumer Reports Money Adviser (USA ISSN 1547-4534) **2637**
Consumer Reports New Car Buying Guide (USA ISSN 1044-3045) **8576**
Consumer Reports New Car Preview (USA ISSN 1551-3009) **8576**
• Consumer Reports on Health (USA ISSN 1058-0832) **6984**
Consumer Reports S U V's, Wagons, Minivans, Trucks (USA ISSN 1555-7464) **8576**
† • Consumer Reports Travel Letter (USA ISSN 0887-8439) **8943**
Consumer Reports Travel Well for Less (USA ISSN 1548-9337) **8695**
Consumer Reports Used Car Buying Guide (USA ISSN 1042-9476) **8576**
† Consumer Reports Used Car Yearbook (USA ISSN 1530-3721) **8943**
Consumer Reports Yard & Garden Equipment Buying Guide (USA) **2637**
Consumer Reports Yard and Garden Equipment Buying Guide *see* Consumer Reports Yard & Garden Equipment Buying Guide **2637**
Consumer Rights and Remedies *see* Texas Practice Series. Consumer Rights and Remedies **2641**
† Consumer Sciences Today (GBR ISSN 1470-8159) **8943**
Consumer Sourcebook (USA ISSN 0738-0518) **2637**
Consumer U S A (Year) (GBR ISSN 0952-9543) **1811**
Consumer Voice (LUX ISSN 1560-263X) **2637**
Consumer Watch (GBR ISSN 1473-978X) **3632**
Consumer Western Europe (Year) (GBR) **1812**
Consumer's Digest (KEN) **2637**
• Consumers Digest (USA ISSN 0010-7182) **2637**
Consumers Federated Groups of the Philippines. Newsletter (PHL) **2637**
• Consumers' Guide to Health Plans (USA) **4500**
• Consumers' Guide to Hospitals (USA ISSN 1070-2644) **2637**
Consumer's Newspaper *see* Xiaofei Xinbao **1196**
Consumers Should Know (USA ISSN 1090-1523) **7587**
• I Consumi Energetici delle Imprese Industriali (ITA ISSN 1825-5876) **3151**
Consumidores y Desarrollo (CHL ISSN 0717-2680) **1448**
Consummate Connecticut (USA ISSN 1558-710X) **8695**
Consumo Industrial de Energia Electrica do Estado da Bahia (BRA) **3297**
Consumo Pecuario Nacional (HND) **178**
Consumptie van Voedingsmiddelen in Nederland (NLD ISSN 0921-4305) **178**
• ➤ Consumption, Markets & Culture (GBR ISSN 1025-3866) **1718**
Conta Mais (BRA ISSN 1518-658X) **3803**
Contabilidad Nacional de Espana (ESP ISSN 0069-9292) **1917**
• Contabilidad Regional de la Comunidad de Madrid (ESP ISSN 1577-1369) **1448**
Contabilidad, Teoria y Practica (CHL) **1285**
Contabilidad y Auditoria (ARG ISSN 1515-2340) **1285**
➤ Contabilitate si Informatica de Gestiune (ROM ISSN 1583-4387) **1285**
Contact (BEL ISSN 0772-6880) **52**
Le Contact *see* L' Inter-action **8047**
Contact (DEU) **2647**
Contact *see* Practical Theology **7670**
Contact (IND) **7635**
Contact *see* Kontakten **2369**
Contact (TCD) **3821**
Contact (Aldershot) (GBR ISSN 1359-1762) **7752**
• Contact (Box Hill) (AUS ISSN 1030-7052) **7752**
Contact (Christchurch) (NZL ISSN 1177-3189) **6644**
Contact (Columbia) (USA) **2839**
Contact (Fortitude Valley) (AUS) **3297**
Contact (Laval) (CAN ISSN 0226-3505) **3807**
Contact (New York) (USA ISSN 1548-1654) **3528**
Contact (Noorden) (NLD) **3263**
Contact (Ottawa) (CAN) **2974**
➤ Contact (Quebec) (CAN ISSN 0832-7556) **3807**
Contact (Richmond) (AUS) **3055**
• Contact (Scoresby) (AUS ISSN 0810-7025) **7793**
Contact (Sheffield) (GBR) **7752**
Contact (Sioux Center) (USA ISSN 1521-9631) **7635**
Contact (Stockport) (GBR) **7635**
Contact (Toronto) (CAN ISSN 1193-7513) **1812**
Contact! (Tucson) (USA) **52**
Contact - Association Canadienne des Professionnels de la Vente *see* Contact (Toronto) **1812**
Contact - Chambre Officielle Franco-Allemande de Commerce et d'Industrie/Zeitschrift der Deutsch-Franzoesischen Wirtschaft (FRA ISSN 0753-5724) **1401**
• ➤ Contact Dermatitis (DNK ISSN 0105-1873) **5873**
• ➤ Contact Dermatitis. Supplement (DNK ISSN 1396-6669) **5873**
Contact Elevage (FRA ISSN 1775-8114) **8289**
Contact Europe (GBR) **2974**
Contact Girls (GBR ISSN 1366-3267) **6288**
• Contact I C C S - C I E C (International Council for Canadian Studies - Conseil International d'Etudes Canadiennes) (CAN ISSN 1681-2883) **4289**
• ➤ Contact in Context (USA ISSN 1547-8890) **573**
• ➤ Contact Lens & Anterior Eye (NLD ISSN 1367-0484) **6040**
Contact Lens Spectrum (USA ISSN 0885-9175) **6040**
Contact Lens Update (USA ISSN 0885-9264) **5742**
Contact Lenses *see* Australian Optometry **6039**
Contact Magazine (GBR) **5804**
Contact Management (CAN ISSN 1498-2145) **1735**
Contact Point (USA ISSN 0010-7301) **5839**
• Contact Point Bulletin (CAN) **8035**
• Contact Quarterly (USA ISSN 0198-9634) **2683**
Contact Sheet (USA ISSN 1064-640X) **6966**
Contact Toronto (CAN) **1086**
Contact Transport & Logistics (BEL) **1735**
Contactblad Spreken bij Uitvaarten (NLD ISSN 1872-535X) **6911**
Contacto *see* Connect **3412**
Contacto (GBR ISSN 1356-0018) **5108**
Contacto (LUX ISSN 1027-7331) **3906**
• Contacto (MEX) **1735**
• Contacto (Burbank) (USA) **3528**
Contacto (Northbrook) (USA ISSN 1526-9744) **5742**
Contacto Turistico (PRY) **8695**
▼ Contacto Vital (COL ISSN 2011-3749) **5600**
Contacts (DEU) **1592**
Contacts (GBR ISSN 1366-4646) **8468**
Contacts (USA ISSN 0738-291X) **23**
Contacts (ZAF ISSN 0250-2003) **8468**
Contacts (Paris, 1949) (FRA ISSN 0045-8325) **7635**
† Contacts A V A (Assurances Vieillesse des Artisans) (FRA ISSN 1166-4231) **8943**
Contacts sans Frontiere (FRA ISSN 1953-762X) **8695**
Contacts. Serie 1: Theatrica (CHE ISSN 0176-2931) **8468**
Contacts. Serie 2: Gallo-Germanica (CHE ISSN 0933-6087) **4212**
Contacts. Serie 3: Etudes et Documents (CHE ISSN 0933-6095) **4212**
▼ Contador Internacional (COL ISSN 2011-4214) **1285**
• Contaduria Universidad de Antioquia (COL ISSN 0120-4203) **1285**
• Contaduria y Administracion (MEX ISSN 0186-1042) **1285**
Contagion (USA ISSN 1075-7201) **8095**
➤ Contagion (USA ISSN 1553-538X) **5812**
Container Age (JPN ISSN 0289-8322) **8494**
Container and Packaging Guide *see* Guia del Envase y Embalaje **6710**
Container Contacts (DEU ISSN 0174-2701) **8494**
Container Intelligence Monthly (GBR ISSN 1467-0488) **8641**
Container Intelligence Quarterly (GBR ISSN 1478-9779) **8641**
Container Management (GBR ISSN 0269-7726) **8641**
Container Management Americas *see* Container Management **8641**
• Container Ship Update (NOR ISSN 1504-2529) **8641**
• Containerisation International (GBR ISSN 0010-7379) **8641**
Containerisation International Reefer Quarterly *see* C I Reefer Quarterly **8640**
Containerisation International World Directory of Liner Shipping Agents *see* World Directory of Liner Shipping Agents (Year) **2035**
Containerisation International Yearbook (GBR ISSN 0305-7402) **8641**
• The Containership Register (London, 2002) (GBR ISSN 1750-3752) **8641**
ConTakt (DEU) **8494**
Contaminacion Ambiental (COL ISSN 0120-0674) **3485**
Contaminated Land Bulletin (GBR ISSN 1751-8377) **3485**
• Contaminated Land Management (GBR ISSN 1478-212X) **3412**
• Contaminated Sites Division. Annual Report (CAN ISSN 1719-9409) **3412**
Contaminated Soil, Sediment & Water *see* Soil Sediment & Water **3467**
† • Contamination Control (USA ISSN 1556-1410) **8943**
Contappunto *see* Contrappunti **6133**
Contas Nacionais Trimestrais (PRT ISSN 0872-1602) **1718**
• Contatto Elettrico (ITA ISSN 1120-2351) **3298**
• Contemplacao (BRA ISSN 1809-1911) **6911**
Contempoary Farm Machinery *see* Dangdai Nong-ji **210**
• Contempora Magazine (USA ISSN 1067-5272) **3528**
• Contemporanea (ITA ISSN 1724-6105) **5278**
• Contemporanea (Bologna) (ITA ISSN 1127-3070) **4212**
Contemporanea (Ravenna) (ITA) **4136**
➤ El Contemporani (ESP ISSN 1133-519X) **4212**
Contemporanul Ideea Europeana (ROM ISSN 1220-9864) **3932**
The Contemporaries *see* Dangdairen **5282**
Contemporary *see* Suvremennik **5383**
Contemporary (GBR ISSN 1475-9853) **483**
Contemporary A Cappella News (USA) **6558**
• ➤ Contemporary Accounting Research/Recherche Comptable Contemporaine (CAN ISSN 0823-9150) **1285**
• ➤ Contemporary Aesthetics (USA ISSN 1932-8478) **6911**
Contemporary African Art *see* Nka **509**
Contemporary Agriculture *see* Savremena Poljoprivreda **154**
• Contemporary American Ethnic Issues (USA ISSN 1543-219X) **333**
Contemporary American History Series (USA ISSN 0069-9357) **4290**
Contemporary Animal Husbandry *see* Dangdai Xumu **284**
▼ • Contemporary Arab Affairs (GBR ISSN 1755-0912) **7228**
Contemporary Architecture (AUS ISSN 1447-8447) **438**
Contemporary Architecture of the World *see* Kindai Kenchiku **447**
• ➤ Contemporary Argumentation and Debate (USA ISSN 1088-498X) **2839**
Contemporary Art Centre of South Australia. Broadsheet (AUS ISSN 0819-677X) **483**
Contemporary Art Review (USA) **483**
Contemporary Artists *see* Dangdai Meishujia **485**
Contemporary Asia-Pacific Studies *see* Dangdai Ya-Tai **547**
Contemporary Austrian Studies (USA ISSN 1074-7184) **4448**
• Contemporary Authors (USA ISSN 0010-7468) **641**
Contemporary Authors. New Revision Series (USA ISSN 0275-7176) **641**
• Contemporary Black Biography (USA ISSN 1058-1316) **641**
Contemporary Brides (USA) **5558**
• ➤ Contemporary British History (GBR ISSN 1361-9462) **4212**
• Contemporary Buddhism (GBR ISSN 1463-9947) **7701**
Contemporary Canadian Authors (CAN ISSN 1203-2816) **5278**
• ➤ Contemporary Cancer Research (USA) **6017**
• ➤ Contemporary Cardiology (USA) **5783**
Contemporary Caribbean Legal Issues (BRB ISSN 1028-9283) **4649**
Contemporary Celebrities *see* Jinri Mingliu **8968**
Contemporary Chemical Industry *see* Dangdai Huagong **3242**
Contemporary China History Studies *see* Dangdai Zhongguoshi Yanjiu **4181**
† Contemporary China Institute Publications (GBR ISSN 0085-2856) **8943**
Contemporary China Series *see* East Asian Institute Contemporary China Series **548**
• ➤ Contemporary Chinese Thought (USA ISSN 1097-1467) **6911**
Contemporary Choice Articles *see* Dangdai Wencui **5282**
Contemporary Christian Music Update *see* C C M Update **6552**
Contemporary Cinema *see* Dangdai Dianying **6495**
Contemporary Cinema (NLD ISSN 1572-3070) **6494**
• ➤ Contemporary Clinical Neuroscience (USA) **6133**
• ➤ Contemporary Clinical Trials (USA ISSN 1551-7144) **5904**
Contemporary Concepts of Condensed Matter Science (NLD ISSN 1572-0934) **7009**
• Contemporary Criminal Procedure (USA) **4886**
• Contemporary Critical Care (USA ISSN 1543-9003) **6058**
Contemporary Critical Concepts and Pre-Enlightenment Literature (USA ISSN 1074-6781) **5278**
Contemporary Dental Assisting *see* Inside Dental Assisting **5848**
† Contemporary Dermatology (USA ISSN 1541-5791) **8943**
• Contemporary Diagnostic Radiology (USA ISSN 0149-9009) **6194**
Contemporary Dialysis & Nephrology (USA ISSN 0899-837X) **6266**
Contemporary Doll Collector (USA ISSN 1075-8674) **4332**
Contemporary Drama in English (DEU) **8468**
Contemporary Drama in English Studies *see* C D E Studies **8467**
Contemporary Dramatists (USA ISSN 1050-3919) **8468**
• ➤ Contemporary Economic Policy (USA ISSN 1074-3529) **1086**
Contemporary Economics *see* Dangdai Jingji **1090**
• ➤ Contemporary Educational Psychology (USA ISSN 0361-476X) **2839**
Contemporary Educational Science *see* Dangdai Jiaoyu Kexue **2841**
• ➤ Contemporary Endocrinology (USA ISSN 0196-8653) **5885**
Contemporary Enterprise *see* Dangdai Qiye **8948**
Contemporary Ergonomics (GBR ISSN 0267-4718) **3186**
Contemporary Esthetics *see* Inside Dentistry **5848**
• Contemporary European History (GBR ISSN 0960-7773) **4212**
• ➤ Contemporary Family Therapy (USA ISSN 0892-2764) **7349**
Contemporary Film Directors (USA ISSN 1933-1878) **6494**
Contemporary Foreign Literature *see* Dangdai Waiguo Wenxue **5282**
• Contemporary French and Francophone Studies (GBR ISSN 1740-9292) **5278**
➤ Contemporary French Civilization (USA ISSN 0147-9156) **4212**
Contemporary German Studies: Occasional Papers (GBR ISSN 0268-1331) **4212**
Contemporary German Writers (GBR) **5278**
† • ➤ Contemporary Gerontology (USA ISSN 1069-0840) **8943**
• ➤ Contemporary Hematology (USA ISSN 1931-2482) **5935**
• Contemporary Heroes and Heroines (USA) **641**
• ➤ Contemporary Herpetology (USA ISSN 1094-2246) **939**
Contemporary Hispanic Biography (USA ISSN 1541-1524) **642**
Contemporary History *see* Soudobe Dejiny **4266**
Contemporary History *see* Historia Contemporanea **4142**
Contemporary History of China *see* Zhongguo Xiandaishi **4191**
• ➤ Contemporary Hypnosis (GBR ISSN 0960-5290) **5942**
• ➤ Contemporary Immunology (USA) **5757**
Contemporary Impressions (USA ISSN 1066-9434) **483**
Contemporary Indian Literature *see* Samakalina Bharatiya Sahitya **5366**
➤ Contemporary Internal Medicine (USA ISSN 1051-1040) **5944**
Contemporary International Relations (CHN ISSN 1003-3408) **7228**
▼ • Contemporary Islam (NLD ISSN 1872-0218) **7710**
Contemporary Issues (AUS ISSN 1832-2514) **4448**
• ➤ Contemporary Issues and Ideas in Social Sciences (IND ISSN 1817-4604) **7956**
Contemporary Issues in Asia and the Pacific (USA) **547**
Contemporary Issues in Clinical Biochemistry (GBR ISSN 0265-6701) **729**
Contemporary Issues in Communication Science & Disorders (USA ISSN 1092-5171) **6079**

Title

Controleprotocol A V R Primair Onderwijs (Aanvraag Vaststelling Rijksvergoeding) (NLD ISSN 1873-8915) **1285**
Controleprotocol O C W vo-bve-hbo *see* Controleprotocol Onderwijs Cultuur en Wetenschappen Voortgezet Onderwijs-Beroepsondederwijs Volwassenen Educatie-Hoger Beroeps Onderwijs-Wetenschappelijk Onderwijs **1285**
Controleprotocol O C W vo-bve-hbo-wo *see* Controleprotocol Onderwijs Cultuur en Wetenschappen Voortgezet Onderwijs-Beroepsondederwijs Volwassenen Educatie-Hoger Beroeps Onderwijs-Wetenschappelijk Onderwijs **1285**
Controleprotocol O C W wo *see* Controleprotocol Onderwijs Cultuur en Wetenschappen Voortgezet Onderwijs-Beroepsondederwijs Volwassenen Educatie-Hoger Beroeps Onderwijs-Wetenschappelijk Onderwijs **1285**
Controleprotocol Onderwijs Cultuur en Wetenschappen Voortgezet Onderwijs-Beroepsondederwijs Volwassenen Educatie-Hoger Beroeps Onderwijs-Wetenschappelijk Onderwijs (NLD ISSN 1873-9687) **1285**
Controleprotocol PO *see* Controleprotocol A V R Primair Onderwijs **1285**
Controlled Clinical Trials *see* Contemporary Clinical Trials **5904**
• Controlled Environments (USA ISSN 1556-9268) **3366**
• Controlled Release Newsletter (USA) **2122**
• Controlled Release Society. Transactions (USA) **2122**
Controlled Substances Regulation (USA) **2692**
The Controller (CAN ISSN 0010-8073) **52**
• Controller (USA) **8539**
Controller Magazin (DEU ISSN 1616-0495) **1735**
• Controller's Business Advisor (Online) (USA) **1286**
Controllers Journaal (NLD ISSN 0926-3004) **1286**
Controllers Magazine (NLD ISSN 0926-7158) **1286**
• The Controller's Report (USA ISSN 0895-2787) **1286**
• Controller's Report Yearbook (USA ISSN 1528-2090) **1286**
• Controller's Tax Letter (USA ISSN 1529-8353) **4650**
• Controllers Update (USA ISSN 8756-5676) **1286**
Controlli della Produttivita del Latte in Italia (ITA ISSN 1971-4076) **262**
Controlling (DEU ISSN 0935-0381) **2460**
Controlling en Auditing in de Praktijk *see* Controlling in de Praktijk **1286**
Controlling i Rachunkowosc Zarzadcza (POL ISSN 1644-4841) **1286**
Controlling in de Praktijk (NLD ISSN 1574-4485) **1286**
Controlling the Volcano Within *see* Anger Management - Controlling the Volcano Within **7334**
• Controlling & Management (DEU ISSN 1614-1822) **1735**
Controllo di Gestione (ITA ISSN 1828-4205) **1735**
• Il Controllo nelle Societa e negli Enti (ITA ISSN 1972-828X) **1286**
• Controls Intelligence & Plant Systems Report (USA ISSN 1528-6312) **2539**
Controspazio/Counterspace (ITA ISSN 0010-809X) **438**
Controtempo (ITA ISSN 1125-4661) **8096**
Controverses (FRA ISSN 1779-2355) **7956**
Controversia (COL ISSN 0120-4165) **7120**
Controversia (USA ISSN 1521-4826) **3055**
Controversial Issues in Public Policy Series (USA) **7120**
Controversies (NLD ISSN 1574-1583) **7228**
Controversy (USA) **3973**
▼ Contr'Un (FRA ISSN 1960-7156) **5279**
Contubernium (DEU ISSN 0340-6857) **7848**
Conturen (AUT) **5212**
▼ Conuco (COL ISSN 2011-4079) **1086**
Conundrum (GBR) **8167**
Convegni B2B (ITA) **8695**
Convegni Giuridici (ITA ISSN 1972-1102) **4650**
Convegni Incentive & Comunicazione (ITA ISSN 1723-4174) **6279**
Convegno di Studi Sulla Magna Grecia. Atti (ITA ISSN 0069-9748) **388**
Convegno di Studi sull'Antico Territorio di Formia. Atti *see* Formianum **8957**
Convegno Internazionale di Studi Italo-Tedeschi. Atti/Internationale Tagung Deutsch-Italienischer Studien. Akten (ITA) **4448**
Convencion Bancaria y de Entidades Financieras. Memoria (COL) **1329**
Convene (USA ISSN 1065-0938) **1735**
Convenience & Fastfood (NOR ISSN 1502-5985) **3632**
Convenience Retailing (GBR ISSN 1470-9988) **3677**
Convenience Shop (DEU ISSN 0948-8855) **3677**
• Convenience Store (GBR ISSN 0267-9361) **3677**
Convenience-Store *see* C-Store **3676**
• Convenience Store Decisions (USA ISSN 1054-7797) **3677**
• Convenience Store News (USA ISSN 0194-8733) **3677**
Convenience Store Petroleum *see* C S P **3676**
Convenience Store Petroleum Independent *see* C S P Independent **3676**
Convenience Store Retailing (ZAF) **1812**
▼ Convenient Care (USA) **5956**
Convenios Centroamericanos de Integration Economica (GTM ISSN 0553-6863) **1593**
• Convenit Internacional (BRA ISSN 1517-6975) **5108**
• Convention Against Torture and Other Cruel, Inhuman or Degrading Treatment or Punishment. Report of Canada (CAN ISSN 1719-9034) **4650**
• Convention & Incentive Marketing (AUS ISSN 1039-1029) **6279**
Convention Centers *see* One+ **6282**
Convention Collective Nationale de Travail des Etablissements et Service pour Personnes Inadaptees et Handicapees du 15 Mars 1966 (FRA ISSN 1773-4312) **1673**
Convention Contre la Torture et Autres Peines ou Traitements Cruels, Inhumains ou Degradants. Rapport du Canada *see* Convention Against Torture and Other Cruel, Inhuman or Degrading Treatment or Punishment. Report of Canada **4650**
Convention Europeenne des Droits de l'Homme. Annuaire *see* European Convention on Human Rights. Yearbook **7206**
• Convention Forum (USA ISSN 1556-1097) **6279**
Convention Herald (USA ISSN 8750-4812) **7635**
Convention Industry *see* T W **6283**
Convention International (DEU) **6279**
Convention Internationale sur l'Elimination de Toutes les Formes de Discrimination Raciale. Rapport du Canada *see* International Convention on the Elimination of All Forms of Racial Discrimination. Report of Canada **7210**
• Convention of Electrical and Electronics Engineers in Israel. Proceedings (USA ISSN 0899-6156) **3298**
Convention on Biological Diversity News *see* C B D News **663**
Convention on International Trade in Endangered Species Control List *see* C I T E S Control List **3408**
Convention on International Trade in Endangered Species Month *see* C I T E S Monthly **3408**
Convention on International Trade in Endangered Species Reports *see* C I T E S Reports **3408**
Convention Program *see* American Christmas Tree Journal **3722**
Conventional Apartments *see* Income - Expense Analysis: Conventional Apartments **7595**
Conventions & Meetings Canada (CAN ISSN 0226-8922) **6279**
ConventionSouth (USA ISSN 1074-0627) **6279**
• Converge Online (USA) **2948**
• Converge Point (USA ISSN 1945-9696) **7752**
• ➤ Convergence (CAN ISSN 0010-8146) **2940**
• Convergence (GBR ISSN 1354-8565) **2379**
Convergence *see* Multichannel News **2385**
Convergence *see* Loci **5509**
• Convergence (London) (GBR ISSN 1817-5694) **4650**
• Convergence: International Congress on Transportation Electronics. Proceedings (USA) **8576**
• Convergence Quarterly (USA) **2415**
▼ Convergence Review (USA ISSN 1943-8230) **5420**
Convergences (CHE ISSN 1421-2854) **5108**
Convergences (FRA ISSN 0293-3292) **7228**
• Convergencia (MEX ISSN 1405-1435) **7432**
Convergencia Lusiada (BRA) **5279**
Converging Evidence in Language and Communication Research (NLD ISSN 1566-7774) **5108**
• Converging Media (GBR ISSN 1750-3906) **2317**
Conversaciones Internacionales de Historia (ESP) **4212**
Conversations (USA ISSN 1548-2057) **7635**
Conversations (USA) **2940**
• Conversations in Religion and Theology (GBR ISSN 1479-2206) **7635**
• Conversations on Philanthropy (USA ISSN 1552-9592) **8035**
Conversations with Filmmakers (USA ISSN 1556-1593) **6495**
Conversely (USA) **7943**
Conversion *see* Konversiya **1142**
Conversion Survey *see* Bonn International Center for Conversion. Jahresbericht **7224**
Converter (GBR ISSN 0010-8189) **6732**
Converter Directory (GBR ISSN 0309-2143) **6733**
Converter Technology & Electric Traction *see* Bianliu Jishu yu Dianli Qianyin **7051**
• Converting Hotline (USA) **7319**
• Converting Magazine (USA ISSN 0746-7141) **6733**
• Converting Magazine Manufacturers Directory (USA) **6733**
Converting Magazine O E M Products and Accessories Guide *see* Converting Magazine O E M Products & Accessories Guide **6733**
• Converting Magazine O E M Products & Accessories Guide (Original Equipment Manufacturer) (USA) **6733**
• Converting Today (GBR ISSN 0264-715X) **6733**
• Convertronic (ESP ISSN 1578-9969) **3186**
• Conveyancer and Property Lawyer (GBR ISSN 0010-8200) **7587**
Conveyancers' Yearbook (GBR ISSN 1462-8201) **4650**
Conveyancing (GBR ISSN 1352-4534) **4650**
Conveyancing and Property Law Journal (IRL ISSN 1393-3213) **4650**
Conveyancing Bulletin (ZAF) **4650**
Conveyancing Manual N S W *see* Conveyancing Manual New South Wales **7587**
• Conveyancing Manual New South Wales (AUS) **7587**
Conveyancing Manual Q L D *see* Conveyancing Manual Queensland **7587**
• Conveyancing Manual Queensland (AUS) **7587**
• Conveyancing Service N S W (AUS) **4650**
Conveyor Equipment Manufacturers Association Bulletin (Online) *see* C E M A Bulletin (Online) **5450**
• Conviction and Sentencing of Offenders in New Zealand (NZL ISSN 1172-0638) **2647**
† ➤ ConVivio (AUS ISSN 1322-7971) **8944**
• Convivium (ESP ISSN 0010-8235) **6912**
Convivium (USA ISSN 1087-8181) **4354**
Convivium Assisiense (ITA ISSN 1828-7743) **7793**
Convocation Speeches of Nigerian Universities *see* Nigeria. National Universities Commission. Convocation Speeches of Nigerian Universities **2996**
Convorbiri Literare (ROM ISSN 0010-8243) **5279**
Conwy Local Transport Plan (GBR) **8630**
Conzema Fortbildungs Journal Diabetes Aktuell fuer die Praxis *see* C F - Journal Diabetes Aktuell fuer die Praxis **5884**
• Conzoom (DNK ISSN 1901-7758) **1222**
Coober Pedy Hospital and Health Services. Annual Report (AUS ISSN 1833-0940) **4091**
• Coober Pedy Regional Times (AUS ISSN 1833-1831) **3793**
Cook & Tell (USA) **4354**
Cook County Financial Malpractice Suit Filing List (USA) **4948**
Cook County Jury Verdict Reporter (USA) **4948**
Cook County Medical Malpractice Suit Filing List (USA) **4948**
Cook County Products Liability Suit Filing List (USA) **4948**
• Cook Islands Herald (COK) **3916**
• Cook Islands News (COK) **3916**
Cook Islands News Online *see* Cook Islands News **3916**
Cook Knowledge *see* Pengtiao Zhishi **4365**
Cook on Costs (Year) (GBR) **4862**
• Cook Political Report (Online Edition) (USA) **7120**
Cook Political Report (Print Edition) *see* Cook Political Report (Online Edition) **7120**
▼ Cook Vegetarian! (GBR) **4354**
Cookbook (GBR ISSN 1472-3107) **4354**
The Cookbook (IRL ISSN 1393-5402) **4354**
Cookbook Digest (USA ISSN 0010-826X) **4354**
Cookbook Review (USA) **4354**
Cookeia (ZWE ISSN 0250-2992) **2174**
Cookia (NZL ISSN 1171-140X) **939**
• Cookie (USA ISSN 1556-410X) **2150**
Cooking and Eating Market Assessment *see* Key Note Market Assessment. Cooking and Eating **1827**
Cooking Club Of America *see* Cooking Pleasures **4354**
Cooking Contest Chronicle (USA ISSN 1092-7867) **3632**
Cooking for 2 *see* Taste of Home's Cooking for 2 **4368**
Cooking for Profit (USA ISSN 0091-861X) **3632**
• Cooking Light (USA ISSN 0886-4446) **4354**
Cooking Pleasures (USA ISSN 1098-1187) **4354**
Cooking Sauces & Food Seasonings *see* Key Note Market Report: Cooking Sauces & Food Seasonings **1828**
Cooking with Paula Deen (USA ISSN 1558-1853) **4354**
• Cook's Country (USA ISSN 1552-1990) **4355**
Cook's Illustrated (USA ISSN 1068-2821) **3632**
• Cook's Index (Online Edition) (USA) **4370**
Cool (RUS ISSN 1560-5485) **2183**
Cool/Liuxing Kubao (TWN ISSN 1028-7094) **3960**
Cool (UKR) **2183**
• Cool (USA ISSN 1941-2525) **483**
Cool and Strange Music! (USA) **6559**
Cool Beans! (USA) **6559**
• Cool Cargoes (USA) **8642**
Cool & Comfort (Dutch Edition) (BEL ISSN 1782-4613) **4118**
Cool & Comfort (French Edition) (BEL ISSN 1782-4621) **4118**
Cool Girl (ROM ISSN 1582-6120) **8856**
Cool Girl (RUS ISSN 1560-5493) **2183**
Cool Girl (UKR) **8856**
Cool Liuxing Kubao *see* Cool **3960**
• Cool News of the Day (USA) **1812**
Cool Player (GBR ISSN 1747-6747) **8167**
Cool Poster (RUS ISSN 1606-8742) **2183**
Cool Toys/Wanju Kubao (TWN ISSN 1562-5338) **2183**
• The Cool Tricks and Trinkets Newsletter (USA) **3973**
Cool'eh (USA) **6559**
• Cooler (GBR ISSN 1746-9171) **8167**
Cooler Innovation (GBR ISSN 1751-4185) **602**
• Cooley Communique (USA) **3763**
Coolia (NLD ISSN 0929-7839) **784**
Coolibri (DEU) **6522**
Cooling Tower Institute. Bibliography of Technical Papers (USA) **6766**
Cooling Tower Institute Journal *see* C T I Journal **6765**
Cooling Tower Institute News (Houston) *see* C T I News (Houston) **6765**
Coon-Hound Corner (USA) **8310**
Coonhound Bloodlines (USA ISSN 1067-0920) **8310**
Coop de France Infos (FRA ISSN 1951-4492) **102**
Coop News (NGA ISSN 0794-7763) **1423**
Coop - Zeitung (CHE) **1423**
Cooper Collection (USA ISSN 1058-4021) **3763**
Cooper Society Newsletter (USA ISSN 1073-0907) **5279**
Cooperacion (MEX) **1593**
Cooperacion Espanola (ESP ISSN 1576-2947) **1593**
Cooperacion Publica Vasca para el Desarrollo. Memoria (Years) (ESP) **1593**
Cooperacion Sur *see* Cooperation South **8096**
• CooperActif (CAN ISSN 1715-8419) **1086**
Cooperateur Agricole (CAN ISSN 0315-1204) **102**
Cooperateur Forestier (CAN) **3711**
Cooperatie (NLD ISSN 1389-7462) **1423**
Cooperatie Rundveeverbetering Magazine (Noord Edition) *see* C R V Magazine (Noord Edition) **864**
Cooperatie Rundveeverbetering Magazine (Oost Edition) *see* C R V Magazine (Oost Edition) **864**
Cooperatie Rundveeverbetering Magazine (Zuid-West Edition) *see* C R V Magazine (Zuid-West Edition) **864**
Cooperatieve Vennootschappen *see* Samsom Cooperatieve Vennootschappen **1170**
Cooperation (CHE) **1423**
Cooperation *see* At- Ta'awin **3912**
• ➤ Cooperation and Conflict (GBR ISSN 0010-8367) **7228**
Cooperation for Development (SDN) **1593**
Cooperation in Turkiye (TUR ISSN 1300-1477) **1423**
Cooperation Internationale (FRA ISSN 1629-7830) **7120**
Cooperation internationale *see* Eurofunding. Cooperation Internationale **7436**
Cooperation South (USA ISSN 0259-3882) **8096**
Cooperation Sud *see* Cooperation South **8096**
† Cooperativa Antigruppo Siciliano (ITA) **8944**
Cooperativa Centro di Documentazione Notiziario *see* C D P. Notiziario **621**
• The Cooperative Accountant (USA ISSN 0010-8391) **1286**
Cooperative and Rural Development Bank. Annual Report and Accounts (TZA) **1329**
Cooperative Bank of Taiwan. Annual Report/Tai-wan Sheng Ho-tso Chin-k'u. Annual Report. (TWN) **1329**
Cooperative Computing and Communication Laboratory Publication *see* C-LAB Publication **2542**
Cooperative e Consorzi (ITA ISSN 1721-5641) **1918**
• Cooperative Education Association Newsletter (Online Edition) (USA) **2839**
Cooperative Education Association Newsletter (Print Edition) *see* Cooperative Education Association Newsletter (Online Edition) **2839**
Cooperative Housing Bulletin (USA ISSN 0097-9759) **4408**
Cooperative Housing Foundation Newsbriefs *see* C H F Newsbriefs **4405**
Cooperative Housing Journal (USA ISSN 0589-6355) **4408**
Cooperative Life/Gekkan Kyodotai (JPN) **8096**
Cooperative Living (Glen Allen) (USA ISSN 1529-4579) **3973**
Cooperative Online Serials Microfiche *see* C O N S E R Microfiche **621**
Cooperative Online Serials Program Cataloging Manual *see* C O N S E R Cataloging Manual **4999**
Cooperative Perspective (IND ISSN 0302-7767) **102**
Cooperative Press in South-East Asia (IND) **4573**
† Cooperative Research Centre for Freshwater Ecology. Identification and Ecology Guide (AUS ISSN 1446-7852) **8944**
Cooperative Research Centre Salinity Bulletin *see* C R C Salinity Bulletin **223**
Cooperative Sugar Press News (IND) **1423**
Cooperative Trade Directory for Southeast Asia (IND ISSN 0069-9837) **1423**
Cooperative Trafipro Umunyamalyango (RWA) **4592**
Cooperative Whole Grain Education Association Newsletter *see* C W G E A Newsletter **3672**
Cooperator (IND ISSN 0010-8464) **1423**
• Cooperator (New York) (USA) **7588**
Cooperazione (CHE) **1423**
Cooperazione di Credito (ITA ISSN 0010-8480) **1423**
Cooperazione Educativa (ITA ISSN 0010-8502) **2839**
Coopoint (CAN ISSN 1715-412X) **1086**
Coordinadora Regional de Investigaciones Economicas y Sociales. Cuadernos (NIC) **1086**
• ➤ Coordinates. Series A (USA ISSN 1553-3247) **4003**
• ➤ Coordinates. Series B (USA ISSN 1553-3255) **4003**
Coordinating Committee for Coastal and Offshore Geoscience Programmes in East and Southeast Asia. Technical Bulletin *see* Coordinating Committee for Geoscience Programmes in East and Southeast Asia. Technical Bulletin **2704**
Coordinating Committee for Earthquake Prediction. Report *see* Jishin Yochi Renrakukai Kaiho **2227**
• Coordinating Committee for Geoscience Programmes in East and Southeast Asia. Annual Session. Proceedings. Part I (THA) **2704**

Title

• ➤ La Coronica (USA ISSN 0193-3892) **5108**
Coros Chronicle *see* C O R O S Chronicle **6892**
Corp! (USA) **1086**
CorpComms (GBR ISSN 1749-1193) **1736**
† Corpo (ITA) **8944**
• Corpo Clip (CAN ISSN 0843-140X) **5004**
Corpo Nazionale Soccorso Alpino e Speleologico. Notizie (ITA) **2226**
• Corpora (GBR ISSN 1749-5032) **5108**
Corporacion Costarricense de Financiamiento Industrial. Memoria Anual (CRI) **1883**
Corporacion de los Andes. Revista (VEN) **1883**
Corporacion Financiera Colombiana. Ejercicio (COL) **1086**
Corporacion Financiera Internacional. Informe Anual *see* International Finance Corporation. Annual Report **1356**
Corporate A V (Year) (DEU) **2317**
• Corporate Accountability & Fraud Daily (USA ISSN 1543-1371) **4863**
• Corporate Accountability Report (USA ISSN 1542-9563) **4651**
Corporate Acquisitions & Mergers (NLD) **4651**
• Corporate Acquisitions and Mergers (USA) **4863**
Corporate Acquisitions, Mergers and Divestitures (USA ISSN 0737-4046) **4863**
Corporate Adviser (GBR ISSN 1756-087X) **1673**
• Corporate Affiliations Plus (USA) **1981**
Corporate Air Travel Survey (CAN) **8540**
Corporate Almanac (USA) **1086**
Corporate & Incentive Travel (USA ISSN 0739-1587) **8695**
Corporate Annual Report Newsletter (USA ISSN 0890-7609) **483**
Corporate Anti-Takeover Defenses: the Poison Pill Device (USA ISSN 0897-6740) **1619**
† Corporate Apparel Magazine (USA ISSN 1941-3548) **8944**
Corporate Aviation Safety Seminar. Proceedings (USA ISSN 0736-4709) **52**
• ➤ Corporate Board (UKR ISSN 1810-8601) **4863**
• Corporate Board (USA ISSN 0746-8652) **1736**
• Corporate Board Member (USA) **1736**
Corporate Bond Market Monthly (USA) **1619**
• Corporate Brief (CAN ISSN 1910-1813) **4863**
Corporate Briefing (GBR ISSN 0950-6209) **4863**
• Corporate Business Taxation Monthly (USA ISSN 1528-5294) **1918**
Corporate Capabilities Report *see* Powder and Bulk Engineering **3215**
Corporate Citizenship Review (USA) **1736**
• ➤ Corporate Communications (GBR ISSN 1356-3289) **2318**
Corporate Communications Handbook (USA) **4863**
Corporate Compass (USA ISSN 1524-508X) **7588**
Corporate Compliance Advisor Magazine *see* Databased Advisor Magazine **2554**
† • Corporate Compliance & Regulatory Newsletter (USA) **8944**
▼ Corporate Compliance Zeitschrift (DEU ISSN 1865-3952) **4863**
• Corporate Control Alert (USA ISSN 0743-0272) **4863**
Corporate Control Newsletter (USA) **4863**
• Corporate Corruption Litigation Reporter (USA ISSN 1546-749X) **4863**
Corporate Counsel (GBR ISSN 1368-972X) **4863**
• Corporate Counsel (Concord) (USA ISSN 0193-4880) **4863**
• Corporate Counsel (New York) (USA ISSN 1524-7597) **4863**
• Corporate Counsel Forum (USA ISSN 1930-3068) **4863**
Corporate Counsel Lawcast (USA ISSN 1087-6707) **4651**
• Corporate Counsel Library (USA ISSN 1549-7461) **4863**
Corporate Counsel Review (USA ISSN 0886-327X) **4863**
• Corporate Counsellor (USA ISSN 0888-5877) **4863**
Corporate Counselor *see* Corporate Counsellor **4863**
Corporate Counsel's Annual Review (USA ISSN 1086-9832) **4863**
Corporate Counsel's Antitrust Deskbook *see* Antitrust Deskbook **4856**
Corporate Counsel's Guide to Alternative Dispute Resolution in the Employment Context (USA) **4863**
Corporate Counsel's Guide to Business-Related Visas (USA) **4863**
• Corporate Counsel's Guide to Copyright Law (USA) **6748**
• Corporate Counsel's Guide to Distribution Counseling (USA) **4863**
Corporate Counsel's Guide to Doing Business in China (USA) **1556**
Corporate Counsel's Guide to Doing Business in India (USA) **1556**
Corporate Counsel's Guide to Doing Business in Russia (USA) **1556**
• Corporate Counsel's Guide to Domestic Joint Ventures (USA) **4863**
Corporate Counsel's Guide to E R I S A (Employee Retirement Income Security Act) (USA) **1673**
Corporate Counsel's Guide to Economic Sanctions and Embargoes (USA) **1556**
• Corporate Counsel's Guide to Employment Contracts (USA) **1673**
Corporate Counsel's Guide to Environmental Compliance Audits (USA) **3412**
Corporate Counsel's Guide to Export Controls (USA) **1556**
Corporate Counsel's Guide to Importing under the U.S. Customs Laws (USA) **1556**
• Corporate Counsel's Guide to Independent Contractors (USA) **1673**
• Corporate Counsel's Guide to Intellectual Property (USA) **6748**
Corporate Counsel's Guide to International Antitrust Laws (USA) **4922**
Corporate Counsel's Guide to Legal Audits and Investigations *see* Corporate Counsel's Guide to Legal Audits & Investigations **4864**
Corporate Counsel's Guide to Legal Audits & Investigations (USA) **4864**
Corporate Counsel's Guide to Letters of Credit (USA) **4864**
• Corporate Counsel's Guide to Nonqualified Deferred Compensation Agreements (USA) **4500**
• Corporate Counsel's Guide to Protecting Trade Secrets (USA) **4864**
Corporate Counsel's Guide to Reductions in Force (USA) **4864**
Corporate Counsel's Guide to Relations with Competitors (USA) **4864**
• Corporate Counsel's Guide to Strategic Alliances (USA) **4864**
• Corporate Counsel's Guide to Technology Management and Transactions (USA) **6748**
Corporate Counsel's Guide to Technology Transactions *see* Corporate Counsel's Guide to Technology Management and Transactions **6748**
Corporate Counsel's Guide to the Americans with Disabilities Act (USA) **1673**
Corporate Counsel's Guide to the Family and Medical Leave Act (USA) **1673**
Corporate Counsel's Guide to the Robinson-Patman Act (USA) **4864**
Corporate Counsel's Guide to the Wage and Hour Laws (USA) **1673**
Corporate Counsel's Guide to Trademark Law (USA) **6748**
Corporate Counsel's Guide to Unfair Competition (USA) **4864**
Corporate Counsel's Guide to White-Collar Crime (USA) **4864**
Corporate Counsel's International Adviser (USA ISSN 0898-9907) **1556**
• Corporate Counsel's International Contract Adviser (USA ISSN 1535-2285) **1556**
Corporate Counsel's Licensing Letter (USA ISSN 1534-455X) **6748**
Corporate Counsel's Monitor (USA ISSN 0898-9923) **4864**
• Corporate Counsel's Primers (USA ISSN 1523-8695) **4864**
• Corporate Counsel's Quarterly (USA ISSN 0897-1617) **4864**
Corporate Counsel's Records Retention Report (USA ISSN 1098-0261) **4864**
† Corporate Counsel's Web Site Review (USA ISSN 1534-4568) **8944**
Corporate Crime Reporter (USA ISSN 0897-4101) **2676**
Corporate Cruise News (USA) **8695**
Corporate Dealmaker (USA ISSN 1547-7584) **1619**
• Corporate Directory of US Public Companies (USA ISSN 1059-7964) **1619**
• Corporate Edge (USA) **4651**
Corporate Elite (CAN) **1086**
Corporate Environmental Data Clearinghouse Reports (USA) **3505**
• Corporate Event (USA ISSN 1553-6998) **1087**
Corporate Event Services (GBR ISSN 1756-6312) **6279**
Corporate Events Guide (NZL ISSN 1177-5734) **1087**
Corporate Examiner (USA ISSN 0361-2309) **1087**
The Corporate Executive (CAN ISSN 1481-2185) **1087**
• Corporate Executive (USA ISSN 1535-962X) **1087**
Corporate Finance *see* Xinlicai **1391**
Corporate Finance *see* Euromoney **1338**
Corporate Finance *see* Corporate Finance Review **1329**
Corporate Finance Directory. Eastern *see* Insider Dealmakers Guides. East of England **1354**
Corporate Finance Directory. United Kingdom *see* Insider Dealmakers Guides. United Kingdom **1354**
• ➤ Corporate Finance Review (USA ISSN 1089-327X) **1329**
Corporate Finance Risk Management and Derivatives Yearbook (GBR ISSN 1359-2394) **1619**
Corporate Finance Sourcebook (USA ISSN 0163-3031) **1087**
• Corporate Financing Week (USA ISSN 1064-1912) **1329**
Corporate Giftware Market Report *see* Key Note Market Report: Corporate Giftware **4060**
Corporate Giving Directory (USA ISSN 1055-0623) **8035**
† Corporate Giving Yellow Pages (USA ISSN 1058-689X) **8944**
† • Corporate Governance (NZL ISSN 1177-6110) **8944**
Corporate Governance *see* Dow Jones Corporate Governance **4866**
Corporate Governance (ZAF ISSN 1024-347X) **4864**
• ➤ Corporate Governance (Bradford) (GBR ISSN 1472-0701) **1736**
Corporate Governance (Kingston) (GBR ISSN 1469-686X) **1736**
Corporate Governance (London) (GBR ISSN 1476-8127) **4864**
• ➤ Corporate Governance (Oxford) (GBR ISSN 0964-8410) **1087**
• Corporate Governance (Sacramento) (USA) **1736**
• The Corporate Governance Advisor (USA ISSN 1067-6163) **4864**
Corporate Governance Bulletin (USA ISSN 1053-5489) **4864**
• ➤ Corporate Governance eJournal (AUS ISSN 1836-1110) **4864**
Corporate Governance Handbook (USA ISSN 1945-6042) **4864**
• ➤ The Corporate Governance Law Review (AUS ISSN 1449-9029) **4864**
• Corporate Governance Library (Online Edition) (USA ISSN 1554-1657) **4651**
Corporate Governance - Meeting Institutional Investors (GBR) **1619**
• Corporate Governance Report (USA ISSN 1520-7625) **4651**
• Corporate Growth Report (USA ISSN 1050-320X) **1619**
Corporate Guide to Green Power Markets (USA ISSN 1935-9934) **3126**
Corporate Handbook: Philippines (USA ISSN 0219-3639) **1619**
Corporate Hospitality Market Report *see* Key Note Market Report: Corporate Hospitality **1828**
Corporate I T Strategy (Information Technology) (GBR) **2535**
• Corporate I T Update (Information Technology) (GBR) **1087**
Corporate Insurance and Risk *see* Continuity Insurance & Risk **4500**
Corporate Intranet Review (Years) (GBR ISSN 1461-0493) **2496**
Corporate Intranet Solutions (USA) **2496**
▼ Corporate Kenya (CHE) **1448**
Corporate Knights (CAN ISSN 1703-2016) **1736**
• Corporate Law Daily (USA ISSN 1532-5164) **4864**
Corporate Law in Quebec *see* Droit des Societes par Actions au Quebec **4866**
• Corporate Law, Partnerships and Trusts (ZAF ISSN 1816-6148) **4864**
Corporate Lawyer (USA) **4864**
† • Corporate Leader (USA ISSN 1939-8085) **8944**
Corporate Legal Times *see* Inside Counsel **4870**
• Corporate Library Benchmarks (USA) **5004**
† • Corporate Library Update Online (USA ISSN 1558-6049) **8944**
(Year) Corporate Loan Market Directory (USA) **1329**
• The Corporate Logo (USA) **23**
• Corporate London (GBR) **1087**
• Corporate Management Tax Conference (CAN ISSN 0070-0282) **1918**
Corporate Meetings & Events (CAN) **6279**
• Corporate Meetings & Incentives (USA ISSN 0745-1636) **6279**
• Corporate Money (GBR ISSN 0951-3639) **1329**
Corporate Networks (GBR ISSN 1369-7382) **2496**
Corporate Nigeria (CHE ISSN 1661-4585) **1448**
• Corporate Northern Ireland (GBR ISSN 1749-4931) **1087**
Corporate Observer (IND) **1087**
Corporate Office (GBR) **1850**
• ➤ Corporate Ownership & Control (UKR ISSN 1727-9232) **4864**
• Corporate Philanthropy Report (USA ISSN 0885-8365) **8035**
Corporate Portfolio Management Gold Yearbook *see* The C P M Gold Yearbook **1614**
• Corporate Practice Commentator (USA ISSN 0010-8995) **4864**
• Corporate Practice Library (Online) (USA ISSN 1537-5102) **4864**
• Corporate Practice Library (Print) (USA) **4864**
• Corporate Practice Series (USA ISSN 0162-5691) **4865**
Corporate Profiles *see* San Diego Daily Transcript **4778**
• Corporate Register (GBR) **1087**
Corporate Registered Bond Interest Record *see* Standard & Poor's Corporate Registered Bond Interest Record **1652**
The Corporate Relocation Quarterly (CAN ISSN 1910-6823) **4651**
Corporate Report Fact Book (USA ISSN 0589-7920) **1981**
• Corporate Report Wisconsin (USA ISSN 0890-4278) **1087**
• ➤ Corporate Reputation Review (GBR ISSN 1363-3589) **1736**
• Corporate Rescue and Insolvency (GBR ISSN 1756-2465) **4651**
• Corporate Responsibility Management (GBR ISSN 1744-0157) **1736**
Corporate Rupee (IND) **1329**
• Corporate Scotland (GBR ISSN 1749-4923) **1087**
• Corporate Secretary (GBR ISSN 1548-7873) **1087**
Corporate Secretary (USA) **4865**
• Corporate Secretary's Guide (USA) **1850**
† • Corporate Security (USA ISSN 1040-4201) **8944**
Corporate Social Investment Handbook *see* The C S I Handbook **1615**
Corporate Social Issues Reporter (USA ISSN 1090-0829) **1619**
Corporate Social Responsibility *see* C S R **3408**
• ➤ Corporate Social Responsibility and Environmental Management (GBR ISSN 1535-3958) **1736**
Corporate Social Responsibility Review (CAN ISSN 1718-2573) **1736**
[corporate] solutions (BEL ISSN 1378-5079) **2492**
Corporate Standard (NGA ISSN 1597-0752) **1087**
• Corporate Statement (USA) **7120**
† Corporate Systems (GBR ISSN 1360-5739) **8944**
Corporate Tanzania (CHE ISSN 1661-8335) **1448**
Corporate Tax *see* International Who's Who of Corporate Tax Lawyers **4871**
Corporate Tax *see* The International Comparative Legal Guide to: Corporate Tax (Year) **1930**
• Corporate Taxation (USA ISSN 1534-715X) **1918**
Corporate Taxation Review (GBR ISSN 1461-2569) **1918**
Corporate Taxes Worldwide Summaries (USA ISSN 1078-3342) **1286**
Corporate Training and Development Advisor *see* Corporate Training & Development Advisor **7559**
• Corporate Training & Development Advisor (USA ISSN 0000-1821) **7559**
• Corporate Training Market (Year): Forecasts & Analysis (USA) **1812**
Corporate Training Market (Year): Forecasts and Analysis *see* Corporate Training Market (Year): Forecasts & Analysis **1812**
Corporate Transfer Agents Association Output *see* C T A Output **1615**
Corporate Travel Management (CAN ISSN 1481-594X) **6279**
Corporate Travel Management *see* Le Guide Annuel des Deplacements Professionnels **8716**
Corporate Traveller *see* Jasons New Zealand Business Traveller: Accomodation Directory **8725**
▼ Corporate U A E (United Arab Emirates) (CHE) **1448**
Corporate Venturing (GBR ISSN 1473-7825) **1736**
Corporate Venturing Report (USA) **1619**
• Corporate Wales (GBR ISSN 1464-2050) **1087**
• Corporate Watch (GBR ISSN 1470-5842) **7120**
• Corporate Watch (USA) **3412**
Corporate Watch Newsletter *see* Corporate Watch **7120**
Corporate Writer & Editor (USA) **2318**
• Corporate Yellow Book (USA ISSN 1058-2908) **1736**
Corporatieinformatie *see* Aedes Corporatie Informatie. Ondernemen **7419**
Corporation, Banking & Business Law Newsletter (USA) **4865**
Corporation de l'Industrie Touristique du Quebec Annual Report *see* C I T Q. Annual Report **8690**
Corporation, Finance and Business Section Journal *see* The Michigan Business Law Journal **4733**
Corporation for Public Broadcasting Today *see* C P B Today **2377**
Corporation of British Columbia Land Surveyors. Report of Proceedings (CAN) **4003**
Corporation of London. Subject Report (GBR) **1087**
Corporation Records *see* Standard Corporation Descriptions (Year) **1653**
Corporation Research *see* Qiye Yanjiu **1965**
• ➤ Corporation, Securities & Business Law (USA) **4865**
Corporation, Securities, and Business Law *see* Corporation, Securities & Business Law **4865**
Corporations *see* B A R - B R I Bar Review. Corporations **4857**
▼ Corporations that Changed the World (USA ISSN 1939-2486) **1087**
• Corporis (BRA ISSN 1516-6023) **8167**
Corps (DEU ISSN 1615-8180) **2279**
Corps (FRA ISSN 1954-1228) **333**
Corps Diplomatique et Representants Consulaires et Autres au Canada *see* Diplomatic, Consular and other Representatives in Canada **7231**
Corps Medical (LUX ISSN 0376-7582) **5600**
Corpse *see* Exquisite Corpse **5215**
Der Corpsstudent *see* Corps **2279**
CorpTech EXPLORE Database (USA) **8419**
† Corpus Antiquitatum Americanensium Italia (ITA) **8944**
Corpus Catholicorum (DEU ISSN 0070-0320) **7793**
Corpus Christi Bay Area Business (USA) **1087**
• The Corpus Christi E-Zine (USA) **3973**
Corpus Christi Lawyer (USA) **4651**
• Corpus Christianorum. Continuatio Mediaevalis (BEL ISSN 0589-7963) **7793**
Corpus Christianorum. Instrumenta Lexicologia Latina *see* Instrumenta Lexicologia Latina **2235**
Corpus Christianorum. Lingua Patrum (BEL ISSN 0777-1673) **5108**
Corpus Christianorum. Series Apocryphorum (BEL ISSN 2031-4876) **7793**
Corpus Christianorum. Series Graeca (BEL ISSN 1781-5967) **7635**
• Corpus Christianorum. Series Latina (BEL ISSN 1780-4582) **7793**
Corpus Consuetudinum Monasticarum (DEU ISSN 0589-7998) **7793**
Corpus de la Peinture des Anciens Pays-Bas Meridionaux et de la Principaute de Liege au Quinzieme Siecle (FRA) **483**
Corpus dei Papiri Filosofici Greci e Latini (ITA ISSN 1122-0872) **2233**

Title

DIRECTORY 2010 COUNCIL OF THE EUROPEAN COMMUNITIES. REVIEW OF THE 10159

Cosmopolitan (Portugal) (PRT) **8857**
Cosmopolitan (Prague) (CZE ISSN 1211-6459) **8857**
Cosmopolitan (Sibir') (RUS) **8857**
Cosmopolitan (Slovenia) (SVN ISSN 1580-6898) **8857**
Cosmopolitan (Sofia) (BGR ISSN 1312-3548) **8857**
• Cosmopolitan (South African Edition) (ZAF ISSN 0256-0283) **8857**
Cosmopolitan (St. Petersburg) (RUS) **8857**
Cosmopolitan (Stockholm) (SWE ISSN 1650-6707) **8857**
Cosmopolitan (Ukraine) (UKR) **8857**
Cosmopolitan (Ural) (RUS) **8857**
Cosmopolitan (Warsaw) (POL ISSN 1428-2542) **8857**
Cosmopolitan (Zud) (CHE ISSN 0941-4118) **8857**
Cosmopolitan Argentina (ARG ISSN 0328-8242) **8857**
Cosmopolitan Bride (AUS) **5558**
Cosmopolitan Bride (GBR) **5558**
• Cosmopolitan en Espanol (USA ISSN 0188-0616) **8857**
Cosmopolitan Hair and Beauty (AUS) **587**
Cosmopolitan Nova *see* Nova **8878**
Cosmopolitan Pregnancy (AUS) **5988**
† Cosmopolitan Shopping (NLD ISSN 1872-3543) **8944**
Cosmopolitan Shopping *see* Cosmo Shopping **8856**
• ➤ Cosmos (AUS ISSN 1832-522X) **7848**
• Cosmos (SGP ISSN 0219-6077) **7009**
• ➤ Cosmos (USA ISSN 1058-2029) **7956**
Cosmos *see* Sky & Telescope **581**
Cosmos (Edinburgh) (GBR ISSN 0269-8773) **6644**
• ➤ Cosmos and History (AUS ISSN 1832-9101) **6912**
Cosmos Club Bulletin (USA ISSN 0742-8995) **7956**
Cosmos Pen *see* Kosmoskyna **5444**
Cosmos tou Tennis/World of Tennis (GRC) **8225**
Cosmos Weekly (HKG) **2379**
• Cosmovaleurs (FRA ISSN 1951-0101) **1619**
COSPAR Information Bulletin *see* Space Research Today **71**
• Cost Accounting Standards Guide (USA ISSN 0162-1165) **1286**
Cost & Logis (DEU) **4384**
• Cost and Management (BGD ISSN 1817-5090) **1286**
Cost Control Strategies for Manufacturing Executives (USA ISSN 1096-4568) **1776**
• ➤ Cost Effectiveness and Resource Allocation (GBR ISSN 1478-7547) **4091**
• ➤ Cost Engineering (Morgantown) (USA ISSN 0274-9696) **3186**
Cost Engineering Series (USA) **3242**
Cost Engineers' Notebook (USA) **3186**
Cost Indices for the Aerospace and Radio and Electronic Capital Goods Industries *see* Aerospace and Electronics Cost Indices **1425**
Cost Management *see* Handbook of Cost Management **1289**
• Cost Management (USA ISSN 1092-8057) **1087**
• Cost Management Update (USA ISSN 1934-3388) **1286**
• Cost of Doing Business for Retail Sporting Goods Stores (USA ISSN 0736-0703) **1427**
Cost of Doing Business Report: Operating Performance Comparisons for Music Product Dealers (USA) **6631**
Cost of Living Ireland Report (GBR ISSN 1748-9377) **1222**
Cost of Living Regional Comparisons (GBR ISSN 1477-6219) **1222**
Cost of Picking and Hauling Florida Citrus Fruits (USA ISSN 0093-6553) **196**
The Cost of Social Security (CHE ISSN 0538-8295) **8035**
Cost Sector Catering (GBR ISSN 1462-4583) **3632**
The Cost Study (USA ISSN 1067-4349) **1329**
• Cost Survey (USA ISSN 1064-4571) **5743**
Cost Survey for Multispecialty Practices (USA ISSN 1558-7061) **4091**
Cost Survey for Obstetrics and Gynecology Practices (USA ISSN 1558-7053) **4091**
Cost Survey for Single Specialty Practices (USA ISSN 1558-707X) **4091**
Cost Survey Report *see* Cost Survey **5743**
Costa Blanca. D K Eyewitness Top 10 Travel Guides (USA ISSN 1930-6032) **8695**
Costa Rica *see* The P R S Group. Country Reports: Costa Rica **1506**
Costa Rica Aktuell (CRI) **3528**
➤ Costa Rica. Archivo Nacional. Revista (CRI ISSN 0034-9003) **4136**
Costa Rica Berlitz Travel Guide *see* Berlitz Costa Rica Pocket Guide **8686**
Costa Rica Calculo de Poblacion (CRI ISSN 1409-0201) **7305**
Costa Rica. Direccion General de Estadistica y Censos. Encuesta de Hogares de Propositos Multiples Modulo de Empleo (CRI ISSN 1409-0198) **1222**
Costa Rica. Direccion General de Estadistica y Censos. Estadisticas Vitales (CRI ISSN 1409-018X) **8365**
Costa Rica. Direccion General de Estadistica y Censos. Inventario de las Estadisticas Nacionales (CRI ISSN 0589-8544) **8365**
Costa Rica. Direccion General de la Tributacion Directa. Estadistica Demografia Fiscal del Impuesto sobre la Renta. Periodos (CRI) **1918**
Costa Rica. Estadisticas de Comercio Exterior (CRI) **1222**
Costa Rica for Dummies (USA ISSN 1933-0774) **8695**
Costa Rica. Instituto Nacional de Estadistica y Censos. Anuario Estadistico (CRI ISSN 1409-1941) **8365**
Costa Rica. Ministerio de Obras Publicas y Transportes. Memorias (CRI) **8630**
Costa Rica Outdoors (CRI) **8310**
Costa Rica y los Libros (CRI) **7559**
Costa Rican Beacon (CRI) **1619**
Costa Smeralda Magazine (ITA) **8695**
Costa Viola Magazine (ITA ISSN 1970-0237) **8695**
CostaGolf (ESP ISSN 1133-7346) **8225**
Costantinian: Magazine for Mature Catholics *see* Hengyi: Chengshu Jiaoyou de Zazhi **7799**
CoStar's Atlanta Property News (USA) **7588**
Costco Auto Buyer's Guide (USA) **8576**
The Costco Connection (USA) **3973**
• Costco Healthy Living with Diabetes (USA) **5885**
Costerus (NLD ISSN 0165-9618) **5108**
Costos y Gestion (ARG ISSN 0327-5345) **1286**
Costruire (ITA ISSN 1121-6336) **1000**
Costruire Impianti (ITA ISSN 1722-3644) **1000**
Costruire in Acciaio *see* Bauen in Stahl **435**
Costruire Stampi (ITA ISSN 1121-8711) **3375**
Costruisci il Rover Sojourner (ITA ISSN 1828-9967) **4332**
Costruttori Romani (ITA ISSN 0010-9657) **1000**
Costruzioni (ITA ISSN 0010-9665) **3263**
Costruzioni Metalliche (ITA ISSN 0010-9673) **3264**
• ➤ Costruzioni Psicoanalitiche (ITA ISSN 1721-9612) **6133**
Costs & Fees Service (GBR) **4651**
Costs and Indexes for Domestic Oil and Gas Field Equipment and Production Operations *see* Oil and Gas Lease Equipment and Operating Costs **1900**
Costs Guide N S W (AUS) **4651**
Costs Guide New South Wales *see* Costs Guide N S W **4651**
Costs Law Reports (GBR ISSN 1366-8617) **1918**
Costs Watch (AUS ISSN 1323-6164) **1286**
Costume (DNK ISSN 1601-9865) **2253**
• ➤ Costume (GBR ISSN 0590-8876) **2253**
† Costume (ITA ISSN 1593-1498) **8944**
The Costume - Halloween Catalog (USA) **2246**
Costume Journal (CAN) **2253**
Costume Society of America Bibliography (USA) **2250**
Costume Society of America News (Earleville) *see* C S A News (Earleville) **2252**
Costume Society of America. Symposia Abstracts (USA) **2250**
▼ • The Costumer (USA ISSN 1940-0233) **2253**
The Costumer (USA) **8468**
Costumes et Coutumes *see* Tracht und Brauch **4274**
† Cosun in Business (NLD ISSN 1568-3184) **8944**
Cosun Magazine (NLD ISSN 1572-6541) **225**
Cosy Style *see* Cosystyle **4536**
Cosystyle (FRA ISSN 1951-1477) **4536**
Cota Zero (ESP ISSN 0213-4640) **388**
Cote (FRA ISSN 1152-6351) **3840**
• Cote & Provence (NLD ISSN 1569-4283) **8576**
Cote Bebe (FRA ISSN 1954-9709) **2150**
Cote Coiffure (FRA ISSN 1954-2763) **587**
La Cote des Vins (FRA ISSN 1257-2187) **602**
Cote d'Ivoire *see* The P R S Group. Country Reports: Cote d'Ivoire **1506**
▼ The Cote d'Ivoire Business Forecast Report Annual (GBR ISSN 1753-6871) **1088**
Cote d'Ivoire en Chiffres (SEN) **4174**
Cote-d'Ivoire Selection (FRA ISSN 0221-5780) **1556**
† Cote Femme (FRA ISSN 1299-3573) **8944**
† Cote Officielle (FRA ISSN 0220-6358) **8944**
Coteau Heritage (USA) **4290**
• ➤ El Cotidiano (MEX ISSN 0186-1840) **3908**
El Cotidiano en Linea *see* El Cotidiano **3908**
Cotidianul (ROM ISSN 1220-692X) **3932**
Cotinga (GBR ISSN 1353-985X) **905**
Cotistics Bi-annual Cotton Statistical Bulletin (PAK) **8449**
Cotswold Archaeological Trust Series (GBR) **388**
Cotswold Life (GBR ISSN 0010-9746) **3863**
Cottage (Victoria) *see* Cottage Magazine **3808**
Cottage Connection (Chicago) (USA) **1959**
The Cottage Gardener (GBR) **3727**
Cottage Industries (IND ISSN 0970-7387) **1959**
Cottage Life (CAN ISSN 0838-2395) **5068**
† Cottage Living (USA ISSN 1550-2562) **8944**
Cottage Magazine (CAN ISSN 1701-7688) **3808**
Cottage Style (USA) **4536**
† Cottager (AUS ISSN 1032-9609) **8944**
▼ Cottages & Bungalows (USA ISSN 1941-4056) **4408**
Cottbuser Studien zur Geschichte von Technik, Arbeit und Umwelt (DEU ISSN 1430-2659) **4212**
• Cottet Magazine (ESP) **6040**
† Cotton & Quail Antique Gazette (USA ISSN 1540-059X) **8944**
Cotton and Quail Antique Gazette *see* Cotton & Quail Antique Gazette **8944**
Cotton & Quail Antique Trail *see* Cotton & Quail Antique Gazette **8944**
Cotton and Wool Outlook *see* Situation & Outlook Report. Cotton and Wool Outlook **206**
Cotton and Wool Yearbook *see* Situation & Outlook Report. Cotton and Wool Yearbook **206**
Cotton Corporation of India. Annual Report (IND ISSN 0304-6907) **196**
Cotton Directory of the World (GBR ISSN 1473-6365) **1981**
Cotton Economic Review (USA ISSN 0199-1779) **225**
Cotton Farming (USA ISSN 0746-8385) **225**
Cotton Gin and Oil Mill Press (USA ISSN 0010-9800) **8449**
Cotton Ginnings, A10 *see* U.S. Department of Agriculture. National Agricultural Statistics Service. Cotton Ginnings **188**
• Cotton Grower (USA ISSN 0194-9772) **225**
Cotton Incorporated Technical Bulletin (USA) **8449**
• Cotton International (USA ISSN 0070-0673) **8449**
Cotton International Annual *see* Cotton International **8449**
• Cotton International Magazine (USA ISSN 1934-3566) **8449**
Cotton Lint and Seed Marketing Board. Annual Report and Accounts (KEN) **226**
Cotton Outlook (GBR) **8449**
Cotton Research and Development Corporation. Handbook *see* Spotlight (Narrabri) **254**
• Cotton: Review of the World Situation (USA ISSN 0008-9729) **8449**
Cotton Textile Technology *see* Mian Fangzhi Jishu **8455**
• Cotton: World Statistics (USA ISSN 0010-9754) **178**
Cotton Yearbook *see* Australian Cottongrower. Cotton Yearbook **220**
Cottonwood (USA ISSN 0147-149X) **5279**
• ➤ Cough (GBR ISSN 1745-9974) **6213**
† Couleur Maison (FRA ISSN 1959-0040) **8944**
▼ • Couleure (USA ISSN 1949-3797) **2253**
Couleurs Catalogne (FRA ISSN 1774-7600) **4003**
Couleurs du Temps, Couleurs du Fleurissement (FRA ISSN 1779-8671) **3727**
† Coulisses (FRA ISSN 1775-0040) **8944**
Couloir *see* Backcountry **8305**
The Council (USA) **4064**
† Council and Community (AUS ISSN 0728-5582) **8944**
The Council Chronicle (USA ISSN 1057-4190) **3055**
Council Columns (USA) **8035**
Council Directions (USA) **7490**
Council Fires (USA ISSN 1058-4048) **4290**
Council for Adult and Experiential Learning Forum and News *see* C A E L Forum and News **2939**
Council for Agricultural Science and Technology. Issue Papers (USA ISSN 1070-0021) **102**
Council for Agricultural Science and Technology. Report *see* Council for Agricultural Science and Technology. Task Force Reports **102**
Council for Agricultural Science and Technology. Special Publications (USA ISSN 0194-407X) **102**
Council for Agricultural Science and Technology. Task Force Reports (USA ISSN 1057-7017) **102**
Council for American Private Education Outlook *see* C A P E Outlook **2833**
Council for British Archaeology Annual Report *see* C B A Annual Report **385**
Council for British Archaeology Research Reports *see* C B A Research Reports **385**
• Council for British Research in the Levant. Bulletin (GBR ISSN 1752-7260) **388**
Council for British Research in the Levant. Bulletin. Newsletter *see* Council for British Research in the Levant. Bulletin **388**
Council for Children with Behavioral Disorders Newsletter *see* C C B D Newsletter **3037**
Council for Court Excellence Annual Report (USA) **4651**
Council for Early Childhood Professional Recognition. Council News & Views (USA) **2150**
Council for Geoscience of South Africa. Bulletin (ZAF ISSN 1680-0370) **2730**
Council for Mutual Economic Assistance Foreign Trade Data *see* C O M E C O N Foreign Trade Data **8938**
➤ Council for Research in Music Education. Bulletin (USA ISSN 0010-9894) **6559**
Council for Scientific and Industrial Research Annual Report - Technology Impact *see* C S I R Annual Report - Technology Impact **7843**
Council for Scientific and Industrial Research Building Technology. Complete List of Publications *see* C S I R Building Technology. Complete List of Publications **1045**
Council for Scientific and Industrial Research Handbook *see* C S I R Handbook **7843**
Council for Slavonic and East European Library and Information Services Newsletter *see* C O S E E L I S Newsletter **4999**
Council for the Advancement of Arab-British Understanding Briefings *see* C A A B U Briefings **7224**
Council for the Development of Economic and Social Research in Africa Book Series *see* C O D E S R I A Book Series **7111**
Council for the Development of Social Science Research in Africa Bulletin *see* C O D E S R I A Bulletin **4174**
Council for the Environment. Work Programme *see* V R O M-Raad. Work Programme **3473**
Council for the Social Sciences in East Africa. Social Science Conference. Proceedings (TZA) **7956**
Council for World Mission. Annual Report (GBR) **7752**
• Council-Grams (Online) (USA) **3055**
Council-Grams (Print) *see* Council-Grams (Online) **3055**
Council News & Views *see* Horizons (Winnipeg) **288**
Council News and Views (USA) **1000**
Council of Academic & Professional Publishers Brief *see* C A P P Brief **7557**
Council of Agriculture. Fisheries Series *see* Nongweihui Yuye Tekan **3603**
Council of Archives of New Brunswick Gazette *see* C A N B Gazette **4999**
• Council of Better Business Bureaus. Business Advisory Series (USA) **2637**
Council of Colleges of Arts & Sciences Newsletter *see* C C A S Newsletter **2969**
Council of Europe. Committee of Independent Experts on the European Social Charter. Conclusions (FRA) **7228**
Council of Europe. Documentation Section. Biblio Bulletin. Series: Legal Affairs (FRA) **4821**
Council of Europe. Documentation Section. Biblio Bulletin. Series: Political, Economic and Social Affairs (FRA) **7199**
Council of Europe. European Committee for the Prevention of Torture. Yearbook (GBR) **7204**
Council of Europe. European Convention for the Prevention of Torture and Inhuman or Degrading Treatment or Punishment. Yearbook (GBR ISSN 1369-9865) **7204**
Council of Europe. European Treaty Series (FRA ISSN 0070-105X) **4922**
Council of Europe. Parliamentary Assembly. Documents: Working Papers (FRA ISSN 0252-0656) **4922**
Council of Europe. Parliamentary Assembly. Official Report of Debates (FRA ISSN 0252-0664) **4922**
Council of Europe. Parliamentary Assembly. Orders of the Day, Minutes of Proceedings (FRA ISSN 0377-1962) **4922**
Council of Europe. Parliamentary Assembly. Texts Adopted by the Assembly (FRA ISSN 0377-6093) **4922**
Council of Europe. Standing Committee on the European Convention on Establishment (Individuals). Periodical Report (FRA ISSN 0377-2748) **7204**
Council of Europe. Study Series: Local and Regional Authorities in Europe (FRA ISSN 0252-0699) **7490**
Council of Europe. Symposium on Legal Processing. Proceedings (FRA) **4844**
• Council of Europe. Venice Commission. Bulletin on Constitutional Case-law (FRA ISSN 1025-8116) **4847**
Council of European Aerospace Societies Space Journal *see* C E A S Space Journal **50**
† Council of Financial Regulators. Annual Report (AUS ISSN 1443-6345) **8944**
Council of Forest Industries. Annual Report (CAN) **3686**
Council of Jewish Organizations in Civil Service. Council News (USA) **3528**
Council of Jewish Theatres Newsletter (USA) **8468**
Council of Logistics Management Annual Conference Proceedings (USA ISSN 0898-6614) **1812**
Council of Mortgage Lenders Annual Report *see* C M L Annual Report **7585**
Council of Mortgage Lenders Directory of Members *see* C M L Directory of Members **7585**
Council of Mortgage Lenders Parliamentary Cutting Service *see* C M L Parliamentary Cutting Service **7585**
Council of Mortgage Lenders. Research Papers (GBR) **1330**
Council of Nova Scotia Archives Newsletter (CAN ISSN 0829-7142) **5004**
Council of Ontario Universities. Application Statistics (CAN ISSN 0382-912X) **2931**
Council of Ontario Universities. Resource Document (CAN ISSN 1486-0929) **2974**
Council of Professional Association on Federal Statistics. News (USA ISSN 0890-1627) **8365**
Council of Protocol Executives. Directory (USA) **6279**
Council of Scientific Society Presidents Congressional Sourcebook *see* C S S P Congressional Sourcebook **7425**
Council of Scientific Society Presidents News *see* C S S P News **2833**
Council of Smaller Enterprises Update *see* C O S E Update **1958**
Council of Societies for the Study of Religion Bulletin *see* C S S R Bulletin **7629**
Council of State Governments State Directory. Directory I. Elective Officials *see* C S G State Directory. Directory I. Elective Officials **7425**
Council of State Governments State Directory. Directory II, Legislative Leadership, Committees & Staff *see* C S G State Directory. Directory II, Legislative Leadership, Committees & Staff **7112**
Council of State Governments State Directory. Directory III, Administrative Officials *see* C S G State Directory. Directory III, Administrative Officials **7425**
Council of State Governments. Suggested State Legislation *see* Suggested State Legislation **4852**
Council of Supervisors and Administrators of the City of New York News (Brooklyn) *see* C S A News (Brooklyn) **3018**
Council of the European Communities. Review of the Council's Work (LUX ISSN 0377-466X) **1448**

Title

▼ *new title* † *ceased* • *electronic media* ➤ *refereed*

Title

▼ *new title* † *ceased* ● *electronic media* ➤ *refereed*

10162 COUNTRY REPORT. CANADA ULRICH'S PERIODICALS

• Country Report. Canada (USA ISSN 0269-4166) **1451**
• Country Report. Cape Verde (USA) **1451**
• Country Report. Central African Republic (USA) **1452**
• Country Report. Chad (USA) **1452**
• Country Report. Chile (USA ISSN 0269-5197) **1452**
• Country Report. China (USA ISSN 1473-897X) **1452**
• Country Report. Colombia (USA ISSN 0269-7157) **1452**
• Country Report. Comoros (USA) **1452**
• Country Report. Congo (Brazzaville) (USA ISSN 1749-1088) **1452**
• Country Report. Costa Rica (USA ISSN 1366-4026) **1452**
• Country Report. Cote d'Ivoire (USA ISSN 1473-9089) **1452**
• Country Report. Croatia (USA ISSN 1462-6748) **1452**
• Country Report. Cuba (USA ISSN 1465-6388) **1453**
• Country Report. Cyprus (USA) **1453**
• Country Report. Czech Republic (USA ISSN 1366-4042) **1453**
• Country Report. Democratic Republic of Congo (USA ISSN 1478-0380) **1453**
• Country Report. Denmark (USA ISSN 1473-9046) **1453**
• Country Report. Djibouti (USA) **1453**
• Country Report. Dominican Republic (USA ISSN 1749-933X) **1453**
Country Report. Dominican Republic, Haiti *see* Country Report. Haiti **1455**
Country Report. Dominican Republic, Haiti, Puerto Rico *see* Country Report. Puerto Rico, Bahamas, Bermuda, Turks and Caicos Islands **1088**
• Country Report. Ecuador (USA ISSN 0269-7165) **1453**
• Country Report. Egypt (USA ISSN 0269-526X) **1453**
• Country Report. El Salvador (USA ISSN 1473-9038) **1453**
• Country Report. Equatorial Guinea (USA) **1453**
• Country Report. Eritrea (USA) **1454**
• Country Report. Estonia (USA ISSN 1462-6705) **1454**
• Country Report. Ethiopia (USA ISSN 1745-6061) **1454**
• Country Report. European Union (USA ISSN 1365-3989) **1454**
• Country Report. Fiji (USA) **1454**
• Country Report. Finland (USA ISSN 0269-5901) **1454**
• Country Report. France (USA ISSN 0269-5286) **1454**
• Country Report. Gabon (USA ISSN 1749-107X) **1454**
• Country Report. Georgia (USA ISSN 1478-0313) **1454**
• Country Report. Germany (USA ISSN 0965-1365) **1454**
• Country Report. Ghana (USA ISSN 1350-7052) **1454**
• Country Report. Greece (USA ISSN 0269-591X) **1455**
• Country Report. Guatemala (USA ISSN 1473-902X) **1455**
• Country Report. Guinea (USA) **1455**
• Country Report. Guinea-Bissau (USA) **1455**
• Country Report. Guyana (USA) **1455**
• Country Report. Haiti (USA ISSN 1749-3455) **1455**
• Country Report. Honduras (USA ISSN 1473-9011) **1455**
• Country Report. Hong Kong (USA) **1455**
• Country Report. Hungary (USA ISSN 0269-4301) **1455**
• Country Report. Iceland (USA ISSN 1473-9054) **1456**
• Country Report. India (USA ISSN 1473-8953) **1456**
• Country Report. Indonesia (USA ISSN 0269-5413) **1456**
• Country Report. Iran (USA ISSN 0269-5448) **1456**
• Country Report. Iraq (USA ISSN 0269-5502) **1456**
• Country Report. Ireland (USA ISSN 0269-5278) **1456**
• Country Report. Israel (USA ISSN 1745-3259) **1456**
• Country Report. Italy (USA ISSN 0269-5421) **1456**
• Country Report. Jamaica (USA ISSN 1749-9054) **1456**
• Country Report. Japan (USA ISSN 0269-6681) **1456**
• Country Report. Jordan (USA ISSN 0269-722X) **1456**
• Country Report. Kazakhstan (USA ISSN 1361-147X) **1456**
• Country Report. Kenya (USA ISSN 0269-4239) **1456**
• Country Report. Kuwait (USA ISSN 0269-5715) **1456**
• Country Report. Kyrgyz Republic (USA ISSN 1478-0399) **1456**
• Country Report. Laos (USA ISSN 1745-6134) **1457**
• Country Report. Latvia (USA ISSN 1462-6713) **1457**
• Country Report. Lebanon (USA ISSN 1350-7141) **1457**
• Country Report. Lesotho, Swaziland (USA ISSN 1749-3781) **1457**
• Country Report. Liberia (USA) **1457**
• Country Report. Libya (USA ISSN 0269-4328) **1457**
• Country Report. Lithuania (USA ISSN 1462-6721) **1457**
• Country Report. Luxembourg (USA ISSN 1473-9070) **1457**
• Country Report. Macau (USA) **1457**
• Country Report. Macedonia (USA ISSN 1462-6691) **1457**
• Country Report. Madagascar (USA) **1457**
• Country Report. Malawi (USA ISSN 1478-0283) **1457**
• Country Report. Malaysia (USA) **1458**
• Country Report. Mali (USA ISSN 1748-961X) **1458**
Country Report. Mali, Niger *see* Country Report. Mali **1458**
• Country Report. Malta (USA) **1458**
• Country Report. Mauritania, The Gambia (USA ISSN 1749-110X) **1458**
• Country Report. Mauritius (USA ISSN 1745-610X) **1458**
• Country Report. Mexico (USA ISSN 0269-5936) **1458**
• Country Report. Moldova (USA ISSN 1478-0305) **1458**
• Country Report. Mongolia (USA) **1458**
• Country Report. Morocco (USA ISSN 0269-6126) **1458**
• Country Report. Mozambique (USA ISSN 1478-0275) **1458**
• Country Report. Myanmar (USA ISSN 1361-1445) **1458**
• Country Report. Namibia (USA ISSN 1749-6802) **1458**
• Country Report. Nepal, Mongolia, Bhutan (USA ISSN 1473-8961) **1458**
• Country Report. Netherlands (USA ISSN 0269-6134) **1458**
• Country Report. Netherlands Antilles (USA) **1459**
• Country Report. New Caledonia (USA) **1459**
• Country Report. New Zealand (USA ISSN 0269-7114) **1459**
• Country Report. Nicaragua (USA ISSN 1473-9003) **1459**
• Country Report. Niger (USA) **1459**
• Country Report. Nigeria (USA ISSN 0269-4204) **1459**
• Country Report. North Korea (USA ISSN 1478-033X) **1459**
• Country Report. Norway (USA ISSN 0269-4182) **1459**
• Country Report. Oman (USA ISSN 1462-6667) **1459**
• Country Report. Pakistan (USA ISSN 1478-0356) **1459**
• Country Report. Panama (USA ISSN 1366-4034) **1459**
Country Report. Papua New Guinea *see* Country Report. Papua New Guinea, Timor-Leste **1459**
Country Report. Papua New Guinea, East Timor *see* Country Report. Papua New Guinea, Timor-Leste **1459**
• Country Report. Papua New Guinea, Timor-Leste (USA ISSN 1753-1721) **1459**
• Country Report. Paraguay (USA ISSN 1473-8996) **1460**
Country Report. Peru *see* E I U Country Reports on Disc: The Americas **8952**
• Country Report. Philippines (USA ISSN 0269-428X) **1460**
• Country Report. Poland (USA ISSN 0269-6193) **1460**
• Country Report. Portugal (USA ISSN 0269-5456) **1460**
• Country Report. Puerto Rico (USA) **1460**
• Country Report. Puerto Rico, Bahamas, Bermuda, Turks and Caicos Islands (USA ISSN 1478-3487) **1088**
• Country Report. Qatar (USA ISSN 1473-8945) **1460**
• Country Report. Romania (USA ISSN 1356-4102) **1460**
• Country Report. Russia (USA ISSN 1350-7184) **1460**
• Country Report. Rwanda (USA) **1460**
• Country Report. Samoa (USA) **1460**
• Country Report. Sao Tome and Principe (USA) **1460**
• Country Report. Saudi Arabia (USA ISSN 0269-6215) **1461**
• Country Report. Senegal (USA ISSN 1749-1096) **1461**
• Country Report. Seychelles (USA) **1461**
• Country Report. Sierra Leone (USA) **1461**
• Country Report. Singapore (USA ISSN 0269-6711) **1461**
• Country Report. Slovakia (USA ISSN 1366-4050) **1461**
• Country Report. Slovenia (USA ISSN 1366-4131) **1461**
• Country Report. Solomon Islands (USA) **1461**
• Country Report. Somalia (USA) **1461**
• Country Report. South Africa (USA ISSN 0269-6738) **1461**
• Country Report. South Korea (USA ISSN 1478-0348) **1461**
• Country Report. Spain (USA ISSN 0269-4263) **1461**
• Country Report. Sri Lanka (USA ISSN 0269-4174) **1461**
• Country Report. Sudan (USA ISSN 0269-6150) **1462**
• Country Report. Suriname (USA) **1462**
• Country Report. Swaziland (USA) **1462**
• Country Report. Sweden (USA ISSN 0269-6142) **1462**
• Country Report. Switzerland (USA ISSN 0269-6169) **1462**
• Country Report. Syria (USA ISSN 0269-7211) **1462**
• Country Report. Taiwan (USA ISSN 0269-672X) **1462**
• Country Report. Tajikistan (USA ISSN 1478-0402) **1462**
• Country Report. Tanzania (USA ISSN 1745-6088) **1462**
• Country Report. Thailand (USA ISSN 1356-4056) **1462**
• Country Report. The Gambia (USA) **1462**
• Country Report. The Palestinian Territories (USA) **1462**
• Country Report. Togo (USA) **1462**
• Country Report. Tonga (USA) **1463**
• Country Report. Trinidad & Tobago (USA ISSN 1745-6118) **1463**
Country Report. Trinidad and Tobago, Guyana, Suriname *see* Country Report. Trinidad & Tobago **1463**
• Country Report. Tunisia (USA ISSN 1350-7168) **1463**
• Country Report. Turkey (USA ISSN 0269-5464) **1463**
• Country Report. Turkmenistan (USA ISSN 1462-6764) **1463**
• Country Report. Uganda (USA ISSN 1465-640X) **1463**
• Country Report. Ukraine (USA ISSN 1356-4129) **1463**
• Country Report. United Arab Emirates (USA ISSN 0269-5162) **1463**
• Country Report. United Kingdom (USA ISSN 0269-5472) **1463**
• Country Report. United States of America (USA ISSN 1367-8876) **1463**
• Country Report. Uruguay (USA ISSN 1473-8988) **1463**
• Country Report. Uzbekistan (USA ISSN 1366-4158) **1463**
• Country Report. Vanuatu (USA) **1464**
• Country Report. Venezuela (USA ISSN 1350-7133) **1464**
• Country Report. Vietnam (USA ISSN 1356-403X) **1464**
• Country Report. Windward & Leeward Islands (USA) **1464**
• Country Report. Yemen (USA ISSN 1462-6675) **1464**
• Country Report. Yugoslavia (Serbia-Montenegro) (USA ISSN 1462-6683) **1464**
• Country Report. Zambia (USA ISSN 1478-0372) **1464**
• Country Report. Zimbabwe (USA ISSN 1350-7095) **1464**
• Country Reports (GBR ISSN 1479-2850) **8695**
Country Reports on Human Rights Practices for (Year) (USA ISSN 0198-9669) **7205**
Country Reports: World Service *see* The P R S Group. Country Reports: World Service **1510**
• Country Review. Afghanistan (USA ISSN 1520-2070) **1464**
• Country Review. Albania (USA ISSN 1520-2089) **1464**
• Country Review. Algeria (USA ISSN 1520-2097) **1464**
• Country Review. Andorra (USA ISSN 1520-2100) **1464**
• Country Review. Angola (USA ISSN 1520-2119) **1464**
• Country Review. Antigua Barbuda (USA ISSN 1520-2127) **1464**
• Country Review. Argentina (USA ISSN 1520-2135) **1464**
• Country Review. Armenia (USA ISSN 1520-2143) **1464**
• Country Review. Australia (USA ISSN 1520-2151) **1464**
• Country Review. Austria (USA ISSN 1520-216X) **1464**
• Country Review. Azerbaijan (USA ISSN 1520-2178) **1465**
• Country Review. Bahamas (USA ISSN 1520-2186) **1465**
• Country Review. Bahrain (USA ISSN 1520-2194) **1465**
• Country Review. Bangladesh (USA ISSN 1520-2208) **1465**
• Country Review. Barbados (USA ISSN 1520-2216) **1465**
• Country Review. Belarus (USA ISSN 1520-2224) **1465**
• Country Review. Belgium (USA ISSN 1520-2232) **1465**
• Country Review. Belize (USA ISSN 1520-2240) **1465**
• Country Review. Benin (USA ISSN 1520-2259) **1465**
• Country Review. Bhutan (USA ISSN 1520-2267) **1465**
• Country Review. Bolivia (USA ISSN 1520-2275) **1465**
• Country Review. Bosnia Herzegovina (USA ISSN 1520-2283) **1465**
• Country Review. Botswana (USA ISSN 1520-2291) **1465**
• Country Review. Brazil (USA ISSN 1520-2305) **1465**
• Country Review. Brunei (USA ISSN 1520-2313) **1465**
• Country Review. Bulgaria (USA ISSN 1520-2321) **1465**
• Country Review. Burkina Faso (USA ISSN 1520-233X) **1465**
• Country Review. Burundi (USA ISSN 1520-2348) **1465**
• Country Review. Cambodia (USA ISSN 1520-2356) **1465**
• Country Review. Cameroon (USA ISSN 1520-2364) **1465**
• Country Review. Canada (USA ISSN 1520-2372) **1465**
• Country Review. Cape Verde (USA ISSN 1520-2380) **1465**
• Country Review. Central African Republic (USA) **1465**
• Country Review. Chad (USA ISSN 1520-2402) **1465**
• Country Review. Chile (USA ISSN 1520-2429) **1465**
• Country Review. China (USA ISSN 1520-2437) **1465**
• Country Review. Colombia (USA ISSN 1520-2445) **1465**
• Country Review. Comoros (USA ISSN 1520-2453) **1465**
• Country Review. Congo (USA ISSN 1520-2488) **1465**
• Country Review. Congo Democratic Republic (USA ISSN 1520-2461) **1466**
• Country Review. Costa Rica (USA ISSN 1520-2496) **1466**
• Country Review. Cote d'Ivoire (USA ISSN 1520-250X) **1466**
• Country Review. Croatia (USA ISSN 1520-2410) **1466**
• Country Review. Cuba (USA ISSN 1520-2518) **1466**
• Country Review. Cyprus (USA ISSN 1520-2526) **1466**
• Country Review. Czech Republic (USA ISSN 1520-2534) **1466**
• Country Review. Denmark (USA ISSN 1520-2542) **1466**
• Country Review. Djibouti (USA ISSN 1520-2550) **1466**
• Country Review. Dominica (USA ISSN 1520-2569) **1466**
• Country Review. Dominican Republic (USA ISSN 1520-2577) **1466**
• Country Review. East Timor (USA) **1466**
• Country Review. Ecuador (USA ISSN 1520-1708) **1466**
• Country Review. Egypt (USA ISSN 1520-1716) **1466**
• Country Review. El Salvador (USA ISSN 1520-1724) **1466**
• Country Review. Equatorial Guinea (USA ISSN 1520-1759) **1466**
• Country Review. Eritrea (USA ISSN 1520-1732) **1466**
• Country Review. Estonia (USA ISSN 1520-1740) **1466**
• Country Review. Ethiopia (USA ISSN 1520-1767) **1466**
• Country Review. Fiji (USA ISSN 1520-1775) **1466**
• Country Review. Finland (USA ISSN 1520-1783) **1466**
• Country Review. France (USA ISSN 1520-1791) **1466**
• Country Review. Gabon (USA ISSN 1520-1805) **1466**
• Country Review. Gambia (USA) **1466**
• Country Review. Georgia (USA ISSN 1520-1821) **1466**
• Country Review. Germany (USA ISSN 1520-183X) **1466**
• Country Review. Ghana (USA ISSN 1520-1848) **1466**
• Country Review. Greece (USA ISSN 1520-1856) **1466**
• Country Review. Grenada (USA ISSN 1520-1864) **1466**
• Country Review. Guatemala (USA ISSN 1520-1872) **1467**
• Country Review. Guinea (USA ISSN 1520-1880) **1467**
• Country Review. Guinea-Bissau (USA ISSN 1520-1899) **1467**
• Country Review. Guyana (USA ISSN 1520-1902) **1467**
• Country Review. Haiti (USA ISSN 1520-1910) **1467**
• Country Review. Holy See (USA ISSN 1520-1929) **1467**
• Country Review. Honduras (USA ISSN 1520-1937) **1467**
• Country Review. Hungary (USA ISSN 1520-1945) **1467**
• Country Review. Iceland (USA ISSN 1520-1953) **1467**

▼ *new title*   † *ceased*   • *electronic media*   ➤ *refereed*

Title

10164 **COUNTRY SPORTS CAMPAIGN UPDATE** **ULRICH'S PERIODICALS**

Country Sports Campaign Update *see* Countryside Alliance. Update **8310**
Country Stitch (USA ISSN 1054-3155) **6637**
• Country Style (DEU ISSN 1432-959X) **438**
† Country Style Homes, Plans and Designs (USA ISSN 1538-3911) **8946**
The Country Today (USA) **102**
Country Trade Sourcebook *see* Official Export Guide: Country Trade Sourcebook **1579**
Country Trends (Year) (GBR) **4384**
Country Update (AUS ISSN 1327-0664) **6559**
Country Updates (GBR ISSN 1465-7686) **8695**
• Country ViewsWire (USA) **1475**
Country Walking (GBR ISSN 0953-2757) **8310**
• Country Weekly (USA ISSN 1074-3235) **6559**
Country Western Corner (USA ISSN 1096-1488) **6560**
Country-Wide (Northern Edition) (NZL ISSN 1175-6918) **103**
Country-Wide (Southern Edition) (NZL ISSN 1175-6926) **103**
Country Woman (USA ISSN 0892-8525) **8857**
Country Yossi Family Magazine (USA ISSN 1050-5075) **3528**
Countryman (AUS ISSN 0011-0264) **103**
Countryman *see* Agrotis **88**
The Countryman (GBR ISSN 0011-0272) **3863**
The Countryman's Weekly (GBR ISSN 1350-9683) **8310**
† Countrypolitan Homes & Plans (USA) **8946**
Country's Best Log Homes (USA ISSN 1089-3466) **1000**
Country's Best Top Selling Home Designs (USA) **7588**
Countryside Agency. Report (GBR) **2608**
• Countryside Agency. Research Notes (GBR) **4408**
Countryside Alliance. Update (GBR) **8310**
• Countryside and Small Stock Journal (USA ISSN 8750-7595) **3973**
Countryside Building *see* The R I D B A Journal **455**
Countryside Commission. Advisory Series (GBR ISSN 0140-5357) **2608**
Countryside Commission. Catalogue of Publications (GBR ISSN 0265-4334) **2608**
Countryside Commission. Research Register (GBR ISSN 0307-532X) **2608**
Countryside Commission. Working Papers (GBR ISSN 0142-0062) **2608**
Countryside la Vie (GBR) **3863**
• Countryside Recreation (GBR ISSN 1464-1194) **4977**
Countryside Recreation Research Advisory Group. Abstracts (GBR ISSN 0308-3748) **8778**
Countryside Voice (GBR ISSN 1742-8777) **2608**
• CountrySingles.com (USA) **7943**
The Countrywoman (GBR ISSN 0011-0302) **8857**
County *see* Irish Examiner **3893**
The County Administrator (USA) **7432**
County Agents Directory (USA ISSN 0739-4330) **103**
• County and City Data Book (USA ISSN 0082-9455) **8365**
• County and City Extra (USA ISSN 1059-9096) **8365**
County Bar Update (USA ISSN 0279-9626) **4651**
County Border Times & Mail (GBR) **3863**
† • County Business Patterns (CD-ROM) (USA ISSN 1064-539X) **8946**
• County Business Patterns (Online) (USA) **1222**
County Circular (USA) **4136**
County Compass (USA) **3528**
County Down Spectator (GBR) **3863**
• County Economic Indicators (USA) **1475**
County Executive Summary (USA) **1088**
County Genealogical Bibliographies (GBR) **3788**
† • County Government Finances (USA ISSN 0098-678X) **8946**
† County Guide to Marine Companies (GBR ISSN 0260-7093) **8946**
County Kildare Archaeological Society. Journal (IRL ISSN 0332-0782) **388**
County Law Library Program Bulletin (USA) **4651**
County Legal Reporter (USA) **4651**
County Line (USA) **4651**
County Lines (USA ISSN 0195-4121) **5069**
County Lines Newsletter *see* Alabama. Department of Revenue. County Lines Newsletter **7487**
County Louth Archaeological and Historical Society. Journal (IRL ISSN 0070-1327) **388**
County Magazine (CAN ISSN 0826-3035) **3808**
County News (Statesville) (USA) **3528**
County News (Washington) (USA ISSN 0744-9798) **7490**
County Penetration Reports (USA) **38**
County Planning Department. Surrey County Council. Technical Report (GBR) **4408**
County Progress (USA ISSN 0011-0353) **7432**
Coup de Foudre (BEL ISSN 0776-8656) **5108**
• Coup de Pouce (CAN ISSN 0822-3033) **3808**
Coup de Pouce Cuisine (CAN ISSN 1207-2478) **3632**
Coup de Soleil (CAN ISSN 1911-3900) **2150**
Coup d'Oeil (CAN) **6040**
Coup d'Oeil sur la Biotechnologie *see* Biotech Watch **759**
• Coupe (DEU ISSN 0935-7475) **6288**
† Coupe & Cabrio (ITA ISSN 1591-0288) **8946**
Coupe Magazine (CAN) **5212**
Le Couple et sa Famille (FRA ISSN 1776-6656) **7350**
Coupler (CAN ISSN 0319-8332) **8616**
Couples (USA) **6288**
† Couples d'Aujourd'hui (FRA ISSN 1163-5568) **8946**
Couples Familles et Metamorphoses *see* Le Couple et sa Famille **7350**
Coupon Treasure Hunt Newsletter (USA ISSN 1053-6523) **2637**
Cour de Cassation. Bulletin des Arrets. Chambre Criminelle (FRA ISSN 0298-7538) **4886**
Cour de Cassation. Bulletin des Arrets. Chambres Civiles (FRA ISSN 0242-5645) **4830**
Cour Europeenne des Droits de l'Homme. Recueil des Arrets et Decisions *see* European Court of Human Rights. Reports of Judgements and Decisions **7206**
La Cour Internationale d'Arbitrage de la C C I. Bulletin *see* The I C C International Court of Arbitration Bulletin **1404**
Cour Internationale de Justice. Actes et Documents/International Court of Justice. Acts and Documents (NLD ISSN 0251-1967) **4922**
Cour Internationale de Justice. Annuaire *see* International Court of Justice. Yearbook **4930**
Cour Internationale de Justice. Bibliographie/ International Court of Justice. Bibliography (NLD ISSN 0085-2139) **4821**
Cour Internationale de Justice. Memoires, Plaidoiries et Documents *see* International Court of Justice. Pleadings, Oral Arguments, Documents **4930**
Cour Supreme en Bref (CAN) **4948**
Courage in the Struggle for Justice and Peace (USA) **8096**
• The Courant (USA ISSN 1554-267X) **5004**
▼ • Courant (Washington) (USA ISSN 1947-377X) **3763**
Le Courbageot (FRA ISSN 0220-8768) **905**
Courchevel International (GBR) **8695**
Courcy's Intelligence Review *see* Strategic Intelligence Review **1519**
• The Courier (GBR) **2279**
Courier *see* Manukau Courier **3917**
The Courier (USA ISSN 1541-1974) **4290**
Courier (Beaufort West) (ZAF ISSN 0011-0426) **3948**
• The Courier (Brockton) (USA ISSN 1062-8371) **4332**
Courier (International) (DEU) **226**
Courier (Lexington) (USA ISSN 0279-4489) **8695**
Courier (London) (GBR ISSN 0011-0396) **2354**
Courier (Mequon) (USA) **2279**
• Courier (Muscatine) (USA ISSN 1044-5900) **7228**
Courier (South Holland) (USA) **2279**
The Courier (St. Louis) (USA ISSN 0746-3030) **7752**
Courier (Winona) (USA) **7794**
The Courier. Africa - Caribbean - Pacific - European Union *see* Magazine of A C P - E U Development Co-operation **1601**
The Courier & Advertiser (GBR ISSN 0307-5869) **3863**
Courier & Express Services Market Report *see* Key Note Market Report: Courier & Express Services **1894**
Courier & Parcel Technology International (GBR) **2354**
Courier Forschungsinstitut Senckenberg *see* C F S **8938**
Courier Magazine (USA ISSN 1075-3621) **8494**
• The Courier-Mail (AUS ISSN 1322-5235) **3794**
Courier of Education *see* Kur'yer Obrazovaniya **2881**
The Courier-Post *see* St. Charles Business Record **1179**
Courier Press (CAN ISSN 0834-7514) **3808**
The Courier Times (USA) **8494**
Courir Passion (FRA ISSN 1777-943X) **8168**
Courrent Immunlolgy *see* Xiandai Mianyixue **5767**
Le Courrier (Ste. Therese) (CAN) **3808**
Le Courrier: Afrique - Caraibes - Pacifique - Union Europeenne *see* Magazine of A C P - E U Development Co-operation **1601**
Courrier Ahuntsic (CAN) **3808**
Courrier Bordeaux - Cartierville (CAN) **3808**
Courrier C E R N *see* C E R N Courier **7065**
Courrier C F F *see* S B B Zeitung **8624**
Courrier Cadres (FRA ISSN 0220-6994) **6696**
Courrier Consulaire du Burkina Faso (BFA ISSN 0574-3370) **1401**
Le Courrier de la Coree *see* Korea Herald **3903**
Le Courrier de la Nature (FRA ISSN 0011-0477) **7848**
Courrier de la Nouvelle-Ecosse (CAN ISSN 1184-2008) **3808**
Courrier de la Planete (FRA ISSN 1161-8043) **196**
Le Courrier de la Transplantation (FRA ISSN 1628-8319) **6240**
Le Courrier de l'Algologie (FRA ISSN 1636-3167) **5601**
Le Courrier de l'Environnement *see* Environnement Magazine Hebdo **3430**
• Courrier de l'Environnement de l'I N R A (Institut National de la Recherche Agronomique) (FRA ISSN 1241-3992) **103**
Courrier De l'Escaut (Tournai Regional Edition) *see* Vers l'Avenir **3802**
Courrier de l'Industrie (TUN ISSN 0330-1516) **1088**
Le Courrier des Addictions (FRA ISSN 1294-2561) **6133**
† Le Courrier des Echecs (FRA ISSN 1272-5005) **8946**
Courrier des Employes d'Immeubles (FRA) **1088**
Le Courrier des Maires et des Elus Locaux (FRA ISSN 1252-1574) **7490**
† • Courrier des Pays de l'Est (FRA ISSN 0590-0239) **8946**
Courrier Deux-Montagnes (CAN) **3808**
Courrier du Bois (BEL ISSN 0770-111X) **3711**
Le Courrier du Grand Paris (FRA ISSN 1959-626X) **1401**
Le Courrier du Logement (FRA ISSN 1277-2607) **4408**
Le Courrier du Meuble et de l'Habitat (FRA ISSN 1169-0704) **4555**
Le Courrier du Musee et de ses Amis (BEL ISSN 1783-8509) **6522**
Courrier du Parlement (FRA ISSN 0045-8899) **7432**
Le Courrier du Passant *see* Le Courrier du Musee et de ses Amis **6522**
Courrier du Queyras (FRA ISSN 0154-733X) **8695**
Courrier du Vietnam (VNM ISSN 0045-8902) **7126**
Courrier Economique (MAR ISSN 0752-1855) **1475**
Courrier Fiscal *see* De Fiscale Koerier **1925**
• Courrier Hebdomadaire (BEL ISSN 0577-148X) **7126**
Courrier Hippique (CAN ISSN 0847-2173) **8289**
• Courrier International (FRA ISSN 1154-516X) **3840**
Courrier Laval (CAN ISSN 1180-6052) **3808**
Courrier Laval du Mercredi Est (CAN) **3808**
Courrier Laval du Mercredi Ouest (CAN) **3808**
Courrier S P C A/S P C A Courier (Societe Canadienne de Protection des Animaux) (CAN ISSN 0382-4497) **6806**
Courrier Sportif du Benin (CMR) **8168**
Le Cours de l'Histoire (FRA ISSN 1637-8407) **4136**
Cours de Perfectionnement du Notariat (CAN ISSN 0316-1234) **4652**
➤ Cours Specialises (FRA ISSN 1284-6090) **5481**
Course Calendar *see* Course Guide **2975**
Course Conductor News (CAN ISSN 1701-7173) **6984**
Course Guide (CAN ISSN 1709-8076) **2975**
Course Text of Histochemistry and Cytochemistry *see* Soshiki Saibo Kagaku Koshukai **836**
Course Trends (USA) **2940**
Courses et Elevage (FRA ISSN 0300-5607) **8289**
Court & Commercial Record (USA ISSN 1090-1612) **1088**
Court and Commerical *see* Daily Commercial Record **1090**
• Court Awarded Attorney Fees (USA) **4652**
Court Awareness (USA) **8225**
Court Companion (Year) (USA ISSN 1087-6200) **4908**
Court Decisions Pertaining to the Federal Trade Commission *see* U.S. Federal Trade Commission. Court Decisions Pertaining to the Federal Trade Commission **1433**
Court Excellence (USA) **4948**
• Court Forms, Precedents and Pleadings - N S W (AUS) **4948**
• Court Forms, Precedents and Pleadings - Queensland (AUS) **4948**
• Court Forms, Precedents & Pleadings - Victoria (AUS) **4948**
Court Forms, Precedents and Pleadings - Victoria *see* Court Forms, Precedents & Pleadings - Victoria **4948**
Court Index (USA) **4948**
Court Index *see* Cincinnati Court Index **4947**
Court Management & Administrative Report (USA ISSN 1063-0821) **4948**
Court Manager (USA ISSN 1046-249X) **4948**
• Court-Martial Procedure (USA) **4971**
Court News (USA) **4948**
• Court of Appeals for the Federal Circuit: Practice and Procedure (USA) **6748**
Court of Appeals of Georgia. Reports of Cases (USA ISSN 0886-120X) **4948**
Court of International Trade Rules *see* C I T Rules **4919**
Court of International Trade Test Case Record *see* C I T Test Case Record **4919**
Court of Justice and the Court of First Instance. Reports of Cases before the Court (LUX ISSN 1022-842X) **4922**
Court of Justice of the European Communities. Annual Report (Year) (LUX) **4652**
Court of Protection Practice (GBR) **4652**
• Court Review (USA ISSN 0011-0647) **4948**
Court Rules Pamphlet(s). Arkansas Rules of Court, State (USA ISSN 1930-9554) **4652**
Court Rules Pamphlet(s). California Rules of Court, State and Federal (USA) **4948**
Court Rules Pamphlet(s). Colorado Rules of Court, State & Federal (USA) **4948**
• Court Rules Pamphlet(s). Connecticut Rules of Court, State and Federal (USA) **4948**
Court Rules Pamphlet(s). Florida Rules of Court, State and Federal (USA ISSN 0735-6838) **4652**
• Court Rules Pamphlet(s). Georgia Court Rules and Procedure, State & Federal (USA) **4948**
• Court Rules Pamphlet(s). Iowa Rules of Court, State and Federal (USA ISSN 0742-9967) **4948**
• Court Rules Pamphlet(s). Kentucky Rules of Court, State and Federal (USA ISSN 1058-5222) **4948**
• Court Rules Pamphlet(s). Louisiana Rules of Court, State and Federal (USA ISSN 1066-1484) **4948**
Court Rules Pamphlet(s). Maine Rules of Court, State and Federal (USA) **4948**
• Court Rules Pamphlet(s). Maryland Rules of Court, State and Federal (USA ISSN 1047-5753) **4949**
Court Rules Pamphlet(s). Massachusetts Rules of Court (USA) **4652**
Court Rules Pamphlet(s). McKinney's New York Rules of Court, State & Federal (USA) **4949**
Court Rules Pamphlet(s). Michigan Rules of Court (USA ISSN 8756-3568) **4949**
• Court Rules Pamphlet(s). Montana Rules of Court, State and Federal (USA) **4652**
• Court Rules Pamphlet(s). New Jersey Rules of Court, State and Federal (USA ISSN 1070-6364) **4949**
Court Rules Pamphlet(s). North Carolina Rules of Court, State & Federal (USA) **4949**
Court Rules Pamphlet(s). North Dakota Court Rules, State and Federal (USA) **4949**
• Court Rules Pamphlet(s). Ohio Rules of Court, State and Federal (USA) **4949**
Court Rules Pamphlet(s). Oklahoma Court Rules and Procedure (USA) **4949**
Court Rules Pamphlet(s). Oregon Rules of Court, State and Federal (USA ISSN 8756-3614) **4949**
Court Rules Pamphlet(s). Pennsylvania Rules of Court, State and Federal (USA ISSN 1047-5109) **4949**
• Court Rules Pamphlet(s). Pennsylvania Rules of Court, State & Federal (USA) **4949**
Court Rules Pamphlet(s). South Carolina Rules of Court, State and Federal (USA) **4949**
• Court Rules Pamphlet(s). Tennessee Rules of Court, State and Federal (USA) **4949**
Court Rules Pamphlet(s). Texas Rules of Court, State and Federal (USA ISSN 0736-3435) **4949**
Court Rules Pamphlet(s). Vermont Rules of Court, State and Federal (USA ISSN 1930-8787) **4652**
• Court Rules Pamphlet(s). Virginia Court Rules & Procedure, State and Federal (USA ISSN 1071-488X) **4949**
• Court Rules Pamphlet(s). Washington Court Rules, State & Federal (USA) **4949**
Court Rules Pamphlet(s). West Virginia Rules of Court, State and Federal (USA) **4949**
• Court Rules Pamphlet(s). Wisconsin Court Rules and Procedure, State and Federal (USA) **4949**
Court Technology Bulletin (Online) (USA) **4949**
Courtauld Institute of Art. Courtauld Research Papers (GBR) **6522**
Courtauld Research Papers *see* Courtauld Institute of Art. Courtauld Research Papers **6522**
• Courtenay Comox Valley Record (CAN ISSN 0836-8880) **3808**
Courtenay Library of Reformation Classics (GBR ISSN 0070-1394) **4212**
Courtenay Reformation Facsimiles (GBR) **7752**
Courtenay Studies in Reformation Theology (GBR ISSN 0070-1408) **7752**
Courtier Nautique (BEL) **8642**
• Courtroom Criminal Evidence (USA) **4886**
Courtroom Handbook of Washington Evidence (USA) **4652**
Courtroom Handbook on Federal Evidence (USA ISSN 1080-9457) **4949**
Courtroom Handbook on Georgia Evidence (USA ISSN 1096-4371) **4949**
Courtroom Handbook on Illinois Evidence (USA ISSN 1930-4838) **4652**
† Courtroom Medicine: Abdominal Injuries (USA) **8946**
• Courtroom Medicine: Cancer (USA) **4652**
• Courtroom Medicine: Chest, Heart and Lungs (USA) **4652**
Courtroom Medicine: Death (USA) **5912**
• Courtroom Medicine: Head and Brain (USA) **4652**
• Courtroom Medicine: Hip and Thigh (USA) **4652**
Courtroom Medicine: Pain and Suffering (USA) **4652**
• Courtroom Medicine: Psychic Injuries (USA) **4652**
† Courtroom Medicine: Shoulder and Elbow (USA) **8946**
Courtroom Medicine: The Eye (USA) **4652**
Courtroom Medicine: The Knee and Its Related Structures (USA) **4652**
• Courtroom Medicine: The Low Back (USA) **4652**
Courtroom Medicine: The Neck (USA) **4652**
Courtroom Toxicology (USA) **5601**
• The Courts & Agency Directory (GBR ISSN 1461-3441) **4652**
Courts and C L E Bulletin *see* Courts Bulletin **4949**
Courts Bulletin (USA) **4949**
Court's Charge Reporter *see* Texas Court's Charge Reporter **4965**
Courts Today (USA) **4949**
Courtside (USA ISSN 1522-9483) **8225**
Couse's Ohio Form Book with Tax Analysis (USA) **4949**
• Cousin Avocado's Hideaway (USA) **5212**
Cousin to Cousin (USA) **3763**
Cousins et Cousines (USA ISSN 0740-3046) **3763**
† Cousteau Junior (FRA ISSN 1267-1053) **8946**
Cousteau Kids (USA ISSN 1946-7133) **2184**
• Le Couteau (FRA ISSN 1778-9745) **484**
Les Couts de Distribution des Films Francais (FRA ISSN 1951-4751) **6495**
Les Couts de Production des Films en (Year) (FRA ISSN 1951-4743) **6495**
Couture (HKG) **2253**
Couture (MYS ISSN 1394-7346) **2253**
Couture International Jeweler (USA) **4565**
• Couture Thailand (THA ISSN 1686-5138) **2253**
Couverture Plomberie (FRA ISSN 1157-545X) **4118**
Couvertures & Etancheite *see* Collection C D Metiers **992**
Cove-Atakpame (FRA ISSN 1957-5130) **8096**
• Coven of Angels (USA) **5441**

DIRECTORY 2010 CREATIVE COLLEGE TEACHING JOURNAL 10165

Covenant Companion (USA ISSN 0011-0671) 7734
• Covenant Discipleship Connection (USA) 7753
Covenant Discipleship Quarterly see Covenant Discipleship Connection 7753
The Covenant Quarterly (USA ISSN 0361-0934) 7734
Covenant Viewpoint (GBR) 7734
Covenant Voice (GBR) 7734
Coventry and District Natural History & Scientific Society. Proceedings (GBR ISSN 0962-5372) 843
Coventry & Kenilworth Citizen (GBR) 3863
Coventry & Warwickshire Chamber of Commerce. Training & Enterprise Directory (GBR) 1401
Coventry Citizen (GBR) 3863
Coventry Law Journal see Law Journal 4715
Coventry University. School of the Built Environment. Proceedings (GBR) 3412
Cover (GBR ISSN 1465-8801) 4500
Cover Letter Almanac see Adams Cover Letter Almanac 6691
• Cover Note (AUS ISSN 0312-6757) 4500
Cover Note (Kew) (AUS ISSN 1446-2885) 4500
▼ Cover Point (IRL ISSN 2009-0323) 8226
• Coverage (USA ISSN 1074-1887) 4500
Covered Bridge Topics (USA ISSN 0011-071X) 4290
➤ Covered Wagon (USA ISSN 0574-3680) 4290
Covering the Education Beat (USA) 4573
Coverings (CAN ISSN 1208-7068) 4536
Covert Action Quarterly see CovertAction Quarterly 7126
Covert Intelligence Letter (USA ISSN 1076-8645) 6417
➤ Covert Policing Review (GBR ISSN 1750-0567) 2676
CovertAction Quarterly (USA ISSN 1067-7232) 7126
Covicrier (VIR) 3412
Covjek i Prostor (HRV ISSN 0011-0728) 484
Cow Country (USA ISSN 0279-8204) 284
Cow Neck Peninsula Historical Society. Journal (USA) 4290
Cow News & Bull Views (USA) 284
Coward Family Newsletter (USA) 3763
Cowboy Magazine (USA ISSN 1053-2633) 8289
Cowboy Sports and Entertainment (USA) 5069
Cowboys & Indians (USA ISSN 1069-8876) 3973
Cowboy's Digest (USA) 284
Coweta Courier (USA ISSN 1082-3638) 3763
Cowgirls & Indians (USA) 2246
The Cowl (USA) 2279
• Cowles Foundation. Discussion Paper (Online) (USA) 1475
Cox Heritage (USA ISSN 0895-4062) 3763
Coyote (DEU ISSN 0939-4362) 6634
• ➤ CoyotE (USA) 2975
Coyote (USA) 2279
Coyote Papers (USA ISSN 0894-4539) 5108
• Coyote's Journal (Online) (USA) 5420
Coyote's Journal (Print) see Coyote's Journal (Online) 5420
• Coyuntura Economica de Andalucia (ESP ISSN 0214-7343) 1475
• Coyuntura Economica Valenciana (ESP ISSN 1134-4636) 1475
Coyuntura Industrial. Boletin (ESP) 1401
Coyuntura Social (COL ISSN 0121-2532) 1476
• Cozies, Capers & Crimes (USA) 5413
Cozinha Criativa (BRA ISSN 0104-9100) 8858
Cozinha da Fazenda (BRA ISSN 0104-4044) 4355
▼ Cozy Cabins (USA ISSN 1945-1385) 438
The Cozy Detective Mystery Magazine (USA) 5413
CPA Practice Management Forum see C P A Practice Management Forum 1283
CPAR see Chinese Public Administration Review 7430
CPI.Q see C P I. Q 4
The Crab (USA ISSN 0300-7561) 5004
Crab Creek Review (USA ISSN 0738-7008) 5279
Crab Orchard Review (USA ISSN 1083-5571) 5279
• Craccum (NZL) 2279
Crackdown! (USA) 4500
Cracked (USA ISSN 0883-6361) 5212
The Cracker see Pillars 2898
Cracking the A C T (American College Tests) (USA ISSN 1059-101X) 2975
Cracking the A C T, with Practice Tests on CD-ROM see Cracking the A C T with Sample Tests on CD-ROM 2975
Cracking the A C T with Sample Tests on CD-ROM (American College Tests) (USA) 2975
Cracking the A P Biology Exams (Advanced Placement) (USA ISSN 1092-0080) 2975
Cracking the A P Calculus AB and BC Exams (Advanced Placement) (USA) 2975
Cracking the A P Chemistry Exam (Advanced Placement) (USA ISSN 1092-0102) 2975
Cracking the A P Computer Science A & AB Exams (Advanced Placement) (USA ISSN 1546-9069) 2975
Cracking the A P Economics Macro and Micro Exams (Advanced Placement) (USA ISSN 1546-6914) 2975
Cracking the A P English Language & Composition Exam (Advanced Placement) (USA ISSN 1558-9676) 2975
Cracking the A P English Literature Exam (Advanced Placement) (USA ISSN 1092-0099) 2975
Cracking the A P Environmental Science Exam (Advanced Placement) (USA ISSN 1558-9684) 2975
Cracking the A P European History Exam (Advanced Placement) (USA ISSN 1522-6409) 2975
Cracking the A P Physics B & C Exams (Advanced Placement) (USA ISSN 1545-0988) 2975
Cracking the A P Psychology Exam (Advanced Placement) (USA ISSN 1546-9093) 2975
Cracking the A P Spanish Exam (Advanced Placement) (USA ISSN 1933-1053) 2975
Cracking the A P Statistics Exam (Advanced Placement) (USA ISSN 1546-9085) 2975
Cracking the A P U.S. Government and Politics Exam (Advanced Placement) (USA ISSN 1097-2757) 2975
Cracking the A P U.S. History Exam (Advanced Placement) (USA ISSN 1092-0072) 2975
Cracking the A P World History Exam (Advanced Placement) (USA ISSN 1546-9077) 2975
Cracking the C A H S E E. English-Language Arts (California High School Exit Examination) (USA ISSN 1942-8472) 2840
Cracking the C A H S E E. Mathematics (California High School Exit Examination) (USA ISSN 1942-8464) 5481
Cracking the English Achievements see Cracking the S A T Literature Subject Test 2976
Cracking the French Achievement see Cracking the S A T French Subject Test 2976
Cracking the G E D (General Educational Development) (USA ISSN 1076-5352) 2975
Cracking the G M A T (Graduate Management Admission Test) (USA ISSN 1062-5550) 2975
Cracking the G M A T with CD-ROM see Cracking the G M A T with DVD-ROM 2975
Cracking the G M A T with DVD-ROM (Graduate Management Admission Test) (USA) 2975
Cracking the G M A T, with Practice Tests on CD-ROM see Cracking the G M A T with DVD-ROM 2975
Cracking the G M A T with Sample Tests on CD-ROM see Cracking the G M A T with DVD-ROM 2975
Cracking the G R E see Cracking the New G R E 2975
Cracking the G R E Biology Test (Graduate Record Examination) (USA ISSN 1089-3687) 2975
Cracking the G R E Chemistry Subject Test (Graduate Record Examination) (USA ISSN 1933-2173) 2975
Cracking the G R E Literature in English Subject Test see Cracking the G R E Literature Test 2975
Cracking the G R E Literature Test (Graduate Record Examination) (USA) 2975
Cracking the G R E Math Test (Graduate Record Examination) (USA ISSN 1541-4957) 2975
Cracking the G R E Psychology Test (Graduate Record Examination) (USA ISSN 1075-2978) 7350
Cracking the G R E with CD-ROM see Cracking the New G R E with DVD 2976
Cracking the G R E with Sample Tests on CD-ROM see Cracking the New G R E with DVD 2976
Cracking the L S A T (Law School Admission Test) (USA ISSN 1062-5542) 2975
Cracking the L S A T with CD-ROM see Cracking the L S A T with DVD-ROM 2975
Cracking the L S A T with DVD-ROM (USA ISSN 1935-7567) 2975
Cracking the L S A T, with Practice Tests on CD-ROM see Cracking the L S A T with DVD-ROM 2975
Cracking the L S A T with Sample Tests on CD-ROM see Cracking the L S A T with DVD-ROM 2975
▼ Cracking the M C A T C B T (Medical College Admissions Test Computer Based Test) (USA ISSN 1934-2306) 5601
Cracking the Math Achievements see Cracking the S A T Math 1 & 2 Subject Tests 2976
Cracking the New G R E (Graduate Record Examination) (USA ISSN 1936-4172) 2975
Cracking the New G R E with DVD (Graduate Record Examination) (USA ISSN 1936-4083) 2976
Cracking the New S A T see Cracking the S A T 2976
Cracking the New S A T with CD-ROM see Cracking the S A T with DVD 2976
Cracking the New S A T with Practice Tests on CD-ROM see Cracking the S A T with DVD 2976
Cracking the P S A T / N M S Q T (Preliminary Scholastic Assessment Test / National Merit Scholarship Qualifying Test) (USA ISSN 1549-6120) 2976
Cracking the S A T (USA ISSN 1934-239X) 2976
Cracking the S A T Biology E/M Subject Test (USA ISSN 1556-8431) 2976
Cracking the S A T Chemistry Subject Test (USA ISSN 1556-844X) 2976
Cracking the S A T French Subject Test (USA) 2976
Cracking the S A T II. Biology E/M Subject Test see Cracking the S A T Biology E/M Subject Test 2976
Cracking the S A T II. Biology Subject Test see Cracking the S A T Biology E/M Subject Test 2976
Cracking the S A T II. Chemistry Subject Test see Cracking the S A T Chemistry Subject Test 2976
Cracking the S A T II. English Subject Tests see Cracking the S A T Literature Subject Test 2976
Cracking the S A T II. French Subject Test see Cracking the S A T French Subject Test 2976
Cracking the S A T II. Math Subject Tests see Cracking the S A T Math 1 & 2 Subject Tests 2976
Cracking the S A T II. Physics Subject Test see Cracking the S A T Physics Subject Test 2976
Cracking the S A T II. Spanish Subject Test see Cracking the S A T Spanish Subject Test 2976
Cracking the S A T II. U.S. and World History Subject Tests see Cracking the S A T U.S. & World History Subject Tests 2976
Cracking the S A T II. Writing and Literature Subject Tests see Cracking the S A T Literature Subject Test 2976
Cracking the S A T Literature Subject Test (USA ISSN 1944-379X) 2976
Cracking the S A T Math 1 & 2 Subject Tests (USA ISSN 1556-7095) 2976
Cracking the S A T Physics Subject Test (USA ISSN 1558-0067) 2976
Cracking the S A T Spanish Subject Test (USA ISSN 1558-3406) 2976
Cracking the S A T U.S. & World History Subject Tests (USA ISSN 1558-3120) 2976
Cracking the S A T with DVD (Scholastic Achievement Test) (USA ISSN 1936-4091) 2976
Cracking the T O E F L (Test of English as a Foreign Language) (USA ISSN 1074-2336) 2976
Cracoviana/Marvels of Krakow (POL ISSN 1232-132X) 3928
Cracow Turkological Studies see Studia Turcologica Cracoviensia 561
Cradles of Civilization Series (USA) 4136
Crafoord Lectures (SWE ISSN 1101-2765) 1736
• Craft (USA ISSN 1932-9121) 532
Craft & Design (GBR) 532
• Craft Arts International (AUS ISSN 1038-846X) 533
Craft Business (GBR ISSN 1470-5656) 533
Craft Connection (USA ISSN 1193-3208) 533
Craft Contacts (CAN ISSN 0823-2148) 533
• Craft Culture (AUS ISSN 1447-0829) 484
The Craft Digest see East Coast Artisan 535
The Craft Factor (CAN ISSN 0228-7498) 533
Craft Galleries Guide (GBR ISSN 1756-3054) 533
Craft Journal see Cahiers Metiers d'Art 532
Craft Kingdom (USA ISSN 1550-9575) 7635
Craft Related Newsletters, Periodicals & Publications (USA ISSN 1053-2013) 533
Craft Stamper (GBR ISSN 1469-3992) 533
Craft Times (USA) 533
CraftArt (ZAF ISSN 1023-5248) 533
† Crafting Traditions (USA ISSN 1082-1376) 8946
• Craftmark (AUS ISSN 1442-9233) 533
Craftmaster News (USA ISSN 1061-3064) 533
† • Craftrends (Online) (USA) 8946
Craftrends (Print) see Craftrends (Online) 8946
Craftrends, Sewbusiness see Craftrends (Online) 8946
• Crafts (GBR ISSN 0306-610X) 533
Crafts 4 Kidz (ZAF ISSN 1814-9804) 533
Crafts Beautiful (GBR ISSN 1350-1984) 533
Crafts Council. News (GBR ISSN 0143-6015) 533
Crafts Council. Newsletter see Stopress 540
Crafts Fair Guide (USA ISSN 0273-7957) 533
Crafts Four Kids see Crafts 4 Kidz 533
• Crafts 'n Things (USA ISSN 0146-6607) 533
• Crafts News (USA ISSN 0899-9724) 533
The Crafts Report (USA ISSN 0160-7650) 533
Craftsman (GBR) 3375
Craftsman (USA) 4592
The Craftsman Magazine see Craft & Design 532
CraftSource (CAN) 533
▼ Craftstylish (USA ISSN 1941-8353) 533
Craftworker's Year Book (GBR ISSN 0968-4506) 533
Craig - Links (USA ISSN 1098-688X) 3763
Craighead's Country Reports (USA) 8695
Craighead's International Business, Travel and Relocation Guide (USA ISSN 1058-3904) 8695
• Crain's Chicago Business (USA ISSN 0149-6956) 1959
• Crain's Cleveland Business (USA ISSN 0197-2375) 1476
• Crain's Detroit Business (USA ISSN 0882-1992) 1088
• Crain's New York Business (USA ISSN 8756-789X) 1088
Crainsdetroit.com see Crain's Detroit Business 1088
• Cranberries (USA ISSN 0011-0787) 226
Cranberries see U.S. Department of Agriculture. National Agricultural Statistics Service. Cranberries 188
• Cranberry Winters (USA) 5279
Cranbourne Leader (AUS) 3794
Cranbourne Sun see Cranbourne Leader 3794
Cranbrook Institute of Science, Bloomfield Hills, Michigan. Bulletin (USA ISSN 0070-1416) 7848
Crane see Kuren 3387
Crane Hot Line (USA ISSN 1550-1388) 5451
Crane Works see Lift & Crane Applications and Equipment 5454
• Cranes and Access (GBR ISSN 1467-0852) 1000
Cranes and Lifting Australia (AUS) 1000
• Cranes Today (GBR ISSN 0307-0018) 5451
Cranes Today Handbook (GBR ISSN 0260-745X) 1000
Cranfield School of Management Address Book (GBR ISSN 0308-048X) 2279
• Crania (USA) 5420
Cranial Letter (USA) 6058
▼ • ➤ Cranial Maxillofacial Trauma & Reconstruction (USA ISSN 1943-3875) 6241
† Cranio Clinics International (USA ISSN 1050-009X) 8946
➤ Cranio: Journal of Craniomandibular Practice (USA ISSN 0886-9634) 5601
Craniofacial Growth Series (USA ISSN 0162-7279) 865
Cranium (NLD ISSN 0923-5647) 939
Crank (CAN ISSN 1910-2402) 5279
CrankMail (USA ISSN 1060-085X) 8256
Crap Hound (USA) 484
Crappie World (USA ISSN 1072-9011) 3589
Crash Cinema (GBR ISSN 1743-4459) 6495
Crash Estimating Guide see Motor Early Model Crash Estimating Guide 8592
Crash Test Technology International (GBR) 8576
• Crate (USA ISSN 1558-4895) 4448
Cratschla (CHE ISSN 1021-9706) 2608
Crave New York (USA) 4384
➤ Crawford County Genealogy (USA ISSN 1079-2600) 3763
Crawford Exchange (USA ISSN 1043-7401) 3763
Crawford Perspectives (USA) 1619
• Crawford's Directory of City Connections (GBR ISSN 0953-8089) 1332
Cray Channels (USA) 2506
Crayfish News (USA ISSN 1023-8174) 939
Crayon (USA ISSN 1093-4677) 5279
Crazy for Cross Stitch (USA ISSN 1527-5973) 6637
➤ Crazyhorse (USA ISSN 0011-0841) 5279
C@re Bleibgesund (DEU) 6984
Crea (JPN) 8858
Crea-Deco (FRA ISSN 1298-2113) 533
Creaciones en Gomaeva (ARG ISSN 1850-0730) 4064
Cream (CHE ISSN 1660-7015) 3958
• ➤ Cream City Review (USA ISSN 0884-3457) 5279
Cream Magazine (AUS ISSN 1329-4016) 6560
Cream Separator and Dairy Newsletter (USA) 262
➤ CREArTA (AUS ISSN 1443-5373) 484
• Create & Decorate (USA) 533
Create and Decorate see Create & Decorate 533
Create Living Home see Home 4360
Create Magazine. (Midwest Edition) see Create Magazine (Southeast Edition) 23
Create Magazine. (Northeast Edition) see Create Magazine (Southeast Edition) 23
Create Magazine (Southeast Edition) (USA ISSN 1935-0813) 23
Create Magazine (Southwest Edition) see Create Magazine (Southeast Edition) 23
Create Magazine (West Coast Edition) see Create Magazine (Southeast Edition) 23
Create the Dream! (USA ISSN 1932-3875) 1088
▼ • Create Your Fashion Career (USA ISSN 1947-2471) 2253
Creatie (NLD ISSN 1572-2570) 23
Creatief met Bloemen (NLD ISSN 1573-3866) 3755
Creatief met Foto's (NLD) 534
Creatief met Kaarten (NLD ISSN 1574-0250) 534
Creatif Special Cartes 3 D (FRA ISSN 1767-5863) 4333
▼ Creating Corporate Cultures (USA ISSN 1935-6560) 1736
Creating Excellence (USA ISSN 1045-7011) 3973
Creating Families/Travail en Cours (CAN ISSN 1715-9504) 5885
Creating Homes see New Homes 4547
Creating Keepsakes (USA ISSN 1091-3580) 534
Creating Quality Cities (USA) 7490
• Creating the Digital Library (USA) 5004
▼ Creating Together Journal (USA ISSN 1938-1212) 534
▼ • Creating True Wealth (USA ISSN 1945-9300) 6644
Creation (AUS ISSN 0819-1530) 7635
Creation see Maison Passion Creation 8972
Creation (GBR) 7635
Creation Care (USA ISSN 1521-9704) 3412
Creation Deco (FRA ISSN 1962-4727) 4536
Creation d'Entreprise Magazine (FRA ISSN 1774-8984) 1959
Creation et Arts du Spectacle (FRA ISSN 1254-745X) 8468
Creation Matters (USA ISSN 1094-6632) 7636
† Creation Passion (FRA ISSN 1291-3138) 8946
• ➤ Creation Research Society Quarterly (USA ISSN 0092-9166) 7848
† Creations (FRA ISSN 0293-0196) 8947
Creations (USA) 6644
Creations Florales (FRA ISSN 1769-5015) 3755
Creativ Idee (DEU) 4333
† Creativ Trends (DEU) 8947
Creativ Verpacken (DEU ISSN 1433-8750) 6709
• Creativa (MEX) 1812
Creative (IRL) 23
Creative see Graph Creative 7321
• Creative (USA ISSN 0737-5883) 23
▼ • ➤ Creative Approaches to Research (AUS ISSN 1835-9442) 7956
Creative Beading (AUS) 534
Creative Beading & Jewellery Design (GBR ISSN 1752-0223) 4333
Creative Book see Pub Creative Book 33
Creative Book Selection Index (IND ISSN 0378-7494) 7578
Creative Cardmaking Ideas (GBR) 534
Creative City Guide (NLD ISSN 1872-1338) 8695
Creative College Teaching Journal (USA ISSN 1934-8606) 3055

Title

DIRECTORY 2010 CUADERNOS DE PENSAMIENTO 10169

Cruise Industry News Quarterly (USA) **8696**
Cruise Magazine *see* Cruise Entertainment Magazine **4372**
Cruise Magazine (USA) **8696**
Cruise Reports (USA) **8696**
Cruise Trade (USA) **8696**
• Cruise Travel (USA ISSN 0199-5111) **8696**
Cruise Vacation *see* Stern's Guide to the Cruise Vacation **8758**
• Cruise Weekly (AUS ISSN 1834-5913) **8642**
Cruiser *see* Motorcycle Cruiser **8263**
Cruising Association. Handbook (GBR) **8274**
Cruising Association. Magazine (GBR ISSN 1350-1321) **8274**
Cruising Helmsman (AUS ISSN 0812-4086) **8274**
Cruising in Style (USA) **8696**
• Cruising the Cape (AUS) **8696**
• Cruising World (USA ISSN 0098-3519) **8275**
Crunk (USA) **5069**
Crusade Magazine (USA ISSN 1096-3782) **8096**
Crusader (LCA) **3944**
The Crusader (USA) **2280**
• Crusader (Alpharetta) (USA ISSN 0011-2151) **7753**
The Crusader (Lancaster) (USA) **2280**
• The Crusader (Selinsgrove) (USA ISSN 1082-0523) **2280**
Crusader (Toronto) (CAN ISSN 0382-4314) **7753**
Crusades (GBR ISSN 1476-5276) **4213**
Crustacean Issues (GBR ISSN 0168-6356) **939**
Crustacean Research (JPN) **939**
• ➤ Crustaceana (NLD ISSN 0011-216X) **939**
➤ Crustaceana Monographs (NLD ISSN 1570-7024) **939**
Crustaceana. Supplements *see* Crustaceana Monographs **939**
Crux (GBR) **7753**
Crux (ZAF ISSN 0250-0035) **5281**
Crux (Boucherville) (CAN ISSN 1715-9857) **8168**
Crux (Vancouver) (CAN ISSN 0011-2186) **7636**
Crux Australis (AUS ISSN 0814-5008) **3763**
• Crux Mathematicorum with Mathematical Mayhem (CAN ISSN 1706-8142) **5481**
Crux of the News (USA ISSN 0591-2296) **7636**
Crux with Mayhem *see* Crux Mathematicorum with Mathematical Mayhem **5481**
Cruz Ansata (PRI) **4448**
• Cruz Roja (ESP ISSN 1575-2011) **8036**
Cruz Roja, Media Luna Roja *see* Red Cross, Red Crescent **8064**
Cruzada Eucaristica (PRT ISSN 0011-2194) **2184**
Cruzado (MEX ISSN 0011-2208) **7127**
Cruzin (AUS ISSN 1444-5352) **8576**
▼ Cruzin' South Magazine (USA) **8576**
Cry Wolf (GBR) **2280**
• ➤ Cryo-Letters (GBR ISSN 0143-2044) **921**
• ➤ Cryobiology (USA ISSN 0011-2240) **753**
CryoGas International (USA ISSN 1052-0139) **3375**
Cryogenic Engineering Conference Proceedings *see* Advances in Cryogenic Engineering (Part A & B) **7053**
Cryogenic Society of Japan. Journal *see* Teion Kogaku **7056**
Cryogenics *see* Diwen Gongcheng **7054**
• ➤ Cryogenics (GBR ISSN 0011-2275) **7053**
CryoLetters *see* Cryo-Letters **921**
Cryonics (USA ISSN 1054-4305) **5904**
▼ • The Cryosphere (DEU ISSN 1994-0416) **6351**
▼ • ➤ The Cryosphere Discussions (DEU ISSN 1994-0432) **6351**
Crypt of Cthulhu (USA ISSN 1077-8179) **5441**
• Crypto-Gram (USA) **2512**
Crypto Rights Journal *see* CryptoRights Journal **2512**
Cryptogamica Helvetica (CHE ISSN 0257-9421) **784**
• ➤ Cryptogamie Algologie (FRA ISSN 0181-1568) **784**
• ➤ Cryptogamie Bryologie (FRA ISSN 1290-0796) **784**
• ➤ Cryptogamie Mycologie (FRA ISSN 0181-1584) **785**
▼ • ➤ Cryptography and Communications (USA ISSN 1936-2447) **2415**
• ➤ Cryptologia (GBR ISSN 0161-1194) **2512**
▼ Cryptology and Information Security Series (NLD ISSN 1871-6431) **2512**
• CryptoRights Journal (USA ISSN 1540-3327) **2512**
• Cryptosystems Journal (USA ISSN 0899-8159) **2575**
The Crystal Ball (USA) **5441**
• Crystal Dragon Rumblings Newsletters (AUS ISSN 1833-0010) **308**
• Crystal Growth & Design (USA ISSN 1528-7483) **2109**
Crystal Mirror (USA ISSN 0097-7209) **7701**
Crystal Palace Foundation News *see* Crystal Palace Foundation. News Bulletin **4213**
• Crystal Palace Foundation. News Bulletin (GBR) **4213**
• ➤ Crystal Research and Technology (DEU ISSN 0232-1300) **2110**
Crystal Wright's Hair, Makeup & Fashion Styling Career Guide *see* The Hair, Makeup & Fashion Styling Career Guide **6698**
Crystallographic Society of Japan. Journal *see* Nihon Kessho Gakkaishi **2111**
• ➤ Crystallography Reports (RUS ISSN 1063-7745) **2110**
• ➤ Crystallography Reviews (GBR ISSN 0889-311X) **2110**
• ➤ CrystEngComm (GBR ISSN 1466-8033) **2110**
▼ CS (Ciencias Sociales) (COL ISSN 2011-0324) **7957**
Csaladi Haz (HUN ISSN 0865-0047) **4355**
Csaladi Lap (HUN ISSN 0133-1868) **8858**
CSERGE Working Paper WM *see* Centre for Social and Economic Research on the Global Environment. Working Paper. Waste Management **3504**
Csok es Konny (HUN ISSN 1215-9840) **8858**
• C'T (DEU ISSN 0724-8679) **2415**
C'T (NLD ISSN 1388-0276) **2415**
CT Business Magazine (USA) **1089**
CT. Catastro (ESP ISSN 1138-3488) **7588**
CTdigest.com *see* C T Digest **5779**
Ctenar (CZE ISSN 0011-2321) **5004**
Cthulhu Codex (USA) **5441**
• CTRL_Z Magazine (BGR) **484**
➤ CTS - Ciencia, Tecnologia y Sociedad (ARG ISSN 1668-0030) **7849**
Ctvrtletnik Christian Science. Biblicke Lecke *see* Christian Science Quarterly. Bible Lessons (English Citation Edition) **7734**
• Cu4tro.com (MEX) **3908**
Cua So Van Hoa Viet Nam *see* Vietnam Cultural Window **3995**
• Cuaderno Cultural Primula (ESP ISSN 1699-3853) **8096**
• Cuaderno de Difusion (CHL ISSN 0718-3771) **6417**
Cuaderno de Informacion Oportuna (MEX ISSN 0186-0445) **1476**
Cuaderno de Informacion Oportuna Regional (MEX ISSN 0186-047X) **1476**
• Cuaderno de Investigacion en la Educacion (PRI ISSN 1540-0786) **2840**
El Cuaderno de los Padres (ESP ISSN 1578-3855) **4355**
• ➤ Cuaderno Internacional de Estudios Humanisticos y Literatura/International Journal of Humanistic Studies and Literature (PRI ISSN 1521-8007) **334**
Cuaderno Trimestral de la Christian Science. Lecciones Biblicas *see* Christian Science Quarterly. Bible Lessons (English Citation Edition) **7734**
▼ Cuadernos (COL ISSN 2011-0170) **1737**
Cuadernos (ESP) **4573**
Cuadernos Abulenses (ESP ISSN 0213-0475) **7490**
Cuadernos Africa - America Latina (ESP ISSN 1130-2569) **7957**
• ➤ Cuadernos Americanos (MEX ISSN 0011-2356) **5281**
• Cuadernos Aragoneses de Economia (ESP ISSN 0211-0865) **1476**
Cuadernos Aranzadi de Jurisprudencia Tributaria (ESP ISSN 1988-1630) **4653**
Cuadernos Aranzadi del Tribunal Constitucional (ESP ISSN 1139-7691) **4847**
Cuadernos Argentinos de Historia de la Psicologia (ARG ISSN 0328-364X) **7350**
Cuadernos Azafea *see* Azafea **6907**
Cuadernos C I P C A (Serie Popular) (BOL) **196**
• Cuadernos Cervantes de la Lengua Espanola (ESP ISSN 1134-9468) **5109**
Cuadernos Cinematograficos (ESP ISSN 0214-462X) **6495**
• Cuadernos Civitas de Jurisprudencia Civil (ESP ISSN 0212-6206) **4830**
Cuadernos da Area de Ciencias Marinas (ESP ISSN 0213-6708) **2803**
Cuadernos de Actualidad (ESP ISSN 1133-9470) **1918**
Cuadernos de Actualidad Internacional (VEN ISSN 0798-0841) **8036**
Cuadernos de Actualizacion Tecnica (ARG ISSN 0327-4950) **103**
Cuadernos de Administracion Local (ESP) **7432**
Cuadernos de Administracion Publica (ARG ISSN 0326-0003) **7432**
• Cuadernos de Administracion. Serie Organizaciones (COL ISSN 0120-3592) **1737**
Cuadernos de Agricultura, Pesca y Alimentacion (ESP ISSN 1139-1456) **103**
Cuadernos de Alhambra (ESP ISSN 0590-1987) **484**
Cuadernos de Alzate (ESP ISSN 0213-1862) **5212**
Cuadernos de Antropologia (GTM ISSN 0590-160X) **334**
• Cuadernos de Antropologia (PER ISSN 1682-458X) **334**
• Cuadernos de Antropologia Social (ARG ISSN 0327-3776) **334**
Cuadernos de Anuario Filosofico (ESP ISSN 1137-2176) **6912**
➤ Cuadernos de Aragon (ESP ISSN 0590-1626) **4213**
Cuadernos de Arqueologia de Deusto (ESP ISSN 0210-3710) **388**
Cuadernos de Arqueologia Maritima (ESP ISSN 1133-5645) **388**
Cuadernos de Arquitectura del Paisaje (ESP ISSN 1697-574X) **439**
Cuadernos de Arquitectura Mesoamericana (MEX ISSN 0185-5131) **439**
Cuadernos de Arquitectura Virreinal (MEX ISSN 0185-8572) **439**
• Cuadernos de Arte e Iconografia (ESP ISSN 0214-2821) **484**
Cuadernos de Artroscopia (ESP ISSN 1134-7872) **6241**
Cuadernos de Bibliografia de las Artes Escenicas (ESP ISSN 1135-3503) **8468**
Cuadernos de Bioetica (ARG ISSN 0328-8390) **5601**
• Cuadernos de Bioetica (ESP ISSN 1132-1989) **5601**
Cuadernos de Capacitacion Popular (PER) **7957**
• Cuadernos de Ciencias Economicas y Empresariales (ESP ISSN 0211-4356) **1089**
Cuadernos de Ciencias Humanas (COL) **4448**
• Cuadernos de Cirugia (CHL ISSN 0716-7040) **6241**
Cuadernos de Comunicacion (Bogota) (COL) **4448**
Cuadernos de Conferencias y Articulos (COL) **4653**
Cuadernos de Contabilidad (COL ISSN 0123-1472) **1286**
▼ Cuadernos de Criminologia (ESP ISSN 1888-0665) **2650**
Cuadernos de Cristianismo y Sociedad (ECU ISSN 0590-1731) **7636**
Cuadernos de Critica (ARG ISSN 1668-7620) **5212**
Cuadernos de Cultura (ESP ISSN 1135-1608) **4448**
Cuadernos de Cultura (PRI ISSN 1545-0090) **4290**
Cuadernos de Derecho (MEX ISSN 1405-3020) **4653**
Cuadernos de Derecho Internacional Privado (URY) **4922**
Cuadernos de Derecho Judicial (ESP ISSN 1134-9670) **4949**
Cuadernos de Derecho Local *see* Quaderns de Dret Local **8983**
Cuadernos de Derecho Publico (ESP ISSN 1138-2848) **4653**
Cuadernos de Derecho y Comercio (ESP ISSN 1575-4812) **4653**
➤ Cuadernos de Desarrollo Rural (COL ISSN 0122-1450) **196**
• Cuadernos de Difusion (PER ISSN 1815-6592) **1737**
Cuadernos de Doctrina y Jurisprudencia Penal (ARG ISSN 0328-3909) **4950**
• Cuadernos de Documentacion Multimedia (ESP ISSN 1133-3030) **2485**
• ➤ Cuadernos de Economia (CHL ISSN 0716-0046) **1089**
• ➤ Cuadernos de Economia (COL ISSN 0121-4772) **1539**
Cuadernos de Economia Murciana (ESP ISSN 0214-6002) **1476**
Cuadernos de Economia Politica (ARG ISSN 0327-9693) **1476**
• Cuadernos de Economia y Direccion de la Empresa (ESP ISSN 1138-5758) **1737**
Los Cuadernos de Editur. Tecno Agencias (ESP ISSN 1137-4837) **8696**
Los Cuadernos de Editur. Tecno Hosteleria (ESP ISSN 1137-4829) **8696**
Cuadernos de Educacion (CHL ISSN 0716-0496) **2840**
▼ Cuadernos de Educacion y Practicas Sociales (ARG ISSN 1851-6637) **2840**
Cuadernos de Esclerosis Multiple (ESP ISSN 1695-7377) **6134**
Cuadernos de Espiritu (ESP ISSN 1133-293X) **6912**
Cuadernos de Estadistica Matematica (ESP ISSN 0211-853X) **8365**
Cuadernos de Estudios (ESP ISSN 1133-0813) **4448**
Cuadernos de Estudios Borjanos (ESP ISSN 0210-8224) **4213**
Cuadernos de Estudios Caspolinos (ESP ISSN 0211-7649) **4213**
Cuadernos de Estudios Cooperativos (ESP) **1423**
Cuadernos de Estudios del Siglo XVIII (ESP ISSN 1131-9879) **5281**
• Cuadernos de Estudios Empresariales (ESP ISSN 1131-6985) **1959**
• Cuadernos de Estudios Gallegos (ESP ISSN 0210-847X) **7957**
Cuadernos de Estudios Latinoamericanos (ARG) **7127**
† Cuadernos de Estudios Medievales y Ciencias y Tecnicas Historiograficas (ESP ISSN 1132-7553) **8947**
Cuadernos de Etica (ARG ISSN 0326-9523) **6912**
Cuadernos de Etnologia (ESP) **334**
Cuadernos de Etnologia de Guadalajara (ESP ISSN 0213-7399) **334**
Cuadernos de Etnologia y Etnografia de Navarra (ESP ISSN 0590-1871) **334**
• Cuadernos de Filologia Clasica. Estudios Griegos e Indoeuropeos (ESP ISSN 1131-9070) **5109**
• Cuadernos de Filologia Clasica. Estudios Latinos (ESP ISSN 1131-9062) **5109**
• Cuadernos de Filologia Clasica. Estudios Latinos. Anejos (ESP) **5109**
Cuadernos de Filologia Francesa (ESP ISSN 1135-8637) **5109**
• Cuadernos de Filologia Italiana (ESP ISSN 1133-9527) **5109**
Cuadernos de Filosofia Latinoamericana (COL ISSN 0120-8462) **6912**
Cuadernos de Fitopatologia (ESP ISSN 0213-4128) **785**
Cuadernos de Gastronomia (ESP ISSN 1133-0643) **4355**
Cuadernos de Geografia (COL ISSN 0121-215X) **4003**
➤ Cuadernos de Geografia (ESP ISSN 0210-086X) **4003**
Cuadernos de Geografia (Cadiz) (ESP ISSN 0214-9869) **4003**
➤ Cuadernos de Geohistoria Regional (ARG ISSN 0325-8246) **4003**
• Cuadernos de Gestion (ESP ISSN 1131-6837) **1737**
Cuadernos de Gestion *see* Cuadernos de Gestion para el Profesional de Atencion Primaria **8947**
▼ Cuadernos de Gestion del Conocimiento (COL ISSN 2011-3684) **2840**
† • Cuadernos de Gestion para el Profesional de Atencion Primaria (ESP ISSN 1135-4127) **8947**
Cuadernos de Gobierno y Administracion (ESP ISSN 1576-0529) **7432**
Cuadernos de Grado Medio (ESP ISSN 1131-8074) **2840**
• Cuadernos de Historia (CHL ISSN 0716-1832) **4290**
Cuadernos de Historia *see* Hispania **4227**
• Cuadernos de Historia Contemporanea (ESP ISSN 0214-400X) **4213**
• Cuadernos de Historia de Espana (ARG ISSN 0325-1195) **4213**
• Cuadernos de Historia de la Salud Publica (CUB ISSN 1013-2821) **7513**
• Cuadernos de Historia del Arte (ARG ISSN 0070-1688) **484**
Cuadernos de Historia del Arte (MEX ISSN 0185-1691) **484**
• Cuadernos de Historia del Derecho (ESP ISSN 1133-7613) **4847**
Cuadernos de Historia Jeronimo Zurita *see* Revista de Historia Jeronimo Zurita **4257**
• Cuadernos de Historia Moderna (ESP ISSN 0214-4018) **4136**
• Cuadernos de Historia Moderna. Anejos (ESP) **4136**
Cuadernos de Historia Regional (ARG ISSN 0326-6060) **7957**
Cuadernos de Humanidades (ARG ISSN 0327-8115) **7957**
Cuadernos de Humanitas *see* Humanitas **4455**
Cuadernos de Ilustracion y Romanticismo (ESP ISSN 1132-8304) **5409**
• Cuadernos de Informacion (CHL ISSN 0716-162X) **2318**
• Cuadernos de Informacion Economica (ESP ISSN 1132-9386) **1089**
Cuadernos de Informacion Economica (VEN) **1089**
• Cuadernos de Informacion y Comunicacion (ESP ISSN 1135-7991) **2318**
▼ Cuadernos de Inteligencia Empresarial (COL ISSN 2011-3692) **1737**
• Cuadernos de Investigacion (COL ISSN 1692-0694) **2840**
Cuadernos de Investigacion - Accion (ARG) **1674**
Cuadernos de Investigacion Biologica (ESP ISSN 0211-5700) **667**
• ➤ Cuadernos de Investigacion Filologica (ESP ISSN 0211-0547) **5109**
• Cuadernos de Investigacion Geografica (ESP ISSN 0211-6820) **4003**
Cuadernos de Investigacion Historica (ESP ISSN 0210-6272) **4136**
Cuadernos de Japon *see* Japan Echo **4184**
• Cuadernos de Jazz (ESP ISSN 1134-7457) **6560**
Cuadernos de la Academia (ESP ISSN 1138-2562) **6495**
Cuadernos de la S I E C A *see* Secretaria Permanente del Tratado General de Integracion Economica Centroamericana. Cuadernos **1582**
Cuadernos de Lazarillo (ESP ISSN 1134-5292) **5109**
Cuadernos de Lenguas Modernas (ARG ISSN 1515-1107) **5109**
Cuadernos de Linguistica (MEX) **5109**
Cuadernos de Linguistica de la Universidad de Puerto Rico *see* U P R Working Papers in Linguistics **5190**
Cuadernos de Literatura (COL ISSN 0122-8102) **5281**
Cuadernos de Literatura Infantil y Juvenil *see* C L I J **7557**
Cuadernos de Literatura Inglesa y Norteamericana (ARG ISSN 0328-9184) **5281**
Cuadernos de Maipu (ARG ISSN 0326-7105) **3791**
• Cuadernos de Medicina Forense (ESP ISSN 1135-7606) **5912**
Cuadernos de Medicina Psicosomatica *see* Cuadernos de Medicina Psicosomatica y Psiquiatria **6134**
• Cuadernos de Medicina Psicosomatica y Psiquiatria (ESP ISSN 1695-4246) **6134**
Cuadernos de Medicina Reproductiva (ESP ISSN 1135-0970) **5601**
Cuadernos de Musica (MEX ISSN 0185-1896) **6560**
Cuadernos de Musica, Artes Visuales y Artes Escenicas (COL ISSN 1794-6670) **6560**
Cuadernos de Musica Iberoamericana (ESP ISSN 1136-5536) **6560**
Cuadernos de Negocios Internacionales e Integracion (URY ISSN 0797-8960) **1560**
• Cuadernos de Neurologia (CHL) **6134**
▼ • Cuadernos de Neuropsicologia (CHL ISSN 0718-4123) **7350**
Cuadernos de Nuestra America (CUB ISSN 1016-9504) **7127**
➤ Cuadernos de Nutricion (MEX ISSN 0186-3274) **6657**
Cuadernos de Ocio (COL ISSN 0123-5761) **6984**
• Cuadernos de Pedagogia (ESP ISSN 0210-0630) **2840**
• Cuadernos de Pedagogia (CD-ROM Edition) (ESP ISSN 1137-4241) **2840**
Cuadernos de Pensamiento (ESP ISSN 0214-0284) **6912**

Title

10170 CUADERNOS DE PENSAMIENTO NAVAL ULRICH'S PERIODICALS

Cuadernos de Pensamiento Naval *see* Revista General de Marina **6443**
Cuadernos de Pensamiento Politico (ESP ISSN 1696-8441) **7127**
Cuadernos de Poblacion (MEX ISSN 0187-6171) **7281**
Cuadernos de Politica Criminal (ESP ISSN 0210-4059) **2650**
† Cuadernos de Prehistoria (ESP ISSN 0211-3228) **8947**
Cuadernos de Prehistoria y Arqueologia (ESP ISSN 0211-1608) **388**
Cuadernos de Psicoanalisis (MEX ISSN 0186-9345) **7350**
Cuadernos de Psicologia (COL ISSN 0120-4653) **7350**
Cuadernos de Psicologia/Quaderns de Psicologia (ESP ISSN 0211-3481) **7350**
Cuadernos de Psicologia del Deporte (ESP ISSN 1578-8423) **7350**
• Cuadernos de Psiquiatria Comunitaria (ESP ISSN 1578-9594) **6134**
Cuadernos de Psiquiatria y Psicoterapia del Nino y del Adolescente (ESP ISSN 1575-5967) **6134**
Cuadernos de Realidades Sociales (ESP ISSN 0302-7724) **8096**
Cuadernos de Recienvenido (BRA ISSN 1413-8255) **5281**
• Cuadernos de Relaciones Laborales (ESP ISSN 1131-8635) **1674**
Cuadernos de Restauracion (ESP ISSN 1138-1299) **484**
Cuadernos de Seguridad (ESP ISSN 1698-4269) **2676**
• Cuadernos de Sociomuseologia (PRT ISSN 1646-3714) **6522**
Cuadernos de Teatro Clasico (ESP ISSN 0214-1388) **5281**
• Cuadernos de Teologia (ARG ISSN 0326-6737) **7636**
Cuadernos de Terapia Familiar (ESP ISSN 0213-7941) **7350**
† Cuadernos de Toponimia (ESP ISSN 1130-8079) **8947**
Cuadernos de Trabajo de Flora Micologica Iberica (ESP ISSN 1132-0605) **785**
Cuadernos de Trabajo de Historia (ESP) **4213**
• Cuadernos de Trabajo Social (ESP ISSN 0214-0314) **8036**
Cuadernos de Turismo (ESP ISSN 1139-7861) **8696**
Cuadernos de Urbanismo (MEX ISSN 0188-2171) **4408**
Cuadernos del Archivo Municipal de Ceuta *see* Archivo Municipal de Ceuta. Cuadernos **8931**
Cuadernos del Aula del Cine (ESP) **6495**
Cuadernos del C E A G R O *see* C E A G R O. Cuadernos **98**
Cuadernos del C E D L A (Centrum voor Studie en Documentatie van Latijns Amerika) (NLD ISSN 1872-9967) **4290**
Cuadernos del C I M B A G E *see* C I M B A G E. Cuadernos **1731**
Cuadernos del C I P E (Centro de Investigaciones y Proyectos Especiales) (COL ISSN 1794-7715) **7957**
Cuadernos del C U R I H A M *see* C U R I H A M. Cuadernos **2793**
Cuadernos del Camino (ARG) **5212**
Cuadernos del Cendes *see* Universidad Central de Venezuela. Centro de Estudios del Desarrollo. Cuadernos del C E N D E S **8145**
➤ Cuadernos del CIDS (COL) **8036**
▼ Cuadernos del Habitat (COL ISSN 2011-365X) **4408**
Cuadernos del I E O (Instituto de Europa Oriental) (ESP) **547**
Cuadernos del Minotauro (ESP ISSN 1699-6321) **4448**
Cuadernos del P I E A *see* Revista Interdisciplinaria de Estudios Agrarios **151**
Cuadernos del Sur (ARG ISSN 0070-1769) **4448**
Cuadernos del Sur (MEX ISSN 1405-1966) **7957**
Cuadernos del Suroeste (ESP ISSN 1133-0783) **6523**
Cuadernos del Taller de Folklore (PER) **3616**
Cuadernos del Tercer Mundo *see* Cadernos do Terceiro Mundo **7112**
Cuadernos Derecho Penitenciario (ESP) **4888**
➤ Cuadernos Dieciochistas (ESP ISSN 1576-7914) **4448**
Cuadernos Docentes (ARG ISSN 0326-2766) **4003**
Cuadernos Economicos Trimestrales (CUB) **1539**
Cuadernos Editur (ESP ISSN 1137-4683) **8696**
• Cuadernos Electronicos de Filosofia del Derecho (ESP ISSN 1138-9877) **4653**
Cuadernos Estadisticos de la C E P A L (CHL ISSN 0251-9437) **8365**
➤ Cuadernos Europeos de Deusto (ESP ISSN 1130-8354) **4448**
• Cuadernos Geograficos (ESP ISSN 0210-5462) **4003**
Cuadernos Grial (ESP ISSN 1697-980X) **4448**
Cuadernos Guadalimar (ESP ISSN 0210-3974) **484**
• Cuadernos Hispanoamericanos (ESP ISSN 0011-250X) **5212**
Cuadernos I N T E M A C (ESP ISSN 1133-9365) **8419**
• Cuadernos Interculturales (CHL ISSN 0718-0586) **8096**
Cuadernos Interdisciplinarios de Estudios Literarios *see* Journal of Interdisciplinary Literary Studies **5315**
• Cuadernos Internacionales de Tecnologia para el Desarrollo Humano (ESP ISSN 1697-820X) **8419**
➤ Cuadernos Latinoamericanos (VEN ISSN 1315-4176) **7957**
† Cuadernos Marisqueros. Publicacion Tecnica (ESP ISSN 0213-7208) **8947**
• Cuadernos Medico Sociales (CHL ISSN 0716-1336) **5602**
Cuadernos Mexicanos de Zoologia (MEX ISSN 0188-9508) **939**
➤ Cuadernos Mujer Salud (CHL) **8845**
Cuadernos N T (ESP) **4448**
Cuadernos Nuevo Sur (VEN ISSN 0798-5126) **1476**
Cuadernos para el Estudio de la Estetica y la Literatura (ARG) **5281**
• Cuadernos para Investigacion de la Literatura Hispanica (ESP ISSN 0210-0061) **5281**
Cuadernos para la Historia de la Evangelizacion en America Latina (PER ISSN 1012-2737) **4290**
• Cuadernos Para la Otra Historia (ARG ISSN 0329-9368) **4137**
Cuadernos Politecnicas (MEX) **8096**
Cuadernos Prehispanicos (ESP ISSN 0302-6728) **4290**
• Cuadernos Profesionales (ARG ISSN 1666-6739) **1089**
• Cuadernos Republicanos (ESP ISSN 1131-7744) **7432**
Cuadernos Salmantinos de Filosofia (ESP ISSN 0210-4857) **6913**
Cuadernos Simancas de Investigaciones Historicas: Monografias (ESP) **4213**
Cuadernos sobre Manara (ESP ISSN 1699-180X) **7636**
➤ Cuadernos sobre Vico (ESP ISSN 1130-7498) **6913**
Cuadernos Sociologicos Vascos *see* Soziologiazko Euskal Koadermoak **8141**
• Cuadernos Templarios (ARG ISSN 1666-1222) **3763**
Cuadernos Trimestrales de Poesia (PER ISSN 0011-2550) **5420**
Cuadernos Universitarios (NIC ISSN 0011-2569) **5281**
Cuadernos Valencianos de Historia de la Medicina y de la Ciencia. Serie D. Revista *see* Cronos **5601**
Cuadernos Venezolanos de Filosofia *see* Logoi **6932**
• La Cuarta Cibernetica (CHL) **3821**
• El Cuarto del Quenepon (PRI) **484**
• Cuarto Oscuro (MEX ISSN 1605-4903) **6966**
• Cuarto Poder (MEX ISSN 1605-0355) **1476**
• Cuarto Poder de Michoacan (MEX ISSN 1605-4873) **1476**
• Cuaternario y Geomorfologia (ESP ISSN 0214-1744) **2730**
Cub Magazine (IND) **2184**
Cub T N G (The Next Generation) (GBR) **2280**
Cuba (CAN ISSN 1912-4694) **8696**
Cuba Azucar (CUB ISSN 0590-2916) **227**
• Cuba Bladet (DNK ISSN 0900-8365) **4290**
Cuba. Centro de Informacion y Documentacion Agropecuario. Boletin de Resenas. Serie: Arroz (CUB ISSN 0138-838X) **271**
Cuba. Centro de Informacion y Documentacion Agropecuario. Boletin de Resenas. Serie: Avicultura (CUB) **284**
Cuba. Centro de Informacion y Documentacion Agropecuario. Boletin de Resenas. Serie: Cafe y Cacao (CUB ISSN 0138-8436) **227**
Cuba. Centro de Informacion y Documentacion Agropecuario. Boletin de Resenas. Serie: Citricos (CUB ISSN 0138-8339) **227**
Cuba. Centro de Informacion y Documentacion Agropecuario. Boletin de Resenas. Serie: Economia Agropecuaria (CUB) **196**
Cuba. Centro de Informacion y Documentacion Agropecuario. Boletin de Resenas. Serie: Forestales (CUB ISSN 0138-7782) **3687**
Cuba. Centro de Informacion y Documentacion Agropecuario. Boletin de Resenas. Serie: Ganado Porcino (CUB ISSN 1011-968X) **284**
Cuba. Centro de Informacion y Documentacion Agropecuario. Boletin de Resenas. Serie: Hortalizas, Papas, Granos y Fibras (CUB ISSN 0138-8231) **227**
Cuba. Centro de Informacion y Documentacion Agropecuario. Boletin de Resenas. Serie: Mecanizacion de la Agricultura (CUB ISSN 1016-9512) **210**
Cuba. Centro de Informacion y Documentacion Agropecuario. Boletin de Resenas. Serie: Mejoramiento Animal (CUB) **939**
Cuba. Centro de Informacion y Documentacion Agropecuario. Boletin de Resenas. Serie: Pastos y Forrajes (CUB ISSN 0138-7839) **271**
Cuba. Centro de Informacion y Documentacion Agropecuario. Boletin de Resenas. Serie: Riego y Drenaje (CUB ISSN 0138-788X) **227**
Cuba. Centro de Informacion y Documentacion Agropecuario. Boletin de Resenas. Serie: Suelos y Agroquimica (CUB ISSN 0138-7936) **227**
Cuba. Comite Estatal de Estadisticas. Revista Estadistica (CUB) **8365**
Cuba: Economia Planificada (CUB ISSN 0864-1420) **1718**
Cuba Economica (CUB ISSN 0864-4675) **1089**
Cuba en Cifras (CUB) **1222**
Cuba en el Ballet (CUB ISSN 0864-1307) **2683**
Cuba Foreign Trade (CUB ISSN 0864-3857) **1401**
Cuba Handbook (GBR ISSN 1369-1422) **8696**
Cuba Human Rights Monitor (USA ISSN 1082-2534) **7205**
Cuba Independiente y Democratica *see* C I D **7111**
• Cuba Internacional (CUB ISSN 0011-2593) **7229**
• Cub@: Medio Ambiente y Desarrollo (CUB ISSN 1683-8904) **3412**
Cuba. Ministerio de Comunicaciones. Centro de Informacion de Comunicaciones. Comunicaciones (CUB) **2318**
Cuba. Ministerio de Cultura. Cartelera (CUB ISSN 1013-6207) **7127**
Cuba. Ministerio de Cultura. Tablas (CUB ISSN 0864-1374) **3831**
Cuba. Ministerio de Educacion Superior. Centro Agricola (CUB ISSN 0253-5785) **103**
• Cuba. Ministerio de Educacion Superior. Centro Azucar (CUB ISSN 0253-5777) **227**
Cuba. Ministerio de la Agricultura. Centro de Informacion y Divulgacion Agropecuario. Noticiero Agropecuario. Suplemento (CUB) **103**
Cuba. Ministerio de la Agricultura. Centro de Informacion y Documentacion Agropecuario. Extranjeras (CUB) **103**
Cuba. Ministerio de la Agricultura. Centro de Informacion y Documentacion Agropecuario. Noticiero Agropecuario (CUB) **103**
Cuba. Ministerio de la Agricultura. Centro de Informacion y Documentacion Agropecuario. Noticiero Agropecuario. Suplemento Agrometeorologico (CUB ISSN 0138-6190) **6351**
• Cuba. Ministerio de la Industria Ligera. Info (CUB ISSN 1682-2722) **3186**
• Cuba. Ministerio de Salud Publica. Direccion Nacional de Estadisticas. Anuario Estadistico (CUB ISSN 1561-4425) **5743**
• Cuba. Ministerio de Salud Publica. Unidad de Analisis y Tendencias en Salud. Reporte Semanal (CUB ISSN 1028-4354) **5602**
Cuba. Ministerio del Azucar. Instituto de Investigaciones de la Cana de Azucar. Boletin (CUB) **227**
Cuba. Ministerio del Comercio Exterior. Boletin Semanal de Precios de los Alimentos (CUB) **1560**
Cuba. Ministerio del Comercio Exterior. Reporte Mensual del Azucar (CUB) **3669**
Cuba. Ministerio del Comercio Exterior. Reporte Semanal del Azucar (CUB) **1560**
Cuba News (GRD) **3831**
Cuba Noticias Turisticas (CUB) **8696**
Cuba. Oficina Cubana de la Propiedad Industrial. Boletin Oficial (CUB ISSN 1028-1452) **6748**
▼ Cuba Plus (CAN ISSN 1911-4133) **8696**
Cuba: Political Executions and Human Rights (USA ISSN 1045-4098) **7205**
Cuba Quarterly Economic Report (CUB ISSN 0138-7766) **1222**
Cuba Rebelde Digital *see* Juventud Rebelde **2157**
Cuba Socialista (CUB ISSN 0011-2623) **5213**
Cuba Survey (USA) **7205**
• Cuba Update (USA ISSN 0196-0830) **7229**
Cubabladet *see* Cuba Bladet **4290**
• CubAhora (CUB ISSN 1605-0207) **3831**
• Cubalex (CUB ISSN 1028-8988) **4653**
• ➤ Cuban Affairs (USA ISSN 1931-6011) **3529**
Cuban American National Foundation News *see* C A N F News **7203**
Cuban Economy *see* Economia Cubana **1479**
➤ Cuban Journal of Agricultural Science (CUB ISSN 0864-0408) **103**
• Cuban Studies/Estudios Cubanos (USA ISSN 0361-4441) **4290**
• CubaNews (USA ISSN 1073-7715) **1089**
Cubase (GBR) **2495**
Cubatabaco (CUB ISSN 0138-7456) **8486**
Cubatravel Magazine (USA ISSN 1542-1538) **8696**
Cube (GBR ISSN 1475-1399) **2475**
Cube (USA) **5441**
Cube Solutions (GBR) **2475**
➤ Cubo (CHL ISSN 0716-7776) **5481**
Cubs Vine Line (USA ISSN 1047-3084) **8226**
Cucafera (ESP ISSN 1133-7222) **2184**
† Cucina (Milan) (ITA ISSN 1827-7438) **8947**
Cucina Bella e Buona (ITA ISSN 1125-1344) **4555**
▼ Cucina che Passione (ITA ISSN 1971-8616) **4355**
† • Cucina Creativa (ITA ISSN 1591-1160) **8947**
† La Cucina Deliziosa (ITA ISSN 1827-8485) **8947**
† Cucina Dolci (ITA ISSN 1827-7446) **8947**
Cucina e Tradizioni del Piemonte (ITA ISSN 1824-5994) **4355**
† Cucina & Vini (ITA ISSN 1128-5486) **8947**
• La Cucina Italiana (ITA ISSN 1121-1504) **4355**
La Cucina Italiana (NLD ISSN 1572-025X) **4355**
• La Cucina Italiana (USA ISSN 1090-4484) **4355**
• Cucina Light (ITA ISSN 1824-5749) **4355**
Cucina Moderna (ITA ISSN 1124-7134) **4355**
Cucina Moderna Oro (ITA ISSN 1126-6953) **4355**
Cucina Moderna Serie d'Oro *see* Cucina Moderna Oro **4355**
Cucina Naturale (ITA ISSN 1120-2009) **4355**
• Cucina Naturale (Milano) (ITA ISSN 1592-3568) **3632**
Cucina No Problem (ITA ISSN 1720-7088) **4355**
† Cucina Popolare Italiana (ITA ISSN 1723-4026) **8947**
▼ Cucina Regionale di Mare (ITA ISSN 1971-9094) **4355**
† Cucina Vegetariana (ITA ISSN 1825-9316) **8947**
Cucinare Bene (ITA ISSN 1126-3350) **4355**
Cucine International (ITA ISSN 1720-8025) **4536**
Cucurbit Genetics Cooperative. Report (USA ISSN 1064-5594) **227**
Cuddles (USA) **6288**
Cue Sheet (USA ISSN 0888-9015) **6560**
Cue Up! (USA) **3055**
Cuenca (ESP ISSN 1130-8133) **7490**
Cuenca Agraria (ESP) **103**
La Cuenta (USA) **1286**
Cuenta Que Te Cuento (CRI) **2184**
• Cuenta y Razon (ESP ISSN 1889-1489) **8096**
Cuenta y Razon del Pensamiento Actual *see* Cuenta y Razon **8096**
† Cuentas de las Administraciones Publicas de Madrid (ESP ISSN 1577-855X) **8947**
Cuentas Economicas del Sector Agrario *see* Nekazal Sektorearen Ekonomi Kontuak **204**
• Cuentas Financieras de la Economia Espanola (ESP ISSN 0212-9779) **1476**
Cuentas Nacionales de Chile (CHL ISSN 0716-2383) **1334**
Cuentas Nacionales Oferta y Demanda Globales (ARG ISSN 0328-8951) **1476**
• Cuentas Patrimoniales del Sector de Sociedades no Financieras de la Comunidad de Madrid (ESP ISSN 1579-346X) **1286**
Cuentistas Rosarinos (ARG ISSN 1666-292X) **2976**
El Cuento (MEX ISSN 0185-2477) **3908**
• El Cuento en Red (MEX ISSN 1527-2958) **5281**
Cuentos en Espanol/Short Stories in Spanish (USA ISSN 0164-0143) **5109**
Cuerpo (USA ISSN 1554-3358) **3529**
Cuerpo Positivo *see* Body Positive **5810**
Cuerpomente (ESP ISSN 1130-4421) **6984**
• Cuestion (MEX) **3908**
Cuestion de Estado (PER) **7127**
Cuestiones de Fisioterapia (ESP ISSN 1135-8599) **6108**
Cuestiones de la Economia Planificado (CUB) **1539**
Cuestiones de Sociologia (ARG ISSN 1668-1584) **8097**
Cuestiones Economicas (ECU ISSN 0252-8673) **1334**
Cuestiones Pedagogicas (ESP ISSN 0213-1269) **3055**
➤ Cuestiones Politicas (VEN ISSN 0798-1406) **7127**
Cuestiones Teologicas y Filosoficas (COL ISSN 0120-131X) **7636**
Cuget Liber/Free Thinking (ROM) **3932**
Cuicuilco (MEX ISSN 0185-1659) **334**
• ➤ Cuihua Xuebao/Journal of Catalysis (CHN ISSN 0253-9837) **2115**
Le Cuir Paris (FRA ISSN 0011-2690) **4973**
Cuir Underground (USA) **7943**
Cuisine *see* Coup de Pouce Cuisine **3632**
Cuisine (NZL ISSN 0113-1206) **4355**
Cuisine Actuelle (FRA ISSN 0989-3091) **4355**
Cuisine at Home (USA ISSN 1537-8225) **4355**
▼ Cuisine by Cyril Lignac (FRA ISSN 1954-1732) **4355**
Cuisine Collective Magazine (FRA ISSN 0985-7303) **4384**
Cuisine Concept *see* Cuisine et Salle de Bains Concept **1000**
Cuisine Contemporaine (FRA ISSN 1950-0262) **4355**
† Cuisine Creative (FRA ISSN 1760-0057) **8947**
▼ Cuisine & Jeux (FRA ISSN 1957-617X) **4355**
Cuisine et Salle de Bains Concept (FRA ISSN 1774-1319) **1000**
† Cuisine et Terroirs (FRA ISSN 1620-1566) **8947**
Cuisine et Vins de France (FRA ISSN 0337-8810) **3632**
Cuisine Gourmande *see* Prima Cuisine Gourmande **3660**
Cuisine Magazine (FRA ISSN 1761-4694) **4355**
Cuisine Revue (FRA ISSN 1635-1207) **4355**
▼ Cuisine Tendances (FRA ISSN 1960-8470) **1000**
Cuisine Tours Magazine (USA) **4384**
Cuisiner au Jour le Jour (FRA ISSN 1777-8840) **4355**
▼ Cuisiner Special Desserts (FRA ISSN 1961-3709) **4355**
Cuisines et Bains *see* Cuisines & Bains Confort Magazine **1000**
Cuisines & Bains Confort Magazine (FRA ISSN 1286-9007) **1000**
Cuisines et Salles de Bains (CAN) **4536**
Cuisines Vegetariennes du Monde *see* Recettes Vegetariennes du Monde **4366**
▼ Cuisinez Comme un Chef (FRA ISSN 1955-9402) **4355**
Le Cuisinier (FRA ISSN 1259-346X) **4384**
† Cuisinons Sante (FRA ISSN 1957-4622) **8947**
Cuivre Canadien *see* Canadian Copper **6308**
Cuiyuan/Green Garden Literary Magazine (CHN ISSN 1005-5282) **5281**
Cuizine Magazine *see* Fervor Magazine **3975**
Cukiernictwo i Piekarstwo (POL ISSN 1643-9988) **3673**
Cukoripar (HUN ISSN 0011-2720) **3632**
Cukurova Universitesi Tip Fakultesi Dergisi (TUR ISSN 0250-5150) **5602**
Cul Sport (IRL ISSN 1649-0266) **8226**
Culfordian (GBR) **2280**
† Culinair Jaarboek (NLD ISSN 1574-3918) **8947**
Culinaire Kalender (NLD ISSN 1574-5058) **4355**
Culinaria Passe Bem (BRA ISSN 1676-7691) **4355**
Culinaria Passe Bem Especial (BRA ISSN 1676-7705) **4355**

Title

➤ Current Issues in Catholic Higher Education (USA) **2976**
• Current Issues in Comparative Education (CISE) (USA ISSN 1523-1615) **2840**
• ➤ Current Issues in Criminal Justice (AUS ISSN 1034-5329) **2650**
Current Issues in Economics (GBR ISSN 0961-0340) **1089**
• Current Issues in Economics and Finance (USA) **1089**
• ➤ Current Issues in Education (USA ISSN 1099-839X) **2840**
Current Issues in Electronic Modeling (NLD ISSN 1381-3951) **3091**
Current Issues in Food Safety *see* Food Safety Handbook **3641**
Current Issues in Intestinal Microbiology *see* Current Issues in Molecular Biology **883**
• Current Issues in Language Planning (GBR ISSN 1466-4208) **5110**
• ➤ Current Issues in Middle Level Education (USA ISSN 1059-7107) **2840**
• ➤ Current Issues in Molecular Biology (GBR ISSN 1467-3037) **883**
➤ Current Issues in Production Ecology (NLD ISSN 0929-7006) **8419**
Current Issues in Real Estate Finance & Economics (NLD) **7588**
Current Issues in the Family Series (USA) **4356**
Current Issues in the Financial Services Industries (USA) **1287**
• ➤ Current Issues in Tourism (GBR ISSN 1368-3500) **8696**
Current Issues on Consumer Law *see* Ajankohtaista Kuluttajaoikeudesta **2634**
Current Issues: Reference Shelf Plus (USA) **7957**
Current Japanese Periodicals for (Year) (JPN) **7578**
Current Labour Law (ZAF) **1674**
• Current Law Index (USA ISSN 0196-1780) **4822**
Current Law Monthly Digest (GBR ISSN 0968-3194) **4653**
Current Law Service (ZAF) **4653**
Current Law Week (Print) *see* Current Law Weekly (Online) **4653**
• Current Law Weekly (Online) (GBR ISSN 2040-8730) **4653**
Current Leasing Law and Techniques: Forms (USA) **7588**
• Current Legal Forms with Tax Analysis (USA) **1918**
• Current Legal Information (GBR ISSN 1361-6196) **4653**
Current Legal Issues (GBR) **4654**
• Current Legal Problems (GBR ISSN 0070-1998) **4654**
Current Legal Sociology (ESP ISSN 1017-4559) **4822**
Current Literature on Science of Science (IND ISSN 0379-4504) **7936**
➤ Current Mammalogy (USA ISSN 0899-577X) **939**
Current Management Literature (IND ISSN 0376-7604) **1223**
➤ Current Management of Pain (NLD ISSN 0923-2354) **6134**
Current Market Perspectives *see* Standard & Poor's Trendline Current Market Perspectives **1653**
• Current Mathematical Publications (USA ISSN 0361-4794) **5548**
• ➤ Current Medical Diagnosis and Treatment (USA ISSN 0092-8682) **5602**
• ➤ Current Medical Imaging Reviews (NLD ISSN 1573-4056) **6194**
Current Medical Issues (IND ISSN 0973-4651) **5602**
• ➤ Current Medical Literature. Breast Cancer (GBR ISSN 0956-6511) **6017**
Current Medical Literature. Cardiologia *see* Current Medical Literature. Cardiology **5784**
• ➤ Current Medical Literature. Cardiology (GBR ISSN 1354-0122) **5784**
• ➤ Current Medical Literature. Colorectal Cancer (GBR ISSN 1364-4831) **6017**
Current Medical Literature. Dermatologie *see* Current Medical Literature. Dermatology **5873**
• ➤ Current Medical Literature. Dermatology (GBR ISSN 1361-4215) **5873**
• ➤ Current Medical Literature. Diabetes (GBR ISSN 0265-797X) **5885**
Current Medical Literature. G H and Growth Factors *see* Current Medical Literature. Growth, Growth Hormone, & Metabolism **5885**
• ➤ Current Medical Literature. Gastroenterology (GBR ISSN 0263-2659) **5922**
• ➤ Current Medical Literature. Growth, Growth Hormone, & Metabolism (GBR ISSN 1750-8673) **5885**
• ➤ Current Medical Literature. Gynaecology and Obstetrics (GBR ISSN 1356-742X) **5988**
Current Medical Literature. Kardiologie *see* Current Medical Literature. Cardiology **5784**
• ➤ Current Medical Literature. Leukaemia and Lymphoma (GBR ISSN 0969-7063) **6017**
• ➤ Current Medical Literature. Lung Cancer (GBR ISSN 1469-6886) **5743**
• ➤ Current Medical Literature. Lysosomal Storage Disease (GBR ISSN 1473-0901) **5885**
Current Medical Literature. Lysosomal Storage Disorders *see* Current Medical Literature. Lysosomal Storage Disease **5885**
Current Medical Literature: Medecine Respiratoire *see* Current Medical Literature. Respiratory Medicine **6213**
• ➤ Current Medical Literature. Neurology (GBR ISSN 1356-6237) **6134**
• ➤ Current Medical Literature. Ophthalmology (GBR ISSN 0963-0112) **5743**
• ➤ Current Medical Literature. Paediatrics (GBR ISSN 0951-9610) **6090**
➤ Current Medical Literature. Pain Medicine (GBR ISSN 1751-3804) **6058**
Current Medical Literature. Perspectives in Depression (GBR ISSN 1361-634X) **5743**
Current Medical Literature. Psychiatrie (French Edition) *see* Current Medical Literature. Psychiatry **6134**
Current Medical Literature. Psychiatrie (German Edition) *see* Current Medical Literature. Psychiatry **6134**
• ➤ Current Medical Literature. Psychiatry (GBR ISSN 0957-770X) **6134**
• ➤ Current Medical Literature. Respiratory Medicine (GBR ISSN 1361-6706) **6213**
• ➤ Current Medical Literature. Rheumatology (GBR ISSN 0261-3360) **6223**
• ➤ Current Medical Literature. Urology (GBR ISSN 1357-1532) **6266**
• ➤ Current Medical Research and Opinion (GBR ISSN 0300-7995) **5602**
Current Medical Research and Opinion. Supplement *see* Current Medical Research and Opinion **5602**
• ➤ Current Medicinal Chemistry (NLD ISSN 0929-8673) **2059**
Current Medicinal Chemistry. Anti-Cancer Agents *see* Anti-Cancer Agents in Medicinal Chemistry **6008**
Current Medicinal Chemistry. Anti-Infective Agents *see* Anti-Infective Agents in Medicinal Chemistry **6821**
Current Medicinal Chemistry. Anti-Inflammatory & Anti-Allergy Agents *see* Anti-Inflammatory & Anti-Allergy Agents in Medicinal Chemistry **6821**
Current Medicinal Chemistry. Cardiovascular & Hematological Agents *see* Cardiovascular & Hematological Agents in Current Medicinal **5780**
Current Medicinal Chemistry. Central Nervous System Agents *see* Central Nervous System Agents in Medicinal Chemistry **6130**
Current Medicinal Chemistry. Immunology, Endocrine and Metabolic Agents *see* Immunology, Endocrine and Metabolic Agents in Medicinal Chemistry **5894**
Current Medicine *see* Gendai Igaku **5618**
Current Methods (USA ISSN 1541-7689) **3264**
• Current Methods in Inorganic Chemistry (NLD ISSN 1873-0418) **2115**
• ➤ Current Microbiology (USA ISSN 0343-8651) **883**
• ➤ Current Molecular Medicine (NLD ISSN 1566-5240) **884**
▼ • ➤ Current Molecular Pharmacology (NLD ISSN 1874-4672) **6831**
Current Municipal Problems (USA ISSN 0011-3727) **7491**
• ➤ Current Musicology (USA ISSN 0011-3735) **6560**
• ➤ Current Nanoscience (NLD ISSN 1573-4137) **3186**
Current Nematology (IND ISSN 0971-0116) **939**
Current Neurologic Drugs (USA ISSN 1083-9429) **6831**
• Current Neurology and Neuroscience Reports (USA ISSN 1528-4042) **6134**
• Current Neuropharmacology (NLD ISSN 1570-159X) **6134**
• Current Neurovascular Research (NLD ISSN 1567-2026) **6134**
Current News (USA) **3156**
• Current News in Medicine (AUT ISSN 1608-2222) **5602**
• Current Nursing in Geriatric Care (USA ISSN 1932-8710) **4043**
• ➤ Current Nutrition & Food Science (NLD ISSN 1573-4013) **6657**
Current Objectives of Postgraduate American Studies *see* C O P A S **5102**
Current Obstetrics & Gynaecology *see* Obstetrics, Gynecology and Reproductive Medicine **6001**
† Current Obstetrics and Gynaecology (Italian Edition) (ITA ISSN 1123-8178) **8947**
Current Occupational & Environmental Medicine (USA) **6675**
• ➤ Current Oncology (Toronto) (CAN ISSN 1198-0052) **6018**
• ➤ Current Oncology Reports (Online) (USA ISSN 1534-6269) **6018**
• Current Opinion in Allergy and Clinical Immunology (USA ISSN 1528-4050) **5757**
Current Opinion in Allergy and Clinical Immunology (Ceske a Slovenske Vyd.) (CZE ISSN 1214-472X) **5757**
• Current Opinion in Anaesthesiology (USA ISSN 0952-7907) **5771**
Current Opinion in Anesthesiology, with Evaluated MEDLINE *see* Current Opinion in Anaesthesiology **5771**
• ➤ Current Opinion in Biotechnology (GBR ISSN 0958-1669) **762**
• ➤ Current Opinion in Cardiology (USA ISSN 0268-4705) **5784**
Current Opinion in Cardiology, with Evaluated MEDLINE *see* Current Opinion in Cardiology **5784**
• ➤ Current Opinion in Cell Biology (GBR ISSN 0955-0674) **831**
• ➤ Current Opinion in Chemical Biology (GBR ISSN 1367-5931) **730**
• ➤ Current Opinion in Clinical Experimental Research (AUT ISSN 1563-311X) **5905**
• ➤ Current Opinion in Clinical Nutrition and Metabolic Care (USA ISSN 1363-1950) **6657**
• ➤ Current Opinion in Colloid & Interface Science (GBR ISSN 1359-0294) **2134**
• Current Opinion in Critical Care (USA ISSN 1070-5295) **6058**
• Current Opinion in Drug Discovery & Development (GBR ISSN 1367-6733) **6831**
Current Opinion in Endocrinology & Diabetes *see* Current Opinion in Endocrinology, Diabetes and Obesity **5885**
Current opinion in Endocrinology & Diabetes, with Evaluated MEDLINE *see* Current Opinion in Endocrinology, Diabetes and Obesity **5885**
• ➤ Current Opinion in Endocrinology, Diabetes and Obesity (GBR ISSN 1752-296X) **5885**
▼ ➤ Current Opinion in Environmental Sustainability (GBR ISSN 1877-3435) **3413**
➤ Current Opinion in European Medicine (AUT ISSN 1607-6524) **5602**
• ➤ Current Opinion in Gastroenterology (USA ISSN 0267-1379) **5922**
Current Opinion in Gastroenterology, with Evaluated MEDLINE *see* Current Opinion in Gastroenterology **5922**
• ➤ Current Opinion in Genetics & Development (GBR ISSN 0959-437X) **865**
• Current Opinion in Hematology (USA ISSN 1065-6251) **5935**
• Current Opinion in HIV and AIDS (USA ISSN 1746-630X) **5812**
• ➤ Current Opinion in Immunology (GBR ISSN 0952-7915) **5743**
• ➤ Current Opinion in Infectious Diseases (USA ISSN 0951-7375) **5812**
† • Current Opinion in Internal Medicine (USA ISSN 1535-5942) **8947**
• Current Opinion in Investigational Drugs (GBR ISSN 1472-4472) **6831**
• ➤ Current Opinion in Lipidology (GBR ISSN 0957-9672) **5784**
Current Opinion in Lipidology, with Evaluated MEDLINE *see* Current Opinion in Lipidology **5784**
• ➤ Current Opinion in Microbiology (GBR ISSN 1369-5274) **884**
• Current Opinion in Molecular Therapeutics (GBR ISSN 1464-8431) **6831**
• ➤ Current Opinion in Nephrology & Hypertension (GBR ISSN 1062-4821) **6266**
Current Opinion in Nephrology & Hypertension, with Evaluated MEDLINE *see* Current Opinion in Nephrology & Hypertension **6266**
• ➤ Current Opinion in Neurobiology (GBR ISSN 0959-4388) **6134**
• ➤ Current Opinion in Neurology (USA ISSN 1350-7540) **6135**
• ➤ Current Opinion in Obstetrics & Gynecology (USA ISSN 1040-872X) **5988**
Current Opinion in Obstetrics & Gynecology, with Evaluated MEDLINE *see* Current Opinion in Obstetrics & Gynecology **5988**
▼ Current Opinion in Oncology (CZE ISSN 1801-2671) **6018**
• Current Opinion in Oncology (USA ISSN 1040-8746) **6018**
• Current Opinion in Ophthalmology (USA ISSN 1040-8738) **6041**
Current Opinion in Ophthalmology, with Evaluated MEDLINE *see* Current Opinion in Ophthalmology **6041**
• Current Opinion in Organ Transplantation (USA ISSN 1087-2418) **5602**
Current Opinion in Orthopaedics *see* Current Orthopaedic Practice **6058**
• Current Opinion in Otolaryngology & Head and Neck Surgery (USA ISSN 1068-9508) **6079**
Current Opinion in Otolaryngology & Head and Neck Surgery, with Evaluated MEDLINE *see* Current Opinion in Otolaryngology & Head and Neck Surgery **6079**
• Current Opinion in Pediatrics (USA ISSN 1040-8703) **6090**
Current Opinion in Pediatrics. Current World Literature *see* Current Opinion in Pediatrics **6090**
Current Opinion in Pediatrics, with Evaluated MEDLINE *see* Current Opinion in Pediatrics **6090**
• Current Opinion in Pharmacology (GBR ISSN 1471-4892) **6831**
• ➤ Current Opinion in Plant Biology (GBR ISSN 1369-5266) **785**
• ➤ Current Opinion in Psychiatry (USA ISSN 0951-7367) **6135**
Current Opinion in Psychiatry, with Evaluated MEDLINE *see* Current Opinion in Psychiatry **6135**
• Current Opinion in Pulmonary Medicine (USA ISSN 1070-5287) **6213**
Current Opinion in Pulmonary Medicine (Ceske a Slovenske Vyd.) (CZE ISSN 1214-4738) **6213**
• Current Opinion in Rheumatology (USA ISSN 1040-8711) **6223**
Current Opinion in Rheumatology, with Evaluated MEDLINE *see* Current Opinion in Rheumatology **6223**
• ➤ Current Opinion in Solid State & Materials Science (GBR ISSN 1359-0286) **3298**
• ➤ Current Opinion in Structural Biology (GBR ISSN 0959-440X) **730**
▼ • Current Opinion in Supportive and Palliative Care (GBR ISSN 1751-4258) **5602**
• Current Opinion in Urology (USA ISSN 0963-0643) **6267**
• ➤ Current Organic Chemistry (NLD ISSN 1385-2728) **2122**
• Current Organic Synthesis (NLD ISSN 1570-1794) **2122**
➤ Current Ornithology (USA ISSN 0742-390X) **906**
• ➤ Current Orthopaedic Practice (USA ISSN 1940-7041) **6058**
Current Orthopaedics *see* Orthopaedics and Trauma **6069**
• ➤ Current Osteoporosis Reports (Online) (USA ISSN 1544-2241) **6058**
Current Paediatrics *see* Paediatrics and Child Health **6098**
• Current Pain and Headache Reports (USA ISSN 1531-3433) **6135**
Current Pain Reports (USA ISSN 1548-596X) **6135**
Current Papers in Physics (GBR ISSN 0011-3786) **7048**
Current Pediatric Diagnosis and Treatment (USA ISSN 0093-8556) **6090**
• ➤ Current Pediatric Research (IND ISSN 0971-9032) **6091**
• ➤ Current Pediatric Reviews (NLD ISSN 1573-3963) **6091**
Current Pediatric Therapy (USA ISSN 1934-5119) **6091**
• Current Perspectives in Healthcare Computing (Year) (GBR) **5830**
• Current Perspectives in Social Theory (USA ISSN 0278-1204) **8097**
• ➤ Current Pharmaceutical Analysis (NLD ISSN 1573-4129) **6831**
• ➤ Current Pharmaceutical Biotechnology (NLD ISSN 1389-2010) **763**
• ➤ Current Pharmaceutical Design (NLD ISSN 1381-6128) **6831**
Current Pharmacogenomics *see* Current Pharmacogenomics and Personalized Medicine **6831**
• ➤ Current Pharmacogenomics and Personalized Medicine (NLD ISSN 1875-6921) **6831**
• Current Physics Index (USA ISSN 0098-9819) **7048**
➤ Current Physics - Sources and Comments (NLD ISSN 0922-503X) **7009**
➤ Current Plant Science and Biotechnology in Agriculture (NLD ISSN 0924-1949) **763**
▼ Current Politics and Economics of Africa (USA ISSN 1098-4070) **7127**
Current Politics and Economics of Asia *see* Current Politics and Economics of Asia and China **7127**
• Current Politics and Economics of Asia and China (USA) **7127**
Current Politics and Economics of China *see* Current Politics and Economics of Asia and China **7127**
• ➤ Current Politics and Economics of Europe (USA ISSN 1057-2309) **7127**
• Current Politics and Economics of Russia, Eastern and Central Europe (USA ISSN 1524-1688) **7229**
▼ • Current Politics and Economics of South and Central America (USA ISSN 1935-2549) **7127**
▼ Current Politics and Economics of the Caucasus Region (USA ISSN 1937-5492) **7127**
▼ Current Politics and Economics of the Middle East (USA ISSN 1939-5809) **7127**
Current Politics and Economics of the United States *see* Current Politics and Economics of the United States, Canada and Mexico **7127**
• Current Politics and Economics of the United States, Canada and Mexico (USA) **7127**
† • Current Population Reports: Black Population in the United States (USA) **8947**
• Current Population Reports. Consumer Income. Income, Poverty, and Health Insurance Coverage in the United States (USA) **8036**
† • Current Population Reports. Hispanic Population in the United States (USA) **8947**
• Current Population Reports. Population Characteristics. Educational Attainment in the United States (USA) **2840**
• Current Population Reports. Population Characteristics. Fertility of American Women (USA ISSN 0272-6505) **7281**
Current Population Reports: Population Characteristics. Geographical Mobility *see* U.S. Bureau of the Census. Current Population Reports. Population Characteristics. Geographical Mobility **8995**
† • Current Population Reports. Population Characteristics. Residents of Farms and Rural Areas (USA) **8947**
• Current Population Reports. Population Characteristics. School Enrollment in the United States (USA) **7305**
Current Population Reports. Population Characteristics. School Enrollment in the United States. Social and Economic Characteristics of Students *see* Current Population Reports. Population Characteristics. School Enrollment in the United States **7305**

Title

10174 CURRENT POPULATION REPORTS: POPULATION CHARACTERISTICS ULRICH'S PERIODICALS

Current Population Reports: Population Characteristics. Social and Economic Characteristics of the Black Population *see* Current Population Reports: Black Population in the United States **8947**
• Current Population Reports. Population Characteristics. The Foreign-Born Population in the United States (USA) **7281**
• Current Population Reports. Population Characteristics. Voting and Registration in the Election (USA) **7127**
• Current Population Reports: Series P-20, Population Characteristics (Print) (USA ISSN 0363-6836) **7305**
• Current Population Reports. Series P-23, Special Studies (USA ISSN 0498-8485) **7305**
• Current Population Reports: Series P-25, Population Estimates and Projections (USA ISSN 0738-453X) **7305**
• Current Population Reports: Series P-60, Consumer Income (USA ISSN 0730-4803) **7305**
• Current Population Reports. Series P-70, Household Economic Studies (USA ISSN 0886-5698) **7305**
Current Population Survey. Geographical Mobility *see* Geographical Mobility **7307**
➤ Current Practice (CAN ISSN 1499-2329) **5839**
➤ Current Practice. Dental Hygiene (CAN ISSN 1499-8033) **5839**
• Current Practice Guidelines in Primary Care (Year) (USA ISSN 1559-4319) **5602**
Current Practice of Medicine (USA ISSN 1079-980X) **5602**
Current Practise of Medicine (GBR) **5602**
Current Primary Care Reports. Arthritis and Pain (USA ISSN 1550-6851) **6223**
Current Primary Care Reports. Cardiovascular Risk Factors (USA ISSN 1550-686X) **5603**
Current Primate References (USA ISSN 0590-4102) **715**
• ➤ Current Problems in Cancer (USA ISSN 0147-0272) **6018**
Current Problems in Cancer (Spanish Edition) (ESP ISSN 1137-196X) **6018**
• ➤ Current Problems in Cardiology (USA ISSN 0146-2806) **5785**
Current Problems in Cardiology (Spanish Edition) (ESP ISSN 1133-1992) **5785**
• ➤ Current Problems in Dermatology (CHE ISSN 1421-5721) **5874**
• ➤ Current Problems in Diagnostic Radiology (USA ISSN 0363-0188) **6194**
Current Problems in Epilepsy (FRA ISSN 0950-4591) **6135**
• ➤ Current Problems in Pediatric and Adolescent Health Care (USA ISSN 1538-5442) **6091**
• Current Problems in Pharmacovigilance (GBR) **6831**
• ➤ Current Problems in Surgery (USA ISSN 0011-3840) **6241**
Current Procedural Terminology *see* C P T **5590**
• Current Prostate Reports (USA ISSN 1544-1865) **6267**
• ➤ Current Protein and Peptide Science (NLD ISSN 1389-2037) **730**
• Current Proteomics (NLD ISSN 1570-1646) **730**
• Current Protocols in Bioinformatics (USA) **825**
• Current Protocols in Cell Biology (USA ISSN 1934-2500) **831**
• Current Protocols in Cytometry (USA) **831**
• Current Protocols in Human Genetics (USA) **865**
• Current Protocols in Immunology (USA ISSN 1934-3671) **5757**
• Current Protocols in Magnetic Resonance Imaging (USA) **6195**
• Current Protocols in Microbiology (USA) **884**
• Current Protocols in Molecular Biology (USA) **730**
• Current Protocols in Neuroscience (USA) **6135**
• Current Protocols in Nucleic Acid Chemistry (USA) **730**
• Current Protocols in Pharmacology (USA ISSN 1934-8282) **6831**
• Current Protocols in Protein Science (USA ISSN 1934-3655) **730**
▼ • Current Protocols in Stem Cell Biology (USA ISSN 1941-7322) **831**
• Current Protocols in Toxicology (USA) **730**
Current Psychiatry (USA ISSN 1537-8276) **6135**
• Current Psychiatry in Primary Care (USA ISSN 1556-3162) **6135**
• Current Psychiatry Reports (USA ISSN 1523-3812) **6135**
• ➤ Current Psychiatry Reviews (NLD ISSN 1573-4005) **6135**
• ➤ Current Psychology (New York) (USA ISSN 1046-1310) **7350**
• ➤ Current Psychology Letters (Online) (FRA ISSN 1379-6100) **7350**
Current Psychology Letters (Print) *see* Current Psychology Letters (Online) **7350**
Current Psychology of Cognition *see* Cahiers de Psychologie Cognitive **7343**
• Current Psychosis & Therapeutics Reports (USA ISSN 1545-8083) **6135**
Current Publications in Legal and Related Fields (USA ISSN 0011-3859) **4822**
▼ • ➤ Current Radiopharmaceuticals (NLD ISSN 1874-4710) **6832**
▼ • ➤ Current Research in Bacteriology (PAK ISSN 1994-5426) **884**
• Current Research in Britain. Social Sciences (GBR ISSN 0267-1964) **8020**
• ➤ Current Research in Earth Sciences (USA) **2705**
Current Research in French Studies at Universities in the United Kingdom and Ireland (GBR ISSN 1350-9209) **5201**
Current Research in Iranian Universities and Research Centers *see* Chikidah-i Tazahha-yi Tahqiq dar Danishgahha va Marakiz-i Tahqiqati Iran **7845**
Current Research in Physical Sciences in Finland (FIN ISSN 0788-6012) **8168**
• ➤ Current Research in Social Psychology (USA ISSN 1088-7423) **7350**
Current Research in the Geological Sciences in Canada (CAN ISSN 0526-4553) **6461**
➤ Current Research in the Pleistocene (USA ISSN 8755-898X) **389**
Current Research in the Semantics - Pragmatics Interface (GBR ISSN 1566-5895) **5110**
• Current Research in Tuberculosis (USA ISSN 1819-3366) **6213**
Current Research on Occupations and Professions (USA ISSN 1043-3287) **8097**
Current Research Reporter (IND ISSN 0256-6885) **104**
• ➤ Current Respiratory Medicine Reviews (NLD ISSN 1573-398X) **6213**
Current Review of Allergic Diseases *see* Current Review of Rhinitis **5757**
Current Review of Asthma (USA ISSN 1542-1007) **6213**
Current Review of Cerebrovascular Disease (USA ISSN 1068-2252) **6135**
Current Review of Interventional Cardiology (USA ISSN 1068-4115) **5785**
Current Review of M R I (Magnetic Resonance Imaging) (USA ISSN 1072-8392) **5603**
Current Review of Rhinitis (USA ISSN 1535-6582) **5757**
Current Review of Sports Medicine (USA ISSN 1069-5842) **6229**
Current Reviews for Nurse Anesthetists (USA ISSN 0164-310X) **5771**
Current Reviews for PeriAnesthesia Nurses (USA ISSN 1940-2953) **5771**
▼ • Current Reviews in Musculoskeletal Medicine (USA ISSN 1935-973X) **6058**
Current Rheumatology Diagnosis and Treatment (USA ISSN 1547-8998) **6223**
• ➤ Current Rheumatology Reports (Online) (USA ISSN 1534-6307) **6223**
• ➤ Current Rheumatology Reviews (NLD ISSN 1573-3971) **6223**
The Current Sauce (USA) **2280**
• ➤ Current Science (IND ISSN 0011-3891) **7849**
• Current Science (USA ISSN 0011-3905) **2184**
Current Science (Large Print) (USA) **2184**
• Current Science and Technology Research in Japan (JPN ISSN 0288-6022) **7936**
Current Sentencing Practice (GBR) **4888**
Current Sentencing Practice News (GBR ISSN 0964-8461) **4888**
Current Separations *see* Current Separations and Drug Development **2099**
➤ Current Separations and Drug Development (USA) **2099**
† • Current Sexual Health Reports (USA ISSN 1548-3584) **8947**
• ➤ Current Signal Transduction Therapy (NLD ISSN 1574-3624) **5812**
• Current Social Issues (AUS ISSN 1037-728X) **7958**
• ➤ Current Sociology/Sociologie Contemporaine (GBR ISSN 0011-3921) **8098**
• Current Sports Medicine Reports (USA ISSN 1537-890X) **6229**
The Current State of the Ugandan Economy *see* State of the Uganda Economy **1519**
Current Statistical Survey *see* Statisticheskoe Obozrenie **1268**
• Current Statistics (CAN) **1223**
➤ Current Status of Clinical Cardiology (NLD) **5785**
• ➤ Current Stem Cell Research & Therapy (NLD ISSN 1574-888X) **730**
• ➤ Current Studies in Hematology and Blood Transfusion (CHE ISSN 0258-0330) **5936**
• ➤ Current Studies in Librarianship (USA ISSN 0742-8227) **5004**
Current Studies in Linguistics (USA) **5110**
Current Surgery *see* Journal of Surgical Education **6250**
• Current Surgical Diagnosis & Treatment (USA ISSN 0894-2277) **6241**
• Current Surgical Therapy (USA ISSN 0835-3689) **6241**
Current Sweden (SWE ISSN 1101-6345) **3955**
➤ Current Swedish Archaeology (SWE ISSN 1102-7355) **389**
Current Swedish Periodicals *see* Svensk Periodicafoerteckning. (Online) **636**
Current Tax Reporter (IND ISSN 0971-0043) **1919**
Current Techniques in Arthroscopy (USA ISSN 1068-4107) **6058**
Current Techniques in Interventional Radiology (USA ISSN 1068-3879) **6195**
Current Techniques in Neurosurgery (USA ISSN 1068-4093) **6135**
Current Techniques in Ophthalmic Laser Surgery (USA ISSN 1078-7283) **6041**
Current Techniques in Surgical Profiles (USA ISSN 1540-7004) **6241**
• ➤ Current Therapeutic Research (USA ISSN 0011-393X) **6832**
Current Therapy *see* Karento Terapi **5656**
Current Therapy in Allergy, Immunology, and Rheumatology (USA ISSN 0831-5027) **5757**
Current Therapy in Neurologic Disease (USA ISSN 0891-7922) **6135**
Current Therapy in Vascular Surgery (USA ISSN 1051-8452) **6241**
Current Titles in Electrochemistry (IND ISSN 0300-4376) **2094**
Current Topics in Acoustical Research (IND ISSN 0972-4818) **7009**
Current Topics in Analytical Chemistry (IND ISSN 0972-4451) **2099**
Current Topics in Biochemical Research (IND ISSN 0972-4583) **730**
• Current Topics in Biophysics (POL ISSN 1232-9630) **753**
➤ Current Topics in Biotechnology (IND ISSN 0972-821X) **763**
Current Topics in Catalysis (IND ISSN 0972-4508) **2134**
• ➤ Current Topics in Cellular Regulation (USA ISSN 0070-2137) **667**
Current Topics in Colloid & Interface Science (IND ISSN 0972-4494) **2134**
Current Topics in Crystal Growth Research (IND ISSN 0972-4834) **2110**
• ➤ Current Topics in Developmental Biology (USA ISSN 0070-2153) **667**
Current Topics in Electrochemistry (IND ISSN 0972-4443) **2112**
† ➤ Current Topics in General Thoracic Surgery (NLD ISSN 1063-2581) **8947**
Current Topics in Management (USA ISSN 1529-2088) **1737**
• ➤ Current Topics in Medicinal Chemistry (NLD ISSN 1568-0266) **5603**
• ➤ Current Topics in Membranes (USA ISSN 1063-5823) **831**
➤ Current Topics in Microbiology and Immunology (USA ISSN 0070-217X) **884**
➤ Current Topics in Nutraceutical Research (USA ISSN 1540-7535) **6657**
Current Topics in Photovoltaics (USA ISSN 1053-122X) **3126**
Current Topics in Phytochemistry (IND ISSN 0972-4796) **785**
† Current Topics in Radiography (GBR) **8947**
Current Topics in Steroid Research (IND ISSN 0972-4788) **2122**
Current Topics in Transport (GBR ISSN 1464-1380) **8630**
➤ Current Topics in Veterinary Medicine and Animal Science (NLD ISSN 0166-2333) **8796**
Current Topics in Wetland Biogeochemistry (USA ISSN 1076-4674) **2730**
• Current Treatment Options in Cardiovascular Medicine (USA ISSN 1092-8464) **5785**
Current Treatment Options in Gastroenterology (Online) *see* Current Treatment Options in Gastroenterology (Print) **8947**
† • Current Treatment Options in Gastroenterology (Print) (USA ISSN 1092-8472) **8947**
• Current Treatment Options in Neurology (USA ISSN 1092-8480) **6135**
• Current Treatment Options in Oncology (USA ISSN 1527-2729) **6018**
Current Treaty Index (USA ISSN 0731-8189) **4822**
• Current Trends in Islamist Ideology (USA ISSN 1940-834X) **7710**
Current Trends in Life Sciences (IND ISSN 0378-7540) **667**
Current Trends in Polymer Science (IND ISSN 0972-446X) **2122**
Current Trends in Psychoanalysis and Psychotherapy (USA ISSN 1554-1940) **7350**
Current Trends in Virology (IND ISSN 0972-4591) **884**
▼ • Current Urology (CHE ISSN 1661-7649) **6267**
• Current Urology Reports (USA ISSN 1527-2737) **6267**
• Current Vascular Pharmacology (NLD ISSN 1570-1611) **5785**
• ➤ Current Women's Health Reviews (NLD ISSN 1573-4048) **5989**
Current World Leaders Almanac (USA ISSN 0192-6802) **7229**
➤ Current Writing (ZAF ISSN 1013-929X) **5281**
• ➤ Current Zoology (CHN ISSN 1674-5507) **939**
Currently: Ontario Museum News (CAN ISSN 0384-9627) **6523**
Currents (CAN ISSN 0715-7045) **3529**
• Currents (NZL ISSN 1177-6315) **1593**
Currents (PHL) **7229**
• ➤ Currents (SWE ISSN 1403-6304) **104**
Currents *see* Colorado Language Arts Society. Currents **5107**
• ➤ Currents (Calgary) (CAN ISSN 1499-6073) **8036**
Currents (Chicago) (USA) **4372**
Currents (Colorado Springs) (USA) **8275**
• Currents (Columbia) (USA) **2803**
• Currents (Los Alamos) (USA ISSN 1946-2503) **7849**
Currents (New York, NY) (USA) **8696**
Currents (Ship Bottom) (USA) **4977**
Currents (Washington) (USA ISSN 0748-478X) **2976**
Currents & Eddies (USA) **2608**
• Currents in Biblical Research (GBR ISSN 1476-993X) **7636**
Currents in Comparative Romance Languages and Literatures (USA ISSN 0893-5963) **5281**
• Currents in Electronic Literacy (USA ISSN 1524-6493) **2415**
• Currents in Emergency Cardiovascular Care (USA ISSN 1054-917X) **5785**
▼ • ➤ Currents in Teaching and Learning (USA ISSN 1945-3043) **3056**
• Currents in Theology and Mission (USA ISSN 0098-2113) **7753**
Currents: International Trade Law Journal (USA ISSN 1534-388X) **4922**
Currents: News of the Utah State Historical Society (USA) **4290**
➤ Currents of Encounter (NLD ISSN 0923-6201) **7636**
Curricula in the Atmospheric, Oceanic, Hydrologic and Related Sciences (USA) **2803**
• ➤ Curriculo sem Fronteiras (PRT ISSN 1645-1384) **2976**
Curriculum Administrator *see* District Administration **3058**
➤ Curriculum and Teaching (AUS ISSN 0726-416X) **3056**
• Curriculum and Teaching Dialogue (USA ISSN 1538-750X) **3056**
Curriculum Briefing (GBR ISSN 1477-7975) **3056**
Curriculum Close-Up *see* Insight (London, 2006) **4082**
Curriculum Connections *see* School Library Journal **5046**
Curriculum Council - Syllabus Manual Year 11 and Year 12 Subjects (AUS) **2840**
➤ Curriculum Forum/Kecheng Luntan (HKG ISSN 1024-0276) **2976**
• Curriculum Handbook for Parents. Grade 1 (CAN ISSN 1483-1694) **3056**
• Curriculum Handbook for Parents. Grade 1 (Catholic School Version) (CAN ISSN 1483-1783) **3056**
Curriculum Handbook for Parents. Grade 2 (CAN ISSN 1483-1686) **3056**
• Curriculum Handbook for Parents. Grade 2 (Catholic School Version) (CAN ISSN 1483-1775) **3056**
• Curriculum Handbook for Parents. Grade 3 (CAN ISSN 1483-1678) **3056**
• Curriculum Handbook for Parents. Grade 3 (Catholic School Version) (CAN ISSN 1483-1767) **3056**
• Curriculum Handbook for Parents. Grade 4 (CAN ISSN 1483-166X) **3056**
• Curriculum Handbook for Parents. Grade 4 (Catholic School Version) (CAN ISSN 1483-1759) **3056**
• Curriculum Handbook for Parents. Grade 5 (CAN ISSN 1483-1651) **3056**
• Curriculum Handbook for Parents. Grade 5 (Catholic School Version) (CAN ISSN 1483-1740) **3056**
• Curriculum Handbook for Parents. Grade 6 (CAN ISSN 1483-1643) **3056**
• Curriculum Handbook for Parents. Grade 6 (Catholic School Version) (CAN ISSN 1483-1732) **3056**
• Curriculum Handbook for Parents. Grade 7 (CAN ISSN 1483-1635) **3056**
• Curriculum Handbook for Parents. Grade 7 (Catholic School Version) (CAN ISSN 1483-1724) **3056**
• Curriculum Handbook for Parents. Grade 8 (CAN ISSN 1483-1627) **3056**
• Curriculum Handbook for Parents. Grade 8 (Catholic School Version) (CAN ISSN 1483-1716) **3056**
• Curriculum Handbook for Parents. Grade 9 (CAN ISSN 1483-1619) **3056**
• Curriculum Handbook for Parents. Grade 9 (Catholic School Version) (CAN ISSN 1483-1708) **3056**
• Curriculum Handbook for Parents. Kindergarten (CAN) **3056**
• Curriculum Handbook for Parents. Kindergarten (Catholic School Version) (CAN) **3056**
• Curriculum Handbook for Parents. Senior High School (CAN ISSN 1487-203X) **3057**
• Curriculum Handbook for Parents. Senior High School (Catholic School Version) (CAN ISSN 1481-9406) **3057**
• Curriculum Handbooks for Parents. French Immersion (CAN) **3057**
• ➤ Curriculum Inquiry (USA ISSN 0362-6784) **3057**
• ➤ Curriculum Journal (GBR ISSN 0958-5176) **3057**
Curriculum Management Update (GBR ISSN 1468-9553) **3057**
• Curriculum Matters (AUS ISSN 1832-4495) **2840**
Curriculum Matters (NZL ISSN 1177-1828) **3057**
Curriculum Perspectives (Journal Edition) (AUS ISSN 0159-7868) **2976**
Curriculum Perspectives (Newsletter Edition) (AUS) **3057**
• Curriculum Review (USA ISSN 0147-2453) **3057**
Curriculum, Teaching Materials, and Method *see* Kecheng - Jiaocai - Jiaofa **3069**
† Curriculum Update/Korero Marautanga (NZL ISSN 1174-9385) **8947**
Curriculum Vitae News *see* C V News **22**
Curry County Echoes (USA) **4290**
Cursillo (AUT ISSN 0011-4057) **7753**
• Cursiv (DNK ISSN 1901-8878) **3057**

DIRECTORY 2010 CYPRUS. OFFICIAL GAZETTE 10175

Curso de Direito. Revista (BRA ISSN 0102-1397) **4654**
▼ Curso de Memorizacao (BRA ISSN 1981-3252) **7351**
• Cursor (NLD ISSN 0920-6876) **2280**
Cursos de Derecho Internacional y Relaciones Internacionales de Vitoria-Gasteiz (ESP ISSN 1577-533X) **4922**
• ➤ Cursus (CAN ISSN 1201-7302) **5004**
Cursus (DEU) **5281**
Cursus Belastingrecht. Vennootschapsbelasting (Studenten Editie) (NLD ISSN 1873-3611) **1919**
Curt Magazin Nuernberg (DEU) **3846**
Curtains (GBR) **5281**
• CurtainUp (USA) **8468**
Curtido y Calzado (GBR ISSN 1473-3811) **4973**
Curtin University of Technology. Department of Environmental Biology. Bulletin (AUS) **667**
▼ • Curtin University of Technology. School of Economics and Finance. Area of Research Excellence in Oil & Gas Management. Working Paper Series (AUS ISSN 1834-6766) **6766**
• Curtin University of Technology. School of Economics and Finance. Working Paper Series (AUS ISSN 1035-901X) **1089**
Curtin University of Technology. School of Marketing. Working Paper Series *see* Marketing Insights **1832**
CurtinCalls (USA ISSN 1534-2778) **5956**
Curtis (GBR) **4865**
• ➤ Curtis's Botanical Magazine (GBR ISSN 1355-4905) **785**
CurtoCo's Digital T V & Sound (USA ISSN 1557-315X) **2379**
• Curve (USA ISSN 1087-867X) **4372**
The Cusan (USA) **7636**
Cusanus-Gesellschaft. Buchreihe (DEU ISSN 0070-2234) **7636**
Cusanus-Gesellschaft. Kleine Schriften (DEU ISSN 0590-4501) **7794**
Cusanus-Gesellschaft. Mitteilungen und Forschungsbeitraege (DEU ISSN 0590-451X) **7794**
Cushitic Language Studies *see* Kuschitische Sprachstudien **5138**
Cushman Foundation for Foraminiferal Research. Special Publication (USA ISSN 0070-2242) **6724**
Cuspide (ARG ISSN 1668-1541) **5839**
• Custom Builder (USA ISSN 1931-4329) **1000**
Custom Builders and Their Communities (USA) **7588**
Custom Car (GBR ISSN 0591-2334) **8576**
• Custom Classic Trucks (USA ISSN 1544-4813) **8670**
Custom Electronics Pro *see* C E Pro **3090**
Custom Electronics Pro Showroom *see* C E Pro Showroom **3090**
Custom Electronics Professional *see* C E Pro **3090**
† Custom Gift Retailer (USA ISSN 1544-0745) **8947**
• Custom Home (USA ISSN 1055-3479) **1000**
Custom Home Outdoors (USA) **1001**
Custom Kitchens & Baths (USA ISSN 1550-4611) **4555**
Custom Kitchens and Baths *see* Custom Kitchens & Baths **4555**
Custom Machines *see* Kustom **8260**
Custom P C (GBR ISSN 1740-7443) **2575**
Custom P C South Africa (ZAF ISSN 1818-3689) **2575**
Custom Planes *see* Private Pilot **8550**
▼ Custom Rigs (USA ISSN 1941-4595) **8670**
† Custom Rodder (USA ISSN 1076-3678) **8947**
Custom Storage (USA ISSN 1935-1666) **4536**
Custom Tailor (USA ISSN 0011-412X) **2246**
Custom Tailors and Designers Association of America. Magazine (USA) **2253**
• Custom Toll and Contract Services Directory (GBR ISSN 1362-4563) **1981**
• Custom Wood Homes (USA ISSN 1943-6610) **1001**
• Custom Woodworking Business (USA ISSN 1058-403X) **1050**
Custombike (DEU ISSN 1614-9378) **8256**
Customer Assistance Handbook (USA ISSN 1089-5663) **6417**
Customer Chat (AUS ISSN 1834-2450) **4408**
• Customer Circular (AUS ISSN 1832-8016) **6675**
• The Customer Communicator (USA ISSN 0145-8450) **1859**
Customer Connect (SGP) **2367**
• Customer Contact Management Report (USA ISSN 1536-5336) **1737**
➤ The Customer Driven Quality Journal (USA) **1089**
• Customer Inter@ction Solutions (USA ISSN 1533-3078) **2318**
• Customer Loyalty Today (USA ISSN 1352-0415) **1812**
Customer Magazines & Contract Publishing Market Assessment *see* Key Note Market Assessment. Customer Magazines & Contract Publishing **1891**
Customer Management *see* Customer Strategy **1859**
• Customer Management Insight (Online) (USA) **1812**
† • Customer Management Insight (Print) (USA) **8947**
Customer Relations Management Buyer *see* C R M Buyer **1078**
Customer Relationship Management (GBR ISSN 1466-8866) **1089**
Customer Relationship Management *see* C R M Magazine **1731**
Customer Relationship Management eWeekly *see* C R M eWeekly **1731**
Customer Relationship Management Expert *see* C R M Expert **1078**
Customer Relationship Management Market Assessment *see* Key Note Market Assessment. Customer Relationship Management **1891**
Customer Relationship Management Profi *see* C R M Profi **1731**
Customer Relationship Technology in Finance (GBR ISSN 1464-9454) **1334**
• The Customer Report (GBR) **1812**
Customer Satisfaction in Tourism and Hospitality *see* Journal of Vacation Marketing **8726**
➤ Customer Service (USA) **1089**
The Customer Service Advantage (USA ISSN 1092-8014) **1812**
Customer Service News (GBR ISSN 1366-9680) **1416**
• Customer Service Newsletter (USA ISSN 0145-8442) **1737**
Customer Service Representative Advisor *see* The C S R Advisor **4497**
Customer Strategy (GBR ISSN 1757-3688) **1859**
CustomerBase *see* C C M. Customer Contact Magazine **1809**
• Customers First (USA ISSN 1525-1047) **1737**
Customers First in Hospitality (USA ISSN 1527-6554) **1737**
• CustomRetailer (USA ISSN 1541-7735) **1089**
• Customretailer E-Weekly (USA ISSN 1930-5850) **1089**
Customs and Border Protection Today *see* Frontline **1566**
Customs and International Trade Bar Association Newsletter *see* C I T B A Newsletter **4919**
• Customs Bulletin and Decisions (USA ISSN 0162-6442) **1919**
Customs Imports and Exports Journal (PAK ISSN 0011-4154) **1560**
Customs Law Handbook (USA) **4922**
Customs Officer's Association of Australia. Fourth Division. Customs Officer (AUS) **1560**
Customs Record (USA ISSN 1063-7443) **1919**
Customs Regulations of the United States (USA) **7432**
• Customs Release (NZL ISSN 0114-0213) **1560**
Customs Tariff Schedules (JPN) **1919**
• Custos e @gronegocio Online (BRA ISSN 1808-2882) **104**
Cut (DNK ISSN 1901-1601) **6495**
▼ Cut! (NLD ISSN 1877-105X) **6495**
The Cut (NZL ISSN 1175-0545) **8226**
• Cut (Online) (DEU) **4573**
Cut (Print) *see* Cut (Online) **4573**
Cut & Dog (DEU) **6806**
The Cut Flowers and Foliage Market in the E U (NLD) **3755**
• ➤ Cutaneous and Ocular Toxicology (USA ISSN 1556-9527) **6832**
➤ CutBank (USA ISSN 0734-9963) **5420**
Cuthbert Asset & Project Finance *see* Asset & Project Finance **1309**
• Cutis (USA ISSN 0011-4162) **5874**
• Cutter Benchmark Review (USA ISSN 1542-0906) **2519**
• Cutter I T Journal (Information Technology) (USA ISSN 1522-7383) **2506**
Cutthroat (USA ISSN 1555-6042) **5281**
• The Cutting Edge (GBR ISSN 1740-0376) **1050**
Cutting Edge (GBR) **587**
Cutting Edge (New York) (USA) **6638**
Cutting Edge (Washington) (USA) **5451**
Cutting Horse Chatter (USA ISSN 1081-0951) **8290**
• Cutting Tool Engineering (USA ISSN 0011-4189) **5451**
Cuvantul Liber (ROM) **3932**
Cuyahoga Review (USA ISSN 0737-139X) **5281**
Cuyo (ARG ISSN 1514-9935) **6913**
• CxO (Chief Executive Officer) (CAN ISSN 1703-0080) **2496**
• Cyber Aspect (GBR) **2553**
▼ Cyber Autodefinidos (ARG ISSN 1851-3859) **8168**
Cyber-Crime Fighter (USA ISSN 1540-0891) **2512**
Cyber Gra (POL ISSN 1895-3638) **2475**
• Cyber Humanitatis (CHL ISSN 0717-2869) **4449**
• Cyber Insurance News (USA) **4500**
Cyber Mycha (POL ISSN 1640-307X) **2184**
Cyber Mycha Extra *see* Cyber Mycha **2184**
• Cyber Oasis (USA) **5213**
• Cyber Periodico 2000 (MEX ISSN 1605-4911) **2977**
• Cyber-Plantsman (USA) **3727**
Cyber-Psychos A O D (USA ISSN 1084-3752) **5441**
• Cyber Review (CAN) **2553**
Cyber Review of Modern Historiography *see* C R O M O H S **4133**
Cyber Star *see* CyberStar **6741**
Cyber Therapy (USA ISSN 1545-8644) **6135**
• Cyber Times (GBR) **8419**
• ➤ Cyberbanking & Law (DEU ISSN 1681-9616) **1334**
• Cybercrime Law Report (USA ISSN 1535-5853) **4844**
• CyberGEO/European Journal of Geography (FRA ISSN 1278-3366) **4003**
• Cyberjournal for Pentecostal-Charismatic Research (USA ISSN 1523-1216) **7636**
• Cyberkids (USA) **2184**
• CyberKino (DEU ISSN 1438-0218) **6495**
• CyberKoch (DEU ISSN 1438-0102) **4356**
Cybermax *see* Max **3897**
• ➤ Cybermetrics (ESP ISSN 1137-5019) **5004**
Cybernetica (BEL ISSN 0011-4227) **2526**
Cybernetics *see* Kybernetika **5508**
Cybernetics *see* Saibanetikusu **8624**
• ➤ Cybernetics & Human Knowing (GBR ISSN 0907-0877) **2526**
Cybernetics and Information Technologies (BGR ISSN 1311-9702) **2526**
• ➤ Cybernetics and Systems (USA ISSN 0196-9722) **2526**
• ➤ Cybernetics and Systems Analysis (USA ISSN 1060-0396) **2526**
Cybernetics: Documents de Travail *see* Cybernetics: Works in Progress **2526**
Cybernetics: Works in Progress/Cybernetics: Documents de Travail (BEL) **2526**
• Cyberonline (USA) **2553**
▼ • Cyberpsychology (CZE ISSN 1802-7962) **7351**
• ➤ CyberPsychology & Behavior (USA ISSN 1094-9313) **2554**
• Cyberpulse (CAN) **2554**
Cyberskeptic's guide *see* The CyberSkeptic's Guide to Internet Research **2554**
The CyberSkeptic's Guide to Internet Research (USA ISSN 1085-2417) **2554**
• Cybersocket Web Magazine (USA) **4372**
Cyberspace Infringement Litigation Reporter (USA) **2554**
• Cyberspace Lawyer (USA ISSN 1088-0593) **2554**
• CyberStar (THA) **6741**
• Cyberteens (USA) **2184**
• Cyberwest Magazine (USA) **8696**
• CyberWire Dispatch (USA) **2554**
➤ Cybium (FRA ISSN 0399-0974) **3589**
† • CYbiz (DEU ISSN 1439-6610) **8947**
Cybiz (POL ISSN 1642-8951) **1416**
• CYbiz.de (DEU ISSN 1439-538X) **1416**
• Cybrarians Journal (EGY ISSN 1687-2215) **5004**
Cycad Society Newsletter (USA) **785**
Cyclamen Journal (GBR ISSN 0143-3571) **3727**
Le Cycle (FRA ISSN 0184-1238) **8256**
Cycle (GBR) **8256**
Cycle 1 (CAN ISSN 0835-0612) **8256**
Cycle California (USA) **8256**
Cycle Canada (CAN ISSN 0319-2822) **8256**
• Cycle News (USA ISSN 1933-9720) **8257**
Cycle Projections (USA ISSN 1055-1700) **1334**
Cycle Sport (GBR ISSN 0969-2576) **8168**
Cycle Sport (American edition) *see* Cycle Sport America **8257**
Cycle Sport America (USA ISSN 1545-0538) **8257**
Cycle Sports (JPN) **8257**
• Cycle World (USA ISSN 0011-4286) **8257**
Cycle World's Motorcycle Travel and Adventure *see* Cycle World's Motorcycle Travel & Adventure **8257**
Cycle World's Motorcycle Travel & Adventure (USA ISSN 1534-5173) **8257**
Cycle World's Power & Performance Harley-Davidson (Year) Buyer's Guide (USA ISSN 1532-5067) **8257**
• Cyclic Defrost (AUS ISSN 1832-4835) **6560**
Cycling: B.C. News (CAN) **8257**
Cycling on One (USA ISSN 0000-0744) **8257**
Cycling Plus (GBR ISSN 0964-6868) **8257**
Cycling Today (GBR ISSN 1351-0142) **8257**
Cycling Utah (USA ISSN 1535-9069) **8257**
• Cycling Weekly (GBR ISSN 0951-5852) **8257**
Cyclists Touring Club Cycling Yearbook *see* C T C Cycling Yearbook **8256**
Cyclists' Yellow Pages (USA) **8257**
Cyclo Sante (FRA ISSN 1775-819X) **6229**
Cyclopedia Medical Dictionary *see* Taber's Cyclopedia Medical Dictionary **5719**
CycloSport (FRA ISSN 1779-1480) **8257**
Cyclotourisme (FRA ISSN 0981-101X) **8257**
▼ Cyclotourisme Sante (FRA ISSN 1957-2492) **6229**
Cyclotron Conference (Year). Proceedings *see* International Conference on Cyclotrons and Their Applications. Proceedings **3169**
Cyclotron Radioisotope Center Annual Report *see* C Y R I C Annual Report **6193**
Cyclotron Radioisotope Center News *see* C Y R I C News **3166**
• ➤ Cycnos (FRA ISSN 0992-1893) **5282**
Cyfeiriadur Mudiadau Gwirfoddol Yng Nghymru: Csysylltiadau Cenedlaethol *see* Directory of Voluntary Organisations in Wales: National Contacts **8037**
➤ Cyfrwng (GBR ISSN 1742-9234) **2318**
➤ Le Cygne (USA ISSN 1087-9501) **5282**
The Cygnet (USA ISSN 1936-7201) **5282**
Cygnus (IND) **5282**
• Cykelbranchen (DNK ISSN 0106-3529) **8257**
Cykelkalendern *see* Svenska Cykelfoerbundets Officiella Kalender **8269**
Cykeltidningen *see* Nya Cykeltidningen **8265**
† Cykle-Jul (DNK ISSN 0107-7805) **8947**
Cyklen (DNK ISSN 0109-4211) **8257**
Cykling (SWE ISSN 0280-3038) **8257**
Cyklister (DNK ISSN 0109-2790) **8257**
Y Cylchgrawn Efengylaidd (GBR ISSN 0143-0076) **7753**
Cylchgrawn Hanes Cymru *see* Welsh History Review **4166**
Cylchgrawn Llyfrgell Genedlaethol Cymru/National Library of Wales Journal (GBR ISSN 0011-4421) **5004**
Cylinder Head & Block Identification Guide (USA) **8576**
• Cymbiosis (USA ISSN 0895-6936) **6560**
Cymro Llundain/London Welshman (GBR ISSN 0024-6204) **5213**
Cymru (GBR) **7127**
Cyngor Gweithredu Gwirfoddol Cymru Cyfres. Adroddiadau *see* Wales Council for Voluntary Action. Report Series **8077**
Cyngor Gweithredu Gwirfoddol Cymru. Paparau Crynhoi *see* Wales Council for Voluntary Action. Briefing Paper **8077**
Cyperaceae Newsletter (GBR ISSN 0775-1400) **785**
Cyphers (IRL ISSN 1393-2985) **5213**
Cypress Basin Genealogical and Historical Society Reporter (USA) **3763**
• ➤ Cypriot Journal of Educational Sciences (TUR ISSN 1305-905X) **2840**
Cypriot Woman *see* Kypria **8870**
• Cypris (USA ISSN 0886-3806) **6724**
Cyprus American Archaeological Research Institute Monograph Series (CYP ISSN 1933-1924) **389**
Cyprus. Budget: Estimates of Revenue and Expenditure (CYP ISSN 0070-2323) **1919**
Cyprus Chamber of Commerce and Industry Directory (CYP ISSN 0070-2331) **1981**
Cyprus. Department of Antiquities. Annual Report (CYP ISSN 1010-1136) **389**
Cyprus. Department of Antiquities. Report (CYP ISSN 0070-2374) **389**
Cyprus. Department of Fisheries. Annual Report on the Department of Fisheries and the Cyprus Fisheries (CYP ISSN 0379-086X) **3589**
Cyprus. Department of Statistics and Research. Agricultural Statistics (CYP ISSN 0379-0924) **178**
Cyprus. Department of Statistics and Research. Census of Agriculture (CYP) **178**
Cyprus. Department of Statistics and Research. Census of Cottage Industry (CYP) **1223**
Cyprus. Department of Statistics and Research. Census of Industrial Production (CYP) **1223**
Cyprus. Department of Statistics and Research. Census of Poultry (CYP) **178**
Cyprus. Department of Statistics and Research. Census of Wholesale and Retail Trade (CYP) **1223**
Cyprus. Department of Statistics and Research. Construction and Housing Statistics (CYP) **1045**
Cyprus. Department of Statistics and Research. Criminal Statistics (CYP ISSN 0253-8695) **2674**
Cyprus. Department of Statistics and Research. Demographic Report (CYP ISSN 0590-4846) **7305**
Cyprus. Department of Statistics and Research. Demographic Survey (Years) (CYP) **7305**
Cyprus. Department of Statistics and Research. Economic Report (CYP ISSN 0070-2412) **1223**
Cyprus. Department of Statistics and Research. Education Statistics (CYP) **2931**
Cyprus. Department of Statistics and Research. Functions and Services (CYP) **7480**
Cyprus. Department of Statistics and Research. Household Income and Expenditure Survey (CYP) **1223**
Cyprus. Department of Statistics and Research. Imports and Exports Statistics (CYP ISSN 0253-858X) **1223**
Cyprus. Department of Statistics and Research. Industrial Statistics (CYP ISSN 1010-1160) **1223**
Cyprus. Department of Statistics and Research. Labour Statistics (CYP) **1223**
Cyprus. Department of Statistics and Research. Monthly Economic Indicators (CYP ISSN 0253-8555) **1476**
Cyprus. Department of Statistics and Research. Multi-Round Demographic Survey. Migration in Cyprus (CYP) **7305**
Cyprus. Department of Statistics and Research. Questionnaires for Censuses and Surveys (CYP) **8365**
Cyprus. Department of Statistics and Research. Statistical Abstract (CYP ISSN 0253-875X) **8020**
Cyprus. Department of Statistics and Research. Statistics of Imports and Exports (CYP ISSN 0070-2420) **1223**
Cyprus. Department of Statistics and Research. Tourism, Migration and Travel Statistics (CYP ISSN 0253-8709) **8778**
Cyprus Development Bank. Annual Report (CYP) **1334**
Cyprus Diplomatist (CYP ISSN 1015-2873) **7229**
Cyprus. Five Year Plans (CYP) **1476**
Cyprus. Geological Survey Department. Bulletin (CYP) **2705**
Cyprus. Geological Survey Department. Memoirs (CYP ISSN 0574-8259) **2705**
Cyprus International Institute of Management (C I I M) Management Review *see* C I I M Management Review **1731**
Cyprus. Ministry of Finance. Annual Report (CYP) **7432**
Cyprus. Ministry of Health. Annual Report (CYP) **7547**
Cyprus. Ministry of Labour and Social Insurance. Annual Report (CYP ISSN 0070-2390) **1674**
• Cyprus. Official Gazette (CYP) **3831**

Title

DIRECTORY 2010 D H LAWRENCE SOCIETY OF NORTH AMERICA. NEWSLETTER 10177

D & B Business Register. Munster see D & B Business Register. Munster, Connaught & Border Regions **1982**
D & B Business Register. Munster, Connaught & Border Regions (Dun & Bradstreet) (GBR ISSN 1740-6331) **1982**
D & B Business Register. Norfolk, Suffolk (Dun & Bradstreet) (GBR ISSN 1365-3350) **1982**
D & B Business Register. Northern Ireland (Dun & Bradstreet) (GBR ISSN 1466-8467) **1982**
D & B Business Register. Northumberland, Tyne & Wear, Cumbria, Isle of Man (Dun & Bradstreet) (GBR ISSN 1365-3482) **1982**
D & B Business Register. Nottinghamshire, Lincolnshire (Dun & Bradstreet) (GBR ISSN 1365-1870) **1982**
D & B Business Register. Oxfordshire, Berkshire, Wiltshire (Dun & Bradstreet) (GBR ISSN 1365-3377) **1982**
D & B Business Register. Scotland. North. Lothians, Fife, Tayside, Grampian, Central, Highlands & Islands see D & B Business Register. Edinburgh & North of Scotland **1982**
D & B Business Register. Scotland. South. Strathclyde, Borders, Dumfries & Galloway see D & B Business Register. Glasgow & South of Scotland **1982**
D & B Business Register. Shropshire, Hereford & Worcester, Gloucestershire (Dun & Bradstreet) (GBR ISSN 1365-3539) **1982**
D & B Business Register. Somerset, Dorset, Bath & Bristol (Dun & Bradstreet) (GBR ISSN 1748-8001) **1983**
D & B Business Register. South Yorkshire, East Yorkshire & North East Lincolnshire (Dun & Bradstreet) (GBR ISSN 1748-8044) **1983**
D & B Business Register. South Yorkshire, Humberside see D & B Business Register. South Yorkshire, East Yorkshire & North East Lincolnshire **1983**
D & B Business Register. Surrey (Dun & Bradstreet) (GBR ISSN 1365-3385) **1983**
D & B Business Register. Wales (Dun & Bradstreet) (GBR ISSN 1365-1889) **1983**
D & B Business Register. West Midlands, Warwickshire (Dun & Bradstreet) (GBR ISSN 1365-3555) **1983**
D & B Business Register. West Yorkshire (Dun & Bradstreet) (GBR ISSN 1363-2213) **1983**
D & B Consultants Directory (Dun & Bradstreet) (USA ISSN 1524-9743) **1983**
D & B Directory of Service Companies (Dun & Bradstreet) (USA) **1983**
D & B Employment Opportunities Directory - Career Guide (Dun & Bradstreet) (USA) **6696**
D & B Europa (Dun & Bradstreet) (GBR ISSN 1472-3166) **1812**
† The D & B Gazette. New South Wales (AUS ISSN 1445-7660) **8947**
• D & B Million Dollar Directory (Dun & Bradstreet) (USA ISSN 1093-4812) **1983**
• D & B Reference Book of Corporate Managements (Dun & Bradstreet) (USA ISSN 1098-7266) **1737**
D & B's Regional Business Directory. Kansas City Area (Dun and Bradstreet) (USA ISSN 1930-6644) **1983**
D & C - Development and Cooperation see D + C **1593**
D & C - Developpement et Cooperation see Developpement et Cooperation **1594**
D & M D Newsletter see Scrip Drug Market Developments **5711**
• D & O Advisor (Director & Officer) (USA ISSN 1546-3966) **4865**
D & O Liability Handbook: Law, Sample Documents, Forms (Director & Officer) (USA) **1620**
D & O Liability Litigation News (Director & Officer) (USA) **4865**
D & P see D & P. Drogueria & Perfumeria **8948**
D & R see Disciplinari e Regolamenti del Libro Genealogico dei Bovini di Razza Bruna **285**
D & V Kompendium see E & E Kompendium **3290**
D & V Test Kompendium (Design and Verification) (DEU) **3290**
† D Ang Vers (Die Angestelltenversicherung) (DEU) **8947**
D B see Deutsche Bauzeitung **440**
D B see Det Baesta **3954**
D B 2 Magazine see I B M Database Magazine **2531**
D B 3 Billedkunst (Danmarks Billedkunstlaerere) (DNK ISSN 0909-5926) **3057**
D B A see Das Bahn-Adressbuch **8615**
† D B B Magazin - Ausgabe Hamburg (Deutscher Beamtenbund) (DEU ISSN 0945-0424) **8947**
D B B Magazin - Ausgabe Komba Bayern (Deutscher Beamtenbund) (DEU ISSN 0945-0416) **4592**
D B B Regional-Magazin (Deutscher Beamtenbund) (DEU ISSN 1438-146X) **4592**
D B B - Report (Deutscher Beamtenbund) (DEU ISSN 1867-8254) **7432**
D B C C Photographic Society. Newsletter (Daytona Beach Community College) (USA) **6966**
D B C P Technical Document Series (Data Buoy Cooperation Panel) (CHE) **6351**
D B E - Aktuelt see Samfunnssikkerhet **2228**
D B E Informerer om Farlig Gods see Farlig Gods-Info **2226**
D B Mobil (Deutsche Bahn) (DEU ISSN 1615-0295) **8616**
D B R see Daily Bankruptcy Review **4865**
D B S see Domestic Broadcasting Survey **2358**
D B S A Development Fund. Activities Report see Development Bank of Southern Africa. Activities **1920**
† • D B S Image Processing Newsletter (DEU) **8947**
† • The D B S Report (Direct Broadcast Satellite) (USA ISSN 1054-0814) **8947**
D B S V Jahrbuch see Weitersehen **4086**
D B - Select (Deutsche Bahn) (DEU) **8524**
D B T see Drug Benefit Trends **6833**
D B V Informationen (Deutscher Bauernverband e.V.) (DEU ISSN 0173-654X) **104**
D B V Jahrbuch (Deutscher Bibliotheksverband) (DEU) **5004**
D B W see Die Betriebswirtschaft **1728**
D B Z (Deutsche Bauzeitschrift) (DEU ISSN 0011-4782) **439**
D B Z see Deutsche Behindertenzeitschrift **3038**
D B Z see Deutsche Baecker Zeitung **3673**
D B Z Magazin (Deutsche Baecker Zeitung) (DEU) **3673**
D B Z - S E (Deutsche Briefmarken Zeitung - Sammler Express) (DEU ISSN 1438-2830) **6894**
• D C (Departament Composicio) (ESP ISSN 1139-5559) **439**
D C see Decisions Marketing **1813**
D C 2000 (BRA ISSN 0104-2947) **2184**
• D C A A Contract Audit Manual (Defense Contract Audit Agency) (USA ISSN 1058-076X) **1919**
D C A A -Nyt (Dansk Center vedroerende Alkoholisme og andre Afhaengighedsygdomme) (DNK ISSN 1901-8029) **2693**
• D C A A Offices. Directory (Defense Contract Audit Agency) (USA ISSN 1058-0158) **1919**
• ➤ D C A M M Report (Danish Center for Applied Mathematics and Mechanics) (DNK ISSN 0106-6366) **5481**
D C A News (Distribution Contractors Association) (USA) **6766**
D C B A see Death Care Business Advisor **3719**
D C B A Brief (DuPage County Bar Association) (USA) **4654**
D C Beverage Journal see Washington D.C. Beverage Journal **612**
D C C - Camping Fuehrer Europa (Deutscher Camping Club e.V.) (DEU ISSN 1430-0192) **8696**
D C C - Caravan und Motorcaravan Modellfuehrer (Deutscher Camping Club e.V.) (DEU ISSN 1430-0966) **8576**
• ➤ D C C Digital Curation Manual (Digital Curation Centre) (GBR ISSN 1747-1524) **2542**
D C C N see Dimensions in Critical Care Nursing **5957**
D C C - Touristik Service (Deutscher Camping Club e.V.) (DEU) **8696**
D C C Trade Directory (Delhi Chamber of Commerce) (IND) **1401**
D.C. Code Updater (District of Columbia) (USA ISSN 0740-1744) **7491**
D C D I S Journal see Dynamics of Continuous, Discrete and Impulsive Systems. Series A: Mathematical Analysis **5484**
D + C - Desarrollo y Cooperacion see Desarrollo y Cooperacion **1593**
D + C - Development and Cooperation see D + C **1593**
D + C - Developpement et Cooperation see Developpement et Cooperation **1594**
D C G Informationen (Deutsche Cichliden-Gesellschaft e.V.) (DEU ISSN 0724-7435) **939**
D C H E see Disability Compliance for Higher Education **7205**
D C I see Developmental & Comparative Immunology **5757**
D C i see Dry Cargo International **8643**
D C I see Complete Directory for People with Chronic Illness **5599**
• D C I D O B (Centre d'Informacio i Documentacio Internacionals a Barcelona) (ESP ISSN 1132-6107) **7229**
D C M see D C M Magazine **2475**
D C M see Data Center Management **2492**
D C M Magazine (Data Center Managers) (USA) **2475**
• D C Magazine (District of Columbia) (USA) **5069**
D C N see District Court Procedure N S W **4660**
• D C Plan News & Analysis (Defined Contribution) (USA ISSN 1554-3110) **1334**
D C Plan News and Analysis see D C Plan News & Analysis **1334**
D.C. Real Estate Reporter (District of Columbia) (USA ISSN 0738-6931) **7588**
D C S see Data Centre Solutions **2533**
D C S Manila Teachers of Secondary English English Quarterly see M S T English Quarterly **3071**
D C S P A see Defined Contribution & Savings Plan Alert **1620**
D C Style (District of Columbia) (USA ISSN 1557-2366) **5069**
D.C. Tracts (Doctor of Chiropractic) (USA ISSN 1041-469X) **5804**
D C U B S Research Papers (Dublin City University Business School) (IRL ISSN 1393-290X) **1089**
D C Velocity (Distribution Center) (USA ISSN 1543-3587) **1812**
D Cuore (ITA ISSN 1827-8256) **5409**
D D A Magazine see Dakota **52**
D D B Design Diffusion Bagno (ITA ISSN 1592-3452) **439**
D D D (KGZ) **3903**
• D D D Express (Division on Developmental Disabilities) (USA) **3038**
D D Guiden (Dagens Dubbel) (SWE) **8290**
D D H see Das Dachdecker-Handwerk **1001**
D D I see Display & Design Ideas **4538**
D D I N International (Diemaking Diecutting Intelligence Newsletter) (USA ISSN 1078-6902) **5451**
D D N see Design Diffusion News **440**
D D N Luce International see Luce International **8972**
† • D D Newsletter (Deutsch Daenischen) (DNK ISSN 1397-7229) **8947**
D D P see Doctors for Disaster Preparedness Newsletter **5606**
D D Q see Digital Document Quarterly **2571**
D D R Studien/East German Studies (GBR ISSN 0882-7095) **4137**
D D S (Die Deutsche Schule) (DEU ISSN 1431-2158) **3019**
D D S see Drug Delivery System **6834**
D D S - Das Magazin fuer Moebel und Ausbau (DEU ISSN 1434-4777) **4555**
D D W see Dian Jiang Ying Shi **8950**
D D W see Drug Discovery World **6835**
† D D W - Die Weinwissenschaft (DEU ISSN 0944-4645) **8947**
D D Z see D W Z - D D Z **6832**
D D Z see Deutsche Dartsport Zeitung **8169**
D D Z - Deutsche Drogisten Zeitung see D W Z - D D Z **6832**
D Dallas/Fort Worth see D **3973**
D D_B see D D B Design Diffusion Bagno **439**
D E (Data Extract) (AUS ISSN 1445-159X) **2379**
D E A Directory of Universities, Scientific and Cultural Institutions in Italy see Annuario D E A delle Universita e Istituti di Studio e Ricerca in Italia **8930**
D E A Progress Report see H M Treasury Economic Briefing **1489**
D E A Registration File - Active see Drug Enforcement Administration Registration File - Active **5607**
D E C Computing (Digital Equipment Corporation) (GBR ISSN 0950-5482) **2573**
D E C H E M A Biotechnology Conferences (DEU ISSN 0934-3792) **763**
D E C Today (Digital Equipment Corporation) (GBR ISSN 0269-0489) **2573**
• D E C U S Magazine (Digital Equipment Computer Users Society, Communications Organization) (USA) **2416**
D E D Brief (Deutscher Entwicklungsdienst) (DEU) **1593**
D E - der Elektro- und Gebaeudetechniker (Der Elektromeister) (DEU ISSN 1617-1160) **3298**
D E E D Digest (Demonstrate Energy Efficient Developments) (USA) **3156**
D E E S see Idees - C N D P **1543**
D E F see Australian Defamation Law and Practice **4827**
D E G A (DEU ISSN 1862-2046) **3727**
D E G A - Deutscher Gartenbau see D E G A **3727**
• D E H K O - Raportti (Diabeteksen Ehkaisyn ja Hoidon Kehittamisohjelma) (FIN ISSN 1459-1065) **5886**
D E H O G A Jahrbuch (Deutscher Hotel- und Gaststaettenverband e.V.) (DEU) **4384**
D E H O G A Magazin (Deutscher Hotel- und Gaststattenverband) (DEU) **4384**
D E H O G A Magazin Schleswig-Holstein (Deutscher Hotel- und Gaststattenverband) (DEU) **4384**
D E - Hausgeraete (Der Elektromeister) (DEU ISSN 1860-7489) **4555**
D E I see Die Ernaehrungsindustrie **3634**
D E - Journal of Dental Engineering (JPN ISSN 0385-0129) **5839**
D E K R A - Fachschriftenreihe (DEU ISSN 0721-7315) **8576**
D E K R A Solutions (DEU) **8576**
D E L T A see Documentacao de Estudos em Linguistica Teorica e Aplicada **5112**
† Delta Akustik & Vibration (Dansk Elektronik, Lys og Akustik) (DNK ISSN 1397-6508) **8948**
D E L T A Portfolio (Demonstration and Evaluation of Lighting Technologies and Applications) (USA ISSN 1075-3966) **4536**
D E M M (Digest of Equipment, Materials and Management) (NZL ISSN 1172-4536) **3186**
D e P see Doctrina et Pietas **4215**
D E P A N A en Accio (Defensa del Patrimoni Natura en Accio) (ESP ISSN 1134-9247) **4449**
• D E P Deportate Esuli Profughe (ITA ISSN 1824-4483) **8895**
D E R P see Diabetes Education Reimbursements & Policy Report **4657**
D E S see Discovery and Excavation in Scotland **390**
D E S Action Voice (Diethylstilbestrol) (USA ISSN 1522-0389) **7513**
D E S Activities Report (Arizona Department of Economic Security) (USA) **7432**
D E S C O Resumen Semanal see Resumen Semanal **7177**
† D E S G Inform (Deutsch-Europaeischen Studiengesellschaft) (DEU) **8948**
D E S I D O C Bulletin of Information Technology see D E S I D O C Journal of Library & Information Technology **5004**
• D E S I D O C Journal of Library & Information Technology (Defence Scientific Information & Documentation Centre) (IND ISSN 0974-0643) **5004**
† • D E S Litigation Reporter (Diethylstilbestrol) (USA ISSN 0276-5675) **8948**
D E S W O S - Brief (Deutsche Entwicklungshilfe fuer Soziales Wohnungs- und Siedlungswesen e.V.) (DEU ISSN 0935-1809) **1593**
D E S Y (Year) (Deutsches Elektronen-Synchrotron) (DEU ISSN 0418-9833) **7009**
D E T C News (Distance Education & Training Council) (USA) **3057**
D E T R - A C R E Guidance Note see Great Britain. Department of the Environment, Transport and the Regions. Advisory Committee on Releases to the Environment Guidance Note **3434**
D E V Plus (Deutsche Einheitsverfahren) (DEU ISSN 1613-4257) **3485**
D E W R Job Outlook see Australian Jobs **1666**
D F A see Diamond Fields Advertiser **3948**
D F A Leader (Dairy Farmers of America) (USA) **262**
D F. Beitraege zur Dialogforschung see Beitraege zur Dialogforschung **5098**
D F G - Graduiertenkolleg Lebenstile, Soziale Differenzen, Gesundheitsfoerderung. Berichte (DEU ISSN 1611-1834) **6984**
• D F I Bogen (Danske Filminstitut) (DNK ISSN 1601-6432) **6495**
▼ • D F I Journal (Deep Foundations Institute) (USA ISSN 1937-5247) **3186**
D F M A R see Design Firm Management & Administration Report **1738**
D F N I Guide to New Airline Listings see Duty Free News International **8783**
D F N Mitteilungen (Verein zur Foerderung eines Deutschen Forschungsnetzes) (DEU ISSN 0177-6894) **2533**
D F O Mag (Des Filles en Ovalie) (FRA ISSN 1954-4758) **8226**
• D F Revy (Danmarks Forskningsbiblioteksforening) (DNK ISSN 0106-0503) **5004**
D F V - Familie (Deutscher Familienverband) (DEU ISSN 0949-4669) **2150**
D F W People - The Airport Newspaper (Dallas - Fort Worth) (USA) **8778**
D G A A E Nachrichten (Deutsche Gesellschaft fuer Allgemeine und Angewandte Entomologie) (DEU ISSN 0931-4873) **843**
D G A Magazine (Directors Guild of America) (USA) **4592**
D G G Journal (Deutsche Glastechnische Gesellschaft e.V.) (DEU ISSN 1618-8721) **2040**
D G I P - Intern (Deutsche Gesellschaft fuer Individualpsychologie) (DEU ISSN 0935-2066) **7351**
• D G Insight (Distributed Generation) (USA ISSN 1545-410X) **3156**
D G L R Bericht (Deutsche Gesellschaft fuer Luft- und Raumfahrt) (DEU ISSN 0178-6326) **52**
D G L R Jahrbuecher (Deutsche Gesellschaft fuer Luft- und Raumfahrt) (DEU ISSN 0070-4083) **52**
D G M K Tagungsbericht (Deutsche Gesellschaft fuer Mineraloelwissenschaft und Kohlechemie) (DEU ISSN 1433-9013) **6766**
D G P C see Developments in Government Policy, Compliance, Lab Strategy and Diagnostic Testing **7514**
D G R see American Chemical Society. Directory of Graduate Research **2049**
D G R Web see American Chemical Society. Directory of Graduate Research **2049**
D G S Intern (Deutsche Gefluegelwirtschaft und Schweineproduktion) (DEU ISSN 0948-4221) **284**
D G S Magazin (Deutsche Gefluegelwirtschaft und Schweineproduktion) (DEU ISSN 0947-5664) **284**
D G S P Schriftenreihe (Deutsche Gesellschaft fuer Soziale Psychiatrie) (DEU ISSN 0176-1218) **6135**
D G U Nachrichten (Deutsche Gesellschaft fuer Umwelterziehung) (DEU ISSN 0939-804X) **3413**
D G V Informationen (Deutsche Gesellschaft fuer Volkskunde) (DEU) **3616**
D G Z - Deutsche Gewerkschafts-Zeitung (DEU ISSN 1434-1581) **4592**
• D H B Hospital Benchmark Information (District Health Board) (NZL ISSN 1176-9858) **4113**
D H B Magazin (Deutscher Hausfrauen Bund e.V.) (DEU) **8858**
D H D (ITA ISSN 1824-3746) **4384**
D H D Hotel Design Diffusion see D H D **4384**
D H F see D H F Intralogistik **5451**
D H F Actuell see D H F Intralogistik **5451**
D H F Intralogistik (Deutsche Hebe- und Foerdertechnik) (DEU) **5451**
D H H S Publication (Department of Health and Human Services) (USA ISSN 0276-4733) **4092**
D H K Magazin (Deutsche Handelskammer in Oesterreich) (AUT) **1401**
• ➤ D H Lawrence Review (David Herbert) (USA ISSN 0011-4936) **5282**
D H Lawrence Society. Journal (David Herbert) (GBR ISSN 0308-7662) **5282**
D H Lawrence Society of North America. Newsletter (David Herbert) (USA) **5282**

▼ *new title* † *ceased* • *electronic media* ➤ *refereed*

Title

D H M see Dairy Herd Management 263
D H Magazine see Detailhandel Magazine 8949
D H Q see Digital Humanities Quarterly 4485
D H S (Diensthabendes System) (DEU ISSN 1435-831X) 6417
• D H S Daily Open Source Infrastructure Report (U.S. Department of Homeland Security) (USA) 7432
D H Z Markt (NLD ISSN 0165-3555) 4437
D Home see D Home and Garden 3727
D Home and Garden (Dallas Home and Garden) (USA ISSN 1536-8300) 3727
† D I A Forum (Drug Information Association) (USA ISSN 1540-6539) 8948
▼ • D I A Global Forum (Drug Information Association) (USA ISSN 1944-1991) 6832
D I A Instructor's Manual see Driving Instructor's Manual 8578
D I A L M - P O M see Joint Workshop on Foundations of Mobile Computing. Proceedings 2328
D I A M see Hansten and Horn's Drug Interactions Analysis and Management 6845
➤ D I A S Technology Review (Delhi Institute of Advanced Studies) (IND ISSN 0972-9658) 1089
D I Analysis see Global Benchmark Report 1114
• D I B T Mitteilungen (Deutsches Institut fuer Bautechnik) (DEU ISSN 1438-7778) 1001
D I B T Mitteilungen. Sonderheft see Bauregelliste A, Bauregelliste B und Liste C 981
• D I Business (Dansk Industri) (DNK ISSN 1604-0708) 1883
D I C Boletin see Universidad Autonoma de Santo Domingo. Direccion de Investigaciones. D I C Boletin 7925
D I C E Report (Database for Institutional Comparisons in Europe) (DEU ISSN 1612-0663) 1089
• D I C Technical Review (English Online Edition) (JPN) 3242
• D I C Technical Review (Japanese Online Edition) (JPN) 3242
• D I C Technical Review (Print Edition) (Dainippon Ink and Chemicals) (JPN ISSN 1341-3201) 3242
D I E (Deutsches Institut fuer Erwachsenenbildung) (DEU ISSN 0945-3164) 2940
D I F U - Arbeitshilfe (Deutsches Institut fuer Urbanistik) (DEU ISSN 1863-6292) 4408
D I F U - Berichte (Deutsches Institut fuer Urbanistik) (DEU ISSN 1439-6343) 4409
D I F U - Impulse (Deutsches Institut fuer Urbanistik) (DEU ISSN 1863-7728) 4409
D I F U - Materialien see D I F U - Impulse 4409
• D I G E M I D. Boletin Informativo (Direccion General de Medicamentos Insumos y Drogas) (PER ISSN 1990-6528) 6832
D I I D see Disegno Industriale Industrial Design 8950
D I I R - Forum (Deutsches Institut fuer Interne Revision) (DEU ISSN 1866-9271) 1737
D I I R - Schriftenreihe (Deutsches Institut fuer Interne Revision) (DEU) 1737
D I J see Drug Information Journal 6835
D I K - Forum (SWE ISSN 0281-6873) 5004
D I K U Technical Reports see Koebenhavns Universitet. Datalogisk Institut. Rapport 2430
D I M see Didactica, Innovacion y Multimedia 3057
D I M A see Die Maschine 5456
D I M A C S Series in Discrete Mathematics and Theoretical Computer Science (Discrete Mathematics and Theoretical Computer Science) (USA ISSN 1052-1798) 5481
D I M E S White Papers (Delft Institute of Microsystems and Nanoelectronics) (NLD ISSN 1872-3462) 3091
† D I N (Dealers International News) (ITA ISSN 1121-8746) 8948
† D I N Catalogue of Technical Rules. Supplement (Deutsches Institut fuer Normung) (DEU ISSN 0936-0530) 8948
D I N - Catalogue of Technical Rules. Vol. 1: German Standards and Technical Rules see D I N - Katalog fuer Technische Regeln. Band 1: Deutsche Normen und Technische Regeln 8419
D I N - Catalogue of Technical Rules. Vol. 2: International Standards and Technical Rules see D I N - Katalog fuer Technische Regeln. Band 2: Internationale Normen und Ausgewaehlte Auslaendische Normen 8419
D I N Handbook (Deutsches Institut fuer Normung) (DEU ISSN 0722-7337) 6401
D I N - Katalog fuer Technische Regeln. Band 1: Deutsche Normen und Technische Regeln (Deutsches Institut fuer Normung) (DEU ISSN 0722-9313) 8419
D I N - Katalog fuer Technische Regeln. Band 2: Internationale Normen und Ausgewaehlte Auslaendische Normen (Deutsches Institut fuer Normung) (DEU ISSN 0945-1080) 8419
D I N Mitteilungen & Elektronorm (Deutsches Institut fuer Normung) (DEU ISSN 0722-2912) 6401
D I N - Taschenbuecher (Deutsches Institut fuer Normung) (DEU ISSN 0342-801X) 6401
D I P P R Data Series (Design Institute for Physical Properties) (USA ISSN 1064-2714) 3242
D I R Annual Report see Division of Intramural Research Annual Research Report 7514
D I R E en A P S (Democratiser, Innover, Rechercher, Eduquer en Activite Physique et Sportive) (FRA ISSN 0293-4086) 8168
D I S A M Journal see The Management of Security Assistance 7251
• ➤ D I S P (Dokumente und Informationen zur Schweizerischen Orts-, Regional- und Landesplanung) (CHE ISSN 0251-3625) 4409
D I T (Drustvo Inzenjera i Tehnicara) (SRB ISSN 0352-0870) 6766
D I T Independent (Dublin Institute of Technology) (IRL) 2977
D I T R Info (Deutsches Institut fuer Normung e.V., Deutsches Informationszentrum fuer Technische Regeln) (DEU) 6401
D I W Magazine (Devil in the Woods) (USA) 6560
• D I W P A News Letter (DIVERSITAS in Western Pacific and Asia) (JPN) 3413
D I W P A Series (DIVERSITAS in Western Pacific and Asia) (JPN) 3413
D I W Wochenbericht see Deutsches Institut fuer Wirtschaftsforschung. Wochenbericht 1476
D I Y (Do It Yourself) (DEU ISSN 0932-9218) 4437
• D I Y & Home Improvements Industry (Do It Yourself) (GBR ISSN 1478-8535) 4536
D I Y Boat Owner (Do It Yourself) (USA ISSN 1201-5598) 8275
D I Y Buyers' Guide International (Do It Yourself) (DEU ISSN 1863-7183) 4437
D I Y Einkaufsfuehrer fuer Bau- und Heimwerkermaerkte see D I Y Buyers' Guide International 4437
D I Y in Europe see D I Y International 4437
D I Y International (Do It Yourself) (DEU ISSN 1868-0038) 4437
D I Y Retailing see Hardware Retailing (Indianapolis) 4438
D I Y Superstore see D I Y Superstore International 4438
D I Y Superstore International (Do It Yourself) (GBR ISSN 1476-0614) 4438
† D I Y Trade Buyers' Guide (Do It Yourself) (GBR ISSN 0967-2257) 8948
D I Y Trade News (Do It Yourself) (ZAF ISSN 1021-9137) 4438
• D I Y Week (Do It Yourself) (GBR ISSN 0954-8823) 4438
D I Z Schriften (Dokumentations und Informations Zentrum Emslandlager) (DEU) 6417
▼ D-Inside (CHE ISSN 1662-338X) 6832
D J see Discipleship Journal 7754
D J B Z (Deutscher Juristinnenbund Zeitschrift) (DEU ISSN 1866-377X) 4654
D J C see Daily Journal of Commerce (Portland) 1427
D J C L see The Delaware Journal of Corporate Law 4865
D J G see Geografisk Tidsskrift 4009
D J G Magazin (Deutsche Justiz-Gewerkschaft) (DEU ISSN 1438-1397) 4654
• D J I - Bulletin (Deutsches Jugendinstitut e.V.) (DEU ISSN 0930-7842) 2150
D J I L P see Denver Journal of International Law and Policy 4922
D J K - Das Magazin (Deutsche Jugendkraft) (DEU) 8168
D J K - Sportmagazin see D J K - Das Magazin 8168
D J K Sportmagazin (Deutsche Jugendkraft) (DEU) 8168
D J L I T see D E S I D O C Journal of Library & Information Technology 5004
D J Magazine (Disc Jockey) (GBR ISSN 0965-4364) 6560
• D J OE F - Bladet (Danmarks Jurist-og Oekonomforbund) (DNK ISSN 0107-6981) 4592
• D J Times (Disc Jockey) (USA ISSN 1045-9693) 6560
D J V - Journal (Deutscher Journalisten-Verband) (DEU ISSN 0178-6806) 4574
D J V - Kurier (Deutscher Journalisten-Verband) (DEU ISSN 0946-218X) 4574
D Journal see Diabetes Journal 5605
D K Find Out! (Dorling Kindersley) (GBR ISSN 1478-2243) 2184
D K Find Out! ... Special (Dorling Kindersley) (GBR ISSN 1747-0420) 2184
D K Find Out Special see D K Find Out! ... Special 2184
D K G Journal (Deutsche Killifisch Gemeinschaft) (DEU ISSN 0179-4957) 939
D K K F - Nyt (Danmarks Katolske Kvindeforening) (DNK ISSN 0109-1476) 7794
D K N T see Dansk Kommentar til det Nye Testamente 7637
• D K N V S 's Meddelelser (Det Kongelige Norske Videnskabers Selskab) (NOR ISSN 1890-081X) 7849
D K Newsletter (IND ISSN 0971-4448) 623
D K Nieuwsbrief (Directie Kennis) (NLD ISSN 1871-9724) 104
• D K V - Tagungsbericht (Deutscher Kaelte- und Klimatechnischer Verein) (DEU ISSN 0172-8849) 4118
D K World Soccer Yearbook (Dorling Kindersley) (USA ISSN 1552-2962) 8226
D L A N Y Newsletter (Dental Laboratory Association of State of New York) (USA) 5839
• D L A P S (Defense Logistics Agency Publishing System) (USA) 7480
D L D Times (Division for Learning Disabilities) (USA) 3038
† D L F Jahrbuch (Deutschlandfunk) (DEU ISSN 0344-3108) 8948
D L G - Mitteilungen (Deutsche Landwirtschafts-Gesellschaft e.V.) (DEU ISSN 0341-0412) 104
D L G Plantevaern see Plantevaern Landbrug 248
• D L Magasinet (Dansk Laegesekretaerforening) (DNK ISSN 1903-3125) 4592
D L O see Development and Learning in Organizations 1859
D L R see Deakin Law Review 4655
D L R G - Aktuell (Deutsche Lebens-Rettungs-Gesellschaft) (DEU) 8168
† D L R Magazine (Distributeurs Loueurs Reparateurs) (FRA ISSN 1167-0991) 8948
D L R - Mitteilungen (Deutsches Zentrum fuer Luft- und Raumfahrt) (DEU ISSN 0939-298X) 52
D L R - Nachrichten (Deutsches Zentrum fuer Luft- und Raumfahrt e.V.) (DEU ISSN 0937-0420) 52
D L S U Business & Economics Review (De La Salle University) (PHL ISSN 0116-7111) 1089
D L S U Dialogue (De La Salle University) (PHL ISSN 0115-6594) 4449
➤ D L S U Engineering Journal (De La Salle University) (PHL ISSN 0116-7103) 3186
D L S U Journal of Science see Manila Journal of Science 7881
D L W see Delaware Law Weekly 4655
• D L Z Agrarmagazin (Deutsche landtechnische Zeitschrift) (DEU ISSN 0340-787X) 104
• D - Lib Magazine (Digital - Library) (USA ISSN 1082-9873) 5061
D Lire (FRA ISSN 1629-9744) 2184
D M see Distrofia Muscolare 6136
D M see Il Dentista Moderno 5842
D M see Disease-A-Month 5605
D M A see Dance Music Authority 6561
D M A Statistical Fact Book (Direct Marketing Association) (USA ISSN 1049-6092) 1813
D M Business (Direct Marketing) (GBR) 1813
D M C - Bladet (Danske Motorcyklisters Raad) (DNK ISSN 0109-3649) 8257
D M D see Dans les Media, Demain 4574
D M D see Drug Metabolism and Disposition 6835
D M D. Documentacion en Medicina del Deporte see Revista Andaluza de Medicina del Deporte 6232
D M Euro see Euro 1816
D M I Colour + Man (Deutsches Mode-Institut) (DEU) 2253
D M I J see Journal of Research in Interactive Marketing 1826
• D M I News (Dansk Maritimt Institut) (DNK ISSN 0905-3549) 8642
D M I Review see Design Management Review 1738
D M J see Diabetes Management Journal 5888
D M K - Die Moderne Kueche (DEU ISSN 1431-8407) 4555
D M M see Der Medienmarkt 2333
D M M see Disease Models and Mechanisms 5812
D M M P see Direct Marketing Market Place 1813
† D M M V Special (Deutscher Multimedia Verband) (DEU) 8948
D M Magazine (De Morgen) (BEL ISSN 1378-5915) 3801
• D M News (Direct Marketing) (USA ISSN 0194-3588) 1813
• D M News International (Direct Marketing) (USA) 1561
† D M P F Medlemmer (Dansk Musikpaedagogisk Forening) (DNK ISSN 0108-9188) 8948
D M R see Disaster Management & Response 5957
D M Review see Information Management (Brookfield) 2531
D M S Market Intelligence Reports: Airborne Electronics Forecast see Market Intelligence Reports: Airborne Electronics Forecast 3108
D M S Market Intelligence Reports: Airborne Retrofit and Modernization Forecast see Market Intelligence Reports: Airborne Retrofit and Modernization Forecast 65
D M S Market Intelligence Reports: Electro-Optical Systems Forecast see Market Intelligence Reports: Electro-Optical Systems Forecast 3108
D M S Market Intelligence Reports: International Contractors see Market Intelligence Reports: International Contractors 6433
D M S Market Intelligence Reports: International Military Markets - Asia, Australia & Pacific Rim see Market Intelligence Reports: International Military Markets - Asia, Australia & Pacific Rim 6433
D M S Market Intelligence Reports: International Military Markets - Latin America & Caribbean see Market Intelligence Reports: International Military Markets - Latin America & Caribbean 6433
D M S Market Intelligence Reports: International Military Markets - Middle East & Africa see Market Intelligence Reports: International Military Markets - Middle East & Africa 6433
D M S Market Intelligence Reports: International Military Markets - N A T O & Europe see Market Intelligence Reports: International Military Markets - Europe 6433
D M S Market Intelligence Reports: Land and Sea-Based Electronics Forecast see Market Intelligence Reports: Land and Sea-Based Electronics Forecast 3108
D M S Market Intelligence Reports: Military Force Structures of the World see Market Intelligence Reports: Military Force Structures of the World 6433
D M S Market Intelligence Reports: Ordnance & Munitions Forecast see Market Intelligence Reports: Ordnance & Munitions Forecast 6433
D M S Market Intelligence Reports: Space Systems Forecast see Market Intelligence Reports: Space Systems Forecast 6433
D M S Market Intelligence Reports: U S Defense Budget Forecast see Market Intelligence Reports: U S Defense Budget Forecast 6434
D M S Market Intelligence Reports: Unmanned Vehicles Forecast see Market Intelligence Reports: Unmanned Vehicles Forecast 6434
D M S Market Intelligence Reports: World Airline Maintenance Forecast see Market Intelligence Reports: World Airline Maintenance Forecast 8972
D M S Market Intelligence Reports: World Commercial Aircraft - Engine Orders & Options see Market Intelligence Reports: World Commercial Aircraft - Engine Orders & Options 65
• ➤ D M T (Dansk Musik Tidsskrift) (DNK ISSN 0106-5629) 6560
D M T C S see Discrete Mathematics and Theoretical Computer Science (Online Edition) 5483
• D M U Nyt (Online) (Danmarks Miljoundersogelser) (DNK ISSN 1397-7008) 3413
D M U Nyt (Print) see D M U Nyt (Online) 3413
D M V - Mitteilungen (Deutsche Mathematiker Vereinigung) (DEU ISSN 0947-4471) 5482
D M V - Seminar see Oberwolfach Seminars 5522
D M W see Digital Media World 4574
• D M W Disk-Archiv (Deutsche Medizinische Wochenschrift) (DEU ISSN 3002-1472) 5744
D M W Praxis plus (Deutsche Medizinische Wochenschrift) (DEU ISSN 1617-5964) 5603
D M Z (Deutsche Molkerei Zeitung) (DEU ISSN 1617-2795) 262
D N A (Deoyxribose Nucleic Acid) (AUS ISSN 1443-1122) 4372
D N A (London) (Deoyxribose Nucleic Acid) (GBR ISSN 1365-9375) 4372
• ➤ D N A and Cell Biology (Deoyxribose Nucleic Acid) (USA ISSN 1044-5498) 730
D N A Newsletter (Deoyxribose Nucleic Acid) (USA) 4654
• ➤ D N A Repair (Deoxyribose Nucleic Acid) (NLD ISSN 1568-7864) 731
• D N A Reporter (Delaware Nurses' Association) (USA) 5956
• ➤ D N A Research (Deoxyribonucleic Acid) (GBR ISSN 1340-2838) 731
D N A Sequence see Mitochondrial D N A 738
D N C see Dakota Nurse Connection 5957
D N Extra see Disability Now 4077
D N H K Markt (Deutsch-Niederlaendische Handelskammer) (NLD ISSN 1871-2800) 1718
D N I see Miro 1024
• D N J (Online) (Developer Network Journal) (GBR) 2570
D N Magazine (Dendrobatidae Nederland) (NLD ISSN 1574-3640) 940
D N O C S - Fins e Atividades (Departamento Nacional de Obras Contra as Secas) (BRA) 227
D N O Nieuws (Diabetes and Nutrition Organization) (NLD ISSN 1875-4422) 5886
• D N R (Daily News Record) (USA ISSN 1092-5511) 8449
D N R Menswear see D N R 8449
• D N S S E C This Month (Domain Name System Security) (USA ISSN 1932-6564) 2676
D N V (Der Neue Vertrieb) (DEU ISSN 0343-5598) 7559
• D N V Forum (Det Norske Veritas) (NOR ISSN 0803-7108) 8642
D N W E Schriftenreihe (Deutsche Netzwerk Wirtschaftsethik - EBEN e.V.) (DEU ISSN 0948-9533) 1674
D N Z International (Die Naehmaschinen-Zeitung) (DEU ISSN 0011-507X) 5451
The D O (Doctor of Osteopathy) (USA ISSN 0011-5088) 5805
† • D O C News (Diabetes, Obesity, Cardiovascular Disease) (USA ISSN 1552-2024) 8948
D O C P A L Latin American Population Abstracts see D O C P A L Resumenes sobre Poblacion en America Latina 7305
D O C P A L Resumenes sobre Poblacion en America Latina/D O C P A L Latin American Population Abstracts (CHL ISSN 0378-5378) 7305
• ➤ D O C Research and Development Series (Department of Conservation) (NZL ISSN 1176-8886) 2608
D O C Science Internal Series see D O C Research and Development Series 2608
D O E and C I R I A Piling Development Group. Report P G (Department of the Environment - Construction Industry Research and Information Association) (GBR ISSN 0308-924X) 1001
D o E E P S Co R H R D & Louis Stokes Louisiana Alliance for Minority Participation Student Research Conference. Proceedings (Department of Energy / Experimental Program to Stimulate Competitive Research) (USA ISSN 1554-7604) 2841
D O E Marine Research Programme. Report see United Kingdom. Department of the Environment. Marine Research Programme. Report 2819

DIRECTORY 2010 DADOS ESTATISTICOS DA MOVIMENTACAO DE CARGA E PASSAGEIROS 10179

● D O E This Month (Department of Energy) (USA ISSN 1057-5782) **3126**
D O F E *see* Directory of Further Education **2978**
D O J Alert (Department of Justice) (USA ISSN 1056-2230) **4950**
D O M E S *see* Digest of Middle East Studies **548**
D O Magazine *see* Design Only Magazine **4538**
D O N G Magasinet *see* Stroemninger **6793**
D o P P *see* Directory of Published Proceedings (Online) **5744**
D O P S - Nyt (Dansk Optisk Selskab) (DNK ISSN 0901-4632) **7075**
D o Q (DEU ISSN 1612-0957) **1416**
D O S B Presse (Deutscher Olympischer Sportbund) (DEU) **8168**
D O S E *see* The Dictionary of Substances and Their Effects **3495**
D O S S U Journal (Dogs on Stamps Study Unit) (USA ISSN 0882-0236) **6894**
D O S T Annual Report *see* Science and Technology Information Institute. Department of Science and Technology. Annual Report **7908**
D O S World (Disk Operating System) (USA ISSN 1078-876X) **2589**
D O T *see* The Directory of the Turf Handbook (Year) **8290**
D O T News (Department of Transport) (GBR) **8494**
D Oe V *see* Die Oeffentliche Verwaltung **4751**
D P A (Documents de Projectes d'Arquitectura) (ESP ISSN 1577-0265) **439**
D P A. Design Products & Applications *see* Design Products and Application **3187**
● D P A Membership Book (Data Publishers Association) (GBR) **1983**
D P A News (Directory & Database Publishers Association) (GBR ISSN 1351-251X) **1983**
D P F News Notes (Disciples Peace Fellowship) (USA) **7229**
D P F Newsletter (Diaper Pail Friends) (USA) **2150**
● D P H Aktualne (Dan z Pridane Hodnoty) (CZE ISSN 1214-7540) **1919**
D P H D Newsletter (Division for Physical & Health Disabilities) (USA) **3038**
D P I & F Publication (AUS) **104**
● D P I C Reports (Death Penalty Information Center) (USA) **7205**
D P I Forestry. Yearbook (Department of Primary Industries) (AUS) **3687**
D P I Programme Update *see* United Nations. Department of Public Information. Programme Update **7270**
D P M *see* Disaster Prevention and Management **7514**
D P N (Deutsche Pensions- und Investmentnachrichten) (DEU ISSN 1476-3028) **1620**
The D P P Collection (CD-ROM) *see* Design Philosophy Papers **440**
The D P P Collection (Print) *see* Design Philosophy Papers **440**
D P P Working Paper (Development Policy & Practice) (GBR ISSN 0958-1383) **1476**
D P R *see* Development Policy Review **1594**
D P R K *see* Democratic People's Republic of Korea **547**
D P V Kom Magazin (Deutscher Postverband) (DEU ISSN 1438-0633) **2354**
D-Photo *see* New Zealand D-Photo **6971**
D Pol Bl *see* Deutsches Polizeiblatt **2650**
● D Q R Studies in Literature (Dutch Quarterly Review) (NLD ISSN 0921-2507) **5282**
D R *see* Disaster Research **7959**
D R A M (Drinks Retailing and Marketing) (GBR ISSN 1470-241X) **1983**
D R & A Brief *see* Defence Research & Analysis. Briefs **6418**
D R C Book & Monograph Series (Disaster Research Center) (USA ISSN 0164-1875) **2226**
D R C C *see* Driving Radio Control Canada **4334**
D R C Historical and Comparative Disasters Series (Disaster Research Center) (USA ISSN 0164-1867) **8036**
D R C Mississippi Newsletter (Delta Resources Committee, Inc.) (USA) **7753**
D R C News (Dutch Reformed Church) (ZAF) **7753**
D R D O Newsletter (Defence Research & Development Organization) (IND ISSN 0971-4391) **6417**
D R G A *see* Revue de Geographie Alpine. Dossiers **4027**
● D R G Handbook (Diagnosis Related Group) (USA ISSN 1069-482X) **4092**
D R I - McGraw-Hill U S Markets Review: Regional Forecast Summary (Data Resources Inc.) (USA ISSN 1056-6058) **1883**
D R I - McGraw-Hill U S Markets Review: Regional Preview (Data Resources Inc.) (USA ISSN 1056-6066) **1883**
D R J *see* Dance Research Journal **2684**
D R N *see* Development Research News **1594**
D R N *see* Dance Retailer News **2684**
D R Q *see* Design Research Quarterly **7319**
D R S Magazine (De Reformatorische School) (NLD ISSN 1872-4930) **2841**
● D R S News (Design Research Society) (GBR) **7319**
D R T *see* Dispute Resolution Times **4593**
● D R U I D Working Paper (Danish Research Unit for Industrial Dynamics) (DNK ISSN 1601-7684) **1737**
▼ ● D R Z E Newsletter (Deutsches Referenzzentrum fuer Ethik in den Biowissenschaften) (DEU) **6913**
D S *see* Derecho y Salud **7514**
D S (De Societe) (FRA ISSN 1281-0789) **8858**
D S *see* Dagens Socialfoersaekring **8036**
D S A *see* Dickens Studies Annual **5284**
D S B (Die Schweizer Baustoff-Industrie) (DEU ISSN 0174-5336) **1001**
† D S B Bladet (Danske Statsbaner) (DNK ISSN 0900-3665) **8948**
D S B i Dag (De danske Statsbaner) (DNK ISSN 1397-9418) **8494**
D S B Kommunikation *see* D S B Bladet **8948**
D S B Presse *see* D O S B Presse **8168**
D S B - Report (Deutscher Schwerhoerigenbund) (DEU ISSN 0172-7753) **4073**
D S Bedre Avisen *see* D S B Bladet **8948**
● D S-Bladet (Dansk Smedemesterforening) (DNK ISSN 1602-7213) **6309**
D S C A Facts Book (Online Edition) *see* U.S. Department of Defense. Defense Security Cooperation Agency. D S C A Facts Book. Foreign Military Sales, Foreign Military Construction Sales and Military Assistance Facts (Online Edition) **6450**
D S I *see* Defense et Securite Internationale **6419**
D S I. Aarsberetning *see* Dansk Sundhedsinstitut. Beretning **4092**
● D S I-Rapport (Dansk Sundhedsinstitut) (DNK ISSN 0904-1737) **4092**
● D S K B-Nyt (DNK ISSN 1902-1526) **5603**
D S M med Know How *see* Den Svenska Marknaden **3957**
D S - Magazin (Der Selbstaendige) (DEU) **1959**
D S N A Newsletter (Dictionary Society of North America) (USA) **5005**
D S N Retail Fax (Discount Store News) (USA ISSN 1079-641X) **2246**
● D S P & F P G A Product Resource Guide (Digital Display Processing & Field Programmable Gate Array) (USA) **2416**
D S P Engineering *see* D S P - F P G A.com **3091**
D S P Engineering Magazine *see* D S P & F P G A Product Resource Guide **2416**
D S P - F P G A Com *see* D S P - F P G A.com **3091**
● D S P - F P G A.com (Digital Signal Processing - Field Programmable Gate Array) (USA) **3091**
● D S P Siteings (Digital Signal Processing) (USA) **2466**
D S R I. Report (Danish Space Research Institute) (DNK ISSN 1602-527X) **52**
D S S Newsletter (Department of Social Services) (USA) **8036**
D S T *see* Jornal Brasileiro de Doencas Sexualmente Transmissiveis **5878**
D S T (Dansk Skovbrugs Tidsskrift) (DNK ISSN 0905-295X) **3687**
D S T Beitraege zum Kommunalrecht *see* Deutscher Staedtetag. Reihe B: Beitraege zum Kommunalrecht **7491**
D S T Beitraege zur Bildungspolitik *see* Deutscher Staedtetag. Reihe C: Beitraege zur Bildungspolitik **7491**
D S T Beitraege zur Finanzpolitik *see* Deutscher Staedtetag. Reihe G: Beitraege zur Finanzpolitik **7491**
D S T Beitraege zur Kommunalpolitik *see* Deutscher Staedtetag. Reihe A: Beitraege zur Kommunalpolitik **7491**
D S T Beitraege zur Sozialpolitik *see* Deutscher Staedtetag. Reihe D: Beitraege zur Sozialpolitik **7491**
D S T Beitraege zur Stadtentwicklung *see* Deutscher Staedtetag. Reihe E: Beitraege zur Stadtentwicklung **7433**
D S T Beitraege zur Statistik und Stadtforschung *see* Deutscher Staedtetag. Reihe H: Beitraege zur Statistik und Stadtforschung **7491**
D S T Beitraege zur Wirtschafts- und Verkehrspolitik *see* Deutscher Staedtetag. Reihe F: Beitraege zur Wirtschafts- und Verkehrspolitik **7491**
D S T G Magazin (Deutsche Steuer-Gewerkschaft) (DEU) **7432**
D S U'eren (Danmarks Socialdemokratiske Ungdom) (DNK ISSN 0905-5525) **7128**
D S V Aktiv Ski & Sportmagazin (Deutscher Skilehrerverband) (DEU) **8310**
D S W '12 Nachrichten (Darmstaedter Schwimm- und Wassersportclub) (DEU ISSN 1431-3707) **8168**
D St R *see* DStR - Deutsches Steuerrecht **1920**
D T *see* Daily Telegraph **3864**
D T & G *see* Journal of Design, Typography & Graphics **2487**
● D T C Perspectives (Direct-to-Customer) (USA) **6832**
● D T - DownTown (ESP ISSN 1575-3360) **6288**
▼ ● D T I (Defence Technology International) (USA ISSN 1935-6269) **6417**
D T J *see* Dance Theatre Journal **2685**
● D T L Magasinet (Dansk Transport og Logistik) (DNK ISSN 1902-5173) **8670**
● D T L - Nyt (Online) (Dansk Transport og Logistik) (DNK) **8670**
D T M C B *see* Dreams That Money Can Buy **5214**
D T P Digetale Medier *see* Digetale Medier Professionel **7579**
● D T P Techniques (Desktop Publishing) (USA) **2570**
● D T T P (Documents to the People) (USA ISSN 0091-2085) **5005**
D T T R *see* Diagnostic Testing and Technology Report **5605**
● D T U Avisen (Danmarks Tekniske Universitet) (DNK ISSN 1604-1232) **8419**
● ➤ D T W (Deutsche Tieraerztliche Wochenschrift) (DEU ISSN 0341-6593) **8796**
D T Z Shop (Die Tabak Zeitung) (DEU) **8486**
D T Z Tabakjahrbuch (Die Tabak Zeitung) (DEU ISSN 0932-4534) **8486**
D U *see* Ducks Unlimited **2609**
D u D *see* Datenschutz und Datensicherheit **2513**
D U E L *see* Dansk Uddannelses & Erhvervs Leksikon **2955**
● D U F, Dansk Ungdoms Faellesraad. Aarsberetning (DNK ISSN 0106-696X) **8098**
▼ D U F Fokus (Dansk Ungdoms Faellesraad) (DNK ISSN 1902-5807) **8098**
● The D U I Report (California Ed.) (Driving Under the Influence) (USA ISSN 1559-5579) **2650**
▼ ● The D U I Report (Pennsylvania Ed.) (Driving Under the Influence) (USA ISSN 1948-4720) **2650**
D U L J *see* Dar es Salaam University Law Journal **4655**
D U M A C (Ducks Unlimited de Mexico, A.C.) (MEX) **3413**
D U Z *see* D U Z Magazin **2977**
D U Z Europa Kompakt (Deutsche Universitaets Zeitung) (DEU ISSN 1867-9595) **2977**
D U Z Magazin (Deutsche Universitaets Zeitung) (DEU ISSN 1613-1290) **2977**
D U Z Nachrichten *see* D U Z Europa Kompakt **2977**
† D V (Digital Video) (CZE ISSN 1214-6692) **8948**
D V (Dagbladid Visir) (ISL ISSN 1021-8254) **3877**
● D V (Digital Video) (USA ISSN 1541-0943) **2379**
D V 8 (USA ISSN 1543-0960) **6561**
† D V Bogen (Danske Vognm aend) (DNK ISSN 0901-6945) **8948**
D V Communicatief *see* Donorvoorlichting Communicatief **6242**
● D V D & Blu-ray Review (Digital Video Disc) (GBR) **6495**
D V D & Surround Test (Digital Video Disc) (DEU) **2400**
† D V D Branden (Digital Versatile Disc) (NLD ISSN 1872-6402) **8948**
D V D Buyer (Digital Video Disc) (GBR ISSN 1468-1250) **2400**
D V D Etc. (Digital Video Disc) (USA ISSN 1543-6144) **2400**
D V D Guide (Digital Video Disc) (USA) **2400**
D V D Hohto *see* Episodi **6497**
● D V D Intelligence (Digital Video Disc) (GBR ISSN 1367-4498) **2400**
D V D - Laser Disc Newsletter (Digital Video Disc) (USA) **8419**
D V D mag *see* D V Dmag (Online) **8948**
D V D mag *see* D V Dmag (Print) **8948**
D V D Magazin (Digital Video Disc) (DEU) **2400**
D V D Magazine (Digital Video Disc) (FRA ISSN 1628-870X) **2400**
Der D V D Markt und Medien Insight Video (Digital Video Disc) (DEU) **2400**
● D V D News (Digital Video Disc) (USA ISSN 1098-2523) **2400**
D V D og Hemmekino *see* Hjemmekino **8153**
D V D Plus (Digital Video Disc) *see* Digital Movie **2401**
† D V D Premiere (Digital Video Disc) (DEU ISSN 1610-7330) **8948**
● D V D Preview (Digital Video Disc) (USA) **2400**
D V D Replication Directory (Digital Video Disc) (USA) **2400**
D V D Resources Directory (Digital Video Disc) (USA) **2400**
D V D Review *see* D V D & Blu-ray Review **6495**
D V D Review (Digital Video Disc) (ITA ISSN 1592-8772) **2400**
D V D Review Presenta (Digital Video Disc) (ITA ISSN 1722-0300) **2401**
D V D Special (Digital Video Disc) (DEU) **2401**
● D V D Statistical Report (Digital Video Disc) (USA) **2347**
D V D Style *see* Svet D V D **8991**
D V D Valley (Digital Video Disc) *see* Filmvalley **6501**
D V D Vision *see* Widescreen Vision **6517**
D V D Welt (Digital Video Disc) (DEU) **2401**
D V D World (Digital Video Disc) (GRC) **2401**
D V Dialog (DEU) **2520**
† ● D V Dmag (Online) (Digital Video Disc) (CZE ISSN 1213-8703) **8948**
† ● D V Dmag (Print) (Digital Video Disc) (CZE ISSN 1214-5467) **8948**
D V F Journal *see* Photographie **6974**
D V G W - Schriftenreihe Wasser (Deutscher Verein des Gas- und Wasserfaches) (DEU ISSN 0342-5630) **8820**
D V I Q *see* Division on Visual Impairments Quarterly **4081**
D V I R C Quarterly (Domestic Violence & Incest Resource Centre) (AUS ISSN 1834-366X) **8036**
● D V M (Doctor of Veterinary Medicine) (USA ISSN 0012-7337) **8796**
D V R *see* Domestic Violence Report **2651**
D.V.R.P.C. Annual Report *see* Delaware Valley Regional Planning Commission. Annual Report **8494**
D V R Report (Deutscher Verkehrssicherheitsrat e.V.) (DEU ISSN 0940-9025) **8630**
D V S Berichte (Deutscher Verband fuer Schweissen und verwandte Verfahren) (DEU ISSN 0418-9639) **3298**
● D V S Guide (E-mail Edition) (Descriptive Video Service) (USA) **2379**
D V V - Kurier (Deutscher Volkssportverband e.V.) (DEU ISSN 0177-7149) **8310**
D V W Landesvereine Hessen und Thueringen. Mitteilungen (Deutscher Verein fuer Vermessungswesen) (DEU ISSN 0949-7900) **3264**
● D V Z (Deutsche Verkehrs - Zeitung) (DEU ISSN 0342-166X) **8630**
D V Z Brief (Deutsche Verkehrs - Zeitung) (DEU) **8494**
D W *see* Dialectes de Wallonie **5111**
D W *see* Derivatives Week **1620**
D W & B P *see* Drinking Water & Backflow Prevention **3265**
D W B *see* Dietsche Warande en Belfort **5213**
D W D Newsletter (Dying with Dignity) (CAN ISSN 0847-1797) **4043**
D W: Drogisten Weekblad (NLD ISSN 0165-6112) **6832**
● D W F (Donna Woman Femme) (ITA ISSN 0393-9014) **8858**
D W I Journal: Law & Science (Driving While Intoxicated) (USA ISSN 0889-0234) **4654**
† D W I Reports (Deutsches Wollforschungsinstitut) (DEU ISSN 0942-301X) **8948**
D W J - Deutsches Waffen-Journal (DEU ISSN 0341-8936) **4333**
D W M *see* Door & Window Manufacturer **1005**
➤ D W P S (Doctoral Working Paper Series) (GBR) **1737**
D W R News (California Department of Water Resources) (USA) **8820**
D W - Schriftenreihe (Deutsche Welle) (DEU) **2358**
D W Z *see* Die Winzer Zeitschrift **613**
▼ D W Z - D D Z (Drogerie Waren Zeitung - Deutsche Drogisten Zeitung) (DEU) **6832**
▼ D X N Magazine (Diversity Exchange Network) (GBR ISSN 1755-4721) **5420**
† D & P. Drogueria & Perfumeria (ESP ISSN 1695-7210) **8948**
D Z M Aktuell (Deutsche Zeltmission) (DEU) **7753**
D Z W Orale Implantologie (Die Zahnarzt Woche) (DEU) **5839**
D Z W Spezial (Die Zahnarzt Woche) (DEU) **5839**
D Z W Zahntechnik (Die Zahnarzt Woche) (DEU) **5839**
D-Zone (NLD ISSN 1389-7888) **7579**
† D'A (ITA ISSN 1120-5822) **8948**
Da-Ai Monthly *see* Da-ai Zhiyou **7701**
Da-ai Zhiyou/Da-Ai Monthly (TWN) **7701**
● Da-Capo (USA) **2977**
Da Capo (Braunschweig) (DEU ISSN 1611-7107) **3846**
Da Capo (Eystrup) (DEU) **8468**
D'A - d'Architectures (FRA ISSN 1145-0835) **439**
D'A. D'Architettura (ITA ISSN 1720-0342) **439**
● Da Dianji Jishu/Large Electric Machine and Hydraulic Turbine (CHN ISSN 1000-3983) **3376**
Da Libro a Libro (ITA ISSN 1828-9533) **7559**
● ➤ Daam, Kesht Va San'at/Livestock, Cultivation & Industry (IRN) **3891**
Daat *see* Da'at **7720**
Da'at (ISR ISSN 0334-2336) **7720**
● Dabien (TWN) **485**
DaCabrio (DEU ISSN 1617-7290) **8577**
Dacapo (JPN) **3900**
Dacca Visva Vidyalaya Patrika *see* Dhaka Bisvabidyalaya Patrika **3799**
Dach und Gruen (DEU ISSN 0943-5271) **3728**
Dach und Wand (CHE) **1001**
Dach und Wand Abdichtung (AUT) **1001**
Dacha (UKR) **4977**
● Dachang-Gangmenbing Waike Zazhi/Journal of Coloproctological Surgery (CHN ISSN 1009-8771) **5603**
Dachauer Hefte (DEU ISSN 0257-9472) **4213**
Dachausbau (DEU) **4555**
Dachbau-Magazin (DEU ISSN 1618-9612) **1001**
Das Dachdecker-Handwerk (DEU ISSN 0172-1003) **1001**
Der Dachdeckermeister *see* Dachbau-Magazin **1001**
Dachniki (RUS) **4977**
Der Dachshund (DEU ISSN 0011-5231) **6806**
Dacia: Revue d'Archeologie et d'Histoire Ancienne (ROM ISSN 0070-251X) **389**
➤ Dacoromania (Cluj-Napoca, 1998) (ROM ISSN 1582-4438) **5110**
Dacorum Heritage Trust. Annual Review (GBR ISSN 1750-9394) **6523**
● Dad eTips (USA) **8098**
Dada (FRA ISSN 1261-4858) **2184**
Dada - Surrealism (USA ISSN 0084-9537) **5282**
● DADAm@g (ITA) **3897**
Dadi/Great Earth (CHN ISSN 1004-0587) **3823**
● Dadi Celiang yu Diqiu Donglixue/Journal of Geodesy and Geodynamics (CHN ISSN 1671-5942) **2779**
● ➤ Dadi Gouzao yu Chengkuangxue (CHN ISSN 1001-1552) **2730**
● DadMag.com (USA) **6288**
● ➤ Dados (BRA ISSN 0011-5258) **7958**
Dados Estatisticos da Movimentacao de Carga e Passageiros (BRA) **8642**

Title

10180 DADOS ESTATISTICOS DA NAVEGACAO ULRICH'S PERIODICALS

Dados Estatisticos da Navegacao *see* Dados Estatisticos da Movimentacao de Carga e Passageiros **8642**
Dados Sobre a Situacao da Agropecuaria Municipal no Estado do Parana (BRA ISSN 0100-9605) **196**
• Dadou Kexue/Soybean Science (CHN ISSN 1000-9841) **227**
Dadushi/Metropolis B I B A (CHN ISSN 1007-8142) **8858**
Dadushi (Nanshi Ban)/Metropolis (CHN) **6288**
Dadushi (Nushi Ban) *see* Dadushi **8858**
Dadushi B I B A *see* Dadushi **8858**
Daedalian (USA ISSN 1092-8111) **6913**
• ➤ Daedalus (USA ISSN 0011-5266) **4449**
• Daedalus (Online) (ITA ISSN 1970-2175) **8098**
Daedalus (Print) *see* Daedalus (Online) **8098**
• ➤ Daedalus (Stockholm) (SWE ISSN 0070-2528) **6523**
Daedalus Flyer (USA ISSN 1083-2831) **2265**
Daegu Chamber of Commerce and Industry. Monthly Daegu - Gyeongbook Economic Trend *see* Wolgan Daegu Gyeongbuk Gyeongje Donghyang **1413**
• Daehan An'gwa Hag'hoeji/Korean Ophthalmological Society. Journal (KOR ISSN 0378-6471) **6041**
Daehan Bangsa'seon Gi'sul Haghoeji/Korean Society of Radiological Science. Journal (KOR ISSN 1226-2854) **6195**
Daehan Bangsaseon Yihag Hoeji/Korean Radiological Society. Journal *see* Daehan Yeongsang ui Haghoeji **6195**
Daehan Ci'gwa Yisa Hyeob'hoeji/Korean Dental Association. Journal (KOR ISSN 0376-4672) **5839**
Daehan Eung'geub Yihaghoeji/Korean Society of Emergency Medicine. Journal (KOR ISSN 1226-4334) **6058**
➤ Daehan Ganho Haghoeji/Korean Society of Nursing Science. Journal (KOR ISSN 1598-2874) **5956**
➤ Daehan Geumsog Haghoeji/Korean Institute of Metals and Materials. Journal (KOR ISSN 0253-3847) **6310**
Daehan Gigye Haghoe Nonmunjib. A/Korean Society of Mechanical Engineers. Transactions. A (KOR ISSN 1226-4873) **3376**
Daehan Gigye Haghoe Nonmunjib. B/Korean Society of Mechanical Engineers. Transactions. B (KOR ISSN 1226-4881) **3376**
• Daehan Haeg Yihag Hoeji/Korean Journal of Nuclear Medicine (KOR ISSN 1225-6714) **6195**
Daehan Hwahak Hoe Jee *see* Korean Chemical Society. Journal **2071**
Daehan Nae'gwa Haghoeji *see* The Korean Journal of Medicine **5947**
Daehan Sin'gyeong Oe'gwa Hag'hoeji *see* Korean Neurosurgical Society. Journal **6158**
Daehan Sohwa'gi'byeong Haghoe Jabji *see* Korean Journal of Gastroenterology **5928**
Daehan Suhaghoe Nonmunjib *see* Korean Mathematical Society. Communications **5508**
• Daehan Suhaghoe Sosig/Korean Mathematical Society. The Newsletter (KOR) **5482**
Daehan Yeongsang ui Haghoeji (KOR ISSN 1738-2637) **6195**
Daehan'yi Jin'gyun Haghoeji/Korean Journal of Medical Mycology (KOR ISSN 1226-4709) **5603**
Daehne Informationsdienst (DEU) **4438**
Daemm Journal (DEU) **1001**
• Daena (MEX ISSN 1870-557X) **6913**
Daenischer Handelskalender *see* Trade Directory for Denmark **8994**
Daenisches Orgeljahrbuch *see* Dansk Orgelaarbog **8948**
• ➤ Daf L'tarbut Yehudit (ISR) **7720**
• The Daffodil Journal (USA ISSN 0011-5290) **3728**
Daffodils and Tulips (GBR) **3728**
† DAFSA des Administrateurs (FRA ISSN 1258-6900) **8948**
Daftar Koleksi Majalah Pusat Dokumentasi dan Informasi Ilmiah Lembaga ilmu Pengetahuan Indonesia *see* Katalog Induk Majalart **10**
Daftar Pengadaan Bahan Indonesia *see* Indonesian Acquisitions List (Online) **627**
• Daftar Terbitan Berkala Indonesia Yang Telah Mempunyai ISSN/List of Indonesian Serials Having ISSN (IDN ISSN 0854-0306) **6**
Dag Allemaal (BEL ISSN 0772-6732) **3801**
• Dag og Tid (NOR ISSN 0803-334X) **3922**
Dagbladen *see* De Nederlandse Dagbladpers. Jaarverslag **4580**
• Dagbladet (NOR ISSN 0805-3766) **3922**
Dagbladet (SWE ISSN 1103-9159) **3955**
Dagbladid Visir *see* D V **3877**
Dagbladid Visir *see* D V **3877**
Dagelijks Beleid (NLD ISSN 1380-6521) **1737**
Dagen (NOR) **3922**
• Dagens Arbete (SWE ISSN 1402-2974) **4592**
† Dagens Danmark (DNK ISSN 0109-7644) **8948**
Dagens Dubbel Guiden *see* D D Guiden **8290**
Dagens E T C *see* E T C **3955**
• Dagens Handel (SWE ISSN 1403-2759) **1427**
• Dagens I T (NOR ISSN 0809-9030) **2318**
• Dagens Industri (SWE ISSN 0346-640X) **1089**
▼ Dagens Ledare (SWE ISSN 1654-4587) **1737**
• Dagens Media (SWE ISSN 1403-8498) **1813**
• Dagens Medicin (DNK ISSN 1397-3290) **5603**
• Dagens Medicin (SWE ISSN 1104-7488) **5603**
Dagens Medier (NOR ISSN 1503-2841) **4574**
• Dagens Medisin (NOR ISSN 1501-4290) **7513**
Dagens Miljoe *see* Miljoeaktuellt **3453**
• Dagens Naeringsliv (NOR ISSN 0803-9372) **3922**
• Dagens Nyheter (SWE ISSN 1101-2447) **3955**
• Dagens Samhaelle (SWE ISSN 1652-6511) **7491**
Dagens Sekreterare (SWE ISSN 0349-3725) **1850**
Dagens Socialfoersaekring (SWE ISSN 1652-9472) **8036**
Dagerotyp (POL ISSN 1233-2445) **6966**
Dagestanskaya Pravda (RUS) **3935**
Dagestanskii Etnograficheskii Sbornik (RUS ISSN 0137-0545) **3529**
Dagjournaal Ordina Open (NLD) **8226**
Dagkalender Astrologie (NLD ISSN 1874-8139) **565**
Dagligvaru Affaerer (SWE) **3677**
Dagningen (NOR) **3922**
• Dagobert's Revenge (Online Edition) (USA) **2265**
Dagobert's Revenge (Print Edition) *see* Dagobert's Revenge (Online Edition) **2265**
Dagongzu (CHN ISSN 1009-8151) **3823**
Dagsavisen (NOR ISSN 1503-2892) **3922**
Dagspressens Detaljspridning (SWE ISSN 0564-7568) **7578**
• Dagsverket (SWE ISSN 0349-6139) **4213**
Dagtilbud til Boern og Unge. Nyhedsbrev *see* Boern, Unge, Familier **8937**
Daguan Weekly *see* Daguan Zhoukan **3823**
Daguan Zhoukan/Daguan Weekly (CHN ISSN 1008-925X) **3823**
Daguerreian Society. Annual (USA) **6966**
Daguerreian Society Newsletter (USA ISSN 1072-8600) **6966**
Dahe Bao/Dahe Daily (CHN) **3824**
Dahe Daily *see* Dahe Bao **3824**
Daheim bei der W A G (Wohnungsaktiengesellschaft Linz) (AUT ISSN 0011-5320) **4409**
Dahesh Voice (USA ISSN 1530-8731) **4449**
Dahlias of Today (USA) **3728**
• Dahuilang Huabao/Big Grey Wolf Pictorial (CHN ISSN 1006-1746) **2184**
Dai Doan Ket/Great Unity (VNM ISSN 1022-8829) **7128**
Dai Nippon Construction Co., Ltd. Technical Materials *see* Dainippon Koboku K.K. Gijutsu Shiryo **1001**
Dai Nippon Construction. Technical Report *see* Dainippon Doboku Gijutsu Kenkyujoho **3264**
Daido Kogyo Daigaku Kiyo (JPN ISSN 0285-5372) **3186**
Daidzhest Marketing (RUS) **1813**
Daidzhest Press (TJK) **3961**
Daietto & Byuuti *see* Diet & Beauty **6657**
➤ Daigaku Toshokan Mondai Kenkyuukaishi/Japan Academic Librarians' Association. Bulletin (JPN ISSN 1348-9186) **5005**
Daigakuin Kokusai Kouhou Media Kenkyuuka Gengo Bunkabu Kiyou/Media, Language and Culture (JPN ISSN 1347-0280) **5110**
• Daihan Binyogigwa Haghoi Ji/Korean Journal of Urology (KOR ISSN 0494-4747) **6267**
Daiichi Kogyo Seiyaku. Review *see* Daiichi Kogyo Seiyaku. Shaho **2122**
Daiichi Kogyo Seiyaku. Shaho/Daiichi Kogyo Seiyaku. Review (JPN ISSN 0011-5355) **2122**
Daikikyu Shinpojumu (JPN) **574**
The Dailies (CAN ISSN 0838-9365) **1620**
• Daily Aardvark (NZL) **1090**
Daily Action Stock Charts (Weekly) *see* Trendline Daily Action Stock Charts (Weekly) **1656**
• Daily Assistant (USA) **5069**
• The Daily Athenaeum (USA ISSN 0011-5371) **2280**
The Daily Aztec (USA) **2280**
Daily Bankruptcy Reporter *see* Daily Bankruptcy Review **4865**
• Daily Bankruptcy Review (USA) **4865**
• Daily Bankruptcy Review Small-Cap (USA) **4865**
• The Daily Barometer (USA ISSN 1080-6814) **2977**
• Daily Bible Study (USA ISSN 0742-065X) **7753**
Daily Blessing (USA ISSN 0011-538X) **7753**
Daily Bread (USA ISSN 0092-7147) **7734**
• Daily Bread (London) (GBR ISSN 0963-4797) **7753**
Daily Bread (Peterborough) (GBR) **7753**
Daily Bread Magazine (USA ISSN 1086-9557) **8310**
Daily Bruin (USA ISSN 1080-5060) **2280**
Daily Bulletin (Brooklyn) (USA) **4654**
• Daily Bulletin (Chapel Hill) (USA) **7432**
• Daily Bulletin - M T I (Magyar Tavirati Iroda) (HUN ISSN 1218-5051) **3876**
• Daily Business Review (Broward Edition) (USA ISSN 1538-1757) **1090**
• Daily Business Review (Online Edition) (USA) **1090**
• Daily Business Review (Palm Beach Edition) (USA ISSN 1538-2311) **1090**
• Daily Bytes (USA) **3974**
• Daily Californian (USA ISSN 1050-2300) **3974**
• The Daily Campus (Dallas) (USA) **2280**
Daily Campus (Storrs Mansfield) (USA) **2280**
• Daily Canadian Oil Report (CAN ISSN 1715-4944) **6766**
• Daily Cardinal (USA ISSN 0011-5398) **2280**
The Daily Challenge (USA) **3529**
Daily Champion (NGA ISSN 0795-5146) **3920**
• The Daily Charge (IRQ ISSN 1943-0442) **6417**
Daily Chronicle (NZL) **3917**
Daily Collegian *see* The Collegian (Fresno) **2278**
Daily Collegian (Fresno) (USA) **2280**
Daily Collegian (University Park) (USA) **2280**
Daily Commerce (USA ISSN 0279-4195) **7588**
• Daily Commercial News and Construction Record (CAN ISSN 0317-3178) **1001**
Daily Commercial Record (USA ISSN 0889-2431) **1090**
Daily Commercial Recorder (USA ISSN 8750-734X) **1090**
• Daily Compilation of Presidential Documents (USA ISSN 1946-6986) **7128**
The Daily Construction News (KOR) **1001**
Daily Construction Report *see* Michigan Contractor & Builder **1024**
Daily Construction Service (USA ISSN 0011-5401) **1001**
Daily Construction Service - Southern California (USA) **1001**
The Daily Cougar (USA) **2280**
• The Daily Courier (CAN ISSN 0842-0092) **3808**
Daily Court Reporter (USA) **4654**
Daily Court Review (USA ISSN 0740-1949) **4865**
• Daily Cow (USA) **262**
• Daily Customer Service Newsletter (USA) **1737**
• The Daily Deal (USA ISSN 1545-830X) **1090**
The Daily Deal Digital *see* The Daily Deal **1090**
The Daily Deal E-Newsletters *see* The Daily Deal **1090**
The Daily Deal Wireless *see* The Daily Deal **1090**
• Daily Defense News Capsule (USA) **6417**
Daily Depository Shipping List (USA ISSN 0145-0646) **5005**
• Daily Deshonnati (IND) **3880**
Daily Devotions *see* African American History Month **7782**
• Daily Devotions for the Deaf (USA ISSN 0744-9100) **4073**
Daily Dispatch (ZAF ISSN 1024-3496) **3948**
• Daily Eastern News (USA ISSN 0894-1599) **2280**
Daily Egyptian (USA) **3529**
Daily Electricity News *see* Nikkan Denki Tsushin **3326**
• Daily Environment Report (Online) (USA ISSN 1521-9402) **3413**
The Daily Events (USA) **4654**
Daily Evergreen (USA) **2280**
Daily Excelsior (IND) **3880**
• Daily Express (GBR) **3863**
• The Daily Fake News (USA) **5213**
• Daily Free Press (USA ISSN 1094-7337) **2280**
• Daily-From Stats Can. (CAN) **1223**
• Daily Gleaner (CAN ISSN 0821-6983) **3808**
Daily Gleaner - Food Supplement (JAM ISSN 0011-5428) **3633**
• Daily Grain Review (USA ISSN 1931-4434) **178**
Daily Graphic (CAN ISSN 0832-4298) **3808**
Daily Graphs. N A S D A Q (O T C). - American Stock Exchange - O.T.C. (USA) **1620**
Daily Graphs. N.Y.S.E. (New York Stock Exchange) (USA) **1620**
Daily Graphs. New York Stock Exchange *see* Daily Graphs. N.Y.S.E. **1620**
Daily Graphs. Option Guide (USA) **1620**
Daily Guide (ZAF) **7636**
Daily Guideposts (USA ISSN 0190-5457) **7636**
Daily Haq Parast (IND) **3880**
The Daily Helmsman (USA) **2280**
Daily Herald *see* Sun (London) **3871**
Daily Herald-Tribune (Grande Prairie) (CAN ISSN 0839-4873) **3808**
Daily Hindi Milap (IND) **3880**
Daily Illini (USA) **2280**
Daily Information Bulletin (GBR ISSN 1356-353X) **7432**
• Daily Inqilab (BGD) **3799**
Daily Insurance Reporter (USA) **4500**
The Daily Iowan (USA) **2280**
• Daily Jagran/Dainik Jagran (IND) **3880**
The Daily Jang (PAK) **3926**
The Daily Jang Lahore *see* Ruznamah-i Jang **3926**
Daily Jang London (GBR ISSN 1352-7541) **7710**
• Daily Journal of Commerce (Metairie) (USA) **1001**
• Daily Journal of Commerce (Portland) (USA ISSN 0896-8012) **1427**
Daily Kansan *see* University Daily Kansan **2306**
• Daily Kent Stater (USA ISSN 0011-5444) **2280**
• Daily Labor Report (USA ISSN 0418-2693) **1674**
Daily Lasso *see* The Lasso **2289**
† • Daily Law Reports Index (GBR ISSN 0955-0798) **8948**
Daily Legal News (Cleveland) (USA) **4654**
The Daily Legal News (Shreveport) (USA) **4654**
The Daily Legal News (Youngstown) (USA) **4654**
Daily Legislative Report (Baton Rouge) (USA) **7432**
Daily Legislative Report (Jackson) (USA) **7432**
Daily Legislative Report (Springfield) (USA ISSN 0277-4917) **7433**
Daily Legislative Reporter (USA) **7433**
• Daily Mail (GBR ISSN 0307-7578) **3863**
Daily Mail and Guardian *see* Mail & Guardian **3949**
• Daily Mail & Guardian (ZAF) **3948**
Daily Mail Ski (GBR ISSN 0960-6157) **8310**
Daily Market Report (USA) **1620**
Daily Mashal Bahawalpur *see* Mashal **3926**
Daily Meillat *see* Dainik Meillat **3799**
The Daily Mercury *see* The Guelph Mercury **3810**
Daily Milap (IND) **3880**
Daily Miner and News (CAN ISSN 0839-4989) **3808**
Daily Mississippian (USA ISSN 1077-8667) **2280**
Daily Monitor (ETH) **3837**
Daily Monitor (MWI) **3906**
Daily Munger Oilgram (USA ISSN 0276-5934) **6766**
Daily Nadeem (IND) **3880**
Daily Nara-e-Haq *see* Nara-e-Haq **3926**
• Daily Nation (KEN ISSN 1025-1227) **3902**
Daily Nation on the Web *see* Daily Nation **3902**
Daily Nawan Zamana (IND) **3880**
Daily Nebraskan (USA ISSN 1090-4085) **2280**
• Daily News/Dikgang tsa Gompieno (BWA) **3803**
• Daily News (NPL) **3913**
Daily News *see* Taranaki Daily News **3919**
• Daily News (POL ISSN 1230-3739) **3928**
Daily News (TZA ISSN 0856-3810) **3961**
• Daily News (ZAF ISSN 1016-8184) **3948**
Daily News (Botswana) *see* Daily News **3803**
• Daily News (Halifax) (CAN ISSN 0715-4321) **3808**
• Daily News (Harare) (ZWE ISSN 1607-3762) **3996**
• Daily News (Nanaimo) (CAN) **3808**
▼ • Daily News Briefing (USA ISSN 1947-8011) **3974**
Daily News Record *see* D N R **8449**
• Daily NewsFax (USA ISSN 1079-6436) **4384**
The Daily Northwestern (USA ISSN 1523-5033) **2280**
• The Daily Observer (CAN) **3808**
• The Daily Observer (GMB ISSN 0796-0832) **3842**
• Daily Observer (USA) **3529**
The Daily O'Collegian (USA) **2280**
The Daily of the University of Washington (USA) **2281**
Daily Oil Bulletin *see* Nickle's Daily Oil Bulletin **6780**
Daily Online Prices *see* Commodities Online Daily **1617**
Daily Orange (USA) **2281**
• Daily Pacific Builder (USA ISSN 1084-970X) **1001**
Daily Panth Khalsa (IND) **7707**
Daily Pasban (IND) **3880**
• Daily Pennsylvanian (USA) **2281**
The Daily PLAnet (USA) **5005**
The Daily Post (NZL ISSN 1170-0254) **3917**
Daily Power (ZAF) **7636**
• Daily Press (CAN ISSN 0841-6966) **3808**
• The Daily Princetonian (USA ISSN 0885-7601) **2281**
Daily Producer *see* The Farmer (Minnesota) **111**
The Daily Purbanchal (BGD) **3799**
Daily Racing Form (Gardena) (USA ISSN 1069-8795) **8310**
• Daily Radio Newsline (USA ISSN 1946-2697) **104**
• The Daily Reckoning Australia (AUS ISSN 1834-3104) **1620**
• Daily Record (GBR ISSN 0956-8069) **3967**
Daily Record (Baltimore) (USA) **4654**
Daily Record (Kansas City) (USA) **1090**
The Daily Record (Little Rock) (USA) **4654**
The Daily Record (Omaha) (USA) **1090**
The Daily Recorder (USA ISSN 0197-8055) **1090**
• Daily Report (Atlanta) (USA ISSN 1063-6439) **4654**
• Daily Report for Executives (USA ISSN 0148-8155) **1737**
• The Daily Reporter (Columbus) (USA ISSN 0011-5487) **4654**
Daily Reporter (Lincoln) (USA) **1090**
• The Daily Reporter (Milwaukee) (USA ISSN 0749-7113) **4592**
• Daily Reporter (Milwaukee) (USA) **1001**
Daily Reveille *see* The Reveille **2298**
Daily Reveille (USA) **2281**
Daily Rover (IND) **3880**
Daily Sada-e-Pakistan *see* Sada-e-Pakistan **3926**
Daily Sagar (IND) **3880**
Daily Salar (IND) **3880**
Daily Shipping News (USA) **8642**
Daily Siyasat Jadid (IND) **3880**
• The Daily Star (BGD) **3799**
• Daily Star (GBR ISSN 0957-6231) **3967**
Daily Stock Price Index *see* Standard & Poor's Daily Stock Price Record. American Stock Exchange **1652**
Daily Stock Price Record. American Stock Exchange *see* Standard & Poor's Daily Stock Price Record. American Stock Exchange **1652**
Daily Stock Price Record: N A S D A Q *see* Standard & Poor's. Daily Stock Price Record. N A S D A Q **1652**
• Daily Sugar Report (GBR) **3673**
Daily Summary of the Japanese Press (JPN ISSN 0499-2814) **4586**
Daily Sun (ZAF ISSN 1683-5654) **3948**
• The Daily Swing Trade (USA) **1620**
• Daily Tar Heel (USA ISSN 1070-9436) **2281**
• Daily Targum (USA) **2281**
• Daily Tax Report (USA ISSN 0092-6884) **1919**
Daily TaxFax (USA) **1919**
Daily Telegraph (AUS) **3794**
• Daily Telegraph (GBR ISSN 0307-1235) **3864**
Daily Telegraph Seasons (GBR) **8696**
Daily Tender Bulletin (ZAF ISSN 0258-8986) **1334**
• Daily Territorial (USA ISSN 0743-8397) **1090**
• The Daily Texan (USA ISSN 1090-1108) **2281**
Daily Thanthi *see* Dinathanthi **3881**
Daily Times (MWI) **3906**
• Daily Tips for Entrepreneurs (USA) **1090**
Daily Tir-Kuman (IND) **3880**
Daily Titan (USA) **2281**
The Daily Toreador (USA) **2281**
Daily Trade News (KOR) **1561**
Daily Transcript (USA) **7588**
Daily Treasury Statement *see* U.S. Department of the Treasury. Financial Management Service. Daily Treasury Statement **1953**
Daily Tribune (BGD) **3799**
Daily Trojan (USA) **2281**
The Daily Universe (USA) **2281**

DIRECTORY 2010 DAMASCUS ROAD 10181

Daily University Star (USA) **2281**
The Daily Utah Chronicle (USA) **2281**
Daily Vanguard *see* Vanguard (Portland) **2308**
Daily Variety (Gotham Edition) *see* Daily Variety (Los Angeles) **2379**
Daily Variety (Hollywood Edition) *see* Daily Variety (Los Angeles) **2379**
• Daily Variety (Los Angeles) (USA ISSN 0011-5509) **2379**
Daily Vidette (USA) **2281**
Daily Walk *see* Navigators Daily Walk **7768**
Daily Washington Law Reporter (USA ISSN 1066-6095) **4654**
Daily Watchwords (GBR) **7753**
Daily Weather Maps *see* Tenkizu **6396**
• Daily Weather Maps (Weekly Series) (USA) **6351**
Daily Word (USA ISSN 0011-5525) **7753**
The Daily Yomiuri *see* Yomiuri Shimbun (Satellite Edition) **3901**
➤ Daimon (ESP ISSN 1130-0507) **6913**
† Dainamikkusu ni Kansaru Odio Bijuaru Shinpojiumu/Audio Visual Symposium on Dynamics (JPN) **8948**
Dainik Alok (IND) **3880**
Dainik Asam (IND) **3880**
Dainik Azad Rajasthan (IND) **3880**
Dainik Basumati (IND) **3880**
Dainik Bhaskar (IND) **3880**
Dainik Ganadoot (IND) **3880**
Dainik Hamara Yug (IND) **3880**
Dainik Jagran *see* Daily Jagran **3880**
Dainik Jagran (Agra Edition) *see* Dainik Jagran (Kanpur Edition) **3880**
Dainik Jagran (Aligarh Edition) *see* Dainik Jagran (Kanpur Edition) **3880**
Dainik Jagran (Allahabad Edition) *see* Dainik Jagran (Kanpur Edition) **3880**
Dainik Jagran (Bareilly Edition) *see* Dainik Jagran (Kanpur Edition) **3880**
Dainik Jagran (Bhopal Edition) *see* Dainik Jagran (Kanpur Edition) **3880**
Dainik Jagran (Dehradun Edition) *see* Dainik Jagran (Kanpur Edition) **3880**
Dainik Jagran (Gorakhpur Edition) *see* Dainik Jagran (Kanpur Edition) **3880**
Dainik Jagran (Hisar Edition) *see* Dainik Jagran (Kanpur Edition) **3880**
Dainik Jagran (Jallandar Edition) *see* Dainik Jagran (Kanpur Edition) **3880**
Dainik Jagran (Jhansi Edition) *see* Dainik Jagran (Kanpur Edition) **3880**
• Dainik Jagran (Kanpur Edition) (IND ISSN 0972-1835) **3880**
Dainik Jagran (Lucknow Edition) *see* Dainik Jagran (Kanpur Edition) **3880**
Dainik Jagran (Meerut Edition) *see* Dainik Jagran (Kanpur Edition) **3880**
Dainik Jagran (Moradabad Edition) *see* Dainik Jagran (Kanpur Edition) **3880**
Dainik Jagran (New Delhi Edition) *see* Dainik Jagran (Kanpur Edition) **3880**
Dainik Jagran (Patna Edition) *see* Dainik Jagran (Kanpur Edition) **3880**
Dainik Jagran (Rewa Edition) *see* Dainik Jagran (Kanpur Edition) **3880**
Dainik Jagran (Varanasi Edition) *see* Dainik Jagran (Kanpur Edition) **3880**
Dainik Janambhumi (IND) **3880**
Dainik Jugasankha (IND) **3880**
Dainik Kamal Netra (IND) **3880**
Dainik Kashmir Times *see* Kashmir Times **3884**
Dainik Lipi (IND) **3880**
Dainik Lokmat (IND) **3880**
Dainik Lokpath (IND) **3880**
Dainik Mahasagar *see* Mahasagar (Nagpur) **3885**
Dainik Meillat (BGD) **3799**
Dainik Navajyoti (IND) **3881**
Dainik Niranjan (IND) **3881**
Dainik Prabhat (IND) **3881**
Dainik Rajpath (IND) **3881**
Dainik Saamana (IND) **3881**
Dainik Sambad (IND) **3881**
Dainik Sandhya Prachar (IND) **3881**
Dainik Sandhya Prakash (IND) **3881**
Dainik Sonar Cachar (IND) **3881**
Dainik Tribune (IND) **3881**
Dainik Vishwa Pariwar (IND) **3881**
Dainippon Doboku Gijutsu Kenkyujoho/Dai Nippon Construction. Technical Report (JPN ISSN 0915-7093) **3264**
Dainippon Ink and Chemicals Technical Review (Print Edition) *see* D I C Technical Review (Print Edition) **3242**
Dainippon Koboku K.K. Gijutsu Shiryo/Dai Nippon Construction Co., Ltd. Technical Materials (JPN ISSN 0914-3890) **1001**
Daintith U K Oil & Gas Law *see* U K Oil & Gas Law **6795**
• Daiqi Kexue/Chinese Journal of Atmospheric Science (CHN ISSN 1006-9895) **6351**
Dairy *see* New Mexico State University. Cooperative Extension Service. Guide D **294**
Dairy and Field Crop Digest (USA) **262**
Dairy & Food Industries Magazine (IRL ISSN 1393-8738) **262**
Dairy & Food Industries Yearbook (IRL ISSN 1393-8746) **262**
Dairy & Ice Cream Industries Directory *see* Dairy Industries International **3633**
Dairy & Liquid Foods Technology (GBR ISSN 1471-8707) **3633**
• Dairy Australia (AUS ISSN 1448-6849) **262**
Dairy Australia *see* The Dairy Australian (International Edition) **263**
• Dairy Australia. Annual Report (AUS ISSN 1449-860X) **262**
• Dairy Australian (Farm Edition) (AUS ISSN 1448-6830) **262**
• The Dairy Australian (International Edition) (AUS ISSN 1448-708X) **263**
Dairy Connection *see* Food Connect **7517**
• Dairy Council Digest (USA ISSN 0011-5568) **6657**
The Dairy Council. Topical Update (GBR) **263**
Dairy - Deli - Bake Digest (USA) **3633**
Dairy Executive (IRL ISSN 0790-732X) **263**
Dairy Executive. Directory and Diary (IRL) **263**
Dairy Facts and Figures (GBR ISSN 1461-9229) **263**
Dairy Facts and Figures at a Glance (CAN ISSN 0317-6207) **178**
• Dairy Farmer (GBR ISSN 1475-6994) **263**
Dairy Farmers of America Leader *see* D F A Leader **262**
Dairy Field *see* Dairy Foods **3633**
Dairy, Food and Environmental Sanitation *see* Food Protection Trends **3641**
• Dairy Foods (USA ISSN 0888-0050) **3633**
Dairy Foods' Buyer's Guide and Sourcebook (USA) **3633**
Dairy Goat Journal (USA ISSN 0011-5592) **284**
Dairy Goat Society of Australia. Victorian Branch Newsletter (AUS ISSN 0815-9769) **284**
Dairy Guide (IND ISSN 0970-3438) **263**
• Dairy Herd Management (USA ISSN 0011-5614) **263**
Dairy Hot Line (USA) **263**
Dairy India Yearbook (IND ISSN 0970-9932) **263**
• Dairy Industries International (GBR ISSN 0308-8197) **3633**
Dairy Industry and Retail Directory Europe *see* Jahrbuch Europaeischer Hersteller und Vermarkter von Milcherzeugnissen **266**
Dairy Innovation (GBR) **263**
Dairy Ireland (IRL) **263**
The Dairy Mail (ZAF ISSN 1561-4301) **263**
Dairy Mail Africa (ZAF ISSN 1818-9083) **263**
• Dairy Market News (USA ISSN 0744-1282) **263**
Dairy Market Statistics: Annual Summary (USA ISSN 0098-6690) **178**
• Dairy Markets (GBR ISSN 1475-0686) **263**
• Dairy Monthly Imports (USA) **179**
Dairy News (IRL) **263**
• Dairy Pipeline (USA) **263**
Dairy Policy (CAN ISSN 0318-2967) **263**
Dairy Producer Highlights (USA) **263**
Dairy Products *see* U.S. Department of Agriculture. National Agricultural Statistics Service. Dairy Products (Print) **8995**
Dairy Products: A World Survey *see* The World Market for Dairy Products **269**
Dairy Profit Weekly (USA ISSN 1051-645X) **263**
• Dairy Projects (AUS ISSN 1832-2042) **263**
Dairy Roundup (USA) **263**
• Dairy Science Abstracts (GBR ISSN 0011-5681) **179**
• ➤ Dairy Science & Technology (FRA ISSN 1958-5586) **884**
• Dairy Statistics (NZL ISSN 0114-975X) **179**
• Dairy Today (USA ISSN 1056-1382) **263**
▼ Dairy Trade Review (GBR ISSN 1757-3173) **263**
Dairy Update (GBR ISSN 1756-4727) **263**
Dairy World (USA ISSN 0736-4962) **263**
Dairy3 Conference. Proceedings (NZL ISSN 1176-2101) **263**
Dairying Today (NZL ISSN 1171-0772) **263**
The Dairyman (NZL ISSN 0114-1473) **264**
Dairymen's Digest (USA) **264**
Dairymen's Digest (North Central Region Edition) (USA ISSN 0745-9033) **264**
Daisaku Ikeda Studies (NLD) **6913**
Daisy (GBR ISSN 1747-1044) **2184**
Daito Bunka Comparative Law and Political Science Review (JPN ISSN 1346-6941) **4654**
Daito Bunka Daigaku Kiyo. Shizen Kagaku/Daito Bunka University. Bulletin. Natural Sciences (JPN ISSN 0912-2346) **7849**
Daito Bunka University. Bulletin. Natural Sciences *see* Daito Bunka Daigaku Kiyo. Shizen Kagaku **7849**
Daito Hogaku/Journal of Law and Politics (JPN ISSN 0287-0940) **4654**
Daiyamondo Kabushiki-Toshi-Ban *see* Diamond, Stock Investment Edition **1620**
Daiyamondo Shinpojumu Koen Yoshishu/Abstracts of Diamond Symposium (JPN) **2094**
Daiyonki Kenkyu/Quaternary Research (JPN ISSN 0418-2642) **2730**
Daizu Tampakushitsu Kenkyu/Nutritional Science of Soy Protein, Japan (JPN ISSN 1344-4050) **6657**
Dajia/Masters (CHN ISSN 1005-4553) **5282**
Dajia Gushi (CHN ISSN 1672-1489) **5282**
Dajia Jiankang/Good Health for All (CHN ISSN 1009-6019) **6984**
Dajia Lai Shang Wang *see* Hello! Net **2557**
Dajiang Nanbei/South & North of the Yangtse River (CHN ISSN 1004-7891) **4181**
• Dajiang Zhoukan (CHN ISSN 1671-2366) **3824**
Dajnik Agradoot *see* Agradoot **3878**
DAK Magazine (NLD) **4500**
Dak Tar (IND ISSN 0011-5762) **2354**
• Dakar Medical (SEN ISSN 0850-797X) **5603**
Dakenraad (NLD ISSN 1381-2874) **1001**
DAKmagazin AHA! *see* AHA! **2175**
DAKmagazin Fit! *see* Fit! **7517**
DAKmagazin Start *see* Start! **7542**
Dakota (NLD ISSN 1871-6717) **52**
Dakota Collector (USA) **6894**
Dakota Counsel (USA) **3127**
Dakota Country (USA ISSN 0194-5769) **8310**
• Dakota Farmer (USA ISSN 1069-5397) **104**
Dakota Homestead Newsletter (USA ISSN 1520-5053) **3763**
Dakota Norway (NOR ISSN 1504-4181) **8540**
• Dakota Nurse Connection (USA) **5957**
Dakota Outdoors (USA ISSN 0891-902X) **8310**
Dakota Scientist (USA) **7849**
• The Dakota Student (USA ISSN 0274-9262) **2977**
† Dal Comune-Notizie (ITA) **8948**
dal Seme (ITA) **227**
Dalademokraten (SWE ISSN 1103-9183) **3955**
• Dalal Street Journal (IND) **1334**
Dalane Tidende (NOR) **3922**
Dalarna (SWE ISSN 1400-3376) **4213**
Dalarnas Fornminnes- och Hembygdsfoerbund. Skrifter (SWE ISSN 0418-3002) **4213**
Dalarnas Spelmansblad (SWE ISSN 0280-6584) **6561**
Daleel Al Montajat Al Sina'iah: Al Shariqah *see* Directory of Industrial Products: Sharjah, United Arab Emirates **1987**
Daleel Al Sariqah Lil Mosaddireen wa Al-Mostawrideen *see* Sharjah Exporter - Importer Directory **2027**
Dalesman (GBR ISSN 0011-5800) **3864**
Dalhousie Dental Journal (CAN ISSN 0418-3010) **5839**
Dalhousie French Studies (CAN ISSN 0711-8813) **5110**
Dalhousie Gazette (CAN ISSN 0011-5819) **2281**
• Dalhousie Journal of Legal Studies (CAN ISSN 1188-4258) **4654**
• Dalhousie Law Journal (CAN ISSN 0317-1663) **4654**
Dalhousie Magazine (CAN ISSN 1185-4014) **2281**
Dalhousie Peer (CAN ISSN 1912-8045) **3808**
• ➤ The Dalhousie Review (CAN ISSN 0011-5827) **5213**
Dalhousie University. Aquatron Laboratory. Biennial Report (CAN) **667**
Dalhousie University. Department of Oceanography. Biennial Report (CAN ISSN 1202-0974) **2803**
Dalhousie University. School of Information Management. Inform (CAN ISSN 1912-0079) **5005**
Dalhousie University. School of Library and Information Studies. Inform *see* Dalhousie University. School of Information Management. Inform **5005**
Dalhousie University. School of Library and Information Studies. Newsletter *see* Dalhousie University. School of Information Management. Inform **5005**
➤ Dalhousie University. School of Library and Information Studies. Occasional Papers (CAN ISSN 1048-471X) **5005**
Dalhousie University. School of Library and Information Studies. Y-A Hotline (CAN) **5005**
• Dali Yixueyuan Xuebao (Yixue Ban) (CHN ISSN 1004-4442) **5603**
Dalian Daily *see* Dalian Ribao **3824**
Dalian Dalian Polytechnic University. Journal *see* Dalian Gongye Daxue Xuebao **7849**
• Dalian Daxue Xuebao/Dalian University. Journal (CHN) **7958**
Dalian Fisheries College. Journal *see* Dalian Shuichan Xueyuan Xuebao **3589**
• ➤ Dalian Gongye Daxue Xuebao/Dalian Dalian Polytechnic University. Journal (CHN ISSN 1674-1404) **7849**
• Dalian Haishi Daxue Xuebao/Dalian Maritime University. Journal (CHN ISSN 1006-7736) **8642**
• Dalian Haishi Daxue Xuebao (Shehui Kexue Ban)/Dalian Maritime University. Journal (CHN ISSN 1671-7031) **7958**
Dalian Institute of Railway Technology. Journal *see* Dalian Jiaotong Daxue Xuebao **7849**
• Dalian Jiaotong Daxue Xuebao/Dalian Institute of Railway Technology. Journal (CHN ISSN 1673-9590) **7849**
• Dalian Ligong Daxue Xuebao/Dalian University of Technology. Journal (CHN ISSN 1000-8608) **7849**
• Dalian Ligong Daxue Xuebao (Shehui Kexue Ban)/Dalian University of Technology. Journal (Social Sciences) (CHN ISSN 1008-407X) **7958**
Dalian Maritime University. Journal *see* Dalian Haishi Daxue Xuebao **8642**
Dalian Maritime University. Journal *see* Dalian Haishi Daxue Xuebao (Shehui Kexue Ban) **7958**
Dalian Medical University. Journal *see* Dalian Yike Daxue Xuebao **5603**
• Dalian Minzu Xueyuan Xuebao/Dalian Nationalities University. Journal (CHN ISSN 1009-315X) **7849**
Dalian Nationalities University. Journal *see* Dalian Minzu Xueyuan Xuebao **7849**
Dalian Nianjian/Dalian Yearbook (CHN ISSN 1671-3001) **7433**
Dalian Qinggongye Xueyuan Xuebao/Dalian Institute of Light Industry. Journal *see* Dalian Gongye Daxue Xuebao **7849**
• Dalian Ribao/Dalian Daily (CHN) **3824**
• ➤ Dalian Shuichan Xueyuan Xuebao/Dalian Fisheries College. Journal (CHN ISSN 1000-9957) **3589**
Dalian Tiedao Xueyuan Xuebao/Dalian Institute of Railway Technology. Journal *see* Dalian Jiaotong Daxue Xuebao **7849**
Dalian University. Journal *see* Dalian Daxue Xuebao **7958**
Dalian University of Technology. Journal *see* Dalian Ligong Daxue Xuebao **7849**
Dalian University of Technology. Journal (Social Sciences) *see* Dalian Ligong Daxue Xuebao (Shehui Kexue Ban) **7958**
Dalian Yearbook *see* Dalian Nianjian **7433**
• Dalian Yike Daxue Xuebao/Dalian Medical University. Journal (CHN ISSN 1671-7295) **5603**
Ad-Dalil *see* An- Nahar **3905**
Dalil ad-Dawriat li-Dawlat al-Imarat al-Arabiyyah al-Muttahidah/Directory of the Periodicals in the United Arab Emirates (UAE) **623**
➤ Dalil ad-Dawriyat al-Libiya wa Muhtawayatuha/Index of Libyan Periodicals and their Contents (LBY) **623**
Dalil Al-Kuwait al-Yawm (KWT) **4822**
Dalil al-Musaddirin/Directory of Exporters (IND) **1561**
Dalil al-Sharqah al-Tijari *see* Sharjah Commercial Directory **2027**
Dalil el Arab *see* Arab Directory **3519**
Dalili (NLD ISSN 1871-3106) **3529**
Dallas Association of Law Librarians Advance Sheet *see* D A L L Advance Sheet **5004**
• Dallas Business Journal (USA ISSN 0899-4129) **1090**
Dallas Child *see* DallasChild **2150**
Dallas Cowboys Outlook (USA) **8226**
Dallas Family Magazine (USA) **2150**
Dallas/Fort Worth *see* D **3973**
Dallas - Fort Worth Home Buyer's Guide (USA ISSN 0894-0258) **7588**
† The Dallas - Fort Worth JobBank (USA ISSN 1069-5435) **8948**
Dallas / Fort Worth New Homes Guide (USA) **7588**
Dallas - Fort Worth People - The Airport Newspaper *see* D F W People - The Airport Newspaper **8778**
Dallas / Ft. Worth Service Directory *see* Greater Dallas Living **4540**
Dallas/Ft. Worth Service Directory *see* Greater Dallas Living **4540**
Dallas Greensheet (USA) **2637**
Dallas Home Design (USA) **4536**
Dallas Home Improvement (USA) **4536**
Dallas Institute of Humanities and Culture. Institute Newsletter (USA) **4449**
Dallas Job Bank *see* The Dallas - Fort Worth JobBank **8948**
Dallas Journal (USA) **3763**
Dallas Medical Journal (USA ISSN 0011-586X) **5603**
Dallas Meeting Professionals Guide (USA) **6279**
Dallas Official Visitors Guide (USA) **8696**
Dallas Post Tribune (USA ISSN 0746-7303) **3529**
Dallas Semiconductor Maxim Engineering Journal (USA) **3186**
Dallas Tenants News (USA) **4409**
Dallas Weekly (USA ISSN 0885-1271) **3529**
• DallasChild (USA) **2150**
• Dallo Scoglio di Santa Rita (ITA) **7794**
Le Dalloz (FRA ISSN 1298-728X) **4654**
Dalmatian Quarterly (USA ISSN 0893-987X) **6806**
Dal'nevostochnoe Malakologicheskoe Obshchestvo. Byulleten'/Russian Far East Malacological Society. Bulletin (RUS ISSN 1560-8425) **940**
Dal'nii Vostok (RUS ISSN 0130-3023) **4181**
• ➤ Dalton Transactions (GBR ISSN 1477-9226) **2115**
• Dalton Transactions (Online) (GBR ISSN 1477-9234) **2115**
Dalton's Allentown, Bethlehem, Lancaster Reading Metropolitan Directory: Business - Industry (USA) **1983**
Dalton's Baltimore - Washington Metropolitan Directory: Business - Industry (USA) **1983**
Dalton's New York Metropolitan Directory: Business - Industry (USA ISSN 1052-6609) **1983**
• Dalton's Philadelphia Metropolitan Directory: Business - Industry (USA ISSN 1053-685X) **1983**
Daltons Weekly (GBR ISSN 0011-5894) **7588**
Dalu Nongye Zixun *see* Zhongguo Dalu Nongye Zixun **172**
Dalu Zazhi/Continent Magazine (TWN ISSN 0496-6724) **389**
Daluqiao Shiye/Landbridge Horizon (CHN ISSN 1671-9670) **1090**
Dam Digest *see* Damu Nippon **3264**
Dam Engineering (GBR ISSN 0958-9341) **3264**
Dam Engineering *see* Damu Kogaku **3264**
• ➤ Dam Safety (Year). Annual Conference Proceedings (USA ISSN 1526-9191) **3264**
Dam Safety Update (USA) **3264**
Damage Report (USA) **8577**
Damages for Personal Injuries in Scotland *see* McEwan & Paton on Damages for Personal Injuries in Scotland **4730**
• Damages in Tort Actions (USA) **4655**
Damals (DEU ISSN 0011-5908) **4137**
Damals Bei Uns in Westfalen (DEU) **4213**
• Damar Cerrahi Dergisi/Turkish Journal of Vascular Surgery (TUR ISSN 1301-1839) **6241**
Damascus Road (USA) **5282**

Title

▼ *new title*　　† *ceased*　　● *electronic media*　　➤ *refereed*

10186 DECCAN CHRONICLE ULRICH'S PERIODICALS

Deccan Chronicle (IND) **3881**
Deccan College. Postgraduate & Research Institute. Bulletin (IND ISSN 0045-9801) **7958**
➤ The Deccan Geographer (IND ISSN 0011-7269) **4003**
Deccan Herald (IND) **3881**
Deccan Sugar Technologists Association. Annual Convention Proceedings (IND) **3633**
Decedents' Estates in Maryland (USA) **4901**
December (USA ISSN 0070-3141) **5283**
Decennial Digest: American Digest System *see* West's General Digest **4813**
▼ Le Dechaine (FRA ISSN 1963-2487) **7205**
Dechaine ton Corps (FRA ISSN 1774-4687) **4592**
Dechema Monographien (DEU ISSN 0070-315X) **2099**
Decheniana (DEU ISSN 0366-872X) **667**
Decheniana-Beihefte (Bonn) (DEU ISSN 0416-833X) **667**
† Dechets Sciences et Techniques (FRA ISSN 1271-0318) **8949**
† Dech'Infos (FRA ISSN 1774-508X) **8949**
• Decibel (USA) **6561**
Decide *see* Schmuck Magazin **4569**
▼ • Decideur Public (FRA ISSN 1958-5330) **5005**
Decideurs d'Ile-de-France (FRA ISSN 0982-0671) **4409**
• ➤ Decimononica/Journal of Nineteenth Century Hispanic Cultural Production (USA ISSN 1554-6535) **4290**
• ➤ Decision (IND ISSN 0304-0941) **1738**
• Decision (IRL ISSN 1393-2993) **1738**
Decision (MEX ISSN 0185-1985) **1401**
Decision *see* Odlocanje **7500**
• Decision (USA ISSN 0011-7307) **7754**
Decision Achats (FRA ISSN 1960-1379) **1813**
Decision Achats Entreprises et Collectivites *see* Decision Achats **1813**
• ➤ Decision Analysis (USA ISSN 1545-8490) **1738**
Decision & Information *see* Juece yu Xinxi **7149**
Decision Atelier (FRA ISSN 1777-6287) **8577**
Decision Boissons (FRA ISSN 1254-2733) **602**
• Decision Financiera Oportuna (MEX) **1335**
• Decision Line (USA ISSN 0732-6823) **1738**
Decision Making *see* Juece **7449**
➤ Decision Making in Manufacturing and Services (POL ISSN 1896-8325) **1738**
Decision Micro (FRA ISSN 1148-4675) **2570**
Decision Sante (FRA ISSN 1157-6197) **4092**
Decision Sante. Le Pharmacien Hopital (FRA ISSN 1293-8890) **6832**
Decision Sante. Profession Medecin (FRA ISSN 1952-9724) **5603**
• ➤ Decision Sciences (USA ISSN 0011-7315) **1738**
• Decision Sciences Institute. Proceedings (USA) **1738**
• ➤ Decision Sciences Journal of Innovative Education (USA ISSN 1540-4595) **2841**
• ➤ Decision Support Systems (NLD ISSN 0167-9236) **1738**
Decisiones seu Sententiae (VAT ISSN 1022-7288) **4655**
Decisions *see* Australian Financial Review **1309**
Decisions (FRA ISSN 1286-1952) **8310**
Decisions & Developments (USA) **4655**
• Decisions and Orders of the National Labor Relations Board (USA ISSN 0083-2227) **1674**
Decisions, Avis Publics, Circulaires et Communiques en Matiere de Telecommunications/Telecom Decisions, Public Notices, Circulars and News Releases (CAN ISSN 1713-3467) **2318**
Decisions des Chambres de Recours de l'Office Europeen des Brevets *see* Entscheidungen der Beschwerdekammern des Europaeischen Patentamts **8954**
• ➤ Decisions in Economics and Finance (ITA ISSN 1593-8883) **5482**
Decisions in Imaging Economics *see* Imaging Economics **6198**
• ➤ Decisions Marketing (FRA ISSN 0779-7389) **1813**
Decisions of the Boards of Appeal of the European Patent Office *see* Entscheidungen der Beschwerdekammern des Europaeischen Patentamts **8954**
Decisions of the Comptroller General of the United States *see* United States Government Accountability Office. Decisions of the Comptroller General of the United States **7474**
Decisions of the Constitutional Court *see* Repertorio Aranzadi del Tribunal Constitucional (Quarterly Edition) **4768**
Decisions of the Department of the Interior *see* U.S. Department of the Interior. Decisions **7472**
Decisions of the Federal Labor Relations Authority (USA ISSN 0278-7695) **1674**
• Decisions of the Nebraska Court of Appeals (USA ISSN 1066-6451) **4655**
Decisions on Air Transport Licence Applications (GBR) **8540**
Decisions on Geographic Names in the United States *see* U.S. Geological Survey. Board on Geographic Names. Decisions on Geographic Names in the United States **4031**
Deck Chair *see* Deckchair **8697**
▼ Deck, Patio & Pool (USA ISSN 1946-0554) **439**
Deckare, Agent, Science Fiction, Thrillers Magazine *see* D A S T Magazine **5441**
Deckchair (CAN ISSN 1715-8281) **8697**
Deckplate (USA ISSN 0747-072X) **6417**
The Declaration (USA ISSN 1545-0481) **3413**
• Declaration des Emissions de Gaz a Effet de Serre (CAN ISSN 1719-0479) **3485**
• Declassified Documents Reference System (USA) **7199**
Declic (FRA ISSN 1764-1144) **4064**
Declic Photo Magazine (FRA ISSN 1769-9568) **6966**
Le Declin (CAN) **2281**
Deco (DEU) **4536**
Deco (TWN) **4536**
Deco Style (ROM ISSN 1583-9508) **4536**
▼ Decodesign (FRA ISSN 1962-2775) **4536**
Decoletaje (ESP) **1001**
• Decomp (USA ISSN 1947-0436) **5213**
Decomposition Magazine *see* Decomp **5213**
Decor (TUR) **4536**
Decor (Des Moines) (USA ISSN 1935-6390) **4536**
Decor (Maryland Heights) (USA ISSN 0011-7358) **4555**
Decor & Style Magazine (USA) **4536**
Decor Bains (FRA) **4536**
Decor Idees (CAN ISSN 1718-8016) **1001**
Decor International Magazine (THA ISSN 0858-4028) **4536**
Decor Living (ITA ISSN 1826-9168) **4537**
Decor-Magasinet (NOR ISSN 1890-2928) **534**
▼ Decoracion (COL ISSN 2011-2254) **4537**
Decoracion Comercial Escaparatismo (ESP) **4537**
Decoracion Comercial Hosteleria (ESP) **4537**
Decoracion Mia *see* Mia Decoracion **4546**
Decorate With Paint (USA ISSN 1540-5435) **4537**
Decoratie (BEL ISSN 1370-9577) **4537**
Decorating *see* Budget Decorating (New York) **4534**
Decorating Digest Craft & Home Projects (USA ISSN 1064-3095) **4537**
Decorating Ideas (USA ISSN 1083-7086) **4537**
Decorating Products Retail Sales Report (USA) **4537**
Decorating Spaces (USA ISSN 1931-7700) **4537**
Decorating with Style (USA) **4537**
Decoration (BEL ISSN 1370-9585) **4537**
† Decoration (DEU ISSN 0938-1635) **8949**
Decoration Chez-Soi (CAN ISSN 0705-1093) **4537**
† Decoration de Reve (FRA ISSN 1772-7022) **8949**
Decorative & Country Painting (ITA ISSN 1970-0288) **534**
† • Decorative Artist's Workbook (USA ISSN 0893-1097) **8949**
Decorative Arts Society, 1850 to the Present. Journal (GBR) **534**
Decorative Arts Society Newsletter (USA ISSN 0884-4011) **485**
† Decorative Crochet (FRA ISSN 0994-2114) **8949**
Decorative Design (JPN ISSN 0289-2847) **4333**
The Decorative Painter (USA ISSN 1096-3278) **534**
The Decorator (GBR) **4537**
• Decormag (CAN ISSN 0315-047X) **4537**
Decoro Io (ITA ISSN 1970-0296) **4537**
† Decoupage Casa (ITA ISSN 1828-1869) **8949**
Decouverte (FRA ISSN 1621-0085) **7849**
Decouverte les Sables d'Olonne (FRA ISSN 1774-7465) **4003**
Decouvrir *see* Association Francophone pour le Savoir. Decouvrir **7837**
Decoy Magazine (USA ISSN 1055-0364) **4333**
• Decree (USA ISSN 1092-0730) **8036**
La Decroissance (FRA ISSN 1767-0187) **7128**
▼ Decryptages (FRA ISSN 1955-5377) **3127**
Dedalo (ITA ISSN 1128-7543) **1001**
Dedalo (PER) **5110**
Dedalus (PRT ISSN 0871-9519) **5283**
Dedica (DEU ISSN 0940-8703) **4059**
• Dedicated Systems Magazine (BEL ISSN 1375-6753) **2520**
• Dedicated Systems Magazine (Online) (BEL) **2520**
Dedicon Bulletin (NLD ISSN 1872-5643) **4081**
• DeDiseno (MEX ISSN 1405-0439) **7319**
Deduct It! (USA ISSN 1941-8248) **1959**
• Deductions (AUS ISSN 1442-1046) **1919**
† Deelname aan Buitenlandse Kansspelen in Nederland (NLD ISSN 1871-3866) **8949**
Deep Drilling and Production Symposium. Proceedings (USA ISSN 0272-9539) **6766**
Deep Focus (IND) **6495**
Deep Foundations Institute Journal *see* D F I Journal **3186**
Deep-Freeze Industry *see* Hutoipar **3646**
Deep Meditation *see* Chan **7700**
• Deep Outside S F F H (Science Fiction, Fantacy, Horrer) (USA) **5441**
† • Deep-Sea Newsletter (DNK ISSN 0903-2533) **8949**
• ➤ Deep-Sea Research. Part 1: Oceanographic Research Papers (GBR ISSN 0967-0637) **2803**
Deep Sea Research. Part 1: Oceanographic Research Papers *see* Deep-Sea Research. Part 1: Oceanographic Research Papers **2803**
• ➤ Deep-Sea Research. Part 2: Topical Studies in Oceanography (GBR ISSN 0967-0645) **2803**
The Deep-Sky Observer (GBR ISSN 0967-6139) **574**
• Deep South (NZL) **5213**
Deep South Genealogical Quarterly (USA ISSN 0418-4904) **3764**
Deep South Jewish Voice (USA) **7720**
Deep South U S A (GBR) **8697**
Deep Thoughts (USA ISSN 1073-4864) **5442**
Deepavali (IND) **3881**
• The Deepening (USA ISSN 1559-7733) **5283**
Deepika (IND) **3881**
• Deeptapioca (USA) **485**
Deepwater (USA) **8642**
Deer (GBR ISSN 0141-4259) **940**
Deer and Deer Hunting *see* Deer & Deer Hunting **8310**
Deer & Deer Hunting (USA ISSN 0164-7318) **8310**
• Deer & Elk Farmers' Digest Newsletter (CAN ISSN 1910-2038) **104**
Deer Course for Veterinarians. Proceedings (NZL ISSN 0112-5265) **8796**
Deer Creek Pilot (USA) **3974**
The Deer Farmer (NZL ISSN 0110-7992) **285**
Deer Farmers' Digest *see* Deer & Elk Farmers' Digest Newsletter **104**
Deer Farming Dnnual *see* New Zealand Deer Farming Annual **294**
Deer Hunter's Almanac (USA) **8311**
➤ Deerghayu International (IND ISSN 0970-3381) **308**
• Defaulted Bonds Newsletter (USA ISSN 1057-7521) **1620**
➤ Defect and Diffusion Forum (CHE ISSN 1012-0386) **6310**
Defective Product: Evidence to Verdict (USA) **4655**
Defectology *see* Defektologiya **3038**
Defectology Theory and Practice *see* Beogradska Defektoloska Skola **3037**
Defektologiya (RUS ISSN 0130-3074) **4064**
➤ Defektologiya/Defectology (UKR) **3038**
Defektoskopiya (RUS ISSN 0130-3082) **3343**
• ➤ Defence and Peace Economics (GBR ISSN 1024-2694) **6417**
Defence & Public Service Helicopter *see* Defence Helicopter **52**
• ➤ Defence and Security Analysis (GBR ISSN 1475-1798) **6417**
• ➤ Defence and Security Studies (NOR ISSN 1504-6532) **2226**
Defence & Strategy *see* Obrana a Strategie **7256**
Defence Asia - Pacific (USA ISSN 1011-2200) **6417**
• Defence Daily International (USA ISSN 1529-4250) **6418**
Defence Digitisation Bulletin (GBR ISSN 1464-8970) **6418**
Defence Equipment Market Report *see* Key Note Market Report: Defence Equipment **6430**
Defence Forces Review (IRL ISSN 1649-7066) **6418**
• Defence Helicopter (GBR ISSN 1741-6043) **52**
• Defence Industry (Hampton) (GBR ISSN 1741-7821) **6418**
Defence Industry Report (GBR ISSN 1465-8313) **6418**
Defence Journal (PAK ISSN 0257-2141) **6418**
Defence Management (IND) **6418**
Defence Management Journal (GBR ISSN 1464-2646) **6418**
• Defence R & D Canada. Annual Report (Research & Development) (CAN ISSN 1702-3599) **6418**
Defence Research & Analysis. Briefs (GBR) **6418**
Defence Research & Development Organization Newsletter *see* D R D O Newsletter **6417**
Defence Review (PAK) **6418**
Defence Science and Technology Department. Materials Research Laboratories. Technical Notes (AUS) **3343**
Defence Science and Technology Organisation. Materials Research Laboratories. Reports (AUS) **3343**
• Defence Science Journal (IND ISSN 0011-748X) **6418**
Defence Scientific Information & Documentation Centre Journal of Library & Information Technology *see* D E S I D O C Journal of Library & Information Technology **5004**
• ➤ Defence Studies (GBR ISSN 1470-2436) **6418**
Defence Systems International (GBR ISSN 0951-9688) **6418**
Defence Technology International *see* D T I **6417**
Defence Today (IND ISSN 0971-4197) **6418**
• ➤ Defender (AUS ISSN 0811-6407) **2226**
The Defender (USA ISSN 1549-8107) **3413**
Defender (Defiance) (USA ISSN 0011-7501) **2281**
Defenders (USA ISSN 0162-6337) **2608**
• Defending D U Is in Washington (Driving Under the Influence) (USA) **4889**
Defending Pesticides in Litigation (USA ISSN 1549-2869) **3495**
Defending Provincial Offence Cases in Ontario *see* Handling Provincial Offence Cases in Ontario (Year) **4684**
Defensa (ESP ISSN 0211-3732) **6418**
Defensa del Patrimoni Natura en Accio en Accio *see* D E P A N A en Accio **4449**
▼ Defensa Judicial (COL ISSN 2011-2785) **4655**
• ➤ Defense A R Journal (Acquisition Review) (USA ISSN 1553-6408) **6418**
• Defense A T & L (Acquisition, Technology & Logistics) (USA ISSN 1547-5476) **2520**
Defense and Aerospace Agencies Briefing (USA) **52**
Defense & Aerospace Companies *see* Market Intelligence Reports: Defense & Aerospace Companies **6432**
Defense and Aerospace Companies Briefing (USA) **52**
Defense and Aerospace Report *see* Defense and Security Report **6418**
Defense and Arms Control Studies Seminar Papers *see* D A C S Seminar Papers **6417**
• Defense & Foreign Affairs Strategic Policy (USA ISSN 0277-4933) **7230**
Defense & Security (RUS ISSN 1608-3520) **6418**
Defense and Security Report (USA ISSN 1934-2543) **6418**
Defense Business Briefing (USA) **6418**
Defense Communities (USA ISSN 1088-9000) **6418**
• Defense Concepts (USA ISSN 1932-3816) **6418**
Defense Consulting & Outsourcing (USA ISSN 1933-5571) **2226**
Defense Contract Audit Agency Contract Audit Manual *see* D C A A Contract Audit Manual **1919**
Defense Contract Audit Agency Offices. Directory *see* D C A A Offices. Directory **1919**
• Defense Contract Awards (USA ISSN 1062-0613) **6418**
• Defense Contracts International (GBR) **6418**
• Defense Counsel Journal (USA ISSN 0895-0016) **4830**
• Defense Daily (USA ISSN 0889-0404) **52**
Defense des Grades de la Police Nationale (FRA) **6418**
• Defense Environment Alert (USA) **3413**
Defense et Securite Internationale (FRA ISSN 1772-788X) **6419**
Defense F A R Supplement (Federal Acquisition Regulation) (USA) **6419**
• Defense Foreign Affairs Handbook (USA ISSN 0160-5836) **6419**
Defense Information Systems Agency. Circulars (USA) **6419**
Defense Information Systems Agency. Notices (USA) **6419**
Defense Intelligence Journal *see* National Intelligence Journal **7254**
Defense International *see* Quanqiu Fangwei Zazhi **6442**
• Defense Law Journal (USA ISSN 0011-7587) **4830**
Defense Logistics Agency Publishing System *see* D L A P S **7480**
Defense Manufacturers & Suppliers Association of America Newsletter (USA) **6419**
Defense Media Review (USA ISSN 0893-0619) **6419**
• Defense Monitor (USA ISSN 0195-6450) **6419**
Defense Nationale *see* Defense Nationale et Securite Collective **6419**
Defense Nationale et Securite Collective (FRA ISSN 1950-3253) **6419**
• Defense News (USA ISSN 0884-139X) **6419**
Defense Nuclear Facilities Safety Board. Report to Congress on Acquisitions Made From Manufacturer Inside and Outside the United States, Fiscal Year (Year) (USA) **6419**
• Defense of Drunk Driving Cases: Criminal, Civil (USA) **4889**
Defense of Equal Employment Claims (USA) **1674**
Defense of Japan (Year) (JPN) **6419**
• Defense of Narcotics Cases (USA) **4889**
Defense of Speeding, Reckless Driving and Vehicular Homicide *see* Defense of Speeding, Reckless Driving & Vehicular Homicide **4889**
Defense of Speeding, Reckless Driving & Vehicular Homicide (USA) **4889**
▼ Defense, Strategie & Relations Internationales (FRA ISSN 1957-9578) **7230**
Defense Systems (USA ISSN 1558-836X) **6419**
• Defense Tech Briefs (USA) **8419**
• Defense Technology Business (USA ISSN 1048-4612) **6419**
Defense Technology Journal *see* Boei Gijutsu Janaru **6413**
Defense Today *see* Defense Daily **52**
• Defense Transportation Journal (USA ISSN 0011-7625) **6419**
Defensive Tactics for Law Enforcement, Public Safety & Correction Officers (USA) **4889**
Defi *see* Challenge (New York) **7115**
Defi (Amancy) (FRA ISSN 1952-8868) **5886**
Defi-Sciences (CAN) **2281**
Defined Benefit Monitor *see* Benefits and Pensions Monitor **1856**
Defined Benefit Pension Plans: Checklist and Illustrative Financial Statement *see* Checklists and Illustrative Financial Statements for Defined Benefit Pension Plans **1285**
'Defined Contribution & Savings Plan Alert *see* Defined Contribution & Savings Plan Alert **1620**
• Defined Contribution & Savings Plan Alert (USA ISSN 1556-3774) **1620**
Defined Contribution Monitor *see* Benefits and Pensions Monitor **1856**
Defined Contribution Plan News & Analysis *see* D C Plan News & Analysis **1334**
Defined Providence (USA ISSN 1066-2197) **5420**
▼ • Defining Ideas (USA ISSN 1947-4962) **7128**
Definitioner av Strukturbegreb inom Varuhandeln (SWE ISSN 1103-1875) **24**
† Defis (FRA ISSN 0759-089X) **8949**
Les Defis du C E A (Commissariat a l'Energie Atomique) (FRA ISSN 1163-619X) **7850**
Defiscience (CAN) **2281**
Deformacion Metalica (ESP ISSN 0210-685X) **6310**
➤ Deformatsiya i Razrushenie Materialov (RUS ISSN 1814-4632) **6310**
Defteros Heri *see* Deuteros Kheri **8257**
Degree Course Guides (Year) (GBR ISSN 0309-0485) **2955**
Degree Course Offers (GBR) **2977**
Degree Student's Guide (FIN ISSN 1795-7877) **2977**
Degrees North (Sunderland) (GBR) **2281**
Degres (BEL ISSN 0376-8163) **5110**
• Deguo Yanjiu/Deutschland-Studien (CHN ISSN 1005-4871) **7230**

Link to your serials resources and content with ulrichsweb.com

Title

Title

• DePaul Business and Commercial Law Journal (USA ISSN 1542-2763) **4656**
▼ DePaul Journal for Social Justice (USA) **4656**
DePaul Journal of Art & Entertainment Law *see* DePaul Journal of Art, Technology & Intellectual Property Law **4656**
• DePaul Journal of Art, Technology & Intellectual Property Law (USA) **4656**
• DePaul Journal of Health Care Law (USA ISSN 1551-8426) **4656**
• DePaul Law Review (USA ISSN 0011-7188) **4656**
Depauw (USA) **2282**
La Depeche A S V (Auxiliaires de Sante Veterinaire) (FRA ISSN 1956-9785) **8796**
Depeche de Tahiti (PYF ISSN 0751-428X) **3842**
• La Depeche du Midi (FRA ISSN 0181-7981) **3840**
Depeche en Ligne *see* La Depeche du Midi **3840**
La Depeche Le Petit Meunier (FRA ISSN 1287-8375) **196**
La Depeche Technique (FRA ISSN 0999-4866) **8796**
Depeche Veterinaire (FRA ISSN 0180-3573) **8796**
• Depenses en Medicaments au Canada (CAN ISSN 1910-0957) **6832**
• Depese (CZE ISSN 1213-5496) **2608**
Deponirovannye Nauchnye Raboty. Bibliograficheskii Ukazatel' (RUS ISSN 0202-6120) **7936**
Deportate Esuli Profughe *see* D E P Deportate Esuli Profughe **8895**
Deporte - Derecho del Pueblo (CUB ISSN 0138-6611) **8169**
Deportes (DOM) **8169**
Deportes (VEN) **8169**
▼ Deportes Quindio (COL ISSN 2011-3048) **8169**
Deportivo (CHL) **8169**
Deportivo 17 *see* Diario 17 **3908**
• Deposit Growth Strategies (USA ISSN 1082-8605) **1335**
Deposit Insurance Corporation. Annual Report: Directors' Report, Balance Sheet and Accounts (IND ISSN 0304-6966) **4501**
Deposition Notebook (USA) **4656**
• Depository and Lending Institutions (USA ISSN 1932-6475) **1335**
Depotredegoerelse om Affaldsdepotomraadet *see* Redegoerelse om Jordforurening **3511**
• Depreciation Handbook (USA) **1920**
Deprem Arastirma Bulteni/Earthquake Research Department. Bulletin (TUR) **2779**
• ➤ Depression and Anxiety (Hoboken) (USA ISSN 1091-4269) **7351**
Depression and Anxiety (New York) (USA ISSN 1542-1880) **6136**
Depression and Primary Care *see* Medical Journal of Australia **5669**
Depression Frontier (JPN ISSN 1347-8893) **6136**
Depression Glass *see* Warman's Depression Glass **369**
➤ Depression: Mind and Body (GBR ISSN 1479-5035) **6136**
Depressive Illness Series (USA ISSN 0893-8636) **7351**
Depth (USA) **6288**
Depthnews (PHL) **4574**
Depthnews Indonesia (IDN ISSN 0376-8201) **3891**
Deputados Brasileiros: Repertorio Biografico (BRA) **7199**
• I Deputati e Senatori del Parlamento Repubblicano. Annuario (ITA) **7433**
Deputatskii Vestnik (RUS) **3935**
Deputazione di Storia Patria per le Antiche Provincie Modenesi. Atti e Memorie (ITA ISSN 0418-7296) **4214**
Deputazione di Storia Patria per l'Umbria. Bollettino (ITA ISSN 0300-4422) **4214**
▼ Deputy and Court Officer (USA ISSN 1948-2612) **2650**
Der Auto-Anzeiger *see* D A Z **8576**
Der Auto-Anzeiger Caravan *see* D A Z Caravan **8576**
Der Auto-Anzeiger Transporter *see* D A Z Transporter **8670**
Der Elektromeister der Elektro- und Gebaeudetechniker *see* D E - der Elektro- und Gebaeudetechniker **3298**
Der Elektromeister Hausgeraete *see* D E - Hausgeraete **4555**
Der Selbstaendige Magazin *see* D S - Magazin **1959**
Der Yid (USA ISSN 0044-040X) **7720**
Derby *see* Jurnal Bihorean **3933**
Derby Diocesan Directory and Clergy List (GBR) **7754**
Derby Diocesan News (GBR ISSN 0953-9301) **7754**
Derby Trader (GBR ISSN 1351-9786) **1561**
Derbyshire & Nottinghamshire Entomological Society. Journal (GBR) **843**
➤ Derbyshire Archaeological Journal (GBR ISSN 0070-3788) **389**
Derbyshire Farmer (GBR ISSN 0954-9684) **105**
• Derbyshire Life and Countryside (GBR ISSN 0011-8990) **3864**
Derdapske Sveske (SRB ISSN 0351-5710) **389**
Derech HaOchel *see* Derekh Ha'Okhel **3633**
Derech Ha'Ochel *see* Derekh Ha'Okhel **3633**
El Derecho (ARG ISSN 1666-8987) **4656**
➤ Derecho (PER ISSN 0251-3412) **4656**
Derecho a Jugar *see* PlayRights Magazine **2165**
▼ Derecho Administrativo (ARG ISSN 1851-328X) **4847**
Derecho de los Negocios (ESP ISSN 1130-5711) **4865**
Derecho del Estado *see* Revista de Derecho del Estado **4770**
Derecho del mar Boletin *see* Law of the Sea Bulletin **4970**
Derecho del Trabajo (ARG ISSN 0325-3627) **1675**
Derecho Europeo de Transportes *see* European Transport Law **8495**
Derecho Internacional Publico (URY) **4923**
Derecho Penal y Criminologia *see* Revista de Derecho Penal y Criminologia **4897**
Derecho Privado y Constitucion (ESP ISSN 1133-8768) **4656**
Derecho y Cambio (ARG ISSN 0329-8434) **105**
Derecho y Ciencias Sociales (MEX) **4656**
† • Derecho y Medio Ambiente (ESP ISSN 1575-8362) **8949**
Derecho y Nuevas Tecnologias (ARG ISSN 1514-1918) **4656**
Derecho y Opinion (ESP ISSN 1133-3278) **4656**
Derecho y Reforma Agraria *see* Revista de Derecho y Reforma Agraria **4771**
▼ Derecho y Religion (ESP ISSN 1887-3243) **4656**
Derecho y Salud (ESP ISSN 1133-7400) **7514**
Derecho y Tecnologias de Informacion y Comunicaciones (CRI ISSN 1659-0430) **5006**
Derechos Humanos (ESP ISSN 1133-3812) **7205**
Derechos Humanos. Serie de Estudios *see* Human Rights. Study Series **7209**
Derechos y Libertades (ESP ISSN 1133-0937) **4657**
➤ Dereito (ESP ISSN 1132-9947) **4657**
• Derekh (ITA) **3529**
• Derekh Ha'Okhel (ISR) **3633**
Derekh Hayyim (ISR) **7514**
Derevoobrabatyvayushchaya Promyshlennost'/Wood Processing Industry (RUS ISSN 0011-9008) **3711**
• Derivatives & Financial Instruments (NLD ISSN 1389-1863) **1620**
• Derivatives and Hedging (USA) **1620**
• Derivatives: Financial Products Report (USA ISSN 1546-6272) **1920**
Derivatives: Law and Practice (GBR) **4657**
Derivatives Use, Trading & Regulation (Print) *see* Journal of Derivatives & Hedge Funds **1635**
• Derivatives Week (USA ISSN 1075-2412) **1620**
• Derive (AUT ISSN 1608-8131) **4409**
Derm (DEU ISSN 0949-7633) **5874**
▼ Derm Products (USA ISSN 1938-9701) **5874**
Derma (JPN ISSN 1343-0831) **5874**
Dermaforum (DEU) **5874**
Dermascope (USA) **587**
• Dermathopathology: Practical and Conceptual (Online) (USA ISSN 1936-9409) **5874**
• ➤ Dermatitis (CAN ISSN 1710-3568) **5874**
▼ • Dermato-Endocrinology (USA ISSN 1938-1972) **5874**
Dermato-Venerologie (ROM ISSN 1220-3734) **5874**
Dermatologen Vademecum (NLD ISSN 1388-4557) **5874**
• ➤ Dermatologia (MEX ISSN 0185-4038) **5874**
Dermatologia Argentina (ARG ISSN 1515-8411) **5874**
Dermatologia Clinica (ITA ISSN 0392-1395) **5874**
Dermatologia Cosmetica, Medica y Quirurgica (MEX ISSN 1665-4390) **5874**
• ➤ Dermatologia Kliniczna/Clinical Dermatology (POL ISSN 1730-7201) **5874**
• Dermatologia Peruana (PER ISSN 1028-7175) **5874**
Dermatologia Practica (ESP ISSN 1130-9407) **5874**
▼ ➤ Dermatologia pre Prax (SVK ISSN 1337-1746) **5874**
• ➤ Dermatologic Clinics (USA ISSN 0733-8635) **5874**
• ➤ Dermatologic Surgery (USA ISSN 1076-0512) **6241**
• Dermatologic Surgery Online (USA ISSN 1524-4725) **6241**
• Dermatologic Therapy (USA ISSN 1396-0296) **5874**
• Dermatologica Helvetica (CHE ISSN 1420-2360) **5875**
Dermatologica Sinica *see* Zhonghua Pifuke Yixue Zazhi **5883**
Dermatological Nursing (GBR ISSN 1477-3368) **5875**
† Dermatologie (CZE ISSN 1802-1719) **8949**
• Dermatologie in Beruf und Umwelt/Occupational and Environmental Dermatology (DEU ISSN 1438-776X) **5875**
Dermatologie Pratique (FRA ISSN 0982-8567) **5875**
Dermatologie-Praxis (CHE ISSN 1661-6200) **5875**
▼ • ➤ Dermatologie pro Praxi (CZE ISSN 1802-2960) **5875**
Dermatologiya i Venerologiya *see* Dermatolohiya ta Venerolohiya **5875**
• Il Dermatologo (ITA ISSN 0391-8912) **5875**
Il Dermatologo Ospedaliero *see* Il Dermatologo **5875**
• ➤ Dermatology (CHE ISSN 1018-8665) **5875**
Dermatology (New York, 1990) (USA ISSN 1051-8258) **5875**
Dermatology and Venereology (Section 13 EMBASE) *see* Excerpta Medica. Section 13: Dermatology and Venereology **5744**
Dermatology Business Management (USA ISSN 1547-6383) **1738**
▼ • Dermatology Coding Alert (USA ISSN 2150-6728) **4501**
• Dermatology Focus (USA) **5875**
Dermatology Health Monitor (USA) **5875**
Dermatology in Practice (GBR ISSN 0262-5504) **5875**
Dermatology Insights (USA ISSN 1527-926X) **5875**
▼ • ➤ Dermatology Nurses' Association. Journal (USA ISSN 1945-760X) **5957**
• ➤ Dermatology Nursing (USA ISSN 1060-3441) **5875**
• ➤ Dermatology Online Journal (USA ISSN 1087-2108) **5875**
▼ • ➤ Dermatology Research and Practice (USA ISSN 1687-6105) **5875**
• Dermatology Times (USA ISSN 0196-6197) **5875**
• Dermatolohiya ta Venerolohiya/Dermatologiya i Venerologiya (UKR) **5875**
Dermatosis and Venereal Disease *see* Pifubing yu Xingbing **5881**
Derniere Guerre ou l'Histoire Controversee de la Deuxieme Guerre Mondiale (CHE) **4214**
• La Derniere Heure (BEL) **3801**
• Dernieres Nouvelles d'Alsace (FRA ISSN 0150-391X) **3840**
Dernieres Nouvelles du Lundi (FRA ISSN 1140-8014) **3840**
▼ • ➤ Derrida Today (GBR ISSN 1754-8500) **7958**
Derriere (GBR) **6288**
• Derry Journal (GBR ISSN 0307-6172) **3864**
Derry People Donegal News (IRL ISSN 1473-6225) **3892**
• Derwent Biotechnology Abstracts (GBR ISSN 0262-5318) **715**
Derwent Directory. Supplementary Protection Certificates. Great Britain (GBR ISSN 1363-4313) **6832**
Derwent Drug File. Profile 33: Drugs Acting on the Respiratory System (GBR ISSN 1358-2666) **6889**
Derwent Drug File. Profile Thirty-Three: Drugs Acting on the Respiratory System *see* Derwent Drug File. Profile 33: Drugs Acting on the Respiratory System **6889**
Dery Archives *see* Dery Archivum **5283**
Dery Archivum/Dery Archives (HUN ISSN 1219-2023) **5283**
Derzhavnyi Visnyk Ukrainy (UKR) **4657**
• Des Affaires Boeuf (CAN ISSN 1702-627X) **3633**
Des Affaires Boeuf. Newsletter (CAN ISSN 1914-5489) **3633**
Des Filles en Ovalie Mag *see* D F O Mag **8226**
• Des Moines Business Record (USA ISSN 1068-6681) **1091**
▼ Des Moines Moms (USA) **4356**
Des Nouvelles d'A S C O D O C P S Y *see* Groupement d'Assistance et de Cooperation Documentaires en Psychiatrie. Nouvelles **6143**
Des Nouvelles d'Ascodocpsy *see* Groupement d'Assistance et de Cooperation Documentaires en Psychiatrie. Nouvelles **6143**
Des Paroles en Actes (FRA ISSN 1950-0378) **7129**
Des Poings et des Roses (FRA ISSN 1952-2452) **7129**
• ➤ Desacatos (MEX ISSN 1607-050X) **335**
Desafio *see* Challenge (New York) **7115**
Desafios *see* Revista Desafios **7262**
▼ Desafios (Ibague) (COL ISSN 2011-3552) **5604**
• ➤ Desalination (NLD ISSN 0011-9164) **8820**
Desarme. Serie de Estudios *see* United Nations Economic and Social Council. Disarmament Study Series **7270**
Desarmement. Serie D'etudes *see* United Nations Economic and Social Council. Disarmament Study Series **7270**
• Desarrollando La Lectura (Escuela Primaria) (USA ISSN 1531-4928) **2841**
• Desarrollando la Lectura (Preparacidon Para la Lectura) (USA ISSN 1531-491X) **2841**
Desarrollo *see* Innovacion **8426**
Desarrollo *see* Development (Basingstoke) **1593**
Desarrollo de Base (USA ISSN 0733-6594) **1593**
➤ Desarrollo Economico (ARG ISSN 0046-001X) **1883**
Desarrollo Indoamericano (COL ISSN 0418-7547) **1883**
Desarrollo Local (ECU) **7491**
Desarrollo Productivo *see* Comision Economica para America Latina y el Caribe. Serie Desarrollo Productivo **1592**
➤ Desarrollo Tecnologico (MEX) **8420**
Desarrollo y Cooperacion (DEU ISSN 0723-7006) **1593**
• Desarrollo y Energia (ARG ISSN 0328-0322) **3127**
• ➤ Desarrollo y Sociedad (COL ISSN 0120-3584) **1476**
• Desastres. Preparativos y Mitigacion en las Americas (USA ISSN 1564-0620) **7514**
Descant (CAN ISSN 0382-909X) **5283**
Descant (USA ISSN 0011-9210) **5283**
The Descendants (USA ISSN 0894-1831) **3788**
Descendants of Chinese Nation *see* Zhonghua Ernu **648**
Descendants of Peter Shaklee (1756-1834) Newsletter (USA ISSN 1044-7873) **3764**
Descendants of Richard Risley in America (USA) **3764**
Descendants of Richard Risley Senior (USA ISSN 1046-4220) **3764**
• Descent (AUS ISSN 0084-9731) **3764**
Descent (GBR ISSN 0046-0036) **8311**
Descriptifs pour la Maison Individuelle (FRA ISSN 1954-4383) **1002**
➤ Descriptions of Ectomycorrhizae (DEU ISSN 1431-4819) **785**
• Descriptions of Fungi and Bacteria (GBR) **667**
Descriptive Video Service Guide (E-mail Edition) *see* D V S Guide (E-mail Edition) **2379**
▼ Descubre (ESP ISSN 1954-8893) **8697**
• Descubrir el Arte (ESP ISSN 1578-9047) **485**
Desde el Sur (MEX ISSN 1405-2040) **2977**
Desde la Gente (ARG ISSN 1851-6009) **1423**
▼ Desde la Rectoria (COL ISSN 2011-3897) **2977**
Desenvolvimento Brasileiro *see* Brazil Development Series **1880**
Desenvolvimento de Base *see* Desarrollo de Base **1593**
Desenvolvimento de Base *see* Grassroots Development **1596**
• Desenvolvimento em Questao (BRA ISSN 1678-4855) **4449**
Deseret News Church Almanac (USA ISSN 0093-786X) **7734**
The Desert Airman (USA) **6419**
➤ Desert Bighorn Council. Transactions (USA ISSN 0418-7598) **2608**
▼ Desert Dog News (USA ISSN 1940-8544) **6806**
Desert Edge (USA) **4593**
Desert Golf Magazine (USA ISSN 1522-9777) **8226**
Desert Guide (USA) **8697**
Desert Home & Garden (USA) **4537**
Desert Living (USA) **3974**
Desert Locust Control Organization for Eastern Africa. Annual Report (ETH ISSN 0418-761X) **227**
➤ Desert Plants (USA ISSN 0734-3434) **786**
• The Desert Real Estate Report (USA) **7588**
Desert Tortoise Council. Proceedings of Symposium (USA ISSN 0191-3875) **940**
Desert Trails (USA) **8311**
• Desert U S A (USA) **4290**
Desert Voice (USA ISSN 1059-9738) **7704**
• Desertification Indicator System For Medeterranean Europe (GBR ISSN 1749-8996) **1091**
Desfile (BRA ISSN 0021-7301) **4356**
Desh (IND) **5283**
Desh Videsh (USA ISSN 1941-2398) **3529**
Deshabhimani (IND) **3881**
Deshabhimani (Calcutta Edition) *see* Deshabhimani **3881**
Deshabhimani (Kannur Edition) *see* Deshabhimani **3881**
Deshabhimani (Kochi Edition) *see* Deshabhimani **3881**
Deshabhimani (Kottayam Edition) *see* Deshabhimani **3881**
Deshabhimani (T'puram Edition) *see* Deshabhimani **3881**
Deshbandhu (IND ISSN 0971-7110) **3881**
Deshbandhu (Bhopal Edition) *see* Deshbandhu **3881**
Deshbandhu (Bilaspur Edition) *see* Deshbandhu **3881**
Deshbandhu (Jabalpur Edition) *see* Deshbandhu **3881**
Deshbandhu (Satna Edition) *see* Deshbandhu **3881**
Deshdoot (IND) **3881**
• Desicio (MEX ISSN 1665-7446) **2940**
• Desidamos (ARG ISSN 0329-7462) **8845**
Desierto Modo (MEX) **5213**
† • Design (DNK ISSN 1602-785X) **8949**
Design (Providence) (USA ISSN 1520-4243) **4574**
• Design and Applied Arts Index (USA ISSN 1353-1298) **530**
Design and Architecture (PHL ISSN 0116-9718) **4537**
Design & Architecture (Arizona Edition) (USA ISSN 1544-3930) **439**
Design & Architecture (Chicago Edition) *see* Design & Architecture (Arizona Edition) **439**
Design & Build (ZAF ISSN 1817-5112) **4356**
▼ • ➤ Design and Culture (GBR ISSN 1754-7075) **485**
• Design & Decor (USA) **4537**
Design & Design (DEU ISSN 0944-0372) **4537**
• Design & Elektronik (DEU ISSN 0933-8667) **2539**
Design & Home Digest (CZE ISSN 1802-2472) **4537**
Design & Manufacture of Diesel Engine *see* Chaiyouji Sheji yu Zhizao **3375**
Design and Nature (GBR ISSN 1478-0585) **7850**
Design and Technology Association Practice *see* D A T A Practice **3057**
Design and Verification *see* Elektronik und Entwicklung **3291**
Design and Verification Test Kompendium *see* D & V Test Kompendium **3290**
Design Annual *see* Graphis Design Annual **492**
Design + Art in Greece/Themata Chorou + Technon (GRC ISSN 0074-1191) **440**
† Design Arts (GBR ISSN 1756-1671) **8949**
Design at Chalmers *see* Design paa Chalmers **8420**
† Design Auswahl (Year)/Design Selection (Year) (DEU) **8949**
The Design Authority *see* Creative Designer **2484**
Design, Automation and Test in Europe Conference *see* Design, Automation, and Test in Europe Conference and Exhibition. Proceedings **2416**
• Design, Automation, and Test in Europe Conference and Exhibition. Proceedings (USA ISSN 1530-1591) **2416**
• ➤ Design Automation for Embedded Systems (USA ISSN 0929-5585) **2460**
• Design - Build (USA ISSN 1096-7095) **3264**

Title

▼ *new title*   † *ceased*   ● *electronic media*   ➤ *refereed*

Deutsches Wirtschaftswissenschaftliches Institut fuer Fremdenverkehr. Sonderreihe (DEU ISSN 0580-6933) **8698**
Deutsches Wollforschungsinstitut Reports *see* D W I Reports **8948**
Deutsches Zentrum fuer Luft- und Raumfahrt e.V. Nachrichten *see* D L R - Nachrichten **52**
Deutsches Zentrum fuer Luft- und Raumfahrt. Forschungsberichte (DEU ISSN 1434-8454) **53**
Deutsches Zentrum fuer Luft- und Raumfahrt Mitteilungen *see* D L R - Mitteilungen **52**
Deutschkanadisches Jahrbuch *see* German-Canadian Yearbook **3535**
Deutschland (Arabic Edition) *see* Deutschland (English Edition) **3846**
Deutschland (English Edition E1) *see* Deutschland (English Edition) **3846**
• Deutschland (English Edition) (DEU ISSN 0945-6791) **3846**
Deutschland (French Edition) *see* Deutschland (English Edition) **3846**
Deutschland (Japanese Edition) *see* Deutschland (English Edition) **3846**
Deutschland (Portuguese Edition) *see* Deutschland (English Edition) **3846**
Deutschland Archiv (DEU ISSN 0012-1428) **7958**
† Deutschland im Globalen Wettbewerb/International Economic Indicators (DEU) **8950**
Deutschland in Geschichte und Gegenwart (DEU ISSN 0340-5710) **4214**
Deutschland in Zahlen (DEU ISSN 1865-6404) **1091**
Deutschland-Journal (DEU ISSN 0944-324X) **3846**
Deutschland Kommunal (DEU) **7491**
Deutschland-Magazin (DEU ISSN 0012-141X) **7129**
Deutschland Spezial Ost (DEU ISSN 1431-4096) **1920**
Deutschland-Studien *see* Deguo Yanjiu **7230**
Deutschland Sucht den Superstar (DEU) **2380**
Deutschlandfunk Jahrbuch *see* D L F Jahrbuch **8948**
Deutschmagazin (DEU ISSN 1613-0693) **5111**
Deutschunterricht (DEU ISSN 0012-1460) **3057**
Der Deutschunterricht (Seelze) (DEU ISSN 0340-2258) **5111**
• ➤ Deutschunterricht im Suedlichen Afrika (ZAF ISSN 1016-4367) **5111**
Deux Mille Cinq Cent Douze *see* 2512 **3932**
Deux-Mille-Un Plus *see* 2001 Plus **7478**
Deuxieme Guerre Mondiale *see* 2e Guerre Mondiale **4281**
• Dev. Developing Software Solutions (ITA ISSN 1124-5468) **2506**
Dev-zine *see* Just Change **8052**
Develop (NLD ISSN 1574-8138) **1859**
Developer (CZE) **1002**
The Developer (UGA) **1593**
Developer (USA ISSN 1946-0961) **1002**
Developer Network Journal (Online) *see* D N J (Online) **2570**
• ➤ Developing Economies (GBR ISSN 0012-1533) **1593**
Developing Highly Qualified Paraeducators (USA ISSN 1930-9058) **3020**
• Developing Mental Health (GBR ISSN 1740-8032) **6136**
• Developing Practice (AUS ISSN 1445-6818) **8037**
Developing Primary R E (Religious Education) (GBR ISSN 1476-6442) **3057**
Developing Secondary R E (Religious Education) (GBR ISSN 1743-0895) **3057**
Developing Software Solutions *see* Dev. Developing Software Solutions **2506**
• Developing World Bioethics (GBR ISSN 1471-8731) **6913**
Development *see* Udvikling **7270**
• ➤ Development (Basingstoke) (GBR ISSN 1011-6370) **1593**
• ➤ Development (Cambridge) (GBR ISSN 0950-1991) **668**
Development (Herndon) (USA ISSN 0888-6067) **1002**
Development and Application of Materials *see* Cailiao Kaifa yu Yingyong **3342**
• ➤ Development and Change (GBR ISSN 0012-155X) **1593**
D + C (DEU ISSN 0723-6980) **1593**
Development & Embryology *see* T S W Development & Embryology **707**
Development and Finance (HUN ISSN 1589-3820) **1335**
• Development and Learning in Organizations (GBR ISSN 1477-7282) **1859**
Development and Policy Research (IND) **1959**
• ➤ Development and Psychopathology (GBR ISSN 0954-5794) **7351**
Development and Research Organisation for Nature, Arts and Heritage. Journal *see* Context **438**
➤ Development and Society (KOR ISSN 1598-8074) **7282**
† Development & Socio-Economic Progress (EGY) **8950**
Development Bank of Japan. Research Report *see* Nippon Seisaku Toshi Ginko. Chosabu. Chosa **1372**
Development Bank of Mauritius. Report and Accounts (MUS) **1335**
Development Bank of Southern Africa. Activities (ZAF ISSN 1992-1748) **1920**
Development Bank of Southern Africa. Annual Report (ZAF ISSN 1728-3213) **1920**
Development Bank of Southern Africa. Development Papers (ZAF) **1593**
Development Bank of Zambia. Annual Report (ZMB) **1335**
• Development Bulletin (Canberra) (AUS ISSN 1035-1132) **7958**
• Development Business (New York, 1978) (USA ISSN 0259-5893) **1593**
Development Business (New York, 1985) (USA) **1561**
Development Connections (USA) **1594**
Development Department Research Programme. Research Findings (GBR) **8037**
Development Dialogue *see* Unnayan Bitarka **5192**
• Development Dialogue (SWE ISSN 0345-2328) **7230**
Development Education (GBR) **3413**
The Development Education Journal (GBR ISSN 1354-0742) **2842**
Development Estimates *see* Kenya. Central Bureau of Statistics. Development Estimates **1247**
Development Finance Company of Kenya. Annual Report and Statement of Accounts (KEN) **1335**
Development Forum (USA ISSN 0251-6632) **1594**
• ➤ Development, Genes and Evolution (DEU ISSN 0949-944X) **668**
• ➤ Development, Growth and Differentiation/Hassei, Seicho, Bunka (AUS ISSN 0012-1592) **668**
Development Handbook (USA) **1427**
• ➤ Development in Practice (GBR ISSN 0961-4524) **1594**
Development ISSues (NLD ISSN 1566-4821) **8098**
Development Issues of Statistics *see* Razvojna Vprasanja Statistike **8396**
Development of Education in Pakistan (PAK ISSN 0080-1321) **2842**
▼ The Development of the Anglo-Saxon Language and Linguistic Universals (NLD ISSN 1877-3451) **5111**
Development Oriented Research in Agriculture (NLD) **105**
• Development Outreach (USA ISSN 1020-797X) **1594**
Development Papers *see* Development Bank of Southern Africa. Development Papers **1593**
Development Policy and Administrative Review (IND ISSN 0251-317X) **7433**
Development Policy & Practice Working Paper *see* D P P Working Paper **1476**
• ➤ Development Policy Review (GBR ISSN 0950-6764) **1594**
• Development Report Card for the States (Online Edition) (USA ISSN 1936-3834) **1477**
Development Research *see* Fazhan Yanjiu **1109**
• Development Research News (PHL ISSN 0115-9097) **1594**
• ➤ Development Review (IRL ISSN 0790-9403) **1594**
• ➤ Development Southern Africa (GBR ISSN 0376-835X) **1594**
Development Studies Journal *see* Estudios del Desarrollo **8100**
Development Studies Working Papers (CAN) **7230**
Development. Supplement *see* Development (Cambridge) **668**
Development Trends in Berkshire (GBR ISSN 0265-2382) **4409**
Development West Coast. Annual Report (Print) *see* Development West Coast. Group Annual Report (Print) **1883**
Development West Coast. Group Annual Report (Online) *see* Development West Coast. Group Annual Report (Print) **1883**
• Development West Coast. Group Annual Report (Print) (NZL ISSN 1178-3338) **1883**
• Development Zambia (ZMB ISSN 1811-7724) **1594**
† Developmental and Cell Biology Series (GBR ISSN 0951-0818) **8950**
• ➤ Developmental & Comparative Immunology (GBR ISSN 0145-305X) **5757**
Developmental Approaches to Psychopathology (USA) **7351**
• ➤ Developmental Biology (USA ISSN 0012-1606) **668**
Developmental Biology and Teratology (Section 21 EMBASE) *see* Excerpta Medica. Section 21: Developmental Biology and Teratology **715**
Developmental Brain Research *see* Brain Research **6128**
• ➤ Developmental Cell (USA ISSN 1534-5807) **832**
Developmental Clinical Psychology and Psychiatry (USA ISSN 0892-8150) **6136**
• ➤ Developmental Disabilities Bulletin (CAN ISSN 1184-0412) **6136**
• ➤ Developmental Disabilities Research Reviews (USA ISSN 1940-5510) **6136**
Developmental Disabilities Special Interest Section Quarterly (USA ISSN 1093-7196) **7351**
• ➤ Developmental Dynamics (USA ISSN 1058-8388) **668**
Developmental Immunology *see* Autoimmunity **5755**
• ➤ Developmental Medicine and Child Neurology (GBR ISSN 0012-1622) **6091**
• ➤ Developmental Microbiology and Molecular Biology (IND) **668**
Developmental Movement Play Journal (GBR ISSN 1756-3429) **2685**
• ➤ Developmental Neurobiology (USA ISSN 1932-8451) **921**
• ➤ Developmental Neuropsychology (USA ISSN 8756-5641) **7351**
• Developmental Neurorehabilitation (GBR ISSN 1751-8423) **6108**
Developmental Neurorehabilitation (Online) *see* Developmental Neurorehabilitation **6108**
• ➤ Developmental Neuroscience (CHE ISSN 0378-5866) **6136**
• Developmental Policy (USA ISSN 1541-4566) **7129**
• ➤ Developmental Psychobiology (USA ISSN 0012-1630) **668**
• ➤ Developmental Psychology (USA ISSN 0012-1649) **7351**
• ➤ Developmental Review (USA ISSN 0273-2297) **7352**
• Developmental Science (GBR ISSN 1363-755X) **7352**
• Developments (GBR ISSN 1461-474X) **1594**
Developments (USA ISSN 1055-8136) **4409**
Developments *see* Housing & Community Developments **1351**
Developments in Aging (USA ISSN 0734-3213) **8037**
➤ Developments in Agricultural and Managed Forest Ecology (NLD ISSN 0166-2287) **3687**
• ➤ Developments in Agricultural Economics (NLD ISSN 0926-5589) **196**
• ➤ Developments in Agricultural Engineering (NLD ISSN 0167-4137) **228**
➤ Developments in Animal and Veterinary Sciences (NLD ISSN 0167-5168) **8796**
Developments in Applied Biology (GBR ISSN 0269-0713) **668**
Developments in Applied Earth Sciences (NLD) **3187**
• ➤ Developments in Aquaculture and Fisheries Science (NLD ISSN 0167-9309) **940**
• ➤ Developments in Atmospheric Science (NLD ISSN 0167-5117) **6352**
➤ Developments in Biogeochemistry (NLD ISSN 0924-5286) **2705**
• ➤ Developments in Biologicals (CHE ISSN 1424-6074) **6401**
Developments in Biotherapy (NLD ISSN 0925-7640) **763**
➤ Developments in Business Simulation & Experiential Exercises (USA ISSN 0278-2375) **2517**
➤ Developments in Cardiovascular Medicine (NLD ISSN 0166-9842) **5785**
Developments in Chemical Engineering and Mineral Processing *see* Asia-Pacific Journal of Chemical Engineering **3236**
➤ Developments in Civil and Foundation Engineering (NLD ISSN 0924-5308) **3264**
➤ Developments in Civil Engineering (NLD ISSN 0167-6288) **3264**
Developments in Clay Science (NLD ISSN 1572-4352) **2730**
➤ Developments in Clinical Biochemistry (NLD ISSN 0167-4978) **731**
➤ Developments in Critical Care Medicine and Anaesthesiology (NLD ISSN 0924-5294) **5771**
• ➤ Developments in Crop Science (NLD ISSN 0378-519X) **228**
Developments in Earth and Environmental Sciences (NLD ISSN 1571-9197) **2705**
• ➤ Developments in Earth Surface Processes (NLD ISSN 0928-2025) **2730**
• ➤ Developments in Economic Geology (NLD ISSN 0168-6178) **2730**
Developments in Economics (GBR ISSN 0951-1407) **1091**
Developments in Ecosystems (NLD) **668**
➤ Developments in Environmental Biology of Fishes (NLD ISSN 0924-5316) **940**
• ➤ Developments in Environmental Economics (NLD ISSN 0927-5207) **3413**
Developments in Environmental Management (NLD) **3413**
• ➤ Developments in Environmental Modelling (NLD ISSN 0167-8892) **3481**
• Developments in Environmental Science (GBR ISSN 1474-8177) **3414**
† Developments in Food Carbohydrate (GBR ISSN 0260-4345) **8950**
† ➤ Developments in Food Preservation (GBR ISSN 0263-4376) **8950**
† ➤ Developments in Food Proteins (GBR ISSN 0263-4708) **8950**
• ➤ Developments in Food Science (NLD ISSN 0167-4501) **2122**
Developments in Fullerene Science (NLD ISSN 1568-2366) **2134**
➤ Developments in Gastroenterology (NLD ISSN 0167-935X) **5922**
➤ Developments in Geomathematics (NLD ISSN 0167-5982) **2779**
• ➤ Developments in Geotechnical Engineering (NLD ISSN 0165-1250) **3264**
• ➤ Developments in Geotectonics (NLD ISSN 0419-0254) **2730**
▼ • Developments in Government Policy, Compliance, Lab Strategy and Diagnostic Testing (USA ISSN 1939-3431) **7514**
Developments in Health Economics and Public Policy (NLD ISSN 0927-4987) **7514**
➤ Developments in Heat Transfer (GBR ISSN 1369-7331) **3376**
➤ Developments in Hematology and Immunology (NLD ISSN 0167-9201) **5936**
➤ Developments in Hydrobiology (NLD ISSN 0167-8418) **668**
▼ Developments in Integrated Environmental Assessment (NLD ISSN 1574-101X) **3414**
➤ Developments in International Law (NLD ISSN 0924-5332) **4923**
➤ Developments in Landscape Management and Urban Planning (NLD ISSN 0923-8131) **4409**
Developments in Life Sciences (GBR ISSN 1467-4912) **668**
• ➤ Developments in Marine Biology (NLD ISSN 0163-6995) **2803**
▼ Developments in Marine Geology (NLD ISSN 1572-5480) **2730**
➤ Developments in Marine Technology (NLD ISSN 0928-2009) **3376**
Developments in Marketing Science (USA ISSN 0149-7421) **1813**
➤ Developments in Medical Virology (NLD ISSN 0924-5367) **5812**
Developments in Mental Health Law (USA ISSN 1063-9977) **4657**
• Developments in Milling and Baking (GBR ISSN 1751-973X) **179**
• ➤ Developments in Mineral Processing (NLD ISSN 0167-4528) **2731**
➤ Developments in Molecular and Cellular Biochemistry (NLD ISSN 0167-9023) **731**
➤ Developments in Molecular Virology (NLD ISSN 0167-8256) **884**
➤ Developments in Nephrology (NLD ISSN 0167-8205) **6267**
Developments in Neurology (NLD ISSN 0166-5960) **6136**
➤ Developments in Nuclear Medicine (NLD ISSN 0167-9074) **6195**
➤ Developments in Oncology (NLD ISSN 0167-4927) **6018**
• ➤ Developments in Ophthalmology (CHE ISSN 0250-3751) **6041**
† ➤ Developments in Oriented Polymers (GBR ISSN 0264-3022) **8950**
• ➤ Developments in Palaeontology and Stratigraphy (NLD ISSN 0920-5446) **6724**
• ➤ Developments in Petroleum Science (NLD ISSN 0376-7361) **6767**
• ➤ Developments in Petrology (NLD ISSN 0167-2894) **2731**
Developments in Pharmacology (NLD ISSN 0167-6431) **6833**
Developments in Plant and Soil Sciences (NLD ISSN 0167-840X) **228**
Developments in Plant Breeding (NLD ISSN 1381-673X) **3728**
• ➤ Developments in Plant Genetics and Breeding (NLD ISSN 0168-7972) **786**
Developments in Plant Pathology (NLD ISSN 0929-1318) **786**
Developments in Politics (GBR ISSN 0961-5431) **7129**
• Developments in Precambrian Geology (NLD ISSN 0166-2635) **2731**
• ➤ Developments in Primatology (NLD ISSN 1574-3489) **940**
• Developments in Quaternary Science (NLD ISSN 1571-0866) **2731**
† Developments in Rubber Technology (GBR ISSN 0262-1584) **8950**
Developments in School Law (USA ISSN 1045-747X) **4657**
• ➤ Developments in Sedimentology (NLD ISSN 0070-4571) **2731**
Developments in Sociology (GBR ISSN 0956-9359) **8098**
Developments in Soil Science (NLD ISSN 0166-0918) **228**
➤ Developments in Solid Earth Geophysics (NLD ISSN 0419-0297) **2779**
Developments in Steelmaking Capacity of Non-O E C D Countries *see* Developments in Steelmaking Capacity of Non-O E C D Economies **6310**
• Developments in Steelmaking Capacity of Non-O E C D Economies/Les Capacites de Production d'Acier dans les Pays Non O C D E (Organisation for Economic Cooperation and Development) (FRA) **6310**
➤ Developments in Structural Geology (NLD) **2731**
Developments in Surgery (NLD ISSN 0167-5079) **6241**
Developments in Transport Studies (NLD ISSN 0924-5324) **8494**
➤ Developments in Volcanology (NLD ISSN 1871-644X) **2779**
• ➤ Developments in Water Science (NLD ISSN 0167-5648) **8820**
Developpement de la Petite Enfance. Rapport *see* Early Childhood Development Report **2151**
• Developpement Durable & Territoires (FRA ISSN 1772-9971) **3414**
Developpement Durable. Rapport (CAN ISSN 1912-0915) **3127**
Developpement et Actualisation des Programmes d'Etudes Professionnelles et Techniques (CAN ISSN 1719-3729) **2842**
Developpement et Civilisations (FRA ISSN 1951-0012) **7958**
Developpement et Cooperation (DEU ISSN 0723-6999) **1594**
Developpement Professionnel (FRA ISSN 1951-7459) **6696**
Developpement Social (CAN ISSN 1488-6499) **8037**
▼ Developpements (FRA ISSN 2103-2874) **7352**

Title

10196 DEVELOPPEUR REFERENCE ULRICH'S PERIODICALS

• Developpeur Reference (FRA ISSN 1628-3368) **2506**
• Devenir (CHE ISSN 1015-8154) **5604**
† Devenir Fonctionnaire (FRA ISSN 1291-6307) **8950**
Devi (IND) **3881**
• Deviajes (ESP) **8698**
• Deviance et Societe (CHE ISSN 0378-7931) **8098**
Deviant (NLD ISSN 1381-0782) **6136**
• ➤ Deviant Behavior (USA ISSN 0163-9625) **8098**
Deviate *see* D V 8 **6561**
• Device Regulation Alert (USA ISSN 1947-8895) **5604**
➤ Device Therapy for Heart Failure (GBR ISSN 1750-8703) **5785**
Devicemed (DEU ISSN 1860-9414) **5905**
• Devices & Diagnostics Letter (USA ISSN 0098-7573) **4486**
Devil Facial Tumour Disease Newsletter (AUS ISSN 1833-4954) **8796**
Devil in the Woods Magazine *see* D I W Magazine **6560**
• Devil Shat (USA ISSN 1097-8534) **3974**
Devil's Artisan (CAN ISSN 0225-7874) **7319**
➤ Devil's Millhopper (USA ISSN 0733-9615) **5420**
Devis de Construction (CAN ISSN 1911-4958) **1002**
DevISSues *see* Development ISSues **8098**
• DeVita, Hellman, and Rosenberg's Cancer, Principles & Practice of Oncology (USA) **6018**
• Le Devoir (CAN ISSN 0319-0722) **3808**
Devon and Cornwall Notes and Queries (GBR ISSN 0012-1681) **4214**
Devon and Cornwall Record Society. New Series (GBR) **4214**
Devon Archaeological Society. Newsletter (GBR) **390**
Devon Archaeological Society. Proceedings (GBR ISSN 0305-5795) **390**
Devon Archaeology (GBR ISSN 0264-7540) **390**
The Devon Closewool Sheep Breeders' Society. Flock Book (GBR ISSN 1746-3556) **285**
Devon Country Gardener (GBR) **3728**
Devon Farmer (GBR ISSN 0012-169X) **105**
➤ Devon Historian (GBR ISSN 0305-8549) **4214**
Devon Life (GBR ISSN 0012-1703) **3864**
Devonshire Association for the Advancement of Science, Literature and the Arts. Report and Transactions (GBR ISSN 0309-7994) **4449**
Devotions (USA) **7754**
• Devo'Zine (USA ISSN 1088-0054) **7754**
Devyat' Mesyatsev *see* 9 Mesyatsev **6007**
Dew Claw (USA) **6806**
Dewan Masyarakat (MYS ISSN 0419-0386) **3906**
Dewan Pelajar (MYS ISSN 0417-3910) **2185**
Dewan Perintis (MYS) **2185**
The DeWeese Report (USA ISSN 1086-7937) **7130**
Dewitt County Genealogical Society. Quarterly (USA ISSN 0890-4456) **3764**
Dex Magazin (DEU) **5069**
Dexter: Ionia County Magazine (USA ISSN 1932-0795) **5069**
Dexter Magazine *see* Dexter: Ionia County Magazine **5069**
• Deyu Xuexi/Wir Lernen Deutsch (CHN ISSN 1002-5545) **5111**
Dez.Eme *see* Dezeme **4137**
Dezeme (ESP ISSN 1576-4044) **4137**
Dezibel (CHE) **8037**
➤ Dezinfektsionnoe Delo (RUS) **5812**
DGiRL *see* Disney Girl **2185**
DGV Informationen *see* D G V Informationen **3616**
Al-Dhafra (UAE) **3966**
Al-Dhaid (UAE) **8169**
Dhaka Bisvabidyalaya Patrika (BGD) **3799**
• Dhaka Courier (BGD) **3799**
Dhaka Law Reports: Civil Digest (BGD) **4657**
• The Dhaka University Journal of Science (BGD ISSN 1022-2502) **7850**
Dhaka University Studies. Part A: Arts, Humanities, and Social Science (BGD ISSN 1013-543X) **4449**
Dhandha (IND ISSN 0300-4309) **5482**
Dhaniram Bhalla Granthamala (IND) **548**
Dharam Narain Memorial Lecture Series (IND) **1091**
▼ Dharana (IND ISSN 0974-0082) **1738**
Dharitri (IND) **3881**
Dharma (MYS ISSN 0012-1746) **7637**
Dharma Beat (USA ISSN 1072-4559) **5284**
† Dharma Life (GBR) **8950**
Dharma - vision *see* The Dharmachaksu **7707**
Dharma World (JPN ISSN 0387-5970) **7701**
The Dharmachaksu/Dharma - vision (THA) **7707**
Dharmaduta (MNG) **7701**
Dharmayug (IND ISSN 0417-3937) **3881**
• Dhaulagiri (NPL ISSN 1994-2664) **8098**
Dhivara (LKA) **3590**
Di *see* Dagens Industri **1089**
Di Biao *see* L P Luxury Properties **7597**
• ➤ Di-Er Jun-Yi Daxue Xuebao/Academic Journal of Second Military Medical University (CHN ISSN 0258-879X) **5604**
Di-er Ketang *see* Guangdong Di-er Ketang **2191**
Di Piu T V Cucina (ITA ISSN 1971-8748) **4356**
Di San Bo/Third Wave Magazine (TWN ISSN 1022-2901) **2589**
• Di-San Junyi Daxue Xuebao/Acta Academiae Medicinae Militaris Tertiae (CHN ISSN 1000-5404) **5604**
• ➤ Di Si Junyi Daxue Xuebao/Fourth Military Medical University. Journal (CHN ISSN 1000-2790) **5604**
• Di-Yi Junyi Daxue Fenxiao Xuebao/First Military Medical University. Branch Campus. Journal (CHN ISSN 1009-1793) **5604**
• Di Yi Junyi Daxue Xuebao/First Military Medical University. Journal (CHN ISSN 1000-2588) **5604**
• Dia (ARG) **3791**
• Dia (PRY) **1092**
El Dia (USA) **3530**
Dia a Dia *see* Forward Day by Day **7758**
Dia Cuatro Que Fuera... (ESP) **8169**
Dia Regno/Divine Kingdom (USA ISSN 0167-9554) **7637**
Dia Spektrum (SVK ISSN 1336-9822) **5886**
Diabc (NLD ISSN 0166-7629) **5886**
• Diabet Bilimi Dergisi (TUR) **5886**
Diabet. Obraz Zhizni (RUS) **6833**
• Il Diabete (ITA ISSN 0394-901X) **5886**
Diabete & Obesite (FRA ISSN 1957-5238) **5886**
Diabete Mondial *see* World Diabetes **5801**
Diabeteksen Ehkaisyn ja Hoidon Kehittamisohjelma Raportti *see* D E H K O - Raportti **5886**
• Diabetes (DNK ISSN 0901-3652) **5886**
Diabetes (ESP ISSN 0417-3988) **5886**
• ➤ Diabetes (FIN ISSN 0046-0192) **5886**
Diabetes (HUN ISSN 1418-4990) **5886**
• Diabetes (SWE ISSN 0419-0459) **5886**
• ➤ Diabetes (USA ISSN 0012-1797) **5886**
Diabetes (Oslo) (NOR ISSN 1502-1424) **5886**
• Diabetes Aktuell (DEU ISSN 1861-6089) **5886**
Diabetes Aktuell, Hallo - Du Auch (DEU ISSN 0931-9379) **5886**
▼ • Diabetes & Metabolic Syndrome (USA ISSN 1871-4021) **5886**
• Diabetes & Metabolism (FRA ISSN 1262-3636) **5886**
Diabetes and Nutrition Organization Nieuws *see* D N O Nieuws **5886**
• Diabetes and Obesity Research Review (NZL ISSN 1178-6116) **5886**
• ➤ Diabetes and Primary Care (GBR ISSN 1466-8955) **5886**
• ➤ Diabetes and Vascular Disease Research (GBR ISSN 1479-1641) **5886**
Diabetes & You (USA) **5886**
† ➤ The Diabetes Annual (NLD ISSN 0168-9282) **8950**
• ➤ Diabetes Care (USA ISSN 0149-5992) **5887**
Diabetes Care and Education Newsletter (USA ISSN 1070-5945) **5887**
Diabetes Care. Supplement (USA ISSN 1064-9131) **5887**
The Diabetes Communicator (CAN ISSN 1912-8851) **5887**
Diabetes Congress Report (DEU ISSN 1617-6529) **5887**
• Diabetes Dateline (USA) **5887**
Diabetes Dialogue (CAN ISSN 0703-5764) **5887**
Diabetes Digest (GBR) **5887**
• Diabetes Digest (USA) **5887**
Diabetes Digest *see* Wal-Mart Diabetes Digest **5901**
Diabetes Education Reimbursements & Policy Report (USA ISSN 1525-7428) **4657**
• ➤ The Diabetes Educator (USA ISSN 0145-7217) **5887**
Diabetes & Leven (NLD ISSN 1566-2756) **5887**
Diabetes en Leven (Journaal Edition) (NLD ISSN 1875-4198) **5887**
Diabetes Explorer (USA) **5887**
Diabetes Focus (USA) **5887**
Diabetes Focus Espanol (USA) **5887**
Diabetes Fonds Nieuwsbrief *see* Dialoog **5890**
Diabetes for Helsepersonell *see* Diabetesforum **5889**
• Diabetes Forecast (USA ISSN 0095-8301) **5887**
Diabetes Forecast en Espanol (USA) **5887**
Diabetes-Forum (DEU ISSN 1614-6476) **5887**
Diabetes Frontier (JPN ISSN 0915-6593) **5887**
Diabetes Health *see* Diabetes Health Professional **5887**
Diabetes Health *see* Kmart Diabetes Health **5896**
Diabetes Health Monitor (USA ISSN 1542-8141) **5887**
Diabetes Health Professional (USA ISSN 1936-9522) **5887**
• Diabetes Hoy (MEX ISSN 0188-6827) **5887**
Diabetes Informatieboek (NLD ISSN 1872-5031) **5887**
Diabetes International (GBR ISSN 1468-6570) **5887**
Diabetes Interview *see* Diabetes Health Professional **5887**
• Diabetes ja Laakari (FIN ISSN 1455-7827) **5887**
Diabetes Journaal *see* Diabetes en Leven (Journaal Edition) **5887**
Diabetes Journal (CHE) **5605**
• ➤ Diabetes-Journal (DEU ISSN 0341-8812) **5888**
Diabetes Journal *see* Diabetes-Journal **5888**
▼ • Diabetes Management (GBR ISSN 1758-1907) **5888**
Diabetes Management Journal (AUS ISSN 1833-5365) **5888**
▼ • ➤ Diabetes, Metabolic Syndrome and Obesity (GBR ISSN 1178-7007) **5888**
• ➤ Diabetes - Metabolism: Research and Reviews (Online) (GBR ISSN 1520-7560) **5888**
• ➤ Diabetes - Metabolism: Research and Reviews (Print) (GBR ISSN 1520-7552) **5888**
Diabetes Newsletter (DEU ISSN 1435-7259) **5888**
• Diabetes, Obesity and Metabolism (GBR ISSN 1462-8902) **5888**
• Diabetes, Obesity and Metabolism Online (GBR ISSN 1463-1326) **5888**
Diabetes, Obesity and Metabolism. Supplement *see* Diabetes, Obesity and Metabolism **5888**
Diabetes, Obesity, Cardiovascular Disease News *see* D O C News **8948**
Diabetes Positive! (USA) **5888**
Diabetes Quarterly *see* The Diabetes Communicator **5887**
† Diabetes-Report (BRD ISSN 0720-0749) **8950**
• ➤ Diabetes Research and Clinical Practice (IRL ISSN 0168-8227) **5888**
Diabetes Research and Clinical Practice. Supplement (IRL ISSN 1572-1671) **5888**
Diabetes Research & Metabolic Syndrome (SGP) **5888**
Diabetes Research and Wellness Direct (USA) **5888**
Diabetes Research: Clinical & Experimental (GBR ISSN 0265-5985) **5888**
Diabetes Self-Management (USA ISSN 0741-6253) **5888**
Diabetes Sourcebook (USA) **5888**
• ➤ Diabetes Spectrum (USA ISSN 1040-9165) **5888**
• Diabetes, Stoffwechsel und Herz (DEU ISSN 1861-7603) **5889**
• ➤ Diabetes Technology & Therapeutics (USA ISSN 1520-9156) **5889**
Diabetes Today (GBR ISSN 1464-5009) **5889**
Diabetes und Stoffwechsel *see* Diabetes, Stoffwechsel und Herz **5889**
Diabetes Vital (USA ISSN 1551-1308) **5889**
• Diabetes Voice (BEL ISSN 1437-4064) **5889**
• Diabetes Week (USA ISSN 1537-1425) **5889**
The DiabetesCare Guide (USA) **5889**
• Diabetesforum (NOR ISSN 1503-9609) **5889**
Diabetesprofi *see* Diabetes-Forum **5887**
DiabetesProfi Aktuell *see* Diabetes-Forum **5887**
▼ Diabetessource (USA ISSN 1940-4948) **5889**
Diabetic *see* Diabetik **5889**
Diabetic Association of India. Journal. Education Section (IND ISSN 0970-4035) **5889**
Diabetic Association of India. Journal. Scientific Section (IND ISSN 0970-4027) **5889**
• Diabetic Cooking (USA ISSN 1526-0291) **5889**
• ➤ The Diabetic Foot (GBR ISSN 1462-2041) **5889**
▼ • ➤ Diabetic Hypoglycaemia (GBR ISSN 1757-2428) **5889**
Diabetic Living (AUS) **6657**
Diabetic Living (USA ISSN 1552-8065) **5889**
▼ Diabetic Living Everyday Cooking (USA ISSN 1943-2615) **4356**
▼ Diabetic Living Favorite Slow Cooker Recipes (USA ISSN 1949-2561) **4356**
▼ Diabetic Living Holiday Cooking (USA ISSN 1943-2887) **4356**
• ➤ Diabetic Medicine (GBR ISSN 0742-3071) **5889**
• ➤ Diabetic Medicine Online (GBR ISSN 1464-5491) **5889**
Diabetic Medicine Supplement *see* Diabetic Medicine **5889**
The Diabetics *see* Al- Sukkaryoun **5900**
Diabetik (SVK ISSN 1336-0426) **5889**
➤ Diabetik/Diabetic (UKR) **5889**
Diabetiker Ratgeber (DEU ISSN 0172-2166) **5889**
Diabetografiya (RUS) **5889**
• Der Diabetologe (DEU ISSN 1860-9716) **5889**
• ➤ Diabetologia (DEU ISSN 0012-186X) **5890**
• ➤ Diabetologia Croatica (HRV ISSN 0351-0042) **5890**
Diabetologia Croatica. Supplement (HRV ISSN 0351-1995) **5890**
Diabetologia Polska (POL ISSN 1233-4723) **5890**
• ➤ Diabetologia Praktyczna (POL ISSN 1640-8497) **5890**
• ➤ Diabetologie, Metabolismus, Endokrinologie, Vyziva (CZE ISSN 1211-9326) **5890**
• ➤ Diabetologie und Stoffwechsel (DEU ISSN 1861-9002) **5890**
• ➤ DiabetologNytt (SWE ISSN 1401-2618) **5890**
Diabetology and Endocrinology *see* Today in Medicine. Diabetology and Endocrinology **5900**
▼ • ➤ Diabetology & Metabolic Syndrome (GBR ISSN 1758-5996) **5890**
Diablo (USA ISSN 1051-3434) **5069**
Diablo Arts Magazine *see* Diablo Magazine **8469**
Diablo Descendents Newsletter (USA) **3764**
Diablo Magazine (USA) **8469**
Diablotexto (ESP ISSN 1134-6302) **5284**
Diabolo (DEU) **5213**
• ➤ Diachronica (NLD ISSN 0176-4225) **5111**
Diac'Infos (FRA ISSN 1775-2531) **5785**
Diaconia Christi (DEU ISSN 0933-0771) **7794**
Diacoon (NLD ISSN 1572-7459) **7754**
Diacritica (PRT ISSN 0870-8967) **5284**
• Diacritics (USA ISSN 0300-7162) **5284**
diacritics *see* Diacritics **5284**
Diadokhe (CHL ISSN 0717-4292) **6914**
Diadora (HRV ISSN 0417-4046) **390**
Diaet und Information (DEU ISSN 1862-0620) **6657**
Diagnose en Therapie (NLD ISSN 1574-3535) **6136**
• Diagnosis (USA) **5111**
Diagnosis and Treatment *see* Shindan To Chiryo **5714**
Diagnosis Coding Pro for Home Health (USA ISSN 1941-8957) **4501**
Diagnosis Related Group Handbook *see* D R G Handbook **4092**
Diagnostic (FRA ISSN 1777-781X) **1477**
• ➤ Diagnostic and Interventional Radiology (TUR ISSN 1305-3825) **6195**
Diagnostic & Invasive Cardiology (USA ISSN 1551-6091) **6195**
• ➤ Diagnostic and Therapeutic Endoscopy (USA ISSN 1070-3608) **5905**
• ➤ Diagnostic Cytopathology (USA ISSN 8755-1039) **832**
Diagnostic Engineering (GBR ISSN 0269-0225) **3376**
• Diagnostic Histopathology (Oxford) (GBR ISSN 1756-2317) **5944**
• Diagnostic Imaging (USA ISSN 0194-2514) **6195**
• Diagnostic Imaging Asia Pacific (USA) **6195**
Diagnostic Imaging Europe (USA ISSN 1461-0051) **6195**
• Diagnostic Imaging Intelligence Report (USA ISSN 1541-2458) **6195**
† Diagnostic Imaging Scan (Online) (USA) **8950**
• Diagnostic Insight (USA ISSN 1098-1012) **5605**
• ➤ Diagnostic Microbiology and Infectious Disease (USA ISSN 0732-8893) **884**
• ➤ Diagnostic Molecular Pathology (USA ISSN 1052-9551) **5605**
Diagnostic News *see* Laboratory News **5908**
• Diagnostic Pathology (GBR ISSN 1746-1596) **5605**
• Diagnostic Testing and Technology Report (USA ISSN 1531-3786) **5605**
Diagnostic Testing & Technology Report *see* Diagnostic Testing and Technology Report **5605**
• ➤ Diagnostica (DEU ISSN 0012-1924) **7352**
Diagnosticians. Proceedings (PAK ISSN 1728-9513) **5605**
Diagnostico (PER ISSN 1018-2888) **5605**
• ➤ Diagnostico & Tratamento (BRA ISSN 1413-9979) **5944**
• Diagnostico y Propuesta (PER ISSN 1682-4350) **1092**
Diagnostics *see* Diagnostic **1477**
Diagnostics & Imaging Update *see* Diagnostics & Imaging Week **5905**
• Diagnostics & Imaging Week (USA ISSN 1932-7757) **5905**
Diagnostics Canada B2B Industry Guide *see* Medical & Assistive Devices & Diagnostics Canada Industry & Buyers Guide **2016**
Diagnostics Intelligence (USA ISSN 1054-9609) **6833**
Diagnostics Today (DEU) **4486**
Diagnostika i Proignozirovanie Razrusheniya Svarnykh Konstruktsii (UKR ISSN 0234-4874) **6342**
Diagnostyka Laboratoryjna (POL ISSN 1509-2305) **5605**
• Diagonal (ESP ISSN 1699-2326) **3951**
Diagonal (FRA ISSN 0338-0610) **4409**
• Diagram (USA ISSN 1543-5784) **5284**
Diagrama Economico (BOL) **1092**
Diagramm (AUT ISSN 0419-9081) **2530**
Diagrammes (FRA ISSN 0224-3911) **5482**
Diagroup (ITA ISSN 0391-545X) **7794**
Diaita (DEU ISSN 1861-955X) **6657**
Diakonia (DEU ISSN 0341-9592) **7794**
Diakonia (NIC) **7794**
• ➤ Diakonian Tutkimus (FIN ISSN 1796-5675) **7637**
Diakonie (AUT) **7754**
† Diakonie im Rheinland (DEU ISSN 0173-9077) **8950**
Diakonie Magazin (DEU ISSN 1864-1628) **7637**
▼ Diakonie-Magazin (DEU ISSN 1864-1660) **8037**
Diakonie Report *see* Diakonie Magazin **7637**
Diakonie Report. Ausgabe Nordelbien, Hamburg *see* Diakonie Magazin **7637**
Diakonieschwester (DEU) **7637**
• Diakonissehjemmets Hoegskole. Arbeidsnotat (NOR ISSN 0809-6813) **5957**
Diakonivetenskapliga Institutet. Skriftserie (SWE ISSN 1404-2924) **7637**
Diakonivetenskapliga Institutet. Temabok (SWE ISSN 1650-2523) **7637**
Diakonos (NOR ISSN 0333-4589) **7637**
Diakonos Magasin *see* Diakonos **7637**
Diakopes (GRC ISSN 1106-8590) **8698**
Diakrisis (DEU ISSN 0174-5506) **7754**
Dial-A-Fax Directory (USA ISSN 1046-7262) **1984**
• Dial-a-Poem Poets (USA) **5420**
Dial. Base de Datos e Imagenes del Diario Oficial de Castilla-La Mancha *see* Diario Oficial de Castilla-La Mancha **4657**
• Dial Electrical - Electronics (GBR ISSN 0953-6949) **3092**
• Dial Engineering (GBR ISSN 0955-4335) **3343**
• Dial Industry. Metals, Metalworking, Mechanical Engineering, Shipbuilding, Aerospace, Marine and Vehicle Industries (GBR ISSN 0263-1628) **6310**
• Dial Info-Link Directory (AUS) **1984**
DIAL M *see* International Workshop on Discrete Algorithms and Methods for Mobile Computing and Communications. Proceedings **2328**
• Dialaesen (SWE ISSN 1104-4616) **6267**
Dialect (CAN ISSN 0383-8528) **8037**
Dialect *see* Fangyan **5118**
Dialectes de Wallonie (BEL ISSN 0773-7688) **5111**
Dialectic (AUS ISSN 0084-9804) **6914**
Dialectica (MEX ISSN 0185-7770) **7959**
• ➤ Dialectica (USA ISSN 0012-2017) **6914**
▼ Dialectica Libertadora (COL ISSN 2011-3501) **7959**
• Dialectical Anthropology (NLD ISSN 0304-4092) **335**
Dialectics *see* Dijalektika **7850**

● ➤ Dialectologia et Geolinguistica (DEU ISSN 0942-4040) **5111**
● Dialegesthai (ITA ISSN 1128-5478) **6914**
Dialekt-, Ortnamns och Folkminnesarkivet i Umeaa Katta *see* D A U M - Katta **5282**
Dialekt-, Ortnamns- och Folkminnesarkivet i Umeaa. Skrifter. Serie A, Dialekter (SWE ISSN 0280-5553) **5111**
Dialekt-, Ortnamns- och Folkminnesarkivet i Umeaa. Skrifter. Serie B, Namn (SWE ISSN 0349-0904) **5111**
Dialekt-, Ortnamns- och Folkminnesarkivet i Umeaa. Skrifter. Serie D, Meddelanden (SWE ISSN 0282-0226) **5111**
Dialekt-, Ortnamns- och Folkminnesarkivet i Umeaa. Skrifter, Serie E, Vaextnamm (SWE ISSN 1402-6783) **5111**
Dialekt-, Ortnamns- och Folkminnesarkivet i Umeaa. Skrifter. Seroe F, Musikliv (SWE ISSN 1650-0326) **3616**
Dialektica (ARG) **6914**
Dialektik *see* Zeitschrift fuer Kulturphilosophie **6962**
Dialektisk Dialog *see* Sociologisk Tidende **8138**
Dialetti d'Italia (ITA ISSN 0012-2025) **5284**
La Dialettica (ITA) **6914**
● Dialisis y Transplante (ESP ISSN 1886-2845) **6267**
Dialog (CAN) **2282**
Dialog (DEU ISSN 0948-1702) **3846**
Dialog *see* Dialogue (Guernes) **8950**
Dialog (MDA) **3912**
Dialog (POL ISSN 0012-2041) **8469**
● Dialog (RUS ISSN 0236-0942) **7130**
The Dialog (USA) **7794**
● Dialog (Berlin) (DEU ISSN 0938-1422) **7230**
Dialog (Essen) (DEU ISSN 1615-7516) **2842**
Dialog (Frankfurt am Main) (DEU) **3299**
Dialog (Hannover, 1973) (DEU) **7637**
Dialog (Hannover, 1994) (DEU ISSN 1619-1064) **1423**
● ➤ Dialog (St Paul) (USA ISSN 0012-2033) **7637**
Dialog (Wilmington) (USA) **7637**
Dialog. Beitraege zur Friedensforschung (AUT) **7959**
● Dialog zzzzh DataStar Database Catalog (USA) **5006**
Dialog der Kirchen (DEU ISSN 0937-1540) **7637**
Dialog Erziehungshilfe (DEU ISSN 1862-0329) **3038**
Dialog on Disc Chemical Business News Base *see* Chemical Business NewsBase **2093**
Dialog on Disc Chemical Engineering and Biotechnology Abstracts *see* Chemical Engineering and Biotechnology Abstracts (Online) **3229**
Dialog on Language Instruction (USA ISSN 1058-3858) **5111**
● Dialog OnDisc Environmental Chemistry, Health and Safety (GBR) **3495**
Dialog Pheniben (POL ISSN 1425-3496) **3530**
† Dialog & Wandel (DEU) **8950**
Dialogas (LTU ISSN 1392-1916) **2842**
Dialoger (SWE ISSN 0283-5207) **8469**
Dialoghi di Diritto Tributario (ITA ISSN 1825-0394) **1920**
Dialoghi fra Dottrina e Giurisprudenza (ITA ISSN 1827-4846) **4657**
▼ ● Dialoghi Tributari (ITA ISSN 1974-1286) **1920**
● Dialogi (FIN ISSN 0789-0346) **8037**
Dialogi (SVN ISSN 0012-2068) **5213**
Dialogikon (POL ISSN 1505-4594) **6914**
Dialogo (AUT) **7230**
Dialogo (PRI) **2282**
Dialogo (USA ISSN 1090-4972) **8098**
● Dialogo Andino (CHL ISSN 0716-2278) **7959**
Dialogo Cientifico (DEU ISSN 0942-2218) **4657**
Dialogo Ecumenico (ESP ISSN 0210-2870) **7637**
Dialogo Filosofico (ESP ISSN 0213-1196) **6914**
Dialogo Mediterraneo (ESP ISSN 1578-6579) **1561**
Dialogo Social (PAN ISSN 0046-0206) **8098**
➤ Dialogos (BRA ISSN 1677-6488) **7959**
● Dialogos (CRI ISSN 1409-469X) **4137**
Dialogos *see* Dialogue (Guernes) **8950**
➤ Dialogos (PRI ISSN 0012-2122) **6914**
Dialogos (El Mansou, Barcelona) (ESP ISSN 1134-7880) **2940**
Dialogos (Maringa) (BRA ISSN 1415-9945) **4290**
Dialogos de la Comunicacion (PER ISSN 1813-9248) **2319**
▼ ● Dialogos de Politicas Publicas (CHL ISSN 0718-4581) **7130**
Dialogos de Saberes (COL ISSN 0124-0021) **6914**
Dialogos Educacionales (CHL ISSN 0716-5722) **2842**
● ➤ Dialogos Latinoamericanos (DNK ISSN 1600-0110) **4291**
Dialogos Pedagogicos (ARG ISSN 1667-2003) **2842**
Dialogue *see* Academy of the Social Sciences in Australia. Dialogue **7945**
Dialogue *see* Canada Asia Commentary **1079**
Dialogue *see* M D Dialogue **5662**
● Dialogue (FRA ISSN 0242-8962) **8098**
Dialogue (GAB) **7130**
● ➤ Dialogue (GBR ISSN 0012-2173) **6914**
Dialogue (IND ISSN 0973-0095) **4657**
● Dialogue (LKA ISSN 0012-2181) **7638**
● ➤ The Dialogue (PAK ISSN 1819-6462) **7959**
● Dialogue (RWA ISSN 0257-0017) **3789**
● Dialogue (TUN ISSN 0330-9436) **3789**
Dialogue (Amsterdam) (NLD ISSN 1574-9630) **5284**
● Dialogue (Chicago) (USA ISSN 1092-2164) **4968**
● Dialogue (Columbus) (USA ISSN 0279-568X) **486**
† Dialogue (Guernes)/Dialog/Dialogos/Dialogus (FRA ISSN 1164-8147) **8950**
Dialogue (Ivry) (FRA ISSN 0223-3592) **3057**
Dialogue (Kingston) (CAN ISSN 1184-6283) **7754**
Dialogue (Logan) *see* Dialogue (Salt Lake City) **7734**
Dialogue (Milwaukee) (USA ISSN 0012-2246) **6914**
▼ ● Dialogue (Monterey) (USA ISSN 1936-1289) **8098**
● Dialogue (Salem) (USA ISSN 1069-6857) **4081**
● ➤ Dialogue (Salt Lake City) (USA ISSN 0012-2157) **7734**
● ➤ Dialogue & Alliance (USA ISSN 0891-5881) **7638**
● ➤ Dialogue and Universalism (POL ISSN 1234-5792) **6914**
Dialogue et Verite (FRA ISSN 1951-5367) **7794**
Dialogue on Campus (USA ISSN 0012-2289) **2977**
Dialogue Sante/Dialoog Gezondheid (BEL ISSN 1377-980X) **5605**
▼ ➤ Dialogue Studies (NLD ISSN 1875-1792) **8098**
Dialogue Today (IND) **8858**
Dialoguer (FRA ISSN 0012-2297) **8098**
● Dialogues (Calgary) (CAN ISSN 1712-8986) **8098**
● Dialogues d'Histoire Ancienne (FRA ISSN 0755-7256) **4137**
Dialogues et Cultures (FRA ISSN 0226-6881) **5112**
Dialogues in Cardiovascular Medicine (FRA ISSN 1272-9949) **5785**
Dialogues in Clinical Neuroscience (FRA ISSN 1294-8322) **6136**
Dialogues in Dermatology (USA) **5875**
Dialogues in Public Policy (USA) **7433**
† Dialogues on Work and Innovation (NLD ISSN 1384-6671) **8950**
Dialogus *see* Dialogue (Guernes) **8950**
Dialogy o Manazmente Podnikania a Veci Verejnych *see* Manazment Podnikania a Veci Verejnych **1778**
Dialoog (NLD ISSN 1871-0719) **5890**
Dialoog Gezondheid *see* Dialogue Sante **5605**
● Dialyse Aktuell (DEU ISSN 1434-0704) **6267**
Dialyse Intern (DEU ISSN 0934-4187) **6267**
➤ Dialyse Journal (DEU ISSN 0932-190X) **6267**
Der Dialysepatient (DEU ISSN 0724-0252) **6267**
Dialysis and Transplant *see* Jinfuzen o Ikiru **6270**
● Dialysis & Transplantation (USA ISSN 0090-2934) **6267**
Diamant Hochleistungswerkzeuge (DEU ISSN 1868-4459) **6461**
Diamanten (DNK ISSN 1399-6142) **5006**
● ➤ Diametros (POL ISSN 1733-5566) **6914**
Diamond (Sioux Center) (USA) **2282**
Diamond & Abrasives Engineering *see* Jin'gangshi yu Moliao Moju Gongcheng **3204**
● ➤ Diamond and Related Materials (CHE ISSN 0925-9635) **2110**
Diamond Box (Year) (JPN ISSN 0388-5119) **3900**
Diamond Fields Advertiser (ZAF) **3948**
Diamond Habado Bijinesu/Diamond Harvard Business (JPN ISSN 0385-4272) **1738**
Diamond Harvard Business *see* Diamond Habado Bijinesu **1738**
Diamond Industria (JPN ISSN 0385-7360) **1427**
● Diamond Intelligence Briefs (ISR) **6461**
Diamond Registry. Bulletin (USA ISSN 0199-9753) **4565**
The Diamond Registry Bulletin (USA) **4565**
Diamond Report (JPN) **1620**
Diamond, Stock Investment Edition/Daiyamondo Kabushiki-Toshi-Ban (JPN) **1620**
Diamond Weekly (JPN) **1738**
Diamond World (IND ISSN 0970-7727) **4565**
Diamond World Review (ISR ISSN 0333-5380) **4565**
The Diamondback (USA) **2282**
Dian Chi Literary Monthly *see* Dianchi **5284**
● ➤ Dian Huaxue/Electrochemistry (CHN ISSN 1006-3471) **2113**
† Dian Jiang Ying Shi/T V and Film Literature (CHN) **8950**
Dian Shijie/Electrical World (CHN ISSN 1000-1344) **3299**
Diana (ITA ISSN 0012-2343) **8311**
Diana Armi (ITA ISSN 0012-2351) **4333**
Diana - Baby (CZE) **6638**
† Diana Baby (DEU ISSN 1434-0534) **8950**
† Diana - Detska Sita Moda (CZE ISSN 1613-3218) **8950**
Diana - Filetove Hackovani (CZE ISSN 1860-1146) **6638**
Diana - Hackovana Moda (CZE ISSN 1433-9188) **6638**
† Diana - Hackovana Moda Pro Deti (CZE ISSN 1860-2983) **8950**
Diana - Hackovani (CZE) **6638**
Diana - Hackovani Special (CZE ISSN 1613-3226) **6638**
▼ Diana - Krajkove Hackovani (CZE ISSN 1864-5844) **6638**
▼ Diana - Kreativni Moda (CZE ISSN 1865-7168) **6638**
Diana - Kreativni Napady (CZE) **534**
Diana - Kreativni Trendy (CZE ISSN 1861-0528) **534**
Diana - Malovane Obrazky (CZE ISSN 1614-4775) **534**
Diana - Moda (CZE) **2253**
Diana - Moda Special (CZE) **2253**
▼ Diana - Muj Kreativni Svet (CZE ISSN 1867-1284) **4356**
Diana Muster Extra *see* Muster Extra **6640**
Diana - Pletena Moda Pro Deti (CZE ISSN 1861-8693) **6638**
▼ Diana - Pletena Moda Pro Zeny (CZE ISSN 1865-7176) **6638**
† Diana - Pro Deti (CZE ISSN 1614-3736) **8950**
Diana - Recepty (CZE) **4356**
Diana - Rucni Prace (CZE) **4356**
Diana - Sita Moda *see* Diana - Moda **2253**
▼ Diana - Skola Hackovani (CZE ISSN 1865-9047) **6638**
Diana Special (DEU ISSN 1434-0437) **534**
▼ Diana - Vysivani (CZE) **6638**
● Diance yu Yibiao/Electronic Measuring and Meters (CHN ISSN 1001-1390) **4486**
Dianchi/Dian Chi Literary Monthly (CHN ISSN 1004-4167) **5284**
● Dianchi (Changsha)/Battery Bi-monthly (CHN ISSN 1001-1579) **3127**
Dianchi Chenbao (CHN) **3824**
● Dianchi Gongye/Chinese Battery Industry (CHN ISSN 1008-7923) **3156**
● Dianci Bileiqi/Insulators and Surge Arresters (CHN ISSN 1003-8337) **3343**
● Diandong Gongju/Electrokinetic Tool (CHN ISSN 1674-2796) **5451**
Diandong Zixingche (CHN ISSN 1672-6936) **8494**
● Diandu yu Huanbao/Electroplating and Pollution Control (CHN ISSN 1000-4742) **3485**
● Diandu yu Jingshi/Plating and Finishing (CHN ISSN 1001-3849) **2113**
● Diandu yu Tushi/Electroplating & Finishing (CHN ISSN 1004-227X) **2113**
Diane (GBR ISSN 0012-236X) **8858**
Diane (USA ISSN 1550-784X) **8845**
● Diangong Cailiao/Electrical Engineering Materials (CHN ISSN 1671-8887) **3299**
● Diangong Dianneng Xinjishu/Advanced Technology of Electrical Engineering and Energy (CHN ISSN 1003-3076) **3299**
● Diangong Jishu Xuebao/Chinese Electrotechnical Society. Transactions (CHN ISSN 1000-6753) **3300**
● Diangong Jishu Zazhi/Journal of Electronics Technology (CHN ISSN 1001-7194) **3092**
Diangong Wenzhai/Electrician Abstracts (CHN ISSN 1673-8845) **3229**
● Dianguang yu Kongzhi/Electronics Optics & Control (CHN ISSN 1671-637X) **7075**
● Dianhanji/Electric Welding Machine (CHN ISSN 1001-2303) **6342**
● Diani yu Fengzhuang/Electronics and Packaging (CHN ISSN 1681-1070) **6709**
Dianji Gongcheng Xuekan *see* International Journal of Electrical Engineering **3320**
● Dianji yu Kongzhi Xuebao/Electric Machines and Control (CHN ISSN 1007-449X) **3300**
● Dianli Dianrongqi yu Wugong Buchang/Power Capacitor & Reactive Power Compensation (CHN ISSN 1674-1757) **3127**
● Dianli Dianzi Jishu/Power Electronics (CHN ISSN 1000-100X) **3092**
Dianli Jiche Jishu/Technology for Electric Locomotives *see* Dianli Jiche yu Chenggui Cheliang **8616**
● Dianli Jiche yu Chenggui Cheliang/Electric Locomotives & Mass Transit Vehicles (CHN ISSN 1672-1187) **8616**
● Dianli Jishu Jingji/Electric Power Technologic Economics (CHN ISSN 1008-1682) **1092**
● Dianli Kexue yu Gongcheng/Electric Power Science and Engineering (CHN ISSN 1672-0792) **3156**
● Dianli Kexue yu Jishu Xuebao/Journal of Electric Power Science and Technology (CHN ISSN 1673-9140) **7850**
Dianli Qingbao/Information on Electric Power *see* Dianli Kexue yu Gongcheng **3156**
● ➤ Dianli Xitong Baohu yu Kongzhi/Power System Protection and Control (CHN ISSN 1674-3415) **3300**
● Dianli Xitong Jiqi Zidong Huaxue Bao/C S U - E P S A. Proceedings (CHN ISSN 1003-8930) **7850**
● Dianli Xitong Zidonghua/Automation of Electric Power Systems (CHN ISSN 1000-1026) **3156**
● Dianli Xuebao/Journal of Electric Power (CHN ISSN 1005-6548) **3156**
● Dianli Zidonghua Shebei/Electric Power Automation Equipments (CHN ISSN 1006-6047) **3300**
Dianlu yu Xitong Xuebao/Journal of Circuits and Systems (CHN ISSN 1007-0249) **3092**
Diannao Aihaozhe/Computer Fan (CHN ISSN 1005-0043) **2416**
● Diannao Biancheng Jiqiao yu Weihu/Computer Programming Skills & Maintenance (CHN ISSN 1006-4052) **2506**
● Diannao Jishu/Computer Technology (CHN ISSN 1006-5202) **2416**
● Diannao Kaifa yu Yingyong/Computer Development & Applications (CHN ISSN 1003-5850) **2416**
● Diannao Youxi Xin Ganxian (CHN ISSN 1672-0148) **2475**
Diannao yu Tongxun Yingyong/Journal of Computer and Communication Applications (TWN ISSN 1992-237X) **2416**
Diannao yu Xinyongka/Computer & Credit Card *see* Zhongguo Xinyongka **1392**
Diannao Zhishi yu Jishu/Computer Knowledge and Technology (CHN ISSN 1009-3044) **2416**
● Diannaomi/P C Fan (CHN ISSN 1672-528X) **2416**
● ➤ Dianoia (MEX ISSN 0185-2450) **6914**
● Dianpo Kexue Xuebao/Chinese Journal of Radio Science (CHN ISSN 1005-0388) **2358**
● Dianqi/China Appliance (CHN ISSN 1672-8823) **4356**
Dianqi & Zhineng Jianzhu *see* Dianqi yu Zhineng Jianzhu **3300**
● Dianqi Chuandong/Electric Drive (CHN ISSN 1001-2095) **3300**
● Dianqi Gongye/China Electrical Equipment Industry (CHN ISSN 1009-5578) **3300**
● Dianqi Pingjie/Consumer Electronics Review (CHN ISSN 1672-1594) **3092**
● Dianqi Shidai/Electric Age (CHN ISSN 1000-453X) **3156**
Dianqi yu Zhineng Jianzhu/Building Electrical & Intelligent System (CHN) **3300**
Dianqi Zhineng Jianzhu *see* Dianqi yu Zhineng Jianzhu **3300**
Dianqi Zidonghua (CHN ISSN 1000-3886) **2460**
Dianshi Dianying Wenxue *see* Dian Jiang Ying Shi **8950**
● Dianshi Yanjiu/T V Research (CHN ISSN 1007-3930) **2380**
Dianshi Yuekan/Television Monthly (CHN ISSN 1003-8558) **2380**
● Dianwang Jishu/Power System Technology (CHN ISSN 1000-3673) **3300**
● Dianwang yu Qingjie Nengyuan/Power System and Clean Energy (CHN ISSN 1674-3814) **3127**
Dianwang yu Shuili Fadian Jinzhan/Advances of Power System & Hydroelectric Engineering *see* Dianwang yu Qingjie Nengyuan **3127**
Dianxin Jianshe/Telecommunication Construction *see* Wangkuan Shidai **8998**
● Dianxin Jishu/Telecommunication Technology (CHN ISSN 1000-1247) **2367**
● Dianxin Kexue/Telecommunications Science (CHN ISSN 1000-0801) **2319**
Dianxin Yanjiu/T L Technical Journal (TWN ISSN 1015-0730) **3300**
● Dianying/Film (CHN ISSN 1671-2528) **6496**
● Dianying Chuangzuo/Cinematic Creation (CHN ISSN 0257-0173) **6496**
Dianying Gushi/Film Stories (CHN ISSN 0493-2374) **6496**
Dianying Jieshao (CHN) **6496**
Dianying Shijie/The Movie Show (CHN ISSN 1006-6756) **6496**
Dianying Wenxue/Film Literature (CHN ISSN 0495-5692) **6496**
Dianying Xinzuo/New Films (CHN ISSN 1005-6777) **6496**
● Dianying Yishu/Film Art (CHN ISSN 0257-0181) **6496**
† Dianying Yuebao/Film Monthly (CHN ISSN 1003-5834) **8950**
† Dianying zhi You/Film's Friends (CHN ISSN 1006-4478) **8950**
Dianying Zuopin/Film Scripts (CHN ISSN 1001-5582) **6496**
● ➤ Dianyuan Jishu/Chinese Journal of Power Sources (CHN ISSN 1002-087X) **3300**
Dianzhi Chanpin yu Jishu/World Products and Technology (CHN) **3092**
● Dianzi Celiang yu Yiqi Xuebao/Journal of Electronic Measurement and Instrument (CHN ISSN 1000-7105) **6401**
Dianzi Duikang Jishu *see* Dianzi Xinxi Duikang Jishu **6419**
● Dianzi Gongcheng Zhuanji. China (SGP ISSN 1684-1115) **3187**
● Dianzi Gongcheng Zhuanji. Taiwan (SGP ISSN 1684-1131) **3187**
● Dianzi Jishu/Electronic Technology (CHN ISSN 1000-0755) **3092**
● Dianzi Jishu Yingyong/Applications of Electronic Technique (CHN ISSN 0258-7998) **3092**
● Dianzi Keji/I T Age (CHN ISSN 1007-7820) **3092**
● Dianzi Keji Daxue Xuebao/University of Electronic Science and Technology of China. Journal (CHN ISSN 1001-0548) **8420**
● Dianzi Keji Daxue Xuebao (Shehui Kexue Xuebao)/University of Electronic Science and Technology of China. Journal (Social Sciences Edition) (CHN) **7959**
Dianzi Kexue Jishu Pinglun *see* Zhongguo Dianzi Kexue Yanjiuyuan Xuebao **3116**
Dianzi Kexue Xuekan *see* Dianzi Yu Xinxi Xuebao **3092**
● Dianzi Qijian/Chinese Journal of Electron Devices (CHN ISSN 1005-9490) **3092**
Dianzi Shangwu/E-Business Journal (CHN ISSN 1009-6108) **1092**
➤ Dianzi Shangwu Yanjiu/Electronic Commerce Studies (TWN ISSN 1726-2364) **1092**
● Dianzi Sheji Jishu/E D N China (CHN ISSN 1023-7364) **3092**
● Dianzi Sheji Yingyong/Electronic Design & Application World-Nikkei Electronics China (CHN ISSN 1672-139X) **2554**
Dianzi Shichang/Electronics Market (CHN ISSN 1991-8895) **3092**
● Dianzi Shijie/Electronic World (CHN ISSN 1003-0522) **3092**
● Dianzi Wenzhaibao/Electronics Digest (CHN) **3092**
● ➤ Dianzi Xianwei Xuebao/Chinese Electron Microscopy Society. Journal (CHN ISSN 1000-6281) **7010**
Dianzi Xinxi Duikang Jishu/Electronic Information Warfare Technology (CHN ISSN 1674-2230) **6419**
Dianzi Xitong Sheji/Electronic Design - China (SGP) **3092**

Title

10198 DIANZI XUEBAO ULRICH'S PERIODICALS

• Dianzi Xuebao/Acta Electronica Sinica (CHN ISSN 0372-2112) **3092**
Dianzi Youxi Ruanjian/Game Software (CHN ISSN 1006-5032) **2475**
• Dianzi yu Diannao/Compotech China (CHN ISSN 1000-1077) **2416**
Dianzi yu Jin Xilie Gongcheng Xinxi/Electronics & Golden Projects Collection *see* Shuzi Jishu yu Yingyong **8438**
➤ Dianzi Yu Xinxi Xuebao (CHN ISSN 1009-5896) **3092**
• Dianzi yu Zidonghua/Electronics and Automation (CHN ISSN 1004-2792) **3093**
• Dianzi Yuanjian yu Cailiao/Electronic Components & Materials (CHN ISSN 1001-2028) **3093**
Dianzi Yuanqijian Zixun/Electronic Component and Device Information (CHN ISSN 1673-9892) **3093**
• Dianzi Zhengwu/e-Government (CHN ISSN 1672-7223) **7485**
• Dianzi Zhiliang/Electronics Quality (CHN ISSN 1003-0107) **3093**
• Dianzi Zhishi Chanquan (CHN ISSN 1004-9517) **6749**
• Diao-yan Shijie/The World of Survey and Research (CHN ISSN 1004-7794) **8366**
Diapason (FRA ISSN 1292-0703) **6561**
Diapason (RWA) **2282**
• The Diapason (USA ISSN 0012-2378) **6561**
Diapason Catalogue Classique (FRA ISSN 1636-5135) **6561**
Diaper Pail Friends Newsletter *see* D P F Newsletter **2150**
• Diari d'Andorra (AND) **3790**
Diari del Diumenge *see* Diari d'Andorra **3790**
• El Diario (BOL ISSN 0254-7457) **3802**
• El Diario (MEX) **3908**
El Diario (El Paso) (USA) **3530**
Diario 17 (MEX) **3908**
Diario A B C *see* A B C **3950**
• Diario Catarinese (BRA) **3803**
El Diario Contigo (USA) **3530**
• Diario da Borborema (BRA) **3803**
• Diario da Justicia. Secao 1 (BRA ISSN 1677-7018) **2650**
• Diario da Justicia. Secao 2 (BRA ISSN 1677-7026) **2650**
Diario da Republica. 1a Serie (PRT ISSN 0870-9963) **3931**
Diario da Republica. 2a Serie (PRT ISSN 0870-9971) **3931**
Diario da Republica. 3a Serie (PRT ISSN 0870-998X) **3931**
Diario de Avui *see* Avui **3951**
• Diario de Centro America (GTM) **7433**
Diario de Congresos Medicos (ESP ISSN 0210-5578) **6279**
• El Diario de Hoy (SLV ISSN 1605-1823) **3821**
• Diario de Justicia. Secao 3 (BRA ISSN 1677-7034) **2651**
Diario de la Bolsa *see* Bolsa de Valores de Caracas. Diario **1613**
• Diario de la Colonia (MEX) **2554**
Diario de las Chicas (ARG) **8895**
• Diario de Mallorca (ESP ISSN 1131-9518) **3951**
• Diario de Morelia (MEX ISSN 1605-0568) **3908**
• Diario de Morelos (MEX ISSN 1607-0313) **3908**
Diario de Noticias (ESP) **3951**
• Diario de Noticias (Las Rozas) (ESP ISSN 1139-5095) **4657**
• Diario de Noticias da Madeira (PRT) **3931**
• Diario de Nuevo Laredo (MEX) **3908**
Diario de Sesiones del Parlamento de Navarra (ESP) **7433**
• Diario de Suzano (BRA) **3803**
• El Diario de Tampico (MEX ISSN 1607-0321) **3908**
• Diario de Yucatan (MEX) **3908**
El Diario del Fin del Mundo (ARG) **3791**
• Diario del Otun (COL) **3830**
Diario del Pueblo en linea *see* Renminwang **3827**
Diario della Settimana (ITA) **3897**
Diario Diecisiete *see* Diario 17 **3908**
• Diario Digital (MEX ISSN 1563-8936) **3908**
• El Diario Digit@al. Chihuahua (MEX ISSN 1563-8944) **3908**
• Diario do Alentejo (PRT) **3931**
• Diario do Povo (BRA) **3803**
• Diario Economico (PRT ISSN 0872-1696) **1092**
• Diario Extra (CRI) **3830**
• Diario Hoy (ECU) **3835**
• El Diario Internet (CHL) **3821**
• Diario Juridico Aranzadi (ESP ISSN 1575-5940) **4657**
Diario La Ley *see* La Ley (Daily Edition) **4723**
Diario la Prensa (HND) **3875**
• El Diario La Prensa (USA ISSN 0742-9428) **3530**
Diario Las Americas (USA ISSN 0744-3234) **3530**
Diario Latino (SLV) **3836**
Diario Los Andes *see* Los Andes **3790**
Diario Medico (ESP) **5605**
• El Diario Montanes (ESP) **3951**
Diario Norte *see* Norte (Chaco) **3791**
• Diario Oficial da Uniao. Secao 1 (BRA ISSN 1677-7042) **4657**
• Diario Oficial da Uniao. Secao 2 (BRA ISSN 1677-7050) **4657**
• Diario Oficial da Uniao. Secao 3 (BRA ISSN 1677-7069) **4657**
• Diario Oficial de Castilla-La Mancha (ESP ISSN 1575-0051) **4657**
• Diario Oficial de Chile (CHL) **4657**
• Diario Oficial de Galicia (Galician Edition) (ESP ISSN 1130-9210) **4657**
• Diario Oficial de Galicia (Spanish Edition) (ESP ISSN 1130-9229) **4658**
• Diario Oficial de la Republica Oriental del Uruguay (URY ISSN 1510-3749) **4658**
• Diario Oficial de la Union Europea (LUX ISSN 1725-4159) **4923**
• Diario Oficial de las Comunidades Europeas. S: Licitaciones y Contratos Publicos (LUX ISSN 1027-6505) **4923**
• Diario Oficial de las Comunidades Europeas. Anexo Debates/Amtsblatt der Europaeischen Gemeinschaften. Anhang. Verhandlungen/ Episeme Efemerida ton Europaikon Koinoteton. Parartema. Suzeteseis/Euroopan Yhteisojen Virallinen Lehti. Liitteet. Taysistuntokeskustelut/ De Europaeiske Faelleskabers Tidende. Tillaeg. Forhandlinger/Europeiska Gemenskapernas Officiella Tidning. Bilaga. Oeverlaeggningar/ Gazzetta Ufficiale delle Comunita Europee. Allegato. Discussioni/Jornal Oficial das Comunidades Europeias. Anexo. Debates/Journal Officiel des Communautes Europeennes. Annexe. Debats/Official Journal of the European Communities. Annex. Debates/Publicatieblad van de Europese Gemeenschappen. Bijlage. Handelingen (LUX ISSN 1609-1213) **4923**
• Diario Oficial de las Comunidades Europeas. C: Comunicaciones e Informaciones (LUX ISSN 0257-7763) **4923**
Diario Oficial de las Comunidades Europeas. L & C: Legislacion, Comunicaciones e Informaciones *see* Official Journal of the European Union. L & C Series: Legislation and Information Notices (Quarterly Edition) **4937**
Diario Oficial de las Comunidades Europeas. L & C: Legislacion, Comunicaciones e Informaciones *see* Diario Oficial de las Comunidades Europeas. C: Comunicaciones e Informaciones **4923**
Diario Oficial de las Comunidades Europeas. L: Legislacion *see* Official Journal of the European Union. L Series: Legislation **7256**
Diario Oficial de las Comunidades Europeas. Suplemento *see* Diario Oficial de las Comunidades Europeas. S: Licitaciones y Contratos Publicos **4923**
Diario Oficial S: Licitaciones y Contratos Publicos *see* Diario Oficial de las Comunidades Europeas. S: Licitaciones y Contratos Publicos **4923**
• Diario Olmeca (MEX ISSN 1605-4954) **3908**
• Diario Perfil (ARG) **3791**
Diario Popular (PRY) **3927**
Diario Regional Viseu (PRT) **3931**
Diario Rio Negro *see* Rio Negro **3792**
• DiarioHoy.net (ARG) **3791**
• Diariomedico.com (ESP) **5605**
Diarist's Journal (USA ISSN 1056-4861) **5284**
Diary (GBR) **2253**
• ➤ Diaspora (CAN ISSN 1044-2057) **7959**
▼ • ➤ Diaspora, Indigenous, and Minority Education (USA ISSN 1559-5692) **2842**
Diaspora le Lien *see* Le Lien Israel-Diaspora.info **3548**
Diaspora - M I V A (Motorisierende Innerdeutsche Verkehrs-Arbeitsgemeinschaft) (DEU) **7794**
▼ Diaspora Studies (IND ISSN 0973-9572) **7230**
† ➤ Diastema (ITA ISSN 1122-3200) **8950**
Diatom (JPN ISSN 0911-9310) **786**
• ➤ Diatom Research (GBR ISSN 0269-249X) **786**
• Diatoms (USA) **6724**
Diatra Journal (DEU ISSN 0940-5623) **6267**
➤ Diatribe (GBR ISSN 1352-4828) **4449**
Dibattiti Storici in Parlamento (ITA ISSN 1827-5575) **7130**
Dibattito (ITA ISSN 1722-6759) **5957**
Dibevo Vakblad dier tuin *see* Dier Tuin **6806**
Al-Diblomasi/Diplomat (UAE) **7230**
Dibrugarh University. Department of Anthropology. Bulletin (IND) **335**
Dic-Agri *see* Dictionnaire - Annuaire de l'Agriculture et de l'Agro-Alimentaire **105**
Dicas & Truques para PlayStation (BRA ISSN 1516-6260) **2475**
Diccionario de Especialidades Agroquimicas (MEX) **105**
Diccionario de Especialidades en Analisis Clinicos (MEX) **2100**
Diccionario de Especialidades Farmaceuticas (MEX) **6833**
Diccionario de Especialidades para la Industria Alimentaria (MEX) **3633**
• Dicenda - Cuadernos de Filologia Hispanica (ESP ISSN 0212-2952) **5284**
• ➤ Dicengxue Zazhi/Journal of Stratigraphy (CHN ISSN 0253-4959) **2731**
Dichten (USA ISSN 1077-4203) **5284**
Dichters in de Prinsentuin (NLD ISSN 1871-0646) **5420**
Dichtung der Englischsprachigen Welt (DEU) **5420**
➤ Dichtung und Sprache (DEU) **5112**
Dichtungsring (DEU ISSN 0724-6412) **5284**
Dichtungstechnik (DEU ISSN 1436-526X) **3366**
Diciotto Karati Gold and Fashion *see* 18 Karati Gold & Fashion **4570**
Dick Berggren's Speedway Illustrated (USA ISSN 1528-4182) **8169**
• Dick Davis Digest (USA ISSN 0890-0957) **1620**
Dick Documents (USA) **3764**
Dick Young's Intelligence Report *see* Richard C. Young's Intelligence Report **1648**
Das Dicke Deutsche Hausbuch (DEU) **1002**
Dickens Companions (GBR) **5284**
The Dickens Magazine (GBR ISSN 1476-1335) **5284**
• ➤ Dickens Quarterly (USA ISSN 0742-5473) **5284**
➤ Dickens Studies Annual (USA ISSN 0084-9812) **5284**
➤ Dickensian (GBR ISSN 0012-2440) **5284**
Dickerchen Hitparade (DEU) **6288**
Dickin' Around (USA) **2265**
Dickinson County Heritage Center. Gazette (USA) **4291**
Dickinson's D T C Marketer (Direct-To-Consumer) (USA) **1813**
Dickinson's F D A Marketer *see* Dickinson's D T C Marketer **1813**
Dickinson's F D A Review (Food and Drug Administration) (USA ISSN 1073-4414) **6833**
Dickinson's F D A Updates (Federal Drug Administration) (USA) **7433**
Dickson Precinct Community Group. Newsletter (AUS ISSN 1328-6404) **5006**
Dickursby Meddelanden *see* Tikkurilan Viesti **1040**
Dicle Medical Journal *see* Dicle Tip Dergisi **5605**
• Dicle Tip Dergisi/Dicle Medical Journal (TUR ISSN 1300-2945) **5605**
Dico - Plus (FRA ISSN 0399-7081) **5112**
• El Dictamen (MEX ISSN 1606-7363) **3908**
➤ Dictionaire des Racines Semitiques (BEL) **548**
Dictionaries (USA ISSN 0197-6745) **5006**
▼ • Dictionary of Australian Artists Online (AUS ISSN 1835-7652) **642**
Dictionary of Canadian Biography/Dictionnaire Bibliographique du Canada (CAN ISSN 0070-4717) **642**
• Dictionary of Contemporary Quotations (USA ISSN 0360-215X) **5285**
Dictionary of Criminal Justice (USA) **2651**
A Dictionary of Human Rights (GBR) **7205**
• Dictionary of Inorganic and Organometallic Compounds on CD-ROM (GBR ISSN 1359-785X) **2060**
Dictionary of Inorganic Compounds. Supplement (USA ISSN 0964-2463) **2115**
Dictionary of International Biography (GBR ISSN 0419-1137) **642**
• Dictionary of Literary Biography (USA ISSN 1096-8547) **642**
Dictionary of Literary Biography: Documentary Series (USA) **642**
Dictionary of Mauritian Biography *see* Dictionnaire de Biographie Mauricienne **642**
A Dictionary of Modern Politics (GBR) **7130**
• Dictionary of Natural Products on CD-ROM (GBR ISSN 0966-2146) **6833**
Dictionary of Old English. Publications (CAN ISSN 0826-8134) **5112**
• Dictionary of Organic Compounds on CD-ROM (GBR ISSN 0967-6686) **2122**
• The Dictionary of Substances and Their Effects (GBR) **3495**
Dictionary Society of North America Newsletter *see* D S N A Newsletter **5005**
Dictionnaire Amoureux (FRA ISSN 1634-9377) **5213**
Dictionnaire - Annuaire de l'Agriculture et de l'Agro-Alimentaire (FRA) **105**
Dictionnaire Bibliographique du Canada *see* Dictionary of Canadian Biography **642**
Dictionnaire de Biographie Francaise (FRA) **648**
Dictionnaire de Biographie Mauricienne/Dictionary of Mauritian Biography (MUS ISSN 1025-367X) **642**
Dictionnaire des Communes (Lavauzelle et Cie) (FRA) **7433**
Dictionnaire des Valeurs des Meubles et Objets d'Art (FRA ISSN 0070-4776) **486**
Dictionnaire d'Histoire et de Geographie Ecclesiastiques (FRA) **7638**
Dictionnaire Joly Bourse et Produits Financiers *see* Juri-Dictionnaire Joly. Bourse et Produits Financiers **1636**
Dictionnaire Joly Concurrence (FRA ISSN 1764-0555) **1092**
Dictionnaire Joly Pratique des Contrats Internationaux (FRA ISSN 1244-443X) **1561**
• Dictionnaire Joly Societes (FRA) **1738**
Dictionnaire Permanent: Action Sociale (FRA ISSN 1161-2428) **8037**
• Dictionnaire Permanent: Assurances (FRA ISSN 1268-6247) **4501**
Dictionnaire Permanent: Bioethique et Biotechnologies (FRA ISSN 1257-0907) **763**
• Dictionnaire Permanent: Construction et Urbanisme (FRA ISSN 0012-2467) **1002**
• Dictionnaire Permanent: Conventions Collectives (FRA ISSN 1161-2436) **4593**
• Dictionnaire Permanent: Difficultes des Entreprises (FRA ISSN 0767-1555) **1738**
Dictionnaire Permanent: Droit de l'Epargne *see* Dictionnaire Permanent: Epargne et Produits Financiers **1335**
• Dictionnaire Permanent: Droit des Affaires (FRA ISSN 0012-2475) **4658**
Dictionnaire Permanent: Droit des Etrangers (FRA ISSN 1268-6239) **4658**
• Dictionnaire Permanent: Droit du Sport (FRA ISSN 1290-0214) **8169**
• Dictionnaire Permanent: Droit Europeen des Affaires (FRA ISSN 0998-4313) **4923**
• Dictionnaire Permanent: Entreprise Agricole (FRA ISSN 0012-2483) **105**
• Dictionnaire Permanent: Epargne et Produits Financiers (FRA ISSN 1958-4512) **1335**
Dictionnaire Permanent: Fiscal *see* Dictionnaire Permanent: Gestion Fiscale **1920**
• Dictionnaire Permanent: Gestion Fiscale (FRA ISSN 1638-2242) **1920**
• Dictionnaire Permanent: Gestion Immobiliere (FRA ISSN 0758-7309) **1738**
• Dictionnaire Permanent: Recouvrement des Creances et Procedures d'Execution (FRA ISSN 1631-0675) **1287**
• Dictionnaire Permanent: Securite et Conditions de Travail (FRA ISSN 0767-2187) **1675**
• Dictionnaire Permanent: Social (FRA ISSN 0012-2513) **1675**
• Dictionnaire Permanent: Social Agricole (FRA ISSN 1290-6115) **105**
Dictionnaire Permanent Transactions Immobilieres (FRA ISSN 1775-9234) **7588**
• Dictionnaire Societas Criticus (CAN ISSN 1910-0884) **7130**
• Dictionnaire Vidal (FRA ISSN 0419-1153) **6833**
Dictionnaires & References. Serie Histoire du Theatre Francais (FRA ISSN 1951-5294) **8469**
Dictionnaires et References (FRA ISSN 1275-0387) **4214**
• Dictum (NOR ISSN 1504-5307) **5213**
Dictum (USA) **4658**
Didac (MEX ISSN 0185-3872) **2977**
Didacta Varia (FIN ISSN 1239-4963) **2842**
• Didactica (Lengua y Literatura) (ESP ISSN 1130-0531) **5112**
Didactica Classica Gandensia (BEL ISSN 0070-4792) **2233**
Didactica de las Ciencias Experimentales y Sociales (ESP ISSN 0214-4379) **7959**
• Didactica, Innovacion y Multimedia (ESP ISSN 1699-3748) **3057**
▼ Didactica Universitaria (COL ISSN 2011-0790) **2977**
Didactics of Translation *see* Pedagogie de la Traduction **5160**
Didactiques (FRA ISSN 1142-2580) **8420**
▼ Didaje (COL ISSN 2011-3617) **2842**
➤ Didakta (SVN ISSN 0354-0421) **3057**
Didaktief (NLD ISSN 1572-4085) **2842**
Didaktief en School *see* Didaktief **2842**
Didaktik Deutsch (DEU ISSN 1431-4355) **5112**
Didaktik in Forschung und Praxis (DEU ISSN 1616-5586) **2842**
➤ Didaktikens Forum (SWE ISSN 1652-2583) **3057**
Didaktisk Tidskift (Print) *see* Didaktisk Tidskrift (Online) **2842**
• ➤ Didaktisk Tidskrift (Online) (SWE) **2842**
➤ Didaskalia (FRA ISSN 1250-0739) **7850**
• ➤ Didaskalia (GBR ISSN 1321-4853) **2233**
Didaskalia (POL ISSN 1233-0477) **8469**
Didaskalia (PRT ISSN 0253-1674) **7794**
Didattica delle Scienze e Informatica nella Scuola (ITA ISSN 0419-1218) **3058**
Didatticamente (ITA ISSN 1827-0794) **2842**
Diddl Mag' (FRA ISSN 1777-6635) **2185**
Diddls Kaeseblatt (DEU) **2185**
Diderot Studies (CHE ISSN 0070-4806) **6914**
▼ • Didi Magazine (USA ISSN 1944-3811) **2253**
Didsbury Review (CAN ISSN 0836-7132) **3808**
Die and Mould Technology *see* Moju Jishu **6343**
Die Aquarien- und Terrarien-Zeitschrift Aquarien, Terrarien *see* D A T Z. Aquarien, Terrarien **3589**
Die Berufsgenossenschaft *see* Die B G **4494**
• Die Cast Digest (USA ISSN 1066-9221) **4333**
Die Casting Buyers Guide (USA ISSN 1056-6090) **5451**
Die Casting Engineer (USA ISSN 0012-253X) **3343**
Die Casting Management (USA ISSN 0745-449X) **6310**
Die Deutsche Schule *see* D D S **3019**
Die Naehmaschinen-Zeitung International *see* D N Z International **5451**
Die Praxis (CHE ISSN 1017-8147) **4658**
Die Schweizer Baustoff-Industrie *see* D S B **1001**
Die Tabak Zeitung Shop *see* D T Z Shop **8486**
Die Tabak Zeitung Tabakjahrbuch *see* D T Z Tabakjahrbuch **8486**
• Die Witterung in Uebersee (DEU ISSN 0043-7085) **6352**
Die Young (USA) **5420**
Die Zahnarzt Woche Orale Implantologie *see* D Z W Orale Implantologie **5839**
Die Zahnarzt Woche Spezial *see* D Z W Spezial **5839**
Die Zahnarzt Woche Zahntechnik *see* D Z W Zahntechnik **5839**
Diecast Collector (GBR ISSN 1369-5363) **4333**
Diecasting Times (GBR ISSN 1467-0240) **6310**
Diecasting World (GBR ISSN 0965-6111) **6310**
Diecinueve y Veinte Veinte *see* XIX y Veinte **4279**
• ➤ Dieciocho (USA ISSN 0163-0415) **5285**
Dieciseis de Abril *see* 16 de Abril **5739**
Diedut (NOR ISSN 0332-7779) **4214**
Diego (SWE ISSN 1653-5103) **3955**
Diehard (USA ISSN 0896-7970) **8226**
Dielheimer Blaetter zum Alten Testament und Seiner Rezeption in der Alten Kirche (DEU ISSN 1434-0631) **7638**
Dielheimer Blaetter zur Archaeologie und Textueberlieferung der Antike und Spaetantike (DEU) **390**
Diemaking Diecutting Intelligence Newsletter International *see* D D I N International **5451**

Link to your serials resources and content with ulrichsweb.com

DIRECTORY 2010 DIGITAL PRINTER 10199

Diemer Courant (NLD) **3914**
Diena (LVA) **3904**
Diena (USA) **3530**
Dienas Bizness (LVA) **1092**
• Dienst am Wort - Gedanken zur Sonntagspredigt (DEU ISSN 0720-9916) **7638**
Dienst Regelingen. Nieuwsbrief (NLD ISSN 1874-7396) **105**
Das Dienst- und Tarifrecht der Sozialversicherungstraeger (DEU) **7433**
Diensthabendes System *see* D H S **6417**
Das Dienstrecht bei der Deutschen Bundesbank (DEU ISSN 0932-0725) **1336**
Dienststellen des Freistaates Bayern (DEU) **7433**
Dier (NLD ISSN 0165-3172) **319**
➤ Dier - en - Arts (NLD ISSN 0920-2412) **8796**
Dier & Jaar (NLD ISSN 1871-2185) **940**
Dier en Milieu (NLD ISSN 1574-8405) **3414**
Dier Journaal (NLD ISSN 1570-6370) **6806**
Dier Tuin (NLD ISSN 1871-000X) **6806**
Dierenambulance Rotterdam Geluiden *see* D A R - Geluiden **319**
Diesel (ITA ISSN 1973-8781) **3376**
• Diesel & Gas Turbine Worldwide (USA ISSN 0278-5994) **3376**
Diesel Car *see* What Diesel Car **8612**
Diesel Engine *see* Chaiyouji **3375**
• Diesel Engines (USA ISSN 1930-5931) **3376**
• Diesel Forecast (USA) **3127**
Diesel Fuel News *see* Hart's Diesel Fuel News **6772**
Diesel - Lehti (FIN ISSN 0012-2629) **3376**
• Diesel Power (USA ISSN 1934-4988) **8577**
• Diesel Progress International Edition (USA ISSN 1091-3696) **3376**
• Diesel Progress North American Edition (USA ISSN 1091-370X) **3376**
Diesel World (USA ISSN 1559-8632) **8169**
DieselCar (ZAF ISSN 1810-2700) **8577**
Diesseits (DEU ISSN 0932-6162) **7130**
Diet, Adventure, Sport and Health *see* D A S H **6657**
• Diet & Beauty/Daietto & Byuuti (JPN) **6657**
Diet & Fat-Free Foods Market Assessment *see* Key Note Market Assessment. Diet Foods **1891**
Diet & Fitness Magazine (USA) **6984**
Diet & Nutrition *see* Today's Diet & Nutrition **6669**
Diet & Nutrition Sourcebook (USA) **6657**
Diet and Nutrition Sourcebook *see* Diet & Nutrition Sourcebook **6657**
Dieta (CZE ISSN 1214-8784) **6657**
Dietary Guidelines for Americans *see* Nutrition and Your Health: Dietary Guidelines for Americans **6665**
Dietary Manager Magazine (USA ISSN 1062-1121) **6657**
The Dietary Supplement (USA ISSN 1529-2460) **6833**
Dietas (ESP ISSN 1577-9068) **6657**
Dietetique en Action (CAN ISSN 0834-3160) **6657**
Diethylstilbestrol Action Voice *see* D E S Action Voice **7513**
Diethylstilbestrol Litigation Reporter *see* D E S Litigation Reporter **8948**
Dietisten *see* Naeringsvaert **6664**
Dietitian's Edge (USA) **6657**
• Dietrich's Index Philosophicus (DEU) **7698**
➤ Dietsche Warande en Belfort (BEL ISSN 0012-2645) **5213**
Diety Odchudzajace *see* Dobre Rady. Diety Odchudzajace **6657**
Dieux, Hommes et Religions *see* Gods, Humans and Religions **7645**
• Diez Minutos (ESP) **3951**
Al-Difa' al-Arabi/Arab Defense Journal (LBN) **6419**
• Difang Caizheng Yanjiu/Sub National Fiscal Research (CHN ISSN 1672-9544) **1920**
• Difangbing Tongbao/Endemic Diseases Bulletin (CHN ISSN 1000-3711) **5812**
Difesa Sociale (ITA ISSN 0012-2653) **7514**
† The Difference (GBR ISSN 1756-0586) **8950**
Differences (FRA ISSN 0247-9095) **3530**
• ➤ Differences (USA ISSN 1040-7391) **8895**
Different Kind of Parenting (USA ISSN 1533-8886) **7352**
➤ Differential and Integral Equations (USA ISSN 0893-4983) **5482**
• ➤ Differential Equations (RUS ISSN 0012-2661) **5482**
Differential Equations and Applications *see* Journal of Difference Equations and Applications **5502**
Differential Equations and Control Processes *see* Differentsial'nye Uravneniya i Protsessy Upravleniya **5483**
• ➤ Differential Equations and Dynamical Systems (IND ISSN 0971-3514) **5482**
• ➤ Differential Equations and Nonlinear Mechanics (USA ISSN 1687-4099) **5482**
• ➤ Differential Geometry and Its Applications (NLD ISSN 0926-2245) **5482**
• ➤ Differential Geometry - Dynamical Systems (ROM ISSN 1454-511X) **5482**
• ➤ Differentiation (GBR ISSN 0301-4681) **669**
➤ Differentsial'nye Uravneniya (RUS ISSN 0374-0641) **5483**
• Differentsial'nye Uravneniya i Protsessy Upravleniya/Differential Equations and Control Processes (RUS ISSN 1817-2172) **5483**
• Difficolta di Apprendimento (ITA ISSN 1123-928X) **4064**
• ➤ Difficult Airway (AUT ISSN 1609-2961) **6213**
• Diffusion (English Edition) (CHE ISSN 1021-3465) **2358**
• Diffusion (French Edition) (CHE ISSN 1021-3457) **2358**
Diffusion and Defect Data. Part A: Defect and Diffusion Forum *see* Defect and Diffusion Forum **6310**
Diffusion and Defect Data. Part B: Solid State Phenomena *see* Solid State Phenomena **6332**
• ➤ Diffusion Fundamentals (DEU ISSN 1862-4138) **7010**
• Diffusion Sport (ESP) **8169**
• Diffusion Sport Directory (ESP) **1984**
Diffusion Sport Gaceta (ESP) **8169**
• Difono (GRC ISSN 1108-5037) **6561**
Difu-Arbeitshilfe *see* D I F U - Arbeitshilfe **4408**
Difu-Berichte *see* D I F U - Berichte **4409**
Difu-Impulse *see* D I F U - Impulse **4409**
Difusion Economica (ECU ISSN 0012-2696) **1092**
• Dig (USA ISSN 1539-7130) **390**
• Dig B M X (GBR) **8257**
Digest *see* Legal Education Digest **2992**
Digest (DEU ISSN 0171-399X) **2040**
The Digest (GBR) **4822**
Digest *see* Intisari **1631**
• The Digest (USA) **2367**
Digest *see* I E E E Antennas and Propagation Society. International Symposium **3310**
Digest (USA) **3530**
The Digest (Knottingly and Ferrybridge Edition) *see* Digest Magazine **4214**
The Digest (Pontefact Edition) *see* Digest Magazine **4214**
Digest (Year) *see* Turkish Chamber of Civil Engineers. Digest (Year) **3234**
Digest de Securite *see* Safety Digest (Ottawa) **6444**
• ➤ Digest Journal of Nanomaterials and Biostructures (ROM ISSN 1842-3582) **763**
▼ Digest Magazine (GBR ISSN 1755-1269) **4214**
The Digest: National Italian American Bar Association Law Journal *see* Digest **3530**
• Digest of Activities of Congress (USA ISSN 0733-0227) **7433**
Digest of Changes in C U S I P (Committee on Uniform Security Procedures) (USA) **1336**
Digest of Chinese and Foreign Books *see* Zhongwai Shuzhai **7576**
Digest of Chinese Studies (TWN ISSN 1053-5977) **5006**
Digest of Commercial Laws of the World (USA ISSN 0419-1285) **4923**
Digest of Education Statistics *see* U.S. Department of Education. National Center for Education Statistics. Digest of Education Statistics **2936**
• The Digest of Environmental Law (USA ISSN 1073-9521) **4658**
Digest of Environmental Statistics *see* Great Britain. Department of the Environment, Transport and the Regions. Digest of Environmental Statistics **3479**
Digest of Equipment, Materials and Management *see* D E M M **3186**
Digest of Health Newspaper *see* Jiankang Wenzhai Bao **7528**
Digest of Labour Cases (IND ISSN 0012-2750) **4658**
Digest of Law School Transfer Policies (USA) **4658**
Digest of Legal Activities of International Organizations and Other Institutions (USA ISSN 0070-4857) **4923**
Digest of Mangement Science *see* Quanli Kexue Wenzhai **1788**
• ➤ Digest of Middle East Studies (USA ISSN 1060-4367) **548**
Digest of Motor Laws *see* A A A Digest of Motor Laws **8553**
• Digest of Neurology & Psychiatry (Online) (USA) **5744**
Digest of Opinions of the Attorney General (USA ISSN 0012-2777) **4658**
Digest of Papers (Spring) *see* CompCon: I E E E Computer Society International Conference **2410**
Digest of Science of Labour *see* Rodo no Kagaku **6685**
Digest of South African Architecture (ZAF ISSN 1027-3468) **440**
Digest of State Accountancy Laws and State Board Regulations (USA ISSN 0161-4290) **1287**
Digest of Statistics (NGA ISSN 0029-0017) **8366**
• Digest of the L E O S Summer Topical Meetings (Lasers and Electro-Optics Society) (USA ISSN 1099-4742) **3300**
Digest of the Russian Nonproliferation Journal Yaderny Kontrol (RUS) **6419**
Digest of the U F V A (USA) **6496**
Digest of the World Core Medical Journals (Cardiology) *see* Shijie Hexin Yixue Qikan Wenzhai (Xinzangbeingxue Fence) **5799**
Digest of the World Core Medical Journals (Clinical Neurology) *see* Shijie Hexin Yixue Qikan Wenzhai (Shenjingbingxue Fence) **6185**
Digest of the World Core Medical Journals (Dermatology) *see* Shijie Hexin Yixue Qikan Wenzhai (Pifubingxue Fence) **5882**
Digest of the World Core Medical Journals (Gastroenterology) *see* Shijie Hexin Yixue Qikan Wenzhai (Weichangbingxue Fence) **5931**
Digest of the World Core Medical Journals (Obstetrics/Gynecology) *see* Shijie Hexin Yixue Qikan Wenzhai (Fuchang Kexue Fence) **6004**
Digest of the World Core Medical Journals (Ophthalmology) *see* Shijie Hexin Yixue Qikan Wenzhai (Yankexue Fence) **6051**
Digest of the World Core Medical Journals (Pediatrics) *see* Shijie Hexin Yixue Qikan Wenzhai (Erkexue Fence) **5713**
Digest of United Kingdom Energy Statistics (GBR ISSN 0307-0603) **3151**
Digest of Welsh Historical Statistics 1974-1996 (GBR) **8366**
Digest of Welsh Local Area Statistics (GBR ISSN 1362-3583) **8366**
Digest of Welsh Statistics (GBR ISSN 0262-8295) **8366**
Digest of World Events (PAK ISSN 0070-4873) **4137**
Digest on Gay Rights (CAN ISSN 0229-0812) **4658**
Digest Quarterly News (NZL ISSN 1177-3863) **228**
• Digester / Over the Spillway (USA) **3414**
• ➤ Digestion (CHE ISSN 0012-2823) **5922**
Digestion & Absorption *see* Shoka to Kyushu **5931**
Digestion & Diet Health Monitor (USA ISSN 1542-8214) **6657**
Digestion and Diet Health Monitor *see* Digestion & Diet Health Monitor **6657**
• ➤ Digestive and Liver Disease (GBR ISSN 1590-8658) **5922**
Digestive and Liver Disease. Supplement *see* Digestive and Liver Disease **5922**
• ➤ Digestive Diseases (CHE ISSN 0257-2753) **5922**
• ➤ Digestive Diseases and Sciences (USA ISSN 0163-2116) **5922**
Digestive Disorders (USA ISSN 1542-1902) **5922**
• ➤ Digestive Endoscopy (AUS ISSN 0915-5635) **5922**
• Digestive Health & Nutrition (USA ISSN 1524-7759) **5922**
Digestive Medicine *see* Shokakika **5931**
• ➤ Digestive Surgery (CHE ISSN 0253-4886) **6241**
Digesto *see* Vitalia **5932**
Digesto Economico (BRA ISSN 0101-4218) **1477**
Digetale Medier *see* Digetale Medier Professionel **7579**
• Digetale Medier Professionel (DNK ISSN 1902-6757) **7579**
Digger (USA) **3728**
• Diggin' for Davises (USA ISSN 1096-4339) **3764**
Digging Stick (ZAF ISSN 1013-7521) **390**
Diggings *see* Diggings Journal **390**
Diggings *see* Archaeological Diggings **376**
Diggings Journal (AUS ISSN 1320-4424) **390**
Diggin's (USA) **4291**
Digi Revue (SVK ISSN 1336-5754) **6966**
▼ • DIGIfoto (CZE) **6966**
• digifoto (DEU ISSN 1617-643X) **6979**
Digifoto *see* Focus (Haarlem) **6967**
Digifoto/Foto+ *see* Focus (Haarlem) **6967**
• Digihouse Newsletter (AUS ISSN 1442-7613) **2554**
† Digimon (DEU) **8950**
Digimon (SWE ISSN 1650-5670) **2185**
Digimon Collector *see* Beckett Digimon Collector **4329**
† Digimon Magazine (ITA ISSN 1591-4941) **8950**
Digit! (DEU) **6979**
• Digit (GBR ISSN 1461-3816) **2416**
• Digit (POL ISSN 1509-6882) **2485**
Digitaal Beeld *see* F+D Fotografie **6967**
Digitaal Bestuur (NLD ISSN 1871-4285) **2416**
† Digitaal Filmen en Fotograferen (NLD ISSN 1871-9260) **8950**
Digitaalgids (NLD ISSN 1874-5040) **2416**
Digital Africa (ZAF ISSN 1818-930X) **2416**
Digital & Micrographic Imaging *see* Shuzi Yu Suowei Yingxiang **6980**
Digital Asset Management *see* Journal of Digital Asset Management **1765**
• Digital Avionics Systems Conference. Proceedings (USA) **53**
Digital Base Line *see* Base Line **4000**
Digital Battlespace (GBR ISSN 1748-6297) **6419**
Digital Broadcaster (GBR ISSN 1460-1354) **2380**
Digital Business Magazin (DEU ISSN 1861-5597) **2589**
Digital Buying Guide (USA ISSN 1547-5662) **2576**
Digital Camera (GBR ISSN 1477-1721) **6979**
Digital Camera (USA ISSN 1523-844X) **6966**
Digital Camera Buyer (GBR ISSN 1475-0538) **6966**
• Digital Camera Magazin (DEU) **6979**
Digital Camera Magazine (ITA ISSN 1721-6893) **6979**
Digital Camera. Photo & Video (RUS ISSN 1684-0135) **3093**
† Digital Camera Shopping (ITA ISSN 1824-8152) **8950**
Digital Camera Special (DEU) **6979**
Digital Chicago (USA) **2571**
• Digital Cinematography (USA ISSN 1555-6719) **6496**
Digital Classroom Resources *see* Loci **5509**
• Digital Coast Daily (USA) **2554**
Digital Coast Reporter (USA ISSN 1531-1015) **2554**
Digital Communication *see* Shuzi Tongxin **3113**
Digital Communication (USA) **2319**
• Digital Comprehensive Summaries of Uppsala Dissertations from the Faculty of Social Sciences (SWE ISSN 1652-9030) **7959**
• Digital Content Producer (USA ISSN 1931-499X) **2401**
• ➤ Digital Creativity (GBR ISSN 1462-6268) **2485**
Digital Curation Centre Digital Curation Manual *see* D C C Digital Curation Manual **2542**
• Digital Dealer (USA) **8577**
Digital Demand (GBR ISSN 1471-5694) **7319**
Digital Directions *see* Education Week's Digital Directions **2948**
• Digital Discovery & e-Evidence (USA ISSN 1537-5099) **4844**
Digital Discovery and e-Evidence *see* Digital Discovery & e-Evidence **4844**
Digital Display for Retail (GBR) **3093**
Digital Display Printing *see* Screen Process & Digital Imaging **7327**
Digital Display Processing & Field Programmable Gate Array Product Resource Guide *see* D S P & F P G A Product Resource Guide **2416**
• Digital Document Quarterly (USA ISSN 1547-8610) **2571**
The Digital Economy (NLD ISSN 1871-9759) **2416**
Digital Engineering Magazin (DEU ISSN 1618-002X) **3290**
Digital Equipment Computer Users Society, Communications Organization Magazine *see* D E C U S Magazine **2416**
Digital Equipment Corporation Computing *see* D E C Computing **2573**
Digital Equipment Corporation Today *see* D E C Today **2573**
• ➤ Digital Evidence and Electronic Signature Law Review (GBR ISSN 1756-4611) **2554**
Digital Evidence Journal *see* Digital Evidence and Electronic Signature Law Review **2554**
Digital Fashion *see* Shuma Shishang **3113**
Digital Fernsehen (DEU ISSN 1610-997X) **2380**
• ➤ Digital Forensics, Security and Law. Journal (USA ISSN 1558-7215) **2651**
Digital Formations (USA ISSN 1526-3169) **2319**
• Digital Fortune China (CHN) **1416**
Digital Future Report *see* Surveying the Digital Future **2567**
• Digital Graphics Magazine (USA ISSN 1097-5926) **530**
Digital Home (DEU) **2380**
Digital Home (GBR) **2416**
▼ • Digital Humanities Quarterly (USA ISSN 1938-4122) **4485**
Digital Imaging (DEU) **1850**
Digital Imaging & Publishing (ZAF ISSN 1024-8552) **2571**
• Digital Imaging Digest (USA) **6966**
• Digital Imaging Techniques (USA ISSN 1557-2811) **2485**
Digital Information Network (USA) **1850**
Digital Insider (DEU) **2380**
Digital Insurance News *see* Cyber Insurance News **4500**
• ➤ Digital Investigation (GBR ISSN 1742-2876) **5913**
• ➤ Digital Journal of Ophthalmology (USA ISSN 1542-8958) **6041**
• ➤ Digital Kompetanse/Nordic Journal for Digital Literacy (NOR ISSN 0809-6724) **3058**
Digital Learning (IND ISSN 0973-4139) **2842**
Digital Libraries *see* Dijitaru Toshokan **5061**
• Digital Library Communication (IND ISSN 0973-6638) **5061**
Digital - Library Lib Magazine *see* D - Lib Magazine **5061**
Digital Lifestyle Magazin (DEU) **2380**
Digital Living (DEU ISSN 1863-3676) **2380**
Digital Machinist (USA ISSN 1933-3773) **5451**
▼ Digital Magazines (USA ISSN 2150-2196) **7559**
• Digital Marketing (Toronto, 2000) (CAN ISSN 1495-5636) **1813**
▼ • Digital Marketing Buzz (USA ISSN 1949-2804) **1813**
Digital Media (GBR ISSN 1355-6606) **1620**
• Digital Media: A Seybold Report (USA ISSN 1056-7038) **2571**
Digital Media World (AUS ISSN 1447-543X) **4574**
• ➤ Digital Medievalist (CAN ISSN 1715-0736) **4137**
Digital Military Industry *see* Shuzi Jungong **70**
• Digital Mirror (DEU) **2554**
• Digital Movie (NLD ISSN 1574-1281) **2401**
Digital Music (ITA ISSN 1824-4173) **6633**
Digital Music Maker (GBR ISSN 1473-1819) **6633**
• Digital Music Weekly (USA) **2554**
▼ • Digital Obscura (GBR ISSN 1756-3046) **5420**
Digital Oman/Digital 'uman (OMN ISSN 1815-753X) **8420**
• Digital Output (USA ISSN 1083-5121) **6966**
Digital Photo (DEU) **6979**
Digital Photo (GBR ISSN 1474-6883) **6979**
• Digital Photo (USA ISSN 1948-5557) **6979**
Digital Photo Magazine (FRA) **6979**
Digital Photo Pro (GBR ISSN 1752-2242) **6966**
Digital Photo Pro (USA ISSN 1545-8520) **6966**
Digital Photographer (GBR ISSN 1477-6650) **6980**
Digital Photographer (USA ISSN 1532-6012) **6980**
Digital Photographer's Guide to Digital Cameras *see* Digital Photographer **6980**
Digital Photography *see* Yingxiang Shijue **6978**
Digital Photography + Design (AUS ISSN 1327-9432) **6966**
• Digital Photography and Imaging (AUS) **6966**
Digital Photography Buyer & User *see* Digital Photography User **8950**
Digital Photography Made Easy (GBR ISSN 1471-1184) **6980**
Digital Photography Techniques (GBR) **6980**
† Digital Photography User (GBR ISSN 1742-7398) **8950**
• Digital Power Report (USA) **2416**
Digital Prepress (USA) **7329**
Digital Printer (GBR ISSN 1749-9186) **7329**

Title

▼ *new title* † *ceased* • *electronic media* ➤ *refereed*

Title

10202 DIRECTORY OF BUILDING AND EQUIPMENT GRANTS ULRICH'S PERIODICALS

Directory of Building and Equipment Grants (USA ISSN 1062-6492) **8037**
Directory of Building Codes & Regulations (USA) **4409**
Directory of Building Products & Hardlines Distributors (USA ISSN 1085-259X) **1985**
The Directory of Business Information Resources (USA ISSN 1549-7224) **1985**
Directory of Business to Business Catalogs *see* The Directory of Mail Order Catalogs with Business to Business Catalogs **1987**
Directory of C A A Approved Organisations (Civil Aviation Authority) (GBR) **8540**
Directory of California Justice Agencies (USA ISSN 1081-6933) **2651**
• Directory of California Manufacturers (USA) **1985**
Directory of California Wholesalers and Service Companies (USA ISSN 1093-6270) **1985**
Directory of Canadian Chartered Accountants (CAN ISSN 0527-9275) **1287**
Directory of Canadian Map Collections (CAN ISSN 0070-5217) **4004**
Directory of Canadian Municipalities *see* Scott's Directory of Canadian Municipalities **7502**
Directory of Canadian Search and Rescue Organizations (CAN ISSN 1207-3644) **8037**
The Directory of Canadian Universities (Year)/Repertoire des Universites Canadiennes (Year) (CAN ISSN 0706-2338) **2955**
Directory of Cartoonists - Gagwriters - Short Humor Markets (USA) **486**
Directory of Catholic Diocese of Spokane (USA) **7795**
Directory of Certified Companies *see* Directory of Certified Companies in Singapore **1884**
Directory of Certified Companies & Green Labelled Companies *see* Directory of Certified Companies in Singapore **1884**
• Directory of Certified Companies in Singapore (SGP) **1884**
Directory of Certified Dehumidifiers (USA) **4118**
Directory of Certified Products and Process in Malawi (MWI) **6401**
Directory of Certified Refrigerators and Freezers (USA) **4118**
Directory of Certified Room Air Conditioners (USA) **4118**
• Directory of Chain Restaurant Operators (Year) (USA ISSN 0411-7085) **1985**
• Directory of Chemical Producers - Canada (USA ISSN 1045-5256) **2060**
• Directory of Chemical Producers - China (USA ISSN 1535-2978) **2060**
• Directory of Chemical Producers - East Asia (USA ISSN 1049-6068) **2060**
• Directory of Chemical Producers - Europe (USA ISSN 1520-0558) **2060**
• Directory of Chemical Producers - India (USA ISSN 1535-296X) **2060**
• Directory of Chemical Producers - Mexico (USA ISSN 1535-2986) **2060**
• Directory of Chemical Producers - Middle East (USA ISSN 1535-2951) **2060**
• Directory of Chemical Producers - South America (USA ISSN 1082-1163) **2060**
• Directory of Chemical Producers - United States (USA ISSN 0012-3277) **2060**
Directory of Chemical Products & Buyers Guide (GBR ISSN 0961-270X) **2060**
• Directory of Chemical Products and Producers in China (Year) (CHN) **3242**
Directory of China's Foreign Trade (CHN) **1561**
Directory of Chinese Enterprises for Foreign Economic Relations and Trades (CHN) **1986**
Directory of Chinese External Economic Organizations & Industrial - Commercial Enterprises (HKG ISSN 0259-1146) **1986**
Directory of Chinese Government Organs (HKG ISSN 1021-691X) **7434**
Directory of City Policy Officials (USA ISSN 1046-2686) **7491**
Directory of Coconut Traders and Equipment Manufacturers (IDN) **1986**
† Directory of College & University Administrators (USA ISSN 1546-7759) **8950**
Directory of College and University Administrators *see* Directory of College & University Administrators **8950**
Directory of College and University Libraries in New York State (USA ISSN 0070-5276) **5006**
Directory of College Stores (USA ISSN 0084-988X) **1814**
• Directory of Colleges and Universities with Accredited Social Work Degree Programs (USA ISSN 1049-5657) **2955**
Directory of Colorado Manufacturers (USA ISSN 0084-9898) **1986**
Directory of Commerce & Industry (SYR) **1986**
Directory of Commercial Computer Software for Civil Engineering (CAN ISSN 1483-5223) **3290**
Directory of Community Blood Centers *see* Directory of Community Blood Centers and Hospital Blood Banks **4092**
Directory of Community Blood Centers and Hospital Blood Banks (USA ISSN 1930-692X) **4092**
Directory of Community Health Services (Years) (GBR ISSN 1755-490X) **5957**
• Directory of Community Legislation in Force (LUX ISSN 0257-5256) **4658**
Directory of Community Nursing (Years) *see* Directory of Community Health Services (Years) **5957**
Directory of Community Resources and Services (USA) **8037**
Directory of Community Services of Greater Montreal/Repertoire des Services Communautaires du Grand Montreal (CAN ISSN 0319-258X) **8037**
Directory of Companies Offering Dividend Reinvestment Plans (USA ISSN 1045-0041) **1986**
Directory of Company Secretaries (IND ISSN 0070-5322) **1739**
Directory of Composite Manufacturers, Suppliers, and Services (Year) (USA) **3343**
• Directory of Computer and Consumer Electronics Retailers (USA ISSN 1067-1072) **2494**
• Directory of Computer V A R's & System Integrators (Year) (Value Added Resellers) (USA) **1986**
Directory of Consultants and Translators for Engineered Materials (USA ISSN 1053-6833) **1986**
Directory of Consulting Engineering Services in North Carolina (USA) **3187**
Directory of Contacts (ZAF) **2319**
• Directory of Corporate Affiliations (USA ISSN 0736-9778) **1986**
Directory of Corporate Archives in the United States and Canada (USA) **5006**
Directory of Corporate Counsel *see* Law & Business Directory of Corporate Counsel **4874**
Directory of Countertrade & Offset Services (USA) **1561**
Directory of Courses and Materials for Training in Distance Education (CAN ISSN 1208-171X) **2842**
Directory of Crematoria (GBR ISSN 0143-3164) **3719**
Directory of Custom Coasters (Year) (USA) **3343**
Directory of Day Schools in the United States and Canada *see* Day School Directory **7720**
Directory of Defence Suppliers *see* Australian & New Zealand Defence Business Directory of Suppliers **1973**
† Directory of Demographic Research Centers/Annuaire des Centres de Recherche Demographique (FRA ISSN 0152-9757) **8950**
• Directory of Department Stores (USA ISSN 1097-7023) **1986**
Directory of Departments and Programs of Religious Studies in North America (USA) **7638**
Directory of Designations of National Historic Significance (CAN) **4137**
† Directory of Designers (GBR ISSN 0959-1710) **8950**
Directory of Development and Training Institutes in Africa (SEN) **2842**
Directory of Diplomatic Corps and International Organizations *see* Kenya. Ministry of Foreign Affairs. Directory of Diplomatic Corps & International Organizations **7249**
• Directory of Directors (GBR ISSN 0070-5438) **1739**
Directory of Directors (IND ISSN 0070-542X) **642**
Directory of Disability Organizations in Canada (CAN ISSN 1207-7267) **4064**
Directory of Discount and General Merchandise Stores (Year) *see* Directory of Discount Stores & Specialty Retailers **1986**
• Directory of Discount Stores & Specialty Retailers (USA ISSN 1937-4240) **1986**
Directory of Distance Education Institutions Part II (Pakistan & Sri Lanka) (IND) **2955**
Directory of Dividend Reinvestment Plans *see* Standard & Poor's Directory of Dividend Reinvestment Plans **8990**
• Directory of Drug Store and H B C Chains (Year) (Health and Beauty Care) (USA ISSN 1084-8878) **1986**
• Directory of E U Information Sources (European Union) (BEL ISSN 1025-6733) **5006**
Directory of Economic Research Centres in India (IND) **1986**
Directory of Editors (CAN ISSN 1702-3114) **7559**
Directory of Editors (USA) **7559**
Directory of Educational Organisations and Contacts in Australia and New Zealand *see* Australasian Education Directory **2828**
Directory of Educational Programs in Gerontology and Geriatrics (USA) **4043**
• The Directory of Egyptian Research Periodicals (D E R P) (EGY ISSN 1110-158X) **624**
Directory of Electric Utilities in Latin America, Bermuda and the Caribbean Islands *see* Electrical World Directory of Electric Utilities in Latin America, Bermuda and the Caribbean Islands **3157**
Directory of Electric Utility Industry (USA ISSN 1084-4961) **3156**
Directory of Employers Associations, Trade Unions, and Other Employees' Associations (GBR ISSN 1360-6255) **1675**
Directory of Engineering and Engineering Technology Undergraduate Programs (USA ISSN 1057-5286) **3187**
Directory of Engineering Capacity (GBR) **1986**
• Directory of Engineering Graduate Studies and Research (USA ISSN 1067-9022) **3187**
The Directory of English Regional Government (GBR ISSN 1471-3586) **7434**
Directory of English - Speaking Churches Abroad (GBR ISSN 1466-6855) **7638**
Directory of Environmental Organizations (USA ISSN 0270-1111) **2608**
Directory of Environmental Websites on the Internet (USA ISSN 1096-3316) **3414**
Directory of European Dyers, Printers and Finishers (GBR ISSN 0965-6030) **1986**
Directory of European Industrial & Trade Associations (GBR ISSN 0952-3626) **1986**
† Directory of European Jazz Festivals and Related Major Jazz Events (DNK ISSN 1397-1999) **8950**
Directory of European Medical Organisations (GBR ISSN 1352-321X) **5744**
Directory of European Professional & Learned Societies (GBR ISSN 0957-0748) **7851**
Directory of European Sports Organisations (GBR ISSN 1352-3201) **8218**
• The Directory of Executive and Professional Recruiters (USA) **1986**
Directory of Executive Recruiters *see* The Directory of Executive and Professional Recruiters **1986**
Directory of Executive Recruiters (Personal Ed.) *see* The Directory of Executive and Professional Recruiters **1986**
Directory of Expert Witnesses & Consultants (National Medical Edition) *see* A L M Experts. National Medical Directory **5564**
Directory of Experts & Legal Services *see* Martindale-Hubbell Directory of Experts & Legal Services **4728**
Directory of Exporters *see* Dalil al-Musaddirin **1561**
Directory of Exporters (LKA) **1401**
Directory of Exporters (Year) (PAK) **1561**
Directory of Extramural Research and Development Projects Approved for Funding by Central Government (IND) **8420**
Directory of Faculty Contracts and Bargaining Agents in Institutions of Higher Education (USA ISSN 0276-7805) **4593**
Directory of Fairs, Festivals and Expositions *see* Directory of North American Fairs, Festivals and Expositions **8950**
Directory of Family Associations (USA) **3764**
Directory of Federal Health Care Facilities (USA) **4092**
• Directory of Fetal Alcohol Spectrum Disorder (F A S D) Information and Support Services in Canada/Repertoire Canadien des Services d'Information et de Soutien sur l'Ensemble des Troubles Causes par l'Alcoolisme Foetale (E T C A F) (CAN ISSN 1715-4200) **8037**
Directory of Financial Aids for Women (USA ISSN 0732-5215) **3020**
Directory of Firms (GBR ISSN 0968-0152) **1986**
Directory of Flower & Herb Buyers (USA ISSN 1931-6305) **3755**
• Directory of Foodservice Distributors (Year) (USA ISSN 0271-7662) **1986**
• Directory of Foreign Firms Operating in the United States (USA ISSN 0070-5543) **1986**
Directory of Freight Accounting Offices and Overcharge Claims (USA) **8616**
Directory of French Speaking Health Care Providers in Newfoundland and Labrador *see* Repertoire des Fournisseurs de Services de Sante en Francais de Terre-Neuve-et-Labrador **4110**
Directory of Fulbright Alumni (IND ISSN 0084-9936) **2978**
Directory of Funding Sources (Computer File) (AUS) **2978**
† Directory of Funparks & Attractions (USA ISSN 1094-3005) **8950**
Directory of Further Education (GBR) **2978**
Directory of Gay and Lesbian Library Workers *see* Directory of Gay, Lesbian, Bisexual and Transgendered Library Workers **4372**
• Directory of Gay, Lesbian, Bisexual and Transgendered Library Workers (USA) **4372**
Directory of Georgia Municipal Officers and Associate Members (USA) **7491**
Directory of Geoscience Departments (USA) **2955**
Directory of Geoservices in Ireland (IRL) **2731**
Directory of Ghostly Websites (USA) **6741**
Directory of Government Document Collections and Librarians (USA ISSN 0276-959X) **5006**
Directory of Government Prime Contractors *see* Government Prime Contractors Directory **1997**
Directory of Graduate Law Programs in the United States (USA) **4658**
Directory of Graduate Studies *see* Postgrad Series - The Directory **2998**
• Directory of Grants in the Humanities (USA ISSN 0887-0551) **2978**
Directory of health and medical resources *see* Detwiler's Directory of Health and Medical Resources (Year) **5744**
The Directory of Health Bodies (GBR ISSN 1479-1544) **4092**
• Directory of Health Care Group Purchasing Organizations (USA ISSN 1064-8496) **1986**
Directory of Healthcare Group Purchasing Organizations *see* Directory of Health Care Group Purchasing Organizations **1986**
Directory of Healthcare Management Education (USA ISSN 1930-8361) **2955**
• Directory of High Volume Independent Restaurants (Year) (USA ISSN 0888-0166) **1986**
Directory of Higher Education *see* Illinois. Board of Higher Education. Directory of Higher Education **2986**
Directory of Higher Education Institutions in the European Community (GBR) **2978**
Directory of Historical Organizations in the United States and Canada (USA ISSN 1045-456X) **4291**
Directory of History Departments and Organizations (Year) (USA ISSN 1077-8500) **2955**
A Directory of History of Medicine Collections (USA ISSN 1559-5323) **4137**
• Directory of Home Center Operators & Hardware Chains (Year) (USA ISSN 0272-0167) **1987**
Directory of Home Furnishings Retailers (Year) (USA ISSN 0888-0158) **1987**
Directory of Hong Kong Industrial Suppliers (Year) (HKG) **1987**
Directory of Hong Kong Industries (HKG) **1987**
Directory of Hospice and Palliative Care Services *see* Hospice and Palliative Care Directory **4099**
• Directory of Hospital Personnel (USA ISSN 0885-9671) **1987**
Directory of Hotel and Motel Companies (USA) **4385**
Directory of Humor Magazines & Humor Organizations in America (and Canada) (USA) **624**
Directory of Idaho Government Officials (USA) **7434**
Directory of Illustration *see* Graphic Artists Guild. Directory of Illustration **491**
Directory of Independent Investment Research (USA ISSN 1547-1071) **1621**
Directory of Indian Engineering Exporters (IND ISSN 0417-5964) **1987**
Directory of Indian Exporters (IND) **1561**
Directory of Industrial Establishments in Punjab (PAK) **1987**
Directory of Industrial Mineral Based Industries (MYS ISSN 1511-645X) **6461**
• Directory of Industrial Products: Sharjah, United Arab Emirates/Daleel Al Montajat Al Sina'iah: Al Shariqah (UAE) **1987**
Directory of Industries *see* Kenya. Central Bureau of Statistics. Directory of Industries **2010**
Directory of Institutional Investment Funds (USA ISSN 1050-3218) **1987**
Directory of Institutions *see* Freedom of Information and Privacy Branch. Directory of Institutions, Ontario **7438**
Directory of Insurance Companies Licensed in New York State (USA ISSN 0070-5691) **4501**
† Directory of Intellectual Property Attorneys (USA ISSN 1064-0355) **8950**
Directory of Interior Designers & Furniture Makers (IND) **4538**
Directory of International Coconut Research Workers (IDN) **1987**
• Directory of International Film and Video Festivals (Year) (GBR ISSN 0268-5256) **6496**
† Directory of Internships Available in Victorian Hospitals (Victorian Medical Postgraduate Foundation) (AUS ISSN 1448-1332) **8950**
Directory of Investment Research *see* Nelson Information's Directory of Investment Research **2019**
Directory of Iranian Periodicals and Newspapers/Rahnamay-i Majallah-ha va Ruznameha-yi Iran (IRN ISSN 1028-7035) **624**
Directory of Iron and Steel Plants (USA) **1987**
Directory of Japanese Addresses in Europe (DEU) **1987**
Directory of Japanese Affiliated Companies in Asia (Year) (JPN) **1987**
Directory of Japanese Affiliated Companies in the E U (Year) (JPN) **1987**
Directory of Japanese Affiliated Companies in the U S A and Canada (JPN) **1987**
Directory of Japanese Publishing Industry (JPN) **7559**
Directory of Japanese Scientific Periodicals (Online) *see* Nihon Kagaku Gijutsu Kankei Chikuji Kankobutsu Soran (Online) **7578**
Directory of Jewish Life *see* Jewish Journal **7723**
• Directory of Justice Issues in the States (USA) **2651**
Directory of Kansas Businesses (USA) **1987**
Directory of Kentucky Labor Organizations (USA) **4593**
Directory of Key Bulgarian Government and Party Officials (BGR) **7130**
Directory of L Ps *see* Directory of Limited Partners **1621**
Directory of Labour Organizations in Canada/Repertoire des Organisations de Travailleurs et Travailleuses au Canada (CAN ISSN 0711-1703) **4593**
Directory of Law - Related CD-ROMs (USA ISSN 1065-0334) **4845**
• Directory of Law Reviews (Online) (USA) **4658**
† • Directory of Law Reviews (Print) (USA ISSN 1932-1910) **8950**
Directory of Law Teachers/Annuaire des Professeurs de Droit (CAN ISSN 0383-8358) **4658**
Directory of Leading Chain Stores (Year) *see* Directory of Leading Chain Tenants **1987**
• Directory of Leading Chain Tenants (USA ISSN 1551-2495) **1987**
Directory of Legal Aid and Defender Offices in the United States and Territories (USA) **4968**
Directory of Legislative Leaders (Year) (USA ISSN 1051-4988) **7434**
• Directory of Libraries and Library Systems in the South Central Regional Library Council Region (USA) **5006**

Link to your serials resources and content with ulrichsweb.com

DIRECTORY 2010 DIRECTORY OF WIRE COMPANIES OF NORTH AMERICA 10203

• Directory of Libraries in Canada (CAN ISSN 1191-1603) **5006**
Directory of Library Automation Software, Systems, and Services (USA ISSN 1071-264X) **5061**
Directory of Library Systems in New York State (USA) **5006**
Directory of Licensed Products (USA) **1002**
Directory of Limited Partners (USA) **1621**
Directory of Listed Plumbing Products (USA) **4118**
Directory of Listed Plumbing Products for Manufactured Housing and Recreational Vehicles (USA) **4118**
Directory of Literary Magazines *see* The Literary Press and Magazine Directory **5407**
The Directory of London Government (GBR ISSN 1468-4179) **7434**
Directory of Long Island Libraries and Media Centers (USA) **5006**
Directory of Long Island Libraries and Media Centers, Including MarketPlace *see* Directory of Long Island Libraries and Media Centers **5006**
Directory of Louisiana Manufacturers *see* Harris Directory. Louisiana Manufacturing **2000**
Directory of M and A intermediaries *see* Directory of M & A Intermediaries **1987**
Directory of M & A Intermediaries (Mergers & Acquisitions) (USA ISSN 1066-9744) **1987**
Directory of Mail Order Catalogs *see* The Directory of Mail Order Catalogs with Business to Business Catalogs **1987**
• The Directory of Mail Order Catalogs with Business to Business Catalogs (USA) **1987**
Directory of Mailing List Companies (USA) **24**
• Directory of Major Mailers & What They Mail (Year) (USA ISSN 1045-6201) **1987**
Directory of Major Mailers avd What They Mail (Year) *see* Directory of Major Mailers & What They Mail (Year) **1987**
• Directory of Major Malls (USA ISSN 0732-5983) **7588**
The Directory of Management Consultants (USA ISSN 0743-6890) **1739**
Directory of Management Consultants in the U K (GBR ISSN 0268-375X) **1739**
Directory of Manufacturers & Dealers of Building Industry (IND) **1987**
Directory of Manufacturers and Distributors (USA) **3728**
Directory of Marine Diesel Engines (GBR ISSN 1369-7587) **8642**
Directory of Marine Technology (GBR ISSN 0144-9702) **2803**
Directory of Market Comparability Programs & Membership (USA) **7559**
Directory of MasterCard & VISA Credit Card Sources (USA ISSN 1061-3358) **1336**
Directory of Medical and Health Care Libraries in the United Kingdom and Republic of Ireland (GBR) **5006**
Directory of Member Benefits *see* The American Gardener **3722**
Directory of Membrane & High Tech Separations (Year) (USA) **8420**
Directory of Mental Health Services (GBR) **4092**
Directory of Metropolitan Planning Organizations (USA) **7434**
Directory of Mexican Corporations (MEX) **1987**
Directory of Michigan Libraries (USA) **5006**
Directory of Michigan Municipal Officials (USA ISSN 0148-7442) **7491**
Directory of Mines and Quarries (GBR ISSN 0957-266X) **6461**
Directory of Ministries in Higher Education (USA) **2978**
Directory of Minnesota City Officials (USA ISSN 0890-1651) **7491**
(Year) Directory of Minority Doctoral Recipients and Candidates in New York State (USA) **2978**
Directory of Minority Ph.D. and M.F.A. Candidates and Recipients (USA) **2978**
Directory of Montana Schools (USA) **3020**
Directory of Municipal and County Officials in Colorado (Year) (USA) **7491**
Directory of Museums and Special Collections in the United Kingdom (GBR) **6523**
• Directory of Music Faculties in Colleges & Universities U S and Canada (USA ISSN 0098-664X) **6561**
• Directory of National Statistical Offices and Societies (Year) (NLD) **8366**
Directory of Nebraska Manufacturers (USA ISSN 0070-5926) **1987**
Directory of New Jersey Labor, Employment, and Immigration Law Practices *see* New Jersey Law Journal **4743**
Directory of New Mexico Municipal Officials (USA) **7434**
Directory of Nominees (GBR ISSN 0967-9626) **1621**
• Directory of Nonpublic Schools and Administrators, New York State (USA) **3020**
† Directory of North American Fairs, Festivals and Expositions (USA ISSN 1521-1304) **8950**
Directory of North Carolina Municipal Officials (USA) **7491**
• Directory of North Dakota Manufacturers and Food Processors (USA) **1987**
The Directory of Northern Ireland Government (GBR ISSN 1465-4768) **7434**
Directory of Nurse-Midwifery Practices (Year) (USA ISSN 1062-8835) **5957**
• Directory of Nursing Homes (Online Edition) (USA) **8037**
• Directory of Obsolete Securities (USA ISSN 0085-0551) **1621**
Directory of Official New Jersey (USA) **7434**
Directory of Official Statistical Agencies (Year) (Online Edition) *see* Directory of National Statistical Offices and Societies (Year) **8366**
Directory of Official Statistical Agencies (Year) (Print Edition) *see* Directory of National Statistical Offices and Societies (Year) **8366**
† • Directory of Online Services (USA ISSN 1081-2024) **8950**
Directory of Ontario Lumber & Building Materials Retailers. Buyer's Guide & Product Directory (CAN ISSN 0827-1194) **1988**
Directory of Operating Grants (USA ISSN 1071-6726) **8037**
Directory of Operating Theatres and Departments of Surgery (Year) (GBR) **4092**
Directory of Organizations Concerned with Scientific Research and Technical Services in Zimbabwe (ZWE) **7851**
• Directory of Organizations in Educational Management (USA ISSN 1044-0453) **3020**
• Directory of Osteopathic Postdoctoral Education (USA) **5805**
Directory of Outplacement Firms and Career Management Firms *see* Directory of Outplacement Firms & Career Management Firms **1675**
Directory of Outplacement Firms & Career Management Firms (USA) **1675**
Directory of Overseas Summer Jobs (GBR ISSN 0070-6051) **1988**
Directory of Pakistani Scholars Abroad (PAK ISSN 0070-606X) **3012**
• Directory of Participating Dialysis Centres, Transplant Centres and Organ Procurement Organizations in Canada/Repertoire des Centres de Dialyse Participants au Canada (CAN ISSN 1486-1410) **6267**
Directory of Pathology Training Programs (Year) (USA ISSN 0070-6086) **2978**
• Directory of Periodicals ONLINE: Humanities and Religion (USA ISSN 1554-2165) **4484**
• Directory of Periodicals ONLINE: Medical and Pharmaceutical (USA ISSN 1554-2173) **5744**
• Directory of Periodicals ONLINE: Science and Technology (USA ISSN 1554-2157) **7936**
Directory of Periodicals Published in India (IND ISSN 0970-9266) **7560**
Directory of Personnel Responsible for Radiological Health Programs (USA ISSN 0149-8304) **3495**
Directory of Philippine Garment & Textile Exporters (PHL) **2246**
Directory of Physics & Astronomy Staff (Year) (USA ISSN 0361-2228) **7010**
Directory of Poetry Publishers (USA) **5421**
Directory of Polish Officials (USA ISSN 0090-9955) **642**
Directory of Premium, Incentive & Travel Buyers (USA ISSN 0196-8262) **1621**
• Directory of Primes (USA ISSN 0887-4042) **1988**
Directory of Privately-Owned: Community Hospitals, Hospital Management Companies and Health Systems, Residential Treatment Facilities and Centers, and Key Management Personnel (USA) **4092**
Directory of Products and Services for the Vacuum Industry (USA) **1988**
• Directory of Professional Appraisers (USA) **7589**
Directory of Professional Genealogists (Year) (USA ISSN 1055-6710) **3764**
Directory of Professional Puppeteers (GBR ISSN 0142-3681) **8469**
Directory of Psychiatry Residency Training Programs (USA ISSN 0740-8250) **6136**
Directory of Public Accounting Firm (IDN) **1287**
Directory of Public Relations Firms *see* O'Dwyer's Directory of Public Relations Firms **2022**
Directory of Public School Systems in the United States (USA) **2955**
• Directory of Public Schools and Administrators, New York State (USA) **3020**
Directory of Public Schools in the U S *see* Directory of Public School Systems in the United States **2955**
Directory of Publicly Owned Natural Gas Systems (USA) **6767**
• Directory of Published Proceedings (Online) (USA) **5744**
Directory of Published Proceedings. Series M L S - Medical, Life Sciences (Print) *see* Directory of Published Proceedings (Online) **5744**
Directory of Published Proceedings. Series P C E - Pollution Control & Ecology (USA ISSN 0093-5816) **3478**
Directory of Published Proceedings. Series S S H - Social Sciences - Humanities (USA ISSN 0012-3307) **4484**
Directory of Publishing in Scotland *see* Publishing Scotland Yearbook (Year) **7571**
Directory of Quarries, Pits and Quarry Equipment (GBR ISSN 1356-7586) **6461**
Directory of R I B A Members *see* Royal Institute of British Architects. Members **456**
Directory of Regional Councils in the United States (Year) (USA) **7434**
Directory of Religious Media (USA) **1988**
Directory of Research and Development Institutions (IND) **8420**
Directory of Research and Special Libraries in Ghana (GHA) **5006**
• Directory of Research Grants (USA ISSN 0146-7336) **2978**
Directory of Residential Camps *see* Directory of Residential Camps. New Zealand **8311**
Directory of Residential Camps. Lower North Island *see* Directory of Residential Camps. New Zealand **8311**
Directory of Residential Camps. Lower North Island and South Island *see* Directory of Residential Camps. New Zealand **8311**
Directory of Residential Camps. New Zealand (NZL ISSN 1177-0392) **8311**
Directory of Residential Camps. South Island, New Zealand *see* Directory of Residential Camps. New Zealand **8311**
Directory of Residential Camps. Upper North Island *see* Directory of Residential Camps. New Zealand **8311**
Directory of Restaurant & Fast Food Chains in Canada (CAN ISSN 0227-4302) **3634**
• Directory of Retail Chains in Canada (CAN ISSN 0225-9443) **1988**
• Directory of Rubber Organizations (Year) (GBR) **1988**
† Directory of Russian Space Industry (FRA) **8950**
Directory of San Francisco Attorneys (USA ISSN 0092-9174) **4659**
Directory of Scientific and Technical Libraries in Thailand (THA ISSN 0858-1630) **5006**
Directory of Scientific Meetings Held in Iran *see* Rahnama-yi Siminarha-yi Iran **7901**
Directory of Scientific Periodicals of Pakistan (PAK) **7936**
Directory of Scientific Research in Nigeria (NGA ISSN 0070-6280) **7851**
The Directory of Scottish Government (GBR ISSN 1465-4776) **7434**
Directory of Selected Early Childhood Programs (USA ISSN 1067-9049) **3038**
Directory of Service Providers to the Insurance Industry in Asia (SGP) **1988**
Directory of Services for People with a Disability (AUS ISSN 1449-0587) **4064**
Directory of Services for Victims of Crime/Repertoire des Services aux Victimes d'Actes Criminels (CAN ISSN 0847-3668) **8037**
Directory of Shopping Centres. Queensland (Year) *see* Shopping Centre Directory. NSW/ ACT (Year) **7618**
Directory of Shopping Centres. South Australia (Year) *see* Shopping Centre Directory. NSW/ ACT (Year) **7618**
Directory of Shopping Centres. Victoria (Year) *see* Shopping Centre Directory. NSW/ ACT (Year) **7618**
Directory of Shopping Centres. Western Australia (Year) *see* Shopping Centre Directory. NSW/ ACT (Year) **7618**
Directory of Simulation Software (USA) **2517**
Directory of Singapore Process & Chemicals Industries (SGP) **1988**
Directory of Singapore Shipbuilding & Offshore Industries (Year) *see* Singapore Shiprepairing, Shipbuilding & Offshore Industries Directory **2028**
Directory of Single Unit Supermarket Operators (Year) (USA ISSN 0896-2162) **1988**
Directory of Small Press & Magazine Editors & Publishers (USA ISSN 0277-1519) **7560**
Directory of South African Publishers (ZAF ISSN 1018-7626) **7560**
† Directory of Special Collections in Western Europe (DEU) **8950**
• Directory of Special Libraries and Information Centers (USA ISSN 0731-633X) **5006**
Directory of Special Libraries and Information Sources in Indonesia (Year) *see* Direktori Perpustakaan Khusus dan Sumber Infomasi di Indonesia **5007**
Directory of Special Libraries in Eastern Canada/Repertoire des Bibliotheques Specialisees dans l'Est du Canada (CAN) **5007**
Directory of Spiritualist Organizations in Canada (CAN ISSN 1187-7227) **6741**
Directory of Sport in London (GBR) **8169**
Directory of Sport in the South East (GBR) **8169**
Directory of Staff Bargaining Agents in Institutions of Higher Education (USA) **1675**
Directory of State, County, and Federal Officials (USA ISSN 0440-4947) **7434**
Directory of State Court Clerks and County Courthouses (Year) *see* Directory of State Court Clerks & County Courthouses (Year) **4950**
• Directory of State Court Clerks & County Courthouses (Year) (USA ISSN 1042-4172) **4950**
Directory of Steel Foundries and Buyer's Guide (USA ISSN 1538-3458) **1988**
Directory of Suicide Prevention and Crisis Intervention Centers (USA) **7352**
Directory of Summer Jobs Abroad (GBR ISSN 0308-7123) **1988**
Directory of Summer Jobs in Britain (GBR ISSN 0143-3490) **1988**
Directory of Superannuation Related Statistics *see* Australia. Bureau of Statistics. Directory of Superannuation Related Statistics **1203**
• Directory of Supermarket, Grocery & Convenience Store Chains (Year) (USA ISSN 0196-1845) **1988**
Directory of Suppliers Serving the Distributor-Served Bakery Industry *see* Modern Baking **3675**
Directory of Support Services (NZL ISSN 1177-2522) **8037**
Directory of Taiwan/Taiwan Zhinan (TWN ISSN 1607-923X) **624**
• (Year) Directory of Taiwan's Leading Manufacturers and Exporters (TWN) **1988**
Directory of Tennessee Municipal Officials (USA) **7491**
Directory of the American Psychological Association *see* American Psychological Association. Directory **639**
Directory of the Arts (CAN ISSN 0832-865X) **486**
Directory of the Canadian Trade Commissioner Service (CAN ISSN 0845-1656) **1988**
Directory of the Canning, Freezing, Preserving Industries (USA ISSN 1063-9756) **3634**
Directory of the French Nuclear Industry (FRA ISSN 0066-2593) **3166**
Directory of the National Productivity Organizations in A P O Member Countries (JPN) **1884**
▼ Directory of the New Urbanism (USA ISSN 1942-9444) **441**
Directory of the Periodicals in the United Arab Emirates *see* Dalil ad-Dawriat li-Dawlat al-Imarat al-Arabiyyah al-Muttahidah **623**
Directory of the Refractories Industry (Year) (USA) **2040**
Directory of the Scientists, Technologists, and Engineers of the P C S I R (PAK) **7851**
Directory of the Spanish Chemical Industry *see* Repertorio de la Industria Quimica Espanola **2078**
Directory of the Spanish Cotton-System Textile Enterprises/Directoire Enterprises Textiles de Processus Cotonnier/Directori Empreses Textils de Proces Cotoner/Directorio Empresas Textiles de Proceso Algodonero (ESP) **8450**
• The Directory of the Turf (Year) (GBR ISSN 1463-8460) **8290**
The Directory of the Turf Handbook (Year) (GBR) **8290**
Directory of Theatre Training Programs (USA ISSN 1041-5211) **8469**
(Year) Directory of Think Tanks in Japan (JPN) **7959**
Directory of Timber Trade (MYS ISSN 0126-6330) **1988**
Directory of Top Computer Executives (USA ISSN 0193-9920) **2416**
Directory of Top Computer Executives (Canada Edition) *see* Directory of Top Computer Executives **2416**
Directory of Top Computer Executives (East Edition) *see* Directory of Top Computer Executives **2416**
Directory of Top Computer Executives (West Edition) *see* Directory of Top Computer Executives **2416**
Directory of Trade and Professional Associations in the European Union - The Blue Book (BEL) **1988**
† Directory of Traditional Music (USA ISSN 0893-3065) **8950**
Directory of Training (GBR) **2416**
Directory of Training Posts in Dermatology (GBR) **5875**
Directory of Training Posts in Ophthalmology (GBR) **6041**
Directory of Treasury Services *see* Treasury Management International **1799**
Directory of Trust Banking (USA ISSN 1085-1240) **1988**
The Directory of U K Associations *see* A S K Hollis **1970**
• The Directory of U K Parliaments and Assemblies (GBR ISSN 1477-3023) **7434**
Directory of U.S. Government Datafiles for Mainframes and Microcomputers (USA ISSN 1061-9623) **1988**
• Directory of U.S. Labor Organizations (Year) (USA ISSN 0734-6786) **4593**
Directory of U.S. Meat Suppliers (USA) **1988**
Directory of UK and Irish Book Publishers *see* The Red Book **7572**
Directory of Undergraduate Political Science Faculty (Year) *see* A P S A Directory of Political Science Faculty (Year) **7101**
• Directory of United States Exporters (USA ISSN 1057-6878) **1561**
• Directory of United States Importers (USA ISSN 1057-5111) **1561**
Directory of University Libraries in Europe (GBR) **5007**
Directory of V A Rs *see* Directory of Computer V A R's & System Integrators (Year) **1986**
Directory of Video Dealers (USA) **1988**
Directory of Visiting Fulbright Scholars and Occasional Lecturers *see* Visiting Scholar Directory **3015**
Directory of Vocational and Further Education (GBR) **2955**
Directory of Voluntary Organisations in Wales: National Contacts/Cyfeiriadur Mudiadau Gwirfoddol Yng Nghymru: Csysylltiadau Cenedlaethol (GBR) **8037**
• Directory of Water and Wildland Expertise and Facilities in the University of California System (USA) **8821**
The Directory of Welsh Government (GBR ISSN 1465-4784) **7434**
• Directory of Wholesale Grocers (Year) (USA ISSN 1068-7157) **1988**
Directory of Wire Companies of North America (USA) **1988**

Title

▼ new title   † ceased   ● electronic media   ➤ refereed

DIRECTORY 2010 DOCUMENTOS DE TRABAJO. SERIE DOCUMENTOS DE POLITICA 10207

Do So'maeeob Tong'gye Jo'sa Bo'go'seo/Korea (Republic). National Statistical Office. Report on the Survey of Wholesale and Retail Trade (KOR ISSN 1599-5194) **1224**
Do Vostrebovaniya (LVA) **3904**
Doane's Agricultural Report (USA ISSN 0093-5271) **196**
▼ Doane's Strategic Planning Quarterly (USA ISSN 1948-2728) **196**
• Doba (UKR) **3964**
Doba Senioru (CZE ISSN 1801-5859) **4043**
Dobar Tek (HRV ISSN 1331-4181) **4356**
Dobbit Magazine (Dutch Edition) *see* Dobbit Magazine (French Edition) **1002**
Dobbit Magazine (French Edition) (BEL ISSN 0771-176X) **1002**
Dobbit Professional (Dutch Edition) *see* Dobbit Professional (French Edition) **1003**
Dobbit Professional (French Edition) (BEL ISSN 0774-1421) **1003**
Doberman (RUS ISSN 1562-756X) **6806**
The Dobie Connection (USA) **4138**
Doboku Gakkai Hokkaido Shibu Ronbun Hokokushu/Japan Society of Civil Engineers. Hokkaido Branch. Research Reports at the Annual Meeting (JPN ISSN 0913-4921) **3264**
Doboku Gakkai Kansai Shibu Nenji Gakujutsu Koenk Ai Koen Gaiyo/Japan Society of Civil Engineers. Kansai Branch. Proceedings of Annual Conference on Civil Engineers (JPN ISSN 0285-7324) **3264**
Doboku Gakkai Nenji Koenkai Koen Gaiyoshu/Japan Society of Civil Engineers. Proceedings of the Annual Conference (JPN ISSN 0285-760X) **3264**
Doboku Gakkai Rombunshuu. A (CD-ROM) *see* Doboku Gakkai Rombunshuu. A (DVD-ROM) **3264**
• Doboku Gakkai Rombunshuu. A (DVD-ROM) (JPN ISSN 1883-4760) **3264**
Doboku Gakkai Rombunshuu. B (CD-ROM) *see* Doboku Gakkai Rombunshuu. B (DVD-ROM) **3361**
• Doboku Gakkai Rombunshuu. B (DVD-ROM) (JPN ISSN 1883-4779) **3361**
Doboku Gakkai Rombunshuu. C (CD-ROM) *see* Doboku Gakkai Rombunshuu. C (DVD-ROM) **2732**
• Doboku Gakkai Rombunshuu. C (DVD-ROM) (JPN ISSN 1883-4787) **2732**
Doboku Gakkai Rombunshuu. D (CD-ROM) *see* Doboku Gakkai Rombunshuu. D (DVD-ROM) **3265**
• Doboku Gakkai Rombunshuu. D (DVD-ROM) (JPN ISSN 1883-4795) **3265**
Doboku Gakkai Rombunshuu. E (CD-ROM) *see* Doboku Gakkai Rombunshuu. E (DVD-ROM) **1003**
• Doboku Gakkai Rombunshuu. E (DVD-ROM) (JPN ISSN 1883-4809) **1003**
Doboku Gakkai Rombunshuu. F (CD-ROM) *see* Doboku Gakkai Rombunshuu. F (DVD-ROM) **1003**
• Doboku Gakkai Rombunshuu. F (DVD-ROM) (JPN ISSN 1883-4817) **1003**
Doboku Gakkai Rombunshuu. G (CD-ROM) *see* Doboku Gakkai Rombunshuu. G (DVD-ROM) **3414**
• Doboku Gakkai Rombunshuu. G (DVD-ROM) (JPN ISSN 1883-4825) **3414**
Doboku Gakkai Ronbunshu/Japan Society of Civil Engineers. Proceedings (Print) *see* Doboku Gakkai Rombunshuu. A (DVD-ROM) **3264**
Doboku Gakkai Ronbunshu/Japan Society of Civil Engineers. Proceedings (Print) *see* Doboku Gakkai Rombunshuu. C (DVD-ROM) **2732**
Doboku Gakkai Ronbunshu/Japan Society of Civil Engineers. Proceedings (Print) *see* Doboku Gakkai Rombunshuu. E (DVD-ROM) **1003**
Doboku Gakkai Ronbunshu/Japan Society of Civil Engineers. Proceedings (Print) *see* Doboku Gakkai Rombunshuu. F (DVD-ROM) **1003**
Doboku Gakkai Ronbunshu/Japan Society of Civil Engineers. Proceedings (Print) *see* Doboku Gakkai Rombunshuu. B (DVD-ROM) **3361**
Doboku Gakkai Ronbunshu/Japan Society of Civil Engineers. Proceedings (Print) *see* Doboku Gakkai Rombunshuu. G (DVD-ROM) **3414**
Doboku Gakkai Ronbunshu/Japan Society of Civil Engineers. Proceedings (Print) *see* Doboku Gakkai Rombunshuu. D (DVD-ROM) **3265**
Doboku Gakkaishi/Japan Society of Civil Engineers. Journal (JPN ISSN 0021-468X) **3265**
Doboku Gijutsu/Civil Engineering (JPN ISSN 0285-5046) **3265**
Doboku Gijutsu Shiryo/Civil Engineering Journal (JPN ISSN 0386-5886) **3265**
Doboku Joho Shisutemu Shinpojumu Koenshu/Symposium on Engineering Processing System. Proceedings (JPN ISSN 0915-5333) **3265**
Doboku Keikakugaku Kenkyu Koenshu/Proceedings of Infrastructure Planning (JPN ISSN 0913-4026) **3265**
Doboku Keikakugaku Kenkyu Ronbunshu/ Infrastructure Planning Review (JPN ISSN 0913-4034) **3265**
Doboku Keikakugaku Shinpojumu/Symposium on Civil Engineering Planning. Proceedings (JPN ISSN 0913-4050) **3265**
Doboku Kenchiku Gyosei no Gaiyo/Public Works and Constructions in Oita Prefecture. Outline (JPN) **3265**
Doboku Kenkyujo Hokoku/Public Works Research Institute. Report (JPN ISSN 0386-4995) **3265**
Doboku Kenkyujo Iho/Public Works Research Institute. Technical Note (JPN ISSN 0386-586X) **3265**
Doboku Kenkyujo Kenkyu Happyokai Ronbunshu/Public Works Research Institute. Proceedings of Meeting (JPN) **3265**
Doboku Kenkyujo Koenkai Koenshu/Public Works Research Institute. Proceedings (JPN) **3265**
Doboku Kenkyujo Nenpo/Public Works Research Institute. Annual Report (JPN ISSN 0419-4926) **3265**
Doboku Kenkyujo Shiryo/Public Works Research Institute. Technical Memorandum (JPN ISSN 0386-5878) **3265**
Doboku Seko (JPN ISSN 0387-0790) **3265**
Dobokubu Gaiyo/Japan. Shizuoka Prefectural Government. Civil Engineering Division. Annual Report (JPN) **3265**
Dobokushi Kenkyu/Historical Studies in Civil Engineering (JPN ISSN 0916-7293) **3265**
Dobra Gra (POL ISSN 1642-2104) **2475**
Dobra Kuhinja (SVN) **4356**
Dobre Jedlo (SVK ISSN 1336-1066) **4356**
Dobre Rady (POL ISSN 1643-8264) **8858**
Dobre Rady. Diety Odchudzajace (POL ISSN 1643-6202) **6657**
Dobre Rady. Fryzury (POL ISSN 1509-6858) **587**
Dobre Rady. Horoskop (POL ISSN 1506-0403) **566**
Dobre Rady. Kwiaty w Domu (POL ISSN 1509-6033) **3728**
Dobre Rady. Piekna i Zdrowa (POL ISSN 1643-0867) **8858**
Dobre Rady. Recepty (POL) **4356**
• Dobre Wnetrze (POL ISSN 1429-3226) **4538**
Dobromysl (UKR) **5214**
Dobrudschabote (DEU) **335**
Dobrye Sovety *see* Liza. Dobrye Sovety **8872**
Dobrye Sovety *see* Liza. Dobrye Sovety **8872**
Dobrye Sovety. Luchshie Retsepty *see* Liza. Dobrye Sovety. Luchshie Retsepty **4363**
Dobutsu Iden Ikushu Kenkyu/Journal of Animal Genetics (JPN ISSN 1345-9961) **866**
Dobutsu Iyakuhin Kensajo Nenpo/Japan. Ministry of Agriculture, Forestry and Fisheries. National Veterinary Assay Laboratory. Annual Report (JPN ISSN 0388-7421) **8796**
Dobutsu Shinrigaku Kenkyu/Japanese Journal of Animal Psychology (JPN ISSN 0916-8419) **940**
Dobutsu to Dobutsuen/Animals and Zoos (JPN ISSN 0288-4887) **940**
Dobutsuen Suizokukan Zasshi/Japanese Association of Zoological Gardens and Aquariums. Journal (JPN ISSN 0386-7498) **940**
Doc *see* Doc Toscana **7231**
Doc' Domicile (FRA ISSN 1952-8531) **8038**
Doc Italia (ITA ISSN 0391-5018) **2978**
Doc Toscana (ITA ISSN 1593-2176) **7231**
• Doc Warren Online (USA) **8290**
Docavia (FRA ISSN 0764-9185) **53**
• Doce Notas (ESP ISSN 1136-6273) **6562**
Doce Notas Preliminares (ESP ISSN 1138-3984) **6562**
Docencia (CHL ISSN 0718-4212) **2842**
• Docencia e Investigacion (ESP ISSN 1133-9926) **2978**
Docencia, Investigacion, Extension (VEN ISSN 1316-5399) **2842**
Docencia Postsecundaria (MEX ISSN 0185-3597) **2978**
Docentraal (NLD) **2842**
Docete (ITA ISSN 0391-6324) **2843**
• DOCHIS. Documentacao Historica (BRA ISSN 1809-0737) **4138**
Dochodi, Raschodi i Potreblenie na Domakinstvata (BGR ISSN 1311-2287) **8366**
The Docket (Atlanta) (USA) **4660**
Docket (Sacramento) (USA) **4660**
Docket Call (Richmond) (USA) **4660**
† • Docklands News (GBR ISSN 0264-9691) **8951**
Dockside (USA) **8275**
Docma (DEU) **2485**
DOCOMOMO Journal (Documentation and Conservation of Buildings, Sites and Neighbourhoods of the Modern Movement) (FRA ISSN 1380-3204) **441**
▼ DocSciences (FRA ISSN 1957-3367) **7851**
• Docteurs & Co. (FRA ISSN 1766-974X) **5606**
• DocTom's Online Self-Care Journal (USA) **6984**
• Doctor (GBR ISSN 0046-0451) **5606**
Doctor (IND) **6041**
The Doctor (JPN) **5606**
Doctor *see* New Zealand Doctor **5685**
Doctor (USA) **5606**
• Doctor Ebiz (USA ISSN 1529-3203) **1959**
Doctor Jazz Magazine (NLD ISSN 0166-2309) **6562**
Doctor of Chiropractic Tracts *see* D.C. Tracts **5804**
Doctor of Dentistry (USA) **5842**
Doctor of Osteopathy *see* The D O **5805**
Doctor of Veterinary Medicine *see* D V M **8796**
➤ Doctor Os (ITA ISSN 1120-7140) **5842**
Doctor - Patient Studies (USA) **5606**
Doctor Salon Library *see* Dokuta Saron **5606**
• Doctor Virtualis (ITA ISSN 2035-7362) **6914**
Doctor Who Magazine (GBR ISSN 0963-1275) **2380**
➤ Doctoral Forum (USA ISSN 1559-2804) **2978**
Doctoral Working Paper Series *see* D W P S **1737**
Doctors' Digest *see* Alberta Doctors' Digest **5571**
• Doctor's Digest (USA ISSN 1554-6195) **5606**
▼ • Doctor's Digest, Oncology (USA) **6018**
Doctors for Disaster Preparedness Newsletter (USA) **5606**
Doctors Magazine *see* Laegemagasinet **5659**
• Doctors N S (Nova Scotia) (CAN) **5606**
• The Doctor's Office (USA ISSN 0733-2262) **4092**
Doctor's Review (CAN ISSN 0821-5758) **8698**
• Doctor's Shopper (USA) **5606**
doctorsNS *see* Doctors N S **5606**
Doctrina (ESP ISSN 1137-6341) **4950**
Doctrina et Pietas (DEU) **4215**
Doctrina Mercantil (COL) **1401**
Doctrina - Sala de lo Social del Tribunal Supremo *see* Doctrina **4950**
➤ Doctrine and Life (IRL ISSN 0012-446X) **7795**
Docuforms International *see* Documents International **7319**
• The Doculabs Report (USA) **2554**
• Document (USA) **7319**
• Document & Image Automation (USA ISSN 1071-6130) **5007**
† Document Brut (FRA ISSN 1958-8143) **8951**
Document de Travail (FRA ISSN 0183-701X) **8099**
• Document Design (USA) **7319**
Document Design Companion Series (NLD ISSN 1568-1963) **2319**
Document d'Information et Fiche de Presentation des Projets *see* Le Concours des Prix Essor. Document d'Information et Fiche de Presentation **2839**
• Document Imaging Report (USA ISSN 1071-1295) **2533**
Document Management Directory *see* Content and Document Management Guide and Directory **2529**
Document Management Guide and Directory *see* Content and Document Management Guide and Directory **2529**
Document Management Update (GBR ISSN 1360-6786) **2530**
• Document Manager (GBR ISSN 1351-3222) **2535**
• Document Numerique (FRA ISSN 1279-5127) **2447**
Document Skateboard Magazine (GBR ISSN 1473-2998) **8170**
Document Survie *see* Planete Survie **3841**
Document Systems Outlook (GBR ISSN 1365-6619) **2530**
➤ Documenta (BEL ISSN 0771-8640) **8469**
Documenta (BRA) **2843**
Documenta (SWE ISSN 0347-5719) **7851**
Documenta Arabica (DEU ISSN 1613-6403) **4321**
Documenta Arabica Antiqua (DEU ISSN 0945-5639) **548**
Documenta Archaeobiologiae (DEU ISSN 1611-7484) **390**
Documenta Augustana (DEU) **7959**
• Documenta et Instrumenta (ESP ISSN 1697-4328) **390**
Documenta et Monumenta Orientis Antiqui *see* Culture and History of the Ancient Near East **4320**
Documenta Ethnographica (AUT) **3616**
Documenta Homoeopathica (AUT ISSN 0343-6640) **5606**
Documenta Iranica et Islamica (DEU) **548**
Documenta Linguistica. Studienreihe (DEU ISSN 0175-873X) **5112**
• ➤ Documenta Mathematica (DEU ISSN 1431-0635) **5484**
➤ Documenta Missionalia (ITA) **7735**
Documenta Missionalia *see* Documenta Missionalia **7735**
Documenta Mundi (SWE ISSN 1104-3199) **4321**
Documenta Naturae (DEU ISSN 0723-8428) **2732**
Documenta Naturae. Sonderband (DEU ISSN 1433-1705) **2732**
• ➤ Documenta Ophthalmologica (NLD ISSN 0012-4486) **6041**
Documenta Ophthalmologica Proceedings Series (NLD ISSN 0303-6405) **6041**
Documenta Orthographica (DEU ISSN 1434-8489) **5112**
Documenta Paediatrie (DEU) **6091**
➤ Documenta Q (BEL) **7638**
Documenta Romaniae Historica. Serie A: La Moldavie (ROM ISSN 0070-6825) **4215**
Documenta Romaniae Historica. Serie B: La Valachie (ROM ISSN 0070-6833) **4215**
Documenta Septentrionalia (FIN ISSN 0359-6788) **4215**
• ➤ Documentacao de Estudos em Linguistica Teorica e Aplicada (BRA ISSN 0102-4450) **5112**
Documentacao e Direito Comparado (PRT ISSN 0870-8002) **4830**
Documentacao Europeia *see* Documentation Europeene **8366**
Documentacion Administrativa (ESP ISSN 0012-4494) **7434**
Documentacion Cervantina (USA) **5285**
Documentacion CINTERFOR (Documentacion Centro Interamericano de Investigacion y Documentacion Sobre Formacion Profesional) (URY ISSN 1020-2625) **5007**
Documentacion de la Seguridad Social Americana (CHE ISSN 0250-6041) **4501**
• Documentacion de las Ciencias de la Informacion (ESP ISSN 0210-4210) **2543**
Documentacion Laboral (ESP ISSN 0211-8556) **1676**
Documentacion Latinoamericana. Boletin Bibliografico *see* Dokumentationsdienst Lateinamerika. Ausgewaehlte Neuere Literatur **8951**
Documentacion Social (ESP ISSN 0417-8106) **7959**
• Documentaliste - Sciences de l'Information (FRA ISSN 0012-4508) **5007**
Documentary Credit World (USA ISSN 1520-0221) **1092**
Documentary Credits Insight (FRA ISSN 1024-008X) **1336**
➤ Documentary Editing (USA ISSN 0196-7134) **4450**
Documentary Reference Collections (USA) **4138**
Documentatie Orgaan Sociale Verzekering (NLD ISSN 1568-8992) **4501**
Documentatie Revue (NLD) **1814**
➤ Documentatieblad Nadere Reformatie (NLD ISSN 0165-4349) **7754**
Documentatieblad voor de Nederlandse Kerkgeschiedenis na 1800 (NLD ISSN 0923-7771) **7754**
Documentation and Conservation of Buildings, Sites and Neighbourhoods of the Modern Movement Journal *see* DOCOMOMO Journal **441**
Documentation and Registration of Rock Art in Tanum (SWE ISSN 1400-6235) **390**
Documentation Bulletin for South-East Asia (IND) **624**
• La Documentation Catholique (FRA ISSN 0012-4613) **7795**
Documentation et Bibliotheques (CAN ISSN 0315-2340) **5007**
Documentation Europea *see* Documentation Europeene **8366**
Documentation Europeene (LUX ISSN 0251-2998) **8366**
Documentation in Public Administration (IND ISSN 0377-7081) **7480**
Documentation Legislative Africaine (SEN ISSN 0378-0783) **4660**
Documentation List: Africa (IND ISSN 0418-582X) **4169**
Documentation on Women's Concerns (IND ISSN 0971-166X) **8858**
Documentation par l'Image (FRA ISSN 0046-0478) **7851**
Documentation Photographique (FRA ISSN 0419-5361) **6966**
Documentation Politique Internationale *see* International Political Science Abstracts **7200**
Documentation Services Index (USA) **1989**
Documentation sur la Recherche Feministe *see* Resources for Feminist Research **8902**
Documentazione Europea *see* Documentation Europeene **8366**
† • Documenter (AUS ISSN 1442-844X) **8951**
Documenti della Scuola (ITA) **2843**
Documenti di Storia Italiana (ITA ISSN 1825-361X) **4215**
Documenti e Informazioni. Bollettino - Scuola Superiore della Pubblica Informazione *see* Scuola Superiore della Pubblica Amministrazione. Bollettino. Documenti e Informazioni **8987**
Documenti e Ricerche d'Arte Alessandrina (ITA) **390**
Documenti e Studi sulla Tradizione Filosofica Medievale (ITA ISSN 1122-5750) **6914**
Documenti sulle Arti del Libro (ITA ISSN 0070-6906) **624**
• Documenting E-Commerce Transactions (USA) **4866**
• Documenting Employee Discipline (USA) **1859**
Documento de Trabajo - MECEP *see* Mejoramiento de la Calidad de la Educacion. Documento de Trabajo **2886**
Documento International Work Group for Indigenous Affairs *see* I W G I A Documento **342**
Documento Tecnico - Instituto Nacional de Salud *see* Instituto Nacional de Salud. Documento Tecnico **5636**
Documentos B U C L M (Biblioteca Universidad de Castilla-La Mancha) (ESP ISSN 1698-3203) **5007**
Documentos C E R E S *see* Universidad del Norte. Centro de Estudios Regionales. Documentos **359**
Documentos de Arquitectura (ESP ISSN 0214-9249) **441**
➤ Documentos de Arquitectura Nacional y Americana (ARG ISSN 0326-8640) **441**
Documentos de Geohistoria Regional (ARG) **4291**
Documentos de Literatura (PER ISSN 1022-0771) **5285**
Documentos de Reinado de Fernando VII (ESP) **4215**
Documentos de Trabajo *see* Pontificia Universidad Catolica de Chile. Instituto de Economia. Documentos de Trabajo **1160**
• Documentos de Trabajo Biltoki (ESP ISSN 1134-8984) **8367**
Documentos de Trabajo en Analisis Economico *see* Economic Analysis Working Papers **1479**
• Documentos de Trabajo Politica y Gestion (ESP ISSN 1698-2894) **7130**
Documentos de Trabajo. Serie Antropologia *see* Instituto de Estudios Peruanos. Documentos de Trabajo. Serie Antropologia **343**
Documentos de Trabajo. Serie Documentos de Politica *see* Instituto de Estudios Peruanos. Documentos de Trabajo. Serie Documentos de Politica **7143**

Title

Title

Dream Factory (AUT) 8783
Dream Gardens Across America (USA ISSN 1935-8679) 3728
Dream Home Source see Dream House Plans 1005
Dream Homes International (USA) 7589
Dream Homes Los Angeles (USA) 7589
Dream Homes San Diego (USA) 7589
Dream Homes San Francisco (USA) 7589
Dream House (CAN ISSN 1712-8129) 441
Dream House Plans (USA ISSN 1931-5708) 1005
▼ Dream Italian Weddings (GBR ISSN 1753-5514) 5558
Dream Kitchens (USA ISSN 1936-4482) 4356
Dream-Machines Harley-Davidson (DEU ISSN 1613-0731) 8258
• Dream Network Journal (USA ISSN 1054-6707) 6644
Dream Pools & Spas (USA ISSN 1936-2218) 1005
Dream Storage see Custom Storage 4536
➤ Dream Time (USA) 7352
▼ Dream Water Gardens (USA ISSN 1941-3246) 3728
Dream Whip (USA) 5286
• Dream World Cruise Destinations (GBR ISSN 1351-640X) 8642
Dreamboys (DEU) 4372
Dreamcast (FRA ISSN 1621-773X) 2475
† Dreamcast (GBR ISSN 1466-2388) 8951
Dreamcast Magazine (GBR) 2476
• The Dreamers Edge (USA ISSN 1930-0190) 7352
• ➤ Dreaming (USA ISSN 1053-0797) 7353
• Dreampop (USA) 6562
Dreams and Nightmares (USA ISSN 0897-0238) 5421
Dreams & Visions (CAN ISSN 0843-445X) 5286
Dreams of Decadence (USA ISSN 1097-2854) 5286
Dreams That Money Can Buy (GBR ISSN 1746-7411) 5214
• Dreamscape (USA) 6496
Dreamstreet (USA) 6562
• DreamSuccess (GBR) 6915
Dreamwest (FRA ISSN 1950-1935) 6562
▼ DreamWorks Magazin (HUN ISSN 2060-1786) 2187
Drecera (ESP) 106
Drechseln (DEU ISSN 0942-6019) 534
• Dredging & Port Construction (GBR ISSN 0264-4835) 8642
Dredging Research (USA) 3361
Dredging Seminar. Proceedings (USA) 8821
• Dregs from the Keg (USA ISSN 1945-1342) 602
Drehen in Deutschland (Year)/Shooting in Germany (Year) (DEU) 6496
Drehscheibe (Bonn) (DEU) 4574
Drehscheibe (Cologne) (DEU ISSN 0934-2230) 8616
Das Drehscheiben Magazin (DEU) 4574
Drehteil und Drehmaschine (DEU) 3366
Die Drei (DEU ISSN 0012-6063) 7735
Drei R International see 3 R - International 3288
Dreihundertsechzig see 360 2482
Dreikoenigsbote (DEU ISSN 0012-608X) 7755
Dreloma (IND) 7701
Drents Heideschaap see Schoone Drent 299
Drents Ondernemers Kontakt see Het Ondernemersbelang Drenthe 1782
Dreptul (ROM ISSN 1018-0435) 4661
Dresdener Beitraege zur Geschichte der Technikwissenschaft (DEU ISSN 0232-5349) 8420
Dresdener Kunstblaetter (DEU ISSN 0418-0615) 6523
Dresdner (DEU) 3846
Dresdner Beitraege zur Hethitologie (DEU) 548
Dresdner Beitraege zur Musikforschung (DEU) 6562
Dresdner Hefte (DEU ISSN 0863-2138) 4215
Dresdner Historische Studien (DEU) 4215
Dresdner Kind (DEU) 2150
• ➤ Dress (USA ISSN 0361-2112) 2253
➤ Dress, Body, Culture (GBR ISSN 1360-466X) 335
Dressage see Dressage Today 8290
Dressage Magazine (GBR ISSN 0958-1804) 8290
• Dressage Today (USA ISSN 1079-1167) 8290
Drevarsky Vyskum see Wood Research 3718
Drevneishie Gosudarstva Vostocnoi Evropy/Ancient States in the Territory of the U.S.S.R. (RUS ISSN 1560-1382) 391
Drevo/Wood (SVK ISSN 0012-6144) 1050
Drew (USA ISSN 0889-0153) 2282
➤ Drewno/Wood (POL ISSN 1644-3985) 1050
• The Drewry Monthly (GBR) 8524
Drexel Faculty Publication (USA) 7851
De Drie Steden (NLD ISSN 0169-4650) 4215
Driebandennieuws (NLD ISSN 1569-4984) 8226
Dried Fruits News see The Vine 3667
Driehoeksverhouding (NLD ISSN 1574-6194) 4409
Driemaandelijks Bulletin (BEL) 335
Driemaandelijks Tijdschrift van de Auschwitz Stichting see La Memoire d'Auschwitz. Bulletin Trimestriel 4244
† Drift (DEU) 8951
Drift (DNK ISSN 1398-7801) 7353
Drift og Vedlikehold see Forvaltning, Drift, Vedlikehold 1746
Drift og Vedlikehold see Byggaktuelt 987
Driftsgranskinger i Jord- og Skogbruk (NOR ISSN 0333-2500) 196
Driftsmagasinet (NOR ISSN 1890-2561) 1814
† Driftsteknikerbogen (DNK ISSN 0108-6707) 8951
The Driftwood (USA ISSN 1520-9873) 5286
Driftwood, Information Guide (CAN ISSN 1710-6699) 8699
▼ DriftyTips (USA ISSN 1940-6096) 2637
Drill (USA) 6288
Drilling Activity Report (CAN ISSN 0228-5630) 6767
Drilling and Production Technology see Zuancai Gongyi 6798
Drilling and Well Servicing Contractors see Drilling & Well Servicing Contractors 6767
Drilling & Well Servicing Contractors (USA) 6767
Drilling Completion and Plugging Summary (USA) 6767
Drilling Contractor (USA ISSN 0046-0702) 6767
Drilling Fluid & Completion Fluid see Zuanjing Ye yu Wanjing Ye 6798
Drilling, Oil, Gas see Wiernictwo, Nafta, Gaz 6797
Drilling Permit Index see Texas. Railroad Commission. Oil and Gas Division. Drilling Permit Index 6794
Drilling Permits (USA) 6767
Drilling Reports (USA) 6767
Drilling Wire. Alaska Region Report (USA) 6767
• Drilling Wire. Wyoming Report (USA) 6767
† The Drink Forecast (GBR ISSN 0951-7723) 8951
† Drink Pocket Book (Year) (GBR ISSN 0965-5360) 8951
• Drink Smart (CAN) 2693
Drink Technology and Marketing (DEU ISSN 1433-1594) 602
Drink World see Jiu Shijie 605
The Drinking Driver in Minnesota (USA) 4661
Drinking / Driving Law Letter (USA ISSN 0730-2568) 8577
Drinking Water and Backflow Prevention see Drinking Water & Backflow Prevention 3265
Drinking Water & Backflow Prevention (USA ISSN 1055-2782) 3265
• ➤ Drinking Water Engineering and Science (DEU ISSN 1996-9457) 8821
• ➤ Drinking Water Engineering and Science Discussions (DEU ISSN 1996-9473) 8821
• Drinking Water Research (USA ISSN 1055-9140) 8821
Drinking Water Safety see Drinking Water Safety in Newfoundland and Labrador 3414
Drinking Water Safety in Newfoundland and Labrador (CAN ISSN 1914-0525) 3414
Drinking Water Surveillance Program Annual Report (Year) Plant Summaries (CAN ISSN 0846-7471) 8821
Drinking Water Surveillance Program Annual Report. Ajax Water Supply Plant (CAN ISSN 0843-8277) 8821
Drinking Water Surveillance Program Annual Report. Alvinston Water System (CAN ISSN 0839-8992) 8821
Drinking Water Surveillance Program Annual Report. Amherstburg Area Water System (CAN ISSN 0839-900X) 8821
Drinking Water Surveillance Program Annual Report. Atikokan Water Treatment Plant (CAN ISSN 0843-8331) 8821
Drinking Water Surveillance Program Annual Report. Bayside School Water Treatment Plant (CAN ISSN 0840-5603) 8821
Drinking Water Surveillance Program Annual Report. Belle River Water Treatment Plant (CAN ISSN 1183-6105) 8821
Drinking Water Surveillance Program Annual Report. Belleville Water Treatment Plant (CAN ISSN 0840-5123) 8821
Drinking Water Surveillance Program Annual Report. Brantford Water Treatment Plant (CAN ISSN 0840-5344) 8821
Drinking Water Surveillance Program Annual Report. Britannia Water Treatment Plant, Ottawa (CAN ISSN 0839-9026) 8821
Drinking Water Surveillance Program Annual Report. Burlington Water Treatment Plant (CAN ISSN 0840-5247) 8821
Drinking Water Surveillance Program Annual Report. Casselman Water Treatment Plant (CAN ISSN 1180-2138) 8821
Drinking Water Surveillance Program Annual Report. Cayuga Water Treatment Plant (CAN ISSN 0843-8323) 8821
Drinking Water Surveillance Program Annual Report. Central Haldimand - Norfolk Water Treatment Plant (CAN ISSN 1180-2162) 8821
Drinking Water Surveillance Program Annual Report. Chatham Water Treatment Plant (CAN ISSN 0843-8315) 8821
Drinking Water Surveillance Program Annual Report. Cornwall Water Treatment Plant (CAN ISSN 0840-5298) 8821
Drinking Water Surveillance Program Annual Report. Delhi Water Supply System (CAN ISSN 1183-613X) 8821
Drinking Water Surveillance Program Annual Report. Deseronto Water Treatment Plant (CAN ISSN 0840-5131) 8821
Drinking Water Surveillance Program Annual Report. Dresden Water Treatment Plant (CAN ISSN 0839-8984) 8821
Drinking Water Surveillance Program Annual Report. Dryden Water Treatment Plant (CAN ISSN 0843-8293) 8821
Drinking Water Surveillance Program Annual Report. Dunnville Water Treatment Plant (CAN ISSN 1192-1196) 8821
Drinking Water Surveillance Program Annual Report. Easterly Water Treatment Plant, Toronto (CAN ISSN 0840-5166) 8821
Drinking Water Surveillance Program Annual Report. Elmire Well Supply (CAN ISSN 0843-8382) 8821
Drinking Water Surveillance Program Annual Report. Fort Erie Treatment Plant (CAN ISSN 0840-5182) 8821
Drinking Water Surveillance Program Annual Report. Fort Frances Water Treatment Plant (CAN ISSN 0843-8358) 8821
Drinking Water Surveillance Program Annual Report. Grimsby Water Treatment Plant (CAN ISSN 0840-5174) 8821
Drinking Water Surveillance Program Annual Report. Guelph Well Supply (CAN ISSN 1192-120X) 8822
Drinking Water Surveillance Program Annual Report. Hamilton Water Treatment Plant (CAN ISSN 0839-9034) 8822
Drinking Water Surveillance Program Annual Report. Harrow - Colchester South Water Supply System (CAN ISSN 0840-5239) 8822
Drinking Water Surveillance Program Annual Report. Hawkesbury Water Treatment Plant (CAN ISSN 1180-2146) 8822
Drinking Water Surveillance Program Annual Report. Kenora Water Treatment Plant (CAN ISSN 0843-8307) 8822
Drinking Water Surveillance Program Annual Report. Kingston Water Treatment Plant (CAN ISSN 0839-9050) 8822
Drinking Water Surveillance Program Annual Report. Kitchener Water Supply Systems (CAN ISSN 0840-5190) 8822
Drinking Water Surveillance Program Annual Report. Lake Huron Water Supply System (CAN ISSN 0840-5271) 8822
Drinking Water Surveillance Program Annual Report. Lambton Area Supply, Sarnia (CAN ISSN 0840-5107) 8822
Drinking Water Surveillance Program Annual Report. Lemieux Island Water Treatment Plant, Ottawa (CAN ISSN 0840-5204) 8822
Drinking Water Surveillance Program Annual Report. Mitchell's Bay Water Treatment Plant (CAN ISSN 0840-531X) 8822
Drinking Water Surveillance Program Annual Report. Niagara Falls Water Treatment Plant (CAN ISSN 0839-8925) 8822
Drinking Water Surveillance Program Annual Report. North Bay Water Treatment Plant (CAN ISSN 0840-5212) 8822
Drinking Water Surveillance Program Annual Report. Odessa Water Treatment Plant (CAN ISSN 0843-8366) 8822
Drinking Water Surveillance Program Annual Report. Owen Sound Water Supply System (CAN ISSN 1183-6172) 8822
Drinking Water Surveillance Program Annual Report. Peterborough Water Treatment Plant (CAN ISSN 0840-514X) 8822
Drinking Water Surveillance Program Annual Report. Port Colborne Water Treatment Plant (CAN ISSN 1183-6180) 8822
Drinking Water Surveillance Program Annual Report. Port Dover - Doan's Hollow Water Treatment Plant (CAN ISSN 0840-5328) 8822
Drinking Water Surveillance Program Annual Report. Port Stanley Water Treatment Plant (CAN ISSN 0839-8968) 8822
Drinking Water Surveillance Program Annual Report. R.C. Harris Water Treatment Plant, Toronto (CAN ISSN 0839-8941) 8822
Drinking Water Surveillance Program Annual Report. R.L. Clark Water Treatment Plant, Toronto (CAN ISSN 0839-8976) 8822
Drinking Water Surveillance Program Annual Report. Renfrew Water Treatment Plant (CAN ISSN 1180-2111) 8822
Drinking Water Surveillance Program Annual Report. St. Catharines Water Treatment Plant (CAN ISSN 0840-528X) 8822
Drinking Water Surveillance Program Annual Report. St. Thomas (Elgin) Water Supply System (CAN ISSN 0840-5255) 8822
Drinking Water Surveillance Program Annual Report. Sault Ste. Marie Wells and Water Treatment Plant (CAN ISSN 0840-5158) 8822
Drinking Water Surveillance Program Annual Report. Simcoe Well Supply (CAN ISSN 1183-6202) 8822
Drinking Water Surveillance Program Annual Report. South Peel (Lakeview) Water Treatment Plant (CAN ISSN 0839-9069) 8822
Drinking Water Surveillance Program Annual Report. South Peel (Lorne Park) Water Supply System (CAN ISSN 1187-6824) 8822
Drinking Water Surveillance Program Annual Report. Stoney Point Water Treatment Plant (CAN ISSN 0839-8933) 8822
Drinking Water Surveillance Program Annual Report. Stouffville Water Supply System (CAN ISSN 0840-5301) 8822
Drinking Water Surveillance Program Annual Report. Sudbury (Ramsey Lake) Water Treatment Plant (CAN ISSN 0840-5336) 8822
Drinking Water Surveillance Program Annual Report. Sudbury (Wanapitei) Water Treatment Plant (CAN ISSN 0840-5220) 8822
Drinking Water Surveillance Program Annual Report. Tecumseh Water Treatment Plant (CAN ISSN 1183-6210) 8822
Drinking Water Surveillance Program Annual Report. Thamesville Water Supply System (CAN ISSN 0843-8374) 8822
Drinking Water Surveillance Program Annual Report. Thunder Bay (Bare Point) Water Treatment Plant (CAN ISSN 0843-8285) 8822
Drinking Water Surveillance Program Annual Report. Thunder Bay (Loch Lomond) Water Treatment Plant (CAN ISSN 0843-834X) 8822
Drinking Water Surveillance Program Annual Report. Trenton Water Treatment Plant (CAN ISSN 1180-212X) 8822
Drinking Water Surveillance Program Annual Report. Union Water Treatment Plant (CAN ISSN 0840-5115) 8823
Drinking Water Surveillance Program Annual Report. Wallaceburg Water Treatment Plant (CAN ISSN 0839-9018) 8823
Drinking Water Surveillance Program Annual Report. Walpole Island Water Treatment Plant (CAN ISSN 0839-8917) 8823
Drinking Water Surveillance Program Annual Report. Welland Water Supply System (CAN ISSN 1180-2103) 8823
Drinking Water Surveillance Program Annual Report. Windsor Water Treatment Plant (CAN ISSN 0839-895X) 8823
Drinks (CHE) 602
Drinks (USA) 602
• Drinks Bulletin (GBR ISSN 1477-8017) 602
• The Drinks Business (GBR ISSN 1477-7495) 602
Drinks Business Brands Report see Brands Report 600
Drinks Buyer Americas see The Drinks Network 602
Drinks Buyer Asia-Pacific see The Drinks Network 602
Drinks Buyer Europe see The Drinks Network 602
Drinks Industry Ireland (IRL) 602
• Drinks International (GBR ISSN 0012-625X) 602
Drinks International Bulletin see Drinks Bulletin 602
Drinks Market see Key Note Market Review: Drinks Market 606
The Drinks Network (GBR ISSN 1752-0983) 602
Drinks Retailing and Marketing see D R A M 1983
Drinks Slijtersvakblad (NLD ISSN 1876-4258) 603
• Drip Investor (USA ISSN 1093-2518) 1621
Driscoll Housing Law & Precedents see Housing Law & Precedents 7593
Drita (ALB) 5214
Dritte Welt Materialien (DEU) 4138
Driva (NOR) 3922
Driva Eget (SWE ISSN 2000-0049) 1740
Drive! (IRL ISSN 1393-8576) 8577
Drive (USA) 5070
Drive! (USA) 8577
Drive America (USA ISSN 1534-5726) 8699
† Drive and Control (DEU ISSN 0939-8007) 8951
Drive Ford Scene International (DEU) 8577
Drive-In see Herald Express 3866
Drive On (GBR ISSN 1461-9423) 8495
Drive Performance (USA) 8578
Drive System Technique see Chuandong Jishu 3184
† Drive und Control (DEU ISSN 0939-7663) 8951
▼ Driven (FRA ISSN 1957-4223) 8578
Driver (NZL ISSN 1175-7388) 8578
▼ Driver and Traffic Safety Briefing (USA ISSN 1939-8476) 8630
Driver Letter (USA) 8495
Driver's World see Jiashi Yuan 8587
Drives and Controls (GBR ISSN 0950-5490) 3361
Drives & Motion (DEU ISSN 1610-9864) 8420
Driving (GBR ISSN 0265-7716) 8578
Driving Costs (CAN) 8578
Driving Force see America's Driving Force 8668
Driving Instructor (GBR ISSN 0265-8747) 8578
Driving Instructor's Manual (GBR) 8578
Driving Magazine see Driving 8578
Driving Radio Control Canada (CAN ISSN 1712-5707) 4334
Driving Under the Influence Report (California Ed.) see The D U I Report (California Ed.) 2650
Driving Under the Influence Report (Pennsylvania Ed.) see The D U I Report (Pennsylvania Ed.) 2650
Driving While Intoxicated Journal: Law & Science see D W I Journal: Law & Science 4654
An Drochaid/Bridge (CAN ISSN 0703-1491) 3530
Droemhem & Traedgaard (SWE ISSN 1652-8824) 4538
Droemmefangeren see Droemmefanger'n 4215
Droemmefanger'n (NOR ISSN 0809-9774) 4215
Droemmen om Elin (SWE ISSN 0283-636X) 1093
Droemskrinet (SWE ISSN 0283-6750) 5286
As Drogas em Destaque see Drugs in Focus 2693
Las Drogas en el Punto de Mira see Drugs in Focus 2693
Drogen im Blickpunkt see Drugs in Focus 2693
Drogerie Journal (AUT) 6833
Drogerie & Parfuemerie (DEU ISSN 0945-4500) 6833
Drogerie Waren Zeitung see D W Z - D D Z 6832
Drogerie Waren Zeitung - Deutsche Drogisten Zeitung see D W Z - D D Z 6832
Drogheda Independent (IRL ISSN 0791-699X) 3892
➤ Drogi i Mosty (POL ISSN 1643-1618) 3265
Drogisten Associatie Leve je Lijf Blad see D A Leve je Lijf Blad 6832
Drogisten Associatie Magazine see D A Leve je Lijf Blad 6832

10214 DUANKUAI YOUQITIAN ULRICH'S PERIODICALS

➤ Duankuai Youqitian/Fault-Block Oil & Gas Field (CHN ISSN 1005-8907) **6767**
Duanpian Xiaoshuo/Short Stories (CHN ISSN 1003-1561) **5286**
• Duanya Jishu/Forging & Stamping Technology (CHN ISSN 1000-3940) **6310**
Duanya Jixie/Metalforming Machine Tools *see* Duanya Zhuangbei yu Zhizao Jishu **5451**
• Duanya Zhuangbei yu Zhizao Jishu/China Metalforming Equipment & Manufacturing Technology (CHN ISSN 1672-0121) **5451**
• Duazary (COL) **5607**
• Dub Magazine (USA ISSN 1536-3562) **8578**
Dub Missive (USA ISSN 1072-8686) **6563**
Dubai External Trade Statistics/Ihsa'iyyat Dubai lil-Tijarah al-Kharijiyyah (UAE) **1225**
Dubai. Government of Dubai. Official Gazette *see* Dubai. Hukumat Dubai. Al-Jaridah al-Rasmiyyah **7434**
Dubai. Hukumat Dubai. Al-Jaridah al-Rasmiyyah/Dubai. Government of Dubai. Official Gazette (UAE) **7434**
Dubai International Airport *see* Matar Dubai al-Dawli **8733**
Dubao Cankao/Background of World News (CHN ISSN 1009-4407) **3824**
Dubfly (IRL) **2685**
Dublin City University Business School Research Papers *see* D C U B S Research Papers **1089**
Dublin Historical Record (IRL ISSN 0012-6861) **4215**
Dublin Institute for Advanced Studies. Communications. Series A (IRL ISSN 0070-7414) **7010**
Dublin Institute for Advanced Studies. Communications. Series D *see* Dublin Institute for Advanced Studies. School of Cosmic Physics. Geophysical Bulletin **2780**
Dublin Institute for Advanced Studies. School of Cosmic Physics. Geophysical Bulletin (IRL ISSN 0070-7422) **2780**
Dublin Institute of Technology Independent *see* D I T Independent **2977**
Dublin Life (USA) **5070**
Dublin Port and Docks Yearbook (IRL) **8643**
➤ Dublin Seminar for New England Folklife. Annual Proceedings (USA ISSN 0888-3165) **3616**
• ➤ Dublin University Law Journal (IRL ISSN 0332-3250) **4661**
• The Dubliner (IRL ISSN 1649-0428) **3892**
Dublin's Evening Classes (IRL ISSN 0791-7392) **2940**
Dublin's Motor Trader (IRL ISSN 1649-6361) **8578**
Dubrovnik (HRV ISSN 0353-8559) **5286**
• Dubrovnik Annals (HRV ISSN 1331-3878) **4215**
Dubuque Leader (USA ISSN 0012-6918) **1676**
Duca Post (CAN ISSN 0012-6934) **1336**
Ducas (USA ISSN 0196-7819) **4216**
▼ Duck Out (NLD ISSN 1875-1970) **8227**
Duck Soup (USA) **5286**
Duckburg Times (USA ISSN 0887-2155) **4334**
Ducks Unlimited (USA ISSN 0012-6950) **2609**
Ducks Unlimited de Mexico, A.C. *see* D U M A C **3413**
• Duckworks Magazine (USA) **8275**
Ductile Iron Pipe News (USA ISSN 1071-0469) **4118**
• Ductus (NOR ISSN 1504-0895) **5785**
Dude (USA ISSN 1521-8686) **6288**
Dude Ranch Vacations & Horseback Adventures (USA ISSN 1546-2072) **8699**
Dude Rancher - Directory (USA ISSN 1073-8533) **8699**
Due Diligence & Risk Management (GBR ISSN 1469-3844) **4661**
Due Diligence Law & Practice (GBR) **4661**
† Due Ruote (ITA ISSN 1121-5534) **8951**
Due South (GBR) **534**
† Duel Masters (SWE ISSN 1652-9758) **8951**
† Duel Masters Magazin (DEU) **8951**
• The Duelist (USA ISSN 1082-8621) **8170**
Duelmasters *see* Duel Masters **8951**
Duelul Mintii (ROM ISSN 1224-3957) **2187**
Duemila *see* 2000 Rivista Europea **4281**
Duemila (NLD ISSN 1385-1489) **8578**
Duenn- und Dickschichttechnik *see* Informationsdienst F I Z Technik. Duenn- und Dickschichttechnik **3116**
Duerrnberg-Forschungen (DEU ISSN 1437-8841) **391**
Duesseldorfer Amtsblatt (DEU ISSN 0012-7019) **7491**
Duesseldorfer Arbeiten zur Geschichte der Medizin (DEU ISSN 0419-800X) **5607**
Duesseldorfer Beitraege aus Anglistik und Amerikanistik *see* Beitraege aus Anglistik und Amerikanistik **5261**
Duesseldorfer Drachen-Post (DEU) **3824**
Duesseldorfer Familienkunde (DEU ISSN 0935-2503) **3764**
Duesseldorfer Hefte (DEU ISSN 0012-7027) **3846**
Duesseldorfer Jahrbuch (DEU ISSN 0342-0019) **4216**
Duesseldorfer Schriften zum Energie- und Kartellrecht (DEU) **3127**
Duesseldorfer Uni-Zeitung (DEU ISSN 0937-3780) **2282**
Duffle Bag (USA) **2265**
Dufu Academic Research Journal *see* Dufu Yanjiu Xuekan **5214**
• Dufu Yanjiu Xuekan/Dufu Academic Research Journal (CHN ISSN 1003-5702) **5214**
Dugandia (COL ISSN 0121-3199) **7851**
Dugdale Society. Occasional Papers (GBR ISSN 0306-3364) **5286**
• Dugesiana (MEX ISSN 1028-3420) **843**
Dugnad (Oslo) *see* Tidsskrift for Kulturforskning **358**
Duhui Jiaren *see* Citta Bella **8855**
DuikMagazine (NLD ISSN 1572-1868) **8170**
Duiken (NLD ISSN 0923-7607) **8311**
• Duilian - Minjian Duilian Gushi/Antithetical Couplet - Folk Stories about Antithetical Couplet (CHN ISSN 1004-1427) **5286**
Duin (NLD ISSN 0168-7948) **2609**
Der Duisburger (DEU) **3846**
Duisburger Beitraege zur Arbeitspsychologie (DEU ISSN 1614-936X) **7353**
Duisburger Journal (DEU ISSN 0343-3277) **4216**
Duisburger Studien (DEU) **6915**
Duitse Kroniek *see* Deutsche Chronik **5284**
Duiwai Dachuanbo/International Communication (CHN ISSN 1671-8038) **2319**
Duiwai Jingji Maoyi/Journal of Foreign Economics and Trade (CHN) **1562**
Duiwai Jingji Maoyi Daxue Xuebao/University of International Business and Economics. Journal *see* Guoji Shangwu - Duiwai Jingji Maoyi Daxue Xuebao **1568**
Duiwai Jingmao/International Economics and Trade (CHN) **1562**
• Duiwai Jingmao Shiwu/Practice in Foreign Economic Relations and Trade (CHN ISSN 1003-5559) **1562**
Dujia Luyou (CHN ISSN 1672-7517) **8699**
Duke Endowment. Annual Report (USA ISSN 0419-8050) **4450**
Duke Endowment. Issues (USA) **4450**
• Duke Environmental Law & Policy Forum (USA ISSN 1064-3958) **4661**
• Duke Gifted Letter (USA ISSN 1530-8774) **2843**
• Duke Journal of Comparative and International Law (USA ISSN 1053-6736) **4923**
• Duke Journal of Constitutional Law & Public Policy (USA ISSN 1937-9439) **7434**
• Duke Journal of Gender Law & Policy (USA ISSN 1090-1043) **7205**
• Duke Law & Technology Review (USA) **4661**
• ➤ Duke Law Journal (USA ISSN 0012-7086) **4661**
• ➤ Duke Mathematical Journal (USA ISSN 0012-7094) **5484**
The Duke Series in Child Development & Public Policy (USA) **2150**
Duke University Libraries (USA ISSN 0895-4909) **5007**
Dukes County Intelligencer (USA ISSN 0418-1379) **4291**
Dukhovna Kultura (BGR) **7704**
Dukhovno-Nravstvennoe Vospitanie (RUS) **7704**
Dulcelandia (MEX) **3673**
Dulces Noticias ... y Algo Mas (ESP ISSN 1134-5640) **3673**
Dulcimer Players News (USA ISSN 0098-3527) **6563**
Dulcypas (ESP ISSN 0212-7725) **3673**
• Dull Men's Club (USA) **6288**
Dulraen Malefni (ISL ISSN 1670-5270) **6741**
Duluth Area Chamber of Commerce Official Business & Community Guide (USA) **1401**
• Duluthian (USA ISSN 0012-7116) **1401**
Duma (RUS) **3935**
Dumbarton and Vale of Leven Reporter (GBR ISSN 1356-8647) **3864**
Dumbarton Oaks Conference Proceedings (USA) **391**
• Dumbarton Oaks Papers (USA ISSN 0070-7546) **391**
Dumbarton Oaks Studies (USA ISSN 0070-7554) **391**
Dumbarton Oaks Texts (USA ISSN 0070-7562) **4138**
Dumbo (BGR) **2187**
Dumbo (HUN ISSN 1215-7163) **2187**
Dumbo Feather *see* Dumbo Feather, Pass it On **5286**
• Dumbo Feather, Pass it On (AUS ISSN 1449-6011) **5286**
Dumjahn's Jahrbuch fuer Eisenbahnliteratur (DEU ISSN 0936-3475) **8616**
• Dummies Daily America Online Newsletter (USA) **2555**
• Dummies Daily Computing Basics Newsletter (USA) **2417**
• Dummies Daily FrontPage Newsletter (USA) **2555**
• Dummies Daily Internet Search Tips Newsletter (USA) **2555**
• Dummies Daily Internet Tips Newsletter (USA) **2555**
• Dummies Daily Microsoft Excel 97 Newsletter (USA) **2589**
• Dummies Daily Microsoft Word 97 Newsletter (USA) **2601**
• Dummies Daily Nerd Word of the Day Newsletter (USA) **2601**
• Dummies Daily Online Shopping Tips Newsletter (USA) **2555**
• Dummies Daily Outlook Express Newsletter (USA) **2555**
• Dummies Daily Quicken Newsletter (USA) **1336**
• Dummies Daily Web After Five: Reviews Newsletter (USA) **2555**
• Dummies Daily Windows Newsletter (USA) **2589**
• Dummy (Online) (GBR) **6563**
Dummy (Print) *see* Dummy (Online) **6563**
Dumortiera (BEL ISSN 0251-1134) **786**
Dun & Bradstreet Business Rankings *see* D & B Business Rankings **1981**
Dun & Bradstreet Business Register. Bedfordshire, Hertfordshire *see* D & B Business Register. Bedfordshire, Hertfordshire **1089**
Dun & Bradstreet Business Register. Birmingham *see* D & B Business Register. Birmingham **1981**
Dun & Bradstreet Business Register. Cheshire *see* D & B Business Register. Cheshire **1981**
Dun & Bradstreet Business Register. Derbyshire, Staffordshire *see* D & B Business Register. Derbyshire, Staffordshire **1982**
Dun & Bradstreet Business Register. Devon, Cornwall, Isles of Scilly, Channel Isles *see* D & B Business Register. Devon, Cornwall, Isles of Scilly, Channel Isles **1982**
Dun & Bradstreet Business Register. Dublin *see* D & B Business Register. Dublin **1982**
Dun & Bradstreet Business Register. Durham, Cleveland, North Yorkshire *see* D & B Business Register. Durham, Cleveland, North Yorkshire **1982**
Dun & Bradstreet Business Register. East & West Sussex *see* D & B Business Register. East & West Sussex **1982**
Dun & Bradstreet Business Register. Edinburgh & North of Scotland *see* D & B Business Register. Edinburgh & North of Scotland **1982**
Dun & Bradstreet Business Register. Essex *see* D & B Business Register. Essex **1982**
Dun & Bradstreet Business Register. Glasgow & South of Scotland *see* D & B Business Register. Glasgow & South of Scotland **1982**
Dun & Bradstreet Business Register. Greater Manchester & Merseyside *see* D & B Business Register. Greater Manchester & Merseyside **1982**
Dun & Bradstreet Business Register. Hampshire, Isle of Wright *see* D & B Business Register. Hampshire, Isle of Wright **1982**
Dun & Bradstreet Business Register. Kent *see* D & B Business Register. Kent **1982**
Dun & Bradstreet Business Register. Lancashire *see* D & B Business Register. Lancashire **1982**
Dun & Bradstreet Business Register. Leicestershire, Northamptonshire, Cambridgeshire *see* D & B Business Register. Leicestershire, Northamptonshire, Cambridgeshire **1982**
Dun & Bradstreet Business Register. Leinster *see* D & B Business Register. Leinster **1982**
Dun & Bradstreet Business Register. London. W C, E C, E, N *see* D & B Business Register. London. W C, E C, E, N **1982**
Dun & Bradstreet Business Register. Middlesex, Buckinghamshire *see* D & B Business Register. Middlesex, Buckinghamshire **1982**
Dun & Bradstreet Business Register. Munster, Connaught & Border Regions *see* D & B Business Register. Munster, Connaught & Border Regions **1982**
Dun & Bradstreet Business Register. Norfolk, Suffolk *see* D & B Business Register. Norfolk, Suffolk **1982**
Dun & Bradstreet Business Register. Northern Ireland *see* D & B Business Register. Northern Ireland **1982**
Dun & Bradstreet Business Register. Northumberland, Tyne & Wear, Cumbria, Isle of Man *see* D & B Business Register. Northumberland, Tyne & Wear, Cumbria, Isle of Man **1982**
Dun & Bradstreet Business Register. Nottinghamshire, Lincolnshire *see* D & B Business Register. Nottinghamshire, Lincolnshire **1982**
Dun & Bradstreet Business Register. Oxfordshire, Berkshire, Wiltshire *see* D & B Business Register. Oxfordshire, Berkshire, Wiltshire **1982**
Dun & Bradstreet Business Register. Shropshire, Hereford & Worcester, Gloucestershire *see* D & B Business Register. Shropshire, Hereford & Worcester, Gloucestershire **1982**
Dun & Bradstreet Business Register. Somerset, Dorset, Bath & Bristol *see* D & B Business Register. Somerset, Dorset, Bath & Bristol **1983**
Dun & Bradstreet Business Register. South Yorkshire, East Yorkshire & North East Lincolnshire *see* D & B Business Register. South Yorkshire, East Yorkshire & North East Lincolnshire **1983**
Dun & Bradstreet Business Register. Surrey *see* D & B Business Register. Surrey **1983**
Dun & Bradstreet Business Register. Wales *see* D & B Business Register. Wales **1983**
Dun & Bradstreet Business Register. West Midlands, Warwickshire *see* D & B Business Register. West Midlands, Warwickshire **1983**
Dun & Bradstreet Business Register. West Yorkshire *see* D & B Business Register. West Yorkshire **1983**
Dun & Bradstreet Consultants Directory *see* D & B Consultants Directory **1983**
Dun and Bradstreet Directory of Service Companies *see* D & B Directory of Service Companies **1983**
Dun & Bradstreet Directory of Service Companies *see* D & B Directory of Service Companies **1983**
Dun & Bradstreet Employment Opportunities Directory - Career Guide *see* D & B Employment Opportunities Directory - Career Guide **6696**
Dun & Bradstreet Europa *see* D & B Europa **1812**
Dun & Bradstreet Looks at Business (USA) **1478**
Dun & Bradstreet Million Dollar Directory *see* D & B Million Dollar Directory **1983**
Dun & Bradstreet Monthly Business Failures (USA ISSN 1082-1937) **1478**
Dun & Bradstreet, North West, West Business Register. London. N W, W *see* D & B Business Register. London. N W, W **1982**
Dun & Bradstreet Reference Book of Corporate Managements *see* D & B Reference Book of Corporate Managements **1737**
Dun & Bradstreet Regional Business Directory. Kansas City Area *see* D & B's Regional Business Directory. Kansas City Area **1983**
Dun and Bradstreet - Seyd's Register *see* Dun & Bradstreet Standard Register **1989**
Dun & Bradstreet, South West, South East Business Register. London. S W, S E *see* D & B Business Register. London. S W, S E **1982**
Dun & Bradstreet Standard Register (USA) **1989**
Dun & Bradstreet's Guide to Your Investments (Year) *see* Dunnan's Guide to Your Investments **1621**
Dun & Bradstreet's Key Business Ratios (USA ISSN 0270-7713) **1093**
Dun and Bradstreet's Regional Business Directory. Kansas City Area *see* D & B's Regional Business Directory. Kansas City Area **1983**
"Dunarea de Jos" University of Galati. Annals. Fascicle IX. Metallurgy and Material Science *see* Universitatea "Dunarea de Jos" din Galati. Analele. Fascicula IX. Metalurgie si Stiinta Materialelor **6336**
Dunarea de Jos University of Galati. Annals. Fascicle X. Applied Mechanics *see* Universitatea "Dunarea de Jos" din Galati. Analele. Fascicula X. Mecanica Aplicata **3359**
Dunaujvarosi Hirlap (HUN ISSN 1219-8153) **3876**
Duncan's Radio Market Guide (USA ISSN 0743-7498) **1989**
Dundalk Argus (IRL ISSN 0791-6981) **3892**
Dundalk Democrat (IRL) **3892**
Dundalk Democrat and People's Journal *see* Dundalk Democrat **3892**
Dundas Star *see* Dundas Star News **3809**
Dundas Star Journal *see* Dundas Star News **3809**
• Dundas Star News (CAN ISSN 1707-1364) **3809**
Dundee and Tayside Chamber of Commerce and Industry. Buyer's Guide and Trade Directory (GBR) **1401**
▼ Dundrum Gazette (IRL ISSN 1649-9700) **3892**
Dundrum Magazine (IRL ISSN 1649-9077) **3892**
Dune Buggies & Hot V Ws (USA ISSN 0012-7132) **8578**
▼ Dune Magazine (USA ISSN 1936-3982) **5070**
Dunedin Family Times (NZL ISSN 1176-7952) **2151**
Dungarvan Leader (IRL) **3892**
Dungarvan Observer (IRL) **3892**
Dunhill Liability Loss Bulletin (CAN ISSN 1495-0464) **4501**
Dunhill Personal Injury & Death Bulletin (CAN) **4501**
Dunhuang Studies *see* Dunhuang Yanjiu **391**
• Dunhuang Yanjiu/Dunhuang Studies (CHN ISSN 1000-4106) **391**
† Dunia (ESP ISSN 1130-409X) **8951**
Dunia Wanita (IDN ISSN 0852-5900) **8859**
Dunkerque Expansion (FRA ISSN 0243-2633) **1401**
Dunlap - Hanna Pennsylvania Forms (USA) **4662**
Dunmow Broadcast & District Advertiser (GBR) **3864**
Dunnan's Guide to Your Investments (USA ISSN 1526-5919) **1621**
• Dunnell Minnesota Digest (USA) **4662**
• The Dunnville Chronicle (CAN ISSN 0841-310X) **3809**
• Dunoon Observer & Argyllshire Standard (GBR) **3864**
Dunrobin Piper (USA ISSN 0741-5273) **3530**
Dun's Business Rankings *see* D & B Business Rankings **1981**
Dun's Industrial Guide - The Metalworking Directory (USA ISSN 0278-8799) **1989**
Dun's Regional Business Directory. Alabama Area (USA ISSN 1061-0723) **1989**
Dun's Regional Business Directory. Atlanta Area (USA ISSN 1051-3876) **1989**
Dun's Regional Business Directory. Boston Area (USA ISSN 1051-1326) **1989**
Dun's Regional Business Directory. Central Indiana Area (USA ISSN 1061-1126) **1989**
Dun's Regional Business Directory. Central Pennsylvania Area (USA ISSN 1061-0820) **1989**
Dun's Regional Business Directory. Charlotte - Greensboro Area (USA ISSN 1061-1134) **1989**
Dun's Regional Business Directory. Chicago Metropolitan Area (USA ISSN 1061-074X) **1989**
Dun's Regional Business Directory. Chicago Suburban Area (USA ISSN 1051-161X) **1989**
Dun's Regional Business Directory. Cincinnati Area (USA ISSN 1051-1288) **1989**
Dun's Regional Business Directory. Cleveland (USA ISSN 1051-1083) **1989**
Dun's Regional Business Directory. Columbus Area (USA ISSN 1061-0758) **1989**
Dun's Regional Business Directory. Dallas - Fort Worth Area (USA ISSN 1051-1180) **1989**
Dun's Regional Business Directory. Denver Area (USA ISSN 1061-1142) **1989**
Dun's Regional Business Directory. Detroit (USA ISSN 1051-1628) **1989**

Title

Title

Title

E J H P (German Edition) *see* E J H P Practice **6837**
E J H P Practice (European Journal of Hospital Pharmacy) (BEL ISSN 1781-9989) **6837**
E J H P Science (European Journal of Hospital Pharmacy) (BEL ISSN 1781-7595) **6837**
• ➤ e J I F C C (Electronic Journal of the International Federation of Clinical Chemistry and Laboratory Medicine) (ITA) **2060**
The e J I H *see* Electronic Journal of International History **4138**
E J I L *see* European Journal of International Law **4925**
E J I M *see* European Journal of Innovation Management **1742**
E J I R *see* European Journal of International Relations **7234**
E J I S *see* European Journal of Information Systems **2543**
E J I S D C *see* The Electronic Journal of Information Systems in Developing Countries **2417**
E J M *see* European Journal of Marketing **1816**
• ➤ e j m p & e p (The European Journal of Mineral Processing and Environmental Protection) (TUR ISSN 1303-0868) **3366**
E J M S *see* European Journal of Mass Spectrometry **2100**
E J N *see* European Journal of Neuroscience **6139**
E J O B A *see* European Journal of Behavior Analysis **7355**
E J O P *see* European Journal of Oncology Pharmacy **6019**
e J O V *see* Electronic Journal of Organizational Virtualness **2556**
E J P *see* European Journal of Philosophy **6918**
E J P *see* European Journal of Phycology **787**
E J P *see* European Journal of Pain **5611**
E J P C E *see* Eurasian Journal of Physics and Chemistry Education **2855**
E.J.P.D. *see* European Journal of Paediatric Dentistry **5844**
E J P E *see* Erasmus Journal for Philosophy and Economics **1105**
E J P H *see* European Journal of Public Health **7516**
E J P R *see* European Journal of Political Research **7134**
E J P R D *see* European Journal of Prosthodontics and Restorative Dentistry **5844**
E J S E *see* Electronic Journal of Structural Engineering **3266**
E J S O *see* European Journal of Surgical Oncology **6019**
E J S S *see* European Journal of Soil Science **229**
E J S S *see* European Journal of Sport Science **8171**
E J S S M *see* Electronic Journal of Severe Storms Metereology **6352**
E J T E *see* European Journal of Teacher Education **2855**
• ➤ E J V E S Extra (European Journal of Vascular and Endovascular Surgery) (GBR ISSN 1533-3167) **5785**
E J W *see* Econ Journal Watch **1539**
E-Jay (GBR) **6563**
E-journal - C I G R *see* Agricultural Engineering International **83**
• ➤ E - Journal of Applied Psychology (AUS ISSN 1832-7931) **7353**
• E-Journal of Chemistry (IND ISSN 0973-4945) **2060**
E-Journal of Instructional Science and Technology *see* Australasian Journal of Educational Technology (Online) **3051**
• ➤ E-Journal of Land and Water (AUS ISSN 1832-5149) **3187**
E-Journal of Music in China *see* Journal of Music in China **6580**
• E-Journal of Nondestructive Testing & Ultrasonics (DEU ISSN 1435-4934) **3343**
• E Journal of Organizational Learning and Leadership (USA) **1740**
• ➤ E-journal of Portuguese History (PRT ISSN 1645-6432) **4174**
• ➤ E - Journal of Reservoir Engineering (CAN ISSN 1715-4677) **3242**
• e-Journal of Science & Technology (GRC ISSN 1790-5613) **7852**
• e-Journal of Soft Materials (JPN ISSN 1349-7308) **7824**
• E-Journal of Solidarity, Sustainability, and Nonviolence (USA) **7960**
• The E-Journal of Student Research (USA) **2843**
• e-Journal of Surface Science and Nanotechnology (JPN ISSN 1348-0391) **7010**
• ➤ E-Journal of Teaching and Learning in Diverse Settings (USA ISSN 1545-9055) **2843**
E-journal of the American Hungarian Educators Association *see* American Hungarian Educators Association. E-journal **2826**
• ➤ E-Journal on Hong Kong Cultural and Social Studies (HKG) **548**
• e-Journal Philosophie der Psychologie (AUT ISSN 1813-7784) **6915**
• E-justice (ESP ISSN 1988-7590) **4662**
• E K (BGR ISSN 1310-2028) **3805**
E K B B *see* The Essential Kitchen Bathroom Bedroom Magazine **4539**
• E K C (Online Edition) (Explore Kansas City) (USA) **5070**
E K C (Print Edition) *see* E K C (Online Edition) **5070**
E K - Experte Aktuell (Einkaufs) (DEU ISSN 1867-0083) **1815**
E K R Magazine (Elisabeth Kuebler-Ross) (NLD ISSN 1871-4315) **7353**
E K R Nieuws *see* E K R Magazine **7353**
E K U *see* Egitimde Kuram ve Uygulama **2852**
• ➤ E-Keltoi (USA ISSN 1540-4889) **7735**
E L *see* The Electronic Library **5061**
E L *see* Educational Leadership **3059**
E L A *see* Mid-Atlantic Executive Legal Adviser **4876**
E L A Briefing (Employment Lawyers Association) (GBR) **4662**
E L A Brooklyn - Belvedere Comet (USA) **3531**
E L A Notes (Education Law Association) (USA) **2843**
E L and P *see* Electric Light and Power **3302**
E L B W Umwelttechnik (Energie, Luft, Boden, Wasser) (AUT) **3415**
E L C A *see* Evangelical Lutheran Church in America (Year) **7756**
E L C A Scientific Journal/Al- Magallat al-'ilmiyyat li-l-Gam'iyyat al-Misriyyat li-Istshari al-Ridha'at al-Tabi'iyyat/Al- Majallat al-'ilmiyyat li-l-Jam'iyyat al-Misriyyat li-Istshari al-Ridha'at al-Tabi'iyyat (Egyptian Lactation Consultant Association) (EGY ISSN 1687-8388) **5989**
E L C A Yearbook *see* Evangelical Lutheran Church in America (Year) **7756**
• ➤ E L C V I A (Electronic Letters on Computer Vision and Image Analysis) (ESP ISSN 1577-5097) **2417**
E L D R *see* E L D R Magazine **4043**
▼ • E L D R Magazine (USA) **4043**
E L E X *see* I E I C E Electronics Express **2544**
E L G News (Education Librarians Group) (GBR ISSN 0267-3614) **5007**
• E L Gazette (English Language) (GBR ISSN 1368-2628) **5113**
• ➤ E L H (English Literary History) (USA ISSN 0013-8304) **5286**
➤ E L I A (Estudios de Linguistica Inglesa Aplicada) (ESP ISSN 1576-5059) **5113**
E L J *see* Energy Law Journal **4665**
E L J *see* Stanford Environmental Law Journal **4787**
E L J *see* New York University Environmental Law Journal **3456**
E L J *see* Brigham Young University Education and Law Journal **4632**
E L K *see* Studien zur Englischen Literatur- und Kulturwissenschaft **5380**
The E L M Bulletin *see* Advocate (Boston) **3401**
• E L M Magazine (ESP) **3531**
E L M R *see* Economic & Labour Market Review **1676**
E L P R *see* William & Mary Environmental Law and Policy Review **3475**
E L Q *see* Ecology Law Quarterly **4663**
E L Q *see* English Leadership Quarterly **3061**
E L R *see* Edinburgh Law Review **4924**
E L R *see* Environmental Law Reporter **3426**
E L R *see* U C L A Entertainment Law Review **4799**
E L R *see* Loyola of Los Angeles Entertainment Law Review **4726**
E L R R *see* The Economic and Labour Relations Review **1676**
E L S A Leiden Magazine (European Law Students' Association) (NLD ISSN 1573-6490) **4924**
• E L S A Selected Papers on European Law (European Law Students' Association) (BEL ISSN 1373-2196) **4662**
➤ E L S Monograph Series (English Literary Studies) (CAN ISSN 0829-7681) **5287**
E L SNews (GBR ISSN 1350-990X) **2447**
• ➤ E L T Journal (English Language Teaching) (GBR ISSN 0951-0893) **5113**
E L T Newsletter *see* C E L E A Journal **5102**
e - lab *see* Energy Futures **3131**
e - lab research reports *see* Energy Futures **3131**
• e-l@tina (ARG ISSN 1666-9606) **7960**
• E-Law (GBR ISSN 1475-7176) **4662**
E Law Murdoch *see* eLaw Journal **4663**
e-LC *see* Electronic Liquid Crystal Communications **2110**
• E-Leader (USA ISSN 1935-4800) **3531**
E-Leader Conference *see* E-Leader **3531**
E-Leader Leadership Conference *see* E-Leader **3531**
e-Learn Magazine *see* eLearn Magazine **2469**
• ➤ E-Learning (GBR ISSN 1741-8887) **3058**
• E.Learning Age (GBR ISSN 1474-5127) **1416**
E Learning Age *see* E.Learning Age **1416**
• ➤ E-Learning and Education (DEU ISSN 1860-7470) **2948**
• E-learning Brasil News (BRA ISSN 1678-0728) **2843**
• E-learning Papers (ESP ISSN 1887-1542) **2843**
E-Learning Research Reeks (NLD ISSN 1871-2703) **2417**
e-Legal History Review (ESP ISSN 1699-5317) **4662**
• E-letter on Systems, Control, & Signal Processing (USA) **2520**
e-Life *see* Newsweek e-Life **2565**
• ➤ E-Logos (CZE ISSN 1211-0442) **6915**
E M *see* Eletricidade Moderna **3306**
E M (Expertise Magazine) (NLD ISSN 1875-4236) **4501**
• E M (Environmental Manager) (USA ISSN 1088-9981) **3505**
E M A *see* Emergency Medicine Australasia (Print) **6059**
E M A Bulletin (Early Music America) (USA) **6563**
E M A - Elektrische Maschinen (DEU ISSN 0013-5445) **3301**
E M A Network (Engineers' and Managers' Association) (GBR) **3187**
E M A News (Environmental Management Association) (USA) **7514**
E M A P Monitor (Environmental Monitoring and Assessment Program) (USA) **3415**
E M A Reporter (Employment Management Association) (USA) **1676**
• E M A S (E-Mail Alert Service) (USA) **7639**
E M A Today (Employers Association Newsletter) *see* Today **8993**
E M & P *see* Electronic Materials and Packaging **3095**
E M B Magazine (Embroidery Monogram Business) (USA) **2246**
• ➤ The E M B O Journal (European Molecular Biology Organization) (GBR ISSN 0261-4189) **731**
▼ • ➤ E M B O Molecular Medicine (European Molecular Biology Organization) (GBR ISSN 1757-4676) **5607**
• ➤ E M B O Reports (European Molecular Biology Organization) (GBR ISSN 1469-221X) **866**
E M B Online *see* Evidence - Based Medicine **5612**
E M B R A P A - C N P F. Circular Tecnica *see* Empresa Brasileira de Pesquisa Agropecuaria. Centro Nacional de Pesquisa de Florestas. Circular Tecnica **3687**
E M B R A P A - C N P F. Documentos *see* Embrapa Florestas. Documentos **3687**
E M C *see* Electrical & Mechanical Contractor **3302**
E M C and Compliance Journal *see* The E M C Journal **3301**
E M C & Compliance Journal *see* The E M C Journal **3301**
E M C C *see* The Earthmover and Civil Contractor **3266**
E M C + Compliance Journal *see* The E M C Journal **3301**
• E M C Connect (USA) **2530**
• The E M C Journal (Electro Magnetic Compatibility) (GBR) **3301**
• ➤ E M C - Neurologie (Online) (Encyclopedie Medico Chirurgicale) (FRA ISSN 1778-6959) **6137**
E M C - Neurologie (Print) *see* E M C - Neurologie (Online) **6137**
• E M C - Psychiatrie (Online) (Encyclopedie Medico-Chirurgicale) (FRA) **6137**
E M C - Psychiatrie (Print) *see* E M C - Psychiatrie (Online) **6137**
E M D M *see* European Medical Device Manufacturer **4486**
E M Directory *see* Ethnic Minorities Directory **3532**
E M E *see* Explorations in Media Ecology **7964**
E M F Bulletin (USA) **3301**
E M F Critiques (Early Modern France) (USA) **5287**
E M F Health Report (Electric and Magnetic Field) (USA ISSN 1070-4027) **6676**
E M F: Studies in Early Modern France (Early Modern France) (USA ISSN 1064-5020) **5287**
E M I *see* Educational Media International **3059**
The E M I E Bulletin (Ethnic and Multicultural Information Exchange Round Table) (USA ISSN 0737-9021) **3531**
E M I S Datareviews *see* Electronic Materials Information Service Datareviews **3095**
E M I S E-Law Service (Egton Medical Information Systems) (GBR ISSN 1741-2544) **4950**
E M I S Personal Injury Service *see* Personal Injury Brief Update Law Journal **4840**
E M I S Processing Series (Electronic Materials Information Service) (GBR) **3301**
E M I S Property Service *see* Property Service **4762**
E M J *see* European Management Journal **1742**
E M J *see* Engineering Management Journal **3190**
E M J B *see* EuroMed Journal of Business **1106**
E M J - Environmental Manager's Journal (GBR ISSN 0964-6035) **3415**
E M J Online *see* Emergency Medicine Journal **6059**
E M L *see* Entertainment Marketing Letter **1815**
▼ • E M L A Laser Health Journal (European Medical Laser Association) (FIN ISSN 1796-8631) **5905**
E M L S *see* Early Modern Literary Studies **5421**
E M M E *see* International Journal of Multicultural Education **2870**
e m mittelstand *see* entscheider magazin mittelstand **1416**
• E M O T A - A E V P C Position Papers (European Mail Order and Distance Selling Trade Association) (BEL) **1815**
E M R *see* European Management Review **1743**
E M R O Technical Publication *see* E M R O Technical Publications Series **7514**
E M R O Technical Publications Series (Regional Office for the Eastern Mediterranean) (EGY ISSN 1020-0428) **7514**
E M S B *see* E P M Entertainment Marketing Sourcebook **1815**
E M S - Impulse (Evangelisches Missionswerk in Suedwestdeutschland e.V.) (DEU) **7755**
• E M S Insider (Emergency Medical Services) (USA ISSN 1081-4507) **6058**
E M S - Jahrbuch *see* E M S - Impulse **7755**
• E M S Magazine (Emergency Medical Services) (USA ISSN 1946-4967) **6058**
• E M S Management Journal (Emergency Medical Services) (USA ISSN 1547-8459) **7514**
• E M S Manager and Supervisor (Emergency Medical Service) (USA ISSN 1532-1576) **6058**
E M S P N *see* E M S Product News **7514**
• E M S Product News (USA ISSN 1935-1445) **7514**
E M T-Basic (Emergency Medical Technician) (USA ISSN 1930-6040) **5607**
E M T-Basic Exam *see* E M T-Basic **5607**
E M U *see* European Monetary Union **1107**
• E M U - The News Bulletin (European Monetary Union) (GBR ISSN 1465-3141) **1096**
E M Update *see* Environmental Management Update **3426**
E M W - Informationen (Evangelisches Missionswerk in Deutschland) (DEU ISSN 0175-7695) **7639**
E M W J *see* Early Modern Women **8895**
• E M X 95 (GBR) **1225**
• E-Magasinet EVAluering (DNK ISSN 1901-5593) **2843**
e Magazine (UAE) **1416**
E Magazine *see* E **3414**
E-Mail Alert Service *see* E M A S **7639**
E-Mail Maledicta (USA ISSN 1540-3882) **2555**
† • E-mail Noviny Bankovni Aktuality (CZE ISSN 1801-268X) **8952**
E-mail Noviny Byty a Nemovitosti (CZE ISSN 1803-7844) **7589**
• E-mail Noviny H R Servis pro Personalisty a Management (Human Resources) (CZE ISSN 1214-4541) **1859**
• E-mail Noviny Kalendar Seminaru (CZE ISSN 1801-5387) **1096**
E-mail Noviny Kalendar Seminaru, Kalendar Seminaru *see* E-mail Noviny Kalendar Seminaru **1096**
• E-mail Noviny Portal pro Skoly (CZE ISSN 1214-6161) **2844**
• E-mail Noviny pro Bezpecnost Prace a Pozarni Ochranu (CZE ISSN 1214-2352) **3576**
• E-mail Noviny pro Dane a Ucetnictvi (CZE ISSN 1213-6158) **1921**
• E-mail Noviny pro Ekologii a Zivotni Prostredi (CZE ISSN 1214-0473) **3415**
• E-mail Noviny pro Logistiku a Dopravu (CZE ISSN 1214-3073) **8495**
• E-mail Noviny pro Management Jakosti a Certifikaci Vyrobku (CZE ISSN 1214-0597) **1884**
• E-mail Noviny pro Mesta a Obce (CZE ISSN 1213-6344) **7435**
• E-mail Noviny pro Mezinarodni Ucetnictvi (CZE ISSN 1802-2049) **1287**
• E-mail Noviny pro Mzdove Ucetni a Personalisty (CZE ISSN 1213-6387) **1859**
• E-mail Noviny pro Podnikatele, Jednatele a Reditele (CZE ISSN 1213-6093) **1740**
• E-mail Noviny pro Stavebnictvi (CZE ISSN 1213-7200) **1005**
• E-mail Noviny pro Technicky Management (CZE ISSN 1213-8975) **1740**
• E-mail Noviny pro Ucetni v Neziskove Sfere (CZE ISSN 1213-6263) **1287**
• E-mail Noviny pro Uzivatele P C (Personal Computer) (CZE ISSN 1214-2360) **2576**
• E-mail Noviny pro Vyrobce a Prodejce Potravin (CZE ISSN 1214-3596) **3634**
• E-mail Noviny pro Zivnostniky a Drobne Podnikatele (CZE ISSN 1214-5564) **1959**
E-mail Noviny Zdravotnicke Listy (CZE ISSN 1213-6255) **5608**
E-MainStream *see* A W W A Streamlines **8817**
E-Mainstream *see* A W W A Mainstream **8927**
• e-media (AUT) **2555**
E Media Buyer's Guide *see* EMedia Buyer's Guide **2556**
e-Memoires de l'Academie Nationale de Chirurgie *see* Academie Nationale de Chirurgie. E-Memoires **6234**
• E-merge (CAN ISSN 1488-240X) **7231**
E-Merging Business (USA ISSN 1531-0612) **1959**
• E-mmerce (GBR ISSN 1469-0462) **1096**
• E-motion (GBR ISSN 1460-1281) **2685**
E N *see* Electronics News **3097**
• E N A (Economic News from Austria) (USA) **1478**
E N A. Encuesta Nacional Agropecuaria Provincia de Entre Rios (ARG ISSN 0329-8159) **106**
E N A S A R C O. Notiziario (Ente Nazionale Assistenza Agenti e Rappresentanti di Commercio) (ITA ISSN 0391-0121) **1096**
• E N A Update (Energy Networks Association) (AUS ISSN 1832-9004) **3127**
E N B News (English National Board for Nursing, Midwifery, and Health Visiting) *see* N M C News **5970**
• E N C Focus (Eisenhower National Clearinghouse for Mathematics and Science Education) (USA) **3058**
E N C Reporter (Engineering and Construction) (USA) **1621**
• The E N D S Directory (Environmental Data Services) (GBR) **3415**
E N D S Environment Daily *see* E N D S Europe Daily **3415**
• E N D S Europe Daily (Environmental Data Services) (GBR ISSN 1751-0376) **3415**
• The E N D S Report (Environmental Data Services) (GBR ISSN 0966-4076) **3415**

E N E A (Rapporti Tecnici) R T - AMB (Ente per le Nuove Tecnologie l'Energia e l'Ambiente (E N E A)) (ITA ISSN 1120-5555) 3166
E N E A (Rapporti Tecnici) R T - E R G (Ente per le Nuove Tecnologie l'Energia e l'Ambiente (E N E A)) (ITA ISSN 1124-7932) 3166
E N E A (Rapporti Tecnici) R T - GEN (ITA ISSN 1120-5571) 3166
E N E A (Rapporti Tecnici) R T - I N N (Ente per le Nuove Tecnologie l'Energia e l'Ambiente (E N E A)) (ITA ISSN 1120-558X) 3166
E N E A (Rapporti Tecnici) R T - NUCL (Ente per le Nuove Tecnologie l'Energia e l'Ambiente (E N E A)) (ITA ISSN 1120-5598) 3166
E N E A (Rapporti Tecnici) R T - STUDI (ITA ISSN 0393-6317) 3166
E N E A Report see Energia Ambiente e Innovazione 3128
• E - N F A I S Notes (USA) 6
E N F O Newsletter (THA ISSN 0125-1783) 3415
E N I Annual Report (Ente Nazionale Idrocarburi (E N I)) (ITA) 3127
• E N I Bulletin (Ecumenical News International) (CHE ISSN 1420-4126) 7639
E N I Bulletin. Edition Francaise see E N I Bulletin 7639
E N I S A Quarterly (European Network and Information Security Agency) (GRC ISSN 1830-3609) 2513
E N L B see Emergency Nurse Legal Bulletin 5957
E N P A T Newsletter (Environmental Potential Atlases) (ZAF) 3415
• E N P Gaceta (Escuela Nacional Preparatoria) (MEX ISSN 0186-176X) 2978
• E N R (Engineering News Record) (USA ISSN 0891-9526) 3265
• E N T (Online) (USA ISSN 1085-2395) 2589
E N T (Print) see E N T (Online) 2589
E N T Journal see Ear, Nose & Throat Journal 6079
• E N T News (Ear Nose and Throat) (GBR ISSN 1368-8944) 6079
E N T News Espanol see E N T News 6079
• E N Today (Ear Nose and Throat) (USA ISSN 1559-4939) 6079
E N V I S Centre on Environmental Biotechnology Newsletter and Abstract (Environmental Information System) (IND ISSN 0974-2476) 3415
▼ E N V I S Kerala (Environmental Information System) (IND ISSN 0973-9815) 3415
E N V I S Newsletter (Environmental Information System) (IND ISSN 0974-1364) 2732
E N V I S Newsletter (Howrah) (Environmental Information System) (IND ISSN 0974-1992) 3415
E N V L see Environmental Law 3425
E N W Info Stroom (Expertise Netwerk Waterveiligheid) (NLD ISSN 1872-0277) 8823
• E-News (New York) (USA) 4574
• E-News (Newton) (USA) 4409
E-Newsletter see The Griffin Report of Food Marketing 3645
E-Newsletter for Science and Technology (BEL ISSN 1784-0732) 7852
• E.nz Magazine (NZL ISSN 1175-2025) 3187
E O I see Equality, Diversity and Inclusion 8895
E O L see Ethnomusicology Online 6565
• The E O L Observer (Earth Observing Laboratory) (USA) 6352
E O M see Earth Observation Magazine (Online Edition) 2706
E O News (Elettronica Oggi) (ITA ISSN 0394-6681) 3094
E O S (Earth Observing System) (USA ISSN 0096-3941) 2780
E O S - E S D Technology (Electrical Overstress - Electrostatic Discharge) (USA) 8420
E O S O A A Option Alert see Michael Gray C P A's Option Alert 1639
e O T see Oral Tradition (Online) 3621
E O T R see The Exempt Organization Tax Review 1923
• E O W A News Alert (Equal Opportunity for Women in the Workplace Agency) (AUS ISSN 1833-6957) 8859
† e.Office (Year) (NZL ISSN 1175-1932) 8952
E P see Economic Society of Australia. Economic Papers 1101
E P see Europace 5786
E P (NZL) 8170
E P see Endocrine Pathology 5891
E P see Environmental Protection 3427
E P A Administrative Law Reporter (Environmental Protection Agency) (USA ISSN 1072-8635) 3415
E P A FastSearch (Environmental Protection Agency) (USA) 3415
• E P A Newsletter (European Photochemistry Association) (FRA ISSN 1011-4246) 2134
E P A Publications Bibliography Quarterly Abstracts Bulletin (Environmental Protection Agency) (USA ISSN 0196-0091) 3478
E P & C see Energy Procurement & Conservation 3133
E P & T (Electronic Products and Technology) (CAN ISSN 0708-4366) 3094
E P & T's Electrosource Product Reference Guide & Telephone Directory (Electronic Products and Technology) (CAN) 3094
E P C M J see A L I - A B A Estate Planning Course Materials Journal 4607
† • E P D A Focus (European Parkinson's Disease Association) (GBR ISSN 1726-0620) 8952
• E P D A Plus (European Parkinson's Disease Association) (GBR) 6137
• E P D Congress (Extraction and Processing Division) (USA ISSN 1079-7580) 6310
E P D Film (Evangelischen Publizistik) (DEU ISSN 0176-2044) 6496
E P D Medien (Evangelischer Pressedienst) (DEU ISSN 1439-6041) 2319
E P D Sozial (Evangelischer Pressedienst) (DEU ISSN 1612-2216) 7755
E P D Wochenspiegel. Ausgabe Ost (Evangelischer Pressedienst) (DEU) 7755
E P E (European Production Engineering) (DEU ISSN 0940-2470) 3376
➤ E P E Journal (European Power Electronics) (BEL ISSN 0939-8368) 3094
E P F Newsletter (Episcopal Peace Fellowship) (USA) 7755
E P I B see European Pharmaceutical Intelligence Bulletin 6838
E P I C Journal (Evidence Photographers International Council) (USA ISSN 1554-8317) 6966
E P I Centre see Epicentre 2853
E P I Information (Europaeischen Patentamt Institut) (DEU ISSN 1434-8853) 6749
E P I Newsletter see Immunization Newsletter 5759
• E P I - Nyt (DNK ISSN 1396-8599) 5608
E P I Vision (Epidemiologia) (CHL ISSN 0717-3911) 5608
E P J see European Polymer Journal 2123
E P J Direct see European Physical Journal Direct 7011
E P L see Europhysics Letters 7012
E P L B see Emergency Physician Legal Bulletin 5609
E P L I C see Employment Practices Liability Consultant 1679
E P L J see Environmental and Planning Law Journal 4666
➤ E P Lab Digest (Electrophysiology) (USA ISSN 1535-2226) 5785
• E P M Datafile (USA ISSN 1933-7388) 1815
• E P M Entertainment Marketing Sourcebook (USA ISSN 1539-7386) 1815
• E.P. Magazine (Extended Play) (GBR) 6563
E P Magazine see E P 8170
E P N see Electronic Product News 3096
E P N - European Pensions & Investment News see European Pensions News 4502
E P N France (Electronic Products News) (FRA ISSN 1957-5580) 3094
E P News (European Parliament) (LUX ISSN 0250-5754) 4924
E P O Applied Technology Series (European Patent Office) (NLD ISSN 1389-1057) 7058
E P O: Catalogo de Equipos para Oficina (Equipos para Oficina) (VEN) 1850
E P O M E X Serie Cientifica (MEX ISSN 0188-4840) 2803
E P P (Elektronik Produktion und Prueftechnik) (DEU ISSN 0943-0962) 3094
E P P Europe (Elektronik Produktion & Prueftechnik) (DEU ISSN 1618-5587) 3094
E P P I see European Promotional Products Industry 25
• E P P I C Information Sheet (Early Psychosis Prevention and Intervention Centre) (AUS ISSN 1326-2610) 6137
• ➤ E P P O Bulletin (European and Mediterranean Plant Protection Organization) (GBR ISSN 0250-8052) 228
A E P R see Asian Economic Policy Review 1438
E P R (Emory Political Review) (USA ISSN 1541-8057) 7131
E P R I-AP (Electric Power Research Institute) (USA) 3301
E P R I-CS (Electric Power Research Institute) (USA) 3301
E P R I-CU (Electric Power Research Institute) (USA) 3301
E P R I-EA (Electric Power Research Institute) (USA ISSN 1051-0532) 3301
E P R I-EL (Electric Power Research Institute) (USA ISSN 0276-0681) 3301
E P R I-EM (Electric Power Research Institute) (USA) 3301
E P R I-EN (Electric Power Research Institute) (USA) 3301
E P R I-ER (Electric Power Research Institute) (USA) 3301
E P R I-GS (Electric Power Research Institute) (USA) 3301
E P R I-NP (Electric Power Research Institute) (USA ISSN 1051-0478) 3301
E P R I-P (Electric Power Research Institute) (USA) 3301
E P R I-TR (Electric Power Research Institute) (USA) 3301
E P R U Papers (European Policy Research Unit) (GBR ISSN 0960-071X) 7131
E P S see El Pais Semanal 3953
E P S see European Political Science 7134
E P S 1 see Education Physique et Sportive au 1er Degre 8171
E P S I G News (Electronic Publishing Special Interest Group) (USA ISSN 1042-3737) 7560
E P V A Monthly Report (Eastern Paralyzed Veterans Association) (USA ISSN 0195-2293) 4065
E P V C see Early Popular Visual Culture 8099
• e-Pasaule (LVA ISSN 1407-7299) 2417
• ➤ e - Perimetron (GRC ISSN 1790-3769) 4004
† E - Permanence Bulletin (AUS ISSN 1833-0711) 8952
E-perspectives see Banking and Community Perspectives 1317
• ➤ e-Polymers (FRA ISSN 1618-7229) 3242
• E-Poradca (SVK ISSN 1336-8877) 1096
• ➤ e-Preservation Science (SVN ISSN 1854-3928) 3415
E.Punkt N R W (DEU ISSN 1616-9387) 2380
E Q (JPN) 5413
E Q see Educause Quarterly 2980
• E Q (New York) (Equalization) (USA ISSN 1050-7868) 8152
E Q (Three Lakes) (Equipment) (USA) 1005
• E Q Australia (Education Quarterly) (AUS ISSN 1320-2944) 3058
• E Q Dispatch (USA) 2844
E Q M see Enterprise Management Quarterly 1741
E Q R see Equestrian Retailer 8290
• E Q Review (USA) 2844
• E-quality (USA ISSN 1551-9325) 7639
E-Quality Matters (NLD ISSN 1389-9430) 8859
E R see The Economic Record 1100
E R see Employee Relations 1677
E R see European Review 7853
E R see Europe Review (London) 1992
E R (Elektrotehniska Revija) (SVN ISSN 1580-3589) 3301
E R A see Engine Reconditioner Australia 8579
E R A see Educational Research Abstracts Online 2932
E R A (Elektricitetens Rationella Anvaending) (SWE ISSN 0013-9939) 3157
E R A - A M S see Electronic Research Announcements in Mathematical Sciences 5486
E R A E see European Review of Agricultural Economics 197
• E R A Forum (Europaeische Rechtsakademie) (DEU ISSN 1612-3093) 4924
E R A News see EURALex 6838
E R A Report (Electrical Research Association) (GBR ISSN 0306-6215) 8420
E R A S M E see Etudes, Recherches, Actions en Sante Mentale en Europe 6139
E R A Technology News (Electrical Research Association) (GBR ISSN 0144-476X) 1815
E R B C see Education Review of Business Communication 1740
E R B E D U. Working Papers (European Regional Business and Economic Development Unit) (GBR ISSN 1369-2054) 1096
E R B Engineers News Brief (Engineers Registration Board) (TZA ISSN 1821-5092) 3187
• E R C E S Quarterly Review (European and International Resarch Group on Crime, Ethics and Social Philosophy) (FRA ISSN 1811-9123) 2651
• E R C I M News (European Research Consortium for Informatics and Mathematics) (FRA ISSN 0926-4981) 2350
E R C O F T A C Bulletin (European Research Community on Flow Turbulence and Combustion) (CHE) 7058
E R C O F T A C Series (European Research Community on Flow, Turbulence and Combustion) (NLD ISSN 1382-4309) 7058
E R C O Lichtbericht (DEU) 4556
• E R C Working Papers (Economic Research Center) (TUR ISSN 1302-5252) 1096
• E R D Technical Note Series (Economics and Research Department) (PHL ISSN 1655-5236) 1478
• E R D Working Paper Series (Economics and Research Department) (PHL ISSN 1655-5252) 1478
E R E see Educational Research and Evaluation 2851
• E R I C (Education Resource Information Center) (USA) 2932
E R I C Clearinghouse for Community Colleges Digest (Educational Resources Information Center) (USA) 2978
E R I C Identifier Authority List (Educational Resources Information Center) (USA ISSN 1062-0508) 2932
E R I C Information Bulletin (USA) 2978
E R I C on CD-ROM see E R I C 2932
E R i E see Evaluation and Research in Education 2855
† E R I S A and Benefits Law Journal (Employee Retirement Income Security Act) (USA ISSN 1068-3542) 8952
• E R I S A Litigation (Employee Retirement Income Security Act) (USA ISSN 1933-477X) 4662
• E R I S A Litigation Alert (Employee Retirement Income Security Act) (USA ISSN 1083-6268) 1676
• E R I S A Litigation Reporter (Employee Retirement Income Security Act) (USA ISSN 1055-5307) 2555
E R I S A Newsletter (Employee Retirement Income Security Act) (USA ISSN 8755-5379) 1676
E R I S A: The Law and the Code (Employee Retirement Income Security Act) (USA ISSN 1050-4230) 1676
E R J see European Rubber Journal 7824
E R L S see Environmental Responsibilities Law NSW 4667
• E R M (Electrical Retailing Magazine) (GBR ISSN 1474-2713) 3301
E R M (Elektro Retail Magazine) (NLD ISSN 0928-1525) 1815
E R N see Executive Recruiter News 1743
• E R News (Energy Resources) (USA) 3127
E R O see European Rail Outlook 8955
E R Online see Educational Researcher 2851
▼ • E R P Expert (Enterprise Resource Planning) (USA ISSN 1942-5104) 2417
E R P Management (Enterprise Resource Planning) (DEU ISSN 1860-6725) 1416
• E R P Software Selection Guide (CD-ROM) (Enterprise Resource Planning) (AUS ISSN 1445-0291) 2417
E R R see European Romantic Review 5293
E R R see Education Research and Reviews 2848
E R R see Educational Research and Reviews 2851
E R S Spectrum (Educational Research Service) (USA ISSN 0740-7874) 2844
E R T Directory (Year) (Electrical & Radio Trading) (GBR) 3094
• E R T Weekly (Electrical and Radio Trading) (GBR ISSN 1740-1615) 2358
e-radio (USA) 2555
e-response see Response (Los Angeles) 7728
▼ E-Revista (COL ISSN 2011-1827) 7852
• E-rural (CHL ISSN 0717-9898) 2844
E S see Engineered Systems 4118
E S A see Elektrohandwerke Sachsen-Anhalt 3305
• E S A A News (Online) (Energy Supply Association of Australia) (AUS ISSN 1832-9403) 3127
• E S A Annual Report (European Space Agency) (ITA ISSN 0258-025X) 53
E S A - B R (European Space Agency) (ITA ISSN 0250-1589) 53
• E S A Bulletin (European Space Agency) (ITA ISSN 0376-4265) 53
E S A Bulletin see Epiphyllum Bulletin 787
E S A Directory (Environmental Services Association) (GBR ISSN 1364-8861) 3505
E S A I M Actes de Congres see E S A I M: Proceedings 5485
• ➤ E S A I M: Control, Optimisation and Calculus of Variations/Controle, Optimisation et Calcul des Variations (European Series in Applied and Industrial Mathematics) (FRA ISSN 1292-8119) 5485
• ➤ E S A I M: Mathematical Modelling and Numerical Analysis/Modelisation Mathematique et Analyse Numerique (European Series in Applied and Industrial Mathematics) (FRA ISSN 0764-583X) 5485
E S A I M: P & S see E S A I M: Probability & Statistics 5485
E S A I M: Probabilites et Statistique see E S A I M: Probability & Statistics 5485
• E S A I M: Probability & Statistics/E S A I M: Probabilites et Statistique (European Series in Applied and Industrial Mathematics) (FRA ISSN 1292-8100) 5485
• ➤ E S A I M: Proceedings/E S A I M Actes de Congres (European Series in Applied and Industrial Mathematics) (FRA ISSN 1270-900X) 5485
• E S A Newsletter (Entomological Society of America) (USA ISSN 0273-7353) 843
• E S A R B I C A Journal (Eastern and Southern Africa Regional Branch International Council on Archives) (ZAF ISSN 0376-4753) 5007
E S A R B I C A Newsletter (Eastern and Southern Africa Regional Branch International Council on Archives) (ZAF) 5007
➤ E S A R D A Bulletin (European Safeguard Research and Development Association) (ITA ISSN 0392-3029) 7514
E S A Rapport Annuel see E S A Annual Report 53
• E S A - S P (European Space Agency - Special Publication) (ITA ISSN 0379-6566) 574
E S A - S T M see European Space Agency. Scientific and Technical Memoranda 53
E S A - S T R see European Space Agency. Scientific and Technical Reports 53
E S & D Database (Year) (Electricity Supply & Demand) (USA) 3157
E S B see Elektro- und Solarmobilbrief 8579
E S B see Economisch-Statistische Berichten 1481
• E S B N Online (Entrepreneur - Small Business Newsletter) (USA) 1096
• E S B Notizie (E.S.Burioni Ricerche Bibliografiche) (ITA ISSN 1592-288X) 5007
E.S.Burioni Ricerche Bibliografiche Notizie see E S B Notizie 5007
E S C A Voice (Exposition Service Contractors Association) (USA) 6279
E S C O L Proceedings (Eastern States Conference on Linguistics) (USA) 5113
E S C W A Population Bulletin (United Nations, Economic and Social Commission for Western Asia) (USA ISSN 1011-4793) 7282
• E S D Report Series (Ecologically Sustainable Development) (AUS ISSN 1448-3599) 3590
E S E see Estudios Sobre Educacion 2854
E S E M News (European Society for Engineering and Medicine) (BEL) 5608
• E S E Notes (Environmental Sciences and Engineering) (USA ISSN 0546-4552) 3415
• E S F Communications (European Science Foundation) (FRA ISSN 0293-082X) 7852

† E S H H S. European Society for the History of the Human Sciences (NLD ISSN 1387-0904) **8952**
• The E S H R E Monographs (European Society of Human Reproduction and Embryology) (GBR ISSN 1477-741X) **921**
E S I A M *see* Electronic Series on Integrated Assessment Modeling **8953**
E S I Africa (Electricity Supply Industry) (ZAF) **3127**
• E S I C Market (Escuela Superior de Gestion Comercial y Marketing) (ESP ISSN 0212-1867) **1740**
E S I C Press (Escuela Superior de Gestion Comercial y Marketing) (ESP) **1740**
E S I S Publication (European Structural Integrity Society) (GBR ISSN 1566-1369) **3377**
E S J *see* The Egyptian Statistical Journal **8367**
E S J *see* The Elementary School Journal **2852**
E S L Grammar Intermediate & Advanced (English as a Second Language) (USA ISSN 1938-6257) **5113**
E S L J *see* Entertainment and Sports Law Journal **4666**
• E S L Magazine (English as a Second Language) (USA ISSN 1098-6553) **5113**
E S L Writing Intermediate & Advanced (English as a Second Language) (USA ISSN 1938-6265) **5113**
E S M *see* Espana Seguridad Minera **6462**
E S M (Entertainment Struggle Magazine) (USA) **5070**
E S M Magazine *see* Employee Services Management **1741**
E S M News. M K E (Engineers and Scientists of Milwaukee Inc.) (USA) **3188**
E S M Q *see* European Sport Management Quarterly **8172**
• E S O A A Options Alert (USA) **1621**
E S O Astrophysics Symposia (European Southern Observatory) (DEU ISSN 1431-2433) **574**
• E S O M A R Directory (Year) (E S O M A R - The World Association of Research Professionals) (NLD) **1815**
E S O M A R - The World Association of Research Professionals Directory (Year) *see* E S O M A R Directory (Year) **1815**
E S O P *see* Epigraphic Society. Occasional Papers **392**
E S O P Report (Employee Stock Ownership Plan) (USA) **1740**
E S P *see* English for Specific Purposes **5114**
• E. S. P. (USA) **7589**
E S P C Weekly List (Edinburgh Solicitors Property Centre) (GBR) **7589**
• E S P Cadernos (Escola de Saude Publica Cadernos) (BRA ISSN 1809-0893) **7515**
• e - S P E N (NLD ISSN 1751-4991) **6657**
• E S P E R Newsletter (Ebony Society of Philatelic Events and Reflections) (USA) **6894**
E S P N Deportes (Entertainment Sports Programming Network) (USA ISSN 1933-947X) **8170**
E S P N Information Please Sports Almanac (Year) *see* E S P N Sports Almanac (Year) **8170**
E S P N Special: Dick Vitale's College Basketball (Year) Preview (Entertainment Sports Programming Network) (USA) **8227**
• E S P N Sports Almanac (Year) (Entertainment Sports Programming Network) (USA ISSN 1555-8304) **8170**
• E S P N The Magazine (Entertainment Sports Programming Network) (USA ISSN 1097-1998) **8170**
E S P Now! (GBR ISSN 1465-9581) **7852**
• ➤ E S Q (Emerson Society Quarterly) (USA ISSN 0093-8297) **5287**
E S R (Electronic - Science - Radio) (AUS) **2358**
E S R *see* European Sociological Review **8101**
E S R C Research Centre on Micro-social Change in Britain. Technical Papers (Economic & Social Research Council) (GBR ISSN 0962-7782) **7960**
E S R C Research Centre on Micro-social Change in Britain. Working Papers (Economic & Social Research Council) (GBR ISSN 0962-1318) **7960**
E S R C Research Group on Wellbeing in Developing Countries. Newsletter (Economic & Social Research Council) (GBR ISSN 1479-9693) **8038**
E S R C Studentship Handbook (Economic and Social Research Council) (GBR ISSN 0269-2554) **7960**
• E S R F News (European Synchrotron Radiation Facility) (FRA) **7065**
E S R F Newsletter *see* E S R F News **7065**
E S R I Accounts and Balance Sheet (Economic and Social Research Institute) (IRL) **1097**
E.S.R. Magazine *see* Empire State Report **7132**
• E S R Review (Economic Self-Reliance) (USA ISSN 1932-9075) **1336**
• E S R Review (Economic and Social Rights) (ZAF ISSN 1684-260X) **7205**
E S S C I R C. Proceedings (European Solid-State Circuits Conference) (USA ISSN 1930-8833) **3094**
E S S Employment Opportunities (Executive Search Service) (USA) **6696**
E S S H *see* European Studies in Sports History **8172**
E S T *see* Empirical Studies in Theology **8099**
• E-S T A (FRA ISSN 1954-3522) **3377**
E S V G H *see* Entscheidungssammlung des Hessischen Verwaltungsgerichtshofs und des Verwaltungsgerichtshofs Baden-Wuerttemberg mit Entscheidungen der Staatsgerichtshofe beider Laender **4950**
E-Scape (USA ISSN 1084-9912) **5442**
E-Sciences et Technologies de l'Automatique *see* E-S T A **3377**
E-Scrap News (USA ISSN 1536-3856) **3505**
• ➤ e-Service Journal (USA ISSN 1528-8226) **2543**
E-Shidai Quanfangwei Qingbao Zhi *see* 3 C Mall **2569**
E-Shopping (Market Assessment) *see* Key Note Market Assessment. E-Shopping **1891**
• E-Source (USA ISSN 1545-5742) **2978**
• E - Spania (FRA ISSN 1951-6169) **4216**
• E-Spectrum (USA) **5785**
• L'E-ssentiel (FRA) **8038**
• E-Streams (USA ISSN 1098-4399) **106**
E T *see* Education Today **2849**
E + T *see* Education & Training **2940**
E T *see* Education & Training **2940**
E T A *see* Elektrowaerme International. Edition A. Elektrowaerme und Technischer Ausbau **4118**
E-T-A-Hoffmann Jahrbuch (Ernst-Theodor-Amadeus) (DEU ISSN 0944-5277) **5287**
E T A I *see* Electronic Transactions on Artificial Intelligence **2448**
E T B A Investment Guide *see* Hellenic Industrial Development Bank. Investment Guide **1628**
E T C (Ensayo Teoria Critica) (ARG ISSN 0327-7089) **6915**
• E T C (SWE ISSN 0348-6567) **3955**
E T C *see* Education & Treatment of Children **2847**
E T Cetera (Early Typewriter Collectors Association) (USA ISSN 1062-9645) **1850**
• ➤ E T D Educacao Tematica Digital (BRA ISSN 1676-2592) **2844**
▼ • E T D Online (ZAF ISSN 1998-7250) **6696**
E T E P *see* European Transactions on Electrical Power **3308**
E T. Energiewirtschaftliche Tagesfragen *see* Energiewirtschaftliche Tagesfragen **3129**
E T F O Voice (Elementary Teachers' Federation of Ontario) (CAN ISSN 1481-4072) **2844**
• E T F R N News (European Tropical Forest Research Network) (NLD ISSN 1876-5866) **669**
E T F R N Series (European Tropical Forest Research Network) (NLD ISSN 1567-4762) **3687**
E T Fs 100 *see* Morningstar E T Fs 150 **1641**
• e T G Complete (AUS ISSN 1447-1868) **5608**
E T G - Fachberichte (Energietechnische Gesellschaft) (DEU ISSN 0341-3934) **3301**
E T H - Bibliothek. A: Wissenschaftsgeschichte (CHE ISSN 1423-6958) **7852**
E T H - Bibliothek. B: Bibliothekswesen (Eidgenoessische Technische Hochschule) (CHE ISSN 1423-6966) **5057**
E T H Globe (Eidgenoessische Technische Hochschule) (CHE ISSN 1661-9323) **2978**
E T H Institut fuer Informationssysteme. Departement Informatik (CHE) **2530**
• E T H O S Newsletter (European Telematics Horizontal Observatory Service) (GBR ISSN 1363-9072) **2350**
E T H Series in Information Processing (Eidgenoessische Technische Hochschule) (DEU ISSN 0942-3044) **2543**
E T H Series in Information Theory and its Applications (Eidgenoessische Technische Hochschule) (DEU ISSN 1860-1081) **2543**
• e - T I (MAR ISSN 1114-8802) **2417**
E T - Lehti (FIN ISSN 0785-0913) **4043**
E T M R *see* European Trade Mark Reports **6749**
E.T.N. *see* E.T.N. Revue de l'Entretien des Textiles et Nettoyage **8450**
E.T.N. Revue de l'Entretien des Textiles et Nettoyage (FRA ISSN 0181-8120) **8450**
E T P C Report (Energy Technology and Thermal Process Chemistry) (SWE ISSN 1653-0551) **3377**
E T R and D *see* Educational Technology Research & Development **3059**
• ➤ E T R I Journal (Electronics and Telecommunications Research Institute) (KOR ISSN 1225-6463) **3094**
E T R News (CAN ISSN 1494-0051) **2319**
E T - Ristikot (FIN ISSN 1795-8938) **8170**
E T S Bulletin *see* Institute of Metal Finishing. Bulletin **6315**
E T S Developments (Educational Testing Service) (USA ISSN 0046-1547) **2978**
E T S Innovations *see* Innovations (Princeton) **2867**
E T S Policy Information Report (Educational Testing Service) (USA) **3020**
E T S Policy Notes (Educational Testing Service) (USA) **3020**
E T S Research Reporter (Educational Testing Service) (USA) **2844**
E T S Today (Educational Testing Service) (USA) **2844**
E T S, Tour d'Horizon des Technologies de la Sante *see* Tour d'Horizon des Technologies de la Sante **5723**
E T S U Special (East Texas State University) (USA) **2282**
• E T Z (Elektrotechnische Zeitschrift) (DEU ISSN 0948-7387) **3301**
• The E-Tactics Letter (USA) **1815**
• E-Tailer's Digest (USA ISSN 1522-6891) **1815**
E-tbt *see* The Baltic Times **3904**
E: The Environment Magazine *see* E **3414**
The E Ticket Magazine (USA) **4291**
• e-tid.com (GBR) **8699**
E Tijdschrift *see* Revue E **3329**
• E-topia (PRT ISSN 1645-958X) **5287**
E-Tradewinds *see* Tradewinds - The Network for Portugal **1585**
† E-Trading and E-Services Market (AUS ISSN 1447-0896) **8952**
E U (Europaeiske Union) (DNK ISSN 1603-3566) **1097**
E U and Competition Law Newsletter (European Union) (GBR) **4866**
• E U Baggrund (European Union) (DNK ISSN 1603-1121) **7231**
E U C C Coastal News (European Union for Coastal Conservation) (NLD) **2609**
E U Dairy Monitor (European Union) (GBR ISSN 1364-7407) **264**
▼ • E U Defence Markets (European Union) (GBR ISSN 1753-9048) **6420**
▼ E U E C. Online Journal (Electric Utilities Environment Conference) (USA ISSN 1941-9848) **3127**
• E U Energy (European Union) (GBR ISSN 1473-7450) **3127**
• E U. Escuela Abierta (Escuela Universitaria) (ESP ISSN 1138-6908) **2844**
• E U Fakta (Europaeiske Union) (DNK ISSN 1602-1169) **7231**
E U Focus (European Focus) (GBR ISSN 1368-907X) **1562**
E U Food Law *see* E U Food Law **4924**
E U Food Law (European Union) (GBR ISSN 1741-6914) **4924**
E U I Law Working Papers (European University Institute) (ITA) **4662**
E U I Papers in Political and Social Sciences (European University Institute) (ITA ISSN 1028-3633) **7131**
E U I. R S C. Policy Papers *see* European University Institute. Robert Schuman Centre for Advanced Studies. Policy Papers **4670**
• E U I Review (European University Institute) (ITA) **7131**
• E U I Working Papers in Economics (European University Institute) (ITA ISSN 1126-2354) **1478**
E U Info (European Union) (CAN ISSN 1488-2787) **1562**
The E U Institutions' Register (European Union) (BEL ISSN 1029-4147) **1991**
E U L E P - E U R A D O S - U I R Newsletter (European Late Effects Project Group - European Radiation Dosimetry Group - Union Internationale de R) (FRA) **3166**
E U Magazin (Europaeische Union) (DEU ISSN 0946-4689) **1478**
E U Market Survey. Cut Flowers and Foliage *see* The Cut Flowers and Foliage Market in the E U **3755**
E U Nu! *see* E U Fakta **7231**
E U-Orientering *see* Erhvervspolitisk Fokus **264**
E U P *see* European Union Politics **7234**
E U R (Europe) (LUX ISSN 1018-5593) **5608**
E U R E D I A *see* Euredia - Revue Europeene de Droit Bancaire et Financier **1338**
E U R O D L *see* European Journal of Open, Distance and E-Learning **3061**
E U R O F I M A Annual Report *see* European Company for the Financing of Railway Rolling Stock. Annual Report **8617**
• E U R O H A R P Newsletter (European Harmonised Procedures) (NOR ISSN 0809-8778) **8823**
• E U R O H A R P Report (European Harmonised Procedures) (NOR ISSN 0809-8751) **8823**
E U R O M A P Economic Survey (European Plastics and Rubber Machinery Manufacturers Association) (GBR ISSN 1352-223X) **7092**
• E U R O S L A Yearbook (European Second Language Association) (NLD ISSN 1568-1491) **5113**
• ➤ E U-Ret & Menneskeret (DNK ISSN 1395-220X) **4924**
E U S A Review (European Union Studies Association) (USA ISSN 1535-7031) **4216**
E U T Report *see* Eindhoven University of Technology. Department of Technology Management. Research Report **8953**
E U T Reports *see* Eindhoven University of Technology. Faculty of Electrical Engineering. Annual Research Report **3301**
E U Tax Journal (European Union) (GBR) **1921**
† • E U Tip (Evropska Unie) (CZE ISSN 1214-7346) **8952**
E U Trend Report (European Union) (NLD ISSN 1874-7531) **1921**
Der E U Umsatz-Steuer-Berater (European Union) (DEU ISSN 1862-9210) **1921**
E & W P.O.S. (Elektro und Wirtschaft) (AUT) **1815**
E & Z (Entwicklung und Zusammenarbeit) (DEU ISSN 0721-2178) **7231**
E V *see* eV **8955**
E V C J *see* European Venture Capital & Private Equity Journal **1622**
E V E *see* Equine Veterinary Education **8797**
E V J *see* Equine Veterinary Journal **8797**
The E V M S Chronicle (Eastern Virginia Medical School) (USA ISSN 1543-8112) **5608**
E V M S Now (Eastern Virginia Medical School) (USA ISSN 1543-4699) **2282**
E V O *see* Egitto e Vicino Oriente **4174**
E V O Magazine (Eigen Vervoer Organisatie) (NLD ISSN 1383-2247) **8578**
• E V World (Electric Vehicles) (USA) **8578**
E Ve N T *see* Electric Vehicle News & Technology **8495**
E-voice *see* ONEvoice (Anderson) **7739**
E W *see* Engineering World **3190**
E W *see* Estates West **4539**
• E W - Elektrizitaetswirtschaft (DEU ISSN 1619-5795) **3301**
E W G - Warenhandel (DEU ISSN 0014-3871) **1562**
E W I S *see* Enterprise and Work Innovation Studies **7961**
E W P A L *see* Edinburgh Working Papers in Applied Linguistics **5113**
E W R (DEU ISSN 0172-391X) **603**
E W Reference and Source Guide (Electronic Warfare) (USA) **3188**
• E W S R A Annual Buyer's Guide (Eastern Winter Sports Reps Association) (USA) **8311**
• E W S R A Newsletter (Eastern Winter Sports Reps Association) (USA) **8311**
† E W Special (NLD) **8952**
E W W *see* English World-Wide **5115**
• E-water (DEU ISSN 1994-8549) **3485**
• ➤ E X C L I Journal (Experimental and Clinical) (DEU ISSN 1611-2156) **669**
➤ E X S (Experientia Supplementum) (CHE ISSN 1023-294X) **669**
E Y *see* E Y Z H N **3874**
E Y Z H N (GRC) **3874**
• E z A - Entscheidungssammlung zum Arbeitsrecht (DEU ISSN 0938-2283) **4866**
E z A Schnelldienst (Entscheidungssammlung zum Arbeitsrecht) (DEU ISSN 0938-2143) **4866**
E Z Tech Guides (Easy) (USA ISSN 1541-5961) **2417**
E Z W - Texte (Evangelische Zentralstelle fuer Weltanschauungsfragen) (DEU ISSN 0344-9106) **7639**
• The E-zine Adsource Directory Weekly (USA) **24**
E-Zine Magazine (USA) **1621**
E22-Projektet 1998-2001. Rapport *see* Kalmar Laens Museums Arkeologiska Rapporter **402**
eAction News *see* E O W A News Alert **8859**
Eads Bridge (USA) **5287**
Eagle (Milwaukee) *see* Eagle Magazine **2265**
Eagle (New York) (USA) **6420**
The Eagle (Price) (USA) **2282**
• Eagle (Washington) (USA ISSN 0012-8082) **2282**
Eagle Eye (USA) **2282**
• Eagle Feather/Plume d'Aigle (CAN ISSN 1704-5061) **3531**
Eagle Leader (USA ISSN 0194-9047) **2265**
• Eagle Magazine (USA) **2265**
• Eagle Valley News (CAN ISSN 0828-833X) **3809**
Eagle's Eye (USA ISSN 0046-0915) **3531**
Eagle's Voice *see* Wanbli Ho **3571**
• eAI Journal (e-Business and Application Integration) (USA) **2555**
• eAI Journal Online (e-Business and Application Integration) (USA) **2555**
Ealing & Acton Gazette (GBR ISSN 0968-3860) **3864**
E&M *see* Economia & Management **1740**
➤ The Ear (USA ISSN 1091-9368) **5287**
• ➤ Ear and Hearing (USA ISSN 0196-0202) **6079**
• ➤ Ear, Nose & Throat Journal (USA ISSN 0145-5613) **6079**
Ear Nose and Throat News *see* E N T News **6079**
Ear Nose and Throat Today *see* E N Today **6079**
Ear Piece *see* The Listening Professional **4463**
• Earl of Seacliff Christmas Surprise (NZL ISSN 1177-7141) **5421**
• The Early America Review (USA ISSN 1090-4247) **4291**
Early American Homes Christmas *see* Early American Life **4556**
Early American Homes Decorates *see* Early American Life **4556**
• Early American Industries Association. Chronicle (USA ISSN 0012-8147) **1884**
• Early American Life (USA ISSN 1534-2042) **4556**
• ➤ Early American Literature (USA ISSN 0012-8163) **5287**
Early American Literature and Culture Through the American Renaissance (USA ISSN 1085-4541) **5287**
• ➤ Early American Studies (USA ISSN 1543-4273) **4291**
The Early Bird (USA) **4291**
➤ Early Book Society. Journal (USA ISSN 1525-6790) **7560**
• ➤ Early Child Development and Care (GBR ISSN 0300-4430) **2151**
Early Childhood and Elementary Literacy (USA ISSN 1554-2548) **2844**
Early Childhood Australia Inc. Research in Practice Series *see* E C A Research in Practice Series **2151**
Early Childhood Australia Inc. Voice *see* E C A Voice **2151**
Early Childhood Connections (USA ISSN 1085-522X) **2151**
Early Childhood Curriculum *see* Xueqian Kecheng Yanjiu **3088**
Early Childhood Development Initiative. Annual Reports *see* Early Childhood Development Report **2151**

Early Childhood Development Report/ Developpement de la Petite Enfance. Rapport (CAN ISSN 1912-8037) **2151**
➤ Early Childhood Education (CAN ISSN 0012-8171) **2844**
Early Childhood Education *see* Prime Minister's Awards for Excellence in Early Childhood Education, Exemplary Practice **2899**
Early Childhood Education and Care *see* Nordisk Barnehageforskning **2892**
• ➤ Early Childhood Education Journal (NLD ISSN 1082-3301) **2844**
• Early Childhood Education Update (NZL ISSN 1177-0716) **2844**
Early Childhood Law and Policy Reporter (USA ISSN 1055-4157) **3058**
Early Childhood Learning (USA) **3058**
• Early Childhood NEWS (USA ISSN 1080-3564) **2151**
• Early Childhood Report (USA ISSN 1058-6482) **3038**
• ➤ Early Childhood Research & Practice (USA ISSN 1524-5039) **2844**
• ➤ Early Childhood Research Quarterly (GBR ISSN 0885-2006) **2844**
▼ ➤ Early Childhood Services (USA ISSN 1559-9647) **2151**
• Early Childhood Today (Online) (USA ISSN 1070-1214) **3058**
➤ Early China (USA ISSN 0362-5028) **4181**
Early China. Supplement *see* Early China **4181**
Early Colorectal Cancer *see* Soki Daichogan **6034**
Early Days (AUS ISSN 0312-6145) **4191**
• Early Developments (USA ISSN 1536-4739) **2151**
Early Drama, Art, and Music Monograph Series (USA) **8469**
† Early Drama, Art, and Music Reference Series (USA ISSN 1059-1168) **8952**
Early Education (Art Edition) *see* Zaoqi Jiaoyu (Meishu Ban) **2928**
Early Education (Home School Edition) *see* Zaoqi Jiaoyu (Jiajiao Ban) **2928**
Early Education (Teacher's Edition) *see* Zaoqi Jiaoyu (Jiaoshi Ban) **2928**
• Early Education and Development (USA ISSN 1040-9289) **2844**
Early English Text Society. Original Series (GBR ISSN 0070-7872) **5287**
Early English Text Society. Supplementary Series (GBR) **5287**
Early Estimates of Public Elementary and Secondary Education Statistics *see* U.S. Department of Education. National Center for Education Statistics. Early Estimates of Public Elementary and Secondary Education Statistics **2921**
Early Evidence of the Impact of the (Years) Reforms in Florida *see* Baselines for Evaluating the Impact of the Reforms in Florida **1666**
• ➤ Early Human Development (IRL ISSN 0378-3782) **5989**
Early Intervention (USA ISSN 1058-8396) **3039**
• Early Intervention & School Special Interest Section Quarterly (USA ISSN 2150-3370) **3039**
▼ • ➤ Early Intervention in Psychiatry (AUS ISSN 1751-7885) **6137**
Early Irish Law Series (IRL ISSN 0790-4657) **5113**
Early Judaism and its Literature (NLD ISSN 1569-3597) **7720**
➤ Early Keyboard Journal (USA ISSN 0899-8132) **6563**
† Early Learnings (AUS ISSN 1832-1364) **8952**
Early Learnings Research Report *see* Early Learnings **8952**
• ➤ Early Medieval China (GBR ISSN 1529-9104) **4181**
• Early Medieval Europe (GBR ISSN 0963-9462) **4216**
Early Model Crash Estimating Guide *see* Motor Early Model Crash Estimating Guide **8592**
Early Modern and Modern Studies (ITA ISSN 1828-2164) **487**
• Early Modern Culture (USA ISSN 1939-0246) **4138**
Early Modern France Critiques *see* E M F Critiques **5287**
Early Modern France Studies in Early Modern France *see* E M F: Studies in Early Modern France **5287**
• Early Modern Japan (USA ISSN 1940-7947) **4181**
• ➤ Early Modern Literary Studies (GBR ISSN 1201-2459) **5421**
Early Modern Literature in History (GBR) **5287**
• Early Modern Women (USA ISSN 1933-0065) **8895**
Early Morn African Violet Group Newsletter (AUS ISSN 1033-0003) **3728**
• ➤ Early Music (GBR ISSN 0306-1078) **6563**
• Early Music America (USA ISSN 1083-3633) **6563**
Early Music America Bulletin *see* E M A Bulletin **6563**
• ➤ Early Music History (GBR ISSN 0261-1279) **6563**
Early Music Newsletter (USA) **6563**
Early Music Performer (GBR ISSN 1477-478X) **6563**
Early Music Record Services. Monthly Review (GBR ISSN 0144-8072) **6563**
Early Music Review (GBR ISSN 1355-3437) **6563**
Early Music Today (GBR ISSN 1352-0059) **6564**
The Early Music Yearbook (GBR ISSN 0967-6619) **6564**
• ➤ Early Popular Visual Culture (GBR ISSN 1746-0654) **8099**
• Early Psychosis News (AUS ISSN 1326-0871) **6137**
Early Psychosis Prevention and Intervention Centre Information Sheet *see* E P P I C Information Sheet **6137**
• ➤ Early Science and Medicine (NLD ISSN 1383-7427) **5608**
• ➤ Early Theatre (CAN ISSN 1206-9078) **8470**
Early Typewriter Collectors Association Cetera *see* E T Cetera **1850**
• Early Warning: Bulgaria Beyond the Facts (Monthly Edition) (BGR) **7231**
• ➤ Early Years (GBR ISSN 0957-5146) **3058**
Early years (Winchester) (USA ISSN 1540-5567) **7755**
Early Years Update (GBR ISSN 1478-3444) **2844**
➤ The Earnings Analyst (USA ISSN 1547-240X) **1097**
Earnings and Employment Data for Workers Covered under Social Security, by State and County (USA) **8038**
• Earnings and Employment Trends (CAN ISSN 1207-4888) **1225**
Earnings Guide (GBR) **1336**
Earnings - Industry and Services (LUX ISSN 0259-0492) **1225**
• Earnings Ticker (USA) **1097**
• Earnshaw's Review (USA) **2246**
Earshot Jazz (USA ISSN 1077-0984) **6564**
• Earth/Chijo (JPN ISSN 0913-7815) **106**
• Earth (USA ISSN 1943-345X) **2706**
Earth (Los Angeles) (USA) **1005**
Earth Almanac (USA ISSN 1533-0605) **2780**
• Earth & E-nvironment (GBR ISSN 1744-2893) **2706**
Earth & Environment *see* Earth & E-nvironment **2706**
Earth and Mineral Sciences (USA ISSN 0026-4539) **2706**
• ➤ Earth and Planetary Science Letters (NLD ISSN 0012-821X) **2706**
Earth Corps: The Daily Planet (USA) **7852**
• Earth First! (USA ISSN 1055-8411) **2609**
• Earth Focus (USA ISSN 1029-1784) **2706**
Earth Garden (AUS ISSN 0310-222X) **6644**
Earth Heritage (GBR ISSN 1350-6331) **2609**
The Earth in Our Hands (GBR) **2732**
• ➤ Earth Interactions (USA ISSN 1087-3562) **2706**
• Earth Island Journal (USA ISSN 1041-0406) **3415**
▼ Earth Jurisprudence Student Series (USA ISSN 1941-7357) **3415**
Earth Matters (GBR ISSN 0956-6651) **3415**
• ➤ Earth, Moon, and Planets (NLD ISSN 0167-9295) **574**
• Earth Observation Magazine (Online Edition) (USA) **2706**
Earth Observation Magazine (Print Edition) *see* Earth Observation Magazine (Online Edition) **2706**
• Earth Observer (USA) **53**
Earth Observing Laboratory Observer *see* The E O L Observer **6352**
Earth Observing System *see* E O S **2780**
• ➤ Earth, Planets and Space (JPN ISSN 1343-8832) **2706**
• Earth Quarterly (USA ISSN 1098-9536) **3974**
Earth Resources Mapping in Africa (KEN) **4005**
Earth Science *see* Diqiu Kexue **2705**
Earth Science *see* Chikyu Kagaku **2704**
Earth Science Computer Applications (USA) **2722**
Earth Science Frontiers *see* Dixue Qianyuan **2705**
▼ • Earth Science Informatics (DEU ISSN 1865-0473) **2722**
• ➤ Earth - Science Reviews (NLD ISSN 0012-8252) **2706**
Earth Science Software Directory (USA ISSN 1087-4720) **6488**
• ➤ Earth Sciences History (USA ISSN 0736-623X) **2706**
• ➤ Earth Sciences Research Journal (COL ISSN 1794-6190) **2780**
Earth Sciences Series (FRA ISSN 0070-7910) **2706**
Earth Song *see* Earthsong Journal **7735**
Earth Speaks *see* Planeta.com **8748**
• ➤ Earth Surface Processes and Landforms (GBR ISSN 0197-9337) **2732**
Earth System Monitor (USA ISSN 1068-2678) **2803**
▼ • ➤ Earth System Science Data (DEU ISSN 1866-3508) **2706**
▼ • ➤ Earth System Science Data Discussions (DEU ISSN 1866-3591) **2706**
Earth: Where Do We Go from Here? (USA) **7960**
Earthhuman (USA ISSN 1544-5275) **3974**
EarthLight (USA ISSN 1050-0413) **7639**
• Earthmatters (AUS ISSN 1448-336X) **2732**
The Earthmover and Civil Contractor (AUS ISSN 0314-4224) **3266**
Earthmovers (GBR ISSN 1743-0372) **5451**
Earthmovers & Excavators (AUS ISSN 1449-6518) **5451**
Earthmoving *see* Infrarakentaja **3270**
Earthquake *see* Dizhen **2779**
Earthquake Engineering *see* Seismostoikoe Stroitel'stvo. Bezopasnost' Sooruzhenii **2789**
• Earthquake Engineering Abstracts (USA) **3229**
• Earthquake Engineering and Engineering Seismology (TWN ISSN 1562-7969) **2732**
• ➤ Earthquake Engineering and Engineering Vibration (USA ISSN 1671-3664) **2780**
• ➤ Earthquake Engineering & Structural Dynamics (GBR ISSN 0098-8847) **3266**
Earthquake Engineering Research Institute Newsletter *see* E E R I Newsletter **2706**
• Earthquake History of the United States (USA) **2780**
Earthquake Research Department. Bulletin *see* Deprem Arastirma Bulteni **2779**
Earthquake Research in China *see* Zhongguo Dizhen **2792**
Earthquake Research in Shanxi *see* Shanxi Dizhen **2789**
• ➤ Earthquake Spectra (USA ISSN 8755-2930) **2780**
• Earthquakes and the Built Environment Index (USA ISSN 1082-4588) **3229**
Earth's Daughters (USA ISSN 0163-0989) **8859**
Earthsong (USA ISSN 1070-8618) **6523**
Earthsong Journal (AUS ISSN 1449-8367) **7735**
EarthSpirit (USA) **6644**
• Earthwatch (USA ISSN 8750-0183) **7852**
• Earthwatch Institute. Research & Exploration (USA ISSN 1526-4092) **2609**
Earthwatch Oregon (USA ISSN 0890-1201) **3415**
† Earwig (NZL) **8952**
The Easingwold Advertiser and Weekly News (GBR ISSN 1749-5962) **3967**
Easingwold Papers (GBR) **2226**
Easingwold Times *see* The Easingwold Advertiser and Weekly News **3967**
East (JPN ISSN 0012-8295) **3900**
East Africa Analysis (UGA) **7131**
• East Africa Journal of Public Health (TZA ISSN 0856-8960) **7515**
▼ ➤ East Africa Journal of Sciences (ETH ISSN 1992-0407) **7852**
East Africa Natural History Society Bulletin *see* E A N H S Bulletin **669**
The East African (KEN ISSN 1024-1418) **3902**
• ➤ East African Agricultural and Forestry Journal (KEN ISSN 0012-8325) **106**
East African Community. Economic and Statistical Review (KEN ISSN 0012-9992) **1225**
East African Development Bank. Annual Report (UGA ISSN 1015-0676) **1336**
East African Freight Forwarding (KEN) **8495**
• East African Journal of Human Rights and Democracy (KEN ISSN 1682-900X) **7205**
• ➤ East African Journal of Ophthalmology (KEN ISSN 1992-5832) **6041**
➤ East African Journal of Peace and Human Rights (UGA ISSN 1021-8858) **7205**
➤ East African Languages and Dialects (DEU) **5113**
East African Law Journal (KEN ISSN 0070-797X) **4662**
The East African Lawyer (TZA ISSN 0856-9940) **4663**
East African Management Journal (KEN ISSN 0012-8341) **1740**
• ➤ The East African Medical Journal (KEN ISSN 0012-835X) **5608**
East African Regional Seas Technical Report Series (SYC) **2803**
• The East African Standard (KEN) **3902**
East Africana Accessions Bulletin (TZA ISSN 0856-0455) **4169**
East and Bays Courier (NZL ISSN 1172-529X) **3917**
• East and Central African Journal of Pharmaceutical Sciences (KEN ISSN 1026-552X) **6837**
• ➤ East and Central African Journal of Surgery (ZMB ISSN 1024-297X) **6242**
East and Central European Journal on Crime and Criminal Law (NLD ISSN 1386-4726) **2651**
East and Maghreb *see* Mi-Mizrah Umi-Ma'arav **7726**
➤ East and West (ITA ISSN 0012-8376) **548**
East & West *see* Dorno, Orno **548**
East and West Series (IND ISSN 0012-8384) **7639**
East Anglia Guide (GBR) **8699**
East Anglia Salary Survey (GBR) **1676**
➤ East Anglian Archaeology. Report (GBR ISSN 0307-2460) **391**
† East Anglian Bibliography (GBR ISSN 0046-0958) **8952**
East Anglian Daily Times (Essex Edition) (GBR ISSN 0958-3904) **3864**
East Anglian Farmer & Grower (GBR) **106**
• East Asia (NLD ISSN 1096-6838) **4181**
East Asia and Pacific Food Report (GBR) **3634**
East Asia Bibliography (GBR) **1225**
East Asia Economy and Trade News *see* Dongya Jingmao Xinwen **1093**
East Asia Intercultural Studies/Interkulturelle Ostasienstudien (DEU ISSN 1861-101X) **548**
East Asia Journal (GBR ISSN 1464-0414) **336**
• East Asian Business Intelligence (USA ISSN 0888-580X) **1562**
East Asian Economic and Socio-cultural Studies (DEU) **548**
East Asian Economic Perspectives (JPN ISSN 1348-0936) **1478**
• East Asian Executive Reports (USA ISSN 0272-1589) **1478**
➤ East Asian History (AUS ISSN 1036-6008) **4182**
East Asian Institute Contemporary China Series (SGP) **548**
East Asian Institute. Occasional Paper Series *see* East Asian Institute Contemporary China Series **548**
East Asian Institute Series *see* Columbia University. East Asian Institute. Studies **547**
East Asian Library Journal (USA ISSN 1079-8021) **548**
• East Asian Library Resources Group of Australia. Newsletter (Canberra, 2005) (AUS ISSN 1832-7648) **5007**
East Asian Pastoral Review (PHL ISSN 0116-0257) **7795**
East Asian Research Aids and Translations (USA) **548**
East Asian Review (JPN ISSN 1342-8047) **548**
East Asian Review (KOR ISSN 1227-4631) **548**
➤ East Asian Science, Technology, and Medicine (DEU ISSN 1562-918X) **548**
▼ • East Asian Science, Technology and Society (NLD ISSN 1875-2160) **7852**
† East Asian Social Science Monographs (GBR) **8952**
• East Asia's Millions (USA ISSN 0012-8406) **7755**
East Bay Business Times *see* San Francisco Business Times **1432**
East Bay Labor Journal (USA ISSN 0012-8422) **4593**
East Bay Living (USA) **4539**
The East Bay Monthly (USA) **24**
▼ • East Bay Quarterly (USA ISSN 1934-6379) **7131**
East Bay Service Directory *see* East Bay Living **4539**
• East Caribbean Business Forecast Report (GBR ISSN 1745-0543) **1097**
The East Carolinian (USA) **2282**
▼ ➤ East Central and Eastern Europe in the Middle Ages, 450-1450 (NLD ISSN 1872-8103) **4216**
• ➤ East Central Europe/Europe du Centre Est (NLD ISSN 0094-3037) **4216**
East China Electric Power *see* Huadong Dianli **3159**
East China Institute of Technology. Journal *see* Donghua Ligong Xueyuan Xuebao **2732**
East China Normal University. Journal (Education Edition) *see* Huadong Shifan Daxue Xuebao (Jiaoyu Ban) **2864**
East China Normal University. Journal (Natural Science Edition) *see* Huadong Shifan Daxue Xuebao (Ziran Kexue Ban) **7862**
• East China Normal University. Journal. (Social Science Edition)/Huadong Shifan Daxue Xuebao (Zhexue Shehui Kexue Ban) (CHN ISSN 1000-5579) **7960**
East China Science and Technology *see* Huadong Keji **7862**
East China Tourism News *see* Huadong Luyou Bao **8720**
East China University of Politics and Law. Journal *see* Huadong Zheng-Fa Xueyuan Xuebao **4688**
East China University of Science and Technology. Journal (Natural Science Edition) *see* Huadong Ligong Daxue Xuebao **3245**
East Coast Artisan (USA) **535**
East Coast Bike Culture Magazine *see* BikeCulture Magazine **8255**
East Coast Ryders (USA) **8578**
East End Life (GBR) **3864**
East End Lights (USA) **6564**
• East European Business Information Searcher (GBR) **5007**
East European Business Law Review (USA ISSN 1568-7260) **4663**
East European Case Reporter of Constitutional Law (USA ISSN 1381-2351) **4848**
East European Clothing & Textile Industry Directory (GBR) **1991**
† East European Constitutional Review (USA ISSN 1075-8402) **8952**
East European Human Rights Review (USA ISSN 1382-7987) **7205**
• East European Insurance Report (GBR ISSN 0965-9676) **4501**
• ➤ East European Jewish Affairs (GBR ISSN 1350-1674) **4216**
East European Monographs (USA ISSN 1083-2890) **3974**
• ➤ East European Politics & Societies (USA ISSN 0888-3254) **7131**
East European Privatisation News (GBR ISSN 0968-6355) **7131**
† • ➤ East European Quarterly (USA ISSN 0012-8449) **8952**
East European, Russian & Central Asian Market Studies *see* Eluosi Zhongya Dongou Shichang **1563**
East European Telecoms (GBR ISSN 1465-0029) **2367**
East European Trade (IND ISSN 0012-8457) **1562**
East-Florida Gazette (USA) **4291**
East German Studies *see* D D R Studien **4137**
East Japan Railway Company. Semi-Annual Report (JPN) **8616**
➤ East Journal on Approximations (BGR ISSN 1310-6236) **5485**
East Kent Mercury (GBR ISSN 0964-1408) **3864**
The East Kentuckian (USA ISSN 0424-107X) **3764**
East Lakes Geographer (USA ISSN 0070-8127) **4005**
East London Advertiser (GBR ISSN 0963-245X) **3864**
East London Directory *see* Braby's East London Directory **1976**
East Lothian Life (GBR) **3864**
East Mercia Chamber of Commerce & Industry Directory (GBR) **1401**
East Midland Historian (GBR ISSN 1350-1615) **4216**
East Midlands Bibliography (GBR ISSN 0029-2885) **4169**

Title

10226 ECONOMIA DE MOCAMBIQUE ULRICH'S PERIODICALS

Economia de Mocambique (MOZ ISSN 0012-9755) **1479**
• ➤ Economia dei Servizi (ITA ISSN 1970-4860) **1884**
Economia della Cultura (ITA ISSN 1122-2417) **1098**
• L'Economia della Marca Trevigiana (ITA) **1402**
L'Economia dell'Abruzzo Montano (ITA ISSN 1971-4424) **1402**
• Economia delle Fonti di Energia e dell'Ambiente (ITA ISSN 1125-1263) **3127**
• L'Economia delle Regioni Italiane (ITA ISSN 1971-4505) **1479**
Economia E C (PRT ISSN 0870-4635) **1479**
• Economia e Diritto Agroalimentare (ITA ISSN 1826-0373) **106**
• Economia e Diritto del Terziario (ITA ISSN 1593-9464) **1098**
Economia & Gestao (BRA ISSN 1678-8982) **1479**
• Economia & Lavoro (ITA ISSN 0012-978X) **1676**
• Economia & Management (ITA ISSN 1120-5032) **1740**
Economia & Politica del Farmaco (ITA ISSN 1970-0474) **6837**
• Economia e Politica Industriale (ITA ISSN 0391-2078) **1098**
• Economia e Sociedade (BRA ISSN 0104-0618) **1098**
Economia e Societa Regionale (ITA ISSN 1827-2479) **1479**
➤ Economia e Sociologia (PRT ISSN 0870-6026) **1479**
➤ Economia em Revista (BRA ISSN 1413-6090) **1479**
† Economia Emilia-Romagna (ITA) **8952**
• Economia Exterior (ESP ISSN 1137-4772) **1718**
Economia Fondiaria (CHE) **7589**
• Economia, Gestion y Desarrollo (COL ISSN 1657-5946) **1479**
Economia Global e Gestao (PRT ISSN 0873-7444) **1740**
† Economia Guipuzcoana (ESP ISSN 0211-4763) **8952**
Economia, Impresa e Mercati Finanziari (ITA ISSN 1970-0911) **1098**
Economia Industrial (ESP ISSN 0422-2784) **1884**
Economia Informa (MEX ISSN 0185-0849) **1098**
Economia Institucional *see* Revista de Economia Institucional **1167**
† Economia Internacional (ESP ISSN 0012-9801) **8952**
Economia Internazionale/Inrenational Economics (ITA ISSN 0012-981X) **1402**
• Economia Mexicana (MEX ISSN 0185-0458) **1098**
Economia Mexicana en Cifras *see* Statistics on the Mexican Economy **1268**
• Economia Nacional (MEX ISSN 0186-8470) **1098**
Economia Politica (HND ISSN 0424-2483) **1098**
• Economia Politica (ITA ISSN 1120-2890) **1098**
Economia Politica (MEX ISSN 0531-8203) **1098**
• Economia Pubblica (ITA ISSN 0390-6140) **1884**
Economia Rural (BRA ISSN 0103-6580) **1479**
• ➤ Economia. Seria Management (ROM ISSN 1454-0320) **1740**
Economia, Sociedad y Territorio (MEX ISSN 1405-8421) **7960**
Economia, Societa e Istituzioni (ITA ISSN 1593-9456) **8099**
Economia: Teoria y Practica (MEX ISSN 0188-3380) **1479**
Economia, Trabajo y Sociedad (ESP ISSN 1136-9221) **1676**
Economia Trentina (ITA ISSN 0012-9879) **1402**
Economia y Administracion (CHL ISSN 0716-0100) **1098**
• Economia y Desarrollo (CUB ISSN 0252-8584) **1098**
▼ Economia y Salud (CHL ISSN 0718-5294) **7515**
• Economia y Sociedad (PER ISSN 1682-4342) **1479**
Economia y Trabajo en Chile (CHL ISSN 0717-0033) **1098**
• Economic Accounts (Online Edition) (CAN) **1225**
Economic Accounts for Agriculture *see* O E C D Agriculture Statistics **184**
• ➤ Economic Affairs (GBR ISSN 0265-0665) **1098**
Economic Affairs (IND ISSN 0424-2513) **1098**
Economic Age (IND) **1479**
• ➤ Economic Analysis and Policy (AUS ISSN 0313-5926) **1098**
Economic Analysis of United States Ski Areas (USA ISSN 1070-9231) **8311**
• Economic Analysis Working Papers/Documentos de Trabajo en Analisis Economico (ESP ISSN 1579-1475) **1479**
Economic and Business Review *see* Ain Shams University. Economic and Business Review **1057**
Economic & Business Review (IND ISSN 0012-995X) **1099**
• ➤ Economic and Business Review/Ekonomska in Poslovna Revija (SVN ISSN 1580-0466) **1099**
Economic and Commercial News (IND ISSN 0970-0560) **1479**
Economic and Environmental Geology *see* Jaweon Hwan'Gyeong Ji'jil **2749**
Economic & Financial Bulletin *see* Kuwait & Gulf Economic and Financial Bulletin **1496**
Economic and Financial Bulletin - K B C *see* K B C Economic and Financial Bulletin **1363**
Economic & Financial Computing (GBR ISSN 0962-2780) **1416**
Economic and Financial Data on CD-ROM *see* Bank of Japan. Economic and Financial Data on CD-ROM **1213**
Economic & Financial Modelling (GBR ISSN 1350-7419) **1416**
Economic and Financial Prospects (CHE ISSN 0256-3525) **1479**
Economic & Financial Quarterly (KWT) **1479**
Economic and Financial Report (CHL ISSN 0716-2421) **1336**
➤ Economic & Financial Review (GBR ISSN 1351-3621) **1099**
• Economic and Financial Review (Dallas) (USA ISSN 1526-3940) **1336**
Economic and Fiscal Policy (CAN) **1479**
• ➤ Economic and Industrial Democracy (GBR ISSN 0143-831X) **7131**
Economic and Industrial Publications Economic Forecasting Service *see* E I P Economic Forecasting Service **1478**
Economic and Industrial Publications Industrial Research Service *see* E I P Industrial Research Service **1884**
▼ • ➤ Economic & Labour Market Review (GBR ISSN 1751-8326) **1676**
➤ The Economic and Labour Relations Review (AUS ISSN 1035-3046) **1676**
Economic and Management Quarterly Journal of the Islamic Azad University *see* Iqtisad va Mudiriyat **1762**
Economic and Market Brief (CAN ISSN 1910-9024) **1621**
Economic and Market Brief, R Funds *see* Economic and Market Brief **1621**
Economic and Market Brief, R Funds, I A Funds, Distinction Portfolios *see* Economic and Market Brief **1621**
• ➤ Economic and Political Weekly (IND ISSN 0012-9976) **1099**
Economic and Scientific Research Foundation. Annual Report (IND ISSN 0070-8437) **1099**
Economic and Social Commission for Asia and the Pacific. Annual Report (THA ISSN 0252-2284) **1595**
Economic and Social Development *see* Jingji yu Shehui Fazhan (Nanning) **1494**
Economic and Social Development of Indigenous Small Nationalities of the Far North *see* Ekonomicheskoe i Sotsial'noe Razvitie Korennykh Malochislennykh Narodov Severa **1225**
Economic and Social Progress in Latin America. Report (USA ISSN 0095-2850) **1479**
Economic & Social Research Council Research Centre on Micro-social Change in Britain. Technical Papers *see* E S R C Research Centre on Micro-social Change in Britain. Technical Papers **7960**
Economic & Social Research Council Research Centre on Micro-social Change in Britain. Working Papers *see* E S R C Research Centre on Micro-social Change in Britain. Working Papers **7960**
Economic & Social Research Council Research Group on Wellbeing in Developing Countries. Newsletter *see* E S R C Research Group on Wellbeing in Developing Countries. Newsletter **8038**
Economic and Social Research Council Studentship Handbook *see* E S R C Studentship Handbook **7960**
Economic and Social Research Institute Accounts and Balance Sheet *see* E S R I Accounts and Balance Sheet **1097**
Economic and Social Research Institute. Annual Report and Review of Research (IRL ISSN 1649-7031) **1099**
➤ Economic and Social Research Institute. General Research Series (IRL) **1099**
Economic and Social Research Institute. Medium Term Review (IRL ISSN 0790-9470) **1099**
Economic and Social Research Institute. Memorandum Series (IRL) **1099**
Economic and Social Research Institute. Policy Research Series (IRL) **1099**
Economic and Social Research Institute. Technical Series (IRL) **1099**
• ➤ Economic and Social Review (IRL ISSN 0012-9984) **1099**
Economic and Social Rights Review *see* E S R Review **7205**
Economic and Social Statistics of Sri Lanka (LKA ISSN 1391-3611) **1225**
• Economic and Social Survey of Asia and the Pacific (THA ISSN 0252-5704) **1479**
Economic and Social Survey of Jamaica (JAM ISSN 0256-5013) **1099**
• ➤ Economic Botany (USA ISSN 0013-0001) **786**
Economic Briefing (GBR) **1427**
† • ➤ Economic Bulletin (DEU ISSN 0343-754X) **8952**
Economic Bulletin *see* Bank of Jamaica Quarterly Monetary Policy Report **1314**
• Economic Bulletin (KOR) **1099**
Economic Bulletin (LBY) **1099**
Economic Bulletin (San Diego) (USA ISSN 1075-8631) **1479**
Economic Bulletin of the Senshu University *see* Senshu Keizaigaku Ronshu **1172**
Economic Census *see* U.S. Census Bureau. Economic Census **1272**
• ➤ Economic Change and Restructuring (USA ISSN 1573-9414) **1479**
• Economic Commentary (USA ISSN 0428-1276) **1099**
Economic Commission for Europe. Annual Report (CHE ISSN 0251-0197) **1099**
Economic Commission for Europe. Statistical Yearbook *see* Trends in Europe and North America **1550**
• Economic Compass (AUS) **1479**
Economic Computation and Economic Cybernetics Studies and Research *see* Studii si Cercetari de Calcul Economic si Cibernetice Economice **1520**
Economic Cooperation Series/Keizai-Kyoryoku Series (JPN) **1595**
Economic Daily *see* Jingji Ribao **1131**
Economic Daily News *see* Jingji Ribao **1132**
Economic Database. Household Database (USA ISSN 1542-7242) **1099**
Economic Debate *see* Ekonomisk Debatt **1103**
• ➤ Economic Development and Cultural Change (USA ISSN 0013-0079) **1595**
• Economic Development Digest (USA) **1479**
Economic Development Institute Development Policy Case Series *see* E D I Development Policy Case Series **1096**
Economic Development Institute Policy Seminar Report *see* E D I Policy Seminar Report **1096**
• Economic Development Journal (USA ISSN 1539-1922) **1099**
Economic Development Management in Asia and the Pacific Joint Policy Studies *see* E D A P Joint Policy Studies **8952**
Economic Development Now (USA ISSN 1539-2503) **1884**
• ➤ Economic Development Quarterly (USA ISSN 0891-2424) **1539**
• Economic Development Review (USA ISSN 0742-3713) **1884**
• Economic Development - State Capitals (USA) **1480**
Economic Dossier "Legislative Support of Business in Russia" *see* Ekonomicheskoe Dos'e "Zakonodatel'noe Obespechenie Biznesa v Rossii" **1103**
• Economic Edge (USA) **1480**
Economic Education *see* Ediyn Dzasgiyn Bolovsrol **1102**
Economic Education Bulletin (USA ISSN 0424-2769) **1099**
Economic Fact Book on Metropolitan Milwaukee *see* Metropolitan Milwaukee Economic Fact Book **1498**
Economic, Financial and Industry Sector Reports (GBR) **3188**
• Economic Focus (GBR ISSN 1751-4339) **1562**
Economic Forecast and Information *see* Jingji Yuce yu Xinxi **1132**
Economic Forum *see* Shanghai Zonghe Jingji **1721**
• Economic Freedom of North America (CAN ISSN 1717-8703) **1099**
• Economic Freedom of the World Annual Report (CAN ISSN 1482-471X) **1480**
Economic Geography *see* Jingji Dili **4016**
• ➤ Economic Geography (USA ISSN 0013-0095) **4005**
Economic Geology *see* Economic Geology and the Bulletin of the Society of Economic Geologists **2732**
• ➤ Economic Geology and the Bulletin of the Society of Economic Geologists (USA ISSN 0361-0128) **2732**
▼ ➤ Economic Growth Centre Research Monograph Series (SGP) **1099**
Economic Growth in Tennessee, Annual Report (USA ISSN 0739-8956) **1884**
Economic Handbook of the Machine Tool Industry (USA ISSN 0070-8550) **5451**
Economic Herald *see* Privredni Vjesnik **1161**
Economic History *see* Hospodarske Dejiny **1543**
• ➤ The Economic History Review (GBR ISSN 0013-0117) **1539**
Economic Horizons *see* Afaq Iqtisadiyyah **1394**
Economic Ideas Leading to the 21st Century/Economic Ideas Leading to the Twenty-First Century (SGP ISSN 0219-9815) **1099**
Economic Ideas Leading to the Twenty-First Century *see* Economic Ideas Leading to the 21st Century **1099**
Economic Impact of Indian Gaming *see* Casino City's Indian Gaming Industry Report **8165**
Economic Indicators (PHL) **1225**
Economic Indicators (Charleston) (USA ISSN 0278-8381) **1480**
• Economic Indicators (Washington) (USA ISSN 0013-0125) **1480**
Economic Indicators Handbook (USA ISSN 1075-3834) **1225**
Economic Indicators of the Development of the Far North and Other Similar Areas *see* Ekonomicheskie Pokazateli Razvitiya Rayonov Krainego Severa i Priravnennykh k nim Mestnostei **1225**
Economic Indicators of Turkey (TUR ISSN 1300-9265) **1718**
Economic Indicators. Upper Hunter Region (AUS ISSN 1834-1225) **1099**
Economic Information Bulletin. Structure and Finances of U.S. Farms *see* U.S. Department of Agriculture. Economic Research Service. Structure and Finances of U.S. Farms **207**
Economic Information Daily *see* Jingji Cankao Bao **1131**
Economic Information Report *see* University of Florida. Food and Resource Economics Department. Economic Information Report **208**
• ➤ Economic Inquiry (USA ISSN 0095-2583) **1100**
▼ Economic Insights (USA ISSN 1937-1977) **1100**
Economic Intelligence Review (GBR ISSN 1350-1070) **7131**
Economic Intelligence Review *see* Asiaint Economic Intelligence Review **1062**
• ➤ Economic Issues (GBR ISSN 1363-7029) **1539**
• ➤ The Economic Journal (GBR ISSN 0013-0133) **1100**
Economic Journal of Chiba University *see* Chiba Daigaku Keizai Kenkyu **1082**
Economic Journal of Hokkaido University (JPN) **1100**
Economic Journal of Nepal (NPL ISSN 1018-631X) **1595**
Economic Justice Report *see* Global Justice Report **7238**
Economic Legislation *see* Legislacion Economica **4722**
Economic Legislation Review *see* Przeglad Ustawodawstwa Gospodarczego **1513**
Economic Letter (LBN) **1480**
Economic Logic (USA) **1621**
Economic Management *see* Jingji Guanli **1762**
Economic Management Digest *see* Jingji Guanli Wenzhai **1763**
Economic Message *see* Mensagem Economica **1367**
• ➤ Economic Modelling (NLD ISSN 0264-9993) **1539**
Economic Monthly *see* Jingji Yuekan **1132**
Economic Monthly *see* Jingji **1131**
Economic Monthly (DNK) **1480**
Economic News from Austria *see* E N A **1478**
Economic News from Russia and Commonwealth *see* Ekonomicheskie Novosti Rossii i Sodruzhestva **1103**
Economic News Weekly: Business Taiwan/Chung-kuo Ching Chi Chou Kan (TWN) **1100**
• Economic Notes (GBR ISSN 0391-5026) **1100**
• Economic Opportunity Report (USA ISSN 0013-0206) **1480**
• Economic Outlook (AUS) **1100**
▼ • Economic Outlook (FIN ISSN 1797-3775) **1336**
• ➤ Economic Outlook (GBR ISSN 0140-489X) **1480**
Economic Outlook (PAK) **1480**
Economic Outlook (SWE) **1718**
Economic Outlook (USA) **1336**
Economic Outlook for Iceland *see* The Icelandic Economy **1121**
Economic Outlook Round the Bohai Sea *see* Huan Bohai Jingji Liaowang **1119**
Economic Outlook Update as of (Year) (USA ISSN 1558-4062) **1480**
Economic Panorama *see* Panorama Economico **1510**
Economic Perspectives *see* Jingjixue Dongtai **1132**
Economic Perspectives (JOR) **1100**
• Economic Perspectives (Chicago) (USA ISSN 1048-115X) **1480**
• Economic Perspectives (Washington, D.C.) (USA) **1100**
• ➤ Economic Policy (GBR ISSN 0266-4658) **1100**
• Economic Policy Reforms (FRA ISSN 1813-2715) **1100**
Economic Portrait of the European Union (LUX ISSN 1680-1687) **1423**
• Economic Principals (USA) **1480**
• Economic Profile of Oregon (USA) **1480**
Economic Progress *see* Progreso Economico **1376**
Economic Progress Report *see* H M Treasury Economic Briefing **1489**
Economic Prospects (Stellenbosch) *see* University of Stellenbosch. Bureau for Economic Research. Economic Prospects **1523**
Economic Prospects in Denmark *see* Dansk Oekonomi **1476**
• ➤ Economic Quality Control (DEU ISSN 0940-5151) **1884**
• ➤ The Economic Record (AUS ISSN 0013-0249) **1100**
• Economic Reform Today (USA ISSN 1058-661X) **1100**
• Economic Report of the President Transmitted to the Congress (USA ISSN 0193-1180) **1480**
Economic Report on Scottish Agriculture (GBR ISSN 0262-9135) **196**
Economic Reporter *see* Jingji Daobao (Jinan) **1131**
Economic Reporter *see* Jingji Daobao (Wanchai) **1494**
Economic Research *see* Ekonomska Istrazivanja **1104**
Economic Research Center Working Papers *see* E R C Working Papers **1096**
Economic Research Journal *see* Jingji Yanjiu **1544**
Economic Research Journal (PHL ISSN 0424-2904) **1100**
Economic Research Reports on Machine Industry *see* Kikai Kogyo Keizai Kenkyu Hokokusho **5454**

Title

Title

DIRECTORY 2010 EGYPTIAN SOCIETY OF PHARMACOLOGY AND EXPERIMENTAL THERAPEUTICS 10231

• Eesti Tootervishoid/Estonian Newsletter on Occupational Health and Safety (EST ISSN 1406-7110) **6676**
Eeva (FIN ISSN 0358-8351) **8859**
Ef (JPN) **8859**
Efemerides Astronomicas (PRT ISSN 0870-1199) **574**
Efemeridy Malykh Planet/Ephemerides of Minor Planets (RUS ISSN 0201-7806) **574**
Efermerides Astronomicas (ESP ISSN 0080-5971) **574**
Effecten-Spiegel (DEU) **1621**
Effectengids (NLD ISSN 1567-4703) **1621**
† • Effective Communication (ISR) **8953**
▼ • ➤ Effective Education (GBR ISSN 1941-5532) **2852**
• Effective Entrepreneur (USA ISSN 1933-1525) **1959**
• ➤ Effective Health Care (GBR ISSN 0965-0288) **5608**
† Effective Health Care (Italian Edition) (ITA ISSN 1722-7690) **8953**
Effective Law Enforcement Report Writing (USA) **4663**
• Effective Legal Negotiation and Settlement (USA) **4663**
Effective Phrases for Performance Appraisals (USA ISSN 1933-6047) **1860**
• Effective Practices for Academic Leaders (USA ISSN 1554-0464) **3022**
Effective School Practices *see* Direct Instruction News **3058**
• Effective Teaching (USA ISSN 1079-610X) **3060**
Effective Telephone Techniques (USA ISSN 1525-1039) **1740**
Effective Use of G M's Labor Time Guide (General Motors) (USA) **8578**
Effective Youth Transitions *see* Manu Matauranga **8972**
• EFFector (USA ISSN 1062-9424) **7205**
• Effektivt Landbrug/Productive Farming (DNK ISSN 0013-2187) **106**
• Effeta (ITA ISSN 0013-2195) **4074**
▼ • Efficiency in Practice (USA ISSN 1948-5174) **5608**
The Efficient Banker (USA ISSN 1074-6560) **1337**
Efficient Frontier (USA) **1621**
The Efficient House Sourcebook (USA) **1006**
• Efficient Purchasing (SWE ISSN 1653-2066) **1815**
Efoyta (ETH) **3837**
• Efrydiau Athronyddol (GBR ISSN 0142-3371) **6915**
• Efs.nu (Evangeliska Fosterlandsstiftelsen) (SWE ISSN 1651-2820) **7755**
Eg J A *see* Egyptian Journal of Anaesthesia **5771**
L'Egalite des Chances pour les Femmes et les Hommes dans l'Union Europeenne *see* Equal Opportunities for Women and Men in the European Union **1680**
EGambling *see* Journal of Gambling Issues **5946**
† eGames (DEU) **8953**
eGaming Review (GBR ISSN 1742-2450) **2476**
Egan (ESP ISSN 0422-7328) **5288**
Ege Academic Review *see* Ege Akademik Bakis **1102**
• Ege Akademik Bakis/Ege Academic Review (TUR ISSN 1303-099X) **1102**
Ege Ingiliz ve Amerikan Incelemeleri Dergisi/Interactions (TUR ISSN 1300-574X) **5113**
Ege Journal of Medicine *see* Ege Tip Dergisi **5608**
Ege Tip Dergisi/Ege Journal of Medicine (TUR ISSN 1016-9113) **5608**
Ege Universitesi. Ziraat Fakultesi. Dergisi (TUR ISSN 1018-8851) **106**
Ege Universitesi. Ziraat Fakultesi. Yayinlari (TUR ISSN 0367-1577) **106**
Ege University. Medical Journal *see* Ege Tip Dergisi **5608**
Egemen Kazakhstan (KAZ) **3902**
Egenmeldingen *see* Helse Finnmark. Nythetsbrev **8044**
Egerer Zeitung (DEU ISSN 0013-2241) **3846**
➤ Egerton Journal (KEN ISSN 1021-1128) **4450**
Egeszsegfejlesztes (HUN ISSN 1786-2434) **6984**
Egeszsegneveles *see* Egeszsegfejlesztes **6984**
Egeszsegtudomany (HUN ISSN 0013-2268) **5608**
➤ Egeszsegugyi Gazdasagi Szemle (HUN ISSN 0013-2276) **4092**
Eget Foeretag (SWE ISSN 1653-4816) **1740**
Egg (Bar Harbor) (USA) **6564**
• Egg Industry (USA ISSN 0896-2804) **285**
• Egg Industry Insider (USA) **285**
Eggcup Collectors' Corner (USA) **4334**
Egin (ESP) **3951**
† Egitim Bulteni/Education Bulletin (TUR) **8953**
Egitim ve Bilim/Education and Science (TUR ISSN 1300-1337) **2852**
• ➤ Egitimde Kuram ve Uygulama/Journal of Theory and Practice in Education (TUR ISSN 1304-9496) **2852**
Egitto (ITA ISSN 1827-2908) **4174**
Egitto e Vicino Oriente (ITA ISSN 0392-6885) **4174**
▼ Egitto. Nuove Scoperte e Antichi Mestieri (ITA ISSN 1971-0402) **4174**
Eglise a Lyon (FRA ISSN 0992-6887) **7796**
L'Eglise Canadienne (CAN ISSN 0013-2322) **7640**
Eglise Catholique a Madagascar (MDG) **7796**
Eglise Catholique. Diocese de Gaspe. Annuaire (CAN ISSN 1719-8658) **7796**
Eglise Catholique. Diocese de Gaspe. Annuaire Diocesain *see* Eglise Catholique. Diocese de Gaspe. Annuaire **7796**
L'Eglise dans le Monde (FRA ISSN 1620-9001) **7796**
Eglise dans les Hautes-Alpes (FRA ISSN 1775-013X) **7796**
Eglise de Gap *see* Eglise dans les Hautes-Alpes **7796**
Eglise du Mans *see* Eglise en Sarthe **7796**
Eglise en Alsace (FRA ISSN 0013-2330) **7796**
Eglise en Sarthe (FRA ISSN 1777-3245) **7796**
EGM *see* Electronic Gaming Monthly en Espanol **2476**
Egmondse Studien (NLD ISSN 0929-9793) **4216**
• Egmont Fonden. Aarsskrift (DNK ISSN 1601-5649) **4450**
• Egmont Foundation. Annual Report (DNK ISSN 1604-875X) **4450**
▼ Egmont Posztermagazin (HUN ISSN 2060-6036) **2187**
Egnatia (GRC ISSN 1105-5421) **4216**
Egnshistorisk Forening i Grundsoe. Aarsskrift (DNK ISSN 0109-0194) **4216**
Ego (GRC ISSN 1108-569X) **8859**
Ego (NLD ISSN 1574-339X) **7354**
Ego (PRT ISSN 0873-3996) **6288**
• EGO (New York) (USA) **3531**
Ego Magazine (USA ISSN 1553-5533) **2282**
Ego Miami (USA) **5070**
▼ Ego, Moi, Mes Cheveux (FRA ISSN 1955-6004) **587**
Egodocumenten (NLD ISSN 0929-9807) **642**
▼ Egodocuments and History Series (NLD ISSN 1873-653X) **7560**
Egoist (RUS) **6288**
egov (IND ISSN 0973-161X) **2536**
• eGovernment Computing (DEU ISSN 1860-2584) **7485**
▼ eGovernment Review (AUT ISSN 1997-4051) **7485**
Egregious Steamboat Journal (USA ISSN 1058-3556) **8275**
Egretta (AUT ISSN 0013-2373) **906**
Egretta *see* Iguretta **908**
Egton Medical Information Systems Law Service *see* E M I S E-Law Service **4950**
Eguzkilore (ESP ISSN 0210-9700) **4663**
Egyhazi Kronika (HUN ISSN 0133-0047) **7704**
Egypt *see* The P R S Group. Country Reports: Egypt **1506**
Egypt and the Levant *see* Aegypten und Levante **371**
• Egypt Autos Report (GBR ISSN 1748-9873) **8578**
• The Egypt Busniness Forecast Report (GBR ISSN 1744-8840) **1482**
• Egypt Chemicals Report (GBR ISSN 1749-2025) **2061**
• Egypt Defence & Security Report (GBR ISSN 1749-1371) **6420**
Egypt Exploration Society. Monographs (GBR) **391**
Egypt Freight Transport Report (GBR ISSN 1752-5780) **8495**
Egypt Handbook (GBR ISSN 1363-7983) **8700**
Egypt Information Technology Report *see* Business Monitor International. Information Technology Country Reports **2491**
Egypt. J. Cataract Refract. Surg. *see* The Egyptian Journal of Cataract and Refractive Surgery **6041**
Egypt Magazine (EGY) **3835**
Egypt. Meteorological Authority. Meteorological Research Bulletin (EGY ISSN 1687-1014) **6352**
Egypt News (IND) **7232**
• Egypt: On the March of Development (EGY ISSN 1687-6512) **1427**
Egypt Petrochemicals Report (GBR ISSN 1749-2238) **6767**
Egypt Quarterly Forecast Report *see* The Egypt Busniness Forecast Report **1482**
Egypt Today (EGY) **3835**
L'Egypte Contemporaine (EGY ISSN 0013-239X) **7199**
➤ Egypte - Monde Arabe (EGY ISSN 1110-5097) **7132**
▼ Egyptian Academic Journal of Biological Sciences/Al Magallat al-Akadimiyyat al-Misriyyat li-l-'Ulum al-Bayulugiyyat/Al Majallat al-Akadimiyyat al-Misriyyat li-l-'Ulum al-Bayulujiyyat (EGY ISSN 1687-8809) **670**
† The Egyptian Academy of Sciences. Proceedings (EGY ISSN 1110-0532) **8953**
Egyptian Archaeology (GBR ISSN 0962-2837) **391**
Egyptian Association of Physical Medicine and Rehabilitation. Journal *see* Egyptian Rheumatology and Rehabilitation **6223**
Egyptian Computer Journal (EGY ISSN 0377-7154) **2417**
Egyptian Computer Science Journal/Al-Magallat AL-Missriyyat lil-hasibat AL-Ilmiyyat (EGY ISSN 1110-2586) **2417**
Egyptian Cotton Gazette (EGY ISSN 0367-0392) **8450**
Egyptian Dental Journal/Magallat Tib al-Asnaan al-Misriyyat (EGY ISSN 0070-9484) **5842**
• ➤ Egyptian Dermatology Online Journal (EGY ISSN 1687-3831) **5875**
Egyptian Gazette (EGY) **3836**
Egyptian German Society for Zoology. Journal. A, Comparative Zoology/Magallat al-Gam'iyyat al-Misriyyat al-Almaaniyyat li-'Ilm al-Hayyawaan. 'Ilm al-Fisyulugia al-Muqaran (EGY ISSN 1110-5321) **941**
Egyptian German Society for Zoology. Journal. B, Anatomy and Embryology/Magallat al-Gam'iyyat al-Misriyyat al-Almaaniyyat li-'Ilm al-Hayyawaan. al-Tasrih wa 'Im al-Aginat (EGY ISSN 1110-533X) **941**
Egyptian German Society for Zoology. Journal. C, Histology and Histochemistry (EGY ISSN 1110-5348) **941**
Egyptian German Society for Zoology. Journal. D, Invertebrate Zoology and Parasitology/Magallat al-Gam'iyyat al-Misriyyat al-Almaaniyyat li-'Ilm al-Hayyawaan. 'Ilm al-Haywan al-Faqqary wa al-Tufayliat (EGY ISSN 1110-5356) **941**
Egyptian German Society for Zoology. Journal. E, Entomology/Magallat al-Gam'iyyat al-Misriyyat al-Almaaniyyat li-'Ilm al-Hayyawaan. 'Ilm al-Hasharat (EGY ISSN 1110-5364) **941**
• The Egyptian Heart Journal/Magallat al-Qalb al-Misriyyat (EGY ISSN 1110-2608) **5785**
† The Egyptian Hospitals Association. Bulletin (EGY ISSN 1110-6573) **8953**
Egyptian Journal for Remote Sensing *see* Egyptian Journal of Remote Sensing and Space Sciences **2707**
Egyptian Journal of Agricultural Research *see* Egyptian Journal of Applied Agriculture Research **106**
Egyptian Journal of Agronematology/Al-Magallat al-Misriyyat lil-NimatuLugiya al-Zira'iyyat (EGY ISSN 1110-6158) **106**
➤ Egyptian Journal of Agronomy/Al-Magallat al-Misriyyat li-l-Mahasil (EGY ISSN 0379-3575) **106**
• Egyptian Journal of Anaesthesia (EGY ISSN 1110-1849) **5771**
Egyptian Journal of Animal Production (EGY ISSN 0302-4520) **285**
Egyptian Journal of Applied Agriculture Research (EGY ISSN 1687-837X) **106**
Egyptian Journal of Applied Endocrinology/Al-Magallat al-Tibbiyat li-Gam'iyyat al-Ghudad al-Sama' al-Tatbiqiyyat (EGY ISSN 1110-7812) **5890**
Egyptian Journal of Applied Science/Al-Magallat al-Misriyyat lil-'lum al-Tatbiiqiyyat (EGY ISSN 1110-1571) **106**
Egyptian Journal of Aquatic Biology and Fisheries/Al-Magallat al-Misriyyat lil-Bayulugiya al-Maiyyat wa-Almasa (EGY ISSN 1110-6131) **670**
The Egyptian Journal of Biochemistry/Magallat al-Gamieyat al-Missriyyat lil-Kimiyaa al-Hayaweyyat (EGY ISSN 1012-554X) **731**
The Egyptian Journal of Biochemistry & Molecular Biology *see* The Egyptian Journal of Biochemistry **731**
• ➤ Egyptian Journal of Biology (EGY ISSN 1110-6859) **670**
Egyptian Journal of Biomedical Sciences/Al-Magallat al-Misriyyat lil-'ulum al-Tibiyyat al-Hayawiyyat (EGY ISSN 1110-6379) **5905**
Egyptian Journal of Biophysics (EGY ISSN 1110-6565) **753**
Egyptian Journal of Biotechnology/Al-Magallat al-Misriyyat lil-TiknuluGya al-Hayawiyyat (EGY ISSN 1110-6093) **763**
▼ The Egyptian Journal of Bronchology (EGY ISSN 1687-8426) **6213**
The Egyptian Journal of Cataract and Refractive Surgery (EGY ISSN 1687-6997) **6041**
➤ Egyptian Journal of Chemistry/Al-Magalla al-Misriyya li-l-Ktmiya' (EGY ISSN 0449-2285) **2061**
The Egyptian Journal of Chest Diseases and Tuberculosis (EGY ISSN 0422-7638) **6213**
Egyptian Journal of Comparative Pathology and Clinical Pathology/Al-Magallat al-Misriyyat lil-Bathologia wa-al-Bathologia al-'iklinikiat al Moqaranat (EGY ISSN 1110-7537) **5608**
➤ Egyptian Journal of Dairy Science (EGY ISSN 0378-2700) **264**
Egyptian Journal of Dermatology and Andrology (EGY ISSN 1110-7650) **5875**
➤ Egyptian Journal of Desert Research/Magallat Ma'had al-Sahraa (EGY ISSN 1687-8043) **107**
Egyptian Journal of E N T and Allied Sciences/Al-Magallat al-'ilmiyyat lil-Gam'iyyat al-Misriyyat lil-Uuzun wa-al-Anf wa-al-Hangarat wa-al-'ulum al-Mushtarakat (Ear, Nose, Throat) (EGY ISSN 1110-6670) **6079**
• ➤ Egyptian Journal of Food Science/Al-Majallah al-Misriyyah li-Ulum al-Aghdhiya (EGY ISSN 1110-0192) **3634**
The Egyptian Journal of Gastroenterology (EGY ISSN 0304-4831) **5922**
Egyptian Journal of Genetics and Cytology (EGY ISSN 0046-161X) **866**
Egyptian Journal of Geology/Al-Magalla al-Misriyya li-Ilm al-Giyulugiya (EGY ISSN 0258-3704) **2732**
The Egyptian Journal of Haematology (EGY ISSN 1110-1067) **5936**
The Egyptian Journal of Histology/Al-Magallat al-Misriyyat li-'Ilm al-Ansigat (EGY ISSN 1110-0559) **832**
The Egyptian Journal of Hypertension and Cardiovascular Risk (EGY ISSN 1687-5338) **5786**
Egyptian Journal of Immunology (EGY) **5757**
The Egyptian Journal of Internal Medicine (EGY ISSN 1110-7782) **5945**
• Egyptian Journal of Medical Laboratory Sciences/Al-Magallat al-Misriyyat lil-'ulum al-Tibiyyat al-Ma'maliyyat (EGY ISSN 1110-5593) **5905**
➤ The Egyptian Journal of Medical Sciences/Al-Magallat al-Misriyyat lil-'lum al-Tibiyyat (EGY ISSN 1110-0540) **5608**
The Egyptian Journal of Mental Health (EGY ISSN 1110-1075) **6137**
➤ Egyptian Journal of Microbiology/Magallah al-Misriyah lil-Mikrubiyulugiya (EGY ISSN 0022-2704) **884**
• Egyptian Journal of Natural History (EGY ISSN 1110-6867) **670**
• ➤ The Egyptian Journal of Neurology, Psychiatry, and Neurosurgery (EGY ISSN 1110-1083) **6137**
Egyptian Journal of Nutrition *see* Egyptian Journal of Nutrition and Feed **6658**
Egyptian Journal of Nutrition and Feed (EGY ISSN 1110-6360) **6658**
Egyptian Journal of Nutrition and Health/Al- Magallat al-Misriyyat li-l-Taghziyyat wa-al-Sihhat/Al-Majallat al-Misriyyat li-l-Taghziyyat wa-al-Sihhat (EGY ISSN 1687-7950) **6658**
Egyptian Journal of Occupational Medicine (EGY ISSN 1110-1881) **5609**
The Egyptian Journal of Otolaryngology (EGY ISSN 1012-5574) **6079**
Egyptian Journal of Petroleum (EGY) **6767**
• ➤ Egyptian Journal of Pharmaceutical Sciences/Al-Magallat al-Misriyya lil-'ulum al Saydaliyyat (EGY ISSN 0301-5068) **6837**
➤ Egyptian Journal of Physics/Al-Magallat al-Misriyyat lil-Fiiziqaa (EGY ISSN 1110-0214) **7010**
➤ Egyptian Journal of Physiological Science/Al-Magallat al-Missriyat lil-'lum al-Fisiulugiyyat (EGY ISSN 0301-8660) **921**
Egyptian Journal of Phytopathology/Al-Magallat al-Miriyyat li-Amradh al-Nabat (EGY ISSN 1110-0230) **786**
The Egyptian Journal of Psychiatry (EGY ISSN 1110-1105) **6137**
Egyptian Journal of Rabbit Science (EGY ISSN 1110-2594) **941**
➤ Egyptian Journal of Radiation Sciences & Applications/Al-Magallat al-Misriyyat Lil-'ulum Al-is'aa'iyyat wa Tatbiqatihaa (EGY ISSN 1110-0303) **6195**
Egyptian Journal of Remote Sensing and Space Sciences (EGY ISSN 1110-9823) **2707**
• Egyptian Journal of Solids (EGY ISSN 1012-5566) **7010**
• ➤ The Egyptian Journal of Surgery/Magallat al-Giraahat al-Misriyyat/Majallat al-Jiraahat al-Misriyyat (EGY ISSN 1110-1121) **6242**
Egyptian Journal of Textile & Polymer Science & Technology (EGY ISSN 1110-600X) **8450**
• ➤ Egyptian Journal of Tourism and Hospitality (ZAF ISSN 1997-163X) **8700**
Egyptian Journal of Urology (EGY ISSN 1110-5712) **6267**
† Egyptian Journal of Wildlife and Natural Resources (EGY ISSN 1110-113X) **8953**
Egyptian Journal of Zoology/Al-Magallah al-Misriyyah li-'Ilm al-Hayawan (EGY ISSN 1110-6344) **941**
Egyptian Lactation Consultant Association Scientific Journal *see* E L C A Scientific Journal **5989**
Egyptian Mathematical Society. Journal (EGY ISSN 1110-256X) **5485**
Egyptian Medical Journal of the National Research Center/Al-Magallat al-Tibbiyyat lil-Markaz al-Qawmi lil-Buhuth (EGY ISSN 1687-1278) **5609**
Egyptian Mineralogist/Al-Magallat al-Misriyyat li-'Im al-Ma'adin (EGY ISSN 1110-1466) **6461**
• Egyptian National Cancer Institute. Journal/Magallat Ma'had al-Awraam al-Qawmi al-Misri (EGY ISSN 1110-0362) **6018**
• Egyptian Orthopaedic Journal/Al-Majallah Al-Misriyyah li-Jirahat al-'Itham (EGY ISSN 1110-1148) **6058**
Egyptian Paediatric Association. Gazette (EGY ISSN 1110-6638) **6091**
The Egyptian Population and Family Planning Review (EGY ISSN 1110-1156) **972**
Egyptian Poultry Science (EGY ISSN 1110-5623) **285**
Egyptian Prehistory Monographs (BEL) **392**
The Egyptian Rheumatologist (EGY ISSN 1110-1164) **6223**
Egyptian Rheumatology and Rehabilitation (EGY ISSN 1110-161X) **6223**
Egyptian Society of Cardiology. Bulletin *see* The Egyptian Heart Journal **5785**
Egyptian Society of Cataract and Corneal Diseases. Journal *see* Cataract and Cornea **6039**
Egyptian Society of Endocrinology, Metabolism and Diabetes. Journal (EGY ISSN 1110-1245) **5890**
Egyptian Society of Engineers. Journal (EGY ISSN 1110-1253) **3188**
Egyptian Society of Obstetrics & Gynecology. Journal (EGY ISSN 0258-3216) **5989**
Egyptian Society of Parasitology. Journal (EGY ISSN 1110-0583) **5813**
Egyptian Society of Pharmacology and Experimental Therapeutics. Journal/Magallat al-Gami'iat al-Misriyyat lil-Adwiyyat wa-al-'ilag al-Tagribi (EGY ISSN 1110-7510) **6837**

Title

10232 EGYPTIAN SOCIETY OF TOXICOLOGY. JOURNAL ULRICH'S PERIODICALS

Egyptian Society of Toxicology. Journal (EGY ISSN 1110-127X) 3496
† Egyptian Society of Ultrasonics in Medicine. Journal (EGY ISSN 1110-7669) 8953
The Egyptian Statistical Journal/Al- Majallah al-Ihsa'iyyah al-Misriyyah (EGY ISSN 0542-1748) 8367
Egyptian Veterinary Medical Association. Journal/Magallat al-Gam'iyyat al-Tibiyyat al-Baytariyyat al-Misriyyat (EGY ISSN 1110-1288) 8797
• Egyptian Women's Dermatological Society. Journal (EGY ISSN 1687-1537) 5876
Egyptological Memoirs (NLD ISSN 1387-2710) 392
Egyptological Publications see Egyptologische Uitgaven 4321
➤ Egyptologische Uitgaven/Egyptological Publications (NLD ISSN 0927-0043) 4321
Egyptology and Ancient Near Eastern Studies see Athlone Publications in Egyptology and Ancient Near Eastern Studies 382
Eh! (MYS ISSN 1511-5631) 8859
Eh! Lisez-moi (FRA ISSN 1774-0436) 5288
Ehe und Familie (AUT ISSN 0013-2470) 3797
Ehe- und Familienrecht Zeitschrift see E F - Z 4909
Ehe- und Familienrechtliche Entscheidungen (AUT) 4663
• eHealth (IND ISSN 0973-8959) 7515
• eHealth (USA) 6985
• eHealth.com (USA) 6985
• ➤ eHealth International (USA ISSN 1476-3591) 5830
eHealthcare Strategy & Trends (USA ISSN 1526-0593) 4092
Ehealthcom see E-Health-Com 5830
Ehime College of Health Sciences. Bulletin see Ehime Kenritsu Iryo Gijutsu Tanki Daigaku Kiyo 5609
Ehime Daigaku Nogakubu Enshurin Hokoku/Ehime University Forest. Bulletin (JPN ISSN 0424-6845) 3687
Ehime Daigaku Nogakubu Kiyo/Ehime University. Memoirs. Section 6 (JPN ISSN 0424-6829) 107
Ehime Daigaku Rigakubu Kiyo/Ehime University. Faculty of Science. Memoirs (JPN ISSN 0919-5203) 7852
Ehime Igaku/Ehime Medical Journal (JPN ISSN 0286-3677) 5609
Ehime Journal of Medicine see Ehime Kenritsu Byoin Gakkai Kaishi 5609
Ehime Kenritsu Byoin Gakkai Kaishi/Ehime Journal of Medicine (JPN ISSN 0289-5463) 5609
Ehime Kenritsu Iryo Gijutsu Tanki Daigaku Kiyo/Ehime College of Health Sciences. Bulletin (JPN ISSN 0915-3012) 5609
Ehime Medical Journal see Ehime Igaku 5609
Ehime Prefecture. Monthly Report of Meteorology see Ehimeken Kisho Geppo 6352
Ehime University. College of Agriculture. Memoirs see Ehime Daigaku Nogakubu Kiyo 107
Ehime University. Faculty of Science. Memoirs see Ehime Daigaku Rigakubu Kiyo 7852
Ehime University Forest. Bulletin see Ehime Daigaku Nogakubu Enshurin Hokoku 3687
Ehime University. Memoirs. Section 6 see Ehime Daigaku Nogakubu Kiyo 107
Ehimeken Construction Laboratory. Report see Ehimeken Kensetsu Kenkyujo Kenkyujoho 3266
➤ Ehimeken Kensetsu Kenkyujo Kenkyujoho/Ehimeken Construction Laboratory. Report (JPN ISSN 0289-5617) 3266
Ehimeken Kisho Geppo/Ehime Prefecture. Monthly Report of Meteorology (JPN ISSN 0916-5061) 6352
EhsCompliance Newsletter see E H S Compliance Newsletter 3414
EhsJustice Newsletter see E H S Justice Newsletter 3414
• ➤ EHumanista (USA ISSN 1540-5877) 4216
Ei-Beibungaku see Studies in British & American Literature 5380
• Ei EnCompassLit (USA) 6799
• Ei Magazine (GBR) 2556
ei8hg (GBR ISSN 1476-6817) 4575
Ei8ht Magazine (USA ISSN 1931-8286) 2380
Eibe (DEU) 2852
Eibungaku Hyoron/Review of English Literature (JPN ISSN 0420-8641) 5288
➤ Eibungaku Kenkyu/Studies in English Literature (JPN ISSN 0039-3649) 5288
Eibungaku Shicho/Current Ideas in English Literature (JPN ISSN 0910-500X) 5114
Eibungaku to Eigogaku/English Literature and Language (JPN ISSN 0289-1050) 5288
Eichler Network Home Maintenance Directory see Eichler Network Newsletter 1006
• Eichler Network Newsletter (USA) 1006
Eichstaetter Antrittsvorlesungen (DEU ISSN 1617-4003) 3060
Eichstaetter Materialien (DEU ISSN 0722-1010) 3060
Eichstaetter Universitaetsreden (DEU ISSN 1617-3996) 7796
Eid & Ramadan Magazine (GBR) 7710
Die Eidechse (DEU ISSN 0945-5183) 941
Eidfaxi (ISL ISSN 1021-7169) 8290
Eidgenoessische Anstalt fuer Wasserversorgung, Abwasserreinigung und Gewaesserschutz News see E A W A G News 8823
• Eidgenoessische Finanzverwaltung. Oekonomenteam. Working Paper (CHE ISSN 1660-8240) 1102
Eidgenoessische Forschungsanstalt fuer Wald, Schnee und Landschaft. Mitteilungen see Forest Snow and Landscape Research 2611
Eidgenoessische Forschungsanstalt W S L. Jahresbericht (CHE ISSN 1424-2699) 2610
Eidgenoessische Technische Hochschule Bibliothek. B: Bibliothekswesen see E T H - Bibliothek. B: Bibliothekswesen 5057
Eidgenoessische Technische Hochschule Globe see E T H Globe 2978
Eidgenoessische Technische Hochschule. Institut fuer Orts-, Regional- und Landesplanung. Lehrmittel (CHE) 4409
Eidgenoessische Technische Hochschule Series in Information Processing see E T H Series in Information Processing 2543
Eidgenoessische Technische Hochschule Series in Information Theory and its Applications see E T H Series in Information Theory and its Applications 2543
Eidgenoessische Technische Hochschule Zuerich. Bulletin see E T H Globe 2978
➤ Eidgenoessische Technische Hochschule Zuerich. Institut fuer Baustatik und Konstruktion. Allgemeine Berichte (CHE) 3343
➤ Eidgenoessische Technische Hochschule Zuerich. Institut fuer Baustatik und Konstruktion. Versuchsberichte (CHE) 3343
Eidgenoessische Technische Hochschule Zuerich. Institut fuer Geodaesie und Photogrammetrie. Mitteilungen (CHE ISSN 0252-9335) 2780
Eidgenoessische Technische Hochschule Zuerich. Versuchsanstalt fuer Wasserbau, Hydrologie und Glaziologie. Jahresbericht (CHE) 2794
Eidgenoessische Technische Hochschule Zuerich. Versuchsanstalt fuer Wasserbau, Hydrologie und Glaziologie. Mitteilungen (CHE ISSN 0374-0056) 2794
Eidgenossische Technische Hoschschule Zurich. Geobotanisches Institut. Bulletin see Geobotanical Institute E T H. Bulletin 791
• Eido Electa (ITA ISSN 1121-8800) 6195
• Eidola (ITA ISSN 1824-6192) 487
† Eidolon (AUS ISSN 1038-5657) 8953
➤ Eidos (CAN ISSN 0707-2287) 6915
Eidos (SWE ISSN 1650-5298) 487
Eidos: Studies in Classical Kinds (USA) 2233
Eidsvold Blad - Ullensaker Blad (NOR) 3922
Eiendomsmegleren (NOR ISSN 0803-7345) 7589
Eier-Wild-Gefluegel-Markt (DEU ISSN 0013-2500) 3634
Eigen Aard (BEL ISSN 0775-4779) 8859
Eigen Huis & Interiur (NLD ISSN 0165-3083) 4539
Eigen Huis Magazine (NLD ISSN 1569-3503) 1006
Eigen Perk (NLD ISSN 0929-8584) 4217
Eigen Vervoer Organisatie Magazine see E V O Magazine 8578
Das Eigene Haus (DEU) 7589
• Die Eigentumswohnung (DEU ISSN 0722-2815) 4409
eight see ei8hg 4575
Eight Ball (USA) 4575
Eight Days see 8 Days 4984
Eight Hundred and Five Living see 805 Living 5087
Eight Hundred and Five Weddings see 805 Weddings 5562
Eight Magazine see Ei8ht Magazine 2380
Eight Ways to Avoid Probate see 8 Ways to Avoid Probate 4906
Eighteen-Eleven (USA) 2651
Eighteen Nineties Society. Journal (GBR ISSN 0144-008X) 5288
Eighteen Sixty Nine Times see 1869 Times 6901
➤ The Eighteenth Century Current Bibliography (USA ISSN 1930-1812) 624
• ➤ Eighteenth-Century Fiction (CAN ISSN 0840-6286) 5288
Eighteenth-Century French Intellectual History (USA ISSN 1073-8657) 4217
Eighteenth-Century Ireland/Iris an da Chultur (IRL ISSN 0790-7915) 4217
• ➤ Eighteenth-Century Life (USA ISSN 0098-2601) 4217
Eighteenth Century Life see Eighteenth-Century Life 4217
• ➤ Eighteenth-Century Music (GBR ISSN 1478-5706) 6564
Eighteenth Century Music see Eighteenth-Century Music 6564
• ➤ The Eighteenth-Century Novel (USA ISSN 1528-3631) 5288
Eighteenth-Century Novels by Women (USA) 5288
• ➤ Eighteenth-Century Studies (USA ISSN 0013-2586) 4138
• Eighteenth Century: Theory and Interpretation (USA ISSN 0193-5380) 4217
➤ Eighteenth-Century Thought (USA ISSN 1545-0449) 6915
➤ Eighteenth-Century Women (USA ISSN 1529-5966) 8099
8th District Dental Society. Bulletin (USA ISSN 0190-0277) 5842
Eighty Twenty Europa see 8020 Europa 2441
Eigo Eibungaku Kenkyu/Hiroshima Studies in English Language and Literature (JPN ISSN 0288-2876) 5288
Eigo Eibungaku Kenkyujo Kiyou (JPN ISSN 0385-8855) 5288
Eigo Eibungaku Ronso/Studies in English Language and Literature (JPN ISSN 0422-7891) 5289
Eigo Seinen/Rising Generation (JPN ISSN 0287-2706) 5114
Eigse (IRL ISSN 0013-2608) 5114
Eigse Cheol Tire see Irish Folk Music Studies 6578
Eijingu ando Herusu/Aging & Health (JPN) 4044
Eiju General Hospital. Journal see Eiju Sogo Byoin Kiyo 5905
Eiju Sogo Byoin Kiyo/Eiju General Hospital. Journal (JPN ISSN 0915-5422) 5905
Eikasmos (ITA ISSN 1121-8819) 5114
Eikestadnuus (ZAF) 3948
• Eikon (AUT ISSN 1024-1922) 6966
➤ Eikon (DEU) 2233
Eikon (ITA ISSN 1970-7789) 487
Eikones (GRC) 3874
Eilbote (DEU) 210
Eildienst: Bundesgerichtliche Entscheidungen E B E - B A G (DEU ISSN 0935-0608) 4663
Eildienst: Bundesgerichtliche Entscheidungen E B E - B G H (DEU ISSN 0935-8455) 4663
Eileen Magazine (NLD ISSN 1872-1389) 8578
Ein Rhaglen ar Gyfer Cefn Gwlad see Our Programme for the Countryside 2623
Ein000 (DEU) 5070
Eina (ESP ISSN 0211-0946) 107
Einayim (ISR ISSN 0793-1891) 2187
Einblick (Berlin) (DEU) 6696
Einblick (Heidelberg) (DEU ISSN 0933-128X) 6018
Einblicke (Frankfurt am Main) (DEU ISSN 1619-5248) 1102
Einblicke (Oldenburg) (DEU ISSN 0930-8253) 2282
Einblicke in die Wissenschaft (DEU ISSN 1615-5971) 7852
Eindexamen Academieboek A K V/St Joost see A K V/St Joost. Academieboek 2822
Eindhoven-Helmond Zakelijk see Zakelijk (Regio Eindhoven-Helmond) 1802
Eindhoven-Helmond Zakelijk see Zakelijk (Regio den Bosch) 1802
† Eindhoven University of Technology. Department of Technology Management. Research Report (NLD ISSN 0929-8479) 8953
• ➤ Eindhoven University of Technology. Faculty of Electrical Engineering. Annual Research Report (NLD) 3301
Eine fuer Alle (DEU) 2187
EineWelt (DEU ISSN 0949-216X) 7755
† Einfach Frau (DEU) 8953
Einfach Gut Kochen (DEU) 4357
Einfach Leben (DEU ISSN 1862-3700) 7796
Einfach Tierisch see Disney's Einfach Tierisch 2185
Einfamilienhaeuser (CHE ISSN 1423-6516) 4539
Einfamilienhaeuser (DEU) 1006
Das Einfamilienhaus (CHE ISSN 1422-8467) 1006
Das Einfamilienhaus (DEU) 1006
Einhard Intern (DEU) 2852
Einhorn-Jahrbuch (DEU ISSN 0723-0877) 4217
Einhorn Newsletter (USA) 1102
Einigkeit (DEU ISSN 0420-8854) 4593
Einkaeufer im Markt see Dow Jones Einkaeufer im Markt 1814
Einkauf see E K - Experte Aktuell 1815
Einkauf - Materialwirtschaft - Logistik (CHE ISSN 1421-864X) 1815
Einkaufen auf dem Bauernhof in Deutschland (DEU ISSN 1430-8223) 107
Einkaufs Experte Aktuell see E K - Experte Aktuell 1815
Einkaufsfuehrer Druck und Publishing (DEU ISSN 1434-2529) 7320
Einkaufsfuehrer fuer den Strassenbau Deutschland (DEU) 8630
Einkaufsfuehrer fuer Wissenschaft und Forschung (AUT) 1884
Eins Eins Zwei - Magazin der Feuerwehr see Feuerwehr Fachzeitschrift 3576
Eins mal Eins Ihr Partner see 1 x 1 Ihr Partner 173
Einsatz (Kissing) (DEU ISSN 1613-7949) 3576
Einsatz (Stuttgart) (DEU) 6059
Einsichten (DEU ISSN 0941-3642) 2980
• Einstein (BRA ISSN 1679-4508) 5609
Einstein Institution Monograph Series see Albert Einstein Institution. Monograph Series 7104
• ➤ Einstein Journal of Biology and Medicine (USA ISSN 1559-5501) 670
Einstein Quarterly Journal of Biology and Medicine see Einstein Journal of Biology and Medicine 670
Eintracht (USA) 3531
Eintracht-Aktuell (DEU) 8227
Eintracht Frankfurt (DEU) 8227
Der Einwurf (DEU) 4081
† Einzelhandels Berater (DEU ISSN 0722-4850) 8953
EIR Strategic Alert see E I R Strategic Alert. Deutsche Ausgabe 5214
• Eire - Ireland (USA ISSN 0013-2683) 4450
➤ Eirene (CZE ISSN 0046-1628) 2233
Eisbericht (DEU ISSN 0013-2705) 2732
➤ Eisei Dobutsu/Medical Entomology and Zoology (JPN ISSN 0424-7086) 941
Eisei Kagaku see Journal of Health Science 3499
Eisei Tsushin Kenkyu/Satellite Communications Study see Jouhou Tsuushin Bulletin 2329
Eisei Tsushin Nenpo/Annual Report of Satellite Communication (JPN) 2319
• Die Eisen, Blech und Metall Verarbeitende Industrie, Stahlverformung (DEU) 6311
Eisen und Stahl (DEU) 6338
Eisen und Stahl - Jaehrliche Statistiken (LUX ISSN 1609-4107) 6338
Eisenbahn-Amateur (CHE ISSN 0013-2764) 4334
† Eisenbahn-Befoerderungsrecht (DEU) 8953
Eisenbahn Geschichte (DEU ISSN 1611-6283) 8616
Eisenbahn Ingenieur Kalender (Year) (DEU ISSN 0934-5930) 8616
Eisenbahn-Journal (DEU ISSN 0720-051X) 8616
Eisenbahn-Kurier (DEU ISSN 0170-5288) 4334
Eisenbahn-Kurier Special (DEU ISSN 1434-3045) 4334
Eisenbahn-Landwirt (DEU ISSN 0013-2772) 3728
Eisenbahn Modellbahn Magazin (DEU ISSN 0342-1902) 8616
Eisenbahn Oesterreich (CHE ISSN 1421-2900) 8616
Eisenbahn Revue International (CHE ISSN 1421-2811) 8617
Eisenbahner (AUT ISSN 0013-2799) 8617
Eisenbahner-Rundschau see G D B A Magazin 1682
Der Eisenbahningenieur (DEU ISSN 0013-2810) 8617
Eisenbahntechnische Rundschau (DEU ISSN 0013-2845) 8617
Eisenhower National Clearinghouse for Mathematics and Science Education Focus see E N C Focus 3058
Eisenwaren Zeitung (DEU) 1053
Eisenwerkstoffe, Legierte und Unlegierte Staehle see Informationsdienst F I Z Technik. Eisenwerkstoffe, Legierte und Unlegierte Staehle 3230
† Eishockey Live (DEU) 8953
• Eishockey News (DEU) 8171
Eiskanal (DEU ISSN 1610-8477) 8311
Eisma's Schildersblad (NLD ISSN 1567-1852) 6717
Eisma's Vakpers see Eisma's Schildersblad 6717
Der Eisstocksport (DEU ISSN 1438-0420) 8171
Eisteach (IRL ISSN 1393-3582) 6137
➤ Eiszeitalter und Gegenwart: E & G (DEU ISSN 0424-7116) 6724
Eivissa (ESP ISSN 1130-7803) 4450
Eiyo Nippon/Nutrition of Japan (JPN ISSN 0013-6492) 6658
Eiyo Seiri Kenkyukaiho/Japanese Society for Animal Nutrition and Metabolism. Proceedings (JPN ISSN 0286-4754) 286
Eiyo Shokuryo Gakkaishi/Japanese Society of Food and Nutrition. Journal see Nippon Eiyo Shokuryo Gakkaishi 6664
Eiyogaku Zasshi/Japanese Journal of Nutrition and Dietetics (JPN ISSN 0021-5147) 6658
Eiyou Hyoka to Chiryo/Japanese Journal of Nutritional Assessment (JPN ISSN 0915-759X) 6658
Eizo Joho Industrial/Monthly Journal of Imaging and Information Technology (JPN ISSN 1346-1362) 6195
Eizo Joho Media Gakkaishi/Institute of Image Information and Television Engineers (JPN ISSN 1342-6907) 2319
Eizo Joho Medical/Monthly Journal of Medical Imaging and Information (JPN ISSN 1346-1354) 6195
Eizo Joho Medikaru see Eizo Joho Medical 6195
Eizou Joho Media Gakkai Gijutsu Hokoku/I T E Technical Report (JPN ISSN 1342-6893) 2319
Eizou Joho Media Gakkai Nenji Taikai Koen Yokoshu/Institute of Image Information and Television Engineers. Proceedings of Annual Convention (JPN ISSN 1343-1846) 2319
Ejecutivos de Finanzas (MEX) 1740
Ejecutivos Financieros (ESP) 1102
• Ejendomsmaegleren (DNK ISSN 0013-2896) 7589
Ejercito (ESP ISSN 0013-2918) 6420
eJIFCC see e J I F C C 2060
Ejobios see EurAsian Journal of Biosciences 672
• eJour (DNK ISSN 1901-3183) 2533
• Ejournal (USA ISSN 1054-1055) 2497
• eJournal of Health Informatics (AUS ISSN 1446-4381) 7515
• ➤ eJournal of Tax Research (AUS ISSN 1448-2398) 1921
Ejournal Tecnica Administrativa see Tecnica Administrativa 1182
▼ • Ejournal USA (USA ISSN 1948-4399) 7232
• ➤ Ejournalist (AUS ISSN 1444-741X) 2320
EjournalUSA. Economic Perspectives see Ejournal USA 7232
EjournalUSA. Global Issues see Ejournal USA 7232
EjournalUSA. Issues of Democracy see Ejournal USA 7232
EjournalUSA. U.S. Foreign Policy Agenda see Ejournal USA 7232
EjournalUSA. U.S. Society & Values see Ejournal USA 7232
Ek Bacharer Srestha Kabita (IND) 5421
EK-Experte Aktuell see E K - Experte Aktuell 1815
Ekach Shatkar (IND) 8227
• Ekaia (ESP ISSN 0214-9001) 7852
Ekeloefet (SWE ISSN 1650-8432) 5289
Ekho Kavkaza (RUS ISSN 0869-3250) 7282
Ekho Litvy (LTU ISSN 1392-0367) 3905
Ekho Osha (KGZ) 3903
Ekho Planety (RUS ISSN 0234-1670) 3935
Ekisho Disupurei Sangyo Nenkan/Annual of Liquid Crystal Display Industries (JPN) 2110
Ekisho Toronkai Koen Yokoshu/Preprints of Symposium on Liquid Crystals (JPN) 2110
Ekistic Index of Periodicals (GRC ISSN 0013-2934) 4435
• ➤ Ekistics (GRC ISSN 0013-2942) 4409
Ekisupato Nasu see Expert Nurse 5958
Ekitai Kuromatogurafu Kenkyukai Koen Yoshishu/Research Group of Liquid Chromatography. Proceedings (JPN) 2061

Ekko see Filmmagasinet Ekko 6500
Ekko see Filmmagasinet Ekko 6500
• Eklectique (USA) 6644
• Eklem Hastaliklan ve Cerrahisi/Joint Diseases & Related Surgery (TUR ISSN 1305-8282) 6059
Eko (RUS ISSN 0131-7652) 1102
Eko. Ekologie a Spolecnost (CZE ISSN 1210-4728) 670
Eko i My (POL ISSN 1232-4531) 3418
Ekobrevet (SWE) 3418
Ekoland (NLD ISSN 0926-9142) 107
Ekoland (POL ISSN 1426-2940) 107
Ekolink (RUS) 1102
• ➤ Ekologia/Ecology (SVK ISSN 1335-342X) 670
Ekologia i Technika/Ecology and Technology (POL ISSN 1230-462X) 3418
Ekologicheskaya Khimiya/Ecological Chemistry (RUS ISSN 1025-6709) 3496
Ekologicheskaya Situatsiya (RUS) 2610
Ekologicheskie Sistemy i Pribory (RUS) 3418
Ekologicheskii Vestnik Moskvy (RUS) 671
Ekologicheskii Vestnik Nauchnykh Tsentrov Chernomorskogo Ekonomicheskogo Sotrudnichestva see Nauchnye Tsentry Chernomorskogo Ekonomicheskogo Sotrudnichestva. Ekologicheskii Vestnik 3456
Ekologicheskii Vestnik Rossii (RUS ISSN 0868-7420) 2610
† Ekologie v Podnikove Praxi (CZE ISSN 1801-6324) 8953
Ekologija (LTU ISSN 0235-7224) 671
Ekologija see Acta Biologica Iugoslavica. Serija D: Ekologija 649
• Ekologiskt Lantbruk (SWE ISSN 1102-6758) 107
• ➤ Ekologiya (RUS ISSN 0367-0597) 3419
Ekologiya Cheloveka (RUS) 3496
Ekologiya i Promyshlennost' Rossii (RUS) 2610
• ➤ Ekologiya Morya/Marine Ecology (UKR ISSN 0203-4646) 2803
Ekologiya Promyshlennogo Proizvodstva (RUS) 3419
• ➤ Ekoloji (TUR ISSN 1300-1361) 3419
Ekoloji Cevre Dergisi see Ekoloji 3419
• Ekoloji Magazin (TUR ISSN 1304-5407) 3419
Ekoloji Magazin Dergisi see Ekoloji Magazin 3419
• Ekoloji Teknik Dergisi (TUR) 3419
Ekonom (CZE ISSN 1210-0714) 1102
▼ • ➤ Ekonometri ve Istatistik E-Dergisi/Istanbul University Econometrics and Statistics e-Journal (TUR ISSN 1308-7215) 1102
† Ekonomi/Economy (TUR) 8953
Ekonomi dan Keuangan Indonesia (IDN ISSN 0126-155X) 1102
Ekonomi dan Pembangunan (IDN) 1102
Ekonomi Indonesia (IDN ISSN 0216-3659) 1102
➤ Ekonomia (CYP ISSN 1025-5508) 1540
Ekonomia i Srodowisko (POL ISSN 0867-8898) 3419
➤ Ekonomia Menedzerska (POL ISSN 1898-1143) 1740
• Ekonomia On-line (POL ISSN 1641-750X) 1225
• Ekonomiaz (ESP ISSN 0213-3865) 1482
Ekonomicheskaya Gazeta (RUS) 1102
Ekonomicheskaya i Social'naya Komissiya Dlya Azii i Tikhogo Okeana. Godovoi Doklad see Economic and Social Commission for Asia and the Pacific. Annual Report 1595
• ➤ Ekonomicheskaya Sotsiologiya (RUS ISSN 1726-3247) 1102
Ekonomicheskie i Pravovye Voprosy Nedropol'zovaniya v Rossii (RUS) 1103
Ekonomicheskie i Sotsial'nye Problemy Rossii (RUS) 1103
Ekonomicheskie Novosti Rossii i Sodruzhestva/Economic News from Russia and Commonwealth (RUS) 1103
Ekonomicheskie Pokazateli Razvitiya Rayonov Krainego Severa i Priravnennykh k nim Mestnostei/Economic Indicators of the Development of the Far North and Other Similar Areas (RUS) 1225
Ekonomicheskoe Dos'e "Zakonodatel'noe Obespechenie Biznesa v Rossii"/Economic Dossier "Legislative Support of Business in Russia" (RUS) 1103
Ekonomicheskoe i Sotsial'noe Razvitie Korennykh Malochislennykh Narodov Severa/Economic and Social Development of Indigenous Small Nationalities of the North (RUS) 1225
Ekonomicheskoe Obozrenie Logos Press (MDA) 1103
Ekonomicheskoe Obozrenie Tadzhikistana (TJK) 1103
• Ekonomicke Spektrum (SVK ISSN 1336-9105) 1103
• Ekonomicke Vysledky Prumyslu C R v Letech (Years) (Ceska Republika) (CZE) 1225
Ekonomicky Casopis/Journal of Economics (SVK ISSN 0013-3035) 1103
Ekonomika (LTU ISSN 1392-1258) 1103
▼ Ekonomika a Management/Economics and Management (CZE ISSN 1802-3975) 1103
Ekonomika APK (UKR) 197
Ekonomika, Finansy, Pravo (UKR) 1337
Ekonomika i Finansy Elektroenergetiki (RUS) 3301
• Ekonomika i Matematicheskie Metody (RUS ISSN 0424-7388) 1103
• Ekonomika i Organizacja Przedsiebiorstwa/Economics and Organization of Enterprise (POL ISSN 0860-6846) 1741
Ekonomika i Politika Rossii i Gosudarstv Blizhnego Zarubezh'ya (RUS) 3935
Ekonomika i Uchet Truda (RUS) 1287
Ekonomika i Upravlenie (UKR) 1741
Ekonomika i Vremya (RUS) 1103
• Ekonomika i Zhizn' (RUS ISSN 1607-0615) 1103
Ekonomika i Zhizn'. Dos'ye (RUS) 4848
Ekonomika i Zhizn'. Gostinyi Ryad (RUS) 1103
Ekonomika i Zhizn'. Moskovskii Vypusk see Ekonomika i Zhizn'. Gostinyi Ryad 1103
Ekonomika i Zhizn'. Moskovskii Vypusk see Ekonomika i Zhizn'. Rus' 1103
Ekonomika i Zhizn'. Moskovskii Vypusk see Ekonomika i Zhizn'. Sankt-Peterburgskii Vypusk 1103
Ekonomika i Zhizn'. Moskovskii Vypusk see Ekonomika i Zhizn' 1103
Ekonomika i Zhizn'. Rus' (RUS) 1103
Ekonomika i Zhizn'. Sankt-Peterburgskii Vypusk (RUS) 1103
• Ekonomika i Zhizn'. Sibir (RUS ISSN 1609-7122) 1103
Ekonomika i Zhizn'. Vopros - Otvet (RUS) 1287
Ekonomika i Zhizn'. Yurist (RUS) 4663
Ekonomika Poljoprivreda (SRB ISSN 0352-3462) 197
Ekonomika. Predprinimatel'stvo. Okruzhayushchaya Sreda (RUS) 1103
Ekonomika Sel'skogo Khozyaistva Rossii (RUS) 197
Ekonomika Sel'skokhozyaistvennykh i Pererabatyvayushchikh Predpriyatii (RUS ISSN 0235-2494) 1103
Ekonomika Sibiri i Dal'nego Vostoka (RUS) 1225
➤ Ekonomika Ukrainy/Ukraine's Economy (UKR ISSN 0131-7741) 1540
Ekonomika. Voprosy Shkol'nogo Ekonomicheskogo Obrazovaniya (RUS ISSN 1560-6937) 1103
Ekonomiko-Pravovoi Byulleten' (RUS) 1287
Ekonomirapporten (SWE ISSN 1653-0853) 1921
Ekonomisk Debatt/Economic Debate (SWE ISSN 0345-2646) 1103
Ekonomiska Forskningsinstitutet Nytt see E F I - Nytt 1225
Ekonomiska Meddelanden see Svenska Bankfoereningen. Ekonomiska Meddelanden 1521
➤ Ekonomiska Samfundets Tidskrift/Journal of the Economic Society of Finland (FIN ISSN 0013-3183) 1103
Ekonomiska Utsikter (SWE) 1718
Ekonomist (HRV ISSN 1332-2788) 1103
Ekonomist (RUS ISSN 0869-4672) 1884
Ekonomist (SRB ISSN 0354-5253) 1103
➤ Ekonomista (POL ISSN 0013-3205) 1103
➤ Ekonomska i Ekohistorija (HRV ISSN 1845-5867) 1540
Ekonomska in Poslovna Revija see Economic and Business Review 1099
Ekonomska Istrazivanja/Economic Research (HRV ISSN 1331-677X) 1104
• Ekonomska Misao i Praksa/Economic Thought and Practice (HRV ISSN 1330-1039) 1104
Ekonomska Politika (SRB ISSN 0013-3248) 1482
Ekonomski Anali (SRB ISSN 0013-3264) 1104
• Ekonomski Fakultet u Rijeci. Zbornik Radova/Rijeka School of Economics. Proceedings (HRV ISSN 1331-8004) 1104
• Ekonomski Pregled (HRV ISSN 0424-7558) 1104
Ekonomski Vjesnik (HRV ISSN 0353-359X) 1104
Ekonomsko Ogledalo (SVN ISSN 1318-3818) 1482
Ekopartner (POL ISSN 1230-2961) 3419
Ekota (BGD) 3799
Ekotechnika (POL ISSN 1428-2852) 8421
Ekotekhnologii i Resursosberezhenie (UKR ISSN 1027-3247) 3243
• Ekotekunoroji Kenkyu/Journal of Ecotechnology Research (JPN ISSN 1341-1187) 3419
Ekphrasis (USA ISSN 1095-841X) 5421
Ekran (RUS ISSN 0868-9024) 8470
• Ekran (SVN ISSN 0013-3302) 6497
Ekran i Stsena (RUS) 6497
Ekskluzivnyi Marketing (RUS) 1815
Eksperiment see Experiment 3533
Eksperimental'naya i Klinicheskaya Dermatokosmetologiya (RUS) 5876
Eksperimental'naya i Klinicheskaya Farmakologiya (RUS ISSN 0869-2092) 6837
➤ Eksperimental'naya i Klinicheskaya Gastroenterologiya (RUS ISSN 1682-8658) 5922
Eksperimental'naya i Klinicheskaya Meditsina see Eksperimentuli da Klinikuri Meditsina 5905
Eksperimental'naya Onkologiya see Experimental Oncology 6019
Eksperimentuli da Klinikuri Meditsina/Eksperimental'naya i Klinicheskaya Meditsina/Experimental and Clinical Medicine (GEO ISSN 1512-0392) 5905
Ekspert (RUS) 1337
Eksplitsitnoe Opisanie Yazyka i Avtomaticheskaya Obrabotka Tekstov see Explizite Beschreibung der Sprache und Automatische Textbearbeitung 8955
Eksport Kontakt see Dansk Export 1883
• Eksportaktuelt.no (NOR ISSN 1502-9964) 1563
Eksportstatistikk/Export Statistics (NOR ISSN 1504-2030) 3613
Ekspres (SRB ISSN 1451-0758) 3944
Ekspress Gazeta (RUS) 3935
Ekspress-Informatsiya. Geologicheskoe Izuchenie Nedr (RUS) 2733
Ekspress-Informatsiya. Geologiya, Metody Poiskov, Razvedki i Otsenki Mestorozhdenii Tverdykh Poleznykh Iskopaemykh (RUS ISSN 0236-3674) 2733
Ekspress-Informatsiya. Konservatsiya i Restavratsiya Pamyatnikov Istorii i Kul'tury (RUS ISSN 0869-8023) 3119
Ekspress Informatsiya. Kontrol'no-Izmeritel'naya Tekhnika (RUS ISSN 0131-0224) 4490
Ekspress-Informatsiya. Marketing Nefti i Nefteproduktov (RUS) 1815
Ekspress-Informatsiya po Zarubezhnoi Elektronnoi Tekhnike (RUS) 3094
Ekspress Informatsiya. Pravovye Voprosy Okhrany Okruzhayushchei Sredy (RUS ISSN 0320-765X) 4822
Ekspress Informatsiya. Resursosberegayushchie Tekhnologii (RUS ISSN 0132-7410) 3478
Ekspress Informatsiya. Tara i Upakovka. Konteinery (RUS ISSN 0131-0526) 6715
Ekspress Informatsiya. Upravlenie, Logistika i Informatika na Transporte (RUS) 8524
• Ekspress K Online (KAZ ISSN 1607-1891) 3902
• Ekspress-Klub (UKR) 3964
Ekspress Novosti (BLR) 3800
Ekspress - Zakon (RUS ISSN 0869-7302) 1921
• Eksternt Notat (Online Edition) (DNK) 3266
Eksternt Notat (Print Edition) see Eksternt Notat (Online Edition) 3266
• Ekstra Bladet (DNK) 3833
Ekstrennaya Meditsinskaya Pomoshch' v Moskve (RUS) 5609
Ekubo (JPN) 2187
Ekumenismo (ITA ISSN 1127-2554) 7640
El-Arabi (EGY) 3836
EL-E-PHANT (USA) 5289
• El Empaque (USA) 6709
El Ha'ayin see Sources of Contemporary Jewish Thought 8989
• El-Hi Textbooks and Serials in Print (USA ISSN 0000-0825) 2933
El & Energi (DNK ISSN 0107-3931) 3301
El Paso Archaeological Society. Special Reports (USA ISSN 0070-9573) 392
El Paso Archaeology (USA ISSN 0013-4023) 392
El Paso Economic Review (USA ISSN 8750-6033) 1104
El Salvador: Coyuntura Economica (SLV) 1104
El Salvador. Direccion General de Estadistica y Censos. Anuario Estadistico (SLV ISSN 0080-5661) 8367
El Salvador. Direccion General de Estadistica y Censos. Boletin Estadistico (SLV ISSN 0013-404X) 8367
El Salvador, Informe Economico y Social (SLV) 1482
El Salvador. Ministerio de Comercio Exterior. Directorio de Oferta Exportable (Year)/El Salvador. Ministry of Foreign Commerce. Exportable Offer Directory (SLV) 1563
El Salvador. Ministerio de Comercio Exterior. Estadisticas (SLV) 1225
El Salvador. Ministerio de Planificacion y Coordinacion del Desarrollo Economico y Social. Encuesta Nacional de Ingresos y Gastos de los Hogares Urbanos (SLV) 4370
El Salvador. Ministerio de Planificacion y Coordinacion del Desarrollo Economico y Social. Indicadores Economicos y Sociales (SLV ISSN 0581-4111) 8367
El Salvador. Ministerio de Planificacion y Coordinacion del Desarrollo Economico y Social. Memoria de Labores (SLV) 1482
El Salvador. Ministerio de Trabajo y Prevision Social. Estadisticas del Trabajo (SLV) 1225
El Salvador. Ministerio del Interior. Memoria de Labores (SLV) 7435
El Salvador. Ministry of Foreign Commerce. Exportable Offer Directory see El Salvador. Ministerio de Comercio Exterior. Directorio de Oferta Exportable (Year) 1563
El Salvador Proceso see Proceso 7173
El-Sharouk Journal for Commercial Studies see Magallat al-Shuruq li-l-'Ulum al-Tigariyyat 1146
Elainmaailma (FIN ISSN 1459-6954) 6808
Elakevaen Ristikot Extra see Kultaristikot Extra 8185
Elan (FRA ISSN 0397-0051) 5289
Elan (USA) 487
• Elan (USA) 3531
Elan (Deventer) see Management Scope 1776
▼ • Elan Money (GBR ISSN 1752-6779) 1337
Elanto (FIN) 1423
elaphe (DEU ISSN 0943-2485) 941
An Elasticthinking Project (NZL ISSN 1177-5610) 4450
Elastomery (POL ISSN 1427-3519) 3243
• Elava Helsinki (FIN ISSN 1455-1233) 7132
• ➤ eLaw Journal (AUS ISSN 1321-8247) 4663
Elbe Wochenblatt (DEU) 3846
Elbinger Nachrichten (DEU ISSN 0933-7334) 4217
Elbogen (Aarskrift) (SWE ISSN 1102-2892) 4217
Elbranschen (SWE ISSN 0013-4007) 3302
Elcina Electronics Directory (IND) 3094
Elde (DEU) 7132
Elder see Eldr 4044
• Elder Client Planner (USA ISSN 1550-0470) 1921
Elder Law Advisory (USA ISSN 1070-4825) 4664
Elder Law and Finance (GBR ISSN 1473-7043) 4664
• Elder Law Attorney (USA ISSN 1070-4817) 4664
Elder Law Bulletin (USA) 7435
• Elder Law in Maryland (USA) 4664
Elder Law Institute see Annual Elder Law Institute 4040
Elder Law Institute, Annual see Annual Elder Law Institute 4040
• ➤ The Elder Law Journal (USA ISSN 1070-1478) 4664
Elder Law News (USA) 4664
Elder Law Practice see Fundamentals of an Elder Law Practice 4678
• The Elder Law Report (USA ISSN 1047-7055) 4664
• ➤ Elder Law Review (AUS) 4664
• Elder Law Weekly (USA ISSN 1551-5117) 8038
▼ Elder Mountain (USA ISSN 1946-0511) 4291
ElderCare (USA ISSN 1548-2219) 4044
Eldercare Activities Guide see Current Activities in Longterm Care 4043
Eldercare Quarterly (CAN ISSN 1480-7912) 4044
† Eldercare Reporter (USA ISSN 1550-9745) 8953
Elderhostel (USA ISSN 1543-4710) 2940
Elderhostel Catalog see Elderhostel 2940
Elderhostel. International Catalog (USA ISSN 1092-6895) 8700
Elderly Chinese see Zhongguo Laonian 4058
• Elderly Client Advisor (GBR ISSN 1361-2700) 4044
Elderly Gazette see Laonianbao 4050
• Elderly Health Services Letter (USA ISSN 0891-9275) 4044
Elderly Latinos (USA ISSN 1069-0530) 4044
Elderly World see Laoren Tiandi 4050
Elder's Advisor see Marquette Elder's Advisor 4904
▼ • Eldr (USA ISSN 1937-5883) 4044
• Eldrimner. Nyhetsblad (SWE ISSN 1653-6460) 3634
Eldritch Tales (USA ISSN 1076-7991) 5442
Ele e Ela (BRA ISSN 0531-9153) 8859
• eLearn Magazine (USA ISSN 1535-394X) 2469
Elearning! (USA) 1416
Eleazer and Weissenberger Florida Evidence Courtroom Manual see Florida Evidence Courtroom Manual 4951
• Elecciones (PER ISSN 1994-5272) 7132
Elected and Appointed Black Judges in the United States (USA ISSN 0889-3179) 4950
Election Administration Reports (USA ISSN 0145-8124) 7132
Election and Related Laws and Rules and Regulations of North Carolina (USA) 7132
Election Archives and International Politics (IND ISSN 0971-2291) 7132
The Election Book (USA) 7492
Election Directory (USA ISSN 0163-5441) 7132
• Election Funding Authority of New South Wales. Annual Report (AUS ISSN 1320-8616) 7435
• ➤ Election Law Journal (USA ISSN 1533-1296) 4848
Election Law Review see Election Law Journal 4848
Election Laws of Arkansas and Constitution of the State of Arkansas of 1874 (USA ISSN 1933-267X) 4664
Election Laws of Arkansas and Constitution of the State of Arkansas of Eighteen Seventy Four see Election Laws of Arkansas and Constitution of the State of Arkansas of 1874 4664
• Election Talk (ZAF) 7132
Elections au Conseil National (Year) see Nationalratswahlen (Year) 7482
Elections Manitoba. Annual Report (CAN ISSN 1704-8389) 7132
Elections of Local Administrations see Turkey. Turkiye Istatistik Kurumu. Mahalli Idareler Secimi 7485
Elections to the Althing see Althingiskosningar 7198
• Elections Today (USA ISSN 1073-6719) 7132
Electoral Commission. Report see New Zealand. Electoral Commission, Te Kaitiaki Taki Kowhiri. Annual Report 7159
Electoral Insight (CAN ISSN 1488-3538) 7132
Electoral Reform Society News (GBR ISSN 0962-7979) 7205
Electoral Registers Since 1832 and Burgess Rolls (USA) 3764
• ➤ Electoral Studies (GBR ISSN 0261-3794) 7132
• Electra (DNK ISSN 0106-4703) 3302
Electra (ESP ISSN 0212-6222) 3157
Electra (FRA ISSN 0424-7701) 3302
• The Electra Buzz (USA) 8859
Electre Biblio see CD-ROM Electre 8940
Electric Age see Dianqi Shidai 3156
Electric and Hybrid Vehicle Technology International (GBR ISSN 1467-5560) 8578
• Electric & Hybrid Vehicles Today (USA) 8578
Electric and Magnetic Field Health Report see E M F Health Report 6676
Electric Blue (GBR ISSN 0959-1060) 6288
Electric Boat Journal (USA) 8275
• Electric Consumer (USA ISSN 0745-4651) 3157
Electric Control Engineering see Denki Kanri Gijutsu 3299
• Electric Dreams (USA ISSN 1089-4284) 7354
Electric Drive see Dianqi Chuandong 3300
• Electric Edge (USA) 4065
Electric Furnace Steel see Denki Seiko 6310
• Electric Light and Power (USA ISSN 0013-4120) 3302
Electric Light & Power see Electric Light and Power 3302
Electric Locomotives & Mass Transit Vehicles see Dianli Jiche yu Chenggui Cheliang 8616
Electric Machine see Denki 3298

Title

DIRECTORY 2010 ELECTRONIC PRODUCTS 10235

Electromedica (German Edition) see Medical Solutions 5671
➤ Electromotion (ROM ISSN 1223-057X) 3157
• Electromusications (GBR ISSN 1749-382X) 2380
Electromyography and Clinical Neurophysiology (BEL ISSN 0301-150X) 6137
Electron (NLD ISSN 0013-4767) 2358
The Electron (USA ISSN 0740-1922) 3095
Electron Devices for Microwave and Optoelectronic Applications see E D M O 3301
Electron - Engineering Review see Eletron: Revista de Engenharia 3306
• Electron Paramagnetic Resonance (GBR ISSN 1464-4622) 2122
• ➤ Electroneurobiologia (ARG ISSN 0328-0446) 6137
Electronic Actuell Magazin (DEU ISSN 0933-596X) 3095
• The Electronic African Bookworm: A Web Navigator (GBR) 2556
Electronic and Atomic Collisions see International Conference on the Physics of Electronic and Atomic Collisions. Abstracts of Contributed Papers and Invited Papers 7067
Electronic and Communications in Japan. Part 1: Communications see Electronics and Communications in Japan 3096
Electronic and Communications in Japan. Part 2: Electronics see Electronics and Communications in Japan 3096
Electronic and Communications in Japan. Part 3: Fundamental Electronic Science see Electronics and Communications in Japan 3096
Electronic & Computer Design World (CHN) 2417
Electronic & Electrical Engineering Research Studies. Communications Systems, Techniques and Applications Series see Next Generation Communications Systems Series 3326
Electronic & Electrical Engineering Research Studies. Pattern Recognition and Image Processing Series (GBR ISSN 0278-825X) 3304
• ➤ Electronic Antiquity (USA ISSN 1320-3606) 2233
Electronic Application News (IND ISSN 0013-4813) 3095
Electronic Article Number Portugal see E A N Portugal 6401
Electronic Auto Volt (FRA ISSN 1630-7062) 8578
Electronic Banking Law & Commerce Report see Electronic Banking Law and Commerce Report 2556
• Electronic Banking Law and Commerce Report (USA ISSN 1090-8420) 2556
Electronic Banking Market Assessment see Key Note Market Assessment. Electronic Banking 1364
† Electronic Banking News (FRA ISSN 1630-9553) 8953
• ➤ The Electronic Book Review (USA ISSN 1553-1139) 5214
• Electronic Boxing Weekly (USA) 8171
Electronic Bulletin of the Dante Society of America see The Dante Society of America. Electronic Bulletin 5283
• Electronic Business and Technology Law (NZL) 1104
• Electronic Business Information (TWN) 1104
Electronic Business Information/Japan Directory CD see Electronic Business Information 1104
• Electronic Business Law (GBR ISSN 1464-9624) 4866
• Electronic Business Law Reports (GBR ISSN 1473-0235) 4664
Electronic Card Industry Directory see Card Industry Directory 1324
Electronic Chart Display and Information System Today see E C D I S Today 8643
Electronic chemicals (USA ISSN 1940-7289) 3095
• Electronic Colloquium on Computational Complexity (DEU ISSN 1433-8092) 3095
Electronic Commerce (CAN) 1427
Electronic Commerce and Communications (GBR ISSN 1361-2727) 2556
• Electronic Commerce & Law Report (USA ISSN 1098-5190) 4830
Electronic Commerce and Law Report see Electronic Commerce & Law Report 4830
Electronic Commerce Briefing (GBR ISSN 1470-3904) 1416
Electronic Commerce Law & Policy see E-commerce Law & Policy 1096
Electronic Commerce Law Daily see E-Commerce Law Daily 4662
Electronic Commerce Management Mgt.com Ezine see E C Mgt.com Ezine 2555
Electronic Commerce News see Electronic Payments Week 1393
• Electronic Commerce Research (USA ISSN 1389-5753) 2556
• ➤ Electronic Commerce Research and Applications (NLD ISSN 1567-4223) 2543
Electronic Commerce Studies see Dianzi Shangwu Yanjiu 1092
• ➤ Electronic Communication Law Review (NLD ISSN 1570-2294) 2533
• ➤ Electronic Communications in Probability (USA ISSN 1083-589X) 5485
Electronic Component and Device Information see Dianzi Yuanqijian Zixun 3093
Electronic Component Distribution Market Report see Key Note Market Report: Electronic Component Distribution 3107
Electronic Component Distributors see Business Ratio. Electronic Component Distributors 3090
Electronic Component Industries Association. Electronics Directory see Elcina Electronics Directory 3094
Electronic Component Manufacturing Market Report see Key Note Market Report: Electronic Component Manufacturing 3107
Electronic Components & Materials see Dianzi Yuanjian yu Cailiao 3093
• Electronic Components & Technology Conference. Proceedings (Institute of Electrical and Electronics Engineers) (USA) 3095
Electronic Cultural Atlas Initiative Echo see E C A I Echo 4004
• Electronic Current Contents of Periodicals on the Middle East (ISR) 4170
Electronic-Data and Research see E-Data & Research 2536
Electronic Data Interchange Barcoding News see E D I & Barcoding News 2417
Electronic Data Management Report see e D M Report 2530
Electronic Data Processing Audit, Control and Security see E D P A C S 2513
Electronic Data Processing Auditing see E D P Auditing 2536
Electronic Data Processing Weekly see E D P Weekly 2536
• Electronic Design (USA ISSN 0013-4872) 3095
Electronic Design & Application World see Electronic Design & Application World - Nikkei Electronics 3095
Electronic Design & Application World - Nikkei Electronics (CHN) 3095
Electronic Design & Application World-Nikkei Electronics China see Dianzi Sheji Yingyong 2554
Electronic Design Automation see E D A 3093
Electronic Design - China see Dianzi Xitong Sheji 3092
Electronic Design Europe (GBR ISSN 1479-9782) 3095
Electronic Device Failure Analysis (USA ISSN 1537-0755) 2485
• Electronic Display World Online (USA) 3095
Electronic Distribution Show Directory (USA) 1991
Electronic Distribution Today (USA ISSN 1066-5773) 3095
• Electronic Education Report (USA ISSN 1077-9949) 2949
• Electronic Engineering Design (GBR) 3095
Electronic Engineering Times see E E Times 3094
Electronic Engineering Times Europe see E E Times Europe 3094
Electronic Engineering Times Japan see E E Times Japan 3187
Electronic Engineering Times U K see E E Times U K 3094
Electronic Engineers see Denki Gijutsusha 3091
Electronic Engineers Master see E E M 3094
Electronic Frontiers Australia Inc. News see E F A News 8952
Electronic Frontiers Australia Update see E F A Update 2417
Electronic Funds Transfer Data Book see E F T Data Book 1336
Electronic Games Market Report see Key Note Market Report: Electronic Games 2478
† • Electronic Gaming Monthly (USA ISSN 1058-918X) 8953
Electronic Gaming Monthly en Espanol (MEX) 2476
Electronic Gaming Monthly Turkiye (TUR) 2476
• Electronic Gay Community Magazine (USA) 4373
• ➤ Electronic Government (GBR ISSN 1740-7494) 7485
• ➤ Electronic Green Journal (USA ISSN 1076-7975) 3419
Electronic Health Record Newsletter see Health e Link 5625
Electronic Health Records Briefing (USA ISSN 1554-3293) 4114
• Electronic House (USA ISSN 0886-6643) 3095
† • Electronic Industry Telephone Directory (Year) (USA ISSN 0422-9053) 8953
• Electronic Information Partnerships (CAN ISSN 1207-8603) 2530
• Electronic Information Report (USA ISSN 1076-0490) 2417
Electronic Information Warfare Technology see Dianzi Xinxi Duikang Jishu 6419
Electronic Journal for History of Probability and Statistics see Journ@l Electronique d'Histoire des Probabilites et de la Statistique 8382
• ➤ Electronic Journal for Inclusive Education (USA ISSN 1545-0473) 3039
• ➤ Electronic Journal for the Integration of Technology in Education (USA ISSN 1556-5378) 2852
• ➤ The Electronic Journal of Academic and Special Librarianship (CAN ISSN 1704-8532) 5008
• ➤ Electronic Journal of Africana Bibliography (USA ISSN 1092-9576) 4170
• ➤ Electronic Journal of Analytic Philosophy (USA ISSN 1071-5800) 6915
▼ • ➤ Electronic Journal of Applied Statistical Analysis (JOR ISSN 2070-5948) 8367
• ➤ The Electronic Journal of Australian and New Zealand History (AUS ISSN 1324-2342) 4191
• Electronic Journal of Biomedicine/Revista Electronica de Biomedicina (ESP ISSN 1697-090X) 5609
• ➤ Electronic Journal of Biotechnology (CHL ISSN 0717-3458) 763
• ➤ Electronic Journal of Boundary Elements (USA ISSN 1542-3891) 3188
• ➤ Electronic Journal of Business Ethics and Organization Studies (FIN ISSN 1239-2685) 1104
• ➤ Electronic Journal of Business Research Methods (GBR ISSN 1477-7029) 1741
The Electronic Journal of Combinatorics see The Journal of Combinatorics 5501
• ➤ Electronic Journal of Communication/La Revue Electronique de Communication (USA ISSN 1183-5656) 7961
Electronic Journal of Communication Online see Electronic Journal of Communication 7961
• ➤ The Electronic Journal of Communicative Psychoanalysis (CAN ISSN 1492-1103) 7354
• ➤ Electronic Journal of Comparative Law (NLD ISSN 1387-3091) 4664
• ➤ Electronic Journal of Computational Kinematics (CAN) 7010
• ➤ Electronic Journal of Contemporary Japanese Studies (GBR ISSN 1476-9158) 549
• ➤ Electronic Journal of Differential Equations (USA ISSN 1072-6691) 5485
• Electronic Journal of e-Government (GBR ISSN 1479-439X) 7132
• Electronic Journal of E-Learning (GBR ISSN 1479-4403) 3060
Electronic Journal of Educational Research see Revista Electronica de Investigacion Educativa 3000
Electronic Journal of Educational Research, Assessment and Evaluation see R E L I E V E: Revista Electronica de Investigacion y Evaluacion Educativa 2902
• Electronic Journal of Endodontics Rosario (ARG ISSN 1666-6143) 5843
• Electronic Journal of Environmental, Agricultural and Food Chemistry (ESP ISSN 1579-4377) 228
• ➤ Electronic Journal of Evolutionary Modeling and Economic Dynamics (FRA ISSN 1298-0137) 1104
▼ • ➤ Electronic Journal of Family Business Studies (FIN ISSN 1796-9360) 1104
• ➤ Electronic Journal of Foreign Language Teaching (SGP ISSN 0219-9874) 5114
• ➤ Electronic Journal of Geotechnical Engineering (USA ISSN 1089-3032) 3266
• The Electronic Journal of Hand Surgery (GBR) 6242
Electronic Journal of Health Informatics see eJournal of Health Informatics 7515
• ➤ The Electronic Journal of Human Sexuality (USA ISSN 1545-5556) 5609
• Electronic Journal of Information Systems Evaluation (GBR ISSN 1566-6379) 1104
• The Electronic Journal of Information Systems in Developing Countries (HKG ISSN 1681-4835) 2417
Electronic Journal of Information Technology in Construction (Online Edition) see Journal of Information Technology in Construction 2548
• ➤ Electronic Journal of International History (GBR ISSN 1471-1443) 4138
• ➤ Electronic Journal of Knowledge Management (GBR ISSN 1479-4411) 5008
• The Electronic Journal of Linear Algebra (USA ISSN 1081-3810) 5485
• ➤ Electronic Journal of Literacy through Science (USA ISSN 1934-6670) 2852
• ➤ Electronic Journal of Mathematical and Physical Sciences (USA ISSN 1538-263X) 5485
➤ Electronic Journal of Mathematical and Physical Sciences. Conference and Seminar Edition (USA ISSN 1538-3318) 5485
▼ • ➤ The Electronic Journal of Mathematics & Technology (USA ISSN 1933-2823) 5485
• Electronic Journal of Natural Sciences (ARM ISSN 1728-791X) 7852
Electronic Journal of Oncology see Bulletin du Cancer (Online) 6010
• Electronic Journal of Operational Meteorology (USA) 6352
• ➤ Electronic Journal of Organizational Virtualness (CHE ISSN 1422-9331) 2556
• ➤ The Electronic Journal of Pediatric Gastroenterology, Nutrition, and Liver Diseases (BRA) 5923
• ➤ Electronic Journal of Polish Agricultural Universities (POL ISSN 1505-0297) 7852
• ➤ Electronic Journal of Probability (USA) 5485
• ➤ Electronic Journal of Qualitative Theory of Differential Equations (HUN ISSN 1417-3875) 5486
• ➤ The Electronic Journal of Radical Organisation Theory (NZL ISSN 1173-6631) 7961
The Electronic Journal of Radical Organization Theory see The Electronic Journal of Radical Organisation Theory 7961
Electronic Journal of Research in Educational Psychology see Revista Electronica de Investigacion Educativa y Psicopedagogica 2906
▼ • ➤ Electronic Journal of Science and Mathematics Education (TUR ISSN 1307-6086) 2949
• ➤ Electronic Journal of Science Education (USA ISSN 1087-3430) 2852
• ➤ Electronic Journal of Severe Storms Metereology (USA ISSN 1559-5404) 6352
• ➤ Electronic Journal of Sociology (CAN ISSN 1198-3655) 8099
▼ • ➤ Electronic Journal of Statistics (USA ISSN 1935-7524) 8367
• ➤ Electronic Journal of Structural Engineering (AUS ISSN 1443-9255) 3266
▼ • ➤ Electronic Journal of Sustainable Development (GBR ISSN 1753-3104) 3419
Electronic Journal of the International Federation of Clinical Chemistry and Laboratory Medicine see e J I F C C 2060
• ➤ Electronic Journal of Theoretical Physics (UAE ISSN 1729-5254) 7010
• ➤ Electronic Journal of Vedic Studies (USA ISSN 1084-7561) 549
• ➤ The Electronic Journal of Virtual Culture (USA ISSN 1081-3055) 2556
• Electronic Journal on Networks and Distributed Processing (FRA ISSN 1262-3261) 2497
Electronic Law see eLaw Journal 4663
Electronic Letters on Computer Vision and Image Analysis see E L C V I A 2417
• ➤ The Electronic Library (GBR ISSN 0264-0473) 5061
• ➤ Electronic Liquid Crystal Communications (USA ISSN 1942-0013) 2110
• Electronic Literature Collection (USA ISSN 1932-2011) 5289
Electronic Magazine of Multicultural Education see International Journal of Multicultural Education 2870
• Electronic Market Data Book (USA ISSN 0270-0093) 3095
• Electronic Market Trends (USA ISSN 0886-8506) 3095
Electronic Marketing Directory (USA ISSN 0070-7589) 1991
The Electronic Marketplace (Year) (USA ISSN 1087-7843) 2556
• ➤ Electronic Markets/Elektronische Maerkte (GBR ISSN 1019-6781) 1815
† Electronic Mass Media Age (ITA ISSN 0393-9170) 8953
• Electronic Materials and Packaging (GBR ISSN 1355-7599) 3095
Electronic Materials Information Service Datareviews (GBR ISSN 0950-1398) 3095
Electronic Materials Information Service Processing Series see E M I S Processing Series 3301
Electronic Materials Letters (KOR ISSN 1738-8090) 3095
Electronic Materials: Science and Technology (NLD) 3095
• Electronic Materials Update (USA) 3096
Electronic Measuring and Meters see Diance yu Yibiao 4486
Electronic Media Buyer's Guide see EMedia Buyer's Guide 2556
• Electronic Media for the School Market (Year): Review, Trends & Forecast (USA) 3060
Electronic Media for the School Market (Year): Review, Trends and Forecast see Electronic Media for the School Market (Year): Review, Trends & Forecast 3060
Electronic Mediations Series (USA) 2350
Electronic Mission Aircraft see Jane's Electronic Mission Aircraft 62
Electronic Monthly (JPN) 3096
• Electronic Musician (USA ISSN 0884-4720) 6564
• ➤ Electronic Musicological Review (BRA ISSN 1415-9538) 6564
Electronic Navigation Review see Denpa Koho 8642
† • The Electronic New Presence (CZE) 8953
▼ • Electronic News (Mahwah) (USA ISSN 1931-2431) 4575
• Electronic News (San Jose) (USA) 3096
Electronic News for China (HKG ISSN 0259-1235) 3096
• Electronic News Journal on Reasoning about Actions and Change (SWE ISSN 1403-2031) 2447
• Electronic Notes in Discrete Mathematics (NLD ISSN 1571-0653) 5486
• Electronic Notes in Theoretical Computer Science (NLD ISSN 1571-0661) 2600
Electronic Parts and Materials see Denshi Zairyo 3092
• Electronic Payments International (GBR ISSN 0954-0393) 1392
Electronic Payments Journal (USA) 1677
• Electronic Payments Week (USA ISSN 1558-7398) 1393
• Electronic Photography News (USA ISSN 0896-0976) 6966
• The Electronic Proceedings of Undergraduate Mathematics Day (USA ISSN 1548-2286) 5486
Electronic Product Design (GBR ISSN 0263-1474) 3304
• Electronic Product News (FRA ISSN 1763-7384) 3096
Electronic Production see Global S M T & Packaging 1886
Electronic Production & TEST see Global S M T & Packaging 1886
• Electronic Products (USA ISSN 0013-4953) 3096

Title

▼ new title † ceased • electronic media ➤ refereed

DIRECTORY 2010 EMBASSY'S COMPLETE BOATING GUIDE TO RHODE ISLAND AND 10237

Elementary Teachers Guide to Free Curriculum Materials (USA ISSN 0070-9980) **3060**
● ➤ Elemente der Mathematik (CHE ISSN 0013-6018) **5486**
Elemente der Metapolitik zur Europaeischen Neugeburt (DEU ISSN 0177-2430) **7132**
● Elementos (MEX ISSN 0187-9073) **4450**
Elementos de Matematica (ARG ISSN 0326-8888) **5486**
● Elementos para la Accion Legislativa (ARG ISSN 0328-607X) **4848**
● Elements (IRL) **2187**
Elements (NLD) **3914**
Elements *see* Our Region **8745**
Elements (Dresden) (CAN ISSN 0830-856X) **3060**
● ➤ Elements (Ottawa) (CAN ISSN 1811-5209) **6461**
Elements (Roslyn) (USA ISSN 1542-2550) **5070**
Elements Pour la Civilisation Europeenne (FRA ISSN 1251-8441) **5215**
Elenchos (ITA ISSN 0392-7342) **6915**
Elenchus of Biblica (ITA ISSN 1123-5608) **7698**
Elenchus of Biblical Bibliography *see* Elenchus of Biblica **7698**
Elentrepenoeren *see* Elmagasinet **3307**
Elepaio (USA ISSN 0013-6069) **906**
Elephant *see* EL-E-PHANT **5289**
Elephant Managers Association. Journal (USA ISSN 1535-0592) **941**
Elephant's Child (ZAF ISSN 1011-193X) **6523**
Eleqtroniqa *see* Electronics **3096**
Eleria (ESP ISSN 1137-1951) **4664**
Eles & Elas (PRT ISSN 0870-8932) **3931**
▼ ● Elestirel Psikoloji Bulteni (AUT ISSN 1998-2410) **7354**
Elet es Irodalom/Life and Literature (HUN ISSN 0424-8848) **5215**
● Elet es Tudomany (HUN ISSN 0013-6077) **7852**
Eletricidade Moderna (BRA ISSN 0100-2104) **3306**
Eletron: Revista de Engenharia/Electron - Engineering Review (BRA) **3306**
A Eletronica em Foco (BRA ISSN 0046-1814) **3099**
Eletronica para Todos (BRA) **3306**
Elettricita *see* Strom **3331**
Elettrificazione (ITA ISSN 0013-6093) **3158**
● Elettro (ITA ISSN 1129-9584) **3306**
● Elettronica e Telecomunicazioni (ITA ISSN 0013-6123) **3099**
Elettronica Flash (ITA ISSN 1124-8912) **3099**
† Elettronica Industriale (ITA ISSN 1591-7185) **8953**
Elettronica Oggi (ITA ISSN 0391-6391) **3099**
Elettronica Oggi News *see* E O News **3094**
† Elettronica Professionale (ITA ISSN 1121-8835) **8953**
Elettroradio Informazioni *see* E I - Elettroradio Informazioni **8952**
Eleusis (DEU ISSN 1439-7536) **6915**
● Eleutheria (GTM ISSN 1990-2433) **6915**
▼ Elevations (USA) **5070**
Elevator Constructor (USA ISSN 0013-614X) **1006**
Elevator Technology (GBR ISSN 1029-6840) **1006**
● Elevator World (USA ISSN 0013-6158) **1006**
● Elevator World Source Directory (USA) **1006**
Elevatori (ITA ISSN 1121-7995) **8495**
Eleven/Irebun (JPN) **8227**
Eleven by Thirty - Broadside *see* 11 x 30 - Broadside **5439**
Eleven Eleven (USA ISSN 1548-243X) **487**
Eleventh Circuit Review (USA) **4950**
The Eleventh Muse (USA ISSN 1559-0542) **5421**
The Eleventh St. Ruse *see* 11th St. Ruse **5439**
Elevernes Katalog for Skolebiblioteker *see* Katalog for Skolebiblioteker. Eleverne **8969**
Eleveur de France (FRA ISSN 0396-0102) **197**
L'Eleveur de Lapins (FRA ISSN 0220-5149) **286**
L'Eleveur Laitier (FRA ISSN 1634-8273) **286**
Eleveur Maine Anjou (FRA ISSN 0046-1822) **286**
Elevforum (SWE ISSN 0283-3395) **2853**
Elf *see* Elf Voetbal **8227**
Elf-Aquitaine. Centres de Recherches Exploration-Production. Bulletin. Memoire (FRA ISSN 0181-0901) **6767**
† Elf Exploration Production. Centres de Recherches. Bulletin (FRA ISSN 1279-8215) **8953**
Elf Voetbal (NLD ISSN 1875-0222) **8227**
Elforbrugeren *see* Energiforbrugeren **3158**
Elfsborgs Laens Allehanda (SWE ISSN 1103-9205) **3955**
Elgar (FRA ISSN 0996-0805) **3531**
Elgar Society. Journal (GBR ISSN 0143-1269) **6564**
Elgar Society. News (GBR ISSN 1368-5163) **6564**
Elhuyar: Zientzia eta Teknika (ESP ISSN 0213-3687) **7852**
ELIA *see* E L I A **5113**
● eLibrary Canada (USA) **2853**
● eLibrary Canada Curriculum Edition (USA) **3060**
Eligible (USA ISSN 1073-256X) **8859**
Elimu Haina Mwisho (TZA) **3961**
Elinstallatoeren (SWE ISSN 0013-6190) **3306**
● Eli's Home Care Week (USA ISSN 1548-8829) **8038**
Eli's Home Health Care *see* Eli's Home Care Week **8038**
● Eli's Hospice Insider (USA ISSN 1947-170X) **4092**
Eli's Joint Commission Compliance Advisor on Behavioral Health Care *see* J C A H O Advisor for Behavioral Health Care Providers **4103**
● Eli's M D S Alert (Minimum Data Set) (USA ISSN 1548-9841) **4501**
Eli's Medicare Risk *see* Medicine & Health's Managed Care Report **4515**
● Eli's Rehab Report (USA ISSN 1085-5181) **4093**
Elisa di Rivombrosa Magazine (ITA ISSN 1826-3429) **5409**
Elisa di Rivombrosa Magazine Teen (ITA ISSN 1826-3496) **2187**
Elisabeth Elliot Newsletter (USA ISSN 8756-1336) **7640**
Elisabeth Kuebler-Ross Magazine *see* E K R Magazine **7353**
Elisabethbode (NLD ISSN 0013-6212) **7640**
Elisha Mitchell Scientific Society. Journal *see* North Carolina Academy of Science. Journal **7893**
Elite (DEU) **264**
Elite (HKG) **8783**
† Elite (ITA ISSN 1972-2613) **8953**
Elite (VEN) **3994**
Elite Fighter (USA ISSN 1941-1073) **8171**
Elite Home & Lifestyle (USA) **5070**
Elite Traveler (USA ISSN 1536-5387) **8700**
Elite Traveler's Hotels Resorts Spas (USA ISSN 1930-6660) **8700**
Elites (ESP) **1741**
Elites (ITA ISSN 1826-8919) **5289**
● Elixir (SWE ISSN 1401-5374) **6837**
Elixir (New Lebanon) (USA ISSN 1557-5527) **7710**
Elizabethan Club Series (USA ISSN 0085-0225) **4217**
Elizabethan Theatre (CAN ISSN 0317-4964) **8470**
Elk Horn (USA) **4291**
Elkab (BEL) **392**
Elkhound Annual (USA) **6808**
Elkraft Marked *see* Energinet.dk. Markedsrapport **3307**
Elkraft Nyt *see* Om Energi **3326**
● The Elks Magazine (USA ISSN 0013-6263) **2265**
Ellas kai Diednis Metaphores *see* Greece and International Transport **8497**
Elle *see* Elle Argentina **8861**
● Elle (American Edition) (USA ISSN 0888-0808) **8860**
Elle (Bucharest) (ROM ISSN 1453-6145) **8860**
Elle (Croatia) (HRV ISSN 1333-7963) **8860**
Elle (Flemish Edition) *see* Elle Belgie **8861**
Elle (Greek Edition) (GRC ISSN 1108-8907) **8860**
Elle (Hong Kong) (HKG ISSN 1018-1148) **8860**
Elle (Istanbul) (TUR ISSN 1302-1982) **8860**
Elle (Johannesburg) (ZAF ISSN 1025-9791) **8860**
Elle (Lisbon) (PRT ISSN 0873-3570) **8860**
● Elle (Madrid) (ESP ISSN 0214-3364) **8860**
Elle (Milan) (ITA ISSN 1120-4397) **8860**
Elle (Moscow) (RUS ISSN 1560-3180) **8860**
Elle (Munich) (DEU ISSN 0935-462X) **8860**
Elle (Netherlands) (NLD ISSN 0926-9398) **8860**
Elle (Oslo) (NOR ISSN 0808-5366) **8860**
Elle (Paris) (FRA ISSN 0013-6298) **8860**
Elle (Prague) (CZE ISSN 1210-8480) **8860**
● Elle (Sao Paolo) (BRA ISSN 0104-1703) **8860**
● Elle (Seoul) (KOR ISSN 1228-0798) **8860**
Elle (Serbia) (SRB) **8860**
Elle (Singapore) (SGP ISSN 0218-6136) **8860**
● Elle (Slovenia) (SVN ISSN 1854-1585) **8860**
● Elle (Stockholm) (SWE ISSN 0284-6969) **8860**
Elle (Sydney) (AUS) **8860**
Elle (Taiwan) (TWN ISSN 1018-8649) **8860**
Elle (Tokyo) (JPN) **8860**
Elle (U K Edition) (GBR ISSN 0269-2597) **8860**
Elle (U K Travel Edition) (GBR ISSN 1744-4772) **8860**
Elle (Wydanie Polskie) (POL ISSN 1232-8308) **8860**
Elle a la Carte *see* Elle Mat & Vin **3634**
ELLE a Seoul *see* Elle Seoul **8861**
Elle a Table (FRA ISSN 1293-5948) **4357**
● Elle Accessories (USA ISSN 1556-5831) **8860**
● Elle Argentina (ARG ISSN 1514-7355) **8861**
Elle Belgie (BEL ISSN 1379-9991) **8861**
Elle Belgique *see* Elle Belgie **8861**
Elle Bistro (DEU ISSN 1434-3983) **4357**
● Elle Canada (CAN ISSN 1496-5186) **8861**
Elle China *see* Shijie Shizhuang Zhiyuan **8883**
Elle Deco *see* Elle Decoracion **4556**
Elle Deco (GRC) **4556**
Elle Deco (JPN) **4556**
Elle Decor (ITA ISSN 1120-4400) **4556**
Elle Decor (RUS) **4556**
● Elle Decor (USA ISSN 1046-1957) **4556**
Elle Decoracion (ARG ISSN 1514-7371) **4539**
● Elle Decoracion (ESP ISSN 1133-7141) **4556**
Elle Decoration (BEL) **4556**
Elle Decoration *see* Jiajulang **4544**
Elle Decoration (DEU ISSN 0941-7303) **4556**
Elle Decoration (FRA ISSN 0988-1476) **4556**
Elle Decoration (GBR ISSN 0957-8943) **4556**
Elle Decoration (HKG ISSN 1018-9432) **4556**
Elle Decoration *see* Elle Deco **4556**
▼ Elle Decoration (KOR ISSN 1976-8842) **4539**
Elle Decoration (ROM ISSN 1842-3140) **4539**
Elle Decoration (ZAF ISSN 1028-9240) **4539**
Elle Dekor (HRV) **4556**
Elle Donichef (JPN) **4357**
Elle. Eten (NLD ISSN 1389-1618) **3634**
Elle Extra (ITA ISSN 1825-6333) **8861**
† Elle Girl (DEU ISSN 1614-9726) **8953**
● Elle Girl/Elleu Geol (KOR ISSN 1599-7731) **8861**
Elle Girl (RUS ISSN 1727-2130) **2187**
Elle Interioer (NOR ISSN 1501-0562) **4556**
● Elle Interioer (SWE ISSN 1103-8802) **4556**
Elle Interioer Sommarstaellet (SWE ISSN 1653-5405) **4556**
● Elle Mat & Vin (SWE ISSN 1653-9206) **3634**
Elle Novias (ARG ISSN 1514-7363) **2254**
Elle Online *see* Elle (American Edition) **8860**
● Elle Quebec (CAN ISSN 0843-6363) **8861**
Elle Seoul (KOR) **8861**
Elle Wonen (NLD ISSN 0926-941X) **4556**
Elle Wonen (Belgium Edition) *see* Elle Decoration **4556**
Ellen (SVK ISSN 1336-8664) **8845**
Ellen Glasgow Newsletter (USA ISSN 0160-7545) **5289**
Ellenike Gastroenterologia *see* Annals of Gastroenterology **5920**
Ellenike Nefrologia/Hellenic Nephrology (GRC ISSN 1105-140X) **6267**
● ➤ Ellenike Orthodontike Epitheorese/Hellenic Orhodontic Review (GRC ISSN 1108-1279) **5843**
Ellenike Purenike Iatrike - Ellenike Etaireia Purenikes Iatrikes Thessalonikes *see* Hellenic Journal of Nuclear Medicine **5627**
Elleniko Zoologiko Arheio/Hellenic Zoological Archives (GRC ISSN 1106-2134) **941**
Ellenikos Typos *see* Greek Press **3535**
Ellenokanadiko Reportaz *see* Greek Canadian Reportage **3535**
Ellery Queen's Mystery Magazine (Palm O S & Windows C E Edition) *see* Ellery Queen's Mystery Magazine (Print Edition) **5413**
Ellery Queen's Mystery Magazine (Print Edition) (USA ISSN 1054-8122) **5413**
Elles et Eux (FRA ISSN 1775-0997) **4138**
Elleu Geol *see* Elle Girl **8861**
➤ Ellinika (GRC ISSN 0013-6336) **2234**
Ellinikis Ktiniatrikis Eterias. Deltio *see* Hellenic Veterinary Medical Society. Bulletin **8798**
Ellinikos kirikas *see* Greek Herald **3535**
Ellinis (AUS ISSN 0310-6888) **3531**
Ellinoamerikanikon Emborikon Epimelitirion. Business Directory *see* American - Hellenic Chamber of Commerce. Business Directory **1395**
Elliot Gold's Electronic TeleSpan *see* TeleSpan (E-mail Edition) **2535**
Elliot Lake Standard *see* The Standard (Elliot Lake) **3817**
Elliott Wave Theorist (USA ISSN 0742-5252) **1621**
● Elliott's Trial Tips Newsletter (USA ISSN 1559-6044) **4664**
Ellips (NLD ISSN 1570-2057) **7640**
Ellipse (CAN ISSN 0046-1830) **5421**
Die Ellipse (DEU ISSN 0177-6967) **6837**
Ellipsis (USA ISSN 1935-0791) **5289**
Ellis Cousins Newsletter (USA ISSN 0740-1477) **3764**
Ellis Horwood Series in Electrical and Electronic Engineering (GBR ISSN 0271-6143) **3306**
Ellis Horwood Series in Engineering Science (GBR ISSN 0272-0272) **3188**
Ellis Horwood Series in Mathematics & Its Applications (GBR ISSN 0271-6151) **5486**
L'Ellisse (ITA ISSN 1826-0187) **5289**
El-Elm/Sciences Monthly Magazine (EGY) **7852**
Elm Farm Research Centre. Bulletin *see* Elm Farm Research Centre. The Organic Research Centre. Bulletin **107**
Elm Farm Research Centre. The Organic Research Centre. Bulletin (GBR ISSN 1754-4815) **107**
Elm Fork Echoes (USA) **4291**
Elm ve Khayat (AZE ISSN 0134-3386) **7961**
Elmagasinet (NOR ISSN 1503-030X) **3307**
● Elmar Proceedings (HRV ISSN 1334-2630) **3099**
Elmhurst College Magazine (USA ISSN 0897-2303) **2282**
Elmira Independent (CAN ISSN 1194-1030) **3809**
elmundo.es *see* El Mundo **3953**
ElNorte.com *see* El Norte **3910**
Eloge de l'Ombre (FRA ISSN 1778-655X) **5289**
● ➤ Elore (FIN ISSN 1456-3010) **3616**
Elpis (POL ISSN 1508-7719) **7704**
Els Marges (ESP ISSN 0210-0452) **5114**
Elsa (SWE ISSN 1401-7237) **7735**
▼ Else Kroener-Fresnius-Symposia (CHE ISSN 1663-0114) **763**
Elseneur (FRA ISSN 0758-3478) **5289**
● Elsevier (NLD ISSN 0922-3444) **3914**
▼ Elsevier Astrodynamics Series (GBR ISSN 1874-9305) **53**
● Elsevier B T W Almanak (Year) (Belasting Toegevoegde Waarde) (NLD ISSN 0923-4985) **1921**
● Elsevier Belasting Almanak (Year) (NLD ISSN 0924-3518) **1921**
● Elsevier Belasting CD-ROM (Year) (NLD) **1921**
Elsevier Ergonomics Book Series (NLD ISSN 1572-347X) **3188**
Elsevier Fiscaal Advies *see* Fiscaal Advies **1110**
† Elsevier Food International (NLD ISSN 1568-4008) **8953**
Elsevier Geo-Engineering Book Series (GBR ISSN 1571-9960) **3266**
● Elsevier I B Almanak (Inkomstenbelasting) (NLD) **1921**
Elsevier Loon Almanak *see* Elsevier Loonheffing Almanak (Year) **1922**
● Elsevier Loonheffing Almanak (Year) (NLD ISSN 1388-4387) **1922**
Elsevier Ocean Engineering Series (GBR ISSN 1571-9952) **2804**
● ➤ Elsevier Oceanography Series (NLD ISSN 0422-9894) **2804**
● Elsevier Pensioen Almanak (NLD ISSN 1570-3827) **1677**
Elsevier Salarismagazine (NLD ISSN 1874-3323) **1741**
Elsevier Schenken en Erven Almanak *see* Elsevier's Almanak voor Schenken en Erven **4901**
● Elsevier Sociale Verzekeringen Almanak (NLD ISSN 1387-7712) **4501**
Elsevier. Speciale Editie (NLD ISSN 1875-080X) **4450**
Elsevier Subsidie Almanak (NLD ISSN 0923-4977) **1922**
● Elsevier V P B Almanak (Venootschapsbelasting) (NLD ISSN 1386-8179) **1922**
● Elsevier V P B Diskette (Year) (Venootschapsbelasting) (NLD) **1922**
Elsevier Vennootschapsbelasting Almanak *see* Elsevier V P B Almanak **1922**
Elsevier World Capital Markets (USA) **1337**
● Elsevier's Almanak voor Schenken en Erven (NLD ISSN 0925-1987) **4901**
Elseviers B V E-Almanak *see* B V E-Almanak **2939**
Der Elsner (DEU ISSN 0071-0067) **3266**
Elteknik (DNK ISSN 0109-2359) **3307**
Eltern (DEU ISSN 0046-1849) **2151**
Eltern for Family (DEU ISSN 1435-2028) **2151**
Eltern-Info (DEU) **2151**
Eltern Sonderheft Geburt (DEU) **5989**
Eltern Sonderheft Mein Baby (DEU) **2151**
Eltern Sonderheft Schwangerschaft (DEU) **5989**
Eltern Unser Kind (DEU) **2151**
Elternforum (DEU ISSN 0934-8662) **2853**
Eltham & Greenwich Times (GBR ISSN 0968-5812) **3864**
Elton Stephens - Investment Advisor (USA) **1621**
Eltra Magasinet *see* Om Energi **3326**
Elu d'Aujourd'hui (FRA ISSN 0181-2726) **7492**
Elukiri (EST ISSN 1406-5266) **3836**
● Eluosi Wenyi/Russian Literature (CHN ISSN 1005-7684) **5289**
Eluosi Yanjiu/Russia Studies (CHN ISSN 1009-721X) **549**
● Eluosi Zhongya Dongou Shichang/East European, Russian & Central Asian Market Studies (CHN ISSN 1671-8453) **1563**
● Eluosi Zhongya Dongou Yanjiu/Russian, Central Asian & East European Studies (CHN ISSN 1671-8461) **7232**
Elus *see* Revue des Collectivites Locales **7502**
Elvira (GBR) **5442**
Elvis (SWE ISSN 1653-8595) **2187**
Elvis Costello Information Service (NLD) **6564**
Elvis International (USA) **6564**
Elvis International Forum *see* Elvis International **6564**
† Elvis Monthly (GBR ISSN 0013-6484) **8953**
Elvis Now Fan Club (USA) **2266**
▼ Elvis - the Official Collector's Edition (GBR ISSN 1752-8615) **4334**
Elvis World (USA) **6564**
Elysian Fields Quarterly (USA ISSN 1526-6346) **8227**
Elytra (JPN ISSN 0387-5733) **843**
Elytron (ESP ISSN 0214-1353) **843**
● ➤ Em Aberto (BRA ISSN 0104-1037) **2853**
● Em Debate (BRA ISSN 1809-0842) **8038**
● Em Questao (BRA ISSN 1807-8893) **2320**
▼ ● eMag (CZE ISSN 1802-4238) **2418**
Email (DEU ISSN 1438-1818) **1006**
● The Emailian (USA) **2556**
Emajenshi Kea *see* Emergency Care **6059**
Emajl, Keramika, Staklo (HRV ISSN 0350-3607) **2040**
Emakeele Seltsi Aastaraamat (EST ISSN 0206-3735) **5114**
Emakunde (ESP ISSN 0214-8781) **8895**
eManager (DEU ISSN 1612-1015) **1416**
▼ ● The eManager (USA ISSN 1941-4110) **7515**
Emania (GBR ISSN 0951-1822) **392**
● Emantalehti (FIN ISSN 0013-6522) **4357**
● eMarine (GBR) **2804**
● eMarketect Magazine (USA) **2556**
eMarketing & Commerce *see* eMarketing and Commerce **1427**
▼ ● eMarketing and Commerce (USA ISSN 1940-5405) **1427**
Emas *see* E M A S **7639**
● EMB Construccion (CHL ISSN 0718-3461) **3266**
● Embajada de Espana. Londres. Consejeria de Educacion y Ciencia. Boletin (GBR) **3012**
Embajada de la Federacion de Rusia. Boletin Informativo (MEX) **7232**
Embalagem (PRT) **6709**
Emballage Digest (FRA ISSN 0013-6557) **6709**
● Emballages Magazine (FRA ISSN 0754-0590) **6709**
● Emballering (NOR ISSN 0013-6581) **6709**
Embarazo Sano (ESP ISSN 1575-1694) **5989**
Embarazo Sano Extra (ESP ISSN 1576-8945) **5989**
EMBASE *see* Excerpta Medica. Abstract Journals **715**
● EMBASE Alert (NLD) **5744**
EMBASE C D *see* Excerpta Medica. Abstract Journals **715**
● EMBASE. Drugs & Pharmacology (NLD ISSN 1573-000X) **6889**
EMBASE List of Journals Indexed (NLD ISSN 0929-3302) **5744**
Embassy's Coastal Cruising Guide: Atlantic Coast (USA) **8700**
Embassy's Complete Boating Guide to Florida's East Coast (USA) **8275**
Embassy's Complete Boating Guide to Long Island Sound (USA) **8275**
Embassy's Complete Boating Guide to Rhode Island and Massachusetts (USA) **8275**

Title

▼ *new title* † *ceased* ● *electronic media* ➤ *refereed*

DIRECTORY 2010 EMPLOYMENT PROFILE: SUMMARY OF THE EMPLOYMENT EXPERIENCE 10239

Emotional Literacy Update see Raising Achievement Update **2902**
➤ Emotions and Behavior. Monograph (USA ISSN 0734-9890) **6137**
Emotions and Social Behavior (USA) **7354**
Emozioni (ITA ISSN 1828-6100) **4357**
• Empan (FRA ISSN 1152-3336) **8038**
Empangeni - Richards Bay Directory (ZAF ISSN 0259-868X) **1991**
• Empathic Parenting (CAN ISSN 0825-7531) **2151**
Empati (SWE ISSN 1102-3104) **6137**
▼ • ➤ Empedocles (GBR ISSN 1757-1952) **6915**
Emphasis (USA ISSN 1074-5254) **2853**
Emphasis on Faith and Living (USA ISSN 0194-5246) **7640**
Empire (AUS) **6497**
• Empire (GBR ISSN 0957-4948) **6497**
† Empire (New York, 2000) (USA ISSN 1553-4049) **8953**
• Empire (New York, 2002) (USA) **1104**
Empire Club Addresses see Empire Club of Canada. Addresses **4138**
• Empire Club of Canada. Addresses (CAN ISSN 0316-0548) **4138**
Empire Food Service News (USA) **3677**
Empire N Y Newsletter see Empire New York Newsletter **1104**
• Empire New York Newsletter (USA) **1104**
Empire State Builder (USA) **1006**
Empire State Farmer (USA ISSN 0886-9693) **107**
Empire State Food Service News (USA) **4385**
Empire State Geogram (USA ISSN 0013-676X) **2733**
Empire State Mason (USA ISSN 0013-6794) **2266**
Empire State Postal History Society. Bulletin (USA) **6894**
Empire State Report (USA ISSN 0747-0711) **7132**
Empire State Report Magazine see Empire State Report **7132**
Empiria (ESP ISSN 1139-5737) **8099**
• Empirica (USA ISSN 0340-8744) **1483**
➤ Empirical Approaches to Language Typology (DEU ISSN 0933-761X) **5114**
• ➤ Empirical Economics (DEU ISSN 0377-7332) **1104**
• ➤ Empirical Finance Review (USA ISSN 1558-8262) **1337**
• ➤ Empirical Musicology Review (USA ISSN 1559-5749) **6564**
• ➤ Empirical Software Engineering (USA ISSN 1382-3256) **2589**
Empirical Studies in Theology (NLD ISSN 1389-1189) **8099**
• Empirical Study of the Arts (USA ISSN 0276-2374) **487**
➤ Empirische Paedagogik (DEU ISSN 0931-5020) **3060**
Empirische Personal- und Organisationsforschung (DEU ISSN 0942-8984) **1860**
Empirische Studien zur Agraroekonomie (DEU ISSN 0177-0675) **197**
Empirische Wirtschafts- und Sozialforschung (DEU ISSN 0935-0365) **7961**
▼ Empleo para la Inclusion (ARG ISSN 1851-667X) **1677**
Empleo y Desempleo en Puerto Rico/Employment and Unemployment in Puerto Rico (PRI ISSN 0555-6635) **1677**
L'Emploi/Posto/Stelle (CHE) **6696**
L'Emploi en Europe see Employment in Europe **1678**
Emploi et Chomage. Enquete sur les Forces de Travail see Belgium. Institut National de Statistique. Emploi et Chomage. Enquete sur les Forces de Travail (Year) **1214**
Emploi et Immigration Canada. Rapport Annuel see Employment and Immigration Canada. Annual Report **1678**
L'Emploi et le Revenu en Perspective see Perspectives on Labour and Income **1258**
Emploi Plus (CAN ISSN 1180-4092) **5289**
Emploi - Quebec. C A M O - P I. Rapport Annuel see Emploi - Quebec. C A M O - P I. Rapport Annuel de Gestion **6696**
Emploi - Quebec. C A M O - P I. Rapport Annuel de Gestion (CAN ISSN 1910-6866) **6696**
Emploi-Quebec. Rapport Annuel de Gestion see Quebec Province. Ministere de l'Emploi et de la Solidarite Sociale. Rapport Annuel de Gestion **6703**
Employee Assistance see Workplace Assistance & Benefits **1878**
Employee Assistance Program Management Letter (USA ISSN 0896-0941) **1677**
Employee Assistance Programs Digest see E A P Digest **2693**
Employee Assistance Quarterly see Journal of Workplace Behavioral Health **1868**
Employee Assistance Report (USA ISSN 1097-6221) **1860**
• Employee Benefit Adviser (USA ISSN 1545-3839) **1860**
Employee Benefit and Retirement Planning see Tools & Techniques of Employee Benefit and Retirement Planning **1711**
• Employee Benefit Cases (USA ISSN 0273-236X) **1677**
• Employee Benefit News (USA ISSN 1044-6265) **1677**
• Employee Benefit Plan Review (USA ISSN 0013-6808) **1860**
Employee Benefit Research Institute Issue Brief see E B R I Issue Brief **1859**
Employee Benefit Research Institute Notes see E B R I Notes **1676**
• Employee Benefits (GBR ISSN 1366-8722) **1860**
• ➤ Employee Benefits (USA) **1677**
Employee Benefits Actueel see Zorg en Inkomen **1717**
† Employee Benefits and Executive Compensation Counselor (USA ISSN 1090-4220) **8953**
Employee Benefits Compliance Coordinator (USA ISSN 0273-768X) **1860**
Employee Benefits Directory (USA) **4093**
• Employee Benefits Guide (USA) **1677**
Employee Benefits in Mergers and Acquisitions (USA ISSN 1544-2837) **4866**
† Employee Benefits Issues: The Multiemployer Perspective (USA ISSN 1048-2814) **8953**
• Employee Benefits Management (USA) **1741**
Employee Benefits Planner (USA) **4093**
Employee Benefits Report (GBR ISSN 1477-6243) **1677**
Employee Benefits Study see U.S. Chamber of Commerce. (Year) Employee Benefits Study **1877**
• Employee Development Bulletin (GBR ISSN 1351-055X) **1860**
Employee Fringe and Welfare Benefit Plans (USA ISSN 1061-2556) **1677**
Employee Involvement Association. Statistical Report (USA) **1860**
Employee Motivation & Incentive Strategies for Financial Institutions (USA) **1337**
Employee Motivation and Incentive Strategies for Managers and Finance Executives (USA ISSN 1528-0764) **1741**
Employee Motivation and Incentive Strategies for Manufacturing Executives (USA) **1741**
Employee Ownership Report (USA ISSN 0899-8833) **1104**
Employee Recruitment and Retention Strategies for Manufacturing Executives (USA) **1741**
• ➤ Employee Relations (GBR ISSN 0142-5455) **1677**
Employee Relations see Human Resources Management - Employment Relations **1865**
Employee Relations Bulletin (USA ISSN 1080-1871) **1677**
Employee Relations Guide to Federal Laws and Regulations (USA) **1677**
Employee Relations in Action (USA ISSN 0013-6824) **1677**
• Employee Relations Law Journal (USA ISSN 0098-8898) **4664**
• ➤ Employee Responsibilities and Rights Journal (USA ISSN 0892-7545) **1677**
Employee Retirement Income Security Act and Benefits Law Journal see E R I S A and Benefits Law Journal **8952**
Employee Retirement Income Security Act Litigation see E R I S A Litigation **4662**
Employee Retirement Income Security Act Litigation Alert see E R I S A Litigation Alert **1676**
Employee Retirement Income Security Act Litigation Reporter see E R I S A Litigation Reporter **2555**
Employee Retirement Income Security Act Newsletter see E R I S A Newsletter **1676**
Employee Retirement Income Security Act. Report to Congress see U.S. Department of Labor. Employee Retirement Income Security Act. Report to Congress **1711**
Employee Retirement Income Security Act The Law and the Code see E R I S A: The Law and the Code **1676**
Employee Rewards & Benefits (GBR ISSN 1746-9988) **1860**
• Employee Rights and Employment Policy Journal (USA ISSN 1522-2225) **1677**
Employee Rights Litigation: Pleading and Practice (USA) **1677**
Employee Sales Contests & Incentive Plans for Financial Institutions (USA) **1337**
• Employee Security Connection (USA ISSN 0894-2080) **2677**
Employee Services Management (USA ISSN 0744-3676) **1741**
Employee Share Schemes (GBR) **4866**
Employee Stock Ownership Plan Report see E S O P Report **1740**
• Employee Terminations Law Bulletin (USA ISSN 1063-097X) **1860**
† Employer (NZL ISSN 0046-1903) **8953**
The Employer (Howe) (GBR ISSN 1744-148X) **1860**
• Employer Costs for Employee Compensation (USA ISSN 1934-0990) **1226**
Employer Health Register (USA) **6676**
Employer Resources Newsletter (USA) **1677**
Employer's Briefing (GBR ISSN 0963-5343) **4867**
Employer's Compliance Review (Federal) (USA) **1860**
• Employer's Guide to Maternity Online (GBR) **1677**
Employers' Guide to Ontario Workplace Safety & Insurance (CAN ISSN 1910-3824) **6676**
Employer's Guide to the Health Insurance Portability and Accountability Act see Employer's Guide to the Health Insurance Portability & Accountability Act **4501**
Employer's Guide to the Health Insurance Portability & Accountability Act (USA) **4501**
Employer's Health and Safety Manual - Ontario (CAN) **6676**
• Employers Law (GBR ISSN 1364-9493) **1860**
• Employers State Law Alert (USA ISSN 1930-2436) **1677**
Employers State Legislative Alert see Employers State Law Alert **1677**
Employer's Wage Manual (Federal) (USA) **1678**
Employeur Suisse see Schweizer Arbeitgeber **1707**
Employment Agencies see Business Ratio Report. Employment Agencies (Year) **6693**
• Employment and Business Journal (CAN) **1678**
Employment and Earnings (Annual) see Employment and Earnings (Online) **1678**
• Employment and Earnings (Online) (USA ISSN 1943-4022) **1678**
Employment and Earnings: Characteristics of Families (USA) **1483**
Employment and Earnings Characteristics of Families News see Employment and Earnings: Characteristics of Families **1483**
Employment and Earnings in the Modern Sector see Kenya. Central Bureau of Statistics. Employment and Earnings in the Modern Sector **1247**
Employment and Economic Policy Research Programme. Occasional Paper (ZAF ISSN 1814-375X) **1678**
Employment and Immigration Canada. Annual Report/Emploi et Immigration Canada. Rapport Annuel (CAN ISSN 0707-901X) **1678**
Employment & Labor Lawcast (USA ISSN 1087-6677) **4664**
Employment and Labor Relations Law see Employment & Labor Relations Law **1678**
• Employment & Labor Relations Law (USA ISSN 1937-3406) **1678**
• Employment and Labour Law Reporter (CAN ISSN 1183-7152) **1678**
Employment and Labour Market Statistics see O E C D Employment and Labour Market Statistics **1256**
Employment and Payrolls in Washington State by County and Industry (USA) **1226**
Employment and the Economy. Atlantic Coastal Region (USA) **1483**
Employment and the Economy. Northern New Jersey Region (USA) **1483**
Employment and the Economy. Southern New Jersey Region (USA) **1483**
• Employment and Training Reporter (USA ISSN 0146-9673) **1678**
Employment and Unemployment see Zaetost i Bezrabotitsa **8414**
Employment and Unemployment in Puerto Rico see Empleo y Desempleo en Puerto Rico **1677**
Employment and Vacancies Statistics (Detailed Tables) Series A. Services Sector see Hong Kong Special Administrative Region of China. Census and Statistics Department. Employment and Vacancies Statistics (Detailed Tables) Series A. Services Sectors **6706**
Employment and Vacancies Statistics (Detailed Tables) Series B. Wholesale and Retail Trades, Restaurants and Hotels see Hong Kong Special Administrative Region of China. Census and Statistics Department. Employment and Vacancies Statistics (Detailed Tables) Series B. Wholesale and Retail Trades, Restaurants and Hotels **6706**
Employment and Vacancies Statistics (Detailed Tables) Series C. Industrial Sector see Hong Kong Special Administrative Region of China. Census and Statistics Department. Employment and Vacancies Statistics (Detailed Tables) Series C. Industrial Sectors **1237**
Employment and Vacancies Statistics (Detailed Tables) Series D. Import/Export Trades see Hong Kong Special Administrative Region of China. Census and Statistics Department. Employment and Vacancies Statistics (Detailed Tables) Series D. Import/Export Trades **1119**
• Employment and Wages Annual Averages (USA ISSN 0748-5336) **1226**
• Employment Attorney's Client Advisor (USA) **1678**
Employment Benefit News Canada (USA) **1678**
Employment Benefits see Employment Law (Falls Church) **1679**
Employment Briefing (GBR) **1678**
The Employment Bulletin (CAN ISSN 1183-3076) **4664**
Employment Bulletin (USA) **6696**
• Employment Cases Summary (Online Edition) (NZL ISSN 1177-7915) **1678**
Employment Cases Summary (Print Edition) see Employment Cases Summary (Online Edition) **1678**
Employment Contracts Briefing see Guide to Contracts of Employment **1862**
† Employment Cost Indexes (USA) **8953**
• Employment Discrimination (USA ISSN 1529-7691) **1860**
• Employment Discrimination (New York) (USA) **1860**
• Employment Discrimination Verdicts and Settlements (USA ISSN 1529-7926) **1678**
• Employment Equity. A Year-end Review (CAN ISSN 1912-2489) **6696**
Employment Equity Act. Annual Report (CAN ISSN 1189-9719) **1678**
• Employment Equity in the Federal Public Service/Equite en Emploi dans la Fonction Publique Federale (CAN ISSN 1493-4884) **7435**
Employment Equity Report see Employment Equity. A Year-end Review **6696**
• Employment Guide (USA) **1678**
† Employment, Hours, and Earnings: States and Areas (USA) **8953**
Employment in Alberta (CAN) **1678**
Employment in British Columbia (CAN) **1678**
Employment in Europe (LUX ISSN 1016-5444) **1678**
Employment in Florida (USA) **1678**
• Employment in Illinois (USA) **1678**
• Employment in Iowa (USA) **1678**
• Employment in Minnesota (USA) **1678**
• Employment in New York State (USA) **1678**
• Employment in Ohio (USA) **1679**
Employment in Ontario (CAN) **1679**
• Employment in Oregon (USA) **1679**
† Employment in Perspective: Minority Workers (USA) **8953**
† Employment in Perspective: Women in the Labor Force (USA) **8953**
• Employment in Texas (USA) **1679**
• Employment in the Mainstream (USA ISSN 1530-8839) **7206**
Employment in the Netherlands (NLD ISSN 1872-5147) **1679**
• Employment in Washington (USA) **1679**
• Employment in Wisconsin (USA) **1679**
• Employment Information in the Mathematical Sciences (USA ISSN 0163-3287) **5486**
Employment Injuries Rehabilitation Engineering Center Kenkyu Hokokushu see E I R E C Kenkyu Hokokushu **6108**
Employment Insurance Statutes see Annotated Employment Insurance Statutes **4617**
Employment Law (GBR ISSN 1353-3606) **4867**
Employment Law (ZAF) **4867**
• Employment Law (Falls Church) (USA ISSN 1934-1652) **1679**
Employment Law & Litigation (GBR ISSN 1472-5290) **4867**
Employment Law Briefing (USA) **1679**
Employment Law Bulletin (AUS ISSN 1440-4532) **4867**
• Employment Law Bulletin (GBR ISSN 1754-1247) **1679**
Employment Law Counselor (USA ISSN 1052-2964) **1679**
Employment Law Desk Book see Employment Law Desk Book for Tennessee Employers **4665**
Employment Law Desk Book for Tennessee Employers (USA) **4665**
• Employment Law Deskbook (USA) **1679**
Employment Law for People Managers see C I P D Employment Law for People Managers **1668**
Employment Law in Canada (CAN) **1679**
Employment Law Journal (GBR ISSN 1467-0119) **4867**
Employment Law Letter see Nevada Employment Law Letter **4741**
Employment Law Letter see Nebraska Employment Law Letter **4740**
Employment Law Letter see North Dakota Employment Law Letter **4748**
Employment Law Manual (USA) **1860**
Employment Law Report (IRL ISSN 0791-2560) **4665**
Employment Law Report (USA ISSN 1058-1308) **1679**
Employment Law Review (IRL ISSN 1649-718X) **4867**
Employment Law Series. Qualified Retirement Plans (USA) **1860**
• Employment Law Strategist (USA ISSN 1069-7829) **1679**
Employment Law Supplement see I D S Employment Law Supplement **1686**
Employment Law Update (Evansville) (USA ISSN 0890-9253) **4665**
Employment Law Update (New York) (USA ISSN 1523-8679) **4665**
Employment Lawyer (GBR ISSN 1463-0435) **1860**
Employment Lawyers Association Briefing see E L A Briefing **4662**
Employment Line see Editor & Publisher's Employment Line Newsletter **6696**
Employment Litigation News (USA) **4665**
Employment Management Association Reporter see E M A Reporter **1676**
Employment Marketplace (USA) **6696**
Employment News (GBR ISSN 0143-9588) **1679**
Employment News (IND) **6696**
Employment Newsletter (GBR) **1860**
Employment Observatory. Policies (BEL ISSN 1019-4304) **1679**
• Employment Opportunities (New York) (USA) **6696**
• Employment Opportunities (Washington) (USA) **6696**
Employment Outlook Survey (USA ISSN 0737-9633) **1679**
The Employment Paper (Pittsburgh) (USA) **1679**
• Employment Practice Guide (USA) **6696**
• Employment Practice Liability Verdicts and Settlements (USA ISSN 1525-2736) **1679**
Employment Practices Decisions (USA ISSN 0149-6255) **1679**
• Employment Practices Liability Consultant (USA ISSN 1529-840X) **1679**
Employment Practices Update (USA) **1679**
• Employment Precedents and Company Policy Documents (GBR) **4867**
Employment Profile: Summary of the Employment Experience of College Graduates Six Months after Graduation (CAN ISSN 1492-045X) **1679**

Title

10240 EMPLOYMENT RELATIONS BULLETIN ULRICH'S PERIODICALS

Employment Relations Bulletin (USA ISSN 0746-9683) **1679**
▼ Employment Relations Review (ZAF ISSN 1997-0285) **1679**
• Employment Relations Today (USA ISSN 0745-7790) **1680**
The Employment Report (HKG ISSN 1022-4238) **1680**
• Employment Research (USA ISSN 1075-8445) **1680**
Employment Review (Albany) (USA ISSN 0013-6883) **1680**
• Employment Review (Jupiter) (USA) **6697**
• Employment Safety and Health Guide (USA ISSN 0093-1535) **6676**
• Employment Screening (USA) **4665**
Employment Service and Unemployment Insurance Operations (USA) **6697**
Employment Situation *see* Labour Market Monthly **6700**
• The Employment Situation (Online) (USA) **1483**
• Employment Situation of Veterans (USA ISSN 1939-3636) **6420**
Employment Standards Handbook (CAN ISSN 1910-6181) **4665**
Employment Standards Handbook and Digest (CAN) **4665**
Employment Standards in British Columbia (CAN ISSN 1912-0516) **1860**
• Employment Standards Law Reporter (CAN) **4665**
Employment Standards Legislation in Canada (CAN ISSN 1185-2429) **1680**
Employment Statistics *see* O E C D Employment and Labour Market Statistics **1256**
Employment Supplement *see* Accountancy S A **1276**
Employment Tax Forms (USA) **1922**
• Employment Terms and Conditions. Asia - Pacific (USA) **1860**
Employment Terms & Conditions. Asia - Pacific *see* Employment Terms and Conditions. Asia - Pacific **1860**
Employment Terms and Conditions - Europe (USA) **1860**
• ➤ Employment Testing (USA ISSN 1065-2531) **4665**
Employment Tribunal Practice in Scotland (GBR) **4867**
Emporia State Research Studies (USA ISSN 0424-9399) **53**
Emporike Trapeza tes Ellados. Oikonomike Epitheorese *see* Commercial Bank of Greece. Economic Review **1328**
Emporike Trapeza tes Ellados. Oikonomike Deltio/Commercial Bank of Greece. Economic Bulletin (GRC ISSN 1106-658X) **1483**
▼ Emporium (AUS ISSN 1834-6472) **8861**
Empowered (NZL ISSN 1177-0546) **7735**
• The Empowered Parenting Ezine (USA ISSN 1526-2154) **2151**
Empowering Girls (USA) **2187**
Empowering Women (USA) **8861**
Empreintes (FRA ISSN 1779-871X) **3419**
Empreintes (Paris) (FRA ISSN 1951-5073) **642**
Empreintes de l'Homme (FRA ISSN 1257-9343) **336**
• O Empreiteiro (BRA ISSN 0103-7358) **1006**
• Emprendedores (ESP ISSN 1138-9702) **1483**
• Emprendedores (MEX ISSN 0187-7828) **1741**
La Empresa (ESP ISSN 1138-6819) **7435**
Empresa & Limpieza (ESP) **2243**
Empresa Brasileira de Pesquisa Agropecuaria. Centro Nacional de Pesquisa de Florestas. Circular Tecnica (BRA ISSN 1414-3046) **3687**
Empresa Brasileira de Pesquisa Agropecuaria. Centro Nacional de Pesquisa de Florestas. Documentos *see* Embrapa Florestas. Documentos **3687**
Empresa Brasileira de Pesquisa Agropecuaria. Embrapa Algodao. Documentos (BRA ISSN 0103-0205) **229**
Empresa Brasileira de Telecomunicacoes. Relatorio Anual (BRA) **2320**
Empresa Capixaba de Pesquisa Agropecuaria. Comunicado Tecnico (BRA ISSN 0101-7683) **107**
Empresa de Navegacao da Amazonia. Estatistica da Navegacao (BRA) **8643**
Empresa de Pesquisa Agropecuaria do Estado do Rio de Janeiro. Comunicado Tecnico (BRA ISSN 0100-896X) **107**
Empresa de Pesquisa Agropecuaria do Rio de Janeiro. Informe Tecnico (BRA ISSN 0101-3769) **107**
• Empresa e (Empresa Electronica) (MEX) **2556**
Empresa Global (ESP ISSN 1578-3456) **1741**
Empresa Nacional de Electricidad. Memoria (CHL) **3307**
Empresa Nacional de Energia Electrica. Datos Estadisticos (HND) **3152**
Empresa Nacional Mercasa. Informe Anual (ESP) **3634**
Empresario (ESP ISSN 1131-6551) **1104**
El Empresario. Suplemento *see* Empresario **1104**
Empresas Japonesas do Brasil. Annuario/Burajiru Nikkei Kigyo Nenkan (BRA) **1991**
Empresas y Negocios en la Republica Checa *see* Czech Business and Trade **1561**
Empress Chinchilla Breeder (USA ISSN 0094-3282) **4973**
▼ • Emprise Review (USA ISSN 1948-2817) **5289**
Empty Closet (USA) **4373**
The Empty Vessel (USA ISSN 1073-7480) **7735**
Empuries (ESP ISSN 0213-9278) **392**
Emroz (RUS) **3532**
Emschergenossenschaft. Jahresberichte (DEU) **1423**
Emshock Letter (USA) **6644**
Emslaendische Geschichte (DEU ISSN 0947-8582) **4217**
• ➤ Emu (AUS ISSN 0158-4197) **906**
Emu Today & Tomorrow (USA) **286**
Emulsion Magazine (USA ISSN 1933-4125) **6966**
Emulsion Polymer Technologies *see* Dispersion Polymers **6717**
• Emunah (USA ISSN 1053-4113) **7721**
eMusician.com *see* Electronic Musician **6564**
Emzin (SVN ISSN 1318-5497) **487**
• En Accion (ESP) **3419**
En Action *see* F I Q en Action (French Edition) **5958**
En Action *see* F I Q en Action (English Edition) **5958**
En Affaires, J'Aime Mon Boeuf *see* Des Affaires Boeuf **3633**
† En Arrivant (FRA ISSN 1774-7473) **8953**
† En Avant (FRA ISSN 0013-6921) **8953**
▼ En Blanco (ESP ISSN 1888-5616) **441**
Das en Boom *see* Landschappelijk **2617**
▼ En Clave Joven La Revista (COL ISSN 2011-4559) **7961**
• En-Claves del Pensamiento Journal (MEX) **4450**
En Concreto (CHL ISSN 0717-7364) **1006**
En Concreto (MEX) **4409**
En Direct de l'E B S I (Ecole de Bibliotheconomie et des Sciences de l'Information) (CAN ISSN 0840-9102) **5008**
En Eglise (CAN ISSN 0317-851X) **7796**
En France (NLD ISSN 1380-8249) **8700**
En Garde (NLD ISSN 1871-9422) **4357**
• L'En - Je Lacanien (FRA ISSN 1761-2861) **7354**
En Jeux Sport (FRA ISSN 1774-7007) **8171**
En Kicsi Ponim *see* My Little Pony **2204**
En la Calle Recta *see* In de Rechte Straat **7800**
• En la Espana Medieval (ESP ISSN 0214-3038) **4217**
• En la Espana Medieval. Anejos (ESP ISSN 1887-4487) **4217**
En La Traba (DOM) **8171**
En La Vida (USA) **4373**
En Lignes - P F T (Patrimoine Ferroviaire Touristique) (BEL ISSN 0777-933X) **8617**
En Mains Propres (FRA ISSN 0985-3685) **3505**
En Marcha (NIC) **7132**
En Marche (BEL ISSN 0013-6964) **6985**
En Marge (FRA ISSN 1951-5340) **5289**
En Passant (USA) **8171**
• En Primeur (CAN ISSN 1190-836X) **6497**
En Primeur Jeunesse (CAN ISSN 1191-2286) **2187**
En Serigrafia (ESP ISSN 1139-8574) **7320**
En Tete (CAN ISSN 0822-8531) **2282**
En Tete *see* Headway **2983**
En Toch *see* Infocus **6061**
En Toch (NLD ISSN 1872-6518) **7796**
En Voie *see* Movin' **8620**
En Vuelo (ARG) **8783**
Enact *see* Conservation Land Management **2607**
Enact (IND ISSN 0013-6980) **8470**
Enayim *see* Einayim **2187**
• Enbi to Porima/Vinyls and Polymers (JPN ISSN 0013-8460) **2122**
Encapsulator (AUS ISSN 1034-8719) **6837**
▼ Enceinte & Accoucher (FRA ISSN 1960-2731) **8845**
• ➤ L'Encephale (FRA ISSN 0013-7006) **6137**
Encephalitis Surveillance (USA ISSN 0191-6955) **6138**
Enchanting News (USA) **6741**
Enchantment (USA ISSN 0046-1946) **3975**
➤ Enchoria (DEU ISSN 0340-627X) **5114**
Enciclopedia degli Animali National Geographic (ITA ISSN 1970-4593) **941**
Enciclopedia della Salute (ITA ISSN 1970-8610) **6985**
Enciclopedia Nacional del Petroleo Petrolquimica y Gas (ESP) **6767**
▼ • Encinitas (Encinitas, 2008) (USA ISSN 1938-4564) **3975**
Encomia (USA ISSN 0363-4841) **5407**
• EnCompass (USA ISSN 1539-7696) **8701**
Encontro Nacional de Estudos Populacionais (BRA) **7282**
• ➤ Encontros Bibli (BRA ISSN 1518-2924) **5008**
Encor Respondence (USA) **3039**
Encordado (SWE ISSN 1102-5964) **6564**
Endorado (AUS ISSN 0815-2063) **6497**
• Encore! (USA) **2283**
Encore (New York) (USA) **8470**
Encore: A Guide to Life After 55 (USA) **3975**
Encore Directory (AUS ISSN 0817-6469) **6497**
Encore un mot! (FRA ISSN 1775-1373) **5289**
• Encounter (AUS) **2283**
Encounter (GBR ISSN 0958-2797) **7640**
The Encounter (USA) **5070**
• Encounter (Cincinnati) (USA) **7640**
• Encounter (Indianapolis) (USA ISSN 0013-7081) **7640**
Encounter (Joliet) (USA) **2283**
Encounter (Lincoln) (USA) **7640**
• Encounter: Education for Meaning and Social Justice (USA ISSN 1094-3838) **3060**
Encounter with God (South African Edition) (ZAF) **7640**
Encounter with God (UK Edition) (GBR ISSN 1350-5130) **7755**
Encountering Jung (USA) **7354**
Encounters (ITA ISSN 1127-2252) **7710**
Encounters (NZL ISSN 1177-2255) **3060**
Encounters (Burnaby) *see* World Political Science Review **7196**
➤ Encounters (Leicester) (GBR ISSN 1358-5770) **7710**
▼ ➤ Encounters (Oxford) (GBR ISSN 1746-8175) **336**
Encounters on Education/Encuentros sobre Educacion/Rencontres sur l'Education (CAN ISSN 1494-4936) **2853**
Encounters Series (GBR ISSN 1471-0277) **5114**
Encouragement *see* Hagemi **4078**
Encrages (FRA ISSN 1623-457X) **487**
Encres Fraiches (FRA ISSN 1772-3345) **7320**
† Encres Vagabondes (FRA ISSN 1251-0483) **8953**
Encres Vives (FRA ISSN 0013-7103) **5421**
➤ Encrucillada (ESP ISSN 1131-6519) **7640**
Encuadernacion de Arte (ESP ISSN 1133-1860) **7560**
Encuentro (ESP ISSN 1130-7021) **5114**
➤ Encuentro (NIC ISSN 0424-9674) **7961**
Encuentro (Buenos Aires) (ARG ISSN 1666-3535) **7132**
▼ • Encuentro Argentino de Historia de la Psiquiatria, la Psicologia y el Psicoanalisis. Actas (ARG ISSN 1851-4812) **6138**
▼ Encuentro de Avances en Psicologia, Gerontologia y Neurociencias (COL ISSN 2011-1622) **7354**
• Encuentro de la Cultura Cubana (ESP ISSN 1136-6389) **7961**
• Encuentro Educacional (VEN ISSN 1315-4079) **2853**
Encuentros (PRI ISSN 1942-2032) **4451**
Encuentros en Catay (TWN ISSN 1023-6961) **5114**
• Encuentros en la Biologia (ESP ISSN 1134-8496) **671**
Encuentros Multidisciplinares (ESP ISSN 1139-9325) **4451**
Encuentros sobre Educacion *see* Encounters on Education **2853**
Encuesta Agropecuaria (VEN ISSN 0798-6351) **197**
• Encuesta Continua de Hogares (URY ISSN 0797-633X) **4435**
Encuesta de Hogares: Ocupacion y Desocupacion (URY ISSN 0797-6291) **1718**
Encuesta Industrial *see* Guatemala. Direccion General de Estadistica. Encuesta de la Industria Manufacturera Fabril **8375**
Encuesta Industrial Annual *see* Encuesta Industrial Trimestral **1226**
Encuesta Industrial: Resultados Nacionales (VEN ISSN 0259-515X) **1226**
• Encuesta Industrial Trimestral (URY ISSN 0797-3209) **1226**
Encuesta Nacional Agropecuaria. Resultados de la Produccion Agricola (BOL) **179**
Encuesta Nacional de Ingresos y Gastos de los Hogares (MEX) **8367**
Encuesta Nacional del Empleo Total Pais (CHL) **1226**
Encuesta Trimestral sobre la Industria de la Construccion (MEX ISSN 0186-9035) **1046**
• Enculturation (USA ISSN 1525-3120) **8099**
Encyclopaedia Africana. Information Report (GHA ISSN 0013-712X) **4174**
† Encyclopaedia Judaica Year Book (ISR ISSN 0303-7819) **8953**
Encyclopaedia of Economic Development (IND) **3119**
Encyclopaedia of Hong Kong Trade & Industry (Year) (HKG) **3119**
▼ • Encyclopaedia of Islam Three (NLD ISSN 1873-9830) **7710**
Encyclopaedia of Mathematical Sciences (DEU ISSN 0938-0396) **5486**
• Encyclopaideia (ITA ISSN 1590-492X) **2853**
Encyclopedia Medico-Quirurgica. Kinesiterapia - Medicina Fisica *see* Encyclopedie Medico-Chirurgicale. Kinesiterapia - Medicina Fisica **6108**
Encyclopedia of American Industries (USA ISSN 1941-2428) **3119**
• Encyclopedia of American Religions (USA ISSN 1066-1212) **7640**
Encyclopedia of American School Law *see* Deskbook Encyclopedia of American School Law **4657**
• Encyclopedia of American Studies (USA) **4291**
• Encyclopedia of Associations (USA ISSN 0071-0202) **3119**
• Encyclopedia of Associations. International Organizations (USA ISSN 1041-0023) **3119**
• Encyclopedia of Associations. Regional, State, and Local Organizations (USA ISSN 0894-2846) **3119**
† Encyclopedia of Associations Supplement (Encyclopedia of Associations) (USA) **8953**
Encyclopedia of Banking Law (GBR) **4665**
† Encyclopedia of Business (USA ISSN 1086-4768) **8953**
• Encyclopedia of Business Information Sources (USA ISSN 0071-0210) **1741**
Encyclopedia of Canadian Municipal Governments (CAN ISSN 1182-6274) **7492**
Encyclopedia of Competition Law (GBR) **4665**
Encyclopedia of Compulsory Purchase and Compensation (GBR ISSN 0142-2820) **1337**
Encyclopedia of Consumer Credit Law (GBR ISSN 0142-2812) **1337**
Encyclopedia of Consumer Law (GBR) **2637**
Encyclopedia of Data Protection *see* Encyclopedia of Data Protection & Privacy **2637**
Encyclopedia of Data Protection & Privacy (GBR) **2637**
Encyclopedia of Endangered Species (USA ISSN 1077-1352) **2610**
Encyclopedia of Environmental Health Law & Practice (GBR) **3419**
Encyclopedia of Environmental Law (GBR) **3419**
Encyclopedia of European Community Law (GBR ISSN 0142-4564) **4665**
Encyclopedia of European Union Law (GBR) **4665**
Encyclopedia of Exhibitions (USA) **6523**
Encyclopedia of Financial Services Law (GBR) **1337**
Encyclopedia of Global Industries (USA ISSN 1084-8614) **1992**
• Encyclopedia of Governmental Advisory Organizations (USA ISSN 0092-8380) **7435**
Encyclopedia of Health & Safety at Work: Law and Practice (GBR ISSN 0142-2979) **6676**
Encyclopedia of Health & Safety at Work: Law and Practice. Bulletin *see* Encyclopedia of Health & Safety at Work: Law and Practice **6676**
• Encyclopedia of Highways Law and Practice (GBR ISSN 0142-2952) **8630**
• Encyclopedia of Housing Law and Practice (GBR ISSN 0142-2995) **4410**
Encyclopedia of Information Technology (GBR) **5061**
Encyclopedia of Insurance Law (GBR) **4501**
Encyclopedia of International Commercial Litigation (NLD) **4924**
Encyclopedia of Local Government Law (GBR ISSN 0261-3689) **4830**
Encyclopedia of Mathematics and Its Applications (GBR ISSN 0953-4806) **5486**
Encyclopedia of Medical Organizations and Agencies (USA ISSN 0743-4510) **5609**
Encyclopedia of Performance Appraisal (USA) **1861**
Encyclopedia of Planning Law and Practice (GBR ISSN 0142-4920) **4665**
Encyclopedia of Professional Partnerships (GBR) **4867**
Encyclopedia of Rating & Local Taxation (GBR ISSN 0958-6245) **1922**
• Encyclopedia of Road Traffic Law (GBR ISSN 0142-2847) **8630**
Encyclopedia of Social Services & Childcare Law (GBR ISSN 0261-3573) **8038**
• Encyclopedia of Social Work (USA ISSN 0071-0237) **8038**
Encyclopedia of Sports Business Contacts (USA) **1992**
Encyclopedia of Stock Market Techniques (USA) **1622**
Encyclopedia of UK & European Patent Law (GBR ISSN 0142-2987) **6749**
Encyclopedia of Words and Phrases, Legal Maxims *see* Sanagan's Encyclopedia of Words and Phrases, Legal Maxims **4778**
• Encyclopedia of World Biography. Supplement (USA ISSN 1099-7326) **3120**
Encyclopedia Year Book (USA ISSN 0196-0172) **3120**
Encyclopedic Dictionary of Economics (USA) **1741**
Encyclopedic Knowledge *see* Baike Zhishi **7839**
Encyclopedie Berbere (FRA ISSN 1015-7344) **3120**
Encyclopedie des Collectivites Locales (FRA ISSN 1775-9471) **7435**
Encyclopedie des Huissiers de Justice *see* Juris-Classeur Encyclopedie des Huissiers de Justice **4706**
Encyclopedie d'Utovie (FRA ISSN 0396-4957) **7852**
Encyclopedie Juridique (FRA ISSN 1275-2320) **4665**
Encyclopedie Medico-Chirurgicale. Anestesia - Rianimazione (ITA ISSN 1283-0771) **5771**
➤ Encyclopedie Medico-Chirurgicale. Anesthesie - Reanimation (FRA ISSN 0246-0289) **5771**
➤ Encyclopedie Medico-Chirurgicale. Aparato Locomotor (FRA ISSN 1286-935X) **6223**
➤ Encyclopedie Medico-Chirurgicale. Appareil Locomoteur (FRA ISSN 0246-0521) **6223**
• ➤ Encyclopedie Medico-Chirurgicale. Cardiologie (FRA ISSN 1166-4568) **5786**
Encyclopedie Medico-Chirurgicale. Cirugia General (FRA ISSN 1634-7080) **6242**
• ➤ Encyclopedie Medico-Chirurgicale. Dermatologie (FRA ISSN 0246-0319) **5876**
Encyclopedie Medico-Chirurgicale. Endocrinologie - Nutrition *see* Encyclopedie Medico-Chirurgicale. Endocrinologie - Nutrition **5890**
• ➤ Encyclopedie Medico-Chirurgicale. Endocrinologie - Nutrition (FRA) **5890**
Encyclopedie Medico-Chirurgicale. Endocrinologie - Nutrition (Print) *see* Encyclopedie Medico-Chirurgicale. Endocrinologie - Nutrition **5890**
• ➤ Encyclopedie Medico-Chirurgicale. Gastro-Enterologie (FRA ISSN 1155-1968) **5923**
Encyclopedie Medico-Chirurgicale. Ginecologia - Obstetricia (FRA ISSN 1283-081X) **5989**
Encyclopedie Medico-Chirurgicale. Ginecologia - Ostetricia (FRA ISSN 1293-2639) **5989**
• ➤ Encyclopedie Medico-Chirurgicale. Gynecologie (FRA ISSN 0246-1064) **5989**
• ➤ Encyclopedie Medico-Chirurgicale. Hematologie (FRA ISSN 1155-1984) **5936**
Encyclopedie Medico-Chirurgicale. Hematologie *see* Encyclopedie Medico-Chirurgicale. Hematologie **5936**
• ➤ Encyclopedie Medico-Chirurgicale. Hepatologie (FRA ISSN 1155-1976) **5923**

▼ *new title*   † *ceased*   ● *electronic media*   ➤ *refereed*

Title

▼ *new title*　　† *ceased*　　● *electronic media*　　➤ *refereed*

English Folk Dance and Song Society. Report and Financial Accounts (GBR) **2686**
• ➤ English for Specific Purposes (GBR ISSN 0889-4906) **5114**
English Four to Eleven (GBR ISSN 1460-5945) **3061**
The English Garden (GBR ISSN 1361-2840) **3729**
• ➤ English Goethe Society. Publications (GBR ISSN 0959-3683) **5289**
English Guernsey Herd Book (GBR ISSN 0071-0571) **286**
English Heritage. Collections Review (GBR ISSN 1473-7523) **4217**
English Heritage Historical Review (GBR ISSN 1752-0169) **4217**
English Heritage. Occasional Paper (GBR ISSN 0961-544X) **4217**
English Heritage. Research News (GBR ISSN 1750-2446) **4217**
English Heritage Research Transactions (GBR ISSN 1461-8613) **392**
English Heritage Visitors' Handbook (GBR) **4217**
• ➤ The English Historical Review (GBR ISSN 0013-8266) **4217**
The English Home (GBR ISSN 1468-0238) **4539**
The English Home (USA) **4539**
English Homes (GBR ISSN 1464-3197) **4539**
• ➤ English in Africa (ZAF ISSN 0376-8902) **5215**
English in Aotearoa (NZL ISSN 0113-7867) **5114**
• ➤ English in Australia (AUS ISSN 0155-2147) **3061**
• ➤ English in Education (GBR ISSN 0425-0494) **3061**
➤ English in Texas (USA ISSN 0425-0508) **3061**
• ➤ English Journal (USA ISSN 0013-8274) **3061**
• ➤ English Language and Linguistics (GBR ISSN 1360-6743) **5115**
English Language Gazette *see* E L Gazette **5113**
English Language Learning *see* Yingyu Xuexi **5197**
• ➤ English Language Notes (USA ISSN 0013-8282) **5290**
English Language Overseas Perspectives and Enquiries (SVN ISSN 1581-8918) **5115**
English Language Teacher Education and Development (GBR ISSN 1365-3741) **3061**
▼ • ➤ English Language Teaching (CAN ISSN 1916-4742) **5115**
English Language Teaching Journal *see* E L T Journal **5113**
• English Leadership Quarterly (USA ISSN 1054-1578) **3061**
English Linguistic Society of Japan. Journal *see* English Linguistics **5115**
English Linguistics (JPN ISSN 0918-3701) **5115**
English Literary History *see* E L H **5286**
• ➤ English Literary Renaissance (GBR ISSN 0013-8312) **5290**
English Literary Studies Monograph Series *see* E L S Monograph Series **5287**
English Literature and Language *see* Eibungaku to Eigogaku **5288**
• ➤ English Literature in Transition, 1880-1920 (USA ISSN 0013-8339) **5290**
English Monarchs Series (USA ISSN 0071-0628) **4217**
English National Opera Programme (GBR) **8470**
English Nature (GBR ISSN 0966-1166) **2610**
English Nature Research Reports (GBR ISSN 0967-876X) **2610**
English Nature Science (GBR ISSN 1363-3015) **2610**
English Now (FRA ISSN 1772-7383) **5115**
English of Science and Technology Learning *see* Keji Yingyu Xuexi **5136**
English Pages (BEL ISSN 0771-1034) **5115**
English Place-Name Society. Journal (GBR ISSN 1351-3095) **4005**
• English Plus Newsletter (USA) **5115**
English Practice Worksheet *see* Newcomer's Almanac **3983**
English Quarterly *see* English Quarterly Canada **3061**
• ➤ English Quarterly Canada (CAN) **3061**
English Record (USA ISSN 0013-8363) **5290**
• The English Review (GBR ISSN 0955-8950) **5290**
▼ English School (COL ISSN 2011-043X) **2853**
• English Schools Swimming Association Handbook (GBR) **8171**
English Self-Study *see* Yingyu Zixue **5197**
English Setter Association of America. Newsletter (USA) **6808**
An English Speaker's Guide to Life in the Eastern Townships (CAN ISSN 1719-6027) **8100**
English Speaking Union Today (USA) **7232**
English Sports Council. Annual Report (Year) (GBR) **8171**
• ➤ English Studies in Africa (GBR ISSN 0013-8398) **4451**
➤ English Studies in Canada (CAN ISSN 0317-0802) **5290**
† English Teachers' Journal (Israel)/'Alon L'Morim L'Anglit (ISR ISSN 0333-533X) **8953**
English Teaching and Research for Elementary and Secondary Schools/Zhongxiaoxue Yingyu Jiaoxue yu Yanjiu (CHN) **5115**
English Teaching Forum *see* Forum **5119**
• ➤ English Teaching: Practice and Critique (NZL ISSN 1175-8708) **2853**
▼ • English Text Construction (NLD ISSN 1874-8767) **5115**
• English Today (GBR ISSN 0266-0784) **5115**
English Tourist Board. Annual Report (GBR) **8701**
English Westerners' Society. Brand Book (GBR ISSN 0013-8401) **4292**
English Westerners' Tally Sheet (GBR ISSN 0013-841X) **4292**
English Woman's Weekly (AUS) **8861**
• ➤ English World-Wide (NLD ISSN 0172-8865) **5115**
EngNews *see* Engineering News **3190**
Engrami (SRB ISSN 0351-2665) **6138**
Engranajes (ARG) **4593**
Engravers Journal (USA ISSN 0099-0043) **1105**
Engravings (USA) **6650**
Enhancing Quality Assurance in the Animal Feed Sector *see* Versterking Kwaliteitsborging Diervoedersector **168**
Enigma (CUB ISSN 0864-1889) **5215**
Enigmas (ESP ISSN 1136-4696) **53**
Enimerossi/Briefing (CYP) **3831**
ENISA Quarterly *see* E N I S A Quarterly **2513**
Enjeux (FRA ISSN 0223-4866) **6402**
Enjeux Diplomatiques et Strategiques (FRA ISSN 1770-1643) **7232**
Enjeux Geographiques (CAN ISSN 1718-0538) **4005**
Enjeux Internationaux (BEL ISSN 1379-4205) **7232**
• Enjeux les Echos (FRA ISSN 1167-2196) **1105**
Enjeux Mediterranee (FRA ISSN 1953-1605) **7133**
Enjeux Sport *see* En Jeux Sport **8171**
Enjine!-Enjine! (USA ISSN 0362-2487) **3576**
Enjiniasu/Engineers (JPN ISSN 0013-8444) **3191**
Enjoy the Countryside (GBR ISSN 0957-7971) **2610**
Enjoy Your Life (DEU ISSN 1614-9750) **6985**
• Enlace (CUB ISSN 1025-0271) **5486**
• Enlace (MEX ISSN 1605-4210) **8100**
Enlace (San Diego) (USA) **3532**
Enlace (Washington, 1975) (USA ISSN 1059-6402) **7232**
Enlace (Washington) (USA ISSN 0425-0702) **8861**
• Enlaces (ESP ISSN 1695-8543) **4451**
• Enlaces. Revista Venezonala de Informacion, Tecnologia y Conocimiento (VEN ISSN 1690-7515) **2418**
Enlargement (GBR ISSN 1470-5966) **7232**
Enl@ce *see* Enlaces. Revista Venezonala de Informacion, Tecnologia y Conocimiento **2418**
Enlighten Next *see* EnlightenNext **7640**
Enlightenment *see* Qimeng **6536**
Enlightenment/Keihatsu (JPN) **2941**
➤ Enlightenment and Dissent (GBR ISSN 0262-7612) **4138**
• Enlightenment Connoisseurs' Cozy Corner (USA) **7640**
• EnlightenNext (USA ISSN 1946-0805) **7640**
Ennaanin Etto/News From the Past (MHL ISSN 1061-4435) **392**
Ennebi (ITA ISSN 1971-4491) **1105**
• ➤ Ennen ja Nyt (FIN ISSN 1458-1396) **4138**
Enniscorthy Guardian *see* Gorey Guardian **3893**
Enoch Pratt Free Library. Staff Reporter (USA ISSN 0013-8495) **5008**
† Enohobby (ITA ISSN 0390-2048) **8953**
• Enoikos (ARG) **1105**
Enologia (PRT ISSN 0874-3479) **603**
L'Enologo (ITA ISSN 1593-6112) **603**
Enonce de Politique (CAN ISSN 1718-8512) **6461**
Enoteca Wine and Food Magazine (CAN) **4385**
Enotria (ITA ISSN 1827-5435) **603**
Enquete *see* Enquete - Ecole des Hautes Etudes en Sciences Sociales **336**
Enquete Annuelle sur l'Activite des Organismes de Securite Sociale (GRC ISSN 0256-3630) **8082**
Enquete du Musee de la Vie Wallonne (BEL ISSN 0773-4980) **336**
Enquete - Ecole des Hautes Etudes en Sciences Sociales (FRA ISSN 1629-7121) **336**
† Enquete Fonciere et Immobiliere aupres des Etudes Notariales de la Region Nord Pas-de-Calais (FRA ISSN 1770-1791) **8953**
Enquete Nationale De Remuneration *see* National Compensation Survey **1870**
Enquete sur la Consommation les Depenses et les Revenus des Menages Prives *see* Verbrauchserhebung. Ausgaben und Einnahmen der Privaten Haushalte **1273**
• L'Enquete sur la Dynamique du Travail et du Revenu (E R T R) (CAN ISSN 1710-0364) **1483**
• L'Enquete sur la Dynamique du Travail et du Revenu, Dictionnaire Electronique des Donnees (CAN ISSN 1710-7490) **8368**
Enquete sur la Planification Familiale en Milieu Urbain *see* Senegal. Ministere de l'Economie, des Finances et du Plan. Enquete sur la Planification Familiale en Milieu Urbain **973**
Enquete sur les Budgets des Menages - Institut National de Statistique *see* Belgium. Institut National de Statistique. Enquete sur les Budgets des Menages **1214**
Enquete sur les Entreprises Industrielles et Commerciales du Togo (TGO) **1427**
Enquete sur les Terrains Residentiels Vacants en Milieu Urbain, Mise a Jour/Vacant Urban Residential Land Survey (CAN ISSN 1719-6949) **4410**
• Enquete sur l'Hebergement des Voyageurs. Rapport (CAN ISSN 1716-9070) **4410**
Enquetes et Documents d'Histoire Africaine (BEL ISSN 0772-6112) **4174**
Enqueteur *see* Eye Opener **4575**
The Enquirer (MWI) **3906**
Enquires (SGP) **1402**
Enquiry (IND ISSN 0013-8517) **7133**
• ➤ Enrahonar (ESP ISSN 0211-402X) **6915**
Enrich (USA) **5609**
Enrich! (USA) **1402**
Enriching Communications (FRA ISSN 1960-7652) **2367**
• Enriching Communications (French Edition) (FRA ISSN 1960-7636) **2367**
• Enrichment (USA ISSN 1082-1791) **7735**
Enrico Fermi International School of Physics *see* International School of Physics "Enrico Fermi." Proceedings **7018**
Enrolled Actuaries Report (USA) **4501**
Enrolled Agents Journal *see* E A Journal **1921**
• Enrollment Management Report (USA ISSN 1094-3757) **1861**
Enron Litigation Reporter *see* Corporate Corruption Litigation Reporter **4863**
EnRoute (CAN ISSN 0703-0312) **8701**
• ➤ Ensaio (BRA ISSN 0104-4036) **2853**
Ensaios e Ciencia (BRA ISSN 1415-6938) **7852**
➤ Ensaios F E E (BRA ISSN 0101-1723) **1540**
Ensaios Linguisticos (BRA) **5115**
Ensanian Physicochemical Institute. Journal (USA ISSN 0013-8533) **7010**
Ensayo Sobre Arte Contemporaneo en Colombia (COL ISSN 2011-0332) **487**
Ensayo Teoria Critica *see* E T C **6915**
Ensayo y Testimonio (URY ISSN 0071-0679) **5290**
➤ Ensayos (COL ISSN 1692-3502) **487**
• Ensayos (ESP ISSN 0214-4824) **2853**
➤ Ensayos de Economia (COL ISSN 0121-117X) **1483**
Ensayos Economicos (ARG ISSN 0325-3937) **1105**
Ensayos Scriptura (ESP) **5290**
Ensayos sobre Economia Cafetera (COL) **197**
➤ Ensayos Sobre Politica Economica (COL ISSN 0120-4483) **1105**
L'Enseignant de Bourgogne (FRA ISSN 1774-4741) **4593**
Enseignants (CAN ISSN 0046-2101) **2853**
➤ L'Enseignement Mathematique (CHE ISSN 0013-8584) **5486**
L'Enseignement Mathematique *see* Nastava Matematike **5519**
➤ L'Enseignement Mathematique. Monographies (CHE ISSN 0425-0818) **5486**
L'Enseignement Philosophique (FRA ISSN 0986-1653) **6915**
Enseignement Public (FRA ISSN 0223-5986) **2853**
Enseignement SUP. Mathematiques *see* Collection Enseignement Sup. Mathematiques **5478**
Enseignement Superieur en Cote-d'Ivoire (CIV) **2980**
Enseignement superieur en Europe *see* Higher Education in Europe **2984**
Enseigner le Francais (FRA ISSN 1960-873X) **5115**
Enseiukarrean (ESP ISSN 1130-8192) **5115**
• Ensemble (ITA ISSN 0997-0274) **5115**
• Ensemble (Hull) (CAN) **5008**
Ensemble (Montreal) (CAN) **4093**
Ensemble (Montvale) (USA ISSN 1546-184X) **4539**
Ensemble pour Agir (FRA ISSN 1950-4519) **4065**
Ensenanza (ESP ISSN 0212-5374) **2853**
Ensenanza Andaluza *see* Informativo Ensenanza Andaluza **2866**
Ensenanza de la Religion (ESP) **7640**
• Ensenanza de las Ciencias (ESP ISSN 0212-4521) **2853**
Ensenanza de las Ciencias Sociales (ESP ISSN 1579-2617) **7961**
• ➤ Ensenanza e Investigacion en Psicologia (MEX ISSN 0185-1594) **7354**
Ensho to Men'eki/Inflammation & Immunology (JPN ISSN 0918-8371) **5757**
• Enshou, Saisei/Inflammation and Regeneration (JPN ISSN 1346-8022) **5609**
Enshu no Shizen/Nature of Enshu (JPN ISSN 0386-5037) **7853**
The Ensign (NZL ISSN 1170-036X) **3917**
• The Ensign (USA ISSN 0744-3129) **8643**
• Ensign (USA ISSN 0884-1136) **7735**
Ensign Talking Book (USA) **7735**
Ensino em Revista (BRA ISSN 0104-3757) **2853**
Ensovoort (ZAF ISSN 0257-2036) **5421**
Entdecken...Erleben (DEU) **3846**
Entdeckungskiste (DEU ISSN 0935-9869) **2187**
Ente Nazionale Assistenza Agenti e Rappresentanti di Commercio Notiziario *see* E N A S A R C O. Notiziario **1096**
Ente Nazionale Idrocarburi (E N I) Annual Report *see* E N I Annual Report **3127**
Ente per le Nuove Tecnologie l'Energia e l'Ambiente (E N E A) (Rapporti Tecnici) R T - AMB *see* E N E A (Rapporti Tecnici) R T - AMB **3166**
Ente per le Nuove Tecnologie l'Energia e l'Ambiente (E N E A) (Rapporti Tecnici) R T - E R G *see* E N E A (Rapporti Tecnici) R T - E R G **3166**
Ente per le Nuove Tecnologie l'Energia e l'Ambiente (E N E A) (Rapporti Tecnici) R T - I N N *see* E N E A (Rapporti Tecnici) R T - I N N **3166**
Ente per le Nuove Tecnologie l'Energia e l'Ambiente (E N E A) (Rapporti Tecnici) R T - NUCL *see* E N E A (Rapporti Tecnici) R T - NUCL **3166**
Ente per le Nuovo Tecnologie l'Energie e l'Ambiente. Rapporto Tecnico - Energia *see* E N E A (Rapporti Tecnici) R T - E R G **3166**
• Entelequia (ESP ISSN 1885-6985) **7961**
Entente Africaine (CIV ISSN 0013-8630) **3532**
• Entente de Financement Canada - Premieres Nations. Modele National pour les Premieres Nations et les Conseils Tribaux (CAN ISSN 1912-0419) **1922**
Entente de Partenariat Economique Canada - Manitoba. Rapport d'Etape Annuel *see* Canada-Manitoba Economic Partnership Agreement. Annual Progress Report **1426**
• Enter (IRL ISSN 1393-8916) **4977**
Enter (POL ISSN 0867-4566) **2418**
Enter (RUS ISSN 1729-0902) **2418**
▼ Enterar (USA) **3532**
† Enteron & Pharyngos (ITA) **8953**
Enterprise (IND ISSN 0013-8673) **1959**
Enterprise (Coventry) (GBR) **1402**
• Enterprise (London) (GBR ISSN 1350-3030) **1741**
• Enterprise (New York) (USA) **4501**
Enterprise (Ontario) (CAN ISSN 0013-8657) **3809**
• Enterprise (Salt Lake City) (USA) **1105**
Enterprise (Sutton) (GBR) **1959**
Enterprise (Vancouver) (CAN) **1337**
Enterprise 200 (ZAF ISSN 1024-154X) **1741**
Enterprise and Innovation (NZL ISSN 1176-1997) **1105**
• ➤ Enterprise and Society (USA ISSN 1467-2227) **1105**
• Enterprise and Work Innovation Studies (PRT ISSN 1646-1223) **7961**
Enterprise Architect (USA ISSN 1547-4569) **2520**
Enterprise Black Business and Professional Directory *see* Directory of Black Business **1985**
• The Enterprise-Bulletin (CAN ISSN 0834-6097) **3809**
• Enterprise Cape Breton Corporation. Annual Report (CAN ISSN 0848-5267) **7435**
Enterprise Culture *see* Qiye Wenhua **5356**
• ➤ Enterprise Development & Microfinance (GBR ISSN 1755-1978) **1959**
• Enterprise Europe (LUX ISSN 1680-0516) **1483**
Enterprise Imaging and Therapeutic Radiology Management *see* Enterprise Imaging & Therapeutic Radiology Management **6196**
• Enterprise Imaging & Therapeutic Radiology Management (USA ISSN 1941-3610) **6196**
▼ • ➤ Enterprise Information Systems (GBR ISSN 1751-7575) **2543**
Enterprise Management *see* Qiye Guanli **1788**
▼ Enterprise Management Quarterly (USA) **1741**
• Enterprise Matters (NZL ISSN 1177-875X) **1885**
Enterprise Middleware (GBR) **2418**
➤ Enterprise Modelling and Information Systems Architectures (DEU ISSN 1860-6059) **1416**
Enterprise Modelling and Information Systems Architectures *see* Informationssystem-Architekturen **2467**
Enterprise Networking Magazine *see* Enterprise Networks & Servers **2497**
Enterprise Networks & Servers (USA) **2497**
Enterprise Networkz *see* Enterprise Matters **1885**
Enterprise New Zealand Trust *see* Enterprise Matters **1885**
Enterprise News *see* Arthur Enterprise News **3806**
Enterprise Open Source Journal (USA) **2418**
• Enterprise Open Source Magazine (USA) **2418**
• Enterprise Operations Management (USA ISSN 1099-4971) **2534**
Enterprise Partner (RUS ISSN 1606-0229) **2589**
Enterprise Resource Planning Expert *see* E R P Expert **2417**
Enterprise Resource Planning Management *see* E R P Management **1416**
Enterprise Resource Planning Software Selection Guide (CD-ROM) *see* E R P Software Selection Guide (CD-ROM) **2417**
▼ Enterprise Risk (ZAF ISSN 1993-8217) **1741**
Enterprise Search Sourcebook (Year) (USA) **1992**
Enterprise Servers World Japan (JPN) **2556**
Enterprise Solutions for Managers of Windows N T *see* E N T (Online) **2589**
• Enterprise Systems (USA ISSN 1533-8983) **2536**
Enterprise Vitality *see* Qiye Huoli **1162**
Entertainer (CAN) **3809**
▼ The Entertainer Bahrain (BHR ISSN 1752-6019) **4977**
▼ Entertaining (USA ISSN 1946-6358) **4357**
Entertainment: An Industry Overview (USA) **4977**
Entertainment & Media Industry Almanac *see* Plunkett's Entertainment and Media Industry Almanac **2387**
Entertainment & Media Law Reports (GBR ISSN 0966-193X) **4830**
• ➤ Entertainment and Sports Law Journal (GBR ISSN 1748-944X) **4666**
• Entertainment and Sports Lawyer (USA ISSN 0732-1880) **4666**
▼ • Entertainment & Travel (USA ISSN 1944-2246) **8701**
• Entertainment, Arts and Sports Law Journal (USA ISSN 1090-8730) **4666**
Entertainment, Arts & Sports Law Journal *see* Entertainment, Arts and Sports Law Journal **4666**
Entertainment, Arts & Sports Law Newsletter *see* E A S L Newsletter **4662**
Entertainment Business (NLD ISSN 1875-2888) **6565**
Entertainment Business Live *see* E B Live **6563**
▼ • ➤ Entertainment Computing (GBR ISSN 1875-9521) **2476**
Entertainment Design *see* Live Design **8473**
• Entertainment Employment Journal (USA ISSN 1067-3970) **1680**
Entertainment Eyes (USA) **6565**
▼ Entertainment Ideas (ZAF ISSN 1998-2844) **4357**
• Entertainment Industry Contracts (USA) **4666**

Title

Title

● ➤ Epileptic Disorders (FRA ISSN 1294-9361) 6138
➤ Epileptologia (POL ISSN 1230-5294) 6138
† Epileptologicke Listy (CZE ISSN 1801-6375) 8954
Epiloge. Oikonomike Episkopese see Economic Review of the Year - The Greek Economy 1480
Epilogi/Choice (GRC ISSN 1105-2503) 1338
Epimelia (ARG ISSN 0327-8514) 7640
● ➤ Epinorth Journal (NOR ISSN 1502-1246) 5813
▼ ● ➤ Epiphany (BIH ISSN 1840-3719) 7961
● Epiphany (New York) (USA ISSN 1937-9803) 5290
● Epiphany International (USA ISSN 1089-1307) 7640
▼ Epiphany Magazine (USA ISSN 1937-898X) 8861
Epiphyllum Bulletin (USA) 787
Episcopal Clerical Directory (USA) 7756
Episcopal Diocese of Michigan (USA) 7756
The Episcopal Evangelical Journal (USA ISSN 1545-6676) 7756
Episcopal Life (USA ISSN 1050-0057) 7756
The Episcopal New Yorker (USA ISSN 1543-2092) 7756
Episcopal Peace Fellowship Newsletter see E P F Newsletter 7755
The Episcopal Times (USA) 7756
Episeme Efemerida ton Europaikon Koinoteton. C. Anakoinoseis Kai Plerofories see Diario Oficial de las Comunidades Europeas. C: Comunicaciones e Informaciones 4923
Episeme Efemerida ton Europaikon Koinoteton. C. Anakoinoseis Kai Plerofories see Official Journal of the European Union 7256
Episeme Efemerida ton Europaikon Koinoteton. L & C: Nomothesia Anakoinoseis kai Plerofories see Official Journal of the European Union. L & C Series: Legislation and Information Notices (Quarterly Edition) 4937
Episeme Efemerida ton Europaikon Koinoteton. L: Nomothesia see Official Journal of the European Union. L Series: Legislation 7256
Episeme Efemerida ton Europaikon Koinoteton. Parartema. Suzeteseis see Diario Oficial de las Comunidades Europeas. Anexo Debates 4923
Episimos Ephimeris tis Kyriakes Demokratias (CYP) 3831
➤ Episodes (CHN ISSN 0705-3797) 2733
Episodi (FIN ISSN 1459-7381) 6497
Episodi - Teatterikorkeakoulu (FIN ISSN 1459-7349) 8470
Episource (USA) 5610
Epistemata. Reihe Philosophie (DEU ISSN 1434-1492) 6916
● Episteme (BRA ISSN 1413-5736) 6916
● ➤ Episteme (GBR ISSN 1742-3600) 6916
● Episteme (NLD ISSN 0165-0904) 7853
Episteme (PRT ISSN 0874-0437) 6916
Episteme (USA ISSN 1542-7072) 6916
● Episteme (Online) (ITA ISSN 1824-8462) 7853
Episteme kai Tehnologia Galaktos/Greek Journal of Dairy Science and Technology (GRC ISSN 1105-0888) 264
● ➤ Episteme N S (VEN ISSN 0798-4324) 6916
● ➤ Epistemologia (ITA ISSN 0392-9760) 6916
● Epistemologicas (BRA ISSN 1517-7823) 6916
Epistulae Slovenorum Illustrium see Korespondence Pomembnih Slovencev 5318
● Epites- Epiteszettudomany/Architectonics and Architecture (HUN ISSN 0013-9661) 1007
Epitesugyi Szemle (HUN ISSN 0013-967X) 1007
Epitheorese Klinikes Farmakologias kai Farmakokinetikes (International Edition)/Review of Clinical Pharmacology and Pharmacokinetics (International Edition) (GRC ISSN 1011-6583) 6837
Epitheoreseis Klostoufantourgias/Epitheorisis Klostoufantourgias (GRC ISSN 1105-4069) 8450
Epitheoresis Synkoinoniakou Dikaiou (GRC) 8495
Epitheorisis Klostoufantourgias see Epitheoresis Klostoufantourgias 8450
Epitheorisis Koinonikon Erevnon see Greek Review of Social Research 7967
Epitoanyag (HUN ISSN 0013-970X) 1007
Epitrope ton Europaikon Koinoteton. Eggrafa see Commission of the European Communities. Documents 7227
ePlant (USA ISSN 1530-4701) 1105
● ➤ Eplasty (USA ISSN 1937-5719) 5913
ePlay see Diannao Youxi Xin Ganxian 2475
Epoc (DEU ISSN 1865-5718) 392
● Epoca (BRA ISSN 1415-5494) 3803
Epoca (ESP ISSN 0213-1080) 3952
Epoca (PRT) 3931
● Epoca (Mexico D.F.) (MEX) 3908
Epoch (Ithaca) (USA ISSN 0145-1391) 5421
The Epoch Times (New Zealand Edition) (NZL ISSN 1177-1461) 3917
● The Epoch Times (UK Edition) (GBR ISSN 1749-5997) 3967
Epocha (CZE ISSN 1214-9519) 3832
Epoche (USA ISSN 0149-3043) 7640
● ➤ Epoche (USA ISSN 1085-1968) 6916
Epokha (RUS) 7133
L'Epoque Conradienne (FRA ISSN 0294-6904) 5290
● ePosters.net (GBR ISSN 1754-1417) 7853
▼ ● Epping Forest Guardian (GBR ISSN 1753-4593) 3967
Epping Forest Guardian (Epping, Ongar and Villages Edition) see Epping Forest Guardian 3967
Epping Forest Guardian (Loughton, Buckhurst Hill, Chigwell and Waltham Abbey Edition) see Epping Forest Guardian 3967
ePregnancy (USA ISSN 1554-1894) 5989
ePregnancy Magazine see ePregnancy 5989
➤ Epsilon (COL ISSN 1692-1259) 3191
Epsilon (ESP ISSN 1131-9321) 5486
Epta Meres TV see 7 Meres T V 2399
ePub Aux see Publishers' Auxiliary 4582
Epworth Review (GBR ISSN 0308-0382) 7756
Eqtesad-e-Melli (IRN) 1680
Eqtisadiah see Al- Iqtisadiyyah 1359
● EQuad News (USA) 3191
Equal Employment Opportunities Trust Diversity Survey Report see E E O Trust Diversity Survey Report 1676
Equal Employment Opportunities Trust Newsletter see E E O Trust Newsletter 1676
Equal Employment Opportunities Trust Work & Life Awards (Series) see E E O Trust Work & Life Awards (Series) 1676
Equal Employment Opportunity see Human Resources Management - Equal Employment Opportunity 1685
Equal Employment Opportunity and Affirmative Employment for Minorities, Women, and People with Disabilities see U.S. Department of Transportation. National Highway Traffic Safety Administration. Equal Employment Opportunity and Affirmative Employment for Minorities, Women, and People with Disabilities 7217
Equal Employment Opportunity Commission Compliance Manual see E E O C Compliance Manual 1676
Equal Employment Opportunity Insight see E E O Insight 1676
Equal Employment Opportunity Report see U.S. Equal Employment Opportunity Commission. Annual Report 1712
● Equal Opportunities Commission. Annual Report (GBR ISSN 0140-9468) 7206
Equal Opportunities for Women and Men in the European Union (LUX ISSN 1680-2381) 1680
Equal Opportunities International see Equality, Diversity and Inclusion 8895
● Equal Opportunities Review (GBR ISSN 0268-7143) 1680
Equal Opportunity (USA ISSN 0071-1039) 3532
Equal Opportunity for Women in the Workplace Agency News Alert see E O W A News Alert 8859
Equal Opportunity Magazine see Equal Opportunity 3532
Equal Rights (USA) 8861
Equal Rights Advocate (USA) 4667
Equal Times (USA) 4373
● ➤ Equality, Diversity and Inclusion (GBR ISSN 2040-7149) 8895
Equality N O W! (National Organization for Women) (USA) 8861
Equality News (CAN ISSN 1188-908X) 3532
Equality Rights. Annual Report (CAN ISSN 1719-7295) 8100
Equality State Almanac (USA) 1483
● Equality Today! (CAN) 7206
Equalization (New York) see E Q (New York) 8152
Equals (GBR ISSN 1465-1254) 3039
Equator (NLD ISSN 0923-3334) 8797
Equestrian (USA ISSN 1548-873X) 8290
Equestrian N Z see New Zealand Equestrian Federation. Bulletin 8295
The Equestrian News (USA) 8290
● Equestrian Retailer (USA ISSN 1528-5197) 8290
● The Equestrian Times (USA) 8290
Equestrian Trade News (GBR ISSN 1462-9526) 8290
Equestrian Trails (USA ISSN 0013-9831) 8290
Equestrian Vacation Guide see Nationwide Overnight Stabling Directory & Equestrian Vacation Guide 8295
Equidata Investor (USA) 1622
● Equijournal (USA) 8290
Equilibre (BEL ISSN 1783-3019) 5610
Equilibre (FRA ISSN 1764-1934) 8171
● Equilibri (ITA ISSN 1594-7580) 3430
Equilibrium Magazine (USA) 5290
➤ Equilibrium Research/Heiko Shinkei Kagaku (JPN ISSN 0385-5716) 921
Equilibrium Research. Supplement/Equilibrium Research. Supplement (JPN ISSN 0916-0337) 922
Equilibrium Research. Supplement see Equilibrium Research. Supplement 922
Equilife (CAN) 8290
Equilink (CAN ISSN 1712-3380) 7354
Equine and Comparative Exercise Physiology see Comparative Exercise Physiology 8289
Equine Behaviour (GBR) 8290
● Equine Health Report (USA) 286
Equine Images (USA ISSN 1044-0224) 487
Equine Journal (USA) 8290
Equine Times (USA ISSN 1056-8212) 8290
The Equine Trade Journal (USA ISSN 1087-8734) 8290
● ➤ Equine Veterinary Education (GBR ISSN 0957-7734) 8797
● ➤ Equine Veterinary Journal (GBR ISSN 0425-1644) 8797
● Equine Wellness (CAN ISSN 1718-5793) 8797
● Equine World UK Online Magazine (GBR) 8291
Equinews (CAN ISSN 0828-864X) 8291
Equinoxe (CHE ISSN 1013-6002) 7961
Equinus (ESP ISSN 1578-861X) 286
Equip for Ministry (USA) 7756
Equip-Mart (USA) 5451
● Equip4wire.Com (GBR) 6311
Equipack (ESP ISSN 0212-5226) 6709
Equipamiento y Servicios Municipales (ESP) 7492
● L'Equipe (FRA ISSN 0153-1069) 8171
L'Equipe Magazine (FRA ISSN 0245-3312) 8171
† Equipe Odontoiatrica (ITA ISSN 1593-9952) 8954
Equipement Sportif et Piscines see S B 1034
Equipement, Transport et Services Infos (FRA ISSN 1263-5618) 8495
Equipes St. Vincent (FRA ISSN 0763-5184) 7796
Equipment (Three Lakes) see E Q (Three Lakes) 1005
Equipment Catalog (USA) 108
Equipment Construction (BEL ISSN 0775-2075) 1007
Equipment Echoes (USA ISSN 0897-5159) 1007
Equipment Environmental Engineering see Zhuangbei Huanjing Gongcheng 5462
Equipment for Geophysical Prospecting see Wu-tan Zhuangbei 6798
Equipment for Geotechnical Engineering see Dizhi Zhuangbei 4486
Equipment for Parks and Amenity Areas (GBR ISSN 0143-506X) 4410
Equipment for the Disabled Market Report see Key Note Market Report: Equipment for the Disabled 4067
Equipment Journal (CAN ISSN 0710-2720) 1007
Equipment Leasing (GBR) 4667
Equipment Leasing (USA) 4667
Equipment Leasing Market Report see Key Note Market Report: Equipment Leasing 1963
Equipment Leasing Newsletter see L J N's Equipment Leasing Newsletter 4710
● Equipment Leasing Today (USA ISSN 1046-6665) 5451
Equipment Manufacturers Institute. First of the Week Newsletter (USA) 210
Equipment Manufacturers Institute. Retail Sales Reports (USA) 210
Equipment Manufacturers Institute. State of the Industry (USA) 210
Equipment News (GBR) 1007
● Equipment Protection (USA ISSN 1544-7812) 5451
● Equipment Protection e-Report (USA ISSN 1938-0798) 3307
† Equipment Solutions (USA) 8954
● Equipment Today (USA ISSN 0891-141X) 1007
● Equipment World (USA ISSN 1057-7262) 1007
Equipment World Online see Equipment World 1007
Equipo Domestico - Electrodomesticos (ESP ISSN 1133-0317) 4556
Equipo Minero (USA ISSN 1937-9714) 6461
Equipos para Oficina Catalogo de Equipos para Oficina see E P O: Catalogo de Equipos para Oficina 1850
Equipos Productos Electronicos (ESP ISSN 1133-4053) 3099
Equipos Productos Industriales (ESP ISSN 1130-9571) 1885
Equipos y Productos. Tecnologia (CUB) 8421
Equipotel (PRT) 4385
Equipping the Man in the Mirror (USA ISSN 1942-3306) 7640
● Equis X (MEX) 8100
Equit' Infos (FRA ISSN 1951-4115) 8291
Equitable Distribution Journal (USA ISSN 0743-247X) 4667
Equitable Distribution of Property (USA) 4667
Equitas Info (CAN ISSN 1912-032X) 7206
Equitas News see Equitas Info 7206
Equitation Infos see Equit' Infos 8291
Equite en Emploi dans la Fonction Publique Federale see Employment Equity in the Federal Public Service 7435
● L'Equite en Matiere d'Emploi. Bilan (CAN ISSN 1912-2497) 6697
L'Equite en Matiere d'Emploi. Rapport see L' Equite en Matiere d'Emploi. Bilan 6697
● Equities (USA ISSN 1053-2544) 1622
Equitrends (DEU ISSN 0948-6119) 8291
Equity see Al- Insaf 4321
Equity (USA) 2853
Equity (London) (GBR ISSN 1749-4184) 8470
● Equity African, Caribbean, Oriental & Asian Artists Register (GBR ISSN 1746-6733) 1992
● Equity & Excellence in Education (USA ISSN 1066-5684) 2853
Equity Central Europe (HUN ISSN 1418-9496) 1622
● Equity Dialogue (BGD) 8039
Equity, Disability and Accommodation Law (CAN) 4667
Equity Investment Strategy Report (USA) 1622
Equity Journal see Equity (London) 8470
Equity News (USA ISSN 0092-4520) 4593
Equivalence of Foreign Degrees (Year) (IND) 2980
Equivalences (BEL ISSN 0779-5599) 5115
Equivalences see Equivalencias 5421
Equivalencias/Equivalences (ESP ISSN 0211-8181) 5421
● Equus (USA ISSN 0149-0672) 942
Equus International (FRA ISSN 1961-6937) 488
Equus les Chevaux see Equus International 488
Er (DEU ISSN 0342-1872) 6289
† Er (ESP ISSN 0213-1668) 8954
Era (FIN ISSN 0356-3464) 8311
Era Agricola (VEN) 108
● The Era Banner (CAN ISSN 0844-4072) 3809
Era Rossii (RUS) 7133
● Era Solar (ESP ISSN 0212-4157) 3176
L'Erable (BEL ISSN 0773-9400) 671
● ➤ Eranos (SWE ISSN 0013-9947) 5115
● ➤ Eras (AUS ISSN 1445-5218) 4139
Erasmi Opera Omnia (NLD) 7796
Erasmus and Lingua Action II. Directory see Commission of the European Communities. Erasmus and Lingua Action II. Directory 2973
Erasmus and Lingua Action II. Repertoire see Commission of the European Communities. Erasmus and Lingua Action II. Directory 2973
▼ ● ➤ Erasmus Journal for Philosophy and Economics (NLD ISSN 1876-9098) 1105
● Erasmus Law and Economics Review (ITA ISSN 1824-3886) 4667
Erasmus Law Lectures (NLD ISSN 1871-7365) 4667
Erasmus Lezing (NLD ISSN 1384-5934) 7232
Erasmus Medical Historical Papers (NLD ISSN 1571-5191) 5610
● ➤ Erasmus of Rotterdam Society Yearbook (NLD ISSN 0276-2854) 6916
Erasmus Studies (CAN ISSN 0318-3319) 4451
● Erasmus: Superior Court Practice (ZAF ISSN 1561-7475) 4950
Erasmus Universiteit. Faculteit der Historsiche en Kunstwetenschappen. Publikaties (NLD ISSN 0929-9823) 4139
Eravaeltaja (FIN ISSN 1459-952X) 8311
Erba d'Arno (ITA ISSN 0394-5618) 5290
Erba d'Arno. Quaderni (ITA ISSN 1120-4923) 5290
L'Erbamusica (ITA ISSN 1122-9462) 6565
➤ Erbe und Auftrag (DEU ISSN 0013-9963) 7796
Erbfolgebesteuerung (DEU ISSN 0945-3520) 4901
● L'Erborista (ITA ISSN 1121-2896) 6837
Erboristeria Domani (ITA ISSN 1721-5676) 6658
ErbR (DEU ISSN 1862-4790) 4901
Erbrecht Effektiv (DEU ISSN 1611-9533) 4901
● Der Erbschaft-Steuer-Berater (DEU ISSN 1610-4072) 4901
Ercilla (CHL ISSN 0716-1204) 3821
Erciyes Medical Journal see Erciyes Tip Dergisi 5610
● Erciyes Tip Dergisi/Erciyes Medical Journal (TUR ISSN 1300-199X) 5610
L'Erckmann - Chatrian see Litterature Lorraine 8971
ERCO Lichtbericht see E R C O Lichtbericht 4556
Die Erde (DEU ISSN 0013-9998) 4005
Die Erdekruik/The Vessel (ZAF ISSN 1818-9342) 7640
Erdelyi Pszichologiai Szemle (ROM ISSN 1454-797X) 7354
● Erdem (TUR ISSN 1010-867X) 3532
Erdeszeti Lapok (HUN ISSN 1215-0398) 3687
Erdeyi Figyelo (ROM ISSN 1220-9880) 3932
Erdgeschichte Mitteleuropaeischer Regionen (DEU ISSN 1436-6800) 2733
Erdinger Land (DEU) 4218
Erdkunde (DEU ISSN 0014-0015) 4005
Erdkundliches Wissen (DEU ISSN 0425-1741) 4005
Erdoel (AUT) 6768
● Erdoel - Erdgas - Kohle (DEU ISSN 0179-3187) 6768
Erdstall (DEU ISSN 0343-6500) 392
Erdwissenschaftliche Forschung (DEU ISSN 0170-3188) 2707
Eredienst (NLD ISSN 1384-6329) 6565
Eredienstvaardig (NLD ISSN 0169-4677) 6565
Erehwon (USA) 5421
Erekutoro Hito/Electro-Heat (JPN ISSN 0919-9721) 3307
Erekutoronikusu Jisso Gakkaishi (JPN ISSN 1343-9677) 6709
Erekutoronikusu no Rinsho/Electronics in Medical Clinics (JPN ISSN 0913-3887) 5610
Erekutoronikusu Raifu/Electronics Life (JPN ISSN 0911-0038) 3099
Erensia Sefardi/Herencia Sefardi/Heritage Sepharade/Sephardic Heritage (USA) 7721
Eres (USA) 3975
Eres Novia (MEX) 2254
Eres. Serie de Arqueologia see Canarias Arqueologica 386
Eretz-Israel. Archaeological, Historical and Geographical Studies (ISR ISSN 0071-108X) 392
Eretz Magazine (ISR ISSN 0334-9578) 2610
Eretz Va-Teva see Eretz Magazine 2610
Erevan (BGR ISSN 0205-0919) 3532
● Ereview of Tourism Research (USA ISSN 1941-5842) 8701
Erexxxion (DEU) 4373
Erfahrung und Denken (DEU ISSN 0425-1806) 6916
● Erfahrungsheilkunde/Acta Medica Empirica (DEU ISSN 0014-0082) 5610
Erfgoed van Industrie en Techniek (NLD ISSN 0927-3026) 8421
Erfinder und Neuheitendienst (DEU) 6749
Erfolg im Beruf (AUT) 1960
Erfolg Konkret (DEU ISSN 1864-1350) 587
Erfolgreiche Gastronomie Heute (DEU ISSN 1861-2334) 4385
Das Erfrischungsgetraenk see A F G Wirtschaft - Das Erfrischungsgetraenk 597
● Erfurt Electronic Studies in English (DEU ISSN 1430-6905) 5290
● Erga (ESP ISSN 0213-943X) 7516
Erga Noticias (ESP ISSN 0213-7658) 5610
Erga Online see Erga 7516
Ergatiki Phoni/Worker's Voice (CYP) 1680
Ergatiko Vima/Worker's Herald (CYP) 1680

Title

Espaces Tropicaux (FRA ISSN 1147-3991) **4005**
Espaces Verts (BEL) **3729**
Espaces Verts (CAN ISSN 0846-5339) **3729**
• ➤ EspacesTemps.net (FRA ISSN 1777-5477) **6916**
Espacio (ESP) **574**
• ➤ Espacio Abierto (VEN ISSN 1315-0006) **8100**
Espacio de Critica e Investigacion Teatral (ARG) **8470**
Espacio - Espaco Escrito (ESP ISSN 1133-2123) **4451**
▼ Espacio Interior (ESP ISSN 1887-7710) **4539**
▼ • Espacio Pensamiento y Verdad (ARG ISSN 1851-5541) **6916**
Espacio, Tiempo y Forma. Serie I. Prehistoria y Arqueologia (ESP ISSN 1131-7698) **392**
Espacio, Tiempo y Forma. Serie II, Historia Antigua (ESP ISSN 0214-9745) **4139**
Espacio, Tiempo y Forma. Serie III. Historia Medieval (ESP ISSN 1130-1082) **4139**
Espacio, Tiempo y Forma. Serie IV. Historia Moderna (ESP ISSN 1131-768X) **4139**
Espacio, Tiempo y Forma. Serie V. Historia Contemporanea (ESP ISSN 1130-0124) **4139**
Espacio, Tiempo y Forma. Serie VI. Geografia (ESP ISSN 1130-2968) **4005**
Espacio, Tiempo y Forma. Serie VII. Historia del Arte (ESP ISSN 1130-4715) **488**
• Espacio Virtual de la Fisica (CRI) **7010**
➤ Espacio y Desarrollo (PER ISSN 1016-9148) **4451**
Espacios (CRI) **7133**
Espacios (ECU) **6916**
• Espacios (VEN ISSN 0798-1015) **7853**
Espacios de Critica y Produccion (ARG ISSN 0326-7946) **6916**
Espacios en Blanco. Serie Indagaciones (ARG ISSN 1515-9485) **7962**
Espacios Publicos (MEX ISSN 1665-8140) **7133**
Espaco (PRT ISSN 0872-458X) **6985**
• Espaco Academico (BRA ISSN 1519-6186) **4451**
▼ • Espaco Amerindio (BRA ISSN 1982-6524) **336**
• Espaco e Geografia (BRA ISSN 1516-9375) **4005**
➤ Espaco Juridico (BRA ISSN 1519-5899) **4667**
• Espaco para a Saude (BRA ISSN 1517-7130) **7516**
Espaco Pedagogico (BRA ISSN 0104-7469) **2854**
L'Espagne en Chiffres *see* Espana en Cifras **7306**
† Espai de Llibertat (ESP ISSN 1136-1581) **8954**
Espana Contemporanea (USA ISSN 0214-1396) **5291**
Espana Desconocida (ESP ISSN 1577-6700) **8701**
Espana en Cifras (ESP ISSN 1136-1611) **7306**
Espana Hostelera (ESP ISSN 0211-0938) **8701**
Espana Seguridad Minera (ESP) **6462**
• Espanol Actual (ESP ISSN 1135-867X) **5115**
Espansione (ITA ISSN 0014-0554) **1885**
Espansiva (DNK ISSN 0909-9050) **6565**
Esparavel (COL ISSN 0014-0562) **5421**
Espartaco (MEX) **7133**
Especes Canadiennes en Peril *see* Canadian Species at Risk **2605**
Especes Canadiennes en Peril (Online) *see* Canadian Species at Risk (Online) **2605**
Especial Arte y Diseno por Ordenador *see* Arte y Diseno por Ordenador **530**
Especial Autodefinidos Gold (ARG ISSN 1669-8819) **4334**
Especial Autodefinidos Pocket (ARG ISSN 1666-0501) **4334**
Especial Custom (PRT) **8258**
• Especial Directivos. Coyuntura Empresarial (ESP ISSN 1135-5441) **1540**
• Especial Directivos. Estrategias (ESP ISSN 1135-5468) **1105**
• Especial Directivos. Management (ESP ISSN 1135-545X) **1742**
▼ Especial Eutodefinidos Premier (ARG ISSN 1851-5819) **4334**
Especial Labores (ESP) **6638**
Especial Massagens (BRA ISSN 1808-8384) **6985**
Especiales Teenager Internacional (MEX) **2254**
➤ The Especialist (BRA ISSN 0102-7077) **5116**
• El Espectador (COL ISSN 0014-0589) **3830**
• Especulo (ESP ISSN 1139-3637) **5291**
Espejo de Paciencia (ESP ISSN 1136-5390) **488**
Espelho (BRA ISSN 1072-7140) **5291**
Espera (USA) **5989**
Esperanta Ligilo (USA ISSN 0014-0600) **4081**
• Esperantic Studies (CAN) **5116**
• Esperanto (NLD ISSN 0014-0635) **5116**
Esperanto Aktuell (DEU ISSN 0942-024X) **5116**
• Esperanto Book Catalog (USA) **5201**
Esperanto Documents (NLD ISSN 0165-2575) **5116**
Esperanto-Dokumentoj (NLD ISSN 0165-2524) **5116**
Esperanto en Skotlando (GBR ISSN 0014-0643) **5116**
Esperanto Fen-X (NLD ISSN 1384-6515) **5116**
Esperanto-Nytt (NOR ISSN 0802-0442) **5116**
Esperanto Sub la Suda Kruco (AUS ISSN 1039-9380) **5116**
Esperanto Teacher (GBR ISSN 0046-2527) **5116**
Esperanto U S A (USA ISSN 1056-0297) **5116**
Esperanto Update (CAN ISSN 1195-6186) **5116**
Esperiana (DEU ISSN 0949-4529) **847**
Esperienza (ITA ISSN 0014-0678) **8039**
Esperienze Dermatologiche (ITA ISSN 1128-9155) **5876**
Esperienze d'Impresa (ITA ISSN 1971-5293) **1105**
• Esperienze e Progetti (ITA) **2854**
• Esperienze Letterarie (ITA ISSN 0392-3495) **5215**
• Espero (SWE ISSN 0014-0694) **5116**
† L'Esperto Risponde (ITA ISSN 1590-0266) **8954**
L'Espill (ESP ISSN 0210-587X) **5291**
• Espiral (BRA ISSN 1678-1643) **7853**
▼ • Espiral (ESP ISSN 1988-7701) **2854**
• Espiral (MEX ISSN 1665-0565) **7133**
Espiritu (ESP ISSN 0014-0716) **6916**
L'Esplumeoir (FRA ISSN 1959-9161) **5291**
L'Espoir du Monde (CHE ISSN 0014-0732) **7133**
Esporo *see* Spore **207**
† Esportazione (ITA ISSN 0014-0740) **8954**
• Esporte e Sociedade (BRA ISSN 1809-1296) **8171**
Espresso (CHE) **1106**
• L'Espresso (ITA ISSN 0423-4243) **3897**
Espresso (Hofheim am Taunus) (DEU) **7133**
Espresso (Mannheim) (DEU) **4385**
Espresso Magazine (Ontario Edition) *see* Magazine Espresso (Quebec Edition) **3654**
Espresso Magazine (Western Edition) *see* Magazine Espresso (Quebec Edition) **3654**
L'Espresso Mese *see* L' Espresso **3897**
• Esprit (FRA ISSN 0014-0759) **5215**
Esprit (GBR ISSN 1364-9922) **593**
Esprit Bonsai (FRA ISSN 1761-662X) **3729**
▼ Esprit Camping-Car (FRA ISSN 1961-6740) **8579**
• ➤ L'Esprit Createur (USA ISSN 0014-0767) **5291**
• Esprit Critique (CAN) **8100**
Esprit d'Aventure *see* L' Esprit Voyageur **4005**
• Esprit de Corps (CAN ISSN 1194-2266) **6420**
L'Esprit de la Creation (FRA ISSN 1629-7199) **4451**
L'Esprit du Droit (FRA ISSN 1778-3437) **4667**
L'Esprit du Temps (FRA ISSN 1168-0733) **2854**
Esprit et Vie (FRA ISSN 0014-0775) **7641**
Esprit Libre (FRA ISSN 1270-7864) **7354**
Esprit Libre Magazine (FRA ISSN 1769-5104) **7710**
† Esprit Saint (FRA ISSN 0396-969X) **8954**
L'Esprit Simple (CAN) **2283**
Esprit Trail (FRA ISSN 1779-3904) **8312**
L'Esprit Voyageur (FRA ISSN 2101-115X) **4005**
▼ • Esproprionline (ITA ISSN 1971-999X) **7435**
Equi Acuatico y Otros Deportes (VEN) **8312**
Esquimalt News *see* News (Esquimalt) **3814**
Esquire *see* Shishang Xiansheng **6300**
Esquire (CZE ISSN 1211-4006) **6289**
• Esquire (GBR ISSN 0960-5150) **6289**
Esquire (NLD ISSN 0926-8901) **6289**
Esquire (TUR ISSN 1300-8099) **6289**
• Esquire (USA ISSN 0194-9535) **6289**
Esquisse d'Une Philosophie de la Religion (FRA) **7756**
• Essaim (FRA ISSN 1287-258X) **6139**
Essais (FRA ISSN 1298-2032) **5291**
Les Essais du Sport (FRA ISSN 1775-0970) **8171**
Essais et Simulations (FRA) **5905**
Essais Industriels *see* Essais et Simulations **5905**
Essais sur le Discours de l'Europe Eclatee *see* Chroniques Slaves **5273**
Essais sur le Moyen Age (FRA ISSN 1284-6147) **4218**
• Essay and General Literature Index (USA ISSN 0014-083X) **5407**
Essays *see* Chairman of the Joint Chiefs of Staff Strategy Essay Competition Essays **6415**
• Essays and Studies (USA ISSN 0071-1357) **5291**
➤ Essays in Arts and Sciences (USA ISSN 0361-5634) **4451**
• ➤ Essays in Biochemistry (GBR ISSN 0071-1365) **731**
Essays in Church History in Hungary *see* Magyar Egyhaztorteneti Vazlatok **4241**
Essays in Cognitive Psychology (GBR ISSN 0959-4779) **7355**
• ➤ Essays in Criticism (GBR ISSN 0014-0856) **5291**
Essays in Developmental Psychology (GBR ISSN 0959-3977) **7355**
➤ Essays in Economic and Business History (USA ISSN 0896-226X) **1540**
• ➤ Essays in Education (USA ISSN 1527-9359) **2854**
Essays in European Law (GBR) **4924**
Essays in French Literature *see* Essays in French Literature and Culture **5291**
➤ Essays in French Literature and Culture (AUS ISSN 1835-7040) **5291**
• ➤ Essays in History (Online) (USA ISSN 1548-9663) **4139**
• ➤ Essays in Medieval Studies (USA ISSN 1538-4608) **4218**
• ➤ Essays in Philosophy (USA ISSN 1526-0569) **6916**
Essays in Social Psychology (GBR ISSN 1367-5826) **7355**
Essays in Social Psychology Series *see* Essays in Social Psychology **7355**
† Essays in Sound (AUS) **8954**
Essays in the Philosophy of Humanism (USA ISSN 1522-7340) **6916**
➤ Essays in Theatre/Etudes Theatrales (CAN ISSN 0821-4425) **8470**
• Essays on Canadian Writing (CAN ISSN 0316-0300) **5291**
Essays on the Economy and Society of the Sudan (SDN) **1483**
Esse (CAN ISSN 0831-859X) **488**
• Essecome (ITA ISSN 0394-8625) **2677**
• Essecome International (ITA) **2677**
Essen und Trinken (DEU ISSN 0721-9776) **4357**
Essen und Trinken fuer Jeden Tag (DEU ISSN 1612-3859) **4357**
• Essence (New York) (USA ISSN 0014-0880) **8861**
Essences of Japan *see* Kokka **500**
Essener Studien zur Semiotik und Kommunikationsforschung (DEU ISSN 1439-4162) **5116**
Essens *see* Skov og Natur **7917**
Essential (ROM ISSN 1454-8372) **8861**
Essential Air and Space Law (NLD ISSN 1872-2180) **53**
Essential Book of Kitchens, Bedrooms & Bathrooms *see* Kitchens, Bedrooms & Bathrooms Magazine **4560**
Essential Brass (GBR ISSN 1744-716X) **6565**
The Essential Cinema (USA ISSN 0363-0900) **6497**
Essential Connection *see* E C **7755**
• Essential Drugs Monitor (CHE ISSN 1015-0919) **6838**
• Essential Family Practice (Year) (GBR) **4909**
Essential Fireplace Book (GBR) **4539**
The Essential Guide to Cycling (ZAF ISSN 1991-6108) **8258**
Essential Guide to the New England States (GBR ISSN 1360-7278) **8701**
Essential Guides for Managers (GBR ISSN 0951-1458) **1742**
Essential Home Cinema (GBR) **3099**
• The Essential Kitchen Bathroom Bedroom Magazine (GBR ISSN 1354-0726) **4539**
Essential PlayStation (GBR ISSN 1365-411X) **2476**
➤ Essential Psychopharmacology (USA ISSN 1087-495X) **6139**
▼ Essential Slow Cooker (USA ISSN 1944-2068) **4357**
The Essential Subwoofer Buyer's Guide (USA) **2380**
Essential Superbike (GBR) **8258**
• ➤ Essential Teacher (USA ISSN 1545-6501) **5116**
Essential Water Garden (GBR ISSN 1465-7678) **3729**
Essential Wildlife & Conservation Biology Abstracts (USA ISSN 1093-3344) **2634**
Essential X-Men (GBR ISSN 1360-5186) **2188**
Essentialis (FRA ISSN 1264-157X) **7355**
Essentially America (GBR ISSN 1352-2825) **8701**
Essentially Food (NZL ISSN 1175-5180) **4357**
Essentially Home (NZL) **4539**
Essentially Quebec (GBR) **8701**
Essentials (GBR ISSN 0953-6337) **8861**
• Essentials (USA) **3022**
Essentials (ZAF ISSN 1023-3768) **3948**
Essentials (Hong Kong) (HKG) **8861**
Essentials for Production (GBR) **3191**
Essentials of Managed Health Care (USA) **4501**
• L'Essentiel (FRA ISSN 1961-7291) **3022**
L'Essentiel *see* L' E-ssentiel **8038**
L'Essentiel de la Coiffure (FRA ISSN 1284-9715) **587**
L'Essentiel de la Couture *see* Burda L'Essentiel de la Couture **8938**
▼ L'Essentiel de la Deco (FRA ISSN 1961-0769) **4539**
L'Essentiel de la Moto (FRA ISSN 1767-4883) **8258**
L'Essentiel de l'Auto (FRA ISSN 1620-5154) **8579**
▼ L'Essentiel de l'Immobilier (FRA ISSN 1955-6969) **7589**
L'Essentiel des Piscines et des Spas (FRA ISSN 1770-1759) **4977**
▼ L'Essentiel du Quad (FRA ISSN 1960-1964) **8258**
L'Essentiel sur... (FRA ISSN 1773-729X) **5008**
Essentiels. Recettes Tendances *see* Recettes Tendances **4366**
Essenze, Derivati Agrumari (ITA ISSN 0014-0902) **2122**
† Essere & Benessere (ITA ISSN 1720-1845) **8954**
Essex Archaeological & Historical Congress. Newsletter (GBR) **392**
Essex Archaeology and History (GBR ISSN 0308-3462) **392**
Essex Archaeology and History News (GBR ISSN 1356-7144) **392**
Essex Bird Report (GBR ISSN 0963-2085) **906**
Essex Birding (GBR) **906**
Essex Business Magazine (GBR) **1402**
Essex Chronicle (GBR ISSN 0961-7167) **3864**
Essex Countryside *see* Essex Life & Countryside **3864**
• Essex County Council. Planning. Applications & Decisions (Waste & Minerals) (Online) (GBR) **7492**
Essex County Family *see* New Jersey Family (Mountainside) **2162**
Essex County Medical Society. Bulletin (USA ISSN 0014-0937) **5610**
Essex Family Historian (GBR ISSN 0140-7503) **3765**
Essex Genealogist (USA ISSN 0279-067X) **3765**
Essex Guide to Environmental Assessment (GBR) **7492**
• ➤ Essex Human Rights Review (GBR ISSN 1756-1957) **7206**
Essex Journal (GBR ISSN 0014-0961) **392**
Essex Life & Countryside (GBR ISSN 1475-8768) **3864**
Essex Magazine *see* Essex Style **5070**
Essex Magazine and East Anglian Life *see* Essex Style **5070**
Essex Naturalist (GBR ISSN 0071-1489) **671**
Essex Papers in Politics and Government (GBR ISSN 1369-006X) **7133**
Essex Papers in Politics and Government. Sub-Series in Ideology and Discourse Analysis (GBR ISSN 1367-2088) **7133**
Essex Record Office Publication (GBR) **7435**
• Essex Research Reports in Linguistics (GBR) **5116**
• Essex Style (GBR ISSN 1753-6790) **5070**
Essex Succulent Review (GBR) **3729**
Essex Wildlife Magazine (GBR ISSN 0961-6004) **2610**
Essex Young Farmer (GBR) **108**
Esskapaden (DEU) **4385**
Esslinger Studien - Jahrbuch (DEU ISSN 0174-4445) **4218**
Esslinger Studien - Schriftenreihe (DEU ISSN 0425-3086) **4218**
Esslinger Zeitung (DEU) **3846**
Esso in Malaysia (MYS ISSN 0127-0710) **6768**
L'Essor (MLI ISSN 0421-4889) **3907**
L'Essor de la Gendarmerie Nationale (FRA ISSN 0338-1595) **2651**
Essor Rural (BFA) **4410**
L'Est Agricole et Viticole (FRA ISSN 0425-3124) **108**
L'Est Republicain (FRA ISSN 0240-4958) **3840**
Est Sesia (ITA ISSN 0014-1100) **229**
Esta (NLD ISSN 1573-6148) **3914**
Establecimientos Manufactureras en Puerto Rico (PRI) **1226**
• Estac@o (BRA ISSN 1678-1317) **2854**
• Estacao Cientifica (BRA ISSN 1809-046X) **7853**
Estacion Experimental Agropecuaria San Pedro. Boletin de Divulgacion Tecnica (ARG ISSN 0327-3237) **108**
Estacion Experimental Agropecuaria El Colorado. Boletin de Divulgacion (ARG ISSN 1666-552X) **108**
Estacion Experimental Agropecuaria El Colorado. Boletin Tecnico (ARG ISSN 0328-6258) **108**
Estacion Experimental Agropecuaria Marcos Juarez. Hoja Informativa (ARG ISSN 0327-6732) **108**
† ➤ Estacion Experimental de Aula Dei. Anales (ESP ISSN 0365-1800) **8954**
Estacion Experimental Region Agropecuaria Pergamino. Informe Tecnico (ARG ISSN 0325-1799) **108**
• Estaciones de Servicio (ESP ISSN 1888-7864) **8579**
Estaciones de Servicio Digital *see* Estaciones de Servicio **8579**
Estadio (ECU) **8171**
Estadistica Basica del Sistema Educativo Nacional (MEX) **2933**
Estadistica de Accidentes de Trabajo (ESP ISSN 1139-4412) **1226**
Estadistica de Criminalidad (COL) **2674**
Estadistica de Energia Electrica (ESP) **3152**
Estadistica de Huelga y Cierres Patronales (ESP ISSN 1138-1566) **1226**
Estadistica de la Industria Maquiladora de Exportacion (MEX ISSN 0187-4845) **1226**
Estadistica de la Produccion Editorial de Libros (ESP ISSN 1136-3495) **5058**
Estadistica de Prospeccion y Produccion de Hidrocarburos (ESP) **6799**
Estadistica de Regulacion de Empleo (ESP ISSN 0213-0386) **4822**
Estadistica del Cemento (ESP) **1046**
Estadistica del Suicidio en Espana (ESP ISSN 0213-3423) **7306**
Estadistica Espanola *see* Instituto Nacional de Estadistica. Estadistica Espanola **8379**
Estadistica Mensual de Faena y Exportacion (URY) **3669**
Estadistica Panamena. Avance de Cifras (PAN) **8368**
Estadistica Panamena. Indicadores Economicos. Seccion 011 (PAN ISSN 1023-3318) **1226**
Estadistica Panamena. Indicadores Sociales. Seccion 012 (PAN ISSN 1023-330X) **8082**
Estadistica Panamena. Situacion Cultural. Seccion 511. Educacion (PAN ISSN 0378-4967) **2933**
Estadistica Panamena. Situacion Demografica. Seccion 221. Estadisticas Vitales (PAN ISSN 0379-4237) **7306**
Estadistica Panamena. Situacion Demografica. Seccion 231. Movimiento Internacional de Pasajeros (PAN ISSN 1022-6605) **7306**
Estadistica Panamena. Situacion Economica. Seccion 312. Produccion Pecuaria (PAN ISSN 0378-2581) **179**
Estadistica Panamena. Situacion Economica. Seccion 312. Superficie Sembrada y Cosecha de Arroz, Maiz y Frijol de Bejuco (PAN ISSN 0378-2565) **179**
Estadistica Panamena. Situacion Economica. Seccion 312. Superficie Sembrada y Cosecha de Cafe y Cana de Azucar (PAN) **179**
Estadistica Panamena. Situacion Economica. Seccion 314, 323, 324, 325, 353. Industria (PAN ISSN 0378-2557) **1226**
Estadistica Panamena. Situacion Economica. Seccion 321. Industria Manufacturera (PAN) **1226**
Estadistica Panamena. Situacion Economica. Seccion 323. Indice de la Produccion de la Industria Manufacturera (PAN) **1226**
Estadistica Panamena. Situacion Economica. Seccion 331. Comercio. Anuario de Comercio Exterior (PAN ISSN 0378-4983) **1226**
Estadistica Panamena. Situacion Economica. Seccion 333. Transporte (PAN ISSN 1012-3555) **8495**
Estadistica Panamena. Situacion Economica. Seccion 334. Comunicaciones (PAN ISSN 1012-3547) **2347**

Title

Estadistica Panamena. Situacion Economica. Seccion 341. Balanza de Pagos (PAN ISSN 0378-7397) **1226**
Estadistica Panamena. Situacion Economica. Seccion 342. Cuentas Nacionales (PAN ISSN 0378-2603) **1226**
Estadistica Panamena. Situacion Economica. Seccion 343. Hacienda Publica (PAN ISSN 1017-4273) **1226**
Estadistica Panamena. Situacion Economica. Seccion 344. Finanzas (PAN ISSN 1017-4281) **1226**
Estadistica Panamena. Situacion Economica. Seccion 351. Indice de Precios al por Mayor y al Consumidor (PAN ISSN 0378-2522) **1226**
Estadistica Panamena. Situacion Economica. Seccion 351. Precios Pagados por el Productor Agropecuario (PAN ISSN 0378-2530) **179**
Estadistica Panamena. Situacion Economica. Seccion 351. Precios Recibidos por el Productor Agropecuario (PAN ISSN 0378-2611) **179**
Estadistica Panamena. Situacion Economica. Seccion 351. Precios Recibidos por el Productor Agropecuario. Compendio (PAN ISSN 0378-2549) **179**
Estadistica Panamena. Situacion Economica. Seccion 352. Hoja de Balance de Alimentos (PAN ISSN 0378-4991) **179**
Estadistica Panamena. Situacion Fisica. Seccion 121. Meteorologia (PAN) **6400**
Estadistica Panamena. Situacion Politica, Administrativa y Justicia. Seccion 631. Justicia (PAN ISSN 0378-259X) **4822**
Estadistica Panamena. Situacion Social. Seccion 431. Servicios de Salud (PAN) **8082**
Estadistica Panamena. Situacion Social. Seccion 441. Estadisticas del Trabajo (PAN) **1226**
Estadistica Panamena. Situacion Social. Seccion 451. Accidentes de Transito (PAN ISSN 0378-6765) **8524**
• Estadisticas Banca Internet (CHL) **1226**
Estadisticas de Convenios Colectivos de Trabajo (ESP ISSN 1138-2791) **1226**
Estadisticas de Educacion Extraescolar (CHL ISSN 0716-0615) **2933**
Estadisticas de la Lesiones Profesionales *see* Laneko Lesioen Estatistikak (Year) **6690**
Estadisticas de Permisos de Trabajo a Estranjeros (ESP ISSN 1138-9001) **7306**
Estadisticas de Transporte de Guatemala (GTM) **8524**
Estadisticas del Cobre y Otros Minerales Anuario (CHL ISSN 0716-8462) **6485**
• Estadisticas del Movimiento Migratorio de la Comunidad de Madrid (ESP ISSN 1139-532X) **7282**
Estadisticas del Movimiento Natural de la Poblacion de la Comunidad de Madrid. Defunciones (ESP ISSN 1696-0459) **7306**
† Estadisticas del Movimiento Natural de la Poblacion de la Comunidad de Madrid. Matrimonios (ESP ISSN 1696-0440) **8954**
† • Estadisticas del Movimiento Natural de la Poblacion de la Comunidad de Madrid. Mortalidad Segun Causas Multiples (ESP ISSN 1696-0467) **8954**
† Estadisticas del Movimiento Natural de la Poblacion de la Comunidad de Madrid. Nacimientos (ESP ISSN 1696-0432) **8954**
Estadisticas del Movimiento Natural de la Poblacion de la Comunidad de Madrid. Nacimientos, Matrimonios, Defunciones, Martalidad Segun Causas Multiples *see* Estadisticas del Movimiento Natural de la Poblacion de la Comunidad de Madrid. Nacimientos **8954**
Estadisticas del Movimiento Natural de Poblacion de la Comunidad de Madrid. Nacimientos, Matrimonios, Defunciones, Mortalidad Segun Causas Multiplas *see* Estadisticas del Movimiento Natural de la Poblacion de la Comunidad de Madrid. Defunciones **7306**
Estadisticas del Movimiento Natural de Poblacion de la Comunidad de Madrid. Nacimientos, Matrimonios, Defunciones, Mortalidad Segun Causas Multiplas *see* Estadisticas del Movimiento Natural de la Poblacion de la Comunidad de Madrid. Matrimonios **8954**
Estadisticas del Movimiento Natural de Poblacion de la Comunidad de Madrid. Nacimientos, Matrimonios, Defunciones, Mortalidad Segun Causas Multiples *see* Estadisticas del Movimiento Natural de la Poblacion de la Comunidad de Madrid. Mortalidad Segun Causas Multiples **8954**
Estadisticas Financieras Internacionales *see* International Financial Statistics **1243**
Estadisticas Financieras Internacionales Anuario *see* International Financial Statistics Yearbook **1243**
Estadisticas Macroeconomicas de Centroamerica (GTM) **1226**
Estadisticas Mineras de Espana (ESP) **6485**
Estadisticas Policiales. Carabineros de Chile (CHL) **2674**
Estadisticas Policiales. Policia de Investigaciones de Chile (CHL) **2674**
Estadisticas Relativas a la Ciencia y a la Tecnologia *see* UNESCO Statistics on Science and Technology **7939**
Estado das Culturas e Previsao de Colheitas (PRT ISSN 0870-2594) **108**
• ➤ Estado, Gobierno, Gestion Publica (CHL ISSN 0717-6759) **7435**
Estado Mundial de la Agricultura y la Alimentacion *see* State of Food and Agriculture **158**
• Estado Mundial de la Infancia (USA ISSN 0251-9119) **8039**
• Estados Financieros Anuales Bancos y Sociedades Financieras (CHL) **1338**
• Estados Financieros Anuales de Sociedades Filiales (CHL) **1227**
• Estados Financieros Comparados (PER ISSN 1682-4326) **1622**
Estafeta (USA ISSN 1088-8136) **7232**
L'Estampille - L'Objet d'Art (FRA ISSN 0998-8041) **488**
Estandarte (ARG) **3765**
Estano (BOL ISSN 0014-1194) **6462**
estarGuapa.com *see* Telva **2262**
• Estate Administration in Massachusetts (USA) **4901**
Estate Agency News (GBR ISSN 1366-4360) **7589**
The Estate Agent (GBR ISSN 0260-1001) **7589**
• Estate Agent (Camberwell) (AUS) **7589**
Estate Agents and Services Market Assessment *see* Key Note Market Assessment. Estate Agents and Services **7597**
Estate Agents Market Report *see* Key Note Market Report: Estate Agents **4903**
Estate Agents' Practice Manual N S W (AUS) **7589**
Estate Agents' Practice Manual New South Wales *see* Estate Agents' Practice Manual N S W **7589**
Estate and Personal Financial Planning (USA) **7589**
Estate Car and Multi-Purpose Vehicle (GBR) **8579**
▼ Estate Law Update (USA ISSN 1946-9020) **4902**
Estate Planner *see* Audio Estate Planner **4901**
• Estate Planner Newsletter (CAN ISSN 1910-1864) **4902**
• Estate Planner's Alert (USA ISSN 1076-819X) **4902**
The Estate Planner's Handbook (CAN ISSN 1910-4111) **4902**
• Estate Planning (New York, 1958) (USA ISSN 0014-1216) **4902**
• Estate Planning (New York, 1973) (USA ISSN 0094-1794) **4902**
Estate Planning and California Probate Reporter (USA ISSN 0273-7027) **4902**
Estate Planning and Taxation Coordinator *see* Estate Planning & Taxation Coordinator **4902**
Estate Planning & Taxation Coordinator (USA ISSN 0195-1238) **4902**
Estate Planning Conference (USA ISSN 1931-1486) **4902**
• Estate Planning for Farmers and Ranchers (USA) **4902**
Estate Planning Forms and Clauses, Anderson's Estate Planning *see* Anderson's Estate Planning Forms and Clauses **4900**
• Estate Planning Review (USA ISSN 0098-2873) **4902**
• Estate Planning: Wills, Trusts and Forms (USA) **4902**
Estates and Trusts Reports (CAN ISSN 0706-5655) **4902**
Estates East (USA) **4539**
Estates Europe Directory *see* EuroProperty **7590**
• Estates Gazette (GBR ISSN 0014-1240) **7589**
Estates Gazette Capital *see* E G Capital **1336**
Estates Gazette Directory (GBR) **7589**
Estates Gazette Law Reports (GBR ISSN 0951-9289) **7590**
Estates Gazette Retail *see* E G Retail **7589**
Estates, Powers and Trusts Law of New York *see* Estates, Powers & Trusts Law of New York **4902**
• Estates, Powers & Trusts Law of New York (USA) **4902**
Estates, Trusts and Pensions Journal (CAN ISSN 1487-3656) **4902**
• Estates West (USA ISSN 1548-436X) **4539**
Estates West Golf Living (USA) **8227**
• EstateTip Review (NLD ISSN 1572-5421) **4902**
Estatistica Brasileira de Energia/Brazilian Energy Statistics (BRA ISSN 0512-350X) **3152**
Estatisticas da Construcao de Edificios (PRT ISSN 0871-9969) **1046**
Estatisticas da Educacao. Continente, Acores e Madeira (PRT) **2854**
Estatisticas da Pesca - Statistiques de la Peche (PRT ISSN 0377-225X) **3613**
Estatisticas da Producao Industrial/Portugal. Statistiques Industrielles: Continent, Acores et Madere. Volume 2: Industries Manufacturieres (PRT ISSN 0872-9298) **1227**
• Estatisticas da Saude: Assistencia Medico-Sanitaria (BRA ISSN 0101-3033) **5744**
Estatisticas das Empresas. Industria (PRT ISSN 0872-8879) **1227**
Estatisticas das Receitas Fiscais (PRT ISSN 0873-6324) **1227**
Estatisticas de Proteccao Social. Associacoes Sindicais e Patronais (PRT ISSN 0870-4406) **8148**
Estatisticas Demograficas (PRT ISSN 0377-2284) **7306**
Estatisticas do Comercio Internacional (PRT ISSN 0873-0687) **1227**
Estatisticas do Emprego (PRT ISSN 0872-7570) **1960**
Estatisticas do Registro Civil *see* Brazil. Fundacao Instituto Brasileiro de Geografia e Estadistica. Estatisticas do Registro Civil **7304**
Estatisticas do Turismo (PRT ISSN 0377-2306) **8779**
Estatisticas dos Transportes e Comunicacoes (PRT ISSN 0870-0451) **8524**
Estatisticas dos Transportes Rodoviarios de Passageiros e de Mercadorias (PRT ISSN 0872-5969) **8524**
Estatisticas Industrais. Suplemento/Portugal. Statistiques Industrielles: Continent, Acores et Madere. Volume 1: Industries Extractives, Electricite, Gaz, Eau. (PRT ISSN 0377-2314) **1227**
• Estatisticas Monetarias e Financieras (PRT ISSN 0377-2322) **1338**
Estcourt - Mooi River Surrounds Directory (ZAF) **1992**
• Este Pais (MEX ISSN 0188-5405) **3908**
• Este Sur (MEX ISSN 1605-0452) **3908**
Estela (ESP ISSN 1888-4679) **574**
Estepa del Nazas (MEX) **4451**
The Ester Republic (USA ISSN 1930-0506) **3975**
Estes Educator News (USA) **3061**
Estestvennoe Dvizhenie Naseleniya Rossiiskoi Federatsii (RUS) **7306**
Estestvennye i Tekhnicheskie Nauki (RUS ISSN 1684-2626) **7853**
Estetica *see* Avantaje **8852**
Estetica (German Edition) (ITA) **587**
Estetica (Torino) *see* Estetica Italia **587**
Estetica Espana (ITA) **587**
Estetica Espana y Sur America (ITA) **587**
Estetica France (ITA ISSN 1244-9709) **587**
• Estetica Italia (ITA ISSN 0421-515X) **587**
La Estetica Profesional *see* Expertos en Estetica **594**
Estetica U.K. (ITA ISSN 1720-9676) **587**
Estetica USA (ITA) **587**
Estetica World (Asia and Oceania) (ITA) **587**
• Esteticheskoe Vospitanie (RUS ISSN 0132-8255) **6962**
Esteticistas, Federacion Nacional (ESP ISSN 1576-351X) **594**
Estetika/Aesthetics (CZE ISSN 0014-1291) **488**
Estetisk Forum (NOR ISSN 1504-5544) **2980**
• ➤ The Estey Centre Journal of International Law and Trade Policy (CAN) **1106**
Esther (USA ISSN 1539-5243) **2188**
† Esthetica Professionnel (FRA ISSN 1146-5794) **8954**
Estheticienne (NLD ISSN 0014-1321) **587**
• Esthetique (DNK ISSN 1396-366X) **587**
† Esthetique (FRA ISSN 0220-1941) **8954**
Esthetique (USA) **8861**
Esthetique & Politique (FRA ISSN 1150-3696) **6916**
Estia (GRC) **3874**
• Estigma (ESP ISSN 1139-1634) **488**
Estimado de Produccion y Consumo de Azucar (CUB) **1563**
Estimados sobre Requerimientos de Importacion de Azucar (CUB) **1563**
The Estimate (USA ISSN 1043-1667) **6420**
• Estimated Use of Water in the United States in (Year) (USA) **8823**
Estimates of Recent Expenditures *see* Kenya. Central Bureau of Statistics. Estimates of Recurrent Expenditures **1247**
Estimates of Revenue Expenditures *see* Kenya. Central Bureau of Statistics. Estimates of Revenue Expenditures **1247**
Estimates. Part I and II. The Government Expenditure Plan and the Main Estimates *see* Budget des Depenses. Partie I et II. Plan de Depenses du Gouvernement et Budget Principal des Depenses **7424**
• Estimations Demographiques Annuelles, Canada, Provinces et Territoires (CAN ISSN 1911-2416) **7306**
• Estimations Preliminaires des Depenses de Sante des Gouvernements Provinciaux et Territoriaux (CAN ISSN 1912-1989) **7516**
Estimo e Territorio (Genio Rurale) (ITA ISSN 1824-8918) **229**
Estiquirin (HND) **7962**
Estirpe (ARG ISSN 0327-7267) **3765**
Estnisches Historisches Archiv *see* Eesti Ajalooarhiivi Toimetised **4216**
• Esto (MEX ISSN 1563-7395) **3908**
Esto Digital *see* Esto **3908**
Estomatologia Integrada (PER ISSN 1680-9289) **5843**
Eston Press (CAN) **3809**
Estonia (EST ISSN 1406-2232) **3836**
• Estonia Autos Report (GBR ISSN 1748-9881) **8579**
Estonia Freight Transport Report (GBR ISSN 1752-5799) **8495**
• ➤ Estonian Academy of Sciences. Proceedings. Biology. Ecology/Eesti Teaduste Akadeemia Toimetised. Bioloogia. Okoloogia (EST ISSN 1406-0914) **671**
• ➤ Estonian Academy of Sciences. Proceedings. Chemistry/Akademiya Nauk Estonii. Izvestiya. Khimiya/Eesti Teaduste Akadeemia Toimetised. Keemia (EST ISSN 1406-0124) **2061**
• ➤ Estonian Academy of Sciences. Proceedings. Engineering/Eesti Teaduste Akadeemia Toimetised. Tehnikateadused (EST ISSN 1406-0175) **3191**
Estonian Academy of Sciences. Proceedings. Geology *see* Estonian Journal of Earth Sciences **2733**
• ➤ Estonian Academy of Sciences. Proceedings. Physics. Mathematics/Akademiya Nauk Estonii. Izvestiya. Fizika, Matematika/Eesti Teaduste Akadeemia Toimetised. Fuusika. Matemaatika (EST ISSN 1406-0086) **7011**
Estonian Agricultural University. Transactions *see* Eesti Pollumajandusulikooli. Teadustoode Kogumik **106**
• Estonian Art (EST) **488**
Estonian Environment *see* Keskkond **3449**
Estonian Geographical Society. Yearbook *see* Eesti Geograafia Seltsi. Aastaraamat **4005**
The Estonian Historical Archives *see* Eesti Ajalooarhiivi Toimetised **4216**
• ➤ Estonian Journal of Earth Sciences/Akademiya Nauk Estonii. Izvestiya. Geologiya/Eesti Teaduste Akadeemia Toimetised. Geoloogia (EST ISSN 1736-4728) **2733**
Estonian Legislation in Translation (EST ISSN 1406-0639) **4667**
Estonian Life *see* Eesti Elu **3836**
Estonian Marine Institute. Report Series (EST ISSN 1406-023X) **2804**
Estonian National Museum Yearbook *see* Eesti Rahva Muuseumi Aastaraamat **336**
Estonian Naturalists' Society. Yearbook *see* Eesti Looduseuurijate Seltsi. Aastaraamat **670**
Estonian Nature *see* Eesti Loodus **7852**
Estonian News *see* Eesti Haal **3531**
Estonian Newsletter on Occupational Health and Safety *see* Eesti Tootervishoid **6676**
Estonian Papers in Applied Linguistics *see* Eesti Rakenduslingvistika Uhingu. Aastaraamat **5113**
Estonian Philatelic Society in U.S.A. (USA) **6894**
Estonian Philatelist *see* Eesti Filatelist **6894**
Estoniya (EST) **3836**
Estonskoe Geograficheskoe Obshchestvo. Ezhegodnik *see* Eesti Geograafia Seltsi. Aastaraamat **4005**
Estonskoye Obshchestvo Estestvoispytatelei. Ezhegodnik *see* Eesti Looduseuurijate Seltsi. Aastaraamat **670**
Estrada (BGR ISSN 0204-8329) **8470**
• Estrada i Studio (POL ISSN 1427-0404) **8152**
Estrat (ESP ISSN 1130-3441) **392**
• Estrategia (CHL ISSN 0716-1255) **1338**
Estrategia Economia y Financiera (COL ISSN 0121-4802) **1106**
▼ Estrategia Energetica (ARG ISSN 1851-491X) **3134**
Estrategia Financiera (ESP ISSN 1130-8753) **1338**
Estrategia Global (ESP ISSN 1697-0764) **7232**
Estrategica sobre Nuevo Leon en una Epoca de Cambio (MEX) **8421**
• eStrategies. Asia-Pacific (GBR ISSN 1752-6736) **2320**
• eStrategies. Central & Eastern Europe (GBR ISSN 1744-3601) **2320**
• eStrategies. Middle East (GBR ISSN 1747-7972) **2320**
Estratos (ESP ISSN 1133-5777) **7853**
La Estrella de Esperanza (USA) **7735**
• La Estrella de Puerto Rico (PRI) **3931**
• La Estrella Digital (ESP ISSN 1696-8662) **3952**
➤ Estreno (USA ISSN 0097-8663) **8470**
Estreno (USA) **8470**
EstrichTechnik und Fussbodenbau (DEU ISSN 1614-6735) **1007**
Estuaire (CAN ISSN 0700-365X) **5421**
L'Estuaire (CAN ISSN 1484-6969) **4292**
L'Estuaire Genealogique (CAN ISSN 0824-4936) **3765**
Estuaries *see* Estuaries and Coasts **671**
• Estuaries and Coastal Waters of the British Isles (GBR ISSN 0261-0663) **3479**
• ➤ Estuaries and Coasts (USA ISSN 1559-2723) **671**
Estuarine and Coastal Sciences Association. Bulletin (GBR ISSN 1352-4615) **2804**
• ➤ Estuarine, Coastal and Shelf Science (GBR ISSN 0272-7714) **2804**
Estudes des Caraibes *see* Caribbean Studies **7953**
Estudia y Ahorra (ESP) **1338**
L'Estudiant *see* Diari d'Andorra **3790**
L'Estudiant (AND) **3790**
Estudio Agustiniano (ESP ISSN 0425-340X) **7796**
• Estudio Economico de America Latina y el Caribe (CHL ISSN 0257-2176) **1484**
Estudio F A O. Alimentacion y Nutricion *see* F A O Food and Nutrition Paper **3635**
Estudio F A O, Produccion y Proteccion Vegetal *see* F A O Plant Production and Protection Papers **229**
Estudio F A O, Produccion y Sanidad Animal *see* F A O Animal Production and Health Papers **286**
Estudio F A O, Riego y Drenaje (USA ISSN 1020-4393) **8823**
Estudio Sistematico de la Jurisprudencia Recaida en Unificacion de Doctrina (ESP ISSN 1139-062X) **4668**
➤ Estudios (GTM) **336**
Estudios (PRY ISSN 1012-2478) **4451**
Estudios (VEN ISSN 0798-958X) **5291**
Estudios Africanos (ESP ISSN 0214-2309) **7962**
• Estudios Afroamericanos Virtual (ESP ISSN 1697-4255) **4174**
• Estudios Agrarios (Mexico, D.F.) (MEX ISSN 1405-2466) **108**
Estudios Andinos (Lima) (PER ISSN 0014-1429) **7133**
• Estudios Atacamenos (CHL ISSN 0716-0925) **392**
• Estudios Avanzados (CHL ISSN 0718-5022) **7962**

DIRECTORY 2010 ETHANOL & BIODIESEL NEWS 10253

Estudios Avanzados Interactivos *see* Estudios Avanzados **7962**
Estudios Aymaras Boletin de Idea (PER) **7962**
Estudios Biblicos (ESP ISSN 0014-1437) **7641**
Estudios Biblicos LifeWay para Adultos. Manual para el Lider (USA ISSN 1555-3108) **7756**
Estudios C E P A *see* Comite Ejecutivo de la Pobreza en la Argentina. Estudios **8034**
Estudios Canarios (ESP ISSN 0423-4804) **4218**
• ➤ Estudios Centroamericanos (SLV ISSN 0014-1445) **7962**
Estudios Clasicos (ESP ISSN 0014-1453) **2234**
• Estudios Constitucionales (CHL ISSN 0718-0195) **4848**
Estudios Cubanos *see* Cuban Studies **4290**
Estudios de Administracion (CHL ISSN 0717-0653) **1106**
Estudios de Antropologia Biologica (MEX) **336**
• Estudios de Arqueologia Alavesa (CD-ROM) (ESP ISSN 1695-1611) **392**
Estudios de Arte y Estetica (MEX ISSN 0071-1659) **488**
Estudios de Asia y Africa (MEX ISSN 0185-0164) **549**
Estudios de Caso. Serie Estados Unidos (MEX ISSN 0185-5271) **1484**
Estudios de Ciencias Sociales (ESP ISSN 1131-6632) **7962**
Estudios de Construccion y Transportes (ESP ISSN 1576-7108) **8495**
Estudios de Coyuntura (VEN ISSN 0798-9733) **1106**
Estudios de Cultura Maya (MEX ISSN 0185-2574) **4292**
• Estudios de Cultura Nahuatl (MEX ISSN 0071-1675) **4292**
Estudios de Cultura Otopame/Studies of Otopame Culture (MEX) **336**
Estudios de Derecho (COL ISSN 0120-1867) **4668**
Estudios de Derecho Judicial (ESP ISSN 1137-3520) **4950**
Estudios de Deusto (ESP ISSN 0423-4847) **7962**
Estudios de Dialectologia Norteafricana y Andalusi *see* E D N A **5113**
• ➤ Estudios de Economia (CHL ISSN 0304-2758) **1106**
• Estudios de Economia Aplicada (ESP ISSN 1133-3197) **1484**
Estudios de Filosofia (ARG ISSN 0325-4933) **6917**
➤ Estudios de Filosofia (COL ISSN 0121-3628) **6917**
Estudios de Folklore (MEX ISSN 0188-0845) **3616**
Estudios de Fonetica Experimental (ESP ISSN 1575-5533) **5116**
▼ Estudios de Gestalt (ESP ISSN 1888-3893) **7355**
Estudios de Gestion Turistica (ESP ISSN 1137-4705) **8701**
• Estudios de Historia Moderna y Contemporanea de Mexico (MEX ISSN 0185-2620) **4292**
• Estudios de Historia Novohispana (MEX ISSN 0185-2523) **4292**
Estudios de Historia Social y Economica de America (ESP ISSN 0214-2236) **1484**
Estudios de Historia y Arqueologia Medievales (ESP ISSN 0212-9515) **392**
Estudios de la Fundacion ONCE sobre el Estado de Bienestar (ESP ISSN 1698-9937) **4065**
Estudios de Lengua y Literatura Francesas (ESP ISSN 0214-9850) **5291**
Estudios de Linguistica (ESP ISSN 0212-7636) **5116**
• Estudios de Linguistica Applicada (MEX ISSN 0185-2647) **5116**
• Estudios de Linguistica Chibcha (CRI ISSN 1409-245X) **336**
Estudios de Linguistica del Espanol *see* Estudios de Linguistica Espanola **5116**
• Estudios de Linguistica Espanola (ESP ISSN 1139-8736) **5116**
Estudios de Linguistica Inglesa Aplicada *see* E L I A **5113**
Estudios de Literatura (MEX ISSN 0188-0853) **5291**
• Estudios de Literatura Colombiana (COL ISSN 0123-4412) **5291**
Estudios de Literatura Contemporanea (ESP ISSN 0071-1705) **5291**
Estudios de Pedagogia y Psicologia (ESP ISSN 1132-8479) **2854**
Estudios de Poblacion (COL) **7282**
Estudios de Poblacion y Desarrollo (BOL) **7282**
Estudios de Prehistoria y Arqueologia Madrilenas/Studies of Madrilenian Prehistory and Archaeology (ESP ISSN 0213-0246) **393**
Estudios de Promocion Femenina (BOL) **8895**
• ➤ Estudios de Psicologia (ESP ISSN 0210-9395) **7355**
Estudios de Recursos Humanos (BOL) **1861**
Estudios de Sociolinguistica *see* Sociolinguistic Studies **5175**
Estudios de Sociologia Familiar (BOL) **8100**
Estudios del Caribe *see* Caribbean Studies **7953**
Estudios del Desarrollo/Development Studies Journal (VEN ISSN 1013-4069) **8100**
Estudios del Habitat (ARG ISSN 0328-929X) **442**
Estudios del Hombre (MEX ISSN 1405-1117) **336**
Estudios del Ministerio Fiscal (ESP ISSN 1135-7509) **1922**
Estudios del Museo de Ciencias Naturales de Alava *see* Museo de Ciencias Naturales de Alava. Estudios **7883**
▼ • Estudios del Patrimonio Cultural (ESP ISSN 1988-8015) **4218**
➤ Estudios del Trabajo (ARG ISSN 0327-5744) **1680**
• ➤ Estudios Demograficos y Urbanos (MEX ISSN 0186-7210) **7283**
Estudios e Informes de la C E P A L (CHL ISSN 0256-9795) **1595**
Estudios Eclesiasticos (ESP ISSN 0210-1610) **7641**
➤ Estudios Economicos (ARG ISSN 0425-368X) **1106**
Estudios Economicos *see* Instituto de Estudios Economicos. Revista **1491**
Estudios Economicos (MEX ISSN 0188-6916) **1541**
• Estudios Economicos de Desarrollo International (ESP ISSN 1578-4479) **1484**
▼ Estudios Economicos de los Sistemas de Produccion y los Recursos Naturales (ARG ISSN 1851-5525) **197**
• Estudios Economicos Regionales y Sectoriales/Regional and Sectoral Economic Studies (ESP ISSN 1578-4460) **1484**
Estudios Empresariales (ESP ISSN 0425-3698) **1742**
Estudios en Educacion Matematica *see* Studies in Mathematics Education Series **5539**
Estudios en el Extranjero *see* Study Abroad **3015**
Estudios Etnohistoricos del Ecuador (ECU) **4292**
Estudios Etnologicos del Valle de Chancay *see* Instituto de Estudios Peruanos. Proyecto de Estudios Etnologicos del Valle de Chancay. Monografia **343**
Estudios Europeos *see* European Studies **4219**
• ➤ Estudios Filologicos (CHL ISSN 0071-1713) **5116**
Estudios Filologicos Alemanes (ESP ISSN 1578-9438) **5116**
Estudios Filosoficos (ESP ISSN 0210-6086) **6917**
Estudios Financieros. Revista de Contabilidad y Tributacion. Comentarios, Casos Practicos (ESP ISSN 1138-9540) **1287**
Estudios Financieros. Revista de Contabilidad y Tributacion. Legislacion, Consultas, Jurisprudencia (ESP ISSN 1138-9613) **4950**
Estudios Financieros. Revista de Trabajo y Seguridad Social. Comentarios, Casos Practicos (ESP ISSN 1138-9532) **1680**
Estudios Financieros. Revista de Trabajo y Seguridad Social. Legislacion, Jurisprudencia (ESP ISSN 1138-9605) **1680**
Estudios Folkloricos Paraguayos (PRY) **3616**
• Estudios Fronterizos (MEX ISSN 0187-6961) **7283**
• Estudios Geograficos (ESP ISSN 0014-1496) **4005**
• ➤ Estudios Geologicos (ESP ISSN 0367-0449) **2707**
• Estudios Gerenciales (COL ISSN 0123-5923) **1742**
Estudios Hispanicos *see* Seu'pein Eo'munhag **5173**
Estudios Historicos (PER ISSN 1019-4533) **4292**
Estudios Historicos sobre San Sebastian. Boletin (ESP ISSN 0210-2889) **4218**
Estudios Humanistas (ESP ISSN 1139-5818) **4451**
Estudios Humanisticos: Filologia (ESP ISSN 0213-1382) **5116**
Estudios Humanisticos: Geografia, Historia, Arte (ESP ISSN 0213-1390) **4005**
Estudios, Informes y Dictamenes (ESP ISSN 1576-9712) **4668**
Estudios Ingleses de la Universidad Complutense *see* Universidad Complutense. Estudios Ingleses **5190**
• ➤ Estudios Interdisciplinarios de America Latina y el Caribe (ISR ISSN 0792-7061) **4451**
➤ Estudios Internacionales (CHL ISSN 0716-0240) **7232**
Estudios Internacionales de la Complutense (ESP ISSN 1575-7056) **7232**
• Estudios Irlandeses (ESP ISSN 1699-311X) **4218**
➤ Estudios Jaliscienses (MEX) **4451**
Estudios Josefinos (ESP ISSN 0210-7074) **7796**
Estudios Latinoamericanos (CHL ISSN 0718-3372) **4451**
Estudios Latinoamericanos *see* Studi Latinoamericani **5179**
Estudios Latinoamericanos (MEX ISSN 0187-1811) **4451**
Estudios Latinoamericanos (POL ISSN 0137-3080) **4292**
▼ Estudios Masonicos (COL ISSN 2011-169X) **1007**
Estudios Mexicanos *see* Mexican Studies **4464**
Estudios Michoacanos (MEX) **4292**
Estudios Migratorios (ESP ISSN 1136-0291) **8100**
➤ Estudios Migratorios Latinoamericanos (ARG ISSN 0326-7458) **7283**
• Estudios Mindonienses (ESP ISSN 0213-4357) **4218**
Estudios Mirandeses (ESP ISSN 0212-1875) **4451**
Estudios Nietzsche (ESP ISSN 1578-6676) **6917**
• Estudios Norteamericanos (CHL ISSN 0716-1468) **7133**
• ➤ Estudios Oceanologicos (CHL ISSN 0071-173X) **2804**
Estudios Paraguayos (PRY ISSN 0251-2483) **7962**
• Estudios Pedagogicos (CHL ISSN 0716-050X) **2980**
Estudios Politicos (COL ISSN 0121-5167) **7133**
Estudios Politicos (MEX ISSN 0185-1616) **7133**
Estudios Politicos Militares (CHL ISSN 0717-6392) **7133**
• Estudios Publicos (CHL ISSN 0716-1115) **7962**
• Estudios Rurales Latinoamericanos/Latin American Rural Studies (COL ISSN 0120-0747) **1484**
Estudios Segovianos (ESP ISSN 0210-7260) **4451**
Estudios sobre Consumo (ESP ISSN 0212-9469) **1816**
• Estudios Sobre Educacion (ESP ISSN 1578-7001) **2854**
• Estudios sobre el Mensaje Periodistico (ESP ISSN 1134-1629) **4575**
Estudios sobre la Elaboracion, la Comercializacion y la Distribucion de los Productos Basicos *see* Studies in the Processing, Marketing and Distribution of Commodities **8991**
Estudios sobre la Mujer (MEX) **8896**
• ➤ Estudios sobre las Culturas Contemporaneas (MEX ISSN 1405-2210) **4451**
Estudios sobre Patrimonio, Cultura y Ciencias Medievales (ESP ISSN 1575-3840) **4451**
Estudios Sobre Teoria y Critica Teatral (ESP) **8470**
Estudios Sociales (CHL ISSN 0716-0321) **7962**
Estudios Sociales (DOM ISSN 1017-0596) **8100**
Estudios Sociales (GTM ISSN 0254-1696) **7133**
• ➤ Estudios Sociales (MEX ISSN 0188-4557) **7962**
Estudios Sociologicos (MEX ISSN 0185-4186) **8100**
Estudios Socioterritoriales (ARG ISSN 1515-6206) **4005**
Estudios Trinitarios (ESP ISSN 0210-0363) **7641**
Estudios Turisticos (ESP ISSN 0423-5037) **8701**
Estudios Urbanos (BOL) **8100**
• Estudios Visuales (ESP ISSN 1698-7470) **488**
Estudios y Debates Regionales Andinos (PER) **7962**
Estudios y Fuentes del Arte en Mexico (MEX ISSN 0185-1845) **488**
Estudios y Perspectivas en Turismo (ARG ISSN 0327-5841) **8701**
Estudis (ESP ISSN 0210-9093) **4218**
Estudis Balearics (ESP ISSN 0212-3703) **7962**
† Estudis Castellonencs (ESP ISSN 1130-8788) **8954**
➤ Estudis d'Historia Agraria (ESP ISSN 0210-4830) **108**
Estudis d'Historia Contemporania del Pais Valencia (ESP ISSN 0210-8704) **4218**
Estudis d'Historia Economica (ESP ISSN 0214-1590) **1484**
Estudis Historics i Documents dels Arxius de Protocols (ESP ISSN 0211-5425) **4668**
Estudis Romanics (ESP ISSN 0211-8572) **5116**
• ➤ Estudos Afro-Asiaticos (BRA ISSN 0101-546X) **7962**
Estudos Anglo-Americanos (BRA ISSN 0102-4906) **5291**
• Estudos Avancados (BRA ISSN 0103-4014) **7962**
Estudos Baianos (BRA) **5291**
Estudos Biblicos (BRA ISSN 1676-4951) **7641**
Estudos Brasileiros (BRA) **7962**
Estudos da lingua(gem) (BRA ISSN 1808-1355) **5116**
Estudos de Antropologia Cultural e Social (PRT ISSN 0870-4457) **336**
Estudos de Biologia (BRA ISSN 0102-2067) **671**
Estudos de Cinema (BRA ISSN 1415-5907) **6497**
▼ • Estudos de Direito Cooperativo e Cidadania (BRA ISSN 1982-4882) **4668**
Estudos de Geografia das Regioes Tropicais (PRT) **4005**
Estudos de Geografia Fisica (PRT) **4005**
Estudos de Geografia Humana e Regional (PRT) **4006**
• Estudos de Gestao/Portuguese Journal of Management Sciences (PRT ISSN 0872-5284) **1742**
▼ • Estudos de Linguistica Galega (ESP ISSN 1889-2566) **5116**
Estudos de Literatura Brasileira Contemporanea (BRA ISSN 1518-0158) **5291**
• ➤ Estudos de Psicologia (Campinas) (BRA ISSN 0103-166X) **7355**
• Estudos de Psicologia (Natal) (BRA ISSN 1413-294X) **7355**
Estudos de Sociologia (BRA ISSN 1414-0144) **8100**
Estudos Demograficos (PRT ISSN 0871-875X) **7306**
Estudos do Quaternario (PRT ISSN 0874-0801) **2707**
Estudos do Seculo XX (PRT ISSN 1645-3530) **4218**
Estudos do Seculo Vinte *see* Estudos do Seculo XX **4218**
• ➤ Estudos Economicos (BRA ISSN 0101-4161) **1106**
Estudos em Avaliacao Educacional (BRA ISSN 0103-6831) **2854**
• Estudos em Design (BRA ISSN 0104-4249) **488**
• Estudos em Jornalismo e Midia (BRA ISSN 1806-6496) **4575**
• Estudos Feministas (BRA ISSN 0104-026X) **8896**
Estudos Germanicos (BRA ISSN 0101-837X) **5291**
Estudos Historicos (BRA ISSN 0103-2186) **4292**
• Estudos Ibero-Americanos (BRA ISSN 0101-4064) **3532**
Estudos Italianos em Portugal (PRT ISSN 0870-8584) **488**
Estudos Italianos em Portugal. Quaderno *see* Estudos Italianos em Portugal **488**
Estudos Juridicos (BRA ISSN 0100-2538) **4668**
Estudos Leopoldenses. Serie Educacao (BRA ISSN 1415-2800) **2854**
Estudos Leopoldenses. Serie Historia (BRA ISSN 1415-2819) **4139**
Estudos Linguisticos (Sao Paulo) (BRA ISSN 1413-0939) **5116**
Estudos Linguisticos e Literarios (BRA) **5117**
Estudos para o Planeamento Regional e Urbano (PRT) **4006**
➤ Estudos Politicos e Sociais (PRT ISSN 0014-1623) **7133**
Estudos Portugueses (BRA ISSN 0104-0049) **4451**
➤ Estudos Portugueses e Africanos (BRA ISSN 0103-1821) **7962**
• Estudos Semioticos (BRA ISSN 1980-4016) **5117**
Estudos Sociedade e Agricultura (BRA) **108**
Estudos Tecnologicos (BRA ISSN 0101-5303) **7853**
➤ Estudos Teologicos (BRA ISSN 0101-3130) **7756**
Estudos Universitarios (BRA ISSN 0425-4082) **2980**
Estylo (USA ISSN 1095-3302) **3532**
Estyn Newsletter/Newyddlen Estyn (GBR) **8039**
Eswau Huppeday (USA ISSN 0747-5810) **3765**
• eSwimmer (AUS) **8171**
eSystemist *see* The Systemist **8009**
Esztetika (HUN ISSN 1216-8114) **587**
Et Cetera (BGR ISSN 0861-9697) **488**
Et Cetera (CHL ISSN 0717-4667) **6917**
Et Cetera *see* Etc. (Fort Worth) **5117**
Et Cetera (USA ISSN 1930-0514) **5291**
Et Maelk *see* & Maelk **268**
ET-Ristikot *see* E T - Ristikot **8170**
L'Eta dell'Acquario (ITA) **6645**
Eta Evolutiva (ITA ISSN 0392-0658) **7355**
† Etage (DEU ISSN 0721-7072) **8954**
Il Etait une Fois (FRA ISSN 1774-3184) **4139**
• Il Etait une Fois l'Imaginaire de Paule Doyon (CAN ISSN 1910-183X) **5421**
Etanim *see* Derekh Hayyim **7514**
Etapes: (FRA ISSN 1774-5160) **7320**
Etapes Graphiques *see* Etapes: **7320**
Etapes: International (FRA ISSN 1767-4751) **7320**
Etat de la Francophonie dans le Monde *see* Francophonie dans le Monde **8103**
Etat de la Migration dans le Monde *see* World Migration **7295**
Etat de la Petite Entreprise at de l'Entrepreneuriat dans la Region de l'Atlantique *see* State of Small Business and Entrepreneurship in Atlantic Canada **1968**
Etat de l'Opinion (FRA ISSN 0984-774X) **1816**
• Etat du Monde (FRA ISSN 0757-6714) **1106**
L'Etat du Monde (Year) (CAN ISSN 0712-1180) **1563**
Etat du Monde sur CD-ROM *see* Etat du Monde **1106**
L'Etat en Vendee *see* La Lettre de l'Etat en Vendee **7451**
L'Etat et les Besoins de l'Education. Rapport Annuel (CAN ISSN 0842-6678) **2854**
Etat-Kalkulator (DEU) **25**
ETAtech Magazine *see* Entrepreneurs des Territoires **4593**
• Etats des Realisations. Mise en Oeuvre de l'Article 41 de la Loi sur les Langues Officielles (CAN ISSN 1910-7668) **2320**
Les Etats Unis d'Europe *see* Gli Stati Uniti d'Europa (Bari) **7266**
Etc. *see* E T C **6915**
Etc... (Denton) (USA ISSN 1559-9310) **5291**
• ➤ Etc. (Fort Worth) (USA ISSN 0014-164X) **5117**
• Etc. Montreal (CAN ISSN 0835-7641) **488**
Etceter@ *see* Etcetera **5215**
• Etcetera (MEX ISSN 1560-7402) **5215**
ETCetera *see* E T Cetera **1850**
Etch a Sketch Club. Newsletter (USA) **2188**
Etchings (AUS ISSN 1833-9654) **5292**
ETDonline *see* E T D Online **6696**
▼ Etela-Karjalan Ammattikorkeakoulu. Julkaisuja, Keittokirjoja (FIN ISSN 1796-8755) **4357**
• Etela-Karjalan Ammattikorkeakoulu. Julkaisuja. Sarja A, Raportteja ja Tutkimuksia/South Carelia Polytechnic. Publications. Series A, Reports and Research Papers (FIN ISSN 1239-8306) **2980**
• Etela-Karjalan Ammattikorkeakoulu. Julkaisuja. Sarja B, Oppimateriaaleja/South Carelia Polytechnic. Publications. Series B, Study Materials (FIN ISSN 1239-8314) **2980**
• Etela-Karjalan Ammattikorkeakoulu. Julkaisuja. Sarja C, Opinnaytteita/South Carelia Polytechnic. Publications. Series C, Theses (FIN ISSN 1239-8322) **2980**
• Etela-Karjalan Ammattikorkeakoulu. Julkaisuja. Sarja D, Muita Julkaisuja/South Carelia Polytechnic. Publications. Series D, Other Publications (FIN ISSN 1459-6881) **2980**
Etela-Karjalan Ammattikorkeakoulun Julkaisuja. Sarja, Keittokirjoja *see* Etela-Karjalan Ammattikorkeakoulu. Julkaisuja, Keittokirjoja **4357**
Etela - Pohjanmaa (FIN ISSN 0356-1682) **3838**
Etela-Saimaa (FIN ISSN 0357-0975) **3838**
Etela-Suomen Sanomat (FIN ISSN 0359-5056) **3838**
† Eten in de Nederlandse Horeca (NLD ISSN 1872-0013) **8954**
L'Etendard de la Bible et Heraut du Royaume de Christ (FRA ISSN 0245-9329) **7641**
Eter-Aktuellt (SWE ISSN 0014-1658) **2380**
Etera (ARM) **3792**
Eternelle (USA) **8861**
Etesia Ekthese Shetika me ten Katastase tou Problematos ton Narkotikon sten Europaike Enose *see* State of the Drugs Problem in the European Union. Annual Report **2699**
Etesia Statistike. Erevna tou Karkinou/Annual Statistical Survey of Cancer (GRC ISSN 0302-9697) **5744**
'Etgar *see* Challenge **7226**
Ethanol and Biodiesel News *see* Ethanol & Biodiesel News **3134**
• Ethanol & Biodiesel News (USA) **3134**

Title

• Ethanol Producer Magazine (USA ISSN 1935-7613) **197**
▼ Ethanol Retailer (USA) **6768**
• ethic@ (BRA ISSN 1677-2954) **6917**
• ➤ Ethica (BRA ISSN 1413-8093) **6917**
Ethica (DEU) **6917**
Ethica - Wissenschaft und Verantwortung (AUT ISSN 1021-8122) **7853**
• Ethical Consumer (GBR ISSN 0955-8608) **2637**
• ➤ Ethical Human Psychology and Psychiatry (USA ISSN 1559-4343) **6139**
• ➤ Ethical Perspectives (BEL ISSN 1370-0049) **6917**
➤ Ethical Perspectives Monograph Series (BEL) **6917**
Ethical Record (GBR ISSN 0014-1690) **6917**
• ➤ Ethical Space (GBR ISSN 1742-0105) **2320**
• Ethical Spectacle (USA) **6838**
• ➤ Ethical Theory and Moral Practice (NLD ISSN 1386-2820) **6917**
• Ethicomp (GBR ISSN 1743-3010) **2418**
Ethics *see* Lunlixue **6933**
• ➤ Ethics (USA ISSN 0014-1704) **6917**
Ethics (Chicago) (USA ISSN 1940-5553) **4501**
Ethics Abstracts on Cards *see* Lunlixue Wenzhai Ka **6933**
• ➤ Ethics & Behavior (USA ISSN 1050-8422) **7355**
➤ Ethics and Critical Thinking Journal (USA ISSN 1547-5425) **6917**
• ➤ Ethics and Education (GBR ISSN 1744-9642) **8100**
▼ • ➤ Ethics & Global Politics (SWE ISSN 1654-4951) **7133**
• ➤ Ethics and Information Technology (NLD ISSN 1388-1957) **5008**
• ➤ Ethics & International Affairs (USA ISSN 0892-6794) **7232**
• ➤ Ethics and Justice (AUS ISSN 1441-5860) **4668**
• ➤ Ethics & Medicine (USA ISSN 0266-688X) **5610**
• Ethics and Medics (USA ISSN 1071-3778) **7796**
Ethics & Policy (USA ISSN 1065-0113) **8100**
Ethics & Politics *see* Etica & Politica **6918**
Ethics and Public Policy Center Newsletter (USA) **7133**
▼ • ➤ Ethics and Social Welfare (GBR ISSN 1749-6535) **8039**
• ➤ Ethics & the Environment (USA ISSN 1085-6633) **6917**
Ethics at Work (USA ISSN 1939-7682) **4501**
Ethics Counsellor Annual Report *see* Report of the Ethics Counsellor on the Activities of the Office of the Ethics Counsellor **7465**
Ethics, Excellence and Leadership. Occasional Papers (GBR) **1106**
Ethics for the Insurance Professional (USA ISSN 1939-8204) **4501**
Ethics in Government Reporter (USA ISSN 0279-2869) **7435**
• ➤ Ethics in Science and Environmental Politics (DEU ISSN 1611-8014) **3430**
• Ethics in Tourism (ESP ISSN 1816-3521) **8701**
▼ The Ethics of American Foreign Policy (USA ISSN 1939-0203) **7232**
• ➤ Ethics, Place and Environment (GBR ISSN 1366-879X) **6917**
Ethics Series *see* Dental Ethics **5840**
• Ethics Today (USA) **2854**
Ethiek & Maatschappij (BEL ISSN 1373-0975) **6917**
Ethik im Unterricht (DEU ISSN 1615-9497) **6917**
Ethik in den Biowissenschaften (DEU) **6917**
Ethik in den Wissenschaften (DEU ISSN 1862-2410) **6917**
• ➤ Ethik in der Medizin (DEU ISSN 0935-7335) **6918**
Ethik in Forschung und Praxis (DEU ISSN 1610-5966) **6918**
Ethik und Politische Philosophie (CHE ISSN 1422-4496) **6918**
Ethik und Recht/Ethique et Droit/Etica e Diritto (CHE) **4668**
Ethik und Unterricht (DEU ISSN 0936-7772) **6918**
Ethikon Series in Comparative Ethics (USA) **6918**
• Ethikos (USA ISSN 0895-5026) **6918**
Ethiope Law Series (NGA) **4668**
➤ Ethiope Research (NGA ISSN 1595-6180) **7962**
Ethiopia (ETH) **3837**
▼ • The Ethiopia Business Forecast Report Annual (GBR ISSN 1753-688X) **1106**
Ethiopia. Customs Head Office. External Trade Statistics (ETH ISSN 0425-4309) **1227**
• Ethiopia Food Security Update (ETH ISSN 1946-6803) **1595**
Ethiopian Herald (ETH) **3837**
Ethiopian Journal of Agricultural Sciences (ETH ISSN 0257-2605) **108**
Ethiopian Journal of Biological Sciences (ETH ISSN 1819-8678) **671**
▼ Ethiopian Journal of Crop Science (ETH ISSN 2072-8506) **229**
Ethiopian Journal of Development Research (ETH ISSN 0378-0813) **1885**
Ethiopian Journal of Economics (ETH ISSN 1993-3681) **1106**
➤ Ethiopian Journal of Education (ETH ISSN 0425-4414) **2854**
▼ Ethiopian Journal of Environmental Studies and Management (ETH ISSN 1998-0507) **3430**
• ➤ The Ethiopian Journal of Health Development (ETH ISSN 1021-6790) **7516**
The Ethiopian Journal of Science and Technology *see* Ethiopian Journal of Technology, Education and Sustainable Development **8421**
Ethiopian Journal of Technology, Education and Sustainable Development (ETH) **8421**
➤ Ethiopian Journal of the Social Sciences and Humanities (ETH ISSN 1810-4487) **7962**
Ethiopian Library Association. Bulletin (ETH ISSN 0014-1747) **5008**
• ➤ Ethiopian Medical Journal (ETH ISSN 0014-1755) **5610**
• Ethiopian Mirror (USA ISSN 1553-2682) **3532**
• ➤ Ethiopian Pharmaceutical Journal (ETH ISSN 1029-5933) **6838**
Ethiopian Publications: Books, Pamphlets, Annuals and Periodical Articles (ETH ISSN 0071-1772) **624**
Ethiopian Trade Directory (ETH) **1992**
Ethiopian Trade Journal (ETH) **1402**
Ethiopian Wildlife and Natural History Society. Newsletter (ETH) **2611**
Ethiopiques (SEN ISSN 0850-2005) **4174**
Ethioscope (ETH) **3837**
Ethique et Droit *see* Ethik und Recht **4668**
• Ethique & Sante (FRA ISSN 1765-4629) **6985**
Ethique Publique (CAN ISSN 1488-0946) **6918**
• ➤ Ethische Perspectieven (BEL ISSN 0778-6069) **6918**
▼ Ethisphere (USA) **1742**
† Ethnic American Voluntary Organizations (USA ISSN 0737-1411) **8954**
Ethnic and Multicultural Information Exchange Round Table Bulletin *see* The E M I E Bulletin **3531**
• ➤ Ethnic and Racial Studies (GBR ISSN 0141-9870) **7962**
Ethnic Arts Quarterly *see* Minzu Yishu **506**
Ethnic Education Studies *see* Minzu Jiaoyu Yanjiu **2887**
Ethnic Foods Plus *see* Key Note Plus Market Report. Ethnic Foods **3653**
Ethnic Groups in California (USA) **3532**
Ethnic Groups of the World *see* Shijie Minzu **355**
Ethnic Interiors *see* Pine & Ethnic Interiors **4561**
Ethnic Links (NZL ISSN 1177-2530) **8039**
Ethnic Media & Markets (CAN ISSN 1205-7142) **25**
Ethnic Minorities Directory (GBR ISSN 1351-8070) **3532**
Ethnic Music *see* Minzu Yinyue **6588**
• Ethnic NewsWatch (USA) **3574**
Ethnic Reporter (USA ISSN 0893-7362) **3532**
Ethnic Review (USA) **3532**
➤ Ethnic Studies Report (LKA ISSN 1010-5832) **3532**
• ➤ Ethnic Studies Review (USA ISSN 1555-1881) **3532**
Ethnic Woman (USA ISSN 0897-4683) **8896**
Ethnica (HUN ISSN 1419-8177) **336**
• ➤ Ethnicities (GBR ISSN 1468-7968) **7962**
• ➤ Ethnicity & Disease (USA ISSN 1049-510X) **5610**
• ➤ Ethnicity and Health (GBR ISSN 1355-7858) **7516**
➤ Ethnicity and Identity Series (GBR ISSN 1354-3628) **336**
Ethnies (FRA ISSN 0295-9151) **3532**
Ethnike Trapeza tes Hellados. Apologismos *see* National Bank of Greece. Annual Report **1370**
Ethnikos Kirix *see* National Herald **3552**
Ethno (CHL ISSN 0717-2958) **2854**
Ethno - Cultural Networker (CAN) **3532**
Ethno-Indology (DEU ISSN 1860-2053) **549**
Ethno-Islamica (DEU ISSN 1432-0266) **549**
Ethno-Lore (HUN ISSN 1787-9396) **8100**
Ethno-National Studies *see* Minzu Yanjiu (Beijing, 1979) **556**
Ethno Reporter *see* Etno Reporter **7206**
▼ • ➤ Ethnoarchaeology (USA ISSN 1944-2890) **393**
EthnoArts Index (USA ISSN 0893-0120) **362**
➤ Ethnobotany (IND ISSN 0971-1252) **787**
• ➤ Ethnobotany Research and Applications (USA ISSN 1547-3465) **787**
Ethnografia Espanola (ESP ISSN 0211-772X) **336**
Ethnographia (HUN ISSN 0014-1798) **336**
• Ethnographic Library on CD (DEU) **336**
Ethnographic Museum in Belgrade. Bulletin *see* Etnografski Muzej u Beogradu. Glasnik **338**
• Ethnographic Praxis in Industry Conference. Conference Proceedings (USA ISSN 1559-890X) **336**
Ethnographic Review *see* Neprajzi Ertesito **350**
Ethnographica et Folkloristica Carpathica *see* Muveltseg es Hagyomany **349**
Ethnographical Studies *see* Neprajzi Tanulmanyok **350**
L'Ethnographie (BEL ISSN 0336-1438) **336**
• Ethnographiques.org (FRA ISSN 1961-9162) **336**
Ethnographisch-Archaeologische Zeitschrift *see* E A Z **336**
• ➤ Ethnography (GBR ISSN 1466-1381) **337**
• ➤ Ethnography and Education (GBR ISSN 1745-7823) **2854**
Ethnography in the San Francisco Bay Area (USA ISSN 1935-3723) **337**
• ➤ Ethnohistory (USA ISSN 0014-1801) **337**
➤ Ethnologia Balkanica (DEU) **337**
Ethnologia Bulgarica (BGR ISSN 1311-0918) **3616**
➤ Ethnologia Europaea/Journal of European Ethnology (DNK ISSN 0425-4597) **337**
Ethnologia Fennica/Finnish Studies in Ethnology (FIN ISSN 0355-1776) **337**
Ethnologia Polona (POL ISSN 0137-4079) **337**
➤ Ethnologia Scandinavica (SWE ISSN 0348-9698) **337**
Ethnologia Slovaca et Slavica (SVK ISSN 1335-4116) **3616**
Ethnologie de l'Europe (FRA ISSN 1771-9615) **337**
Ethnologie Francaise/French Ethnology (FRA ISSN 0046-2616) **337**
• ➤ Ethnologies (CAN ISSN 1481-5974) **3616**
Ethnologisches Museum. Veroeffentlichungen (DEU) **337**
Ethnology (IND) **337**
• ➤ Ethnology (USA ISSN 0014-1828) **337**
Ethnology Monographs (USA) **337**
➤ Ethnomusicologie (BEL ISSN 0299-3201) **6565**
• ➤ Ethnomusicology (USA ISSN 0014-1836) **6565**
• ➤ Ethnomusicology Forum (GBR ISSN 1741-1912) **6565**
• ➤ Ethnomusicology Online (USA ISSN 1092-7336) **6565**
• Ethnomusicology Research Digest (USA ISSN 1054-1624) **337**
▼ Ethnopharmacognosy Series (USA ISSN 1944-8228) **6838**
• ➤ Ethnopolitics (GBR ISSN 1744-9057) **7133**
Ethnopsychoanalyse (DEU ISSN 0937-4523) **7355**
Ethnopsychologie (FRA ISSN 1281-5578) **7355**
• Ethnorema (ITA ISSN 1826-8803) **8101**
Ethnos (AUT ISSN 0425-4600) **3532**
Ethnos (BRA ISSN 1415-4706) **3532**
• ➤ Ethnos (GBR ISSN 0014-1844) **337**
Ethnos (GRC ISSN 1108-8699) **3874**
Ethnos-Julkaisu (FIN ISSN 0781-9021) **3616**
• Ethnos-Tiedote (FIN ISSN 1796-0959) **3616**
Ethnos-Toimite (FIN ISSN 0357-511X) **3616**
Ethnosciences (BEL ISSN 0299-1098) **337**
Ethnozootechnie (FRA ISSN 0397-6572) **942**
Ethnozootechnie. Hors-Serie (FRA) **942**
• ➤ Ethology (DEU ISSN 0179-1613) **942**
• ➤ Ethology Ecology & Evolution (ITA ISSN 0394-9370) **942**
Ethology Ecology & Evolution. Special Issue (ITA ISSN 1120-6705) **942**
• Ethology Online (DEU ISSN 1439-0310) **942**
Ethos (ARG ISSN 0325-5387) **6918**
Ethos (POL ISSN 0860-8024) **7797**
• Ethos (Ames) (USA ISSN 1074-2174) **2283**
Ethos (Canberra) (AUS) **4668**
• ➤ Ethos (Carlton) (AUS ISSN 1448-1324) **3061**
• ➤ Ethos (Malden) (USA ISSN 0091-2131) **337**
• Ethos (Online Edition) (SWE) **8101**
Ethos - Die Zeitschrift fuer die Ganze Familie (CHE) **7641**
Ethos Educativo (MEX ISSN 1405-7255) **2855**
Ethylene Industry *see* Yixi Gongye **6798**
• Ethylene Producers Conference. Proceedings (USA ISSN 1066-1557) **3243**
▼ • Etica de los Ciudadanos (ESP ISSN 1988-7973) **6918**
Etica e Diritto *see* Ethik und Recht **4668**
• Etica & Politica/Ethics & Politics (ITA ISSN 1825-5167) **6918**
Etica & Ciencia (ARG ISSN 0326-9442) **7853**
Etienne Gilson Series (CAN ISSN 0708-319X) **6918**
Etiketten-Labels (DEU ISSN 0949-9695) **7320**
▼ • ➤ Etikk i Praksis (NOR ISSN 1890-3991) **6918**
Etin (USA) **5008**
L'Etincelle (FRA ISSN 1952-9864) **6565**
Etincelle (GLP ISSN 0755-2947) **7133**
Etincelle (USA ISSN 0791-9433) **5117**
Etiq et Pack (FRA ISSN 1951-0330) **6709**
Etiqueta de Ediciones Marco Real (ESP) **603**
Etiquettes Plus (FRA ISSN 1765-4602) **6733**
Etniker Bizkaia (ESP ISSN 1132-0729) **338**
Etno Reporter (BGR ISSN 1311-0276) **7206**
Etnofolk (BOL) **338**
Etnofoor (NLD ISSN 0921-5158) **338**
▼ • Etnografia e Ricerca Qualitativa (ITA ISSN 1973-3194) **8101**
Etnografia Polska (POL ISSN 0071-1861) **338**
Etnografia Shqiptare/The Albanian Ethnography (ALB ISSN 0425-466X) **338**
• Etnografica (PRT ISSN 0873-6561) **338**
• Etnograficheskoe Obozrenie (RUS ISSN 0869-5415) **338**
Etnografija Hrvata u Madarskoj (HUN ISSN 1219-5804) **3532**
Etnografski Muzej u Beogradu. Glasnik/Ethnographic Museum in Belgrade. Bulletin (SRB ISSN 0350-0322) **338**
Etnolog. Nova Vrsta (SVN ISSN 0354-0316) **338**
Etnologia i Antropologia Kulturowa (POL ISSN 1230-8595) **3616**
Etnologia y Folklore (CUB) **338**
Etnologicke Rozpravy (SVK ISSN 1335-5074) **338**
Etnologiska Skrifter (SWE ISSN 1103-6516) **338**
Etnologiska Studier (SWE ISSN 0374-7530) **338**
Etnologiske Studier (DNK ISSN 1398-8980) **338**
➤ Etnoloska Tribina (HRV ISSN 0351-1944) **338**
Etnomusikologian Vuosikirja (FIN ISSN 0783-6821) **3617**
Etnopoliticheskii Vestnik (RUS) **338**
• Etobicoke Guardian (CAN ISSN 1181-3040) **3809**
L'Etoile Absinthe (FRA ISSN 0750-9219) **5292**
Etoiles *see* Yllkat **2223**
▼ Etoiles Passion (FRA ISSN 1963-2347) **4334**
Etologia *see* Acta Ethologica **929**
Etop (UGA) **3963**
• Etoy Tanksystem (CHE) **2556**
E*Trade (USA) **1563**
Etranger *see* Lo Straniero **5240**
Etre Parents *see* Lihyot Mishpaha **8118**
e!trend (AUT) **2556**
eTrend *see* Trend **1184**
• Etruscan News (USA ISSN 1933-9674) **4218**
➤ Etruscan Studies (USA ISSN 1080-1960) **2234**
Ett Trykk (NOR ISSN 1504-4386) **6650**
Ettela' Resani/Journal of Information Sciences (IRN ISSN 1022-7822) **7853**
• Ettela'at (GBR ISSN 1353-8829) **3532**
Ettelaat *see* Ettela'at **3532**
Ettela'at-e Elmi (IRN) **7853**
Ettela'at-e Siyassi Eqtesadi (IRN ISSN 1017-4141) **7133**
Ettela'at Haftegi (IRN) **3891**
• Ettela'at Newspaper (IRN) **3891**
• Etude de la Population Africaine/African Population Studies (SEN ISSN 0850-5780) **7283**
Etude des Conditions Economiques et Sociales en Afrique *see* Survey of Economic and Social Conditions in Africa **1605**
Etude F A O. Alimentation et Nutrition *see* F A O Food and Nutrition Paper **3635**
Etude F A O, Production et Sante Animales *see* F A O Animal Production and Health Papers **286**
Etude F A O, Production Vegetale et Protection des Plantes *see* F A O Plant Production and Protection Papers **229**
Etude sur les Permis d'Exercice de la Profession d'Infirmiere Delivres (CAN ISSN 1910-7838) **5958**
Etude sur les Transports Maritimes *see* Review of Maritime Transport **8658**
• Etudes (FRA ISSN 0014-1941) **7797**
Etudes a l'Etranger *see* Study Abroad **3015**
Etudes Africaines Hambourgeoises *see* Hamburg African Studies **8961**
• Etudes Anglaises (FRA ISSN 0014-195X) **5292**
Etudes Arabes (ITA ISSN 1722-943X) **7710**
Etudes Asiatiques *see* Asiatische Studien **544**
Etudes Balkaniques (BGR ISSN 0324-1645) **4218**
➤ Etudes Britanniques Contemporaines (FRA ISSN 1168-4917) **5292**
Etudes Byzantines *see* Byzantine Studies **4445**
Etudes Canadiennes/Canadian Studies (BEL ISSN 1781-3867) **7962**
Etudes Canadiennes/Canadian Studies (FRA ISSN 0153-1700) **4451**
Etudes Canadiennes de Lange et Litterature Allemandes *see* Canadian Studies in German Language and Literature **5270**
• Etudes Caribeennes (MTQ ISSN 1779-0980) **4006**
Etudes Celtiques (FRA ISSN 0373-1928) **5117**
Etudes Chinoises (FRA ISSN 0755-5857) **549**
Etudes Christiniennes (FRA ISSN 1279-8193) **5292**
Etudes Chypriotes (GRC ISSN 0424-2246) **2234**
➤ Les Etudes Classiques (BEL ISSN 0014-200X) **2234**
Etudes Cognitives *see* Studia Kognitywne **5180**
Etudes Corses (FRA ISSN 0338-361X) **338**
Etudes Creoles (FRA ISSN 0708-2398) **5117**
Etudes Dahomeennes (BEN ISSN 0014-2018) **4174**
Etudes d'Antiquites Africaines (FRA ISSN 0768-2352) **4174**
Etudes Danubiennes (FRA ISSN 0769-3656) **4218**
• ➤ Etudes de Communications (FRA ISSN 1270-6841) **2320**
Etudes de Droit International (NLD) **4924**
Les Etudes de la Documentation Francaise (FRA ISSN 1763-6191) **1484**
Etudes de Langue et Litterature Francaises (JPN ISSN 0425-4929) **5117**
Etudes de Lettres (CHE ISSN 0014-2026) **5292**
• Etudes de Linguistique Appliquee (FRA ISSN 0071-190X) **5117**
Etudes de l'Institut Pierre Bayle, Nimegue *see* Institut Pierre Bayle. Studies **4232**
Etudes de Musicologie/Musicological Studies (BEL) **6565**
Etudes de Paleographie Hebraique (FRA ISSN 0395-8108) **5117**
Etudes de Philologie, d'Archeologie et d'Histoire Ancienne (BEL ISSN 0071-1926) **5117**
Etudes de Philosophie Interculturelle *see* Studien zur Interkulturellen Philosophie **6954**
Etudes d'Histoire de l'Art (BEL ISSN 0071-1969) **488**
Etudes d'Histoire Economique et Sociale (BEL ISSN 0071-1977) **1541**
Etudes d'Histoire et de Philosophie Religieuses (FRA ISSN 0992-6488) **7641**
Etudes d'Histoire Medievale (FRA ISSN 1278-3854) **4218**
Etudes d'Histoire Religieuse (CAN ISSN 1193-199X) **7797**
Etudes Economiques de l'O C D E *see* O C D E. Etudes Economiques **1502**
Etudes Economiques de l'O C D E : Coree *see* O E C D Economic Surveys: Korea **1155**
Etudes Economiques de l'O C D E. Espagne *see* O E C D Economic Surveys: Spain **1504**
Etudes Economiques de l'O C D E: Etats-Unis *see* O E C D Economic Surveys: United States **1504**
Etudes Economiques de l'O C D E. Federation de Russie *see* O E C D Economic Surveys: Russian Federation **1155**
Etudes Economiques de l'O C D E: Mexique *see* O E C D Economic Surveys: Mexico **1503**
Etudes Economiques de l'O C D E: Norvege *see* O E C D Economic Surveys: Norway **1504**

▼ new title   † ceased   ● electronic media   ➤ refereed

Title

10256 EUROASIA SEMICONDUCTOR ULRICH'S PERIODICALS

EuroAsia Semiconductor (GBR ISSN 1751-1135) **3099**
Euroasian Entomological Journal *see* Evraziatskii Entomologicheskii Zhurnal **847**
† Euroasiatica (ITA) **8954**
• Euroavain (FIN ISSN 1237-203X) **8368**
Eurobalkans (GRC ISSN 1105-9176) **4219**
• Eurobarometer (English Edition) (LUX ISSN 1012-2249) **7283**
Eurobarometre (French Edition) *see* Eurobarometer (English Edition) **7283**
Eurobarometro (Italian Edition) *see* Eurobarometer (English Edition) **7283**
Eurobarometro (Portuguese Edition) *see* Eurobarometer (English Edition) **7283**
Eurobarometro (Spanish Edition) *see* Eurobarometer (English Edition) **7283**
Eurobjet Conso Magazine (FRA ISSN 1957-4819) **25**
Eurobjet Magazine *see* Eurobjet Conso Magazine **25**
Eurobjet Magazine *see* Eurobjet Pro Magazine **25**
Eurobjet Pro Magazine (FRA ISSN 1957-4827) **25**
Eurobond Market in E C U - Monthly Statistics *see* Le Marche Euro-Obligataire en E C U - Statistiques Mensuelles **1251**
EuroBus (DEU) **8495**
Eurocalcio (ITA ISSN 1591-254X) **8171**
Eurocamp.nl (NLD ISSN 1871-9783) **8312**
Eurocancer (Year) (FRA ISSN 1253-0727) **6019**
Eurocargo *see* Logistra **8503**
• Eurocarne (ESP ISSN 1132-2675) **3634**
• Eurocarni (ITA ISSN 0394-2910) **3634**
Eurochem Monitor (GBR ISSN 0967-7844) **2061**
• ➤ EuroChoices (GBR ISSN 1478-0917) **108**
EuroCity (AUT) **8701**
Eurocity (HRV ISSN 1330-0555) **8617**
EuroCity Survey (GBR) **4385**
Euroclio Bulletin (NLD ISSN 1871-3386) **4219**
Euroclio. Etudes et Documents (BEL ISSN 0944-2294) **7962**
Euroclio. References (BEL ISSN 0946-9737) **7962**
† EuroComputer (DNK) **8954**
EuroCriminology (POL ISSN 0860-3723) **2651**
EuroDecor (DEU ISSN 0942-9638) **1106**
EuroEquipos & Obras (ESP) **5451**
Eurofach Electronica (ESP ISSN 0211-2973) **3099**
Eurofi Guide to European Community Grants and Loans *see* Guide to European Community Grants and Loans **1596**
Eurofile *see* The Banker **1316**
Eurofinas. Annual Report *see* European Federation of Finance House Associations. Annual Report **1339**
Eurofinas. Newsletter *see* European Federation of Finance House Associations. Newsletter **1339**
Eurofish Magazine (DNK) **3590**
• Eurofood (GBR ISSN 0955-5404) **3634**
• Eurofood Monitor (GBR ISSN 0960-7943) **3635**
Eurofotbal (ROM) **8227**
• Eurofound News/Fondation Europeenne pour l'Amelioration des Conditions de Vie et de Travail. Communique (IRL ISSN 1830-7108) **7516**
Eurofruit Magazine (GBR ISSN 1359-7515) **3677**
Eurofunding. Cooperation Internationale (FRA ISSN 1778-8358) **7436**
Eurofunding. Education Formation Recherche (FRA ISSN 1778-834X) **7436**
Eurofunding. International Cooperation (FRA ISSN 1778-8331) **7436**
Eurofunding. Public Sector (FRA ISSN 1778-8366) **7436**
Eurogast (AUT) **8702**
† Eurogay (DEU ISSN 1439-653X) **8954**
➤ Eurogermanistik (DEU ISSN 0941-6870) **5117**
Eurographics (AUT ISSN 0946-2767) **2485**
• Eurohealth (GBR ISSN 1356-1030) **7516**
Euroheat & Power (DEU) **4118**
EuroHedge (GBR ISSN 1473-3153) **1622**
• EurOhs (GBR ISSN 1475-388X) **6676**
➤ EuroIntervention (FRA ISSN 1774-024X) **6242**
Eurolaser (DEU ISSN 1430-8274) **3366**
† • EuroLex (DEU) **8954**
Eurolinguistische Arbeiten (DEU ISSN 1613-1118) **5117**
• Euroman (DNK ISSN 0906-9690) **6289**
Euromarket Decisions (GBR ISSN 1467-0046) **1622**
Euromarket Directory (GBR ISSN 0265-2633) **1484**
Euromat *see* F E M S News **3344**
Euromaterials *see* F E M S News **3344**
Euromecum (DEU ISSN 0939-4494) **2980**
▼ • ➤ EuroMed Journal of Business (GBR ISSN 1450-2194) **1106**
† Euromedia (ITA) **8954**
• Euromedia Acquisitions & Finance (USA ISSN 1083-8880) **1338**
• Euromicro Conference on Real-Time Systems. Proceedings (USA) **2536**
• Euromicro Conference. Proceedings (USA ISSN 1089-6503) **2589**
• Euromicro Workshop on Parallel and Distributed Processing (USA ISSN 1066-6192) **2466**
† EuroMilcomp (Year) (GBR) **8954**
EuroMold Special (DEU) **3366**
• Euromoney (GBR ISSN 0014-2433) **1338**
Euromoney Capital Markets Directory (US & Canada Edition) *see* Fincareer Euromoney Capital Markets Directory (Year) **1995**
Euromoney Capital Markets Guide (GBR) **1338**
Euromoney Derivatives Handbook (Year) (GBR ISSN 1368-2792) **1622**
Euromoney Foreign Exchange and Treasury Management Handbook (GBR ISSN 1472-2868) **1338**
The Euromoney Foreign Exchange Handbook (Year) (GBR) **1338**
Euromoney Global M & A Handbook (Mergers and Acquisitions) (GBR ISSN 1462-7825) **1338**
The Euromoney International Equity Capital Markets Handbook (Year) (GBR ISSN 1478-2588) **1622**
Euromoney Online *see* Euromoney **1338**
Euromoney Syndication Guide. Weekly Fact Sheet *see* Euromoney Capital Markets Guide **1338**
Euromoney Trade Finance Report (GBR ISSN 0264-6706) **1338**
▼ • Euromoney Weekly FiX (GBR) **1338**
Euromoney's Regulation and Case Alert (GBR ISSN 0962-2551) **1106**
Euromoto (ITA ISSN 1827-0131) **8258**
Euromueble (ESP ISSN 0210-5489) **4556**
Euronetwork (GBR) **8039**
Euronews on Special Needs Education (DNK ISSN 1029-8142) **3039**
• Euronomics (USA ISSN 1524-6515) **1106**
Euronova (FRA ISSN 1145-0339) **1106**
Euroopan Investointipankki. Tiedote *see* European Investment Bank. Information **1622**
Euroopan Keskuspankki. Kuukausikatsaus (DEU ISSN 1561-0322) **1338**
Euroopan Keskuspankki. Vuosikertomous *see* European Central Bank. Annual Report **1339**
• Euroopan Tiede ja Teknologia (FIN ISSN 1459-4862) **53**
Euroopan Unionin Tiedote *see* European Union. Bulletin **1485**
Euroopan Unionin Tiedotteessa *see* European Commission. European Union. Bulletin **7233**
Euroopan Unionin Verolait (FIN ISSN 1795-777X) **1922**
Euroopan Yhteisojen Komissio. Asiakirjat *see* Commission of the European Communities. Documents **7227**
Euroopan Yhteisojen Virallinen Lehti. C: Tiedonantoja ja Ilmoituksia *see* Diario Oficial de las Comunidades Europeas. C: Comunicaciones e Informaciones **4923**
Euroopan Yhteisojen Virallinen Lehti. C: Tiedonantoja ja Ilmoituksia *see* Official Journal of the European Union **7256**
Euroopan Yhteisojen Virallinen Lehti. L & C: Lainsaadanto, Tiedonantoja ja Ilmoituksia *see* Official Journal of the European Union. L & C Series: Legislation and Information Notices (Quarterly Edition) **4937**
Euroopan Yhteisojen Virallinen Lehti. L: Lainsaadanto *see* Official Journal of the European Union. L Series: Legislation **7256**
Euroopan Yhteisojen Virallinen Lehti. Liitteet. Taysistuntokeskustelut *see* Diario Oficial de las Comunidades Europeas. Anexo Debates **4923**
Euroopan Yhtheison Kilpailupolitiikka. Kilpailupolitiikkaa Koskeva Kertomus *see* European Community Competition Policy. Report on Competition Policy **1885**
▼ • Eurooppalainen Suomi. Raportteja (FIN ISSN 1796-8542) **7233**
Europ Magazine (FRA ISSN 0180-7897) **7134**
Europa *see* Journal Europa **2288**
Europa (GBR ISSN 1350-4770) **7233**
Europa (NLD) **4219**
Europa *see* Nei til EU. Aarbok **4936**
• Europa (Online) (DNK ISSN 1609-9400) **1563**
Europa (Print) *see* Europa (Online) **1563**
Europa Aktuell (DEU ISSN 1614-6883) **1622**
† Europa Blaetter (DEU ISSN 1435-3253) **8954**
Europa Camping und Caravaning. Internationaler Fuehrer (DEU ISSN 0071-2272) **8312**
† L'Europa della C E E (Comunita Economica Europea) (ITA) **8954**
Europa Directory of International Organizations (GBR ISSN 1465-4628) **7233**
• Europa Dokumentaro (DEU ISSN 1439-216X) **4219**
Europa Dwadziescia Jeden *see* Europa XXI **7283**
Europa e Diritto Privato (ITA ISSN 1720-4542) **4924**
Europa Ethnica (AUT ISSN 0014-2492) **3533**
† Europa Europe (ITA) **8954**
Europa Forum (HUN ISSN 1215-4504) **7963**
Europa Forum (LUX ISSN 1016-572X) **4924**
The Europa International Foundation Directory (Year) (GBR ISSN 1752-2676) **3012**
Europa-Jahrbuch Oel und Gas *see* European Oil and Gas Yearbook **6768**
Europa Kommunal (DEU ISSN 1433-7428) **7233**
The Europa Magazine (Colorado Springs) (USA) **8171**
Europa Magazine (Lawrenceville) (USA ISSN 1939-3423) **5070**
Europa Medicophysica *see* European Journal of Physical and Rehabilitation Medicine **6109**
Europa Mediterranea - Quaderni (ITA) **4219**
Europa Mediterranea - Quaderni G I S E M *see* Europa Mediterranea - Quaderni **4219**
Europa Nostra (NLD ISSN 1871-417X) **4451**
Europa Nostra. Annual Report (NLD ISSN 1875-290X) **7436**
Europa Nostra. Scientific Bulletin (NLD ISSN 1875-2896) **442**
Europa Noter *see* European File **1563**
Europa Oggi (LUX ISSN 1016-5738) **4924**
Europa ohne Grenzen *see* Frontier-Free Europe **1566**
➤ Europa Regional (DEU ISSN 0943-7142) **4006**
Europa sem Fronteiras *see* Frontier-Free Europe **1566**
Europa Senza Frontiere *see* Frontier-Free Europe **1566**
Europa sin Fronteras *see* Frontier-Free Europe **1566**
• Europa Star (European Edition) (CHE ISSN 0014-2603) **4565**
Europa Star (International Edition) (CHE ISSN 1660-9425) **4565**
Europa Star Couture Jeweler Magazine (CHE) **4565**
Europa Star Espana, Hora Latina (CHE ISSN 1661-3457) **4565**
• Europa Star International Jeweler's (Year) Yearbook (CHE) **4565**
Europa Transport (LUX) **8495**
† • Europa van Morgen (NLD ISSN 0165-7070) **8954**
Europa Verde *see* Green Europe **116**
The Europa World of Learning *see* World of Learning (Year) **2963**
Europa World Year Book (Year) (GBR ISSN 0956-2273) **3120**
Europa XXI (POL ISSN 1429-7132) **7283**
• Europa XXI (ROM ISSN 1222-6084) **4219**
Europa zonder Grenzen *see* Frontier-Free Europe **1566**
Europabrevet (NOR ISSN 1501-6145) **1563**
• ➤ Europace (GBR ISSN 1099-5129) **5786**
Europace. Supplement *see* Europace **5786**
• Europaea (ITA ISSN 1124-5425) **338**
Europaea Memoria. Reihe I: Studien (DEU ISSN 1613-7388) **4219**
Europaeische Aufklaerung in Literatur und Sprache (DEU ISSN 0935-5677) **5293**
Europaeische Bibliographie Oesteuropastudien *see* European Bibliography of Slavic and East European Slavonic Studies **4170**
Europaeische Bildung im Dialog (DEU ISSN 0947-6849) **2855**
Europaeische Diktaturen und Ihre Ueberwindung (DEU) **4139**
Europaeische Dokumentation *see* Documentation Europeene **8366**
Europaeische Ex Libris *see* Bibliografi over Europaeiske Kunstneres Ex Libris **8935**
Europaeische Freihandelsassoziation. Jahresbericht (CHE ISSN 0258-3852) **1563**
Europaeische Gegenwart (DEU ISSN 0931-5233) **1484**
Europaeische Gemeinschaft Kartellrecht *see* E G - Kartellrecht **4866**
Europaeische Gemeinschaft Umweltrecht *see* E G - Umweltrecht **3414**
Europaeische Geschichtsdarstellungen (AUT) **4219**
Europaeische Gesellschaft fuer die Theologische Forschung von Frauen. Jahrbuch *see* European Society of Women in Theological Research. Journal **7641**
Europaeische Gesellschaft fuer Katholische Theologie. Bulletin (BEL ISSN 0939-3897) **7797**
† Europaeische Gesetze gegen Wettbewerbsbeschraenkungen (DEU ISSN 0933-8314) **8954**
Europaeische Gesundheitsgespraeche (AUT) **5610**
Europaeische Grundrechte Zeitschrift (DEU ISSN 0341-9800) **4668**
Europaeische Hochschulschriften. Reihe 1: Deutsche Sprache und Literatur/European University Studies. Series 1: German Language and Literature (DEU ISSN 0721-3301) **5293**
Europaeische Hochschulschriften. Reihe 11: Paedagogik/European University Studies. Series 11: Education (DEU ISSN 0531-7398) **2855**
Europaeische Hochschulschriften. Reihe 13: Franzoesische Sprache und Literatur/European University Studies. Series 13: French Language and Literature (DEU ISSN 0721-3360) **5293**
Europaeische Hochschulschriften. Reihe 14: Angelsaechsische Sprache und Literatur/European University Studies. Series 14: Anglo-Saxon Language and Literature (DEU ISSN 0721-3387) **5293**
Europaeische Hochschulschriften. Reihe 16: Slawische Sprachen und Literaturen (DEU ISSN 0721-3441) **5117**
Europaeische Hochschulschriften. Reihe 18: Vergleichende Literaturwissenschaft/European University Studies. Series 18: Comparative Literature (DEU ISSN 0721-3425) **5293**
Europaeische Hochschulschriften. Reihe 19: Volkskunde/Ethnologie. Abteilung A: Volkskunde/European University Studies. Series 19: Anthropology, Ethnology. Section A: Anthropology (DEU ISSN 0721-3522) **338**
Europaeische Hochschulschriften. Reihe 19: Volkskunde/Ethnologie. Abteilung B: Ethnologie/European University Studies. Series 19: Anthropology/Ethnology. Section B: Ethnology (DEU ISSN 0721-3549) **338**
Europaeische Hochschulschriften. Reihe 2: Rechtswissenschaft/European University Studies. Series 2: Law (DEU ISSN 0531-7312) **4668**
Europaeische Hochschulschriften. Reihe 21: Linguistik/European University Studies. Series 21: Linguistics (DEU ISSN 0721-3352) **5117**
Europaeische Hochschulschriften. Reihe 23: Theologie *see* European University Studies. Series 23: Theology **7963**
Europaeische Hochschulschriften. Reihe 24: Ibero-Romanische Sprachen und Literaturen/European University Studies. Series 24: Ibero-Romance Languages and Literature (DEU ISSN 0721-3565) **5293**
Europaeische Hochschulschriften. Reihe 27: Asiatische und Afrikanische Studien/European University Studies. Series 27: Asian and African Studies (DEU ISSN 0721-3581) **549**
Europaeische Hochschulschriften. Reihe 3: Geschichte und Ihre Hilfswissenschaften/European University Studies. Series 3: History and Allied Studies (DEU ISSN 0531-7320) **4139**
Europaeische Hochschulschriften. Reihe 30: Theater-, Film- und Fernsehwissenschaften/European University Papers. Series 30: Theatre, Film and Television (DEU ISSN 0721-3662) **8470**
Europaeische Hochschulschriften. Reihe 31: Politikwissenschaft/European University Studies. Series 31: Political Sciences (DEU ISSN 0721-3654) **7134**
Europaeische Hochschulschriften. Reihe 7: Medizin. Abteilung B: Geschichte der Medizin (DEU ISSN 0721-3344) **5610**
Europaeische Hochschulschriften. Reihe 9: Italienische Sprache und Literatur/European University Studies. Series 9: Italian Language and Literature/Publications Universitaires Europeennes. Serie 9: Lingua e Letteratura Italiana (DEU ISSN 0531-7371) **5117**
Europaeische Investitionsbank. Informationen *see* European Investment Bank. Information **1622**
Europaeische Kinder- und Jugendliteratur im Interkulturellen Kontext *see* European Literature for Children and Young Adults in an Inter-Cultural Context **5293**
Europaeische Kulturstudien (DEU) **4219**
Europaeische Migrationsforschung (DEU ISSN 1430-0095) **7283**
Europaeische Rechtsakademie Forum *see* E R A Forum **4924**
Europaeische Religionsgeschichte (DEU) **7641**
Europaeische Rundschau (AUT ISSN 0304-2782) **7233**
Europaeische Schriften (DEU ISSN 0071-2329) **7233**
Europaeische Sicherheit (DEU ISSN 0940-4171) **6420**
Europaeische Sozialistik. Sozialschutz. Ausgaben und Einnahmen *see* European Social Statistics. Social Protection. Expenditure and Receipts **8082**
Europaeische Studien *see* European Studies **4219**
Europaeische und Internationale Studien (DEU) **7963**
Europaeische Union. Bulletin *see* European Union. Bulletin **1485**
Europaeische Union Magazin *see* E U Magazin **1478**
Europaeische Zeitschrift Berufsbildung *see* European Journal Vocational Training **2855**
▼ Europaeische Zeitschrift fuer Arbeitsrecht/European Journal of Labour Law (DEU ISSN 1865-3030) **1680**
Europaeische Zeitschrift fuer Kinder- und Jugendforschung *see* European Journal on Child and Youth Research **2152**
Europaeische Zeitschrift fuer Kinder- und Jugendpolitik *see* Forum 21. European Journal of Child and Youth Policy **2153**
Europaeische Zeitschrift fuer Kombinatorik *see* European Journal of Combinatorics **5487**
Europaeische Zeitschrift fuer Politische Oekonomie *see* European Journal of Political Economy **7134**
Europaeische Zeitschrift fuer Privatrecht *see* European Review of Private Law **4925**
Europaeische Zeitschrift fuer Unternehmensfuehrung und Betriebswirtschaft *see* Revista Europea de Direccion y Economia de la Empresa **1581**
Europaeische Zeitschrift fuer Wirtschaftsrecht (DEU ISSN 0937-7204) **4867**
† Europaeische Zeitung (DEU) **8954**
Europaeische Zentralbank. Jahresbericht *see* European Central Bank. Annual Report **1339**
Europaeische Zentralbank. Monatsbericht (DEU ISSN 1561-0292) **1338**
Europaeischen Patentamt Institut Information *see* E P I Information **6749**
Europaeischer Arbeitskreis fuer Prae- und Postnatale Entwicklungsforschung. Schriftenreihe (DEU ISSN 1435-6945) **5989**
Europaeischer Informationsbrief Bildung und Beschaeftigung (DEU ISSN 0949-8567) **1106**
Europaeischer Informationsbrief Gesundheit (DEU ISSN 1860-6636) **7516**
Europaeischer Kongress fuer Chronometrie *see* Congres Europeen de Chronometrie. Actes **3375**
• Europaeischer Wetterbericht (Online) (DEU ISSN 1614-0761) **6352**
Europaeischer Wirtschaftsdienst. Eildienst Holz (DEU) **3711**
Europaeischer Wirtschaftsdienst. Facility Management (DEU) **1851**
Europaeischer Wirtschaftsdienst. Holz *see* Europaeischer Wirtschaftsdienst. Holz und Holzwerkstoffe **3711**
Europaeischer Wirtschaftsdienst. Holz und Holzwerkstoffe (DEU) **3711**

† Europaeischer Wirtschaftsdienst. Informationsbrief Holz - Zellstoff - Papier (DEU) **8954**
Europaeischer Wirtschaftsdienst. Kunststoff (DEU) **7092**
Europaeischer Wirtschaftsdienst. Laubholz (DEU) **3711**
Europaeischer Wirtschaftsdienst. Moebel (DEU) **4556**
Europaeischer Wirtschaftsdienst. Papier und Zellstoff (DEU) **6733**
• Europaeischer Wirtschaftsdienst. Pulp and Paper (DEU) **6733**
• Europaeischer Wirtschaftsdienst. Recycling and Waste Management (DEU) **3506**
Europaeischer Wirtschaftsdienst. Recycling und Entsorgung (DEU) **3506**
Europaeischer Wirtschaftsdienst. Service Papier et Pate (DEU) **6733**
† Europaeischer Wirtschaftsdienst. Timber (DEU) **8954**
Europaeischer Wirtschaftsdienst. Verpackung (DEU) **6709**
Europaeischer Wirtschaftsdienst. Wasser und Abwasser (DEU) **8823**
• Europaeischer Wirtschaftsdienst. Wood Products and Panels (DEU) **3711**
Europaeisches Archiv fuer Soziologie *see* Archives Europeennes de Sociologie **8088**
Europaeisches Forum (DEU ISSN 0721-3018) **7233**
▼ • Europaeisches Journal fuer Minderheitenfragen (AUT ISSN 1865-1089) **7206**
• Europaeisches Patentamt. Amtsblatt/European Patent Office. Official Journal (DEU ISSN 0170-9291) **6749**
• Europaeisches Patentblatt (Online) (DEU) **6749**
† • Europaeisches Patentblatt (Print)/Bulletin Europeen des Brevets/European Patent Bulletin (DEU ISSN 0170-9305) **8954**
Europaeisches Transportrecht *see* European Transport Law **8495**
Europaeisches Uebereinkommen ueber die Internationale Befoerderung Gefaehrlicher Gueter auf der Strasse (A D R) (DEU ISSN 0173-0037) **8524**
Europaeisches Wirtschafts- und Steuerrecht (DEU ISSN 0938-3050) **4924**
Europaeisches Zuckerjournal *see* F.O. Licht's Europaeisches Zuckerjournal **109**
Europaeisk Debat *see* Europaeisk Politik **4924**
Europaeisk Dokumentation *see* Documentation Europeene **8366**
Europaeisk Fiskeri *see* Fisheries and Aquaculture in Europe **3592**
• Europaeisk Politik (DNK ISSN 0909-1076) **4924**
Europaeiske Centralbank. Arsberetning *see* European Central Bank. Annual Report **1339**
Europaeiske Centralbank. Manedsoversigt (DEU ISSN 1561-0241) **1339**
De Europaeiske Faelleskabers Tidende. Tillaeg. Forhandlinger *see* Diario Oficial de las Comunidades Europeas. Anexo Debates **4923**
De Europaeiske Faellesskabers Konkurrencepolitik. Beretning om Konkurrencepolitikken *see* European Community Competition Policy. Report on Competition Policy **1885**
De Europaeiske Faellesskabers Tidende. L & C: Retsforskrifter, Meddelelser og Oplysninger *see* Official Journal of the European Union. L & C Series: Legislation and Information Notices (Quarterly Edition) **4937**
Europaeiske Faellesskabers Tidende. L: Retsforskrifter *see* Official Journal of the European Union. L Series: Legislation **7256**
Europaeiske Investeringsbank. Information *see* European Investment Bank. Information **1622**
Europaeiske Unie. Bulletin *see* European Union. Bulletin **1485**
Europaeiske Union *see* E U **1097**
Europaeiske Union Fakta *see* E U Fakta **7231**
† • Europages (FRA ISSN 0762-4468) **8954**
• Europages (FRA ISSN 1638-1548) **1992**
Az Europai Unio Agrargazdasaga (HUN ISSN 1416-6194) **108**
Europaika Keimena *see* Documentation Europeene **8366**
Europaika Themata *see* European File **1563**
Europaike Kentrike Trapeza. Etesia Ekthese *see* European Central Bank. Annual Report **1339**
Europaike Kentrike Trapeza. Meniaio Deltio (DEU ISSN 1561-025X) **1339**
Europaike Trapeza Ependuseon. Plerofories *see* European Investment Bank. Information **1622**
Europaikes Enoses. Deltio *see* European Union. Bulletin **1485**
Europaische Gemeinschaft Wirtschaftsrecht Aussenwirtschaft *see* E G Wirtschaftsrecht Aussenwirtschaft **8952**
De Europaiske Fallesskabers Tidende. C: Meddelelser og Oplysninger *see* Official Journal of the European Union **7256**
De Europaiske Fallesskabers Tidende. C: Meddelelser og Oplysninger *see* Diario Oficial de las Comunidades Europeas. C: Comunicaciones e Informaciones **4923**
Europaraettslig Tidskrift (SWE ISSN 1403-8722) **4668**
Europarecht (DEU ISSN 0531-2485) **4924**
Europarecht. Beiheft *see* Europarecht **4924**
EuroParking (DEU ISSN 1862-1724) **8579**
Europastimme (AUT ISSN 0014-2727) **7233**
Europastudier *see* European Studies **4219**
• Europavegen (NOR ISSN 1500-0303) **8101**
• Europe (FRA ISSN 0014-2751) **5215**
L'Europe (FRA ISSN 1775-9501) **4668**
Europe *see* E U R **5608**
Europe (LUX) **3837**
• Europe (Paris, 1991) (FRA ISSN 1163-8184) **4668**
Europe (Year) (USA ISSN 0883-2498) **8702**
• Europe & Americas Petrochemical Scan (USA ISSN 1931-1796) **6768**
Europe and Americas Petrochemical Scan *see* Europe & Americas Petrochemical Scan **6768**
Europe and Americas Petrochemicalscan *see* Platt's Petrochemicalscan (Online) **6789**
Europe and the Balkans International Network (ITA ISSN 1721-3363) **7233**
Europe Asia Studies *see* Europe - Asia Studies **1106**
• ➤ Europe - Asia Studies (GBR ISSN 0966-8136) **1106**
Europe Bulletin (GBR ISSN 0967-618X) **1742**
Europe. Bulletin Quotidien (BEL ISSN 0423-6386) **7233**
Europe Buyout Review (Year) (GBR ISSN 0965-2698) **1622**
Europe by Eurail (USA ISSN 1548-6788) **8702**
• Europe - Corporate Taxation (NLD) **1922**
Europe Day May 9th *see* Ad- Dustour **3901**
Europe de Tradition Orale (BEL ISSN 0755-9313) **5117**
Europe. Diplomatie & Defense (BEL ISSN 1784-0759) **7233**
Europe. Documents (BEL ISSN 1026-3012) **7233**
Europe du Centre Est *see* East Central Europe **4216**
Europe du Sud-Est *see* Southeastern Europe **4266**
• Europe-Echecs (FRA ISSN 0014-2794) **8171**
Europe Echecs (FRA ISSN 0763-5982) **4334**
Europe Energie *see* Europe Energy **3134**
• Europe Energy (BEL ISSN 1021-4259) **3134**
Europe Entreprises *see* European Intelligence **1484**
Europe Environment *see* Europolitics Environment **3431**
Europe Environnement *see* European Information Environnement **3430**
L'Europe et les Europes (BEL ISSN 1422-9846) **4219**
† Europe et Liberte Magazine (FRA ISSN 1164-7957) **8954**
Europe Federale (FRA ISSN 1958-3672) **7233**
Europe for Business Travelers (USA ISSN 0749-4815) **8702**
Europe horis Sunora *see* Frontier-Free Europe **1566**
• Europe - Individual Taxation (NLD) **1922**
Europe Information *see* Europolitics **1340**
Europe Information Development (LUX ISSN 1012-2184) **1595**
Europe Information Developpement *see* Europe Information Development **1595**
• Europe Information Social (English Edition) (BEL ISSN 1811-4148) **7233**
• Europe Information Social (French Edition) (BEL ISSN 1811-413X) **7233**
Europe Locale (FRA ISSN 1265-3292) **7492**
Europe Metal *see* Revue Europe Metal **6331**
▼ Europe - New Zealand Research Series (NZL ISSN 1177-8229) **8101**
• Europe/North America - Corporate Investment Income (NLD) **1922**
• Europe/North America - Private Investment Income (NLD) **1922**
Europe on Forty Dollars a Day (USA) **8702**
Europe: Personnel and Development (GBR ISSN 1369-7404) **1861**
Europe Plurielle *see* Multiple Europes **7253**
† Europe Plurilingue (FRA ISSN 1161-8884) **8954**
• Europe Real Estate Yearbook (NLD ISSN 1871-4633) **7590**
• Europe Review (London) (GBR ISSN 1461-4014) **1992**
• Europe Review (Saffron Walden) (GBR ISSN 0269-3852) **1484**
Europe sans Frontieres *see* Frontier-Free Europe **1566**
Europe Telecom East and West *see* European Telecom East & West **2367**
• Europe Today (USA) **7641**
Europe Transports *see* Transport Europe **8514**
Europe TravelBook (USA ISSN 1074-7516) **8702**
Europe Verte *see* Green Europe **116**
Europea de Derecho. Avance Normativo (ESP ISSN 1576-9879) **4950**
Europea Elite Jurisprudencial. Colleccion Juridica (ESP ISSN 1697-3666) **4668**
Europea: Ethnomusicologies and Modernities (USA) **6565**
• ➤ European Academy of Dermatology and Venereology. Journal (GBR ISSN 0926-9959) **5876**
• ➤ European Academy of Dermatology and Venereology. Journal. Supplement (GBR ISSN 0929-0168) **5876**
European Academy of Legal Theory Series (GBR) **4668**
• The European Academy of Sciences. Annals (BEL ISSN 1784-0686) **7853**
European Accounting Focus (GBR ISSN 0955-4882) **1287**
• ➤ The European Accounting Review (GBR ISSN 0963-8180) **1287**
• ➤ European Addiction Research (CHE ISSN 1022-6877) **2694**
• European Adhesives and Sealants (GBR ISSN 1478-9574) **6311**
European Adhesives & Sealants Yearbook and Directory (GBR ISSN 0966-8268) **6717**
▼ ➤ European Administrative Law Series (NLD) **4668**
• European Advertising & Media Forecast (GBR ISSN 0951-7758) **25**
• European Affairs (USA ISSN 1527-8158) **7233**
• European Agency for Safety and Health at Work. Annual Report (ESP ISSN 1681-0155) **6676**
• European Agency for Safety and Health at Work. Conference Proceedings (ESP) **6676**
European Agency for Safety and Health at Work. Fact Sheets *see* European Agency for Safety and Health at Work. Facts **6676**
• European Agency for Safety and Health at Work. Facts (ESP ISSN 1681-2123) **6676**
• European Agency for Safety and Health at Work. Forum (ESP ISSN 1681-4398) **6676**
• European Agency for Safety and Health at Work. Magazine (ESP ISSN 1608-4144) **6677**
† • European Agency for Safety and Health at Work. Newsletter (ESP ISSN 1029-7022) **8954**
European Agency News *see* European Agency for Safety and Health at Work. Newsletter **8954**
European Agenda (DEU) **7134**
European AIDS Directory (GBR) **5813**
European Air Law (NLD) **8540**
European Air Law Association Conference Papers (NLD) **8540**
▼ European Alternative Investments Journal (FRA ISSN 1957-4045) **1339**
European Aluminium Association. Aluminium Quarterly Report (BEL) **6311**
European and American Painting, Sculpture and Decorative Arts, Volume 1: 1300-1800 (CAN) **6523**
European and International Criminal Law Series (NLD) **4889**
European and International Resarch Group on Crime, Ethics and Social Philosophy Quarterly Review *see* E R C E S Quarterly Review **2651**
European and Mediterranean Plant Protection Organization Bulletin *see* E P P O Bulletin **228**
European and Transatlantic Studies (DEU ISSN 1431-3006) **1106**
European Annals of Allergy and Clinical Immunology (ITA ISSN 1764-1489) **5758**
European Antitrust Review (GBR ISSN 1466-6065) **4668**
European Aquaculture in (Year) (LUX) **3590**
European Aquaculture Society. Special Publications (BEL ISSN 0774-0689) **3590**
• ➤ European Archives of Oto-Rhino-Laryngology (DEU ISSN 0937-4477) **6079**
European Archives of Oto-Rhino-Laryngology. Supplement *see* European Archives of Oto-Rhino-Laryngology **6079**
• ➤ European Archives of Paediatric Dentistry (GBR ISSN 1818-6300) **5843**
• ➤ European Archives of Psychiatry and Clinical Neuroscience (DEU ISSN 0940-1334) **6139**
European Aspects, Law Series (FRA ISSN 0531-2671) **4668**
European Aspects, Social Studies Series (FRA ISSN 0531-2663) **8101**
European Association for Animal Production. Annual Meeting. Book of Abstracts (NLD ISSN 1382-6077) **179**
➤ European Association for Animal Production. Scientific Series (NLD ISSN 0071-2477) **286**
European Association for Animal Production. Technical Series (NLD ISSN 1570-7318) **286**
• European Association for Health Information and Libraries. Journal (NLD ISSN 1841-0715) **5610**
European Association for International Education Forum *see* E A I E Forum **3012**
European Association for International Education Occasional Paper *see* E A I E Occasional Paper **3012**
European Association for International Education Professional Development Series for International Educators *see* E A I E Professional Development Series for International Educators **3012**
European Association for Personnel Management. Congress Reports (FRA ISSN 0071-2493) **1861**
European Association for Potato Research Abstracts of Conference Papers, Posters and Demonstrations *see* E A P R Abstracts of Conference Papers, Posters and Demonstrations **228**
European Association for Research on Plant Breeding. Report of the Congress (DEU ISSN 0071-2515) **3729**
➤ European Association for Theoretical Computer Science. Bulletin (GRC ISSN 0252-9742) **2600**
• European Association of Development Research and Training Institutes. Annual Report (DEU) **1595**
European Association of Development Research and Training Institutes Newsletter *see* E A D I Newsletter **1594**
European Association of Fish Pathologists. Bulletin (GBR ISSN 0108-0288) **942**
† European Association of Fisheries Economists. Bulletin (DNK ISSN 0967-5795) **8954**
European Association of Geoscientists and Engineers. Conference and Technical Exhibition (NLD ISSN 1028-3668) **2733**
European Association of Geoscientists and Engineers Special Publication *see* E A G E Special Publication **2732**
European Association of Remote Sensing Laboratories Se L Newsletter *see* E A R Se L Newsletter **2705**
European Association of Tax Law Professors International Tax Series *see* E A T L P International Tax Series **1921**
European Association of Urology - European Board of Urology Update Series *see* E A U - E B U Update Series **6267**
European Association of Zoos and Aquaria Conference. Proceedings (NLD ISSN 1876-2832) **942**
European Association of Zoos and Aquaria News *see* E A Z A News **941**
European Association of Zoos and Aquaria Yearbook *see* E A Z A Yearbook **941**
European Astronomical Society Publications Series *see* E A S Publications Series **574**
European Automotive Components News (GBR ISSN 1747-5279) **8579**
• European Automotive Design (GBR ISSN 1368-552X) **8579**
European Aviation Safety Seminar. Proceedings (USA ISSN 1533-5038) **53**
European Baker (GBR ISSN 1351-0762) **3673**
• European Bank for Reconstruction and Development. Working Paper (GBR ISSN 0969-8906) **1595**
• European Banker (GBR ISSN 0953-8399) **1339**
The European Banking Review (GBR) **1339**
European Bibliography of Slavic and East European Slavonic Studies/Bibliographie Europeenne des Travaux sur l'ex-URSS et l'Europe de l'Est/Europaeische Bibliographie Oesteuropastudien (FRA ISSN 1259-458X) **4170**
European Biopatent Watch *see* New Genetics and Society **876**
European BioPharmaceutical Review (GBR ISSN 1369-0663) **6838**
• ➤ European Biophysics Journal (DEU ISSN 0175-7571) **753**
The European Biotechnology Directory *see* BioCommerce Data's Business Profile Series. Volume 2. The European Biotechnology Directory **757**
• The European Biotechnology Directory (Year) (GBR ISSN 1462-9976) **763**
• European Biotechnology Science & Industry News (DEU ISSN 1618-8276) **764**
European Book Plates *see* Bibliografi over Europaeiske Kunstneres Ex Libris **8935**
• European Book World (GBR ISSN 1351-8275) **7560**
European Borzoi (DEU) **6808**
† • European Brewery Convention. Proceedings of the Congress (DEU ISSN 0367-018X) **8954**
• European Broadband (USA ISSN 1537-0011) **2381**
European Broadcasting Union Technical Review *see* E B U Technical Review **2319**
European Building Magazine *see* T R E - European Building Magazine **1039**
European Bulletin and Press (GBR ISSN 0309-474X) **7134**
➤ European Bulletin of Himalayan Research (DEU ISSN 0943-8254) **339**
European Business (LUX) **1106**
European Business Air News (GBR ISSN 0959-1311) **8540**
• European Business Forum (GBR ISSN 1469-6460) **1106**
European Business Information Conference (Year) Proceedings (GBR) **1107**
• ➤ European Business Journal (DEU ISSN 0955-808X) **1107**
• ➤ European Business Law Review (NLD ISSN 0959-6941) **4668**
• European Business Organization Law Review (NLD ISSN 1566-7529) **4668**
• ➤ European Business Review (Bingley) (GBR ISSN 0955-534X) **1107**
European Business Review (London) (GBR ISSN 1741-9433) **1107**
• European Buyouts Daily (USA) **1339**
• European C E O (Chief Executive Officer) (GBR ISSN 1755-2206) **1742**
• The European Campaigner (GBR ISSN 1353-0011) **7233**
European Can Makers Report (GBR) **603**
• European Car (USA ISSN 1056-8476) **8579**
European Card Review *see* Payments Cards and Mobile **1374**
• European Cardiovascular Disease (GBR ISSN 1752-9794) **5786**
European Catering Report (GBR) **3635**
• ➤ European Cells & Materials (CHE ISSN 1473-2262) **731**
European Cement Association. European Annual Review (BEL ISSN 1010-7185) **1007**
European Cement Association. World Statistical Review (BEL ISSN 0777-611X) **1046**
• European Central Bank. Annual Report (DEU ISSN 1561-4573) **1339**
† European Central Bank. Compendium: Collection of Legal Instruments (DEU) **8954**
• European Central Bank. Convergence Report (DEU ISSN 1725-9312) **1339**
• European Central Bank. Financial Stability Review (DEU ISSN 1830-2017) **1339**
• European Central Bank. Monthly Bulletin (DEU ISSN 1561-0136) **1339**

Title

10258 EUROPEAN CENTRAL BANK. OCCASIONAL PAPERS ULRICH'S PERIODICALS

• European Central Bank. Occasional Papers (DEU ISSN 1607-1484) **1339**
European Central Bank. Payment and Securities Settlement Systems in the European Union and in the Acceding Countries *see* European Central Bank. Statistics on Payments, and Securities Trading, Clearing and Settlement **1339**
European Central Bank. Payment Systems in the European Union *see* European Central Bank. Statistics on Payments, and Securities Trading, Clearing and Settlement **1339**
• European Central Bank. Statistics on Payments, and Securities Trading, Clearing and Settlement (DEU) **1339**
• European Central Bank. Working Papers (Online) (DEU ISSN 1725-2806) **1339**
European Central Bank. Working Papers (Print) *see* European Central Bank. Working Papers (Online) **1339**
European Centre for Development Policy Management Discussion Paper *see* E C D P M Discussion Paper **1562**
European Centre for Development Policy Management Occasional Paper *see* E C D P M Occasional Paper **7435**
European Centre for Ecotoxicology and Toxicology of Chemicals Document *see* E C E T O C Document **3496**
European Centre for Ecotoxicology and Toxicology of Chemicals Monograph *see* E C E T O C Monograph **3496**
European Centre for Ecotoxicology and Toxicology of Chemicals Special Report (New Series) *see* E C E T O C Special Report (New Series) **3496**
European Centre for Ecotoxicology and Toxicology of Chemicals Technical Report *see* E C E T O C Technical Report **3496**
† • European Centre for Medium-Range Weather Forecasts. Technical Report (GBR ISSN 1012-6899) **8954**
European Centre for Minority Issues Journal on Ethnopolitics and Minority Issues in Europe *see* E C M I Journal on Ethnopolitics and Minority Issues in Europe **3530**
• ➤ European Centre for Minority Issues. Working Paper (DEU ISSN 1435-9812) **3533**
European Centre for Space News *see* E C S L News **53**
European Centre for the Development of Vocational Training. Annual Report (GRC) **6697**
• ➤ European Ceramic Society. Journal (GBR ISSN 0955-2219) **2040**
European Chemical News Chemscope *see* E C N Chemscope **3242**
European Chemical Risks & Environment Law (GBR ISSN 1464-9802) **4668**
• ➤ European Child & Adolescent Psychiatry (DEU ISSN 1018-8827) **6139**
European Cigar Cult Journal (AUT ISSN 1728-3574) **8486**
European Civil Aviation Conference (Report of Session) (FRA ISSN 0071-2558) **8540**
† European Clinical Laboratory (GBR ISSN 1047-5354) **8954**
European Clinical Laboratory. Buyers' Guide *see* European Clinical Laboratory **8954**
The European Clothing Retail Handbook (GBR) **2246**
European Co-Operation (FRA ISSN 0589-9575) **4925**
European Coal and Steel Community Financial Report *see* E C S C Financial Report **1921**
European Coatings Journal (DEU ISSN 0930-3847) **6717**
European Coffee Report (NLD ISSN 1027-748X) **3635**
European Coil Coating Association Directory (GBR ISSN 0964-8666) **6717**
European College of Sport Science News Bulletin *see* E C S S News Bulletin **8170**
▼ • ➤ European Comic Art (GBR ISSN 1754-3797) **488**
European Commercial Cases (GBR ISSN 0141-7266) **4668**
European Commission and International Tax Law Series *see* E C and International Tax Law Series **4662**
European Commission. Background Briefing (LUX) **7134**
European Commission Competition Policy Newsletter *see* E C Competition Policy Newsletter **7231**
European Commission Corporate Tax Law *see* E C Corporate Tax Law **8952**
European Commission. Directorate-General for Agriculture and Rural Development. Newsletter (BEL ISSN 1560-1862) **108**
• European Commission. European Union. Bulletin (LUX) **7233**
European Commission Inform Transport *see* E C Inform Transport **8952**
• European Commission. Joint Research Center. Annual Report (BEL ISSN 0376-5482) **7134**
European Commission. Report on Competition Policy *see* European Community Competition Policy. Report on Competition Policy **1885**
European Commission. Tacis Programme. Contract Information Update (LUX) **1595**
• European Communications (GBR ISSN 1367-9996) **2320**
European Communities. Asylum-Seekers (LUX ISSN 1029-354X) **7233**
European Communities. Cost (LUX ISSN 1015-8642) **1922**
• European Communities. Court of Justice and Court of First Instance. Proceedings (LUX ISSN 1018-5933) **4950**
European Communities. Economic and Social Committee. Bulletin. (LUX ISSN 0256-5846) **1107**
European Communities. Economic and Social Committee. Commission Documents (LUX) **1107**
European Communities. Economic and Social Consultative Assembly. Annual Report (LUX ISSN 1011-5269) **1107**
European Communities Economic Data Pocketbook *see* E C Economic Data Pocketbook **1478**
European Communities Environmental Policy Series (NLD ISSN 0927-5886) **3430**
• European Communities. European Environment Agency. Annual Report (LUX ISSN 1561-2120) **3430**
European Communities Fisheries Cooperation Bulletin *see* E C Fisheries Cooperation Bulletin **3590**
European Communities Legislation: Current Status (GBR ISSN 0950-7361) **4669**
European Communities Legislation Implementator *see* E C Legislation Implementator **4924**
European Communities. Official Journal. C: Information and Notices *see* Official Journal of the European Union **7256**
European Communities. Official Journal. C Series *see* Justis CD-ROM Official Journal. C Series **4934**
European Communities Tax Review *see* E C Tax Review **1921**
European Communities Tenders *see* E C Tenders **1814**
European Community Cases (GBR ISSN 0954-710X) **4669**
European Community Competition Law Handbook *see* E C Competition Law Handbook **4923**
European Community Competition Law Report *see* E C Competition Law Report **4662**
European Community Competition Law Reporter *see* E C Competition Law Reporter **4662**
European Community Competition Policy. Report on Competition Policy (LUX ISSN 1609-5111) **1885**
European Community Humanitarian Office. Annual Report (LUX) **1595**
European Community Humanitarian Office News *see* E C H O News **1594**
European Community Law Series (GBR) **4925**
European Community Merger Control Reporter *see* E C Merger Control Reporter **4866**
European Community Shipowners' Associations. Annual Report (BEL) **8643**
European Community Shipowners' Associations. Newsletter (BEL) **8643**
European Community Tax Journal *see* E C Tax Journal **1921**
European Companies (GBR ISSN 0071-2582) **1227**
• ➤ European Company and Financial Law Review (DEU ISSN 1613-2548) **4867**
European Company for the Financing of Railway Rolling Stock. Annual Report (CHE ISSN 0071-2264) **8617**
• European Company Law (NLD ISSN 1572-4999) **4867**
European Company Profiles *see* P P I's European Company Profiles **6735**
• ➤ European Competition Journal (GBR ISSN 1744-1056) **4669**
European Competition Law Annual (GBR ISSN 1467-744X) **4669**
European Competition Law Review *see* E C L R: European Competition Law Review **4924**
• European Competitiveness Report (LUX ISSN 1682-0800) **1107**
European Computer Manufacturers Association Memento *see* E C M A Memento **2492**
European Conference on Computer Supported Cooperative Work. Proceedings (NLD) **2418**
European Conference on Optical Communication. Proceedings (USA) **3192**
• European Conference on Software Maintenance and Reengineering. Proceedings (USA ISSN 1534-5351) **2589**
† European Congress of Cardiology. Abstracts of Papers (GBR ISSN 0421-7527) **8954**
• European Congress of Cardiology. Proceedings (Online) (FRA) **5786**
European Congress of Cardiology. Proceedings (Print) *see* European Congress of Cardiology. Proceedings (Online) **5786**
European Congress of Perinatal Medicine. Proceedings (CHE ISSN 0071-2698) **5989**
European Congress on Electron Microscopy. Proceeding (CZE ISSN 0071-2647) **899**
European Connections (GBR ISSN 1424-3792) **5293**
• ➤ European Constitutional Law Review (NLD ISSN 1574-0196) **4848**
European Construction Institute. Publication (GBR ISSN 1367-8140) **1007**
European Contributions to American Studies (NLD ISSN 1387-9332) **4292**
European Convention on Human Rights. Yearbook/Convention Europeenne des Droits de l'Homme. Annuaire (NLD ISSN 0071-2701) **7206**
• European Converting Industry Directory (GBR ISSN 0961-7507) **6733**
European Copyright and Designs Report (GBR ISSN 1467-6656) **6749**
European Corporate Finance Directory (GBR ISSN 1460-7158) **1339**
• European Cosmetic Markets (GBR ISSN 0957-1515) **594**
European Council of Information Associations Views *see* E C I A Views **2319**
European Council of International Schools Higher Education Directory *see* E C I S Higher Education Directory **2955**
European Court of Human Rights. Reports of Judgements and Decisions/Cour Europeenne des Droits de l'Homme. Recueil des Arrets et Decisions (FRA ISSN 1682-7449) **7206**
European Court Reports. Reports of European Community Staff Cases (LUX ISSN 1023-4209) **4669**
European Critical Traditions Series (GBR) **5293**
• European Cross-Border Estate Planning (GBR) **1922**
European Cultural Heritage Review *see* Europa Nostra **4451**
European Cultural Heritage Review. Special Edition: Awards (NLD ISSN 1875-2918) **442**
European Cultures (DEU) **4451**
European Currency Unit Eurobond Market *see* E C U - E U R O Eurobond Market **1225**
European Current Law (GBR ISSN 0964-0037) **4669**
European Current Law Yearbook (GBR ISSN 1351-9123) **4925**
European Cycle Routes (GBR ISSN 1368-8421) **8258**
• European Cytokine Network (Online) (FRA ISSN 1952-4005) **866**
The European D I Y Retailing Handbook (Do-it-Yourself) (GBR) **1816**
European Daily Carbon Markets (GBR ISSN 1750-290X) **3134**
European Dairy Magazine (DEU ISSN 0936-6318) **264**
† European Dance News (USA) **8954**
European Democracy Series (SWE ISSN 1652-5345) **7134**
• European Dermatology Review (GBR ISSN 1754-369X) **5876**
† • European Design Automation Conference. Proceedings (USA) **8954**
• European Development Policy Study Group Discussion Papers (GBR ISSN 1749-4591) **7963**
• ➤ European Diabetes Nursing (GBR ISSN 1551-7853) **5958**
The European Directory of Management Consultants (GBR ISSN 1355-0292) **1742**
European Directory of Sustainable and Energy Efficient Building - Components Services Materials (GBR) **1053**
▼ • European Distributed Institute of Taxonomy. Newsletter (FRA ISSN 1962-3402) **672**
• European Diversity and Autonomy Papers (ITA ISSN 1827-8361) **7134**
• ➤ European Document Series (IRL ISSN 0791-8097) **7233**
European Documentation *see* Documentation Europeene **8366**
• ➤ European Early Childhood Education Research Journal (GBR ISSN 1350-293X) **2855**
† European Earthquake Engineering (ITA ISSN 0394-5103) **8954**
• ➤ European Eating Disorders Review (GBR ISSN 1072-4133) **7355**
• ➤ European Economic Association. Journal (USA ISSN 1542-4766) **1563**
• European Economic Perspectives (GBR ISSN 1351-7937) **1541**
• ➤ European Economic Review (NLD ISSN 0014-2921) **1107**
European Economy (LUX ISSN 0379-0991) **1484**
• European Economy. Series A: Recent Economic Trends (LUX) **1484**
• European Economy. Series B: Business and Consumer Survey Results (LUX) **1484**
European Economy. Special Report *see* European Economy **1484**
• ➤ European Education (USA ISSN 1056-4934) **2855**
European Educational Research Association Bulletin *see* E E R A Bulletin **2843**
• ➤ European Educational Research Journal (GBR ISSN 1474-9041) **2855**
European Electoral Studies *see* Evropska Volebni Studia **7134**
European Electric Motors (GBR) **3307**
• European Electronics Engineer (GBR ISSN 1742-9579) **3099**
• European Electronics Markets Forecasts (GBR ISSN 1364-2197) **3099**
European Employment Law Review (NLD ISSN 1385-1748) **1680**
• European Employment Review (GBR ISSN 1754-0143) **1680**
• European Endocrine Disease (GBR ISSN 1753-397X) **5892**
• ➤ European Energy and Environmental Law Review (NLD) **4669**
▼ European Energy Review (NLD ISSN 1875-3744) **3134**
European English Messenger (CHE ISSN 0960-4545) **5117**
European Entomology Journal *see* Linneana Belgica **854**
European Entrepreneur (GBR) **1107**
European Environment *see* Environmental Policy and Governance **3427**
• European Environment & Packaging Law Weekly (GBR ISSN 1750-0079) **3506**
European Environment Law for Industry (GBR ISSN 1353-3525) **3430**
European Environmental Education Newsletter ~ n *see* e e e ~ n **3414**
European Environmental Law (NLD) **3430**
European Environmental Law Annual (NLD ISSN 1566-5429) **4669**
European Environmental Law Review *see* European Energy and Environmental Law Review **4669**
European Equipment Index (GBR) **1007**
European Essay (GBR) **7134**
• European Executive Education Directory (Online Edition) (NLD) **1742**
European Executive Education Directory (Print Edition) *see* European Executive Education Directory (Online Edition) **1742**
▼ ➤ European Expansion and Indigenous Response (NLD ISSN 1873-8974) **4452**
European Federation of Corrosion. Newsletter (GBR) **6311**
European Federation of Corrosion. Publications (GBR ISSN 1354-5116) **6311**
European Federation of Finance House Associations. Annual Report (BEL ISSN 0071-2787) **1339**
European Federation of Finance House Associations. Newsletter (BEL ISSN 0300-4252) **1339**
European Fiber Optics Report (USA) **2497**
European File (BEL ISSN 0379-3133) **1563**
• ➤ European Financial Management (GBR ISSN 1354-7798) **1339**
European Financial Management & Marketing Association Magazine (English Edition) *see* E F M A Magazine (English Edition) **1740**
European Financial Management and Marketing Association Magazine (French Edition) *see* E F M A Magazine (French Edition) **1336**
European Fine Wine Magazine *see* Fine **603**
European Fish Price Report *see* Globefish. European Fish Price Report **3595**
European Fish Price Report (MYS) **3590**
European Fish Trader *see* Fish Update **8313**
European Focus (GBR ISSN 1357-8030) **1339**
European Focus Focus *see* E U Focus **1562**
➤ European Food and Feed Law Review (DEU ISSN 1862-2720) **3635**
European Food Databook *see* World Food Data & Statistics **3668**
European Food Marketing Directory *see* World Food Marketing Directory **3668**
• ➤ European Food Research and Technology (DEU ISSN 1438-2377) **3669**
The European Forecourt Retailing Handbook (GBR) **1816**
• ➤ European Foreign Affairs Review (NLD ISSN 1384-6299) **7233**
• European Foreign Policy Bulletin Online (ITA) **7233**
European Foreign Policy Unit Working Papers *see* E F P U Working Papers **7231**
European Forest Institute. Discussion Paper (FIN ISSN 1455-6936) **3687**
European Forest Institute News *see* E F I News **3687**
European Forest Institute Proceedings *see* E F I Proceedings **3687**
➤ European Forest Institute. Research Reports (FIN ISSN 1238-8785) **3687**
European Foundation. Briefing Paper (GBR) **7233**
European Foundation for the Improvement of Living and Working Conditions. Annual Report (IRL ISSN 1016-5614) **1680**
European Foundation for the Improvement of Living and Working Conditions. Bulletin from the Foundation (IRL ISSN 1028-5962) **7963**
European Foundation for the Improvement of Living and Working Conditions. Communique *see* Eurofound News **7516**
• European Foundation for the Improvement of Living and Working Conditions. Information Booklet Series (LUX) **1680**
European Foundations (GBR ISSN 1460-3187) **3266**
European Franchising (GBR ISSN 1469-3070) **1816**
European Free Trade Association. Annual Report (CHE ISSN 0258-3844) **1563**
European Free Trade Association Bulletin *see* E F T A Bulletin **1562**
European Fuel Price Service (USA ISSN 1938-7644) **6768**
▼ European Fuel Price Service. Germany and Italy (USA ISSN 1943-8435) **6768**
▼ European Fuel Price Service. United Kingdom (USA ISSN 1943-8443) **6768**
European Furniture (HKG ISSN 1018-6034) **4556**
European Gen-Set Directory *see* European Generating Set Directory **3307**
European Generating Set Directory (GBR) **3307**
† European Geophysical Society Series on Hydrological Sciences (NLD ISSN 0928-9542) **8954**

Title

10260 EUROPEAN JOURNAL OF ORAL IMPLANTOLOGY ULRICH'S PERIODICALS

▼ • European Journal of Oral Implantology (GBR ISSN 1756-2406) **5843**
• ➤ European Journal of Oral Sciences (DNK ISSN 0909-8836) **5844**
• European Journal of Oral Sciences Online (DNK ISSN 1600-0722) **5844**
• ➤ European Journal of Organic Chemistry (DEU ISSN 1434-193X) **2122**
• European Journal of Oriental Medicine (GBR ISSN 1351-6647) **309**
• ➤ European Journal of Orthodontics (GBR ISSN 0141-5387) **5844**
• ➤ European Journal of Orthopaedic Surgery & Traumatology (FRA ISSN 1633-8065) **6060**
• ➤ European Journal of Paediatric Dentistry (ITA ISSN 1591-996X) **5844**
• European Journal of Paediatric Neurology (GBR ISSN 1090-3798) **6091**
• ➤ European Journal of Pain (GBR ISSN 1090-3801) **5611**
European Journal of Pain Supplements *see* European Journal of Pain **5611**
• European Journal of Palliative Care (GBR ISSN 1352-2779) **5945**
➤ European Journal of Parapsychology (GBR ISSN 0168-7263) **6741**
➤ European Journal of Parenteral Sciences (GBR ISSN 0964-4679) **6838**
European Journal of Pediatric Dermatology (English Edition) (ITA ISSN 1122-7672) **5876**
• European Journal of Pediatric Dermatology (Italian Edition) (ITA ISSN 1122-7788) **5876**
• ➤ European Journal of Pediatric Surgery (DEU ISSN 0939-7248) **6243**
European Journal of Pediatric Surgery. Supplement (DEU ISSN 0939-6764) **6243**
• ➤ European Journal of Pediatrics (DEU ISSN 0340-6199) **6091**
European Journal of Pediatrics. Supplement (DEU ISSN 0943-9676) **6091**
• ➤ European Journal of Personality (GBR ISSN 0890-2070) **7355**
• ➤ European Journal of Pharmaceutical Sciences (NLD ISSN 0928-0987) **6838**
• ➤ European Journal of Pharmaceutics and Biopharmaceutics (NLD ISSN 0939-6411) **6838**
• ➤ European Journal of Pharmacology (NLD ISSN 0014-2999) **6838**
• ➤ European Journal of Philosophy (GBR ISSN 0966-8373) **6918**
• ➤ European Journal of Phycology (GBR ISSN 0967-0262) **787**
• ➤ European Journal of Physical and Rehabilitation Medicine (ITA) **6109**
• ➤ European Journal of Physics (GBR ISSN 0143-0807) **7011**
European Journal of Physiology *see* Pfluegers Archiv **5695**
• ➤ European Journal of Plant Pathology (NLD ISSN 0929-1873) **787**
▼ The European Journal of Plant Science and Biotechnology (GBR ISSN 1752-3842) **787**
• ➤ European Journal of Plastic Surgery (DEU ISSN 0930-343X) **6243**
• ➤ European Journal of Political Economy/Europaeische Zeitschrift fuer Politische Oekonomie (NLD ISSN 0176-2680) **7134**
• ➤ European Journal of Political Research (GBR ISSN 0304-4130) **7134**
• ➤ European Journal of Political Theory (GBR ISSN 1474-8851) **7134**
• ➤ European Journal of Population/Revue Europeenne de Demographie (NLD ISSN 0168-6577) **7306**
European Journal of Prosthodontics and Restorative Dentistry (GBR ISSN 0965-7452) **5844**
• ➤ European Journal of Protistology (DEU ISSN 0932-4739) **6724**
• ➤ The European Journal of Psychiatry (ESP ISSN 0213-6163) **6139**
• The European Journal of Psychiatry (Spanish Edition) (ESP ISSN 1579-699X) **6139**
• ➤ European Journal of Psychological Assessment (USA ISSN 1015-5759) **7356**
▼ • The European Journal of Psychology Applied to Legal Context (ESP ISSN 1889-1861) **7356**
• ➤ European Journal of Psychology of Education/Journal Europeen de Psychologie de l'Education (PRT ISSN 0256-2928) **2855**
• ➤ European Journal of Psychotherapy and Counselling (GBR) **6139**
• ➤ European Journal of Public Health (GBR ISSN 1101-1262) **7516**
▼ • ➤ European Journal of Pure and Applied Mathematics (TUR ISSN 1307-5543) **5487**
▼ • European Journal of Radiography (GBR ISSN 1756-1175) **6196**
• ➤ European Journal of Radiology (IRL ISSN 0720-048X) **6196**
• European Journal of Radiology Extra (USA ISSN 1571-4675) **6196**
• ➤ European Journal of Scientific Research (AUT ISSN 1450-216X) **7853**
• ➤ European Journal of Social Psychology (GBR ISSN 0046-2772) **7356**
• ➤ European Journal of Social Quality (GBR ISSN 1461-7919) **4452**
• ➤ The European Journal of Social Sciences (AUT ISSN 1450-2267) **7963**
• ➤ European Journal of Social Security (BEL ISSN 1388-2627) **4502**
• ➤ European Journal of Social Theory (GBR ISSN 1368-4310) **8101**
• ➤ European Journal of Social Work (GBR ISSN 1369-1457) **8039**
European Journal of Sociology *see* Archives Europeennes de Sociologie **8088**
• ➤ European Journal of Soil Biology (FRA ISSN 1164-5563) **672**
• ➤ European Journal of Soil Science (GBR ISSN 1351-0754) **229**
• ➤ European Journal of Spatial Development (SWE ISSN 1650-9544) **4410**
• ➤ European Journal of Special Needs Education (GBR ISSN 0885-6257) **3039**
• ➤ European Journal of Sport Science (GBR ISSN 1746-1391) **8171**
• ➤ European Journal of Surgical Oncology (GBR ISSN 0748-7983) **6019**
• ➤ European Journal of Teacher Education (GBR ISSN 0261-9768) **2855**
• ➤ The European Journal of Technology and Advanced Engineering Research (AUT ISSN 1450-202X) **8421**
† The European Journal of Teleworking (GBR ISSN 0966-7458) **8954**
• ➤ European Journal of the History of Economic Thought (GBR ISSN 0967-2567) **1541**
• European Journal of Theology (GBR ISSN 0960-2720) **7756**
European Journal of Traditional Chinese Medicine (NLD ISSN 1572-4875) **309**
• ➤ European Journal of Transport and Infrastructure Research (NLD ISSN 1567-7133) **8422**
European Journal of Trauma *see* European Journal of Trauma and Emergency Surgery **6060**
• ➤ European Journal of Trauma and Emergency Surgery (DEU ISSN 1863-9933) **6060**
† The European Journal of Trauma and Emergency Surgery (ITA ISSN 1828-440X) **8954**
• European Journal of Turkish Studies (FRA ISSN 1773-0546) **4321**
• ➤ European Journal of Ultrasound (IRL ISSN 0929-8266) **6196**
† European Journal of Underwater and Hyperbaric Medicine (DEU ISSN 1605-9204) **8955**
• ➤ European Journal of Vascular and Endovascular Surgery (GBR ISSN 1078-5884) **5786**
European Journal of Vascular and Endovascular Surgery Extra *see* E J V E S Extra **5785**
• ➤ European Journal of Wildlife Research (DEU ISSN 1612-4642) **319**
• ➤ European Journal of Women's Studies (GBR ISSN 1350-5068) **8896**
European Journal of Wood and Wood Industries (Online) *see* European Journal of Wood and Wood Industries (Print) **3711**
• European Journal of Wood and Wood Industries (Print) (DEU) **3711**
• ➤ European Journal of Work and Organizational Psychology (GBR ISSN 1359-432X) **7356**
▼ • European Journal on Child and Youth Research/Europaeische Zeitschrift fuer Kinder- und Jugendforschung/Revue Europeenne de Recherche sur l'Enfance et la Jeunesse (GBR) **2152**
• European Journal on Criminal Policy and Research (NLD ISSN 0928-1371) **2651**
European Journal on Mental Disability *see* Revue Europeenne du Handicap Mental **6182**
➤ European Journal Vocational Training (GRC) **2855**
European Journalism Review Series (DEU ISSN 1434-0976) **4575**
• European Joyce Studies (NLD ISSN 0923-9855) **5293**
• ➤ European Judaism (GBR ISSN 0014-3006) **7721**
European Juornal of International Review *see* Ouzhou Guoji Pinglun **7257**
European Kidney & Urological Disease *see* European Renal & Genito-Urinary Disease **6268**
European Late Effects Project Group - European Radiation Dosimetry Group - Union Internationale de R Newsletter *see* E U L E P - E U R A D O S - U I R Newsletter **3166**
• ➤ European Law Journal (GBR ISSN 1351-5993) **4925**
• European Law Reports (GBR ISSN 1091-3297) **4830**
• European Law Review (GBR ISSN 0307-5400) **4669**
European Law Students' Association Leiden Magazine *see* E L S A Leiden Magazine **4924**
European Law Students' Association Selected Papers on European Law *see* E L S A Selected Papers on European Law **4662**
• The European Lawyer (GBR ISSN 1470-9279) **4925**
European League for Economic Cooperation. Publications (BEL ISSN 0071-2884) **1595**
European League for Economic Cooperation. Report of the Secretary General on the Activities of E.L.E.C. (BEL ISSN 0531-7436) **1595**
• ➤ The European Legacy (GBR ISSN 1084-8770) **6918**
European Legal 500 *see* The Legal 500 - Europe, Middle East & Africa **2013**
European Legal Book Index (USA ISSN 1381-1002) **4669**
European Legal Business (GBR ISSN 1474-6239) **4867**
The European Legal Forum. Section I/Forum Iuris Communis Europae (DEU ISSN 1861-8383) **4925**
The European Legal Forum. Section II/Forum Iuris Communis Europae (DEU ISSN 1861-8391) **4925**
European Lenses & Technology (USA) **6041**
▼ European Literature for Children and Young Adults in an Inter-Cultural Context/Europaeische Kinder- und Jugendliteratur im Interkulturellen Kontext (CHE ISSN 1660-7538) **5293**
European Long-Term Insurance Market Assessment *see* Key Note Market Assessment. European Long-Term Insurance **4511**
European Mail Order and Distance Selling Trade Association Position Papers *see* E M O T A - A E V P C Position Papers **1815**
• ➤ European Management Journal (GBR ISSN 0263-2373) **1742**
• ➤ European Management Review (GBR ISSN 1740-4754) **1743**
European Marketing Data and Statistics (Year) (GBR ISSN 0071-2930) **1227**
European Marketing Forecasts (GBR) **1227**
European Marketing Pocket Book (Year) (GBR ISSN 0966-7717) **1816**
European Marketplace (USA) **4502**
European Markets: A Guide to Company and Industry Information Sources (USA ISSN 1044-9280) **1563**
European Marketscan (USA ISSN 0149-5836) **6768**
➤ European Materials Research Society. Symposia Proceedings (NLD ISSN 0927-5002) **3344**
• ➤ European Mathematical Society. Journal (CHE ISSN 1435-9855) **5487**
European Mathematical Society. Newsletter (CHE ISSN 1027-488X) **5487**
European Media Art Festival (DEU) **6497**
European Media Directory (GBR ISSN 0968-2694) **1992**
• European Medical Device Manufacturer (USA) **4486**
European Medical Laser Association. Journal *see* E M L A Laser Health Journal **5905**
European Medical Laser Association Laser Health Journal *see* E M L A Laser Health Journal **5905**
• ➤ European Medieval Drama (BEL ISSN 1378-2274) **5293**
➤ European Meetings in Ethnomusicology (ROM ISSN 1582-5841) **6565**
The European Mergers & Acquisitions Handbook (Years) (GBR ISSN 1366-283X) **1107**
European Microwave Association. Proceedings *see* International Journal of Microwave and Wireless Technologies **3321**
European Microwave Conference Proceedings (USA) **3308**
European Microwave Integrated Circuits Conference. Proceedings (USA) **2465**
European Molecular Biology Organization Journal *see* The E M B O Journal **731**
European Molecular Biology Organization Molecular Medicine *see* E M B O Molecular Medicine **5607**
European Molecular Biology Organization Reports *see* E M B O Reports **866**
• European Monetary Union (GBR ISSN 1462-320X) **1107**
European Monetary Union The News Bulletin *see* E M U - The News Bulletin **1096**
European Monographs (NLD ISSN 0926-9657) **4925**
European Monographs in Social Psychology (GBR ISSN 0892-7286) **7356**
European Mosquito Bulletin (GBR ISSN 1460-6127) **229**
• European Musculoskeletal Review (GBR ISSN 1754-5072) **6060**
European Music Directory. Vol. 1: Orchestras, Competitions and Prizes, Festivals, Agencies, Radio and Television, Associations and Foundations, Teaching and Instruction, Documentation and Research *see* International Music Directory. Vol. 1: Performed Music, Concert Management and Promotion Agencies, Teaching and Instruction **6577**
European Music Directory. Volume 2: Music Industry, Trade, Studios and Record Companies, Music Publishers, Indexes *see* International Music Directory. Volume 2: Radio and Television, Music Publishers, Documentation and Research, National Music Councils, Associations and Foundations, Indexes **6577**
European Network and Information Security Agency Quarterly *see* E N I S A Quarterly **2513**
European Network of Scientific and Technical Cooperation. Journal *see* Pact **410**
• European Neurological Disease (GBR ISSN 1753-3953) **6140**
• ➤ European Neurology (CHE ISSN 0014-3022) **6140**
• ➤ European Neuropsychopharmacology (NLD ISSN 0924-977X) **6140**
European Newsletter (GBR ISSN 1473-7868) **1563**
† European Newsletter of Southeast Asian Studies (NLD ISSN 0929-6727) **8955**
† European Observatory for S M Es. Annual Report (Small to Medium Enterprises) (NLD) **8955**
European Observatory on Health Systems and Policies *see* Euro Observer **7516**
European Occupational Health and Safety *see* EurOhs **6676**
• European Offshore Petroleum Newsletter (GBR ISSN 0332-5210) **6768**
European Oil and Gas Yearbook/Annuaire Europeen du Petrole et du Gaz/Europa-Jahrbuch Oel und Gas (DEU) **6768**
• The European Ombudsman. Annual Report (LUX ISSN 1680-3809) **4669**
• European Oncological Disease (GBR ISSN 1753-4100) **6019**
European Ophthalmological Society. Congress (SWE ISSN 0301-326X) **6041**
European Optical Society. Annual Meetings Digest Series (DEU ISSN 1022-0151) **7075**
• ➤ European Optical Society. Journal. Rapid Publications (DEU ISSN 1990-2573) **7075**
European Organization for Nuclear Research. List of Scientific Publications/Conseil Europeen pour la Recherche Nucleaire. Liste des Publications Scientifiques (CHE ISSN 0304-2871) **7048**
European Organization for Quality. Conference Proceedings (CHE) **8422**
▼ • European Orthopaedics and Traumatology (DEU) **6060**
European Packaging *see* PackReport **1837**
European Packaging (GBR ISSN 0966-4734) **6709**
European Packaging & Waste Law *see* European Environment & Packaging Law Weekly **3506**
• European Paint and Resin News (GBR ISSN 0266-7800) **6717**
European Panel Analysis Group. Working Paper (GBR) **1107**
European Papers on the New Welfare *see* Quaderni Europei sul Nuovo Welfare **8064**
European Parkinson's Disease Association Focus *see* E P D A Focus **8952**
European Parkinson's Disease Association Plus *see* E P D A Plus **6137**
European Parliament. Bulletin (LUX ISSN 0423-7846) **7134**
European Parliament. Group of the European People's Party. Christian Democrat Group. Report on the Activities (LUX) **7134**
European Parliament News *see* E P News **4924**
European Parliament's Official Handbook (LUX ISSN 0250-7781) **7134**
European Patent Bulletin *see* Europaeisches Patentblatt (Print) **8954**
European Patent Decisions (GBR) **6749**
• European Patent Office. Annual Report (DEU ISSN 0724-7729) **6749**
European Patent Office Applied Technology Series *see* E P O Applied Technology Series **7058**
European Patent Office. Official Journal *see* Europaeisches Patentamt. Amtsblatt **6749**
European Patent Office Reports (GBR ISSN 0269-0802) **6749**
European Patents Handbook (GBR) **6749**
European Patents Sourcefinder (GBR) **6749**
European Pattern Book (GBR) **8291**
▼ European Pensions (GBR ISSN 1753-5859) **1622**
• European Pensions News (GBR ISSN 1462-7973) **4502**
➤ European Pentecostal Theological Association. Journal (GBR ISSN 1812-4461) **7756**
European Perspectives: A Series in Social Thought and Cultural Criticism (USA) **339**
European Perspectives on Rural Development (NLD) **108**
• European Pharmaceutical Contractor (GBR ISSN 1364-369X) **6838**
European Pharmaceutical Executive *see* Pharmaceutical Executive Europe (Print) **8980**
European Pharmaceutical Intelligence Bulletin (GBR) **6838**
• European Pharmaceutical Review (GBR ISSN 1360-8606) **6839**
European Photochemistry Association Newsletter *see* E P A Newsletter **2134**
• European Photography (DEU ISSN 0172-7028) **6967**
European Photography (GBR) **6967**
• ➤ European Physical Education Review (GBR ISSN 1356-336X) **3061**
• ➤ European Physical Journal A. Hadrons and Nuclei (DEU ISSN 1434-6001) **7065**
• ➤ The European Physical Journal - Applied Physics (FRA ISSN 1286-0042) **7011**
• ➤ European Physical Journal B. Condensed Matter and Complex Systems (DEU ISSN 1434-6028) **7011**
• ➤ European Physical Journal C. Particles and Fields (DEU ISSN 1434-6044) **7011**
• ➤ European Physical Journal D. Atomic, Molecular, Optical and Plasma Physics (DEU ISSN 1434-6060) **7011**
• ➤ European Physical Journal Direct (DEU ISSN 1435-3725) **7011**
• ➤ European Physical Journal E. Soft Matter (DEU ISSN 1292-8941) **7011**
• ➤ European Physical Journal H (DEU) **7011**
• ➤ The European Physical Journal. Special Topics (DEU ISSN 1951-6355) **7012**
The European Physical Journal. Special Topics (Online) *see* The European Physical Journal. Special Topics **7012**
• ➤ European Planning Studies (GBR ISSN 0965-4313) **4410**
European Plastic Laminates Forum. Proceedings (USA) **7092**

Link to your serials resources and content with ulrichsweb.com

DIRECTORY 2010 EUROPEAN UNIVERSITY INSTITUTE PAPERS IN POLITICAL AND 10261

• European Plastics and Rubber Directory (GBR ISSN 1749-5571) **7092**
European Plastics and Rubber Machinery Manufacturers Association Economic Survey *see* E U R O M A P Economic Survey **7092**
European Plastics Directory *see* European Plastics and Rubber Directory **7092**
• European Plastics News (GBR ISSN 0306-3534) **7092**
European Players' Directory *see* Annuario degli Attori **6489**
European Policy/Cite Europeenne (BEL ISSN 1376-0890) **7436**
• European Policy Analyst (USA ISSN 1364-2758) **1484**
The European Policy Centre. Annual Report (BEL) **1484**
The European Policy Centre. Conference Reports (BEL) **1484**
• The European Policy Centre. Newsletter (BEL) **1484**
The European Policy Centre. Occasional Papers (BEL) **1484**
The European Policy Centre. Position Papers (BEL) **1484**
European Policy Focus (GBR) **7234**
• European Policy Research Papers (GBR) **7134**
European Policy Research Unit Papers *see* E P R U Papers **7131**
• ➤ European Political Science (GBR ISSN 1680-4333) **7134**
▼ • ➤ European Political Science Review (GBR ISSN 1755-7739) **7134**
• ➤ European Polymer Journal (GBR ISSN 0014-3057) **2123**
European Potato Markets Monthly (GBR ISSN 1360-4392) **197**
European Powder Coatings *see* Polymers Paint Color Year Book (Year) **6720**
European Powder Coatings *see* European Adhesives and Sealants **6311**
European Powder Coatings *see* P P C J **6719**
European Power Electronics Journal *see* E P E Journal **3094**
European Power News *see* Power (Houston) **3393**
European Power Watch (USA ISSN 1931-650X) **3134**
European Practice in Gynaecology and Obstetrics (NLD ISSN 1625-1180) **5990**
European Private Law (NLD ISSN 1874-8325) **4925**
European Procurement Directory (GBR ISSN 1356-9678) **1992**
European Production Engineering *see* E P E **3376**
European Promotional Products Industry (DEU ISSN 1435-5264) **25**
• ➤ European Psychiatry (FRA ISSN 0924-9338) **6140**
European Psychiatry (Spanish Edition) (ESP ISSN 1134-0665) **6140**
• ➤ European Psychologist (USA ISSN 1016-9040) **7356**
• European Psychotherapy (DEU ISSN 1435-9464) **7356**
The European Public Affairs Directory (Year) (GBR ISSN 0777-5814) **1564**
• ➤ European Public Law (NLD ISSN 1354-3725) **4925**
European Public Private Partnership Law Review (DEU ISSN 1863-0987) **4669**
European Pumps & Pumping (GBR) **3366**
• European Qualifying Examination (DEU ISSN 1022-4025) **6749**
European Quality (GBR ISSN 0969-059X) **8422**
European Quality Today (GBR) **1885**
European Quantum Electronics Conference. Proceedings (USA) **7075**
• European R T D Insight (BEL) **7853**
• European Race Bulletin (GBR ISSN 1463-9696) **3533**
• ➤ European Radiology (DEU ISSN 0938-7994) **6196**
European Radiology. Supplements *see* European Radiology **6196**
† European Rail Outlook (USA ISSN 1746-5427) **8955**
European Rail Timetable (GBR ISSN 1748-0817) **8495**
• European Railway Review (GBR ISSN 1351-1599) **8617**
European Real Estate Quarterly (USA ISSN 1065-3635) **7590**
European Regional Business and Economic Development Unit Working Papers *see* E R B E D U. Working Papers **1096**
European Regional Planning Study Series (FRA ISSN 0252-0990) **7492**
European Regional Prospects (GBR ISSN 1747-3756) **1484**
European Regional Prospects (Abridged Edition) (GBR ISSN 0969-4595) **1485**
European Regulation of Company and Securities Law (NLD ISSN 1871-7632) **4669**
• European Renal & Genito-Urinary Disease (GBR ISSN 1752-9034) **6268**
European Rental News *see* International Rental News **1890**
European Report *see* Europolitics **1340**
European Research Community on Flow Turbulence and Combustion Bulletin *see* E R C O F T A C Bulletin **7058**
European Research Community on Flow, Turbulence and Combustion Series *see* E R C O F T A C Series **7058**
European Research Consortium for Informatics and Mathematics News *see* E R C I M News **2350**
† ➤ European Research in Regional Science (GBR ISSN 0960-6130) **8955**
European Research on Cetaceans (DEU ISSN 1028-3412) **3590**
• European Respiratory Disease (GBR ISSN 1754-5552) **6213**
• ➤ The European Respiratory Journal (CHE ISSN 0903-1936) **6214**
European Respiratory Journal. Supplement (CHE ISSN 0904-1850) **6214**
European Respiratory Monograph (CHE ISSN 1025-448X) **6214**
• ➤ European Respiratory Review (CHE ISSN 0905-9180) **6214**
European Respiratory Topic (GBR ISSN 1355-493X) **6214**
European Retail Digest *see* The Retail Digest **1903**
European Retail Finance (GBR ISSN 1748-9172) **1340**
The European Retail Handbook (GBR) **1816**
European Retail Space (USA ISSN 1742-2566) **1816**
• ➤ European Review (GBR ISSN 1062-7987) **7853**
European Review for Medical and Pharmacological Sciences (ITA ISSN 1128-3602) **5611**
• European Review of Aging and Physical Activity (DEU ISSN 1813-7253) **4044**
• ➤ European Review of Agricultural Economics (GBR ISSN 0165-1587) **197**
European Review of Applied Psychology *see* Revue Europeene de Psychologie Appliquee **7405**
• European Review of Contract Law (DEU ISSN 1614-9920) **4669**
• ➤ European Review of Economic History (GBR ISSN 1361-4916) **1541**
• ➤ European Review of History/Revue Europeene d'Histoire (GBR ISSN 1350-7486) **4219**
➤ European Review of Latin American and Caribbean Studies/Revista Europea de Estudios Latinoamericanos y del Caribe (NLD ISSN 0924-0608) **7963**
European Review of Management and Business Economics *see* Revista Europea de Direccion y Economia de la Empresa **1581**
➤ European Review of Native American Studies (AUT ISSN 0238-1486) **6634**
• ➤ European Review of Private Law/Europaeische Zeitschrift fuer Privatrecht/Revue Europeenne de Droit Prive (NLD ISSN 0928-9801) **4925**
The European Review of Public Law (GRC ISSN 1105-1590) **4669**
• ➤ European Review of Social Psychology (Online Edition) (GBR ISSN 1479-277X) **7356**
• ➤ European Review of Social Psychology (Print Edition) (GBR ISSN 1046-3283) **7356**
• ➤ European Romantic Review (GBR ISSN 1050-9585) **5293**
• European Rubber Journal (GBR ISSN 0266-4151) **7824**
European Safeguard Research and Development Association Bulletin *see* E S A R D A Bulletin **7514**
European Savings Bank. Activity Report (BEL) **1340**
European School of Oncology. Scientific Updates (NLD ISSN 1387-6589) **6019**
▼ • European Science and Technology Review (USA ISSN 1937-3198) **7853**
➤ European Science Editing (GBR ISSN 0258-3127) **7560**
• European Science Foundation. Annual Report/European Science Foundation. Rapport Annuel (FRA) **7853**
European Science Foundation Communications *see* E S F Communications **7852**
European Science Foundation. Rapport Annuel *see* European Science Foundation. Annual Report **7853**
European Science Foundation. Scientific Papers and Position Papers (FRA) **7853**
• European Science Policy Briefing (FRA ISSN 1560-7623) **7853**
European Scientific Working Group on Influenza. Bulletin (GBR) **5813**
The European Screen Printer & Digital Images Magazine (GBR) **7320**
European Second Language Association Yearbook *see* E U R O S L A Yearbook **5113**
• European Securities Trading (USA ISSN 1092-0854) **1622**
• ➤ European Security (GBR ISSN 0966-2839) **7234**
European Security and Defence (DEU ISSN 1617-7983) **6420**
• European Semi Bulletin (GBR) **3099**
European Semiconductor *see* EuroAsia Semiconductor **3099**
European Semiotics (CHE ISSN 1423-5587) **5117**
European Series in Applied and Industrial Mathematics Control, Optimisation and Calculus of Variations *see* E S A I M: Control, Optimisation and Calculus of Variations **5485**
European Series in Applied and Industrial Mathematics Mathematical Modelling and Numerical Analysis *see* E S A I M: Mathematical Modelling and Numerical Analysis **5485**
European Series in Applied and Industrial Mathematics Probability & Statistics *see* E S A I M: Probability & Statistics **5485**
European Series in Applied and Industrial Mathematics Proceedings *see* E S A I M: Proceedings **5485**
European Services Industry (USA) **1885**
European Short Breaks Market Assessment *see* Key Note Market Assessment. European Short Breaks **1891**
European Sign Magazine (GBR ISSN 0924-5855) **25**
European Single Financial Market (Years) (GBR ISSN 1461-9326) **1340**
European Social Fund. Evaluation Unit. Impact of Evaluations (Year) (IRL ISSN 1029-8630) **8039**
European Social Statistics. Social Protection. Expenditure and Receipts (LUX ISSN 1681-9365) **8082**
• ➤ European Societies (GBR ISSN 1461-6696) **8101**
European Society for Engineering and Medicine News *see* E S E M News **5608**
European Society for Medical Oncology. Abstracts of the Congress (CHE ISSN 0937-8723) **6019**
European Society for Opinion and Marketing Research. Monograph Series (NLD) **1816**
European Society for Surgical Research. Congress Proceedings (ITA) **6243**
• European Society of Cardiology. Annual Report (FRA) **5786**
• European Society of Cardiology. Newsletter (FRA) **5786**
European Society of Human Reproduction and Embryology Monographs *see* The E S H R E Monographs **921**
• ➤ European Society of Women in Theological Research. Journal/Association Europeenne des Femmes pour la Recherche Theologique. Annuaire/Europaeische Gesellschaft fuer die Theologische Forschung von Frauen. Jahrbuch (BEL ISSN 1783-2454) **7641**
• ➤ European Sociological Review (GBR ISSN 0266-7215) **8101**
European Solid-State Circuits Conference Proceedings *see* E S S C I R C. Proceedings **3094**
European Solid State Device Research Conference. Proceedings (USA ISSN 1930-8876) **7087**
European Sourcebook of Crime and Criminal Justice Statistics (NLD ISSN 1874-4931) **2674**
• European Southern Observatory. Annual Report (DEU ISSN 0531-4496) **574**
European Southern Observatory Astrophysics Symposia *see* E S O Astrophysics Symposia **574**
European Space Agency *see* E S A - B R **53**
European Space Agency Annual Report *see* E S A Annual Report **53**
European Space Agency. Brochure *see* E S A - B R **53**
European Space Agency Bulletin *see* E S A Bulletin **53**
European Space Agency. Scientific and Technical Memoranda (ITA ISSN 0379-4075) **53**
European Space Agency. Scientific and Technical Reports (ITA ISSN 0379-4067) **53**
European Space Agency - Special Publication *see* E S A - S P **574**
European Space Directory (FRA ISSN 0765-0574) **53**
European Spatial Research and Policy (POL ISSN 1231-1952) **3430**
European Specialist Publishers Directory (GBR) **1992**
• ➤ European Spine Journal (DEU ISSN 0940-6719) **6243**
• ➤ European Sport Management Quarterly (GBR ISSN 1618-4742) **8172**
European Stainless Steel Directory (GBR) **6311**
European State Aid Law Quarterly (DEU ISSN 1619-5272) **4925**
European Steel Review (GBR ISSN 1369-8583) **1564**
European Steel Review Supplement *see* European Steel Review **1564**
European Structural Integrity Society Publication *see* E S I S Publication **3377**
European Studies (DNK ISSN 0906-0308) **4219**
• European Studies (NLD ISSN 1568-1858) **7234**
European Studies Amsterdam. Working Papers (NLD ISSN 1871-1693) **7963**
European Studies in Education (DEU ISSN 0946-6797) **2855**
European Studies in Philosophy of Medicine (NLD ISSN 1381-1150) **5611**
▼ ➤ European Studies in Private Law (NLD) **4669**
➤ European Studies in Sports History (ITA) **8172**
European Studies in the History of Science and Ideas (DEU ISSN 0948-7255) **7963**
European Studies Newsletter (USA ISSN 0046-2802) **7963**
European Studies of Population (NLD ISSN 1381-3579) **7283**
• ➤ European Surgery (AUT ISSN 1682-8631) **6243**
European Surgery. Acta Chirurgica Austriaca *see* European Surgery **6243**
European Surgery. Acta Chirurgica Austriaca Online *see* European Surgery Online **6243**
• ➤ European Surgery Online (AUT ISSN 1682-4016) **6243**
European Surgery. Supplement *see* European Surgery **6243**
• ➤ European Surgical Research (CHE ISSN 0014-312X) **6243**
European Synchrotron Radiation Facility News *see* E S R F News **7065**
European Tableware Buyers Guide (GBR ISSN 0264-5041) **535**
European Tax Handbook (Year) (NLD ISSN 0925-9759) **1922**
European Tax Service *see* Tax Planning International European Tax Service **1949**
• European Tax Service (GBR ISSN 1751-4746) **1922**
• European Taxation (NLD ISSN 0014-3138) **1922**
European Taxation Data Base on CD-ROM *see* European Taxation Database **1922**
• European Taxation Database (NLD) **1922**
European Technology Review (DEU) **4118**
• European Telecom East & West (USA) **2367**
European Telecom's Intelligence Bulletin (GBR ISSN 1468-4543) **2320**
European Telematics Horizontal Observatory Service Newsletter *see* E T H O S Newsletter **2350**
† • European Television (USA ISSN 1052-5068) **8955**
European Textiles *see* D N R **8449**
European Tool & Mould Making (DEU) **3366**
European Trade Mark Reports (GBR ISSN 1363-4542) **6749**
European Trade Union Institute. Discussion & Working Papers (BEL ISSN 1025-2533) **4593**
• ➤ European Transactions on Electrical Power (GBR ISSN 1430-144X) **3308**
European Transport Law/Derecho Europeo de Transportes/Diritto Europeo dei Trasporti/Droit Europeen des Transports/Europaeisches Transportrecht/Europees Vervoerrecht (BEL ISSN 0014-3154) **8495**
▼ • European Transport Research Review (DEU ISSN 1867-0717) **8495**
➤ European Transport - Trasporti Europei (ITA ISSN 1825-3997) **8495**
European Trash Cinema (USA) **6497**
European Travel and Entertainment Magazine (USA) **8702**
European Travel Guide for Jews *see* Guide Touristique Europeen pour Israelites **3536**
European Tropical Forest Research Network News *see* E T F R N News **669**
European Tropical Forest Research Network Series *see* E T F R N Series **3687**
European Truck + Bus Technology (GBR ISSN 1755-1625) **3192**
European Union Activities on Environmental Matters (BEL) **3431**
European Union and Competition Law Newsletter *see* E U and Competition Law Newsletter **4866**
European Union Baggrund *see* E U Baggrund **7231**
• European Union. Bulletin (LUX ISSN 1025-4005) **1485**
European Union. Bulletin. Supplement (LUX ISSN 1027-6424) **1485**
European Union Dairy Monitor *see* E U Dairy Monitor **264**
European Union Defence Markets *see* E U Defence Markets **6420**
The European Union Encyclopedia and Directory (Year) (GBR ISSN 1363-7045) **7234**
European Union Energy *see* E U Energy **3127**
European Union. Financial Report (LUX) **1107**
European Union Focus *see* European Tax Service **1922**
European Union Food Law *see* E U Food Law **4924**
European Union for Coastal Conservation Coastal News *see* E U C C Coastal News **2609**
European Union Info *see* E U Info **1562**
• European Union Institute for Security Studies. Occasional Papers/Union de l'Europe Occidentale. Institut d'Etudes de Securite. Publications Occasionelles (FRA ISSN 1608-5000) **7234**
European Union Institutions' Register *see* The E U Institutions' Register **1991**
• European Union Law Library (GBR) **4925**
European Union Law Reporter (GBR) **4669**
European Union Legislation *see* Evropsko Zakonodavstvo **7234**
European Union Policy Papers (GBR ISSN 1362-0541) **7134**
• ➤ European Union Politics (GBR ISSN 1465-1165) **7234**
European Union Prize for Cultural Heritage. Europa Nostra Awards *see* European Cultural Heritage Review. Special Edition: Awards **442**
The European Union Review (ITA ISSN 1606-8963) **7234**
European Union Studies Association Review *see* E U S A Review **4216**
European Union Tax Journal *see* E U Tax Journal **1921**
European Union Trend Report *see* E U Trend Report **1921**
European Union Umsatz-Steuer-Berater *see* Der E U Umsatz-Steuer-Berater **1921**
European University Institute. Academic Year (LUX ISSN 1016-5428) **2855**
European University Institute Law Working Papers *see* E U I Law Working Papers **4662**
European University Institute Papers in Political and Social Sciences *see* E U I Papers in Political and Social Sciences **7131**

Title

European University Institute Review *see* E U I Review **7131**
• European University Institute. Robert Schuman Centre for Advanced Studies. Distinguished Lectures (ITA) **4670**
• European University Institute. Robert Schuman Centre for Advanced Studies. Policy Papers (ITA) **4670**
• European University Institute. Robert Schuman Centre for Advanced Studies. Working Papers (ITA) **4670**
European University Institute Working Papers in Economics *see* E U I Working Papers in Economics **1478**
European University News *see* Nouvelles Universitaires Europeennes **2892**
European University Papers. Series 30: Theatre, Film and Television *see* Europaeische Hochschulschriften. Reihe 30: Theater-, Film- und Fernsehwissenschaften **8470**
European University Studies. Series 1: German Language and Literature *see* Europaeische Hochschulschriften. Reihe 1: Deutsche Sprache und Literatur **5293**
European University Studies. Series 11: Education *see* Europaeische Hochschulschriften. Reihe 11: Paedagogik **2855**
European University Studies. Series 13: French Language and Literature *see* Europaeische Hochschulschriften. Reihe 13: Franzoesische Sprache und Literatur **5293**
European University Studies. Series 14: Anglo-Saxon Language and Literature *see* Europaeische Hochschulschriften. Reihe 14: Angelsaechsische Sprache und Literatur **5293**
European University Studies. Series 15: Classics (CHE ISSN 0721-3433) **2234**
European University Studies. Series 18: Comparative Literature *see* Europaeische Hochschulschriften. Reihe 18: Vergleichende Literaturwissenschaft **5293**
European University Studies. Series 19: Anthropology, Ethnology. Section A: Anthropology *see* Europaeische Hochschulschriften. Reihe 19: Volkskunde/Ethnologie. Abteilung A: Volkskunde **338**
European University Studies. Series 19: Anthropology/Ethnology. Section B: Ethnology *see* Europaeische Hochschulschriften. Reihe 19: Volkskunde/Ethnologie. Abteilung B: Ethnologie **338**
European University Studies. Series 2: Law *see* Europaeische Hochschulschriften. Reihe 2: Rechtswissenschaft **4668**
European University Studies. Series 21: Linguistics *see* Europaeische Hochschulschriften. Reihe 21: Linguistik **5117**
European University Studies. Series 23: Theology/Europaeische Hochschulschriften. Reihe 23: Theologie/Publications Universitaires Europeennes. Serie 23: Theologie (CHE ISSN 0721-3409) **7963**
European University Studies. Series 24: Ibero-Romance Languages and Literature *see* Europaeische Hochschulschriften. Reihe 24: Ibero-Romanische Sprachen und Literaturen **5293**
European University Studies. Series 27: Asian and African Studies *see* Europaeische Hochschulschriften. Reihe 27: Asiatische und Afrikanische Studien **549**
European University Studies. Series 3: History and Allied Studies *see* Europaeische Hochschulschriften. Reihe 3: Geschichte und Ihre Hilfswissenschaften **4139**
European University Studies. Series 31: Political Sciences *see* Europaeische Hochschulschriften. Reihe 31: Politikwissenschaft **7134**
European University Studies. Series 9: Italian Language and Literature *see* Europaeische Hochschulschriften. Reihe 9: Italienische Sprache und Literatur **5117**
• European Update (BEL) **1922**
• ➤ European Urban and Regional Studies (GBR ISSN 0969-7764) **7963**
• ➤ European Urology (NLD ISSN 0302-2838) **6268**
➤ European Urology (Italian Edition) (ITA ISSN 1828-6569) **6268**
• European Urology Supplements (NLD ISSN 1569-9056) **6268**
European Urology Update Series *see* European Urology Supplements **6268**
European Utilities Procurement Directory (GBR ISSN 1356-9686) **1992**
• European Utility Retail (GBR) **3135**
European Values Studies (NLD ISSN 1568-5926) **7963**
European Valves (GBR) **3366**
European Vehicle Leasing (GBR ISSN 1352-2027) **8579**
European Venture Capital and Private Equity Journal *see* European Venture Capital & Private Equity Journal **1622**
• European Venture Capital & Private Equity Journal (USA ISSN 1742-9501) **1622**
European Venture Capital Association. Directory (BEL ISSN 1561-9273) **1992**
European Venture Capital Association. Yearbook (BEL ISSN 1368-8340) **1622**
† European Veterinary Dissertations (NLD ISSN 1569-0229) **8955**
• European View (DEU ISSN 1781-6858) **7234**
• European Voice (GBR ISSN 1370-6012) **3837**
European Water Management Online *see* E-water **3485**
European Women Writers Series (USA) **5293**
European Woodworking (DEU) **4556**
European Works Councils Bulletin (GBR ISSN 1361-312X) **1681**
European Workshop on Periodontology. Proceedings (DEU) **5844**
European Yearbook/Annuaire Europeen (NLD ISSN 0167-6717) **4925**
European Yearbook of Minority Issues (NLD ISSN 1570-7865) **3533**
Europees Belasting Toegevoegde Waarde-Nieuws *see* B T W Bulletin **1912**
Europees Parlement (LUX ISSN 0250-5738) **4925**
Europees Recht voor Decentrale Overheden (NLD ISSN 1573-3858) **4926**
Europees Strafprocesrecht (NLD ISSN 1574-5155) **4889**
Europees Vervoerrecht *see* European Transport Law **8495**
Europeesrechtelijke Actualiteiten (NLD ISSN 1569-7282) **4926**
Europeisk Dokumentation *see* Documentation Europeene **8366**
Europeiska Centralbanken. Arsrapport *see* European Central Bank. Annual Report **1339**
Europeiska Centralbanken. Manadsrapport (DEU ISSN 1561-0144) **1340**
Europeiska Gemenskapens Konkurrenspolitik. Rapporten om Konkurrenspolitiken *see* European Community Competition Policy. Report on Competition Policy **1885**
Europeiska Gemenskapernas Kommission. Dokument *see* Commission of the European Communities. Documents **7227**
Europeiska Gemenskapernas Officiella Tidning. Bilaga. Oeverlaeggningar *see* Diario Oficial de las Comunidades Europeas. Anexo Debates **4923**
Europeiska Gemenskapernas Officiella Tidning. C: Oplysninger *see* Diario Oficial de las Comunidades Europeas. C: Comunicaciones e Informaciones **4923**
Europeiska Gemenskapernas Officiella Tidning. C: Oplysninger *see* Official Journal of the European Union **7256**
Europeiska Gemenskapernas Officiella Tidning. L & C: Lagstiftning, Meddelanden och Upplysningar *see* Official Journal of the European Union. L & C Series: Legislation and Information Notices (Quarterly Edition) **4937**
Europeiska Gemenskapernas Officiella Tidning. L: Lagstiftning *see* Official Journal of the European Union. L Series: Legislation **7256**
Europeiska Gemenskapernas Officiella Tidning. S: Anbudsinfordringar foer Offentlig Upphandling *see* Official Journal of the European Union. S Series: Tendering Procedures for Public Contracts **4937**
Europeiska Investeringsbanken. Information *see* European Investment Bank. Information **1622**
Europeiska Unionens. Bulletin *see* European Union. Bulletin **1485**
Europeiska Unionens Bulletin *see* European Commission. European Union. Bulletin **7233**
Europeiskt Fiske *see* Fisheries and Aquaculture in Europe **3592**
L'Europeo (ITA ISSN 0014-3189) **3897**
† El Europeo de las Cuatro Estaciones (ESP ISSN 1135-0482) **8955**
Europe's 15,000 Largest Companies *see* Europe's 15000 Largest Companies (Year) **1885**
• Europe's 15000 Largest Companies (Year) (GBR ISSN 0956-1447) **1885**
Europe's 15,000 Largest Companies on CD-ROM *see* Europe's 15000 Largest Companies (Year) **1885**
Europe's Automotive Components Business (USA ISSN 0960-5436) **8579**
Europe's Top 70 Food Groups (GBR) **3635**
Europe's Wonderful Little Hotels and Inns: The Continent *see* Europe's Wonderful Little Hotels & Inns: The Continent (Year) **4385**
Europe's Wonderful Little Hotels & Inns: The Continent (Year) (USA) **4385**
• Europe's World (BEL ISSN 1782-0642) **7134**
Europese Centrale Bank. Jaarverslag *see* European Central Bank. Annual Report **1339**
Europese Centrale Bank. Maandbericht (DEU ISSN 1561-0314) **1340**
Europese Documentatie *see* Documentation Europeene **8366**
• Europese Gemeenschap Recht CD (NLD ISSN 1567-5025) **4926**
Europese Investeringsbank. Mededelingen *see* European Investment Bank. Information **1622**
Het Europese Mededingingsbeleid. Verslag over het Mededingingsbeleid *see* European Community Competition Policy. Report on Competition Policy **1885**
† Europese Monografieen (NLD ISSN 1572-3593) **8955**
Europese Unie. Bulletin *see* European Union. Bulletin **1485**
EuroPetroleum (GBR ISSN 1470-434X) **6768**
Europhil News (LUX) **6894**
EuroPhonics (USA ISSN 1091-6083) **7075**
Europhysics Conference Abstracts (FRA ISSN 0378-2271) **7048**
• ➤ Europhysics Letters (FRA ISSN 0295-5075) **7012**
• Europhysics News (FRA ISSN 0531-7479) **7012**
Europiano (CHE) **6565**
EuroPiano (DEU ISSN 0014-2387) **6566**
➤ Europolis - N U R E C Working Papers (DEU ISSN 1022-534X) **4410**
• Europolitics (BEL) **1340**
• Europolitics Environment (BEL) **3431**
Europolitique (Bruxelles) (BEL ISSN 1021-4275) **7234**
Europoort Kringen (NLD ISSN 1568-881X) **8643**
• Europower (NOR ISSN 1503-9013) **3135**
Europower Nytt *see* Europower **3135**
• EuroProperty (GBR ISSN 0961-9712) **7590**
Europski Glasnik (HRV ISSN 1331-0232) **5293**
Euroreport Plus (SVK ISSN 1336-8796) **1564**
• Eurorett (NOR ISSN 0805-1232) **4926**
Eurosat (ITA) **2381**
Euroseil (DEU ISSN 0945-1943) **8450**
Eurosemi Magazine *see* EuroAsia Semiconductor **3099**
EuroShell Club News (DEU) **8579**
EUROSIM - Simulation News Europe (AUT ISSN 0929-2268) **2517**
Euroslot (GBR ISSN 0966-0259) **1816**
† Eurosoccer (CHE ISSN 1661-822X) **8955**
Eurosocial Reports (AUT ISSN 0258-6193) **8039**
Eurosource (GBR) **624**
▼ • Eurosphere Working Paper Series (NOR ISSN 1890-5986) **4926**
Eurosport MotorMagazin (DEU) **8172**
† Eurostar (FRA ISSN 1276-7816) **8955**
Eurostat. Agrarpreise. Preisindizes und Absolute Preise *see* Eurostat Agricultural Prices. Price Indices and Absolute Prices. **108**
Eurostat Agricultural Prices. Price Indices and Absolute Prices./Eurostat. Agrarpreise. Preisindizes und Absolute Preise/Eurostat. Prix Agricoles. Indices de Prix et Prix Absolus (LUX ISSN 1015-9924) **108**
Eurostat Consumer Price Index (Monthly Edition) (LUX ISSN 1013-3402) **2642**
Eurostat Consumer Price Index (Quarterly Edition) *see* Eurostat Consumer Price Index (Monthly Edition) **2642**
EUROSTAT. Directory of Community Legislation in Force *see* Directory of Community Legislation in Force **4658**
Eurostat. ECU-EMS Information *see* Eurostat ECU-EMS Information and Central Bank Interest Rates **1340**
Eurostat ECU-EMS Information and Central Bank Interest Rates (LUX ISSN 1024-4239) **1340**
Eurostat ECU-EWS Information und Zinssatze der Zentralbanken *see* Eurostat ECU-EMS Information and Central Bank Interest Rates **1340**
• Eurostat. Energy Statistics Monthly (LUX ISSN 0258-3569) **3152**
EUROSTAT. European Union Direct Investment. Yearbook (LUX ISSN 1605-2935) **1622**
Eurostat. External Trade and Balance of Payments. Monthly Statistics (LUX ISSN 1560-8492) **1427**
• Eurostat Geld, Finanzen und der Euro: Statistiken (LUX ISSN 1562-3041) **1227**
Eurostat. Geonomenclature (LUX ISSN 1015-3071) **1227**
• Eurostat International Transport by Air. Intra - and Extra - EU (LUX ISSN 1028-348X) **8540**
EUROSTAT. Methods and Nomenclatures (LUX ISSN 1725-0056) **1227**
Eurostat. Prix Agricoles. Indices de Prix et Prix Absolus *see* Eurostat Agricultural Prices. Price Indices and Absolute Prices. **108**
Eurostat Publications and Databases *see* Publications et Bases de Donnees **1259**
Eurostat Schnellberichte. Aussenhandel *see* Eurostat Statistics in Focus. External Trade **1227**
Eurostat Statistics in Focus. Agriculture and Fisheries (LUX ISSN 1562-1340) **179**
Eurostat Statistics in Focus. Economy and Finance (LUX ISSN 1024-4298) **1227**
Eurostat Statistics in Focus. Environment and Energy (LUX ISSN 1562-3106) **3479**
Eurostat Statistics in Focus. External Trade (LUX ISSN 1024-6878) **1227**
Eurostat Statistics in Focus. General Statistics (LUX ISSN 1561-4875) **1227**
Eurostat Statistics in Focus. Industry, Trade and Services (LUX ISSN 1561-4840) **1227**
Eurostat Statistics in Focus. Population and Social Conditions (LUX ISSN 1024-4352) **1227**
Eurostat Statistics in Focus. Science and Technology (LUX ISSN 1609-5995) **1227**
Eurostat Statistics in Focus. Transport (LUX ISSN 1562-1324) **8524**
Eurostat Statistik Kurz Gefasst. Allgemeine Statistik *see* Eurostat Statistics in Focus. General Statistics **1227**
Eurostat Statistik Kurz Gefasst. Bevoelkerung und Soziale Bedingungen (LUX ISSN 1024-4379) **1227**
Eurostat Statistik Kurz Gefasst. Industrie, Handel und Dienstleistungen (LUX ISSN 1561-4832) **1227**
Eurostat Statistik Kurz Gefasst. Landwirtschaft und Fischerei (LUX ISSN 1562-1359) **179**
Eurostat Statistik Kurz Gefasst. Umwelt und Energie *see* Eurostat Statistics in Focus. Environment and Energy **3479**
Eurostat Statistik Kurz Gefasst. Wirtschaft und Finanzen (LUX ISSN 1024-431X) **1227**
Eurostat Statistik Kurz Gefasst. Wissenschaft und Technologie (LUX ISSN 1609-6002) **1228**
Eurostat Statistiques en Bref. Agriculture et Peche (LUX ISSN 1561-8455) **179**
Eurostat Statistiques en Bref. Economie et Finances (LUX ISSN 1024-4301) **1228**
Eurostat Statistiques en Bref. Environnement et Energie *see* Eurostat Statistics in Focus. Environment and Energy **3479**
Eurostat Statistiques en Bref. Industrie, Commerce et Services (LUX ISSN 1561-4859) **1228**
Eurostat Statistiques en Bref. Population et Conditions Sociales (LUX ISSN 1024-4360) **1228**
Eurostat Statistiques en Bref. Science et Technologie (LUX ISSN 1609-5987) **1228**
Eurostat Statistiques en Bref. Statistiques Generales *see* Eurostat Statistics in Focus. General Statistics **1227**
Eurostat Statistiques Rapides. Commerce Exterieur *see* Eurostat Statistics in Focus. External Trade **1227**
Eurostat Verbraucherpreisindex *see* Eurostat Consumer Price Index (Monthly Edition) **2642**
Eurostat Veroeffentlichungen und Datenbanken *see* Publications et Bases de Donnees **1259**
Eurostat Yearbook (LUX ISSN 1681-4789) **8368**
• Eurostatistics. Data for Short Term Economic Analysis (LUX ISSN 1725-8111) **1228**
Eurostatistik. Daten zuer Konjunkturanalyse (LUX ISSN 0252-8266) **8368**
† Eurostitch Magazine (NLD ISSN 1387-0076) **8955**
• Eurostyle (DNK ISSN 1901-8819) **5070**
Eurosuites (ESP) **4385**
Eurosun (CYP) **8783**
• Eurosurveillance (Online Edition) (FRA ISSN 1560-7917) **5813**
• Eurosurveillance (Print Edition) (FRA ISSN 1025-496X) **5813**
Eurotax - Auto - Information (CHE) **8579**
EuroTB Newsletter *see* Euro T B Newsletter **5813**
• Eurotec (CHE ISSN 0014-3243) **8422**
Eurotech - Katalogus (BEL ISSN 1371-6972) **3366**
Eurotelevizia (SVK ISSN 1336-4006) **2381**
Eurotrade Computer & Communication Magazine (NLD ISSN 1572-2147) **2418**
Eurotransport (GBR ISSN 1478-8217) **8495**
• Eurotuner (USA ISSN 1538-2079) **8579**
Eurotutkimus *see* Euroopan Tiede ja Teknologia **53**
EuroUniversity. Series. International Relations (EST ISSN 1406-4812) **7234**
Euroveletrhy (CZE ISSN 1802-436X) **6279**
Eurovin - News (FRA ISSN 1626-6838) **109**
• EuroWatch (USA ISSN 1063-6323) **7234**
• EuroWeek (GBR ISSN 0952-7036) **1340**
† Eurowings Magazin (DEU) **8955**
EuroWire (GBR ISSN 1463-2438) **3366**
• EuroWired (GBR ISSN 1470-2126) **1743**
• Eurowoman (DNK ISSN 1398-1099) **3833**
• eurozine (AUT ISSN 1684-4637) **7963**
EurUP *see* Eur U P **4924**
Euskal Arrantzu-Flotaren Aurkibidea/Directorio de la Flota Pesquera Vasca (ESP ISSN 0214-6991) **3590**
Euskaldunak *see* Vascos **4481**
Euskera (ESP ISSN 0210-1564) **5293**
• Euskonews & Media (ESP ISSN 1139-3629) **8101**
Euthanasia Roses (USA) **5421**
† Eutopia (ITA ISSN 1121-1628) **8955**
† Eutopias. Documentos de Trabajo (ESP ISSN 0213-246X) **8955**
Eutrophia *see* Norsk Tidsskrift for Ernaering **6664**
† eV (USA) **8955**
Eva (DOM ISSN 0014-3286) **8861**
Eva (SVK ISSN 0139-8717) **2254**
Eva (SVN ISSN 1580-6308) **8861**
Eva (Hilversum) (NLD ISSN 1385-9889) **8861**
Eva Tremila (ITA) **3897**
Eva, Your Guide to Tonga (TON) **8702**
Evaluace a Diagnostika pro Reditele na ZS (CZE ISSN 1801-8424) **3022**
L'Evaluateur Canadien *see* Canadian Property Valuation **7586**
Evaluating Eden Series (GBR ISSN 1561-8382) **5293**
Evaluating Your Regional Council (USA) **7436**
• ➤ Evaluation (GBR ISSN 1356-3890) **7963**
• ➤ Evaluation and Program Planning (GBR ISSN 0149-7189) **7963**
• ➤ Evaluation and Research in Education (GBR ISSN 0950-0790) **2855**
• ➤ Evaluation and the Health Professions (USA ISSN 0163-2787) **5612**
Evaluation des Technologies de la Sante, Tour d'Horizon des Technologies de la Sante *see* Tour d'Horizon des Technologies de la Sante **5723**
Evaluation of New Canal Point Sugarcane Clones (USA ISSN 0899-3270) **229**
Evaluation Results for... - World Bank *see* Annual Review of Development Effectiveness **1590**
• ➤ Evaluation Review (USA ISSN 0193-841X) **7963**
• Evaluations of Drug Interactions (USA ISSN 0090-6654) **6839**
The Evaluator (London) (GBR ISSN 1743-954X) **8101**

DIRECTORY 2010 EVROPSKA VOLEBNI STUDIA 10263

Evam (IND ISSN 0972-6160) **5293**
Evandale's Directory of World Underwriters (GBR ISSN 1461-314X) **4502**
• Evangel (GBR ISSN 0265-4547) **7641**
Evangel (USA ISSN 0162-1890) **7756**
Evangelical Alliance Mission Horizons *see* T E A M Horizons **7687**
Evangelical & Reformed Historical Society Newsletter (USA ISSN 1529-4773) **7641**
Evangelical Baptist (CAN ISSN 0014-3324) **7756**
Evangelical Baptist Churches in Canada. Fellowship Yearbook (CAN ISSN 0317-266X) **7756**
Evangelical Beacon (USA ISSN 0014-3332) **7756**
Evangelical Catholic (USA) **7641**
Evangelical Church of West Africa Theological Seminary. Journal *see* E C W A Theological Seminary. Journal **7638**
Evangelical Homiletics Society. Journal (USA ISSN 1534-7478) **7756**
• Evangelical Journal (USA ISSN 0741-1758) **7641**
Evangelical Lutheran Church in America (Year) (USA ISSN 1058-3696) **7756**
The Evangelical Magazine (GBR ISSN 1743-4092) **7756**
• Evangelical Missions Quarterly (USA ISSN 0014-3359) **7641**
Evangelical Morning *see* Yevanhelskyj Ranok **7781**
• Evangelical Quarterly (GBR ISSN 0014-3367) **7756**
▼ • ➤ Evangelical Review of Society and Politics (GBR ISSN 1750-2217) **7735**
• Evangelical Review of Theology (GBR ISSN 0144-8153) **7641**
Evangelical Studies Bulletin (USA ISSN 0890-703X) **7756**
• ➤ Evangelical Theological Society. Journal (USA ISSN 0360-8808) **7756**
Evangelicals & Society from 1750 Series (GBR) **7756**
Evangelicky Casopis Cesky Bratr (CZE ISSN 1211-6793) **7756**
Evangelikale Missiologie (DEU ISSN 0177-8706) **7641**
Evangelikus Elet (HUN ISSN 0133-1302) **7757**
Evangelio y Mision (ESP) **7641**
Evangelisch-Lutherische Landeskirche Sachsens. Amtsblatt (DEU ISSN 0423-8346) **7757**
Evangelisch-Lutherisches Missionswerk in Niedersachsen. Jahrbuch (Year) (DEU) **7757**
Evangelische Arbeitsgemeinschaft fuer Kirchliche Zeitgeschichte. Mitteilungen (DEU ISSN 0949-5908) **7641**
Der Evangelische Buchberater (DEU ISSN 0930-8873) **7735**
Evangelische Fachhochschule Nuernberg. Vorlesungs-Verzeichnis (DEU) **2955**
Evangelische Fachhochschulen Darmstadt, Freiburg, Ludwigshafen, Reutlingen. Hochschulbrief (DEU ISSN 0344-1466) **2856**
Evangelische Kinderkirche (DEU ISSN 0342-2763) **7757**
Evangelische Kirche der Kirchenprovinz Sachsen. Amtsblatt (DEU ISSN 0232-6310) **7757**
Evangelische Kirche in Deutschland. Amtsblatt (DEU ISSN 0014-343X) **7757**
Evangelische Kirchenzeitung *see* Evangelische Sonntags-Zeitung **7757**
Evangelische Landeskirche in Wuerttemberg. Amtsblatt (DEU ISSN 0014-3529) **7757**
Evangelische Lutherische Kirche in Bayern. Pfarrer- und Pfarrerinnenverein. Korrespondenzblatt (DEU) **7757**
Evangelische-Lutherische Kirche in Thueringen. Amtsblatt (DEU ISSN 0014-326X) **7757**
Evangelische Orientierung (DEU) **7757**
Evangelische Sammlung (DEU) **7641**
Evangelische Sonntags-Zeitung (DEU ISSN 1862-8249) **7757**
Evangelische Theologie (DEU ISSN 0014-3502) **7641**
Evangelische Zeitung fuer Niedersachsen (DEU) **7757**
Evangelische Zentralstelle fuer Weltanschauungsfragen Texte *see* E Z W - Texte **7639**
Evangelischen Publizistik Film *see* E P D Film **6496**
Evangelischer Bund in Oesterreich. Schriftenreihe (AUT ISSN 0036-6943) **7757**
Evangelischer Digest *see* Christlicher Digest **7633**
Evangelischer Kirchenbote (DEU) **7757**
Evangelischer Kirchenbote Linz (AUT) **7757**
Evangelischer Pressedienst Medien *see* E P D Medien **2319**
Evangelischer Pressedienst Sozial *see* E P D Sozial **7755**
Evangelischer Pressedienst Wochenspiegel. Ausgabe Ost *see* E P D Wochenspiegel. Ausgabe Ost **7755**
Evangelisches Gemeindeblatt fuer Wuerttemberg (DEU ISSN 0014-360X) **7757**
Evangelisches Missionswerk in Deutschland Informationen *see* E M W - Informationen **7639**
Evangelisches Missionswerk in Suedwestdeutschland e.V. Impulse *see* E M S - Impulse **7755**
Evangelisches Sonntagsblatt aus Bayern (DEU ISSN 0174-3376) **7641**
• Evangelisk Alliance. Nyhedsbrev (DNK ISSN 1901-533X) **7757**
Evangelisk-Luthersk Barntidning Droppen *see* Droppen **7755**
Evangelisk-Lutherska Kyrkan i Finland. Cirkulaer (Online) *see* Suomen Evankelis-Luterilainen Kirkko. Kirkkohallituksen Yleiskirje (Online) **7776**
Evangeliska Fosterlandsstiftelsen Missionstidning Budbaeraren *see* E F S Missionstidning Budbaeraren **7755**
Evangeliska Oestasienmissionen (SWE ISSN 0280-6339) **7642**
Evangelist (Albany) (USA ISSN 0738-8489) **7735**
Evangelist (Pasadena) (USA ISSN 0014-3626) **7735**
• Evangeliumi Hirnok/Gospel Messenger (USA) **7735**
• Evangeliums Posaune (USA) **7757**
Evangelizing Today's Child *see* Teach Kids! **7776**
Evangelizzare (ITA) **7642**
Evangile et Liberte (FRA ISSN 1146-4771) **7757**
Evanjelicky Hlasnik (SRB ISSN 0014-3642) **7757**
† • Evans-Novak Political Report (USA ISSN 0014-3650) **8955**
• Evans Report (CAN ISSN 1180-3711) **2492**
Evansville Living (USA ISSN 1533-0613) **3975**
Evansville - Vanderburgh County Public Libraries. Staff News Bulletin (USA) **5009**
Eve (DEU) **6985**
Eve *see* Hawa'a **8867**
† • Eve (GBR ISSN 1471-5023) **8955**
Eve/Xia Wa (HKG) **8861**
Eve Essentials (HKG) **2254**
Evean Plus (NLD ISSN 1871-790X) **6985**
Evean Zorg Plus *see* Evean Plus **6985**
Eveil du Travailleur Togolais (TGO) **1681**
• Eveil & Evolution (FRA ISSN 1779-5567) **6918**
• ➤ Evelyn Waugh Newsletter and Studies (Online) (USA) **5293**
Evelyn Waugh Newsletter and Studies (Print) *see* Evelyn Waugh Newsletter and Studies (Online) **5293**
L'Evenement Immobilier (BEL ISSN 0778-4899) **1107**
Evenement Sportif *see* Bo **8162**
L'Evenement Syndical. Ed. Unia (CHE ISSN 1661-1748) **6733**
Evenementenlocaties (NLD ISSN 1874-1770) **1816**
L'Evenementiel (FRA ISSN 1145-6167) **25**
• Evenimentul Zilei (ROM ISSN 1222-328X) **3932**
Evening (JPN) **6289**
Evening Echo (IRL ISSN 0332-4788) **3892**
† Evening Echo, Bournemouth (GBR ISSN 0307-2711) **8955**
• Evening Express (GBR ISSN 0962-2284) **3864**
• Evening Gazette (GBR ISSN 0964-3095) **3864**
• Evening Guide (CAN ISSN 1184-5511) **3809**
Evening Herald (IRL ISSN 0791-6892) **3893**
• Evening News (CAN ISSN 0839-0355) **3809**
• Evening News (Edinburgh) (GBR ISSN 0307-5761) **3865**
Evening News (Norwich) (GBR ISSN 0964-4946) **3865**
Evening News of Tianjin *see* Jinwanbao **3826**
Evening Out (CAN ISSN 1911-1495) **8470**
Evening Post (ZAF) **3948**
Evening Sentinel (Stoke-on-Trent) (GBR ISSN 0307-0999) **3865**
Evening Standard (City Prices) (GBR ISSN 1472-5223) **3865**
Evening Standard (Late Prices Extra Edition) (GBR ISSN 1472-5231) **3865**
Evening Standard (News Extra Edition) (GBR ISSN 1472-524X) **3865**
• Evening Standard (West End Final Edition) (GBR ISSN 1472-5215) **3865**
Evening Star (GBR ISSN 0958-4056) **3865**
Evening Telegram (St. John's, 1882) *see* The Telegram **3818**
Evening Telegraph and Post (GBR ISSN 0262-3048) **3865**
Evening Times Wee Red Book (GBR) **8227**
Evensongs/Yeh Ko (TWN) **5215**
Event (CAN ISSN 0315-3770) **5293**
Event. (DEU) **6566**
EVeNT *see* Electric Vehicle News & Technology **8495**
• Event (GBR ISSN 1477-738X) **6279**
Event & Expo (SWE ISSN 1652-0602) **25**
• Event D V (USA ISSN 1554-2009) **2557**
Event Design Magazine (USA ISSN 1936-1025) **1816**
• The Event Guide (IRL) **3893**
Event Horizon (USA ISSN 1099-3738) **7853**
• ➤ Event Management (USA ISSN 1525-9951) **8702**
• Event Marketer (USA ISSN 1930-2266) **1816**
Event Organiser (GBR) **1816**
Event Partner (DEU ISSN 0949-9504) **6566**
• Event Solutions (USA ISSN 1098-9102) **6279**
eVentage (ZAF ISSN 1814-3903) **1816**
• EventD V Spotlight (Digital Video) (USA) **2401**
† Eventi (ITA) **8955**
† Eventi e Interventi (ITA) **8955**
Eventing (GBR ISSN 0267-5358) **8172**
† • Eventline (NLD) **8955**
▼ Eventos Empresariales (COL ISSN 2011-2335) **1743**
Events (USA ISSN 1082-3441) **8039**
Events (Frankfurt am Main) (DEU) **6279**
Events (Logan) *see* Campus Events Professional **2276**
Events (Potsdam) (DEU) **3846**
Events Guide (CAN ISSN 1491-4638) **8702**
Events in Academe *see* The Chronicle of Higher Education **2972**
Evenwicht *see* Antroposana **307**
The Ever Dancing Muse (USA ISSN 1070-0889) **5215**
Ever - Ready *see* Eso - Etimos **3832**
• Everba (ARG ISSN 1668-1002) **4452**
Everest (CZE ISSN 1213-1849) **8312**
Everett & McCracken's Banking and Financial Institutions Law *see* Studies in Australian Banking & Finance Series. Banking and Financial Institutions Law **1384**
• The Everett Business Journal (USA ISSN 1528-0160) **1485**
Everglades National Park and the Surrounding Area *see* A FalconGuide to Everglades National Park and the Surrounding Area **8680**
• Evergreen (GBR ISSN 0269-123X) **3865**
• Evergreen (IND ISSN 0254-6426) **3688**
▼ EverGreen (USA) **4093**
Evergreen Monthly (TWN) **6985**
Evergreen Monthly (USA) **6645**
• Evergreen Review (Online Edition) (USA) **5293**
Everket *see* Energi & Ledelse **3307**
Everlasting Circle (GBR) **535**
Evermore (USA ISSN 1087-4976) **5293**
Everson Museum of Art Bulletin (USA ISSN 1068-2317) **6523**
The Evertonian (GBR ISSN 1357-3500) **8227**
Everton's Family History Magazine *see* Everton's Genealogical Helper **3765**
• Everton's Genealogical Helper (USA ISSN 1554-2645) **3765**
Every Child (AUS ISSN 1322-0659) **2856**
Every Day with Rachael Ray (USA ISSN 1932-0590) **5070**
Every Landlord's Tax Deduction Guide (USA ISSN 1945-8770) **7590**
Every Place *see* Kol Atar **8969**
† Every Second Counts (USA ISSN 1525-1667) **8955**
Every Wednesday (USA) **3533**
Every Woman (USA ISSN 1932-1171) **8845**
Everybody is Doing Outrageous Sex *see* E I D O S **8859**
• Everybody's (USA ISSN 0164-9329) **3533**
Everyday Food (USA ISSN 1544-6395) **3635**
▼ Everyday Healthy Food (NZL ISSN 1178-1831) **4357**
• Everyday Practical Electronics (GBR ISSN 1367-398X) **3099**
Everyday with Rachael Ray *see* Every Day with Rachael Ray **5070**
• Everyman (CAN ISSN 1199-1461) **6289**
Everyman's Science (IND ISSN 0531-495X) **7853**
• Everyone's Backyard (USA ISSN 0749-3940) **3506**
† Everyone's United Nations (USA ISSN 0251-690X) **8955**
Everything (GBR ISSN 1361-7699) **488**
Everything for Men (USA) **6289**
Everything for Women (USA) **8861**
• The Everything Get a Job Book (USA) **6697**
▼ Everywhere (USA ISSN 1940-9613) **8702**
• Eve's Magazine (USA) **3975**
Eve's Weekly (IND ISSN 0014-3812) **8861**
Evidence *see* B A R - B R I Bar Review. Evidence **4624**
Evidence: A Structured Approach (USA ISSN 1557-3818) **4950**
• ➤ Evidence and Policy (GBR ISSN 1744-2648) **7964**
• ➤ Evidence - Based Cardiovascular Medicine (GBR ISSN 1361-2611) **5787**
• Evidence-Based Child Health (GBR ISSN 1557-6272) **6092**
▼ • Evidence-Based Communication Assessment and Intervention (GBR ISSN 1748-9539) **5612**
• ➤ Evidence - Based Complementary and Alternative Medicine (GBR ISSN 1741-427X) **309**
• Evidence - Based Dentistry (GBR ISSN 1462-0049) **5844**
Evidence - Based Eye Care *see* Evidence - Based Ophthalmology **6041**
† • ➤ Evidence - Based Gastroenterology (USA ISSN 1527-8557) **8955**
• ➤ Evidence Based Library and Information Practice (CAN ISSN 1715-720X) **5009**
• Evidence - Based Medicine (GBR ISSN 1356-5524) **5612**
Evidence - Based Medicine (Ed. Espanola) (ESP ISSN 1578-598X) **5612**
• Evidence - Based Mental Health (GBR ISSN 1362-0347) **6140**
• Evidence - Based Nursing (GBR ISSN 1367-6539) **5958**
• ➤ Evidence - Based Obstetrics & Gynaecology (GBR ISSN 1361-259X) **5990**
• Evidence - Based Ophthalmology (USA ISSN 1555-9203) **6041**
Evidence Based Practice (USA ISSN 1095-4120) **5612**
† • ➤ Evidence - Based Preventive Medicine (NZL ISSN 1176-2349) **8955**
• Evidence-Based Spine-Care Surgery (USA) **6243**
Evidence-Based Spine Surgery *see* Evidence-Based Spine-Care Surgery **6243**
• Evidence in America: The Federal Rules in the States (USA) **4950**
• Evidence in Health Care Reports (AUS ISSN 1449-8286) **5612**
Evidence into Policy in Australian Primary Health Care *see* Medical Journal of Australia **5669**
Evidence Law and Practice (USA) **4670**
Evidence Laws of New York (USA) **4950**
Evidence Photographers International Council Journal *see* E P I C Journal **6966**
Evidence Report - Technology Assessment (Summary) (USA ISSN 1530-440X) **5612**
Evidence Science *see* Zhengju Kexue **4820**
Evidence Technology Magazine (USA ISSN 1555-998X) **2652**
➤ Evidencia (BRA ISSN 1519-5287) **764**
Evidencia Odontologica (PER ISSN 1813-2022) **5844**
▼ • Evidens (SWE ISSN 1654-8825) **8039**
Evidensbaserad Sjukgymnastisk Behandling (SWE ISSN 1404-0670) **5612**
• Evidentia (ESP ISSN 1697-638X) **5958**
• Evidentiary Foundations (USA) **4950**
• Eviran Kaari (FIN ISSN 1796-9182) **6658**
Evita (BEL ISSN 1377-3607) **8862**
Evlenme Istatistikleri *see* Turkey. Turkiye Istatistik Kurumu. Evlenme Istatistikleri (Year) **5563**
Evliya Celebi's Book of Travels (NLD ISSN 0922-7768) **549**
Evo (FRA ISSN 1774-5187) **8172**
Evo (GBR ISSN 1464-2786) **8579**
Evo (ITA ISSN 1590-8461) **8579**
• Evocations Rurales (CAN ISSN 1716-2866) **197**
▼ Evoke (USA ISSN 1935-5386) **7356**
• Evolucion Bancaria (CHL) **1340**
Evolucion de la Economia en (Year) y Perspectivas para (Year) (CHL) **1107**
La Evolucion Fonologica del Protovaltuat (MEX) **5117**
• ➤ Evolution (GBR ISSN 0014-3820) **866**
Evolution *see* Wireless Evolution **2504**
• Evolution (SWE ISSN 1104-8158) **3377**
Evolution (American Edition) *see* Evolution **3377**
Evolution (Chinese Edition) *see* Evolution **3377**
Evolution (Czech Edition) *see* Evolution **3377**
Evolution (English Edition) *see* Evolution **3377**
Evolution (French Edition) *see* Evolution **3377**
Evolution (German Edition) *see* Evolution **3377**
Evolution (Italian Edition) *see* Evolution **3377**
Evolution (Polish Edition) *see* Evolution **3377**
Evolution (Russian Edition) *see* Evolution **3377**
Evolution (Spanish Edition) *see* Evolution **3377**
➤ Evolution and Cognition (AUT ISSN 0938-2623) **7356**
• ➤ Evolution & Development (USA ISSN 1520-541X) **672**
• Evolution & Development Online (USA ISSN 1525-142X) **672**
• ➤ Evolution and Human Behavior (USA ISSN 1090-5138) **942**
Evolution de la Situation dans le Sectuer Secondaire *see* Geschaeftsgang im Sekunden Sektor **1234**
Evolution Demographique Recente en Europe et en Amerique du Nord *see* Recent Demographic Developments in Europe and North America **7291**
• L'Evolution du Climat et Votre Sante (CAN ISSN 1710-2014) **7517**
▼ • ➤ Evolution: Education & Outreach (USA ISSN 1936-6426) **867**
• ➤ L'Evolution Psychiatrique (FRA ISSN 0014-3855) **6140**
• ➤ Evolutionary Anthropology (USA ISSN 1060-1538) **339**
▼ • Evolutionary Applications (USA ISSN 1752-4563) **672**
• ➤ Evolutionary Bioinformatics (NZL ISSN 1176-9343) **748**
• ➤ Evolutionary Biology (USA ISSN 0071-3260) **867**
• ➤ Evolutionary Computation (USA ISSN 1063-6560) **2418**
• ➤ Evolutionary Ecology (NLD ISSN 0269-7653) **3431**
• ➤ Evolutionary Ecology Research (USA ISSN 1522-0613) **3431**
➤ Evolutionary Foundations of Human Behavior (USA) **7356**
▼ • Evolutionary Intelligence (DEU ISSN 1864-5909) **2448**
➤ Evolutionary Monographs (USA ISSN 0272-0809) **672**
• ➤ Evolutionary Psychology (USA ISSN 1474-7049) **7356**
Evolve! (USA ISSN 1942-5627) **6645**
Evolving Woman (USA) **8862**
Evonik-Magazin (DEU) **3135**
Evonik Magazine (DEU) **3243**
Evphrosyne (PRT ISSN 0870-0133) **2234**
Evraziatskii Entomologicheskii Zhurnal/Euroasian Entomological Journal (RUS ISSN 1684-4866) **847**
Evrei i Evreiski Narod - Peticii Pis'ma i Obraseni Evreev S S S R *see* Jews and the Jewish People - Petitions, Letters and Appeals from Soviet Jews **8967**
Evreiski Vesti (BGR) **3533**
Evreiskie Vesti (UKR) **4452**
Evreiskii Universitet v Moskve. Vestnik (RUS) **3533**
Evreyskaya Gazeta (DEU) **3533**
Evrika (KAZ) **3902**
Evropa (POL ISSN 1643-0360) **7234**
• Evropa 2001 (BGR ISSN 1310-3989) **3837**
Evropa Ekspress (DEU ISSN 1619-1196) **3846**
Evropeiskoe Kachestvo (RUS) **6402**
Evropska Unie Tip *see* E U Tip **8952**
• ➤ Evropska Volebni Studia/European Electoral Studies (CZE ISSN 1801-6545) **7134**

Title

Title

Title

10268 F A O LAND AND WATER DEVELOPMENT SERIES ULRICH'S PERIODICALS

F A O Land and Water Development Series (Food and Agriculture Organization) (ITA ISSN 0259-2568) **109**

F A O Legislative Study (Food and Agriculture Organization of the United Nations) (USA ISSN 1014-6679) **109**

F A O Orientaciones Tecnicas para la Pesca Responsable *see* F A O Technical Guidelines for Responsible Fisheries **3591**

• F A O Plant Production and Protection Papers (Food and Agriculture Organization of the United Nations) (ITA ISSN 0259-2517) **229**

F A O Plant Protection Bulletin (Multilingual Edition) (Food and Agriculture Organization of the United Nations) (ITA ISSN 0254-9727) **787**

F A O Regional Conference for Africa. Report (Food and Agriculture Organization of the United Nations) (USA ISSN 0429-9353) **109**

F A O Regional Conference for Asia and the Pacific. Report (Food and Agriculture Organization of the United Nations) (USA ISSN 1010-0997) **109**

F A O Regional Conference for Europe. Report (Food and Agriculture Organization of the United Nations) (USA ISSN 1010-1403) **109**

F A O Regional Conference for Latin America and the Caribbean. Report (Food and Agriculture Organization of the United Nations) (USA ISSN 1020-2889) **109**

F A O Regional Conference for the Near East. Report (Food and Agriculture Organization of the United Nations) (USA ISSN 0427-8089) **109**

• F A O S. Aarbog (Forskningscenter for Arbejdsmarkeds- og Organisationsstudier) (DNK ISSN 1901-3442) **1681**

F A O S. Beretning (Forskningscenter for Arbejdsmarkeds- og Organisationsstudier) (DNK ISSN 1604-6838) **1681**

• F A O S Information (Forskningscenter for Arbejdsmarkeds- og Organisationsstudier) (DNK ISSN 1603-5593) **1681**

F A O Serie Informatique. Peche *see* F A O Computerized Information Series. Fisheries **3590**

F A O Soils Bulletin (Food and Agriculture Organization of the United Nations) (USA ISSN 0253-2050) **230**

F A O Statistical Development Series (Food and Agriculture Organization) (ITA ISSN 1014-3378) **8369**

F A O Technical Guidelines for Responsible Fisheries (ITA ISSN 1020-5292) **3591**

F A O Terminology Bulletin (Food and Agriculture Organization) (USA ISSN 0532-0313) **109**

• F A O Today (Finance and Accounting Outsourcing) (USA ISSN 1556-6196) **1340**

† F A O Training Series (Food and Agriculture Organization) (ITA ISSN 0259-2533) **8955**

F A O Yearbook. Fertilizer (Food and Agriculture Organization of the United Nations) (USA ISSN 1014-7675) **230**

F A O Yearbook. Fishery Statistics. Capture Production (ITA ISSN 1020-6663) **3613**

F A O Yearbook. Fishery Statistics. Commodities (ITA ISSN 1014-7667) **3613**

F A O Yearbook. Production (Food and Agriculture Organization of the United Nations) (USA ISSN 1014-7640) **197**

F A O Yearbook, Trade (Food and Agriculture Organization of the United Nations) (USA ISSN 1014-7632) **197**

F A P C C I Review (Federation of Andhra Pradesh Chambers of Commerce & Industry) (IND) **1402**

F A P E Review (Fund for Assistance to Private Education) (PHL ISSN 0115-8090) **2856**

F A P I G (First Atomic Power Industry Group) (JPN ISSN 0014-5645) **3167**

F A P Journal (Fine Arts Philatelists) (USA) **6894**

F A Q, Frequently Asked Questions About Public Broadcasting (USA ISSN 1936-2315) **2381**

F A R *see* Federal Acquisition Regulation (Washington) **7436**

F A R *see* Federal Acquisition Regulation (Chicago) **6421**

F A R Archives *see* Federal Acquisition Regulation (Chicago) **6421**

F A R FastSearch (Federal Acquisition Regulations) (USA) **1288**

F A R M Report (Farm Animal Report Movement) (USA) **6658**

• ➤ The F A R M S Review (Foundation for Ancient Research and Mormon Studies) (USA ISSN 1550-3194) **7735**

F A R M S Review of Books *see* The F A R M S Review **7735**

• F A R Skatt & Redovisning (Online Edition) (Foereningen Auktoriserade Revisorer) (SWE ISSN 1653-4905) **1288**

F A Rendement (NLD ISSN 1568-1130) **1288**

F A Rs Normsamling foer den Offentliga Sektion (Foereningen Autoriserade Revisorer) (SWE ISSN 1653-509X) **1288**

F A Rs Regelsamling *see* Vaerdepapper **4806**

F A Rs Regelsamling *see* Boers **4630**

F A Rs Regelsamling *see* Bank & Foersaekring **4626**

F A S A Update (Federated Ambulatory Surgery Association) (USA ISSN 1559-6990) **6243**

F A S B Interpretation (Financial Accounting Standards Board) (USA ISSN 0193-7855) **1288**

F A S B Technical Bulletin (Financial Accounting Standards Board) (USA ISSN 0886-4535) **1288**

• ➤ The F A S E B Journal (Federation of American Societies for Experimental Biology) (USA ISSN 0892-6638) **672**

F A S E B News (Federation of American Societies for Experimental Biology) (USA) **672**

F A S/E S R I Manpower Forecasting Studies (Foras Aiseanna Saothair/Economic and Social Research Institute) (IRL) **1485**

F A S - F A X: Canadian Daily Newspapers (USA ISSN 1082-4634) **38**

F A S - F A X Reports: Business Publications (USA) **38**

F A S - F A X Reports: Magazine, Farm and Religious Publications (USA) **38**

F A S - F A X: United States and Canadian Weekly Newpapers (USA) **38**

F A S - F A X: United States Daily Newspapers (USA) **38**

• F A S G O Ciencia (Federacion Argentina de Sociedades de Ginecologia y Obstetrica) (ARG) **5990**

• F A S G O Informa (Federacion Argentina de Sociedades de Ginecologia y Obstetrica) (ARG) **5990**

F A S Handbook (Federation of Astronomical Societies) (GBR) **574**

• F A S Public Interest Report (Federation of American Scientists) (USA ISSN 0092-9824) **7854**

F A S S *see* F A S S - Laekemedel i Sverige **6840**

F A S S - Laekemedel i Sverige (Farmacevtiska Specialiteter i Sverige) (SWE ISSN 1400-6588) **6840**

F A S S Vet (Farmaceutiska Specialiteter i Sverige) (SWE ISSN 0347-1136) **6840**

• F A S T (Flight, Airworthiness, Support and Techology) (FRA ISSN 1293-5476) **54**

• F A S T Conference Papers (Fast Sea Transportation) (AUS) **8643**

• F A S Worldwide (Foreign Agricultural Service) (USA ISSN 1559-6648) **197**

F A T - Berichte *see* A R T - Berichte **78**

➤ F A T E in Review (Foundations in Art Theory and Education) (USA ISSN 1090-3372) **489**

• F A U-Conferenen (Foreningen af Udviklingsforskere i Danmark) (DNK ISSN 1903-5829) **1595**

F A U Free Press (Florida Atlantic University) (USA) **2283**

• F A U Nyt (Foreningen af Udviklingsforskere) (DNK ISSN 1395-4911) **1595**

• F A V E. Seccion Ciencias Agrarias (Facultad de Ciencias Agrarias. Seccion Ciencias Agrarias) (ARG ISSN 1666-7719) **109**

F A V E. Seccion Ciencias Veterinarias (Facultad de Ciencias Veterinarias. Seccion Ciencias Veterinarias) (ARG ISSN 1666-938X) **8797**

† F A Z Weekly (Frankfurter Allgemeine Zeitung) (DEU) **8955**

F & A Actueel (Financieel en Administratief) (NLD ISSN 1568-5802) **1744**

▼ F & B (Food & Beverage Business) (USA ISSN 1943-0256) **197**

F & B J *see* The Food and Beverage Journal **3637**

F & F Select *see* Facility and Finance Select **8955**

F & H - Foerdern und Heben (DEU ISSN 0341-2636) **3377**

• F & I Management and Technology (Finance & Insurance) (USA ISSN 1529-5656) **8580**

F & I News (Finance & Insurance) (ZAF ISSN 1814-1374) **1340**

F & J *see* Flotsam & Jetsam **944**

F & L Primo *see* Primo **3559**

F and M *see* F & M **6311**

• F & M (Fabricating & Metalworking) (USA ISSN 1541-2415) **6311**

F & O *see* Fusie & Overname **1112**

F & O S Motor Carrier Annual Report *see* Motor Carrier Annual Reports **8527**

F & P *see* Fundraising & Philanthropy Australasia **1746**

F & P *see* Feminism & Psychology **7357**

F & S Index. United States (Annual) (Funk and Scott) (USA ISSN 1076-4941) **1228**

F & T Weekly (Finansies en Tegniek) (ZAF ISSN 1024-7408) **1340**

F & V News *see* Fruit & Vegetable News **3730**

• F & W - Fuehren und Wirtschaften im Krankenhaus (DEU ISSN 0175-4548) **4093**

F B G Forum (Fleischerei Berufsgenossenschaft) (DEU ISSN 0946-705X) **3635**

F B - I E (Fortschrittliche Betriebsfuehrung und Industrial Engineering) (DEU ISSN 1431-2271) **1744**

• F B I Law Enforcement Bulletin (Federal Bureau of Investigation) (USA ISSN 0014-5688) **2652**

F B N *see* Fiscale Berichten voor het Notariaat **4674**

F B N *see* Food Business News **3638**

• F B News (Firumu Badji) (JPN ISSN 1349-6395) **7517**

F B News *see* Tennessee Farm Bureau News **161**

F B S. Adult Leader Guide K J V *see* Bible Studies for Life: Life Words K J V Leader Guide **7625**

F B S. Adult Learner Guide H C S B *see* Bible Studies for Life: Life Lessons Learner Guide **7625**

F B S. Advanced Bible Study Commentary *see* Bible Studies for Life: Holman Christian Standard Bible Advanced Bible Study Commentary **7625**

F B S. All Youth Learner Guide H C S B *see* Bible Studies for Life: Life Focus All Youth Learner Guide Holman C S B **7625**

F B S. Collegiate Learner Guide *see* Collegiate+ **7634**

F B S. Older Youth Learner Guide *see* Bible Studies for Life: LifeFX Older Youth Learner **7626**

F B V A Berichte (Forstliche Bundesversuchsanstalt) (AUT ISSN 1013-0713) **3688**

F B W-Information (Filmbewertungsstelle Wiesbaden) (DEU ISSN 0427-8186) **6497**

F C *see* Full Contact **6568**

F C *see* Voetbal Magazine **8250**

• F C & S (Fire, Casualty & Surety) (USA) **4502**

F C B *see* Fuel Cells Bulletin **3135**

• F C C Daily Digest (Federal Communications Commission) (USA) **1485**

F C C. I N F Bulletins *see* U.S. Federal Communications Commission. I N F Bulletins **2343**

F C C Record (U.S. Federal Communications Commission) (USA ISSN 1057-5766) **2320**

• F C C Report (Federal Communications Commission) (USA ISSN 1081-9541) **2320**

F C C Telephone Equipment Registration List (Federal Communications Commission) (USA) **2367**

F C E *see* Folia Cryptogamica Estonica **789**

F C Groningen Presentatiegids (NLD ISSN 1873-6645) **8227**

F C H *see* Family & Community History **4139**

F C I *see* Farm Chemicals International **230**

F C I *see* Floor Covering Installer **1050**

F C I B Country Report (Finance, Credit and International Business - National Association of Credit Management) (USA) **1565**

F C I B Credit Reports (Financial, Credit and International Business) (USA) **1565**

F C I B International Bulletin (Finance, Credit and International Business - National Association of Credit Management) (USA) **1565**

F C I B Minutes of Round Table Conference (Finance, Credit and International Business) (USA) **1565**

F C I L Newsletter (Foreign, Comparative and International Law) (USA) **5009**

F C L J *see* Federal Communications Law Journal **4672**

F C L Newsletter (Friends Committee on Legislation of California) (USA ISSN 0532-7091) **7135**

• F C N L Washington Newsletter (Friends Committee on National Legislation) (USA ISSN 0014-5734) **7135**

F C P R A C Annual Review of Research (Online Edition) *see* F C P R A C Annual Review of Research (Print Edition) **230**

• F C P R A C Annual Review of Research (Print Edition) (Florida Citrus Production Research Advisory Council) (USA ISSN 1935-7974) **230**

F C R *see* The Federal Court Reports **4951**

F C Report *see* Fine Ceramics Report **2041**

F C S Publication (Fish Culture Section) (USA ISSN 0731-065X) **3591**

F C T *see* Food and Chemical Toxicology **3497**

F C W *see* Floor Covering Weekly **4557**

f d (Food Development) (GBR ISSN 1741-7031) **3635**

F D A Approved Animal Drug Products (Food and Drug Administration) (USA ISSN 1064-0258) **6840**

F D A Compliance Policy Guidance. Manual (Food and Drug Administration) (USA) **3635**

• F D A Enforcement Manual (Food and Drug Administration) (USA) **7517**

• F D A Enforcement Report (Online Edition) (USA) **7517**

• F D A Law Weekly (USA ISSN 1551-5079) **4670**

• F D A News Drug Daily Bulletin (Federal Drug Administration) (USA) **6840**

• F D A News Nutraceutical Weekly Bulletin (Federal Drug Administration) (USA ISSN 1554-0049) **6840**

F D A Surveillance Index for Pesticides (Food and Drug Administration) (USA) **3243**

• F D A Veterinarian (Food & Drug Administration) (USA ISSN 1057-6223) **8797**

• F D A Week (Food and Drug Administration) (USA) **2637**

• F D C C Quarterly (Federation of Defense and Corporate Counsel) (USA ISSN 1544-9947) **4867**

• F D C Control Newsletter (Online) (Food, Drug, and Cosmetics) (USA) **3635**

F D C H *see* Front Desk Chicago **3976**

F D I C Data Book 5 - IA, KS, MN, MO, NE, ND, SD *see* Operating Banks and Branches. Data Book 5: Iowa, Kansas, Minnesota, Missouri, Nebraska, North Dakota, South Dakota **1373**

• F D I C Enforcement Decisions and Orders (Online) (U.S. Federal Deposit Insurance Corp.) (USA) **1340**

F D I C Enforcement Decisions and Orders (Print) *see* F D I C Enforcement Decisions and Orders (Online) **1340**

• F D I C Quarterly (U.S. Federal Deposit Insurance Corp.) (USA ISSN 1944-8880) **1340**

▼ • F D I C State Profile, Alabama (U.S. Federal Deposit Insurance Corp.) (USA ISSN 1942-1494) **1228**

▼ • F D I C State Profile, Alaska (U.S. Federal Deposit Insurance Corp.) (USA ISSN 1942-1508) **1228**

▼ • F D I C State Profile, Arizona (U.S. Federal Deposit Insurance Corp.) (USA ISSN 1942-1516) **1228**

▼ • F D I C State Profile, Arkansas (U.S. Federal Deposit Insurance Corp.) (USA ISSN 1942-1524) **1228**

▼ • F D I C State Profile, California (U.S. Federal Deposit Insurance Corp.) (USA ISSN 1942-1532) **1228**

▼ • F D I C State Profile, Colorado (U.S. Federal Deposit Insurance Corp.) (USA ISSN 1942-1540) **1228**

▼ • F D I C State Profile, Connecticut (U.S. Federal Deposit Insurance Corp.) (USA ISSN 1942-1559) **1228**

▼ • F D I C State Profile, Delaware (Federal Deposit Insurance Corporation) (USA ISSN 1942-1567) **1228**

▼ • F D I C State Profile, Florida (Federal Deposit Insurance Corporation) (USA ISSN 1942-1575) **1228**

▼ • F D I C State Profile, Georgia (Federal Deposit Insurance Corporation) (USA ISSN 1942-1583) **1228**

▼ • F D I C State Profile, Hawaii (U.S. Federal Deposit Insurance Corp.) (USA ISSN 1942-1591) **1229**

▼ • F D I C State Profile, Idaho (U.S. Federal Deposit Insurance Corp.) (USA ISSN 1942-1605) **1229**

▼ • F D I C State Profile, Illinois (U.S. Federal Deposit Insurance Corp.) (USA ISSN 1942-1613) **1229**

▼ • F D I C State Profile, Indiana (U.S. Federal Deposit Insurance Corp.) (USA ISSN 1942-1621) **1229**

▼ • F D I C State Profile, Iowa (U.S. Federal Deposit Insurance Corp.) (USA ISSN 1942-163X) **1229**

▼ • F D I C State Profile, Kansas (U.S. Federal Deposit Insurance Corp.) (USA ISSN 1942-1648) **1229**

▼ • F D I C State Profile, Kentucky (U.S. Federal Deposit Insurance Corp.) (USA ISSN 1942-1656) **1229**

▼ • F D I C State Profile, Louisiana (U.S. Federal Deposit Insurance Corp.) (USA ISSN 1942-1664) **1229**

▼ • F D I C State Profile, Maine (U.S. Federal Deposit Insurance Corp.) (USA ISSN 1942-1672) **1229**

▼ • F D I C State Profile, Maryland and Washington, D.C. (U.S. Federal Deposit Insurance Corp.) (USA ISSN 1942-1680) **1229**

▼ • F D I C State Profile, Massachusetts (U.S. Federal Deposit Insurance Corp.) (USA ISSN 1942-1699) **1229**

▼ • F D I C State Profile, Michigan (U.S. Federal Deposit Insurance Corp.) (USA ISSN 1942-1702) **1229**

▼ • F D I C State Profile, Minnesota (U.S. Federal Deposit Insurance Corp.) (USA ISSN 1942-1710) **1229**

▼ • F D I C State Profile, Mississippi (U.S. Federal Deposit Insurance Corp.) (USA ISSN 1942-1729) **1229**

▼ • F D I C State Profile, Missouri (U.S. Federal Deposit Insurance Corp.) (USA ISSN 1942-1737) **1229**

▼ • F D I C State Profile, Montana (U.S. Federal Deposit Insurance Corp.) (USA ISSN 1942-1745) **1229**

▼ • F D I C State Profile, Nebraska (U.S. Federal Deposit Insurance Corp.) (USA ISSN 1942-1753) **1229**

▼ • F D I C State Profile, Nevada (U.S. Federal Deposit Insurance Corp.) (USA ISSN 1942-1761) **1229**

▼ • F D I C State Profile, New Hampshire (U.S. Federal Deposit Insurance Corp.) (USA ISSN 1942-177X) **1229**

▼ • F D I C State Profile, New Jersey (U.S. Federal Deposit Insurance Corp.) (USA ISSN 1942-1788) **1229**

▼ • F D I C State Profile, New Mexico (U.S. Federal Deposit Insurance Corp.) (USA ISSN 1942-1796) **1229**

▼ • F D I C State Profile, New York (U.S. Federal Deposit Insurance Corp.) (USA ISSN 1942-180X) **1229**

▼ • F D I C State Profile, North Carolina (U.S. Federal Deposit Insurance Corp.) (USA ISSN 1942-1818) **1229**

▼ • F D I C State Profile, North Dakota (U.S. Federal Deposit Insurance Corp.) (USA ISSN 1942-1826) **1229**

▼ • F D I C State Profile, Ohio (U.S. Federal Deposit Insurance Corp.) (USA ISSN 1942-1834) **1229**

▼ • F D I C State Profile, Oklahoma (U.S. Federal Deposit Insurance Corp.) (USA ISSN 1942-1842) **1229**

▼ • F D I C State Profile, Oregon (U.S. Federal Deposit Insurance Corp.) (USA ISSN 1942-1850) **1229**

▼ • F D I C State Profile, Pennsylvania (U.S. Federal Deposit Insurance Corp.) (USA ISSN 1942-1869) **1229**

▼ • F D I C State Profile, Puerto Rico and the U.S. Virgin Islands (U.S. Federal Deposit Insurance Corp.) (USA ISSN 1942-1877) **1229**

DIRECTORY 2010 F I J ACTIVIST 10269

▼ • F D I C State Profile, Rhode Island (U.S. Federal Deposit Insurance Corp.) (USA ISSN 1942-1885) **1229**
▼ • F D I C State Profile, South Carolina (U.S. Federal Deposit Insurance Corp.) (USA ISSN 1942-1893) **1229**
▼ • F D I C State Profile, South Dakota (U.S. Federal Deposit Insurance Corp.) (USA ISSN 1942-1907) **1229**
▼ • F D I C State Profile, Tennessee (U.S. Federal Deposit Insurance Corp.) (USA ISSN 1942-1915) **1229**
▼ • F D I C State Profile, Texas (U.S. Federal Deposit Insurance Corp.) (USA ISSN 1942-1923) **1229**
▼ • F D I C State Profile, Utah (U.S. Federal Deposit Insurance Corp.) (USA ISSN 1942-1931) **1229**
▼ • F D I C State Profile, Vermont (U.S. Federal Deposit Insurance Corp.) (USA ISSN 1942-194X) **1108**
▼ • F D I C State Profile, Virginia (U.S. Federal Deposit Insurance Corp.) (USA ISSN 1942-1958) **1229**
▼ • F D I C State Profile, Washington (U.S. Federal Deposit Insurance Corp.) (USA ISSN 1942-1966) **1229**
▼ • F D I C State Profile, West Virginia (U.S. Federal Deposit Insurance Corp.) (USA ISSN 1942-1974) **1229**
▼ • F D I C State Profile, Wisconsin (U.S. Federal Deposit Insurance Corp.) (USA ISSN 1942-1982) **1229**
▼ • F D I C State Profile, Wyoming (U.S. Federal Deposit Insurance Corp.) (USA ISSN 1942-1990) **1230**
• F D I C Statistics on Banking (U.S. Federal Deposit Insurance Corp.) (USA) **1230**
• F D I C. Summary of Deposits. Bank & Thrift Branch Office Data Book. Central Region (U.S. Federal Deposit Insurance Corp., Division of Insurance and Research) (USA) **1340**
• F D I C. Summary of Deposits. Bank & Thrift Branch Office Data Book. Midwest Region (U.S. Federal Deposit Insurance Corp., Division of Insurance and Research) (USA) **1340**
• F D I C. Summary of Deposits. Bank & Thrift Branch Office Data Book. National (U.S. Federal Deposit Insurance Corp., Division of Insurance and Research) (USA) **1341**
• F D I C. Summary of Deposits. Bank & Thrift Branch Office Data Book. Northeast Region (U.S. Federal Deposit Insurance Corp., Division of Insurance and Research) (USA) **1341**
• F D I C. Summary of Deposits. Bank & Thrift Branch Office Data Book. Southeast Region (U.S. Federal Deposit Insurance Corp., Division of Insurance and Research) (USA) **1341**
• F D I C. Summary of Deposits. Bank & Thrift Branch Office Data Book. Southwest Region (U.S. Federal Deposit Insurance Corp., Division of Insurance and Research) (USA) **1341**
F D I World (Federation Dentaire Internationale) (GBR ISSN 1025-403X) **5844**
F D L *see* The Food & Drug Letter **6842**
• F D Legal (Financial Director) (GBR ISSN 1752-8011) **1341**
F D M *see* Food Distribution Magazine **3638**
• F D M (Furniture Design & Manufacturing) (USA ISSN 1098-6812) **4556**
F D M Asia (Furniture Design & Manufacturing) (SGP ISSN 0218-7663) **4556**
F D M P *see* Fluid Dynamics & Materials Processing **7058**
F D N Z Newsletter *see* Folkdancers' Own **2686**
F D O *see* For Dickheads Only **5442**
F D Outlook (Financieele Dagblad) (NLD ISSN 1877-2374) **1744**
F D P Law Series (Fourth Dimension Publishing Co. Ltd.) (NGA) **4670**
F D Persoonlijk (Financieele Dagblad) (NLD ISSN 1872-5872) **1108**
F D Q Fashion Doll Quarterly (USA) **4334**
F D Strategie *see* F D Outlook **1744**
➤ F D U Magazine (Fairleigh Dickinson University) (USA) **2283**
F D V *see* Forvaltning, Drift, Vedlikehold **1746**
F D Y *see* The Finance Director's Yearbook **1343**
F E *see* Feminist Economics **1109**
F E *see* Fleet Equipment **8670**
F E *see* Food Engineering **3638**
F E & S *see* Foodservice Equipment & Supplies **4386**
F E B Bulletin (Federation des Entreprises de Belgique) (BEL ISSN 0771-2987) **1885**
F E B E L G R A Tijdschrift (Federatie van de Belgische Industrie) (BEL) **7320**
• ➤ The F E B S Journal (Federation of European of Biochemical Societies) (GBR ISSN 1742-464X) **732**
• The F E B S Journal (Online) (Federation of European Biochemical Societies) (GBR ISSN 1742-4658) **732**
• ➤ F E B S Letters (Federation of European Biochemical Societies) (NLD ISSN 0014-5793) **732**
F E D A News & Views (Foodservice Equipment Distributors Association) (USA ISSN 0746-9675) **4385**
• F E D M A - Membership News (Federation of European Direct Marketing) (BEL) **25**
F E D R I P Database *see* Federal Research in Progress Database **3192**
F.E.D.S. (USA) **6566**
F E E M Series on Economics, Energy and Environment (Fondazione ENI Enrico Mattei) (NLD ISSN 1380-6866) **3135**
• F E F C Corporate Plan (Further Education Funding Council) (GBR) **2980**
F E L A Reporter & Railroad Liability Monitor (Federal Employees Liability Act) (USA ISSN 1044-6648) **4670**
F E M *see* Forbrugerelektronik Magasinet **8957**
F E M Business *see* F E M Business and Finance **1341**
• F E M Business and Finance (Financieel Economisch Magazine) (NLD) **1341**
F E M De Week *see* F E M Business and Finance **1341**
• F E M E D E. Boletin (Federacion Espanola de Medicina del Deporte) (ESP) **6229**
F E M M *see* Foundation & Endowment Money Management **1625**
• ➤ F E M S Immunology and Medical Microbiology (Federation of European Microbiological Societies) (GBR ISSN 0928-8244) **885**
† ➤ F E M S Microbiology (Federation of European Microbiological Societies) (GBR ISSN 0921-8254) **8955**
• ➤ F E M S Microbiology Ecology (Federation of European Microbiological Societies) (GBR ISSN 0168-6496) **885**
• ➤ F E M S Microbiology Letters (Federation of European Microbiological Societies) (GBR ISSN 0378-1097) **885**
• ➤ F E M S Microbiology Reviews (Federation of European Microbiological Societies) (GBR ISSN 0168-6445) **885**
• F E M S News (Federation of European Materials Societies) (DEU) **3344**
F E M S Symposium (Federation of European Microbiological Societies) (USA ISSN 0163-9188) **886**
• ➤ F E M S Yeast Research (Federation of European Microbiological Societies) (GBR ISSN 1567-1356) **886**
• F E N (AUS ISSN 0728-9413) **8422**
F E N *see* Fabricating Equipment News **6311**
F E N S A News (Fenestration Self-Assessment Scheme) (GBR) **2041**
F E O R *see* Federal Equal Opportunity Reporter **1681**
F E P A G R O Boletim (Fundacao Estadual de Pesquisa Agropecuaria, Secretaria da Ciencia e Tecnologia) (BRA ISSN 0104-9089) **109**
F E P C Briefing Note (Federation of Electric Power Companies) (JPN) **3308**
F E P N *see* Fire / E M S Product News **3577**
F E R C Report *see* S N L - F E R C Report **3147**
The F E R C Report (Financial Enforcement Regulation Compliance) (USA) **1341**
F E R N Journal (Further Education Research Network) (GBR ISSN 0260-5058) **2980**
The F E S P A Magazine *see* F E S P A World **7320**
F E S P A World (Federation of European Screen Printers Associations) (GBR) **7320**
F E Supplied-Reference Handbook *see* Fundamentals of Engineering Supplied-Reference Handbook **3193**
F E V S *see* Fuersorgerechtliche Entscheidungen der Verwaltungs- und Sozialgerichte **8041**
F E W A Membership Directory (Farm Equipment Wholesalers Association) (USA) **210**
F E W A Tips (Farm Equipment Wholesalers Association) (USA) **210**
F E W Journal *see* Freemen of England & Wales Journal **7207**
• F E W's News and Views (Federally Employed Women Inc.) (USA ISSN 0895-3619) **7436**
F E Z A N A Journal (Federation of Zoroastrian Associations of North America) (USA ISSN 1068-2376) **7735**
F en D *see* F+D Fotografie **6967**
F+D Fotografie (NLD) **6967**
† F F (Fremdsprachen Fruehbeginn) (DEU ISSN 1613-2009) **8955**
▼ F F 3 C Informations (Federation Francaise des Combustibles Carburants et Chauffage) (FRA ISSN 1962-9214) **6768**
F F A *see* Foundation & Corporate Funding Advantage **8041**
F F A *see* Family Foundation Advisor **4671**
• F F A Advisors Making a Difference (Future Farmers of America) (USA) **109**
• F F A New Horizons (Future Farmers of America) (USA ISSN 1069-806X) **109**
F F A News Digest *see* M C S Newsletter **3601**
F F A Report (South Pacific Forum Fisheries Agency) (SLB) **3591**
F F A-V M S Newsletter *see* M C S Newsletter **3601**
F F C *see* Films for the Feminist Classroom **8863**
▼ F F C G E A. La Lettre (Federation Francaise des Associations de Gestion et de Comptabilite et des Centres de Gestion et d'E) (FRA ISSN 1955-5237) **1960**
➤ F F Communications (Folklore Fellows) (FIN ISSN 0014-5815) **3617**
F F F S *see* Finansinspektionens Foerfattningssamling **7437**
F F - Forum Familien- und Erbrecht *see* Forum Familienrecht **4910**
• F F I - Fokus (Forsvarets Forskningsinstitutt) (NOR ISSN 1503-4399) **6420**
F F I Publication (Forsvarets Forskningsinstitutt) (NOR) **7854**
F F I Rapport (Forsvarets Forskningsinstitutt) (NOR ISSN 0802-2437) **6420**
F F Journal (Fabricating & Forming) (USA ISSN 1551-1006) **6311**
• F. F. M. Annuaire - Ligues, Comites Departementaux et Clubs (Federation Francaise de Motocyclisme (F F M)) (FRA) **8172**
F F Magazin (Frauenfussball) (DEU) **8227**
• F F Network (FIN ISSN 0789-0249) **3617**
• f f - Suedtiroler Wochenmagazin (ITA) **3897**
F F T C Book Series (Food and Fertilizer Technology Center) (TWN ISSN 0253-9616) **230**
• F F T C Newsletter (Food and Fertilizer Technology Center) (TWN) **230**
• F F T C Technical Bulletin (Food and Fertilizer Technology Center) (TWN) **230**
F G *see* La France Graphique **7321**
F G *see* Farmers Guide **112**
▼ F G (Formal Grammar) (USA ISSN 1935-1569) **5118**
F G A *see* Fucking Good Art **490**
F G B G (For Girls by Girls) (USA ISSN 1554-5253) **2188**
F G C S The International Journal of Grid Computing: Theory, Methods and Applications *see* Future Generation Computer Systems **2520**
• F G D & DeNOx Newsletter (USA) **3158**
F G D and DeNOx Newsletter *see* F G D & DeNOx Newsletter **3158**
• F G D C Newsletter (Federal Geographic Data Committee) (USA ISSN 1073-0613) **4006**
F G G B Rundbriefe (Forschungsgemeinschaft Grossbritannien) (BEL ISSN 1437-4382) **6894**
F G M News (Functionally Gradient Materials) (JPN) **8422**
F G Prax *see* Praxis der Freiwilligen Gerichtsbarkeit **4840**
F G S Delegate Digest (Federation of Genealogical Societies) (USA) **3765**
• F G V. Boletim Cenarios (Fundacao Getulio Vargas) (BRA) **1485**
F G W Schriftenreihe (Forschungsgesellschaft fuer Wohnen Bauen und Planen) (AUT) **1007**
F H *see* Scen & Salong **4982**
F H A Home Mortgage Insurance Operations *see* U.S. Department of Housing and Urban Development. F H A Home Mortgage Insurance Operations: State, County and M S A - P M S A **4437**
F H A Homes *see* U.S. Department of Housing and Urban Development. F H A Homes **4437**
F H A Homes (Supplement) *see* U.S. Department of Housing and Urban Development. F H A Homes (Supplement) **4437**
F H A Monthly Report of Operations. Project Insurance Programs *see* U.S. Department of Housing and Urban Development. F H A Monthly Report of Operations. Project Insurance Programs **4437**
F H A Report of Insurance Operations Under Home Mortgage Programs for (Month) *see* U.S. Department of Housing and Urban Development. F H A Report of Insurance Operations under Home Mortgage Programs for (Month) **4437**
F H A Trends of Home Mortgage Characteristics *see* U.S. Department of Housing and Urban Development. F H A Trends of Home Mortgage Characteristics **4437**
F H D W Fachbericht (Fachhochschule der Wirtschaft) (DEU) **1108**
F H D W Schriftenreihe (Fachhochschule der Wirtschaft) (DEU ISSN 1610-1650) **2981**
F.H.I. Annual: Fresh and Industrialized Fruits and Vegetables *see* Anuario F.H.I. Argentina: Frutas y Hortalizas Industrializadas y Frescas **218**
F H I Chicago (For Her Information) (USA ISSN 1557-9123) **8862**
F H M (Australia) (For Him Magazine) (AUS ISSN 1440-3358) **6289**
F H M (Bejing) *see* Nanrenzhuang **6296**
† F H M (Denmark) (For Him Magazine) (DNK ISSN 1603-3736) **8955**
F H M (Estonia) (For Him Magazine) (EST ISSN 1736-1443) **6289**
F H M (France) (For Him Magazine) (FRA ISSN 1295-9138) **6289**
F H M (Germany) (For Him Magazine) (DEU ISSN 1860-0026) **6289**
F H M (Greece) (GRC) **6289**
F H M (Hungary) (Ferfiak Himek Magazinja) (HUN ISSN 1586-4839) **6289**
F H M (Indonesia) (IDN) **6289**
F H M (Latvia) (For Him Magazine) (LVA ISSN 1691-094X) **6289**
F H M (Lithuania) (For Him Magazine) (LTU ISSN 1648-9837) **6289**
F H M (Malaysia) (For Him Magazine) (MYS ISSN 1511-3248) **6289**
F H M (Mexico) (For Him Magazine) (MEX) **6289**
F H M (Netherlands) (For Him Magazine) (NLD ISSN 1568-184X) **6289**
F H M (Norway) (For Him Magazine) (NOR ISSN 1504-0100) **6289**
F H M (Philippines) (For Him Magazine) (PHL) **6289**
F H M (Portugal) (For Him Magazine) (PRT) **6289**
F H M (Romania) (For Him Magazine) (ROM ISSN 1583-6517) **6289**
F H M (Russia) (For Him Magazine) (RUS) **6290**
F H M (Singapore) (For Him Magazine) (SGP) **6290**
F H M (Slovenia) (For Him Magazine) (SVN) **6290**
F H M (South Africa) (ZAF ISSN 1562-4692) **6290**
F H M (Spain) (For Him Magazine) (ESP) **6290**
F H M (Sweden) (For Him Magazine) (SWE) **6290**
F H M (Taiwan) (For Him Magazine) (TWN ISSN 1606-6995) **6290**
F H M (Thailand) (For Him Magazine) (THA ISSN 0859-2527) **6290**
F H M (Turkey) (For Him Magazine) (TUR) **6290**
F H M (Ukraine) (UKR) **6290**
• F H M (United Kingdom) (GBR ISSN 0966-0933) **6290**
† F H M Collections (For Him Magazine) (AUS ISSN 1448-2452) **8955**
F H M Collections (For Him Magazine) (DEU) **2254**
F H M Collections (For Him Magazine) (GBR ISSN 1463-3949) **2254**
F H O *see* Freehouse Owner **4386**
F H Presse (Fachhochschule Dortmund) (DEU) **2856**
F H S *see* Coaching Edge **8167**
F I *see* Forum Italicum **5297**
F I *see* Free Inquiry **6921**
F I A B C I Press (International Real Estate Federation (FIABCI)) (FRA ISSN 0767-0192) **7590**
• F I A F International FilmArchive CD-ROM (International Federation of Film Archives) (BEL ISSN 1355-1671) **6518**
F I A F International FilmArchive Database *see* International Index to Film Periodicals **6518**
F I A F International Index to Film Periodicals *see* International Index to Film Periodicals **6518**
F I A Kenkyu Kondankai Kaishi *see* Journal of Flow Injection Analysis **2102**
F I A S - Report (Forschungsgemeinschaft Internationale Antwortscheine) (DEU) **6894**
F I A T A Review (Federation Internationale des Associations de Transitaires et Assimiles) (CHE) **8496**
F I B A Basketball (Federation Internationale de Basketball Amateur) (GBR ISSN 0959-888X) **8227**
F I B Bulletin (Federation Internationale du Beton) (CHE ISSN 1562-3610) **1007**
▼ • F I B E R (Fashion International Business Education Response) (USA ISSN 1946-1534) **2247**
F I C E (Federation Internationale des Communautes d'Enfants) (DNK ISSN 1901-5062) **2152**
F I / C O Expert *see* S A P Financials Expert **2524**
• F I D I C International Directory of Consulting Engineers (Federation Internationale des Ingenieurs Conseils) (GBR) **1993**
F I D I Focus (Federation Internationale des Demenageurs Internationaux) (GBR) **8643**
† F I D Publication/Federation International de Documentation. Publication/Internationalen Verbandes fuer Dokumentation. Veroeffentlichungen (International Federation for Information and Documentation) (NLD ISSN 0168-6224) **8955**
F I F A - Coca-Cola Cup *see* F I F A World Youth Championship **8227**
F I F A Handbook (Federation Internationale de Football Association) (CHE) **8227**
† F I F A Magazine (Federation Internationale de Football Association) (DEU) **8955**
F I F A News (Federation Internationale de Football Association) (CHE) **8227**
F I F A O *see* Institut Francais d'Archeologie Orientale du Caire. Fouilles **398**
F I F A Olympic Football Tournament (Federation Internationale de Football Association) (CHE) **8227**
F I F A Technical Reports (Federation Internationale de Football Association) (CHE) **8227**
F I F A U-17 World Championship (Federation Internationale de Football Association) (CHE) **8227**
F I F A World Cup (Federation Internationale de Football Association) (CHE) **8227**
F I F A World Youth Championship (Federation Internationale de Football Association) (CHE) **8227**
F I. Fondazione Liberal *see* Fondazione Liberal **8957**
F I G A Magazine (Fretted Instrument Guild of America) (USA ISSN 0196-187X) **6566**
• F I I Annual Guide to Bonds (Financial Information Incorporated) (USA) **1623**
• F I I Annual Guide to Stocks (Financial Information Incorporated) (USA) **1623**
F I I Q en Action *see* F I Q en Action (English Edition) **5958**
F I I Q en Action *see* F I Q en Action (French Edition) **5958**
F I I R O Industrial Abstracts (Federal Institute of Industrial Research Oshodi) (NGA) **1230**
F I I R O Technical Information Bulletin for Industry (Federal Institute of Industrial Research Oshodi) (NGA) **1885**
F I IQ Women's Network. Le Reseau (CAN ISSN 1911-5288) **5958**
F I J Activist (Fully Informed Jury Association) (USA) **4670**

Title

Title

Title

10276 FAYETTE COUNTY (KY.) GENEALOGICAL SOCIETY QUARTERLY ULRICH'S PERIODICALS

Fayette County (Ky.) Genealogical Society Quarterly (USA ISSN 0892-5194) **3766**
Fayette Legal Journal (USA ISSN 0196-4194) **4671**
• Fayin/The Voice Dharma (CHN ISSN 1004-2636) **7701**
• ➤ Fayixue Zazhi/Journal of Forensic Medicine (CHN ISSN 1004-5619) **5913**
Fayoum Journal of Agricultural Research and Development/Magallat al-Fayyum al-Bihuth wa-al-Tanmiyyat al-Zira'iyyat (EGY ISSN 1110-7790) **112**
• Fayu Xuexi/Apprenons le Francais (CHN ISSN 1002-1434) **5118**
Fayyum Sudies (ITA ISSN 1827-3831) **393**
▼ • Faz (CHL ISSN 0718-526X) **489**
Faze Magazine (CAN ISSN 1706-0745) **2188**
Fazenda (UKR) **4977**
• Fazhan Yanjiu/Development Research (CHN ISSN 1003-0670) **1109**
Fazhi (CHN) **4671**
Fazhi (Ha'erbin) (CHN ISSN 1009-802X) **4671**
Fazhi Liaowang/Legal Outlook (CHN) **2652**
Fazhi Rensheng/Law Life (CHN ISSN 1673-4661) **4671**
• Fazhi Ribao/Legal Daily (CHN) **4671**
Fazhi Tiandi (CHN ISSN 1003-5818) **4671**
Fazhi Yanjiu/Law Research (CHN ISSN 1674-1455) **4671**
• Fazhi yu Shehui/Legal System and Society (CHN ISSN 1009-0592) **4671**
• Fazhi yu Shehui Fazhan (CHN ISSN 1006-6128) **4671**
Fazhi yu Wenming/Legal System and Civilization (CHN) **4671**
Fazhi yu Xinwen/Law and News (CHN ISSN 1006-5555) **4671**
Fazhi Yuekan/Legality Monthly (CHN ISSN 1003-8663) **4671**
• FDAnews Drug Drug Pipeline Alert (USA) **6842**
Fearnleys Monthly Report (NOR) **8643**
• Fearnleys Weekly Report (NOR) **8643**
Feaschan Staidrimh *see* Ireland. Central Statistics Office. Statistical Bulletin **1245**
Feast of Hate and Fear (USA) **5216**
Feasta (IRL ISSN 0014-8946) **3893**
• Feasting with Fiction (USA ISSN 1552-8006) **5295**
Feather Fancier (CAN ISSN 0380-352X) **286**
• Feathers & Fur (AUS ISSN 1323-4854) **8312**
The Feathertale Review (CAN ISSN 1911-2734) **5295**
Feature *see* Movie Entertainment **6507**
Feature Edition (USA ISSN 1548-1840) **2283**
Featured Reviews in Mathematical Reviews (USA ISSN 1094-3706) **5487**
Febox-Boxeo (ESP) **8172**
• FeBR - Frontiers of e-Business Research (FIN ISSN 1459-0131) **1817**
Fechten/Escrime/Scherma (CHE) **8172**
Fechtsport (DEU ISSN 0720-2229) **8172**
Fed Fiscale Brochures (NLD) **1923**
FED Fiscale Studieserie *see* Fiscale Studieserie **1925**
• Fed in Print (Online) (USA) **1230**
Fed in Print (Print) *see* Fed in Print (Online) **1230**
Fed Rate Watch (Email) *see* Fed Watch **1341**
Fed Tech Magazine (USA ISSN 1552-6976) **7486**
The Fed Tracker (USA ISSN 0889-9223) **1109**
• Fed Watch (USA) **1341**
FEDActueel (NLD ISSN 1872-6526) **3378**
Fedayie (NOR ISSN 1504-0704) **4321**
• FedCon (GBR) **7436**
• ➤ Feddes Repertorium (DEU ISSN 0014-8962) **787**
Fedelec (Dutch Edition) (BEL ISSN 1379-6429) **3308**
Fedelec (French Edition) (BEL ISSN 1379-6437) **3308**
† Fedelta (ITA) **8956**
Fedelta del Suono (ITA ISSN 1121-5313) **6566**
Feder Pesca (ESP) **3591**
Federaal Agentschap voor Nucleaire Controle. Jaarverslag (BEL ISSN 1784-018X) **7066**
Federacio Esperantista Fervojista Austria Sekcio. Bulteno *see* I F E F Austria Sekcio. Bulteno **8618**
• Federacion Argentina de Cardiologia. Revista (ARG ISSN 0326-646X) **5787**
Federacion Argentina de Sociedades de Ginecologia y Obstetrica Ciencia *see* F A S G O Ciencia **5990**
Federacion Argentina de Sociedades de Ginecologia y Obstetrica Informa *see* F A S G O Informa **5990**
Federacion Argentina de Sociedades de Otorrinolaringologia. Revista (ARG ISSN 1666-9398) **6080**
• Federacion. Diario Oficial (Online Edition) (MEX ISSN 1563-7468) **7436**
Federacion Espanola de Medicina del Deporte Boletin *see* F E M E D E. Boletin **6229**
Federacion Espanola de Municipios y Provincias. Revista (ESP) **7492**
Federacion Medica Venezolana. Revista (VEN ISSN 1315-1789) **5613**
Federacion Nacional de Cafeteros de Colombia. Boletin de Informacion Estadistica Sobre Cafe (COL ISSN 0084-7941) **603**
Federacion Nacional de Cafeteros de Colombia. Informe de Labores de los Comites Departamentales de Cafeteros (COL) **3636**
• Federacion Odontologica Colombiana. Revista (COL ISSN 0046-354X) **5844**
Federacion Panamericana de Asociaciones de Facultades de Medicina. Boletin (VEN ISSN 0533-0327) **5613**
Federacja (POL) **2266**
Federacja Polskich Zwiazkow Obroncow Ojczyzny. Biuletyn (POL) **2266**
Federal A D P and Telecommunications Standards Index (USA) **2534**
• Federal Acquisition Regulation (Chicago) (USA ISSN 1084-7898) **6421**
• Federal Acquisition Regulation (Washington) (USA ISSN 1068-7386) **7436**
Federal Acquisition Regulations FastSearch *see* F A R FastSearch **1288**
• Federal Action Affecting the States - State Capitals (USA) **4671**
• Federal Administrative Law (AUS) **4848**
Federal Advertising and Marketing Law Guide (USA) **4672**
Federal Aid to States for Fiscal Year (USA) **7436**
• Federal Air Surgeon's Medical Bulletin (USA ISSN 1545-1518) **5613**
• Federal and Armed Forces Libraries (USA) **5009**
Federal and Florida Evidence Rules (USA ISSN 1930-0964) **4672**
Federal and Foundation Assistance Monitor *see* Federal & Foundation Assistance Monitor **4672**
• Federal & Foundation Assistance Monitor (USA ISSN 1934-5054) **4672**
Federal Appeals: Jurisdiction & Practice *see* Federal Appeals: Jurisdiction and Practice **4951**
Federal Appeals: Jurisdiction and Practice (USA) **4951**
Federal Arbitration Advocate's Handbook (USA ISSN 1071-7617) **4594**
Federal Archeological Programs and Activities: The Secretary of the Interior's Report to Congress (USA) **393**
Federal Assistance Monitor *see* Federal & Foundation Assistance Monitor **4672**
Federal Audit Guides (USA) **1288**
Federal Aviation Administration Aviation Safety Journal *see* F A A Aviation Safety Journal **8540**
Federal Aviation Adinistration. Safety Journal *see* F A A Aviation Safety Journal **8540**
Federal Aviation Administration Airworthiness Directives. Book 2, Large Aircraft (USA) **54**
Federal Aviation Administration Airworthiness Directives. Book 2, Small Aircraft, Rotorcraft, Gliders, and Balloons (USA) **54**
Federal Aviation Administration Aviation Forecasts *see* F A A Aviation Forecasts **54**
Federal Aviation Administration: High Altitude Pollution Program (USA) **8540**
Federal Aviation Administration, Office of Aviation Policy and Plans Long-Range Aerospace Forecasts, Fiscal Years (Year) *see* F A A Long-Range Aerospace Forecasts, Fiscal Years (Year) **54**
Federal Aviation Administration Statistical Handbook of Aviation *see* F A A Statistical Handbook of Aviation **8524**
• Federal Aviation Regulations. Part 1, Definitions and Abbreviations (USA) **54**
• Federal Aviation Regulations. Part 11, General Rule-Making Procedures (USA) **54**
Federal Aviation Regulations. Part 119, Certification: Air Carriers and Commercial Operators (USA) **54**
Federal Aviation Regulations. Part 121, Certification and Operations: Domestic, Flag, and Supplemental Air Carriers and Commercial Operators of Large Aircraft (USA) **54**
Federal Aviation Regulations. Part 125, Certification and Operations: Airplanes Having a Seating Capacity of 20 or More Passengers or a Maximum Payload Capacity of 6,000 Pounds or More (USA) **54**
Federal Aviation Regulations. Part 129, Operations: Foreign Air Carriers and Foreign Operators of United States-Registered Aircraft Engaged in Common Carriage (USA) **54**
Federal Aviation Regulations. Part 13, Investigative and Enforcement Procedures (USA) **54**
Federal Aviation Regulations. Part 135, Air Taxi Operators and Commercial Operators (USA) **54**
Federal Aviation Regulations. Part 145, Repair Stations (USA) **54**
Federal Aviation Regulations. Part 21, Certification Procedures for Products and Parts (USA) **54**
Federal Aviation Regulations. Part 23, Airworthiness Standards: Normal, Utility, Acrobatics, and Commuter Category Airplanes (USA) **54**
Federal Aviation Regulations. Part 25, Airworthiness Standards: Transport Category Airplanes (USA) **54**
Federal Aviation Regulations. Part 27, Airworthiness Standards: Normal Category Rotorcraft (USA) **54**
Federal Aviation Regulations. Part 29, Airworthiness Standards: Transport Category Rotorcraft (USA) **54**
Federal Aviation Regulations. Part 33, Airworthiness Standards: Aircraft Engines (USA) **54**
Federal Aviation Regulations. Part 61, Certification: Pilots, Flight Instructors, and Ground Instructors (USA) **54**
Federal Aviation Regulations. Part 65, Certification: Airmen Other Than Flight Crewmembers (USA) **55**
Federal Aviation Regulations. Part 71, Designation of Federal Airways, Area Low Routes, Controlled Airspace, Reporting Points, Jet Routes, and Area High Routes (USA) **55**
Federal Aviation Regulations. Part 91, General Operating and Flight Rules (USA) **55**
Federal Aviation Regulations. Part 93, Special Air Traffic Rules and Airport Traffic Patterns (USA) **55**
• Federal Banking Law Reporter (USA ISSN 0162-1157) **1341**
Federal Bankruptcy Law Handbook (USA) **4672**
• Federal Bar Association. Section of Taxation. Report (USA ISSN 0742-5317) **1923**
Federal Bar Council News (USA ISSN 1075-8534) **4672**
• Federal Benefits for Veterans and Dependents (USA ISSN 0883-3370) **6421**
Federal Bio-Technology Transfer Directory (USA) **764**
Federal Budget Report (USA ISSN 0898-0071) **7436**
Federal Bureau of Investigation Law Enforcement Bulletin *see* F B I Law Enforcement Bulletin **2652**
Federal Buyers Guide (USA ISSN 1043-7568) **1993**
• Federal Capital Improvements Program for the National Capital Region (USA ISSN 0275-6404) **7436**
• Federal Career Opportunities (USA ISSN 0279-2230) **6697**
Federal Carriers Reporter (USA) **8496**
Federal Carriers Reports *see* Federal Carriers Reporter **8496**
† • Federal Cases (Disk 1) (AUS ISSN 1443-5527) **8956**
† • Federal Cases (Disk 2) (AUS ISSN 1443-5535) **8956**
Federal Circuit Annual Review (USA ISSN 1933-4516) **4672**
• Federal Circuit Bar Journal (USA ISSN 1055-8195) **4672**
▼ Federal Circuit Historical Society. Journal (USA ISSN 1942-9487) **4951**
Federal Circuit Yearbook (USA ISSN 1532-6632) **4951**
Federal Civil Judicial Procedure and Rules (USA ISSN 1080-7578) **4830**
• Federal Civil Litigation Precedents (AUS) **4831**
Federal Civil Procedure Handbook (USA) **4831**
Federal Civil Procedure Litigation Manual *see* Weissenberger's Federal Civil Procedure (Year) Litigation Manual **4844**
Federal Civilian Workforce Statistics. Affirmative Employment Statistics (USA) **1230**
Federal Civilian Workforce Statistics. Employment and Trends (USA ISSN 1058-0859) **1230**
Federal Civilian Workforce Statistics. Occupations of Federal White-Collar and Blue-Collar Workers *see* U.S. Office of Personnel Management. Personnel Systems and Oversight Group. Federal Civilian Workforce Statistics. Occupations of Federal White-Collar and Blue-Collar Workers **1272**
Federal Civilian Workforce Statistics. Pay Structure of the Federal Civil Service (USA) **1230**
Federal Civilian Workforce Statistics. Work Years and Personnel Costs. Executive Branch, United States Government (USA ISSN 0277-3325) **1230**
Federal Claims Reporter (USA ISSN 1067-4934) **4951**
Federal Claims Reporter. Bound Volumes *see* Federal Claims Reporter **4951**
Federal Coal Management Report (USA ISSN 0192-3862) **6462**
Federal Communications Commission Daily Digest *see* F C C Daily Digest **1485**
Federal Communications Commission Report *see* F C C Report **2320**
Federal Communications Commission Reports (USA ISSN 0098-3942) **2321**
Federal Communications Commission Telephone Equipment Registration List *see* F C C Telephone Equipment Registration List **2367**
• ➤ Federal Communications Law Journal (USA ISSN 0163-7606) **4672**
• Federal Computer Market Report (USA ISSN 1042-721X) **2513**
• Federal Computer Week (USA ISSN 0893-052X) **7486**
• Federal Contract Disputes (USA ISSN 0747-9700) **4867**
Federal Contract Management: A Manual for the Contract Professional (USA) **1745**
• Federal Contracts Daily (USA ISSN 1534-441X) **7436**
• Federal Contracts Report (USA ISSN 0014-9063) **7436**
Federal Court Clerks' News (USA) **4831**
• Federal Court Management Statistics (USA ISSN 0741-692X) **4951**
• Federal Court of Canada Service (CAN) **4951**
• Federal Court Practice (AUS) **4951**
Federal Court Practice (CAN ISSN 1187-5089) **4951**
Federal Court Procurement Decisions (USA ISSN 0734-9513) **4672**
• The Federal Court Reports (AUS ISSN 0813-7803) **4951**
Federal Courtroom Evidence (USA) **4951**
• The Federal Courts Law Review (USA ISSN 1936-2471) **4831**
Federal Credit Union (USA ISSN 1043-7789) **1341**
• Federal Criminal Code and Rules (USA ISSN 1080-5516) **4889**
• Federal Criminal Law (AUS) **4889**
Federal Criminal Law Handbook (USA) **4889**
Federal Criminal Practice. Seventh Circuit Handbook (USA ISSN 1932-0531) **4889**
Federal Criminal Rules Handbook (USA) **4889**
Federal Criminal Trials (USA) **4889**
Federal Data Base Finder (USA ISSN 0897-4810) **2530**
Federal Deposit Insurance Corporation State Profile, Delaware *see* F D I C State Profile, Delaware **1228**
Federal Deposit Insurance Corporation State Profile, Florida *see* F D I C State Profile, Florida **1228**
Federal Deposit Insurance Corporation State Profile, Georgia *see* F D I C State Profile, Georgia **1228**
The Federal Directory (USA ISSN 0360-3512) **7436**
• Federal Discovery News (USA ISSN 1082-4782) **4672**
Federal Drug Administration News Drug Daily Bulletin *see* F D A News Drug Daily Bulletin **6840**
Federal Drug Administration News Nutraceutical Weekly Bulletin *see* F D A News Nutraceutical Weekly Bulletin **6840**
• Federal E E O Advisor (USA ISSN 1098-9307) **4672**
Federal Election Campaign Financing Guide (USA ISSN 0195-5330) **1341**
• Federal Election Commission. Record (USA ISSN 0145-8566) **7135**
Federal Elections (USA ISSN 8756-4890) **7135**
Federal Employee (USA ISSN 0014-9071) **7436**
• Federal Employees Almanac (USA ISSN 0071-4127) **7436**
Federal Employees Liability Act Reporter & Railroad Liability Monitor *see* F E L A Reporter & Railroad Liability Monitor **4670**
• Federal Employees News Digest (USA ISSN 1065-0970) **7436**
Federal Employment Law (CAN) **4672**
Federal Employment Law Insider (USA ISSN 1545-617X) **4848**
Federal Employment Statistics. Biennial Report of Employment by Geographic Area (USA ISSN 8756-7156) **7436**
Federal Energy Regulatory Commission. Annual Report (USA ISSN 0195-9069) **3135**
• Federal Energy Regulatory Commission Reports. Opinions, Orders & Decisions (USA) **3135**
Federal Environmental Laws (USA ISSN 1045-408X) **4672**
Federal Equal Opportunity Reporter (USA ISSN 1043-7274) **1681**
Federal Equal Opportunity Year Book (USA) **1681**
• Federal Estate and Gift Tax Reports (USA ISSN 0162-1114) **4902**
Federal Estate & Gift Taxation *see* Federal Estate and Gift Taxation **1923**
• Federal Estate and Gift Taxation (USA) **1923**
Federal Estate and Gift Taxation. Supplement *see* Federal Estate and Gift Taxation **1923**
Federal Ethics Report (USA ISSN 1080-210X) **7436**
Federal Evidence Courtroom Manual (USA) **4951**
• Federal Evidence Practice Guide (USA) **4672**
Federal Evidence Practice Guide Reporter (USA) **4672**
Federal Excise Tax Reporter *see* Federal Excise Tax Reports **1923**
• Federal Excise Tax Reports (USA ISSN 0414-0141) **1923**
• Federal Firearms Regulations Reference Guide (USA ISSN 1930-451X) **4672**
Federal Funds Information for States Newsletter (USA) **7437**
Federal Geographic Data Committee Newsletter *see* F G D C Newsletter **4006**
• ➤ Federal Governance (CAN) **7135**
Federal Grant Deadline Calendar (USA ISSN 1080-5575) **7492**
Federal Grant Deadline Calendar. A Supplement to the Guide to Federal Funding for Education (USA ISSN 1080-5583) **3022**
• Federal Grants & Contracts Weekly (USA ISSN 0194-2247) **4672**
• Federal Grants Management Handbook (USA ISSN 0195-2617) **1745**
• Federal Guidebook (CAN ISSN 1205-6294) **7437**
• Federal Habeas Corpus Practice and Procedure (USA) **4951**
▼ ➤ Federal History (USA ISSN 1943-8036) **7135**
Federal Home Loan Bank of Atlanta. Annual Report (USA) **1341**
▼ • Federal Home Loan Bank of Boston. Results (USA ISSN 1946-2875) **1341**
Federal Home Loan Bank of Chicago. Annual Report (USA) **1341**
Federal Home Loan Bank of Dallas. Annual Report (USA) **1341**
Federal Home Loan Bank of Des Moines. Annual Report (USA) **1341**
Federal Home Loan Bank of Des Moines. Weekly Financial Bulletin (USA) **1341**
Federal Home Loan Bank of Indianapolis. Annual Report (USA) **1341**
Federal Home Loan Bank of San Francisco. Annual Report. (USA ISSN 0098-2830) **1341**
Federal Home Loan Bank of Seattle. Annual Report (USA) **1341**

▼ new title   † ceased   ● electronic media   ➤ refereed

10278 FEDERATIE VAN DE CHEMISCHE INDUSTRIE VAN BELGIE. ACTIVITEITENVERSLAG ULRICH'S PERIODICALS

• Federatie van de Chemische Industrie van Belgie. Activiteitenverslag Fedichem (BEL) 1487
Federatie van Nederlandse Blindenbibliotheken. Bulletin see Dedicon Bulletin 4081
Federatie van Nederlandse Officieren. Bulletin (NLD ISSN 1871-6083) 6421
Federatie van Ondernemers in het Schilders-, Afwerkings- en Glaszetbefrijf Visie see F O S A G Visie 6697
Federation (GBR ISSN 1350-8598) 4575
Federation Canadienne des Amis de Musees. Newsletter see Au Courant (French Edition) 6520
Federation Colombophile Francaise. Bulletin National (FRA ISSN 1637-5505) 6808
Federation d'Associations de Techniciens des Industries des Peintures, Vernis, Emaux et Encres d'Imprimerie de l'Europe Continentale. Annuaire Officiel. Official Yearbook. Amtliches Jahrbuch/Amtliches Jahrbuch/Official Yearbook (FRA ISSN 1026-1923) 6717
Federation d'Associations de Techniciens des Industries des Peintures, Vernis, Emaux et Encres d'Imprimerie de l'Europe Continentale. Congress Proceedings see Congress F A T I P E C 6716
Federation de l'Industrie Horlogere Suisse. Annual Report (CHE ISSN 1421-7384) 4566
Federation de l'Industrie Horlogere Suisse. Revue (CHE) 4566
Federation de l'Informatique du Quebec. Info see L'Info F I Q 2431
Federation Dentaire Internationale World see F D I World 5844
Federation des Carrossiers Romands. Journal (CHE) 8580
Federation des Chambres de Commerce du Quebec. Rapport Annuel (CAN ISSN 1910-6637) 1402
Federation des Chambres de Commerce du Quebec. Rapport d'Activites see Federation des Chambres de Commerce du Quebec. Rapport Annuel 1402
▼ Federation des Employes et Cadres Force Ouvriere. Journal (FRA ISSN 1963-238X) 4594
Federation des Entrepreneurs de Nettoyage de France. Annuaire Officiel (FRA) 2243
Federation des Entreprises de Belgique Bulletin see F E B Bulletin 1885
Federation des Entreprises de Belgique. Rapport Annuel (BEL ISSN 0773-1884) 1885
Federation des Entreprises du Congo. Annuaire des Entreprises du Zaire (COD) 1402
Federation des Entreprises du Congo. Circulaire d'Information (COD) 1402
Federation des Industries Chimiques de Belgique. Annuaire/Federatie der Chemische Nyverheid van Belgie. Directory (BEL ISSN 0425-9076) 1993
• Federation des Industries Chimiques de Belgique. Rapport d'Activites (BEL) 1487
Federation des Industries Mecaniques en Ligne see F I M en Ligne 8955
Federation des Ingenieurs de Telecommunications de la Communaute Europeenne Forum see F I T C E Forum 3308
Federation Feminine Franco-Americaine. Bulletin (USA) 3533
• The Federation Flash (USA ISSN 1524-0452) 6645
Federation Focus see Housing Scotland 4414
Federation Francaise de la Franchise. Lettre (FRA ISSN 0992-7425) 1565
Federation Francaise de Natation. Annuaire (FRA ISSN 0071-4194) 8275
Federation Francaise des Associations de Gestion et de Comptabilite et des Centres de Gestion et d'E La Lettre see F F C G E A. La Lettre 1960
Federation Francaise des Combustibles Carburants et Chauffage 3 C Informations see F F 3 C Informations 6768
Federation Hospitaliere de France. Circulaire see Federation Hospitaliere de France. La Lettre 4093
Federation Hospitaliere de France. La Lettre (FRA ISSN 1630-3555) 4093
Federation International de Documentation. Publication see F I D Publication 8955
Federation International des Associations de Bibliothecaires et des Bibliotheques. Project Report (SEN ISSN 1023-8212) 5009
Federation Internationale de Basketball Amateur Basketball see F I B A Basketball 8227
Federation Internationale de Football Association 17 World Championship see F I F A U-17 World Championship 8227
Federation Internationale de Football Association Handbook see F I F A Handbook 8227
Federation Internationale de Football Association Magazine see F I F A Magazine 8955
Federation Internationale de Football Association News see F I F A News 8227
Federation Internationale de Football Association Olympic Football Tournament see F I F A Olympic Football Tournament 8227
Federation Internationale de Football Association Technical Reports see F I F A Technical Reports 8227
Federation Internationale de Football Association World Cup see F I F A World Cup 8227
Federation Internationale de Football Association World Youth Championship see F I F A World Youth Championship 8227
Federation Internationale de Gymnastique. Bulletin (CHE ISSN 0428-1659) 8172
Federation Internationale de Laiterie. Bulletin see International Dairy Federation. Bulletin 265
Federation Internationale de Laiterie. Newsletter see International Dairy Federation. Newsletters 265
Federation Internationale de Laiterie. Norme Internationale see International Dairy Federation. International Standard 265
Federation Internationale de Rugby Amateur. Annuaire (FRA ISSN 0071-4267) 8228
Federation Internationale des Associations de Transitaires et Assimiles Review see F I A T A Review 8496
Federation Internationale des Communautes d'Enfants see F I C E 2152
Federation Internationale des Demenageurs Internationaux Focus see F I D I Focus 8643
Federation Internationale des Ingenieurs Conseils International Directory of Consulting Engineers see F I D I C International Directory of Consulting Engineers 1993
Federation Internationale des Producteurs de Jus de Fruits. Compte-Rendu du Congres/International Federation of Fruit Juice Producers. Proceedings of Congress (FRA ISSN 0074-5952) 603
Federation Internationale des Producteurs de Jus de Fruits. Rapport Annuel d'Activite (FRA) 3636
Federation Internationale des Professeurs de Langues Vivantes World News see F I P L V World News 5118
Federation Internationale des Traducteurs Monograph Series/Collection see F I T Monograph Series/Collection 5118
Federation Internationale du Beton Bulletin see F I B Bulletin 1007
Federation Internationale Laitiere. Catalogue des Publications see International Dairy Federation. Catalogue of I D F Publications 182
Federation Internationale Motocycliste. Annuaire (CHE ISSN 0071-4283) 8258
Federation Internationale pour la Recherche Theatrale Bulletin see F I R T - I F T R - S I B M A S Bulletin 8470
Federation Interprofessionnelle de la Sante du Quebec en Action (English Edition) see F I Q en Action (English Edition) 5958
Federation Jazz (USA ISSN 1081-5988) 6566
Federation Nationale de Medecine Traditionnelle Chinoise. Bulletin d'Information (FRA ISSN 1770-9652) 309
• Federation Nationale des Agences de Presse. Annuaire (Online) (FRA) 4575
Federation Nationale des Agriculteurs Multiplicateurs de Semences. Bulletin (FRA ISSN 0396-8936) 113
Federation Nationale des Associations de Directeurs d'Etablissements et de Services pour Personnes A Express see F N A D E P A Express 8039
Federation Nationale des Infirmieres de Belgique Flash-Info see F N I B Flash-Info 5959
Federation Nationale du Credit Agricole. Rapport d'Activite (Year) (FRA ISSN 0998-0164) 1342
Federation News (GBR ISSN 0014-9411) 4594
Federation News (Chicago) (USA ISSN 0014-942X) 4594
Federation of American Scientists Public Interest Report see F A S Public Interest Report 7854
Federation of American Societies for Experimental Biology Journal see The F A S E B Journal 672
Federation of American Societies for Experimental Biology News see F A S E B News 672
Federation of Andhra Pradesh Chambers of Commerce & Industry Review see F A P C C I Review 1402
Federation of Astronomical Societies Handbook see F A S Handbook 574
Federation of Bangladesh Chambers of Commerce and Industry. Federation Journal (BGD) 1403
Federation of British Tape Recordists. Recording News (GBR) 8152
Federation of Canadian Archers. Rules Book (CAN ISSN 0226-773X) 8173
Federation of Catholic Parent-Teacher Associations of Ontario. Newsletter (CAN ISSN 0700-9070) 2856
Federation of Defense and Corporate Counsel Quarterly see F D C C Quarterly 4867
Federation of Egyptian Industries. Year Book see Ittihad al-Sinaat al-Misriyah. Year Book 8967
Federation of Electric Power Companies Briefing Note see F E P C Briefing Note 3308
Federation of European Biochemical Societies Journal (Online) see The F E B S Journal (Online) 732
Federation of European Biochemical Societies Letters see F E B S Letters 732
Federation of European Direct Marketing Membership News see F E D M A - Membership News 25
Federation of European Materials Societies News see F E M S News 3344
Federation of European Microbiological Societies Immunology and Medical Microbiology see F E M S Immunology and Medical Microbiology 885
Federation of European Microbiological Societies Microbiology see F E M S Microbiology 8955
Federation of European Microbiological Societies Microbiology Ecology see F E M S Microbiology Ecology 885
Federation of European Microbiological Societies Microbiology Letters see F E M S Microbiology Letters 885
Federation of European Microbiological Societies Microbiology Reviews see F E M S Microbiology Reviews 885
Federation of European Microbiological Societies Symposium see F E M S Symposium 886
Federation of European Microbiological Societies Yeast Research see F E M S Yeast Research 886
Federation of European Microbiological Societies Yeast Research Online see F E M S Yeast Research 886
Federation of European of Biochemical Societies Journal see The F E B S Journal 732
Federation of European Screen Printers Associations World see F E S P A World 7320
Federation of Genealogical Societies Delegate Digest see F G S Delegate Digest 3765
Federation of Genealogical Societies Forum (USA ISSN 1531-720X) 3766
• Federation of Jordanian Chambers of Commerce. Magazine (JOR) 1403
Federation of Kenya Employers. Newsletter (KEN) 4594
Federation of Manufactured Home Owners of Florida News see F M O News 7590
Federation of Migros Cooperatives. Documentation and Information (CHE) 1423
Federation of Nepalese Chambers of Commerce and Industry. Newsletter (NPL) 1403
Federation of Oils Seeds and Fats Associations International. Newsletter see F O S F A International. Newsletter 230
Federation of Pakistan Chambers of Commerce and Industry. Annual Report (PAK) 1403
Federation of Pakistan Chambers of Commerce and Industry. Brief Report of Activities (PAK ISSN 0071-4429) 1403
Federation of Pakistan Chambers of Commerce and Industry. Directory of Exporters (PAK) 1993
Federation of Pakistan Chambers of Commerce and Industry. Trade Bulletin (PAK) 1403
Federation of Private Residents Associations. Newsletter (GBR) 7590
Federation of Southern Cooperatives Monthly Bulletin see F S C Monthly Bulletin 8039
Federation of State Medical Boards Handbook see F S M B Handbook 5612
Federation of State Medical Boards Newsline see F S M B Newsline 5613
Federation of the Electricity Companies in Belgium B F E - F P E. Facts and Figures (BEL) 3152
Federation of Women's Institutions News see F W I News 2856
Federation of Workers' Educational Associations. Newsletter (NZL ISSN 1177-150X) 2941
Federation of Zoroastrian Associations of North America Journal see F E Z A N A Journal 7735
Federation Professionnelle des Producteurs et Distributeurs d'Electricite de Belgique. Rapport Annuel. Jaarverslag (BEL ISSN 0071-4453) 3158
Federation Professionnelle du Secteur Electrique. Annuaire Statistique (Year) (BEL) 3152
Federation Protestante de France. Annuaire (FRA ISSN 0240-5164) 7758
Federation Quebecoise de la Faune. Nouvelles (CAN ISSN 0046-3590) 943
Federation Quebecoise des Directeurs et Directrices d'Ecole. Revue Information (CAN) 2856
Federation Quebecoise du Loisir Litteraire. Bulletin (CAN ISSN 1910-7684) 5295
Federation Roundtable (USA) 4292
Federation Series on Coatings Technology (USA ISSN 0099-801X) 6717
Federation Universitaire et Polytechnique de Lille. Annuaire (FRA ISSN 0181-4516) 3022
Federatsiya Nezavisimykh Profsoyuzov Rossii. Vesti (RUS) 4594
Federauto Magazine (BEL) 8580
Federazione Autotraportatori Italiani see F A I 8955
† • Federazione delle Societa Medico - Scientifiche Italiane. Congressi (Year) (ITA) 8956
† Federfarma Notizie (ITA) 8956
Federmobili (ITA ISSN 1122-0457) 4556
• Fedgazette: Federal Reserve Bank of Minneapolis Regional Business & Economics Newspaper (USA ISSN 1045-3334) 1487
Fedlink Technical Notes (USA ISSN 0737-4178) 5061
Fednews (USA ISSN 0430-2761) 4594
• Fee-Help Information (AUS ISSN 1449-9282) 2856
Fee Schedule for Citizenship and Immigration Services/Bareme des Frais pour les Services de Citoyennete et Immigration (CAN ISSN 1910-7943) 7283
Feed Additive Compendium (USA ISSN 0071-450X) 271
Feed and Feeding Digest (USA ISSN 0886-5884) 271
• Feed & Grain (USA ISSN 1055-3223) 271
Feed and Grain see Feed & Grain 271
• Feed Bulletin (USA ISSN 0014-9543) 271
Feed China see Siliao Guangjiao 275
Feed Compounder (GBR ISSN 0950-771X) 271
Feed Compounder. Pet Food Supplement (GBR ISSN 1744-9294) 6808
Feed Control Comment (USA) 271
Feed Facts Quarterly (GBR ISSN 0965-2558) 271
• Feed for Thought (USA) 271
Feed Industry Review (GBR) 272
• Feed International (USA ISSN 0274-5771) 272
Feed Legislation (GBR ISSN 0969-0735) 272
Feed Lot (USA ISSN 1083-5385) 286
Feed Magazine see Kraftfutter 240
• Feed Management (USA ISSN 0014-956X) 272
Feed Mix (NLD ISSN 0928-124X) 272
Feed Outlook see Situation & Outlook Report. Feed Outlook 275
Feed Panorama see Siliao Bolan 275
Feed Research see Siliao Yanjiu 275
Feed Tech (NLD ISSN 1387-1978) 3636
Feed Trade (JPN ISSN 0014-9586) 272
Feed Yearbook see Situation & Outlook Report. Feed Yearbook 275
Feedback (USA ISSN 0147-4871) 2381
• Feedback (North Sydney) (AUS ISSN 1441-6557) 286
• Feedback (Online Edition) (NLD) 272
• Feedback (Surry Hills) (AUS ISSN 1446-2001) 2188
Feedback (Wembley) (GBR ISSN 1745-4824) 2321
Feedback from Fujitsu (USA) 2418
Feedgram (USA) 272
• FeedRoom (USA) 3975
Feedstock Wire see Refiner 6790
• Feedstuffs (USA ISSN 0014-9624) 272
• Feel Free to Prosper (USA ISSN 1949-9175) 4673
FeelGood see Irish Examiner 3893
Feeling (BEL ISSN 0777-3439) 8862
† Feeling Sports Magazine (USA) 8956
Feeling Wonen (BEL ISSN 1373-4989) 4539
• Feeries (FRA ISSN 1766-2842) 339
Fees, Utilization, and Other Key Metrics (USA ISSN 1940-364X) 1745
Feestelijk Vieren (NLD) 4386
Feestelijk Zakendoen see F Z 339
FEhS - Institut fuer Baustoff-Forschung. Schriftenreihe (Forschungsgemeinschaft Eisenhuettenschlacken) (DEU ISSN 0948-4787) 3506
• Fei Tian/Flying Apsaras (CHN ISSN 1002-803X) 5295
Feichang Xilie Xinli Ceyan (TWN) 7357
• Feidie Tansuo/Journal of U F O Research (CHN ISSN 1001-7674) 55
Feierabend (DEU ISSN 0343-7205) 7797
† Feierabend-Raetsel (DEU) 8956
• Feihang Daodan/Winged Missiles Journal (CHN ISSN 1009-1319) 55
Feilding Herald (NZL ISSN 1170-0408) 3917
Feilding Herald Rangitikei Mail see Rangitikei Mail 3918
• Feile - Festa (USA ISSN 1931-7263) 5295
Feinbearbeitung, Schleifen, Raeumen, Honen, Laeppen, Polieren see Informationsdienst F I Z Technik. Feinbearbeitung, Schleifen, Raeumen, Honen, Laeppen, Polieren 3230
Feine Adressen Berlin see Feine Adressen Berlin, Potsdam 3847
Feine Adressen Berlin, Potsdam (DEU ISSN 1861-0870) 3847
Feine Adressen Bodensee (DEU ISSN 1430-5755) 3847
Feine Adressen Braunschweig see Feine Adressen Braunschweig, Wolfsburg, Harz und Heide 3847
Feine Adressen Braunschweig, Wolfsburg, Harz und Heide (DEU ISSN 1861-7859) 3847
Feine Adressen Bremen - Weser-Ems (DEU ISSN 0947-0409) 3847
Feine Adressen Dortmund (DEU ISSN 0949-9768) 3847
Feine Adressen Duisburg - Essen - Muelheim (DEU ISSN 0949-9776) 3847
Feine Adressen Frankfurt - Rhein-Main (DEU ISSN 0942-1092) 3847
Feine Adressen Hamburg (DEU ISSN 0943-1667) 3847
Feine Adressen Hannover (DEU ISSN 0943-3120) 3847
Feine Adressen Hof - Oberfranken - Plauen (DEU ISSN 0949-9784) 3847
Feine Adressen International (DEU ISSN 0949-9792) 3847
Feine Adressen Kassel - Kurhessen (DEU ISSN 1618-3738) 3847
Feine Adressen Koeln (DEU ISSN 1438-8138) 3847
Feine Adressen Metropolregion Nuernberg (DEU ISSN 1865-1321) 3847
Feine Adressen Muenchen (DEU ISSN 0944-4769) 3847
Feine Adressen Nuernberg - Franken see Feine Adressen Metropolregion Nuernberg 3847
Feine Adressen Stuttgart (DEU ISSN 1861-9193) 3847
Feine Adressen Stuttgart - Schwaben see Feine Adressen Stuttgart 3847
Feine Adressen Sylt (DEU ISSN 0949-9814) 3847
Feine Kueche (AUT) 3636
Der Feinschmecker (DEU ISSN 0342-2739) 3636
Der Feinschmecker Wein Gourmet see Wein Gourmet 612
• Feinspitz (AUT ISSN 1605-8585) 3636
† Feit & Fictie (NLD ISSN 0929-2411) 8956

Title

Finland. Forsknings- och Utvecklingscentralen foer Social- och Haelsovaarden. Aeldreomsorgen *see* Finland. Sosiaali- ja Terveysalan Tutkimus- ja Kehittamiskeskus. Ikaantyneiden Sosiaali- ja Terveyspalvelut **4058**

Finland. Forsknings- och Utvecklingscentralken foer Social- och Haelsovaarden. Statistikrapport *see* Finland. Sosiaali- ja Terveysalan Tutkimus- ja Kehittamiskeskus. Tilastoraportti **8082**

Finland. Forsknings- och Utveclingscentralen foer Social- och Haelsoevaarden. Privat Serviceproduktion inom Socialvaarden och Haelso- och Sjukvaarden *see* Finland. Sosiaali- ja Terveysalan Tutkimus- ja Kehittamiskeskus. Yksityinen Palvelutuotanto Sosiaali- ja Terveydenhuollossa **8082**

• Finland. Huoltovarmuuskeskus. Julkaisu (FIN ISSN 1795-7842) **1885**

Finland. Jord- och Skogsbruksministeriet. Informationstjanstcentral. Jordbruksstatistisk Rapport *see* Finland. Maa- ja Metsatalousministerio. Tietopalvelukeskus. Maataloustilastotiedote **113**

Finland. Jord- och Skogsbruksministeriets Informationstjanstcentral. Fraan Aakern till Bordet:Statistik oever Livsmedelskedjan och Tillsyn *see* Finland. Maa- ja Metsatalousministerio. Tietopalvelukeskus. Pellolta Poytaan **113**

• Finland. Kansanelakelaitos. Kelan Tilastollinen Vuosikirja/Finland. Folkpensionsanstalten. F P As Statistiska Aarsbok/Finland. Social Insurance Institution. Statistical Yearbook (FIN ISSN 1796-5659) **4529**

Finland. Kansanelakelaitos. Tilastollinen Vuosikirja *see* Finland. Kansanelakelaitos. Kelan Tilastollinen Vuosikirja **4529**

Finland. Kansantalousosasto. Kansantalouden Kehitysarvio. Summary: National Budget for Finland (FIN ISSN 0533-1099) **1925**

Finland. Kasvintuotannon Tarkastuskeskus. Julkaisuja. B 2, Luomutuotanto *see* Finland. Elintarviketurvallisuusvirasto Evira. Julkaisu **7517**

Finland. Konsumentverket. Publikationsserie *see* Finland. Kuluttajaviraston. Julkaisu **2638**

Finland. Kuluttaja-Asiain Osaston. Julkaisu. Sarja B *see* Finland. Kuluttajaviraston. Julkaisu **2638**

• Finland. Kuluttajaviraston. Julkaisu/Finland. Finnish Consumer Agency and Consumer Ombudsman. Publication Series/Finland. Konsumentverket. Publikationsserie (FIN ISSN 0788-544X) **2638**

Finland. Laakintohallitus. Hammarslaakarit (FIN ISSN 0780-1807) **5844**

Finland. Laakintohallitus. Laakarit/Finland. Medicinalstyrelsen. Laekare (FIN ISSN 0780-1785) **5614**

Finland Levererar *see* Forum Finland **1403**

Finland. Maa- ja Metsatalousministerio. Tietopalvelukeskus. Eurojyva/Jord- och Skogsbruksministeriet. Informationstjaenstcentral. Lantbrukslagenheter i Finland och EU/Ministry of Agriculture and Forestry. Information Centre. Farms in Finland and EU (FIN ISSN 1795-3898) **113**

Finland. Maa- ja Metsatalousministerio. Tietopalvelukeskus. Maataloustilastotiedote/ Finland. Jord- och Skogsbruksministeriet. Informationstjanstcentral. Jordbruksstatistisk Rapport/Finland. Ministry of Agriculture and Forestry. Information Centre. Agricultural Statistical Bulletin (FIN ISSN 1796-1238) **113**

▼ • Finland. Maa- ja Metsatalousministerio. Tietopalvelukeskus. Pellolta Poytaan/Finland. Jord- och Skogsbruksministeriets Informationstjanstcentral. Fraan Aakern till Bordet:Statistik oever Livsmedelskedjan och Tillsyn/Finland. Ministry of Agriculture and Foresty. Information Centre. From Farm to Fork:Statistics on Food Chain and Control (FIN ISSN 1796-6930) **113**

• Finland. Maa- ja Metsatalousministerio. Tietopalvelukeskus Tietokappa (Online) (FIN ISSN 1796-7759) **180**

Finland. Maa- ja Metsatalousministerio. Tietopalvelukeskus. Tietokappa (Print) *see* Finland. Maa- ja Metsatalousministerio. Tietopalvelukeskus Tietokappa (Online) **180**

Finland. Medicinalstyrelsen. Laekare *see* Finland. Laakintohallitus. Laakarit **5614**

Finland. Ministerio de los Asuntos Extranjeros. Publicaciones *see* Finland. Ulkoasiainministerio. Julkaisuja **7234**

Finland. Ministry for Foreign Affairs. Publications *see* Finland. Ulkoasiainministerio. Julkaisuja **7234**

Finland. Ministry of Agriculture and Forestry. Information Centre. Agricultural Statistical Bulletin *see* Finland. Maa- ja Metsatalousministerio. Tietopalvelukeskus. Maataloustilastotiedote **113**

Finland. Ministry of Agriculture and Forestry. Information Centre. Statistics. Maatilatilastollinen Vuosikirja/Yearbook of Farm Statistics (FIN ISSN 0786-2857) **180**

Finland. Ministry of Agriculture and Foresty. Information Centre. From Farm to Fork:Statistics on Food Chain and Control *see* Finland. Maa- ja Metsatalousministerio. Tietopalvelukeskus. Pellolta Poytaan **113**

• Finland. Ministry of Foreign Affairs. Helsinki Process. Publication Series (FIN ISSN 1795-8628) **1718**

Finland. Ministry of Justice, Data System Unit. D *see* Finland. Oikeusministerio. Tietojarjestelmayksikko. D **4674**

Finland. Ministry of Social Affairs and Health. Publications *see* Finland. Sosiaali- ja Terveysministerio. Julkaisuja **8040**

Finland. National Agency for Welfare and Health. Home Help *see* Finland. Sosiaali- ja Terveyshallitus. Kotipalvelu **8040**

Finland. National Board of Customs. Foreign Trade of Goods *see* Finland. Tullihallitus. Tavaroiden Ulkomaankauppa **1232**

Finland. National Research and Development Centre for Welfare and Health. Care and Services for Older People *see* Finland. Sosiaali- ja Terveysalan Tutkimus- ja Kehittamiskeskus. Ikaantyneiden Sosiaali- ja Terveyspalvelut **4058**

Finland. National Research and Development Centre for Welfare and Health. Private Service Provision in Social and Health Care *see* Finland. Sosiaali- ja Terveysalan Tutkimus- ja Kehittamiskeskus. Yksityinen Palvelutuotanto Sosiaali- ja Terveydenhuollossa **8082**

Finland. National Research and Development Centre for Welfare and Health. Statistical Report *see* Finland. Sosiaali- ja Terveysalan Tutkimus- ja Kehittamiskeskus. Tilastoraportti **8082**

• Finland. Oikeusministerio. Julkaisu (FIN ISSN 1458-6444) **4674**

Finland. Oikeusministerio. Tietohallintotoimisto. A (FIN ISSN 0789-0893) **7437**

Finland. Oikeusministerio. Tietojarjestelmayksikko. B (FIN ISSN 0359-6729) **7437**

Finland. Oikeusministerio. Tietojarjestelmayksikko. D/Finland. Ministry of Justice, Data System Unit. D (FIN ISSN 0789-2918) **4674**

• Finland. Oikeusministerio. Tyoryhmamietinto (FIN ISSN 1458-6452) **4674**

• Finland. Patentti- ja Rekisterihallitus. Mallioikeuslehti/Moenster Raetts Tidning (FIN ISSN 0355-4481) **6750**

Finland. Patentti- ja Rekisterihallitus. Patenttilehti/Patenttidning (FIN ISSN 0031-2916) **6750**

• Finland. Patentti- ja Rekisterihallitus. Tavaramerkkilehti/Varumaerkestidning (FIN ISSN 0039-9922) **6750**

• Finland. Rikosseuraamusvirasto. Julkaisu (FIN ISSN 1458-4131) **4890**

Finland. Rikosseuraamusvirasto. Kriminaalihuoltolaitos ja Vankeinhoitolaitos. Vuosikertomus *see* Finland. Rikosseuraamusvirasto. Vuosikertomus **4890**

• Finland. Rikosseuraamusvirasto. Vuosikertomus (FIN ISSN 1796-9905) **4890**

Finland. Riksdagens Kansli. Publikationer *see* Finland. Eduskunnan Kanslia. Julkaisu **7437**

Finland. Social Insurance Institution. Statistical Yearbook *see* Finland. Kansanelakelaitos. Kelan Tilastollinen Vuosikirja **4529**

Finland. Social- och Haelsovaardsministeriet. Publikationer *see* Finland. Sosiaali- ja Terveysministerio. Julkaisuja **8040**

Finland. Social- og Haelsostyrelsen. Hemservice *see* Finland. Sosiaali- ja Terveyshallitus. Kotipalvelu **8040**

• Finland. Sosiaali- ja Terveysalan Tutkimus- ja Kehittamiskeskus. Discussion Papers (FIN ISSN 1795-6897) **8040**

Finland. Sosiaali- ja Terveysalan Tutkimus- ja Kehittamiskeskus. Ikaantyneiden Sosiaali- ja Terveyspalvelut/Finland. Forsknings- och Utvecklingscentralen foer Social- och Haelsovaarden. Aeldreomsorgen/Finland. National Research and Development Centre for Welfare and Health. Care and Services for Older People (FIN ISSN 1459-7071) **4058**

Finland. Sosiaali- ja Terveysalan Tutkimus- ja Kehittamiskeskus. Themes *see* Finland. Sosiaali- ja Terveysalan Tutkimus- ja Kehittamiskeskus. Discussion Papers **8040**

Finland. Sosiaali- ja Terveysalan Tutkimus- ja Kehittamiskeskus. Tilastoraportti/Finland. Forsknings- och Utvecklingscentralken foer Social- och Haelsovaarden. Statistikrapport/Finland. National Research and Development Centre for Welfare and Health. Statistical Report (FIN ISSN 1455-7460) **8082**

▼ Finland. Sosiaali- ja Terveysalan Tutkimus- ja Kehittamiskeskus. Yksityinen Palvelutuotanto Sosiaali- ja Terveydenhuollossa/Finland. Forsknings- och Utvecklingscentralen foer Social- och Haelsovaarden. Privat Serviceproduktion inom Socialvaarden och Haelso- och Sjukvaarden/Finland. National Research and Development Centre for Welfare and Health. Private Service Provision in Social and Health Care (FIN ISSN 1796-7848) **8082**

Finland. Sosiaali- ja Terveyshallitus. Kotipalvelu/Finland. National Agency for Welfare and Health. Home Help/Finland. Social- og Haelsostyrelsen. Hemservice (FIN ISSN 0788-6098) **8040**

• Finland. Sosiaali- ja Terveysministerio. Julkaisuja/Finland. Ministry of Social Affairs and Health. Publications/Finland. Social- och Haelsovaardsministeriet. Publikationer (FIN ISSN 1236-2050) **8040**

Finland. Statistics Finalnd. Consumer Barometer *see* Finland. Tilastokeskus. Kuluttajabarometri **1231**

Finland. Statistics Finland. Aliens and International Migration *see* Finland. Tilastokeskus. Ulkomaalaiset ja Siirtolaisuus **7306**

Finland. Statistics Finland. Building and Dwelling Production *see* Finland. Tilastokeskus. Rakennus- ja Asuntotuotanto **1046**

Finland. Statistics Finland. Building Cost Index *see* Finland. Tilastokeskus. Rakennuskustannusindeksi (Kuukausitilasto) **1046**

Finland. Statistics Finland. Buildings, Dwellings and Housing Conditions *see* Finland. Tilastokeskus. Rakennukset, Asunnot ja Asuinolot **4435**

Finland. Statistics Finland. Bulletin of Statistics *see* Finland. Tilastokeskus. Tilastokatsauksia **8372**

Finland. Statistics Finland. Business Enterprises - Net Results and Balance Sheets *see* Finland Tilastokeskus. Yritysten Rakenteet -Tilastopalvelu **1232**

Finland. Statistics Finland. Causes of Death *see* Finland. Tilastokeskus. Kuolemansyyt **7306**

Finland. Statistics Finland. Construction and Housing. Yearbook *see* Finland. Tilastokeskus. Rakentaminen ja Asuminen: Vuosikirja **4435**

Finland. Statistics Finland. Consumer Price Index *see* Finland. Tilastokeskus. Kuluttajahintaindeksi **1231**

Finland. Statistics Finland. Corporate Enterprises and Personal Businesses in Finland *see* Finland. Tilastokeskus. Suomen Yritykset **1232**

Finland. Statistics Finland. Cost Index for Road Transport of Goods *see* Finland. Tilastokeskus. Kuorma-Autoliikenteen Kustannusindeksi **8524**

Finland. Statistics Finland. Cost Index of Civil Engineering Works *see* Finland. Tilastokeskus. Maarakennuskustannusindeksi **1046**

Finland. Statistics Finland. Cost of Hour Worked. Labour Cost Index *see* Finland. Tilastokeskus. Tyotunnin Kustannus. Tyovoimakustannusindeksi **1232**

Finland. Statistics Finland. Cultural Statistics *see* Finland. Tilastokeskus. Kulttuuritilasto **8149**

Finland. Statistics Finland. Elections for the European Parliament *see* Finland. Tilastokeskus. Europarlamenttivaalit, Ennakkotilasto **7199**

Finland. Statistics Finland. Elections for the European Parliament *see* Finland. Tilastokeskus. Europarlamenttivaalit **7199**

• Finland. Statistics Finland. Energy in Finland (FIN ISSN 1457-0491) **3152**

Finland. Statistics Finland. Energy Statistics *see* Finland. Tilastokeskus. Energiatilastot **3152**

Finland. Statistics Finland. Environment Statistics *see* Finland. Tilastokeskus. Ymparistotilasto **3479**

Finland. Statistics Finland. Families *see* Finland. Tilastokeskus. Perheet **7306**

Finland. Statistics Finland. Finances of Agricultural and Forestry Enterprises *see* Finland. Tilastokeskus. Maa- ja Metsatalousyritysten Taloustilasto **180**

Finland. Statistics Finland. Financial Leasing *see* Finland. Tilastokeskus. Rahoitusleasing **1232**

Finland. Statistics Finland. Finnish Mass Media *see* Finland. Tilastokeskus. Joukkoviestimet **8149**

Finland. Statistics Finland. Finnish Travel *see* Finland. Tilastokeskus. Suomalaisten Matkailu **8779**

Finland. Statistics Finland. Flow-of-Funds Accounts *see* Finland. Tilastokeskus. Rahoitustilinpito **1232**

Finland. Statistics Finland. Free-time Residences *see* Finland. Tilastokeskus. Kesamokit **4435**

Finland. Statistics Finland. Gender Equality in Finland *see* Finland. Tilastokeskus. Sukupuolten Tasa-Arvo **8149**

Finland. Statistics Finland. General Government Deficit and Gross Debt according to EMU Criteria *see* Finland. Tilastokeskus. Julkisyhteisojen Alijaama ja Bruttovelka EMU-Kriteerien Mukaisina (Online) **1231**

Finland. Statistics Finland. Government R&D Funding in the State Budget *see* Finland. Tilastokeskus. Tutkimus- ja Kehittamisrahoitus Valtion Talousarviossa **1232**

Finland. Statistics Finland. Handbooks *see* Finland. Tilastokeskus. Kasikirjoja **8370**

Finland. Statistics Finland. House Prices *see* Finland. Tilastokeskus. Asuntojen Hinnat. Vuositilasto **4435**

Finland. Statistics Finland. Income Distribution Statistics *see* Finland. Tilastokeskus. Tulonjakotilasto **1232**

Finland. Statistics Finland. Index of Real Estate Maintenance Costs *see* Finland. Tilastokeskus. Kiinteiston Yllapidon Kustannusindeksi **4435**

Finland. Statistics Finland. Index of Wage and Salary Earnings *see* Finland. Tilastokeskus. Ansiotasoindeksi **1231**

Finland. Statistics Finland. Internationalisation of Enterprises *see* Finland. Tilastokeskus. Yritysten Kansainvalistyminen **1232**

Finland. Statistics Finland. Investment Service Companies *see* Finland. Tilastokeskus. Sijoituspalveluyritykset **1232**

Finland. Statistics Finland. Labour Cost Index *see* Finland. Tilastokeskus. Tyotunnin Kustannus. Tyovoimakustannusindeksi **1232**

Finland. Statistics Finland. Labour Force Statistics *see* Finland. Tilastokeskus. Tyovoimatilasto **1232**

Finland. Statistics Finland. Labour Force Statistics *see* Finland. Tilastokeskus. Tyovoimatilasto **1232**

Finland. Statistics Finland. Monetary Financial Institutions *see* Finland. Tilastokeskus. Rahalaitokset **1231**

Finland. Statistics Finland. Motor Vehicles *see* Finland. Tilastokeskus. Moottoriajoneuvot **8524**

Finland. Statistics Finland. Moving Images in Finland *see* Finland. Tilastokeskus. Suomessa Liikkuvat Liikkuvat Kuvat **2347**

Finland. Statistics Finland. Municipal Elections *see* Finland. Tilastokeskus. Kunnallisvaalit **7480**

Finland.Statistics Finland. Municipal Finances *see* Finland. Tilastokeskus. Kuntien Talousarviot **7480**

Finland. Statistics Finland. Mutual Funds *see* Finland. Tilastokeskus. Sijoitusrahastot **1232**

Finland. Statistics Finland. National Accounts. Tables *see* Finland. Tilastokeskus. Kansantalouden Tilinpito. Taulukot **1231**

Finland. Statistics Finland. Occupational Accident Statistics *see* Finland. Tilastokeskus. Tyotapaturmat **1232**

Finland. Statistics Finland. Official Statistics of Finland *see* Finland. Tilastokeskus. Suomen Virallinen Tilasto **8371**

Finland. Statistics Finland. Outstanding Credit *see* Finland. Tilastokeskus. Luottokanta **1231**

Finland. Statistics Finland. Parliamentary Elections *see* Finland. Tilastokeskus. Eduskuntavaalit **7199**

Finland. Statistics Finland. Population Projection *see* Finland. Tilastokeskus. Vaestoennusteet **7306**

Finland. Statistics Finland. Population Structure and Vital Statistics by Municipality *see* Finland. Tilastokeskus. Vaestorakenne ja Vaestonmuutokset Kunnittain **7306**

Finland. Statistics Finland. Preliminary Energy Statistics *see* Finland. Tilastokeskus. Energiaennakko **3152**

Finland. Statistics Finland. Presidential Election *see* Finland. Tilastokeskus. Presidentin Vaalit **7199**

Finland. Statistics Finland. Prices and Wages Review *see* Finland. Tilastokeskus. Hinta- ja Palkkatiedote **1231**

Finland. Statistics Finland. Producer Price Indices *see* Finland. Tilastokeskus. Tuottajahintaindeksit **1232**

Finland. Statistics Finland. Providers of Education and Educational Institutions *see* Finland. Tilastokeskus. Koulutuksen Jarjestajat ja Oppilaitokset **2933**

Finland. Statistics Finland. Rents *see* Finland. Tilastokeskus. Vuokratilasto **4435**

Finland. Statistics Finland. Road Accidents in Finland *see* Finland. Tilastokeskus. Tieliikenneonnettomuudet **8524**

Finland. Statistics Finland. Road Freight Transport *see* Finland. Tilastokeskus. Tieliikenteen Tavarankuljetustilasto **8779**

Finland. Statistics Finland. Science, Technology, and Information Society *see* Finland. Tilastokeskus. Tiede, Teknologia ja Tietoyhteiskunta **7854**

Finland. Statistics Finland. Statistical Yearbook of Finland *see* Finland. Tilastokeskus. Suomen Tilastollinen Vuosikirja **8371**

Finland. Statistics Finland. Statistics of Income and Property *see* Finland. Tilastokeskus. Tulo- ja Varallisuustilasto **1232**

Finland. Statistics Finland. Structure of Earnings *see* Finland. Tilastokeskus. Palkkarakenne **1231**

Finland. Statistics Finland. Studies *see* Finland. Tilastokeskus. Tutkimuksia **8372**

Finland. Statistics Finland. Tourism Statistics *see* Finland. Tilastokeskus. Matkailutilasto **8779**

Finland. Statistics Finland. Tourism Statistics *see* Finland. Tilastokeskus. Matkailutilasto **8779**

Finland. Statistics Flnland. Trade *see* Finland. Tilastokeskus. Kauppa **1231**

Finland. Statistics Finland. Transport and Communications Statistical Yearbook for Finland *see* Finland. Tilastokeskus. Liikennetilastollinen Vuosikirja **8524**

Finland. Statistics Finland. Vital Statistics *see* Finland. Tilastokeskus. Vaestonmuutokset **7306**

Finland. Statistics Finland. Wholesale and Retail Trade *see* Finland. Tilastokeskus. Tukku- ja Vahittaiskauppa **1232**

Finland. Statistics Finland. Women and Men in Finland *see* Finland. Tilastokeskus. Naiset ja Miehet Suomessa **8149**

Finland. Statistics Finland. Yearbook of Justice Statistics *see* Finland. Tilastokeskus. Oikeustilastollinen Vuosikirja **2674**

Finland. Statistikcentalen. Raettsstatististisk Aarsbok *see* Finland. Tilastokeskus. Oikeustilastollinen Vuosikirja **2674**

Finland. Statistikcentralen. Arbetskraftskostnadsindex *see* Finland. Tilastokeskus. Tyotunnin Kustannus. Tyovoimakustannusindeksi **1232**

Finland. Statistikcentralen. Arbetskraftsstatistik *see* Finland. Tilastokeskus. Tyovoimatilasto **1232**

Finland. Statistikcentralen. Arbetskraftsstatistik *see* Finland. Tilastokeskus. Tyovoimatilasto **1232**

▼ *new title*   † *ceased*   ● *electronic media*   ➤ *refereed*

Title

10286 FINLAND. TILASTOKESKUS. LUONNONVARAT JA YMPARISTO ULRICH'S PERIODICALS

Finland. Tilastokeskus. Luonnonvarat ja Ymparisto (FIN ISSN 1238-0261) **3479**

• Finland. Tilastokeskus. Luottokanta/Finland. Statistics Finland. Outstanding Credit/Finland. Statistikcentralen. Kreditbestaandet (FIN ISSN 1459-5451) **1231**

• Finland. Tilastokeskus. Luottokortit/Finland. Statistikcentralen. Kreditkort (FIN ISSN 0785-7934) **1231**

▼ • Finland. Tilastokeskus. Maa- ja Metsatalousyritysten Taloustilasto/Finland. Statistics Finland. Finances of Agricultural and Forestry Enterprises/Finland. Statistikcentralen. Jord- och Skogsbruksfoeretagens Ekonomi (FIN ISSN 1797-304X) **180**

• Finland. Tilastokeskus. Maailma Numeroina. Suomen Tilastollinen Vuosikirjan...Kansainvalinen Osa/Finland. Statitikcentralen. Vaerlden i Siffror. Statistical Yearbook of Finland...Internationella Oeversikter (FIN ISSN 0787-8516) **8371**

• Finland. Tilastokeskus. Maarakennuskustannusindeksi/Finalnd. Statistikcentralen. Jordbyggnadskostnadsindex/ Finland. Statistics Finland. Cost Index of Civil Engineering Works (FIN ISSN 1236-9942) **1046**

Finland. Tilastokeskus. Maatilatalouden Tulo- ja Verotustiedot *see* Finland. Tilastokeskus. Maa- ja Metsatalousyritysten Taloustilasto **180**

Finland. Tilastokeskus. Maatilatalouden Yritys- ja Tulotilasto (Print) *see* Finland. Tilastokeskus. Maa- ja Metsatalousyritysten Taloustilasto **180**

• Finland. Tilastokeskus. Matkailutilasto/Finland. Statistics Finland. Tourism Statistics/Finland. Statistikcentralen. Turismstatistik (FIN ISSN 1238-7150) **8779**

• Finland. Tilastokeskus. Matkailutilasto/Finland. Statistics Finland. Tourism Statistics (FIN ISSN 1238-7169) **8779**

• Finland. Tilastokeskus. Moottoriajoneuvot/Finland. Statistics Finland. Motor Vehicles/Finland. Statistikcentralen. Motorfordon (FIN ISSN 0785-613X) **8524**

• Finland. Tilastokeskus. Naiset ja Miehet Suomessa (FIN ISSN 1456-2618) **8149**

Finland. Tilastokeskus. Naturresurserna och Miljoen *see* Finland. Tilastokeskus. Luonnonvarat ja Ymparisto **3479**

Finland. Tilastokeskus. Oikeustilastollinen Vuosikirja/Finland. Statistics Finland. Yearbook of Justice Statistics/Finland. Statistikcentalen. Raettsstatististisk Aarsbok (FIN ISSN 1236-2638) **2674**

• Finland. Tilastokeskus. Oppilaitostilastot (FIN ISSN 1455-4402) **2933**

Finland. Tilastokeskus. Oulun Aluepalvelu. Pohjois-Suomen Katsaus (FIN ISSN 1238-9064) **7480**

• Finland. Tilastokeskus. Palkkarakenne/Finland. Statistics Finland. Structure of Earnings/Finland. Statistikcentralen. Loenestrukturstatistik (FIN ISSN 1457-5973) **1231**

Finland. Tilastokeskus. Pankit: Vuositilasto *see* Finland. Tilastokeskus. Rahalaitokset **1231**

Finland. Tilastokeskus. Perheet/Finland. Statistics Finland. Families/Finland. Statistikcentralen. Familjer (FIN ISSN 0785-8205) **7306**

• Finland. Tilastokeskus. Poliisin Tietoon Tullut Rikollisuus/Finland. Statistikcentralen. Brottslighet som Kommit till Polisens Kaennedom (FIN ISSN 0784-882X) **2674**

• Finland. Tilastokeskus. Presidentin Vaalit/Ffinland. Statistikcentralen. Presidentvalet/Finland. Statistics Finland. Presidential Election (FIN ISSN 1237-6779) **7199**

Finland. Tilastokeskus. Rahalaitokset/Finland. Statistics Finland. Monetary Financial Institutions/Finland. Statistikcentralen. Monetaera Finansinstitut (FIN ISSN 1795-2050) **1231**

• Finland. Tilastokeskus. Rahoitusleasing/Finland. Statistics Finland. Financial Leasing/Finland. Statistikcentralen. Finansieringsleasing (FIN ISSN 1237-024X) **1232**

• Finland. Tilastokeskus. Rahoitustilinpito/Finland. Statistics Finland. Flow-of-Funds Accounts/Finland. Statistikcentralen. Finansraekenskaper (FIN ISSN 0784-9672) **1232**

Finland. Tilastokeskus. Rakennukset, Asunnot ja Asuinolot/Finland. Statistics Finland. Buildings, Dwellings and Housing Conditions/Finland. Statistikcentralen. Byggnader, Bostaeder och Boendefoerhaallanden (FIN ISSN 1455-3724) **4435**

• Finland. Tilastokeskus. Rakennus- ja Asuntotuotanto/Finland. Statistics Finland. Building and Dwelling Production/Finland. Statistikcentralen. Byggnads- och Bostadsproduktion (FIN ISSN 1238-4623) **1046**

• Finland. Tilastokeskus. Rakennuskustannusindeksi (Kuukausitilasto)/Finland. Statistics Finland. Building Cost Index/Finland. Statistikcentralen. Byggnadskostnadsindex (FIN ISSN 0784-8196) **1046**

• Finland. Tilastokeskus. Rakentaminen ja Asuminen: Vuosikirja/Finland. Statistics Finland. Construction and Housing. Yearbook (FIN ISSN 0787-572X) **4435**

Finland. Tilastokeskus. Science and Technology in Finland (FIN ISSN 0785-885X) **7854**

Finland. Tilastokeskus. Seutukunta- ja Maakuntakatsaus (FIN ISSN 1456-2480) **8371**

• Finland. Tilastokeskus. SijoittumisCD (FIN ISSN 1239-467X) **2933**

• Finland. Tilastokeskus. Sijoituspalveluyrittykset/ Finland. Statistics Finland. Investment Service Companies/Finland. Statistikcentralen. Vaerdepappersfoeretag (FIN ISSN 1457-148X) **1232**

• Finland. Tilastokeskus. Sijoitusrahastot/Finland. Statistics Finland. Mutual Funds/Finland. Statistikcentralen. Investeringsfonder (FIN ISSN 0784-994X) **1232**

• Finland. Tilastokeskus. Sukupuolten Tasa-Arvo/Finalnd. Statistikcentralen. Jaemstaelldheten mellan Kvinnor och Maen i Finland/Finland. Statistics Finland. Gender Equality in Finland (FIN ISSN 1457-5604) **8149**

• Finland. Tilastokeskus. Suomalaisten Matkailu/Finland. Statistics Finland. Finnish Travel/Finland. Trafikcentralen. Finlaendarnas Resor (FIN ISSN 1239-7342) **8779**

Finland. Tilastokeskus. Suomen Lahialueet (FIN ISSN 1239-2669) **1232**

• Finland. Tilastokeskus. Suomen Tilastollinen Vuosikirja/Finland. Statistics Finland. Statistical Yearbook of Finland/Finland. Statistikcentralen. Statistisk Aarsbok foer Finland (FIN ISSN 0081-5063) **8371**

• Finland. Tilastokeskus. Suomen Virallinen Tilasto/FInland. Statistics Finland. Official Statistics of Finland/Finland. Statistikcentralen. Finlands Officiella Statistik (FIN ISSN 1795-5165) **8371**

• Finland. Tilastokeskus. Suomen Virallinen Tilasto (FIN ISSN 1796-0479) **8371**

• Finland. Tilastokeskus. Suomen Yritykset/Finland. Statistics Finland. Corporate Enterprises and Personal Businesses in Finland/Finland. Statistikcentralen. Finlands Foeretag (FIN ISSN 0788-1738) **1232**

Finland. Tilastokeskus. Suomessa Liikkuvat Liikkuvat Kuvat/Finland. Statistics Finland. Moving Images in Finland (FIN ISSN 1237-4407) **2347**

• Finland. Tilastokeskus. Suomi CD (FIN ISSN 1236-7877) **8371**

Finland. Tilastokeskus. Suomi Lukuina (FIN ISSN 1795-732X) **8371**

Finland. Tilastokeskus. Tasa-Arvobarometri (FIN ISSN 1456-3096) **8082**

Finland. Tilastokeskus. Taskutilasto *see* Finland. Tilastokeskus. Suomi Lukuina **8371**

Finland Tilastokeskus. Teollisuuden, Rakennusalan ja Liikenteen Tyontekijoiden Palkat *see* Finland. Tilastokeskus. Yksityisen Sektorin Palkat **1232**

Finland. Tilastokeskus. Tiede ja Teknologia (FIN ISSN 0785-0719) **7854**

• Finland. Tilastokeskus. Tiede, Teknologia ja Tietoyhteiskunta/Finland. Statistics Finland. Science, Technology, and Information Society/Finland. Statistikcentralen. Vetenskap, Teknologi och Informationssamhaelle (FIN ISSN 1795-536X) **7854**

Finland. Tilastokeskus. Tiede, Teknologia ja Tutkimus *see* Finland. Tilastokeskus. Tiede, Teknologia ja Tietoyhteiskunta **7854**

• Finland. Tilastokeskus. Tieliikenneonnettomuudet/ Finland. Statistics Finland. Road Accidents in Finland/Finland. Statistikcentralen. Vaegtrafikolykor (FIN ISSN 0785-6245) **8524**

• Finland. Tilastokeskus. Tieliikenteen Tavarankuljetustilasto/Finland. Statistics Finland. Road Freight Transport/Finland. Statistikcentralen. Varutransporter med Lastbil (FIN ISSN 0786-1877) **8779**

Finland. Tilastokeskus. Tilastokatsauksia/Finland. Statistics Finland. Bulletin of Statistics/Finland. Statistikcentralen. Statistiska Oeversikter (FIN ISSN 0015-2390) **8372**

Finland. Tilastokeskus. Tilastokatsaus *see* Finland. Tilastokeskus. Tilastokatsauksia **8372**

Finland. Tilastokeskus. Tilastollisia Tiedonantoja/Finland. Central Statistical Office. Statistical Surveys/Finland. Statistikcentralen. Statistiska Meddelanden (FIN ISSN 0355-208X) **8372**

• Finland. Tilastokeskus. Tukku- ja Vahittaiskauppa/Finland. Statistics Finland. Wholesale and Retail Trade/Finland. Statistikcentralen. Parti- och Detaljhandeln (FIN ISSN 0785-6288) **1232**

• Finland. Tilastokeskus. Tulo- ja Varallisuustilasto/Finland. Statistics Finland. Statistics of Income and Property/Finland. Statistikcentralen. Inkomst- och Foermoegenhetstatistik (FIN ISSN 0785-6016) **1232**

• Finland. Tilastokeskus. Tulonjakotilasto/Finland. Statistics Finland. Income Distribution Statistics/Finland. Statistikcentralen. Inkomstfoerdelingsstatistik (FIN ISSN 0785-9880) **1232**

• Finland. Tilastokeskus. Tuottajahintaindeksit/ Finland. Statistics Finland. Producer Price Indices/Finland. Statistikcentralen. Producentprisindex (FIN ISSN 0784-817X) **1232**

Finland. Tilastokeskus. Tuottavuuskatsaus (FIN ISSN 1239-3975) **1232**

Finland. Tilastokeskus. Tutkimuksia/Finland. Statistics Finland. Studies/Finland. Statistikcentralen. Undersoekningar (FIN ISSN 0355-2071) **8372**

• Finland. Tilastokeskus. Tutkimus- ja Kehittamisrahoitus Valtion Talousarviossa/ Finland. Statistics Finland. Government R&D Funding in the State Budget/Finland. Statistikcentralen. Forsknings- och Utvecklingsfinansiering i Statsbudgeten (FIN ISSN 1459-9066) **1232**

• Finland. Tilastokeskus. Tutkimus- ja Kehittamistoiminta Suomessa/Finland. Central Statistical Office. Research Activity/Finland. Statistikcentralen. Forskningsverksamheten (FIN ISSN 1457-4101) **7937**

• Finland. Tilastokeskus. Tyossakaynti/Finand. Statistics Finland. Employment Statistics/Finland. Statistikcentralen. Sysselsaettningsstatistik (FIN) **1232**

Finland. Tilastokeskus. Tyossakayntitilasto (Print) *see* Finland. Tilastokeskus. Tyossakaynti **1232**

Finland. Tilastokeskus. Tyotaistelut (Neljannesvuositilasto) (FIN ISSN 0785-0204) **1232**

• Finland. Tilastokeskus. Tyotapaturmat/Finland. Statistics Finland. Occupational Accident Statistics/Finland. Statistikcentralen. Olycksfall i Arbete (FIN ISSN 0789-1180) **1232**

• Finland. Tilastokeskus. Tyotunnin Kustannus. Tyovoimakustannusindeksi/Finland. Statistics Finland. Cost of Hour Worked. Labour Cost Index/Finland. Statistikcentralen. Arbetskraftskostnadsindex (FIN ISSN 1457-084X) **1232**

Finland. Tilastokeskus. Tyovoimakustannusindeksi *see* Finland. Tilastokeskus. Tyotunnin Kustannus. Tyovoimakustannusindeksi **1232**

• Finland. Tilastokeskus. Tyovoimatilasto/Finland. Statistikcentralen. Arbetskraftsstatistik (FIN ISSN 0784-7998) **1232**

Finland. Tilastokeskus. Tyovoimatilasto/Finland. Statistics Finland. Labour Force Statistics/Finland. Statistikcentralen. Arbetskraftsstatistik (FIN ISSN 0785-0050) **1232**

Finland. Tilastokeskus. Ulkomaalaiset ja Siirtolaisuus/Finland. Statistics Finland. Aliens and International Migration (FIN ISSN 1239-9663) **7306**

• Finland. Tilastokeskus. Vaestoennusteet/Finland. Statistics Finland. Population Projection/Finland. Statistikcentralen. Befolkningsprognoser (FIN ISSN 1236-5483) **7306**

Finland. Tilastokeskus. Vaeston Koulutusrakenne Kunnittain (FIN ISSN 0785-0743) **2933**

Finland. Tilastokeskus. Vaestonmuutokset/Finland. Statistics Finland. Vital Statistics/Finland. Statistikcentralen. Befolkningsroerelsen (FIN ISSN 0788-5245) **7306**

Finland. Tilastokeskus. Vaestonmuutokset Kunnittain *see* Finland. Tilastokeskus. Vaestorakenne ja Vaestonmuutokset Kunnittain **7306**

Finland Tilastokeskus. Vaestorakenne *see* Finland. Tilastokeskus. Vaestorakenne ja Vaestonmuutokset Kunnittain **7306**

• Finland. Tilastokeskus. Vaestorakenne ja Vaestonmuutokset Kunnittain/Finland. Statistics Finland. Population Structure and Vital Statistics by Municipality/Finland. Statistikcentralen. Befolkningens Sammansaettning och Befolkningsfoeraendringar Kommunvis (FIN ISSN 1795-1887) **7306**

• Finland. Tilastokeskus. Valtion Kuukausipalkat/Finland. Statistikcentralen. Maanadsloener inom Staten (FIN ISSN 0785-8884) **1232**

• Finland. Tilastokeskus. Vuokratilasto/Finland. Statistics Finland. Rents/Finland. Statistikcentralen. Hyresstatistik (FIN ISSN 0784-9346) **4435**

Finland. Tilastokeskus. Yksityisen Sektorin Kuukausipalkat *see* Finland. Tilastokeskus. Yksityisen Sektorin Palkat **1232**

▼ • Finland. Tilastokeskus. Yksityisen Sektorin Palkat/Finland. Statistikcentralen. Loener inom den Privata Sektorn (FIN ISSN 1797-0776) **1232**

• Finland. Tilastokeskus. Ymparistotilasto/Finland. Statistics Finland. Environment Statistics (FIN ISSN 0785-0387) **3479**

Finland. Tilastokeskus. Yritysten Kansainvalistyminen/Finland. Statistics Finland. Internationalisation of Enterprises/Finland. Statistikcentralen. Foeretagens Internationalisering (FIN ISSN 1459-7713) **1232**

• Finland Tilastokeskus. Yritysten Rakenteet -Tilastopalvelu/Finland. Statistics Finland. Business Enterprises - Net Results and Balance Sheets/Finland. Statistikcentralen. Foeretagsverksamhetens Resultat och Balansraeknig (FIN) **1232**

Finland. Tilastokeskus. Yritystoiminnan Talous ja Tasset (Print) *see* Finland Tilastokeskus. Yritysten Rakenteet -Tilastopalvelu **1232**

Finland. Trafikcentralen. Finlaendarnas Resor *see* Finland. Tilastokeskus. Suomalaisten Matkailu **8779**

Finland. Tullihallitus. Tavaroiden Ulkomaankauppa/Finland. National Board of Customs. Foreign Trade of Goods/Finland. Tullstyrelsen. Utrikeshandel med Varor (FIN ISSN 1796-9344) **1232**

Finland. Tullihallitus. Ulkomaankauppa *see* Finland. Tullihallitus. Tavaroiden Ulkomaankauppa **1232**

Finland. Tullstyrelsen. Utrikeshandel med Varor *see* Finland. Tullihallitus. Tavaroiden Ulkomaankauppa **1232**

Finland. Ulkoasiainministerio. Julkaisuja/Finland. Ministerio de los Asuntos Extranjeros. Publicaciones/Finland. Ministry for Foreign Affairs. Publications/Finland. Utrikesministeriet. Publikationer (FIN ISSN 0358-1489) **7234**

Finland. Utrikesministeriet. Publikationer *see* Finland. Ulkoasiainministerio. Julkaisuja **7234**

• Finland. Valtioneuvoston Kanslia. Julkaisusarja (FIN ISSN 0782-6028) **7437**

Finland. Valtiovarainministerio. Economic Survey (FIN ISSN 0430-5221) **1487**

Finland. Valtiovarainministerio. Ekonomisk Oeversikt *see* Finland. Valtiovarainministerio. Taloudellinen Katsaus **1487**

Finland. Valtiovarainministerio. Ekonomisk Oeversikt *see* Finland. Valtiovarainministerio. Economic Survey **1487**

Finland. Valtiovarainministerio. Taloudellinen Katsaus (FIN ISSN 0071-5271) **1487**

• Finland. Ymparistoministerio. Raportteja (FIN ISSN 1796-1696) **3486**

• Finland. Ymparistoministerio. Ymparistohallinnon Ohjeita (FIN ISSN 1796-1645) **7437**

• Finland. Tilastokeskus. La Finlande en Chiffres (FIN ISSN 0782-7326) **8372**

Finland's Balance of Payments *see* Suomen Maksutase (Online) **1904**

Finland's Balance of Payments. Annual Statistics *see* Suomen Maksutase. Vuositilasto **1904**

• Finlands Bank. Aarsberaettelse (FIN ISSN 1239-9337) **1347**

Finlands Bank. Statistisk Oeversikt. Finansmarknaden *see* Suomen Pankki. Rahoitusmarkkinat. Tilastokatsaus **1269**

Finlands Betalingsbalans *see* Suomen Maksutase (Online) **1904**

Finlands Betalningsbalans *see* Suomen Maksutase. Vuositilasto **1904**

Finlands Industrifoerbund. Medlemsfoerteckning *see* Teollisuuden Keskusliitto. Jasenluettelo **2030**

• Finlands Kommuntidning (FIN ISSN 1235-9343) **7437**

Finlands Laekartidning *see* Suomen Laakarilehti **5718**

Finlands Medicinhistoriska Saellskap. Aarsskrift *see* Hippokrates **5628**

Finlands Natur (FIN ISSN 0356-4509) **788**

Finlands Press *see* Suomen Lehdisto **4584**

Finlands Tandlaekartidning *see* Suomen Hammaslaakarilehti **5866**

Finlanf. Statistikcentralen. Konsumentbarometern *see* Finland. Tilastokeskus. Kuluttajabarometri **1231**

Finnair Lento (FIN) **8541**

Finnam Newsletter (USA) **3533**

Finnboat News (FIN ISSN 0789-7332) **8275**

Finnisch-Ugrische Forschungen (FIN ISSN 0355-1253) **5119**

Finnisch - Ugrische Mitteilungen (DEU ISSN 0341-7816) **5119**

Finnisches Geodaetisches Institut. Veroeffentlichungen *see* Suomen Geodeettisen Laitos. Julkaisuja **2790**

Finnish American Club of Saima, Inc. Newsletter *see* F A C S Newsletter **3975**

• The Finnish American Reporter (USA ISSN 1078-0025) **3533**

Finnish Anthropological Society. Journal *see* Suomen Antropologi **357**

Finnish Anthropological Society. Transactions *see* Suomen Antropologisen Seura. Toimituksia **357**

Finnish Architectural Review *see* Arkkitehti **433**

➤ Finnish Association for Aerosol Research. Report Series in Aerosol Science (FIN ISSN 0784-3496) **2100**

➤ Finnish Association for Aerosol Research. Report Series. Part B (FIN ISSN 1456-226X) **2100**

Finnish Association on Intellectual and Developmental Disabilities. Studies *see* Kehitysvammaliitto. Tutkimuksia **8052**

Finnish Boatbuilding Industry (FIN ISSN 0356-7753) **8275**

Finnish Bond Issues *see* Suomen Joukkovelkakirjalainat **1654**

Finnish Broadcasting Company. Annual Report *see* Yleisradio. Annual Report **2399**

Finnish Chemical Journal *see* Kemia - Kemi **2069**

Finnish Civil Engineering and Construction Journal *see* Rakennustekniikka **3281**

Finnish Construction Magazine *see* Rakennustaito **1031**

Finnish Dance in Focus (FIN ISSN 1795-9837) **2686**

Finnish Dental Journal *see* Suomen Hammaslaakarilehti **5866**

• Finnish Documentary Films (FIN ISSN 1795-9977) **6501**

Finnish Economic Journal *see* Kansantaloudellinen Aikakauskirja **1139**

• Finnish Economic Papers (FIN ISSN 0784-5197) **1110**

Finnish Educational Research Association. Research in Educational Sciences *see* Suomen Kasvatustieteellinen Seura. Kasvatusalan Tutkimuksia **2916**

Finnish Environment *see* Suomen Ymparisto **3468**

Finnish Environment Institute. Reports *see* Suomen Ympariskeskus. Raportteja **3491**

• Finnish Films (FIN ISSN 1796-0738) **6501**

Title

Firsts (USA ISSN 1066-5471) **7561**
• FirstSurf (DEU) **2557**
Firth Derivatives Law and Practice *see* Derivatives: Law and Practice **4657**
➤ Firudo Baiorojisuto/Field Biologist (JPN ISSN 0917-4850) **673**
Firumu Badji News *see* F B News **7517**
Fisc *see* F & A Actueel **1744**
Fiscaal Advies (NLD ISSN 1383-7060) **1110**
Fiscaal Jaarboek (BEL ISSN 0775-0781) **1925**
Fiscaal Ondernemingsrecht (NLD ISSN 0927-5746) **1925**
• Fiscaal Praktijkblad (NLD ISSN 1569-4151) **1288**
Fiscaal Praktijkboek Directe Belastingen (BEL) **1925**
Fiscaal Recht *see* Weekblad voor Fiscaal Recht **4811**
Fiscaal Recht (Year) (NLD ISSN 1876-4215) **1925**
Fiscaal Rendement (NLD ISSN 1567-6897) **1925**
Fiscaal Tijdschrift FED (NLD ISSN 1574-1737) **1925**
Fiscaal Tijdschrift Vermogen (NLD ISSN 1566-6697) **1925**
• Fiscaal Up to Date (NLD ISSN 0925-4552) **1110**
Fiscaal Weekblad Fed *see* Fiscaal Tijdschrift FED **1925**
The Fiscal Monitor (CAN ISSN 0839-8224) **1925**
• Fiscal Notes (USA) **1110**
• ➤ Fiscal Studies (USA ISSN 0143-5671) **1925**
Fiscal Year (Year) Performance and Accountability Report *see* U.S. Department of Veterans Affairs. Fiscal Year (Year) Performance and Accountability Report **6450**
Fiscale Berichten voor het Notariaat (NLD ISSN 0925-6822) **4674**
Fiscale Jurisprudentie/Jurisprudence Fiscale (BEL ISSN 0772-733X) **1925**
De Fiscale Koerier (BEL ISSN 0774-658X) **1925**
Fiscale Praktijkvragen (NLD ISSN 1382-3507) **1925**
Fiscale Studieserie (NLD ISSN 1572-4239) **1925**
Fiscale Wenken *see* Samsom Fiscale Wenken **1942**
FiscAlert Magazine (NLD ISSN 1388-2538) **1925**
Fiscalita Internazionale (ITA ISSN 1723-4263) **1925**
Fiscalite *see* Source O C D E. Fiscalite **1943**
Fiscalite Europeenne (FRA ISSN 0242-5599) **1925**
Fiscalite Europeenne: Droit International des Affaires (FRA) **1925**
Fiscaliteit. Monografieen (BEL) **1347**
Der Fisch (DEU) **2857**
Fisch und Fang (DEU ISSN 0015-2838) **8312**
Fisch und Fliege (DEU) **8312**
Fisch und Umwelt Mecklenburg-Vorpommern. Jahresheft (DEU) **3431**
Fischelner Woche (DEU) **3847**
Fischer Film Almanach (Year) (DEU ISSN 0173-542X) **6501**
Fischer und Teichwirt (DEU ISSN 0342-5703) **3591**
Das Fischerblatt (DEU ISSN 0015-2854) **3591**
Fischerei in Baden-Wuerttemberg (DEU) **3591**
Fischerei in Europa *see* Fisheries and Aquaculture in Europe **3592**
Fischerei. Jahrbuch *see* Fisheries. Yearbook **3613**
Fischer's Archiv (DEU) **1817**
Fischers Gueterttransport Nachrichten Informationen fuer den Gueterverkehr (DEU ISSN 0945-6732) **8617**
Fischmagazin (DEU ISSN 0930-6544) **3591**
Fischoekologie (DEU ISSN 0934-4225) **3591**
Fischoekologie Aktuell *see* Fischoekologie **3591**
Fischwaid (DEU ISSN 0722-706X) **8312**
• Il Fisco (ITA ISSN 1124-9307) **1925**
Fiscolex B T W (BEL ISSN 0774-3289) **1925**
Fiscolex C I R *see* Fiscolex B T W **1925**
Fiscolex Impots Regioniaux et Provinciaux *see* Fiscolex Regionale Belastingen **1925**
Fiscolex Regionale Belastingen/Fiscolex Impots Regioniaux et Provinciaux (BEL ISSN 1378-6814) **1925**
Fiscolex Regionale en Provinciale Belastingen *see* Fiscolex Regionale Belastingen **1925**
Le Fiscologue (BEL ISSN 0772-4845) **1925**
Le Fiscologue International (BEL ISSN 0772-1463) **1925**
Fiscus (POL ISSN 0867-3748) **1288**
• Fish (AUS) **3591**
Fish (GBR) **3591**
Fish Aggregating Devices (NCL ISSN 1026-2032) **3591**
• Fish & Chips and Fast Food (GBR ISSN 0969-2037) **3636**
Fish and Fish Egg Distribution Report *see* National Fish Hatchery System. Fish and Fish Egg Distribution Report (Online) **3602**
Fish & Fish Products *see* Key Note Market Report: Fish & Fish Products **1894**
• ➤ Fish and Fisheries (GBR ISSN 1467-2960) **943**
Fish & Fisheries (NLD ISSN 1367-8396) **3591**
• Fish & Fisheries Worldwide (USA ISSN 1069-9309) **716**
Fish & Fly (USA ISSN 1535-6353) **8312**
Fish & Game New Zealand (NZL ISSN 1172-434X) **8312**
Fish & Hunt *see* Nation's Best Sports **8324**
• ➤ Fish and Shellfish Immunology (GBR ISSN 1050-4648) **943**
Fish and Wildlife Research (USA ISSN 1040-2411) **943**
Fish and Wildlife Research Institute Technical Reports (USA ISSN 1930-1448) **673**
† Fish Boats (ITA ISSN 1970-5573) **8956**
Fish Culture *see* Yoshoku **3612**
Fish Culture Section Publication *see* F C S Publication **3591**
Fish Culturist (USA ISSN 0015-2919) **3591**
Fish Drum (USA ISSN 1051-1695) **5296**
• Fish Farmer (GBR ISSN 0262-9615) **3591**
Fish Farming *see* Fiskeopdrett **3613**
Fish Farming and Fishing *see* Rybovodstvo i Rybolovstvo **3606**
• Fish Farming International (GBR ISSN 0262-0820) **3591**
Fish Farming News (USA) **3591**
Fish Farming Today *see* Fish Update **8313**
• Fish Health Newsletter (USA) **3592**
Fish Immunology - Technical Communications (USA) **673**
The Fish Industry (GBR ISSN 1474-5232) **3592**
Fish Industry *see* Rybnaya Promyshlennost' **3606**
Fish Magazine *see* Fisshu Magajin **3594**
Fish Pathology *see* Gyobyo Kenkyu **945**
• Fish Physiology (USA ISSN 1546-5098) **943**
• ➤ Fish Physiology & Biochemistry (NLD ISSN 0920-1742) **943**
• Fish Piss (CAN ISSN 1206-3355) **5296**
The Fish Sniffer (USA ISSN 0747-3397) **8313**
Fish Technology Newsletter (IND ISSN 0971-0167) **3592**
Fish Trader (Edinburgh) (GBR) **3592**
Fish Trader (Redhill) (GBR ISSN 0143-7771) **3592**
Fish Trader Yearbook (GBR ISSN 0953-8860) **3592**
• Fish Update (GBR ISSN 1750-4023) **8313**
FishBoats (CAN ISSN 1202-0265) **8275**
• ➤ Fisheries (USA ISSN 0363-2415) **3592**
Fisheries and Aquaculture in Europe (BEL) **3592**
Fisheries and Fishbreeding in Israel *see* Dayig u-Midgeh be-Yisrael **3590**
Fisheries Bulletin (IRL ISSN 0332-4338) **943**
Fisheries Bulletin *see* Malawi. Fisheries Department. Fisheries Bulletin **3601**
Fisheries Census Report *see* Eoeob Chong Jo'sa Bunseog Bo'go'seo **3613**
Fisheries Centre Research Reports (CAN ISSN 1198-6727) **3592**
• Fisheries Draft Policy (AUS ISSN 1441-4007) **3592**
Fisheries Education and Training (NCL ISSN 1025-7438) **3592**
Fisheries Engineering *see* Suisan Kogaku **3609**
Fisheries Extension *see* Yuye Tuiguang **3612**
• Fisheries Improvement Loans Act. Annual Report (CAN ISSN 0700-1576) **1926**
Fisheries Journal (PHL ISSN 0115-950X) **3592**
• ➤ Fisheries Management and Ecology (GBR ISSN 0969-997X) **3592**
• ➤ Fisheries Management & Ecology Online (GBR ISSN 1365-2400) **3592**
† • Fisheries Market News Report (USA) **8956**
Fisheries Newsletter (NCL ISSN 0248-076X) **3592**
Fisheries Notice (GBR ISSN 0436-4430) **3592**
Fisheries Occasional Publications *see* Western Australia. Fisheries Department. Occasional Publications **3611**
• ➤ Fisheries Oceanography (GBR ISSN 1054-6006) **3592**
• ➤ Fisheries Oceanography Online (GBR ISSN 1365-2419) **3592**
Fisheries Oceanography. Supplement *see* Fisheries Oceanography **3592**
Fisheries of the United States (USA) **3592**
Fisheries R & D News *see* Fish **3591**
• ➤ Fisheries Research (NLD ISSN 0165-7836) **3592**
Fisheries Research Agency. Bulletin *see* Suisan Sougou Kenkyuu Senta Kenkyuu Houkoku **3609**
Fisheries Research Bulletin of Tonga (TON ISSN 1173-3012) **673**
• Fisheries Research Data Report (GBR ISSN 0264-5130) **3593**
• Fisheries Research Technical Report (GBR ISSN 0963-4916) **3593**
Fisheries Research Technical Report *see* Fisheries Research Technical Report **3593**
Fisheries Resource Conservation Council. Report (CAN) **2611**
Fisheries Resource Series (IRL ISSN 1649-5357) **3593**
• ➤ Fisheries Science (JPN ISSN 0919-9268) **3593**
Fisheries Science Research *see* Su'san Gwahag Yeon'gu **8991**
Fisheries Society of Taiwan. Journal *see* Taiwan Shuichan Xuehui Kan **3609**
Fisheries Statistical Yearbook. Taiwan, Kinmen and Matsu Area *see* Zhonghua Minguo Taimin Diqu Yuye Tongji Nianbao **3614**
Fisheries Statistics *see* Kuwait. Central Statistical Office. Fishing Statistics Bulletin **3613**
Fisheries Statistics of Indonesia (IDN ISSN 0301-7222) **3613**
Fisheries Statistics of Japan (JPN ISSN 0071-5581) **3593**
Fisheries Technical Publications Catalogue (AUS ISSN 1833-4148) **3593**
Fisheries World *see* Suisan Kai **3609**
• Fisheries. Yearbook/Fischerei. Jahrbuch/Peche. Annuaire (LUX ISSN 1609-4085) **3613**
Fisherman (CAN ISSN 0015-2986) **3593**
The Fisherman (GHA) **3593**
The Fisherman (Delaware, Maryland, Virgina Edition) (USA ISSN 1040-0133) **8313**
The Fisherman (Florida Edition) (USA ISSN 1059-5295) **8313**
The Fisherman (Long Island, Metropolitan New York Edition) (USA ISSN 1040-0109) **8313**
The Fisherman (New England Edition) (USA ISSN 1040-0125) **8313**
The Fisherman (New Jersey, Delaware Bay, Edition) (USA ISSN 1040-0117) **8313**
Fisherman Union of Indonesia. Central Governing Board. Annual Report/Himpunan Nelayan Selurah Indonesia. Dewan Pimpanan Pusat. Laporan Kegiatan (IDN) **3593**
Fisherman's Manual (GBR) **3593**
Fishermen's News (USA ISSN 0015-2994) **3593**
Fishery and Aquaculture in Lithuania *see* Zuvininkyste Lietuvoje **3612**
• ➤ Fishery Bulletin (USA ISSN 0090-0656) **3593**
Fishery Committee for the Eastern Central Atlantic. ECAF Series *see* C E C A F/E C A F Series **8938**
Fishery Committee for the Eastern Central Atlantic Series *see* C E C A F/E C A F Series **8938**
• Fishery Leaflet (IRL ISSN 0332-1789) **3593**
Fishery Management Strategies Performance Report (AUS ISSN 1832-3383) **3593**
Fishery Modernization *see* Yuye Xiandaihua **3612**
Fishery Research Bulletin *see* Alaska Fishery Research Bulletin **3583**
Fishery Statistical Bulletin for South China Sea Area (THA ISSN 0857-748X) **3613**
Fishery Statistics *see* Fisheries. Yearbook **3613**
Fishery Survey of India. Annual Report (IND) **3593**
Fishery Survey of India. Bulletin (IND) **3593**
Fishery Survey of India. Occasional Paper (IND) **3593**
Fishery Technology (IND ISSN 0015-3001) **3593**
Fishes *see* Uo **966**
Fishes of Sahul (AUS ISSN 0813-3778) **3593**
Fishes of the Western North Atlantic. Memoirs (USA) **673**
▼ • Fishfarming Xpert (NOR ISSN 1504-9558) **3593**
Fishin' Boats (AUS) **8313**
Fishing *see* Halaszat **3596**
▼ • The Fishing Almanac (AUS ISSN 1833-7430) **8313**
Fishing and Hunting News (USA ISSN 0015-301X) **8313**
Fishing Boat and System Engineering Association of Japan. Journal *see* Kaiyou Suisan Enjiniaringu **3600**
Fishing Boat World *see* Work Boat World **8665**
Fishing Chimes/Visakhapatnam (IND ISSN 0971-4529) **3593**
Fishing Facts (USA) **8313**
• Fishing Florida Magazine (USA) **8275**
• Fishing Future (AUS ISSN 1447-9818) **3593**
Fishing Guru (USA) **8313**
Fishing in Britain (GBR) **8313**
Fishing in Europe *see* Fisheries and Aquaculture in Europe **3592**
Fishing in Maryland (USA ISSN 0164-0941) **8313**
Fishing Industry Handbook (ZAF) **3593**
Fishing Industry Handbook: South Africa, Namibia and Mozambique (ZAF) **3593**
Fishing Industry News Southern Africa (ZAF) **3593**
Fishing Industry Research Institute. Annual Report of the Director/Visnywerheid-Navorsingsinstituut. Jaarverslag van die Direkteur (ZAF ISSN 0250-2372) **3636**
The Fishing Journal (ZAF ISSN 1562-9120) **8313**
Fishing Magazine *see* Yaoxue Shijian Zazhi **6886**
Fishing Magazine for Young Boy (JPN) **2189**
Fishing Monthly *see* Fish Update **8313**
Fishing Murman *see* Rybnyi Murman **3606**
• The Fishing Network Web-Zine (CAN ISSN 1488-0717) **8313**
Fishing News (GBR ISSN 0015-3036) **3593**
Fishing News *see* Alieftika Nea **3583**
• Fishing News International (GBR ISSN 0015-3044) **3594**
Fishing Queensland (AUS ISSN 1447-2228) **8313**
Fishing Tackle Retailer (USA ISSN 8750-1287) **8313**
Fishing Tips & Techniques *see* Australian Adventure Angler **8304**
Fishing Today (AUS ISSN 1031-7368) **3594**
Fishing Victoria Annual (AUS ISSN 1448-756X) **8313**
Fishing World (AUS ISSN 1320-2839) **3594**
Fishing World's Boat Fishing *see* Fishing World **3594**
Fishkeeping Answers (GBR ISSN 0965-3805) **3594**
FishLines (USA) **3594**
Fishtail West (CAN) **8258**
Fisica (ARG ISSN 0326-7512) **7012**
Fisica (ITA) **7012**
• ➤ Fisica de la Tierra (ESP ISSN 0214-4557) **2780**
FISIO Active/Fisioterapia (CHE ISSN 1660-5209) **6109**
Fisioterapia *see* FISIO Active **6109**
• ➤ Fisioterapia (ESP ISSN 0211-5638) **5959**
• Fisioterapia (ESP ISSN 1579-7864) **6060**
Fisioterapia Actual (ESP ISSN 1576-141X) **6109**
Fisioterapia. Monografico (ESP ISSN 1578-2069) **5959**
➤ Fisioterapia y Calidad de Vida (ESP ISSN 1575-4847) **6109**
• Fisk (NOR ISSN 0808-6559) **3594**
Fisk og Fri (DNK ISSN 0108-2000) **8313**
• Fisk & Hav (DNK ISSN 0105-9211) **3594**
• Fiskaren (NOR ISSN 0015-3095) **3594**
Fiske-Feber (Copenhagen) (DNK ISSN 1600-1664) **8313**
Fiske-Feber (Helsingborg) (SWE ISSN 1652-2540) **8313**
Fiske foer Alla (SWE ISSN 1100-3626) **8313**
Fiske Nailing the New S A T *see* Nailing the New S A T **2889**
Fiskehandleren (DNK ISSN 1903-4350) **3594**
Fiskejournalen (SWE ISSN 1403-7300) **8313**
Fisken og Havet (NOR ISSN 0071-5638) **3594**
Fisken og Havet. Saernummer *see* Fisken og Havet **3594**
• Fiskeopdrett/Fish Farming (NOR ISSN 0809-4527) **3613**
• Fiskerbladet (DNK ISSN 1396-4194) **3594**
• Fiskeri Tidende (DNK ISSN 0909-7325) **3594**
Fiskeriaarbogen (DNK ISSN 0900-9787) **3594**
• Fiskeribladet (NOR ISSN 0805-5289) **3594**
• Fiskeriets Oekonomi/Economic Situation of the Danish Fishery (DNK ISSN 1601-5568) **3594**
Fiskeriforskning Info (NOR ISSN 1500-6891) **1885**
Fiskeriforskning Informerer (NOR ISSN 1500-130X) **1885**
Fiskeriforskning. Rapport *see* Nofima Marked. Rapport **3603**
Fiskerioekonomiske Smaaskrifter/Papers on Fisheries Economics (NOR ISSN 0332-8643) **3594**
Fiskeriteknisk Fagblad (NOR ISSN 1502-9808) **3594**
Fiskeritidskrift foer Finland (FIN ISSN 0015-3125) **3594**
• Fiskeriverket Informerar (Online Edition) (SWE ISSN 1404-8590) **3594**
• Fiskets Gang (Online Edition) (NOR ISSN 1503-1993) **3594**
Fiskifrettir (ISL ISSN 1017-3536) **3594**
Fiskoloog *see* Le Fiscologue **1925**
Fiskoloog (English Edition) *see* Le Fiscologue International **1925**
Fiskoloog Internationaal *see* Le Fiscologue International **1925**
Fisshu Magajin/Fish Magazine (JPN ISSN 1348-6683) **3594**
Fit (BLR) **3800**
Fit! (DEU) **7517**
• Fit & Fun Magazine (USA) **6985**
• The Fit Christian (USA ISSN 1933-9305) **6985**
Fit durch Tip (DEU) **7798**
Fit en Gezond *see* Evita **8862**
• Fit for Fun (DEU ISSN 0946-9680) **6985**
Fit for Fun (ITA ISSN 1125-6737) **6985**
Fit for Life (CHE ISSN 1423-5137) **8313**
• Fit im Job (CHE ISSN 1661-6650) **1861**
▼ Fit Living (DNK ISSN 1903-3176) **6985**
Fit / Low Carb (USA) **6659**
Fit mit Walking *see* Laufzeit **6991**
• Fit Pregnancy (USA ISSN 1079-3615) **5990**
Fit Pregnancy (ZAF ISSN 1812-3058) **5991**
Fit und Fuenfzig (DEU ISSN 1611-8448) **6985**
Fit Yoga (USA ISSN 1932-8842) **6985**
Fitech International (GBR ISSN 0307-2118) **3578**
Fitlink Australia (AUS) **6986**
• FITNE Healthnet (Fuld Institute for Technology in Nursing Education) (USA) **5959**
Fitness (CHN) **6986**
Fitness *see* New Zealand Fitness **6994**
• Fitness (USA ISSN 1060-9237) **6986**
Fitness (ZAF ISSN 1816-2452) **8845**
• Fitness America (USA) **8173**
Fitness and Beauty *see* Jian yu Mei **6990**
• Fitness & Performance Journal (BRA ISSN 1519-9088) **6986**
Fitness and Physique (USA ISSN 1549-9030) **6986**
• Fitness and Wellness Business Week (USA ISSN 1552-9118) **6986**
Fitness & Wellness Business Week *see* Fitness and Wellness Business Week **6986**
Fitness Appraisal Certification and Accreditation News *see* Course Conductor News **6984**
• Fitness Business Canada (CAN ISSN 1494-9318) **5614**
▼ Fitness Business News (USA) **1110**
Fitness Business Pro *see* Club Industry's Fitness Business Pro **6984**
Fitness Cycling (USA ISSN 1046-1701) **8313**
Fitness Life *see* FitnessLife **6986**
Fitness Management (USA ISSN 0882-0481) **6986**
Fitness Management International (DEU) **6986**
Fitness Plus Magazine (USA) **6986**
Fitness Product News (USA ISSN 1095-4929) **6986**
• Fitness Rx (USA ISSN 1543-3730) **8845**
Fitness Rx for Men (USA ISSN 1543-8406) **6986**
Fitness Trainer Canada *see* Fitness Business Canada **5614**
Fitness Update (NLD ISSN 1572-7599) **8173**
FitnessLife (NZL ISSN 1175-8430) **6986**
FitnessLink (USA) **6986**
➤ Fitopatologia (PER ISSN 0430-6155) **788**
Fitopatologia Brasileira *see* Tropical Plant Pathology **821**
Fitopatologia Colombiana (COL ISSN 0120-0143) **788**
Fitopatologia Venezolana (VEN ISSN 0798-0035) **788**
• Fitosanidad (CUB ISSN 1562-3009) **231**
Fitosociologia (ITA ISSN 1125-9078) **788**
➤ Fitossanidade (BRA ISSN 0100-4204) **788**
Fitotecnia Colombia (COL ISSN 0123-1286) **231**
• ➤ Fitoterapia (NLD ISSN 1971-551X) **788**
FitPregnancy *see* Fit Pregnancy **5991**
Fitt Mama (HUN ISSN 1586-4936) **8845**
The Fitzhugh Directory of Independent Healthcare and Long Term Care. Financial Information (GBR) **5614**
Five (DEU ISSN 1614-9297) **8228**
Five AM *see* 5 AM **5439**

Flits see V O-Flits 3035
Flo' (NLD ISSN 1871-8531) 2189
Floating Island (USA ISSN 0147-1686) 5297
† Flock (DEU ISSN 0933-2316) 8956
Flock Book of Devon Cornwall Longwool Sheep (GBR) 287
Flock Book of Oxford Down Sheep (GBR) 287
Floete Aktuell (DEU ISSN 0930-8563) 6567
Floh (DEU ISSN 0943-8157) 2189
Flohkiste (DEU ISSN 0943-7797) 2189
Flohs Ideenkiste see Ideenkiste 3064
• Flomsonekart (NOR ISSN 1504-5161) 8823
Floodlight (GBR ISSN 0956-3709) 2941
Floodtide (USA) 7643
• Floor Covering Installer (USA ISSN 1099-9647) 1050
Floor Covering News (USA ISSN 1079-4174) 4540
Floor Covering Weekly (USA ISSN 0015-3761) 4557
Floor Covering Weekly. Product Source Guide (USA) 4557
• Floor Focus (USA ISSN 1064-7627) 4540
Flooring (London) (GBR ISSN 1461-3999) 1050
• The Flooring Contractor (USA) 4557
Floors (GBR ISSN 0263-7693) 4540
Floors & Walls (DEU ISSN 1614-6743) 1008
Floors Buyers Guide (ZAF) 1008
Floors in Africa see Schalk Burger's Floors in Africa 1034
Flor-Ala (USA) 2283
• ➤ Flora (DEU ISSN 0367-2530) 788
Flora (ECU ISSN 0015-380X) 788
Flora (RUS) 788
Flora (Hamburg) see Flora Garten 3729
Flora Agaricina Neerlandica (USA) 788
Flora de Colombia (COL ISSN 0120-4351) 788
Flora de Venezuela (VEN ISSN 0798-8613) 788
• Flora de Veracruz (MEX ISSN 0187-425X) 788
• Flora del Bajio y de Regiones Adyacentes (MEX ISSN 0188-5170) 788
Flora del Paraguay (CHE ISSN 0254-8453) 788
Flora et Vegetatio Mundi (DEU ISSN 0071-576X) 788
Flora, Fauna y Areas Silvestres (ITA ISSN 1014-2800) 7854
Flora Fukushima see Furora Fukushima 3730
• Flora Garten (DEU ISSN 1610-3157) 3729
Flora Garten-Praxis see Flora Garten 3729
Flora Garten Spezial see Flora Garten 3729
Flora International (GBR ISSN 1479-3954) 3756
Flora Liquenologica Iberica (ESP ISSN 1696-0513) 788
Flora Magazine (USA ISSN 1556-6358) 3756
Flora Malesiana Bulletin (NLD ISSN 0071-5778) 788
➤ Flora Malesiana. Series 1: Seed Plants (NLD ISSN 1872-924X) 788
➤ Flora Malesiana. Series 2: Pteridophyta (Ferns & Fern Allies) (NLD ISSN 0071-5786) 789
• Flora Montiberica (ESP ISSN 1138-5952) 7854
Flora Neotropica (USA ISSN 0071-5794) 789
Flora of Australia (AUS ISSN 0726-3449) 789
Flora of Ecuador (DNK ISSN 0347-8742) 789
Flora of Poland: Fungi see Flora Polski: Grzyby 789
Flora of Poland: Vascular Plants see Flora Polski: Rosliny Naczyniowe 789
Flora of Southern Africa (ZAF) 789
➤ Flora og Fauna (DNK ISSN 0015-3818) 7854
• Flora Online (DEU) 3729
Flora Palaestina (ISR) 789
➤ Flora Polski: Grzyby/Flora of Poland: Fungi (POL) 789
Flora Polski: Rosliny Naczyniowe/Flora of Poland: Vascular Plants (POL) 789
➤ Flora Slodkowodna Polski/Freshwater Flora of Poland (POL ISSN 0071-5840) 789
FloraCulture International (USA ISSN 1051-9076) 3729
Florae Polonicae Terrarunique Adiacentium Sconographia see Atlas Flory Polskiej i Ziem Osciennych 777
Florafacts (USA ISSN 0046-4082) 3756
Floral Design (NZL ISSN 1176-9726) 3756
Floral Lifestyles (USA) 3756
Floral Management (USA ISSN 1067-4772) 3756
Floral Marketing Association Directory and Buyer's Guide see F M A Directory and Buyer's Guide 3755
Floral Mass Marketing (USA) 3756
Floral Retailing see Super Floral Retailing 3757
Floral Underawl & Gazette Times (USA ISSN 0149-7499) 4335
Floraline (USA) 3756
Flore d'Afrique Centrale (Zaire - Rwanda - Burundi) (BEL ISSN 0779-116X) 789
Flore de la Nouvelle Caledonie et Dependances (FRA ISSN 0430-666X) 789
Flore de Madagascar et des Comores (FRA) 789
Flore du Cambodge, du Laos et du Vietnam (FRA ISSN 0071-5867) 789
Flore du Cameroun (CMR ISSN 0071-5875) 789
Flore du Gabon (FRA ISSN 0071-5883) 789
Flore Illustree des Champignons d'Afrique Centrale (BEL ISSN 0379-1890) 789
Flore Pratique des Algues d'Eau Douce de Belgique (BEL ISSN 0779-1089) 789
Florence (Year) (USA ISSN 1056-4489) 8703
Florence Black Sun (USA) 3534
• Florence Directions (USA ISSN 1933-0790) 8703
Florensia (ITA ISSN 1123-573X) 7643
Florentia Iliberritana (ESP ISSN 1131-8848) 2234
• ➤ Floresta (BRA ISSN 0015-3826) 3688
Floresta e Ambiente (BRA ISSN 1415-0980) 3431
Florian Hessen (DEU ISSN 0936-5370) 3578
Floribella (PRT) 2189
▼ Floriculture and Ornamental Biotechnology (GBR ISSN 1749-0294) 789
Floriculture Crops see U.S. Department of Agriculture. National Agricultural Statistics Service. Floriculture Crops 188
Floriculture Indiana (USA ISSN 1052-5416) 3729
• Floriculture News (AUS ISSN 1444-1810) 3756
Floriculture Newsletter see Floriculture News 3756
Floriculture, Ornamental and Plant Biotechnology (GBR) 789
Florida see Florida & Caribbean 8703
Florida A & M University Law Review (Agricultural / Mechanical) (USA ISSN 1935-5173) 4674
Florida Administrative Law Reports (USA ISSN 0194-4800) 4674
Florida Administrative Practice (USA) 7437
Florida Administrative Weekly (USA ISSN 0098-874X) 4674
Florida Agricultural Market Research Center Industry Report see F A M R C Industry Report 197
Florida Agricultural Research (USA) 113
Florida: All-Industries see Harris Directory. Florida All-Industries 1999
Florida Almanac (USA ISSN 0361-9796) 8703
Florida & Caribbean (GBR ISSN 1748-6866) 8703
Florida and the Nation (USA) 8372
Florida Anthropological Society. Newsletter (USA ISSN 1949-2073) 339
➤ Florida Anthropologist (USA ISSN 0015-3893) 339
Florida Appellate Practice (USA) 4674
Florida Archaeology (USA ISSN 0888-4277) 393
• The Florida Archivist (USA) 5009
Florida Association of Voluntary Agencies for Caribbean Action. Annual Report (USA) 1596
Florida Atlantic University Free Press see F A U Free Press 2283
Florida Avocado Administrative Committee. Annual Report (USA) 231
Florida Avocado Administrative Committee. Meeting Minutes (USA) 231
Florida Avocado Administrative Committee. Shipments Report (USA) 180
• Florida Banking (USA ISSN 1064-0673) 1348
Florida Bankruptcy Casenotes (USA) 4674
Florida Bar. Administrative Law Section. Newsletter (USA) 4674
Florida Bar. Appellate Practice and Advocacy Section. Record (USA) 4675
Florida Bar. Business Law Section. Quarterly Report (USA) 4868
Florida Bar. City County & Local Government Law Section Agenda (USA) 7492
Florida Bar. Elder Law Advocate (USA) 4675
Florida Bar. Environmental and Land Use Law Section. Reporter (USA) 3431
Florida Bar. Florida Criminal Law Journal (USA) 4890
Florida Bar. Government Lawyer Section Reporter (USA) 4675
Florida Bar. Health Law Section Newsletter (USA) 4675
• The Florida Bar Journal (USA ISSN 0015-3915) 4675
• Florida Bar News (USA ISSN 0360-0114) 4675
Florida Bar. Public Interest Law Section Newsletter (USA) 4675
Florida Bar. State of the Art News (USA) 4675
Florida Bar. Tax Section Bulletin (USA) 1926
Florida Bernard Shaw Series (USA) 5297
Florida Business (USA ISSN 1042-590X) 1110
• Florida Business Credit Directory (USA) 1995
• Florida Business Directory (USA ISSN 1048-7093) 1995
• Florida C P A Today (Certified Public Accountant) (USA) 1288
Florida/Caribbean Architect (USA) 442
Florida Catholic (Miami Edition) (USA ISSN 0746-4584) 7798
Florida Catholic (Orlando Edition) see Florida Catholic (Miami Edition) 7798
Florida Catholic (Orlando Edition) see Gathered 7798
Florida Catholic (Palm Beach Edition) see Florida Catholic (Miami Edition) 7798
Florida Catholic (Palm Beach Edition) see Gathered 7798
Florida Catholic (Pensacola - Tallahassee Edition) see Florida Catholic (Miami Edition) 7798
Florida Catholic (Pensacola - Tallahassee Edition) see Gathered 7798
Florida Catholic (St. Petersburg Edition) see Gathered 7798
Florida Catholic (Venice Edition) see Florida Catholic (Miami Edition) 7798
Florida Catholic (Venice Edition) see Gathered 7798
Florida Cattleman and Livestock Journal (USA ISSN 0015-3958) 287
Florida Cities & Counties Graphic Performance Analysis (USA ISSN 1935-5858) 7480
Florida Cities and Counties Graphic Performance Analysis see Florida Cities & Counties Graphic Performance Analysis 7480
Florida Citrus Production Research Advisory Council. Annual Report see F C P R A C Annual Review of Research (Print Edition) 230
Florida Citrus Production Research Advisory Council Annual Review of Research (Print Edition) see F C P R A C Annual Review of Research (Print Edition) 230
† • Florida Civil Practice Guide (USA) 8956
Florida Civil Practice Motions (USA) 4831
• Florida Civil Procedure (USA ISSN 1554-5156) 4831
† Florida Civil Procedure Litigation Manual (USA) 8956
Florida Classic Home (USA) 4540
Florida Coastal Home (USA) 4540
Florida Coastal Law Journal (USA ISSN 1528-056X) 4675
• Florida Commercial Landlord - Tenant Law (USA) 4675
▼ Florida Commercial Properties (USA ISSN 1936-8003) 7591
Florida Commission for Independent Education. Annual Report (USA) 2981
➤ Florida Communication Journal (USA ISSN 1050-3366) 2321
Florida Community Association Journal (USA) 7591
Florida Community Studies Weekly see World Community Studies Weekly 2926
Florida: Compass American Guides see Compass American Guides: Florida 8694
• Florida Condominium Law Manual (USA) 4675
Florida Construction Law Manual (USA ISSN 1558-1632) 1008
• Florida Construction Lien Manual (USA) 1008
• Florida Construction News Covering Northwest Florida (USA ISSN 1085-2255) 1008
Florida Construction News Covering Orlando and Vicinity see Florida Construction News Covering Orlando & Vicinity 1008
• Florida Construction News Covering Orlando & Vicinity (USA ISSN 1085-2239) 1008
† • Florida Construction News Weekly Covering Miami & Vicinity (USA ISSN 1084-9548) 8956
• Florida Construction News Weekly Covering West Palm Beach and Vicinity (USA ISSN 1084-9564) 1008
Florida Contractor (USA ISSN 0046-4112) 4119
Florida Cooperative Extension Service. Circular (USA ISSN 0099-7676) 113
• Florida Corporations Manual (USA) 4868
Florida County Age, Sex and Race Population Estimates (USA) 7307
Florida County Migration Flows 1981-1996 (USA) 1487
• Florida County Rankings (USA) 7307
• Florida Creditors' Rights Manual (USA) 4868
Florida Criminal and Traffic Court Rules of Procedure (USA ISSN 1930-1634) 4890
• Florida Criminal Defense Trial Manual (USA) 4890
Florida Criminal Law & Motor Vehicle Handbook see Florida Criminal Law and Motor Vehicle Handbook 4890
• Florida Criminal Law and Motor Vehicle Handbook (USA) 4890
• Florida Criminal Laws (USA) 2652
Florida Criminal Sentencing Law (USA) 4890
Florida Curiosities (USA ISSN 1541-7824) 8703
Florida. Department of Agriculture and Consumer Services. Botany Circular (USA) 789
Florida. Department of Agriculture and Consumer Services. Division of Plant Industry. Bulletin Series (USA ISSN 0428-6294) 789
Florida. Department of Agriculture and Consumer Services. Entomology Circular (USA ISSN 0013-8932) 847
Florida. Department of Agriculture and Consumer Services. Nematology Circular (USA ISSN 0360-7550) 943
Florida. Department of Agriculture and Consumer Services. Plant Pathology Circular (USA ISSN 0032-0870) 789
Florida. Department of Corrections. Annual Report (USA) 8040
Florida Department of Education. Professional Practices Council. Report (USA) 2857
Florida. Department of Health. Vital News (USA) 7307
Florida Design (USA ISSN 1082-3891) 4540
▼ Florida Designers Review (USA ISSN 1939-8409) 4540
Florida Design's Miami Home & Decor (USA ISSN 1935-9055) 4540
Florida Design's Palm Beach Home & Decor (USA ISSN 1936-7996) 4540
Florida Directory (USA) 7437
Florida. Division of Motor Vehicles. Tags and Revenue (USA ISSN 0092-0177) 8496
Florida. Division of Plant Industry. Biennial Report (USA ISSN 0071-5948) 113
Florida Education Advocate (USA) 2857
Florida Education Directory (USA) 2955
Florida Educational Research Council. Research Bulletin (USA) 2857
• Florida Employment Law (USA ISSN 1934-1636) 1682
• Florida Employment Law Letter (USA ISSN 1041-3537) 4675
Florida Employment Law Manual (USA) 4675
Florida Engineering Society. Journal (USA ISSN 0015-4032) 3192
Florida English (USA ISSN 1940-6088) 5297
• ➤ Florida Entomologist (USA ISSN 0015-4040) 847
• Florida Estates Practice Guide (USA) 4902
Florida Estimates of Population (Year) (USA ISSN 1524-234X) 7307
Florida Evidence Courtroom Manual (USA ISSN 1069-0611) 4951
• Florida Evidence Manual (USA) 4951
• Florida Evidentiary Foundations (USA) 4952
Florida Facts (USA ISSN 0895-8084) 3120
• Florida Family Law (USA) 4910
Florida Family Law Handbook (USA ISSN 1931-4647) 4910
• Florida Family Law Practice Manual (USA) 4910
• Florida Family Law Reporter (USA ISSN 1048-0595) 4910
• Florida Family Living (Central Florida Edition) (USA) 2153
Florida Family Living (Gulf Coast Edition) see Florida Family Living (Central Florida Edition) 2153
Florida Family Living (Tampa Bay Edition) see Florida Family Living (Central Florida Edition) 2153
➤ Florida Field Naturalist (USA ISSN 0738-999X) 907
Florida Fireman (USA ISSN 0274-8797) 3578
• Florida Fish and Game Finder Magazine (USA ISSN 1081-910X) 8314
Florida Fish and Wildlife News (USA ISSN 1520-8214) 2611
Florida Food and Resource Economics (USA ISSN 0886-5868) 3636
Florida Football (USA) 8228
Florida Foreclosures, Remedies, Defenses, and Lender Liability (USA) 4868
• Florida Forms of Jury Instruction (USA) 4675
Florida Forum (USA ISSN 0191-4618) 1008
Florida Fossil Invertebrates (USA ISSN 1536-5557) 944
Florida Friends of Bluegrass Society. Newsletter (USA ISSN 0160-5119) 6567
Florida Funeral Director (USA ISSN 0273-9747) 3719
Florida Game & Fish (USA ISSN 0889-3322) 8314
Florida Gardening (USA ISSN 1086-3087) 3730
Florida Genealogical Society Journal (USA ISSN 0374-6240) 3766
Florida Genealogical Society Newsletter (USA) 3766
Florida Genealogist (USA ISSN 0161-4932) 3766
Florida General Practice, Solo & Small Firm, Journal (USA) 4675
➤ Florida Geographer (USA ISSN 0739-0041) 4006
Florida Geological Survey. Biennial Report (USA ISSN 1052-6536) 2734
Florida Geological Survey. Bulletin (USA ISSN 0271-7832) 2734
Florida Geological Survey. Information Circular (USA) 2734
Florida Geological Survey. Map Series (USA) 2734
Florida Geological Survey. Report of Investigations (USA ISSN 1053-0533) 2734
• Florida Grower (USA ISSN 1531-2356) 113
Florida Historical Quarterly (USA ISSN 0015-4113) 4292
Florida History and Culture (USA) 4292
Florida Homes & Lifestyles (USA ISSN 1549-4748) 4540
Florida Hotel & Motel Journal see Southern Hospitality Magazine 4398
Florida Independent Accountant (USA) 1289
Florida InsideOut (USA) 4540
Florida Institute of Phosphate Research. Publications (USA) 6462
Florida International Magazine (USA ISSN 1098-0636) 3975
Florida International Planner (USA) 8703
Florida International University, College of Law Law Review see F I U Law Review 4670
Florida International University Hospitality Review see F I U Hospitality Review 4385
Florida James Joyce Series (USA) 5297
† The Florida JobBank (USA ISSN 1069-8981) 8956
Florida Journal of Anthropology see The University of Florida Journal of Anthropology 359
▼ • ➤ Florida Journal of Educational Administration & Policy (USA ISSN 1942-3497) 3023
• ➤ Florida Journal of Educational Research (Online Edition) (USA) 2857
• Florida Journal of International Law (USA ISSN 1556-2670) 4926
Florida Jury Verdict Reporter (USA ISSN 1059-6275) 4675
Florida Jury Verdict Review and Analysis (USA ISSN 1058-8604) 4675
The Florida Keys and Key West (GBR ISSN 1359-1576) 8703
Florida Keys Coconut Telegraph see The Conch Republic Coconut Telegraph 3973
Florida Kitchen & Bath (USA) 4540
† Florida Land Use and Growth Management Law (USA) 8956
• Florida Law Review (USA ISSN 1045-4241) 4675
• Florida Law Weekly (USA ISSN 0274-8533) 4675
Florida Lawyer (USA ISSN 1549-5205) 4675
• Florida Libraries (USA ISSN 0046-4147) 5009
Florida Life (USA) 5071
Florida Lime Administrative Committee. Annual Report (USA) 231
Florida Lime Administrative Committee. Meeting Minutes (USA) 231
Florida Lime Administrative Committee. Shipments Report (USA) 180
Florida Long-Term Economic Forecast (USA) 1233
• Florida Manufacturers Register (USA ISSN 0882-9438) 1995
Florida: Manufacturing see Harris Florida Manufacturers Directory 2003
Florida Mariner (USA) 8275
Florida Market Bulletin (USA ISSN 0046-4120) 113
Florida Medical Business (USA) 5614

Title

▼ *new title*   † *ceased*   • *electronic media*   ➤ *refereed*

Folia Philosophica *see* Uniwersytet Slaski w Katowicach. Prace Naukowe. Folia Philosophica **6959**
● ➤ Folia Phoniatrica et Logopaedica (CHE ISSN 1021-7762) **6080**
Folia Praehistorica Posnaniensia (POL ISSN 0239-8524) **393**
● ➤ Folia Primatologica (CHE ISSN 0015-5713) **944**
Folia Quaternaria (POL ISSN 0015-573X) **6724**
Folia Scandinavica Posnaniensia (POL ISSN 1230-4786) **4220**
Folia Scientiarum Universitatis Technicae Resoviensis *see* Politechnika Rzeszowska. Zeszyty Naukowe. Matematyka **5525**
Folia Turistica (POL ISSN 0867-3888) **8710**
➤ Folia Universitatis Agriculturae Stetinensis. Oeconomica (POL ISSN 1506-1965) **7964**
➤ Folia Universitatis Agriculturae Stetinensis. Piscaria (POL ISSN 1506-168X) **3595**
➤ Folia Universitatis Agriculturae Stetinensis. Zootechnica (POL ISSN 1506-1698) **287**
➤ Folia Universitatis Agriculturae Stetinesis. Agricultura (POL ISSN 1506-1973) **231**
Folia Veterinaria (SVK ISSN 0015-5748) **8797**
● ➤ Folia Zoologica (CZE ISSN 0139-7893) **944**
Folia Zoologica Monographs (CZE ISSN 1213-1164) **944**
● Foliaca (AUT ISSN 1028-0332) **790**
Folio *see* Discover N L S **5007**
Folio (NLD ISSN 1381-205X) **5297**
● Folio: (USA ISSN 0046-4333) **7561**
Folio *see* Vocare **7779**
Folio (Brockport) (USA ISSN 0882-3030) **4452**
Folio (North Hollywood) (USA) **2358**
Folio (Oklahoma City) (USA) **1110**
Folio (Washington) (USA ISSN 1547-4151) **5297**
● Folio: First Day (USA) **7561**
Folio: First Day Financial Report (USA) **7561**
Folio Physician Directory. Connecticut and Rhode Island *see* Folio Physician Directory with Healthcare Facilities. Connecticut and Rhode Island **5615**
Folio Physician Directory. Maine, New Hampshire and Vermont *see* Folio Physician Directory with Healthcare Facilities. Maine, New Hampshire and Vermont **5615**
Folio Physician Directory. Massachusetts *see* Folio Physician Directory with Healthcare Facilities. Massachusetts **5615**
Folio Physician Directory. New Jersey *see* Folio Physician Directory with Healthcare Facilities. New Jersey **5615**
Folio Physician Directory. New York City and Long Island *see* Folio Physician Directory with Healthcare Facilities. New York City and Long Island **5615**
Folio Physician Directory. New York Upstate *see* Folio Physician Directory with Healthcare Facilities. New York Upstate **5615**
Folio Physician Directory. Ohio *see* Folio Physician Directory with Healthcare Facilities. Ohio **5615**
● Folio Physician Directory with Healthcare Facilities. Connecticut and Rhode Island (USA ISSN 1559-7660) **5615**
● Folio Physician Directory with Healthcare Facilities. Maine, New Hampshire and Vermont (USA ISSN 1559-7679) **5615**
● Folio Physician Directory with Healthcare Facilities. Massachusetts (USA ISSN 1559-7652) **5615**
● Folio Physician Directory with Healthcare Facilities. New Jersey (USA ISSN 1559-6419) **5615**
● Folio Physician Directory with Healthcare Facilities. New York City and Long Island (USA ISSN 1559-4351) **5615**
● Folio Physician Directory with Healthcare Facilities. New York Upstate (USA ISSN 1559-436X) **5615**
● Folio Physician Directory with Healthcare Facilities. Ohio (USA ISSN 1559-7687) **5615**
Folio: Sourcebook *see* Folio: SuperBook **7561**
● Folio: SuperBook (USA) **7561**
Folio Weekly (USA) **3975**
Folios (COL ISSN 0123-1022) **8102**
Folios (Bogota) (COL ISSN 0123-4870) **7964**
† Folk (DNK ISSN 0085-0756) **8957**
Folk Art (USA ISSN 1067-3067) **489**
Folk Art and Artists (USA) **489**
➤ Folk Art Messenger (USA ISSN 1043-5026) **490**
Folk Dance Directory (USA ISSN 0163-528X) **2686**
Folk Dance New Zealand Newsletter *see* Folkdancers' Own **2686**
Folk Dance Phone Book and Group Directory (Year) (USA ISSN 1081-2695) **2686**
Folk Dance Problem Solver (Year) (USA ISSN 1081-7654) **2686**
Folk Dancer (CAN) **2686**
Folk Directory (GBR) **2686**
Folk Era Today! (USA ISSN 1076-4119) **6567**
Folk Fortaeller (DNK ISSN 0109-8365) **4220**
Folk Harp Journal (USA ISSN 0094-8934) **6567**
● Folk Life (GBR ISSN 0430-8778) **339**
Folk Literature *see* Minjian Wenxue **3620**
Folk Literature *see* Literatura Ludowa **5225**
● ➤ Folk Music Journal (GBR ISSN 0531-9684) **6567**
Folk North-West (GBR ISSN 1350-8083) **6567**
Folk och Foersvar *see* Perspektiv **6441**
Folk och Musik (FIN ISSN 0789-6549) **3617**
Folk & Spraak (SWE ISSN 1651-8365) **7643**
Folk og Kultur (DNK ISSN 0105-1024) **3617**
Folk og Minder fra Nordsjaelland (DNK ISSN 0105-9610) **4220**
Folk og Musik *see* Roots Zone (Print) **8986**
Folk on the Delaware General Corporation Law: Fundamentals (USA ISSN 1084-7707) **4868**
Folk Song *see* Canu Gwerin **6554**
Folk Song Weekly *see* Caifeng Bao **6553**
Folk Tales *see* Minjian Gushi **3620**
Folkdancers' Own (NZL ISSN 1176-628X) **2686**
Folke Bernadotte Academy. Conference Proceedings (SWE ISSN 1652-2664) **8102**
Folke Bernadotte Academy. Handbook (SWE ISSN 1652-9456) **8102**
Folke Bernadotte Academy. Research Report (SWE ISSN 1652-7887) **7235**
Folkebladet (DNK ISSN 1902-0090) **3833**
Folkebladet (Sydjylland) (DNK) **3833**
Folkens Museum - National Museum of Ethnography (SWE ISSN 1102-6502) **339**
Folkeoplysnings- og Voksenundervisningsarbejde Dialog *see* F O V U Dialog **2941**
Folkepensionistanstalten Bladet *see* F P A - Bladet **4502**
Folker! (DEU) **6567**
● Folkeskolen (DNK ISSN 0015-5837) **2858**
† ● Folkeskolen. Katalog (DNK ISSN 0909-6477) **8957**
Folkesocialisten *see* F! **7135**
Folkestone and Dover K M Extra (GBR) **3865**
● Folket i Bild - Kulturfront (SWE ISSN 0345-3073) **3955**
● Folketidende (DNK) **3833**
Folketinget efter Valget (DNK ISSN 0906-4893) **7438**
● Folkets Framtid (NOR ISSN 0805-5300) **7136**
Folkets Historia (Aarsbok) (SWE ISSN 1652-2842) **4220**
● Folkevirke (DNK ISSN 0015-5845) **5216**
The FolkFire (USA) **6568**
Folkhaelsoinstitutet. Rapport *see* Statens Folkhaelsoinstitut. Rapport **7542**
Folkhaelsorapport (SWE ISSN 1402-0327) **7517**
Folkhoegskolan (SWE ISSN 0348-4769) **2941**
Folkkulturdarkivet. Meddelanden (FIN ISSN 0355-9963) **3617**
● Folklife Center News (USA ISSN 0149-6840) **3617**
Folklivsskildringar och Bygdestudier (SWE ISSN 0071-6766) **3617**
Folklivsstudier (FIN ISSN 0085-0764) **339**
Fol'klor Urala (RUS) **3617**
● Folklore (CAN ISSN 0824-3085) **3617**
Folklore *see* Shan Hai Jing **3622**
● ➤ Folklore (EST ISSN 1406-0949) **3617**
● ➤ Folklore (GBR ISSN 0015-587X) **3617**
● Folklore Americano (MEX ISSN 0071-6774) **3617**
Folklore de France (FRA ISSN 0015-5918) **3617**
Folklore du Monde (BEL) **3617**
Folklore Fellows Communications *see* F F Communications **3617**
Folklore Fellows Network *see* F F Network **3617**
Folklore Fellows of India. News Bulletin (IND) **3617**
● ➤ Folklore Forum (Online Edition) (USA) **3617**
Folklore Forum (Print Edition) *see* Folklore Forum (Online Edition) **3617**
Folklore Historian (USA ISSN 1041-8644) **3618**
Folklore in the Carolinas (USA) **3618**
Folklore of American Holidays (USA) **3618**
Folklore of World Holidays (USA) **3618**
Folklore Research Journal (IND) **3618**
Folklore Society Children's Folklore Newsletter *see* F L S - Children's Folklore Newsletter **5294**
Folklore Society of Greater Washington Newsletter (USA ISSN 0015-5950) **3618**
Folklore Society of Ireland. Journal *see* Bealoideas **3615**
Folklore Studies *see* Minsu Yanjiu **7986**
Folklore Studies *see* Tautosakos Darbai **3623**
Folklore Suisse *see* Schweizer Volkskunde (Deutsch - Franzosisch - Italienische Ausgabe) **3622**
Folklore Svizzero *see* Schweizer Volkskunde (Deutsch - Franzosisch - Italienische Ausgabe) **3622**
Folklores and Folk Cultures of Eastern Europe (USA) **3618**
FolkMagazin (DEU) **6568**
Folktales of the World (USA ISSN 0071-6804) **3618**
Folkwang Studien (DEU ISSN 1861-3047) **6568**
FolkwangStudien *see* Folkwang Studien **6568**
Folletos de Divulgacion (URY) **393**
Follies (GBR ISSN 0963-9004) **442**
The Follies Journal (GBR ISSN 1474-7669) **442**
● Follow (AUS ISSN 1832-4231) **2255**
Follow Up File (USA ISSN 0888-3955) **4575**
Folsom El Dorado Hills Style *see* FolsomElDoradoHillsStyle **5071**
FolsomElDoradoHillsStyle (USA) **5071**
Fomento Agropecuario (VEN) **113**
● Fomento de la Produccion (ESP ISSN 0015-6035) **1886**
● Fomento de la Produccion. Espana 30000 (ESP ISSN 1578-7729) **1886**
Fomento del Trabajo. Horizonte Empresarial (ESP ISSN 1137-4128) **1487**
Fomento Literario (USA) **5297**
Fomento y Produccion (ECU) **1348**
Fomrhi Quarterly *see* F O M R H I Quarterly **6566**
FoNalAp Divulga (VEN) **113**
† Fonaments (ESP ISSN 0210-2366) **8957**
Fonarik (RUS) **4452**
Fonction Publique (CHE) **4594**
Fonctionnaire Magazine (FRA ISSN 1622-3071) **7438**
Fond za Naucna Istrazivanja. Bilten (SRB ISSN 0352-2385) **4452**
† Fondamenti (ITA ISSN 1122-102X) **8957**
Fondation Africaine pour les Technologies Agricoles. Annual Report (KEN ISSN 1993-4173) **113**
Fondation de la France Libre (FRA ISSN 1630-5078) **6421**
Fondation de l'Armee du Salut. Le Magazine (FRA ISSN 1636-1377) **8040**
Fondation de l'Hopital Sainte-Justine. Annual Report (CAN ISSN 1910-6408) **4093**
Fondation de l'Hopital Sainte-Justine. Rapport Annuel *see* Fondation de l'Hopital Sainte-Justine. Annual Report **4093**
Fondation de Recherche et d'Editions de Philosophie Neohellenique. Serie Recherches (GRC ISSN 1105-221X) **6920**
● Fondation des Maladies Mentales. Bulletin (CAN ISSN 1712-8021) **6141**
Fondation des Maladies Mentales. Rapport d'Activites *see* Mental Illness Foundation. Activity Report **6160**
Fondation Europeenne pour l'Amelioration des Conditions de Vie et de Travail. Communique *see* Eurofound News **7516**
Fondation Fyssen. Annales (FRA ISSN 0980-157X) **7855**
Fondation Louis de Broglie. Annales (FRA ISSN 0182-4295) **7013**
Fondation Maurice Careme (BEL ISSN 0779-0732) **5297**
Fondation pour l'Etude des Processus de Gouvernement au Canada. Rapport Annuel *see* Foundation for the Study of Processes of Government in Canada. Annual Report **7136**
● Fondation pour l'Innovation Politique. Newsletter (FRA ISSN 1777-9014) **7136**
● Fondation Quebecoise des Maladies Mentales. Rapport d'Activites (CAN ISSN 1910-0973) **6141**
Fondazione B N C. Studi e Ricerche (Banca Nazionale delle Comunicazioni) (ITA ISSN 1970-7231) **4452**
Fondazione Basso. Annali (ITA ISSN 0392-0003) **4139**
Fondazione Carlo Marchi. Studi (ITA ISSN 1122-4290) **4452**
Fondazione Cassa di Risparmio di Roma. Notiziario (ITA ISSN 1828-4760) **1110**
Fondazione ENI Enrico Mattei Series on Economics, Energy and Environment *see* F E E M Series on Economics, Energy and Environment **3135**
Fondazione Giangiacomo Feltrinelli. Annali (ITA ISSN 0393-3954) **7964**
Fondazione Giangiacomo Feltrinelli. Quaderni (ITA) **7561**
● ➤ Fondazione Giorgio Ronchi. Atti (ITA ISSN 0391-2051) **7075**
Fondazione Giuseppe Di Vittorio. Annali (ITA) **7964**
Fondazione Guarasci. Bollettino (ITA ISSN 1122-3960) **7136**
Fondazione Istituto Gramsci. Annali (ITA ISSN 1972-2818) **7136**
Fondazione Italiana per il Notariato. Quaderni (ITA ISSN 1971-5285) **4676**
† Fondazione Liberal (ITA ISSN 1721-2812) **8957**
● Fondazione Luigi Einaudi. Annali (ITA ISSN 0531-9870) **7964**
Fondazione Luigi Firpo. Studi e Testi (ITA ISSN 1122-4312) **7136**
Fondazione Luigi Micheletti. Annali (ITA ISSN 1121-7448) **4220**
Fondazione Mariano Rumor. Annali (ITA ISSN 1828-4493) **7136**
Fondazione Ugo La Malfa. Annali (ITA ISSN 1826-8854) **7136**
Fondements des Sciences (FRA ISSN 0295-6977) **7855**
● Fonderia (ITA ISSN 0015-6078) **6312**
Fonderie, Fondeur d'Aujourd'hui (FRA ISSN 0249-3136) **6312**
Fonderie sous Pression International (FRA ISSN 1775-2523) **6312**
Fondo de Cohesion. Informe Anual *see* Cohesion Fund. Annual Report (Year) **1083**
Fondo de Cultura. Serie de Lecturas (MEX) **1110**
Fondo de Promocion de Exportaciones. Directorio de Exportadores/Export Directory (COL) **1565**
Fondo Monetario Internacional. Informe Anual del Directorio Ejectivo *see* International Monetary Fund. Annual Report of the Executive Board **1358**
● Fondo Monetario Internacional. Serie de Folletos (USA ISSN 0252-2993) **1348**
Fondo Monetario Internacional. Temas de Economia *see* International Monetary Fund. Economic Issues **1571**
Fondo Nacional de Investigaciones Agropecuarias Divulga *see* FoNalAp Divulga **113**
Fondo Veinte Mas Uno (ESP ISSN 1699-0102) **1487**
Fondov Pazar/Stock Market (BGR) **1624**
Fondovye Novosti (RUS) **1110**
Fondovyi Rynok (UKR) **1110**
Der Fonds (DEU ISSN 1439-3344) **1624**
Fonds Africain de Developpement. Rapport Annuel *see* African Development Fund. Annual Report **1590**
Fonds de Cohesion. Rapport Annuel *see* Cohesion Fund. Annual Report (Year) **1083**
Fonds de Developpement Economique et Social. Conseil de Direction. Rapport (FRA ISSN 0071-6847) **1886**
Fonds de la Musique du Canada. Programme d'Aide aux Associations Sectorielles. Rapport Annuel *see* Canada Music Fund. Support to Sector Associations Program. Annual Report **1079**
Fonds de la Musique du Canada. Programme de suivi de la Politique. Rapport Annuel *see* Canada Music Fund. Policy Monitoring Program. Annual Report **6553**
Fonds de la Musique du Canada. Rapport Annuel *see* Canada Music Fund. Annual Report **6553**
Fonds d'Indemnisation des Services Financiers. Rapport Annuel *see* Quebec Province. Autorite des Marches Financiers. Rapport Annuel **1646**
Fonds et Sicav (BEL ISSN 0779-9411) **1348**
Fonds Monetaire International. Dossiers Economiques *see* International Monetary Fund. Economic Issues **1571**
Fonds Monetaire International. Etudes Economiques et Financieres (USA ISSN 1020-5101) **1348**
Fonds Monetaire International. Rapport Annuel du Conseil d'Administration *see* International Monetary Fund. Annual Report of the Executive Board **1358**
Fonds Monetaire International. Serie des Brochures (USA ISSN 0252-2985) **1348**
Fonds pour l'Etude de l'Environnement. Rapport Annuel *see* Environmental Studies Research Funds. Annual Report **3429**
Fonds Professionell (DEU) **1624**
Fonds Psychische Gezondheid. Nieuwsbrief (NLD ISSN 1875-2551) **6141**
Fonds & Co. (DEU ISSN 1614-3256) **1624**
Fondsen en Sicav *see* Fonds et Sicav **1348**
Fondsmagazin (DEU ISSN 1434-0259) **1624**
● ➤ Fonetica si Dialectologie (ROM ISSN 0071-6855) **5119**
FonoForum (DEU ISSN 0015-6140) **6568**
● Fonorama (POL ISSN 0867-0501) **6568**
Fons and Porter's Love of Quilting (USA ISSN 1525-1284) **6639**
Fons & Porter's Love of Quilting *see* Fons and Porter's Love of Quilting **6639**
● The Font Site (USA) **7320**
Fontane-Blaetter (DEU ISSN 0015-6175) **5297**
➤ Fontanus (CAN ISSN 0838-2026) **4453**
Fontanus Monograph Series (CAN ISSN 1183-1774) **4453**
Fontes *see* Towarzystwo Naukowe w Toruniu. Fontes **4274**
Fontes Archaeologicae Moravicae (CZE) **393**
● ➤ Fontes Archaeologici Posnanienses/Annales Musei Archaeologici Posnaniensis (POL ISSN 0071-6863) **393**
Fontes Archaeologici Pragenses (CZE ISSN 0015-6183) **393**
● Fontes Artis Musicae (USA ISSN 0015-6191) **6631**
Fontes Linguae Vasconum (ESP ISSN 0046-435X) **5119**
Fontes Rerum Austriacarum. Reihe 1. Scriptores (AUT ISSN 0071-6871) **4220**
Fontes Rerum Austriacarum. Reihe 2. Diplomataria et Acta (AUT ISSN 0071-688X) **4220**
Fontes Rerum Austriacarum. Reihe 3. Fontes Juris (AUT ISSN 0071-6898) **4220**
Fonti (ITA ISSN 1724-2355) **7855**
Fonti di Storia Toscana (ITA) **4220**
Fonti e Studi Francescani (ITA) **7698**
Fonti per la Storia dell'Umbria (ITA) **4220**
† Fonti sui Comuni Rurali Toscani (ITA ISSN 0071-6901) **8957**
Fontilles. Revista de Leprologia (ESP ISSN 0367-2743) **5814**
FOOCUS *see* FOCUS Journal for Respiratory Care & Sleep Medicine **6214**
▼ Food (GBR ISSN 1749-7140) **3637**
Food *see* Mazon Plus **3655**
Food *see* Ahan **3625**
Food 2 Go *see* Food to Go **4386**
Food Additive Intake Studies (IRL ISSN 1029-8614) **6659**
Food Additives and Contaminants *see* Food Additives and Contaminants. Part B. Surveillance Communications **6842**
Food Additives and Contaminants *see* Food Additives & Contaminants: Part A - Chemistry, Analysis, Control, Exposure & Risk Assessment **6842**
● ➤ Food Additives & Contaminants: Part A - Chemistry, Analysis, Control, Exposure & Risk Assessment (GBR ISSN 1944-0049) **6842**
● ➤ Food Additives and Contaminants. Part B. Surveillance Communications (GBR ISSN 1939-3210) **6842**
Food, Agriculture and the Environment (USA ISSN 1029-8622) **113**
Food Aid Needs Assessment *see* World Food Aid Needs and Availabilities. Food Aid Needs Assessment **1608**
Food Aid Shipments *see* International Grains Council. Food Aid Shipments **1599**
Food Allergy and Intolerance Journal (GBR ISSN 1468-8530) **5758**
Food Allergy News (USA ISSN 1075-4318) **5758**
▼ ● Food Analytical Methods (USA ISSN 1936-9751) **3637**
Food and Agricultural Export Directory (USA ISSN 0083-0976) **198**

Title

Title

Foreign Medical Sciences (Orthopaedics) *see* Guowai Yixue (Gukexue Fence) **6061**
Foreign Medical Sciences (Otolaryngology) *see* Guowai Yixue (Er Bi Yanhou Kexue Fence) **6080**
Foreign Medical Sciences (Parasitosis) *see* Guowai Yixue (Jishengbing Fence) **886**
Foreign Medical Sciences (Pediatrics) *see* Guowai Yixue (Erkexue Fence) **6092**
Foreign Medical Sciences (Physical Medicine & Rehabilitation) *see* Guowai Yixue (Wuli Yixue yu Kangfuxue Fence) **6109**
Foreign Medical Sciences (Prevention, Diagnosis & Biologicals for Medical Treatment) *see* Guowai Yixue (Yufang, Zhenduan, Zhiliao Yong Shengwu Zhipin Fence) **5622**
Foreign Medical Sciences (Psychiatry) *see* Guowai Yixue (Jingshenbingxue Fence) **6143**
Foreign Medical Sciences (Radiology & Nuclear Medicine) *see* Guowai Yixue (Fangshe Yixue Heyixue Fence) **6197**
Foreign Medical Sciences (Respiratory Systems) *see* Guowai Yixue (Huxi Xitong Fence) **6214**
Foreign Medical Sciences (Sanitation Economics) *see* Guowai Yixue (Weisheng Jingji Fence) **7520**
Foreign Medical Sciences (Social Medicine) *see* Guowai Yixue (Shehui Yixue Fence) **5622**
Foreign Medical Sciences (Surgery) *see* Guowai Yixue (Waikexue Fence) **6244**
Foreign Medical Sciences (Urologic System) *see* Guowai Yixue (Miniao Xitong Fence) **6268**
Foreign Medical Sciences (Women & Children Health Care) *see* Guowai Yixue (Fu-you Baojian Fence) **5991**
Foreign Medicine (Neurology, Neurosurgery) *see* Guowai Yixue (Shenjingbingxue Shenjing Waikexue Fence) **6143**
Foreign Medicines (Plant Medicine) *see* Guowai Yiyao (Zhiwuyao Fence) **6845**
Foreign Military Literature Index *see* Inostrannaya Voennaya Literatura **6455**
Foreign Military Sales, Foreign Military Construction Sales and Military Assistance Facts (Online Edition) *see* U.S. Department of Defense. Defense Security Cooperation Agency. D S C A Facts Book. Foreign Military Sales, Foreign Military Construction Sales and Military Assistance Facts (Online Edition) **6450**
Foreign Oil Field Engineering *see* Guowai Youtian Gongcheng **6772**
Foreign Philosophy *see* Waiguo Zhexue **6960**
Foreign Policy *see* Politica Externa **7167**
Foreign Policy (French Edition) (FRA ISSN 1957-5335) **7235**
• Foreign Policy (Spanish Edition) (ESP ISSN 1697-1515) **7235**
• ➤ Foreign Policy (Washington) (USA ISSN 0015-7228) **7235**
• ➤ Foreign Policy Analysis (USA ISSN 1743-8586) **7235**
• Foreign Policy Association. Headline Series (USA ISSN 0017-8780) **7235**
Foreign Policy Briefing (USA ISSN 1054-0083) **7235**
• ➤ Foreign Policy Bulletin (GBR ISSN 1052-7036) **7235**
• Foreign Policy in Focus (USA ISSN 1524-1939) **7236**
Foreign Policy Research Institute. Monograph Series (USA ISSN 0196-0334) **7236**
Foreign Policy Review *see* Kulugyi Szemle **7250**
Foreign Policy Review (USA) **7236**
Foreign Production, Supply and Distribution of Agricultural Commodities (USA) **180**
Foreign Relations of the United States (USA ISSN 0071-7355) **7236**
• Foreign Representatives in the U.S. Yellow Book (USA ISSN 1089-5833) **7236**
Foreign Science and Technology Catalogue (Geology) *see* Guowai Keji Ziliao Mulu (Dizhixue) **2720**
Foreign Science and Technology Catalogue (Medical Health) *see* Guowai Keji Ziliao Mulu (Yiyao Weisheng) **8960**
Foreign Service *see* Overseas Diplomat **7257**
• Foreign Service Journal (USA ISSN 0146-3543) **7236**
Foreign Silk *see* Guowai Sichou **8451**
• Foreign Tax and Trade Briefs (USA) **1926**
Foreign Trade *see* Handel Zagraniczny **1568**
Foreign Trade *see* Vneshnaya Torgovlya **1586**
Foreign Trade Bulletin (IND ISSN 0015-7317) **1566**
Foreign Trade Economics and International Trade *see* Waimao Jingji, Guoji Maoyi **1587**
Foreign Trade Fairs New Products Newsletter (USA ISSN 0883-4687) **1566**
Foreign Trade in the Republic of Bulgaria *see* Vunshna Turgovia na Republika Bulgaria **8413**
Foreign Trade of Romania *see* Comertul Exterior al Romaniei **1221**
Foreign Trade of the Democratic People's Republic of Korea (PRK) **1566**
• Foreign Trade Reports. U.S. Waterborne Exports and General Imports (Online Edition) (USA) **1566**
Foreign Trade Review (IND ISSN 0015-7325) **1566**
Foreign Trade Statistics of Africa. Series A: Direction of Trade (ETH ISSN 0071-7398) **1233**
Foreign Trade Statistics of Africa. Series C: Summary Tables/Statistiques Africaines du Commerce Exterieur. Serie C: Tableaux Recapitulatifs (ETH ISSN 0252-2012) **1233**
Foreign Trade Statistics of Asia and the Pacific (THA ISSN 1011-4858) **1233**
Foreign Trade Statistics of Bangladesh (BGD) **1233**
Foreign Trade Statistics of Iran/Amar-e Bazargani-Ye Khareji-Ye Iran (IRN) **1233**
Foreign Trade Statistics of the Philippines (PHL ISSN 0116-1822) **1233**
Foreign Trade Statistics of Yemen Arab Republic (YEM ISSN 0376-5695) **1233**
Foreign Trade - Trends & Tidings (IND) **1566**
• Foreign-Trade Zones Board. Annual Report to Congress (USA ISSN 1544-2322) **1566**
Foreign Travel & Immunization Guide (USA) **5758**
• Foreign Voices (DEU ISSN 1862-3913) **1596**
Foreign Wire *see* ForeignWire.com **3865**
• ForeignWire.com (GBR) **3865**
Foreldre og Barn (NOR ISSN 0332-513X) **2153**
• Foreningen af Danske Doevblinde. Medlemsnyt (DNK ISSN 1902-6587) **4081**
Foreningen af Kommunale Chefer Nyt *see* K C Nyt **7494**
Foreningen af Statsautoriserede Revisorer Rs Afgiftslove *see* F S Rs Afgiftslove **1923**
Foreningen af Statsautoriserede Revisorer Rs Skatte- og Afgiftslove. Supplement *see* F S Rs Skatte- og Afgiftslove. Supplement **1923**
Foreningen af Statsautoriserede Revisorer Rs Skattelove med Noter *see* F S Rs Skattelove med Noter **1923**
Foreningen af Udviklingsforskere i Danmark Conference *see* F A U-Conference **1595**
Foreningen af Udviklingsforskere Nyt *see* F A U Nyt **1595**
• Foreningen Baeredygtige Byer og Bygninger. Nyhedsbrev (DNK ISSN 1902-4789) **3431**
† Foreningen Danmarks Folkeminder. Skrifter (DNK ISSN 1396-0660) **8957**
Foreningen Hexis. Nyhedsbrev *see* Praktiske Grunde **4470**
Foreningen Musikk fra Livets Begynnelse. Medlemsblad *see* Musikk fra Livets Begynnelse **6596**
• Foreningen Sex & Samfund. Nyhedsbrev (DNK) **972**
Foreningen til Norske Fortidsminnesmerkers Bevaring. Aarbok (NOR ISSN 0071-7436) **4220**
Foreningsaarsskrift (DNK ISSN 1902-3367) **4220**
Forensic Drug Abuse Advisor (USA ISSN 1048-8731) **2694**
• Forensic Echo (USA) **5913**
• ➤ Forensic Examiner (USA ISSN 1084-5569) **5913**
Forensic Focus (GBR) **6141**
Forensic Medicine Bulletin *see* Adli Tip Bulteni **5912**
• The Forensic of Pi Kappa Delta (USA ISSN 0015-735X) **2321**
• Forensic Pathology Reviews (USA ISSN 1556-5661) **5615**
The Forensic Quarterly (USA ISSN 0196-304X) **2858**
• ➤ Forensic Science and Medicine (USA) **5913**
Forensic Science and Technology *see* Xingshi Jishu **5917**
• ➤ Forensic Science Communications (USA ISSN 1528-8005) **5913**
• ➤ Forensic Science International (IRL ISSN 0379-0738) **5913**
▼ • ➤ Forensic Science International: Genetics (NLD ISSN 1872-4973) **5913**
• ➤ Forensic Science, Medicine, and Pathology (USA ISSN 1547-769X) **5913**
▼ • Forensic Science Policy & Management (USA ISSN 1940-9044) **5913**
➤ Forensic Science Review (USA ISSN 1042-7201) **4676**
Forensic Sciences (USA) **5913**
• Forensic Scientist (CAN ISSN 1201-0790) **5913**
• Forensic Services Directory (USA ISSN 0192-3145) **4676**
The Forensic Teacher (USA ISSN 1936-3397) **2653**
• Forensic Toxicology/Ho Chudoku (JPN ISSN 1860-8965) **5913**
• FORENSICnetBASE (USA ISSN 1538-0874) **5913**
▼ • ➤ Forensische Psychiatrie, Psychologie, Kriminologie (DEU ISSN 1862-7072) **6141**
➤ Forensische Psychiatrie und Psychotherapie (DEU ISSN 0945-2540) **6141**
ForePlay (GBR ISSN 1746-7527) **6290**
Forerunners (USA ISSN 1076-2612) **6895**
▼ • Foresight (IND) **1111**
• ➤ Foresight (USA ISSN 1555-9068) **1746**
Foresight (USA) **1289**
• ➤ Foresight (Cambridge) (GBR ISSN 1463-6689) **8422**
Foresight (London) (GBR ISSN 0141-2027) **4503**
• Foresight (Peterborough) (GBR) **4902**
▼ • Foresight: International Journal of Business Economy and Society (IND) **1111**
• Foresight Update (USA ISSN 1078-9731) **3192**
Forest & Bird (NZL ISSN 0015-7384) **2611**
Forest and Human Kind *see* Senlin yu Renlei **3702**
Forest and Hunting Magazine *see* Lisovyi i Myslyvs'kyi Zhurnal **8321**
Forest and Nature *see* Denmark. Miljoe- og Energiministeriet. Skov- og Naturstyrelsen. Aarsberetning **3687**
Forest Chemicals Review (USA ISSN 1520-0191) **6733**
• ➤ Forest Ecology and Management (NLD ISSN 0378-1127) **3688**
Forest Engineering *see* Senlin Gongcheng **3715**
Forest Engineering Research Institute of Canada. Special Report (CAN ISSN 0381-7733) **3688**
Forest Engineering Research Institute of Canada. Technical Note (CAN ISSN 0381-7741) **3688**
Forest Engineering Research Institute of Canada. Technical Report (CAN ISSN 0318-7063) **3711**
Forest Experiments Herald *see* Glasnik za Sumske Pokuse **3692**
Forest, Farm, and Community Tree Research Reports (USA) **3688**
Forest Fire Prevention *see* Senlin Fanghuo **3581**
• Forest Genetic Resources (ITA ISSN 1020-4431) **3688**
Forest Genetics *see* International Journal of Forest Genetics **3694**
Forest Genetics Council of British Columbia. Tree Improvement Program. Project Report (CAN ISSN 1912-3779) **3688**
• Forest Health Bulletin (CAN) **3688**
Forest Health in Canada (CAN ISSN 1481-8868) **3689**
• Forest Health News (NZL ISSN 1175-9755) **3689**
Forest History Today (USA) **3689**
Forest Insect and Disease Leaflets (USA ISSN 0197-8500) **3689**
Forest Investment Account, Land Base Investment Program. Annual Update (CAN ISSN 1912-6832) **1625**
Forest Landowner (USA ISSN 1087-9110) **3689**
Forest Landowner Manual *see* Forest Landowner **3689**
† Forest Logger & Sawmiller Monthly (AUS) **8957**
Forest Machine Journal *see* Forestry Journal **3712**
Forest Magazine (USA) **3689**
Forest Notes (USA ISSN 0015-7457) **3689**
Forest of Education/Kyoiku-No-Mori (JPN) **3689**
Forest Operations Review (USA ISSN 1948-6960) **3689**
Forest Participation Series (GBR ISSN 1026-6887) **3689**
• ➤ Forest Pathology/Journal de Pathologie Forestiere/Zeitschrift fuer Forstpathologie (DEU ISSN 1437-4781) **3689**
• ➤ Forest Pathology Online (DEU ISSN 1439-0329) **3689**
Forest Pest and Disease *see* Zhongguo Senlin Bingchong **861**
Forest Pests/Shinrin Boeki (JPN ISSN 0288-3740) **3689**
• ➤ Forest Policy and Economics (NLD ISSN 1389-9341) **3689**
• Forest Products Abstracts (GBR ISSN 0140-4784) **3709**
Forest Products Carrier (CAN) **3689**
• Forest Products Equipment (USA) **3711**
Forest Products Industries *see* Linchan Gongye **3696**
• ➤ Forest Products Journal (USA ISSN 0015-7473) **3711**
Forest Products Research and Development Institute Journal *see* F P R D I Journal **3711**
Forest Products Research and Industries Development Commission. Annual Report (PHL ISSN 0115-0251) **3712**
Forest Products Technoflow (PHL ISSN 0116-1784) **3712**
Forest Research *see* Linye Kexue Yanjiu **3696**
Forest Research *see* Shinrin Kenkyu **3702**
Forest Research Biennial Report (MYS) **3689**
Forest Research Bulletin (IDN) **3689**
Forest Research Bulletin (NZL ISSN 1174-5096) **3689**
Forest Research Institute and Colleges, Dehra Dun. Quarterly News Letter (IND ISSN 0015-7481) **3689**
Forest Research Institute: Research Pamphlet (MYS ISSN 0126-8198) **3689**
Forest Resource Development Agreement Report (CAN ISSN 0835-0752) **3689**
➤ Forest Resources Series (AUS ISSN 1033-1220) **3689**
• Forest Sangha Newsletter (GBR) **7701**
• ➤ Forest Science (USA ISSN 0015-749X) **3689**
Forest Science And Technology (KOR) **3690**
Forest Service Employees for Environmental Ethics Activist *see* F S E E E Activist **3688**
➤ Forest Snow and Landscape Research (CHE ISSN 1424-5108) **2611**
Forest Tree Breeding *see* Rinboku no Ikushu **3701**
➤ Forest, Trees and Livelihoods (GBR ISSN 1472-8028) **3690**
Forest Up-Close (CAN ISSN 1715-0027) **2611**
➤ Forest Usufructs (IND ISSN 0972-1134) **3690**
Forest Vegetation Management Conference. Proceedings (USA ISSN 1057-2147) **3690**
Forest Voice (USA ISSN 1069-2002) **3431**
• Forest@ (ITA ISSN 1824-0119) **3690**
Foresta Veracruzana (MEX ISSN 1405-7247) **3690**
The Forester (USA) **2284**
• The Forester Miscellany (GBR) **2266**
The Foresters' Miscellany *see* The Forester Miscellany **2266**
• ➤ Forestry (GBR ISSN 0015-752X) **3690**
• Forestry Abstracts (GBR ISSN 0015-7538) **3709**
Forestry and British Timber *see* Forestry Journal **3712**
Forestry and Forest Products Research Institute. Hokkaido Research Center. Annual Report *see* Shinrin Sogo Kenkyujo Hokkaido Shisho Nenpo **3702**
Forestry Authority. Research Division. Information Note (GBR) **3690**
• ➤ Forestry Chronicle (CAN ISSN 0015-7546) **3690**
Forestry Commission. Bulletin (GBR ISSN 0950-6470) **3690**
Forestry Commission. Field Book (GBR ISSN 0963-4924) **3690**
Forestry Commission. Practice Note (GBR) **3690**
Forestry Commission. Technical Paper (GBR ISSN 1460-8758) **3690**
Forestry Conservation Conference, Aichi Prefecture. Proceedings *see* Chisan Kenkyu Happyokai Ronbunshu **3686**
Forestry in China *see* Zhongguo Linye **3708**
▼ Forestry Journal (GBR ISSN 1756-3275) **3712**
Forestry Journal *see* Lesnicky Casopis **3696**
Forestry Labour Safety *see* Linye Laodong Anquan **3696**
Forestry Machinery *see* Linye Jixie **3696**
Forestry, Minerals, Parks & Wildlife in Nova Scotia *see* Nature's Resources **2621**
Forestry Monthly *see* Linye Yuekan **3696**
Forestry Prospect and Design *see* Linye Kancha Sheji **3696**
Forestry Research Institute of Malawi. Research Record (MWI) **3690**
Forestry Science and Technology *see* Linye Shiyong Jishu **3696**
• Forestry Sciences (NLD ISSN 0924-5480) **3690**
The Forestry Source (USA ISSN 1084-5496) **3690**
Forestry Statistics *see* Norway. Statistisk Sentralbyraa. Skogstatistikk **3709**
Forestry Studies *see* Metsanduslikud Uurimused **3696**
• Forestry Studies in China (CHN ISSN 1008-1321) **3690**
Forestry. Supplement *see* Forestry **3690**
Forestry Update (USA) **3690**
Forests & People (USA ISSN 0015-7589) **3690**
La Foret (CHE ISSN 0015-7597) **3712**
Foret de Gascogne (FRA ISSN 0992-955X) **3690**
Foret - Entreprise (FRA ISSN 0752-5974) **3690**
Foret et le Bois en Suisse. Annuaire *see* Wald und Holz in der Schweiz. Jahrbuch **3709**
Foret Mediterraneenne (FRA ISSN 0245-484X) **3691**
Foret Mediterraneenne. Hors - Serie *see* Foret Mediterraneenne **3691**
La Foret Privee (FRA ISSN 0153-0216) **3691**
Foretaksnytt *see* Helse Finnmark. Nythetsbrev **8044**
Forets de France et Action Forestiere (FRA ISSN 0046-4619) **3691**
Les Forets Vues de Pres (CAN ISSN 1715-0043) **2611**
Forever Young (CAN ISSN 1487-2412) **4045**
• ForeverSkim (USA) **8315**
ForeWord (USA ISSN 1099-2642) **7561**
ForexCast. Quarterly Strategy Outlook *see* Foreign Exchange Strategy. Quarterly Strategy Outlook **1566**
ForexCast. Special Alert *see* Foreign Exchange Strategy. Special Alert **1566**
ForexCast. Weekly Bulletin *see* Foreign Exchange Strategy. Weekly Bulletin **1566**
Forfaitair (NLD ISSN 0925-4110) **1926**
Forge (Year) (GBR ISSN 0955-5293) **6312**
Forge Press (GBR) **2284**
Forge Supplement *see* Industrial Heating **3368**
• Forging (USA ISSN 1054-1756) **6312**
Forging & Stamping Technology *see* Duanya Jishu **6310**
• Forgiveness and Freedom Ezine with Brenda Adelman (USA ISSN 1947-0444) **6645**
Forgiveness and Freedom News *see* Forgiveness and Freedom Ezine with Brenda Adelman **6645**
• Forinf@ (ESP ISSN 1695-6869) **5010**
Forintek Canada Corp., Western Laboratory. Special Publications (CAN ISSN 0824-2119) **3712**
Forja *see* Semanario Universidad **2300**
Forja (ESP) **2858**
Fork in the Road (USA) **4386**
▼ Forkirurgisk Tidskrift (SWE ISSN 1654-8388) **6060**
Forktail (GBR ISSN 0950-1746) **907**
† • Forlagsvejviser (DNK ISSN 0109-405X) **8957**
Form (CHE ISSN 0015-7678) **4540**
Form (NOR ISSN 0805-9144) **535**
Form (SWE ISSN 0015-766X) **4540**
Form & Function (USA ISSN 0015-7686) **442**
Form and Style (USA ISSN 1559-2200) **2255**
Form & Werkzeug (DEU ISSN 1439-667X) **5452**
Form & Zweck (DEU ISSN 0429-1050) **1008**
Form Book Flat Annual (GBR) **8291**
Form Function Finland *see* Pap **452**
Form: Pioneering Design (USA ISSN 1931-5643) **442**
Forma (GRC ISSN 1109-5202) **8845**
➤ Forma (JPN ISSN 0911-6036) **7855**
Forma Italiae. Serie I (ITA) **393**
Forma Italiae. Serie II. Documenti (ITA) **393**
Forma & Furniture (FIN ISSN 1795-3715) **4540**
Forma Uutiset *see* Forma & Furniture **4540**
• Forma y Funcion (COL ISSN 0120-338X) **5119**
Formacion Continuada en Nutricion y Obesidad *see* Revista Espanola de Obesidad **6669**
Formacion de Seguridad Laboral (ESP ISSN 1130-9148) **2677**
Formacion Medica Continuada *see* Formacion Medica Continuada en Atencion Primaria **5615**
• Formacion Medica Continuada en Atencion Primaria (ESP ISSN 1134-2072) **5615**
▼ • ➤ Formacion Universitaria (CHL ISSN 0718-5006) **3192**

Title

Title

France. Direction de la Balance des Paiements. La Balance des Paiements et la Position Exterieure de la France (FRA) **1926**
France. Direction de l'Animation de la Recherche, des Etudes et des Statistiques. Dossiers (FRA ISSN 1263-1973) **1233**
France. Direction de l'Espace Rural et de la Foret. Rapport sur le Fonds Forestier National (FRA ISSN 1249-4232) **3691**
France. Direction des Affaires Economiques et Internationales. Etudes sur la Construction et l'Equipement *see* France. Ministere de l'Equipement, des Transports, du Logement et du Tourisme. Donnees Detaillees du S E S. Construction **4435**
France. Direction Generale de la Concurrence, de la Consommation et de la Repression des Fraudes. Actualites (FRA ISSN 0995-3531) **1111**
France. Direction Generale de l'Aviation Civile. Bulletin Statistique (FRA ISSN 0181-1517) **76**
France. Direction Generale des Douanes et Droits Indirects. Statistiques du Commerce Exterieur: Importations - Exportations. Nomenclature: N.G.P. (Nomenclature Generale des Produits) (FRA ISSN 0071-8688) **1233**
France. Direction Generale des Impots. Bulletin Officiel d'Annonces des Domaines (FRA) **1926**
France. Direction Generale des Impots. Precis de Fiscalite (FRA ISSN 0767-1237) **1926**
France. Direction Nationale des Douanes et Droits Indirects. Tableau General des Transports (FRA ISSN 0071-8726) **1566**
France. Direction Nationale des Douanes et Droits Indirects. Transport du Commerce Exterieur (FRA ISSN 0071-8718) **1566**
France Eco - Peche (FRA ISSN 1156-8496) **3595**
France. Electricite de France International (FRA) **3308**
France Energie Avenir (FRA ISSN 1775-8076) **1596**
France Environnement (FRA ISSN 1283-8403) **3432**
France - Etats-Unis (FRA ISSN 0995-8622) **7236**
▼ France Fiction (FRA ISSN 1958-1122) **490**
• France Food & Drink Report (GBR ISSN 1749-2696) **1111**
France Football (FRA ISSN 0015-9557) **8229**
France Forum (FRA ISSN 0046-4910) **7136**
France Freight Transport Report (GBR ISSN 1752-5802) **1886**
La France Graphique (FRA ISSN 0015-9565) **7321**
France Horlogere (FRA ISSN 0015-9573) **4566**
France. Imprimerie Nationale. Annuaire. (FRA ISSN 0078-9666) **7561**
• France Insider's News (USA) **8710**
France. Inspection Generale des Finances. Annuaire (FRA ISSN 0071-8742) **1926**
France. Institut National de la Statistique et des Etudes Economiques. Annales d'Economie et de Statistique (FRA ISSN 0769-489X) **1233**
France. Institut National de la Statistique et des Etudes Economiques. Bulletin Mensuel de Statistique (FRA ISSN 0007-4713) **8373**
France. Institut National de la Statistique et des Etudes Economiques. Conjoncture in France (FRA ISSN 1152-9776) **1233**
France. Institut National de la Statistique et des Etudes Economiques. Courrier des Statistiques (FRA ISSN 0151-9514) **8373**
• France. Institut National de la Statistique et des Etudes Economiques. Economie et Statistique (FRA ISSN 0336-1454) **1233**
France. Institut National de la Statistique et des Etudes Economiques. Informations Rapides (FRA ISSN 0151-1475) **1233**
France. Institut National de la Statistique et des Etudes Economiques. Note de Conjoncture (FRA ISSN 0766-6268) **1111**
France. Institut National de la Statistique et des Etudes Economiques. Note de Conjoncture Internationale (FRA ISSN 0990-9435) **1111**
France. Institut National de la Statistique et des Etudes Economiques. Recueil d'Etudes Sociales (FRA ISSN 1259-4261) **1541**
France. Institut National de l'Environnement Industriel et des Risques. Rapport Annuel (FRA ISSN 1777-6147) **3497**
France. Institut National d'Etudes Demographiques. Cahiers de Travaux et Documents (FRA ISSN 0071-8823) **7283**
France Italie (FRA ISSN 1146-0024) **1403**
➤ France Japon Eco (JPN ISSN 1342-369X) **1403**
France. Laboratoire Central des Ponts et Chaussees. Rapport General d'Activite (FRA ISSN 0337-1573) **3267**
France. Laboratoires des Ponts et Chaussees. Bulletin (FRA ISSN 1269-1496) **3267**
La France Latine (FRA ISSN 0222-0334) **5120**
France Magazine (USA ISSN 0886-2478) **5216**
France. Mediateur. Rapport Annuel du Mediateur (FRA ISSN 0182-7502) **7236**
France. Ministere de l' Equipement, des Transports, du Logement, du Tourisme et de la Mer. Annales de la Recherche Urbaine (FRA ISSN 0180-930X) **4410**
France. Ministere de la Culture et Communication. Developpement Culturel (FRA ISSN 0294-8451) **5010**
France. Ministere de la Culture et des Affaires Sociales. Lectures (BEL ISSN 0251-7388) **5010**
France. Ministere de la Culture. Lettre d'Information (FRA ISSN 1255-6270) **5010**
France. Ministere de la Defense Nationale. Bulletin Officiel (FRA ISSN 0015-9727) **6422**
France. Ministere de la Mer. Bulletin Officiel (FRA ISSN 0988-4386) **8644**
France. Ministere de l'Agriculture et de la Foret. Bulletin d'Information (FRA ISSN 0152-3295) **114**
France. Ministere de l'Agriculture et de la Peche. Agreste Animaux Hebdo (FRA) **198**
France. Ministere de l'Agriculture et de la Peche. Agreste. Cahiers (FRA ISSN 1274-1116) **180**
France. Ministere de l'Agriculture et de la Peche. Agreste. Chiffres et Donnees. Agriculture (FRA ISSN 1624-9011) **199**
France. Ministere de l'Agriculture et de la Peche. Agreste Conjoncture (FRA) **199**
France. Ministere de l'Agriculture et de la Peche. Agreste Info (FRA) **180**
France. Ministere de l'Agriculture et de la Peche. Agreste. L'Agriculture, la Foret et les Industries Agroalimentaires (FRA ISSN 1763-7023) **114**
France. Ministere de l'Agriculture et de la Peche. Agreste Le Bulletin (FRA) **180**
France. Ministere de l'Agriculture et de la Peche. Agreste Primeur (FRA ISSN 1283-4858) **199**
France. Ministere de l'Agriculture et de la Peche. Conjoncture Commerce Exterieur Agro-Alimentaire (FRA) **1566**
France. Ministere de l'Agriculture et de la Peche. Conjoncture Fruits (FRA) **199**
France. Ministere de l'Agriculture et de la Peche. Conjoncture Grandes Cultures (FRA) **199**
France. Ministere de l'Agriculture et de la Peche. Conjoncture Lait et Produits Laitiers (FRA) **264**
France. Ministere de l'Agriculture et de la Peche. Conjoncture Legumes (FRA) **199**
France. Ministere de l'Agriculture et de la Peche. Conjoncture Productions Animales (FRA) **199**
France. Ministere de l'Agriculture et de la Peche. Conjoncture Viticulture (FRA) **199**
France. Ministere de l'Agriculture et de la Peche. Donnees Chiffres. I A A (FRA) **180**
France. Ministere de l'Agriculture et de la Peche. Graph-Agri (FRA) **199**
France. Ministere de l'Agriculture et de la Peche. Graph-Agri (Regions) (FRA) **180**
France. Ministere de l'Amenagement du Territoire et de l'Environnement. Bulletin de Documentation de l'Environnement (FRA ISSN 0980-949X) **3479**
France. Ministere de l'Ecologie, de l'Energie, du Developpement Durable, et de l'Amenagement du Territoire. Activite et Emploi dans le B T P (Batiment et Travaux Publics) (FRA ISSN 1252-3097) **4411**
• France. Ministere de l'Economie, des Finances et de l'Industrie. Direction Generale des Entreprises (FRA ISSN 1772-1407) **1111**
• France. Ministere de l'Economie, des Finances et de l'Industrie. Economie et Prevision (FRA ISSN 0249-4744) **1541**
France. Ministere de l'Economie, des Finances et de l'Industrie. Note Trimestrielle de Conjoncture (FRA) **1487**
France. Ministere de l'Economie, des Finances et de l'Industrie. Revue de la Concurrence et de la Consommation (FRA ISSN 0220-9896) **1428**
France. Ministere de l'Economie, des Finances et du Budget. Bulletin Officiel de l'Administration Centrale (FRA ISSN 0760-0305) **7438**
France. Ministere de l'Education Nationale, de la Recherche et de la Technologie. Direction de la Programmation et du Developpement. Note d'Information *see* France. Ministere de l'Education Nationale, de l'Enseignement Superieur et de la Recherche. Direction de l'Evaluation et de la Prospective. Note d'Information **2933**
France. Ministere de l'Education Nationale, de l'Enseignement Superieur et de la Recherche. Direction de l'Evaluation et de la Prospective. Note d'Information (FRA) **2933**
† France. Ministere de l'Emploi, du Travail, et de la Cohesion Sociale. Bulletin Officiel (FRA ISSN 1768-0611) **8958**
France. Ministere de l'Emploi et de la Solidarite. Annuaire des Statistiques Sanitaires et Sociales (FRA ISSN 0755-3374) **7518**
† France. Ministere de l'Emploi et de la Solidarite. Bulletin Mensuel des Statistiques du Travail (FRA ISSN 1161-8205) **8958**
France. Ministere de l'Environnement. Bilan d'Activite des Agences Financieres de Bassin (FRA) **3432**
† France. Ministere de l'Equipement, des Transports, du Logement, du Tourisme et de la Mer. Statistiques de la Construction (FRA ISSN 1274-8668) **8958**
France. Ministere de l'Equipement, des Transports, du Logement et du Tourisme. Donnees Detaillees du S E S. Construction (FRA ISSN 1274-865X) **4435**
France. Ministere de l'Equipement, des Transports et du Logement. S E S Infos Rapides. Transport (FRA ISSN 1277-4561) **8373**
France. Ministere de l'Equipement, du Logement, des Transports et du Tourisme. Bulletin Officiel (FRA) **8496**
France. Ministere de l'Interieur. Repertoire Mensuel (FRA ISSN 0240-4729) **7438**
France. Ministere de l'Urbanisme et du Logement. Statistiques et Etudes Generales *see* France. Ministere de l'Equipement, des Transports, du Logement et du Tourisme. Donnees Detaillees du S E S. Construction **4435**
France. Ministere Delegue a la Promotion de l'Egalite des Chances. Lettre (FRA ISSN 1950-4918) **1682**
France. Ministere des Affaires Etrangeres. Documents d'Actualite Internationale (FRA ISSN 0338-4454) **4926**
France. Ministere des Affaires Etrangeres. La Politique Etrangere de la France (FRA ISSN 0180-9563) **7236**
France. Ministere des Affaires Sociales, du Travail et de la Solidarite; Ministere de la Sante, de la Famille et des Personnes Handicapees. Bulletin Officiel *see* France. Ministere de l'Emploi, du Travail, et de la Cohesion Sociale. Bulletin Officiel **8958**
France. Ministere des Affaires Sociales et de la Solidarite Nationale. Ministere Charge de l'Emploi. Conventions Collectives (FRA ISSN 0759-0083) **7438**
France. Ministere des Armees. Bulletin Officiel des Armees (FRA) **6422**
† France. Ministere des Armees. Bulletin Officiel des Armees. Edition Chronologique (FRA ISSN 0755-2289) **8958**
† France. Ministere des Armees. Bulletin Officiel des Armees. Edition Chronologique. Partie Principale (FRA ISSN 0755-2270) **8958**
France Mutualite (FRA ISSN 0015-9670) **3840**
France Nature (FRA ISSN 1762-8830) **309**
France.Office National d'Etudes et de Recherches Aerospatiales. Scientific and Technical Activities *see* O N E R A. Activites Scientifiques et Techniques **67**
La France Papetiere (FRA) **6733**
France. Parlement. Assemblee Nationale. Bulletin *see* France. Assemblee Nationale. Bulletin. Bilan de Session **7136**
France - Pays Arabes (FRA ISSN 0533-0866) **4321**
France - Photographie (FRA ISSN 1625-6433) **6968**
France Protestante et les Eglises de Langue Francaise (FRA) **7758**
France Routes (FRA ISSN 0993-1953) **8496**
France. Service Economique et Statistique. Memento de Statistiques des Transports (FRA ISSN 0758-9719) **8524**
• France-Soir (FRA ISSN 0182-5860) **3840**
France Soir *see* France-Soir **3840**
France Stamp Catalogue (GBR ISSN 0142-9809) **6895**
France Tabac (FRA ISSN 0296-3361) **8486**
France Telecom (FRA) **2321**
• France Telexport (FRA ISSN 1270-8054) **1996**
France Tennis de Table Journal (FRA ISSN 1156-4954) **8229**
• France Today (USA ISSN 0895-3651) **5216**
France - USA *see* France - Etats-Unis **7236**
Franceguide (Year) (USA) **8710**
Francesco il Volto Secolare (ITA ISSN 1828-4671) **7798**
FranceVision - Hit Parade (USA) **6568**
Franche-Comte. Annales Litteraires *see* Universite de Besancon. Annales Litteraires **5393**
Franche Comte Batiment et Travaux Publics (FRA) **1008**
Franchir les Lignes *see* Cross the Lines **7205**
▼ Franchise (Year) (GBR ISSN 1752-3338) **1428**
Franchise Annual (USA ISSN 0318-8752) **1996**
• Franchise Bulletin (AUS ISSN 1834-285X) **1111**
Franchise Canada (CAN ISSN 1497-1488) **1111**
Franchise-Chancen fuer Deutschland, Oesterreich und die Schweiz (DEU ISSN 1863-6276) **1961**
• The Franchise Handbook (USA ISSN 0882-5505) **1961**
• Franchise International (GBR ISSN 1363-7274) **1817**
• ➤ Franchise Law Journal (USA ISSN 8756-7962) **4677**
• The Franchise Lawyer (USA ISSN 1092-2598) **4677**
Franchise Magazine (FRA ISSN 0221-7821) **1112**
The Franchise Magazine (GBR ISSN 0268-8395) **1817**
Franchise Market (USA) **1961**
Franchise Networks (GBR ISSN 1351-4822) **8581**
Franchise News (USA) **1817**
• Franchise Opportunities Guide (USA) **1961**
Franchise Times (Roseville) (USA ISSN 1530-3748) **1886**
† Franchise und Kooperation (DEU ISSN 1614-3868) **8958**
Franchise Update (USA) **1112**
Franchise World (GBR ISSN 0144-0543) **1961**
• Franchising (AUS ISSN 1321-408X) **1961**
Franchising *see* Key Note Market Report: Franchising **1963**
Franchising in Britain Report *see* I F R C - Lloyds Bank Plc Franchising in Britain Report **1629**
• Franchising Law and Practice (AUS) **4677**
Franchising Law & Practice (GBR) **4677**
• Franchising.mag (DEU) **1961**
Franchising Research *see* Journal of Consumer Marketing **1823**
• Franchising World (USA ISSN 1524-4814) **1817**
Francis Bacon Research Trust (GBR ISSN 0262-8228) **6921**
Francis - Leatherhead Food Research Abstracts (GBR) **3670**
Franciscaans Leven (NLD ISSN 0015-9794) **7798**
Franciscaans Leven Special (NLD) **7798**
Franciscaans Maandblad (Utrecht) *see* F M (Utrecht) **7797**
• Franciscan (GBR ISSN 0532-579X) **7798**
Franciscan Institute. Philosophy Series (USA ISSN 0080-5432) **7798**
Franciscan Institute. Text Series (USA ISSN 0080-5440) **7798**
• Franciscan Studies (USA ISSN 0080-5459) **7798**
Franciscanum (COL ISSN 0120-1468) **6921**
Franco-British Chamber of Commerce and Industry. Trade Directory (FRA ISSN 0995-2209) **1403**
Franco-British Studies (GBR ISSN 0952-8571) **4221**
Franco-British Trade Directory (GBR ISSN 0071-917X) **1996**
Franco - Italica (ITA ISSN 1121-7189) **5297**
Franco Maria Ricci (Italian Edition) *see* F M R (Italian Edition) **489**
Francofonia (ESP ISSN 1132-3310) **5298**
• Francofonia (ITA ISSN 1121-953X) **5298**
Francofonia. Quaderni (ITA ISSN 1122-0740) **5298**
Francographies (USA ISSN 1069-1200) **5422**
Francophone Cultures and Literatures (USA ISSN 1077-0186) **5298**
Francophonie (GBR ISSN 0957-1744) **5120**
Francophonie dans le Monde (FRA ISSN 1773-9209) **8103**
Francophonie Nord-Americaine (CAN ISSN 1206-5188) **3120**
† • Francophonies d'Amerique (CAN ISSN 1183-2487) **8958**
Francophonies du Sud (FRA ISSN 1631-4786) **5120**
• Francopolyphonies (NLD ISSN 1574-2032) **5298**
Francoscopie (Year) (FRA ISSN 1956-7332) **8103**
▼ Frank (USA ISSN 1939-7992) **7438**
Frank Lloyd Wright Quarterly (USA) **443**
Frank M. Covey, Jr., Loyola Lectures in Political Analysis (USA ISSN 1555-8681) **7137**
Frankel Center for Judaic Studies News *see* Jean & Samuel Frankel Center for Judaic Studies. News **3542**
Frankenland (DEU ISSN 0015-9905) **4221**
Frankenpost (DEU) **3848**
Frankenthal, Einst und Jetzt (DEU) **3848**
Frankfurt am Main. Buergeramt, Statistik und Wahlen. Statistisches Jahrbuch (DEU) **8373**
Frankfurt Geht Aus! (Year) (DEU ISSN 1437-9996) **4386**
Frankfurt Kauft Ein! (DEU ISSN 1438-0005) **5071**
Frankfurt Pur (DEU) **5071**
Der Frankfurter (DEU ISSN 1615-7214) **3848**
Frankfurter Abhandlungen zur Slavistik (DEU ISSN 0473-5277) **5120**
Frankfurter Adorno Blaetter (DEU ISSN 0943-4666) **6921**
Frankfurter Afrikanistische Blaetter (DEU ISSN 0937-3039) **5120**
• Frankfurter Allgemeine (DEU ISSN 0174-4909) **3848**
Frankfurter Allgemeine Magazin (DEU) **3848**
Frankfurter Allgemeine. Sonntagszeitung (Ausg. D) (DEU ISSN 1611-3993) **3848**
Frankfurter Allgemeine Zeitung Weekly *see* F A Z Weekly **8955**
Frankfurter Althistorische Beitraege (DEU ISSN 1432-542X) **2234**
Frankfurter Archaeologische Schriften (DEU) **394**
Frankfurter Beitraege zur Biologischen Bildung (DEU ISSN 1437-6059) **673**
Frankfurter Beitraege zur Germanistik (DEU ISSN 0071-9226) **5298**
Frankfurter Beitraege zur Geschichte, Theorie und Ethik der Medizin (DEU ISSN 0179-0668) **5616**
Frankfurter Beitraege zur Lateinamerikanistik (DEU ISSN 0940-1598) **5298**
Frankfurter Bibliotheksschriften (DEU ISSN 1612-7714) **5010**
• Frankfurter Elektronische Rundschau zur Altertumskunde (DEU ISSN 1862-8478) **394**
Frankfurter Finanzmarkt Bericht (DEU) **1348**
Frankfurter Forschungen zu Suedostasien (DEU ISSN 1613-9690) **549**
Frankfurter Forschungen zur Kultur- und Sprachwissenschaft (DEU ISSN 1433-3252) **5120**
Frankfurter Frauenschule. Materialienband (DEU ISSN 1439-4340) **8897**
Frankfurter Gastronomie (DEU ISSN 0015-9964) **4386**
† Frankfurter Geowissenschaften Arbeiten. Serie A. Geologie Palaeontologie (DEU ISSN 0173-1742) **8958**
Frankfurter Geowissenschaften Arbeiten. Serie B. Meteorologie und Geophysik (DEU ISSN 0173-1769) **6352**
Frankfurter Geowissenschaften Arbeiten. Serie C. Mineralogie (DEU ISSN 0173-1785) **6462**
Frankfurter Geowissenschaften Arbeiten. Serie D. Physische Geographie (DEU ISSN 0173-1807) **4006**
Frankfurter Historische Abhandlungen (DEU ISSN 0170-3226) **4221**
Frankfurter Kirchliches Jahrbuch (DEU) **4221**
▼ Frankfurter Kulturwissenschaftliche Beitraege (DEU) **4453**
Frankfurter Lehrerzeitung (DEU) **3023**
Frankfurter Neue Presse (DEU) **3848**
Frankfurter Reihe (DEU ISSN 0930-9985) **4503**
Frankfurter Rundschau (DEU ISSN 0940-6980) **3848**

Title

10304 FRANKFURTER STATISTISCHE BERICHTE ULRICH'S PERIODICALS

Frankfurter Statistische Berichte (DEU ISSN 0177-7351) **8373**
Frankfurter Vortraege zum Versicherungswesen (DEU ISSN 0936-2045) **4503**
Frankfurter Wirtschafts- und Sozialwissenschaftliche Studien (DEU ISSN 0532-6028) **1746**
• Frankfurter Zeitschrift fuer Musikwissenschaft (CHE ISSN 1438-857X) **6568**
Frankie (AUS ISSN 1449-7794) **8864**
Franklin Advocate (USA) **4677**
Franklin and Marshall (USA) **2284**
▼ • The Franklin County Explorer (USA) **3976**
Franklin County News (NZL ISSN 1170-0416) **3917**
Franklin County Watchman (USA) **4677**
Franklin Express (USA) **4293**
Franklin Flyer (USA ISSN 1087-8114) **4293**
• ➤ Franklin Institute. Journal (GBR ISSN 0016-0032) **7013**
Franklin Pierce Times (USA ISSN 1060-5312) **642**
Franklin Research's Insight (USA ISSN 1085-6765) **1625**
Franklintonian (USA ISSN 1059-4051) **3767**
Frankreich Erleben (DEU ISSN 1861-4256) **8710**
Frankreich Jahrbuch (DEU ISSN 0935-6649) **5216**
Frankreich-Zentrum. Veroeffentlichungen (DEU ISSN 1431-0694) **4221**
† Frankrig Information (DNK ISSN 0900-2995) **8958**
Franky (Bamberg) (DEU) **3848**
Franky (Bayreuth) (DEU) **3848**
Franquicias Hoy (ESP ISSN 1135-6359) **1428**
• De Franse Nederlanden/Pays-Bas Francais (BEL ISSN 0251-2408) **5216**
Franz-Fischer-Jahrbuch fuer Philosophie und Paedagogik *see* Franz-Fischer-Jahrbuecher **6921**
Franz-Fischer-Jahrbuecher (DEU ISSN 1431-1119) **6921**
Franz Liszt Studies Series (USA) **6568**
Franziskaner Mission (DEU) **7798**
Franzoesisch Heute (DEU ISSN 0342-2895) **3062**
Franzz (DEU) **3848**
Frary Family Journal (USA ISSN 0887-6320) **3767**
Frary Family Newsletter (USA ISSN 0887-6312) **3767**
• Fraser Forum (CAN ISSN 0827-7893) **1487**
Fraser River Panel. Report to the Pacific Salmon Commission on the (Year) Fraser River Sockeye Salmon Fishing Season (CAN ISSN 0846-3689) **3595**
• Fraser's Canadian Trade Directory (CAN ISSN 0071-9277) **1996**
Fraser's Potato Newsletter (CAN ISSN 0384-7322) **231**
The Frat (USA ISSN 0739-9243) **4074**
Frate Indovino (ITA ISSN 0393-5671) **3120**
Frater of Psi Omega (USA ISSN 0071-9285) **5845**
Fraternal Herald *see* Bratrsky Vestnik **4496**
Fraternal Law (USA) **4677**
The Fraternal Leader *see* Direction **2265**
Fraternal Monitor (USA ISSN 0016-0105) **4503**
Fraternite (BEN) **3802**
Fraternite (CAN ISSN 1719-5985) **4594**
Fraternite 299 *see* Fraternite **4594**
Fraternite - Hebdo (CIV) **7137**
• Fraternite Matin (CIV) **7137**
Fraternity *see* Srpsko Bratstvo **3566**
Fraternity Monthly Magazines (JPN) **8451**
Fraters C M M (Congregatie Mater Misericordiae) (NLD ISSN 1574-9193) **7644**
Frati Minori Cappuccini. Istituto Storico. Varia (ITA) **7798**
• Fratricide (USA) **5216**
▼ • Frattura e Integrita Strutturale (ITA ISSN 1971-8993) **3345**
Frau (JPN) **8864**
Frau Aktuell (AUT) **8864**
Frau Aktuell (DEU ISSN 0174-0423) **8864**
Frau & Gesund (DEU) **8845**
Frau im Blick (DEU) **8864**
Frau im Leben (DEU ISSN 0016-0148) **8864**
Frau im Spiegel (DEU ISSN 0046-497X) **8864**
† Frau im Spiegel Legenden (DEU) **8958**
Frau im Spiegel Raten und Gewinnen (DEU) **8173**
Frau im Trend (DEU) **8864**
Frau im Trend Gute Kueche (DEU) **4358**
Frau im Trend Wohnen und Wohlfuehlen (DEU) **8864**
Frau mit Herz (DEU ISSN 0948-650X) **8864**
Frau und Kultur (DEU ISSN 0344-0745) **8864**
Frau und Mutter (DEU ISSN 0722-8120) **7644**
Frau und Politik (DEU ISSN 0016-0202) **7137**
Frau von Heute (DEU ISSN 1614-4902) **8864**
Fraud Intelligence (GBR ISSN 1462-1401) **2653**
Fraud International *see* Crackdown! **4500**
Fraud Magazine (USA ISSN 1553-6645) **2677**
Fraud Report (GBR ISSN 1360-4740) **1348**
• Fraud Watch (GBR ISSN 0966-7334) **1348**
Frauen - Apotheken - Magazin (DEU ISSN 1861-1192) **8845**
Frauen - Forschung - Archaeologie (DEU ISSN 1619-8328) **8897**
Frauen - Genderforschung in Rheinland-Pfalz (DEU ISSN 1436-4751) **8897**
Frauen in der Einen Welt (DEU ISSN 0937-5848) **8897**
Frauen Lesemagazin (DEU) **8864**
Frauen und Film (DEU ISSN 0343-7736) **6501**
Der Frauenarzt (DEU ISSN 0016-0237) **5991**
Frauenbildungs- und Ferienhaus Osteresch (DEU) **8864**
Frauenfussball Magazin *see* F F Magazin **8227**
Frauengesundheit (DEU) **8845**
▼ • Frauenheilkunde up2date (DEU ISSN 1439-3719) **8845**
Fraueninformationsblatt (DEU ISSN 0935-9710) **8897**
Frauenland (CHE ISSN 1660-2617) **114**
• frauennews (DEU ISSN 1437-5001) **8864**
Frauenrat (DEU ISSN 1438-3667) **8864**
Frauensolidaritaet (AUT ISSN 1023-1943) **8897**
Frauensolidaritaet. Annotierte Bibliographie (AUT) **8906**
Frauenzeitung (CHE ISSN 1420-8458) **8864**
Fraunhofer Institut fuer Chemische Technologie International Jahrestagungen *see* I C T. International Jahrestagungen **3246**
Fraunhofer-Institute fuer Produktionstechnik und Automatisierung Forschung und Praxis *see* I P A - Forschung und Praxis **3196**
• Fraunhofer Magazin (DEU ISSN 1434-7113) **3135**
Fraunhofer Magazine *see* Fraunhofer Magazin **3135**
Fraunhofer Series in Information and Communication Technology (DEU ISSN 1612-4863) **2543**
Fraza (POL ISSN 1230-4832) **5298**
▼ Freche Maedchen - Freches Magazin (DEU) **2189**
Frecuencia L (ESP ISSN 1136-5080) **5120**
• Frecuencia Latinoamerica (USA ISSN 1555-855X) **2368**
Fred och Frihet (SWE ISSN 0016-0288) **7236**
Fred og Frihed (DNK ISSN 0902-9273) **7236**
Fred Trost's Practical Sportsman *see* Practical Sportsman **8329**
Il Freddo (ITA ISSN 0016-0296) **4119**
Frederick Findings (USA ISSN 0899-4188) **3767**
Frederick Forerunners (USA ISSN 0887-2139) **3767**
Frederick Magazine (USA ISSN 1058-3270) **3976**
Fredericksburg History and Biography (USA ISSN 1541-5120) **4293**
Frederiksberg Gennem Tiderne (DNK ISSN 0108-8777) **4221**
Fredriksstad Blad (NOR) **3922**
Fredrikstad-Avisa Demokraten (NOR) **3922**
• Fredstidningen Pax (SWE ISSN 1403-1442) **7236**
• Free Access (AUS ISSN 1440-7949) **2557**
† • Free Associations (GBR ISSN 0267-0887) **8958**
Free Church of Scotland. Monthly Record (GBR ISSN 0016-0334) **7758**
• Free Content (USA) **3976**
• Free E-Book About Free E-Books (USA ISSN 1552-7093) **7580**
Free Estonia *see* Vaba Eestlane **3570**
Free Estonian Word *see* Vaba Eesti Sona **3570**
Free Flight/Vol Libre (CAN ISSN 0827-2557) **56**
Free - Floating Subdivisions: An Alphabetic Index *see* U.S. Library of Congress. Free - Floating Subdivisions: An Alphabetic Index **637**
• Free Focus (USA) **5422**
Free Grace Broadcaster (USA) **7644**
Free House *see* PubChef **4396**
Free House Innovations *see* PubChef **4396**
Free in America Catalog (USA) **1996**
• Free Inquiry (USA ISSN 0272-0701) **6921**
➤ Free Inquiry in Creative Sociology (USA ISSN 0736-9182) **8103**
Free Lance (USA ISSN 0016-0369) **5298**
Free Life (GBR ISSN 0260-5112) **7137**
Free Lunch (USA ISSN 1041-0945) **5422**
Free Magazines for Libraries (USA) **7561**
The Free Market (USA ISSN 1051-4333) **1541**
Free Market Environmental Bibliography (USA) **3479**
Free Methodist World Mission People (USA ISSN 1081-8898) **7758**
Free Mind (USA) **6921**
Free on Board Colon Free Zone *see* F O B Colon Free Zone **1565**
Free Online Scholarship Newsletter *see* S P A R C Open Access Newsletter **3000**
† Free Palestine (AUS ISSN 0157-3845) **8958**
• Free Penny Poems (USA) **5422**
• Free Pint (GBR ISSN 1460-7239) **2557**
The Free Press (AUS ISSN 1832-3758) **3794**
• Free Press (CAN ISSN 0834-6933) **3810**
• The Free Press (USA ISSN 1063-1267) **5216**
Free Press Journal (IND) **3882**
Free Radical (GBR) **7137**
• ➤ Free Radical Biology & Medicine (USA ISSN 0891-5849) **673**
• ➤ Free Radical Research (GBR ISSN 1071-5762) **732**
• Free Radicals (GBR ISSN 1474-2101) **8422**
Free Rock (ESP) **6568**
Free Sons Reporter (USA) **2266**
Free Speech (USA) **7206**
• Free Speech Journal (USA) **5202**
Free Speech Monitor (CAN ISSN 1182-008X) **5298**
Free Spirit (Brooklyn) (USA) **6921**
• Free Spirit Journal (USA) **309**
Free State Educational News/Vrystaatse Onderwysnuus (ZAF ISSN 0042-9228) **2858**
Free State Libraries (ZAF ISSN 0016-0458) **5010**
• Free State Provincial Legislation Library (ZAF ISSN 1683-2612) **4677**
Free State Warrior (USA) **2266**
Free Thinking *see* Cuget Liber **3932**
Free Thinking School *see* Svobodna Skola **5383**
Free Times (USA) **3976**
Free-Trade Update *see* Bulletin du Libre - Echange **4858**
Free Verse (USA ISSN 1935-4703) **5422**
• Free World Press (CAN) **7137**
Free Zone *see* Svobodnaya Zona **1433**
• Freebies (Online) (USA) **2638**
Freebies (Print) *see* Freebies (Online) **2638**
Freedom *see* Azadi **3521**
Freedom (GBR ISSN 0016-0504) **7206**
Freedom *see* Foroyaa **3842**
Freedom *see* Szabadsag **3934**
• Freedom (USA) **7644**
• Freedom B M X (DEU) **8259**
▼ The Freedom Center Journal (USA ISSN 1942-5856) **4677**
Freedom Digest (KOR ISSN 1028-8341) **7206**
Freedom First (IND ISSN 0016-0547) **7206**
Freedom for Man *see* Yancin Dan Adam **3921**
Freedom Forum Media Studies Center. Occasional Paper (USA) **8103**
Freedom House Monitor *see* Freedom Monitor **7207**
Freedom in the World (Year) (USA ISSN 0732-6610) **7207**
Freedom Isn't Free (USA) **5216**
Freedom Journal (USA) **3534**
Freedom Monitor (USA ISSN 0898-9265) **7207**
Freedom Network News (USA) **7207**
Freedom of Expression (USA) **5216**
Freedom of Expression in Hong Kong: Annual Report (GBR) **7207**
• Freedom of Information (GBR ISSN 1745-1825) **4678**
Freedom of Information Act Annual Report for Fiscal Year (Year) *see* U.S. Department of Homeland Security. Privacy Office. (Year) Annual Freedom of Information Act Report to the Attorney General of the United States **4800**
Freedom of Information Act Update *see* F O I A Update **4575**
Freedom of Information and Privacy Branch. Directory of Institutions, Ontario (CAN ISSN 0845-096X) **7438**
• Freedom of Information and Protection of Privacy Act. Annual Report (CAN ISSN 1491-3690) **4678**
† ➤ Freedom of Information Review (AUS ISSN 0817-3532) **8958**
• Freedom of Spirit (GBR ISSN 1361-5580) **6808**
• Freedom Organisation for the Right to Enjoy Smoking Tobacco (GBR) **7207**
Freedom Socialist (USA ISSN 0272-4367) **8864**
Freedom to Read (CAN ISSN 1711-9367) **2858**
Freedom to Read Foundation News (USA ISSN 0046-5038) **5010**
Freedom to Read Week *see* Freedom to Read **2858**
Freedom Today (GBR ISSN 0957-3070) **7207**
Freedonia Gazette (USA ISSN 0748-5247) **6501**
FreeFall (CAN ISSN 1203-9586) **5216**
Freeflow (GBR ISSN 1747-048X) **8315**
Freehouse Owner (GBR ISSN 1745-7491) **4386**
Freekick (USA) **8229**
Freelance (CAN ISSN 0705-1379) **5298**
Freelance Informer (GBR ISSN 1361-4436) **2418**
Freelance Market News (GBR) **4575**
Freelance New York (USA) **6697**
• Freelance Photographer (GBR ISSN 1465-2781) **6968**
• Freelance Register (AUS ISSN 1834-5026) **7561**
• Freelance Success (USA ISSN 1067-2524) **5298**
Freelance Writer's Report (USA ISSN 0731-549X) **4575**
The Freelancer (USA ISSN 1094-4567) **7561**
Freelancer's Business Bulletin *see* Get Great Clients **1961**
Freelancer's News (USA) **490**
• Freelancing 4 Money Newsletter (USA) **4575**
Freeland and Allied Families (USA ISSN 0738-484X) **3767**
• The Freeman (USA ISSN 1559-1638) **7207**
Freeman of England & Wales. Newsletter *see* Freemen of England & Wales Journal **7207**
Freemarket Gold & Money Report (USA ISSN 1073-0796) **1625**
Freemen of England & Wales Journal (GBR ISSN 1749-4095) **7207**
• Freemuse Report (DNK ISSN 1601-2127) **6568**
† Freenet.de (DEU ISSN 1616-7155) **8958**
• Freenews Marketineras (PRY ISSN 1607-2871) **1817**
The Freeport News (BHS) **3799**
Freer Gallery of Art, Washington, D.C. Occasional Papers (USA ISSN 0071-9382) **490**
Freeride (DEU ISSN 1866-7724) **8259**
Freerider M X Magazine (AUS ISSN 1443-1998) **8259**
Freerider M X Photo Annual *see* Freerider M X Magazine **8259**
Freeskier (USA) **8173**
Freestone Frontiers (USA ISSN 0735-3278) **3767**
Freestyle Motocross (FRA ISSN 1634-3735) **8259**
Freesun News Magazine (BEL ISSN 0779-5696) **8710**
Freethinker (GBR ISSN 0016-0687) **6921**
The Freethinker's Press (CAN ISSN 1912-7510) **6921**
Freethought History (USA ISSN 1071-7269) **4453**
• Freethought Today (USA ISSN 0882-8512) **6921**
Freeway Magazine (FRA ISSN 1167-3559) **8259**
Freeway Magazine (ITA ISSN 1125-4696) **8259**
Freeway Magazine. Hors Serie *see* Freeway Magazine **8259**
▼ Freewheel (IRL ISSN 1649-9875) **8259**
FreeXpresSion (AUS ISSN 1320-9337) **5298**
Freeze Frame (CAN ISSN 0704-9536) **6501**
Freezer Burn (USA) **5442**
• Freezerbox (USA ISSN 1936-0657) **7965**
† • Frei-literarisch Orientierte Beitraege (DEU ISSN 1864-3256) **8958**
• ➤ Freiberg Online Geoscience (DEU ISSN 1434-7512) **2734**
Freiberger Beitraege zur Interkulturellen und Wirtschaftskommunikation (DEU ISSN 1612-989X) **7965**
• Freiberufler Info (DEU ISSN 1433-7924) **2492**
Freiburg Aktuell (DEU) **3848**
Freiburger Altorientalische Studien (DEU ISSN 0170-3307) **549**
Freiburger Altorientalische Studien. Beihefte: Altassyrische Texte und Untersuchungen *see* Freiburger Altorientalische Studien **549**
Freiburger Archaeologie *see* Archeologie Fribourgeoise **379**
Freiburger Archaeologische Studien (DEU ISSN 1437-3327) **394**
Freiburger Beitraege zur Archaeologie und Geschichte des Ersten Jahrtausends (DEU ISSN 1437-1707) **394**
Freiburger Beitraege zur Musikermedizin (DEU ISSN 1863-1932) **5616**
Freiburger Beitraege zur Wissenschafts- und Universitaetsgeschichte (DEU ISSN 0408-8263) **4221**
Freiburger Dioezesan-Archiv (DEU ISSN 0342-0213) **7798**
Freiburger Fernoestliche Forschungen (DEU ISSN 0724-4703) **549**
Freiburger Geographische Hefte (DEU ISSN 0071-9447) **4006**
Freiburger Hausbesitzer Zeitung (DEU) **4411**
Freiburger Islamstudien (DEU ISSN 0170-3285) **7710**
Freiburger Literaturpsychologische Gespraeche (DEU ISSN 0721-8907) **5298**
▼ Freiburger Mediaevistische Vortraege (CHE) **6921**
Freiburger Rechtsgeschichtliche Abhandlungen (DEU ISSN 0720-6704) **4678**
Freiburger Theologische Studien (DEU ISSN 0174-5875) **7644**
Freiburger Uni-Magazin (DEU ISSN 0947-1251) **2284**
Freiburger Universitaetsblaetter (DEU ISSN 0016-0717) **2284**
Freiburger Zeitschrift fuer Philosophie und Theologie (CHE ISSN 0016-0725) **7798**
Freiburger Zeitschrift fuer Philosophie und Theologie. Oekumenische Beihefte *see* Studia Oecumenica Friburgensia **7818**
Freidenker (CHE ISSN 0256-8993) **5216**
Freidenker der Europaeischen Aufklaerung (DEU) **4221**
Freie Assoziation (DEU) **7357**
Die Freie Deutsche Jugend (DEU) **4221**
Freie Fahrt (AUT) **8581**
Freie Meinung (AUT) **3062**
Freie Presse (DEU) **3848**
Freie Universitaet Berlin. Institut fuer Staatslehre, Staats- und Verwaltungsrecht. Studien und Gutachten (DEU ISSN 0409-1426) **7438**
Freie Universitaet Berlin. John F. Kennedy-Institut fuer Nordamerika Studien. Materialien (DEU ISSN 0948-9428) **4293**
Freie Universitaet Berlin Nachrichten *see* F U: Nachrichten **2283**
Freie Universitaet Berlin. Osteuropa-Institut. Arbeitspapiere. Bereich Geschichte und Kultur (DEU ISSN 1437-1499) **4140**
Freie Universitaet Berlin. Osteuropa-Institut. Arbeitspapiere. Bereich Politik und Gesellschaft (DEU ISSN 1434-419X) **7137**
Freie Universitaet Berlin. Osteuropa-Institut. Arbeitspapiere. Bereich Recht und Wirtschaft (DEU ISSN 1437-1502) **4678**
Freie Universitaet Berlin. Osteuropa-Institut. Balkanologische Veroeffentlichungen (DEU ISSN 0170-1533) **5120**
Freie Universitaet Berlin. Osteuropa-Institut. Bibliographische Mitteilungen (DEU ISSN 0067-5881) **4170**
Freie Universitaet Berlin. Osteuropa-Institut. Erziehungswissenschaftliche Veroeffentlichungen (DEU ISSN 0067-589X) **7137**
Freie Universitaet Berlin. Osteuropa-Institut. Historische Veroeffentlichungen (DEU ISSN 0067-5903) **4221**
Freie Universitaet Berlin. Osteuropa-Institut. Interdisziplinaere Arbeitspapiere (DEU ISSN 1436-2430) **7137**
Freie Universitaet Berlin. Osteuropa-Institut. Philosophische und Soziologische Veroeffentlichungen (DEU ISSN 0067-5911) **6921**
Freie Universitaet Berlin. Osteuropa-Institut. Rechtswissenschaftliche Veroeffentlichungen (DEU ISSN 0343-835X) **4678**
Freie Universitaet Berlin. Osteuropa-Institut. Slavistische Veroeffentlichungen (DEU ISSN 0067-592X) **5298**
Freie Universitaet Berlin. Osteuropa-Institut. Wirtschaftswissenschaftliche Veroeffentlichungen (DEU ISSN 0067-5938) **1112**
• Freie Universitaet Berlin. Zentraleinrichtung Studienberatung und Psychologische Beratung. Studienhandbuch (DEU ISSN 0941-0155) **2284**
Die Freie Wohnungswirtschaft *see* Die Private Immobilienwirtschaft **7604**
Der Freie Zahnarzt (DEU ISSN 0340-1766) **5845**
• Freies China (USA ISSN 1013-0896) **3960**
• Freies Deutsches Hochstift. Jahrbuch (DEU ISSN 0071-9463) **5298**

Title

Title

Title

G A A R Interpreted (General Anti-avoidance Rule) (CAN ISSN 1719-1270) **1349**
G A A S (Year) Conference Proceedings: European Gallium Arsenide and Other Compound Semiconductors Application Symposium *see* European Microwave Integrated Circuits Conference. Proceedings **2465**
G A A S Guide *see* Miller G A A S Guide **1296**
G A B A L *see* Global Accumulative Bibliography of Action Learning **2933**
G A B A R (Growth and Biology of African Raptors) (ZAF) **907**
• G A C I A C Bulletin (Guidance and Control Information Analysis Center) (USA) **56**
G A C S Today (Georgia Association of Convenience Stores) (USA) **1961**
G A Document (Global Architecture) (JPN ISSN 0389-0066) **443**
G A E A. Anales de la Sociedad Argentina de Estudios Geograficos *see* Sociedad Argentina de Estudios Geograficos. Anales **4028**
▼ G A E Mag (Global Artist Exchange) (USA ISSN 1940-6614) **490**
G A F A *see* Geometric and Functional Analysis **5490**
G A F F Magazine (Gulf Atlantic Florida Fishing) (USA ISSN 1930-0468) **8315**
G A Houses (Global Architecture) (JPN) **443**
G A L R O Bulletin (Guardians ad Litem and Reporting Officers) (GBR) **4678**
• G A L T Upate (Global Agreements, Legislation, and Trade) (IND) **1596**
➤ G A M (Graz Architecture Magazine) (AUT ISSN 1612-9482) **443**
G A M A International Journal (General Agents and Managers Association) (USA ISSN 1095-7367) **4503**
Le G A M Info (Groupement Archeologique du Maconnais) (FRA ISSN 0994-6837) **395**
• G A M M Mitteilungen (Gesellschaft fuer Angewandte Mathematik und Mechanik) (DEU ISSN 0936-7195) **5489**
▼ • ➤ G A M S Journal of Mathematical Biosciences (Gwalior Academy of Mathematical Sciences) (IND ISSN 0974-2689) **5489**
G A M S Journal of Mathematics and Mathematical Biosciences *see* G A M S Journal of Mathematical Biosciences **5489**
G A N I L. Nouvelles (Grand Accelerateur National d'Ions Lourds) (FRA ISSN 0769-1343) **7014**
G A N P A C Brief (German-American National Public Affairs Committee) (USA ISSN 1062-3868) **3534**
G A News *see* G A (Sheffield) **4007**
G A O Abstracts of Reports and Testimony: Fiscal Year (Year) *see* United States Government Accountability Office. Abstracts of Reports and Testimony: Fiscal Year (Year) **7474**
G A O Month in Review *see* United States Government Accountability Office. Month in Review **7474**
G A O Newsletter *see* U.S. General Accounting Office. Office of Public Affairs. Month in Review (Online) **7485**
G A O Reports and Testimony *see* United States Government Accountability Office. Reports and Testimony **7474**
G A O Today's Reports *see* United States Government Accountability Office. Today's Reports **7474**
G A P *see* Good Autism Practice **4066**
G A P Dergisi (Guneydogu Anadolu Projesi) (TUR ISSN 1301-5745) **8042**
G A P P Magazin (German - American Partnership Program) (DEU ISSN 0940-3116) **3012**
• G A P S S/Rangahau Tane Ai Tane (Gay Auckland Periodic Sex Surveys) (NZL ISSN 1177-8474) **8103**
G A Pilot *see* Australian Pilot **47**
G A Press Bulletin *see* Georgia Press Bulletin **2321**
G A S B Technical Bulletin *see* Governmental Accounting Standards Board. Technical Bulletin **1927**
G A T A Report (Guia Argentina de Trafico Aereo) (ARG) **8541**
• G A T F World (Graphic Arts Technical Foundation) (USA ISSN 1048-0293) **7321**
G A World (Girls in Action) (USA ISSN 1083-3277) **7759**
G A Z *see* Generalanzeiger **8959**
• G. Advocacy (USA ISSN 1933-4176) **867**
G & A *see* Guns & Ammo **8316**
G & D *see* Genes & Development **867**
G & H *see* Gastroenterology & Hepatology **5924**
G & H - Gebaeudetechnik und Handwerk (DEU ISSN 1434-8063) **1009**
G. & M. Gestion Minera (CHL ISSN 0718-3577) **6462**
G & P *see* Genomics & Proteomics **764**
G & T Update (Gifted & Talented) (GBR ISSN 1479-795X) **3040**
G & V *see* Gestalten und Verkaufen **3733**
G B (DEU ISSN 1618-4769) **3730**
G B A Kwaliteitsbrochure *see* Basisadministratie Persoonsgegevens en Reisdocumenten Kwaliteitsbrochure **7422**
G B H (USA) **2381**
Het G B I O & de O R *see* Het Gemeenschappelijk BegeleidingsInstituut Ondernemingsraden en de Ondernemingsraad **6697**
De G B I O Krant *see* Het Gemeenschappelijk BegeleidingsInstituut Ondernemingsraden en de Ondernemingsraad **6697**
G B J *see* G B Journal **6895**
G B Journal (Great Britain) (GBR ISSN 0430-8913) **6895**
G B R Challenge (GBR) **8275**
G B S *see* Goettinger Beitraege zur Sprachwissenschaft **5123**
G B U Reporter (Greater Beneficial Union of Pittsburgh) (USA ISSN 1523-4819) **4503**
G Baby (ITA ISSN 1591-4844) **2190**
G C *see* Gran Cuenta **2492**
G C A *see* Geochimica et Cosmochimica Acta **2735**
G C B *see* Global Change Biology **675**
G C Bulletin *see* Gold Coast Bulletin **3794**
G C California (General Counsel) (USA ISSN 1557-0061) **4678**
G C D: La Revista de la Seguridad (MEX ISSN 1405-7697) **7438**
G C Government Communications (USA ISSN 1067-1722) **4575**
G C I C Annual Report (Grenada Chamber of Industry and Commerce) (GRD) **1403**
G C Magazine *see* Government Computing **7486**
• G C Mid-Atlantic (General Counsel) (USA ISSN 1933-5881) **4678**
• G C N (Government Computer News) (USA ISSN 0738-4300) **7486**
G C N (Year) Contracts Sourcing Guide *see* G C N **7486**
G C N A Bulletin (Guild of Carillonneurs in North America (San Antonio)) (USA ISSN 0827-5955) **6568**
G C N Contracts Sourcing Guide *see* Government Computer News. Contracts Sourcing Guide **7486**
G C New England (General Counsel) (USA ISSN 1554-0871) **4678**
• G C New York (General Counsel) (USA ISSN 1933-186X) **4678**
G C R *see* Global Construction Review **1009**
G C R *see* Global Corruption Report **7237**
G C R *see* G-Two Compliance Report **4678**
G C S A A Membership Directory *see* Golf Course Superintendents Association of America. Membership Directory **8231**
G-Cube SolutionZone (GBR) **2476**
G D *see* Government Digest **7493**
G D B A Magazin (Gewerkschaft Deutscher Bundesbahnbeamten und Anwaerter) (DEU ISSN 1861-4809) **1682**
G d E D Inform (Gewerkschaft der Eisenbahner Deutschlands) (DEU) **1682**
G d F *see* Il Giornale del Farmacista **6844**
G D F *see* Global Development Finance **1596**
G D I Book Series (German Development Institute) (GBR ISSN 1460-4175) **1596**
G D I Impuls (Gottlieb Duttweiler Institut) (CHE ISSN 1422-0482) **1112**
G D L Magazin Voraus (Gewerkschaft Deutscher Lokomotivfuehrer) (DEU ISSN 1438-0099) **8617**
G D L Taschenbuch (Gewerkschaft Deutscher Lokomotivfuehrer) (DEU) **8617**
G d M *see* Giornale del Medico **5619**
G d O *see* Giornale dell'Odontoiatra **5845**
• G D O Week (Grande Distribuzione Organizzata) (ITA ISSN 1123-7260) **1112**
G D - Oficialni Ceska Verze Golf Digest *see* Golf Digest **8231**
G D R (ZAF) **7321**
G D S *see* Going Down Swinging **5301**
G D S *see* Il Giornale del Serramento **1009**
G D S Archiv fuer Hochschul- und Studentengeschichte (Gemeinschaft fuer Deutsche Studentengeschichte) (DEU ISSN 0938-6173) **2859**
G D S Archiv fuer Hochschul- und Studentengeschichte. Beihefte (Gemeinschaft fuer Deutsche Studentengeschichte) (DEU ISSN 0938-6688) **2859**
G D S - Info (Goer Det Selv) (DNK ISSN 1395-5411) **1428**
G D S - Magazin (Gewerkschaft der Sozialversicherung) (DEU ISSN 1437-983X) **4594**
G d'A *see* Il Giornale dell'Arredamento **4540**
G: Documentation Technique et Commerciale des Vendeurs de Gaz (FRA ISSN 0072-0046) **3136**
G E *see* Ground Engineering **3268**
G E *see* Jornal Portugues de Gastrenterologia **5927**
G E A *see* Giornale Europeo di Aerobiologia **5758**
G E A Advocate (Grossmont Education Association) (USA) **2859**
G E A Educator *see* G E A Advocate **2859**
G.E.A.R. *see* Gaming Equipment and Reviews **2477**
G E C A M I N E S Annual Report *see* G E C A M I N E S Rapport Annuel **6462**
G E C A M I N E S Rapport Annuel/G E C A M I N E S Annual Report (Generale des Carrieres et des Mines) (COD) **6462**
G E C. Boletin (Grupo de Estudios Sobre la Critica Literaria) (ARG ISSN 1515-6117) **5299**
• G E C H S News (Global Environmental Change and Human Security) (NOR ISSN 0809-909X) **3432**
▼ • G E C H S Report (Global Environmental Change and Human Security) (NOR ISSN 1504-5749) **3432**
G E C O. Collection (Groupe d'Etude pour la Chirurgie Osseuse) (FRA ISSN 1951-5839) **6060**
G E D (Gastroenterologia e Endoscopia Digestiva) (BRA ISSN 0101-7772) **5923**
G E D Basico *see* G E D Basics **2941**
G E D Basics (General Educational Development) (USA ISSN 1544-7227) **2941**
G E D en Espanol (General Education Development) (USA ISSN 1945-9289) **2941**
G E D I S S T. Cahiers *see* Cahiers du Genre **8092**
G E D Items (General Educational Development) (USA ISSN 0896-0518) **2941**
G E D Language Arts, Reading *see* The Best Study Series for G E D. Language Arts, Reading **2830**
G E D. Rapport Public *see* G O L Public Report **7518**
G E D Science *see* The Best Study Series for G E D. Science **2830**
G E. Diritto ed Economia dello Stato Sociale (ITA ISSN 1592-8624) **4678**
G E E (Games Entertainment Education) (DEU) **2476**
• ➤ G E F A D/Gazi University. Gazi Educational Faculty. Journal (Gazi Egitim Fakultesi Dergisi) (TUR ISSN 1300-1876) **2859**
• G E F A M E (USA ISSN 1558-7274) **4175**
G E I C O Direct (USA) **4503**
G E - I R C Current Awareness Service (Geotechnical Engineering International Resources Center) (THA) **2707**
G E K K O (DEU) **8042**
G E L N E. Revista (Grupo de Estudos Linguisticos do Nordeste) (BRA ISSN 1517-7874) **5121**
G E M *see* Gulf Economic Monitor **1115**
G E M A Jahrbuch (Gesellschaft fuer Musikalische Auffuehrungs- und Mechanische Vervielfaeltigungsrechte) (DEU ISSN 0945-8867) **6568**
G E M A Nachrichten (Gesellschaft fuer Musikalische Auffuehrungs- und Mechanische Vervielfaeltigungsrechte) (DEU ISSN 0946-0055) **6568**
• ➤ G E M A Online Journal of Language Studies (MYS ISSN 1675-8021) **5299**
G E N (Georgian Engineering News) (GEO ISSN 1512-0287) **3267**
G E N (Gastroenterologia, Endocrinologia y Nutricion) (VEN ISSN 0016-3503) **5923**
G E O *see* Grassroots Economic Organizing Newsletter **6698**
G E O S. Circular on Eclipsing Binaries (Groupe Europeen d'Observation Stellaire) (FRA ISSN 1148-6252) **574**
G E O S. Circular on RR Lyr Type Variables (Groupe Europeen d'Observation Stellaire) (FRA) **574**
G E O S. Note Circulaire (Groupe Europeen d'Observation Stellaire) (FRA) **575**
G E O Yearbook (Year) *see* U N E P Year Book **3471**
G E P *see* Gene Expression Patterns **867**
G E P *see* Global Environmental Politics **3434**
G E P *see* Global Economics Prospects (Year) **1596**
G E R *see* Global Engineering Review **3367**
G E R *see* German Economic Review **1488**
G E R M E (Groupe d'Etudes et de Recherche sur les Mouvements Etudiants) (FRA ISSN 1951-5952) **7137**
G E S Boletin de Informacion (General Espanola de Seguros) (ESP) **4503**
G E S T A *see* A L A R M Course Syllabus **5985**
G E T *see* Guia Espanola del Transporte **8497**
G E T E A. Cuadernos (Grupo de Estudios de Teatro Argentino e Iberoamericano) (ARG ISSN 1851-5991) **8471**
G E T: Graduate Employment and Training (Year) (GBR ISSN 0309-894X) **6697**
• G E W E X News (Global Energy and Water Cycle Experiment) (USA) **2794**
G E W Lehrerkalender Nordrhein-Westfalen (Gewerkschaft Erziehung und Wissenschaft) (DEU) **2859**
G E W - Zeitung Rheinland-Pfalz (Gewerkschaft Erziehung und Wissenschaft) (DEU ISSN 0946-6002) **3023**
G: Echo (Guildhall) (GBR) **2284**
• ➤ G F A (Goettinger Forum fuer Altertumswissenschaft) (DEU ISSN 1437-9082) **4140**
G F A News (Georgia Forestry Association, Inc.) (USA) **3691**
G F E - Dokumentation (Gesellschaft fuer Forschung und Entwicklungsprojektierung) (DEU ISSN 0721-8141) **8103**
G F F (Glas, Fenster, Fassade) (DEU ISSN 1432-6264) **2041**
➤ G F F (Geografiska Foereningens i Stockholm Foerhandlingar) (SWE ISSN 1103-5897) **2734**
G F L *see* German as a Foreign Language **5122**
• G F M S Precious Metals Quarterly (Gold Fields Mineral Services Ltd) (GBR) **6462**
▼ G F N P (English Edition) (Guide du Futur et Nouveau Proprietaire) (FRA ISSN 1957-6137) **7591**
G F N P (National Edition) (Guide du Futur et Nouveau Proprietaire) (FRA ISSN 1769-843X) **7591**
G F O A Newsletter (Government Finance Officers Association) (USA ISSN 1051-6964) **7492**
G F S *see* Government Food Service **3645**
G F S R *see* International Monetary Fund. Global Financial Stability Report **1358**
G.F. Unger (CZE ISSN 1212-9224) **5410**
G F W *see* Golf for Women **8960**
G F W C Clubwoman (General Federation of Women's Clubs) (USA ISSN 0745-2209) **2266**
G F W C of Minnesota News (General Federation of Women's Clubs of Minnesota, Inc.) (USA) **2266**
▼ G for Women (USA ISSN 1944-4389) **8230**
G G *see* 2 G **461**
G G *see* Gaaf Goed **4557**
G G D-News *see* G **7518**
G G E *see* Gerontology & Geriatrics Education **4046**
G G S Retailer (Greetings Gifts Stationery) (GBR) **4059**
G G U Journal of Business (Guru Ghasidas University) (IND ISSN 0973-5887) **1112**
G G Z in Tabellen (NLD ISSN 1875-3868) **6142**
G - Geschichte (DEU ISSN 1617-9412) **4140**
• G H A Today Newsletter (Georgia Hospital Association) (USA) **4093**
• G H C C Forecast (Global Hydrology and Climate Center) (USA) **6353**
† • G H E X I S Newsletter (Greenland Hydrocarbon Exploration Information Service) (DNK ISSN 0909-0630) **8958**
G H Gastrotel (Gastronomie und Hotellerie) (DEU) **4386**
G H I *see* Geneve Home Informations **3958**
G H I Bulletin *see* German Historical Institute. Bulletin **4223**
G H J *see* Gippsland Heritage Journal **4192**
G H K Publik (Gesamt Hochschule Kassel) (DEU) **2955**
G H S Foot-Notes *see* Georgia History Today **4293**
G I A M. Boletin (Grupo Iberico de Aves Marinas) (ESP ISSN 1134-5543) **907**
G I A Quarterly (Gregorian Institute of America) (USA ISSN 1070-7794) **6568**
G I Aktuell (Goethe-Institut) (DEU) **490**
▼ G I & Hepatology News (USA ISSN 1934-3450) **5923**
G I E L R *see* Georgetown International Environmental Law Review **3433**
• G I E Media's Snow (USA ISSN 1930-2479) **8315**
G I F A S Info *see* Groupement des Industries Francaises Aeronautiques et Spatiales. Info **57**
G I F A S Newsletter *see* Groupement des Industries Francaises Aeronautiques et Spatiales. Info **57**
• G I G A Focus. Afrika (German Institute of Global and Area Studies) (DEU ISSN 1862-3603) **7236**
G I G A Focus. Asien (German Institute of Global and Area Studies) (DEU ISSN 1862-359X) **7236**
• G I G A Focus. Global (German Institute of Global and Area Studies) (DEU ISSN 1862-3581) **7236**
G I G A Focus. Lateinamerika (Online Edition) *see* G I G A Focus. Lateinamerika (Print Edition) **7236**
• G I G A Focus. Lateinamerika (Print Edition) (German Institute of Global and Area Studies) (DEU ISSN 1862-3352) **7236**
G I G A Focus. Nahost (German Institute of Global and Area Studies) (DEU ISSN 1862-3611) **7236**
• G I G A Working Papers (German Institute of Global and Area Studies) (DEU) **7236**
G I G Newsletter (Gluten Intolerance Group of North America) (USA ISSN 0890-570X) **6659**
➤ G I - Gesundheits Ingenieur (DEU ISSN 0932-6200) **7518**
A G I Grafguide *see* Grafguide **7321**
G I H Aktuell *see* Kontinenz Aktuell **6271**
G I Jobs (USA ISSN 1545-9527) **6697**
G I M a R *see* Giornale Italiano di Malattie Reumatiche **6223**
G I M International (Geomatics Info Magazine) (NLD ISSN 1566-9076) **4007**
G I M Journal of Management (Guruvayurappan Institute of Management) (IND ISSN 0974-0708) **1747**
• G I M M O C (Giornale Italiano di Microbiologia Medica Odontoiatrica e Clinica) (ITA) **886**
G I M T *see* Giornale Italiano delle Malattie del Torace **6214**
G I Oncology Review & Outlook (Gastrointestinal) (USA) **6020**
G I P A M R *see* Global Intellectual Property Asset Management Report **6750**
G I P O *see* Giornale Italiano di Psicologia dell'Orientamento **7358**
G I P S (Government Imprinted Penalty Stationery Society) (USA) **6895**
G.I. Research (Gastrointestinal) (JPN ISSN 0918-9408) **5923**
G I S Business (DEU) **2722**
G I S Magazine (Geographic Information Systems) (NLD ISSN 1571-7194) **4007**
• G I S News (Geographic Information Systems) (USA) **4037**
G I S Newsletter (Geoscience Information Society) (USA ISSN 1062-791X) **2707**
G I S - Obozrenie (RUS) **1112**
G I S R U K *see* Innovations in G I S **4015**
G I S T Global Information on Science and Technology (GBR ISSN 1366-7831) **7856**
G I T (Glas und Instrumenten Technik) (DEU ISSN 0016-3538) **5905**
G I T Imaging & Microscopy *see* Imaging & Microscopy **899**
G I T Inspect *see* Inspect **8426**
• G.I.T. Laboratory Journal Europe (Glas und Instrumenten Technik) (DEU ISSN 1611-6038) **5617**
G I T ReinRaum Technik *see* ReinRaumTechnik **3371**
• G I T Security & Management (Glas und Instrumenten Technik) (DEU) **6677**

Title

G I T Sicherheit & Management *see* G I T Spezial Sicherheit und Management **6677**
G I T Spezial Separation (Glas und Instrumenten Technik) (DEU ISSN 0940-032X) **2100**
G I T Spezial Sicherheit und Management (Glas und Instrumenten Technik) (DEU ISSN 0948-9487) **6677**
G I T SterilTechnik *see* SterilTechnik **3371**
• G Info - Gazeta de Informatica (ROM ISSN 1222-7129) **1417**
G - Invest (BEL ISSN 0778-7170) **1626**
G J *see* The Geographical Journal **4010**
G J E *see* Griffith Journal of the Environment **3436**
G J G L *see* The Georgetown Journal of Gender and the Law **4679**
G J I *see* Geophysical Journal International **2782**
G J L E *see* Georgetown Journal of Legal Ethics **4680**
G J L P P *see* Georgetown Journal of Law & Public Policy **4679**
• G K E (DEU) **6569**
G K Round-Up (IND) **1851**
G K S S (Gesellschaft fuer Kernenergieverwertung in Schiffbau und Schiffahrt) (DEU ISSN 0344-9629) **7856**
G K S S Forschungszentrum. Jahresbericht (Gesellschaft fuer Kernenergieverwertung in Schiffbau und Schiffahrt) (DEU ISSN 1430-7278) **7856**
G K T Gazette (Guy's, King's and St. Thomas's) (GBR ISSN 1476-9964) **4093**
G K Traumgarten (DEU ISSN 1614-2578) **3730**
G L *see* Girls' Life **2191**
G L A A D Dispatch (Gay & Lesbian Alliance Against Defamation) (USA) **4373**
G L B *see* Geistliche Literatur der Barockzeit **5299**
G L B Ames Newsletter (Gays, Lesbians and Bisexuals) (USA ISSN 1059-065X) **4373**
G L B T R T Newsletter (Gay, Lesbian, Bisexual and Transgendered Round Table) (USA ISSN 1533-7219) **4373**
• G L C S Ink (Gay and Lesbian Counselling Service) (AUS) **4373**
▼ G L Compendium (Grey Literature) (NLD ISSN 1876-2476) **7561**
G L I B News (Gaymen and Lesbians in Brookhaven) (USA) **4373**
G L I P Review *see* Gay and Lesbian Issues and Psychology Review **4374**
G L Kompakt (Gladbach) (DEU ISSN 1615-4223) **3849**
G L M *see* Gulfshore Life **5072**
G L P Journal *see* Government, Law and Policy Journal **4682**
• ➤ G L Q (Gay and Lesbian Quarterly) (USA ISSN 1064-2684) **4373**
G L R *see* Griffith Law Review **4683**
G L S *see* Grazer Linguistische Studien **5123**
G L S G American Musicological Society. Newsletter *see* American Musicological Society. L G B T Q Study Group. Newsletter **4370**
G L T O Nieuws *see* Oogst Landbouw **144**
G L W *see* Green Left Weekly **7139**
G M *see* Gambling Matters **6142**
G M *see* Green Markets **116**
• G M A Forum (Grocery Manufacturers of America) (USA) **3678**
G M A T *see* Barron's G M A T **2968**
G M A T *see* Master the G M A T **2993**
G M B Direct (General Municipal Boilermakers and Allied Trades Union) (GBR) **4594**
G M C *see* Global Media and Communication **2321**
G M C Directions (General Motors Corporation) (USA) **8581**
▼ • ➤ G M Crops (Genetically Modified) (USA ISSN 1938-1999) **232**
G M D A Journal (Greater Milwaukee Dental Association) (USA) **5845**
• G M D Geschaeftsbericht (Gesellschaft fuer Mathematik und Datenverarbeitung) (DEU ISSN 0949-2283) **2419**
† G M D - Spiegel (Gesellschaft fuer Mathematik und Datenverarbeitung) (DEU ISSN 0724-4339) **8958**
G M H C Treatment Issues *see* Achieve **5807**
G M High Tech Performance (General Motors) (USA ISSN 1523-9454) **8581**
G M M *see* Global Money Management **1626**
G M P Horizons (Glass, Molders, Pottery, Plastics and Allied Workers) (USA ISSN 1065-1640) **4594**
• The G M P Letter (Good Manufacturing Practice) (USA ISSN 0196-626X) **4487**
G M P Regulations of Japan (JPN) **6843**
G M P Review (Good Medical Practice) (GBR ISSN 1476-4547) **6843**
• G M P Trends (Good Manufacturing Practice) (USA ISSN 1047-6555) **1886**
G M Pro *see* Greenhouse Management & Production **3734**
G M R Genetics and Molecular Research *see* Genetics and Molecular Research **869**
• G M S Current Posters in Otorhinolaryngology, Head and Neck Surgery (German Medical Science) (DEU ISSN 1865-1038) **6080**
• G M S Current Topics in Otorhinolaryngology - Head and Neck Surgery (German Medical Science) (DEU ISSN 1865-1011) **6080**
• G M S. Health Technology Assessment (German Medical Science) (DEU ISSN 1861-8863) **5617**
• ➤ G M S Krankenhaushygiene Interdisziplinaer (German Medical Science) (DEU ISSN 1863-5245) **7518**
• ➤ G M S Medizin - Bibliothek - Information (German Medical Science) (DEU ISSN 1865-066X) **5617**
G M S Medizinische Informatik, Biometrie und Epidemiologie *see* Medizinische Informatik, Biometrie und Epidemiologie **5635**
• ➤ G M S Psycho - Social - Medicine (German Medical Science) (DEU ISSN 1860-5214) **6142**
• ➤ G M S Thoracic Surgical Science (German Medical Science) (DEU ISSN 1862-4006) **6244**
• G M S Zeitschrift fuer Medizinische Ausbildung (German Medical Science) (DEU ISSN 1860-7446) **5617**
G Magazine *see* G **4359**
• G - Mail (CAN) **1113**
G-Man Jerry Cotton (DEU) **5414**
➤ G N A Journal of Management and Technology (IND ISSN 0974-5726) **1747**
• G N I F Brain Blogger (Global Neuroscience Initiative Foundation) (USA ISSN 1931-6224) **674**
G N P *see* Encyclopedie Pratique du Medicament **6837**
G N S Science Consultancy Report *see* G N S Science Report **2734**
G N S Science Miscellaneous Series (Geological and Nuclear Sciences) (NZL ISSN 1177-2441) **2734**
➤ G N S Science Monograph (NZL ISSN 1177-2433) **2734**
G N S Science Report (Geological and Nuclear Sciences) (NZL ISSN 1177-2425) **2734**
G.O. *see* Scinexx **2766**
G O A L Gazette (Gay Officers Action League) (USA) **4373**
• g-o.de Wissen Online (Geoscience Online) (DEU) **7857**
G O - Giovane Odontoiatra *see* Giovane Odontoiatra **5845**
• G.O.L.F.-Time (DEU) **8230**
G.O.L.F. Time Online *see* G.O.L.F.-Time **8230**
• G O L Public Report (Government On-Line) (CAN ISSN 1910-1872) **7518**
G O R *see* Global Outsourcing Review **5620**
• G O R P Travel Newsletter (USA) **8712**
G O T R *see* Greek Orthodox Theological Review **7704**
• G P (General Practitioner) (GBR ISSN 0268-8417) **5617**
G P A Ports Guide & Directory (Georgia Ports Authority) (USA) **8644**
G P Gazette (General Practice) (USA) **4678**
G P I *see* Gesundheitspolitische Informationen **7519**
G P I A G *see* Primary Care Respiratory Journal **6217**
G P I R *see* Group Processes & Intergroup Relations **8105**
G P L Actualite (Gaz de Petrole Liquefie) (FRA ISSN 0985-200X) **6769**
• G P L Informazioni (Gas di Petrolio Liquefatti) (ITA) **6769**
G P L L A Newsletter (Greater Philadelphia Law Library Association) (USA ISSN 1061-3072) **5010**
G P Light *see* Gwiazda Polarna **3536**
G P M U Journal (Graphic Paper & Media Union) (GBR) **7321**
G P Management Report (General Partners) (USA ISSN 1544-9319) **1747**
• G P N (Greenhouse Product News) (USA ISSN 1529-5524) **3756**
• G P N Educational Media Catalog (Great Plains National) (USA) **2859**
G P N R J *see* Great Plains Natural Resources Journal **3434**
G P N T B Rossii. Algoritmy i Programmy (Gosudarstvennaya Publichnaya Nauchno-tekhnicheskaya Biblioteka Rossii) (RUS ISSN 0320-7420) **2590**
G P News (General Practice) (USA) **4678**
G P O Annual Report *see* U.S. Government Printing Office. Annual Report **7328**
G P O New Sales Publications (Government Printing Office) (USA ISSN 1058-0891) **7438**
G P O Sales Publications Reference File: Magnetic Tape (U.S. Government Printing Office) (USA) **625**
G P O Style Manual *see* U.S. Government Printing Office. Style Manual **7575**
G P P *see* Geneva Papers on Risk and Insurance - Issues and Practice **4503**
G P R *see* Gander Press Review **5422**
G P R - Zeitschrift fuer Gemeinschaftsprivatrecht (DEU ISSN 1612-9229) **4678**
▼ • G P Research Review (General Practitioner) (NZL ISSN 1178-6124) **5617**
G P S A Engineering Data Book (Gas Processors Suppliers Association) (USA) **6769**
G P S C *see* Kuangshan Yali yu Dingban Guanli **6468**
• ➤ G P S Solutions (Global Positioning System) (DEU ISSN 1080-5370) **4007**
• G P S User Magazine (Global Positioning System) (USA ISSN 1545-9039) **3193**
• G P S World (Global Positioning System) (USA ISSN 1048-5104) **4007**
G P S World Online *see* G P S World **4007**
G P Solo (General Practice) (USA ISSN 1528-638X) **4678**
▼ • G P W A Times (Gambling Portal Webmasters Association) (USA ISSN 1941-9872) **8174**
G Q (British Edition) (Gentlemen's Quarterly) (GBR ISSN 0954-8750) **6291**
▼ G Q (French Edition) (Gentlemen's Quarterly) (FRA ISSN 1959-7800) **6291**
G Q (Milano) (Gentlemen's Quarterly) (ITA ISSN 1129-3780) **6291**
G Q (Moscow) (Gentlemen's Quarterly) (RUS) **6291**
G Q (Munich) (Gentlemen's Quarterly) (DEU ISSN 1434-5560) **6291**
• G Q (New York) (Gentlemen's Quarterly) (USA ISSN 0016-6979) **6291**
• G Q (Spanish Edition) (Gentlemen's Quarterly) (ESP ISSN 1134-6884) **6291**
G Q Active (Gentlemen's Quarterly) (GBR ISSN 1362-4431) **6291**
G Q Australia (Gentlemen's Quarterly) (AUS ISSN 1440-7795) **6291**
† G Q Cars (Gentlemen's Quarterly) (DEU ISSN 1862-4561) **8958**
G Q Cars (Gentlemen's Quarterly) (ZAF ISSN 1812-1373) **8581**
G Q Style (Gentlemen's Quarterly) (DEU ISSN 1610-4315) **6291**
G Q Style (Gentlemen's Quarterly) (GBR ISSN 1748-2895) **2255**
G R *see* Generations Review **4045**
G R *see* Genome Research **870**
G R A C E *see* Genetic Resources and Crop Evolution **869**
G R A F Newsletter (Groupe de Recherches sur l'Afrique Francophone) (USA ISSN 1948-6928) **4175**
G R A L. Bulletin (Groupe de Recherches Archeologiques de la Loire) (FRA ISSN 1154-6646) **395**
G R A M (Gemeentereiniging en Afvalmanagement) (NLD ISSN 1569-0458) **3506**
G R A P P A F. Cahiers (Groupe de Recherche et d'Application des Concepts Psychanalytiques a la Psychiatrie en Afrique Franc) (FRA ISSN 1636-2667) **6142**
G R A Reporter (Governmental Research Association, Inc.) (USA ISSN 0016-3619) **7438**
▼ • G R C Expert (Goverance, Risk and Compliance) (USA ISSN 1940-0853) **2419**
G R C News (Gerontology Research Centre) (CAN ISSN 1188-181X) **4045**
G R C Revue Trimestrielle *see* Royal Canadian Mounted Police. Quarterly **2667**
G R E (Exam Cram) (Graduate Record Exam) (USA ISSN 1931-5902) **2982**
• G R E E N Lines (GrassRoots Environmental Effectiveness Network) (USA) **3432**
G R E Exam (Graduate Record Examinations) (USA) **2982**
G R E S. Cahiers (Groupe de Recherche Etnicite et Societe) (CAN ISSN 1499-0431) **3534**
G R F *see* Government Recreation & Fitness **4978**
G R H I S. Cahiers (Groupe de Recherche d'Histoire) (FRA ISSN 1773-7931) **340**
G R I H L. Les Dossiers *see* Groupe de Recherches Interdisciplinaires sur l'Histoire du Litteraire. Les Dossiers **5218**
G R I R *see* The Geneva Risk and Insurance Review **4503**
G R Infos Sentiers (BEL ISSN 0776-3646) **8315**
G R L *see* Geophysical Research Letters **2782**
G R M A News (Ghana Registered Midwives Association) (GHA ISSN 0855-0948) **5959**
G R M-Beiheft *see* Germanisch-Romanische Monatsschrift. Beiheft **5300**
G R M U G Newsletter (Great River Microcomputer Users Group) (USA) **2576**
• G R R - Global Retail Review (GBR ISSN 1471-4221) **1113**
G R S Bericht (Gesellschaft fuer Anlagen- und Reaktorsicherheit mbH) (DEU ISSN 0170-1991) **3193**
G R S - F (Gesellschaft fuer Anlagen- und Reaktorsicherheit mbH) (DEU ISSN 0944-5021) **3193**
G R S - S (Gesellschaft fuer Anlagen- und Reaktorsicherheit mbH) (DEU ISSN 0172-8903) **3193**
G R U R *see* Gewerblicher Rechtsschutz und Urheberrecht **6750**
G R U R - D V D *see* Gewerblicher Rechtsschutz und Urheberrecht **6750**
G R U R - Rechtsprechungs-Report (Gewerblicher Rechtsschutz und Urheberrecht) (DEU ISSN 1616-2277) **6750**
G-Raadmeter *see* Network Newsletter **7533**
G S *see* Gay Scotland **4374**
• G S 1 Fokus (Global Standard) (NOR ISSN 0809-8700) **6402**
G S 1 Info (Global Standards) (FIN ISSN 1795-8083) **6402**
G S 1 Magazin (Global Standards) (DEU) **6402**
G S 1 Sweden Fokus (Global Standards) (SWE ISSN 1653-2775) **6402**
G S A Specialty Meetings: Abstracts with Programs *see* Geological Society of America. Specialty Meetings, Abstracts with Programs **2739**
G S A Supply Catalog (General Services Administration) (USA ISSN 0095-5620) **7438**
• G S A Today (Geological Society of America) (USA ISSN 1052-5173) **2734**
The G S A Travel Agents' Sales Guide (ZAF) **8712**
G S A Travel Magazine (CAN) **8712**
G S B Chicago (Graduate School of Business) (USA ISSN 1072-7612) **1113**
G S C Newsletter *see* Ghana Studies Council. Newsletter **7966**
G S E Today *see* Ground Support Worldwide **57**
G S F - Bericht (Gesellschaft fuer Strahlenforschung) (DEU ISSN 0721-1694) **3432**
G S F - Forschungszentrum fuer Umwelt und Gesundheit. Jahresbericht (DEU ISSN 0941-3847) **3432**
➤ G S F Mensch und Umwelt Spezial (DEU ISSN 0949-0663) **3432**
G S I Groundwater Newsletter *see* Geological Survey of Ireland. Groundwater Newsletter **2740**
G S I Report (Gesellschaft fuer Schwerionenforschung mbH) (DEU ISSN 0171-4546) **7066**
G S I S *see* Gerontology Special Interest Section Quarterly **4046**
• G S I Scientific Report (Online) (Gesellschaft fuer Schwerionenforschung mbH) (DEU) **7066**
G S I Scientific Report (Print) *see* G S I Scientific Report (Online) **7066**
G S J *see* Gray's Sporting Journal **8316**
G S M Chronicle (University of Dallas, Graduate School of Management) (USA) **2284**
G S M Quarterly (Global System for Mobile) (GBR ISSN 1360-6603) **2321**
G S M World Focus (Global System for Mobile) (GBR ISSN 1462-2262) **2321**
G S N: Government Security News (USA ISSN 1548-940X) **4890**
G S N J Newsletter (Genealogical Society of New Jersey) (USA ISSN 1938-5803) **3767**
G S News Technical Report (JPN ISSN 0385-7204) **3309**
G S O C News (Genealogical Society of Okaloosa County, Florida) (USA) **3767**
G S P *see* Genocide Studies and Prevention **340**
G S P *see* Global Social Policy **8042**
G S P C A Shorthair (German Shorthaired Pointer Club of America) (USA) **6808**
G S P News (Geological Survey of Pakistan) (PAK) **2735**
G S R (Gakki Shoho Review) (JPN) **6569**
• G S R - Global Security Review/Internationale Zeitschrift fur Schutz und Sicherheit/Revista Internacional de la Seguridad/Revue Internationale de la Surete et de la Securite (GBR ISSN 1475-9330) **2677**
G S S Newsletter *see* Genealogical Society of Sarasota. Newsletter **3768**
G S T *see* Golf and Sports Turf Australia **233**
G S T & Commodity Tax (Goods and Services Tax) (CAN ISSN 0847-3528) **1926**
G S T Bulletin/Bulletin S V S (Gesellschaft Schweizer Tieraerztinnen und Tieraerzte) (CHE) **8797**
G S T Guide for Business (Goods and Services Tax) (CAN) **1926**
G S U Review (Georgia State University) (USA ISSN 1078-3121) **5217**
G S W *see* GeoScienceWorld **2720**
• G T (Giurisprudenza Tributaria) (ITA ISSN 1591-3961) **1926**
G T A V News (Geography Teachers Association of Victoria) (AUS ISSN 1329-7783) **4007**
G T E Network Systems World-Wide Communications Journal (General Telephone & Electronics) (USA ISSN 0742-6151) **2350**
• G T I Paper Series (Great Transition Initiative) (USA ISSN 1935-3251) **8103**
G T O (Gran Turismo Omologato) (NLD ISSN 1571-5256) **8581**
G T Purely Porsche (GBR ISSN 1474-6549) **8582**
G T R *see* Global Trade Review **1567**
G T R-W O *see* U.S. Forest Service. General Technical Report W O **3706**
G T S Advisor (Government Technical Services) (USA) **1626**
• G T S J Gasu Tabin Semina Shiryoshu/Gas Turbine Society of Japan. Seminar Report (Gas Turbine Society of Japan) (JPN ISSN 1341-8491) **3378**
G T T *see* Glastuinbouwtechniek Magazine **2042**
G T V Bulletin (Groupements Techniques Veterinaires) (FRA ISSN 0399-2519) **8797**
G Three *see* G3 **8671**
G U E D E - J. Fac. Pharm. Gazi *see* Gazi Universitesi Eczacilik Fakultesi Dergisi **6843**
• G U Fen Bilimleri Dergisi/G U Journal of Science (Gazi Universitesi) (TUR ISSN 1303-9709) **7857**
G u G *see* Grundstuecksmarkt und Grundstueckswert **7592**
➤ G u G Aktuell (Grundstuecksmarkt und Grundstueckswert) (DEU ISSN 0945-9243) **7591**
• G U Gaceta Universitaria (ESP) **2284**
• G U I Program News (Graphic User Interface) (USA) **2590**
G U J G E F *see* G E F A D **2859**
G U Journal of Science *see* G U Fen Bilimleri Dergisi **7857**
G U P (Guide to Unique Photography) (NLD ISSN 1871-8450) **6969**
G U - Spegeln (Goeteborgs Universitet) (SWE ISSN 1653-3941) **2982**
G & D Report (DEU) **1393**
† G V B Nieuws (Gementevervoerbedryf Amsterdam) (NLD) **8958**

Title

DIRECTORY 2010 GAY AND LESBIAN COUNSELLING SERVICE INK 10315

Garden Products and Planning Guide see Better Homes and Gardens Garden Products and Planning Guide 3724
• Garden Railways (USA ISSN 0747-0622) 4335
Garden Retail (GBR ISSN 1746-6644) 3731
Garden Rooms (USA ISSN 1933-334X) 3731
Garden Shed (USA ISSN 1088-3177) 3731
• Garden State EnviroNews (USA) 2612
Garden State Golf (USA ISSN 1532-8996) 8174
Garden State Parkway Traffic Report (USA) 8631
▼ Garden State Town & Country Living (USA ISSN 1936-8011) 5071
Garden State Woman (USA ISSN 1530-7077) 8865
Garden Structures (USA ISSN 1940-8846) 3731
Garden Style (DEU ISSN 1614-8312) 3731
† Garden Style (USA) 8958
Garden to Kitchen Newsletter (NCL ISSN 1022-9221) 6659
Garden Trade News (GBR) 3732
Garden Trade News International see Garden Trade News 3732
The Gardener (ZAF ISSN 1810-794X) 3732
The Gardener (Torrington) (USA ISSN 1533-8932) 3732
Gardener News (USA) 3732
Gardener. Supplement see Come Gardening. Supplement 4080
Gardener's Companion see The Old Farmer's Almanac All-Seasons Garden Guide 3746
Gardener's Guide to Pest Prevention and Control in the Home and Garden (CAN ISSN 0832-6509) 3732
Gardenia (ITA ISSN 0393-585X) 3732
Gardening and Beekeeping see Darzs un Drava 3728
Gardening and Deck Design see Gardening & Deck Design 3732
Gardening & Deck Design (USA ISSN 1550-6371) 3732
Gardening and Outdoor Living see Gardening & Outdoor Living 3732
Gardening & Outdoor Living (USA) 3732
Gardening How-To (USA ISSN 1087-0083) 3732
• Gardening Life (CAN ISSN 1203-858X) 3732
• Gardening Newsletter (USA) 3732
• Gardening Which? (GBR) 3732
• GardenRail (GBR ISSN 0969-952X) 8617
➤ Gardens' Bulletin, Singapore (SGP ISSN 0374-7859) 791
Gardens Illustrated (GBR ISSN 0968-8927) 3732
Gardens Made Easy see Gardens Monthly 3732
Gardens Monthly (GBR ISSN 1476-7791) 3732
• Gardens of England and Wales Open for Charity (Year) (GBR ISSN 1365-0572) 3732
Gardens West (CAN ISSN 0863-4947) 3732
• GardenWeb (USA) 3732
Gargoyle (CAN ISSN 0318-0107) 2284
Gargoyle (Ann Arbor) (USA) 5217
Gargoyle (Washington, DC) (USA ISSN 0162-1149) 5299
Garibaldi (URY ISSN 0797-6313) 5217
Garland Medieval Casebooks see Routledge Medieval Casebooks 4260
Garland Reference Library of the Humanities (USA ISSN 1059-3454) 4453
Garment Manufacturer's Index (USA ISSN 1065-1330) 2247
Garments & Textiles see Global Sources Garments & Textiles 8451
Garments Imports America Directory (CAN) 2247
• Garner's Environmental Law (GBR) 4679
Garnet Letter (USA) 2284
Garser Kulturbrief (AUT) 4222
Garston Docks Tide Table (GBR) 8644
Garten (CHE) 3732
Garten (DEU) 5072
Garten & Lifestyle (DEU ISSN 1865-6064) 3732
Garten Idee (DEU) 3732
Garten Spass see Gartenspass 3733
Garten Traeume see Gartentraeume 3733
Garten- und Freizeitmarkt (DEU ISSN 0342-4650) 3732
• Garten und Haus (AUT) 3732
Garten und Landschaft (DEU ISSN 0016-4720) 3732
Garten und Wohnen see Wohnen & Garten 4552
• Garten Zeitung (DEU ISSN 0944-9248) 3732
Der Gartenbau/Horticulture (CHE ISSN 0016-4747) 3732
Gartenbau in Baden see Gartenbau in Baden-Wuerttemberg 3733
Gartenbau in Baden-Wuerttemberg (DEU ISSN 1862-3840) 3733
Gartenbau in Niedersachsen und Bremen (DEU) 3733
Gartenbauwissenschaft see European Journal of Horticultural Science 3729
Gartencenterwissen (DEU ISSN 1618-6931) 1818
Gartenfreund/Jardin Familial (CHE) 3733
Gartenidee (CHE ISSN 1424-0092) 3733
Gartenidee see Garten Idee 3732
Die Gartenkunst (DEU ISSN 0935-0519) 3733
Gartenkurier see G K Traumgarten 3730
Gartenmagazin (AUT) 3733
Gartenpraxis (DEU ISSN 0341-2105) 3733
Gartenspass (DEU) 3733
Gartenteich (DEU ISSN 1615-3448) 3733
Gartentraeume (DEU) 3733
Garth Analysis (USA ISSN 0745-6468) 7138
Gartner Connect see GartnerConnect 2506
Gartner Group. Research Review (USA) 2543
• Gartner Tidende (DNK ISSN 0106-8393) 3733
• GartnerConnect (USA) 2506
Gartneren see Groent 3 F Punkt 3734
• Gartneri - Regnskabsstatistik/Horticultural Accounts Statistics (DNK) 181
Gartnertidende see Gartner Tidende 3733
Gartneryrket (NOR ISSN 0046-5437) 3733
Garuda Magazine (IDN) 8783
Garun (ARM) 4453
Gary Life (USA ISSN 1559-3193) 5072
Gary North's Remnant Review (USA ISSN 1053-5527) 1113
Gas see Plyn 6789
Gas (DEU ISSN 0343-2092) 6769
Gas and Electricity Market Statistics (LUX ISSN 1830-0472) 3152
Gas and Heat see Meiqi yu Reli 3325
Gas and Oil Equipment Directory (USA) 4119
Gas and Water Statistics see Turkey. Turkiye Istatistik Kurumu. Gaz ve Su Istatistikleri 8994
Gas Appliances (GBR) 4119
Gas Briefing Europe (GBR ISSN 1464-3928) 6769
• The Gas Carrier Register (GBR ISSN 1478-4610) 8644
Gas Consumers Council. Annual Report (GBR ISSN 0951-8592) 6769
• Gas Daily (USA ISSN 0885-5935) 6770
• Gas Daily Europe (GBR ISSN 1466-8874) 6770
• Gas Daily's Gas Transportation & Storage Week (USA ISSN 1524-0398) 6770
Gas Daily's N G (Natural Gas) (USA ISSN 1068-1299) 6770
Gas di Petrolio Liquefatti Informazioni see G P L Informazioni 6769
Gas Digest (USA ISSN 0161-4851) 6770
Gas Distribution Industry Performance Indicators see Gas Statistics Australia 6800
Gas e-Matters see Gas Matters 6770
Gas Engine Magazine (USA ISSN 0435-1304) 4335
➤ Gas Engineering (GBR ISSN 1755-5477) 6770
Gas Facts (USA ISSN 0361-4298) 6770
† Gas Industry Directory (Year) (GBR ISSN 0954-853X) 8958
Gas Installer (GBR ISSN 0964-6825) 6770
Gas Leads see Gas Leads for Suppliers of Products and Services to the World Gas Community 6770
• Gas Leads for Suppliers of Products and Services to the World Gas Community (USA ISSN 1930-0646) 6770
Gas Lease Index see Texas. Railroad Commission. Oil and Gas Division. Gas Lease Index 6794
Gas Market (NOR) 8644
Gas Market Report see Inside F E R C's Gas Market Report 6773
• Gas Market Trends (CYP) 3136
• Gas Matters (GBR ISSN 0964-8496) 6770
• Gas Matters Today (GBR ISSN 1746-8213) 6770
• Gas Matters Today Asia (GBR ISSN 1746-8205) 6770
• Gas Processes Handbook (USA ISSN 1939-8344) 6770
• Gas Processors Association. Annual Convention. Proceedings (USA ISSN 0096-8870) 6770
Gas Processors Association. Research Reports (USA) 6770
• Gas Processors Association. Technical Publications (USA) 6770
• Gas Processors Report (USA ISSN 0740-5278) 6770
Gas Processors Suppliers Association Engineering Data Book see G P S A Engineering Data Book 6769
Gas Production Ledger see Texas. Railroad Commission. Oil and Gas Division. Gas Production Ledger 6794
Gas Purchaser see Texas. Railroad Commission. Oil and Gas Division. Gas Purchaser 6794
Gas Regulation (GBR ISSN 1740-7826) 4679
Gas Statistics Australia (AUS ISSN 1327-4627) 6800
Gas Supply and Demand Study (AUS) 6770
Gas Technology Institute. Annual Report (USA) 6770
• Gas-Teknik (DNK ISSN 0106-4355) 6770
Gas-to-Liquids News see Gasification News 6770
• Gas Transactions Report (USA ISSN 1072-5113) 6770
Gas Transportation & Storage Week see Gas Daily's Gas Transportation & Storage Week 6770
Gas Turbine Experiment and Research see Ranqi Wolun Shiyan yu Yanjiu 3217
Gas Turbine Society of Japan. Bulletin (JPN ISSN 1341-6618) 3378
Gas Turbine Society of Japan Gasu Tabin Semina Shiryoshu see G T S J Gasu Tabin Semina Shiryoshu 3378
Gas Turbine Society of Japan. Journal see Nihon Gasu Tabin Gakkaishi 3391
Gas Turbine Society of Japan. Seminar Report see G T S J Gasu Tabin Semina Shiryoshu 3378
Gas Turbine World (USA ISSN 0747-7988) 3136
Gas Turbine World Handbook (USA ISSN 0883-458X) 3136
Gas- und Wasserfach Wasser, Abwasser see G W F - Wasser, Abwasser 8823
Gas Utility Industry (USA) 6770
• Gas Utility Report (USA ISSN 1074-3723) 6770
Gas Utility Week see S N L Energy Gas Utility Week 6791
Gas - Wasser - Abwasser see G W A 6769
Gas, Wasser, Waerme Aktuell see G W W Aktuell 6769
• Gas Week (Email) (AUS ISSN 1444-9064) 6770
Gas Week Brief (Email) see Gas Week (Email) 6770
Gasbag (USA) 56
Gascon Magazine (FRA ISSN 1245-1606) 115
Gaseous Dielectrics (USA ISSN 1523-3472) 7051
▼ • Gases & Instrumentation (USA ISSN 1937-6774) 3244
• The Gases & Welding Distributor (USA ISSN 1079-3909) 6342
• Gasification News (USA) 6770
The Gaskell Society Journal (GBR ISSN 0951-7200) 5299
Gaskiya ta fi Kwabo (NGA) 3920
Gaslines (USA) 6771
• Gaslini (ITA ISSN 0390-5845) 6092
Gasnytt see Energigas 6767
Gasoil (IND ISSN 0971-0191) 6771
Gasoline Magazine (SWE ISSN 1653-3771) 8582
† • Gasp (ESP) 8958
Gasparilla Magazine (USA) 5072
The Gaspereau Review (CAN ISSN 1206-7040) 5217
Gaspesie Gourmande (CAN ISSN 1911-0006) 4386
Gaspreise. Preissysteme see Gas and Electricity Market Statistics 3152
▼ Gass! (ESP ISSN 1888-3966) 8174
• Gassmagasinet (NOR ISSN 1502-1645) 6771
Gastein Aktuell Interessengemeinschaft (AUT) 4386
Gastgewerbe (DEU) 4386
Das Gasthaus (DEU) 4386
Gasthaus Hamburg (DEU) 4386
† • GasTIPS (USA ISSN 1078-3954) 8958
• ➤ Gastric and Breast Cancer (GRC ISSN 1109-7655) 6020
• ➤ Gastric Cancer (JPN ISSN 1436-3291) 6020
Gastro (DNK ISSN 1901-2187) 3644
• Der Gastroenterologe (DEU ISSN 1861-9681) 5924
† Gastroenterologia Clinica (ITA ISSN 1120-3757) 8958
Gastroenterologia e Endoscopia Digestiva see G E D 5923
Gastroenterologia, Endocrinologia y Nutricion see G E N 5923
• Gastroenterologia Integrada (ESP ISSN 1576-0839) 5924
▼ Gastroenterologia Internacional (ESP ISSN 1888-3605) 5924
Gastroenterologia Latinoamericana (CHL ISSN 0716-8594) 5924
• Gastroenterologia Polska/Polish Gastroenterology (POL ISSN 1232-9886) 5924
Gastroenterologia Practica (ESP ISSN 1130-9431) 5924
➤ Gastroenterologia pre Prax (SVK ISSN 1336-1473) 5924
• Gastroenterologia y Hepatologia (ESP ISSN 0210-5705) 5924
• Gastroenterologia y Hepatologia Continuada (ESP ISSN 1578-1550) 5924
Gastroenterologia y Hepatologia. Monografias see Gastroenterologia y Hepatologia 5924
➤ Gastroenterological Endoscopy (JPN ISSN 0387-1207) 5924
Gastroenterological Society of Taiwan. Journal see Taiwan Xiaohua Xiyi Xuehui Zazhi 5931
Gastroenterological Surgery see Shokaki Geka 5931
Gastroenterological Surgery Nursing see Shokaki Geka Nursing 5981
Gastroenterologie see Les Actualites en Gastroenterologie 5919
• ➤ Gastroenterologie Clinique et Biologique (FRA ISSN 0399-8320) 5924
• Gastroenterologie up2date (DEU ISSN 1616-9670) 5924
Il Gastroenterologo (ITA ISSN 0391-8939) 5924
• ➤ Gastroenterology (USA ISSN 0016-5085) 5924
Gastroenterology see Today in Medicine. Gastroenterology 5932
• Gastroenterology and Endoscopy News (USA ISSN 0883-8348) 5924
➤ Gastroenterology & Hepatology (USA ISSN 1554-7914) 5924
• ➤ Gastroenterology Clinics of North America (USA ISSN 0889-8553) 5924
• Gastroenterology Coder's Pink Sheet (USA ISSN 1941-806X) 5924
• Gastroenterology Coding Alert (USA ISSN 1527-831X) 4503
• Gastroenterology Hepatology Annual Review (USA ISSN 1932-8001) 5925
Gastroenterology in Perspective see Gastroenterology in Primary Care 5925
• Gastroenterology in Primary Care (GBR ISSN 1752-8763) 5925
• Gastroenterology Nursing (USA ISSN 1042-895X) 5925
▼ • ➤ Gastroenterology Research and Practice (USA ISSN 1687-6121) 5925
Gastroenterology Today (GBR ISSN 0969-0131) 5925
Gastroenterology Today (IND) 5925
• Gastroenterology Week (USA ISSN 1543-6756) 5925
Gastroenteropatoloski Arhiv (SRB) 5925
• GastroHep (GBR ISSN 1478-1239) 5925
▼ • Gastrointestinal Cancer Research (USA ISSN 1934-7820) 6020
• ➤ Gastrointestinal Endoscopy (USA ISSN 0016-5107) 5925
• Gastrointestinal Endoscopy Clinics of North America (USA ISSN 1052-5157) 5925
Gastrointestinal Nursing (GBR ISSN 1479-5248) 5925
Gastrointestinal Oncology Review & Outlook see G I Oncology Review & Outlook 6020
Gastrointestinal Physiology (USA ISSN 1556-1267) 5925
Gastrointestinal Research see G.I. Research 5923
▼ Gastromania (BEL ISSN 1784-3243) 4386
Gastronomia Book Buen Vivir see El Buen Vivir Magazine 3830
• Gastronomica (USA ISSN 1529-3262) 7966
Gastronomie (DEU ISSN 0323-4762) 4359
Gastronomie & Tourisme (CHE) 8713
• Gastronomie-Report (DEU) 4386
Gastronomie und Hotel (DEU) 4386
Gastronomie und Hotellerie Gastrotel see G H Gastrotel 4386
▼ Gastronomie und Recht Aktuell (DEU ISSN 1863-7086) 4387
Der Gastronomiefuehrer von A-Z (DEU) 4387
Gastrotour (LUX) 4359
Gastrum (ESP ISSN 0211-058X) 5925
Gastwirt (DEU ISSN 0016-5158) 4387
Gastwirt, Hotelier & Cafetier (AUT) 4387
Gaswaerme International (DEU ISSN 0020-9384) 4119
gate (DEU ISSN 0723-2225) 8423
The Gate (USA ISSN 0886-6791) 6741
The Gate to Turkey (TUR) 3962
Gateaux/Gatou (JPN) 3673
• Gateavisa (NOR ISSN 0802-2216) 5217
Gatebil (NOR) 8582
The Gated Wye (USA) 3578
▼ Gategate (GBR ISSN 1754-4866) 5299
• Gatekeeper Series (GBR ISSN 1018-7235) 2612
Gatelodge (GBR) 2653
Gatepost see Viewpoint (London, 1995) 6189
The Gatepost (USA) 2284
Gateway (CAN ISSN 0016-5190) 2284
Gateway see Nanfang Hangkong 8785
Gateway (Middlesboro) (USA) 4293
Gateway (New York) (USA) 5072
Gateway Antarctica Special Publication Series (NZL ISSN 1177-0481) 8713
Gateway Heritage (USA ISSN 0198-9375) 4293
Gateway Magazine (DEU) 3534
• Gateway Monthly (GBR) 5442
Gateway to Medicine see Iyaku no Mon 6851
Gateways see National Library of Australia Gateways (Print) 8976
Gateways (Brookfield) (USA ISSN 1947-4385) 944
Gathered (USA) 7798
Gathered View (USA ISSN 1077-9965) 5618
Gatherer Stripout see Texas. Railroad Commission. Oil and Gas Division. Gatherer Stripout 6794
Gathering Gibsons (USA ISSN 0893-3162) 3767
• A Gathering of the Tribes (USA ISSN 1058-9112) 491
Gato Negro (ARG) 5414
Gatopardo (MEX ISSN 0124-616X) 3909
Gator Bait Magazine (USA ISSN 1531-7463) 8174
Gatou see Gateaux 3673
Gatsby (CHE) 5072
Gatskrikan (SWE) 5217
Gatt (ISL ISSN 1670-5386) 2941
Gattefosse. Bulletin Technique (FRA ISSN 0183-1224) 5618
Gatto Magazine (ITA ISSN 1594-5782) 6808
Gatwick News (GBR) 56
Gauchebdo (CHE) 4595
Gaucher Disease Newsletter (USA) 5618
Gaudeamus (SWE ISSN 0016-5247) 2284
† Gaudeamus Information (English Edition) (NLD ISSN 0923-6244) 8958
Gaudie (GBR) 2284
Gauer Distinguished Lecture in Law and Public Policy (USA ISSN 1054-4674) 4679
Gauheria (FRA ISSN 0764-6488) 4222
Gauke's Jahrbuch (DEU ISSN 0720-2520) 5299
Gaulim Teacher's College Magazine (PNG) 5442
† Gault Millau (DEU) 8958
Gault Millau Guide Deutschland (DEU) 4387
Gault Millau WeinGuide Deutschland (DEU) 604
▼ GaultMillau (NLD ISSN 1872-6666) 4387
Gauntlet (CAN) 2285
Gauntlet (USA ISSN 1047-4463) 5217
• Gausac (ESP ISSN 1139-6830) 4222
Gauss-Gesellschaft. Mitteilungen (DEU ISSN 0435-1452) 575
Gaussenia (FRA ISSN 0761-3067) 3691
Gauteng Business (ZAF ISSN 1814-1625) 1747
Gauteng Companies (ZAF ISSN 1990-6021) 1997
Gauteng Directory (ZAF) 1997
• Gauteng Provincial Legislation Library (ZAF ISSN 1683-2620) 4679
Gavagai (ESP ISSN 0213-4403) 5121
Gavakari (IND) 3882
Gavea - Brown (USA ISSN 0276-7910) 5299
The Gavin Report (USA) 6569
Gavroche (FRA ISSN 0242-9705) 4222
Gawalo (NLD ISSN 1385-3112) 4119
Gawler Community Information & Business Directory (AUS ISSN 1833-5977) 8042
Gay Airline & Travel Club Newsletter (USA ISSN 1072-8074) 4373
Gay & Lesbian Alliance Against Defamation Dispatch see G L A A D Dispatch 4373
Gay and Lesbian Counselling Service Ink see G L C S Ink 4373

Title

DIRECTORY 2010 GENEALOGIE 10317

Gegenschein (USA) 5299
Gegenseitigkeit see Mutualite 4515
Gegenwart (CHE ISSN 0016-5867) 5217
Die Gegenwart (DEU ISSN 0016-5859) 4081
Die Gegenwart see Neue Gegenwart 5078
Gegenwartszeit der Unicycle see Re-Unicycling the Past 368
Gegenworte (DEU ISSN 1435-571X) 7857
Geghjuk see Azat Artsakh 3792
➤ De Geheel-Onthouder (NLD ISSN 0166-2880) 2694
Geheim (DEU ISSN 0930-8571) 7237
Gehet Hin! - Missionsblatt (DEU ISSN 1437-1146) 7759
Gehirn und Geist (DEU ISSN 1618-8519) 7358
Gehoor in Onderzoek (NLD ISSN 1874-6993) 6080
• Geiger (DNK ISSN 1600-8871) 6569
Geiger Report (USA) 25
Geijutsu Shincho (JPN ISSN 0435-1657) 491
Geiken Tsushin (JPN ISSN 1340-9409) 944
Geino no Kagaku/Tokyo National Research Institute of Cultural Properties. Department of Performing Arts. Journal (JPN ISSN 0919-0600) 8471
Geiriadur Prifysgol Cymru (GBR ISSN 0072-0542) 5121
• Geisha (BOL ISSN 1609-672X) 5299
Geist (CAN ISSN 1181-6554) 5299
Geist, Erkenntnis, Kommunikation (DEU ISSN 1612-7919) 6921
Geist und Auftrag (DEU) 7799
Geist und Leben (DEU ISSN 0016-5921) 7644
Geist und Wort (DEU ISSN 1615-3669) 7799
Geisterjaeger John Sinclair (DEU) 5443
Die Geistesgeschichte und Ihre Methoden (DEU ISSN 0177-9389) 5443
Geisteskultur Indiens (DEU ISSN 1619-4470) 8103
Geistig Fit (DEU ISSN 0941-0767) 7358
Der Geistig Schaffende (AUT) 5217
Geistige Behinderung see Teilhabe 3048
Geistliche Literatur der Barockzeit (NLD ISSN 1570-2456) 5299
Geitenhouderij (NLD ISSN 1386-5048) 287
Geka/Surgery (JPN ISSN 0016-593X) 6244
Geka Chiryo/Surgical Therapy (JPN ISSN 0433-2644) 6244
Geka Shudankai Shorokushu/Tokyo Surgical Society. Abstracts (JPN) 5747
Geka to Taisha Eiyo/Japanese Journal of Surgical Metabolism and Nutrition (JPN ISSN 0389-5564) 6244
Gekiryu (JPN ISSN 0385-0722) 1113
Gekkan Akua Raifu/Aqual Life (JPN) 2804
Gekkan Asahi/Monthly Asahi (JPN ISSN 0916-1929) 3900
Gekkan Bakodo/Monthly Bar Code see Gekkan Jidou Ninshiki 2460
Gekkan Bijutsu see Monthly Art 506
➤ Gekkan Chiiki Igaku/Monthly Community Medicine (JPN ISSN 0914-4277) 5618
Gekkan Chikyu/Chikyu Monthly (JPN ISSN 0387-3498) 2707
Gekkan Chusho-Kigyo/Monthly Smaller Businesses (JPN ISSN 0285-8460) 1961
Gekkan Ebui Furonto/Audio Video Front (JPN) 8153
Gekkan Eko Indasutori/Eco Industry (JPN ISSN 1342-3037) 3433
Gekkan Fukushi (JPN ISSN 1341-6669) 8042
Gekkan Gasorin Stutando/Monthly Gas Station (JPN ISSN 0016-5069) 6771
Gekkan Gendai (JPN) 1747
Gekkan Hoken Shinryo/Monthly Review of Insurance Treatment (JPN ISSN 0385-8588) 5618
Gekkan Hoso Janaru/Monthly Broadcasting Journal (JPN ISSN 0385-3810) 2381
Gekkan I M/Journal of Image & Information Management (JPN ISSN 0913-2708) 6969
Gekkan Iryo Joho/Medical News of the Month (JPN ISSN 0913-9443) 5618
Gekkan Jidou Ninshiki (JPN) 2460
Gekkan Kaiyo/Oceanography Monthly (JPN ISSN 0916-2011) 2804
Gekkan Keidanren (JPN ISSN 0918-0591) 1113
Gekkan Kendo Nippon/Monthly Japanese Fencing (JPN) 8175
Gekkan Kokogaku Journal/Archaeological Journal (JPN ISSN 0454-1634) 395
Gekkan Kyodotai see Cooperative Life 8096
Gekkan Kyoiku Journal see Monthly Education Journal 2887
Gekkan Kyuyusho Nihon see Monthly Journal of Gasoline Service Stations 6778
Gekkan Media Deeta/Monthly Media Data (JPN ISSN 0387-7019) 1997
Gekkan Mikusu/Medical Information Express (JPN ISSN 1341-3864) 5618
Gekkan Musen Shuchi/Monthly News on Radio (JPN) 2358
Gekkan Nashingu/Japanese Journal of Nursing (JPN ISSN 0389-8326) 5959
Gekkan Pishi Warudo Japan see P C World Japan 2581
Gekkan Rikujyo Kyogi (JPN) 6291
Gekkan Ryutsu Netto Wakingu see Ryutsu Netto Wakingu 1841
Gekkan Saibo/Cell (JPN ISSN 0386-4766) 832
Gekkan Shakaiminshu (JPN) 7138
Gekkan Shin Iryo/New Medical Treatment (JPN ISSN 0910-7991) 5618
Gekkan Shonen-Champion see Monthly Boy's Champion 2203
Gekkan Shonen Magazine (JPN) 2190
Gekkan Sogo Kea/Japanese Journal of Total Care (JPN ISSN 0916-7013) 5618
Gekkan Syokudo/The Food Service Management (JPN) 4387
Gekkan Tenmon (JPN ISSN 0288-4216) 575
Gekkan Tenmon Gaido see Tenmon Gaido 582
Gekkan Toraiboroji/Tribology (JPN ISSN 0914-6121) 3378
• Gekkan Yakuji/Pharmaceuticals Monthly (JPN ISSN 0016-5980) 6843
Gekko see G E K K O 8042
Het Gekrookte Riet see Hervormd Kerkblad 7760
Gelatiere Italiano (ITA ISSN 0016-5999) 3644
Gelato Artigianale (ITA) 3644
Gelbe Liste Identa (DEU ISSN 1616-198X) 6843
Gelbe Liste Pharmindex (DEU ISSN 0942-2951) 6843
Gelbe Liste Pharmindex. Dermatologen (DEU ISSN 0942-3117) 6844
Gelbe Liste Pharmindex. Gynaekologen (DEU ISSN 0942-3125) 6844
Gelbe Liste Pharmindex. H N O-Aerzte (Hals-Nasen-Ohren) (DEU ISSN 0942-3133) 6844
Gelbe Liste Pharmindex. Internisten (DEU ISSN 1431-6072) 6844
Gelbe Liste Pharmindex. Neurologen, Psychiater (DEU ISSN 0942-3141) 6844
Gelbe Liste Pharmindex. Ophthalmologen (DEU ISSN 0942-3168) 6844
Gelbe Liste Pharmindex. Orthopaeden (DEU ISSN 0942-3176) 6844
Gelbe Liste Pharmindex. Paediater (DEU ISSN 0942-3184) 6844
Gelbe Liste Pharmindex. Phytopharmaka und Homoeopathika (DEU ISSN 0942-3192) 6844
Gelbe Liste Pharmindex. Urologen (DEU ISSN 0942-315X) 6844
Gelbe Liste Vademecum (DEU ISSN 1436-1906) 6844
Gelbvieh World (USA ISSN 1084-5100) 287
Geld (NLD) 2638
Geld en Onderneming see Samsom Geld en Onderneming 1381
Geld-Profi (DEU ISSN 0171-6018) 1349
Geld und Kapital (DEU ISSN 1616-0185) 1349
Geldanlage Berater (DEU ISSN 0939-4966) 1626
➤ Gelders Erfgoed (NLD ISSN 0927-7749) 4223
Gelders Landschap see Mooi Gelderland 4246
Gelderse Historische Reeks (NLD) 4223
De Gelderse Roos (NLD ISSN 1873-5762) 3914
Geldgeschichtliche Nachrichten (DEU ISSN 0435-1835) 4335
Geldgids see ConsumentenGeldgids 1329
Geldidee (DEU ISSN 1861-9584) 1349
Geldinstitute (DEU ISSN 0343-8740) 1349
Geldprofi see Geld-Profi 1349
Der Geldscheinsammler (DEU ISSN 0931-0681) 6651
Geldtipps Konkret! (DEU) 1626
Gele Katern see Regelingen Onderwijs 3030
➤ Gelfand Mathematical Seminars (USA ISSN 1068-7122) 5490
Geliebte Katze (DEU ISSN 0946-6215) 6808
Gelijke Behandeling (NLD ISSN 1567-4924) 1683
Gelijke Kansen voor Vrouwen en Mannen in de Europese Unie see Equal Opportunities for Women and Men in the European Union 1680
Gelin (TUR ISSN 1300-8110) 5558
Geliotekhnika/Solar Technics (UZB ISSN 0130-0997) 3176
Gellis & Kagan's Current Pediatric Therapy see Current Pediatric Therapy 6091
Gelosophist (USA ISSN 8756-2898) 5217
Gelre see Vereeniging tot Beofening van Geldersche Geschiedenis, Oudheidkunde en Recht. Werken 4276
Gelsenkirchen im Spiegel der Statistik (DEU) 7480
Das Geltende Seevoelkerrecht in Einzeldarstellungen (DEU ISSN 0174-1845) 4926
Geluid (NLD ISSN 0925-9406) 3433
Gem & Jewellery News see Gems & Jewellery 4566
Gem & Jewellery Yearbook (IND) 4566
Gema Jusan (IDN) 3891
➤ Gematologiya i Transfusiologiya/Hematology and Transfusiology (RUS ISSN 0234-5730) 5936
Gemeenschap van Zendings-Diaconessen in Nederland. Nieuwsbrief (NLD ISSN 1871-9694) 7644
Het Gemeenschappelijk BegeleidingsInstituut Ondernemingsraden en de Ondernemingsraad (NLD ISSN 1871-8442) 6697
Gemeente Facilitair see Weekblad Facilitair & Gebouwbeheer 1801
Gemeente-stem see De Gemeentestem 7438
Gemeentekrediet van Belgie. Driemaandelijks Tijdschrift see Credit Communal de Belgique. Bulletin Trimestriel 1333
Gemeenteleven (NLD ISSN 0016-6065) 7644
Gemeentereiniging en Afvalmanagement see G R A M 3506
• De Gemeentestem (NLD ISSN 0165-7895) 7438
Gemeentewet Actueel (NLD ISSN 1571-361X) 4952
Die Gemeinde (AUT ISSN 0021-2334) 7721
Die Gemeinde (Cologne) (DEU) 7492
Die Gemeinde (Kassel) (DEU ISSN 0016-6073) 7759
Die Gemeinde (Stuttgart) (DEU) 7438
Gemeinde Cleebronn. Mitteilungsblatt (DEU) 3849
Gemeinde Creativ (DEU ISSN 1618-8322) 7799
Gemeinde Leingarten. Amtsblatt (DEU) 3849
Gemeinde Schoenaich - Rueckspiegel (DEU) 7492
Gemeinde Talheim. Mitteilungsblatt (DEU) 3849
Gemeinde Zaberfeld. Mitteilungsblatt (DEU) 3849
Gemeindebote (AUT ISSN 0016-609X) 7492
Gemeindebrief (DEU ISSN 0936-0107) 7759
Der Gemeindehaushalt (DEU ISSN 0340-3645) 7492
Die Gemeindekasse Baden-Wuerttemberg (DEU ISSN 0174-2612) 7492
Die Gemeindekasse Bayern (DEU ISSN 0341-2245) 7492
Die Gemeindekasse Hessen, Niedersachsen, Nordrhein-Westfalen, Schleswig-Holstein (DEU ISSN 1618-7679) 7492
Gemeindekurier (AUT ISSN 0016-6146) 3797
Gemeinden Nordrhein-Westfalens (DEU) 8373
Gemeindeordnung fuer das Land Sachsen-Anhalt (DEU ISSN 0943-7878) 7438
Gemeindeordnung fuer den Freistaat Sachsen (DEU ISSN 0944-1131) 7438
† Gemeindeordnung und Amtsordnung fuer das Land Brandenburg (DEU ISSN 0942-1653) 8958
Der Gemeinderat (DEU ISSN 0723-8274) 7492
Die Gemeindeverwaltung Rheinland-Pfalz (DEU ISSN 0016-6170) 7492
Gemeinnuetzigkeit und Management see Sozialmarkt Aktuell 1794
➤ Gemeinsam Leben (DEU ISSN 0943-8394) 3062
Gemeinsames Amtsblatt des Landes Baden-Wuerttemberg (DEU ISSN 1434-4025) 7492Gemeinsames Ministerialblatt des Auswaertigen Amtes, des Bundesministers des Innern, des Bundesministers fuer Ernaehrung, Landwirtschaft und Forsten, des Bundesministers fuer Innerdeutsche Beziehungen, des Bundesministers fuer Jugend, Familie, Frauen und Gesundheit, des Bundesministers fuer Umwelt, Naturschutz und Reaktorsicherheit, des Bundesministers fuer Raumordnung, Bauwesen und Staedtebau (DEU ISSN 0939-4729) 7438
Gemeinschaft fuer Deutsche Studentengeschichte Archiv fuer Hochschul- und Studentengeschichte see G D S Archiv fuer Hochschul- und Studentengeschichte 2859
Gemeinschaft fuer Deutsche Studentengeschichte Archiv fuer Hochschul- und Studentengeschichte. Beihefte see G D S Archiv fuer Hochschul- und Studentengeschichte. Beihefte 2859
Gemeinschaftliches Sortenamt. Jahresbericht see Community Plant Variety Office. Annual Report 3411
Gemeinschafts- und Sozialkunde (DEU ISSN 0936-1111) 2190
Gemeinschafts Verpflegung Kompakt see G V Kompakt 3644
Gemengde Branche (NLD) 2041
Gemenskapens Vaxtsortsmyndighet. Aarsrapport see Community Plant Variety Office. Annual Report 3411
Gementevervoerbedryf Amsterdam Nieuws see G V B Nieuws 8958
• Gemini (NOR ISSN 0802-085X) 3193
Gemini Observatory Newsletter see GeminiFocus 575
GeminiFocus (USA ISSN 1930-9740) 575
Der Gemischtwarenhandel (DEU ISSN 0016-6243) 3678
Gemma's Homestyle Italian Cooking (USA) 3644
Gemmologie (DEU ISSN 0948-7395) 4566
Gemmology Queensland (AUS ISSN 1443-1688) 4566
Gems & Gemology (USA ISSN 0016-626X) 4566
Gems & Jewellery (GBR ISSN 1746-8043) 4566
• Gems in Israel (ISR ISSN 1527-9812) 8713
Gems of Culture and History see Wenshi Jinghua 4167
Gems of Genealogy (USA) 3767
Gems Series (GBR) 4926
Gemse (DEU) 4045
• The Gemstone Forecaster (USA) 6462
The Gemstone Forecaster Online see The Gemstone Forecaster 6462
Gemuese (DEU ISSN 0016-6286) 3733
Gemuesebau (CHE) 3733
The Gen (GBR) 3158
▼ Gen 7 (USA ISSN 1949-9248) 7518
Gen-Etik i Praksis see Bio-Etik i Praksis 6907
Gen Seven see Gen 7 7518
Gen Sheet (GBR ISSN 1749-1134) 6422
Genau (DEU ISSN 0948-4914) 7092
Genava (CHE ISSN 0072-0585) 395
Gendai (JPN) 3900
Gendai Igaku/Current Medicine (JPN ISSN 0433-3047) 5618
Gendai Kagaku/Chemistry Today (JPN ISSN 0386-961X) 2062
Gendai Kagaku. Zokan/Chemistry Today. Special Number (JPN ISSN 0910-4747) 2062
Gendai no Chuto see The Contemporary Middle East 7119
Gendai no Me (JPN ISSN 0435-219X) 6524
Gendai no Toshokan see Libraries Today 5026
Gendai Nogyo (JPN ISSN 0289-3517) 115
Gendai Ringyo/Current Forestry (JPN ISSN 0386-2321) 3691
Gendarmerie Royale du Canada. Gazette see Royal Canadian Mounted Police. Gazette (Print) 2667
Gendarmerie Royale du Canada. Gazette see Royal Canadian Mounted Police. Gazette (Online) 2667
Genden no Genkyo/Japan Atomic Power Company. Annual Report (JPN) 3167
• Gender & Behaviour (NGA ISSN 1117-7322) 7358
Gender and Culture Series (USA) 8103
• Gender and Development (GBR ISSN 1355-2074) 8897
Gender and Development Directory. Australia (AUS) 8897
• Gender and Development in Brief (GBR ISSN 1750-6425) 8103
• ➤ Gender and Education (GBR ISSN 0954-0253) 2859
• ➤ Gender and History (GBR ISSN 0953-5233) 4140
• Gender and Language (GBR ISSN 1747-6321) 5121
➤ Gender & Psychoanalysis (USA ISSN 1091-6318) 7358
• ➤ Gender & Society (USA ISSN 0891-2432) 8104
Gender Equality Magazine (LUX ISSN 1680-2144) 8865
• Gender Forum (DEU ISSN 1613-1878) 4374
• ➤ Gender in Management (GBR ISSN 1754-2413) 1747
Gender in World Religions (CAN ISSN 1183-3491) 7645
• ➤ Gender Issues (USA ISSN 1098-092X) 8898
• Gender Journal: Men and Women Working Together (USA) 1683
Gender Matters Quarterly (USA) 8865
• ➤ Gender Medicine (USA ISSN 1550-8579) 5618
• Gender Newsletter (ITA ISSN 1564-3506) 1596
• ➤ Gender, Place and Culture (GBR ISSN 0966-369X) 8898
• Gender, Rovne Prilezitosti, Vyzkum (CZE ISSN 1213-0028) 8104
Gender Studies (DEU ISSN 1612-5142) 8104
• Gender Studies and Policy Review (KOR) 8898
• ➤ Gender, Technology & Development (IND ISSN 0971-8524) 8898
• ➤ Gender, Work and Organization (GBR ISSN 0968-6673) 1747
• Gendereview (KEN ISSN 1027-9237) 8865
• ➤ Gendernye Issledovaniya (UKR ISSN 1682-3265) 340
• ➤ Genders (Online Edition) (USA ISSN 1936-3249) 340
• GenderWatch (USA) 8149
Gend'Info (FRA ISSN 1161-1715) 6422
• ➤ Gene (NLD ISSN 0378-1119) 764
Gene & Medicine see Idenshi Igaku 872
Gene - C O M B I S see Gene 764
• Gene Conserve (BRA ISSN 1808-1878) 232
• ➤ Gene Expression (USA ISSN 1052-2166) 867
• Gene Expression Patterns (NLD ISSN 1567-133X) 867
Gene Function & Disease see Comparative and Functional Genomics 729
Gene Perret's Round Table (USA) 2381
▼ ➤ Gene Regulation and Systems Biology (NZL ISSN 1177-6250) 867
Gene Regulatory Mechanisms see Biochimica et Biophysica Acta. Gene Regulatory Mechanisms 864
Gene Talk see GeneTalk 868
• ➤ Gene Therapy (Basingstoke) (GBR ISSN 0969-7128) 5618
• Gene Therapy & Molecular Biology (GRC ISSN 1529-9120) 675
• ➤ Gene Therapy and Regulation (SGP ISSN 1388-9532) 867
• Gene Therapy Business News (USA) 867
• Gene Therapy Weekly (USA ISSN 1078-2842) 5618
Geneagram (USA ISSN 8756-7989) 3767
Genealogen (NOR ISSN 0807-2191) 3767
Genealogia (USA ISSN 1096-6757) 3767
† Genealogical Computing (USA ISSN 0277-5913) 8958
Genealogical Forum of Oregon. Bulletin (USA) 3767
Genealogical Gems (USA ISSN 0882-1623) 3767
Genealogical Goldmine (USA ISSN 0738-3770) 3767
Genealogical Helper see Everton's Genealogical Helper 3765
The Genealogical Inquirer (USA ISSN 1940-1337) 3767
Genealogical Journal of Jefferson County, New York (USA ISSN 1045-8166) 3767
Genealogical Magazine of New Jersey (USA ISSN 0016-6367) 3767
Genealogical Research Directory: National & International (AUS) 3767
Genealogical Society of New Jersey Newsletter see G S N J Newsletter 3767
Genealogical Society of Okaloosa County, Florida News see G S O C News 3767
Genealogical Society of Okaloosa County. Journal (USA ISSN 0884-2086) 3767
Genealogical Society of Old Tryon County. Bulletin (USA ISSN 0092-7953) 3768
Genealogical Society of Sarasota. Newsletter (USA) 3768
Genealogical Society of Vermont. Newsletter (USA ISSN 1087-4550) 3768
Genealogical Speakers Guild. Speakers Directory (USA) 3768
Genealogie (DEU ISSN 0016-6383) 3768

Title

10318 GENEALOGIE ULRICH'S PERIODICALS

Genealogie (NLD ISSN 1381-6985) **3768**
Genealogie en Computer (BEL ISSN 0771-713X) **2419**
Genealogie Facile (FRA ISSN 1779-8701) **3768**
Genealogie Franc-Comtoise (FRA) **3768**
Genealogie Lorraine (FRA ISSN 0221-1777) **3768**
Genealogies de la Psychologie (FRA ISSN 1775-1187) **7358**
Genealogisches Handbuch des Bayerischen Adels (DEU ISSN 0085-0934) **3768**
Genealogisches Jahrbuch (DEU ISSN 0514-3292) **3768**
Genealogiska Samfundet i Finland. Skrifter *see* Suomen Sukututkimusseura. Julkaisuja **4272**
The Genealogist (AUS ISSN 0311-1776) **3768**
➤ The Genealogist (USA ISSN 0197-1468) **3768**
Genealogists' Magazine (GBR ISSN 0016-6391) **3768**
• Genealogy Bulletin (USA ISSN 1049-9571) **3768**
Genealogy Club of Albuquerque Quarterly (USA) **3768**
Genealogy Guidebook *see* Family Tree Magazine **3766**
Genealogy Workshop Bulletin (USA ISSN 1069-6210) **3768**
Genealogysk Jierboek (NLD ISSN 0928-0480) **3768**
Geneeskunde en Sport *see* Sport & Geneeskunde **6233**
Geneeskundig Adresboek Nederland (NLD ISSN 0302-864X) **5618**
Geneeskundig Jaarboek (NLD ISSN 0302-6752) **5618**
Geneesmiddelen, Zwangerschap en Borstvoeding (NLD ISSN 1871-0239) **6844**
• ➤ Geneesmiddelenbulletin (NLD ISSN 0304-4629) **6844**
• ➤ Genel Tip Dergisi (TUR) **5618**
Genera (GBR) **5422**
Generacion (ARG ISSN 0326-4378) **3791**
Generacion '83 *see* Generacion **3791**
General *see* Avalon Hill General **8160**
General Acts Affecting Arkansas Municipalities (USA ISSN 1559-9248) **4679**
General Agents and Managers Association International Journal *see* G A M A International Journal **4503**
General Agreement on Tariffs and Trade. Basic Instruments and Selected Documents Series. Supplement (CHE ISSN 0072-0623) **1567**
General American Solutions (USA) **4503**
➤ General and Applied Entomology (AUS ISSN 0158-0760) **848**
• ➤ General and Applied Plant Physiology (BGR ISSN 1312-8183) **3733**
• ➤ General and Comparative Endocrinology (USA ISSN 0016-6480) **5893**
• General Anthropology (USA ISSN 1537-1727) **340**
General Anti-avoidance Rule Interpreted *see* G A A R Interpreted **1349**
General-Anzeiger (DEU) **3849**
General Aviation Aircraft Shipment Report (USA) **8541**
General Aviation Business Report (USA ISSN 1529-8841) **8542**
General Aviation News (USA ISSN 1536-8513) **56**
General Aviation Statistical Databook (USA) **8524**
General Conference of the New Church. Yearbook (GBR ISSN 0072-0666) **7736**
General Conference of Weights and Measures *see* Conference Generale des Poids et Mesures. Comptes Rendus des Seances **6401**
General Counsel California *see* G C California **4678**
General Counsel Mid-Atlantic *see* G C Mid-Atlantic **4678**
General Counsel New England *see* G C New England **4678**
General Counsel New York *see* G C New York **4678**
• General Dental Council. Dentists Register (GBR ISSN 0072-0674) **5845**
General Dental Council. Minutes of the Proceedings (GBR ISSN 0072-0682) **5845**
➤ General Dentistry (USA ISSN 0363-6771) **5845**
General Directory of the Perfume and Cosmetic Industry *see* Guide International des Fournisseurs de la Beaute **8960**
General Economics & Future Studies *see* Source O E C D. General Economics & Future Studies **1177**
General Education Development en Espanol *see* G E D en Espanol **2941**
General Educational Development Basics *see* G E D Basics **2941**
General Educational Development Items *see* G E D Items **2941**
General Educator (GBR) **2982**
General Espanola de Seguros Boletin de Informacion *see* G E S Boletin de Informacion **4503**
General Federation of Women's Clubs Clubwoman *see* G F W C Clubwoman **2266**
General Federation of Women's Clubs of Minnesota, Inc. of Minnesota News *see* G F W C of Minnesota News **2266**
General Fisheries Commission for the Mediterranean (USA ISSN 1020-7236) **3595**
General Fisheries Commission for the Mediterranean. Studies and Reviews (USA ISSN 1020-9549) **3595**
General - Flag Officer Worldwide Roster (USA ISSN 1058-0131) **6422**
General Guidebook on Industrial Safety (JPN) **6677**
General History of the Caribbean (FRA) **4293**
• ➤ General Hospital Psychiatry (USA ISSN 0163-8343) **6143**
General Household Survey *see* Great Britain. General Household Survey **7307**
General Information Concerning Patents (USA ISSN 0160-9491) **6750**
General Information Program - U N I S I S T Newsletter (UNESCO Programme of International Cooperation in Scientific and Technological Information) (FRA ISSN 0379-2218) **5010**
General Insurance (GBR ISSN 0953-2749) **4503**
General Insurance in Japan. Fact Book (JPN) **4503**
• General Insurance in Korea (KOR) **4503**
General Insurance in Korea Factbook *see* General Insurance in Korea **4503**
General Insurance Market Assessment *see* Key Note Market Assessment. General Insurance **4511**
† General Insurance Outlook (GBR ISSN 1361-9756) **8958**
General Knowledge Digest *see* Dogar's General Knowledge Digest **7130**
• General Laws of Massachusetts (USA) **4952**
➤ General Linguistics (USA ISSN 0016-6553) **5121**
• ➤ General Mathematics (ROM ISSN 1221-5023) **5490**
General Medical Council. Annual Review (GBR ISSN 1464-9853) **5618**
• General Medical Council. Medical Register (GBR ISSN 0072-0763) **5618**
General Medical Council. Minutes (GBR) **5618**
General Medicine *see* Obshta Meditsina **5689**
General Merchandise Distributors Council. Marketing Conference Transcripts (USA) **6280**
General Minutes of the Annual Conferences of the United Methodist Church *see* United Methodist Church. General Minutes of the Annual Conferences **7778**
General Motors Corporation Directions *see* G M C Directions **8581**
General Motors High Tech Performance *see* G M High Tech Performance **8581**
General Motors Research Laboratories Symposia Series (USA) **8582**
General Municipal Boilermakers and Allied Trades Union Direct *see* G M B Direct **4594**
• ➤ General Music Today (Online) (USA ISSN 1931-3756) **6569**
General Ophthalmology *see* Vaughan & Asbury's General Ophthalmology **6052**
General Partners Management Report *see* G P Management Report **1747**
➤ General Physiology and Biophysics (SVK ISSN 0231-5882) **922**
General Practice Gazette *see* G P Gazette **4678**
General Practice News *see* G P News **4678**
• ➤ General Practice On-Line (GBR ISSN 1359-7639) **5618**
General Practice Section Gazette *see* G P Gazette **4678**
General Practice Section Newsletter *see* One on One (Albany) **4753**
General Practice Solo *see* G P Solo **4678**
• General Practice Update (GBR ISSN 1753-9773) **5619**
General Practitioner *see* Prakticky Lekar **5699**
General Practitioner *see* G P **5617**
General Practitioner Research Review *see* G P Research Review **5617**
General Practitioner's Sourcebook (CAN ISSN 0844-1138) **5619**
• ➤ General Relativity and Gravitation (USA ISSN 0001-7701) **7014**
General Report on the Activities of the European Communities (LUX ISSN 0259-3963) **1488**
General Report on the Activities of the European Union (LUX ISSN 1608-7321) **3837**
General Requirements for Applications in Commercial Offset Lithography *see* Graphic Arts Monthly **7322**
General Review of The Communist Party of China *see* Dangshi Bolan **7128**
• General Science Abstracts (USA ISSN 1092-1443) **7937**
• General Science Abstracts - Full Text (USA) **7937**
• General Science Index (USA ISSN 0162-1963) **7937**
General Semantics Bulletin (USA ISSN 0072-0771) **5121**
General Services Administration Supply Catalog *see* G S A Supply Catalog **7438**
General Social Surveys (USA ISSN 0161-3340) **8149**
General Store Magazine (USA) **8713**
General Structures (USA ISSN 1935-0325) **443**
General Structures. Questions & Answers (USA ISSN 1935-035X) **443**
General Stud Book (GBR ISSN 0072-078X) **8291**
General Studies Newsletter (USA) **2285**
• General Surgery Coder's Pink Sheet (USA ISSN 1941-840X) **6244**
• General Surgery Coding Alert (USA ISSN 1526-0356) **4503**
• General Surgery News (USA ISSN 1099-4122) **6244**
• General Systems Bulletin (GBR ISSN 0016-6588) **7857**
General Systems, International Journal *see* International Journal of General Systems **2522**
General Technical Report P S W *see* U.S. Department of Agriculture Forest Service. Pacific Southwest Research Station. General Technical Report P S W **3706**
General Technical Report R M R S *see* U S D A Forest Service. Rocky Mountain Research Station. General Technical Report **3705**
General Technical Report S R S (USA) **3691**
General Telephone & Electronics Network Systems World-Wide Communications Journal *see* G T E Network Systems World-Wide Communications Journal **2350**
• General Thoracic and Cardiovascular Surgery (JPN ISSN 1863-6705) **6244**
General Treaty for Central American Economic Integration. Permanent Secretariat. Newsletter (GTM ISSN 0553-6898) **1596**
General Urology *see* Smith's General Urology **6274**
General Wage Determinations Issued Under the Davis-Bacon and Related Acts: Volume 1 (USA) **1683**
General Wage Determinations Issued Under the Davis-Bacon and Related Acts: Volume 2 (USA) **1683**
General Wage Determinations Issued Under the Davis-Bacon and Related Acts: Volume 3 (USA) **1683**
General Wage Determinations Issued Under the Davis-Bacon and Related Acts: Volume 4 (USA) **1683**
General Wage Determinations Issued Under the Davis-Bacon and Related Acts: Volume 5 (USA) **1683**
General Wage Determinations Issued Under the Davis-Bacon and Related Acts: Volume 6 (USA) **1683**
General Wage Determinations Issued Under the Davis-Bacon and Related Acts: Volume 7 (USA) **1683**
† Generalanzeiger (DEU) **8959**
Generalanzeiger *see* General-Anzeiger **3849**
Generale Bank. Bulletin (BEL) **1349**
Generale Bank. Report (BEL) **1349**
Generale des Carrieres et des Mines. Monographie (COD) **6462**
Generale des Carrieres et des Mines Rapport Annuel *see* G E C A M I N E S Rapport Annuel **6462**
† Generali-Lloyd-Versicherungen. News (DEU) **8959**
Le Generaliste (BEL ISSN 0777-7426) **5619**
† • Generalitat de Catalunya. Diari Oficial (Catalan Edition) (ESP ISSN 0213-3539) **8959**
Generalitat de Catalunya. Diari Oficial (Spanish Edition) *see* Generalitat de Catalunya. Diari Oficial (Catalan Edition) **8959**
• Generalitat Valenciana. Diari Oficial (ESP ISSN 0212-8195) **7493**
Generally Accepted Accounting Practice. A South African Viewpoint (Student Edition) (ZAF) **1289**
Generally Accepted Accounting Principles Guide Level A *see* G A A P Guide Level A **1289**
Generally Accepted Accounting Principles Handbook of Policies and Procedures *see* G A A P Handbook of Policies and Procedures **1289**
Generally Accepted Auditing Standards Guide *see* Miller G A A S Guide **1296**
• Generating Availability Report (Year) (USA ISSN 1072-2017) **3158**
• Generating Unit Statistics (Year) (USA) **3158**
Generation (FRA ISSN 1766-0246) **3535**
Generation 125 (FRA ISSN 1286-3661) **8259**
Generation After (USA) **4140**
Generation Camping Car (FRA ISSN 1953-650X) **8582**
Generation Cent-Vingt-Cinq *see* Generation 125 **8259**
Generation Speed (USA ISSN 1542-7870) **8175**
Generation, Transmission and Distribution *see* I E T Generation, Transmission and Distribution **3317**
Generation Urbaine (FRA ISSN 1952-0298) **8104**
• Generation Woman (USA) **8865**
Generations (Fredericton) (CAN ISSN 0821-5359) **3768**
• ➤ Generations (San Francisco) (USA ISSN 0738-7806) **4045**
Generations (Wayzata) (USA) **6143**
Generations (Winnipeg) (CAN ISSN 0226-6105) **3768**
Generations Femme (FRA ISSN 1638-7929) **7799**
• Generations Review (GBR ISSN 0965-2000) **4045**
Generative Grammar in Geneva (CHE) **5121**
Generator (USA ISSN 0896-7431) **5422**
Generazioni (ITA ISSN 1825-7631) **6697**
• Generic Companies Analysis (GBR ISSN 1746-7829) **6844**
• Generic Line (USA ISSN 1076-884X) **6844**
Generic Rx Product Report (USA) **6844**
Generics Bulletin (GBR ISSN 1742-0784) **6844**
▼ Generique(s) (FRA ISSN 1956-7049) **2381**
Genero (SRB ISSN 1451-2203) **8898**
Genero y Sociedad (DOM) **7966**
Genes (USA ISSN 1462-6438) **867**
• ➤ Genes & Development (USA ISSN 0890-9369) **867**
• Genes and Environment/Environmental Mutagen Research (JPN) **867**
• ➤ Genes & Genetic Systems (JPN ISSN 1341-7568) **867**
➤ Genes and Genomics/Han'gug Yujeon Haghoeji (KOR ISSN 1976-9571) **867**
• ➤ Genes and Immunity (GBR ISSN 1466-4879) **868**
• ➤ Genes & Nutrition (DEU ISSN 1555-8932) **868**
• ➤ Genes, Brain and Behavior (DNK ISSN 1601-1848) **868**
• ➤ Genes, Chromosomes & Cancer (USA ISSN 1045-2257) **868**
▼ Genes, Genomes and Genomics (GBR ISSN 1749-0383) **868**
• ➤ Genes to Cells (GBR ISSN 1356-9597) **868**
Genesee Country (USA ISSN 1080-9805) **4293**
• Geneses (FRA ISSN 1155-3219) **7966**
Genesis (FRA ISSN 1167-5101) **5299**
• Genesis (ITA ISSN 1594-9281) **8865**
Genesis (Paramus) (USA) **6291**
Genesis ... a Caravan (IND ISSN 0973-3043) **1747**
• Genesis Report - M Cx (USA) **5619**
• ➤ Genesis: The Journal of Genetics and Development (USA ISSN 1526-954X) **868**
GeneTalk (USA) **868**
Genetic Algorithms and Evolutionary Computation *see* Genetic and Evolutionary Computation **868**
• Genetic and Evolutionary Computation (USA ISSN 1932-0167) **868**
➤ Genetic Counseling (CHE ISSN 1015-8146) **868**
Genetic Disorder (USA) **5217**
• Genetic Drift (USA) **868**
➤ Genetic Engineering (USA ISSN 0196-3716) **764**
• Genetic Engineering and Biotechnology News (USA ISSN 1935-472X) **868**
Genetic Engineering News *see* Genetic Engineering and Biotechnology News **868**
• ➤ Genetic Epidemiology (USA ISSN 0741-0395) **869**
Genetic Epistemologist (USA ISSN 0740-9583) **7358**
• ➤ Genetic Programming and Evolvable Machines (USA ISSN 1389-2576) **2448**
• ➤ Genetic Resources and Crop Evolution (NLD ISSN 0925-9864) **869**
Genetic Resources Communication (AUS ISSN 0159-6071) **232**
• Genetic Technology News (USA ISSN 0272-9032) **869**
Genetic Testing *see* Genetic Testing and Molecular Biomarkers **869**
• ➤ Genetic Testing and Molecular Biomarkers (USA ISSN 1945-0265) **869**
Genetic Testing and Molecular Biomarkers (Online) *see* Genetic Testing and Molecular Biomarkers **869**
• ➤ Genetic Vaccines and Therapy (GBR ISSN 1479-0556) **869**
• ➤ Genetica (NLD ISSN 0016-6707) **869**
Genetical Research *see* Genetics Research **870**
Genetically Modified Crops *see* G M Crops **232**
• ➤ Genetics (USA ISSN 0016-6731) **869**
• Genetics Abstracts (USA ISSN 0016-674X) **716**
Genetics and Breeding (BGR) **869**
• Genetics & Environmental Business Week (USA ISSN 1552-5651) **1113**
Genetics and Environmental Business Week *see* Genetics & Environmental Business Week **1113**
• Genetics & Environmental Health Week (USA ISSN 1552-2547) **869**
Genetics and Environmental Health Week *see* Genetics & Environmental Health Week **869**
• Genetics & Environmental Law Weekly (USA ISSN 1551-5095) **869**
Genetics and Environmental Law Weekly *see* Genetics & Environmental Law Weekly **869**
Genetics and Genetic Engineering *see* Information Plus Reference Series. Genetics and Genetic Engineering **872**
• ➤ Genetics and Molecular Biology (BRA ISSN 1415-4757) **869**
• ➤ Genetics and Molecular Research (BRA ISSN 1676-5680) **869**
• ➤ Genetics In Medicine (USA ISSN 1098-3600) **870**
Genetics Law Monitor (GBR ISSN 1471-3624) **870**
Genetics Newsletter/Genetika Nuusbrief (ZAF ISSN 0259-0301) **870**
• ➤ Genetics Research (GBR ISSN 0016-6723) **870**
Genetics Resource Book *see* The Australasian Genetics Resource Book **713**
• ➤ Genetics Selection Evolution (GBR ISSN 0999-193X) **870**
Genetics Society. Newsletter (GBR) **870**
Genetics Society of Canada Bulletin (CAN ISSN 0316-4357) **870**
Genetics Society of Japan. Abstracts of the Annual Meeting/Nihon Iden Gakkai Taikai Puroguramu Yokoshu (JPN) **716**
• Genetika (RUS ISSN 0016-6758) **870**
Genetika *see* Acta Biologica Iugoslavica. Serija F: Genetika **861**
Genetika Nuusbrief *see* Genetics Newsletter **870**
Geneva International Peace Research Institute. Cahiers (FRA ISSN 1954-9229) **7237**
• Geneva Lakes Area Visitors Guide (USA) **8713**
Geneva News and International Report (CHE) **3958**
• ➤ Geneva Papers on Risk and Insurance - Issues and Practice (GBR ISSN 1018-5895) **4503**
The Geneva Post Quarterly (CHE ISSN 1422-2248) **7237**
Geneva Reporter (CHE) **7237**
Geneva Reports on the World Economy (GBR ISSN 1607-8616) **1488**
• ➤ The Geneva Risk and Insurance Review (USA ISSN 1554-964X) **4503**
Geneve Home Informations (CHE) **3958**
Geneve le Mensuel (CHE ISSN 1421-1343) **3958**

Geneve. Office Cantonal de la Statistique. Bulletin Statistique Mensuel (CHE ISSN 1423-1387) **8373**
Genevieve (NGA ISSN 1596-6844) **3920**
➤ Genewatch (USA ISSN 0740-9737) **870**
Gengo Bunka/Doshisha Studies in Language and Culture (JPN ISSN 1344-1418) **5121**
Gengo Bunka Ronkyu (JPN ISSN 1341-0032) **5121**
Gengo Kenkyu *see* Linguistic Society of Japan. Journal **5146**
Gengo Sentau Kouhou *see* Language Studies **5141**
Gengo to Bunka/Language and Culture (JPN ISSN 1345-1642) **5121**
Gengo to Bunka (Nishinomiya)/Language and Culture (JPN ISSN 1343-8530) **5121**
• ➤ Gengo to Kyoiku no Kenkyu/Journal of Japanese Language Teaching (JPN ISSN 0912-6015) **3062**
Genie (USA) **3768**
Le Genie des Biosystemes au Canada *see* Canadian Biosystems Engineering **210**
† Genie Educatif (FRA ISSN 1162-6496) **8959**
† Genie Logiciel (FRA ISSN 1265-1397) **8959**
Geniessen & Mehr (DEU ISSN 1861-2601) **3849**
Genieten (BEL ISSN 1374-7002) **5072**
Genii (USA ISSN 0016-6855) **4335**
Genii Ortopedii (RUS ISSN 1028-4427) **6060**
Genike Ekthese epi tes Drasteriotetas tes Europaikes Enoses *see* General Report on the Activities of the European Union **3837**
Genio Rurale *see* Estimo e Territorio **229**
Genki (JPN) **2190**
Genocidas ir Rezistencija (LTU ISSN 1392-3463) **4223**
• ➤ Genocide Studies and Prevention (CAN ISSN 1911-0359) **340**
• ➤ Genome (CAN ISSN 0831-2796) **870**
• ➤ Genome Biology (Online) (GBR ISSN 1474-760X) **675**
† • ➤ Genome Biology (Print) (GBR ISSN 1474-7596) **8959**
• ➤ Genome Dynamics (CHE ISSN 1660-9263) **870**
Genome Informatics Workshop. Proceedings (JPN ISSN 0919-9454) **870**
Genome Letters (Print Edition) *see* Journal of Genome Science and Technology (Print Edition) **874**
▼ • ➤ Genome Medicine (GBR) **5619**
Genome Medicine *see* Genomu Igaku **5619**
• ➤ Genome Research (USA ISSN 1088-9051) **870**
• Genome Technology (USA ISSN 1530-7107) **764**
GenomeBiology.com (Online) *see* Genome Biology (Online) **675**
Genomic Medicine *see* The H U G O Journal **5622**
† Genomic Proteomic Technology (USA ISSN 1544-6778) **8959**
• ➤ Genomics (USA ISSN 0888-7543) **870**
• Genomics & Genetics Weekly (USA ISSN 1531-6467) **871**
Genomics and Genetics Weekly *see* Genomics & Genetics Weekly **871**
• Genomics & Proteomics (USA ISSN 1536-7495) **764**
Genomics and Proteomics *see* Genomics & Proteomics **764**
• Genomics - Based Drug Data Report Regenerative Therapy (ESP ISSN 1579-0363) **871**
Genomics Investing (USA ISSN 1535-2420) **1626**
• Genomics Proteomics & Bioinformatics (GBR ISSN 1672-0229) **871**
• ➤ Genomics, Society and Policy (GBR ISSN 1746-5354) **871**
Genomu Igaku/Genome Medicine (JPN ISSN 1346-4671) **5619**
Genootschap Amstelodamum. Jaarboek (NLD ISSN 0923-0254) **4223**
Genos (FIN ISSN 0016-6898) **3768**
Genossenschaften in Baden (DEU ISSN 1432-4369) **1349**
Genossenschaftliches Mitteilungsblatt Weser-Ems *see* Genossenschafts-Magazin Weser-Ems **1349**
Genossenschafts-Handbuch (DEU ISSN 0933-9477) **1423**
Genossenschafts-Kurier (DEU ISSN 0947-0115) **1747**
Genossenschafts-Magazin Weser-Ems (DEU ISSN 1610-630X) **1349**
Genossenschaftsblatt (DEU ISSN 1433-4267) **1349**
Genous, First Peoples Art of Canada (CAN ISSN 1488-1063) **491**
➤ Genre (Norman) (USA ISSN 0016-6928) **5299**
Le Genre Human (FRA ISSN 0293-0277) **4453**
† • Genre Magazine (USA ISSN 1074-5246) **8959**
• The Genre Traveler (USA ISSN 1557-7198) **5299**
Genreflecting Advisory Series (USA) **5299**
• Genryu (JPN ISSN 1345-3610) **7857**
Des Gens Constructifs/Constructive People (CAN ISSN 1910-8869) **3193**
Gens-Dunia (NLD ISSN 1872-390X) **3768**
Gens Nostra, "Ons Geslacht" (NLD ISSN 0016-6936) **3768**
Gensan Monthly (JPN) **3167**
Gensan Nenji Taikai Ronbun Kopishu/Japan Atomic Industrial Forum. Conference (JPN) **3167**
Gensei/Entomological Society of Kochi. Journal (JPN ISSN 0433-3950) **848**
Gensei Dobutsugaku Zasshi/Japanese Journal of Protozoology (JPN ISSN 0388-3752) **944**
Genshi Nenryo Saikuru Shisetsu Kankyo Hoshasento Jizen Chosa Hokokusho/Report of Environmental Radiology of Nuclear Fuel Cycle Facilities (JPN) **3506**
Genshi Shototsu Sakyura/Society for Atomic Collision Research. Circular (JPN ISSN 0912-4063) **7066**
Genshikaku Kenkyu/Nuclear Study (JPN ISSN 0367-4169) **7066**
Genshiro Jikkenjo Dayori/Research Reactor Institute. News (JPN ISSN 0915-4418) **7066**
Genshiryoku Anzen Hakusho/White Paper of Nuclear Safety (JPN) **7066**
Genshiryoku Anzen Iinkai Geppo/Nuclear Safety Commission. Monthly Report (JPN ISSN 0387-9674) **7066**
Genshiryoku Anzensei Kenkyu no Genjo/Progress of Nuclear Safety Research (JPN) **7066**
➤ Genshiryoku Bakku Endo Kenkyu/Journal of Nuclear Fuel Cycle and Environment (JPN ISSN 1343-4446) **3167**
Genshiryoku Dayori Kagoshima/Kagoshima Nuclear Power News (JPN) **3167**
Genshiryoku Dayori Miyagi/Miyagi Nuclear Power News (JPN) **3167**
Genshiryoku Eye/Genshiryoku Kogyo (JPN ISSN 1343-3563) **3167**
Genshiryoku Hakusho/White Paper of Atomic Energy (JPN) **3167**
Genshiryoku Hatsuden (JPN ISSN 0433-4000) **3167**
Genshiryoku Hatsudensho *see* Nuclear Power Plants in the World **3172**
Genshiryoku Iinkai Geppo/Atomic Energy Commission. Journal (JPN ISSN 0433-4019) **3167**
Genshiryoku Kaigai Information (JPN) **7066**
Genshiryoku Kogaku Kenkyu Shisetsu Nenpo/Nuclear Engineering Research Laboratory. Annual Report (JPN) **3167**
Genshiryoku Kogyo *see* Genshiryoku Eye **3167**
Genshiryoku Koho Sendai/Sendai Nuclear Power News (JPN) **3167**
Genshiryoku Nenkan/Nuclear Almanac (JPN) **3167**
Genshiryoku Nyusu/Atomic Energy News (JPN) **3167**
Genshiryoku Riyo Jisseki Hokoku/Rikkyo University. Institute for Atomic Energy. Annual Report of Reactor Facilities (JPN) **7066**
Genshiryoku Seisaku. Joho Fairu Circular (JPN ISSN 0913-8609) **3167**
Genshiryoku Shiryo/Nuclear Power Information (JPN ISSN 0387-0928) **3167**
Genshiryoku Shiryo Johoshitsu Tsushin/Citizens' Nuclear Information Center News (JPN) **3168**
Genshiryoku Sogo Shinpojiumu Yokoshu/National Symposium on Atomic Energy. Proceedings (JPN) **3168**
• Gente (ARG ISSN 0328-8560) **3791**
Gente (ITA ISSN 0016-6944) **3897**
Gente (MEX ISSN 0016-6952) **3909**
• Gente (PER ISSN 1605-3133) **3927**
Gente de Aztlan (USA) **3535**
Gente de Minnesota (USA) **3535**
Gente Enigmistica (ITA ISSN 1592-5013) **8175**
Gente Libre (ESP) **3952**
† Gente Mese (ITA ISSN 0393-7941) **8959**
† Gente Money (ITA ISSN 0393-7925) **8959**
Gente Motori (ITA ISSN 0393-7860) **8582**
• Gente Sur (MEX) **1488**
Gente Viaggi (ITA ISSN 0393-7895) **8713**
Gente Viaggi Collection (ITA ISSN 1720-1624) **8713**
• Gentes (ITA ISSN 0016-6960) **7645**
Genti e Provincie d'Italia (ITA ISSN 1828-8243) **8104**
• Gentleman (IND) **5072**
Gentleman (ITA ISSN 1722-2222) **6291**
Gentleman (Dutch Edition) (BEL ISSN 1783-3086) **6291**
Gentleman (French Edition) (BEL ISSN 1783-3094) **6291**
Gentlemen Drivers (FRA ISSN 1950-4616) **8582**
Gentlemen's Quarterly (British Edition) *see* G Q (British Edition) **6291**
Gentlemen's Quarterly (French Edition) *see* G Q (French Edition) **6291**
Gentlemen's Quarterly (Milano) *see* G Q (Milano) **6291**
Gentlemen's Quarterly (Moscow) *see* G Q (Moscow) **6291**
Gentlemen's Quarterly (Munich) *see* G Q (Munich) **6291**
Gentlemen's Quarterly (New York) *see* G Q (New York) **6291**
Gentlemen's Quarterly (Spanish Edition) *see* G Q (Spanish Edition) **6291**
Gentlemen's Quarterly Active *see* G Q Active **6291**
Gentlemen's Quarterly Australia *see* G Q Australia **6291**
Gentlemen's Quarterly Cars *see* G Q Cars **8958**
Gentlemen's Quarterly Cars *see* G Q Cars **8581**
Gentlemen's Quarterly Style *see* G Q Style **6291**
Gentlemen's Quarterly Style *see* G Q Style **2255**
Gentry Magazine (USA ISSN 1545-7664) **3976**
• ➤ Gentse Bijdragen tot de Interieurgeschiedenis (BEL ISSN 1780-7212) **491**
Gentse Bijdragen tot de Kunstgeschiedenis *see* Gentse Bijdragen tot de Interieurgeschiedenis **491**
Genus (POL ISSN 0867-1710) **791**
Genus (SWE ISSN 1403-8943) **8898**
• Genus (Online) (ITA ISSN 2035-5556) **7283**
Genus (Print) *see* Genus (Online) **7283**
Genus: Gender in Modern Culture (NLD ISSN 1568-1602) **8104**
Genusperspektiv (SWE ISSN 1652-3768) **8865**
▼ • Genusstudier vid Mittuniversitetet (SWE ISSN 1654-5753) **8104**
Genys (LTU ISSN 0132-649X) **2190**
Geo (CZE ISSN 1801-3201) **4007**
• Geo (DEU ISSN 0342-8311) **3433**
Geo (ESP ISSN 0213-7755) **3952**
▼ Geo (FIN ISSN 1797-3600) **4007**
• Geo (FRA ISSN 0220-8245) **4007**
Geo (HRV ISSN 1845-7681) **4007**
Geo (HUN ISSN 1787-2723) **4007**
Geo (ITA ISSN 1826-8307) **4007**
Geo (ROM) **4007**
Geo (RUS ISSN 1029-5828) **3433**
Geo (SVK ISSN 1336-8001) **4007**
Geo (SVN ISSN 1854-4479) **8713**
Geo (TUR) **4007**
• GEO (Godmanchester) (GBR ISSN 1748-5487) **4037**
Geo Ado (FRA ISSN 1634-3956) **4007**
Geo.Alp (AUT ISSN 1824-7741) **6725**
Geo - Archeologia (ITA ISSN 0390-2196) **395**
• Geo.br (BRA ISSN 1519-5708) **2735**
Geo.br (English Edition) *see* Geo.br **2735**
Geo.brief (NLD ISSN 1876-231X) **2735**
GEO: Connexion *see* GEO (Godmanchester) **4037**
Geo-Eco-Trop (BEL ISSN 1370-6071) **675**
Geo Epoche (DEU ISSN 1861-6097) **4140**
Geo Focus (RUS ISSN 1814-5000) **4007**
Geo Histoire (FRA ISSN 1956-7855) **4140**
Geo Hors-Serie *see* Geo **4007**
Geo-Information Science *see* Diqiu Xinxi Kexue **2705**
Geo - Informations - Systeme *see* G I S Business **2722**
Geo Kompakt (DEU ISSN 1614-6913) **7857**
Geo Lenok (RUS) **2190**
Geo Lino (DEU) **2190**
Geo Lino Extra (DEU) **2190**
• ➤ Geo-Marine Letters (DEU ISSN 0276-0460) **2735**
† Geo Media (ITA ISSN 1128-8132) **8959**
Geo-Oeko (DEU ISSN 1616-0983) **4007**
Geo Plein-Air (CAN ISSN 1194-5303) **8315**
Geo Saison (DEU ISSN 0946-8773) **8713**
Geo Saison fuer Geniesser (DEU) **8713**
• ➤ Geo-Spatial Information Science/Diqiu Kongjian Xinxi Kexue Xuebao (Yingwenban) (CHN ISSN 1009-5020) **4007**
Geo Special (DEU ISSN 0723-5194) **4007**
Geo Traveller (RUS ISSN 1814-5140) **4007**
Geo - U N A M (Universidad Nacional Autonoma de Mexico) (MEX ISSN 0188-8064) **4008**
Geo Wissen (DEU ISSN 0933-9736) **4008**
• Geo World (USA ISSN 1528-6274) **4037**
Geoacta (ARG ISSN 0326-7237) **2707**
GeoActa (ITA ISSN 1721-8039) **2707**
Geoactive (GBR ISSN 0956-0629) **4008**
• ➤ Geoadria (HRV ISSN 1331-2294) **4008**
➤ GeoArabia (BHR ISSN 1025-6059) **6771**
GeoArabia Special Publication *see* GeoArabia **6771**
• ➤ Geoarchaeology (USA ISSN 0883-6353) **395**
GEOBASE *see* Oceanographic Literature Review **2720**
GEOBASE *see* Geographical Abstracts: Physical Geography **4036**
GEOBASE *see* Geomechanics Abstracts **2719**
GEOBASE *see* Geological Abstracts **2719**
GEOBASE *see* Ecological Abstracts **715**
GEOBASE *see* International Development Abstracts **4036**
GEOBASE *see* Geographical Abstracts: Human Geography **4035**
• ➤ Geobiology (GBR ISSN 1472-4677) **2735**
• ➤ Geobios (FRA ISSN 0016-6995) **6725**
➤ Geobios (IND ISSN 0251-1223) **675**
Geobios. Memoire Speciale *see* Geobios **6725**
Geobios New Reports (IND ISSN 0253-3340) **675**
GeoBIT *see* G I S Business **2722**
Geobotanical Institute E T H. Bulletin (CHE ISSN 1420-6803) **791**
Geobotanisches Institut E T H, Stiftung Ruebel, Zurich. Veroeffentlichungen (CHE ISSN 0254-9433) **791**
Geobotany *see* Plant and Vegetation **2762**
Geobulletin *see* Geological Society of South Africa. Geobulletin **2739**
• Geobuzon (CRI ISSN 1409-4851) **2735**
Geocarrefour (FRA ISSN 1627-4873) **4008**
• ➤ Geocarto International (GBR ISSN 1010-6049) **4008**
Geochemica *see* Diqiu Huaxue **2731**
• ➤ Geochemical Journal (JPN ISSN 0016-7002) **2707**
• The Geochemical News (USA) **2735**
Geochemical Society of India. Journal (IND ISSN 0368-2323) **2735**
Geochemical Society of Japan. Abstracts of Reports on Annual Meeting *see* Nihon Chikyu Kagakkai Nenkai Koen Yoshishu **2720**
Geochemical Society of Japan. News *see* Nihon Chikyu Kagakkai Nyusu **2714**
• Geochemical Society. Special Publication (USA ISSN 1873-9881) **2735**
• ➤ Geochemical Transactions (GBR ISSN 1467-4866) **2708**
Geochemistry *see* Chemie der Erde / Geochemistry **2728**
Geochemistry *see* Chikyu Kagaku **2704**
• ➤ Geochemistry: Exploration, Environment, Analysis (GBR ISSN 1467-7873) **2735**
• ➤ Geochemistry International (RUS ISSN 0016-7029) **2708**
• ➤ Geochimica et Cosmochimica Acta (GBR ISSN 0016-7037) **2735**
• Geochimica et Cosmochimica Acta. Supplement (GBR ISSN 0046-564X) **2735**
Geochronique (FRA ISSN 0292-8477) **2735**
• ➤ Geochronometria (POL ISSN 1733-8387) **7857**
➤ Geociencias (BRA ISSN 0101-9082) **2708**
Geociencias (PRT ISSN 0871-3529) **2736**
GeoConnections. Annual Report (CAN ISSN 1912-8290) **4008**
Geocosmic Journal (USA) **566**
Geocritica *see* Scripta Nova **4028**
Geodaesie (DEU ISSN 1438-4566) **3267**
• Geodate (Online) (AUS) **4008**
Geodate (Print) *see* Geodate (Online) **4008**
Geode (USA) **2285**
Geodemos (ARG ISSN 0328-0527) **4008**
• ➤ Geoderma (NLD ISSN 0016-7061) **232**
Geodesia (NLD ISSN 1385-7517) **4008**
• Geodesia Online (BRA ISSN 1415-1111) **2736**
Geodesy and Carthography *see* Geodezja i Kartografia **2781**
Geodesy and Cartography *see* Geodezia es Kartografia **4008**
Geodesy and Cartography *see* Geodezija ir Kartografija **4008**
Geodetic Society of Japan. Journal *see* Sokuchi Gakkaishi **4029**
Geodeticky a Kartograficky Obzor (CZE ISSN 0016-7096) **4008**
Geodetska Sluzba (SRB ISSN 1451-0561) **4008**
➤ Geodetski List (HRV ISSN 0016-710X) **2708**
• Geodetski Vestnik (SVN ISSN 0351-0271) **2781**
Geodetski Zurnal (SRB ISSN 1451-2602) **4008**
Geodezia es Kartografia/Geodesy and Cartography (HUN ISSN 0016-7118) **4008**
Geodezija ir Kartografija/Geodesy and Cartography (LTU ISSN 1392-1541) **4008**
Geodeziya, Aeros'emka, Kartografiya: Sostoyanie i Perspektivy Razvitiya Tsifrovogo Kartografii (RUS ISSN 0201-5137) **2781**
Geodeziya i Kartografiya (RUS ISSN 0016-7126) **2781**
Geodeziya, Topografiya, Kartografiya. Seriya: Distantsionnoe Zondirovanie Zemli dlya Ekologii i Prirodopol'zovaniya (RUS ISSN 0201-890X) **2781**
Geodeziya, Topografiya, Kartografiya. Seriya: Distantsionnoe Zondirovanie Zemli v Raionakh Slozhnykh Ekologicheskikh Situatsii (RUS) **2781**
Geodeziya, Topografiya, Kartografiya. Seriya: Geodeziya, Topografiya, Fototopografiya (RUS ISSN 0869-6802) **2781**
Geodeziya, Topografiya, Kartografiya. Seriya: Kartografiya i Geograficheskie Informatsionnye Sistemy (RUS ISSN 0202-6619) **2781**
Geodeziya, Topografiya, Kartografiya. Seriya: Prikladnaya Geodeziya (RUS) **2781**
➤ Geodezja (POL ISSN 1234-6608) **6462**
Geodezja i Kartografia/Geodesy and Carthography (POL ISSN 0016-7134) **2781**
• ➤ Geodinamica Acta (FRA ISSN 0985-3111) **2736**
Geodiversitas *see* Museum National d'Histoire Naturelle. Geodiversitas **2756**
Geodrilling International (GBR ISSN 0969-3769) **3267**
† • ➤ Geodynamics Series (USA ISSN 0277-6669) **8959**
Geoecological Research (DEU ISSN 0170-3250) **2708**
• Geoecomarina (ROM ISSN 1224-6808) **2736**
• Geoekologiya, Inzhenernaya Geologiya, Gidrogeologiya, Geokriologiya (RUS ISSN 0869-7809) **2736**
• Geoensenanza (VEN ISSN 1316-6077) **2859**
Geofile (GBR ISSN 0267-7563) **4008**
Geofisica Colombiana *see* Earth Sciences Research Journal **2780**
Geofisica dell'Ambiente e del Territorio (ITA) **2781**
• ➤ Geofisica Internacional (MEX ISSN 0016-7169) **2781**
Geofizicheskii Byulleten' *see* Geophysical Transactions **2782**
Geofizicheskii Zhurnal/Journal of Geophysics (UKR ISSN 0203-3100) **2781**
• ➤ Geofizika (HRV ISSN 0352-3659) **2781**
Geofizikai Kozlemenyek *see* Geophysical Transactions **2782**
• Geofluids (GBR ISSN 1468-8115) **2736**
• ➤ Geofluids Online (GBR ISSN 1468-8123) **2736**
• ➤ Geofocus (ESP ISSN 1578-5157) **4008**
GeoFocus *see* Geo Focus **4007**
• Geofoorumi (FIN ISSN 1796-1475) **2736**
• ➤ Geoforum (GBR ISSN 0016-7185) **4008**
• Geoforum.dk (DNK ISSN 1602-4435) **4008**
• ➤ Geoforum Perspektiv (DNK ISSN 1601-8796) **4008**
Geogaceta (ESP ISSN 0213-683X) **2736**
• Geografi i Bergen (NOR ISSN 1503-2701) **7966**
➤ Geografia (BRA ISSN 0100-7912) **4008**
Geografia (VEN ISSN 1316-5437) **4009**
• ➤ Geografia Fisica e Dinamica Quaternaria (ITA ISSN 0391-9838) **2736**
Geografia w Szkole (POL ISSN 0137-7566) **4009**
• Geografias. Espacios y Sociedades (ESP ISSN 1885-7183) **4009**
Geografica (ARG ISSN 0325-4097) **4009**

▼ *new title* † *ceased* • *electronic media* ➤ *refereed*

Title

10320 GEOGRAFICA ULRICH'S PERIODICALS

Geografica (CHL ISSN 0718-2988) **4009**
Geografica Digital *see* Geografica **4009**
Geografica Universal (BRA) **3804**
Geograficando (ARG ISSN 1850-1885) **4009**
➤ Geograficky Casopis/Geographical Journal (SVK ISSN 0016-7193) **4009**
➤ Geografie/Czech Geographical Society. Journal (CZE ISSN 1212-0014) **4009**
• Geografie (NLD ISSN 0926-3837) **4009**
Geografija (LTU ISSN 1392-1096) **4009**
Geografija v Soli (SVN ISSN 1318-4717) **4009**
• ➤ Geografijos Metrastis/Geographical Yearbook (LTU ISSN 0132-3156) **4009**
Geografikes Uperesias Stratou. Deltio/Hellenic Military Geographical Service. Bulletin (GRC ISSN 1105-1531) **4009**
• ➤ Geografisk Tidsskrift/Danish Journal of Geography (DNK ISSN 0016-7223) **4009**
➤ Geografisk Tidsskrift. Special Issue/Danish Journal of Geography. Special Issue (DNK ISSN 1399-0179) **4009**
• ➤ Geografiska Annaler. Series A. Physical Geography (GBR ISSN 0435-3676) **4009**
• Geografiska Annaler. Series B. Human Geography (GBR ISSN 0435-3684) **340**
Geografiska Foereningens i Stockholm Foerhandlingar *see* G F F **2734**
Geografiska Notiser (SWE ISSN 0016-724X) **4009**
Geografiya (RUS) **4009**
Geografiya i Prirodnye Resursy (RUS ISSN 0206-1619) **4009**
Geografiya v Shkole (RUS ISSN 0016-7207) **4009**
Geografski Glasnik *see* Hrvatski Geografski Glasnik **4014**
Geografski Horizont (HRV ISSN 0016-7266) **4009**
Geografski List (BIH ISSN 0350-0985) **4009**
• ➤ Geografski Obzornik/Geographic Horizon (SVN ISSN 0016-7274) **4010**
Geografski Obzornik. Povzetki *see* Geografski Obzornik **4010**
Geografski Vestnik (SVN ISSN 0350-3895) **4010**
Geografski Zbornik *see* Acta Geographica Slovenica **3997**
Geographe Canadien *see* The Canadian Geographer **4001**
Geographer (IND ISSN 0072-0909) **4010**
Geographers (GBR ISSN 0308-6992) **4010**
• Geographia Antiqua (ITA ISSN 1121-8940) **4010**
• ➤ Geographia Polonica (POL ISSN 0016-7282) **4010**
† Geographia Religionum (DEU ISSN 0933-0356) **8959**
Geographic Distribution of V A Expenditures (Veterans Administration) (USA ISSN 0741-0611) **6422**
Geographic Horizon *see* Geografski Obzornik **4010**
• Geographic Information and Decision Analysis Research Group. Newsletter (CAN) **4010**
Geographic Information Sciences (USA ISSN 1082-4006) **4010**
Geographic Information Systems Magazine *see* G I S Magazine **4007**
Geographic Information Systems News *see* G I S News **4037**
Geographic Information Systems Research U K *see* Innovations in G I S **4015**
• Geographic Profile of Employment and Unemployment (USA ISSN 0145-7330) **1683**
Geographic Reference Report (Year) (USA ISSN 1061-7469) **1861**
Geographic Report on Engineering, Design, and Drafting Personnel Compensation *see* Survey Report on Engineering, Design & Drafting Personnel Compensation **1709**
Geographic Report on Sales and Marketing Personnel Compensation *see* Survey Report on Sales Personnel Compensation **1709**
Geographic Report on Sales and Marketing Personnel Compensation *see* Survey Report on Marketing Personnel Compensation **1709**
Geographic Thesaurus (USA ISSN 0894-9190) **6800**
Geographica (NGA ISSN 0016-7290) **4010**
Geographica Hafniensia. Publications A *see* Geographica Hafniensia. Skrifter A **4010**
Geographica Hafniensia. Publications C *see* Geographica Hafniensia. Skrifter C **4010**
Geographica Hafniensia. Skrifter A/Geographica Hafniensia. Publications A (DNK ISSN 0908-6625) **4010**
Geographica Hafniensia. Skrifter C/Geographica Hafniensia. Publications C (DNK ISSN 0908-6633) **4010**
➤ Geographica Helvetica (CHE ISSN 0016-7312) **4010**
Geographica Historica (DEU ISSN 1381-0472) **2234**
Geographica Pannonica *see* International Scientific Journal Geographica Pannonica **4016**
Geographica Slovenica *see* Acta Geographica Slovenica **3997**
• Geographical (GBR ISSN 0016-741X) **4010**
• Geographical Abstracts: Human Geography (GBR ISSN 0953-9611) **4035**
• Geographical Abstracts: Physical Geography (GBR ISSN 0954-0504) **4036**
• ➤ Geographical Analysis (USA ISSN 0016-7363) **4010**
Geographical Association (Sheffield) *see* G A (Sheffield) **4007**
Geographical Association. Annual Review (GBR) **4010**
Geographical Association of Tanzania Journal (TZA ISSN 0016-738X) **4010**
Geographical Association of Western Australia. Bulletin (AUS) **4010**
➤ Geographical Bulletin (USA ISSN 0731-3292) **4010**
Geographical Bulletin of India (IND) **4010**
Geographical Chronicles *see* Geographika Chronika **4012**
Geographical Code of Greece (GRC) **7480**
Geographical Distribution of Assets and Liabilities of Major Foreign Branches of U.S. Banks (USA) **1349**
• ➤ Geographical Education (AUS ISSN 0085-0969) **3063**
Geographical Education Magazine (ZWE) **4010**
• ➤ The Geographical Journal (GBR ISSN 0016-7398) **4010**
Geographical Journal *see* Czasopismo Geograficzne **4003**
Geographical Journal *see* Geograficky Casopis **4009**
➤ Geographical Journal of Zimbabwe (ZWE ISSN 1011-5919) **4011**
Geographical Knowledge *see* Zhongguo Guojia Dili **4035**
Geographical Magazine *see* Geographical **4010**
• Geographical Mobility (USA) **7307**
Geographical Observer (IND ISSN 0072-0925) **4011**
Geographical Papers *see* University of Karachi. Department of Geography. Geographical Papers **4032**
• ➤ Geographical Research (AUS ISSN 1745-5863) **4011**
Geographical Research *see* Dili Yanjiu **4004**
Geographical Research *see* Faslnamah-i Tahqiqat-i Jughrafiya-i **4006**
Geographical Review *see* Przeglad Geograficzny **4025**
• ➤ Geographical Review (USA ISSN 0016-7428) **4011**
➤ Geographical Review of India (IND ISSN 0375-6386) **4011**
Geographical Review of Japan *see* Chirigaku Hyouron **4002**
Geographical Review of Japan. Series B *see* Chirigaku Hyouron **4002**
➤ Geographical Society of China. Bulletin (TWN ISSN 1025-1464) **4011**
Geographical Survey Institute, Tokyo. Bulletin/Kokudo Chiriin Hokoku (JPN ISSN 0373-7160) **4011**
➤ Geographical View Point (IND ISSN 0046-5712) **4011**
Geographical Viewpoint (IRL ISSN 0332-4877) **4011**
Geographical Yearbook *see* Geografijos Metrastis **4009**
Geographicalia (ESP ISSN 0210-8380) **4011**
Geographicalia. Serie Monographica (ESP ISSN 0211-1179) **4011**
La Geographie (FRA ISSN 1627-4911) **4011**
Geographie de la Sante (FRA) **4011**
Geographie - Ecologie - Environnement (BEL) **4011**
• Geographie, Economie, Societe (FRA ISSN 1295-926X) **4011**
Geographie et Cultures (FRA ISSN 1165-0354) **4011**
Geographie et Teledetection. Bulletin de Recherche (CAN ISSN 0710-0868) **4011**
Geographie Heute (DEU ISSN 0721-8400) **4011**
• ➤ Geographie Physique et Quaternaire (CAN ISSN 0705-7199) **4011**
➤ Geographie und Ihre Didaktik (DEU ISSN 0343-7256) **4012**
Geographie und Schule (DEU ISSN 0171-8649) **4012**
Les Geographies du Monde (FRA ISSN 1279-8428) **5299**
Geographika Chronika/Geographical Chronicles (CYP) **4012**
Geographische Gesellschaft in Hamburg. Mitteilungen (DEU ISSN 0374-9061) **4012**
➤ Geographische Gesellschaft Muenchen. Mitteilungen (DEU ISSN 0072-0941) **4012**
Geographische Gesellschaft von Bern. Jahrbuch (CHE) **4012**
Geographische Hochschulmanuskripte (DEU ISSN 0723-175X) **4012**
Geographische Hochschulmanuskripte. Diskussionspapiere (DEU ISSN 0723-1679) **4012**
Geographische Rundschau (DEU ISSN 0016-7460) **4012**
Geographische Rundschau (International Edition) *see* Geographische Rundschau **4012**
• ➤ Geographische Zeitschrift (DEU ISSN 0016-7479) **4012**
Geographisches Taschenbuch (DEU ISSN 0072-0968) **4012**
Geography *see* Dili (Beijing) **4004**
Geography *see* Dili (Chengdu) **4004**
• ➤ Geography (GBR ISSN 0016-7487) **4012**
Geography and Geo-Information Science *see* Dili yu Dili Xinxi Kexue **2731**
• Geography and Natural Resources (NLD ISSN 1875-3728) **4012**
▼ • ➤ Geography Compass (GBR ISSN 1749-8198) **4012**
Geography-Ecology-Tropical *see* Geo-Eco-Trop **675**
• Geography Review (GBR ISSN 0950-7035) **4012**
• The Geography Teacher (USA ISSN 1933-8341) **4012**
Geography Teachers Association of New South Wales. Geography Bulletin (AUS ISSN 0156-9236) **4012**
Geography Teachers Association of Victoria News *see* G T A V News **4007**
Geography Teaching/Dili Jiaoxue (CHN ISSN 1000-078X) **3063**
• GeoHealth. Proceedings (NZL ISSN 1177-6773) **7518**
▼ • ➤ Geoheritage (DEU ISSN 1867-2477) **2736**
• Geoinfo (CUB ISSN 1028-8961) **2781**
† Geoinfo (CZE ISSN 1212-4311) **8959**
Geoinformatica (ITA ISSN 1828-4477) **2722**
• ➤ Geoinformatica (USA ISSN 1384-6175) **2722**
• Geoinformatics (JPN) **2736**
Geoinformatics (NLD ISSN 1387-0858) **2708**
Geoinformatika (RUS) **2736**
• ➤ GeoJournal (NLD ISSN 0343-2521) **4012**
➤ Geojournal Library (NLD ISSN 0924-5499) **2736**
GeoKatalog 2 - Geosciences (DEU) **4012**
Geokhimiia, Mineralogiia i Petrologiia (BGR ISSN 0324-1718) **2708**
• ➤ Geokhimiya (RUS ISSN 0016-7525) **2736**
Geokhimiya i Rudoobrazovanie (UKR ISSN 0130-1128) **2736**
Geokompakt *see* Geo Kompakt **7857**
Geolenok *see* Geo Lenok **2190**
• Geolines (CZE ISSN 1210-9606) **2736**
➤ Geolinguistics (USA ISSN 0190-4671) **5121**
Geolinguistique (FRA ISSN 0761-9081) **5121**
GeoLino *see* Geo Lino **2190**
Geolino Extra *see* Geo Lino Extra **2190**
Geolnova (PRT ISSN 0874-6540) **4012**
Geolog (CAN ISSN 0227-3713) **2736**
Geologi (FIN ISSN 0046-5720) **2736**
Geologi - Nyt fra GEUS *see* Geoviden **2709**
➤ Geologia (POL ISSN 0138-0974) **2736**
† Geologia Applicata e Idrogeologia (ITA ISSN 0435-3870) **8959**
Geologia Colombiana (COL ISSN 0072-0992) **2737**
• ➤ Geologia Croatica (HRV ISSN 1330-030X) **2737**
Geologia na Balkanite *see* Geologica Balcanica **2737**
➤ Geologia Sudetica (POL ISSN 0072-100X) **2737**
Geologia Tecnica & Ambientale (ITA ISSN 1722-0025) **2737**
Geologiai es Geofizikai Szakirodalmi Tajekoztato/Geology and Geophysics Abstracts (HUN ISSN 0230-7065) **2719**
Geologian Tutkimuskeskus. Kertomus Toiminnasta/Geological Survey of Finland. Annual Report/Geologiska Forskningscentralen. Verksamhetsberaettelse (FIN ISSN 1239-3177) **2737**
➤ Geologian Tutkimuskeskus. Opas/Geological Survey of Finland. Guide (FIN ISSN 0781-643X) **2737**
Geologian Tutkimuskeskus. Toimintakertomus/Geological Survey of Finland. Annual Report (FIN) **2737**
• ➤ Geologian Tutkimuskeskus. Tutkimusraportti/Geological Survey of Finland. Report of Investigation (FIN ISSN 0781-4240) **2737**
• Geologian Tutkimuskeskus. Ydinjatteiden Sijoitustutkimukset. Tiedonanto Y S T/Geological Survey of Finland. Nuclear Waste Disposal Research. Report Y S T (FIN ISSN 0783-3555) **2737**
• ➤ Geologica Acta (ESP ISSN 1695-6133) **2737**
Geologica Balcanica (BGR ISSN 0324-0894) **2737**
Geologica Bavarica (DEU ISSN 0016-755X) **2737**
➤ Geologica Belgica (BEL ISSN 1374-8505) **2708**
Geologica Carpathica (SVK ISSN 1335-0552) **2737**
➤ Geologica et Palaeontologica (DEU ISSN 0072-1018) **2737**
➤ Geologica Hungarica. Series Geologica (HUN ISSN 0367-4150) **2737**
➤ Geologica Hungarica. Series Palaeontologica (HUN ISSN 0374-1893) **6725**
Geologica Macedonica (MKD ISSN 0352-1206) **2737**
Geologica Romana (ITA ISSN 0435-3927) **2737**
• ➤ Geologica Ultraiectina (NLD ISSN 0072-1026) **2737**
• Geological Abstracts (GBR ISSN 0954-0512) **2719**
Geological and Geophysical Bibliography of Romania *see* Bibliografia Geologica si Geofizica a Romaniei **2719**
Geological and Nuclear Sciences Science Miscellaneous Series *see* G N S Science Miscellaneous Series **2734**
Geological and Nuclear Sciences Science Report *see* G N S Science Report **2734**
• Geological Association of Canada. Miscellaneous Publication (CAN ISSN 1706-936X) **2708**
Geological Association of Canada. Short Course Notes (CAN ISSN 1189-6094) **2738**
Geological Association of Canada. Special Paper (CAN ISSN 0072-1042) **2738**
Geological Bulletin of China *see* Dizhi Tongbao **2732**
➤ Geological Bulletin of Turkey (TUR ISSN 1300-6827) **2738**
Geological Conservation Review Series (GBR ISSN 0965-9994) **2738**
Geological Correlation (FRA ISSN 0302-069X) **2738**
Geological Curator (IRL ISSN 0144-5294) **6524**
Geological Curator. Supplement (IRL ISSN 0265-0126) **6524**
Geological Fieldwork (CAN ISSN 0381-243X) **2738**
Geological Guidebooks *see* Virginia Polytechnic Institute and State University. Department of Geological Sciences. Geological Guidebooks **2773**
Geological Hazards and Environment Preservation *see* Dizhi Zaihai yu Huanjing Baohu **3414**
• ➤ Geological Journal (GBR ISSN 0072-1050) **2738**
Geological Journal of China Universities *see* Gaoxiao Dizhi Xuebao **2735**
Geological Journal - Special Issues (GBR ISSN 0435-3951) **2738**
• ➤ Geological Magazine (GBR ISSN 0016-7568) **2738**
Geological Map Commentary *see* 1:100 000 Geological Map Commentary **2776**
Geological Map Series. Explanatory Notes *see* 1:100 000 Geological Map Series. Explanatory Notes **2776**
Geological Materials Research *see* The American Mineralogist (Online) **6456**
Geological, Mining and Metallurgical Society of India. Bulletin (IND ISSN 0016-7576) **2738**
• ➤ Geological Quarterly (POL ISSN 1641-7291) **2738**
Geological Reference Book (CAN) **2738**
Geological Review *see* Dizhi Lun-Ping **2732**
Geological Review *see* Przeglad Geologiczny **2763**
Geological Science and Technology Information *see* Dizhi Keji Qingbao **2731**
• ➤ Geological Society. Journal (GBR ISSN 0016-7649) **2738**
Geological Society of America. Abstracts with Programs (USA ISSN 0016-7592) **2719**
• ➤ Geological Society of America Bulletin (USA ISSN 0016-7606) **2738**
† Geological Society of America, Inc. Proceedings Volume (USA ISSN 0096-4271) **8959**
➤ Geological Society of America. Map and Chart Series (USA ISSN 0272-0795) **2738**
• ➤ Geological Society of America. Memoirs (USA ISSN 0072-1069) **2738**
Geological Society of America. Memorials (USA ISSN 0091-5041) **2739**
• ➤ Geological Society of America. Special Papers (USA ISSN 0072-1077) **2739**
Geological Society of America. Specialty Meetings, Abstracts with Programs (USA ISSN 1556-4800) **2739**
Geological Society of America Today *see* G S A Today **2734**
Geological Society of Australia. Abstracts Series (AUS ISSN 0729-011X) **2719**
Geological Society of Australia. Special Publication (AUS ISSN 0072-1085) **2739**
➤ Geological Society of China. Journal (TWN ISSN 1018-7057) **2739**
• ➤ Geological Society of Denmark. Bulletin/Dansk Geologisk Forening. Meddelelser (DNK ISSN 0011-6297) **2739**
Geological Society of Egypt. Annual Meeting. Abstracts of Papers (EGY ISSN 0446-4648) **2719**
Geological Society of Finland. Bulletin (FIN ISSN 0367-5211) **2739**
Geological Society of Greece. Bulletin/Deltio tes Ellenikes Geologikes Etaireias (GRC ISSN 0438-9557) **2739**
Geological Society of Greece. Special Paper (GRC) **2739**
• ➤ Geological Society of India. Journal (IND ISSN 0016-7622) **2739**
Geological Society of India. Memoir (IND ISSN 0435-4001) **2739**
Geological Society of Jamaica. Journal *see* Caribbean Journal of Earth Science **2727**
Geological Society of Japan. Abstracts of Kanto Branch Symposium *see* Nihon Chishitsu Gakkai Kanto Shibu Shinpojumu Koen Yoshishu **2720**
Geological Society of Japan. Journal *see* Chishitsugaku Zasshi **2729**
Geological Society of Japan. Kansai Branch. Proceedings *see* Nihon Chishitsu Gakkai Kansai Shibu Kaiho **2759**
Geological Society of Japan. Memoirs *see* Chishitsugaku Ronshu **2729**
Geological Society of London. Memoirs (GBR ISSN 0435-4052) **2739**
Geological Society of London. Miscellaneous Paper (GBR ISSN 0305-0394) **2739**
Geological Society of London. Professional Handbook Series (GBR) **2739**
➤ Geological Society of Malaysia. Bulletin (MYS ISSN 0126-6187) **2739**
Geological Society of Malaysia Newsletter *see* Warta Geologi **2774**
Geological Society of Norfolk. Bulletin (GBR ISSN 0143-9286) **2739**
Geological Society of Norfolk. Newsletter (GBR) **2739**
Geological Society of South Africa. Geobulletin/Geologiese Vereniging van Suid-Africa. Geobulletin (ZAF ISSN 0256-3029) **2739**
Geological Society of South Africa. Special Publication (ZAF) **2739**
Geological Society of the Oregon Country. Geological Newsletter (USA ISSN 0270-5451) **2739**
Geological Society of Yamaguchi. Reports *see* Yamaguchi Chigakkaishi **2718**

Link to your serials resources and content with ulrichsweb.com

DIRECTORY 2010 GEORGETOWN LAW JOURNAL 10321

Geological Society of Zimbabwe (NLD ISSN 0921-4054) **2739**
Geological Society Special Publication (GBR ISSN 0305-8719) **2739**
Geological Survey and Research *see* Dizhi Diaocha yu Yanjiu **2731**
Geological Survey of Alabama. Bulletin (USA ISSN 0097-3262) **2739**
Geological Survey of Alabama. Circular (USA ISSN 0097-3149) **2739**
Geological Survey of Alabama. Geology and Ground Water Resources Report (USA) **2739**
Geological Survey of Alabama. Monograph (USA ISSN 0886-7526) **2739**
Geological Survey of Alabama. Oil and Gas Report (USA ISSN 0364-2984) **6771**
Geological Survey of Belgium. Memoirs/Belgische Geologische Dienst. Verhandeling (BEL ISSN 1373-5438) **2740**
▼ Geological Survey of Canada. Technical Note (CAN ISSN 1914-525X) **2740**
• ➤ Geological Survey of Denmark and Greenland Bulletin (DNK ISSN 1811-4598) **2740**
• ➤ Geological Survey of Denmark and Greenland Map Series (DNK ISSN 1604-9780) **4012**
Geological Survey of Finland. Annual Report *see* Geologian Tutkimuskeskus. Kertomus Toiminnasta **2737**
Geological Survey of Finland. Annual Report *see* Geologian Tutkimuskeskus. Toimintakertomus **2737**
Geological Survey of Finland. Bulletin (FIN ISSN 0367-522X) **2740**
Geological Survey of Finland. Guide *see* Geologian Tutkimuskeskus. Opas **2737**
Geological Survey of Finland. Nuclear Waste Disposal Research. Report Y S T *see* Geologian Tutkimuskeskus. Ydinjatteiden Sijoitustutkimukset. Tiedonanto Y S T **2737**
Geological Survey of Finland. Report of Investigation *see* Geologian Tutkimuskeskus. Tutkimusraportti **2737**
• ➤ Geological Survey of Finland. Special Paper (FIN ISSN 0782-8535) **2740**
Geological Survey of Hokkaido. Report (JPN) **2740**
Geological Survey of India. News (IND ISSN 0378-4029) **2740**
Geological Survey of Ireland. Bulletin (IRL ISSN 0085-0985) **2740**
Geological Survey of Ireland. Groundwater Newsletter (IRL ISSN 0790-7753) **2740**
Geological Survey of Ireland. Guide Series (IRL ISSN 0790-0260) **2740**
Geological Survey of Ireland. Information Circulars (IRL ISSN 0085-0993) **2740**
Geological Survey of Ireland. Report Series (IRL ISSN 0790-0279) **2740**
Geological Survey of Ireland. Special Papers (IRL ISSN 0085-1019) **2740**
Geological Survey of Japan. Annual Report *see* Chishitsu Chosajo Nenpo **2729**
Geological Survey of Japan. Bulletin *see* Chishitsu Chousa Kenkyuu Houkoku **2729**
Geological Survey of Japan. Cruise Report (JPN ISSN 0288-5980) **2740**
Geological Survey of Japan. Report *see* Chishitsu Chosajo Hokoku **2729**
Geological Survey of N.S.W. Mineral Resources *see* New South Wales. Geological Survey. Mineral Resources Series **6474**
Geological Survey of Namibia. Communications (NAM ISSN 1026-2954) **2740**
Geological Survey of Namibia. Memoirs (NAM) **2740**
Geological Survey of Namibia. Reports on Open File. C D M Mineral Surveys (NAM) **2740**
Geological Survey of Namibia. Reports on Open File. Economic Geology (NAM) **2740**
Geological Survey of Namibia. Reports on Open File. Engineering Geology (NAM) **2740**
Geological Survey of Namibia. Reports on Open File. Geophysics (NAM) **2781**
Geological Survey of Namibia. Reports on Open File. Mineral Resource Series (NAM) **2740**
Geological Survey of Namibia. Reports on Open File. Regional Geology (NAM) **2740**
Geological Survey of New South Wales. 1:250000 Geological Sheets Series. Explanatory Notes (AUS ISSN 1321-828X) **2740**
Geological Survey of Pakistan News *see* G S P News **2735**
Geological Survey of South Australia. Bulletin (AUS ISSN 0365-4400) **2740**
Geological Survey of South Australia. Explanatory Notes (AUS ISSN 0572-0125) **2740**
Geological Survey of South Australia. Report of Investigations (AUS ISSN 0016-7681) **2740**
Geological Survey of Sweden. Geomagnetic Publications *see* Sveriges Geologiska Undersoekning. Serie Cb. Jordmagnetiska Publikationer **2770**
Geological Survey of Sweden. Series C. Research Papers *see* Sveriges Geologiska Undersoekning. Serie C. Forskningsrapporter **2770**
Geological Survey of Sweden. Series Ca. Notices in Folio and Quarto *see* Sveriges Geologiska Undersoekning. Serie Ca. Avhandlingar och Uppsatser i Kvarto **2770**
• Geological Survey of Victoria. Report (AUS ISSN 1446-7895) **2740**
Geological Technoeconomic Management *see* Dizhi Jishu Jingji Guanli **1092**
Geologicheskii Zhurnal Armenii/Gitutsunner Erkry Massin (ARM ISSN 0016-769X) **2740**
Geologicheskoe Izuchenie i Ispol'zovanie Nedr (RUS) **2741**
Geologichnyi Zhurnal (UKR ISSN 1025-6814) **2741**
• Geologie de la France/Geology of France and Surrounding Areas (FRA ISSN 1638-5977) **2741**
Geologie de la France (Print) *see* Geologie de la France **2741**
† Geologie Mediterraneenne (FRA ISSN 0397-2844) **8959**
Geologie und Palaeontologie in Westfalen (DEU ISSN 0176-148X) **2741**
Geologiese Vereniging van Suid-Africa. Geobulletin *see* Geological Society of South Africa. Geobulletin **2739**
Geologija (LTU ISSN 1392-110X) **2741**
• ➤ Geologija (SVN ISSN 0016-7789) **2741**
Geologisch-Palaeontologische Mitteilungen Innsbruck *see* Geo.Alp **6725**
Geologische Abhandlungen Hessen (DEU ISSN 0341-4043) **2741**
Geologische Beitraege Hannover (DEU ISSN 1615-6684) **2741**
Geologische Blaetter fuer Nordost-Bayern und Angrenzende Gebiete (DEU ISSN 0016-7797) **2741**
Geologische Bundesanstalt. Abhandlungen (AUT ISSN 0378-0864) **2741**
Geologische Bundesanstalt. Berichte (AUT ISSN 1017-8880) **2741**
Geologische Bundesanstalt. Bundeslaenderserie (AUT) **2741**
Geologische Bundesanstalt. Fuehrer zu den Arbeitstagungen (AUT ISSN 1015-6208) **2741**
• Geologische Bundesanstalt. Jahrbuch (AUT ISSN 0016-7800) **2741**
Geologische Bundesanstalt. Jahresbericht (AUT ISSN 1013-0349) **2741**
Geologische Bundesanstalt. Populaerwissenschaftliche Veroeffentlichungen (AUT) **2741**
Geologisches Jahrbuch Hessen (DEU ISSN 0341-4027) **2741**
➤ Geologisches Jahrbuch. Reihe A: Allgemeine und Regionale Geologie B.R. Deutschland und Nachbargebiete, Tektonik, Stratigraphie, Palaeontologie (DEU ISSN 0341-6399) **2741**
➤ Geologisches Jahrbuch. Reihe B: Regionale Geologie Ausland (DEU ISSN 0341-6402) **2741**
➤ Geologisches Jahrbuch. Reihe C: Hydrogeologie. Ingenieurgeologie (DEU ISSN 0341-6410) **2741**
➤ Geologisches Jahrbuch. Reihe D: Mineralogie. Petrographie, Geochemie, Lagerstaettenkunde (DEU ISSN 0341-6429) **2741**
➤ Geologisches Jahrbuch. Reihe E: Geophysik (DEU ISSN 0341-6437) **2742**
➤ Geologisches Jahrbuch. Reihe F: Bodenkunde (DEU ISSN 0341-6445) **2742**
➤ Geologisches Jahrbuch. Reihe G: Informationen aus den Bund - Laender-Arbeitsgruppen der Geologischen Dienste (DEU ISSN 1431-5084) **2742**
➤ Geologisches Jahrbuch. Reihe H: Wirtschaftsgeologie, Berichte zur Rohstoffwirtschaft (DEU ISSN 1431-5092) **2742**
• ➤ Geologisk Tidsskrift (DNK ISSN 1395-0150) **2742**
Geologiska Forskningscentralen. Verksamhetsberaettelse *see* Geologian Tutkimuskeskus. Kertomus Toiminnasta **2737**
Geologiskt Forum (SWE ISSN 1104-4721) **2742**
Geologists' Association (London) *see* G A (London) **2734**
• ➤ Geologists' Association. Proceedings (GBR ISSN 0016-7878) **2742**
Geologist's Directory (GBR ISSN 0260-0463) **2742**
Geologiya, Geofizika i Razrabotka Neftyanykh Mestorozhdenii (RUS ISSN 0234-1581) **2742**
➤ Geologiya i Geofizika (RUS ISSN 0016-7886) **2742**
Geologiya Nefti i Gaza (RUS ISSN 0016-7894) **6771**
• Geologiya Rudnykh Mestorozhdenii (RUS ISSN 0016-7770) **6463**
Geologoj Demokratiaj *see* Chigaku Dantai Kenkyukai. Sokuho **2728**
Geologues (FRA ISSN 0016-7916) **2742**
Geology *see* Ti Chih **2717**
• ➤ Geology (Boulder) (USA ISSN 0091-7613) **2742**
Geology Abroad *see* Guowai Dizhi **2745**
Geology and Geochemistry of Combustible Minerals *see* Heolohiya i Heokhimiya Horiuchykh Kopalyn **2746**
Geology and Geophysics Abstracts *see* Geologiai es Geofizikai Szakirodalmi Tajekoztato **2719**
Geology and Mineral Resources of Japan/Nihon Chishitsu Kosanshi (JPN) **2742**
Geology and Mineral Resources of South China *see* Hua'nan Dizhi yu Kuangchan **2746**
Geology and Mining *see* Netherlands Journal of Geosciences **2757**
• Geology and Ore (GRL ISSN 1602-818X) **2742**
Geology and Prospecting *see* Dizhi yu Kantan **2732**
Geology and Resources *see* Zizhi yu Ziyuan **2776**
Geology - Geochemistry *see* Dizhi Diqiu Huaxue **2731**
Geology in China *see* Zhongguo Dizhi **2776**
Geology News *see* Chishitsu Nyusu **2729**
Geology of France and Surrounding Areas *see* Geologie de la France **2741**
• ➤ Geology of Ore Deposits (RUS ISSN 1075-7015) **6463**
Geology of Poland (POL ISSN 0138-0389) **2742**
Geology of the Pacific Ocean *see* Russian Journal of Pacific Geology **2765**
Geology Science and Technology Development *see* Dizhi Keji Dongtai **2731**
• ➤ Geology Today (GBR ISSN 0266-6979) **2742**
• ➤ Geology Today Online (GBR ISSN 1365-2451) **2742**
Geoloski Anali Balkanskoga Poluostrva/Annales Geologiques de la Peninsule Balkanique (SRB ISSN 0350-0608) **2742**
Geomagnetic Bulletin *see* Great Britain. Natural Environment Research Council. British Geological Survey. Geomagnetic Bulletin **2783**
Geomagnetic Indices Bulletin (USA) **2781**
Geomagnetic, Ionospheric and Auroral Data from Finland (FIN ISSN 1455-867X) **2781**
Geomagnetic Observations at Mizusawa and Kanozan *see* Chikyu Jiki Kansoku Hokoku **2779**
• ➤ Geomagnetism and Aeronomy (RUS ISSN 0016-7932) **2781**
• ➤ Geomagnetizm i Aeronomiya (RUS ISSN 0016-7940) **2781**
➤ Geomatica (CAN ISSN 1195-1036) **2708**
Geomatica Svizzera *see* Geomatik Schweiz **3267**
➤ Geomatics and Environmental Engineering (POL ISSN 1898-1135) **3433**
Geomatics and Information Science of Wuhan University *see* Wuhan Daxue Xuebao (Xinxi Kexue Ban) **4034**
Geomatics & Spatial Information Technology *see* Cehui yu Kongjian Dili Xinxi **4002**
Geomatics Canada *see* Canada. Earth Sciences Sector. Annual Review **2703**
▼ Geomatics Canada. Technical Note (CAN ISSN 1914-4229) **4012**
Geomatics Info Magazine International *see* G I M International **4007**
Geomatics World (GBR ISSN 1567-5882) **4013**
Geomatik Schweiz/Geomatica Svizzera/Geomatique Suisse (CHE ISSN 1660-4458) **3267**
Geomatique Suisse *see* Geomatik Schweiz **3267**
Geomax (DEU) **2742**
Geombinatorics (USA ISSN 1065-7371) **5490**
• Geomechanics Abstracts (GBR ISSN 1365-1617) **2719**
▼ • Geomechanics and Engineering (KOR ISSN 2005-307X) **3378**
• ➤ Geomechanics and Geoengineering (GBR ISSN 1748-6025) **3267**
Geomechanics Research Series (GBR ISSN 0929-4856) **2742**
• ➤ Geomechanik und Tunnelbau (DEU ISSN 1865-7362) **2743**
Geometre (FRA ISSN 0016-7967) **3268**
† Geometri Informazione (ITA) **8959**
† Geometria (ESP ISSN 0213-4780) **8959**
• ➤ Geometriae Dedicata (NLD ISSN 0046-5755) **5490**
• ➤ Geometric and Functional Analysis (CHE ISSN 1016-443X) **5490**
• ➤ Geometry & Topology (GBR ISSN 1465-3060) **5490**
• Geometry & Topology Monographs (GBR ISSN 1464-8989) **5490**
• ➤ Geomicrobiology Journal (USA ISSN 0149-0451) **886**
Geomimet (MEX ISSN 0185-1314) **6463**
Geominas (VEN ISSN 0016-7975) **2708**
Geomorfologiya (RUS ISSN 0435-4281) **2708**
• ➤ Geomorphologie (FRA ISSN 1266-5304) **2743**
• ➤ Geomorphology (NLD ISSN 0169-555X) **2743**
Geomundo (ARG) **4013**
• Geomundo (USA ISSN 0256-7253) **4013**
Geonchug Munhwa/Architecture and Culture (KOR ISSN 1227-0903) **443**
• GeoNet News (NZL ISSN 1176-0567) **2708**
Geonome Letters (Online Edition) *see* Journal of Genome Science and Technology (Online Edition) **874**
Geonotas (BRA ISSN 1415-0646) **4013**
Geonovas (PRT ISSN 0870-7375) **2743**
• Geonseol'eob Tong'gye Jo'sa Bo'go'seo/Korea (Republic). National Statistical Office. Report on the Construction Work Survey (KOR ISSN 1599-1407) **1046**
Geooeko *see* Geo-Oeko **4007**
† Geophilos (GBR ISSN 1472-6300) **8959**
• ➤ Geophysica (FIN ISSN 0367-4231) **2781**
Geophysical Activity in Japan *see* Butsuri Tansa Chosa Kenkyu Ichiran **2778**
• ➤ Geophysical and Astrophysical Fluid Dynamics (GBR ISSN 0309-1929) **2781**
Geophysical and Geochemical Exploration *see* Wutan yu Huatan **6484**
Geophysical Directory (USA) **2782**
Geophysical Exploration *see* Butsuri Tansa **2778**
• ➤ Geophysical Journal International (GBR ISSN 0956-540X) **2782**
➤ Geophysical Monographs Book Series (USA ISSN 0065-8448) **2782**
• ➤ Geophysical Prospecting (GBR ISSN 0016-8025) **2782**
Geophysical Prospecting for Petroleum *see* Shiyou Wutan **6792**
• Geophysical Research Abstracts (DEU ISSN 1607-7962) **2719**
• ➤ Geophysical Research Letters (USA ISSN 0094-8276) **2782**
Geophysical Review *see* Kisho Yoran **2786**
➤ Geophysical Transactions/Geofizicheskii Byulleten'/Geofizikai Kozlemenyek (HUN ISSN 0016-7177) **2782**
• ➤ Geophysics (USA ISSN 0016-8033) **2782**
➤ Geophysics and Astrophysics Monographs (NLD ISSN 0165-1307) **575**
➤ Geophytology (IND ISSN 0376-5156) **6725**
Geoplace.com *see* Geo World **4037**
➤ Geopolitical Studies (POL ISSN 1429-009X) **4013**
• ➤ Geopolitics (GBR ISSN 1465-0045) **7237**
Geopolitics and Conflict Resolution *see* Geopolitique et Resolution des Conflits **7237**
▼ Geopolitics, History, and International Relations (USA ISSN 1948-9145) **7237**
Geopolitics of Energy (CAN ISSN 0273-1371) **7237**
Geopolitique (FRA ISSN 0752-1693) **7237**
Geopolitique (English Edition) *see* Geopolitique **7237**
Geopolitique et Resolution des Conflits/Geopolitics and Conflict Resolution (BEL ISSN 1780-5848) **7237**
Georama (BEL) **3268**
• GeoRef (USA ISSN 0197-7482) **2719**
• GeoRef Serials List (USA ISSN 1069-1022) **2720**
• GeoReport (USA) **2743**
GeoResearch Forum (CHE) **2743**
Georesources *see* Georesursy **2743**
• Georesursy (RUS ISSN 1608-5043) **2743**
Georg-August-Universitaet Goettingen. Spektrum (DEU ISSN 0945-3512) **7857**
• Georg Buechner Jahrbuch (DEU ISSN 0722-3420) **5299**
Georg Forsters Werke (DEU) **5300**
George (NLD ISSN 1875-1989) **6291**
George - Anne (USA) **2285**
The George B. Pegram Lecture Series (USA ISSN 0435-4389) **7857**
† George Best's United Monthly (GBR ISSN 1461-6335) **8959**
George C. Marshall Foundation. Topics (USA) **4293**
George Eastman House - International Museum of Photography and Film. Annual Report (USA) **6969**
George Eastman House Newsletter *see* Close-up **6965**
George Eliot - George Henry Lewes Newsletter *see* George Eliot - George Henry Lewes Studies **5217**
➤ George Eliot - George Henry Lewes Studies (USA ISSN 0953-0754) **5217**
➤ George Eliot Review (GBR ISSN 1358-345X) **5300**
• ➤ George Herbert Journal (USA ISSN 0161-7435) **5423**
• George-Jahrbuch (DEU ISSN 1430-2519) **5300**
• ➤ George Mason Law Review (USA ISSN 1088-5625) **4679**
• George Mason University. Civil Rights Law Journal (USA ISSN 1049-4766) **4831**
George Meany Memorial Archives Library Current Acquisitions (USA) **4606**
• George Research (AUS ISSN 1833-3656) **7518**
• The George Washington International Law Review (USA ISSN 1534-9977) **4926**
• ➤ George Washington Law Review (USA ISSN 0016-8076) **4679**
George Washington Magazine *see* G W Magazine **2284**
George Washington University Hatchet *see* G W Hatchet **2284**
George Washington University, Medical Center Department of Biochemistry and Molecular Biology. Annual Spring Symposia Series *see* G W U M C. Department of Biochemistry and Molecular Biology. Annual Spring Symposia Series **733**
George Washington University Review *see* G W Review **5299**
• George Wells' Washington Beverage Insight (USA ISSN 1074-0759) **604**
• George Wright Forum (USA ISSN 0732-4715) **2612**
Georges Pompidou - Archives (BEL ISSN 1783-0710) **4223**
Georges Pompidou - Etudes (BEL ISSN 1782-4931) **4223**
Georges Yared's Game Changers *see* Game Changers **1626**
Georgeson Report (USA ISSN 1044-7121) **1626**
• ➤ Georgetown Immigration Law Journal (USA ISSN 0891-4370) **4679**
• ➤ Georgetown International Environmental Law Review (USA ISSN 1042-1858) **3433**
Georgetown Journal (USA) **5300**
• The Georgetown Journal of Gender and the Law (USA ISSN 1525-6146) **4679**
• Georgetown Journal of International Affairs (USA ISSN 1526-0054) **7237**
• Georgetown Journal of International Law (USA ISSN 1550-5200) **4926**
• Georgetown Journal of Law & Public Policy (USA ISSN 1536-5077) **4679**
• ➤ Georgetown Journal of Legal Ethics (USA ISSN 1041-5548) **4680**
• Georgetown Journal on Poverty Law and Policy (USA ISSN 1524-3974) **8042**
Georgetown Law *see* Res Ipsa Loquitur **4769**
• ➤ Georgetown Law Journal (USA ISSN 0016-8092) **4680**

Title

10322 THE GEORGETOWN LAW JOURNAL ANNUAL REVIEW OF CRIMINAL ULRICH'S PERIODICALS

The Georgetown Law Journal Annual Review of Criminal Procedure (USA ISSN 1551-059X) **4890**
Georgetown Magazine (USA ISSN 0745-9009) **2285**
The Georgetown Public Policy Review (USA ISSN 1083-7523) **7966**
Georgetown Studies in Romance Linguistics (USA) **5121**
Georgetown University. Center for Latin American Studies. Occasional Paper Series (USA) **4293**
Georgetown University Round Table on Languages and Linguistics (USA ISSN 0196-7207) **5122**
Georgia Administrative Law Digest of Environmental Decisions (USA ISSN 1548-1743) **4680**
• Georgia Advance Sheets (USA ISSN 8750-0515) **4680**
Georgia Advocate *see* Georgia Law Advocate **2285**
Georgia: All-Industries *see* Harris Directory. Georgia All-Industries **1999**
Georgia Alumni Record (USA ISSN 0016-8130) **2285**
Georgia AnchorAge (USA ISSN 0016-8149) **8644**
Georgia Association of Convenience Stores Today *see* G A C S Today **1961**
➤ Georgia Association of Historians. Journal (USA) **4293**
Georgia Association of Historians. Newsletter (USA) **4293**
Georgia Athlete (USA) **8175**
Georgia Augusta (DEU ISSN 0016-8157) **2982**
Georgia Backroads (USA) **8713**
• ➤ Georgia Bar Journal (USA ISSN 1085-1437) **4680**
Georgia Beat (USA) **7138**
• Georgia Beekeepers Association. Newsletter (USA) **115**
The Georgia Bulletin (USA) **7799**
Georgia Business and Economic Conditions (USA ISSN 0279-3857) **1113**
• Georgia Business Credit Directory (USA) **1997**
• Georgia Business Directory (USA ISSN 1048-7220) **1997**
Georgia Cattleman (USA ISSN 0744-4451) **287**
Georgia Cities & Counties Graphic Performance Analysis (USA ISSN 1935-584X) **7480**
Georgia Cities and Counties Graphic Performance Analysis *see* Georgia Cities & Counties Graphic Performance Analysis **7480**
▼ Georgia Civil Discovery (USA ISSN 1943-8508) **4831**
• Georgia Civil Practice (USA) **4831**
Georgia Civil Procedure Forms (USA) **4831**
Georgia Civil Rights Report (USA) **7207**
Georgia College Alumni News Quarterly (USA) **2285**
Georgia Commercial Properties (USA ISSN 1934-8169) **7591**
Georgia Conservation Law Handbook (USA) **2612**
Georgia Corporate Forms (USA) **4868**
† Georgia Corporations, Partnerships and Associations Law Annotated (USA) **8959**
• Georgia County Government (USA ISSN 1066-0119) **7439**
The Georgia County Guide (USA ISSN 1044-0976) **8373**
Georgia Courts Journal (USA ISSN 0147-7161) **4952**
• Georgia Criminal and Traffic Law Manual (USA ISSN 1540-4234) **4890**
• Georgia Criminal Law and Motor Vehicle Handbook (USA) **4890**
Georgia Criminal Law Case Finder (USA ISSN 1558-8378) **4890**
Georgia Criminal Trial Practice *see* Daniel's Georgia Criminal Trial Practice **4888**
Georgia Curiosities (USA ISSN 1542-1252) **8713**
• Georgia. Department of Law. Attorney General's Office. Opinions of the Attorney General (USA ISSN 0431-2716) **4680**
• Georgia Domestic Relations Case Finder (USA) **4910**
• Georgia Domestic Relations Forms (USA) **4910**
Georgia Economic Outlook (USA ISSN 0884-1179) **1113**
Georgia Employment Law (USA ISSN 1934-1628) **1683**
• Georgia Employment Law Letter (USA ISSN 1040-4813) **4680**
Georgia Engineer (USA) **3193**
† • Georgia Environmental Law Letter (USA ISSN 1044-2324) **8959**
Georgia Estate Planning, Will Drafting and Estate Administration Forms (USA) **4903**
Georgia F O P News *see* The Watchful Eye **2671**
Georgia Facts (USA ISSN 1044-9086) **3120**
Georgia Farm Bureau News (USA ISSN 0735-696X) **115**
Georgia Food Connection (USA ISSN 1091-479X) **3678**
Georgia Football (USA) **8230**
Georgia Forestry (USA) **3692**
Georgia Forestry Association, Inc. News *see* G F A News **3691**
Georgia Future Farmer (USA ISSN 0016-8262) **115**
Georgia Gardening Magazine (USA ISSN 1541-8405) **3733**
Georgia Genealogical Society Quarterly (USA ISSN 0435-5393) **3768**
Georgia Geologic Survey. Bulletin (USA) **2743**
Georgia Geologic Survey. Circular (USA) **2743**
Georgia Geologic Survey. Circular 1. List of Publications (USA) **2720**
Georgia Geologic Survey. Circular 2. Mining Directory of Georgia (USA) **6463**
Georgia Geologic Survey. Circular 3. The Mineral Industry of Georgia (USA) **6463**
Georgia Geologic Survey. Educational Series (USA) **3433**
Georgia Geologic Survey. Geologic Guide (USA) **2743**
Georgia Geologic Survey. Geologic Report (USA) **2743**
Georgia Geologic Survey. Guidebook (USA) **2743**
Georgia Geologic Survey. Information Circular (USA ISSN 0433-5473) **6463**
Georgia Geologic Survey. Miscellaneous Publication (USA) **2743**
Georgia Geologic Survey. Open File Report (USA) **2743**
Georgia Geologic Survey. Project Report (USA) **2743**
Georgia Geological Survey. Bulletin (USA ISSN 0277-9420) **2743**
Georgia Geological Survey. Information Circular (USA ISSN 0278-3398) **2743**
Georgia Golf (USA ISSN 1930-773X) **8230**
Georgia Green Industry Association Newsletter (USA) **3733**
Georgia Guardian and Ward (USA ISSN 1942-2946) **4910**
• ➤ Georgia Historical Quarterly (USA ISSN 0016-8297) **4293**
Georgia History Today (USA) **4293**
Georgia Holiday Guide (GBR ISSN 1360-726X) **8713**
Georgia Hospital Association Today Newsletter *see* G H A Today Newsletter **4093**
Georgia Humanities (USA) **4453**
• ➤ Georgia Journal of International and Comparative Law (USA ISSN 0046-578X) **4926**
Georgia Journal of Professional Counseling (USA ISSN 1541-7557) **7358**
• ➤ Georgia Journal of Science (GAJSCI) (USA ISSN 0147-9369) **7857**
Georgia Labor Market Trends (USA ISSN 0147-9865) **1683**
• Georgia Law Advocate (USA ISSN 1557-1025) **2285**
• Georgia Law Review (USA ISSN 0016-8300) **4680**
Georgia Legislative Review (USA ISSN 0362-5931) **4680**
• ➤ Georgia Library Quarterly (USA) **5011**
Georgia Livestock (USA) **287**
Georgia Living *see* Southern Living **3988**
• Georgia Magazine (USA ISSN 1061-5822) **3976**
• Georgia Manufacturers Register (USA ISSN 0896-4009) **1997**
Georgia: Manufacturing *see* Harris Directory. Georgia Manufacturing **1999**
Georgia Manufacturing Directory (USA ISSN 0435-5482) **1997**
Georgia Marine Science Center. Technical Report Series (USA ISSN 0275-6269) **675**
Georgia Museum of Art. Bulletin (USA ISSN 0147-1902) **491**
Georgia Museum of Art Newsletter (USA) **6524**
Georgia Music Magazine (USA ISSN 1939-8158) **6569**
Georgia Music News (USA ISSN 0046-5798) **6569**
Georgia Neighbors (USA) **115**
Georgia, North Carolina, South Carolina *see* TourBook: Georgia, North Carolina, South Carolina **8762**
Georgia, North Carolina, South Carolina TourBook *see* TourBook: Georgia, North Carolina, South Carolina **8762**
• Georgia Nursing (USA ISSN 0016-8335) **5959**
Georgia Outdoor News (USA ISSN 0895-3295) **8315**
• Georgia Pest Management Newsletter (USA) **233**
Georgia Pharmacist Quarterly *see* U G A - R X **6883**
➤ Georgia Philological Association. Journal (USA ISSN 1946-2107) **5122**
Georgia Ports Authority Ports Guide & Directory *see* G P A Ports Guide & Directory **8644**
Georgia Practice, with Forms. Handbook (USA ISSN 1930-5990) **4680**
Georgia Press Bulletin (USA ISSN 1067-2931) **2321**
Georgia Probate and Related Laws and Rules Annotated *see* Georgia Probate and Related Laws & Rules Annotated **4903**
Georgia Probate and Related Laws & Rules Annotated (USA) **4903**
Georgia Real Estate Forms (USA) **7591**
Georgia Real Estate Law Letter (USA ISSN 1040-4805) **4680**
• Georgia Real Estate Licensing and Appraiser Laws and Regulations Annotated (USA ISSN 1546-8380) **4680**
Georgia Realtor (USA ISSN 0433-6070) **7591**
Georgia Recall Act of 1989 (USA) **7138**
• The Georgia Review (USA ISSN 0016-8386) **5300**
Georgia Rules of Court Annotated (USA ISSN 0747-6973) **4952**
Georgia School Directory *see* M D R's School Directory. Georgia **2958**
Georgia School Law Decisions (USA) **3023**
Georgia Sea Grant College Program. Marine Extension Bulletin (USA) **2804**
Georgia Sportsman (USA ISSN 0199-6517) **8315**
Georgia State Literary Studies (USA ISSN 0884-8696) **5300**
• Georgia State University Law Letter (USA) **4680**
• ➤ Georgia State University Law Review (USA ISSN 8755-6847) **4680**
Georgia State University Review *see* G S U Review **5217**
• Georgia State University Signal (USA ISSN 0016-8424) **2285**
• Georgia Statistical Abstract (USA ISSN 0085-1043) **1233**
Georgia Straight (CAN ISSN 1485-1318) **3810**
Georgia Strait Alliance. Annual Report (CAN ISSN 1910-6459) **7439**
Georgia Studies Weekly. Democracy (USA ISSN 1933-3285) **2859**
▼ Georgia Studies Weekly. My State (USA ISSN 1941-9619) **2859**
Georgia Super Lawyers (USA ISSN 1556-2093) **4680**
Georgia Superior Court Domestic Violence Benchbook *see* Domestic Violence Benchbook **4660**
Georgia Tech Alumni Magazine (USA ISSN 1061-9747) **2285**
• Georgia Trend (USA ISSN 0882-5971) **1349**
The Georgia Veterinarian (USA ISSN 0886-5760) **8797**
• Georgia Vital Statistics Report (Online Edition) (USA) **7307**
Georgia Vital Statistics Report (Print Edition) *see* Georgia Vital Statistics Report (Online Edition) **7307**
Georgia Voyager Magazine (USA ISSN 1554-5008) **2190**
Georgia Workers' Compensation Laws, Rules and Regulations Annotated *see* Georgia Workers' Compensation Laws, Rules & Regulations Annotated **1683**
• Georgia Workers' Compensation Laws, Rules & Regulations Annotated (USA ISSN 1534-5440) **1683**
Georgian Academy of Sciences. Bulletin/Sakartvelos Metsnierebata Akademia. Moambe (GEO ISSN 0132-1447) **7857**
Georgian Annual (USA) **7736**
Georgian Bay Today (CAN ISSN 0849-5696) **3810**
Georgian Engineering News *see* G E N **3267**
➤ Georgian Geophysical Society. Journal (GEO ISSN 1512-1127) **2782**
Georgian Group Journal (GBR ISSN 0963-1070) **443**
Georgian Group. Symposium Proceedings (GBR) **443**
Georgian Group. Town Reports (GBR) **443**
▼ Georgian International Journal of Science, Technology and Medicine (USA ISSN 1939-5825) **5619**
Georgian Journal of Radiology (GEO ISSN 1512-0031) **6197**
• Georgian Law Review (GEO) **4680**
• ➤ Georgian Mathematical Journal (DEU ISSN 1072-947X) **5490**
➤ Georgian Medical News (GEO ISSN 1512-0112) **5619**
Georgian Monthly (USA) **7736**
Georgian Times (GEO) **3843**
Georgia's Cities (USA) **7493**
Georgia's Colleges, Universities and Technical Colleges (USA) **2956**
Georgia's Outdoor Adventures (USA ISSN 1939-5418) **8315**
Georgia's Postsecondary Schools *see* Georgia's Colleges, Universities and Technical Colleges **2956**
Georgica (DEU ISSN 0232-4490) **4223**
Georgica (ESP ISSN 1132-810X) **115**
Georgike Statistike tes Ellados *see* Agricultural Statistics of Greece **174**
Georgist Journal (USA ISSN 0887-6290) **1542**
▼ • ➤ Georisk (GBR ISSN 1749-9518) **2743**
GEOS *see* Cahiers de Geographie de la Sante **5591**
Geos (VEN ISSN 0435-5601) **2743**
Geosaison *see* Geo Saison **8713**
• Geosanidad (ESP ISSN 1699-227X) **2638**
Geoscience *see* Xiandai Dizhi **2775**
Geoscience *see* Meddelelser om Groenland. Geoscience **2754**
• Geoscience Australia. Record (AUS ISSN 1448-2177) **2743**
• ➤ Geoscience Canada (CAN ISSN 0315-0941) **2743**
➤ Geoscience Canada Reprint Series (CAN ISSN 0821-381X) **2708**
• Geoscience Documentation (GBR ISSN 0016-8483) **2720**
Geoscience Education (USA) **2743**
Geoscience in South-West England (GBR) **2743**
Geoscience Information Society Newsletter *see* G I S Newsletter **2707**
➤ Geoscience Information Society. Proceedings (USA ISSN 0072-1409) **2708**
Geoscience Journal (IND ISSN 0252-1970) **2743**
Geoscience Magazine *see* Chigaku Kenkyu **2728**
Geoscience Online de Wissen Online *see* g-o.de Wissen Online **7857**
† Geoscience Texts (GBR ISSN 0278-7091) **8959**
• Geoscience Wisconsin (USA ISSN 0164-2049) **2744**
Geosciences (FRA ISSN 1772-094X) **2744**
• ➤ Geosciences Journal (DEU ISSN 1226-4806) **2708**
• GeoScienceWorld (USA) **2720**
▼ • ➤ Geoscientific Model Development (DEU ISSN 1991-959X) **2782**
▼ • ➤ Geoscientific Model Development Discussions (DEU ISSN 1991-9611) **2782**
Geoscientist (GBR ISSN 0961-5628) **2744**
• Geosources (GBR) **2720**
• Geospatial Health (ITA ISSN 1827-1987) **6197**
† • Geospatial Solutions (USA ISSN 1529-7403) **8959**
• Geosphere (USA ISSN 1553-040X) **2744**
• ➤ Geostandards and Geoanalytical Research (USA ISSN 1639-4488) **2744**
Geostoria del Territorio (ITA ISSN 1970-7193) **7966**
Geosul (BRA ISSN 0103-3964) **2744**
Geosur (URY ISSN 0250-7609) **7237**
• Geosynthetics (USA ISSN 1931-8189) **8451**
† • ➤ Geosynthetics International (GBR ISSN 1072-6349) **8959**
• ➤ Geosynthetics International (Online) (GBR ISSN 1751-7613) **8451**
Geosynthetics World (AUT ISSN 1359-5253) **3433**
† Geotec (ITA) **8959**
• ➤ Geotechnical and Geological Engineering (NLD ISSN 0960-3182) **6463**
Geotechnical Engineering (THA ISSN 0046-5828) **3268**
Geotechnical Engineering Bulletin (THA ISSN 0858-4869) **2708**
Geotechnical Engineering International Resources Center Current Awareness Service *see* G E - I R C Current Awareness Service **2707**
Geotechnical News (CAN ISSN 0823-650X) **2744**
Geotechnical Research Institute. Technical Reports *see* Jiban Kogaku Kenkyujo Hokoku **2749**
Geotechnical Science Laboratories. Publications, Reports, and Theses (CAN ISSN 0831-5000) **2720**
Geotechnical Special Publications (USA ISSN 0895-0563) **2744**
• ➤ Geotechnical Testing Journal (USA ISSN 0149-6115) **3268**
• ➤ Geotechnik (DEU ISSN 0172-6145) **3193**
Geotechnika (NLD ISSN 0926-5074) **2744**
• ➤ Geotechnique (GBR ISSN 0016-8505) **3268**
Geotecnia (PRT ISSN 0379-9522) **2744**
• Geotectonic Research (DEU ISSN 1864-5658) **2782**
Geotectonica et Metallogenia *see* Dadi Gouzao yu Chengkuangxue **2730**
• Geotectonics (RUS ISSN 0016-8521) **2782**
Geotehnika (HRV) **2744**
• Geotektonika (RUS ISSN 0016-853X) **2744**
Geotektonika, Tektonofizika i Geodinamika (BGR ISSN 0324-1661) **2744**
Geotema (ITA ISSN 1126-7798) **4013**
Geotemas (ESP ISSN 1576-5172) **2744**
• Geotermia (MEX ISSN 0186-5897) **3162**
➤ GEOtext (CAN ISSN 1208-2260) **2708**
• ➤ Geotextiles and Geomembranes (GBR ISSN 0266-1144) **8451**
Geothermal Energy (USA ISSN 0896-6257) **3152**
Geothermal Energy Research and Development Co., Ltd. Journal *see* Chinetsu Gijutsu **3162**
Geothermal Hotline (USA ISSN 0735-0503) **3162**
Geothermal Research Society of Japan. Journal *see* Nihon Chinetsu Gakkaishi **2787**
• Geothermal Resources Council. Bulletin (USA ISSN 0160-7782) **3162**
Geothermal Resources Council. Special Report (USA ISSN 0149-8991) **2782**
Geothermal Resources Council. Transactions (USA ISSN 0193-5933) **2783**
Geothermal Training in Iceland (ISL ISSN 1670-7400) **2783**
• ➤ Geothermics (GBR ISSN 0375-6505) **2708**
Geotimes *see* Earth **2706**
• Geotitles (GBR ISSN 0952-2700) **2720**
Geotraveler (USA ISSN 1067-4527) **8713**
• ➤ GeoTropico (COL ISSN 1692-0791) **4013**
• Geoviden (DNK ISSN 1604-6935) **2709**
GeoWissen *see* Geo Wissen **4008**
Geowissen Kompakt (DEU ISSN 0341-7522) **2744**
Geowissenschaften Online *see* Scinexx **2766**
Geowissenschaftliche Mitteilungen (DEU ISSN 1616-3931) **2744**
GeoWorld *see* Geo World **4037**
Gep/Machine (HUN ISSN 0016-8572) **5452**
Gepeszeti Szakirodalmi Tajekoztato/Machinery Abstracts (HUN ISSN 0231-0686) **3230**
Gepgyartas (HUN ISSN 1587-4648) **5452**
Gepgyartastechnologiai es Szerszamgepipari Szakirodalmi Tajekoztato/Mechanical Engineering & Machine Tool Abstracts (HUN ISSN 0231-0694) **3230**
Geppo Furudo Pawa/Fluid Power (JPN) **3361**
Geppo Hatsumei/Monthly Report of Invention (JPN) **6750**
Gequ/Songs Monthly (CHN ISSN 0454-0816) **6569**
Geraete- und Produktsicherheitsgesetz (DEU) **3100**
Geraniums Around the World (USA ISSN 0016-8599) **3733**
Gerardus (NLD ISSN 1878-8718) **7799**
Gerardus Klok *see* Gerardus **7799**
Gerbil (USA ISSN 1086-5624) **4374**
Gerechtelijk Wetboek (BEL) **4952**
Gerechtelijk Zakboekje (Bilingual Edition)/Memento Judiciaire (BEL ISSN 1374-1136) **4952**
De Gerechtsdeurwaarder *see* Executief **4950**
De Gerechtsdeurwaarder - Digest/Le Huissier de Justice - Digest (BEL ISSN 0774-9732) **4952**
† ➤ Gereformeerd Theologisch Tijdschrift (NLD ISSN 0016-8610) **8959**

DIRECTORY 2010 GERMANY. STATISTISCHES BUNDESAMT. FACHSERIE 17, PREISE 10323

Gereformeerde Vroueblad (ZAF ISSN 0378-407X) **7759**
• Geren Diannao/P C Magazine (CHN ISSN 1006-3145) **2419**
• Gerencia (CHL ISSN 0718-350X) **1747**
Gerencia & Sistemas (CHL) **2543**
Gerencia de Riesgos (ESP ISSN 0213-4314) **4504**
Gerencia de Viajes (COL ISSN 0121-9227) **8713**
Gerencia Tecnologica Informatica (COL ISSN 1657-8236) **2419**
Gerentologia Polska (POL) **4045**
Gerer et Comprendre/To Manage and to Understand (FRA ISSN 0295-4397) **6463**
Gerer un Service d'Aide a Domicile (FRA ISSN 1957-6269) **4094**
Gerhard-Mercator-Universitaet Duisburg. Duisburger Universitaets-Report (DEU) **2982**
Geriatria (ITA ISSN 1122-5807) **4045**
Geriatria (PRT ISSN 0871-5386) **4045**
• Geriatrianet.com (ESP ISSN 1575-3166) **4045**
➤ Geriatric and Medical Intelligence/Medicina e Anziani (ITA ISSN 1121-8460) **4045**
Geriatric Care (USA ISSN 1524-2870) **4045**
• ➤ Geriatric Medicine (GBR ISSN 0268-201X) **4045**
• ➤ Geriatric Nursing (USA ISSN 0197-4572) **4045**
Geriatric Psychiatry *see* American Journal of Geriatric Psychiatry **4040**
• ➤ Geriatrics (USA ISSN 0016-867X) **4045**
• ➤ Geriatrics and Aging (CAN ISSN 1488-8408) **4045**
• ➤ Geriatrics & Gerontology International (AUS ISSN 1444-1586) **4045**
▼ • Geriatrics Research Review (NZL ISSN 1172-0557) **4045**
• Geriatrics Review Syllabus (USA) **4045**
Geriatrics Today *see* Canadian Journal of Geriatrics **4042**
Het Geriatrie Formularium (NLD ISSN 1386-6168) **4045**
Geriatrie Journal (DEU ISSN 1439-1139) **4045**
Geriatrie Pratique *see* Geriatrie-Praxis **4045**
Geriatrie-Praxis (CHE ISSN 1661-9382) **4045**
Geriatrie Praxis Oesterreich (AUT) **4046**
† Geriatrie und Rehabilitation (BRD ISSN 0934-5086) **8959**
Geriatries *see* Reperes en Geriatrie **4054**
Gerichtsnotizen (DEU ISSN 1618-1883) **4680**
• Gerion (ESP ISSN 0213-0181) **4140**
• Gerion. Anejos (ESP ISSN 1576-2564) **4140**
Germain's Transnational Law Research: A Guide for Attorneys (USA) **4927**
German American Genealogy (USA) **3768**
German American Journal (USA ISSN 0273-5261) **3535**
German-American National Public Affairs Committee Brief *see* G A N P A C Brief **3534**
German - American Partnership Program Magazin *see* G A P P Magazin **3012**
German American Trade (CAN ISSN 1182-803X) **1567**
German and American Studies in Sport (DEU) **8175**
German Arab Trade (EGY ISSN 0072-1433) **1403**
• ➤ German as a Foreign Language (GBR ISSN 1470-9570) **5122**
German-Australian Studies/Deutsch-Australische Studien (CHE ISSN 1421-7902) **5300**
German Blues Circle Info (DEU) **6569**
German Books in Print *see* Verzeichnis Lieferbarer Buecher **638**
German Books in Print on CD-ROM *see* Verzeichnis Lieferbarer Buecher - CD-ROM **638**
† • German Brief (DEU ISSN 1616-0940) **8959**
▼ • German Business Review (USA ISSN 1937-3201) **1113**
German-Canadian Yearbook/Deutschkanadisches Jahrbuch (CAN ISSN 0316-8603) **3535**
German Chapter of the A C M. Berichte (Association for Computing Machinery) (DEU ISSN 0724-9764) **2419**
➤ German Connection (USA ISSN 8755-1756) **3768**
German Development Institute Book Series *see* G D I Book Series **1596**
• German Economic Review (GBR ISSN 1465-6485) **1488**
German Films Quarterly (DEU) **6502**
German Financial Markets Yearbook (Year) (GBR) **1626**
German Historical Institute. Annual Lecture (GBR ISSN 0269-8560) **4223**
German Historical Institute. Bulletin (USA ISSN 1048-9134) **4223**
German Historical Institute London. Bulletin (GBR ISSN 0269-8552) **4223**
➤ German Historical Perspectives (GBR ISSN 0953-363X) **4223**
• ➤ German History (GBR ISSN 0266-3554) **4223**
German Institute of Global and Area Studies Focus. Afrika *see* G I G A Focus. Afrika **7236**
German Institute of Global and Area Studies Focus. Asien *see* G I G A Focus. Asien **7236**
German Institute of Global and Area Studies Focus. Global *see* G I G A Focus. Global **7236**
German Institute of Global and Area Studies Focus. Lateinamerika (Print Edition) *see* G I G A Focus. Lateinamerika (Print Edition) **7236**
German Institute of Global and Area Studies Focus. Nahost *see* G I G A Focus. Nahost **7236**
German Institute of Global and Area Studies Working Papers *see* G I G A Working Papers **7236**
German Journal for Evidence and Quality in Health Care *see* Zeitschrift fuer Evidenz, Fortbildung und Qualitaet im Gesundheitswesen **5734**
German Journal of Acupuncture *see* Deutsche Zeitschrift fuer Akupunktur **5604**
German Journal of Hydrography *see* Ocean Dynamics **2814**
German Journal of Hydrography. Supplement *see* Deutsche Hydrographische Zeitschrift. Ergaenzungsheft **8949**
German Journal of Oncology *see* Deutsche Zeitschrift fuer Onkologie **6018**
• ➤ German Journal of Psychiatry (DEU ISSN 1433-1055) **6143**
German Journal of Urban Studies *see* Deutsche Zeitschrift fuer Kommunalwissenschaften **7491**
• German Law Journal (USA) **4680**
• German Life (USA ISSN 1075-2382) **3535**
German Life and Civilization (GBR ISSN 0899-9899) **4223**
• ➤ German Life and Letters (GBR ISSN 0016-8777) **5300**
German Linguistic and Cultural Studies (GBR ISSN 1422-1454) **5122**
• ➤ German Medical Science (DEU ISSN 1612-3174) **5619**
German Medical Science Current Posters in Otorhinolaryngology, Head and Neck Surgery *see* G M S Current Posters in Otorhinolaryngology, Head and Neck Surgery **6080**
German Medical Science Current Topics in Otorhinolaryngology - Head and Neck Surgery *see* G M S Current Topics in Otorhinolaryngology - Head and Neck Surgery **6080**
German Medical Science Health Technology Assessment *see* G M S. Health Technology Assessment **5617**
German Medical Science Krankenhaushygiene Interdisziplinaer *see* G M S Krankenhaushygiene Interdisziplinaer **7518**
German Medical Science Medizin - Bibliothek - Information *see* G M S Medizin - Bibliothek - Information **5617**
German Medical Science Psycho - Social - Medicine *see* G M S Psycho - Social - Medicine **6142**
German Medical Science Thoracic Surgical Science *see* G M S Thoracic Surgical Science **6244**
German Medical Science Zeitschrift fuer Medizinische Ausbildung *see* G M S Zeitschrift fuer Medizinische Ausbildung **5617**
German Medical Weekly *see* Deutsche Medizinische Wochenschrift **5604**
German Merchant Fleet (DEU ISSN 0723-2667) **8644**
• ➤ German Monitor (NLD ISSN 0927-1910) **5217**
† German Motor Directory (DEU ISSN 1860-1111) **8959**
German Motor Tribune *see* German Motor Directory **8959**
German News/German Samachar (IND ISSN 0016-8793) **1488**
• ➤ German Policy Studies/Politikfeldanalyse (USA ISSN 1523-9764) **7439**
• ➤ German Politics (GBR ISSN 0964-4008) **7237**
• ➤ German Politics and Society (USA ISSN 1045-0300) **7138**
German Postal Specialist (USA ISSN 0016-8823) **6895**
• ➤ The German Quarterly (USA ISSN 0016-8831) **5122**
• German Research (DEU ISSN 0172-1526) **7857**
† German Research Service. Special Science Reports (DEU ISSN 0949-7811) **8959**
▼ • German Review (USA ISSN 1937-3171) **3535**
• ➤ German Risk and Insurance Review (DEU ISSN 1860-5400) **4504**
German Samachar *see* German News **1488**
German Shepherd Dog Review (USA ISSN 0046-5852) **6808**
German Shepherd Quarterly (USA ISSN 0745-1849) **6808**
German Shorthaired Pointer Club of America Shorthair *see* G S P C A Shorthair **6808**
German Shorthaired Pointer News (USA ISSN 1065-0830) **6808**
German Society for General and Applied Entomology. Proceedings *see* Deutsche Gesellschaft fuer Allgemeine und Angewandte Entomologie. Mitteilungen **843**
German Studies Library Group Newsletter (GBR ISSN 0951-2616) **5011**
• ➤ German Studies Review (USA ISSN 0149-7952) **4223**
➤ German Studies Series (GBR ISSN 1354-3571) **1113**
German Tax News (DEU ISSN 0947-658X) **1926**
• German-Thai Chamber of Commerce Handbook and Directory (THA) **1403**
• ➤ German Working Papers in Law and Economics (USA ISSN 1933-8627) **4680**
• German World (USA ISSN 1558-7568) **3535**
German Yearbook of International Law (DEU ISSN 0344-3094) **4927**
Germana Esperanta Fervojista Asocio. Bulteno (DEU ISSN 0016-8866) **8617**
Germania (DEU ISSN 0016-8874) **395**
➤ Germania Sacra (DEU ISSN 0435-5857) **4223**
Germanic Genealogy Journal (USA ISSN 1548-3150) **3768**
Germanic Linguistics and Semiotic Analysis *see* Interdisciplinary Journal for Germanic Linguistics and Semiotic Analysis **5128**
➤ Germanic Notes and Reviews (USA) **5122**
• ➤ The Germanic Review (USA ISSN 0016-8890) **5122**
Germanic Studies in America (CHE ISSN 0721-3727) **5300**
Germanica (FRA ISSN 0984-2632) **5300**
Germanica Pacifica Studies (NZL ISSN 1176-8606) **8104**
Germanisch-Romanische Monatsschrift (DEU ISSN 0016-8904) **5300**
Germanisch-Romanische Monatsschrift. Beiheft (DEU ISSN 0178-4390) **5300**
Germanische Denkmaeler der Voelkerwanderungszeit. Series B (DEU ISSN 0418-9779) **395**
Germanistische Arbeitshefte. Erganzungsreihe *see* Germanistische Arbeitshefte **5122**
Germanistik (Berlin, 2005) (DEU ISSN 1860-8345) **5300**
• Germanistik (Tuebingen) (DEU ISSN 0016-8912) **5407**
Germanistische Arbeiten zu Sprache und Kulturgeschichte (DEU ISSN 0723-3191) **5122**
Germanistische Arbeiten zur Sprachgeschichte (DEU) **5122**
Germanistische Arbeitshefte (DEU ISSN 0344-6697) **5122**
• Germanistische Beitraege (ROM ISSN 1454-5144) **4453**
Germanistische Linguistik (DEU ISSN 0072-1492) **5122**
Germanistische Linguistik. Varia *see* Germanistische Linguistik **5122**
Germanistische Mitteilungen (BEL ISSN 0771-3703) **5122**
Germanistische Schlaglichter (SWE ISSN 1403-6142) **5122**
Germanistische Symposien (DEU ISSN 0936-3890) **5300**
Germanistische Texte und Studien (DEU ISSN 0175-9388) **5122**
• ➤ Germano-Slavica (CAN ISSN 0317-4956) **5300**
Germanoslavica (CZE ISSN 1210-9029) **5300**
➤ Germantown Crier (USA ISSN 0742-6631) **4293**
• Germany Auto Reports (GBR ISSN 1748-9903) **8582**
The Germany Autos Report *see* Germany Auto Reports **8582**
Germany. Bundesagentur fuer Arbeit. Amtliche Nachrichten (DEU ISSN 1613-9429) **1683**
† Germany. Bundesagentur fuer Arbeit. Berufsberatung (DEU) **8959**
Germany. Bundesanstalt fuer Arbeit. Foerderung der Beruflichen Weiterbildung (DEU ISSN 1439-9350) **3063**
Germany. Bundesanstalt fuer Gewaesserkunde. Jahresbericht (DEU ISSN 0170-5156) **8823**
Germany. Bundesanstalt fuer Materialforschung und -pruefung. Jahresbericht (DEU ISSN 0934-9456) **3345**
Germany. Bundesanstalt fuer Strassenwesen. Berichte: Strassenbau (DEU ISSN 0943-9323) **3268**
Germany. Bundesministerium fuer Bildung, Wissenschaft, Forschung und Technologie. Bundesbericht Forschung *see* Bundesministerium fuer Bildung und Forschung. Bundesbericht Forschung und Innovation **7425**
† Germany. Bundesministerium fuer Verkehr. Strassenbaubericht (DEU) **8959**
• Germany Defence & Security Report (GBR ISSN 1749-1398) **6422**
Germany. Deutscher Bundestag. Wissenschaftliche Dienste. Aktuelle Bibliographien der Bibliothek (DEU ISSN 1435-4039) **625**
† Germany. Deutscher Bundestag. Wissenschaftliche Dienste. Materialien (DEU ISSN 0344-9130) **8959**
Germany. Deutscher Bundestag. Wissenschaftliche Dienste. Neue Aufsaetze in der Bibliothek *see* Germany. Deutscher Bundestag. Wissenschaftliche Dienste. Neue Buecher und Aufsaetze in der Bibliothek **7937**
Germany. Deutscher Bundestag. Wissenschaftliche Dienste. Neue Buecher und Aufsaetze in der Bibliothek (DEU) **7937**
Germany. Deutscher Bundestag. Wissenschaftliche Dienste. Neuerwerbungen der Bibliothek (DEU ISSN 0931-3397) **625**
• Germany Food & Drink Report (GBR ISSN 1749-270X) **1113**
Germany Freight Transport Report (GBR ISSN 1752-5810) **8497**
• Germany Info (USA) **3535**
Germany. Kraftfahrt-Bundesamt. Fahr- und Fahrlehrerlaubnisstatistiken (DEU ISSN 0943-1527) **8524**
Germany. Kraftfahrt-Bundesamt. Fahrerlaubnis auf Probe (DEU ISSN 0943-1519) **8524**
Germany. Kraftfahrt-Bundesamt. Fahrzeuguntersuchungen (DEU) **8524**
Germany. Kraftfahrt-Bundesamt. Grenzueberschreitender Strassenverkehr (DEU ISSN 0949-9636) **8524**
Germany. Kraftfahrt-Bundesamt. Kraftfahrzeugstatistiken (DEU ISSN 0943-1470) **8524**
Germany. Kraftfahrt-Bundesamt. Neuzulassungen - Besitzumschreibungen - Loeschungen von Kraftfahrzeugen und Kraftfahrzeuganhaengern (DEU ISSN 0943-1497) **8524**
Germany. Kraftfahrt-Bundesamt. Verkehrsstatistiken (DEU ISSN 0943-1543) **8524**
Germany. Kraftfahrt-Bundesamt. Verkehrszentralregister (DEU ISSN 0943-1500) **8524**
Germany Petrochemicals Report (GBR ISSN 1749-2246) **6771**
▼ Germany Real Estate Yearbook (NLD ISSN 1872-7301) **7591**
Germany. Sachverstaendigenrat zur Begutachtung der Gesamtwirtschaftlichen Entwicklung. Jahresgutachten (DEU ISSN 0072-159X) **1886**
Germany Stamp Catalogue (GBR ISSN 0142-9817) **6895**
Germany. Statistisches Bundesamt. Alphabetisches Laenderverzeichnis fuer die Aussenhandelsstatistik (DEU ISSN 0072-1638) **1233**
Germany. Statistisches Bundesamt. Ausgewaehlte Zahlen fuer die Bauwirtschaft (DEU ISSN 0072-1719) **1046**
Germany. Statistisches Bundesamt. Ausgewahlte Zahlen zur Energiewirtschaft (DEU ISSN 0721-653X) **3153**
Germany. Statistisches Bundesamt. Bevoelkerung und Erwerbstaetigkeit. Reihe 1: Gebiet und Bevoelkerung (DEU) **7307**
Germany. Statistisches Bundesamt. Fachserie 1, Bevoelkerung und Erwerbstaetigkeit, Reihe 1: Gebiet und Bevoelkerung (DEU ISSN 0072-1794) **7307**
Germany. Statistisches Bundesamt. Fachserie 1, Bevoelkerung und Erwerbstaetigkeit, Reihe 3: Haushaelte und Familien (DEU) **7307**
Germany. Statistisches Bundesamt. Fachserie 1, Bevoelkerung und Erwerbstaetigkeit, Reihe 4: Erwerbstaetigkeit (DEU ISSN 0072-1832) **1233**
Germany. Statistisches Bundesamt. Fachserie 11: Bildung und Kultur (DEU ISSN 0072-1778) **2933**
Germany. Statistisches Bundesamt. Fachserie 12, Gesundheitswesen, Reihe 1: Ausgewaehlte Zahlen fuer das Gesundheitswesen (DEU ISSN 0172-9551) **7548**
Germany. Statistisches Bundesamt. Fachserie 13, Reihe 2: Sozialhilfe; Reihe 3: Kriegsopferfuersorge (DEU ISSN 0072-3754) **8083**
Germany. Statistisches Bundesamt. Fachserie 13, Sozialleistungen, Reihe 6: Jugendhilfe (DEU ISSN 0072-3762) **8083**
Germany. Statistisches Bundesamt. Fachserie 14: Finanzen und Steuern (DEU) **1233**
Germany. Statistisches Bundesamt. Fachserie 15, Wirtschaftsrechnungen, Reihe 1: Einnahmen und Ausgaben Ausgewaehlter Privater Haushalte (DEU ISSN 0176-9405) **1233**
Germany. Statistisches Bundesamt. Fachserie 16, Loehne und Gehaelter, Reihe 1: Arbeiterverdienste in der Landwirtschaft (DEU ISSN 0176-7445) **181**
Germany. Statistisches Bundesamt. Fachserie 16, Loehne und Gehaelter, Reihe 2.1: Arbeiterverdienste in der Industrie (DEU ISSN 0177-2473) **1233**
Germany. Statistisches Bundesamt. Fachserie 16, Loehne und Gehaelter, Reihe 2.2: Angestelltenverdienst in Industrie und Handel (DEU) **1233**
Germany. Statistisches Bundesamt. Fachserie 16, Loehne und Gehaelter, Reihe 3: Arbeiterverdienste im Handwerk (DEU ISSN 0072-3797) **1233**
Germany. Statistisches Bundesamt. Fachserie 16, Loehne und Gehaelter, Reihe 4: Tarifloehne und Tarifgehaelter (DEU ISSN 0072-3843) **1234**
Germany. Statistisches Bundesamt. Fachserie 16, Loehne und Gehaelter, Reihe 5: Loehne, Gehaelter und Arbeitskosten im Ausland (DEU ISSN 0941-3685) **1234**
Germany. Statistisches Bundesamt. Fachserie 17, Preise, Reihe 1: Preise und Preisindizes fuer die Land- und Forstwirtschaft (DEU ISSN 0072-3894) **181**
Germany. Statistisches Bundesamt. Fachserie 17, Preise, Reihe 10: Internationaler Vergleich der Preise fuer die Lebenshaltung (DEU ISSN 0072-3827) **1234**
Germany. Statistisches Bundesamt. Fachserie 17, Preise, Reihe 11: Preise und Preisindizes im Ausland (DEU ISSN 0072-3940) **1234**
Germany. Statistisches Bundesamt. Fachserie 17, Preise, Reihe 2: Preise und Preisindizes fuer Gewerbliche Produkte. Erzeugerpreise (DEU ISSN 0721-121X) **1234**
Germany. Statistisches Bundesamt. Fachserie 17, Preise, Reihe 3: Preisindex fuer den Wareneingang des Produzierenden Gewerbes (DEU ISSN 0940-3949) **1234**
Germany. Statistisches Bundesamt. Fachserie 17, Preise, Reihe 4: Messzahlen fuer Bauleistungspreise und Preisindizes fuer Bauwerke (DEU ISSN 0720-4221) **1234**
Germany. Statistisches Bundesamt. Fachserie 17, Preise, Reihe 5: Kaufwerte fuer Bauland (DEU ISSN 0720-4124) **1046**

Title

10324 GERMANY. STATISTISCHES BUNDESAMT. FACHSERIE 17, PREISE ULRICH'S PERIODICALS

Germany. Statistisches Bundesamt. Fachserie 17, Preise, Reihe 7: Preisindices fuer die Lebenshaltung (DEU) **1234**
Germany. Statistisches Bundesamt. Fachserie 17, Preise, Reihe 8: Preisindizes fuer die Ein- und Ausfuhr (DEU) **1234**
Germany. Statistisches Bundesamt. Fachserie 17, Preise, Reihe 9: Preise und Preisindizes fuer Verkehr und Nachrichtenuebermittlung (DEU) **8525**
Germany. Statistisches Bundesamt. Fachserie 18, Volkswirtschaftliche Gesamtrechnungen, Reihe 1: Konten und Standardtabellen (DEU ISSN 0072-4009) **1234**
Germany. Statistisches Bundesamt. Fachserie 19, Umweltschutz, Reihe 2: Wasserversorgung und Abwasserbeseitigung (DEU) **8843**
Germany. Statistisches Bundesamt. Fachserie 2, Unternehmen und Arbeitsstaetten, Reihe 3: Abschluesse der Oeffentlichen Versorgungs-, Entsorgungs- und Verkehrsunternehmen (DEU) **1234**
Germany. Statistisches Bundesamt. Fachserie 2, Unternehmen und Arbeitsstaetten, Reihe 4.1: Insolvenzverfahren (DEU) **1234**
Germany. Statistisches Bundesamt. Fachserie 3, Land- und Forstwirtschaft, Fischerei; Reihe 2: Betriebs-, Arbeits- und Einkommensverhaeltnisse (DEU ISSN 0072-3681) **181**
Germany. Statistisches Bundesamt. Fachserie 3, Land- und Forstwirtschaft, Fischerei; Reihe 3: Landwirtschaftliche Bodennuetzung und Pflanzliche Erzeugung (DEU) **181**
Germany. Statistisches Bundesamt. Fachserie 3, Land- und Forstwirtschaft, Fischerei; Reihe 4.5: Fischerei (DEU ISSN 0072-3673) **3613**
Germany. Statistisches Bundesamt. Fachserie 3, Land- und Forstwirtschaft, Fischerei; Reihe 4: Viehbestand und Tierische Erzeugung (DEU) **181**
Germany. Statistisches Bundesamt. Fachserie 4, Produzierendes Gewerbe, Reihe 2.1: Indizes der Produktion und Produktion ausgewaehlter Erzeugnisse im Produzierenden Gewerbe (DEU) **1234**
Germany. Statistisches Bundesamt. Fachserie 4, Produzierendes Gewerbe, Reihe 2.2: Auftragseingang und Umsatz im Verarbeitenden Gewerbe, Auftragseingang und Auftragsbestand im Bauhauptgewerbe. Indices (DEU) **1234**
Germany. Statistisches Bundesamt. Fachserie 4, Produzierendes Gewerbe, Reihe 3.1: Produktion im Produzierenden Gewerbe (DEU) **1234**
Germany. Statistisches Bundesamt. Fachserie 4, Produzierendes Gewerbe, Reihe 5: Baugewerbe (DEU) **1046**
Germany. Statistisches Bundesamt. Fachserie 4, Produzierendes Gewerbe, Reihe 7.1: Handwerk. Beschaeftigte und Umsatz im Handwerk (DEU) **1234**
Germany. Statistisches Bundesamt. Fachserie 5, Bautaetigkeit und Wohnungen, Reihe 1: Bautaetigkeit (DEU ISSN 0072-1735) **1046**
Germany. Statistisches Bundesamt. Fachserie 5, Bautaetigkeit und Wohnungen, Reihe 2: Bewilligungen im Sozialen Wohnungsbau (DEU ISSN 0072-1743) **1046**
Germany. Statistisches Bundesamt. Fachserie 5, Bautaetigkeit und Wohnungen, Reihe 3: Bestand an Wohnungen (DEU ISSN 0072-1751) **1046**
Germany. Statistisches Bundesamt. Fachserie 6, Binnenhandel, Gastgewerbe, Tourismus; Reihe 1: Grosshandel (DEU) **1234**
Germany. Statistisches Bundesamt. Fachserie 6, Binnenhandel, Gastgewerbe, Tourismus; Reihe 3: Einzelhandel (DEU) **1234**
Germany. Statistisches Bundesamt. Fachserie 6, Binnenhandel, Gastgewerbe, Tourismus; Reihe 7: Reiseverkehr (DEU) **8779**
Germany. Statistisches Bundesamt. Fachserie 7, Aussenhandel, Reihe 1: Zusammenfassende Uebersichten fuer den Aussenhandel (DEU ISSN 0072-1646) **1234**
Germany. Statistisches Bundesamt. Fachserie 7, Aussenhandel, Reihe 2: Aussenhandel nach Waren und Laendern (Spezialhandel) (DEU ISSN 0072-1654) **1234**
Germany. Statistisches Bundesamt. Fachserie 7, Aussenhandel, Reihe 3: Aussenhandel Nach Laendern und Warengruppen (Spezialhandel) (DEU ISSN 0072-1662) **1234**
Germany. Statistisches Bundesamt, Fachserie 7, Aussenhandel, Reihe 4. Aussenhandel mit Ausgewaehlten Waren (DEU) **1234**
Germany. Statistisches Bundesamt. Fachserie 7, Aussenhandel, Reihe 7: Aussenhandel nach Laendern und Guetergruppen der Produktionsstatistiken (Spezialhandel) (DEU) **1234**
Germany. Statistisches Bundesamt. Fachserie 8, Verkehr, Reihe 2: Eisenbahnverkehr (DEU ISSN 0072-4041) **8525**
Germany. Statistisches Bundesamt. Fachserie 8, Verkehr, Reihe 3: Strassenpersonenverkehr (DEU ISSN 0935-7726) **8525**
Germany. Statistisches Bundesamt. Fachserie 8, Verkehr, Reihe 4: Binnenschiffahrt (DEU ISSN 0072-4017) **8525**
Germany. Statistisches Bundesamt. Fachserie 8, Verkehr, Reihe 5: Seeschiffahrt (DEU ISSN 0072-4025) **8525**
Germany. Statistisches Bundesamt. Fachserie 8, Verkehr, Reihe 6: Luftverkehr (DEU ISSN 0072-4033) **8525**
Germany. Statistisches Bundesamt. Fachserie 8, Verkehr, Reihe 7: Verkehrsunfaelle (DEU ISSN 0937-8294) **8525**
Germany. Statistisches Bundesamt. Fremdsprachige Veroeffentlichungen Nr. 6370010: Foreign Trade According to Standard International Trade Classification (SITC) - Special Trade (DEU) **1234**
Germany. Statistisches Bundesamt. Warenverzeichnis fuer die Aussenhandelsstatistik (DEU ISSN 0072-4106) **1234**
Germany. Statistisches Bundesamt. Zahlenkompass (DEU ISSN 0072-4114) **8374**
† • Germany's Top 500 (DEU) **8959**
Germination (CAN ISSN 0704-6286) **5423**
• ➤ Gerodontology (DNK ISSN 0734-0664) **5845**
• ➤ Gerokomos (ESP ISSN 1134-928X) **4046**
Geroldsecker Land (DEU ISSN 1614-1407) **3849**
➤ Geron (NLD ISSN 1389-143X) **4046**
Geronimo de Uztariz (ESP ISSN 1697-5081) **4223**
• Geronius (Online Edition) (NOR ISSN 0809-7275) **4046**
• ➤ Gerontechnology (NLD ISSN 1569-1101) **4046**
Gerontologi (DNK ISSN 1604-8644) **4046**
Gerontologi og Samfund *see* Gerontologi **4046**
• ➤ Gerontologia (BRA ISSN 0104-1258) **4046**
Gerontologia (FIN ISSN 0784-0039) **4046**
Gerontological Nursing *see* Journal of Gerontological Nursing **4049**
Gerontologie et Societe (FRA ISSN 0151-0193) **4046**
Gerontologie Pratique (FRA ISSN 0990-5669) **4046**
Gerontologija (SRB ISSN 0354-415X) **4046**
• ➤ The Gerontologist (USA ISSN 0016-9013) **4046**
• ➤ Gerontology (CHE ISSN 0304-324X) **4046**
• ➤ Gerontology (ISR ISSN 0334-2360) **4046**
Gerontology *see* Jerontoroji **4048**
• ➤ Gerontology & Geriatrics Education (USA ISSN 0270-1960) **4046**
• Gerontology News (USA ISSN 1083-222X) **4046**
Gerontology Research Centre News *see* G R C News **4045**
Gerontology Special Interest Section Quarterly (USA ISSN 1093-717X) **4046**
Gerontophile *see* Vie et Vieillissement **4057**
• ➤ GeroPsych (DEU ISSN 1662-9647) **4046**
Geroscopie *see* Geroscopie Magazine **4046**
Geroscopie Magazine (FRA ISSN 1770-362X) **4046**
Gerson Healing Newsletter (USA) **5619**
Gesamt Hochschule Kassel Publik *see* G H K Publik **2955**
Gesamtausgaben (CAN ISSN 0537-9423) **6569**
Gesamtbericht ueber die Taetigkeit der Europaeischen Union *see* General Report on the Activities of the European Union **3837**
Gesamte Oeffentliche Dienstrecht (DEU ISSN 0943-8289) **1683**
• Gesamtfahrplan (DEU) **8497**
Gesamtkatalog der Wiegendrucke (DEU) **625**
Gesamtkommentar Oeffentliches Dienstrecht. Band I: Beamtenrecht des Bundes und der Laender Richterrecht und Wehrrecht (DEU) **1683**
Gesamtkommentar Oeffentliches Dienstrecht. Band II: Disziplinarrecht des Bundes und der Laender (DEU) **1683**
Gesamtkommentar Oeffentliches Dienstrecht. Band III: Besoldungsrecht des Bundes und der Laender (DEU) **1683**
Gesamtkommentar Oeffentliches Dienstrecht. Band IV: Recht der Arbeitnehmer im Oeffentlichen Dienst (DEU) **1683**
Gesamtkommentar Oeffentliches Dienstrecht. Band V: Personalvertretungsrecht des Bundes und der Laender (DEU) **1683**
Gesamtregister mit den Rechtssaetzen und Fundstellen der Entscheidungen der Zeitschrift fuer Verkehrsrecht (AUT) **4822**
Gesamtschule in Nordrhein-Westfalen (DEU ISSN 1615-2999) **3023**
Gesamtstatistik der Kraftfahrtversicherung (DEU ISSN 0435-7442) **4529**
Gesamtverband Autoteile-Handel. Mitgliederverzeichnis (DEU ISSN 0939-5849) **8582**
Gesamtverband Werbeagenturen e.V. *see* G W A **25**
† Gesamtverzeichnis (Year) (DEU) **8959**
Geschaeftsgang im Sekunden Sektor/Evolution de la Situation dans le Sectuer Secondaire (CHE) **1234**
Die Geschaeftsidee (DEU ISSN 0344-2292) **1961**
Geschaeftsmann und Christ (CHE ISSN 0016-9021) **7759**
Geschaeftspartner Ungarn (HUN ISSN 0237-5478) **1113**
GeschaeftsWelt *see* Profits **1162**
Geschichte (Essen) (DEU) **4140**
Geschichte Betrifft Uns (DEU ISSN 0176-943X) **2859**
Geschichte der Geschichtsschreibung *see* Storia della Storiografia **4268**
Geschichte der Konzentrationslager 1933-1945 (DEU) **4223**
Geschichte der Meteorologie in Deutschland (DEU ISSN 0943-9862) **6353**
Geschichte der Pharmazie (DEU ISSN 0939-334X) **6844**
Geschichte der Sprachtheorie (DEU) **5122**
Geschichte des Arabischen Schrifttums (NLD) **5300**
Geschichte des Buchhandels (DEU ISSN 0941-7877) **7561**
Geschichte des Kirchlichen Lebens (DEU) **7759**
Geschichte in Koeln (DEU ISSN 0720-3659) **4223**
Geschichte in Wissenschaft und Unterricht (DEU ISSN 0016-9056) **4140**
Geschichte Lernen (DEU ISSN 0933-3096) **2860**
Geschichte, Politik und ihre Didaktik (DEU ISSN 0343-4648) **4223**
➤ Geschichte und Gesellschaft (DEU ISSN 0340-613X) **7966**
Geschichte und Philosophie der Medizin (DEU ISSN 1860-6199) **5619**
Geschichte und Politik in Sachsen (AUT ISSN 1611-5139) **4223**
Geschichte und Region/Storia e Regione (AUT ISSN 1121-0303) **4223**
Die Geschichte Unserer Heimat (DEU) **4223**
Geschichtliche Landeskunde (DEU ISSN 0072-4203) **4223**
Geschichtliches Eupen (BEL) **4223**
Geschichtsblaetter des Kreises Coesfeld (DEU ISSN 0723-2098) **4223**
➤ Geschichtsblaetter fuer Waldeck (DEU ISSN 0342-0965) **4223**
Geschichtswissenschaft (DEU ISSN 1860-1960) **4223**
Geschiebekunde Aktuell (DEU ISSN 0178-1731) **6725**
➤ Der Geschiebesammler (DEU ISSN 0340-4056) **2744**
Geschied- en Oudheidkundige Kring van Ronse en het Tenement van Inde. Annalen/Cercle Historique et Archeologique de Renaix et du Tenement d'Inde. Annales (BEL ISSN 0591-1133) **4223**
➤ Geschied- en Oudheidkundige Kring voor Leuven en Omgeving. Jaarboek (BEL ISSN 0774-5435) **4223**
Geschiedenis Actueel *see* Historisch Overijssel **4144**
Geschiedenis der Geneeskunde (BEL ISSN 0929-6824) **5619**
Geschiedenis Magazine (NLD ISSN 1872-0625) **4140**
De Geschiedenis van Hilversum (NLD ISSN 0929-9815) **4224**
Geschmacksmusterblatt (DEU ISSN 0934-7062) **6750**
Geschriften Vanwege de Vereniging Corporate Litigation (NLD ISSN 1574-4957) **4680**
Gesellschaft der Geologie- und Bergbaustudenten in Oesterreich. Mitteilungen (AUT ISSN 1563-0846) **2744**
Gesellschaft fuer Angewandte Mathematik und Mechanik Mitteilungen *see* G A M M Mitteilungen **5489**
Gesellschaft fuer Anlagen- und Reaktorsicherheit. Fortschrittsbericht *see* G R S - F **3193**
Gesellschaft fuer Anlagen- und Reaktorsicherheit. Jahresbericht (DEU ISSN 0944-0577) **3193**
Gesellschaft fuer Anlagen- und Reaktorsicherheit mbH *see* G R S - S **3193**
Gesellschaft fuer Anlagen- und Reaktorsicherheit mbH *see* G R S - F **3193**
Gesellschaft fuer Anlagen- und Reaktorsicherheit mbH Bericht *see* G R S Bericht **3193**
Gesellschaft fuer Bedrohte Voelker. Arbeitsbericht (DEU ISSN 0179-6682) **7207**
Gesellschaft fuer Bergbau, Metallurgie, Rohstoff- und Umwelttechnik. Schriftenreihe (DEU) **6313**
Gesellschaft fuer Bibliothekswesen und Dokumentation des Landbaues. Mitteilungen (DEU ISSN 0433-860X) **181**
Gesellschaft fuer das Buch (DEU ISSN 0948-5007) **5011**
Gesellschaft fuer Deutschlandforschung. Schriftenreihe (DEU ISSN 0935-5774) **4224**
Gesellschaft fuer die Geschichte und Bibliographie des Brauwesens. Jahrbuch *see* Gesellschaft fuer Geschichte des Brauwesens. Jahrbuch **604**
Gesellschaft fuer Forschung und Entwicklungsprojektierung Dokumentation *see* G F E - Dokumentation **8103**
Gesellschaft fuer Fraenkische Geschichte. 8. Reihe: Quellen und Darstellungen zur Fraenkischen Geschichte (DEU ISSN 0435-818X) **4224**
Gesellschaft fuer Fraenkische Geschichte. Veroeffentlichungen. 1. Reihe: Fraenkische Chroniken (DEU ISSN 0930-9926) **4224**
Gesellschaft fuer Fraenkische Geschichte. Veroeffentlichungen. 3. Reihe: Fraenkische Urkundenbuecher und Regestenwerke (DEU ISSN 0931-0134) **4224**
Gesellschaft fuer Fraenkische Geschichte. Veroeffentlichungen. 4. Reihe: Matrikeln Fraenkischer Schulen und Staende (DEU ISSN 0931-0479) **4224**
Gesellschaft fuer Fraenkische Geschichte. Veroeffentlichungen. 5. Reihe: Inventare Fraenkischer Archive (DEU ISSN 0931-0525) **4224**
Gesellschaft fuer Fraenkische Geschichte. Veroeffentlichungen. Reihe 10: Quellen zur Rechts- und Wirtschaftsgeschichte Frankens (DEU ISSN 0931-1726) **4224**
Gesellschaft fuer Fraenkische Geschichte. Veroeffentlichungen. Reihe 11. Abteilung 2: Frankenland (DEU ISSN 0931-2404) **4224**
Gesellschaft fuer Fraenkische Geschichte. Veroeffentlichungen. Reihe 12: Quellen und Forschungen zur Fraenkischen Volkskunde (DEU) **4224**
Gesellschaft fuer Fraenkische Geschichte. Veroeffentlichungen. Reihe 13: Neujahrsblaetter (DEU) **4224**
Gesellschaft fuer Fraenkische Geschichte. Veroeffentlichungen. Reihe 7 A: Fraenkische Lebensbilder (DEU ISSN 0435-8198) **4224**
Gesellschaft fuer Fraenkische Geschichte. Veroeffentlichungen. Reihe 9: Darstellungen aus der Fraenkischen Geschichte (DEU ISSN 0930-8342) **4224**
Gesellschaft fuer Geschichte des Brauwesens. Jahrbuch (DEU ISSN 1860-8922) **604**
Gesellschaft fuer Griechische und Hellenistische Rechtsgeschichte. Akten (AUT ISSN 0340-3149) **4680**
† Gesellschaft fuer Innere Medizin der Deutschen Demokratischen Republik. Tagungsbericht (BRD ISSN 0371-6910) **8959**
Gesellschaft fuer Kernenergieverwertung in Schiffbau und Schiffahrt *see* G K S S **7856**
Gesellschaft fuer Kernenergieverwertung in Schiffbau und Schiffahrt Forschungszentrum. Jahresbericht *see* G K S S Forschungszentrum. Jahresbericht **7856**
Gesellschaft fuer Mathematik und Datenverarbeitung Geschaeftsbericht *see* G M D Geschaeftsbericht **2419**
Gesellschaft fuer Mathematik und Datenverarbeitung Spiegel *see* G M D - Spiegel **8958**
Gesellschaft fuer Medienwissenschaft. Schriftenreihe (DEU ISSN 1619-960X) **8104**
Gesellschaft fuer Musikalische Auffuehrungs- und Mechanische Vervielfaeltigungsrechte Jahrbuch *see* G E M A Jahrbuch **6568**
Gesellschaft fuer Musikalische Auffuehrungs- und Mechanische Vervielfaeltigungsrechte Nachrichten *see* G E M A Nachrichten **6568**
Gesellschaft fuer Natur- und Voelkerkunde Ostasiens. Nachrichten (DEU ISSN 0016-9080) **549**
Gesellschaft fuer Naturkunde in Wuerttemberg. Jahreshefte (DEU ISSN 0368-2307) **675**
➤ Gesellschaft fuer Niedersaechsische Kirchengeschichte. Jahrbuch (DEU ISSN 0072-4238) **7759**
Gesellschaft fuer Oekologie. Verhandlungen (DEU ISSN 0171-1113) **675**
Gesellschaft fuer Praktische Sexualmedizin. Mitteilungen (DEU ISSN 0179-2504) **5619**
Gesellschaft fuer Rheinische Geschichtskunde. Jahresbericht (DEU ISSN 0720-4655) **4224**
Gesellschaft fuer Rheinische Geschichtskunde. Publikationen (DEU ISSN 0930-8822) **4224**
Gesellschaft fuer Salzburger Landeskunde. Mitteilungen (AUT ISSN 0435-8279) **4224**
Gesellschaft fuer Schleswig-Holsteinische Geschichte. Zeitschrift (DEU ISSN 0072-4254) **4224**
Gesellschaft fuer Schwerionenforschung mbH Report *see* G S I Report **7066**
Gesellschaft fuer Schwerionenforschung mbH Scientific Report (Online) *see* G S I Scientific Report (Online) **7066**
Gesellschaft fuer Sozialen Fortschritt. Schriften (DEU ISSN 0435-8287) **7966**
Gesellschaft fuer Strahlenforschung Bericht *see* G S F - Bericht **3432**
Gesellschaft fuer Theatergeschichte. Kleine Schriften (DEU ISSN 0176-8905) **8471**
Gesellschaft fuer Theatergeschichte. Schriften (DEU ISSN 0176-8891) **8471**
Gesellschaft fuer Umweltforschung und Entwicklungsplanung. Schriften (DEU ISSN 0721-8133) **1596**
Gesellschaft fuer Umweltrecht. Tagungen (DEU ISSN 1613-267X) **3433**
Gesellschaft fuer Universitaets- und Wissenschaftsgeschichte. Veroeffentlichungen (CHE ISSN 1660-6388) **2982**
Gesellschaft fuer Unterhaltende Buehnenkunst. Kleine Schriften (DEU) **8471**
Gesellschaft fuer Vergleichende Kunstforschung in Wien. Mitteilungen (AUT ISSN 1013-6800) **6524**
Gesellschaft fuer Westfaelische Wirtschaftsgeschichte. Vortragsreihe (DEU) **1542**
Gesellschaft fuer Wissenschaftliche Gespraechspsychotherapie e.V. Zeitschrift *see* G W G - Zeitschrift **3040**
Gesellschaft - Geschichte - Gegenwart (DEU) **7966**
Gesellschaft mit Beschraenkter Haftung-Tip *see* GmbH-Tip **1927**
Gesellschaft Naturforschender Freunde zu Berlin. Sitzungsberichte. Neue Folge (DEU ISSN 0037-5942) **7857**
Gesellschaft Pro Vindonissa. Jahresbericht (CHE ISSN 0072-4270) **395**
Gesellschaft Pro Vindonissa. Veroeffentlichungen (CHE ISSN 0072-4289) **395**
Gesellschaft Schweizer Tieraerztinnen und Tieraerzte Bulletin *see* G S T Bulletin **8797**
Gesellschaft und Politik (AUT ISSN 0016-9099) **7138**
➤ Gesellschaft, Wirtschaft, Politik (DEU ISSN 1619-6910) **2860**
Gesellschaften und Staaten im Epochenwandel (BEL ISSN 0941-7389) **4224**
Der Gesellschafter (AUT ISSN 0250-6440) **4868**

Title

10326 GHENT ULRICH'S PERIODICALS

• Ghent (USA) 5217
Ghent Port Annual *see* Haven Gent. Jaarboek 8645
Ghexis Newsletter *see* G H E X I S Newsletter 8958
Ghid G S M (ROM ISSN 1582-5256) 2321
Ghid G S M Supliment (ROM ISSN 1582-5264) 2321
Ghost Magazine *see* Ghost! Magazine 6741
Ghost! Magazine (USA ISSN 1552-7646) 6741
• Ghost Sites (USA) 6741
Ghost Trackers Newsletter (USA) 6741
Ghostmasters: Pokemon, Digimon, Dragon Ball Z (USA) 8175
The Ghosts & Scholars M R James Newsletter (Montague Rhodes) (GBR ISSN 1475-3723) 5443
Al-Ghurfa (UAE) 1403
Ghurfat Tijarah wa-Sina'ah Abu Dhabi. Al-Taqrir al-Sanawi *see* Abu Dhabi Chamber of Commerce and Industry. Annual Report 1394
Giallo Polar (FRA ISSN 1779-7322) 5300
Giannini Foundation Information Series (USA ISSN 1081-6526) 199
Giannini Foundation Monograph (USA ISSN 0575-4208) 199
Giannini Foundation Research Report (USA ISSN 0899-3068) 199
† Giano (ITA ISSN 1124-9021) 8959
Giant *see* Juren 8969
Giant (New York) (USA ISSN 1550-6614) 6291
Giant (Oak Brook) (USA) 1009
• Giant Robot (USA ISSN 1534-9845) 3535
Giants (USA) 8230
Giao Thong-Van Tai/Transport (VNM ISSN 0866-8345) 8497
Giao Vien Nhan Dan/People's Theatre (VNM) 8471
Il Giappone (ITA ISSN 0390-6647) 4182
Giardinaggio (ITA ISSN 1594-1892) 3733
Giardini (ITA ISSN 0394-0853) 3733
Giardini e Ambiente *see* Giardini 3733
Giardini e Paesaggio (ITA ISSN 1824-2804) 3733
I Giardini Storici di Roma (ITA ISSN 1825-3512) 491
Giatros Ortho *see* Propraxis Orthopaedie - Rheumatologie 6071
• Gibbons Stamp Monthly (GBR ISSN 0954-8084) 6895
Gibbs - Johnson Family Newsletter (USA ISSN 1075-4806) 3788
Gib'Echos (FRA ISSN 1774-0452) 7439
Gibeciere (USA ISSN 1558-8149) 4335
Gibier et Chasse (FRA ISSN 1261-3436) 287
• Gibraltar Chronicle (GIB) 3861
Gibraltar Nature News (GIB ISSN 1352-8726) 7858
Gibraltar Ornithological & Natural History Society. Journal *see* Gibraltar Nature News 7858
Gibridnye Vychislitel'nye Mashiny i Kompleksy (UKR ISSN 0207-0111) 2526
Gibson County Lines (USA) 4293
Gibson's Guides for Genealogists *see* Location Guides for Family and Local Historians 3774
• Gibson's Suits in Chancery (USA) 4681
Gideon's Trumpet (USA) 8713
Gidravlicheskie Mashiny (UKR ISSN 0130-1152) 7059
➤ Gidrobiologicheskii Zhurnal/Hidrobiolohichnyi Zhurnal (UKR ISSN 0375-8990) 675
Gidromekhanika *see* Prikladnaya Gidromekhanika 7062
Gidrotekhnicheskoe Stroitel'stvo (RUS ISSN 0016-9714) 3361
De Gids (NLD ISSN 0016-9730) 5218
Gids Bedrijfshulpverlening (NLD ISSN 1573-9813) 6677
Gids Content Management Systemen (NLD ISSN 1871-3750) 2536
Gids Geestelijke Gezondheidszorg *see* Sociale Kaart Geestelijke Gezondheidszorg 7542
Gids Gemeentebesturen (NLD) 7493
De Gids op Maatschappelijk Gebied (BEL ISSN 0378-4657) 4595
Gids voor Accountants & Bedrifsrevisoren (BEL ISSN 1373-3346) 1289
Gids voor Belastingstudie *see* Belastingrecht voor Ondernemers 1912
Gids voor Belastingstudie *see* Belastingrecht voor Particulieren 1912
Gids voor Financials (NLD ISSN 1569-5352) 1926
Gids voor Personeelsmanagement (NLD ISSN 0921-1896) 1861
Gids voor Sociale Reglementering in Ondernemingen (BEL ISSN 0778-5208) 4831
Gielda Papierow Wartosciowych. Biuletyn Miesieczny/W S E Monthly Bulletin (POL ISSN 1426-1553) 1626
Gien/Innovative Technology World (JPN ISSN 0285-6301) 8423
Giessener Abhandlungen zur Agrar- und Wirtschaftsforschung des Europaeischen Ostens *see* Osteuropastudien der Hochschulen des Landes Hessen. Reihe 1. Giessener Abhandlungen zur Agrar- und Wirtschaftsforschung des Europaeischen Ostens 204
Giessener Allgemeine (DEU) 3849
Giessener Arbeiten zur Neueren Deutschen Literatur und Literaturwissenschaft (DEU ISSN 0721-7897) 5300
Giessener Beitraege zur Deutschen Philologie *see* Beitraege zur Deutschen Philologie 5098
Giessener Beitraege zur Fremdsprachendidaktik (DEU ISSN 0175-7776) 5122
Giessener Beitraege zur Kunstgeschichte (DEU ISSN 0342-104X) 491
Giessener Magazin-Express (DEU) 3849
Giessener Schriften zur Agrar- und Ernaehrungswirtschaft (DEU ISSN 0179-0145) 115
Giessener Studien zur Transportwirtschaft und Kommunikation (DEU ISSN 0931-8852) 8497
Giesserei (DEU ISSN 0016-9765) 6313
Giesserei - Erfahrungsaustausch (DEU ISSN 0016-9773) 6313
Giesserei Jahrbuch (DEU) 6313
Giesserei-Literaturschau (DEU ISSN 0721-9679) 6338
Giesserei-Praxis (DEU ISSN 0016-9781) 6313
Giesserei Rundschau (AUT ISSN 0016-979X) 6313
Giessereiforschung (DEU ISSN 0046-5933) 6314
Gift Basket Idea Newsletter (USA ISSN 1086-3001) 4060
Gift Basket Products Guide (USA ISSN 1099-8349) 1997
Gift Basket Review (USA ISSN 1050-0316) 535
• Gift Trader (ITA) 4060
Gifted (AUS ISSN 1038-5266) 2860
Gifted and Talented International (CAN ISSN 1533-2276) 3040
Gifted & Talented Update *see* G & T Update 3040
• ➤ Gifted Child Quarterly (USA ISSN 0016-9862) 3040
• ➤ Gifted Child Today (USA) 3040
Gifted Education International (GBR ISSN 0261-4294) 3040
• Gifted Education Press Quarterly (USA ISSN 1064-0053) 3040
† GiftMaker (USA ISSN 1935-7443) 8959
Gifts and Decorative Accessories *see* Gifts & Decorative Accessories 4060
• Gifts & Decorative Accessories (USA) 4060
Gifts & Decorative Accessories Annual Buyer's Guide *see* Gifts & Decorative Accessories 4060
Gifts & Home Products *see* Global Sources Gifts & Home Products 4060
Gifts & Housewares Buyers' Guide (TWN) 1997
• Gifts & Tablewares (CAN ISSN 0700-9380) 4060
Giftware *see* Key Note Market Report: Giftware 4060
• Giftware News (USA ISSN 0193-2551) 4060
Giftware News U K (USA) 4060
Gifu Botanical Society. Bulletin *see* Gifuken Shokubutsu Kenkyukaishi 791
Gifu Daigaku Igakubu Hansha Kenkyu Shisetsu Gyosekishu/Gifu University. School of Medicine. Institute of Equilibrium Research. Bulletin (JPN) 922
Gifu Daigaku Igakubu Kiyo (JPN ISSN 0072-4521) 5619
Gifu Daigaku Kyoikugakubu Kenkyu Hokoku. Shizen Kagaku/Gifu University. Faculty of Education. Science Report. Natural Science (JPN ISSN 0533-9529) 7858
Gifu Daigaku Nogakubu Kenkyu Hokoku/Gifu University. Faculty of Agriculture. Research Bulletin (JPN ISSN 0072-4513) 115
Gifu Dental Society. Journal *see* Gifu Shika Gakkai Zasshi 5845
Gifu Furusato to Dobutsu Tsushin/Mammals' Newsletter in Homeland Gifu (JPN ISSN 0911-0461) 944
Gifu Iryo Gijutsu Tanki Daigaku Kiyo/Gifu University of Medical Science. Bulletin (JPN ISSN 0912-0513) 5619
Gifu-ken Hakubutsukan Chosa Kenkyu Hokoku/Gifu Prefectural Museum. Bulletin (JPN ISSN 0388-550X) 7858
Gifu-ken Hoken Kankyo Kenkyujoho (JPN ISSN 1340-2676) 7519
Gifu Medical Association. Journal *see* Gifuken Ishikai Igaku Zasshi 5619
Gifu Prefectural Museum. Bulletin *see* Gifu-ken Hakubutsukan Chosa Kenkyu Hokoku 7858
Gifu Prefectural Research Institute for Freshwater Fish and Aquatic Environments. Report *see* Gifuken Kasen Kankyou Kenkyuujo Kenkyuu Houkoku 3595
Gifu Prefecture. Monthly Report of Meteorology *see* Gifuken Kisho Geppo 6353
Gifu Shika Gakkai Zasshi/Gifu Dental Society. Journal (JPN ISSN 0385-0072) 5845
Gifu University. Faculty of Agriculture. Research Bulletin *see* Gifu Daigaku Nogakubu Kenkyu Hokoku 115
Gifu University. Faculty of Education. Science Report. Natural Science *see* Gifu Daigaku Kyoikugakubu Kenkyu Hokoku. Shizen Kagaku 7858
Gifu University of Medical Science. Bulletin *see* Gifu Iryo Gijutsu Tanki Daigaku Kiyo 5619
Gifu University. School of Medicine. Institute of Equilibrium Research. Bulletin *see* Gifu Daigaku Igakubu Hansha Kenkyu Shisetsu Gyosekishu 922
Gifuken Ishikai Igaku Zasshi/Gifu Medical Association. Journal (JPN ISSN 0914-9538) 5619
➤ Gifuken Kasen Kankyou Kenkyuujo Kenkyuu Houkoku/Gifu Prefectural Research Institute for Freshwater Fish and Aquatic Environments. Report (JPN ISSN 1880-7437) 3595
Gifuken Kisho Geppo/Gifu Prefecture. Monthly Report of Meteorology (JPN ISSN 0916-507X) 6353
Gifuken Shokubutsu Kenkyukaishi/Gifu Botanical Society. Bulletin (JPN ISSN 0911-422X) 791
The Gig (CAN ISSN 1481-5133) 5423
Gig (DEU) 3849
Gig (GBR ISSN 1744-0904) 6569
† • Gig Magazine (USA ISSN 1093-5657) 8959
• Giga Online (CUB ISSN 1605-9069) 1886
▼ Giga Sopas de Letras (ARG ISSN 1851-3867) 8175
• Gigabit / A T M (USA ISSN 1541-1222) 2497
• Gigabit News (USA ISSN 1094-2793) 2539
Gigabit Newsletter *see* Gigabit News 2539
Gigajoule (ZAF) 3136
Gigantes del Basket (ESP) 8230
Giganti del Basket (ITA ISSN 1122-1801) 8230
• Gigatronic (ESP ISSN 1575-6130) 3193
Gigiena i Sanitariya/Hygiene and Sanitation (RUS ISSN 0016-9900) 6987
Gigs (JPN) 6569
• Gigye Jeoneol/Korean Society of Mechanical Engineers. Journal (KOR ISSN 1226-7287) 3378
• Gi'gye Suju Tong'gye (Online)/Korea (Republic). National Statistical Office. Monthly Report on the Wholesale and Retail Sales Index (KOR ISSN 2005-1743) 1235
Gi'gye Suju Tong'gye (Print) *see* Gi'gye Suju Tong'gye (Online) 1235
Gijutsu Joho Mie. Kikai Kinzoku Hen/Technical Information in Mie Prefecture: Machine and Metal Series (JPN) 5452
Gijutsu Kaihatsu Nyusu/Research and Development News (JPN) 3309
Gijutsu Kenkyujo Dayori/Technical Research Institute News (JPN ISSN 0914-9589) 3309
Gijutsu Kenkyujo Shoho/Institute of Technology and Development. Technical Reports (JPN ISSN 0911-713X) 3268
Gijutsu Kenkyujoho/Technical Research Institute. Technical Reports (JPN ISSN 0388-6999) 3268
Gijutsu Kyoiku Kenkyu Ronbunshi/Journal of Technology and Education (JPN ISSN 0918-1083) 3309
Gijutsu Kyoshitsu/Journal of Technical Education (JPN ISSN 0285-0478) 2860
• Gijutsu Manejimento Kenkyuu/Yokohama Journal of Technology Management Studies (JPN ISSN 1347-3042) 1747
Gijutsubu Gijutsu Kenkyu Hokoku/Technology & Research Report (JPN ISSN 1341-3422) 6314
• Giken Dayori/N H K Science & Technical Research Laboratories. News (JPN) 2381
Giken Jiho (JPN ISSN 0385-6666) 3136
Gila Heritage (USA ISSN 0893-7753) 3768
Gila Monster (USA) 2285
Gila Queen's Guide to the Markets (USA) 7561
• The Gilbane Report (USA ISSN 1067-8719) 2497
Gilbert! (USA ISSN 1542-6602) 5300
Gilbert Law Summaries. Accounting and Finance for Lawyers (USA) 4868
Gilbert Law Summaries. Administrative Law (USA ISSN 0149-3272) 4681
Gilbert Law Summaries. Agency and Partnership (USA) 4868
Gilbert Law Summaries. Agency & Partnership *see* Gilbert Law Summaries. Agency and Partnership 4868
Gilbert Law Summaries. Antitrust (USA) 4869
Gilbert Law Summaries. Bankruptcy (USA ISSN 1078-2079) 4869
Gilbert Law Summaries. Business Law (USA) 4869
Gilbert Law Summaries. California Bar Performance Test Skills (USA) 4681
Gilbert Law Summaries. Civil Procedure (USA ISSN 0161-830X) 4831
Gilbert Law Summaries. Commercial Paper and Payment Law (USA) 4869
Gilbert Law Summaries. Community Property (USA ISSN 0192-561X) 4681
Gilbert Law Summaries. Conflict of Laws (USA ISSN 0270-2908) 4681
Gilbert Law Summaries. Constitutional Law (USA) 4848
Gilbert Law Summaries. Contracts (USA) 4869
Gilbert Law Summaries. Corporations (USA) 4869
Gilbert Law Summaries. Criminal Law (USA ISSN 0193-7200) 4890
Gilbert Law Summaries. Criminal Procedure (USA ISSN 0193-8010) 4890
Gilbert Law Summaries. Estate and Gift Tax (USA) 4903
Gilbert Law Summaries. Evidence (USA) 4952
Gilbert Law Summaries. Federal Courts (USA ISSN 1051-5585) 4952
Gilbert Law Summaries. Future Interests and Perpetuities (USA ISSN 1092-793X) 4681
† Gilbert Law Summaries. Income Tax 1 (Individual) (USA) 8959
Gilbert Law Summaries. Income Tax 2 (Corporate) (USA) 4869
Gilbert Law Summaries. Labor Law (USA) 4869
Gilbert Law Summaries. Legal Ethics (USA) 4681
Gilbert Law Summaries. Legal Research, Writing, & Analysis (USA) 4576
Gilbert Law Summaries. Legal Research, Writing, and Analysis *see* Gilbert Law Summaries. Legal Research, Writing, & Analysis 4576
Gilbert Law Summaries on Accounting & Finance for Lawyers *see* Gilbert Law Summaries. Accounting and Finance for Lawyers 4868
Gilbert Law Summaries. Personal Property (USA) 4681
Gilbert Law Summaries. Property (USA) 4681
Gilbert Law Summaries. Remedies (USA) 4952
† Gilbert Law Summaries. Review for the Multistate Bar Examination (USA) 8959
Gilbert Law Summaries. Sales & Lease of Goods (USA ISSN 1078-2060) 1818
Gilbert Law Summaries. Sales and Lease of Goods *see* Gilbert Law Summaries. Sales & Lease of Goods 1818
Gilbert Law Summaries. Secured Transactions (USA) 4681
Gilbert Law Summaries. Securities Regulation (USA) 1626
Gilbert Law Summaries. Torts (USA) 4831
Gilbert Law Summaries. Trusts (USA) 4903
Gilbert Law Summaries. Wills (USA) 4903
Gilcrease (USA) 6524
The Gilcrease Journal (USA ISSN 1070-7808) 4293
Gildea Review (USA ISSN 0892-1776) 3506
Gildebonden *see* Norturamagasinet 142
Gildebrief (NLD ISSN 1574-6518) 8542
▼ Gildebrief Ambacht en Gereedschap (NLD ISSN 1874-9550) 1053
Gildenweg (AUT ISSN 0016-9986) 2266
• Gilder Technology Report (USA) 8423
• Giliberto-Levy Monitor (USA) 7591
Gillet Gillette Gillett Pride 'n' Joy (USA ISSN 0890-4022) 3768
Gilmore Genealogical Newsletter (USA) 3768
Gilson Studies (NLD) 6921
• Gilson, Trademark Protection and Practice (USA) 6750
Gilt (GBR) 1113
• Gimbernat (ESP ISSN 0213-0718) 5619
Gimik (BEL ISSN 1784-133X) 5072
Gimnasta *see* Sport Aktiv 8203
Gimtoji Kalba (LTU ISSN 0868-5134) 5122
Gina's World (GBR ISSN 1461-1775) 2190
Ginecologia dell'Infanzia e dell'Adolescenza (ITA ISSN 0393-5337) 5991
Ginecologia - Obstetricia *see* Encyclopedie Medico-Chirurgicale. Ginecologia - Obstetricia 5989
Ginecologia - Ostetricia *see* Encyclopedie Medico-Chirurgicale. Ginecologia - Ostetricia 5989
• Ginecologia y Obstetricia (PER ISSN 1015-3047) 5991
Ginecologia y Obstetricia Clinica (ESP ISSN 1695-3827) 5991
• Ginecologia y Obstetricia de Mexico (MEX ISSN 0300-9041) 5991
• Il Ginecologo (ITA ISSN 1827-7152) 5991
• Ginecorama (ITA ISSN 0391-8920) 5991
Ginekologia Polska (POL ISSN 0017-0011) 5991
Ginekologiya (RUS) 5991
Ginekolosko Akuserski Glasnik (SRB) 5991
Ginger (GBR ISSN 0956-3229) 8042
Ginger Series (NZL ISSN 1176-8452) 3917
Gingerbread Annual Report *see* Gingerbread Northern Ireland. Annual Report 1289
Gingerbread Magazine *see* Magazine Pain d'Epices 2201
• Gingerbread Northern Ireland. Annual Report (GBR ISSN 1750-9041) 1289
Ginka *see* Silver Flower 4347
Ginkai (JPN ISSN 0285-1458) 6844
• Il Ginnasta (Online) (ITA ISSN 1973-8110) 8175
Ginseng Studies *see* Renshen Yanjiu 150
Gintong Butil/Golden Grains (PHL) 272
Ginza (JPN) 8865
Giochi per Il Mio Computer (ITA ISSN 1125-601X) 2477
Gioia (ITA ISSN 0017-0062) 8865
Gioia Bambini (ITA ISSN 1594-3917) 2153
Gioia Casa (ITA ISSN 1124-2590) 4540
Gioia Cucina (ITA ISSN 1594-3925) 4359
Gioia Salute (ITA ISSN 1594-3909) 8865
† Giorgio Levi della Vida Conferences. Reports of the Conference (GBR ISSN 0340-6369) 8959
• Giornale (ITA) 3897
Giornale Critico della Filosofia Italiana (ITA ISSN 0017-0089) 6921
Giornale degli Economisti e Annali di Economia (ITA ISSN 0017-0097) 1113
Giornale dei Distillatori *see* Nuovo Giornale dei Distillatori 8978
Il Giornale dei Misteri (ITA ISSN 1122-4940) 6741
• Giornale del Bieticoltore (ITA ISSN 1128-8299) 233
† Giornale del Cacciatore (ITA) 8959
• G E C Il Giornale del Cartolaio (ITA ISSN 0394-8234) 2321
Il Giornale del Colore *see* Progetto Colore 6720
Il Giornale del Farmacista (ITA ISSN 0393-8476) 6844
Giornale del Genio Civile (ITA ISSN 0017-016X) 3268
• Il Giornale del Marmo/International Stone Magazine (ITA ISSN 1123-8259) 1009
Il Giornale del Meccanico (ITA ISSN 1120-8287) 8582
• Giornale del Medico (ITA ISSN 0393-8492) 5619
† Il Giornale del Serramentista e delle Costruzioni in Alluminio (ITA ISSN 1590-9611) 8959
• Il Giornale del Serramento (ITA ISSN 1123-8194) 1009
• G T Il Giornale del Termoidraulico (ITA ISSN 1120-5377) 4119
• Giornale della Libreria (ITA ISSN 1124-9137) 7561
Giornale della Libreria. Quaderni *see* Q G 7571

Link to your serials resources and content with ulrichsweb.com

DIRECTORY 2010 GLASNIK POLJOPRIVREDNE PROIZVODNJE, PRERADE I PLASMANA 10327

• Il Giornale della Musica (ITA ISSN 1120-6195) **6569**
† Giornale della Natura (ITA ISSN 1121-8487) **8959**
Giornale della Natura Illustrato *see* Giornale della Natura **8959**
† Giornale della Soia (ITA ISSN 0393-9200) **8959**
Il Giornale della Subfornitura (ITA ISSN 0392-3622) **6314**
• Il Giornale della Vela (ITA ISSN 1122-3073) **8276**
† Il Giornale dell'Albergatore (ITA ISSN 1593-7941) **8959**
Il Giornale dell'Architettura (ITA ISSN 1721-5463) **443**
Il Giornale dell'Arredamento (ITA ISSN 0393-4500) **4540**
Il Giornale dell'Arredamento International *see* Il Giornale dell'Arredamento **4540**
• Il Giornale dell'Arte (ITA ISSN 0394-0543) **491**
Giornale delle Assicurazioni (ITA ISSN 1120-5105) **4504**
• Il Giornale delle Barche a Motore (ITA ISSN 1120-799X) **8276**
Il Giornale delle Telecomunicazioni (ITA) **2321**
Il Giornale dell'Edilizia Italiana (ITA) **1009**
† Giornale dell'Industria (ITA ISSN 0393-4608) **8959**
• Il Giornale dell'Installatore Elettrico (ITA ISSN 0392-3630) **3309**
Giornale dello Spettacolo (ITA ISSN 0017-0232) **2686**
• ➤ Il Giornale dello Stroke (ITA ISSN 1972-1935) **5787**
Giornale dell'Odontoiatra (ITA ISSN 0393-067X) **5845**
• Il Giornale dell'Umbria (ITA) **3897**
• Giornale di Astronomia (ITA ISSN 0390-1106) **575**
• Giornale di Barga (ITA ISSN 0017-0259) **3897**
• Il Giornale di Chirurgia (ITA ISSN 0391-9005) **6244**
• Giornale di Diritto Amministrativo (ITA ISSN 1591-559X) **4681**
• Giornale di Diritto del Lavoro e di Relazioni Industriali (ITA ISSN 1720-4321) **1684**
• Il Giornale di Filosofia (ITA ISSN 1827-5834) **6921**
• Giornale di Fisica (ITA ISSN 0017-0283) **7014**
† Giornale di Fotologia (ITA) **8959**
Giornale di Gerontologia (ITA ISSN 0017-0305) **4047**
• Giornale di Medicina Militare (ITA ISSN 0017-0364) **5619**
• ➤ Giornale di Metafisica (ITA ISSN 0017-0372) **6921**
Il Giornale di Musicalia (ITA ISSN 1824-8055) **6569**
Giornale di Neuropsichiatria dell'Eta Evolutiva (ITA ISSN 0392-4483) **6143**
• Giornale di Neuropsichiatria Geriatrica (ITA ISSN 1826-008X) **4047**
• ➤ Giornale di Neuropsicofarmacologia (ITA ISSN 0391-9048) **6143**
▼ • Giornale di Psicologia/Journal of Psychology (ITA ISSN 1971-9558) **7358**
Giornale di Storia Contemporanea (ITA) **4224**
• Giornale di Storia Costituzionale (ITA ISSN 1593-0793) **4848**
• ➤ Giornale di Tecniche Nefrologiche e Dialitiche (ITA ISSN 0394-9362) **6268**
Giornale Economico (ITA ISSN 0017-0429) **1403**
Il Giornale Elettro *see* Elettro **3306**
G E Il Giornale Elettro *see* Elettro **3306**
Giornale Esercenti Albergatori Ticino (CHE) **4387**
Giornale Europeo di Aerobiologia (ITA ISSN 1825-2893) **5758**
Giornale Europeo di Aerobiologia, Medicina Ambientale ed Infezioni Aerotrasmesse *see* Giornale Europeo di Aerobiologia **5758**
Giornale Europeo di Oncologia *see* European Journal of Oncology **6019**
• Giornale in Cartoleria (ITA) **1851**
Giornale Italiano del Manitoba (CAN ISSN 1196-3964) **3535**
Giornale Italiano delle Malattie del Torace/Italian Journal of Chest Diseases (ITA ISSN 1127-0810) **6214**
Giornale Italiano delle Malattie del Torace. Supplemento *see* Giornale Italiano delle Malattie del Torace **6214**
Giornale Italiano di Allergologia e Immunologia Clinica/Italian Journal of Allergy and Clinical Immunology (ITA ISSN 1120-6373) **5758**
Giornale Italiano di Anestesia e di Analgesia *see* Minerva Anestesiologica **5772**
• ➤ Giornale Italiano di Aritmologia e Cardiostimolazione (ITA ISSN 1971-730X) **5787**
• Giornale Italiano di Cardiologia (ITA ISSN 1827-6806) **5787**
Giornale Italiano di Cardiologia Invasiva (ITA ISSN 1824-7008) **5787**
Giornale Italiano di Cardiologia Invasiva. Supplemento *see* Giornale Italiano di Cardiologia Invasiva **5787**
Giornale Italiano di Cardiologia. Supplemento *see* Giornale Italiano di Cardiologia **5787**
• Giornale Italiano di Conservativa (ITA ISSN 1724-2908) **5845**
• Giornale Italiano di Dermatologia e Venereologia (ITA ISSN 0392-0488) **5877**
Giornale Italiano di Diabetologia e Metabolismo (ITA ISSN 1593-6104) **5893**
Giornale Italiano di Ecografia *see* Journal of Ultrasound **6201**
• Giornale Italiano di Endodonzia (ITA ISSN 1121-4171) **5845**
Giornale Italiano di Endoscopia Digestiva (ITA ISSN 0394-0225) **5925**
Giornale Italiano di Farmacia Clinica (ITA ISSN 1120-3749) **6844**
Giornale Italiano di Filologia (ITA ISSN 0017-0461) **5122**
Giornale Italiano di Malattie Reumatiche (ITA ISSN 1129-8731) **6223**
• Giornale Italiano di Medicina del Lavoro ed Ergonomia (ITA ISSN 1592-7830) **6677**
Giornale Italiano di Medicina Sessuale e Riproduttiva *see* Journal of Andrological Sciences **5645**
Giornale Italiano di Medicina Tropicale (ITA ISSN 0394-3445) **5814**
Giornale Italiano di Microbiologia Medica Odontoiatrica e Clinica *see* G I M M O C **886**
➤ Giornale Italiano di Nefrologia (ITA ISSN 0393-5590) **6268**
• Giornale Italiano di Oncologia (ITA ISSN 0392-128X) **6020**
Giornale Italiano di Ortopedia e Traumatologia (ITA ISSN 0390-0134) **6061**
• Giornale Italiano di Ostetricia e Ginecologia (ITA ISSN 0391-9013) **5991**
• ➤ Giornale Italiano di Psico-Oncologia (ITA ISSN 1128-5516) **6020**
• Giornale Italiano di Psicologia/Italian Journal of Psychology (ITA ISSN 0390-5349) **7358**
Giornale Italiano di Psicologia dello Sport (ITA ISSN 1722-8530) **6229**
Giornale Italiano di Psicologia dell'Orientamento (ITA ISSN 1720-7681) **7358**
• Giornale Italiano di Psicopatologia (ITA ISSN 1592-1107) **6143**
† Giornale Italiano di Riflessoterapia ed Agopuntura (ITA ISSN 1120-3560) **8959**
Giornale Italiano di Salute Pubblica *see* Italian Journal of Public Health **7528**
† • Giornale Storico della Letteratura Italiana (ITA ISSN 0017-0496) **8959**
Giornale Storico della Lunigiana e del Territorio Lucense (ITA ISSN 0017-050X) **4224**
Giornale Storico di Psicologia Dinamica *see* Centro Studi di Psicologia e Letteratura. Giornale Storico **7344**
Giornale Svizzero degli Impresari Costruttori *see* Schweizer Bauwirtschaft **1035**
Giornale Svizzero di Farmacia *see* PharmaJournal **6874**
Il Giornalino (ITA ISSN 1123-0541) **2190**
Il Giorno (ITA ISSN 1124-2116) **3897**
Giorno Poetry Systems L P's, C D's, Cassettes & Giorno Video Pak Series (USA) **5423**
† Giovane Critica (ITA ISSN 0017-0526) **8959**
Giovane Odontoiatra (ITA) **5845**
† Giovani Amici (ITA ISSN 1120-2564) **8959**
Giovani Genitori (ITA ISSN 1828-9738) **5072**
† Gioventu Passionista/Passionist Youth (ITA ISSN 0072-4548) **8959**
Gippsland Anglican (AUS) **7759**
Gippsland Farmer (AUS ISSN 0158-3840) **115**
Gippsland Heritage Journal (AUS ISSN 0817-9638) **4192**
• Gippsland Heritage Journal Index (Online) (AUS) **4170**
Gippsland Heritage Journal Index (Print) *see* Gippsland Heritage Journal Index (Online) **4170**
• La Girafe (FRA ISSN 1775-965X) **8497**
Giraffe News (USA) **2153**
GirafPost (NLD ISSN 1574-9819) **945**
Girasol (CRI ISSN 1659-1119) **2982**
Girl (SRB ISSN 1451-530X) **2190**
Girl! Hors-Serie *see* Girls! **2191**
Girl Power (AUS ISSN 1449-8529) **2190**
Girl Power *see* Chicks Power **8309**
• Girl Scout Leader (USA ISSN 0017-0577) **2153**
Girl Scout News (USA) **2153**
Girl Scout News *see* The Bridge (Minneapolis) **2180**
• Girl Stuff (USA) **2190**
Girl Talk (GBR ISSN 1357-5538) **2190**
Girl Talk Extra (GBR ISSN 1748-8591) **2190**
Girl Talk Magazine (USA ISSN 1524-5594) **5072**
• Girl Tech (USA) **2190**
• Girlfriend (AUS ISSN 1033-7288) **2190**
• Girlfriend Getaways (USA) **8865**
girlfriends (DEU) **2191**
▼ • ➤ Girlhood Studies (USA ISSN 1938-8209) **8104**
• girliestyle.de (DEU) **2154**
• Girljock (USA) **4374**
Girls! (FRA ISSN 1286-577X) **2191**
Girls (NOR ISSN 1500-7324) **2191**
Girls and Boys Town Journal *see* Boys Town Journal **8028**
▼ Girls and Corpses (USA ISSN 1939-0033) **6292**
Girls and Women in Sport News *see* G W S News **8174**
Girls Brigade International News (GBR) **2191**
† Girl's Club (DEU) **8959**
Girls in Action World *see* G A World **7759**
Girls in Uniform (GBR) **6292**
• Girls' Life (USA ISSN 1078-3326) **2191**
Girls Like Us (NLD) **4374**
• Girls of Gaming (USA) **2477**
Girls of Outlaw Biker (USA ISSN 1060-1422) **6292**
Girls of Penthouse (USA ISSN 0031-4935) **6292**
• Girls Only (USA) **2191**
▼ Die Girls von F H M (For Him Magazine) (DEU) **6292**
Die Girls von FHM *see* Die Girls von F H M **6292**
• A Girl's World (USA) **2191**
Girlz! (NLD ISSN 1570-5285) **2191**
• GIScience and Remote Sensing (USA ISSN 1548-1603) **4013**
Gissing Journal (GBR ISSN 0962-0443) **5300**
Gist (USA ISSN 0732-7781) **7645**
Gistarychna-Arkhealagichny Zbornik/The Historic-Archaeologic Collection (BLR) **395**
➤ Gister en Vandag/Yesterday and Today (ZAF) **4140**
• Gististkyrslur/Tourist Accommodation (ISL ISSN 1024-0012) **8779**
• Gisul Pyojun/The Monthly Technology and Standard (KOR) **6402**
Gitans *see* Zhitan **3573**
Gitara (POL ISSN 1428-0027) **6569**
• Gitara i Bas (POL ISSN 1230-1809) **6569**
Gitara i Bas + Bebny Online *see* Gitara i Bas **6569**
Gitarr och Luta (SWE ISSN 0283-474X) **6569**
Gitarre Aktuell (DEU ISSN 0934-4241) **6569**
Gitarre & Laute (DEU ISSN 0172-9683) **6569**
Gitarre und Bass (DEU ISSN 0937-4213) **6569**
Gite (CAN ISSN 0705-7520) **4387**
Gitelson Peace Papers (ISR ISSN 0793-4114) **7966**
• Gitlin on Divorce (USA) **4911**
Gitutsunner Erkry Massin *see* Geologicheskii Zhurnal Armenii **2740**
Il Giudice di Pace (ITA ISSN 1720-4348) **4831**
Giudice di Pace Oggi (ITA ISSN 1590-6663) **4831**
Giudizio Universale (ITA ISSN 1825-4691) **3897**
Il Giuliano Dalmata (ITA ISSN 1970-5336) **3897**
Giurisdizione Amministrativa (ITA ISSN 1828-4418) **4681**
Giurisprudenza Annotata di Diritto Industriale (ITA ISSN 1720-4356) **4869**
• Giurisprudenza Commerciale (ITA ISSN 0390-2269) **4869**
Giurisprudenza Costituzionale (ITA ISSN 0436-0222) **4848**
• Giurisprudenza delle Imposte (Online) (ITA ISSN 1826-2430) **1926**
• Giurisprudenza di Merito (ITA ISSN 0436-0230) **4831**
• Giurisprudenza Italiana (ITA ISSN 1125-3029) **4681**
Giurisprudenza Milanese *see* Il Corriere del Merito **4651**
Giurisprudenza Napoletana *see* Il Corriere del Merito **4651**
Giurisprudenza Piemontese (ITA ISSN 1720-4380) **4681**
Giurisprudenza Romana *see* Il Corriere del Merito **4651**
Giurisprudenza Tributaria *see* G T **1926**
Gius *see* Il Corriere del Merito **4651**
• Giustizia Civile (ITA ISSN 0017-0631) **4831**
Giustizia Civile. Massimario Annotato della Cassazione (ITA ISSN 0434-0442) **4831**
Giustizia Civile. Repertorio Generale Annuale di Legislazione, Bibliografia, Giurisprudenza (ITA ISSN 1124-6685) **4832**
Il Giusto Processo Civile (ITA ISSN 1828-311X) **4832**
Giv det Stoerste til de Mindste (DNK ISSN 1603-6816) **7759**
▼ Give Magazine (USA) **8042**
Giving U S A (USA ISSN 0436-0257) **8042**
Giving U S A Quarterly (USA) **8042**
Giving U S A Update *see* Giving U S A Quarterly **8042**
Gizarte Ekonomiaren Euskal Aldizkaria *see* Revista Vasca de Economia Social **7998**
Gizi Indonesia (IDN ISSN 0436-0265) **6659**
Gjengangeren (NOR) **3922**
Gjuha Jone (ALB) **5122**
Gjurmime Albanologjike *see* Gjurmime Albanologjike. Seria e Shkencave Filologjike **6921**
Gjurmime Albanologjike: Folklor dhe Etnologji/Albanological Research: Folklore and Ethnology Series (KOS ISSN 0350-7998) **3618**
Gjurmime Albanologjike. Seria e Shkencave Filologjike/Albanologycal Researches: Philological Science Series (KOS ISSN 0351-2223) **6921**
Gjurmime Albanologjike. Seria e Shkencave Historike/Albanological Research: Historical Sciences Series (KOS ISSN 0350-6258) **4140**
Gjuteriet (SWE ISSN 0017-0682) **6314**
GKOeD I *see* Gesamtkommentar Oeffentliches Dienstrecht. Band I: Beamtenrecht des Bundes und der Laender Richterrecht und Wehrrecht **1683**
GL Kompakt *see* G L Kompakt **3849**
Glaamdalen (NOR) **3922**
Glacier (USA ISSN 1933-9313) **8713**
Glacier Park Magazine (USA ISSN 1942-2725) **2612**
Glaciological Data (USA ISSN 0149-1776) **2744**
➤ Glaciology and Quaternary Geology (NLD ISSN 0924-5006) **2744**
Glad Rags (IND) **2255**
Glad Tidings (CAN ISSN 0017-0720) **7759**
Gladbach Kompakt *see* G L Kompakt **3849**
Glades Star (USA ISSN 0431-915X) **4293**
Gladiator *see* Gladiator Magazine **8175**
▼ • Gladiator Magazine (USA) **8175**
Gladiolus Annual (GBR ISSN 0072-4580) **3756**
Gladiolus, Dahlias (CAN ISSN 1187-8673) **3733**
• Gladius (ESP ISSN 0436-029X) **366**
Gladsaxe Lokalhistoriske Forening. Aarbog (DNK ISSN 1903-0916) **4224**
• Glaenta (SWE ISSN 1104-5205) **5218**
Glagol (RUS ISSN 0885-7369) **5300**
Glam (MYS) **8865**
Glam - It (BEL ISSN 1780-6895) **588**
Glamcult (NLD ISSN 1874-1932) **5072**
Glamorgan Family History Society. Journal (GBR ISSN 0264-5440) **3768**
Glamorous (JPN) **8865**
• Glamorous Life (ZAF ISSN 1991-5799) **5072**
Glamour (Athens) (GRC ISSN 1109-3501) **8865**
• Glamour (London) (GBR ISSN 1472-6165) **8865**
• Glamour (Madird) (ESP ISSN 1886-3345) **8865**
Glamour (Milan) (ITA ISSN 1121-5348) **8865**
Glamour (Moscow) (RUS ISSN 1729-8644) **8865**
• Glamour (Munich) (DEU) **8865**
Glamour (Netherlands) (NLD ISSN 1871-4617) **8865**
• Glamour (New York) (USA ISSN 0017-0747) **8865**
Glamour (Stockholm) (SWE ISSN 1653-6762) **8866**
Glamour (Warsaw) (POL ISSN 1730-2781) **8866**
Glamour en Espanol *see* Glamour Latinoamerica **8866**
Glamour Latinoamerica (USA ISSN 1556-2131) **8866**
Glandulas Tiroides y Paratiroides (ARG ISSN 1666-2121) **5893**
Glareana (CHE) **6569**
Glas (AUT) **2041**
Glas (BGR ISSN 0861-1238) **4454**
Glas (DEU ISSN 0949-2720) **443**
• Glas (DNK ISSN 1604-8016) **2041**
Glas (RUS ISSN 0869-3102) **5301**
Glas (USA) **5301**
Glas, Fenster, Fassade *see* G F F **2041**
Glas in Beeld (NLD ISSN 1386-176X) **2041**
Glas Ingenieur *see* GlasIngenieur **2041**
Glas Istre (HRV ISSN 0017-0771) **5218**
• Glas Javnosti (SRB ISSN 1450-7218) **3944**
• Glas Koncila (HRV ISSN 0436-0311) **7799**
Glas Lokalne Samouprave (SRB ISSN 1451-3838) **7493**
Glas och Porslin (SWE ISSN 0017-078X) **2041**
Glas Podravine (HRV ISSN 0017-0801) **5218**
Glas Podrinja (SRB ISSN 0017-081X) **3945**
Glas S G N J *see* Savez Gluvih i Nagluvih Jugoslavije. Glas **4076**
• Glas Slavonije (HRV ISSN 0350-3968) **3831**
Glas und Instrumenten Technik *see* G I T **5905**
Glas und Instrumenten Technik Laboratory Journal Europe *see* G.I.T. Laboratory Journal Europe **5617**
Glas und Instrumenten Technik Security & Management *see* G I T Security & Management **6677**
Glas und Instrumenten Technik Spezial Separation *see* G I T Spezial Separation **2100**
Glas und Instrumenten Technik Spezial Sicherheit und Management *see* G I T Spezial Sicherheit und Management **6677**
Glas und Rahmen (DEU ISSN 0342-5142) **2041**
Glasba v Soli (SVN ISSN 1318-735X) **2860**
Glasbulletin *see* Fjoezzz **489**
Glasenapp-Stiftung (DEU ISSN 0170-3455) **550**
Glasforum (DEU ISSN 0017-0852) **443**
Glasgow & West of Scotland Family History Society. Newsletter (GBR ISSN 0141-8009) **3768**
Glasgow Caledonian University. Caledonian Business School. Working Paper (GBR) **1114**
Glasgow Chamber of Commerce. Annual Report (GBR) **1403**
Glasgow Chamber of Commerce. Information Newsletter (GBR) **1403**
Glasgow Chamber of Commerce. Journal (GBR ISSN 0017-0860) **1403**
Glasgow Directory of Voluntary Organizations (GBR ISSN 0143-7429) **8042**
Glasgow Emblem Studies (GBR) **5301**
➤ Glasgow Introductory Guides to French Literature (GBR ISSN 0955-9590) **5301**
• Glasgow Magazine (GBR) **3865**
• ➤ Glasgow Mathematical Journal (GBR ISSN 0017-0895) **5490**
➤ Glasgow Naturalist (GBR ISSN 0373-241X) **675**
• Glasgow University Guardian (GBR ISSN 0017-0917) **2285**
Glasgow University Students' Handbook (GBR) **2982**
Glasilo *see* Prosveta **3559**
GlasIngenieur (DEU) **2041**
Glaskracht Nederland. Nieuwsbrief (NLD ISSN 1872-3616) **3733**
Glaskunstbeurs *see* Internationale Glaskunstbeurs **2043**
Glasmagasinet *see* Glas **2041**
Glasnik Advokatske Komore Vojvodine *see* Advokatska Komora Vojvodine. Glasnik **4611**
Glasnik Arhiva i Drustva Arhivskih Radnika Bosne i Hercegovine (BIH ISSN 0436-046X) **4224**
Glasnik Bastina *see* Bastina **330**
Glasnik Drustva Konzervatora Srbije *see* Drustvo Konzervatora Srbije. Glasnik **2609**
Glasnik Etnografskog Instituta *see* Srpska Akademija Nauka i Umetnosti. Etnografski Institut. Glasnik **356**
Glasnik H D Z (Hrvatska Demokratska Zajednica) (HRV ISSN 1331-2111) **5218**
Glasnik Hemicara i Tehnologa Bosne i Hercegovine (BIH ISSN 0367-4444) **2062**
Glasnik Hrvatske Seljacke Stranke (CAN ISSN 0837-2071) **3535**
• ➤ Glasnik Matematicki (HRV ISSN 0017-095X) **5490**
Glasnik na Hemicarite i Tehnolozite na Makedonija *see* Macedonian Journal of Chemistry and Chemical Engineering **2072**
Glasnik Poljoprivredne Proizvodnje, Prerade i Plasmana (SRB ISSN 0017-0976) **115**

Title

10328 GLASNIK RIJASETA ISLAMSKE ZAJEDNICE ULRICH'S PERIODICALS

Glasnik Rijaseta Islamske Zajednice *see* Rijaset Islamske Zajednice u Bosni i Hercegovini. Glasnik **7715**
Glasnik S E D *see* Slovensko Etnolosko Drustvo. Glasnik **355**
Glasnik Z R S *see* Znanstveno Raziskovalno Sredisce. Glasnik **4483**
➤ Glasnik za Sumske Pokuse/Forest Experiments Herald (HRV ISSN 0352-3861) **3692**
Glasnik Zastite Bilja (HRV ISSN 0350-9664) **233**
Glasnost' (RUS) **3935**
➤ Glasra (IRL ISSN 0332-0235) **791**
• Glass (USA ISSN 1064-900X) **2041**
The Glass (Northwood) (GBR ISSN 0269-770X) **5301**
• Glass (Redhill) (GBR ISSN 0017-0984) **2041**
† • Glass Age (GBR ISSN 1476-0517) **8959**
Glass Age & Window Construction *see* Glass Age **8959**
† Glass Age Directory (GBR) **8959**
• ➤ Glass and Ceramics (USA ISSN 0361-7610) **2041**
Glass and Ceramics Maker *see* Sklar a Keramik **2045**
Glass & Enamel *see* Boli yu Tangci **2038**
Glass and Glazing News (GBR ISSN 0260-6321) **2041**
Glass & Glazing Products (GBR ISSN 0269-0659) **2041**
Glass and Pottery Collector *see* The Glass and Pottery Review **2041**
• The Glass and Pottery Review (USA) **2041**
Glass Art Society Journal (USA ISSN 0278-9426) **491**
Glass Association. Journal (GBR ISSN 0951-3108) **2042**
The Glass Bead (USA ISSN 1945-8045) **2042**
Glass Canada (CAN ISSN 0843-7041) **2042**
Glass Cone (GBR ISSN 0265-9654) **2042**
† Glass Digest (USA ISSN 0017-1018) **8959**
† Glass Digest Buyer's Guide (USA) **8959**
Glass Directory (Year) (GBR) **2042**
• Glass Factory Directory of North America and U.S. Industry Factbook (USA ISSN 1057-5405) **1997**
Glass Fasade *see* Glass & Fasade **2042**
• Glass International (GBR ISSN 0143-7836) **2042**
• Glass Line Newsletter (USA) **2042**
Glass Machinery Plants & Accessories (ITA ISSN 0394-9893) **2042**
• Glass Magazine (USA ISSN 0747-4261) **2042**
Glass, Molders, Pottery, Plastics and Allied Workers Horizons *see* G M P Horizons **4594**
Glass New England (USA) **2042**
• Glass & Fasade (NOR ISSN 0802-295X) **2042**
➤ Glass on Metal (USA ISSN 1083-6888) **2042**
Glass Patterns Quarterly (USA ISSN 1041-6684) **535**
• ➤ Glass Physics and Chemistry (RUS ISSN 1087-6596) **2042**
Glass Reflections (USA ISSN 1077-517X) **2042**
Glass Science and Technology - Glastechnische Berichte *see* European Journal of Glass Science and Technology. Part A. Glass Technology **2040**
† Glass Style (ITA ISSN 1129-3950) **8959**
Glass Technology *see* European Journal of Glass Science and Technology. Part A. Glass Technology **2040**
Glass Technology International (ITA ISSN 1126-8573) **2042**
Glass Will (USA) **5423**
• Glassonline World Yellow Pages (ITA) **2042**
Glass's Car Checkbook (GBR) **8582**
Glass's Commercial Vehicle Checkbook (GBR) **8497**
Glass's Guide to Car Values (GBR) **8582**
Glass's Guide to Caravan Values (GBR) **4411**
Glass's Guide to Commercial Vehicle Values (GBR) **8582**
Glass's Guide to Company Car Tax (GBR) **8582**
Glass's Guide to Motorcycle Values (GBR) **8259**
Glass's Motorcycle Checkbook (GBR) **8259**
Glassware *see* Key Note Market Report: Glassware **2044**
• Glasteknisk Tidskrift (SWE) **2042**
Glastuinbouw en Bouwen aan de Toekomst (NLD ISSN 1873-3484) **1009**
Glastuinbouwtechniek Magazine (NLD ISSN 1872-549X) **2042**
Glasul Bucovinei (ROM ISSN 1222-5606) **4454**
• Glaswelt (DEU ISSN 0017-1107) **2042**
Glaube Hoffnung Liebe (DEU) **7645**
Glaube in der 2. Welt (CHE ISSN 0254-4377) **7645**
Glaube und Heimat (DEU ISSN 0323-8202) **7759**
Glaube und Leben (DEU ISSN 0935-8889) **7645**
➤ Glaube und Lernen (DEU ISSN 0179-3551) **7645**
Glauben Leben (DEU) **7645**
Glaucom (DNK ISSN 1901-774X) **6042**
➤ Glaucoma Forum (GBR ISSN 1465-5071) **6042**
• Glaucoma Today (USA) **6042**
Glaucoommagazine (NLD ISSN 1872-6658) **6043**
Glaucus (GBR ISSN 0963-9519) **2804**
Glavbukh (RUS) **1114**
Glaven Schetovoditel (BGR) **1289**
Glavnaya Meditsinskaya Sestra (RUS) **5959**
Glavnyi Redaktor (RUS) **4576**
Glazed Expressions (GBR ISSN 0261-0329) **2042**
• Gleams (USA ISSN 1072-7906) **6043**
The Gleaner (CAN) **2285**
• The Gleaner (JAM) **3899**
The Gleaner (Madison) (USA) **4374**
Gleaner Index (JAM ISSN 0259-0336) **4587**
Gleanings (LKA) **7645**
Gleanings (Buhler) (USA ISSN 1932-9601) **6639**
Gleanings (Keokuk) (USA ISSN 1059-1664) **3769**
Gledista (SRB ISSN 0017-1166) **4454**
Gleichheit (DEU ISSN 1434-5617) **7138**
Gleichstellung in der Praxis (DEU ISSN 1614-6085) **8866**
Gleichstellung von Frauen und Mannern *see* Gender Equality Magazine **8865**
Gleitschirm *see* Gleitschirm, Fly and Glide **8315**
▼ Gleitschirm, Fly and Glide (AUT) **8315**
Glenbow Occasional Papers (CAN) **4294**
• Glendale Law Review (USA ISSN 0363-2423) **4681**
Glendora Review (NGA ISSN 1118-146X) **5301**
Glengarry News (CAN ISSN 0834-5694) **3810**
Glenmary Challenge (USA ISSN 0746-3022) **7799**
† GlennGould (CAN ISSN 1201-821X) **8959**
Glenorchy Series (GBR) **4411**
† Glen's Guide (GBR ISSN 1747-5996) **8959**
• ➤ Glia (USA ISSN 0894-1491) **6143**
Glid (SWE ISSN 1652-2737) **8315**
Glid. Laangfaerdsskridskor (SWE ISSN 1653-5553) **8315**
Glimmer Train (USA ISSN 1055-7520) **5301**
• Glimpse (BGD ISSN 0253-7508) **7519**
▼ • Glimpse (USA ISSN 1945-3906) **8104**
Globaal *see* Amnesty.nl **7202**
Globai Views *see* Dongfang Qiyejia **1093**
Global (BRA ISSN 1415-2649) **1428**
Global (FRA ISSN 1774-9565) **3840**
Global (GBR) **8713**
† Global (ITA) **8959**
• Global (NIC) **3821**
• Global Accumulative Bibliography of Action Learning (GBR) **2933**
The Global Advisor (CAN) **1626**
• Global Advisor Newsletter (USA) **1114**
† Global Agenda (GBR ISSN 1479-0289) **8959**
Global Agreements, Legislation, and Trade Upate *see* G A L T Upate **1596**
• ➤ Global and Planetary Change (NLD ISSN 0921-8181) **2744**
• The Global Anti-Dumping Handbook (GBR ISSN 1465-413X) **4869**
• ➤ Global Antiviral Journal (USA ISSN 1556-9047) **5814**
Global Approaches to Extension Practice: A Journal of Agricultural Extension (NGA ISSN 0794-1005) **115**
Global Aquaculture Advocate (USA ISSN 1540-8906) **3595**
Global Arbitration Review (GBR ISSN 1749-611X) **4869**
Global Architecture *see* G A **443**
Global Architecture Document *see* G A Document **443**
Global Architecture Houses *see* G A Houses **443**
Global Artist Exchange Mag *see* G A E Mag **490**
Global Asset Allocation (USA) **1626**
• Global Asset Protection (USA) **1927**
Global Banking & Financial Policy Review (Years) (GBR ISSN 1364-9159) **1349**
• Global Benchmark Report (DNK ISSN 1901-7448) **1114**
• Global Bioethics (ITA ISSN 1128-7462) **675**
• ➤ Global Biogeochemical Cycles (USA ISSN 0886-6236) **7858**
The Global Biotechnology Industry to 2010: Status and Prognosis (USA) **765**
• Global Bits (NZL ISSN 1176-9467) **8104**
Global Books in Print *see* Bowker's Global Books in Print **621**
Global Books in Print on Disc *see* Bowker's Global Books in Print on Disc **621**
• Global Books in Print with Book Reviews (USA) **625**
Global Broadband Market (AUS) **2350**
• ➤ Global Built Environment Review (GBR ISSN 1474-6824) **3433**
➤ Global Business & Economics Anthology (USA ISSN 1553-1392) **1114**
• ➤ Global Business & Economics Review (GBR ISSN 1097-4954) **1114**
Global Business & Economics Review: Anthology *see* Global Business & Economics Anthology **1114**
➤ Global Business & Finance Review (USA ISSN 1088-6931) **1567**
▼ • Global Business and Management Journal (USA ISSN 1946-3324) **1567**
▼ • ➤ Global Business and Management Research (USA ISSN 1947-5667) **1861**
• Global Business and Organizational Excellence (USA ISSN 1932-2054) **1748**
Global Business Jet (GBR ISSN 1466-6510) **8542**
Global Business Magazine (USA ISSN 1528-8161) **1114**
• ➤ Global Business Review (IND ISSN 0972-1509) **1114**
Global C E O (IND ISSN 0972-5318) **1748**
• Global Cement and Lime Magazine (GBR ISSN 1473-1940) **1009**
Global Cement Report (GBR) **1009**
Global Ceramic Review (GBR ISSN 1368-0099) **2042**
• Global Challenge. Report (SWE ISSN 1654-2541) **1596**
• Global Change (USA) **3486**
Global Change and Human Health *see* EcoHealth **3416**
• ➤ Global Change Biology (GBR ISSN 1354-1013) **675**
Global Change Biology. Supplement *see* Global Change Biology **675**
Global Change NewsLetter (SWE ISSN 0284-5865) **2744**
• Global Change, Peace & Security (Online) (GBR ISSN 1478-1166) **7237**
• ➤ Global Change, Peace & Security (Print) (GBR ISSN 1478-1158) **7237**
Global Change Report *see* I G B P Global Change Report **2746**
Global Charity *see* Huanqiu Cishan **8045**
Global Child Health News & Review (CAN ISSN 1192-9073) **6092**
• The Global Child Journal (USA ISSN 1543-298X) **3012**
Global Chinese Medicine *see* Huanqiu Zhongyiyao **5630**
Global Chinese Times (USA) **3535**
• Global Citizenship in Action (CAN ISSN 1492-4099) **1596**
Global City Geography *see* Chengshi Dili **4002**
Global City Review (USA ISSN 1068-0586) **5218**
Global Civil Society (Year) (GBR) **7237**
Global Climate Change (Lexington) (USA ISSN 1936-9484) **6353**
Global Climate Change Digest (USA ISSN 0897-4268) **3433**
Global Commerce (USA) **1567**
The Global Communicator (USA) **2321**
Global Communique (USA ISSN 1055-3940) **1235**
The Global Community (USA ISSN 1535-9468) **4927**
(Year) Global Comparison of Test Methods (USA) **8451**
▼ Global Competition Litigation Review (GBR ISSN 1756-6002) **4681**
• Global Competition Review (GBR ISSN 1369-4561) **4869**
The Global Competitiveness Report (GBR) **1114**
Global Connections (USA) **6280**
• Global Connections (Rochester) (USA) **5011**
Global Constitutional Law Collection (NLD) **4848**
• Global Construction Review (GBR ISSN 1471-2997) **1009**
Global Construction Sourcebook *see* Top 400 Contractors Sourcebook **1041**
Global Construction Sourcebook *see* Design - Build **3264**
Global Construction Sourcebook *see* E N R **3265**
Global Construction Sourcebook *see* The Top 500 Design Firms Sourcebook **3223**
The Global Consulting Marketplace (USA ISSN 1941-644X) **1748**
• Global Contact (NLD ISSN 1386-0194) **6043**
• Global Corruption Report (GBR ISSN 1749-3161) **7237**
• Global Cosmetic Industry (USA ISSN 1523-9470) **594**
Global Counsel 3000 *see* Doing Business In... Handbook **1562**
• ➤ Global Crime (GBR ISSN 1744-0572) **7237**
▼ Global Crime and Justice (USA ISSN 1931-7239) **2653**
▼ Global Crises and the Media (USA ISSN 1947-2587) **4576**
Global Custodian (USA ISSN 1047-8736) **1626**
• Global Development Finance (USA ISSN 1020-5454) **1596**
Global Development Studies (USA ISSN 1093-8281) **1596**
Global Dialogue (CYP ISSN 1450-0590) **7237**
Global Directory of Peace Studies & Conflict Resolution Programs (USA) **7237**
Global Directory of Schools of Law Outside of the United States of America (USA) **4681**
Global Discovery & Development (GBR) **6844**
▼ • Global-e (USA ISSN 1932-8060) **7966**
▼ Global E-Governance Series (NLD ISSN 1874-8511) **2557**
• Global E H S Library (Environment, Health and Safety) (USA) **3433**
• Global Ecology and Biogeography (GBR ISSN 1466-822X) **3433**
Global eCommerce Law and Business Report *see* Global Intellectual Property Asset Management Report **6750**
▼ Global Economic History Series (NLD ISSN 1872-5155) **1718**
Global Economic Justice Report *see* Global Justice Report **7238**
• ➤ Global Economic Review (GBR ISSN 1226-508X) **7138**
Global Economic Trends (USA ISSN 1090-3976) **1567**
• Global Economics Prospects (Year) (USA) **1596**
▼ • Global Economist Review (USA ISSN 1946-7230) **1114**
Global Economy and Development Working Paper (USA ISSN 1939-9383) **1596**
• ➤ Global Economy Journal (USA ISSN 1553-5304) **1718**
Global Education *see* Quanqiu Jiaoyu Zhanwang **2901**
➤ Global Education Journal (USA) **3012**
The Global Educator (CAN ISSN 1719-9603) **7238**
Global Electronics China *see* Shijie Dianzi Yuanqijian **3113**
Global Energy and Water Cycle Experiment News *see* G E W E X News **2794**
Global Energy Policy and Economics (NLD) **3136**
• Global Engineering Review (GBR ISSN 1471-423X) **3367**
The Global Environment (GBR ISSN 1750-7979) **8824**
Global Environment Review (IND ISSN 0972-1932) **3433**
• ➤ Global Environmental Change (GBR ISSN 0959-3780) **3434**
Global Environmental Change and Human Security News *see* G E C H S News **3432**
Global Environmental Change and Human Security Report *see* G E C H S Report **3432**
Global Environmental Change Part B: Environmental Hazards *see* Environmental Hazards **3425**
Global Environmental Law Annual (NLD ISSN 0928-933X) **4681**
Global Environmental Law Collection (NLD ISSN 1386-4688) **4681**
Global Environmental Law Review (NLD) **4927**
• Global Environmental Politics (USA ISSN 1526-3800) **3434**
Global Environmental Research (JPN ISSN 1343-8808) **3434**
Global Estate Planning (NLD) **4903**
• Global Facilitation Network for Security Sector Reform. Newsletter (GBR) **2677**
Global Finance *see* Huanqiu Caijing **1568**
• Global Finance (USA ISSN 0896-4181) **1349**
• ➤ Global Finance Journal (NLD ISSN 1044-0283) **1349**
† Global Financial Services Regulators. Asia Pacific (GBR ISSN 1743-6036) **8959**
† Global Financial Services Regulators. Middle East and Africa (GBR ISSN 1743-601X) **8959**
Global Financial Stability Report *see* International Monetary Fund. Global Financial Stability Report **1358**
Global Focus (BEL ISSN 1784-2344) **1748**
• Global Food and Wine (AUS ISSN 1449-9835) **3644**
• Global Food Contact News (GBR ISSN 1750-2624) **6710**
Global Foodservice (USA ISSN 1529-1189) **1997**
Global Foodservice en Espanol *see* Global Foodservice **1997**
• Global Fuels Magazine (GBR) **6771**
Global Fungicide Directory (USA ISSN 1091-1375) **233**
Global Gaming Business (USA ISSN 1555-922X) **8175**
The Global Gig Guide (NOR ISSN 1356-8280) **6569**
• Global Gourmet (USA) **4359**
• ➤ Global Governance (USA ISSN 1075-2846) **7238**
• Global Gypsum (GBR ISSN 1463-9661) **1009**
• Global H R Report (USA ISSN 1542-5665) **1861**
• Global Health (GBR) **7548**
▼ • ➤ Global Health (USA ISSN 1937-514X) **7519**
▼ • ➤ Global Health Action (SWE ISSN 1654-9880) **5620**
Global Health Directory (USA) **5620**
▼ • ➤ Global Health Governance (USA ISSN 1939-2389) **7519**
• ➤ Global Health Promotion/Promotion et Education (GBR ISSN 1757-9759) **7519**
Global Herbicide Directory (USA ISSN 1079-3275) **233**
Global Human Resources Report *see* Global H R Report **1861**
Global Human Rights Law Collection (NLD ISSN 1384-6523) **7207**
Global Hydrology and Climate Center Forecast *see* G H C C Forecast **6353**
• Global Information Network (USA) **7138**
† Global Innovation Research (TWN) **8959**
Global Insecticide Directory (USA ISSN 1088-8497) **233**
Global Insight (ZAF ISSN 1607-2375) **7238**
Global Insurance Bulletin (GBR) **4504**
• Global Intellectual Property Asset Management Report (USA) **6750**
Global International Courts Review (NLD ISSN 1387-0599) **4927**
Global Internet Geography (USA ISSN 1938-6249) **2557**
Global Investment Services (GBR) **1626**
• Global Investment Technology (USA ISSN 1058-3920) **1349**
• Global Investor (GBR ISSN 0951-3604) **1349**
• Global Issues (NZL ISSN 1175-7655) **7966**
Global Issues (USA ISSN 1559-8047) **7238**
• Global Issues (USA) **7238**
➤ Global Issues Series (GBR ISSN 1354-3644) **340**
• ➤ Global Journal of Agricultural Sciences (NGA ISSN 1596-2903) **115**
▼ Global Journal of Business Research (USA ISSN 1931-0277) **1114**
• ➤ Global Journal of Classical Theology (USA ISSN 1521-6055) **7645**
➤ Global Journal of Educational Research (NGA ISSN 1596-6224) **2860**
▼ • Global Journal of Emerging Market Economies (IND ISSN 0974-9101) **1114**
• ➤ Global Journal of Engineering Education (AUS ISSN 1328-3154) **3193**
• ➤ Global Journal of Engineering Research (NGA ISSN 1596-292X) **3194**
• ➤ Global Journal of Environmental Sciences (NGA ISSN 1596-6194) **3434**
▼ • ➤ Global Journal of Finance and Banking Issues (USA ISSN 1933-3439) **1350**
▼ • ➤ Global Journal of Finance and Management (IND) **1350**

Link to your serials resources and content with ulrichsweb.com

▼ new title   † ceased   • electronic media   ➤ refereed

10332 GONGYE JIARE ULRICH'S PERIODICALS

• Gongye Jiare/Industrial Heating (CHN ISSN 1002-1639) **4119**
Gongye Jingji/Industrial Economy (CHN ISSN 1001-3024) **1115**
• Gongye Kongzhi Jisuanji/Industry Control Computer (CHN ISSN 1001-182X) **2460**
• Gongye Lu/Industrial Furnace (CHN ISSN 1001-6988) **3345**
Gongye Qicai/Machinery & Materials (HKG ISSN 1023-0254) **5452**
Gongye Qiye Guanli/Industrial Enterprise Management (CHN ISSN 1001-2516) **1748**
• Gongye Shui Chuli/Industrial Water Treatment (CHN ISSN 1005-829X) **3486**
• Gongye Weisheng yu Zhiyebin/Industrial Health and Occupational Diseases (CHN ISSN 1000-7164) **6677**
• Gongye Weishengwu/Industrial Microbiology (CHN ISSN 1001-6678) **765**
• Gongye Yongshui yu Feishui/Industrial Water & Wastewater (CHN ISSN 1009-2455) **3506**
Goniec Kujawski (POL ISSN 1426-1677) **5218**
• Gonzaga Journal of International Law (USA ISSN 1942-9193) **4927**
• Gonzaga Law Review (USA ISSN 0046-6115) **4682**
Goo Maral/Beautiful Doe (MNG) **588**
• Good (USA ISSN 1935-1488) **3976**
• The Good 5-Cent Cigar (USA) **2285**
Good Age (USA) **4047**
Good Autism Practice (GBR ISSN 1466-2973) **4066**
• Good Beach Guide (GBR) **3486**
• The Good Bed and Breakfast Guide (GBR) **8714**
Good Beer Guide (GBR ISSN 0265-0681) **604**
• The Good Book Guide (GBR ISSN 1472-2097) **7561**
Good Camps Guide Britain (Year) (GBR ISSN 0963-1135) **8714**
Good Camps Guide Europe (Year) (GBR ISSN 0955-9183) **8714**
Good Camps Guide France (Year) (GBR ISSN 0955-9205) **8714**
Good Children Pictorial *see* Hao Ertong Huabao **2192**
Good Clinical Practice Journal (GBR ISSN 1350-0961) **5620**
Good Company (ZAF) **2191**
Good Country People (USA ISSN 1047-7225) **4294**
Good Day Sunshine *see* Beatles Fan Club: Liverpool Productions **6548**
Good Earth Association. Newsletter (USA) **116**
▼ Good Eating, Good Living (USA) **6659**
The Good Five Cent Cigar *see* The Good 5-Cent Cigar **2285**
• The Good Food Guide (GBR ISSN 0072-5005) **4387**
Good Foot (USA) **5423**
Good Fruit & Vegetables (AUS ISSN 1321-0165) **233**
• Good Fruit Grower (USA ISSN 0046-6174) **3734**
Good Government (AUS ISSN 0818-2493) **1542**
▼ Good Health & Medicine (AUS) **6987**
Good Health for All *see* Dajia Jiankang **6984**
Good Holiday Magazine (GBR ISSN 0955-5994) **8714**
The Good Hotel Guide. Great Britain & Ireland (USA ISSN 1933-5512) **4387**
Good Housekeeping *see* Hao Guanjia **4360**
• Good Housekeeping (GBR ISSN 0017-2081) **8866**
Good Housekeeping (IND) **4359**
Good Housekeeping (PHL) **4359**
Good Housekeeping *see* Domashnii Ochag **4356**
• Good Housekeeping (USA ISSN 0017-209X) **4359**
Good Housekeeping Annual Recipes (USA ISSN 1537-6478) **4359**
Good Housekeeping Holiday Best (USA ISSN 1546-6043) **4359**
Good Life (Austin) (USA) **5072**
The Good Life (Metairie) (USA) **4047**
Good Life (Santa Monica) (USA) **3976**
The Good Life, Central New York Magazine (USA ISSN 1931-194X) **5072**
• Good Life in Vancouver (CAN) **3810**
Good Living Uncorked *see* Sydney Morning Herald **3796**
Good Manufacturing Practice Letter *see* The G M P Letter **4487**
Good Manufacturing Practice Trends *see* G M P Trends **1886**
Good Medical Practice Review *see* G M P Review **6843**
Good Medicine *see* Good Health & Medicine **6987**
• Good Medicine (USA ISSN 1072-8503) **5620**
Good Money (USA ISSN 0742-4515) **1627**
Good Money's Social Funds Guide (USA) **1627**
Good Motoring (GBR ISSN 0017-2111) **8582**
• Good News (CAN ISSN 0848-9076) **1115**
Good News (CHE) **6570**
Good News (GBR) **7645**
Good News/Goeie Nuus (ZAF ISSN 0017-2146) **7645**
• Good News (Birmingham) (GBR ISSN 0262-2874) **7759**
Good News (New Berlin) (USA ISSN 1047-2320) **7645**
Good News (Wilmore) (USA ISSN 0436-1563) **7759**
The Good News Letter (USA ISSN 0738-6419) **7799**
Good-News-Letter (Washington) (USA) **6659**
Good Old Boat (USA ISSN 1099-6354) **8276**
Good Old Days (USA ISSN 0046-6158) **5301**
Good Old Days Looking Back *see* Looking Back **5327**
Good Old Days Specials *see* Looking Back **5327**
Good Practice Case Study (GBR ISSN 1368-0080) **1009**
Good Practice Guide (AUS ISSN 1449-2733) **1289**
Good Practice in Health Social Care and Criminal Justice (GBR) **8042**
Good Practice in Rural Development (GBR) **199**
Good Practice Series *see* Good Practice in Health Social Care and Criminal Justice **8042**
Good Pub Guide (Year) (GBR) **604**
Good Reading in South Australian History *see* Historical Society of South Australia. Guidesheet **626**
Good Retirement Guide (Year) (GBR) **4978**
Good Ski Guide (GBR ISSN 0958-0689) **8316**
Good Ski Guide A-Z of World Resorts (GBR ISSN 0958-0735) **8316**
The Good Skiing and Snowboarding Guide *see* The Great Skiing and Snowboarding Guide (Year) **8316**
• The Good Society (USA ISSN 1089-0017) **7138**
The Good Society - P E G S *see* The Good Society **7138**
Good Start *see* Godt i Gang **2860**
Good Stuff (Grand Forks) (USA ISSN 0882-4746) **5011**
Good Stuff (Malvern) (USA ISSN 1523-4215) **1115**
▼ Good Things for a Healthy Home (USA) **4359**
Good Tidings (CAN ISSN 1481-2282) **7736**
Good Timer (DEU) **2191**
• Good Times (CAN ISSN 0847-1126) **4047**
Good Times (GBR) **4978**
• Good Vibes Magazine (USA) **5301**
Good Vibrations (GBR) **4081**
• Good Woodworking (GBR ISSN 0967-0009) **1050**
Goodenows' Ghosts (USA ISSN 1061-7973) **3769**
Goode's Consumer Credit Legislation (GBR) **4682**
Goode's World Atlas *see* Rand McNally Goode's World Atlas **4026**
Goodfellow Monitor (USA) **6422**
Goodguys Goodtimes Gazette (USA) **8175**
Goodie Bag Mag (GBR ISSN 1741-1475) **2191**
† Goodies (NLD ISSN 1874-544X) **8960**
Goodrich Gospel (USA) **3769**
Goods and Services Bulletin (USA) **1886**
Goods and Services Tax Commodity Tax *see* G S T & Commodity Tax **1926**
Goods and Services Tax Guide for Business *see* G S T Guide for Business **1926**
• Goods in Transit (USA) **4869**
Goodtimes (GBR ISSN 1359-9178) **4978**
Goodwill Dimensions (CAN) **6697**
Goodwin Series. Occasional Papers (ZAF ISSN 0304-3460) **395**
Goodwood Journal (SGP) **4387**
• Google Librarian Newsletter (USA) **2557**
Goose Letter *see* Gan no Tayori **2612**
Goose Study (JPN) **945**
Gopher Music Notes (USA ISSN 0017-2235) **6570**
Gopher Oversea'r (USA) **6422**
Gora (BGR ISSN 0861-7570) **3692**
Gordan J Christensen Clinicians Report (French Edition) (USA) **5846**
† Gordian (DEU ISSN 0017-2243) **8960**
Gordon H. Brown Lecture (NZL ISSN 1177-004X) **491**
Gordon H. Brown Lecture Series *see* Gordon H. Brown Lecture **491**
Gordon Harold Brown Lecture *see* Gordon H. Brown Lecture **491**
Gordon J. Christensen Clinicians Report *see* Gordon J. Christensen Clinicians Report **5595**
Gordon J. Christensen Dental Hygiene Clinicians Report *see* Gordon J. Christensen Dental Hygiene Clinicians Report **5837**
Gordon Office Market Report (USA) **7591**
Gordon Setter News (USA) **6808**
• Gordon's (Year) International Photography Price Annual (USA) **6969**
• Gordon's Print Price Annual (Year) (USA ISSN 0160-6298) **491**
Gorey Guardian (IRL ISSN 1393-2470) **3893**
GoreZone (Northampton) (GBR ISSN 1750-7782) **5443**
Gorge Guide (USA ISSN 1063-7656) **8276**
▼ Gorgias Classic Archaeological Reprints (USA ISSN 1935-4401) **395**
Gorgias Handbooks (USA ISSN 1935-6838) **5123**
▼ Gorgias Historic Travels in the Cradle of Civilization (USA ISSN 1935-3200) **4140**
▼ Gorgias Historical Catalogues (USA ISSN 1935-3197) **4182**
▼ Gorgias Historical Dictionaries (USA ISSN 1935-3189) **5123**
▼ Gorgias Historical Grammars (USA ISSN 1935-3162) **5123**
Gorgias Historical Texts (USA ISSN 1935-6919) **4140**
▼ Gorgias Liturgical Studies (USA ISSN 1937-3252) **7645**
▼ Gorgias Mandaean Studies (USA ISSN 1935-441X) **7736**
▼ Gorgias Occasional Historical Commentaries (USA ISSN 1935-4398) **7645**
▼ Gorgias Ottoman Travelers (USA ISSN 1946-2212) **4321**
▼ Gorgias Precis Portfolios (USA ISSN 1935-3871) **4454**
▼ Gorgias Reference Classics (USA ISSN 1937-3287) **7645**
▼ Gorgias Studies in Philosophy and Theology (USA ISSN 1940-0020) **6922**
Gorgias Theological Library (USA ISSN 1935-6935) **7645**
▼ Gorgias Ugaritic Studies (USA ISSN 1935-388X) **5123**
Gorgo (CHE ISSN 0172-3421) **7358**
Gorilla (USA) **945**
Gorilla Gazette (USA) **319**
Gorilla Journal (DEU) **945**
• Goriva i Maziva/Fuels and Lubricants (HRV ISSN 0350-350X) **3194**
• Gorkhapatra (NPL ISSN 1563-7123) **3913**
Gornaya Promyshlennost' (RUS ISSN 1609-9192) **6463**
➤ Gornictwo i Geoinzynieria (POL ISSN 1732-6702) **6463**
Gornictwo Odkrywkowe (POL ISSN 0043-2075) **6463**
Gornoslaskie Studia Socjologiczne (POL ISSN 0072-5013) **8104**
Gornye Lyzhi/Mountain-Skiing (RUS) **8316**
Gornyi Mir (RUS) **6464**
Gornyi Vestnik (RUS) **6464**
Gornyi Zhurnal/Mining Journal (RUS ISSN 0017-2278) **6464**
• Gorod (UKR) **3964**
Gorod N (RUS) **1115**
Gorodskie Vedomosti (RUS) **3935**
Goroskop (RUS) **4335**
• Gorskys. Comedy (AUS) **5218**
➤ Gortania (ITA ISSN 0391-5859) **7858**
Gorteria (NLD ISSN 0017-2294) **791**
➤ Gorteria. Supplement (NLD ISSN 0928-8228) **791**
Goryachaya Liniya Bukhgaltera (RUS) **1289**
Goryeoa'na *see* Koreana **554**
Goryuchie Slantsy *see* Oil Shale **6475**
Go'saengmul Haghoeji/Paleontological Society of Korea. Journal (KOR ISSN 1225-0929) **6725**
• Gosciniec (POL ISSN 1642-0853) **8714**
Gosei Jushi/Plastics (JPN ISSN 0387-0936) **7092**
Gosei Kozo no Katsuyo ni Kansuru Shinpojumu Koen Ronbunshu/Symposium on Research and Application of Composite Constructions. Proceedings (JPN) **3268**
Goshen College Bulletin (USA ISSN 0017-2308) **2285**
Gospel Advocate (USA ISSN 0195-1297) **7645**
Gospel and Contemporary Christian Music Networking Guide (USA) **6570**
Gospel Entertainment Magazine (USA ISSN 1536-7096) **6570**
Gospel Flava Magazine (USA) **6570**
Gospel Herald (CAN ISSN 0829-4666) **7645**
The Gospel Herald and Sunday School Times (USA ISSN 0746-0880) **7645**
Gospel Magazine (GBR) **7759**
The Gospel Messenger (USA ISSN 0017-2359) **4081**
Gospel Messenger *see* Evangeliumi Hirnok **7735**
Gospel of God *see* Shree Hari Katha **7708**
Gospel Outreach (USA) **7646**
Gospel Standard (GBR ISSN 0017-2367) **7759**
• Gospel Today Magazine (USA ISSN 1081-8162) **6570**
The Gospel Voice (USA ISSN 1087-9153) **6570**
Gospel Voice (Sugarland) (USA ISSN 1545-763X) **6570**
Gospodarka Materialowa i Logistyka (POL ISSN 1231-2037) **1886**
Gospodarka Miesna (POL ISSN 0367-4916) **287**
➤ Gospodarka Narodowa (POL ISSN 0867-0005) **1488**
Gospodarka Paliwami i Energia/Fuel and Energy Management (POL ISSN 0017-2413) **3136**
Gospodarka Surowcami Mineralnymi (POL ISSN 0860-0953) **6464**
Gospodarka Wodna (POL ISSN 0017-2448) **8824**
Gospodarski List (HRV ISSN 0350-3100) **199**
Gospodarstvo i Okolis (HRV ISSN 1330-1152) **2612**
Gospodarstvo Istre *see* Ekonomska Istrazivanja **1104**
Gospodin Narod (RUS) **3935**
Gosport (USA) **6422**
Goss and Crested China (GBR ISSN 0262-8902) **366**
Gossner Mission Information (DEU) **7646**
Gostelow Report (GBR) **8714**
Gosudarstva SNG v Zerkale Rossiiskoi Pressy (RUS) **3935**
Gosudarstvennaya Duma. Stenogramma Zasedanii (RUS) **4682**
Gosudarstvennaya Publichnaya Nauchno-tekhnicheskaya Biblioteka Rossii Rossii. Algoritmy i Programmy *see* G P N T B Rossii. Algoritmy i Programmy **2590**
Gosudarstvennye Standarty (RUS ISSN 0134-8752) **4682**
Gosudarstvennyi Informatsionnyi Byulleten' o Privatizatsii (UKR) **4682**
• Gosudarstvo i Pravo (RUS ISSN 1026-9452) **4682**
▼ • Got Genealogy News (USA ISSN 1941-9236) **3769**
Gotarc. Serie A (SWE ISSN 1403-8293) **395**
Gotarc. Serie B, Gothenburg Archaeological Theses (SWE ISSN 0282-6860) **395**
Gotarc. Serie C, Arkeologiska Skrifter (SWE ISSN 0282-9479) **395**
Gothaer Magazin (DEU) **4504**
Gotham (ESP ISSN 1139-9848) **6502**
Gotham (USA) **3976**
Gotham Baseball (USA) **8234**
Gothenburg Papers in Theoretical Linguistics (SWE ISSN 0349-1021) **5123**
Gothenburg Studies in Art and Architecture (SWE ISSN 0348-4114) **491**
Gothenburg Studies in English (SWE ISSN 0072-503X) **5123**
Gothenburg Studies in Social Anthropology (SWE ISSN 0348-4076) **340**
Gothenburg Studies in the History of Science and Ideas (SWE ISSN 0348-6788) **7858**
Gothic Beauty (USA ISSN 1533-841X) **6570**
• Gothic.net (USA ISSN 1539-6053) **5443**
• ➤ Gothic Studies (GBR ISSN 1362-7937) **5301**
Gothix (USA) **5443**
Gothix (Graphic Novel Compilation) *see* Gothix **5443**
Gothorror (GBR) **5443**
Gotlaendskt Arkiv (SWE ISSN 0434-2429) **4225**
Gotlands Allehanda (SWE) **3955**
Gotlands Tidningar (SWE ISSN 1103-9329) **3955**
Gott & Groent (SWE) **3645**
Gotta Write Network Lit-Mag (USA ISSN 1079-1221) **5301**
Gottes Volk (DEU ISSN 0946-8943) **7799**
Gottes Volk Sonderband *see* Gottes Volk **7799**
Gottes Wort im Kirchenjahr (DEU ISSN 0017-2480) **7646**
Gottesdienst (DEU ISSN 0343-8732) **7799**
Gottesdienst und Kirchenmusik (DEU ISSN 0017-2499) **6570**
Gottesdienste Vorbereiten (DEU ISSN 0945-4667) **7799**
Gottfried Benn Forum (DEU) **5301**
Gottfried Wilhelm Leibniz Bibliothek. Kleine Schriften (DEU) **625**
Gottlieb Duttweiler Institut Impuls *see* G D I Impuls **1112**
Goucher (USA) **2285**
Gould's Alcoholic Beverage Control Law of New York *see* New York Alcoholic Beverage Control Law **608**
Gould's Consolidated Laws of New York *see* New York Consolidated Laws **4957**
Gould's Criminal Law Handbook of New York *see* New York Criminal Law Handbook **4895**
Gould's Family Law Handbook of New York *see* New York Family Law Handbook **4913**
Gould's Maryland Criminal Law and Motor Vehicle Handbook *see* Maryland Criminal Law and Motor Vehicle Handbook **4893**
Gould's New Jersey Civil Practice and Court Rules *see* New Jersey Civil Practice and Court Rules **4839**
Gould's New York City Housing Maintenance Code *see* New York City Housing Maintenance Code **4744**
• Gould's New York Civil Practice Law & Rules Handbook (USA ISSN 1933-429X) **4832**
Gould's New York Civil Service Law *see* N Y Civil Service Law **4838**
Gould's New York Consolidated Laws *see* New York Consolidated Laws **4957**
Gould's New York Court Forms *see* New York Court Forms **4957**
Gould's New York Divorces and Annulments *see* New York Gitlitz on Divorces and Annulments **4913**
Gould's New York Estates, Powers and Trusts Law *see* Estates, Powers & Trusts Law of New York **4902**
Gould's New York Family Law Handbook *see* New York Family Law Handbook **4913**
Gould's New York Multiple Dwelling Law *see* New York Multiple Dwelling Law **4745**
Gould's New York Real Property Law Handbook *see* New York Real Property Law Handbook **4745**
Gould's Penal Code Handbook of California *see* California Penal Code Handbook **4637**
Gour-med (DEU ISSN 0177-3941) **5620**
Gourd (USA ISSN 0888-5672) **3734**
Gourman Report. Rating of Graduate and Professional Programs in American and International Universities (USA ISSN 1049-717X) **2982**
Gourman Report. Rating of Undergraduate Programs in American and International Universities (USA ISSN 1049-7188) **2982**
Le Gourmand (FRA ISSN 1774-4792) **4387**
Gourmand Herald *see* Meishi Daobao **4393**
Gourmed *see* Gour-med **5620**
Gourmet (CHE) **4387**
Gourmet (SWE ISSN 0349-6325) **4359**
• Gourmet (USA ISSN 0017-2553) **3645**
• Gourmet Connection (USA) **3645**
• Gourmet Fare Magazine (USA) **3645**
▼ • Gourmet Insider (USA) **3678**
• Gourmet News (USA ISSN 1052-4630) **3678**
• Gourmet Retailer (USA ISSN 0199-0357) **3645**
Gourmetabaco (ESP) **8486**
GourmetReise (AUT) **3645**
Gourmets Wine Guide/Guia de Vinos Gourmets (ESP) **604**
Gouvernance *see* Source O C D E. Gouvernance **1176**
Gouvernement du Quebec. Ministere des Finances. Comptes Publics (CAN ISSN 0706-2869) **7439**
Goverance, Risk and Compliance Expert *see* G R C Expert **2419**
Governance *see* Source O E C D. Governance **1177**
Governance (GBR ISSN 1358-5142) **1748**

Link to your serials resources and content with ulrichsweb.com

Title

DIRECTORY 2010 GREAT BRITAIN. DEPARTMENT OF THE ENVIRONMENT, TRANSPORT 10335

• Graphic Arts in Finland (Online) (FIN ISSN 1457-9723) **7322**
• Graphic Arts Monthly (USA ISSN 1047-9325) **7322**
Graphic Arts Monthly. Buyers' Guide *see* Graphic Arts Monthly **7322**
Graphic Arts Technical Foundation World *see* G A T F World **7321**
Graphic Communications World (USA ISSN 0884-6901) **7322**
Graphic Communicator (USA) **4595**
Graphic Design in Japan (JPN) **7322**
Graphic Design: U S A (USA ISSN 0274-7499) **7322**
Graphic Designers' Index (GBR) **530**
Graphic Exchange (CAN) **492**
Graphic Facts (Year) (JPN) **3244**
Graphic Fund Forecaster (USA) **1627**
Graphic Interface Conference. Proceedings *see* Graphics Interface. Proceedings **2486**
Graphic Magazine (NLD ISSN 1569-4119) **7322**
Graphic Monthly (CAN ISSN 0227-2806) **7322**
Graphic Monthly Estimators' & Buyers Guide (Ontario Edition) (CAN ISSN 0828-9638) **7322**
Graphic Monthly Estimators' & Buyers Guide (Western Edition) *see* Graphic Monthly Estimators' & Buyers Guide (Ontario Edition) **7322**
Graphic News (USA) **7322**
Graphic Paper & Media Union Journal *see* G P M U Journal **7321**
Graphic Repro (GBR ISSN 0952-4118) **7322**
• Graphic Repro On-Line (ZAF ISSN 1814-2915) **7322**
▼ • Graphic Tips for Students (USA ISSN 1941-5117) **7322**
Graphic User Interface Program News *see* G U I Program News **2590**
Graphic Work of Birger Sandzen (USA) **492**
• ➤ Graphical Models (USA ISSN 1524-0703) **2485**
Graphical Survey of the Economy of Taiwan District, Republic of China *see* Zhongua Minguo Taiwan Diqu Jingji Tongji Tubiao **9000**
• GraphicRepro.Net E-News (ZAF ISSN 1814-2923) **7322**
Graphics *see* Graphics International **492**
Graphics (USA) **7322**
• ➤ Graphics Interface. Proceedings/Interface Graphique. Comptes Rendus (CAN ISSN 0713-5424) **2486**
Graphics International (GBR ISSN 1350-0937) **492**
Graphics Update (USA) **7322**
Graphics World (GBR ISSN 0142-8853) **492**
Graphicus (ITA ISSN 0017-3436) **7322**
• Graphikos (DNK ISSN 1603-6050) **7322**
† Graphing and Charting, Simplified (USA) **8960**
Graphis *see* Graphis Advertising Annual **25**
Graphis *see* Graphis Photography Annual **6969**
Graphis *see* Graphis Design Annual **492**
• Graphis Advertising Annual (USA) **25**
Graphis Advertising Journal *see* Graphis Advertising Annual **25**
Graphis Annual Reports (USA) **492**
Graphis Corporate Identity (CHE) **492**
• Graphis Design Annual (USA) **492**
Graphis Design Journal *see* Graphis Design Annual **492**
Graphis Logo (CHE) **492**
Graphis Photography Annual (USA) **6969**
Graphis Photography Journal *see* Graphis Photography Annual **6969**
Graphis Poster Annual *see* Graphis Posters **492**
Graphis Posters (USA ISSN 1021-2892) **492**
Graphis T - Shirt Design (CHE) **492**
Graphische Kunst (DEU ISSN 0342-3158) **492**
Graphische Revue Oesterreichs (AUT ISSN 0017-3479) **7322**
Graphische Unternehmungen Oesterreichs. Jahrbuch (AUT ISSN 0075-2266) **7322**
Graphix (ZAF ISSN 1816-0786) **7322**
Graphix Direct Response (ZAF) **7322**
• Graphology Digest (GBR) **7359**
• Graphos (BRA ISSN 1516-1536) **5302**
• Graphoscope (CAN ISSN 0046-631X) **1627**
• ➤ Graphs and Combinatorics (JPN ISSN 0911-0119) **5552**
Grappling (USA) **8176**
• ➤ Grasas y Aceites (ESP ISSN 0017-3495) **2123**
Grasduinen (BEL ISSN 0167-2932) **791**
Grasp (GBR) **8176**
De Graspieper *see* Tussen Duin en Dijk **821**
• ➤ Grass and Forage Science (GBR ISSN 0142-5242) **116**
Grass & Grain (USA) **233**
Grass Roots (AUS ISSN 0310-2890) **8104**
Grass Roots Campaigning (USA) **7139**
† Grass Roots Perspectives on American History (USA ISSN 0148-771X) **8960**
Grasses and Herbage Legumes Variety Leaflet (GBR ISSN 1467-6672) **273**
Grasset Noir (FRA ISSN 1760-3285) **5443**
Grassland and Turf *see* Caoyuan yu Caoping **783**
• Grassland Science (GBR ISSN 1744-6961) **116**
➤ Grassland Science/Nippon Sochi Gakkai-shi (JPN) **233**
Grasslands (USA ISSN 1540-6857) **116**
• Grasslands and Forage Abstracts (GBR ISSN 1350-9837) **181**
➤ Grasslands Review (USA ISSN 1066-4742) **5302**
Grassroots (PAK ISSN 1726-0396) **4182**
• Grassroots Development (USA ISSN 0733-6608) **1596**
• Grassroots Economic Organizing Newsletter (USA ISSN 1071-0590) **6698**
• Grassroots Editor (USA ISSN 0017-3541) **4576**
GrassRoots Environmental Effectiveness Network Lines *see* G R E E N Lines **3432**
Grassroots Fundraising Journal (USA ISSN 0740-4832) **8042**
Grassroots Motorsports (USA ISSN 1047-0298) **8583**
Gratia (DEU ISSN 0343-1258) **4225**
• Gratis (ITA) **2557**
Der Graue (DEU) **8714**
Graue Literatur zur Stadt-, Regional- und Landesplanung (DEU ISSN 0948-2970) **4411**
Grauer Panther (DEU ISSN 0178-5109) **4047**
† Graven Images (USA ISSN 1078-3547) **8960**
De Graven Koerier *see* De Koerier **448**
Gravesend K M Extra (GBR) **3865**
Gravesend Messenger (GBR ISSN 1462-1185) **3865**
Gravesend Reporter (GBR ISSN 0968-5758) **3865**
Gravesiana (GBR ISSN 1368-1095) **5302**
Gravid (DNK ISSN 1398-5604) **5991**
Gravid (NOR ISSN 1500-2144) **5991**
• Gravitas (USA) **7646**
• ➤ Gravitation & Cosmology (RUS ISSN 0202-2893) **7014**
• ➤ Gravitational and Space Biology Bulletin (USA ISSN 1089-988X) **56**
• Gravity (Scottdale) (USA ISSN 1524-5470) **5423**
• Gravity (Year) (Boulder) (USA) **2783**
Gravure (USA ISSN 0894-4946) **7322**
The Grawunder and Graffunder Connection (USA ISSN 1081-6240) **3769**
• Gray Areas (Online Edition) (USA) **3976**
Gray Areas (Print Edition) *see* Gray Areas (Online Edition) **3976**
• The Gray Sheet (USA ISSN 1530-1214) **5620**
Gray Sheet - Medical Devices, Diagnostics & Instrumentation Reports *see* The Gray Sheet **5620**
Graybar Outlook (USA ISSN 0017-3592) **3309**
Gray's Sporting Journal (USA ISSN 0273-6691) **8316**
Grayson-Jockey Club Research Today *see* Research Today **8806**
Grayson Report (USA ISSN 1526-8241) **594**
Graz Architecture Magazine *see* G A M **443**
The Graz Schumpeter Lectures (GBR) **1542**
• Der Grazer (AUT) **3797**
➤ Grazer Linguistische Studien (AUT ISSN 1015-0498) **5123**
➤ Grazer Mathematische Berichte (AUT ISSN 1016-7692) **5490**
• ➤ Grazer Philosophische Studien (NLD ISSN 0165-9227) **6922**
Grazer Schriftenreihe Knowledge Management (DEU ISSN 1860-2169) **1748**
Grazhdanskaya Aviatsiya (RUS ISSN 0017-3606) **8542**
Grazhdanskaya Zashchita (RUS ISSN 0869-5881) **7139**
Grazia (BGR) **8866**
Grazia (GBR ISSN 1745-9567) **8866**
Grazia (HRV ISSN 1845-8785) **8866**
Grazia (ITA ISSN 1120-5113) **8866**
Grazia (JPN) **8866**
▼ Grazia (NLD) **8866**
Grazia (SRB ISSN 1452-5038) **8866**
Grazia (UAE ISSN 1817-4280) **8866**
▼ Grazia Casa (ITA ISSN 1971-8322) **4359**
• The Graziadio Business Report (USA ISSN 1939-1633) **1115**
The Grazier (USA ISSN 1057-2430) **3692**
Great Activities (USA ISSN 0886-764X) **2860**
Great Airliners Series (USA) **57**
• Great American Orators (USA ISSN 0898-8277) **4170**
Great American Video Business Newsletter (USA ISSN 1051-6050) **2401**
Great Australian Quilts (AUS ISSN 1832-8121) **6639**
• Great Barrier Reef Marine Park Authority. Annual Report (AUS ISSN 0155-8072) **675**
• ➤ Great Barrier Reef Marine Park Authority Research Publication Series (AUS ISSN 1037-1508) **675**
Great Barrier Reef Marine Park Authority. Research Report *see* Great Barrier Reef Marine Park Authority. Annual Report **675**
† Great Barrier Reef Marine Park Authority. Special Publication Series (AUS ISSN 0810-6983) **8960**
• ➤ Great Barrier Reef Marine Park Authority Technical Memorandum (AUS ISSN 0817-6094) **675**
• Great Barrier Reef Marine Park Authority Workshop Series (AUS ISSN 0156-5842) **2804**
Great Basin Naturalist Memoirs *see* Western North American Naturalist. Monographs **967**
Great Britain (Year) (USA ISSN 0896-8683) **8714**
Great Britain. Agricultural Science Service. Research and Development Report. Agricultural Service (GBR ISSN 0954-4208) **116**
• Great Britain. Air Transport Users Council Annual Report (GBR) **8542**
Great Britain. Board of Inland Revenue. Survey of Personal Incomes (GBR) **1927**
Great Britain. Central Statistical Office. Annual Census of Production Reports (GBR) **1235**
Great Britain. Central Statistical Office. Family Spending (GBR ISSN 0965-1403) **1718**
Great Britain. Central Statistical Office. Guide to Official Statistics (GBR ISSN 0261-1791) **8374**
Great Britain. Central Statistical Office. Key Data (GBR ISSN 0951-9092) **8374**
Great Britain. Central Statistical Office. Regional Trends (GBR ISSN 0261-1783) **8374**
Great Britain. Central Statistical Office. Social Trends (GBR ISSN 0306-7742) **8149**
Great Britain. Central Statistical Office. Standard Industrial Classification of Economic Activities (Year) (GBR) **1235**
• Great Britain. Central Statistical Office. Statistical News (GBR ISSN 0017-3630) **8374**
Great Britain. Central Statistical Office. Studies in Official Statistics (GBR ISSN 0081-8313) **8374**
Great Britain. Central Statistical Office. United Kingdom Balance of Payments (GBR ISSN 0950-7558) **1235**
Great Britain. Central Statistical Office. United Kingdom National Accounts (GBR ISSN 0267-8691) **1235**
• Great Britain. Centre for Environment, Fisheries and Aquaculture Science. Annual Report and Accounts (GBR) **3595**
Great Britain. Centre for Environment, Fisheries and Aquaculture Science. Science Series. Technical Report (GBR ISSN 1467-5609) **3595**
Great Britain. Civil Aviation Authority. Air Travel Trust. Annual Report and Accounts (GBR) **8542**
Great Britain. Civil Aviation Authority. Air Travel Trust Committee. Annual Report (GBR) **8542**
Great Britain. Civil Aviation Authority. Airport Surveys (GBR) **8525**
Great Britain. Civil Aviation Authority. Airworthiness Notices (GBR) **8542**
Great Britain. Civil Aviation Authority. Annual Punctuality Statistics - Full Analysis (Year) (GBR) **8525**
Great Britain. Civil Aviation Authority. Annual Punctuality Statistics - Summary Analysis (Year) (GBR) **8525**
Great Britain. Civil Aviation Authority. Annual Report and Accounts (GBR ISSN 0306-3569) **8542**
Great Britain. Civil Aviation Authority. Approved Aerial Positions (GBR) **8542**
Great Britain. Civil Aviation Authority. Civil Aviation Publications (GBR) **8542**
Great Britain. Civil Aviation Authority. D O R A Communication (GBR) **8542**
Great Britain. Civil Aviation Authority. D O R A Report (GBR) **8542**
Great Britain. Civil Aviation Authority. D R Report (GBR) **8542**
Great Britain. Civil Aviation Authority. Data Sheets (GBR) **8542**
Great Britain. Civil Aviation Authority. Document (GBR) **8542**
Great Britain. Civil Aviation Authority. General Aviation Airmiss Bulletin (GBR) **8542**
Great Britain. Civil Aviation Authority. General Aviation Safety Information Leaflets (GBR ISSN 0309-667X) **8542**
Great Britain. Civil Aviation Authority. General Information Bulletin (GBR) **8542**
Great Britain. Civil Aviation Authority. International Register of Civil Aircraft (GBR) **8542**
Great Britain. Civil Aviation Authority. Navigation Warning Information Bulletin (GBR) **8543**
Great Britain. Civil Aviation Authority. New Reportable Occurrences (GBR) **8543**
Great Britain. Civil Aviation Authority. Notices to A O C Holders (Air Operator's Certificate) (GBR) **8543**
Great Britain. Civil Aviation Authority. Occurrence Digest (GBR) **8543**
Great Britain. Civil Aviation Authority. Official Record Series 1: Licensing Notices (GBR ISSN 0306-4646) **8543**
Great Britain. Civil Aviation Authority. Official Record Series 2: Notices Relating to Air Transport Licenses, Route Licenses and Operating Licenses (GBR ISSN 0306-4654) **8543**
Great Britain. Civil Aviation Authority. Official Record Series 3: Air Travel Organiser Licensing, Part 1 (GBR ISSN 0951-0036) **8543**
Great Britain. Civil Aviation Authority. Official Record Series 3: Air Travel Organiser Licensing, Part 2 (GBR ISSN 0951-0044) **8543**
Great Britain. Civil Aviation Authority. Official Record Series 4: Miscellaneous (GBR ISSN 0306-4670) **8543**
Great Britain. Civil Aviation Authority. Official Record Series 5: Schemes of Changes (GBR ISSN 0306-4689) **8543**
Great Britain. Civil Aviation Authority. Official Record Series 6: Airports - Economic Regulation, Part 1 (GBR ISSN 0951-0052) **8543**
Great Britain. Civil Aviation Authority. Official Record Series 6: Airports - Economic Regulation, Part 2 (GBR ISSN 0951-0060) **8543**
Great Britain. Civil Aviation Authority. Papers (GBR) **8543**
Great Britain. Civil Aviation Authority. Punctuality Statistics Heathrow, Gatwick, Manchester, Birmingham, Luton and Stanstead - Full Analysis (GBR ISSN 0957-5154) **8525**
Great Britain. Civil Aviation Authority. Punctuality Statistics Heathrow, Gatwick, Manchester, Birmingham, Luton and Stanstead - Summary Analysis (GBR ISSN 0957-5162) **8525**
Great Britain. Civil Aviation Authority. Reportable A T C Occurrences (Air Traffic Control) (GBR) **8543**
Great Britain. Civil Aviation Authority. Reportable Occurrences (GBR) **8543**
Great Britain. Civil Aviation Authority. Type Certificate Data Sheets (GBR) **8543**
Great Britain. Civil Aviation Authority. U.K. Airlines Annual Operating, Traffic & Financial Statistics (GBR) **8525**
Great Britain. Civil Aviation Authority. U.K. Airlines Monthly Operating & Traffic Statistics (GBR) **8525**
Great Britain. Civil Aviation Authority. U.K. Airports Annual Statements of Movements, Passengers and Cargo (Year) (GBR) **8525**
Great Britain. Civil Aviation Authority. U.K. Airports Monthly Statements of Movements, Passengers and Cargo (GBR) **8525**
Great Britain Collectors Club. Quarterly Newsletter (USA) **6895**
Great Britain Concise Stamp Catalogue (GBR) **6895**
Great Britain. Contributions Agency. Framework Document (Year) (GBR) **4504**
Great Britain. Department for Children, Schools and Families. Bulletin (GBR) **2933**
Great Britain. Department for Education and Employment. Building Bulletins (GBR) **3024**
Great Britain. Department for Education and Employment. Circular (GBR) **2860**
Great Britain. Department for Education and Skills. Bulletin *see* Great Britain. Department for Children, Schools and Families. Bulletin **2933**
Great Britain. Department for Education and Skills. First Release (GBR) **2933**
Great Britain. Department for Education and Skills. Research Brief (GBR) **2860**
Great Britain. Department for Education. Postgraduate Awards (GBR) **2983**
Great Britain. Department for Education. Statistics of Education. Further and Higher Education. Student - Staff Ratios and Unit Costs (GBR ISSN 0955-9574) **2933**
Great Britain. Department for Transport, Local Government and the Regions. Regeneration Research Summary (GBR) **8631**
Great Britain. Department for Transport, Local Government and the Regions. Roads and Local Transport Research Programme. Summary of Planned Research (GBR) **8631**
Great Britain. Department for Work and Pensions. Social Research Branch. In-House Report (GBR ISSN 1368-244X) **8042**
Great Britain. Department for Work and Pensions. Working Paper (GBR) **8043**
Great Britain. Department of Education and Science. Annual Report (GBR) **2860**
Great Britain. Department of Employment. Research (GBR) **1684**
Great Britain. Department of Energy. Coal Research and Development Programme. Progress Report (Year) (GBR) **3244**
Great Britain. Department of Environment, Food and Rural Affairs. Report (GBR) **3434**
• Great Britain. Department of Health and Social Security. Health Building Notes (GBR ISSN 0952-1054) **4094**
Great Britain. Department of Health and Social Security. Health Equipment Notes (GBR ISSN 0141-1403) **4094**
• Great Britain. Department of Health. On the State of the Public Health (GBR ISSN 0072-6087) **7519**
Great Britain. Department of Health. Physiotherapy Services (GBR) **6109**
Great Britain. Department of Social Security. Social Security Statistics (GBR) **8083**
Great Britain. Department of the Environment. Energy Efficiency Office. Best Practice Programme. Future Practice Report (GBR) **3136**
Great Britain. Department of the Environment. Enterprise Zone Information (GBR ISSN 0956-0769) **2612**
Great Britain. Department of the Environment. Environmental Action Guide Advisory Notes (GBR ISSN 1369-930X) **2612**
Great Britain. Department of the Environment. Local Government Financial Statistics: England and Wales (GBR ISSN 0308-1745) **7480**
Great Britain. Department of the Environment. Planning Inspectorate. Executive Agency. Business and Corporate Plan (GBR) **7442**
Great Britain. Department of the Environment. Price Adjustment Formulae for Construction Contracts: Monthly Bulletin of Indices (GBR ISSN 0964-4571) **1046**
Great Britain. Department of the Environment, Transport and the Regions. Advisory Committee on Releases to the Environment Guidance Note (GBR ISSN 1463-9793) **3434**
• Great Britain. Department of the Environment, Transport and the Regions. Annual Report (GBR) **3434**
• Great Britain. Department of the Environment, Transport and the Regions. Aviation Consultation Papers (GBR) **8543**
Great Britain. Department of the Environment, Transport and the Regions. Digest of Environmental Statistics (GBR) **3479**
Great Britain. Department of the Environment, Transport and the Regions. Environment Circular (GBR) **3434**

Title

▼ *new title* † *ceased* • *electronic media* ➤ *refereed*

10336 GREAT BRITAIN. DEPARTMENT OF THE ENVIRONMENT, TRANSPORT ULRICH'S PERIODICALS

• Great Britain. Department of the Environment, Transport and the Regions. Environmental Protection Consultation Papers (GBR) **3434**
Great Britain. Department of the Environment, Transport and the Regions. Housing and Construction Statistics (GBR) **1046**
• Great Britain. Department of the Environment, Transport and the Regions. Housing Consultation Papers (GBR) **4411**
Great Britain. Department of the Environment, Transport and the Regions. Housing Research Summary (GBR) **4411**
Great Britain. Department of the Environment, Transport and the Regions. Library Services. Publications Issued in (Year) (GBR ISSN 1362-1580) **3479**
Great Britain. Department of the Environment, Transport and the Regions. Library Services. Publications Monthly List (GBR ISSN 1465-1475) **3479**
• Great Britain. Department of the Environment, Transport and the Regions. Local and Regional Government Consultation Papers (GBR) **7493**
Great Britain. Department of the Environment, Transport and the Regions. Local Housing Statistics: England and Wales (GBR) **4435**
• Great Britain. Department of the Environment, Transport and the Regions. Road Network Consultation Paper (GBR) **8631**
• Great Britain. Department of the Environment, Transport and the Regions. Shipping Consultation Papers (GBR) **8644**
• Great Britain. Department of the Environment, Transport and the Regions. Wildlife and Countryside Consultation Papers (GBR) **2612**
Great Britain. Department of Trade and Industry. Assessment Paper (GBR ISSN 0960-7250) **1748**
Great Britain. Department of Trade and Industry. Energy Paper (GBR ISSN 1365-5949) **1428**
Great Britain. Department of Trade and Industry. Insolvency: General Annual Report (GBR) **1350**
Great Britain. Department of Trade. Insurance Business: Annual Report (GBR ISSN 0308-499X) **4504**
Great Britain. Department of Trade. Patents, Design and Trade Marks (Annual Report) (GBR ISSN 0072-5706) **6750**
Great Britain. Department of Transport, Local Government and the Regions. Fire Statistics United Kingdom (GBR ISSN 1476-2021) **3582**
Great Britain. Departments of Health and Social Security. N H S Day Care Facilities (GBR) **8043**
• Great Britain. Economic and Social Research Council. Annual Report (GBR ISSN 0266-2043) **7967**
Great Britain. Energy Technology Support Unit. Energy and the Environment Programme. Unit B-CR. Report (GBR ISSN 1368-843X) **3136**
Great Britain. Energy Technology Support Unit. Energy and the Environment Programme. Unit J. Report (GBR ISSN 1367-8388) **3136**
Great Britain. Energy Technology Support Unit. Energy Technology Best Practice Programme. Case Study Example (GBR) **3506**
Great Britain. Foreign and Commonwealth Office. Treaty Series (GBR ISSN 0072-6397) **7238**
Great Britain. Forestry Commission. Library Review (GBR ISSN 0436-4112) **3692**
• Great Britain. General Household Survey (GBR ISSN 1754-4777) **7307**
Great Britain. Government Statistical Service. Abortion Statistics, England and Wales (Year) (GBR) **973**
• Great Britain. Government Statistical Service. Birth Statistics. England and Wales (GBR ISSN 0140-2587) **7307**
• Great Britain. Government Statistical Service. Cancer Statistics Registrations. England and Wales (GBR ISSN 0143-4829) **5747**
Great Britain. Government Statistical Service. Series FM1. Birth Statistics. England and Wales *see* Great Britain. Government Statistical Service. Birth Statistics. England and Wales **7307**
Great Britain. Greater London Authority. Technical Report (GBR) **4411**
The Great Britain Guide (GBR) **8715**
Great Britain. H M Customs & Excise. Management Plan (GBR) **1927**
• Great Britain. H.M.S.O. Books in Print (GBR ISSN 0267-1727) **625**
• Great Britain. H.M.S.O. Daily List (GBR ISSN 0951-8843) **625**
Great Britain. H.M.S.O. Government Publications (Monthly) *see* Stationery Office Monthly Catalogue **636**
• Great Britain. H.M.S.O. Publications Catalogue (GBR ISSN 0955-7601) **625**
• Great Britain. H.M.S.O. Statutory Instruments List (GBR) **625**
Great Britain. H M Treasury. Civil Service Statistics (GBR ISSN 0267-095X) **7480**
Great Britain. H M Treasury. Forecasts for the U K Economy (GBR) **1488**
Great Britain. H M Treasury. Government Procurement: Progress Report to the Prime Minister (Year) (GBR) **1927**
Great Britain. Health & Safety Executive. Technology and Health Sciences Division. Specialist Inspector Reports (GBR ISSN 1363-0695) **7519**
Great Britain. Home Office. Crime Reduction Programme Guidance Note (GBR) **2653**
Great Britain. Home Office. Criminal Statistics. England and Wales. Supplementary Tables (GBR ISSN 0950-5237) **2674**
Great Britain. Home Office. Development and Practice (GBR ISSN 1477-3120) **7442**
Great Britain. Home Office. Police Research Group. Crime Prevention Unit. Papers (GBR ISSN 0959-597X) **2653**
Great Britain. Home Office. Probation Statistics England & Wales (Year) (GBR ISSN 0265-573X) **2653**
Great Britain. Home Office. Research and Planning Unit. Papers *see* R P U Papers **7464**
Great Britain. Home Office. Research and Planning Unit. Programme (Year) (GBR) **7442**
Great Britain. Home Office. Research and Statistics Department. Research Bulletin (GBR ISSN 0962-0478) **7442**
Great Britain. Home Office. Research, Development and Statistics Directorate. Findings (GBR ISSN 1473-8406) **7442**
Great Britain. Home Office. Research, Development and Statistics Directorate. Research Findings *see* Great Britain. Home Office. Research, Development and Statistics Directorate. Findings **7442**
Great Britain. Home Office. Research Studies (GBR ISSN 0072-6435) **2653**
• Great Britain. House of Commons. Parliamentary Debates (GBR ISSN 0309-8826) **7442**
Great Britain. House of Commons. Parliamentary Debates (Weekly Edition) *see* Great Britain. House of Commons. Parliamentary Debates **7442**
• Great Britain. House of Lords. Parliamentary Debates (GBR ISSN 0309-8834) **7139**
• Great Britain. House of Lords. Parliamentary Debates (CD-ROM Edition) (USA) **7139**
Great Britain. Institute of Terrestrial Ecology. Statistical Checklist (GBR ISSN 0141-6464) **675**
Great Britain Journal *see* G B Journal **6895**
Great Britain. Laboratory of the Government Chemist. Annual Report of the Government Chemist (GBR ISSN 0072-6524) **2062**
Great Britain. Law Commission. Consultation Paper (GBR ISSN 1357-9223) **4682**
Great Britain. Learning and Skills Development Agency. Briefing *see* Great Britain. Learning and Skills Network. Briefing **2941**
Great Britain. Learning and Skills Network. Briefing (GBR ISSN 1754-1115) **2941**
• Great Britain. Medical Research Council. Annual Report and Accounts (Years) (GBR) **5620**
Great Britain. Medicines Act 1968 Advisory Bodies. Annual Report (GBR) **7519**
Great Britain. Ministry of Agriculture, Fisheries and Food. Digest of Agricultural Census Statistics (GBR ISSN 1359-3919) **116**
Great Britain. Ministry of Defence. Navy List (GBR) **6422**
Great Britain. National Crime Squad. Inspection (GBR) **2653**
• Great Britain. National Environment Research Council. British Geological Survey. Annual Report (GBR) **2745**
Great Britain. National Environment Research Council. British Geological Survey. Report *see* Great Britain. National Environment Research Council. British Geological Survey. Annual Report **2745**
Great Britain. National Physical Laboratory. Measurement Note (GBR) **7014**
Great Britain. Natural Environment Research Council. British Geological Survey. British Regional Geology (GBR ISSN 0367-3928) **2745**
Great Britain. Natural Environment Research Council. British Geological Survey. Geomagnetic Bulletin (GBR ISSN 0073-9316) **2783**
Great Britain. Natural Environment Research Council. British Geological Survey. Offshore Regional Reports (GBR) **2745**
Great Britain. Natural Environment Research Council. British Geological Survey. Overseas Geology and Mineral Resources (GBR ISSN 0030-7467) **2745**
Great Britain. Natural Environment Research Council. British Geological Survey. Overseas Memoirs (GBR ISSN 0951-6646) **2745**
Great Britain. Natural Environment Research Council. Center for Ecology and Hydrology. Annual Report (GBR) **3434**
• Great Britain. Natural Resources Institute. Bulletin (GBR) **116**
Great Britain. Office for National Statistics. Annual Abstract of Statistics (GBR) **8375**
Great Britain. Office for National Statistics. Consumer Trends (GBR ISSN 1366-2538) **1115**
Great Britain. Office for National Statistics. Monthly Digest of Statistics *see* Monthly Digest of Statistics **8389**
Great Britain. Office for National Statistics. Mortality Statistics. Cause *see* Great Britain. Office for National Statistics. Mortality Statistics. Deaths Registered in (Year) **7307**
• Great Britain. Office for National Statistics. Mortality Statistics. Deaths Registered in (Year) (GBR ISSN 2040-252X) **7307**
Great Britain. Office for National Statistics. Mortality Statistics. General *see* Great Britain. Office for National Statistics. Mortality Statistics. Deaths Registered in (Year) **7307**
Great Britain. Office for National Statistics. Mortality Statistics. Injury and Poisoning *see* Great Britain. Office for National Statistics. Mortality Statistics. Deaths Registered in (Year) **7307**
Great Britain. Office of Fair Trading. Report (GBR) **1567**
Great Britain. Office of National Statistics. Population Estimates: England and Wales (GBR ISSN 0950-7574) **7284**
Great Britain. Press Complaints Commission. Report (GBR ISSN 1751-0406) **1684**
Great Britain. Public Works Loan Board. Annual Report (GBR ISSN 0072-7032) **7442**
Great Britain. Royal Army Chaplains' Department. Journal (GBR) **6422**
Great Britain. Royal Commission on Historical Manuscripts. Annual Review (GBR ISSN 0957-7149) **4170**
† Great Britain. Schools Council Publications. Curriculum Bulletins (GBR ISSN 0072-7113) **8960**
† Great Britain. Schools Council Publications. Examinations Bulletins (GBR ISSN 0072-7121) **8960**
Great Britain. Scottish Law Commission. Annual Report (GBR ISSN 0080-7915) **4682**
Great Britain. Scottish Law Commission. Discussion Paper (GBR) **4682**
Great Britain. Scottish Office. Economic Research Paper (GBR ISSN 1464-2190) **1115**
• Great Britain. Sea Fish Industry Authority. Annual Report and Accounts (GBR) **3595**
Great Britain. Sea Fish Industry Authority. European Supplies Bulletin (GBR ISSN 0142-937X) **3595**
Great Britain. Sea Fish Industry Authority. Fisheries Economics Newsletter (GBR ISSN 0309-4294) **3596**
Great Britain. Sea Fish Industry Authority. Household Fish Consumption in Great Britain (GBR ISSN 0262-3269) **3596**
Great Britain. Sea Fish Industry Authority. Key Indicators (GBR ISSN 0953-8348) **3596**
Great Britain. Social Services Inspectorate. Registration and Inspection Units in Northern Ireland (IRL) **8043**
Great Britain. Soil Survey of England and Wales. Bulletin (GBR ISSN 0072-7164) **233**
Great Britain. Soil Survey of England and Wales. Special Surveys (GBR ISSN 0072-7202) **233**
Great Britain. Soil Survey of England and Wales. Technical Monographs (GBR ISSN 0072-7210) **233**
Great Britain Specialised Stamp Catalogue (GBR ISSN 0072-7229) **6895**
• Great Britain. Stationery Office. Annual Catalogue (GBR ISSN 1462-0022) **625**
• Great Britain. Stationery Office. Chairmen Reports of Official Committees. Index (GBR) **625**
• Great Britain. Studies on Medical and Population Subjects (GBR ISSN 0072-6400) **7284**
Great Britain. Treasury. Supply Estimates (GBR) **1927**
▼ Great British Food (GBR ISSN 1755-3148) **3645**
Great Cars (GBR ISSN 1354-5795) **8583**
Great Changes to the World *see* Cangsang **4180**
• ➤ The Great Circle (AUS ISSN 0156-8698) **4141**
Great Circumpolar Bear Cult (USA ISSN 0196-3147) **5302**
Great Dane Club of America. Monthly Bulletin (USA) **6808**
Great Dane Reporter (USA ISSN 0889-7727) **6808**
Great Decisions (USA ISSN 0072-727X) **7239**
Great Earth *see* Dadi **3823**
Great European Itineraries *see* Fodor's Touring Europe **8709**
Great Expectations *see* Today's Parent, Pregnancy & Birth **6005**
Great Expeditions (USA ISSN 0706-7682) **8715**
Great Golf Resorts of the World (USA ISSN 1061-3544) **8234**
▼ • Great Health (USA) **5620**
Great Ideas for Long-Term Care *see* Eldercare Reporter **8953**
• The Great Ideas Letter (AUS ISSN 1449-4183) **1115**
Great Laker (USA) **8644**
Great Lakes Advocate (AUS ISSN 1321-554X) **3794**
Great Lakes and Connecting Channels: Water Levels and Depths (USA) **3361**
Great Lakes Angler (USA ISSN 1524-0355) **8316**
Great Lakes Boating (USA ISSN 1937-7274) **8276**
Great Lakes Brewing News (USA) **604**
Great Lakes Bulletin (USA) **6422**
Great Lakes Cruiser (USA) **8715**
➤ The Great Lakes Entomologist (USA ISSN 0090-0222) **848**
• Great Lakes Environmental Directory (USA ISSN 1080-5664) **2612**
• Great Lakes Family (USA) **2154**
Great Lakes Fisherman (CAN ISSN 0847-0685) **3596**
➤ Great Lakes Fishery Commission (United States and Canada) Technical Report Series (USA ISSN 0072-730X) **3596**
• Great Lakes Fishery Commission. Miscellaneous Publications (USA ISSN 1090-106X) **3596**
➤ Great Lakes Fishery Commission. Special Publication (USA ISSN 1090-1051) **3596**
Great Lakes Fishery Commission Technical Report *see* Great Lakes Fishery Commission (United States and Canada) Technical Report Series **3596**
Great Lakes Fitness Extreme Magazine *see* F X M **8172**
▼ Great Lakes Gaming and Poker Magazine (USA) **8176**
• ➤ Great Lakes Geographer (CAN ISSN 1195-3071) **4013**
Great Lakes Log (USA ISSN 1067-4144) **8644**
Great Lakes Navigation (CAN ISSN 0824-8583) **8644**
• Great Lakes News (USA) **2612**
The Great Lakes of North America (GBR) **8715**
• Great Lakes Pilotage Authority. Annual Report (Online Edition) (CAN ISSN 1910-3468) **8644**
• Great Lakes Pilotage Authority. Annual Report (Print Edition) (CAN ISSN 0711-0707) **8644**
Great Lakes Program. Memorial Monograph Series (USA) **3434**
Great Lakes Program. Occasional Paper Series (USA) **3434**
Great Lakes Research Checklist (USA ISSN 0072-7326) **8824**
Great Lakes Research Review (USA) **3434**
Great Lakes Seaway Log *see* Great Lakes/Seaway Review **8644**
Great Lakes/Seaway Review (USA) **8644**
Great Lakes - St. Lawrence River Water Level *see* Level News **8828**
Great Lakes Symposium on V L S I (Very Large Scale Integration) (USA) **2539**
• Great Lakes Symposium on V S L I. Proceedings (USA ISSN 1066-1395) **2471**
Great Lakes Water Quality. Report/La Qualite de l'Eau des Grands Lacs. Rapport (CAN ISSN 0845-0919) **3434**
Great Locations (USA) **8715**
Great Migration Newsletter (USA ISSN 1049-8087) **3769**
Great Minds of the 21st Century (USA ISSN 1545-9225) **642**
Great Model Railroads (USA ISSN 1048-8685) **4335**
Great North Review (GBR ISSN 0307-3319) **8618**
The Great Outdoors (GBR ISSN 0140-7570) **8316**
Great Plains Game & Fish (USA ISSN 1055-6532) **8316**
Great Plains Journal (USA ISSN 0017-3673) **3976**
Great Plains National Educational Media Catalog *see* G P N Educational Media Catalog **2859**
• Great Plains Natural Resources Journal (USA) **3434**
Great Plains Newsletter (USA) **4294**
➤ Great Plains Quarterly (USA ISSN 0275-7664) **4294**
➤ Great Plains Research (USA ISSN 1052-5165) **7858**
The Great Plains Sociologist (USA ISSN 0896-0054) **8104**
Great Restaurants of Long Island (USA) **3645**
Great Restaurants of New York City (West Side Edition) (USA ISSN 1930-6075) **3645**
Great River Microcomputer Users Group Newsletter *see* G R M U G Newsletter **2576**
• Great River Review (USA ISSN 0160-2144) **5302**
Great Scale Modeling (Year) (USA ISSN 1096-3944) **4335**
The Great Skiing and Snowboarding Guide (Year) (GBR ISSN 1750-7103) **8316**
Great Smoky Mountains *see* Insiders' Guide to the Great Smoky Mountains **8722**
Great Smoky Mountains National Park *see* Fodor's in Focus Great Smoky Mountains National Park **8706**
Great Tao (USA) **7736**
Great Times *see* Saskatoon's Magazine **3817**
Great Transition Initiative Paper Series *see* G T I Paper Series **8103**
Great Unity *see* Dai Doan Ket **7128**
▼ Great Walks (AUS ISSN 1835-0321) **8316**
The Great Wall *see* Changcheng **5272**
Great Wall *see* Chang Cheng **5272**
Great West and Indian Series (USA ISSN 0072-7342) **4294**
Great-West Lifeco. Annual Reports (CAN ISSN 0849-6463) **4504**
Great Western Echo (GBR ISSN 1362-2153) **8618**
Great Western Railway Journal (GBR ISSN 0964-6809) **4335**
Great Women of the 21st Century (USA ISSN 1551-1332) **642**
Great Women of the Twenty-First Century *see* Great Women of the 21st Century **642**
Great Yarmouth Port and Industry Handbook (GBR ISSN 0260-9517) **8644**
• The Greater Baton Rouge Business Report (USA ISSN 0747-4652) **1488**
Greater Baton Rouge Manufacturers Directory (USA) **1997**
Greater Beneficial Union of Pittsburgh Reporter *see* G B U Reporter **4503**
• The Greater Boston Builder (USA) **1009**
Greater Chicago Ocean Freight Directory (USA) **8644**
Greater Cincinnati - Northern Kentucky Bride & Groom Magazine (USA) **5558**
Greater Dallas Living (USA) **4540**
▼ Greater Fort Wayne at Home (USA) **3976**
• Greater Fort Wayne Business Weekly (USA ISSN 1940-6509) **1115**
Greater Fort Wayne Family (USA) **2154**
Greater Good (USA ISSN 1553-3239) **6645**
➤ Greater Houston Dental Society. Journal (USA ISSN 1062-0265) **5846**
Greater Houston Home Buyer's Guide (USA) **7591**

DIRECTORY 2010 GREEN'S CIVIL PRACTICE BULLETIN 10337

Greater Johannesburg Library Services. Annual Report (ZAF) **5011**
Greater Kansas City Medical Bulletin (USA ISSN 0894-508X) **5620**
Greater London History and Heritage Handbook (GBR) **4225**
Greater London Papers (GBR ISSN 0072-7350) **7443**
Greater Louisville Home Design & Living (USA ISSN 1935-7087) **4540**
Greater Louisville Ink (USA) **1403**
Greater Louisville Relocation Guide (USA ISSN 1935-7079) **7591**
Greater Milwaukee Dental Association Journal *see* G M D A Journal **5845**
Greater New Orleans Archivists Newsletter (USA) **4294**
Greater North Central Natural Resources Journal *see* Great Plains Natural Resources Journal **3434**
Greater Northern News (USA) **8043**
Greater Orlando Chamber of Commerce Membership Directory (USA) **1997**
▼ • Greater Paris (FRA ISSN 1960-825X) **8715**
Greater Philadelphia House & Home (USA) **4541**
† The Greater Philadelphia JobBank (USA ISSN 1098-982X) **8960**
Greater Philadelphia Law Library Association Newsletter *see* G P L L A Newsletter **5010**
Greater Philadelphia, Southern New Jersey and Delaware Office Buildings (USA) **7592**
• Greater Philly Tails (USA ISSN 1945-6654) **6808**
Greater Phoenix Blue Chip Economic Forecast (USA ISSN 1093-8931) **1488**
The Greater Samui Magazine *see* Samui Magazine **3962**
Greater Seattle InfoGuide (USA ISSN 0749-8128) **3977**
Greater Toronto (Metro & Boundary) *see* Ontario Business Directory **2022**
Greater Toronto Transit Authority. Year in Review (CAN ISSN 1496-0710) **8497**
Greater Vancouver Japanese Canadian Citizens Association. Bulletin/Greater Vancouver Japanese Canadian Citizens Association. Geppo (CAN ISSN 1182-0225) **3535**
Greater Vancouver Japanese Canadian Citizens Association. Geppo *see* Greater Vancouver Japanese Canadian Citizens Association. Bulletin **3535**
Greater Washington Board of Trade News (USA ISSN 0274-5496) **1428**
Greater Washington Board of Trade Progress Report (USA) **1403**
Greater Washington - Maryland Service Station and Automotive Repair Association. Membership Directory & Buyer's Guide (USA) **1998**
The Greater World Newsletter (GBR ISSN 0957-8935) **7736**
The Greatest Game (GBR ISSN 0965-4232) **8234**
▼ Greatest Geniuses of the 21st Century (USA ISSN 1940-8498) **643**
Greatest Geniuses of the Twenty-First Century *see* Greatest Geniuses of the 21st Century **643**
▼ • Greatest Uncommon Denominator Magazine (USA ISSN 1932-8222) **5302**
Greats of the World *see* Stefan University Press Series on the Greats of the World **645**
Gredleriana (ITA ISSN 1593-5205) **7858**
Greece (GBR ISSN 1740-2794) **8715**
Greece (GRC ISSN 0432-6105) **8715**
Greece and International Transport/Ellas kai Diednis Metaphores (GRC) **8497**
• ➤ Greece and Rome (GBR ISSN 0017-3835) **2234**
• Greece Autos Report (GBR ISSN 1748-9911) **8583**
• Greece Defence & Security Report (GBR ISSN 1749-1401) **6422**
Greece Freight Transport Report (GBR ISSN 1752-5829) **8497**
Greece. National Statistical Service. Agricultural and Livestock Production (Year) (GRC ISSN 1107-0129) **181**
Greece. National Statistical Service. Annual Industrial Survey (GRC ISSN 0072-7393) **1235**
Greece. National Statistical Service. Annual Statistical Survey on Mines, Quarries and Salterns (GRC ISSN 0072-7415) **6485**
Greece. National Statistical Service. Building Activity Statistics (GRC ISSN 0256-7970) **1046**
Greece. National Statistical Service. Cultural Statistics (GRC ISSN 0256-3606) **530**
Greece. National Statistical Service. Environmental Statistics (GRC ISSN 1106-1553) **3479**
Greece. National Statistical Service. Greek Industrial Classification *see* Greece. National Statistical Service. Standard Classification of the Branches of Economic Activity **1235**
Greece. National Statistical Service. Household Expenditure Survey (GRC ISSN 1012-2397) **1235**
Greece. National Statistical Service. Labour Force Survey (GRC ISSN 0256-3576) **1235**
Greece. National Statistical Service. Monthly Statistical Bulletin (GRC ISSN 0028-0240) **8375**
Greece. National Statistical Service. Production of Manufactured Items (GRC) **1235**
Greece. National Statistical Service. Provisional National Accounts of Greece (GRC ISSN 0259-997X) **1235**
Greece. National Statistical Service. Public Finance Statistics (GRC ISSN 0256-3568) **1235**
Greece. National Statistical Service. Quarterly National Accounts of Greece (GRC ISSN 1105-2147) **1235**
Greece. National Statistical Service. Results of Sea Fishery Survey by Motor Vessels/Apotelesmata Ereunes Thalassias Alieias dia Mehanokineton Skafon (GRC ISSN 0256-3584) **3613**
Greece. National Statistical Service. Revised Agricultural Price Indices (GRC) **181**
Greece. National Statistical Service. Revised Consumer Price Index (GRC) **1235**
Greece. National Statistical Service. Revised Price Indices of New Building Dwellings Construction (Year) (GRC) **1046**
Greece. National Statistical Service. Shipping Statistics (GRC ISSN 0072-7423) **8525**
Greece. National Statistical Service. Social Welfare and Health Statistics (GRC ISSN 0253-9454) **8083**
Greece. National Statistical Service. Standard Classification of the Branches of Economic Activity (GRC) **1235**
Greece. National Statistical Service. Statistical Bulletin of Public Finance (GRC ISSN 0256-3592) **1235**
Greece. National Statistical Service. Statistics of the Declared Income of Legal Entities and Its Taxation (GRC ISSN 0302-1416) **1235**
Greece. National Statistical Service. Statistics on Civil, Criminal and Reformatory Justice (GRC ISSN 0256-3665) **2674**
Greece. National Statistical Service. Statistics on the Declared Income of Physical Persons and Its Taxation (GRC ISSN 0302-1114) **1235**
Greece. National Statistical Service. Statistiques du Travail (GRC ISSN 1106-1502) **1235**
Greece. National Statistical Service. Tourist Statistics (GRC ISSN 0256-3649) **8779**
Greece. National Statistical Service. Transport and Communication Statistics (GRC ISSN 0256-3657) **8525**
Greek American *see* The GreekAmerican **3535**
Greek - American Trade (GRC ISSN 0046-6379) **1403**
Greek Canadian Action - Drassis (CAN ISSN 0837-1083) **3535**
Greek Canadian Reportage (CAN ISSN 0839-7678) **3535**
Greek Canadian Tribune (CAN ISSN 0046-6387) **3535**
Greek Commission on Irrigation and Drainage. Bulletin (GRC) **8824**
Greek Economy in Figures (Year) (GRC ISSN 0257-7240) **1236**
• Greek Export Directory (GRC) **1404**
• Greek Herald/Ellinikos kirikas (AUS ISSN 1442-6471) **3535**
Greek Index Project Series (CAN ISSN 1183-1286) **4225**
Greek Institute Review (GBR) **5218**
Greek Journal of Dairy Science and Technology *see* Episteme kai Tehnologia Galaktos **264**
Greek Mathematical Society. Bulletin/Hellenike Mathematike Hetaireia. Deltion (GRC ISSN 0072-7466) **5490**
Greek National Committee for Astronomy. Annual Reports of the Astronomical Institutes of Greece (GRC ISSN 0072-7385) **575**
Greek Orthodox Archdiocese of North and South America. Annual Report (USA) **7704**
• ➤ Greek Orthodox Theological Review (USA ISSN 0017-3894) **7704**
Greek Press/Ellenikos Typos (USA ISSN 0745-9645) **3535**
Greek Review of European Law *see* Helliniki Epitheorissis Evropaikou Dikaiou **4927**
Greek Review of Social Research/Epitheorisis Koinonikon Erevnon (GRC ISSN 0013-9696) **7967**
➤ Greek, Roman and Byzantine Monographs (USA ISSN 0072-7474) **2234**
• ➤ Greek, Roman and Byzantine Studies (USA ISSN 0017-3916) **2234**
➤ Greek, Roman, and Byzantine Studies. Scholarly Aids (USA ISSN 0072-7482) **2234**
Greek Speleological Society. Deltion/Societe Speleologique de Grece. Bulletin Trimestriel (GRC ISSN 0374-0390) **2745**
Greek Times *see* Nea Elladas **3553**
Greek Travel Pages (GRC ISSN 1107-3748) **8715**
The GreekAmerican (USA ISSN 0890-0035) **3535**
• Greeley Medical Staff Institute Update (USA ISSN 1947-8852) **4094**
• Green (ITA) **3434**
Green Acre News (USA) **3977**
Green Anarchist (GBR ISSN 0957-5170) **7139**
Green Anarchy (USA) **2613**
• Green and White (CAN ISSN 0017-3924) **2285**
Green at Work *see* Green@Work **1115**
• The Green Bag (USA ISSN 1095-5216) **4682**
The Green Bag Almanac & Reader (Year) (USA ISSN 1931-9711) **4682**
The Green Bag Almanac of Useful and Entertaining Tidbits for Lawyers & Reader of Good Legal Writing from the Past Year Selected by the Luminaries and Sages on Our Board of Advisors *see* The Green Bag Almanac & Reader (Year) **4682**
• Green Base Exchange (GBR) **3486**
Green Bay Catholic Compass (USA ISSN 8755-9323) **7799**
Green Block (USA) **8618**
Green Book (New York City) *see* New York (City). Department of Citywide Administrative Services. Green Book **7499**
The Green Book (Newton) (USA ISSN 1940-2791) **588**
Green Book: The Directory of Natural History and General Stock Photography (USA) **6969**
Green Brigades (POL ISSN 1231-2134) **3435**
• Green Builder Magazine (USA ISSN 1559-4971) **1010**
Green Building Product News (USA) **1010**
▼ • Green Business (CAN) **3435**
▼ Green Business (GBR) **1886**
The Green Business Guide (EGY) **1998**
Green Car Journal (USA ISSN 1059-6143) **3136**
• ➤ Green Chemistry (GBR ISSN 1463-9262) **2062**
▼ • Green Chemistry Letters and Reviews (GBR ISSN 1751-7192) **2062**
Green City Calendar (USA) **3435**
Green Construction Purchasing (USA) **1010**
Green Country Quarterly (USA ISSN 0743-2828) **3769**
Green Cross (English Edition) (USA ISSN 1934-5577) **3535**
Green Cross (Vietnamese Edition) *see* Green Cross (English Edition) **3535**
▼ • Green Customer News (USA ISSN 1940-4441) **3435**
Green Drum (GBR ISSN 0263-0095) **2613**
▼ • Green Electronics Daily (USA ISSN 1943-152X) **3100**
• Green Energy News (USA) **3136**
Green Europe (LUX ISSN 1012-2117) **116**
• Green Futures (GBR ISSN 1366-4417) **3435**
Green Garden Literary Magazine *see* Cuiyuan **5281**
Green Government *see* Sustainable Development U K **3469**
Green Guerilla Vitisvine (USA) **3435**
• The Green Guide (USA ISSN 1942-3403) **3435**
Green Hotelier (GBR ISSN 1367-0379) **4387**
▼ Green Intelligent Buildings (USA) **1010**
Green Island (GBR ISSN 0017-3967) **5423**
The Green Journal *see* Obstetrics and Gynecology **6001**
† Green Keeper (FRA ISSN 0993-3093) **8960**
• Green Left Weekly (AUS ISSN 1036-126X) **7139**
Green Line (GBR ISSN 1352-450X) **3435**
• Green Lines (GBR ISSN 1466-7959) **2613**
• Green List (CAN ISSN 1188-2662) **2613**
Green Magazine (Bee) (USA ISSN 0883-5462) **3734**
The Green Magazine (New York) (USA ISSN 1554-1886) **8234**
• Green Markets (USA) **116**
• Green Markets Dealer Report (USA ISSN 0895-772X) **116**
Green Markets World Directory of the Fertilizer Industry (USA) **1998**
• Green Money Journal (USA) **1350**
• Green Mountain Links (USA) **8234**
• Green Mountain Music Review (USA) **6570**
• Green Mountains Review (USA ISSN 0895-9307) **5302**
• Green Pages (GBR ISSN 0963-1682) **199**
Green Pages: Directory of Non-Government Environmental Groups in Australia (AUS ISSN 0727-0119) **2613**
Green Place Magazine (AUS ISSN 0310-5482) **3794**
• Green Places (GBR ISSN 1742-3716) **443**
Green Places News (GBR ISSN 1742-3724) **443**
▼ • Green + Design (USA) **1010**
Green Politics (USA) **7139**
Green Power *see* Gurin Pawa **3692**
• Green Power (USA ISSN 1544-7804) **3136**
Green Prints (USA ISSN 1064-0118) **3734**
Green Productivity (HKG ISSN 1024-4662) **3435**
Green Products and Technology *see* EcoHome **1005**
Green Profit (USA ISSN 1094-0650) **3734**
Green Revolution (USA ISSN 0017-3983) **6922**
• Green River Current (USA ISSN 0017-3991) **2285**
The Green Scene (USA ISSN 0190-9789) **3734**
Green Seattle (USA ISSN 1544-1253) **7139**
• The Green Sheet (GBR ISSN 1476-3842) **1236**
Green Sheet (Albany) *see* Green Sheet New York **3435**
• The Green Sheet (Chevy Chase) (USA ISSN 1530-6208) **6844**
Green Sheet (Norcross) (USA) **1010**
• Green Sheet New York (USA) **3435**
Green Source *see* GreenSource **1010**
Green Teacher (CAN ISSN 1192-1285) **3063**
▼ • Green Tech News e-Report (USA ISSN 1938-0887) **3136**
• ➤ Green Theory & Praxis (USA ISSN 1941-0948) **3435**
Green Topics (JPN) **3692**
Green Triangle Holiday News (AUS) **8715**
• The Green Tricycle (USA ISSN 1525-9048) **5302**
Green Vision *see* Luse Shiye **3451**
• The Green Voice (AUS) **3435**
Green Week *see* The Green Voice **3435**
Green World (GBR ISSN 1359-110X) **3435**
Green World News (USA) **3734**
▼ Greenability (USA ISSN 1938-5749) **2613**
• GreenBook (USA ISSN 8756-534X) **1818**
Greenbrier Historical Society. Journal (USA ISSN 1064-0711) **4294**
Greenbusiness International (DEU ISSN 1617-2000) **3734**
Greencherry Project (ZAF ISSN 1992-2957) **26**
Greene County Democrat (USA ISSN 0889-518X) **3536**
Greene County Historical Journal (USA ISSN 0894-8135) **4294**
Greene County Medical Society Bulletin (USA) **5620**
Greene Hills of Home (USA) **4294**
• Greener Design Update (USA) **3435**
• Greener I T Update (USA) **3435**
• ➤ Greener Management International (GBR ISSN 0966-9671) **3435**
• Greener Times (AUS ISSN 1324-5740) **2613**
Greenery Research and Information Center. Report (JPN) **3692**
GreenFleet Magazine (GBR) **8497**
Greenford & Northolt Gazette *see* Ealing & Acton Gazette **3864**
GreenGarden (DEU) **3734**
• Greenhouse Business (USA ISSN 1079-9257) **3756**
• Greenhouse Canada (CAN ISSN 0712-4996) **3734**
Greenhouse Gas Emissions in the Netherlands (NLD ISSN 1574-5007) **3435**
• Greenhouse Gas Emissions Reporting (CAN ISSN 1719-0460) **3435**
Greenhouse Grower *see* The Commercial Greenhouse Grower **3727**
• Greenhouse Grower (USA ISSN 0745-7324) **3734**
Greenhouse Issues (GBR ISSN 0967-2710) **3506**
Greenhouse Management & Production (USA ISSN 1080-6679) **3734**
Greenhouse Newsletter (USA ISSN 1051-9025) **3734**
Greenhouse Product News *see* G P N **3756**
Greenhouse Review Press Chapbook Series (USA) **5302**
The Greenhouse Yearbook & Buyer's Guide (GBR ISSN 1748-1201) **3734**
• The Greening Australian (AUS ISSN 1446-6597) **2613**
Greening Waipara (NZL ISSN 1177-5270) **2613**
Greenland Bioscience *see* Meddelelser om Groenland. Bioscience **689**
Greenland Geoscience *see* Meddelelser om Groenland. Geoscience **2754**
Greenland. Groenlands Statistik. Befolkning (GRL ISSN 0904-6860) **7307**
Greenland. Groenlands Statistik. Befolkningens Bevaegelser/Innuttaasut Nikeranerat (GRL ISSN 1397-6966) **7307**
Greenland. Groenlands Statistik. Bygdestatistik (GRL ISSN 1397-0682) **8375**
Greenland. Groenlands Statistik. Fiskeri og Fangst. Opgoerelser fra Groenlands Statistik (GRL ISSN 1396-4402) **3613**
Greenland. Groenlands Statistik. Greenland (Year) - Statistical Yearbook/Kalaallit Nuaat (GRL ISSN 0907-9432) **8375**
Greenland. Groenlands Statistik. Groenland (Year) - Statistisk Aarbog/Kalaallit Nunaat (GRL ISSN 0106-228X) **8375**
Greenland. Groenlands Statistik. Groenlands Befolkning/Kalatdlit Nunane Inuit (GRL ISSN 0105-0885) **7284**
Greenland. Groenlands Statistik. Ilinniartitaaneq *see* Greenland. Groenlands Statistik. Uddannelse **8375**
Greenland. Groenlands Statistik. Konjunkturstatistik (GRL ISSN 0906-3315) **1236**
Greenland. Groenlands Statistik. Nationalregnskab (GRL ISSN 1395-6159) **1236**
Greenland. Groenlands Statistik. Offentlige Finanser (GRL ISSN 1397-2405) **1236**
Greenland. Groenlands Statistik. Uddannelse (GRL ISSN 0907-2225) **8375**
• Greenland. Groenlands Statistik. Udenrigshandel (GRL ISSN 1604-4959) **1567**
• Greenland Guide (DNK) **8715**
Greenland Hydrocarbon Exploration Information Service Newsletter *see* G H E X I S Newsletter **8958**
The Greenland Law Reports *see* Tidsskrift for Groenlands Retsvaesen **4796**
Greenland M I N E X News *see* M I N E X **6469**
Greenland Man and Society *see* Meddelelser om Groenland. Man & Society **347**
• Greenland Mineral Resources. Fact Sheet (GRL ISSN 1602-8171) **6464**
▼ Greenland Today (DNK ISSN 1902-8857) **3874**
The Greenleaf (CAN ISSN 1911-7817) **3734**
GreenLines *see* G R E E N Lines **3432**
Greenmaster (CAN ISSN 0380-3333) **8234**
• GreeNotes (USA ISSN 1092-3896) **3435**
• Greenpeace Business (GBR ISSN 0962-9467) **3435**
Greenpeace en Accion (ARG ISSN 1515-0569) **3435**
Greenpeace-Magazin (DEU ISSN 1611-3462) **3435**
Greenpeace Magazine (FRA ISSN 0241-2926) **3435**
Greenpeace Newsletter (GBR) **7239**
• Greenpeace Update (USA) **2613**
Greenport Duin- en Bollenstreek (NLD) **7493**
Greenprint (ZAF ISSN 1817-9355) **3435**
• Greens (DNK ISSN 0901-6201) **1998**
Green's Business Law Bulletin (GBR ISSN 0967-2540) **4869**
Green's Civil Practice Bulletin (GBR ISSN 1357-2768) **4832**

Title

10338 GREEN'S CONVEYANCING STATUTES ULRICH'S PERIODICALS

Green's Conveyancing Statutes (GBR ISSN 0969-109X) **4832**
Green's Criminal Law Bulletin (GBR ISSN 0967-2532) **4890**
Green's Criminal Statutes (GBR) **4890**
Green's Employment Law Bulletin (GBR ISSN 1352-2159) **4869**
Green's Family Law Bulletin (GBR ISSN 0967-2524) **4911**
Green's Family Law Reports (GBR ISSN 1367-6644) **4911**
Green's Housing Law Reports (GBR ISSN 1364-274X) **4682**
• Green's Litigation Styles (GBR) **4682**
Green's Mercantile Statutes (GBR ISSN 1350-133X) **4832**
• Green's Practice Styles (GBR) **4682**
Green's Property Law Bulletin (GBR ISSN 0967-2516) **4832**
Green's Reparation Law Bulletin (GBR ISSN 1357-2776) **4682**
Green's Reparation Law Reports (GBR ISSN 1362-167X) **4683**
Green's Scottish Human Rights Journal (GBR ISSN 1470-8302) **7207**
Greens Scottish Human Rights Service (GBR) **7207**
Greens Scottish Planning Factbook *see* Scottish Planning Factbook **4781**
Green's Statutes. Family Law, Succession, Trusts and Judicial Factors (GBR ISSN 0969-1103) **4911**
• Green's Weekly Digest (GBR ISSN 0955-4491) **4683**
Greensboro Justice Fund Newsletter (USA) **7207**
• ➤ Greensboro Review (USA ISSN 0017-4084) **5302**
Greenscape Hot Line (USA ISSN 1545-3227) **3734**
Greensheet Logger (USA) **3692**
Greenside (GBR) **8234**
Greenslade on Costs (GBR) **4683**
• Greensleeves (BEL) **3435**
• GreenSource (USA ISSN 1930-9848) **1010**
Greensward (GBR ISSN 0017-4092) **116**
The Greentree Gazette (USA ISSN 1545-4665) **2983**
Greentrees (GBR ISSN 0261-1139) **3769**
Greenville Black Star (USA) **3536**
Greenville Magazine (USA) **3977**
• Greenwich (USA ISSN 1072-2432) **3977**
Greenwich Mercury (GBR) **3865**
Greenwich Time Report (GBR ISSN 0264-4177) **575**
• Greenwire (USA ISSN 1540-787X) **3436**
Greenwood Biographies *see* Greenwood Press Biography Series **643**
The Greenwood Educators' Reference Collection (USA ISSN 1056-2192) **2860**
• The Greenwood Encyclopedia of American Institutions (USA ISSN 0271-9509) **2860**
Greenwood Encyclopedia of Black Music (USA ISSN 0272-0264) **6570**
Greenwood Encyclopedias of Modern World Wars (USA ISSN 1941-4080) **4141**
Greenwood Folklore Handbooks (USA ISSN 1549-733X) **3618**
Greenwood Genetic Center. Proceedings (USA ISSN 0733-124X) **5620**
The Greenwood Guide to American Popular Culture *see* American Popular Culture **4282**
• Greenwood Guides to American Roots Music (USA ISSN 1551-0271) **6571**
▼ Greenwood Guides to Biomes of the World (USA ISSN 1942-4728) **3436**
Greenwood Guides to Business and Economics (USA ISSN 1559-2367) **1115**
Greenwood Guides to Business & Economics *see* Greenwood Guides to Business and Economics **1115**
• Greenwood Guides to Great Ideas in Science (USA ISSN 1559-5374) **7858**
• Greenwood Guides to Shakespeare (USA) **8471**
• Greenwood Guides to the Animal World (USA ISSN 1559-5617) **945**
▼ Greenwood Guides to the Universe (USA ISSN 1944-625X) **575**
† Greenwood Historical Encyclopedia of the World's Political Parties (USA ISSN 1062-9726) **8960**
Greenwood Introduces Literary Masterpieces (USA ISSN 1545-6285) **5302**
▼ Greenwood Living (USA ISSN 1935-2581) **5072**
Greenwood Press Biography Series (USA ISSN 1540-4900) **643**
The Greenwood Press "Literature in Context" Series (USA ISSN 1074-598X) **5302**
• Greenwood Technographies (USA ISSN 1549-7321) **8423**
Greenwood Tree (GBR ISSN 0307-9872) **3769**
Greenwood's Guide to Great Lakes Shipping (USA ISSN 0072-7490) **8645**
• Green@Work (USA ISSN 1529-9139) **1115**
Greenworks (USA) **8824**
Greenworld (AUS) **3734**
Greeting Card Industry *see* Business Ratio Report. The Greeting Card Industry **4059**
• Greeting Card Writer Magazine (USA) **7322**
Greetings (GBR ISSN 0269-9486) **1851**
Greetings *see* Selamta **8785**
Greetings & Gifts (AUS ISSN 1036-5915) **4060**
• Greetings Cards (GBR ISSN 1479-1323) **4060**
• Greetings Etc. (USA) **4060**
Greetings Gifts Stationery Retailer *see* G G S Retailer **4059**
Greffier Municipal (FRA) **7493**
Gregorian Institute of America Quarterly *see* G I A Quarterly **6568**
➤ Gregorianum (ITA ISSN 0017-4114) **7799**
➤ Gregorios O Palamas (GRC ISSN 1011-3010) **7704**
Gregoriusblad (NLD ISSN 0017-4122) **6571**
Gregory's 200 Kilometres Around Sydney *see* Discovering Sydney and Surrounds **8698**
• Gregory's ClearPath - A-Series Technical Journal (USA) **2539**
Gregory's Discovering Sydney and Surrounds *see* Discovering Sydney and Surrounds **8698**
Gregynog Papers (GBR ISSN 1462-6179) **7967**
Der Greif (AUT) **5218**
Greifswalder Beitraege zur Stadtgeschichte, Denkmalpflege, Stadtsanierung (DEU) **4225**
Greifswalder Historische Studien (DEU ISSN 1435-6929) **4225**
▼ Greiti Ratai/Hot Wheels (LTU ISSN 1822-6566) **2191**
Grem (ESP) **7322**
• Gremlins in the Garage (USA) **4335**
Gremo! (SVN ISSN 1580-3783) **8316**
Grenaa og Omegn Foer og Nu (DNK ISSN 0105-7243) **4225**
Grenada Banana Co-operative Society. Annual Report and Financial Statements (GRD) **233**
Grenada. Board of Tourism. Annual Statistical Report (GRD) **8779**
Grenada. Board of Tourism. Monthly Statistical Report (GRD) **8779**
Grenada. Board of Tourism. Quarterly (GRD) **8715**
Grenada. Board of Tourism. Semi-annual Statistical Review (GRD) **8779**
Grenada Breweries Annual Report (GRD) **604**
Grenada Chamber of Industry and Commerce Annual Report *see* G C I C Annual Report **1403**
Grenada. Government Gazette (GRD) **3995**
Grenada Informer (GRD) **3995**
Grenada Planned Parenthood Association. Annual Report (GRD) **972**
Grenada Ports Authority. (Year) Handbook (GRD) **8645**
Grenada Ports Authority Annual Report & Accounts (GRD) **8645**
Grenada School Directory and Basic Educational Statistics (GRD) **2933**
Grenada Today (GRD) **3995**
Grenadian Voice (GRD) **3995**
Grenda (NOR) **3922**
Grenzenlos (DEU) **7799**
Grenzfragen (DEU ISSN 0933-5366) **7858**
Grenzfriedenshefte (DEU) **5218**
Grenzgaenge (DEU ISSN 0944-8594) **5302**
Grenzgebiete der Wissenschaft (AUT ISSN 1021-8130) **7858**
• Grenzland (DNK ISSN 0107-9840) **3833**
Grenzueberschreitungen (DEU ISSN 1863-933X) **6741**
Grenzueberschreitungen - Studien zur Europaeischen Reiseliteratur (DEU) **5302**
Gress-Forum (NOR ISSN 0804-8665) **8316**
Gressitt Center News (USA) **848**
Grey Bibliographies (ZAF) **625**
• Grey Book (Online) (USA) **181**
Grey Book (Print) *see* Grey Book (Online) **181**
• The Grey House Biometric Information Directory (USA ISSN 1933-4435) **2677**
• The Grey House Safety and Security Directory (USA ISSN 1550-1566) **6677**
• The Grey House Transportation Security Directory & Handbook (USA ISSN 1931-6208) **8497**
• The Grey Journal (NLD ISSN 1574-1796) **5302**
Grey Literature Compendium *see* G L Compendium **7561**
• Grey Literature Report (USA ISSN 1931-7050) **7520**
Grey Market in the U K *see* Key Note Market Assessment. The Grey Consumer **1828**
• ➤ Grey Room (USA ISSN 1526-3819) **444**
Greyfriars Review (USA ISSN 1936-4903) **7799**
Greyhound (GBR ISSN 0017-4157) **8176**
Greyhound Owner & Breeder (GBR ISSN 0017-4165) **6809**
The Greyhound Recorder (AUS ISSN 1320-9507) **6809**
Greyhound Review (USA ISSN 1042-4016) **8176**
Greyhound Star (GBR ISSN 0955-047X) **6809**
• Grial (ESP ISSN 0017-4181) **4454**
Gribb Bedrijfsadviseur (NLD ISSN 1874-057X) **4683**
Gribb Belastingadviseur (NLD ISSN 1872-5694) **1927**
Gribb Salarisadviseur (NLD ISSN 1872-5686) **1684**
Grid (AUS ISSN 1324-9428) **7736**
The GRID (GBR ISSN 1743-2308) **7646**
The Grid (GBR) **3158**
Grid (ITA ISSN 1021-268X) **233**
Gridiron Coach (USA ISSN 1071-1902) **8234**
Gridiron Greats (USA) **8234**
Gridley Wave (USA ISSN 0017-419X) **5443**
Griechischen Christlichen Schriftsteller der ersten Jahrhunderte (DEU ISSN 0232-2900) **7646**
Grief Digest (USA ISSN 1559-5064) **7359**
Grief Digest Magazine *see* Grief Digest **7359**
Griephan Berlin Kontakt (DEU) **1998**
Griephan Briefe (DEU ISSN 1860-403X) **6422**
Griephan Executive Summary (DEU ISSN 1619-4403) **6422**
Grier's Almanac (USA) **3977**
• Griffe (ITA ISSN 1973-5537) **588**
La Griffe *see* Griffe **588**
The Griffin (FIN ISSN 1795-2484) **3692**
• Griffin (USA ISSN 0276-1947) **2285**
The Griffin Report of Food Marketing (USA ISSN 0192-4400) **3645**
Griffin's Modern Grocer (USA ISSN 1086-0452) **3679**
Griffin's Tri-State Food News *see* Tri-State Food News **3682**
• Griffith Asia Institute. Newsletter (AUS ISSN 1832-3715) **7967**
• ➤ Griffith Journal of the Environment (AUS ISSN 1832-8520) **3436**
• ➤ Griffith Law Review (AUS ISSN 1038-3441) **4683**
• Griffith News Now (Online) (AUS) **2941**
Griffith Observer (USA ISSN 0195-3982) **575**
• ➤ Griffithiana (ITA ISSN 0393-3857) **6502**
Griffith's 5 Minute Clinical Consult *see* The 5-Minute Clinical Consult **5739**
• Grifo (CHL ISSN 0718-4786) **5302**
Grih Shobha (IND ISSN 0971-152X) **8866**
Grihalakshmi (IND) **3882**
Grihshobha *see* Grih Shobha **8866**
Grill *see* Food Service **3642**
▼ Grill It! (USA ISSN 1941-8728) **4359**
• Grilled Pterodactyl (AUS ISSN 1325-2763) **3794**
Grillen & Party (DEU) **4359**
Grimace et Galipette *see* Parenthese **3557**
Grimes & Battersby Report (USA) **6750**
Grimme (DEU ISSN 1437-2916) **2382**
Grimper (FRA ISSN 1251-4187) **8316**
Grimsby Telegraph (GBR ISSN 1750-9580) **3967**
Grimstad Adressetidende (NOR) **3923**
• Grinder (CHL) **6571**
Grinding & Abrasives Magazine (USA) **5452**
Gringo Grande (SWE ISSN 1653-1051) **3955**
• Gringo's (DEU ISSN 1439-202X) **6292**
† La Grinta (ITA) **8960**
Le Griot (CIV) **3789**
• Griot (USA ISSN 0737-0873) **3536**
Grip (GBR) **5072**
Grip *see* JOP Coach Magazine **2943**
Grip 4 (NLD ISSN 1872-2946) **3578**
† Grip Dirt Bike (GBR ISSN 1465-0207) **8960**
Grip Magazine (Atlanta) (USA) **5072**
• Grip Magazine EduVision (USA) **4576**
Grip op Verzuim en Re-Integratie (NLD ISSN 1874-8678) **1684**
• Griper (USA) **3977**
➤ Gripla (ISL ISSN 1018-5011) **5302**
Gripped (CAN ISSN 1488-0814) **8316**
Gris/Pig (SWE ISSN 1402-8085) **287**
Grist International (GBR) **604**
• Grist Mill (USA) **4294**
• Grit (USA ISSN 0017-4289) **3977**
Grit and Steel (USA ISSN 0017-4297) **8176**
Gritty Business Buzz *see* The Portable Business **1965**
Grizzly (USA) **2285**
▼ • Gro (NOR ISSN 1504-7512) **2191**
Groblad (SWE ISSN 0282-227X) **5302**
• The Grocer (GBR ISSN 0017-4351) **3679**
The Grocer Directory of Manufacturers & Suppliers (European Edition) *see* The Grocer Directory of Manufacturers & Suppliers Europe (Year) **3645**
• Grocer Directory of Manufacturers & Suppliers (UK Edition) (GBR ISSN 1475-9772) **3645**
• The Grocer Directory of Manufacturers & Suppliers Europe (Year) (GBR ISSN 1746-112X) **3645**
The Grocer. Independents Special Issue *see* The Grocer **3679**
Grocer Magazine (IRL) **3645**
Grocer Today Magazine (CAN ISSN 1196-0817) **3679**
Grocergram *see* I G A Grocergram **3679**
Grocers Report (USA ISSN 0160-8894) **3679**
Grocers' Review (NZL ISSN 0113-1850) **3679**
Grocers' Review *see* New Zealand Grocery Who's Who **3670**
• Grocery Headquarters (USA ISSN 1094-1088) **3679**
The Grocery Industry: Past, Present, and Future (USA) **3679**
Grocery Manufacturers of America Forum *see* G M A Forum **3678**
Grocery Retailing (Year) (GBR ISSN 1358-7900) **3679**
Grocery Review *see* Retail News **1840**
Grocery Wholesalers *see* Business Ratio. Grocery Wholesalers **3676**
Grocery Wholesaling (Year) (GBR ISSN 0954-4925) **3679**
Groei en Bloei (NLD ISSN 0017-4475) **3734**
Groen (NLD ISSN 0166-3534) **3734**
Groen & Golf (NLD ISSN 1573-529X) **8234**
Groen Europa *see* Green Europe **116**
Groen Magazine (BEL ISSN 0778-1199) **3734**
Groen Viden, Havebrug (DNK ISSN 0903-0719) **3734**
Groen Viden, Husdyrbrug (DNK ISSN 1397-9868) **116**
Groen Viden, Markbrug (DNK ISSN 1397-985X) **116**
Groena Fakta (SWE ISSN 0284-9798) **444**
• De Groene Amsterdammer (NLD ISSN 0017-4483) **5218**
Groene Band *see* Bosrevue **3685**
Groene Carriere *see* Carriere+ **100**
Groene Krant (BEL) **116**
Groene Maand Magazine (NLD ISSN 1874-0286) **2613**
Groene Markt (NLD ISSN 1381-4826) **3734**
Groenkoepings Veckoblad (SWE ISSN 0017-4548) **5218**
Groenkoepings Veckoblads Aarsbok *see* Aarsbok fraan Groenkoepings Veckoblad **5204**
Groenland (DNK ISSN 0907-1040) **1010**
• Groenland (Charlottenlund) (DNK ISSN 0017-4556) **4013**
Groenlands Fiskeritende *see* Aulisarnermit Nutarsiagssat **3586**
Groenlands Naturinstitut. Aarsberetning *see* Pinngortitaleriffik. Ukiumoortumik Nalunaarusiaq **7898**
Groenlandsposten *see* A G **3874**
• Groenlandsrelateret Forskning og Udvikling (DNK ISSN 1901-4198) **8375**
Groensaken *see* Groent **7139**
Groent (SWE ISSN 1652-1196) **7139**
• Groent 3 F Punkt (DNK ISSN 1902-1496) **3734**
Groent Miljoe (DNK ISSN 0108-4755) **3734**
Groent Traefpunkt *see* Groent 3 F Punkt **3734**
Groenten & Fruit. Algemeen (NLD ISSN 0925-9708) **3735**
Groenyteleverantoererna (SWE) **3735**
Groepen (NLD ISSN 1871-1146) **6143**
Groepspsychotherapie *see* Groepen **6143**
• Grok Newsmagazine (AUS ISSN 1326-2815) **2285**
Grond-, Water- en Wegenbouw Kosten. Kabelwerk (NLD ISSN 1382-5739) **3309**
➤ Grondboor en Hamer (NLD ISSN 0017-4505) **2745**
Grondverzet en Bouwtransport *see* Materieelkrant **1023**
Grondzaken in de Praktijk (NLD) **4683**
➤ Groniek (NLD ISSN 0169-2801) **4225**
Groningen (Groningen) (NLD ISSN 1871-6601) **4225**
Groningen Archaeological Studies (NLD ISSN 1572-1760) **396**
Groningen Oriental Studies (NLD ISSN 0924-8846) **550**
Groninger Arbeiten zur Germanistischen Linguistik (NLD ISSN 0924-655X) **5123**
Groninger Forum Magazine (NLD ISSN 1875-2195) **492**
Groninger Hanze Studies (NLD ISSN 1872-308X) **4225**
Groninger Ondernemers Kontakt *see* Het Ondernemersbelang Groningen **1782**
Gronlands Naturinstitut. Teknisk Rapport *see* Pinngortitaleriffik. Teknisk Rapport **3459**
Gronne Europa *see* Green Europe **116**
Groomer to Groomer (USA) **6809**
Groomer's Voice (USA) **6809**
Groothandel (NLD ISSN 1569-8459) **1961**
Grootkeuken *see* Food Hospitality **3639**
Groove (DEU) **6571**
Groove *see* Rap & Groove **6609**
Groove (ITA ISSN 1592-7814) **6571**
Groove *see* The Real Groove **6609**
• Groove (SWE ISSN 1401-7091) **6571**
• Gros Plan sur la Securite et l'Environnement (CAN ISSN 1716-4230) **3436**
Gross and Taxable Sales Report (USA) **8375**
Gross Domestic Product (Annual Edition) *see* Hong Kong Special Administrative Region of China. Census and Statistics Department. Gross Domestic Product (Annual Edition) **1237**
Gross Domestic Product (Quarterly Edition) *see* Hong Kong Special Administrative Region of China. Census and Statistics Department. Gross Domestic Product (Quarterly Edition) **1238**
Gross Domestic Product by Industry/Produit Interieur Brut par Industrie (CAN ISSN 0711-852X) **8375**
Gross National Product Results, Quarterly *see* Turkey. Turkiye Istatistik Kurumu. Gayri Safi Milli Hasila, Haber Bulteni **1270**
Gross Verbraucher Manager *see* G V Manager **1747**
Gross Wartenberger Heimatblatt (DEU ISSN 0017-4599) **625**
Das Grosse Horoskop - Meine Sternstunden (DEU) **566**
Der Grosse Knigge (DEU) **3849**
Grosse Komponisten und Ihre Zeit (DEU ISSN 0177-4190) **6571**
The Grosse Pointer (USA ISSN 0017-4629) **8276**
Die Grosse Raetsel-Zeitung (DEU) **8176**
Die Grosse Reiseapotheke (DEU) **6845**
Der Grosse Rock & Pop L P - C D Preiskatalog *see* Der Grosse Rock & Pop L P - Preiskatalog **6571**
Der Grosse Rock & Pop L P - Preiskatalog (DEU ISSN 1614-1482) **6571**
• Grosse- und Mittelstaendische Unternehmen in der Tschechischen Republik (AUT) **1998**
• Grosse- und Mittelstaendische Unternehmen in Oesterreich (AUT) **1886**
• Grosse und Mittelstaendische Unternehmen in Ungarn (AUT ISSN 1217-7776) **1887**
• Die Grossen 500 (DEU ISSN 1436-9893) **1998**
Grossenhainer Tageblatt (DEU) **3849**
Die Grosshandelskaufleute (DEU ISSN 1619-2575) **1115**
Die Grosskueche (DEU ISSN 0932-9765) **3645**
Grossmont Education Association Advocate *see* G E A Advocate **2859**
Grossunternehmen der Tschechischen Republik *see* Grosse- und Mittelstaendische Unternehmen in der Tschechischen Republik **1998**
Grossverbraucher Intern (DEU ISSN 0946-6592) **116**

DIRECTORY 2010 GUANGDIANZI - JIGUANG 10339

Grossverpflegung Praxis *see* G V - Praxis **3644**
Grosz (POL) **6651**
De Grote Kennis Scheurkalender (NLD ISSN 1871-7187) **4454**
De Grote Lijsters (NLD ISSN 0925-4617) **5302**
Grote Vuurvlinder in Overijssel (NLD ISSN 1871-8825) **848**
Groter Groeien (NLD ISSN 1384-7511) **2154**
• Grotiana (NLD ISSN 0167-3831) **4683**
Grotius (ITA ISSN 1826-8862) **4927**
† Grotte d'Italia (ITA ISSN 0373-7500) **8960**
Grottkau - Falkenberger Heimatblatt (DEU) **3849**
• Ground Engineering (GBR ISSN 0017-4653) **3268**
Ground Engineering *see* Jiban to Kensetsu **3274**
† Ground Engineering Yearbook (GBR ISSN 0959-9959) **8960**
Ground Force (GBR ISSN 1467-405X) **3735**
• Ground Handling International (GBR ISSN 1364-8330) **8497**
Ground Improvement *see* Institution of Civil Engineers. Proceedings. Ground Improvement **3271**
Ground Pressure and Strata Control *see* Kuangshan Yali yu Dingban Guanli **6468**
• Ground Support Worldwide (USA ISSN 1934-2861) **57**
Ground Up (ZMB ISSN 1992-3015) **2613**
• Ground Warrior (USA) **6422**
• ➤ Ground Water (USA ISSN 0017-467X) **2794**
Ground Water Canada (CAN ISSN 1206-3762) **8824**
Ground Water Management (USA ISSN 1047-9023) **8824**
• ➤ Ground Water Monitoring & Remediation (USA ISSN 1069-3629) **2794**
Ground Water Protection Council. Annual Forum (USA) **3486**
Ground Water Science and Engineering Organizations *see* Compensation in Ground Water Science and Engineering Organizations **1671**
• ➤ The Grounded Theory Review (USA ISSN 1556-1542) **8105**
• Grounding (ITA ISSN 1971-0372) **675**
Groundings (USA) **8866**
Grounds Management Forum (USA ISSN 0742-5511) **3735**
Groundsman (GBR ISSN 0017-4696) **8316**
† Groundwork (AUS ISSN 1832-6986) **8960**
GroundWork (USA ISSN 1085-2751) **3436**
• Group (Loveland) (USA ISSN 0163-8971) **2154**
• ➤ Group (New York) (USA ISSN 0362-4021) **7359**
• ➤ Group Analysis (GBR ISSN 0533-3164) **7359**
• ➤ Group & Organization Management (USA ISSN 1059-6011) **2861**
Group Benefits (USA ISSN 1945-242X) **4504**
Group Circle (USA) **7359**
• ➤ Group Decision and Negotiation (NLD ISSN 0926-2644) **1748**
• ➤ Group Dynamics (USA ISSN 1089-2699) **7359**
Group Dynamics: Theory, Research and Practice *see* Group Dynamics **7359**
Group Economics Research *see* Jituan Jingji Yanjiu **1132**
• Group Facilitation (USA ISSN 1534-5653) **7359**
Group Leisure (GBR ISSN 1363-7797) **4978**
Group of Seven Report Investors Newsmagazine *see* The G-7 Report Investors Newsmagazine **1626**
Group of Thirty. Annual Report (USA ISSN 0735-2034) **1488**
Group of Thirty. Occasional Paper (USA ISSN 0278-1468) **1488**
Group Practice Journal (USA ISSN 0199-5103) **5621**
Group Practice Solutions (USA ISSN 1548-1786) **4094**
• ➤ Group Processes & Intergroup Relations (GBR ISSN 1368-4302) **8105**
Group Solution (USA) **7359**
Group Structure Database *see* Konzern-Strukturen **1142**
Group Tour Magazine (USA) **8715**
Group Tour Magazines Industry Update (USA) **8715**
Group Travel Leader (USA) **8715**
Group Travel Lifestyles (USA) **8715**
• Group Travel Organiser (GBR ISSN 0962-8266) **8715**
Group Travel Planet (USA) **1115**
Groupe Bruxelles Lambert. Annual Reports (BEL) **1627**
Groupe Bruxelles Lambert. Interim Reports (BEL) **1627**
▼ • Groupe de Recherche Archeologique sur le Haut Moyen Age. Cahiers (FRA ISSN 1958-5713) **396**
Groupe de Recherche d'Histoire Cahiers *see* G R H I S. Cahiers **340**
Groupe de Recherche en Economie Financiere et Gestion des Entreprises. Cahiers de Recherche *see* Centre Europeen de Recherche en Economie Financiere et Gestion des Entreprises. Cahier de Recherche **1326**
Groupe de Recherche et d'Action pour l'Enfance. La Lettre *see* La Lettre de l'Enfance et de l'Adolescence **7383**
Groupe de Recherche et d'Application des Concepts Psychanalytiques a la Psychiatrie en Afrique Franc Cahiers *see* G R A P P A F. Cahiers **6142**
Groupe de Recherche et d'Etudes Nord-Americaines. Actes du Colloque (FRA) **5302**
Groupe de Recherche Etnicite et Societe Cahiers *see* G R E S. Cahiers **3534**
Groupe de Recherche pour l'Education et la Prospective. Pour (FRA ISSN 0245-9442) **2861**
Groupe de Recherches Archeologiques de la Loire Bulletin *see* G R A L. Bulletin **395**
▼ • Groupe de Recherches Interdisciplinaires sur l'Histoire du Litteraire. Les Dossiers (FRA ISSN 1958-9247) **5218**
Groupe de Recherches sur l'Afrique Francophone Newsletter *see* G R A F Newsletter **4175**
Groupe de Travail Mondial sur les Rapaces. Circulaire (FRA ISSN 1013-7998) **908**
Groupe des Chambres Syndicales du Batiment et des Travaux Publics du Departement de l'Oise. Monthly Review (FRA) **1010**
Groupe d'Etude pour la Chirurgie Osseuse Collection *see* G E C O. Collection **6060**
Groupe d'Etudes et de Recherche sur les Mouvements Etudiants *see* G E R M E **7137**
▼ Groupe E I D O S. Collection (Etude de l'Image Dans une Orientation Semiotique) (FRA ISSN 1956-5550) **492**
Groupe E S C Grenoble. Papiers de Recherche (FRA ISSN 1632-4366) **1748**
Groupe Europeen d'Observation Stellaire Circular on Eclipsing Binaries *see* G E O S. Circular on Eclipsing Binaries **574**
Groupe Europeen d'Observation Stellaire Circular on RR Lyr Type Variables *see* G E O S. Circular on RR Lyr Type Variables **574**
Groupe Europeen d'Observation Stellaire Note Circulaire *see* G E O S. Note Circulaire **575**
Groupe Interdisciplinaire du Theatre Antique. Cahiers (FRA ISSN 0295-9909) **8471**
Groupe Interdisciplinaire du Theatre Antique. Textes et Documents (FRA ISSN 0993-5835) **8471**
Groupe International d'Etude de la Ceramique Egyptienne. Bulletin de Liaison (EGY ISSN 0255-0903) **396**
Groupe Linguistique d'Etudes Chamito-Semitiques. Comptes Rendus (FRA ISSN 0399-0400) **5123**
Groupement Archeologique du Maconnais Info *see* Le G A M Info **395**
Groupement d'Assistance et de Cooperation Documentaires en Psychiatrie. Nouvelles (FRA ISSN 1952-7519) **6143**
Groupement de Recherches Coordonnees sur l'Administration Locale. Collection (FRA ISSN 0248-0573) **7493**
Groupement des Industries Electroniques. Rapport d'Activites (FRA) **3100**
Groupement des Industries Electroniques. Statistiques Annuelles (FRA) **3100**
Groupement des Industries Francaises Aeronautiques et Spatiales. Info (FRA) **57**
Groupement d'Informations Mutuelles A M P E R E. Bulletin (CHE ISSN 0432-7136) **7014**
• Groupement d'Interet Economique. Systeme d'Information pour les Produits de Sante. Mini Dossier (FRA ISSN 1773-3510) **6845**
Groupement International pour la Recherche Scientifique en Stomatologie & Odontologie. Bulletin (BEL ISSN 0250-4693) **5846**
Groupements Techniques Veterinaires Bulletin *see* G T V Bulletin **8797**
Groupes Therapeutiques (FRA ISSN 1275-3424) **7359**
▼ • Groups, Geometry, and Dynamics (CHE ISSN 1661-7207) **5490**
Groupware Magazin (DEU ISSN 1612-1023) **2350**
Groupwise Advisor *see* Databased Advisor Magazine **2554**
• Groupwork (GBR ISSN 0951-824X) **8043**
The Grove (ESP ISSN 1137-005X) **5123**
The Grove (GBR) **6987**
Grove Biblical Series (GBR ISSN 1365-490X) **7759**
Grove Booklet on Ministry & Worship (GBR ISSN 0305-3067) **7759**
Grove City College Alumni Bulletin (USA) **2285**
Grove Ethics Series (GBR ISSN 1470-854X) **6922**
Grove Evangelism Series (GBR ISSN 1367-0840) **7759**
Grove Liturgical Studies (GBR ISSN 0306-0608) **7759**
Grove Pastoral Series (GBR ISSN 0144-171X) **7646**
Grove Renewal Series (GBR ISSN 1470-8531) **7759**
The Grove Review (USA ISSN 1551-983X) **5302**
Grove Spirituality Series (GBR ISSN 0262-799X) **7646**
Grove Worship Series (GBR ISSN 0144-1728) **7759**
Grove Youth Series (GBR ISSN 1748-3492) **7759**
Grovvarelederen *see* AgroForum **1425**
▼ • Grow a Winning Business (USA ISSN 1949-1107) **1961**
Grow America *see* High Times Grow America **5073**
Grow Dahlias with Us (GBR) **3735**
Grow It! (GBR) **3735**
Grow Letter (USA) **3735**
• Grow Your Own (GBR ISSN 1745-1876) **3735**
The Grower *see* The South Australian Grower **254**
The Grower (CAN ISSN 0017-4777) **233**
Grower *see* Horticulture Week **3737**
The Grower (USA ISSN 0745-1784) **233**
Grower *see* Yankee Grower **259**
• Grower (Wellington) (NZL ISSN 1175-2742) **116**
• Grower Talks Magazine (USA ISSN 0276-9433) **3735**
Growing Affinities (COL ISSN 0122-8048) **117**
Growing Child (USA) **2154**
Growing Edge Magazine (USA ISSN 1043-2906) **3735**
Growing for Market (USA ISSN 1060-9296) **3735**
➤ The Growing Lamp (USA ISSN 1060-4162) **5959**
Growing Native (USA) **791**
Growing Old in America *see* Information Plus Reference Series. Growing Old in America **4047**
Growing Opportunities. The Young Farmers Newsletter *see* The Young Farmers Newsletter **171**
Growing Parent Newsletter (USA ISSN 0193-8037) **2154**
Growing Together (USA) **2154**
Growing Up *see* Hun Boloh Bagaasaa **2864**
▼ Growing Up (USA ISSN 1938-6095) **8105**
Growing Up in America *see* Information Plus Reference Series. Growing Up in America **8107**
Growing Up in North Cambridge (USA ISSN 1939-2540) **4294**
Growl (USA) **2285**
Growth (USA ISSN 1543-3668) **7759**
Growth and Biology of African Raptors *see* G A B A R **907**
• ➤ Growth and Change (USA ISSN 0017-4815) **1887**
Growth Company Investor (GBR ISSN 1756-9796) **1627**
† • ➤ Growth, Development & Aging (USA ISSN 1041-1232) **8960**
• ➤ Growth Factors (GBR ISSN 0897-7194) **922**
Growth Factors and Cytokines in Health and Disease (GBR ISSN 1874-5687) **733**
Growth Fund Guide (USA ISSN 0017-4831) **1628**
• Growth, Genetics & Hormones (USA ISSN 0898-6630) **5893**
• ➤ Growth Hormone & IGF Research (GBR ISSN 1096-6374) **5893**
Growth in Action (BEL) **8423**
• Growth/No Growth (USA ISSN 1551-2150) **4411**
Growth No Growth *see* Growth/No Growth **4411**
Growth Stock Outlook (USA ISSN 1073-7626) **1628**
• Growth Strategies (USA ISSN 0894-1297) **1488**
Groznenskii Rabochii (RUS) **3935**
• Grrowl! Ezine (USA ISSN 1098-1381) **8866**
Grub (CAN) **5302**
Grudnaya i Serdechno-Sosudistaya Khirurgiya/Chest and Cardiovascular Surgery (RUS ISSN 0236-2791) **6244**
Grue Magazine (USA ISSN 0897-9707) **5443**
▼ Gruen (CHE) **5072**
Gruen (DEU ISSN 1863-6306) **3735**
Gruen ist Leben (DEU) **3735**
† Gruenbuch der Kinder- und Jugendmedien (DEU) **8960**
• Gruender (NOR ISSN 1502-055X) **1748**
Gruender Magazin (DEU) **1115**
Die Gruene (CHE ISSN 0255-903X) **3735**
Gruene Blaetter (DEU) **8866**
• Das Gruene Haus (AUT) **8845**
Das Gruene Jahrbuch (DEU ISSN 0935-5405) **6809**
• Gruener Anzeiger (DEU ISSN 1435-3458) **3735**
Gruener Bericht (AUT) **199**
Gruener Markt (DEU ISSN 1437-0069) **3735**
Gruener Weg 31A (DEU ISSN 0943-2949) **2613**
GruenForum.LA *see* T A S P O Gartendesign **458**
Gruenstift (Berlin) (DEU ISSN 0178-1421) **2613**
Gruenstift (Rattingen) (DEU) **3436**
Grund Genug (DEU ISSN 0941-5203) **7592**
Der Grundbesitz *see* A I Z - Das Immobilienmagazin **7581**
Das Grundeigentum (DEU ISSN 0017-4882) **4411**
Grundeigentumsrecht und Bodennutzungsrecht in den Neuen Bundeslaendern (DEU ISSN 0943-0881) **4411**
Grundgesetz der Bundesrepublik Deutschland (DEU ISSN 0934-2621) **4848**
Grundig Report (DEU) **3309**
Grundlagen der Germanistik (DEU ISSN 0533-3350) **5123**
Grundlagen der Medienkommunikation (DEU ISSN 1434-0461) **2322**
Grundlagen der Rechtsphilosophie (DEU ISSN 1612-3654) **4683**
Grundlagen der Weiterbildung *see* Weiterbildung **2925**
Grundlagen und Perspektiven fuer Bildung und Wissenschaft. Berufsbildungsbericht *see* Berufsbildungsbericht **7840**
Grundlagen und Praxis des Bank- und Boersenwesens (DEU ISSN 0340-9392) **1350**
Grundlagen und Praxis des Wirtschaftsrechts (DEU ISSN 0533-3407) **4869**
Grundlehren der Mathematischen Wissenschaften (USA) **5490**
† Grundriss der Literaturgeschichten nach Gattungen (BRD ISSN 0174-0679) **8960**
Das Grundschul-Hausaufgabenheft (DEU) **3063**
Grundschule (DEU ISSN 0533-3431) **3063**
Grundschule Deutsch (DEU ISSN 1614-1040) **5123**
Grundschule Englisch (DEU) **5123**
Grundschule Kunst (DEU ISSN 1616-7104) **3063**
Grundschule Mathematik (DEU) **5490**
Grundschule Musik (DEU ISSN 1436-8447) **6571**
Grundschule Religion (DEU) **7646**
Grundschule Sachunterricht - Themenheft (DEU ISSN 1437-319X) **3063**
Grundschule Sprachen *see* Grundschule Deutsch **5123**
➤ Grundschulmagazin (DEU ISSN 0943-3759) **3063**
Grundschulmagazin Englisch/The Primary English Magazine (DEU ISSN 1610-7918) **5123**
Grundschulunterricht (DEU ISSN 0945-2079) **2861**
Die Grundschulzeitschrift (DEU ISSN 0932-3910) **3063**
Grundskoletidningen (SWE ISSN 1652-7844) **2861**
Der Grundstein (DEU ISSN 0432-7519) **4595**
Grundstuecks- und Gebaeudeservice (DEU ISSN 1433-335X) **4411**
Grundstuecksmarkt und Grundstueckswert (DEU ISSN 0938-0175) **7592**
Grundstuecksmarkt und Grundstueckswert Aktuell *see* G u G Aktuell **7591**
➤ Grundtvig Studier (DNK ISSN 0107-4164) **7759**
Grundtvigstudier *see* Grundtvig Studier **7759**
Grundvandsmoedet *see* Geologisk Tidsskrift **2742**
† • Grundvandsovervaagning (DNK ISSN 1395-248X) **8960**
• ➤ Grundwasser (DEU ISSN 1430-483X) **8824**
Grundwasserbericht (DEU ISSN 0944-0704) **8824**
† Grundzuege des Umweltrechts (DEU ISSN 1433-5328) **8960**
Grunes Europa *see* Green Europe **116**
Grup Catala d'Anellament. Butlleti *see* Revista Catalana d'Ornitologia **913**
• Grupo de Estudios de Politica Criminal (ESP) **4890**
Grupo de Estudios de Teatro Argentino e Iberoamericano Cuadernos *see* G E T E A. Cuadernos **8471**
Grupo de Estudios Masinos. Boletin *see* Mas de las Matas **4152**
Grupo de Estudios Sobre la Critica Literaria Boletin *see* G E C. Boletin **5299**
Grupo de Estudos Linguisticos do Nordeste Revista *see* G E L N E. Revista **5121**
Grupo de Investigacao Arqueologica do Norte. Trabalhos (PRT) **396**
Grupo Entomologico de Madrid. Boletin (ESP ISSN 0213-3873) **848**
Grupo Espanol de la Union Interparlamentaria. Boletin de Informacion (ESP) **7239**
Grupo I C O. Memoria (ESP ISSN 1579-2072) **1927**
Grupo I N I (Resumen de Actividades) (Instituto Nacional de Industria) (ESP ISSN 1130-5185) **1887**
Grupo Iberico de Aves Marinas Boletin *see* G I A M. Boletin **907**
Grupo Santander. Boletin Financiero (ESP) **1350**
Grupo Santander. Boletin la Accion (ESP) **1350**
Grupo Santander. Informe Anual (Year) (ESP) **1350**
Gruppe Berliner Mondbeobachter. Protokoll der Sitzung (DEU) **575**
Gruppe und Spiel (DEU ISSN 0724-3332) **3063**
Gruppenanalyse (DEU ISSN 0939-4273) **7359**
• ➤ Gruppendynamik und Organisationsberatung (DEU ISSN 1618-7849) **7359**
➤ Gruppenpsychotherapie und Gruppendynamik (DEU ISSN 0017-4947) **6143**
➤ Gruppenpsychotherapie und Gruppendynamik. Beihefte (DEU ISSN 0085-1302) **7359**
• Gruppi (ITA ISSN 1826-2589) **7359**
Grus & Guld (SWE ISSN 1650-4704) **1350**
Gruss der Grossheppacher Schwesternschaft (DEU) **7646**
Grutsk (NLD ISSN 1574-3365) **6524**
Gruvarbetaren (SWE ISSN 0432-7632) **6464**
Gruzovik &/Truck & (RUS ISSN 1684-1298) **8497**
Gry (POL ISSN 1640-7180) **2419**
Gryps (SWE ISSN 1101-4628) **4225**
GS1 Info *see* G S 1 Info **6402**
GS1 Magazin *see* G S 1 Magazin **6402**
GS1 Sweden Fokus *see* G S 1 Sweden Fokus **6402**
GTi-Magazine (FIN ISSN 1457-6058) **8583**
GTi Tuning en Design *see* Auto & Tuning **8558**
GTO *see* G T O **8581**
Gu yu Guanjie Sunshang Zazhi/Journal of Bone and Joint Injury *see* Zhongguo Gu yu Guanjie Sunshang Zazhi **6075**
• El Guacharo (VEN ISSN 1011-7407) **2745**
Guadalajara Colony Reporter *see* Guadalajara Reporter **3909**
The Guadalajara Colony Reporter *see* Guadalajara Reporter **3909**
• Guadalajara Reporter (MEX ISSN 1605-072X) **3909**
Guadalbullon (ESP ISSN 0213-2192) **2861**
Guadalimar (ESP ISSN 0210-1254) **492**
Guadeloupe 2000 Magazine (GLP ISSN 0757-7907) **7139**
Guam Business News (GUM ISSN 1045-053X) **1115**
Guam. Department of Revenue and Taxation. Report (GUM ISSN 0072-7873) **1927**
Guam U S O Handbook (GUM) **5218**
Guanabara: O Balanco Economico (BRA) **1488**
• Guanaquin On Line (SLV ISSN 1605-1831) **3821**
• Guancha yu Sikao/Study and Think (CHN ISSN 1008-8512) **7967**
Guang de Shijie/World of Light (CHN) **7075**
• ➤ Guang Tongxin Jishu/Optical Communications Technology (CHN ISSN 1002-5561) **2322**
Guang yu Ying/Light and Shadow (CHN ISSN 1003-3343) **492**
• Guan'gai Paishui Xuebao/Journal of Irrigation and Drainage (CHN ISSN 1672-3317) **117**
• ➤ Guangdian Gongcheng/Opto-Electronic Engineering (CHN ISSN 1003-501X) **3309**
• Guangdian Jishu Yingyong/Electro-Optic Technology Application (CHN ISSN 1673-1255) **7075**
• Guangdianzi - Jiguang/Journal of Optronics-Laser (CHN ISSN 1005-0086) **7075**

▼ *new title* † *ceased* • *electronic media* ➤ *refereed*

Title

Guangdong A I B Polytechnic College. Journal *see* Guangdong Nong-Gong-Shang Zhiye Jishu Xueyuan Xuebao **7967**

Guangdong Architecture Civil Engineering *see* Guangdong Tumu yu Jianzhu **444**

Guangdong Chemical Industry *see* Guangdong Huagong **2062**

Guangdong College of Young Cadres. Journal *see* Guangdong Qingnian Ganbu Xueyuan Xuebao **7967**

Guangdong Communication Polytechnic. Journal *see* Guangdong Jiaotong Zhiye Jishu Xueyuan Xuebao **2322**

Guangdong Di-2 Ketang *see* Guangdong Di-er Ketang **2191**

• Guangdong Di-er Ketang/The Second Class of Guangdong (CHN ISSN 1005-1430) **2191**

• Guangdong Dianli/Guangdong Electric Power (CHN ISSN 1007-290X) **3158**

Guangdong Dianshi/Guangdong Television (CHN) **2382**

• Guangdong Dizhi/Guangdong Geology (CHN ISSN 1001-8670) **2745**

Guangdong Duiwai Jingmao/Guangdong Foreign Economics and Trade (CHN) **1567**

Guangdong Education *see* Guangdong Jiaoyu (Zonghe Ban) **2861**

Guangdong Education (High School Edition) *see* Guangdong Jiaoyu (Gaozong Ban) **2861**

Guangdong Education (Teachers Edition) *see* Guangdong Jiaoyu (Zhijiao Ban) **3063**

Guangdong Education Institute. Journal *see* Guangdong Jiaoyu Xueyuan Xuebao **2861**

Guangdong Electric Power *see* Guangdong Dianli **3158**

Guangdong Food *see* Guangdong Shipin **8960**

Guangdong Foreign Economics and Trade *see* Guangdong Duiwai Jingmao **1567**

Guangdong Geology *see* Guangdong Dizhi **2745**

• Guangdong Gongye Daxue Xuebao/Guangdong Institute of Technology. Journal (CHN) **3194**

• Guangdong Gongye Daxue Xuebao (Shehui Kexue Ban)/Guangdong University of Technology. Journal (CHN ISSN 1671-623X) **7967**

• Guangdong Guangbo Dianshi Daxue Xuebao/Guangdong Radio & Television University. Journal (CHN ISSN 1008-9764) **2358**

• Guangdong Haiyang Daxue Xuebao/Zhanjiang Ocean University. Journal (CHN ISSN 1673-9159) **2709**

Guangdong-Hong Kong Information Daily *see* Yuegang Xinxi Ribao **3829**

Guangdong Huabao/Guangdong Pictorial *see* Cheng Shi Huabao **3823**

• Guangdong Huagong/Guangdong Chemical Industry (CHN ISSN 1007-1865) **2062**

Guangdong Industry Technical College. Journal *see* Guangdong Qinggong Zhiye Jishu Xueyuan Xuebao **7967**

Guangdong Institute of Technology. Journal *see* Guangdong Gongye Daxue Xuebao **3194**

• Guangdong Jianshe Bao (CHN) **3824**

• Guangdong Jiaotong Zhiye Jishu Xueyuan Xuebao/Guangdong Communication Polytechnic. Journal (CHN ISSN 1671-8496) **2322**

• Guangdong Jiaoyu (Gaozong Ban)/Guangdong Education (High School Edition) (CHN) **2861**

• Guangdong Jiaoyu (Zhijiao Ban)/Guangdong Education (Teachers Edition) (CHN) **3063**

• Guangdong Jiaoyu (Zonghe Ban)/Guangdong Education (CHN) **2861**

▼ Guangdong Jiaoyu Nianjian (CHN) **2861**

• Guangdong Jiaoyu Xueyuan Xuebao/Guangdong Education Institute. Journal (CHN ISSN 1007-8754) **2861**

Guangdong Jinrong/Guangdong Finance *see* Nanfang Jinrong **1369**

• Guangdong Jinrong Xueyuan Xuebao/Guangdong University of Finance. Journal (CHN ISSN 1674-1625) **1350**

• ➤ Guangdong Jishu Shifan Xueyuan Xuebao/Guangdong Polytechnic Normal University. Journal (CHN ISSN 1672-402X) **7967**

Guangdong Medical College. Journal *see* Guangdong Yixueyuan Xuebao **5621**

Guangdong Medical Journal *see* Guangdong Yixue **5621**

Guangdong Meteorology *see* Guangdong Qixiang **6353**

• Guangdong Nong-Gong-Shang Zhiye Jishu Xueyuan Xuebao/Guangdong A I B Polytechnic College. Journal (CHN ISSN 1009-931X) **7967**

Guangdong Polytechnic Normal University. Journal *see* Guangdong Jishu Shifan Xueyuan Xuebao **7967**

Guangdong Power Transmission Technology *see* Guangdong Shudian yu Biandian Jishu **3158**

• Guangdong Qinggong Zhiye Jishu Xueyuan Xuebao/Guangdong Industry Technical College. Journal (CHN ISSN 1672-1950) **7967**

• Guangdong Qingnian Ganbu Xueyuan Xuebao/Guangdong College of Young Cadres. Journal (CHN ISSN 1009-5446) **7967**

• Guangdong Qixiang/Guangdong Meteorology (CHN ISSN 1007-6190) **6353**

Guangdong Radio & Television University. Journal *see* Guangdong Guangbo Dianshi Daxue Xuebao **2358**

• Guangdong Shangxueyuan Xuebao/Guangdong University of Business Studies. Journal (CHN ISSN 1008-2506) **1115**

• Guangdong Shehui Kexue/Guangdong Social Science (CHN ISSN 1000-114X) **7967**

† Guangdong Shipin/Guangdong Food (CHN ISSN 1005-5657) **8960**

• Guangdong Shudian yu Biandian Jishu/Guangdong Power Transmission Technology (CHN ISSN 1672-6324) **3158**

• Guangdong Shuili Dianli Zhiye Jishu Xueyuan Xuebao/Guangdong Technical College of Water Resources and Electric Engineering. Journal (CHN ISSN 1672-2841) **2861**

• Guangdong Shuili Shuidian/Guangdong Water Resources and Hydropower (CHN ISSN 1008-0112) **8824**

Guangdong Social Science *see* Guangdong Shehui Kexue **7967**

Guangdong Socioeconomic Statistics Monthly (HKG) **1236**

Guangdong Technical College of Water Resources and Electric Engineering. Journal *see* Guangdong Shuili Dianli Zhiye Jishu Xueyuan Xuebao **2861**

Guangdong Telecommunication Technology *see* Guangdong Tongxin Jishu **2322**

Guangdong Television *see* Guangdong Dianshi **2382**

• Guangdong Tongxin Jishu/Guangdong Telecommunication Technology (CHN ISSN 1006-6403) **2322**

Guangdong Trace Elements Science *see* Guangdong Weiliang Yuansu Kexue **6197**

• Guangdong Tumu yu Jianzhu/Guangdong Architecture Civil Engineering (CHN ISSN 1671-4563) **444**

Guangdong University of Business Studies. Journal *see* Guangdong Shangxueyuan Xuebao **1115**

Guangdong University of Finance. Journal *see* Guangdong Jinrong Xueyuan Xuebao **1350**

Guangdong University of Foreign Studies. Journal *see* Guangdong Waiyu Waimao Daxue Xuebao **7967**

Guangdong University of Technology. Journal *see* Guangdong Gongye Daxue Xuebao (Shehui Kexue Ban) **7967**

• Guangdong Waiyu Waimao Daxue Xuebao/Guangdong University of Foreign Studies. Journal (CHN ISSN 1672-0962) **7967**

Guangdong Water Resources and Hydropower *see* Guangdong Shuili Shuidian **8824**

• Guangdong Weiliang Yuansu Kexue/Guangdong Trace Elements Science (CHN ISSN 1006-446X) **6197**

• Guangdong Xingzheng Xueyuan Xuebao (CHN ISSN 1008-4533) **7139**

Guangdong Yaoxue/Guangdong Pharmaceutical Journal *see* Jinri Yaoxue **6851**

• Guangdong Yaoxueyuan Xuebao/Academic Journal of Guangdong College of Pharmacy (CHN ISSN 1006-8783) **6845**

• Guangdong Yixue/Guangdong Medical Journal (CHN ISSN 1001-9448) **5621**

• Guangdong Yixueyuan Xuebao/Guangdong Medical College. Journal (CHN ISSN 1005-4057) **5621**

Guangdong Yiyao Xueyuan Xuebao/Academic Journal of Guangdong Medical and Pharmaceutical College *see* Guangdong Yaoxueyuan Xuebao **6845**

Guangdong Yousejinshu Xuebao/Journal of Guangdong Non-Ferrous Metals *see* Cailiao Yanjiu yu Yingyong **6307**

Guangdong Zidonghua yu Xinxi Gongcheng/Guangdong Automation & Information Engineering *see* Zidonghua yu Xinxi Gongcheng **2465**

Guanggaozhu *see* Guanggaozhu Shichang Guancha **26**

Guanggaozhu Shichang Guancha/Advertiser Market Observer (CHN ISSN 1674-1315) **26**

Guanghua (Zhong-Yingwen Ban) *see* Sinorama **3960**

Guangjiaojing/Wide Angle (HKG ISSN 1609-2589) **3875**

Guangming Daily *see* Guangming Ribao **3824**

Guangming Daily (Reduced Size Bound Volume) *see* Guangming Ribao (Suoyin Heding Ben) **3824**

Guangming Ribao/Guangming Daily (CHN) **3824**

Guangming Ribao (Suoyin Heding Ben)/Guangming Daily (Reduced Size Bound Volume) (CHN) **3824**

Guangming Ribao. Index *see* Guangming Ribao Suoyin **4587**

Guangming Ribao Suoyin/Guangming Ribao. Index (CHN) **4587**

Guangming Traditional Chinese Medicine *see* Guangming Zhongyi **5621**

• Guangming Zhongyi/Guangming Traditional Chinese Medicine (CHN ISSN 1003-8914) **5621**

• Guangpan Jishu/C D Tecnnology (CHN ISSN 1006-6950) **2419**

• Guangpu Shiyanshi/Chinese Journal of Spectroscopy Laboratory (CHN ISSN 1004-8138) **7014**

• ➤ Guangpuxue yu Guangpu Fenxi/Spectroscopy and Spectral Analysis (CHN ISSN 1000-0593) **7075**

Guangtian Yixue Zazhi/Kuang Tien Medical Journal (TWN ISSN 1819-4567) **5621**

Guanguang Liuyou Yanjiu Xuekan/Journal of Tourism and Travel Research (TWN) **8715**

Guangxi Academy of Science. Journal *see* Guangxi Kexueyuan Xuebao **7859**

Guangxi Administrative Cadre Institute of Politics and Law. Journal *see* Guangxi Zheng-Fa Guanli Ganbu Xueyuan Xuebao **2653**

Guangxi Agricultural and Biological Science. Journal *see* Guangxi Nongye Shengwu Kexue **676**

Guangxi Agricultural Sciences *see* Guangxi Nongye Kexue **117**

Guangxi Audit *see* Guangxi Shenji **1927**

• Guangxi Caijing Xueyuan Xuebao/Guangxi University of Finance and Economics. Journal (CHN ISSN 1673-5609) **1115**

Guangxi Daily *see* Guangxi Ribao **3824**

• Guangxi Daxue Wuzhou Fenxiao Xuebao/Guangxi University. Wuzhou Branch. Journal (CHN ISSN 1009-2633) **7858**

• Guangxi Daxue Xuebao (Zhexue Shehui Kexue Ban)/Guangxi University. Journal (Philosophy and Social Sciences) (CHN ISSN 1001-8182) **7967**

• Guangxi Daxue Xuebao (Ziran Kexue Ban)/Guangxi University. Journal (Natural Science Edition) (CHN ISSN 1001-7445) **7858**

Guangxi Economic & Trade *see* Guangxi Jingmao **8960**

• Guangxi Fangzhi Keji (CHN ISSN 1674-2400) **8451**

Guangxi Flora *see* Guangxi Zhiwu **791**

Guangxi Forestry Science *see* Guangxi Linye Kexue **3692**

Guangxi Geology *see* Nanfang Guotu Ziyuan **2757**

• Guangxi Gongxueyuan Xuebao/Guangxi University of Technology. Journal (CHN ISSN 1004-6410) **8423**

Guangxi Huabao/Guangxi Pictorial (CHN) **3824**

† • Guangxi Jingmao/Guangxi Economic & Trade (CHN ISSN 1008-1712) **8960**

Guangxi Jinrong Yanjiu/Journal of Guangxi Financial Research *see* Quyu Jinrong Yanjiu **1163**

Guangxi Journal of Animal Husbandry & Veterinary Medicine *see* Guangxi Xumu Shouyi **8798**

Guangxi Journal of Traditional Chinese Medicine *see* Guangxi Zhongyiyao **309**

• Guangxi Kexue/Guangxi Sciences (CHN ISSN 1005-9164) **7858**

• Guangxi Kexueyuan Xuebao/Guangxi Academy of Science. Journal (CHN ISSN 1002-7378) **7859**

• Guangxi Linye Kexue/Guangxi Forestry Science (CHN ISSN 1006-1126) **3692**

Guangxi Literature *see* Guangxi Wenxue **5302**

Guangxi Medical Journal *see* Guangxi Yixue **5621**

• Guangxi Minzu Xueyuan Xuebao (Ziran Kexue Ban)/Guangxi University for Nationalities. Journal (Natural Science Edition) (CHN ISSN 1007-0311) **7859**

Guangxi Nianjian/Guangxi Yearbook (CHN) **3120**

• Guangxi Nongxuebao/Journal of Guangxi Agriculture (CHN ISSN 1003-4374) **117**

• Guangxi Nongye Kexue/Guangxi Agricultural Sciences (CHN ISSN 1002-8161) **117**

• Guangxi Nongye Shengwu Kexue/Guangxi Agricultural and Biological Science. Journal (CHN ISSN 1008-3464) **676**

Guangxi Normal University. Journal (Natural Science Edition) *see* Guangxi Shifan Daxue Xuebao (Ziran Kexue Ban) **7859**

Guangxi Normal University. Journal (Philosophy and Social Sciences Edition) *see* Guangxi Shifan Daxue Xuebao (Zhexue Shehui Kexue Ban) **7967**

Guangxi Physics *see* Guangxi Wuli **7014**

Guangxi Pictorial *see* Guangxi Huabao **3824**

• Guangxi Qingnian Ganbu Xueyuan Xuebao/Guangxi Youth Leaders College. Journal (CHN ISSN 1008-5254) **2941**

• Guangxi Qixiang/Journal of Guangxi Meteorology (CHN ISSN 1001-5191) **6353**

• Guangxi Ribao/Guangxi Daily (CHN) **3824**

Guangxi Sciences *see* Guangxi Kexue **7858**

Guangxi Shenji/Guangxi Audit (CHN) **1927**

• Guangxi Shifan Daxue Xuebao (Zhexue Shehui Kexue Ban)/Guangxi Normal University. Journal (Philosophy and Social Sciences Edition) (CHN ISSN 1001-6597) **7967**

• Guangxi Shifan Daxue Xuebao (Ziran Kexue Ban)/Guangxi Normal University. Journal (Natural Science Edition) (CHN ISSN 1001-6600) **7859**

• Guangxi Shifan Xueyuan Xuebao (Ziran Kexue Ban)/Guangxi Teachers College. Journal (Natural Science Edition) (CHN) **7859**

Guangxi Shuiwu/Guangxi Taxation (CHN) **1927**

Guangxi Statistics *see* Guangxi Tongji **8375**

Guangxi Taxation *see* Guangxi Shuiwu **1927**

Guangxi Teachers College. Journal (Natural Science Edition) *see* Guangxi Shifan Xueyuan Xuebao (Ziran Kexue Ban) **7859**

Guangxi Tongji/Guangxi Statistics (CHN) **8375**

Guangxi Traditional Chinese Medical University. Journal *see* Guangxi Zhongyi Xueyuan Xuebao **5621**

Guangxi University for Nationalities. Journal (Natural Science Edition) *see* Guangxi Minzu Xueyuan Xuebao (Ziran Kexue Ban) **7859**

Guangxi University. Journal (Natural Science Edition) *see* Guangxi Daxue Xuebao (Ziran Kexue Ban) **7858**

Guangxi University. Journal (Philosophy and Social Sciences) *see* Guangxi Daxue Xuebao (Zhexue Shehui Kexue Ban) **7967**

Guangxi University of Finance and Economics. Journal *see* Guangxi Caijing Xueyuan Xuebao **1115**

Guangxi University of Medical Sciences. Journal *see* Guangxi Yike Daxue Xuebao **5621**

Guangxi University of Technology. Journal *see* Guangxi Gongxueyuan Xuebao **8423**

Guangxi University. Wuzhou Branch. Journal *see* Guangxi Daxue Wuzhou Fenxiao Xuebao **7858**

Guangxi Wenxue/Guangxi Literature (CHN ISSN 1002-7629) **5302**

• Guangxi Wuli/Guangxi Physics (CHN ISSN 1003-7551) **7014**

• Guangxi Xumu Shouyi/Guangxi Journal of Animal Husbandry & Veterinary Medicine (CHN ISSN 1002-5235) **8798**

Guangxi Yearbook *see* Guangxi Nianjian **3120**

• Guangxi Yike Daxue Xuebao/Acta Academiae Medicinae Guangxi (CHN ISSN 1005-930X) **5621**

• Guangxi Yixue/Guangxi Medical Journal (CHN ISSN 0253-4304) **5621**

• Guangxi Youjiang Minzu Shifan Gaodeng Zhuanke Xuexiao Xuebao/Youjiang Teachers College For Nationalities Guangxi. Journal (CHN ISSN 1008-8113) **2861**

Guangxi Youth Leaders College. Journal *see* Guangxi Qingnian Ganbu Xueyuan Xuebao **2941**

Guangxi Yufang Yixue/Guangxi Journal of Preventive Medicine *see* Yingyong Yufang Yixue **5733**

• Guangxi Zheng-Fa Guanli Ganbu Xueyuan Xuebao/Guangxi Administrative Cadre Institute of Politics and Law. Journal (CHN ISSN 1008-8628) **2653**

• ➤ Guangxi Zhiwu/Guihaia (CHN ISSN 1000-3142) **791**

• Guangxi Zhongyi Xueyuan Xuebao/Guangxi Traditional Chinese Medical University. Journal (CHN ISSN 1008-7486) **5621**

• Guangxi Zhongyiyao/Guangxi Journal of Traditional Chinese Medicine (CHN ISSN 1003-0719) **309**

• Guangxian yu Dianlan/Optical Fibre and Cable (CHN ISSN 1006-1908) **3309**

• Guangxue Jingmi Gongcheng (CHN ISSN 1004-924X) **3194**

• Guangxue Jishu/Optical Technology (CHN ISSN 1002-1582) **7075**

• Guangxue Xuebao/Acta Optica Sinica (CHN ISSN 0253-2239) **7076**

• Guangxue Yiqi/Optical Instruments (CHN ISSN 1005-5630) **4487**

• Guangxue yu Guangdian Jishu/Optics & Optoelectronic Technology (CHN ISSN 1672-3392) **7076**

Guangzhou Chemical Industry and Technology *see* Guangzhou Huagong **3244**

Guangzhou Chemistry *see* Guangzhou Huaxue **2062**

Guangzhou Civil Aviation *see* Guangzhou Minhang **8543**

Guangzhou Daily *see* Guangzhou Ribao **3824**

Guangzhou Daxue Xuebao (Shehui Kexue Ban)/Guangzhou University. Journal (Social Science Edition) (CHN ISSN 1671-394X) **7967**

Guangzhou Daxue Xuebao (Ziran Kexue Ban) (CHN ISSN 1671-4229) **7859**

Guangzhou Digest *see* Guangzhou Wenzhai Bao **3824**

• Guangzhou Huagong/Guangzhou Chemical Industry and Technology (CHN ISSN 1001-9677) **3244**

• Guangzhou Huaxue/Guangzhou Chemistry (CHN ISSN 1009-220X) **2062**

Guangzhou Literature and Art *see* Guangzhou Wenyi **5302**

Guangzhou Medical College. Academic Journal *see* Guangzhou Yixueyuan Xuebao **5621**

Guangzhou Medicine and Pharmacology *see* Guangzhou Yiyao **6845**

Guangzhou Minhang/Guangzhou Civil Aviation (CHN) **8543**

Guangzhou Morning Post *see* Guangzhou Yingwen Zaobao **3824**

Guangzhou Physical Education Institute. Journal *see* Guangzhou Tiyu Xueyuan Xuebao **2861**

Guangzhou Ribao/Guangzhou Daily (CHN) **3824**

Guangzhou Shipin Gongye Keji/Guangzhou Food Science and Technology *see* Xiandai Shipin Keji **3668**

• Guangzhou Tiyu Xueyuan Xuebao/Guangzhou Physical Education Institute. Journal (CHN ISSN 1007-323X) **2861**

Guangzhou University. Journal (Social Science Edition) *see* Guangzhou Daxue Xuebao (Shehui Kexue Ban) **7967**

Guangzhou University of Traditional Chinese Medicine. Journal *see* Guangzhou Zhongyiyao Daxue Xuebao **5621**

Guangzhou Wenyi/Guangzhou Literature and Art (CHN ISSN 0257-022X) **5302**

• Guangzhou Wenzhai Bao/Guangzhou Digest (CHN) **3824**

Guangzhou Yearbook (Year) (HKG) **1488**

• Guangzhou Yingwen Zaobao/Guangzhou Morning Post (CHN) **3824**

• Guangzhou Yixueyuan Xuebao/Academic Journal of Guangzhou Medical College (CHN ISSN 1008-1836) **5621**
• Guangzhou Yiyao/Guangzhou Medicine and Pharmacology (CHN ISSN 1000-8535) **6845**
• Guangzhou Zhongyiyao Daxue Xuebao/Guangzhou University of Traditional Chinese Medicine. Journal (CHN ISSN 1007-3213) **5621**
• Guangzi Xuebao/Acta Photonica Sinica (CHN ISSN 1004-4213) **7076**
• Guanli Gongcheng Xuebao/Journal of Industrial Engineering and Engineering Management (CHN ISSN 1004-6062) **3194**
Guanli Kexue/Management Science (CHN ISSN 1007-0591) **1748**
• Guanli Kexue Yanjiu/Management Sciences Research (TWN ISSN 1813-4564) **1748**
• Guanli Shijie/Management World (CHN ISSN 1002-5502) **1749**
• Guanli Xuebao/Chinese Journal of Management (CHN ISSN 1672-884X) **1749**
Guanli Xuebao (Taipei, 1997)/Journal of Management (TWN) **1749**
Guanli yu Xiaoyi/Management and Benefit (CHN ISSN 1004-5414) **1749**
† Guanli yu Xinxi/Management & Information (CHN ISSN 1007-2268) **8960**
Guanlixue Wenzhai Ka/Science of Management Abstracts on Cards (CHN ISSN 1009-7309) **1236**
• Guanxi (USA ISSN 1931-0641) **1887**
Guanxun Zazhi *see* Taiwan Museum of Art Newsletter **6537**
Guanyu junhei guanzhi he caijun duobian xieding de xiankuang - Lianheguo *see* United Nations Disarmament Yearbook **7270**
• Guanzi Xuekan/Journal of Tube Science (CHN ISSN 1002-3828) **4454**
• Guaraguao (ESP ISSN 1137-2354) **5218**
Guaranteed Winning Lottery Systems Quarterly (USA) **8176**
Guarantor (Chicago) (USA) **7592**
Guard *see* Straz **3566**
Guard Experience *see* G X **6422**
Guard the North (CAN ISSN 0700-9917) **5443**
• Guardia Civil (ESP ISSN 0210-5470) **6422**
Guardia Civil. Cuadernos (ESP ISSN 1136-4645) **6423**
Guardia di Finanza. Archivio Storico. Museo Storico. Bollettino d'Archivio (ITA ISSN 1828-4507) **2653**
Guardia di Finanza. Rivista (ITA ISSN 0035-595X) **1927**
The Guardian (AUS ISSN 1325-295X) **7139**
The Guardian (AUS ISSN 1833-4377) **5218**
Guardian (CAN) **4595**
• The Guardian (GBR ISSN 0261-3077) **3865**
The Guardian (IRL ISSN 1649-0584) **3893**
• Guardian (Charlottetown) (CAN ISSN 0832-2708) **3810**
The Guardian (Dayton) (USA) **2285**
• The Guardian (Los Angeles) (USA ISSN 1059-6224) **7139**
The Guardian (Moody Air Force Base) (USA) **6423**
Guardian Index (USA ISSN 0886-4667) **4587**
Guardian News (NGA) **3920**
Guardian Newsletter (Print Edition) *see* e Guardian **3414**
• The Guardian on CD-ROM (USA ISSN 1354-4322) **3866**
• Guardian Weekly (GBR ISSN 0958-9996) **3866**
Guardiani & Molossi *see* Molossi & Guardiani **6811**
Guardians ad Litem and Reporting Officers Bulletin *see* G A L R O Bulletin **4678**
The Guards Magazine (GBR ISSN 0017-503X) **6423**
The Guardsman (USA) **2286**
Guatemala *see* The P R S Group. Country Reports: Guatemala **1507**
Guatemala. Banco Nacional de Desarrollo Agricola. Memoria (GTM) **199**
Guatemala. Consejo Nacional para la Proteccion de la Antigua Guatemala. Carta Informativa (GTM) **396**
Guatemala. Consejo Nacional para la Proteccion de la Antigua Guatemala. Memoira de Labores *see* Guatemala. Consejo Nacional para la Proteccion de la Antigua Guatemala. Carta Informativa **396**
Guatemala. Direccion General de Estadistica. Encuesta de la Industria Manufacturera Fabril (GTM) **8375**
Guatemala Filatelica (GTM ISSN 0046-6549) **6895**
• Guatemala Flash (GTM ISSN 1563-8405) **3874**
Guatemala. Instituto Nacional de Estadistica. Directorio Nacional de Establecimientos Industriales (GTM) **1236**
Guatemala. Instituto Nacional de Sismologia, Vulcanologia, Meteorologia e Hidrologia. Boletin (GTM) **2709**
Guatemala. Ministerio de Agricultura, Ganaderia y Alimentacion. Direccion General de Servicios Agricolas. Memoria de Labores (GTM) **117**
• Guatemala News Watch (GTM) **3874**
Guberniya (UKR) **3936**
Gubernskie Vedomosti (RUS) **3936**
Guckloch (DEU) **7799**
Gudbrandsdalslaget *see* Gudbrandsdalslaget Centennial Yearbook **3769**
▼ Gudbrandsdalslaget Centennial Yearbook (USA ISSN 1948-0113) **3769**
Gudbrandsdoelen Lillehammer Tilskuer (NOR) **3923**
Gudian Wenxue Zhishi/Classic Literature Knowledge (CHN) **5302**
• Gudili Xuebao/Journal of Palaeogeography (CHN ISSN 1671-1505) **4013**
• Gudok (RUS) **8618**
Guelph Alumnus (CAN ISSN 0830-3630) **2286**
• Guelph Ichthyology Reviews (CAN) **945**
• The Guelph Mercury (CAN) **3810**
• Guelph Tribune (CAN ISSN 1197-4400) **3810**
Guerin Sportivo (ITA ISSN 1122-1712) **8176**
• Guernica (USA) **5218**
Guernsey Breeders' Journal (GBR) **287**
Guernsey Breeders' Journal (USA ISSN 0017-5110) **264**
• Guernsey Evening Press and Star (GBR ISSN 1355-3984) **3967**
Guernsey Museum & Art Gallery. Monographs (GBR ISSN 0958-9864) **6524**
Guernsey News (CAN ISSN 1910-9105) **288**
Guernsey Newsletter *see* Guernsey News **288**
Guerre e Pace (ITA ISSN 1126-7836) **6423**
Guerreros y Batallas (ESP ISSN 1697-9842) **6423**
Guerres Mondiales et Conflits Contemporains (FRA ISSN 0984-2292) **4141**
Guerrilla Girls *see* Hot Flashes from the Guerrilla Girls **8868**
• Guerrilla - Tactics (USA) **1749**
A Guest *see* A Vendeg **4400**
Guest Informant. Fort Myers *see* Where GuestBook. Southwest Florida **8788**
Guest Informant. Memphis *see* Where GuestBook. Tennessee **8788**
Guest Informant. Nashville *see* Where GuestBook. Tennessee **8788**
Guest Informant. Southwest Florida *see* Where GuestBook. Southwest Florida **8788**
GuestLife (USA) **8715**
Gueterbahnen (DEU) **8618**
Gueterkraftverkehrsrecht (DEU ISSN 0935-090X) **8671**
Guetertransport (DEU ISSN 1861-0986) **8645**
Guetertransport im Land-, See- und Luftverkehr *see* Guetertransport **8645**
Gueterverkehr (DEU ISSN 0017-5137) **8671**
▼ Guetteur de l'Aube (FRA ISSN 1959-4275) **6645**
Gug-rib Gisul Pumjil-weon. Yeon-gu Bogo/National Industrial Technology Institute. Annual Report *see* Korean Agency forTechnology and Standards. Annual Report **8430**
➤ Gugje Hoeui Tong'yeog gwa Beon'yeog/ Conference Interpretation and Translation (KOR ISSN 1229-6074) **5123**
Gugje Jeongchi Nonchong/Korean Journal of International Relations (KOR ISSN 1598-4818) **7239**
• ➤ Gugje Jiyeog Yeon'gu/Review of International and Area Studies (KOR ISSN 1226-7317) **1567**
Gugje Sahoe Bojang Donghyang/International Social Security Today (KOR ISSN 1975-017X) **8043**
Gugjejeoneol Muhyeongmunhwa-yusan *see* International Journal of Intangible Heritage **4457**
• Gugong Bowuyuan Yuankan/Palace Museum. Journal (CHN ISSN 0452-7402) **4454**
Gugong Tongxun Yingwen Shuangyuekan *see* National Palace Museum Bulletin **6534**
Gugong Wenwu Yuekan/National Palace Museum. Monthly of Chinese Art (TWN ISSN 1011-9078) **6524**
Gugong Xueshu Jikan/National Palace Museum Research Quarterly (TWN ISSN 1011-9094) **6524**
Gugong Zhanlan Tongxun *see* National Palace Museum. Newsletter **6534**
Gugrib Su-san Jinheung-weon. Yeon-gu Bo-go/National Fisheries Research and Development Agency. Bulletin (KOR ISSN 1225-6358) **3596**
• Guhanyu Yanjiu/Research in Ancient Chinese Language (CHN ISSN 1001-5442) **5124**
Guhrauer Kreiszeitung (DEU) **3849**
Guia (DOM) **1567**
Guia (USA) **1998**
Guia a las Resenas de Libros de y sobre Hispanoamerica *see* Guide to Reviews of Books from and about Hispanic America **7562**
Guia Aerea (PER) **8715**
Guia Aerea de Mexico (MEX) **8543**
Guia Aerea Oficial - Chile (CHL) **8543**
Guia Aerea y Maritima de Venezuela C.A. (VEN) **8497**
Guia Aeronautico (BRA ISSN 0017-5145) **8543**
Guia Argentina de Trafico Aereo (ARG ISSN 0326-1050) **8543**
Guia Argentina de Trafico Aereo Report *see* G A T A Report **8541**
Guia Automotriz (MEX) **8497**
Guia Bolivia (BOL) **1489**
Guia Brasil (BRA) **8715**
• Guia Chip (ESP ISSN 0211-8688) **2494**
Guia Creativity (ESP ISSN 1139-5214) **492**
Guia Cultural de la Actualidad (ESP) **5218**
Guia da Carga Aerea/Air Cargo Guide (BRA ISSN 1415-3971) **8543**
Guia das Analises (BRA) **2100**
Guia das Livrarias e Pontos de Venda de Livros no Brasil (BRA) **7562**
Guia de Aviacao Agricola/Agricultural Aviation Guide (BRA ISSN 0104-4958) **57**
Guia de Centros de Ensenanza Media de la Iglesia *see* Guia de Centros Educativos Catolicos **2956**
Guia de Centros Educativos Catolicos (ESP ISSN 0211-4410) **2956**
Guia de Comercio Exterior Exportadores/Guide to Foreign Trade Exporters (COL ISSN 0121-8018) **1998**
Guia de Distribuidores *see* Anuario Distribucion **1972**
† La Guia de Editores de Espana (ESP ISSN 0212-5242) **8960**
Guia de Embarazo y Parto (ESP ISSN 1138-8412) **5991**
Guia de Estaciones de Servicio, Proveedores y Operadores *see* Estaciones de Servicio **8579**
• Guia de Fornecedores da Construcao (BRA) **1010**
• Guia de Fornecedores Hospitalares (BRA ISSN 1414-1922) **4047**
• Guia de Fornecedores Municipais (BRA ISSN 1414-3461) **7443**
Guia de Fundidores (ESP ISSN 1137-0157) **6314**
• Guia de Informacion Juvenil (ESP ISSN 1130-0566) **2191**
Guia de la Comunicacion Grafica y Creativa (COL) **1998**
Guia de la Cria Caballar (ESP) **8291**
Guia de la Decoracion (ESP ISSN 0212-7083) **4558**
• Guia de la Distribucion en Espana (ESP) **1998**
• Guia de la Industria Alimentaria/Mexican Food & Feed Industry Guide (MEX) **3645**
Guia de la Industria del Caucho (ARG ISSN 0533-4500) **7824**
Guia de la Industria: Equipo y Aparatos/Plant and Laboratory Equipment Guide (MEX) **5452**
Guia de la Industria: Hule, Plasticos y Resinas/Rubber, Plastics and Resins Guide (MEX) **7092**
Guia de la Industria Quimica/Mexican Chemical Industry Guide (MEX) **3244**
Guia de la Industria: Republica del Paraguay (PRY) **1998**
Guia de la Industria y Comercio Aceites Grasas *see* Oleo **3659**
† Guia de la Radioaficion y C B (ESP) **8960**
Guia de las Empresas que Ofrecen Empleo (ESP ISSN 1139-1618) **1684**
La Guia de las Nuevas Tecnologias e Internet *see* Senior Net **2566**
Guia de Oficinas e Manutencao/Workshop and Maintenance Guide (BRA ISSN 0104-4974) **57**
➤ Guia de Productos Terapeuticos (VEN ISSN 1317-9888) **5621**
Guia de Programacao N E T (BRA) **2382**
Guia de Refrigeracion y Aire Acondicionado (ARG ISSN 0325-4798) **4119**
Guia de Reuniones Cientificas y Tecnicas en la Argentina (ARG ISSN 0301-7567) **6280**
Guia de Soluciones *see* Autodesk Noticias **2588**
Guia de Su Primer Ano (ESP ISSN 1138-8404) **2154**
Guia de Turismo y de Servicios (MEX) **8715**
Guia de Viajes (MEX) **8715**
Guia de Vinos Gourmets *see* Gourmets Wine Guide **604**
Guia del Comercio y de la Industria de Madrid (ESP ISSN 0211-4917) **1404**
Guia del Comprador de Casas (ESP) **7592**
Guia del Comprador de Coches (ESP ISSN 0211-657X) **8583**
Guia del Comprador de Furgonetas y Todo Terreno (ESP) **8583**
Guia del Comprador de Ordenadores y Software (ESP) **2511**
Guia del Envase y Embalaje/Container and Packaging Guide (MEX) **6710**
Guia del Marketing (ESP ISSN 1576-7000) **1818**
• Guia del Mundo (URY ISSN 0797-6763) **3120**
Guia del Plastico (ARG) **7092**
Guia del Psicologo (ESP ISSN 1885-8392) **7359**
Guia del Sector Financiero Ecuatoriano (ECU) **1350**
Guia del Sol (CUB) **8715**
Guia del Tour (ESP) **8259**
Guia del Transporte Maritimo (ESP) **8645**
Guia del Viajero Curioso *see* Guida del Viaggiatore Curioso **8716**
† Guia Deusto Laboral (ESP ISSN 1135-660X) **8960**
Guia Distribucion No Agrupada *see* Recambios & Accesorios **8600**
Guia do Acessorio Auto e Servicos (PRT) **8583**
Guia do Aeroclubes e Aerodesportos/Aeroclubs and Air Sports Guide (BRA ISSN 0104-7957) **57**
• Guia do Automovel (PRT) **8583**
Guia do Empreendedor *see* Pequenas Empresas Grandes Negocios **1965**
• Guia do Estudante (BRA ISSN 0104-480X) **2983**
Guia do Helicoptero/Helicopter Guide (BRA ISSN 0104-7949) **8543**
Guia do Laboratorio (BRA) **3244**
Guia do Porto de Lisboa (PRT) **8645**
Guia do Taxi Aereo/Air Taxi Guide (BRA ISSN 0104-4966) **8543**
Guia do Terceiro Mundo *see* Guia del Mundo **3120**
• Guia do Turista (BRA ISSN 1413-9049) **8715**
Guia dos Comerciais *see* Veiculos Comerciais **8610**
Guia dos Editores Associados (BRA) **7562**
Guia dos Terminais Aereos/Airports Guide (BRA) **8544**
Guia Electronica de Consulta. Laboral (ESP ISSN 1579-6566) **4683**
Guia Espanola del Transporte (ESP) **8497**
• Guia Estradas - Quatro Rodas (BRA ISSN 0104-5024) **8715**
Guia Familiar (USA) **6502**
Guia Financiera (URY ISSN 0797-1176) **1350**
Guia Financiera Magui *see* Guia Financiera **1350**
Guia General de las Industrias Ceramicas y Afines de Espana (ESP) **1998**
Guia Geral de Produtos Quimicos (BRA) **3244**
Guia Grupo de Distribucion de Recambios *see* Recambios & Accesorios **8600**
• Guia Industrial de Venezuela (VEN) **1115**
Guia Industrial Mexicana (MEX) **1998**
Guia Integrada de Hosteleria (ESP ISSN 1888-4148) **8715**
Guia Internacional de Trafico (ARG) **8715**
Guia Laboral y de Asuntos Sociales (ESP ISSN 1138-9095) **1684**
Guia Las Energias.com *see* Energias **3128**
Guia Madera de Proveedores y Operadores *see* TecniMadera **3716**
• Guia Maritima (PER ISSN 1726-0841) **8645**
Guia Maritima, Portuaria y de la Industria Naval de Venezuela/Maritime, Port and Naval Industry Guide of Venezuela (VEN ISSN 1315-5792) **1998**
Guia Maritimo (BRA ISSN 1414-0438) **6423**
• Guia nei Brasil (BRA) **5452**
Guia Oficial de Centro-America (HND) **8715**
Guia Panrotas (BRA ISSN 0102-3225) **8715**
Guia para la Emision de Billetes *see* I A T A Ticketing Handbook **8544**
• Guia Polibea de la Discapacidad (ESP ISSN 1136-9353) **4066**
Guia Practica de Legislacion Laboral (ESP ISSN 1137-1455) **4848**
Guia Practica de Seguridad Social (ESP ISSN 1577-7928) **8043**
Guia Practica del Mar (ESP ISSN 1137-2516) **8645**
Guia Praias - Quatro Rodas (BRA ISSN 0104-5067) **8715**
Guia Prevenir *see* Guia Prevenir Salud **6987**
Guia Prevenir Salud (ESP ISSN 1888-0991) **6987**
Guia Puntex. Anuario Dental Espanol (ESP ISSN 1576-1509) **5846**
Guia Puntex. Anuario Espanol de Analitica (ESP ISSN 1576-1487) **5945**
Guia Puntex. Anuario Espanol de E F P y Parafarmacia (Especialidades Farmaceuticas y Publicitarias) (ESP ISSN 1576-1533) **6845**
Guia Puntex. Anuario Espanol de Enfermeria (ESP ISSN 1576-1584) **5959**
Guia Puntex. Anuario Espanol de Optica y Audioprotesis (ESP ISSN 1576-3234) **5621**
Guia Puntex. Anuario Espanol de Ortopedia y Gerontologia (ESP ISSN 1576-1622) **6061**
Guia Puntex. Anuario Espanol de Podologia (ESP ISSN 1576-1649) **6061**
Guia Puntex. Anuario Espanol de Protesis Dental (ESP ISSN 1576-1657) **5846**
Guia Puntex. Anuario Espanol de Veterinaria (ESP ISSN 1136-9345) **8798**
Guia Puntex. Anuario Hospitalario Espanol (ESP ISSN 1131-3978) **5621**
Guia Puntex. Proveedores Medico-Hospitalarios (ESP ISSN 1886-1202) **4094**
Guia Quatro Rodas Brasil (BRA ISSN 0104-4982) **8715**
Guia Quatro Rodas. Rodoviario *see* Guia Rodoviario - Quatro Rodas **8716**
Guia Quatro Rodas. Sao Paulo *see* Guia Sao Paulo - Quatro Rodas **8716**
Guia Quatro Rodas. Sul (BRA) **8715**
Guia Quimica Latinoamericana/Latin American Chemical Guide (MEX) **2062**
Guia Rodoviario - Quatro Rodas (BRA) **8716**
Guia Sao Paulo - Quatro Rodas (BRA ISSN 0104-4990) **8716**
Guia Silber. Directorio de Instituciones Chilenas (CHL ISSN 0717-2966) **1998**
Guia Turistica de Rosario y Sante Fe (ARG) **8716**
Guia Universitaria Salvadorena (SLV) **2956**
Guia Util del Automovil de Coche Actual (ESP) **8583**
Guia Venezolana de Publicidad y Mercadeo (VEN) **26**
Guia Verde Industrial y Comercial (PER) **1998**
• Guia Ya.com/Gourmetour (ESP) **4387**
Las Guias de Editur (ESP ISSN 1137-4764) **8716**
▼ • Guias para Ensenanzas Medias. Biologia y Geologia (ESP ISSN 1988-7760) **676**
▼ • Guias para Ensenanzas Medias. Ciencias de la Naturaleza (ESP ISSN 1988-7485) **7859**
▼ • Guias para Ensenanzas Medias. Educacion Fisica (ESP ISSN 1988-7795) **8176**
▼ • Guias para Ensenanzas Medias. Educacion para la Ciudadania (ESP ISSN 1988-7779) **7139**
▼ • Guias para Ensenanzas Medias. Educacion Plastica (ESP ISSN 1988-7558) **535**
▼ • Guias para Ensenanzas Medias. Etica (ESP ISSN 1988-7507) **6922**
▼ • Guias para Ensenanzas Medias. Fisica y Quimica (ESP ISSN 1988-7752) **2062**
▼ • Guias para Ensenanzas Medias. Geografia e Historia (ESP ISSN 1988-7566) **4013**
▼ • Guias para Ensenanzas Medias. Interdisciplinar (ESP ISSN 1988-7787) **4454**
▼ • Guias para Ensenanzas Medias. Lengua y Literatura (ESP ISSN 1988-7523) **5302**
▼ • Guias para Ensenanzas Medias. Matematicas (ESP ISSN 1988-7531) **5491**
▼ • Guias para Ensenanzas Medias. Musica (ESP ISSN 1988-754X) **6571**
▼ • Guias para Ensenanzas Medias. Tecnologia (ESP ISSN 1988-7493) **8423**
▼ • Guias para Formacion Profesional (ESP ISSN 1988-7809) **2861**
Guida (Year) al Mercato Elettrico (ITA) **1010**

Title

10342 LA GUIDA AGENZIE ULRICH'S PERIODICALS

La Guida Agenzie (ITA ISSN 1123-4148) **1998**
Guida agli Accessori e Componenti Nautici *see* Motonautica **8278**
• Guida agli Acquisti per gli Alberghi (ITA) **4387**
• Guida agli Acquisti per gli Enti Pubblici (ITA) **7443**
† La Guida ai Fuoristrada (ITA ISSN 1827-837X) **8960**
Guida ai Principali Contabili Internazionali (ITA ISSN 1824-8756) **1289**
† Guida ai Vini del Mondo (ITA) **8960**
Guida al Benessere (Year) *see* Suite Benessere **5084**
• Guida al Diritto (ITA ISSN 1590-0282) **4683**
Guida al Mercato dell'Edilizia (ITA) **1010**
Guida al Pubblico Impiego (ITA ISSN 1827-5060) **1684**
Guida al Pubblico Impiego Locale *see* Guida al Pubblico Impiego **1684**
Guida alla Contabilita & Bilancio (ITA ISSN 1826-2651) **1289**
Guida alla Novita Fiscale (ITA ISSN 1827-7489) **1927**
Guida all'Acquisto dello Scooter (ITA ISSN 1971-0259) **8259**
† Guida alle Applicazioni OS-2 Warp (ITA) **8960**
• Guida: Annuario dei Fornitori dell'Industria del Mobile (ITA) **1050**
Guida Bibliografica (ITA) **626**
Guida Camping d'Italia (ITA ISSN 0072-792X) **8316**
Guida del Viaggiatore Curioso (ITA ISSN 1825-5434) **8716**
Guida della Montagna (ITA ISSN 1972-2427) **8316**
Guida della Stampa Periodica Italiana (ITA) **626**
Guida Eurocamping Europa (ITA) **8716**
• Guida Eurocamping Italia e Corsica (ITA) **8716**
• La Guida Italiana del Petrolio (ITA) **6771**
La Guida Marketing (ITA ISSN 1123-4156) **1998**
Guida Monaci. Agenda Nazionale (ITA ISSN 1122-8490) **1749**
Guida Monaci. Annuario della Salute (ITA) **4094**
• Guida Monaci. Annuario Generale (ITA) **1428**
Guida Monaci C D *see* C D Guida Monaci **1977**
La Guida Monaci del Sistema Lazio (ITA ISSN 1828-4639) **8716**
Guida Motonautica *see* Motonautica **8278**
Guida Mutui (ITA ISSN 1827-661X) **7592**
• Guida Normativa (ITA ISSN 1590-0304) **1115**
† La Guida Photocamere Digitali (ITA ISSN 1828-2679) **8960**
• Guida Pratica del Lavoro (ITA ISSN 1590-0088) **1684**
Guida Pratica Fiscale (ITA ISSN 1128-336X) **1927**
Guida Pratica Lavoro *see* Guida Pratica del Lavoro **1684**
† Guida Ragionata alle Scuole d'Inglese in Italia (ITA) **8960**
Guida Software (ITA ISSN 1592-3487) **2590**
† Guida Ufficiale Monovolume (ITA ISSN 1824-2235) **8960**
† Guida Ufficiale S U V (Sports Utility Vehicle) (ITA ISSN 1824-7628) **8960**
• Guida Viaggi (ITA) **8716**
GuidaMutui *see* Guida Mutui **7592**
Guidance and Control (USA ISSN 1057-493X) **57**
Guidance and Control Information Analysis Center Bulletin *see* G A C I A C Bulletin **56**
Guidance and Detonator *see* Zhidao yu Yinxin **6455**
Guidance & Fuze *see* Zhidao yu Yinxin **6455**
Guidance of Infants/Yoji-No-Shido (JPN) **2861**
Guidazzurra Amministrazione Centrale dello Stato *see* Guidazzurra Repertori **7443**
Guidazzurra Repertori (ITA) **7443**
Guide *see* Al- Murshid **3799**
• Guide (CAN ISSN 1197-9992) **3810**
Guide *see* Al- Murshid **8739**
• The Guide (VNM) **8716**
• The Guide (Boston) (USA ISSN 1047-8906) **4374**
Guide (Hagerstown) (USA ISSN 0017-5226) **7760**
The Guide (Peachtree City) (USA) **3977**
The Guide (San Francisco) (USA ISSN 1547-8874) **2322**
The Guide (Toronto) (CAN ISSN 0533-5051) **4595**
The Guide (Year) (HKG) **4387**
Guide ai Classici (ITA ISSN 1970-9609) **5302**
Guide & Directory *see* Food Processing **3640**
The Guide Ankara (TUR ISSN 1303-054X) **8716**
Le Guide Annuel des Deplacements Professionnels (FRA ISSN 1774-9484) **8716**
Guide Annuel des S A M U et S M U R de France (Services d'Aide Medicale Urgente) (FRA) **6061**
The Guide Antalya (TUR ISSN 1303-5762) **8716**
Guide Art Services (FRA ISSN 1771-6853) **492**
• Guide Association. Executive News (GBR) **2154**
Guide Astrologique (FRA) **566**
Guide Aubrey des Meilleurs Vins et Spiritueux *see* Les 100 Meilleurs Vins a Moins de 25$ **614**
Guide Aubry *see* Les 100 Meilleurs Vins a Moins de 25$ **614**
Guide Bel Air (FRA) **8716**
The Guide Bodrum (TUR ISSN 1303-0558) **8716**
The Guide - Bucuresti (ROM ISSN 1224-6689) **8716**
Guide C *see* New Mexico State University. Cooperative Extension Service. Guide C **4365**
Guide Complet de Prix Autos, Fourgonnettes et Camions Usages *see* Guide Complet des Prix, Fourgonnettes, V U S et Camions Usages **8583**
Guide Complet de Prix Autos, Fourgonnettes et Camions Usages *see* Guide Complet des Prix, Automobiles Usagees **8583**
Guide Complet des Prix, Automobiles Usagees (CAN ISSN 1719-7104) **8583**
Guide Complet des Prix, Fourgonnettes, V U S et Camions Usages (CAN ISSN 1719-7112) **8583**
Guide Cuisine (FRA ISSN 0767-8177) **4359**
Guide D *see* New Mexico State University. Cooperative Extension Service. Guide D **294**
Guide D V D (CAN ISSN 1910-2917) **2401**
Guide d'Acces aux Programmes et Produits de Statistique Canada *see* Canada. Statistics Canada. Guide to Statistics Canada's Programs and Products **8361**
Guide d'Application de l'A D R (Accord Europeen Relatif au Transport International des Marchandises Dangereuses par Route) (FRA ISSN 1775-9587) **8497**
Guide d'Application des Exigences Relatives aux Vehicules et Accessoires d'Intervention a l'Intention des Services de Securite Incendie (CAN ISSN 1910-3921) **3578**
Guide de Controle des Mutuelles du Code de la Mutualite Assumant un Risque d'Assurance (FRA ISSN 1775-9455) **4504**
Le Guide de Cotation des Artistes d'Art Zoom (CAN ISSN 1719-5942) **492**
Guide de Donnees Astronomiques pour l'Observation du Ciel (FRA ISSN 1770-1074) **575**
Guide de Donnees sur la Consommation d'Energie *see* Energy Use Data Handbook (Online Edition) **3134**
Guide de France (FRA ISSN 0750-4152) **2191**
Guide de la Chimie (FRA ISSN 1766-7771) **2062**
Le Guide de la Cuisine Etrangere a Paris *see* Le Bottin Gourmand. Le Guide de la Cuisine Etrangere a Paris **4382**
Guide de la Mariee *see* Perfect Match Mariage **8880**
Le Guide de la Protection de l'Enfance (FRA ISSN 1624-6179) **8043**
Guide de la Protection du Vignoble *see* Guide des Vignobles Rhone-Mediterranee **117**
Guide de la Reglementation Sociale pour les Entreprises *see* Gids voor Sociale Reglementering in Ondernemingen **4831**
Guide de la Remuneration et de la Paie des Personnels Medicaux et Hospitaliers (FRA ISSN 1775-9315) **4094**
Guide de la Route: la Caroline du Nord, la Caroline du Sud et la Georgie (CAN) **8716**
Guide de la Route: La Floride (CAN ISSN 0838-0015) **8716**
Guide de la Route: Le Centre de la Cote Atlantique (CAN) **8716**
Guide de la Route: Le Maine, le New Hampshire, et le Vermont (CAN) **8716**
Guide de la Route: Le Quebec et les Provinces de l'Atlantique (CAN) **8716**
Guide de la Route, l'Ontario (CAN ISSN 1193-3569) **8716**
Guide de la Securite des Entreprises et des Collectivites (FRA ISSN 0990-8498) **3579**
Guide de l'Accueil Temporaire (FRA ISSN 1775-9463) **4066**
Guide de l'Acheteur Public (FRA ISSN 1957-6250) **7493**
† Guide de l'Adjoint des Ressources Humaines (FRA ISSN 1773-4142) **8960**
Guide de l'Agriculture du Quebec (CAN) **117**
Guide de l'Amateur (FRA ISSN 1637-0449) **4359**
• Le Guide de l'Eau (FRA ISSN 2101-1680) **8824**
Le Guide de l'Emploi Associatif dans les Alpes de Haute-Provence (FRA ISSN 1773-4258) **1489**
† Guide de l'Equipement et de l'Outillage (FRA ISSN 1157-1888) **8960**
Le Guide de l'Espresso (ITA ISSN 1128-4099) **4387**
Guide de l'Habitat et du Developpement Local (FRA) **4411**
Le Guide de l'Indice de Mission *see* The Guide to the Post Index **1236**
Le Guide de l'Intervention Sociale (FRA ISSN 1291-2484) **8043**
Guide de l'Investisseur Industriel au Senegal (SEN) **1887**
Guide de Montreal-Nord (CAN) **3810**
Guide de Planification. l'Outaouais, Quebec *see* Guide des Planificateurs de Congres et des Voyagistes **8716**
Guide de Subventions et Bourses *see* Medical Research Council of Canada. Grants and Awards Guide **5671**
• Guide de Traitement des Victimes d'Actes Criminels (CAN ISSN 1910-4138) **2654**
Guide Delta des Hotels et Restaurants de Bruxelles (BEL) **8716**
• Guide des Approvisionnements (CAN ISSN 1910-8982) **7443**
Le Guide des Assurances Sociales (FRA ISSN 1243-5082) **8043**
† Guide des Banques de Donnees Factuelles Francaises sur les Materiaux (FRA) **8960**
Le Guide des Bistrots a Paris *see* Le Bottin Gourmand. Le Guide des Bistrots a Paris **4382**
Guide des Centres et des Quincailleries du Quebec (CAN) **1053**
Guide des Couts de Transport (FRA) **8497**
Guide des Declarations Fiscales (FRA ISSN 1144-5777) **1289**
Guide des Donateurs Canadiens *see* Canadian Donor's Guide (Year) **8030**
Guide des Donateurs Canadiens Faisant Etat des Organismes de Souscription de Fonds (CAN ISSN 0849-0104) **8043**
Guide des Etablissements de Sante du Canada *see* Guide to Canadian Healthcare Facilities **4094**
Guide des Etablissements pour Personnes Agees (FRA ISSN 1950-3555) **4047**
Le Guide des Etudes Superieures *see* Que Faire Apres le Bac **2999**
• Guide des Legislations en Restauration (CAN ISSN 1913-3618) **4387**
• Le Guide des Marques de Commerce (CAN ISSN 1912-0745) **4869**
Guide des Merveilles de la Nature (FRA ISSN 1951-3143) **8716**
▼ Le Guide des Methodes de Musique & Recueils Pedagogiques (FRA ISSN 1958-802X) **6571**
Le Guide des Metiers (FRA ISSN 1166-7419) **2861**
Le Guide des Piscines et des Spas *see* L' Essentiel des Piscines et des Spas **4977**
Guide des Planificateurs de Congres et des Voyagistes (CAN ISSN 1912-8096) **8716**
• Guide des Procedures Douanieres (FRA ISSN 1290-3736) **8497**
Le Guide des Produits Corses *see* Nustrale.com **3658**
• Guide des Programmes d'Appui Financier du Patrimoine Canadien (En Ligne) (CAN ISSN 1719-7279) **8043**
• Guide des Programmes Federaux d'Aide Financiere a l'Industrie du Film et de la Video (CAN ISSN 1719-5802) **6502**
Le Guide des Ressources Humaines (FRA ISSN 1773-4304) **1861**
Guide des Revetements et des Finitions *see* Sols, Murs, Plafonds **4562**
Guide des Vignobles Rhone-Mediterranee (FRA ISSN 1770-166X) **117**
Guide di Architettura (ITA ISSN 1970-9617) **444**
Le Guide di Campagna Amica Cibi & Natura (ITA ISSN 1824-0968) **4359**
Le Guide di Campagna Amica Vacanze e Natura (ITA ISSN 1824-0976) **8716**
Le Guide di Mondadori (ITA ISSN 1828-292X) **2638**
Guide di Ricerca Storica e Restauro (ITA) **444**
Guide Dog News (USA) **4081**
Guide du Budget (FRA ISSN 1775-920X) **4094**
Guide du Chauffage *see* Chauffage & Climatisation Magazine **4117**
Guide du Chauffage & de la Climatisation *see* Chauffage & Climatisation Magazine **4117**
Guide du Citoyen (CAN ISSN 1910-3093) **7443**
Guide du Contribuable (BEL) **2638**
Le Guide du Contribuable Canadien (CAN ISSN 0432-9368) **1927**
Le Guide du Cyclotouriste (FRA ISSN 1951-4581) **8259**
Guide du Debutant (FRA ISSN 1775-1195) **2419**
Guide du Directeur (FRA ISSN 1639-7568) **1749**
Guide du Dirigeant d'Entreprise *see* Lamy Droit du Dirigeant d'Entreprise **4873**
Guide du Dirigeant d'Entreprise Actualites *see* Lamy Droit du Dirigeant d'Entreprise **4873**
Guide du Droit de la Formation Professionnelle (FRA ISSN 1773-4215) **4869**
Guide du Feu (FRA ISSN 0337-5781) **3579**
Guide du Futur et Nouveau Proprietaire *see* G F N P (National Edition) **7591**
Guide du Futur et Nouveau Proprietaire *see* G F N P (English Edition) **7591**
Guide du Futur et Nouveau Proprietaire (English Edition) *see* G F N P (English Edition) **7591**
Guide du Futur et Nouveau Proprietaire (National Edition) *see* G F N P (National Edition) **7591**
Guide du Jeune Avocat (FRA) **4683**
Le Guide du Kokin (FRA ISSN 1774-0398) **6292**
Guide du Livre Ancien et des Libraires (FRA) **7562**
Guide du Locataire (CAN ISSN 1719-4954) **4411**
Le Guide du Logement et de l'Habitation (FRA ISSN 1161-1790) **7592**
Guide du Management des Competences (FRA ISSN 1775-9439) **1749**
Guide du Papier Arts Graphiques (FRA) **6733**
Guide du Papier Carton pour la Transformation (FRA) **6733**
Guide du Pouvoir au Quebec (CAN ISSN 1491-6983) **7443**
Guide du Programme des Dons Ecologiques du Canada *see* Canadian Ecological Gifts Program Handbook (Online Edition) **3409**
Guide du Programme des Dons Ecologiques du Canada *see* Canadian Ecological Gifts Program Handbook (Print Edition) **3409**
• Guide du Responsable Comptable et Financier (FRA ISSN 1290-3728) **1289**
Guide du Routard (FRA ISSN 0768-2034) **8716**
Le Guide du Textile et de l'Habillement (FRA ISSN 1956-9599) **2247**
Guide du Transport par Camion (CAN ISSN 0706-9995) **8497**
Le Guide du Travail (FRA ISSN 1255-2917) **1862**
Guide E *see* New Mexico State University. Cooperative Extension Service. Guide E **4365**
Guide Economique de la Tunisie (TUN ISSN 0330-9290) **1998**
Guide Emer (FRA ISSN 0533-5167) **492**
Guide Evenements d'Affaires *see* Business Events Guide (Year) **6278**
Guide F *see* New Mexico State University. Cooperative Extension Service. Guide F **4365**
Le Guide Fiscal Financier: Le Comptable et Budgetaire (FRA ISSN 1773-4193) **4411**
Guide for Biblical Studies (USA) **7760**
Guide for Buyers of Quality Hardwoods (USA) **1998**
Guide for Landlords and Tenants in British Columbia *see* Residential Tenancy Act **4425**
A Guide for Madrichim (ISR) **2861**
• The Guide for Pension Trustees (GBR ISSN 1741-8909) **1684**
Guide for Planning Educational Facilities (USA ISSN 0072-8101) **3024**
• A Guide for Postgraduate Award Holders in the Arts and Humanities (Online) (GBR) **2861**
A Guide for Postgraduate Award Holders in the Arts and Humanities (Print) *see* A Guide for Postgraduate Award Holders in the Arts and Humanities (Online) **2861**
Guide for the Care and Use of Laboratory Animals (USA) **5905**
Guide for the Preparation of Patent Drawings *see* U.S. Patent and Trademark Office. Guide for the Preparation of Patent Drawings **6759**
Guide G *see* New Mexico State University. Cooperative Extension Service. Guide G **4365**
Guide H *see* New Mexico State University. Cooperative Extension Service. Guide H **3745**
Le Guide I Distribution *see* Le Guide Informatique Distribution **1818**
Guide Illustrate (ITA ISSN 1970-3953) **8716**
Le Guide Informatique Distribution (FRA ISSN 1953-5880) **1818**
Guide Insolite (ITA ISSN 1970-3783) **8716**
Guide International de la Parfumerie *see* Guide International des Fournisseurs de la Beaute **8960**
† Guide International des Banques de Donnees sur les Brevets et les Marques (FRA) **8960**
Guide International des Experts & Specialistes (FRA) **492**
† Guide International des Fournisseurs de la Beaute/General Directory of the Perfume and Cosmetic Industry (FRA ISSN 1766-2826) **8960**
The Guide Istanbul (TUR ISSN 1303-0574) **8716**
Le Guide Juridique de l'Elu Local (FRA ISSN 1775-9536) **7443**
† Le Guide Juridique et Fiscal de l'Entreprise (FRA ISSN 1961-5272) **8960**
Guide Lines (Yorktown Heights) (USA) **6809**
Guide Magazine (LBN) **3905**
Le Guide Mode-Textile-Maison *see* Le Guide du Textile et de l'Habillement **2247**
Guide National de Prescription des Medicaments *see* Encyclopedie Pratique du Medicament **6837**
Le Guide Nustrale.com des Produits Corses *see* Nustrale.com **3658**
Guide of Consumer Goods in Greece/Odegos Proionton Eureias Katanaloseos (GRC ISSN 1105-4964) **1818**
Guide of the Disabled Person *see* Belgium. Federaal Ministerie van Sociale Zaken, Volksgezondheid en Leefmilieu. Hanidgids **4064**
Guide Officiel des Etapes de Camping-Car (FRA) **8316**
• The Guide on CD (GBR) **8645**
• The Guide Online (VNM ISSN 1563-8839) **8716**
† Guide P N P (Profession Nouveau Papetier) (FRA ISSN 1764-6499) **8960**
Guide Parlementaire Canadien *see* Canadian Parliamentary Guide (Year) **7113**
Guide Permanent: Paie (FRA ISSN 1290-0222) **1927**
Guide Plastiques et Caoutchouc (FRA ISSN 1281-0657) **1998**
Guide Pocket (ITA ISSN 1724-532X) **2477**
Guide pour les Plans d'Education et la Communication des Resultats (CAN ISSN 1715-2275) **2861**
Guide Pratiche Cavalli *see* Le Guide Pratiche dei Nostri Amici Cavalli **8960**
† Le Guide Pratiche dei Nostri Amici Cavalli (ITA ISSN 1827-9597) **8960**
Guide Pratique - Dalian *see* L' Exploitation Vitivinicole **109**
Le Guide Pratique de la Formation (FRA ISSN 1622-3322) **1862**
Guide Pratique de la Medecine du Travail (FRA ISSN 1957-6242) **5621**
• Guide Pratique de l'Intendant (FRA ISSN 1775-934X) **4683**
Guide Pratique des Alternatives a l'Hospitalisation Traditionnelle (FRA ISSN 1957-6099) **4683**
Guide Pratique des Carrieres d'Avenir au Quebec *see* Carrieres d'Avenir **6695**
Guide Pratique des Centres de Vacances (FRA ISSN 1957-6536) **4978**
Guide Pratique des Etudes Universitaires au Quebec (CAN ISSN 0820-2788) **2956**
▼ Guide Pratique des Medecines Traditionnelles Orientales (FRA ISSN 1959-4569) **309**
Guide Pratique des Medicaments (FRA ISSN 1775-2744) **5621**
• Guide Pratique des Representants du Personnel (FRA ISSN 1770-1112) **4683**
Le Guide Pratique des Solutions Technologiques et Web en Gestion des Ressources Humaines (CAN ISSN 1912-2756) **1862**
Guide Pratique du C L S H (Centre de Loisirs sans Hebergement) (FRA ISSN 1957-6323) **4978**
Guide Pratique du Centre de Loisirs sans Hebergement *see* Guide Pratique du C L S H **4978**
Le Guide Pratique du Chasseur Sous-Marin (FRA ISSN 1951-4034) **8316**
▼ Guide Pratique du Tibet en France (FRA ISSN 1960-9205) **3536**

Link to your serials resources and content with ulrichsweb.com

Title

10344 GUIDE TO THE ITALIAN RUBBER INDUSTRY ULRICH'S PERIODICALS

Guide to the Italian Rubber Industry *see* L' Industria Italiana della Gomma. Guida **7825**
Guide to the Large Goods Vehicle Driving Test and Licences (GBR) **8583**
(Year) Guide to the Licensing World (GBR ISSN 0968-2635) **6750**
Guide to the National Lottery Charities Board (GBR) **8176**
Guide to the National Park Areas: Eastern States (USA ISSN 1537-3320) **8717**
† Guide to the National Park Areas: Western States (USA ISSN 1537-3339) **8960**
Guide to the Ohio Rules of Civil Procedure (USA) **4832**
A Guide to the Personal Information Protection and Electronic Documents Act (CAN ISSN 1495-6047) **4848**
• The Guide to the Post Index (CAN ISSN 1708-6205) **1236**
Guide to the Queen Charlottes (CAN) **8717**
▼ Guide to the Secondary Market (USA ISSN 1945-3566) **1628**
Guide to the Social Services (GBR ISSN 0072-8756) **8043**
Guide to the Textile and Clothing Industries in Denmark *see* Danish Textile and Clothing Industries. Guide (Online) **8449**
Guide to the Top Consumer Products Employers *see* Vault Guide to the Top Consumer Products Employers **1713**
Guide to the Top Government & Nonprofit Employers *see* Vault Guide to the Top Government & Nonprofit Employers **1713**
Guide to the United States Treaties in Force (USA ISSN 0736-5713) **4822**
Guide to the Use of Herbicides (ZAF) **234**
Guide to the Use of Pesticides and Fungicides in the Republic of South Africa (ZAF) **234**
Guide to the Winelands of the Cape (ZAF) **8717**
Guide to Touring & Promotion *see* The Musician's Guide to Touring and Promotion **6594**
Guide to Tourism *see* Luyou Daobao **8731**
• A Guide to Toxic Torts (USA) **4832**
Guide to Toys for Children Who Are Blind or Visually Impaired (USA) **4081**
Guide to Trade-marks *see* Le Guide des Marques de Commerce **4869**
Guide to Training and Benefits to Young People (GBR) **8043**
The Guide to U K Company Giving (Year) (GBR) **8043**
Guide to U N C T A D Publications (CHE ISSN 0255-9358) **1236**
Guide to U.S. Foundations, Their Trustees, Officers & Donors (USA ISSN 1071-202X) **8083**
A Guide to U S Government Information (USA) **626**
Guide to U S Government Publications (USA ISSN 0092-3168) **7480**
Guide to Unique Meeting and Event Facilities (USA ISSN 1066-7679) **8717**
Guide to Unique Photography *see* G U P **6969**
Guide to Universities & Colleges in Canada (BEL ISSN 1561-1965) **2956**
Guide to Virginia's Blue Ridge, including the Shenandoah Valley *see* Insiders' Guide to Virginia's Blue Ridge, Including the Shenandoah Valley **8723**
† Guide to Washington Area Restaurants (USA) **8960**
Guide to Wealth Protection Strategies (USA ISSN 1539-6002) **1350**
A Guide to Women's Health *see* Nursing (Year) **5972**
Guide to World Economy *see* Shijie Jingji Daokan **1173**
Guide to Worldwide Bunkering Services (GBR) **1567**
Guide to Worldwide Maritime Training (GBR) **8645**
Guide to Worldwide Postal-Code and Address Formats (USA ISSN 1072-3862) **2354**
Guide to Yoga Teachers and Classes (USA) **6645**
Guide to Your Career (USA ISSN 1097-6418) **6698**
Guide Touristique Europeen pour Israelites/European Travel Guide for Jews (BEL) **3536**
Guide Touristique, Nord - du - Quebec, Baie - James *see* Baie - James **8685**
Guide Vert (FRA ISSN 0760-4300) **945**
Guide Video *see* Guide D V D **2401**
Guide Video + D V D *see* Guide D V D **2401**
Guide Z *see* New Mexico State University. Cooperative Extension Service. Guide Z **204**
Guide4Grads *see* Australian Optometry **6039**
Guidebook of United States Coins (USA ISSN 0072-8829) **6651**
Guidebook on Environmental Courses and Conferences (USA) **3436**
Guidebook - State of Ohio, Department of Natural Resources, Division of Geological Survey *see* Ohio. Division of Geological Survey. Guidebook **2760**
Guided Reading for Primary School Students *see* Xiaoxuesheng Daodu **2927**
Guideline (IRL) **6698**
Guidelines *see* Pautas **7570**
GuideLines (USA) **2368**
Guidelines for Handling Molten Aluminum (USA) **6314**
Guidelines for Health Supervision (USA) **6092**
Guidelines for Health Supervision Three *see* Guidelines for Health Supervision **6092**
Guidelines for Improving Practice. Architects and Engineers Professional Liability (USA ISSN 0091-8245) **444**
Guidelines for Pastoral Liturgy *see* Ordo **7810**
Guidelines for Perinatal Care (USA) **5991**
Guidelines for Submitting Proposals *see* Canadian International Development Agency. Mass Media Initiative. Development Information Program. Guidelines for Submitting Proposals **1592**
• Guidelines for the Medical Management of Genital HPV and/or Genital Warts in Australia and New Zealand (NZL ISSN 1177-6099) **5814**
Guidelines in the Use of Parenteral and Enteral Nutrition in Adult and Pediatric Patients *see* Journal of Parenteral and Enteral Nutrition **6662**
Guidelines Letter (USA ISSN 1089-2141) **444**
Guidelines Report *see* Environment Bay of Plenty. Guideline **3421**
• Guidepoints (USA ISSN 1070-8200) **6109**
• Guidepost (ESP ISSN 0432-9791) **8717**
Guidepost for Science and Technology Development Quarterly *see* Keji Fazhan Biaogan **7875**
Guideposts (USA ISSN 0017-5331) **7646**
Guideposts for Teens *see* Guideposts Sweet 16 **2191**
Guideposts Sweet 16 (USA ISSN 1551-904X) **2191**
Guides Alpinisme et Randonnee *see* Alpinisme & Randonnee **8302**
Guides de Charme Rivages (FRA ISSN 0991-4781) **8717**
Les Guides des Grossistes Informatiques *see* Distributique **2492**
Guides Pratiques (BEL) **2638**
Guides Pratiques Medicaux (FRA ISSN 1140-0277) **5621**
† Guides to Antiquity Sites (ISR) **8960**
Guides to European Taxation: Taxation & Investment in Central and East European Countries *see* Central/Eastern Europe - Taxation & Investment **1916**
Guides to European Taxation: Taxation of Companies in Europe *see* Europe - Corporate Taxation **1922**
Guides to European Taxation: Taxation of Individuals in Europe *see* Europe - Individual Taxation **1922**
Guides to European Taxation: Taxation of Patent Royalties, Dividends, Interest in Europe *see* Europe/North America - Corporate Investment Income **1922**
Guides to European Taxation: Taxation of Private Investment Income *see* Europe/North America - Private Investment Income **1922**
Guides to Great Ideas in Science *see* Greenwood Guides to Great Ideas in Science **7858**
Guides to Sources for British History (GBR) **5011**
Guides to Suppliers *see* I D S H R Studies **1686**
➤ Guides to the Identification of the Microinvertebrates of the Continental Waters of the World (NLD ISSN 0928-2440) **945**
Guides to the Mesopotamian Textual Record (DEU) **4321**
Guiding (GBR ISSN 0265-2706) **2154**
Guiding Journal of Traditional Chinese Medicine and Pharmacology *see* Zhongyiyao Daobao **5739**
Guihaia *see* Guangxi Zhiwu **791**
• Guijinshu/Precious Metals (CHN ISSN 1004-0676) **6314**
Guijinshu Dizhi/Journal of Precious Metallic Geology *see* Zizhi yu Ziyuan **2776**
Guild and City Gazette (GBR) **2286**
• Guild Briefs (USA) **8043**
Guild Digest (Year) (AUS ISSN 0155-9885) **6889**
Guild Gazette (USA ISSN 1948-1179) **1115**
Guild News (GBR) **57**
Guild News (USA ISSN 1099-2316) **492**
Guild Notes *see* National Lawyers Guild. Guild Notes **4851**
Guild of Agricultural Journalists Year Book (GBR ISSN 0072-8969) **117**
Guild of Book Workers Journal (USA ISSN 0434-9245) **7562**
Guild of Book Workers. Newsletter (USA ISSN 0730-3203) **7562**
Guild of Carillonneurs in North America (San Antonio) Bulletin *see* G C N A Bulletin **6568**
Guild of Freemen of the City of London (GBR) **4225**
• The Guild Practitioner (USA ISSN 0017-5390) **4832**
Guild Reporter (USA ISSN 0017-5404) **4595**
Guild Sourcebooks: The Architect's Sourcebook - Architectural Arts & Sculpture (USA) **444**
Guild Sourcebooks: The Designer's Sourcebook - Art for the Wall, Furniture & Accessories (USA) **4541**
Guildhall Poets (GBR) **5423**
• Guildnotes (USA) **492**
Guildworks (USA) **8471**
Guilford Family Therapy Series (USA) **7359**
Guilford School Practitioner Series (USA) **7359**
Guilford Series on Social and Emotional Development (USA) **7359**
Guilford Substance Abuse Series (USA) **2694**
• Guilfoyle Report (USA ISSN 0889-8235) **6969**
• Guilin Dianzi Gongye Xueyuan Xuebao (CHN ISSN 1001-7437) **3100**
• Guilin Gongxueyuan Xuebao/GuiLin University of Technology. Journal (CHN ISSN 1006-544X) **8423**
Guilin Institute of Electronic Technology. Journal *see* Guilin Dianzi Gongye Xueyuan Xuebao **3100**
Guilin Institute of Tourism. Journal *see* Guilin Luyou Gaodeng Zhuanke Xuexiao Xuebao **8717**
• Guilin Luyou Gaodeng Zhuanke Xuexiao Xuebao/Guilin Institute of Tourism. Journal (CHN ISSN 1008-6080) **8717**
GuiLin University of Technology. Journal *see* Guilin Gongxueyuan Xuebao **8423**
Guilin Yixueyuan Xuebao/Guilin Medical College. Journal *see* Huaxia Yixue **5630**
• Guilt & Pleasure (USA ISSN 1559-7547) **3536**
Guimaraes. Arquivo Municipal "Alfredo Pimenta." Boletim de Trabalhos Historicos (PRT ISSN 0871-7478) **4225**
Guinea *see* The P R S Group. Country Reports: Guinea **1507**
• ➤ Guinea Pig Zero (USA ISSN 1098-0539) **6845**
• Guineana (ESP ISSN 1135-7924) **791**
Guiniguada (ESP ISSN 0213-0610) **2941**
Guinness Book of Knowledge (USA) **3120**
Guinness Globe (GBR) **604**
▼ Guinness World Records (SWE ISSN 1654-6458) **3120**
Guinness World Records (USA ISSN 1475-7419) **3120**
Guiones Liturgicos (ESP) **7799**
• Guisuanyan Tongbao/Chinese Silicate Society. Bulletin (CHN ISSN 1001-1625) **2116**
• ➤ Guisuanyan Xuebao/Chinese Ceramic Society. Journal (CHN ISSN 0454-5648) **2116**
• Guitar (DEU ISSN 1430-9769) **6571**
The Guitar *see* Guitar & Bass **6571**
▼ Guitar Aficionado Magazine (USA ISSN 1949-0690) **6571**
Guitar & Bass (GBR ISSN 1755-3385) **6571**
Guitar & Bass Buyer's Guide (USA ISSN 1075-5039) **6571**
Guitar Buyer's Guide *see* Guitar World **6571**
Guitar Collector's (FRA ISSN 1261-0410) **6571**
Guitar Foundation of America Soundboard *see* Soundboard **6618**
Guitar Legends (USA) **6571**
Guitar Magazine *see* Guitar & Bass **6571**
† Guitar One (USA ISSN 1525-3562) **8960**
Guitar Part (FRA ISSN 1256-737X) **6571**
• Guitar Player (USA ISSN 0017-5463) **6571**
Guitar Review (USA ISSN 0017-5471) **6571**
Guitar Tutor (GBR ISSN 1476-6736) **6571**
• Guitar World (USA ISSN 1045-6295) **6571**
† Guitar World Acoustic (USA ISSN 1549-6376) **8960**
Guitar World's Bass Guitar *see* Bass Guitar **8935**
Guitare Classique (FRA ISSN 1294-8055) **6571**
• Guitare Live (FRA ISSN 1776-0879) **6571**
Guitarist (GBR ISSN 0953-7023) **6571**
Guitarist Australia (AUS) **6571**
Guitarist Magazine (FRA ISSN 0997-3443) **6571**
• La Guitarra Eclectica (ESP) **6571**
Guitarra Magazine (USA ISSN 0434-9350) **6571**
Guitarrista (ESP ISSN 1885-5571) **6571**
• Guitars & Musical Instruments (USA ISSN 1046-3879) **6572**
Guix (ESP ISSN 0213-8581) **3063**
Guix d'Infantil *see* Aula de Infantil **2828**
Guix Dos *see* Guix **3063**
Guiyang Medical College. Journal *see* Guiyang Yixueyuan Xuebao **5621**
• Guiyang Yixueyuan Xuebao/Guiyang Medical College. Journal (CHN ISSN 1000-2707) **5621**
† Guize (ESP) **8960**
Guizhou Agricultural Sciences *see* Guizhou Nongye Kexue **117**
Guizhou Culture and History Collection *see* Guizhou Wenshi Congkan **4182**
• Guizhou Daxue Xuebao (Shehui Kexue Ban)/Guizhou University. Journal (Social Science) (CHN ISSN 1000-5099) **7967**
• Guizhou Daxue Xuebao (Yishu Ban) (CHN ISSN 1671-444X) **492**
• Guizhou Daxue Xuebao (Ziran Kexue Ban)/Guizhou University. Journal (Natural Science Edition) (CHN ISSN 1000-5269) **7859**
Guizhou Ethnic Studies *see* Guizhou Minzu Yanjiu **550**
Guizhou Gongye Daxue Xuebao *see* Guizhou Gongye Daxue Xuebao (Shehui Kexue Ban) **7967**
• Guizhou Gongye Daxue Xuebao (Shehui Kexue Ban)/Guizhou University of Technology. Journal (Social Science Edition) (CHN ISSN 1009-0509) **7967**
• Guizhou Gongye Daxue Xuebao (Ziran Kexue Ban)/Guizhou University of Technology. Journal (CHN ISSN 1009-0193) **7859**
• Guizhou Kexue/Guizhou Science (CHN ISSN 1003-6563) **7859**
Guizhou Medical Journal *see* Guizhou Yiyao **5621**
• Guizhou Minzu Yanjiu/Guizhou Ethnic Studies (CHN ISSN 1002-6959) **550**
• Guizhou Nongye Kexue/Guizhou Agricultural Sciences (CHN ISSN 1001-3601) **117**
Guizhou Normal University. Journal (Natural Science) *see* Guizhou Shifan Daxue Xuebao (Ziran Kexueban) **7859**
Guizhou Normal University. Journal (Social Science Edition) *see* Guizhou Shifan Daxue Xuebao (Shehui Kexue Ban) **7967**
Guizhou Science *see* Guizhou Kexue **7859**
• Guizhou Shehui Kexue/Social Sciences in Guizhou (CHN ISSN 1002-6924) **7967**
• Guizhou Shifan Daxue Xuebao (Shehui Kexue Ban)/Guizhou Normal University. Journal (Social Science Edition) (CHN ISSN 1001-733X) **7967**
• Guizhou Shifan Daxue Xuebao (Ziran Kexueban)/Guizhou Normal University. Journal (Natural Science) (CHN ISSN 1004-5570) **7859**
Guizhou Today *see* Dangdai Guizhou **3824**
Guizhou University. Journal (Natural Science Edition) *see* Guizhou Daxue Xuebao (Ziran Kexue Ban) **7859**
Guizhou University. Journal (Social Science) *see* Guizhou Daxue Xuebao (Shehui Kexue Ban) **7967**
Guizhou University of Technology. Journal *see* Guizhou Gongye Daxue Xuebao (Ziran Kexue Ban) **7859**
Guizhou University of Technology. Journal (Social Science Edition) *see* Guizhou Gongye Daxue Xuebao (Shehui Kexue Ban) **7967**
Guizhou Wenshi Congkan/Guizhou Culture and History Collection (CHN ISSN 1000-8705) **4182**
• Guizhou Yiyao/Guizhou Medical Journal (CHN ISSN 1000-744X) **5621**
Gujarat Agricultural University Research Journal (IND ISSN 0250-5193) **117**
Gujarat Chamber of Commerce and Industry. Annual Report (IND) **1404**
Gujarat Chamber of Commerce and Industry. Bulletin (IND) **1404**
Gujarat Industrial Development Corporation. Annual Report (IND) **1887**
Gujarat Labour Gazette (IND ISSN 0017-5501) **1684**
Gujarat Law Reporter (IND ISSN 0017-551X) **4683**
Gujarat Law Times (IND ISSN 0017-5528) **4683**
Gujarat Research Society. Journal (IND) **7859**
Gujarat Revenue Tribunal Law Reporter (IND ISSN 0017-5536) **4683**
Gujarat Samachar (GBR) **3536**
Gujarat State Financial Corporation. Annual Report (IND ISSN 0533-649X) **1927**
Gujarat Times (IND) **3882**
Gujarat Today (IND) **3882**
Gujaratmitra & Gujaratdarpan (IND) **3882**
• Guji Zhengli Yanjiu Xuekan/Journal of Ancient Books Collation and Studies (CHN ISSN 1009-1017) **5011**
• Gujian Yuanlin Jishu/Traditional Chinese Architecture and Gardens (CHN ISSN 1000-7237) **444**
• ➤ Gujizhui Dongwu Xuebao/Vertebrata Palasiatica (CHN ISSN 1000-3118) **945**
Gujrati Mid-Day (IND) **3882**
Guke Dongtai/Journal of Bone & Joint Surgery (CHN) **6061**
Gukjesaenghwal/International Life (PRK) **7239**
Gula Tidend (NOR) **3923**
Gulab (IND) **3882**
Guld, Soelv, Ure *see* AuClock **4564**
➤ De Gulden Passer/Le Compas d'Or (BEL ISSN 0777-5067) **7562**
† Guldnummeret (DNK ISSN 0905-5878) **8960**
Den Gule Serie (DNK ISSN 0902-9125) **2861**
Gulf Air (HKG) **8783**
➤ Gulf and Caribbean Research (USA ISSN 1528-0470) **2805**
Gulf Association of Geological Societies. Transactions (USA ISSN 0533-6562) **2745**
Gulf Atlantic Florida Fishing Magazine *see* G A F F Magazine **8315**
• Gulf Business (UAE) **1115**
• ➤ Gulf Coast (Houston) (USA ISSN 0896-2251) **5303**
Gulf Coast & Texas Boating (USA) **8276**
Gulf Coast Business Review (USA ISSN 1539-9184) **1115**
Gulf Coast Cattleman (USA ISSN 0017-5552) **288**
Gulf Coast Fisherman (USA ISSN 0164-3746) **8316**
Gulf Coast Golfer (USA ISSN 0889-4825) **8234**
Gulf Coast Oil Directory (USA ISSN 0739-3547) **1998**
Gulf Coast PetroProcess Directory (USA) **6771**
Gulf Coast PetroProcess Directory. Buyer's Guide *see* Gulf Coast PetroProcess Directory **6771**
• Gulf Construction (BHR ISSN 1560-0416) **1010**
Gulf Construction & Saudi Arabia Review Directory (GBR ISSN 0266-2736) **1010**
• Gulf Daily News (BHR ISSN 1729-3456) **3799**
Gulf Directory (BHR) **1998**
Gulf Economic Monitor (BHR ISSN 1353-5528) **1115**
Gulf Industry Manufacturing & Trading (BHR ISSN 0965-2809) **1887**
Gulf Islands Driftwood (CAN) **3810**
• Gulf Marketing Review (UAE ISSN 1350-4746) **1818**
Gulf News (UAE) **3966**
• Gulf of Maine Times (CAN) **2613**
• Gulf of Mexico Drilling Report (USA ISSN 1058-5850) **6771**
Gulf of Mexico Field Development Locator (USA) **6771**
• Gulf of Mexico Newsletter (USA ISSN 1058-5885) **6771**
Gulf of Mexico Rig Locator (USA) **6772**
Gulf of Mexico Rig Report (USA) **6772**
• ➤ Gulf of Mexico Science (USA ISSN 1087-688X) **2805**
Gulf Panorama (BHR) **3799**
Gulf Pine Catholic (USA) **7799**
• Gulf Shipper (USA ISSN 1086-1807) **8645**
The Gulf State Marine Directory (USA) **1998**
Gulf States Marine Yellow Pages *see* The Gulf State Marine Directory **1998**
Gulf States Newsletter (GBR ISSN 0953-5411) **7239**
Gulf Stream Magazine (USA ISSN 1540-8477) **5303**
Gulf T V *see* Tilivisyon al-Khalij **2397**

Link to your serials resources and content with ulrichsweb.com

DIRECTORY 2010 GUOWAI YIXUE (WEISHENG JINGJI FENCE) 10345

Gulf Times (QAT) **3912**
Gulf Tourism Directory (BHR) **8717**
• Gulf War Review (USA) **3497**
• Gulf Weekly (BHR ISSN 1478-9817) **5072**
Gulfshore Homebuyer (USA) **7592**
Gulfshore Life (USA ISSN 0745-0079) **5072**
▼ • Gulfstream Tropical Bonsai Journal (USA ISSN 1938-5153) **3735**
Gulhane Medical Journal *see* Gulhane Tip Dergisi **5621**
• ➤ Gulhane Tip Dergisi/Gulhane Medical Journal (TUR ISSN 1302-0471) **5621**
Guliwer (POL) **2191**
• The Gull (USA ISSN 0164-971X) **908**
▼ Gulli le Mag (FRA ISSN 1967-2152) **2191**
Gulliver (ITA ISSN 1122-0627) **8717**
Gulliver's Gazette (USA) **4336**
Gullsmedkunst (NOR ISSN 0046-6603) **4566**
Guma, Elastomery, Przetwortstwo (POL) **3244**
Gumanitarnye Nauki v Sibiri (RUS ISSN 0869-8651) **4454**
• Gumball Poetry (USA) **5423**
Gumbinner Heimatbrief (DEU) **3618**
Gummi, Fasern, Kunststoffe (DEU ISSN 0176-1625) **7824**
Gummibereifung (DEU ISSN 0017-5609) **7824**
Gumpoldskirchner Nachrichten (AUT) **7493**
Le Gun (GBR) **5303**
Gun (TUR) **3962**
Gun & Accessories Mart (GBR ISSN 0956-6600) **4336**
Gun and Game *see* Ase & Era **8304**
Gun Ay (AZE) **3798**
Gun Control *see* Information Plus Reference Series. Gun Control **2655**
Gun Digest (USA ISSN 0072-9043) **4336**
Gun Dog (USA ISSN 0279-5086) **8316**
• Gun Dogs Online.com (USA) **6809**
• Gun Games Magazine (USA ISSN 1083-8333) **8176**
Gun-Knife Show Calendar (USA ISSN 1522-9572) **366**
† Gun List (USA ISSN 0894-8119) **8960**
The Gun Report (USA ISSN 0017-5617) **4336**
Gun Tests (USA ISSN 1042-6450) **8316**
Gun Traders Guide (USA ISSN 0883-4431) **8176**
Gun World (USA ISSN 0017-5641) **8176**
Guncel Hukuk (TUR) **4683**
• ➤ Guncel Pediatri/The Journal of Current Pediatrics (TUR ISSN 1304-9054) **6092**
Gunderson News (USA) **8618**
Gundogsonline.com *see* Gun Dogs Online.com **6809**
Guneydogu Anadolu Projesi Dergisi *see* G A P Dergisi **8042**
Gunma Biological Education Society. Bulletin *see* Gunma Seibutsu **676**
Gunma Daigaku Iryo Gijutsu Tanki Daigakubu Kiyo/Gunma University. College of Medical Care and Technology. Annual Reports *see* Gunma Hokengaku Kiyo **5621**
Gunma Daigaku Kyoikugakubu Kiyo. Shizen Kagaku Hen/Gunma University. Faculty of Education. Science Reports (JPN ISSN 0017-5668) **7859**
Gunma Hokengaku Kiyo/Gunma University School of Health Science. Annals (JPN ISSN 1343-4179) **5621**
Gunma Igaku/Gunma Medical Association. Journal (JPN ISSN 0285-0656) **5621**
Gunma Journal of Liberal Arts and Sciences (JPN ISSN 0367-4061) **4454**
Gunma Kenritsu Shizenshi Hakubutsukan Kenkyu Hokoku *see* Gunma Museum of Natural History. Bulletin **7859**
Gunma Medical Association. Journal *see* Gunma Igaku **5621**
Gunma Museum of Natural History. Bulletin/Gunma Kenritsu Shizenshi Hakubutsukan Kenkyu Hokoku (JPN ISSN 1342-4092) **7859**
Gunma Prefecture. Monthly Report of Meteorology *see* Gunmaken Kisho Geppo **6353**
Gunma Prefecture. News of Agricultural Meteorology Disaster *see* Gunmaken Nogyo Kisho Saigai Sokuho **6353**
Gunma Seibutsu/Gunma Biological Education Society. Bulletin (JPN ISSN 0288-822X) **676**
Gunma University, Faculty of Education. Annual Report: Art, Technology, Health & Physical Education, and Science of Human Living Series (JPN ISSN 0533-6627) **2983**
Gunma University. Faculty of Education. Annual Report: Cultural Science Series (JPN ISSN 0386-4294) **4454**
Gunma University. Faculty of Education. Science Reports *see* Gunma Daigaku Kyoikugakubu Kiyo. Shizen Kagaku Hen **7859**
Gunma University School of Health Science. Annals *see* Gunma Hokengaku Kiyo **5621**
Gunmaken Kisho Geppo/Gunma Prefecture. Monthly Report of Meteorology (JPN ISSN 0916-5088) **6353**
Gunmaken Nogyo Kisho Saigai Sokuho/Gunma Prefecture. News of Agricultural Meteorology Disaster (JPN) **6353**
Gunmaker (USA ISSN 1050-6616) **1887**
Gunn Salute (USA ISSN 0738-4866) **3769**
➤ Gunneria (NOR ISSN 0332-8554) **7859**
• Guns (Year) (USA) **4336**
Guns and Ammo *see* Guns & Ammo **8316**
• Guns & Ammo (USA ISSN 0017-5684) **8316**
Guns & Ammo Action Series (USA ISSN 0883-9468) **8316**
Guns and Ammo Action Series *see* Guns & Ammo Action Series **8316**
Guns & Ammo Annual *see* Annual Guns & Ammo **8303**
Guns & Gear (USA ISSN 1521-0138) **8316**
Guns and Hunting *see* Guns & Hunting **8316**
Guns & Hunting (USA) **8316**
Guns & Weapons *see* Guns & Weapons for Law Enforcement **2654**
Guns and Weapons *see* Guns & Weapons for Law Enforcement **2654**
Guns and Weapons for Law Enforcement *see* Guns & Weapons for Law Enforcement **2654**
• Guns & Weapons for Law Enforcement (USA ISSN 1058-2975) **2654**
Guns Annual *see* Guns Magazine **8176**
Guns Australia (AUS ISSN 0157-1729) **8176**
Guns Illustrated (Year) (USA ISSN 0072-9078) **4336**
• Guns Magazine (USA ISSN 1044-6257) **8176**
Guns of the Old West (USA) **8316**
Guns Review (GBR ISSN 0017-5692) **4336**
• Gunshot (NZL) **8176**
Gunzo (JPN ISSN 1342-5552) **5303**
Guo Ji You Xian Yu Wei Xing *see* Cable & Satellite International **2377**
• ➤ Guo Moruo Xuekan (CHN ISSN 1003-7225) **643**
• Guocheng Gongcheng Xuebao/Chinese Journal of Process Engineering (CHN ISSN 1009-606X) **3244**
• Guofang Jiaotong Gongcheng yu Jishu/Traffic Engineering and Technology for National Defence (CHN ISSN 1672-3953) **8631**
• Guofang Keji/National Defense Science & Technology (CHN ISSN 1671-4547) **6423**
• Guofang Keji Daxue Xuebao/National University of Defense Technology. Journal (CHN ISSN 1001-2486) **6423**
Guohua Jia (CHN ISSN 1005-6912) **492**
• Guoji Bingduxue Zazhi/International Journal of Virology (CHN ISSN 1673-4092) **5913**
• Guoji Bingli Kexue yu Linchuang Zazhi/Journal of International Pathology and Clinical Medicine (CHN ISSN 1673-2588) **5622**
Guoji Chanye Jingji Jishu (CHN) **1567**
• Guoji Chengshi Guihua/Urban Planning International (CHN) **4411**
Guoji Dianzi Shangqing *see* Electronic News for China **3096**
• Guoji Dizhen Dongtai/Recent Developments of World Seismology (CHN ISSN 0253-4975) **2783**
• Guoji Fangzhi Daobao/Melliand - China (CHN ISSN 1007-6867) **8451**
Guoji Faxue/Studies of International Law (CHN ISSN 1007-0532) **4927**
• ➤ Guoji Fuchan Kexue Zazhi/Journal of International Obstetrics and Gynecology (CHN ISSN 1674-1870) **5991**
Guoji Gongchanzhuyi Yundong/The International Communist Movement (CHN ISSN 1001-3202) **7139**
Guoji Gongcheng yu Laowu/International Project Contracting and Labour Service (CHN ISSN 1672-2884) **1684**
• Guoji Guancha/International Review (CHN ISSN 1005-4812) **7239**
➤ Guoji Guangbo Dianshi Jishu/International Broadcasting Technology (CHN ISSN 1002-4530) **2322**
• Guoji Guanxi Xueyuan Xuebao/Journal of University of International Relations (CHN ISSN 1004-3489) **7239**
• Guoji Hangkong/International Aviation (CHN ISSN 1000-4009) **57**
Guoji Huobi Jijin Zuzhi. Jingji Wenti *see* International Monetary Fund. Economic Issues **1571**
• ➤ Guoji Jianyan Yixue Zazhi/International Journal of Laboratory Medicine (CHN ISSN 1673-4130) **5622**
• Guoji Jingji Hezuo/International Economic Cooperation (CHN ISSN 1002-1515) **1596**
• Guoji Jingji Pinglun/International Economic Review (CHN ISSN 1007-0974) **1115**
• Guoji Jingji Qingshi Zhoubao (Online Edition) (TWN) **1116**
Guoji Jingji Wenzhai Ka/International Economics Abstracts on Cards (CHN ISSN 1009-7384) **1489**
• Guoji Jingmao Tansuo/International Economics and Trade Research (CHN ISSN 1002-0594) **1567**
Guoji Jingmao Xiaoxi/International Trade News *see* Xinnongcun Shangbao **1196**
• Guoji Jingrong Cankao Ziliao (TWN ISSN 1017-9690) **1350**
• Guoji Jinrong Yanjiu/Studies of International Finance (CHN ISSN 1001-9758) **1350**
Guoji Laogong Tongxun/International Labor Bulletin (CHN ISSN 1002-7823) **1684**
Guoji Lianyou yu Shihua *see* Hydrocarbon China **6772**
Guoji Luntan/International Forum (CHN ISSN 1008-1755) **7239**
• Guoji Luntan (TWN ISSN 1029-8010) **7239**
• Guoji Maoyi/Intertrade (CHN ISSN 1002-4999) **1567**
• Guoji Maoyi Wenti/International Trade Journal (CHN ISSN 1002-4670) **1567**
Guoji Mazuipin Guanzhiju (Year) Baogao *see* International Narcotics Control Board. Report for (Year) **6850**
Guoji Nisha Yanjiu *see* International Journal of Sediment Research **2710**
Guoji Qiche Gongcheng/Automotive Engineering International (HKG) **8583**
• Guoji Rencai Jiaoliu/International Talent Magazine (CHN ISSN 1001-0114) **3012**
Guoji Shangbao/International Business Monthly (CHN) **1568**
Guoji Shangwu - Duiwai Jingji Maoyi Daxue Xuebao/International Business - Journal of the University of International Business and Economics (CHN) **1568**
Guoji Shehui Kexue Zazhi/International Social Science Journal (CHN ISSN 1002-4913) **7967**
• ➤ Guoji Shengzhi Jiankang / Jihua Shengyu Zazhi/Foreign Medical Sciences (Family Planning) (CHN ISSN 1674-1889) **972**
• Guoji Shichang/International Market (CHN ISSN 1001-5450) **1568**
Guoji Shipin/Global Food Magazine *see* Meishi yu Meijiu **3656**
• Guoji Wenti Yanjiu/International Studies (CHN ISSN 0452-8832) **7239**
Guoji Xinjingguan *see* International New Landscape **3739**
• Guoji Xinwenjie/International Communication Journal (CHN ISSN 1002-5685) **26**
• Guoji Yanke Zazhi/International Journal of Ophthalmology (CHN ISSN 1672-5123) **6043**
• Guoji Yaoxue Yanjiu Zazhi/International Journal of Pharmaceutical Research (CHN ISSN 1674-0440) **6845**
• ➤ Guoji Yixue Fangshexue Zazhi/International Journal of Medical Radiology (CHN ISSN 1674-1897) **6197**
• Guoji Yiyao Weisheng Daobao/International Medicine and Hygiene Guidance News (CHN ISSN 1007-1245) **5622**
Guoji Yuanzineng Jigou Tongbao *see* I A E A Bulletin **3168**
• Guoji Zaozhi/World Pulp and Paper (CHN ISSN 1006-2599) **6733**
Guoji Zhanwang/International Prospect (CHN ISSN 0452-8778) **7239**
Guoji Zhengzhi/International Politics (CHN ISSN 1005-426X) **7239**
Guoji Zhengzhi Kexue (CHN) **7239**
Guoji Zhengzhi Yanjiu (CHN ISSN 1671-4709) **7239**
• Guoji Zhonghua Shenjing Jingshen Yixue Zazhi/International Chinese Neuropsychiatry Medicine Journal (CHN ISSN 1528-2996) **6143**
• ➤ Guoji Zhongliuxue Zazhi/Journal of International Oncology (CHN ISSN 1673-422X) **6020**
• Guoji Zhongyi Zhongyao Zazhi/International Journal of Traditional Chinese Medicine (CHN ISSN 1673-4246) **5622**
Guojia Fazheng Yanjiu/Journal of National Development Studies (TWN) **4683**
➤ Guojia Tushuguan Guankan/National Central Library Bulletin (TWN ISSN 1026-5279) **5011**
Guojia Tushuguan Xuekan/National Library of China. Journal (CHN ISSN 1009-3125) **5011**
Guoli Bingdong Keji Daxue Xuebao (TWN ISSN 1028-5636) **7859**
• Guoli Chengda Lishi Xuebao (TWN ISSN 1683-9749) **4182**
Guoli Taiwan Bowuguan Xuekan/National Taiwan Museum. Journal (TWN) **340**
Guoli Taiwan Daxue Shehui Xuekan *see* National Taiwan University Journal of Sociology **8122**
Guoli Taiwan Daxue. Wenshi Zhexue Bao/Humanitas Taiwanica (TWN ISSN 1015-2687) **4182**
Guoli Zhengzhi Daxue. Bianzheng Yanjiusuo Nianbao/Institute of China Border Area Studies. Bulletin *see* Minzu Xuebao **3551**
Guomin Jiaoyu Xuebao *see* Journal of Research on Elementary Education **2878**
Guomin Jingji Dongxiang Tongji Jibao - Zhonghua Minguo Taiwan Diqu *see* Taiwan, Republic of China. Executive Yuan. Directorate-General of Budget, Accounting & Statistics. Quarterly National Economic Trends, Taiwan Area **1521**
Guomin Jingji Guanli/Management of National Economy (CHN ISSN 1009-1572) **1116**
• Guonong zhi You/Fruit Growers' Friend (CHN ISSN 1671-7759) **117**
• ➤ Guoshu Xuebao/Journal of Fruit Science (CHN ISSN 1009-9980) **3735**
• Guotu Ziyuan Keji Guanli/Scientific and Technological Management of Land and Resources (CHN ISSN 1009-4210) **1749**
Guotu Ziyuan Xinxihua (CHN) **7592**
• Guotu Ziyuan Yaogan/Remote Sensing for Land & Resources (CHN ISSN 1001-070X) **2709**
Guowai Chengshi Guihua/Urban Planning Overseas *see* Guoji Chengshi Guihua **4411**
• Guowai Dianzi Yuanqijian/International Electronic Elements (CHN ISSN 1006-6977) **3100**
Guowai Dizhi/Geology Abroad (CHN) **2745**
Guowai Dizhi Keji/Foreign Geology Science and Technology (CHN ISSN 1003-2959) **2745**
• Guowai Jiancai Keji/Science and Technology of Overseas Building Materials (CHN ISSN 1006-4575) **1010**
Guowai Jiguang/Foreign Lasers (CHN) **7076**
Guowai Keji Ziliao Mulu (Dizhixue)/Foreign Science and Technology Catalogue (Geology) (CHN ISSN 1003-2924) **2720**
† Guowai Keji Ziliao Mulu (Yiyao Weisheng)/Foreign Science and Technology Catalogue (Medical Health) (CHN ISSN 1003-0387) **8960**
Guowai Naihuo Cailiao (CHN ISSN 1000-7563) **6314**
• ➤ Guowai Shehui Kexue/Social Science Abroad (CHN ISSN 1000-4777) **7968**
• Guowai Shehui Kexue Wenzhai (CHN ISSN 1009-3923) **7968**
Guowai Sichou/Foreign Silk (CHN) **8451**
• Guowai Suliao/World Plastics (CHN ISSN 1002-5219) **7092**
• Guowai Wenxue (CHN ISSN 1002-5014) **5303**
Guowai Yaoxue (Hechengyao Shenghuayao Zhiji Fence) *see* Shijie Linchuang Yaowu **6880**
Guowai Yixue (Bingduxue Fence)/Foreign Medical Sciences (Virology) *see* Guoji Bingduxue Zazhi **5913**
Guowai Yixue (Chuangshang yu Waike Jiben Wenti Fence) *see* Guowai Yixue (Gukexue Fence) **6061**
• Guowai Yixue (Er Bi Yanhou Kexue Fence)/Foreign Medical Sciences (Otolaryngology) (CHN ISSN 1001-1102) **6080**
• Guowai Yixue (Erkexue Fence)/Foreign Medical Sciences (Pediatrics) (CHN ISSN 1001-3512) **6092**
• Guowai Yixue (Fangshe Yixue Heyixue Fence)/Foreign Medical Sciences (Radiology & Nuclear Medicine) (CHN ISSN 1001-098X) **6197**
Guowai Yixue (Fenzi Shengwuxue Fence) *see* Yixue Fenzi Shengwuxue Zazhi **898**
• Guowai Yixue (Fu-you Baojian Fence)/Foreign Medical Sciences (Women & Children Health Care) (CHN ISSN 1008-2514) **5991**
Guowai Yixue (Fuchan Kexue Fence)/Foreign Medical Sciences (Gynecology & Obstetrics) *see* Guoji Fuchan Kexue Zazhi **5991**
• Guowai Yixue (Gukexue Fence)/Foreign Medical Sciences (Orthopaedics) (CHN ISSN 1009-9255) **6061**
• Guowai Yixue (Hulixue Fence)/Foreign Medical Sciences (Nursing) (CHN ISSN 1001-1099) **5959**
• ➤ Guowai Yixue (Huxi Xitong Fence)/Foreign Medical Sciences (Respiratory Systems) (CHN ISSN 1001-1064) **6214**
• Guowai Yixue (Jingshenbingxue Fence)/Foreign Medical Sciences (Psychiatry) (CHN ISSN 1001-120X) **6143**
• Guowai Yixue (Jishengbing Fence)/Foreign Medical Sciences (Parasitosis) (CHN ISSN 1001-1072) **886**
• Guowai Yixue (Kouqiang Yixue Fence)/Foreign Medical Science (Stomatology) (CHN ISSN 1001-1188) **5925**
• Guowai Yixue (Laonan Yixue Fence)/Foreign Medical Sciences (Gerontology) (CHN ISSN 1003-2665) **4047**
Guowai Yixue (Linchuang Fangshexue Fence)/Foreign Medical Sciences (Clinical Radiology) *see* Guoji Yixue Fangshexue Zazhi **6197**
Guowai Yixue (Linchuang Shengwu Huaxue yu Jianyan Fence)/Foreign Medical Sciences (Clinic Biochemistry and Medical Test) *see* Guoji Jianyan Yixue Zazhi **5622**
• Guowai Yixue (Liuxingbingxue Chuanranbingxue Fence)/Foreign Medical Sciences (Epidemiology Lemology) (CHN ISSN 1000-4351) **5814**
• Guowai Yixue (Mazuixue yu Fusu Fence)/Foreign Medical Science (Anesthesiology & Resuscitation) (CHN ISSN 1001-1005) **5771**
• Guowai Yixue (Mianyixue Fence)/Foreign Medical Sciences (Immunology) (CHN ISSN 1001-103X) **5758**
• Guowai Yixue (Miniao Xitong Fence)/Foreign Medical Sciences (Urologic System) (CHN ISSN 1001-4594) **6268**
• Guowai Yixue (Naoxieguan Jibing)/Foreign Medical Sciences (Cerebrovascular Diseases) (CHN ISSN 1004-6690) **6143**
• Guowai Yixue (Neifenmixue Fence)/Foreign Medical Sciences (Endocrinology) (CHN ISSN 1003-5435) **5893**
• Guowai Yixue (Neikexue Fence)/Foreign Medical Sciences (Internal Medicine) (CHN ISSN 1004-2369) **5945**
• Guowai Yixue (Pifubingxue Fence)/Foreign Medical Sciences (Dermatoses) (CHN ISSN 1001-3504) **5877**
• Guowai Yixue (Shehui Yixue Fence)/Foreign Medical Sciences (Social Medicine) (CHN ISSN 1001-1234) **5622**
Guowai Yixue (Shengli Bingli Kexue yu Linchuang Fence)/Foreign Medical Sciences (Phisiology, Pathology & Clinic) *see* Guoji Bingli Kexue yu Linchuang Zazhi **5622**
• Guowai Yixue (Shengwu Yixue Gongcheng Fence)/Foreign Medical Sciences (Biomedical Engineering) (CHN ISSN 1001-1110) **748**
• Guowai Yixue (Shenjingbingxue Shenjing Waikexue Fence)/Foreign Medicine (Neurology, Neurosurgery) (CHN ISSN 1001-1056) **6143**
• Guowai Yixue (Shuxue yu Xueyexue Fence)/Foreign Medical Sciences (Blood Transfusion and Hematology) (CHN ISSN 1001-1013) **5936**
• Guowai Yixue (Waikexue Fence)/Foreign Medical Sciences (Surgery) (CHN ISSN 1000-6877) **6244**
• Guowai Yixue (Weisheng Jingji Fence)/Foreign Medical Sciences (Sanitation Economics) (CHN ISSN 1001-1137) **7520**

Title

▼ *new title* † *ceased* • *electronic media* ➤ *refereed*

10346 GUOWAI YIXUE (WEISHENGWUXUE FENCE) ULRICH'S PERIODICALS

• Guowai Yixue (Weishengwuxue Fence)/Foreign Medical Sciences (Microbiology) (CHN ISSN 1001-1129) **886**
• Guowai Yixue (Weishengxue Fence)/Foreign Medical Sciences (Hygienics) (CHN ISSN 1001-1226) **6987**
• Guowai Yixue (Wuli Yixue yu Kangfuxue Fence)/Foreign Medical Sciences (Physical Medicine & Rehabilitation) (CHN ISSN 1001-117X) **6109**
• Guowai Yixue (Xiaohuaxi Jibing Fence)/Foreign Medical Sciences (Digestive System Diseases) (CHN ISSN 1001-1153) **5925**
• Guowai Yixue (Xinxueguan Jibing Fence)/Foreign Medical Sciences (Cardioangiopathy) (CHN ISSN 1001-0998) **5787**
• Guowai Yixue (Yankexue Fence)/Foreign Medical Sciences (Ophthalmology) (CHN ISSN 1001-1196) **6043**
Guowai Yixue (Yaoxue Fence)/Foreign Medical Sciences (Pharmacy) *see* Guoji Yaoxue Yanjiu Zazhi **6845**
• Guowai Yixue (Yichuanxue Fence)/Foreign Medical Sciences (Genetics) (CHN ISSN 1001-1048) **871**
• Guowai Yixue (Yixue Dili Fence)/Foreign Medical Sciences (Medical Geography) (CHN ISSN 1001-8883) **5622**
• Guowai Yixue (Yufang, Zhenduan, Zhiliao Yong Shengwu Zhipin Fence)/Foreign Medical Sciences (Prevention, Diagnosis & Biologicals for Medical Treatment) (CHN ISSN 1000-6591) **5622**
Guowai Yixue (Zhongliuxue Fence)/Foreign Medical Sciences (Cancer) *see* Guoji Zhongliuxue Zazhi **6020**
• Guowai Yixue Qingbao/Foreign Medical Information (CHN ISSN 1003-0395) **5622**
Guowai Yiyao (Hechengyao, Shenghuayao, Zhiji Fence) *see* Shijie Linchuang Yaowu **6880**
• Guowai Yiyao (Kangshengsu Fence)/World Notes on Antibiotics (CHN ISSN 1001-8751) **6845**
• Guowai Yiyao (Zhiwuyao Fence)/Foreign Medicines (Plant Medicine) (CHN ISSN 1001-6856) **6845**
Guowai Youqi Kantan (CHN ISSN 1001-5825) **2745**
• Guowai Youtian Gongcheng/Foreign Oil Field Engineering (CHN ISSN 1002-641X) **6772**
• Guoyi Luntan/Forum on Traditional Chinese Medicine (CHN ISSN 1002-1078) **6845**
Guoyu Qingshaonan/Mandarin Teenager Monthly (TWN) **5124**
Guoyu Youer/Mandarin Children Monthly (TWN) **5124**
Guoyu Zhoukan/Mandarin Weekly (TWN) **5124**
Guraindingu Akademi Tekisuto/Textbook for Grinding Academy (JPN) **3378**
Gurbe-Rige (NLD ISSN 1875-3302) **5303**
• The Gurdjieff Journal (USA ISSN 1948-0873) **6922**
Gure Artea (ESP) **535**
Gurin Pawa/Green Power (JPN ISSN 0389-0988) **3692**
Gurklisten (SWE ISSN 0281-7411) **8618**
• Gurl (USA) **8866**
Gurmat Sagar (IND) **7707**
Gurobaru Akitekucha *see* G A **443**
Guru Ghasidas University Journal of Business *see* G G U Journal of Business **1112**
Guru Nanak Journal of Sociology (IND ISSN 0970-0242) **8105**
Gurukula Kangri Vijnana Patrika Aryabhata (IND) **7859**
Guruvayurappan Institute of Management Journal of Management *see* G I M Journal of Management **1747**
• ➤ Gushengwu Xuebao/Acta Palaeontologica Sinica (CHN ISSN 0001-6616) **6725**
Gushengwuxue Wenzhai/Palaeontological Abstracts (CHN ISSN 1001-4306) **6731**
† Gushi Daguan/Kingdom of the Stories (CHN ISSN 1002-6401) **8960**
Gushi Dawang/King of Story Tellers (CHN) **5303**
Gushi Dawang Huabao/Ace Story - Teller Pictorial (CHN) **2191**
Gushi Jia/Story Teller (CHN ISSN 1002-8633) **5303**
Gushi Lin (CHN ISSN 1002-2554) **5303**
Gushi Shijie (CHN) **5303**
Gushihui/Story Selection (CHN ISSN 0257-0238) **5303**
Gust (ZAF ISSN 1814-2648) **8276**
Gustaf (SWE ISSN 0282-0005) **2191**
Gustav-Adolf-Blatt (DEU ISSN 0017-5730) **7760**
Gustav Freytag Blaetter (DEU) **5303**
Gusto (AUT ISSN 1013-9478) **4359**
Gusto (FRA ISSN 1952-9155) **4387**
• ➤ Gut (GBR ISSN 0017-5749) **5925**
▼ Gut and Liver (KOR ISSN 1976-2283) **5925**
Gut Kochen & Backen *see* Bild der Frau Gut Kochen & Backen **4353**
Gut Kochen & Geniessen *see* Frau im Trend Gute Kueche **4358**
▼ • Gut Microbes (USA) **5926**
Gut Online *see* Gut **5925**
▼ • ➤ Gut Pathogens (GBR ISSN 1757-4749) **5926**
Gut Reaction (IRL ISSN 1649-6019) **5622**
Gute Arbeit (DEU) **3436**
Gute Besserung (DEU) **7646**
Gute Fahrt (DEU ISSN 0017-5765) **8583**
Gute Laune (DEU) **3849**
Gute Nachrichten (AUT ISSN 0017-5781) **3797**
Gute Pillen - Schlechte Pillen (DEU ISSN 1861-6046) **6845**
Gute Zeiten - Schlechte Zeiten *see* G Z S Z Inside **2381**
† Gute Zeiten - Schlechte Zeiten RaetselSpass (DEU) **8960**
Le Gutenberg (CHE ISSN 0017-5811) **4595**
Gutenberg (POL ISSN 1505-8328) **7323**
Gutenberg-Gesellschaft. Kleine Drucke (DEU ISSN 0933-6230) **7323**
Gutenberg - Jahrbuch (DEU ISSN 0072-9094) **7323**
Guter Rat! (DEU ISSN 0017-582X) **4359**
Guter Start (DEU) **2191**
• Guthrie Journal (USA ISSN 0882-696X) **5622**
Guthrie Theater Program (USA) **8471**
Guthrie Theater Program Magazine *see* Guthrie Theater Program **8471**
• ➤ Guti Dianzixue Yanjiu yu Jinzhan/Research & Progress of Solid State Electronics (CHN ISSN 1000-3819) **3100**
• Guti Huojian Jishu/Journal of Solid Rocket Technology (CHN ISSN 1006-2793) **57**
• ➤ Guti Lixue Xuebao (CHN ISSN 0254-7805) **7059**
• The Guttmacher Report on Public Policy (USA ISSN 1096-7699) **972**
Guyana. Auditor General. Report on the Public Accounts (GUY ISSN 0301-7168) **1236**
Guyana. Hydrometeorological Service. Annual Climatological Data Summary (GUY) **6353**
Guyana Information Bulletin (GUY) **7139**
Guyana Library Association. Bulletin (GUY ISSN 1023-3385) **5011**
Guyana. National Insurance Board. Annual Report: Guyana National Insurance Scheme (GUY) **4529**
Guyana Science Teachers' Association. Newsletter (GUY) **7859**
Guyana. Statistical Bureau. Annual Account Relating to External Trade (GUY ISSN 0533-991X) **1236**
Guyana Sugar Corporation. Annual Reports and Accounts (GUY) **234**
Guyana Trade Directory (GBR) **1999**
Guyanese National Bibliography (GUY ISSN 0376-5202) **626**
Guy's, King's and St. Thomas's Gazette *see* G K T Gazette **4093**
Guzarish *see* Gozaresh **3891**
Guzarishha-yi Dawlati-i Iran *see* Iranian Government Reports **7200**
• G'vanim (USA) **7721**
• G'vanim (Riverdale) (USA ISSN 1944-3528) **7721**
GVonline *see* G V Manager **1747**
GW2K: The Gateway Magazine (USA) **2576**
• Gwahag Dong'a/Donga Science (KOR ISSN 1228-3401) **7859**
Gwalior Academy of Mathematical Sciences Journal of Mathematical Biosciences *see* G A M S Journal of Mathematical Biosciences **5489**
Gwang Gong'eob Tong'gye Jo'sa Bo'go'seo. Jiyeog Pyeon/Korea (Republic). National Statistical Office. Report on Mining and Manufacturing Survey. Whole Country (KOR ISSN 1599-1369) **6485**
Gwang'eob. Jejoeob Tong'gye Josa Bo'goseo. Gi'eobche Pyeon/Korea (Republic). National Statistical Office. Report on Mining and Manufacturing Survey. Enterprise (KOR ISSN 1739-9467) **1236**
Gwang'eob. Jejo'eob Tong'gye Josa Bogoseo. San'eobpyeon-jeon'gug/Korea (Republic). National Statistical Office. Report on Mining and Manufacturing Survey. Industry - National Area (KOR ISSN 1739-9475) **1236**
Gwent Family History Society. Journal (GBR ISSN 0262-4672) **3769**
Gwiazda Polarna/North Star (Stevens Point) (USA ISSN 0740-5944) **3536**
Gwinnett Parents (USA) **4359**
• Gwlad (GBR) **288**
Gwynmercian (USA) **2286**
Gyan (IND ISSN 0972-9992) **2861**
Gybe (GBR) **7076**
• Gyeong'gi Jonghab Ji'su/Korea (Republic). National Statistical Office. Composite Indexes of Business Indicators (KOR ISSN 1228-8071) **1236**
† Gyeongje Hwaldong Ingu Wolbo/Korea (Republic). National Statistical Office. Monthly Report on the Economically Active Population Survey (KOR ISSN 1228-8160) **8960**
Gyeongje Hwaldong Ingu Yeonbo/Korea (Republic). National Statistical Office. Annual Report on the Economically Active Population Survey (KOR ISSN 1228-8411) **1236**
Gyeongje Nonjib/Korean Economic Journal (KOR ISSN 1738-1150) **1116**
Gyeongjehag Munheon Yeonbo/Korean Journal of Economic Literature (KOR ISSN 1226-4733) **1116**
Gyeong'yeong Nonjib *see* Korean Business Journal **1771**
Gyermekgyogyaszat (HUN ISSN 0017-5900) **6092**
Gyermekorvos Tovabbkepzes (HUN ISSN 1589-0309) **6092**
Gym et Sport *see* Sport Aktiv **8203**
• Gymnasieskolen (DNK ISSN 0017-5927) **2861**
† • Gymnasiet og HF (DNK ISSN 0901-9308) **8960**
Gymnasium (DEU ISSN 0342-5231) **2235**
Gymnasium Helveticum (CHE ISSN 0017-5951) **2861**
Das Gymnasium in Bayern (DEU) **2861**
Gymnast Magazine (GBR) **8176**
Le Gymnaste (FRA ISSN 1242-1316) **8176**
Gymnastik (Print) *see* Alt om Gymnastik **8157**
Gymnastik Magasinet (SWE ISSN 1401-5269) **8176**
Gymnastikk og Turn (NOR ISSN 0017-596X) **8176**
† Gymnica (ITA) **8960**
The Gympie Times (AUS ISSN 1321-5353) **3794**
Gyn (DEU ISSN 1432-2870) **5991**
Gyn-Depesche (DEU ISSN 1435-5507) **5992**
† ➤ Gyn Obs - La Medecine et la Femme (FRA ISSN 0240-172X) **8960**
➤ Gynaecologia et Perinatologia (HRV ISSN 1330-0091) **5992**
Gynaecologia et Perinatologia. Supplement *see* Gynaecologia et Perinatologia **5992**
Gynaecology Forum (NLD ISSN 1384-5454) **5992**
• ➤ Der Gynaekologe (DEU ISSN 0017-5994) **5992**
Gynaekologie fuer Hausaerzte (CHE ISSN 1420-6811) **5992**
Gynaekologie-Praxis (CHE ISSN 1661-9390) **5992**
Gynaekologie und Geburtshilfe (DEU ISSN 1439-3557) **5992**
• ➤ Gynaekologisch - Geburtshilfliche Rundschau (CHE ISSN 1018-8843) **5992**
• ➤ Gynaekologische Endokrinologie (DEU ISSN 1610-2894) **5992**
Gynaekologische Nachrichten (DEU ISSN 1439-4898) **5992**
Gynaekologische Praxis (DEU ISSN 0341-8677) **5992**
Gynaika/Woman (GRC ISSN 1105-1493) **8866**
Gyne (DEU ISSN 0179-9185) **5992**
• ➤ Gynecologic and Obstetric Investigation (CHE ISSN 0378-7346) **5992**
Gynecologic and Obstetric Surgery *see* Sanfujinka Shujutsu **6004**
• ➤ Gynecologic Oncology (USA ISSN 0090-8258) **5992**
• ➤ Gynecological Endocrinology (GBR ISSN 0951-3590) **5893**
Gynecological Society of Nagano. Bulletin *see* Naganoken Sanka Fujinka Ikaiho **5999**
• ➤ Gynecological Surgery (DEU ISSN 1613-2076) **6244**
• Gynecologie Obstetrique et Fertilite (FRA ISSN 1297-9589) **5992**
Gynecologie - Obstetrique Pratique (FRA ISSN 0988-6990) **5992**
➤ Gynekologia pre Prax (SVK ISSN 1336-3425) **5992**
Gynekologie po Promoci (CZE ISSN 1213-2578) **5992**
➤ Gyobyo Kenkyu/Fish Pathology (JPN ISSN 0388-788X) **945**
Gyogyasz (HUN ISSN 1419-0974) **3876**
Gyogyszereink, O G Y I Kozlemenyek (Orszagos Gyogyszereszeti Intezet) (HUN ISSN 1787-1204) **6845**
• Gyogyszereszet (HUN ISSN 0017-6036) **6845**
Gyomu Nenpo - Aomori-ken Ringo Shikenjo/Aomori Apple Experiment Station. Annual Report (JPN ISSN 0570-4561) **117**
Gyongy (HUN ISSN 1218-3776) **8866**
Gyosei Journal (GBR ISSN 1354-2893) **1116**
Gypsum (USA ISSN 0193-0001) **6464**
Gypsy (USA ISSN 0176-3148) **5303**
Gypsy Lore Society. Newsletter (USA ISSN 1070-4604) **340**
GyroScope (USA ISSN 0279-6694) **2266**
▼ • Gyroscopy and Navigation (RUS ISSN 2075-1087) **2783**
Gyszereink *see* Gyogyszereink, O G Y I Kozlemenyek **6845**
➤ Gyuje Wanhwa/Journal of Regulation Studies (KOR ISSN 1225-7230) **1116**
Gyulai Naplo *see* Bekes Megyei Hirlap **3876**
A H *see* All Hands **6410**
H A A C P & Food Compliance News (Hazard Analysis and Critical Control Point) (USA) **3645**
H A B - Hamburger Avifaunistische Beitraege (DEU ISSN 0340-5168) **908**
H A B M *see* Housing Association. Building and Maintenance **4412**
H A C News (Housing Assistance Council) (USA ISSN 1093-8036) **4411**
H A H R *see* Hispanic American Historical Review **4295**
H A K (Hrvatski Auto-Klub) (HRV ISSN 1331-2596) **8583**
H A L L Newsletter (Houston Area Law Librarians) (USA) **5011**
H A L O Newsletter (Homophile Association of London Ontario) (CAN) **4374**
H A L - P C Magazine (Houston Area League - Personal Computer) (USA) **2576**
H A P P I *see* Household & Personal Products Industry **1819**
H A P P I Cards *see* Handling and Packaging Product Information Cards **6710**
H A R *see* Housing Affordability Report **4435**
H A S *see* Hospital Accreditation Standards **4099**
▼ • H.A.S. Magazine (Hip Artistic Stylish) (USA ISSN 1938-4041) **2256**
H A S W A Newsletter *see* Health & Safety at Work Act Newsletter **6678**
H A W B R *see* Hecate's Australian Women's Book Review (Online) **8898**
H & A *see* Hospital & Agedcare **4099**
H & E (Hausrat und Eisenwaren) (DEU ISSN 0930-6765) **4558**
H & E *see* Health and Efficiency **6987**
H & H N Online *see* Hospital & Health Networks **4099**
H & H N's Most Wired Magazine *see* Health Care's Most Wired Magazine **4114**
H & H Scientific Consultants Handbook *see* H H S C Handbook **3436**
H & M M *see* Hotel and Motel Management **4389**
H & M Magazine (FRA ISSN 1960-2022) **2256**
H & V News (Heating and Ventilating) (GBR) **4119**
H B *see* Health Business **4095**
H B A Options (Home Builders Association) (USA) **1010**
H B Cientifica (BRA ISSN 1414-6142) **5622**
H B I *see* Healthcare Building Ideas **1011**
H B J *see* Houston Business Journal **1489**
H B L J *see* Hastings Communications and Entertainment Law Journal **4685**
H B L J *see* Hastings Business Law Journal **4685**
H B N *see* Great Britain. Department of Health and Social Security. Health Building Notes **4094**
† H B O Journaal (Hoger Beroepsonderwijs) (NLD ISSN 0167-0468) **8960**
H B O's Guide to Movies on Videocassette and Cable TV (Home Box Office) (USA ISSN 1050-8996) **6502**
H B R *see* Harvard Business Review **1117**
H B S A Newsletter (Historical Breechloading Smallarms Association) (GBR ISSN 0262-4915) **366**
H B S Alumni Bulletin *see* Harvard Business School Alumni Bulletin **1117**
H B T L J *see* Houston Business and Tax Law Journal **4688**
H Bomb (USA) **6292**
H C B *see* Healthcare Brief **4097**
H C B International Drum and I B C Guide (Hazardous Cargo Bulletin) (GBR ISSN 1367-9341) **6710**
H C B Tank Guide (Hazardous Cargo Bulletin) (GBR) **8645**
▼ • The H C C A - A I S Medicaid Compliance News (Health Care Compliance Association - Atlantic Information Services) (USA ISSN 1937-6669) **4504**
H C C Magazine (NLD ISSN 1876-1585) **2419**
H C C Nieuwsbrief *see* H C C Magazine **2419**
The H C C Times (Howard Community College) (USA) **2286**
H C E A Association Alert (Healthcare Convention & Exhibitors Association) (USA) **6280**
H C E A Directory (Healthcare Convention & Exhibitors Association) (USA) **6280**
H C E P *see* Handling Corporate Employment Problems **4870**
H C I *see* Hot Compact & Imports **8584**
H C I M A Quarterly Current Awareness Bulletin for Hospitality Management (Hotel and Catering International Management Association) (GBR) **4401**
H C I - R G *see* eMinds **2320**
H C M *see* Human Capital Management **1863**
H C M S *see* Health Care Management Science **4095**
H C M State Institute of Public Administration (IND) **7443**
H C N *see* Home Channel News **1118**
H C N Newsfax *see* Home Channel News NewsFax **1011**
• H C Pro's Advisor to the A N C C Magnet Recognition Program (USA ISSN 1939-5671) **5959**
H C Pro's Advisor to the American Nurses Credentialing Center Magnet Recognition Program *see* H C Pro's Advisor to the A N C C Magnet Recognition Program **5959**
H C R *see* Hudson's Childrenswear Review **2256**
H C S *see* Arizona Journal of Hispanic Cultural Studies **8088**
H D *see* Hospitality Design **4542**
H d A - Dokumente zur Architektur (Haus der Architektur) (AUT ISSN 1027-9725) **444**
▼ • H D D Guide (Hard Disk Drive) (DEU ISSN 1864-3795) **2539**
• H D I Support World (Help Desk Institute) (USA ISSN 1559-3975) **2419**
H D K Magazin (Hochschule der Kuenste Berlin) (DEU ISSN 0947-3882) **492**
• H D M Week (Health Data Management) (USA) **4094**
HD+TV (DEU) **2382**
H D R *see* Housing and Development Reporter **4412**
H D R I 3 D (High Dynamic Range Image) (USA ISSN 1551-689X) **2486**
H D T *see* Newport's Heavy Duty Trucking **8673**
H D T V Etc. (High Definition Television) (USA ISSN 1550-7858) **2382**
H D T V Guide *see* Sound & Vision H D T V Guide **2391**
• H D T V Insider Newsletter (High Definition Television) (USA) **2382**
• H D T V Retailer (USA ISSN 1930-1642) **2382**
H D: The Journal for Healthcare Design & Development (GBR) **4094**
▼ H D Video Pro (High Definition) (USA ISSN 1936-3206) **2401**
▼ H D World (High Definition) (CZE ISSN 1802-8411) **2486**
H E *see* Health Education **6988**
H E A *see* Highway Engineering in Australia **3269**
H E A P Journal (PHL) **7520**

DIRECTORY 2010 H R MEMO (OAK BROOK) 10347

H E C E A S - Aktuelle Debatte (Heidelberger Centrum fuer Euro-Asiatische Studien e.V.) (DEU) **7239**
• ➤ H E C Forum (HealthCare Ethics Committee) (NLD ISSN 0956-2737) **4094**
H E D U *see* Heat Exchanger Design Update **3195**
The H E D U Bulletin (Higher Education Development Unit) (BWA ISSN 1024-8110) **2983**
• H E F S Bulletin (Huggins' Email Form Script) (USA ISSN 1949-2758) **2419**
H E I *see* Home Electronic Ideas **3101**
H E I A Journal *see* Home Economics Institute of Australia. Journal **4360**
H E I M - Hengelo's Educatief Industrie-Museum *see* HEIMvizier **6525**
• H E I News (Higher Education International) (GBR) **2983**
H E J *see* Health Education Journal **7522**
H E L R *see* Harvard Environmental Law Review **4684**
H E P *see* Higher Education Policy **2984**
• H E P Express (Hepatitis) (USA ISSN 1547-6375) **7520**
H E P L *see* Health Economics, Policy and Law **5625**
H E P Libraries Webzine *see* High Energy Physics Libraries Webzine **7066**
H E P Net News Newsletter (High Energy Physics) (USA) **2497**
H E R *see* Higher Education Review **2985**
H E R *see* Harvard Educational Review **2862**
H E R *see* Health Education Research **8044**
H E R *see* Human Ecology Review **8106**
H E R A Annual Report (Heavy Engineering Research Association) (NZL ISSN 1170-3075) **3194**
H E R A News (Heavy Engineering Research Association) (NZL) **3194**
H E R A Report (Heavy Engineering Research Association) (NZL ISSN 0112-1758) **3194**
H E R D *see* Higher Education Research and Development **2985**
▼ ➤ H E R D (Health Environments Research & Design) (USA ISSN 1937-5867) **5622**
† H E R D S A Gold Guide Series (Higher Education Research and Development Society of Australasia) (AUS ISSN 1323-4021) **8960**
† H E R D S A Green Guide Series (Higher Education Research and Development Society of Australasia) (AUS ISSN 0813-524X) **8960**
• H E R D S A News (Higher Education Research and Development Society of Australasia) (AUS ISSN 0157-1826) **2983**
H E R M I S (Hellenic European Research on Mathematics and Informatics Science) (GRC ISSN 1108-7609) **5552**
H E R S Newsletter (Hysterectomy Educational Resources & Services) (USA ISSN 0892-628X) **5992**
• H E S A Newsletter (Health and Safety) (BEL ISSN 1815-3615) **6677**
H E S D A. Briefing Papers (Higher Education Staff Development Agency) (GBR) **2983**
H E T (Home Entertainment Today) (NLD ISSN 1571-0475) **4978**
H E U N I Papers (Helsinki European Institute for Crime Prevention and Control) (FIN ISSN 1236-8245) **4890**
H E - Videotraileren *see* Home-Entertainment + Videotraileren **2382**
H E - Xtra (USA) **6987**
H et M Magazine *see* H & M Magazine **2256**
H F B *see* Home Furnishings Business **4558**
• H F Business Now (Home Furnishings) (USA ISSN 1930-5834) **4558**
H F H *see* Hobby Farm Home **4360**
H f K S *see* Haeften foer Kritiska Studier **5219**
H F M *see* Healthcare Facilities Management **4097**
H F M (GBR) **5218**
H F M *see* H F M Magazine **4094**
• H F M A Career Opportunities (Healthcare Financial Management Association) (USA) **6698**
• H F M A Wants You to Know (Healthcare Financial Management Association) (USA ISSN 1540-0697) **6698**
▼ • H F M A's Patient Friendly Billing (Healthcare Financial Management Association) (USA ISSN 1934-6700) **4094**
• H F M Magazine (Healthcare Financial Management) (USA) **4094**
• H F N (Home Furnishings News) (USA ISSN 1082-0310) **4558**
H F N *see* H F N **4558**
▼ • ➤ H F S P Journal (Human Frontier Science Program) (FRA ISSN 1955-2068) **676**
H F S P Workshop (Human Frontier Science Program) (FRA ISSN 1026-9819) **5622**
H F V Newsletter *see* Haemophilia Foundation, Victoria. Newsletter **5937**
H G K Info (Hrvatska Gospodarska Komora) (HRV) **1404**
H G R G Research Paper Series *see* Historical Geography Research Paper Series **4014**
H.G. Wells Society Newsletter (GBR ISSN 0306-5480) **5303**
H H *see* Heavy Hitters **8583**
H H C *see* Home Health Care Services Quarterly **4098**
H H D *see* Hvor Hender Det? **7240**
H H L A Report (Hamburger Hafen- und Lagerhaus-Aktiengesellschaft) (DEU) **8645**
• H H M I Bulletin (Howard Hughes Medical Institute) (USA) **5622**
H H M M *see* Healthcare Hazard Management Monitor **5626**
H H R *see* Health and Human Rights **7520**
H H S *see* History of the Human Sciences **7969**
H H S C Handbook (GBR ISSN 1368-6747) **3436**
H I A S Statistical Abstract (Hebrew Immigrant Aid Society) (USA ISSN 0271-0684) **7307**
H I A's Nationwide Craft & Hobby Industry Consumer Survey (Year) (Hobby Industry Association) (USA) **4351**
H I C *see* Health Informatics Conference **5830**
H I C L R *see* Hastings International and Comparative Law Review **4927**
H I C S S *see* Annual Hawaii International Conference on System Sciences. Proceedings **2519**
H I D A Manufacturers Directory (Health Industry Distributors Association) (USA ISSN 1045-6058) **5622**
H I L J *see* Health Information and Libraries Journal (Online) **5012**
H I M S S Insider (Healthcare Information and Management Systems Society) (USA) **4094**
• H i N - Alexander von Humboldt im Netz (DEU ISSN 1617-5239) **7859**
H I P *see* Honors in Practice **3064**
H I P A A Compliance Alert (Health Insurance Portability and Accountability Act) (USA ISSN 1941-7764) **4094**
The H I P A A Privacy Reference (Health Insurance Portability and Accountability Act) (USA) **4504**
H I P A A Regulatory Alert (Health Insurance Portability and Accountability Act) (USA ISSN 1542-9830) **4504**
• H I P A A Training Advisor (Health Insurance Portability and Accountability Act) (USA ISSN 1543-7531) **4504**
H I S Voice (Hudebni Informacni Stredisko) (CZE ISSN 1213-2438) **6572**
H I T Products (Health-care Information Technology) (USA ISSN 1559-8292) **5622**
H I V O S Magazine (Humanistisch Instituut voor Ontwikkelingssamenwerking) (NLD ISSN 1383-0759) **1596**
H J H L P *see* Houston Journal of Health Law & Policy **4101**
H J I L *see* Houston Journal of International Law **4688**
H J S *see* Hypermedia Joyce Studies **5307**
• H J V Magasinet (Hjemmevaernskommandoen) (DNK ISSN 1902-3391) **6423**
• H K Ex Cash and Derivatives Markets Quarterly Report (Hong Kong Exchange) (HKG) **1628**
• H K EX Fact Book (Year) (Hong Kong Exchange) (HKG) **1628**
H K Gebaeudetechnik (Heizung Klima) (CHE) **4119**
H K H Perspektiven (Holz und Kunststoffverarbeitende Handwerk) (DEU) **492**
H K Handel *see* H K Handelsbladet **4595**
• H K Handelsbladet (DNK ISSN 1901-9254) **4595**
• H K Information Technology Times *see* Hong Kong Jingji Ribao **1119**
H K J *see* Hong Kong Journal **7140**
H K J S W *see* Hong Kong Journal of Social Work **8045**
• H K Kommunalbladet (Handels- og Kontorfunktionaerernes Forbund) (DNK ISSN 1901-2209) **4595**
H K-Merkur *see* H K Handelsbladet **4595**
H K Money Times *see* Hong Kong Jingji Ribao **1119**
H K P C Electronics Bulletin (Hong Kong Productivity Council) (HKG) **3100**
H K P C Textile and Clothing Bulletin (Hong Kong Productivity Council) (HKG ISSN 1024-4638) **8451**
• H K Staff (HKG ISSN 1012-7887) **1862**
H K T *see* Handelskammartidningen **1404**
H L *see* Hispanic Linguistics **5125**
H L A B C Forum (Health Libraries Association of British Columbia) (CAN ISSN 0826-0125) **5061**
H L A Newsletter *see* Hawaii Library Association Newsletter (Online) **5011**
• H L H, Heizung, Lueftung, Klima, Haustechnik (DEU ISSN 1436-5103) **4119**
H L I Reports (Human Life International) (USA ISSN 0899-2673) **7284**
H L J *see* Hastings Law Journal **4685**
H L K - Heizung - Lueftung - Klimatechnik (AUT ISSN 0171-564X) **4119**
H L L R *see* Harvard Latino Law Review **4685**
H L Q Three Rivers Resource Guide for Holistic Living (USA) **309**
H L R *see* Hospital Litigation Reporter **4100**
H L R *see* The Honey Land Review **5423**
H L R P *see* Harvard Law & Policy Review **4849**
H L S *see* Holy Land Studies **7648**
▼ H L-Senteret. Temahefte (Senter for Studier av Holocaust og Livssynsminoriteter) (NOR ISSN 1504-758X) **4225**
H L V-Informationen *see* Informationen fuer Mitarbeiter und Vereine **8179**
H L W *see* Health Law Week **4686**
H L Z - Zeitschrift der G E W Hamburg (Hamburger Lehrerzeitung) (DEU ISSN 1431-5335) **2861**
H L Z. Zeitschrift der G E W Hessen fuer Erziehung, Bildung, Forschung (Hessische Lehrerzeitung) (DEU ISSN 0935-0489) **3024**
H M *see* Hotel & Accommodation Management **4389**
H M *see* Health Management **4096**
H M (His Magazine) (KEN ISSN 1991-1017) **6292**
H M A A Q News (Hotel Motel & Accommodation Association of Queensland) (AUS ISSN 1329-5780) **4387**
• H M A T (Hot Mix Asphalt Technology) (USA) **8631**
H M D - Praxis der Wirtschaftsinformatik (Handbuch der Modernen Datenverarbeitung) (DEU) **2419**
• H M E Business (USA ISSN 1940-6479) **5622**
• H M E News (Home Medical Equipment) (USA ISSN 1091-3823) **4047**
• H M E Today (Home Medical Equipment) (USA ISSN 1936-2102) **4095**
H M G *see* Human Molecular Genetics **872**
† H M H. Hygiene en Milieu Hospitalier (FRA ISSN 1276-2172) **8960**
• H M i C (Historia Moderna i Contemporania) (ESP ISSN 1696-4403) **4141**
• H M Info Newsletter (Home Modification) (AUS ISSN 1832-2379) **1010**
H M Inspectorate of Probation. Quality & Effectiveness Inspection Reports (GBR) **2654**
H M L T C *see* Homiletic (Online) **7760**
H M M *see* Hotel and Motel Management **4389**
H M M *see* Home Media Magazine **2401**
H M Magazine (Hard Music) (USA) **6572**
H M N Journal *see* Humanistic Mathematics Network Journal (Online Edition) **5491**
H M O *see* A H I P Coverage **4490**
• H M O - P P O Directory (Health Maintenance Organization - Preferred Provider Organization) (USA ISSN 0887-4484) **1999**
H M Q *see* Health Marketing Quarterly **7522**
H M R *see* Holland Management Review **1118**
H M R *see* Housing Market Report **4413**
H M R G *see* Historische Mitteilungen der Ranke-Gesellschaft **4144**
H M S - Magasinet (NOR ISSN 1501-9144) **6677**
H M S O Agency Catalogue (Her Majesty's Stationery Office) (GBR ISSN 1462-477X) **626**
H.M.S.O. in Print *see* Great Britain. H.M.S.O. Books in Print **625**
H M T (Helse Medisin Teknikk) (NOR ISSN 1501-7729) **4095**
H M T *see* Health Management Technology **5830**
• H M Treasury Economic Briefing (Her Majesty) (GBR) **1489**
H M V Choice (GBR ISSN 1467-6923) **6572**
▼ H Magazine (USA) **3977**
H N A Sonntagszeit (Hessische-Niedersaechsische Allgemeine) (DEU) **3849**
• H N - Hospodarske Noviny (CZE ISSN 0862-9587) **1116**
H N I Annual Report *see* H N I Jahresbericht **3194**
• H N I Jahresbericht (Heinz Nixdorf Institut) (DEU ISSN 1619-3679) **3194**
H N I Nachrichten (Heinz Nixdorf Institut) (DEU ISSN 1619-3687) **3194**
H N Magazine (Harvey Nichols) (GBR ISSN 1357-7360) **3866**
H N-Magazine *see* VolZin **7693**
• ➤ H N O (Berlin) (Hals-, Nasen-, Ohren-Heilkunde) (DEU ISSN 0017-6192) **6080**
H N O Aktuell *see* H N O Kompakt **6080**
➤ H N O Informationen (Hals - Nase - Ohren) (DEU ISSN 0344-9319) **6080**
H N O Kompakt (Hals - Nase - Ohren) (DEU) **6080**
H N O - Mitteilungen (Hals Nase Ohren) (DEU ISSN 0939-6381) **6080**
H N O - Nachrichten (Hals Nase Ohren) (DEU ISSN 0177-1000) **6080**
H N Reality (Hospodarske Noviny) (SVK ISSN 1335-8200) **7592**
• H-Net (USA) **4454**
• H-Net Reviews in the Humanities and Social Sciences (USA ISSN 1538-0661) **4454**
H O B - Die Holzbearbeitung (DEU ISSN 0018-3822) **3712**
H.O.M.E. (DEU) **4541**
H O M E Voice (Hoosier Organic Marketing Education) (USA) **234**
H O O P (Hoger Onderwijs en Onderzoekplan) (NLD ISSN 1872-2393) **2983**
H O P Nyusu/Hokkaido Hospital Pharmacists' Newsletter (JPN ISSN 0917-1681) **6845**
• H O P O S Newsletter (USA ISSN 1544-9912) **7859**
H O R E S C A - Informations (Hoteliers Restaurateurs et Cafetiers) (LUX) **4387**
• H O R N Skriftserie (Health Organization Research Program Norway) (NOR ISSN 1503-8068) **4095**
H O V System Notes (High Occupancy Vehicle) (USA) **8497**
H P *see* H P - Accaparlante **4066**
• H P A C Engineering (Heating, Piping, Air Conditioning) (USA ISSN 1527-4055) **4119**
• H P A C Techlit Selector (Online) (Heating Piping Air Conditioning) (USA) **3378**
H P A Resource (American Physical Therapy Association, Health Policy & Administration Section) (USA ISSN 1931-6313) **4095**
H P - Accaparlante (ITA ISSN 1129-6313) **4066**
• H P B (Hepato Pancreato Biliary) (GBR ISSN 1365-182X) **5926**
H P B Surgery *see* H P B **5926**
• ➤ H P B Surgery (USA ISSN 0894-8569) **6244**
H P C *see* Household and Personal Care Today **6989**
H P C A *see* International Symposium on High-Performance Computer Architecture. Proceedings **2467**
H P C World *see* Health & Personal Care World **588**
H P D C *see* International Symposium on High-Performance Distributed Computing. Proceedings **2467**
H P - De Tijd (NLD ISSN 0924-9648) **3914**
H P I *see* High Performance Imports **8584**
H. P. Lovecraft's Magazine of Horror (USA ISSN 1552-8642) **5443**
† The H P Palmtop Paper (Hewlett-Packard) (USA ISSN 1065-6189) **8960**
H P Q *see* History of Philosophy Quarterly **6923**
H P S eWeekly Report *see* H P S Weekly Report (Online) **5814**
• H P S Weekly Report (Online) (Health Protection Scotland) (GBR ISSN 1753-4224) **5814**
H P T (Hrvatska Posta i Telekomunikacije) (HRV ISSN 1330-8661) **2354**
H P Trasporti Club (ITA ISSN 2035-4215) **8631**
H P - U X - Usr (Hewlett-Packard) (USA) **2574**
• H P V News (Human Powered Vehicle) (USA ISSN 0898-6894) **8176**
H P W *see* Health Plan Week **4505**
▼ H q (Headquarters) (USA ISSN 1944-3862) **444**
▼ H Q: Good Design is Good Business (Headquarters) (USA) **1010**
H Q Poetry Magazine (GBR) **5423**
H R *see* Human Resources **1864**
A H R *see* American Historical Review **4129**
H R *see* History of Religions **7647**
H R *see* Human Rights **8045**
H R A *see* Horse Racing Australia Magazine **8292**
H R Advisor: Legal and Practical Guidance *see* H R Advisor: Legal & Practical Guidance **1862**
H R Advisor: Legal & Practical Guidance (Human Resources) (USA ISSN 1088-5935) **1862**
H R B R *see* Human Resources Business Review **1864**
H R Banker (Austin) (Human Resources) (USA ISSN 1553-8192) **1862**
• H R Banker (Middletown) (Human Resources) (USA) **1350**
H R Bible *see* What to Do about Personnel Problems in (State) **1877**
• H R C D: General Schedule Position Classification and Federal Wage System Job Grading Standards (Human Resources Compact Disk) (USA) **1684**
H R C Imprint Series *see* Harry Ransom Humanities Research Center. Imprint Series **5303**
H R C Monthly Report *see* South African Human Rights Commission. Monthly Report **7215**
• H R C News (Health Research Council of New Zealand) (NZL ISSN 1178-9565) **7520**
H R C System *see* Healthcare Risk Control System **4098**
• H R D Alert (Human Resource Development) (AUS) **1862**
H R D I *see* Human Resource Development International **1863**
• H R Department Benchmarks and Analysis (Human Resources) (USA ISSN 1540-2711) **1862**
• H R Expert (USA ISSN 1546-9832) **1862**
H R F *see* HRfocus **1863**
• H R Florida Review Magazine (Human Resources) (USA) **1862**
H R H *see* Human Resources for Health **5631**
H R Hero's Hiring & Firing (Human Resources) (USA ISSN 1554-0936) **1862**
H R Hero's Hiring & Firing *see* H R Hero's Hiring & Firing 2d **1862**
▼ H R Highway (ZAF ISSN 1993-789X) **1862**
• H R I - Buyers Guide (E-mail) (Hotels, Restaurants, Institutions) (USA) **3645**
† • H R I - Buyers Guide (Print) (Hotels, Restaurants, Institutions) (USA) **8961**
H R I S Q *see* Hampton Roads International Security Quarterly **7239**
H R I T *see* H R Insight (Brentwood) **1862**
H R Insight (Brentwood) (Human Resources) (USA ISSN 1548-4211) **1862**
• H R Insight (Brighton) (Human Resources) (GBR ISSN 1755-8360) **1862**
H R J *see* Hispanic Research Journal **5305**
H R L R *see* Columbia Human Rights Law Review **4645**
H R Leader *see* Human Resources Leader **1865**
H R M (Human Resources Management) (CZE ISSN 1801-4690) **1862**
H R M I D *see* Human Resource Management International Digest **1864**
H R M J *see* Human Resource Management Journal **1864**
H R M Select (Human Resource Management) (NLD ISSN 0923-1420) **1862**
H R Magazine *see* Human Resources **1864**
• H R Magazine (Human Resources) (USA ISSN 1047-3149) **1862**
H R Magazine (Dutch Edition) *see* H R Magazine (French Edition) **1862**
H R Magazine (French Edition) (BEL ISSN 1781-4456) **1862**
H R Management (Human Resource) (NLD ISSN 1567-2786) **1684**
H R Manager's Legal Reporter *see* Human Resource Manager's Legal Reporter **1685**
• H R Memo (Indianapolis) (Human Resources) (USA) **1862**
• H R Memo (Oak Brook) (Human Resources) (USA) **1116**

Title

▼ *new title* † *ceased* • *electronic media* ➤ *refereed*

Hadorom (USA ISSN 0017-6532) **7721**
➤ Hadronic Journal (USA ISSN 0162-5519) **7014**
➤ Hadronic Journal. Supplement (USA ISSN 0882-5394) **7014**
Had'shot Ha-Shomronim *see* A.B. - The Samaritan News **3514**
† Had'shot Pensia Uvittu'ah Sotsiali (ISR) **8961**
Had'shot Sappanut Uteufa - Yidi'on *see* Hadshot Sappanut Uteufah - Yidion **8645**
Hadshot Sappanut Uteufah - Yidion (ISR ISSN 0334-715X) **8645**
Hadtortenelmi Kozlemenyek (HUN ISSN 0017-6540) **6423**
• ➤ Haecceity Papers (GBR ISSN 1832-8229) **444**
Haefft Timer (DEU) **2192**
Haefftmaeg (DEU) **2192**
Haeften foer Kritiska Studier (SWE ISSN 0345-4789) **5219**
Haelge (SWE ISSN 1650-0946) **2192**
Haelsa (SWE ISSN 0345-4797) **6659**
Haelsahoegskolan i Joenkoeping. Avdelingen foer Rehabilitering. Forskningsrapport (SWE ISSN 1650-3732) **6109**
Haelsinge Kuriren (SWE) **3955**
Haelsingerunor (SWE ISSN 0440-0585) **4225**
Haelsinglands Tidning (SWE ISSN 1104-9111) **3955**
Haelsohoegskolan i Joenkoeping. Rapportserie (SWE ISSN 1653-1558) **8043**
• Haema (GRC ISSN 1108-2682) **5936**
Haemato-Onkologische Nachrichten (DEU) **5936**
• Haematologica (ESP ISSN 1138-0381) **5936**
• ➤ Haematologica (ITA ISSN 0390-6078) **5936**
Haematologica Reports *see* Haematology Meeting Reports **5937**
Haematologie und Bluttransfusion *see* Haematology and Blood Transfusion **5937**
Haematology *see* C P D Journal in Haematology **5935**
Haematology and Blood Transfusion/Haematologie und Bluttransfusion (USA ISSN 0171-7111) **5937**
• Haematology Meeting Reports (ITA ISSN 1970-7339) **5937**
• ➤ Haemophilia (GBR ISSN 1351-8216) **5937**
• Haemophilia Foundation, Victoria. Newsletter (AUS) **5937**
• ➤ Haemophilia Online (GBR ISSN 1365-2516) **5937**
• Haemophilia. Supplement (GBR ISSN 1355-0691) **5937**
• ➤ Haemostaseologie (DEU ISSN 0720-9355) **5937**
Haendel-Jahrbuch (DEU ISSN 0440-0615) **6572**
Haent Bild (SWE ISSN 1652-0947) **5072**
Haent Extra (SWE ISSN 0283-7129) **3955**
• Haerbin Gongye Daxue Xuebao (Shehui Kexue Ban)/Harbin Institute of Technology. Journal (Social Sciences Edition) (CHN ISSN 1009-1971) **7968**
• Haerbin Ligong Daxue Xuebao/Harbin University of Science and Technology. Journal (CHN ISSN 1007-2683) **7859**
Ha'erbin Medical Journal *see* Ha'erbin Yiyao **6845**
Haerbin Shangye Daxue Xuebao (Ziran Kexue Ban)/Harbin University of Commerce. Journal (Natural Science Edition) (CHN ISSN 1672-0946) **7859**
Ha'erbin Shangye Daxue Xuebao (Ziran Kexue Ban) *see* Haerbin Shangye Daxue Xuebao (Ziran Kexue Ban) **7859**
• Haerbin Shi-Wei Dangxiao Xuebao/Harbin Committee School of The C C P. Journal (CHN ISSN 1008-8520) **7140**
Haerbin Tiedao Keji/Harebin Railway Science & Technology (CHN ISSN 1674-2451) **8618**
Ha'erbin University of Commerce. Journal (Natural Science Edition) *see* Haerbin Shangye Daxue Xuebao (Ziran Kexue Ban) **7859**
• Ha'erbin Yike Daxue Xuebao/Harbin Medical University. Journal (CHN ISSN 1000-1905) **5622**
• Ha'erbin Yiyao/Ha'erbin Medical Journal (CHN ISSN 1001-8131) **6845**
Haerliga Hund (SWE) **6809**
Haest & Ryttare (SWE ISSN 1653-400X) **8291**
Haesten/Horse (SWE ISSN 0345-486X) **8291**
Haestmagasinet (SWE ISSN 1404-7322) **8291**
Haestsport (SWE ISSN 0280-7777) **8291**
Haeuser (DEU ISSN 0724-6528) **4411**
Haeuser Billiger Bauen (DEU) **1010**
Haeuser Heute (DEU ISSN 1430-7715) **1010**
Haeuser Modernisieren (CHE ISSN 1422-8483) **1010**
Haeusliche Pflege (DEU ISSN 0935-8234) **6268**
Haeyang Jo'sa Yeonbo/Annual Report of Oceanographic Observations (KOR ISSN 1229-8905) **2805**
Haeyang San-eob Yeon-gusobo/Institute of Marine Industry. Journal (KOR ISSN 1226-5101) **3596**
Hafen von Gent. Jahrbuch *see* Haven Gent. Jaarboek **8645**
Hafenbautechnische Gesellschaft. Jahrbuch (USA ISSN 0340-4838) **3268**
Haflinger Aktuell (DEU) **8291**
Haflinger Magazin (DEU ISSN 0945-2117) **8291**
Haflingersport *see* Mensch und Pferd **8294**
† Hafnarposturinn (DNK ISSN 1604-2344) **8961**
Hafnia: Copenhagen Papers in the History of Art (DNK ISSN 0085-1361) **492**
• Hafrannsoknastofnunin. Fjoelrit (ISL ISSN 1015-6119) **3596**
Hafrannsoknir (ISL ISSN 0258-381X) **3596**
• Hafta Sonu (TUR ISSN 1013-6657) **3962**
➤ Hagar (ISR ISSN 1565-3323) **7968**
Hagemi/Encouragement (JPN ISSN 0017-6605) **4078**
Hagerstown Town & Country Almanack *see* J. Gruber's Hagerstown Town and Country Almanack **3120**
Hagerty's (USA) **8583**
• HaGeZe (HRV ISSN 1332-1129) **6572**
➤ Hagiographica (BEL ISSN 1124-1225) **7799**
• Hagskyrslur Islands/Statistics of Iceland (ISL ISSN 0254-4733) **8375**
Hagstroemer Bibliotekets Skriftserie *see* Hagstroemerbibliotekets Skriftserie **5622**
▼ Hagstroemerbibliotekets Skriftserie (SWE ISSN 1654-5354) **5622**
Hagstrom Map and Travel Newsletter (USA) **8717**
• Hagtidindi/Statistical Series (ISL ISSN 0019-1078) **8375**
Hagtoel um Landamak *see* Statistics Across Borders **8990**
Hagtoelur an Landamaera *see* Statistics Across Borders **8990**
The Hague *see* The Hague Chamber of Commerce. Newsletter **1404**
Hague Academy of International Law. Collected Courses *see* Academie de Droit International de la Haye. Recueil des Cours **4916**
The Hague Chamber of Commerce. Newsletter (NLD ISSN 1874-9038) **1404**
Hague Conference on Private International Law. Proceedings *see* Conference de la Haye de Droit International Prive. Actes et Documents **4922**
• The Hague Journal of Diplomacy (NLD ISSN 1871-1901) **7239**
▼ • The Hague Journal on the Rule of Law (GBR ISSN 1876-4045) **4684**
➤ Hague Yearbook of International Law (NLD ISSN 0923-8298) **4927**
Hague-Zagreb Essays *see* Hague-Zagreb-Ghent Essays **4927**
➤ Hague-Zagreb-Ghent Essays (NLD) **4927**
Haguruma/Gear (JPN ISSN 0438-3664) **3378**
Haha Huabao/Haha Pictorial (CHN ISSN 1005-7382) **2192**
Haha Pictorial *see* Haha Huabao **2192**
Hahlo's South African Company Law Through the Cases (ZAF) **4869**
Hahn-Meitner-Institut. Berichte/Hahn-Meitner-Institute. Reports (DEU ISSN 0936-0891) **3168**
Hahn-Meitner-Institute. Reports *see* Hahn-Meitner-Institut. Berichte **3168**
† Al-Hahoma (ISR) **8961**
Hai (IDN) **2192**
Hai-Lights (DEU) **3849**
Hai Shang Culture World *see* Haishang Wentan **8961**
Hai Vi *see* Hivi **8153**
Hai Yan (CHN) **5303**
• Haian Gongcheng/Coastal Engineering (CHN ISSN 1002-3682) **2805**
Haifa Law Review *see* Din Udvarim **4658**
Haifa Time *see* Zman Haifa **3896**
• Haigan (JPN ISSN 0386-9628) **6020**
Haigan no Rinsho/Japanese Journal of Lung Cancer Clinics *see* Mook: Haigan no Rinsho **6028**
Haight Ashbury Literary Journal (USA) **5303**
Haihuyan yu huagong/Sea-lake Salt Industry & Chemical Engineering *see* Yanye yu Huagong **3257**
• Haijun Gongcheng Daxue Xuebao/Naval University of Engineering. Journal (CHN ISSN 1009-3486) **3194**
• Haijun Yuanxiao Jiaoyu/Education of Naval Academies (CHN) **6423**
• Haijun Zongyiyuan Xuebao/People's Liberation Army. Naval General Hospital. Journal (CHN ISSN 1009-3427) **5623**
Haikan Gijutsu/Piping Engineering (JPN ISSN 0385-9894) **3378**
Haikan to Sochi/Piping and Process Equipment (JPN ISSN 0288-2302) **3378**
➤ Haikibutsu Gakkaishi/Waste Management Research (JPN ISSN 0917-0855) **3506**
• Haiku Harvest (USA ISSN 1558-9862) **5423**
Haiku Headlines (USA) **5423**
Haiku Society of America. Member's Anthology (USA ISSN 1544-0974) **5423**
▼ Hail to the Victors (USA ISSN 1942-2717) **8234**
Hainan Daily *see* Hainan Ribao **3824**
• Hainan Daxue Xuebao (Renwen Shehui Kexueban)/Humanities & Social Sciences Journal of Hainan University (CHN) **4454**
• Hainan Daxue Xuebao (Ziran Kexue Ban)/Natural Science Journal of Hainan University (CHN ISSN 1004-1729) **7859**
Hainan Finance *see* Hainan Jinrong **1350**
• Hainan Guangbo Dianshi Daxue Xuebao/Hainan Radio & T V University. Journal (CHN ISSN 1009-9743) **2358**
• Hainan Jinrong/Hainan Finance (CHN ISSN 1003-9031) **1350**
Hainan Jishu Jingji Xinxi (CHN) **1116**
Hainan Medical College. Journal *see* Hainan Yixueyuan Xuebao **5623**
Hainan Medical Journal *see* Hainan Yixue **5623**
Hainan Normal University. Journal (Humanities and Social Sciences) *see* Hainan Shifan Xueyuan Xuebao (Shehui Kexue Ban) **7968**
Hainan Qiaobao/Overseas Chinese News of Hainan (CHN) **3536**
Hainan Radio & T V University. Journal *see* Hainan Guangbo Dianshi Daxue Xuebao **2358**
• Hainan Ribao/Hainan Daily (CHN) **3824**
• Hainan Shifan Xueyuan Xuebao (Shehui Kexue Ban)/Hainan Normal University. Journal (Humanities and Social Sciences) (CHN ISSN 1672-223X) **7968**
Hainan University. Journal (Natural Science Edition) *see* Hainan Daxue Xuebao (Ziran Kexue Ban) **7859**
• Hainan Yixue/Hainan Medical Journal (CHN ISSN 1003-6350) **5623**
• Hainan Yixueyuan Xuebao/Hainan Medical College. Journal (CHN ISSN 1007-1237) **5623**
Hainei yu Haiwai/At Home & Overseas (CHN ISSN 1002-3801) **3824**
Hainyo Shogai Purakutisu (JPN ISSN 0919-5750) **6268**
† Hair + (AUS) **8961**
Hair (GBR ISSN 0143-7968) **588**
Hair & Beauty (GBR ISSN 1360-3701) **588**
Hair & Beauty (JPN) **588**
Hair & Beauty Fashion (ZAF) **588**
Hair and Beauty Magazine *see* Har og Fegurd **588**
Hair Flair *see* HairFlair **588**
Hair Ideas (GBR) **588**
Hair International News (USA ISSN 0887-803X) **588**
The Hair, Makeup & Fashion Styling Career Guide (USA ISSN 1933-3064) **6698**
Hair Now (GBR ISSN 1362-8496) **588**
Hair Plus *see* Hair + **8961**
Hair Style & Beauty (GBR) **588**
Hair Style Forum (HUN) **588**
Hair to Stay (USA) **6292**
Hair und Beauty (DEU ISSN 1614-8347) **5072**
Hairdo Ideas (USA ISSN 1058-0980) **588**
• Hairdressers' Journal International (GBR ISSN 0143-6910) **588**
Hairenik Weekly (USA ISSN 0017-677X) **5219**
HairFlair (GBR ISSN 0954-2787) **588**
Hair's How (USA ISSN 1932-9091) **588**
Hairstyle! (DEU ISSN 1614-8355) **5072**
Hairstyle (USA ISSN 1058-3025) **588**
Hairstyle & Beauty (DNK ISSN 1604-5262) **588**
HairStyle & Beauty (SWE) **588**
† Haishang Wentan/Hai Shang Culture World (CHN ISSN 1005-7536) **8961**
Haiteny, Haisorata, Hairaha (MDG) **5219**
Haiti *see* The P R S Group. Country Reports: Haiti **1507**
Haiti en Marche (USA ISSN 1064-3869) **3536**
Haiti. Institut Haitien de Statistique. Bulletin Trimestriel de Statistique (HTI ISSN 0017-6788) **8375**
Haiti News (USA ISSN 1062-578X) **1597**
• Haiti Observateur (HTI ISSN 1043-3783) **3874**
Haiti Philately (USA) **6895**
Haiti Progres (USA ISSN 1047-1405) **3536**
Haiti. Secretaire d'Etat du Plan. Plan Annuel et Budget de Developpement (HTI) **1542**
Haiwai Xiaoyuan/Overseas Campus (USA ISSN 1072-1053) **7646**
• Haiwai Yingyu/Overseas English (CHN ISSN 1009-5039) **5124**
Haixia/Strait (CHN ISSN 1002-6312) **5303**
• Haixia Daobao/Strait Herald Fujian (CHN) **3824**
• Haixia Dushi Bao/Strait City Daily (CHN) **3824**
• Haixia Keji yu Chanye (CHN ISSN 1006-3013) **1116**
• Haixia Yaoxue/Strait Pharmaceutical Journal (CHN ISSN 1006-3765) **6845**
• Haixia Yufang Yixue Zazhi/Strait Journal of Preventive Medicine (CHN ISSN 1007-2705) **5623**
• Haiyang Dizhi yu Disiji Dizhi/Marine Geology & Quaternary Geology (CHN ISSN 0256-1492) **2745**
• Haiyang Gongcheng/Ocean Engineering (CHN ISSN 1005-9865) **3194**
• Haiyang Huanjing Kexue/Marine Environmental Science (CHN ISSN 1004-1281) **3436**
• Haiyang Huzhao Tongbao/Transactions of Oceanology and Limnology (CHN ISSN 1003-6482) **3596**
• Haiyang Jishu/Ocean Technology (CHN ISSN 1003-2029) **2805**
• Haiyang Kaifa yu Guanli/Ocean Development and Management (CHN ISSN 1005-9857) **2805**
• Haiyang Kexue/Marine Sciences (CHN ISSN 1000-3096) **2805**
Haiyang Kexue Jikan/Studia Marina Sinica (CHN ISSN 0438-380X) **2805**
• Haiyang Kexue Jinzhan/Advances in Marine Science (CHN ISSN 1671-6647) **2805**
Haiyang Shijie/Ocean World (CHN ISSN 1001-5043) **2805**
• Haiyang Shuichan Yanjiu/Marine Fisheries Research (CHN ISSN 1000-7075) **945**
• Haiyang Tongbao/Marine Science Bulletin (CHN ISSN 1001-6392) **2805**
Haiyang Wenzhai/Oceanic Abstracts (CHN ISSN 1001-0157) **2805**
• Haiyang Xinxi/Marine Information (CHN ISSN 1005-1724) **2805**
• ➤ Haiyang Xuebao (CHN ISSN 0253-4193) **2805**
• ➤ Haiyang yu Huzhao/Oceanologia et Limnologia Sinica (CHN ISSN 0029-814X) **2805**
• Haiyang Yubao/Marine Forecasts (CHN ISSN 1003-0239) **2805**
• Haiyang Yuye/Marine Fisheries (CHN ISSN 1004-2490) **3596**
➤ Haizi Tiandi/Children's World (CHN ISSN 1002-4069) **2154**
Hajdu-Bihari Naplo (HUN ISSN 0133-1051) **3876**
Hajj (SAU) **7710**
Hajozasi Szakirodalmi Tajekoztato/Shipping Abstracts (HUN ISSN 0231-1941) **8525**
Hakai Rikigaku Shinpojumu Koen Ronbunshu/Symposium on Fracture and Fracture Mechanics. Proceedings (JPN) **7059**
HakiElimu. Annual Report (TZA ISSN 1821-5017) **3024**
HakiElimu. Working Paper Series (TZA ISSN 1821-5068) **2862**
Hakim Fashion Eyewear Magazine (CAN) **2256**
▼ • Hakimani (KEN ISSN 1995-6339) **8105**
Hakin 9 (POL ISSN 1731-7150) **2513**
• Hakin 9 (USA ISSN 1733-7186) **2513**
Hakin Dziewiec *see* Hakin 9 **2513**
Hakirah (USA ISSN 1532-1290) **3536**
Hakku (FIN ISSN 0017-6796) **6423**
➤ Hakluyt Society (GBR ISSN 0072-9396) **4141**
Hakodate Igakushi/Hokodate Medical Journal (JPN ISSN 0910-0725) **5623**
Hakodate Kaiyo Kishodai. Kaijo Kisho Hokoku/Hakodate Marine Observatory. Marine Meteorological Report (JPN ISSN 0440-1077) **6353**
Hakodate Kaiyo Kishodai. Kaiyo Sokuho/Hakodate Marine Observatory. Oceanographic Observation Report (JPN) **2805**
Hakodate Kaiyo Kishodai. Yoho/Hakodate Marine Observatory. Bulletin (JPN ISSN 0438-4172) **6353**
Hakodate Kogyo Koto Senmon Gakko Kiyo *see* Hakodate Technical College. Research Reports **8423**
Hakodate Marine Observatory. Bulletin *see* Hakodate Kaiyo Kishodai. Yoho **6353**
Hakodate Marine Observatory. Marine Meteorological Report *see* Hakodate Kaiyo Kishodai. Kaijo Kisho Hokoku **6353**
Hakodate Marine Observatory. Oceanographic Observation Report *see* Hakodate Kaiyo Kishodai. Kaiyo Sokuho **2805**
Hakodate Technical College. Research Reports/Hakodate Kogyo Koto Senmon Gakko Kiyo (JPN ISSN 0286-5491) **8423**
Hakomi Forum (USA ISSN 0884-5808) **7359**
Hakoniwa Ryohogaku Kenkyu/Archives of Sandplay Therapy (JPN ISSN 0916-3662) **6143**
Hakubutsukan Dayori/Saito Ho-on Kai Museum of Natural History. News (JPN ISSN 0289-4092) **7860**
Hakubutsukan Kenkyu/Museum Studies (JPN ISSN 0911-9892) **6524**
Hakumaku Denshi Debaisu Nenkan/Thin Film Device (JPN) **3309**
Hakumaku Hyomen Butsuri Semina/Japan Society of Applied Physics. Thin Film and Surface Physics Seminar (JPN) **7014**
Hakusan/Hakusan Nature Conservation Center. News (JPN ISSN 0388-4732) **2613**
Hakusan Nature Conservation Center. Annual Report *see* Ishikawa-ken Hakusan Shizen Hogo Senta Kenkyu Hokoku **2615**
Hakusan Nature Conservation Center. News *see* Hakusan **2613**
Halal Consumer (USA ISSN 1532-351X) **6659**
Halaszat/Fishing (HUN ISSN 0133-1922) **3596**
Halat o Afkar (PAK) **7140**
† ➤ Halbgraue Reihe zur Historischen Fachinformatik. Serie A: Historische Quellenkunden/Half-Gray Series on Historical Information Technology. Series A: Study of Historical Sources (DEU) **8961**
† ➤ Halbgraue Reihe zur Historischen Fachinformatik. Serie B: Softwarebeschreibungen/Half-Gray Series on Historical Information Technology. Series B: Software Descriptions (DEU) **8961**
➤ Halbgraue Reihe zur Historischen Fachinformatik. Serie C: Datenbasen als Editionen/Half-Gray Series on Historical Information Technology. Series C: Databases as Editions (DEU) **4171**
Halbleiter-Materialforschung (DEU ISSN 1610-045X) **3345**
Halden Arbeiderblad (NOR) **3923**
Half-Gray Series on Historical Information Technology. Series A: Study of Historical Sources *see* Halbgraue Reihe zur Historischen Fachinformatik. Serie A: Historische Quellenkunden **8961**
Half-Gray Series on Historical Information Technology. Series B: Software Descriptions *see* Halbgraue Reihe zur Historischen Fachinformatik. Serie B: Softwarebeschreibungen **8961**
Half-Gray Series on Historical Information Technology. Series C: Databases as Editions *see* Halbgraue Reihe zur Historischen Fachinformatik. Serie C: Datenbasen als Editionen **4171**
Half Mask (AUS) **2862**
Half the World *see* Nisf al-Dunya **3836**
▼ • Halftime Magazine (USA ISSN 1939-6171) **6572**
Halfyard Heritage (CAN ISSN 0828-9557) **3769**
Halge *see* Haelge **2192**
Hali (GBR ISSN 0142-0798) **535**
The Hali Annual (Year) (GBR ISSN 1356-7985) **535**
Haliburton County Echo (CAN ISSN 1482-8197) **3810**

Title

10350 HALICARNASSIAN STUDIES ULRICH'S PERIODICALS

Halicarnassian Studies (DNK ISSN 1395-1475) **4182**
Halifax Chamber of Commerce. Business Directory (CAN ISSN 1914-1440) **1404**
Halifax / Equitable Student Book (Year) (GBR) **2956**
Halifax Magazine (USA ISSN 0199-9451) **3977**
Halikhot Sadeh/Institute for Agricultural Research According to the Torah. Bulletin (ISR ISSN 0334-9942) **117**
Haliotis (FRA ISSN 0397-765X) **945**
Halk *see* Hulk **2193**
Hall of Fame News (USA) **8176**
Halland (SWE ISSN 0347-4364) **4225**
Hallands Nyheter (SWE ISSN 1103-9353) **3955**
Halle Year Book (GBR ISSN 0262-7272) **6572**
Hallelujah! (Vancouver) (CAN) **7736**
Hallenser Schriften zur Automatisierungstechnik (DEU ISSN 1616-4679) **2460**
Haller Blatt (AUT) **3797**
Hallesche Beitraege zur Europaeischen Aufklaerung (DEU ISSN 0948-6070) **4225**
Hallesche Diskussionsbeitraege zur Wirtschafts- und Sozialgeographie (DEU ISSN 1618-2111) **4013**
Hallesche Forschungen (DEU ISSN 0949-0086) **4225**
Hallesche Quellenpublikationen und Repertorien (DEU ISSN 1434-0496) **4225**
Hallesche Schriften zur Sprechwissenschaft und Phonetik (DEU ISSN 1437-3890) **5124**
Hallesches Jahrbuch fuer Geowissenschaften. Reihe A: Geographie und Geooekologie (DEU ISSN 1432-3699) **2745**
Hallesches Jahrbuch fuer Geowissenschaften. Reihe B: Geologie, Palaeontologie, Mineralogie (DEU ISSN 1432-3702) **2745**
Hallesches Jahrbuch fuer Geowissenschaften. Reihe B: Geologie, Palaeontologie, Mineralogie. Beiheft *see* Hallesches Jahrbuch fuer Geowissenschaften. Reihe B: Geologie, Palaeontologie, Mineralogie **2745**
Hallingdoelen (NOR) **3923**
Hallinnon Julkaisuja (FIN ISSN 0782-3770) **2983**
Hallinto (FIN ISSN 0355-7448) **7443**
Halliwell's Film Guide (USA ISSN 1552-6992) **6502**
Halliwell's Film, Video and D V D Guide *see* Halliwell's Film Guide **6502**
Hallmark (GBR) **6572**
Hallmark (USA) **3977**
Hallmark Magazine (USA ISSN 1932-4383) **4360**
Hallmark Society Newsletter *see* Preserve **4309**
Hallmarks (USA) **6572**
Hallo Baby (DEU) **2154**
Hallo Sparefroh (AUT) **2192**
Hallo Taxi (DEU ISSN 0949-9288) **8583**
Halloween Celebrations (USA ISSN 1549-5558) **4360**
• ➤ Hallym International Journal of Aging (USA ISSN 1535-6523) **4047**
Hals - Nase - Ohren Informationen *see* H N O Informationen **6080**
Hals - Nase - Ohren Kompakt *see* H N O Kompakt **6080**
Hals Nase Ohren Mitteilungen *see* H N O - Mitteilungen **6080**
Hals Nase Ohren Nachrichten *see* H N O - Nachrichten **6080**
Hals-, Nasen-, Ohren-Heilkunde (Berlin) *see* H N O (Berlin) **6080**
• Halsbury's Laws of Australia (AUS) **4684**
• Halsbury's Laws of England (GBR) **4952**
Halsbury's Laws of England Monthly Review (GBR ISSN 0307-9821) **4952**
Halsbury's Statutes (GBR) **4952**
Halton-Peel KINnections (CAN ISSN 1719-4474) **3769**
Halton-Peel News Letter *see* Halton-Peel KINnections **3769**
De Halve Maen/Journal of Dutch American Colonial History (USA ISSN 0017-6834) **4294**
Halychyna (UKR) **3964**
• Halyts'ki Kontrakty (UKR) **1116**
Ham & High Broadway (GBR ISSN 1366-9192) **3866**
➤ Ham-mizrah He-Hadash/New East (ISR ISSN 0017-7083) **550**
➤ Hamadryad (IND ISSN 0972-205X) **945**
Hamamatsu Seikei Geka Kiyo/Hamamatsu University. Annual of Orthopaedic Surgery (JPN ISSN 0917-365X) **6061**
Hamamatsu University. Annual of Orthopaedic Surgery *see* Hamamatsu Seikei Geka Kiyo **6061**
Hamar Arbeiderblad (NOR) **3923**
Hambai Kakushin (JPN) **7562**
Hambone (USA ISSN 0733-6616) **5303**
Hambros Dealers Directory (Year) (GBR) **1999**
Hambruecker Wochenblatt (DEU) **3849**
† Hamburg African Studies/Etudes Africaines Hambourgeoises (DEU ISSN 0947-4900) **8961**
Hamburg-Bibliographie (DEU ISSN 1430-6344) **626**
Hamburg Fuehrer (DEU) **3849**
Hamburg Geht Aus (DEU) **4387**
Hamburg in Zahlen (DEU ISSN 0017-6877) **7481**
Hamburg - Le Havre Range (NLD) **8645**
Hamburg Nachrichten (DEU) **1749**
Hamburg: Pur (DEU) **3849**
• ➤ Hamburg Review of Social Sciences (DEU ISSN 1862-3921) **7968**
Hamburg State Bureau of Statistics. Facts and Figures *see* Statistisches Landesamt Hamburg. Ein Stadtportraet in Zahlen **7484**
Hamburg Studies in Multiculturalism (NLD ISSN 1571-4934) **7239**
Hamburg Studies on Maritime Affairs (DEU ISSN 1614-2462) **4969**
Hamburger Abendblatt (DEU ISSN 0949-4618) **3849**
Hamburger Aerzteblatt (DEU ISSN 0017-6915) **5623**
Hamburger Beitraege zur Afrika-Kunde (DEU ISSN 0440-1670) **7140**
Hamburger Beitraege zur Archaeologie (DEU ISSN 0341-3152) **396**
Hamburger Beitraege zur Friedensforschung und Sicherheitspolitik (DEU ISSN 0936-0018) **7239**
Hamburger Beitraege zur Geschichte des Oestlichen Europas (DEU ISSN 1435-6910) **4225**
Hamburger Derby-Woche (DEU) **8291**
Hamburger Eyes (USA ISSN 1551-4943) **6969**
Hamburger Gartenfreund (DEU ISSN 0171-7073) **3735**
Hamburger Gesellschaft zur Foerderung des Versicherungswesens. Veroeffentlichungen (DEU ISSN 0947-6067) **4504**
Hamburger Grundeigentum (DEU) **4412**
Hamburger Hafen- und Lagerhaus-Aktiengesellschaft Report *see* H H L A Report **8645**
Hamburger Informationen zur Friedensforschung und Sicherheitspolitik (DEU ISSN 0931-8399) **7239**
Hamburger Jahrbuch fuer Musikwissenschaft (DEU ISSN 0342-8303) **6572**
Hamburger Jahrbuch fuer Wirtschafts- und Gesellschaftspolitik (DEU ISSN 0072-9566) **7860**
Hamburger Kloenschnack (DEU) **3849**
Hamburger Lehrerzeitung Zeitschrift der G E W Hamburg *see* H L Z - Zeitschrift der G E W Hamburg **2861**
Hamburger Morgenpost (DEU) **3849**
Hamburger Notizen (DEU) **7493**
Hamburger Rechtsstudien (DEU ISSN 0072-9590) **4684**
Hamburger Reihe. Reihe A: Rechtswissenschaft (DEU ISSN 0720-4205) **4504**
Hamburger Reihe. Reihe B: Wirtschaftswissenschaft (DEU ISSN 0720-4256) **4504**
Hamburger Reihe. Reihe C: Versicherungs- und Finanzmathematik (DEU ISSN 1439-2240) **4504**
Hamburger Schriften zur Marketingforschung (DEU) **1818**
Hamburger Schriftenreihe zur Schul- und Unterrichtsgeschichte (DEU) **2862**
Hamburger Sport - Mitteilungen (DEU ISSN 0017-6982) **8176**
Hamburger Sport Verein Live *see* H S V Live **8176**
Hamburger Statistische Portraets (DEU ISSN 1433-7991) **7481**
Hamburger Studien zum Europaeischen und Internationalen Recht (DEU ISSN 0945-2435) **4927**
Der Hamburger Tischlermeister (DEU) **1050**
Hamburger Top Info for Visitors (DEU) **8717**
Hamburger Vorschau (DEU ISSN 0017-6990) **1568**
Hamburger Wasserwerke. Fachliche Berichte (DEU ISSN 0722-6462) **8824**
• Hamburger Wirtschaft (DEU ISSN 0935-0594) **1404**
Hamburger Zahnaerzteblatt (DEU ISSN 0933-9299) **5846**
Hamburgische Anstalt fuer Neue Medien. Schriftenreihe (DEU ISSN 0947-4528) **8105**
Hamburgische Geschichts- und Heimatblaetter (DEU ISSN 0931-0185) **4225**
Hamburgische Lebensbilder (DEU) **4225**
Hamburgisches Welt Wirtschafts Archiv Report *see* H W W A - Report **1116**
➤ Hamburgisches Zoologisches Museum und Institut. Mitteilungen (DEU ISSN 0072-9612) **945**
Hamdard Foundation. Report (PAK) **7710**
• Hamdard Islamicus (PAK ISSN 0250-7196) **7710**
• Hamdard Medicus (PAK ISSN 0250-7188) **5623**
Hamdard Naunehal (PAK ISSN 0259-3734) **6659**
Hameen Sanomat (FIN ISSN 0356-2751) **3838**
Hameenmaa (FIN) **4225**
Hames Aircraft Finance *see* Aircraft Finance **8535**
• ➤ Hamevaser (USA ISSN 0017-7040) **7721**
Hamilton Advertiser (GBR ISSN 1353-4351) **3866**
Hamilton Alumni Review (USA ISSN 0017-7067) **2286**
Hamilton Branch (CAN ISSN 1183-7632) **3769**
Hamilton County Genealogical Society. Gazette (USA) **3769**
Hamilton Directory for New Settlers (NZL ISSN 1176-1709) **8105**
▼ • Hamilton Fish Institute News (USA ISSN 1936-6396) **2862**
Hamilton - Halton Homebuilder (CAN ISSN 1910-0604) **1010**
Hamilton Press (NZL ISSN 1170-0491) **3917**
Hamilton This Month (CAN ISSN 0829-1373) **3810**
Hamizrah Hehadash *see* Ham-mizrah He-Hadash **550**
Hamline Journal *see* Water Stone **5397**
• Hamline Journal of Public Law and Policy (USA) **4684**
• Hamline Law Review (USA ISSN 0198-7364) **4684**
Hammaburg (DEU ISSN 0173-0886) **4225**
• Hammer (AUS ISSN 1447-445X) **6525**
• Hammer (SGP) **7140**
† Hammers News Magazine (GBR ISSN 1353-7431) **8961**
Hammersmith, Fulham & Shepherd's Bush Gazette *see* Ealing & Acton Gazette **3864**
Hamodia (Daily Edition) *see* Hamodia (Weekend Edition) **3536**
• Hamodia (Weekend Edition) (USA ISSN 1553-9490) **3536**
Hamodia Magazine *see* Hamodia (Weekend Edition) **3536**
Hamore (FRA ISSN 0046-676X) **3063**
Hamotherapie, Beitrage zur Transfusionsmedizin (DEU) **5937**
Hamotherapie, Beitrage zur Transfusionsmedizin (Baden-Wurttemberg, Hessen Edition) *see* Hamotherapie, Beitrage zur Transfusionsmedizin **5937**
Hamotherapie, Beitrage zur Transfusionsmedizin (Bayern Edition) *see* Hamotherapie, Beitrage zur Transfusionsmedizin **5937**
Hamotherapie, Beitrage zur Transfusionsmedizin (Berlin, Brandenburg Edition) *see* Hamotherapie, Beitrage zur Transfusionsmedizin **5937**
Hamotherapie, Beitrage zur Transfusionsmedizin (Bremen, Niedersachsen, Sachsen-Anhalt, Thuringen Edition) *see* Hamotherapie, Beitrage zur Transfusionsmedizin **5937**
Hamotherapie, Beitrage zur Transfusionsmedizin (Hamburg, Schleswig-Holstein Edition) *see* Hamotherapie, Beitrage zur Transfusionsmedizin **5937**
Hamotherapie, Beitrage zur Transfusionsmedizin (Mecklenburg-Vorpommern Edition) *see* Hamotherapie, Beitrage zur Transfusionsmedizin **5937**
Hamotherapie, Beitrage zur Transfusionsmedizin (Nordrhein-Westfalen, Rheinland-Pfalz, Saarland Edition) *see* Hamotherapie, Beitrage zur Transfusionsmedizin **5937**
Hamotherapie, Beitrage zur Transfusionsmedizin (Sachsen Edition) *see* Hamotherapie, Beitrage zur Transfusionsmedizin **5937**
Hampden Hippocrat (USA) **5623**
Hampden-Sydney Poetry Review (USA ISSN 0190-6135) **5423**
Hampden-Sydney Tiger (USA) **5423**
Hampshire Bird Report (GBR ISSN 0438-4903) **908**
The Hampshire Family Historian (GBR ISSN 0306-6843) **3769**
Hampshire Farmer (GBR ISSN 0017-7121) **117**
Hampshire Field Club and Archaeological Society. Newsletter (GBR) **4225**
Hampshire Field Club and Archaeological Society. Section Newsletters *see* Hampshire Field Club and Archaeological Society. Newsletter **4225**
Hampshire Life (GBR ISSN 1463-1458) **3866**
➤ Hampshire Studies (Year) (GBR) **396**
Hampstead & Highgate Express (GBR ISSN 0961-3323) **3866**
Hampton Family Life (USA) **3977**
• Hampton Roads International Security Quarterly (USA ISSN 1536-9609) **7239**
Hampton Roads Monthly *see* H R Monthly **3977**
Hampton Script (USA) **2286**
The Hampton Sheet (USA) **3977**
Hampton Style *see* Dan's Hampton Style **7588**
HamptonRoads Magazine (USA) **5072**
Hamptons Cottages & Gardens (USA) **3735**
Hamptons Magazine (USA) **3977**
• Hamsun-Nytt (NOR ISSN 0804-5070) **5303**
Hamsun Selskapet. Skriftserie (NOR ISSN 0803-2688) **5303**
HAN-blad (Hogeschool van Arnhem en Nijmegen) (NLD ISSN 1873-0663) **2983**
Han-gug Chugsan Sigpum Hag-hoeji/Korean Society for Food Science of Animal Resources. Journal (KOR ISSN 1225-8563) **3645**
• Han-gug Gugje Gyoryu Jaedan Sosig (KOR ISSN 1225-8091) **550**
• Han-gug Jin-gong Hag-hoeji/Korean Vacuum Society. Journal (KOR ISSN 1225-8822) **7014**
Han-gug Suhag Gyoyug Hag-hoeji. Series B *see* Sunsu Mit Eung-yong Suhag **5540**
Han-gug Yangsig Hag-hoeji/Journal of Aquaculture (KOR ISSN 1226-0193) **3596**
Han' Guk T'onggye Wolbo *see* Han'gug Tong'gye Wolbo **8376**
Han Sheng *see* Echo **3960**
• Han Wei Wushu! Newsletter (USA) **8176**
Hana Arerugi Furontia (JPN ISSN 1346-1966) **5623**
Hana Hou! (USA) **8783**
Hana no Wa/Hiroshima City Park Association. News (JPN ISSN 0388-2845) **792**
Hanaabu/Hoverfly (JPN ISSN 1342-0267) **848**
Hanako (JPN) **2638**
Hanako - West (JPN) **3900**
Hanamaki City Medical Association. News *see* Iho Hanamaki **5632**
• Hanasaari Agenda (FIN ISSN 1795-8830) **7239**
Hanasaari Meny *see* Hanasaari Agenda **7239**
Hanauer Anzeiger (DEU) **3849**
• Hanburyana (GBR ISSN 1749-723X) **792**
Hanby's Texas Rules of Appellate Procedure Annotated (USA ISSN 1091-6628) **4684**
Hancock Heritage (USA) **3769**
• ➤ Hand (New York) (USA ISSN 1558-9447) **6245**
Hand & Nails (DEU ISSN 1615-0694) **594**
Hand and Small Tool Industry *see* Financial Survey. The Hand and Small Tool Industry **1994**
Hand Book on Sugar Statistics (IND) **3670**
• ➤ Hand Clinics (USA ISSN 0749-0712) **6061**
Hand in Hand (CAN) **5959**
Hand in Hand (NLD ISSN 1874-4923) **8043**
Hand Luggage & Leather Goods *see* Key Note Market Report: Hand Luggage & Leather Goods **4973**
H@nd Ouest (FRA ISSN 1774-4865) **8234**
Hand Papermaking (USA ISSN 0887-1418) **6734**
Hand Papermaking Newsletter (USA ISSN 1075-1319) **6734**
• ➤ Hand Surgery (SGP ISSN 0218-8104) **6245**
• ➤ Hand Therapy (GBR ISSN 1758-9983) **6110**
➤ Handai Kagaku Netsugaku Repoto/Osaka University. Research Center for Molecular Thermodynamics. Annual Report (JPN ISSN 0910-6774) **2135**
Handai Nanophotonics (NLD ISSN 1574-0641) **7014**
Handai Nihongo Kenkyu (JPN ISSN 0916-2135) **5124**
Handan Medical College. Journal *see* Handan Yixue Gaodeng Zhuanke Xuexiao Xuebao **8961**
Handan Polytechnic College. Journal *see* Handan Zhiye Jishu Xueyuan Xuebao **2941**
† • Handan Yixue Gaodeng Zhuanke Xuexiao Xuebao/Handan Medical College. Journal (CHN ISSN 1008-3073) **8961**
• Handan Zhiye Jishu Xueyuan Xuebao/Handan Polytechnic College. Journal (CHN ISSN 1009-5462) **2941**
Die Handarbeitsbeilage (DEU) **4081**
Handball (CHE) **8234**
Handball (USA ISSN 0046-6778) **8234**
Handball in Oesterreich (AUT) **8176**
Handball Magazin (DEU ISSN 0178-2983) **8234**
Handball-Report (DEU) **8234**
Der Handball Schiedsrichter (DEU) **8235**
Handballtraining (DEU ISSN 0172-2476) **8235**
Handballwoche (DEU ISSN 0947-8949) **8235**
Handbells (USA ISSN 8756-7407) **6572**
Handboek A D N R *see* Handboek Accord Europeen Relatif au Transport International des Marchandises Dangereuses par voie de Navigation du Rhin **8497**
Handboek Accord Europeen Relatif au Transport International des Marchandises Dangereuses par voie de Navigation du Rhin (NLD ISSN 1872-3969) **8497**
Handboek Arbeidshygiene (NLD ISSN 1874-818X) **6677**
Handboek Arbobesluit (NLD ISSN 1876-293X) **1684**
Handboek Arboregeling (NLD ISSN 1876-3081) **1684**
Handboek Arbowet (NLD ISSN 1574-4949) **1684**
Handboek Auto en Verkeer (NLD) **8717**
Handboek Europa (NLD ISSN 1570-3649) **8717**
Handboek Externe Verslaggeving (NLD ISSN 1574-681X) **1289**
Handboek Fietsen (NLD) **8717**
• Handboek Financiele Verslaggeving. Jaarrekening (NLD ISSN 1871-0204) **1289**
Handboek I C A O (NLD ISSN 1872-3985) **8544**
Handboek I M D G *see* Handboek International Maritime Dangerous Goods **8645**
Handboek International Maritime Dangerous Goods (NLD ISSN 1872-3977) **8645**
Handboek Kamperen (NLD) **8316**
Handboek Muziekdocent (NLD ISSN 1871-7705) **6572**
Handboek Non-Profitorganisaties *see* Handboek Onderwijsinstellingen **2956**
Handboek Non-Profitorganisaties *see* Handboek Woningscorporaties **1423**
Handboek Non-Profitorganisaties *see* Handboek Zorginstellingen **4095**
Handboek Onderwijsinstellingen (NLD ISSN 1876-4703) **2956**
Handboek Personenbelasting (BEL ISSN 1376-6066) **1927**
Handboek Regeling Vervoer over de Spoorweg Gevaarlijke Stoffen / Reglement Concernant le Transport International Ferroviaire des Marchandises Dangereuses (NLD ISSN 1872-3861) **8618**
Handboek Regeling Vervoer over Land van Gevaarlijke Stoffen / Accord Europeen Relatif au Transport International des Marchandises Dangereuses par Route (NLD ISSN 1872-3837) **8671**
Handboek Uitkeringsberekening Wet Werk en Bijstand (NLD ISSN 1871-5729) **7443**
Handboek Uitkeringsberekening WWB *see* Handboek Uitkeringsberekening Wet Werk en Bijstand **7443**
Handboek V L G/A D R *see* Handboek Regeling Vervoer over Land van Gevaarlijke Stoffen / Accord Europeen Relatif au Transport International des Marchandises Dangereuses par Route **8671**
Handboek V S G/R I D *see* Handboek Regeling Vervoer over de Spoorweg Gevaarlijke Stoffen / Reglement Concernant le Transport International Ferroviaire des Marchandises Dangereuses **8618**
• Handboek van de Nederlandse Pers en Publiciteit (NLD ISSN 0440-1875) **626**
Handboek Verre Reizen (NLD) **8717**
Handboek Vervoer Gevaarlijke Stoffen over de Binnenwateren (NLD ISSN 1872-3748) **8497**
Handboek voor Fiscaal Recht (BEL ISSN 0779-1186) **1927**
Handboek Woningscorporaties (NLD ISSN 1876-469X) **1423**
Handboek Zorginstellingen (NLD ISSN 1876-4649) **4095**
▼ Handboekbinden (NLD ISSN 1876-0848) **7562**
Handbok Baenda (ISL ISSN 0251-1940) **117**
Handbok over Finlands Industri och Naeringsliv *see* Kompass Finland **1574**

Title

10352 HANDBUCH LAENDERRISIKEN ULRICH'S PERIODICALS

Handbuch Laenderrisiken (DEU) **1568**
Handbuch Lebensmittelzusatzstoffe (DEU) **3645**
Handbuch Milch (DEU ISSN 0948-9053) **264**
Handbuch Reha- und Vorsorge-Einrichtungen (DEU ISSN 1432-3648) **6061**
➤ Handbuch Translation (DEU) **5124**
Handbuecher zur Sprach- und Kommunikationswissenschaft/Handbooks of Linguistics and Communication Science (DEU ISSN 1861-5090) **5124**
• Handchirurgie - Mikrochirurgie - Plastische Chirurgie (DEU ISSN 0722-1819) **6245**
Handcraft Illustrated (USA ISSN 1072-0529) **535**
Der Handel (DEU ISSN 0017-7229) **1428**
Handel (POL ISSN 1230-9664) **1116**
Handel Heute (CHE) **1818**
Handel im Fokus (DEU) **1428**
Der Handel mit Baumaterial *see* The Trade with Building Materials **1041**
Der Handel mit Chemikalien *see* Chemical Trade **3240**
Der Handel mit Computern *see* Computer Trade **2492**
Der Handel mit Getraenken *see* The Trade with Beverages **611**
Handel Wewnetrzny (POL ISSN 0438-5403) **1428**
Handel Zagraniczny/Foreign Trade (POL ISSN 0017-7245) **1568**
Handel Zagraniczny Produktami Rolno-Spozywczymi (POL ISSN 1234-6292) **199**
Handeln i Sverige (SWE ISSN 1102-917X) **1719**
Handels- og Kontorfunktionaerernes Forbund Kommunalbladet *see* H K Kommunalbladet **4595**
Handels- og Soefartsmuseet paa Kronborg. Aarbog (DNK ISSN 0085-1418) **8645**
• Handels Utredningsinstitut. Forskningsrapport (SWE ISSN 1102-8882) **1818**
• Handels Utredningsinstitut. Working Papers (SWE ISSN 1653-1884) **1428**
Handelsagent (AUT) **1116**
Handelsauskunft (DEU) **1818**
Handelsbestyreren (NOR ISSN 0332-8066) **1749**
Handelsbladet F K (NOR ISSN 1502-9557) **3679**
• Handelsblatt (DEU ISSN 0017-7296) **1428**
De HandelsCourant (NLD ISSN 1875-1776) **1116**
De HandelsCourant (Noord Edition) *see* De HandelsCourant **1116**
De HandelsCourant (Oost Edition) *see* De HandelsCourant **1116**
De HandelsCourant (West Edition) *see* De HandelsCourant **1116**
De HandelsCourant (Zuid Edition) *see* De HandelsCourant **1116**
Handelshoegsskolan vid Goeteborgs Universitet. Ekonomisk-Historiska Institutionen. Meddelanden (SWE ISSN 1403-2864) **1116**
Handelshoehskolen i Koebenhavn. Institut for Afsaetningsoekonomi. Forum for Reklameforskning. Research Paper *see* Handelshoejskolen i Koebenhavn. Institut for Afsaetningsoekonomi. Research Paper **1117**
† Handelshoejskolen i Aarhus. Institut for Erhvervs- og Samfundsbeskrivelse. Skriftserie C (DNK ISSN 0106-4363) **8961**
† Handelshoejskolen i Aarhus. Institut for Finansiering og Kreditvaesen. Kompendium D (DNK ISSN 0105-4058) **8961**
• Handelshoejskolen i Koebenhavn. Aarsberetning (DNK ISSN 0907-2357) **1749**
• Handelshoejskolen i Koebenhavn. Department of Operations Management. Working Paper (DNK ISSN 1398-9480) **1749**
Handelshoejskolen i Koebenhavn. Institut for Afsaetningsoekonomi. Research Paper/Handelshoehskolen i Koebenhavn. Institut for Afsaetningsoekonomi. Forum for Reklameforskning. Research Paper (DNK ISSN 1602-6004) **1117**
Handelshoejskolen i Koebenhavn. Institut for Industrioekonomi og Virksomhedsstrategi. Publikation (DNK ISSN 1396-6723) **1117**
• Handelshoejskolen i Koebenhavn. Institut for Informatik. Working Paper (DNK ISSN 1399-1779) **1749**
Handelshoejskolen i Koebenhavn. Institut for Ledelse, Politik og Filosofi. Working Paper *see* Copenhagen Business School. Department of Management, Politics and Philosophy. Wp **1086**
Handelsjournal (DEU ISSN 0941-0716) **1429**
Handelsjournal. Ausgabe Baden-Wuerttemberg *see* Handelsjournal **1429**
Handelsjournal. Ausgabe Bayern *see* Handelsjournal **1429**
Handelsjournal. Ausgabe Hessen *see* Handelsjournal **1429**
Handelsjournal. Ausgabe Neue Bundeslaender und Berlin *see* Handelsjournal **1429**
Handelsjournal. Ausgabe Norddeutschland *see* Handelsjournal **1429**
Handelsjournal. Ausgabe Rheinland-Pfalz *see* Handelsjournal **1429**
• Handelskammaren (SWE) **1404**
Handelskammartidningen (SWE ISSN 0345-4495) **1404**
Handelskammer Finnland-Schweiz. Bulletin (CHE) **1404**
Handelsmagazin (DEU ISSN 0342-5002) **1819**
† Handelsmagazin B A G (Bundesarbeitsgemeinschaft der Mittel- und Grossbetriebe des Einzelhandels e.V.) (DEU ISSN 1616-1483) **8961**
• Handelsnytt (SWE ISSN 0017-7326) **4595**
Handelspraktijken en Mededinging/Pratique du Commerce et Concurrence (BEL) **4869**
Handelsrechtliche Entscheidungen (AUT) **4869**
Handelsregistertidning *see* Kaupparekisterilehti **6753**
Handelsskole Dansk *see* H S D **5124**
• Handelsskolen (DNK ISSN 0900-4505) **1117**
Handelsvermittlung und Vertrieb Journal *see* H V - Journal **1428**
HandelsZeitung (CHE ISSN 1422-8971) **1117**
Handes Amsorya (AUT ISSN 0017-7377) **5124**
Handfest (DEU) **6698**
Handgunner: Britain's Foremost Firearms Journal (GBR ISSN 0260-8693) **8176**
Handgunner Tactical Annual *see* American Handgunner Tactical Annual **6285**
• Handguns (USA ISSN 1068-2635) **8317**
Handguns (Year) (USA ISSN 1058-3793) **4336**
Handhaving (NLD ISSN 1381-8767) **4412**
De Handhavingskrant (NLD ISSN 1872-5856) **7494**
Handhavingszakboekje (BEL) **3497**
† ➤ Handicap (FRA ISSN 1295-2362) **8961**
Handicap en Beleid *see* W M O Magazine **4070**
Handicap en Beleid. Nieuwsbrief *see* W M O Magazine. Nieuwsbrief **4070**
Handicap Grave (ITA ISSN 1721-4157) **4066**
Handicap Idraet *see* Handicapidraet **4066**
Handicap - Jul (DNK ISSN 1395-4563) **3833**
• Handicap - Nyt (DNK ISSN 0904-8081) **4066**
Handicaphistorisk Tidsskrift (DNK ISSN 1399-4786) **4066**
Handicapidraet (DNK ISSN 0902-5618) **4066**
Handicapped-Kurier (DEU ISSN 1860-5982) **4066**
† • Handicappede, Sindslidende, Aeldre (DNK ISSN 1902-1704) **8961**
• Handicappede, Sindslidende, Aeldre (Online) (DNK) **8043**
Handicappede, Sindslidende, Aeldre (Print) *see* Handicappede, Sindslidende, Aeldre (Online) **8043**
▼ • Handicrafts Through World History (USA ISSN 1552-8952) **535**
Handikids Sport *see* Xsport **8342**
Handiscoop (BEL ISSN 0779-3367) **4066**
Handisport Magazine (FRA ISSN 0753-521X) **8176**
Handledarskap i Aeldre och Handikappomsorg (SWE ISSN 1403-3070) **8043**
Handledarskap i Foerskolan *see* Foerskoletidningen Handledarskap **2857**
Handledarskap i Skolan *see* Grundskoletidningen **2861**
Handledarskap: Tidningen Aeldreomsorg *see* Handledarskap i Aeldre och Handikappomsorg **8043**
Handleren (DNK ISSN 0108-6987) **1117**
Handling (DEU ISSN 0343-8759) **2460**
• Handling a Family Law Matter in Ontario (CAN ISSN 1910-3042) **4911**
Handling and Packaging Product Information Cards (GBR) **6710**
Handling and Storage Solutions (GBR ISSN 1460-7344) **1887**
Handling Child Custody, Abuse, and Adoption Cases (USA) **4911**
Handling Corporate Employment Problems (USA ISSN 1059-0277) **4870**
Handling Federal Tort Claims: Administrative and Judicial Remedies (USA) **4684**
Handling Provincial Offence Cases in Ontario (Year) (CAN ISSN 1719-8283) **4684**
Handloader *see* Rifle's Handloader Ammunition Reloading Journal **8330**
† Handloader's Digest (USA) **8961**
Handlowa (POL ISSN 1425-8242) **1819**
Handlungsbedingungen und Handlungsspielraeume fuer Entwicklungspolitik/Conditions and Scopes of Action in Development Policy (DEU ISSN 0936-3084) **7968**
Handmade (AUS) **6639**
The Handmaiden (USA ISSN 1086-7600) **7704**
Handotai Kenkyu/Semiconductor Research (JPN) **3100**
Handotai Kenkyujo Hokoku/Semiconductor Research Institute. Report (JPN ISSN 0385-7131) **3100**
Handotai Sangyo Shinbun/Semiconductor Industry News (JPN) **3100**
Handotai Shuseki Kairo Gijutsu Shinpojumu Koen Ronbunshu/Symposium on Semiconductors and Integrated Circuits Technology. Proceedings (JPN) **3100**
• Hands On! (Cambridge) (USA ISSN 0743-0221) **2862**
• Hands On Pages (USA) **6502**
HandSchrift (NLD ISSN 1571-4365) **7140**
Handschriften des Altaegyptischen Totenbuches (DEU ISSN 0948-8650) **550**
▼ Handsome (USA ISSN 1935-1674) **5423**
Handvapenguiden (SWE) **8317**
Handwerk Magazin (DEU ISSN 0942-8976) **8423**
Handwerk21 (DEU) **1749**
Handwierk (LUX) **4595**
Handwoven (USA ISSN 0198-8212) **535**
HANDY (USA ISSN 1531-569X) **4438**
Handy Hollis *see* Hollis UK Public Relations Annual **26**
† Handy und Notebook Praxis (DEU) **8961**
Handy - Whitman Index of Public Utility Construction Costs (USA) **1928**
† Handymag (DNK ISSN 1902-9691) **8961**
Hanesydd Cymreig *see* Welsh Historian **4278**
HanfBlatt (DEU) **5072**
Hang Gliding and Paragliding *see* Hang Gliding and Paragliding **8317**
Hang Gliding and Paragliding (USA ISSN 1936-2552) **8317**
• Hang Hai (CHN ISSN 1000-0356) **8645**
• Hangar Happenin's (USA) **57**
• Hanghai Jiaoyu Yanjiu/Maritime Education Research (CHN ISSN 1006-8724) **2862**
• Hanghai Jishu/Marine Technology (CHN ISSN 1006-1738) **8645**
• Hanging Loose (USA ISSN 0440-2316) **5423**
• Hangkong Biaozhunhua yu Zhiliang/Aeronautic Standardization and Quality (CHN ISSN 1003-6660) **57**
• ➤ Hangkong Cailiao Xuebao/Journal of Aeronautical Materials (CHN ISSN 1005-5053) **57**
Hangkong Dang'an/Aeronautics Archives (CHN) **57**
• Hangkong Dongli Xuebao/Journal of Aerospace Power (CHN ISSN 1000-8055) **57**
• Hangkong Fadongji (CHN ISSN 1672-3147) **57**
• Hangkong Hangtian Yiyao/Aerospace Medicine (CHN ISSN 1005-9334) **5623**
• Hangkong Jice Jishu/Aeronautical Metrology and Measurement Technique (CHN ISSN 1002-6061) **57**
• Hangkong Jingmi Zhizao Jishu/Aviation Precision Manufacturing Technology (CHN ISSN 1003-5451) **57**
• Hangkong Junyi/Flight Surgeon (CHN ISSN 1009-5187) **6245**
• Hangkong Kexue Jishu/Aeronautical Science and Technology (CHN ISSN 1007-5453) **57**
Hangkong Moxing/Model Airplane (CHN ISSN 1000-6885) **57**
Hangkong Taikong ji Minhang Xuekan/Journal of Aeronautics Astronautics and Aviation. Series B (TWN ISSN 1990-7729) **57**
Hangkong Weixiu yu Gongcheng/Aviation Maintenance & Engineering (CHN ISSN 1672-0989) **57**
• Hangkong Weiziu yu Gongcheng/Aviation Engineering and Maintenance (CHN) **58**
Hangkong Wenzhai/Aeronautics Abstracts (CHN ISSN 1006-2130) **76**
• Hangkong Xuebao/Acta Aeronautica et Astronautica Sinica (CHN ISSN 1000-6893) **58**
• Hangkong Zhishi/Aerospace Knowledge (CHN ISSN 1000-0119) **58**
• ➤ Hangkong Zhizao Jishu/Aeronautical Manufacturing Technology (CHN ISSN 1671-833X) **58**
† Hangkong Zhoukan/Aviation News Weekly (CHN ISSN 1004-6518) **8961**
Hangkonggang/Airport Journal (CHN ISSN 1006-7310) **8544**
• Hangtian Dianzi Duikang/Aerospace Electronic Warfare (CHN ISSN 1673-2421) **6423**
• Hangtian Fanhui yu Yaogan/Spacecraft Recovery & Remote Sensing (CHN ISSN 1009-8518) **58**
• Hangtian Kongzhi/Aerospace Control (CHN ISSN 1006-3242) **8544**
• Hangtian Yixue yu Yixue Gongcheng/Space Medicine & Medical Engineering (CHN ISSN 1002-0837) **58**
• Hangtianqi Huanjing Gongcheng/Spacecraft Environment Engineering (CHN ISSN 1673-1379) **58**
Han'gug Bu'sig Haghoebo *see* Bu'sig gwa Bangsig **3342**
• Han'gug Dongmul Bunryu Haghoeji/The Korean Journal of Systematic Zoology (KOR ISSN 1018-192X) **945**
Han'gug Dongmul Jawon Gwahag Hoeji/Journal of Animal Science and Technology (KOR ISSN 1598-9429) **288**
• Han'gug Eon'eo Haghoe. Eon'eohag/Linguistic Society of Korea. Journal (KOR ISSN 1225-7494) **5124**
• ➤ Han'gug Eonlon Hagbo/Korean Journal of Journalism and Communication Studies (KOR ISSN 1229-7526) **2322**
• Han'gug Eung'yong Goncung Haghoeji/Korean Journal of Applied Entomology (KOR ISSN 1225-0171) **848**
• ➤ Han'gug Eung'yong Saengmyeong hwa Haghoeji/Korean Society for Applied Biological Chemistry. Journal (KOR ISSN 1738-2203) **234**
Han'gug Gang'gujo Haghoe Nonmunjib/Korean Society of Steel Construction. Journal (KOR ISSN 1226-363X) **1011**
Han'gug Gang'gujo Haghoeji/Korean Society of Steel Construction. Magazine (KOR ISSN 1225-4312) **1011**
• Han'gug Gugje Gyoryu Jaedan. Yeonbo (KOR) **550**
• Han'gug gwa Gug'je Jeong'chi/Korea and World Politics (KOR ISSN 1225-3006) **7239**
Han'gug Gwahagsa Haghoeji/Korean History of Science Society. Journal (KOR ISSN 1229-7895) **4182**
Han'gug Gwanghag Hoeji (KOR ISSN 1225-6285) **7076**
• Han'gug Gyeongje Hagbo/Korean Journal of Economics (KOR ISSN 1738-3234) **1117**
Hangug Gynnhaghoi Ji/Korean Journal of Mycology (KOR ISSN 0253-651X) **792**
➤ Hangug Haeyang Haghoe Ji - Bada/Korean Society of Oceanography. Journal - Sea (KOR ISSN 1226-2978) **2805**
Han'gug Haeyang Haghoeji *see* Ocean Science Journal **2815**
➤ Han'gug Hwan'gyeong Bo'geon Haghoeji/Journal of Environmental Health Sciences (KOR ISSN 1738-4087) **3436**
Han'gug Hwan'gyeong Wisaeng Haghoeji/Korean Journal of Environmental Health Society *see* Han'gug Hwan'gyeong Bo'geon Haghoeji **3436**
• Han'gug Jaeryo Haghoeji/Korean Journal of Materials Research (KOR ISSN 1225-0562) **3345**
• Han'gug Jeongbo Gwahaghoe. Jeongbo Gwahag Hoeji/Korean Institute of Information Scientists and Engineers. Communications (KOR ISSN 1229-6821) **2419**
Han'gug Jujo Gong Haghoeji/Korean Foundrymen's Society. Journal (KOR ISSN 1598-706X) **6314**
• ➤ Han'gug Kitin Kito'san Haghoeji/Journal of Chitin and Chitosan (KOR ISSN 1229-4160) **3244**
Han'gug Mi'saengmul Saengmyeong Gong Haghoeji/Korean Journal of Microbiology and Biotechnology (KOR ISSN 1598-642X) **886**
➤ Han'gug Munheon Jeongbo Haghoeji/Korean Library and Information Science Society. Journal (KOR ISSN 1225-598X) **5011**
Han'gug Sa'sang Sahag/Study of Korean History of Thoughts (KOR ISSN 1226-9441) **4182**
Han'gug Seupoceu Simri Haghoeji/Korean Journal of Sport Psychology (KOR ISSN 1226-685X) **8176**
• ➤ Han'gug Sigpum Yeong'yang Gwahag Hoeji/Korean Society of Food Science and Nutrition. Journal (KOR ISSN 1226-3311) **6659**
Han'gug Simlihag Hoeji. Baldal/Korean Journal of Development Psychology (KOR ISSN 1229-0718) **7359**
Han'gug Simlihag Hoeji. Sahoe mich Seong'gyeog/Korean Journal of Social and Personality Psychology (KOR ISSN 1229-0653) **7359**
Han'gug Simri Haghoeji. Saengmul Mic Saengri/Korean Journal of Biological and Physiological Psychology (KOR ISSN 1226-9875) **7359**
Han'gug Suhag Gyo'yug Haghoeji. Series C *see* Codeung Suhag Gyo'yug **5478**
Han'gug Suhag Gyo'yug Haghoeji. Series D *see* Suhag Gyo'yug Yeon'gu **2916**
Han'gug Suhag Gyo'yug Haghoeji. Series E *see* Suhag Gyo'yug Nonmunjib **2916**
Han'gug Suhag Gyo'yug Haghoeji. Series F *see* Suhag Gyoyug Nonchong - Han'gug Suhag Gyoyug Haghoe **2916**
• Hangug Susan Haghoi Ji/Korean Fisheries Society. Bulletin (KOR ISSN 0374-8111) **3596**
• Han'gug Tong'gye Wolbo/Monthly Statistics of Korea (KOR ISSN 1228-8101) **8376**
• Han'gug Tong'gye Yeon'gam/Korea Statistical Yearbook (KOR ISSN 0075-6873) **7307**
Han'gug ui Sahoe Ji'pyo/Korea (Republic). National Statistical Office. Social Indicators in Korea (KOR ISSN 1599-0907) **7307**
Han'gug Weon'ye Haghoeji/Korean Society for Horticultural Science. Journal *see* Horticulture, Environment and Biotechnology **3737**
• Han'gug Ye'iceu Jeoneol/Yeats Journal of Korea (KOR ISSN 1226-4946) **5303**
Han'gug Yeomsaeg Ga'gong Haghoeji/Journal of the Korean Society of Dyers And Finishers (KOR ISSN 1229-0033) **2243**
Han'gug Yo'eob Haghoe Yoeob/Korean Ceramic Society. Bulletin (KOR) **2042**
• Han'gug yu'a Gyoyug Yeon'gu/Korean Journal of Early Childhood Education (KOR ISSN 1975-7190) **2862**
Han'gug Yujeon Haghoeji *see* Genes and Genomics **867**
Han'gugsa Yeon'gu/Journal of Korean History (KOR ISSN 1226-296X) **4182**
Hanguk Nonghwahakhoechi/Agricultural Chemistry and Biotechnology *see* Han'gug Eung'yong Saengmyeong hwa Haghoeji **234**
➤ Hanguk Sahoehak/Korean Journal of Sociology (KOR ISSN 1225-0120) **8105**
Han'guk Sikp'um Kwahakhoe Chi/Korean Journal of Food Science and Technology (KOR ISSN 0367-6293) **3645**
Hangzhou Daxue Xuebao (Lixue Ban)/Hangzhou University. Journal (Natural Science Edition) *see* Zhejiang Daxue Xuebao (Lixue Ban) **7933**
Hangzhou Daxue Xuebao (Zhexue Shehui Kexue Ban] *see* Zhejiang Daxue Xuebao (Renwen Shehui Kexue Ban) **8018**
Hangzhou Shangxueyuan/Hangzhou University of Commerce. Journal *see* Zhejiang Gongshang Daxue Xuebao **1197**
• Hangzhou Shifan Xueyuan Xuebao (Shehui Kexue Ban)/Hangzhou Teachers College. Journal (Social Science Edition) (CHN ISSN 1000-2146) **7968**
Hangzhou Teachers College. Journal (Social Science Edition) *see* Hangzhou Shifan Xueyuan Xuebao (Shehui Kexue Ban) **7968**
• Hangzhou Zhengbao (CHN ISSN 1674-2540) **7443**
• Hanjie/Welding & Joining (CHN ISSN 1001-1382) **6342**
Hanjie (GBR ISSN 1746-1219) **8176**
• Hanjie Xuebao/China Welding Institution. Transactions (CHN ISSN 0253-360X) **6342**
Hankook Kwanghak Hoeji *see* Han'gug Gwanghag Hoeji **7076**
Hankuk Ch'ulpan Yongam/Korean Publications Yearbook (KOR ISSN 1227-1977) **7562**

DIRECTORY 2010 HARRIS DIRECTORY. CALIFORNIA WHOLESALERS & SERVICE 10353

Hanley-Wood's Tools of the Trade *see* Tools of the Trade **1041**
▼ Hannah Montana (FIN ISSN 1798-0208) **2192**
▼ Hannah Montana (HUN ISSN 2060-1662) **2192**
▼ Hannah Montana (POL) **2192**
▼ Hannah Montana (ROM) **2192**
Hannah Research Institute. Yearbook (GBR ISSN 0960-1252) **264**
Hannema-de Stuers Fundatie. Bulletin *see* Museum de Fundatie. Bulletin **6531**
• Hanneng Cailiao/Energetic Materials (CHN ISSN 1006-9941) **3136**
HannoRad (DEU) **8259**
Hannover-Journal (DEU ISSN 1437-6199) **1429**
Hannover Live (DEU) **3849**
Hannover Vorschau (DEU) **5219**
Der Hannoveraner (DEU ISSN 1433-3457) **8291**
Hannoveraner Reihe (DEU ISSN 0945-9804) **4504**
Hannoversche Allgemeine Zeitung (DEU) **3850**
Hannoversche Berichte zum Qualitaetsmanagement (DEU ISSN 1435-6694) **1887**
Hannoversche Geographische Arbeiten (DEU ISSN 0940-3329) **4013**
Hannoversche Geschichtsblaetter (DEU ISSN 0342-1104) **4225**
Hannoversche Schriften zur Regional- und Lokalgeschichte (DEU ISSN 1439-068X) **4225**
Hannoversche Schuetzenzeitung (DEU) **2266**
Hannoversche Wirtschaftszeitung (DEU) **1489**
• Hanover Post (CAN ISSN 0834-6372) **3811**
Hans Kelsen - Institut. Schriftenreihe (AUT) **4684**
Hans - Pfitzner - Gesellschaft. Mitteilungen (DEU ISSN 0440-2863) **6572**
Hansa (DEU ISSN 0017-7504) **8645**
Hansard (Parliamentary Debates) *see* Parliamentary Debates (Wellington) **7459**
Hansard - House of Commons Official Report *see* Great Britain. House of Commons. Parliamentary Debates **7442**
Hansard - House of Lords Official Report *see* Great Britain. House of Lords. Parliamentary Debates **7139**
Hansard - House of Lords Official Report (CD-ROM Edition) *see* Great Britain. House of Lords. Parliamentary Debates (CD-ROM Edition) **7139**
Hansconian (USA) **6423**
The Hansen Report on Automotive Electronics (USA ISSN 1040-1105) **3194**
Hansenologia Internationalis (BRA ISSN 0100-3283) **5814**
Hanser Automotive (DEU ISSN 1860-5699) **8583**
Hansestadt Luebeck Travemuende Aktuell (DEU) **8717**
• Hanshan Shifan Xueyuan Xuebao/Hanshan Teachers College. Journal (CHN ISSN 1007-6883) **7968**
Hanshan Teachers College. Journal *see* Hanshan Shifan Xueyuan Xuebao **7968**
• Hanshao Jibing Zazhi/Journal of Rare and Uncommon Diseases (CHN ISSN 1009-3257) **5623**
Hanshin Gijutsu Nyusu/Hanshin Technical News (JPN) **3379**
Hanshin Shell Club. Report *see* Kai Nakama **953**
Hanshin Technical News *see* Hanshin Gijutsu Nyusu **3379**
Hanshoku Gijutsu *see* Animal Reproduction Techniques **278**
➤ Hansische Geschichtsblaetter (DEU ISSN 0073-0327) **4225**
Hansische Studien (DEU ISSN 1617-061X) **4225**
Hansoku Kaigi/Top Promotion's (JPN) **26**
Hanson Institute. Annual Report (AUS ISSN 1446-7941) **6020**
Hansten and Horn Managing Clinically Important Drug Interactions *see* Managing Clinically Important Drug Interactions **6860**
Hansten and Horn's Drug Interactions Analysis and Management (USA ISSN 1092-048X) **6845**
Hantkeniana (HUN ISSN 1219-3933) **6725**
Hanxue Yanjiu (TWN ISSN 0254-4466) **4182**
• ➤ Hanyang Medical Reviews (KOR ISSN 1738-429X) **5623**
Hanyu Shangwutong - Zhongji Kouyu Jiaocheng *see* Beida Ban Xin Yidai Duiwai Hanyu Jiaocai. Jichu Jiaocheng Xilie **5098**
• ➤ Hanyu Xuexi/Chinese Language Learning (CHN ISSN 1003-7365) **5124**
Hanzai Shinrigaku Kenkyu/Japanese Journal of Criminal Psychology (JPN ISSN 0017-7547) **7360**
Hanzaigaku Zasshi/Acta Criminologiae et Medicinae Legalis Japonica (JPN ISSN 0302-0029) **2654**
Hanze Magazine (NLD ISSN 1874-1398) **1719**
Hanze Magazine *see* HanzeMag **2862**
† Hanzehogeschool Groningen. Academie van Bouwkunst. Jaarboek (NLD ISSN 1871-4056) **8961**
▼ HanzeMag (NLD ISSN 1876-1909) **2862**
• Hanzi Wenhua/Chinese Character Culture (CHN ISSN 1001-0661) **4454**
• Hao Ertong Huabao/Good Children Pictorial (CHN ISSN 1006-3749) **2192**
Hao Guanjia/Good Housekeeping (CHN ISSN 1009-9999) **4360**
Hao/How *see* Xing Shidai **2263**
Hap Jones Motorcycle Blue Book *see* Motorcycle Blue Book **8263**
Haparandabladet/Haaparannaleh (SWE ISSN 1103-937X) **3955**
† Hapdong Yongam (KOR ISSN 0073-0335) **8961**
Happenings (CAN ISSN 0844-5753) **5011**
Happenings (USA) **8043**
HAPPI *see* Household & Personal Products Industry **1819**
Happiness *see* Jargalan **4361**
Happinez Spirituele Scheurkalender *see* Spirituele Scheurkalender **7409**
Happo Sanso/Wild Flower Lover's Society of Northern Block. Journal (JPN) **3735**
Happy (USA) **5303**
▼ Happy Day (CZE ISSN 1802-8020) **4360**
Happy Day! (DEU) **8866**
Happy Home (NGA ISSN 0331-1457) **8867**
▼ Happy Tails (ZAF ISSN 1996-7438) **6809**
Happy Times (USA) **7760**
Happy Weight Scheurkalender (NLD ISSN 1874-8872) **6659**
Haptics-e (USA ISSN 1545-1143) **2584**
Al Haqq/Droit (EGY) **4684**
Al-Haqq (NGA) **7711**
Al-Haqq - Shari'ah wa-Qanun (UAE) **7711**
Har og Fegurd/Hair and Beauty Magazine (ISL) **588**
Al-Harakah (MYS ISSN 0127-4147) **7140**
Haramata (English Edition) (GBR ISSN 0964-6760) **3436**
Haramata (French Edition) *see* Haramata (English Edition) **3436**
Harambee (KEN) **1423**
Haramsnytt (NOR) **3923**
HarardEx - The Journal *see* HazardEx **3436**
Al-Haras al-Watani/National Guard Magazine (SAU ISSN 1319-2655) **3944**
Haratch (FRA ISSN 0996-133X) **3536**
Harbin Committee School of The C C P. Journal *see* Haerbin Shi-Wei Dangxiao Xuebao **7140**
Harbin Engineering University. Journal *see* Harbin Gongcheng Daxue Xuebao **3194**
• Harbin Gongcheng Daxue Xuebao/Harbin Engineering University. Journal (CHN ISSN 1006-7043) **3194**
• ➤ Harbin Gongye Daxue Xuebao (CHN ISSN 0367-6234) **3194**
• ➤ Harbin Institute of Technology. Journal (CHN ISSN 1005-9113) **8423**
Harbin Institute of Technology. Journal (Social Sciences Edition) *see* Haerbin Gongye Daxue Xuebao (Shehui Kexue Ban) **7968**
• Harbin Jianzhu Daxue Xuebao/Harbin University of Architecture and Engineering. Journal (CHN ISSN 1006-6780) **444**
Harbin Kexue Jishu Daxue Xuebao/Harbin University of Science and Technology. Journal (CHN ISSN 1000-5897) **7860**
Harbin Medical University. Journal *see* Ha'erbin Yike Daxue Xuebao **5622**
• Harbin Shifan Daxue Ziran Kexue Xuebao/Natural Sciences Journal of Harbin University (CHN ISSN 1000-5617) **7860**
Harbin University of Architecture and Engineering. Journal *see* Harbin Jianzhu Daxue Xuebao **444**
Harbin University of Commerce. Journal (Natural Science Edition) *see* Haerbin Shangye Daxue Xuebao (Ziran Kexue Ban) **7859**
Harbin University of Science and Technology. Journal *see* Harbin Kexue Jishu Daxue Xuebao **7860**
Harbin University of Science and Technology. Journal *see* Haerbin Ligong Daxue Xuebao **7859**
Harbinger (Detroit) (USA) **2862**
• Harbinger File (USA ISSN 1073-6824) **3436**
Harbor Branch News (USA) **2805**
Harbor of Literature *see* Wenxue Gang **5397**
Harbor Style (USA ISSN 1938-6303) **5072**
Harbour and Shipping (CAN ISSN 0017-7636) **8645**
• Harbour Authorities Forum/Forum des Administrations Portuaires (CAN ISSN 1203-5564) **8645**
Harbour News *see* Auckland City Harbour News **3916**
• Harburger Anzeigen und Nachrichten (DEU) **3850**
The Harbus (USA ISSN 1932-4006) **2286**
• The Hard Copy Observer (USA ISSN 1058-2444) **2419**
Hard Disk Drive Guide *see* H D D Guide **2539**
Hard Hat Magazine (USA) **1684**
Hard Hat News (USA ISSN 0279-1242) **1011**
Hard i Soft (RUS) **2419**
Hard Music Magazine *see* H M Magazine **6572**
Hard 'n' Fast (USA) **6572**
Hard 'N' Heavy (FRA ISSN 1252-2279) **6572**
Hard 'n' Soft (RUS) **2419**
Hard Rock Magazine (FRA ISSN 0764-1346) **6572**
Hard Row to Hoe (USA ISSN 1085-5351) **5303**
Hard Times (DEU ISSN 0171-1695) **5219**
Hardanger Fartoeyvernsenter. Rapport (NOR ISSN 1503-9927) **8645**
Hardanger Folkeblad (NOR) **3923**
The Hardball Times Baseball Annual (USA ISSN 1940-4484) **8235**
▼ The Hardball Times Season Preview (USA ISSN 1940-798X) **8235**
Hardboiled (USA) **5414**
† Hardcore Delphi (USA ISSN 1543-1282) **8961**
Hardcore Ink (USA) **6572**
† Hardcore International (CZE ISSN 1214-8636) **8961**
† Hardcore Web Services (USA ISSN 1543-222X) **8961**
Harden-in-ing Newsletter (USA) **3769**
Harden Murrumburrah Express (AUS ISSN 1321-5221) **3794**
Harden Murrumburrah Landcare Newsletter (AUS ISSN 1833-6663) **3436**
Hardin County Historical Quarterly (USA ISSN 8755-6073) **4294**
Hardin Herald *see* Big Horn County News **3522**
Hardin - Simmons University Brand *see* H S U Brand **2286**
Hardman's Tax Rates & Tables (GBR ISSN 1467-3258) **1928**
Hardop (NLD) **4081**
Hards Family Newsletter (GBR ISSN 0268-1021) **3769**
Hardsyssels Aarbog (DNK ISSN 0046-6840) **4226**
Hardware *see* Ferretaria **6311**
Hardware and Building Material Buyers' Guide (TWN) **1999**
Hardware & Building Materials World Buyers' Guide (GBR ISSN 1466-6170) **1054**
Hardware & D I Y *see* Global Sources Hardware & D I Y **1053**
Hardware and Garden Review (GBR ISSN 0266-0539) **1054**
• Hardware & Home Centre Magazine (CAN ISSN 0847-9968) **1054**
Hardware.info Magazine (NLD ISSN 1871-0425) **2539**
Hardware Magainze (Philippines) *see* H W M (Philippines) **2539**
Hardware Magazine (Indonesia) *see* H W M (Indonesia) **2539**
Hardware Magazine (Malaysia) *see* H W M (Malaysia) **2539**
Hardware Magazine (Thailand) *see* H W M (Thailand) **2539**
• Hardware Merchandising (CAN ISSN 1199-2786) **1054**
Hardware Retailer (ZAF) **1054**
• Hardware Retailing (Indianapolis) (USA ISSN 1934-8819) **4438**
Hardware Today (GBR) **1054**
Hardware World (TWN) **1054**
Hardwareluxx (DEU) **2539**
• Hardwood Floors (USA ISSN 0897-022X) **1050**
Hardwood Market Report (USA ISSN 0888-9104) **1050**
Hardwood Plywood & Veneer News (USA) **3712**
Hardwood Research *see* Koyoju Kenkyu **3695**
Hardy Plant Journal (GBR ISSN 0969-1901) **3735**
Hardy Plant Society. News Letter (GBR) **3735**
Hardy-Ramanujan Journal (IND) **5491**
• The Hardy Review (GBR ISSN 1934-8908) **5303**
Hare Krishna World (USA ISSN 1093-2372) **7736**
Harebin Railway Science & Technology *see* Haerbin Tiedao Keji **8618**
Hareem (IND) **8867**
• Harford Business Ledger (USA) **1117**
Harford Historical Bulletin (USA ISSN 0741-7802) **4294**
Haridus (EST ISSN 0235-9146) **2862**
Harlan Mountain Roots (USA ISSN 1085-5254) **3769**
• HarlemLive (USA) **2154**
Harlequin Edice Special (CZE ISSN 1212-852X) **5410**
Harlequin World's Best Romances (CAN ISSN 1183-5044) **5410**
Harley-Davidson Magazin (DEU) **8259**
• The Harley Hahn Experience (USA ISSN 1547-6022) **3977**
• Harley Hahn's Guide to Muds (USA ISSN 1547-6057) **2477**
• Harley Hahn's Internet Advisor (USA ISSN 1547-6049) **2557**
• Harley Hahn's Internet Insecurity (USA ISSN 1547-6030) **2513**
• Harley Hahn's Internet Yellow Pages (USA ISSN 1546-4148) **2557**
• Harley Hahn's Tidbits (USA ISSN 1547-6014) **3977**
Harlow and Bishop's Stortford Citizen (GBR) **3866**
• Harlow Report: Geographic Information Systems (Online) (USA) **1417**
Harlow's Wooden Man (USA ISSN 0887-5448) **4294**
• ➤ Harm Reduction Journal (GBR ISSN 1477-7517) **7520**
▼ L'Harmattan Burkina Faso (FRA ISSN 1956-6824) **7140**
• Harmful Algae (NLD ISSN 1568-9883) **886**
Harmful Algae News (FRA ISSN 1020-2706) **676**
Harmonia (JPN ISSN 0914-2541) **6572**
Harmonica (USA) **6572**
Harmonicas de France Federation magazine (FRA ISSN 1775-0121) **6572**
Harmonienachrichten (CHE) **6572**
Harmonika International (DEU ISSN 0938-6629) **6572**
Harmonikales Denken (AUT ISSN 1727-5792) **6572**
Harmonious Harmonica (USA ISSN 9874-5840) **6572**
Harmoniously United *see* Pupukahi **6442**
• Harmonized Tariff Schedule of the United States (USA ISSN 1066-0925) **1928**
Harmonizer (USA ISSN 0017-7849) **6572**
Harmonologia - Studies in Music Theory (USA ISSN 1062-4090) **6572**
Harmony (DEU) **7760**
Harmony (ZAF) **3948**
Harmony (San Francisco) (USA ISSN 0896-243X) **7207**
Harmony Bianca (ITA ISSN 1122-5424) **5410**
Harmony Collezione (ITA ISSN 1122-5459) **5410**
† Harmony Comedy (ITA ISSN 1594-283X) **8961**
† Harmony Desire (ITA ISSN 1123-8437) **8961**
Harmony Destiny (ITA ISSN 1122-5475) **5303**
Harmony Hi! *see* Add-a-Line **6542**
Harmony History (ITA ISSN 1124-7320) **5410**
Harmony History Special (ITA ISSN 1724-5354) **5410**
† Harmony Intrigue (ITA ISSN 1722-070X) **8961**
• Harmony Magazine (USA) **4454**
† Harmony Oasi Donna (ITA ISSN 1721-369X) **8961**
Harmony Oasidonna *see* Harmony Oasi Donna **8961**
Harmony Pack (ITA ISSN 1122-5386) **5410**
Harmony Premium (ITA ISSN 1724-5346) **5410**
† Harmony. Serie Jolly (ITA ISSN 1122-5394) **8961**
Harmony Special (ITA ISSN 1122-5491) **5410**
Harmony Temptation (ITA ISSN 1591-6707) **5410**
Harness Racing *see* New Zealand Harness Racing Weekly **8295**
Harness Racing Weekly (AUS ISSN 1440-0057) **8291**
The Harness Shop News *see* Shop Talk! (Oriental) **4975**
Harnett's Sports Arizona (USA ISSN 1090-1116) **8177**
Haro! (SWE ISSN 1650-5085) **8105**
Haro Chosa Hokokusho/Research Report of Waves (JPN) **2805**
Harold Recorder (GBR ISSN 1362-8321) **3866**
Harold Wells Gulf Coast Fisherman *see* Gulf Coast Fisherman **8316**
† Haroshet (ISR ISSN 0334-8121) **8961**
Harp (USA ISSN 1536-1438) **6572**
Harp-Strings (USA) **5303**
• Harpers (GBR ISSN 1367-9082) **604**
• Harper's (USA ISSN 0017-789X) **5219**
Harpers & Queen (GBR ISSN 0141-0547) **8867**
Harper's Bazaar *see* Shishang Basha **2261**
Harper's Bazaar (RUS ISSN 1562-5095) **8867**
Harper's Bazaar (TUR) **8867**
• Harper's Bazaar (USA ISSN 0017-7873) **2256**
Harper's Bazaar (London) (GBR ISSN 1751-1593) **3967**
Harper's Bazaar (Men's Edition) *see* Shishang Basha - Nanshi **6300**
Harper's Bazaar (Prague) (CZE ISSN 1211-5371) **2256**
Harper's Bazaar Australia (AUS ISSN 0814-8821) **2256**
† Harper's Bazaar Italia (ITA ISSN 1121-7375) **8961**
† Harper's Bazaar Italia Uomo (ITA ISSN 1121-7251) **8961**
Harper's Biochemistry *see* Harper's Illustrated Biochemistry **733**
† Harper's Gran Bazaar (ITA ISSN 0394-1132) **8961**
Harpers Guide to Sports Trade (GBR ISSN 0073-0416) **8177**
Harper's Illustrated Biochemistry (USA ISSN 1547-562X) **733**
Harpers Weekly *see* Harpers **604**
• Harpers Wine and Spirit Directory (GBR ISSN 1367-9090) **604**
Harpoen (NLD ISSN 0017-7911) **2286**
Harpsichord and Fortepiano (GBR ISSN 1463-0036) **6572**
• Harpur Palate (USA ISSN 1532-9046) **5303**
Harrah's World (USA) **8177**
Harriman Review (USA) **5219**
Harrington Family Miscellany (GBR ISSN 0307-0298) **3769**
Harrington Gay Men's Fiction Quarterly *see* Harrington Gay Men's Literary Quarterly **8961**
† • Harrington Gay Men's Literary Quarterly (USA ISSN 1556-9241) **8961**
Harrington Lesbian Fiction Quarterly *see* Harrington Lesbian Literary Quarterly **8961**
† • Harrington Lesbian Literary Quarterly (USA ISSN 1556-9225) **8961**
Harris & Newiss International Intellectual Property Litigation *see* International Intellectual Property Litigation **4694**
Harris Arizona Services Directory (USA ISSN 1538-4977) **1999**
Harris Auction Galleries. Collectors' Auction (USA ISSN 0093-1047) **6525**
Harris Connecticut Manufacturers Directory *see* Harris Directory. Connecticut Manufacturing **1999**
Harris Connecticut Services Directory (USA ISSN 1536-5727) **1999**
Harris Delaware Manufacturers Directory *see* Harris Directory. Delaware Manufacturing **1999**
• Harris Directory. Alabama All-Industries (USA) **1999**
• Harris Directory. Alabama Manufacturing (USA) **1999**
• Harris Directory. Arizona All-Industries (USA) **1999**
• Harris Directory. Arizona Manufacturing (USA) **1999**
• Harris Directory. Arkansas All-Industries (USA) **1999**
• Harris Directory. Arkansas Manufacturing (USA) **1999**
• Harris Directory. California All-Industries (USA) **1999**
• Harris Directory. California Manufacturing (USA) **1999**
• Harris Directory. California Orange County (USA) **1999**
Harris Directory. California San Diego County (USA) **1999**
Harris Directory. California Wholesalers & Service Companies (USA) **1999**

Title

10354 HARRIS DIRECTORY. COLORADO MANUFACTURING ULRICH'S PERIODICALS

• Harris Directory. Colorado Manufacturing (USA) **1999**
• Harris Directory. Connecticut All-Industries (USA) **1999**
• Harris Directory. Connecticut Manufacturing (USA ISSN 1080-2614) **1999**
• Harris Directory. Delaware All-Industries (USA) **1999**
• Harris Directory. Delaware Manufacturing (USA) **1999**
▼ Harris Directory. District of Columbia All-Industries (USA) **1999**
• Harris Directory. Florida All-Industries (USA) **1999**
• Harris Directory. Georgia All-Industries (USA) **1999**
• Harris Directory. Georgia Manufacturing (USA ISSN 1544-4600) **1999**
• Harris Directory. Idaho All-Industries (USA) **2000**
• Harris Directory. Illinois All-Industries (USA) **2000**
• Harris Directory. Illinois Manufacturing (USA) **2000**
• Harris Directory. Indiana All-Industries (USA) **2000**
• Harris Directory. Indiana Manufacturing (USA) **2000**
• Harris Directory. Iowa Manufacturing (USA ISSN 1550-137X) **2000**
• Harris Directory. Kansas All-Industries (USA) **2000**
• Harris Directory. Kentucky All-Industries (USA) **2000**
• Harris Directory. Kentucky Manufacturing (USA ISSN 1533-550X) **2000**
• Harris Directory. Louisiana Manufacturing (USA) **2000**
• Harris Directory. Maryland Manufacturing (USA) **2000**
• Harris Directory. Massachusetts All-Industries (USA) **2000**
• Harris Directory. Massachusetts Manufacturing (USA ISSN 1078-6341) **2000**
• Harris Directory. Michigan All-Industries (USA) **2000**
• Harris Directory. Michigan Manufacturing (USA) **2000**
• Harris Directory. Minnesota All-Industries (USA) **2000**
• Harris Directory. Minnesota Manufacturing (USA) **2000**
• Harris Directory. Mississippi All-Indsutries (USA) **2000**
• Harris Directory. Mississippi Manufacturing (USA ISSN 1078-635X) **2000**
• Harris Directory. Missouri All-Industries (USA) **2000**
• Harris Directory. Missouri Manufacturing (USA) **2000**
• Harris Directory. Montana All-Industries (USA) **2000**
• Harris Directory. Nebraska All-Industries (USA) **2000**
• Harris Directory. Nevada All-Industries (USA) **2000**
• Harris Directory. Nevada Manufacturing (USA) **2000**
Harris Directory. New England All-Industries (USA) **2001**
Harris Directory. New England Manufacturing (USA) **2001**
• Harris Directory. New Hampshire All-Industries (USA) **2001**
• Harris Directory. New Hampshire Manufacturing (USA) **2001**
• Harris Directory. New Jersey All-Industries (USA) **2001**
• Harris Directory. New Jersey Manufacturing (USA ISSN 1551-742X) **2001**
• Harris Directory. New Mexico All-Industries (USA) **2001**
• Harris Directory. New Mexico Manufacturing (USA) **2001**
• Harris Directory. New York All-Industries (USA) **2001**
• Harris Directory. New York Manufacturing (USA) **2001**
• Harris Directory. North Carolina All-Industries (USA) **2001**
• Harris Directory. North Carolina Manufacturing (USA) **2001**
• Harris Directory. North Dakota All-Industries (USA) **2001**
• Harris Directory. North Dakota Manufacturing (USA) **2001**
• Harris Directory. Northern C A Business (California) (USA) **2001**
Harris Directory of Delaware Businesses (USA ISSN 1536-5603) **2001**
Harris Directory of Iowa Manufacturers *see* Harris Directory. Iowa Manufacturing **2000**
• Harris Directory of Kansas Businesses (Online) (USA) **2001**
Harris Directory of Kansas Businesses (Print) *see* Harris Directory of Kansas Businesses (Online) **2001**
• Harris Directory of Maine Businesses (Online) (USA) **2001**
Harris Directory of Maine Businesses (Print) *see* Harris Directory of Maine Businesses (Online) **2001**
Harris Directory of Mississippi Manufacturers *see* Harris Directory. Mississippi Manufacturing **2000**
• Harris Directory of Montana Businesses (Online) (USA) **2001**
Harris Directory of Montana Businesses (Print) *see* Harris Directory of Montana Businesses (Online) **2001**
Harris Directory of Nevada Businesses (USA ISSN 1535-9190) **2001**
• Harris Directory of North Dakota Businesses (Online) (USA) **2001**
Harris Directory of North Dakota Businesses (Print) *see* Harris Directory of North Dakota Businesses (Online) **2001**
• Harris Directory of South Dakota Businesses (Online) (USA) **2001**
Harris Directory of South Dakota Businesses (Print) *see* Harris Directory of South Dakota Businesses (Online) **2001**
Harris Directory of Washington, D.C. Businesses (USA ISSN 1536-5662) **2001**
• Harris Directory. Ohio All-Indsutries (USA) **2001**
• Harris Directory. Ohio Manufacturing (USA) **2001**
• Harris Directory. Oklahoma All-Industries (USA) **2002**
• Harris Directory. Oklahoma Manufacturing (USA) **2002**
• Harris Directory. Oregon All-Industries (USA) **2002**
• Harris Directory. Oregon Manufacturing (USA) **2002**
• Harris Directory. Pennsylvania All-Industries (USA) **2002**
• Harris Directory. Pennsylvania Manufacturing (USA) **2002**
• Harris Directory. Rhode Island All-Industries (USA) **2002**
• Harris Directory. Rhode Island Manufacturing (USA) **2002**
• Harris Directory. San Diego County Commerce and Industry Directory (USA ISSN 1536-9420) **2002**
• Harris Directory. South Carolina All-Industries (USA) **2002**
• Harris Directory. South Carolina Manufacturing (USA ISSN 1065-4747) **2002**
• Harris Directory. South Dakota All-Industries (USA) **2002**
• Harris Directory. South Dakota Manufacturing (USA) **2002**
• Harris Directory. Southern C A Business (California) (USA) **2002**
• Harris Directory. Tennessee All-Industries (USA) **2002**
• Harris Directory. Tennessee Manufacturing (USA) **2002**
• Harris Directory. Texas All-Industries (USA) **2002**
• Harris Directory. Texas Manufacturing (USA) **2002**
Harris Directory. U.S. Midwest All-Industries (USA) **2002**
• Harris Directory. U.S. Midwest Manufacturing (USA) **2002**
Harris Directory. U.S. Northeast All-Industries (USA) **2002**
• Harris Directory. U.S. Northeast Manufacturing (USA) **2002**
• Harris Directory. U.S. Pacific Northwest All-Industries (USA) **2002**
• Harris Directory. U.S. Pacific Northwest Manufacturing (USA) **2002**
Harris Directory. U.S. Southeast All-Industries (USA) **2002**
• Harris Directory. U.S. Southeast Manufacturing (USA) **2002**
• Harris Directory. Utah All-Industries (USA) **2002**
• Harris Directory. Utah Manufacturing (USA) **2003**
• Harris Directory. Vermont All-Industries (USA) **2003**
† • Harris Directory. Vermont Manufacturing (USA) **8961**
• Harris Directory. Virginia All-Industries (USA) **2003**
• Harris Directory. Virginia Manufacturing (USA) **2003**
• Harris Directory. Washington All-Industries (USA) **2003**
• Harris Directory. Washington D.C. All-Industries (USA) **2003**
• Harris Directory. Washington Manufacturing (USA) **2003**
• Harris Directory. West Virginia All-Industries (USA) **2003**
• Harris Directory. West Virginia Manufacturing (USA) **2003**
• Harris Directory. Wisconsin All-Industries (USA) **2003**
• Harris Directory. Wisconsin Manufacturing (USA) **2003**
• Harris Florida Manufacturers Directory (USA ISSN 1550-2589) **2003**
Harris Florida Services Directory (USA ISSN 1532-3846) **2003**
Harris Georgia Services Directory (USA ISSN 1534-3650) **2003**
Harris Illinois Business Service Directory (USA ISSN 1532-1606) **2003**
• Harris Illinois Industrial Directory (Year) (USA ISSN 1550-1973) **2003**
• Harris Indiana Industrial Directory (Year) (USA ISSN 1549-5795) **2003**
Harris Indiana Services Directory (USA ISSN 1532-1584) **2003**
Harris Kentucky Services Directory (USA ISSN 1532-1592) **2003**
Harris Manufacturers Directory (National Edition) *see* Harris U.S. Manufacturers Directory - National Edition **2003**
Harris Maryland Manufacturers Directory *see* Harris Directory. Maryland Manufacturing **2000**
Harris Massachusetts Manufacturers Directory *see* Harris Directory. Massachusetts Manufacturing **2000**
Harris Massachusetts Services Directory (USA ISSN 1536-7452) **2003**
Harris Michigan Services Directory (USA ISSN 1532-1614) **2003**
Harris Minnesota Directory of Manufacturers *see* Harris Directory. Minnesota Manufacturing **2000**
Harris Missouri Directory of Manufacturers *see* Harris Directory. Missouri Manufacturing **2000**
Harris National Manufacturers Directory (Year) *see* Harris U.S. Manufacturers Directory - National Edition **2003**
Harris National Manufacturers Directory. Midwest Edition (Year) *see* Harris Directory. U.S. Midwest Manufacturing **2002**
Harris National Manufacturers Directory. Northeast Edition (Year) *see* Harris Directory. U.S. Northeast Manufacturing **2002**
Harris National Manufacturers Directory. Southeast Edition (Year) *see* Harris Directory. U.S. Southeast Manufacturing **2002**
Harris New England Manufacturers Directory *see* Harris Directory. New England Manufacturing **2001**
Harris New Jersey Manufacturers Directory *see* Harris Directory. New Jersey Manufacturing **2001**
Harris New York Manufacturers Directory *see* Harris Directory. New York Manufacturing **2001**
Harris North Carolina Services Directory (USA ISSN 1533-6964) **2003**
• Harris Poll (Online) (USA ISSN 1946-4525) **8149**
Harris Poll (Print) *see* Harris Poll (Online) **8149**
• Harris Rhode Island Manufacturers Directory (USA ISSN 1078-6333) **2003**
Harris South Carolina Services Directory (USA ISSN 1533-6948) **2003**
Harris Tennessee Manufacturers Directory *see* Harris Directory. Tennessee Manufacturing **2002**
Harris Texas Manufacturers Directory *see* Harris Directory. Texas Manufacturing **2002**
• Harris U.S. Manufacturers Directory - National Edition (USA ISSN 1061-2076) **2003**
Harris Virginia Services Directory (USA ISSN 1533-6972) **2003**
• Harris West Virginia Manufacturing Directory (Year) (USA ISSN 0887-4247) **2003**
Harrisburg Metro Business to Business *see* Harrisburg Metro Business2Business **1749**
• Harrisburg Metro Business2Business (USA) **1749**
HarrisMartin Columns. Silica (USA ISSN 1559-4815) **4684**
Harrison Local Government Precedents and Procedures *see* Local Government Precedents and Procedures **7497**
Harrison on Wills and Administration for Virginia and West Virginia (USA) **4903**
Harrison Post (USA) **6423**
Harrison's Inland Revenue Index to Tax Cases (GBR) **1928**
• Harrison's Principles of Internal Medicine (USA) **5945**
Harrow Observer (GBR ISSN 0964-3168) **3866**
• Harrowsmith Country Life (CAN ISSN 1190-8416) **117**
Harry Ransom Humanities Research Center. Imprint Series (USA) **5303**
▼ Harry und Sein Eimer Voller Dinos (DEU) **2192**
Harstad Tidende (NOR) **3923**
Harsunan Nijeriya (NGA) **5124**
➤ Hart Bulletin (NLD ISSN 0301-8202) **5787**
Hart County Historical Society Quarterly (USA ISSN 1546-7341) **4294**
Hart Monographs in Transnational and International Law (GBR) **4927**
Hart voor Dieren (NLD ISSN 0922-520X) **319**
The Hartford Agent (USA) **4504**
• Hartford Business Journal (USA ISSN 1083-5245) **1117**
Hartford College for Women. Chronicle (USA) **2286**
Hartford Dental Society Newsletter (USA) **5846**
Hartford Inquirer *see* Inquiring News **3539**
Hartford Magazine (USA ISSN 1543-4834) **3977**
Hartlepool Mail (Final Edition) (GBR ISSN 1750-919X) **3967**
Hartlepool Star *see* Washington Star **3872**
Hartlepool Star *see* Houghton Star **2287**
Hartman Institute Axiology Studies (NLD) **7360**
Hartmannbund in Baden - Wuerttemberg (DEU) **7520**
Hartmannbund Magazin (DEU ISSN 0944-7369) **5623**
• Hart's Africa Oil and Gas (GBR ISSN 1469-106X) **6772**
• Hart's Asian Petroleum News (GBR ISSN 1095-0664) **6772**
• Hart's Diesel Fuel News (USA ISSN 1092-2849) **6772**
• Hart's E & P Daily (GBR ISSN 1469-1108) **6772**
† • Hart's Energy Markets (USA ISSN 1090-8706) **8961**
Hart's Euroil *see* E & P **6767**
• Hart's European Petroleum Finance Week (GBR ISSN 1469-1086) **6772**
Hart's Octane Week *see* Octane Week **6782**
Hart's Oil & Gas Interests *see* Oil and Gas Investor's A & D Watch **6783**
Hart's Oxy-Fuel News *see* Ethanol & Biodiesel News **3134**
• Haruah: Breath of Heaven (USA ISSN 1932-7595) **7646**
• Harvard Advocate (USA ISSN 0017-8004) **5303**
Harvard AIDS Institute Update (USA) **5814**
Harvard AIDS Review (USA ISSN 1526-0232) **5814**
➤ Harvard Armenian Texts and Studies (USA ISSN 0073-0459) **4321**
• Harvard Asia Pacific Review (USA ISSN 1522-1113) **7140**
• Harvard Asia Quarterly (USA ISSN 1522-4147) **7239**
• Harvard BlackLetter Law Journal (USA ISSN 1089-2907) **4832**
• The Harvard Brain (USA) **6144**
Harvard Business Manager (DEU ISSN 0945-6570) **1749**
• Harvard Business Review (USA ISSN 0017-8012) **1117**
Harvard Business Review Catalog (Year) (USA) **1236**
Harvard Business Review Russia (RUS) **1117**
Harvard Business School Alumni Bulletin (USA ISSN 1553-1546) **1117**
Harvard Business School. Annual Report (USA ISSN 0749-5072) **1117**
Harvard Business School. Bulletin *see* Harvard Business School Alumni Bulletin **1117**
Harvard Business School Club of London Address Book (GBR ISSN 0308-0463) **2286**
Harvard Celtic Colloquium. Proceedings (USA ISSN 1545-0155) **5124**
• Harvard China Review (USA ISSN 1098-1144) **1117**
• Harvard Civil Rights - Civil Liberties Law Review (USA ISSN 0017-8039) **4832**
• Harvard College Economics Review (USA ISSN 1946-2034) **1542**
Harvard College Economist (USA ISSN 0197-7636) **1719**
Harvard Contemporary China Series (USA ISSN 1051-0311) **4182**
The Harvard Crimson (USA ISSN 1932-4219) **2286**
Harvard Dental Bulletin (USA ISSN 1062-029X) **5846**
• ➤ Harvard Design Magazine (USA ISSN 1093-4421) **444**
Harvard - Deusto Business Review (ESP ISSN 0210-900X) **1117**
Harvard - Deusto Finanzas y Contabilidad (ESP ISSN 1134-0827) **1290**
Harvard - Deusto Marketing y Ventas (ESP ISSN 1133-7672) **1819**
• ➤ Harvard Divinity Bulletin (USA ISSN 1550-2465) **7646**
➤ Harvard East Asian Monographs (USA ISSN 0073-0483) **4182**
➤ Harvard East Asian Series (USA ISSN 0073-0491) **4182**
➤ Harvard Economic Studies (USA ISSN 0073-0505) **1117**
• Harvard Education Letter (USA ISSN 8755-3716) **2862**
• ➤ Harvard Educational Review (USA ISSN 0017-8055) **2862**
Harvard Educational Review. Reprint Series (USA ISSN 0362-8027) **2862**
Harvard English Studies (USA ISSN 0073-0513) **5303**
• ➤ Harvard Environmental Law Review (USA ISSN 0147-8257) **4684**
The Harvard Forest (USA ISSN 0360-7844) **3436**
• The Harvard Health Letter (USA ISSN 1052-1577) **6987**
• Harvard Heart Letter (USA ISSN 1051-5313) **5787**
➤ Harvard Historical Monographs (USA ISSN 0073-0521) **4141**
➤ Harvard Historical Studies (USA ISSN 0073-053X) **4141**
• Harvard Human Rights Journal (USA ISSN 1057-5057) **7207**
The Harvard International Journal of Press / Politics *see* International Journal of Press / Politics **4577**
• ➤ Harvard International Law Journal (USA ISSN 0017-8063) **4927**
• Harvard International Review (USA ISSN 0739-1854) **7239**
➤ Harvard Iranian Series (USA) **4321**
• ➤ Harvard Journal of African American Public Policy (USA ISSN 1081-0463) **7443**
• ➤ Harvard Journal of Asiatic Studies (USA ISSN 0073-0548) **551**
• ➤ Harvard Journal of Hispanic Policy (USA ISSN 1074-1917) **3536**
• Harvard Journal of Law & Gender (USA ISSN 1558-4356) **4684**
• ➤ Harvard Journal of Law and Public Policy (USA ISSN 0193-4872) **4684**
• ➤ Harvard Journal of Law and Technology (USA ISSN 0897-3393) **4684**
➤ The Harvard Journal of World Affairs (USA ISSN 1068-1485) **7239**
• ➤ Harvard Journal on Legislation (USA ISSN 0017-808X) **4685**
Harvard Judaic Monographs (USA) **7721**
Harvard Lampoon (USA ISSN 0017-8098) **2286**
• Harvard Latino Law Review (USA ISSN 1542-460X) **4685**
▼ • Harvard Law & Policy Review (USA ISSN 1935-2077) **4849**

Title

10356 HAWAII. LEGISLATIVE REFERENCE BUREAU. REPORT ULRICH'S PERIODICALS

Hawaii. Legislative Reference Bureau. Report (USA ISSN 0073-1277) **7140**
• Hawaii Library Association Newsletter (Online) (USA ISSN 1551-787X) **5011**
Hawaii Magazine (USA ISSN 1549-2109) **8717**
• Hawaii Manufacturers Directory (USA ISSN 1085-7451) **2003**
➤ Hawaii Medical Journal (USA ISSN 0017-8594) **5623**
Hawaii Notary Law Primer (USA) **4685**
Hawaii. Office of the Ombudsman. Report (USA ISSN 0073-1137) **7494**
Hawaii on 80 Dollars a Day (USA ISSN 1534-8547) **8717**
Hawaii on Eighty Dollars a Day *see* Hawaii on 80 Dollars a Day **8717**
Hawaii Orchid Journal *see* Na Okika O Hawaii **803**
▼ • ➤ Hawaii Pacific Journal of Social Work Practice (USA ISSN 1938-2197) **8044**
➤ Hawaii Pacific Review (USA ISSN 1047-4331) **5304**
• Hawaii Papayas (USA ISSN 1948-6286) **117**
• Hawaii Penal Code, Motor Vehicles & Related Statutes (USA) **4685**
Hawaii Realtor Journal (USA ISSN 0895-8556) **7592**
Hawaii Review (USA ISSN 0093-9625) **5304**
• Hawaii Rules of Evidence Manual (USA ISSN 1943-1082) **4685**
Hawaii School Directory *see* M D R's School Directory. Hawaii **2958**
Hawaii State Bar Association. Annual Directory (USA ISSN 0277-0520) **4685**
Hawaii. State Commission on the Status of Women. Annual Report (USA ISSN 0092-9190) **8898**
• Hawaii Sugarcane Acreage & Production (USA ISSN 1948-6308) **200**
• Hawaii Taro Millings (USA ISSN 1949-5099) **181**
Hawaii, the Big Island *see* Paradise Family Guides: Big Island of Hawaii **8746**
Hawaii, the Big Island Revealed (USA ISSN 1930-5974) **8717**
Hawaii: The Big Island Update (USA ISSN 1042-8046) **8717**
Hawaii TourBook *see* TourBook: Hawaii **8762**
• Hawaii Underground (USA) **3977**
• Hawaii Vegetables (USA ISSN 2150-0711) **181**
Hawaii Westways (USA ISSN 1524-8453) **8717**
Hawaiian Acquisition List (USA) **626**
Hawaiian Church Chronicle (USA ISSN 0274-7154) **7760**
➤ Hawaiian Entomological Society. Proceedings (USA ISSN 0073-134X) **848**
Hawaiian Historical Society. Annual Report (USA ISSN 0363-4760) **4192**
• ➤ Hawaiian Journal of History (USA ISSN 0440-5145) **4192**
• Hawaiian Journal of Law and Politics (USA ISSN 1550-6177) **4686**
Hawaiian Newsletter (USA) **3977**
• Hawaiian Shell News (USA ISSN 0017-8624) **945**
Hawaii's Economy Newsletter (USA) **1887**
Hawaii's International Festival of the Pacific (USA) **1404**
Hawes Fantasy Baseball Guide (USA) **8235**
Hawes Fantasy Football Guide (USA ISSN 1076-2949) **8235**
Hawgs Illustrated (USA ISSN 1066-1239) **8235**
Hawk (USA ISSN 1075-0797) **6292**
▼ Hawk & Whippoorwill (USA ISSN 1938-2618) **5423**
Hawk Migration Studies (USA) **908**
Hawk Mountain News (USA ISSN 1534-9292) **908**
• Hawke Research Institute. Postgraduate Working Paper Series (Online) (AUS ISSN 1833-136X) **7968**
Hawke Research Institute. Postgraduate Working Paper Series (Print) *see* Hawke Research Institute. Postgraduate Working Paper Series (Online) **7968**
Hawke's Bay Today (NZL ISSN 1174-9792) **3917**
• Hawkeye (La Plata) (USA) **2286**
Hawkeye Engineer (USA) **3195**
Hawkeye Heritage (USA ISSN 0440-5234) **3769**
Hawkfrendz (GBR) **5219**
• Hawkhill News (USA) **7860**
Hawkhill Science Newsletter *see* Hawkhill News **7860**
Hawliyah Kulliyah al-Tarbiyyah/Educational Journal (UAE) **2862**
Hawliyat al-'lum al-Zira'iyyat *see* Annals of Agricultural Science **91**
Hawliyyaat al-'ulum al-Zira'iyyat bi-Mustuhur *see* Annals of Agricultural Science, Moshtohor **91**
Hawliyyat Da'irat al-Athar al-'Ammath/Department of Antiquities of Jordan. Annual (JOR ISSN 0449-1564) **4141**
➤ Hawliyyat Kulliyyat al-Adab/Annals of the Arts and Social Sciences (KWT ISSN 1560-5248) **4454**
Hawver's Capitol Report (USA ISSN 1071-5401) **7443**
• ➤ Hawwa (NLD ISSN 1569-2078) **8898**
Hay & Feedstuffs (USA) **234**
• Hay & Forage Grower (USA ISSN 0891-5946) **273**
Hay Balranald Landcare Networks Newsletter (AUS ISSN 1833-7384) **3436**
Hay Dramagitakan Handes *see* Armenian Numismatic Journal **6649**
Hay Market News - National (USA) **200**
Hay There (USA) **234**
Al Hay'a al-Duwaliyyatt li-Muraqaba al-Muhaddirat li'Am (Year). Taqrir *see* International Narcotics Control Board. Report for (Year) **6850**
Al Haya'at al-'arabiyyat li-l-Istithmar wa-al-Inma al-Zira'i. Al-Taqrir al-Sanawi *see* Arab Authority for Agricultural Investment and Development. Annual Report **194**
Hayakawa S F (JPN) **5443**
Hayashibara Museum of Natural Sciences Research Bulletin (JPN ISSN 1345-7225) **7860**
Hayastani Bzhshkagitutyun/Armenian Medical Journal/Meditsinskaya Nauka Armenii (ARM ISSN 1029-6905) **5905**
Hayastani Chimikakan Handes (ARM ISSN 1561-4190) **2063**
Hayastani Gitutsunneri Azgain Academiay Teghekagir Matematika *see* Akademiya Nauk Armenii. Izvestiya. Seriya Matematika **5467**
Hayastani Hanrapetutian Gitutsunneri Azgain Academiay Tegekagir Mechanics *see* Natsional'naya Akademiya Nauk Armenii. Izvestiya. Seriya Mekhanika **3390**
Hayastani Hanrapetutian Gitutsunneri Azgain Academiay Tekhnikakan Gitutsunnery Handes *see* Akademiya Nauk Armenii. Izvestiya. Seriya Tekhnicheskikh Nauk **8415**
Hayastany Guitoutyunnery Azgayin Academia. Teghekagir. Fizika/Akademiya Nauk Armenii. Izvestiya. Seriya Fizika (ARM) **7015**
Hayastany Guitoutyunnery Azgayin Academia Zekuyts'ner/Akademiya Nauk Armenii. Doklady (ARM ISSN 1026-6496) **7860**
Hayastany Hanrapetutyan Titutyunneri Azgayin Akademia Teghekagir. Gitutyunner Erkri Masin (ARM ISSN 1029-7901) **7860**
• Al-Hayat (GBR ISSN 0967-5590) **3912**
• ➤ HAYAT (IRN ISSN 1735-2215) **5959**
Hayden's Ferry Review (USA ISSN 0887-5170) **5219**
➤ Haydn Society Journal (GBR ISSN 1350-1267) **6572**
Haydn - Studien (DEU ISSN 0440-5323) **6572**
▼ The Hayes-A I S Medical Technology Adviser (USA ISSN 1941-2223) **5624**
Hayes of America Herald (USA ISSN 0736-9557) **3769**
Hayit Spezial (DEU) **8717**
Haynes Alloys Digest (USA) **6343**
Hayward Handbook of Land Compensation *see* Handbook of Land Compensation **7592**
• Hayyim Aherim (ISR ISSN 0793-7121) **309**
Hazama Corporation. Report of Special Research *see* Hazamagumi Tokutei Kenkyu Hokoku **3268**
• Hazama Kenkyu Nenpo (CD-ROM)/Technical Research Report of Hazama Corporation (JPN ISSN 1880-2370) **3268**
Hazama Kenkyu Nenpo (Print) *see* Hazama Kenkyu Nenpo (CD-ROM) **3268**
Hazamagumi Tokutei Kenkyu Hokoku/Hazama Corporation. Report of Special Research (JPN) **3268**
• Hazard (AUS ISSN 1320-0593) **7520**
Hazard Analysis and Critical Control Point Food Compliance News *see* H A A C P & Food Compliance News **3645**
Hazard Assessment of Chemicals (USA ISSN 0730-5427) **3245**
Hazard Communication Handbook (USA ISSN 1061-5229) **3507**
Hazard Control Manager (USA) **6677**
Hazard Ex *see* HazardEx **3436**
Hazard Prevention *see* Journal of System Safety **3206**
HazardEx (GBR ISSN 1476-7376) **3436**
• Hazardous Area International (GBR ISSN 1751-780X) **3436**
• Hazardous Cargo Bulletin (GBR ISSN 0143-6864) **8497**
Hazardous Cargo Bulletin International Drum and I B C Guide *see* H C B International Drum and I B C Guide **6710**
Hazardous Cargo Bulletin Tank Guide *see* H C B Tank Guide **8645**
Hazardous Locations Equipment (USA) **3507**
Hazardous Materials (USA ISSN 1559-9086) **3507**
Hazardous Materials Newsletter (USA ISSN 0889-3454) **7520**
Hazardous Materials Regulation Guide (USA) **3497**
Hazardous Materials Transportation Report *see* Keller's Hazardous Materials Transportation Report **8672**
Hazardous Waste and Superfund (USA ISSN 1075-8828) **3507**
• Hazardous Waste Consultant (USA ISSN 0738-0232) **3507**
• Hazardous Waste - Superfund Alert (USA) **3507**
Hazards Magazine (GBR ISSN 0267-7296) **6677**
Hazards of Confined Spaces (CAN ISSN 1712-1442) **7520**
Hazards of Confined Spaces for Food and Beverage Industries (CAN ISSN 1712-1434) **7520**
Hazards of Confined Spaces for Municipalities and the Construction Industry (CAN ISSN 1712-1426) **7520**
Hazards of Confined Spaces for Shipping and Transportation Industries (CAN ISSN 1708-6396) **7520**
Hazelden Voice (USA) **2694**
The Hazen Road Dispatch (USA ISSN 1545-7346) **4294**
Hazi Praktika *see* Praktika **8880**
Hazmat (USA ISSN 1521-7639) **5304**
Hazmat *see* Hazardous Materials **3507**
• HazMat Management (CAN ISSN 1713-9511) **3507**
HazMat News (Box Hill) *see* Fire Australia **3577**
HazMat Packager and Shipper *see* The Journal of HazMat Transportation **3508**
• HazMat Transport News (USA ISSN 1545-8210) **3507**
• HazMat Transportation News (USA ISSN 1539-7661) **8498**
• Haznews (GBR ISSN 0953-5357) **3507**
• HazSafety Training Advisor (USA ISSN 1546-7309) **7520**
HazTech News (USA ISSN 1051-3221) **3507**
HCC!link *see* H C C Magazine **2419**
HD plus TV *see* HD+TV **2382**
HDRI 3D *see* H D R I 3 D **2486**
He (DNK ISSN 1604-7680) **6292**
• He Kexue yu Gongcheng/Chinese Journal of Nuclear Science and Engineering (CHN ISSN 0258-0918) **3168**
He Kohinga Korero *see* Communication Journal of New Zealand **2315**
He Lines (GBR ISSN 0961-1266) **2247**
➤ He Pukenga Korero (NZL ISSN 1173-5767) **3536**
He - She Directory (USA) **6292**
He Thong Giao duc cua New Zealand (NZL ISSN 1176-6069) **2862**
HE-Xtra *see* H E - Xtra **6987**
• ➤ Head & Face Medicine (GBR ISSN 1746-160X) **5624**
• ➤ Head & Neck (USA ISSN 1043-3074) **6245**
Head and Neck Cancer *see* Tokeibu Shuyo **6035**
▼ • ➤ Head & Neck Oncology (GBR ISSN 1758-3284) **6021**
▼ • ➤ Head & Neck Pathology (USA ISSN 1936-055X) **5624**
• Head Start Bulletin (USA) **2862**
Head Teachers Review (GBR ISSN 0017-873X) **2862**
Head Teacher's Special Report (GBR ISSN 1476-5977) **3024**
• ➤ Headache (USA ISSN 0017-8748) **6144**
Headache and Migraine Management Journal (USA) **5624**
• ➤ Headache & Pain (USA ISSN 1545-8261) **6144**
• ➤ Headache Care (GBR ISSN 1742-3430) **6144**
Headache in Practice (GBR ISSN 1741-735X) **6144**
Headache Online (USA ISSN 1526-4610) **6144**
Headings (USA) **4504**
The Headless Way (GBR ISSN 1367-6709) **6645**
Headlight (GBR ISSN 0959-1745) **8631**
Headline News (GBR) **588**
Headliner (NZL ISSN 0110-9790) **1628**
Headliner (USA) **8583**
Headlines (AUS ISSN 1832-2573) **7140**
Headlines (NGA ISSN 0189-3963) **3920**
Headlines (London) (GBR ISSN 0954-9021) **4576**
Headlines & Highlights (USA) **8044**
• Headlines on the Path to Progress (USA ISSN 1949-0593) **6021**
Headmark (AUS ISSN 1833-6531) **6423**
Headpress (GBR ISSN 1353-9760) **493**
Headquarters Good Design is Good Business *see* H Q: Good Design is Good Business **1010**
Headquarters Heliogram (USA) **4294**
Headquarters q *see* H q **444**
Headquarters U S A (USA ISSN 1531-2909) **2004**
Heads (CAN) **5073**
Heads of State and Chief Executives' Award (IRL) **7140**
Headship Matters *see* Secondary Headship **3033**
Headteacher Update (GBR ISSN 1478-5307) **3063**
Headway (CAN ISSN 1911-8112) **2983**
Headwear Institute of America. Newsletter (USA) **2247**
▼ Heal (USA ISSN 1548-5072) **6021**
• Healing Garden Journal (USA ISSN 1942-2768) **309**
Healing Hand (GBR ISSN 0017-8829) **7646**
• Healing Lifestyles & Spas (USA ISSN 1547-5115) **6110**
➤ Healing Ministry (USA ISSN 1087-1586) **7646**
The Healing Muse (USA ISSN 1539-6983) **5304**
▼ Healing Society (USA ISSN 1933-5938) **5624**
• Healing Spirit (USA ISSN 1943-6556) **7646**
Healing Thoughts (USA) **7736**
• ➤ Health (GBR ISSN 1363-4593) **7520**
Health *see* Kenko **6991**
Health *see* Eruul Mend **6985**
• Health (USA ISSN 1059-938X) **6987**
▼ • Health (Irvine) (USA ISSN 1949-4998) **5624**
• Health A to Z News (USA) **5624**
• Health Action (CAN ISSN 1193-2295) **7520**
Health Action (IND ISSN 0970-471X) **4095**
• Health Administrator (IND ISSN 0971-5673) **4095**
Health Advocate (USA ISSN 0897-3598) **6987**
• ➤ Health Affairs (USA ISSN 0278-2715) **7520**
Health after 50 *see* Johns Hopkins Medical Letter Health after 50 **4048**
Health & Ageing (GBR ISSN 1365-4691) **4047**
Health & Beauty *see* Boots Health & Beauty **8854**
• Health & Beauty Salon (GBR) **588**
Health & Care *see* Herusu & Kea **5628**
Health and Clinical Excellence (GBR ISSN 1747-4280) **7520**
Health & Cuisine (THA ISSN 1513-7589) **6659**
• Health and Efficiency (GBR ISSN 0017-8888) **6987**
† Health & Environment in America's Top-Rated Cities: A Statistical Profile (Years) (USA ISSN 1080-4161) **8961**
Health and Fitness (GBR ISSN 0957-5928) **6987**
Health & Fitness Journal *see* A C S M's Health & Fitness Journal **6981**
Health and Fitness Sports Magazine (USA) **6987**
Health and Food (Dutch Edition) *see* Health and Food (French Edition) **6660**
Health and Food (French Edition) (BEL ISSN 1374-626X) **6660**
Health and Happiness *see* Kangle Shijie **8969**
Health & Healing (AUS ISSN 1328-4312) **309**
Health and Healing (GBR ISSN 0265-2021) **6987**
Health & Healing (USA ISSN 1057-9273) **6987**
➤ Health and History (AUS ISSN 1442-1771) **5624**
• Health and Homeopathy (GBR ISSN 0965-1292) **5805**
Health and Hospital Law Section Newsletter *see* New Jersey State Bar Association. Health and Hospital Law Section. Newsletter **4108**
Health & Housing Insight (GBR) **7520**
• ➤ Health and Human Rights (USA ISSN 1079-0969) **7520**
Health and Human Rights Publication Series (CHE ISSN 1684-1700) **7520**
Health & Human Services Directory (USA) **8044**
• ➤ Health & Hygiene (GBR ISSN 0140-2986) **7520**
Health & Hygiene (ZAF) **6987**
• Health & Law Trends (USA) **4686**
Health & Life *see* Baojian yu Shenghuo **6982**
Health and Life Insurance Litigation Reporter *see* Andrews Health and Life Insurance Litigation Reporter **4616**
Health & Lifestyle *see* Conscious Living Fremantle **3412**
Health and medical resources *see* Detwiler's Directory of Health and Medical Resources (Year) **5744**
• Health & Medicine Week (USA ISSN 1531-6459) **5624**
Health and Medicine Week *see* Health & Medicine Week **5624**
Health & Nutrition (IND) **6988**
Health & Nutrition (IRL) **6988**
• Health & Personal Care World (USA) **588**
• Health and Personal Development Learning Area Manual (Year) (AUS ISSN 1440-0545) **2862**
Health & Pharmaceuticals *see* Interfax. Health & Pharmaceuticals **6849**
Health and Physical Education/Hoken Taiiku Kyoshitsu (JPN ISSN 0018-3350) **2862**
• ➤ Health & Place (GBR ISSN 1353-8292) **4014**
• Health and Population: Perspectives and Issues (IND ISSN 0253-6803) **972**
Health & Productivity Management (USA) **5624**
• ➤ Health and Quality of Life Outcomes (GBR ISSN 1477-7525) **7521**
Health and Safety at Work (GBR ISSN 1464-1569) **6677**
Health & Safety @ Work (GBR ISSN 1745-2864) **6677**
• Health & Safety at Work (Croydon) (GBR ISSN 0141-8246) **6677**
• Health and Safety at Work (Kingston) (GBR) **6678**
Health & Safety at Work Act Newsletter (GBR ISSN 0966-8365) **6678**
† Health and Safety at Work Directory (GBR ISSN 1356-1928) **8961**
Health & Safety at Work in S A (ZAF ISSN 1742-6928) **6678**
Health and Safety Briefing (GBR ISSN 0963-5351) **6678**
Health & Safety Bulletin (London) (GBR) **7521**
Health and Safety Bulletin (Sutton) (GBR ISSN 1358-2208) **3497**
Health and Safety Commission Annual Report and the Health and Safety Commission Executive Accounts (GBR ISSN 1469-302X) **7521**
Health & Safety Commission Annual Report and the Health & Safety Commission Executive Accounts (GBR) **6678**
Health and Safety Commission. Newsletter *see* Health and Safety Newsletter **7521**
Health and Safety Executive Agriculture Information Sheet *see* H S E Agriculture Information Sheet **117**
Health and Safety Executive Information Sheet. Construction Information Sheet *see* H S E Information Sheet. Construction Information Sheet **1010**
Health and Safety Executive. News Bulletin Service (GBR ISSN 0956-4977) **6678**
Health and Safety Executive. Research Paper (GBR ISSN 0265-9581) **6678**
Health & Safety Law Reporter (CAN ISSN 1205-5719) **4686**
Health & Safety Manager *see* Croner's Health & Safety Manager **6675**
Health and Safety Matters *see* H S M **6677**
• Health & Safety Monitor (GBR ISSN 0140-8534) **6678**
Health and Safety Newsletter *see* H E S A Newsletter **6677**
Health and Safety Newsletter (GBR ISSN 1751-7850) **7521**
Health & Safety Newsline (GBR ISSN 0142-5021) **7521**
Health and Safety Regulations (NLD) **7521**
Health & Safety Resource (CAN ISSN 1198-1229) **3692**

Link to your serials resources and content with ulrichsweb.com

Title

10358 HEALTH S A GESONDHEID ULRICH'S PERIODICALS

• Health S A Gesondheid (Health South Africa Gesondheid) (ZAF ISSN 1025-9848) **5626**
• Health Science (USA ISSN 0883-8216) **6660**
▼ • ➤ Health Sciences Review (USA ISSN 1941-8310) **5626**
Health Scout News *see* Health Day **5624**
Health Scripts (USA) **5073**
The Health Service Journal (GBR ISSN 0952-2271) **4096**
Health Service Risks. Special Report (GBR ISSN 1364-8497) **4096**
Health Services Administration Education *see* Directory of Healthcare Management Education **2955**
• Health Services and Outcomes Research Methodology (USA ISSN 1387-3741) **5626**
Health Services Journal *see* Yobo Igaku Janaru **5734**
• ➤ Health Services Management Research (GBR ISSN 0951-4848) **5626**
• ➤ Health Services Research (USA ISSN 0017-9124) **4096**
Health Services Research and Development Research Briefs *see* H S R & D Research Briefs **6423**
Health Services Under Siege: the Case for Clinical Process Redesign *see* Medical Journal of Australia **5669**
Health Shopper (USA) **6988**
• ➤ Health Sociology Review (AUS ISSN 1446-1242) **8044**
Health Spa and Resort Newsletter (USA ISSN 1844-9123) **4387**
Health Statistics in the Nordic Countries *see* Helsestatistik for de Nordiske Lande **5747**
• ➤ Health Statistics Quarterly (GBR ISSN 1465-1645) **7284**
Health Statistics Wales/Ystadegau Iechyd Cymru (GBR ISSN 1361-3677) **4113**
• Health Stream Newsletter (AUS) **7523**
Health Systems Trust Annual Report *see* H S T Annual Report **5622**
• ➤ Health Technology Assessment (GBR ISSN 1366-5278) **5830**
Health Technology Assessment Reports *see* Office of Health Technology Assessment Reports **5689**
Health Technology Directions (USA ISSN 0730-8620) **7523**
• Health Technology Trends (USA ISSN 1041-6072) **5626**
• Health, United States (USA ISSN 0361-4468) **5747**
Health Visitor Opportunities *see* Community Practitioner **5956**
Health Vocational Education *see* Weisheng Zhiye Jiaoyu **2925**
• Health Voices (AUS ISSN 1835-5862) **4096**
• Health Watch (Washington D.C.) (USA) **7523**
Health Wisdom for Women (USA ISSN 1084-3442) **8846**
Health Word *see* HealthWord **4047**
Health Workforce in Alberta. Annual Report (CAN ISSN 1195-7506) **7523**
Health World *see* Jiankang Tiandi **6990**
Health World *see* Jiankang Shijie **6990**
• Healthcare Advertising Review (USA ISSN 8756-4513) **26**
• Healthcare Auditing Weekly (USA ISSN 1948-0563) **4097**
• Healthcare Benchmarks and Quality Improvement (USA ISSN 1541-1052) **4097**
• Healthcare Brief (AUS) **4097**
• Healthcare Building Ideas (USA ISSN 1948-9617) **1011**
Healthcare Convention & Exhibitors Association Association Alert *see* H C E A Association Alert **6280**
Healthcare Convention & Exhibitors Association Directory *see* H C E A Directory **6280**
• Healthcare Corporate Finance News (USA ISSN 1556-3642) **4097**
▼ • Healthcare Cost Containment (USA ISSN 1945-6360) **4097**
• Healthcare Counselling and Psychotherapy Journal (GBR ISSN 1475-0724) **4097**
Healthcare Design (USA ISSN 1541-7905) **4097**
Healthcare Directions (USA) **5073**
Healthcare Disparities Report (USA ISSN 1548-8268) **7523**
HealthCare Distributor (USA ISSN 1096-9160) **6846**
Healthcare Engineering Association of Japan. Journal *see* Byoin Setsubi **4089**
† Healthcare Enterprise (USA) **8961**
Healthcare Equipment & Supplies (GBR ISSN 1740-097X) **4097**
† Healthcare Equipment Supplies International (GBR ISSN 1472-5401) **8961**
HealthCare Ethics Committee Forum *see* H E C Forum **4094**
• Healthcare Executive (USA ISSN 0883-5381) **4097**
Healthcare Facilities Management (CAN) **4097**
Healthcare Finance News (USA ISSN 1932-7021) **4097**
• Healthcare Finance Newsweek (USA) **4097**
Healthcare Finance, Tax and Law Weekly *see* Healthcare Finance, Tax & Law Weekly **1351**
• Healthcare Finance, Tax & Law Weekly (USA ISSN 1551-5516) **1351**
Healthcare Financial Management Association Career Opportunities *see* H F M A Career Opportunities **6698**
Healthcare Financial Management Association Wants You to Know *see* H F M A Wants You to Know **6698**
Healthcare Financial Management Association's Patient Friendly Billing *see* H F M A's Patient Friendly Billing **4094**
Healthcare Financial Management Magazine *see* H F M Magazine **4094**
• Healthcare Hazard Control (USA) **5626**
• Healthcare Hazard Management Monitor (USA ISSN 1532-3633) **5626**
Healthcare I T News (Information Technology) (USA ISSN 1547-3139) **4114**
▼ Healthcare Imaging Update (USA ISSN 1940-8684) **4097**
• ➤ Healthcare Infection (AUS ISSN 1835-5617) **5814**
• Healthcare Informatics (USA ISSN 1050-9135) **5830**
Healthcare Information and Management Systems Society Insider *see* H I M S S Insider **4094**
Healthcare Information Management & Communications Canada (CAN ISSN 1485-7375) **7523**
HealthCare Insurance Report (GBR ISSN 1461-5746) **4505**
▼ • Healthcare Journal of Baton Rouge (USA ISSN 1937-7797) **5626**
Healthcare Leadership & Management Report *see* Healthcare Leadership Report **7523**
Healthcare Leadership Report (USA ISSN 1551-8906) **7523**
• Healthcare Leadership Review (USA ISSN 1082-6718) **4097**
Healthcare Leadership Review *see* C O R Healthcare Leadership Review **8938**
The Healthcare Ledger (USA ISSN 1932-8982) **5626**
• Healthcare Life Safety Compliance (USA ISSN 1523-7575) **4097**
The Healthcare Lobbyist *see* EURALex **6838**
Healthcare Management Communicator (USA ISSN 1542-0167) **4097**
Healthcare Management Education *see* Directory of Healthcare Management Education **2955**
• ➤ Healthcare Management Forum (CAN ISSN 0840-4704) **4097**
• Healthcare Market (GBR ISSN 1740-4835) **5626**
• Healthcare Market News (GBR ISSN 1360-9378) **4097**
Healthcare Market Strategist *see* Healthcare Marketing Advisor **4097**
• Healthcare Marketer's Executive Briefing (USA) **5626**
• Healthcare Marketing Advisor (USA ISSN 1931-9894) **4097**
• Healthcare Marketing Report (USA ISSN 0741-9368) **6988**
Healthcare Mergers, Acquisition & Ventures Week *see* Healthcare Mergers, Acquisition and Ventures Week **4097**
• Healthcare Mergers, Acquisition and Ventures Week (USA ISSN 1552-6380) **4097**
Healthcare Network Management *see* Renkei Iryou **4110**
Healthcare Organizations (USA ISSN 1910-6416) **4097**
• Healthcare Packaging (USA) **6710**
• Healthcare Parliamentary Monitor (GBR ISSN 0952-9519) **5626**
• ➤ Healthcare Policy/Politiques de Sante (CAN ISSN 1715-6572) **5626**
Healthcare Product Comparison System: Clinical Laboratory Edition *see* Clinical Laboratory Product Comparison System **5904**
Healthcare Product Comparison System: Hospital Edition *see* Hospital Product Comparison System **4101**
Healthcare Product Comparison System: Imaging and Radiology Edition *see* Imaging & Radiology Product Comparison System **6198**
Healthcare Product Comparison System: Surgical Edition *see* Surgical Product Comparison System **6260**
• Healthcare Purchasing News (USA ISSN 1098-3716) **4097**
• Healthcare Quarterly (CAN ISSN 1710-2774) **5626**
• The Healthcare Registration (USA ISSN 1524-1068) **1749**
Healthcare Resources (USA ISSN 1538-330X) **5747**
Healthcare Restaurant *see* Herusukea Resutoran **6660**
• Healthcare Review (Northern New England Edition) (USA ISSN 1084-130X) **4098**
Healthcare Review (Southern New England Edition) (USA ISSN 1084-1318) **4098**
• Healthcare Review Online (NZL ISSN 1173-7956) **5626**
• Healthcare Review Online: Experience in Practice (NZL ISSN 1175-0928) **4098**
• Healthcare Risk Control System (USA) **4098**
• Healthcare Risk Management (USA ISSN 1081-6534) **4098**
Healthcare Standards *see* Healthcare Standards Directory **5627**
• Healthcare Standards Directory (USA ISSN 1044-4076) **5627**
† Healthcare Standards Update (USA ISSN 1048-8103) **8961**
The Healthcare Strategist (USA ISSN 1097-0819) **4098**
Healthcare Technology Pipeline *see* The Medical Pipeline **5670**
• Healthcare Training Weekly (USA ISSN 1543-7361) **4098**
• Healthcare Traveler (USA ISSN 1077-5676) **4098**
Healthcare Trends & Forecasts (USA ISSN 1931-9754) **7523**
Healthcare Trends Report (USA ISSN 0894-7961) **5627**
• HealthcarePapers (CAN ISSN 1488-917X) **7523**
HealthDirect Agenda Cardiologie *see* HealthDirect Cardiologie **5787**
HealthDirect Agenda Neurologie *see* HealthDirect Neurologie **6144**
HealthDirect Cardiologie (NLD ISSN 1574-8758) **5787**
HealthDirect Diabetes (NLD ISSN 1569-7347) **5893**
HealthDirect Neurologie (NLD ISSN 1574-8731) **6144**
• HealthEX Specialist (GBR ISSN 1744-9375) **6988**
• HealthFacts (USA ISSN 0738-811X) **5627**
HealthFax (USA) **4098**
• HealthLeaders (USA ISSN 1536-1357) **4098**
▼ • HealthLeaders Daily News (USA) **4098**
• HealthLeaders eHealthcare & Technology Weekly News (USA) **4098**
• HealthLeaders Executive Survival Guide (USA) **4098**
HealthLeaders MedFax *see* HealthFax **4098**
HealthLeaders Media Daily News *see* HealthLeaders Daily News **4098**
• HealthLeaders Weekly Healthcare Business News (USA) **4098**
▼ Healthmatters (USA) **5893**
▼ • ➤ HealthMED (BIH ISSN 1840-2291) **5627**
▼ HealthNews (NZL ISSN 1177-8113) **7523**
HealthNews (Norwalk) (USA ISSN 1081-5880) **4098**
• Healthology (USA) **6988**
Healthplan *see* A H I P Coverage **4490**
Healthpoint (USA) **7523**
HealthServe (GBR) **7760**
HealthSmart Today (USA ISSN 1539-1205) **6660**
Healthstate (USA) **5627**
Healthways (USA ISSN 0897-9251) **6660**
Healthwire (USA ISSN 0199-8552) **5959**
Healthwise Handbook (USA ISSN 1051-8770) **6988**
Healthwise Handbook (Canadian Edition) *see* Healthwise Handbook **6988**
• HealthWord (USA ISSN 1554-5997) **4047**
Healthy & Fit (USA) **6988**
Healthy & HeartWise (AUS ISSN 1833-8798) **5627**
• Healthy Animals (USA) **288**
Healthy Canadians/Canadiens en Sante (CAN ISSN 1714-3837) **7523**
Healthy Children's Pictorial *see* Jiankang Shaonian Huabao **6990**
Healthy Companies (USA ISSN 0897-7615) **6678**
Healthy Cooking (USA ISSN 1547-1993) **3646**
Healthy Directions (USA) **7523**
Healthy Eating Market Assessment *see* Key Note Market Assessment. Healthy Eating **3652**
Healthy Family (JPN) **6988**
Healthy Food Guide *see* Australian Healthy Food Guide **3627**
Healthy Food Guide *see* New Zealand Healthy Food Guide **6664**
Healthy for Baby *see* Ertong yu Jiankang **2152**
• Healthy Horizons (USA) **5627**
Healthy Living (DEU) **6988**
Healthy Living *see* Delaware Today **3974**
Healthy Living N Y C (USA) **6988**
Healthy Living with Diabetes *see* Costco Healthy Living with Diabetes **5885**
Healthy Mind, Healthy Body (USA) **6988**
Healthy Minds (GBR ISSN 1462-8260) **2154**
• Healthy Options (NZL ISSN 1170-6058) **6988**
Healthy Pregnancy *see* Parenting's Healthy Pregnancy **6001**
Healthy Smile, Beautiful Smile Newsletter *see* Dental Zone Healthy Smile, Beautiful Smile Newsletter **5841**
Healthy Travel *see* Active Travel News **8253**
Healthy Traveler (USA) **8718**
Healthy Weight Journal *see* Health at Every Size **6660**
Healthy Woman (CAN ISSN 1496-1636) **8846**
• Healthy Women Today (USA) **8846**
Healthy Years (USA ISSN 1551-4617) **4047**
Healthychurch Mag Uk *see* He@lthychurch.mag.uk **7647**
Hear Our Wings (CAN ISSN 0846-3522) **3040**
Hear This (USA ISSN 0017-9175) **2286**
Heard Heritage (USA ISSN 0149-5046) **3769**
† • hEARd Magazine (AUS) **8961**
Heard Museum Journal (USA ISSN 1523-4401) **6525**
Hearing Aid Journal (IND ISSN 0971-0949) **4074**
Hearing Concern (GBR) **4074**
• Hearing Health (USA) **4074**
• Hearing Journal (USA ISSN 0745-7472) **4074**
Hearing Loss (USA ISSN 1090-6215) **4074**
• Hearing Matters (AUS ISSN 1444-5417) **4074**
Hearing News *see* Kuuloviesti **4075**
Hearing Products Report (USA ISSN 1530-6003) **4074**
The Hearing Professional (USA ISSN 1529-1340) **4074**
• ➤ Hearing Research (NLD ISSN 0378-5955) **6080**
▼ • Hearing Review (NZL ISSN 1178-6698) **6080**
• The Hearing Review (USA ISSN 1074-5734) **6080**
† Hearsay (AUS ISSN 0725-6108) **8961**
Hearsay (CAN ISSN 0704-4860) **2286**
Hearsay Handbook (USA) **4952**
Hearsay Magazine (GBR) **6573**
• ➤ Heart (GBR ISSN 1355-6037) **5787**
Heart (ZAF ISSN 1682-5063) **5787**
• Heart (Las Cruces) (USA ISSN 1932-5878) **8867**
Heart (Tokyo) *see* Shinzo **5799**
• Heart Advisor (USA ISSN 1523-9004) **5788**
• ➤ Heart & Lung (USA ISSN 0147-9563) **5959**
• Heart & Soul (USA ISSN 1092-1974) **6988**
Heart and Stroke Foundation of Canada. Annual Report (CAN) **5788**
• ➤ Heart and Vessels (JPN ISSN 0910-8327) **5788**
Heart and Vessels. Supplement *see* Heart and Vessels **5788**
▼ Heart Business Journal for Women (CAN) **1117**
† • Heart Disease (USA ISSN 1521-737X) **8961**
Heart Disease and Stroke in Canada (CAN ISSN 1201-9828) **5788**
• Heart Disease Weekly (USA ISSN 1531-6408) **5788**
Heart Diseases & Disorders Sourcebook (USA) **5788**
Heart Diseases and Disorders Sourcebook *see* Heart Diseases & Disorders Sourcebook **5788**
Heart Drug *see* Cardiology **5779**
• Heart Failure Clinics (USA ISSN 1551-7136) **5788**
• ➤ Heart Failure Monitor (GBR ISSN 1470-8590) **5788**
• ➤ Heart Failure Reviews (USA ISSN 1382-4147) **5788**
Heart, Health & Nutrition (USA ISSN 1554-2467) **5627**
Heart Healthy Cooking (USA ISSN 1537-8853) **4360**
Heart Healthy Living *see* Heart-Healthy Living **6660**
Heart-Healthy Living (USA ISSN 1559-2871) **6660**
▼ Heart Insight (USA ISSN 1934-5917) **5788**
• ➤ Heart International (ITA ISSN 2036-2579) **5788**
• ➤ Heart, Lung and Circulation (Print) (AUS ISSN 1443-9506) **5788**
Heart Nursing/Hato Nashingu (JPN ISSN 0914-2819) **5960**
Heart of America Aquarium Society News (USA ISSN 0193-1997) **6809**
The Heart of Europe *see* Im Herzen Europas **5220**
• Heart of New Hampshire Magazine (USA ISSN 1559-3991) **8718**
Heart of Texas Records (USA ISSN 0093-9854) **3769**
Heart Online *see* Heart **5787**
• Heart Rhythm (USA ISSN 1547-5271) **5788**
Heart Rhythm Society. Newsletter (USA) **5788**
Heart Statistics *see* Hjertestatistik **5747**
• ➤ The Heart Surgery Forum (USA ISSN 1098-3511) **5788**
• The Heart Thread Resource Page on Marriage, Parenting, Family & Society (USA) **8105**
Heart to Heart (NZL ISSN 1178-3923) **5410**
Heart to Heart Newsletter (USA) **7736**
Heart View (JPN ISSN 1342-6591) **5788**
Heart Wise Living *see* Healthy & HeartWise **5627**
† Heartbeat! (DEU) **8961**
Heartbeat (Antioch) (USA) **7760**
Heartbeat (Brainerd) (USA) **4098**
• Heartbeat : FM103.2 Newsletter (AUS) **2358**
Hearth & Home (USA) **4558**
Heartland Beef (NZL ISSN 1175-6438) **117**
Heartland Boating (USA ISSN 1042-1009) **8276**
Heartland Critiques (USA ISSN 1063-1186) **5410**
The Heartland Donor Newsletter (Print Edition) *see* Managing High Blood Pressure (Online Edition) **5664**
Heartland Link (USA) **3436**
Heartland Real Estate Business (USA ISSN 1542-8311) **7592**
Heartland Retailer (USA) **4120**
Heartland Sheep (NZL ISSN 1175-0642) **117**
Heartland U S A (USA) **6292**
• The Heartlander (USA) **8044**
Heartlands (USA) **5304**
The Heartlands Today *see* Heartlands **5304**
• HeartLinx (USA) **5788**
• Hearts at Home Newsletter (CAN) **8867**
Heartwise (IRL ISSN 1393-8207) **5788**
➤ HEAT (AUS ISSN 1326-1460) **5219**
Heat (London) (GBR ISSN 1465-6264) **3866**
• ➤ Heat and Mass Transfer (DEU ISSN 0947-7411) **7054**
Heat and Technology *see* International Journal of Heat and Technology **7055**
Heat Engineering *see* Foster Wheeler Review **3193**
Heat Exchanger Design Handbook *see* Heat Exchanger Design Update **3195**
Heat Exchanger Design Update (USA ISSN 1074-7214) **3195**
Heat Processing (DEU ISSN 1611-616X) **3367**
Heat Transfer and Fluid Mechanics Institute. Proceedings (USA ISSN 0097-059X) **3379**
• Heat Transfer - Asian Research (Online Edition) (USA ISSN 1523-1496) **3379**
• Heat Transfer - Asian Research (Print Edition) (USA ISSN 1099-2871) **3379**
• ➤ Heat Transfer Engineering (USA ISSN 0145-7632) **3245**
Heat Transfer - Fluid Flow Data Books (USA) **3379**
• Heat Transfer - Recent Contents (Online) (USA ISSN 1543-3056) **7048**
• Heat Transfer Research (USA ISSN 1064-2285) **3379**
Heat Transfer Society of Japan. Journal *see* Dennetsu **7053**

Link to your serials resources and content with ulrichsweb.com

Title

• ➤ Hehai Daxue Xuebao (Ziran Kexue Ban)/Hohai University. Journal (Natural Sciences Edition) (CHN ISSN 1000-1980) **2794**
Hehua Dian (CHN) **5304**
• Hehuaxue yu Fangshe Huaxue/Journal of Nuclear and Radiochemistry (CHN ISSN 0253-9950) **2063**
• Heibel-Ticker Plus (DEU ISSN 1862-5436) **1628**
• Heibel-Ticker Standard (DEU ISSN 1862-5428) **1628**
Heidegger-Jahrbuch (DEU ISSN 1612-3166) **6922**
Heidegger Studien *see* Heidegger Studies **6922**
Heidegger Studies/Etudes Heidegger/Heidegger Studien (DEU ISSN 0885-4580) **6922**
Heidelberger Akademie der Wissenschaften. Jahrbuch (DEU ISSN 0341-2865) **7860**
Heidelberger Akademie der Wissenschaften. Mathematisch - Naturwissenschaftliche Klasse. Schriften (DEU) **7860**
Heidelberger Akademie der Wissenschaften. Philosophisch-Historische Klasse. Supplemente zu den Schriften (DEU ISSN 0933-5323) **4141**
Heidelberger Akademie der Wissenschaften. Philosophisch-Historischen Klasse. Schriften (DEU) **6923**
Heidelberger Althistorische Beitraege und Epigraphische Studien (DEU ISSN 0930-1208) **2235**
Heidelberger Centrum fuer Euro-Asiatische Studien e.V. Aktuelle Debatte *see* H E C E A S - Aktuelle Debatte **7239**
Heidelberger Forschungen (DEU ISSN 0440-6044) **4454**
Heidelberger Geographische Arbeiten (DEU ISSN 0440-6052) **4014**
Heidelberger Jahrbuecher (USA ISSN 0073-1641) **7860**
Heidelberger Publikationen zur Slavistik A: Linguistische Reihe (DEU ISSN 0930-7281) **5124**
Heidelberger Publikationen zur Slavistik B: Literaturwissenschaftliche Reihe (DEU ISSN 0930-729X) **5304**
Heidelberger Rechtsvergleichende und Wirtschaftsrechtliche Studien (DEU ISSN 0170-320X) **4686**
Heidelberger Schriften zur Pharmazie- und Naturwissenschaftsgeschichte (DEU) **6846**
• Heidelberger Stadtblatt (DEU) **7494**
Heidelberger Studien zur Naturkunde der Fruehen Neuzeit (DEU ISSN 0935-6576) **7860**
• The Heights (Chestnut Hill) (USA ISSN 0017-9590) **2286**
Heiki to Gijutsu/Ordnance and Technology (JPN) **6423**
Heiko Shinkei Kagaku *see* Equilibrium Research **921**
Heilbad und Kurort (DEU ISSN 0343-768X) **309**
• Heilberufe (DEU ISSN 0017-9604) **5627**
Heilbronner Stimme (DEU) **3850**
Das Heilige Band (DEU ISSN 0017-9612) **3536**
Heiliger Dienst (AUT ISSN 0017-9620) **7646**
• Heilongjian Kejie Xinxi (CHN) **7860**
Heilongjiang Commercial College. Journal *see* Heilongjiang Shangxueyuan Xuebao (Ziran Kexueban) **7861**
Heilongjiang Daily *see* Heilongjiang Ribao **3825**
• Heilongjiang Daxue Ziran Kexue Xuebao/Heilongjiang University. Journal of Natural Sciences (CHN ISSN 1001-7011) **7861**
• Heilongjiang Dizhi/Heilongjiang Geology (CHN ISSN 1002-2325) **2746**
• Heilongjiang Dongwu Fanzhi Zazhi/Heilongjiang Journal of Animal Breeding (CHN ISSN 1005-2739) **288**
Heilongjiang Economy *see* Heilongjiang Jingjibao **1117**
Heilongjiang Education *see* Heilongjiang Jiaoyu **2863**
Heilongjiang Environmental Journal *see* Heilongjiang Huanjing Tongbao **3436**
Heilongjiang Finance *see* Heilongjiang Jingrong **1351**
Heilongjiang Fisheries *see* Heilongjiang Shuichan **3596**
Heilongjiang Geology *see* Heilongjiang Dizhi **2746**
• Heilongjiang Gongcheng Xueyuan Xuebao (Ziran Kexue Ban)/Heilongjiang Institute of Technology. Journal (CHN ISSN 1671-4679) **7861**
Heilongjiang Huabao (CHN ISSN 1004-2784) **3825**
• Heilongjiang Huanjing Tongbao/Heilongjiang Environmental Journal (CHN ISSN 1674-263X) **3436**
Heilongjiang Hydraulic Engineering College. Journal *see* Heilongjiang Shuizhuan Xuebao **3361**
Heilongjiang Institute of Science and Technology. Journal *see* Heilongjiang Keji Xueyuan Xuebao **7861**
Heilongjiang Institute of Technology. Journal *see* Heilongjiang Gongcheng Xueyuan Xuebao (Ziran Kexue Ban) **7861**
Heilongjiang Jiaoyu/Heilongjiang Education (CHN ISSN 0438-9050) **2863**
Heilongjiang Jingjibao/Heilongjiang Economy (CHN) **1117**
• Heilongjiang Jingrong/Heilongjiang Finance (CHN ISSN 1001-0432) **1351**
Heilongjiang Journal of Animal Breeding *see* Heilongjiang Dongwu Fanzhi Zazhi **288**
Heilongjiang Journal of Traditional Chinese Medicine *see* Heilongjiang Zhongyiyao **5627**
• Heilongjiang Keji Xueyuan Xuebao/Heilongjiang Institute of Science and Technology. Journal (CHN ISSN 1671-0118) **7861**
Heilongjiang Medical Journal *see* Heilongjiang Yiyao **5627**
Heilongjiang Medical Sciences *see* Heilongjiang Yixue **5627**
Heilongjiang Medicine and Pharmacy *see* Heilongjiang Yiyao Kexue **5627**
• Heilongjiang Qixiang (CHN ISSN 1002-252X) **6353**
• Heilongjiang Ribao/Heilongjiang Daily (CHN) **3825**
Heilongjiang Ribao Hedingben *see* Heilongjiang Ribao **3825**
• Heilongjiang Shangxueyuan Xuebao (Ziran Kexueban)/Heilongjiang Commercial College. Journal (CHN ISSN 1004-1842) **7861**
Heilongjiang Shiyou Huagong/Heilongjiang Petrochemical Technology *see* Lianyou yu Huagong **6777**
• Heilongjiang Shuichan/Heilongjiang Fisheries (CHN ISSN 1674-2419) **3596**
• Heilongjiang Shuizhuan Xuebao/Heilongjiang Hydraulic Engineering College. Journal (CHN ISSN 1000-9833) **3361**
Heilongjiang University. Journal of Natural Sciences *see* Heilongjiang Daxue Ziran Kexue Xuebao **7861**
• Heilongjiang Yixue/Heilongjiang Medical Sciences (CHN ISSN 1004-5775) **5627**
• Heilongjiang Yiyao/Heilongjiang Medical Journal (CHN ISSN 1006-2882) **5627**
• Heilongjiang Yiyao Kexue/Heilongjiang Medicine and Pharmacy (CHN ISSN 1008-0104) **5627**
• Heilongjiang Zhongyiyao/Heilongjiang Journal of Traditional Chinese Medicine (CHN ISSN 1000-9906) **5627**
Heilpaedagogik (AUT ISSN 0438-9174) **5627**
Heilpaedagogik in Forschung und Praxis (DEU ISSN 1611-3136) **5627**
• Heilpaedagogik Online (DEU ISSN 1610-613X) **3041**
Heilpaedagogische Forschung (DEU ISSN 0017-9647) **6144**
Der Heilpraktiker und Volksheilkunde (DEU ISSN 1432-6256) **309**
Heilsarmee Zeitung (CHE) **7760**
Heilsuhringurinn (ISL ISSN 1563-3128) **309**
• Heim + Pflege (DEU ISSN 0941-8172) **4047**
Heim und Hobby (DEU ISSN 0342-5045) **4360**
Heim und Pflege *see* Heim + Pflege **4047**
Heim und Welt (DEU ISSN 0947-3335) **8867**
Heim und Welt - Mein Horoskop *see* Mein Horoskop **566**
Heima er Bezt (ISL ISSN 0017-9698) **3877**
Die Heimat *see* Natur- und Landeskunde **4247**
Heimat am Inn (DEU) **4226**
Heimat-Chronik - Komotauer Zeitung (DEU ISSN 1431-231X) **3536**
Heimat Dortmund (DEU ISSN 0932-9757) **7494**
Heimat im Weinland (AUT) **4226**
Heimat-Roman (DEU) **5410**
Heimat- und Trachtenbote (DEU) **4226**
Heimat - Zeitung Roemerstaedter Laendchen (DEU ISSN 0017-9752) **4226**
Heimatblaetter des Rhein-Sieg-Kreises (DEU) **4226**
Heimatblaettle (DEU ISSN 0935-364X) **4226**
Heimatbrief der Stadt Germersheim (DEU) **4226**
Heimatbriefe der Stadt Pirmasens (DEU) **7494**
Heimatbuch des Kreises Viersen (DEU ISSN 0948-6631) **4141**
Heimatgruss (DEU ISSN 0440-6230) **4226**
Heimatjahrbuch Kreis Ahrweiler (DEU ISSN 0342-5827) **5304**
Heimatjahrbuch Landkreis Alzey-Worms (DEU) **3850**
Heimatkalender fuer die Lueneburger Heide (DEU ISSN 0945-4942) **3850**
Heimatkunde, Kulturpflege, Stadtgeschichte (AUT) **4226**
Heimatkundliche Nachrichten (AUT) **4226**
Heimatland Lippe (DEU ISSN 0017-9787) **3850**
Das Heimatmuseum Alsergrund (AUT ISSN 0017-9809) **4226**
Heimatpflege in Westfalen (DEU ISSN 0933-6346) **3436**
Der Heimatpfleger (DEU ISSN 0177-2538) **3618**
Heimatschutz/Sauvegarde (CHE ISSN 0017-9817) **2613**
Heimatstimmen aus dem Kreis Olpe (DEU ISSN 0177-2899) **4226**
Heimatzeitung Kreis Koenigsberg - Neumark (DEU) **3850**
† Heimdal (FRA ISSN 0336-030X) **8961**
➤ Heimen (NOR ISSN 0017-9841) **4226**
• Heimevernsbladet (NOR ISSN 0017-985X) **6423**
Heimkino (DEU ISSN 1614-6727) **3100**
Heimtex Orient *see* Carpet X L **4554**
Heimtex Orient (DEU) **4558**
HEIMvizier (NLD ISSN 1875-6034) **6525**
Heimvorteil (DEU) **2983**
Heimwerker Praxis (DEU) **4438**
Heimwerker Test *see* Heimwerker Praxis **4438**
Heimwerkermagazin (AUT) **4438**
Hein Checklist of Statutes (USA) **4686**
Heine A La Carte (AUT) **4387**
Heine-Jahrbuch (DEU ISSN 0073-1692) **5304**
Heine Saekularausgabe: Werke-Briefwechsel-Lebenszeugnisse (DEU) **5304**
Heinrich-Mann-Jahrbuch (DEU ISSN 0176-3318) **5304**
Heinrich Schmid Aktuell *see* H S Aktuell **492**
Heinrichsblatt (DEU) **7647**
Heinz (DEU) **3850**
Heinz Nixdorf Institut Jahresbericht *see* H N I Jahresbericht **3194**
Heinz Nixdorf Institut Nachrichten *see* H N I Nachrichten **3194**
HeinzeBauOffice. Band 1: Firmeninformationen, Produktinformationen, Markennamenverzeichnis (DEU ISSN 1863-4753) **2004**
HeinzeBauOffice. Band 2: Herstellerverzeichnis. Baukonstruktionen (DEU ISSN 1863-4761) **2004**
HeinzeBauOffice. Band 3: Herstellerverzeichnis. Technische Anlagen, Aussenanlagen, Ausstattung (DEU ISSN 1863-477X) **2004**
HeinzeBauOffice Journal *see* Journal (Celle) **1018**
• Heir Lines (USA ISSN 0742-4779) **3770**
The Heirloom Gardener Magazine (USA ISSN 1548-1085) **3736**
Heisey News (USA ISSN 0731-8014) **366**
Heiwa Kenkyu/Peace Studies (JPN ISSN 0385-0749) **7240**
Heizung Klima Gebaeudetechnik *see* H K Gebaeudetechnik **4119**
Heizung und Lueftung/Chauffage et Ventilation (CHE ISSN 0251-1231) **4120**
Heizungs-Ratgeber (DEU) **4120**
Heizungsjournal (DEU ISSN 0722-690X) **4120**
• ➤ Hejishu/Nuclear Techniques (CHN ISSN 0253-3219) **3168**
Hejnal Mariacki (POL ISSN 0017-9914) **7799**
• Hejubian yu Denglizitiwuli/Nuclear Fusion and Plasma Physics (CHN ISSN 0254-6086) **7066**
De Hekkensluiter (NLD ISSN 1573-6466) **4226**
Hel Achau (GBR ISSN 0260-1753) **3770**
Hela Jorden (SWE ISSN 1102-0105) **7647**
Heldia (DEU ISSN 0176-2621) **945**
Heldia. Sonderhefte (DEU ISSN 0932-4143) **945**
Hele Danmarks Familie Journal *see* Familie Journalen **3833**
Helen (USA) **8867**
Helen Hecker's Hotline (USA) **7562**
• Helen K. Mussallem Library Selected Acquisitions (CAN) **5747**
Helen Kellogg Institute for International Studies. Working Paper (USA) **7968**
Helensburgh Advertiser (GBR ISSN 1356-8663) **3866**
Helsestatistikk *see* Norway. Statistisk Sentralbyraa. Helsestatistikk **7548**
Helfen und Retten *see* Rotkreuzmagazin **8066**
† Helfende Haende (DEU) **8962**
Der Helfer *see* KinderSpiel **2159**
Helft Uns Helfen (AUT) **8044**
Helgeland Arbeiderblad (NOR) **3923**
Helgelands Blad (NOR) **3923**
Der Helgolaender (DEU) **3850**
• ➤ Helgoland Marine Research (DEU ISSN 1438-387X) **2806**
Heli Ski - Cat Ski Journal *see* Heliski Catski Journal **8962**
Helia (SRB ISSN 1018-1806) **234**
Heliand Korrespondenz (DEU) **7799**
Helice (ESP ISSN 1133-7451) **5423**
Helice (MEX) **58**
Helico Revue (CHE ISSN 1019-1178) **58**
Helicobacter (Japanese Edition) *see* Helicobacter (Oxford) **887**
• ➤ Helicobacter (Oxford) (GBR ISSN 1083-4389) **887**
• Helicobacter. Supplement (GBR ISSN 1478-4041) **5926**
Helicon (DEU ISSN 0721-2879) **5304**
Heliconia Society International Bulletin *see* H S I Bulletin **3735**
Helicopter Annual (USA ISSN 0739-5728) **8544**
Helicopter Association International. Maintenance Update (USA) **8544**
Helicopter Association International. Operations Update (USA) **8544**
Helicopter Association International. Preliminary Accident Reports (USA) **58**
Helicopter Guide *see* Guia do Helicoptero **8543**
• Helicopter International Magazine (GBR ISSN 1369-7358) **58**
Helicopter Markets and Systems *see* Jane's Helicopter Markets and Systems **62**
• Helicopter News (USA ISSN 0363-8227) **58**
Helicopter Safety *see* AeroSafety World **8533**
Helicopter World. Special Report (GBR ISSN 1744-2605) **8544**
Helicoptere Business Loisirs *see* Helicoptere Magazine **58**
Helicoptere Magazine (FRA ISSN 1957-1372) **58**
Helicopters (CAN ISSN 0227-3160) **8544**
➤ Helictite (AUS ISSN 0017-9973) **2746**
HeliData Classified *see* HeliData News & Classified **58**
HeliData News *see* HeliData News & Classified **58**
• HeliData News & Classified (GBR ISSN 1740-7788) **58**
Helikon (HUN ISSN 0017-999X) **5304**
Helikon (ITA ISSN 0017-9981) **2235**
Helikon (ROM ISSN 1220-6288) **5304**
Heliopolis (ITA) **5423**
• Helios (ITA ISSN 1970-8254) **6245**
• ➤ Helios (USA ISSN 0160-0923) **5304**
Heliotrope (USA ISSN 1541-9908) **5304**
• ➤ Heliotropia (USA ISSN 1542-3352) **5304**
Heliport Development Guide (USA ISSN 0882-6633) **8544**
† Heliski Catski Journal (USA) **8962**
• Helium Report (USA ISSN 1933-6853) **8718**
Helix (AUS ISSN 1033-3096) **7861**
Helix (GBR ISSN 1466-1330) **765**
Hellas (USA ISSN 1044-5331) **5423**
Hellas et Roma (CHE ISSN 1424-7720) **2235**
Hellenews (GRC) **1117**
The Hellenic Calendar (USA) **3536**
Hellenic Canadian Chronicles (CAN) **3536**
Hellenic Conference on Informatics. Proceedings *see* Advances on Informatics **2406**
Hellenic European Research on Mathematics and Informatics Science *see* H E R M I S **5552**
Hellenic Hamilton News (CAN ISSN 0715-4410) **3537**
Hellenic Industrial Development Bank. Investment Guide (GRC) **1628**
Hellenic Journal (USA) **3537**
• ➤ Hellenic Journal of Cardiology/Helleniki Kardiologiki Epitheorisi (GRC ISSN 1011-7970) **5788**
• Hellenic Journal of Nuclear Medicine/Ellenike Purenike Iatrike - Ellenike Etaireia Purenikes Iatrikes Thessalonikes (GRC ISSN 1108-1430) **5627**
Hellenic Journal of Psychology (GRC ISSN 1790-1391) **7360**
• Hellenic Journal of Surgery (AUT) **6245**
Hellenic Medical Journal (GBR ISSN 1365-7291) **5627**
Hellenic Meteorological Society. Bulletin *see* Deltion Ellenikes Meteorologikes Etaireias **6351**
Hellenic Military Geographical Service. Bulletin *see* Geografikes Uperesias Stratou. Deltio **4009**
Hellenic Nephrology *see* Ellenike Nefrologia **6267**
Hellenic News (CAN ISSN 0821-7270) **3537**
Hellenic Numismatic Society. Biblioteca (GRC) **6651**
▼ • ➤ Hellenic Open University Journal of Informatics (GRC ISSN 1791-4701) **2419**
Hellenic Orthodontic Review *see* Ellenike Orthodontike Epitheorese **5843**
Hellenic Philatelic Society of Great Britain. Bulletin (GBR ISSN 0950-3102) **6895**
Hellenic Stomatological Review (GRC ISSN 1011-4181) **5846**
• Hellenic Times (USA ISSN 1059-2121) **3537**
• Hellenic Veterinary Medical Society. Bulletin/Ellinikis Ktiniatrikis Eterias. Deltio (GRC ISSN 0257-2354) **8798**
Hellenic Zoological Archives *see* Elleniko Zoologiko Arheio **941**
Hellenika (DEU ISSN 0018-0084) **5304**
➤ Hellenika (SWE ISSN 0348-0100) **2235**
Hellenike Cheirougike *see* Hellenic Journal of Surgery **6245**
Hellenike Mathematike Hetaireia. Deltion *see* Greek Mathematical Society. Bulletin **5490**
Helleniki Kardiologiki Epitheorisi *see* Hellenic Journal of Cardiology **5788**
➤ Hellenistic Culture & Society (USA ISSN 1054-0857) **2235**
Heller Commercial Property Development Precedents *see* Commercial Property Development Precedents **7587**
Heller Helper (USA ISSN 0882-5882) **3770**
Helliniki Epitheorissis Evropaikou Dikaiou/Greek Review of European Law/Revue Hellenique de Droit Europeen (GRC ISSN 0251-6535) **4927**
Hellmuth-Loening-Zentrum fuer Staatswissenschaften Jena. Schriften (DEU) **7240**
Hellnotes (USA) **5443**
Hello! (CAN) **5073**
• Hello! (GBR ISSN 0214-3887) **5073**
Hello! (GRC) **3874**
Hello! (RUS ISSN 1811-0924) **5073**
Hello (SGP ISSN 0217-3948) **2368**
Hello Again (USA) **2266**
Hello Baby (NLD) **2154**
Hello Bali (IDN ISSN 0216-3489) **3891**
▼ Hello Kitty Magazin (HUN) **2192**
Hello Kitty Magazine (DEU) **2192**
Hello! Net/Dajia Lai Shang Wang (TWN ISSN 1561-0438) **2557**
Hello Southern Africa (ZAF) **8718**
Hellraiser (UKR) **6573**
Helm-Nieuws (NLD ISSN 1384-5500) **3770**
Helmantica (ESP ISSN 0018-0114) **4455**
• ➤ Helminthologia (POL ISSN 0440-6605) **945**
• Helminthological Abstracts (GBR ISSN 0957-6789) **716**
Help Desk Institute Support World *see* H D I Support World **2419**
Help Desk Solutions (USA) **2497**
Help the Aged News (GBR ISSN 1365-7402) **8044**
▼ Helpen (NLD ISSN 1875-1164) **8044**
The Helper (USA ISSN 1064-4873) **5814**
Helper to Trade Union's Members (BGR) **4595**
• Helping Children Learn (Elementary School Edition) (USA ISSN 1526-9264) **2863**
• Helping Children Learn (School Readiness English Edition) (USA ISSN 1526-9256) **2863**
† Helping Children Locally Information Book (GBR ISSN 1751-0937) **8962**
Helping Hand in Bible Study (USA) **7760**
Helping Out in the Outdoors (USA ISSN 8756-310X) **8317**
• Helping Students Learn (High School English Edition) (USA ISSN 1526-9280) **2863**
• Helping Students Learn (Middle School English Edition) (USA ISSN 1526-9272) **2863**
Helpot Ristikot (FIN ISSN 1456-1727) **8177**
Helse *see* Helsejob **6988**
• Helse (DNK ISSN 0018-0149) **6988**
• Helse (NOR ISSN 1503-1780) **8044**

DIRECTORY 2010 HENAN UNIVERSITY OF SCIENCE & TECHNOLOGY. JOURNAL (SOCIAL 10361

• Helse Finnmark. Nythetsbrev (NOR ISSN 1890-1581) **8044**
• Helse i Vest (NOR ISSN 1504-3703) **8044**
Helse Medisin Teknikk *see* H M T **4095**
• Helsejob (DNK ISSN 1903-8461) **6988**
• Helsenytt for Alle (NOR ISSN 0333-2861) **7524**
• Helserevyen Online (NOR ISSN 1890-2979) **7524**
• Helsestatistikk for de Nordiske Lande/Health Statistics in the Nordic Countries (DNK ISSN 0900-7962) **5747**
Helsinfors Laekartidning *see* Helsingin Laakarilehti **5627**
Helsingborgs Dagblad (SWE) **3955**
Helsingfors i Forna Tider (FIN ISSN 0356-875X) **3838**
Helsingfors Slaktforskare. Skrifter *see* Uppsatser **4276**
Helsingfors Stads Faktacentral. Kvartalspublikation *see* Helsingin Kaupungin Tietokeskuksen Neljannesvuosijulkaisu. Kvartti **7444**
Helsingfors Stads Faktacentral. Statistik *see* Helsingin Kaupungin Tietokeskus. Tilastoja **7481**
Helsingfors Universitet. Institutionen foer Ekonomi. Kompendium *see* Helsingin Yliopisto. Taloustieteen Laitos. Monistesarja **1118**
Helsingfors Universitet. Institutionen foer Ekonomi. Publikationer *see* Helsingin Yliopisto. Taloustieteen Laitos. Julkaisuja **1118**
Helsingfors Universitet. Veterinaermedicinska Fakulteten. Publikationer *see* Helsingin Yliopisto. Elainlaaketieteellinen Tiedekunta. Julkaisuja **8798**
Helsingfors Universitets Biblioteks Skrifter *see* Helsingin Yliopiston Kirjaston. Julkaisuja **5012**
Helsingin Kauppakorkeakoulu. Julkaisusarja A. Vaitoskirjat *see* Acta Universitatis Oeconomicae Helsingiensis. A **1056**
• Helsingin Kauppakorkeakoulu. Julkaisusarja B. Tutkimuksia/Helsinki School of Economics. Series B (FIN ISSN 0356-889X) **1117**
Helsingin Kauppakorkeakoulu. Julkaisusarja C. Oppikirjoja./Helsinki School of Economics. C, Textbooks (FIN ISSN 0356-892X) **1117**
Helsingin Kauppakorkeakoulu. Julkaisusarja D./Helsinki School of Economics. Research Notes D. (FIN ISSN 0356-8164) **1236**
Helsingin Kauppakorkeakoulu. Selvityksiae. E (FIN ISSN 1237-5330) **1118**
Helsingin Kauppakorkeakoulu. W. Working Papers (Online) (FIN ISSN 1795-1828) **1118**
Helsingin Kauppakorkeakoulu. W. Working Papers (Print) *see* Helsingin Kauppakorkeakoulu. W. Working Papers (Online) **1118**
• Helsingin Kaupungin Tietokeskuksen Neljannesvuosijulkaisu. Kvartti/City of Helsinki Urban Facts. Quarterly/Helsingfors Stads Faktacentral. Kvartalspublikation (FIN ISSN 0788-1576) **7444**
• Helsingin Kaupungin Tietokeskus. Keskustelualoitteita/Core Indicators for Sustainable Development in Helsinki (FIN ISSN 1455-7258) **7444**
• Helsingin Kaupungin Tietokeskus. Tilastoja/City of Helsinki Urban Facts. Statistics/Helsingfors Stads Faktacentral. Statistik (FIN ISSN 1455-7231) **7481**
Helsingin Kaupungin Tilastollinen Vuosikirja (FIN ISSN 0785-8736) **8376**
Helsingin Kaupungin Ymparistokeskuksen Julkaisuja (FIN ISSN 1235-9718) **3436**
Helsingin Laakarilehti/Helsinfors Laekartidning (FIN ISSN 0437-2468) **5627**
• Helsingin Sanomat (FIN ISSN 0355-2047) **3838**
Helsingin Sanomat. Kuukausiliite (FIN ISSN 0780-0096) **3838**
Helsingin Yliopisto. Biocentri Viikki Universitatis Helsingiensis. Dissertations *see* Helsingin Yliopisto. Biotieteellinen Tiedekunta. Dissertationes Bioscientiarum Molecularium Universitatis Helsingiensis in Viikki **676**
• Helsingin Yliopisto. Biotieteellinen Tiedekunta. Dissertationes Bioscientiarum Molecularium Universitatis Helsingiensis in Viikki (FIN ISSN 1795-7079) **676**
• Helsingin Yliopisto. Elainlaaketieteellinen Tiedekunta. Julkaisuja/Helsingfors Universitet. Veterinaermedicinska Fakulteten. Publikationer/University of Helsinki. Faculty of Veterinary Medicine. Publications (FIN ISSN 1457-1552) **8798**
• Helsingin Yliopisto. Elainlaaketieteellinen Tiedekunta. Oppimateriaalia. (FIN ISSN 1457-1544) **8798**
Helsingin Yliopisto. Kotielaintieteen Laitos. Julkaisuja/University of Helsinki. Department of Animal Science. Publications (FIN ISSN 1236-9837) **288**
Helsingin Yliopisto. Maaseudun Tutkimus- ja Koulutuskeskus. Julkaisuja *see* Helsingin Yliopisto. Ruralia-Instituutti. Julkaisuja **1489**
Helsingin Yliopisto. Maaseudun Tutkimus- ja Koulutuskeskus. Raportteja *see* Helsingin Yliopisto. Ruralia-Instituutti. Raportteja **1489**
Helsingin Yliopisto. Metsaekologian Laitos. Julkaisuja/University of Helsinki. Department of Forest Ecology. Publications (FIN ISSN 1235-4449) **3692**
Helsingin Yliopisto. Metsavarojen Kayton Laitos. Julkaisuja/Helsinki University. Department of Forest Resource Management. Publications (FIN ISSN 1236-1313) **3692**
Helsingin Yliopisto. Opettajankoulutuslaitos. Tutkimuksia *see* Helsingin Yliopisto. Soveltavan Kasvatustieteen Laitos. Tukimuksia **2863**
• Helsingin Yliopisto. Ruralia-Instituutti. Julkaisuja (FIN ISSN 1796-0649) **1489**
• Helsingin Yliopisto. Ruralia-Instituutti. Raportteja (FIN ISSN 1796-0622) **1489**
Helsingin Yliopisto. Soveltavan Biologian Laitos.Julkaisuja *see* Helsingin Yliopisto. Soveltavan Biologian Laitos. Publications **676**
Helsingin Yliopisto. Soveltavan Biologian Laitos. Publications/Helsingin Yliopisto. Soveltavan Biologian Laitos.Julkaisuja (FIN ISSN 1457-8085) **676**
Helsingin Yliopisto. Soveltavan Elaintieteen Laitos. Julkaisuja/University of Helsinki. Department of Applied Zoology. Reports (FIN ISSN 1235-0664) **945**
Helsingin Yliopisto. Soveltavan Kasvatustieteen Laitos. Studia Paedagogica (FIN ISSN 1236-2867) **2863**
Helsingin Yliopisto. Soveltavan Kasvatustieteen Laitos. Tukimuksia/University of Helsinki. Department of Applied Sciences of Education. Research Report (FIN ISSN 1795-2158) **2863**
• Helsingin Yliopisto. Taloustieteen Laitos. Julkaisuja/Helsingfors Universitet. Institutionen foer Ekonomi. Publikationer/University of Helsinki. Department of Economics and Management. Publications (FIN ISSN 1235-2241) **1118**
Helsingin Yliopisto. Taloustieteen Laitos. Monistesarja/Helsingfors Universitet. Institutionen foer Ekonomi. Kompendium (FIN ISSN 1237-2722) **1118**
• Helsingin Yliopisto. Taloustieteen Laitos. Selvityksia/University of Helsinki. Department of Economics and Management. Working Papers (FIN ISSN 1455-8211) **1118**
Helsingin Yliopisto, Vasa Nation. Aarsbok (FIN ISSN 1795-5211) **2983**
• Helsingin Yliopisto. Viikin Normaalikoulu. Julkaisu (FIN ISSN 1795-0589) **2863**
Helsingin Yliopiston Kirjaston. Julkaisuja/Helsingfors Universitets Biblioteks Skrifter/Helsinki University Library. Publications (FIN ISSN 0355-1350) **5012**
• Helsingoer Dagblad (DNK) **3834**
Helsingoer Kommunes Museer *see* Helsingoer Kommunes Museer. Aarbog **6525**
Helsingoer Kommunes Museer. Aarbog (DNK ISSN 1902-6447) **6525**
Helsinki European Institute for Crime Prevention and Control Papers *see* H E U N I Papers **4890**
Helsinki In Your Pocket (FIN) **8718**
Helsinki Monitor *see* Security and Human Rights **7215**
Helsinki Papers in Archaeology (FIN ISSN 0783-2842) **396**
Helsinki Quarterly *see* Helsingin Kaupungin Tietokeskuksen Neljannesvuosijulkaisu. Kvartti **7444**
Helsinki School of Economics. C, Textbooks *see* Helsingin Kauppakorkeakoulu. Julkaisusarja C. Oppikirjoja. **1117**
Helsinki School of Economics. Research Notes D. *see* Helsingin Kauppakorkeakoulu. Julkaisusarja D. **1236**
Helsinki School of Economics. Series B *see* Helsingin Kauppakorkeakoulu. Julkaisusarja B. Tutkimuksia **1117**
▼ • Helsinki Times (FIN ISSN 1796-8321) **3838**
Helsinki University. Department of Forest Resource Management. Publications *see* Helsingin Yliopisto. Metsavarojen Kayton Laitos. Julkaisuja **3692**
Helsinki University Library. Publications *see* Helsingin Yliopiston Kirjaston. Julkaisuja **5012**
• Helsinki University of Technology. Laboratory of Industrial Management. Report (FIN ISSN 1459-806X) **1749**
Helsinki University of Technology. Laboratory of Paper and Printing Technology. Reports. Series A (FIN ISSN 1796-7414) **6734**
Helsinki University of Technology. Laboratory of Paper and Printing Technology. Reports. Series B (FIN ISSN 1797-0008) **6734**
Helsinki University of Technology. Laboratory of Paper Technology. Reports. Series A *see* Helsinki University of Technology. Laboratory of Paper and Printing Technology. Reports. Series A **6734**
Helsinki University of Technology. Laboratory of Paper Technology. Reports. Series B *see* Helsinki University of Technology. Laboratory of Paper and Printing Technology. Reports. Series B **6734**
Helsinki University of Technology. Laboratory of Structural Engineering and Building Physics. Publications/Teknillinen Korkeakoulu. Talonrakennustekniikan Laboratorio. Julkaisu (FIN ISSN 1456-4297) **3268**
• Helsinki University of Technology. Laboratory of Work Psychology and Leadership. Report/Teknillinen Korkeakoulu. Tyopsykologian Laboratorio. Report (FIN ISSN 1459-8035) **7360**
Helsinki University of Technology. Radio Laboratory Publications. Report S *see* T T K Radio Science and Engineering Publications **2364**
Helsinki University of Technology. Signal Processing Laboratory. Report (FIN ISSN 1458-6401) **2570**
• He@lthychurch.mag.uk (GBR ISSN 1748-8028) **7647**
Helvetia Sacra (CHE) **7647**
• ➤ Helvetica Chimica Acta (CHE ISSN 0018-019X) **2063**
Helvetische Muenzen-Zeitung *see* Numis-Post und H M Zeitung **6652**
Helwan University. Science & Arts. Research Studies/Magallat Ulum wa Fonoun. Dirasat wa Behouth (EGY ISSN 1110-1369) **5304**
Hem Aware (USA ISSN 1088-7008) **5937**
• Hem & Hyra/Our Dwelling (SWE ISSN 1654-2576) **4412**
Hem och Samhaelle (SWE ISSN 0018-0254) **4360**
• ➤ Hem/Onc Today (USA ISSN 1526-0488) **5937**
• ➤ Hematologia, Citoquinas, Inmunoterapia y Terapia Celular (ESP ISSN 1138-6029) **5937**
Hematologia Practica (ESP ISSN 1886-4325) **5937**
• ➤ Hematological Oncology (GBR ISSN 0278-0232) **5937**
• ➤ Hematologie (FRA ISSN 1264-7527) **5937**
• ➤ Hematology (GBR ISSN 1024-5332) **5937**
Hematology *see* Hematology Education **5937**
• Hematology (USA ISSN 1520-4391) **5937**
Hematology & Oncology *see* Ketsueki Shuyoka **5939**
Hematology and Transfusiology *see* Gematologiya i Transfusiologiya **5936**
Hematology Education (NLD ISSN 1872-5503) **5937**
Hematology Frontier *see* Ketsueki Furontia **5939**
• The Hematology Journal (GBR ISSN 1466-4860) **5789**
▼ • ➤ Hematology - Oncology and Stem Cell Therapy (SAU ISSN 1658-3876) **5937**
• ➤ Hematology / Oncology Clinics of North America (USA ISSN 0889-8588) **6021**
➤ Hematology Oncology News & Issues (USA ISSN 1538-6902) **6021**
Hematology. Proceedings (PAK ISSN 1728-9467) **5938**
▼ • ➤ Hematology Reviews (ITA ISSN 1970-6804) **5938**
• Hematology Week (USA ISSN 1543-673X) **5938**
Hembygden (SWE ISSN 0346-9018) **2686**
Hemecht (LUX ISSN 0018-0270) **4141**
Hemi - Sync Journal (USA) **7087**
➤ Hemijska Industrija (SRB ISSN 0367-598X) **3245**
Hemijski Pregled/Chemical Review (SRB ISSN 0440-6826) **2063**
Hemingway Newsletter (USA ISSN 0739-7801) **5304**
• ➤ The Hemingway Review (USA ISSN 0276-3362) **5305**
Hemipterological Society of Japan. Transactions *see* Rostria **858**
• Hemisphere (USA ISSN 0898-3038) **7240**
Hemispheres (USA) **8783**
Hemkundskap i Skolan *see* Hushaalsvetaren **4361**
Hemlock Timelines *see* Compassion and Choices Magazine **5599**
Hemma i H S B (Hyresgaesternes Sparkasse- och Byggnadsfoereningars Riksfoerbund) (SWE) **4412**
HemmaBio (SWE ISSN 1402-7402) **6502**
Hemmets Journal (SWE ISSN 0018-0327) **3955**
Hemmets Vaen (SWE ISSN 0018-0335) **7647**
Hemmets Veckotidning (SWE ISSN 0345-4630) **3955**
Hemmings Classic Car (USA ISSN 1550-8730) **8583**
Hemmings Collector-Car Almanac (USA ISSN 1543-7213) **366**
• Hemmings Motor News (USA) **8583**
Hemmings Muscle Machines (USA ISSN 1550-0691) **8177**
Hemmings Rods & Performance (USA) **8583**
Hemmings Sports & Exotic Car (USA ISSN 1555-6867) **8177**
• Hemodialysis International (USA ISSN 1492-7535) **5938**
• ➤ Hemoglobin (GBR ISSN 0363-0269) **5938**
• Hemophilia Symposium (DEU) **5938**
• Hemophilia Today (CAN ISSN 0046-7251) **5938**
L'Hemophilie de Nos Jours *see* Hemophilia Today **5938**
▼ Hemostasis Laboratory (USA ISSN 1941-8493) **5938**
• L'Hemovigilance (FRA ISSN 1630-7399) **5938**
• Hempels Strassenmagazin (DEU) **3850**
Hempstead County Historical Society. Journal (USA) **4294**
Hemsloejden (SWE ISSN 0345-4649) **536**
Hemtraedgaarden (SWE ISSN 0018-0343) **3736**
Hemvaernet (SWE ISSN 0018-0351) **6423**
Henan Agricultural University. Journal *see* Henan Nongye Daxue Xuebao **118**
Henan Chemical Industry *see* Henan Huagong **1118**
Henan Daily *see* Henan Ribao **3825**
• Henan Daxue Xuebao (Shehui Kexue Ban)/Henan University. Journal (Social Science Edition) (CHN ISSN 1000-5242) **4455**
• Henan Daxue Xuebao (Yixue Kexue Ban)/Henan University. Journal (Medical Edition) (CHN) **5627**
• Henan Daxue Xuebao (Ziran Kexue Ban)/Henan University. Journal (Natural Science Edition) (CHN ISSN 1003-4978) **7861**
• Henan Gongcheng Xueyuan Xuebao (Shehui Kexue Ban)/Henan Institute of Engineering. Journal (Social Science Edition) (CHN ISSN 1674-3318) **1118**
• Henan Gongcheng Xueyuan Xuebao (Ziran Kexue Ban)/Hennan Institute of Engineering. Journal (Natural Science Edition) (CHN ISSN 1674-330X) **7861**
• Henan Gongye Daxue Xuebao (Shehui Kexue Ban)/Henan University of Technology. Journal (Social Science Edition) (CHN ISSN 1673-1751) **7968**
• Henan Gongye Daxue Xuebao (Ziran Kexue Ban)/Henan University of Technology. Journal (Natural Science Edition) (CHN ISSN 1673-2383) **7861**
• He'nan Guangbo Dianshi Daxue Xuebao/Henan Radio & TV University. Journal (CHN ISSN 1671-2862) **2359**
Henan Huabao (CHN ISSN 1003-6237) **3825**
• Henan Huagong/Henan Chemical Industry (CHN ISSN 1003-3467) **1118**
Henan Institute of Education. Journal (Natural Science) *see* He'nan Jiaoyu Xueyuan Xuebao (Ziran Kexue Ban) **7861**
Henan Institute of Engineering. Journal (Social Science Edition) *see* Henan Gongcheng Xueyuan Xuebao (Shehui Kexue Ban) **1118**
Henan Institute of Financial Management. Journal *see* He'nan Jinrong Guanli Ganbu Xueyuan Xuebao **1118**
• He'nan Jiaoyu Xueyuan Xuebao (Ziran Kexue Ban)/Henan Institute of Education. Journal (Natural Science) (CHN ISSN 1007-0834) **7861**
• He'nan Jinrong Guanli Ganbu Xueyuan Xuebao/Henan Institute of Financial Management. Journal (CHN ISSN 1008-7796) **1118**
Henan Journal of Practical Nervous Diseases *see* Henan Shiyong Shenjing Jibing Zazhi **6144**
Henan Journal of Preventive Medicine *see* Henan Yufang Yixue Zazhi **5628**
Henan Judicial Police Vocational College. Journal *see* He'nan Sifa Jingguan Zhiye Xueyuan Xuebao **2863**
• Henan Keji Daxue Xuebao (Shehui Kexue Ban)/Henan University of Science & Technology. Journal (Social Science) (CHN ISSN 1672-3910) **7861**
• Henan Keji Daxue Xuebao (Yixue Ban)/Henan University of Science & Technology. Journal (CHN ISSN 1672-688X) **5627**
• Henan Keji Daxue Xuebao (Ziran Kexue Ban)/Henan University of Science & Technology. Journal (Natural Science) (CHN ISSN 1672-6871) **8423**
• Henan Kexue/Henan Science (CHN ISSN 1004-3918) **7861**
He'nan Kunchong Fenlei Quxi Yanjiu (CHN ISSN 1007-3450) **848**
• Henan Ligong Daxue Xuebao (Shehui Kexue Ban)/Henan Polytechnic University. Journal (Social Sciences). Journal (CHN) **7968**
• Henan Ligong Daxue Xuebao (Ziran Kexue Ban) (CHN) **7861**
Henan Medical College for Staff and Workers. Journal *see* He'nan Zhigong Yixueyuan Xuebao **7969**
Henan Medical Research *see* Henan Yixue Yanjiu **5628**
Henan Nongcun Bao/Henan Rural Daily (CHN) **3825**
• Henan Nongye Daxue Xuebao/Henan Agricultural University. Journal (CHN ISSN 1000-2340) **118**
Henan Normal University. Journal (Natural Science Edition) *see* Henan Shifan Daxue Xuebao (Ziran Kexue Ban) **7861**
Henan Normal University. Journal (Social Science Edition) *see* Henan Shifan Daxue Xuebao (Shehui Kexue Ban) **7969**
Henan Polytechnic University. Journal (Social Sciences). Journal *see* Henan Ligong Daxue Xuebao (Shehui Kexue Ban) **7968**
Henan Radio & TV University. Journal *see* He'nan Guangbo Dianshi Daxue Xuebao **2359**
Henan Ribao/Henan Daily (CHN) **3825**
Henan Rural Daily *see* Henan Nongcun Bao **3825**
Henan Science *see* Henan Kexue **7861**
• Henan Shifan Daxue Xuebao (Shehui Kexue Ban)/Henan Normal University. Journal (Social Science Edition) (CHN ISSN 1000-2359) **7969**
• Henan Shifan Daxue Xuebao (Ziran Kexue Ban)/Henan Normal University. Journal (Natural Science Edition) (CHN ISSN 1000-2367) **7861**
• Henan Shiyong Shenjing Jibing Zazhi/Henan Journal of Practical Nervous Diseases (CHN ISSN 1008-2360) **6144**
• He'nan Sifa Jingguan Zhiye Xueyuan Xuebao/Henan Judicial Police Vocational College. Journal (CHN ISSN 1672-2663) **2863**
Henan University. Journal (Medical Edition) *see* Henan Daxue Xuebao (Yixue Kexue Ban) **5627**
Henan University. Journal (Natural Science Edition) *see* Henan Daxue Xuebao (Ziran Kexue Ban) **7861**
Henan University. Journal (Social Science Edition) *see* Henan Daxue Xuebao (Shehui Kexue Ban) **4455**
Henan University of Science & Technology. Journal *see* Henan Keji Daxue Xuebao (Yixue Ban) **5627**
Henan University of Science & Technology. Journal (Natural Science) *see* Henan Keji Daxue Xuebao (Ziran Kexue Ban) **8423**
Henan University of Science & Technology. Journal (Social Science) *see* Henan Keji Daxue Xuebao (Shehui Kexue Ban) **7861**

Title

10362 HENAN UNIVERSITY OF TECHNOLOGY. JOURNAL (NATURAL SCIENCE ULRICH'S PERIODICALS

Henan University of Technology. Journal (Natural Science Edition) see Henan Gongye Daxue Xuebao (Ziran Kexue Ban) 7861
Henan University of Technology. Journal (Social Science Edition) see Henan Gongye Daxue Xuebao (Shehui Kexue Ban) 7968
He'nan Yike Daxue Xuebao see Zhengzhou Daxue Xuebao (Yixue Ban) 5735
• Henan Yixue Yanjiu/Henan Medical Research (CHN ISSN 1004-437X) 5628
• Henan Yufang Yixue Zazhi/Henan Journal of Preventive Medicine (CHN ISSN 1006-8414) 5628
• He'nan Zhigong Yixueyuan Xuebao/Henan Medical College for Staff and Workers. Journal (CHN ISSN 1008-9276) 7969
Henares: Revista de Geologia (ESP ISSN 0214-6088) 2746
Henceforth (USA ISSN 0895-7622) 7647
Henderson Community College Literary Magazine (USA) 5423
Henderson Electronic Market Forecast (USA ISSN 1074-6544) 3100
Henderson's Casting Directors Guide (USA ISSN 1098-948X) 8471
Hendes Verden (DNK ISSN 0907-4732) 4360
▼ Hendricks County Magazine (USA) 3977
Heneng Tiandi/Nuclear Climate Monthly (TWN ISSN 1021-4577) 3168
Heng Ngan (LAO) 1429
Hengelo Toen & Nu (NLD ISSN 1876-4606) 4226
Hengelsport Nieuws (NLD) 8317
▼ Hengelsport Special (NLD ISSN 1874-7213) 8317
Hengitys ja Terveys Ry. Vuosikirja (FIN ISSN 1455-528X) 6214
Hengste see Stodhestar 8299
Hengyang Yixueyuan Xuebao (Shehui Kexue Ban)/Hengyang Medical College. Journal (Social Science Edition) see Nanhua Daxue Xuebao (Shehui Kexue Ban) 7987
Hengyi: Chengshu Jiaoyou de Zazhi/Costantinian: Magazine for Mature Catholics (TWN) 7799
• Henke's California Law Guide (USA) 4687
Henkimaailma (FIN ISSN 1459-3432) 6741
• The Henlein-Heinlein Chanticleer (USA ISSN 1057-008X) 3770
† • Henley Manager Update (GBR ISSN 1745-7866) 8962
Henley Standard (GBR ISSN 0962-6514) 3866
Hennan Institute of Engineering. Journal (Natural Science Edition) see Henan Gongcheng Xueyuan Xuebao (Ziran Kexue Ban) 7861
Henne (NOR ISSN 0804-7464) 2256
† Henne Interior (NOR ISSN 1500-6034) 8962
The Hennepin Lawyer (USA) 4687
Hennes/Her Journal (SWE ISSN 1403-8064) 8867
Hennes and Mauritz Magazine see H & M Magazine 2256
Hennes Serier (SWE ISSN 1101-9581) 3955
Henoch (ITA ISSN 0393-6805) 7721
• Henong Xuebao/Acta Agriculturae Nucleatae Sinica (CHN ISSN 1000-8551) 118
Henry (SWE) 8044
Henry County Historicalog (USA) 3770
Henry George Newsletter (USA ISSN 0734-4031) 2286
• ➤ The Henry James Review (USA ISSN 0273-0340) 5305
➤ Henry Martyn Institute. Journal (IND) 7711
Henry McBride Series in Modernism and Modernity (USA) 5305
Henry Miller Library Newsletter (USA) 5219
Henry Street (CAN ISSN 1204-9689) 5305
Henry Sweet Society for the History of Linguistic Ideas. Bulletin see Language and History 5139
Henry Sweet Society Studies in the History of Linguistics (DEU ISSN 0947-210X) 5124
Henry Williamson Society Journal (GBR ISSN 0144-9338) 5305
Henry Williamson Society. Publications Newsletter (GBR) 5305
Henry's Auktionen (DEU) 366
• Henry's Indiana Probate Law and Practice (USA) 4903
Henshu Kaigi/Web & Publishing (JPN) 7562
The Henston Companion Animal Veterinary Vade Mecum see Henston Small Animal Veterinary Vade Mecum (Peterborough, 2005) 8798
Henston Large Animal and Equine Veterinary Vade Mecum (GBR ISSN 1460-6666) 8798
Henston Small Animal Veterinary Vade Mecum (Peterborough, 2005) (GBR) 8798
➤ Heohrafiya ta Osnovy Ekonomiky v Shkoli (UKR) 4014
Heoloh Ukrainy (UKR ISSN 1727-835X) 2746
➤ Heolohiya i Heokhimiya Horiuchykh Kopalyn/Geology and Geochemistry of Combustible Minerals (UKR ISSN 0869-0774) 2746
Hepatic, Pancreatic, and Biliary Surgery see H P B Surgery 6244
Hepatitis (USA) 5814
• ➤ Hepatitis B Annual (IND ISSN 0972-9747) 5814
Hepatitis C (CAN ISSN 1719-766X) 7548
Hepatitis C (GBR ISSN 1461-8052) 5815
Hepatitis Express see H E P Express 7520
Hepatitis Hoy (ESP ISSN 1698-9279) 5628
• ➤ Hepatitis Monthly (IRN ISSN 1735-143X) 5926
▼ • Hepatitis Research Review (NZL ISSN 1170-3202) 5926
• Hepatitis Weekly (USA ISSN 1086-0223) 5815
• Hepato - Gastro (FRA ISSN 1253-7020) 5926
➤ Hepato-Gastroenterology (GRC ISSN 0172-6390) 5926
Hepato Pancreato Biliary see H P B 5926
➤ Hepatobiliary & Pancreatic Diseases International (CHN ISSN 1499-3872) 5926
Hepatologia Polska (POL ISSN 1232-9878) 5926
• ➤ Hepatology (USA ISSN 0270-9139) 5926
▼ • ➤ Hepatology International (USA ISSN 1936-0533) 5893
• ➤ Hepatology Research (GBR ISSN 1386-6346) 5926
Hephaistos (DEU ISSN 0942-7511) 493
Hephaistos (Hamburg) (DEU ISSN 0174-2086) 396
Hepple, Matthews & Howarth: Tort - Cases and Materials (GBR) 4832
Her (USA) 8867
Her Business see Her Magazine 8867
Her Journal see Hennes 8867
Her Magazine (NZL ISSN 1177-9438) 8867
Her Magazine Who's Who see Who's Who 2035
Her Majesty Treasury Economic Briefing see H M Treasury Economic Briefing 1489
Her Majesty's Stationery Office Agency Catalogue see H M S O Agency Catalogue 626
Her og Na (NOR ISSN 1502-5853) 3923
• Her & Nu (DNK ISSN 1397-503X) 3834
Her Own Words (USA ISSN 0898-0241) 8898
Her Sports see Her Sports + Fitness 8177
Her Sports + Fitness (USA) 8177
Her Voice (USA) 8867
Her World (MYS ISSN 0127-0079) 8867
• Her World (SGP ISSN 0046-7278) 8867
▼ • Her Yonuyle Dernekler (TUR ISSN 1307-5942) 7969
• HERA Update (AUS ISSN 0819-484X) 4170
Herademing (NLD ISSN 0929-7154) 7647
Herald see Kirykas 4597
• The Herald (GBR) 3866
Herald (PAK ISSN 0018-0467) 3926
Herald see Visnyk 5244
• The Herald (ZWE ISSN 0255-6227) 3996
Herald (Alliston) (CAN ISSN 0834-5740) 3811
• The Herald (Conroe) (USA ISSN 0730-6520) 3770
The Herald (Hamilton) (CAN ISSN 1480-0462) 4294
Herald (Herbert) (CAN ISSN 1197-9917) 3811
Herald (Independence) (USA ISSN 1541-6143) 7736
The Herald (St. Augustine) (USA) 3041
Herald (Winnipeg)/Visnyk (CAN ISSN 0701-8290) 7704
Herald Business see Heroldu Gyeongje 1118
The Herald Business Journal see Snohomish County Business Journal 1176
• Herald Express (GBR ISSN 0961-4419) 3866
Herald Leader Press (CAN ISSN 0841-355X) 3811
† • The Herald of Christian Science (USA ISSN 0146-7174) 8962
Herald of Europe (GBR ISSN 1740-3790) 7969
Herald of Health (IND ISSN 0018-0491) 6988
Herald of His Coming (USA) 7647
➤ Herald of Library Science (IND ISSN 0018-0521) 5012
Herald of Social Sciences see Lraber Hasarakakan Gitut'yunneri 4464
Herald of the Russian Academy of Sciences see Russian Academy of Sciences. Herald 7906
Herald of the Serbian Orthodox Church in Western Europe (GBR) 7704
Herald of the Supreme Islamic Authorities see Rijaset Islamske Zajednice u Bosni i Hercegovini. Glasnik 7715
Herald Sun see Herald-Sun News-Pictorial 3794
• Herald-Sun News-Pictorial (AUS ISSN 1038-3433) 3794
Herald Tribune - The Asahi Shimbun (JPN) 3900
Heraldika a Genealogie (CZE ISSN 0232-0304) 3770
Heraldique au Canada see Heraldry in Canada 3770
Heraldisch - Genealogische Gesellschaft Adler. Jahrbuch (AUT ISSN 0073-1897) 3770
Heraldisk Tidsskrift (DNK ISSN 0440-6966) 3770
Heraldiske Studier (DNK ISSN 0109-3061) 3770
O Heraldo (IND) 3882
El Heraldo Catolico/The Catholic Herald (USA ISSN 0746-4185) 7799
El Heraldo Community News (USA) 3537
Heraldo Cristiano (CUB ISSN 0864-0270) 7760
• El Heraldo de Aragon (ESP) 3952
Heraldo de Broward (USA) 3537
Heraldo De Brownsville, El see El Nuevo Heraldo 3555
• El Heraldo de Chihuahua (MEX) 3909
Heraldo de la Christian Science see Le Heraut de la Christian Science 7736
Heraldo de la Christian Science see The Herald of Christian Science 8962
• El Heraldo de Leon (MEX ISSN 1563-7328) 3909
• El Heraldo de Mexico (MEX) 3909
• Heraldo de Saltillo (MEX) 3909
• Heraldo de San Luis Potosi (MEX) 3909
Heraldo Episcopal (CUB) 7760
Heraldo.es see El Heraldo de Aragon 3952
Heraldo Escolar see El Heraldo de Aragon 3952
• The Heraldry Gazette (GBR ISSN 0437-2980) 3770
Heraldry in Canada/Heraldique au Canada (CAN ISSN 0441-6619) 3770
Heraldry Society of Ireland. Newsletter (IRL) 3770
Heraldry Society of Scotland. Journal (GBR ISSN 0141-4534) 3770
Le Heraut de la Christian Science (USA ISSN 1520-7072) 7736
• The Herb Companion (USA ISSN 1040-581X) 3736
Herb Federation of New Zealand Inc. see Herb News 3736
Herb News (NZL ISSN 1176-970X) 3736
Herb Quarterly (USA ISSN 0163-9900) 3736
• Herb, Spice and Medicinal Plant Digest (USA ISSN 1048-3160) 3736
• ➤ Herba Polonica (POL ISSN 0018-0599) 792
Herbage Varieties Recommended List see Ireland. Department of Agriculture and Food. Herbage Varieties Recommended List (Year) 238
HerbAir see Caobenfeng 6644
• Herbal Medicines (GBR ISSN 1752-4105) 309
• HerbalGram (USA ISSN 0899-5648) 792
Herbalia (FRA ISSN 1250-6273) 792
• ➤ Herbals and Complementary Medicine (AUT ISSN 1609-4573) 310
Herbarist (USA ISSN 0740-5979) 3736
Herbarium Pacificum News (USA) 792
Herbert Read Series (GBR ISSN 0073-1927) 5305
Herbertia (USA ISSN 8756-9418) 3736
Herbes Rouges (CAN ISSN 0441-6627) 5423
➤ Herbolgia (BIH ISSN 1840-0809) 792
➤ Herbology Magazine (AUS ISSN 0729-560X) 310
Herbs (GBR ISSN 0961-5873) 3736
Herbs for Health (USA ISSN 1086-1955) 310
Hercegnok (HUN ISSN 1589-4592) 2192
Hercules Moderno (MEX) 6988
➤ Hercynia (DEU ISSN 0018-0637) 7861
Herd Book of Hereford Cattle (GBR ISSN 0073-1943) 288
Herder Jahrbuch (DEU ISSN 0948-5279) 4226
Herder - Korrespondenz (DEU ISSN 0018-0645) 7800
Herders Bibliothek der Philosophie des Mittelalters (DEU) 6923
Here! (USA ISSN 1936-8518) 4412
Here (USA) 8718
Here (Atlanta) (USA ISSN 1934-2764) 4412
Here and Now (CAN ISSN 0085-1493) 7360
▼ Here Come the Irish (USA ISSN 1942-1478) 8235
• Here Comes the Guide (USA) 5558
Here Is Las Vegas (USA) 8718
Here Is Your Indiana Government (USA ISSN 0894-6434) 1404
➤ Hereditary Cancer in Clinical Practice (GBR ISSN 1731-2302) 6021
Hereditary Society Blue Book (USA ISSN 1068-3569) 3770
Hereditas see Yichuan 879
• ➤ Hereditas (USA ISSN 0018-0661) 871
• ➤ Heredity (GBR ISSN 0018-067X) 871
Heredity see Iden 872
Hereford (DNK ISSN 0108-9692) 288
▼ Hereford Advantage (Northern Edition) (AUS) 288
Hereford Advantage (Southern Edition) see Hereford Advantage (Northern Edition) 288
Hereford Breed Journal (GBR ISSN 0073-1951) 288
Hereford World (USA ISSN 1085-9896) 288
Hereford's (GBR ISSN 1462-0693) 8544
Herefords Australia see Hereford Advantage (Northern Edition) 288
Herefordshire Family History Society. Journal (GBR ISSN 0260-1044) 3770
Herefordshire Farmer (GBR ISSN 0018-0688) 118
Herefordshire Ornithological Club. Annual Report (GBR ISSN 0962-5895) 908
La Herencia (USA ISSN 1531-0442) 3537
Herencia Sefardi see Erensia Sefardi 7721
Here's Health (GBR ISSN 0018-0696) 6988
Here's Help (USA ISSN 1064-2080) 4047
Heresbach Stiftung Kalkar. Schriften (DEU ISSN 1439-8761) 4226
Heresis (FRA ISSN 0758-3737) 4226
Herforder Forschungen (DEU ISSN 1439-0698) 4226
Herikarukei no Tojikome/Confinement of Helical System (JPN) 7066
Herion - Informationen (DEU ISSN 0440-7059) 3361
Heriot-Watt University. Department of Economics. Discussion Paper in Economics (GBR ISSN 1469-4816) 1489
† Herisson (FRA) 8962
Heritage (AUS ISSN 0155-2716) 4192
Heritage see Spadcyna 4266
Heritage (DEU ISSN 1613-2068) 4226
L'Heritage (FRA ISSN 1763-5853) 7140
Heritage (GBR ISSN 0950-5245) 3866
Heritage (NGA ISSN 0794-3415) 3537
L'Heritage (USA ISSN 0162-0851) 3770
Heritage see Morasha 3775
Heritage see Union County Heritage 3786
• Heritage (Austin) (USA ISSN 1047-5613) 4294
Heritage (Cooperstown) (USA ISSN 8755-9064) 4294
Heritage (Lawrenceville) (USA ISSN 8756-5242) 4294
Heritage (Loughborough) (GBR ISSN 0260-4957) 4226
Heritage (Ottawa) (CAN ISSN 1480-6924) 4294
• Heritage (Waltham) (USA ISSN 0732-0914) 7721
• Heritage 365 (GBR) 6525
Heritage Amruth (IND ISSN 0973-2764) 310
Heritage and Arts see Turath wa-Funun 3623
Heritage and History (USA) 4294
• Heritage Business (GBR) 6525
Heritage Commercials (GBR ISSN 1476-2110) 8498
• Heritage Council of New South Wales. Annual Report (AUS ISSN 0157-9231) 4192
• Heritage Education (USA ISSN 1933-6349) 4294
Heritage Florida Jewish News (USA ISSN 0199-0721) 7721
The Heritage Foundation see The Heritage Members Newsletter 7140
Heritage Group Journal (GBR ISSN 1369-4138) 8618
The Heritage Guide see Steam Heritage Guide (Year) 8511
• Heritage International Newswatch. Bulletin (CAN ISSN 1712-3925) 4576
▼ Heritage Iron (USA ISSN 1945-3639) 211
• ➤ Heritage Language Journal (USA ISSN 1550-7076) 5124
Heritage Learning (GBR ISSN 1355-7572) 2863
• Heritage Lectures (USA ISSN 0272-1155) 7444
Heritage Living (AUS) 4192
Heritage Magazine (USA) 4294
▼ Heritage Magazine for the Intelligent Collector (USA ISSN 1941-1790) 4336
▼ • ➤ Heritage Management (USA ISSN 1940-8420) 340
Heritage Matters (CAN ISSN 1198-2454) 4295
Heritage Matters (NZL ISSN 1176-7413) 4192
• Heritage Matters (USA ISSN 1942-6194) 4295
The Heritage Members Newsletter (USA) 7140
Heritage N S W (New South Wales) (AUS ISSN 1321-1099) 444
• Heritage New Zealand (NZL ISSN 1175-9615) 4192
Heritage News (Manitowoc) (USA) 4295
Heritage News (San Francisco) (USA) 4295
• Heritage News (Washington, D.C.) (USA ISSN 1555-2748) 4295
The Heritage of Naples see Valori di Napoli 4276
➤ Heritage of the Great Plains (USA ISSN 0739-4772) 4295
Heritage of Vermilion County (USA ISSN 0018-0718) 4295
Heritage of Zimbabwe (ZWE) 4175
• Heritage Post Interactive (CAN) 4295
Heritage Quest Magazine (USA ISSN 1074-5238) 3770
• Heritage Railway (GBR ISSN 1466-3562) 8618
Heritage Railway Association. Information Papers (GBR) 8618
Heritage Railway. Journal (GBR) 8618
Heritage Retail (GBR ISSN 1471-8081) 6525
Heritage Review (USA ISSN 0162-8267) 3537
Heritage Seeker (USA) 3770
Heritage Seekers (CAN ISSN 0707-0780) 3770
Heritage Sepharade see Erensia Sefardi 7721
Heritage: The Yorker Scene see Heritage (Cooperstown) 4294
Heritage Today (GBR ISSN 1356-0824) 4226
Heritage Travel see Family Tree Magazine 3766
▼ Heritages Magazine (FRA ISSN 1956-7553) 4903
• Herizons (CAN ISSN 0711-7485) 8867
Herlevend Verleden - Archeologische Gidsen (BEL ISSN 0779-6080) 396
Hermaea (DEU ISSN 0440-7164) 5305
Herman Hedning (SWE ISSN 1403-543X) 2192
Herman, Russ M. Louisiana Personal Injury see Louisiana Personal Injury 4835
Hermann (DEU) 3850
• Hermann-Hesse-Jahrbuch (DEU ISSN 1614-1423) 5305
• Hermaphrodites with Attitudes (USA ISSN 1084-5771) 4374
Hermathena (IRL ISSN 0018-0750) 4455
• ➤ Hermenaut (USA ISSN 1523-8717) 6923
Hermeneia (CHE ISSN 1661-8505) 6923
Hermeneus (ESP ISSN 1139-7489) 5124
Hermeneus (NLD ISSN 0165-8158) 4141
Hermeneutica (BRA ISSN 1518-9724) 7647
Hermeneutica (ITA ISSN 1590-6833) 7647
Hermeneutics of Art (USA ISSN 0899-9856) 493
• Hermeneutische Blaetter (CHE ISSN 1660-5403) 7647
Hermeneutische Untersuchungen zur Theologie (DEU ISSN 0440-7180) 7647
• ➤ Hermes (DEU ISSN 0018-0777) 2235
• Hermes (DNK ISSN 0904-1699) 2322
Hermes (FRA ISSN 0767-9513) 7969
Hermes (JPN ISSN 0910-3023) 4455
➤ Hermes Americanus (USA ISSN 0741-1286) 2235
Hermes - Einzelschriften (DEU ISSN 0341-0064) 2235
Hermes International (CYP ISSN 1025-4692) 3832
Hermit Kingdom Studies in Christianity and Judaism (USA ISSN 1932-6718) 7647
Hermit Kingdom Studies in History and Religion (USA ISSN 1932-6696) 7647
Hermit Kingdom Studies in Identity and Society (USA ISSN 1932-6726) 8105
† Hermit Press Pamphlets (AUS ISSN 0729-2449) 8962
Herne in Zahlen. Jahrbuch (Year) (DEU ISSN 1437-7365) 1236
Herne in Zahlen. Monatsbericht (DEU) 1236
Herne in Zahlen. Vierteljahresberichte (DEU ISSN 1437-7357) 1236
• ➤ Hernia (FRA ISSN 1265-4906) 6245
Herning-Bogen (DNK ISSN 0108-8017) 4226
• Herning Folkeblad (DNK) 3834
Herodot (DEU ISSN 1437-7837) 340

DIRECTORY 2010 HISTOIRE GENERALE DE L'AFRIQUE 10365

Hindustan Latex. Annual Reports see Hindustan Latex. Varshika Riporta **7092**
Hindustan Latex. Varshika Riporta/Hindustan Latex. Annual Reports (IND) **7092**
• The Hindustan Times (IND) **3882**
Hindustan Times Evening News (IND) **3882**
Hindvasi (IND) **3882**
Hine's Directory of Insurance Adjusters, Appraisers and Investigators (USA) **4505**
Hine's Insurance Counsel (USA) **4687**
Hinkan Jiho (JPN) **8646**
Hinman Heritage (USA ISSN 0885-2367) **3770**
Hinnerk (DEU) **4374**
Hinshitsu/Journal of the Japanese Society for Quality Control (JPN ISSN 0386-8230) **1750**
Hinshitsu Kanri see Kuoriti Manejimento **1771**
Hinshitsu Kogaku/Quality Engineering Society. Journal (JPN) **3195**
Hint (IND) **3882**
• Hint (USA) **2256**
Hints to Potato Growers (USA ISSN 0018-1986) **234**
Hinyoki Geka/Japanese Journal of Urological Surgery (JPN ISSN 0914-6180) **6268**
Hinyokika Kiyo/Acta Urologica Japonica (JPN ISSN 0018-1994) **6268**
Hinyouki Kea (JPN ISSN 1349-6549) **6268**
• Hinz & Kunzt (DEU) **3850**
Hip Artistic Stylish Magazine see H.A.S. Magazine **2256**
Hip Compass Escapes see HipCompass Escapes **8718**
▼ Hip Hop Business Journal (USA) **6573**
Hip-Hop Connection (GBR ISSN 1465-4407) **6573**
Hip-Hop Ireland see Rap Ireland **6609**
▼ Hip Hop Weekly (USA ISSN 1932-5177) **6573**
• ➤ Hip International (ITA ISSN 1120-7000) **5628**
Hip Joint (JPN ISSN 0389-3634) **6061**
Hip Mama (USA ISSN 1074-195X) **5219**
▼ • HipCompass Escapes (USA ISSN 1947-6205) **8718**
Hiper Disney (PRT) **2193**
Hipertension (Print) see Hipertension y Riesgo Vascular **5789**
• Hipertension y Riesgo Vascular (ESP ISSN 1889-1837) **5789**
• Hipertexto (USA ISSN 1553-3018) **5124**
Hipodromo (VEN) **8177**
De Hippische Ondernemer (NLD) **8291**
Hippo News (BEL ISSN 1377-2201) **8292**
• ➤ The Hippocampus (USA ISSN 1050-9631) **5628**
Hippocrates (GRC ISSN 0250-5215) **5628**
Hippokrat Daidzhest (UKR) **5628**
Hippokrates (DEU ISSN 1435-6309) **5628**
Hippokrates/Finlands Medicinhistoriska Saellskap. Aarsskrift/Societatis Historiae Medicinae Fenniae. Annales (FIN ISSN 0781-5859) **5628**
Hiradastechnika/Journal on Communications, Computers, Convergence, Contents, Companies (HUN ISSN 0018-2028) **2322**
• Hiragana Times (JPN ISSN 0915-9975) **3900**
• ➤ Hiram Poetry Review (USA ISSN 1547-8416) **5423**
Hirasaki University. Snow and Ice Observatory. Science Reports see Hirosaki Daigaku Rigakubu Setsugai Kansokujo Hokoku **6353**
Hirata Municipal Hospital. Journal see Izumo Shiritsu Sougou Iryou Senta Nempou **4103**
Hirata Shiritsu Byoin Nenpo/Hirata Municipal Hospital. Journal see Izumo Shiritsu Sougou Iryou Senta Nempou **4103**
Hire South Africa (ZAF ISSN 1607-9604) **1011**
▼ • Hire Up! (USA ISSN 1944-3935) **1685**
• Hir@gana e-Times (JPN) **3900**
• Hiring the Best (USA ISSN 1526-2987) **1863**
Hirmagazin - Magyar Iparszovetseg (HUN ISSN 1217-0992) **4595**
Hirosaki Daigaku Nogakubu Gakujutsu Hokoku see Hirosaki University. Faculty of Agriculture. Bulletin **118**
Hirosaki Daigaku Rigakubu Fuzoku Fukaura Rinkai Jisshujo Hokoku/Hirosaki University. Fukaura Marine Biological Laboratory. Report (JPN ISSN 0285-9416) **2806**
Hirosaki Daigaku Rigakubu Kanchi Kisho Jikkenshitsu Hokoku/Hirosaki University. Faculty of Science. Laboratory of Cold Regions Meteorology. Annual Report (JPN ISSN 0916-2038) **6353**
Hirosaki Daigaku Rigakubu Setsugai Kansokujo Hokoku/Hirasaki University. Snow and Ice Observatory. Science Reports (JPN ISSN 0285-6840) **6353**
Hirosaki Daigaku Rika Hokoku see Hirosaki University. Faculty of Science and Technology. Bulletin **7861**
Hirosaki Igaku/Hirosaki Medical Journal (JPN ISSN 0439-1721) **5628**
Hirosaki Medical Association. Journal see Hirosakishi Ishikaiho **5628**
Hirosaki Medical Journal see Hirosaki Igaku **5628**
Hirosaki University. Faculty of Agriculture. Bulletin/Hirosaki Daigaku Nogakubu Gakujutsu Hokoku (JPN ISSN 0073-229X) **118**
Hirosaki University. Faculty of Science and Technology. Bulletin/Hirosaki Daigaku Rika Hokoku (JPN ISSN 1344-2139) **7861**
Hirosaki University. Faculty of Science. Laboratory of Cold Regions Meteorology. Annual Report see Hirosaki Daigaku Rigakubu Kanchi Kisho Jikkenshitsu Hokoku **6353**
Hirosaki University. Fukaura Marine Biological Laboratory. Report see Hirosaki Daigaku Rigakubu Fuzoku Fukaura Rinkai Jisshujo Hokoku **2806**
Hirosakishi Ishikaiho/Hirosaki Medical Association. Journal (JPN ISSN 0912-5930) **5628**
Hiroshima Botanical Garden. Bulletin see Hiroshimashi Shokubutsu Koen Kiyo **792**
Hiroshima Botanical Garden. Investigation see Hiroshimashi Shokubutsu Koen Saibai Kiroku **792**
Hiroshima City Medical Association. Journal see Hiroshimashi Ishikai Dayori **5628**
Hiroshima City Medical Association. Medical Laboratory Center. News see Hiroshimashi Ishikai Rinsho Kensa Senta Dayori **5628**
Hiroshima City Park Association. News see Hana no Wa **792**
Hiroshima Daigaku Bungakubu Kiyo see Hiroshima Daigaku Daigakuin Bungaku Kenkyuuka Ronshuu **5305**
Hiroshima Daigaku Chigaku Kenkyu Hokoku/Hiroshima University. Geological Report (JPN ISSN 0073-2303) **2746**
Hiroshima Daigaku Daigakuin Bungaku Kenkyuuka Ronshuu/Hiroshima University. Graduate School of Letters. Studies (JPN ISSN 1347-7013) **5305**
Hiroshima Daigaku Daigakuin Kougaku Kenkyuuka Kenkyuu Houkoku (JPN ISSN 1347-7218) **3195**
Hiroshima Daigaku Daigakuin Kyouikugaku Kenkyuuka Kiyou. Dai 2 Bu, Bunka Kyouiku Kaihatsu Kanren Ryouiki/Hiroshima University. Graduate School of Education. Bulletin. Part. 2, Arts and Science Education (JPN ISSN 1346-5554) **2985**
Hiroshima Daigaku Gembaku Houshasen Ikagaku Kenkyuujo Nempou/Hiroshima University. Research Institute for Radiation Biology and Medicine. Proceedings (JPN ISSN 1348-3765) **6197**
Hiroshima Daigaku Igaku Zasshi (JPN ISSN 0018-2087) **5628**
Hiroshima Daigaku Keizai Kenkyu Sosho (JPN ISSN 0917-0030) **1118**
Hiroshima Daigaku Keizai Ronso (JPN ISSN 0386-2704) **1118**
Hiroshima Daigaku Seibutsu Gakkaishi/Biological Society of Hiroshima University. Bulletin (JPN ISSN 0367-5912) **676**
Hiroshima Daigaku Shigaku Zasshi/Hiroshima University Dental Society. Journal (JPN ISSN 0046-7472) **5846**
Hiroshima Economic Review see Hiroshima Daigaku Keizai Ronso **1118**
Hiroshima Economic Studies see Nenpo Keizaigaku **1152**
Hiroshima Heiwa Kagaku/Hiroshima Peace Science (JPN ISSN 0386-3565) **7140**
Hiroshima Institute of Technology. Bulletin. Education Volume see Hiroshima Kougyou Daigaku Kiyou. Kyouiku Hen **8424**
Hiroshima Institute of Technology. Bulletin. Research Volume see Hiroshima Kougyou Daigaku Kiyou. Kenkyuu Hen **8424**
Hiroshima Journal of International Studies see Hiroshima Kokusai Kenkyu **7240**
➤ Hiroshima Journal of Mathematics Education/Sugaku Kyoiku Gakujutsu Zasshi (JPN ISSN 0919-1720) **5491**
Hiroshima-ken Shibu Nenpo/Wild Bird Society of Japan. Hiroshima Prefecture Branch. Annual Report (JPN ISSN 1340-9263) **908**
Hiroshima Kenritsu Byoin Ishi/Hiroshima Prefectural Hospital. Medical Journal (JPN ISSN 0387-6454) **5628**
Hiroshima Kenritsu Seibu Kogyo Gijutsu Senta Kenkyu Hokoku (JPN ISSN 0915-194X) **1887**
Hiroshima Kokusai Kenkyu/Hiroshima Journal of International Studies (JPN ISSN 1341-3546) **7240**
Hiroshima Kougyou Daigaku Kiyou. Kenkyuu Hen/Hiroshima Institute of Technology. Bulletin. Research Volume (JPN ISSN 1346-9975) **8424**
Hiroshima Kougyou Daigaku Kiyou. Kyouiku Hen/Hiroshima Institute of Technology. Bulletin. Education Volume (JPN ISSN 1346-9983) **8424**
• Hiroshima Mathematical Journal (JPN ISSN 0018-2079) **5491**
Hiroshima Mushi no Kai Kaiho/Entomological Society of Hiroshima. Journal (JPN ISSN 0389-827X) **848**
Hiroshima Peace Science see Hiroshima Heiwa Kagaku **7140**
Hiroshima Prefectural Hospital. Medical Journal see Hiroshima Kenritsu Byoin Ishi **5628**
Hiroshima Prefecture. Monthly Report of Meteorology see Hiroshimaken Kisho Geppo **6353**
Hiroshima Society of Hospital Pharmacists. Annual Research Report see Hiroshimaken Byoin Yakuzaishikai Gakujutsu Nenpo **6846**
Hiroshima Studies in English Language and Literature see Eigo Eibungaku Kenkyu **5288**
Hiroshima University Dental Society. Journal see Hiroshima Daigaku Shigaku Zasshi **5846**
Hiroshima University. Faculty of Integrated Arts and Science. Bulletin see Ningen Bunka Kenkyu **4466**
Hiroshima University. Faculty of Integrated Arts and Sciences. Bulletin. I, Studies in Area Culture see Chiiki Bunka Kenkyu **7954**
Hiroshima University. Faculty of Science. Botanical Institute. Research Report (JPN) **792**
Hiroshima University. Geological Report see Hiroshima Daigaku Chigaku Kenkyu Hokoku **2746**
Hiroshima University. Graduate School of Education. Bulletin. Part. 2, Arts and Science Education see Hiroshima Daigaku Daigakuin Kyouikugaku Kenkyuuka Kiyou. Dai 2 Bu, Bunka Kyouiku Kaihatsu Kanren Ryouiki **2985**
Hiroshima University. Graduate School of Letters. Studies see Hiroshima Daigaku Daigakuin Bungaku Kenkyuuka Ronshuu **5305**
Hiroshima University. Journal of Science. Series A. Physics and Chemistry (JPN ISSN 0386-3034) **7015**
Hiroshima University. Journal of Science. Series C. Earth and Planetary Sciences (JPN) **2746**
Hiroshima University. Mukaishima Marine Biological Station. Contributions (JPN ISSN 0289-2197) **2806**
Hiroshima University. Research Institute for Radiation Biology and Medicine. Proceedings see Hiroshima Daigaku Gembaku Houshasen Ikagaku Kenkyuujo Nempou **6197**
Hiroshimaken Byoin Yakuzaishikai Gakujutsu Nenpo/Hiroshima Society of Hospital Pharmacists. Annual Research Report (JPN ISSN 0388-2616) **6846**
Hiroshimaken Hospital Pharmacists Association. Drug Information News (JPN ISSN 0389-4061) **6846**
Hiroshimaken Kisho Geppo/Hiroshima Prefecture. Monthly Report of Meteorology (JPN ISSN 0385-7158) **6353**
Hiroshimashi Asa Dobutsu Koen Nenpo/Asa Zoological Park of Hiroshima. Annual Report (JPN) **946**
Hiroshimashi Ishikai Dayori/Hiroshima City Medical Association. Journal (JPN) **5628**
Hiroshimashi Ishikai Rinsho Kensa Senta Dayori/Hiroshima City Medical Association. Medical Laboratory Center. News (JPN) **5628**
Hiroshimashi Shokubutsu Koen Kiyo/Hiroshima Botanical Garden. Bulletin (JPN ISSN 0386-5304) **792**
Hiroshimashi Shokubutsu Koen Saibai Kiroku/Hiroshima Botanical Garden. Investigation (JPN ISSN 0387-8597) **792**
Hirschmannbrief (DEU) **8317**
Hirundo (CAN ISSN 1718-8296) **2235**
Hirundo (EST ISSN 1406-2062) **908**
Hiryo Kagaku/Fertilizer Science (JPN ISSN 0387-2718) **234**
His see Shishang Caifu **8988**
His & Hers (USA ISSN 1559-5560) **5073**
His Magazine see H M **6292**
• Hislop's Art Sales Index (GBR) **493**
• Hislop's Fine Art Sales Index (USA) **530**
➤ Hispamerica (USA ISSN 0363-0471) **5305**
• Hispania (ESP ISSN 0018-2141) **4227**
• ➤ Hispania (USA ISSN 0018-2133) **5124**
Hispania Antiqua (ESP ISSN 1130-0515) **4227**
• Hispania Epigraphica (ESP ISSN 1132-6875) **4227**
Hispania Judaica Bulletin (ISR ISSN 1565-0073) **4183**
• Hispania Nova (ESP ISSN 1138-7319) **4227**
• Hispania Sacra (ESP ISSN 0018-215X) **7647**
• Hispanic (USA ISSN 0898-3097) **3537**
† Hispanic - American Almanac (USA) **8962**
Hispanic American Almanac see Hispanic - American Almanac **8962**
• ➤ Hispanic American Historical Review (USA ISSN 0018-2168) **4295**
• Hispanic American Periodicals Index (USA ISSN 0270-8558) **4170**
Hispanic Books Bulletin (USA ISSN 0894-2358) **7562**
• Hispanic Business Magazine (USA ISSN 0199-0349) **1118**
Hispanic Career World (USA) **6698**
• Hispanic Engineer & Information Technology (USA ISSN 1088-3452) **3195**
• Hispanic Enterprise (USA ISSN 1938-1077) **3537**
Hispanic Focus (USA ISSN 0737-7029) **3574**
• ➤ Hispanic Health Care International (USA ISSN 1540-4153) **5960**
Hispanic Horizon (IND ISSN 0970-7522) **5305**
Hispanic Issues (USA ISSN 0893-2395) **5305**
• ➤ Hispanic Issues Online (USA ISSN 1931-8006) **3537**
➤ Hispanic Journal (Indiana) (USA ISSN 0271-0986) **3537**
• ➤ Hispanic Journal of Behavioral Sciences (USA ISSN 0739-9863) **7360**
Hispanic Linguistics (USA ISSN 0742-5287) **5125**
Hispanic Link Weekly Report (USA) **3537**
➤ Hispanic Literature (USA) **5305**
Hispanic Market News (USA ISSN 0898-4174) **3679**
• Hispanic Market Weekly (USA) **1819**
Hispanic Network Magazine (USA ISSN 1550-6444) **3537**
Hispanic Outlook see Hispanic Outlook in Higher Education **2985**
• ➤ Hispanic Outlook in Higher Education (USA ISSN 1054-2337) **2985**
Hispanic Poetry Review (USA ISSN 1531-0167) **5423**
Hispanic Population in the United States see Current Population Reports. Hispanic Population in the United States **8947**
Hispanic Research Center. Research Bulletin (USA) **5125**
• ➤ Hispanic Research Journal (GBR ISSN 1468-2737) **5305**
Hispanic Resource Directory (USA ISSN 1085-276X) **3537**
• ➤ Hispanic Review (USA ISSN 0018-2176) **5125**
Hispanic Studies (GBR) **5305**
• Hispanic Today (USA ISSN 1524-279X) **3537**
Hispanic Trends see Hispanic Enterprise **3537**
Hispanic Yearbook see Anuario Hispano **6692**
Hispanic Yellow Pages (Atlanta)/Paginas Amarillas Hispanas (USA) **2004**
Hispanic Yellow Pages (Fairfax) (USA) **2004**
Hispanica Posnaniensia (POL ISSN 0867-020X) **5306**
• HispanicAd.com (USA) **26**
Hispanisms (USA) **5306**
Hispanistica (IND ISSN 0971-4111) **5306**
Hispanistische Studien (DEU ISSN 0170-8570) **5125**
El Hispano (Sacramento) (USA) **3537**
El Hispano (Upper Darby) (USA) **3537**
El Hispano News (Albuquerque) (USA) **3537**
El Hispano News (Dallas) (USA) **3537**
➤ Hispanofila (USA ISSN 0018-2206) **5306**
Hispanorama (DEU ISSN 0720-1168) **5306**
Hispanos Unidos (USA) **3537**
Hissu Aminosan Kenkyu/Research Committee of Essential Amino Acids. Reports (JPN ISSN 0387-4141) **733**
Histocar Revue (BEL ISSN 1784-2816) **366**
The Histochemical Journal see Journal of Molecular Histology **834**
• ➤ Histochemistry and Cell Biology (DEU ISSN 0948-6143) **833**
L'Histoire (FRA ISSN 0182-2411) **4141**
Histoire (FRA ISSN 1635-2238) **4141**
Histoire (La Rochelle) see Collection Histoire (La Rochelle) **4135**
Histoire (Paris) (FRA ISSN 1953-2172) **4141**
L'Histoire a l'Oeuvre (FRA ISSN 1775-1411) **4141**
Histoire Antique (FRA ISSN 1632-0859) **4141**
Histoire Antique et Medievale see Histoire Antique **4141**
Histoire Biographique de l'Enseignement (FRA ISSN 0298-5632) **3064**
Histoire Comparee des Litteratures en Langues Europeennes see Comparative History of Literatures in European Languages **5277**
† L'Histoire de la Marine (FRA ISSN 1774-0401) **8962**
Histoire de la Pensee (FRA ISSN 0073-2362) **7861**
➤ Histoire de l'Art (FRA ISSN 0992-2059) **493**
Histoire de l'Education (FRA ISSN 0221-6280) **2863**
Histoire de l'Historiographie see Storia della Storiografia **4268**
Histoire d'Entreprises (FRA ISSN 1960-9302) **1118**
Histoire des Arts (Aix-en-Provence) see Universite de Provence. Arts. Histoire des Arts **523**
Histoire des Bibliotheques Medievales (FRA ISSN 1773-7257) **5012**
Histoire des Idees et Critique Litteraire (CHE ISSN 0073-2397) **5306**
Histoire des Sciences (FRA ISSN 1258-116X) **7861**
† Histoire des Sciences et des Techniques (FRA ISSN 1141-4588) **8962**
Histoire des Sciences Medicales (FRA ISSN 0440-8888) **5628**
• Histoire, Economie et Societe (FRA ISSN 0752-5702) **1542**
Histoire Economique et Financiere de la France. Animation de la Recherche (FRA ISSN 1248-6620) **1542**
Histoire Economique et Financiere de la France. Etudes et Documents (FRA ISSN 1241-3496) **1542**
Histoire Economique et Financiere de la France. Etudes Generales (FRA ISSN 1251-5140) **1542**
Histoire Economique et Financiere de la France. Memoire (FRA ISSN 1251-5132) **643**
Histoire Economique et Financiere de la France. Recueils de Documents (FRA ISSN 1151-9037) **1542**
Histoire Economique et Financiere de la France. Sources (FRA ISSN 1248-6221) **1542**
L'Histoire en Savoie (FRA ISSN 0046-7510) **4227**
• ➤ Histoire Epistemologie Langage (FRA ISSN 0750-8069) **5125**
Histoire et Archeologie (FRA ISSN 1273-3563) **4227**
† Histoire et Archives (FRA ISSN 1278-382X) **8962**
Histoire et Civilisation du Livre (CHE ISSN 0073-2419) **4141**
Histoire et Civilisations (FRA ISSN 1284-5655) **4141**
Histoire et Images Medievales (FRA ISSN 1777-9103) **4227**
Histoire et Images Medievales. Thematique (FRA ISSN 1779-059X) **4227**
• Histoire et Mesure (FRA ISSN 0982-1783) **4141**
▼ Histoire & Missions Chretiennes (FRA ISSN 1957-5246) **7800**
† Histoire et Nature (FRA ISSN 0396-9681) **8962**
Histoire et Patrimoine de Villers-Semeuse (FRA ISSN 1774-4938) **4227**
Histoire et ses Representations (FRA ISSN 0766-1827) **4227**
Histoire & Societes (FRA ISSN 1633-2784) **4227**
Histoire et Societes de l'Amerique Latine see Histoire(s) de l'Amerique Latine **4295**
• ➤ Histoire et Societes Rurales (FRA ISSN 1254-728X) **340**
Histoire Generale de l'Afrique see UNESCO General History of Africa **4178**

Title

▼ *new title*   † *ceased*   ● *electronic media*   ➤ *refereed*

Title

Hoja Divulgativa - REDFRUIT see Red de Desarrollo Tecnologico de Frutales. Hoja Divulgativa **150**
• Hoja Informativa (ARG) **7360**
• Hoja Informativa Electronica (ARG ISSN 1666-6097) **118**
Hoja Trinitaria (ESP) **7800**
Hojas de Lectura (COL ISSN 0121-3563) **2193**
Hojas de Sal (MEX) **4455**
Hojas Universitarias (COL ISSN 0120-1301) **2985**
Hojin Kigyo no Jittai see Zeimu Tokei Kara Mita Hojin Kigyo no Jittai **1955**
Hoken Butsuri/Japanese Journal of Health Physics (JPN ISSN 0367-6110) **7524**
Hoken Kanri Senta Dayori (JPN ISSN 0912-1420) **2942**
Hoken no Kagaku/Health Care (JPN ISSN 0018-3342) **6988**
Hoken Sangyo Jiho/Medical Instrument News (JPN) **5628**
Hoken Taiiku Kyoshitsu see Health and Physical Education **2862**
Hokenfu no Kekkaku Tenbo/Review of Tuberculosis for Public Health Nurse (JPN ISSN 0018-3369) **5960**
Hokenfu Zasshi see The Japanese Journal for Public Health Nurse **5963**
Hokkai Gakuen Daigaku Hogaku Kenkyu (JPN ISSN 0385-7255) **4687**
Hokkai Gakuen Law Journal see Hokkai Gakuen Daigaku Hogaku Kenkyu **4687**
Hokkaido Association of Medical Service for Workers. Medical Journal see Hokkaido Kinrosha Iryo Kyokai Igaku Zasshi **5629**
Hokkaido Branch Journal see Hokkaidou Shibu Kaishi **946**
Hokkaido Brown Bear see Higuma **946**
Hokkaido Byoin Yakuzaishikaishi/Hokkaido Society of Hospital Pharmacists. Journal (JPN ISSN 0917-0936) **6846**
Hokkaido Daigaku. Aisotopu Sogo Senta Nyusu/Hokkaido University. Central Institute of Isotope Science. News (JPN) **3168**
Hokkaido Daigaku Bungaku Kenkyuka Kiyo/Annual Report on Cultural Science (JPN ISSN 1346-0277) **5306**
Hokkaido Daigaku Chikyu Butsurigaku Kenkyu Hokoku/Hokkaido University. Geophysical Bulletin (JPN ISSN 0439-3503) **2783**
Hokkaido Daigaku Daigakuin Nogaku Kenkyuka Hobun Kiyo/Hokkaido University. Graduate School of Agriculture. Memoirs (JPN ISSN 1345-661X) **118**
Hokkaido Daigaku Daigakuin Nogaku Kenkyuka Kiyo see Hokkaido University. Graduate School of Agriculture. Journal **119**
Hokkaido Daigaku Nogakubu Fuzoku Shokubutsuen Nenpo/Hokkaido University. Faculty of Agriculture. Botanic Garden. Annual Report (JPN) **792**
Hokkaido Daigaku Nogakubu Hobun Kiyo/Hokkaido University. Faculty of Agriculture. Memoirs see Hokkaido Daigaku Daigakuin Nogaku Kenkyuka Hobun Kiyo **118**
Hokkaido Daigaku Oyo Denki Kenkyujo Gijutsu Hokoku/Hokkaido University. Research Institute of Applied Electricity. Technical Bulletin (JPN ISSN 0286-3189) **3310**
Hokkaido Daigaku Rigakubu Kaiso Kenkyujo Obun Hokoku see Hokkaido University. Institute of Algological Research. Scientific Papers **2806**
Hokkaido Daigaku Shokubai Kagaku Kenkyu Center Nenpo see Hokkaido University. Catalysis Research Center. Annual Report (Year) **2135**
Hokkaido Denryoku K.K. Sogo Kenkyujo Kenkyu Nenpo/Hokkaido Electric Power Co. General Research Center. Annual Report (JPN ISSN 0915-2938) **3310**
Hokkaido Dental Association. Journal see Hokkaido Shikaishikaishi **5846**
Hokkaido Eiyo Syokuryo Gakkaishi/Hokkaido Society of Food and Nutrition. Journal (JPN ISSN 0285-1806) **264**
Hokkaido Electric Power Co. General Research Center. Annual Report see Hokkaido Denryoku K.K. Sogo Kenkyujo Kenkyu Nenpo **3310**
Hokkaido Electric Power. Department of Research and Development. News see Hokuden Soken Nyusu **3310**
Hokkaido Fisheries Experimental Station. Journal see Hokusuishi Dayori **3597**
Hokkaido Fisheries Experimental Station. Scientific Reports see Hokkaidoritsu Suisan Shikenjo Kenkyu Hokoku **3596**
Hokkaido Forestry Research Institute. Annual Report see Hokkaido Ringyo Shikenjo Nenpo **3692**
Hokkaido Forestry Research Institute. Bulletin see Hokkaido Ringyo Shikenjo Kenkyu Hokoku **3692**
Hokkaido Geka Zasshi/Hokkaido Journal of Surgery (JPN ISSN 0288-7509) **6245**
Hokkaido Genshiryoku Kankyo Dayori/Hokkaido Nuclear Energy Environmental Research Center. News (JPN ISSN 0913-1760) **3168**
Hokkaido Hatsumei Koan Nenpo/Annual Report of Invention in Hokkaido (JPN) **6751**
Hokkaido Hoshasen Gijutsu Zasshi/Journal of Hokkaido Radiological Technology (JPN ISSN 0912-0327) **6197**
Hokkaido Hospital Pharmacists' Newsletter see H O P Nyusu **6845**
➤ Hokkaido Igaku Zasshi/Hokkaido Journal of Medical Science (JPN ISSN 0367-6102) **5628**
• Hokkaido Iho/Hokkaido Medical Association. News (JPN ISSN 0913-0217) **5628**
Hokkaido Institute of Environmental Sciences. Report (JPN ISSN 0916-8656) **3486**
Hokkaido Institute of Public Health. Report see Hokkaidoritsu Eisei Kenkyushoho **7524**
Hokkaido Institute of Technology. Memoirs see Hokkaido Kogyo Daigaku Kenkyu Kiyo **8424**
Hokkaido Jishin Kazan Geppo/Seismological and Volcanological Monthly Report in Hokkaido (JPN) **2783**
Hokkaido Jishin Kazan Nenpo/Seismological and Volcanological Annual Report in Hokkaido (JPN) **2783**
Hokkaido Journal of Agricultural Meteorology see Hokkaido no Nogyo Kisho **6354**
Hokkaido Journal of Medical Science see Hokkaido Igaku Zasshi **5628**
Hokkaido Journal of Occupational Therapy see Hokkaidou Sagyou Ryouhou **6110**
Hokkaido Journal of Orthopaedics and Traumatology see Hokkaido Seikei Saigai Geka Gakkai Zasshi **6061**
Hokkaido Journal of Physical Therapy see Hokkaido Rigaku Ryoho **6110**
Hokkaido Journal of Primary Care see Hokkaido Puraimari Kea Kenkyukai Kaiho **5629**
Hokkaido Journal of Surgery see Hokkaido Geka Zasshi **6245**
Hokkaido Juishikai Zasshi see Hokkaido Veterinary Medical Association. Journal **8798**
Hokkaido Kaitaku Kinenkan Chosa Hokoku (JPN ISSN 0915-5511) **6525**
Hokkaido Kaitaku Kinenkan Kenkyu Kiyo/Historical Museum of Hokkaido. Bulletin (JPN ISSN 1341-2795) **6525**
Hokkaido Kinrosha Iryo Kyokai Igaku Zasshi/Hokkaido Association of Medical Service for Workers. Medical Journal (JPN ISSN 0285-0664) **5629**
Hokkaido Kisho Geppo/Hokkaido Monthly Report of Meteorology (JPN ISSN 0916-5096) **6354**
Hokkaido Kogyo Daigaku Kenkyu Kiyo/Hokkaido Institute of Technology. Memoirs (JPN ISSN 0385-0862) **8424**
Hokkaido Kogyo Gijutsu Kenkyujo Shiryoh see Hokkaido National Industrial Research Institute. Technical Data **8424**
Hokkaido Kyoiku Daigaku Kiyo. Jimbun Kagaku, Shakai Kagaku-Hen/Hokkaido University of Education. Journal. Humanities and Social Sciences (JPN ISSN 1344-2562) **4455**
Hokkaido Kyoiku Daigaku Kiyo. Kyoiku Kagaku-Hen/Hokkaido University of Education. Journal. Education (JPN ISSN 1344-2554) **2864**
Hokkaido Kyoiku Daigaku Kiyo. Shizen Kagaku-hen/Hokkaido University of Education. Journal. Natural Sciences (JPN ISSN 1344-2570) **7862**
➤ Hokkaido Kyoiku Daigaku Taisetsuzan Shizen Kyoiku Kenkyu Shisetsu Kenkyu Hokoku/Hokkaido University of Education. Taisetsuzan Institute of Science. Reports (JPN ISSN 0386-4464) **7862**
Hokkaido Law Review (Sapporo, 1961) see Hokudai Hogaku Ronshu **4687**
Hokkaido Librarians Study Circle. Bulletin see Hokkaido Toshokan Kenkyukai. Kaiho **5012**
➤ Hokkaido Mathematical Journal (JPN ISSN 0385-4035) **5491**
Hokkaido Medical Association. News see Hokkaido Iho **5628**
Hokkaido Monthly Report of Meteorology see Hokkaido Kisho Geppo **6354**
Hokkaido Museum of Northern Peoples. Bulletin see Hokkaidoritsu Hoppo Minzoku Hakubutsukan Kenkyu Kiyo **6525**
Hokkaido National Industrial Research Institute. Technical Data/Hokkaido Kogyo Gijutsu Kenkyujo Shiryoh (JPN) **8424**
Hokkaido no Chusho Kasen/Medium and Small Scale River in Hokkaido (JPN) **8824**
Hokkaido no Kisho see Meteorological Data of Hokkaido **6391**
Hokkaido no Nogyo Kisho/Hokkaido Journal of Agricultural Meteorology (JPN ISSN 0915-6062) **6354**
Hokkaido no Seppyo/Snow and Ice in Hokkaido (JPN) **6354**
Hokkaido no Shizen/Nature in Hokkaido (JPN ISSN 0286-0627) **2613**
• Hokkaido Nogyo Shikenjo Kenkyu Hokoku/National Agricultural Research Center for Hokkaido Region. Research Bulletin (JPN ISSN 0367-5955) **118**
Hokkaido Nogyo Shikenjo Kenkyu Shiryo/National Agricultural Research Center for Hokkaido Region. Miscellaneous Publication (JPN ISSN 0386-2224) **118**
Hokkaido Nogyo Shikenjo Nenpo/National Agricultural Research Center for Hokkaido Region. Annual Reports (JPN ISSN 0441-0750) **119**
Hokkaido Nuclear Energy Environmental Research Center. News see Hokkaido Genshiryoku Kankyo Dayori **3168**
Hokkaido Orthopaedic Traumatology Association. Journal see Hokkaido Seikei Saigai Geka Gakkai Kenkyukai Kaishi **6061**
Hokkaido Prefectural Midorigaoka Hospital. Annual Report see Hokkaidoritsu Midorigaoka Byoin Nenpo **4098**
Hokkaido Puraimari Kea Kenkyukai Kaiho/Hokkaido Journal of Primary Care (JPN) **5629**
Hokkaido Rehabilitation Association. Journal see Hokkaido Rihabiriteshon Gakkai Zasshi **6110**
Hokkaido Rigaku Ryoho/Hokkaido Journal of Physical Therapy (JPN ISSN 0912-1455) **6110**
Hokkaido Rihabiriteshon Gakkai Zasshi/Hokkaido Rehabilitation Association. Journal (JPN ISSN 0304-2081) **6110**
Hokkaido Ringyo Shikenjo Kenkyu Hokoku/Hokkaido Forestry Research Institute. Bulletin (JPN ISSN 0910-3945) **3692**
Hokkaido Ringyo Shikenjo Nenpo/Hokkaido Forestry Research Institute. Annual Report (JPN ISSN 0910-3937) **3692**
Hokkaido Salmon Hatchery. Technical Report (JPN) **3596**
Hokkaido Seikei Geka Gaisho Kenkyukai Kaishi/Hokkaido Orthopaedic Traumatology Association. Journal (JPN ISSN 0914-6083) **6061**
Hokkaido Seikei Saigai Geka Gakkai Zasshi/Hokkaido Journal of Orthopaedics and Traumatology (JPN ISSN 1343-3873) **6061**
Hokkaido Shikaishikaishi/Hokkaido Dental Association. Journal (JPN ISSN 0073-2915) **5846**
Hokkaido Society for Dialysis Therapy. Proceedings of Symposium see Hokkaido Toseki Ryoho Gakkai Shinpojumu **6268**
Hokkaido Society for Dialysis Therapy. Program and Abstracts see Hokkaido Toseki Ryoho Gakkai Puroguramu Endai Shoroku **5747**
Hokkaido Society of Food and Nutrition. Journal see Hokkaido Eiyo Syokuryo Gakkaishi **264**
Hokkaido Society of Hospital Pharmacists. Journal see Hokkaido Byoin Yakuzaishikaishi **6846**
Hokkaido Toseki Ryoho Gakkai Puroguramu Endai Shoroku/Hokkaido Society for Dialysis Therapy. Program and Abstracts (JPN) **5747**
Hokkaido Toseki Ryoho Gakkai Shinpojumu/ Hokkaido Society for Dialysis Therapy. Proceedings of Symposium (JPN) **6268**
Hokkaido Toshokan Kenkyukai. Kaiho/Hokkaido Librarians Study Circle. Bulletin (JPN ISSN 0018-3431) **5012**
Hokkaido University. Bulletin of Fisheries Sciences (JPN ISSN 1346-1842) **3596**
Hokkaido University. Catalysis Research Center. Annual Report (Year)/Hokkaido Daigaku Shokubai Kagaku Kenkyu Center Nenpo (JPN ISSN 0915-8170) **2135**
Hokkaido University. Central Institute of Isotope Science. News see Hokkaido Daigaku. Aisotopu Sogo Senta Nyusu **3168**
Hokkaido University. Economic Journal (JPN ISSN 0916-4650) **1118**
Hokkaido University. Faculty of Agriculture. Botanic Garden. Annual Report see Hokkaido Daigaku Nogakubu Fuzoku Shokubutsuen Nenpo **792**
Hokkaido University. Faculty of Agriculture. Journal see Hokkaido University. Graduate School of Agriculture. Journal **119**
Hokkaido University. Faculty of Engineering. Memoirs (JPN ISSN 0368-9379) **3195**
Hokkaido University. Faculty of Fisheries. Data Record of Oceanographic Observations and Exploratory Fishing/Kaiyo Chosa Gyogyo Shiken Yoho (JPN ISSN 0439-3511) **2806**
➤ Hokkaido University. Faculty of Science. Journal. Series 7: Geophysics (JPN ISSN 0441-067X) **2783**
Hokkaido University Forests. Research Bulletin see Hokkaidou Daigaku Enshuurin Henkyuu Houkoku **3692**
Hokkaido University. Geophysical Bulletin see Hokkaido Daigaku Chikyu Butsurigaku Kenkyu Hokoku **2783**
Hokkaido University. Graduate School of Agriculture. Journal/Hokkaido Daigaku Daigakuin Nogaku Kenkyuka Kiyo (JPN ISSN 1345-6601) **119**
Hokkaido University. Graduate School of Agriculture. Memoirs see Hokkaido Daigaku Daigakuin Nogaku Kenkyuka Hobun Kiyo **118**
Hokkaido University. Graduate School of Fisheries Sciences. Memoirs (JPN ISSN 1346-3306) **3596**
Hokkaido University. Institute for Genetic Medicine. Collected Papers (JPN ISSN 1346-3837) **6214**
Hokkaido University. Institute of Algological Research. Scientific Papers/Hokkaido Daigaku Rigakubu Kaiso Kenkyujo Obun Hokoku (JPN ISSN 0385-6054) **2806**
• Hokkaido University Medical Library Series (JPN ISSN 0385-6089) **5629**
Hokkaido University Museum. Bulletin see Hokkaidou Daigaku Sougou Hakubutsukan Kenkyuu Houkoku **6525**
Hokkaido University of Education. Journal. Education see Hokkaido Kyoiku Daigaku Kiyo. Kyoiku Kagaku-Hen **2864**
Hokkaido University of Education. Journal. Humanities and Social Sciences see Hokkaido Kyoiku Daigaku Kiyo. Jimbun Kagaku, Shakai Kagaku-Hen **4455**
Hokkaido University of Education. Journal. Natural Sciences see Hokkaido Kyoiku Daigaku Kiyo. Shizen Kagaku-hen **7862**
Hokkaido University of Education. Taisetsuzan Institute of Science. Reports see Hokkaido Kyoiku Daigaku Taisetsuzan Shizen Kyoiku Kenkyu Shisetsu Kenkyu Hokoku **7862**
Hokkaido University. Research Institute of Applied Electricity. Technical Bulletin see Hokkaido Daigaku Oyo Denki Kenkyujo Gijutsu Hokoku **3310**
➤ Hokkaido Veterinary Medical Association. Journal/Hokkaido Juishikai Zasshi (JPN ISSN 0018-3385) **8798**
Hokkaido Wakkanai Fisheries Experimental Station. Annual Report (JPN) **3596**
Hokkaido Wild Birds Association. News see Yacho Dayori **917**
Hokkaidoritsu Eisei Kenkyushoho/Hokkaido Institute of Public Health. Report (JPN ISSN 0441-0793) **7524**
Hokkaidoritsu Hoppo Minzoku Hakubutsukan Kenkyu Kiyo/Hokkaido Museum of Northern Peoples. Bulletin (JPN ISSN 0918-3159) **6525**
Hokkaidoritsu Midorigaoka Byoin Nenpo/Hokkaido Prefectural Midorigaoka Hospital. Annual Report (JPN ISSN 0916-9547) **4098**
Hokkaidoritsu Suisan Shikenjo Kenkyu Hokoku/Hokkaido Fisheries Experimental Station. Scientific Reports (JPN ISSN 0914-6830) **3596**
Hokkaidou Daigaku Daigakuin Bungaku Kenkyuuka Kenkyuu Ronshuu/Research Journal of Graduate Students of Letters (JPN ISSN 1347-0132) **5306**
Hokkaidou Daigaku Enshuurin Henkyuu Houkoku/Hokkaido University Forests. Research Bulletin (JPN ISSN 1347-0981) **3692**
Hokkaidou Daigaku Sougou Hakubutsukan Kenkyuu Houkoku/Hokkaido University Museum. Bulletin (JPN ISSN 1348-169X) **6525**
Hokkaidou Kaihatsu Doboku Kenkyuujo Geppou/Civil Engineering Research Institute. Monthly Report (JPN ISSN 1346-6747) **3269**
Hokkaidou Sagyou Ryouhou/Hokkaido Journal of Occupational Therapy (JPN ISSN 1349-4317) **6110**
Hokkaidou Shibu Kaishi/Hokkaido Branch Journal (JPN ISSN 1349-8142) **946**
Hokke Bunka Kenkyu see Institute for the Comprehensive Study of Lotus Sutra. Journal **7701**
Hokkohken News (JPN) **1887**
Hokkyokusei Hoikakuhyo/Polaris Almanac for Azimuth Determination (JPN ISSN 0389-7605) **575**
Hokodate Medical Journal see Hakodate Igakushi **5623**
Hokouk (AFG) **4687**
• Hokouk Newsletter (LBN ISSN 1811-9603) **3538**
Hokubei Hochi see North American Post **3555**
Hokubei Mainichi (USA) **3538**
Hokudai Hogaku Ronshu/Hokkaido Law Review (Sapporo, 1961) (JPN ISSN 0385-5953) **4687**
Hokuden Gijutsu Kaihatsu Nyusu/Hokuriku Electric Power. Technical Development News (JPN ISSN 0389-4983) **3310**
Hokuden Soken Nyusu/Hokkaido Electric Power. Department of Research and Development. News (JPN) **3310**
Hokuno see Agriculture in Hokkaido **86**
Hokuriku Daigaku Kiyo/Hokuriku University. Bulletin (JPN ISSN 0387-074X) **2864**
• Hokuriku Denki to Kogyo/Electricity and Industry in Hokuriku District (JPN) **3310**
Hokuriku Denryoku K.K. Gijutsu Kenkyujo Gijutsu Kenkyu Hokoku/Hokuriku Electric Power. Technical Research Institute. Report (JPN ISSN 0389-6390) **3310**
Hokuriku Denryoku Shaho/Hokuriku Electric Power. News (JPN) **3310**
Hokuriku Electric Power. News see Hokuriku Denryoku Shaho **3310**
Hokuriku Electric Power. Technical Development News see Hokuden Gijutsu Kaihatsu Nyusu **3310**
Hokuriku Electric Power. Technical Research Institute. Report see Hokuriku Denryoku K.K. Gijutsu Kenkyujo Gijutsu Kenkyu Hokoku **3310**
➤ Hokuriku Geka Gakkai Zasshi/Hokuriku Journal of Surgery (JPN ISSN 0913-7629) **6245**
Hokuriku Ishi/Hokuriku Medical History (JPN ISSN 0389-3928) **5629**
Hokuriku Journal of Anesthesiology see Hokuriku Masuigaku Zasshi **5771**
Hokuriku Journal of Public Health see Hokuriku Koshu Eisei Gakkaishi **7524**
Hokuriku Journal of Surgery see Hokuriku Geka Gakkai Zasshi **6245**
Hokuriku Koshu Eisei Gakkaishi/Hokuriku Journal of Public Health (JPN ISSN 0386-3530) **7524**
Hokuriku Masuigaku Zasshi/Hokuriku Journal of Anesthesiology (JPN ISSN 0367-5947) **5771**
Hokuriku Medical History see Hokuriku Ishi **5629**
Hokuriku no Denki to Kogyo/Electricity and Industry in Hokuriku (JPN) **3153**
Hokuriku University. Bulletin see Hokuriku Daigaku Kiyo **2864**
Hokushin'etsu Chikusan Gakkaihou/Hokushinetsu Journal of Animal Science (JPN ISSN 1347-7544) **946**
Hokushinetsu Journal of Animal Science see Hokushin'etsu Chikusan Gakkaihou **946**
Hokusuishi Dayori/Hokkaido Fisheries Experimental Station. Journal (JPN ISSN 0914-6849) **3597**
• Hola (ESP ISSN 0214-3895) **3952**
Hola Pages (USA) **6502**
➤ Holarctic Lepidoptera (USA ISSN 1070-4140) **848**

Title

10370 HOLAS CARKVY ULRICH'S PERIODICALS

Holas Carkvy/Voice of the Church (USA ISSN 0437-6749) **7704**
Holbo Herreds Kulturhistoriske Centre, Gilleleje og Omegns Museumsforening, Arkiv- og Museumsforeningen i Helsinge. Aarbog (DNK ISSN 1604-4886) **4230**
• Holbrook Happenings (AUS ISSN 1832-0198) **5073**
• Hold Pusten (NOR ISSN 0332-9410) **6197**
• Holding Companies (NLD) **1928**
Holdsworth Law Review (GBR ISSN 0260-5864) **4687**
• Holgyvilag (HUN ISSN 1585-4310) **8867**
Holiday (BGD) **3799**
Holiday *see* Jiari **8725**
Holiday 100 *see* Jiari Yibiatian **5074**
Holiday & Business in Austria (AUT) **8718**
Holiday Baking (Des Moines) (USA ISSN 1939-1587) **4360**
Holiday Baking (New York) (USA ISSN 1550-9893) **4360**
Holiday Celebrations *see* Better Homes and Gardens Holiday Celebrations **4353**
Holiday Cookies (USA) **4360**
Holiday Cooking *see* Better Homes and Gardens Holiday Cooking **3671**
Holiday Cooking *see* Holiday Cooking with America's Top Chefs **4360**
Holiday Cooking and Entertaining *see* Holiday Cooking & Entertaining **3673**
Holiday Cooking & Entertaining (USA) **3673**
Holiday Cooking with America's Top Chefs (USA ISSN 1557-7570) **4360**
Holiday Crafts *see* Better Homes and Gardens Holiday Crafts **531**
Holiday Decorating (USA ISSN 1521-5806) **536**
Holiday Guide O F S/Vakansiegids O V S (ZAF) **8718**
Holiday Guide. Winter (GBR ISSN 1472-7110) **8718**
Holiday Hotspots *see* N Z Holiday Hotspots **8739**
Holiday One Hundred *see* Jiari Yibiatian **5074**
Holiday Parks and Campgrounds *see* Jasons Holiday Parks and Campgrounds Accommodation Directory **8725**
Holiday Purchasing Patterns Market Assessment *see* Key Note Market Assessment. Holiday Purchasing Patterns **8727**
Holiday Resorts & Destinations (ZAF ISSN 1995-9753) **8718**
Holiday Special (AUS ISSN 1832-2336) **5306**
Holiday & Lifestyle (DEU ISSN 1614-8827) **5073**
• Holiday Villas Magazine (GBR ISSN 1461-4170) **8718**
Holiday Weekly (PAK) **8719**
Holiday West Highland (GBR) **8719**
Holiday Which? (GBR) **8719**
† Holiday's (FRA ISSN 1959-0857) **8962**
Holidays (USA) **8719**
Holidays (ZAF) **8719**
Holidays at the Kindergarten (RUS) **2193**
Holidays, Festivals and Celebrations of the World Dictionary (USA) **341**
Holistic Health & Medicine *see* T S W Holistic Health & Medicine **315**
▼ • Holistic Health Luminary (USA ISSN 1947-251X) **310**
Holistic Health Sourcebook (USA) **6645**
Holistic Life/Vida Holistica (USA ISSN 1060-2615) **310**
Holistic Management In Practice (USA ISSN 1098-8157) **2613**
• ➤ Holistic Nursing Practice (USA ISSN 0887-9311) **5960**
Holland (NLD ISSN 0166-2511) **4230**
• Holland Exports (NLD ISSN 1380-846X) **1568**
Holland Film (NLD ISSN 1385-0504) **6502**
Holland Flower (NLD ISSN 1388-9567) **3756**
Holland Genetics Highlights *see* Highlights **871**
The Holland Handbook (NLD ISSN 1871-9899) **8105**
Holland Herald (NLD ISSN 0018-3563) **8784**
Holland in Congres (NLD ISSN 1574-7921) **6280**
Holland Management Review (NLD ISSN 0927-4375) **1118**
Holland Real Estate Yearbook (NLD ISSN 1572-820X) **7592**
Holland Shipbuilding (NLD ISSN 1877-1661) **8646**
Holland - U S A (USA) **1404**
Hollandiai Magyar Hirek (NLD ISSN 1572-5200) **3538**
▼ Hollands Diep (NLD ISSN 1874-0324) **3915**
Hollands Maandblad (NLD ISSN 0018-3601) **5219**
Hollandse Studien (NLD ISSN 0929-9718) **4230**
• ➤ Hollins Critic (USA ISSN 0018-3644) **5219**
Hollis Business Entertainment (Year) (GBR ISSN 1364-5382) **1819**
Hollis Europe (GBR ISSN 0962-3590) **26**
Hollis Media Guide (GBR ISSN 1741-7368) **26**
Hollis Sponsorship & Donations Yearbook (GBR ISSN 1351-5691) **26**
Hollis Sponsorship Newsletter (GBR ISSN 1354-2397) **26**
• Hollis UK Public Relations Annual (GBR ISSN 1753-9072) **26**
• Hollow Ear (USA) **5423**
Hollowell Heritage (USA ISSN 0891-270X) **3771**
▼ • Holly Rose Review (USA ISSN 1944-6675) **5423**
Holly Society Journal (USA ISSN 0738-2421) **3736**
Hollywood (HRV ISSN 1330-9471) **6502**
Hollywood Acting Coaches and Teachers Directory (USA ISSN 1069-3874) **3064**
Hollywood Aftermarket (USA ISSN 1533-4813) **6502**
Hollywood Call Sheet (USA ISSN 1091-8760) **4595**
Hollywood Dog (USA) **6809**
Hollywood Happenings (USA) **3538**
Hollywood Jesus Reviews (USA ISSN 1942-5554) **6502**
Hollywood Life (USA ISSN 1557-7228) **6502**
Hollywood Music Industry Directory (USA ISSN 1559-5471) **6573**
Hollywood Philatelist (USA) **6895**
• The Hollywood Reporter (USA ISSN 0018-3660) **6502**
• The Hollywood Reporter. International Edition (USA) **6502**
Hollywood Reporter Magazine *see* The Hollywood Reporter **6502**
Hollywood Reporter: Premier Edition *see* The Hollywood Reporter **6502**
• Hollywood Scriptwriter (USA ISSN 1097-8577) **6502**
Hollywood Worldwide Black Hairstyles & Trends (USA ISSN 1533-8789) **589**
Holman Christian Standard Bible Advanced Bible Study Commentary *see* Bible Studies for Life: Holman Christian Standard Bible Advanced Bible Study Commentary **7625**
• Holmes Safety Association. Bulletin (USA ISSN 0271-3888) **6678**
Holocaust and Genocide Studies (NLD) **4230**
• ➤ Holocaust and Genocide Studies (USA ISSN 8756-6583) **4230**
Holocaust Education and Memorial Centre of Toronto. Newsletter (CAN) **4230**
• ➤ Holocaust Studies (GBR ISSN 1750-4902) **4146**
➤ Holocaust Studies Series (NLD ISSN 0924-5022) **4146**
• ➤ The Holocene (GBR ISSN 0959-6836) **3437**
• Hologramatica (ARG ISSN 1668-5024) **2323**
• Holography News (USA ISSN 0895-9080) **7076**
• Holos (BRA ISSN 1518-1634) **3269**
• Holos Environment (BRA ISSN 1519-8634) **3437**
Holos Ukrainy/Golos Ukrainy (UKR) **3964**
Holos Ukrainy-Tyzhden'/Golos Ukrainy-Nedelya (UKR) **3964**
➤ HolQeD (USA ISSN 1061-2327) **6502**
Holstebro Museum. Aarsskrift (DNK ISSN 1395-5284) **4230**
Holstebro Museum. Skriftraekke (DNK ISSN 0907-9556) **4230**
Holstein International (NLD ISSN 1380-2879) **264**
▼ Holstein International Plus! (NLD ISSN 1877-1653) **288**
Holstein Journal (CAN ISSN 0710-1309) **265**
Holstein Journal (GBR ISSN 1466-0733) **265**
Holstein News *see* Ohio News **268**
Holstein World (USA ISSN 0199-4239) **265**
Holsteinische Courier (DEU) **3850**
Holston Pastfinder (USA ISSN 0887-3135) **3771**
Holt Happenings (USA) **3771**
• The Holy Cross Journal of Law & Public Policy (USA) **4849**
Holy Cross. Newsletter (USA) **7800**
Holy Land Postal History (ISR ISSN 0333-6875) **6895**
Holy Land Review (ISR ISSN 0333-7189) **7721**
• ➤ Holy Land Studies (GBR ISSN 1474-9475) **7648**
Holy TitClamps (USA) **4375**
• Holyrood News (GBR) **7444**
Holz (DEU ISSN 0945-1994) **1050**
Holz *see* Puu **1051**
Holz als Roh- und Werkstoff *see* European Journal of Wood and Wood Industries (Print) **3711**
Holz Journal (DEU ISSN 0945-8158) **3692**
• Holz Kurier (AUT ISSN 0018-3784) **3712**
Holz und Agrar im Spiegel (AUT) **3712**
Holz und Kunststoff (DEU ISSN 0722-6829) **3712**
Holz und Kunststoffverarbeitende Handwerk Perspektiven *see* H K H Perspektiven **492**
Holz- und Kunststoffverarbeitung (DEU ISSN 0947-6237) **4558**
Holz- und Moebelindustrie Deutschland (DEU ISSN 1614-6514) **4558**
Holz-Zentralblatt (DEU ISSN 0018-3792) **3712**
• Holzbau (DEU ISSN 1860-8841) **1011**
Holzbau - Report (DEU ISSN 0723-4856) **1050**
Holzb!ts (DEU ISSN 1439-1945) **1011**
HolzDesign (AUT) **4558**
• ➤ Holzforschung (DEU ISSN 0018-3830) **3712**
Holzforum (DEU ISSN 0947-6512) **3712**
HolzKurier *see* Holz Kurier **3712**
Holzpraxis Exklusiv (DEU ISSN 1430-788X) **1050**
Holzpreise/Prix du Bois (CHE) **3709**
Holztechnologie (DEU ISSN 0018-3881) **3712**
Die Holzzucht (DEU ISSN 0437-7168) **3692**
Hombre (New York) (USA) **6292**
Hombre y Ambiente (ECU ISSN 1021-044X) **8105**
Hombre y Cultura (PAN ISSN 0439-397X) **341**
Hombre y Desierto (CHL ISSN 0716-5897) **341**
• El Hombre y la Maquina (COL ISSN 0121-0777) **8424**
Hombre y Trabajo (CUB) **1685**
Home (CZE ISSN 1214-3960) **4541**
Home *see* H.O.M.E. **4541**
Home (ITA) **4541**
Home (JOR) **4541**
† • Home (USA ISSN 0278-2839) **8962**
Home (ZAF ISSN 1814-165X) **4360**
• Home Accents Today (USA ISSN 1093-0337) **4541**
Home and Architecture Trends (USA ISSN 1933-7671) **445**
Home & Away *see* A A A Living (Iowa Edition) **8679**
Home & Away (USA) **8719**
Home & Away (Findlay, Ohio) *see* Home & Away **8719**
Home & Away (Indianapolis Edition) (USA ISSN 8750-5649) **8719**
Home & Away (Minneapolis Edition) (USA ISSN 0274-8266) **8719**
Home & Away (Minnesota/Iowa Edition) *see* A A A Living (Minnesota Edition) **8679**
Home & Away (North Dakota Edition) (USA) **8719**
• Home & Away (Ohio Edition) (USA ISSN 0889-4078) **8719**
Home & Building Automation Quarterly *see* iHomes & Buildings **3318**
• Home and Community Care South Australia (AUS ISSN 1832-7796) **8044**
Home & Community Health Special Interest Section Newsletter *see* Home & Community Health Special Interest Section Quarterly **7524**
Home & Community Health Special Interest Section Quarterly (USA ISSN 1093-7218) **7524**
Home & Condo (USA) **3977**
Home and Country (GBR ISSN 1355-4735) **8867**
Home & Country (NZL ISSN 0018-3938) **8867**
Home & Decor (SGP ISSN 0129-0029) **4558**
Home & Design *see* Washington Maryland Virginia Home & Design **4552**
Home & Design *see* Arizona Home & Design **4531**
Home and Family (GBR ISSN 0018-3946) **8867**
Home & Family Finance (USA ISSN 1090-042X) **1351**
Home & Fire (USA ISSN 1547-2434) **3579**
Home and Garden *see* Toronto Life **3818**
Home and Garden (NLD ISSN 1569-3376) **3736**
Home & Garden *see* Baltimore Magazine **5065**
Home & Garden *see* Boston Home **4353**
Home and Garden Bulletin *see* U.S. Department of Agriculture. Home and Garden Bulletin **3753**
Home & Living Trends (USA ISSN 1933-7663) **4541**
Home & Studio Recording (GBR ISSN 0957-6614) **8153**
• Home & Towne (USA ISSN 1935-150X) **5073**
Home Art (TUR ISSN 1300-8056) **4541**
Home Automation News (USA ISSN 1057-8536) **2460**
• Home-Based Travel Agent (USA ISSN 1933-2262) **8719**
Home Beautiful *see* Australian Home Beautiful **5065**
Home Box Office's Guide to Movies on Videocassette and Cable TV *see* H B O's Guide to Movies on Videocassette and Cable TV **6502**
Home Builder Magazine (CAN ISSN 0840-4348) **1011**
Home Builders Association Options *see* H B A Options **1010**
† Home Building (USA ISSN 1550-5715) **8962**
• Home Business Connection (USA) **1118**
• The Home Business Files (USA ISSN 1522-7731) **1961**
Home Business Idea Possibility Newsletter (USA ISSN 0738-7490) **1750**
• Home Business Magazine (USA ISSN 1092-4779) **1961**
• Home Business Newsletter (USA) **1961**
Home Business Report *see* S O H O Business Report **1170**
• Home Business Tax Deductions (USA ISSN 1932-2402) **1961**
Home Care and Hospice Update (USA ISSN 1527-6821) **5960**
Home Care Family Newsletter (USA) **8044**
Home Care Outcomes (USA ISSN 1941-8965) **4098**
• Home Channel News (USA ISSN 1538-7348) **1118**
• Home Channel News NewsFax (USA) **1011**
† Home Cinema (CZE ISSN 1801-5441) **8962**
Home Cinema (ITA ISSN 1593-4349) **2401**
Home Cinema & Hi-Fi Living (AUS ISSN 1442-2824) **8153**
Home Cinema Choice (GBR ISSN 1359-6276) **2401**
Home Cinema Test (DEU) **3101**
† Home Cooking (USA ISSN 1071-4782) **8962**
• ➤ Home Cultures (GBR ISSN 1740-6315) **7969**
Home Dairy News *see* Cheese Enthusiast **262**
Home Decor & Furnishings (GBR) **6718**
Home Decor Buyer (USA ISSN 1528-4328) **4541**
The Home Decorating & Craft Catalog (USA) **4541**
Home Design (USA ISSN 1939-2265) **4541**
Home Digest (CAN) **4558**
• ➤ Home Economics Institute of Australia. Journal (AUS ISSN 1322-9974) **4360**
Home Economics Research Report *see* U.S. Department of Agriculture. Home Economics Research Report **4368**
Home Education Magazine (USA ISSN 0888-4633) **3064**
Home Educator's Family Times (USA) **2864**
Home Electronic Ideas (USA ISSN 1931-9959) **3101**
▼ Home Emotion (NLD ISSN 1875-3272) **8153**
• Home Energy (USA ISSN 0896-9442) **3137**
• Home Entertainment (GBR ISSN 0967-8239) **6502**
Home Entertainment *see* Robb Report Home Entertainment **3112**
Home Entertainment Market Assessment *see* Key Note Market Assessment. Home Entertainment **4979**
Home-Entertainment + Videotraileren (DNK ISSN 1398-5590) **2382**
Home Entertainment Today *see* H E T **4978**
Home Equity Lines of Credit Report (USA ISSN 1051-4902) **1351**
Home Equity News (USA ISSN 1085-0902) **1351**
• Home Equity Strategies & Advise (USA) **1351**
Home Fashion & Furniture Trends (USA) **4558**
Home from Home *see* Oldham Evening Chronicle **3869**
• Home Furnishings (GBR ISSN 0954-1071) **4558**
• Home Furnishings Business (USA ISSN 1558-9285) **4558**
Home Furnishings Business Now *see* H F Business Now **4558**
Home Furnishings Business NOW! *see* H F Business Now **4558**
• Home Furnishings Executive (USA ISSN 1073-5585) **4558**
Home Furnishings News *see* H F N **4558**
Home Furnishings Review (USA) **4558**
Home Graphic/Katei-Gaho (JPN) **4360**
Home Ground (USA ISSN 1053-0762) **4412**
Home - Grown Cereals Authority. Cereals R & D Conference. Proceedings (GBR) **234**
Home - Grown Cereals Authority. Cereals Statistics (GBR ISSN 1350-3057) **181**
Home - Grown Cereals Authority. Progress Reports on Research and Development (GBR ISSN 0951-0958) **273**
Home - Grown Cereals Authority. Project Report (GBR ISSN 1368-6739) **234**
Home - Grown Cereals Authority. Research Review (GBR ISSN 1367-1812) **234**
▼ Home Gym Magazine (USA) **6989**
The Home Handyman (ZAF ISSN 1022-1247) **4438**
Home Health Business Quarterly *see* Hospital Home Health **4100**
Home Health Care Dealer/Provider *see* H M E Today **4095**
• ➤ Home Health Care Management and Practice (USA ISSN 1084-8223) **4098**
• ➤ Home Health Care Services Quarterly (USA ISSN 0162-1424) **4098**
Home Health Care Technology Report (USA ISSN 1547-4550) **5629**
• Home Health Digest (USA ISSN 1077-9531) **5629**
• Home Health I C D-9 Alert (International Classification of Diseases) (USA ISSN 1558-6413) **5629**
Home Health I C D-Nine Alert *see* Home Health I C D-9 Alert **5629**
• Home Health Line (USA ISSN 1078-2389) **6989**
Home Health Line's Private Duty Insider (USA ISSN 1941-9309) **4098**
Home Health Products *see* H M E Business **5622**
Home Healthcare Magazine (GBR ISSN 1465-0436) **4099**
• ➤ Home Healthcare Nurse (USA ISSN 0884-741X) **5629**
Home Help (GBR) **4081**
Home Improvement Ideas (USA ISSN 1939-4705) **1011**
Home Improvement Retailing (CAN ISSN 1204-3044) **1054**
Home Improver Magazine (USA) **4541**
Home Journal/Meihao Jiaju (HKG) **4541**
Home Journal Buyer's Guide (HKG) **4541**
Home Journal Hardcover Book - Interior Images (HKG) **4541**
Home Journal of Knowledge *see* Jiating Baishitong **4361**
Home Lawn & Leisure (USA ISSN 1093-7102) **3736**
Home - Life Magazine (GBR) **4360**
Home Lighting & Accessories (USA ISSN 0162-9077) **4558**
Home Loan Affordability Report *see* Housing Affordability Report **4435**
Home Magazine (FRA ISSN 1950-1846) **4541**
• Home Magazine's Best Kitchen & Bath (USA ISSN 1050-494X) **1011**
Home Makeover (CAN ISSN 1719-8712) **1011**
Home Management *see* New Mexico State University. Cooperative Extension Service. Guide G **4365**
Home Meal Replacement *see* FoodService Director **3643**
• Home Media Magazine (USA ISSN 1934-9882) **2401**
Home Media Retailing *see* Home Media Magazine **2401**
Home Medical Equipment News *see* H M E News **4047**
Home Medical Equipment Today *see* H M E Today **4095**
Home Miniaturist (GBR ISSN 0143-554X) **4336**
Home Modification Info Newsletter *see* H M Info Newsletter **1010**
• Home Networking News (USA ISSN 1521-236X) **1119**
Home Networks *see* Home Networks Newsletter **2323**
• Home Networks Newsletter (USA ISSN 1531-4847) **2323**
Home New Zealand (NZL ISSN 1178-4148) **1012**
Home of Dramas *see* Xiju Zhijia **8485**
Home Office *see* Entrepreneur's Home Office **1960**
Home Office Circular (GBR ISSN 1366-2627) **7444**
Home Office List of Publications (GBR ISSN 0143-3237) **7562**
Home Office. National Advisory Council for the Boards of Visitors of England and Wales. Annual Report (GBR) **8719**

Home Office Research and Statistics Department. Research Bulletin see Great Britain. Home Office. Research and Statistics Department. Research Bulletin **7442**
• Home Office. Research and Statistics Directorate. Statistical Bulletin (GBR ISSN 1358-510X) **7481**
Home Office Research Studies see Great Britain. Home Office. Research Studies **2653**
Home Organization Products (USA ISSN 1945-189X) **1887**
Home Owner Building & Improvements Buyers Guide (ZAF ISSN 1023-2451) **1012**
Home P C see Domashnii P K **2576**
Home P C World China (CHN) **2576**
Home Page (Waikato Edition) see U N O (Waikato Edition) **5085**
Home Page. Tauranga Region see U N O **5085**
Home Planet News (USA ISSN 0273-303X) **5423**
Home Planner (USA ISSN 1040-547X) **1012**
Home Planners Outdoor Living see HomePlanners Outdoor Living **3736**
Home Planners Presents: Vacation & Second Homes (USA ISSN 1529-0646) **4541**
Home Planning Ideas see New Home (Des Moines) **4364**
• Home Power (USA ISSN 1050-2416) **3137**
Home Products Guide see Better Homes and Gardens Home Products Guide **982**
The Home Railway Journal (USA ISSN 1937-6790) **8618**
Home Recording Magazine (USA ISSN 1526-419X) **6573**
Home Remodeling & Makeovers see Remodeling & Makeovers **455**
Home Remodeling New Product Ideas (USA) **1012**
➤ Home School Researcher (USA ISSN 1054-8033) **2864**
Home Shop Machinist (USA ISSN 0744-6640) **5452**
The Home Show Magazine (GBR ISSN 1359-2653) **4541**
Home Studies (NGA ISSN 0331-3778) **3920**
Home Textile see Exports Home Textile **1565**
• Home Textiles Today (USA ISSN 0195-3184) **8451**
Home Theater see Homu Shiata **8153**
• Home Theater (USA ISSN 1096-3065) **2382**
Home Theater Buyer's Guide (USA ISSN 1092-731X) **3101**
▼ Home Theater Design (USA ISSN 1946-8156) **2382**
Home Times (USA) **7648**
• Home to Hill (USA ISSN 1946-5424) **1351**
Home to Home (CAN) **7593**
Home Trader (GBR) **8584**
Home Trends of Tampa Bay Magazine (USA) **7593**
Home Voice see H O M E Voice **234**
▼ Home Wellness (ITA ISSN 1970-4852) **6989**
• Homebuilding & Renovating (GBR ISSN 1464-1054) **1012**
• HomeBusiness Journal (USA ISSN 1097-2420) **1961**
Homec - Home Economics Yearbook (GBR) **4360**
Homecare Administrator (USA ISSN 1541-2490) **5960**
Homecare Direction (USA ISSN 1069-4560) **5960**
▼ • Homecare Insider Q & A (Question & Answer) (USA ISSN 1947-8917) **4099**
• HomeCare Magazine (USA ISSN 1529-1715) **5960**
• HomeCare Monday (USA ISSN 1525-982X) **5960**
Homecare News (USA ISSN 1045-1242) **5960**
Homecare Professional see Patient Centre Care **4109**
Homecoming Magazine (USA ISSN 1542-6637) **7648**
• Homeland Defense & Security Monitor (USA ISSN 1553-3301) **3507**
• Homeland Defense Journal (USA ISSN 1546-7368) **6424**
Homeland Protection Professional (USA ISSN 1556-0031) **2677**
Homeland Response see Responder Safety **7538**
Homeland Security (DEU ISSN 1614-3523) **2226**
• ➤ Homeland Security Affairs (USA ISSN 1558-643X) **7524**
▼ • Homeland Security and National Defense Newsletter (USA ISSN 1939-7070) **2226**
Homeland Security & Resilience Monitor (GBR ISSN 1746-1960) **2226**
• Homeland Security Briefing (USA ISSN 1543-4427) **2654**
Homeland Security Business Connection & Buyers Guide see Homeland Security Buyers Guide **2004**
Homeland Security Buyers Guide (USA) **2004**
Homeland Security Funding Week (USA ISSN 1554-737X) **7444**
Homeland Security Review see Jane's Homeland Security Review **2227**
• ➤ The Homeland Security Review (USA ISSN 1554-3234) **7444**
Homeland Security Today see H S Today **7443**
Homeland Security Today see H S Today **7443**
• Homeland Security Weekly (USA) **2677**
Homelife (PHL ISSN 0115-2971) **3928**
HomeLife (USA ISSN 0018-4071) **7760**
Homemaker (GBR) **4541**
• Homemaker's/Madame au Foyer (CAN ISSN 1491-8978) **4360**
Homemakers Network Newsletter (USA) **8867**
Homemarket Trends (USA) **4558**
Homenajes (USA) **5306**

The Homeopath (GBR ISSN 0263-3256) **5805**
Homeopathie see Homeopathie Magazine **5805**
L'Homeopathie Europeenne (FRA ISSN 1244-2356) **5805**
Homeopathie Magazine (NLD) **5805**
Homeopathy (Online) see Homeopathy (Print) **5805**
• ➤ Homeopathy (Print) (GBR ISSN 1475-4916) **5805**
Homeopathy International (GBR ISSN 0953-1203) **5805**
Homeopatia (ARG ISSN 0325-7282) **5805**
Homeostasis see Activitas Nervosa Superior **6119**
Homeowners Association and Planned Unit Development and Practice: Forms (USA) **7593**
• Homepage Helpers (USA) **2557**
Homepages see The Source **7574**
• HomePlanners Outdoor Living (USA ISSN 1548-1824) **3736**
HomePlanners Ultimate Home Plan Collection see Big Book of House Plans **435**
Homes (GBR ISSN 1740-3421) **1012**
Homes 24 (GBR ISSN 1750-0826) **7593**
Homes & Buildings see iHomes & Buildings **3318**
Homes & Gardens (DEU ISSN 0947-6547) **5073**
Homes and Gardens (GBR ISSN 0018-4233) **4542**
Homes & Gardens (RUS ISSN 1813-8926) **4558**
Homes & Land Magazine (USA) **7593**
Homes & Living (AUS ISSN 0817-4296) **1012**
Homes & Living see Dream House **441**
• Homes of Color (USA ISSN 1540-0034) **4360**
Homes Overseas (GBR ISSN 0018-4241) **7593**
Homes Twenty Four see Homes 24 **7593**
Homes Worldwide (GBR ISSN 1743-2669) **7593**
• Homescapes (CAN) **4542**
Homeschooler's Guide to Free Teaching Aids (USA ISSN 1535-7260) **3064**
Homeschooler's Guide to Free Videotapes (USA) **2864**
Homeschoolers' Support Association Happenings see H S A Happenings **2862**
• Homeschooling Horizons Magazine (CAN ISSN 1499-187X) **2864**
Homeschooling Today (USA ISSN 1073-2217) **2864**
• The Homeseeker (GBR ISSN 1749-1037) **1012**
The Homeseeker Scotland see The Homeseeker **1012**
Homespun see Australian Homespun **4352**
Homestead Hotline (USA) **5559**
Homesteader (USA) **3771**
Homestorys (DEU) **3850**
HomeStyle (GBR ISSN 1355-2996) **4558**
Homestyle (NZL ISSN 1177-0015) **4360**
† Homestyles Home Plans (USA ISSN 0897-621X) **8962**
▼ Hometown Cooking (Des Moines) (USA ISSN 1940-9109) **4360**
Hometown Favorites (USA ISSN 1944-6349) **4360**
Hometown Potluck Favorites see Hometown Favorites **4360**
HomeVision see Video-HomeVision **2398**
HomeWorld Business (USA ISSN 1048-0641) **4558**
• Homicide in California (USA ISSN 0098-8537) **2654**
• ➤ Homicide Studies (USA ISSN 1088-7679) **2654**
• Homicide Trends in the United States (USA ISSN 1931-8340) **2654**
• ➤ Homiletic (Online) (USA) **7760**
† • ➤ Homiletic (Print) (USA ISSN 0738-0534) **8962**
Homiletic and Pastoral Review (USA ISSN 0018-4268) **7800**
• Homiletica (ESP ISSN 0439-4208) **7648**
Homiletics (USA ISSN 1040-6255) **7760**
➤ Homiletische Monatshefte (DEU ISSN 0018-4276) **7648**
• Homily Helps (USA) **7648**
• Homily Service (USA ISSN 0732-1872) **7648**
Homin Ukrainy/Ukrainian Echo (CAN ISSN 0018-4284) **3538**
Homines (PRI ISSN 0252-8908) **7969**
Homing World Stud Book (GBR ISSN 0073-3164) **8178**
Hominid Remains see Anthropologica et Praehistorica **325**
L'Homme (AUT ISSN 1016-362X) **8898**
➤ L'Homme (FRA ISSN 0439-4216) **341**
L'Homme et la Societe (Paris, 1966) (FRA ISSN 0018-4306) **8105**
L'Homme et la Societe (Paris, 1993) (FRA ISSN 1242-9945) **8105**
L'Homme et l'Oiseau (BEL ISSN 0770-1365) **908**
L'Homme Nouveau (FRA ISSN 0018-4322) **7648**
L'Homme Nouveau Magazine (FRA ISSN 1955-1878) **7648**
Hommes & Libertes see Hommes et Libertes **7208**
Hommes de Dieu et Revolution (BEL ISSN 1258-2697) **7648**
Hommes et Fonderie (FRA ISSN 0018-4357) **6314**
† Hommes et la Terre (FRA ISSN 0073-3202) **8962**
• Hommes et Libertes (FRA ISSN 0180-8524) **7208**
Hommes & Migrations (FRA ISSN 1142-852X) **7284**
Hommes et Terres du Nord see Territoire en Movement **4031**
Hommes Street Hommes (FRA ISSN 1958-3494) **6292**
• ➤ HOMO (DEU ISSN 0018-442X) **341**
† ➤ Homo (FRA ISSN 0563-9743) **8962**
Homo Dei (POL ISSN 0208-757X) **7800**
† Homo Faber (ITA ISSN 0439-4291) **8962**
† Homo Sociologicus (ESP) **8962**
Homo Xtra Magazine see H X Magazine **8961**

Homo Xtra Philadelphia see H X Philadelphia **4374**
Homoeopathic Heritage see Homoeopathic Heritage International **5805**
➤ Homoeopathic Heritage International (IND) **5805**
• Homoeopathic Links (DEU ISSN 1019-2050) **5805**
Homoeopathic Update (IND ISSN 0971-4839) **5805**
Homoeopathy (IND ISSN 0046-7820) **5805**
Homoeopathy Heritage Nine see Homoeopathic Heritage International **5805**
Homoeopathy News see Homoeopathy NewZ **5805**
Homoeopathy NewZ (NZL ISSN 1171-1159) **5805**
Homoeopathy Today (USA ISSN 0886-1676) **310**
Homoeopatisk Tidsskrift (NOR ISSN 0333-0044) **5805**
Homoh (DEU) **4375**
• ➤ Homology, Homotopy and Applications (USA ISSN 1532-0073) **5491**
Homon Kango to Kaigo/Japanese Journal of Home Care Nursing (JPN ISSN 1341-7045) **5960**
Homophile Association of London Ontario Newsletter see H A L O Newsletter **4374**
• Homopolitan (MEX ISSN 1606-7851) **4375**
Homu Shiata/Home Theater (JPN ISSN 1346-0390) **8153**
Hon (JPN ISSN 0385-0366) **5306**
Hon Viet Magazine (USA ISSN 1066-6311) **3538**
➤ Honam Mathematical Journal/Honam Suhag Hagsulji (KOR ISSN 1225-293X) **5491**
Honam Suhag Hagsulji see Honam Mathematical Journal **5491**
Honar-ha-ye-ziba/Journal of Faculty of Fine Arts (IRN ISSN 1025-9570) **493**
† • Honcho (USA ISSN 0733-5865) **8962**
Honda Tuning (USA) **8584**
HondenManieren (NLD ISSN 1569-9129) **6809**
Hondensport & Sporthonden (NLD ISSN 1389-1960) **6809**
Hondenwereld (NLD ISSN 0018-4527) **6809**
Honduras see The P R S Group. Country Reports: Honduras **1507**
Honduras (Year) (HND) **3875**
Honduras al Dia (HND) **3875**
Honduras and the Bay Islands (USA ISSN 1523-9497) **8719**
Honduras. Congreso Nacional. Boletin (HND) **7444**
Honduras. Consejo Superior de Planificacion Economica. Plan Operativo Anual. Sector Industrial (HND) **1119**
Honduras. Consejo Superior de Planificacion Economica. Plan Operativo Anual. Sector Turismo (HND) **8719**
Honduras en Cifras (HND) **8376**
Honduras Rotaria (HND) **2266**
Honduras. Secretaria de Hacienda y Credito Publico. Direccion General de Presupuesto. Presupuesto General de Ingresos y Egresos de la Republica (HND) **8376**
Honduras. Secretaria de Planificacion, Coordinacion y Presupuesto. Anuario Estadistico (HND) **8376**
Honduras. Secretaria de Planificacion Coordinacion y Presupuesto. Direccion General de Estadistica y Censos. Encuesta Permanente de Hogares de Propositos Multiples (HND) **4435**
Honduras. Secretaria de Trabajo y Prevision Social. Boletin de Estadisticas Laborales (HND) **8044**
• Honduras This Week (HND) **3875**
Honduras. Universidad Nacional Autonoma. Revista de la Universidad (HND) **2985**
El Hondureno (USA) **6895**
Hone Report (USA) **1628**
Honest Ulsterman see H U **8961**
• Honestly Woman (AUS ISSN 1833-3621) **8867**
Honey (LKA) **4360**
▼ • The Honey Land Review (USA ISSN 1946-1283) **5423**
Honeybee Science see Mitsubachi Kagaku **855**
Honeyguide (ZWE ISSN 0018-456X) **908**
Honeywell Instrumentatie Nieuws (NLD ISSN 0020-4358) **4487**
Hong Dou (CHN) **5306**
Hong Kong see The P R S Group. Country Reports: Hong Kong **1507**
Hong Kong (Year) (HKG ISSN 1011-4521) **7284**
Hong Kong (Year) Population By-Census see Hong Kong Special Administrative Region of China. Census and Statistics Department. Hong Kong (Year) Population By-Census **7308**
Hong Kong (Year) Population By-Census. Basic Tables for Constituency Areas: Hong Kong Island see Hong Kong Special Administrative Region of China. Census and Statistics Department. Hong Kong (Year) Population By-Census. Basic Tables for Constituency Areas: Hong Kong Island **7308**
Hong Kong (Year) Population By-Census. Basic Tables for Constituency Areas: Kowloon see Hong Kong Special Administrative Region of China. Census and Statistics Department. Hong Kong (Year) Population By-Census. Basic Tables for Constituency Areas: Kowloon **7308**
Hong Kong (Year) Population By-Census. Basic Tables for Constituency Areas: New Territories see Hong Kong Special Administrative Region of China. Census and Statistics Department. Hong Kong (Year) Population By-Census. Basic Tables for Constituency Areas: New Territories **7308**
Hong Kong (Year) Population By-Census. Basic Tables for District Board Districts see Hong Kong Special Administrative Region of China. Census and Statistics Department. Hong Kong (Year) Population By-Census. Basic Tables for District Board Districts **7308**

Hong Kong (Year) Population By-Census. Basic Tables for Tertiary Planning Units: Hong Kong Island see Hong Kong Special Administrative Region of China. Census and Statistics Department. Hong Kong (Year) Population By-Census. Basic Tables for Tertiary Planning Units: Hong Kong Island **7308**
Hong Kong (Year) Population By-Census. Basic Tables for Tertiary Planning Units: Kowloon see Hong Kong Special Administrative Region of China. Census and Statistics Department. Hong Kong (Year) Population By-Census. Basic Tables for Tertiary Planning Units: Kowloon **7308**
Hong Kong (Year) Population By-Census. Basic Tables for Tertiary Planning Units: New Territories see Hong Kong Special Administrative Region of China. Census and Statistics Department. Hong Kong (Year) Population By-Census. Basic Tables for Tertiary Planning Units: New Territories **7308**
Hong Kong (Year) Population By-Census. Boundary Maps Complementary to Tables for District Board Districts and Constituency Areas see Hong Kong Special Administrative Region of China. Census and Statistics Department. Hong Kong (Year) Population By-Census. Boundary Maps Complementary to Tables for District Board Districts and Constituency Areas **7308**
Hong Kong (Year) Population By-Census. Graphic Guide see Hong Kong Special Administrative Region of China. Census and Statistics Department. Hong Kong (Year) Population By-Census. Graphic Guide **7308**
Hong Kong (Year) Population By-Census. Main Report see Hong Kong Special Administrative Region of China. Census and Statistics Department. Hong Kong (Year) Population By-Census. Main Report **7308**
Hong Kong (Year) Population By-Census. Main Tables see Hong Kong Special Administrative Region of China. Census and Statistics Department. Hong Kong (Year) Population By-Census. Main Tables **7308**
Hong Kong (Year) Population By-Census. MAP on CD-ROM see Hong Kong Special Administrative Region of China. Census and Statistics Department. Hong Kong (Year) Population By-Census. MAP on CD-ROM **7308**
Hong Kong (Year) Population By-Census. Summary Results see Hong Kong Special Administrative Region of China. Census and Statistics Department. Hong Kong (Year) Population By-Census. Summary Results **7308**
Hong Kong (Year) Population By-Census T A B on CD-ROM see Hong Kong Special Administrative Region of China. Census and Statistics Department. Hong Kong (Year) Population By-Census T A B on CD-ROM **7308**
Hong Kong (Year) Population By-Census. Tables for District Board Districts and Constituency Areas: Quarters, Households and Population by Type of Quarters see Hong Kong Special Administrative Region of China. Census and Statistics Department. Hong Kong (Year) Population By-Census. Tables for District Board Districts and Constituency Areas: Quarters, Households and Population by Type of Quarters **7308**
Hong Kong (Year) Population By-Census. Tables for Tertiary Planning Units: Population by Age and Sex see Hong Kong Special Administrative Region of China. Census and Statistics Department. Hong Kong (Year) Population By-Census. Tables for Tertiary Planning Units: Population by Age and Sex **7309**
Hong Kong & Macau Airline Timetable (HKG) **8544**
• Hong Kong Annual Digest of Statistics (HKG ISSN 1011-4033) **7307**
• Hong Kong Apparel (HKG ISSN 1021-8939) **2247**
• Hong Kong Autos Report (GBR ISSN 1748-992X) **8584**
Hong Kong Best Restaurants (Chinese Edition) (HKG) **4387**
Hong Kong Best Restaurants (English Edition) (HKG) **4388**
Hong Kong Bird Report (HKG ISSN 1017-1118) **908**
• Hong Kong Builder Directory (Hong Kong Edition) (HKG) **1012**
Hong Kong. Building Development Department. Building Statistics (HKG) **8376**
• Hong Kong Business (HKG) **1119**
Hong Kong Business Annual (HKG) **1119**
• Hong Kong Cases (HKG ISSN 1358-037X) **4687**
Hong Kong Catholic Church Directory/Hsiang-Kang T'ien Chu Chiao Shou Ts'e (HKG ISSN 0073-3210) **7800**
Hong Kong. Civil Aviation Department. Director's Annual Report (HKG) **8544**
• ➤ Hong Kong College of Cardiology. Journal (HKG ISSN 1027-7811) **5789**
➤ Hong Kong College of Radiologists. Journal (HKG ISSN 1029-5097) **6197**
Hong Kong. Commissioner of Banking. Annual Report (HKG) **1236**
Hong Kong Compensation Report see Compensation Report - Hong Kong **1858**
Hong Kong Computer Directory (Year) (HKG) **2004**
Hong Kong Computer Journal (HKG) **2419**
Hong Kong Convention & Exhibtion Directory (HKG) **2004**

Title

10372 THE HONG KONG COURT OF FINAL APPEAL REPORTS ULRICH'S PERIODICALS

The Hong Kong Court of Final Appeal Reports/Xianggang Zhongshen Fayuan Anli Huibao (HKG ISSN 1561-4247) **4687**
Hong Kong Customs *see* Xianggang Fengqing **8147**
Hong Kong Daily News *see* Xin Bao **3876**
Hong Kong Dermatology & Venereology Bulletin *see* Hong Kong Journal of Dermatology & Venereology **5877**
Hong Kong Digest (USA) **3875**
Hong Kong Directory to 10,000 Exporters & Importers (USA) **1819**
Hong Kong Economic Journal/Xinbao Caijing Yuekan (HKG ISSN 1018-6751) **1543**
Hong Kong Economic Times *see* Hong Kong Jingji Ribao **1119**
• Hong Kong Economic Trends (HKG) **1237**
Hong Kong Economic Yearbook (HKG) **1119**
Hong Kong Electronic Components and Parts/Xianggang Dianzi Lingjian (HKG ISSN 1026-6712) **3101**
Hong Kong Electronics (HKG ISSN 1021-8866) **3101**
Hong Kong Energy Statistics Annual Report *see* Hong Kong Special Administrative Region of China. Census and Statistics Department. Hong Kong Energy Statistics Annual Report **3153**
Hong Kong Energy Statistics Quarterly Report *see* Hong Kong Special Administrative Region of China. Census and Statistics Department. Hong Kong Energy Statistics Quarterly Report **3153**
Hong Kong Engineer (HKG ISSN 1607-9183) **3195**
• Hong Kong Enterprise (HKG ISSN 1021-5611) **4060**
Hong Kong Exchange Ex Cash and Derivatives Markets Quarterly Report *see* H K Ex Cash and Derivatives Markets Quarterly Report **1628**
Hong Kong Exchange EX Fact Book (Year) *see* H K EX Fact Book (Year) **1628**
Hong Kong Exchanges and Clearing Ltd. Monthly Market Data (Main Board and Stock Options Market) (HKG) **1351**
• Hong Kong Exchanges and Clearing Ltd. Monthly Market Statistics (HKG) **1628**
• Hong Kong Exchanges and Clearing Ltd. Weekly Quotations (HKG) **1628**
Hong Kong Export Credit Insurance Corporation. Annual Report (HKG) **1351**
Hong Kong External Trade *see* Hong Kong Special Administrative Region of China. Census and Statistics Department. Hong Kong External Trade **1238**
Hong Kong External Trade (CD-ROM Edition) *see* Hong Kong Special Administrative Region of China. Census and Statistics Department. Hong Kong External Trade **1238**
• Hong Kong Fabrics & Accessories (HKG ISSN 1025-7802) **8451**
Hong Kong Family Law Reports (HKG ISSN 1749-7930) **4911**
Hong Kong Financial Services (HKG ISSN 1027-6335) **1351**
• Hong Kong Food & Drink Report (GBR ISSN 1749-2726) **1119**
• Hong Kong Footwear (HKG) **7941**
Hong Kong Freight Transport Report (GBR ISSN 1752-5837) **8498**
Hong Kong General Chamber of Commerce. Annual Report (HKG) **1404**
Hong Kong General Chamber of Commerce Bulletin (HKG) **1404**
Hong Kong Geologist (HKG ISSN 1024-669X) **2746**
• Hong Kong Gifts, Premiums & Stationery (HKG) **4060**
Hong Kong. Government Publication Centre. Economic Background (HKG) **1719**
Hong Kong. Government Publication Centre. Economic Prospects (HKG) **1719**
Hong Kong. Government Publication Centre. Economic Report (HKG) **1719**
Hong Kong. Government Publication Centre. Inquiry Reports (HKG) **7444**
Hong Kong Guide (Year) (HKG) **8719**
Hong Kong Harmonized Commodity Description and Coding System Handbook *see* Hong Kong Special Administrative Region of China. Census and Statistics Department. Hong Kong Harmonized Commodity Description and Coding System Handbook **1238**
• Hong Kong Household (HKG ISSN 1021-8882) **1054**
Hong Kong Importers' Directory (Year) (HKG) **2004**
The Hong Kong Imports and Exports Classification LIst (Harmonized System). Volume One *see* Hong Kong Special Administrative Region of China. Census and Statistics Department. The Hong Kong Imports and Exports Classification LIst (Harmonized System). Volume One **1240**
The Hong Kong Imports and Exports Classification LIst (Harmonized System). Volume Three *see* Hong Kong Special Administrative Region of China. Census and Statistics Department. The Hong Kong Imports and Exports Classification List (Harmonized System). Volume Three **1240**
The Hong Kong Imports and Exports Classification List (Harmonized System). Volume Two *see* Hong Kong Special Administrative Region of China. Census and Statistics Department. The Hong Kong Imports and Exports Classification List (Harmonized System). Volume Two **1240**
• Hong Kong in Figures (HKG) **8376**
• Hong Kong Industrialist (HKG) **1429**
Hong Kong Information Technology Report *see* Business Monitor International. Information Technology Country Reports **2491**
• Hong Kong Institution of Engineers, Transactions (HKG ISSN 1023-697X) **3195**
• Hong Kong Jewellery Collection (HKG) **4566**
Hong Kong Jewellery Magazine (HKG) **4566**
Hong Kong Jingji Ribao/Hong Kong Economic Times (HKG) **1119**
• Hong Kong Journal (USA ISSN 1947-0983) **7140**
➤ Hong Kong Journal of Applied Linguistics (HKG ISSN 1028-4435) **5125**
• Hong Kong Journal of Dermatology & Venereology (HKG ISSN 1814-7453) **5877**
• Hong Kong Journal of Emergency Medicine (HKG ISSN 1024-9079) **6061**
Hong Kong Journal of Gerontology (HKG ISSN 1608-2346) **4047**
➤ Hong Kong Journal of Modern Chinese History (HKG ISSN 1727-8147) **4183**
• Hong Kong Journal of Nephrology (HKG ISSN 1561-5413) **6268**
• Hong Kong Journal of Occupational Therapy (NLD ISSN 1569-1861) **6110**
Hong Kong Journal of Orthopaedic Surgery (HKG ISSN 1028-2637) **6061**
• Hong Kong Journal of Paediatrics (HKG ISSN 1013-9923) **6092**
➤ Hong Kong Journal of Psychiatry (HKG ISSN 1026-2121) **6145**
• Hong Kong Journal of Social Sciences (HKG ISSN 1021-3619) **7969**
• ➤ Hong Kong Journal of Social Work/Hong Kong Shehui Gongzuo Xuebao (SGP ISSN 0219-2462) **8045**
Hong Kong Journal of Sociology (HKG ISSN 1606-8610) **8105**
The Hong Kong Journal of Sports Medicine and Sports Science *see* Journal of Exercise Science and Fitness **6230**
Hong Kong Law Digest (HKG ISSN 1017-7817) **4688**
• Hong Kong Law Journal (HKG ISSN 0378-0600) **4688**
Hong Kong. Law Reform Commission. Report (HKG) **4688**
Hong Kong Law Yearbook (HKG) **4688**
• Hong Kong Lawyer/Hong Kong Lushi (HKG ISSN 1464-6595) **4688**
Hong Kong Leather Goods and Bags (HKG ISSN 1021-8955) **4973**
Hong Kong Legends (GBR ISSN 1748-0094) **6503**
Hong Kong. Legislative Council. Finance Committee. Report (HKG) **7444**
Hong Kong. Legislative Council. Proceedings (HKG) **7444**
Hong Kong. Legislative Council. Public Works Sub-Committee. Report (HKG) **7444**
• Hong Kong Library Association. Newsletter (HKG) **5012**
Hong Kong Life Tables *see* Hong Kong Special Administrative Region of China. Census and Statistics Department. Hong Kong Life Tables **7309**
Hong Kong Linkage Industry Directory (Year) (HKG) **2004**
Hong Kong Lushi *see* Hong Kong Lawyer **4688**
Hong Kong Manager (HKG ISSN 0018-4594) **1750**
Hong Kong Manufacturers and Exporters Register (HKG ISSN 0073-3245) **2004**
Hong Kong Mechatronics Directory (Year) (HKG) **2004**
• ➤ Hong Kong Medical Journal (HKG ISSN 1024-2708) **5629**
Hong Kong Meteorological Society. Bulletin (HKG ISSN 1024-4468) **6354**
• Hong Kong Monthly Digest of Statistics (HKG ISSN 0300-418X) **7308**
Hong Kong Muslim Herald (HKG) **7711**
• Hong Kong Narcotics Report (HKG) **2694**
Hong Kong Now! (Print) *see* e-Hong Kong **8699**
• ➤ Hong Kong Nursing Journal/Hsiang Kang Hu Li Tsa Chih (HKG ISSN 0073-3253) **5960**
Hong Kong Observatory Almanac (HKG) **6354**
Hong Kong Observatory. Daily Weather Chart (HKG) **6354**
Hong Kong Observatory. Historical Publications (HKG) **6354**
Hong Kong Observatory. Hong Kong Tide Tables (HKG) **6354**
Hong Kong Observatory. Marine Climatological Summary Charts for the South China Sea (HKG) **6354**
Hong Kong Observatory. Monthly Weather Summary (HKG) **6354**
• Hong Kong Observatory. Newsletter for Friends of Observatory (HKG) **6354**
• Hong Kong Observatory. Newsletter for Hong Kong Voluntary Observating Ships (HKG) **6354**
• Hong Kong Observatory. Newsletter for the Aviation Community (HKG) **6354**
Hong Kong Observatory. Occasional Paper (HKG) **6354**
Hong Kong Observatory. Technical Note (HKG) **6354**
Hong Kong Observatory. Technical Notes (Local) (HKG) **6354**
Hong Kong Observatory. Technical Reports on Environmental Radiation Monitoring in Hong Kong (HKG) **3437**
• Hong Kong Observatory. Tropical Cyclones (Year) (HKG) **6354**
• Hong Kong Optical (HKG ISSN 1021-8947) **6043**
Hong Kong Packaging (HKG ISSN 1026-6720) **6710**
Hong Kong Pharmaceutical Journal (HKG ISSN 1727-2874) **6846**
• Hong Kong Physiotherapy Journal (HKG ISSN 1013-7025) **6110**
Hong Kong Population Projections (Year-Year) *see* Hong Kong Special Administrative Region of China. Census and Statistics Department. Hong Kong Population Projections (Year-Year) **7309**
Hong Kong Practitioner/Xianggang Uankeyixueyuan Yuekan (HKG ISSN 1027-3948) **5629**
Hong Kong Productivity Council Annual Report (HKG) **1887**
Hong Kong Productivity Council Electronics Bulletin *see* H K P C Electronics Bulletin **3100**
Hong Kong Productivity Council Textile and Clothing Bulletin *see* H K P C Textile and Clothing Bulletin **8451**
Hong Kong Productivity News (HKG) **1887**
• Hong Kong Property Review (HKG) **7593**
Hong Kong. Public Service Commission. Chairman's Report (HKG) **7444**
Hong Kong Radiographers Journal *see* Xianggang Fangshe Jishi Zazhi **6210**
• Hong Kong Revenue Legislation (SGP) **4688**
Hong Kong Shehui Gongzuo Xuebao *see* Hong Kong Journal of Social Work **8045**
Hong Kong Shipping Statistics *see* Hong Kong Special Administrative Region of China. Census and Statistics Department. Hong Kong Shipping Statistics **1238**
• Hong Kong Shipping Statistics (CD-ROM Edition) (HKG) **1237**
• Hong Kong Social and Economic Trends (HKG) **1489**
Hong Kong Source Book for Architects, Designers & Building Contractors/Caiku (HKG) **1012**
• Hong Kong Special Administrative Region of China. Audit Commission. Director of Audit's Reports (HKG) **8376**
• Hong Kong Special Administrative Region of China. Census and Statistics Department. An Outline of Statistical Development (HKG) **7308**
• Hong Kong Special Administrative Region of China. Census and Statistics Department. Annual Report on the Consumer Price Index (HKG) **8376**
• Hong Kong Special Administrative Region of China. Census and Statistics Department. Annual Review of Hong Kong External Trade (HKG) **1237**
• Hong Kong Special Administrative Region of China. Census and Statistics Department. Annual Survey of Wholesale, Retail and Import and Export Trades, Restaurants and Hotels (HKG) **1237**
• Hong Kong Special Administrative Region of China. Census and Statistics Department. Average Daily Wages of Workers Engaged in Government Building and Construction Projects (HKG) **1237**
• Hong Kong Special Administrative Region of China. Census and Statistics Department. Average Wholesale Prices of Selected Building Materials (HKG) **1046**
Hong Kong Special Administrative Region of China. Census and Statistics Department. Balance of Payments Statistics of Hong Kong (HKG) **1237**
Hong Kong Special Administrative Region of China. Census and Statistics Department. Balance of Payments Statistics of Hong Kong (Cumulative Edition) (HKG) **1237**
Hong Kong Special Administrative Region of China. Census and Statistics Department. Consumer Price Index (HKG) **1237**
Hong Kong Special Administrative Region of China. Census and Statistics Department. Crime and Its Victims in Hong Kong (HKG) **2674**
• Hong Kong Special Administrative Region of China. Census and Statistics Department. Demographic Trends in Hong Kong (HKG) **7284**
Hong Kong Special Administrative Region of China. Census and Statistics Department. Domestic Exports of Manufactured Goods Classified by Industrial Origin (HKG) **1237**
• Hong Kong Special Administrative Region of China. Census and Statistics Department. Employment and Vacancies Statistics (Detailed Tables) Series A. Services Sectors (HKG) **6706**
• Hong Kong Special Administrative Region of China. Census and Statistics Department. Employment and Vacancies Statistics (Detailed Tables) Series B. Wholesale and Retail Trades, Restaurants and Hotels (HKG) **6706**
• Hong Kong Special Administrative Region of China. Census and Statistics Department. Employment and Vacancies Statistics (Detailed Tables) Series C. Industrial Sectors (HKG) **1237**
• Hong Kong Special Administrative Region of China. Census and Statistics Department. Employment and Vacancies Statistics (Detailed Tables) Series D. Import/Export Trades (HKG) **1119**
• Hong Kong Special Administrative Region of China. Census and Statistics Department. External Direct Investment Statistics of Hong Kong (Year) (HKG) **1237**
• Hong Kong Special Administrative Region of China. Census and Statistics Department. External Trade Figures (HKG) **1237**
Hong Kong Special Administrative Region of China. Census and Statistics Department. Gross Domestic Product (Annual Edition) (HKG) **1237**
• Hong Kong Special Administrative Region of China. Census and Statistics Department. Gross Domestic Product (Quarterly Edition) (HKG) **1238**
• Hong Kong Special Administrative Region of China. Census and Statistics Department. Hong Kong (Year) Population By-Census (HKG) **7308**
Hong Kong Special Administrative Region of China. Census and Statistics Department. Hong Kong (Year) Population By-Census. Basic Tables for Constituency Areas: Hong Kong Island (HKG) **7308**
Hong Kong Special Administrative Region of China. Census and Statistics Department. Hong Kong (Year) Population By-Census. Basic Tables for Constituency Areas: Kowloon (HKG) **7308**
Hong Kong Special Administrative Region of China. Census and Statistics Department. Hong Kong (Year) Population By-Census. Basic Tables for Constituency Areas: New Territories (HKG) **7308**
Hong Kong Special Administrative Region of China. Census and Statistics Department. Hong Kong (Year) Population By-Census. Basic Tables for District Board Districts (HKG) **7308**
Hong Kong Special Administrative Region of China. Census and Statistics Department. Hong Kong (Year) Population By-Census. Basic Tables for Tertiary Planning Units: Hong Kong Island (HKG) **7308**
Hong Kong Special Administrative Region of China. Census and Statistics Department. Hong Kong (Year) Population By-Census. Basic Tables for Tertiary Planning Units: Kowloon (HKG) **7308**
Hong Kong Special Administrative Region of China. Census and Statistics Department. Hong Kong (Year) Population By-Census. Basic Tables for Tertiary Planning Units: New Territories (HKG) **7308**
Hong Kong Special Administrative Region of China. Census and Statistics Department. Hong Kong (Year) Population By-Census. Boundary Maps Complementary to Tables for District Board Districts and Constituency Areas (HKG) **7308**
Hong Kong Special Administrative Region of China. Census and Statistics Department. Hong Kong (Year) Population By-Census. Boundary Maps Complementary to Tables for Tertiary Planning Units and Constituency Areas (HKG) **7308**
Hong Kong Special Administrative Region of China. Census and Statistics Department. Hong Kong (Year) Population By-Census. Graphic Guide (HKG) **7308**
Hong Kong Special Administrative Region of China. Census and Statistics Department. Hong Kong (Year) Population By-Census. Main Report (HKG) **7308**
Hong Kong Special Administrative Region of China. Census and Statistics Department. Hong Kong (Year) Population By-Census. Main Tables (HKG) **7308**
Hong Kong Special Administrative Region of China. Census and Statistics Department. Hong Kong (Year) Population By-Census. MAP on CD-ROM (HKG) **7308**
Hong Kong Special Administrative Region of China. Census and Statistics Department. Hong Kong (Year) Population By-Census. Summary Results (HKG) **7308**
• Hong Kong Special Administrative Region of China. Census and Statistics Department. Hong Kong (Year) Population By-Census T A B on CD-ROM (HKG) **7308**
Hong Kong Special Administrative Region of China. Census and Statistics Department. Hong Kong (Year) Population By-Census. Tables for District Board Districts and Constituency Areas: Quarters, Households and Population by Type of Quarters (HKG) **7308**
Hong Kong Special Administrative Region of China. Census and Statistics Department. Hong Kong (Year) Population By-Census. Tables for Tertiary Planning Units: Population by Age and Sex (HKG) **7309**
Hong Kong Special Administrative Region of China. Census and Statistics Department. Hong Kong (Year) Population By-Census. Tables for Tertiary Planning Units: Quarters, Households and Population by Type of Quarters (HKG) **7309**
Hong Kong Special Administrative Region of China. Census and Statistics Department. Hong Kong Energy Statistics Annual Report (HKG) **3153**
Hong Kong Special Administrative Region of China. Census and Statistics Department. Hong Kong Energy Statistics Quarterly Report (HKG) **3153**
• Hong Kong Special Administrative Region of China. Census and Statistics Department. Hong Kong External Trade (HKG) **1238**
• Hong Kong Special Administrative Region of China. Census and Statistics Department. Hong Kong Harmonized Commodity Description and Coding System Handbook (HKG) **1238**
Hong Kong Special Administrative Region of China. Census and Statistics Department. Hong Kong Life Tables (HKG) **7309**
Hong Kong Special Administrative Region of China. Census and Statistics Department. Hong Kong Population Projections (Year-Year) (HKG) **7309**

Title

10374 HORIZONREEKS ULRICH'S PERIODICALS

Horizonreeks (NLD ISSN 1574-2318) **4230**
▼ • Horizons (GBR ISSN 1756-2422) **5125**
Horizons (Blacksburg) (USA ISSN 1075-9255) **200**
Horizons (Columbus) (USA) **7444**
Horizons (Cumbria) (GBR ISSN 1462-0677) **8317**
Horizons (Elmwood Park) (USA) **536**
Horizons (Kingston) (USA) **2286**
Horizons (Livingston) (USA) **6989**
Horizons (Metuchen) (USA ISSN 1548-2227) **5629**
Horizons (Montreal) (CAN ISSN 0704-2965) **3811**
Horizons (Newport) (GBR ISSN 1366-0101) **7284**
Horizons (Perth) (AUS) **8584**
Horizons (Shawano) (USA) **265**
Horizons (Toronto) (CAN ISSN 0381-3789) **2985**
Horizons (Torrance) (USA) **58**
• ➤ Horizons (Villanova) (USA ISSN 0360-9669) **7800**
Horizons (Winnipeg) (CAN ISSN 1719-6388) **288**
Horizons Banquaires/Agricultural Economics and Finance (FRA ISSN 1626-5246) **200**
Horizons Centre Ile-de-France (Edition Eure et Loir) (FRA ISSN 1147-7598) **119**
Horizons Centre Ile-de-France (Edition Loir-et-Cher) (FRA ISSN 1147-758X) **119**
Horizons Centre Ile-de-France (Edition Seine-et-Marne) (FRA ISSN 1147-7563) **119**
• Horizons & Conseils. Bi-Hebdomadaire (FRA ISSN 1765-3061) **1629**
• Horizons & Conseils. Mensuel (FRA ISSN 1765-3053) **1629**
• ➤ Horizons in Biblical Theology (NLD ISSN 0195-9085) **7648**
Horizons in Geography *see* Ofaqim B'geografiya **4023**
Horizons in Medicine (GBR ISSN 0957-5804) **5629**
Horizons Magazine (USA) **3977**
Horizons Maghrebins (FRA ISSN 0984-2616) **341**
Horizons.mw. Annual Plan *see* Horizons Regional Council. Annual Plan **7494**
Horizons.mw. Annual Report *see* Horizons Regional Council. Annual Report **7494**
Horizons Nature (FRA ISSN 1778-8137) **8719**
Horizons Newsletter (CAN) **8045**
Horizons of Psychology *see* Psiholoska Obzorja **7394**
Horizons Philosophiques (CAN ISSN 1181-9227) **6923**
Horizons Regional Council. Annual Plan (NZL ISSN 1176-9750) **7494**
Horizons Regional Council. Annual Report (NZL ISSN 1176-9548) **7494**
• Horizons Strategiques (FRA ISSN 1958-3370) **7444**
Horizons Unlimited (PHL ISSN 0018-5019) **2864**
Horizons Unlimited (USA ISSN 1041-5270) **7760**
• Horizont (AUT) **26**
Horizont (HUN ISSN 0139-1380) **2266**
• Horizont (Frankfurt) (DEU ISSN 0175-7989) **26**
Horizont Bestseller *see* Bestseller **8935**
• Horizont Sport Business (DEU ISSN 1617-125X) **8178**
Horizonte (BRA ISSN 1679-9615) **7648**
Horizonte (PRT) **6989**
Horizonte (Trier) (DEU) **5306**
Horizonte (Tuebingen) (DEU ISSN 1430-3922) **5306**
Horizonte de Enfermeria (CHL ISSN 0716-8861) **5960**
Horizonte Geografico (BRA ISSN 0104-6365) **4014**
Horizonte Medico (PER ISSN 1727-558X) **5629**
• Horizontes (BRA ISSN 0103-7706) **341**
• ➤ Horizontes (PRI ISSN 0018-5027) **4455**
• Horizontes Antropologicos (BRA ISSN 0104-7183) **341**
Le Horla (FRA ISSN 1264-532X) **5306**
Horme (DEU ISSN 0935-2880) **5993**
• Hormigon Preparado (ESP ISSN 1133-1380) **1012**
➤ Hormigon y Acero (ESP ISSN 0439-5689) **1012**
• ➤ Hormone and Metabolic Research (DEU ISSN 0018-5043) **5893**
• Hormone and Metabolic Research. Supplement (DEU ISSN 0170-5903) **5893**
Hormone Frontier in Gynecology (JPN ISSN 1340-220X) **5993**
▼ • ➤ Hormone Molecular Biology and Clinical Investigation (DEU ISSN 1868-1883) **5894**
Hormone Research *see* Hormone Research in Paediatrics **5894**
• ➤ Hormone Research in Paediatrics (CHE ISSN 1663-2818) **5894**
Hormone Research in Paediatrics (Online) *see* Hormone Research in Paediatrics **5894**
Hormones (GRC ISSN 1109-3099) **5894**
• ➤ Hormones and Behavior (USA ISSN 0018-506X) **5894**
▼ • ➤ Hormones and Cancer (USA ISSN 1868-8497) **5894**
Hormones and Signaling (USA ISSN 1094-0103) **5894**
Hormos (ITA ISSN 1972-2672) **4146**
Horn & Whistle (USA) **4336**
• Horn Book Guide to Children's and Young Adult Books (USA ISSN 1044-405X) **7562**
• The Horn Book Magazine (USA ISSN 0018-5078) **7562**
• The Horn Call (USA ISSN 0046-7928) **6573**
➤ Horn Call Annual (USA) **6573**
The Horn Magazine *see* The Horn Player **6573**
Horn of Africa (USA ISSN 0161-4703) **4014**
Horn of Africa Bulletin (SWE ISSN 1100-2840) **4175**
Horn of Africa Journal of AIDS (USA ISSN 1930-3645) **5816**
The Horn Player (GBR) **6573**
Horn Speaker (USA ISSN 0898-6959) **366**
• Hornbill (IND ISSN 0441-2370) **676**
▼ Hornby Magazine (GBR ISSN 1753-2469) **4336**
• ➤ El Hornero (ARG ISSN 0073-3407) **908**
Hornet (USA ISSN 0018-5086) **2286**
Hornsey & Crouch End Journal (GBR ISSN 1364-5951) **3866**
Hornsey Historical Society. Bulletin (GBR ISSN 0955-8071) **4230**
Horny Housewives (GBR ISSN 1369-3468) **6292**
Horological Institute of Japan. Bulletin *see* Maikuromekatoronikusu **2572**
Horological Journal (GBR ISSN 0018-5108) **4566**
Horological Times (USA ISSN 0145-9546) **4566**
Horoscope (CAN ISSN 1910-0590) **566**
Horoscope (GBR ISSN 0954-9587) **566**
Horoscope Guide (USA ISSN 8750-3042) **566**
Horoscope Quotidien (CAN) **566**
Horoscopo (BRA ISSN 0104-1576) **566**
Horoshie Roditeli (UKR ISSN 1817-454X) **2154**
Horoskop *see* Dobre Rady. Horoskop **566**
Horoskop im Monat (DEU) **566**
Horowhenua-Kapiti Chronicle *see* Daily Chronicle **3917**
Horowhenua Mail (NZL ISSN 1172-5842) **3917**
Horreyati/My Liberty (EGY) **3836**
Horrible Imaginings (GBR) **5443**
▼ The Horror Collection (GBR ISSN 1752-9972) **6503**
Horror Cult (ITA ISSN 1723-3488) **2402**
Horror Garage (USA) **5443**
Horror Writers Association Newsletter (USA) **5443**
Hors-Bord Magazine (FRA ISSN 1774-1505) **8276**
• Hors Champ (CAN ISSN 1712-9567) **3811**
Horse *see* Haesten **8291**
• The Horse (USA ISSN 1081-9711) **8292**
Horse & Country Canada (CAN) **8292**
Horse and Hound (GBR ISSN 0018-5140) **8292**
Horse + Pony (GBR) **8292**
Horse & Pony (USA) **8292**
▼ Horse & Pony Collection (GBR ISSN 1755-2974) **4336**
Horse & Rider (GBR ISSN 0955-5366) **8292**
• Horse & Rider (USA ISSN 0018-5159) **8292**
The Horse, Backstreet Choppers (USA ISSN 1523-8857) **8259**
Horse Brass (GBR) **4336**
Horse Canada (CAN ISSN 1702-8299) **8292**
Horse-Canada.com *see* Horse Canada **8292**
Horse Deals (AUS ISSN 1446-6287) **8292**
Horse Illustrated (USA ISSN 0145-9791) **8292**
Horse Industry Directory (USA ISSN 0890-233X) **8292**
Horse International (NLD ISSN 1383-0732) **8292**
Horse Journal (USA ISSN 1097-6949) **8292**
▼ • Horse Lover Journal (USA ISSN 1935-2433) **8292**
Horse Magazine (GBR ISSN 1368-6453) **8292**
• Horse News (USA) **8292**
• The Horse of Delaware Valley (USA) **8292**
Horse Owners and Breeders Tax Handbook (USA) **8292**
• Horse Previews Magazine (USA) **8292**
Horse Property *see* Bit and Bridle (National Edition) **8288**
• Horse Racing Australia Magazine (AUS ISSN 1833-3427) **8292**
Horse Racing Quiz Book (GBR) **8292**
The Horse Report (USA) **8798**
Horse Shows (AUS ISSN 1832-4819) **8293**
Horse Source (CAN ISSN 1205-5433) **8293**
Horse Trader *see* New Zealand Monthly Horse Trader **1964**
Horse World (USA ISSN 0018-5191) **8293**
▼ Horseland (DEU) **2193**
Horseless Carriage Gazette (USA ISSN 0018-5213) **366**
HorseLife (CAN ISSN 1495-5563) **8293**
• Horseman and Fair World (USA ISSN 0018-523X) **8293**
Horseman's News (USA) **8293**
Horsemen's Journal (USA ISSN 0018-5256) **8293**
Horse'n Around (USA) **8293**
• Horsens Folkeblad (DNK) **3834**
Horses (USA ISSN 0046-7936) **8293**
Horses All (CAN ISSN 0225-4913) **8293**
Horses in Training (Year) (GBR ISSN 0081-3761) **8293**
Horses to Follow (GBR) **8293**
Horses U S A (USA ISSN 1093-9385) **8293**
Horseshoe Crab *see* Nihon Kabutogani o Mamoru Kai Kaiho **958**
• The Horsethief's Journal (USA ISSN 1525-903X) **5424**
The Horsetrader (USA ISSN 0018-5264) **8293**
Horsewyse *see* Australian Horsewyse **8287**
Horsimo (NLD ISSN 1570-6354) **8293**
Horsin' Around *see* Delmarva Farmer **104**
Horsing Around *see* Horse'n Around **8293**
Hort Expo Northwest (USA) **234**
Hort Notes (Print) (USA ISSN 1933-8708) **3736**
Hort West (CAN ISSN 0847-9763) **3736**
• Horticom (ESP ISSN 1696-1129) **3737**
Horticulteurs et Maraichers Romands (CHE) **3737**
• Horticultura (ESP ISSN 1132-2950) **3737**
Horticultura (ROM ISSN 1017-155X) **3737**
• Horticultura Brasileira (BRA ISSN 0102-0536) **234**
Horticultura Internacional (ESP ISSN 1134-4881) **3737**
Horticultura Mexicana (MEX ISSN 0188-9761) **3737**
Horticultural Abstracts *see* Horticultural Science Abstracts **3755**
Horticultural Accounts Statistics *see* Gartneri - Regnskabsstatistik **181**
Horticultural and Viticultural Science *see* Gradinarska i Lozarska Nauka **3734**
Horticultural Business Data (GBR ISSN 0962-3639) **3737**
Horticultural Directory (GBR ISSN 1368-9762) **2004**
• Horticultural Forum (CAN ISSN 1719-590X) **3737**
Horticultural Guide to Australian Plants (AUS) **3737**
Horticultural Industry *see* Greenbusiness International **3734**
Horticultural News (USA ISSN 0886-5779) **3737**
Horticultural Quarterly Review (ZWE) **3737**
Horticultural Research International (BEL ISSN 0441-7461) **3737**
Horticultural Retailing *see* Key Note Market Report: Horticultural Retailing **3740**
Horticultural Reviews (USA ISSN 0163-7851) **3737**
➤ Horticultural Science (CZE) **3737**
• Horticultural Science Abstracts (GBR) **3755**
Horticultural Societies' Newsletter (CAN) **3737**
Horticultural Society of Ethiopia. Bulletin (ETH) **3737**
Horticultural Society of New York. Newsletter (USA) **3737**
Horticulture *see* Der Gartenbau **3732**
Horticulture *see* International Journal of Horticultural Science **3739**
• Horticulture (USA ISSN 0018-5329) **3737**
▼ • Horticulture and Arable Monitoring Report (NZL ISSN 1178-2757) **200**
• Horticulture & Home Pest News (USA) **3737**
Horticulture, Environment and Biotechnology (KOR) **3737**
Horticulture Facts & Figures *see* Fresh Facts **3755**
L'Horticulture Francaise (FRA ISSN 1767-9915) **3737**
Horticulture Monitoring Report *see* Horticulture and Arable Monitoring Report **200**
Horticulture News (NZL ISSN 0110-8530) **3737**
Horticulture Research Institute. Annual Report. Part 1. Horticultural Research Centre (ZWE) **234**
Horticulture Research International. Annual Report (GBR ISSN 0963-3235) **234**
Horticulture Review (CAN ISSN 0823-8472) **3737**
Horticulture Viniculture *see* Kerteszet es Szoleszet **3740**
• Horticulture Week (GBR ISSN 0269-9478) **3737**
➤ The Horticulturist (GBR ISSN 0964-8992) **3738**
• HortIdeas (USA ISSN 0742-8219) **3738**
HortResearch *see* Shoku to Midori no Kagaku **3750**
• ➤ HortScience (USA ISSN 0018-5345) **3738**
• ➤ HortTechnology (USA ISSN 1063-0198) **3738**
Hortus (GBR ISSN 0950-1657) **3738**
• Hortus Artium Medievalium (HRV ISSN 1330-7274) **4230**
Hortus Botanicus Catalogue Series (NLD ISSN 1389-4749) **792**
† Hortus Musicus (ITA ISSN 1129-4965) **8962**
Horumon to Rinsho/Clinical Endocrinology (JPN ISSN 0045-7167) **5894**
Horus (DEU ISSN 0724-7389) **4081**
Hosadigantha (IND) **3882**
• Hoseasons Boating Holidays in UK and Europe (GBR) **8276**
Hoseasons Holiday Parks and Lodges (GBR) **8719**
Hosei Daigaku Ion Bimu Kogaku Kenkyujo Hokoku/Hosei University. Research Center of Ion Beam Technology. Report (JPN ISSN 0286-0201) **3310**
Hosei Daigaku Keisan Senta Kenkyu Hokoku/Hosei University. Computer Center. Bulletin (JPN ISSN 0913-8420) **2419**
Hosei Daigaku Kogakubu Kenkyu Shuho/Hosei University. College of Engineering. Bulletin (JPN ISSN 0441-2494) **3195**
Hosei Ronshu/Journal of Law and Political Science (Nagoya) (JPN ISSN 0439-5905) **4688**
Hosei University. College of Engineering. Bulletin *see* Hosei Daigaku Kogakubu Kenkyu Shuho **3195**
Hosei University. Computer Center. Bulletin *see* Hosei Daigaku Keisan Senta Kenkyu Hokoku **2419**
Hosei University Economic Review *see* Keizai Shirin **1140**
Hosei University. Research Center of Ion Beam Technology. Report *see* Hosei Daigaku Ion Bimu Kogaku Kenkyujo Hokoku **3310**
Hoseiken Nyusu/Radiation Biology Center News (JPN) **753**
Hosha Kagaku Toronkai Koen Yokoshu *see* Symposium on Radiochemistry. Abstracts of Papers **2096**
Hoshano Chosa Kenkyu Hokokusho/National Institute of Radiological Sciences. Survey Report (JPN) **6197**
Hoshasen/Ionizing Radiation (JPN ISSN 0285-3604) **7066**
Hoshasen Eikyo Kenkyusho Kaisetsu Sosetsu Shu *see* Radiation Effects Research Foundation. Commentary and Review Series **6205**
Hoshasen Eikyo Kenkyusho Nenpo *see* Radiation Effects Research Foundation. Annual Report **6205**
Hoshasen Igaku Butsuri/Japanese Journal of Medical Physics *see* Igaku Butsuri **6198**
• Hoshasen Igaku Sogo Kenkyujo Nenpo (JPN ISSN 0439-5948) **6197**
Hoshasen Jikkenjo Dayori/Radiation Laboratory News (JPN ISSN 0912-5116) **7066**
Hoshasen Kagaku (Chiba)/Radiological Sciences (JPN ISSN 0441-2540) **6197**
Hoshasen Kagaku (Tokyo)/Radiation Chemistry (JPN ISSN 0286-6722) **2063**
Hoshasen Kagaku Toronkai Koen Yoshishu/Proceedings of Symposium on Radiation Chemistry (JPN) **2135**
Hoshasen Kanrishitsu Nenpo/Radiological Health Office. Annual Report (JPN) **7066**
Hoshasen Riyo Kenkyu Seika Hokokukai Koen Yoshi/Abstracts of Research Results of Radiation Utilization (JPN) **7048**
Hoshasen Riyo Kenkyukai Hokokusho, Aisotopu Riyo Gurupu/Research Report of Utilization of Radiation by Isotope User's Group (JPN) **7066**
Hoshasen Riyo Kenkyukai Hokokusho, Igaku Riyo Gurupu/Research Report of Utilization of Radiation by Medical User's Group (JPN) **6198**
Hoshasen Riyo Kenkyukai Hokokusho, Shosha Riyo Gurupu/Research Report of Utilization of Radiation by Irradiation Therapy Group (JPN) **7066**
➤ Hoshasen Seibutsu Kenkyu/Radiation Biology Research Communication (JPN ISSN 0441-747X) **753**
➤ Hoshasen to Sangyo/Radiation and Industries (JPN ISSN 0286-8873) **7066**
Hoshi (JPN) **575**
Hoshi College of Pharmacy. Annual Report *see* Hoshi Yakka Daigaku Kiyo **6846**
Hoshi General Hospital. Annual Report *see* Hoshi Sogo Byoin Nenpo **4099**
Hoshi no Techo (JPN ISSN 0389-2131) **575**
Hoshi no Tomo/Friend of Stars (JPN ISSN 0389-0341) **575**
Hoshi Sogo Byoin Nenpo/Hoshi General Hospital. Annual Report (JPN ISSN 0915-7344) **4099**
Hoshi Yakka Daigaku Kiyo/Hoshi College of Pharmacy. Annual Report (JPN ISSN 0441-2559) **6846**
Hoshruba Da'ijist (PAK) **5306**
Hosiery and Textile Journal (IND ISSN 0018-5388) **2247**
Hosiery Report Weekly (IND) **8452**
Hoso Gijutsu/Japan Packaging Institute. Journal (JPN ISSN 0385-728X) **6710**
Hoso Kikai Shinbun/Packaging Machinery News (JPN) **6710**
Hospersa Update (ZAF) **4099**
• Hospice and Palliative Care Directory (GBR ISSN 1749-558X) **4099**
Hospice Bulletin *see* Hospice Information Bulletin **4099**
Hospice Information Bulletin (GBR ISSN 1476-7864) **4099**
• Hospice Letter (USA ISSN 0193-6816) **4099**
• Hospice Management Advisor (USA ISSN 1087-0288) **4099**
Hospice Today (USA) **8045**
Hospitais Civis de Lisboa. Boletim Clinico (PRT ISSN 0374-6070) **5629**
Hospital *see* Korhaz **4105**
Hospital *see* Byoin **4089**
• El Hospital (Coral Gables) (USA ISSN 0018-5485) **5629**
• Hospital Access Management (USA ISSN 1079-0365) **4099**
• The Hospital Accounts Receivable Analysis (USA ISSN 1078-8123) **4099**
• Hospital Accreditation Standards (USA ISSN 1522-1083) **4099**
Hospital Address Directory (GBR) **4099**
• Hospital Administration (IND ISSN 0018-5531) **4099**
Hospital Administration *see* Byoin Kanri **4089**
Hospital Administration Journal of Chinese People's Liberation Army *see* Jiefangjun Yiyuan Guanli Zazhi **4103**
Hospital & Agedcare (AUS ISSN 1835-663X) **4099**
Hospital and Health Care Law Conference (USA ISSN 1934-4724) **4099**
• Hospital & Health Networks (USA ISSN 1068-8838) **4099**
Hospital and Healthcare *see* Hospital & Agedcare **4099**
• Hospital & Nursing Home Week (USA ISSN 1552-5309) **4099**
Hospital Auxiliaries Association of Ontario. Quarterly Newsletter *see* Hospital Auxiliaries Association of Ontario. Volunteer **5960**
Hospital Auxiliaries Association of Ontario. Volunteer (CAN) **5960**
• Hospital Blue Book (Official National Edition) (USA ISSN 1047-6903) **4099**
• Hospital Blue Book (Official Southern Edition) (USA ISSN 1047-6911) **4099**
Hospital Business (CAN) **4100**
• Hospital Business Week (USA ISSN 1552-9053) **4100**
• Hospital Case Management (USA ISSN 1087-0652) **4100**
Hospital Caterers Yearbook (GBR) **4388**
• Hospital Central (PER) **5629**
Hospital Code Chek *see* HospitalCodeChek **4101**
Hospital Conduct & Technology *see* Hospital Drift & Teknologi **4100**
Hospital Contracts Manual (USA ISSN 0734-0028) **4100**
➤ Hospital de Ninos. Revista (ARG ISSN 0521-517X) **6092**
Hospital de Pronto Socorro. Revista (BRA ISSN 0103-6475) **6110**
Hospital Dentistry & Oral-Maxillofacial Surgery (JPN ISSN 0915-1664) **5846**

10376 HOURLY PRECIPITATION DATA. ARIZONA ULRICH'S PERIODICALS

• Hourly Precipitation Data. Arizona (USA ISSN 0364-6084) **6354**
• Hourly Precipitation Data. Arkansas (USA ISSN 0090-2683) **6354**
• Hourly Precipitation Data. California (USA ISSN 0364-6092) **6354**
• Hourly Precipitation Data. Colorado (USA ISSN 0364-6106) **6354**
• Hourly Precipitation Data. Florida (USA ISSN 0364-6114) **6354**
• Hourly Precipitation Data. Georgia (USA ISSN 0364-6122) **6354**
• Hourly Precipitation Data. Hawaii, Alaska and Pacific Islands (USA) **6354**
• Hourly Precipitation Data. Idaho (USA ISSN 0364-6149) **6354**
• Hourly Precipitation Data. Illinois (USA ISSN 0364-6157) **6354**
• Hourly Precipitation Data. Indiana (USA ISSN 0364-6165) **6355**
• Hourly Precipitation Data. Iowa (USA ISSN 0364-6173) **6355**
• Hourly Precipitation Data. Kansas (USA ISSN 0364-6181) **6355**
• Hourly Precipitation Data. Kentucky (USA ISSN 0364-5401) **6355**
• Hourly Precipitation Data. Louisiana (USA ISSN 0364-5398) **6355**
• Hourly Precipitation Data. Maryland & Delaware (USA ISSN 0364-538X) **6355**
• Hourly Precipitation Data. Michigan (USA ISSN 0364-6203) **6355**
• Hourly Precipitation Data. Minnesota (USA ISSN 0364-6211) **6355**
• Hourly Precipitation Data. Mississippi (USA ISSN 0364-622X) **6355**
• Hourly Precipitation Data. Missouri (USA ISSN 0364-6238) **6355**
• Hourly Precipitation Data. Montana (USA ISSN 0364-6246) **6355**
• Hourly Precipitation Data. Nebraska (USA ISSN 0364-6254) **6355**
• Hourly Precipitation Data. Nevada (USA ISSN 0364-6262) **6355**
• Hourly Precipitation Data. New England (USA ISSN 0364-6270) **6355**
• Hourly Precipitation Data. New Jersey (USA ISSN 0364-6289) **6355**
• Hourly Precipitation Data. New Mexico (USA ISSN 0364-6297) **6355**
• Hourly Precipitation Data. New York (USA ISSN 0364-6300) **6355**
• Hourly Precipitation Data. North Carolina (USA ISSN 0364-6319) **6355**
• Hourly Precipitation Data. North Dakota (USA ISSN 0364-6327) **6355**
• Hourly Precipitation Data. Ohio (USA ISSN 0364-6335) **6355**
• Hourly Precipitation Data. Oklahoma (USA ISSN 0364-6343) **6356**
• Hourly Precipitation Data. Oregon (USA ISSN 0364-6351) **6356**
• Hourly Precipitation Data. Pennsylvania (USA ISSN 0364-619X) **6356**
• Hourly Precipitation Data. Puerto Rico & Virgin Islands (USA ISSN 1058-5079) **6356**
• Hourly Precipitation Data. South Carolina (USA ISSN 0364-636X) **6356**
• Hourly Precipitation Data. South Dakota (USA ISSN 0364-6378) **6356**
• Hourly Precipitation Data. Tennessee (USA ISSN 0364-6386) **6356**
• Hourly Precipitation Data. Texas (USA ISSN 0364-6882) **6356**
• Hourly Precipitation Data. Utah (USA ISSN 0364-6920) **6356**
• Hourly Precipitation Data. Virginia (USA ISSN 0364-6874) **6356**
• Hourly Precipitation Data. Washington (USA ISSN 0364-6912) **6356**
• Hourly Precipitation Data. West Virginia (USA ISSN 0364-6904) **6356**
• Hourly Precipitation Data. Wisconsin (USA ISSN 0364-6939) **6356**
• Hourly Precipitation Data. Wyoming (USA ISSN 0364-6890) **6356**
House (TWN) **445**
House (USA ISSN 1074-4274) **3977**
House & Garden (London) (GBR ISSN 0043-5759) **4542**
House & Garden Design (AUS) **4542**
House & Gardening (DEU) **4542**
House & Home (AUS ISSN 1324-6798) **4438**
House and Home (IRL ISSN 1393-3043) **4542**
House & Home (JPN) **4542**
House and Household Insect Pests *see* Kaoku Gaichu **240**
House and Household Insect Pests Society of Japan. Abstracts of Meeting *see* Nihon Kaoku Gaichu Gakkai Taikai Kenkyu Happyo Yoshishu **717**
House and Leisure (ZAF ISSN 1021-9773) **3948**
• House and More (DEU) **4542**
• House Beautiful (GBR ISSN 0955-3533) **4559**
• House Beautiful (USA ISSN 0018-6422) **4542**
House Beautiful Home Building (USA ISSN 1532-8597) **1012**
House Beautiful Houses & Plans (USA ISSN 1532-8716) **445**
• House Beautiful Premier Homes (USA ISSN 1553-281X) **1012**
House Builder *see* Housebuilder **1012**
House Buyer (GBR ISSN 0018-6473) **7593**
House Committee on Rules. Survey of Activities (USA ISSN 0740-8269) **7444**
House, Home & Garden (USA ISSN 1073-7502) **3977**
House Hunters in the Sun *see* R T E House Hunters in the Sun **7606**
House Law *see* HouseLaw **7593**
House Magazine (GBR ISSN 0309-0426) **7444**
House Magazine (USA) **1012**
House of Business (USA) **1119**
House of Commons. Library. Research Paper (GBR ISSN 1368-8456) **7444**
House of Questions *see* Eichler Network Newsletter **1006**
House of Roses (USA ISSN 1524-3265) **6292**
House of the Year. Canterbury, South Canterbury, Ashburton, Otago, Southland, Gore *see* House of the Year. South Island **1012**
House of the Year. North Island *see* House of the Year. North Island **1012**
▼ House of the Year. North Island (NZL ISSN 1178-7872) **1012**
House of the Year. Northland, Auckland, Coromandel *see* House of the Year. North Island **1012**
House of the Year. South Island (NZL) **1012**
House of the Year. Taranaki, Manawatu, Wanganui, Wairarapa, Wellington, Nelson, Marlborough *see* House of the Year. North Island **1012**
House of the Year. Upper North Island *see* House of the Year. North Island **1012**
House of the Year. Waikato, Tauranga, Rotorua, Taupo, Bay of Plenty, Gisborne, Hawkes Bay *see* House of the Year. North Island **1012**
House of the Year. Winners Wellington Region *see* House of the Year. North Island **1012**
House Plan Favorites (USA) **4542**
Houseboat Magazine (USA) **8276**
Houseboating Adventures (USA) **8276**
Housebuilder (GBR ISSN 0951-1334) **1012**
Housebuilders. Intermediate *see* Business Ratio Report. Housebuilders. Intermediate (Year) **987**
Housebuilders. Major *see* Business Ratio Report. Housebuilders. Major (Year) **987**
Housecalls (USA) **5073**
• Household and Personal Care Today (ITA ISSN 2035-4614) **6989**
• Household & Personal Products Industry (USA ISSN 0090-8878) **1819**
Household Appliance *see* Jiayong Dianqi **1890**
Household Appliances (White Goods) *see* Key Note Market Report: Household Appliances (White Goods) **4559**
Household Appliances News *see* Kaden Shinbun **3107**
Household Economic Studies *see* Current Population Reports. Series P-70, Household Economic Studies **7305**
Household Expenditure Survey and the Rebasing of the Consumer Price Indices *see* Hong Kong Special Administrative Region of China. Census and Statistics Department. Household Expenditure Survey and the Rebasing of the Consumer Price Indices **1238**
• Household Food Security in the United States (USA) **6671**
Household Furniture *see* Key Note Market Report: Household Furniture **4559**
• Household Income and Income Distribution, Australia (Online) (AUS) **1240**
Household Labour Force Survey (ROM ISSN 1223-7566) **8376**
Household Projections *see* Janglae Ga'gu Chu'gye **7311**
• Housekeeping Solutions (USA) **2243**
Housekeeping Today (GBR) **4361**
Houseki - Kikinzoku Ichiba Nenkan/Market Directory for Jewelry and Precious Metal Wholesalers and Manufacturers (JPN) **2004**
Houseki no Shiki/Four Seasons of Jewelry (JPN) **4566**
• HouseLaw (USA) **7593**
• Houses (AUS ISSN 1440-3382) **445**
Houses and Housing *see* R I B A Sector Review. Houses and Housing **455**
Houses N Z *see* Houses New Zealand **445**
Houses N Z: Kitchens + Bathrooms *see* Houses New Zealand **445**
Houses New Zealand (NZL ISSN 1177-1739) **445**
Houses Style: Kitchens + Bathrooms (AUS ISSN 1833-5241) **4542**
• Housewares Canada (CAN ISSN 0829-9889) **4559**
Housewares Focus (GBR ISSN 1357-9517) **4559**
• Housewares Magazine (GBR ISSN 0264-8563) **4559**
▼ • Housewares Magazine (USA) **4559**
Housewives and Living (JPN) **8868**
Housing (AUS ISSN 1444-1128) **1012**
Housing *see* Jutaku **4418**
Housing Abstracts (H A B S) (GBR ISSN 0952-8156) **4435**
The Housing Advocate (USA) **4412**
• Housing Affairs Letter (USA ISSN 0018-6554) **4412**
Housing Affordability Report (AUS) **4435**
Housing Agenda (GBR ISSN 1467-0151) **4412**
Housing Aid Update *see* Shelter's Housing Law Update **4783**
Housing and Communities (USA) **4412**
• Housing & Community Developments (USA ISSN 1946-2700) **1351**
Housing and Development Reporter (USA ISSN 0091-5939) **4412**
Housing & Finance - Jamaica (JAM) **4412**
Housing and Planning Year Book (GBR) **4412**
Housing and Society (USA ISSN 0888-2746) **4412**
Housing and Urban Policy Studies (NLD ISSN 0926-6240) **4412**
Housing Assistance Council News *see* H A C News **4411**
Housing Association. Building and Maintenance (GBR ISSN 1757-5788) **4412**
Housing Authority Journal (USA ISSN 0018-6627) **4412**
† • Housing Bond Report (USA ISSN 1536-6847) **8962**
• Housing, Care and Support (GBR ISSN 1460-8790) **8045**
Housing Characteristics *see* Current Housing Reports. Series H-121, Homeownership Trends **8947**
Housing Cheap or on a Budget Newsletter (USA) **2638**
• Housing Construction (CZE) **1047**
Housing Consultation Papers *see* Great Britain. Department of the Environment, Transport and the Regions. Housing Consultation Papers **4411**
Housing Court Reporter (USA) **7593**
Housing Facts & Findings (USA ISSN 1525-2833) **4412**
Housing Finance (GBR ISSN 0955-3800) **7593**
• Housing Finance, Australia (Online) (AUS ISSN 1449-5953) **1240**
Housing Finance Company of Kenya. Annual Report and Accounts (KEN) **4412**
• Housing Finance International (BEL ISSN 1534-8784) **1351**
Housing Finance Review (GBR ISSN 1359-4672) **1012**
• Housing for Seniors Report (USA ISSN 1551-6598) **4412**
Housing in Southern Africa (ZAF) **4413**
Housing Industry Association. Buyer's Guide *see* Housing **1012**
• Housing Information Monthly/Bulletin Mensuel d'Information sur le Logement (CAN ISSN 1719-4423) **4413**
Housing Law (GBR) **7593**
Housing Law & Precedents (GBR) **7593**
Housing Law Bulletin (USA ISSN 0277-8491) **4413**
Housing Law Monitor (GBR ISSN 1352-2191) **4688**
Housing Law Reports (GBR ISSN 0263-7537) **4688**
Housing Legislation Manual (GBR) **7444**
Housing Magazine (GBR) **4413**
Housing Manufacturers Directory *see* Building Systems Magazine **987**
• Housing Market Outlook. Calgary (Online) (CAN ISSN 1719-5381) **7593**
• Housing Market Outlook. Canada (CAN ISSN 1719-9123) **7593**
• Housing Market Outlook. Charlottetown (Online) (CAN ISSN 1719-4571) **7593**
• Housing Market Outlook. Edmonton (CAN ISSN 1719-5403) **7593**
• Housing Market Outlook. Gatineau (CAN ISSN 1719-4652) **7593**
• Housing Market Outlook. Hamilton (CAN ISSN 1719-4679) **7593**
• Housing Market Outlook. Kelowna (CAN ISSN 1719-4695) **7593**
• Housing Market Outlook. Kitchener C M A (Census Metropolitan Areas) (CAN ISSN 1719-4725) **7593**
• Housing Market Outlook. London (CAN ISSN 1719-4741) **7593**
• Housing Market Outlook. Metro Victoria (CAN ISSN 1713-4129) **7593**
• Housing Market Outlook. Montreal (Online) (CAN ISSN 1719-542X) **7593**
• Housing Market Outlook. Northern Ontario (CAN ISSN 1719-5748) **7593**
• Housing Market Outlook. Oshawa (CAN ISSN 1719-4792) **7593**
• Housing Market Outlook. Ottawa (CAN ISSN 1719-5454) **7593**
• Housing Market Outlook. Quebec (CAN ISSN 1719-4814) **7594**
• Housing Market Outlook. Regina (CAN ISSN 1719-4830) **7594**
• Housing Market Outlook. Saguenay (CAN ISSN 1719-4857) **7594**
• Housing Market Outlook. Saint John, Moncton and Fredericton (CAN ISSN 1719-5764) **7594**
• Housing Market Outlook. Saskatoon (CAN ISSN 1719-4873) **7594**
• Housing Market Outlook. Sherbrooke (CAN ISSN 1719-4911) **7594**
• Housing Market Outlook. St. Catharines - Niagara C M A (Census Metropolitan Areas) (CAN ISSN 1719-4938) **7594**
• Housing Market Outlook. St. John's (Online) (CAN ISSN 1719-4962) **7594**
• Housing Market Outlook. Toronto (CAN ISSN 1719-5489) **7594**
• Housing Market Outlook. Trois-Rivieres (Online) (CAN ISSN 1719-4989) **7594**
• Housing Market Outlook. Vancouver (CAN ISSN 1713-4102) **7594**
Housing Market Outlook. Victoria *see* Housing Market Outlook. Metro Victoria **7593**
• Housing Market Outlook. Windsor (Online) (CAN ISSN 1719-5039) **7594**
• Housing Market Outlook. Winnipeg (CAN ISSN 1719-5055) **7594**
• Housing Market Report (USA ISSN 0363-4744) **4413**
Housing Needs and Resources (Year) (GBR) **4435**
Housing New Zealand. Annual Report *see* Housing New Zealand Corporation. Annual Report **4413**
• Housing New Zealand Corporation. Annual Report (NZL ISSN 1175-7248) **4413**
Housing New Zealand Corporation. Statement of Intent (NZL ISSN 1176-0966) **4413**
Housing New Zealand Limited. Statement of Corporate Intent *see* Housing New Zealand Corporation. Statement of Intent **4413**
Housing Now *see* Actualites Habitation. Charlottetown **4402**
Housing Now (British Columbia) *see* Actualites Habitation. Colombie-Britannique **4402**
Housing Now (Gatineau) *see* Actualites Habitation. Gatineau **4402**
Housing Now (Kitchener) *see* Actualites Habitation. Kitchener **4402**
Housing Now (Province of Quebec) *see* Actualites Habitation. Province de Quebec **4432**
Housing Now (Quebec) *see* Actualites Habitation. Quebec **4432**
Housing Now (Regina) *see* Actualites Habitation. Regina **4432**
Housing Now (Saguenay) *see* Actualites Habitation. Saguenay **4432**
Housing Now (Saint John, Moncton and Fredericton) *see* Actualites Habitation. Saint John, Moncton et Fredericton **4432**
Housing Now (Saskatoon) *see* Actualites Habitation. Saskatoon **4432**
Housing Now. Alberta *see* Housing Now. Prairies **4413**
• Housing Now. Atlantic Canada (CAN ISSN 1719-7058) **4413**
• Housing Now. British Columbia (CAN ISSN 1719-7414) **4413**
• Housing Now. Charlottetown (CAN ISSN 1719-7031) **4413**
• Housing Now. Gatineau (CAN ISSN 1719-7511) **4413**
• Housing Now. Hamilton (CAN ISSN 1495-3099) **4413**
Housing Now. Kitchener (CAN ISSN 1496-1091) **4413**
Housing Now. Manitoba *see* Housing Now. Prairies **4413**
Housing Now. Metropolitan Kitchener *see* Housing Now. Kitchener **4413**
• Housing Now. Metropolitan London (CAN ISSN 1495-3129) **7594**
Housing Now. Metropolitan Windsor (CAN ISSN 1495-3226) **7594**
Housing Now. New Brunswick (Online Edition) *see* Housing Now. Atlantic Canada **4413**
Housing Now. Newfoundland and Labrador *see* Housing Now. Atlantic Canada **4413**
• Housing Now. Northern Ontario (CAN ISSN 1719-5128) **7594**
• Housing Now. Ontario (CAN ISSN 1719-7554) **4413**
• Housing Now. Oshawa (CAN ISSN 1495-3145) **4413**
• Housing Now. Prairies (CAN ISSN 1910-3409) **4413**
Housing Now. Prince Edward Island *see* Housing Now. Atlantic Canada **4413**
• Housing Now. Province of Quebec (CAN ISSN 1719-7996) **4413**
• Housing Now. Quebec (CAN ISSN 1719-7562) **4413**
• Housing Now. Regina (CAN ISSN 1719-8011) **4413**
• Housing Now. Saguenay (CAN ISSN 1719-7597) **4413**
• Housing Now. Saint John, Moncton and Fredericton (CAN ISSN 1719-7465) **4413**
Housing Now. Saskatchewan *see* Housing Now. Prairies **4413**
• Housing Now. Saskatoon (CAN ISSN 1719-7627) **4413**
• Housing Now. Sherbrooke (CAN ISSN 1719-8038) **4413**
• Housing Now. St. John's (CAN ISSN 1719-7481) **4413**
• Housing Now. Trois-Rivieres (CAN ISSN 1719-8054) **4413**
Housing Now. Windsor *see* Housing Now. Metropolitan Windsor **7594**
Housing Operations Manager (USA) **4413**
• ➤ Housing Policy Debate (USA ISSN 1051-1482) **4413**
Housing Research Findings *see* Findings (York) **4410**
Housing Research Review (GBR ISSN 1359-1002) **4414**
• Housing Research Summary (GBR) **4414**
Housing Rights Service. Briefing Paper (GBR) **8045**
• Housing Scotland (GBR ISSN 1743-4238) **4414**
• Housing Service Newsletter (GBR) **8045**
Housing Statistics (CAN ISSN 1192-0955) **4435**
• ➤ Housing Studies (GBR ISSN 0267-3037) **4414**
• ➤ Housing, Theory and Society (NOR ISSN 1403-6096) **4414**
Housing Times (IND) **4414**
Housing Today (GBR ISSN 1365-6309) **4414**
• Housing Units Authorized by Building Permits (Online) (USA) **4414**

Link to your serials resources and content with ulrichsweb.com

Title

Title

• Human Resources Abstracts (USA ISSN 0099-2453) **1240**
Human Resources Advisor: Legal & Practical Guidance *see* H R Advisor: Legal & Practical Guidance **1862**
• Human Resources Advisor Newsletter (Atlantic Edition) (CAN ISSN 1492-6032) **1864**
• Human Resources Advisor Newsletter (Ontario Edition) (CAN ISSN 1203-1151) **1864**
• Human Resources Advisor Newsletter (Western Edition) (CAN ISSN 1206-8977) **1864**
Human Resources and Industrial Relations Directory *see* Van Zyl, Rudd Industrial Relations and Human Resources Diary **1713**
Human Resources and the Law *see* The Complete Guide to Human Resources and the Law **1858**
Human Resources: Answers to Your Top 25 Questions (USA ISSN 1933-4826) **1864**
Human Resources Banker (Austin) *see* H R Banker (Austin) **1862**
Human Resources Banker (Middletown) *see* H R Banker (Middletown) **1350**
▼ • Human Resources Business Review (BEL ISSN 1949-1050) **1864**
Human Resources Compact Disk General Schedule Position Classification and Federal Wage System Job Grading Standards *see* H R C D: General Schedule Position Classification and Federal Wage System Job Grading Standards **1684**
Human Resources Department Benchmarks and Analysis *see* H R Department Benchmarks and Analysis **1862**
Human Resources Development and Management *see* Renli Ziyuan Kaifa Guanli **1874**
Human Resources Director *see* The HRdirector **1863**
The Human Resources Directory (HKG) **1685**
Human Resources Florida Review Magazine *see* H R Florida Review Magazine **1862**
• ➤ Human Resources for Health (GBR ISSN 1478-4491) **5631**
• Human Resources Guide (USA ISSN 1079-5081) **1864**
Human Resources Hero's Hiring & Firing *see* H R Hero's Hiring & Firing **1862**
Human Resources Insight (Brentwood) *see* H R Insight (Brentwood) **1862**
Human Resources Insight (Brighton) *see* H R Insight (Brighton) **1862**
Human Resources Jobs Report (USA ISSN 1089-8158) **6698**
Human Resources Leader (AUS) **1865**
• Human Resources Library (USA ISSN 1941-3513) **1865**
• Human Resources Library (Lawyers' Edition) (USA) **1865**
Human Resources Magazine *see* H R Magazine (French Edition) **1862**
Human Resources Magazine *see* H R Magazine **1862**
Human Resources Management *see* H R M **1862**
• Human Resources Management - Compensation (USA ISSN 0745-063X) **1865**
• Human Resources Management - Employment Relations (USA ISSN 0745-2179) **1865**
• Human Resources Management - Equal Employment Opportunity (USA ISSN 0745-2187) **1685**
Human Resources Management - Ideas and Trends (USA) **1750**
• Human Resources Management - O S H A Compliance (USA) **6678**
• Human Resources Management - Personnel Practices & Communications (USA ISSN 0745-0621) **1865**
• Human Resources Management - State Employment Laws (USA) **1489**
The Human Resources Memo *see* H R Memo (Oak Brook) **1116**
Human Resources Memo (Indianapolis) *see* H R Memo (Indianapolis) **1862**
Human Resources Memo (Oak Brook) *see* H R Memo (Oak Brook) **1116**
Human Resources Monthly *see* H R Monthly **1862**
Human Resources News *see* H R News **1862**
Human Resources on Campus *see* H R on Campus **1862**
Human Resources - Organizational Dynamics *see* H R - O D **1862**
• Human Resources Outsourcing Europe (USA ISSN 1556-3278) **1865**
• Human Resources Outsourcing Today (USA ISSN 1541-3551) **1865**
Human Resources Performance *see* H R - Performance **2419**
Human Resources PolicyPro (Alberta Edition) *see* Human Resources PolicyPro (Ontario Edition) **1865**
Human Resources PolicyPro (British Columbia Edition) *see* Human Resources PolicyPro (Ontario Edition) **1865**
• Human Resources PolicyPro (Ontario Edition) (CAN) **1865**
Human Resources Professional *see* H R Professional **1863**
Human Resources Rendement *see* H R Rendement **1863**
Human Resources Report *see* H R Report **1863**
Human Resources Report *see* C B I. Human Resources Report **1668**
• Human Resources Report (USA ISSN 1095-6239) **1685**
Human Resources Series: Compensation & Benefits *see* H R Series: Compensation & Benefits **1863**
Human Resources Series: Policies and Practices *see* H R Series: Policies and Practices **1863**
Human Resources Services *see* H R Services **1863**
Human Resources South West & Wales *see* H R South West & Wales **1863**
Human Resources Specialist *see* The H R Specialist **1863**
Human Resources Strategic Advisor *see* H R Strategic Advisor **1863**
Human Resources Yorkshire & Humber *see* H R Yorkshire & Humber **1863**
Human Rights (CHE ISSN 1020-6507) **7208**
Human Rights *see* Huniy Erh **7209**
• ➤ Human Rights (USA) **8045**
Human Rights (Bristol) (GBR ISSN 1473-7051) **4832**
• Human Rights (Chicago) (USA ISSN 0046-8185) **7208**
Human Rights (London) (GBR) **7208**
Human Rights Alerter (GBR ISSN 1470-3254) **7208**
Human Rights & Charter Law (CAN) **4689**
Human Rights and Constitutionalism Series (ZWE ISSN 1992-1543) **4849**
• Human Rights & Globalization Law Review (USA) **4689**
• Human Rights & Human Welfare (USA ISSN 1533-0834) **7208**
• ➤ Human Rights and International Legal Discourse (BEL ISSN 1783-7014) **7208**
Human Rights & Peace Law Docket (USA ISSN 1064-4016) **4849**
Human Rights & U K Practice (GBR ISSN 1468-3997) **7208**
• Human Rights Brief (USA ISSN 1932-4073) **4832**
Human Rights Bulletin (New York) (USA) **7208**
† • Human Rights Case Digest (NLD ISSN 0965-934X) **8962**
• Human Rights Centre. Occasional Papers (GBR ISSN 1368-132X) **7208**
Human Rights Code of British Columbia (CAN) **7208**
Human Rights Commission. Report (NZL) **7208**
Human Rights Country Reports *see* Country Reports on Human Rights Practices for (Year) **7205**
The Human Rights Defender *see* Amnesty International Australia. Newsletter **2643**
• Human Rights Dialogue (USA ISSN 1540-0123) **7208**
• Human Rights Digest (CAN ISSN 1492-0719) **7208**
Human Rights Fact Sheet (CHE ISSN 1014-5567) **7208**
Human Rights Forum (PHL ISSN 0117-5521) **7208**
➤ Human Rights in Development (NLD ISSN 1569-528X) **4832**
• Human Rights Information Bulletin (FRA ISSN 1608-9618) **7208**
† ➤ Human Rights Law and Practice (NZL ISSN 1173-5252) **8962**
Human Rights Law in Africa (NLD ISSN 1385-3716) **4849**
Human Rights Law in Perspective (GBR) **4832**
• Human Rights Law Journal (DEU ISSN 0174-4704) **4849**
Human Rights Law Reports - UK Cases (GBR ISSN 1470-1669) **7208**
• Human Rights Law Review (GBR ISSN 1461-7781) **7208**
Human Rights Organizations & Periodicals Directory (USA ISSN 0098-0579) **7199**
Human Rights Practice (GBR) **7208**
• ➤ Human Rights Quarterly (USA ISSN 0275-0392) **7208**
Human Rights Reports of New Zealand (NZL ISSN 1173-356X) **4849**
Human Rights Research and Education Bulletin *see* Universite d'Ottawa. Centre de Recherche et d'Enseignement sur les Droits de la Personne. Droits de la Personne **7218**
• Human Rights Review (NLD ISSN 1524-8879) **7209**
Human Rights. Study Series (USA ISSN 1014-5680) **7209**
Human Rights Tribunal Decisions (CAN) **7209**
• Human Rights Tribune (Online)/Tribune des Droits Humains (CAN ISSN 1192-3822) **7209**
Human Rights Tribune (Print) *see* Human Rights Tribune (Online) **7209**
† • Human Rights Watch. A (USA) **8962**
† • Human Rights Watch. B (USA) **8962**
† • Human Rights Watch. C (USA) **8962**
† • Human Rights Watch. D (USA ISSN 1552-7042) **8962**
† • Human Rights Watch. E (USA) **8962**
Human Rights Watch Publications on Asia *see* Human Rights Watch. C **8962**
Human Rights Watch Publications on Europe and Central Asia *see* Human Rights Watch. D **8962**
Human Rights Watch Publications on Sub-Saharan Africa *see* Human Rights Watch. A **8962**
Human Rights Watch Publications on the Americas and the Caribbean *see* Human Rights Watch. B **8962**
Human Rights Watch Publications on the Middle East and North Africa *see* Human Rights Watch. E **8962**
Human Rights Watch Women's Rights Project (USA) **7209**
• Human Rights Watch World Report (USA ISSN 1054-948X) **7209**
† Human Rights Worldwide (DEU ISSN 1015-5945) **8962**
Human Science (IND ISSN 0970-3411) **342**
Human Sciences Research Council. Annual Report (ZAF) **4455**
Human Sciences Research Council Review (ZAF ISSN 1726-9709) **8106**
• Human Security & Development (USA ISSN 1554-3617) **3196**
• Human Security Report (USA ISSN 1557-914X) **2677**
Human Serve Campaign Newsletter (USA) **8045**
➤ Human Service Education (USA ISSN 0890-5428) **8045**
Human Service Yellow Pages of Massachusetts Rhode Island (Year) (USA) **8045**
Human Services Reporter (USA ISSN 0164-6079) **8045**
Human Settlements Basic Statistics (KEN) **4435**
➤ Human Sexualities (USA ISSN 1943-9814) **7361**
Human Sexuality Supplement (USA ISSN 0196-061X) **3064**
Human Stress: Current Selected Research (USA ISSN 0885-1174) **7361**
• ➤ Human Studies (NLD ISSN 0163-8548) **6923**
➤ Human Systems (GBR ISSN 0960-9830) **7361**
• Human Systems I A C Gateway (Information Analysis Center) (USA) **6678**
• ➤ Human Systems Management (NLD ISSN 0167-2533) **1750**
• ➤ Human Technology (FIN ISSN 1795-6889) **2323**
• ➤ Human Vaccines (USA ISSN 1554-8600) **6846**
▼ • ➤ Human-Wildlife Conflicts (USA ISSN 1934-4392) **3438**
Humana Iura (ESP ISSN 1132-7294) **7209**
Humane Gesellschaft (DEU) **7141**
Humane News (USA) **319**
Humane Slaughter Association Newsletter (GBR ISSN 0263-1407) **319**
Humane Slaughter Association Report and Accounts (GBR ISSN 0264-8741) **319**
Humanes Leben - Humanes Sterben (DEU ISSN 0938-9717) **5631**
• Humanetten (SWE ISSN 1403-2279) **5307**
Humanidades (BRA ISSN 0102-9479) **4455**
Humanidades (GTM ISSN 0018-7356) **4455**
• Humanidades (Mexico, D.F.) (MEX ISSN 0188-6959) **342**
• Humaniora (DNK ISSN 0903-2401) **4455**
• Humanising Language Teaching (GBR ISSN 1755-9715) **5125**
Humanisme (FRA ISSN 0018-7364) **2266**
Humanisme et Entreprise (FRA ISSN 0018-7372) **1685**
• Humanismus Aktuell (DEU ISSN 1433-514X) **7970**
• Humanist (DNK ISSN 0107-9573) **2986**
Humanist *see* Human **6923**
• Humanist (NOR ISSN 0801-6283) **6923**
• The Humanist (USA ISSN 0018-7399) **6923**
• Humanist Discussion Group (GBR) **4485**
Humanist in Canada *see* Humanist Perspectives **6924**
• Humanist-Info (SWE) **6924**
Humanist News (GBR) **6924**
Humanist News & Views (USA ISSN 1054-9633) **6924**
Humanist Outlook (IND ISSN 0018-7429) **6924**
• Humanist Perspectives (CAN ISSN 1719-6337) **6924**
Humanist Post *see* South Australian Humanist Post **6953**
The Humanist Sociologist (USA) **8106**
Humanist Viewpoints (AUS) **6924**
• Humanistdag-Boken (SWE ISSN 1400-4496) **2986**
Humanistdagboken *see* Humanistdag-Boken **2986**
• Humanisten (SWE ISSN 1401-8691) **6924**
Humanistic Judaism (USA ISSN 0441-4195) **7722**
• Humanistic Mathematics Network Journal (Online Edition) (USA) **5491**
Humanistic Mathematics Network Journal (Print Edition) *see* Humanistic Mathematics Network Journal (Online Edition) **5491**
• ➤ The Humanistic Psychologist (USA ISSN 0887-3267) **7361**
• Humanistica (ITA ISSN 1828-2334) **4455**
➤ Humanistica (LTU ISSN 1392-5628) **4455**
Humanistica (Rome) (ITA ISSN 1724-0956) **4455**
Humanistica e Teologia (PRT ISSN 0870-080X) **7648**
Humanistica Lovaniensia (BEL ISSN 0774-2908) **2235**
Humanistica Lovaniensia. Supplementa (BEL) **2235**
Humanistica Oerebroensia. Artes et Linguae (SWE ISSN 1403-6525) **4455**
Humanistics University Press Proefschriftenreeks *see* HUP Proefschriftenreeks **6924**
Humanistisch Erfgoed (NLD ISSN 1568-1785) **6924**
Humanistisch Instituut voor Ontwikkelingssamenwerking Magazine *see* H I V O S Magazine **1596**
Humanistische Bibliothek. Reihe I: Abhandlungen (DEU ISSN 0177-9478) **626**
Humanistische Bibliothek. Reihe II: Texte (DEU ISSN 0177-9486) **626**
Humanistische Bibliothek. Reihe III: Skripten (DEU ISSN 0177-9494) **626**
Humanistische Union. Mitteilungen (DEU ISSN 0046-824X) **6924**
Humanistisen Tiedekunnan Jatko-Opiskelijan Opinto-Opas (FIN ISSN 1796-3176) **2986**
Humanistisen Tiedekunnan Jatkotutkinto-Opas *see* Humanistisen Tiedekunnan Jatko-Opiskelijan Opinto-Opas **2986**
Humanistisk Serie *see* Acta Jutlandica. Humanistisk Serie **4441**
Humanistiske Studier (CD-ROM Edition) *see* Humanistiske Studier (Print Edition) **2986**
Humanistiske Studier (Print Edition) (DNK ISSN 1901-4821) **2986**
➤ Humanistyka i Przyrodoznawstwo (POL ISSN 1234-4087) **7863**
Humanitaeres Voelkerrecht (DEU ISSN 0937-5414) **4928**
• The Humanitarian (AUS ISSN 1833-8666) **8045**
The Humanitarian (USA) **8045**
Humanitas (ARG ISSN 0441-4217) **4455**
• Humanitas (CHL ISSN 0717-2168) **342**
▼ Humanitas (COL ISSN 2011-4591) **4455**
Humanitas (ESP ISSN 1695-8713) **4455**
• Humanitas (ITA ISSN 0018-7461) **5220**
Humanitas (MEX ISSN 0441-4209) **4455**
• ➤ Humanitas (USA ISSN 1066-7210) **4455**
• Humanitas, Humanidades Medicas (ESP ISSN 1886-1601) **5631**
Humanitas. Revista do ICH *see* Instituto de Ciencias Humanas. Humanitas **7973**
Humanitas Taiwanica *see* Guoli Taiwan Daxue. Wenshi Zhexue Bao **4182**
• Humanities (USA ISSN 0018-7526) **4455**
The Humanities (Yokohama, 1998) *see* Yokohama Kokuritsu Daigaku Kyoiku Ningen Kagakubu Kiyo. II, Jimbun Kagaku **4483**
• Humanities Abstracts (USA) **4484**
• Humanities Abstracts Full Text (USA) **4484**
Humanities Aitia (USA ISSN 1522-1121) **4455**
Humanities & Social Sciences Journal of Hainan University *see* Hainan Daxue Xuebao (Renwen Shehui Kexueban) **4454**
Humanities and Social Sciences. Latvia (LVA ISSN 1022-4483) **7970**
Humanities: Christianity and Culture *see* Jinbun Kagaku Kenkyu **4459**
➤ Humanities Diliman (PHL ISSN 1655-1532) **4455**
Humanities in the South (USA ISSN 0018-7577) **4456**
• Humanities Index (USA ISSN 0095-5981) **4484**
• Humanities International Index (USA) **4484**
• ➤ Humanities Research (AUS ISSN 1440-0669) **4456**
Humanities Review (IND) **4456**
Humanities Review *see* Jimbun Ronkyu **4458**
• Humanities Review Journal (NGA ISSN 1596-0749) **4456**
➤ Humanity & Society (USA ISSN 0160-5976) **8106**
Humanizacja Pracy/Humanization of Work (POL ISSN 1643-7446) **1685**
Humanizacja Pracy. Zarzadzanie Zasobami Ludzkimi *see* Humanizacja Pracy **1685**
Humanization of Work *see* Humanizacja Pracy **1685**
• ➤ Humanomics (GBR ISSN 0828-8666) **1543**
Humans and Nature *see* Hito to Shizen **341**
Humanwirtschaft (DEU ISSN 1617-9153) **5220**
Humber Etc... (CAN) **2287**
Humboldt (Portuguese Edition) (DEU ISSN 0018-7623) **5220**
Humboldt (Spanish Edition) (DEU ISSN 0018-7615) **5220**
Humboldt Historian (Eureka) (USA) **4297**
Humboldt Historian (Winnemucca) (USA) **4297**
➤ Humboldt Journal of Social Relations (USA ISSN 0160-4341) **7970**
Humboldt Kosmos (DEU) **4456**
Humboldt Society Newsletter (USA ISSN 0898-2805) **4375**
Humboldt-Spektrum (DEU ISSN 0946-641X) **4456**
Humboldt-Universitaet zu Berlin. Institut fuer Mathematik. Preprint (DEU) **5491**
Humboldt-Universitaet zu Berlin. Institut fuer Mathematik. Seminarberichte (DEU) **5491**
Humboldt-Universitaet zu Berlin. Institut fuer Rehabilitationswissenschaften. Schriften (DEU ISSN 1619-8107) **3041**
Humboldt-Universitaet zu Berlin. Landwirtschaftlich-Gaertnerische Fakultaet. Schriftenreihe (DEU ISSN 1433-4569) **200**
Humboldt-Universitaet zu Berlin. Universitaetsbibliothek. Schriftenreihe (DEU ISSN 0522-9898) **5012**
Humboldt-Universitaet zu Berlin. Vorlesungsverzeichnis (DEU) **3024**
Hume Occasional Papers (GBR ISSN 0955-3169) **7141**
• ➤ Hume Studies (ISL ISSN 0319-7336) **6924**
Hummer (AUS ISSN 0816-0368) **4146**
Humo (BEL ISSN 0771-8179) **2382**
Humor (ARG) **5220**
• ➤ Humor (DEU ISSN 0933-1719) **8106**
HumOr (IDN ISSN 0852-8225) **5220**
Humor & Satire *see* Renmin Ribao **3827**
Humor Defense (USA) **5220**
† Humor Graphic (ITA) **8962**
Humor Registrado *see* Humor **5220**
➤ Humor Research (DEU ISSN 1861-4116) **5125**
Humor Special *see* K I H **4337**
Humor Times (USA ISSN 1937-299X) **5220**
Humor - Verdade *see* H V **3804**
Humoresques (FRA ISSN 0996-9942) **5307**

Title

Title

• I B M System User (International Business Machines) (GBR ISSN 0950-303X) **2520**
I B M Systems Journal (Online) *see* I B M Systems Journal (Print) **8963**
† • ➤ I B M Systems Journal (Print) (International Business Machines) (USA ISSN 0018-8670) **8963**
I B M Systems Magazine (i5 Business Systems Edition) (International Business Machines) (USA ISSN 1935-1097) **2420**
I B M Systems Magazine (iFive Business Systems Edition) *see* I B M Systems Magazine (i5 Business Systems Edition) **2420**
I B M Systems Magazine (Mainframe Edition) (International Business Machines) (USA ISSN 1933-1312) **2520**
I B M Systems Magazine (Open Systems Edition) (International Business Machines) (USA ISSN 1935-0929) **2520**
I B N (Internationale Bodensee & Boot Nachrichten) (DEU ISSN 0020-921X) **8276**
I B N S Journal (International Bank Note Society) (USA) **6651**
• I B O Publications Catalogue (International Baccalaureate Organisation) (CHE) **2986**
I B P A Independent (Independent Book Publishers Association) (USA) **7563**
I B R *see* Internationale Bibliographie der Rezensionen Geistes- und Sozialwissenschaftlicher Literatur **7937**
I B R *see* International Business Review **1126**
I B R A Conference on Tropical Bees (International Bee Research Association) (GBR) **119**
I B R O News (International Brain Research Organization) (FRA ISSN 0361-0713) **6145**
I B R R *see* Index to Book Reviews in Religion **7698**
• I B Revija (SVN ISSN 1318-2803) **1489**
I B S *see* Immunoanalyse et Biologie Specialisee **677**
I B S A Bulletin (Indigenous Bulb Association of South Africa) (ZAF) **3738**
I B S Aktuell (Interessenvereins des Bayerischen Staatsopernpublikums e.V.) (DEU) **6574**
I B S J O S *see* I B Scientific Journal of Science **7864**
I B S Journal *see* International Banking Systems **1355**
I B S Journal of Science *see* I B Scientific Journal of Science **7864**
• I B S Newsletter Baltic States (International Business Statistics) (FIN ISSN 1796-2757) **1241**
• I B S Newsletter Central and Western Europe (International Business Statistics) (FIN ISSN 1796-2765) **1241**
• I B S Newsletter Russia (International Business Statistics) (FIN ISSN 1796-2749) **1241**
I B S R A M Proceedings (International Board for Soil Research and Management) (THA ISSN 1015-8650) **234**
I B S S: Anthropology *see* International Bibliography of the Social Sciences. Anthropology **362**
• I B S S CD-ROM (International Bibliography of the Social Sciences) (USA ISSN 1544-9289) **8020**
I B S S: Economics *see* International Bibliography of the Social Sciences. Economics **1243**
I B S S: Political Science *see* International Bibliography of Political Science **7200**
I B S S: Sociology *see* International Bibliography of the Social Sciences. Sociology **8149**
• I B S World Newsletter (International Business Statistics) (FIN ISSN 1459-1219) **1241**
• ➤ I B Scientific (GBR ISSN 1751-0716) **7864**
• ➤ I B Scientific Journal of Science (Ibn Badis) (GBR ISSN 1751-0724) **7864**
I B T D *see* International Bibliography of Theatre & Dance **8485**
I B W *see* Internet Bookwatch **627**
I B W A News (International Bottled Water Association) (USA ISSN 1058-3289) **604**
I B W A Technical Bulletin (International Bottled Water Association) (USA) **604**
I B World (International Baccalaureate) (GBR ISSN 1560-5795) **2986**
I B Z *see* I B Z - Internationale Bibliographie der Geistes- und Sozialwissenschaftlichen Zeitschriftenliteratur **626**
• I B Z - Internationale Bibliographie der Geistes- und Sozialwissenschaftlichen Zeitschriftenliteratur/International Bibliography of Periodical Literature from All Fields of Knowledge (DEU ISSN 1618-923X) **626**
I B Z - Internationaler Betriebswirtschaftlicher Zeitschriften-Report (DEU ISSN 0340-871X) **4870**
I-bunpi Kenkyukai Kiroku *see* I-bunpi Kenkyukaishi **5894**
I-bunpi Kenkyukaishi/Japanese Society of Gastric Secretion Research. Proceedings (JPN ISSN 0289-2057) **5894**
I C *see* Index Chemicus (Online) **2094**
† I C 2 Management and Management Science Series (USA ISSN 1058-5036) **8963**
I C A A C Program and Abstracts *see* Interscience Conference on Antimicrobial Agents and Chemotherapy. Abstracts **888**
I C A A News (International Council on Alcohol and Addictions) (CHE ISSN 1012-8360) **2694**
I C A A Publications (International Council on Alcohol and Addictions) (CHE) **2694**
I C A C Commissioner's Annual Report (Independent Commission Against Corruption) (HKG) **7445**
• I C A C Recorder (International Cotton Advisory Committee) (USA ISSN 1022-6303) **8452**
I C A D E la Empresa *see* La Empresa **7435**
I C A D T S Reporter (International Council on Alcohol, Drugs and Traffic Safety) (USA ISSN 1016-0477) **2694**
I C A Documents (Institute of Contemporary Arts) (GBR ISSN 0957-2465) **493**
I C A E Bulletin (International Council for Adult Education) (CAN ISSN 1029-709X) **2942**
I C A Gazette *see* InColor **4566**
I - C A H T A's Newsletter (Informatiu - Catalan Agency for Health Technology Assessment) (ESP ISSN 1697-039X) **5631**
I C A L P Revista (Instituto de Cultura e Lingua Portuguesa) (PRT ISSN 0870-8436) **4456**
I C A M (VEN) **5307**
• I C A M E Journal (International Computer Archive of Modern and Medieval English) (NOR ISSN 0801-5775) **5126**
I C A Monthly Bulletin (Institute of Contemporary Arts) (GBR) **493**
▼ • ➤ I C A N (Infant, Child & Adolescent Nutrition) (USA ISSN 1941-4064) **6660**
I C A N Communicate (Invalid Children's Aid Nationwide) (GBR) **3041**
• I C A News (International Co-Operative Alliance) (CHE ISSN 1013-1221) **7240**
• I C A Newsletter (Online Edition) (International Communication Association) (USA) **8106**
I C A Newsletter (Print Edition) *see* I C A Newsletter (Online Edition) **8106**
• I C A Nyheter (SWE ISSN 1652-5590) **1819**
I C A O Abbreviations and Codes (International Civil Aviation Organization) (CAN) **8544**
I C A O Circulars (International Civil Aviation Organization) (CAN ISSN 1014-4412) **8544**
The I C A O Financial Regulations (International Civil Aviation Organization) (CAN) **8544**
• I C A O Journal (International Civil Aviation Organization) (CAN ISSN 1014-8876) **59**
• I C A O Publications and Audio Visual Training Aids Catalogue (International Civil Aviation Organization) (CAN ISSN 1014-5834) **8526**
I C A O Publications Regulations (International Civil Aviation Organization) (CAN) **8544**
I C A O's Policies on Taxation in the Field of International Air Transport (International Civil Aviation Organization) (CAN) **59**
I C A R D A. Annual Report *see* International Center for Agricultural Research in the Dry Areas. Annual Report **122**
• I C A R News (Indian Council of Agricultural Research) (IND) **119**
• I C A R Reporter (Indian Council of Agricultural Research) (IND) **119**
I C A Regional Bulletin (International Cooperative Alliance) (IND) **1423**
I C A Regional Womens Forum (International Co-operative Alliance) (IND) **8899**
I C A Review (International Chiropractors Association) (USA ISSN 0899-9260) **5805**
I C A S A L S Annual Report (International Center for Arid and Semi-Arid Land Studies) (USA) **2614**
I C A S A L S Newsletter (International Center for Arid and Semiarid Land Studies) (USA ISSN 0018-8808) **2614**
• I C A S A News (International Consortium for Agricultural Systems Applications) (USA ISSN 1084-3736) **234**
➤ I C A S E - L A R C Interdisciplinary Series in Science and Engineering (Institute for Computer Applications in Science and Engineering - Langley Research Center) (NLD ISSN 1381-1339) **7864**
I C A S Fact Facts *see* Fast Facts **54**
I C A S T Buyer's Guide (International Convention of Allied Sportfishing Trades) (USA) **3597**
I C A Update (Chicago) (International Carwash Association) (USA) **8584**
I C A Update (Rockville) (Interstitial Cystitis Association) (USA) **6268**
I C Alternate Sources & Replacements D.A.T.A. Digest (Integrated Circuits) (USA ISSN 1049-2682) **3101**
I C B *see* Integrative & Comparative Biology **947**
I C B Digital *see* Investigacion Clinica y Bioetica **6850**
I C B L Reports *see* Institute for Computer Based Learning. Reports **2987**
† I C B Newsletter (International Correspondent Banker) (GBR ISSN 1355-8447) **8963**
I C B P Monographs (International Council for Bird Preservation) (GBR ISSN 1012-6201) **908**
I C B Settlements Report (International Correspondent Banker) (GBR ISSN 1355-8455) **1629**
A I C Bollettino (Associazione Italiana di Cartografia) (ITA ISSN 0044-9733) **4014**
I C C A Congress Series (International Council for Commercial Arbitration) (NLD ISSN 1572-4441) **4870**
I C C A D *see* I C C A D - I E E E - A C M International Conference on Computer-Aided Design. Proceedings **3291**
• I C C A D - I E E E - A C M International Conference on Computer-Aided Design. Proceedings (International Conference on Computer Aided Design / Institute of Electrical and Electronics Engineer) (USA ISSN 1933-7760) **3291**
I C C A Journal on Community Corrections (International Community Corrections Association) (USA ISSN 1546-7627) **2654**
I C C Annual Report (International Chamber of Commerce) (FRA) **1404**
• I C C. Bulletin (Institut Canadien de Conservation) (CAN ISSN 1719-5861) **4297**
I C C Bulletins Techniques *see* C C I Technical Bulletins **6521**
I C C D *see* I E E E International Conference on Computer Design. V L S I in Computers & Processors. Proceedings **2471**
I C C E *see* I E E E International Conference on Consumer Electronics. Digest of Technical Papers **3101**
I C C E S *see* International Conference on Computational & Experimental Engineering and Sciences. Proceedings **2471**
I C C F A Magazine (International Cemetery, Cremation and Funeral Association) (USA ISSN 1936-2099) **3719**
The I C C International Court of Arbitration Bulletin (International Chamber of Commerce) (FRA ISSN 1017-284X) **1404**
• I C C Journal (Intercultural Communications College) (USA) **5126**
I C C L R *see* International Company and Commercial Law Review **4930**
I C C O Annual Report (International Cocoa Organization) (GBR) **3646**
I C C O P S Newsletter (International Centre for Coastal and Ocean Policy Studies (I C C O P S)) (ITA ISSN 1027-4529) **2806**
I C C O World Cocoa Directory (International Cocoa Organization) (GBR) **3646**
I C C Performance Code For Buildings And Facilities (International Code Council) (USA ISSN 1935-6064) **1013**
I C C S Contact *see* Contact I C C S - C I E C **4289**
I C C S R Research Paper Series *see* University of Nottingham. International Centre for Corporate Social Responsibility. Research Paper Series **1189**
• I C C T E Journal (International Community of Christians in Teacher Education) (USA ISSN 1932-7846) **2865**
I C C V - International Conference on Computer Vision (USA) **2448**
I C C W Journal (Indian Council for Child Welfare) (IND) **8045**
I C D C *see* Inside Consumer-Directed Care **4102**
I C D C News (Industrial and Commercial Development Corporation) (KEN) **1429**
I C D Globe *see* The Globe **5846**
I C D Journaal (Implantable Cardioverter-Defibrillator) (NLD ISSN 1572-5278) **5789**
I C D L *see* International Conference on Conduction and Breakdown in Dielectric Liquids. Proceedings **3320**
I C E (Internal Combustion Engine) (USA ISSN 1066-5048) **3379**
I C E A *see* International Civil Engineering Abstracts **3232**
I C E C A P Report (Integrated Circuit Engineering Corporation) (USA) **3101**
I C E C E News (Innovation Centers in Eastern and Central Europe) (DEU ISSN 1433-8025) **1750**
I C E Economico. Boletin (Informacion Comercial Espanola) (ESP ISSN 0214-8307) **1429**
I C E L References (International Council of Environmental Law) (DEU) **3479**
I C E Magazine *see* Inner Circle Elite Magazine **5074**
† I C E Revista de Instrumentacion, Componentes y Equipos Electronicos (ESP ISSN 1136-2065) **8963**
I C E S Annual Report *see* International Council for the Exploration of the Sea. Annual Report **2808**
• I C E S Cooperative Research Report/Conseil International pour l'Exploration de la Mer Rapport des Recherches Collectives (International Council for the Exploration of the Sea) (DNK ISSN 1017-6195) **3597**
• I C E S Council Meeting (International Council for the Exploration of the Sea) (DNK ISSN 1015-4744) **3597**
• I C E S Identification Leaflets for Diseases and Parasites of Fish and Shellfish/Fiches d'Identification des Maladies et Parasites des Poissons, Crustaces et Mollusques (International Council for the Exploration of the Sea) (DNK ISSN 0109-2510) **947**
• I C E S Identification Leaflets for Plankton/Fiches d'Identification du Plancton (International Council for the Exploration of the Sea) (DNK ISSN 1019-1097) **3438**
• I C E S Insight (International Council for the Exploration of the Sea) (DNK ISSN 1995-7815) **2806**
• ➤ I C E S Journal of Marine Science (International Council for the Exploration of the Sea) (GBR ISSN 1054-3139) **2806**
I C E S Marine Science Symposia (International Council for the Exploration of the Sea) (DNK ISSN 0906-060X) **3597**
I C E S Newsletter *see* I C E S Insight **2806**
• ➤ I C E S Techniques in Marine Environmental Sciences (International Council for the Exploration of the Sea) (DNK ISSN 0903-2606) **677**
I C F A (International Custody & Fund Administration) (GBR ISSN 1478-727X) **1629**
The I C F A I Journal of Accounting Research (Institute of Chartered Financial Analysts of India) (IND ISSN 0972-690X) **1290**
The I C F A I Journal of Alternative Dispute Resolution (Institute of Chartered Financial Analysts of India) (IND ISSN 0972-6969) **4689**
The I C F A I Journal of Applied Economics (Institute of Chartered Financial Analysts of India) (IND ISSN 0972-6861) **1120**
The I C F A I Journal of Audit Practice (Institute of Chartered Financial Analysts of India) (IND ISSN 0972-9070) **1290**
The I C F A I Journal of Bank Management (Institute of Chartered Financial Analysts of India) (IND ISSN 0972-6918) **1352**
The I C F A I Journal of Banking Law (Institute of Chartered Financial Analysts of India) (IND ISSN 0972-7884) **4870**
The I C F A I Journal of Behavioral Finance (Institute of Chartered Financial Analysts of India) (IND ISSN 0972-9089) **1750**
The I C F A I Journal of Brand Management (Institute of Chartered Financial Analysts of India) (IND ISSN 0972-9097) **1819**
The I C F A I Journal of Business Strategy (Institute of Chartered Financial Analysts of India) (IND ISSN 0972-9259) **1750**
The I C F A I Journal of Corporate and Securities Law (Institute of Chartered Financial Analysts of India) (IND ISSN 0973-2640) **4870**
The I C F A I Journal of Corporate Governance (Institute of Chartered Financial Analysts of India) (IND ISSN 0972-6853) **1750**
The I C F A I Journal of Cyber Law (Institute of Chartered Financial Analysts of India) (IND ISSN 0972-6934) **4689**
The I C F A I Journal of Derivatives Markets (Institute of Chartered Financial Analysts of India) (IND ISSN 0972-9119) **1629**
The I C F A I Journal of Employment Law (Institute of Chartered Financial Analysts of India) (IND ISSN 0972-7868) **4689**
The I C F A I Journal of Entrepreneurship Development (Institute of Chartered Financial Analysts of India) (IND ISSN 0973-2659) **1750**
The I C F A I Journal of Environmental Economics (Institute of Chartered Financial Analysts of India) (IND ISSN 0972-9313) **3438**
The I C F A I Journal of Environmental Law (Institute of Chartered Financial Analysts of India) (IND ISSN 0972-6942) **4689**
The I C F A I Journal of Financial Economics (Institute of Chartered Financial Analysts of India) (IND ISSN 0972-9151) **1352**
The I C F A I Journal of Financial Risk Management (Institute of Chartered Financial Analysts of India) (IND ISSN 0972-916X) **1750**
The I C F A I Journal of Healthcare Law (Institute of Chartered Financial Analysts of India) (IND ISSN 0972-785X) **7524**
The I C F A I Journal of Industrial Economics (Institute of Chartered Financial Analysts of India) (IND ISSN 0972-9208) **1120**
The I C F A I Journal of Information Technology (Institute of Chartered Financial Analysts of India) (IND ISSN 0973-2896) **2420**
The I C F A I Journal of Infrastructure (Institute of Chartered Financial Analysts of India) (IND ISSN 0972-9194) **1750**
The I C F A I Journal of Insurance Law (Institute of Chartered Financial Analysts of India) (IND ISSN 0972-7876) **4870**
The I C F A I Journal of Intellectual Property Rights (Institute of Chartered Financial Analysts of India) (IND ISSN 0972-6926) **6751**
The I C F A I Journal of International Business Law (Institute of Chartered Financial Analysts of India) (IND ISSN 0972-6950) **4928**
The I C F A I Journal of Knowledge Management (Institute of Chartered Financial Analysts of India) (IND ISSN 0972-9216) **1751**
The I C F A I Journal of Management Research (Institute of Chartered Financial Analysts of India) (IND ISSN 0972-5342) **1751**
The I C F A I Journal of Managerial Economics (Institute of Chartered Financial Analysts of India) (IND ISSN 0972-9305) **1751**
The I C F A I Journal of Marketing Management (Institute of Chartered Financial Analysts of India) (IND ISSN 0972-6845) **1819**
The I C F A I Journal of Mergers and Acquisitions (Institute of Chartered Financial Analysts of India) (IND ISSN 0972-9232) **1120**
The I C F A I Journal of Monetary Economics (Institute of Chartered Financial Analysts of India) (IND ISSN 0972-9291) **1719**
The I C F A I Journal of Operations Management (Institute of Chartered Financial Analysts of India) (IND ISSN 0972-6888) **1751**
The I C F A I Journal of Organizational Behavior (Institute of Chartered Financial Analysts of India) (IND ISSN 0972-687X) **1865**
The I C F A I Journal of Public Administration (Institute of Chartered Financial Analysts of India) (IND ISSN 0973-225X) **7445**
The I C F A I Journal of Public Finance (Institute of Chartered Financial Analysts of India) (IND ISSN 0972-9356) **1928**

The I C F A I Journal of Risk and Insurance (Institute of Chartered Financial Analysts of India) (IND ISSN 0972-933X) **4505**
➤ The I C F A I Journal of Science and Technology (Institute of Chartered Financial Analysts of India) (IND ISSN 0973-2268) **7864**
The I C F A I Journal of Services Marketing (Institute of Chartered Financial Analysts of India) (IND ISSN 0972-9224) **1819**
The I C F A I Journal of Supply Chain Management (Institute of Chartered Financial Analysts of India) (IND ISSN 0972-9267) **1819**
The I C F A I Journal of Systems Management (Institute of Chartered Financial Analysts of India) (IND ISSN 0972-6896) **1751**
▼ I C F A I University Journal of Physics (IND ISSN 0974-1380) **7015**
I C F A Instrumentation Bulletin (International Committee for Future Accelerators) (USA) **4487**
I C F Bugle (International Crane Foundation) (USA) **908**
I C F Quarterly Papers (Industry Churches Forum) (GBR) **7736**
I C F R Annual Research Report (Institute for Commercial Forestry Research) (ZAF) **3692**
I C F T U - O R I T Inter-American Labor News (Organizacion Regional Interamericana de Trabajadores) (MEX) **4595**
• I C F T U Online (International Confederation of Free Trade Unions) (BEL) **4595**
➤ I C G A Journal (International Computer Games Association) (NLD ISSN 1389-6911) **2477**
I C G Magazine *see* International Cinematographers Guild Magazine **6970**
I C H A Buyers' Guide to Manufacturers (Year) (International Cargo Handling Co-ordination Association) (GBR ISSN 1366-2473) **8646**
I C H C A News and Cargo Management (International Cargo Handling Co-ordination Association) (GBR ISSN 1028-8821) **8646**
I C H C A News and Cargo Today (International Cargo Handling Co-ordination Association) (GBR ISSN 1029-1768) **8526**
I C H E5 Handbook (Year) (JPN) **6846**
• I C H F Newsletter (International Council for Health Freedom) (USA ISSN 1093-1376) **7524**
I C H P E R - S D Congress Proceedings (International Council on Health, Physical Education, Recreation, Sport and Dance) (USA) **6989**
I C H P E R - S D Journal *see* I C H P E R - S D Journal of Research in Health, Physical Education, Recreation, Sport and Dance **6989**
➤ I C H P E R - S D Journal of Research in Health, Physical Education, Recreation, Sport and Dance (International Council for Health, Physical Education, Recreation, Sport and Dance) (USA ISSN 1930-4595) **6989**
I C H R Newsletter (Indian Council of Historical Research) (IND ISSN 0376-9682) **4183**
I C I A S F Record *see* International Congress on Instrumentation in Aerospace Simulation Facilities. Record **60**
I C I D Bibliography *see* Bibliography on Irrigation, Drainage, River Training and Flood Control **8843**
I C I D C A. Sobre los Derivados de la Cana de Azucar (Instituto Cubano de Investigaciones de los Derivados de la Cana de Azucar) (CUB ISSN 1727-0286) **235**
I C I Journal (Indian Concrete Institute) (IND ISSN 0972-2998) **1013**
• I C I M: International Conference on Multimodal Interfaces. Proceedings (USA) **2420**
I C J Mice Magazine (Incentive Congress Journal) (DEU ISSN 1862-8672) **1819**
I C J Newsletter (International Commission of Jurists) (CHE ISSN 0252-0346) **4928**
I C J Review (International Commission of Jurists) (CHE ISSN 0020-6393) **4928**
I C L *see* Illness, Crisis, and Loss **8107**
I C L A Bulletin (International Comparative Literature Association) (USA ISSN 0887-3615) **5307**
I C L G News (Print) *see* C L S I G News (Online) **4999**
I C L Q *see* International and Comparative Law Quarterly **4929**
† ➤ I C L Systems Journal (International Computers Ltd.) (GBR ISSN 1364-310X) **8963**
• I C M A B Newsletter (Institute of Cost and Management Accountants of Bangladesh) (BGD) **1290**
I C M A Newsletter (International City/County Management Association) (USA ISSN 0047-0651) **7494**
• I C M A Public Management Magazine (International City/County Management Association) (USA) **7494**
I C M E Manual for Cars (Institute of Consulting Motor Engineers) (GBR) **8584**
I C M E Manual for Heavy Goods Vehicles (Institute of Consulting Motor Engineers) (GBR) **8584**
I C M E Manual for Light Commercial Vehicles (Institute of Consulting Motor Engineers) (GBR) **8584**
I C M I Proceedings *see* International Conference on Multimodal Interfaces. Proceedings **2424**
I C M J's Prospecting and Mining Journal *see* International California Mining Journal **6466**
I C M M Newsletter *see* International Council on Mining and Metals. Newsletter **6316**
I C M R *see* Islam and Christian - Muslim Relations **7711**
• I C M R Bulletin (Indian Council of Medical Research) (IND ISSN 0377-4910) **5631**
• I C Master (Online) (Integrated Circuits) (USA) **3101**
I C N *see* International Cosmetique News **589**
I C N A Message *see* The Message (Jamaica) **7714**
I C N-Informatie (Instituut Collectie Nederland) (NLD ISSN 1566-760X) **6525**
I C N-Information (Instituut Collectie Nederland) (NLD ISSN 1873-0396) **6525**
I.C. Nachrichten (Institutum Canarium) (AUT) **397**
I C O Den Iconographiske Post *see* Iconographisk Post **8963**
I C O - Information Christlicher Orient (AUT) **7761**
I C O M Cahiers d'Etude *see* I C O M Study Series **6525**
I C O M News (English Edition) (International Council of Museums) (FRA ISSN 1020-6418) **6525**
I C O M Newsletter (International Communications Agency Network) (USA) **26**
I C O M. Noticias *see* I C O M News (English Edition) **6525**
I C O M. Nouvelles *see* I C O M News (English Edition) **6525**
I C O M O S News *see* I C O M O S Nouvelles **445**
I C O M O S Nouvelles/I C O M O S News (International Council on Monuments and Sites) (FRA ISSN 1019-679X) **445**
I C O M Study Series/I C O M Cahiers d'Etude (International Council of Museums) (FRA ISSN 1020-5543) **6525**
• I C O N D A: International Construction Database (International Construction Database) (USA) **8**
I C O O L (International Conference on Open and Online Learning) (MUS ISSN 1694-0202) **2497**
▼ • I C O S A (USA ISSN 1938-2081) **1751**
I C O T S *see* International Conference on Teaching Statistics. Proceedings **3065**
I C P (Industria Chimica e Petrolifera) (ITA ISSN 0390-2358) **3246**
▼ I C P Advanced Texts in Mathematics (Imperial College Press) (GBR ISSN 1753-657X) **5491**
I C P D Newsletter (Institution for Continuing Professional Development) (GBR ISSN 1465-0134) **2986**
I C P E A C Abstracts of Contributed Papers and Invited Papers *see* International Conference on the Physics of Electronic and Atomic Collisions. Abstracts of Contributed Papers and Invited Papers **7067**
• I C P Information Newsletter (Online Edition) (Inductively Coupled Plasma) (USA) **2064**
I C P S Newsletter (International Centre for Policy Studies) (UKR) **7445**
I C P S R Bulletin (Inter-University Consortium for Political and Social Research) (USA ISSN 0198-6848) **7971**
I C Q M Quarterly Review (Institute for Compliance and Quality Management) (LIE ISSN 1609-6290) **1352**
I C R A - Agrimissio Information (International Catholic Rural Association) (VAT) **7800**
I C R A. Research Monographs *see* International Centre for Research and Assessment. Research Monographs **3025**
I C R Annual Report (Institute for Chemical Research) (JPN ISSN 1342-0321) **2064**
I C R. Bollettino (Istituto Centrale del Restauro) (ITA ISSN 1594-2562) **493**
I C R C *see* International Classical Record Collector **6576**
I C R Coal Statistics Monthly (International Coal Report) (GBR ISSN 0268-0343) **6464**
I C R G *see* International Country Risk Guide **1492**
I C R G *see* International Country Risk Guide Annual. Vol. 1, The Americas **1492**
I C R G *see* International Country Risk Guide Annual. Vol. 2, Europe (European Union) **1492**
I C R G *see* International Country Risk Guide Annual. Vol. 3, Europe (Non-European Union) **1492**
I C R G *see* International Country Risk Guide Annual. Vol. 5, Sub-Saharan Africa **1492**
I C R G *see* International Country Risk Guide Annual. Vol. 6, Asia & the Pacific **1492**
I C R G *see* International Country Risk Guide Annual. Vol. 7, Risk Ratings & Statistics **1492**
I C R I S A T Report (International Crops Research Institute for the Semi-Arid Tropics) (IND ISSN 1017-9933) **235**
I C R R Annual Report (Institute for Cosmic Ray Research) (JPN ISSN 0919-8296) **575**
I C R R Hokoku (Institute for Cosmic Ray Research) (JPN) **575**
I C R R News (Institute for Cosmic Ray Research) (JPN) **575**
I C R: The International Cookbook Revue (ESP ISSN 1136-2073) **4361**
• ➤ I C R U Journal (International Commission on Radiation Units and Measurements) (GBR ISSN 1473-6691) **7066**
I C R W Reports and Publications (International Center for Research on Women) (USA) **8868**
I C S *see* Information, Communication and Society **2545**
I C S A News (International Customer Service Association) (USA) **1120**
• I C S A Newsletter (International Christian Studies Association) (USA ISSN 1051-2772) **2986**
• I C S C Research Review (International Council of Shopping Centers) (USA) **7594**
I C S Cahiers (ICS, Forum voor Geloof, Wetenschap en Samenleving) (NLD) **7648**
• I C S Cleaning Specialist (Installation and Cleaning Specialist) (USA ISSN 1522-4708) **4559**
I C S D *see* I E E E International Conference on Solid Dielectrics. Proceedings **3312**
• I C S I D Review (International Centre for Settlement of Investment Disputes) (USA ISSN 0258-3690) **1629**
I C S I M Newsletter (Istituto per la Cultura e la Storia d'Impresa Franco Momigliano) (ITA ISSN 1828-4655) **1120**
I C S M Biennial Report *see* Australia. Intergovernmental Committee on Surveying and Mapping. Biennial Report **3999**
I C S News *see* I C S News and Prayer Diary **7648**
• I C S News and Prayer Diary (GBR ISSN 1755-294X) **7648**
I C S Newsletter (Indian Coin Society) (IND ISSN 0973-1938) **6651**
I C S Newsletter (International Catacomb Society) (USA) **493**
I C S Prayer Diary *see* I C S News and Prayer Diary **7648**
I C S S Newsletter (Illinois Council for the Social Studies) (USA) **2865**
I C S S P E Bulletin (Print) *see* Sport Science & Physical Education Bulletin **6997**
I C S S R Journal of Abstracts and Reviews: Economics (Indian Council of Social Science Research) (IND ISSN 0250-9695) **1241**
I C S S R Journal of Abstracts and Reviews: Geography (Indian Council of Social Science Research) (IND ISSN 0250-9687) **4036**
I C S S R Journal of Abstracts and Reviews: Political Science (Indian Council of Social Science Research) (IND ISSN 0250-9660) **7199**
I C S S R Journal of Abstracts and Reviews: Sociology & Social Anthropology (Indian Council of Social Science Research) (IND) **362**
I C S S R Newsletter (Indian Council of Social Science Research) (IND ISSN 0018-9049) **7971**
I C S S R Union Catalogue of Social Science Periodicals (Indian Council of Social Science Research) (IND) **8020**
• I C S T I Forum (International Council for Scientific and Technical Information) (FRA ISSN 1018-9580) **5012**
I C S U Newsletter (International Council for Science) (FRA) **7864**
I C T *see* Industrial and Commercial Training **1866**
I C T A Update (Institute of Certified Travel Agents) (USA) **8720**
• I C T & S Research Paper Series (Information and Communication Technologies and Society) (AUT ISSN 1990-8563) **2350**
I C T Coordinator's File (Information and Communications Technology) (GBR ISSN 1474-2462) **3064**
I C T for Education (Information and Communications Technology) (GBR ISSN 1742-7827) **3064**
I C T in het Amerikaans Hoger Onderwijs *see* EDUCAUSE **2980**
I C T. International Jahrestagungen (Fraunhofer Institut fuer Chemische Technologie) (DEU) **3246**
I C T P Series in Theoretical Physics (International Centre for Theoretical Physics) (SGP ISSN 0218-0243) **7015**
I C T Professional (Information and Communication Technology) (ITA ISSN 1828-2865) **1751**
I C T Rendement (Informatie- en Communicatie Technologie) (NLD ISSN 1574-1680) **2420**
I C T Update (English Edition) (Information Communication Technology) (NLD ISSN 1569-7568) **119**
I C T Update (French Edition) (Information Communication Technology) (NLD ISSN 1569-7576) **119**
I C U D *see* Index to Current Urban Documents **7481**
▼ • ➤ I C U Director (Intensive Care Unit) (USA ISSN 1944-4516) **4102**
I C U M S A Methods Book (International Commission of Uniform Methods of Sugar Analysis) (GBR) **3646**
• ➤ I C U s and Nursing Web Journal (Intensive Care Units) (GRC ISSN 1108-7366) **5961**
I C Week *see* Insurance Compliance Week **4506**
I C Y R A N A Directory (Intercollegiate Yacht Racing Association of North America) (USA) **8276**
I CAHTA's Newsletter *see* I - C A H T A's Newsletter **5631**
I Can (GBR ISSN 1477-366X) **6021**
• I Can Do That! (GBR) **4066**
• I Can Make it Myself (AUS ISSN 1832-6331) **536**
• i-com (DEU ISSN 1618-162X) **2350**
I-CON *see* International Journal of Constitutional Law **4849**
i-D (GBR ISSN 0262-3579) **2256**
I D *see* Interior Design (Watford) **4543**
I D *see* Information Display **2487**
• I.D. (International Design) (USA ISSN 0894-5373) **4542**
I D *see* Illinois Director **3719**
i D (Dutch Edition) (Informatie Documentatie) (BEL ISSN 1370-6500) **2193**
I D (French Edition) *see* i D (Dutch Edition) **2193**
• I D 3 Podcast Magazine (USA) **2350**
I D A Downtown Newsbriefs (International Downtown Association) (USA ISSN 1526-3053) **4414**
▼ • ➤ I D A Journal on Desalination and Water Reuse (International Desalination Association) (USA) **8825**
I D A Magazine *see* In Defense of Animals Magazine **320**
I D A Membership and Survival Guide (International Documentary Association) (USA) **6503**
I D A Newsletter (International Desalination Association) (USA) **8825**
I D A Q P *see* Infinite Dimensional Analysis, Quantum Probability and Related Topics **5493**
I D A S (Year) *see* International Directory of Automotive Suppliers & Vehicle Manufacturers **8586**
I D A Working Papers (Institute for Development Anthropology) (USA ISSN 1059-8316) **342**
I D B America (Online) (Inter-American Development Bank) (USA ISSN 1932-409X) **1352**
I D B America (Print) *see* I D B America (Online) **1352**
I D B Extra *see* I D B America (Online) **1352**
• I D B Projects (Inter-American Development Bank) (USA ISSN 1076-8424) **1352**
I D C *see* Industrie du Cuir **4973**
I D C Impact (Industrial Development Corporation) (BRB) **1597**
• I D C Japan Report (International Data Corporation) (USA) **2493**
I D C Newsletter *see* I D C Quarterly **4689**
• I D C Quarterly (Illinois Association of Defense Trial Counsel) (USA ISSN 1094-9542) **4689**
I D Checking Guide (International Edition) (USA) **2654**
I D Checking Guide (U.S. & Canada Edition) (USA ISSN 1557-6043) **2654**
I D D *see* Investment Dealers' Digest **1632**
I D D *see* Intellectual and Developmental Disabilities **3041**
I D D B A LegisLetter (International Dairy - Deli - Bakery Association) (USA) **3646**
I D D B A WrapUp (International Dairy - Deli - Bakery Association) (USA) **3646**
I D E (Informacion de Envase y Embalaje) (ESP ISSN 0300-4171) **6710**
I D E A *see* Interinstitutional Directory. Who's Who in the European Union? **643**
• I D E A Compliance Alert (Individuals with Disabilities Education Act) (USA ISSN 1947-1971) **3041**
• I D E A Compliance Insider (Individuals with Disabilities Education Improvement Act) (USA ISSN 1551-2231) **3041**
• I D E A Conference Papers (USA) **8452**
• I D E A Fitness Journal (International Dance-Exercise Association) (USA ISSN 1548-419X) **6989**
I D E A Fitness Manager Newsletter (International Dance-Exercise Association) (USA ISSN 1073-7952) **6989**
I D E A Health & Fitness Source *see* I D E A Fitness Journal **6989**
I D E A News (Individuals with Disabilities Education Act) (USA) **3041**
I D E A Personal Trainer *see* I D E A Fitness Journal **6989**
I D E A S Bulletin (Investment Diversification & Economic Analysis) (GBR) **1629**
I D E A T *see* Ideat **4543**
I D E A Trainer Success (International Dance-Exercise Association) (USA) **6989**
I D E Informe de un Seminario de Politica *see* E D I Policy Seminar Report **1096**
I D E International Joint Research Project Series (Institute of Developing Economies) (JPN) **1120**
I D E L R *see* Individuals with Disabilities Education Law Report **3041**
➤ I D E Occasional Papers Series (Institute of Developing Economies) (JPN ISSN 0537-9202) **1120**
➤ I D E Research Series/Kenkyu-Sosho (Institute of Developing Economies) (JPN) **1120**
I D E Spot Survey (Institute of Developing Economies) (JPN) **1120**
I D E Statistical Data Series (Institute of Developing Economies) (JPN) **1241**
I D E Symposium Proceedings (Institute of Developing Economies) (JPN) **1120**
• I D E X Magazine (International Diamond Exchange) (ISR) **1120**
• I D F A Magazine (International Documentary Filmfestival Amsterdam) (NLD) **6503**
I D F Law review *see* Israel Defense Forces Law Review **6425**
• I D F - Nyt (Immun Defekt Foreningen) (DNK ISSN 1601-7862) **5759**
I D G *see* Ingenieria del Gas **6773**
• I D G News Service (International Data Group) (GBR) **1417**
I D H *see* Interior Decorators' Handbook **4543**
• I D Handbook of Foodservice Distribution CD-ROM (Institutional Distribution) (USA) **3646**
• I D I I Software Newsletter (Industrial Data & Information Inc.) (USA ISSN 1533-435X) **1888**
• I D I S (Iowa Drug Information Service) (USA ISSN 0891-8511) **6889**
I D J (International Disc Jockey) (GBR ISSN 1471-0641) **6574**
I D - L'Information Dentaire (FRA ISSN 0297-8350) **5846**

Title

10386 I D M A ANNUAL PUBLICATION ULRICH'S PERIODICALS

I D M A Annual Publication (Indian Drug Manufacturers' Association) (IND) **6846**
I D M A Bulletin (Indian Drug Manufacturers' Association) (IND ISSN 0970-6054) **6846**
I D Magazine (FRA ISSN 1959-5360) **7141**
I D N *see* International Defence Newsletter **6425**
I D N *see* Integrated Dealer News **2326**
I D N (International Designers Network) (HKG ISSN 1029-4805) **2534**
† I D O C Internazionale (International Documentation and Communication Center) (ITA ISSN 0250-7641) **8963**
I D P *see* Revista de Internet, Derecho y Politica **4771**
I D P M Discussion and Working Papers (Institute for Development Policy and Management) (GBR) **1597**
• I D P News (International Dunhuang Project) (GBR ISSN 1354-5914) **4183**
I D Profile *see* Who's Who in International Development **1607**
I D R *see* Diamant Hochleistungswerkzeuge **6461**
I D R *see* Indian Drug Review **6847**
I D R *see* International Dredging Review **3362**
I D R A Newsletter (Intercultural Development Research Association) (USA ISSN 1069-5672) **3064**
• I D R C Reports (International Development Research Centre) (CAN ISSN 0315-9981) **1597**
I D R Extra *see* International Defense Review Extra **6425**
I D R. Industrial Diamond Review *see* Industrial Diamond Review **8425**
I D R - Journal of International Dispute Resolution *see* Recht der Internationalen Wirtschaft **4938**
A I D R O M. Proceedings *see* A I D R O M. Actas **4607**
I D R Online *see* The Infectious Disease Review **5817**
I D S Brief *see* I D S Employment Law Brief **1685**
• I D S Bulletin (Institute of Development Studies) (GBR ISSN 0265-5012) **1597**
I D S Discussion Paper (Institute of Development Studies) (GBR ISSN 0308-5864) **1597**
• I D S Diversity at Work (Incomes Data Services) (GBR ISSN 1743-7350) **1865**
• I D S Employment Law Brief (Incomes Data Services) (GBR ISSN 1748-2828) **1685**
I D S Employment Law Handbooks (Incomes Data Services) (GBR) **1685**
• I D S Employment Law Supplement (Incomes Data Services) (GBR ISSN 1752-7694) **1686**
I D S Executive Compensation Review (Incomes Data Services Ltd.) (GBR ISSN 1746-1847) **1686**
• I D S H R Studies (Incomes Data Services Ltd.) (GBR) **1686**
I D S Handbook Series (Incomes Data Services) (GBR ISSN 0308-7085) **1686**
• I D S Pay Benchmark (Incomes Data Services Ltd.) (GBR ISSN 1474-1792) **1686**
I D S Pay Directory *see* I D S Pay Benchmark **1686**
• I D S Pay Report (Incomes Data Services) (GBR ISSN 1745-3739) **1686**
I D S Pensions Bulletin (Incomes Data Services) (GBR ISSN 1748-0981) **1686**
I D S Pensions Law Reports (Incomes Data Services) (GBR ISSN 0959-8014) **1686**
I D S Policy Briefing (Institute of Development Studies) (GBR ISSN 1360-4724) **1597**
I D S Report *see* I D S Pay Report **1686**
I D S Report. Labour Market Supplement (Incomes Data Services) (GBR ISSN 0958-2673) **1686**
I D S Research Reports (Institute of Development Studies) (GBR ISSN 0141-1314) **1597**
I D S Studies *see* I D S H R Studies **1686**
I D S Working Paper (Institute of Development Studies) (GBR ISSN 1353-6141) **1597**
I D Systems Buyers Guide (Indentification) (USA ISSN 1043-8319) **1417**
I D U *see* Impaired Driving Update **8585**
I D U G Solutions Journal (International DB2 Users Group) (USA ISSN 1078-8093) **2590**
I D U N. Noticiero (Instituto de Desarrollo Urbano) (COL) **4414**
I D W Fachnachrichten (Institut der Wirtschaftspruefer in Deutschland e.V.) (DEU ISSN 0937-4019) **1290**
• I DNewswire (USA) **1352**
I Do (USA) **5559**
I Do I Do Creations Magazine (AUS ISSN 1449-5945) **8868**
• I Drugs: the Investigational Drugs Journal (GBR ISSN 1369-7056) **6846**
I E *see* Independent Education **2986**
I E (ZAF ISSN 1816-1251) **445**
I E A Clean Coal Centre. Annual Report (International Energy Agency) (GBR) **3137**
I E A Clean Coal Centre. Newsletter (International Energy Agency) (GBR) **3137**
I E A Clean Coal Centre. Profiles (International Energy Agency) (GBR) **3137**
I E A Clean Coal Centre. Reports (International Energy Agency) (GBR) **3137**
I E A Coal Information *see* Coal Information **6460**
I E A Coal Research. Annual Report *see* I E A Clean Coal Centre. Annual Report **3137**
I E A Coal Research. Newsletter *see* I E A Clean Coal Centre. Newsletter **3137**
I E A Coal Research. Profiles *see* I E A Clean Coal Centre. Profiles **3137**
I E A Energy Prices and Taxes *see* Energy Prices and Taxes (Print) **3133**
• I E A Energy Prices and Taxes (Online) (International Energy Agency) (FRA ISSN 1683-626X) **3137**
I E A Final Reports (Institute of European Affairs) (IRL) **7240**
I E A Interim Reports (Institute of European Affairs) (IRL) **7240**
• ➤ The I E A Journal of Ergonomics (International Ergonomics Association) (SGP) **3196**
I E A Natural Gas Information *see* Natural Gas Information **6779**
I E A News (Institute of European Affairs) (IRL) **7240**
I E A Oil Information *see* Oil Information **6784**
• I E A Oil Market Report (International Energy Agency) (GBR) **3137**
I E A Reporter (Year) (Idaho Education Association) (USA ISSN 1059-7743) **2865**
I E A Seminar Papers (Institute of European Affairs) (IRL) **7240**
I E A Seminar Reports (Institute of European Affairs) (IRL) **7240**
I E A Studies on the Environment (Institute of Economic Affairs) (GBR ISSN 1368-9584) **3438**
I E & S News *see* International Environment and Safety News **3441**
• I E C Bulletin (International Electrotechnical Commission) (CHE ISSN 0018-9138) **3310**
I E C C *see* International Energy Conservation Code (Year) **1016**
• I E C Catalogue of Publications (International Electrotechnical Commission) (CHE) **3101**
I E C Quarterly (Independent Electrical Contractors) (USA) **3101**
• I E Comunicaciones (Informatica Educativa) (ESP ISSN 1699-4574) **2949**
I E E - Automatisierung und Datentechnik (Industrie Elektrik und Elektronik) (DEU ISSN 1434-2898) **3310**
I E E Circuits, Devices and Systems Series *see* The I E T Circuits, Devices and Systems Series **3316**
I E E Conference Publication Series *see* The I E T Conference Publication Series **3316**
I E E Control Series *see* The I E T Control Series **3317**
• I E E E / A C M International Conference on Automated Software Engineering (Institute of Electrical and Electronics Engineers / Association for Computing Machinery) (USA ISSN 1938-4300) **2590**
I E E E - A C M - S I G G R A P H Symposium on Volume Visualization and Graphics. Proceedings (Institute of Electrical and Electronics Engineering - Association for Computing Machinery) (USA ISSN 1727-8376) **2486**
• I E E E - A C M Transactions on Computational Biology and Bioinformatics (Institute of Electrical and Electronics Engineers - Association for Computing Machinery) (USA ISSN 1545-5963) **825**
• ➤ I E E E - A C M Transactions on Networking (Institute of Electrical and Electronics Engineers - Association for Computing Machinery) (USA ISSN 1063-6692) **2497**
• I E E E - A E S C O N Aerospace and Electronics Conference. Record (Institute of Electrical and Electronics Engineers - Aerospace and Electronics Systems Society) (USA) **3310**
• I E E E - A E S S Dayton Chapter Symposium (Institute of Electrical and Electronics Engineers - Aerospace and Electronic Systems Society) (USA) **59**
• I E E E - A I A A Digital Avionics Systems Conference. Proceedings (Institute of Electrical and Electronics Engineers - American Institute of Aeronautics and Astronauti) (USA) **59**
I E E E / A S M E International Conference on Advanced Intelligent Mechatronics *see* Advanced Intelligent Mechatronics **2457**
• I E E E - A S M E Joint Rail Conference. Proceedings (Institute of Electrical and Electronics Engineers - American Society of Mechanical Engineers) (USA ISSN 1559-9531) **8618**
• ➤ I E E E - A S M E Transactions on Mechatronics (Institute of Electrical and Electronics Engineers - American Society of Mechanical Engineers) (USA ISSN 1083-4435) **3367**
I E E E A S S P Workshop on Applications of Signal Processing to Audio and Acoustics *see* I E E E Workshop on Applications of Signal Processing to Audio and Acoustics **7087**
• I E E E - A T M Workshop. Proceedings (Institute of Electrical and Electronics Engineers) (USA ISSN 1098-7789) **2497**
• ➤ I E E E Aerospace and Electronic Systems Magazine (Institute of Electrical and Electronics Engineers) (USA ISSN 0885-8985) **3101**
I E E E Aerospace Applications Conference. Digest (Institute of Electrical and Electronics Engineers) (USA) **59**
• I E E E Aerospace Conference. Proceedings (Institute of Electrical and Electronics Engineers) (USA ISSN 1095-323X) **59**
I E E E Almanack (Institute of Electrical and Electronics Engineers) (USA ISSN 0018-9154) **3310**
I E E E America Latina. Revista/I E E E Latin America Transactions (Institute of Electrical and Electronics Engineers) (USA ISSN 1548-0992) **3362**
• ➤ I E E E Annals of the History of Computing (Institute of Electrical and Electronics Engineers) (USA ISSN 1058-6180) **2420**
• ➤ I E E E Antennas and Propagation Magazine (Institute of Electrical and Electronics Engineers) (USA ISSN 1045-9243) **3310**
• I E E E Antennas and Propagation Society. International Symposium (Institute of Electrical and Electronics Engineers) (USA) **3310**
• I E E E Antennas and Propagation Society. International Symposium (CD-ROM) (Institute of Electrical and Electronics Engineers) (USA) **2323**
I E E E Antennas and Propagation Society. International Symposium Digest *see* I E E E Antennas and Propagation Magazine **3310**
• I E E E Antennas and Wireless Propagation Letters (Institute of Electrical and Electronics Engineers) (USA ISSN 1536-1225) **2323**
• I E E E Applied Power Electronics Conference and Exposition. Conference Proceedings (Institute of Electrical and Electronics Engineers) (USA ISSN 1048-2334) **3101**
• I E E E Asia-Pacific Conference on A S I C. Proceedings (Institute of Electrical and Electronics Engineers) (USA) **2465**
I E E E Asia - Pacific Conference on Circuits and Systems. Proceedings (Institute of Electrical and Electronics Engineers) (USA) **2465**
• I E E E Autotestcon (Institute of Electrical and Electronics Engineers) (USA) **3311**
I E E E - C O M P S A C *see* I E E E International Computer Software and Applications Conference. Proceedings **2590**
• I E E E - C P M T Electronics Manufacturing Technology (I E M T) (Institute of Electrical and Electronics Engineers - Components, Packaging, and Manufacturing Technol) (USA ISSN 1089-8190) **3101**
I E E E Canadian Review (Institute of Electrical and Electronic Engineers) (CAN ISSN 1481-2002) **3311**
• I E E E Cement Industry Technical Conference. Proceedings (Institute of Electrical and Electronics Engineers) (USA) **1013**
• I E E E Circuits and Systems Magazine (Institute of Electrical and Electronics Engineers) (USA ISSN 1531-636X) **2465**
• I E E E Communications Letters (Institute of Electrical and Electronics Engineers) (USA ISSN 1089-7798) **2323**
• ➤ I E E E Communications Magazine (Institute of Electrical and Electronics Engineers) (USA ISSN 0163-6804) **3311**
• I E E E Communications Surveys and Tutorials (Institute of Electrical and Electronics Engineers) (USA ISSN 1553-877X) **2323**
I E E E Communications Theory Mini-Conference. Proceedings (Institute of Electrical and Electronics Engineers) (USA ISSN 1086-5195) **2323**
• I E E E Compound Semiconductor Integrated Circuit Symposium. Technical Digest (Institute of Electrical and Electronics Engineers) (USA ISSN 1550-8781) **3101**
• I E E E Computational Intelligence Magazine (Institute of Electrical and Electronics Engineers) (USA ISSN 1556-603X) **2449**
I E E E Computational Systems Bioinformatics Conference. Proceedings *see* C S B. Conference Proceedings **2409**
• I E E E Computer Architecture Letters (Institute of Electrical and Electronics Engineers) (USA ISSN 1556-6056) **2467**
• ➤ I E E E Computer Graphics and Applications (Institute of Electrical and Electronics Engineers) (USA ISSN 0272-1716) **2486**
I E E E Computer Magazine *see* Computer (New York) **2411**
• I E E E Computer Security Foundations Symposium. Proceedings (USA ISSN 1940-1434) **2513**
• I E E E Computer Society Annual Symposium on V L S I. Proceedings (Institute of Electrical and Electronics Engineers) (USA) **2539**
I E E E Computer Society Bioinformatics Conference. Proceedings *see* C S B. Conference Proceedings **2409**
• I E E E Computer Society Conference on Computer Vision and Pattern Recognition. Proceedings (Institute of Electrical and Electronics Engineers) (USA ISSN 1063-6919) **2449**
I E E E Computer Society. D C C *see* Data Compression Conference. Proceedings **2533**
I E E E Computer Society International Conference *see* CompCon: I E E E Computer Society International Conference **2410**
• I E E E Conference on Computational Complexity. Proceedings (Institute of Electrical and Electronics Engineers) (USA ISSN 1093-0159) **5491**
I E E E Conference on Computational Intelligence for Financial Engineering. Proceedings (Institute of Electrical and Electronics Engineers) (USA) **2449**
• I E E E Conference on Control Applications. Proceedings (Institute of Electrical and Electronics Engineers) (USA ISSN 1085-1992) **2460**
• I E E E Conference on Decision and Control. Proceedings (Institute of Electrical and Electronics Engineers) (USA ISSN 0743-1546) **8424**
I E E E Conference on Electron Devices and Solid-State Circuits (Institute of Electrical and Electronics Engineers) (USA) **2465**
I E E E Conference on Information Visualization *see* I E E E International Conference on Information Visualisation (Year) **2486**
• I E E E Conference on Visualization (Institute of Electrical and Electronics Engineers) (USA ISSN 1070-2385) **2449**
I E E E ConferenceSearch (Institute of Electrical and Electronics Engineers) (USA) **3311**
I E E E Congress on Evolutionary Computation. Proceedings (Institute of Electrical and Electronics Engineers) (USA) **2449**
I E E E coNNections (Institute of Electrical and Electronics Engineers) (USA ISSN 1543-4281) **2471**
• I E E E Control Systems (Institute of Electrical and Electronics Engineers) (USA ISSN 1066-033X) **3311**
• I E E E Custom Integrated Circuits Conference. Proceedings (Institute of Electrical and Electronics Engineers) (USA) **3311**
• ➤ I E E E Design & Test of Computers (Institute of Electrical and Electronics Engineers) (USA ISSN 0740-7475) **2471**
• I E E E Device Research Conference. Proceedings (Institute of Electrical and Electronics Engineers) (USA ISSN 1548-3770) **3101**
• I E E E Distributed Systems Online (Institute of Electrical and Electronics Engineers) (USA ISSN 1541-4922) **2520**
I E E E - E M B S Conference on Information Technology Applications in Biomedicine. Proceedings (Institute of Electrical and Electronics Engineers - Engineering in Medicine and Biology Society) (USA ISSN 1049-3565) **2420**
I E E E - E M C Society Newsletter (Institute of Electrical and Electronics Engineers - Electromagnetic Compatibility) (USA ISSN 1089-0785) **3311**
• ➤ I E E E Electrical Insulation Magazine (Institute of Electrical and Electronics Engineers) (USA ISSN 0883-7554) **3311**
• ➤ I E E E Electron Device Letters (Institute of Electrical and Electronics Engineers) (USA ISSN 0741-3106) **3101**
▼ • I E E E Embedded Systems Letters (USA ISSN 1943-0663) **2471**
I E E E Emerging Technologies Symposium (Institute of Electrical and Electronics Engineers) (USA) **2359**
• ➤ I E E E Engineering in Medicine and Biology Magazine (Institute of Electrical and Electronics Engineers) (USA ISSN 0739-5175) **748**
• I E E E Engineering in Medicine and Biology Society. Conference Proceedings (Institute of Electrical and Electronics Engineers) (USA ISSN 1557-170X) **5830**
I E E E Engineering in Medicine and Biology Society. International Conference *see* I E E E Engineering in Medicine and Biology Society. Conference Proceedings **5830**
• I E E E Engineering Management Review (Institute of Electrical and Electronics Engineers) (USA ISSN 0360-8581) **3196**
• I E E E European Test Workshop. Proceedings (Institute of Electrical and Electronics Engineers) (USA ISSN 1530-1877) **2471**
I E E E Ga As I C Symposium *see* I E E E Compound Semiconductor Integrated Circuit Symposium. Technical Digest **3101**
• I E E E Geoscience and Remote Sensing Letters (Institute of Electrical and Electronics Engineers) (USA ISSN 1545-598X) **3311**
I E E E Geoscience and Remote Sensing Society Newsletter (Institute of Electrical and Electronics Engineers) (USA ISSN 0274-6638) **3311**
I E E E German Microwave Theory and Techniques Society - Antennas and Propagation Joint Chapter. International Workshop Digest (Institute of Electrical and Electronics Engineers) (DEU ISSN 0938-8028) **3311**
I E E E Grid (Institute of Electrical and Electronics Engineers) (USA ISSN 0018-9189) **3311**
I E E E History Center (Institute of Electrical and Electronics Engineers) (USA) **3311**
I E E E Hong Kong Electron Devices Meeting (Institute of Electrical and Electronics Engineers) (USA) **3101**
• I E E E - I F I P Network Operations and Management Symposium (Institute of Electrical and Electronics Engineers - International Federation for Information Process) (USA ISSN 1542-1201) **2520**
• I E E E - I O N Position Location and Navigation Symposium. Record (Institute of Electrical and Electronics Engineers - Institute of Navigation) (USA) **3311**
▼ • I E E E Industrial Electronics Magazine (Institute of Electrical and Electronics Engineers) (USA ISSN 1932-4529) **3101**

• I E E E Industrial Electronics Society. Annual Conference. Proceedings (Institute of Electrical and Electronics Engineers) (USA ISSN 1553-572X) **4487**
I E E E Industrial Electronics Society Conference *see* I E E E Industrial Electronics Society. Annual Conference. Proceedings **4487**
I E E E Industry Applications Conference. Conference Record (Institute of Electrical and Electronics Engineers) (USA) **2493**
• I E E E Industry Applications Magazine (Institute of Electrical and Electronics Engineers) (USA ISSN 1077-2618) **3311**
• I E E E Infocom. Proceedings (Institute of Electrical and Electronics Engineers) (USA ISSN 0743-166X) **2350**
I E E E Information Technology Conference. Proceedings (Institute of Electrical and Electronics Engineers) (USA) **2520**
I E E E Information Theory and Communications Workshop (Institute of Electrical and Electronics Engineers) (USA) **2543**
I E E E Institute Newsletter *see* The Institute (New York) **3319**
• I E E E Instrumentation and Measurement Magazine (Institute of Electrical and Electronics Engineers) (USA ISSN 1094-6969) **6402**
• I E E E Instrumentation and Measurement Technology Conference. Proceedings (Institute of Electrical and Electronics Engineers) (USA ISSN 1091-5281) **4487**
I E E E Intelligent Network Workshop (Institute of Electrical and Electronics Engineers) (USA) **2323**
• ➤ I E E E Intelligent Systems (Institute of Electrical and Electronics Engineers) (USA ISSN 1541-1672) **2471**
I E E E Intelligent Transportation Systems Conference. Proceedings (Institute of Electrical and Electronics Engineers) (USA) **8498**
▼ • ➤ I E E E Intelligent Transportation Systems Magazine (Institute of Electrical and Electronics Engineers) (USA ISSN 1939-1390) **8498**
• I E E E Intelligent Vehicles Symposium (Institute of Electrical and Electronics Engineers) (USA ISSN 1931-0587) **8498**
I E E E International Automated Software Engineering Conference *see* I E E E / A C M International Conference on Automated Software Engineering **2590**
• I E E E International Carcas Conference on Devices Circuits and Systems. Proceedings (Institute of Electrical and Electronics Engineers) (USA ISSN 1541-6275) **3101**
• I E E E International Computer Software and Applications Conference. Proceedings (Institute of Electrical and Electronics Engineers) (USA ISSN 0730-3157) **2590**
• I E E E International Conference on Acoustics, Speech and Signal Processing. Proceedings (Institute of Electrical and Electronics Engineers) (USA ISSN 1520-6149) **3311**
I E E E International Conference on Advanced Robotics. Proceedings *see* International Conference on Advanced Robotics. Proceedings **2585**
• I E E E International Conference on Cluster Computing. Proceedings (Institute of Electrical and Electronics Engineers) (USA ISSN 1552-5244) **2497**
• I E E E International Conference on Communications (Institute of Electrical and Electronics Engineers) (USA ISSN 1550-3607) **2323**
• I E E E International Conference on Computer Design. V L S I in Computers & Processors. Proceedings (Institute of Electrical and Electronics Engineers) (USA ISSN 1063-6404) **2471**
• I E E E International Conference on Computer Vision. Proceedings (Institute of Electrical and Electronics Engineers) (USA ISSN 1550-5499) **2449**
• I E E E International Conference on Consumer Electronics. Digest of Technical Papers (Institute of Electrical and Electronics Engineers) (USA ISSN 0747-668X) **3101**
I E E E International Conference on Electronics, Circuits and Systems. Proceedings (Institute of Electrical and Electronics Engineers) (USA) **3101**
I E E E International Conference on Emerging Technologies and Factory Automation. Proceedings (Institute of Electrical and Electronics Engineers) (USA) **2460**
I E E E International Conference on Engineering of Complex Computer Systems. Proceedings (Institute of Electrical and Electronics Engineers) (USA) **2590**
• I E E E International Conference on Hardware-Software Codesign and System Synthesis (Institute of Electrical and Electronics Engineers) (USA) **2540**
I E E E International Conference on Industrial Informatics (Institute of Electrical and Electronics Engineers) (USA ISSN 1935-4576) **1751**
• I E E E International Conference on Information Visualisation (Year) (Institute of Electrical and Electronics Engineers) (USA ISSN 1550-6037) **2486**
• I E E E International Conference on Innovative Systems in Silicon (Institute of Electrical and Electronics Engineers) (USA ISSN 1094-7116) **2520**
I E E E International Conference on Intelligent Robots and Systems. Proceedings (Institute of Electrical and Electronics Engineers) (USA) **2584**
I E E E International Conference on Microelectronic Test Structures. Proceedings (Institute of Electrical and Electronics Engineers) (USA ISSN 1071-9032) **2465**
• I E E E International Conference on Microelectronics for Neural, Fuzzy and Bio-inspired Systems. Proceedings (Institute of Electrical and Electronics Engineers) (USA) **2498**
I E E E International Conference on Microelectronics Systems Education. Proceedings *see* International Conference on Microelectronic Systems Education. Proceedings **2540**
I E E E International Conference on Mobile Data Management. Mobile Data Management *see* I E E E International Conference on Mobile Data Management. Proceedings **2350**
I E E E International Conference on Mobile Data Management. Proceedings (Institute of Electrical and Electronic Engineers) (USA ISSN 1551-6245) **2350**
• I E E E International Conference on Multimedia Computing and Systems. Proceedings (Institute of Electrical and Electronics Engineers) (USA ISSN 1530-2032) **2467**
I E E E International Conference on Networking, Sensing and Control. Conference Proceedings (Institute of Electrical and Electronics Engineers) (USA ISSN 1810-7869) **2498**
I E E E International Conference on Networks. Proceedings *see* I E E E International Conference on Networks. Proceedings **2498**
• I E E E International Conference on Networks. Proceedings (USA ISSN 1556-6463) **2498**
I E E E International Conference on Personal Wireless Communications. Proceedings (Institute of Electrical and Electronics Engineers) (USA ISSN 1541-1354) **2359**
• I E E E International Conference on Plasma Science (Institute of Electrical and Electronics Engineers) (USA ISSN 0730-9244) **3311**
I E E E International Conference on Power Electronics, Drives and Energy for Industrial Growth. Proceedings (Institute of Electrical and Electronics Engineers) (USA) **3101**
• I E E E International Conference on Robotics and Automation. Proceedings (Institute of Electrical and Electronics Engineers) (USA ISSN 1050-4729) **2460**
I E E E International Conference on Semiconductor Electronics. Proceedings (Institute of Electrical and Electronics Engineers) (USA) **7051**
I E E E International Conference on Solid Dielectrics. Proceedings (Institute of Electrical and Electronics Engineers) (USA ISSN 1553-5282) **3312**
I E E E International Electric Machines and Drives Conference. Proceedings (Institute of Electrical and Electronics Engineers) (USA) **5452**
I E E E International Engineering Management Conference. Proceedings (Institute of Electrical and Electronics Engineers) (USA ISSN 1029-6735) **3196**
• I E E E International Frequency Control Symposium & Exposition. Proceedings (Institute of Electrical and Electronics Engineers) (USA ISSN 1932-2380) **3102**
I E E E International Frequency Control Symposium & P D A Exhibition. Proceedings *see* I E E E International Frequency Control Symposium & Exposition. Proceedings **3102**
• I E E E International Fuzzy Systems Conference. Proceedings (Institute of Electrical and Electronics Engineers) (USA ISSN 1544-5615) **2449**
I E E E International High-Level Design Validation and Test Workshop. Proceedings (Institute of Electrical and Electronics Engineers) (USA ISSN 1552-6674) **2471**
I E E E International Information Theory Workshop (Institute of Electrical and Electronics Engineers) (USA) **2543**
I E E E International Integrated Reliability Workshop *see* I E E E International Integrated Reliability Workshop Final Report **2420**
I E E E International Integrated Reliability Workshop Final Report (Institute of Electrical and Electronics Engineers) (USA ISSN 1930-8841) **2420**
I E E E International Nonvolatile Memory Technology Conference. Proceedings (Institute of Electrical and Electronics Engineers) (USA) **2531**
• I E E E International Performance, Computing, and Communications Conference. Proceedings (Institute of Electrical and Electronics Engineers) (USA ISSN 1097-2641) **2534**
I E E E International Power Electronics Congress (Institute of Electrical and Electronics Engineers) (USA) **3102**
I E E E International Reliability Physics Proceedings *see* I E E E International Reliability Physics Symposium. Proceedings **6402**
I E E E International Reliability Physics Symposium. Proceedings (Institute of Electrical and Electronics Engineers) (USA) **6402**
• I E E E International S O C Conference. Proceedings (Institute of Electrical and Electronics Engineers) (USA) **2465**
• ➤ I E E E International S O I Conference Proceedings (Institute of Electrical and Electronics Engineers, Silicon-On-Insulator) (USA ISSN 1078-621X) **3312**
• I E E E International Semiconductor Laser Conference. Conference Digest (Institute of Electrical and Electronics Engineers) (USA ISSN 0899-9406) **7076**
• I E E E International Solid State Circuits Conference. Digest of Technical Papers (Institute of Electrical and Electronics Engineers) (USA ISSN 0193-6530) **3102**
• I E E E International Symposium on Applications of Ferroelectrics (Institute of Electrical and Electronics Engineers) (USA ISSN 1099-4734) **7015**
I E E E International Symposium on Assembly and Manufacturing (USA) **2584**
I E E E International Symposium on Assembly and Task Planning *see* I E E E International Symposium on Assembly and Manufacturing **2584**
• I E E E International Symposium on Circuits and Systems. Proceedings (Institute of Electrical and Electronics Engineers) (USA ISSN 0271-4302) **3102**
I E E E International Symposium on Computational Intelligence in Robotics and Automation (Institute of Electrical and Electronics Engineers) (USA) **2449**
• I E E E International Symposium on Computers and Communications (Institute of Electrical and Electronics Engineers) (USA ISSN 1530-1346) **2590**
I E E E International Symposium on Defect and Fault - Tolerance in V L S I Systems. Proceedings *see* International Symposium on Defect and Fault - Tolerance in V L S I Systems. Proceedings **2540**
• I E E E International Symposium on Distributed Simulation and Real-Time Applications. Proceedings (Institute of Electrical and Electronics Engineers) (USA ISSN 1550-6525) **2517**
• I E E E International Symposium on Electrical Insulation. Conference Record (Institute of Electrical and Electronics Engineers) (USA ISSN 0164-2006) **3312**
• I E E E International Symposium on Electromagnetic Compatibility. Symposium Record (Institute of Electrical and Electronics Engineers) (USA ISSN 1077-4076) **3312**
• I E E E International Symposium on Electronics and the Environment (Institute of Electrical and Electronics Engineers) (USA ISSN 1095-2020) **3102**
• I E E E International Symposium on High-Assurance Systems Engineering (Institute of Electrical and Electronics Engineers) (USA ISSN 1530-2059) **2590**
• I E E E International Symposium on Information Theory. Proceedings (Institute of Electrical and Electronics Engineers) (USA) **2544**
I E E E International Symposium on Intelligent Control. Proceedings (Institute of Electrical and Electronics Engineers) (USA) **2449**
• I E E E International Symposium on Phased Array Systems and Technology (Institute of Electrical and Electronics Engineers) (USA ISSN 1554-8422) **2520**
I E E E International Symposium on Semiconductor Manufacturing Conference Proceedings (Institute of Electrical and Electronics Engineers) (USA ISSN 1523-553X) **2471**
• I E E E International Symposium on V L S I Technology. Proceedings of Technical Papers (Institute of Electrical and Electronics Engineers, Very-Large-Scale Integration) (USA ISSN 1930-8868) **2465**
I E E E International Symposium on V L S I Technology, Systems and Applications. Proceedings of Technical Papers *see* I E E E International Symposium on V L S I Technology. Proceedings of Technical Papers **2465**
• I E E E International Symposium on Workload Characterization. Proceedings (Institute of Electrical and Electronics Engineers) (USA) **3312**
I E E E International Symposium Personal, Indoor and Mobile Radio Communications (Institute of Electrical and Electronics Engineers) (USA) **2359**
I E E E International Symposium Spread Spectrum Techniques and Applications (Institute of Electrical and Electronics Engineers) (USA) **2359**
I E E E International Telecommunications Symposium (Institute of Electrical and Electronics Engineers) (USA) **2323**
• I E E E International Ultrasonics Symposium. Proceedings (Institute of Electrical and Electronics Engineers) (USA) **7087**
I E E E International Vacuum Nanoelectronics Conference (Institute of Electrical and Electronics Engineers) (USA) **2465**
I E E E International Vehicle Electronics Conference Proceedings (Institute of Electrical and Electronics Engineers) (USA) **8498**
I E E E International Workshop on Current and Defect Based Testing (Institute of Electrical and Electronics Engineers) (USA) **2540**
• I E E E International Workshop on Imaging Systems and Techniques (Institute of Electrical and Electronics Engineers) (USA ISSN 1558-2809) **2420**
I E E E International Workshop on Integrated Power Packaging (Institute of Electrical and Electronics Engineers) (USA) **2420**
• I E E E International Workshop on Memory Technology, Design and Testing (Institute of Electrical and Electronics Engineers) (USA ISSN 1087-4852) **2540**
I E E E International Workshop on Mobile Commerce and Services. Proceedings (USA ISSN 1933-7965) **3312**
I E E E International Workshop on Source Code Analysis and Manipulation. Proceedings *see* IEEE International Working Conference on Source Code Analysis and Manipulation. Proceedings **2507**
I E E E International Workshop on Workload Characterization. Proceedings *see* I E E E International Symposium on Workload Characterization. Proceedings **3312**
• I E E E International Workshops on Enabling Technologies: Infrastructure for Collaborative Enterprises. Proceedings (Institute of Electrical and Electronics Engineers) (USA ISSN 1524-4547) **3312**
• ➤ I E E E Internet Computing (Institute of Electrical and Electronics Engineers) (USA ISSN 1089-7801) **2557**
• ➤ I E E E Journal of Microelectromechanical Systems (Institute of Electrical and Electronics Engineers) (USA ISSN 1057-7157) **3312**
• ➤ I E E E Journal of Oceanic Engineering (Institute of Electrical and Electronics Engineers) (USA ISSN 0364-9059) **3312**
• ➤ I E E E Journal of Quantum Electronics (Institute of Electrical and Electronics Engineers) (USA ISSN 0018-9197) **3102**
▼ • I E E E Journal of Selected Topics in Applied Earth Observations and Remote Sensing (Institute of Electrical and Electronics Engineers) (USA ISSN 1939-1404) **3196**
• ➤ I E E E Journal of Solid State Circuits (Institute of Electrical and Electronics Engineers) (USA ISSN 0018-9200) **3312**
I E E E Journal of Solid-State Circuits CD-ROM *see* I E E E Journal of Solid State Circuits **3312**
† • ➤ I E E E Journal of Technology Computer Aided Design (Institute of Electrical and Electronics Engineers) (USA) **8963**
• ➤ I E E E Journal on Selected Areas in Communications (Institute of Electrical and Electronics Engineers) (USA ISSN 0733-8716) **2323**
• ➤ I E E E Journal on Selected Topics in Quantum Electronics (Institute of Electrical and Electronics Engineers) (USA ISSN 1077-260X) **3102**
▼ • I E E E Journal on Selected Topics in Signal Processing (Institute of Electrical and Electronics Engineers) (USA ISSN 1932-4553) **3312**
• I E E E Knowledge and Data Exchange Workshop. Proceedings (Institute of Electrical and Electronics Engineers) (USA ISSN 1530-096X) **2534**
I E E E L E O S (Institute Of Electrical And Electronics Engineers Lasers & Electro-Optics Society) (USA) **7076**
I E E E L E O S Newsletter *see* I E E E Photonics Society News **7076**
• I E E E Lasers and Electro-Optics Society. Annual Meeting (Institute of Electrical and Electronics Engineers) (USA ISSN 1092-8081) **7076**
I E E E Lasers & Electro-Optics Society. Newsletter *see* I E E E L E O S **7076**
I E E E Latin America Transactions *see* I E E E America Latina. Revista **3362**
• I E E E Lester Eastman Conference on High Performance Devices (Institute of Electrical and Electronics Engineers) (USA ISSN 1550-4905) **3312**
• I E E E - M T T S International Microwave Symposium. Digest (Institute of Electrical and Electronics Engineers - Microwave Theory and Techniques Society) (USA ISSN 0149-645X) **3312**
I E E E - M T T S International Topical Symposium on Technologies for Wireless Applications (Institute of Electrical and Electronics Engineers, Microwave Theory and Techniques Society) (USA) **2359**
• ➤ I E E E Micro (Institute of Electrical and Electronics Engineers) (USA ISSN 0272-1732) **2571**
• I E E E Microwave and Wireless Components Letters (Institute of Electrical and Electronics Engineers) (USA ISSN 1531-1309) **3312**
• I E E E Microwave Magazine (Institute of Electrical and Electronics Engineers) (USA ISSN 1527-3342) **3312**
I E E E Midnight - Sun Workshop on Soft Computing in Industrial Applications (Institute of Electrical and Electronics Engineers) (USA) **2420**

• I E E E Military Communications Conference. Conference Record (Institute of Electrical and Electronics Engineers) (USA) **3313**

I E E E Military Communications Conference. Proceedings *see* I E E E Military Communications Conference. Conference Record **3313**

• I E E E Multidisciplinary Engineering Education Magazine (Institute of Electrical and Electronics Engineers) (USA ISSN 1558-7908) **3313**

• ➤ I E E E MultiMedia Magazine (Institute of Electrical and Electronics Engineers) (USA ISSN 1070-986X) **2486**

• ➤ I E E E - N P S S Symposium on Fusion Engineering. Proceedings (Institute of Electrical and Electronics Engineers, Nuclear and Plasma Sciences Society) (USA ISSN 1078-8891) **3168**

▼ • ➤ I E E E Nanotechnology Magazine (Institute of Electrical and Electronics Engineers) (USA ISSN 1932-4510) **2571**

• I E E E National Radar Conference. Proceedings (Institute of Electrical and Electronics Engineers) (USA ISSN 1097-5659) **3313**

• ➤ I E E E Network (Institute of Electrical and Electronics Engineers) (USA ISSN 0890-8044) **2498**

I E E E Neural Networks for Signal Processing *see* Machine Learning for Signal Processing **2454**

I E E E Neural Networks Society. Connections *see* I E E E coNNections **2471**

I E E E Normen Nachrichten *see* I E E E StandardsWire **6402**

I E E E Nouvelle des Normes *see* I E E E StandardsWire **6402**

• I E E E Nuclear Science Symposium Conference Record (Institute of Electrical and Electronics Engineers) (USA ISSN 1095-7863) **6198**

I E E E - O S A Journal of Display Technology *see* Journal of Display Technology **3106**

I E E E Oceanic Engineering Society. Newsletter (USA ISSN 0746-7834) **3313**

I E E E Open Architectures and Network Programming (Institute of Electrical and Electronics Engineers) (USA) **2323**

• I E E E Optical Communications (Institute of Electrical and Electronics Engineers) (USA) **2323**

I E E E Orlando Section Monthly (Institute of Electrical and Electronics Engineers) (USA) **3313**

• I E E E Pacific Rim Conference on Communications, Computers and Signal Processing. Conference Proceedings (Institute of Electrical and Electronics Engineers) (USA ISSN 1555-5798) **2350**

I E E E Pacific Rim International Symposium on Dependable Computing. Proceedings (Institute of Electrical and Electronics Engineers) (USA ISSN 1555-094X) **2420**

• I E E E Particle Accelerator Conference. Conference Record (Institute of Electrical and Electronics Engineers) (USA ISSN 1063-3928) **3313**

• ➤ I E E E Pervasive Computing (Institute of Electrical and Electronics Engineers) (USA ISSN 1536-1268) **2420**

▼ • I E E E Photonics Journal (USA ISSN 1943-0655) **7076**

• I E E E Photonics Society News (Institute of Electrical and Electronics Engineers) (USA ISSN 1949-128X) **7076**

• ➤ I E E E Photonics Technology Letters (Institute of Electrical and Electronics Engineers) (USA ISSN 1041-1135) **7076**

• I E E E Photovoltaic Specialists Conference. Conference Record (Institute of Electrical and Electronics Engineers) (USA ISSN 0160-8371) **3313**

I E E E Position Location and Navigation Symposium. Record *see* I E E E - I O N Position Location and Navigation Symposium. Record **3311**

• I E E E Potentials (Institute of Electrical and Electronics Engineers) (USA ISSN 0278-6648) **3313**

• I E E E Power & Energy Magazine (Institute of Electrical and Electronics Engineers) (USA ISSN 1540-7977) **7015**

• I E E E Power Electronics Letters (Institute of Electrical and Electronics Engineers) (USA ISSN 1540-7985) **7015**

I E E E Power Electronics Specialists Conference. Conference Proceedings *see* I E E E Power Electronics Specialists Conference. Proceedings **59**

• I E E E Power Electronics Specialists Conference. Proceedings (Institute of Electrical and Electronics Engineers) (USA) **59**

I E E E Power Engineering Society. Discussions and Closures of Abstracted Papers from the Summer Meeting (Institute of Electrical and Electronics Engineers) (USA ISSN 0160-0141) **3196**

I E E E Power Engineering Society General Meeting (Institute of Electrical and Electronics Engineers) (USA ISSN 1932-5517) **3313**

† • I E E E Power Engineering Society. Summer Meeting. Preprints (Institute of Electrical and Electronics Engineers) (USA) **8963**

† • I E E E Power Engineering Society. Winter Meeting. Preprints (Institute of Electrical and Electronics Engineers) (USA ISSN 0073-9154) **8963**

• I E E E Publication Services and Products Board. Quarterly Newsletter (Institute of Electrical and Electronics Engineers) (USA) **3230**

• I E E E Pulsed Power Conference. Digest of Technical Papers (Institute of Electrical and Electronics Engineers) (USA) **3159**

• ➤ I E E E - R I T A (ESP ISSN 1932-8540) **2865**

• I E E E Radar Conference. Proceedings (Institute of Electrical and Electronics Engineers) (USA ISSN 1097-5764) **59**

I E E E Radio and Wireless Conference. Proceedings *see* I E E E Radio and Wireless Symposium. Proceedings **2359**

I E E E Radio and Wireless Symposium. Proceedings (Institute of Electrical and Electronics Engineers) (USA) **2359**

I E E E Radio Communications *see* I E E E Communications Magazine **3311**

• I E E E Radio Frequency Integrated Circuits Symposium. Digest of Papers (Institute of Electrical and Electronics Engineers) (USA ISSN 1529-2517) **2465**

• I E E E Real-Time Systems Education Workshop (Institute of Electrical and Electronics Engineers) (USA ISSN 1530-132X) **2520**

I E E E Real-Time Systems Symposium. Proceedings *see* Real-Time Systems Symposium **2524**

• I E E E Real-Time Technology and Applications Symposium. Proceedings (Institute of Electrical and Electronics Engineers) (USA ISSN 1545-3421) **3291**

▼ • ➤ I E E E Reviews in Biomedical Engineering (Institute of Electrical and Electronics Engineers) (USA ISSN 1937-3333) **5631**

I E E E. Revista Mexicana de Electricidad/Mexican Electricity Review (Institute of Electrical and Electronics Engineers) (MEX ISSN 0187-5736) **3313**

• ➤ I E E E Robotics and Automation Magazine (Institute of Electrical and Electronics Engineers) (USA ISSN 1070-9932) **2584**

• ➤ I E E E - S E M I Advanced Semiconductor Manufacturing Conference and Workshop (Institute of Electrical and Electronics Engineers, Semiconductor Equipment and Materials Institute) (USA ISSN 1078-8743) **3313**

I E E E - S P International Symposium on Time-Frequency and Time-Scale Analysis (Institute of Electrical and Electronics Engineers) (USA) **2534**

I E E E / S P Workshop on Statistical Signal and Array Processing (Institute of Electrical and Electronics Engineers. Signal Processing Society) (USA) **2471**

▼ • I E E E S S C S News (Institute of Electrical and Electronics Engineers Solid-State Circuits Society) (USA) **3313**

• I E E E Security & Privacy Magazine (Institute of Electrical and Electronics Engineers) (USA ISSN 1540-7993) **2513**

I E E E Semiconducting and Insulating Materials Conference. Proceedings (Institute of Electrical and Electronics Engineers) (USA) **7051**

• I E E E Semiconductor Thermal Measurement and Management Symposium (Institute of Electrical and Electronics Engineers) (USA ISSN 1065-2221) **7051**

I E E E Sensor Array and Multichannel Signal Proceeding Workshop Proceedings *see* Sensor Array and Multichannel Signal Processing. I E E E Workshop **2466**

• ➤ I E E E Sensors Journal (Institute of Electrical and Electronics Engineers) (USA ISSN 1530-437X) **4487**

I E E E Sensors. Proceedings (Institute of Electrical and Electronics Engineers) (USA ISSN 1930-0395) **2421**

• ➤ I E E E Signal Processing Letters (Institute of Electrical and Electronics Engineers) (USA ISSN 1070-9908) **3313**

• ➤ I E E E - Signal Processing Magazine (Institute of Electrical and Electronics Engineers) (USA ISSN 1053-5888) **7087**

I E E E Signal Processing on Higher Order Statistics (Institute of Electrical and Electronics Engineers) (USA) **2540**

• ➤ I E E E Software (Institute of Electrical and Electronics Engineers) (USA ISSN 0740-7459) **2590**

• I E E E Solid State Circuits Magazine (Institute of Electrical and Electronics Engineers) (USA ISSN 1943-0582) **3102**

I E E E Solid - State Circuits Society News *see* I E E E Solid State Circuits Magazine **3102**

• I E E E Solid-State Sensor and Actuator Workshop. Technical Digest (Institute of Electrical and Electronics Engineers) (USA) **3313**

I E E E South African Symposium on Communications and Signal Processing (Institute of Electrical and Electronics Engineers) (USA) **2324**

I E E E Southeastcon. Proceedings (Institute of Electrical and Electronics Engineers) (USA ISSN 1091-0050) **3313**

• I E E E Southwest Symposium on Image Analysis and Interpretation. Proceedings (Institute of Electrical and Electronics Engineers) (USA ISSN 1550-5782) **2421**

• ➤ I E E E Spectrum (Institute of Electrical and Electronics Engineers) (USA ISSN 0018-9235) **3313**

I E E E Standards Bearer *see* I E E E StandardsWire **6402**

I E E E Standards Bearer (British Edition) *see* I E E E StandardsWire **6402**

• I E E E StandardsWire (Institute of Electrical and Electronics Engineers) (USA) **6402**

I E E E Student Papers (Institute of Electrical and Electronics Engineers) (USA ISSN 0362-4536) **3313**

• I E E E Symposium on Autonomous Underwater Vehicle Technology (Institute of Electrical and Electronics Engineers) (USA ISSN 1522-3167) **2806**

• I E E E Symposium on Computer - Based Medical Systems. Proceedings (Institute of Electrical and Electronics Engineers) (USA ISSN 1063-7125) **5831**

• I E E E Symposium on Information Visualization (Institute of Electrical and Electronics Engineers) (USA ISSN 1093-9547) **2486**

• I E E E Symposium on Mass Storage Systems. Digest of Papers (Institute of Electrical and Electronics Engineers) (USA ISSN 1051-9173) **2421**

• I E E E Symposium on Parallel and Distributed Processing. Proceedings (Institute of Electrical and Electronics Engineers) (USA ISSN 1063-6374) **2536**

• I E E E Symposium on Security and Privacy. Proceedings (Institute of Electrical and Electronics Engineers) (USA ISSN 1081-6011) **2513**

• ➤ I E E E Symposium on V L S I Circuits (Institute of Electrical and Electronics Engineers) (USA) **3314**

I E E E Symposium on V L S I Technology (Institute of Electrical and Electronics Engineers, Very Large Scale Integration) (USA ISSN 0743-1562) **2540**

• I E E E Symposium on Visual Languages and Human-Centric Computing. Proceedings (Institute of Electrical and Electronics Engineers) (USA) **5202**

▼ • I E E E Systems Journal (Institute of Electrical and Electronics Engineers) (USA ISSN 1932-8184) **2520**

• ➤ I E E E Technology and Society Magazine (Institute of Electrical and Electronics Engineers) (USA ISSN 0278-0097) **8424**

• I E E E Textile, Fiber and Film Industry Technical Conference. Proceedings (Institute of Electrical and Electronics Engineers) (USA ISSN 1049-3328) **8452**

• ➤ I E E E Transactions on Advanced Packaging (Institute of Electrical and Electronics Engineers) (USA ISSN 1521-3323) **3314**

• ➤ I E E E Transactions on Aerospace and Electronic Systems (Institute of Electrical and Electronics Engineers) (USA ISSN 0018-9251) **3314**

• ➤ I E E E Transactions on Antennas and Propagation (Institute of Electrical and Electronics Engineers) (USA ISSN 0018-926X) **3314**

• ➤ I E E E Transactions on Applied Superconductivity (Institute of Electrical and Electronics Engineers) (USA ISSN 1051-8223) **3102**

• ➤ I E E E Transactions on Audio, Speech and Language Processing (Institute of Electrical and Electronics Engineers) (USA ISSN 1558-7916) **2351**

• ➤ I E E E Transactions on Automatic Control (Institute of Electrical and Electronics Engineers) (USA ISSN 0018-9286) **3314**

• I E E E Transactions on Automation Science and Engineering (Institute of Electrical and Electronics Engineers) (USA ISSN 1545-5955) **3314**

▼ • I E E E Transactions on Autonomous Mental Development (Institute of Electrical and Electronics Engineers) (USA ISSN 1943-0604) **7361**

▼ • I E E E Transactions on Biomedical Circuits and Systems (Institute of Electrical and Electronics Engineers) (USA ISSN 1932-4545) **748**

• ➤ I E E E Transactions on Biomedical Engineering (Institute of Electrical and Electronics Engineers) (USA ISSN 0018-9294) **749**

• ➤ I E E E Transactions on Broadcasting (Institute of Electrical and Electronics Engineers) (USA ISSN 0018-9316) **2382**

• ➤ I E E E Transactions on Circuits and Systems for Video Technology (Institute of Electrical and Electronics Engineers) (USA ISSN 1051-8215) **3102**

I E E E Transactions on Circuits and Systems Part 1: Fundamental Theory and Applications *see* I E E E Transactions on Circuits and Systems Part 1: Regular Papers **3102**

• ➤ I E E E Transactions on Circuits and Systems Part 1: Regular Papers (Institute of Electrical and Electronics Engineers) (USA ISSN 1549-8328) **3102**

I E E E Transactions on Circuits and Systems Part 2: Analog and Digital Signal Processing *see* I E E E Transactions on Circuits and Systems. Part 2: Express Briefs **3102**

• ➤ I E E E Transactions on Circuits and Systems. Part 2: Express Briefs (Institute of Electrical and Electronics Engineers) (USA ISSN 1549-7747) **3102**

• ➤ I E E E Transactions on Communications (Institute of Electrical and Electronics Engineers) (USA ISSN 0090-6778) **2324**

• ➤ I E E E Transactions on Components and Packaging Technology (Institute of Electrical and Electronics Engineers) (USA ISSN 1521-3331) **3314**

▼ • I E E E Transactions on Computational Intelligence and A I in Games (Institute of Electrical and Electronics Engineers) (USA ISSN 1943-068X) **2449**

• ➤ I E E E Transactions on Computer - Aided Design of Integrated Circuits and Systems (Institute of Electrical and Electronics Engineers) (USA ISSN 0278-0070) **3117**

• ➤ I E E E Transactions on Computers (Institute of Electrical and Electronics Engineers) (USA ISSN 0018-9340) **2421**

• ➤ I E E E Transactions on Consumer Electronics (Institute of Electrical and Electronics Engineers) (USA ISSN 0098-3063) **3102**

• ➤ I E E E Transactions on Control Systems Technology (Institute of Electrical and Electronics Engineers) (USA ISSN 1063-6536) **3314**

• I E E E Transactions on Dependable and Secure Computing (Institute of Electrical and Electronics Engineers) (USA ISSN 1545-5971) **2513**

• I E E E Transactions on Device and Materials Reliability (Institute of Electrical and Electronics Engineers) (USA ISSN 1530-4388) **3103**

• ➤ I E E E Transactions on Dielectrics and Electrical Insulation (Institute of Electrical and Electronics Engineers) (USA ISSN 1070-9878) **3314**

• ➤ I E E E Transactions on Education (Institute of Electrical and Electronics Engineers) (USA ISSN 0018-9359) **3314**

• ➤ I E E E Transactions on Electromagnetic Compatibility (Institute of Electrical and Electronics Engineers) (USA ISSN 0018-9375) **3103**

• ➤ I E E E Transactions on Electron Devices (Institute of Electrical and Electronics Engineers) (USA ISSN 0018-9383) **3103**

• I E E E Transactions on Electronics Packaging Manufacturing (Institute of Electrical and Electronics Engineers) (USA ISSN 1521-334X) **3315**

• ➤ I E E E Transactions on Energy Conversion (Institute of Electrical and Electronics Engineers) (USA ISSN 0885-8969) **3159**

• ➤ I E E E Transactions on Engineering Management (Institute of Electrical and Electronics Engineers) (USA ISSN 0018-9391) **3315**

• I E E E Transactions on Evolutionary Computation (Institute of Electrical and Electronics Engineers) (USA ISSN 1089-778X) **2421**

• ➤ I E E E Transactions on Fuzzy Systems (Institute of Electrical and Electronics Engineers) (USA ISSN 1063-6706) **2449**

• ➤ I E E E Transactions on Geoscience and Remote Sensing (Institute of Electrical and Electronics Engineers) (USA ISSN 0196-2892) **3315**

▼ I E E E Transactions on Haptics (Institute of Electrical and Electronics Engineers) (USA ISSN 1939-1412) **2584**

• ➤ I E E E Transactions on Image Processing (Institute of Electrical and Electronics Engineers) (USA ISSN 1057-7149) **2486**

• ➤ I E E E Transactions on Industrial Electronics (Institute of Electrical and Electronics Engineers) (USA ISSN 0278-0046) **3103**

• I E E E Transactions on Industrial Informatics (Institute of Electrical and Electronics Engineers) (USA ISSN 1551-3203) **3315**

• ➤ I E E E Transactions on Industry Applications (Institute of Electrical and Electronics Engineers) (USA ISSN 0093-9994) **3315**

• I E E E Transactions on Information Forensics and Security (Institute of Electrical and Electronics Engineers) (USA ISSN 1556-6013) **2513**

• I E E E Transactions on Information Technology in Biomedicine (Institute of Electrical and Electronics Engineers) (USA ISSN 1089-7771) **765**

• ➤ I E E E Transactions on Information Theory (Institute of Electrical and Electronics Engineers) (USA ISSN 0018-9448) **2544**

• ➤ I E E E Transactions on Instrumentation and Measurement (Institute of Electrical and Electronics Engineers) (USA ISSN 0018-9456) **6402**

• ➤ I E E E Transactions on Intelligent Transportation Systems (Institute of Electrical and Electronics Engineers) (USA ISSN 1524-9050) **8498**

• ➤ I E E E Transactions on Knowledge & Data Engineering (Institute of Electrical and Electronics Engineers) (USA ISSN 1041-4347) **3315**

Title

I F U. Informe Anual *see* I F U. Annual Report **1597**
I F U. Rapport Annuel *see* I F U. Annual Report **1597**
I F - Zeitschrift fuer Internationale Freimaurer-Forschung *see* Internationale Freimaurer-Forschung **2267**
• I Form (DNK ISSN 0902-1620) **6989**
• I G (Infoglis) (SWE ISSN 1652-7992) **4375**
I G A B Newsletter Bureau Talk (International Group of Agencies and Bureaus) (USA) **2324**
I G A Grocergram (Independent Grocers Alliance) (USA ISSN 0018-9766) **3679**
I G A R S S *see* International Geoscience and Remote Sensing Symposium Digest **4016**
I G B *see* Indian Gaming Business **8179**
• I G B Berichte (Leibniz-Institut fuer Gewaesseroekologie und Binnenfischerei) (DEU ISSN 1432-508X) **677**
I G B P Book Series (International Geosphere-Biosphere Programme) (SWE ISSN 1368-8766) **2746**
I G B P Directory (International Geosphere-Biosphere Programme) (SWE) **2746**
➤ I G B P Global Change Report (International Geosphere-Biosphere Programme) (SWE ISSN 0284-8015) **2746**
I G B P Science (International Geosphere - Biosphere Programme) (SWE ISSN 1650-7770) **7971**
I G D R *see* Indian Growth and Development Review **1122**
I G e L Aktiv (Individuelle Gesundheitsleistungen) (DEU ISSN 1612-1902) **5631**
• I G E L Newsletter (Online) (DEU) **2521**
I G E L Newsletter (Print) *see* I G E L Newsletter (Online) **2521**
I G e L Plus (Individuelle Gesundheitsleistungen) (DEU ISSN 1866-282X) **5631**
I G E R Annual Report & Accounts (Institute of Grassland and Environmental Research) (GBR ISSN 1463-6255) **235**
• I G E R Innovations (Institute of Grassland and Environmental Research) (GBR ISSN 1368-5503) **235**
I G E R Technical Advisory Report *see* Institute of Grassland and Environmental Research (UK). Technical Advisory Report **237**
I G E R Technical Review (Institute of Grassland and Environmental Research) (GBR ISSN 1358-5991) **235**
I G F - Journal (International Graphical Federation) (BEL ISSN 0018-9782) **7323**
I G I V Insights & Viewpoints (Immune Globulin) (GBR ISSN 1751-6218) **5938**
• I G Living (Immune Globulin) (USA ISSN 1949-4548) **6847**
I G Medien Forum *see* Druck und Papier **7320**
• I G O Report (Intergovernmental Organizations) (USA) **1568**
• I G P C Newsletter (International Guild of Professional Consultants) (USA) **1961**
I G S *see* International Gambling Studies **7363**
• ➤ I G T na Rede (Instituto de Gestalt - Terapia) (BRA ISSN 1807-2526) **7361**
I G T R *see* International Game Theory Review **8426**
• I G U Bulletin/Bulletin de l'U G I (International Geographical Union) (DEU ISSN 0018-9804) **4014**
I G - U S P. Boletim. Publicacao Especial (Instituto de Geociencias - Universidade de Sao Paulo) (BRA ISSN 0102-6275) **2709**
I G - U S P. Boletim. Serie Cientifica (Instituto de Geociencias - Universidade de Sao Paulo) (BRA ISSN 0102-6283) **2709**
I G - U S P. Boletim. Serie Didatica (Instituto de Geociencias - Universidade de Sao Paulo) (BRA ISSN 0102-6291) **2709**
➤ I G W M C Conference. Proceedings (International Ground Water Modeling Center) (USA) **2795**
• I G W M C Ground Water Modeling Newsletter (International Ground Water Modeling Center) (USA ISSN 0741-8507) **2795**
• I Garden (GBR) **3738**
I H *see* Hosteleria y Turismo **4388**
I H *see* Industrial Heating **3368**
I H 3 P A Newsletter *see* International Home and Private Poker Players Newsletter **8180**
I H A News (CHE) **1820**
I H D Frontier *see* Ischemic Heart Disease Frontier **5791**
• I H D P Update (International Human Dimensions Programme on Global Environmental Change) (DEU ISSN 1727-155X) **7971**
I H E Delft Lecture Note Series (International Institute for Infrastructural, Hydraulic and Environmental Engineering) (NLD ISSN 1567-7052) **3362**
• I H E Information (Institutet foer Haelso- och Sjukvaardsekonomi) (SWE ISSN 0349-5175) **5631**
• I H E Rapport (Institutet foer Haelso- och Sjukvaardsekonomi) (SWE ISSN 1651-7598) **1888**
I H F Management Handbooks (International Hospital Federation) (GBR) **4102**
I H F Reference Book *see* The International Hospital Federation. Reference Book **4102**
I H F Yearbook *see* Hospital Management International **4100**
I H F Yearbook *see* The International Hospital Federation. Reference Book **4102**
I H I Engineering Review (Ishikawajima-Harima Heavy Industries Co. Ltd.) (JPN ISSN 0018-9820) **8646**
I H J Bulletin (International House of Japan Inc.) (JPN ISSN 0285-2608) **7240**
I H K Journal Koblenz (Industrie- und Handelskammer) (DEU ISSN 0936-4579) **1404**
I H K Lippe Info (Industrie- und Handelskammer Lippe zu Detmold) (DEU) **1404**
I H K Magazin Erfurt (Industrie- und Handelskammer) (DEU) **1404**
I H K Magazin Krefeld, Moenchengladbach, Neuss und Viersen (Industrie- und Handelskammer) (DEU ISSN 1864-4406) **1404**
• I H K Plus (Industrie- und Handelskammer) (DEU) **1404**
I H K Report Suedhessen (Industrie- und Handelskammer) (DEU ISSN 1433-8610) **1404**
I H K Wirtschaft (Industrie- und Handelskammer) (DEU ISSN 1434-5072) **1404**
I H K WirtschaftsForum (Industrie- und Handelskammer) (DEU) **1404**
I H K Wirtschaftsspiegel (Industrie- und Handelskammer) (DEU) **1404**
I H K - Zeitung (Industrie- und Handelskammer) (DEU ISSN 1438-5740) **1405**
I H L I A Nieuwsbrief (International Homo/Lesbisch Informatiecentrum en Archief) (NLD ISSN 1872-1494) **4375**
• I H M F News (International Herpes Management Forum) (GBR ISSN 1750-1253) **5816**
I H M Yearbook *see* The Health and Social Care Yearbook **7521**
I H N *see* International Humanist News **6925**
I H N News (International Handicapper's Net) (USA ISSN 1042-4334) **4066**
I H P Humid Tropics Programme Series (International Hydrological Programme) (FRA) **3438**
I H R *see* Internationales Handelsrecht **1572**
I H R I M *see* Institute of Health Record Information & Management. Journal **5635**
I H R I M e-Journal *see* International Association for Human Resource Information Management e-Journal **1866**
I H R I M Journal *see* International Association for Human Resource Information Management Journal **1866**
➤ I H R I M.link (International Association for Human Resource Information Management) (USA ISSN 1089-991X) **1865**
I H R R *see* International Human Rights Reports **7210**
I H S J *see* Italian Historical Society Journal **4233**
I H S M Health and Social Services Database CD-ROM *see* The Health and Social Care Yearbook **7521**
• I H S Primary Care Provider (Indian Health Service) (USA ISSN 1063-4398) **8045**
• I Hate Computers (USA ISSN 1076-7967) **2421**
▼ I Heart Magazine (USA ISSN 1942-9436) **6969**
• I I (International Institute) (USA ISSN 1074-9055) **7240**
I I A S A Annual Report (International Institute for Applied Systems Analysis) (AUT ISSN 0304-7121) **3482**
I I A S A Reports (International Institute for Applied Systems Analysis) (AUT ISSN 0250-7625) **3482**
• I I A S Newsletter (International Institute for Asian Studies) (NLD ISSN 0929-8738) **4183**
I I A S Publications Series (International Institute for Asian Studies) (NLD) **551**
I I B P Full Text *see* International Index to Black Periodicals Full Text **3574**
I I C A Documentacao (Instituto de Investigacao Cientifica de Angola, Departamento de Documentacao e Informacao) (AGO ISSN 0018-9863) **7937**
I I C Annual *see* International and Intercultural Communication Annual **8108**
I I C Annual Report (Inter-American Investment Corporation) (USA) **1352**
I I C Bulletin (Institute of Inorganic Chemistry) (CZE) **2116**
I I C I T News (International Institute of Connector and Interconnection Technology, Inc.) (USA) **3104**
• ➤ I I C - International Review of Intellectual Property and Competition Law (DEU) **6751**
• I I C S Newsline (International Interactive Communications Society) (USA) **2351**
I I C Studies (GBR ISSN 0930-2395) **6751**
I I E C E-Notes (International Institute for Energy Conservation - Africa) (ZAF) **3438**
I I E Network Memberhip Directory (Institute of International Education) (USA ISSN 1933-3331) **2865**
IIENetworker Magazine (USA ISSN 1937-0946) **3013**
• I I E P Newsletter (International Institute for Educational Planning) (FRA ISSN 1564-2356) **2865**
I I E P Occasional Papers (International Institute for Educational Planning) (FRA ISSN 0074-6401) **3024**
I I E P Research Reports (International Institute for Educational Planning) (FRA) **3024**
I I E P Seminar Papers (International Institute for Educational Planning) (FRA) **3024**
I I E P Studies Series (International Institute for Educational Planning) (FRA) **3024**
I I E Revista (Universidad Boliviana Tecnica de Oruro, Instituto de Investigaciones Economicas) (BOL) **1121**
I I E S Exchange (Institute for the International Education of Students) (USA) **3013**
• ➤ I I E Transactions (Institute of Industrial Engineers) (USA ISSN 0740-817X) **3367**
• I I F Newsletter (Indian Institute of Finance) (IND ISSN 0970-3780) **1352**
I.I. Grekov Annals of Surgery *see* Vestnik Khirurgii im. I.I. Grekova **6262**
I I H R Report (Iowa Institute of Hydraulic Research) (USA ISSN 0578-6444) **3362**
I.I.I. Insurance Daily (Insurance Information Institute) (USA) **4505**
• I + I Informe de Investigacion (CHL ISSN 0718-4271) **2865**
I I M C News Digest (International Institute of Municipal Clerks) (USA ISSN 0145-2290) **7494**
• ➤ I I M Metal News (Indian Institute of Metals) (IND ISSN 0972-0480) **6315**
I I M P *see* International Index to Music Periodicals **6631**
I I P A *see* International Index to the Performing Arts **8485**
I I P A Newsletter (Indian Institute of Public Administration) (IND) **7445**
I I P Occasional Paper (International Institute for Peace) (AUT) **7240**
I I P S Newsletter (International Institute for Population Sciences) (IND) **7284**
I I R A Bulletin (International Industrial Relations Association) (CHE) **1686**
I I R B Congress Proceedings *see* International Institute for Beet Research. Congress Proceedings **237**
I I R - Forum *see* D I I R - Forum **1737**
The I I R Newsletter (International Institute of Refrigeration) (FRA) **4120**
I I R R Report (International Institute of Rural Reconstruction) (USA ISSN 1011-8721) **1597**
I I T C Bulletin (Indian International Trade Center) (IND ISSN 0019-4980) **1568**
I I T C Directory (Indian International Trade Center) (IND ISSN 0073-6546) **1568**
I I T Research Institute, Reliability Analysis Center Journal *see* R A C Journal **3217**
I I U M Journal of Economics and Management (International Islamic University Malaysia) (MYS ISSN 1394-7680) **1751**
I I U M Law Journal (International Islamic University Malaysia) (MYS) **4689**
I J A *see* International Journal of Andrology **6269**
I J A *see* International Journal of Auditing **1292**
I J A C *see* The International Journal of Architectural Computing **462**
I J A D E *see* International Journal of Art & Design Education **3065**
I J A D R *see* The I C F A I Journal of Alternative Dispute Resolution **4689**
I J A E *see* The I C F A I Journal of Applied Economics **1120**
I J A E S *see* International Journal of Arabic-English Studies **5310**
I J A I *see* International Journal of Aerospace Innovations **6629**
I J A I M *see* International Journal of Accounting and Information Management **1292**
I J A I S L *see* International Journal of Accounting Information Science and Leadership **1292**
I J A I T *see* International Journal on Artificial Intelligence Tools **2452**
I J A L *see* International Journal of American Linguistics **5129**
I J A M C *see* International Journal of Advanced Media and Communication **2326**
I J A P *see* International Journal of Alternative Propulsion **3138**
I J A P *see* The I C F A I Journal of Audit Practice **1290**
I J A P S *see* International Journal of Asia - Pacific Studies **4457**
I J A R *see* The I C F A I Journal of Accounting Research **1290**
I J A R G E *see* International Journal of Agricultural Resources, Governance and Ecology **123**
I J A R G E *see* International Journal of Management and Decision Making **1759**
I J A S *see* International Journal of Asian Studies **551**
I J A T M *see* International Journal of Automotive Technology and Management **8586**
I J B *see* International Journal of the Book **2327**
I J B C B *see* The International Journal of Biochemistry & Cell Biology **734**
I J B C T *see* International Journal of Behavioral and Consultation Therapy **7364**
I J B D *see* International Journal of Behavioral Development **7364**
I J B F *see* International Annual Bibliography of Festschriften **627**
I J B F *see* The I C F A I Journal of Behavioral Finance **1750**
I J B K *see* Internationale Jahresbibliographie der Kongressberichte **628**
I J B L *see* The I C F A I Journal of Banking Law **4870**
I J B M *see* International Journal of Bank Marketing **1356**
I J B M *see* The I C F A I Journal of Bank Management **1352**
I J B P M *see* International Journal of Business Performance Management **1755**
I J B R *see* International Journal of Business Research **1755**
I J B - Report (Internationale Jugendbibliothek) (DEU ISSN 1013-0071) **5307**
I J B S *see* International Journal of Business Studies **1127**
I J B S *see* The I C F A I Journal of Business Strategy **1750**
I J B S *see* International Journal of Business Strategy **1755**
I J B S *see* International Journal of Business Studies **1571**
I J B S A M *see* International Journal of Business Science and Applied Management **1755**
I J B T *see* International Journal of Biotechnology **765**
I J Br M *see* The I C F A I Journal of Brand Management **1819**
I J C A *see* International Journal for Computers and Their Applications **2424**
I J C A I. Proceedings *see* International Joint Conference on Artificial Intelligence. Proceedings **2450**
I J C C M *see* International Journal of Cross Cultural Management **1867**
I J C C M *see* Indian Journal of Critical Care Medicine **5633**
I J C E H *see* International Journal of Clinical and Experimental Hypnosis **5943**
I J C F D *see* International Journal of Computational Fluid Dynamics **7059**
I J C G *see* The I C F A I Journal of Corporate Governance **1750**
I J C G A *see* International Journal of Computational Geometry and Applications **5552**
I J C H M *see* International Journal of Contemporary Hospitality Management **4391**
• I J C H R News Letter (Independent Jamaica Council for Human Rights) (JAM) **7209**
I J C I A *see* International Journal of Computational Intelligence and Applications **2451**
I J C I M *see* International Journal of Computer Integrated Manufacturing **3292**
I J C I R *see* International Journal of Computing and Information and Communication Technology Research **2425**
I J C I S *see* International Journal of Critical Infrastructures **3139**
I J C I S *see* International Journal of Cooperative Information Systems **2546**
I J C L *see* The I C F A I Journal of Cyber Law **4689**
I J C L P *see* International Journal of Communications Law and Policy **2424**
I J C M *see* International Journal of Computer Mathematics **5552**
I J C M A *see* International Journal of Conflict Management **1756**
I J C O M A *see* International Journal of Commerce and Management **1756**
I J C P *see* International Journal of Cultural Property **497**
I J C P *see* International Journal of Clinical Practice **5638**
I J C P O L *see* International Journal of Computer Processing of Oriental Languages **5202**
I J C R A *see* International Journal of Case Method Research & Application **2868**
I J C S *see* International Journal of Cosmetic Science **594**
I J C S *see* International Journal of Children's Spirituality **7364**
I J C S *see* International Journal of Cultural Studies **8109**
I J C S N S *see* International Journal of Computer Science and Network Security **2425**
I J C S S *see* International Journal of Computers, Systems and Signals **2522**
I J C S T *see* International Journal of Clothing Science and Technology **2247**
I J C T H R *see* International Journal of Culture, Tourism and Hospitality Research **8723**
I J D *see* Indian Journal of Dermatology **5877**
I J D B *see* International Journal of Development Banking **1599**
I J D C *see* International Journal of Digital Curation **5019**
I J D D E *see* International Journal of Disability, Development and Education **3041**
I J D E *see* International Journal of Digital Earth **2722**
I J D H D *see* International Journal on Disability and Human Development **5895**
I J D L (International Journal of Dravidian Linguistics) (IND ISSN 0378-2484) **5126**
I J D M *see* The I C F A I Journal of Derivatives Markets **1629**
I J D N *see* International Journal of Developmental Neuroscience **6146**
I J D S *see* International Journal for Dialogical Science **8108**
I J D S *see* International Journal of Doctoral Studies **4457**
I J D T *see* International Journal of Dairy Technology **266**
I J E B *see* International Journal of Electronic Business **1418**

Title

DIRECTORY 2010 INSCAN 10393

• i L E A P S. Newsletter (Intergrated Land Ecosystem-Atmosphere Processes Study) (FIN ISSN 1796-0363) **7864**
I L E I A Boletin *see* L E I S A **241**
I L E Quarterly Progress Report (Institute of Laser Engineering) (JPN ISSN 0289-1549) **3318**
I L G A Bulletin (International Lesbian and Gay Association) (BEL ISSN 0281-627X) **4375**
I L J *see* Insurance Law Journal **4693**
I L J *see* Boston University International Law Journal **4918**
I L J *see* North Carolina Journal of International Law and Commercial Regulation **4937**
I L J *see* Fordham International Law Journal **4926**
I L J *see* International Leadership Journal **8110**
I L L A *see* Indigenous Languages of Latin America **5127**
I L M *see* International Legal Materials **4932**
I L M *see* Inside Laboratory Management **2100**
I L M D A Advantage *see* Advantage (Springfield) **975**
I L M P *see* International Literary Market Place **7563**
I L N *see* International Law News **4931**
I L O Committee on Salaried Employees and Professional Workers. Report (International Labour Office) (CHE ISSN 0251-3803) **1686**
I L O Joint Committee on the Public Service. Report (International Labour Office) (CHE ISSN 0253-7834) **1686**
I L O Judgements of the Administrative Tribunal (International Labour Office) (CHE ISSN 0378-7362) **4689**
• I L O LEX CD-ROM (International Labour Organization) (CHE) **1686**
I L O Metal Trades Committee. Report (International Labour Office) (CHE ISSN 1010-2388) **1686**
I L O Multinational Enterprises Programme. Working Paper (International Labour Office) (CHE ISSN 1011-4971) **1490**
I L O Training Papers in Population and Family Welfare Education in the Worksetting (International Labour Office) (CHE ISSN 1014-9287) **1686**
I L P E S Cuadernos (Instituto Latinoamericano y del Caribe de Planificacion Economica y Social) (CHL ISSN 0020-4080) **1719**
I L R *see* Iowa Law Review **4696**
I L R *see* Penn State International Law Review **4937**
I L R *see* The Loyola University Chicago International Law Review **4935**
I L R *see* Internet Law & Regulation **4845**
I L R *see* Industrial Literature Review **1242**
The I L R Journal *see* Northwestern University School of Continuing Studies. Osher Lifelong Learning Institute. Journal **5343**
I L R Review *see* Industrial and Labor Relations Review **1687**
I L S (Institut fuer Landes- und Stadtentwicklungsforschung und Bauwesen des Landes N R W) (DEU ISSN 1434-2545) **4414**
• ➤ I L S A Journal of International and Comparative Law (International Law Students Association) (USA ISSN 1082-944X) **4928**
I L S A Quarterly (International Law Students Association) (USA) **4928**
I L S I Monograph (International Life Sciences Institute) (USA ISSN 1432-0010) **6660**
I.L.S.L. Cahiers *see* University of Lausanne. Institut de Linguistique et des Sciences du Langage. Cahiers **5192**
I L S News Digest (Institute for Labor Studies) (PHL ISSN 0118-0169) **4595**
I L T *see* Industrial Lubrication & Tribology **3379**
I L Vehicle Code *see* Illinois Vehicle Code **4690**
I L W C H *see* International Labor and Working-Class History **1689**
I Love Animals. Albo Magico (ITA ISSN 1970-1535) **2193**
I Love Animals. Colori (ITA ISSN 1970-1527) **2193**
I Love Animals. Giochi (ITA ISSN 1970-1543) **2193**
• I Love Cats (USA ISSN 0899-9570) **6809**
I Love English (ESP ISSN 0214-2864) **5126**
• I Love English (FRA ISSN 1765-4750) **2193**
I Love English Junior (DEU) **2193**
I Love English Junior (ESP ISSN 1131-5288) **2193**
I Love English Junior *see* I Love English **2193**
• I Love My Job! (USA) **6698**
I Love New York: The Finger Lakes Travel Guide (USA) **8720**
• I Love New York Travel Guide (USA) **8720**
• I Love New York Winter Travel and Ski Guide (USA) **8318**
I Love Orlando (USA) **8720**
I Love Pop *see* I Love Stars **2193**
I Love Pop Special *see* I Love Pop ... Special **2193**
I Love Pop ... Special (GBR ISSN 1477-9544) **2193**
I Love Puppets (ITA ISSN 1123-0517) **8471**
I Love Stars (GBR) **2193**
I Luften (SWE ISSN 1404-5591) **59**
I M *see* Interactive Media **6504**
I M (Information Management) (DEU ISSN 1616-1017) **2558**
I M/Teen Magazine (Ifjusagi Magazin) (HUN) **2194**
I M *see* Italia Missionaria **2194**
I M *see* Medmaensklighet **1601**
I M *see* Internal Medicine **5945**
I M A C *see* International Conference on Image Management and Communication in Patient Care. Proceedings **2424**
I M A C S Symposium on Theoretical Computational Acoustics. Proceedings *see* Theoretical and Computational Acoustics **7050**
▼ • I M A Educational Case Journal (Institute of Management Accountants) (USA ISSN 1940-204X) **1290**
• ➤ I M A J (Israel Medical Association Journal) (ISR ISSN 1565-1088) **5631**
• ➤ I M A Journal of Applied Mathematics (Institute of Mathematics and Its Applications) (GBR ISSN 0272-4960) **5492**
• ➤ I M A Journal of Management Mathematics (Institute of Mathematics and Its Applications) (GBR ISSN 1471-678X) **5492**
• ➤ I M A Journal of Mathematical Control & Information (Institute of Mathematics and Its Applications) (GBR ISSN 0265-0754) **5492**
I M A Journal of Mathematics Applied in Medicine & Biology (Online) *see* Mathematical Medicine and Biology (Online) **5513**
• ➤ I M A Journal of Numerical Analysis (Institute of Mathematics and Its Applications) (GBR ISSN 0272-4979) **5492**
• I M A Numerical Analysis Newsletter (Institute of Mathematics and Its Applications) (GBR) **5492**
I M A S Bulletin (Institutul de Marketing si Sondaje) (ROM ISSN 1221-6992) **1820**
I M A Volumes in Mathematics and Its Applications (Institute of Mathematics and Its Applications) (USA ISSN 0940-6573) **5492**
I M Advantage (Print) *see* I M Advantage Papers (Online) **5945**
• I M Advantage Papers (Online) (Internal Medicine) (USA) **5945**
I M B *see* International Medieval Bibliography **4170**
I M B *see* Insect Molecular Biology **849**
I M C *see* International Mechanical Code **3383**
I M C (Year) *see* A C M SIGCOMM Internet Measurment Conference. Proceedings **2552**
I M C H Newsletter (Institute of Maternal and Child Health) (PHL) **2154**
I M C P *see* Israel Mathematical Conference Proceedings **5498**
I M C S *see* Information Management & Computer Security **1752**
▼ I.M. Cowgirl (USA ISSN 1940-0551) **8868**
I M D *see* Information Marketplace Directory **7563**
I M D A Journal *see* Instruments India **4488**
I M D S *see* Industrial Management + Data Systems **1418**
I M E F M *see* International Journal of Islamic and Middle Eastern Finance and Management **1357**
▼ I M E Journal (Institute of Management Education) (IND ISSN 0974-0716) **1751**
I M Environnement (l'Industrie Minerale) (FRA) **6464**
I M F C Review (Institute of Marriage and Family Canada) (CAN ISSN 1715-5711) **5559**
• I M F Committee on Balance of Payments Statistics. Annual Report (International Monetary Fund) (USA ISSN 1020-1637) **1352**
I M F Economic Forums and International Seminars (International Monetary Fund) (USA) **1490**
I M F. Economic Reviews. Press Information Notices (International Monetary Fund) (USA ISSN 1020-6779) **1490**
• I M F Financial Resources and Liquidity Position (International Monetary Fund) (USA) **1490**
I M F Heavily Indebted Poor Countries Country Documents (International Monetary Fund) (USA) **1597**
I M F in Focus *see* International Monetary Fund Survey **1244**
I M F News (International Metalworkers Federation) (CHE) **6315**
I M F Newsletter (Industrial Materials for the Future) (USA) **3367**
• I M F Policy Discussion Papers (International Monetary Fund) (USA ISSN 1564-5193) **1490**
• I M F Poverty Reduction Strategy Papers (International Monetary Fund) (USA) **1597**
• I M F Quarterly Report on the Assessments of Standards and Codes (International Monetary Fund) (USA) **1490**
I M F Research Bulletin *see* International Monetary Fund. Research Bulletin **1358**
I M F S P *see* International Monetary Fund. Staff Papers **1358**
I M F Staff Country Report (International Monetary Fund) (USA ISSN 1564-5169) **1490**
I M F Staff Papers *see* International Monetary Fund. Staff Papers **1358**
I M F Survey *see* International Monetary Fund Survey **1244**
I M F U F A Tekst *see* Institut for Studiet af Matematik og Fysik samt deres Funktioner i Undervisning Forskning og Anvendelse. Tekster **5493**
I M F Views and Commentaries (International Monetary Fund) (USA) **1490**
• I M F Working Paper (International Monetary Fund) (USA ISSN 1018-5941) **1490**
• I M G Magazine (CAN ISSN 1719-8100) **5307**
I M H A on the Move! *see* L' I A L A en Action! **6223**
• I M H E (Informacion de Maquinas - Herramienta Equipos y Accesorios) (ESP ISSN 0210-1777) **5452**
I M I Monitor (GBR) **1686**
I M I S - Beitraege (Institut fuer Migrationsforschung und Interkulturelle Studien) (DEU ISSN 0949-4723) **7284**
I M I S C O E Dissertations (International Migration, Integration and Social Cohesion in Europe) (NLD) **7284**
I M I S C O E Research (International Migration, Integration and Social Cohesion in Europe) (NLD) **7141**
I M I S Journal (Institute for the Management of Information Systems) (GBR) **2531**
• I M Industrial Minerals Directory (GBR ISSN 1363-2779) **6464**
I M - Information Management *see* I M **2558**
I M IS C O E Reports (International Migration, Integration and Social Cohesion in Europe) (NLD) **7284**
I M J *see* Internal Medicine Journal (Print) **5946**
• I M J (Irish Marketing Journal) (IRL ISSN 0791-6809) **1820**
I M J *see* International Medical Journal **5640**
I M M *see* Australian Immigration Law **4846**
I M M *see* International Musculoskeletal Medicine **6062**
I M M *see* Injection Molding **7092**
• I M M Abstracts (Institution of Mining and Metallurgy) (GBR ISSN 0019-0020) **6485**
I M M Abstracts. Index *see* I M M Abstracts **6485**
• I M M E Boletin Tecnico (Instituto de Materiales y Modelos Estructurales) (VEN ISSN 0376-723X) **3269**
I M M O International Magazine *see* Mondi Personal **1639**
• I M M-T R (Informatik og Matematisk Modellering - Teknisk Rapport) (DNK ISSN 1601-2321) **8377**
I M M-Thesis (DNK ISSN 1601-233X) **5492**
• ➤ I M O, F A O, Unesco - I O C, W M O, W H O, I A E A, U N, U N E P - G E S A M P Reports and Studies (GBR ISSN 1020-4873) **3487**
I M O - I P I E C A Report Series (International Maritime Organization, International Petroleum Industry Environmental Conservation As) (GBR) **3438**
• I M O News (International Maritime Organization) (GBR ISSN 0253-8199) **8646**
I M P *see* Inside Mortgage Profitability **1354**
I M P A C T News (Irish Municipal Public and Civil Trade Union) (IRL) **7445**
I M P I Newsletter (International Microwave Power Institute) (USA ISSN 0318-0883) **3318**
I M P P *see* Innovation: Management, Policy & Practice **1753**
• I M P: the Magazine on Information Impacts (USA) **7141**
I M R *see* International Marketing Review **1822**
I M R *see* International Materials Reviews **3348**
I M R *see* International Migration Review **7285**
I M R *see* Internet Marketing Report **2561**
I M R N *see* International Mathematics Research Notices **5498**
I M R O News (Irish Music Rights Organisation) (IRL) **6574**
I M R Open Report *see* University of Zimbabwe. Institute of Mining Research. Report **6483**
I M S A Journal (International Municipal Signal Association) (USA ISSN 1064-2560) **8631**
I M S Bulletin (Institute of Materials Science) (USA ISSN 0019-0063) **3345**
• I M S Bulletin (Institute of Mathematical Statistics) (USA ISSN 1544-1881) **5492**
• I M S Company Profiles (Intelligence Marketing Services) (GBR) **6847**
I M S Lecture Notes - Monograph Series (Institute of Mathematical Statistics) (USA ISSN 0749-2170) **5492**
I M S Lifecycle New Product Focus *see* New Product Focus **6863**
I M S Lifecycle R & D Focus *see* R & D Focus **6877**
• I M S Magazine (IP Multimedia Subsystem) (USA) **2324**
I M S New Product Focus *see* New Product Focus **6863**
• I M S Newsletter (International Marine Science) (FRA ISSN 0020-7918) **2806**
I M S Retail Drug Monitor (USA) **6847**
I M T *see* Indre Missions Tidende **7761**
I M T C *see* I E E E Instrumentation and Measurement Technology Conference. Proceedings **4487**
I M W *see* Investment Management Weekly **1632**
I-Manager's Journal of Education Technology (IND ISSN 0973-0559) **2865**
I mas S *see* Informatica y Salud **5016**
i MD *see* images.MD **5633**
I Mech E Seminar Publication *see* Institution of Mechanical Engineers Seminar Publication **8965**
• I Mpact (Philadelphia) (Online) (Internal Medicine) (USA) **5632**
I Mu *see* Ingenieria Municipal **3270**
I N A Casopis (Industrija Nafte) (HRV ISSN 1331-6095) **6773**
• I N A Fagreport (Institutt for Naturforvaltning) (NOR ISSN 1503-9439) **2614**
I N A G E Q. Actas (Instituto Nacional de Geoquimica) (MEX) **2746**
• I N A Glasnik (Industrija Nafte) (HRV ISSN 1331-9132) **6773**
• I N A H T A Briefs (International Network of Agencies for Health Technology Assessment) (SWE ISSN 1653-5316) **5632**
I N A I L Dati (Istituto Nazionale per l'Assicurazione Contro gli Infortuni sul Lavoro) (ITA) **6690**
I N A I L Notiziario Statistico (Istituto Nazionale per l'Assicurazione Contro gli Infortuni sul Lavoro) (ITA ISSN 1592-6818) **6690**
I N A M E News *see* Newspaper Marketing **1836**
I N A M I Bulletin d'Information *see* Belgium. Institut National d'Assurance Maladie Invalidite. I N A M I Bulletin d'Information **4494**
I N A Newsletter (International Nannoplankton Association) (USA ISSN 0255-013X) **2806**
I N A Quarterly (Institute of Nautical Archaeology) (USA) **397**
I N A S P Health Directory (Year) (International Network for the Availability of Scientific Publications) (GBR) **5632**
• I N A S P Newsletter (International Network for the Availability of Scientific Publications) (GBR ISSN 1028-0790) **5014**
I N C Hebdo Consommateurs Actualites (Institut National de la Consommation) (FRA ISSN 1145-0673) **2638**
• I N D A Association of the Nonwoven Fabrics Industry. I N T C Papers (International Nonwovens Technical Conference) (USA) **8452**
I N D A C Magazine (Indianapolis Athletic Club) (USA ISSN 0019-3569) **2266**
I N D E C Documentos de Trabajo (Instituto Nacional de Estadistica y Censos) (ARG ISSN 0326-6230) **8377**
I N D E C Estudios (Instituto Nacional de Estadistica y Censos) (ARG ISSN 0326-6249) **8377**
I N D E C Informa (Instituto Nacional de Estadistica y Censos) (ARG ISSN 0328-5804) **8377**
I N D E C Informacion de Prensa (Instituto Nacional de Estadistica y Censos) (ARG) **8377**
I N D E C Metodologias (Instituto Nacional de Estadistica y Censos) (ARG ISSN 0326-6222) **8377**
I N D E C Normas (Instituto Nacional de Estadistica y Censos) (ARG) **8377**
I N D E C Recopilaciones (Instituto Nacional de Estadistica y Censos) (ARG) **8377**
I N E. Cifras (Instituto Nacional de Estadistica) (ESP ISSN 1579-2277) **8377**
I N F A D (Infancia y Adolescencia) (ESP ISSN 0214-9877) **7361**
I N F A Press and Advertisers Year Book (India News and Feature Alliance) (IND ISSN 0073-4284) **26**
I N F - Die Information fuer Steuerberater und Wirtschaftspruefer (DEU) **1928**
I N F F O - Flash (FRA ISSN 0397-3301) **1751**
• I N F L I B N E T Newsletter (Information and Library Network Centre) (IND ISSN 0971-9849) **5014**
I N F O Journal (International Fortean Organization) (USA ISSN 0019-0144) **7864**
• I N F O L A C. Boletin (Sociedad de la Informacion para America Latina y el Caribe) (VEN) **5014**
• ➤ I N F O R Journal (CAN ISSN 0315-5986) **2536**
• ➤ I N F O R M S Journal on Computing (Institute for Operations Research and the Management Sciences) (USA ISSN 1091-9856) **2421**
• ➤ I N F O R M S Transactions on Education (Institute for Operations Research and the Management Sciences) (USA ISSN 1532-0545) **1751**
I N G Belgique. Bulletin Financier (BEL) **1629**
I N G Scorecard (USA) **8235**
I N G Shareholder (Internationale Nederlanden Groep) (NLD ISSN 1874-0472) **1928**
➤ I N I D E P Informe Tecnico (Instituto Nacional de Investigacion y Desarrollo Pesquero) (ARG ISSN 0327-9642) **3597**
• I N I S Atomindex (Online Edition) (International Nuclear Information System) (AUT) **7048**
I N I S Reference Series (International Nuclear Information System) (AUT ISSN 1014-1561) **5014**
I N: Inside Innovation (USA) **8425**
I N M R Quarterly Review *see* Insulator News and Market Report. Quarterly Review **3159**
I N O Journal of Nursing Research (Irish Nurses' Organisation) (IRL) **5961**
I N P R A Latina (Industrias de Pinturas, Revestimientos, Adhesivos y Tintas) (COL) **6718**
I N P R E K O R R (Internationale Pressekorrespondenz) (DEU ISSN 0256-4416) **7240**
I N Q U A Newsletter *see* Quaternary Perspective **2763**
I N R *see* Industrie Report International **5453**
I N R *see* International Nursing Review **5962**
I N R A. Colloques (Institut National de la Recherche Agronomique) (FRA ISSN 0293-1915) **119**
I N R A Magazine *see* Institut National de la Recherche Agronomique. Magazine **122**
Les Cahiers de l'I N R A P *see* Institut National de Recherches Archeologiques Preventives. Cahiers **398**
I N R A Sciences Sociales (Institut National de la Recherche Agronomique, Departement d'Economie et de Sociologie Rurales) (FRA ISSN 0988-3266) **200**
• I N R S - E T E. Rapport Annuel (Institut National de la Recherhce Scientifique - Eau, Terre et Environnement) (CAN ISSN 1719-5586) **3438**
I N S C A N (International Settlement Canada) (CAN ISSN 0845-2466) **7284**

Title

▼ *new title* † *ceased* • *electronic media* ➤ *refereed*

Title

DIRECTORY 2010 IBERO-AMERICANA 10397

I T Professional (Dutch Edition) *see* I T Professional (French Edition) **2544**
I T Professional (French Edition) (Information Technology) (BEL ISSN 1783-1989) **2544**
I T Project Management Essentials (Information Technology) (USA ISSN 1935-1852) **1751**
I T Q *see* Irish Theological Quarterly **7651**
I T Qualifikation (Informations Technik) (DEU ISSN 1612-2607) **1417**
I T R (International Transport Revue) (AUT ISSN 0019-0845) **8671**
I T R O W News (Institute for Teaching & Research on Women) (USA ISSN 1063-8725) **2865**
• The I T R Report (International Traders Research) (USA) **1629**
• I T R U Report (Interdisciplinary Trauma Research Unit) (NZL ISSN 1177-4347) **6061**
Der I T - Rechtsberater (DEU ISSN 1617-1527) **2514**
• I T Reseller (Information Technology) (GBR ISSN 1475-3332) **2493**
I T Reseller Magazine *see* I T Reseller **2493**
I T Review *see* Information Technology Review **2534**
I T Review (Information Technology) (GBR ISSN 1025-2592) **5014**
I T Review *see* Information Technology Review **2423**
• I T - Revision (Informations Technologie) (DEU ISSN 1615-8091) **1417**
I T Rewards (Information Technology) (GBR ISSN 1472-9857) **1686**
I T S E *see* Interactive Technology and Smart Education **8426**
I T S International (Intelligent Transport Systems) (GBR ISSN 1463-6344) **8498**
I T S Journal *see* Journal of Intelligent Transportation Systems **2329**
I T S Magazine *see* I E E E Intelligent Transportation Systems Magazine **8498**
I T S Quarterly (Intelligent Transportation Society of America) (USA) **8498**
I T S S A *see* International Transactions on Systems Science and Applications **2427**
I T S Textile Leader *see* Textile Leader **8460**
I T Security (Informations Technik) (DEU ISSN 1438-5503) **2514**
I T Service Magazine (Information Technology) (NLD ISSN 1566-5275) **2498**
• I T Services Business Report (Online) (Information Technology) (USA) **2493**
I T Sicherheit (Information Technology) (DEU) **4689**
• I T Solutions Guide (Information Technology) (USA) **2544**
I T - Sources (Information Technology) (DEU ISSN 1435-7054) **1417**
I T - Sources Weekly (Information Technology) (DEU) **1417**
I T T R *see* Industry, Trade, and Technology Review **1569**
• I T Today (Online Edition) (GBR) **2422**
• I T Training (Information Technology) (GBR ISSN 0954-7940) **1866**
I T Training *see* Key Note Market Report: I T Training **1894**
• I T Trends (Information Technology) (USA) **3024**
• I T Trends in Local Government (Information Technology) (GBR) **2544**
I T U Global Directory (International Telecommunication Union) (CHE ISSN 1027-7420) **2325**
I T U Jyanaru (JPN ISSN 0916-7544) **2325**
I T U News (International Telecommunication Union) (CHE ISSN 1020-4148) **2325**
I T U Statistical Yearbook/Annuaire Statistique des l'U I T (International Telecommunication Union) (CHE) **2347**
I T U Weekly Circular and Special Sections (International Telecommunication Union) (CHE) **2325**
• I T University. Technical Report Series (DNK ISSN 1600-6100) **2422**
I T Viikko (Information Technology) (FIN ISSN 1457-0025) **1417**
I T Week *see* Computing (London, 2008) **2415**
I T Week *see* Zixun Chuanzhen Zhoukan **2441**
I Tavisen Business *see* Dagens I T **2318**
• I-Tips Newsletter (USA) **2558**
• I Tjaenst foer Riksdagen (SWE ISSN 1653-8307) **7141**
• I to Cho/Stomach and Intestine (JPN ISSN 0536-2180) **5926**
I U A E S Commission on Urgent Anthropological Research. Newsletter (International Union of Anthropological and Ethnological Research) (AUT) **342**
• ➤ I U B M B Life (International Union of Biochemistry and Molecular Biology) (GBR ISSN 1521-6543) **733**
I U B S Monograph Series (International Union of Biological Sciences) (GBR ISSN 0952-2204) **677**
I U C N Environmental Policy and Law Papers (CHE) **3438**
I U F News Bulletin (International Union of Food, Agricultural, Hotel, Restaurant, Catering, Tobacco and Allied Workers) (CHE) **4595**
I U F R O Occasional Papers (International Union of Forestry Research Organizations) (AUT ISSN 1024-414X) **3693**
I U F R O Research Series (International Union of Forestry Research Organizations) (GBR) **3693**
I U F R O World Congress. Congress Reports (International Union of Forestry Research Organizations) (AUT) **3693**
I U F R O World Series (International Union of Forestry Research Organizations) (AUT ISSN 1016-3263) **3693**
I U G G Year Book/Annuaire U G G I (International Union of Geodesy and Geophysics) (USA) **2783**
I U G S. UNESCO. I C G P. Project 133. Bulletin de Liaison et Information see International Union of Geological Sciences. United Nations Educational, Scientific and Cultural Organization. International Geological Correlation Programme. Projet 133. Bulletin de Liaison et Information **2784**
I U I Dissertation Series (Year) (Industriens Utrednings Institut) (SWE ISSN 1404-0700) **1751**
• I U I: International Conference on Intelligent User Interfaces. Proceedings (USA) **2422**
I U I. Yearbook *see* Institutet foer Naeringslivsforskning. Aarsbok **1889**
• I U L News (Indiana University Libraries) (USA) **5014**
• I U Newsletter (Online Edition) (USA) **6214**
I U O M A Magazine (International Union of Mail Artists) (NLD) **494**
I U P A C Chemistry for the Twenty First Century Series *see* Chemistry for the 21st Century Series **2057**
I U P A C Experimental Thermodynamics Series *see* Experimental Thermodynamics Series **2134**
• I U P A C Handbook (Year) (International Union of Pure and Applied Chemistry) (USA) **2100**
I U P A C Nomenclature Series *see* Nomenclature Series **2117**
I U P A C Series on Analytical and Physical Chemistry of Environmental Systems (International Union of Pure and Applied Chemistry) (GBR ISSN 1528-2503) **3497**
I U P A C Solubility Data Series *see* Solubility Data Series **2081**
I U P I W Views (International Union of Petroleum & Industrial Workers) (USA ISSN 0199-5685) **6773**
➤ I U P Stress and Health Series (International Universities Press) (USA ISSN 0899-403X) **6145**
I U S S P. Newsletter/U I E S P. Bulletin (International Union for the Scientific Study of Population) (FRA ISSN 0771-2022) **7284**
I U S T International Journal of Engineering Science (Iran University of Science and Technology) (IRN ISSN 1681-066X) **3196**
I U S Y Newsletter (International Union of Socialist Youth) (AUT) **7141**
• I U V S T A News Bulletin (International Union for Vacuum Science Technique and Applications) (GBR) **7016**
• L'I V A (Imposta sul Valore Aggiunto) (ITA ISSN 1593-2443) **1929**
• I V A - aktuellt (Kungliga Ingenjoersvetenskapsakademien) (SWE ISSN 1401-1999) **3196**
I V C A Update (International Visual Communications Association) (GBR) **1751**
I V D T *see* I V D Technology **5632**
• I V D Technology (In Vitro Diagnostic) (USA ISSN 1093-5207) **5632**
• I V L - Nyheter (Online Edition) (Institutet foer Vatten- och Luftvaardsforskning) (SWE) **3438**
I V L - Nyheter (Print Edition) *see* I V L - Nyheter (Online Edition) **3438**
• I V L Rapport. B (SWE ISSN 0283-877X) **3487**
I V L Referat (Institutet foer Vatten- och Luftvaardsforskning) (SWE ISSN 0283-1511) **3487**
I V Neurologie Psychiatrie (DEU) **6145**
I V R Interventional Radiology (JPN ISSN 1340-4520) **6198**
I V S *see* Information Visualization **2450**
I V S (Index of Veterinary Specialists) (ZAF ISSN 0019-0918) **8798**
• I V S Annual (AUS ISSN 1033-2863) **8816**
I V S Desk Reference (Index of Veterinary Specialists) (ZAF) **8798**
I V S L A Series *see* Istituto Veneto di Scienze, Lettere ed Arti Series **4458**
I V T B Corporate Plan (Industrial and Vocational Training Board) (MUS ISSN 1694-0482) **1686**
I V T International *see* Industrial Vehicle Technology International **8671**
I V T International. Lift Truck & Materials Handling *see* Industrial Vehicle Technology. Lift Truck & Materials Handling **8671**
I V U N News *see* Ventilator-Assisted Living **5728**
I W *see* IronWorks **8260**
I W *see* Industrial Wastewater (Online) **3487**
I W B *see* Internationale Wirtschafts-Briefe **1931**
I W D (Institut der Deutschen Wirtschaft) (DEU ISSN 0344-919X) **1121**
I W F A Yearbook (International Women's Fishing Association) (USA) **8318**
I W G I A Document (International Work Group for Indigenous Affairs) (DNK ISSN 0105-4503) **342**
I W G I A Documento (International Work Group for Indigenous Affairs) (DNK ISSN 0108-9927) **342**
I W G O Newsletter (International Working Group on Ostrinia Nubilalis) (AUT) **235**
I W J *see* International Wound Journal **6062**
I W J *see* The Internet Writing Journal **5310**
I W K (Internationale Wissenschaftliche Korrespondenz zur Geschichte der Deutschen Arbeiterbewegung) (DEU ISSN 0046-8428) **4596**
I W M Publication *see* C I W M Publication **3504**
I W M Scientific & Technical Review (Institute of Wastes Management) *see* Communications in Waste and Resource Management **3505**
I W O Journal (Institution of Water Officers) (GBR) **8825**
I W P A News (International Wood Products Association) (USA) **3712**
I W - Positionen (DEU) **1888**
I W R *see* International Woodfiber Report **6734**
I W R C Proceedings (International Wildlife Rehabilitation Council) (USA) **947**
I W R C Skills Seminars (International Wildlife Rehabilitation Council) (USA) **947**
I W Trends (DEU ISSN 0941-6838) **1490**
I W Z *see* Illustrierte Wochenzeitung **2382**
• I W Z Online (Illustrierte Wochenzeitung) (DEU) **2382**
• I - Watch Newsletter (AUS) **2558**
• I-Ways (NLD ISSN 1084-4678) **2558**
i - Weekly (SGP) **3945**
i World *see* iWorld **2562**
I Y F *see* Ignite Your Faith **2194**
I Z *see* Informatore Zootecnico **289**
I Z A (CHE ISSN 0376-9410) **6678**
I Z Ph *see* Internationale Zeitschrift fuer Philosophie **6926**
I Z R G Schriftenreihe (Institut fuer Schleswig-Holsteinische Zeit- und Regionalgeschichte) (DEU ISSN 1616-2781) **4231**
• i4D - Information for Development (IND ISSN 0972-804X) **2325**
▼ iA (Interactive Architecture) (NLD ISSN 1875-0133) **445**
iA Bookzine Series *see* iA **445**
• Iablis (DEU ISSN 1610-6261) **7971**
Iacobus (ESP ISSN 1137-2397) **4146**
IAEA Tecdoc *see* I A E A Technical Documents Series **3168**
I'Afrika (DNK ISSN 1395-0118) **4175**
• iAmericanSpirit (USA) **2194**
Ian Ramsey Centre. Publications (GBR) **6924**
• ianorth&south (NZL ISSN 1177-2344) **1290**
Iaponia Insula (DEU) **551**
• Iasi Polytechnic Magazine (ROM ISSN 1013-5278) **3196**
Iasi - What, Where, When (ROM) **8720**
• Iatreia (COL ISSN 0121-0793) **5632**
Iatrika Chronika/Medical Annals (GRC ISSN 0303-4925) **5632**
Iatriki (GRC ISSN 0019-0950) **5632**
Iaw! (GBR ISSN 1359-7396) **2194**
Ibaraki Daigaku Kogakubu Kenkyu Shuho/Ibaraki University. Faculty of Engineering. Journal (JPN ISSN 0367-7389) **3197**
➤ Ibaraki Daigaku Kyoikugakubu Kiyo. Shizen Kagaku/Ibaraki University. Faculty of Education. Bulletin. Natural Sciences (JPN ISSN 0386-7668) **7864**
Ibaraki Daigaku Rigakubu Kiyo. Sugaku *see* Ibaraki University. Mathematical Journal **5492**
Ibaraki Insect Society. News *see* Okera **856**
Ibaraki Journal of Nuclear Medicine *see* Ibaraki Kaku Igaku **6198**
Ibaraki Kaku Igaku/Ibaraki Journal of Nuclear Medicine (JPN ISSN 0915-308X) **6198**
Ibaraki-ken Kyukyu Igakkai Zasshi (JPN ISSN 0912-2125) **6061**
Ibaraki-ken Shizen Hakubutsukan Kenkyu Hokoku/Ibaraki Nature Museum. Bulletin (JPN ISSN 1343-8921) **6525**
Ibaraki Kenritsu Byoin Igaku Zasshi/Ibaraki Prefectural Hospital. Medical Journal (JPN ISSN 0912-9952) **5632**
Ibaraki Medical Association. Journal *see* Ibarakiken Ishikaiho **5632**
Ibaraki Nature Museum. Bulletin *see* Ibaraki-ken Shizen Hakubutsukan Kenkyu Hokoku **6525**
Ibaraki Prefectural Hospital. Medical Journal *see* Ibaraki Kenritsu Byoin Igaku Zasshi **5632**
Ibaraki Prefecture Industrial Research Information: Machine and Metal Section *see* Ibarakiken Kogyo Gijutsu Joho. Kikai Kenzoku Hen **5452**
Ibaraki Prefecture. Monthly Report of Meteorology *see* Ibarakiken Kisho Geppo **6356**
Ibaraki Society of Rural Medicine. Journal *see* Ibarakiken Noson Igakkai Zasshi **5632**
Ibaraki University. Faculty of Education. Bulletin. Natural Sciences *see* Ibaraki Daigaku Kyoikugakubu Kiyo. Shizen Kagaku **7864**
Ibaraki University. Faculty of Engineering. Journal *see* Ibaraki Daigaku Kogakubu Kenkyu Shuho **3197**
Ibaraki University. Itako Hydrobiological Station. Publications (JPN ISSN 0289-9531) **2795**
Ibaraki University. Mathematical Journal/Ibaraki Daigaku Rigakubu Kiyo. Sugaku (JPN ISSN 1343-3636) **5492**
Ibaraki University. Natural History Bulletin (JPN ISSN 1343-0955) **7864**
Ibarakiken Ishikaiho/Ibaraki Medical Association. Journal (JPN ISSN 0914-4501) **5632**
Ibarakiken Kisho Geppo/Ibaraki Prefecture. Monthly Report of Meteorology (JPN ISSN 0916-5304) **6356**
Ibarakiken Kogyo Gijutsu Joho. Kikai Kenzoku Hen/Ibaraki Prefecture Industrial Research Information: Machine and Metal Section (JPN) **5452**
Ibarakiken Noson Igakkai Zasshi/Ibaraki Society of Rural Medicine. Journal (JPN ISSN 0915-1982) **5632**
• Ibarske Novosti (SRB ISSN 0019-0977) **3945**
iBasekhaya (ZAF ISSN 1816-5486) **4391**
iBau Informationsdienst fuer den Tiefbau. Regionalausgabe Baden-Wuerttemberg (DEU) **1013**
iBau Informationsdienst fuer den Tiefbau. Regionalausgabe Bayern (DEU) **1013**
iBau Informationsdienst fuer den Tiefbau. Regionalausgabe Hessen, Rheinland-Pfalz, Saarland (DEU) **1013**
iBau Informationsdienst fuer den Tiefbau. Regionalausgabe Mecklenburg-Vorpommern, Brandenburg, Sachsen-Anhalt, Berlin (DEU) **1013**
iBau Informationsdienst fuer den Tiefbau. Regionalausgabe Niedersachsen, Bremen, Hamburg, Schleswig-Holstein (DEU) **1013**
iBau Informationsdienst fuer den Tiefbau. Regionalausgabe Nordrhein-Westfalen (DEU) **1013**
iBau Informationsdienst fuer den Tiefbau. Regionalausgabe Thueringen, Sachsen (DEU) **1013**
iBau Planungsinformationen. Regionalausgabe Aachen (DEU ISSN 0723-6387) **4414**
iBau Planungsinformationen. Regionalausgabe Arnsberg (DEU ISSN 0723-6360) **4414**
iBau Planungsinformationen. Regionalausgabe Berlin (DEU ISSN 0178-1936) **4414**
iBau Planungsinformationen. Regionalausgabe Brandenburg (DEU ISSN 0944-0895) **4414**
iBau Planungsinformationen. Regionalausgabe Braunschweig (DEU ISSN 0723-645X) **4414**
iBau Planungsinformationen. Regionalausgabe Darmstadt (DEU ISSN 0723-6441) **4414**
iBau Planungsinformationen. Regionalausgabe Detmold (DEU ISSN 0723-6395) **4414**
iBau Planungsinformationen. Regionalausgabe Duesseldorf (DEU ISSN 0723-6379) **4414**
iBau Planungsinformationen. Regionalausgabe Freiburg (DEU ISSN 0178-1820) **4415**
iBau Planungsinformationen. Regionalausgabe Grossraum Muenchen (DEU ISSN 0942-7201) **4415**
iBau Planungsinformationen. Regionalausgabe Hamburg (DEU ISSN 0178-1839) **4415**
iBau Planungsinformationen. Regionalausgabe Hannover (DEU ISSN 0723-6425) **4415**
iBau Planungsinformationen. Regionalausgabe Hildesheim (DEU ISSN 0723-6468) **4415**
iBau Planungsinformationen. Regionalausgabe Karlsruhe (DEU ISSN 0723-6484) **4415**
iBau Planungsinformationen. Regionalausgabe Kassel (DEU ISSN 0723-6433) **4415**
iBau Planungsinformationen. Regionalausgabe Koblenz - Trier (DEU ISSN 0178-1847) **4415**
iBau Planungsinformationen. Regionalausgabe Koeln (DEU ISSN 0723-3914) **4415**
iBau Planungsinformationen. Regionalausgabe Mecklenburg-Vorpommern, Brandenburg, Sachsen-Anhalt (DEU ISSN 0941-7737) **4415**
iBau Planungsinformationen. Regionalausgabe Muenster (DEU ISSN 0723-6352) **4415**
iBau Planungsinformationen. Regionalausgabe Oldenburg (DEU ISSN 0723-6417) **4415**
iBau Planungsinformationen. Regionalausgabe Osnabrueck (DEU ISSN 0723-6409) **4415**
iBau Planungsinformationen. Regionalausgabe Regierungsbezirk Niederbayern und Noerdliches Oberbayern (DEU ISSN 0942-5586) **4415**
iBau Planungsinformationen. Regionalausgabe Regierungsbezirk Oberfranken - Oberpfalz (DEU ISSN 0942-5578) **4415**
iBau Planungsinformationen. Regionalausgabe Rheinhessen-Pfalz (DEU ISSN 0723-6476) **4415**
iBau Planungsinformationen. Regionalausgabe Schleswig-Holstein (DEU ISSN 0178-1863) **4415**
iBau Planungsinformationen. Regionalausgabe Schwaben (DEU ISSN 0178-188X) **4415**
iBau Planungsinformationen. Regionalausgabe Stuttgart (DEU ISSN 0178-1812) **4415**
iBau Planungsinformationen. Regionalausgabe Thueringen - Sachsen (DEU ISSN 0941-7745) **4415**
iBau Planungsinformationen. Regionalausgabe Tuebingen (DEU ISSN 0178-1855) **4415**
iBau Planungsinformationen. Regionalausgabe Unter-/Mittelfranken (DEU ISSN 0942-7198) **4415**
† Ibda'/Innovation (EGY) **8963**
IBDigest *see* I B D Digest **5926**
Iber (ESP ISSN 1133-9810) **7971**
Iberia (ESP ISSN 1575-0221) **2235**
† ➤ Iberian Studies (GBR ISSN 0307-3262) **8963**
• Iberica (ESP ISSN 1139-7241) **5126**
Iberica (USA ISSN 1056-5000) **8471**
Iberiul-Kavkasiuli Enatmetsnierebis Tselitsdeuli/Annual of Iberian-Caucasian Linguistics/Yezhegodnik Iberiisko-Kavkazskogo Yazykoznaniya (GEO ISSN 0134-9899) **5126**
• Iberlex B O E - Boletin Oficial del Estado (ESP ISSN 1132-0451) **4849**
➤ Ibero-Americana (SWE ISSN 0046-8444) **4170**

▼ *new title* † *ceased* • *electronic media* ➤ *refereed*

Title

DIRECTORY 2010 ILLINOIS. LEGISLATIVE REFERENCE BUREAU. LEGISLATIVE 10399

Identite, Culture et Politique see Identity, Culture and Politics **8106**
Identitet (HRV ISSN 1331-386X) **3538**
• ➤ Identities (GBR ISSN 1070-289X) **3538**
Identity (IRL ISSN 1649-1033) **5894**
Identity (Coral Springs) (USA ISSN 1555-3914) **3978**
• Identity (Philadelphia) (USA ISSN 1528-3488) **8106**
➤ Identity, Culture and Politics/Identite, Culture et Politique (SEN ISSN 0851-2914) **8106**
▼ • ➤ Identity in the Information Society (NLD ISSN 1876-0678) **2514**
• ➤ Identity, Self & Symbolism (GBR ISSN 1748-8621) **342**
• Idenyt, Vi i Villa (DNK ISSN 1903-184X) **4543**
Idenyt, Vi med Hus og Have see Idenyt, Vi i Villa **4543**
† Ideo Mag (FRA ISSN 1953-6720) **8963**
Ideologia y Politica (PER ISSN 1019-455X) **7141**
Ideological and Political Education see Sixiang Zhengzhi Jiaoyu **2913**
Ideological Front see Sixiang Zhanxian **8002**
Ideologies of Desire (GBR) **5220**
Ideology and Politics Teaching see Sixiang Zhengzhike Jiaoxue **2913**
• ➤ Idesia (CHL ISSN 0073-4675) **120**
• Ide@sostenible (ESP ISSN 1887-2379) **7971**
† Idet News (CZE ISSN 1211-8702) **8963**
• iDetour (USA) **8868**
idFX see id F X **4542**
Idiom (AUS ISSN 0046-8568) **3064**
Idiom 23 (AUS ISSN 1032-1640) **5424**
Idiomania (ARG ISSN 0327-9758) **5126**
Idiomatica (DEU ISSN 0344-6719) **5126**
Idiot Wind (USA ISSN 1081-8073) **5308**
Idle-free Zone see Action Contre la Marche au Ralenti **3400**
The Idler (CAN ISSN 0828-1289) **3811**
Ido no Nippon/Journal of Japanese Acupuncture & Moxibustion (JPN ISSN 0287-6760) **310**
➤ Idojaras/Quarterly Journal of the Hungarian Meteorological Service (HUN ISSN 0324-6329) **6356**
Idol of My Heart Elvis Presley Fan Club Newsletter (USA) **2266**
▼ Idols. West Africa (ZAF ISSN 1994-165X) **4978**
Idraetshistorisk Aarbog (DNK ISSN 0900-8632) **8178**
• Idraetsliv (DNK ISSN 0109-3835) **8178**
Idrett & Anlegg (NOR ISSN 1503-0628) **8178**
➤ Idrijski Razgledi (SVN ISSN 0019-1523) **4146**
Idrott, Historia och Samhaelle (SWE ISSN 0280-2775) **8178**
Idrott & Haelse (SWE) **8178**
Idrott & Kunskap (SWE) **8178**
Idrottsbladet (SWE ISSN 0345-5106) **8178**
Idrottsbladet. Special (SWE ISSN 0345-5114) **8178**
Idrottsboken (SWE ISSN 0347-2744) **8235**
Idrottsforskaren (SWE ISSN 0348-9787) **8235**
• idrottsforum.org (SWE ISSN 1652-7224) **8178**
• Idrottslaeraren (SWE ISSN 1101-6892) **8235**
IDrugs see I Drugs: the Investigational Drugs Journal **6846**
Idryma Meleton Chersonesou Aimou. Ekdoseis see Institute for Balkan Studies. Publications **4232**
Idunna (USA ISSN 1937-397X) **7736**
Ie-no-Hikari/Light of Home (JPN ISSN 0913-7823) **120**
IEEE International Working Conference on Source Code Analysis and Manipulation. Proceedings (Institute of Electrical and Electronics Engineers) (USA ISSN 1942-5430) **2507**
IEEE/OSA Journal of Optical Communications and Networking see Journal of Optical Communications and Networking **7079**
IEEE Solid State Circuits Magazine see I E E E Solid State Circuits Magazine **3102**
IEEE Transactions on Autonomous Mental Development see I E E E Transactions on Autonomous Mental Development **7361**
IEEE Transactions on Dependable and Secure Computing see I E E E Transactions on Dependable and Secure Computing **2513**
IeJNART see International e-Journal of Numerical Analysis and Related Topics **5494**
Ieva (LTU ISSN 1648-3804) **2256**
Ieva (LVA ISSN 1407-2033) **8868**
▼ If My People (USA ISSN 1937-3856) **7649**
Ife Journal of Agriculture (NGA ISSN 0331-6351) **120**
Ife Journal of History (NGA ISSN 1116-4689) **4175**
• ➤ Ife Journal of Science (NGA ISSN 0794-4896) **7864**
Ife Studies in English Language (NGA ISSN 0794-9804) **5126**
Ifigea (ESP ISSN 0213-0149) **4015**
Ifjusagi Magazin see I M **2194**
▼ • ➤ iForest (ITA ISSN 1971-7458) **3693**
iFotoVideo see FotoVideo **6968**
Iga Bonchi Kasekishu/Atlas of Fossils from Iga Basin (JPN) **6725**
Igaku Butsuri/Japanese Journal of Medical Physics (JPN ISSN 1345-5354) **6198**
• Igaku Chuo Zasshi/Japana Centra Revuo Medicina (JPN ISSN 0387-0006) **5632**
Igaku Chuo Zasshi Personal Web see Igaku Chuo Zasshi **5632**
Igaku Chuo Zasshi Web (Corporate Edition) see Igaku Chuo Zasshi **5632**
Igaku Hyoron/Japana Medicina Revuo (JPN ISSN 0019-1574) **5632**
Igaku Kenkyusha Meibo/Japanese Medical Researchers Directory (JPN ISSN 0536-3489) **5632**
Igaku Kyoiku/Medical Education (JPN ISSN 0386-9644) **5632**
Igaku no Ayumi/Journal of Clinical and Experimental Medicine (JPN ISSN 0039-2359) **5632**
Igaku Seibutsugaku Kenkyu Kiyo see Acta Medica et Biologica **5566**
Igaku to Fukuin/Medicine and the Gospel (JPN ISSN 0019-1582) **5632**
Igaku to Seibutsugaku/Medicine and Biology (JPN ISSN 0019-1604) **5632**
Igaku to Yakugaku/Journal of Medicine and Pharmaceutical Science (JPN ISSN 0389-3898) **6847**
• Igaku Toshokan/Japan Medical Library Association. Journal (JPN ISSN 0445-2429) **5014**
Igakushi Kenkyu/Studium Historiae Medicae (JPN ISSN 0019-1612) **5632**
Igamehe Ristsonad (EST) **8178**
IGeL Aktiv see I G e L Aktiv **5631**
Igen (HUN ISSN 0864-8557) **7800**
Igeret (Louisville) (USA ISSN 1045-9898) **5126**
Iggeret see Igeret (Louisville) **5126**
Igiene Alimenti. Disinfestazione & Igiene Ambientale (ITA ISSN 1721-5366) **7524**
Igiene e Salute Orale (ITA ISSN 1824-9787) **5847**
Igiene e Sanita Pubblica (ITA ISSN 0019-1639) **7524**
• Igiene & Sicurezza del Lavoro (ITA ISSN 1592-5633) **7524**
• Igiene e Sicurezza del Lavoro. I Corsi (ITA ISSN 1129-5864) **7524**
Igitur Revista Literaria (ARG ISSN 0019-1663) **5308**
Iglesia de Sevilla (ESP) **7800**
• Ignaziana (ITA ISSN 1828-2377) **7800**
Ignite (USA ISSN 1533-8819) **6574**
• Ignite Your Faith (USA ISSN 1558-7770) **2194**
Ignition Magazine (AUS ISSN 1834-0717) **8585**
Igo (JPN ISSN 1345-8809) **8178**
• Igorota (PHL ISSN 1655-2245) **8868**
Igra (ISR ISSN 0334-5572) **5308**
Igra i Deti (RUS) **2155**
Igra'a (Guddat) see Iqraa **3944**
➤ Igreja Luterana (BRA ISSN 0103-779X) **7761**
Igualdad de Oportunidades entre Mujeres y Hombres en la Union Europea see Equal Opportunities for Women and Men in the European Union **1680**
Igualdade de Oportunidades entre Mulheres e Homens na Uniao Europeia see Equal Opportunities for Women and Men in the European Union **1680**
Iguana (DEU) **947**
Iguana (USA ISSN 1554-916X) **2194**
Iguana Magazine (NLD ISSN 1876-4193) **947**
Iguana-Rundschreiben see Iguana **947**
Iguretta/Egretta (JPN) **908**
• iHealthCare Weekly (USA) **2558**
➤ Iheringia. Serie Botanica (BRA ISSN 0073-4705) **793**
• ➤ Iheringia. Serie Zoologia (BRA ISSN 0073-4721) **947**
Ihitza (ESP ISSN 1135-6391) **3439**
Iho Hanamaki/Hanamaki City Medical Association. News (JPN) **5632**
• iHomes & Buildings (CAN ISSN 1719-4563) **3318**
Ihos kai Hi Fi see Echos kai Hi Fi **6564**
Ihr Reiseplan (DEU) **8618**
Ihsa'at al-Anshitah al-'Ilmiyyah wal-Teknolojiyyah fi Dawlat al-Kuwayt see Statistics on Scientific and Technological Activities **7939**
Ihsa'iyyat Dubai lil-Tijarah al-Kharijiyyah see Dubai External Trade Statistics **1225**
Iines (FIN ISSN 1459-6261) **2194**
Iisalmen Sanomat (FIN ISSN 0356-2298) **3838**
Iiyama Memoirs see Iiyama Ronso **2986**
Iiyama Ronso/Iiyama Memoirs (JPN ISSN 0289-3762) **2986**
Ija Webonere (TZA ISSN 0856-1931) **7761**
IJIDEM see I J I D E M **3379**
Ijslandse Paarden (NLD ISSN 1384-4334) **8293**
IJsselakademie see Historisch Overijssel **4144**
Ijsselmeer Krant see Ijsselmeerberichten **7864**
Ijsselmeerberichten (NLD ISSN 1571-9448) **7864**
IJsselmeerziekenhuizen Magazine see I J Z Magazine **5631**
Ik Ga Bouwen see Casas (Dutch Edition) **990**
Ika Kikaigaku/Japanese Journal of Medical Instrumentation (JPN ISSN 0385-440X) **5632**
Ikaalisten Kasi- ja Taideteollisuusoppilaitos. Julkaisu (FIN ISSN 1795-7834) **495**
Ikagaku Oyo Kenkyu Zaidan Kenkyu Hokoku/Suzuken Memorial Foundation. Research Papers (JPN ISSN 0914-5117) **7524**
Ikala (COL ISSN 0123-3432) **5126**
Ikarie (CZE ISSN 1210-6798) **5443**
Ikastaria (ESP ISSN 1137-4446) **2865**
▼ • ➤ Ikastorratza (ESP ISSN 1988-5911) **2865**
IKEA Family Live (DEU) **4543**
IKEA Room see IKEA Family Live **4543**
IKEA Space see Space **4562**
Ikenga (NGA ISSN 0331-0205) **3538**
Iki Sahil (AZE) **3798**
Ikia & Diakosmisi (GRC) **4543**
Ikkare Yisra'el (ISR ISSN 0333-9025) **120**
Ikomayama Uchu Kagakukan Nyusu (JPN) **6525**
▼ • Ikon (BEL ISSN 1846-8551) **6924**
Ikon (DEU ISSN 0941-911X) **5993**
• Ikon (ITA ISSN 0019-1744) **2325**
▼ Ikon (NOR ISSN 1504-7814) **3923**
Ikonenkalender (DEU) **495**
• Ikoner (SWE ISSN 1403-7211) **5014**
Ikonomicheska Misul (BGR ISSN 0013-2993) **1121**
Ikonomicheski Izsledvania/Studies of Economics (BGR ISSN 0205-3292) **1121**
Ikonomicheski Zhivot (BGR ISSN 0205-0994) **1121**
Ikonomika (BGR ISSN 0204-711X) **1352**
Ikonomika i Finansi (BGR ISSN 1311-2376) **8377**
Ikonomika i Upravlenie na Selskoto Stopanstvo (BGR ISSN 0205-3845) **200**
➤ Ikonotheka (POL ISSN 0860-5769) **495**
Ikoro (NGA) **4175**
Ikusgaiak (ESP ISSN 1137-4438) **6503**
• ➤ Ikushugaku Kenkyu/Breeding Research (JPN ISSN 1344-7629) **677**
Ikushugaku Zasshi/Japanese Journal of Breeding see Ikushugaku Kenkyu **677**
Il-Kampanja (MLT) **2614**
Ilahiyat Fakultesi Dergisi see Ataturk Universitesi. Ilahiyat Fakultesi. Dergisi **7709**
▼ The Ilan Stavans' Library of Latino Civilization (USA ISSN 1938-615X) **3538**
Ilanga (ZAF ISSN 0019-1779) **3948**
Ilanga LangeSonto (ZAF ISSN 1816-0972) **3948**
Ilanga le Theku (ZAF ISSN 1816-8892) **3948**
Ilco-Praxis (DEU ISSN 0724-8016) **6021**
Ildfisken (DNK ISSN 0906-5202) **5308**
• Ile de France (FRA ISSN 1779-4331) **4978**
Ile-de-France see Adventure Guide. Paris & Ile-de-France **8681**
Ile-de-France Regards sur... (FRA ISSN 1775-0326) **8377**
Ileostomy and Internal Pouch Support Group Quarterly Journal see I A Quarterly Journal **6021**
Ilerda. Ciencies (ESP ISSN 1130-7900) **7864**
Ilerda. Humanitats (ESP ISSN 1130-7897) **4456**
Les Iles see Le Magazine les Iles **7497**
† Iles (FRA ISSN 1012-8107) **8963**
Ilex (DEU ISSN 0937-3691) **677**
Ilford & Redbridge Post (GBR ISSN 1469-2317) **3866**
Ilford Recorder (GBR ISSN 0961-3331) **3866**
➤ Ilha do Desterro (BRA ISSN 0101-4846) **5308**
Ilhicac (MEX ISSN 0188-4093) **4146**
Ilia Vekuas Saxelobis Gamoqenebit'i Mat'ematikis Institutis Seminaris Gap'art'oebuli Sxdomebis Moxsenebebi/Javakhishvili Tbilisi State University. Ilia Vekua Institute of Applied Mathematics. Reports of Enlarged Sessions of the Seminar (GEO ISSN 1512-0066) **5492**
Ilia Vekuas Saxelobis Gamoqenebit'i Mat'ematikis Institutis Seminaris Moxsenebebi/Tbilisi Ivane Javakhishvili State University. Seminar of Ilia Vekua Institute of Applied Mathematics. Reports (GEO ISSN 1512-0058) **5492**
▼ • Ilinois Employment Law (USA ISSN 1934-1598) **1687**
Iliria (ALB ISSN 1727-2548) **397**
Ilkka (FIN ISSN 0356-1283) **3838**
• ➤ Ilkoegretim Online/Elementary Education Online (TUR ISSN 1305-3515) **2865**
Ilkoegretim Online E-Dergi see Ilkoegretim Online **2865**
Ill Eagle (GBR ISSN 1466-9005) **6293**
• Illawarra Unity (AUS ISSN 1327-8126) **4596**
Illegal Drugs (Farmington Hills) see Information Plus Reference Series. Alcohol, Tobacco, and Illicit Drugs **2695**
Illiana Genealogist (USA ISSN 0019-1809) **3771**
Illiana News (USA) **7722**
• Illiesia (SVN ISSN 1854-0392) **849**
Illinois A F L - C I O Laborletter see LaborLetter **4597**
Illinois. Administrative Office of Illinois Courts. Annual Report to the Supreme Court of Illinois (USA ISSN 0536-3713) **4952**
Illinois Advance (USA ISSN 0745-1539) **4074**
Illinois Agri News (USA ISSN 0194-7443) **120**
Illinois: All-Industries see Harris Directory. Illinois All-Industries **2000**
Illinois Alumni (USA) **2287**
Illinois Appellate Reports (USA ISSN 0884-0482) **4690**
Illinois Archaeological Survey. Bulletin Series (USA) **397**
Illinois Archaeological Survey. Circular Series (USA) **397**
Illinois Archaeological Survey. Monographs (USA) **397**
Illinois Archaeological Survey. Special Publications (USA) **397**
Illinois Archaeology (USA ISSN 1050-8244) **397**
Illinois Association of Defense Trial Counsel Quarterly see I D C Quarterly **4689**
Illinois Attorney General's Report and Opinions (USA) **4690**
Illinois Audubon (USA ISSN 1061-9801) **2614**
Illinois Aviation (USA ISSN 0276-640X) **8544**
• Illinois Banker (USA ISSN 0019-185X) **1352**
• Illinois Banking Act and Related Laws (USA ISSN 1551-0700) **1352**
Illinois Baptist (USA ISSN 0019-1868) **7761**
• ➤ Illinois Bar Journal (USA ISSN 0019-1876) **4690**
Illinois Beef (USA) **288**
Illinois Beverage Guide (USA) **604**
Illinois Blue Book (USA ISSN 0191-104X) **7445**
• Illinois. Board of Higher Education. Directory of Higher Education (USA ISSN 0094-8322) **2986**
• Illinois Braille Messenger (USA ISSN 0019-1906) **4082**
Illinois. Bureau of Air. Annual Air Quality Report (USA) **3487**
Illinois Business (USA) **1405**
• Illinois Business Credit Directory (USA) **2005**
• Illinois Business Directory (USA ISSN 1048-504X) **2005**
Illinois Chicago see Chicago Area Business Directory **1979**
• Illinois Child Welfare (USA ISSN 1934-3612) **8046**
Illinois Cities and Counties Graphic Performance Analysis see Illinois Cities & Counties Graphic Performance Analysis **7481**
Illinois Cities & Counties Graphic Performance Analysis (USA ISSN 1935-5823) **7481**
Illinois Civil Litigation Guide see Illinois Practice Series. Civil Litigation Guide **4832**
Illinois Civil Trial Guide (USA) **4832**
Illinois Classical Studies (USA ISSN 0363-1923) **2235**
Illinois Commercial Financing Forms with Practice Commentary (USA) **1352**
Illinois. Community College Board. Biennial Report (USA) **2986**
Illinois. Community College Board. Data and Characteristics (USA) **2986**
Illinois Compiled Statutes (USA ISSN 1069-5613) **4952**
Illinois Conservation Law (USA) **2614**
Illinois Council for the Social Studies. Journal (USA) **2865**
Illinois Council for the Social Studies Newsletter see I C S S Newsletter **2865**
Illinois Country Living (USA ISSN 1086-8062) **3978**
Illinois Court Rules and Procedure (USA) **4690**
➤ Illinois Courts Bulletin (USA ISSN 0019-1957) **4690**
• Illinois Criminal and Traffic Law Manual (USA ISSN 1530-163X) **4891**
• Illinois Criminal Defense Motions (USA) **4891**
• Illinois Criminal Law (USA) **4891**
• Illinois Criminal Law and Motor Vehicle Handbook (USA) **4891**
• Illinois Criminal Procedure (USA) **4891**
Illinois Dealer Directory and Buyer's Guide (USA) **1013**
Illinois Deer & Turkey Show Preview (USA) **8318**
Illinois Dental News (USA ISSN 1084-8282) **5847**
Illinois. Department of Human Services. Division of Disability and Behavioral Health Services. Illinois Statistics (USA) **8083**
Illinois Director (USA) **3719**
Illinois' Divorce Magazine (CAN ISSN 1492-2045) **8106**
Illinois Domestic Relations and Related Laws Annotated (USA ISSN 1542-930X) **4911**
Illinois Domestic Relations Forms (USA) **4911**
Illinois Downstate see Downstate Illinois Business Directory **1989**
• Illinois Employment Law Letter (USA ISSN 1049-9385) **4870**
Illinois Engineer (USA ISSN 0019-2015) **3197**
Illinois English Bulletin (USA ISSN 0019-2023) **3064**
• Illinois Entertainer (USA ISSN 1078-1986) **6575**
Illinois Environmental Protection Agency. Division of Water Pollution Control. Report (USA) **3487**
Illinois Estate Planning Will Drafting and Estate Administration Forms (USA) **4903**
† Illinois Evidentiary Foundations (USA) **8963**
Illinois Facts (USA ISSN 1041-2778) **3120**
Illinois FarmWeek (USA) **120**
Illinois Federation of Teachers Insight see I F T Insight **2865**
Illinois Food Retailers' Association (USA) **3646**
Illinois Food Service News (USA ISSN 0279-9618) **4391**
• Illinois Forest Management (USA ISSN 1057-2236) **3693**
Illinois Forms of Jury Instruction (USA) **4690**
Illinois Game & Fish (USA ISSN 0897-9014) **8318**
➤ Illinois Geographical Society. Bulletin (USA ISSN 0019-2031) **4015**
Illinois Guard Chronicle (USA) **6424**
Illinois Heritage (USA ISSN 1094-0596) **4297**
• Illinois History (Online) (USA) **4297**
• Illinois History Teacher (USA) **2865**
Illinois. Housing Development Authority. Annual Report (USA ISSN 0090-3248) **4415**
Illinois, Indiana, Ohio TourBook see TourBook: Illinois, Indiana, Ohio **8762**
Illinois-Indiana Sea Grant College Program. Report (USA) **677**
Illinois Insurance (USA ISSN 0094-7660) **4505**
• Illinois Insurance Laws (USA) **4690**
Illinois Issues (USA ISSN 0738-9663) **7141**
➤ Illinois Journal of Health, Physical Education, Recreation and Dance (USA ISSN 1062-2764) **6989**
• ➤ Illinois Journal of Mathematics (USA ISSN 0019-2082) **5492**
Illinois Journal of Technology Education (USA ISSN 1545-6684) **8425**
Illinois Jury Verdict Reporter (USA) **4832**
Illinois Labor History Society Reporter (USA ISSN 0085-1728) **1687**
Illinois Law Office Practice Forms (USA) **4870**
Illinois Leave to Appeal Table (USA ISSN 1048-2148) **4952**
Illinois. Legislative Reference Bureau. Legislative Synopsis and Digest (USA) **4690**

Title

▼ *new title* † *ceased* • *electronic media* ➤ *refereed*

10400 ILLINOIS LEGISLATIVE SERVICE ULRICH'S PERIODICALS

Illinois Legislative Service (USA ISSN 1076-7517) **4690**
† • Illinois Libraries (USA ISSN 0019-2104) **8963**
• Illinois Libraries (Online) (USA) **5014**
Illinois Library Association Reporter *see* I L A Reporter **5014**
† Illinois Limitations Manual (USA) **8963**
• Illinois Literacy (USA) **3024**
• The Illinois Manufacturer (USA) **1888**
• The Illinois Manufacturers Association. Annual Reports. Benefits Report (USA) **1121**
• The Illinois Manufacturers Association. Annual Reports. Compensation Report (USA) **1121**
• Illinois Manufacturers Directory (USA ISSN 0160-3302) **2005**
Illinois: Manufacturing *see* Harris Directory. Illinois Manufacturing **2000**
Illinois Master Plumber Magazine (USA ISSN 0019-2112) **4120**
▼ Illinois Meetings + Events (USA) **6280**
Illinois Minerals (USA) **6464**
Illinois Mining Institute. Proceedings (USA) **6464**
▼ • Illinois Motions in Limine (USA ISSN 1944-8503) **4952**
Illinois Municipal Review (USA ISSN 0019-2139) **7494**
• Illinois Municipal Tort Liability (USA) **4690**
• ➤ Illinois Music Educator (USA ISSN 0019-2147) **6575**
➤ Illinois Natural History Survey. Biological Notes (USA ISSN 1076-4712) **677**
➤ Illinois Natural History Survey. Bulletin (USA ISSN 0073-4918) **677**
• Illinois Natural History Survey Reports (USA ISSN 0536-4132) **2614**
Illinois. Natural History Survey. Special Publication (USA ISSN 0888-9546) **677**
Illinois Objections at Trial (USA) **4952**
Illinois Optometric Association. Journal (USA ISSN 0279-6422) **6043**
▼ Illinois Outdoor News (USA ISSN 1942-6461) **8318**
Illinois Parks & Recreation (USA ISSN 0019-2155) **8318**
Illinois Petroleum (USA ISSN 0073-5108) **6773**
Illinois Pharmacist (USA ISSN 0195-2099) **6847**
Illinois Police Association. Official Journal (USA ISSN 0019-2171) **2654**
Illinois Postal Historian (USA) **6895**
Illinois Practice Series. Civil Litigation Guide (USA ISSN 1930-4889) **4832**
• Illinois Prairie Farmer (USA ISSN 0032-6615) **120**
Illinois PressLines (USA ISSN 1074-5009) **4576**
Illinois Probate Act and Related Laws Annotated (USA) **4903**
Illinois Probate Laws Annotated *see* Illinois Probate Act and Related Laws Annotated **4903**
Illinois Property Tax Statistics (USA) **1241**
The Illinois Public Employee Relations Report (USA ISSN 1559-9892) **1687**
Illinois Public Employment Library on CD-ROM *see* Public Employee Reporter for Illinois **4763**
Illinois Public Sector *see* Illinois Staff Directory **7445**
Illinois Racing News (USA ISSN 1083-8309) **8293**
• Illinois Reading Council Journal (USA ISSN 1082-555X) **2865**
• Illinois Real Estate Forms (USA) **7594**
Illinois Real Estate Journal (USA) **7594**
Illinois Real Estate Leasing Forms with Practice Commentary (USA) **7594**
Illinois Reporter (USA) **1352**
Illinois Reports (USA ISSN 0160-1199) **4690**
Illinois Reports *see* West's Jury Verdicts. Illinois Reports **4967**
Illinois School Board Journal (USA ISSN 0019-221X) **3024**
Illinois School Directory *see* M D R's School Directory. Illinois **2958**
Illinois Schools Journal (USA ISSN 0019-2236) **2865**
• Illinois Services Directory (USA ISSN 0092-3818) **2005**
Illinois Snowmobiler (USA ISSN 0745-0915) **8318**
➤ Illinois Speech and Theatre Association. Journal (USA ISSN 0145-5516) **2325**
Illinois Staff Directory (USA ISSN 1938-4890) **7445**
➤ Illinois State Academy of Science. Transactions (USA ISSN 0019-2252) **7864**
Illinois State Alumni Magazine (USA) **2287**
Illinois State Bar Association Bar News *see* I S B A Bar News **4689**
• ➤ Illinois State Bar Association. Education Law (USA) **4690**
Illinois State Bar Association. Human Rights Law Section. Newsletter *see* Human Rights **8045**
• Illinois. State Board of Education. Annual Report (USA ISSN 0147-2860) **3024**
Illinois State Genealogical Society Quarterly (USA ISSN 0046-8622) **3771**
Illinois. State Geological Survey. Bulletin (USA ISSN 0073-5051) **2746**
Illinois. State Geological Survey. Circular (USA ISSN 0073-506X) **2746**
Illinois. State Geological Survey. Cooperative Groundwater Report (USA ISSN 0731-7662) **8825**
Illinois. State Geological Survey. Environmental Geology (USA ISSN 1060-1988) **2747**
Illinois. State Geological Survey. Guidebook Series (USA ISSN 0073-5094) **2747**
• ➤ Illinois State Historical Society. Journal (USA ISSN 1522-1067) **4297**
Illinois. State Library, Springfield. Publications of the State of Illinois. (USA ISSN 0191-1058) **7199**
Illinois. State Museum. Handbook of Collections (USA ISSN 0445-3387) **495**
➤ Illinois. State Museum. Inventory of the Collections (USA ISSN 0095-2893) **6525**
➤ Illinois. State Museum. Popular Science Series (USA ISSN 0360-0297) **7864**
Illinois. State Museum. Reports of Investigations (USA ISSN 0360-0270) **7864**
➤ Illinois. State Museum. Scientific Papers Series (USA ISSN 0445-3395) **7864**
Illinois State Water Survey. Bulletin (USA ISSN 0360-9804) **8825**
Illinois State Water Survey. Circular (USA ISSN 0097-5524) **8825**
• Illinois Statistical Abstract (Online) (USA ISSN 1933-5709) **8377**
Illinois Steward (USA ISSN 1058-9309) **2614**
Illinois Super Lawyers (USA ISSN 1930-5443) **4690**
Illinois T E S O L - B E Newsletter *see* Illinois Teachers of English to Speakers of Other Languages - Bilingual Education Newsletter **5126**
Illinois Teachers of English to Speakers of Other Languages - Bilingual Education Newsletter (USA) **5126**
• Illinois Technograph (USA ISSN 0745-6476) **3197**
• Illinois Technology (USA) **8425**
• Illinois Tort Law (USA ISSN 1555-1660) **4690**
Illinois Truck News (USA ISSN 0019-2309) **8671**
Illinois Valley Archaeological Program Research Papers (USA) **397**
• Illinois Vehicle Code (USA) **4690**
Illinois Voter (USA ISSN 1041-1283) **7141**
Illinois Workers' Compensation Digest (USA) **4505**
• Illinois Workers' Compensation Law Bulletin (USA ISSN 1067-2338) **4505**
• ➤ Illness, Crisis, and Loss (USA ISSN 1054-1373) **8107**
Illtop Journal (USA) **5220**
Illum (MLT) **3907**
Illume Magazine (USA ISSN 1942-244X) **7711**
Illuminating Engineering Institute of Japan. Journal *see* Shomei Gakkai Shi **3331**
• Illuminating Engineering Society. Journal (USA ISSN 0099-4480) **3318**
Illuminating Engineering Society of North America Lighting Handbook *see* I E S Lighting Handbook **3316**
Illuminations (USA ISSN 0736-4725) **5424**
L'Illuminista (ITA ISSN 1720-5395) **4456**
Illuminotecnica (ITA ISSN 0019-2384) **3318**
Illusions (NZL ISSN 0112-9341) **6503**
Illustoria (FRA ISSN 1778-6878) **4231**
Illustrated Flora of Hokkaido *see* Miyabea **801**
Illustrated Periodical for Kindergarteners *see* Wawa Huabao **2221**
Illustrated Report of Communications *see* Zusetsu Tsushin Hakusho **2346**
Illustrated Weekly of India (IND ISSN 0019-2430) **3883**
Illustration (USA ISSN 1543-4737) **495**
Illustration in Japan (JPN) **495**
Illustratofiat (ITA) **8585**
Illustrator (USA ISSN 0019-2465) **495**
The Illustrator Collectors News (USA) **4337**
Illustrazione Ticinese (CHE) **3958**
L'Illustre (CHE ISSN 1420-5165) **3958**
Illustrerad Vetenskap (DNK ISSN 0281-9341) **7864**
• Illustreret Bunker (DNK) **4576**
Illustreret Videnskab (DNK ISSN 0109-2456) **7865**
Illustrert Vitenskap (NOR ISSN 0800-3955) **7865**
Illustrierte Neue Welt (AUT) **3538**
• Illustrierte Wochenzeitung (DEU) **2382**
Illustrierte Wochenzeitung Online *see* I W Z Online **2382**
➤ Al-Ilm (ZAF ISSN 0258-932X) **7711**
Ilmailu (FIN ISSN 0019-252X) **59**
Ilmanlaadun Julkaisuja/Finnish Meteorological Institute. Publications on Air Quality (FIN ISSN 1456-789X) **3487**
➤ Ilmansuojeluyhdistys (FIN ISSN 1239-8950) **3487**
Ilmastotilastoja Suomesta/Climatological Statistics of Finland (FIN ISSN 1458-4530) **6400**
Ilmatieteen Laitos. Geofysikaalisia Julkaisuja *see* Finnish Meteorological Institute. Geophysical Publications **2780**
Ilmatieteen Laitos. Meteorologisia Julkaisuja/Finnish Meteorological Institute. Publications (FIN ISSN 0782-6109) **6356**
Ilmavoimalainen (FIN ISSN 1795-7672) **6424**
Ilmenauer Uni-Nachrichten (DEU) **2287**
Ilmiocamper (ITA ISSN 1970-6065) **8318**
Ilmu Alam (MYS ISSN 0126-7000) **4015**
Ilocos Review (PHL ISSN 0019-2538) **4183**
Ilot (FRA ISSN 1768-546X) **5308**
• Ilta - Sanomat (FIN ISSN 0355-2055) **3838**
Ilta-Sanomat Plussa *see* Ilta - Sanomat **3838**
Ilta-Sanomat T V *see* Ilta - Sanomat **3838**
• Iltalehti (FIN ISSN 0783-0025) **3838**
Iltalehti Areena *see* Iltalehti **3838**
• 'Ilu (ESP ISSN 1135-4712) **7649**
'Ilu. Anejos (ESP ISSN 1578-1305) **7649**
'Ilu. Cuadernos *see* 'Ilu. Anejos **7649**
'Ilu. Monografias *see* 'Ilu. Anejos **7649**
Iluminace (CZE ISSN 0862-397X) **6503**
• La Ilustracion Liberal (ESP ISSN 1139-8051) **5220**
Ilustre Colegio de Abogados de Madrid. Boletin (ESP ISSN 0413-2963) **4690**
• Ilustre Consejo General de Colegios de Ondotologos y Estomatologos de Espana. Revista (ESP ISSN 1138-123X) **5847**
Ilustrovana Politika (SRB ISSN 0019-2570) **3945**
Im Dienst der Kirche (DEU ISSN 0939-4656) **7800**
Im Einsatz (DEU ISSN 1617-4283) **5632**
Im Focus Onkologie (DEU ISSN 1435-7402) **6021**
Im Garten (DEU ISSN 0946-3313) **3738**
Im Herzen Europas (CZE ISSN 1211-9296) **5220**
Im Lande der Bibel (DEU ISSN 0019-2597) **7649**
Im Medium Fremder Sprachen und Kulturen (DEU ISSN 1439-5894) **5126**
Im Ruhestand *see* Aktiv im Ruhestand **4039**
Ima Focus *see* Strategic Technotes **1180**
Imafronte (ESP ISSN 0213-392X) **495**
Image (AUS ISSN 0728-5701) **6969**
Image (DEU ISSN 0176-8565) **7649**
Image (IND) **551**
• Image (IRL ISSN 0791-7570) **8868**
The Image (USA) **2155**
Image (ZAF) **6969**
• Image (Cologne) (DEU ISSN 1614-0885) **495**
Image (London) (GBR ISSN 1361-2050) **6969**
• ➤ Image (Rochester, 1952) (USA ISSN 0536-5465) **6969**
Image (Seattle) (USA ISSN 1087-3503) **7649**
Image (Suffolk) (USA) **4120**
• ➤ Image Analysis and Stereology (SVN ISSN 1580-3139) **677**
• ➤ Image & Narrative (BEL ISSN 1780-678X) **4456**
➤ Image & Text (ZAF ISSN 1021-1497) **495**
• ➤ Image and Vision Computing (NLD ISSN 0262-8856) **2487**
Image Communication *see* Signal Processing: Image Communication **2535**
Image de la Mauricie (CAN ISSN 0704-7428) **2638**
Image File (USA ISSN 1046-6614) **4297**
Image Hifi (DEU ISSN 0947-8922) **3104**
Image Home Entertainment (DEU ISSN 1435-2982) **3104**
Image: I L A S Bulletin (International Linear Algebra Society) (USA) **5492**
Image Interiors (IRL ISSN 1393-4406) **4543**
Image Lab *see* Gazo Rabo **6969**
Image Magazine (AUS) **7323**
The Image Makers Source (USA) **6969**
Image Processing Europe *see* Vision Systems Design **3226**
Image Reports (GBR ISSN 1478-338X) **7329**
Image-Scene (DEU ISSN 0937-101X) **6980**
Image Source *see* imageSource **1851**
Image Technology *see* Yingxiang Jishu **6978**
† • Image Technology (GBR ISSN 0950-2114) **8963**
• Image Technology (GBR) **6503**
ImageMakers (CAN) **1121**
• Imagen (MEX) **3909**
Imagen (PRI ISSN 0890-6548) **3931**
Imagen (VEN ISSN 0797-3233) **4456**
• Imagen Vasca Online (ESP) **1429**
Imagenes *see* La Opinion **3830**
Imagenes (URY) **3994**
Imagenes de Actualidad (ESP ISSN 1137-6546) **6503**
Imagenes de la Fe (ESP ISSN 0211-5441) **7649**
Imagens da Amazonia (BRA) **2614**
Imagepack (USA) **6969**
• Imagerie de la Femme (FRA ISSN 1776-9817) **5633**
Imagery Today (USA ISSN 1041-8377) **7361**
▼ • Images (NLD ISSN 1871-7993) **495**
ImageS *see* Vadeboncoeur Collection of Images **524**
• Images (Kansas City) (USA) **3978**
Images (London) (GBR) **26**
Images (New York) (USA) **4375**
Images (Pensacola) *see* Journal of Radiology Nursing **5967**
Images Doc (FRA ISSN 0995-1121) **2194**
Images Documentaires (FRA ISSN 1255-3468) **6503**
Images du Mois (FRA ISSN 0750-3407) **7800**
Images en Bibliotheques. La Lettre (FRA ISSN 1952-8752) **6503**
▼ Images en Ophtalmologie (FRA ISSN 1961-3172) **6043**
Images Images (FRA ISSN 1951-5960) **495**
• Images in Paediaric Cardiology (MLT ISSN 1729-441X) **6092**
• Images Inscript (USA) **5220**
• images.MD (USA ISSN 1537-8926) **5633**
• Images Newsletter (USA) **2487**
Images of Excellence (USA ISSN 0899-1138) **643**
• ➤ Images Re - Vues (FRA ISSN 1778-3801) **342**
▼ Images Spectacles Photo (FRA ISSN 1955-6063) **6969**
• Images Yearbook (IND ISSN 0972-9739) **2256**
imageSource (USA) **1851**
• ➤ ImageTexT (USA ISSN 1549-6732) **5126**
• Imaginaire & Inconscient (FRA ISSN 1628-9676) **7361**
Imaginaire et Inconscient *see* Imaginaire & Inconscient **7361**
Imaginaires (Reims) (FRA ISSN 1270-931X) **5308**
• Imaginaria (MEX) **5424**
• Imaginario (BRA ISSN 1413-666X) **7361**
• ➤ Imagination, Cognition and Personality (USA ISSN 0276-2366) **7362**
Imagine (GBR ISSN 1748-1244) **6503**
† • Imagine (ITA) **8963**
Imagine (NLD ISSN 1875-2942) **6924**
▼ Imagine (ZAF ISSN 1996-2797) **4337**
• Imagine (Baltimore) (USA ISSN 1071-605X) **3041**
Imagine (Cambridge) (USA ISSN 1930-6016) **7563**
Imagine (Spokane) (USA ISSN 1549-4314) **6645**
Imagine Animation Directory (GBR ISSN 1755-0718) **6503**
Imagine Demain le Monde (BEL ISSN 1782-0758) **1598**
Imagine F X (GBR ISSN 1748-930X) **2487**
Imagined South Africa (NLD) **4175**
Imagines Medii Aevi (DEU) **4231**
• ➤ Imaging (GBR ISSN 0965-6812) **6198**
• Imaging Abstracts (GBR ISSN 0896-100X) **6979**
Imaging and Machine Vision Europe (GBR ISSN 1745-5758) **3367**
• Imaging & Microscopy (DEU ISSN 1439-4243) **899**
• Imaging & Radiology Product Comparison System (USA) **6198**
• ➤ Imaging Decisions M R I (Magnetic Resonance Imaging) (DEU ISSN 1433-3317) **6198**
Imaging Diagnosis in Nuclear Medicine *see* Kaku Igaku Gazo Shindan **6202**
• Imaging Economics (USA) **6198**
▼ • Imaging in Medicine (GBR ISSN 1755-5191) **6198**
Imaging Science and Photochemistry *see* Yingxiang Kexue yu Guanghuaxue **6978**
• ➤ The Imaging Science Journal (GBR ISSN 1368-2199) **6969**
Imaging Society of Japan. Journal *see* Nihon Gazo Gakkaishi **6971**
Imaging Spectrum Magazine (USA ISSN 1540-5044) **3318**
Imaging Technology News *see* M E N Imaging Technology News **6202**
Imaging Technology Report (USA ISSN 1041-4320) **3318**
Imaging und Foto-Contact (DEU ISSN 1430-1121) **6970**
Imagining America News *see* I A News **2865**
Imagining America. Newsletter *see* I A News **2865**
• ➤ Imago Mundi (GBR ISSN 0308-5694) **4146**
Imago Musicae (ITA ISSN 0255-8831) **6575**
Imago Shop & Fair (ITA ISSN 1824-2421) **4543**
Imago Vitae (DEU ISSN 1614-4449) **643**
Imanet (USA) **1121**
Al-Imarat fil-Ajwa'/Emirates Inflight (UAE) **8784**
▼ • iMarketing Magazine (USA ISSN 1949-4084) **1820**
Imarsiornermik Quppersagaq/Haandbog for Fiskeri (GRL ISSN 1603-3485) **3597**
• ImasD (Online) (ESP ISSN 1696-2427) **8425**
• iMassJazz Ezine (USA) **6575**
Imatge (ESP ISSN 1135-2167) **6503**
Imbibe (USA ISSN 1557-7082) **604**
Imbila (ZMB) **3995**
Imbonezamulyango *see* Rwanda. Office National de la Population. Famille, Sante, Developpement **7292**
Imbongi Yenkosi (ZAF ISSN 0378-4088) **7761**
• Imbottigliamento (ITA ISSN 0392-792X) **6710**
iMD *see* images.MD **5633**
IMechE Seminar Publication *see* Institution of Mechanical Engineers Seminar Publication **8965**
Imenem Zakonu (UKR) **4690**
Imfama (Braille Edition) (ZAF) **4082**
Imfama (Inkprint Edition) (ZAF ISSN 0019-2724) **4082**
Imfama (Tape Edition) (ZAF) **4082**
➤ Imhotep (CMR ISSN 1608-9324) **5492**
iMira! *see* Mira! **3982**
Imkerfreund (DEU ISSN 0019-2732) **120**
Immaculate Conception College. La Salle Journal (PHL) **342**
L'Immaginazione (ITA) **5308**
iMMAgine *see* Imagine (Cambridge) **7563**
L'Immagine Riflessa (ITA ISSN 0391-2973) **5308**
Immagini Foto - Pratica *see* Immagini Fotopratica **6970**
Immagini Fotopratica (ITA ISSN 1592-341X) **6970**
† Immaginifico (ITA ISSN 1593-9286) **8963**
† Immanuel (ISR ISSN 0302-8127) **8963**
Immediate Arts - Writers' Directory (GBR) **7563**
▼ Immediate Care Business (USA) **4102**
Immer Gruen (DEU) **7761**
Immersed Magazine (USA) **8178**
Immersion Journal *see* Le Journal de l'Immersion **3066**
Immigrant Communities & Ethnic Minorities in the United States & Canada (USA ISSN 0749-5951) **7284**
Immigrant Genealogical Society. Newsletter (USA) **3771**
• ➤ Immigrants and Minorities (GBR ISSN 0261-9288) **4146**
• Immigrant's Weekly (USA) **4849**
Immigranty (RUS) **7209**
Immigration and Asylum Law and Policy in Europe (NLD ISSN 1568-2749) **4849**
The Immigration and Ethnic History. Newsletter (USA ISSN 1949-9671) **7284**
Immigration and Illegal Aliens (Farmington Hills) *see* Information Plus Reference Series. Immigration and Illegal Aliens **7241**
Immigration & Nationality Law Handbook (USA ISSN 1072-4257) **4849**
Immigration and Nationality Law Reports (GBR ISSN 1460-423X) **4928**
• ➤ Immigration and Nationality Law Review (USA ISSN 0149-9807) **4928**

Title

Title

Title

Title

Inferno! (GBR ISSN 1369-8648) 5443
Inferno Magazine (FIN ISSN 1796-7600) 6575
Infeuro (LUX ISSN 1027-930X) 4928
Le Infezioni in Medicina (ITA ISSN 1124-9390) 5817
An Infiltrated Enemy see Un Nemico Infiltrato 1026
Infiltration (CAN) 5221
• InFinance (AUS ISSN 1834-4232) 1353
L'Infini (FRA ISSN 0754-023X) 5221
• ➤ Infinite Dimensional Analysis, Quantum Probability and Related Topics (SGP ISSN 0219-0257) 5493
Infinite Energy (USA ISSN 1081-6372) 3138
• The Infinite Matrix (USA) 5443
InFinsia see InFinance 1353
Infirmiere Autochtone see Aboriginal Nurse 5950
L'Infirmiere Canadienne see Canadian Nurse 5954
L'Infirmiere Liberale Magazine (FRA ISSN 1267-9925) 5961
L'Infirmiere Magazine (FRA ISSN 0981-0560) 5635
• ➤ Inflammation (USA ISSN 0360-3997) 5635
Inflammation & Allergy see Inflammation & Allergy - Drug Targets 5761
• ➤ Inflammation & Allergy - Drug Targets (NLD ISSN 1871-5281) 5761
➤ Inflammation and Drug Therapy Series (NLD ISSN 0923-9405) 6848
Inflammation & Immunology see Ensho to Men'eki 5757
Inflammation and Regeneration see Enshou, Saisei 5609
• ➤ Inflammation Research (CHE ISSN 1023-3830) 6848
Inflammatory Bowel Disease Digest see I B D Digest 5926
➤ Inflammatory Bowel Disease Monitor (GBR ISSN 1466-7401) 5927
Inflammatory Bowel Disease Research Review see I B D Research Review 5926
• ➤ Inflammatory Bowel Diseases (USA ISSN 1078-0998) 5927
Inflammatory Disease and Therapy (USA ISSN 1047-5028) 5927
• ➤ Inflammopharmacology (CHE ISSN 0925-4692) 6848
Inflation Report see Bangko Sentral ng Pilipinas. Inflation Report 1065
Inflation Report (SWE ISSN 1401-3967) 1353
• Inflation Watch (USA) 1491
Inflationsrapport see Penningpolitisk Rapport 1374
• infLect (AUS ISSN 1448-0581) 5308
Inflexions (FRA ISSN 1772-3760) 6424
Inflight (Burnham) (GBR ISSN 1356-1715) 8544
Inflight Hospitality see Onboard Hospitality 4395
Inflight Review (RUS) 8784
▼ • Inflow (CZE ISSN 1802-9736) 5015
• The Influential Executive (USA) 26
Influenza see Infuruenza 5818
• Influenza and Other Respiratory Viruses (GBR ISSN 1750-2640) 5817
• Inf@ncia (ESP ISSN 1988-7612) 2155
▼ +info (Plusinfo) (ARG ISSN 1851-1287) 4337
† • Info (AUS) 8964
Info see Verband Angestellter Akademiker und Leitender Angestellter der Chemischen Industrie. Info 1411
Die Info (DEU) 3693
• ➤ Info (Bingley) (GBR ISSN 1463-6697) 2325
Info (London) (GBR) 1405
Info (Year) (GBR) 8378
Info 7 (DEU ISSN 0930-5483) 5015
Info A A U (Amateur Athletic Union of the United States) (USA ISSN 0279-9863) 8179
Info A C C S see C H A C Info 4089
† Info A L S (Amyotrophic Lateral Sclerosis) (CAN ISSN 0715-3120) 8964
Info A M P see M A P News 8054
• Info - A S E A N & Pacific Rim (USA) 1242
Info Accueillant(e)s (BEL ISSN 1781-2631) 2866
Info - Affaires (CAN ISSN 1194-8973) 1123
Info Also (DEU ISSN 1862-0469) 8046
Info at Library.une see info@library.une 5015
Info-Atlas: Schule Unterwegs (DEU) 3064
• Info-Autorite (CAN ISSN 1710-5838) 1123
Info Biznes (RUS) 1123
Info Buitenschoolse Opvang see Info Buitenschoolse Opvang, Brede School en Dagarrangementen 2866
Info Buitenschoolse Opvang, Brede School en Dagarrangementen (NLD ISSN 1875-0753) 2866
Info Buitenschoolse Opvang en Brede School see Info Buitenschoolse Opvang, Brede School en Dagarrangementen 2866
• Info Buro Mag. (FRA ISSN 1264-6253) 1851
• Info - C I S (Commonwealth of Independent States) (USA) 1242
Info.ca de l'Agence (CAN ISSN 1718-1704) 8046
Info Chimie Magazine (FRA ISSN 1286-0921) 2065
† Info D G A (Delegation Generale pour l'Armement) (FRA ISSN 0299-8459) 8964
▼ ➤ InFo Diabetologie (DEU ISSN 1865-5459) 5894
• Info Direct (NZL ISSN 1177-858X) 3197
Info Drei see Info3 7736
Info en Detail see L' Information en Detail 1491
Info en Sante (FRA ISSN 1957-4959) 4102
• Info Exame (BRA ISSN 1415-3270) 2422
Info F C D P see Equitas Info 7206
Info Femmes Chirurgiens Dentistes see Lettre Info Femmes Chirurgiens Dentistes 5855
Info Formatie Budget Systeem en Rrechtspositie see Info Lumpsum Primair Onderwijs 3025
Info Franchise Newsletter (USA ISSN 0147-5924) 1962
• Info - Genealogie (CAN ISSN 1183-0840) 3771
Info Generation Humanitaire (FRA ISSN 1622-9789) 8046
Info-Guide Montreal Scope (CAN) 3811
Info Intern (DEU) 2655
L'Info Journal (FRA ISSN 1165-0729) 320
L'Info Journal Junior (FRA ISSN 1770-4359) 320
Info Komputer (IDN ISSN 0215-2118) 5061
Info La Peche (CAN ISSN 1911-7787) 7445
Info-lands/Info-terres (CAN ISSN 1715-586X) 7595
• Info - Latinoamerica (USA) 1242
• Info-Link (NZL ISSN 1176-7189) 1014
Info-Link Architectural (AUS) 445
▼ • Info-Link Hardware+ (NZL ISSN 1178-1807) 1054
Info-Link Hardware Plus see Info-Link Hardware+ 1054
Info-Link Magazine (CAN ISSN 1192-2168) 445
Info-Link S E Asia (AUS) 1014
• Info-Link The Book (AUS) 1014
Info-Link the Hospitality Book (AUS) 2005
Info Lumpsum P O see Info Lumpsum Primair Onderwijs 3025
Info Lumpsum Primair Onderwijs (NLD ISSN 1875-2373) 3025
Info Magazine (USA) 8618
Info-Markt Informationsdienst (DEU ISSN 0177-1159) 1418
Info-Markt Ratgeber Computer Peripherie, Seitendrucker, Monitore, Scanner (DEU ISSN 0945-1714) 1851
Info-Markt Ratgeber Kopierer (DEU ISSN 0179-9452) 1851
Info-Markt Ratgeber Schneider-Liste (DEU ISSN 0943-8378) 1123
Info-Markt Ratgeber Telekommunikation (DEU ISSN 1617-7231) 2325
Info Matin (MLI) 3907
INFO: Mededelingenblad van de Vlaamse Vereniging voor Bibliotheek-, Archief- en Documentatiewezen (BEL ISSN 0771-7148) 5015
Info Media Net (Flemish Edition) (BEL ISSN 1371-3817) 2576
Info Media Net (French Edition) see Info Media Net (Flemish Edition) 2576
Info - MIL see Cuba. Ministerio de la Industria Ligera. Info 3186
• Info-N O V A (Norsk Institutt for Forskning om Opvekst, Velferd og Aldring) (NOR ISSN 1502-1041) 8107
InFo Neurologie und Psychiatrie (CHE ISSN 1661-2671) 6145
InFo Neurologie und Psychiatrie (DEU ISSN 1437-062X) 6145
• Info-News Newsletter (USA) 1866
Info-Niveau see Level News 8828
Info-Nursing (BEL) 5961
Info Nursing (CAN ISSN 0846-524X) 5961
• InFo Onkologie (DEU ISSN 1613-3633) 6022
Info P O E Ms for Hospitalists see Journal of Hospital Medicine 5650
Info P V see Les Cahiers de P V 4828
Info-parents, Colombie-Britannique see Parenthese 3557
Info Parkinson (CAN ISSN 1910-0469) 6146
Info Phare (LUX) 1598
Info Pharma Magazine (FRA) 6848
Info-Pilote (FRA ISSN 0761-0718) 59
† • Info Point (GBR ISSN 1741-2188) 8964
Info Presse Communications see Infopresse 26
Info R I S M (Online) (Repertoire International des Sources Musicales) (DEU) 6575
Info R I S M (Print) see Info R I S M (Online) 6575
▼ • Info R U V I D (Red de Universidades Valencianas para el Fomento de la Investigacion, el Desarrollo y la Innovacion) (ESP ISSN 1988-8155) 7865
Info Regio (Dutch Edition) (NLD ISSN 1572-7858) 3915
Info Regio (Editie De Meerlanden) (NLD ISSN 1573-9627) 3915
Info Regio (Editie Kennemerland en de IJmond) (NLD ISSN 1573-9619) 3915
Info Ressources Humaines (FRA ISSN 1774-4954) 1688
• Info - S A A R C (South Asian Association of Regional Cooperation) (USA) 1242
Info S Ö L O G (Schweizerische Offiziersgesellschaft der Logistik) (CHE ISSN 1422-5794) 6424
Info Satelit see T V Satelit 2394
Info Sein (CAN ISSN 1718-553X) 8846
Info - Seri (FRA ISSN 0980-9112) 7323
Info Source Bulletin (CAN ISSN 0825-2238) 4849
Info Source. Directory of Federal Government Databases see Info Source. Sources of Federal Government Information 7445
Info Source. Directory of Federal Government Enquiry Points (CAN ISSN 1205-5166) 7445
Info Source. Guide des Sources de Renseignements Federaux see Info Source. Guide to Sources of Federal Government Information 7445
Info Source. Guide to Sources of Federal Government Information/Info Source. Guide des Sources de Renseignements Federaux (CAN ISSN 1188-7907) 7445
Info Source. Source de Renseignements Federaux (CAN ISSN 1184-8111) 7445
Info Source. Sources of Federal Employee Information (CAN ISSN 1188-7893) 7445
Info Source. Sources of Federal Government Information (CAN ISSN 1184-8103) 7445
• Info Svin (DNK ISSN 1602-4168) 289
Info Tech & Telecom News (USA) 2422
Info Terre (FRA ISSN 1771-8120) 2710
Info-terres see Info-lands 7595
Info Trend see InfoTrend 1418
Info U E see E U Info 1562
Info-Vente (CHE) 1123
Info Wet Maatschappelijke Ondersteuning (NLD ISSN 1874-5598) 7445
Info21 (DEU ISSN 1433-7150) 2544
Info3 (DEU ISSN 1437-1898) 7736
Infobebes (FRA ISSN 1277-2542) 2155
InfoBrief: Film (DEU) 6504
InfoBrief: Fotografie (DEU) 6970
Infobulletin Gemeenschappelijk Landbouwbeleid see Dienst Regelingen. Nieuwsbrief 105
Infobusiness - Economic News of Bulgaria (BGR ISSN 1310-9332) 1405
† Infocab (AUS ISSN 0725-5489) 8964
• Infochannel (MEX) 2558
• infoChem (GBR ISSN 1752-0533) 2065
Infocomm Development Authority of Singapore. Annual Report (SGP ISSN 0219-7286) 2368
• InfoCommerce Report (USA ISSN 1533-8746) 1418
• ➤ InfoComp (BRA ISSN 1807-4545) 2422
InfoCongres (CAN ISSN 1198-189X) 6280
• Infoconomist (GBR ISSN 1473-0960) 1491
• Infocop (ESP ISSN 1138-364X) 7362
InfoCotonou (NLD ISSN 1571-7453) 4928
Infocus (NLD ISSN 1871-2789) 6061
• InFocus (Owings Mills) (USA) 6043
Infocus (Philadelphia) (USA ISSN 0889-6836) 2521
Infocus (Portland) (USA ISSN 1040-2179) 1418
• Infocus Magazine (GBR ISSN 1750-4740) 899
† Infocus News Magazine (AUS ISSN 0815-6905) 8964
• Infocusco.com (PER ISSN 1684-1786) 3927
Infodent International (ITA) 5848
InfoDienst I A S - I F R S (DEU ISSN 1861-356X) 1290
Infodienst Reisemedizin Aktuell (DEU ISSN 1430-8495) 5635
• Infodienst Schulleitung (DEU ISSN 1861-8758) 3025
† Infodigital (DEU) 8964
Infodirect see Info Direct 3197
• Infodiversidad (ARG ISSN 1514-514X) 5015
INFOdoc (DEU ISSN 0941-6048) 2571
Infodomus (ESP ISSN 1886-8762) 1014
• InfoElectro (CAN) 3318
Infoenviro (ESP ISSN 1699-2520) 3439
Infofish Fullnet: Globefish Highlight (MYS) 3597
Infofish Fullnet: Trade News (MYS ISSN 0127-9114) 3597
Infofish International (MYS ISSN 0127-2012) 3597
Infofish Technical Handbook (MYS) 3597
Infoglis see I G 4375
• Infoil Newsletter (DEU) 6315
• Infokara (CHE ISSN 1021-9056) 5635
• info@library.une (AUS ISSN 1833-7260) 5015
• Infoline (USA ISSN 8755-9269) 2942
Infolingua (CAN ISSN 1198-1083) 5201
• Infolink P C World (LKA) 2576
• Infolkus (AUS) 3618
• InfoMagazine - P C World (MAR) 2493
InfoManage (USA ISSN 1070-0013) 2544
• L'Infomane (CAN ISSN 0229-2068) 2287
Infomarine (ESP ISSN 1135-9099) 4969
Infomatics Digest (GBR ISSN 1367-966X) 2537
• Infomed, Anuario Estadistico (CUB ISSN 1680-7677) 5747
• Infomed Screen (CHE ISSN 1422-0059) 5635
Infomercial Marketing Report (USA ISSN 1058-0344) 1821
Infomet (USA) 6315
• Infomusa (English Edition) (FRA ISSN 1023-0076) 236
• Infomusa (French Edition) (FRA ISSN 1023-0068) 236
• Infomusa (Spanish Edition) (FRA ISSN 1729-0996) 236
• Infonet (AUS ISSN 1036-3882) 2866
Infonetics (USA ISSN 0895-8726) 2571
• Infonomics (USA) 2544
Infopack E & E (ESP ISSN 1136-3053) 6710
InfoParkinson see Info Parkinson 6146
InfoParkinson Bulletin see Info Parkinson 6146
Infopeche. Nouvelle Commerciales (CIV) 3597
Infopeche Trade News (African Edition) (CIV) 3597
Infopesca Internacional (URY ISSN 1510-3625) 3597
Infopesca. Noticias Comerciales (URY) 121
Infopesca. Publicaciones Especiales (URY) 3597
• Infoportalsocial.net (ESP ISSN 1988-7604) 8046
Infopost (DEU) 6424
Infopower (ESP ISSN 1138-5073) 3138
Infopresse (CAN ISSN 1709-6618) 26
Infor-Business see Prawo Przedsiebiorcy 1161
Infor Marechalerie-Der Huf/The Farriers Journal (BEL ISSN 0777-916X) 8293
Infor Mascalcia see Infor Marechalerie-Der Huf 8293
Inforegio News (Danish Edition) see Inforegio News (English Edition) 7241
Inforegio News (Dutch Edition) see Inforegio News (English Edition) 7241
Inforegio News (English Edition) (LUX ISSN 1025-7039) 7241
Inforegio News (Finnish Edition) see Inforegio News (English Edition) 7241
Inforegio News (French Edition) see Inforegio News (English Edition) 7241
Inforegio News (German Edition) see Inforegio News (English Edition) 7241
Inforegio News (Greek Edition) see Inforegio News (English Edition) 7241
Inforegio News (Italian Edition) see Inforegio News (English Edition) 7241
Inforegio News (Portuguese Edition) see Inforegio News (English Edition) 7241
Inforegio News (Spanish Edition) see Inforegio News (English Edition) 7241
Inforegio News (Swedish Edition) see Inforegio News (English Edition) 7241
Inforegio Panorama (English Edition) (LUX ISSN 1608-389X) 7241
Inforegio Panorama (French Edition) see Inforegio Panorama (English Edition) 7241
Inforegio Panorama (German Edition) see Inforegio Panorama (English Edition) 7241
Inforegio Panorama (Italian Edition) see Inforegio Panorama (English Edition) 7241
Inforegio Panorama (Spanish Edition) see Inforegio Panorama (English Edition) 7241
Inforespace (BEL) 59
InfoRISM see Info R I S M (Online) 6575
Inform (DEU ISSN 1863-8031) 8499
▼ Inform (GBR ISSN 1758-8944) 4978
Inform (ZAF) 2544
• Inform (Champaign) (USA ISSN 1528-9303) 2065
Inform (Lincoln) (USA ISSN 1539-4360) 445
Inform (London, 1994) (GBR ISSN 1354-8204) 3064
Inform (Richmond) (USA ISSN 1047-8353) 445
Inform-Progulka (BLR) 3800
Inform Reports (USA ISSN 0275-522X) 3439
Inform Special Reports (USA ISSN 1050-8953) 3439
• Informa (CHL) 8179
Inform'A P P I P C (CAN ISSN 0820-3938) 3064
• Informa Sicilia (ITA ISSN 1724-9007) 3897
Informa Tuttorario see Tuttorario 8770
➤ Informaa Quarterly (AUS ISSN 0816-200X) 1851
Informaatiotutkimus (FIN ISSN 1239-3614) 5015
Informacao & Informacao (Online) (BRA ISSN 1981-8920) 5015
Informacao & Informacao (Print) see Informacao & Informacao (Online) 5015
• Informacao & Sociedade (BRA ISSN 0104-0146) 5015
• Informacao Economica (PRT ISSN 0871-7338) 1491
Informacao Psiquiatrica (BRA ISSN 0101-4331) 6146
• Informace (CZE ISSN 1210-8502) 5015
Informace na Dlani (CD-ROM) see Inforum Sbornik 5017
➤ Informacije MIDEM (SVN ISSN 0352-9045) 3104
† Informacije Z P M S (Zveza Prijateljev Mladine Slovenije) (SVN ISSN 1318-3877) 8964
• Informacijos Mokslai/Information Sciences (LTU ISSN 1392-0561) 2544
➤ Informacines Technologijos ir Valdymas/Information Technology and Control (LTU ISSN 1392-124X) 2422
Informacio-Elektronika (HUN ISSN 0019-9753) 2537
• Informacio Psicologica (ESP ISSN 0214-347X) 7362
Informacion (ESP) 1429
La Informacion (Bronx) (USA) 3978
La Informacion (Houston) (USA) 3539
Informacion Agricola Panamena (PAN) 121
Informacion Agropecuaria (ESP) 289
Informacion Cientifica y Tecnologica see ICyT 7864
Informacion Civil (ESP ISSN 1135-5123) 4833
Informacion Comercial Espanola. Cuadernos Economicos (ESP ISSN 0210-2633) 1491
Informacion Comercial Espanola Economico. Boletin see I C E Economico. Boletin 1429
Informacion Comercial Espanola. Revista de Economia (ESP) 1429
Informacion Comercial Espanola. Sector Exterior (Year) (ESP) 1242
• ➤ Informacion, Cultura y Sociedad (ARG ISSN 1514-8327) 5015
• Informacion de Entidades Financieras (ARG ISSN 1851-4928) 1353
Informacion de Envase y Embalaje see I D E 6710
Informacion de Maquinas - Herramienta Equipos y Accesorios see I M H E 5452
Informacion de Patentes (CUB) 6751
Informacion de Publicidad y Marketing Mark see I.P. Mark 1820
• Informacion Dinamica de Consulta (MEX ISSN 1405-0145) 4870
Informacion Estadistica Regional Cochabamba (BOL) 8378
Informacion Express. Serie: Apicultura (CUB ISSN 0138-7685) 289
Informacion Express. Serie: Arroz (CUB ISSN 0138-7731) 273
Informacion Express. Serie: Avicultura (CUB ISSN 0138-7383) 289
Informacion Express. Serie: Cafe y Cacao (CUB ISSN 0138-7634) 236
Informacion Express. Serie: Citricos y Otros Frutales (CUB ISSN 0138-743X) 236
Informacion Express. Serie: Economia y Organizacion del Trabajo Agropecuario (CUB ISSN 0138-7480) 200
Informacion Express. Serie: Forestales (CUB ISSN 0138-6735) 3693
Informacion Express. Serie: Ganado Equino (CUB ISSN 0138-7537) 289

Title

DIRECTORY 2010 INFORMATIONSDIENST NATURSCHUTZ NIEDERSACHSEN 10413

Information und Forschung Studien zur Entwicklungsforschung. Sonderreihe Information und Dokumentation *see* I F O Studien zur Entwicklungsforschung. Sonderreihe Information und Dokumentation **1597**
Information und Forschung Studien zur Europaeischen Wirtschaft *see* I F O Studien zur Europaeischen Wirtschaft **1490**
Information und Forschung Studien zur Finanzpolitik *see* I F O Studien zur Finanzpolitik **1352**
Information und Forschung Studien zur Industriewirtschaft *see* I F O Studien zur Industriewirtschaft **1888**
Information und Forschung Studien zur Innovationsforschung *see* I F O Studien zur Innovationsforschung **1120**
Information und Forschung Studien zur Japanforschung *see* I F O Studien zur Japanforschung **1490**
Information und Forschung Studien zur Osteuropa- und Transformationsforschung *see* I F O Studien zur Osteuropa- und Transformationsforschung **1490**
Information und Forschung Studien zur Regional- und Stadtoekonomie *see* I F O Studien zur Regional- und Stadtoekonomie **1490**
Information und Forschung Studien zur Strukturforschung *see* I F O Studien zur Strukturforschung **1120**
Information und Forschung Studien zur Umweltoekonomie *see* I F O Studien zur Umweltoekonomie **1120**
Information und Forschung Studien zur Verkehrswirtschaft *see* I F O Studien zur Verkehrswirtschaft **8498**
• ➤ Information Visualization (GBR ISSN 1473-8716) **2450**
• Information Week (German Edition) (DEU ISSN 1436-0829) **2558**
• Information Week (US Edition) (USA ISSN 8750-6874) **2531**
Information Week Online *see* Information Week (US Edition) **2531**
• Information - Wissenschaft und Praxis (DEU ISSN 1434-4653) **5017**
Information Work *see* Qingbao Ziliao Gongzuo **5041**
Information World *see* Bilgi Dunyasi **4997**
• Information World Review (GBR ISSN 0950-9879) **2351**
Information x-III (USA) **2287**
• InformationAge (AUS ISSN 1324-5945) **2498**
Informational Guide to Passover Medicines & Cosmetics and Star-K Passover Directory (USA ISSN 1559-4742) **3539**
• Informationen aus der Fischereiforschung (DEU ISSN 1860-9902) **3597**
Informationen aus der Forschung des B B R *see* B B S R - Info **4404**
• Informationen aus Orthodontie und Kieferorthopaedie (DEU ISSN 0020-0336) **5848**
Informationen Deutsch als Fremdsprache (DEU ISSN 0724-9616) **2986**
Informationen fuer Auslaendische Studierende in Oesterreich (AUT) **3013**
Informationen fuer den Geschichts- und Gemeinschaftskundelehrer (DEU ISSN 0930-7672) **3064**
Informationen fuer den Verkaufs Innendienst (DEU ISSN 0940-7707) **1821**
Informationen fuer die Fischwirtschaft aus der Fischereiforschung *see* Informationen aus der Fischereiforschung **3597**
Informationen fuer die Wirtschaft (DEU) **1405**
Informationen fuer Einelternfamilien (DEU ISSN 0938-0124) **8107**
Informationen fuer Erziehungsberatungstellen (DEU) **2155**
Informationen fuer Mitarbeiter und Vereine (DEU) **8179**
Informationen fuer Regensburger Studentinnen und Studenten (DEU) **2987**
Informationen fuer Religionslehrerinnen und Religionslehrer *see* Eulenfisch **7797**
Informationen und Berichte (DEU ISSN 0937-0994) **4231**
Informationen zum Arbeitslosenrecht und Sozialhilferecht *see* Info Also **8046**
Informationen zur Akademischen Mobilitaet (AUT) **2987**
Informationen zur Deutschdidaktik (AUT ISSN 0721-9954) **5127**
Informationen zur Modernen Stadtgeschichte (I M S) (DEU ISSN 0340-1774) **4415**
Informationen zur Politischen Bildung (AUT) **7142**
Informationen zur Politischen Bildung/Information for Civic Education (DEU ISSN 0046-9408) **7142**
Informationen zur Politischen Bildung - Aktuell (DEU) **7142**
➤ Informationen zur Raumentwicklung (DEU ISSN 0303-2493) **4415**
Informationes Theologiae Europae (CHE ISSN 0942-4822) **7649**
Informations C N C *see* C N C. Dossier **6491**
Informations - Chimie *see* Info Chimie Magazine **2065**
Informations Chirurgicales Veterinaires (FRA ISSN 1777-8255) **8799**
Informations Concernant la Peche *see* Mitteilungen zur Fischerei **3601**
Informations Constitutionnelles et Parlementaires (FRA ISSN 0251-3617) **7142**
Informations Entreprise (FRA ISSN 0292-4765) **1962**
Informations Fleuristes (FRA ISSN 0290-683X) **3756**
Informations M M M (FRA ISSN 0766-6241) **1123**
Informations Ophtalmologiques Veterinaires (FRA ISSN 1777-8263) **8799**
Informations Pharmaceutiques O M S (Organisation Mondiale de la Sante) (CHE ISSN 1011-5706) **7525**
Informations Rapides de la Copropriete (FRA ISSN 0750-8042) **7595**
Informations Sociales (FRA ISSN 0046-9459) **8046**
Informations Statistiques *see* Statistische Information **7483**
Informations Statistiques sur la Conjoncture *see* Algeria. Office National des Statistiques. Informations Statistiques sur la Conjoncture **8344**
Informations Systeme Report *see* I S Report **1417**
Informations Technik Qualifikation *see* I T Qualifikation **1417**
Informations Technik Security *see* I T Security **2514**
Informations Technologie Administrator *see* I T Administrator **1417**
Informations Technologie Revision *see* I T - Revision **1417**
Informations U F O L E P - U S E P (FRA) **6989**
Informations- und Kommunikationstechnologien Report *see* I K T - Report **1490**
Informations- und Telekommunikationstechnik (DEU ISSN 1613-9364) **2351**
Informations V S I G *see* V S I G - Mitteilungen **1586**
Informationsblatt Forschungsbereich Landschaft *see* Informationsblatt Landschaft **2614**
• Informationsblatt Forschungsbereich Wald (CHE ISSN 1424-5701) **2614**
• Informationsblatt Landschaft (CHE ISSN 1661-5824) **2614**
Informationsbrief Auslaenderrecht (DEU ISSN 0174-2108) **4928**
Informationsbrief fuer Fuehrungskraefte *see* Informationsbrief fuer Fuehrungskraefte in der Chemischen Industrie **3246**
Informationsbrief fuer Fuehrungskraefte in der Chemischen Industrie (DEU ISSN 1860-9228) **3246**
Informationsbulletin Kurdistan (DEU) **3539**
Informationsdienst Altersfragen (DEU) **4047**
Informationsdienst Bauen und Energie (DEU ISSN 1862-0973) **1014**
➤ Informationsdienst Europaeisches Arbeits- und Sozialrecht (DEU ISSN 0943-1799) **4870**
Informationsdienst F I Z Technik. Allgemeine Messtechnik, Messen und Pruefen Elektrischer und Magnetischer Groessen, Nachrichtenmesstechnik, Masssysteme, Messumformer, Anzeigegeraete *see* Informationsdienst F I Z Technik. Messen und Pruefen Elektrischer und Magnetischer Groessen **3231**
Informationsdienst F I Z Technik. Alternative Energien (DEU ISSN 0179-0269) **3153**
Informationsdienst F I Z Technik. Analysenmesstechnik und Messtechnik im Umweltschutzbereich (DEU) **3230**
Informationsdienst F I Z Technik. Antriebstechnik, Maschinenelemente und -baugruppen, Getriebe (DEU ISSN 0938-0892) **3230**
Informationsdienst F I Z Technik. Batterien und Akkumulatoren (DEU) **3153**
Informationsdienst F I Z Technik. Bekleidungstechnik, Management, Wirtschaft (DEU) **8463**
Informationsdienst F I Z Technik. Beschichten, Beschichtungsanlagen, Oberflaechenbehandlung (DEU) **3230**
Informationsdienst F I Z Technik. Bilderkennung und -verarbeitung (DEU) **2443**
Informationsdienst F I Z Technik. Biomaterialen, Implantatwerkstoffe (DEU) **3230**
Informationsdienst F I Z Technik. Blechbearbeitung (DEU) **6315**
Informationsdienst F I Z Technik. Brennstoffzellen (DEU) **3153**
Informationsdienst F I Z Technik. C A D - Schaltungsentwurf (DEU) **3116**
Informationsdienst F I Z Technik. Diskrete Halbleiterbauelemente (DEU ISSN 0176-5868) **3230**
Informationsdienst F I Z Technik. Drahtherstellung und Drahterzeugnisse (DEU) **3230**
Informationsdienst F I Z Technik. Duenn- und Dickschichttechnik (DEU) **3116**
Informationsdienst F I Z Technik. Eisenwerkstoffe, Legierte und Unlegierte Staehle (DEU ISSN 0179-5198) **3230**
Informationsdienst F I Z Technik. Elektrisch Abtragende Fertigungsverfahren (DEU) **6315**
Informationsdienst F I Z Technik. Elektrische Isolierstoffe (DEU) **3230**
Informationsdienst F I Z Technik. Elektrische Maschinen, Stromrichter und Transformatoren *see* Informationsdienst F I Z Technik. Elektrische Maschinen und Transformatoren **3153**
Informationsdienst F I Z Technik. Elektrische Maschinen und Transformatoren (DEU) **3153**
Informationsdienst F I Z Technik. Elektrische Steuerungs- und Regelungstechnik (DEU) **3230**
Informationsdienst F I Z Technik. Elektrowaerme, Elektrochemie, Elektrophysik (DEU ISSN 0176-5795) **3230**
Informationsdienst F I Z Technik. Energieuebertragung und -verteilung (DEU ISSN 0176-5590) **3153**
Informationsdienst F I Z Technik. Energiewirtschaft, Energietechnik, Elektrizitaetswirtschaft, Kraftwerkstechnik (DEU ISSN 0947-6059) **3153**
Informationsdienst F I Z Technik. Feinbearbeitung, Schleifen, Raeumen, Honen, Laeppen, Polieren (DEU) **3230**
Informationsdienst F I Z Technik. Fluidtechnik, Oelhydraulik, Pneumatik (DEU ISSN 0937-4299) **3230**
Informationsdienst F I Z Technik. Foerder- und Lagertechnik (DEU ISSN 0176-6368) **3230**
Informationsdienst F I Z Technik. Industrieroboter und Handhabungssysteme (DEU ISSN 1431-3790) **3230**
Informationsdienst F I Z Technik. Instandhaltung (DEU) **3230**
Informationsdienst F I Z Technik. Integrierte Schaltungen (DEU) **3116**
Informationsdienst F I Z Technik. Kalt- und Warmmassivumformung (DEU ISSN 1437-451X) **6339**
Informationsdienst F I Z Technik. Keramik, Grundlagen, Technologien, Werkstoffe, Produkte (DEU) **3231**
Informationsdienst F I Z Technik. Klima-, Reinraum-, Entstaubungs- und Trocknungstechnik, Kaelte- und Waermepumpentechnik (DEU ISSN 0937-4329) **3479**
Informationsdienst F I Z Technik. Konstruktionstechnik, Fertigungsorganisation und Arbeitsschutz im Maschinen- und Anlagenbau *see* Informationsdienst F I Z Technik. Wirtschaftlichkeit in Konstruktion und Fertigung im Maschinen- und Anlagenbau **3231**
Informationsdienst F I Z Technik. Kunststoffe, Kunststofftechnologien und Kunststoffverarbeitungsmaschinen (DEU ISSN 0933-2634) **3231**
Informationsdienst F I Z Technik. L S I-, V L S I- und U L S I-Schaltungen (DEU) **3116**
Informationsdienst F I Z Technik. Laerm (DEU ISSN 0176-5442) **3231**
Informationsdienst F I Z Technik. Laserstrahltechnik (DEU) **3231**
Informationsdienst F I Z Technik. Lasertechnologien in der Medizin (DEU) **5747**
Informationsdienst F I Z Technik. Leistungselektronik und Stromrichter (DEU) **3153**
Informationsdienst F I Z Technik. Lichtleiter und Glasfaserkabel (DEU) **2347**
Informationsdienst F I Z Technik. Logistik Aktuell (DEU) **1242**
Informationsdienst F I Z Technik. Magnetwerkstoffe (DEU) **3231**
Informationsdienst F I Z Technik. Mechanische Verbindungstechnik (DEU) **3231**
Informationsdienst F I Z Technik. Medizinische Technik (DEU ISSN 0932-6324) **5747**
Informationsdienst F I Z Technik. Messen und Pruefen Elektrischer und Magnetischer Groessen (DEU) **3231**
Informationsdienst F I Z Technik. Mikroprozessoren (DEU ISSN 0179-2474) **3116**
Informationsdienst F I Z Technik. Mikrosystemtechnik (DEU) **3231**
Informationsdienst F I Z Technik. Mikrowellentechnik (DEU) **2347**
Informationsdienst F I Z Technik. Mobilfunk (DEU) **2347**
Informationsdienst F I Z Technik. Nachrichtenleitungen und Antennen (DEU ISSN 1439-8206) **2348**
Informationsdienst F I Z Technik. Nachrichtentechnische Schaltungen, Verstaerker, Oszillatoren, Netzwerke *see* Informationsdienst F I Z Technik. Verstaerker, Oszillatoren und Filter **2348**
Informationsdienst F I Z Technik. Nachrichtenuebertragung *see* Informationsdienst F I Z Technik. Nachrichtenuebertragung, Verfahren, Geraete und Systeme **2348**
Informationsdienst F I Z Technik. Nachrichtenuebertragung, Verfahren, Geraete und Systeme (DEU) **2348**
Informationsdienst F I Z Technik. Nachrichtenvermittlung, Netze, Teilnehmereinrichtungen (DEU ISSN 0176-5620) **2348**
Informationsdienst F I Z Technik. Neue Fertigungsverfahren (DEU ISSN 0720-9878) **6339**
Informationsdienst F I Z Technik. Neue Werkstoffe und Innovative Werkstoffanwendungen (DEU) **3231**
Informationsdienst F I Z Technik. Nichteisenmetalle und Ihre Legierungen (DEU ISSN 0179-5201) **3231**
Informationsdienst F I Z Technik. Optoelektronik (DEU) **3116**
Informationsdienst F I Z Technik. Physiologische Optik und Optometrie (DEU) **5747**
Informationsdienst F I Z Technik. Pumpen (DEU) **3231**
Informationsdienst F I Z Technik. Qualitaetsmanagement (DEU ISSN 0947-6032) **3231**
Informationsdienst F I Z Technik. Rechner und Rechnernetze (DEU) **2443**
Informationsdienst F I Z Technik. Recycling und Entsorgung von Abfallstoffen (DEU) **3479**
† Informationsdienst F I Z Technik. Regelungstechnik (DEU ISSN 0179-0811) **8964**
Informationsdienst F I Z Technik. Regelungstheorie (DEU) **3231**
Informationsdienst F I Z Technik. Regelungstheorie, Technische Kybernetik *see* Informationsdienst F I Z Technik. Regelungstheorie **3231**
Informationsdienst F I Z Technik. S M D - Oberflaechenmontage-Technologie (DEU) **3117**
Informationsdienst F I Z Technik. Schmieden und Pressen (DEU) **6339**
Informationsdienst F I Z Technik. Schmierungstechnik und Schmierstoffe (DEU ISSN 0176-6171) **3231**
Informationsdienst F I Z Technik. Schwingungsverhalten von Maschinen und Baugruppen (DEU) **3231**
Informationsdienst F I Z Technik. Software Engineering (DEU) **2443**
Informationsdienst F I Z Technik. Spanende Fertigungsverfahren, Drehen, Fraesen, Hobeln, Bohren, Schleifen, Abtragen *see* Informationsdienst F I Z Technik. Spanende Fertigungsverfahren und Werkzeugmaschinen, Drehen, Fraesen, Hobeln, Bohren, Abtragen **3231**
Informationsdienst F I Z Technik. Spanende Fertigungsverfahren und Werkzeugmaschinen, Drehen, Fraesen, Hobeln, Bohren, Abtragen (DEU) **3231**
Informationsdienst F I Z Technik. Spracherkennung und -verarbeitung (DEU) **5201**
Informationsdienst F I Z Technik. Steuern, Regeln und Automatisieren von Maschinen und Anlagen (DEU ISSN 0937-4302) **3231**
Informationsdienst F I Z Technik. Steuerungs- und Regelungstechnik *see* Informationsdienst F I Z Technik. Elektrische Steuerungs- und Regelungstechnik **3230**
Informationsdienst F I Z Technik. Strangpressen von Metallen (DEU) **6339**
Informationsdienst F I Z Technik. Stroemungs- und Kolbenmaschinen (DEU) **3231**
Informationsdienst F I Z Technik. Stroemungsmaschinen und Kolbenmaschinen *see* Informationsdienst F I Z Technik. Stroemungs- und Kolbenmaschinen **3231**
Informationsdienst F I Z Technik. System-Software und Software Engineering *see* Informationsdienst F I Z Technik. Software Engineering **2443**
Informationsdienst F I Z Technik. Technische Textilien (DEU) **8463**
Informationsdienst F I Z Technik. Textil- und Bekleidungstechnik, Textilveredlung, Textilmaschinenbau (DEU) **8463**
Informationsdienst F I Z Technik. Textilveredlung (DEU) **8463**
Informationsdienst F I Z Technik. Umformtechnik, Pressen, Schmieden, Waelzen, Biegen, Sintern *see* Informationsdienst F I Z Technik. Umformtechnik und Werkzeugmaschinen - Pressen, Schmieden, Waelzen, Ziehen, Biegen, Sintern **3231**
Informationsdienst F I Z Technik. Umformtechnik und Werkzeugmaschinen - Pressen, Schmieden, Waelzen, Ziehen, Biegen, Sintern (DEU) **3231**
Informationsdienst F I Z Technik. Umweltschutz und Umwelttechnik, Luftreinhaltung, Gewaesserschutz, Abfallentsorgung, Messtechnik (DEU) **3479**
Informationsdienst F I Z Technik. Umwelttechnik *see* Informationsdienst F I Z Technik. Umweltschutz und Umwelttechnik, Luftreinhaltung, Gewaesserschutz, Abfallentsorgung, Messtechnik **3479**
Informationsdienst F I Z Technik. Verbundwerkstoffe und Faserverstaerkte Werkstoffe (DEU) **3231**
Informationsdienst F I Z Technik. Verschleiss und Lebensdauer, Reibung (DEU) **3231**
Informationsdienst F I Z Technik. Verstaerker, Oszillatoren und Filter (DEU) **2348**
Informationsdienst F I Z Technik. Waelzlager (DEU) **3231**
Informationsdienst F I Z Technik. Waermebehandlung von Werkstoffen (DEU) **3231**
Informationsdienst F I Z Technik. Werkstoff- und Materialpruefung (DEU) **3231**
Informationsdienst F I Z Technik. Werkstoffpruefung, Materialpruefung *see* Informationsdienst F I Z Technik. Werkstoff- und Materialpruefung **3231**
Informationsdienst F I Z Technik. Wirtschaftlichkeit in Konstruktion und Fertigung im Maschinen- und Anlagenbau (DEU) **3231**
Informationsdienst F I Z Technik. Zahnraeder und Zahnradgetriebe (DEU) **3231**
Informationsdienst Gross- und Aussenhandel (DEU) **1569**
Informationsdienst Kaltmassivumformung *see* Informationsdienst F I Z Technik. Kalt- und Warmmassivumformung **6339**
• Informationsdienst Krankenhauswesen/Health Care Information Service (DEU ISSN 0341-0595) **4102**
Informationsdienst Kunst (DEU ISSN 0939-9259) **496**
Informationsdienst Naturschutz Niedersachsen (DEU ISSN 0934-7135) **2614**

Title

▼ • Infrastructure Investment & Policy Report (Weekly Edition) (USA ISSN 1947-4660) **1630**
• Infrastructure Journal (GBR ISSN 1460-468X) **1123**
Infrastructure Planning Review *see* Doboku Keikakugaku Kenkyu Ronbunshu **3265**
Infrastructure Yearbook (GBR) **1123**
Infrastructuur, Transport en Logistiek (NLD ISSN 0924-8609) **4416**
InfrastrukturRecht (DEU ISSN 1612-7803) **4692**
InFurniture *see* Home Furnishings Business **4558**
Infuruenza/Influenza (JPN ISSN 1345-8345) **5818**
Infusion (Alexandria) (USA ISSN 1080-3858) **6022**
Infusion (Cambridge) (USA ISSN 1084-659X) **7142**
Infusion Nurses Society Newsline *see* I N S Newsline **5961**
Infusionstherapie und Transfusionsmedizin. Supplement (CHE ISSN 1421-5799) **5635**
• -ing (FIN ISSN 1795-7850) **3270**
• ING Direct - Melbourne Institute Household Saving and Investment Report (AUS ISSN 1832-4371) **1719**
Ingaang (SWE ISSN 1401-8616) **7649**
• Ingede (ZAF ISSN 1815-3933) **2866**
Ingegneri Architetti Costruttori (ITA ISSN 0391-6537) **3270**
Ingegneri e Architetti Svizzeri *see* Tec21 **458**
Ingegneria Alimentare - Le Carni (ITA ISSN 1825-9758) **3647**
• Ingegneria Ambientale (ITA ISSN 0394-5871) **7525**
Ingegneria Ambientale Quaderni (ITA) **7525**
Ingegneria dell'Autoveicolo (ITA) **8585**
Ingegneria Ferroviaria (ITA ISSN 0020-0956) **8619**
Ingegneria Sanitaria Ambientale *see* I S A Ingegneria Sanitaria Ambientale **7524**
Ingegneria Sismica (ITA ISSN 0393-1420) **3197**
Ingelise (DNK ISSN 1398-9154) **4361**
Ingelise *see* Allt om Handarbete **4351**
Ingenerare (CHL ISSN 0718-1442) **3197**
• Ingenia (GBR ISSN 1472-9768) **3197**
• ➤ Ingeniare (CHL ISSN 0718-3291) **3379**
La Ingenieria (ARG ISSN 0325-2701) **3197**
Ingenieria (COL ISSN 0121-750X) **3197**
Ingenieria (CRI ISSN 1409-2441) **3197**
Ingenieria (MEX ISSN 1665-529X) **3197**
Ingenieria Aeronautica y Astronautica (ESP ISSN 0020-1006) **59**
Ingenieria Agronomica (MEX) **121**
Ingenieria al Dia (CHL ISSN 0718-073X) **7866**
Ingenieria Alimentaria (ARG ISSN 0328-865X) **3647**
Ingenieria Civil (CUB ISSN 0020-1022) **3270**
Ingenieria Civil (ESP ISSN 0213-8468) **3270**
Ingenieria Civil/Civil Engineering (MEX) **3270**
Ingenieria de Costos (MEX) **1753**
Ingenieria de Sistemas *see* La Revista Ingenieria de Sistemas **3218**
Ingenieria del Agua (ESP ISSN 1134-2196) **3439**
Ingenieria del Gas (ESP ISSN 1134-3168) **6773**
• Ingenieria e Investigacion (COL ISSN 0120-5609) **3197**
• Ingenieria Electronica, Automatica y Comunicaciones (CUB ISSN 0258-5944) **3104**
• Ingenieria Energetica (CUB ISSN 0253-5645) **3138**
Ingenieria Estructural (CUB ISSN 0258-5952) **3379**
Ingenieria Hidraulica *see* Ingenieria Hidraulica y Ambiental **3362**
➤ Ingenieria Hidraulica en Mexico (MEX ISSN 0186-4076) **3362**
• Ingenieria Hidraulica y Ambiental (CUB ISSN 1680-0338) **3362**
• Ingenieria Hospitalaria (ESP ISSN 1133-7419) **4102**
• Ingenieria Industrial (CUB ISSN 0258-5960) **3198**
• Ingenieria Informatica (CHL ISSN 0717-4195) **2423**
Ingenieria, Investigacion y Tecnologia (MEX ISSN 1405-7743) **3198**
• Ingenieria Mecanica (CUB ISSN 1029-516X) **3379**
Ingenieria Mecanica, Tecnologia y Desarrollo (MEX ISSN 1665-7381) **3379**
Ingenieria Mecanica y Electrica (MEX ISSN 0374-339X) **3379**
Ingenieria Municipal (ESP ISSN 0213-795X) **3270**
➤ Ingenieria Naval (ESP ISSN 0020-1073) **8646**
Ingenieria Petrolera (MEX ISSN 0185-3899) **6773**
Ingenieria Quimica (ARG ISSN 0325-5395) **3246**
• Ingenieria Quimica (ESP ISSN 0210-2064) **3246**
• Ingenieria Quimica (URY ISSN 0797-4930) **3246**
Ingenieria Sanitaria (BRA ISSN 0446-2424) **7525**
• Ingenieria Sismica (MEX ISSN 0185-092X) **2710**
• ➤ Ingenieria U C (Universidad de Carabobo) (VEN) **3198**
Ingenieria y Arquitectura (PAN) **3270**
• Ingenieria y Ciencia (COL ISSN 1794-9165) **3198**
Ingenieria y Competitividad (COL ISSN 0123-3033) **3198**
• Ingenieria y Desarrollo (COL ISSN 0122-3461) **3198**
• Ingenieria y Gestion de Mantenimiento (ESP ISSN 1695-3754) **1290**
Ingenieria y Sociedad (ESP ISSN 1133-3707) **3198**
Ingenieria y Territorio (ESP ISSN 1695-9647) **3270**
• ➤ Ingenieria y Universidad (COL ISSN 0123-2126) **3198**
• Ingenierias (MEX ISSN 1405-0676) **7866**
Ingenierie, Conseil, Informatique (FRA ISSN 1955-9232) **3270**
Ingenierie des Systemes d'Information/Networking and Information Systems (FRA ISSN 1633-1311) **2521**
Ingenierie et Conseil *see* Ingenierie, Conseil, Informatique **3270**
Ingenierie et Recherche BioMedicale *see* I R B M News **765**
Ingenierie International (FRA ISSN 1167-1793) **3198**
Ingenieries (FRA ISSN 1264-9147) **121**
Ingeniero Andino (CHL ISSN 0717-0572) **6465**
Ingeniero Latinoamericano (COL) **3198**
Ingenieros (CHL ISSN 0716-4610) **3198**
Der Ingenieur (AUT) **3198**
De Ingenieur (NLD ISSN 0020-1146) **3198**
Ingenieur Civil Canadien *see* Canadian Civil Engineer **3261**
Ingenieur et Industrie (BEL ISSN 0775-2962) **3198**
Ingenieurbauten (USA ISSN 0172-8008) **3270**
Ingenieurgeodaesie - T U Graz *see* Engineering Geodasy - T U Graz **3266**
Ingenieurnews (DEU ISSN 1860-0573) **3198**
Ingenieurs de la Vie *see* Agro Mag **86**
Ingenieurs de l'Automobile (FRA ISSN 0020-1200) **8585**
Ingenieurs E S M E (FRA ISSN 0980-8434) **3319**
Ingenieurs et Architectes Suisses *see* Tec21 **458**
Ingenieurs sans Frontieres *see* Altercatif **3180**
Het Ingenieursblad (BEL ISSN 0020-1235) **3198**
Das Ingenieurstudium (DEU) **2957**
• Ingenio (NZL ISSN 1176-211X) **2287**
Ingenioer - Hvorfor, Hvordan (DNK ISSN 0905-2143) **3198**
• Ingenioeren/Engineer (DNK ISSN 0105-6220) **3198**
Ingenioeren - Job *see* Ingenioeren **3198**
• Ingenioerens Indkoebsbog (DNK ISSN 0446-2491) **1889**
IngenioerNytt/Engineering News (NOR ISSN 0332-611X) **3198**
Ingenium (ESP ISSN 1133-7486) **7866**
• Ingenium (PRT ISSN 0870-5968) **3198**
Ingenjoeren (SWE ISSN 1101-8704) **3198**
Ingenjoersvetenskapsakademien. I V A - M (SWE ISSN 1102-8254) **8426**
Ingens Bulletin (ZWE ISSN 1016-524X) **794**
Ingenue (USA ISSN 1546-7457) **6504**
Inglewood Public Library Quarterly Report (USA ISSN 0020-1308) **5017**
Ingmar *see* Allt om Film **6489**
Ingmar (SWE) **6504**
• Ingram's (USA ISSN 1046-9958) **1123**
Ingredienti Alimentari (ITA ISSN 1594-0543) **3647**
Ingredients Extra *see* Feed Tech **3636**
Ingu Dongtae Tong'gye Yeonbo. Chong'gwal Chulsaeng Sa'mang Pyeon/Korea (Republic). National Statistical Office. Annual Report on the Vital Statistics. Volume 1. On Live Births and Deaths (KOR ISSN 1599-046X) **7309**
Ingu Dongtae Tong'gye Yeonbo. Hon'in Ihon Pyeon/Korea (Republic). National Statistical Office. Annual Report on the Vital Statistics. Volume 2. On Marriages and Divorces (KOR ISSN 1599-0478) **7309**
In'gu Idong Tong'gye Yeonbo/Korea (Republic). National Statistical Office. Annual Report on the Internal Migration Statistics (KOR ISSN 1228-9019) **7309**
In'gu Jutaeg Chong Jo'sa Jamjeong Bo'go'seo/Korea (Republic). National Statistical Office. Population and Housing Census Report (KOR ISSN 1599-1717) **7309**
Inguirer *see* Ordet **6509**
▼ • Inhalation (USA ISSN 1937-0717) **6849**
• ➤ Inhalation Toxicology (USA ISSN 0895-8378) **3498**
Inhaled Particles (GBR ISSN 0301-1577) **4102**
➤ Inhenyeriya (PHL ISSN 0118-7473) **3198**
• Inherit (AUS ISSN 1448-6261) **3771**
Inheritance (GBR) **3967**
Inheritance, Estate and Gift Tax Reports - All States *see* Inheritance, Estate and Gift Tax Reports - Federal and All States **1929**
Inheritance, Estate and Gift Tax Reports - Federal *see* Inheritance, Estate and Gift Tax Reports - Federal and All States **1929**
Inheritance, Estate and Gift Tax Reports - Federal and All States (USA) **1929**
• ➤ Iniciacao Cientifica CESUMAR (Centro Universitario de Maringa) (BRA ISSN 1518-1243) **7866**
• Iniciacom (BRA ISSN 1980-3494) **2326**
• Iniciativa Socialista (ESP ISSN 1130-829X) **7142**
Iniciativas en Politicas sobre la Salud Reproductiva *see* Initiatives in Reproductive Health Policy **8846**
Iniciativas para el Desarrollo de Espacios Solidarios (ARG) **7972**
Inima si Literatura *see* Gazeta de Transilvania **3932**
Initial Attack (CAN) **3693**
Initiales/Initials (CAN ISSN 0710-4278) **5127**
Initials *see* Initiales **5127**
Initiation a la Linguistique. Serie A. Lectures (FRA ISSN 0073-8018) **5127**
Initiation a la Linguistique. Serie B. Problemes et Methodes (FRA ISSN 0073-8026) **5127**
Initiations et Etudes Africaines *see* Institut Fondamental d'Afrique Noire. Initiations et Etudes Africaines **4175**
Initiativ (DEU) **3850**
Initiative (AUT) **2194**
Initiative (GBR) **1569**
Initiative for Policy Dialogue Series (GBR ISSN 1754-6869) **7242**
Initiativen zum Umweltschutz (DEU ISSN 1438-5023) **3440**
Initiatives (FRA ISSN 1962-5766) **7142**
• Initiatives (USA) **5017**
Initiatives Education (FRA ISSN 1952-1146) **2866**
Initiatives en Immunisation *see* Immunization Initiatives **7524**
Initiatives in Reproductive Health Policy (USA ISSN 1086-4350) **8846**
Initiatives Magazine *see* Le Nouvel Entrepreneur **1964**
Initiatives Magazine & le Nouvel Entrepreneur *see* Le Nouvel Entrepreneur **1964**
Initiators & Pyrotechnics *see* Huogongpin **6424**
Initium (ESP ISSN 1137-8069) **4692**
▼ • Initium (USA ISSN 1938-7350) **7142**
Iniziative (ITA ISSN 1825-1552) **4596**
Le Iniziative del Corriere della Sera *see* Corriere della Sera. Iniziative **3896**
L'Injecteur (CAN ISSN 1719-8348) **2695**
• Injection Molding (USA ISSN 1071-362X) **7092**
• Injection Moulding Asia (GBR ISSN 1462-0278) **7093**
• ➤ Injury (GBR ISSN 0020-1383) **6061**
Injury, Collision and Theft Losses (USA) **7525**
Injury Experience in Sand and Gravel Mining (USA ISSN 0270-2053) **6690**
Injury Extra *see* Injury **6061**
• Injury Facts (Year) (USA ISSN 1538-5337) **7525**
• ➤ Injury Prevention (GBR ISSN 1353-8047) **6093**
• ➤ Injustice Studies (USA) **4692**
Injuve *see* Guia de Informacion Juvenil **2191**
Ink (FRA ISSN 1957-1674) **7323**
Ink (Idaho Springs) (USA) **7563**
• Ink 19 (USA ISSN 1075-8933) **6575**
• Ink & Ashes (USA ISSN 1554-0294) **5309**
Ink & Gall (USA ISSN 0894-0479) **7563**
• Ink & Print (GBR) **7323**
Ink Blot Magazine (USA) **6575**
Ink Disease (USA) **6575**
▼ • Ink Filled Page (USA ISSN 1940-2031) **5309**
† • Ink Maker (USA ISSN 1545-813X) **8964**
Ink Nineteen *see* Ink 19 **6575**
Ink Review *see* Polymers Paint Color Year Book (Year) **6720**
Ink Review *see* European Adhesives and Sealants **6311**
Ink Review *see* P P C J **6719**
• Ink World (USA ISSN 1093-328X) **7323**
Inkanyamba: Tornadoes in South Africa (ZAF) **6357**
Inkasso-Praxis (CHE) **1630**
• Inked (USA ISSN 1555-8630) **496**
Inkijk (NLD ISSN 1382-0044) **8047**
† Inking (GBR) **8964**
Inkling (GBR ISSN 0968-1876) **2942**
Inklings (DEU ISSN 0176-3733) **5443**
Inklusief (NLD ISSN 0041-2562) **2155**
Inklusion - Exklusion (DEU ISSN 1860-899X) **4231**
Inkomstskattelagen (SWE ISSN 1651-095X) **1929**
• Inkoop en Aanbesteding in de Publieke Sector (NLD ISSN 1385-5875) **4692**
Inkoop en Logistiek Kennisbanken *see* I & L Kennisbanken **1819**
Inksherds (USA) **397**
• Inksider (USA) **7323**
Inktpatroon *see* Ho! **2985**
• L'Inkulth (FRA ISSN 1776-2529) **4456**
• Inkwel (AUS ISSN 1036-871X) **8868**
Inkwell (USA ISSN 1085-0287) **5309**
• Inkworld (IND ISSN 0377-0087) **4596**
Inky Fingers (NZL) **7323**
Inky Trail News (USA ISSN 1533-1504) **4337**
• Inland Architect (USA ISSN 0020-1472) **445**
Inland Empire Family (USA) **2155**
Inland Empire Magazine (USA ISSN 0199-5073) **3978**
The Inland Episcopalian (USA ISSN 2150-5780) **7761**
The Inland Fisheries News (IND) **3597**
➤ Inland Fisheries Society of India. Journal (IND ISSN 0379-3435) **3598**
Inland Home (USA) **4543**
Inland Index Grade Price Average *see* Western Wood Products Association. Inland Index Grade Price Average **3717**
• Inland Lumber Price Index (USA) **3709**
Inland Register (USA ISSN 0020-1510) **7800**
• Inland Revenue Department. Tax Information Bulletin (NZL ISSN 0114-7161) **1929**
Inland Revenue Practices and Concessions (GBR) **1929**
Inland Revenue Practices and Concessions Yearbook (GBR ISSN 1350-410X) **1929**
Inland River Guide (USA ISSN 0198-859X) **8646**
Inland River Record (USA) **8646**
• Inland Seas (USA ISSN 0020-1537) **4298**
▼ • Inland Water Biology (RUS ISSN 1995-0829) **678**
Inland Waterways Handbook (GBR ISSN 1471-1370) **8646**
Inleiding tot die Sakereg *see* Introduction to the Law of Property **4696**
• InLife (GRC ISSN 1108-8192) **2558**
• Inline (English Edition) (FIN ISSN 1795-3588) **1054**
• Inline (Finnish Edition) (FIN ISSN 1795-357X) **1054**
• Inline (German Edition) (FIN ISSN 1795-360X) **1054**
• Inline (Polish Edition) (FIN ISSN 1796-0495) **1054**
• Inline (Swedish Edition) (FIN ISSN 1795-3596) **1054**
† Inline Magazin (DEU ISSN 1612-1627) **8964**
Inline Skate *see* Inline Magazin **8964**
Inmersion (ESP) **8318**
▼ La Inmigracion en Espana (ESP ISSN 1888-251X) **7285**
Inmobiliaria Industrial y Logistica (ESP ISSN 1695-7415) **7595**
• Inmolandia.com (ESP ISSN 1699-3284) **7595**
• InMotion (AUS ISSN 1447-1132) **7059**
inMotion (USA ISSN 1529-6350) **4066**
† Inmun Gwahag/Journal of Humanities (KOR ISSN 1229-6201) **8964**
Inmunologia (ESP ISSN 0213-9626) **5761**
Inn Focus *see* Innfocus **4391**
Inn Marketing Digest (USA) **4391**
Inn Room Visitors Magazine (USA) **8784**
Inn Times (USA) **4391**
Inn Touch (USA) **4391**
• INN-Touch (Online) (USA) **5017**
• ➤ Innate Immunity (GBR ISSN 1753-4259) **5894**
▼ • Innate Immunity (USA ISSN 1940-3011) **678**
➤ Innen und Aussen (BEL ISSN 1382-4279) **7649**
Innenpolitik (DEU ISSN 0179-4108) **7445**
➤ Inner Asia (GBR ISSN 1464-8172) **4456**
Inner Circle (NZL) **8179**
▼ Inner Circle Elite Magazine (USA ISSN 1947-4563) **5074**
Inner Circle Letter (USA) **4337**
The Inner Ear Report (CAN ISSN 0842-6376) **3104**
Inner Mongolia Agricultural University. Journal (Social Science Edition) *see* Neimenggu Nongye Daxue Xuebao (Shehui Kexue Ban) **7988**
Inner Mongolia Finance and Economics College. Journal *see* Neimenggu Caijing Xueyuan Xuebao **1152**
Inner Mongolia Forestry Science and Technology *see* Neimenggu Linye Keji **3698**
Inner Mongolia Medical Journal *see* Neimenggu Yixue Zazhi **5684**
Inner Mongolia Normal University. Journal (Education Science Edition) *see* Nei Menggu Shifan Daxue Xuebao (Jiaoyu Kexue Ban) **2890**
Inner Mongolia Normal University. Journal (Natural Science Edition) *see* Nei Menggu Shifan Daxue Xuebao (Ziran Kexue Ban) **7891**
Inner Mongolia Normal University. Journal (Philosophy & Social Science Chinese Edition) *see* Nei Menggu Shifan Daxue Xuebao (Zhexue Shehui Kexue Hanwen Ban) **6935**
Inner Mongolia Radio & T V University. Journal *see* Neimenggu Dian-Daxue Kan **7988**
Inner Mongolia Theory Research of United Front *see* Neimenggu Tongzhan Lilun Yanjiu **7988**
Inner Mongolia University for Nationalities. Journal (Natural Sciences) *see* Neimenggu Minzu Daxue Xuebao (Ziran Kexue Ban) **7891**
Inner Mongolia University for Nationalities. Journal (Social Sciences) *see* Neimenggu Minzu Daxue Xuebao (Shehui Kexue Ban) **7988**
Inner Mongolia University. Journal (Humanities & Social Sciences Edition) *see* Nei Menggu Daxue Xuebao (Renwen - Shehui Kexue Ban) **7988**
Inner Mongolian Social Sciences *see* Nei Menggu Shehui Kexue **7988**
Inner Mongolian Women *see* Nei Menggu Funu **8877**
Inner Nets (USA) **8236**
Inner Paths (USA ISSN 0149-6026) **6645**
• Inner Self (USA) **6645**
Inner Strength (USA) **5894**
Inner Swine (USA ISSN 1527-7704) **3978**
Inner Voice *see* Forest Magazine **3689**
Inner West Courier (AUS) **3794**
Inner West Courier (Inner City Edition) *see* Inner West Courier **3794**
Inner West Courier (Inner West Edition) *see* Inner West Courier **3794**
• InnerCity Magazine (USA) **6575**
Innervision (JPN ISSN 0913-8919) **6198**
▼ • Innerworldaudio (FIN ISSN 1797-030X) **8153**
• ➤ The Innes Review (GBR ISSN 0020-157X) **7800**
Innfocus (CAN ISSN 1193-1922) **4391**
Innherreds Folkeblad og Verdalingen (NOR) **3923**
Innis Herald (CAN) **2287**
Innisfail Booster (CAN) **3811**
The Innisfil Enterprise (CAN ISSN 1719-9735) **3811**
Innisfil Scope (CAN ISSN 0225-1604) **3811**
The Innkeepers' Register (USA ISSN 1052-794X) **8721**
• Innominate (AUS ISSN 0020-1618) **2287**
▼ • ➤ Innov A i T (Associates in Training) (GBR ISSN 1755-7380) **5635**
Innova (CHL ISSN 0717-9812) **446**
• Innovacion (CHL ISSN 0716-6311) **8426**
➤ Innovacion Educativa (ESP ISSN 1130-8656) **2866**
• Innovacion Tecnologica (CUB ISSN 1025-6504) **8426**
Innovacion y Ciencia (COL ISSN 0121-5140) **7866**
Innovaciones Educativas (CRI ISSN 1022-9825) **2942**
InNOVAcorp. Annual Report (CAN ISSN 1205-9331) **8426**
InnovAiT *see* Innov A i T **5635**
• Innovate (NOR ISSN 1503-9676) **8426**
Innovate (ZAF ISSN 1818-443X) **3198**
Innovate (Boston) (USA ISSN 1932-7749) **1753**
• ➤ Innovate (North Miami) (USA ISSN 1552-3233) **2867**
• Innovating (USA ISSN 1053-2587) **1753**
Innovation (CAN ISSN 1206-3622) **3198**
Innovation *see* Ibda' **8963**
• ➤ Innovation (SGP ISSN 0219-4023) **7866**

Title

Title

DIRECTORY 2010 INSTITUT PIERRE BAYLE. STUDIES 10419

Institut Francais de Recherche en Afrique Documents in Social Sciences and Humanities *see* I F R A Documents in Social Sciences and Humanities **7240**
Institut Francais de Recherche en Afrique Occasional Publications *see* I F R A Occasional Publications **7240**
Institut Francais de Recherche pour l'Exploitation de la Mer. Actes de Colloques (FRA ISSN 0761-3962) **2807**
Institut Francais de Recherche pour l'Exploitation de la Mer Centre de Brest. Bilans & Prospectives *see* I F R E M E R Centre de Brest. Bilans & Prospectives **2806**
Institut Francais de Recherche Scientifique pour le Developpement en Cooperation. Colloques et Seminaires (FRA ISSN 0767-2896) **7866**
Institut Francais de Recherche Scientifique pour le Developpement en Cooperation. Etudes et Theses (FRA ISSN 0767-2888) **7866**
▼ Institut Francais des Relations Internationales. Etudes (FRA ISSN 1962-610X) **7242**
• Institut Francais des Relations Internationales. Notes (FRA ISSN 1272-9914) **7242**
• Institut Francais d'Etudes Andines. Bulletin/Instituto Frances de Estudios Andinos. Boletin (PER ISSN 0303-7495) **7973**
Institut Francais d'Etudes Andines. Travaux (PER ISSN 0768-424X) **7973**
Institut Francais du Petrole. Collection Colloques et Seminaires (FRA ISSN 0073-8360) **6773**
Institut Francais du Petrole. Rapport Annuel (FRA ISSN 0073-8379) **6773**
Institut fuer Afrika-Kunde. Arbeiten (DEU ISSN 0945-3601) **7142**
Institut fuer Allgemeine Botanik und Botanischer Garten. Mitteilungen (DEU ISSN 0344-5615) **794**
Institut fuer Angewandte Geodaesie. Mitteilungen (DEU ISSN 0071-9196) **4015**
Institut fuer den Wissenschaftlichen Film. Beitraege zu Zeitgeschichtlichen Filmquellen (DEU ISSN 0944-3215) **6504**
• ➤ Institut fuer Deutsche Sprache. Jahrbuch (DEU ISSN 0537-7900) **5128**
Institut fuer Deutsche Sprache. Schriften (DEU ISSN 1861-566X) **5128**
Institut fuer Deutsches, Europaeisches und Internationales Medizinrecht, Gesundheitsrecht und Bioethik der Universitaeten Heidelberg und Mannheim. Veroeffentlichungen (DEU) **4693**
Institut fuer die Paedagogik der Naturwissenschaften Blaetter *see* I P N - Blaetter **7864**
Institut fuer Donauschwaebische Geschichte und Landeskunde. Materialien (DEU ISSN 0945-425X) **4231**
Institut fuer Donauschwaebische Geschichte und Landeskunde. Schriftenreihe (DEU ISSN 1611-2083) **4231**
Institut fuer Eisenhuettenkunde. Berichte (DEU ISSN 0943-4631) **6315**
Institut fuer Empirische Wirtschaftsforschung. Arbeitspapiere (DEU ISSN 0720-6852) **1124**
Institut fuer Empirische Wirtschaftsforschung. Veroeffentlichungen (DEU ISSN 0720-7239) **1124**
Institut fuer Entwicklungsforschung, Wirtschafts- und Sozialplanung. Schriften (DEU ISSN 0721-8125) **8107**
Institut fuer Europaeische Geschichte, Mainz. Veroeffentlichungen. Abteilung Universalgeschichte. Beihefte (DEU ISSN 0170-365X) **4146**
Institut fuer Europaeische Geschichte, Mainz. Veroeffentlichungen. Abteilung Universalgeschichte und Abteilung fuer Abendlaendische Religionsgeschichte (DEU) **4146**
Institut fuer Europaeische Geschichte, Mainz. Vortraege. Abteilung Universalgeschichte und Abteilung fuer Abendlaendische Religionsgeschichte (DEU) **4146**
Institut fuer Europaeische Wirtschaftsstudien Schriftenreihe *see* I E W S Schriftenreihe **1120**
Institut fuer Festkoerperforschung Bulletin *see* I F F Bulletin **8963**
Institut fuer Festkoerperforschung Ferienkurses. Vorlesungsmanuskripte *see* I F F - Ferienkurses. Vorlesungsmanuskripte **7015**
Institut fuer Finanzwirtschaft und Finanzrecht. Schriftenreihe (CHE) **1354**
Institut fuer Finanzwissenschaft und Steuerrecht. Gelbe Briefe (AUT) **1929**
Institut fuer Finanzwissenschaft und Steuerrecht. Mitteilungsblatt (AUT) **1929**
Institut fuer Foederalismus. Berichte (AUT) **7143**
Institut fuer Foederalismus. Schriftenreihe (AUT) **7143**
Institut fuer Interdisziplinaere Forschung und Fortbildung Texte *see* I F F Texte **8106**
Institut fuer Interdisziplinaere Zypern-Studien. Schriften (DEU) **4321**
Institut fuer Internationale Begegnungen. Schriften (DEU ISSN 0720-5899) **8107**
Institut fuer Kolbenmaschinen. Forschungsberichte (DEU ISSN 1615-2980) **3380**
Institut fuer Konstruktiven Ingenieurbau. Schriftenreihe (DEU ISSN 1614-4384) **3270**
Institut fuer Landes- und Stadtentwicklungsforschung und Bauwesen des Landes N R W *see* I L S **4414**
Institut fuer Landes- und Stadtentwicklungsforschung und Bauwesen des Landes N R W. Journal (DEU ISSN 1612-9660) **4416**
Institut fuer Migrationsforschung und Interkulturelle Studien Beitraege *see* I M I S - Beitraege **7284**
Institut fuer Migrationsforschung und Interkulturelle Studien. Schriften (DEU) **7285**
Institut fuer Oeffentliche Dienstleistungen und Tourismus. Schriftenreihe *see* Beitraege zum Oeffentlichen Management **8686**
➤ Institut fuer Oesterreichische Geschichtsforschung. Mitteilungen (DEU ISSN 0073-8484) **4232**
Institut fuer Orthodoxe Theologie. Veroeffentlichungen (DEU) **7704**
Institut fuer Ostrecht. Studien (DEU ISSN 0073-8492) **4693**
Institut fuer Rehabilitationsmedizin und Balneologie Bad Wildungen. Wissenschaftliche Schriftenreihe (DEU ISSN 1435-6902) **5635**
Institut fuer Saechsische Geschichte und Volkskunde. Bausteine (DEU) **4232**
Institut fuer Schleswig-Holsteinische Zeit- und Regionalgeschichte Schriftenreihe *see* I Z R G Schriftenreihe **4231**
Institut fuer Schweizerisches Arbeitsrecht. Mitteilungen (CHE ISSN 1022-5625) **1688**
Institut fuer Sozial- und Wirtschaftswissenschaften Forschungsarbeiten *see* I S W - Forschungsarbeiten **7971**
Institut fuer Sportpublizistik. Beitraege (DEU ISSN 0947-4501) **8179**
Institut fuer Stadt- und Regionalforschung Forschungsberichte *see* I S R - Forschungsberichte **4414**
Institut fuer Steuerungstechnik der Werkzeugmaschinen und Fertigungseinrichtungen Forschung und Praxis *see* I S W Forschung und Praxis **5452**
Institut fuer Technikfolgen-Abschaetzung Berichte *see* I T A - Berichte **8425**
† Institut fuer Technologie der Gesundheitsbauten Berlin. Mitteilungen (DDR ISSN 0323-4738) **8965**
† Institut fuer Textiltechnik der Rheinisch-Westfaelischen Technischen Hochschule Aachen. Mitteilungen (DEU ISSN 0515-0582) **8965**
Institut fuer Theoretische Chemie. Universitaet Stuttgart. Arbeitsbericht (DEU) **2065**
Institut fuer Thermische Stroemungsmaschinen. Forschungsberichte (DEU ISSN 1615-4983) **3380**
Institut fuer Umformtechnik *see* I F U **8424**
Institut fuer Verkehr und Stadtbauwesen. Veroeffentlichungen (DEU) **8631**
Institut fuer Verkehrswesen. Schriftenreihe (AUT) **8499**
Institut fuer Verwaltung und Verwaltungsrecht in den Neuen Bundeslaendern. Schriften (DEU) **7446**
Institut fuer Wasserwirtschaft, Hydrologie und Landwirtschaftlichen Wasserbau. Mitteilungen (DEU ISSN 0343-8090) **8825**
Institut fuer Weltwirtschaft. Annual Report (DEU) **1491**
Institut fuer Werkzeugmaschinen und Betriebstechnik Forschungsberichte *see* W B K Forschungsberichte **3226**
Institut fuer Westslawische Musikforschung. Schriften (DEU ISSN 1862-6173) **6575**
Institut fuer Wirtschafts- und Sozialgeography Discussion Papers *see* W S G Discussion Papers **4034**
➤ Institut fuer Wissenschaft und Kunst. Mitteilungen (AUT ISSN 0020-2320) **2987**
Institut Geographique du Zaire. Rapport Annuel (COD ISSN 0443-3173) **4015**
Institut Geographique National. Bulletin d'Information (FRA ISSN 0427-2218) **4036**
• ➤ l'Institut Henri Poincare. Annales (B). Probabilites et Statistiques (USA ISSN 0246-0203) **5493**
• ➤ l'Institut Henri Poincare. Annales (C). Analyse Non Lineaire (FRA ISSN 0294-1449) **5493**
Institut Historique Archeologique Neerlandais de Stamboul. Publications/Nederlands Historisch-Archaeologisch Instituut te Istanbul. Uitgaven (NLD ISSN 0926-9568) **4321**
Institut Historique Belge de Rome. Bibliotheque (BEL ISSN 0073-8522) **4232**
Institut Historique Belge de Rome. Bulletin (BEL ISSN 0073-8530) **4232**
Institut International d'Administration Publique. Dossiers et Debats (FRA ISSN 1152-5096) **7446**
Institut International du Froid. Bulletin/International Institute of Refrigeration. Bulletin (FRA ISSN 0020-6970) **4121**
Institut International du Froid. Comptes Rendus de Reunions de Commissions/International Institute of Refrigeration. Proceedings of Commission Meetings (FRA ISSN 0074-6541) **4121**
Institut International J. Maritain. Notes et Documents (ITA ISSN 0393-6503) **7143**
Institut Interregional de Recherche des Nations Unies sur la Criminalite et la Justice. Serie Themes et Rapports *see* United Nations Interregional Crime and Justice Research Institute. Issues and Reports Series **2670**
Institut Jean Vigo. Archives (FRA ISSN 0985-2395) **6504**
Institut Jules Destree. Collection: Etudes et Documents *see* Institut Jules Destree. Etudes et Documents **4232**
Institut Jules Destree. Etudes et Documents (BEL ISSN 0073-8557) **4232**
Institut Matematiki. Trudy *see* Matematicheskie Trudy **5511**
• ➤ Institut Mathematique. Publications (SRB ISSN 0350-1302) **5494**
Institut National de la Consommation Hebdo Consommateurs Actualites *see* I N C Hebdo Consommateurs Actualites **2638**
Institut National de la Recherche Agronomique Colloques *see* I N R A. Colloques **119**
Institut National de la Recherche Agronomique de Tunisie. Annales (TUN ISSN 0365-4761) **122**
Institut National de la Recherche Agronomique de Tunisie. Documents Techniques (TUN ISSN 0020-238X) **122**
Institut National de la Recherche Agronomique de Tunisie. Rapport d'Activite (TUN ISSN 1737-7188) **122**
Institut National de la Recherche Agronomique. Departement d'Economie et de Sociologie Rurales Sciences Sociales *see* I N R A Sciences Sociales **200**
▼ Institut National de la Recherche Agronomique. Magazine (FRA ISSN 1958-3923) **122**
Institut National de la Recherche Agronomique. Station d'Amelioration des Plantes Maraicheres d'Avignon - Montfavet. Rapport d'Activite (FRA ISSN 0762-1167) **794**
Institut National de la Recherhce Scientifique - Eau, Terre et Environnement Rapport Annuel *see* I N R S - E T E. Rapport Annuel **3438**
Institut National de la Sante et de la Recherche Medicale. Actualites (FRA ISSN 0755-4168) **7525**
Institut National de la Sante et de la Recherche Medicale Atelier *see* I N S E R M. Atelier **5632**
Institut National de la Sante et de la Recherche Medicale Collection Grandes Enquetes en Sante Publique et Epidemiologie *see* I N S E R M. Collection Grandes Enquetes en Sante Publique et Epidemiologie **5632**
Institut National de la Sante et de la Recherche Medicale. Colloques (FRA ISSN 0768-3154) **5635**
Institut National de la Sante et de la Recherche Medicale Symposia *see* I N S E R M Symposia **5632**
Institut National de la Statistique et des Etudes Economiques Actualites *see* I N S E E Actualites **1490**
Institut National de la Statistique et des Etudes Economiques Bulletin Mensuel Statistique *see* I N S E E Bulletin Mensuel Statistique **1241**
Institut National de la Statistique et des Etudes Economiques Ile-de-France a la Page *see* I N S E E Ile-de-France a la Page **1241**
Institut National de la Statistique et des Etudes Economiques Methodes *see* I N S E E Methodes **1241**
Institut National de la Statistique et des Etudes Economiques Picardie Dossiers *see* I N S E E Picardie Dossiers **1241**
Institut National de la Statistique et des Etudes Economiques Picardie Premiere *see* I N S E E Picardie Premiere **1241**
Institut National de la Statistique et des Etudes Economiques Premiere *see* I N S E E Premiere **1241**
Institut National de la Statistique et des Etudes Economiques Resultats *see* I N S E E Resultats **1241**
Institut National de la Statistique et des Etudes Economiques Resultats: Economie Generale *see* I N S E E Resultats: Economie Generale **1241**
Institut National de la Statistique et des Etudes Economiques Resultats: Systeme Productif *see* I N S E E Resultats: Systeme Productif **1241**
Institut National de la Statistique et des Etudes Economiques Statistiques et Etudes: Midi-Pyrenees *see* I N S E E Statistiques et Etudes: Midi-Pyrenees **1241**
Institut National de Recherche en Informatique et en Automatique. Collection Didactique (FRA ISSN 0299-0733) **2537**
• Institut National de Recherche en Informatique et en Automatique. Rapports de Recherche (FRA ISSN 0249-6399) **2423**
Institut National de Recherche en Informatique et en Automatique. Rapports Techniques (FRA ISSN 0249-0803) **2461**
▼ Institut National de Recherches Archeologiques Preventives. Cahiers (FRA ISSN 1960-307X) **398**
Institut National de Sante Publique du Quebec. Programmation (CAN ISSN 1910-6300) **7525**
Institut National de Statistique. Accidents de la Circulation sur la Voie Publique avec Tues et Blesses *see* Belgium. Institut National de Statistique. Sante. Accidents de la Circulation sur la Voie Publique avec Tues et Blesses en (Annee) **8522**
Institut National de Statistique. Annuaire de Statistiques Regionales *see* Belgium. Institut National de Statistique. Annuaire de Statistiques Regionales **1214**
Institut National de Statistique. Annuaire Statistique de Poche *see* Belgium. Communaute Francaise de Belgique. Institut National de Statistique. Annuaire Statistique **1214**
Institut National de Statistique. Catalogue des Produits et Services *see* Belgium. Institut National de Statistique. Catalogue des Produits et Services **8357**
Institut National de Statistique. Communique Hebdomadaire *see* Belgium. Institut National de Statistique. Communique Hebdomadaire **1214**
Institut National de Statistique. Enquete sur les Budgets des Menages *see* Belgium. Institut National de Statistique. Enquete sur les Budgets des Menages **1214**
Institut National de Statistique. Enquete sur les Forces de Travail *see* Belgium. Institut National de Statistique. Emploi et Chomage. Enquete sur les Forces de Travail (Year) **1214**
Institut National de Statistique. Etudes Statistiques *see* Belgium. Institut National de Statistique. Etudes Statistiques **8357**
Institut National de Statistique. Navigation Interieure *see* Belgium. Institut National de Statistique. Transport. Navigation Interieure **8522**
Institut National de Statistique. Nombre de Licences d'Appareils de Radio sur Vehicule et de Television au 31 Decembre *see* Belgium. Institut National de Statistique. Media. Nombre de Licences d'Appareils de Radio sur Vehicule et de Television **1214**
Institut National de Statistique. Nouvelles Economiques *see* Belgium. Institut National de Statistique. Nouvelles Economiques **1214**
Institut National de Statistique. Parc de Vehicules a Moteur *see* Belgium. Institut National de Statistique. Statistiques du Transport. Parc des Vehicules a Moteur au (Year) **8522**
Institut National de Statistique. Perspectives de Population *see* Belgium. Institut National de Statistique. Perspectives de Population **7303**
Institut National de Statistique. Statistique du Tourisme et de l'Hotellerie *see* Belgium. Institut National de Statistique. Statistique du Tourisme et de l'Hotellerie **8778**
Institut National de Statistique. Statistiques Agricoles *see* Belgium. Institut National de Statistique. Agriculture. Statistiques Agricoles **175**
Institut National de Statistique. Statistiques de la Construction et du Logement *see* Belgium. Institut National de Statistique. Industrie et Construction. Construction et Logement **4434**
Institut National de Statistique. Statistiques Demographiques *see* Belgium. Institut National de Statistique. Demographie Mathematique. Tables de Mortalite **7303**
Institut National de Statistique. Statistiques Industrielles *see* Belgium. Institut National de Statistique. Industrie et Construction **1214**
Institut National de Statistique. Statistiques Sociales *see* Belgium. Institut National de Statistique. Statistiques Sociales **8081**
Institut National des Appellations d'Origine. Bulletin (FRA) **605**
Institut National des Langues et Civilisations Orientales. Livret de l'Etudiant (FRA ISSN 0765-1899) **4184**
Institut National des Techniques de la Documentation. Bulletin Bibliographique (FRA ISSN 0398-9577) **5058**
Institut National d'Etudes Demographiques. Congres et Colloques (FRA ISSN 1144-7648) **7285**
• Institut National du Cancer. Lettre (FRA ISSN 1950-9308) **6022**
Institut National Genevois. Acts (CHE) **4457**
Institut National pour l'Etude et la Recherche Agronomique. Rapport Annuel (COD) **122**
Institut Oceanographique. Bulletin (MCO ISSN 0304-5722) **2807**
Institut Oceanographique. Memoires (MCO ISSN 0304-5714) **2807**
Institut Oceonographique. Bulletin. Numero Special (MCO ISSN 1606-1160) **2807**
Institut of National History, Skopje. Review *see* Institut za Nacionalna Istorija, Skopje. Glasnik **4232**
Institut Panafricain pour le Developpement. Centre de Formation au Management des Projets. Bilan des Activites (CMR) **1598**
Institut Panafricain pour le Developpement. Centre d'Etudes et de Recherches Appliquees. Evaluation du Seminaire sur la Methodologie du Management des Projets (CMR) **1598**
Institut Panafricain pour le Developpement. Travaux d'Etudiants. Bulletin Analytique (CMR) **1598**
Institut Panafricain pour le Developpement. Travaux Manuscrits (CMR) **200**
Institut Pasteur d'Algerie. Archives (DZA ISSN 0020-2460) **887**
Institut Pasteur de Bangui. Rapport Annuel (CAF) **5635**
Institut Pasteur de Dakar. Rapport sur le Fonctionnement Technique (SEN ISSN 0377-3418) **887**
• Institut Pasteur de Tunis. Archives (TUN ISSN 0020-2509) **5635**
Institut Pasteur. Lettre (FRA ISSN 1243-8863) **5635**
Institut Phytopathologique Benaki. Annales. Nouvelle Serie (GRC ISSN 0365-5814) **122**
Institut Pierre Bayle. Studies (NLD ISSN 0927-1864) **4232**

Title

10420 INSTITUT PO OKEANOLOGIIA. TRUDOVE ULRICH'S PERIODICALS

Institut po Okeanologiia. Trudove/Institute of Oceanology. Proceedings (BGR) **2807**
Institut Polonais des Arts et des Sciences au Canada et la Bibliotheque Polonaise. Bulletin *see* Polski Instytut Naukowy w Kanadzie i Biblioteka Polska im. Wandy Stachiewicz. Biuletyn **4469**
▼ • Institut pour la Prevention de la Criminalite. Revue/Institute for the Prevention of Crime. Review (CAN ISSN 1913-1941) **2655**
Institut pour la Surveillance et la Recherche Environnementales. Rapport Annuel *see* Institute for Environmental Monitoring and Research. Annual Report **3440**
Institut pour l'Egalite des Femmes et des Hommes. Rapport d'Activites (BEL ISSN 1784-1410) **8868**
Institut Prikladnoi Astronomii. Trudy/I A A Transactions (RUS) **575**
Institut Professionel de la Fonction Publique du Canada *see* Professional Institute of the Public Service of Canada. Communications **7460**
Institut Provincial d'Etudes et Recherches Bibliotheconomiques. Memoires (BEL) **627**
Institut Quimic de Sarria Tesis Doctorales. Trabajos de Fin de Carrera. Tesis de Master *see* I.Q.S. Tesis Doctorales. Trabajos de Fin de Carrera. Tesis de Master **2064**
➤ Institut Razi. Archives (IRN ISSN 0365-3439) **5818**
Institut Royal des Sciences Naturelles de Belgique. Bulletin. Serie Biologie (BEL ISSN 0374-6429) **678**
Institut Royal des Sciences Naturelles de Belgique. Bulletin. Serie Entomologie (BEL ISSN 0374-6232) **850**
Institut Royal des Sciences Naturelles de Belgique. Bulletin. Serie Sciences de la Terre (BEL ISSN 0374-6291) **2747**
Institut Royal des Sciences Naturelles de Belgique. Documents de Travail *see* Koninklijk Belgisch Instituut voor Natuurwetenschappen. Studiedocumenten **686**
Institut Royal du Patrimoine Artistique. Bulletin/Koninklijk Instituut voor het Kunstpatrimonium. Bulletin (BEL ISSN 0085-1892) **496**
Institut Royal du Patrimoine Artistique. Rapport (BEL ISSN 1784-5211) **496**
Institut Royal Meteorologique de Belgique. Annuaire: Magnetisme Terrestre/Koninklijk Meteorologisch Instituut van Belgie. Jaarboek: Aardmagnetisme (BEL ISSN 0770-4569) **2747**
Institut Royal Meteorologique de Belgique. Bulletin Mensuel: Observations Climatologiques/Koninklijk Meteorologische Instituut van Belgie. Maandbulletin: Klimatologische Waarnemingen (BEL ISSN 0029-7682) **6357**
Institut Royal Meteorologique de Belgique. Bulletin Mensuel: Observations Geophysiques/Koninklijk Meteorologisch Instituut van Belgie. Maandbulletin. Geofysische Waarnemingen (BEL ISSN 0020-2525) **2783**
Institut Royal Meteorologique de Belgique. Bulletin Mensuel: Observations Ionospheriques et du Rayonnement Cosmique/Koninklijk Meteorologische Instituut van Belgie. Maandbulletin: Waarnemingen van de Ionosfeer en de Kosmische Straling (BEL ISSN 0020-2533) **6357**
Institut Royal Meteorologique de Belgique. Bulletin Quotidien du Temps/Koninklijk Meteorologisch Instituut van Belgie. Dagelijks Weerbulletin (BEL ISSN 0007-5280) **6357**
Institut Royal Meteorologique de Belgique. Bulletin Trimestriel: Observations d'Ozone/Koninklijk Meteorologische Instituut van Belgie. Driemaandelijks Bulletin: Ozon Waarnemingen (BEL ISSN 0770-0164) **6357**
Institut Royal Meteorologique de Belgique. Miscellanea. Serie A/Koninklijk Meteorologisch Instituut van Belgie. Miscellanea. Serie A (BEL ISSN 0770-0261) **6357**
Institut Royal Meteorologique de Belgique. Publications. Serie B/Koninklijk Meteorologisch Instituut van Belgie. Publicaties. Reeks B (BEL ISSN 0770-4615) **6357**
Institut Scientifique. Bulletin (MAR ISSN 0253-3243) **7866**
• Institut Scientifique. Bulletin. Section Sciences de la Terre (MAR ISSN 1114-6834) **2710**
• Institut Scientifique. Bulletin. Section Sciences de la Vie (MAR ISSN 1114-8500) **678**
Institut Stomatologii (RUS) **5848**
Institut Suisse de Droit Compare. Publications (CHE ISSN 1015-9746) **4693**
Institut Syndical Europeen. Rapport d'Activites (BEL) **4596**
Institut Technique du Batiment et des Travaux Publics. Annales *see* Annales du Batiment et des Travaux Publics **976**
Institut Technique Francais de la Betterave Industrielle. Compte Rendu des Travaux Effectues (FRA ISSN 1250-6893) **236**
Institut Universitaire d'Etudes du Developpement. Les Nouveaux Cahiers (CHE ISSN 1260-8971) **1598**
Institut Wiener Kreis. Veroeffentlichung (AUT) **6925**
• Institut za Archeologiju. Annales (HRV ISSN 1845-4046) **398**
• ➤ Institut za Archeologiju u Zagrebu. Prilozi (HRV ISSN 1330-0644) **398**
Institut za Arhitekturu i Urbanizam Srbije. Zbornik Radova (SRB) **446**
• ➤ Institut za Hrvatski Jezik i Jezikoslovlje. Rasprave (HRV ISSN 1331-6745) **5128**
➤ Institut za Istoriju u Sarajevu. Prilozi/Historical Institute. Contributions (BIH ISSN 0350-1159) **4232**
Institut za Nacionalna Istorija, Skopje. Glasnik/Institut of National History, Skopje. Review (MKD ISSN 0583-4961) **4232**
Institut za Nuklearne Nauke, Vinca. Bibliografija Radova (SRB ISSN 0354-107X) **3153**
Institut za Oceanografiju i Ribarstvo Split. Biljeske/Institute of Oceanography and Fisheries Split. Notes (HRV ISSN 0561-6360) **2807**
• Institut za Povijest Umjetnosti. Radovi (HRV ISSN 0350-3437) **496**
• The Institute (New York) (USA ISSN 1050-1797) **3319**
Institute for Advanced Research in Arts and Social Sciences. Occasional Paper *see* University of Birmingham. Institute for Advanced Research in Arts and Social Sciences. Occasional Paper **4480**
Institute for Agricultural Research According to the Torah. Bulletin *see* Halikhot Sadeh **117**
Institute for American Indian Studies. Occasional Paper and Books (USA) **6635**
Institute for Animal Health (GBR ISSN 1463-998X) **320**
Institute for Animal Health. Report *see* Institute for Animal Health **320**
Institute for Archaeo-Metallurgical Studies Journal *see* I A M S Journal **397**
Institute for Balkan Studies. Publications/Idryma Meleton Chersonesou Aimou. Ekdoseis (GRC ISSN 0073-862X) **4232**
Institute for Briquetting and Agglomeration. Proceedings (USA ISSN 0145-8701) **6465**
• Institute for Canadian Music. Newsletter (CAN ISSN 1705-1452) **6575**
Institute for Certification of Computing Professionals. Annual Report (USA ISSN 0098-2431) **2423**
Institute for Chemical Research Annual Report *see* I C R Annual Report **2064**
Institute for Civil Justice. Annual Report (USA ISSN 1041-4940) **7209**
Institute for Commercial Forestry Research Annual Research Report *see* I C F R Annual Research Report **3692**
Institute for Comparative Studies of Culture. Annals (JPN ISSN 0563-8186) **7973**
Institute for Compliance and Quality Management Quarterly Review *see* I C Q M Quarterly Review **1352**
Institute for Comprehensive Studies of Buddhism. Annual *see* Taisho Daigaku Sogo Bukkyo Kenkyujo Nenpo **7702**
Institute for Computer Applications in Science and Engineering - Langley Research Center Interdisciplinary Series in Science and Engineering *see* I C A S E - L A R C Interdisciplinary Series in Science and Engineering **7864**
Institute for Computer Based Learning. Reports (GBR ISSN 0965-5298) **2987**
Institute for Cosmic Ray Research Annual Report *see* I C R R Annual Report **575**
Institute for Cosmic Ray Research Hokoku *see* I C R R Hokoku **575**
Institute for Cosmic Ray Research News *see* I C R R News **575**
Institute for Defence Studies and Analyses. Strategic Digest (IND ISSN 0970-017X) **2226**
• ➤ Institute for Defence Studies and Analysis. Strategic Analysis (GBR ISSN 0970-0161) **2226**
Institute for Development Anthropology Working Papers *see* I D A Working Papers **342**
Institute for Development Policy and Management Discussion and Working Papers *see* I D P M Discussion and Working Papers **1597**
Institute for Employment Studies Annual Review *see* I E S Annual Review **1686**
Institute for Employment Studies. Report (GBR ISSN 1369-4987) **1688**
Institute for Environment and Health. Assessments (GBR) **3440**
Institute for Environment and Health. Reports (GBR) **3440**
Institute for Environment and Health. Special Reports (GBR) **3440**
Institute for Environmental Monitoring and Research. Annual Report/Institut pour la Surveillance et la Recherche Environnementales. Rapport Annuel (CAN ISSN 1911-1908) **3440**
• Institute for European Environmental Policy. Annual Report (GBR) **3440**
Institute for Financial Management and Research Publications *see* I F M R Publications **1751**
Institute for Financial Research Working Papers (GBR ISSN 1367-5796) **1124**
• Institute for Fiscal Studies. Commentary (GBR ISSN 0961-3153) **1929**
Institute for Fiscal Studies. Working Paper Series *see* Institute for Fiscal Studies. Working Papers (Print) **8965**
• Institute for Fiscal Studies. Working Papers (Online) (GBR ISSN 1742-0415) **1929**
† • Institute for Fiscal Studies. Working Papers (Print) (GBR ISSN 1369-4685) **8965**
• Institute for Foreign Policy Analysis. Conference and Workshop Reports (USA) **7242**
• Institute for Foreign Policy Analysis. Special Reports and Monographs (USA) **7242**
Institute for Fusion Studies Newsletter *see* I F S Newsletter **3168**
The Institute For Genomic Research. International Genome Sequencing and and Analysis Conference (USA) **872**
Institute for Grassland and Animal Production. Report (GBR ISSN 0963-5246) **236**
Institute for Information Law (Proceedings) *see* Information Law Series **4692**
Institute for Japanese - European Technology Studies. Paper (GBR ISSN 1369-7919) **8426**
Institute for Jewish Studies Studies in Judaica *see* I J S Studies in Judaica **7722**
Institute for Labor Studies. Annual Report (PHL) **1688**
Institute for Labor Studies. Monograph Series (PHL ISSN 0118-3877) **1688**
Institute for Labor Studies News Digest *see* I L S News Digest **4595**
Institute for Laboratory Animal Research Journal *see* I L A R Journal **947**
Institute for Laser Technology. Annual Progress Report *see* Reza Gijutsu Sogo Kenkyujo Nenpo **7084**
Institute for Laser Technology. Report *see* Reza Gijutsu Sogo Kenkyujo Jigyo Hokokusho **7084**
Institute for Logic, Language and Computation. Prepublication Series (NLD) **5128**
Institute for Management Education and Development. Report (IDN) **1754**
Institute for Mesoamerican Studies. Monograph Series *see* State University of New York at Albany. Institute for Mesoamerican Studies. Monograph Series **356**
Institute for Microstructural Sciences. Annual Activities Report (CAN ISSN 1193-9400) **6315**
Institute for Molecular Science. Annual Review (JPN) **7067**
Institute for Molecular Science. Computer Center Report/Okazaki Kokuritsu Kyodo Kenkyu Kiko Bunshi Kagaku Kenkyujo Denshi Keisanki Senta Repoto (JPN) **7067**
Institute for Molecular Science. Letters *see* Bunshiken Retazu **7065**
The Institute for Nuclear Theory. Proceedings (SGP) **7016**
Institute for Objective Measurement Newsletter *see* I O M Newsletter **6402**
Institute for Operations Research and the Management Sciences Journal on Computing *see* I N F O R M S Journal on Computing **2421**
Institute for Operations Research and the Management Sciences Transactions on Education *see* I N F O R M S Transactions on Education **1751**
Institute for Orgonomic Science. Annals (USA ISSN 8755-3252) **6146**
Institute for Palestine Studies. Israeli Knesset Series (LBN) **4321**
Institute for Palestine Studies. Monograph Series (LBN ISSN 0073-8816) **4321**
Institute for Palestine Studies. Zionist Congress Series (LBN) **4321**
Institute for Philosophy and Public Policy. Report *see* Philosophy and Public Policy Quarterly **6942**
The Institute for Reformed Theology. Bulletin (USA ISSN 1543-1975) **7761**
Institute for Research in English Acquisition and Development Perspectives *see* R E A D Perspectives **2902**
Institute for Research of Christian Culture. Bulletin *see* Kirisutokyo Ronso **7658**
• Institute for Research on Public Policy. Annual Report (CAN ISSN 1719-9093) **7446**
Institute for Research on Women and Gender. Newsletter (USA) **8899**
Institute for Safe Medication Practices Medication Safety Alert! *see* I S M P Medication Safety Alert! **6847**
Institute for Sea Training. Journal (JPN ISSN 0386-1198) **8646**
Institute for Social and Economic Change Monograph *see* I S E C Monograph **1490**
Institute for Social and Economic Research Fact Paper *see* I S E R Fact Paper **7971**
Institute for Social and Economic Research Occasional Paper *see* I S E R Occasional Paper **7971**
Institute for Social and Economic Research Report *see* I S E R Report **7971**
Institute for Social & Economic Research Reports *see* I S E R Reports **7971**
Institute for Social and Economic Research Special Publication *see* I S E R Special Publication **7971**
Institute for Social Research Newsletter (CAN ISSN 0834-1729) **7973**
Institute for Social Research. Report *see* Institutt for Samfunnsforskning. Rapport **8107**
Institute for Socioeconomic Studies. Journal (USA ISSN 0364-0779) **7143**
Institute for Solid State Physics. News *see* Busseiken Dayori **7007**
➤ Institute for Strategic Studies. Bulletin/Instituut vir Strategiese Studies. Bulletin (ZAF ISSN 0257-1447) **7242**
Institute for Studies in American Music. Monographs (USA) **6575**
Institute for Studies in American Music. Newsletter *see* American Music Review **6544**
Institute for Study of the Earth's Interior Technical Report. Series C *see* I S E I Technical Report. Series C **2709**
Institute for Teaching & Research on Women News *see* I T R O W News **2865**
➤ Institute for the Comprehensive Study of Lotus Sutra. Journal/Hokke Bunka Kenkyu (JPN ISSN 0287-1513) **7701**
Institute for the International Education of Students Exchange *see* I I E S Exchange **3013**
Institute for the Management of Information Systems Journal *see* I M I S Journal **2531**
Institute for the Prevention of Crime. Review *see* Institut pour la Prevention de la Criminalite. Revue **2655**
Institute for the Study of Earth and Man Newsletter (USA) **398**
Institute for the Study of Genocide Newsletter (USA ISSN 1078-1706) **8107**
Institute for the Study of International Problems in Education. Publications *see* Institutionen for Internationell Pedagogik. Publications **2867**
Institute for the Study of Man in Africa Occasional Papers *see* I S M A Occasional Papers **342**
Institute for the Study of Man in Africa Papers *see* I S M A Papers **342**
Institute for Theological Encounter with Science and Technology Bulletin *see* I T E S T Bulletin **7648**
Institute for Theological Encounter with Science and Technology Conference Proceedings *see* I T E S T Conference Proceedings **7648**
Institute for Tropical and Subtropical Crops. Bulletin (ZAF) **236**
• Institute for Women's Policy Research. Conference Proceedings (USA) **8899**
• Institute for World Economics. Working Papers (HUN ISSN 1215-5241) **1124**
Institute Items (USA) **496**
Institute Newspaper *see* The Institute (New York) **3319**
Institute of Acoustics. Proceedings (GBR ISSN 0309-8117) **7087**
Institute of Administration and Commerce of South Africa. Journal (ZAF) **1754**
Institute of Advertising Practitioners in Ireland Business Readership Survey *see* I A P I Business Readership Survey **26**
• ➤ Institute of African Studies Research Review (GHA ISSN 0855-4412) **7973**
Institute of Aging. Annual Report of Activities *see* Canadian Institutes of Health Research. Institute of Aging. Biennial Report **8092**
➤ Institute of Agriculture and Animal Science. Journal (NPL ISSN 1018-6182) **8799**
Institute of Agriculture. Research Reports *see* R D A Journal of Agricultural Science **8983**
Institute of Applied Manpower Research Report *see* I A M R Report **1685**
Institute of Applied Manpower Research Working Paper *see* I A M R Working Paper **1685**
Institute of Arable Crops Research. Annual Report (GBR) **236**
Institute of Arable Crops Research. Report *see* Institute of Arable Crops Research. Annual Report **236**
• Institute of Asian Studies. Journal (IND ISSN 0970-2814) **8107**
Institute of Automotive Engineer Assessors. Journal (GBR ISSN 0309-1430) **8585**
Institute of Bankers in Pakistan. Council. Report and Accounts (PAK ISSN 0073-8999) **1354**
➤ Institute of Bankers. Journal. (BGD ISSN 1684-0054) **1354**
Institute of Bankers of Sri Lanka. Journal (LKA) **6698**
Institute of Biology. Symposia (GBR ISSN 0537-9032) **678**
➤ Institute of Brewing. Journal (GBR ISSN 0046-9750) **605**
Institute of British Foundrymen. Annual Conference Proceedings (GBR) **6315**
• ➤ Institute of British Geographers. Transactions (GBR ISSN 0020-2754) **4015**
Institute of Business, Ideas on Solutions Best Solutions *see* I.B.I.S. Best Solutions **1750**
Institute of Cemetery & Crematorium Management. Journal (GBR ISSN 1747-129X) **3720**
Institute of Certified Travel Agents Update *see* I C T A Update **8720**
† Institute of Chartered Accountants in Australia. Annual Report and Accounts (AUS) **8965**
Institute of Chartered Accountants in Australia. Annual Report on Professional Conduct (AUS ISSN 1833-9476) **1291**
• The Institute of Chartered Accountants in Australia. Report to Members (AUS ISSN 1834-0423) **1291**
Institute of Chartered Accountants in England and Wales. Accounting Standards Board. Papers (GBR) **1291**
Institute of Chartered Accountants in England and Wales. Adding Value: For the General Practitioner Supporting Small Business (GBR ISSN 1369-0175) **1291**
Institute of Chartered Accountants in England and Wales. Business Digest (GBR) **1291**
Institute of Chartered Accountants in England and Wales. Internal Control Newsletter (GBR ISSN 1367-2517) **1291**
Institute of Chartered Accountants in England and Wales. International Accounting Standards Committee. Papers (GBR) **1291**

Institute of Chartered Accountants in England and Wales. Tax Digest (GBR ISSN 0260-6496) **1929**

Institute of Chartered Accountants in England and Wales. Update (GBR ISSN 0266-7053) **1291**

● Institute of Chartered Accountants of Alberta. C A Monthly Statement (CAN) **1291**

● Institute of Chartered Accountants of British Columbia. Beyond Numbers (CAN ISSN 1208-5499) **1291**

Institute of Chartered Accountants of Scotland. Official Directory (GBR ISSN 0073-9057) **1291**

Institute of Chartered Financial Analysts of India Journal of Accounting Research see The I C F A I Journal of Accounting Research **1290**

Institute of Chartered Financial Analysts of India Journal of Alternative Dispute Resolution see The I C F A I Journal of Alternative Dispute Resolution **4689**

Institute of Chartered Financial Analysts of India Journal of Applied Economics see The I C F A I Journal of Applied Economics **1120**

Institute of Chartered Financial Analysts of India Journal of Audit Practice see The I C F A I Journal of Audit Practice **1290**

Institute of Chartered Financial Analysts of India Journal of Bank Management see The I C F A I Journal of Bank Management **1352**

Institute of Chartered Financial Analysts of India Journal of Banking Law see The I C F A I Journal of Banking Law **4870**

Institute of Chartered Financial Analysts of India Journal of Behavioral Finance see The I C F A I Journal of Behavioral Finance **1750**

Institute of Chartered Financial Analysts of India Journal of Brand Management see The I C F A I Journal of Brand Management **1819**

Institute of Chartered Financial Analysts of India Journal of Business Strategy see The I C F A I Journal of Business Strategy **1750**

Institute of Chartered Financial Analysts of India Journal of Corporate and Securities Law see The I C F A I Journal of Corporate and Securities Law **4870**

Institute of Chartered Financial Analysts of India Journal of Corporate Governance see The I C F A I Journal of Corporate Governance **1750**

Institute of Chartered Financial Analysts of India Journal of Cyber Law see The I C F A I Journal of Cyber Law **4689**

Institute of Chartered Financial Analysts of India Journal of Derivatives Markets see The I C F A I Journal of Derivatives Markets **1629**

Institute of Chartered Financial Analysts of India Journal of Employment Law see The I C F A I Journal of Employment Law **4689**

Institute of Chartered Financial Analysts of India Journal of Entrepreneurship Development see The I C F A I Journal of Entrepreneurship Development **1750**

Institute of Chartered Financial Analysts of India Journal of Environmental Economics see The I C F A I Journal of Environmental Economics **3438**

Institute of Chartered Financial Analysts of India Journal of Environmental Law see The I C F A I Journal of Environmental Law **4689**

Institute of Chartered Financial Analysts of India Journal of Financial Economics see The I C F A I Journal of Financial Economics **1352**

Institute of Chartered Financial Analysts of India Journal of Financial Risk Management see The I C F A I Journal of Financial Risk Management **1750**

Institute of Chartered Financial Analysts of India Journal of Healthcare Law see The I C F A I Journal of Healthcare Law **7524**

Institute of Chartered Financial Analysts of India Journal of Industrial Economics see The I C F A I Journal of Industrial Economics **1120**

Institute of Chartered Financial Analysts of India Journal of Information Technology see The I C F A I Journal of Information Technology **2420**

Institute of Chartered Financial Analysts of India Journal of Infrastructure see The I C F A I Journal of Infrastructure **1750**

Institute of Chartered Financial Analysts of India Journal of Insurance Law see The I C F A I Journal of Insurance Law **4870**

Institute of Chartered Financial Analysts of India Journal of Intellectual Property Rights see The I C F A I Journal of Intellectual Property Rights **6751**

Institute of Chartered Financial Analysts of India Journal of International Business Law see The I C F A I Journal of International Business Law **4928**

Institute of Chartered Financial Analysts of India Journal of Knowledge Management see The I C F A I Journal of Knowledge Management **1751**

Institute of Chartered Financial Analysts of India Journal of Management Research see The I C F A I Journal of Management Research **1751**

Institute of Chartered Financial Analysts of India Journal of Managerial Economics see The I C F A I Journal of Managerial Economics **1751**

Institute of Chartered Financial Analysts of India Journal of Marketing Management see The I C F A I Journal of Marketing Management **1819**

Institute of Chartered Financial Analysts of India Journal of Mergers and Acquisitions see The I C F A I Journal of Mergers and Acquisitions **1120**

Institute of Chartered Financial Analysts of India Journal of Monetary Economics see The I C F A I Journal of Monetary Economics **1719**

Institute of Chartered Financial Analysts of India Journal of Operations Management see The I C F A I Journal of Operations Management **1751**

Institute of Chartered Financial Analysts of India Journal of Organizational Behavior see The I C F A I Journal of Organizational Behavior **1865**

Institute of Chartered Financial Analysts of India Journal of Public Administration see The I C F A I Journal of Public Administration **7445**

Institute of Chartered Financial Analysts of India Journal of Public Finance see The I C F A I Journal of Public Finance **1928**

Institute of Chartered Financial Analysts of India Journal of Risk and Insurance see The I C F A I Journal of Risk and Insurance **4505**

Institute of Chartered Financial Analysts of India Journal of Science and Technology see The I C F A I Journal of Science and Technology **7864**

Institute of Chartered Financial Analysts of India Journal of Services Marketing see The I C F A I Journal of Services Marketing **1819**

Institute of Chartered Financial Analysts of India Journal of Supply Chain Management see The I C F A I Journal of Supply Chain Management **1819**

Institute of Chartered Financial Analysts of India Journal of Systems Management see The I C F A I Journal of Systems Management **1751**

Institute of Chemotherapy. Bulletin see Kagaku Ryoho Kenkyujo Kiyo **5997**

Institute of Comparative Studies of International Cultures and Societies. Bulletin see Hikaku Bunka Kenkyu **7240**

Institute of Consulting Engineers. Journal (IND ISSN 0020-2800) **3199**

Institute of Consulting Motor Engineers Manual for Cars see I C M E Manual for Cars **8584**

Institute of Consulting Motor Engineers Manual for Heavy Goods Vehicles see I C M E Manual for Heavy Goods Vehicles **8584**

Institute of Consulting Motor Engineers Manual for Light Commercial Vehicles see I C M E Manual for Light Commercial Vehicles **8584**

Institute of Contemporary Arts Documents see I C A Documents **493**

Institute of Contemporary Arts Monthly Bulletin see I C A Monthly Bulletin **493**

● Institute of Cost and Management Accountants of Bangladesh. Annual Report (BGD) **1291**

Institute of Cost and Management Accountants of Bangladesh Newsletter see I C M A B Newsletter **1290**

Institute of Criminal Studies. Occasional Papers (GBR) **2655**

Institute of Criminology and Justice. Research Series (GBR) **4929**

Institute of Criminology. Occasional Papers (AUS) **2655**

Institute of Developing Economics. Annual Report (JPN) **1598**

Institute of Developing Economies International Joint Research Project Series see I D E International Joint Research Project Series **1120**

Institute of Developing Economies Occasional Papers Series see I D E Occasional Papers Series **1120**

Institute of Developing Economies Research Series see I D E Research Series **1120**

Institute of Developing Economies Spot Survey see I D E Spot Survey **1120**

Institute of Developing Economies Statistical Data Series see I D E Statistical Data Series **1241**

Institute of Developing Economies Symposium Proceedings see I D E Symposium Proceedings **1120**

Institute of Development Management. Report of the Activities of the Institute (TZA) **1754**

Institute of Development Studies. Annual Report (GBR) **1598**

Institute of Development Studies Bulletin see I D S Bulletin **1597**

Institute of Development Studies. Development Bibliography Series (GBR ISSN 0955-0569) **1243**

Institute of Development Studies Discussion Paper see I D S Discussion Paper **1597**

Institute of Development Studies Policy Briefing see I D S Policy Briefing **1597**

Institute of Development Studies Research Reports see I D S Research Reports **1597**

Institute of Development Studies Working Paper see I D S Working Paper **1597**

Institute of Diving. Newsletter (USA) **8179**

➤ Institute of Economic Affairs. Occasional Papers (GBR ISSN 0073-909X) **1124**

➤ Institute of Economic Affairs. Research Monographs (GBR ISSN 0073-9103) **1125**

Institute of Economic Affairs Studies on the Environment see I E A Studies on the Environment **3438**

Institute of Economic Geography, India. Journal (IND) **1125**

Institute of Economic Growth. Book Review List (IND) **627**

Institute of Economic Growth. Census Studies (IND ISSN 0070-3311) **7285**

Institute of Economic Growth. List of Periodical Holding in the I E G Library (IND) **627**

Institute of Economic Growth. List of Periodicals Currently Received in the I E G Library (IND) **627**

Institute of Economic Growth. Micro Document List (IND) **627**

Institute of Economic Growth. Selective List of Books and Documents Added to the Library (IND) **627**

Institute of Economic Growth. Working Papers (IND) **1125**

Institute of Economic Research. Journal (IND ISSN 0020-2851) **1125**

Institute of Economic Research. Publications on Demography (IND) **7285**

Institute of Economic Research. Publications on Economics (IND) **1125**

Institute of Ecosystem Studies Newsletter see I E S Newsletter **3438**

Institute of Education. Nuffield Series (GBR) **3025**

Institute of Educational Research Flambeau see I E R Flambeau **2865**

Institute of Educational Research Newsletter see I E R Newsletter **2865**

Institute of Electrical and Electronic Engineers Canadian Review see I E E E Canadian Review **3311**

Institute of Electrical and Electronic Engineers Computer Society Workshop on Very Large Scale Integration. Proceedings see I E E E Computer Society Annual Symposium on V L S I. Proceedings **2539**

Institute of Electrical and Electronic Engineers International Conference on Mobile Data Management. Proceedings see I E E E International Conference on Mobile Data Management. Proceedings **2350**

Institute of Electrical and Electronics Engineering - Association for Computing Machinery Symposium on Volume Visualization and Graphics. Proceedings see I E E E - A C M - S I G G R A P H Symposium on Volume Visualization and Graphics. Proceedings **2486**

Institute of Electrical and Electronics Engineers Aerospace and Electronic Systems Magazine see I E E E Aerospace and Electronic Systems Magazine **3101**

Institute of Electrical and Electronics Engineers - Aerospace and Electronic Systems Society Dayton Chapter Symposium see I E E E - A E S S Dayton Chapter Symposium **59**

Institute of Electrical and Electronics Engineers - Aerospace and Electronics Systems Society Aerospace and Electronics Conference. Record see I E E E - A E S C O N Aerospace and Electronics Conference. Record **3310**

Institute of Electrical and Electronics Engineers Aerospace Applications Conference. Digest see I E E E Aerospace Applications Conference. Digest **59**

Institute of Electrical and Electronics Engineers Aerospace Conference. Proceedings see I E E E Aerospace Conference. Proceedings **59**

Institute of Electrical and Electronics Engineers Almanack see I E E E Almanack **3310**

Institute of Electrical and Electronics Engineers America Latina. Revista see I E E E America Latina. Revista **3362**

Institute of Electrical and Electronics Engineers - American Institute of Aeronautics and Astronauti Digital Avionics Systems Conference. Proceedings see I E E E - A I A A Digital Avionics Systems Conference. Proceedings **59**

Institute of Electrical and Electronics Engineers - American Society of Mechanical Engineers Joint Rail Conference. Proceedings see I E E E - A S M E Joint Rail Conference. Proceedings **8618**

Institute of Electrical and Electronics Engineers - American Society of Mechanical Engineers Transactions on Mechatronics see I E E E - A S M E Transactions on Mechatronics **3367**

Institute of Electrical and Electronics Engineers Annals of the History of Computing see I E E E Annals of the History of Computing **2420**

Institute of Electrical and Electronics Engineers Antennas and Propagation Magazine see I E E E Antennas and Propagation Magazine **3310**

Institute of Electrical and Electronics Engineers Antennas and Propagation Society. International Symposium see I E E E Antennas and Propagation Society. International Symposium **3310**

Institute of Electrical and Electronics Engineers Antennas and Propagation Society. International Symposium (CD-ROM) see I E E E Antennas and Propagation Society. International Symposium (CD-ROM) **2323**

Institute of Electrical and Electronics Engineers Antennas and Wireless Propagation Letters see I E E E Antennas and Wireless Propagation Letters **2323**

Institute of Electrical and Electronics Engineers Applied Power Electronics Conference and Exposition. Conference Proceedings see I E E E Applied Power Electronics Conference and Exposition. Conference Proceedings **3101**

Institute of Electrical and Electronics Engineers Asia-Pacific Conference on A S I C. Proceedings see I E E E Asia-Pacific Conference on A S I C. Proceedings **2465**

Institute of Electrical and Electronics Engineers Asia - Pacific Conference on Circuits and Systems. Proceedings see I E E E Asia - Pacific Conference on Circuits and Systems. Proceedings **2465**

Institute of Electrical and Electronics Engineers / Association for Computing Machinery / A C M International Conference on Automated Software Engineering see I E E E / A C M International Conference on Automated Software Engineering **2590**

Institute of Electrical and Electronics Engineers - Association for Computing Machinery Transactions on Computational Biology and Bioinformatics see I E E E - A C M Transactions on Computational Biology and Bioinformatics **825**

Institute of Electrical and Electronics Engineers - Association for Computing Machinery Transactions on Networking see I E E E - A C M Transactions on Networking **2497**

Institute of Electrical and Electronics Engineers Autotestcon see I E E E Autotestcon **3311**

Institute of Electrical and Electronics Engineers Cement Industry Technical Conference. Proceedings see I E E E Cement Industry Technical Conference. Proceedings **1013**

Institute of Electrical and Electronics Engineers Circuits and Systems Magazine see I E E E Circuits and Systems Magazine **2465**

Institute of Electrical and Electronics Engineers Communications Letters see I E E E Communications Letters **2323**

Institute of Electrical and Electronics Engineers Communications Magazine see I E E E Communications Magazine **3311**

Institute of Electrical and Electronics Engineers Communications Surveys and Tutorials see I E E E Communications Surveys and Tutorials **2323**

Institute of Electrical and Electronics Engineers Communications Theory Mini-Conference. Proceedings see I E E E Communications Theory Mini-Conference. Proceedings **2323**

Institute of Electrical and Electronics Engineers - Components, Packaging, and Manufacturing Technol Electronics Manufacturing Technology (I E M T) see I E E E - C P M T Electronics Manufacturing Technology (I E M T) **3101**

Institute of Electrical and Electronics Engineers Compound Semiconductor Integrated Circuit Symposium. Technical Digest see I E E E Compound Semiconductor Integrated Circuit Symposium. Technical Digest **3101**

Institute of Electrical and Electronics Engineers Computational Intelligence Magazine see I E E E Computational Intelligence Magazine **2449**

Institute of Electrical and Electronics Engineers Computer Architecture Letters see I E E E Computer Architecture Letters **2467**

Institute of Electrical and Electronics Engineers Computer Graphics and Applications see I E E E Computer Graphics and Applications **2486**

Institute of Electrical and Electronics Engineers Computer Society Annual Symposium on V L S I. Proceedings see I E E E Computer Society Annual Symposium on V L S I. Proceedings **2539**

Institute of Electrical and Electronics Engineers Computer Society Conference on Computer Vision and Pattern Recognition. Proceedings see I E E E Computer Society Conference on Computer Vision and Pattern Recognition. Proceedings **2449**

Institute of Electrical and Electronics Engineers Conference on Computational Complexity. Proceedings see I E E E Conference on Computational Complexity. Proceedings **5491**

Institute of Electrical and Electronics Engineers Conference on Computational Intelligence for Financial Engineering. Proceedings see I E E E Conference on Computational Intelligence for Financial Engineering. Proceedings **2449**

Institute of Electrical and Electronics Engineers Conference on Control Applications. Proceedings see I E E E Conference on Control Applications. Proceedings **2460**

Institute of Electrical and Electronics Engineers Conference on Decision and Control. Proceedings see I E E E Conference on Decision and Control. Proceedings **8424**

Institute of Electrical and Electronics Engineers Conference on Electron Devices and Solid-State Circuits see I E E E Conference on Electron Devices and Solid-State Circuits **2465**

Institute of Electrical and Electronics Engineers Conference on Visualization see I E E E Conference on Visualization **2449**

Institute of Electrical and Electronics Engineers ConferenceSearch see I E E E ConferenceSearch **3311**

Institute of Electrical and Electronics Engineers Congress on Evolutionary Computation. Proceedings see I E E E Congress on Evolutionary Computation. Proceedings **2449**

Institute of Electrical and Electronics Engineers coNNections see I E E E coNNections **2471**

Institute of Electrical and Electronics Engineers Control Systems see I E E E Control Systems **3311**

Title

10422 INSTITUTE OF ELECTRICAL AND ELECTRONICS ENGINEERS CUSTOM ULRICH'S PERIODICALS

Institute of Electrical and Electronics Engineers Custom Integrated Circuits Conference. Proceedings *see* I E E E Custom Integrated Circuits Conference. Proceedings **3311**

Institute of Electrical and Electronics Engineers Design & Test of Computers *see* I E E E Design & Test of Computers **2471**

Institute of Electrical and Electronics Engineers Device Research Conference. Proceedings *see* I E E E Device Research Conference. Proceedings **3101**

Institute of Electrical and Electronics Engineers Distributed Systems Online *see* I E E E Distributed Systems Online **2520**

Institute of Electrical and Electronics Engineers Electrical Insulation Magazine *see* I E E E Electrical Insulation Magazine **3311**

Institute of Electrical and Electronics Engineers - Electromagnetic Compatibility Society Newsletter *see* I E E E - E M C Society Newsletter **3311**

Institute of Electrical and Electronics Engineers Electron Device Letters *see* I E E E Electron Device Letters **3101**

Institute of Electrical and Electronics Engineers Emerging Technologies Symposium *see* I E E E Emerging Technologies Symposium **2359**

Institute of Electrical and Electronics Engineers Engineering in Medicine and Biology Magazine *see* I E E E Engineering in Medicine and Biology Magazine **748**

Institute of Electrical and Electronics Engineers - Engineering in Medicine and Biology Society Conference on Information Technology Applications in Biomedicine. Proceedings *see* I E E E - E M B S Conference on Information Technology Applications in Biomedicine. Proceedings **2420**

Institute of Electrical and Electronics Engineers Engineering in Medicine and Biology Society. Conference Proceedings *see* I E E E Engineering in Medicine and Biology Society. Conference Proceedings **5830**

Institute of Electrical and Electronics Engineers Engineering Management Review *see* I E E E Engineering Management Review **3196**

Institute of Electrical and Electronics Engineers European Test Workshop. Proceedings *see* I E E E European Test Workshop. Proceedings **2471**

Institute of Electrical and Electronics Engineers Geoscience and Remote Sensing Letters *see* I E E E Geoscience and Remote Sensing Letters **3311**

Institute of Electrical and Electronics Engineers Geoscience and Remote Sensing Society Newsletter *see* I E E E Geoscience and Remote Sensing Society Newsletter **3311**

Institute of Electrical and Electronics Engineers German Microwave Theory and Techniques Society - Antennas and Propagation Joint Chapter. International Workshop Digest *see* I E E E German Microwave Theory and Techniques Society - Antennas and Propagation Joint Chapter. International Workshop Digest **3311**

Institute of Electrical and Electronics Engineers Grid *see* I E E E Grid **3311**

Institute of Electrical and Electronics Engineers History Center *see* I E E E History Center **3311**

Institute of Electrical and Electronics Engineers Hong Kong Electron Devices Meeting *see* I E E E Hong Kong Electron Devices Meeting **3101**

Institute of Electrical and Electronics Engineers Industrial Electronics Magazine *see* I E E E Industrial Electronics Magazine **3101**

Institute of Electrical and Electronics Engineers Industrial Electronics Society. Annual Conference. Proceedings *see* I E E E Industrial Electronics Society. Annual Conference. Proceedings **4487**

Institute of Electrical and Electronics Engineers Industry Applications Conference. Conference Record *see* I E E E Industry Applications Conference. Conference Record **2493**

Institute of Electrical and Electronics Engineers Industry Applications Magazine *see* I E E E Industry Applications Magazine **3311**

Institute of Electrical and Electronics Engineers Infocom. Proceedings *see* I E E E Infocom. Proceedings **2350**

Institute of Electrical and Electronics Engineers Information Technology Conference. Proceedings *see* I E E E Information Technology Conference. Proceedings **2520**

Institute of Electrical and Electronics Engineers Information Theory and Communications Workshop *see* I E E E Information Theory and Communications Workshop **2543**

Institute of Electrical and Electronics Engineers - Institute of Navigation Position Location and Navigation Symposium. Record *see* I E E E - I O N Position Location and Navigation Symposium. Record **3311**

Institute of Electrical and Electronics Engineers Instrumentation and Measurement Magazine *see* I E E E Instrumentation and Measurement Magazine **6402**

Institute of Electrical and Electronics Engineers Instrumentation and Measurement Technology Conference. Proceedings *see* I E E E Instrumentation and Measurement Technology Conference. Proceedings **4487**

Institute of Electrical and Electronics Engineers Intelligent Network Workshop *see* I E E E Intelligent Network Workshop **2323**

Institute of Electrical and Electronics Engineers Intelligent Systems *see* I E E E Intelligent Systems **2471**

Institute of Electrical and Electronics Engineers Intelligent Transportation Systems Conference. Proceedings *see* I E E E Intelligent Transportation Systems Conference. Proceedings **8498**

Institute of Electrical and Electronics Engineers Intelligent Transportation Systems Magazine *see* I E E E Intelligent Transportation Systems Magazine **8498**

Institute of Electrical and Electronics Engineers Intelligent Vehicles Symposium *see* I E E E Intelligent Vehicles Symposium **8498**

Institute of Electrical and Electronics Engineers International Carcas Conference on Devices Circuits and Systems. Proceedings *see* I E E E International Carcas Conference on Devices Circuits and Systems. Proceedings **3101**

Institute of Electrical and Electronics Engineers International Computer Software and Applications Conference. Proceedings *see* I E E E International Computer Software and Applications Conference. Proceedings **2590**

Institute of Electrical and Electronics Engineers International Conference on Acoustics, Speech and Signal Processing. Proceedings *see* I E E E International Conference on Acoustics, Speech and Signal Processing. Proceedings **3311**

Institute of Electrical and Electronics Engineers International Conference on Cluster Computing. Proceedings *see* I E E E International Conference on Cluster Computing. Proceedings **2497**

Institute of Electrical and Electronics Engineers International Conference on Communications *see* I E E E International Conference on Communications **2323**

Institute of Electrical and Electronics Engineers International Conference on Computer Design. V L S I in Computers & Processors. Proceedings *see* I E E E International Conference on Computer Design. V L S I in Computers & Processors. Proceedings **2471**

Institute of Electrical and Electronics Engineers International Conference on Computer Vision. Proceedings *see* I E E E International Conference on Computer Vision. Proceedings **2449**

Institute of Electrical and Electronics Engineers International Conference on Consumer Electronics. Digest of Technical Papers *see* I E E E International Conference on Consumer Electronics. Digest of Technical Papers **3101**

Institute of Electrical and Electronics Engineers International Conference on Electronics, Circuits and Systems. Proceedings *see* I E E E International Conference on Electronics, Circuits and Systems. Proceedings **3101**

Institute of Electrical and Electronics Engineers International Conference on Emerging Technologies and Factory Automation. Proceedings *see* I E E E International Conference on Emerging Technologies and Factory Automation. Proceedings **2460**

Institute of Electrical and Electronics Engineers International Conference on Engineering of Complex Computer Systems. Proceedings *see* I E E E International Conference on Engineering of Complex Computer Systems. Proceedings **2590**

Institute of Electrical and Electronics Engineers International Conference on Hardware-Software Codesign and System Synthesis *see* I E E E International Conference on Hardware-Software Codesign and System Synthesis **2540**

Institute of Electrical and Electronics Engineers International Conference on Industrial Informatics *see* I E E E International Conference on Industrial Informatics **1751**

Institute of Electrical and Electronics Engineers International Conference on Information Visualisation (Year) *see* I E E E International Conference on Information Visualisation (Year) **2486**

Institute of Electrical and Electronics Engineers International Conference on Innovative Systems in Silicon *see* I E E E International Conference on Innovative Systems in Silicon **2520**

Institute of Electrical and Electronics Engineers International Conference on Intelligent Robots and Systems. Proceedings *see* I E E E International Conference on Intelligent Robots and Systems. Proceedings **2584**

Institute of Electrical and Electronics Engineers International Conference on Microelectronic Test Structures. Proceedings *see* I E E E International Conference on Microelectronic Test Structures. Proceedings **2465**

Institute of Electrical and Electronics Engineers International Conference on Microelectronics for Neural, Fuzzy and Bio-inspired Systems. Proceedings *see* I E E E International Conference on Microelectronics for Neural, Fuzzy and Bio-inspired Systems. Proceedings **2498**

Institute of Electrical and Electronics Engineers International Conference on Multimedia Computing and Systems. Proceedings *see* I E E E International Conference on Multimedia Computing and Systems. Proceedings **2467**

Institute of Electrical and Electronics Engineers International Conference on Networking, Sensing and Control. Conference Proceedings *see* I E E E International Conference on Networking, Sensing and Control. Conference Proceedings **2498**

Institute of Electrical and Electronics Engineers International Conference on Personal Wireless Communications. Proceedings *see* I E E E International Conference on Personal Wireless Communications. Proceedings **2359**

Institute of Electrical and Electronics Engineers International Conference on Plasma Science *see* I E E E International Conference on Plasma Science **3311**

Institute of Electrical and Electronics Engineers International Conference on Power Electronics, Drives and Energy for Industrial Growth. Proceedings *see* I E E E International Conference on Power Electronics, Drives and Energy for Industrial Growth. Proceedings **3101**

Institute of Electrical and Electronics Engineers International Conference on Robotics and Automation. Proceedings *see* I E E E International Conference on Robotics and Automation. Proceedings **2460**

Institute of Electrical and Electronics Engineers International Conference on Semiconductor Electronics. Proceedings *see* I E E E International Conference on Semiconductor Electronics. Proceedings **7051**

Institute of Electrical and Electronics Engineers International Conference on Solid Dielectrics. Proceedings *see* I E E E International Conference on Solid Dielectrics. Proceedings **3312**

Institute of Electrical and Electronics Engineers International Electric Machines and Drives Conference. Proceedings *see* I E E E International Electric Machines and Drives Conference. Proceedings **5452**

Institute of Electrical and Electronics Engineers International Engineering Management Conference. Proceedings *see* I E E E International Engineering Management Conference. Proceedings **3196**

Institute of Electrical and Electronics Engineers - International Federation for Information Process Network Operations and Management Symposium *see* I E E E - I F I P Network Operations and Management Symposium **2520**

Institute of Electrical and Electronics Engineers International Frequency Control Symposium & Exposition. Proceedings *see* I E E E International Frequency Control Symposium & Exposition. Proceedings **3102**

Institute of Electrical and Electronics Engineers International Fuzzy Systems Conference. Proceedings *see* I E E E International Fuzzy Systems Conference. Proceedings **2449**

Institute of Electrical and Electronics Engineers International High-Level Design Validation and Test Workshop. Proceedings *see* I E E E International High-Level Design Validation and Test Workshop. Proceedings **2471**

Institute of Electrical and Electronics Engineers International Information Theory Workshop *see* I E E E International Information Theory Workshop **2543**

Institute of Electrical and Electronics Engineers International Integrated Reliability Workshop Final Report *see* I E E E International Integrated Reliability Workshop Final Report **2420**

Institute of Electrical and Electronics Engineers International Nonvolatile Memory Technology Conference. Proceedings *see* I E E E International Nonvolatile Memory Technology Conference. Proceedings **2531**

Institute of Electrical and Electronics Engineers International Performance, Computing, and Communications Conference. Proceedings *see* I E E E International Performance, Computing, and Communications Conference. Proceedings **2534**

Institute of Electrical and Electronics Engineers International Power Electronics Congress *see* I E E E International Power Electronics Congress **3102**

Institute of Electrical and Electronics Engineers International Reliability Physics Symposium. Proceedings *see* I E E E International Reliability Physics Symposium. Proceedings **6402**

Institute of Electrical and Electronics Engineers International S O C Conference. Proceedings *see* I E E E International S O C Conference. Proceedings **2465**

Institute of Electrical and Electronics Engineers International Semiconductor Laser Conference. Conference Digest *see* I E E E International Semiconductor Laser Conference. Conference Digest **7076**

Institute of Electrical and Electronics Engineers International Solid State Circuits Conference. Digest of Technical Papers *see* I E E E International Solid State Circuits Conference. Digest of Technical Papers **3102**

Institute of Electrical and Electronics Engineers International Symposium on Applications of Ferroelectrics *see* I E E E International Symposium on Applications of Ferroelectrics **7015**

Institute of Electrical and Electronics Engineers International Symposium on Circuits and Systems. Proceedings *see* I E E E International Symposium on Circuits and Systems. Proceedings **3102**

Institute of Electrical and Electronics Engineers International Symposium on Computational Intelligence in Robotics and Automation *see* I E E E International Symposium on Computational Intelligence in Robotics and Automation **2449**

Institute of Electrical and Electronics Engineers International Symposium on Computers and Communications *see* I E E E International Symposium on Computers and Communications **2590**

Institute of Electrical and Electronics Engineers International Symposium on Distributed Simulation and Real-Time Applications. Proceedings *see* I E E E International Symposium on Distributed Simulation and Real-Time Applications. Proceedings **2517**

Institute of Electrical and Electronics Engineers International Symposium on Electrical Insulation. Conference Record *see* I E E E International Symposium on Electrical Insulation. Conference Record **3312**

Institute of Electrical and Electronics Engineers International Symposium on Electromagnetic Compatibility. Symposium Record *see* I E E E International Symposium on Electromagnetic Compatibility. Symposium Record **3312**

Institute of Electrical and Electronics Engineers International Symposium on Electronics and the Environment *see* I E E E International Symposium on Electronics and the Environment **3102**

Institute of Electrical and Electronics Engineers International Symposium on High-Assurance Systems Engineering *see* I E E E International Symposium on High-Assurance Systems Engineering **2590**

Institute of Electrical and Electronics Engineers International Symposium on Information Theory. Proceedings *see* I E E E International Symposium on Information Theory. Proceedings **2544**

Institute of Electrical and Electronics Engineers International Symposium on Intelligent Control. Proceedings *see* I E E E International Symposium on Intelligent Control. Proceedings **2449**

Institute of Electrical and Electronics Engineers International Symposium on Phased Array Systems and Technology *see* I E E E International Symposium on Phased Array Systems and Technology **2520**

Institute of Electrical and Electronics Engineers International Symposium on Semiconductor Manufacturing Conference Proceedings *see* I E E E International Symposium on Semiconductor Manufacturing Conference Proceedings **2471**

Institute of Electrical and Electronics Engineers International Symposium on Time-Frequency and Time-Scale Analysis *see* I E E E - S P International Symposium on Time-Frequency and Time-Scale Analysis **2534**

Institute of Electrical and Electronics Engineers International Symposium on Workload Characterization. Proceedings *see* I E E E International Symposium on Workload Characterization. Proceedings **3312**

Institute of Electrical and Electronics Engineers International Symposium Personal, Indoor and Mobile Radio Communications *see* I E E E International Symposium Personal, Indoor and Mobile Radio Communications **2359**

Institute of Electrical and Electronics Engineers International Symposium Spread Spectrum Techniques and Applications *see* I E E E International Symposium Spread Spectrum Techniques and Applications **2359**

Institute of Electrical and Electronics Engineers International Telecommunications Symposium *see* I E E E International Telecommunications Symposium **2323**

Institute of Electrical and Electronics Engineers International Ultrasonics Symposium. Proceedings *see* I E E E International Ultrasonics Symposium. Proceedings **7087**

Institute of Electrical and Electronics Engineers International Vacuum Nanoelectronics Conference *see* I E E E International Vacuum Nanoelectronics Conference **2465**

Institute of Electrical and Electronics Engineers International Vehicle Electronics Conference Proceedings *see* I E E E International Vehicle Electronics Conference Proceedings **8498**

Institute of Electrical and Electronics Engineers International Working Conference on Source Code Analysis and Manipulation. Proceedings *see* IEEE International Working Conference on Source Code Analysis and Manipulation. Proceedings **2507**

Title

Institute of Electronics, Information and Communication Engineers Transactions on Information and Systems (Japanese Edition) *see* Denshi Jouhou Tsuushin Gakkai Rombunshi. D, Jouhou Shisutemu **2542**

Institute of Electrostatics. Proceedings of Annual Meeting *see* Seidenki Gakkai Koen Ronbunshu **7039**

Institute of Energy Yearbook and Directory (GBR) **3138**

• Institute of Environmental Sciences and Technology. Annual Technical Meeting. Proceedings (USA) **3440**

• ➤ Institute of Environmental Sciences and Technology. Journal (USA ISSN 1098-4321) **3440**

Institute of Environmental Sciences and Technology. Tutorial Series (USA ISSN 0090-0729) **3440**

Institute of European Affairs Final Reports *see* I E A Final Reports **7240**

Institute of European Affairs Interim Reports *see* I E A Interim Reports **7240**

Institute of European Affairs News *see* I E A News **7240**

Institute of European Affairs. Occasional Papers (IRL) **7242**

Institute of European Affairs Seminar Papers *see* I E A Seminar Papers **7240**

Institute of European Affairs Seminar Reports *see* I E A Seminar Reports **7240**

Institute of European Finance. School of Accounting, Banking and Economics. Research Papers in Banking and Finance (GBR ISSN 0269-3933) **1355**

Institute of Ferrous Metallurgy. Transactions *see* Instytut Metalurgii Zelaza. Prace **6316**

Institute of Finance Management. Prospectus (TZA) **1355**

Institute of Fire Prevention Officers Journal *see* I F P O Journal **3579**

Institute of Food Technologists Meeting. Book of Abstracts (USA ISSN 1082-1236) **3647**

Institute of Freshwater Ecology. Report *see* Natural Environment Research Council. Centre for Ecology and Hydrology. Report **2797**

Institute of Geological and Nuclear Sciences. Geological Map (NZL ISSN 1171-9168) **2747**

Institute of Geological and Nuclear Sciences. Information Series *see* G N S Science Miscellaneous Series **2734**

Institute of Geological and Nuclear Sciences. Monograph *see* G N S Science Monograph **2734**

Institute of Geological and Nuclear Sciences. Science Report *see* G N S Science Report **2734**

• Institute of Grassland and Environmental Research (UK). Annual Report (GBR ISSN 1460-3144) **236**

Institute of Grassland and Environmental Research (UK). Technical Advisory Report (GBR) **237**

Institute of Grassland and Environmental Research Annual Report & Accounts *see* I G E R Annual Report & Accounts **235**

Institute of Grassland and Environmental Research Innovations *see* I G E R Innovations **235**

Institute of Grassland and Environmental Research Technical Review *see* I G E R Technical Review **235**

Institute of Guidance Counsellors. Journal (IRL ISSN 0332-3641) **6699**

Institute of Health Record Information & Management. Journal (GBR ISSN 1364-6974) **5635**

Institute of Hydrology. Report (GBR ISSN 0264-8709) **2795**

Institute of Image Information and Television Engineers *see* Eizo Joho Media Gakkaishi **2319**

Institute of Image Information and Television Engineers. Proceedings of Annual Convention *see* Eizou Joho Media Gakkai Nenji Taikai Koen Yokoshu **2319**

Institute of Indian Geographers. Transactions (IND ISSN 0970-9851) **4015**

† Institute of Industrial Engineers. Integrated Systems Conference. Proceedings (USA ISSN 1069-367X) **8965**

Institute of Industrial Engineers Transactions *see* I I E Transactions **3367**

Institute of Industrial Geological Sciences. Annual Report *see* Sangyo Chishitsu Kagaku Kenkyujo Kenkyu Nenpo **2765**

Institute of Inorganic Chemistry Bulletin *see* I I C Bulletin **2116**

Institute of International Education. Annual Report (USA ISSN 0160-0079) **3013**

Institute of International Education Network Memberhip Directory *see* I I E Network Memberhip Directory **2865**

Institute of International Sociology. Journal *see* Kokusai Shakaigaku Kenkyujo Kenkyu Kiyo **8117**

• Institute of Justice and International Studies. Journal (USA ISSN 1538-7909) **2655**

Institute of Laser Engineering Quarterly Progress Report *see* I L E Quarterly Progress Report **3318**

Institute of Living and Environmental Sciences. Annual Report *see* Seikatsu Kankyou Kagaku Kenkyuujo Kenkyuu Houkoku **704**

Institute of Local Television. Research Monograph (GBR ISSN 0969-9872) **2383**

Institute of Logistics. Members' Directory (GBR) **1430**

Institute of Macao Civil Aviation. Journal *see* Aomen Minhang Xuekan **47**

Institute of Malacology of Tokyo. Bulletin (JPN ISSN 0288-1527) **947**

Institute of Management Accountants Educational Case Journal *see* I M A Educational Case Journal **1290**

Institute of Management & Administration's Complete Guide to Best Practices in Performance Management *see* I O M A's Complete Guide to Best Practices in Performance Management **1865**

Institute of Management & Administration's Human Resources Department Management Report *see* I O M A's Human Resources Department Management Report **1865**

Institute of Management & Administration's Payroll Manager's Report *see* I O M A's Payroll Manager's Report **1290**

Institute of Management & Administration's Report on Compensation & Benefits for Law Offices *see* I O M A's Report on Compensation & Benefits for Law Offices **1865**

Institute of Management & Administration's Report on Customer Relationship Management *see* I O M A's Report on Customer Relationship Management **8963**

Institute of Management & Administration's Report on Financial Analysis, Planning & Reporting *see* I O M A's Report on Financial Analysis, Planning & Reporting **1751**

Institute of Management & Administration's Report on Managing 401k Plans *see* I O M A's Report on Managing 401k Plans **1865**

Institute of Management & Administration's Report on Managing Accounts Payable *see* I O M A's Report on Managing Accounts Payable **1290**

Institute of Management & Administration's Report on Managing Benefits Plans *see* I O M A's Report on Managing Benefits Plans **1865**

Institute of Management & Administration's Report on Managing Credit, Receivables and Collections *see* I O M A's Report on Managing Credit, Receivables and Collections **1352**

Institute of Management & Administration's Report on Managing Exports & Imports *see* I O M A's Report on Managing Exports & Imports **1568**

Institute of Management & Administration's Report on Managing Training & Development *see* I O M A's Report on Managing Training & Development **1865**

Institute of Management & Administration's Report on Salary Surveys *see* I O M A's Report on Salary Surveys **1866**

Institute of Management & Administration's Safety Director's Report *see* I O M A's Safety Director's Report **8963**

Institute of Management & Administration's Security Director's Report *see* I O M A's Security Director's Report **2382**

Institute of Management Education Journal *see* I M E Journal **1751**

➤ Institute of Marine Engineering, Science & Technology. Conference Proceedings (GBR) **8646**

Institute of Marine Engineering, Science & Technology. Conference Proceedings. Part D *see* Institute of Marine Engineering, Science & Technology. Conference Proceedings **8646**

Institute of Marine Engineering, Science and Technology. Proceedings. Part A *see* Journal of Marine Engineering and Technology **8648**

Institute of Marine Engineering, Science and Technology. Proceedings. Part B *see* Journal of Marine Design and Operations **8648**

Institute of Marine Engineering, Science and Technology. Proceedings. Part C *see* Journal of Operational Oceanography **2809**

Institute of Marine Industry. Journal *see* Haeyang San-eob Yeon-gusobo **3596**

Institute of Marriage and Family Canada Review *see* I M F C Review **5559**

• ➤ Institute of Materials, Minerals and Mining. Transactions. Section A: Mining Technology (GBR ISSN 1474-9009) **6465**

• ➤ Institute of Materials, Minerals and Mining. Transactions. Section B: Applied Earth Science (GBR ISSN 0371-7453) **6465**

• ➤ Institute of Materials, Minerals and Mining. Transactions. Section C: Mineral Processing & Extractive Metallurgy (GBR ISSN 0371-9553) **6465**

Institute of Materials Science. Annual Report (USA) **3346**

Institute of Materials Science Bulletin *see* I M S Bulletin **3345**

Institute of Maternal and Child Health Newsletter *see* I M C H Newsletter **2154**

➤ Institute of Mathematical Geography. Monograph Series (USA) **5494**

Institute of Mathematical Sciences, Madras. Reports (IND) **5494**

Institute of Mathematical Statistics Bulletin *see* I M S Bulletin **5492**

• Institute of Mathematical Statistics. Joint Directory of Members (USA) **8378**

Institute of Mathematical Statistics Lecture Notes - Monograph Series *see* I M S Lecture Notes - Monograph Series **5492**

† Institute of Mathematics and Its Applications. Conference Series (GBR ISSN 0960-2526) **8965**

Institute of Mathematics and Its Applications Journal of Applied Mathematics *see* I M A Journal of Applied Mathematics **5492**

Institute of Mathematics and Its Applications Journal of Management Mathematics *see* I M A Journal of Management Mathematics **5492**

Institute of Mathematics and Its Applications Journal of Mathematical Control & Information *see* I M A Journal of Mathematical Control & Information **5492**

Institute of Mathematics and Its Applications Journal of Numerical Analysis *see* I M A Journal of Numerical Analysis **5492**

Institute of Mathematics and Its Applications Numerical Analysis Newsletter *see* I M A Numerical Analysis Newsletter **5492**

Institute of Mathematics and Its Applications Volumes in Mathematics and Its Applications *see* I M A Volumes in Mathematics and Its Applications **5492**

• Institute of Mathematics of Jussieu. Journal (GBR ISSN 1474-7480) **5494**

Institute of Maya Studies. Journal (USA) **343**

• ➤ Institute of Measurement and Control. Transactions (GBR ISSN 0142-3312) **4487**

Institute of Medical and Veterinary Science. Annual Report (AUS ISSN 0159-2254) **5636**

Institute of Medicine. Journal (NPL ISSN 0259-0972) **5636**

➤ Institute of Medicine of Chicago. Proceedings (USA ISSN 0091-746X) **5636**

Institute of Metal Finishing. Bulletin (GBR ISSN 0443-3726) **6315**

• ➤ Institute of Metal Finishing. Transactions (GBR ISSN 0020-2967) **6316**

Institute of Meteorology and Water Management. Reports *see* Instytut Meteorologii i Gospodarki Wodnej. Wiadomosci **6357**

Institute of Meteorology and Water Management. Research Papers. Series: Hydrology and Oceanology *see* Instytut Meteorologii i Gospodarki Wodnej. Materialy Badawcze. Seria: Hydrologia i Oceanologia **2795**

Institute of Meteorology and Water Management. Research Papers. Series: Meteorology *see* Instytut Meteorologii i Gospodarki Wodnej. Materialy Badawcze. Seria: Meteorologia **6357**

Institute of Meteorology and Water Management. Research Papers. Series: Water Engineering *see* Instytut Meteorologii i Gospodarki Wodnej. Materialy Badawcze. Seria: Inzynieria Wodna **3362**

Institute of Meteorology and Water Management. Research Papers. Series: Water Management and Water Protection *see* Instytut Meteorologii i Gospodarki Wodnej. Materialy Badawcze. Seria: Gospodarka Wodna i Ochrona Wod **8826**

Institute of Mine Surveyors of South Africa. Journal/Instituut van Mynopmeters van Suid-Afrika. Joernaal (ZAF ISSN 0020-2983) **6466**

Institute of Mining and Metallurgy. Transactions: Metallurgical Series *see* Vysoka Skola Banska - Technicka Univerzita Ostrava. Sbornik Vedeckych Praci: Rada Hutnicka **6336**

Institute of Mining Research. Report *see* University of Zimbabwe. Institute of Mining Research. Report **6483**

Institute of Modern Russian Culture Newsletter (USA ISSN 0738-7105) **8107**

Institute of Nature Education in Shiga Heights. Bulletin *see* Shiga Shizen Kyoiku Kenkyu Shisetsu Kenkyu Gyoseki **2716**

Institute of Nautical Archaeology Quarterly *see* I N A Quarterly **397**

Institute of Navigation. National Technical Meeting Proceedings (USA) **60**

Institute of Navigation. Proceedings of the Annual Meeting (USA) **8646**

Institute of Noise Control Engineering. Journal (JPN ISSN 0386-8761) **7087**

• Institute of Nuclear Materials Management. Proceedings of Annual Meeting (USA ISSN 0073-9472) **3169**

Institute of Nuclear Materials Management Proceedings Online *see* Institute of Nuclear Materials Management. Proceedings of Annual Meeting **3169**

Institute of Nuclear Safety System Journal *see* I N S S Journal **3168**

Institute of Oceanographic and Fisheries Research. Special Publication *see* Institouton Okeanografikon kai Alieutikon Ereunon. Eidike Ekdose **2807**

Institute of Oceanography and Fisheries Split. Notes *see* Institut za Oceanografiju i Ribarstvo Split. Biljeske **2807**

Institute of Oceanology. Proceedings *see* Institut po Okeanologiia. Trudove **2807**

Institute of Patent and Trade Mark Attorneys of Australia. Annual Proceedings (AUS) **6751**

Institute of Petroleum (GBR ISSN 0309-1880) **6773**

• Institute of Petroleum Statistics Service (GBR) **6800**

Institute of Pharmacy Management International. Institute News (GBR ISSN 1369-8540) **6849**

➤ Institute of Physics and Engineering in Medicine. Report (GBR ISSN 1468-7232) **6198**

➤ Institute of Physics Conference Series (GBR ISSN 0951-3248) **7016**

Institute of Physics Conference Series: Earth and Environment *see* I O P Conference Series: Earth and Environment **3438**

Institute of Physics Conference Series: Materials Science and Engineering *see* I O P Conference Series: Materials Science and Engineering **7059**

Institute of Plant Breeding and Acclimatization. Bulletin *see* Instytut Hodowli i Aklimatyzacji Roslin. Biuletyn **181**

▼ • Institute of Policy Studies. Working Paper (NZL ISSN 1178-3656) **7143**

Institute of Political and Social Studies Bulletin *see* I P S S Bulletin **7141**

Institute of Postgraduate Medicine and Research. Journal (BGD ISSN 1017-9216) **5636**

Institute of Public Administration Australia Byte *see* I P A A Byte **1121**

Institute of Public Administration, Dublin. Administration Yearbook and Diary (IRL ISSN 0073-9596) **7446**

Institute of Public Administration, Dublin. Annual Report (IRL ISSN 0073-9588) **7446**

Institute of Public Administration, Dublin. Discussion Paper (IRL ISSN 1393-6190) **7446**

Institute of Public Administration, Dublin. Research Report (IRL ISSN 1393-9424) **7446**

Institute of Public Administration, Khartoum. Occasional Papers (SDN ISSN 0073-9618) **7446**

Institute of Public Administration, Khartoum. Proceedings of the Annual Round Table Conference (SDN ISSN 0073-9626) **7446**

Institute of Public Administration Report *see* I P A Report **1121**

• Institute of Public Affairs. Review (AUS ISSN 1329-8100) **1125**

Institute of Public Enterprise. Journal (IND ISSN 0971-1864) **1754**

Institute of Public Finance and Accountancy International Public Sector Guideline (No.) *see* I F A C International Public Sector Guideline (No.) **1928**

Institute of Public Health. Annual Report/Kokuritsu Koshu Eisei-in Nenpo (JPN) **7525**

Institute of Public Relations. Handbook (Year) (GBR ISSN 1351-4598) **27**

Institute of Pure and Applied Physics Conference Series *see* I P A P Conference Series **7016**

Institute of Quarrying, Northern Ireland. Year Book (GBR) **6466**

Institute of Race Relations. Annual Report (GBR) **3540**

Institute of Radiation Breeding. Technical News (JPN ISSN 0285-1962) **7067**

Institute of Refrigeration. Conference & Seminar Proceedings (GBR) **4121**

Institute of Refrigeration. Proceedings (GBR ISSN 0073-9677) **4121**

Institute of Revenues Rating and Valuation Insight *see* I R R V Insight **7594**

Institute of River and Basin Integrated Communications. Report *see* Kasen Joho Kenkyujo Hokoku **8828**

Institute of Scrap Recycling Industries, Inc. Digest *see* I S R I Digest **3507**

• Institute of Secretariat Training and Management. Annual Report (IND ISSN 0304-7083) **1866**

Institute of Social and Economic Research Conference Paper *see* I S E R Conference Paper **8106**

Institute of Social and Economic Research Occasional Papers *see* I S E R Occasional Papers **7971**

Institute of Social and Economic Research. Reports (USA) **1125**

Institute of Social and Economic Research Reprint Series *see* I S E R Reprint Series **1121**

Institute of Social and Economic Research Research and Policy Papers *see* I S E R Research and Policy Papers **8106**

Institute of Social and Economic Research. Social and Economic Papers (CAN) **1125**

Institute of Southeast Asian Studies. Annual Report (SGP) **4184**

Institute of Southeast Asian Studies, Asia-Pacific Economic Cooperation Series on A P E C *see* I S E A S Series on A P E C **4183**

Institute of Southeast Asian Studies Current Economic Affairs Series *see* I S E A S Current Economic Affairs Series **1121**

Institute of Southeast Asian Studies Environment and Development Series *see* I S E A S Environment and Development Series **3438**

Institute of Southeast Asian Studies. Field Reports Series (SGP ISSN 0217-7099) **7973**

Institute of Southeast Asian Studies. Library. Accessions List (SGP ISSN 0046-984X) **564**

Institute of Southeast Asian Studies. Local History and Memoirs (SGP) **4184**

Institute of Southeast Asian Studies. Monographs Series (SGP) **7973**

Institute of Southeast Asian Studies. Occasional Paper (SGP ISSN 0073-9731) **7973**

Institute of Southeast Asian Studies. Proceedings of International Conferences (SGP) **1491**

Institute of Southeast Asian Studies. Research Notes and Discussion Series (SGP ISSN 0129-8828) **7973**

Title

Institution of Railway Signal Engineers. Proceedings (GBR ISSN 0073-9839) **8619**

Institution of Structural Engineers. Sessional Yearbook and Directory of Members (GBR) **3272**

Institution of Water Officers Journal *see* I W O Journal **8825**

Institutional Change in Agriculture and Natural Resources *see* Institutioneller Wandel der Landwirtschaft und Ressourcennutzung **200**

Institutional Distribution Handbook of Foodservice Distribution CD-ROM *see* I D Handbook of Foodservice Distribution CD-ROM **3646**

Institutional Equity Research *see* Standard & Poor's Institutional Equity Research **1653**

Institutional Holdings of Oil Stocks (USA) **1630**

▼ • Institutional Investing in Infrastructure (USA ISSN 1941-2630) **1630**

Institutional Investment Review (Year) (GBR) **1630**

• Institutional Investor (America's Edition) (USA ISSN 0020-3580) **1630**

• Institutional Investor (International Edition) (USA ISSN 0192-5660) **1630**

Institutional Investor Directory (USA ISSN 0735-9098) **1630**

Institutional Investor Platinum *see* Institutional Investor (America's Edition) **1630**

Institutional Investor's Alpha *see* Alpha (New York) **8929**

Institutional Pharmacy Practice. Handbook (USA ISSN 1932-2410) **6849**

▼ • Institutional Real Estate Dealmakers (USA ISSN 1941-3858) **7596**

Institutional Real Estate Fund Tracker *see* Fund Tracker **7591**

• The Institutional Real Estate Letter (USA ISSN 1044-1662) **7596**

• Institutional Real Estate Newsline (USA) **7596**

Institutional Review Board A Review of Human Subjects Research *see* I R B: A Review of Human Subjects Research **5906**

Institutional Review Board Advisor *see* I R B Advisor **4102**

Institutioneller Wandel der Landwirtschaft und Ressourcennutzung/Institutional Change in Agriculture and Natural Resources (DEU ISSN 1617-4828) **200**

Institutionen for Internationell Pedagogik. Publications/Institute for the Study of International Problems in Education. Publications (SWE ISSN 0348-8381) **2867**

Institutions and Economic Development *see* Istituzioni e Sviluppo Economico **1130**

Institutionskatalog. Vem gor Vad i Europeiska Unionen? *see* Interinstitutional Directory. Who's Who in the European Union? **643**

➤ Instituto Adolfo Lutz. Revista (BRA ISSN 0073-9855) **887**

Instituto Americano de Estudios Vascos. Boletin (ARG ISSN 0020-3637) **4298**

Instituto Antartico Argentino. Contribuciones (ARG ISSN 0524-9376) **2710**

Instituto Antartico Argentino. Publicacion (ARG ISSN 0521-520X) **2710**

Instituto Antartico Chileno. Contribution. Serie Cientifica (CHL ISSN 0073-9871) **2710**

• Instituto Antonio de Nebrija de Estudios sobre la Universidad. Cuadernos (ESP ISSN 1139-6628) **2987**

Instituto Argentino de Ciencias Genealogicas. Boletin Interno (ARG ISSN 0579-3599) **3771**

Instituto Argentino de Normalizacion y Certificacion Boletin *see* I R A M. Boletin **6402**

Instituto Bacteriologico de Camara Pestana. Arquivos (PRT ISSN 0365-2998) **887**

➤ Instituto Barraquer. Anales (ESP ISSN 0020-3645) **6043**

Instituto Biologico. Arquivos (BRA ISSN 0020-3653) **122**

Instituto Brasil - Estados Unidos. Boletim (BRA ISSN 0020-367X) **2867**

Instituto Brasileiro do Patrimonio Cultural. Government Cultural Publications (BRA) **4457**

Instituto Butantan. Memorias (BRA ISSN 0073-9901) **947**

Instituto Camoes. Boletim. (PRT ISSN 0872-4296) **5128**

Instituto Canario de Ciencias Marinas. Informes Tecnicos (ESP ISSN 1136-193X) **2807**

Instituto Caro y Cuervo. Boletin *see* Thesaurus **5187**

Instituto Caro y Cuervo. Noticias Culturales (COL ISSN 0020-370X) **5309**

Instituto Caro y Cuervo. Publicaciones (COL) **4457**

Instituto Caro y Cuervo. Seminario Andres Bello. Cuadernos (COL) **5128**

Instituto Caro y Cuervo. Serie Bibliografica (COL ISSN 0073-991X) **627**

Instituto Caro y Cuervo. Serie Granada Entreabierta (COL) **5309**

Instituto Caro y Cuervo. Serie Minor (COL ISSN 0073-9928) **5309**

Instituto Colombiano Agropecuario. Boletin Tecnico (COL ISSN 0538-0391) **122**

Instituto Colombiano de Cultura. Gaceta (COL ISSN 0121-7194) **7973**

Instituto Comunitario das Variedades Vegetais. Relatorio Anual *see* Community Plant Variety Office. Annual Report **3411**

Instituto Costarricense de Turismo. Memoria Anual (CRI) **8723**

Instituto Cubano de Investigaciones de los Derivados de la Cana de Azucar Sobre los Derivados de la Cana de Azucar *see* I C I D C A. Sobre los Derivados de la Cana de Azucar **235**

Instituto Cultural Italo-Brasileiro. Caderno (BRA) **7242**

Instituto Cultural Peruano Norteamericano. Newsletter (PER) **2867**

➤ Instituto de Astronomia y Geodesia. Publicacion (ESP ISSN 0213-6198) **576**

Instituto de Botanica. Boletim (BRA ISSN 0074-0055) **794**

• Instituto de Catalisis y Petroleoquimica. Memoria (ESP) **2065**

Instituto de Censores Jurados de Cuentas de Espagna. Revista Technica (ESP) **1291**

Instituto de Chile. Anales (CHL ISSN 0716-6117) **4457**

Instituto de Ciencia de Materiales de Madrid. Memoria (ESP) **3346**

Instituto de Ciencia Politica Rafael Bielsa. Anuario (ARG ISSN 0074-0063) **7143**

Instituto de Ciencia y Tecnologia de Polimeros. Memoria (ESP) **7093**

➤ Instituto de Ciencias Humanas. Cadernos (BRA ISSN 0104-1525) **7973**

➤ Instituto de Ciencias Humanas. Humanitas (BRA) **7973**

Instituto de Ciencias para la Familia (ESP) **4911**

Instituto de Contabilidad y Auditoria de Cuentas. Boletin (ESP ISSN 1130-3883) **1291**

Instituto de Credito Oficial. Annual Report (ESP ISSN 1579-2102) **1929**

Instituto de Cultura e Lingua Portuguesa Revista *see* I C A L P Revista **4456**

Instituto de Cultura Puertorriquena. Revista (PRI ISSN 0020-3815) **4457**

Instituto de Derecho Comparado. Anuario (VEN ISSN 1316-5852) **4693**

Instituto de Desarrollo Urbano Noticiero *see* I D U N. Noticiero **4414**

Instituto de Economia Agricola. Informacoes Economicas (BRA) **200**

Instituto de Economia do Setor Publico. Notas Tecnicas (BRA) **1491**

Instituto de Economia y Producciones Ganaderas del Ebro. Comunicaciones (ESP ISSN 0374-8189) **122**

Instituto de Economia y Producciones Ganaderas del Ebro. Trabajos (ESP ISSN 0375-3417) **122**

Instituto de Estudios Almeriense. Boletin. Ciencias (ESP ISSN 1133-1488) **4146**

Instituto de Estudios Asturianos. Boletin *see* Real Instituto de Estudios Asturianos. Boletin **4256**

Instituto de Estudios con Iberoamerica y Portugal. Seminarios Tematicos. Seminario Iberoamericano de Matematicas *see* Seminario Iberoamericano de Matematicas. Publicaciones **5534**

• Instituto de Estudios del Pacifico. Boletin (CHL ISSN 0717-2443) **1491**

Instituto de Estudios Economicos. Revista (ESP ISSN 0210-9565) **1491**

Instituto de Estudios Gerundenses. Serie Monografica (ESP ISSN 0211-2477) **3540**

Instituto de Estudios Giennenses. Boletin (ESP ISSN 0561-3590) **4232**

Instituto de Estudios Historico-Sociales Anuario *see* I E H S. Anuario **4231**

† Instituto de Estudios Madrilenos. Anales (ESP ISSN 0584-6374) **8965**

Instituto de Estudios Peruanos. Analisis Economico (PER ISSN 1019-4509) **1492**

Instituto de Estudios Peruanos. Coleccion Minima (PER ISSN 1019-4479) **7973**

Instituto de Estudios Peruanos. Documentos de Trabajo (PER ISSN 1022-0356) **7973**

Instituto de Estudios Peruanos. Documentos de Trabajo. Serie Antropologia (PER ISSN 1022-0364) **343**

Instituto de Estudios Peruanos. Documentos de Trabajo. Serie Documentos de Politica (PER ISSN 1022-0372) **7143**

Instituto de Estudios Peruanos. Documentos de Trabajo. Serie Economia (PER ISSN 1022-0399) **1125**

Instituto de Estudios Peruanos. Documentos de Trabajo. Serie Etnohistoria (PER ISSN 1022-0380) **343**

Instituto de Estudios Peruanos. Documentos de Trabajo. Serie Historia (PER ISSN 1022-0402) **4298**

Instituto de Estudios Peruanos. Documentos de Trabajo. Serie Linguistica (PER ISSN 1022-0410) **5128**

Instituto de Estudios Peruanos. Documentos de Trabajo. Serie Sociologia, Politica (PER ISSN 1022-0429) **8107**

Instituto de Estudios Peruanos. Documentos de Trabajo. Serie Talleres (PER ISSN 1022-0437) **1889**

Instituto de Estudios Peruanos. Estudios de la Sociedad Rural (PER ISSN 1019-4517) **8107**

Instituto de Estudios Peruanos. Miscelanea (PER) **343**

Instituto de Estudios Peruanos. Proyecto de Estudios Etnologicos del Valle de Chancay. Monografia (PER ISSN 1019-4525) **343**

Instituto de Estudios sobre la Realidad Argentina y Latinoamericana. Estudios (ARG) **1492**

Instituto de Estudios Tarraconenses Ramon Berenguer IV. Publicacion (ESP ISSN 0534-3364) **4232**

Instituto de Estudios Zamoranos "Florian de Ocampo". Anuario (ESP ISSN 0213-8212) **4232**

Instituto de Filosofia del Derecho Dr. Jose Manuel Delgado Ocando. Boletin (VEN ISSN 1315-3269) **4693**

Instituto de Filosofia del Derecho Dr. Jose Manuel Delgado Ocando. Coleccion de Cursos y Lecciones (VEN) **4693**

Instituto de Filosofia del Derecho Dr. Jose Manuel Delgado Ocando. Coleccion de Monografias (VEN) **4693**

Instituto de Filosofia del Derecho Dr. Jose Manuel Delgado Ocando. Cuaderno de Trabajo (VEN ISSN 1315-3072) **4693**

Instituto de Filosofia del Derecho Dr. Jose Manuel Delgado Ocando. Revista (VEN) **4693**

• Instituto de Geociencias. Anuario (BRA ISSN 0101-9759) **2710**

Instituto de Geociencias - Universidade de Sao Paulo Boletim. Publicacao Especial *see* I G - U S P. Boletim. Publicacao Especial **2709**

Instituto de Geociencias - Universidade de Sao Paulo Boletim. Serie Cientifica *see* I G - U S P. Boletim. Serie Cientifica **2709**

Instituto de Geociencias - Universidade de Sao Paulo Boletim. Serie Didatica *see* I G - U S P. Boletim. Serie Didatica **2709**

Instituto de Gestalt - Terapia na Rede *see* I G T na Rede **7361**

Instituto de Higiene e Medicina Tropical. Anais (PRT ISSN 0303-7762) **7525**

Instituto de Historia Argentina. Anuario (ARG ISSN 1668-950X) **4298**

• Instituto de Historia Argentina y Americana Doctor Emilio Ravignani. Boletin (ARG ISSN 0524-9767) **4298**

➤ Instituto de Informatica da PUC Campinas. Revista (BRA ISSN 0104-4869) **2546**

Instituto de Investigacao Agronomica de Mocambique. Centro de Documentacao Agraria. Memorias (MOZ ISSN 0077-1791) **122**

Instituto de Investigacao Agronomica de Mocambique. Comunicacoes *see* Agronomia Mocambicana **88**

Instituto de Investigacao Cientifica de Angola. Bibliograficas Tematicas (AGO ISSN 0074-008X) **7937**

Instituto de Investigacao Cientifica de Angola. Boletim (AGO ISSN 0020-3912) **7866**

Instituto de Investigacao Cientifica de Angola, Departamento de Documentacao e Informacao Documentacao *see* I I C A Documentacao **7937**

Instituto de Investigacao Cientifica de Angola. Memorias e Trabalhos (AGO ISSN 0074-0098) **7866**

Instituto de Investigacao Cientifica de Angola. Relatorios e Comunicacoes (AGO ISSN 0003-343X) **7866**

Instituto de Investigacao Cientifica Tropical. Centro de Estudos de Historia e Cartografia Antiga. Serie Separatas (PRT ISSN 0870-6735) **4147**

Instituto de Investigacao Cientifica Tropical. Centro de Estudos de Historia e Cartografia Antiga. Studia (PRT ISSN 0870-0028) **4147**

Instituto de Investigacao Cientifica Tropical. Comunicacoes. Serie de Ciencias Agrarias (PRT ISSN 0871-1763) **122**

Instituto de Investigacao Cientifica Tropical. Comunicacoes. Serie de Ciencias Biologicas (PRT ISSN 0871-1755) **678**

Instituto de Investigacao Cientifica Tropical. Comunicacoes. Serie de Ciencias da Engenharia Geografica (PRT ISSN 0871-1747) **4015**

Instituto de Investigacao Cientifica Tropical. Comunicacoes. Serie de Ciencias da Terra (PRT ISSN 0871-1798) **2710**

Instituto de Investigacao Cientifica Tropical. Comunicacoes. Serie de Ciencias Etnologicas e Etnomuseologicas (PRT ISSN 0871-178X) **3540**

Instituto de Investigacao Cientifica Tropical. Estudos de Historia e Cartografia Antiga - Memorias (PRT ISSN 0870-5879) **4147**

Instituto de Investigacao Cientifica Tropical. Estudos, Ensaios e Documentos (PRT ISSN 0870-001X) **7866**

Instituto de Investigacao Cientifica Tropical. Index Seminum Quae Hortus et Musaeum Agricolum Tropicum (PRT ISSN 0872-315X) **3755**

Instituto de Investigacao Cientifica Tropical. Memorias (PRT ISSN 0870-0036) **7866**

Instituto de Investigacao Pesqueira. Boletim de Divulgacao (MOZ) **3598**

Instituto de Investigacion e Informacion Geocientifica, Minero-Ambiental y Nuclear Ingeominas. Informe Anual de Actividades (COL) **2747**

Instituto de Investigacion e Information Geocientifica, Minero-Ambiental y Nuclear Ingeominas. Publicaciones Geologicas Especiales del Ingeominas (COL ISSN 0120-078X) **2747**

Instituto de Investigacion Musicologica Carlos Vega. Revista (ARG ISSN 1515-050X) **6576**

• Instituto de Investigacion Textil y de Cooperacion Industrial. Boletin Intexter (ESP ISSN 1131-6756) **8453**

Instituto de Investigaciones Economicas. Revista (BOL) **1543**

Instituto de Investigaciones Educativas. Boletin (ARG ISSN 0328-3852) **2867**

Instituto de Investigaciones Educativas. Boletin. Numero Especial *see* Instituto de Investigaciones Educativas. Boletin **2867**

• ➤ Instituto de Investigaciones Electricas. Boletin (MEX ISSN 0185-0059) **3319**

• ➤ Instituto de Investigaciones Electricas. Informe Anual (MEX) **3319**

• ➤ Instituto de Investigaciones Esteticas. Anales (MEX ISSN 0185-1276) **496**

Instituto de Investigaciones Historicas Juan Manuel de Rosas. Revista (ARG ISSN 0327-5574) **4147**

• ➤ Instituto de Investigaciones Literarias. Anuario (VEN ISSN 1316-4945) **5309**

• Instituto de Investigaciones Pesqueras. Boletin (URY ISSN 0797-1478) **3598**

Instituto de la Mujer. Revista (URY ISSN 0797-552X) **8899**

Instituto de la Patagonia. Anales. Serie Ciencias Humanas *see* Magallania **7984**

Instituto de la Patagonia. Anales. Serie Ciencias Naturales (CHL ISSN 0716-6486) **678**

➤ Instituto de la Patagonia. Anales. Serie Ciencias Sociales (CHL ISSN 0716-6478) **7973**

Instituto de la Vivienda. Boletin *see* Instituto Nacional de la Vivienda. Revista **446**

Instituto de Laticinios Candido Tostes. Revista (BRA ISSN 0100-3674) **265**

Instituto de Lengua y Cultura Espanola para Extranjeros. Coleccion (ESP ISSN 0552-9832) **5128**

Instituto de Lengua y Cultura Espanolas. Revista *see* R I L C E **5165**

Instituto de Matematica Beppo Levi. Cuadernos (ARG ISSN 0326-0690) **5494**

Instituto de Materiales y Modelos Estructurales Boletin Tecnico *see* I M M E Boletin Tecnico **3269**

• Instituto de Medicina Tropical de Sao Paulo. Revista (BRA ISSN 0036-4665) **5818**

Instituto de Nutricion de Centro America y Panama (I N C A P). Informe Anual (GTM ISSN 0533-4179) **6660**

Instituto de Optica "Daza de Valdes". Memoria (ESP) **7077**

Instituto de Optica "Daza de Valdes". Publicacion (ESP ISSN 0304-9957) **7077**

• Instituto de Pesca. Boletim Tecnico (Online Edition) (BRA ISSN 1678-2291) **3598**

• Instituto de Pesca. Boletim Tecnico (Print Edition) (BRA ISSN 0103-1767) **3598**

• Instituto de Pesca, Sao Paulo. Boletim (BRA ISSN 0046-9939) **3598**

Instituto de Pesca, Sao Paulo. Boletim. Serie de Divulgacao (BRA) **3598**

• ➤ Instituto de Pesquisa e Estudos. Revista (BRA ISSN 1413-7100) **4693**

Instituto de Pesquisa Economica Aplicada. Boletim Conjuntural (BRA ISSN 1415-4250) **1125**

▼ • Instituto de Posturologia y Podoposturologia. Revista (ESP ISSN 1988-8198) **6229**

Instituto de Recursos Naturales y Agrobiologia de Sevilla. Memoria (ESP ISSN 1134-4903) **122**

Instituto de Resseguros do Brasil Revista *see* I R B Revista **4505**

Instituto de Salud Publica de Chile. Boletin (CHL ISSN 0716-1387) **7526**

Instituto de Seguridad y Servicios Sociales de los Trabajadores al Servicio del Estado. Boletin Medico (MEX ISSN 0187-1447) **5636**

Instituto de Seguridad y Servicios Sociales de los Trabajadores al Servicio del Estado. Revista Medica (MEX ISSN 0186-8985) **5636**

Instituto de Tecnologia de Alimentos. Estudos Economicos. Alimentos Processados (BRA ISSN 0100-4964) **3647**

Instituto de Teologia para Religiosos Revista de Teologia *see* I T E R Revista de Teologia **7648**

Instituto del Mar del Peru. Boletin (PER ISSN 0378-7699) **3598**

Instituto del Mar del Peru. Informe (PER ISSN 0378-7702) **3598**

Instituto del Mar del Peru. Informe Progresivo (PER) **678**

Instituto do Desenvolvimento Economico-Social do Para. Boletim de Pesquisa Emprego e Desemprego na Regiao Metropolitana de Belem (BRA) **1688**

Instituto do Desenvolvimento Economico-Social do Para. Comercio Varejista (BRA) **1492**

Instituto do Desenvolvimento Economico-Social do Para. Indicadores da Socio-Economia Paraense (BRA ISSN 0103-5282) **1492**

Instituto do Desenvolvimento Economico-Social do Para. Indice do Custo de Vida (BRA) **1492**

Instituto do Desenvolvimento Economico-Social do Para. Para Agrario (BRA ISSN 0103-5215) **122**

Instituto do Desenvolvimento Economico-Social do Para. Para Desenvolvimento (BRA ISSN 0553-1721) **1492**

Instituto dos Advogados Brasileiros. Revista (BRA ISSN 0100-1752) **4693**

Instituto dos Advogados de Sao Paulo. Revista (BRA ISSN 1415-7683) **4693**

Instituto Ecuatoriano de Ciencias Naturales. Contribuciones (ECU ISSN 0010-7972) **7866**

Instituto Egipcio de Estudios Islamicos en Madrid. Revista (ESP ISSN 1132-3485) **7711**

Instituto Espanol de Oceanografia. Boletin (ESP ISSN 0074-0195) **2807**

Title

▼ *new title* † *ceased* • *electronic media* ➤ *refereed*

10428 INSTITUTO ESPANOL DE OCEANOGRAFIA. INFORMES TECNICOS ULRICH'S PERIODICALS

Instituto Espanol de Oceanografia. Informes Tecnicos (ESP ISSN 0212-1565) **2807**
Instituto Espanol de Oceanografia. Microfichas *see* Instituto Espanol de Oceanografia. Tesis Doctorales **2807**
Instituto Espanol de Oceanografia. Publicaciones Especiales (ESP ISSN 0214-7378) **2807**
• Instituto Espanol de Oceanografia. Tesis Doctorales (ESP ISSN 1578-410X) **2807**
Instituto Estadual de Hematologia Arthur de Siqueira Cavalcanti. Revista (BRA ISSN 0103-3263) **5938**
Instituto Frances de Estudios Andinos. Boletin *see* Institut Francais d'Etudes Andines. Bulletin **7973**
• ➤ Instituto Franciscano de Antropologia. Cadernos (BRA ISSN 0104-2300) **343**
Instituto Gemologico Espanol. Boletin (ESP ISSN 0210-7228) **4566**
• Instituto Geografico Militar. Boletin Informativo (ARG ISSN 1851-3697) **6425**
Instituto Geografico Nacional. Monografias (ESP ISSN 0213-1749) **4015**
Instituto Geografico Nacional. Publicacion Tecnica (ESP ISSN 0213-4454) **4015**
Instituto Geologico. Boletim (BRA ISSN 0100-431X) **2747**
Instituto Geologico e Mineiro. Memorias (PRT ISSN 0873-9498) **2710**
• Instituto Geologico Minero y Metalurgico. Boletin. Serie D. Estudios Regionales (PER ISSN 1607-5617) **6466**
Instituto Geologico. Revista (BRA ISSN 0100-929X) **2747**
Instituto Geronimo de Uztariz. Boletin *see* Geronimo de Uztariz **4223**
Instituto Goiano de Pre-historia e Antropologia. Cadernos de Pesquisa (BRA) **398**
Instituto Hidrografico. Anais (PRT ISSN 0870-3884) **8826**
➤ Instituto Historico e Geografico Brasileiro. Revista (BRA ISSN 0101-4366) **4298**
• Instituto Historico e Geografico de Sao Paulo. Revista (BRA ISSN 0100-2953) **4015**
Instituto Historico e Geografico do Espirito Santo. Revista (BRA) **4147**
Instituto Hondureno de Antropologia e Historia. Estudios Antropologicos (HND) **343**
Instituto Hondureno de Seguridad Social. Departamento de Estadistica y Procesamiento de Datos. Anuario Estadistico (HND ISSN 0074-0233) **4506**
Instituto Interamericano de Derechos Humanos. Boletin (CRI) **7209**
Instituto Interamericano de Derechos Humanos. Boletin Documental (CRI) **7209**
Instituto Interamericano de Derechos Humanos. Revista (CRI ISSN 1015-5074) **7209**
Instituto Latinoamericano y del Caribe de Planificacion Economica y Social Cuadernos *see* I L P E S Cuadernos **1719**
Instituto Linguistico de Verano. Documentos de Trabajo (PER ISSN 1022-1522) **5128**
Instituto Linguistico de Verano en Colombia. Bibliografia (COL) **5201**
Instituto Linguistico de Verano. Serie de Gramaticas de Lenguas Indigenas de Mexico (MEX) **5128**
Instituto Maritimo Portuario. Boletim *see* Mar (Lisboa) **8651**
Instituto Medico Sucre. Revista (BOL ISSN 1561-8374) **7866**
Instituto Mexicano de Tecnologia dele Agua. Tablas de Contenido (MEX ISSN 0187-8336) **3362**
Instituto Mexicano del Seguro Social. Revista de Enfermeria (MEX ISSN 0188-431X) **5961**
• Instituto Mexicano del Seguro Social. Revista Medica (MEX ISSN 0443-5117) **5636**
Instituto Nacional de Administracion Publica. Servicio de Biblioteca y Documentacion. Boletin de Informacion Bibliografica (ESP) **627**
Instituto Nacional de Antropologia e Historia. Coleccion Cientifica (MEX ISSN 0076-7611) **343**
Instituto Nacional de Antropologia y Pensamiento Latinoamericano. Cuadernos (ARG) **343**
Instituto Nacional de Cancerologia. Revista *see* Cancerologia **6015**
Instituto Nacional de Colonizacao e Reforma Agraria. Procuradoria Geral. Boletim. Pareceres (BRA) **4693**
• Instituto Nacional de Enfermedades Neoplasticas. Boletin (PER ISSN 1017-0642) **6022**
• ➤ Instituto Nacional de Enfermedades Respiratorias. Revista (MEX ISSN 0187-7585) **6215**
Instituto Nacional de Estadistica *see* INEbase **7309**
• Instituto Nacional de Estadistica. Anuario Estadistico (URY ISSN 1688-101X) **8379**
• Instituto Nacional de Estadistica. Anuario Estadistico de Espana: Edicion Extensa (ESP ISSN 0066-5177) **8379**
Instituto Nacional de Estadistica. Boletim Mensal de Estadistica (AGO ISSN 1010-4151) **7481**
• Instituto Nacional de Estadistica. Boletin Mensual de Estadistica (ESP ISSN 1132-0516) **8379**
Instituto Nacional de Estadistica Cifras *see* I N E. Cifras **8377**
• Instituto Nacional de Estadistica. Encuesta de Poblacion Activa (CD-ROM Edition) (ESP ISSN 1698-4595) **7309**
Instituto Nacional de Estadistica. Encuesta de Poblacion Activa. Principales Resultados (ESP ISSN 0212-6532) **1243**
Instituto Nacional de Estadistica. Encuesta Industrial (ESP) **1243**
Instituto Nacional de Estadistica. Estadistica Espanola (ESP ISSN 0014-1151) **8379**
Instituto Nacional de Estadistica, Geografia e Informatica. Catalogo de Publicaciones (MEX ISSN 0186-0437) **8379**
Instituto Nacional de Estadistica, Geografia e Informatica. Gaceta Informativa (MEX) **1492**
Instituto Nacional de Estadistica. Indices de Precios de Consumo. Boletin Informativo (ESP ISSN 0213-7410) **8379**
Instituto Nacional de Estadistica y Censos Documentos de Trabajo *see* I N D E C Documentos de Trabajo **8377**
Instituto Nacional de Estadistica y Censos Estudios *see* I N D E C Estudios **8377**
Instituto Nacional de Estadistica y Censos Informa *see* I N D E C Informa **8377**
Instituto Nacional de Estadistica y Censos Informacion de Prensa *see* I N D E C Informacion de Prensa **8377**
Instituto Nacional de Estadistica y Censos Metodologias *see* I N D E C Metodologias **8377**
Instituto Nacional de Estadistica y Censos Normas *see* I N D E C Normas **8377**
Instituto Nacional de Estadistica y Censos Recopilaciones *see* I N D E C Recopilaciones **8377**
Instituto Nacional de Geoquimica Actas *see* I N A G E Q. Actas **2746**
Instituto Nacional de Higiene Rafael Rangel. Revista (VEN ISSN 0798-0477) **7526**
Instituto Nacional de Investigacao Cientifica. Textos Classicos (PRT) **6925**
Instituto Nacional de Investigacao Cientifica. Textos de Linguistica (PRT) **5128**
Instituto Nacional de Investigacao Cientifica. Textos Humanisticos Portugueses (PRT) **4457**
Instituto Nacional de Investigacion y Desarrollo Pesquero Informe Tecnico *see* I N I D E P Informe Tecnico **3597**
Instituto Nacional de Investigacion y Desarrollo Pesquero. Revista *see* Revista de Investigacion y Desarrollo Pesquero **3606**
Instituto Nacional de Investigacion y Desarrollo Pesqueros. Departamento de Aguas Continentales. Informes Tecnicos (ARG ISSN 0326-8659) **3598**
Instituto Nacional de Investigaciones Forestales, Agricolas y Pecuarias. Boletin Divulgativo (MEX ISSN 1405-356X) **850**
Instituto Nacional de Investigaciones Forestales, Agricolas y Pecuarias. Boletin Tecnico (MEX ISSN 1405-3551) **850**
Instituto Nacional de Investigaciones Forestales, Agricolas y Pecuarias. Catalogo (MEX) **3693**
Instituto Nacional de Investigaciones Forestales, Agricolas y Pecuarias. Folletos de Investigacion (MEX) **122**
Instituto Nacional de Investigaciones Forestales, Agricolas y Pecuarias. Publicacion Especial (MEX ISSN 1405-3578) **850**
Instituto Nacional de Investigaciones Forestales, Agricolas y Pecuarias. Temas Didacticos (MEX) **122**
• Instituto Nacional de la Vivienda. Revista (CHL ISSN 0718-1299) **446**
➤ Instituto Nacional de Medicina Legal de Colombia. Revista (COL ISSN 0120-0097) **5914**
Instituto Nacional de Pesca del Ecuador. Boletin Cientifico y Tecnico (ECU ISSN 0374-6097) **3598**
Instituto Nacional de Pesca. Informe Tecnico (URY ISSN 0797-3306) **3598**
• Instituto Nacional de Salud. Boletin (PER ISSN 1606-6979) **5636**
• Instituto Nacional de Salud. Documento Tecnico (PER ISSN 1683-7452) **5636**
Instituto Nacional de Seguros Memoria Anual (CRI) **4506**
Instituto Nacional de Tecnologia Agropecuaria. Estacion Experimental Regional Agropecuaria. Boletin de Divulgacion Tecnica (ARG ISSN 0325-1772) **122**
• Instituto Nacional del Carbon. Memoria (ESP ISSN 0490-2602) **2123**
Instituto Nacional del Teatro. Coleccion (ARG ISSN 1851-6017) **8471**
➤ Instituto Oceanografico de Venezuela. Boletin (VEN ISSN 0798-0639) **2807**
• ➤ Instituto Oswaldo Cruz, Rio de Janeiro. Memorias (BRA ISSN 0074-0276) **678**
Instituto Panamericano de Geografia e Historia. Boletin Aereo (MEX ISSN 0020-4188) **6280**
Instituto Panamericano de Geografia e Historia. Serie Inmigracion (MEX) **7285**
Instituto para el Desarrollo de Ejecutivos en la Argentina. Revista (ARG ISSN 0325-9072) **1754**
Instituto para la Integracion de America Latina y el Caribe Carta Mensual (Online Edition) *see* I N T A L Carta Mensual (Online Edition) **1568**
Instituto para la Integracion de America Latina y el Caribe Documentos de Divulgacion *see* I N T A L Documentos de Divulgacion **1597**
Instituto para la Integracion de America Latina y el Caribe Documentos de Trabajo *see* I N T A L Documentos de Trabajo **1597**
Instituto Pau Brasil de Historia Natural. Publicacoes Avulsas (BRA ISSN 1516-4926) **8020**
Instituto Peruano de Polemologia (PER) **7143**
† Instituto Pirenaico de Ecologia. Monografias (ESP ISSN 0214-0861) **8965**
• ➤ Instituto Politecnico Nacional. Escuela Nacional de Ciencias Biologicas. Anales (MEX ISSN 0185-0946) **678**
Instituto Portugues de Investigacao Maritima. Relatorios Cientificos e Tecnicos (PRT ISSN 0872-9123) **7866**
➤ Instituto Riva-Aguero. Boletin (PER ISSN 0459-410X) **4457**
Instituto Rosario de Investigacion en Ciencias de la Educacion. Revista (ARG ISSN 0327-392X) **2867**
Instituto Superior de Agronomia. Anais (PRT ISSN 0365-2971) **122**
• Instituto Superior de Correlacion Geologica. Serie Correlacion Geologica (ARG ISSN 1514-4186) **2747**
• ➤ Instituto Superior de Correlacion Geologica. Serie Miscelanea (ARG ISSN 1514-4836) **2747**
Instituto Tecnologico de Santo Domingo. Biblioteca. Boletin de Adquisiciones (DOM) **627**
Instituto Tecnologico de Santo Domingo. Biblioteca. Boletin de Analiticas (DOM) **8426**
Instituto Tecnologico de Santo Domingo. Boletin (DOM) **2987**
Instituto Tecnologico de Santo Domingo. Documentos (DOM ISSN 0378-956X) **7866**
Instituto Tecnologico Pesquero del Peru. Boletin de Investigacion (PER ISSN 1023-7070) **3598**
Instituto Venezolano de Genealogia. Boletin (VEN) **3771**
Instituts de Recherche en Sante du Canada, Institut du Vieillissement. Rapport Biennal *see* Canadian Institutes of Health Research. Institute of Aging. Biennial Report **8092**
Instituts de Recherche en Sante du Canada. Institut du Vieillissement. Rapport Annuel des Activites *see* Canadian Institutes of Health Research. Institute of Aging. Annual Report of Activities **8092**
Instituts de Recherche en Sante du Canada. Rapport Annuel *see* Canadian Institutes of Health Research. Annual Report **5591**
Instituts de Recherche en Sante du Canada. Rapport sur le Rendement *see* Canadian Institutes of Health Research. Performance Report **7428**
Instituts zur Erforschung der Europaeischen Arbeiterbewegung. Mitteilungsblatt (DEU ISSN 0934-4500) **4596**
Institutt for Naturforvaltning Fagreport *see* I N A Fagreport **2614**
Institutt for Samfunnsforskning. Aarsmelding (NOR ISSN 0801-8863) **8107**
• Institutt for Samfunnsforskning. I S F Sammendrag (NOR ISSN 0804-6832) **8149**
• Institutt for Samfunnsforskning. Rapport/Institute for Social Research. Report (NOR ISSN 0333-3671) **8107**
Institutul de Arheologie - Cluj-Napoca. Anuarul (ROM) **398**
Institutul de Cercetare si Productie pentru Cultura si Industrializarea Sfeclei de Zahar si a Substantelor Dulci-Fundulea. Lucrari Stiintifice. Sfecla si Zahar (ROM ISSN 1016-4839) **237**
Institutul de Cercetare si Projectare pentru Electrotehnica. Lucrarile (ROM ISSN 1224-094X) **3319**
Institutul de Cercetari pentru Cereale si Plante Tehnice. Laborator Sfecla de Zahar. Anale. Lucrari Stiintifice (ROM) **237**
Institutul de Cercetari pentru Protectia Plantelor. Analele/Research Institute for Plant Protection. Annals (ROM ISSN 0365-575X) **794**
Institutul de Cercetari Socio-Umane -Sibiu. Anuarul (ROM ISSN 1223-1088) **7973**
Institutul de Etnografie si Folclor Constantin Ibrailoiu. Anuarul (ROM ISSN 1220-5230) **3618**
• Institutul de Istorie "A.D. Xenopol". Anuarul (ROM ISSN 1221-3705) **398**
• Institutul de Istorie - Cluj-Napoca. Anuarul (ROM ISSN 1220-5176) **4147**
Institutul de Marketing si Sondaje Bulletin *see* I M A S Bulletin **1820**
Institutul de Studii si Proiectari Energetice. Buletinul (ROM ISSN 1220-4145) **3138**
Institutul de Subingineri Oradea. Lucrari Stiintifice: Seria Chimie (ROM) **2065**
Institutul de Subingineri Oradea. Lucrari Stiintifice: Seria Fizica (ROM) **7016**
Institutul de Subingineri Oradea. Lucrari Stiintifice: Seria Geografie (ROM) **4015**
Institutul de Subingineri Oradea. Lucrari Stiintifice: Seria Istorie (ROM) **4147**
Institutul de Subingineri Oradea. Lucrari Stiintifice: Seria Lingvistica (ROM) **5128**
Institutul de Subingineri Oradea. Lucrari Stiintifice: Seria Literatura (ROM) **5309**
Institutul de Subingineri Oradea. Lucrari Stiintifice: Seria Matematica (ROM) **5494**
Institutul de Subingineri Oradea. Lucrari Stiintifice: Seria Stiinte Sociale (ROM) **7973**
Institutul Geologic al Romaniei. Anuarul (ROM ISSN 1453-357X) **2747**
Institutul Geologic al Romaniei. Memoire (ROM) **2710**
Institutul Politehnic din Iasi. Buletinul. Sectia 1: Matematica, Mecanica, Fizica (ROM ISSN 1220-0549) **5494**
Institutul Politehnic din Iasi. Buletinul. Sectia 2: Chimie (ROM ISSN 1223-8147) **2065**
Institutul Politehnic din Iasi. Buletinul. Sectia 3: Electrotehnica, Energetica, Electronica (ROM ISSN 1223-8139) **3319**
Institutul Politehnic din Iasi. Buletinul. Sectia 4. Automatica si Calculateare (ROM ISSN 1220-2169) **2461**
➤ Institutul Politehnic din Iasi. Buletinul. Sectia 5: Constructii de Masini (ROM) **3346**
Institutul Politehnic din Iasi. Buletinul. Sectia 6: Constructii, Arhitectura (ROM ISSN 1223-8120) **1014**
Institutul Politehnic din Iasi. Buletinul. Sectia 7: Hidrotehnica (ROM ISSN 1223-5083) **2795**
Institutul Politehnic din Iasi. Buletinul. Sectia 8: Textile, Pielarie (ROM) **8453**
Institutului National de Cercetare-Dezvoltare in Sudura. Buletinul (ROM ISSN 1453-0392) **6316**
Institutum Canarium Nachrichten *see* I.C. Nachrichten **397**
Institutum Canarium Yearbook. Almogaren (AUT) **398**
Institutum Romanum Finlandiae. Acta (ITA ISSN 0538-2270) **398**
Instituut Collectie Nederland Informatie *see* I C N-Informatie **6525**
Instituut Collectie Nederland Information *see* I C N-Information **6525**
Instituut van Mynopmeters van Suid-Afrika. Joernaal *see* Institute of Mine Surveyors of South Africa. Journal **6466**
Instituut vir Strategiese Studies. Bulletin *see* Institute for Strategic Studies. Bulletin **7242**
† Instituut voor Planteziektenkundig Onderzoek. Jaarverslag/Research Institute for Plant Protection. Annual Report (NLD ISSN 0074-0446) **8965**
Instituut voor Publiek en Politiek. Nieuwsbrief (NLD ISSN 1871-9767) **7143**
Instituut voor Studie en Stimulering van Onderzoek ThemaTech *see* I S S O ThemaTech **3269**
• Instore Buyer (USA ISSN 1554-348X) **3647**
Instruct-o-gram (USA) **3579**
• Instruction Manual. Chronic Renal Failure Patients on Renal Replacement Therapy (Online) (CAN ISSN 1910-8370) **6269**
• Instruction Manual. Chronic Renal Failure Patients on Renal Replacement Therapy (Print) (CAN ISSN 1498-8100) **6269**
• Instruction Section Newsletter (USA ISSN 1085-0724) **5018**
• Instructional Leadership Abstracts (Online Edition) (USA ISSN 1551-7756) **2942**
Instructional Leadership Abstracts (Print Edition) *see* Instructional Leadership Abstracts (Online Edition) **2942**
• ➤ Instructional Science (NLD ISSN 0020-4277) **3065**
Instructional Strategies: An Applied Research Series *see* Journal of Applied Research for Business Instruction **3067**
Instructional Telecommunications Council News *see* I T C News **2942**
Instructions Nautiques (FRA ISSN 0223-534X) **8646**
Instructor *see* Fudao Yuan **7137**
• Instructor (New York) (USA ISSN 1532-0200) **2867**
• Instructor New Teacher (USA) **2867**
Instruktoermagasinet Krumspring *see* Udspil **8214**
• Instrument Business Outlook (USA ISSN 1061-2203) **4487**
Instrument Design & Technology (USA ISSN 1930-7780) **4487**
• Instrument Design & Technology e-Report (USA ISSN 1938-0801) **4487**
Instrument Engineer's Yearbook (GBR) **4487**
Instrument Flight Rule *see* I F R **59**
Instrument-Making and Automation Equipment *see* Priborostroenie i Sredstva Avtomatizatsii **5458**
• Instrument Pilot (GBR ISSN 1747-0382) **8545**
Instrument Society of America Directory of Automation *see* I S A Directory of Automation **4487**
Instrument Society of America Expo (Year). Technology Update *see* I S A Expo (Year). Technology Update **4487**
Instrument Technique and Sensor *see* Yibiao Jishu yu Chuanganqi **4490**
Instrument Technique Sensor *see* Yibiao Jishu yu Chuanganqi **4490**
• Instrumenta (GBR ISSN 1474-0710) **4488**
Instrumenta Lexicologia Latina (BEL ISSN 0771-5463) **2235**
Instrumenta Patristica et Mediaevalia (BEL ISSN 1379-9878) **7650**
Instrumentacion y Desarrollo (MEX ISSN 0187-8549) **6403**
• The Instrumentalist (USA ISSN 0020-4331) **6576**
The Instrumentality (AUS ISSN 0314-7177) **5443**
Instrumentation (Tokyo) *see* Keiso **4488**
Instrumentation and Automation *see* Keisoku Gijutsu **2462**
Instrumentation and Automation News Inside Products *see* I A N Inside Products **4487**
Instrumentation for the Process Industries (USA) **4488**
Instrumentation Newsletter (USA) **4488**
• ➤ Instrumentation Science & Technology (USA ISSN 1073-9149) **2100**
Instrumentation Solutions (GBR) **8426**
The Instrumentation, Systems and Automation Society Technology Update *see* I S A Technology Update **4487**

Title

10430 INTEGRATION ULRICH'S PERIODICALS

Integration (DEU ISSN 0720-5120) **7242**
Integration (GBR) **2498**
• ➤ Integration (NLD ISSN 0167-9260) **3319**
Integration and Trade *see* Integracion y Comercio **1598**
• Integration Insights (AUS ISSN 1834-304X) **7867**
Integration: Mathematical Theory and Applications (USA) **5494**
• Integration of Speech and Image Understanding. Proceedings (USA ISSN 1530-079X) **2351**
Integrationspaedagogik in Forschung und Praxis (DEU ISSN 1860-0603) **3065**
• Integrationsstatus (DNK ISSN 1600-8936) **7285**
• ➤ Integrative & Comparative Biology (GBR ISSN 1540-7063) **947**
▼ • Integrative Biology (GBR ISSN 1757-9694) **678**
Integrative Biosciences *see* Animal Cells and Systems **932**
• Integrative Cancer Therapies (USA ISSN 1534-7354) **6022**
• ➤ Integrative Medicine (USA ISSN 1546-993X) **310**
• Integrative Medicine Consult (USA ISSN 1522-5062) **310**
• ➤ Integrative Medicine Insights (NZL ISSN 1177-3936) **310**
Integrative Nursing (USA ISSN 1542-3344) **5961**
Integrative Physiological and Behavioral Science *see* Integrative Psychological & Behavioral Science **6146**
• ➤ Integrative Psychological & Behavioral Science (USA ISSN 1932-4502) **6146**
Integrative Therapie (DEU ISSN 0342-6831) **7363**
† • Integrative Zoology (GBR ISSN 1749-4869) **8965**
▼ • Integrative Zoology Online (GBR ISSN 1749-4877) **948**
L'Integratore Nutrizionale (ITA ISSN 1127-6320) **6660**
L'Integrazione Scolastica e Sociale (ITA ISSN 1720-996X) **2867**
Integrierte Schaltungen *see* Informationsdienst F I Z Technik. Integrierte Schaltungen **3116**
• Integrirovannaya Logistika. Nauchnyi Informatsionnyi Zhurnal (RUS) **8526**
• Integrite (USA ISSN 1547-0474) **7761**
• The Integrity Journal (USA) **6645**
Integrity Online Magazine (USA) **5221**
• Integrovany System Rizeni (CZE ISSN 1801-8165) **1754**
Intekrant *see* Integrand Magazine **2987**
• Intel Channel News (USA) **2540**
Intel Microprocessor Forecast (USA) **2467**
• Intel Owner's Club (USA) **2591**
▼ • Intel Premier I T Magazine (Information Technology) (USA ISSN 1939-6503) **2423**
• Intel Technology Journal (USA ISSN 1535-864X) **2423**
Intele-CardNews (USA) **2326**
Intelektualna Sobstvenost/Intellectual Property (BGR) **6751**
➤ Intelektual'na Vlasnist' (UKR ISSN 1608-6422) **6752**
• Inteligencia Artificial (ESP ISSN 1137-3601) **2450**
Inteligencia Emocional (BRA ISSN 1809-8002) **7363**
Intellect Quarterly *see* I Q **5307**
▼ • ➤ Intellectbase International Consortium. Conference Proceedings (USA ISSN 1940-1876) **2987**
Intellectica (FRA ISSN 0769-4113) **7363**
• ➤ Intellector (BRA ISSN 1807-1260) **7143**
The Intellectual Activist (USA ISSN 0730-2355) **6925**
• ➤ Intellectual and Developmental Disabilities (USA ISSN 1934-9491) **3041**
Intellectual and Industrial Property Rights Info *see* I P R Info **6751**
Intellectual and Industrial Property Rights University Center. Julkaisija. I P R Series A *see* I P R University Center. Julkaisija. I P R Series A **6751**
Intellectual and Industrial Property Rights University Center. Publications. I P R Series B *see* I P R University Center. Publications. I P R Series B **6751**
Intellectual and Industrial Property Rights University Centerin. Julkaisuja *see* I P R University Centerin. Julkaisuja **6751**
Intellectual and Industrial Property Section Newsletter *see* Washington State Bar Association. Intellectual and Industrial Property Section. Newsletter **6760**
Intellectual Asset Management (GBR ISSN 1741-1424) **1754**
➤ Intellectual Discourse (MYS ISSN 0128-4878) **7711**
Intellectual Freedom Action News (USA) **5018**
Intellectual Freedom Manual (USA) **5018**
Intellectual Freedom Round Table Report *see* I F R T Report **5014**
• ➤ Intellectual History Review (GBR ISSN 1749-6977) **4147**
Intellectual News *see* Intellectual History Review **4147**
Intellectual Property *see* Intelektualna Sobstvenost **6751**
Intellectual Property (Blaine) (USA) **6752**
• ➤ Intellectual Property (Springfield) (USA) **6752**
Intellectual Property and Antitrust Law (USA) **6752**
Intellectual Property and Information Technology Law (GBR ISSN 1463-7006) **6752**
• Intellectual Property and Technology Forum (USA) **6752**
• Intellectual Property and Technology Law Journal (USA ISSN 1534-3618) **6752**
Intellectual Property Asia *see* I P Asia **6751**
Intellectual Property Asia Law Reports *see* I P Asia Law Reports **4689**
Intellectual Property Business *see* I P Business **6751**
• Intellectual Property Counseling and Litigation (USA) **6752**
Intellectual Property Counselor (USA ISSN 1092-5864) **6752**
Intellectual Property Decisions (GBR ISSN 0141-7584) **1569**
• Intellectual Property Forum (AUS ISSN 0815-2098) **6752**
Intellectual Property Institute of Canada Bulletin *see* I P I C Bulletin **6751**
• Intellectual Property Journal (CAN ISSN 0824-7064) **4693**
Intellectual Property Law & Business *see* I P Law & Business **6751**
Intellectual Property Law Bulletin (USA ISSN 1554-9607) **6752**
Intellectual Property Law Institute *see* Annual Intellectual Property Law Institute **6745**
Intellectual Property Law Library (NLD ISSN 1871-6725) **6752**
Intellectual Property Law News (USA) **6752**
Intellectual Property Law Newsletter (GBR) **6752**
• Intellectual Property Law Review (USA ISSN 0193-4864) **6752**
Intellectual Property Law Section Newsletter *see* Bright Ideas (Albany) **4632**
Intellectual Property Law Section Newsletter *see* I P L Newsletter **6751**
Intellectual Property Lawcast (USA ISSN 1087-6685) **4694**
• Intellectual Property Library (USA ISSN 1526-8535) **4694**
Intellectual Property: Licensing and Joint Venture Profit Strategies. Cumulative Supplement (USA) **6752**
• Intellectual Property Licensing Today (USA ISSN 1931-9703) **4694**
• Intellectual Property Litigation (USA ISSN 1936-7619) **4694**
Intellectual Property Litigation Reporter *see* Andrews Litigation Reporter: Intellectual Property **1552**
Intellectual Property Litigation Yearbook *see* I P Litigation Yearbook **6751**
Intellectual Property Litigator *see* The I P Litigator **6751**
Intellectual Property Magazine *see* I P Magazine **4689**
▼ Intellectual Property Marketing Advisor (USA ISSN 1948-0423) **6752**
Intellectual Property Newsletter (GBR ISSN 1350-1976) **1570**
Intellectual Property Pleadings (USA ISSN 1553-6491) **6752**
Intellectual Property Protection in Asia (USA) **4929**
Intellectual Property Quarterly (GBR ISSN 1364-906X) **6752**
• Intellectual Property Reports (AUS ISSN 0812-2024) **6752**
Intellectual Property Research Institute of Australia Report *see* I P R I A Report **4689**
• Intellectual Property Review (USA) **6752**
• Intellectual Property Strategist (USA ISSN 1079-2422) **6752**
Intellectual Property Strategy Yearbook (GBR ISSN 1460-2334) **6752**
• Intellectual Property Today (USA ISSN 1521-7256) **1570**
• Intellectual Property Update (USA) **6752**
• Intellectual Property Update (ZAF) **4833**
Intellectual Property Value *see* I P Value **6751**
Intellectual Property World Desk Reference (NLD) **6752**
Intellectual Property Worldwide *see* I P Worldwide **4689**
Intellectuals' Rendezvous (IND) **3883**
• Intellectuele Eigendom & Reclamerecht (NLD ISSN 0169-1074) **6753**
• Intellectum (GRC ISSN 1790-8426) **4457**
Intellektual'naya Sobstvennost' (RUS ISSN 0869-6993) **4694**
Intellektual'nye Resursy Rossii (RUS) **2710**
Intelligence *see* Zhili **3830**
Intelligence (USA ISSN 1042-4296) **2423**
• Intelligence (ZAF ISSN 1022-8314) **1492**
• ➤ Intelligence (Kidlington) (GBR ISSN 0160-2896) **7363**
• ➤ Intelligence and National Security (GBR ISSN 0268-4527) **7242**
Intelligence and Security Command Journal *see* I N S C O M Journal **6424**
Intelligence and the Quest for Security (USA ISSN 1932-3492) **6425**
Intelligence & Strategie (FRA ISSN 1765-582X) **7242**
The Intelligence Gap (GBR) **1570**
• Intelligence in Industry (GBR ISSN 1465-4210) **2450**
Intelligence Informatique *see* Computational Intelligence **2410**
• Intelligence Insights (USA ISSN 1930-0441) **7363**
Intelligence Marketing Services Company Profiles *see* I M S Company Profiles **6847**
Intelligence Profession Series (USA) **2678**
Intelligence Report *see* Richard C. Young's Intelligence Report **1648**
• Intelligence Report (USA) **7209**
▼ • Intelligence Reports (USA ISSN 1940-7009) **5961**
• Intelligence Watch Report (GBR ISSN 1524-3885) **7242**
Intelligence Weekly *see* Jane's Intelligence Weekly **7247**
• Intelligencer (Belleville, 1930) (CAN ISSN 0839-1904) **3811**
Intelligences de la Nature (FRA ISSN 1771-6101) **6925**
Intelligens Epuelet/Intelligent Building (HUN ISSN 1587-4621) **1015**
L'Intelligent *see* Jeune Afrique **7247**
Intelligent Automation and Soft Computing (USA ISSN 1079-8587) **2461**
Intelligent Autonomous Systems (NLD ISSN 1873-1139) **2471**
Intelligent Build & Design Innovations (GBR) **1015**
Intelligent Building *see* Intelligens Epuelet **1015**
▼ • ➤ Intelligent Buildings International (GBR ISSN 1750-8975) **1015**
• ➤ Intelligent Data Analysis (NLD ISSN 1088-467X) **2450**
▼ • ➤ Intelligent Decision Technologies (NLD ISSN 1872-4981) **2450**
† Intelligent E A I (Enterprise Application Integration) (USA) **8965**
Intelligent Engineering Systems Through Artificial Neural Networks (USA) **3199**
• Intelligent Enterprise (Online) (USA) **1418**
Intelligent Glass Solutions (GBR ISSN 1742-2396) **2043**
• Intelligent Highway (USA ISSN 0959-6631) **8631**
▼ ➤ Intelligent Information Systems (SGP ISSN 1793-4990) **2423**
Intelligent Investor *see* Outlook Money **1373**
• Intelligent Life (GBR) **5074**
Intelligent Logistik (SWE ISSN 1653-9451) **1754**
Intelligent Robot Symposium. Proceedings *see* Chino Ido Robotto Shinpojumu Shiryo **2584**
• Intelligent Service Robotics (DEU ISSN 1861-2776) **2585**
• ➤ Intelligent Systems in Accounting, Finance & Management (GBR ISSN 1550-1949) **1418**
• Intelligent Systems Report (USA ISSN 1054-8696) **2450**
• Intelligent Times (TWN) **2423**
Intelligent Transport Systems International *see* I T S International **8498**
Intelligent Transportation Society of America Quarterly *see* I T S Quarterly **8498**
Intelligent Transportation Systems Journal *see* Journal of Intelligent Transportation Systems **2329**
▼ • Intelligent Utility (USA ISSN 1944-4583) **3159**
Intelligent Verpacken (DEU ISSN 1860-9708) **6710**
Intelligente Architektur (DEU ISSN 0949-2356) **446**
IntelligentEAI *see* Intelligent E A I **8965**
Intelligenter Produzieren (DEU) **1754**
Intelligentutility *see* Intelligent Utility **3159**
Intel's Merced and IA-64: Technology and Market Forecast (USA) **2467**
InteNet (USA) **2498**
▼ • Intensetimes (GBR ISSN 1755-8816) **5636**
• Intensities (GBR ISSN 1471-5031) **6504**
Intensity (USA) **6576**
• ➤ Intensiv (DEU ISSN 0942-6035) **5636**
Intensiv- und Notfallbehandlung (DEU ISSN 0947-5362) **5636**
Intensive Agriculture (IND ISSN 0020-4919) **122**
• ➤ Intensive and Critical Care Nursing (GBR ISSN 0964-3397) **5961**
Intensive Care & Emergency Medicine *see* Medycyna Intensywna i Ratunkowa **6067**
• ➤ Intensive Care Medicine (DEU ISSN 0342-4642) **5636**
Intensive Care Medicine. Supplement *see* Intensive Care Medicine **5636**
Intensive Care Monitor (GBR ISSN 1360-306X) **5636**
• Intensive Care Society. Journal (GBR ISSN 1751-1437) **6061**
Intensive Care Unit Director *see* I C U Director **4102**
Intensive Care Units and Nursing Web Journal *see* I C U s and Nursing Web Journal **5961**
➤ Intensive Care World (GBR ISSN 0266-7037) **5636**
Intensive French Resource List (CAN ISSN 1912-7278) **5128**
Intensive Therapy *see* Neotlozhnaya Terapiya **5684**
• ➤ Intensivmedizin und Notfallmedizin (DEU ISSN 0175-3851) **5636**
Intensivmedizin und Notfallmedizin. Supplementum *see* Intensivmedizin und Notfallmedizin **5636**
• ➤ Intensivmedizin up2date (DEU ISSN 1614-4856) **5636**
➤ Intensivmedizinisches Seminar (AUT ISSN 0936-8507) **5945**
Intentions d'Achat des Consommateurs. Halifax *see* Intentions d'Achat ou de Renovation des Consommateurs. Halifax **1430**
Intentions d'Achat des Consommateurs. Region Metropolitaine de Montreal *see* Intentions d'Achat ou de Renovation des Consommateurs. Montreal **1430**
Intentions d'Achat des Consommateurs. Vancouver *see* Intentions d'Achat ou de Renovation des Consommateurs. Vancouver **1430**
Intentions d'Achat ou de Renovation des Consommateurs (Print Edition) *see* Intentions d'Achat ou de Renovation des Consommateurs. Calgary **1430**
• Intentions d'Achat ou de Renovation des Consommateurs. Calgary (CAN ISSN 1912-712X) **1430**
• Intentions d'Achat ou de Renovation des Consommateurs. Halifax (CAN ISSN 1912-7162) **1430**
• Intentions d'Achat ou de Renovation des Consommateurs. Montreal (CAN ISSN 1912-7200) **1430**
• Intentions d'Achat ou de Renovation des Consommateurs. Toronto (CAN ISSN 1912-7227) **1430**
• Intentions d'Achat ou de Renovation des Consommateurs. Vancouver (CAN ISSN 1912-7243) **1430**
Intentions de Renovation des Consommateurs. Halifax *see* Intentions d'Achat ou de Renovation des Consommateurs. Halifax **1430**
• InTents (USA ISSN 1090-8366) **8453**
L'Inter (CIV ISSN 1563-5961) **3899**
Inter-Acao (BRA ISSN 0101-7136) **2987**
L'Inter-action (CAN ISSN 1719-8542) **8047**
Inter Alia (GBR ISSN 1461-3964) **4694**
Inter - America Series (USA) **8108**
Inter-American Bar Association. Conference Proceedings (USA) **4694**
Inter-American Bar Association. Newsletter (USA) **4694**
Inter-American Center of Tax Administrators. Informativo - Newsletter (PAN ISSN 1684-9833) **1929**
• Inter-American Commission on Human Rights. Annual Report (USA) **7209**
Inter-American Council of Commerce and Production. Uruguayan Section. Publicaciones (URY ISSN 0538-3048) **1598**
Inter-American Development Bank America (Online) *see* I D B America (Online) **1352**
Inter-American Development Bank. Annual Report (USA) **1355**
Inter-American Development Bank. Board of Governors. Proceedings of the Meeting (USA ISSN 0074-0861) **1355**
Inter-American Development Bank. Occasional Papers (USA) **1355**
Inter-American Development Bank Projects *see* I D B Projects **1352**
Inter-American Development Bank. Working Papers Series (USA) **1355**
Inter-American Foundation. Year in Review (USA) **1598**
Inter-American Investment Corporation Annual Report *see* I I C Annual Report **1352**
• Inter-American Law Review (USA ISSN 0884-1756) **4929**
• Inter-American Music Review (USA ISSN 0195-6655) **6576**
Inter-American Newsletter *see* Revista Interamerica **1300**
Inter American Press Association. Freedom of the Press Annual Report (USA) **7210**
Inter American Press Association News *see* I A P A News **4576**
• Inter-American Trade Report (USA ISSN 1097-2838) **4929**
Inter-American Tropical Tuna Commission. Annual Report/Comision Interamericana del Atun Tropical. Informe Anual (USA ISSN 0074-1000) **3598**
Inter-American Tropical Tuna Commission. Bulletin/Comision Interamericana del Atun Tropical. Boletin (USA ISSN 0074-0993) **3598**
Inter-American Tropical Tuna Commission. Data Report (USA ISSN 0538-3609) **3598**
Inter-American Tropical Tuna Commission. Quarterly Report/Comision Interamericana del Atun Tropical. Informe Trimestral (USA ISSN 1048-6259) **3598**
Inter-American Tropical Tuna Commission. Special Report (USA ISSN 0749-8187) **3598**
Inter-American Tropical Tuna Commission. Stock Assessment Report (USA ISSN 1532-7337) **2807**
Inter-American Yearbook on Human Rights *see* Anuario Interamericano de Derechos Humanos **4917**
Inter - Art Actuel (CAN ISSN 0825-8708) **446**
• Inter-Asia Cultural Studies (GBR ISSN 1464-9373) **3540**
Inter Automatique (FRA) **4978**
• Inter Bloc (FRA ISSN 0242-3960) **5961**
Inter-business Issues (USA) **1125**
• Inter - C D I (FRA ISSN 0242-2999) **2957**
Inter-Cambio (MEX ISSN 0020-5192) **1405**
Inter - Canadian (CAN) **2638**
The Inter-City Express (USA) **1125**
Inter Football Club (ITA) **8236**
Inter Forain (FRA ISSN 0154-1617) **27**
• Inter-Forum Newsletter (DOM ISSN 1680-6190) **3835**
Inter Marium *see* Intermarium **4232**
Inter-Mecanique du Batiment (CAN ISSN 0831-411X) **4121**
Inter Medios de la Comunicacion *see* Intermedios de la Comunicacion **2326**
Inter National Ist (USA) **1821**
Inter-Noise (Year) *see* Inter-Noise Proceedings **3487**

Link to your serials resources and content with ulrichsweb.com

▼ new title   † ceased   ● electronic media   ➤ refereed

Title

10432 INTERFAX. RUSSIA & C I S BANKING & FINANCE WEEKLY ULRICH'S PERIODICALS

• Interfax. Russia & C I S Banking & Finance Weekly (Commonwealth of Independent States) (RUS) **1355**
• Interfax. Russia & C I S Business and Financial Daily (Commonwealth of Independent States) (RUS) **1126**
• Interfax. Russia & C I S Business & Investment Weekly (Commonwealth of Independent States) (RUS) **1630**
• Interfax. Russia & C I S Business Law Weekly (Commonwealth of Independent States) (RUS) **1126**
• Interfax. Russia & C I S Diplomatic Panorama (Commonwealth of Independent States) (RUS) **7242**
• Interfax. Russia & C I S Energy Daily (RUS) **6774**
• Interfax. Russia & C I S IT & Telecom Weekly (Commonwealth of Independent States) (RUS) **2326**
• Interfax. Russia & C I S Military Daily (Commonwealth of Independent States) (RUS) **6425**
• Interfax. Russia & C I S Military Information Weekly (Commonwealth of Independent States) (RUS) **6425**
• Interfax. Russia & C I S Oil & Gas Weekly (Commonwealth of Independent States) (RUS) **6774**
• Interfax. Russia & C I S Presidential Bulletin (Commonwealth of Independent States) (RUS) **1126**
• Interfax. Russia & C I S Statistics Weekly (Commonwealth of Independent States) (RUS) **1243**
• Interfax. Russia & F S U Business Report Weekly (Former Soviet Union) (RUS) **1126**
• Interfax. Russia & F S U General News (Former Soviet Union) (RUS) **1126**
• Interfax. Russia Defense Industry Weekly (RUS) **2226**
• Interfax. Russia Insurance Weekly (RUS) **4509**
• Interfax. Russia Metals & Mining Weekly (RUS) **6466**
• Interfax. Russia Precious Metals & Gems Weekly (RUS) **6466**
† Interfax. Russian Company News (RUS) **8965**
• Interfax. T M T China Weekly (Telecom, Media, Technology) (HKG) **2326**
• Interfax. Ukraine Business Daily (RUS) **1126**
Interfax. Ukraine Business Weekly (RUS) **1126**
† Interfax Vremya (RUS) **8965**
Interference on the Brain Screen (USA) **5443**
Interference Technology (USA) **3319**
Interferences: Series Etudes et Travaux (FRA ISSN 0154-5590) **5309**
† Interferenzen (DEU ISSN 0940-0117) **8965**
Interferon (USA ISSN 0276-1076) **887**
Interflo (USA ISSN 0748-4631) **1570**
Interflow (NZL ISSN 1172-1219) **8826**
Interfraternity Bulletin *see* N I F Notes **2293**
InterGame (GBR ISSN 1356-966X) **8180**
InterGaming (GBR ISSN 1357-7891) **8180**
• Intergovernmental Oceanographic Commission. Annual Report (FRA ISSN 1020-4040) **2807**
Intergovernmental Oceanographic Commission. Manuals and Guides (FRA ISSN 0251-6020) **2807**
Intergovernmental Oceanographic Commission. Report of Meetings of Experts and Equivalent Bodies (FRA ISSN 1014-9538) **678**
Intergovernmental Oceanographic Commission. Reports of Governing and Major Subsidiary Bodies (FRA ISSN 1564-1813) **1126**
Intergovernmental Oceanographic Commission. Technical Series (FRA ISSN 0074-1175) **2808**
Intergovernmental Oceanographic Commission. Training Course Reports (FRA ISSN 1014-2568) **2808**
Intergovernmental Oceanographic Commission. Workshop Report (FRA ISSN 0251-9569) **2808**
Intergovernmental Organizations Report *see* I G O Report **1568**
Intergrated Land Ecosystem-Atmosphere Processes Study Newsletter *see* i L E A P S. Newsletter **7864**
Interieur (DNK ISSN 0903-3033) **4543**
Interieur (NLD) **4543**
Interieur & Etalage (NLD ISSN 0926-4744) **2256**
† Interieur Systemes (FRA ISSN 1267-0669) **8965**
• Interights Bulletin (GBR ISSN 0268-3709) **7210**
➤ Interim (ZAF ISSN 1684-498X) **8426**
Interim (Las Vegas) (USA ISSN 0888-2452) **5309**
Interim Decisions (Online) *see* Board of Immigration Appeals. Interim Decisions (Online) **4846**
Interim Manager Today *see* Project Manager Today **1787**
• Interinstitutional Directory. Who's Who in the European Union? (LUX ISSN 1680-3698) **643**
Interinstitutioneel Jaarboek. Wie is Wie in de Europese Unie *see* Interinstitutional Directory. Who's Who in the European Union? **643**
Interinstitutionelles Verzeichnis. Who's Who in der Europaischen Union? *see* Interinstitutional Directory. Who's Who in the European Union? **643**
Interinvest Review and Outlook (USA) **1630**
Interioer *see* Interieur **4543**
Interioer-Magasinet (NOR ISSN 0801-7212) **4543**
Interior *see* International Textiles Interior **8453**
The Interior Budget in Brief (USA ISSN 0743-2844) **7446**
Interior Construction (USA ISSN 0888-0387) **1015**
• Interior Decorators' Handbook (USA ISSN 1086-5543) **4543**
Interior Design *see* Shinei Sheji **4550**
• Interior Design (USA ISSN 0020-5508) **4543**
Interior Design (Watford) (GBR ISSN 1474-7197) **4543**
• Interior Design Buyers Guide (USA) **4543**
Interior Design Construction *see* Shinei Sheji yu Zhuangxiu **4550**
† Interior Design Handbook (GBR ISSN 0956-988X) **8965**
† Interior Design Market (USA) **8965**
Interior Detail Book Series (KOR) **4543**
Interior Landscape (USA ISSN 1063-1607) **3739**
• Interior Motives (London) (GBR ISSN 1476-2838) **8585**
Interior Plan *see* Plan **453**
Interiormotives (GBR) **4543**
Interiors *see* R I B A Sector Review. Interiors **455**
• Interiors & Sources (USA ISSN 1943-8648) **4559**
▼ Interiors Deco (FRA ISSN 1958-7821) **4543**
Interiorscape (USA ISSN 0744-8635) **4543**
Interjeunes *see* Youthlink **2223**
• ➤ InterJournal (USA ISSN 1081-0625) **2987**
Interkulturell *see* Interkulturell und Global **2868**
Interkulturell und Global (DEU ISSN 1613-1266) **2868**
➤ Interkulturelle Bildungsforschung (DEU ISSN 1432-8186) **8108**
Interkulturelle Bildungsgaenge (DEU ISSN 1438-0196) **8108**
Interkulturelle Ostasienstudien *see* East Asia Intercultural Studies **548**
Interlabor News *see* Interlabor-Parameter **3648**
Interlabor-Parameter (CHE ISSN 1661-6545) **3648**
Interlangues: Civilisations (FRA) **4147**
Interleaf (USA ISSN 0892-9793) **6896**
• ➤ Interlending & Document Supply (GBR ISSN 0264-1615) **5018**
Interlenguajes (COL) **4457**
Interline Settlement System Rules (USA) **8619**
• Interlink Headline News (ARG ISSN 1514-349X) **3791**
Interlit (USA ISSN 0020-5575) **7650**
Interlitteraria (EST ISSN 1406-0701) **5309**
Interlochen Review (USA ISSN 1544-0567) **5309**
Interlocking Concrete Pavement Magazine (USA ISSN 1087-9862) **1015**
• Intermag Asia (USA) **7016**
• Intermarium (USA ISSN 1537-7822) **4232**
• Intermarket Review (USA ISSN 1096-1747) **1821**
• InterMedia (GBR ISSN 0309-118X) **2383**
Intermediair (NLD ISSN 0020-5605) **1355**
L'Intermediaire des Casanovistes (CHE ISSN 0259-4366) **5309**
L'Intermediaire des Chercheurs et Curieux (FRA ISSN 0994-4532) **3120**
Intermediaire des Genealogistes/Middelaar Tussen de Genealogische Navorsers (BEL ISSN 0020-5621) **3771**
IntermediairPW (NLD ISSN 1872-3179) **1866**
The Intermediairy *see* Entremetteur **2283**
• Intermedialites (CAN ISSN 1705-8546) **496**
• Intermediateswire (USA ISSN 1931-1915) **6774**
Intermedios de la Comunicacion (ESP ISSN 1134-0533) **2326**
Intermedium (NLD ISSN 1574-6615) **4509**
• ➤ Intermetallics (GBR ISSN 0966-9795) **6316**
Intermezzo (IRL ISSN 1649-9069) **4361**
Intermezzo (Lexington) (USA) **5074**
Intermission (Alexandria) (USA) **8471**
Intermission (Long Beach) (USA) **6576**
Intermodal Business (USA) **8499**
Intermodal Surface Transportation Act: Flexible Funding Opportunities for Transit (Year) (USA) **8631**
Intermountain Acoustic Musician (USA ISSN 1933-4974) **6576**
Intermountain Catholic (USA ISSN 0273-6187) **7801**
• Intermountain Contractor (USA ISSN 0020-5656) **1015**
Intermountain Farmers Association Cooperator *see* I F A Cooperator **119**
Intermountain Flora (USA) **794**
Intermountain Jewish News (USA ISSN 0047-0511) **7722**
➤ Intermountain Journal of Sciences (USA ISSN 1081-3519) **7867**
The Intermountain Retailer (USA ISSN 1040-578X) **3679**
Intern (AUT ISSN 1817-1044) **27**
• Intern (HUN ISSN 1785-8100) **1821**
Intern Transport *see* Transport-Magasinet **8515**
➤ Interna Medicina (SVK ISSN 1335-8359) **5945**
Internacional de la Educacion *see* Education International Quarterly Magazine **2848**
Internacional de Relaciones Publicas *see* Revista Internacional de Comunicacion y Relaciones Publicas **34**
• ➤ Internal and Emergency Medicine (ITA ISSN 1828-0447) **5945**
Internal and Intercountry Adoption Laws (NLD) **4911**
Internal Auditing (GBR ISSN 1757-0999) **1291**
• Internal Auditing (USA ISSN 0897-0378) **1291**
Internal Auditing & Business Risk *see* Internal Auditing **1291**
• ➤ Internal Auditor (USA ISSN 0020-5745) **1291**
Internal Auditor Alert (USA ISSN 1553-8222) **1291**
Internal Combustion Engine *see* Nainen Kikan **3390**
Internal Combustion Engine *see* I C E **3379**
Internal Combustion Engine Symposium. Proceedings *see* Nainen Kikan Godo Shinpojumu Koen Ronbunshu **3390**
Internal Combustion Engines *see* Neiranji **8595**
Internal Communication (GBR ISSN 1472-9741) **1754**
Internal Control Newsletter *see* Institute of Chartered Accountants in England and Wales. Internal Control Newsletter **1291**
Internal Medicine *see* Audio-Digest Internal Medicine **5944**
• Internal Medicine (USA ISSN 1056-9286) **5945**
Internal Medicine (Online) *see* Internal Medicine (Tokyo, 1992) **5945**
Internal Medicine (Section 6 EMBASE) *see* Excerpta Medica. Section 6: Internal Medicine **5746**
Internal Medicine (Tokyo, 1958) *see* Naika **5947**
• ➤ Internal Medicine (Tokyo, 1992) (JPN ISSN 0918-2918) **5945**
Internal Medicine Advantage Papers (Online) *see* I M Advantage Papers (Online) **5945**
• Internal Medicine Alert (USA ISSN 0195-315X) **5945**
Internal Medicine. Clinical and Laboratory (ITA ISSN 1590-9271) **5946**
• Internal Medicine Coding Alert (USA ISSN 1522-7480) **4509**
• ➤ Internal Medicine Journal (Online) (AUS ISSN 1445-5994) **5946**
• ➤ Internal Medicine Journal (Print) (AUS ISSN 1444-0903) **5946**
• Internal Medicine News (USA ISSN 1097-8690) **5946**
Internal Medicine Report *see* Today in Medicine. Internal Medicine Report **5949**
▼ • Internal Medicine Research Review (NZL ISSN 1178-6140) **5946**
Internal Revenue Acts (USA ISSN 0885-0437) **1929**
Internal Revenue Code (USA ISSN 0163-7177) **1930**
Internal Revenue Cumulative Bulletin (USA ISSN 0364-0620) **1930**
Internal Revenue Manual *see* Internal Revenue Manual - Abridged and Annotated **1930**
Internal Revenue Manual *see* Internal Revenue Manual - Audit and Administration **1930**
Internal Revenue Manual - Abridged and Annotated (USA) **1930**
• Internal Revenue Manual - Audit and Administration (USA) **1930**
Internal Revenue Service Letter Rulings and Memoranda (CD-ROM) *see* I R S Letter Rulings and Memoranda (CD-ROM) **1928**
Internal Revenue Service Letter Rulings Reporter *see* I R S Letter Rulings Reporter **1928**
Internal Revenue Service Practice Adviser Report *see* I R S Practice Adviser Report **1928**
Internal Revenue Service Publications *see* I R S Publications **1928**
Internal Trade of Iran (IRN ISSN 0074-1213) **1430**
➤ Internasjonal Politikk (NOR ISSN 0020-577X) **7242**
▼ • ➤ The Internatioanl Journal of Research and Review (AUS ISSN 2094-1420) **7974**
Internationaal Ondernemen (NLD ISSN 1569-7495) **1570**
The International (USA) **6293**
The International (London, 1990) (GBR ISSN 0960-1503) **7242**
➤ The International Abraham Lincoln Journal (USA ISSN 1528-7211) **7242**
International Abstracts. Alzheimer's Disease & Other Dementias (CAN ISSN 1700-411X) **5747**
International Abstracts in Analytical Psychology (USA ISSN 1040-2144) **7417**
• ➤ International Abstracts in Operations Research (GBR ISSN 0020-580X) **2443**
• International Abstracts of Human Resources (USA ISSN 1542-8397) **1243**
• ➤ International Academy for Case Studies. Journal (USA ISSN 1078-4950) **4871**
International Academy for Marital Spirituality Review *see* I N T A M S Review **7648**
International Academy for the Study of Tourism. Newsletter (USA ISSN 1012-8042) **8723**
International Academy of Business and Economics Annual Conference. Proceedings (Online) *see* I A B E Annual Conference. Proceedings (Online) **1120**
➤ International Academy of Indian Culture. Satapitaka Series (IND ISSN 0074-123X) **4184**
International Academy of Legal Medicine. Congress Reports (CHE) **5914**
International Academy of Legal Medicine. Newsletter (CHE) **5914**
➤ International Academy of Periodontology. Journal (GBR ISSN 1466-2094) **5848**
International Academy of Periodontology. Newsletter (USA ISSN 0963-5742) **5848**
International Academy of Trial Lawyers. Dean's Address (USA) **4694**
• International Accountant (GBR ISSN 1465-5144) **1291**
International Accounting and Reporting Issues (USA ISSN 1014-4633) **1291**
• International Accounting Bulletin (GBR ISSN 0265-0223) **1291**
International Accounting Standards Board Insight *see* I A S B Insight **1290**
International Accounting Standards Board Update *see* I A S B Update **1290**
International Accreditation New Zealand. Technical Guide (NZL ISSN 1178-332X) **4488**
• ➤ International Advances in Economic Research (USA ISSN 1083-0898) **1126**
International Advertising Association World News *see* I A A World News **26**
International Aerial Lift Review *see* Internationale Seilbahn-Rundschau **8500**
• International Aerospace Abstracts (USA ISSN 0020-5842) **76**
International Affairs *see* Kokusai Mondai **7250**
• International Affairs (USA ISSN 0130-9641) **7242**
• ➤ International Affairs (London) (GBR ISSN 0020-5850) **7243**
• International African Bibliography (DEU ISSN 0020-5877) **627**
International African Institute. Bulletin (GBR ISSN 0308-2717) **4175**
• International Agency and Distribution Agreements (USA) **4929**
International Agency and Distribution Law (USA) **4929**
International Agency for Research on Cancer Biennial Report *see* I A R C Biennial Report **6021**
International Agency for Research on Cancer Handbooks of Cancer Prevention *see* I A R C Handbooks of Cancer Prevention **6021**
International Agency for Research on Cancer Monographs on the Evaluation of Carcinogenic Risks to Humans *see* I A R C Monographs on the Evaluation of Carcinogenic Risks to Humans **6021**
International Agency for Research on Cancer Scientific Publications *see* I A R C Scientific Publications **6021**
International Agency for Research on Cancer Technical Reports *see* I A R C Technical Reports **6021**
International Agricultural Policy *see* Politica Agricola Internazionale **147**
• ➤ International Agrophysics (POL ISSN 0236-8722) **237**
International Aids Vaccine Initiative Report *see* I A V I Report **5816**
International Air Power Review (USA ISSN 1473-9917) **6425**
• International Air Safety Seminar. Proceedings (USA ISSN 1932-1317) **60**
International Air Transport Association Annual Report *see* I A T A Annual Report **8544**
International Air Transport Association City Code Directory *see* I A T A City Code Directory **8544**
International Air Transport Association Environmental Review (Online) *see* I A T A Environmental Review (Online) **3438**
International Air Transport Association List of Ticket and Airport Taxes and Fees (Online) *see* I A T A List of Ticket and Airport Taxes and Fees (Online) **8544**
International Air Transport Association Monthly International Statistics *see* I A T A Monthly International Statistics **8526**
International Air Transport Association Ticketing Handbook *see* I A T A Ticketing Handbook **8544**
International Airborne Remote Sensing Conference and Exhibition. Proceedings (USA ISSN 1076-7924) **3199**
• International Aircraft Price Guide (GBR ISSN 1366-669X) **8545**
• International Airline Guide (GBR) **8545**
• International Airport Review (GBR ISSN 1366-6339) **8545**
International Alliance for Women in Music Journal *see* I A W M Journal **6574**
International Alliance of Theatrical Stage Employes, Moving Picture Technicians, Artists and Allied Crafts of the U.S., Its Territories and Canada. Official Bulletin. (USA) **4596**
• International Aluminium Journal (DEU) **6316**
International Amateur - Professional Photoelectric Photometry. Communication (USA ISSN 0886-6961) **576**
† International Amusement Industry Buyers Guide (USA ISSN 1083-9399) **8965**
• ➤ International and Comparative Corporate Law Journal (GBR ISSN 1388-7084) **4871**
International and Comparative Criminal Law Series (NLD ISSN 1873-6629) **4891**
International and Comparative Criminology (USA ISSN 1548-4173) **2655**
• ➤ International and Comparative Law Quarterly (GBR ISSN 0020-5893) **4929**
• International & Comparative Law Review (USA ISSN 1551-3289) **4929**
International and Comparative Social History (CHE ISSN 1420-5297) **4147**
• International and Intercultural Communication Annual (USA ISSN 0270-6075) **8108**
International and National Water Law and Policy Series (NLD ISSN 1387-6880) **4929**
• ➤ International Anesthesiology Clinics (USA ISSN 0020-5907) **5771**
• ➤ International Angiology (ITA ISSN 0392-9590) **5790**
International Angler (USA ISSN 0257-1420) **8319**
International Annals of Criminology *see* Annales Internationales de Criminologie **2643**
International Annual Bibliography of Congress Proceedings *see* Internationale Jahresbibliographie der Kongressberichte **6283**

Link to your serials resources and content with ulrichsweb.com

Title

Title

† International Conference of Building Officials. Uniform Housing Code (USA ISSN 0501-1213) **8965**
† International Conference of Building Officials. Uniform Mechanical Code (USA ISSN 0896-9671) **8965**
International Conference of Eastern Studies. Transactions (JPN ISSN 1349-9181) **551**
International Conference of Ethiopian Studies. Proceedings (ETH ISSN 0074-2945) **4175**
International Conference of Social Security Actuaries and Statisticians. Reports (CHE ISSN 0444-1583) **4509**
• International Conference of the Chilean Computer Science Society. Proceedings (USA ISSN 1522-4902) **2424**
International Conference of Women Engineers and Scientists. Proceedings (JPN) **8868**
• International Conference on 3-D Digital Imaging and Modeling. Proceedings (USA ISSN 1550-6185) **2517**
International Conference on A T M. Proceedings (USA) **2498**
International Conference on Adhesives Joining and Coating Technology in Electronics Manufacturing. Proceedings (USA) **3104**
• International Conference on Advanced Information Networking and Applications. Proceedings (USA ISSN 1550-445X) **2498**
• International Conference on Advanced Robotics. Proceedings (USA) **2585**
International Conference on Advanced Semiconductor Devices and Microsystems. Proceedings (USA) **2465**
• International Conference on Application of Concurrency to System Design. Proceedings (USA ISSN 1550-4808) **2521**
• International Conference on Application-Specific Systems, Architecture and Processors. Proceedings (USA) **2471**
• The International Conference On Array-Prog Language. Proceedings (USA) **2507**
International Conference on Aspect-Oriented Software Development. Proceedings *see* Aspect-Oriented Software Development **2588**
International Conference on Asphalt Pavements. Proceedings (USA) **8632**
International Conference on Assessment Administration. Proceedings (USA) **1126**
International Conference on Automated Software Engineering. Proceedings *see* I E E E / A C M International Conference on Automated Software Engineering **2590**
• International Conference on Autonomous Agents. Proceedings (USA ISSN 1534-4797) **2450**
• International Conference on Cement Microscopy. Proceedings (CD-ROM Edition) (USA) **3346**
International Conference on Cement Microscopy. Proceedings (Print Edition) *see* International Conference on Cement Microscopy. Proceedings (CD-ROM Edition) **3346**
International Conference on Chemical Vapor Deposition. Proceedings (USA ISSN 1056-9480) **2065**
International Conference on Cloud Physics. Proceedings (CAN ISSN 0074-3011) **6357**
▼ • International Conference on Computational & Experimental Engineering and Sciences. Proceedings (USA ISSN 1933-2815) **2471**
International Conference on Computational Electromagnetics and its Application. Proceedings (USA) **7052**
• International Conference on Computational Linguistics. Proceedings (USA ISSN 1525-2477) **2424**
International Conference on Computational Molecular Biology. Annual. Proceedings (USA) **678**
International Conference on Computer Aided Design / Institute of Electrical and Electronics Engineer International Conference on Computer-Aided Design. Proceedings *see* I C C A D - I E E E - A C M International Conference on Computer-Aided Design. Proceedings **3291**
• International Conference on Computer Animation and Social Agents. Proceedings (USA ISSN 1550-3623) **2487**
• International Conference on Computer Communications and Networks. Proceedings (USA ISSN 1095-2055) **2498**
International Conference on Computing Fixed Points with Applications. Proceedings (USA) **5494**
• International Conference on Conduction and Breakdown in Dielectric Liquids. Proceedings (USA ISSN 1012-0351) **3320**
• International Conference on Cooperative Information Systems. Proceedings (USA ISSN 1530-1095) **2498**
International Conference on Cosmic Rays. Proceedings (IND ISSN 0074-3046) **7067**
• International Conference on Creating, Connecting and Collaborating through Computing. Proceedings (USA ISSN 1556-0082) **2499**
International Conference on Cyclotrons and Their Applications. Proceedings (USA) **3169**
• International Conference on Data Engineering. Proceedings (USA ISSN 1084-4627) **2471**
International Conference on Data Processing in the Field of Social Security. Reports (CHE ISSN 0251-7469) **4509**
International Conference on Database Systems for Advanced Applications. Proceedings (USA) **2521**
International Conference on Dependable Systems and Networks. Proceedings (USA ISSN 1530-0889) **462**
• International Conference on Distributed Computing Systems. Proceedings (USA ISSN 1063-6927) **2467**
International Conference on Distributed Computing Systems Workshop. Proceedings (USA ISSN 1533-9610) **2521**
International Conference on Ecological Agriculture: Proceedings: Towards Sustainable Agriculture (IND) **3440**
International Conference on Education. Final Report/Conference International de l'Education. Rapport Final (CHE) **2868**
International Conference on Electricity Distribution. Special Reports (BEL ISSN 1025-9074) **3159**
International Conference on Electromagnetic Interference and Compatibility. Proceedings (USA) **7052**
• International Conference on Embedded and Real-Time Computing Systems and Applications. Proceedings (USA) **2521**
International Conference on Engineering Psychology and Cognitive Ergonomics (GBR) **3200**
International Conference on Experimental Meson Spectroscopy. Proceedings (USA) **7077**
International Conference on Fertilizers. Proceedings (GBR) **237**
International Conference on Fibonacci Numbers and Their Applications. Proceedings *see* Applications of Fibonacci Numbers **5471**
International Conference on Fluid Sealing. Papers Presented (GBR ISSN 0263-4112) **3381**
International Conference on Formal Engineering Methods. Proceedings (USA) **2467**
• International Conference on G R I D Computing. Proceedings (USA ISSN 1550-5510) **2499**
International Conference on Genetic Algorithms. Proceedings (USA) **2450**
† International Conference on Grey Literature. Conference Memorandum (NLD ISSN 1574-1214) **8965**
International Conference on Harmonics and Quality of Power. Proceedings (USA) **3104**
• International Conference on Head-Driven Phrase Structure Grammar. Proceedings (USA ISSN 1535-1793) **5129**
• International Conference on High-Performance Computing. Proceedings (USA ISSN 1094-7256) **2467**
International Conference on High Power Particle Beams. Proceedings (USA) **7052**
International Conference on Hydropower. Proceedings *see* Waterpower **3287**
International Conference on Image Management and Communication in Patient Care. Proceedings (USA) **2424**
• International Conference on Image Processing. Proceedings (USA ISSN 1522-4880) **2487**
• International Conference on Indium Phosphide and Related Materials. Proceedings (USA ISSN 1092-8669) **7077**
International Conference on Information and Communications Technology. Proceedings (USA) **2326**
International Conference on Information Technology: Coding and Computing. Proceedings (USA) **2507**
International Conference on Information Technology Interfaces. Proceedings (USA) **2472**
International Conference on Integrated Circuits Yields. Proceedings (USA ISSN 1096-4789) **2465**
International Conference on Integrated Optics and Optical Fiber Communication. Proceedings (USA) **7077**
International Conference on Intelligent Systems for Molecular Biology. Proceedings (USA ISSN 1553-0833) **826**
International Conference on Intelligent User Interfaces. Proceedings *see* I U I: International Conference on Intelligent User Interfaces. Proceedings **2422**
International Conference on Ion Implantation Technology. Proceedings (USA) **2465**
International Conference on Large High Voltage Electric Systems. Proceedings (FRA ISSN 0074-3151) **3159**
International Conference on Lasers. Proceedings (Year) (USA ISSN 0190-4132) **7077**
International Conference on Lead. Proceedings (GBR ISSN 0074-316X) **6316**
International Conference on Lighthouses and Other Aids to Navigation. Reports (FRA ISSN 0538-6128) **8646**
International Conference on Liquefied Natural Gas. Papers (USA ISSN 0197-2782) **6774**
International Conference on Livestock in the Tropics (USA) **289**
International Conference on Mathematical Methods in Electromagnetic Theory. Proceedings (USA) **3320**
• International Conference on Micro Electro Mechanical Systems (USA) **3320**
• International Conference on Microelectronic Systems Education. Proceedings (USA ISSN 1530-2024) **2540**
International Conference on Microelectronics for Neural, Fuzzy, and Bio-Inspired Systems. Proceedings (USA) **2540**
International Conference on Microelectronics. Proceedings (USA) **3104**
International Conference on Microwave and Millimeter Wave Technology. Proceedings (USA) **3104**
International Conference on Mobile Business *see* International Conference on Mobile Business. Proceedings **1126**
International Conference on Mobile Business. Proceedings (USA ISSN 1935-4908) **1126**
• International Conference On Mobile Systems, Applications And Services (USA ISSN 1931-0137) **2424**
International Conference on Multichip Modules. Proceedings (USA) **3104**
• International Conference on Multimodal Interfaces. Proceedings (USA ISSN 1550-5480) **2424**
International Conference on Multimodal Interfaces. Proceedings *see* I C I M: International Conference on Multimodal Interfaces. Proceedings **2420**
• International Conference on Network Protocols. Proceedings (USA ISSN 1092-1648) **2499**
• International Conference on Neural Networks. Proceedings (USA ISSN 1098-7576) **2450**
• International Conference on Offshore Mechanics and Arctic Engineering. Proceedings (USA) **3381**
International Conference on Open and Online Learning *see* I C O O L **2497**
• International Conference on Parallel and Distributed Systems. Proceedings (USA ISSN 1521-9097) **2467**
• International Conference on Parallel Architecture and Compilation Techniques. Proceedings (USA ISSN 1089-795X) **2467**
• International Conference on Parallel Interconnects. Proceedings (USA ISSN 1530-1397) **2472**
• International Conference on Parallel Processing. Proceedings (USA ISSN 0190-3918) **2467**
• International Conference on Parallel Processing Workshop. Proceedings (USA ISSN 1530-2016) **2467**
• International Conference on Pattern Recognition (USA ISSN 1051-4651) **2450**
International Conference on Port and Ocean Engineering under Arctic Conditions Proceedings *see* P O A C. Proceedings **3214**
International Conference on Power Electronics and Drive Systems. Proceedings (USA) **3104**
International Conference on Power System Technology. Proceedings (USA) **3138**
International Conference on Pressure Surges. Proceedings (GBR ISSN 0269-655X) **3381**
International Conference on Quality of Service in Heterogeneous Wired/Wireless Networks. Proceedings (USA ISSN 1931-2385) **3320**
International Conference on Radar (Publication) *see* International Radar Conference. Record **2327**
International Conference on Sawing Technology. Proceedings (USA) **3713**
• International Conference on Scientific and Statistical Database Management. Proceedings (USA ISSN 1551-6393) **2591**
International Conference on Signal Processing. Proceedings (USA) **2326**
International Conference on Simulation of Semiconductor Processes and Devices. Proceedings (USA) **3104**
International Conference on Social Welfare. Conference Proceedings (CAN ISSN 0074-2961) **8047**
† International Conference on Software Engineering: Education and Practice. Proceedings (USA ISSN 1523-4479) **8965**
• International Conference on Software Engineering. Proceedings (USA ISSN 0270-5257) **2591**
International Conference on Software Maintenance. Proceedings (USA) **2591**
International Conference on Solid-State and Integrated Circuit Technology (USA) **2465**
• (Year) International Conference on Solid Waste Technology. Proceedings (USA ISSN 1091-8043) **3507**
• International Conference on Teaching Statistics. Proceedings (NLD) **3065**
▼ • International Conference on Technology, Communication and Education. Proceedings (KWT ISSN 1997-7697) **8426**
International Conference on Telecommunications in Modern Satellite, Cable and Broadcasting Services. Proceedings (USA) **2499**
International Conference on Terahertz Electronics. Proceedings (USA) **3104**
International Conference on the Physics of Electronic and Atomic Collisions. Abstracts of Contributed Papers and Invited Papers (USA) **7067**
International Conference on the Study of Shamanism and Alternative Modes of Healing. Proceedings (USA) **310**
• International Conference on Thermoelectrics (USA ISSN 1094-2734) **7052**
International Conference on Thermoelectronics. Proceedings (USA) **3138**
• International Conference on Transmission and Distribution Construction, Operation and Live-Line Maintenance. Conference Papers (USA) **3320**
International Conference on V L S I and C A D. Proceedings (Very Large Scale Integration and Computer-Aided Design) (USA) **3320**
• International Conference on V L S I Design. Proceedings (Very Large Scale Integration) (USA ISSN 1063-9667) **2540**
International Conference on Vehicle Structural Mechanics. Proceedings (USA) **8585**
➤ International Conference on Very Large Data Bases. Proceedings (USA ISSN 1047-7349) **2531**
International Conference on Web Information Systems Engineering. Proceedings *see* International Conference on Web Information Systems Engineering Workshops. Proceedings **2472**
International Conference on Web Information Systems Engineering Workshops. Proceedings (USA ISSN 1550-6010) **2472**
International Conference Transparent Optical Network. Proceedings (USA) **7077**
• International Congregational Journal (GBR ISSN 1472-2089) **7650**
International Congress Calendar (BEL ISSN 0538-6349) **6280**
International Congress for Analytical Psychology. Proceedings (CHE ISSN 0074-3364) **7363**
International Congress for Cybernetics. Proceedings/Congres International de Cybernetique. Actes (BEL ISSN 0074-3380) **2527**
International Congress for Papyrology. Proceedings (BEL ISSN 0074-3429) **398**
† International Congress for Statistics, Computer Science (EGY ISSN 1110-7707) **8965**
➤ International Congress for Stereology. Proceedings (ESP ISSN 0074-3437) **3346**
International Congress for the Study of Pre-Columbian Cultures of the Lesser Antilles. Proceedings (CAN ISSN 0538-6381) **343**
International Congress of Comparative Law. Israel Reports (ISR) **4694**
International Congress of Electroencephalography and Clinical Neurophysiology (Proceedings) (IRL ISSN 0074-3631) **6146**
International Congress of Entomology (AUS ISSN 0074-364X) **850**
International Congress of Food Science and Technology. Proceedings *see* World Congress of Food Science and Technology. Proceedings **3668**
International Congress of Histochemistry and Cytochemistry. Proceedings (USA ISSN 0074-3690) **734**
International Congress of Linguists. Proceedings (NLD ISSN 0074-3755) **5129**
➤ International Congress of Occupational Therapy. Proceedings (AUS ISSN 0074-3828) **6679**
➤ International Congress of Ophthalmology. Abstracts (USA) **6043**
International Congress of Parasitology. Proceedings (TUR ISSN 0074-3860) **948**
International Congress of Pharmaceutical Sciences. Proceedings (NLD ISSN 0074-3879) **6849**
International Congress of Primatology. Proceedings (DEU ISSN 0074-3895) **948**
➤ International Congress of Psychology. Proceedings (GBR ISSN 0085-2112) **7363**
International Congress of Radiology. Reports (USA ISSN 0074-3933) **6198**
International Congress of Refrigeration. Proceedings *see* Congres International du Froid. Actes **4117**
International Congress of Sugarcane Technologists. Proceedings (IDN ISSN 0074-3968) **3648**
International Congress of Verdi Studies. Proceedings *see* Congresso Internazionale di Studi Verdiani. Atti **6558**
International Congress on Alcoholism and Drug Dependence. Proceedings (CHE) **2695**
International Congress on Animal Reproduction. Proceedings (AUS) **8799**
International Congress on Archives. Proceedings (FRA) **5018**
International Congress on Canned Foods. Texts of Papers Presented and Resolutions/Congres International de la Conserve. Textes des Communications (FRA ISSN 0534-9257) **3648**
➤ International Congress on Combustion Engines. Proceedings (DEU ISSN 0074-4077) **3381**
• International Congress on Experimental Mechanics. Proceedings (CD-ROM) (USA) **3346**
International Congress on High Speed Photography and Photonics. Proceedings (USA ISSN 1018-9181) **6970**
International Congress on Instrumentation in Aerospace Simulation Facilities. Record (USA ISSN 0730-2010) **60**
International Congress on Irrigation and Drainage. Transactions (IND ISSN 1025-9058) **8826**
International Congress on Meat Science and Technology. Proceedings (USA ISSN 1025-904X) **3648**
International Congress on Mushroom Science. Proceedings *see* Mushroom Science **802**
International Congress on Technology and Technology Exchange. Proceedings (USA ISSN 1045-585X) **3200**
International Congress on the History of Art. Proceedings (FRA ISSN 0074-4190) **496**
International Congress Science Series (BEL ISSN 0538-6772) **6280**

DIRECTORY 2010 THE INTERNATIONAL DIRECTORY OF ENVIRONMENTAL PROTECTION 10437

† • ➤ International Congress Series (NLD ISSN 0531-5131) **8965**
International Congress, Symposium and Seminar Series (GBR ISSN 0969-2622) **6280**
International Connection (GBR) **6504**
International Connection (USA ISSN 1522-2136) **8546**
International Consortium for Agricultural Systems Applications News *see* I C A S A News **234**
• International Construction (GBR ISSN 0020-6415) **3272**
International Construction Database International Construction Database *see* I C O N D A: International Construction Database **8**
• International Construction Law Review (GBR ISSN 0265-1416) **4930**
International Construction Management Series (CHE ISSN 1020-0142) **1015**
International Consultants' Guide (GBR ISSN 1460-4124) **1754**
• International Consultative Forum on Education for All. Status and Trends (FRA ISSN 1020-0908) **2868**
International Consumer Protection (NLD) **2638**
International Contact (DEU ISSN 0939-8619) **6970**
International Contact Lens Clinic *see* Contact Lens & Anterior Eye **6040**
† International Container Directory (USA) **8965**
• International Container Review (GBR ISSN 1352-2515) **8647**
International Contract Design (USA ISSN 1043-4100) **4544**
† International Contract Manual (NLD) **8965**
International Contractors *see* Market Intelligence Reports: International Contractors **6433**
International Contributions to Hydrogeology (NLD ISSN 0936-3912) **2795**
International Convention of Allied Sportfishing Trades Buyer's Guide *see* I C A S T Buyer's Guide **3597**
International Convention on the Elimination of All Forms of Racial Discrimination. Report of Canada (CAN ISSN 0839-4407) **7210**
International Cooper Series in English Language and Literature (CHE) **5129**
International Cooperation *see* Kokusai Kyoryoku **7250**
International Cooperative Alliance. Cooperative Series (IND ISSN 0074-4255) **1423**
International Cooperative Alliance Regional Bulletin *see* I C A Regional Bulletin **1423**
International Copyright and Neighbouring Rights (USA) **6753**
• International Copyright Law and Practice (USA) **6753**
International Coronelli Society. News (AUT ISSN 1680-5356) **4016**
• International Corporate Rescue (GBR ISSN 1572-4638) **4871**
International Corporate Responsibility Series (USA ISSN 1935-1178) **1754**
International Correspondent Banker Newsletter *see* I C B Newsletter **8963**
International Correspondent Banker Settlements Report *see* I C B Settlements Report **1629**
International Correspondent Banking Review (Years) (GBR ISSN 1361-6048) **1356**
International Corrugated Containers Conference. Proceedings *see* T A P P I International Corrugated Containers Conference and Trade Fair. Proceedings **6738**
• International Cosmetique News (FRA ISSN 1264-6539) **589**
International Cotton Advisory Committee. Proceedings (USA ISSN 1022-629X) **8453**
International Cotton Advisory Committee Recorder *see* I C A C Recorder **8452**
International Cotton Industry Statistics (CHE ISSN 0538-6829) **8463**
International Council for Adult Education Bulletin *see* I C A E Bulletin **2942**
International Council for Bird Preservation Monographs *see* I C B P Monographs **908**
International Council for Commercial Arbitration Congress Series *see* I C C A Congress Series **4870**
International Council for Health Freedom Newsletter *see* I C H F Newsletter **7524**
International Council for Health, Physical Education, Recreation, Sport and Dance Journal of Research in Health, Physical Education, Recreation, Sport and Dance *see* I C H P E R - S D Journal of Research in Health, Physical Education, Recreation, Sport and Dance **6989**
International Council for Science Newsletter *see* I C S U Newsletter **7864**
International Council for Science. Year Book (FRA) **7867**
International Council for Scientific and Technical Information Forum *see* I C S T I Forum **5012**
• International Council for the Exploration of the Sea. Annual Report/Conseil International pour l'Exploration de la Mer. Annual Report (DNK ISSN 2070-7185) **2808**
International Council for the Exploration of the Sea. C.M. *see* I C E S Council Meeting **3597**
International Council for the Exploration of the Sea Cooperative Research Report *see* I C E S Cooperative Research Report **3597**
International Council for the Exploration of the Sea Council Meeting *see* I C E S Council Meeting **3597**
International Council for the Exploration of the Sea Identification Leaflets for Diseases and Parasites of Fish and Shellfish *see* I C E S Identification Leaflets for Diseases and Parasites of Fish and Shellfish **947**
International Council for the Exploration of the Sea Identification Leaflets for Plankton *see* I C E S Identification Leaflets for Plankton **3438**
International Council for the Exploration of the Sea Insight *see* I C E S Insight **2806**
International Council for the Exploration of the Sea Journal of Marine Science *see* I C E S Journal of Marine Science **2806**
International Council for the Exploration of the Sea Marine Science Symposia *see* I C E S Marine Science Symposia **3597**
International Council for the Exploration of the Sea Techniques in Marine Environmental Sciences *see* I C E S Techniques in Marine Environmental Sciences **677**
• International Council for Traditional Music. Bulletin (AUS ISSN 0739-1390) **6576**
International Council of Aircraft Owner and Pilot Associations Bulletin (USA) **61**
International Council of Environmental Law References *see* I C E L References **3479**
International Council of Museums News (English Edition) *see* I C O M News (English Edition) **6525**
International Council of Museums Study Series *see* I C O M Study Series **6525**
International Council of Onomastic Sciences. Congress Proceedings (BEL) **5129**
International Council of Shopping Centers Research Review *see* I C S C Research Review **7594**
International Council on Alcohol and Addictions News *see* I C A A News **2694**
International Council on Alcohol and Addictions Publications *see* I C A A Publications **2694**
International Council on Alcohol, Drugs and Traffic Safety Reporter *see* I C A D T S Reporter **2694**
International Council on Health, Physical Education, Recreation, Sport and Dance Congress Proceedings *see* I C H P E R - S D Congress Proceedings **6989**
• International Council on Large High Voltage Electric Systems. Proceedings (FRA) **3320**
International Council on Metals and the Environment. Newsletter *see* International Council on Mining and Metals. Newsletter **6316**
• International Council on Mining and Metals. Newsletter (GBR) **6316**
International Council on Monuments and Sites Nouvelles *see* I C O M O S Nouvelles **445**
• International Country Risk Guide (USA ISSN 0278-6680) **1492**
International Country Risk Guide Annual. Vol. 1, The Americas (USA ISSN 1539-9699) **1492**
International Country Risk Guide Annual. Vol. 2, Europe (European Union) (USA ISSN 1539-9788) **1492**
International Country Risk Guide Annual. Vol. 3, Europe (Non-European Union) (USA ISSN 1539-9796) **1492**
International Country Risk Guide Annual. Vol. 4, The Middle East & North Africa (USA ISSN 1551-9252) **1492**
International Country Risk Guide Annual. Vol. 5, Sub-Saharan Africa (USA ISSN 1539-9818) **1492**
International Country Risk Guide Annual. Vol. 6, Asia & the Pacific (USA ISSN 1539-9826) **1492**
International Country Risk Guide Annual. Vol. 7, Risk Ratings & Statistics (USA ISSN 1539-9834) **1492**
International Court of Justice. Acts and Documents *see* Cour Internationale de Justice. Actes et Documents **4922**
International Court of Justice. Bibliography *see* Cour Internationale de Justice. Bibliographie **4821**
International Court of Justice. Pleadings, Oral Arguments, Documents/Cour Internationale de Justice. Memoires, Plaidoiries et Documents (NLD ISSN 0074-4433) **4930**
International Court of Justice: Reports of Judgments, Advisory Opinions and Orders/Recueils des Arrets, Avis Consultatifs et Ordonnances (NLD ISSN 0074-4441) **4953**
International Court of Justice. Yearbook (NLD ISSN 0074-445X) **4930**
International Crane Foundation Bugle *see* I C F Bugle **908**
International Cranes *see* International Cranes and Specialized Transport **1015**
International Cranes and Specialized Transport (GBR ISSN 1747-700X) **1015**
• ➤ International Criminal Justice Review (USA ISSN 1057-5677) **4891**
• International Criminal Law Review (NLD ISSN 1567-536X) **4891**
International Criminal Tribunal for the Former Yugoslavia. Basic Documents *see* Tribunal Penal International pour l'ex-Yougoslavie. Documents de Reference **8994**
International Criminal Tribunal for the Former Yugoslavia. Judicial Reports *see* Tribunal Penal International pour l'ex-Yougoslavie. Recueils Judiciaires **4899**
• International Criminal Tribunal for the Former Yugoslavia. Yearbook (NLD ISSN 1020-3907) **4930**
➤ International Crisis Behavior (USA ISSN 1549-0432) **7243**
International Crops Research Institute for the Semi-Arid Tropics Report *see* I C R I S A T Report **235**
• International Cruise and Ferry Review (GBR ISSN 0957-7696) **8647**
International Currency Review (GBR ISSN 0020-6490) **1356**
International Custody & Fund Administration *see* I C F A **1629**
International Customer Service Association News *see* I C S A News **1120**
International Customs Journal/Bulletin International des Douanes (BEL ISSN 1378-4048) **1930**
International Cycle Sport (GBR ISSN 0020-6504) **8259**
International Daily News (USA ISSN 0741-126X) **3540**
International Dairy - Deli - Bakery Association LegisLetter *see* I D D B A LegisLetter **3646**
International Dairy - Deli - Bakery Association WrapUp *see* I D D B A WrapUp **3646**
International Dairy Federation. Bulletin/Federation Internationale de Laiterie. Bulletin (BEL ISSN 0259-8434) **265**
International Dairy Federation. Catalogue of I D F Publications/Federation Internationale Laitiere. Catalogue des Publications (BEL ISSN 0538-7086) **182**
International Dairy Federation. International Standard/Federation Internationale de Laiterie. Norme Internationale (BEL ISSN 0538-7094) **265**
International Dairy Federation. Newsletters/ Federation Internationale de Laiterie. Newsletter (BEL ISSN 1011-9027) **265**
International Dairy Federation. Special Issue *see* International Dairy Federation. Bulletin **265**
• ➤ International Dairy Journal (NLD ISSN 0958-6946) **265**
International Dairy Topics (GBR ISSN 1745-7785) **265**
International Dance-Exercise Association Fitness Journal *see* I D E A Fitness Journal **6989**
International Dance-Exercise Association Fitness Manager Newsletter *see* I D E A Fitness Manager Newsletter **6989**
International Dance-Exercise Association Trainer Success *see* I D E A Trainer Success **6989**
International Data Corporation Japan Report *see* I D C Japan Report **2493**
International Data Group News Service *see* I D G News Service **1417**
International Data Series. Selected Data on Mixtures. Series A. Thermodynamic Properties of Non-reacting Binary Systems of Organic Substances (USA ISSN 0147-1503) **2136**
• International Database Engineering and Applications Symposium (USA ISSN 1098-8068) **2521**
International DB2 Users Group Solutions Journal *see* I D U G Solutions Journal **2590**
International Dealer News (GBR ISSN 1354-4047) **8260**
• International Debates (USA ISSN 1542-0345) **7243**
International Defence Newsletter (GBR ISSN 0950-3714) **6425**
International Defense Review Extra (GBR ISSN 1362-3974) **6425**
International Deliverance Magazine (USA ISSN 1559-9191) **7650**
• ➤ International Dental Journal (GBR ISSN 0020-6539) **5848**
International Dentistry South Africa (ZAF ISSN 1818-6734) **5848**
International Desalination and Water Reuse Quarterly (USA ISSN 1022-5404) **8826**
International Desalination Association Journal on Desalination and Water Reuse *see* I D A Journal on Desalination and Water Reuse **8825**
International Desalination Association Newsletter *see* I D A Newsletter **8825**
International Design *see* I.D. **4542**
International Design Yearbook (GBR ISSN 0883-7155) **4544**
International Designers Network *see* I D N **2534**
International Designs Bulletin (CHE ISSN 0250-7730) **6753**
International Developer (AUS) **2424**
• International Development Abstracts (GBR ISSN 0262-0855) **4036**
International Development in Space Station and Space Technologies (USA) **61**
• ➤ International Development Planning Review (GBR ISSN 1474-6743) **4416**
International Development Policies (GBR ISSN 0964-699X) **1598**
• International Development Research Centre. Annual Report/Centre de Recherches pour le Developpement International. Rapport Annuel (CAN ISSN 0704-7584) **1126**
International Development Research Centre Reports *see* I D R C Reports **1597**
† International Development Resource Books (USA ISSN 0738-1425) **8965**
International Development Review (Manchester) (GBR ISSN 1743-5641) **1598**
• International Diabetes Monitor (NLD ISSN 0924-3623) **5894**
International Dialogue on Migration (CHE ISSN 1726-2224) **7285**
International Diamond Exchange Magazine *see* I D E X Magazine **1120**
• International Dictionary of Films and Filmmakers (USA) **6504**
International Dimensions of U.S. Securities Law *see* International Dimensions of United States Securities Law **4871**
International Dimensions of United States Securities Law (USA ISSN 1933-8104) **4871**
International Diplomatic Review (TZA) **7243**
International Direct Investment Statistics *see* O E C D International Direct Investment Statistics (Online) **1256**
International Directions in Education *see* Directions in Education **3012**
International Directory/Repertoire International (CHE) **2226**
International Directory (Year) *see* The Global Environment **8824**
International Directory of Agents, Distributors and Wholesalers *see* The International Directory of Agents, Distributors & Wholesalers **2006**
The International Directory of Agents, Distributors & Wholesalers (USA ISSN 1095-161X) **2006**
• The International Directory of Agricultural Machinery and Implements Importers (USA) **2006**
• The International Directory of Aircraft and Aviation Equipment & Accessories Importers (USA) **2006**
International Directory of Aircraft and Aviation Equipment and Accessories Importers *see* The International Directory of Aircraft and Aviation Equipment & Accessories Importers **2006**
International Directory of Antiquarian Booksellers/Repertoire International de la Librairie Ancienne (GBR ISSN 0538-7159) **7563**
• The International Directory of Apparel and Clothing Importers (USA) **2006**
International Directory of Arts (DEU ISSN 0074-4565) **496**
• International Directory of Arts & Museums of the World CD-ROM (DEU) **496**
• The International Directory of Automotive Equipment, Parts and Accessories Importers (USA) **2006**
International Directory of Automotive Suppliers & Vehicle Manufacturers (FRA) **8586**
• The International Directory of Beauty Supplies, Cosmetics and Toiletries Importers (USA) **2006**
• The International Directory of Bicycles, Mopeds and Motorcycles Importers (USA) **2006**
• The International Directory of Building and Construction Materials & Supplies Importers (USA) **2006**
International Directory of Building and Construction Materials and Supplies Importers *see* The International Directory of Building and Construction Materials & Supplies Importers **2006**
• International Directory of Business and Management Scholars and Research (USA ISSN 1079-9508) **6699**
The International Directory of Business Information Sources & Services (GBR) **1570**
• The International Directory of Chemicals and Allied Products Importers (USA) **2006**
International Directory of Civil Aircraft (Year) (AUS) **8546**
• The International Directory of Communications Equipment and Supplies Importers (USA) **2006**
• The International Directory of Computers and Data Processing Equipment and Supplies Importers (USA) **2006**
• The International Directory of Construction and Building Equipment Importers (USA) **2006**
• The International Directory of Consumer Electronics, Audio / Video, T V and C D's Importers (USA) **2006**
International Directory of Consumer Electronics, Audio / Video, Television and Compact Discs Importers *see* The International Directory of Consumer Electronics, Audio / Video, T V and C D's Importers **2006**
• The International Directory of Control Equipment and Switches Importers (USA) **2006**
International Directory of Control Equipment and Switches Importers *see* The International Directory of Control Equipment and Switches Importers **2006**
• International Directory of Design (USA ISSN 1068-7688) **496**
† International Directory of Distinguished Leadership (USA ISSN 1087-3988) **8965**
• The International Directory of Drugs and Pharmaceuticals Importers (USA) **2006**
International Directory of Eighteenth-Century Studies/Repertoire International des Dix-Huitiemistes (GBR ISSN 0066-3247) **4457**
• The International Directory of Electrical Equipment and Supplies Importers (USA) **2006**
• The International Directory of Electronic and Computer Components & Parts Importers (USA) **2006**
International Directory of Electronic and Computer Components and Parts Importers *see* The International Directory of Electronic and Computer Components & Parts Importers **2006**
• The International Directory of Environmental Protection Equipment Importers (USA) **2006**

Title

▼ *new title* † *ceased* • *electronic media* ➤ *refereed*

10440 INTERNATIONAL FORUM ON INFORMATION AND DOCUMENTATION ULRICH'S PERIODICALS

International Forum on Information and Documentation *see* Mezhdunarodnyi Forum po Informatsii **5032**
International Foundation for Art Research, Inc. Journal *see* I F A R Journal **494**
International Foundry Congress. Papers and Communications (USA ISSN 0074-6118) **6316**
International Franchise Association Insider *see* I F A Insider **1568**
International Franchise Research Centre Lloyds Bank Plc Franchising in Britain Report *see* I F R C - Lloyds Bank Plc Franchising in Britain Report **1629**
International Freediving and Spearfishing News (AUS ISSN 1446-3636) **8319**
• International Freighting Weekly (GBR ISSN 0032-5007) **8647**
• International Frequency List/Lista Internacional de Frecuencias/Liste Internationale des Frequences (CHE ISSN 0252-7235) **2383**
International Frequency List. Preface (CHE ISSN 0252-1725) **2383**
International Fund for Agricultural Development Update *see* I F A D Update **1597**
International Fund Investment (GBR) **1356**
International Futures & Options Databook (Online) (GBR ISSN 1749-5393) **1631**
International Futures & Options Databook (Print) *see* International Futures & Options Databook (Online) **1631**
International Gallerie (IND ISSN 0973-2314) **4457**
• ➤ International Gambling Studies (GBR ISSN 1445-9795) **7363**
• ➤ International Game Theory Review (SGP ISSN 0219-1989) **8426**
International Games Magazine (DEU) **2477**
• International Gaming & Wagering Business (USA ISSN 1066-145X) **8180**
International Gas Engineering and Management *see* Gas Engineering **6770**
• International Gas Report (GBR ISSN 0266-9382) **6774**
International Gas Union. Proceedings of World Gas Conferences (CHE) **6774**
• International Gateways eNewsletter (USA ISSN 1931-5066) **3540**
International Geographical Bibliography *see* Bibliographie Geographique Internationale (Paris, 1996) **4035**
International Geographical Union Bulletin *see* I G U Bulletin **4014**
• ➤ International Geology Review (USA ISSN 0020-6814) **2748**
• International Geophysics Series (USA ISSN 0074-6142) **2783**
• International Geoscience and Remote Sensing Symposium Digest (USA) **4016**
International Geosphere-Biosphere Programme Book Series *see* I G B P Book Series **2746**
International Geosphere-Biosphere Programme Directory *see* I G B P Directory **2746**
International Geosphere-Biosphere Programme Global Change Report *see* I G B P Global Change Report **2746**
International Geosphere - Biosphere Programme Science *see* I G B P Science **7971**
International Geosynthetics Society. Symposium Proceedings *see* Jiosinsetikkusu Shinpojumu Happyo Ronbunshu **2749**
• International Gestalt Journal (USA ISSN 1545-7516) **7364**
• International Glass Review (GBR ISSN 1359-4974) **2043**
• International Government Contractor (USA) **7446**
† International Grafik (DNK ISSN 0020-6830) **8966**
International Grains Council. Food Aid Shipments (GBR) **1599**
International Grains Council. Grain Market Report (GBR) **201**
International Grains Council. Ocean Freight Rates (GBR) **8647**
International Grains Council. Report for Fiscal Year (GBR) **273**
International Grains Council. Wheat and Coarse Grain Shipments (GBR) **273**
International Grains Council. World Grain Statistics (Year) (GBR) **182**
International Graphical Federation Journal *see* I G F - Journal **7323**
International Graphical Federation. Report of Activities (BEL ISSN 0074-6177) **4596**
International Grassland Congress. Proceedings (RUS ISSN 0074-6185) **237**
International Gravimetrique Bureau. Bulletin d'Information (FRA) **2783**
International Ground Water Modeling Center Conference. Proceedings *see* I G W M C Conference. Proceedings **2795**
International Ground Water Modeling Center Ground Water Modeling Newsletter *see* I G W M C Ground Water Modeling Newsletter **2795**
International Group of Agencies and Bureaus Newsletter Bureau Talk *see* I G A B Newsletter Bureau Talk **2324**
† The International Guide to Advance Rulings (NLD) **8966**
International Guide to Mergers and Acquisitions *see* Mergers and Acquisitions **1934**
• International Guide to Microform Masters (DEU) **627**
The International Guide to Partnerships *see* Partnerships **1938**
International Guide to Qualifications in Education (GBR) **3013**
International Guide to Scientific Instruments & Chemicals (GBR) **4488**
The International Guide to Taxation of Life Assurance and Mutual Funds (GBR) **1930**
• International Guide to the Coalfields (GBR ISSN 1364-7512) **6466**
The International Guide to the Taxation of Holding Companies *see* Holding Companies **1928**
† The International Guide to the Taxation of Real Estate (NLD) **8966**
† The International Guide to the Taxation of Sportsmen and Sportswomen (NLD) **8966**
† The International Guide to the Taxation of Transfers of Technology (NLD) **8966**
The International Guide to the Taxation of Trusts *see* Trusts **1953**
The International Guide to Universities & 4-year Colleges in the U S A (BEL ISSN 1561-7564) **2957**
The International Guide to Universities & Four-year Colleges in the U S A *see* The International Guide to Universities & 4-year Colleges in the U S A **2957**
International Guide to Unmanned Vehicles (USA) **61**
International Guild of Professional Consultants Newsletter *see* I G P C Newsletter **1961**
• International Gymnast (USA ISSN 0891-6616) **8180**
International Gymnast Magazine Online *see* International Gymnast **8180**
International H R Journal (Human Resources) (USA ISSN 1081-4876) **1866**
International Hajji Baba Society. Newsletter (USA) **8453**
International Handbook of Universities *see* International Handbook of Universities **2987**
International Handbook of Universities (GBR) **2987**
International Handbook on Commercial Arbitration (NLD) **4931**
International Handbook on Contracts of Employment (NLD) **1688**
International Handbooks of Education *see* Springer International Handbooks of Education Series **2914**
International Handbooks of Religion and Education (NLD ISSN 1874-0049) **7650**
• International Handbooks on Information Systems (DEU) **2546**
International Handicapper's Net News *see* I H N News **4066**
International Handwriting Analysis Review (USA ISSN 1552-8138) **7364**
International Hardware & D I Y News *see* Home Channel News **1118**
International Hatchery Practice (GBR ISSN 0959-9363) **289**
International Health Data Reference Guide *see* U.S. Department of Health and Human Services. National Center for Health Statistics. International Health Data Reference Guide **5751**
International Health News (CAN ISSN 1203-1925) **5637**
International Healthcare Ethics (USA ISSN 1073-5771) **5637**
• ➤ International Heart Journal (JPN ISSN 1349-2365) **5790**
▼ • International Heat Treatment and Surface Engineering (GBR ISSN 1749-5148) **6316**
• International Helsinki Federation for Human Rights. Annual Report (AUT) **7210**
• International Herald Tribune (FRA ISSN 0294-8052) **3841**
• International Herald Tribune - The Asahi Shimbun (JPN) **1493**
International Herpes Management Forum News *see* I H M F News **5816**
International High Flyer (GBR) **8546**
International High Temperature Electronics Conference. Proceedings (USA) **3346**
• ➤ The International History Review (CAN ISSN 0707-5332) **4147**
International Home and Private Poker Players Newsletter (USA ISSN 1078-0807) **8180**
• International Home Plans (CAN ISSN 1198-113X) **4416**
International Homo/Lesbisch Informatiecentrum en Archief Nieuwsbrief *see* I H L I A Nieuwsbrief **4375**
† International Horisont (DNK ISSN 0109-2650) **8966**
International Horn Society. Directory (USA) **6576**
International Horn Society. Newsletter (USA) **6576**
• International Horticultural Congress. Proceedings (BEL ISSN 0074-6231) **3739**
• International Hospital Equipment & Solutions (BEL) **5637**
International Hospital Federation Management Handbooks *see* I H F Management Handbooks **4102**
The International Hospital Federation. Reference Book (GBR ISSN 1751-0767) **4102**
International House of Japan Inc. Bulletin *see* I H J Bulletin **7240**
International Human Dimensions Programme on Global Environmental Change Update *see* I H D P Update **7971**
International Human Powered Vehicle Association. News *see* H P V News **8176**
• International Human Resources Guide (USA) **1866**
• International Human Rights Reports (GBR ISSN 1351-542X) **7210**
• International Humanist News (GBR ISSN 0929-4589) **6925**
International Humanitarian Affairs (USA ISSN 1541-7409) **7210**
International Humanitarian Law *see* C D - I H L **4919**
International Humanitarian Law Series (NLD ISSN 1389-6776) **4931**
International Hydrocarbon (GBR ISSN 1464-0309) **6774**
International Hydrographic Conference. Reports of Proceedings (MCO ISSN 0074-6274) **2808**
International Hydrographic Organization. Annual Report (MCO) **2795**
International Hydrographic Organization. Yearbook (MCO) **2808**
International Hydrological Programme Humid Tropics Programme Series *see* I H P Humid Tropics Programme Series **3438**
International Immigration and Nationality Law (NLD) **4931**
• ➤ International Immunology (GBR ISSN 0953-8178) **5761**
• ➤ International Immunopharmacology (GBR ISSN 1567-5769) **6849**
International Income Tax & Estate Planning (USA) **4903**
International Income Tax Rules of the United States (USA) **1930**
• International Index to Black Periodicals Full Text (USA ISSN 1528-3143) **3574**
• International Index to Film Periodicals (BEL ISSN 0000-0388) **6518**
• International Index to Music Periodicals (USA ISSN 1087-6871) **6631**
• International Index to the Performing Arts (USA ISSN 1528-3119) **8485**
International Industrial Relations Association Bulletin *see* I I R A Bulletin **1686**
• ➤ International Information and Library Review (GBR ISSN 1057-2317) **5018**
➤ International Information, Communication and Education (IND ISSN 0970-1850) **5019**
† International Information Directory (USA ISSN 1098-3333) **8966**
International Insider (GBR ISSN 0953-2714) **1631**
International Insights *see* Regards sur l'International **7261**
➤ International Insights (CAN ISSN 0829-321X) **7243**
• International Insolvency (USA) **1356**
• ➤ International Insolvency Review (GBR ISSN 1180-0518) **1356**
International Institute *see* I I **7240**
International Institute for Applied Systems Analysis Annual Report *see* I I A S A Annual Report **3482**
International Institute for Applied Systems Analysis Reports *see* I I A S A Reports **3482**
International Institute for Applied Systems Analysis. Research Reports (AUT ISSN 0378-9004) **3482**
International Institute for Asian Studies. Annual Report (NLD) **4184**
International Institute for Asian Studies Newsletter *see* I I A S Newsletter **4183**
International Institute for Asian Studies Publications Series *see* I I A S Publications Series **551**
International Institute for Beet Research. Congress Proceedings (BEL) **237**
• International Institute for Conservation of Historic and Artistic Works. Bulletin of the American Group (USA ISSN 0535-0867) **497**
International Institute for Educational Planning Newsletter *see* I I E P Newsletter **2865**
International Institute for Educational Planning Occasional Papers *see* I I E P Occasional Papers **3024**
International Institute for Educational Planning Research Reports *see* I I E P Research Reports **3024**
International Institute for Educational Planning Seminar Papers *see* I I E P Seminar Papers **3024**
International Institute for Educational Planning Studies Series *see* I I E P Studies Series **3024**
International Institute for Energy Conservation - Africa Notes *see* I I E C E-Notes **3438**
➤ International Institute for Environment and Development. Discussion Paper (GBR ISSN 1560-2192) **122**
International Institute for Environment and Development. Drylands Paper (GBR ISSN 1357-9266) **3441**
• International Institute for Environment and Development. Environmental Economics Programme. Discussion Paper (GBR ISSN 1357-9282) **1127**
International Institute for Environment and Development. Pastoral Land Tenure Series (GBR ISSN 1357-9274) **3441**
• International Institute for Environment and Development. Sustainable Agriculture Programme. Gatekeeper Series (GBR ISSN 1357-9258) **123**
➤ International Institute for Environment and Development. Sustainable Agriculture Programme. Hidden Harvest Research Series. (GBR) **201**
International Institute for Environment and Development. Wildlife and Development Series (GBR ISSN 1361-8628) **2615**
International Institute for Geo-Information Science and Earth Observation Jaarverslag *see* I T C Jaarverslag **2709**
International Institute for Geo-Information Science and Earth Observation News *see* I T C News **2709**
International Institute for Infrastructural, Hydraulic and Environmental Engineering Delft Lecture Note Series *see* I H E Delft Lecture Note Series **3362**
International Institute for Labour Studies. Bibliography Series (CHE ISSN 1014-8620) **8108**
International Institute for Labour Studies. Research Series (CHE) **1689**
† International Institute for Land Reclamation and Improvement. Annual Report (NLD ISSN 0165-1803) **8966**
† International Institute for Land Reclamation and Improvement. Bibliography (NLD ISSN 0074-6436) **8966**
International Institute for Land Reclamation and Improvement. Publication (NLD ISSN 0074-6452) **237**
International Institute for Peace Occasional Paper *see* I I P Occasional Paper **7240**
International Institute for Population Sciences. Director's Report (IND) **7285**
International Institute for Population Sciences Newsletter *see* I I P S Newsletter **7284**
International Institute for the Study of Islam in the Modern World Dissertations *see* I S I M Dissertations **7711**
International Institute for the Study of Islam in the Modern World Papers *see* I S I M Papers **7711**
International Institute for the Study of Islam in the Modern World Review *see* I S I M Review **8963**
➤ International Institute of Administrative Sciences Monographs (NLD ISSN 1382-4414) **7446**
International Institute of Administrative Sciences. Reports of the International Congress (BEL ISSN 0074-6479) **7446**
International Institute of Applied Aesthetics. Series (FIN ISSN 1239-193X) **497**
International Institute of Connector and Interconnection Technology. Annual Connector Symposium. Proceedings (USA) **3320**
International Institute of Connector and Interconnection Technology, Inc. News *see* I I C I T News **3104**
International Institute of Fisheries Economics and Trade Newsletter (USA ISSN 1048-9509) **3598**
International Institute of Ibero-American Literature. Congress Proceedings. Memoria (USA ISSN 0074-6495) **5310**
International Institute of Municipal Clerks News Digest *see* I I M C News Digest **7494**
International Institute of Philosophy. Actes (FRA ISSN 0074-6525) **6926**
International Institute of Refrigeration. Bulletin *see* Institut International du Froid. Bulletin **4121**
International Institute of Refrigeration Newsletter *see* The I I R Newsletter **4120**
International Institute of Refrigeration. Proceedings of Commission Meetings *see* Institut International du Froid. Comptes Rendus de Reunions de Commissions **4121**
International Institute of Rural Reconstruction Report *see* I I R R Report **1597**
International Institute of Seismology and Earthquake Engineering. Bulletin (JPN ISSN 0074-655X) **2783**
International Institute of Seismology and Earthquake Engineering. Individual Studies by Participants at I I S E E (JPN) **2784**
International Institute of Seismology and Earthquake Engineering. Year Book (JPN ISSN 0074-6614) **2784**
International Institute of Sociology. Annals (New Series) (NLD ISSN 1568-1548) **8108**
• International Institute of Synthetic Rubber Producers. Proceedings Annual General Meeting (USA ISSN 1070-6488) **7825**
International Institute of Tropical Agriculture. Annual Report and Research Highlights (NGA ISSN 1013-0322) **123**
International Institute of Tropical Forestry. Annual Letter (PRI) **3693**
International Institute on the Prevention and Treatment of Dependencies. Selected Papers (CHE) **2695**
• International Instrumentation Symposium. Proceedings (CD-ROM) (USA ISSN 1558-8041) **61**
International Instrumentation Symposium. Proceedings (Print) *see* International Instrumentation Symposium. Proceedings (CD-ROM) **61**
† International Insurance Law Review (GBR ISSN 0968-2090) **8966**
• International Insurance Monitor (USA ISSN 0020-6997) **4509**
International Intellectual Property Litigation (GBR) **4694**
• ➤ International Interactions (USA ISSN 0305-0629) **7243**
International Interactive Communications Society Newsline *see* I I C S Newsline **2351**

Link to your serials resources and content with ulrichsweb.com

▼ *new title*   † *ceased*   ● *electronic media*   ➤ *refereed*

International Journal of Applied Sports Sciences (KOR ISSN 1598-2939) **8180**
• International Journal of Applied Strategic Management (GBR ISSN 1744-8204) **1755**
• ➤ International Journal of Applied Sustainable Development (GBR ISSN 1742-2620) **1755**
▼ • ➤ International Journal of Applied Systemic Studies (GBR ISSN 1751-0589) **2521**
International Journal of Applied Thermodynamics *see* International Journal of Thermodynamics **7055**
• International Journal of Applied Training and Development (GBR ISSN 1745-5731) **1755**
• ➤ International Journal of Approximate Reasoning (USA ISSN 0888-613X) **2450**
▼ • ➤ International Journal of Aquatic Research and Education (USA ISSN 1932-9997) **6989**
▼ • ➤ International Journal of Arab Culture, Management and Sustainable Development (GBR ISSN 1753-9412) **3540**
➤ International Journal of Arabic-English Studies (LBN ISSN 1680-0982) **5310**
International Journal of Arbitration (IND ISSN 0020-7098) **4695**
• ➤ The International Journal of Architectural Computing (GBR ISSN 1478-0771) **462**
▼ • International Journal of Architectural Heritage (USA ISSN 1558-3058) **446**
† The International Journal of Architectural Management Practice & Research (GBR ISSN 1026-3454) **8966**
International Journal of Architectural Research *see* ArchNet - I J A R **432**
International Journal of Aromatherapy *see* The International Journal of Essential Oil Therapeutics **310**
• ➤ International Journal of Art & Design Education (GBR ISSN 1476-8062) **3065**
• ➤ International Journal of Art Therapy (GBR ISSN 1745-4832) **6110**
▼ • ➤ International Journal of Artificial Intelligence and Soft Computing (GBR ISSN 1755-4950) **2450**
• ➤ International Journal of Artificial Intelligence in Education (NLD ISSN 1560-4292) **2450**
• ➤ The International Journal of Artificial Organs (ITA ISSN 0391-3988) **5637**
▼ • ➤ International Journal of Arts and Technology (GBR ISSN 1754-8853) **530**
• International Journal of Arts Management (CAN ISSN 1480-8986) **497**
• ➤ International Journal of Asia - Pacific Studies (MYS ISSN 1823-6243) **4457**
• ➤ International Journal of Asian Studies (GBR ISSN 1479-5914) **551**
International Journal of Assistive Robotics and Mechatronics (KOR ISSN 1975-0153) **2585**
• International Journal of Astrobiology (GBR ISSN 1473-5504) **678**
• The International Journal of Atherosclerosis (BRA ISSN 1809-2942) **5790**
• ➤ International Journal of Audiology (GBR ISSN 1499-2027) **6081**
• ➤ International Journal of Auditing (GBR ISSN 1090-6738) **1292**
▼ • ➤ International Journal of Auditing Technology (GBR ISSN 1757-8752) **2592**
• ➤ International Journal of Automation and Computing (CHN ISSN 1476-8186) **2461**
▼ • ➤ International Journal of Automation and Control (GBR ISSN 1740-7516) **2461**
▼ • ➤ International Journal of Automation Technology (JPN ISSN 1881-7629) **2461**
• ➤ International Journal of Automotive Technology (DEU ISSN 1229-9138) **8586**
• ➤ International Journal of Automotive Technology and Management (GBR ISSN 1470-9511) **8586**
▼ • ➤ International Journal of Autonomic Computing (GBR ISSN 1741-8569) **2424**
▼ • ➤ International Journal of Autonomous and Adaptive Communications Systems (GBR ISSN 1754-8632) **2351**
▼ • ➤ International Journal of Aviation Management (GBR ISSN 1755-9901) **8546**
▼ • ➤ International Journal of Aviation Management and Logistics (GBR ISSN 1744-2796) **8546**
• ➤ The International Journal of Aviation Psychology (USA ISSN 1050-8414) **8546**
• ➤ International Journal of Ayurveda Research (IND ISSN 0974-7788) **310**
• International Journal of Baltic Law (USA ISSN 1648-9349) **4695**
• ➤ International Journal of Bank Marketing (GBR ISSN 0265-2323) **1356**
▼ • ➤ International Journal of Banking, Accounting and Finance (GBR ISSN 1755-3830) **1292**
• International Journal of Baudrillard Studies (CAN ISSN 1705-6411) **5310**
• International Journal of Behavioral and Consultation Therapy (USA ISSN 1555-7855) **7364**
• ➤ International Journal of Behavioral Development (GBR ISSN 0165-0254) **7364**
• ➤ International Journal of Behavioral Medicine (USA ISSN 1070-5503) **7364**
• ➤ The International Journal of Behavioral Nutrition and Physical Activity (GBR ISSN 1479-5868) **7364**
▼ • ➤ International Journal of Behavioural Accounting and Finance (GBR ISSN 1753-1969) **1292**
▼ • ➤ International Journal of Behavioural and Healthcare Research (GBR ISSN 1755-3539) **5637**
International Journal of Behavioural Sciences (IND ISSN 0971-3190) **7364**
• ➤ International Journal of Bifurcation and Chaos in Applied Sciences and Engineering (SGP ISSN 0218-1274) **3200**
• ➤ International Journal of Bilingual Education and Bilingualism (GBR ISSN 1367-0050) **2868**
• ➤ International Journal of Bilingualism (GBR ISSN 1367-0069) **5129**
▼ • ➤ International Journal of Bio-Inspired Computation (GBR ISSN 1758-0366) **826**
• ➤ The International Journal of Biochemistry & Cell Biology (GBR ISSN 1357-2725) **734**
• ➤ The International Journal of Biodiversity Science & Management (GBR ISSN 1745-1590) **2615**
• International Journal of Bioelectromagnetism (FIN ISSN 1456-7865) **753**
International Journal of Bioethics *see* Journal International de Bioethique **6927**
• ➤ International Journal of Bioinformatics Research and Applications (GBR ISSN 1744-5485) **826**
▼ • ➤ International Journal of Biological and Medical Sciences (TUR ISSN 1307-7457) **5637**
• International Journal of Biological Chemistry (USA ISSN 1819-155X) **734**
• ➤ International Journal of Biological Macromolecules (NLD ISSN 0141-8130) **734**
• ➤ The International Journal of Biological Markers (ITA ISSN 0393-6155) **678**
• ➤ International Journal of Biological Sciences (AUS ISSN 1449-2288) **678**
▼ • ➤ International Journal of Biology (CAN ISSN 1916-9671) **679**
International Journal of Biology and Biotechnology (PAK ISSN 1810-2719) **765**
▼ • ➤ International Journal of Biomaterials (USA ISSN 1687-8787) **749**
▼ • International Journal of Biomathematics (SGP ISSN 1793-5245) **5495**
▼ • ➤ International Journal of Biomechatronics and Biomedical Robotics (GBR ISSN 1757-6792) **5637**
International Journal of Biomechatronics and Robotics *see* International Journal of Biomechatronics and Biomedical Robotics **5637**
▼ International Journal of Biomedical and Pharmaceutical Sciences (GBR ISSN 1752-3788) **5637**
▼ • ➤ International Journal of Biomedical Engineering and Technology (GBR ISSN 1752-6418) **749**
• ➤ International Journal of Biomedical Imaging (USA ISSN 1687-4188) **5637**
▼ • ➤ International Journal of Biomedical Nanoscience and Nanotechnology (GBR ISSN 1756-0799) **679**
• ➤ International Journal of Biomedical Science (USA ISSN 1550-9702) **749**
• ➤ International Journal of Biomedical Sciences (TUR ISSN 1306-1216) **679**
• ➤ International Journal of Biometeorology (DEU ISSN 0020-7128) **6357**
▼ • ➤ International Journal of Biometrics (GBR ISSN 1755-8301) **2424**
▼ • International Journal of Biometrics and Informatics (MYS ISSN 1985-2347) **679**
• ➤ The International Journal of Biostatistics (USA ISSN 1557-4679) **679**
• ➤ International Journal of Biotechnology (GBR ISSN 0963-6048) **765**
• ➤ International Journal of Biotechnology and Biochemistry (IND ISSN 0973-2691) **766**
➤ International Journal of Body Composition Research (GBR ISSN 1479-456X) **5637**
▼ • ➤ International Journal of Border Security and Immigration Policy (GBR ISSN 1755-2419) **4849**
• ➤ International Journal of Botany (PAK ISSN 1811-9700) **794**
➤ International Journal of Business (USA ISSN 1083-4346) **1571**
▼ ➤ International Journal of Business, Accounting, and Finance (USA ISSN 1936-699X) **1127**
International Journal of Business and Economics (TWN ISSN 1607-0704) **1127**
➤ International Journal of Business and Economics Perspectives (USA ISSN 1931-907X) **1127**
▼ • ➤ International Journal of Business and Emerging Markets (GBR ISSN 1753-6219) **1127**
▼ The International Journal of Business and Finance Research (USA ISSN 1931-0269) **1631**
▼ • ➤ International Journal of Business and Globalisation (GBR ISSN 1753-3627) **1127**
International Journal of Business and Globalization *see* International Journal of Business and Globalisation **1127**
➤ International Journal of Business and Information (TWN ISSN 1728-8673) **1127**
• ➤ International Journal of Business and Management (CAN ISSN 1833-3850) **1755**
➤ International Journal of Business and Public Administration (USA ISSN 1547-4844) **7446**
• ➤ International Journal of Business and Society (MYS ISSN 1511-6670) **1127**
▼ • ➤ International Journal of Business and Systems Research (GBR ISSN 1751-200X) **1127**
• ➤ International Journal of Business Data Communications and Networking (USA ISSN 1548-0631) **2534**
➤ International Journal of Business, Economy & Industry Studies (CAN ISSN 1206-7873) **1127**
• ➤ International Journal of Business Environment (GBR ISSN 1740-0589) **1755**
▼ • ➤ International Journal of Business Excellence (GBR ISSN 1756-0047) **1127**
▼ • ➤ International Journal of Business Forecasting and Market Intelligence (GBR ISSN 1744-6635) **1821**
• ➤ International Journal of Business Governance and Ethics (GBR ISSN 1477-9048) **1127**
• ➤ International Journal of Business Information Systems (GBR ISSN 1746-0972) **1755**
• ➤ International Journal of Business Innovation and Research (GBR ISSN 1751-0252) **1127**
• ➤ International Journal of Business Intelligence and Data Mining (GBR ISSN 1743-8195) **1418**
▼ International Journal of Business, Marketing, and Decision Sciences (USA ISSN 1942-8162) **1821**
▼ • ➤ International Journal of Business Performance and Supply Chain Modelling (GBR ISSN 1758-9401) **1127**
• ➤ International Journal of Business Performance Management (GBR ISSN 1368-4892) **1755**
• International Journal of Business Process Integration and Management (GBR ISSN 1741-8763) **1755**
• ➤ International Journal of Business Research (USA ISSN 1554-5466) **1755**
International Journal of Business Research (Hayward) (USA ISSN 1931-7980) **1571**
• International Journal of Business Science and Applied Management (GBR ISSN 1753-0296) **1755**
• ➤ International Journal of Business Strategy (USA ISSN 1553-9563) **1755**
• ➤ International Journal of Business Studies (AUS ISSN 1320-7156) **1127**
➤ International Journal of Business Studies (USA ISSN 1555-7715) **1571**
➤ International Journal of C O M A D E M (Condition Monitoring and Diagnostic Engineering Management) (GBR ISSN 1363-7681) **8426**
International Journal of C O P D *see* The International Journal of Chronic Obstructive Pulmonary Disease (Online) **5790**
The International Journal of C O P D *see* The International Journal of Chronic Obstructive Pulmonary Disease (Print) **8966**
• International Journal of Call Centre Management (GBR ISSN 1463-1415) **1755**
• ➤ International Journal of Canadian Studies/Revue Internationale d'Etudes Canadiennes (CAN ISSN 1180-3991) **8108**
• ➤ International Journal of Cancer/Journal International du Cancer (USA ISSN 0020-7136) **6022**
• ➤ International Journal of Cancer Prevention (USA ISSN 1554-1134) **6022**
• ➤ International Journal of Cancer Research (USA ISSN 1811-9727) **6022**
International Journal of Cancer. Supplement (USA ISSN 0898-6924) **6023**
• ➤ International Journal of Cardiology (IRL ISSN 0167-5273) **5790**
• ➤ International Journal of Cardiovascular Imaging (NLD ISSN 1569-5794) **5790**
International Journal of Cardiovascular Interventions (Online Edition) *see* Acute Cardiac Care (Online Edition) **5775**
International Journal of Cardiovascular Interventions (Print Edition) *see* Acute Cardiac Care (Print Edition) **5775**
• International Journal of Care Pathways (GBR ISSN 2040-4026) **4509**
International Journal of Care Pathways (Online) *see* International Journal of Care Pathways **4509**
• International Journal of Case Method Research & Application (USA ISSN 1554-7752) **2868**
• International Journal of Cases on Electronic Commerce (USA ISSN 1548-0623) **1418**
• ➤ The International Journal of Cast Metals Research (GBR ISSN 1364-0461) **6316**
▼ • ➤ International Journal of Cell Biology (USA ISSN 1687-8876) **833**
• International Journal of Central Banking (USA ISSN 1815-4654) **1357**
International Journal of Chaos Theory and Applications (ROM ISSN 1453-1437) **5495**
International Journal of Chem Tech Research *see* International Journal of ChemTech Research **2065**
▼ • ➤ International Journal of Chemical and Biomolecular Engineering (TUR ISSN 1307-7449) **3247**
▼ • ➤ International Journal of Chemical Engineering (USA ISSN 1687-806X) **3247**
▼ • ➤ International Journal of Chemical Engineering Research (IND) **3247**
• ➤ International Journal of Chemical Kinetics (USA ISSN 0538-8066) **2136**
▼ ➤ International Journal of Chemical Modeling (USA ISSN 1941-3955) **2065**
• ➤ International Journal of Chemical Reactor Engineering (USA ISSN 1542-6580) **3247**
International Journal of Chemical Sciences (IND) **2065**
▼ • ➤ International Journal of Chemistry (CAN ISSN 1916-9698) **2065**
▼ • International Journal of ChemTech Research (IND ISSN 0974-4290) **2065**
▼ ➤ International Journal of Child and Adolescent Health (USA ISSN 1939-5930) **6093**
➤ International Journal of Child & Family Welfare (Leuven) (BEL ISSN 1378-286X) **8108**
International Journal of Child & Family Welfare (Utrecht) *see* International Journal of Child & Family Welfare (Leuven) **8108**
▼ International Journal of Child Health and Human Development (USA ISSN 1939-5965) **6093**
• ➤ International Journal of Childbirth Education (USA ISSN 0887-8625) **5993**
➤ International Journal of Children & Adolescents (CAN ISSN 1206-8330) **2155**
• ➤ The International Journal of Children's Rights (NLD ISSN 0927-5568) **7210**
• ➤ International Journal of Children's Spirituality (GBR ISSN 1364-436X) **7364**
➤ International Journal of Chinese & Comparative Philosophy (HKG) **5637**
▼ • ➤ International Journal of Chinese Culture and Management (GBR ISSN 1752-1270) **8108**
• ➤ The International Journal of Chronic Obstructive Pulmonary Disease (Online) (GBR ISSN 1178-2005) **5790**
† • ➤ The International Journal of Chronic Obstructive Pulmonary Disease (Print) (NZL ISSN 1176-9106) **8966**
• ➤ International Journal of Circuit Theory and Applications (GBR ISSN 0098-9886) **3320**
• ➤ International Journal of Circumpolar Health (FIN ISSN 1239-9736) **5637**
➤ International Journal of Circumpolar Health. Supplement (FIN ISSN 1239-9744) **5638**
▼ ➤ International Journal of Civil Engineering Research (IND) **3272**
• International Journal of Civil Society Law (USA ISSN 1943-1260) **4833**
▼ • ➤ The International Journal of Climate Change: Impacts and Responses (AUS ISSN 1835-7156) **3441**
▼ • ➤ International Journal of Climate Change Strategies and Management (GBR ISSN 1756-8692) **6357**
• ➤ International Journal of Climatology (GBR ISSN 0899-8418) **6357**
➤ International Journal of Clinical Acupuncture (USA ISSN 1047-1979) **310**
• ➤ International Journal of Clinical and Experimental Hypnosis (GBR ISSN 0020-7144) **5943**
▼ • ➤ International Journal of Clinical and Experimental Medicine (USA ISSN 1940-5901) **5906**
▼ • ➤ International Journal of Clinical and Experimental Pathology (USA ISSN 1936-2625) **5638**
• International Journal of Clinical and Health Psychology (ESP ISSN 1697-2600) **7364**
➤ International Journal of Clinical Aromatherapy (FRA) **310**
▼ International Journal of Clinical Dentistry (USA ISSN 1939-5833) **5848**
• ➤ International Journal of Clinical Investigation (ITA ISSN 1590-7120) **5638**
• ➤ The International Journal of Clinical Leadership (GBR ISSN 1757-207X) **5638**
• ➤ International Journal of Clinical Legal Education (GBR ISSN 1467-1069) **2869**
• ➤ International Journal of Clinical Oncology (JPN ISSN 1341-9625) **6023**
• ➤ International Journal of Clinical Oncology (Online) (JPN ISSN 1437-7772) **6023**
• ➤ International Journal of Clinical Pharmacology and Therapeutics (DEU ISSN 0946-1965) **6849**
➤ International Journal of Clinical Pharmacology Research (CHE ISSN 0251-1649) **6849**
• ➤ International Journal of Clinical Practice (GBR ISSN 1368-5031) **5638**
International Journal of Clinical Practice. Supplement *see* International Journal of Clinical Practice **5638**
• ➤ International Journal of Clinical Rheumatology (GBR ISSN 1758-4272) **6224**
• ➤ International Journal of Clothing Science and Technology (GBR ISSN 0955-6222) **2247**
▼ International Journal of Coaching Science (KOR ISSN 1975-8286) **8180**
• ➤ International Journal of Coal Geology (NLD ISSN 0166-5162) **2748**
• ➤ International Journal of Coal Preparation and Utilization (USA ISSN 1939-2699) **6466**
• ➤ International Journal of Coatings Science (USA ISSN 1537-3207) **2124**
▼ • ➤ International Journal of Cognitive Informatics and Natural Intelligence (USA ISSN 1557-3958) **2450**
▼ • International Journal of Cognitive Perfomance Support (GBR ISSN 1742-7207) **1867**
▼ • ➤ International Journal of Cognitive Therapy (USA ISSN 1937-1209) **7364**
▼ • ➤ International Journal of Collaborative Engineering (GBR ISSN 1745-0039) **3200**
▼ • ➤ International Journal of Collaborative Enterprise (GBR ISSN 1740-2085) **1418**
▼ • ➤ International Journal of Collaborative Research on Internal Medicine & Public Health (BIH ISSN 1840-4529) **7526**

• ➤ International Journal of Colorectal Disease (DEU ISSN 0179-1958) **6246**
▼ • ➤ International Journal of Combinatorics (USA ISSN 1687-9163) **5495**
• ➤ International Journal of Commerce and Management (GBR ISSN 1056-9219) **1756**
➤ International Journal of Communication (IND) **2326**
▼ • ➤ International Journal of Communication (USA ISSN 1932-8036) **8108**
▼ • ➤ International Journal of Communication Networks and Distributed Systems (GBR ISSN 1754-3916) **2499**
▼ • International Journal of Communication Networks and Information Security (PAK ISSN 2073-607X) **2424**
• ➤ International Journal of Communication Systems (GBR ISSN 1074-5351) **3320**
▼ • International Journal of Communication Technologies and Human Development (USA ISSN 1935-5661) **2326**
• ➤ International Journal of Communications Law and Policy (GBR ISSN 1439-6262) **2424**
The International Journal of Communicative Psychoanalysis & Psychotherapy (USA ISSN 1062-3051) **6146**
• International Journal of Community Currency Research (GBR ISSN 1325-9547) **1357**
▼ • ➤ International Journal of Community Music (GBR ISSN 1752-6299) **6576**
• ➤ International Journal of Community Music (USA ISSN 1550-7327) **6576**
➤ International Journal of Comparative and Applied Criminal Justice (USA ISSN 0192-4036) **2655**
• ➤ International Journal of Comparative Criminology (CAN ISSN 1201-9607) **2655**
• ➤ The International Journal of Comparative Labour Law and Industrial Relations (NLD ISSN 0952-617X) **4695**
• ➤ International Journal of Comparative Psychology (USA ISSN 0889-3667) **7364**
• ➤ International Journal of Comparative Sociology (GBR ISSN 0020-7152) **8108**
International Journal of Complexity *see* International Journal of Complexity in Applied Science and Engineering **8426**
▼ • ➤ International Journal of Complexity in Applied Science and Engineering (GBR ISSN 1740-0546) **8426**
▼ • ➤ International Journal of Complexity in Leadership and Management (GBR ISSN 1759-0256) **1756**
• ➤ International Journal of Computational and Applied Mathematics (IND ISSN 1819-4966) **5495**
➤ International Journal of Computational and Numerical Analysis and Applications (BGR ISSN 1311-6789) **5495**
▼ • ➤ International Journal of Computational Biology and Drug Design (GBR ISSN 1756-0756) **679**
• ➤ International Journal of Computational Cognition (USA ISSN 1542-8060) **2450**
▼ • ➤ International Journal of Computational Economics and Econometrics (GBR ISSN 1757-1170) **1127**
International Journal of Computational Engineering Science *see* International Journal for Computational Methods in Engineering Science & Mechanics **5494**
• ➤ International Journal of Computational Fluid Dynamics (GBR ISSN 1061-8562) **7059**
• ➤ International Journal of Computational Geometry and Applications (SGP ISSN 0218-1959) **5552**
• ➤ International Journal of Computational Intelligence (TUR ISSN 1304-4508) **2451**
• ➤ International Journal of Computational Intelligence and Applications (GBR ISSN 1469-0268) **2451**
▼ • ➤ International Journal of Computational Intelligence in Bioinformatics and Systems Biology (GBR ISSN 1755-8034) **2451**
• ➤ International Journal of Computational Intelligence Research (IND ISSN 0973-1873) **2425**
▼ • ➤ International Journal of Computational Intelligence Studies (GBR ISSN 1755-4977) **2451**
International Journal of Computational Linguistics and Chinese Language Processing (TWN ISSN 1027-376X) **5202**
▼ • ➤ International Journal of Computational Materials Science and Surface Engineering (GBR ISSN 1753-3465) **3346**
▼ • ➤ International Journal of Computational Medical Engineering (GBR ISSN 1755-4500) **5831**
• International Journal of Computational Methods (SGP ISSN 0219-8762) **5495**
▼ • ➤ International Journal of Computational Physical Sciences (IND) **7939**
• ➤ International Journal of Computational Science and Engineering (GBR ISSN 1742-7185) **2472**
▼ • ➤ International Journal of Computational Vision and Robotics (GBR ISSN 1752-9131) **2585**
▼ • ➤ International Journal of Computer Aided Engineering and Technology (GBR ISSN 1757-2657) **3292**
International Journal of Computer Algebra in Mathematics Education *see* The International Journal for Technology in Mathematics Education **5552**
▼ • ➤ International Journal of Computer and Information Science and Engineering (TUR ISSN 1307-4164) **2546**
• ➤ International Journal of Computer Applications in Technology (GBR ISSN 0952-8091) **2592**
• ➤ International Journal of Computer Assisted Radiology and Surgery (DEU ISSN 1861-6410) **6198**
▼ • International Journal of Computer Games Technology (USA ISSN 1687-7047) **2477**
▼ ➤ International Journal of Computer, Information, and Systems Science, and Engineering (TUR ISSN 1307-2331) **2472**
• ➤ International Journal of Computer Integrated Design and Construction (GBR ISSN 1466-5115) **1016**
• ➤ International Journal of Computer Integrated Manufacturing (GBR ISSN 0951-192X) **3292**
• ➤ International Journal of Computer Mathematics (GBR ISSN 0020-7160) **5552**
• ➤ International Journal of Computer Processing of Oriental Languages (SGP ISSN 0219-4279) **5202**
• International Journal of Computer Research (USA ISSN 1535-6698) **2425**
• ➤ International Journal of Computer Science (TUR ISSN 1306-4428) **2425**
• International Journal of Computer Science & Applications (IND ISSN 0972-9038) **2425**
▼ • ➤ International Journal of Computer Science and Engineering (TUR ISSN 1307-3699) **2472**
• International Journal of Computer Science and Network Security (KOR ISSN 1738-7906) **2425**
▼ • ➤ International Journal of Computer Science and Security (MYS ISSN 1985-1553) **2514**
• ➤ International Journal of Computer-Supported Collaborative Learning (USA ISSN 1556-1607) **2949**
➤ International Journal of Computer Systems Science and Engineering (GBR ISSN 0267-6192) **2522**
▼ • ➤ International Journal of Computer Systems Science and Engineering (TUR ISSN 1307-430X) **2472**
• ➤ International Journal of Computer Vision (USA ISSN 0920-5691) **2451**
International Journal of Computerized Dentistry (DEU ISSN 1463-4201) **5848**
➤ International Journal of Computers and Applications (CAN ISSN 1206-212X) **2571**
• International Journal of Computers, Communications and Control (ROM ISSN 1841-9836) **2425**
• ➤ International Journal of Computers for Mathematical Learning (NLD ISSN 1382-3892) **5553**
▼ • ➤ International Journal of Computers in Healthcare (GBR ISSN 1755-3199) **5831**
International Journal of Computers, Systems and Signals (ZAF ISSN 1608-5655) **2522**
International Journal of Computing and I C T Research *see* International Journal of Computing and Information and Communication Technology Research **2425**
▼ • ➤ International Journal of Computing and Information and Communication Technology Research (UGA ISSN 1818-1139) **2425**
• International Journal of Computing and Information Sciences (CAN ISSN 1708-0460) **2425**
▼ • ➤ International Journal of Computing & Information Technology (IND ISSN 0974-696X) **2425**
▼ • ➤ International Journal of Computing Science and Mathematics (GBR ISSN 1752-5055) **2425**
• International Journal of Condensed Matter Research and Internet Reviews (USA ISSN 1523-9063) **2110**
• ➤ International Journal of Conflict and Violence/Journal of Conflict and Violence Research (DEU ISSN 1864-1385) **7143**
• ➤ International Journal of Conflict Management (GBR ISSN 1044-4068) **1756**
• International Journal of Constitutional Law (GBR ISSN 1474-2640) **4849**
• ➤ International Journal of Construction Education and Research (Online) (GBR ISSN 1550-3984) **1016**
• ➤ International Journal of Construction Education and Research (Print) (GBR ISSN 1557-8771) **1016**
▼ ➤ International Journal of Construction Project Management (USA ISSN 1944-1436) **1016**
• ➤ International Journal of Consumer Studies (GBR ISSN 1470-6423) **2638**
• ➤ International Journal of Contemporary Hospitality Management (GBR ISSN 0959-6119) **4391**
▼ • ➤ International Journal of Contemporary Iraqi Studies (GBR ISSN 1751-2867) **5310**
• ➤ International Journal of Contemporary Mathematical Sciences (BGR ISSN 1312-7586) **5496**
➤ International Journal of Contemporary Sociology (FIN ISSN 0019-6398) **8109**
• ➤ International Journal of Continuing Engineering Education and Life-Long Learning (GBR ISSN 1560-4624) **3200**
• ➤ International Journal of Control (GBR ISSN 0020-7179) **3200**
• International Journal of Control, Automation and Systems (DEU ISSN 1598-6446) **2461**
• ➤ International Journal of Cooperative Information Systems (SGP ISSN 0218-8430) **2546**
▼ • ➤ International Journal of Corporate Governance (GBR ISSN 1754-3037) **1756**
• ➤ International Journal of Corpus Linguistics (NLD ISSN 1384-6655) **5129**
• ➤ International Journal of Corrosion (USA ISSN 1687-9325) **3346**
• ➤ International Journal of Cosmetic Science (GBR ISSN 0142-5463) **594**
• International Journal of Cow Science (IND ISSN 0973-2241) **289**
• ➤ International Journal of Crashworthiness (GBR ISSN 1358-8265) **8499**
• The International Journal of Creativity & Problem Solving (KOR) **7364**
• ➤ International Journal of Criminal Justice Sciences (IND ISSN 0973-5089) **2655**
▼ • ➤ International Journal of Critical Accounting (GBR ISSN 1757-9848) **1292**
▼ • ➤ International Journal of Critical Computer-Based Systems (GBR ISSN 1757-8779) **2425**
▼ ➤ International Journal of Critical Infrastructure Protection (NLD ISSN 1874-5482) **2499**
• ➤ International Journal of Critical Infrastructures (GBR ISSN 1475-3219) **3139**
International Journal of Critical Sociology (IND ISSN 0377-0141) **8109**
• ➤ International Journal of Cross Cultural Management (GBR ISSN 1470-5958) **1867**
▼ • International Journal of Cuban Studies (GBR ISSN 1756-3461) **4457**
▼ • ➤ International Journal of Cultural Management (GBR ISSN 1756-5669) **7974**
• ➤ The International Journal of Cultural Policy (GBR ISSN 1028-6632) **7974**
• ➤ International Journal of Cultural Property (GBR ISSN 0940-7391) **497**
• ➤ International Journal of Cultural Studies (GBR ISSN 1367-8779) **8109**
▼ • ➤ International Journal of Culture and Mental Health (GBR ISSN 1754-2863) **7364**
▼ • International Journal of Culture, Tourism and Hospitality Research (GBR ISSN 1750-6182) **8723**
• International Journal of Customer Relationship Management (GBR ISSN 1461-4561) **1756**
▼ • ➤ International Journal of Cyber Criminology (IND ISSN 0974-2891) **2655**
• ➤ International Journal of Dairy Science (USA ISSN 1811-9743) **265**
• ➤ International Journal of Dairy Technology (GBR ISSN 1364-727X) **266**
• ➤ International Journal of Dairy Technology Online (GBR ISSN 1471-0307) **1127**
• ➤ International Journal of Damage Mechanics (GBR ISSN 1056-7895) **3346**
▼ • ➤ International Journal of Data Analysis Techniques and Strategies (GBR ISSN 1755-8050) **1756**
• ➤ International Journal of Data Mining and Bioinformatics (GBR ISSN 1748-5673) **2546**
▼ • ➤ International Journal of Data Mining, Modelling and Management (GBR ISSN 1759-1163) **2537**
• ➤ International Journal of Data Warehousing and Mining (USA ISSN 1548-3924) **2531**
▼ International Journal of Decision Science and Information Technology (USA ISSN 1937-9013) **1756**
▼ • ➤ International Journal of Decision Sciences, Risk and Management (GBR ISSN 1753-7169) **1756**
▼ • International Journal of Decision Support System Technology (USA ISSN 1941-6296) **2451**
▼ • ➤ International Journal of Defense Acquisition Management (USA ISSN 1940-3445) **2227**
• ➤ International Journal of Dental Hygiene (DNK ISSN 1601-5029) **5848**
International Journal of Dental Symposia (USA) **5848**
▼ • ➤ International Journal of Dentistry (USA ISSN 1687-8728) **5848**
• ➤ International Journal of Dermatology (GBR ISSN 0011-9059) **5877**
International Journal of Dermatology. Supplement *see* International Journal of Dermatology **5877**
▼ • ➤ International Journal of Design (TWN ISSN 1991-3761) **27**
International Journal of Design & Dynamics *see* International Journal of Design & Nature and Ecodynamics **3200**
▼ • ➤ International Journal of Design & Nature and Ecodynamics (GBR ISSN 1755-7437) **3200**
▼ • ➤ International Journal of Design Engineering (GBR ISSN 1751-5874) **3201**
International Journal of Design Sciences & Technology/Revue des Sciences et Techniques de la Conception (FRA ISSN 1630-7267) **8427**
International Journal of Development Banking (IND ISSN 0970-1044) **1599**
• ➤ International Journal of Development Issues (GBR ISSN 1446-8956) **7243**
International Journal of Development Studies (USA ISSN 1934-8339) **1599**
• ➤ The International Journal of Developmental Biology (ESP ISSN 0214-6282) **679**
• ➤ International Journal of Developmental Neuroscience (GBR ISSN 0736-5748) **6146**
International Journal of Diabetes *see* International Journal of Diabetes and Metabolism **5894**
International Journal of Diabetes and Metabolism (SWE ISSN 1606-7754) **5894**
• International Journal of Diabetes in Developing Countries (IND ISSN 0973-3930) **5894**
• ➤ International Journal of Difference Equations (IND) **5496**
▼ • ➤ International Journal of Differential Equations (USA ISSN 1687-9643) **5496**
➤ International Journal of Differential Equations and Applications (BGR ISSN 1311-2872) **5496**
• The International Journal of Digital Accounting Research (ESP ISSN 1577-8517) **1292**
▼ • International Journal of Digital Crime and Forensics (USA ISSN 1941-6210) **5914**
▼ • ➤ International Journal of Digital Culture and Electronic Tourism (GBR ISSN 1753-5212) **2425**
• ➤ International Journal of Digital Curation (GBR ISSN 1746-8256) **5019**
▼ • ➤ International Journal of Digital Earth (GBR ISSN 1753-8947) **2722**
▼ • ➤ International Journal of Digital Enterprise Technology (GBR ISSN 1756-2554) **3382**
• International Journal of Digital Evidence (USA ISSN 1938-0917) **2655**
▼ • ➤ International Journal of Digital Multimedia Broadcasting (USA ISSN 1687-7578) **2351**
• International Journal of Digital Philology (ITA ISSN 1826-0144) **5203**
• ➤ International Journal of Disability, Community & Rehabilitation (CAN ISSN 1703-3381) **3041**
• ➤ International Journal of Disability, Development and Education (GBR ISSN 1034-912X) **3041**
• ➤ International Journal of Disability Management Research (AUS ISSN 1833-8550) **4066**
• International Journal of Disaster Medicine (GBR ISSN 1503-1438) **5638**
▼ • ➤ International Journal of Disaster Resilience in the Built Environment (GBR ISSN 1759-5908) **1016**
• ➤ International Journal of Disclosure and Governance (GBR ISSN 1741-3591) **1756**
➤ International Journal of Discrimination and the Law (GBR ISSN 1358-2291) **7210**
• ➤ International Journal of Distance Education Technologies (USA ISSN 1539-3100) **2869**
➤ International Journal of Distributed Energy Resources (DEU ISSN 1614-7138) **3159**
• International Journal of Distributed Sensor Networks (USA ISSN 1550-1329) **2499**
• ➤ The International Journal of Diversity in Organisations, Communities and Nations (AUS ISSN 1447-9532) **3540**
• ➤ International Journal of Doctoral Studies (USA ISSN 1556-8881) **4457**
International Journal of Dravidian Linguistics *see* I J D L **5126**
• ➤ International Journal of Drug Policy (NLD ISSN 0955-3959) **2695**
▼ • ➤ International Journal of Dynamical Systems and Differential Equations (GBR ISSN 1752-3583) **5496**
• International Journal of Dynamics of Fluids (IND ISSN 0973-1784) **3382**
▼ • ➤ The International Journal of E-Adoption (USA ISSN 1937-9633) **2559**
International Journal of E-Business (USA ISSN 1553-4685) **1418**
▼ • ➤ International Journal of e-Business Management (AUS ISSN 1835-5412) **1756**
• International Journal of E-Business Research (USA ISSN 1548-1131) **1418**
• International Journal of E-business Strategy Management (GBR ISSN 1467-0305) **1756**
• International Journal of E-Collaboration (USA ISSN 1548-3673) **2537**
▼ • International Journal of e-Services and Mobile Applications (USA ISSN 1941-627X) **2327**
• ➤ International Journal of Early Childhood (HKG ISSN 0020-7187) **2155**
➤ International Journal of Early Childhood Education (KOR ISSN 1226-9557) **2869**
• ➤ International Journal of Early Years Education (GBR ISSN 0966-9760) **2869**
• ➤ International Journal of Earth Sciences (DEU ISSN 1437-3254) **2748**
International Journal of Earthquake Engineering and Structural Dynamics *see* Earthquake Engineering & Structural Dynamics **3266**
• ➤ International Journal of Eating Disorders (USA ISSN 0276-3478) **6660**
International Journal of Ecodynamics *see* International Journal of Design & Nature and Ecodynamics **3200**
• ➤ International Journal of Ecological Economics & Statistics (IND ISSN 0973-1385) **679**
➤ International Journal of Ecology and Environmental Sciences (IND ISSN 0377-015X) **3441**
• ➤ International Journal of Economic Development (USA ISSN 1523-9748) **1493**
▼ • ➤ International Journal of Economic Perspectives (TUR ISSN 1307-1637) **1543**
▼ • ➤ International Journal of Economic Policy and Emerging Economies (GBR ISSN 1752-0452) **1599**

Title

10444 INTERNATIONAL JOURNAL OF ECONOMIC RESEARCH ULRICH'S PERIODICALS

International Journal of Economic Research (IND ISSN 0972-9380) **1128**
• ➤ International Journal of Economic Theory (GBR ISSN 1742-7355) **1543**
▼ • ➤ International Journal of Economics and Accounting (GBR ISSN 2041-868X) **1292**
▼ • ➤ International Journal of Economics and Business Research (GBR ISSN 1756-9850) **1128**
▼ • ➤ International Journal of Economics and Finance (CAN ISSN 1916-971X) **1357**
• International Journal of Education and Development Using Information and Communication Technology (BRB ISSN 1814-0556) **2869**
International Journal of Education and Religion *see* Journal of Empirical Theology **7655**
• ➤ International Journal of Education and the Arts (USA ISSN 1529-8094) **2869**
▼ • ➤ International Journal of Education Economics and Development (GBR ISSN 1759-5673) **2869**
• ➤ International Journal of Education Policy and Leadership (USA ISSN 1555-5062) **3025**
➤ International Journal of Education Research (USA ISSN 1932-8443) **2869**
• ➤ International Journal of Education Through Art (GBR ISSN 1743-5234) **2869**
▼ • ➤ International Journal of Educational Administration (IND) **3025**
• ➤ International Journal of Educational Advancement (GBR ISSN 1744-6503) **2869**
• ➤ International Journal of Educational Advancement (Online) (GBR ISSN 1744-6511) **2869**
• ➤ The International Journal of Educational and Psychological Assessment (AUS ISSN 2094-0734) **2869**
• ➤ International Journal of Educational Development (GBR ISSN 0738-0593) **2869**
• ➤ International Journal of Educational Integrity (AUS ISSN 1833-2595) **2869**
• ➤ International Journal of Educational Management (GBR ISSN 0951-354X) **1756**
➤ International Journal of Educational Reform (USA ISSN 1056-7879) **2869**
• ➤ International Journal of Educational Research (GBR ISSN 0883-0355) **2869**
International Journal of Educational Sciences (IND ISSN 0252-8576) **2870**
International Journal of Educational Telecommunications *see* International Journal on E-learning **2560**
• ➤ International Journal of Educology (CD-ROM) (AUS ISSN 1449-7255) **2870**
• ➤ International Journal of Effective Management (USA ISSN 1547-3686) **1756**
▼ • ➤ International Journal of Electric and Hybrid Vehicles (GBR ISSN 1751-4088) **3159**
▼ • International Journal of Electrical and Power Engineering (PAK ISSN 1990-7958) **3159**
▼ • ➤ International Journal of Electrical, Computer, and Systems Engineering (TUR ISSN 1307-5179) **3320**
International Journal of Electrical Engineering/Dianji Gongcheng Xuekan (TWN ISSN 1812-3031) **3320**
• ➤ International Journal of Electrical Engineering Education (GBR ISSN 0020-7209) **3320**
International Journal of Electrical Engineering in Transportation (FRA ISSN 1773-9357) **3321**
➤ International Journal of Electrical Machining (JPN ISSN 1341-7908) **3321**
• ➤ International Journal of Electrical Power & Energy Systems (GBR ISSN 0142-0615) **3321**
▼ • ➤ International Journal of Electrical Systems Science and Engineering (TUR ISSN 1307-8917) **3321**
• ➤ International Journal of Electrochemical Science (SRB ISSN 1452-3981) **2114**
▼ • ➤ International Journal of Electronic Banking (GBR ISSN 1753-5239) **1357**
• ➤ International Journal of Electronic Business (GBR ISSN 1470-6067) **1418**
• ➤ International Journal of Electronic Business Management (TWN ISSN 1728-2047) **1756**
• ➤ International Journal of Electronic Commerce (USA ISSN 1086-4415) **1418**
International Journal of Electronic Commerce and Business Media *see* Electronic Markets **1815**
† International Journal of Electronic Commerce Law & Practice (GBR ISSN 1468-9685) **8966**
▼ • ➤ International Journal of Electronic Customer Relationship Management (GBR ISSN 1750-0664) **1756**
▼ • ➤ International Journal of Electronic Democracy (GBR ISSN 1742-4224) **7143**
• ➤ International Journal of Electronic Finance (GBR ISSN 1746-0069) **1357**
▼ • ➤ International Journal of Electronic Governance (GBR ISSN 1742-7509) **7446**
• ➤ International Journal of Electronic Government Research (USA ISSN 1548-3886) **7446**
• ➤ International Journal of Electronic Healthcare (GBR ISSN 1741-8453) **4102**
• ➤ International Journal of Electronic Marketing and Retailing (GBR ISSN 1741-1025) **1821**
▼ • ➤ International Journal of Electronic Security and Digital Forensics (GBR ISSN 1751-911X) **2514**
▼ • ➤ International Journal of Electronic Trade (GBR ISSN 1742-7525) **1128**
▼ • ➤ International Journal of Electronic Transport (GBR ISSN 1742-6952) **8499**
• ➤ International Journal of Electronics (GBR ISSN 0020-7217) **3105**
▼ • ➤ International Journal of Electronics, Circuits and Systems (TUR ISSN 1307-4156) **2465**
▼ • ➤ International Journal of Electronics Engineering Research (IND) **3321**
† International Journal of Elevator Engineering (GBR ISSN 1029-6646) **8966**
• ➤ International Journal of Embedded Systems (GBR ISSN 1741-1068) **2425**
• ➤ International Journal of Emergency Management (GBR ISSN 1471-4825) **1757**
▼ • International Journal of Emergency Medicine (Online) (USA ISSN 1865-1380) **6062**
† • International Journal of Emergency Medicine (Print) (USA ISSN 1865-1372) **8966**
➤ International Journal of Emergency Mental Health (USA ISSN 1522-4821) **6146**
• International Journal of Emerging Electric Power Systems (USA ISSN 1553-779X) **3159**
• ➤ International Journal of Emerging Markets (GBR ISSN 1746-8809) **1571**
▼ • ➤ International Journal of Emerging Multidisciplinary Fluid Sciences (GBR ISSN 1756-8315) **7059**
• ➤ The International Journal of Emerging Technologies and Society (AUS ISSN 1835-8780) **7867**
➤ International Journal of Emotional Psychology and Sport Ethics (NGA ISSN 1119-7048) **7364**
International Journal of Employment Studies (AUS ISSN 1039-6993) **1689**
International Journal of Endocrinology *see* Mizhnarodnyi Endokrynolohichnyi Zhurnal **5897**
▼ • ➤ International Journal of Endocrinology (USA ISSN 1687-8337) **5895**
• International Journal of Endocrinology and Metabolism (IRN ISSN 1726-913X) **5895**
• International Journal of Energy, Environment and Economics (USA ISSN 1054-853X) **3139**
• ➤ International Journal of Energy Research (GBR ISSN 0363-907X) **3139**
▼ • ➤ International Journal of Energy Sector Management (GBR ISSN 1750-6220) **3139**
• ➤ International Journal of Energy Technology and Policy (GBR ISSN 1472-8923) **3139**
• ➤ International Journal of Engine Research (GBR ISSN 1468-0874) **3382**
International Journal of Engineering *see* International Journal of Engineering. Transactions B: Applications **3201**
International Journal of Engineering *see* International Journal of Engineering. Transactions A: Basics **3201**
▼ • International Journal of Engineering (MYS ISSN 1985-2312) **3201**
• ➤ International Journal of Engineering Education (IRL ISSN 0949-149X) **3201**
▼ • ➤ International Journal of Engineering Management and Economics (GBR ISSN 1756-5154) **3201**
International Journal of Engineering Negotiation *see* International Journal of Collaborative Engineering **3200**
International Journal of Engineering Science *see* I U S T International Journal of Engineering Science **3196**
• ➤ International Journal of Engineering Science (USA ISSN 0020-7225) **3201**
• International Journal of Engineering Simulation (GBR ISSN 1468-1137) **3201**
▼ • ➤ International Journal of Engineering Systems Modelling and Simulation (GBR ISSN 1755-9758) **3292**
• International Journal of Engineering. Transactions A: Basics (IRN ISSN 1728-1431) **3201**
International Journal of Engineering. Transactions B: Applications (IRN ISSN 1728-144X) **3201**
• ➤ International Journal of English Studies (ESP ISSN 1578-7044) **5129**
• International Journal of Enterprise Information Systems (USA ISSN 1548-1115) **2522**
• ➤ International Journal of Enterprise Network Management (GBR ISSN 1748-1252) **1757**
▼ • ➤ International Journal of Enterprise Systems Integration and Interoperability (GBR ISSN 1745-3143) **1757**
▼ • ➤ International Journal of Entertainment Technology and Management (GBR ISSN 1475-8954) **1757**
• ➤ International Journal of Entrepreneurial Behaviour & Research (GBR ISSN 1355-2554) **1962**
▼ • ➤ International Journal of Entrepreneurial Venturing (GBR ISSN 1742-5360) **1757**
• ➤ International Journal of Entrepreneurship (USA ISSN 1099-9264) **1757**
• ➤ International Journal of Entrepreneurship and Innovation (GBR ISSN 1465-7503) **1128**
• ➤ International Journal of Entrepreneurship and Innovation Management (GBR ISSN 1368-275X) **1757**
• ➤ International Journal of Entrepreneurship and Small Business (GBR ISSN 1476-1297) **1757**
• International Journal of Entrepreneurship Education (IRL) **1128**
International Journal of Environment and Development (IND ISSN 0973-3574) **3441**
▼ • ➤ International Journal of Environment and Health (GBR ISSN 1743-4955) **3441**
• ➤ International Journal of Environment and Pollution (GBR ISSN 0957-4352) **3487**
• ➤ International Journal of Environment and Sustainable Development (GBR ISSN 1474-6778) **3441**
• ➤ International Journal of Environment and Waste Management (GBR ISSN 1478-9876) **3507**
• ➤ International Journal of Environment, Workplace and Employment (GBR ISSN 1741-8437) **1689**
• ➤ International Journal of Environmental Analytical Chemistry (GBR ISSN 0306-7319) **2101**
• ➤ International Journal of Environmental and Science Education (TUR ISSN 1306-3065) **2870**
• ➤ The International Journal of Environmental, Cultural, Economic and Social Sustainability (AUS ISSN 1832-2077) **3442**
▼ • ➤ International Journal of Environmental Engineering (GBR ISSN 1756-8463) **3442**
• ➤ International Journal of Environmental Health Research (GBR ISSN 0960-3123) **3442**
▼ • ➤ International Journal of Environmental Policy and Marketing (GBR ISSN 1752-6906) **3442**
International Journal of Environmental Pollution *see* Revista Internacional de Contaminacion Ambiental **3463**
▼ • International Journal of Environmental Research (IRN ISSN 1735-6865) **3442**
• ➤ International Journal of Environmental Research and Public Health (CHE ISSN 1660-4601) **3442**
• ➤ International Journal of Environmental Science and Technology (IRN ISSN 1735-1472) **3442**
• ➤ International Journal of Environmental Studies (GBR ISSN 0020-7233) **3442**
• ➤ International Journal of Environmental Studies (USA ISSN 1097-7104) **3442**
The International Journal of Environmental Studies. Section B, Environmental Science and Technology *see* International Journal of Environmental Studies **3442**
• ➤ International Journal of Environmental Technology and Management (GBR ISSN 1466-2132) **3442**
• ➤ International Journal of Environmentally Conscious Design and Manufacturing (USA ISSN 1095-807X) **3442**
• ➤ International Journal of Epidemiology (GBR ISSN 0300-5771) **5638**
The International Journal of Erotica (GBR ISSN 1740-3545) **6293**
• ➤ The International Journal of Essential Oil Therapeutics (GBR) **310**
• ➤ International Journal of Ethics (USA ISSN 1556-4444) **7143**
▼ • International Journal of Event and Festival Management (GBR) **1757**
• ➤ International Journal of Evidence & Proof (GBR ISSN 1365-7127) **4891**
• ➤ International Journal of Evidence Based Coaching and Mentoring (GBR ISSN 1741-8305) **2870**
• ➤ International Journal of Evidence-Based Healthcare (AUS ISSN 1744-1595) **5638**
• ➤ International Journal of Evolution Equations (USA ISSN 1549-2907) **5496**
▼ • ➤ International Journal of Evolutionary Biology (USA ISSN 2090-052X) **872**
▼ • ➤ International Journal of Exercise Science (USA ISSN 1939-795X) **6989**
• ➤ International Journal of Exergy (GBR ISSN 1742-8297) **3201**
† • International Journal of Experimental and Clinical Chemotherapy (CHE ISSN 0933-0453) **8966**
▼ • International Journal of Experimental and Computational Biomechanics (GBR ISSN 1755-8735) **749**
▼ • ➤ International Journal of Experimental Design and Process Optimisation (GBR ISSN 2040-2252) **3368**
International Journal of Experimental Diabetes Research *see* Experimental Diabesity Research **5758**
• ➤ International Journal of Experimental Pathology (GBR ISSN 0959-9673) **5638**
▼ • ➤ International Journal of Fashion Design, Technology and Education (GBR ISSN 1754-3266) **2257**
• ➤ International Journal of Fatigue (GBR ISSN 0142-1123) **3346**
▼ • International Journal of Feminist Approaches to Bioethics (USA ISSN 1937-4585) **6926**
▼ • ➤ International Journal of Feminist Technoscience (SWE ISSN 1654-6792) **8899**
➤ International Journal of Fertility and Women's Medicine (USA ISSN 1534-892X) **5638**
• International Journal of Finance (USA ISSN 1041-2743) **1357**
• ➤ International Journal of Finance & Economics (GBR ISSN 1076-9307) **1357**
▼ • ➤ International Journal of Financial Markets and Derivatives (GBR ISSN 1756-7130) **1357**
• ➤ International Journal of Financial Services Management (GBR ISSN 1460-6712) **1357**
➤ International Journal of Fitness (IND ISSN 0973-2152) **6990**
International Journal of Flexible Manufacturing Systems *see* Flexible Services and Manufacturing Journal **3344**
▼ • ➤ International Journal of Flow Control (GBR ISSN 1756-8250) **7059**
• ➤ International Journal of Fluid Dynamics (AUS ISSN 1327-1660) **7059**
• International Journal of Fluid Mechanics Research (USA) **3382**
➤ International Journal of Fluid Power (DEU ISSN 1439-9776) **3362**
International Journal of Food, Agriculture and Environment *see* Journal of Food, Agriculture and Environment **127**
• ➤ International Journal of Food Engineering (USA ISSN 1556-3758) **3648**
• ➤ International Journal of Food Microbiology (NLD ISSN 0168-1605) **887**
• International Journal of Food Properties (USA ISSN 1094-2912) **679**
International Journal of Food Safety *see* International Journal of Food Safety, Nutrition and Public Health **3648**
▼ • ➤ International Journal of Food Safety, Nutrition and Public Health (GBR ISSN 1479-3911) **3648**
• ➤ International Journal of Food Science and Technology (GBR ISSN 0950-5423) **3648**
• ➤ International Journal of Food Science & Technology Online (GBR ISSN 1365-2621) **3648**
• ➤ International Journal of Food Sciences and Nutrition (GBR ISSN 0963-7486) **6660**
• ➤ International Journal of Forecasting (NLD ISSN 0169-2070) **1493**
▼ • ➤ International Journal of Forensic Engineering (GBR ISSN 1744-9944) **3201**
▼ • ➤ International Journal of Forensic Engineering and Management (GBR ISSN 1478-1476) **1757**
International Journal of Forensic Mental Health (CAN ISSN 1499-9013) **7526**
• ➤ International Journal of Forensic Psychology (AUS ISSN 1448-4374) **5914**
▼ • ➤ International Journal of Forensic Software Engineering (GBR ISSN 1743-5099) **2592**
• ➤ International Journal of Foresight and Innovation Policy (GBR ISSN 1740-2816) **7446**
• ➤ International Journal of Forest Engineering (CAN ISSN 1494-2119) **3694**
➤ International Journal of Forest Genetics (SVK ISSN 1335-048X) **3694**
• ➤ International Journal of Forestry Research (USA ISSN 1687-9368) **3694**
International Journal of Forming Processes (FRA ISSN 1292-7775) **6316**
• ➤ International Journal of Foundations of Computer Science (SGP ISSN 0129-0541) **2425**
• ➤ International Journal of Fracture (NLD ISSN 0376-9429) **3347**
• ➤ International Journal of Franchising Law (GBR ISSN 1741-7392) **4871**
• ➤ International Journal of Francophone Studies (GBR ISSN 1368-2679) **7974**
International Journal of Frontier Missions (USA ISSN 0743-2429) **7650**
• International Journal of Fruit Science (USA ISSN 1553-8362) **237**
▼ • ➤ International Journal of Functional Informatics and Personalised Medicine (GBR ISSN 1756-2104) **5638**
International Journal of Fuzzy Systems (TWN ISSN 1562-2479) **2522**
• ➤ International Journal of Game Theory (DEU ISSN 0020-7276) **5496**
▼ • ➤ International Journal of Gaming and Computer-Mediated Simulations (USA ISSN 1942-3888) **2477**
▼ • International Journal of Gandhi Studies (USA ISSN 1941-2266) **7143**
International Journal of Gastrointestinal Cancer *see* Journal of Gastrointestinal Cancer **5896**
▼ • ➤ International Journal of Gender and Entrepreneurship (GBR ISSN 1756-6266) **1128**
▼ • ➤ International Journal of General Medicine (GBR ISSN 1178-7074) **5639**
International Journal of General Orthodontics (USA ISSN 1539-1450) **5849**
International Journal of General Practice and Primary Care *see* General Practice On-Line **5618**
• ➤ International Journal of General Systems (GBR ISSN 0308-1079) **2522**
▼ International Journal of General Topology (IND ISSN 0973-6751) **5496**
• International Journal of Generic Drugs (ISR ISSN 0793-694X) **6849**
• ➤ International Journal of Geographical Information Science (GBR ISSN 1365-8816) **4037**
International Journal of Geoinformatics (THA ISSN 1686-6576) **4016**
• ➤ International Journal of Geomagnetism and Aeronomy (USA ISSN 1524-4423) **2784**
• ➤ International Journal of Geomechanics (USA ISSN 1532-3641) **2748**
• International Journal of Geometric Methods in Modern Physics (SGP ISSN 0219-8878) **7016**
▼ • ➤ International Journal of Geophysics (USA ISSN 1687-885X) **2784**

Title

10446 INTERNATIONAL JOURNAL OF ISLAMIC AND MIDDLE EASTERN ULRICH'S PERIODICALS

▼ • International Journal of Islamic and Middle Eastern Finance and Management (GBR ISSN 1753-8394) **1357**
• International Journal of Islamic Financial Services (USA) **1128**
➤ International Journal of Islamic Studies (CAN ISSN 1206-789X) **552**
• ➤ International Journal of Jaina Studies (GBR ISSN 1748-1074) **7736**
International Journal of Japanese Society of Pediatric Dentistry *see* Pediatric Dental Journal **5860**
• ➤ International Journal of Japanese Sociology (AUS ISSN 0918-7545) **8109**
▼ • ➤ The International Journal of Jungian Studies (GBR ISSN 1940-9052) **7365**
• ➤ International Journal of Knowledge and Learning (GBR ISSN 1741-1009) **1758**
▼ • ➤ International Journal of Knowledge and Web Intelligence (GBR ISSN 1755-8255) **2559**
• International Journal of Knowledge-Based and Intelligent Engineering Systems (NLD ISSN 1327-2314) **2451**
▼ • ➤ International Journal of Knowledge-Based Development (GBR ISSN 2040-4468) **8109**
• ➤ International Journal of Knowledge, Culture and Change Management (AUS ISSN 1447-9524) **1128**
▼ • ➤ International Journal of Knowledge Engineering and Soft Data Paradigms (GBR ISSN 1755-3210) **2452**
• International Journal of Knowledge Management (USA ISSN 1548-0666) **1758**
▼ • ➤ International Journal of Knowledge Management in Tourism and Hospitality (GBR ISSN 1756-0322) **4391**
• ➤ International Journal of Knowledge Management Studies (GBR ISSN 1743-8268) **1758**
▼ • The International Journal of Korean Art and Archaeology (KOR ISSN 2005-1115) **398**
• International Journal of Korean History (KOR ISSN 1598-2041) **4184**
International Journal of Korean Unification Studies (KOR ISSN 1229-6902) **552**
• ➤ International Journal of Kurdish Studies (USA ISSN 1073-6697) **4321**
• International Journal of Laboratory Hematology (Online) (GBR ISSN 1751-553X) **5938**
• ➤ International Journal of Laboratory Hematology (Print) (GBR ISSN 1751-5521) **5938**
International Journal of Laboratory Medicine *see* Guoji Jianyan Yixue Zazhi **5622**
• ➤ International Journal of Lakes and Rivers (IND ISSN 0973-4570) **8826**
International Journal of Language and Communication *see* Rask **5165**
• ➤ International Journal of Language and Communication Disorders (GBR ISSN 1368-2822) **6081**
International Journal of Lateral Computing (IND ISSN 0973-208X) **2426**
• ➤ International Journal of Law and Information Technology (GBR ISSN 0967-0769) **4695**
• ➤ International Journal of Law and Management (GBR ISSN 1754-243X) **1689**
• ➤ International Journal of Law and Psychiatry (GBR ISSN 0160-2527) **4695**
• ➤ International Journal of Law Crime and Justice (GBR ISSN 1756-0616) **4695**
• International Journal of Law in Context (GBR ISSN 1744-5523) **4695**
▼ • ➤ International Journal of Law in the Built Environment (GBR ISSN 1756-1450) **3442**
• ➤ International Journal of Law, Policy and the Family (GBR ISSN 1360-9939) **4911**
• ➤ International Journal of Leadership in Education (GBR ISSN 1360-3124) **2870**
• The International Journal of Leadership in Public Service (GBR ISSN 1754-8187) **7447**
• ➤ International Journal of Leadership Studies (USA ISSN 1554-3145) **8109**
▼ • ➤ International Journal of Lean Enterprise Research (GBR ISSN 1754-2294) **1128**
▼ • ➤ International Journal of Lean Six Sigma (GBR) **1758**
• ➤ The International Journal of Learning (AUS ISSN 1447-9494) **2870**
• ➤ International Journal of Learning and Change (GBR ISSN 1740-2875) **1758**
• ➤ International Journal of Learning and Intellectual Capital (GBR ISSN 1479-4853) **1867**
▼ • International Journal of Learning and Media (USA ISSN 1943-6068) **8109**
• ➤ International Journal of Learning Technology (GBR ISSN 1477-8386) **8427**
• International Journal of Legal Information (USA ISSN 0731-1265) **5019**
▼ • ➤ International Journal of Legal Information Design (GBR ISSN 1750-8142) **4695**
• ➤ International Journal of Legal Medicine (Print) (DEU ISSN 0937-9827) **5914**
▼ • ➤ International Journal of Leisure and Tourism Marketing (GBR ISSN 1757-5567) **8723**
• ➤ International Journal of Leprosy and Other Mycobacterial Diseases (USA ISSN 0148-916X) **5818**
• ➤ International Journal of Lexicography (GBR ISSN 0950-3846) **5129**
▼ • ➤ International Journal of Liability and Scientific Enquiry (GBR ISSN 1741-6426) **7867**
• ➤ International Journal of Life Cycle Assessment (DEU ISSN 0948-3349) **3443**
• ➤ International Journal of Lifelong Education (GBR ISSN 0260-1370) **2942**
• ➤ International Journal of Listening (USA ISSN 1090-4018) **4457**
• ➤ International Journal of Logistics (GBR ISSN 1367-5567) **1128**
▼ • ➤ International Journal of Logistics Economics and Globalisation (GBR ISSN 1741-5373) **8499**
• ➤ The International Journal of Logistics Management (GBR ISSN 0957-4093) **1758**
• ➤ International Journal of Logistics Systems and Management (GBR ISSN 1742-7967) **1758**
• ➤ International Journal of Low-Carbon Technologies (GBR ISSN 1748-1317) **3443**
• ➤ International Journal of Low Energy and Sustainable Buildings (SWE ISSN 1403-2147) **3272**
• ➤ International Journal of Low Radiation (GBR ISSN 1477-6545) **3443**
• ➤ International Journal of Lower Extremity Wounds (USA ISSN 1534-7346) **5639**
International Journal of Luxury Intelligence *see* Luxury Intelligence **1145**
• ➤ International Journal of M S Care (Multiple Sclerosis) (USA ISSN 1537-2073) **6146**
• ➤ International Journal of Machine Tools and Manufacture (USA ISSN 0890-6955) **3369**
• ➤ International Journal of Machining and Machinability of Materials (GBR ISSN 1748-5711) **5453**
• International Journal of Magnetic Resonance Imaging (GBR ISSN 1749-8023) **6198**
• ➤ International Journal of Management (GBR ISSN 0813-0183) **1759**
• ➤ International Journal of Management and Decision Making (GBR ISSN 1462-4621) **1759**
• ➤ International Journal of Management and Enterprise Development (GBR ISSN 1468-4330) **1759**
▼ International Journal of Management and Innovation (TWN) **1759**
▼ International Journal of Management and Marketing Research (USA ISSN 1933-3153) **1759**
▼ • ➤ International Journal of Management and Network Economics (GBR ISSN 1754-2316) **1759**
International Journal of Management and Systems (IND ISSN 0970-7328) **1759**
• ➤ International Journal of Management Concepts and Philosophy (GBR ISSN 1478-1484) **1759**
▼ • ➤ International Journal of Management Development (GBR ISSN 1752-8240) **1759**
The International Journal of Management Education (GBR ISSN 1472-8117) **1759**
▼ • ➤ International Journal of Management in Education (GBR ISSN 1750-385X) **3013**
• International Journal of Management in Small and Medium Sized Enterprises (AUS ISSN 1441-5410) **1759**
▼ • ➤ International Journal of Management Perspectives (UKR ISSN 1307-1629) **1759**
• ➤ International Journal of Management Practice (GBR ISSN 1477-9064) **1759**
• International Journal of Management Reviews (GBR ISSN 1460-8545) **1759**
• International Journal of Management Science and Engineering Management (GBR ISSN 1750-9653) **3202**
International Journal of Management Sciences (IND ISSN 0973-2101) **1759**
➤ International Journal of Management Studies (RUS ISSN 1931-1400) **1759**
▼ • ➤ International Journal of Managerial and Financial Accounting (GBR ISSN 1753-6715) **1292**
• ➤ International Journal of Managerial Finance (GBR ISSN 1743-9132) **1357**
▼ • ➤ International Journal of Managing Projects in Business (GBR ISSN 1753-8378) **1759**
• ➤ International Journal of Manpower (GBR ISSN 0143-7720) **1689**
• ➤ International Journal of Manufacturing Research (GBR ISSN 1750-0591) **3382**
• ➤ International Journal of Manufacturing Technology and Management (GBR ISSN 1368-2148) **3382**
• ➤ The International Journal of Marine and Coastal Law (NLD ISSN 0927-3522) **4969**
International Journal of Maritime Engineering *see* Royal Institution of Naval Architects. Transactions. Part A. International Journal of Maritime Engineering **8659**
➤ International Journal of Maritime History (CAN ISSN 0843-8714) **8647**
• ➤ International Journal of Market Research (GBR ISSN 1470-7853) **1821**
➤ International Journal of Marketing Research (USA ISSN 1559-5048) **1821**
• ➤ International Journal of Mass Customisation (GBR ISSN 1742-4208) **1889**
➤ International Journal of Mass Emergencies and Disasters (USA ISSN 0280-7270) **8047**
• ➤ International Journal of Mass Spectrometry (NLD ISSN 1387-3806) **7077**
▼ • ➤ International Journal of Material Forming (FRA ISSN 1960-6206) **3347**
• ➤ International Journal of Materials and Product Technology (GBR ISSN 0268-1900) **3347**
▼ • ➤ International Journal of Materials and Structural Integrity (GBR ISSN 1745-0055) **3202**
▼ • ➤ International Journal of Materials Engineering Innovation (GBR ISSN 1757-2754) **3347**
• International Journal of Materials Research (DEU ISSN 1862-5282) **6316**
• ➤ International Journal of Materials Science (IND ISSN 0973-4589) **3347**
▼ • ➤ International Journal of Mathematical Analysis (BGR ISSN 1312-8876) **5496**
➤ International Journal of Mathematical and Statistical Sciences (BRA ISSN 1055-7490) **5496**
▼ • ➤ International Journal of Mathematical Combinatorics (USA ISSN 1937-1055) **5496**
▼ • ➤ International Journal of Mathematical Education (IND) **5496**
• ➤ International Journal of Mathematical Education in Science and Technology (GBR ISSN 0020-739X) **5496**
International Journal of Mathematical Inequalities and Applications (IND) **5496**
▼ • ➤ International Journal of Mathematical Modelling and Numerical Optimisation (GBR ISSN 2040-3607) **5496**
▼ • ➤ International Journal of Mathematical, Physical and Engineering Sciences (TUR ISSN 1307-7465) **5496**
International Journal of Mathematical Sciences (IND ISSN 0972-754X) **5496**
• ➤ International Journal of Mathematics (SGP ISSN 0129-167X) **5497**
International Journal of Mathematics and Analysis (IND ISSN 0973-3604) **5497**
• ➤ International Journal of Mathematics and Computer Science (LBN ISSN 1814-0424) **5553**
• ➤ International Journal of Mathematics and Mathematical Sciences (USA ISSN 0161-1712) **5497**
• International Journal of Mathematics, Game Theory and Algebra (USA ISSN 1099-1859) **5497**
▼ • ➤ International Journal of Mathematics in Operational Research (GBR ISSN 1757-5850) **5497**
International Journal of Mathematics Sciences *see* International Journal of Mathematical, Physical and Engineering Sciences **5496**
▼ • ➤ International Journal of Meat Science (PAK ISSN 2071-7113) **3648**
International Journal of Mechanical Diagnosis and Therapy (NZL ISSN 1902-8016) **6062**
• International Journal of Mechanical Engineering Education (GBR ISSN 0306-4190) **3202**
• ➤ International Journal of Mechanical Sciences (GBR ISSN 0020-7403) **3347**
▼ • ➤ International Journal of Mechanical Systems Science and Engineering (TUR ISSN 1307-7473) **3292**
• International Journal of Mechanics and Materials in Design (NLD ISSN 1569-1713) **3347**
• ➤ International Journal of Mechanics and Solids (IND ISSN 0973-1881) **3347**
▼ • ➤ International Journal of Mechatronics and Manufacturing Systems (GBR ISSN 1753-1039) **3382**
• International Journal of Media and Cultural Politics (GBR ISSN 1740-8296) **2327**
▼ • ➤ International Journal of Media & Foreign Affairs (USA ISSN 1940-9311) **7243**
The International Journal of Media Justice (GBR ISSN 1471-4426) **2870**
• International Journal of Medical and Biological Frontiers (USA ISSN 1081-3829) **5639**
▼ • ➤ International Journal of Medical Engineering and Informatics (GBR ISSN 1755-0653) **5831**
• ➤ International Journal of Medical Informatics (IRL ISSN 1386-5056) **5831**
International Journal of Medical Marketing (Online) *see* Journal of Medical Marketing (Online) **6854**
International Journal of Medical Marketing (Print) *see* Journal of Medical Marketing (Print) **6854**
• ➤ International Journal of Medical Microbiology (DEU ISSN 1438-4221) **5818**
International Journal of Medical Radiology *see* Guoji Yixue Fangshexue Zazhi **6197**
• International Journal of Medical Robotics and Computer Assisted Surgery (GBR ISSN 1478-5951) **5906**
• ➤ International Journal of Medical Sciences (AUS ISSN 1449-1907) **5639**
• International Journal of Medical Toxicology and Legal Medicine (IND ISSN 0972-0448) **3498**
• ➤ International Journal of Medicinal Mushrooms (USA ISSN 1521-9437) **794**
International Journal of Medicine *see* Shijie Yixue Zazhi **5713**
International Journal of Medicine *see* Medicine On-Line **5674**
International Journal of Medicine (London) (GBR ISSN 1468-3814) **5639**
International Journal of Medicine and Science of Physical Activity and Sport *see* Revista Internacional de Medicina y Ciencias de la Actividad Fisica y del Deporte **6232**
• ➤ International Journal of Men's Health (USA ISSN 1532-6306) **6284**
• ➤ International Journal of Mental Health (USA ISSN 0020-7411) **7365**
• International Journal of Mental Health and Addiction (USA ISSN 1557-1874) **7365**
• ➤ International Journal of Mental Health Nursing (AUS ISSN 1445-8330) **6146**
• ➤ The International Journal of Mental Health Promotion (GBR ISSN 1462-3730) **7526**
▼ • ➤ International Journal of Mental Health Systems (GBR ISSN 1752-4458) **6147**
• ➤ International Journal of Metadata, Semantics and Ontologies (GBR ISSN 1744-2621) **2559**
▼ • International Journal of Metaheuristics (GBR ISSN 1755-2176) **2426**
▼ International Journal of Metalcasting (USA ISSN 1939-5981) **6317**
➤ The International Journal of Meteorology (GBR ISSN 1748-2992) **6358**
• ➤ International Journal of Methods in Psychiatric Research (GBR ISSN 1049-8931) **6147**
▼ • ➤ International Journal of Micro Air Vehicles (GBR ISSN 1756-8293) **61**
▼ • ➤ International Journal of Micro-Nano Scale Transport (GBR ISSN 1759-3093) **3382**
▼ • ➤ International Journal of Microbiology (USA ISSN 1687-918X) **888**
• ➤ International Journal of Micrographics & Optical Technology (GBR ISSN 0958-9961) **2487**
• ➤ International Journal of Microstructure and Materials Properties (GBR ISSN 1741-8410) **3347**
• ➤ International Journal of Microwave and Optical Technology (USA ISSN 1553-0396) **7077**
• International Journal of Microwave and Wireless Technologies (GBR ISSN 1759-0787) **3321**
▼ • ➤ International Journal of Microwave Science and Technology (USA ISSN 1687-5826) **3321**
• ➤ International Journal of Middle East Studies (GBR ISSN 0020-7438) **552**
• International Journal of Migration, Health and Social Care (GBR ISSN 1747-9894) **8047**
• ➤ International Journal of Mineral Processing (NLD ISSN 0301-7516) **6466**
▼ • ➤ International Journal of Mining and Mineral Engineering (GBR ISSN 1754-890X) **6466**
• ➤ International Journal of Mining, Reclamation and Environment (GBR ISSN 1748-0930) **6466**
▼ • International Journal of Mobile and Blended Learning (USA ISSN 1941-8647) **2949**
• ➤ International Journal of Mobile Communications (GBR ISSN 1470-949X) **2327**
▼ • International Journal of Mobile Computing and Multimedia Communications (USA ISSN 1937-9412) **2426**
▼ • International Journal of Mobile Human Computer Interaction (USA ISSN 1942-390X) **2452**
• ➤ International Journal of Mobile Learning and Organisation (GBR ISSN 1746-725X) **1759**
International Journal of Mobile Marketing (USA ISSN 1939-1161) **1822**
• ➤ International Journal of Mobile Network Design and Innovation (GBR ISSN 1744-2869) **2351**
➤ International Journal of Modelling & Simulation (CAN ISSN 0228-6203) **3347**
• ➤ International Journal of Modelling, Identification and Control (GBR ISSN 1746-6172) **2462**
• International Journal of Modern Engineering (USA ISSN 1930-6628) **3202**
• International Journal of Modern Mathematics (USA ISSN 1559-3894) **5497**
• ➤ International Journal of Modern Physics A (SGP ISSN 0217-751X) **7017**
• ➤ International Journal of Modern Physics B (SGP ISSN 0217-9792) **7017**
• ➤ International Journal of Modern Physics C: Physics and Computers (SGP ISSN 0129-1831) **7017**
• ➤ International Journal of Modern Physics D: Gravitation, Astrophysics and Cosmology (SGP ISSN 0218-2718) **7017**
• ➤ International Journal of Modern Physics E (SGP ISSN 0218-3013) **7067**
▼ • ➤ International Journal of Molecular Engineering (GBR ISSN 1743-8241) **749**
▼ • ➤ International Journal of Molecular Genetics (IND) **873**
• ➤ International Journal of Molecular Medicine (GRC ISSN 1107-3756) **5639**
• International Journal of Molecular Sciences (CD-ROM) (CHE ISSN 1424-6783) **2124**
• ➤ International Journal of Molecular Sciences (Online) (CHE ISSN 1422-0067) **2124**
▼ • ➤ International Journal of Monetary Economics and Finance (GBR ISSN 1752-0479) **1357**
▼ • ➤ International Journal of Mormon Studies (GBR ISSN 1757-5532) **7737**
• ➤ International Journal of Morphology (CHL ISSN 0717-9367) **5639**
The International Journal of Morse Telegraphy *see* Morsum Magnificat **2370**
• ➤ International Journal of Motorcycle Studies (USA ISSN 1931-275X) **8260**
▼ • ➤ International Journal of Multicriteria Decision Making (GBR ISSN 2040-106X) **2452**
• ➤ International Journal of Multicultural Education (USA ISSN 1934-5267) **2870**
▼ • ➤ International Journal of Multidisciplinary Research (USA ISSN 1934-6840) **2870**
• The International Journal of Multilingualism (GBR ISSN 1479-0718) **5129**
• ➤ International Journal of Multiphase Flow (GBR ISSN 0301-9322) **3382**
▼ • ➤ The International Journal of Multiphysics (GBR ISSN 1750-9548) **7017**

▼ • International Journal of Multiple Research Approaches (AUS ISSN 1834-0806) **1760**
• International Journal of Multiscale Computational Engineering (USA ISSN 1543-1649) **3272**
International Journal of Mushroom Research and Development *see* Mushroom Research **802**
• ➤ International Journal of Music Education (GBR ISSN 0255-7614) **6577**
International Journal of Musicology (DEU ISSN 0941-9535) **6577**
▼ • International Journal of Myriapodology (NLD ISSN 1875-2535) **850**
▼ • ➤ International Journal of Nano and Biomaterials (GBR ISSN 1752-8933) **7867**
• ➤ International Journal of Nanomanufacturing (GBR ISSN 1746-9392) **3382**
▼ ➤ International Journal of Nanomechanics Science and Technology (USA ISSN 1947-5748) **3202**
• ➤ International Journal of Nanomedicine (Online) (GBR ISSN 1178-2013) **6849**
† • ➤ International Journal of Nanomedicine (Print) (NZL ISSN 1176-9114) **8966**
▼ • ➤ International Journal of Nanoparticles (GBR ISSN 1753-2507) **766**
• ➤ International Journal of Nanoscience (SGP ISSN 0219-581X) **2571**
• ➤ International Journal of Nanotechnology (GBR ISSN 1475-7435) **3347**
▼ • International Journal of Nanotechnology and Applications (IND ISSN 0973-631X) **3347**
▼ • International Journal of Nanotechnology and Molecular Computation (USA ISSN 1941-6318) **7017**
• ➤ International Journal of Narrative Therapy and Community Work (AUS ISSN 1446-5019) **7365**
➤ International Journal of Natural and Applied Sciences (NGA ISSN 0794-4713) **7867**
▼ • ➤ International Journal of Natural and Engineering Sciences (TUR ISSN 1307-1149) **7867**
▼ • ➤ International Journal of Natural Products and Pharmaceutical Sciences (MYS ISSN 1985-0735) **6849**
• ➤ International Journal of Nautical Archaeology (GBR ISSN 1057-2414) **398**
• International Journal of Naval History (USA ISSN 1932-6556) **4147**
▼ • ➤ International Journal of Navigation and Observation (USA ISSN 1687-5990) **4037**
➤ International Journal of Nematology (GBR ISSN 1368-8774) **948**
▼ • ➤ International Journal of Nephrology and Renovascular Disease (GBR ISSN 1178-7058) **6269**
• ➤ International Journal of Network Management (GBR ISSN 1055-7148) **2327**
• International Journal of Network Security (TWN ISSN 1816-353X) **2515**
▼ • ➤ International Journal of Networking and Computer Engineering (IND) **2499**
• ➤ International Journal of Networking and Virtual Organisations (GBR ISSN 1470-9503) **2499**
• ➤ International Journal of Neural Systems (SGP ISSN 0129-0657) **2452**
• ➤ International Journal of Neuropsychopharmacology (GBR ISSN 1461-1457) **6850**
• ➤ International Journal of Neuroscience (GBR ISSN 0020-7454) **6147**
• International Journal of New Product Development & Innovation Management (GBR ISSN 1464-6684) **1760**
➤ International Journal of Non-Equilibrium Processing (GBR ISSN 1368-9290) **6317**
• ➤ International Journal of Non-Linear Mechanics (GBR ISSN 0020-7462) **3347**
• ➤ International Journal of Nonlinear Modelling in Science and Engineering (GBR ISSN 1472-085X) **5497**
• International Journal of Nonlinear Science (GBR ISSN 1749-3889) **7017**
International Journal of Nonlinear Sciences and Numerical Simulation (ISR ISSN 1565-1339) **5497**
• ➤ International Journal of Nonprofit and Voluntary Sector Marketing (GBR ISSN 1465-4520) **1822**
International Journal of Nonviolence (USA ISSN 1069-2541) **8109**
• International Journal of Not-for-Profit Law (USA ISSN 1556-5157) **4695**
• ➤ International Journal of Nuclear Desalination (GBR ISSN 1476-914X) **8826**
• ➤ International Journal of Nuclear Energy Science and Technology (GBR ISSN 1741-6361) **3169**
• ➤ International Journal of Nuclear Governance, Economy and Ecology (GBR ISSN 1742-4186) **3169**
• ➤ International Journal of Nuclear Hydrogen Production and Applications (GBR ISSN 1743-4939) **3169**
• ➤ International Journal of Nuclear Knowledge Management (GBR ISSN 1479-540X) **3169**
• ➤ International Journal of Nuclear Law (GBR ISSN 1741-6388) **4695**
• ➤ International Journal of Number Theory (SGP ISSN 1793-0421) **5497**
➤ International Journal of Numerical Analysis and Modeling (CAN ISSN 1705-5105) **5497**
• ➤ International Journal of Numerical Methods for Heat and Fluid Flow (GBR ISSN 0961-5539) **3272**
• ➤ International Journal of Numerical Modelling: Electronic Networks, Devices and Fields (GBR ISSN 0894-3370) **3292**
• ➤ International Journal of Nursing Education Scholarship (USA ISSN 1548-923X) **5962**
• ➤ International Journal of Nursing in Intellectual and Developmental Disabilities (USA ISSN 1941-2800) **5962**
• ➤ International Journal of Nursing Practice (AUS ISSN 1322-7114) **5962**
• ➤ International Journal of Nursing Studies (GBR ISSN 0020-7489) **5962**
• ➤ The International Journal of Nursing Terminologies and Classifications (USA ISSN 1541-5147) **5962**
• ➤ International Journal of Obesity (GBR ISSN 0307-0565) **6660**
International Journal of Obesity and Related Metabolic Disorders *see* International Journal of Obesity **6660**
• ➤ International Journal of Obstetric Anesthesia (GBR ISSN 0959-289X) **5994**
• ➤ International Journal of Occupational and Environmental Health (USA ISSN 1077-3525) **6679**
• ➤ International Journal of Occupational Medicine and Environmental Health (POL ISSN 1232-1087) **6679**
• ➤ International Journal of Occupational Safety and Ergonomics (POL ISSN 1080-3548) **6679**
▼ • ➤ International Journal of Ocean and Climate Systems (GBR ISSN 1759-3131) **2808**
▼ • ➤ International Journal of Ocean Systems Management (GBR ISSN 1752-6582) **8647**
• ➤ International Journal of Oceanography (USA ISSN 1687-9406) **2808**
• ➤ International Journal of Oceans and Oceanography (IND ISSN 0973-2667) **2808**
➤ International Journal of Odonatology (GBR ISSN 1388-7890) **850**
▼ • International Journal of Odontostomatology (CHL ISSN 0718-3801) **5849**
• ➤ International Journal of Offender Therapy and Comparative Criminology (USA ISSN 0306-624X) **2655**
➤ International Journal of Offshore and Polar Engineering (USA ISSN 1053-5381) **3383**
▼ • ➤ International Journal of Oil, Gas and Coal Technology (GBR ISSN 1753-3309) **6774**
• International Journal of Oil Palm (IND ISSN 0972-5806) **123**
• ➤ International Journal of Older People Nursing (GBR ISSN 1748-3735) **5962**
• ➤ International Journal of Oncology (GRC ISSN 1019-6439) **6023**
• ➤ International Journal of Online Engineering (DEU ISSN 1861-2121) **8427**
▼ • ➤ International Journal of Open Problems in Complex Analysis (JOR ISSN 2074-2827) **5497**
▼ • ➤ International Journal of Open Problems in Computer Science and Mathematics (JOR ISSN 1998-6262) **2426**
▼ • ➤ International Journal of Open Source Software & Processes (USA ISSN 1942-3926) **2592**
• ➤ International Journal of Operational Research (GBR ISSN 1745-7645) **1760**
• ➤ International Journal of Operations and Production Management (GBR ISSN 0144-3577) **1760**
• ➤ International Journal of Operations and Quantitative Management (USA ISSN 1082-1910) **1760**
International Journal of Ophthalmology *see* Guoji Yanke Zazhi **6043**
International Journal of Opportunity, Growth and Value Creation *see* International Journal of Entrepreneurial Venturing **1757**
• ➤ International Journal of Optics (USA ISSN 1687-9384) **7077**
▼ • ➤ International Journal of Optomechatronics (USA ISSN 1559-9612) **3383**
• ➤ International Journal of Oral & Maxillofacial Implants (USA ISSN 0882-2786) **5849**
• ➤ International Journal of Oral and Maxillofacial Surgery (GBR ISSN 0901-5027) **5849**
International Journal of Oral and Maxillofacial Surgery. Supplement *see* International Journal of Oral and Maxillofacial Surgery **5849**
International Journal of Oral Biology (KOR ISSN 1226-7155) **5849**
• ➤ International Journal of Organisational Behaviour (AUS ISSN 1440-5377) **7365**
▼ • ➤ International Journal of Organisational Design and Engineering (GBR ISSN 1758-9797) **1128**
• ➤ International Journal of Organization Theory and Behavior (USA ISSN 1093-4537) **7447**
• ➤ International Journal of Organizational Analysis (GBR ISSN 1934-8835) **1760**
▼ • ➤ International Journal of Organizational Innovation (USA ISSN 1943-1813) **1760**
International Journal of Ornithology *see* Lundiana **687**
The International Journal of Orofacial Myology (USA ISSN 0735-0120) **5849**
• ➤ International Journal of Osteoarchaeology (GBR ISSN 1047-482X) **343**
• ➤ International Journal of Osteopathic Medicine (GBR ISSN 1746-0689) **6062**
▼ • ➤ International Journal of Osteoporosis and Metabolic Disorders (PAK ISSN 1994-5442) **6062**
▼ • ➤ International Journal of Otolaryngology (USA ISSN 1687-9201) **6081**
International Journal of Ozone Therapy (ITA ISSN 1972-3539) **310**
International Journal of P E P E Inc *see* International Journal of Practical Experiences in Professional Education **2870**
• ➤ International Journal of P I X E (Particle-Induced X-ray Emission) (SGP ISSN 0129-0835) **7067**
• ➤ International Journal of Paediatric Dentistry (Online) (GBR ISSN 1365-263X) **5849**
• ➤ International Journal of Paediatric Dentistry (Print) (GBR ISSN 0960-7439) **5849**
• ➤ International Journal of Palliative Nursing (GBR ISSN 1357-6321) **5962**
• ➤ International Journal of Parallel, Emergent and Distributed Systems (GBR ISSN 1744-5760) **2507**
• ➤ International Journal of Parallel Programming (USA ISSN 0885-7458) **2507**
International Journal of Parasychology (USA ISSN 0553-206X) **6742**
• ➤ International Journal of Pattern Recognition and Artificial Intelligence (SGP ISSN 0218-0014) **2452**
• ➤ The International Journal of Pavement Engineering (GBR ISSN 1029-8436) **3272**
➤ The International Journal of Pavement Engineering & Asphalt Technology (GBR ISSN 1464-8164) **3273**
• ➤ International Journal of Peace Studies (TWN ISSN 1085-7494) **7143**
• ➤ International Journal of Pedagogies and Learning (AUS ISSN 1833-4105) **3065**
▼ • International Journal of Pediatric Endocrinology (USA ISSN 1687-9848) **5895**
• ➤ International Journal of Pediatric Obesity (GBR ISSN 1747-7166) **6661**
• ➤ International Journal of Pediatric Otorhinolaryngology (GBR ISSN 0165-5876) **6081**
International Journal of Pediatric Otorhinolaryngology Extra *see* International Journal of Pediatric Otorhinolaryngology **6081**
▼ • International Journal of Pediatrics (USA ISSN 1687-9740) **6093**
• ➤ International Journal of Peptide Research and Therapeutics (NLD ISSN 1573-3149) **734**
• ➤ International Journal of Performability Engineering (IND ISSN 0973-1318) **3202**
• International Journal of Performance Analysis in Sport (GBR) **8180**
• ➤ International Journal of Performance Arts and Digital Media (GBR ISSN 1479-4713) **8471**
• ➤ International Journal of Periodontics & Restorative Dentistry (USA ISSN 0198-7569) **5849**
• ➤ International Journal of Pervasive Computing and Communications (GBR ISSN 1742-7371) **2426**
• ➤ International Journal of Pest Management (GBR ISSN 0967-0874) **237**
▼ • ➤ International Journal of Petroleum Engineering (GBR ISSN 1754-8888) **6774**
▼ • ➤ International Journal of Petroleum Science and Technology (IND ISSN 0973-6328) **6774**
▼ • ➤ International Journal of Pharmaceutical and Healthcare Marketing (GBR ISSN 1750-6123) **1822**
• ➤ International Journal of Pharmaceutical Compounding (USA ISSN 1092-4221) **6850**
International Journal of Pharmaceutical Medicine *see* Pharmaceutical Medicine **6869**
International Journal of Pharmaceutical Research *see* Guoji Yaoxue Yanjiu Zazhi **6845**
• ➤ International Journal of Pharmaceutics (NLD ISSN 0378-5173) **6850**
• ➤ International Journal of Pharmacology (PAK ISSN 1811-7775) **6850**
▼ • International Journal of Pharmacy and Pharmaceutical Sciences (IND) **6850**
• ➤ International Journal of Pharmacy Education (USA ISSN 1557-1017) **6850**
• ➤ International Journal of Pharmacy Practice (GBR ISSN 0961-7671) **6850**
▼ International Journal of PharmTech Research (IND ISSN 0974-4304) **6850**
• International Journal of Philosophical Practice (USA ISSN 1531-7900) **6926**
• ➤ International Journal of Philosophical Studies (GBR ISSN 0967-2559) **6926**
International Journal of Philosophical Studies Online *see* International Journal of Philosophical Studies **6926**
• ➤ International Journal of Photoenergy (USA ISSN 1110-662X) **2136**
• ➤ International Journal of Physical Distribution & Logistics Management (GBR ISSN 0960-0035) **8671**
• International Journal of Physical Education/Internationale Zeitschrift fuer Sportpaedagogik (DEU ISSN 0341-8685) **3065**
➤ International Journal of Physical Modelling in Geotechnics (JPN ISSN 1346-213X) **3273**
• ➤ International Journal of Physical Sciences (USA ISSN 1992-1950) **7017**
▼ • ➤ International Journal of Physiology, Pathophysiology and Pharmacology (USA ISSN 1944-8171) **5639**
▼ • ➤ International Journal of Physiotherapy and Life Physics (GBR ISSN 2040-4549) **311**
• ➤ International Journal of Phytoremediation (USA ISSN 1522-6514) **3443**
▼ International Journal of Plant Breeding (GBR ISSN 1752-3478) **794**
• International Journal of Plant Breeding and Genetics (USA ISSN 1819-3595) **794**
▼ International Journal of Plant Developmental Biology (GBR ISSN 1749-4753) **794**
International Journal of Plant Engineering and Management (CHN ISSN 1007-4546) **3202**
• ➤ International Journal of Plant Genomics (USA ISSN 1687-5370) **873**
• ➤ International Journal of Plant Production (IRN ISSN 1735-6814) **795**
• ➤ International Journal of Plant Sciences (USA ISSN 1058-5893) **795**
▼ • ➤ International Journal of Plasma Science and Engineering (USA ISSN 1687-6245) **7017**
• ➤ International Journal of Plasticity (GBR ISSN 0749-6419) **3348**
• ➤ International Journal of Plastics Technology (IND ISSN 0972-656X) **7093**
• ➤ International Journal of Play Therapy (USA ISSN 1555-6824) **7365**
▼ • ➤ International Journal of Pluralism and Economics Education (GBR ISSN 1757-5648) **1128**
➤ International Journal of Poetry & Poets (CAN ISSN 1206-7881) **5424**
• International Journal of Police Science and Management (GBR ISSN 1461-3557) **2655**
• ➤ International Journal of Political Economy (USA ISSN 0891-1916) **7144**
International Journal of Political Thought *see* Revista Internacional de Pensamiento Politico **7178**
International Journal of Politics and Ethics *see* International Journal of Ethics **7143**
• ➤ International Journal of Politics, Culture, and Society (USA ISSN 0891-4486) **7243**
• ➤ International Journal of Polymer Analysis & Characterization (USA ISSN 1023-666X) **3247**
• ➤ International Journal of Polymer Science (USA ISSN 1687-9422) **3247**
• ➤ International Journal of Polymeric Materials (USA ISSN 0091-4037) **3247**
• ➤ International Journal of Postharvest Technology and Innovation (GBR ISSN 1744-7550) **201**
• ➤ International Journal of Poultry Science (PAK ISSN 1682-8356) **289**
International Journal of Powder Metallurgy (USA ISSN 0888-7462) **6317**
▼ • ➤ International Journal of Power and Energy Conversion (GBR ISSN 1757-1154) **3159**
International Journal of Power and Energy Systems (CAN ISSN 1078-3466) **3139**
▼ • ➤ International Journal of Power Electronics (GBR ISSN 1756-638X) **3105**
▼ • International Journal of Power Management Electronics (USA ISSN 1687-6679) **3105**
▼ International Journal of Power Systems & Power Electronics (IND ISSN 0973-8886) **3383**
▼ • ➤ International Journal of Powertrain (GBR ISSN 1742-4267) **8619**
International Journal of Practical Approaches to Disability *see* International Journal of Disability, Community & Rehabilitation **3041**
• International Journal of Practical Experiences in Professional Education (AUS ISSN 1832-276X) **2870**
• ➤ International Journal of Practical Theology (DEU ISSN 1430-6921) **7650**
• ➤ International Journal of Precision Engineering and Manufacturing (KOR ISSN 1229-8557) **3348**
▼ • ➤ International Journal of Precision Technology (GBR ISSN 1755-2060) **3202**
• ➤ International Journal of Press / Politics (USA ISSN 1940-1612) **4577**
• ➤ International Journal of Pressure Vessels and Piping (GBR ISSN 0308-0161) **3383**
▼ • ➤ International Journal of Prevention Practice and Research (USA ISSN 1941-8418) **5639**
▼ • International Journal of Primary Research (GBR ISSN 2040-8110) **1128**
• ➤ International Journal of Primatology (USA ISSN 0164-0291) **948**
• International Journal of Prisoner Health (USA ISSN 1744-9200) **7527**
▼ • ➤ International Journal of Private Law (GBR ISSN 1753-6235) **4695**
➤ International Journal of Probiotics & Prebiotics (USA ISSN 1555-1431) **888**
• ➤ International Journal of Process Management and Benchmarking (GBR ISSN 1460-6739) **1760**
▼ • ➤ International Journal of Process Systems Engineering (GBR ISSN 1757-6342) **3202**
▼ • ➤ International Journal of Procurement Management (GBR ISSN 1753-8432) **1760**
International Journal of Product Design and Manufacture for Sustainability *see* International Journal of Sustainable Manufacturing **3383**
• ➤ International Journal of Product Development (GBR ISSN 1477-9056) **1760**
• ➤ International Journal of Product Lifecycle Management (GBR ISSN 1743-5110) **1822**

Title

10448 INTERNATIONAL JOURNAL OF PRODUCT SOUND QUALITY ULRICH'S PERIODICALS

▼ • ➤ International Journal of Product Sound Quality (GBR ISSN 1742-6758) **8153**
• ➤ International Journal of Production Economics (NLD ISSN 0925-5273) **3369**
• ➤ International Journal of Production Research (GBR ISSN 0020-7543) **1889**
• ➤ International Journal of Productivity and Performance Management (GBR ISSN 1741-0401) **1760**
• ➤ International Journal of Productivity and Quality Management (GBR ISSN 1746-6474) **1760**
• ➤ International Journal of Progressive Education (USA ISSN 1554-5210) **2870**
• ➤ International Journal of Project Management (GBR ISSN 0263-7863) **1419**
▼ • ➤ International Journal of Project Organisation and Management (GBR ISSN 1740-2891) **1760**
• ➤ International Journal of Prosthodontics (USA ISSN 0893-2174) **5849**
▼ • International Journal of Protective Structures (GBR ISSN 2041-4196) **3273**
† • ➤ The International Journal of Psychiatric Nursing Research (GBR ISSN 0968-0624) **8966**
• ➤ International Journal of Psychiatry in Clinical Practice (GBR ISSN 1365-1501) **6147**
• ➤ The International Journal of Psychiatry in Medicine (USA ISSN 0091-2174) **6147**
• ➤ The International Journal of Psychoanalysis (GBR ISSN 0020-7578) **7365**
• International Journal of Psychoanalytic Self Psychology (USA ISSN 1555-1024) **7365**
• ➤ International Journal of Psychology/Journal International de Psychologie (GBR ISSN 0020-7594) **7365**
▼ • ➤ International Journal of Psychology: A Biopsychosocial Approach (LTU ISSN 1941-7233) **7365**
International Journal of Psychology and Psychological Therapy *see* Revista Internacional de Psicologia y Terapia Psicologica **7404**
• International Journal of Psychology Research (USA ISSN 1098-4127) **7365**
• ➤ International Journal of Psychopathology, Psychopharmacology, and Psychotherapy (USA ISSN 1088-6710) **7365**
• ➤ International Journal of Psychophysiology (NLD ISSN 0167-8760) **7365**
• ➤ International Journal of Psychosocial Rehabilitation (GBR ISSN 1475-7192) **7366**
• ➤ International Journal of Public Administration (USA ISSN 0190-0692) **7447**
• ➤ International Journal of Public Health/Medecine Sociale et Preventive/Social and Preventive Medicine (CHE ISSN 1661-8556) **5639**
• International Journal of Public Information Systems (SWE ISSN 1653-4360) **2426**
• ➤ International Journal of Public Opinion Research (GBR ISSN 0954-2892) **7144**
• ➤ International Journal of Public Policy (GBR ISSN 1740-0600) **7447**
• ➤ International Journal of Public Sector Management (GBR ISSN 0951-3558) **1761**
▼ • ➤ International Journal of Public Sector Performance Management (GBR ISSN 1741-1041) **7447**
International Journal of Public Services, Economics and Management *see* International Journal of Services, Economics and Management **1761**
▼ • International Journal of Public Theology (NLD ISSN 1872-5171) **7650**
• ➤ The International Journal of Punishment and Sentencing (AUS ISSN 1449-9045) **4953**
International Journal of Punjab Studies *see* Journal of Punjab Studies **7979**
• International Journal of Pure and Applied Mathematical Sciences (IND ISSN 0972-9828) **5497**
➤ International Journal of Pure and Applied Mathematics (BGR ISSN 1311-8080) **5497**
• ➤ International Journal of Pure and Applied Physics (IND ISSN 0973-1776) **7017**
• ➤ International Journal of Qualitative Methods (CAN ISSN 1609-4069) **7974**
• ➤ International Journal of Qualitative Studies in Education (GBR ISSN 0951-8398) **2870**
• International Journal of Qualitative Studies on Health and Well-Being (GBR ISSN 1748-2623) **5639**
▼ • ➤ International Journal of Quality and Innovation (GBR ISSN 1756-6975) **1128**
• International Journal of Quality and Productivity Management (USA ISSN 1935-8032) **1761**
• ➤ International Journal of Quality & Reliability Management (GBR ISSN 0265-671X) **1761**
▼ • ➤ International Journal of Quality and Service Sciences (GBR ISSN 1756-669X) **1890**
▼ • The International Journal of Quality and Standards (GBR ISSN 1753-9439) **2987**
▼ • ➤ International Journal of Quality, Statistics, and Reliability (USA ISSN 1687-7144) **3202**
• ➤ International Journal of Quantum Chemistry (USA ISSN 0020-7608) **2065**
• ➤ International Journal of Quantum Information (SGP ISSN 0219-7499) **7017**
International Journal of R F and Microwave Computer-Aided Engineering (Online) *see* International Journal of R F and Microwave Computer-Aided Engineering (Print) **3292**
• ➤ International Journal of R F and Microwave Computer-Aided Engineering (Print) (USA ISSN 1096-4290) **3292**
▼ • ➤ International Journal of R F Technologies (Radio Frequency) (GBR ISSN 1754-5730) **2359**
• ➤ International Journal of Radiation Biology (GBR ISSN 0955-3002) **6023**
International Journal of Radiation Medicine *see* Mezhdunarodnyi Zhurnal Radiatsionnoi Meditsiny **6203**
• ➤ International Journal of Radiation: Oncology - Biology - Physics (USA ISSN 0360-3016) **6199**
International Journal of Radiation: Oncology - Biology - Physics. Supplement *see* International Journal of Radiation: Oncology - Biology - Physics **6199**
• ➤ International Journal of Radio Frequency Identification Technology and Applications (GBR ISSN 1745-3216) **2359**
▼ • ➤ International Journal of Rapid Manufacturing (GBR ISSN 1757-8817) **3202**
▼ • ➤ International Journal of Reacting Systems (USA ISSN 1687-6016) **7055**
• ➤ International Journal of Reality Therapy (USA ISSN 1099-7717) **7366**
▼ • ➤ International Journal of Reasoning-Based Intelligent Systems (GBR ISSN 1755-0556) **2452**
▼ • ➤ International Journal of Reconfigurable Computing (USA ISSN 1687-7195) **2472**
• ➤ International Journal of Refractory Metals and Hard Materials (GBR ISSN 0958-0611) **6317**
• ➤ International Journal of Refrigeration/Revue Internationale du Froid (GBR ISSN 0140-7007) **4122**
• ➤ International Journal of Refugee Law (GBR ISSN 0953-8186) **7243**
• ➤ The International Journal of Regional and Local Studies (GBR ISSN 1750-0478) **4232**
• International Journal of Regulation and Governance (IND ISSN 0972-4907) **7243**
• ➤ International Journal of Rehabilitation Research (USA ISSN 0342-5282) **6110**
➤ International Journal of Reliability and Applications (KOR ISSN 1598-0073) **3202**
• ➤ International Journal of Reliability and Safety (GBR ISSN 1479-389X) **3202**
• ➤ International Journal of Reliability, Quality & Safety Engineering (SGP ISSN 0218-5393) **3202**
▼ • International Journal of Religion and Society (USA ISSN 1935-2409) **8109**
• ➤ International Journal of Remote Sensing (GBR ISSN 0143-1161) **2710**
▼ • ➤ International Journal of Renewable Energy Technology (GBR ISSN 1757-3971) **3139**
• ➤ International Journal of Research and Method in Education (GBR ISSN 1743-727X) **2870**
• International Journal of Research and Method in Education (Online) (GBR ISSN 1743-7288) **2870**
• ➤ International Journal of Research in Marketing (NLD ISSN 0167-8116) **1822**
International Journal of Research in Physical Chemistry and Chemical Physics *see* Zeitschrift fuer Physikalische Chemie **2142**
International Journal of Respiratory Care (GBR ISSN 1747-1273) **6215**
• International Journal of Retail & Distribution Management (GBR ISSN 0959-0552) **1822**
• ➤ International Journal of Revenue Management (GBR ISSN 1474-7332) **1357**
• ➤ International Journal of Rheumatic Diseases (AUS ISSN 1756-1841) **6224**
▼ • ➤ International Journal of Rheumatology (USA ISSN 1687-9260) **6224**
• ➤ The International Journal of Risk and Safety in Medicine (NLD ISSN 0924-6479) **4509**
• ➤ International Journal of Risk Assessment and Management (GBR ISSN 1466-8297) **1761**
• ➤ International Journal of River Basin Management (ESP ISSN 1571-5124) **3362**
International Journal of Robotics and Automation (CAN ISSN 0826-8185) **2462**
• ➤ International Journal of Robotics Research (GBR ISSN 0278-3649) **2585**
• ➤ International Journal of Robust and Nonlinear Control (GBR ISSN 1049-8923) **3321**
• ➤ International Journal of Rock Mechanics and Mining Sciences (GBR ISSN 1365-1609) **6466**
➤ International Journal of Rope Science and Technology (GBR ISSN 1997-6461) **3273**
• ➤ International Journal of Rotating Machinery (USA ISSN 1023-621X) **5453**
• ➤ International Journal of Rural Management (IND ISSN 0973-0052) **4016**
➤ International Journal of Rural Studies (IND ISSN 1023-2001) **8109**
• ➤ International Journal of S T D & AIDS (Sexually Transmitted Diseases & Acquired Immune Deficiency Syndrome) (GBR ISSN 0956-4624) **5818**
• ➤ International Journal of Satellite Communications and Networking (GBR ISSN 1542-0973) **2383**
▼ • ➤ International Journal of Satellite Communications Policy and Management (GBR ISSN 1742-7568) **2327**
International Journal of Scholarly Academic Intellectual Diversity (USA ISSN 1091-3610) **2871**
International Journal of Science & Engineering (IND ISSN 0257-7828) **7867**
• ➤ International Journal of Science and Mathematics Education (NLD ISSN 1571-0068) **7868**
International Journal of Science and Research (AUS ISSN 1832-1011) **7868**
International Journal of Science and Technology of the University of Kashan (IRN ISSN 1680-144X) **7868**
• ➤ International Journal of Science Education (GBR ISSN 0950-0693) **2871**
➤ International Journal of Scientific America & Middle East Studies (CAN ISSN 1206-7849) **552**
• ➤ International Journal of Scottish Theatre (GBR ISSN 1471-5198) **8472**
▼ • International Journal of Security (MYS ISSN 1985-2320) **2426**
• ➤ International Journal of Security and Networks (GBR ISSN 1747-8405) **2499**
• International Journal of Sediment Research/Guoji Nisha Yanjiu (CHN ISSN 1001-6279) **2710**
• ➤ International Journal of Selection and Assessment (GBR ISSN 0965-075X) **1867**
• ➤ International Journal of Self-Directed Learning (USA ISSN 1934-3701) **2987**
• ➤ International Journal of Self-Help and Self-Care (USA ISSN 1091-2851) **7366**
• ➤ International Journal of Self-Propagating High-Temperature Synthesis (USA ISSN 1061-3862) **7055**
▼ • International Journal of Semantic Computing (SGP ISSN 1793-351X) **2426**
▼ • ➤ International Journal of Semiconductor Science & Technology (IND) **3105**
• ➤ International Journal of Sensor Networks (GBR ISSN 1748-1279) **2499**
➤ International Journal of Servant-Leadership (USA) **6926**
International Journal of Service Industry Management *see* Journal of Service Management **1769**
• ➤ International Journal of Services and Operations Management (GBR ISSN 1744-2370) **1761**
• ➤ International Journal of Services and Standards (GBR ISSN 1740-8849) **1129**
▼ • ➤ International Journal of Services, Economics and Management (GBR ISSN 1753-0822) **1761**
• ➤ International Journal of Services Operations and Informatics (GBR ISSN 1741-539X) **1761**
▼ • ➤ International Journal of Services Sciences (GBR ISSN 1753-1446) **1761**
• ➤ International Journal of Services Technology and Management (GBR ISSN 1460-6720) **1419**
• ➤ International Journal of Sexual Health (USA ISSN 1931-7611) **7366**
International Journal of Sexual Health (Online) *see* International Journal of Sexual Health **7366**
• ➤ International Journal of Shaping Modeling (SGP ISSN 0218-6543) **2487**
• ➤ International Journal of Sheep and Wool Science (AUS ISSN 1832-8679) **290**
▼ • ➤ International Journal of Shipping and Transport Logistics (GBR ISSN 1756-6517) **8647**
▼ • ➤ International Journal of Shoulder Surgery (IND ISSN 0973-6042) **6246**
▼ • ➤ International Journal of Signal and Imaging Systems Engineering (GBR ISSN 1748-0698) **3321**
• ➤ International Journal of Signal Processing (TUR ISSN 1304-4494) **2462**
• ➤ International Journal of Simulation and Process Modelling (GBR ISSN 1740-2123) **1419**
➤ International Journal of Simulation Modelling (AUT ISSN 1726-4529) **2472**
• International Journal of Simulation. Systems, Science and Technology (GBR ISSN 1473-8031) **2517**
• ➤ International Journal of Six Sigma and Competitive Advantage (GBR ISSN 1479-2494) **3369**
• ➤ International Journal of Slavic Linguistics and Poetics (USA ISSN 0538-8228) **5129**
• ➤ The International Journal of Sleep and Wakefulness (USA ISSN 1754-307X) **6147**
• ➤ The International Journal of Sleep and Wakefulness. Primary Care Edition (USA ISSN 1754-3088) **6147**
The International Journal of Sleep and Wakefulness. Specialist Edition *see* The International Journal of Sleep and Wakefulness **6147**
International Journal of Small Craft Technology *see* Royal Institution of Naval Architects. Transactions. Part B. International Journal of Small Craft Technology **8659**
▼ • ➤ International Journal of Social and Management Sciences (NOR ISSN 1504-8446) **7974**
▼ • ➤ International Journal of Social Computing and Cyber-Physical Systems (GBR ISSN 2040-0721) **2522**
• ➤ International Journal of Social Economics (GBR ISSN 0306-8293) **1129**
• ➤ International Journal of Social Education (USA ISSN 0889-0293) **7974**
▼ • International Journal of Social Health Information Management (USA ISSN 1942-9665) **7527**
▼ • ➤ International Journal of Social Humanistic Computing (GBR ISSN 1752-6124) **7974**
▼ • ➤ International Journal of Social Network Mining (GBR ISSN 1757-8485) **2499**
• ➤ International Journal of Social Psychiatry (GBR ISSN 0020-7640) **6147**
• ➤ International Journal of Social Research Methodology (GBR ISSN 1364-5579) **7974**
▼ • ➤ International Journal of Social Robotics (NLD ISSN 1875-4805) **2585**
➤ International Journal of Social Sciences (CAN ISSN 1192-2664) **7974**
▼ • ➤ International Journal of Social Sciences (TUR ISSN 1306-973X) **7974**
▼ • ➤ International Journal of Social Security and Workers Compensation (AUS ISSN 1836-9022) **1930**
• ➤ International Journal of Social Welfare (GBR ISSN 1369-6866) **8047**
▼ • ➤ International Journal of Society Systems Science (GBR ISSN 1756-2511) **7975**
• ➤ International Journal of Sociology (USA ISSN 0020-7659) **8109**
• ➤ International Journal of Sociology and Social Policy (GBR ISSN 0144-333X) **8109**
• ➤ International Journal of Sociology of Agriculture and Food/Revista Internacional de Sociologia Sobre Agricultura y Alimentos (JPN ISSN 0798-1759) **8109**
International Journal of Sociology of the Family (IND ISSN 0020-7667) **8110**
▼ • International Journal of Sociotechnology and Knowledge Development (USA ISSN 1941-6253) **8110**
• International Journal of Soft Computing (PAK ISSN 1816-9503) **2472**
▼ International Journal of Soft Computing Techniques (IND ISSN 0973-8878) **2426**
• ➤ International Journal of Software Engineering and Knowledge Engineering (SGP ISSN 0218-1940) **2592**
▼ • International Journal of Software Science and Computational Intelligence (USA ISSN 1942-9045) **2592**
• International Journal of Soil Science (USA ISSN 1816-4978) **237**
▼ • The International Journal of Soil, Sediment and Water (USA ISSN 1940-3259) **237**
• ➤ International Journal of Solids and Structures (GBR ISSN 0020-7683) **7059**
▼ • International Journal of South American Archeology (COL ISSN 2011-0626) **398**
• ➤ International Journal of Space Structures (GBR ISSN 0956-0599) **1016**
• ➤ International Journal of Spatial Data Infrastructures Research (ITA ISSN 1725-0463) **2426**
• ➤ International Journal of Special Education (Online Edition) (CAN) **3041**
▼ • ➤ International Journal of Spectroscopy (USA ISSN 1687-9449) **7077**
• ➤ International Journal of Speech, Language and the Law (GBR ISSN 1748-8885) **4695**
• ➤ International Journal of Speech-Language Pathology (GBR ISSN 1754-9507) **5129**
• ➤ International Journal of Speech Technology (USA ISSN 1381-2416) **5203**
• ➤ International Journal of Speleology (ITA ISSN 0392-6672) **2748**
• International Journal of Sport and Exercise Psychology (USA ISSN 1612-197X) **7366**
• ➤ International Journal of Sport and Health Science (JPN ISSN 1348-1509) **6990**
▼ • ➤ International Journal of Sport Communication (USA ISSN 1936-3915) **8180**
• ➤ International Journal of Sport Finance (USA ISSN 1558-6235) **8180**
➤ International Journal of Sport Management (USA ISSN 1546-234X) **1761**
International Journal of Sport Management and Marketing *see* International Journal of Sports Management and Marketing **1761**
• ➤ International Journal of Sport Nutrition & Exercise Metabolism (USA ISSN 1526-484X) **6661**
▼ • International Journal of Sport Policy (GBR ISSN 1940-6940) **8180**
• ➤ International Journal of Sport Psychology (ITA ISSN 0047-0767) **6230**
▼ • The International Journal of Sports and Entertainment Business (USA ISSN 1947-4342) **1822**
• ➤ International Journal of Sports Management and Marketing (GBR ISSN 1475-8962) **1761**
• ➤ International Journal of Sports Marketing & Sponsorship (GBR ISSN 1464-6668) **8180**
• ➤ International Journal of Sports Medicine (DEU ISSN 0172-4622) **6230**
• International Journal of Sports Medicine. Supplement (DEU ISSN 0943-917X) **6230**
• International Journal of Sports Physiology and Performance (USA ISSN 1555-0265) **6990**
• ➤ International Journal of Sports Science and Coaching (GBR ISSN 1747-9541) **8180**
• International Journal of Sports Science and Engineering (GBR ISSN 1750-9823) **7868**
➤ International Journal of Sports, Tourism & Physical Education (CAN ISSN 1206-7857) **6990**
▼ • ➤ International Journal of Spray and Combustion Dynamics (GBR ISSN 1756-8277) **61**
• ➤ International Journal of Statistics and Systems (IND ISSN 0973-2675) **8379**

International Journal of Steel Structures (KOR ISSN 1598-2351) 1016
▼ • ➤ International Journal of Stomatology & Occlusion Medicine (AUT ISSN 1867-2221) 5849
▼ • ➤ International Journal of Strategic Business Alliances (GBR ISSN 1756-6444) 1129
• ➤ International Journal of Strategic Change Management (GBR ISSN 1740-2859) 1761
▼ • ➤ International Journal of Strategic Communication (USA ISSN 1553-118X) 1129
▼ • ➤ International Journal of Strategic Engineering Asset Management (GBR ISSN 1759-9733) 3202
➤ International Journal of Strategic Management (RUS ISSN 1555-2411) 1761
• International Journal of Strategic Property Management (LTU ISSN 1648-715X) 7596
• ➤ International Journal of Stress Management (USA ISSN 1072-5245) 5640
• ➤ International Journal of Stroke (AUS ISSN 1747-4930) 5790
▼ • International Journal of Structural Integrity (GBR ISSN 1757-9864) 3273
• ➤ International Journal of Structural Stability and Dynamics (SGP ISSN 0219-4554) 3383
➤ International Journal of Structures (IND ISSN 0253-4754) 3273
▼ • ➤ International Journal of Sudan Research, Policy and Sustainable Development (GBR ISSN 2040-4247) 7868
▼ • ➤ International Journal of Surface Science and Engineering (GBR ISSN 1749-785X) 3348
• International Journal of Surgery (GBR) 6246
• ➤ International Journal of Surgical Pathology (USA ISSN 1066-8969) 6246
• ➤ International Journal of Sustainability in Higher Education (GBR ISSN 1467-6370) 2987
• ➤ International Journal of Sustainability in Higher Education (Online) (GBR ISSN 1758-6739) 2988
▼ • ➤ International Journal of Sustainable Design (GBR ISSN 1743-8284) 1129
• ➤ International Journal of Sustainable Development (GBR ISSN 0960-1406) 3443
• ➤ International Journal of Sustainable Development and Planning (GBR ISSN 1743-7601) 3443
• ➤ International Journal of Sustainable Development and World Ecology (GBR ISSN 1350-4509) 3443
International Journal of Sustainable Development Law and Policy *see* McGill International Journal of Sustainable Development Law and Policy 4730
▼ • ➤ International Journal of Sustainable Economy (GBR ISSN 1756-5804) 1129
• ➤ International Journal of Sustainable Energy (GBR ISSN 1478-6451) 3176
▼ • International Journal of Sustainable Engineering (GBR ISSN 1939-7038) 3202
▼ • ➤ International Journal of Sustainable Manufacturing (GBR ISSN 1742-7223) 3383
▼ • ➤ International Journal of Sustainable Society (GBR ISSN 1756-2538) 8110
▼ • ➤ International Journal of Sustainable Strategic Management (GBR ISSN 1753-3600) 1761
▼ • International Journal of Sustainable Transportation (GBR ISSN 1556-8318) 8499
International Journal of System (IND) 2522
▼ • ➤ International Journal of System Control and Information Processing (GBR ISSN 1759-9334) 2462
➤ International Journal of System Dynamics and Policy Planning (IND) 3202
▼ • ➤ International Journal of System of Systems Engineering (GBR ISSN 1748-0671) 3202
• ➤ International Journal of Systematic and Evolutionary Microbiology (GBR ISSN 1466-5026) 888
• ➤ International Journal of Systematic Theology (GBR ISSN 1463-1652) 7651
International Journal of Systemics, Cybernetics and Informatics *see* I J S C I 2527
▼ • International Journal of Systems Assurance Engineering and Management (IND) 2472
▼ • ➤ International Journal of Systems, Control and Communications (GBR ISSN 1755-9340) 2522
• ➤ International Journal of Systems Science (GBR ISSN 0020-7721) 3203
▼ • ➤ International Journal of Systems Signal Control & Engineering Applications (PAK ISSN 1997-5422) 3203
➤ International Journal of Tantric Studies (USA ISSN 1084-7553) 6926
• International Journal of Tea Science (IND ISSN 0972-544X) 3648
International Journal of Tea Science Including Tea Science Abstracts *see* International Journal of Tea Science 3648
▼ • ➤ International Journal of Teacher Leadership (USA ISSN 1934-9726) 2871
▼ • ➤ International Journal of Teaching and Case Studies (GBR ISSN 1749-9151) 2871
• ➤ International Journal of Teaching and Learning in Higher Education (USA ISSN 1812-9129) 2988
▼ • ➤ International Journal of Technoentrepreneurship (GBR ISSN 1746-5370) 1761
▼ • ➤ International Journal of Technological Learning, Innovation and Development (GBR ISSN 1753-1942) 8427
International Journal of Technology Advances (CAN ISSN 1192-2575) 8427
• ➤ International Journal of Technology and Design Education (NLD ISSN 0957-7572) 3065
• ➤ International Journal of Technology and Globalisation (GBR ISSN 1476-5667) 8427
• ➤ International Journal of Technology and Human Interaction (USA ISSN 1548-3908) 8427
• ➤ International Journal of Technology Assessment in Health Care (GBR ISSN 0266-4623) 5906
▼ • ➤ International Journal of Technology Enhanced Learning (GBR ISSN 1753-5255) 3065
• ➤ International Journal of Technology in Teaching and Learning (USA ISSN 1551-2576) 2871
• ➤ International Journal of Technology Intelligence and Planning (GBR ISSN 1740-2832) 8427
• ➤ International Journal of Technology, Knowledge and Society (AUS ISSN 1832-3669) 8427
• ➤ International Journal of Technology Management (GBR ISSN 0267-5730) 8427
• ➤ International Journal of Technology Management & Sustainable Development (GBR ISSN 1474-2748) 8427
• ➤ International Journal of Technology Marketing (GBR ISSN 1741-878X) 1822
▼ • ➤ International Journal of Technology Policy and Law (GBR ISSN 1742-4240) 4871
• ➤ International Journal of Technology Policy and Management (GBR ISSN 1468-4322) 8427
• ➤ International Journal of Technology Transfer and Commercialisation (GBR ISSN 1470-6075) 8428
▼ • International Journal of Telemedicine and Applications (USA ISSN 1687-6415) 5831
▼ • ➤ International Journal of Telerehabilitation (USA ISSN 1945-2020) 6110
▼ ➤ International Journal of Terraspace Science and Engineering (USA ISSN 1943-3514) 2710
• International Journal of Terrorism and Political Hot Spots (USA ISSN 1932-7889) 7244
• International Journal of Testing (USA ISSN 1530-5058) 7366
▼ • The International Journal of the Academic Business World (USA ISSN 1942-6089) 1129
• ➤ The International Journal of the Arts in Society (AUS ISSN 1833-1866) 4457
• ➤ International Journal of the Book (AUS ISSN 1447-9516) 2327
• ➤ International Journal of the Classical Tradition (NLD ISSN 1073-0508) 2236
▼ • International Journal of the Commons (NLD ISSN 1875-0281) 7144
• ➤ International Journal of the Economics of Business (GBR ISSN 1357-1516) 1129
• ➤ The International Journal of the History of Sport (GBR ISSN 0952-3367) 4147
• ➤ International Journal of the Humanities (AUS ISSN 1447-9508) 4458
▼ ➤ The International Journal of the Inclusive Museum (AUS ISSN 1835-2014) 6526
• ➤ International Journal of the Legal Profession (GBR ISSN 0969-5958) 4695
▼ • ➤ International Journal of the Platonic Tradition (NLD ISSN 1872-5082) 6926
• ➤ International Journal of the Sociology of Language (DEU ISSN 0165-2516) 5130
International Journal of the Sociology of Law *see* International Journal of Law Crime and Justice 4695
International Journal of Theoretical and Applied Computer Sciences (IND) 2426
• ➤ International Journal of Theoretical and Applied Finance (SGP ISSN 0219-0249) 1357
• ➤ International Journal of Theoretical and Applied Mechanics (IND ISSN 0973-6085) 3383
▼ • ➤ International Journal of Theoretical and Applied Multiscale Mechanics (GBR ISSN 1755-9995) 3348
• ➤ International Journal of Theoretical Physics (USA ISSN 0020-7748) 7018
• International Journal of Theoretical Physics, Group Theory and Nonlinear Optics (USA ISSN 1525-4674) 7018
▼ • ➤ International Journal of Therapeutic Massage & Bodywork (USA ISSN 1916-257X) 6990
• International Journal of Therapy and Rehabilitation (GBR ISSN 1741-1645) 6110
• ➤ International Journal of Thermal Sciences (FRA ISSN 1290-0729) 7055
➤ International Journal of Thermodynamics (TUR ISSN 1301-9724) 7055
• ➤ International Journal of Thermophysics (USA ISSN 0195-928X) 7055
• ➤ International Journal of Tomography & Statistics (IND ISSN 0972-9976) 6199
▼ • ➤ International Journal of Tourism Anthropology (GBR ISSN 1759-0442) 8723
▼ • ➤ International Journal of Tourism Policy (GBR ISSN 1750-4090) 8723
International Journal of Tourism Policy and Research *see* International Journal of Tourism Policy 8723
• ➤ International Journal of Tourism Research (GBR ISSN 1099-2340) 8723
• ➤ International Journal of Toxicology (USA ISSN 1091-5818) 3498
▼ • ➤ International Journal of Trade and Global Markets (GBR ISSN 1742-7541) 1762
• ➤ International Journal of Training & Development (GBR ISSN 1360-3736) 1867
➤ International Journal of Training Research (AUS ISSN 1448-0220) 2871
• ➤ The International Journal of Transgenderism (USA ISSN 1434-4599) 7366
▼ • ➤ International Journal of Transitional Justice (GBR ISSN 1752-7716) 4695
▼ • ➤ International Journal of Transitions and Innovation Systems (GBR ISSN 1745-0071) 2462
➤ International Journal of Translation (IND ISSN 0970-9819) 5130
• ➤ International Journal of Transpersonal Studies (USA ISSN 1321-0122) 7366
• ➤ International Journal of Transport Economics/Rivista Internazionale di Economia dei Trasporti (ITA ISSN 0303-5247) 8499
• ➤ International Journal of Transport Phenomena (USA ISSN 1028-6578) 3203
➤ International Journal of Transportation, Privatization & Public Policy (JOR ISSN 1682-2587) 8499
• International Journal of Trichology (IND ISSN 0974-7753) 5878
International Journal of Triditional Chinese Medicine *see* Guoji Zhongyi Zhongyao Zazhi 5622
International Journal of Tropical Agriculture (IND ISSN 0254-8755) 123
• ➤ International Journal of Tropical Insect Science (GBR ISSN 1742-7584) 850
• International Journal of Tropical Medicine (PAK ISSN 1816-3319) 5819
International Journal of Tropical Plant Diseases (IND ISSN 0254-0126) 795
▼ • ➤ International Journal of Tryptophan Research (NZL ISSN 1178-6469) 5640
• ➤ International Journal of Tuberculosis and Lung Disease (FRA ISSN 1027-3719) 6215
➤ International Journal of Turbo and Jet Engines (ISR ISSN 0334-0082) 61
International Journal of Turkish Studies (USA ISSN 0272-7919) 4321
▼ • ➤ International Journal of Ultra Wideband Communications and Systems (GBR ISSN 1758-728X) 2327
• ➤ International Journal of Uncertainty, Fuzziness and Knowledge-Based Systems (SGP ISSN 0218-4885) 2452
• ➤ International Journal of Unconventional Computing (USA ISSN 1548-7199) 2426
• ➤ International Journal of Urban and Regional Research (GBR ISSN 0309-1317) 4416
• International Journal of Urban Labour and Leisure (GBR) 7975
▼ • ➤ International Journal of Urban Sustainable Development (GBR ISSN 1756-5723) 4416
▼ • ➤ International Journal of Urological Nursing (GBR ISSN 1749-7701) 5962
• ➤ International Journal of Urology (AUS ISSN 0919-8172) 6269
International Journal of Value-Based Management *see* Journal of Business Ethics 1134
• ➤ International Journal of Value Chain Management (GBR ISSN 1741-5357) 1762
• ➤ International Journal of Vegetable Science (USA ISSN 1931-5260) 237
• ➤ International Journal of Vehicle Autonomous Systems (GBR ISSN 1471-0226) 8499
• ➤ International Journal of Vehicle Design (GBR ISSN 0143-3369) 8499
International Journal of Vehicle Design. Heavy Vehicle Systems *see* International Journal of Heavy Vehicle Systems 8499
• ➤ International Journal of Vehicle Information and Communication Systems (GBR ISSN 1471-0242) 8500
• ➤ International Journal of Vehicle Noise and Vibration (GBR ISSN 1479-1471) 8500
▼ • ➤ International Journal of Vehicle Performance (GBR ISSN 1745-3194) 8586
• ➤ International Journal of Vehicle Safety (GBR ISSN 1479-3105) 8500
• ➤ International Journal of Vehicle Systems Modelling and Testing (GBR ISSN 1745-6436) 8586
▼ • ➤ International Journal of Vehicular Technology (USA ISSN 1687-5702) 3383
• International Journal of Ventilation (GBR ISSN 1473-3315) 4122
The International Journal of Veterinary Medicine *see* Vet On-Line 8810
International Journal of Virology *see* Guoji Bingduxue Zazhi 5913
• International Journal of Virology (USA ISSN 1816-4900) 5819
▼ • International Journal of Virtual Communities and Social Networking (USA ISSN 1942-9010) 2559
▼ • ➤ International Journal of Virtual Technology and Multimedia (GBR ISSN 1741-1874) 2351
➤ International Journal of Vocational Education and Training (USA ISSN 1075-2455) 2871
International Journal of Volleyball Research (USA ISSN 1524-4652) 8236
• ➤ International Journal of Water (GBR ISSN 1465-6620) 8826
• ➤ International Journal of Water Resources Development (GBR ISSN 0790-0627) 8826
• ➤ International Journal of Wavelets, Multiresolution and Information Processing (SGP ISSN 0219-6913) 5497
• ➤ International Journal of Web and Grid Services (GBR ISSN 1741-1106) 2559
• ➤ International Journal of Web Based Communities (GBR ISSN 1477-8394) 2559
• International Journal of Web-Based Learning and Teaching Technologies (USA ISSN 1548-1093) 2469
• ➤ International Journal of Web Engineering and Technology (GBR ISSN 1476-1289) 2547
• ➤ International Journal of Web Information Systems (GBR ISSN 1744-0084) 2560
▼ • ➤ International Journal of Web Portals (USA ISSN 1938-0194) 2560
• ➤ International Journal of Web Services Research (USA ISSN 1545-7362) 2560
➤ International Journal of Weight Engineering (USA) 61
• ➤ International Journal of Whole Schooling (USA ISSN 1710-2146) 2871
The International Journal of Wild Life and Environmental Research (PAK ISSN 1728-6328) 3694
International Journal of Wilderness (USA ISSN 1086-5519) 2615
• ➤ International Journal of Wildland Fire (AUS ISSN 1049-8001) 3579
• ➤ International Journal of Wine Business Research (GBR ISSN 1751-1062) 605
The International Journal of Wine Marketing *see* International Journal of Wine Business Research 605
▼ • ➤ International Journal of Wine Research (GBR ISSN 1179-1403) 5640
• ➤ International Journal of Wireless and Mobile Computing (GBR ISSN 1741-1084) 2351
• ➤ International Journal of Wireless Information Networks (USA ISSN 1068-9605) 2327
▼ • ➤ International Journal of Women's Health (GBR ISSN 1179-1411) 5994
• ➤ International Journal of Work Organisation and Emotion (GBR ISSN 1740-8938) 1867
▼ • ➤ International Journal of Workplace Health Management (GBR ISSN 1753-8351) 6679
▼ • ➤ International Journal of Yoga (IND ISSN 0973-6131) 6990
• ➤ International Journal of Yoga Therapy (USA ISSN 1531-2054) 6990
▼ • ➤ International Journal of Zizek Studies (GBR ISSN 1751-8229) 8110
• ➤ International Journal of Zoological Research (USA ISSN 1811-9778) 948
▼ • ➤ International Journal of Zoology (USA ISSN 1687-8477) 948
• ➤ International Journal on Algae (USA ISSN 1521-9429) 795
• ➤ International Journal on Artificial Intelligence Tools (SGP ISSN 0218-2130) 2452
▼ • International Journal on Computer Science and Engineering (IND ISSN 0975-3397) 2426
• ➤ International Journal on Digital Libraries (DEU ISSN 1432-5012) 5062
➤ International Journal on Disability and Human Development (ISR) 5895
• ➤ International Journal on Document Analysis and Recognition (DEU ISSN 1433-2833) 2427
• ➤ International Journal on E-learning (USA ISSN 1537-2456) 2560
➤ The International Journal on Hydropower & Dams (GBR ISSN 1352-2523) 3163
International Journal on Immunorehabilitation (RUS ISSN 1562-3629) 5761
International Journal on Interactive Design and Manufacturing *see* I J I D E M 3379
International Journal on Media Management *see* J M M 2328
• ➤ International Journal on Minority and Group Rights (NLD ISSN 1385-4879) 7210
• International Journal on Multicultural Societies (FRA ISSN 1817-4574) 8110
• ➤ The International Journal on School Disaffection (GBR ISSN 1478-8497) 3065
• International Journal on Semantic Web and Information Systems (USA ISSN 1552-6283) 2547
▼ • ➤ International Journal on Smart Sensing and Intelligent Systems (NZL ISSN 1178-5608) 2452
• ➤ International Journal on Software Tools for Technology Transfer (DEU ISSN 1433-2779) 2592
• International Journal on Wireless & Optical Communications (SGP ISSN 1548-548X) 2327
• ➤ International Journal on World Peace (USA ISSN 0742-3640) 7244
The International Journalist (USA) 4577
• International Judicial Monitor (USA ISSN 1931-3667) 4931
International Juridical Organization for Environment and Development Newsletter *see* I J O Newsletter 8963
International Justice Tribune (English Edition) (FRA ISSN 1767-8889) 4931
• International Justice Tribune (French Edition) (FRA ISSN 1767-8862) 4931
International Kemps Film, T V and Video (GBR ISSN 1466-1721) 6504
International Kernekraftstatus *see* Kernekraft og Nuklear Sikkerhed 3207
International Key Personnel List (USA ISSN 1058-8914) 3348

Title

• ➤ International N G O Journal (Non Governmental Organizations) (USA ISSN 1993-8225) **8048**
International Nannoplankton Association Newsletter *see* I N A Newsletter **2806**
International Narcotic Enforcement Officers Association Directory (USA) **2655**
• International Narcotics Control Board. Psychotropic Substances (USA ISSN 1564-8753) **6889**
• International Narcotics Control Board. Report for (Year) (USA ISSN 0257-3717) **6850**
• International Narcotics Control Strategy Report (USA ISSN 1939-4314) **2656**
International Naturist Information Center Newsletter (NLD) **6990**
International Navigation Association. Bulletin *see* On Course **8656**
International Navigation Association. Newsletter *see* Sailing Ahead **8659**
• International Navigation Association. Technical Briefs (BEL) **8647**
International Navigation Congress. Papers (BEL ISSN 1015-9568) **8647**
• ➤ International Negotiation (NLD ISSN 1382-340X) **7244**
➤ International Negotiation Series (NLD ISSN 1871-3319) **7244**
International Network for the Availability of Scientific Publications Health Directory (Year) *see* I N A S P Health Directory (Year) **5632**
International Network for the Availability of Scientific Publications Newsletter *see* I N A S P Newsletter **5014**
International Network of Agencies for Health Technology Assessment Briefs *see* I N A H T A Briefs **5632**
• International Network on Participatory Irrigation Management. Newsletter (USA) **201**
• ➤ International Neuropsychological Society. Journal (GBR ISSN 1355-6177) **6147**
International New Landscape/Guoji Xinjingguan (CHN ISSN 1833-0673) **3739**
• International New Product Report (GBR) **3679**
• International News (USA) **4696**
▼ • International News Services.com (GBR ISSN 1756-5499) **4577**
International Newsletter on Rock Art/Lettre Internationale d'Informations sur l'Art Rupestre (FRA ISSN 1022-3282) **398**
International Nonwovens Technical Conference Association of the Nonwoven Fabrics Industry. I N T C Papers *see* I N D A Association of the Nonwoven Fabrics Industry. I N T C Papers **8452**
International Notebook of Poetry *see* Caiete Internationale de Poezie **5418**
International Notices to Airmen (USA ISSN 0364-6742) **61**
International Nubian Breeders Association Newsletter (USA) **290**
• International Nuclear Energy Research Initiative. Annual Report (USA) **3169**
International Nuclear Information System Atomindex (Online Edition) *see* I N I S Atomindex (Online Edition) **7048**
International Nuclear Information System Reference Series *see* I N I S Reference Series **5014**
International Nursing and Midwifery Link-up *see* Link-up **5969**
International Nursing Perspectives (ITA ISSN 1592-6478) **5962**
• ➤ International Nursing Review (GBR ISSN 0020-8132) **5962**
International Nursing Review en Espanol *see* International Nursing Review **5962**
• ➤ International Nursing Review Online (GBR ISSN 1466-7657) **5962**
International Oaks (USA ISSN 1941-2061) **795**
International Observer (USA ISSN 1061-0324) **7244**
International Observer Political Report (USA ISSN 1554-2181) **7244**
International Ocean-Colour Coordinating Group Report *see* I O C C G Report **2806**
International Ocean Institute. Occasional Papers (MLT) **2808**
International Ocean Institute. Pacem in Maribus. Proceedings (MLT) **2808**
International Ocean Systems (GBR ISSN 1471-0188) **2808**
International Odd Fellow and Rebekah (USA) **2266**
International Office of Cocoa, Chocolate and Sugar Confectionery. Annual Statistical Bulletin *see* International Confectionery Association. Statistical Bulletin Review (Year) **3674**
International Offices Activity Report (CAN ISSN 1911-2602) **1571**
International Offices Annual Report *see* International Offices Activity Report **1571**
• ➤ International Offshore and Polar Engineering Conference. Proceedings (USA ISSN 1098-6189) **3383**
International Offshore Oil Company Directory (USA ISSN 1059-7816) **6774**
International Oil & Gas Finance Review (Year) (GBR ISSN 1364-9167) **6774**
• International Oil Daily (USA ISSN 1540-8108) **6774**
International Oil News (USA) **6774**
International Oil Scouts Association Directory (USA) **2009**
International Oil Spill Control Directory (USA) **6774**
International Oil Spill Database (USA) **6800**
International Oil Spill Statistics *see* Oil Spill Intelligence Report **3490**
International Old Lacers, Inc. Bulletin (USA ISSN 0740-6746) **6639**
International Olympic Academy. Report of the Sessions (GRC ISSN 0074-7181) **8181**
International Ombudsman Institute. Newsletter (CAN ISSN 0229-2181) **4696**
International Ombudsman Institute. Occasional Paper Series (CAN) **4696**
International Ombudsman Journal *see* The International Ombudsman Yearbook **4696**
The International Ombudsman Yearbook (CAN ISSN 1387-1846) **4696**
† International One- and Two-Family Dwelling Code (USA) **8966**
• International Online Conference on Second and Foreign Language Teaching and Research. Proceedings (USA ISSN 1550-8501) **5130**
International Online Information Meeting (Proceedings) (GBR) **2560**
International Online Markets (Year): Strategic Outlook & Forecasts *see* International Online Markets (Year): Strategic Outlook and Forecasts **1571**
• International Online Markets (Year): Strategic Outlook and Forecasts (USA) **1571**
International Opera Collector (GBR ISSN 1361-925X) **6577**
International Operating Engineer (USA ISSN 0020-8159) **4596**
International Operations Bulletin (USA) **61**
• ➤ International Ophthalmology (NLD ISSN 0165-5701) **6044**
• ➤ International Ophthalmology Clinics (USA ISSN 0020-8167) **6044**
International Optical Communications (GBR ISSN 1740-6471) **2327**
The International Orem Society Newsletter *see* Self-Care, Dependent-Care & Nursing **5981**
International Organisation for the Study of the Endurance of Wire Ropes. Bulletin *see* International Journal of Rope Science and Technology **3273**
• ➤ International Organization (GBR ISSN 0020-8183) **7244**
International Organization for Cooperation in Health Care. General Assembly. Report (BEL) **5640**
International Organization for Migration. Annual Report (CHE) **7285**
International Organization for Migration Migration Research Series *see* I O M Migration Research Series **7284**
➤ International Organization for Septuagint and Cognate Studies. Bulletin (USA ISSN 0145-3890) **4458**
International Organization for Standardization 9000 + I S O 14000 + po Materialam I S O *see* I S O 9000 + I S O 14000 + po Materialam I S O **6402**
International Organization for Standardization 9000 Registered Firms Directory *see* I S O 9000 Registered Firms Directory **1888**
International Organization for Standardization Catalogue (English Edition) *see* I S O Catalogue (English Edition) **6402**
International Organization for Standardization Catalogue. Supplement *see* I S O Catalogue. Supplement **6402**
International Organization for Standardization Focus (English Edition) *see* I S O Focus (English Edition) **6402**
International Organization for Standardization, International Electrotechnical Commission. Guide (CHE ISSN 1029-371X) **6403**
International Organization for Standardization, Maintenance Agency Maintenance Agency. Annual Report *see* I S O Maintenance Agency. Annual Report **6402**
International Organization for Standardization Management Systems (Swiss Edition) *see* I S O Management Systems (Swiss Edition) **6402**
International Organization for Standardization Memento *see* I S O Memento **6402**
International Organization for Standardization Technical Programme *see* I S O Technical Programme **6403**
International Organization for the Study of the Old Testament. Triennial Congress Volume *see* Vetus Testamentum. Supplements **7731**
International Organization of Plant Biosystematists. Newsletter (USA ISSN 0254-8844) **795**
† ➤ International Organizations and the Law of the Sea (Year) (NLD ISSN 0920-7767) **8966**
• International Organizations Law Review (NLD ISSN 1572-3739) **4932**
International Ornithological Congress. Proceedings (USA ISSN 0074-7211) **908**
• International Orthodontics (FRA ISSN 1761-7227) **5849**
• ➤ International Orthopaedics (DEU ISSN 0341-2695) **6062**
International Outlook. Wages, Salaries, Labour Costs *see* International Utblick. Loener och Arbetskraftskostnader **1690**
International P.E.N. Writers-in-Exile Center's Newsletter (USA) **7210**
International Pacific Halibut Commission. Annual Report (USA ISSN 0074-7238) **3598**
International Pacific Halibut Commission. Report *see* International Pacific Halibut Commission. Scientific Report **3598**
International Pacific Halibut Commission. Scientific Report (USA ISSN 0304-016X) **3598**
• International Pacific Halibut Commission. Technical Report (USA ISSN 0579-3920) **3599**
International Packaging Abstracts *see* Packaging Month **6715**
International Pan Pacific Conference. Proceedings *see* T A P P I International Pan Pacific Conference. Proceedings **6739**
• International Paper Board Industry (USA ISSN 0020-8191) **6710**
International Paper History *see* Paper History **6736**
International Paperworld (DEU ISSN 1615-1720) **6734**
International Parallel and Distributed Processing Symposium Proceedings *see* I P D P S Proceedings **2471**
• International Parallel Processing Symposium. Proceedings (USA ISSN 1063-7133) **2467**
International Patent Litigation. Supplement (USA) **6753**
International Payments (GBR ISSN 1740-1852) **1358**
• International Peace Update (CHE) **7244**
• ➤ International Peacekeeping (GBR ISSN 1353-3312) **7244**
International Peacekeeping *see* Journal of International Peacekeeping **7248**
➤ International Peat Journal (FIN ISSN 0782-7784) **795**
International Pediatric Association. Proceedings of Congress (CHE ISSN 0074-7300) **6093**
International Pediatrics (USA ISSN 0885-6265) **6246**
• International Pension Funds and Their Advisors (GBR ISSN 1470-5680) **1631**
The International Permaculture Solutions Journal (USA ISSN 1046-8366) **2615**
International Personal Finance (ZAF) **1358**
International Personnel Management Association News *see* I P M A News **1866**
International Perspectives on Child and Adolescent Mental Health (USA ISSN 1874-5911) **6147**
• International Perspectives on Education and Society (GBR ISSN 1479-3679) **2871**
➤ International Perspectives on Europe (GBR ISSN 0956-2583) **8110**
• International Perspectives on Higher Education Research (GBR ISSN 1479-3628) **2988**
• International Perspectives on Inclusive Education (GBR ISSN 1479-3636) **2871**
• ➤ International Perspectives on Sexual and Reproductive Health (USA ISSN 1944-0391) **5994**
• International Pest Control (GBR ISSN 0020-8256) **851**
• International Pesticide Directory (GBR ISSN 1351-346X) **237**
International Pet Industry News (USA ISSN 1074-780X) **6810**
• International Petroleum Encyclopedia (USA ISSN 0148-0375) **6774**
• International Petroleum Finance (USA ISSN 0193-9270) **6774**
International Petroleum Industry (USA) **6774**
International Petroleum Industry Environmental Conservation Association. Report Series (GBR ISSN 1367-1359) **6774**
International Petroleum Monthly (Online) *see* U.S. Department of Energy. Energy Information Administration. International Petroleum Monthly (Online) **6795**
International Petroleum Statistics Report (Online) *see* U.S. Department of Energy. Energy Information Administration. International Petroleum Monthly (Online) **6795**
† International Pharma News (FRA ISSN 1289-0146) **8966**
• International Pharmaceutical Abstracts (USA ISSN 0020-8264) **6889**
International Pharmaceutical Intelligence *see* Kokusai Iyakuhin Joho **6858**
▼ • International Pharmaceutical Quality (USA ISSN 1937-6898) **6850**
International Pharmaceutical Regulatory Monitor (USA ISSN 1934-600X) **6850**
International Pharmaceutical Students Federation News Bulletin *see* I P S F News Bulletin **6847**
International Pharmacy Journal (NLD ISSN 1010-0423) **6850**
International Philatelic Federation. General Assembly. Proces-Verbal (CHE ISSN 0074-7343) **6896**
International Philatelic Press Club. Report to Members (USA) **6896**
International Philosophical Bibliography *see* Repertoire Bibliographique de la Philosophie **6963**
• ➤ International Philosophical Quarterly (USA ISSN 0019-0365) **6926**
• International Phonetic Association. Journal (GBR ISSN 0025-1003) **5130**
International Photo Magazine *see* C International Photo Magazine (English-Chinese Edition) **6965**
International Photo Magazine *see* C International Photo Magazine (Spanish-Japanese Edition) **6965**
• International Photo Processing Industry Report (USA ISSN 1084-2233) **6979**
International Piano (GBR) **6577**
International Pig Topics (GBR ISSN 0963-5866) **290**
International Pipe Line and Offshore Contractors Association Yearbook *see* The I P L O C A Yearbook **6773**
† International Pipe Line Industry (USA ISSN 0272-1090) **8966**
International Pittsburgh Coal Conference. Proceedings (USA ISSN 1075-7961) **6467**
International Planned Parenthood Federation Annual Report *see* I P P F Annual Report **972**
International Planned Parenthood Federation Medical Bulletin *see* I P P F Medical Bulletin **972**
International Planned Parenthood Federation News *see* I P P F News **2154**
• International Planning Studies (GBR ISSN 1356-3475) **4416**
➤ International Plant Propagators' Society. Combined Proceedings of Annual Meetings (USA ISSN 0538-9143) **3739**
International Plastic Modelers' Society - U S A. Journal (USA ISSN 1083-7981) **4337**
International Plastic Modellers Society (UK) Magazine *see* I P M S Magazine **4337**
International Plastic Modellers Society. Magazine *see* I P M S Magazine **4337**
• International Plastics (GBR ISSN 1367-2711) **7093**
International Plastics Directory *see* Handbuch der Internationalen Kunststoffindustrie **7092**
International Plastics Engineering & Technology (IND) **7093**
• International Plumbing Code (USA ISSN 1083-4109) **4122**
International Poetry (USA) **5424**
International Poetry Review (USA ISSN 0145-0786) **5424**
International Police Association Aktuell *see* I P A Aktuell **2654**
International Policing Technology (GBR ISSN 1470-6784) **2678**
International Policy Report (USA ISSN 0738-6508) **7244**
International Policy Review (USA ISSN 1088-7326) **7244**
International Political Economy Yearbook (USA ISSN 8755-8335) **7244**
• International Political Science Abstracts/Documentation Politique Internationale (GBR ISSN 0020-8345) **7200**
International Political Science Association. World Congress (CAN) **7144**
• ➤ International Political Science Review/Revue Internationale de Science Politique (GBR ISSN 0192-5121) **7244**
▼ • ➤ International Political Sociology (GBR ISSN 1749-5679) **8110**
International Politics *see* Guoji Zhengzhi **7239**
• ➤ International Politics (GBR ISSN 1384-5748) **7244**
International Politics of the Middle East. Series (GBR) **7244**
➤ International Polymer Processing (DEU ISSN 0930-777X) **7093**
• International Polymer Science and Technology (GBR ISSN 0307-174X) **7093**
• International Population Reports (USA) **7309**
• ➤ International Poster Journal of Dentistry and Oral Medicine (DEU ISSN 1612-7749) **5849**
International Potash Institute Bulletin *see* I P I Bulletin **235**
International Potash Institute. Congress Proceedings (CHE) **238**
International Potash Institute. Proceedings of Colloquium, Congresses, Workshops, Seminars (CHE) **238**
International Potash Institute Research Topics *see* I P I Research Topics **235**
• International Poultry Exposition Guide (USA) **290**
International Poultry Production (GBR) **290**
International Power Generation *see* Power (Houston) **3393**
International Power Generation Directory of Equipment Manufacturers (GBR ISSN 1361-8105) **2009**
International Power Modulator Symposium and High-Voltage Workshop. Conference Record *see* International Power Modulator Symposium and High-Voltage Workshop. Proceedings **3321**
• International Power Modulator Symposium and High-Voltage Workshop. Proceedings (USA ISSN 1930-885X) **3321**
International Practice Law Newsletter (USA) **4932**
International Practice News (USA) **4932**
International Practitioners' Workshop Series (USA ISSN 1080-3238) **4932**
International Prepress Association Bulletin *see* I P A Bulletin **7323**
• International Preservation News (FRA ISSN 0890-4960) **5019**
International Press Cutting Service: Central Excise Notifications and News (IND) **1930**
International Press Cutting Service: Import - Export - Licenses (IND ISSN 0047-0953) **1571**
International Press Cutting Service: Labour Welfare - Industrial Legislation and Personnel Management (IND ISSN 0047-097X) **1689**
International Press Cutting Service: List of New Industries Approved by Government (IND) **1129**
International Press Cutting Service: Taxation - Finance - Company Law (IND ISSN 0047-1097) **1930**

Title

10452 INTERNATIONAL PRESS CUTTING SERVICE: TENDER NOTIFICATIONS ULRICH'S PERIODICALS

International Press Cutting Service: Tender Notifications (Indian & Global) (IND ISSN 0047-1127) **1571**
International Press Institute Global Journalist *see* I P I Global Journalist **4576**
International Press Telecommunications Council Spectrum *see* I P T C Spectrum **2368**
International Primate Protection League News *see* I P P L News **2614**
International Privaatrecht (NLD ISSN 1568-6426) **4932**
International Private Label Directory (Year) (USA) **2009**
International Private Sewage Disposal Code (USA ISSN 1085-1151) **1016**
International Problems *see* Medjunarodni Problemi **7252**
International Process & Product Quality Conference Proceedings (Year) *see* T A P P I International Process & Product Quality Conference Proceedings (Year) **6739**
The International Procurement Reporter (USA ISSN 1077-3290) **4696**
• International Product Alert (USA ISSN 1086-1238) **1822**
International Production Cost Comparison (CHE ISSN 1017-270X) **8453**
• International Productivity Monitor (CAN ISSN 1492-9759) **7285**
• International Professional Communication Conference. Conference Record. (USA) **2327**
International Programme for Technology and Research in Irrigation and Drainage Issues Paper *see* I P T R I D Issues Paper **235**
International Project Contracting and Labour Service *see* Guoji Gongcheng yu Laowu **1684**
International Property (GBR ISSN 1351-0746) **7596**
International Prospect *see* Guoji Zhanwang **7239**
• ➤ International Psychiatry (GBR ISSN 1749-3676) **6147**
• International Psychoanalysis (GBR ISSN 1564-0361) **7366**
• ➤ International Psychogeriatrics (GBR ISSN 1041-6102) **6148**
International Psychologist (USA ISSN 0047-116X) **7366**
▼ ➤ International Public Health Journal (USA ISSN 1947-4989) **7527**
• ➤ International Public Management Journal (USA ISSN 1096-7494) **7447**
International Public Management Network Newsletter *see* I P M N Newsletter **1751**
• ➤ International Public Policy Review (GBR ISSN 1748-5207) **7144**
➤ International Public Relations Review (CAN ISSN 0269-0357) **7244**
▼ • International Publications of the National Audit Office of Finland (FIN ISSN 1797-0598) **1292**
International Publishers Association. Proceedings of Congress (CHE ISSN 0074-7556) **7563**
International Publishing Handbook (GBR) **7564**
International Pulp Bleaching Conference. Proceedings (USA ISSN 1076-2043) **6734**
International Quantum Electronics Conference (USA) **3321**
• International Quarterly (USA ISSN 1041-3855) **4871**
• ➤ International Quarterly of Community Health Education (USA ISSN 0272-684X) **7527**
▼ • ➤ International Quarterly of Sport Science (HUN ISSN 2060-9469) **8181**
• International Radar Conference. Record (USA) **2327**
International Radcure Directory *see* International Radiation Curing Yearbook & Directory (Year) **3247**
International Radiation Curing Yearbook & Directory (Year) (GBR ISSN 1355-073X) **3247**
International Radio Consultative Committee. Plenary Assembly. Proceedings (CHE) **2359**
• The International Radioactive Exchange (USA ISSN 1558-3384) **3508**
• International Railway Journal (USA) **8619**
International Railway Statistics (Year) (FRA ISSN 0074-7580) **8526**
International Railway Traveler (USA ISSN 0891-7655) **8724**
International Rangeland Congress. Proceedings *see* Society for Range Management. International Rangeland Congress. Abstracts of Papers **186**
International Rayon and Synthetic Fibres Committee. Statistical Yearbook (BEL ISSN 0074-7599) **8463**
International Real Estate Federation (FIABCI) Press *see* F I A B C I Press **7590**
International Reconciliation (NLD) **7210**
International Reference Annual for Building and Equipment of Sports, Tourism, Recreation Installations (FRA ISSN 0074-7645) **8181**
International Refractories Handbook & Directory (GBR) **2043**
• ➤ International Regional Science Review (USA ISSN 0160-0176) **7975**
International Register of Civil Aircraft *see* Great Britain. Civil Aviation Authority. International Register of Civil Aircraft **8542**
International Registry of Organization Development Professionals and Organization Development Handbook (USA ISSN 0749-2685) **1867**
International Rehabilitation Review (USA ISSN 0020-8477) **5640**
• ➤ International Relations (GBR ISSN 0047-1178) **7245**
International Relations Center News *see* I R C News **7241**
• ➤ International Relations of the Asia-Pacific (GBR ISSN 1470-482X) **7245**
International Relations Research Directory (GBR) **7245**
International Relations Studies Series (NLD ISSN 1570-6451) **7245**
• International Rental News (GBR ISSN 1749-5040) **1890**
International Reporter (IND ISSN 0020-8493) **3883**
• International Requirements Engineering Conference. Proceedings (USA) **2592**
International Rescue Committee. Annual Report (USA ISSN 0538-9461) **8048**
International Rescue Committee at Work *see* The I R C at Work **8045**
International Research Center for Energy and Economic Development. Annual Conference. Proceedings (USA) **3139**
International Research Center for Energy and Economic Development. Occasional Papers (USA) **3139**
International Research Center for Japanese Studies. Bulletin *see* Nihon Kenkyu (Kyoto) **4186**
International Research Centers Directory (USA ISSN 0278-2731) **2871**
International Research for Image Selection *see* I R I S **6969**
▼ • ➤ International Research in Children's Literature (GBR ISSN 1755-6198) **2194**
• ➤ International Research in Geographical and Environmental Education (GBR ISSN 1038-2046) **4016**
• International Research in the Business Disciplines (USA ISSN 1074-7877) **1129**
International Research Journal of Arts & Humanities (PAK) **497**
• ➤ International Research Journal of Finance and Economics (AUT ISSN 1450-2887) **1129**
International Residental Code Study Companion (USA ISSN 1948-6340) **1016**
• International Residential Code for One- and Two-Family Dwellings (USA) **1016**
International Review *see* Guoji Guancha **7239**
International Review for Business Education/Internationale Zeitschrift fuer Kaufmaennisches Bildungswesen/Revista Internacional para la Ensenanza Comercial/Revue Internationale pour l'Enseignement Commercial/Rivista Internazionale per la Cultura Commerciale (USA ISSN 0035-354X) **1129**
• ➤ International Review for Environmental Strategies (JPN ISSN 1345-7594) **3443**
International Review for Social Sciences *see* Kyklos **8117**
• ➤ International Review for the Sociology of Sport (GBR ISSN 1012-6902) **8110**
• ➤ International Review of Administrative Sciences (GBR ISSN 0020-8523) **7447**
• ➤ International Review of African American Art (USA ISSN 1045-0920) **497**
• ➤ International Review of Allergology and Clinical Immunology (POL ISSN 1232-9142) **5761**
• ➤ International Review of Applied Economics (GBR ISSN 0269-2171) **1129**
International Review of Biblical Studies/Internationale Zeitschriftenschau fuer Bibelwissenschaft und Grenzgebiete (NLD ISSN 0074-9745) **7698**
• ➤ International Review of Business Research Papers (AUS ISSN 1832-9543) **1129**
• ➤ International Review of Cell and Molecular Biology (USA ISSN 1937-6448) **833**
➤ International Review of Child Neurology Series (GBR ISSN 0899-3653) **6148**
International Review of Comenius Studies and Early Modern Intellectual History *see* Acta Comeniana **4440**
International Review of Comparative Public Policy (USA ISSN 1051-4694) **7144**
International Review of Constitutionalism (USA ISSN 1569-3074) **4849**
International Review of Cytology *see* International Review of Cell and Molecular Biology **833**
• International Review of Economics (DEU ISSN 1865-1704) **1130**
• ➤ International Review of Economics & Finance (NLD ISSN 1059-0560) **1493**
• ➤ International Review of Economics Education (GBR ISSN 1477-3880) **1130**
• ➤ International Review of Education/ Internationale Zeitschrift fuer Erziehungswissenschaft/Revue Internationale de l'Education (NLD ISSN 0020-8566) **2871**
▼ • International Review of Eighteenth-Century Studies/Revue Internationale d'Etude du Dix-Huitieme Siecle (FIN ISSN 1797-0091) **4147**
• ➤ International Review of Electrical Engineering (USA ISSN 1827-6660) **3321**
• International Review of Environmental and Resource Economics (USA ISSN 1932-1465) **1130**
• ➤ International Review of Finance (AUS ISSN 1369-412X) **1358**
• ➤ International Review of Financial Analysis (NLD ISSN 1057-5219) **1359**
International Review of Graphic Design and Visual Communications *see* Lineagrafica **8971**
† International Review of Health Psychology (GBR) **8966**
International Review of History Education (GBR ISSN 1461-8141) **4147**
• ➤ International Review of Hydrobiology (DEU ISSN 1434-2944) **679**
➤ International Review of Industrial and Organizational Psychology (GBR ISSN 0886-1528) **7366**
International Review of Industrial Property and Copyright Law Studies *see* I I C Studies **6751**
• ➤ International Review of Information Ethics (DEU) **6926**
International Review of Korean Studies (AUS ISSN 1449-7395) **3540**
• ➤ International Review of Law and Economics (USA ISSN 0144-8188) **4696**
• ➤ International Review of Law, Computers & Technology (GBR ISSN 1360-0869) **4845**
• ➤ International Review of Mechanical Engineering (USA ISSN 1970-8734) **3383**
• International Review of Mission (GBR ISSN 0020-8582) **7651**
International Review of Modern Sociology (IND ISSN 0970-4841) **8110**
The International Review of Modern Surgery (GBR ISSN 1465-8747) **6246**
• ➤ International Review of Neurobiology (USA ISSN 0074-7742) **6148**
International Review of Neurobiology. Supplement *see* International Review of Neurobiology **6148**
International Review of Nuclear Physics (SGP ISSN 0217-9474) **7067**
International Review of Patient Care (GBR) **5640**
▼ • International Review of Physics (USA ISSN 1971-680X) **7018**
▼ • ➤ International Review of Pragmatics (NLD ISSN 1877-3095) **5203**
† ➤ International Review of Professional Issues in Selection and Assessment (GBR ISSN 1067-9987) **8966**
• ➤ International Review of Psychiatry (GBR ISSN 0954-0261) **6148**
International Review of Psychiatry (USA ISSN 1066-3657) **6148**
International Review of Public Administration (KOR ISSN 1229-4659) **7447**
International Review of Pure and Applied Mathematics (IND ISSN 0973-1350) **5498**
▼ • International Review of Qualitative Research (USA ISSN 1940-8447) **7975**
• ➤ International Review of Research in Mental Retardation (USA ISSN 0074-7750) **6148**
• ➤ International Review of Research in Open and Distance Learning (CAN ISSN 1492-3831) **2942**
• ➤ The International Review of Retail, Distribution and Consumer Research (GBR ISSN 0959-3969) **1822**
• ➤ International Review of Social History (GBR ISSN 0020-8590) **4147**
International Review of Social Psychology *see* Revue Internationale de Psychologie Sociale **7405**
• ➤ International Review of Sociology (GBR ISSN 0390-6701) **8110**
▼ • ➤ International Review of Sport and Exercise Psychology (GBR ISSN 1750-984X) **7366**
• International Review of the Aesthetics and Sociology of Music (HRV ISSN 0351-5796) **6577**
• ➤ International Review of the Red Cross (GBR ISSN 1816-3831) **4932**
International Review of Third World Culture and Issues (USA) **8110**
• ➤ International Review of Victimology (GBR ISSN 0269-7580) **2656**
• ➤ International Review of Women and Leadership (AUS ISSN 1323-1685) **8899**
• ➤ International Review on Computers and Software (USA ISSN 1828-6003) **2427**
• International Review on Public and Non Profit Marketing (DEU ISSN 1865-1984) **1822**
• ➤ International Reviews in Physical Chemistry (GBR ISSN 0144-235X) **2136**
• ➤ International Reviews of Immunology (GBR ISSN 0883-0185) **5761**
International Rice Industry Guide (USA) **238**
International Rice Research Institute Corporate Reports *see* I R R I Corporate Reports **273**
International Rice Research Institute Program Report *see* I R R I Program Report **273**
• International Rice Research Notes (PHL ISSN 0117-4185) **273**
• International Rig Report (USA ISSN 1368-9118) **6774**
International Risk Management Institute Workers Comp *see* I R M I Workers Comp **4505**
International Rivers and Lakes (USA ISSN 0257-6236) **2796**
International Road Congresses. Proceedings (FRA ISSN 0074-7815) **8632**
• International Road Haulage by United Kingdom Registered Vehicles (GBR ISSN 0262-6195) **8671**
International Road Weather Conference. Proceedings *see* S I R W E C. Proceedings **6394**
• International Roundup (AUS ISSN 1832-7249) **1762**
• International Roundup News (AUS ISSN 1834-4437) **1762**
International Rubber Digest *see* Rubber Industry Report **7826**
International Rubber Directory *see* Handbuch der Internationalen Kautschukindustrie **7824**
• International Rubber Forum (GBR) **7825**
International Rubber Study Group. Secretariat Papers (GBR) **7825**
International Rubber Study Group Staff Papers *see* I S R G Staff Papers **7824**
International Rugby News (GBR ISSN 1742-7908) **8236**
International Rural Sociology Association Items *see* I R S A Items **8106**
International S A M P E Symposium and Exhibition (Society for the Advancement of Material and Process Engineering) (USA ISSN 0891-0138) **3348**
• International S A M P E Technical Conference Series (Society for the Advancement of Material and Process Engineering) (USA ISSN 0892-2624) **3348**
International Safe Transit Association Resource Book *see* I S T A Resource Book **6710**
International SafetyNet Manual (GBR) **2327**
International Sales Voice (DEU ISSN 1615-0619) **1822**
International Sanitary Supply Association, Inc. Today *see* I S S A Today **7524**
• International Satellite Directory (USA ISSN 1041-4541) **2327**
➤ International Satellite Symposium on Acute Renal Failure. Proceedings (GRC) **6269**
International School for Advanced Studies Lecture Series (SGP) **7018**
International School Magazine *see* I S. International School **3013**
International School of Hydrocarbon Measurement. Proceedings (USA ISSN 0145-7594) **6774**
International School of Physics "Enrico Fermi." Proceedings (NLD ISSN 0074-784X) **7018**
International School of Plasma Physics Piero Caldirola. Proceedings (ITA) **7018**
International School of Solid State Physics. Proceeding of the (Number) Course of *see* The Science and Culture Series - Physics **7039**
International Schools Directory (Year) (GBR) **2957**
➤ International Schools Journal (GBR ISSN 0264-7281) **3013**
International Schools Services Directory of International Schools *see* I S S Directory of International Schools **2956**
• International Schools, the Database (GBR ISSN 1470-4862) **2957**
International Science Policy: Press Review *see* Internationale Wissenschaftspolitik: Presseschau **7937**
• ➤ International Scientific Journal Geographica Pannonica (SRB ISSN 0354-8724) **4016**
International Scrap Directory (GBR) **6317**
➤ International Seaweed Symposium. Proceedings (BRA ISSN 0074-7874) **795**
International Section International News *see* A S A E International News **1722**
International Section of the I S S A for the Prevention of Occupational Risks Due to Electricity. Bulletin *see* Internationale Sektion der I V S S fuer die Verhuetung von Arbeitsunfaellen und Berufskrankheiten durch Elektrizitaet. Bulletin **8966**
International Securities and Financial Reporting Update (USA ISSN 1939-6759) **1631**
• International Securities Finance (GBR ISSN 1470-4005) **1359**
International Securities Service - Capital Event File (GBR) **1631**
International Securities Service - Coding and Prices File (GBR) **1631**
International Securities Service - Dividend File (GBR) **1631**
International Securitization & Structured Finance Report (USA ISSN 1523-262X) **1571**
• ➤ International Security (USA ISSN 0162-2889) **7245**
International Security Review (GBR ISSN 1469-3909) **6425**
International Sedimentological Congress. Guidebook (ESP ISSN 0074-7904) **2748**
• International Seismological Centre. Bulletin (GBR ISSN 0020-8671) **2784**
• International Seismological Centre. Regional Catalogue of Earthquakes (GBR ISSN 0034-334X) **2784**
International Semiconductor Conference. Proceedings (USA) **7052**
International Semiconductor Laser Conference. Proceedings (USA) **7077**
International Semiconductor-on-Insulator Conference Proceedings *see* I E E E International S O I Conference Proceedings **3312**
• International Seminars in Paediatric Gastroenterology and Nutrition (CAN ISSN 1188-4525) **5927**
• International Seminars in Surgical Oncology (GBR ISSN 1477-7800) **6023**
➤ International Sephardic Journal (USA ISSN 1547-5808) **3540**
➤ International Series in Economic Modeling (NLD ISSN 0924-5235) **1419**
➤ International Series in Intelligent Technologies (NLD ISSN 1382-3434) **2452**

Link to your serials resources and content with ulrichsweb.com

10454 INTERNATIONAL STUDIES ULRICH'S PERIODICALS

• ➤ International Studies (IND ISSN 0020-8817) **7245**
International Studies *see* Kokusai Kenkyu **7250**
➤ International Studies (POL ISSN 1641-4233) **7975**
▼ • International Studies in Catholic Education (GBR ISSN 1942-2539) **7801**
➤ International Studies in Economics and Econometrics (NLD ISSN 0924-5170) **1130**
• International Studies in Educational Administration (CYP ISSN 1324-1702) **3013**
International Studies in Folklore and Ethnology (GBR ISSN 1662-0615) **3618**
➤ International Studies in Human Rights (NLD ISSN 0924-4751) **7210**
➤ International Studies in Philosophy (USA ISSN 0270-5664) **6926**
International Studies in Population (NLD ISSN 1871-0395) **7285**
International Studies in Religion and Society (NLD ISSN 1573-4293) **8110**
➤ International Studies in Sociology and Social Anthropology (NLD ISSN 0074-8684) **8110**
• ➤ International Studies in Sociology of Education (GBR ISSN 0962-0214) **3066**
• International Studies in the Philosophy of Science (GBR ISSN 0269-8595) **6926**
➤ International Studies in the Service Economy (NLD ISSN 0924-6363) **1890**
International Studies in the Theory of Private Law (GBR) **4833**
† International Studies. Nordic Seminar on Human Rights. Proceedings (NLD ISSN 0903-9961) **8966**
• ➤ International Studies of Management and Organization (USA ISSN 0020-8825) **1762**
➤ International Studies on Childhood and Adolescence (DEU ISSN 1432-4873) **2155**
International Studies on Social Security (GBR) **4509**
• ➤ International Studies Perspectives (USA ISSN 1528-3577) **7245**
• ➤ International Studies Quarterly (USA ISSN 0020-8833) **7245**
• International Studies Review (KOR ISSN 1226-8240) **7245**
• ➤ International Studies Review (USA ISSN 1521-9488) **7245**
International Study Programs at the Universiteit van Amsterdam (NLD) **2988**
International Study Report on the Earthquake and Earthquake Engineering *see* Kokusai Jishingaku Oyobi Jishin Kogaku Kenshu Nenpo **2712**
International Sugar and Sweetener Report *see* F.O. Licht's International Sugar and Sweetener Report **110**
International Sugar Journal (GBR ISSN 0020-8841) **3649**
• International Sugar Organization. Market Report and Press Summary (GBR) **3649**
International Sugar Organization. Monthly Market Report and Press Summary *see* International Sugar Organization. Market Report and Press Summary **3649**
International Sugar Organization. Monthly Statistical Bulletin *see* International Sugar Organization. Statistical Bulletin **3670**
International Sugar Organization. Proceedings (GBR) **3649**
• International Sugar Organization. Quarterly Market Outlook (GBR) **3674**
• International Sugar Organization. Quarterly Market Review (GBR) **3649**
International Sugar Organization. Statistical Bulletin (GBR ISSN 0020-885X) **3670**
International Sugar Organization. Studies (GBR) **3674**
International Sugar Organization. Sugar Year Book (GBR) **3649**
International Superconductivity Technology Center Journal *see* I S T E C Journal **3104**
➤ International Surgery (USA ISSN 0020-8868) **6246**
• International Survey of Business Expectations (USA) **1599**
➤ The (Year) International Survey of Family Law (GBR ISSN 1384-623X) **4911**
International Swimming Hall of Fame Headlines (USA) **8181**
International Symposia on Asian Studies. Proceedings (HKG) **552**
International Symposium on Acoustical Holography and Imaging. Proceedings *see* Acoustical Imaging **7085**
International Symposium on Advanced Packaging Materials: Processes, Properties and Interfaces. Proceedings (USA) **6711**
• International Symposium on Advanced Research in Asynchronous Circuits and Systems (USA ISSN 1522-8681) **3105**
International Symposium on Advanced Science Research. Proceedings *see* Physical Society of Japan. Journal **7032**
• International Symposium on Agent Systems and Applications. Proceedings (USA ISSN 1530-2008) **2522**
International Symposium on Automated Cartography. Proceedings (USA) **4016**
• International Symposium on Automation and Robotics in Construction. Proceedings (NLD) **2585**
International Symposium on Autonomous Decentralized Systems (USA ISSN 1541-0056) **2467**
• International Symposium on Biomedical Imaging. Proceedings (USA ISSN 1945-7928) **6199**
International Symposium on Ceramics in Medicine. Proceedings (CHE) **5640**
International Symposium on Chemical Reaction Engineering. Proceedings (USA ISSN 0071-3112) **3247**
International Symposium on Circuits and Systems *see* I E E E International Symposium on Circuits and Systems. Proceedings **3102**
International Symposium on Code Generation and Optimization (USA ISSN 1931-0544) **2507**
International Symposium on Cold Regions Engineering. Proceedings (USA ISSN 0270-546X) **3273**
International Symposium on Combustion. Proceedings *see* Combustion Institute. Proceedings **2134**
International Symposium on Compound Semiconductors (USA) **2466**
International Symposium on Concrete Roads. Reports (BEL) **3273**
International Symposium on Crop Protection. Proceedings (BEL) **238**
• International Symposium on Defect and Fault - Tolerance in V L S I Systems. Proceedings (Very Large Scale Integration) (USA ISSN 1550-5774) **2540**
• International Symposium on Discharges and Electrical Insulation in Vacuum. Proceedings (USA ISSN 1093-2941) **3321**
International Symposium on Dry Process. Proceedings/Dorai Purosesu Shinpojumu (JPN) **3321**
International Symposium on Electrets. Proceedings (USA) **7052**
International Symposium on Electrical Insulating Materials. Proceedings/Denki Zetsuen Zairyo Shimpojumu Yokoshu (JPN) **3348**
• International Symposium on Electromagnetic Compatibility and Electromagnetic Ecology. Proceedings (USA ISSN 1938-5358) **7018**
International Symposium on Electron Devices for Microwave and Optoelectronic Applications (USA) **2427**
International Symposium on Environmentally Conscious Design and Inverse Manufacturing (USA) **2540**
International Symposium on Fault-Tolerant Computing Fast Abstracts (USA) **2592**
International Symposium on Fingerprint Detection and Identification. Proceedings (USA) **2656**
• International Symposium on High-Performance Computer Architecture. Proceedings (USA ISSN 1530-0897) **2467**
• International Symposium on High Performance Computing Systems and Applications. Proceedings (USA ISSN 1550-5243) **2522**
• International Symposium on High-Performance Distributed Computing. Proceedings (USA ISSN 1082-8907) **2467**
International Symposium on Industrial Robots. Symposium Proceedings (FRA) **2585**
• International Symposium on Information Processing in Sensor Networks. Proceedings (USA) **2427**
• International Symposium on Low Power Electronics and Design. Proceedings (USA ISSN 1533-4678) **3105**
International Symposium on Micro Mechatronics and Human Science *see* International Symposium on Micro-NanoMechatronics and Human Science. Proceeedings **2466**
International Symposium on Micro-NanoMechatronics and Human Science. Proceeedings (USA) **2466**
• International Symposium on Microarchitecture. Proceedings (USA ISSN 1072-4451) **2467**
• International Symposium on Microelectronics. Proceedings (USA ISSN 1085-8024) **3105**
International Symposium on Mini and Microcomputers. Proceedings (CAN) **2574**
International Symposium on Mixed and Augmented Reality (I S M A R). Proceedings (USA ISSN 1554-7868) **2472**
• International Symposium on Modeling, Analysis, and Simulation of Computer and Telecommunication Systems. Proceedings (USA ISSN 1526-7539) **2472**
International Symposium on Multimedia Software Engineering (USA) **2592**
• International Symposium on Multiple-Valued Logic (USA ISSN 0195-623X) **2472**
▼ • International Symposium on Networks-on-Chip. Proceedings (USA) **2540**
International Symposium on New Materials for Electrochemical Systems. Extended Abstracts (CAN) **3321**
International Symposium on Object-Oriented Real-Time Distributed Computing (USA ISSN 1555-0885) **2531**
• International Symposium on Parallel Architectures, Algorithms, and Networks (USA ISSN 1087-4089) **2522**
International Symposium on Photofinishing Technology. Proceedings (USA) **6970**
International Symposium on Plasma Process-Induced Damage (USA) **7018**
• International Symposium on Power Semiconductor Devices and ICs (USA ISSN 1063-6854) **3105**
International Symposium on Regional Development. Papers and Proceedings (JPN ISSN 0074-8897) **4416**
International Symposium on Remote Sensing of the Environment. Proceedings (CAN) **2784**
International Symposium on Science and Technology Society (USA) **6699**
International Symposium on Semiconductor Manufacturing. Proceedings *see* I E E E International Symposium on Semiconductor Manufacturing Conference Proceedings **2471**
International Symposium on Signals, Systems, and Electronics (USA) **2462**
International Symposium on Software Engineering for Parallel and Distributed Systems (USA) **2592**
• International Symposium on Software Engineering Standards (USA ISSN 1530-1613) **2592**
• International Symposium on Software Metrics (USA) **2592**
• International Symposium on Software Reliability Engineering. Proceedings (USA ISSN 1071-9458) **2593**
International Symposium on String Processing and Information Retrieval (USA) **2468**
International Symposium on Surfactants in Solution. Proceedings *see* Surfactants in Solution **3256**
International Symposium on Symbolic and Algebraic Computation (USA ISSN 1532-1029) **2601**
• International Symposium on System Synthesis. Proceedings (USA ISSN 1080-1820) **2593**
International Symposium on the Aerodynamics and Ventilation of Vehicle Tunnels. Papers Presented (GBR ISSN 0263-4317) **3273**
• International Symposium on Uncertainty Modeling and Analysis. Proceedings (USA ISSN 1068-2228) **3321**
International Symposium on V L S I Design. Proceedings (USA) **2472**
• International Symposium on Wearable Computers. Digest of Papers (USA ISSN 1530-0811) **2427**
International Symposium on Wearable Computers. Proceedings *see* International Symposium on Wearable Computers. Digest of Papers **2427**
The International System of Units *see* Comite International des Poids et Mesures. Systeme International d'Unites **6401**
International System Safety Conference. Proceedings (USA) **7527**
International Talent and Touring Directory *see* Billboard International Talent and Touring Directory (Year) **6549**
International Talent Magazine *see* Guoji Rencai Jiaoliu **3012**
International Tattoo Art (USA ISSN 1065-643X) **497**
International Tax Agreements (USA ISSN 0074-896X) **1930**
• ➤ International Tax and Public Finance (USA ISSN 0927-5940) **1930**
International Tax Havens (USA) **1930**
• International Tax Journal (USA ISSN 0097-7314) **1930**
International Tax Law Reports (GBR ISSN 1464-7117) **1930**
• International Tax Monitor (USA ISSN 1535-7783) **1930**
• International Tax Report (GBR ISSN 0300-1628) **1930**
• International Tax Review (GBR ISSN 0958-7594) **1571**
International Tax Systems and Planning Techniques (GBR) **1930**
International Taxation *see* Journal of International Taxation **1931**
International Taxation in China *see* Shewai Shuiwu **1943**
International Taxation of Low Tax Transactions (GBR) **1930**
International Taxation Series (USA ISSN 1550-0845) **1930**
International Technical Conference on Coal Utilization & Fuel Systems. Proceedings (USA) **3139**
International Technical Literature Guide *see* I T L **8425**
• International Technology and Business Opportunities. Catalogue (IND ISSN 0972-0693) **8428**
International Technology Exchange - International Battery Materials Association Letters on Batteries, New Technologies & Medicine (with News for Research) *see* I T E - I B A Letters on Batteries, New Technologies & Medicine (with News for Research) **7051**
International Technology Law Review (GBR ISSN 1475-4320) **4932**
International Telecom Directory (USA ISSN 1047-8744) **2368**
International Telecommunication Union. Booklets (CHE) **2328**
International Telecommunication Union. Central Library. List of Periodicals/Union Internacional de Telecomunicaciones. Biblioteca Central. Lista de Revistas/Union Internationale des Telecommunications. Bibliotheque Centrale. Liste des Periodiques (CHE) **2348**
International Telecommunication Union. Central Library. List of Recent Acquisitions/Union Internacional de Telecomunicaciones. Biblioteca Central. Lista de Adquisiciones Recientes/Union Internationale des Telecommunications. Bibliotheque Centrale. Liste des Acquisitions Recentes (CHE) **2348**
International Telecommunication Union Global Directory *see* I T U Global Directory **2325**
International Telecommunication Union. List of Annuals/Union Internacional de Telecomunicaciones. Lista de Publicaciones Anuales/Union Internationale des Telecommunications. Listes des Publications Annuelles (CHE) **2348**
International Telecommunication Union. List of Telegraph Offices Open for International Service (CHE ISSN 0074-9044) **2368**
International Telecommunication Union News *see* I T U News **2325**
• International Telecommunication Union. Operational Bulletin (CHE ISSN 0047-1224) **2368**
International Telecommunication Union. Report on the Activities (CHE ISSN 0085-2201) **2368**
International Telecommunication Union. Seminars (CHE) **2328**
International Telecommunication Union Statistical Yearbook *see* I T U Statistical Yearbook **2347**
International Telecommunication Union Weekly Circular and Special Sections *see* I T U Weekly Circular and Special Sections **2325**
• International Telecommunications Energy Conference. Proceedings (USA ISSN 0275-0473) **2328**
• International Telecommunications Intelligence (GBR ISSN 0268-9960) **2328**
International Telecoms Review (GBR ISSN 1361-603X) **2328**
International Telegraph and Telephone Consultative Committee. Plans (CHE) **2368**
International Telegraph and Telephone Consultative Committee. Plenary Assembly. Proceedings (CHE) **2368**
International Television & Video Almanac (USA ISSN 0895-2213) **2383**
International Test & Evaluation Association Journal of Test and Evaluation *see* I T E A Journal of Test and Evaluation **8425**
International Test Commission. Bulletin *see* International Journal of Testing **7366**
• International Test Conference. Proceedings (USA ISSN 1089-3539) **2427**
International Textbook Research *see* Internationale Schulbuchforschung **3066**
International Textile and Apparel Association Monographs *see* I T A A Monographs **2247**
International Textile and Apparel Association Newsletter *see* I T A A Newsletter **2247**
International Textile and Apparel Association Proceedings (Online) *see* I T A A Proceedings (Online) **2251**
International Textile Bulletin (CHE ISSN 1029-8525) **8453**
International Textile Bulletin: Nonwovens - Industrial Textiles (CHE ISSN 1024-6592) **8453**
International Textile Calendar (GBR ISSN 0263-5879) **8453**
International Textile Machinery Shipment Statistics (CHE) **8463**
International Textile Magazine *see* Tekstil & Teknik **8458**
International Textile Manufacturers Federation. Annual Conference Report (Year) (CHE ISSN 1727-4761) **8453**
International Textile Manufacturers Federation Country Statements *see* I T M F Country Statements **8452**
International Textile Manufacturers Federation Directory *see* I T M F Directory **8452**
International Textile Manufacturers Federation State of Trade Report *see* I T M F State of Trade Report **8452**
International Textile Reports *see* Melliand Textilberichte **8455**
International Textiles (GBR ISSN 0020-8914) **8453**
International Textiles Bodywear *see* Active Sports and Bodywear **2245**
International Textiles Interior (GBR ISSN 1740-4053) **8453**
International Theatre Institute of the United States. Newsletter (USA) **8472**
▼ • International Theory (GBR ISSN 1752-9719) **7245**
International Thermal Spraying Conference. Preprint of Papers (USA) **6343**
International Thermonuclear Experimental Reactor - Co-ordinated Technical Activities Newsletter *see* I T E R - C T A Newsletter **3168**
International Thermonuclear Experimental Reactor. Documentation Series (AUT ISSN 1018-6298) **3169**
➤ International Third World Studies - Journal and Review (USA ISSN 1041-3944) **7246**
The International Ticketing Association Newsletter *see* I N T I X Newsletter **1820**
International Tin Research Institute. Annual Report (GBR) **6317**
• ➤ International Tinnitus Journal (USA ISSN 0946-5448) **6081**
International Titanium Association. (Year) Buyers Guide (USA) **6317**

▼ *new title*   † *ceased*   • *electronic media*   ➤ *refereed*

Title

Interne Rapportenreeks Communicatie Research en Semiotiek (NLD ISSN 1567-8989) **8110**
† • Internet (CZE ISSN 1211-6351) **8966**
Al-Internet *see* An- Nahar **3905**
Internet Access Made Easy Guide to A O L (America Online) (GBR) **2560**
Internet Advertising Market Assessment *see* Key Note Market Assessment. Internet Advertising **1892**
Internet Advisor (GBR) **2560**
L'Internet Agricole *see* Agriculture & Nouvelles Technologies **85**
• Internet and E-Commerce Law in Canada (CAN ISSN 1494-4146) **2560**
• Internet and Electronic Commerce Strategies (USA ISSN 1092-1303) **2560**
• ➤ The Internet and Higher Education (GBR ISSN 1096-7516) **2560**
• Internet & Personal Computing Abstracts (Online) (USA) **2443**
• Internet & Technology Finance (GBR ISSN 1474-2012) **2328**
• ➤ Internet Archaeology (GBR ISSN 1363-5387) **399**
Internet Atlas of Websites (USA) **2560**
Internet Banking Commentary (USA ISSN 1553-8206) **1393**
Internet Banking Growth Strategies (USA ISSN 1533-9939) **1393**
• Internet Bookwatch (USA) **627**
Internet Broadcaster (GBR ISSN 1470-4188) **2560**
• Internet Business (GBR ISSN 1366-2821) **2560**
Internet Business *see* Internet Business Newsletter **2368**
• Internet Business News (GBR ISSN 1363-9919) **2560**
• Internet Business Newsletter (USA ISSN 1541-1249) **2368**
▼ • Internet Business Newsweekly (USA ISSN 1944-2300) **2560**
• Internet Business Report (USA) **2560**
Internet Business Review *see* Journal of Internet Business **1137**
Internet Business Strategies (USA) **2560**
Internet.by (RUS) **2560**
• Internet Connection (Little Falls) (USA ISSN 1080-8493) **2560**
• Internet Daily News (USA) **2560**
Internet Developer's Journal *see* Java Developer's Journal **2507**
Internet Dimensions (USA ISSN 1542-8699) **2561**
The Internet Directory of the Turf *see* The Directory of the Turf (Year) **8290**
• ➤ Internet Electronic Journal of Molecular Design (USA ISSN 1538-6414) **734**
Internet en Belgique (BEL ISSN 1375-3991) **2561**
Internet Facile (ITA ISSN 1127-1663) **2561**
▼ • Internet Fact Finding for Lawyers (USA ISSN 1936-1882) **4696**
The Internet for Dummies (USA ISSN 1931-4698) **2527**
† Internet fuer Einsteiger (DEU) **8966**
Internet Garden *see* I Garden **3738**
• The Internet Gazette Newsletter (USA ISSN 1533-1377) **2561**
• Internet Genealogy (USA ISSN 1718-0414) **3771**
† Internet Genius (ITA ISSN 1828-7840) **8966**
▼ • The Internet Guide for the Legal Researcher Newsletter (USA ISSN 1558-6227) **4845**
• The Internet Guide to Baby Health (USA ISSN 1537-9140) **6093**
† • ➤ Internet He@lth (IND) **8966**
Internet Homesteader. Series A: Library and Information Science (USA ISSN 1076-4143) **5019**
Internet in Belgie *see* Internet en Belgique **2561**
Internet Job Search Almanac *see* Adams Internet Job Search Almanac **8928**
• Internet Journal (USA ISSN 1937-3805) **2561**
• ➤ The Internet Journal of Academic Physician Assistants (USA ISSN 1092-4078) **5640**
• ➤ The Internet Journal of Advanced Nursing Practice (USA ISSN 1523-6064) **5962**
▼ • ➤ The Internet Journal of Aesthetic and Antiaging (USA) **311**
• ➤ The Internet Journal of Allied Health Sciences and Practice (USA ISSN 1540-580X) **5640**
• ➤ The Internet Journal of Alternative Medicine (USA ISSN 1540-2584) **311**
• ➤ The Internet Journal of Anesthesiology (USA ISSN 1092-406X) **5771**
• ➤ The Internet Journal of Asthma, Allergy and Immunology (USA ISSN 1532-0642) **5761**
• ➤ The Internet Journal of Bioengineering (USA ISSN 1937-8246) **749**
▼ • ➤ The Internet Journal of Biological Anthropology (USA ISSN 1939-4594) **680**
• ➤ The Internet Journal of Cardiology (USA ISSN 1528-834X) **5790**
• ➤ The Internet Journal of Cardiovascular Research (USA ISSN 1540-2592) **5790**
The Internet Journal of Caribbean and Third World Medicine *see* The Internet Journal of Third World Medicine **5640**
➤ Internet Journal of Criminology (GBR) **2656**
• ➤ The Internet Journal of Dental Science (USA ISSN 1937-8238) **5849**
• ➤ The Internet Journal of Dermatology (USA ISSN 1531-3018) **5878**
• ➤ Internet Journal of e-Language Learning and Teaching (MYS) **2949**
• ➤ The Internet Journal of Emergency and Intensive Care Medicine (USA ISSN 1092-4051) **6062**
• ➤ The Internet Journal of Emergency Medicine (USA ISSN 1935-9551) **6062**
• ➤ The Internet Journal of Endocrinology (USA ISSN 1540-2606) **5895**
▼ • The Internet Journal of Endovascular Medicine (USA ISSN 1937-822X) **5790**
• ➤ The Internet Journal of Entrepreneurship (USA) **1962**
• ➤ The Internet Journal of Epidemiology (USA ISSN 1540-2614) **7527**
• ➤ The Internet Journal of Family Practice (USA ISSN 1528-8358) **5946**
• ➤ The Internet Journal of Forensic Sciences (USA ISSN 1540-2622) **5914**
• ➤ The Internet Journal of Gastroenterology (USA ISSN 1528-8323) **5927**
• ➤ The Internet Journal of Genomics and Proteomics (USA ISSN 1540-2630) **766**
• ➤ The Internet Journal of Geriatrics and Gerontology (USA ISSN 1937-8211) **4048**
• ➤ The Internet Journal of Gynecology and Obstetrics (USA ISSN 1528-8439) **5994**
▼ • ➤ The Internet Journal of Hand Surgery (USA ISSN 1937-8203) **6246**
▼ • ➤ The Internet Journal of Head and Neck Surgery (USA ISSN 1937-819X) **6246**
• ➤ The Internet Journal of Health (USA ISSN 1528-8315) **7527**
• ➤ The Internet Journal of Healthcare Administration (USA ISSN 1531-2933) **4102**
• ➤ The Internet Journal of Hematology (USA ISSN 1540-2649) **5939**
• ➤ The Internet Journal of Infectious Diseases (USA ISSN 1528-8366) **5640**
• ➤ The Internet Journal of Internal Medicine (USA ISSN 1528-8382) **5946**
• ➤ The Internet Journal of Laboratory Medicine (USA ISSN 1937-8181) **5906**
Internet Journal of Language, Culture and Society *see* Language, Culture and Society **5140**
▼ • ➤ The Internet Journal of Laserneedle Medicine (USA ISSN 1937-8173) **5640**
• ➤ The Internet Journal of Law, Healthcare and Ethics (USA ISSN 1528-8250) **5914**
• ➤ The Internet Journal of Medical Informatics (USA ISSN 1937-8300) **5640**
• ➤ The Internet Journal of Medical Simulation (USA ISSN 1559-4734) **5640**
The Internet Journal of Medical Simulation and Technology *see* The Internet Journal of Medical Simulation **5640**
• ➤ The Internet Journal of Medical Technology (USA ISSN 1559-4610) **8428**
• ➤ Internet Journal of Medical Update (MUS ISSN 1694-0423) **5640**
• ➤ The Internet Journal of Mental Health (USA ISSN 1531-2941) **7366**
• ➤ The Internet Journal of Microbiology (USA ISSN 1937-8289) **888**
▼ • ➤ The Internet Journal of Minimally Invasive Spinal Technology (USA ISSN 1937-8254) **6246**
• ➤ The Internet Journal of Nanotechnology (USA ISSN 1937-8262) **8428**
• ➤ The Internet Journal of Nephrology (USA ISSN 1540-2665) **6269**
• ➤ The Internet Journal of Neurology (USA ISSN 1531-295X) **6148**
• ➤ The Internet Journal of Neuromonitoring (USA ISSN 1531-300X) **6148**
• ➤ The Internet Journal of Neurosurgery (USA ISSN 1528-8285) **6246**
• ➤ The Internet Journal of Nuclear Medicine (USA ISSN 1539-4638) **6199**
• ➤ The Internet Journal of Nutrition and Wellness (USA ISSN 1937-8297) **6661**
• ➤ The Internet Journal of Oncology (USA ISSN 1528-8331) **6023**
• ➤ The Internet Journal of Ophthalmology and Visual Science (USA ISSN 1528-8269) **6044**
• ➤ The Internet Journal of Orthopedic Surgery (USA ISSN 1531-2968) **6062**
• ➤ The Internet Journal of Otorhinolaryngology (USA ISSN 1528-8420) **6081**
• ➤ The Internet Journal of Pain, Symptom Control and Palliative Care (USA ISSN 1528-8277) **5771**
• ➤ The Internet Journal of Parasitic Diseases (USA ISSN 1559-4629) **5819**
• ➤ The Internet Journal of Pathology (USA ISSN 1528-8307) **5640**
• ➤ The Internet Journal of Pediatrics and Neonatology (USA ISSN 1528-8374) **6093**
• ➤ The Internet Journal of Perfusionists (USA ISSN 1531-3026) **5790**
• ➤ The Internet Journal of Pharmacology (USA ISSN 1531-2976) **6850**
• ➤ The Internet Journal of Plastic Surgery (USA ISSN 1528-8293) **6246**
• Internet Journal of Public Health Education (DNK ISSN 1437-9619) **7527**
• ➤ The Internet Journal of Pulmonary Medicine (USA ISSN 1531-2984) **6215**
• ➤ The Internet Journal of Radiology (USA ISSN 1528-8404) **6199**
• ➤ The Internet Journal of Rescue and Disaster Medicine (USA ISSN 1531-2992) **6062**
• ➤ The Internet Journal of Rheumatology (USA ISSN 1528-8412) **6224**
† • Internet Journal of Science - Biological Chemistry (GBR ISSN 1462-2149) **8966**
• ➤ The Internet Journal of Spine Surgery (USA ISSN 1937-8270) **6246**
• ➤ The Internet Journal of Strategy (USA) **1762**
• ➤ The Internet Journal of Surgery (USA ISSN 1528-8242) **6246**
• ➤ The Internet Journal of Third World Medicine (USA ISSN 1539-4646) **5640**
• ➤ The Internet Journal of Thoracic and Cardiovascular Surgery (USA ISSN 1524-0274) **6247**
• ➤ The Internet Journal of Toxicology (USA ISSN 1559-3916) **6850**
• ➤ The Internet Journal of Tropical Medicine (USA ISSN 1540-2681) **5819**
• ➤ The Internet Journal of Urology (USA ISSN 1528-8390) **6269**
• ➤ The Internet Journal of Veterinary Medicine (USA ISSN 1937-8165) **8799**
• Internet Journal of Vibrational Spectroscopy (GBR ISSN 1362-671X) **2065**
• ➤ The Internet Journal of World Health and Societal Politics (USA ISSN 1540-269X) **7527**
Internet Law and Business (USA ISSN 1529-6369) **2561**
• Internet Law & Regulation (USA) **4845**
• Internet Law & Strategy (USA ISSN 1544-1911) **2561**
Internet Law Bulletin (AUS ISSN 1329-9735) **2561**
• Internet Law Researcher (USA ISSN 1087-7703) **2561**
• Internet Lawyer (USA ISSN 1087-7223) **2561**
The Internet Leisure and Entertainments Market *see* Key Note Market Assessment. E-Commerce: The Internet Leisure and Entertainments Market **1891**
Internet Librarian (Year) Conference Proceedings (USA) **5062**
Internet Librarian International (Year) Conference Proceedings (USA) **5062**
Internet Made Easy (GBR ISSN 1465-6965) **2561**
• Internet Magazin (DEU ISSN 1433-3511) **2561**
† • Internet Magazine (NZL ISSN 1175-3811) **8966**
Internet Magazine (THA) **2561**
Internet Marketing & Technology Report (USA ISSN 1082-1945) **2561**
Internet Marketing Report (USA ISSN 1099-0143) **2561**
• Internet Marketing Tips (USA) **2047**
• Internet Marketing Update (USA) **2561**
Internet Markets *see* Converging Media **2317**
• Internet Mathematics (USA ISSN 1542-7951) **2561**
Internet Media Directory *see* Bacon's Internet Media Directory **2552**
• Internet Media Review (USA) **2561**
Internet Medicina *see* Masson Newsletter de Internet Medicina **5832**
Internet Medicine *see* Disease Management Advisor **4092**
• The Internet Mole (GBR) **2561**
▼ • Internet, Networks & Communications (USA ISSN 1944-1819) **2561**
• Internet Newsroom (USA ISSN 1542-5312) **2561**
• Internet-on-a-Disk (USA) **2561**
Internet on a Disk *see* Internet-on-a-Disk **2561**
• Internet Panorama (NLD) **2427**
• Internet Photochemistry and Photobiology (GBR) **2136**
Internet Popsoft *see* Dazhong Ruanjian **2554**
† Internet Pratico (ITA ISSN 1591-6995) **8966**
Internet Pratique (FRA ISSN 1635-2610) **2561**
Internet - Praxis und Zukunftsanwendungen (DEU ISSN 1611-8634) **2561**
† Internet.pro (ITA ISSN 1824-8403) **8966**
† • Internet Professionell (DEU ISSN 1619-6481) **8966**
Internet Protocol Journal (USA) **2561**
Internet Protocol Video Surveillance Market Info Articles *see* I P Video Surveillance Market Info Articles **2402**
Internet Protocol Wireline and Wireless Week *see* I P Wireline and Wireless Week **2324**
Internet Quotient *see* i Q: **2558**
• ➤ Internet Reference Services Quarterly (USA ISSN 1087-5301) **5019**
• ➤ Internet Research (GBR ISSN 1066-2243) **2561**
The Internet Resource Directory for K-12 Teachers and Librarians (USA ISSN 1084-5798) **2561**
• Internet Resources Newsletter (GBR ISSN 1361-9381) **2561**
• Internet Retailer (USA ISSN 1527-7089) **2562**
Internet Retailing (GBR ISSN 1759-0582) **2562**
• The Internet Review of Science Fiction (USA ISSN 1547-819X) **5443**
• Internet Roadstop: Mac Zine and Information (USA) **2562**
• Internet ScamBusters (USA) **2562**
Internet Scams Ezine (USA) **2562**
Internet Security Advisor *see* Databased Advisor Magazine **2554**
Internet Service Provider World *see* I S P World **2558**
Internet Service Providers Business Monthly Newsletter *see* I S P Business Monthly Newsletter **2368**
Internet Service Providers Market Assessment *see* Key Note Market Assessment. Internet Service Providers **1892**
• Internet Standard (POL ISSN 1641-2575) **2562**
• Internet - Stock Watch (USA) **1631**
• Internet Surfer (USA) **2562**
• Internet Surveys (USA) **2562**
• Internet Tax Advisor (USA ISSN 1532-8805) **1393**
• Internet Telephony Magazine (USA ISSN 1098-0008) **2369**
• The Internet Times (USA) **2562**
† Internet Tips & Trucs (NLD ISSN 1570-9175) **8966**
Internet Travel Planner (USA ISSN 1540-0603) **8724**
• Internet Trend Watch for Libraries (USA) **2562**
Internet Usage in Business *see* Key Note Market Report: Internet Usage in Business **1894**
• Internet Watchdog (CAN) **2562**
• The Internet Web Source (USA) **2562**
▼ • Internet Weekly News (USA ISSN 1944-2327) **2562**
Internet Works (GBR ISSN 1460-1214) **2562**
• Internet World (ARG ISSN 0329-2967) **2562**
Internet World *see* Internet World Business **2562**
Internet World (GBR ISSN 1365-439X) **2562**
Internet World Business (DEU ISSN 1862-4901) **2562**
Internet World en Espanol (MEX) **2562**
Internet World Online (DEU) **2562**
• Internet World Sweden (SWE ISSN 1401-6125) **2562**
• The Internet Writing Journal (USA ISSN 1095-3973) **5310**
Internet Yellow Pages (Year): Business Models & Market Opportunities *see* Internet Yellow Pages (Year): Business Models and Market Opportunities **1419**
• Internet Yellow Pages (Year): Business Models and Market Opportunities (USA ISSN 1548-9019) **1419**
Internetid (ISL ISSN 1024-8730) **2562**
Internetmercado (USA) **2562**
InternetTelephony *see* Telephony **2373**
InternetWorld *see* Internet World Sweden **2562**
Internews *see* Orphans International Worldwide Internews **8061**
Internews Network Armenia. Newsletter (ARM) **3792**
• Internews Network Azerbaijan. Bulletin (AZE) **3799**
Internewsletter Afrique (USA) **7246**
Interni *see* Interni. La Rivista dell'Arredamento **4544**
Interni Annual *see* Interni. La Rivista dell'Arredamento **4544**
Interni Guida *see* Interni. La Rivista dell'Arredamento **4544**
Interni International *see* Interni. La Rivista dell'Arredamento **4544**
Interni. La Rivista dell'Arredamento (ITA ISSN 1122-3650) **4544**
• ➤ Interni Medicina pro Praxi (CZE ISSN 1212-7299) **5946**
• ➤ Der Internist (DEU ISSN 0020-9554) **5946**
➤ L'Internista (ITA ISSN 1121-9017) **5946**
Internisten Vademecum (NLD ISSN 1384-6620) **5946**
Internistische Praxis (DEU ISSN 0020-9570) **5946**
Die Internistische Welt *see* Onkologische Welt **5948**
Die Internistische Welt Onkologie *see* Onkologische Welt **5948**
Internships in Psychology (USA ISSN 1933-3315) **7366**
InterPark (GBR ISSN 1359-6284) **8181**
▼ • ➤ Interpersona (BRA ISSN 1981-6472) **7366**
Interpersonal Commtext Series (USA) **8110**
Interphex U S A. Proceedings of the Technical Program (USA ISSN 1066-7474) **6850**
Interplanetary News (GBR ISSN 0020-9597) **61**
• Interplay (GBR ISSN 1475-4703) **2155**
Interplay (Hillsdale) (USA) **6577**
Interplay (Malibu) (USA ISSN 0742-1176) **5310**
• Interpres (ITA ISSN 0392-0224) **4458**
Interpretatie (NLD ISSN 0929-015X) **7651**
➤ Interpretation (Flushing) (USA ISSN 0020-9635) **7144**
• ➤ Interpretation (Richmond) (USA ISSN 0020-9643) **7651**
Interpretation and Application of International Accounting Standards (USA ISSN 1099-5765) **1293**
Interpretation and Translation (NLD) **6926**
Interpretation Studies *see* Tsuuyaku Kenkyuu **5189**
▼ Interpretation und Quellen (DEU) **6926**
Interpretazioni (ITA) **6926**
† Interpretazioni Tendenziose (ITA) **8966**
L'Interprete (CHE ISSN 0047-1291) **5130**
L'Interprete (ITA) **5310**
• The Interpreter (Durham) (USA ISSN 0020-9651) **4510**
• Interpreter (Nashville) (USA ISSN 0020-9678) **7762**
▼ ➤ The Interpreter and Translator Trainer (GBR ISSN 1750-399X) **5130**
• Interpreter Releases (USA ISSN 0020-9686) **4696**
• ➤ Interpreting (NLD ISSN 1384-6647) **5130**
➤ Interpreting the Past (USA) **399**
• Interracial Voice (USA) **3540**
• ➤ Interreligious and Intercultural Investigation (ITA) **7801**
Interreligious Foundation for Community Organization News *see* I F C O News **8045**
Interreligious Insight (GBR ISSN 1742-1888) **7651**
InterReview (USA ISSN 1944-0634) **497**
• Interrobang (CAN) **2288**
L'Interrogation Philosophique (FRA ISSN 1159-6120) **6927**

Title

Interscholastic Athletic Administration (USA ISSN 0097-871X) **3025**
➤ Interscience Conference on Antimicrobial Agents and Chemotherapy. Abstracts (USA ISSN 1532-0227) **888**
Intersec (GBR ISSN 0963-0058) **2678**
• Intersecciones en Antropologia (ARG ISSN 1666-2105) **343**
Intersecoes (BRA ISSN 1517-6088) **7975**
Intersection (GBR ISSN 1473-7620) **8586**
• Intersection (NZL ISSN 1176-421X) **8110**
Intersection (USA ISSN 1542-9695) **7651**
• ➤ Intersections (AUS ISSN 1440-9151) **8899**
➤ Intersections/Revue de Musique des Universites Canadiennes (CAN ISSN 1911-0146) **6577**
➤ Intersections (NLD ISSN 1568-1181) **4148**
Intersections in Communications and Culture (USA ISSN 1528-610X) **8110**
Intersedes (CRI ISSN 1409-4746) **2871**
• Intersezioni (ITA ISSN 0393-2451) **4458**
➤ Intersight (USA ISSN 1049-6564) **446**
Intersociety Conference on Thermal Phenomena in Electronic Systems. Proceedings (USA ISSN 1087-9870) **2466**
Interspace - Link Confidential Newsletter (USA) **61**
Interspecies Newsletter (USA) **2328**
Interstandox (DEU) **6718**
Interstandox Extra (DEU) **6718**
• ➤ InterStat (USA ISSN 1941-689X) **8380**
• Interstate Commission on the Potomac River Basin. Technical Reports (USA) **3443**
Interstate Manufacturers & Industrial Classified Directory & Buyers Guide (USA) **2009**
Interstate Oil and Gas Compact Commission Members and Oil and Gas Agencies Directory *see* I O G C C Members and Oil and Gas Agencies Directory **2004**
Intersticios (URY) **7975**
Interstitial Cystitis Association Update (Rockville) *see* I C A Update (Rockville) **6268**
Intersubjetivo (ESP ISSN 1575-6483) **6148**
• ➤ Intertax (NLD ISSN 0165-2826) **1572**
• InterText (USA ISSN 1071-7676) **5443**
• ➤ Intertexts (USA ISSN 1092-0625) **5310**
Intertrade *see* Guoji Maoyi **1567**
Intertrade (CHN) **1572**
InterTruckNews (ITA ISSN 1970-6251) **8671**
Interuniversitair Centrum voor Hedendaagse Geschiedenis. Mededelingen *see* Centre Interuniversitaire d'Histoire Contemporaine. Cahiers **4210**
Interuniversity Programme in Demography Working Papers *see* I P D Working Papers **7309**
Intervac U S (USA) **8724**
Interval (CAN) **8472**
Interval World (USA) **8724**
Interval(le)s *see* Intervalles **497**
Intervalle (DEU ISSN 0579-8353) **6578**
• Intervalles (BEL ISSN 1784-8180) **497**
• Intervalli (Online) (FIN ISSN 1796-7392) **6578**
Intervalli (Print) *see* Intervalli (Online) **6578**
• Intervencion Psicosocial (ESP ISSN 1132-0559) **7366**
• Intervencni a Akutni Kardiologie (CZE ISSN 1213-807X) **5790**
Intervenor (CAN ISSN 0820-3458) **3443**
Interventi Classensi (ITA) **497**
Intervention (CAN ISSN 0047-1321) **8048**
Intervention (GBR ISSN 1571-8883) **8048**
• ➤ Intervention in School and Clinic (USA ISSN 1053-4512) **3042**
• Intervention Research (NLD ISSN 1573-417X) **7975**
▼ • Interventional Cardiology (GBR ISSN 1755-5302) **5791**
➤ Interventional Cardiology (NLD ISSN 0926-9649) **5790**
• ➤ Interventional Neuroradiology (ITA ISSN 1123-9344) **6199**
• Interventional Procedure Coder's Pink Sheet (USA ISSN 1941-8620) **5641**
The Interventionalist (USA ISSN 1533-5364) **6199**
• ➤ Interventions (GBR ISSN 1369-801X) **5310**
• Intervet Agenda Magasin (NOR ISSN 0809-9014) **3599**
Interview (NLD) **6775**
• Interview (New York) (USA ISSN 0149-8932) **3979**
• Interview & Reading Guide Roundup (USA ISSN 1937-593X) **7564**
• Intervir (PRT ISSN 1645-2194) **2871**
• ➤ Intervirology (CHE ISSN 0300-5526) **888**
Interviu (ESP) **3952**
Interweave Crochet (USA ISSN 1937-0008) **6639**
Interweave Knits (USA ISSN 1088-3622) **6639**
Interzona Latinoamericana (ARG ISSN 1851-2216) **4298**
Interzone (GBR ISSN 0264-3596) **5443**
Intestinal Research (KOR ISSN 1598-9100) **5927**
• Intheblack (AUS ISSN 1832-0899) **1293**
➤ Inti (USA ISSN 0732-6750) **5310**
Intiem *see* Candlelight Magazine **8854**
Intiem (ZAF ISSN 1994-1137) **3949**
Intihar Istatistikleri *see* Turkey. Turkiye Istatistik Kurumu. Intihar Istatistikleri (Year) **7317**
Intima (ESP) **2257**
Intima France (ITA) **2247**
Intimacy (USA ISSN 0747-380X) **5410**
▼ Intimacy (ZAF ISSN 1997-5082) **8846**
Intimita (ITA) **8869**
Intimo Piu Mare (ITA ISSN 1127-0497) **2257**
Intisari/Digest (IDN ISSN 0535-4900) **1631**
Intix Newsletter *see* I N T I X Newsletter **1820**
Into the Blue (AUS ISSN 0815-077X) **8319**
• Into the Dark (USA ISSN 1099-856X) **6742**
Into the Game (NLD ISSN 1872-0781) **8181**
• Into the Light (USA ISSN 1092-5708) **7651**
Into View (GBR) **7762**
• Intouch (AUS ISSN 1833-8941) **7527**
InTouch (DEU ISSN 1862-1945) **3850**
InTouch (IRL ISSN 1393-4813) **2988**
InTouch *see* In Touch (Melville) **6022**
InTouch (Chicago) (USA) **605**
InTouch (Jackson) (USA ISSN 1535-7937) **1359**
Intoxications Alimentaires et Maladies d'Origine Hydrique au Canada *see* Foodborne and Waterborne Disease in Canada **3643**
• Intra (GBR ISSN 1476-6140) **4544**
Intra-Ocular Lens & Refractive Surgery *see* I O L & R S **6043**
• Intrafish (NOR ISSN 1502-7287) **1572**
• Intralinea (ITA ISSN 1827-000X) **5130**
Intralinea Online Translation Journal *see* Intralinea **5130**
Intramural Bulletin (JPN) **3900**
Intramuros (ESP ISSN 0329-3416) **643**
Intramuros (FRA ISSN 0769-3710) **446**
• Intranet Digest (USA) **2562**
Intranet Management (GBR) **2562**
Intranet Strategist *see* Ei Magazine **2556**
Intranets (USA ISSN 1546-3087) **1419**
Intranets and Advanced Networking (USA) **2562**
Intravenous Medications (USA ISSN 1556-7443) **6850**
• Intrep (USA ISSN 1557-4687) **6425**
Intrigue (USA ISSN 0743-3077) **2678**
Intro (DEU) **6578**
Intro (USA) **1130**
Introducing... (USA) **7801**
Introducing Computers: Concepts, Systems, and Applications (USA ISSN 1051-9246) **2427**
An Introduction to Australian Book Publishing (AUS) **7564**
Introduction to Federal Income Taxation in Canada (Year) (CAN ISSN 0821-5340) **1931**
Introduction to Federal Income Taxation in Canada. Instructor's Sample Exams *see* Introduction to Federal Income Taxation in Canada (Year) **1931**
Introduction to Gravitation Chemistry (USA) **2066**
Introduction to Japanese Medicine *see* Riben Yixue Jieshao **5706**
Introduction to Mail Order (USA) **1962**
Introduction to the American Political System *see* U.S. Policy & Politics **7190**
Introduction to the Law of Property/Inleiding tot die Sakereg (ZAF) **4696**
Introductions to Older Languages (USA ISSN 1099-0313) **5130**
Introductory Psychology *see* The Best Test Preparation for the C L E P. Introductory Psychology **2969**
▼ Introductory Series in Medicine (SGP) **5641**
Introduktsiya i Akklimatyzatsiya Rastenii (UKR ISSN 0257-9936) **795**
Intron - Canadian Molecular Biology (CAN) **766**
• Introspection (USA) **2478**
Intrum Info *see* Credit Management Magazine **8947**
Intrus (BFA) **5221**
Intuitive Flash (USA ISSN 1528-588X) **2710**
Intus (ESP ISSN 0214-7424) **6148**
• Inua. Revista Philologica Romanica (ESP ISSN 1616-413X) **5130**
Inuit Art Quarterly (CAN ISSN 0831-6708) **497**
Inuit Studies *see* Etudes Inuit Studies **3532**
• Inuktitut (CAN ISSN 0020-9872) **4298**
• Inussuk (GRL ISSN 1397-7431) **5641**
Invading Nature (NLD ISSN 1874-7809) **680**
Invalid Children's Aid Nationwide Communicate *see* I C A N Communicate **3041**
Invalide Belge (BEL) **6425**
Invalidiliiton Julkaisuja M (FIN ISSN 1457-8298) **4066**
Invalidityoe *see* I T - Invalidityoe **8046**
Invaluable & Trace Magazine (GBR ISSN 1471-3497) **497**
Invandrare & Minoriteter *see* I & M **7284**
Invandrare och Minoriteter *see* I & M **7284**
Invandraren (SWE ISSN 0348-145X) **3956**
Invandrarkvinnan (SWE ISSN 0348-6435) **7285**
† Invandrartidningen pa Franska Information (SWE ISSN 0349-5574) **8966**
▼ • Invasive Plant Science and Management (USA ISSN 1939-7291) **238**
• Invasor (CUB ISSN 0864-1110) **7144**
Invasor Digital *see* Invasor **7144**
Invatamintul Primar *see* Revista de Pedagogie **2906**
• Invenio (ARG ISSN 0329-3475) **7975**
Inventaire Canadien des Gaz a Effet de Serre *see* Le Rapport d'Inventaire National **3462**
Inventaire des Archives Historiques/Inventaris van het Historisch Archief (BEL) **4175**
Inventaire des Programmes d'Aide Financiere aux Individus, Entreprises et Organismes (CAN ISSN 1489-761X) **8048**
Inventaire des Trouvailles Monetaires Suisses. Bulletin *see* Inventar der Fundmuenzen der Schweiz. Bulletin **1359**
Inventaire General des Monuments et des Richesses Artistiques de la France (FRA ISSN 0075-0018) **446**
Inventar der Fundmuenzen der Schweiz. Bulletin/Inventaire des Trouvailles Monetaires Suisses. Bulletin/Inveratrio dei Ritrovamenti Monetali Svizzeri. Bulletin (CHE ISSN 1024-1663) **1359**
Inventare Nichtstaatlicher Archive (DEU ISSN 0535-5079) **628**
Inventari dei Manoscritti delle Biblioteche d'Italia (ITA ISSN 0075-0026) **5058**
Inventario Antropologico *see* Alteridades **323**
Inventario del Planeamiento Urbanisticointegral de los Municipios (ESP) **4416**
Inventaris van het Historisch Archief *see* Inventaire des Archives Historiques **4175**
▼ Invented Languages (USA ISSN 1945-1261) **5130**
➤ Inventio (USA) **3066**
Invention *see* Hatsumei **6750**
Invention and Contrivance Information *see* Hatsumei Koan no Shokai **6750**
Invention & Life *see* Hatsumei to Seikatsu **6751**
Invention Intelligence (IND ISSN 0970-0056) **7868**
▼ Invention Passion (FRA ISSN 1959-4631) **6753**
• ➤ Inventiones Mathematicae (DEU ISSN 0020-9910) **5498**
Inventions *see* Izobreteniya **6753**
• Inventor Magazin (DEU ISSN 1619-2974) **2593**
• Inventories of Natural Gas Liquids & Liquified Refinery Gases (USA) **6800**
• Inventors' Digest (USA ISSN 0883-9859) **6753**
Inventor's News (USA) **7868**
• Inventory Management Report (USA ISSN 1541-1141) **1851**
Inventory Newsletter (USA) **5019**
Inventory of Health Workforce in Alberta (CAN) **7527**
Inveratrio dei Ritrovamenti Monetali Svizzeri. Bulletin *see* Inventar der Fundmuenzen der Schweiz. Bulletin **1359**
Inveresk Play Series (AUS ISSN 1833-3362) **8472**
Inverness Courier (GBR ISSN 0020-9929) **3867**
Inverse and Ill-Posed Problems Series (NLD ISSN 1381-4524) **5498**
• ➤ Inverse Problems (GBR ISSN 0266-5611) **5553**
▼ • Inverse Problems and Imaging (USA ISSN 1930-8337) **5498**
• ➤ Inverse Problems in Science and Engineering (GBR ISSN 1741-5977) **3203**
Inversion Extranjera en America Latina y el Caribe (CHL ISSN 1020-5144) **1599**
Inversion y Capital *see* Mi Cartera de Inversion **1639**
Inversion y Finanzas/Finance and Investment (MEX ISSN 1405-0595) **1631**
Inversiones, Venezuela (VEN) **1631**
Inversionista Mexicano (MEX ISSN 1405-0811) **1631**
• ➤ Invertebrate Biology (USA ISSN 1077-8306) **948**
• ➤ Invertebrate Neuroscience (DEU ISSN 1354-2516) **949**
• ➤ Invertebrate Survival Journal (ITA ISSN 1824-307X) **949**
• ➤ Invertebrate Systematics (AUS ISSN 1445-5226) **949**
Inverted-A Horn (USA ISSN 0894-7910) **3979**
• Invesbreu Criminologia (ESP ISSN 1138-5014) **4891**
Invest-Immobilien *see* Finanz und Wirtschaft **1624**
Invest in Britain Annual Report (GBR) **1130**
Invest in Ecuador *see* Invierta en el Ecuador **1634**
• Invest in Korea (KOR) **1572**
• Invest Korea Journal (Online) (KOR) **1572**
• Invest Korea Journal (Print) (KOR) **1572**
Invest Romania Magazine (ROM ISSN 1224-810X) **1631**
Invest Romania Newsletter (ROM) **1631**
InvesTech Market Analyst (USA ISSN 0896-4157) **1631**
InvesTech Mutual Fund Advisor (USA ISSN 0896-4165) **1631**
InvestHedge (GBR) **1631**
Investicije (SRB ISSN 0351-4129) **1244**
• Investigacao Operacional (PRT ISSN 0874-5161) **2427**
• ➤ Investigacion Agraria. Sistemas y Recursos Forestales (ESP ISSN 1131-7965) **3694**
• Investigacion & Desarrollo (COL ISSN 0121-3261) **7975**
• ➤ Investigacion Bibliotecologica (MEX ISSN 0187-358X) **5019**
† Investigacion Cardiovascular (ESP ISSN 1139-2096) **8966**
• ➤ Investigacion Clinica (VEN ISSN 0535-5133) **5641**
Investigacion Clinica. Suplemento (VEN ISSN 0259-0395) **5641**
• Investigacion Clinica y Bioetica (ESP ISSN 1131-8910) **6850**
• Investigacion Clinica y Farmaceutica (ESP ISSN 1697-2554) **5641**
Investigacion Economica (MEX ISSN 0185-1667) **1543**
➤ Investigacion en Enfermeria (COL ISSN 0124-2059) **5641**
Investigacion en la Escuela (ESP ISSN 0213-7771) **2871**
• Investigacion en Salud (MEX ISSN 1405-7980) **5641**
Investigacion mas Desarrollo *see* ImasD (Online) **8425**
Investigacion Medica Internacional (MEX ISSN 0185-2108) **5641**
• ➤ Investigacion Operacional (CUB ISSN 0257-4306) **5498**
Investigacion Pesquera (CHL ISSN 0716-1328) **949**
➤ Investigacion y Ciencia (ESP ISSN 0210-136X) **7868**
• Investigacion y Ciencia (MEX ISSN 1665-4412) **7975**
➤ Investigacion y Desarrollo (CHL ISSN 0717-0610) **7868**
• Investigacion y Desarrollo (MEX ISSN 1606-8165) **7868**
• Investigacion y Educacion en Enfermeria (COL ISSN 0120-5307) **5962**
Investigacion y Marketing (ESP ISSN 1131-6144) **1823**
Investigacion y Progreso Agropecuario Kampenaike (CHL) **123**
• Investigacion y Reflexion (COL ISSN 0121-6805) **1130**
Investigacion y Tecnica del Papel (ESP ISSN 0368-0789) **6734**
† Investigaciones Arqueologicas (ESP ISSN 1132-2446) **8966**
Investigaciones de Historia Economica (ESP ISSN 1698-6989) **1543**
• Investigaciones Economicas (ESP ISSN 0210-1521) **1130**
• Investigaciones en Psicologia (ARG ISSN 0329-5893) **7366**
Investigaciones en Sociologia (ARG ISSN 0020-9961) **8111**
Investigaciones Europeas de Direccion y Economia de la Empresa (ESP ISSN 1135-2523) **1762**
• Investigaciones Geograficas (ESP ISSN 0213-4691) **4016**
Investigaciones Geograficas *see* Universidad Nacional Autonoma de Mexico. Instituto de Geografia. Investigaciones Geograficas **4032**
Investigaciones Historicas (ESP ISSN 0210-9425) **4232**
Investigaciones Marinas *see* Revista Investigaciones Marinas **701**
Investigaciones Regionales (ESP ISSN 1695-7253) **1543**
Investigaciones y Ensayos Geograficos (ARG ISSN 1668-9070) **4016**
• ➤ Investigaciones y Postgrado (VEN ISSN 1316-0087) **7975**
• ➤ Investigacoes em Ensino de Ciencias (BRA ISSN 1518-9384) **7868**
Investigate (AUS ISSN 1832-2794) **7144**
Investigated in Russia *see* Issledovano v Rossii **7869**
Investigating Concepts of Success *see* Profiles of Business Success. Hamilton - Niagara Edition **7604**
Investigating Concepts of Success *see* Profiles of Business Success. Ontario North Edition **7604**
Investigating Concepts of Success *see* Profiles of Business Success. Ottawa Edition **7604**
Investigating Concepts of Success *see* Profiles of Business Success. Toronto East Edition **7604**
Investigating Concepts of Success *see* Profiles of Business Success. Vancouver Edition **7604**
Investigating Concepts of Success *see* Profiles of Business Success. Burlington - Oakville Edition **7604**
Investigating Concepts of Success *see* Profiles of Business Success. Southwestern Ontario Edition **7604**
Investigating Concepts of Success *see* Profiles of Business Success. Toronto West, Toronto North Edition **7604**
Investigating Concepts of Success *see* Profiles of Business Success. Vancouver West Edition **7604**
Investigation of Landslides and Their Control *see* Jisuberi Kyukeishachi no Chosa to Taisaku Koza **2784**
Investigational Drug Information. Medical and Dental *see* Chiken Ishiyaku Joho **6828**
• ➤ Investigational New Drugs (USA ISSN 0167-6997) **6851**
• ➤ Investigationes Linguisticae (Online Edition) (POL ISSN 1733-1757) **5130**
Investigationes Linguisticae (Print Edition) *see* Investigationes Linguisticae (Online Edition) **5130**
• ➤ Investigations in Mathematics Learning (USA ISSN 1947-7503) **5498**
Investigative and Operational Report Writing *see* Effective Law Enforcement Report Writing **4663**
Investigative Fund Magazine *see* I F Magazine **3978**
• ➤ Investigative Ophthalmology & Visual Science (USA ISSN 0146-0404) **6044**
• ➤ Investigative Radiology (USA ISSN 0020-9996) **6199**
Investigative Reporters & Editors Journal *see* I R E Journal **4576**
▼ • ➤ The Investigative Sciences Journal (USA ISSN 1942-7794) **7868**
• Investigative Stops Law Bulletin (USA ISSN 1544-6409) **2656**
Investigator (AUS ISSN 0021-0013) **4192**
Investigator's International All-in-One Directory of the Investigative Industry (USA) **2656**
Investimento e Tecnologia (PRT ISSN 0870-4805) **1631**
• Investing for Growth (GBR ISSN 1476-8429) **1631**
Investing in KwaZulu Natal (ZAF) **1631**

Investing in Radio Market Report (USA ISSN 1933-3625) **1631**
Investing In Television Market Report (USA ISSN 1933-4354) **1632**
• Investing, Licensing and Trading. Global Edition (USA) **1572**
Investing, Licensing and Trading. Mexico *see* Country Commerce. Mexico **1558**
• Investir (FRA ISSN 0759-7673) **1359**
Investissements Prives et Publics, Quebec et ses Regions. Perspectives (Year) *see* Bulletin Flash. Investissements Prives et Publics, Quebec et ses Regions. Perspectives (Year) **1614**
Investitsii v Rossii (RUS) **1632**
Investitsionnaya Deyatel'nost' v Rossii: Usloviya, Faktory, Tendentsii (Year)/Investment Activity in Russia: Conditions, Factors and Tendencies (RUS) **1244**
Investitsionnye Proekty Predpriyatii Rossii (RUS) **1632**
Investitsionnyi Ekspert (RUS) **1632**
Investment (Aarbergen) (DEU) **1632**
Investment (Berlin) (DEU ISSN 0935-1744) **1632**
Investment Activity in Russia: Conditions, Factors and Tendencies *see* Investitsionnaya Deyatel'nost' v Rossii: Usloviya, Faktory, Tendentsii (Year) **1244**
Investment Advice/Toshi Sodan (JPN) **1632**
• Investment Adviser (GBR ISSN 1361-1593) **1632**
Investment Adviser Week *see* I A Week **1629**
Investment Advisor *see* Elton Stephens - Investment Advisor **1621**
• Investment Advisor (USA ISSN 1069-1731) **1632**
Investment Analysts Journal/Beleggingsontleders Tydskrif (ZAF ISSN 1029-3523) **1632**
Investment and Development Bank of Malawi. Annual Report and Accounts (MWI) **1359**
Investment and Management of Financial Transactions *see* Touzi yu Licai **1656**
Investment & Marketing (PAK ISSN 0021-0064) **1823**
Investment and Operating Cost in the Philippines (PHL) **1632**
• Investment and Pensions Europe (GBR ISSN 1369-3727) **1632**
Investment & Savings Handbook (CHE ISSN 1748-0825) **1632**
Investment and Securities *see* Touzi yu Zhengquan **1656**
Investment and Tax Guide *see* Report on Business Magazine **1165**
Investment Bank Diversity Programs *see* Vault - S E O Guide to Investment Bank Diversity Programs **6705**
Investment Bulletin (USA) **4510**
The Investment Calendar (GBR ISSN 0951-3736) **1632**
Investment Column Quarterly (USA ISSN 0739-6449) **1632**
• Investment.com (CAN) **1632**
Investment.com Magazine *see* Planning for Profits Magazine **1644**
Investment Companies, with Conforming Changes (USA) **1293**
Investment Company Fact Book (USA ISSN 1938-6729) **1632**
Investment Company Institute. Annual Report to Members (USA ISSN 1938-8594) **1632**
• Investment Dealers' Digest (USA ISSN 0021-0080) **1632**
Investment Diversification & Economic Analysis Bulletin *see* I D E A S Bulletin **1629**
Investment Economics/Toshi Keizai (JPN) **1632**
• Investment Executive (CAN ISSN 1202-7405) **1632**
Investment Fund Index - Investment Trusts (GBR ISSN 0954-2485) **1632**
• Investment Funds (Online Edition) (NLD) **1931**
† • Investment Funds (Print Edition) (NLD) **8966**
• Investment Guide (USA ISSN 0739-9138) **1632**
• Investment International (GBR ISSN 0950-6195) **1632**
• The Investment Lawyer (USA ISSN 1075-4512) **1632**
Investment Management (GBR ISSN 0267-3770) **1359**
• ➤ Investment Management & Financial Innovations (UKR ISSN 1810-4967) **1632**
Investment Management and Study *see* Touzi Guanli yu Yanjiu **1656**
• Investment Management Weekly (USA ISSN 0896-8500) **1632**
• Investment Monitor (AUS) **1633**
Investment News (KEN ISSN 1814-6996) **1633**
• Investment News (USA ISSN 1098-1837) **1633**
Investment Newsletter Contacts (USA ISSN 1051-1512) **4577**
Investment Performance Digest (USA ISSN 1050-6551) **1130**
Investment Planning and Project Evaluation Bibliography (IND) **628**
Investment Planning Guide *see* Investment Reporter **1633**
Investment Policy Review Series (CHE) **1633**
• Investment Portfolio Guide (USA ISSN 0883-1661) **1633**
▼ • The Investment Professional (USA ISSN 1945-3655) **1633**
Investment Projects (AUS) **1633**
Investment Property (USA) **7596**
Investment Property Databank United Kingdom Annual Property Index *see* I P D U K Annual Property Index **7594**
Investment Property Databank United Kingdom Monthly Index *see* I P D U K Monthly Property Index **1629**
Investment Property Databank United Kingdom Monthly Property Index *see* I P D U K Monthly Property Index **1629**
• Investment Quality Trends (USA ISSN 0021-0110) **1633**
Investment Reporter (CAN ISSN 0700-5539) **1633**
The Investment Reporter (USA ISSN 1062-4678) **1633**
Investment Strategy (USA) **1633**
Investment Strategy and Recommendations for All Asset Classes in the Euro Area, the U.K., Sweden and Switzerland *see* European Investment Strategy **1622**
Investment Strategy and Recommendations for the U.S. Fixed Income Market *see* U.S. Bond Strategy **1657**
• Investment Strategy Quarterly (USA) **1633**
Investment Trust Handbook (GBR) **1633**
Investment Trusts (GBR ISSN 0959-9568) **1633**
• Investment Week (GBR ISSN 1469-1876) **1633**
Investments and Credit Corporation of Oyo State. Industrial Directory (NGA) **2009**
▼ • Investments & Pensions Asia (GBR ISSN 1753-8882) **1633**
Investments in Emerging Markets (GBR) **3649**
Investor (DEU) **1633**
The Investor (IND) **1633**
• Investor (SVK ISSN 1335-8235) **1633**
Investor (THA ISSN 0021-0153) **1633**
▼ Investor Concepts (USA) **1633**
• Investor Relations Guide (USA) **1633**
• Investor Relations Magazine (GBR ISSN 0958-6679) **1633**
• Investor Relations Newsletter (USA ISSN 1535-5802) **1633**
Investor Relations Update *see* I R Update **1629**
Investor Responsibility Research Center. Annual Report (USA) **1633**
• Investor Weekly (AUS ISSN 1834-8602) **1633**
Investor's Advisor *see* I F A **1629**
Investor's Almanac (USA ISSN 1933-9240) **1633**
• Investor's Business Daily (USA ISSN 1061-2890) **1633**
The Investor's Choice (JAM) **1634**
• Investors Chronicle (London, 1860) (GBR ISSN 0261-3115) **1634**
• Investor's Digest of Canada (CAN ISSN 0047-1356) **1634**
Investor's Guide (CAN) **1634**
• The Investors' Guide (ZAF ISSN 0250-1732) **1634**
The Investor's Guide to Closed-End Funds (USA) **1634**
Investors' Guide to Hungary (HUN ISSN 0865-6746) **1634**
Investor's Guide to Low-Cost Mutual Funds (USA) **1634**
Investors' Guide to Nepal (NPL) **1634**
Investor's Guide to Singapore (SGP ISSN 0129-5276) **1634**
Investors Intelligence (USA) **1634**
Investors Update (USA) **1634**
• ➤ InVet (ARG ISSN 1514-6634) **8799**
Invierta en el Ecuador (ECU) **1634**
Invisible City (USA ISSN 0147-4936) **5424**
• ➤ Invitation (USA) **7711**
Inviting Arkansas (USA ISSN 1930-2452) **5074**
Invito all'Opera (ITA ISSN 1824-6699) **8472**
InVo - Insolvenz und Vollstreckung *see* Forderung und Vollstreckung **1348**
▼ • Involve (USA ISSN 1944-4176) **5498**
Involvement of Participation Association Magazine *see* I P A Magazine **1686**
Involvency & Restructuring (GBR ISSN 1468-3180) **4872**
Inwater (ZAF ISSN 1727-3382) **8319**
Inwater Africa *see* Inwater **8319**
Inwater Africa Outdoor Explorer Sport Fishing & Boating *see* Inwater **8319**
Inwestor Finansowy (POL ISSN 1641-5280) **1634**
Inwood International *see* Inwood Magazine **3713**
• Inwood Magazine (NZL ISSN 1176-9785) **3713**
Inzage (NLD ISSN 0925-0689) **7564**
Inzenerna Geologiia i Khidrogeologiia (BGR ISSN 0204-7934) **2710**
Inzenyrska Mechanika *see* Engineering Mechanics **7058**
Inzet *see* Vieren **7692**
Inzhener (RUS ISSN 0868-443X) **3203**
Inzhenernaya Ekologiya (RUS ISSN 0204-3483) **3203**
Inzhenernaya Fizika (RUS) **7018**
Inzhenernaya Gazeta (RUS) **3203**
Inzhenerno-Fizicheskii Zhurnal (BLR ISSN 0021-0285) **3203**
Inzicht (NLD ISSN 0021-0307) **2871**
Inzicht in de Ondernemingsraad (NLD ISSN 1574-4868) **1690**
Inzicht in Verzorging, Verzorging in Zicht (NLD ISSN 1871-1189) **7527**
Inzichten *see* Voortschrijdende Inzichten **8998**
• ➤ Inzinerine Ekonomika/Engineering Economics (LTU ISSN 1392-2785) **1130**
• Inzinierska Pedagogika (SVK ISSN 1336-8990) **2988**
Inzinierske Stavby/Civil Engineering (SVK ISSN 1335-0846) **3273**
➤ Inzynieria Biomaterialow/Engineering of Biomaterials (POL ISSN 1429-7248) **749**
➤ Inzynieria Chemiczna i Procesowa (POL ISSN 0208-6425) **3247**
Inzynieria i Aparatura Chemiczna (POL ISSN 0368-0827) **3247**
• Inzynieria i Budownictwo (POL ISSN 0021-0315) **3273**
Inzynieria i Ochrona Srodowiska/Engineering and Protection of Environment (POL ISSN 1505-3695) **3443**
Inzynieria Materialowa (POL ISSN 0208-6247) **3203**
➤ Inzynieria Morska i Geotechnika (POL ISSN 0867-4299) **8647**
• Inzynieria Powierzchni/Surface Engineering (POL ISSN 1426-1723) **7059**
➤ Inzynieria Srodowiska (POL ISSN 1426-2908) **3480**
Io (USA ISSN 0021-0331) **497**
Io Cucino (ITA ISSN 1723-4670) **4361**
Io e il Mio Bambino (ITA ISSN 1123-8062) **2155**
Io e il Mio Bambino. La Guida (ITA ISSN 1123-8089) **2155**
† Io e Mio Figlio (ITA) **8966**
Io Energy's Power Daily Northeast *see* Power Daily Northeast **3144**
Io Programmo (ITA ISSN 1128-594X) **2507**
Ioana (ROM ISSN 1453-2417) **8869**
Ioana Frizuri (ROM) **589**
Ion Chunyu Hyoso Shori Shinpojumu Yokoshu/Symposium on Surface Layer Modification by Ion Implantation. Proceedings (JPN ISSN 0917-1460) **3321**
Ion Exchange and Adsorption *see* Lizi Jiaohuan yu Xifu **2072**
➤ Ion Exchange and Solvent Extraction (USA ISSN 0092-0193) **2136**
▼ • ➤ Ion Exchange Letters (CZE ISSN 1803-4039) **2066**
• Ionian (USA ISSN 0021-0358) **2288**
• ➤ Ionics (DEU ISSN 0947-7047) **7018**
Ionizing Radiation *see* Hoshasen **7066**
Ionnye Rasplavy i Tverdye Elektrolity (UKR ISSN 0234-4483) **2117**
Ionosfera (UKR) **2710**
Ionospheric Data at Showa Station (Antarctica) (JPN ISSN 0389-8237) **6358**
Ionospheric Data in Japan/Denriso Geppo (JPN ISSN 0021-0382) **6358**
IOP Conference Series: Earth and Environment *see* I O P Conference Series: Earth and Environment **3438**
Iota (CAN ISSN 0229-7493) **2288**
Iota (GBR ISSN 0266-2922) **5310**
Iowa A F L - C I O News (USA ISSN 0273-1770) **4596**
• ➤ Iowa Academy of Science. Journal (USA ISSN 0896-8381) **7868**
Iowa Advocate (USA ISSN 0578-6533) **4696**
• Iowa Ag Review (USA ISSN 1080-2193) **201**
Iowa Agriculture and Home Economics Experiment Station. Research Bulletin (USA ISSN 0097-3416) **123**
Iowa Agriculture and Home Economics Experiment Station. Special Report (USA ISSN 0361-199X) **123**
Iowa Alumni Quarterly (USA ISSN 1079-0985) **2288**
Iowa Archaeological Society. Newsletter (USA ISSN 1940-7122) **399**
Iowa Archeological Society. Journal (USA ISSN 0535-5729) **399**
Iowa Archeology News *see* Iowa Archaeological Society. Newsletter **399**
Iowa Architect (USA ISSN 0021-0439) **446**
Iowa Bird Life (USA ISSN 0021-0455) **909**
Iowa Board of Nursing. Newsletter (USA) **5963**
• Iowa Business Directory (USA ISSN 1048-7263) **2009**
Iowa Cattleman (USA ISSN 0279-4608) **290**
Iowa Cities & Counties Graphic Performance Analysis (USA ISSN 1935-5831) **7481**
Iowa Civil Rights Commission. Annual Report (USA) **7210**
Iowa Civil Rights Commission. Case Reports (USA) **7210**
Iowa Commerce (USA ISSN 8750-6645) **1430**
Iowa Conservation Commission. Completion Report *see* Iowa Department of Natural Resources. Completion Report **2615**
Iowa Conservationist *see* Iowa Outdoors **2615**
The Iowa County (USA ISSN 0892-3795) **7494**
Iowa Crops & Weather (USA ISSN 1041-9268) **182**
Iowa Curiosities (USA ISSN 1551-7985) **8724**
Iowa Dental Journal (USA ISSN 0021-0498) **5849**
Iowa. Department of Employment Services. Annual Report (USA) **1690**
Iowa Department of Natural Resources. Completion Report (USA) **2615**
Iowa Drug Information Service *see* I D I S **6889**
Iowa Educational Leadership (Online Edition) (USA) **3066**
Iowa Educational Leadership (Print Edition) *see* Iowa Educational Leadership (Online Edition) **3066**
• Iowa Employment Law Letter (USA ISSN 1075-962X) **4696**
➤ Iowa English Bulletin (USA ISSN 0444-4663) **5130**
Iowa Facts (USA ISSN 0895-8092) **3120**
• Iowa Family Physician (USA) **5641**
Iowa Farm Bureau Spokesman (USA ISSN 0021-051X) **123**
Iowa Farmer Today (USA) **123**
Iowa Game & Fish (USA ISSN 0897-9197) **8319**
Iowa Gardening (USA ISSN 1545-0457) **3739**
Iowa Genealogical Society Newsletter (USA) **3771**
Iowa Geological Survey Bureau. Aeromagnetic Survey Series (USA) **2748**
Iowa Geological Survey Bureau. Annual Report (USA) **2748**
Iowa Geological Survey Bureau. Educational Series (USA) **2748**
Iowa Geological Survey Bureau. Guidebook Series (USA) **2748**
Iowa Geological Survey Bureau. Miscellaneous Publications (USA) **2748**
Iowa Geological Survey Bureau. Open-File County Groundwater Resources Report Series (USA) **8826**
Iowa Geological Survey Bureau. Open-File Report Series (USA) **2748**
Iowa Geological Survey Bureau. Public Information Circular (USA) **2748**
Iowa Geological Survey Bureau. Special Report (USA) **2748**
Iowa Geological Survey Bureau. Technical Information Series (USA) **2748**
Iowa Geological Survey Bureau. Technical Papers (USA) **2748**
Iowa Geological Survey Bureau. Water Supply Bulletin (USA) **8826**
Iowa Geology (USA ISSN 0193-4856) **2748**
Iowa Grocer (USA) **3679**
Iowa Heritage Illustrated (USA ISSN 1088-5943) **4298**
The Iowa Historian (USA) **4298**
Iowa Institute of Hydraulic Research Report *see* I I H R Report **3362**
➤ Iowa Journal of Communication (USA ISSN 1537-1824) **5130**
➤ Iowa Journal of Cultural Studies (USA) **7975**
Iowa Journal of Literary Studies *see* Iowa Journal of Cultural Studies **7975**
Iowa Jury Verdict Reporter *see* West's Jury Verdicts. Iowa Reports **4813**
• ➤ Iowa Law Review (USA ISSN 0021-0552) **4696**
The Iowa Lawyer (USA ISSN 1052-5327) **4697**
Iowa Legionnaire (USA ISSN 0021-0560) **2267**
• Iowa Legislative News Service Bulletin (USA ISSN 0738-9450) **7447**
Iowa Legislative News Service Bulletin (Interim Report Edition) *see* Iowa Legislative News Service Bulletin **7447**
• Iowa Manufacturers Register (USA ISSN 0737-7940) **2009**
Iowa: Manufacturing *see* Harris Directory. Iowa Manufacturing **2000**
Iowa Medicine (USA ISSN 0746-8709) **5641**
The Iowa Music Educator (USA ISSN 0021-0609) **6578**
Iowa Official Register (USA) **7481**
Iowa Optometric Association News *see* I O A News **6043**
• ➤ The Iowa Orthopaedic Journal (USA ISSN 1541-5457) **6062**
Iowa Outdoors (USA ISSN 1936-2080) **2615**
Iowa Parent (USA) **2155**
Iowa Parks & Recreation (USA) **4978**
Iowa Pharmacy Association. Journal (USA ISSN 1525-7894) **6851**
† Iowa Pleading and Causes of Action (USA) **8966**
Iowa Police Journal (USA ISSN 0021-0633) **2656**
Iowa Pork Producer (USA) **290**
Iowa Pork Today (USA ISSN 1043-9676) **290**
Iowa Practice Series. Methods of Practice (USA ISSN 1930-8604) **4697**
Iowa R E C News (Rural Electric Cooperative) (USA ISSN 0162-2412) **3159**
• The Iowa Review (USA ISSN 0021-065X) **5310**
Iowa School Directory *see* M D R's School Directory. Iowa **2958**
Iowa Seed News (USA) **238**
Iowa Sierran (USA) **2615**
Iowa Smoke-Eater (USA) **3579**
Iowa State Archaeologist. Report (USA ISSN 0085-2252) **399**
Iowa State Daily (USA) **2288**
Iowa State Education Association Communique *see* I S E A Communique **2865**
Iowa State University. Center for Agricultural and Rural Development. Staff Report (USA ISSN 1059-2504) **8111**
Iowa State University. Statistical Laboratory. Annual Report (USA) **5548**
➤ Iowa State University Veterinarian (USA ISSN 0099-5851) **8799**
Iowa Stater (USA ISSN 0746-2204) **2288**
Iowa Studies in African Art (USA ISSN 0897-8573) **343**
Iowa Trucking Lifeliner (USA) **8671**
The Iowan (USA ISSN 0021-0722) **3979**
IowaParent *see* Iowa Parent **2155**
IP Multimedia Subsystem Magazine *see* I M S Magazine **2324**
Ipari Formatervezesi Szakirodalmi Tajekoztato/Industrial Design Abstracts (HUN ISSN 0231-195X) **3232**
Iparmuveszet *see* Ars Decorativa **6519**
IPC Pro (HKG) **2427**
• Ipertensione & Prevenzione Cardiovascolare (ITA ISSN 1122-8601) **5791**
IPFA *see* International Pension Funds and Their Advisors **1631**

Title

Islensk Fraedi *see* Studia Islandica **5180**
Islensk Fyrirtaeki/Icelandic Firms (ISL ISSN 1011-5323) **2009**
Islensk Hljodritaskra/Bibliography of Icelandic Sound Recordings (ISL ISSN 0254-4067) **8156**
Islenskt Maal og Almenn Maalfraedi (ISL ISSN 0256-842X) **5130**
Islenskur Idnadur (ISL ISSN 1022-7741) **4596**
Hid Islenzka Fornleifafelag. Arbok (ISL ISSN 0256-8462) **4233**
Isles Works! (USA) **3444**
▼ • ➤ Islets (USA ISSN 1938-2014) **5895**
Islington Gazette (GBR ISSN 0964-9778) **3867**
Islington Gazette (EC1 Edition) (GBR ISSN 1478-5161) **3867**
• Isn't It Romantic? (USA) **5410**
• ISO 14001: Environmental Management Systems: A Complete Implementation Guide (USA) **3482**
Iso-Hymo *see* Hymy **3838**
• ➤ Isokinetics and Exercise Science (NLD ISSN 0959-3020) **6230**
Isola d'Elba e Arcipelago Toscano Grand Tour (ITA ISSN 1825-3121) **8724**
Isolation (Kalamazoo) (USA) **6578**
Isolier-Technik (DEU ISSN 0938-1899) **1017**
Isoplan-Schriften *see* Institut fuer Entwicklungsforschung, Wirtschafts- und Sozialplanung. Schriften **8107**
Isotope (USA ISSN 1544-8479) **5311**
Isotope and Radiation Research/Buhuth al-Naza'ir Wa-al-Ish'a' (EGY ISSN 0021-1907) **6199**
Isotope News (JPN ISSN 0285-5518) **7067**
• ➤ Isotopes in Environmental and Health Studies (GBR ISSN 1025-6016) **2066**
† • iSource Business (USA) **8966**
Ispat (Chittagong) (BGD) **6318**
Ispat (Kushtia) (BGD) **3799**
Ispat Vihangam *see* B S P Magazine **6306**
Israel (DNK ISSN 0021-194X) **7144**
Israel *see* Fodor's Israel **8707**
Israel *see* The P R S Group. Country Reports: Israel **1507**
Israel Academy of Sciences and Humanities. Proceedings (ISR ISSN 0578-9230) **4458**
† Israel Academy of Sciences and Humanities. Section of Sciences. Proceedings (ISR ISSN 0333-6190) **8966**
• ➤ Israel Affairs (GBR ISSN 1353-7121) **7246**
Israel Air Force Magazine *see* Bit'on Hel ha-Avir **49**
➤ Israel Annual Conference on Aerospace Sciences. Proceedings (ISR) **61**
Israel Antiquities Authority Reports *see* I A A Reports **8962**
• Israel Autos Report (GBR ISSN 1748-9970) **8586**
Israel Aviation and Space Magazine *see* Biaf **49**
Israel Book Trade Directory (ISR ISSN 0333-6018) **7564**
Israel. Central Bureau of Statistics. Construction in Israel/Ha-Binui Be-Yisrael (ISR ISSN 0069-9195) **1047**
Israel. Central Bureau of Statistics. Energy in Israel (ISR ISSN 0333-9491) **3153**
Israel. Central Bureau of Statistics. Foreign Trade Statistics (Annual) - Exports (ISR ISSN 0333-8436) **1245**
Israel. Central Bureau of Statistics. Foreign Trade Statistics (Annual) - Imports (ISR ISSN 0333-8487) **1245**
Israel. Central Bureau of Statistics. Hotels (ISR) **4402**
Israel. Central Bureau of Statistics. Immigrant Population from Former U S S R - Demographic Trends/Ukhlusiyyat 'Ole B'rit Ha-Mo'atsot L'She'avar. M'gamot Demografiyyot (ISR ISSN 0793-3606) **7310**
Israel. Central Bureau of Statistics. Immigration to Israel/Statistiqa shel 'Aliyya (ISR ISSN 0302-816X) **7310**
Israel. Central Bureau of Statistics. Judicial Statistics (ISR ISSN 0075-1030) **4823**
Israel. Central Bureau of Statistics. Labour Force Surveys/Siq're Ko'ah 'Adam (ISR ISSN 0075-1049) **1245**
Israel. Central Bureau of Statistics. Monthly Bulletin of Statistics/Yarhon Statisti L'Yisra'el (ISR ISSN 0021-1982) **8381**
Israel. Central Bureau of Statistics. National Accounts of Israel (ISR ISSN 0793-2235) **1245**
Israel. Central Bureau of Statistics. National Expenditure on Culture, Recreation and Sports/Ha-Hotsa'a Ha-L'umit L'Tarbut, L'Viddur, U-l'Sport (ISR ISSN 0793-0275) **7481**
Israel. Central Bureau of Statistics. New Statistical Projects and Publications in Israel/Pe'ulot Ufirsuimim Statistiyyim Hadashim b'Yisra'el (ISR ISSN 0334-3278) **8381**
Israel. Central Bureau of Statistics. Price Statistics Monthly/Yarhon L'Statistiqa Shel M'hirim (ISR ISSN 0021-2008) **1245**
Israel. Central Bureau of Statistics. Road Accidents with Casualties. Part 1 (ISR ISSN 0333-6050) **8527**
Israel. Central Bureau of Statistics. Road Accidents with Casualties. Part 2/T'unot D'rakhim 'im Nifga'im (ISR ISSN 0333-6107) **8527**
Israel. Central Bureau of Statistics. Statistical Abstract of Israel/Shenaton Statisti le-Yisrael (ISR ISSN 0081-4679) **8381**
Israel. Central Bureau of Statistics. Survey of Travelling Habits/Seqer Herg'le N'si'a. Heleq A (ISR ISSN 0333-6603) **8779**
Israel. Central Bureau of Statistics. Survey of Trucks/Seqer Masa'iyot (ISR ISSN 0333-8266) **8527**
Israel. Central Bureau of Statistics. Tourism/Tayyarut (ISR ISSN 0333-6204) **8779**
Israel. Central Bureau of Statistics. Tourism and Hotel Services Statistics Quarterly/Riv'on Statisti L'tayyarut Ul'sherute Hr'hh (ISR ISSN 0334-2476) **8779**
Israel. Central Bureau of Statistics. Transport Statistics Quarterly/Riv'on L'statistiqa shel Ha-Tahbura (ISR ISSN 0334-2220) **8527**
Israel. Central Bureau of Statistics. Victimization Survey (ISR ISSN 0333-7634) **2674**
Israel. Central Bureau of Statistics. Vital Statistics (ISR ISSN 0075-1111) **7310**
Israel Chemical Society. Bulletin (ISR) **2066**
† Israel. Commissioner for Complaints from the Public (Ombudsman). Annual Report (ISR ISSN 0302-8976) **8966**
† Israel Conventions, Trade Shows, Festivals & Special Events (ISR ISSN 0793-4947) **8966**
† Israel Dance Quarterly (ISR) **8966**
• Israel Defence & Security Report (GBR ISSN 1749-1460) **6425**
Israel Defense Forces Law Review (ISR) **6425**
Israel Dental Association. Journal *see* Refu'at Happe Vehashinnayim **5863**
• Israel Environment Bulletin (ISR ISSN 0334-3804) **3444**
Israel Equality Monitor/Meda' 'al Shivyon (ISR ISSN 0792-7029) **7210**
➤ Israel Exploration Journal (ISR ISSN 0021-2059) **399**
• Israel Faxx (USA ISSN 1074-2255) **3541**
† Israel Film Centre Information Bulletin (ISR ISSN 0792-8610) **8966**
• Israel Food & Drink Report (GBR ISSN 1749-2769) **1130**
Israel Freight Transport Report (GBR ISSN 1752-5888) **8500**
Israel. Geological Survey. Current Research (ISR ISSN 0333-6425) **2748**
Israel Handbook (GBR ISSN 1368-4280) **8724**
Israel Heute (DEU) **7651**
Israel High-Tech & Investment Report (ISR ISSN 0334-6307) **8428**
• Israel Horizons (USA ISSN 0021-2083) **7246**
† Israel Information (DNK) **8966**
Israel Information Technology Report *see* Business Monitor International. Information Technology Country Reports **2491**
† Israel Institute of Applied Social Research. Research Report (ISR ISSN 0075-1227) **8966**
• ➤ Israel Journal of Chemistry (ISR ISSN 0021-2148) **2066**
• ➤ Israel Journal of Earth Sciences (ISR ISSN 0021-2164) **2711**
• ➤ Israel Journal of Ecology & Evolution (ISR ISSN 1565-9801) **949**
➤ Israel Journal of Entomology (ISR ISSN 0075-1243) **851**
• ➤ Israel Journal of Mathematics (USA ISSN 0021-2172) **5498**
Israel Journal of Mathematics *see* Journal d'Analyse Mathematique **5499**
• ➤ Israel Journal of Plant Sciences (ISR ISSN 0792-9978) **795**
• ➤ Israel Journal of Psychiatry and Related Sciences (ISR ISSN 0333-7308) **6148**
• Israel Journal of Veterinary Medicine (ISR ISSN 0334-9152) **8800**
Israel Journal of Zoology *see* Israel Journal of Ecology & Evolution **949**
Israel, Kamisar & LaFave's Criminal Procedure and the Constitution (USA) **4891**
• Israel. Knesset. Divrei ha-Knesset (ISR ISSN 0334-0309) **7144**
Israel. Knesset. Finance Committee. Data on Activities *see* Israel. Knesset. Va'adat ha-Kesafim. Misparim al Avodat Va'adat ha-Kesafim **1931**
Israel. Knesset. Va'adat ha-Kesafim. Misparim al Avodat Va'adat ha-Kesafim/Israel. Knesset. Finance Committee. Data on Activities (ISR) **1931**
• ➤ Israel Law Review (ISR ISSN 0021-2237) **4697**
➤ Israel Mathematical Conference Proceedings (ISR ISSN 0792-4119) **5498**
Israel Medical Association Journal *see* I M A J **5631**
➤ Israel Meteorological Society/Meteorologia b'Yisra'el (ISR ISSN 0026-1122) **6358**
Israel. Ministry of Agriculture. Department of Fisheries. Dayig u-Midgeh be-Yisrael - Fisheries and Fishbreeding in Israel *see* Dayig u-Midgeh be-Yisrael **3590**
† Israel. Ministry of Labour and Social Affairs. Department of International Relations. The Press on Welfare (ISR) **8966**
† Israel. Ministry of Labour. Registrar of Cooperative Societies. Report on the Cooperative Movement in Israel (ISR ISSN 0080-1313) **8966**
Israel Museum Journal (ISR ISSN 0333-7499) **6526**
Israel Museum Studies in Archaeology (ISR ISSN 1565-3617) **399**
Israel Numismatic Journal *see* Israel Numismatic Research **6651**
Israel Numismatic Research (ISR) **6651**
† Israel Oil News (ISR ISSN 0047-1585) **8966**
➤ Israel Oriental Studies (USA ISSN 0334-4401) **552**
Israel Petrochemicals Report (GBR ISSN 1749-2297) **6775**
Israel Philatelist (USA ISSN 0161-0074) **6896**
† Israel Physical Society. Annals (ISR ISSN 0309-8710) **8967**
Israel Physical Society. Bulletin (ISR ISSN 0374-2687) **7018**
Israel Prehistoric Society. Journal (ISR) **399**
Israel Securities Authority. Annual Report *see* Rashut Neyarot Erekh. Annual Report **1377**
Israel Shipping *see* Ha-Sapanut ha-Yisre'elit **8961**
Israel South Africa Business Opportunities Newsletter (ZAF) **1573**
† Israel Studies (ISR) **8967**
• ➤ Israel Studies (USA ISSN 1084-9513) **7976**
• ➤ Israel Studies Forum (USA ISSN 1557-2455) **4322**
Israel Studies in Criminology (CAN ISSN 0075-1391) **2656**
The Israel Telecommunications Report (GBR ISSN 1748-4618) **2328**
▼ • Israel Today (ISR ISSN 1875-256X) **4322**
† Israel Tourist News (ISR) **8967**
Israel und Palaestina (DEU ISSN 0175-7024) **7246**
† Israel Update (ISR) **8967**
Israel Yearbook on Human Rights (NLD ISSN 0333-5925) **7211**
† Israeli Academic Center in Cairo. Bulletin (ISR) **8967**
Israeli History, Politics and Society (GBR ISSN 1368-4795) **7246**
➤ Israeli Journal of Aquaculture - Bamidgeh (ISR ISSN 0792-156X) **3599**
The Israeli Journal of Occupational Therapy/Ketav 'Et Yisre'eli Le-Rippuy be-'Issuq (ISR ISSN 0792-7002) **6110**
Israeli Tax Review *see* Ha-Riv'on ha-Yisre'eli l'Missim **1927**
Israels and Guttman's Modern Securities Transfers. Cumulative Supplement *see* Modern Securities Transfers **1639**
† Israel's Foreign Trade (ISR) **8967**
IssacharFile (USA ISSN 1092-4973) **7737**
Isskustvo (RUS) **497**
Issledovanie, Konstruirovanie i Raschet Rezbovykh Soedinenii (RUS) **3203**
Issledovaniya Fauny Morey/Explorations of the Fauna of the Seas (RUS ISSN 0368-007X) **2808**
Issledovaniya v Oblasti Khimii Redkozemel'nykh Elementov (RUS) **2711**
• Issledovano v Rossii/Investigated in Russia (RUS ISSN 1819-4192) **7869**
Issue (New York) (USA) **497**
• Issues (AUS ISSN 1833-7856) **2656**
• Issues (Camberwell) (AUS ISSN 0819-8101) **3066**
Issues (Chicago) (USA ISSN 0885-0046) **5963**
Issues (San Francisco) (USA ISSN 0741-0352) **7737**
† Issues (Toowong) (AUS ISSN 0814-303X) **8967**
Issues (Topeka) (USA) **2872**
Issues (Year) *see* National Association of Insurance Commissioners. Issues **4516**
† Issues and Answers in Sales Management (USA ISSN 1096-9446) **8967**
Issues and Controversies on File (USA ISSN 1081-941X) **7976**
Issues and Debates Series (USA) **5221**
• Issues and Letters (PHL ISSN 0117-4800) **7976**
Issues and Studies *see* Wenti yu Yanjiu **7273**
➤ Issues & Studies (TWN ISSN 1013-2511) **7246**
• Issues & Views. Update (USA) **3541**
Issues Current in the Social Studies (USA ISSN 1086-2005) **2872**
• Issues de la Grossesse (CAN ISSN 1712-4085) **8381**
Issues, Events & Ideas (CAN ISSN 0704-6936) **2872**
• ➤ Issues in Accounting Education (USA ISSN 0739-3172) **1293**
Issues in Agricultural Economy *see* Nongye Jingji Wenti **204**
➤ Issues in Applied Linguistics (USA ISSN 1050-4273) **5130**
Issues in Aviation Law and Policy (USA ISSN 1934-7170) **4697**
➤ Issues in Business Ethics (NLD ISSN 0925-6733) **6927**
• ➤ Issues in Child Abuse Accusations (Online Edition) (USA) **2155**
Issues in Christian Education (USA ISSN 0278-0216) **2872**
Issues in Clinical Child Psychology (NLD ISSN 1574-0471) **7367**
• ➤ Issues in Comprehensive Pediatric Nursing (GBR ISSN 0146-0862) **5963**
Issues in Constitutional Law (NLD) **4849**
▼ Issues in Contemporary Chinese Thought and Culture (NLD ISSN 1874-0588) **552**
Issues in Development. Discussion Paper (CHE ISSN 1020-3877) **1599**
• ➤ Issues in Ecology (USA ISSN 1092-8987) **3444**
Issues in Education Series (GBR ISSN 1367-0174) **2872**
• ➤ Issues in Educational Research (AUS ISSN 0313-7155) **2872**
• Issues in Emerging Health Technologies (CAN ISSN 1488-6316) **5642**
Issues in English (GBR) **5311**
• Issues in Environmental Science and Technology (GBR ISSN 1350-7583) **3444**
Issues in Ethics (USA ISSN 1091-7772) **6927**
➤ Issues in Forensic Psychology (GBR ISSN 1468-4748) **7367**
• Issues in Global Education. Occasional Paper Series (Online Edition) (USA) **3013**
Issues in Global Education. Occasional Paper Series (Print Edition) *see* Issues in Global Education. Occasional Paper Series (Online Edition) **3013**
• ➤ Issues in Infectious Diseases (CHE ISSN 1660-1890) **5819**
• ➤ Issues in Informing Science & Information Technology (USA ISSN 1547-5840) **8428**
➤ Issues in Innovation (USA ISSN 1943-4820) **8428**
• ➤ Issues in Integrative Studies (USA ISSN 1081-4760) **2988**
▼ ➤ Issues in Intercultural Communications (USA ISSN 1941-7195) **5130**
Issues in International Business (USA ISSN 1056-3024) **1573**
• Issues in Labor Statistics (USA) **1690**
Issues in Language Education (USA) **5130**
➤ Issues in Language Program Direction (USA) **3066**
• ➤ Issues in Law and Medicine (USA ISSN 8756-8160) **5642**
Issues in Mathematics Education (USA ISSN 1047-398X) **5498**
• ➤ Issues in Mental Health Nursing (USA ISSN 0161-2840) **5963**
Issues in Nigerian Development Series (NGA ISSN 1115-0017) **3920**
• ➤ Issues in Political Discourse Analysis (USA ISSN 1941-7209) **7145**
• ➤ Issues in Political Economy (USA) **7145**
Issues in Practice (GBR ISSN 1476-6868) **2872**
Issues in Psychoanalytic Psychology (USA ISSN 1075-0754) **7367**
• ➤ Issues in Science and Technology (USA ISSN 0748-5492) **7869**
• ➤ Issues in Science and Technology Librarianship (USA ISSN 1092-1206) **5019**
Issues in Southeast Asian Security (SGP) **7246**
Issues in Systematic Theology (USA ISSN 1081-9479) **7651**
• Issues in Teacher Education (USA ISSN 1536-3031) **3066**
Issues in the Practice of Psychology (USA ISSN 1567-7346) **7367**
• ➤ Issues in the Undergraduate Mathematics Preparation of School Teachers (USA) **2872**
• Issues in Toxicology (GBR ISSN 1757-7179) **3498**
➤ Issues in Urology (USA ISSN 1559-4637) **6269**
• ➤ Issues in Writing (USA ISSN 0897-0696) **4577**
• Issues Magazine (USA) **3979**
Issues of Contemporary World Socialism *see* Dangdai Shijie Shehuizhuyi Wenti **7128**
• Issues of Democracy (USA) **7145**
• Issues of Teaching and Learning (AUS ISSN 1329-2285) **3066**
Issues of the American Council for Judaism *see* American Council for Judaism. Issues **7717**
Issues on Juvenile Crimes and Delinquency *see* Qingshaonian Fanzui Wenti **4764**
Issues Paper (CAN ISSN 0838-0511) **4697**
Issyk-Kul Kabarlary (KGZ) **3903**
• Istanbul Life (TUR ISSN 1301-0514) **3962**
➤ Istanbul Medical Faculty. Medical Bulletin/Istanbul Tip Fakultesi. Mecmuasi (TUR ISSN 0378-6358) **5642**
Istanbul Stock Exchange Review *see* I S E Review **1352**
Istanbul Tip Fakultesi. Mecmuasi *see* Istanbul Medical Faculty. Medical Bulletin **5642**
Istanbul Universitesi Eczacilik Fakultesi Mecmuasi (TUR ISSN 0367-7524) **6851**
† Istanbul Universitesi. Fen Fakultesi. Matematik Dergisi/University of Istanbul. Faculty of Science. The Journal of Mathematics (TUR ISSN 1300-0713) **8967**
• ➤ Istanbul Universitesi Isletme Fakultesi Dergisi (TUR ISSN 1303-1732) **1130**
Istanbul Universitesi. Istanbul Tip Fakultesi. Mecmuasi *see* Istanbul Medical Faculty. Medical Bulletin **5642**
➤ Istanbul Universitesi Orman Fakultesi Dergisi, Seri A/Universitat Istanbul. Forstlichen Fakultaet. Zeitschrift/Universite d'Istanbul. Faculte Forestiere. Revue/University of Istanbul. Faculty of Forestry. Review (TUR ISSN 0535-8418) **3694**
• ➤ Istanbul Universitesi. Veteriner Fakultesi Dergisi/University of Istanbul. Faculty of Veterinary Medicine. Journal (TUR ISSN 0378-2352) **8800**
Istanbul University Econometrics and Statistics e-Journal *see* Ekonometri ve Istatistik E-Dergisi **1102**
Istanbul University. Faculty of Pharmacy. Journal *see* Istanbul Universitesi Eczacilik Fakultesi Mecmuasi **6851**
Istanbuler Mitteilungen (DEU ISSN 0341-9142) **399**
Istanbuler Mitteilungen. Beihefte (DEU ISSN 0418-9701) **4322**
Istanbuler Texte und Studien (DEU ISSN 1863-9461) **4322**
Istatistiklerle Turkiye (Year) (TUR ISSN 1300-431X) **8381**
Isthmia (GRC ISSN 0362-8108) **399**
Istina (FRA ISSN 0021-2423) **7652**
Isti'rau al-Naql al-Bauri 'am *see* Review of Maritime Transport **8658**

Title

Istituto Accademico di Roma. Acta (ITA ISSN 1827-4870) **4458**
Istituto Centrale del Restauro Bollettino *see* I C R. Bollettino **493**
Istituto di Diritto Processuale Civile. Pubblicazioni (ITA ISSN 0485-4098) **4833**
Istituto di Diritto Romano. Bullettino (ITA ISSN 0391-1810) **4697**
Istituto di Diritto Romano. Pubblicazioni (ITA ISSN 1971-1050) **4833**
Istituto di Fisica dell'Atmosfera, Rome. Pubblicazioni Scientifiche (ITA ISSN 0075-1936) **6358**
† Istituto di Idrobiologia e Acquacoltura G. Brunelli. Quaderni (ITA ISSN 1120-3080) **8967**
Istituto di Psicoterapia del Bambino e dell'Adolescente. Quaderno (ITA ISSN 1128-3963) **6148**
Istituto di Ricerca sulle Acque. Quaderni (ITA ISSN 0390-6329) **8826**
Istituto di Scienze Amministrative e Sociali. Collana (ITA ISSN 1824-1255) **7976**
➤ Istituto di Scienze Religiose. Saggi. Nuova Serie (ITA) **7801**
Istituto di Sociologia Internazionale di Gorizia Trimestrale di Sociologia Internazionale *see* I S I G Trimestrale di Sociologia Internazionale **8106**
Istituto di Storia dell'Arte Medioevale e Moderna. Quaderni (ITA ISSN 0391-3813) **497**
Istituto e Museo di Storia della Scienza. Biblioteca (ITA ISSN 0075-1499) **7869**
Istituto Elettrotecnico Nazionale Galileo Ferraris *see* Istituto Nazionale di Ricerca Metrologica. Rapporto Annuale **6403**
Istituto Ellenico di Studi Bizantini e Postbizantini di Venezia. Biblioteca (ITA ISSN 0075-1502) **4233**
Istituto Giangiacomo Feltrinelli. Annali *see* Fondazione Giangiacomo Feltrinelli. Annali **7964**
† Istituto Giapponese di Cultura, Rome. Notiziario. (ITA ISSN 0080-3928) **8967**
• Istituto Gramsci Emilia-Romagna. Annali (ITA ISSN 1128-9279) **7145**
Istituto Gramsci Marche. Quaderni (ITA) **4458**
Istituto Italiano degli Attuari. Giornale (ITA ISSN 0390-5780) **4510**
Istituto Italiano di Navigazione. Atti (ITA ISSN 1120-6977) **61**
Istituto Italiano di Numismatica. Annali (ITA ISSN 0578-9923) **6651**
Istituto Italiano di Preistoria e Protostoria. Atti della Riunione Scientifica (ITA) **4148**
Istituto Italiano per gli Studi Filosofici. Saggi (ITA ISSN 1824-5080) **6927**
Istituto Italiano per gli Studi Storici. Annali (ITA ISSN 0578-9931) **4148**
Istituto Italiano per l'Africa e l'Oriente. Reports and Memoirs (ITA ISSN 1827-6334) **399**
Istituto Lombardo. Accademia di Scienze e Lettere. Memorie. Classe di Lettere e Scienze Morali e Storiche. (ITA ISSN 1124-1969) **5131**
Istituto Lombardo. Accademia di Scienze e Lettere. Rendiconti. A: Scienze Matematiche e Applicazioni (ITA ISSN 0392-9523) **7869**
Istituto Lombardo. Accademia di Scienze e Lettere. Rendiconti. B: Scienze Chimiche e Fisiche, Geologiche, Biologiche e Mediche. (ITA ISSN 0392-9531) **7869**
† Istituto Mobiliare Italiano. Annual Report (ITA ISSN 0075-1529) **8967**
Istituto Nazionale d' Archeologia e Storia dell'Arte. Rivista (ITA ISSN 0392-5285) **399**
Istituto Nazionale d' Archeologia e Storia dell'Arte. Rivista. Supplemento *see* Istituto Nazionale d' Archeologia e Storia dell'Arte. Rivista **399**
• Istituto Nazionale della Previdenza Sociale. Atti Ufficiali (ITA ISSN 0021-2520) **4510**
Istituto Nazionale di Ricerca Metrologica. Annual Report *see* Istituto Nazionale di Ricerca Metrologica. Rapporto Annuale **6403**
Istituto Nazionale di Ricerca Metrologica. Rapporto Annuale/Istituto Nazionale di Ricerca Metrologica. Annual Report (ITA) **6403**
Istituto Nazionale di Studi Romani. Rassegna d'Informazioni (ITA) **4458**
Istituto Nazionale di Studi sul Rinascimento. Atti di Convegni (ITA) **4233**
Istituto Nazionale di Studi sul Rinascimento. Studi e Testi (ITA ISSN 0394-4409) **4233**
Istituto Nazionale di Studi Verdiani. Bollettino (ITA) **6578**
Istituto Nazionale per l'Assicurazione Contro gli Infortuni sul Lavoro Dati *see* I N A I L Dati **6690**
Istituto Nazionale per l'Assicurazione Contro gli Infortuni sul Lavoro Notiziario Statistico *see* I N A I L Notiziario Statistico **6690**
Istituto per i Beni Culturali *see* I B C **493**
Istituto per la Cultura e la Storia d'Impresa Franco Momigliano Newsletter *see* I C S I M Newsletter **1120**
Istituto per la Documentazione Giuridica. Bibliografia. Diritto Civile (ITA ISSN 0392-7571) **4823**
Istituto per la Documentazione Giuridica. Bibliografia. Diritto Internazionale (ITA) **4823**
Istituto per la Vigilanza sulle Assicurazioni Private e di Interesse Collettivo Bollettino *see* I S V A P Bollettino **4505**
Istituto per lo Sviluppo della Formazione Professionale dei Lavoratori Orienta *see* I S F O L Orienta **1686**
† Istituto Ricerche Pesca Marittima. Quaderni (ITA ISSN 0393-3571) **8967**
Istituto Siciliano di Studi Bizantini e Neoellenici. Monumenti (ITA ISSN 0393-0904) **497**
Istituto Siciliano di Studi Bizantini e Neoellenici. Quaderni (ITA ISSN 0075-1545) **4233**
Istituto Siciliano di Studi Bizantini e Neoellenici. Testi e Monumenti. Testi (ITA ISSN 0075-1553) **4233**
† Istituto Sieroterapico Milanese. Bollettino (ITA ISSN 0021-2547) **8967**
Istituto Sperimentale per la Selvicoltura. Annali (ITA ISSN 0390-0010) **3694**
Istituto Sperimentale per l'Enologia Asti. Annali (ITA ISSN 0374-5791) **605**
Istituto Storico Artistico Orvietano. Bollettino (ITA ISSN 0391-8211) **4233**
† Istituto Storico e di Cultura dell'Arma del Genio. Bollettino (ITA) **8967**
➤ Istituto Storico Italiano per il Medio Evo. Bullettino (ITA ISSN 1127-6096) **4233**
Istituto Storico Italiano per il Medio Evo. Nuovi Studi Storici (ITA) **4233**
Istituto Storico Italiano per l'Eta Moderna e Contemporanea. Annuario (ITA ISSN 0391-7010) **4233**
Istituto Storico Italo-Germanico in Trento. Annali/Italienisch-Deutschen Historischen Instituts in Trento. Jahrbuch (ITA ISSN 0392-0011) **4233**
• ➤ Istituto Superiore di Sanita. Annali (ITA ISSN 0021-2571) **7527**
Istituto Superiore di Sanita. Congressi (ITA ISSN 0393-5620) **7527**
• Istituto Superiore di Sanita. Notiziario (ITA ISSN 0394-9303) **7527**
Istituto Superiore di Sanita. Rapporti (ITA ISSN 1123-3117) **7528**
Istituto Superiore di Studi Medievali Cecco d'Ascoli. Atti e Memorie (ITA ISSN 1828-6283) **4233**
Istituto Universitario Navale. Facolta di Scienze Nautiche, Naples. Annali *see* Universita degli Studi di Napoli Parthenope. Facolta di Scienze e Tecnologie. Annali **7926**
Istituto Universitario Orientale. Annali (ITA ISSN 0393-3180) **4458**
Istituto Universitario Orientale di Napoli. Annali (ITA ISSN 1720-1721) **5131**
Istituto Universitario Orientale di Napoli. Annali. Slavistica (ITA ISSN 1122-195X) **4458**
• Istituto Universitario Orientale di Napoli. Dipartimento di Studi del Mondo Classico e del Mediterraneo Antico. Sezione Filologico - Letteraria. Annali (ITA ISSN 1128-7209) **2236**
Istituto Universitario Orientale di Napoli. Dipartimento di Studi dell'Europa Orientale. Sezione Storico - Politico - Sociale (ITA ISSN 1120-8422) **4148**
Istituto Universitario Orientale di Napoli. Seminario di Studi dell'Europa Orientale. Arte e Letteratura. (ITA ISSN 0394-0411) **497**
Istituto Universitario Orientale di Napoli. Seminario di Studi dell'Europa Orientale. Sezione Linguistico - Filologica. Annali (ITA ISSN 0394-0403) **5131**
Istituto Universitario Orientale. Dipartimento di Filosofia e Politica. Quaderni (ITA) **6927**
Istituto Universitario Orientale. Dipartimento di Scienze Sociali. Monografie (ITA) **4148**
Istituto Universitario Orientale. Dipartimento di Scienze Sociali. Quaderni (ITA) **7976**
Istituto Universitario Orientale. Dipartimento di Studi Asiatici. Series Minor (ITA) **552**
Istituto Universitario Orientale. Dipartimento di Studi Asiatici. Sezione Orientale. Annali (ITA) **552**
Istituto Universitario Orientale. Dipartimento di Studi Letterari e Linguistici dell'Occidente. Anglistica. Annali (ITA ISSN 1125-1077) **5311**
Istituto Universitario Orientale. Sezione Germanica. Annali (ITA ISSN 1124-3724) **5131**
Istituto Universitario Orientale. Sezione Romanza. Annali (ITA ISSN 0547-2121) **5311**
Istituto Veneto di Scienze, Lettere ed Arti. Atti. Classe di Scienze Fisiche, Matematiche e Naturali (ITA ISSN 0392-6680) **7869**
Istituto Veneto di Scienze, Lettere ed Arti. Atti. Classe di Scienze Morali, Lettere ed Arti (ITA ISSN 0392-1336) **5311**
Istituto Veneto di Scienze, Lettere ed Arti. Atti. Classe Scienze Morali e Fisiche. Memorie (ITA ISSN 1122-3642) **7869**
Istituto Veneto di Scienze, Lettere ed Arti. Atti. Classe Scienze Morali, Fisiche e Parte Generale e Atti Ufficiali (ITA ISSN 0373-2541) **7869**
Istituto Veneto di Scienze, Lettere ed Arti. Biblioteca Luzzattiana. Fonti e Studi (ITA) **5311**
Istituto Veneto di Scienze, Lettere ed Arti. Monumenta Veneta (ITA) **497**
Istituto Veneto di Scienze, Lettere ed Arti. Saggi (ITA) **7869**
➤ Istituto Veneto di Scienze, Lettere ed Arti Series (NLD ISSN 1387-6864) **4458**
Istituto Veneto di Scienze, Lettere ed Arti. Storia della Scienze. Seminari (ITA) **7869**
Istituto Veneto di Scienze, Lettere ed Arti. Studi di Arte Veneta (ITA) **497**
Istituto Veneto di Scienze, Lettere ed Arti. Summer School of Environmental Dynamics. Environmental Series (ITA) **3444**
† Istituzioni Culturali Piemontesi. Pubblicazioni (ITA) **8967**
Le Istituzioni del Federalismo (ITA ISSN 1126-7917) **7494**
† Istituzioni e Societa (ITA ISSN 1724-1316) **8967**
• Istituzioni e Sviluppo Economico/Institutions and Economic Development (ITA ISSN 1828-518X) **1130**
➤ Istmica (CRI ISSN 1023-0890) **4458**
• ➤ Istmo (MEX ISSN 1405-602X) **3909**
➤ Istochnik (RUS) **4233**
Istochnikovedenie Otechestvennoi Istorii (RUS ISSN 0321-2858) **4233**
• IstoE (BRA ISSN 0104-3943) **3804**
Istoria (BGR) **4148**
Istoricheskaya Gazeta (RUS) **4233**
Istoricheskaya Genealogiya/Historical Genealogy (RUS) **3772**
Istoricheski Pregled (BGR ISSN 0323-9748) **4148**
Istoricheskie Zapiski (RUS ISSN 0130-6685) **4148**
Istoricheskii Arkhiv/Historical Archives (RUS ISSN 0869-6322) **4233**
Istorichesko Budeshte/Historical Future (BGR ISSN 1311-0144) **4233**
Istorie si Civilizatie (ROM ISSN 0075-1626) **4148**
Istorija (LTU ISSN 1392-0456) **4233**
Istorijski Casopis (SRB ISSN 0350-0802) **4233**
Istorijski Zapisi (MNE ISSN 0021-2652) **4233**
Istoriko-filologicheskii Zhurnal *see* Patma-banasirakan Andes **4253**
Istoriko-Matematicheskie Issledovaniya (RUS ISSN 0136-0949) **5498**
Istoriya (RUS) **4148**
➤ Istoriya 20 Veka/History of 20th Century (SRB ISSN 0352-3160) **4233**
Istoriya Dvadesetogo Veka *see* Istoriya 20 Veka **4233**
Istoriya i Istoriki (RUS) **4233**
Istoriya i Obshchestvoznanie dlya Shkol'nikov (RUS) **4148**
• Istoriya. Istorychni Nauky (UKR) **4170**
Istoriya Narodnoho Hospodarstva ta Ekonomichnoi Dumky Ukrainy (UKR ISSN 0320-4421) **1543**
Istoriya Nauki i Tekhniki (RUS) **7869**
Istoriya Sibiri i Dal'nego Vostoka (RUS ISSN 0869-2599) **4170**
Istratigiyyat al-Hay'at al-'arabiyyat li-l-istithmar wa-al-Inma al-Zira'i li-l-A'wam *see* Strategy (Khartoum) **1605**
Istropolitan (SVK ISSN 1337-0049) **3946**
Isturitz (ESP ISSN 1137-4489) **399**
Isuma (CAN ISSN 1492-0611) **7145**
Isurv Knowledge Alert (GBR ISSN 1746-8248) **3232**
• It (AUS) **8319**
IT-Branchen *see* I T Branchen **8963**
IT Consultant (Information Technology) (GBR ISSN 1366-9435) **1419**
It Goes on the Shelf (USA) **5443**
• IT Marketing News (GBR) **1823**
I T & Co (SWE) **2537**
IT-Partner Denmark *see* I T Partner Denmark **8963**
IT.Services *see* Iconomy **1751**
It Starts on the Frontline *see* PRincipal Communicator **2899**
It-Torca (MLT ISSN 0021-2725) **4596**
Ita - Savo (FIN ISSN 0356-4444) **3838**
Itaca (ESP ISSN 0213-6643) **4148**
Itaici (BRA) **3541**
Itaici Revista de Espiritualidade Inaciana (BRA ISSN 1517-7807) **7801**
Italcommerce (CAN ISSN 0225-1140) **1405**
Italia/Studi e Ricerche sulla Storia, la Cultura e la Letteratura degli Ebrei d'Italia (ISR ISSN 0334-360X) **3541**
† Italia (ITA ISSN 0535-9031) **8967**
Italia Benedettina (ITA) **7801**
• Italia Casa (ITA) **4361**
Italia Contemporanea (ITA ISSN 0392-3568) **4233**
• L'Italia Cooperativa (ITA ISSN 0391-7150) **1423**
L'Italia dei Comuni (ITA ISSN 1828-468X) **7494**
L'Italia Dialettale (ITA ISSN 0085-2295) **5131**
Italia Forestale e Montana (ITA ISSN 0021-2776) **3694**
Italia Francescana (ITA ISSN 0391-7509) **6927**
L'Italia Grafica *see* Italia Grafica **7324**
• Italia Grafica (ITA ISSN 0021-2784) **7324**
Italia Imballaggio (ITA) **6711**
L'Italia in Cucina (ITA ISSN 1129-8332) **4361**
• Italia Medievale e Umanistica (ITA ISSN 0391-7495) **4233**
† Italia Meravigliosa (ITA ISSN 1828-2881) **8967**
Italia Missionaria (ITA ISSN 0021-2806) **2194**
Italia Nostra (ITA ISSN 0021-2822) **6526**
† Italia Nostra. Sezione di Trento. Bollettino (ITA) **8967**
• Italia Publishers Magazine (ITA) **7580**
L'Italia Scacchistica (ITA ISSN 0021-2849) **8181**
† Italia Turistica (ITA ISSN 1972-6074) **8967**
† Italia Viva (ITA) **8967**
Italiamondo *see* Voce dell'Emigrante **8077**
Italian (USA ISSN 1939-2273) **4361**
Italian Academy Lectures (USA ISSN 1555-7057) **5311**
• Italian America (USA ISSN 1089-5043) **3541**
Italian American Chamber of Commerce of Chicago. Bulletin (USA ISSN 0021-2903) **1405**
Italian-American Digest (USA) **3541**
The Italian American Review (USA ISSN 0535-9120) **3541**
➤ Italian Americana (USA ISSN 0096-8846) **3541**
Italian Astronomical Society. Journal *see* Societa Astronomica Italiana. Memorie **581**
Italian Beverage Technology *see* Italian Food and Beverage Technology **3649**
Italian Books and Periodicals *see* Libri e Riviste d'Italia **7566**
Italian Books in Print *see* Catalogo dei Libri in Commercio **622**
Italian Books in Print on CD-ROM *see* Catalogo dei Libri in Commercio (CD-ROM) **622**
Italian Building and Construction (ITA ISSN 0393-8069) **1017**
Italian Canadiana (CAN ISSN 0827-6129) **4298**
Italian Cinema (ITA) **6504**
Italian Cooking & Living (USA ISSN 1539-8633) **4391**
• ➤ Italian Culture (GBR ISSN 0161-4622) **5311**
† Italian Dental Economist (ITA ISSN 1593-4977) **8967**
Italian Dental Journal (ITA ISSN 1970-7428) **5850**
Italian Design Selection Milano (ITA ISSN 1720-8041) **4544**
Italian Food and Beverage Technology (ITA ISSN 1590-6515) **3649**
† Italian Food Machines (ITA) **8967**
• Italian Food Materials and Machinery (ITA ISSN 1970-9684) **6711**
Italian Food Technology *see* Italian Food and Beverage Technology **3649**
Italian Geotechnical Journal *see* Rivista Italiana di Geotecnica **2764**
Italian Heart Journal *see* Giornale Italiano di Cardiologia **5787**
Italian Heart Journal *see* Journal of Cardiovascular Medicine (Hagerstown) **5792**
• Italian Historical Society Journal (AUS ISSN 1321-3881) **4233**
Italian History & Culture (ITA ISSN 1123-2463) **4233**
• Italian Home News (ITA) **4544**
• ➤ Italian Journal of Agronomy (ITA ISSN 1125-4718) **124**
Italian Journal of Agronomy/Rivista di Agronomia *see* Italian Journal of Agronomy **124**
Italian Journal of Allergy and Clinical Immunology *see* Giornale Italiano di Allergologia e Immunologia Clinica **5758**
Italian Journal of Anatomy and Embryology (ITA ISSN 1122-6714) **680**
• ➤ Italian Journal of Animal Science (ITA ISSN 1594-4077) **290**
➤ Italian Journal of Biochemistry (ITA ISSN 0021-2938) **734**
Italian Journal of Chest Diseases *see* Giornale Italiano delle Malattie del Torace **6214**
Italian Journal of Engineering Geology and Environment (ITA ISSN 1825-6635) **2748**
• ➤ Italian Journal of Food Science (ITA ISSN 1120-1770) **3649**
Italian Journal of Gynaecology & Obstetrics (ITA ISSN 1121-8339) **5994**
Italian Journal of Laboratory Medicine *see* La Rivista Italiana della Medicina di Laboratorio **5910**
Italian Journal of Linguistics *see* Rivista di Linguistica **5169**
Italian Journal of Maxillofacial Surgery *see* Rivista Italiana di Chirurgia Maxillo-Facciale **5864**
The Italian Journal of Medicine *see* Italian Journal of Medicine **5642**
Italian Journal of Medicine (ITA ISSN 0393-8166) **5642**
• ➤ Italian Journal of Mineral & Electrolyte Metabolism (ITA ISSN 1121-1709) **734**
Italian Journal of Osseointegration *see* European Journal of Implant Prosthodontics **5843**
• The Italian Journal of Pediatrics (Online) (GBR ISSN 1824-7288) **6094**
† • The Italian Journal of Pediatrics (Print) (ITA ISSN 1720-8424) **8967**
† The Italian Journal of Psychiatry and Behavioural Sciences (ITA ISSN 1122-2247) **8967**
Italian Journal of Psychology *see* Giornale Italiano di Psicologia **7358**
• Italian Journal of Public Health/Giornale Italiano di Salute Pubblica (ITA ISSN 1723-7807) **7528**
➤ Italian Journal of Pure and Applied Mathematics (ITA ISSN 1126-8042) **5499**
Italian Journal of Regional Science *see* Scienze Regionali **1549**
• ➤ Italian Journal of Vascular and Endovascular Surgery (ITA ISSN 1824-4777) **6247**
• Italian Journal of Zoology (GBR ISSN 1125-0003) **949**
• ➤ Italian Labour Law e-Journal (ITA ISSN 1561-8048) **4697**
† Italian Life (ITA ISSN 1122-4029) **8967**
Italian Lighting (ITA) **3322**
Italian Magazine (GBR) **8724**
▼ Italian Modernities (GBR) **5131**
Italian Oral Surgery (ITA ISSN 1827-2452) **5850**
Italian Physical Society. Conference Proceedings *see* Societa Italiana di Fisica. Atti di Conferenze **7040**
➤ Italian Poetry Review (ITA ISSN 1557-5012) **5424**
Italian Pointers *see* P O I N T ers **3778**
Italian Politics (GBR ISSN 1086-4946) **1130**
Italian Psychoanalytical Society. Journal *see* Rivista di Psicoanalisi **7405**
Italian Sons and Daughters of America Unione *see* I S D A Unione **3538**
Italian Statistical Abstract (ITA ISSN 1126-8603) **8381**
• ➤ Italian Studies (GBR ISSN 0075-1634) **5311**
Italian Studies in Southern Africa (ZAF ISSN 1012-2338) **4233**
Italian Technology (ITA ISSN 0391-738X) **8428**
Italian Technology Machine Tools *see* Italian Technology **8428**
Italian Texts (GBR) **5131**
Italian Tribune News (USA) **3541**
Italian Voice/Voce Italiana (USA) **3541**
† Italian Wines & Spirits (UK Edition) (ITA) **8967**
† Italian Wines & Spirits (US and Canada Edition) (ITA) **8967**

Title

J A R P *see* Journal of Art and Record Production **8153**
J A R Q *see* Japan Agricultural Research Quarterly **125**
J A R Verklaard (Jurisprudentie Arbeidsrecht) (NLD ISSN 1574-7379) **4698**
J A S *see* Journal of Applied Statistics **8382**
J A S A *see* Acoustical Society of America. Journal **7086**
J A S A *see* American Statistical Association. Journal **8344**
J A S A - E L *see* J A S A Express Letters **7088**
• ➤ J A S A Express Letters (Journal of the Acoustical Society of America) (USA) **7088**
J A S A L *see* Association for the Study of Australian Literature. Journal **5257**
J A S A M *see* Australasian Society of Aerospace Medicine. Journal **5581**
J A S, Australia's Public Intellectual Forum *see* Journal of Australian Studies **4192**
J A S C O Report (Japan Spectroscopic Corporation) (JPN ISSN 0916-3492) **7077**
J A S E M *see* Journal of Applied Sciences and Environmental Management **3488**
J A S I S *see* American Society for Information Science and Technology. Journal **4989**
J A S Joho (Japanese Agricultural Standards Association) (JPN) **124**
J A S Journal (Japan Audio Society) (JPN ISSN 0388-158X) **8153**
J A S M A: Journal of the Japan Society of Microgravity Application (JPN ISSN 0915-3616) **7018**
J A S N *see* American Society of Nephrology. Journal **6265**
J A S N A News (Jane Austen Society of North America) (USA ISSN 0892-8665) **5312**
J A S O *see* Anthropological Society of Oxford. Journal **326**
J A S O Occasional Papers (Journal of the Anthropological Society of Oxford) (GBR ISSN 1369-7900) **343**
J A S P *see* Journal of Aging & Social Policy **4048**
J A S S *see* Journal of Artificial Societies and Social Simulation **8111**
• J A S S A (Journal of the Australian Society of Security Analysts) (AUS ISSN 0313-5934) **1634**
J A S S A *see* Journal of Applied Science in Southern Africa **7871**
• ➤ J A S T (Journal of Aerospace Science and Technology) (IRN ISSN 1735-2134) **62**
• ➤ J A S T (Journal of American Studies of Turkey) (TUR ISSN 1300-6606) **4298**
J A S T R O Newsletter (JPN ISSN 0918-399X) **6199**
J A T *see* Journal of Analytical Toxicology **3498**
J A T A *see* American Taxation Association. Journal **1910**
J A T E News *see* J A T E Tsushin **2328**
J A T E Tsushin/J A T E News (Japan Approvals Institute for Telecommunications Equipment) (JPN ISSN 0913-8293) **2328**
J A T I P *see* DePaul Journal of Art, Technology & Intellectual Property Law **4656**
J A T I T *see* Journal of Theoretical and Applied Information Technology **2430**
J A V A *see* Journal of Animal and Veterinary Advances **8800**
J A V A *see* Association for Vascular Access. Journal **5778**
J A V M A *see* American Veterinary Medical Association. Journal **8791**
J A - Zenchu News (JPN) **1423**
J & K Research Biannual (Jammu and Kashmir) (IND) **4458**
• J & W Banking International. International Banking and Finance Communications Directory (DEU) **2009**
A J B *see* Australian Journal of Botany **777**
J B *see* Journal of Biochemistry **735**
J B *see* Journal of Bisexuality **4375**
J B A *see* J B A. Jornal Brasileiro de A T M, Oclusao & Dor Orofacial **5850**
J B A *see* British Archaeological Association. Journal **384**
J B A *see* Journal of Biomaterials Applications **6247**
J B A *see* Journal of Building Appraisal **1018**
J B A *see* Juniorway Bible Activities **7657**
J B A H S F M *see* Journal of Behavior Analysis in Health, Sports, Fitness and Medicine **7528**
A J B A S *see* Australian Journal of Basic and Applied Sciences **7838**
J B B *see* Journal of Biomedicine and Biotechnology **5646**
J B B M *see* Journal of Business-to-Business Marketing **1823**
J B C *see* Jornal Brasileiro de Clinica Odontologica Integrada **5850**
J B C C *see* Jornal Brasileiro de Ciencias da Comunicacao **2328**
J B C. Jornal Brasileiro de Clinica & Estetica em Odontologia (BRA ISSN 1516-7550) **5850**
• J B C Papers in Press (Journal of Biological Chemistry) (USA) **734**
J B D Q *see* Jornal Brasileiro de Dependencias Quimicas **2695**
J B E *see* Jornal Brasileiro de Endodontia **5850**
J B E *see* Journal of Business & Entrepreneurship **1133**
J B E *see* Journal of Buddhist Ethics **7701**
J B E E *see* Journal of Business Ethics Education **6928**
J B E S *see* Journal of Business and Economic Statistics **1247**
J B F *see* Jornal Brasileiro de Fitoterapia **6852**
J B F A *see* Journal of Business Finance & Accounting **1294**
J B F L *see* Journal of Business & Finance Librarianship **5020**
J B G *see* Jornal Brasileiro de Odontogeriatria **5850**
J B I A Directory (Japan Book Importers Association) (JPN) **2009**
• J B I Best Practice Technical Report (Joanna Briggs Institute) (AUS ISSN 1833-7732) **5643**
J B I C *see* Journal of Biological Inorganic Chemistry **2117**
J B I C I Review (Japan Bank for International Cooperation Institute) (JPN) **1359**
J B I C Today (Japan Bank for International Cooperation) (JPN) **1599**
J B I Journal (Jamaica Bauxite Institute) (JAM ISSN 0254-5241) **6467**
J B I M *see* Journal of Business & Industrial Marketing **1823**
• J B I Quarterly (Jamaica Bauxite Institute) (JAM ISSN 1018-2160) **6467**
J B I Reports *see* International Journal of Evidence-Based Healthcare **5638**
J B I S *see* British Interplanetary Society Journal **50**
J - B I S C *see* Nihon Zenkoku Shoshi **632**
J B J S *see* Journal of Bone and Joint Surgery: British Volume **6063**
J B L *see* Journal of Biblical Literature **7654**
J B L *see* University of Pennsylvania. Journal of Business Law **4882**
J B M *see* Jornal Brasileiro de Medicina **5645**
J B M R S *see* Journal of the Book of Mormon & Restoration Scripture **7737**
J B N *see* Juridische Berichten voor het Notariaat **4705**
J B P (BRA ISSN 1415-4846) **5850**
J B P C *see* Journal of Biological Physics and Chemistry **753**
J B R *see* Journal of Biological Rhythms **6149**
J B R - B T R (Journal Belge de Radiologie - Belgisch Tijdschrift voor Radiologie) (BEL ISSN 1780-2393) **6199**
J B R M R *see* The Journal of Business and Retail Management Research **1764**
J B S *see* Journal of Biosocial Science **8112**
J B S *see* Journal of Business Strategy **1764**
J B S *see* Journal of British Studies **4235**
• J B S Bulletin (John Birch Society) (USA ISSN 0449-0754) **7246**
J B S G E *see* Journal of Business Systems, Governance and Ethics **1764**
J B S L *see* Journal of Business and Securities Law **4872**
J B S P *see* British Society for Phenomenology. Journal **6908**
J B S W *see* Journal of Baccalaureate Social Work **8048**
J B T *see* Jornal Brasileiro de Transplantes **6247**
J C 2 M *see* Journal for Crime, Conflict and Media Culture **4699**
J C A *see* Journal of Chinese Australia **3544**
J C A *see* Journal of Computational Acoustics **7050**
J C A B *see* Journal of Cell and Animal Biology **833**
• J C A H O Advisor for Behavioral Health Care Providers (Joint Commission on Accreditation of Healthcare Organizations) (USA ISSN 1520-8265) **4103**
• J C A H O Advisor for Health Care Human Resources (Joint Commission on the Accreditation of Healthcare Organizations) (USA ISSN 1521-8317) **1867**
J C A H O Update for Infection Control *see* Hospital Infection Control & Prevention **5816**
J C A Janaru *see* J C A Journal **1573**
J C A Journal (Japan Commercial Arbitration Association) (JPN ISSN 0386-3042) **1573**
J C A L *see* Journal of Computer Assisted Learning **2469**
J C A P *see* Journal of Cosmology and Astroparticle Physics **7020**
J C A P N *see* Journal of Child and Adolescent Psychiatric Nursing **5964**
J C A S *see* Journal of Contemporary African Studies **7978**
J C A S A *see* Journal of Child & Adolescent Substance Abuse **2695**
J C B *see* Journal of Commercial Biotechnology **767**
J C B *see* The Journal of Cell Biology **833**
J C C *see* The Journal of Corporate Citizenship **1765**
J C C A *see* Canadian Chiropractic Association. Journal **5803**
J C C A *see* Journal of Child-Care Administration **3025**
J C C Circle (Jewish Community Centers Association of North America) (USA) **7722**
J C C P *see* Journal of Clinical Chiropractic Pediatrics **5806**
J C D *see* Journal of Cosmetic Dermatology **5878**
J C D *see* Journal of Clinical Densitometry **5647**
J C D T *see* Journal of Dual Diagnosis **2696**
J C E *see* Journal of Chemical Education **2067**
J C E B S *see* Journal of Chinese Economics and Business Studies **1494**
J C E F T S *see* Journal of Chinese Economic and Foreign Trade Studies **1573**
J C E M *see* Journal of Clinical Endocrinology and Metabolism **5895**
J C E R *see* Journal of Contemporary European Research **7247**
J C F S *see* Journal of Chronic Fatigue Syndrome **8968**
J C G S *see* Journal of Computational and Graphical Statistics **5502**
J C H *see* Journal of Contemporary History **4149**
J C I *see* Journal of Clinical Investigation **5647**
J C I News (Junior Chamber International) (USA) **2267**
• J C K (USA ISSN 1534-2719) **4567**
J C K Luxury (Jewelers' Circular Keystone) (USA ISSN 1559-5900) **1823**
J C K's Annual Directory of Suppliers and Services (Jewelers' Circular Keystone) (USA) **4567**
J C K's High Volume Jeweler *see* J C K **4567**
J C K's Jewelers' Directory *see* J C K's Annual Directory of Suppliers and Services **4567**
J C K's Luxury International *see* J C K Luxury **1823**
J C L *see* Journal of Commonwealth Literature **5314**
J C L *see* The Journal of Corporation Law **4872**
J C I. Administratif *see* Juris-Classeur Administratif **4706**
J C I. Bail a Loyer *see* Juris-Classeur des Loyers et de la Propriete Commerciale **4706**
J C I. Banque - Credit - Bourse *see* Juris-Classeur Banque Credit Bourse **4872**
J C I. Baux Ruraux *see* Juris-Classeur des Baux. Baux Ruraux **4873**
J C I. Brevets *see* Juris-Classeur Brevets **4706**
J C L C *see* Journal of Criminal Law & Criminology **2657**
J C I. Commercial *see* Juris-Classeur Commercial **4873**
J C I. Concurrence - Consommation *see* Juris-Classeur Concurrence-Consommation **4873**
J C I. Construction - Urbanisme *see* Juris-Classeur Construction Urbanisme **4873**
J C I. Contrats - Distribution *see* Juris-Classeur Contrats-Distribution **4873**
J C I. Copropriete *see* Juris-Classeur Copropriete **4873**
J C I. Divorce *see* Juris-Classeur Divorce **4911**
J C L E *see* Journal of Competition Law and Economics **4700**
J C I. Encyclopedie des Huissiers de Justice *see* Juris-Classeur Encyclopedie des Huissiers de Justice **4706**
J C I. Environnement *see* Juris-Classeur Environnement **4706**
J C I. Fonctions Publiques *see* Juris-Classeur Fonctions Publiques **4850**
J C L I *see* The Journal of Contemporary Legal Issues **4700**
J C I. Impot sur la Fortune *see* Juris-Classeur Impot sur la Fortune **4903**
J C I. Procedure Civile *see* Juris-Classeur de Procedure Civile **4706**
J C I. Procedures Collectives *see* Juris-Classeur Procedures Collectives **4706**
J C I. Procedures Formulaire *see* Juris-Classeur Procedures Formulaire **4706**
J C I. Propriete Litteraire et Artistique *see* Juris-Classeur Propriete Litteraire et Artistique **4706**
J C I. Protection Sociale. Traite *see* Juris-Classeur. Protection Sociale Traite **4706**
J C I. Responsabilite Civile et Assurances *see* Juris-Classeur de la Responsabilite Civile et des Assurances **4706**
J C I. Rural *see* Juris-Classeur Rural **4706**
J C I. Transport *see* Juris-Classeur Transport **4706**
J C I. Travail. Traite *see* Juris-Classeur Travail Traite **4706**
➤ J C M C C (Journal of Combinatorial Mathematics and Combinatorial Computing) (CAN ISSN 0835-3026) **5499**
J C M S Annual Review of the European Union in ... (GBR) **7145**
J C M S Newsletter (Jefferson County Medical Society) (USA) **5643**
J C M T Newsletter (GBR) **576**
J C N *see* Journal of Clinical Nursing **5964**
J C O *see* Journal of Clinical Oncology **6024**
J C O M *see* Journal of Communication Management **1765**
J C O M *see* Journal of Science Communication **2330**
J C O M *see* Journal of Clinical Outcomes Management **4103**
J C P A *see* Journal of Comparative Policy Analysis **7448**
▼ • J C P: Biochemical Physics (Journal of Chemical Physics) (USA ISSN 1931-9223) **7018**
J C P C N S Capsules (Journal Clinical Pyschiatry Central Nervous System) (USA ISSN 1548-7040) **6148**
J C P E S Congressional District Fact Book (Joint Center for Political and Economic Studies) (USA) **7145**
J C P Online *see* Journal of Clinical Pathology **5647**
J C P P *see* Journal of Child Psychology and Psychiatry **7370**
J C P S P *see* College of Physicians and Surgeons Pakistan. Journal **5599**
J C R *see* Journal of Construction Research **1018**
J C R *see* Journal of Consumer Research **1823**
J C R *see* Journal of Clinical Rheumatology **6224**
J C R E *see* Journal of Corporate Real Estate **7596**
J C R R *see* Journal of Cardiothoracic-Renal Research **5792**
• J C R Science Edition (Journal Citation Reports) (USA ISSN 1524-5047) **7869**
• ➤ J C R Social Sciences Edition (Journal Citation Reports) (USA ISSN 1524-5055) **8020**
J C R T *see* Journal of Cancer Research and Therapeutics **6024**
J C R Web Science Edition *see* J C R Science Edition **7869**
J C R Web Social Science Edition *see* J C R Social Sciences Edition **8020**
J C S *see* Journal of Canadian Studies **4460**
J C S *see* Journal of Cell Science **833**
J C S *see* Journal of Classical Sociology **8112**
J C S *see* Journal of Civil Society **7146**
J C S *see* Journal of Chromatographic Science **2101**
J C S *see* Journal of Church and State **7654**
J C S *see* Journal of Cuneiform Studies **400**
J C S A *see* Journal of Child Sexual Abuse **8049**
J C S E *see* The Journal of Corrosion Science and Engineering **6319**
J C S E Online *see* Journal for Computing Teachers **2428**
J C S P *see* Journal of College Student Psychotherapy **7371**
J C S U News (Johnson C. Smith University) (USA) **2288**
J C T *see* The Journal of Chemical Thermodynamics **2136**
• ➤ J C T (Journal of Curriculum Theorizing) (USA ISSN 1057-896X) **3066**
• J C T CoatingsTech (Journal of Coatings Technology) (USA ISSN 1547-0083) **6718**
J C T: Journal of Coatings Technology *see* J C T CoatingsTech **6718**
J C T R *see* Journal of Coatings Technology and Research **6718**
• J C T R Bulletin (Jesuit Centre for Theological Reflection) (ZMB ISSN 1990-4479) **7801**
J C U L *see* Journal of College and University Law **4700**
J C W I Annual Report and Policy Review (Joint Council for the Welfare of Immigrants) (GBR) **4698**
J C W I Bulletin (Joint Council for the Welfare of Immigrants) (GBR) **4698**
J C W I Immigration, Nationality and Refugee Law Handbook (Joint Council for the Welfare of Immigrants) (GBR) **4850**
J C W S *see* Journal of Cold War Studies **7247**
J D *see* Journal of Documentation **5020**
† J D (Junior Dental) (ITA ISSN 0393-800X) **8967**
J D B P *see* Journal of Developmental and Behavioral Pediatrics **6094**
J D C *see* Journal of Digital Contents **2571**
J D D G (Online Edition) *see* J D D G (Print Edition) **5878**
• ➤ J D D G (Print Edition) (Journal der Deutschen Dermatologischen Gesellschaft) (DEU ISSN 1610-0379) **5878**
J D D G Supplement *see* J D D G (Print Edition) **5878**
J D D S T *see* Journal of Drug Delivery Science and Technology **6853**
J D E A *see* Journal of Difference Equations and Applications **5502**
J D I (Journal des Instituteurs) (FRA ISSN 1969-3303) **2872**
J D I 2 *see* J D I **2872**
J D I Q *see* A C M Journal of Data and Information Quality **2528**
J D J *see* Java Developer's Journal **2507**
J D Journal (John Deere) (USA) **212**
J D Jungle *see* Jungle Law **4705**
J D Q: Journal Dentaire du Quebec *see* J O D Q: Journal de l'Ordre des Dentistes du Quebec **5850**
J D R *see* Journal of Divorce & Remarriage **5559**
Le J D S *see* Le Journal du S I D A **5819**
J D S D E *see* The Journal of Deaf Studies and Deaf Education **4075**
J D T *see* Journal of Dental Technology **5851**
J E A *see* Journal of Egyptian Archaeology **400**
J E A *see* Journal of Educational Administration **3026**
J E A B *see* Journal of the Experimental Analysis of Behavior **7381**
J E A D V *see* European Academy of Dermatology and Venereology. Journal **5876**
J E A D V Supplement *see* European Academy of Dermatology and Venereology. Journal. Supplement **5876**
J E A N *see* Journal of Elder Abuse & Neglect **4049**
J E A P *see* Journal of English for Academic Purposes **3067**
J E A P M *see* Journal of Environmental Assessment Policy and Management **3445**
J E B *see* The Journal of Experimental Biology **682**
J E B *see* Journal of Evolutionary Biology **873**
J E B D *see* Journal of Emotional and Behavioral Disorders **6151**
J E B E *see* The Journal for Education in the Built Environment **447**
J E B P S *see* Journal of Evidence-Based Practices for Schools **2876**
J E B S *see* Journal of Educational and Behavioral Statistics **2934**
J E C *see* Journal of Enterprising Communities **1136**
J E C *see* Japan Economic Currents (Online) **1131**
J E C A R *see* Journal of Experimental & Clinical Assisted Reproduction **5995**

Title

J J S P C *see* Japan Society of Pain Clinics. Journal **4103**
▼ J Journal (USA ISSN 1941-5230) **2656**
J K (Jesuskvinner) (NOR ISSN 1504-1573) **7652**
J K - Beslut (SWE ISSN 0281-0883) **4698**
J. K. Lasser's 1001 Deductions and Tax Breaks (Year) (USA ISSN 1559-9000) **1931**
J. K. Lasser's Homeowner's Tax Breaks (Year) (USA ISSN 1930-6083) **1931**
J.K. Lasser's Monthly Tax Letter (USA ISSN 1056-3121) **1931**
J.K. Lasser's Your Income Tax (Year) (USA ISSN 0084-4314) **1931**
J.K. Lasser's Your Income Tax, Professional Edition (USA ISSN 0075-2061) **1931**
J K M *see* Journal of Knowledge Management **1767**
J K M P *see* Journal of Knowledge Management Practice **6928**
J K Magazine *see* MGZN **1407**
● ➤ J K Practitioner (IND ISSN 0971-8834) **5819**
● ➤ J K Science (Jammu & Kashmir) (IND ISSN 0972-1177) **5643**
J K T R *see* Journal of Knot Theory and Its Ramifications **5504**
J L A *see* Journal of Library Administration **5022**
J L A G *see* Journal of Latin American Geography **4017**
J L A M S *see* Library Administration and Management Section. Journals **5026**
J L A News (Jamaica Library Association) (JAM) **5019**
● J L B Smith Institute of Ichthyology. Ichthyological Bulletin (ZAF ISSN 0251-1258) **949**
J L B Smith Institute of Ichthyology. Special Publication *see* Smithiana. Special Publication **963**
J L F S *see* Journal of Law & Family Studies **4702**
J L I S *see* Journal of Library and Information Science **5022**
J L L *see* Lingua et Linguistica **5145**
J L L *see* The John Liner Letter **4510**
J L P *see* Journal of Legal Pluralism and Unofficial Law **4703**
J L P P *see* Journal of Law & Public Policy **4702**
J L R *see* Journal of Lipid Research **736**
J L R *see* The John Liner Review **4510**
J L R E L *see* Journal of Land, Resources, & Environmental Law **3140**
J L S *see* The Journal of Legal Studies (Chicago) **4703**
J L S *see* Journal of Lesbian Studies **4375**
J L S C *see* Journal of Law & Social Challenges **4702**
J L S D E *see* The Journal of Library Services for Distance Education **5022**
J/M *see* J/M voor Geweldige Ouders met Kinderen van 2 tot 14+ **2156**
J M *see* Journal of Marketing **1825**
J M 2 *see* Journal of Modelling in Management **1768**
J M A *see* Journal of Maintenance in the Addictions **8968**
J M A C *see* Ayub Medical College. Journal **5581**
J M A Janaru/Japan Management Association. Journal (JPN ISSN 0287-5802) **1762**
J M B *see* Journal of Molecular Biology **736**
J M B *see* Journal of Motor Behavior **7376**
J M B *see* The Journal of Mind and Behavior **7376**
J M B A *see* Marine Biological Association of the United Kingdom. Journal **688**
J M B Online *see* Journal of Molecular Biology **736**
J M C *see* Journal of Marketing Channels **1825**
J M D *see* Journal of Management Development **1767**
J M D *see* The Journal of Molecular Diagnostics **5653**
J M D O *see* Journal of Marine Design and Operations **8648**
J M E *see* Journal of Mediterranean Ecology **3448**
J M E I S A *see* Journal of Middle Eastern and Islamic Studies in Asia **553**
J M E Online *see* Journal of Medical Ethics **5651**
J M E T *see* Journal of Marine Engineering and Technology **8648**
J M E W S *see* Journal of Middle East Women's Studies **8900**
J M G Online *see* Journal of Medical Genetics **874**
J M H *see* Journal of Management History **1768**
J M H *see* The Journal of Modern History **4149**
J M H E *see* Journal of Marketing for Higher Education **2991**
J M H G *see* Journal of Men's Health **6284**
● The J M I (Journal of Music in Ireland) (IRL ISSN 1649-0215) **6578**
J M I *see* Journal of Managerial Issues **1768**
J M I S *see* Journal of Modern Italian Studies **5315**
J M I S *see* Journal of Medieval Iberian Studies **4236**
J M I S *see* Journal of Management Information Systems **2548**
J M L *see* Lebanese Medical Journal **5660**
J M L *see* Journal of Modern Literature **5315**
J M L A *see* Medical Library Association. Journal **5669**
J M L C *see* Journal of Money Laundering Control **1362**
J M L L *see* Journal of Mesoamerican Languages and Linguistics **5134**
J M M *see* The Journal of Music and Meaning **6580**
J M M *see* Journal of Micromechanics and Microengineering **3386**
J M M *see* Journal of Medical Marketing (Print) **6854**
J M M *see* Journal of Mathematics and Music **5505**
J M M (Jag, Mats, Mentzoni) (SWE ISSN 1652-5914) **5312**
● J M M (Journal on Media Management) (USA ISSN 1424-1277) **2328**
J M M A R *see* Journal of Mentored Management Accounting Research **1295**
J M M H *see* The Journal for MultiMedia History **2351**
J M N *see* Journal of Molecular Neuroscience **6153**
J M N R (Journal of Military Nursing & Research) (USA ISSN 1070-4329) **5963**
J M O *see* Journal of Modern Optics **7078**
J M P *see* Journal of Management Practice **1768**
J M P *see* Journal of Managerial Psychology **1768**
J M P *see* Journal of Manufacturing Processes **1890**
J M P *see* Journal of Musculoskeletal Pain **6064**
J M P R *see* Journal of Medicinal Plant Research **311**
J M P T *see* Journal of Manipulative and Physiological Therapeutics **5806**
J/M Pubers *see* J/M voor Geweldige Ouders met Kinderen van 2 tot 14+ **2156**
J M R *see* Journal of Marine Research **2809**
J M R *see* Journal of Marketing Research **1825**
J M R *see* Journal of Materials Research **3350**
J M R *see* Journal of Multidisciplinary Research **7979**
J M R I *see* The Medical Research Institute. Journal **5671**
J M R I *see* Journal of Magnetic Resonance Imaging **6200**
J M S *see* Journal of Management Studies **1768**
J M S R *see* Journal of Medical Sciences Research **5652**
J M S Y *see* Journal of Manufacturing Systems **3386**
J M T M *see* Journal of Manufacturing Technology Management **3292**
J M T P *see* Journal of Marketing Theory and Practice **1826**
▼ J/M voor Geweldige Ouders met Kinderen van 2 tot 14+ (NLD ISSN 1875-1865) **2156**
J/M voor Ouders *see* J/M voor Geweldige Ouders met Kinderen van 2 tot 14+ **2156**
● J M W W (Jen Michalski's Written World) (USA) **5312**
J M W W Anthology (Jen Michalski's Written World) (USA ISSN 1933-6136) **5312**
J. Michael Pinson's Investment Digest (USA) **1634**
J N *see* Journal of Neurophysiology **924**
J N A A *see* Journal of Numismatic Association of Australia **6651**
J N A S *see* The Journal of North African Studies **4176**
J N C *see* Journal of Neurochemistry **736**
J N C C *see* Journal of the New Comprehensive College **2991**
J N C C Reports (Joint Nature Conservation Committee) (GBR ISSN 0963-8091) **2615**
J N C Fashion Trend Magazine *see* J'N'C Fashion Trend Magazine **2257**
● J N C Z Marketing Newsletter (GBR) **1823**
J N E *see* Journal of Negro Education **2877**
J N E *see* Journal of Nutrition for the Elderly **4049**
J N E R *see* Journal of NeuroEngineering and Rehabilitation **6153**
† J N F Illustrated (Jewish National Fund) (ISR ISSN 0021-3705) **8967**
J N F M F *see* Journal of Dietary Supplements **6853**
J N I R S *see* Journal of Near Infrared Spectroscopy **2102**
J N: Journal of Nephrology *see* Journal of Nephrology **6270**
J N K V V News (Jawaharlal Nehru Krishi Vishwa Vidyalaya) (IND ISSN 0021-3713) **124**
J N K V V Research Journal (Jawaharlal Nehru Krishi Vishwa Vidyalaya) (IND ISSN 0021-3721) **124**
J N M A *see* Nepal Medical Association. Journal **5685**
J N M M *see* Journal of Nuclear Materials Management **3170**
J N M Online *see* The Journal of Nuclear Medicine **6201**
J N M R *see* Journal of New Music Research **2495**
J N N P Online *see* Journal of Neurology, Neurosurgery and Psychiatry **6154**
J N O P M *see* Journal of Nonlinear Optical Physics and Materials **7079**
J N P S M *see* Journal of Nonprofit & Public Sector Marketing **1826**
J N R *see* Journal of Nursing Research **5966**
J N R E L *see* Journal of Natural Resources & Environmental Law **3448**
J N S *see* Journal of New Seeds **239**
J N S P *see* Nigeria Society of Physiotherapy. Journal **6113**
J N T: Journal of Narrative Theory *see* Journal of Narrative Theory **5315**
J O (Junge Ortskrankenkasse) (DEU) **8048**
J O B (Job Opportunities Bulletin) (USA ISSN 1074-956X) **7494**
J O B M *see* Journal of Organizational Behavior Management **7377**
J O C E P S *see* The Growing Lamp **5959**
J O C M *see* Journal of Organizational Change Management **1769**
J O C N *see* Journal of Optical Communications and Networking **7079**
J O D *see* The Journal of Derivatives **1360**
J O D C Catalogue (Japan Oceanographic Data Center) (JPN) **2808**
J O D C News (Japan Oceanographic Data Center) (JPN ISSN 0287-2609) **2808**
J o D I *see* Journal of Digital Information **2548**
➤ J O D Q: Journal de l'Ordre des Dentistes du Quebec (CAN ISSN 1718-1569) **5850**
J O E *see* Journal of Ecotourism **8725**
J O E *see* Journal of Extension (Online) **2876**
J O F A Journal (Jewish Orthodox Feminist Alliance) (USA ISSN 1538-0777) **7722**
J O G C *see* Journal of Obstetrics and Gynaecology Canada **5996**
J O G N N *see* Journal of Obstetric, Gynecologic, and Neonatal Nursing **5966**
J O H A R (Journal of Hospitality Application and Research) (IND ISSN 0973-4538) **4391**
J O H N S: Journal of Otolaryngology, Head and Neck Surgery/Jibi Inkoka, Tokeibu Geka (JPN ISSN 0910-6820) **6081**
J O I *see* The Journal of Investing **1635**
J O I C *see* Journal of Investment Compliance **1635**
J O I C F P News (Japanese Organization for International Cooperation in Family Planning Inc.) (JPN ISSN 0911-0755) **972**
J O I D *see* Journal of Intellectual Disabilities **3042**
J O I D E S Journal (Joint Oceanographic Institutions for Deep Earth Sampling) *see* Scientific Drilling **6791**
J O I E *see* Journal of Institutional Economics **1137**
J O I N *see* Journal of Interconnection Networks **2500**
J O K Verenigingsblad *see* Waffel **7218**
J O L E *see* Journal of Labor Economics **1691**
J O L L A S *see* The Journal of Latino-Latin American Studies **7248**
J O L L E *see* Journal of Language and Literacy Education **5134**
J O L P *see* Journal of the Legal Profession **4704**
J O L T *see* The Richmond Journal of Law & Technology **4775**
J O L T *see* U C L A Journal of Law and Technology **4799**
J O M *see* Journal of Offender Monitoring **2657**
● ➤ J O M (Journal of Metals) (USA ISSN 1047-4838) **6318**
J O M F P *see* Journal of Oral and Maxillofacial Pathology **5852**
J O N A *see* The Journal of Nursing Administration **5965**
➤ J O N A S (Journal of Nordic Archeological Science) (SWE ISSN 1650-1519) **399**
● J O N A's Healthcare Law, Ethics, and Regulation (Journal of Nursing Administration) (USA ISSN 1520-9229) **5963**
J O P *see* Journal of the Pancreas **5928**
J O P E (BRA ISSN 1677-6755) **5850**
J O P E R D *see* Journal of Physical Education, Recreation and Dance **3068**
J O P S O M (Journal of Preventive and Social Medicine) (BGD ISSN 1012-8697) **7528**
J O R *see* Journal of Oral Rehabilitation **5852**
J O R *see* Journal of Offender Rehabilitation **2657**
J O R S *see* Operational Research Society. Journal **2433**
J O R S E N *see* The Journal of Research in Special Educational Needs **3042**
J O S *see* Journal of Sociology **8116**
J O S *see* Journal of Simulation **2429**
J O S A *see* Journal of Oriental Society of Australia **553**
J O S A A *see* Optical Society of America. Journal A: Optics, Image Science, and Vision **7082**
J O S E *see* International Journal of Occupational Safety and Ergonomics **6679**
J O S P T *see* Journal of Orthopaedic and Sports Physical Therapy **6230**
J O T (Journal fuer Oberflaechentechnik) (DEU ISSN 0940-8789) **5453**
J O T *see* Journal of Turbulence **7023**
J O T *see* Journal of Optical Technology **7079**
J O T *see* The Journal of Trading **1636**
● J O Y (Journal of Yoga) (USA ISSN 1541-5910) **6645**
J P 4 Mensile di Aeronautica (Jet Petrol Quattro) (ITA ISSN 0394-3437) **62**
J - P A E *see* Journal of Public Affairs Education **7448**
J - P A R T *see* Journal of Public Administration Research and Theory **7448**
● J P Airline Fleets International (CHE) **8546**
J P B M *see* Journal of Product and Brand Management **1826**
J P C L *see* Journal of Protective Coatings & Linings **6718**
J P C N *see* Journal of Police Crisis Negotiations **4892**
J P E *see* Journal of Plant Ecology **798**
J P E *see* Journal of Political Economy **1138**
J P E *see* The Journal of Private Equity **1635**
J P E F *see* Journal of Pension Economics and Finance **1868**
J P E N: Journal of Parenteral and Enteral Nutrition *see* Journal of Parenteral and Enteral Nutrition **6662**
J P E T *see* The Journal of Pharmacology and Experimental Therapeutics **6855**
J P F *see* Jurisprudentie Personen- en Familierecht **4912**
J P G *see* Journal of Petroleum Geology **6776**
● J P G (Joint Photographic Experts Group) (USA ISSN 1935-0414) **6970**
J P G Letter (Japan Publications Guide Service) (JPN ISSN 0387-3927) **7564**
J P G M *see* Journal of Postgraduate Medicine **5654**
J P H *see* The Journal of Practical Hygiene **5853**
J P H P *see* Journal of Public Health Policy **7529**
J P H S *see* International Journal of Sexual Health **7366**
J P I *see* Journal of Plant Interactions **798**
J P I C *see* Journal of Prevention and Intervention in the Community **7417**
J P I F *see* Journal of Property Investment & Finance **7596**
† J P I - Jugend Presse Informationen (DEU) **8967**
J P I O *see* Journal de Parodontologie et d'Implantologie Orale **5850**
J P I Petroleum Refining Conference *see* Sekiyu Gakkai Seisei Koenkai **6791**
J P Journal of Algebra and Number Theory *see* J P Journal of Algebra, Number Theory and Applications **5499**
● J P Journal of Algebra, Number Theory and Applications (IND ISSN 0972-5555) **5499**
● ➤ J P Journal of Biostatistics (IND ISSN 0973-5143) **8381**
● ➤ J P Journal of Fixed Point Theory and Applications (IND ISSN 0973-4228) **5499**
● ➤ J P Journal of Geometry and Topology (IND ISSN 0972-415X) **5499**
● ➤ J P Journal of Heat and Mass Transfer (IND ISSN 0973-5763) **3140**
▼ ● ➤ J P Journal of Solids and Structures (IND ISSN 0973-5615) **3273**
J P K E. Journal of Post Keynesian Economics *see* Journal of Post Keynesian Economics **1545**
J P M *see* Journal of Property Management **7596**
J P M *see* The Journal of Portfolio Management **1635**
J P M *see* Journal of Promotion Management **27**
J P M A *see* Pakistan Medical Association. Journal **5692**
J P M D *see* Journal of Place Management and Development **1769**
J P M I *see* Postgraduate Medical Institute. Journal **5698**
J P M M *see* Journal of Pharmaceutical Marketing and Management **8968**
J P Master Magazine *see* Jyllands-Posten **3834**
J P N *see* Journal of Psychiatry and Neuroscience **6156**
J P O *see* Journal of Psychosocial Oncology **6025**
J P O *see* Journal of Prosthetics and Orthotics **6065**
J P P *see* Journal of Perioperative Practice **5967**
J P P & M *see* Journal of Public Policy & Marketing **1826**
J P P R *see* Journal of Pharmacy Practice and Research **6856**
J P P S *see* Pakistan Psychiatric Society. Journal **6173**
J P P T *see* Journal of Pediatric Pharmacology and Therapeutics **6095**
J P R *see* Journal of Peace Research **7249**
J P R *see* Journal of Population Research **7286**
J P R H C *see* Journal of Pharmaceutiocal Research and Health Care **6855**
J P R P *see* Journal of Pacific Rim Psychology **7377**
● J P R Reports and Policy Papers (Jewish Policy Research) (GBR) **3541**
J P S *see* The Journal of Peasant Studies **8115**
● ➤ J P S (Journal of the Polynesian Society) (NZL ISSN 0032-4000) **344**
J P S *see* Journal of the Philosophy of Sport **8183**
J P S *see* Journal of Palestine Studies **4322**
J P S W *see* Pharmacy Society of Wisconsin. Journal **6874**
J P T *see* Journal of Poetry Therapy **7378**
● J P T (Journal of Petroleum Technology) (USA ISSN 0149-2136) **6775**
J P T *see* Journal of Pharmacy Teaching **8968**
J P T *see* Journal of Pharmacy Technology **6856**
J Pov *see* Journal of Poverty **8050**
J Pro *see* Journal of Progressive Human Services **8050**
J Q *see* Justice Quarterly **2658**
J Q *see* Jewelers Quarterly **4567**
J Q A S *see* Journal of Quantitative Analysis in Sports **8182**
J Q L *see* Journal of Quantitative Linguistics **5203**
J Q M E *see* Journal of Quality in Maintenance Engineering **3369**
J Q Magazine *see* Jewelers Quarterly **4567**
J Q Magazine (Jewelry Quorum) (USA) **4567**
J Q P *see* Journal for Quality and Participation **1867**
J Q R *see* The Jewish Quarterly Review **7723**
J Q S *see* Journal of Quaternary Science **2751**
J Q S *see* Journal of Qur'anic Studies **7713**
J Q T *see* Journal of Quality Technology **3351**
J R A *see* Journal of Roman Archaeology **401**
J R A A S *see* Journal of the Renin-Angiotensin-Aldosterone System **5655**
J R A H S *see* Royal Australian Historical Society. Journal **4194**
➤ J R A - The Supplementary Series (Journal of Roman Archaeology) (USA ISSN 1063-4304) **399**
J R C *see* Journal of Research for Consumers **2639**
J R C Annual Report *see* European Commission. Joint Research Center. Annual Report **7134**

Title

J R C D see Journal of Rural and Community Development 3448
J R C I see Journal of Rehabilitation Council of India 8051
J R C Review see Nihon Musen Giho 2361
J R D H see Journal of Religion, Disability & Health 7656
J R E see Japanese Railway Engineering 8619
J R E A (Japan Railway Engineers Association) (JPN ISSN 0447-2322) 8619
J R E P P see Rural Education Policy and Practice. Journal 2908
J R F see The Journal of Risk Finance 1636
J R I E see Journal of Research in International Education 3014
J R I P see Journal of Reproductive and Infant Psychology 7379
J R M see Journal of Relationship Marketing 1138
J R M E S see Journal of Roman Military Equipment Studies 6429
J R M S see Journal of Research in Medical Sciences 5654
J R N see Journal of Research in Nursing 5967
J R P see Journal fuer Rechtspolitik 4699
J R P S see Journal of Roman Pottery Studies 2236
J R S see Journal of Raman Spectroscopy 2103
J R S A Forum (Justice Research and Statistics Association, Inc.) (USA) 2656
J R T E see Journal of Research on Technology in Education 2950
J R T I see Journal of Religious & Theological Information 7656
J R T P H see Journal of Rural and Tropical Public Health 3448
J S A see Journal of Social Archaeology 401
J S A see Journal of Sustainable Agriculture 128
J S A C see Societe Algerienne de Chimie. Journal 2080
J S A E Review see Review of Automotive Engineering 8601
J S A H see Society of Architectural Historians. Journal 457
J S A M see Society for American Music. Journal 6617
J S A M S see Journal of Science and Medicine in Sport 6230
J S A P see Journal of Small Animal Practice 8801
J S A P International (Japan Society of Applied Physics) (JPN) 7019
J S A S see Society for Armenian Studies. Journal 3565
J S & T see Journal of Sport and Tourism 4978
J S B E D see Journal of Small Business and Enterprise Development 1962
J S B Journal (Judicial Studies Board) (GBR ISSN 1368-8901) 4953
J S C see Journal of School Counseling 3068
J S C S see Journal of Statistical Computation and Simulation 2443
J S D L P see McGill International Journal of Sustainable Development Law and Policy 4730
J S - das Magazin fuer Leute beim Bund (Junge Soldaten) (DEU) 7762
J S E see Journal of Scientific Exploration 7873
J S E see Journal of Statistics Education 8383
J S E A S Special Publication Series (Journal of Southeast Asian Studies) (SGP) 552
J S E B see Journal of Social and Ecological Boundaries 4461
J S E E B S S see Journal of Southeast European and Black Sea Studies 7249
J S E P see Journal of Sport and Exercise Psychology 7381
J S F see Journal of Sustainable Forestry 3695
J S F see The Journal of Structured Finance 1363
J S I J see Jewish Studies, an Internet Journal 7724
J S I M see Journal of Service Management 1769
J S I T see Journal of Systems and Information Technology 2549
J S L see The Journal of Symbolic Logic 5507
J S L P - A B A see The Journal of Speech and Language Pathology and Applied Behavior Analysis 7380
J S L P A - R O A see Canadian Journal of Speech-Language Pathology and Audiology 3037
J S L S see Society of Laparoendoscopic Surgeons. Journal 6259
J S L W see Journal of Second Language Writing 5135
J S M see Journal of Services Marketing 1827
J S M see Journal of Sport Management 8182
J S M E / A S M E International Conference on Materials and Processing (Year). Program and Abstract/Kikai Zairuo Zairuo Kako Gijutsu Koenkai Koen Ronbunshu (Japan Society of Mechanical Engineers / American Society of Mechanical Engineers) (JPN) 3383
J S M E Annual Meeting (Japan Society of Mechanical Engineers) (JPN) 3383
• ➤ J S M E International Journal. Series A: Solid Mechanics and Material Engineering (Japan Society of Mechanical Engineers) (JPN ISSN 1344-7912) 3384
• ➤ J S M E International Journal. Series B: Fluids and Thermal Engineering (Japan Society of Mechanical Engineers) (JPN ISSN 1340-8054) 3384
J S M E International Journal. Series C: Dynamics, Control, Robotics, Design and Manufacturing see J S M E International Journal. Series C, Mechanical Systems, Machine Elements and Manufacturing 3384
• ➤ J S M E International Journal. Series C, Mechanical Systems, Machine Elements and Manufacturing (Japan Society of Mechanical Engineers) (JPN ISSN 1344-7653) 3384
J S M E News (Japan Society of Mechanical Engineers) (JPN ISSN 1340-8763) 3384
J S M P News (Japan Society of Medical Physics) (JPN) 5643
J S O A see Journal of Surgical Orthopaedic Advances 6066
J S P see Journal of Scholarly Publishing 7564
J S P see Journal of School Psychology 7380
J S P see Journal for the Study of the Pseudepigrapha 7653
J S P see Journal of Scottish Philosophy 6929
J S P see Journal of Ship Production 8648
J S P E Publication Series (Japan Society for Precision Engineering) (JPN) 3204
J S P Mag (Jeunes Sapeurs-Pompiers Magazine) (FRA ISSN 1952-3831) 3579
J S P N see Journal for Specialists in Pediatric Nursing 5963
J S P P Newsletter (Japanese Society of Plant Physiologists) (JPN ISSN 0912-2214) 795
J S P R see Journal of Social and Personal Relationships 7380
J S P S see Journal of Social and Psychological Sciences 7980
J S R see Journal of Sleep Research 5654
J S R see Journal of Ship Research 8649
J S R see Journal of Sport Rehabilitation 6230
J S R I see Journal for the Study of Religious and Ideologies 7653
J S S see Journal of Separation Science 2103
J S S C Bulletin (Japanese Society of Steel Construction) (JPN) 1017
J S S C Journal of Constructional Steel (Japanese Society of Steel Construction) (JPN) 1017
J S S C Technical Report see J S S C Tekunikaru Repoto 1017
J S S C Tekunikaru Repoto/J S S C Technical Report (Japanese Society of Steel Construction) (JPN) 1017
J S S E see Journal of the Short Story in English 5316
J S S P see Journal of Scholarly and Scientific Perspectives 7980
J S S R see Journal of Social Service Research 8051
J S S T Symposium on Calculations in Electrical and Electronics Engineering. Proceedings see Keisan Denki Denshi Kogaku Shinpojumu Ronbunshu 3323
J S T A T see Journal of Statistical Mechanics: Theory and Experiment 7060
J S T L see The Journal of Science & Technology Law 4704
J S V see Journal of Sound and Vibration 7088
J S W see Journal of Social Work 8051
J S W C see Journal of Sino-Western Communications 7656
J S W V E see Journal of Social Work Values and Ethics 8052
J-SPOT see Journal of Social and Political Thought 7148
J T see Journal du Textile 8454
J T see Journal of Targeting, Measurement and Analysis for Marketing 1890
J T A Community News Reporter see Community News Reporter 7720
J T A T E see Journal of Technology and Teacher Education 2950
J T A Weekly News Digest (Jewish Telegraphic Agency) (USA ISSN 0021-6763) 7722
• J T A World Report (Email Edition) (USA) 3541
J T C C see Journal of Tourism & Cultural Change 8726
J T C I see Journal of Tax Credit Investing 1636
J T E see Journal of Testing and Evaluation 3351
J T E P see Journal of Transport Economics and Policy 8501
J T H see Journal of Thrombosis and Haemostasis 5939
J T H S see Journal of Technology in Human Services 8151
J T I see Journal of Taxation of Investments 1932
J T I B see Journal of Teaching in International Business 1574
J T I P see Tulane Journal of Technology & Intellectual Property 4798
• J T I - Rapport. Kretslopp & Avfall (SWE ISSN 1401-4955) 125
• J T I - Rapport. Lantbruk & Industri (SWE ISSN 1401-4963) 125
J T L R see Juta's Tax Law Report 1932
J T M C see Journal of Technology Management in China 8429
J T M D see Journal of Transnational Management 1574
J T M O see Journal of Trauma Management & Outcomes 6066
J T N Monthly see Asian Textile Business 8448
J T News (USA) 7722
J T N's Asian Textile Weekly see Asian Textile Weekly 8448
J T P see Journal of Theoretical Politics 7148
J T P R see Job Training and Placement Report 1763
J T P R Plus see Job Training and Placement Report 1763
J T S Academic Newsletter (Jewish Theological Seminary) (USA ISSN 1547-2418) 7722
• J T S Magazine (Jewish Theological Seminary) (USA) 7722
J T S W see Journal of Teaching in Social Work 3068
J Taylor's Gold & Technology Stocks (USA) 1634
J-tuner (GBR ISSN 1744-4721) 8586
• ➤ J U C M (Journal of Urgent Care Medicine) (USA ISSN 1938-0011) 6062
J U F News (Jewish United Fund) (USA) 7722
† J U M A (DEU ISSN 0940-4961) 8967
J U M - Jugend und Medien (AUT) 2156
J U M R see Journal of Undergraduate Materials Research 3351
J U Magazine (Jacksonville University) (USA) 2288
J U N E see Journal of Undergraduate Neuroscience Education 6157
J U S E K Tidningen (Foerbundet foer Jurister Samhaellsvetare och Ekonomer) (SWE ISSN 1100-620X) 4698
J u S - Magazin see Juristische Schulung 4707
J U T L P see Journal of University Teaching & Learning Practice 2991
J U V see Juvenile Justice Update 2658
J U V A T-dag see Juristenvereniging voor Afgestudeerden in Tilburg Dag 4707
J U V E Rechtsmarkt (Juristische Verlag) (DEU ISSN 1435-4578) 4698
J V B L see The Journal of Values Based Leadership 8116
J V B - Presse (Justizvollzugsbediensteten) (DEU) 7447
J V C see Journal of Vibration and Control 7088
J V C P see International Journal of Vegetable Science 237
J V E see Journal of Vector Ecology 685
J V H see Journal of Viral Hepatitis 5928
J V I R see Journal of Vascular and Interventional Radiology 6201
J V M see Journal of Vacation Marketing 8726
J V M E see Journal of Veterinary Medical Education 8801
J V P see Journal of Vertebrate Paleontology 6726
J V R B see Journal of Virtual Reality and Broadcasting 2488
J V S see Journal of Vietnamese Studies 553
J V S R see Journal of Vertebral Subluxation Research (Online Edition) 5806
J V T see Journal of Validation Technology 4488
J Vibe see JVibe 2196
J W A see Journal of Women and Aging 8900
J W C see The Journal of Workers Compensation 4510
J.W. Dawes Family Newsletter (USA) 3772
J W E. Journal of Wind Engineering (JPN ISSN 0912-1935) 3273
J W H see Journal of World History 4150
J W I P see The Journal of World Intellectual Property 6753
J W L see Journal of Workplace Learning 1868
J W M see The Journal of Wealth Management 1636
J W R see Journal of Workplace Rights 1691
J W R D see Journal of Whiplash & Related Disorders 8968
J W V A Bulletin (Jewish War Veterans of the U.S.A.) (USA ISSN 0021-3799) 7722
J. Wayne and Elsie M. Gunn Center for the Study of Science Fiction Newsletter (USA) 5444
J X see Journal X 5316
J Z W M see Journal of Zoo and Wildlife Medicine 8802
• J3eA (FRA ISSN 1638-5705) 7869
Ja (DEU ISSN 0342-6505) 7652
Ja, das Wort fuer Alle (DEU ISSN 0342-6513) 7652
Ja Mag (FRA ISSN 1639-0091) 125
Ja Zum Baby (DEU ISSN 1619-3911) 6094
• Jaakartta/Ice Chart/Iskarta (FIN ISSN 1238-3724) 2784
Jaapani Moistatused (EST) 8181
Jaar in Cijfers (Year) (NLD ISSN 0927-4634) 8382
Jaarbeeld Zorg (NLD ISSN 1574-3829) 7528
Jaarbericht Bevolkingsonderzoek (NLD ISSN 1876-6358) 7528
Jaarbericht Brede Scholen in Nederland see Brede Scholen in Nederland 2832
Jaarbericht "Ex Oriente Lux" see Vooraziatisch-Egyptisch Genootschap "Ex Oriente Lux". Jaarbericht 4326
Jaarbijlage Facility Management see Facility Management Magazine Jaarboek 1744
Jaarboek Achterhoek en Liemers (NLD ISSN 0923-070X) 4234
Jaarboek Afvalstoffenkaarten see Praktijkgids Afvalstoffenkaarten 3510
Jaarboek Arbeidsomstandigheden see Praktijkboek Arbeidsomstandigheden 4759
Jaarboek Arbo en Binnenmilieu see Handboek Arbeidshygiene 6677
Jaarboek Bijzondere Vormen van Arbeidsrelaties (NLD ISSN 1872-2431) 1690
Jaarboek Corporate Performance Management (NLD ISSN 1574-5910) 1762
Jaarboek CustomerBase see C C M. Customer Contact Magazine 1809
Jaarboek der Schone Kunsten/Algemeen Jaarboek der Schone Kunsten (BEL ISSN 0066-3174) 498
Jaarboek Ecologische Geschiedenis (NLD ISSN 1375-5692) 7869
Jaarboek Flexibiliteit in Arbeidsrelaties (NLD ISSN 1573-9945) 1690
Jaarboek Heemkunde Wahlwiller see Heemkunde Wahlwiller 4226
Jaarboek I T Beheer en Informatiebeveiliging (NLD ISSN 1874-7728) 2515
Jaarboek Informatie Technologie en Informatiebeveiliging see Jaarboek I T Beheer en Informatiebeveiliging 2515
Jaarboek Integrale Aanpak Preventie, Verzuim en Reintegratie see Grip op Verzuim en Re-Integratie 1684
➤ Jaarboek Integrale Geneeskunde (NLD ISSN 1874-0251) 311
Jaarboek Integrale Verzuimaanpak Casemanagement en Reintegratie see Grip op Verzuim en Re-Integratie 1684
Jaarboek KennisSamenleving (NLD ISSN 1871-0034) 7447
Jaarboek Minderheden see Jaarboek Multiculturele Samenleving in Ontwikkeling 7286
Jaarboek Monitor Nieuwe Woningen (NLD ISSN 1872-3799) 1017
Jaarboek Monumentenzorg (NLD ISSN 0925-7845) 446
Jaarboek Multiculturele Samenleving in Ontwikkeling (NLD ISSN 1875-8916) 7286
Jaarboek Nederlandse Frisdrankenindustrie (NLD ISSN 1871-5753) 605
Jaarboek Nederlandse Postzegels (NLD ISSN 1872-0420) 6896
† Jaarboek Nederlandse Vormgeving (NLD ISSN 1574-3888) 8967
Jaarboek Numaga (NLD ISSN 0927-4626) 4234
Jaarboek Onderwijs (NLD ISSN 1388-9737) 2934
Jaarboek Onderwijs in Cijfers see Jaarboek Onderwijs 2934
Jaarboek Personeelsverzekeringen & Subsidies (NLD ISSN 1872-0595) 1690
Jaarboek Personenbelasting see Handboek Personenbelasting 1927
Jaarboek Sport (NLD ISSN 1571-3490) 8181
Jaarboek Sterrenkunde (NLD ISSN 1574-4272) 576
Jaarboek Vaarreglementen Nederland (NLD ISSN 1573-1235) 4970
Jaarboek van de Christelijke Gereformeerde Kerken in Nederland (NLD) 7762
Jaarboek van het Rijksinstituut voor Oorlogsdocumentatie see Nederlands Instituut voor Oorlogsdocumentatie. Jaarboek 6439
Jaarboek voor Liturgie - Onderzoek (NLD ISSN 0924-042X) 7801
➤ Jaarboek voor Middeleeuwse Geschiedenis (NLD ISSN 1388-6649) 4234
Jaarboek voor Munt- en Penningkunde (NLD ISSN 0920-380X) 6651
Jaarboek voor Vrouwengeschiedenis (NLD ISSN 1574-2334) 8899
Jaarboekje BTW en Overdrachtsbelasting in de Vastgoedsector see Belasting Toegevoegde Waarde en Overdrachtsbelasting in de Vastgoedsector 1912
Jaarkrant Botanische Tuinen Utrecht see Botanische Tuinen Utrecht 781
Jaarlikse Ekonomiese Verslag - Suid-Afrikaanse Reserwebank see South African Reserve Bank. Annual Economic Report 1518
Jaaroverzicht Boekenvak (NLD ISSN 1874-5539) 7564
Jaarraport de Rijn (NLD ISSN 1871-9007) 8827
• Jaarrapport Integratie (NLD ISSN 1872-1354) 7211
Jaarrapportage van de Wet Afbreking Zwangerschap (NLD ISSN 1871-5745) 5994
Jaarrekening Kleinbedrijf see Zakboekje Jaarrekening Kleinbedrijf 8999
Jaaruitgave Inkoop van Energie (NLD ISSN 1573-9805) 3140
Jaaruitgave Stralingsbescherming (NLD ISSN 1574-4191) 7528
Jaarverslag A B - D L O see Research Institute for Agrobiology and Soil Fertility. Annual Report 250
Jaarverslag K D D see Keuringsdienst Diervoedersector 130
Jaarverslag over de Stand van de Drugsproblematiek in de Europese Unie see State of the Drugs Problem in the European Union. Annual Report 2699
Jabalpur Law Journal (IND ISSN 0448-1054) 4698
Jabatan Mineral dan Geosains Malaysia. Lapuran Tahunan/Malaysia. Minerals and Geoscience Department Malaysia. Annual Report (MYS) 2749
Jabatan Perikanan. Buletin Perikanan/Department of Fisheries Malaysia. Fisheries Bulletin (MYS) 3599
Jabberwock Review (USA ISSN 1541-3705) 5312
Jabberwocky (Rockville) (USA) 5312
Jabbok (SWE ISSN 0283-3484) 7652
➤ Jabega (ESP ISSN 0210-8496) 3952
Jacaranda (USA) 5424
Jacetania (ESP ISSN 0021-3810) 8725
J'Achete Mieux (CHE) 2639
Jachtbouw Nederland (NLD ISSN 1871-1561) 3384
† Jack (GBR) 8967
Jack (ITA ISSN 1591-1047) 6293

10472 JAHRESBERICHT UBER DEN STAND DER DROGENPROBLEMATIK ULRICH'S PERIODICALS

Jahresbericht uber den Stand der Drogenproblematik in der Europaischen Union *see* State of the Drugs Problem in the European Union. Annual Report **2699**
† Jahresbericht ueber die Deutsche Fischwirtschaft (DEU ISSN 0075-2851) **8967**
Jahresberichte aus Augst und Kaiseraugst (CHE ISSN 1018-5259) **400**
Jahresberichte fuer Deutsche Geschichte (DEU ISSN 0075-286X) **4234**
Jahresbilanz der Landesforstverwaltung (DEU ISSN 1614-2640) **3709**
Jahresschrift fuer Mitteldeutsche Vorgeschichte (DEU ISSN 0075-2932) **4234**
Jahrestagung (Year) Suvaziavimo Darbai (DEU ISSN 0931-9921) **3850**
Jahrestagung Kerntechnik (DEU ISSN 0720-9207) **3170**
Jahreszeiten Raetsel (DEU) **8182**
Jai Hind (IND) **3883**
J'ai la Terre qui Tourne (FRA ISSN 1952-5486) **2194**
J'ai Lu. Bien-Etre (FRA ISSN 1159-7623) **5643**
J'ai Lu. Cuisine (FRA ISSN 1950-0173) **4361**
J'ai Lu. Fantasy (FRA ISSN 1290-6697) **5444**
J'ai Lu. Policier *see* J'ai Lu. Roman Policier **5414**
J'ai Lu. Roman Policier (FRA ISSN 0768-0627) **5414**
J'ai Lu. Science Fiction (FRA ISSN 0768-0635) **5444**
J'ai Lu. Thriller (FRA ISSN 0988-0895) **5414**
Jai Rajasthan (IND) **3883**
Jai Rajasthan (Banswara Edition) *see* Jai Rajasthan **3883**
Jai Rajasthan (Pali Edition) *see* Jai Rajasthan **3883**
Jai Rajasthan (Udaipur Edition) *see* Jai Rajasthan **3883**
• Jail and Prisoner Law Bulletin (USA ISSN 0739-0998) **4892**
Jail Operations Bulletin (USA) **2656**
• Jails in Indian Country (USA) **2674**
J'aime et Je Cuisine (FRA ISSN 1951-7165) **4361**
J'aime Lire (CAN ISSN 0835-7714) **2194**
J'aime Lire (FRA ISSN 0399-4600) **2194**
Jain Journal (IND ISSN 0021-4043) **7737**
Jain Spirit (GBR ISSN 1532-0472) **7737**
Jaina (MEX ISSN 0188-4700) **2808**
• Jak na Pocitac (CZE ISSN 1214-1917) **2428**
Jak Prowadzic Ksiege Przychodow i Rozchodow? (POL ISSN 1428-8184) **1293**
Jakarta Business Directory (IDN ISSN 0215-8590) **2009**
Jakarta Java Kini (IDN ISSN 0216-3446) **3891**
Jakarta Metropolitan Buyers' Guide (IDN) **2009**
• Jakarta Post (IDN ISSN 0215-3432) **3891**
Jake Hardy (USA ISSN 1550-1272) **5312**
Jakin/Saber (ESP ISSN 0211-495X) **6927**
• Jakob Nielsen Hakushino Alertbox (JPN) **2499**
Jakobstads Tidning *see* Oesterbottens Tidning **3839**
Jakobus-Studien (DEU ISSN 0934-8611) **7802**
Jakosc i Uzytkowanie Energii Elektrycznej (POL ISSN 1234-6799) **3159**
Jakt (NOR ISSN 1503-1233) **8319**
Jakt och Fiske *see* Jaktmarker och Fiskevatten **8320**
Jakt och Jaegare (SWE ISSN 1401-8306) **8319**
Jakt & Fiske (NOR ISSN 0800-3041) **8182**
Jakt & Fiske, Friluftsliv (NOR ISSN 0809-6201) **8319**
Jaktdebatt (SWE ISSN 1102-5026) **8320**
Jaktjournalen (SWE ISSN 0345-5637) **8320**
Jaktkamraten (SWE ISSN 1102-1217) **8320**
Jaktmarker och Fiskevatten (SWE ISSN 0021-406X) **8320**
• Jaktstatistikk (Year)/Hunting Statistics (NOR ISSN 0550-0400) **8219**
Jaktvapenguiden (SWE ISSN 1103-2731) **8320**
Jala' Medical Journal *see* Galaa Medical Journal **5617**
Jalan Jalan (IDN ISSN 0216-3497) **8725**
Jalgaon Tarun Bharat (IND) **3883**
Jalkine (FIN ISSN 0021-4078) **7941**
Jalons (FRA ISSN 0184-8100) **5424**
Jalouse (FRA ISSN 1281-0282) **2257**
Jalte Deep (IND) **3883**
Jam (Bishkek) (KGZ) **3903**
Jam Rag (USA ISSN 1094-9488) **6578**
Al-Jamahiriya (LBY) **3905**
Jamaica *see* The P R S Group. Country Reports: Jamaica **1507**
Jamaica Agricultural Society. Minutes of the Half-Yearly Meeting (JAM) **125**
Jamaica Bauxite Institute Journal *see* J B I Journal **6467**
Jamaica Bauxite Institute Quarterly *see* J B I Quarterly **6467**
Jamaica Beat (JAM) **3995**
Jamaica Chamber of Commerce Journal (JAM ISSN 0021-4094) **1405**
Jamaica Churchman (JAM ISSN 0047-1720) **7762**
Jamaica Dental Association. Newsletter (JAM) **5850**
Jamaica Handbook *see* Moon Handbooks: Jamaica **8738**
Jamaica Journal (JAM ISSN 0021-4124) **3995**
Jamaica Library Association. Bulletin (JAM) **5019**
Jamaica Library Association News *see* J L A News **5019**
Jamaica. Ministry of Construction (Works). Jamaica Budget (Year) (JAM) **1017**
Jamaica. Ministry of Social Security. Report (JAM) **4510**
Jamaica Naturalist (JAM ISSN 1018-1261) **2615**
Jamaica Philatelic Society. Newsletter (JAM) **6896**
Jamaica Plain Gazette (USA) **3542**
Jamaica Port News (JAM) **8648**
Jamaica. Urban Development Corporation. Annual Report (JAM ISSN 0304-8373) **4416**
Jamaica Vacation Guide (JAM) **8725**
Jamaican Association of Sugar Technologists. Proceedings (JAM) **238**
Jamaican Bar Association. Annual Report (JAM) **4698**
Jamaican Exporter (JAM) **1573**
Jamaican Geographer (JAM ISSN 1017-4753) **4016**
Jamaican Historical Review (JAM ISSN 1010-6367) **4298**
Jamaican Historical Society. Bulletin (JAM ISSN 0447-3302) **4148**
➤ Jamaican Journal of Science and Technology (JAM ISSN 1016-2054) **7870**
• Jamaican Law Reports (ZAF ISSN 1683-2582) **4698**
Jamaican National Bibliography (JAM ISSN 0075-2991) **628**
Jamaican Nurse (JAM ISSN 0021-4140) **5963**
• Jamaican Weekly Gleaner (CAN ISSN 1018-2330) **3542**
Jamail Center for Legal Research Annual Report *see* Report of the Tarlton Law Library **5043**
Jamana (MLI ISSN 1011-6591) **3789**
• Jamba (ZAF ISSN 1996-1421) **2227**
The Jambar (USA) **2288**
Jame-e-Jamshed (IND) **3883**
▼ James (NLD) **6293**
James Arthur Lecture on the Evolution of the Human Brain (USA ISSN 0447-3353) **873**
James Bay *see* Baie - James **8685**
James Bay and Northern Quebec Agreement. Annual Report (CAN ISSN 0838-8814) **7145**
• James Cook University. Course and Subject Handbook (AUS) **2988**
• James Cook University. Department of Computer Science. Technical Report (AUS ISSN 1326-4524) **2428**
• ➤ James Cook University Law Review (AUS ISSN 1321-1072) **4698**
James Cook University. Student Handbook *see* James Cook University. Course and Subject Handbook **2988**
• James Dickey Newsletter (USA ISSN 0749-0291) **5312**
James Fenimore Cooper Society Miscellaneous Papers (USA ISSN 1072-9585) **5312**
James Joyce Broadsheet (GBR ISSN 0143-6333) **5312**
James Joyce Journal *see* Jeimseu Joi'seu Jeo'neol **5313**
James Joyce Literary Supplement (USA ISSN 0899-3114) **5312**
James Joyce Newestlatter (USA) **5312**
• ➤ James Joyce Quarterly (USA ISSN 0021-4183) **5313**
James MacGregor Burns Lectureship in Leadership Studies and Biography (USA ISSN 1555-8142) **4148**
James S. Coleman Memorial Papers Series (USA) **4175**
† The James Sprunt Studies in History and Political Science (USA ISSN 0361-6169) **8967**
James Taylor's Shocked and Amazed *see* Shocked and Amazed **5083**
• James White Review (USA ISSN 0891-5393) **4375**
Jamestown College. Alumni & Friends (USA) **2288**
➤ Jami'at al-Imam Muhammad Ibn Sa'ud al-Islamiyyah. Imadat al-Bahth al-Ilmi. Majallah/Islamic University of Imam Muhammad Ibn Saud. Deanery of Academic Research. Journal (SAU) **7713**
Jami'at al-Imarat al-Arabiyyah al-Muttahidah. Kulliyyat al-Ulum. Majallah *see* United Arab Emirates University. Faculty of Science. Journal **7925**
Jami'at al-Malik Sa'ud. Majallah. Al-'Ulum al-Hasib wal-Ma'lumat *see* King Saud University Journal. Computer and Information Sciences **2430**
Jami'at al-Malik Sa'ud. Majallah. Al-'Ulum al-Tarbawiyyah wal-Dirasat al-Islamiyyah *see* King Saud University Journal. Educational Sciences and Islamic Studies **7713**
Jami'at Qatar. Al-Taqrir al-Ihsa'i al-Sanawi lil-Aam al-Jami'i/University of Qatar. Annual Statistical Report for the School Year (QAT) **2934**
Jami'at Umm al-Qura. Kulliyyat al-Lughah al-Arabiyyah. Muhadarat al-Mawsim al-Thaqafi (SAU) **5131**
Jami'i (UAE) **2288**
Al Jamila (SAU) **8869**
Jamila (Doha) (QAT ISSN 1997-8499) **8869**
Jaminraitu (IND) **5424**
Jammu and Kashmir. Directorate of Economics and Statistics. Digest of Statistics (IND ISSN 0303-9234) **1246**
Jammu and Kashmir Law Reporter (IND) **4698**
Jammu and Kashmir. Legislative Council. Committee on Privileges. Report (IND ISSN 0448-2433) **7145**
Jammu & Kashmir Minerals Limited. Annual Report (IND ISSN 0304-7164) **6467**
Jammu and Kashmir Research Biannual *see* J & K Research Biannual **4458**
Jammu & Kashmir Science *see* J K Science **5643**
Jana (EST) **8869**
Jana (SVN ISSN 0350-9125) **8869**
Janakavi (LKA) **7145**
Janaman (IND ISSN 0021-4213) **7145**
Janasatta (IND) **3883**
Janashakti (Jalgaon) (IND) **3883**
Janashakti (Patna) (IND) **3883**
Janashakti News Weekly (IND) **3883**
Janata (IND ISSN 0021-4221) **7145**
Janatha (LKA) **3954**
Janavarta (IND) **3883**
† • Jane (USA ISSN 1093-8737) **8967**
Jane and Jane (USA ISSN 1933-2777) **4375**
Jane Austen Society of Melbourne. Observations (AUS) **5313**
Jane Austen Society of North America News *see* J A S N A News **5312**
Jane Greenoff's Cross Stitch (GBR ISSN 1463-5461) **6639**
• Jane's Aero-Engines (GBR ISSN 1748-2534) **62**
• Jane's Air and Systems Library (GBR) **6426**
• Jane's Air-Launched Weapons (GBR ISSN 0954-3848) **6426**
• Jane's Air Traffic Control (GBR ISSN 1357-339X) **8546**
Jane's Airborne Electronic Mission Systems *see* Jane's Electronic Mission Aircraft **62**
• Jane's Aircraft Component Manufacturers (GBR) **62**
• Jane's Aircraft Upgrades (GBR ISSN 1361-6684) **62**
• Jane's Airport Review (GBR ISSN 0954-7649) **8546**
• Jane's Airports and Handling Agents. Central Latin America Including the Caribbean (GBR ISSN 0969-1243) **8546**
• Jane's Airports and Handling Agents. Europe (GBR ISSN 0952-4673) **8546**
• Jane's Airports and Handling Agents. Far East, Asia and Australasia (GBR ISSN 0952-469X) **8546**
• Jane's Airports and Handling Agents. Middle East and Africa (GBR ISSN 0952-4665) **8546**
• Jane's Airports and Handling Agents. United States and Canada (GBR ISSN 1365-7836) **8547**
• Jane's Airports, Equipment and Service (GBR) **8547**
• Jane's All the World's Aircraft (GBR ISSN 0075-3017) **62**
• Jane's Ammunition Handbook (GBR ISSN 1369-7277) **6426**
• Jane's Amphibious and Special Forces (GBR ISSN 1748-2577) **6426**
Jane's Amphibious Warfare Capabilities *see* Jane's Amphibious and Special Forces **6426**
• Jane's Armour and Artillery (GBR ISSN 0143-9952) **6426**
• Jane's Armour and Artillery Upgrades (GBR ISSN 1360-5682) **6426**
Jane's Asian Infrastructure *see* Asian Infrastructure **8490**
Jane's Asian Infrastructure Monthly *see* Asian Infrastructure **8490**
• Jane's Avionics (GBR ISSN 0264-794X) **62**
Jane's Beat Officer's Companion (GBR) **2227**
• Jane's C 4 I Systems (GBR ISSN 1357-0226) **6426**
• Jane's Defence Equipment Library (GBR) **6426**
• Jane's Defence Industry (GBR ISSN 1755-4314) **6426**
Jane's Defence Upgrades *see* Jane's International Defence Review **6427**
• Jane's Defence Weekly (GBR ISSN 0265-3818) **6426**
• Jane's Electro-Optic Systems (GBR ISSN 1367-5044) **6426**
• Jane's Electronic Mission Aircraft (GBR ISSN 1748-2569) **62**
• Jane's Explosive Ordnance Disposal (GBR) **2227**
• Jane's Fighting Ships (GBR ISSN 0075-3025) **6426**
Jane's Foreign Report *see* Jane's Intelligence Weekly **7247**
Jane's Geopolitical Library *see* Jane's Security Library **2678**
Jane's Geopolitical Library *see* Jane's Sentinel Security Assessments **2678**
• Jane's Helicopter Markets and Systems (GBR ISSN 1748-2542) **62**
• Jane's High-Speed Marine Transportation (GBR ISSN 1364-9647) **8648**
▼ Jane's Homeland Security Review (GBR ISSN 1759-7439) **2227**
▼ Jane's Industry Quarterly (GBR ISSN 1758-521X) **6427**
• Jane's Infantry Weapons (GBR ISSN 0306-3410) **6427**
Jane's Intelligence Digest *see* Jane's Intelligence Weekly **7247**
• Jane's Intelligence Review (GBR ISSN 1350-6226) **6427**
Jane's Intelligence Review. Special Report *see* Jane's Intelligence Review **6427**
▼ • Jane's Intelligence Weekly (GBR ISSN 2040-8315) **7247**
• Jane's International A B C Aerospace Directory (GBR ISSN 1467-1662) **62**
• Jane's International Defence Directory (GBR ISSN 1368-8359) **6427**
• Jane's International Defence Review (GBR ISSN 1476-2129) **6427**
Jane's International Defense Review Extra *see* International Defense Review Extra **6425**
• Jane's Islamic Affairs Analyst (GBR ISSN 0969-4234) **7145**
Jane's Land and Systems Library *see* Jane's Defence Equipment Library **6426**
• Jane's Land-Based Air Defence (GBR ISSN 0959-5821) **6427**
• Jane's Marine Propulsion (GBR ISSN 1748-2550) **8648**
• Jane's Merchant Ships (GBR ISSN 0263-7030) **8648**
• Jane's Military Communications (GBR ISSN 0144-0004) **6427**
• Jane's Military Vehicles and Logistics (GBR ISSN 1369-5967) **6427**
• Jane's Mines and Mine Clearance (GBR ISSN 1366-5103) **6427**
• Jane's Missiles and Rockets (GBR ISSN 1365-4187) **6427**
Jane's N B C Defence Systems *see* Jane's Nuclear, Biological and Chemical Defence **6428**
• Jane's Naval Construction and Retrofit Markets (GBR) **1017**
• Jane's Naval Weapon Systems (GBR ISSN 0960-4448) **6427**
• Jane's Navy International (GBR ISSN 1358-3719) **6428**
• Jane's Nuclear, Biological and Chemical Defence (GBR ISSN 1464-8210) **6428**
• Jane's Police and Homeland Security Equipment (Years) (GBR) **2678**
Jane's Police and Security Equipment (Years) *see* Jane's Police and Homeland Security Equipment (Years) **2678**
Jane's Police and Security Library *see* Jane's Security Library **2678**
• Jane's Police Review (GBR ISSN 0309-1414) **2656**
Jane's Policing Today *see* Policing Today **2664**
• Jane's Radar and Electronic Warfare Systems (GBR ISSN 0959-5759) **6428**
• Jane's Security Library (GBR) **2678**
• Jane's Sentinel Security Assessments (GBR) **2678**
• Jane's Simulation and Training Systems (GBR ISSN 1361-9675) **6428**
Jane's Space Directory *see* Jane's Space Systems & Industry **62**
• Jane's Space Systems & Industry (GBR) **62**
• Jane's Strategic Weapon Systems (GBR ISSN 0958-6032) **6428**
• Jane's Terrorism & Security Monitor (GBR ISSN 1367-0409) **7247**
• Jane's Terrorism Watch Report (GBR ISSN 1524-3877) **7247**
• Jane's Transport Finance (GBR ISSN 1351-1211) **1359**
• Jane's Transport Library (GBR) **8500**
• Jane's Underwater Security Systems & Technology (GBR) **2809**
Jane's Underwater Technology *see* Jane's Underwater Security Systems & Technology **2809**
• Jane's Underwater Warfare Systems (GBR ISSN 0959-6283) **6428**
• Jane's Unmanned Aerial Vehicles and Targets (GBR ISSN 1748-250X) **63**
▼ • Jane's Unmanned Ground Vehicles and Systems (GBR ISSN 1759-7161) **6428**
• Jane's Urban Transport Systems (GBR ISSN 0263-8460) **8500**
• Jane's World Air Forces (GBR ISSN 1748-2526) **6428**
• Jane's World Airlines (GBR ISSN 1748-2518) **8547**
• Jane's World Armies (GBR ISSN 1748-2607) **6428**
• Jane's World Defence Industry (GBR ISSN 1748-2593) **1131**
• Jane's World Insurgency and Terrorism (GBR ISSN 1748-2585) **2678**
▼ • Jane's World Navies (GBR ISSN 1757-5710) **6428**
• Jane's World Railways (GBR ISSN 0075-3084) **8619**
Jane's World Railways and Rapid Transit Systems *see* Jane's World Railways **8619**
• Jane's Xine (USA) **6578**
Janes's International Defense Review Quarterly Report *see* International Defense Review Extra **6425**
Janes's International Defense Review Quarterly Report *see* Jane's International Defence Review **6427**
Jang Digest (PAK) **5313**
Jangal va Marta' (IRN) **3444**
Jangan (IND) **3883**
Janglae Ga'gu Chu'gye/Korea (Republic). National Statistical Office. Household Projections (KOR ISSN 1599-6484) **7311**
Janglae In'gu Chu'gye/Korea (Republic). National Statistical Office. Population Projections by Provinces (KOR ISSN 1599-4384) **7311**
Janhit Darshan (IND) **3883**
Janmabhoomi (IND) **3883**
Janmabhoomi Khagol Siddha Sukshma Nirayana Bharatiya Panchang (Gujarati Edition) (IND) **566**
Janmabhoomi Khagol Siddha Sukshma Nirayana Bharatiya Panchang (Hindi Edition) (IND) **566**
Janmabhoomi Panchang (IND) **566**
Janmabhoomi Pravasi (IND) **3883**
Janmabhumi (IND) **3883**
Janmat (IND) **3883**

10474 JAPAN MARINE SCIENCE AND TECHNOLOGY CENTER. REPORT ULRICH'S PERIODICALS

Japan Marine Science and Technology Center. Report *see* Kaiyo Kagaku Gijutsu Senta Shiken Kenkyu Hokoku **2810**
Japan Marine Science and Technology Center. Research Report on Oceans *see* Oceans Chosa Hokoku **2815**
Japan Marine Science and Technology Center, Scientific Information Service Journal of Deep Sea Research *see* J A M S T E C Journal of Deep Sea Research **2808**
Japan Maritime Daily *see* Nihon Kaiji Shimbun **8655**
Japan Maritime Research Institute. Bulletin *see* Kaiji Sangyo Kenkyujoho **8649**
Japan. Maritime Safety Agency. Hydrographic Department. Notices to Mariners/Suiro Tsuho (JPN ISSN 0447-3728) **8648**
Japan. Maritime Safety Agency. Hydrographic Department. Report of Hydrographic Research (JPN ISSN 0373-3602) **2711**
Japan Marketing Data (JPN) **1823**
Japan Matrix (Collagen) Club. Proceedings of the Annual Meeting of Japan Matrix Club (JPN) **5643**
Japan Meat Processing Journal (JPN ISSN 0386-2372) **3649**
Japan Medical Association. Journal *see* Nihon Ishikai Zasshi **5687**
Japan Medical Journal *see* Nihon Iji Shinpo **5686**
Japan Medical Library Association. Journal *see* Igaku Toshokan **5014**
Japan Medical Society of Paraplegia. Journal *see* Nihon Sekizui Shougai Igakkai Zasshi **6068**
• Japan Metal Bulletin (Online Edition) (JPN) **6318**
Japan Metal Bulletin (Print Edition) *see* Japan Metal Bulletin (Online Edition) **6318**
Japan Meteorological Agency *see* Kazan Hokoku **2786**
Japan Meteorological Agency. Annual Report/Kishocho Nenpo Zenkoku Kishohyo (JPN ISSN 0448-3758) **6358**
Japan Meteorological Agency. Monthly Report. Meteorological Observations *see* Kishocho Geppo Zenkoku Kishohyo **6359**
Japan Meteorological Agency. Report of Magnetic Pulsations (JPN ISSN 1342-3800) **2784**
Japan Meteorological Agency. Technical Data Series *see* Kishocho Kansoku Gijutsu Shiryo **6359**
Japan Meteorological Agency. Technical Report *see* Kishocho Gijutsu Hokoku **2786**
▼ Japan Mining Report (GBR ISSN 1755-7984) **6467**
Japan. Ministry of Agriculture and Forestry. Annual Report *see* Japan. Norin-sho Nenpo **125**
Japan. Ministry of Agriculture, Forestry and Fisheries. National Research Institute of Agricultural Engineering. Abstracts from Research Reports (JPN ISSN 0386-5126) **212**
Japan. Ministry of Agriculture, Forestry and Fisheries. National Research Institute of Agricultural Engineering. Technical Report (JPN ISSN 0287-0029) **212**
Japan. Ministry of Agriculture, Forestry and Fisheries. National Veterinary Assay Laboratory. Annual Report *see* Dobutsu Iyakuhin Kensajo Nenpo **8796**
Japan. Ministry of Education. National Science Museum. Institute for Nature Study. Miscellaneous Reports *see* Shizen Kyoikuen Hokoku **7916**
Japan. Ministry of Health, Labour and Welfare. Handbook of Health and Welfare Statistics *see* Kouseiroudoushou. Kosei Tokei Yoran **7548**
Japan. Ministry of Health, Labour and Welfare. Monthly Report on Vital Statistics *see* Kouseiroudoushou. Jinko Dotai Tokei Geppo, Gaisu **8384**
Japan. Ministry of Health, Labour and Welfare, National Health and Nutrition Survey in Japan *see* Kousei Roudoushou. Kokumin Kenko - Eiyo Chosa Hokoku **6662**
Japan. Ministry of Health, Labour and Welfare. Occupational and Industrial Aspects: Special Report of Vital Statistics in (Year) *see* Kouseiroudoushou. Jinkou Doutai Shokuguon. SangyouToukei: Jinkou Doutai Toukei Tokushu Houkoku **6706**
Japan. Ministry of Health, Labour and Welfare. Report on Activities of Public Health Centers *see* Chiiki Hoken Roujin Hoken Jigyou Houkoku **5742**
Japan. Ministry of Health, Labour and Welfare. Report on Survey of National Medical Care Insurance Services *see* Kouseiroudoushou. Shakai Iryo Shinryo Koibetsu Chosa Hokoku **4530**
Japan. Ministry of Health, Labour and Welfare. Report on Survey of Public Assistance *see* Kouseiroudoushou. Seikatsu Hogo Dotai Chosa Hokoku **8083**
Japan. Ministry of Health, Labour and Welfare. Report on Survey of Social Welfare Institutions *see* Kouseiroudoushou. Shakai Fukushi Shisetsu Tou Chosa Hokoku **8083**
Japan. Ministry of Health, Labour and Welfare. Report on Survey of Socio-Economic Aspects on Vital Events *see* Kouseiroudoushou. Jinko Dotai Shakai Keizaimen Chosa Hokoku **7311**
Japan. Ministry of Health, Labour and Welfare. Statistical Report on Food Poisonings *see* Kouseiroudoushou. Shokuchudoku Tokei **7548**
Japan. Ministry of Health, Labour and Welfare. Statistical Report on Social Welfare Administration and Services *see* Kouseiroudoushou. Shakai Fukushi Gyosei Gyomu Hokoku **8083**
Japan. Ministry of Health, Labour and Welfare. Vital Statistics *see* Kouseiroudoushou. Jinko Dotai Tokei **8384**
Japan. Ministry of Labour. Yearbook of Labour Statistics (JPN) **1246**
Japan. Ministry of Posts and Telecommunications. Communications Research Laboratory. News *see* N I C T News **2334**
➤ Japan Mission Journal (JPN ISSN 1344-7297) **7652**
Japan Monkey Centre. Annual Report *see* Nihon Monki Senta Nenpo **958**
Japan Motor Industry (JPN ISSN 0289-6087) **8587**
Japan N P O Research Association. Journal *see* Nonpurofitto Rebyu **8059**
Japan National Conference on Soil Mechanics and Foundation Engineering. Proceedings *see* Doshitsu Kogaku Kenkyu Happyokai Happyo Koenshu **3265**
Japan. National Institute of Animal Health. Bulletin *see* Doubutsu Eisei Kenkyuujo Kenkyuu Houkoku **8796**
Japan. National Museum News (JPN ISSN 0040-8948) **6526**
Japan Nematology News *see* Nihon Senchu Gakkai Nyusu **958**
Japan-Netherlands Institute. Journal (JPN ISSN 0915-4981) **7247**
Japan Neurosurgical Society. Abstracts of the Annual Meeting (CD-ROM) *see* Nihon Nou Shinkei Geka Gakkai Soukai Shourokushuu (CD-ROM) **5749**
Japan Nonprofit Organization Research Association NewsLetter *see* J A N P O R A NewsLetter **8048**
Japan Nonwovens Report *see* Fushokufu Joho **6733**
Japan. Norin-sho Nenpo/Japan. Ministry of Agriculture and Forestry. Annual Report (JPN ISSN 0446-5458) **125**
Japan Ocean Development Construction Association. News *see* Kaiyo Kyokaiho **2810**
Japan Oceanographic Data Center Catalogue *see* J O D C Catalogue **2808**
Japan Oceanographic Data Center News *see* J O D C News **2808**
Japan Ophthalmologists Association. Journal *see* Nihon no Ganka **6046**
Japan/Pacific Rim Fiber Optics Report (USA) **2499**
Japan Packaging Institute. Journal *see* Hoso Gijutsu **6710**
Japan Pancreas Society. Journal *see* Suizo **5949**
Japan Petrochemicals Report (GBR ISSN 1749-2300) **6775**
Japan Petroleum and Energy Trends (JPN ISSN 0916-2623) **6775**
• ➤ The Japan Petroleum Institute. Journal (JPN ISSN 1346-8804) **6775**
Japan Pharmaceutical Abstracts *see* Nihon Iyaku Bunken Shorokushu **6890**
Japan Pharmaceutical Association. Journal *see* Nippon Yakuzaishikai Zasshi **6864**
Japan. Pocket Size Statistics of Sugar Products (JPN) **3670**
• Japan Policy and Politics (USA) **7145**
Japan Political Research (USA ISSN 1051-1776) **7145**
Japan Port Information (JPN) **8648**
Japan Precious Metals and Watch News *see* Nippon Kikinzoku Tokei Shinbun **4568**
Japan Press Weekly: News & Comments (JPN ISSN 0287-7112) **3900**
Japan Printer *see* Insatsu Zasshi **7324**
Japan Printing Art Annual *see* Nihon Insatsu Nenkan **7325**
Japan Printing News *see* Nippon Insatsu Shinbun **7325**
Japan Prosthodontic Society. Journal *see* Journal of Prosthodontic Research **5853**
Japan Publications Guide Service Letter *see* J P G Letter **7564**
Japan Radio News *see* Nihon Rajio Shinbun **2361**
Japan Railway Engineers Association *see* J R E A **8619**
Japan Refrigeration and Air Conditioning News *see* Nihon Reito Reibo Shinbun **4124**
Japan Refrigeration and Airconditioning Industry Association. Journal *see* Reito to Kucho **4126**
Japan Register of Ships I *see* Nihon Senpaku Meisaisho I **8655**
Japan Register of Ships II (of Japanese flag, under 100 GT) *see* Nihon Senpaku Meisaisho II **8655**
Japan Research Association for Textile End-Uses. Journal *see* Sen'i Seihin Shohi Kagaku **8457**
Japan Research Group of Electrical Discharges. Journal *see* Hoden Kenkyu **7051**
Japan Research Institute for Screw Threads and Fasteners. Journal *see* Nihon Neji Kenkyu Kyokaishi **3391**
Japan Research Review *see* Business & Economic Review **1070**
Japan Review of International Affairs (JPN ISSN 0913-8773) **7247**
Japan Revolutionary Communist League. Journal *see* Shinseiki **7182**
Japan Rhinologic Society. Journal *see* Nihon Bika Gakkai Kaishi **5686**
Japan S I D S Research Society. Journal *see* Nihon S I D S Gakkai Zasshi **6097**
Japan Salivary Gland Society. Journal *see* Nihon Daekisen Gakkaishi **926**
Japan Select Magazine (JPN) **3900**
Japan Sewage Works Association. Journal *see* Gesuido Kyokaishi **7518**
Japan Sewage Works Association. Research Journal *see* Gesuido Kyokaishi Ronbunshu **3268**
Japan. Shizuoka Prefectural Government. Civil Engineering Division. Annual Report *see* Dobokubu Gaiyo **3265**
Japan Society for Aeronautical and Space Sciences *see* Nihon Koku Uchu Gakkai Rombunshu **67**
• ➤ Japan Society for Aeronautical and Space Sciences. Transactions (JPN ISSN 0549-3811) **63**
• Japan Society for Aeronautical and Space Sciences. Transactions. Space Technology Japan (JPN ISSN 1347-3840) **63**
Japan Society for Analytical Chemistry. Abstracts of the Annual Meeting *see* Nihon Bunseki Kagakkai Koen Yoshishu **2095**
Japan Society for Archaebacteriology. Abstracts of Annual Meeting *see* Nihon Archaebacteria Kenkyukai Koenkai Yoshishu **894**
Japan Society for Atmospheric Environment *see* Taiki Kankyo Gakkaishi **3491**
Japan Society for Cell Biology. Abstracts of the Meeting *see* Nihon Saibo Seibutsu Gakkai Taikai Koen Yoshishu **717**
Japan Society for Clinical Anesthesia. Journal *see* Nihon Rinsho Masui Gakkaishi **5772**
Japan Society for Comparative Endocrinology. Newsletter *see* Nihon Hikaku Naibunpi Gakkai Nyusu **5898**
Japan Society for Comparative Endocrinology. Proceedings (JPN ISSN 0913-9036) **5895**
Japan Society for Composite Materials. Journal *see* Nihon Fukugo Zairyo Gakkaishi **3355**
➤ Japan Society for Composite Materials. Transactions (JPN ISSN 0385-2571) **3348**
• Japan Society for Computational Engineering and Science. Transactions (JPN ISSN 1344-9443) **3292**
Japan Society for Controlled Ecological and Life Support Systems Journal *see* C E L S S Journal **663**
Japan Society for Controlled Ecological and Life Support Systems News *see* C E L S S News **663**
Japan Society for Earthquake Engineering Promotion News *see* Jishin Kogaku Shinkokai Nyusu **2784**
Japan Society for Endoscopic Surgery. Journal *see* Nihon Naishikyo Geka Gakkai Zasshi **6253**
Japan Society for Fuzzy Theory and Intelligent Informatics. Journal *see* Chinou to Jouhou **5478**
Japan Society for Head and Neck Surgery. Journal *see* Toukeibu Geka **6261**
Japan Society for Heat Treatment. Journal *see* Netsu Shori **6327**
Japan Society for Industrial and Applied Mathematics. Transactions *see* Nihon Oyo Suri Gakkai Ronbunshi **5520**
Japan Society for Infectious Diseases in Otolaryngology. Journal *see* Nihon Jibi Inkoka Kansensho Kenkyukai Kaishi **6083**
Japan Society for Intellectual Production. Journal *see* Sangaku Renkeigaku **7907**
Japan Society for Laser Medicine. Journal *see* Nippon Laser Igakkaishi **5687**
Japan Society for Marine Surveys and Technology. Journal *see* Kaiyo Chosa Gijutsu **2810**
Japan Society for Oral Tumors. Journal *see* Nihon Koku Shuyo Gakkaishi **6029**
Japan Society for Photoelasticity. Journal *see* Nihon Kodansei Gakkai Kaiho **7081**
Japan Society for Photoelasticity. Proceedings *see* Kodanseigaku Ronbunshu **7079**
Japan Society for Power Electronics. Transactions *see* Pawa Erekutoronikusu Kenkyukai Ronbunshi **3110**
The Japan Society for Precision Engineering. Journal *see* Seimitsu Kogakkaishi **3219**
The Japan Society for Precision Engineering. Proceedings of the Meeting *see* Seimitsu Kogakkai Taikai Gakujutsu Koenkai Koen Ronbunshu **3219**
Japan Society for Precision Engineering Publication Series *see* J S P E Publication Series **3204**
Japan Society for Respiratory Endoscopy. Journal *see* Kikanshigaku **6215**
Japan Society for Safety Engineering. Journal *see* Anzen Kogaku **3181**
Japan Society for Simulation Technology. Journal *see* Shimyureshon **2518**
Japan Society for Software Science and Technology. Internet Conference. Proceedings. *see* Kenkyukai Shiryo Shirizu **2593**
Japan Society for Surgery of the Foot. Journal *see* Nihon Ashi no Geka Gakkai Zasshi **6253**
Japan Society for Technology of Plasticity. Journal *see* Sosei to Kako **8439**
Japan Society for the History of Industrial Technology. Annual Conference. Proceedings *see* Nihon Sangyo Gijutsushi Gakkai Nenkai Koen Gaiyoshu **8447**
Japan Society for the Promotion of Machine Industry. Technical News *see* Kikai Shinko Kyokai. Gijutsu Kenkyujo. Giken Nyusu **5454**
Japan Society of Aesthetic Plastic Surgery. Journal *see* Nihon Biyo Geka Gakkai Kaiho **6253**
Japan Society of Aesthetic Surgery. Journal *see* Nippon Biyo Geka Gakkaishi **6253**
Japan Society of Applied Electromagnetics and Mechanics. Journal *see* Nihon A E M Gakkaishi **3326**
Japan Society of Applied Physics. Autumn Meeting. Extended Abstracts *see* Oyo Butsuri Gakkai Gakujutsu Koenkai ko en Yokoshu **7029**
Japan Society of Applied Physics International *see* J S A P International **7019**
Japan Society of Applied Physics. Solid State Physics and Application Division. Bulletin *see* Oyo Denshi Bussei Bunkakai Kenkyu Hokoku **7029**
Japan Society of Applied Physics. Thin Film and Surface Physics Division. Newsletter (JPN) **7019**
Japan Society of Applied Physics. Thin Film and Surface Physics Seminar *see* Hakumaku Hyomen Butsuri Semina **7014**
Japan Society of Blood Transfusion. Journal *see* Nippon Yuketsu Gakkai Zasshi **5940**
Japan Society of Civil Engineers. Earthquake Engineering Symposium. Proceedings *see* Jishin Kogaku Kenkyu Happoyokai Koen Gaiyo **2784**
Japan Society of Civil Engineers. Hokkaido Branch. Research Reports at the Annual Meeting *see* Doboku Gakkai Hokkaido Shibu Ronbun Hokokushu **3264**
Japan Society of Civil Engineers. Journal *see* Doboku Gakkaishi **3265**
Japan Society of Civil Engineers. Kansai Branch. Proceedings of Annual Conference on Civil Engineers *see* Doboku Gakkai Kansai Shibu Nenji Gakujutsu Koenk Ai Koen Gaiyo **3264**
Japan Society of Civil Engineers. Proceedings of the Annual Conference *see* Doboku Gakkai Nenji Koenkai Koen Gaiyoshu **3264**
Japan Society of Colo-Proctology. Journal *see* Nippon Daicho Komonbyo Gakkai Zasshi **5930**
Japan Society of Colour Material. Journal *see* Shikizai Kyokaishi **6721**
Japan Society of Cranio-Maxillo-Facial Surgery. Journal *see* Nihon Togai Gaku Ganmen Geka Gakkaishi **6253**
Japan Society of Electrical - Machining Engineers. Journal *see* Denki Kako Gakkaishi **3299**
Japan Society of Energy and Resources. Proceedings of the Meeting *see* Kenkyu Happyokai Koen Ronbunshu - Enerugi, Shigen Kenkyukai **3141**
Japan Society of Engineering Geology. Journal *see* Oyo Chishitsu **2761**
Japan Society of Engineering Geology. Kyushu Branch Report *see* Nihon Oyo Chishitsu Gakkai Kyushu Shibu Kaiho **2759**
Japan Society of Engineering Geology. Proceedings of Meeting *see* Nihon Oyo Chishitsu Gakkai Kenkyu Happyokai Koen Ronbunshu **2759**
Japan Society of Erosion Control Engineering. Journal *see* Sabo Gakkaishi **3282**
Japan Society of Fluid Mechanics. Journal *see* Nagare **3363**
Japan Society of Fluid Mechanics. Proceedings (JPN) **3362**
Japan Society of Gynecologic Oncology. Journal *see* Nihon Fujinka Shuyou Gakkai Zasshi **5999**
Japan Society of Heat and Fluid Engineering. Transactions *see* Nihon Netsu Ryutai Kogakkai Ronbunshu **7056**
Japan Society of Human Genetics. Abstracts of the Annual Meeting *see* Nihon Jinrui Iden Gakkai Taikai Shorokushu **717**
Japan Society of Hydrology and Water Resources. Journal *see* Suimon Mizu Shigen Gakkaishi **2798**
Japan Society of Hydrology and Water Resources News *see* Suimon Mizu Shigen Gakkai Nyusu **2798**
Japan Society of Infrared Science and Technology. Journal *see* Nihon Sekigaisen Gakkaishi **7056**
Japan Society of Laser Technology. Winter Seminar *see* Reza Kyokai Uinta Semina **7084**
Japan Society of Library and Information Science. Journal *see* Nippon Toshokan Joho Gakkai-shi **5036**
Japan Society of Mechanical Engineers / American Society of Mechanical Engineers / A S M E International Conference on Materials and Processing (Year). Program and Abstract *see* J S M E / A S M E International Conference on Materials and Processing (Year). Program and Abstract **3383**
Japan Society of Mechanical Engineers Annual Meeting *see* J S M E Annual Meeting **3383**
Japan Society of Mechanical Engineers International Journal. Series A: Solid Mechanics and Material Engineering *see* J S M E International Journal. Series A: Solid Mechanics and Material Engineering **3384**
Japan Society of Mechanical Engineers International Journal. Series B: Fluids and Thermal Engineering *see* J S M E International Journal. Series B: Fluids and Thermal Engineering **3384**
Japan Society of Mechanical Engineers International Journal. Series C, Mechanical Systems, Machine Elements and Manufacturing *see* J S M E International Journal. Series C, Mechanical Systems, Machine Elements and Manufacturing **3384**
Japan Society of Mechanical Engineers. Journal (JPN ISSN 0021-4728) **3384**

Japan Society of Mechanical Engineers News *see* J S M E News **3384**
Japan Society of Mechanical Engineers. Preprints of the Meeting *see* Nihon Kikai Gakkai. Koenkai Koen Ronbunshu **3391**
Japan Society of Mechanical Engineers. Transactions. Series A *see* Nihon Kikai Gakkai Ronbunshu. A Hen **3391**
Japan Society of Mechanical Engineers. Transactions. Series B *see* Nihon Kikai Gakkai Ronbunshu. B Hen **3391**
Japan Society of Mechanical Engineers. Transactions. Series C *see* Nihon Kikai Gakkai Ronbunshu. C Hen **3391**
Japan Society of Medical Entomology and Zoology (JPN) **851**
Japan Society of Medical History. Journal *see* Nihon Ishigaku Zasshi **5687**
Japan Society of Medical History. Kansai Branch. Journal *see* Itan **5642**
Japan Society of Medical Physics News *see* J S M P News **5643**
Japan Society of Medical Physics. Official Journal *see* Igaku Butsuri **6198**
Japan Society of Microgravity Application. Journal *see* J A S M A: Journal of the Japan Society of Microgravity Application **7018**
Japan Society of Naval Architects and Ocean Engineers. Bulletin *see* Kanrin **8649**
Japan Society of Naval Architects and Ocean Engineers. Journal *see* Nihon Sempaku Kaiyou Kougakkai Rombunshuu **8655**
Japan Society of Obstetrics and Gynecology. Chugoku and Shikoku Districts Journal *see* Nihon Sanka Fujinka Gakkai Chugoku Shinkoku Godo Chiho Bukai Zasshi **5999**
Japan Society of Obstetrics and Gynecology. Kanagawa District Journal *see* Nihon Sanka Fujinka Gakkai Kanagawa Chiho Bukai Kaishi **5999**
Japan Society of Obstetrics and Gynecology. Kumamoto District Journal *see* Nihon Sanka Fujinka Gakkai Kumamoto Chiho Bukai Zasshi **6000**
Japan Society of Obstetrics and Gynecology. Kyushu District Journal *see* Nihon Sanka Fujinka Gakkai Kyushu Rengo Chiho Bukai Zasshi **6000**
Japan Society of Obstetrics and Gynecology. Niigata Districts Journal *see* Nihon Sanka Fujinka Gakkai Niigata Chiho Bukai Kaisshi **6000**
Japan Society of Obstetrics and Gynecology. Saitama District Journal *see* Nihon Sanka Fujinka Gakkai Saitama Chiho Bukai Kaishi **6000**
• Japan Society of Pain Clinics. Journal/Nihon Pein Kurinikku Gakkaishi (JPN ISSN 1340-4903) **4103**
Japan Society of Perinatal and Neonatal Medicine. Journal *see* Nihon Shuusanki Shinseiji Igakkai Zasshi **6097**
Japan Society of Perinatology. Year Book *see* Shusankigaku Shimpojiumu **6004**
Japan Society of Plant Taxonomists. Proceeding of the Annual Meeting *see* Nihon Shokubutsu Bunrui Gakkai Taikai Happyo Yoshishu **805**
Japan Society of Plasma Sciences and Nuclear Fusion Research. Preprints of Annual Meeting *see* Purazuma Kaku Yugo Gakkai Nenkai Yokai Yokoshu **7071**
Japan Society of Plastic and Reconstructive Surgery. Annual Meeting *see* Nihon Keisei Geka Gakkai Gakujutsu Shukai **6253**
Japan Society of Plastic and Reconstructive Surgery. Journal *see* Nihon Keisei Geka Gakkai Kaishi **6253**
Japan Society of Polymer Processing. Journal *see* Seikei Kakou **7099**
Japan Society of Powder and Powder Metallurgy *see* Funtai Oyobi Funmatsuyakin **6313**
Japan Society of Refrigeration and Air Conditioning Engineers. Proceedings of Annual Conference *see* Nihon Reito Kuchou Gakkai Gakujutsu Koenkai Koen Ronbunshu **4124**
Japan Society of Refrigeration and Air Conditioning Engineers. Transactions *see* Nihon Reito Kucho Gakkai Rombunshu **4124**
Japan Society of Reproductive Surgery. Journal *see* Nihon Seishoku Geka Gakkai Zasshi **6000**
Japan Society on Adsorption. Abstracts of the Meeting *see* Nihon Kyuchaku Gakkai Kenkyu Happyokai Koen Yoshishu **2095**
Japan Society on Water Environment. Journal *see* Mizu Kankyo Gakkaishi **3453**
Japan Society. Proceedings (GBR ISSN 0952-2050) **7247**
Japan Society. Review *see* Japan Society. Proceedings **7247**
Japan Solar Energy Society. Journal *see* Taiyo Enerugi **3178**
Japan. Sorifu. Tokeikyoku. News Bulletin *see* Japan. Statistics Bureau. Management and Coordination Agency. News Bulletin **7311**
Japan Special Libraries Association. Bulletin *see* Senmon Toshokan **5047**
Japan Spectroscopic Corporation Report *see* J A S C O Report **7077**
Japan Spine Research Society. Journal *see* Nihon Sekitsui Sekizuibyou Gakkai Zasshi **6068**
Japan Spinners' Association. Monthly Report *see* Nihon Boseki Geppo **8455**
• Japan Spotlight: Economy, Culture & History (JPN ISSN 1348-9216) **1131**
Japan Spring Manufacturers Association *see* Bane Ronbunshu **3374**
Japan Statistical Association. Facts and Findings About Japan by Statistical Data (Year) *see* Nihon Tokei Kyokai. Tokei de Miru Nippon (Year) **8391**
Japan Statistical Association. Index to Statistical Data Sources (Year) *see* Nihon Tokei Kyokai. Tokei Joho Indekkusu (Year) **8391**
Japan Statistical Association. International Statistical Compendia (Year) *see* Nihon Tokei Kyokai. Sekai No Tokei (Year) **8391**
Japan Statistical Association. Statistics of Japan (Year) *see* Nihon Tokei Kyokai. Nihon No Tokei (Year) **8391**
Japan Statistical Society. Journal *see* Nihon Tokei Gakkaishi (Tokyo, 1971) **1255**
Japan. Statistics Bureau. Management and Coordination Agency. Annual Report on Current Population Estimates (JPN) **7311**
Japan. Statistics Bureau. Management and Coordination Agency. Annual Report on Family Income and Expenditure Survey (Year)/Nihon Tokei Kyokai. Kakei Chosa Nenpo (JPN) **4370**
Japan. Statistics Bureau. Management and Coordination Agency. Annual Report on the Consumer Price Index (Year)/Nihon Tokei Kyokai. Shohisha Bukka Shisu Nenpo (JPN ISSN 0289-1336) **2642**
Japan. Statistics Bureau. Management and Coordination Agency. Annual Report on the Internal Migration in Japan Derived from the Basic Resident Registers (Year)/Nihon Tokei Kyokai. Jumin Kihon Daicho Jinko Ido Hokoku Nenpo (JPN ISSN 0286-1410) **7311**
Japan. Statistics Bureau. Management and Coordination Agency. Annual Report on the Labour Force Survey/Nihon Tokei Kyokai. Rodoryoku Chosa Nenpo (JPN ISSN 0289-1344) **1246**
Japan. Statistics Bureau. Management and Coordination Agency. Annual Report on the Retail Price Survey/Nihon Tokei Kyokai. Kouri Bukka Tokei Chosa Nenpo (JPN ISSN 0289-1301) **1246**
Japan. Statistics Bureau. Management and Coordination Agency. Annual Report on the Unincorporated Enterprise Survey (Year)/Nihon Tokei Kyokai. Kojin Kigyo Keizai Chosa Nenpo (JPN ISSN 0448-7141) **1246**
Japan. Statistics Bureau. Management and Coordination Agency. Employment Status Survey (Year) (JPN) **1246**
Japan. Statistics Bureau. Management and Coordination Agency. Family Savings Survey (Year)/Nihon Tokei Kyokai. Chochiku Doko Chosa Hokoku (JPN ISSN 0448-7109) **1246**
Japan. Statistics Bureau. Management and Coordination Agency. Housing and Land Survey of Japan (Year) (JPN) **4436**
• Japan. Statistics Bureau. Management and Coordination Agency. Japan Statistical Yearbook/Nihon Tokei Nenkan (JPN ISSN 0389-9004) **8382**
Japan. Statistics Bureau. Management and Coordination Agency. Monthly Report of Retail Prices Survey/Nihon Tokei Kyokai. Kouri Bukka Tokei Chosa Hokoku (JPN ISSN 0448-7176) **1246**
Japan. Statistics Bureau. Management and Coordination Agency. Monthly Report on the Consumer Price Index/Nihon Tokei Kyokai. Shohisha Bukka Shisu Geppo (JPN ISSN 0288-920X) **2642**
Japan. Statistics Bureau. Management and Coordination Agency. Monthly Report on the Family Income and Expenditure Survey/Nihon Tokei Kyokai. Kakei Chosa Hokoku (JPN) **1246**
Japan. Statistics Bureau. Management and Coordination Agency. Monthly Report on the Labour Force Survey (JPN) **1246**
Japan. Statistics Bureau. Management and Coordination Agency. Monthly Statistics of Japan/Nihon Tokei Kyokai. Nihon Tokei Geppo (JPN ISSN 0549-4680) **8382**
Japan. Statistics Bureau. Management and Coordination Agency. News Bulletin (JPN ISSN 0449-5314) **7311**
• Japan. Statistics Bureau. Management and Coordination Agency. Population Census of Japan (Year) (JPN) **7311**
Japan. Statistics Bureau. Management and Coordination Agency. Population Estimates Series (JPN ISSN 0448-7117) **7311**
Japan. Statistics Bureau. Management and Coordination Agency. Quarterly Report on the Internal Migration in Japan Derived from the Basic Resident Registers/Nihon Tokei Kyokai. Jumin Kihon Daicho Jinko Ido Hokoku Kiho (JPN ISSN 0285-3140) **7311**
Japan. Statistics Bureau. Management and Coordination Agency. Quarterly Report on the Unincorporated Enterprise Survey/Nihon Tokei Kyokai. Kojin Kigyo Keizai Chosa Kiho (JPN ISSN 0448-715X) **1246**
Japan. Statistics Bureau. Management and Coordination Agency. Report on the Special Survey of the Labour Force Survey (Year)/Nihon Tokei Kyokai. Rodoryoku Chosa Tokubetsu Chosa Hokoku (JPN ISSN 0448-7214) **1246**
Japan. Statistics Bureau. Management and Coordination Agency. Report on the Survey of Research and Development (Year)/Nihon Tokei Kyokai. Kagaku Gijutsu Kenkyu Chosa Hokoku (JPN ISSN 0447-5089) **8428**
• Japan. Statistics Bureau. Management and Coordination Agency. Social Indicators By Prefecture (Year) (JPN) **8083**
Japan. Statistics Bureau. Management and Coordination Agency. Statistical Handbook of Japan (Year) (JPN ISSN 0081-4792) **8382**
Japan Steel Works Technical News (JPN ISSN 0368-444X) **6318**
Japan Steel Works Technical Review *see* Nihon Seikosho Giho **6327**
Japan Stomatological Society. Journal *see* Kokubyo Gakkai Zasshi **5928**
➤ Japan Studies Review (USA ISSN 1550-0713) **4458**
Japan Surgical Association. Journal *see* Nihon Rinsho Geka Gakkai Zasshi **6253**
Japan Surgical Society. Journal *see* Nippon Geka Gakkai Zasshi **6253**
Japan Synchrotron Radiation Research Institute. News *see* Spring Eito Nyusu **7072**
Japan T A P P I. Annual Meeting. Proceedings *see* Kami Paupu Gijutsu Kyokai. Nenji Taikai. Kouen Yokoshu **6734**
Japan T A P P I Journal *see* Kami Pa Gikyoshi **6734**
Japan Technical Association of Pulp and Paper Industry. Annual Meeting. Proceedings *see* Kami Paupu Gijutsu Kyokai. Nenji Taikai. Kouen Yokoshu **6734**
• Japan Telecom (USA ISSN 1081-9983) **2328**
Japan Telecom Newsletter *see* Japan Telecom **2328**
Japan Textile Industry. Directory *see* Sen-i Kougyo Yoran **8464**
Japan Thermal Spraying Society. Journal *see* Yosha **6721**
• The Japan Times (JPN ISSN 0289-1956) **3900**
• The Japan Times International (JPN ISSN 1345-1189) **3900**
Japan Times Online *see* The Japan Times **3900**
• Japan Today (JPN) **3900**
Japan Toy and Game Journal (JPN) **8182**
Japan Toy and Game Software Journal *see* Japan Toy and Game Journal **8182**
Japan Trade Directory (Year)/Nihon Boeki Shinkokai (JPN) **2010**
• Japan Travel View (USA ISSN 1539-7467) **8725**
Japan Typography Annual/Nihon Taipogurafi Nenkan (JPN) **7324**
Japan - U.S. Bridge Engineering Workshop. Proceedings *see* Nichibei Kyoryo Wakushoppu Ronbunshu **3279**
Japan University Network Earthquake Catalog/Kokuritsu Daigaku Kansokumo Jishin Katarogu (JPN) **2784**
Japan Washington Watch. Section A *see* Asia Policy Calendar **7222**
• Japan Weekly Monitor (USA) **1131**
Japan Welding Society. Journal/Yosetsu Gakkaishi (JPN ISSN 0021-4787) **6343**
Japan Welding Society. Quarterly Journal *see* Yosetsu Gakkai Ronbunshu **6345**
Japan Women's University. Faculty of Humanities. Journal *see* Nihon Joshi Daigaku Kiyo. Bungakubu **4466**
Japan Women's University. Faculty of Science. Journal *see* Nihon Joshi Daigaku Kiyo. Rigakubu **7892**
Japan Women's University. Graduate School of Humanities. Journal *see* Nihon Joshi Daigaku Daigakuin Bungaku Kenkyuka Kiyo **4466**
Japan Wood Research Society. Journal *see* Mokuzai Gakkaishi (Japanese Edition) **3714**
Japana Centra Revuo Medicina *see* Igaku Chuo Zasshi **5632**
Japana Medicina Revuo *see* Igaku Hyoron **5632**
JapanContact (DEU) **1573**
Japanese Academy of Home Care Physicians. Journal *see* Nihon Zaitaku Igakkai Zasshi **5687**
Japanese Academy of Maxillofacial Prosthetics. Journal *see* Gaku Ganmen Hotetsu **6244**
Japanese Agricultural Standards Association Joho *see* J A S Joho **124**
Japanese Animal Hospital Association. Proceedings *see* J A H A Shorei Happyokai **8800**
• Japanese Annual of International Law (JPN ISSN 0448-8806) **4933**
Japanese Antarctic Research Expedition Data Reports (JPN ISSN 0075-3343) **2711**
Japanese Antarctic Research Report to S C A R (Scientific Committee on Antarctic Research) (JPN) **2711**
Japanese Archaeological Association. Bulletin (JPN) **400**
Japanese Archaeological Association. Journal *see* Nihon Kokogaku **408**
Japanese Archaeologists Association. Annual Report *see* Nihon Kokogaku Nenpo **408**
Japanese Association for Acute Medicine. Journal *see* Nihon Kyukyu Igakkai Zasshi **5948**
Japanese Association for Chest Surgery. Journal *see* Nihon Kokyuki Geka Gakkai Zasshi **6253**
Japanese Association for Chromosome and Gene Analysis. Abstract of Annual Meeting *see* Nihon Senshokutai Idenshi Kensa Gakkai Shorokushu **717**
Japanese Association for Chromosome and Gene Analysis. Official Journal *see* Nihon Senshokutai Idenshi Kensa Gakkai Zasshi **740**
Japanese Association for Critical Care Medicine. Journal *see* Nihon Kyumei Iryo Gakkai Zasshi **5687**
• Japanese Association for Dental Research. Newsletter (JPN) **5850**
Japanese Association for Ecological Nutrition Research. Annals *see* Seitaigakuteki Eiyogaku Kenkyu **704**
Japanese Association for Heat Pipes. Journal *see* Hito Paipu Gijutsu **3379**
Japanese Association for Infectious Diseases. Journal *see* Kansenshogaku Zasshi **5821**
Japanese Association for Laboratory Animal Science. Abstracts of General Meeting *see* Nihon Jikken Dobutsu Gakkai Sokai Koen Yoshishu **717**
Japanese Association for Operative Medicine. Journal *see* Nihon Shujutsu Igakkaishi **6253**
Japanese Association for Petroleum Technology. Journal *see* Sekiyu Gijutsu Kyokaishi **6791**
Japanese Association for the Surgery of Trauma. Journal *see* Nihon Gaisho Gakkai Zasshi **6067**
Japanese Association of Animal Models for Human Diseases. Proceedings *see* Nihon Shikkan Moderu Gakkai Kiroku **926**
Japanese Association of Behavior Therapy. Newsletter *see* Nihon Kodo Ryoho Gakkai Nyuzu Reta **7388**
Japanese Association of Benthology. Abstracts of Annual Meeting *see* Nihon Bentosu Gakkai Taikai **717**
Japanese Association of Crystal Growth. Journal *see* Nihon Kessho Seicho Gakkaishi **2111**
Japanese Association of External Fixation and Limb Lengthening. Journal *see* Nihon Sogai Kotei, Kotsu Encho Gakkai Zasshi **6068**
Japanese Association of Germfree Life and Gnotobiology. Abstracts of Meeting *see* Nihon Mukin Seibutsu Noto Baioroji Gakkai Sokai Nittei to Shoroku **717**
Japanese Association of Hydrological Sciences. Journal *see* Nihon Suimon Kagaku Kaishi **2797**
Japanese Association of Physical Medicine, Balneology, and Climatology. Journal *see* Nihon Onsen Kiko Butsuri Igakkai Zasshi **5687**
Japanese Association of Regenerative Dentistry. Journal *see* Nihon Saisei Shikaigakkai Zasshi **5857**
Japanese Association of Rural Medicine. Journal *see* Nihon Noson Igakkai Zasshi **5687**
Japanese Association of Strabismus and Amblyopia. Bulletin *see* Nihon Jakushi Shashi Gakkaiho **6046**
Japanese Association of Strabismus and Amblyopia. Journal *see* Nihon Jakushi Shashi Gakkai Zasshi **6046**
Japanese Association of Yogo Teacher Education. Journal *see* Nihon Yougo Kyouyu Kyouiku Gakkaishi **3044**
Japanese Association of Zoological Gardens and Aquariums. Annual Report *see* Nihon Dobutsuen Suizokukan Nenpo **958**
Japanese Association of Zoological Gardens and Aquariums. Journal *see* Dobutsuen Suizokukan Zasshi **940**
Japanese Biblical Institute. Annual (JPN ISSN 0912-9243) **7652**
Japanese Biochemical Society. Journal *see* Seikagaku **745**
Japanese Biochemical Society. Kinki Branch Office. Abstracts of Meeting *see* Nihon Seikagakkai Kinki Shibu Reikai Yoshishu **3613**
Japanese Bird Banding Association. Bulletin *see* Nihon Chorui Hyoshiki Kyokaishi **911**
Japanese Book News (JPN ISSN 0918-9580) **7564**
• Japanese Books in Print (Year) (JPN) **628**
Japanese Breast Cancer Society. Journal *see* Breast Cancer **6009**
Japanese Bulletin of Arts Therapy *see* Nippon Geijutsu Ryoho Gakkaishi **509**
Japanese Car Culture *see* J-tuner **8586**
Japanese Carbohydrate Symposium. Abstracts *see* Toshitsu Shinpojumu Koen Yoshishu **2096**
Japanese Chamber of Commerce and Industry of Hawaii. Newsbulletin (USA) **1405**
• Japanese Circulation Journal Supplement (JPN) **5791**
Japanese Clinical Orthopaedic Association. Journal *see* Nihon Rinsho Seikei Gekaikai Kaishi **6067**
Japanese Cognitive Linguistics Association. Annual Meetings. Proceedings *see* Nihon Ninchi Gengo Gakkai Rombunshu **5155**
Japanese College of Angiology. Journal *see* Myakkangaku **5796**
Japanese College of Surgeons. Journal *see* Nihon Gekakei Rengo Gakkaishi **5749**
Japanese Conference of Remote Sensing. Proceedings *see* Gakujutsu Koenkai Ronbunshu **4007**
Japanese Conference on the Biochemistry of Lipids. Circular *see* Shishitsu Seikagaku Kenkyu Circular **745**
Japanese Conference on the Biochemistry of Lipids. Proceedings *see* Shishitsu Seikagaku Kenkyu **745**
Japanese Congress for Testing Materials. Proceedings *see* Japan Congress on Materials Research. Proceedings **3348**

Title

10476 JAPANESE CONSTRUCTION METHOD AND MACHINERY RESEARCH ULRICH'S PERIODICALS

Japanese Construction Method and Machinery Research Institute. Report of Performance Tests *see* Kensetsu Kikaikai Kenkyujo Seino Shiken Hokoku **1019**
Japanese Coronary Association. Journal *see* Nihon Kan Shikkan Gakkai Zasshi **5796**
Japanese Cosmetic Science Society. Journal (JPN ISSN 0287-1238) **594**
Japanese Council for Advanced Food Ingredients Research. Journal *see* Nihon Shokuhin Shinsozai Kenkyukaishi **3658**
Japanese Cyperaceae Newsletter *see* Suge no Kai Kaiho **819**
Japanese Deaf News (JPN) **4074**
• Japanese Dental Science Review (GBR ISSN 1882-7616) **5850**
Japanese Dental Society of Anesthesiology. Journal *see* Nihon Shika Masui Gakkai Zasshi **5772**
• ➤ The Japanese Economic Review (AUS ISSN 1352-4739) **1131**
• ➤ The Japanese Economy (USA ISSN 1097-203X) **1131**
Japanese Economy & Labor Series (JPN) **1690**
Japanese Films (JPN ISSN 0448-8830) **6504**
† Japanese Finance and Industry: Quarterly Survey (JPN ISSN 0385-2369) **8967**
Japanese Forest Society. Journal *see* Nihon Shinrin Gakkaishi **3698**
Japanese Geomorphological Union. Transactions *see* Chikei **2729**
Japanese Geotechnical Society. Journal *see* Jiban Kogakkai Ronbun Hokokushu **3274**
Japanese Guide to Hawaii (USA ISSN 1545-8970) **8725**
Japanese Heart Journal (Print) *see* International Heart Journal **5790**
Japanese Hospital Directory *see* Byoin Yoran **4089**
Japanese Industrial Standards Yearbook (Year) *see* J I S Yearbook (Year) **6403**
Japanese Institue of Anatolian Archaeology. Bulletin (DEU) **552**
Japanese Institute of Landscape Architecture. Journal *see* Randosukepu Kenkyu **3748**
Japanese International Taxation (USA) **1931**
Japanese Journal for Midwives *see* Josan Zasshi **5994**
The Japanese Journal for Public Health Nurse (JPN ISSN 1348-8333) **5963**
Japanese Journal of Acute Medicine *see* Kyukyu Igaku **5659**
Japanese Journal of Addiction & Family *see* Adikushon to Kazoku **2690**
Japanese Journal of Aerospace and Environmental Medicine *see* Uchu Koku Kankyo Igaku **5725**
Japanese Journal of Alcohol Studies and Drug Dependence (Kyoto, 1996) *see* Nihon Arukoru, Yakubutsu Igakkai Zasshi **2697**
Japanese Journal of Allergology *see* Arerugi **5754**
• Japanese Journal of American Studies (JPN ISSN 0288-3570) **4298**
Japanese Journal of Anesthesiology *see* Masui **5772**
Japanese Journal of Animal Psychology *see* Dobutsu Shinrigaku Kenkyu **940**
Japanese Journal of Antibiotics (JPN ISSN 0368-2781) **5643**
Japanese Journal of Apheresis *see* Nihon Afereshisu Gakkai Zasshi **5940**
Japanese Journal of Applied Entomology and Zoology *see* Nihon Oyo Dobutsu Konchu Gakkaishi **856**
• Japanese Journal of Applied I T Healthcare (JPN ISSN 1881-4808) **5831**
• ➤ Japanese Journal of Applied Physics (JPN) **7019**
Japanese Journal of Applied Physics: Part 1. Regular Papers & Short Notes *see* Japanese Journal of Applied Physics **7019**
Japanese Journal of Applied Physics. Part 2, Letters & Express Lettres *see* Applied Physics Express **7006**
Japanese Journal of Applied Physics Series *see* J J A P Series **7019**
Japanese Journal of Applied Psychology *see* Oyo Shinrigaku Kenkyu **7389**
Japanese Journal of Applied Statistics *see* Oyo Tokeigaku **8393**
Japanese Journal of Artificial Organs *see* Jinko Zoki **5644**
Japanese Journal of Autogenic Therapy *see* Jiritsu Kunren Kenkyu **7367**
Japanese Journal of Autologous Blood Transfusion *see* Jikoketsu Yuketsu **5791**
Japanese Journal of Bacteriology *see* Nihon Saikingaku Zasshi **5823**
Japanese Journal of Behavior Analysis *see* Kodo Bunsekigaku Kenkyu **7382**
Japanese Journal of Behavior Therapy *see* Kodo Ryoho Kenkyu **7382**
Japanese Journal of Behaviormetrics *see* Kodo Keiryogaku **8149**
Japanese Journal of Biofeedback Research *see* Baiofidobakku Kenkyu **7338**
Japanese Journal of Biological Education *see* Seibutsu Kyoiku **703**
Japanese Journal of Biometeorology *see* Nihon Seikisho Gakkai Zasshi **6392**
➤ Japanese Journal of Biometrics (JPN ISSN 0918-4430) **680**
Japanese Journal of Breast Cancer *see* Nyugan no Rinsho **6029**
Japanese Journal of Cancer and Chemotherapy *see* Gan To Kagaku Ryoho **6020**
Japanese Journal of Cancer Care *see* Gan Kango **6020**
Japanese Journal of Cancer Clinics *see* Gan No Rinsho **6020**
Japanese Journal of Cancer Research *see* Cancer Science **6014**
Japanese Journal of Cardiovascular Surgery *see* Nihon Shinzo Kekkan Geka Gakkai Zasshi **6253**
Japanese Journal of Cataract and Refractive Surgery *see* I O L & R S **6043**
Japanese Journal of Chemotherapy *see* Nihon Kagaku Ryoho Gakkai Zasshi **6864**
Japanese Journal of Chest Diseases *see* Nihon Kyobu Rinsho **5796**
Japanese Journal of Child & Adolescent Psychiatry/Jido Seinen Seishin Igaku to Sono Kinsetsu Ryoiki (JPN ISSN 0289-0968) **6149**
Japanese Journal of Child Nursing, Monthly *see* Shoni Kango **5981**
Japanese Journal of Circulation Research *see* Kekkan **5795**
Japanese Journal of Clinical and Experimental Medicine *see* Rinsho to Kenkyu **5910**
Japanese Journal of Clinical Chemistry *see* Rinsho Kagaku **5707**
Japanese Journal of Clinical Dermatology *see* Rinsho Hifuka **5881**
Japanese Journal of Clinical Dialysis *see* Rinsho Toseki **6274**
Japanese Journal of Clinical Hematology *see* Rinsho Ketsueki **5941**
Japanese Journal of Clinical Immunology *see* Nihon Rinsho Men'eki Gakkai Kaishi **5764**
Japanese Journal of Clinical Medicine *see* Nippon Rinsho **5687**
Japanese Journal of Clinical Nursing, Monthly *see* Rinsho Kango **5980**
Japanese Journal of Clinical Nutrition *see* Rinsho Eiyo **6669**
• ➤ Japanese Journal of Clinical Oncology (GBR ISSN 0368-2811) **6023**
Japanese Journal of Clinical Ophthalmology *see* Rinsho Ganka **6051**
Japanese Journal of Clinical Pathology/Rinsho Byori (JPN ISSN 0047-1860) **5643**
Japanese Journal of Clinical Pharmacology and Therapeutics *see* Rinsho Yakuri **6879**
Japanese Journal of Clinical Physiology *see* Nihon Rinsho Seiri Gakkai Zasshi **5687**
Japanese Journal of Clinical Psychiatry *see* Rinsho Seishin Igaku **6183**
Japanese Journal of Clinical Psychology *see* Rinshou Shinrigaku Kenkyuu **7405**
Japanese Journal of Clinical Psychology *see* Rinsho Shinrigaku **6183**
Japanese Journal of Clinical Radiology *see* Rinsho Hoshasen **6207**
Japanese Journal of Clinical Urology *see* Rinsho Hinyokika **6274**
Japanese Journal of Communication Disorders *see* Kominikeisyon Syogaigaku **6082**
• Japanese Journal of Complementary and Alternative Medicine (JPN ISSN 1348-7922) **311**
Japanese Journal of Computer Science *see* Komputa Saiensu **2430**
Japanese Journal of Conservation Ecology *see* Hozen Seitaigaku Kenkyu **2613**
Japanese Journal of Conservative Dentistry *see* Nihon Shika Hozongaku Zasshi **5857**
Japanese Journal of Constitutional Medicine *see* Nihon Taishitsu Igakkai Zasshi **926**
Japanese Journal of Counseling Science *see* Kaunseringu Kenkyu **7382**
Japanese Journal of Criminal Psychology *see* Hanzai Shinrigaku Kenkyu **7360**
Japanese Journal of Crop Science *see* Nihon Sakumotsu Gakkai Kiji **243**
Japanese Journal of Dermatology: Series A *see* Nihon Hifuka Gakkai Zasshi **5880**
Japanese Journal of Developmental and Therapeutic Pharmacology *see* Nihon Shoni Rinsho Yakuri Gakkai Zasshi **6864**
Japanese Journal of Developmental Psychology *see* Hattatsu Shinrigaku Kenkyu **7360**
Japanese Journal of Diabetes Master Clinician *see* Tounyoubyou Shinryou Masuta **5900**
The Japanese Journal of Diabetic Caring *see* Tounyoubyou Kea **5900**
Japanese Journal of Diagnostic Imaging *see* Gazo Shindan **6197**
Japanese Journal of Ecology *see* Nippon Seitai Gakkaishi **3456**
Japanese Journal of Education of the Handicapped *see* Shitai Fujiyu Kyoiku **3046**
Japanese Journal of Educational Psychology *see* Kyoiku Shinrigaku Kenkyu **7382**
Japanese Journal of Educational Research *see* Kyoikugaku Kenkyu **2881**
Japanese Journal of Electoral Studies *see* Senkyo Kenkyu **7182**
Japanese Journal of Entomology. New Series/Konchu. Nyu Shirizu (JPN ISSN 1343-8794) **851**
Japanese Journal of Environment, Entomology and Zoology *see* Kandokon **853**
Japanese Journal of Ergonomics *see* Ningen Kogaku **1700**
Japanese Journal of Ethnology/Minzokugaku Kenkyu (JPN ISSN 0021-5023) **344**
Japanese Journal of Experimental Social Psychology *see* Jikken Shakai Shinrigaku Kenkyu **7367**
Japanese Journal of Family Psychology *see* Kazoku Shinrigaku Kenkyu **7382**
Japanese Journal of Family Sociology *see* Kazoku Shakaigaku Kenkyu **7981**
Japanese Journal of Food Chemistry *see* Nihon Shokuhin Kagaku Gakkaishi **3658**
Japanese Journal of Food Microbiology *see* Nihon Shokuhin Biseibutsu Gakkai Zasshi **894**
Japanese Journal of Forensic Science and Technology *see* Nihon Hou Kagaku Gijutsu Gakkaishi **5916**
Japanese Journal of Forensic Toxicology *see* Forensic Toxicology **5913**
Japanese Journal of Gastroenterological Surgery *see* Nihon Shokaki Geka Gakkai Zasshi **5929**
Japanese Journal of Gastroenterology *see* Nihon Shokakibyo Gakkai Zasshi **5929**
Japanese Journal of Geriatric Psychiatry *see* Ronen Seishin Igaku Zasshi **4055**
Japanese Journal of Geriatrics *see* Nihon Ronen Igakkai Zasshi **4052**
Japanese Journal of Gynecologic and Obstetric Endoscopy *see* Nihon Sanka Fujinka Naishikyo Gakkai Zasshi **6000**
Japanese Journal of Health and Human Ecology *see* Minzoku Eisei **689**
Japanese Journal of Health Physics *see* Hoken Butsuri **7524**
Japanese Journal of Health Psychology *see* Kenko Shinrigaku Kenkyu **7382**
Japanese Journal of Herpetology *see* Current Herpetology **939**
Japanese Journal of Historical Botany *see* Shokuseishi Kenkyu **817**
Japanese Journal of Home Care Nursing *see* Homon Kango to Kaigo **5960**
Japanese Journal of Hospital and Community Psychiatry *see* Byoin, Chiiki Seishin Igaku **6129**
Japanese Journal of Hygiene *see* Nihon Eiseigaku Zasshi **6994**
Japanese Journal of Hyperthermic Oncology *see* Thermal Medicine **6035**
Japanese Journal of Hypnosis *see* Saimingaku Kenkyu **7406**
Japanese Journal of Impotence Research *see* Nihon Sei Kino Gakkai Zasshi **6273**
• ➤ Japanese Journal of Infectious Diseases (JPN ISSN 1344-6304) **5643**
Japanese Journal of Interventional Cardiology (JPN ISSN 0914-8922) **5791**
Japanese Journal of Jaw Deformities *see* Nihon Gaku Henkeisho Gakkai Zasshi **5857**
Japanese Journal of Language in Society *see* Shakai Gengo Kagaku **5173**
Japanese Journal of Leprosy *see* Nihon Hansenbyo Gakkai Zasshi **5823**
Japanese Journal of Limnology *see* Rikusui Gaku Zasshi **2798**
Japanese Journal of Lymphology *see* Rinpagaku **5900**
Japanese Journal of Maternal Health *see* Bosei Eisei **8844**
• ➤ Japanese Journal of Mathematics (JPN ISSN 0289-2316) **5499**
Japanese Journal of Medical and Psychological Study of Infants *see* Nyuuyouji Igaku, Shinrigaku Kenkyu **7388**
Japanese Journal of Medical Imaging *see* Nihon Gazo Igaku Zasshi **6204**
Japanese Journal of Medical Imaging and Information Sciences *see* Iyo Gazo Joho Gakkai Zasshi (Online) **6199**
Japanese Journal of Medical Instrumentation *see* Ika Kikaigaku **5632**
Japanese Journal of Medical Mycology *see* Nippon Ishinkin Gakkai Zasshi **894**
Japanese Journal of Medical Physics *see* Igaku Butsuri **6198**
Japanese Journal of Medical Social Work *see* Iryo to Fukushi **5642**
Japanese Journal of Medical Ultrasound Technology *see* Chouompa Kensa Gijutsu **6193**
Japanese Journal of Molecular Psychiatry *see* Bunshi Seishin Igaku **6129**
Japanese Journal of Nematology *see* Nihon Senchu Gakkaishi **958**
Japanese Journal of Nephrology *see* Nihon Jinzo Gakkaishi **6273**
Japanese Journal of Neuropsychology *see* Shinkei Shinrigaku **6185**
Japanese Journal of Neurosurgery *see* No Shinkei Geka Janaru **7388**
Japanese Journal of Nuclear Medicine *see* Kaku Igaku **6202**
Japanese Journal of Nuclear Medicine Technology *see* Kaku Igaku Gijutsu **6202**
Japanese Journal of Nursing *see* Kango **5968**
Japanese Journal of Nursing *see* Kangogaku Zasshi **5968**
Japanese Journal of Nursing *see* Gekkan Nashingu **5959**
Japanese Journal of Nursing Arts *see* Kango Gijutsu **5968**
Japanese Journal of Nursing Education *see* Kango Kyoiku **5968**
Japanese Journal of Nursing Research *see* Kango Kenkyu **5968**
Japanese Journal of Nursing Science *see* Kango Tenbo **5968**
Japanese Journal of Nursing Special *see* J J N Supesharu **5963**
Japanese Journal of Nutrition and Dietetics *see* Eiyogaku Zasshi **6658**
Japanese Journal of Nutritional Assessment *see* Eiyou Hyoka to Chiryo **6658**
Japanese Journal of Obstetrical, Gynecological and Neonatal Hematology *see* Nihon Sanfujinka Shinseiji Ketsueki Gakkaishi **5999**
Japanese Journal of Occupational Therapy *see* Sagyo Ryoho Janaru **6686**
Japanese Journal of Ocular Pharmacology *see* Gan Yakuri **6042**
Japanese Journal of Ophthalmic Caring *see* Ganka Kea **6042**
• ➤ Japanese Journal of Ophthalmology (JPN ISSN 0021-5155) **6044**
Japanese Journal of Optics *see* Kogaku **7079**
Japanese Journal of Oral and Maxillofacial Surgery *see* Nippon Koku Geka Gakkai Zasshi **5857**
Japanese Journal of Oral Hygiene *see* Koku Eisei Gakkai Zasshi **5854**
Japanese Journal of Orthopedic Nursing *see* Seikei-geka Kango **5981**
Japanese Journal of Orthopedic Sports Medicine *see* Nihon Seikei Geka Supotsu Igakkaishi **6067**
Japanese Journal of Palynology *see* Nihon Kafun Gakkai Kaishi **6727**
Japanese Journal of Paper Technology *see* Kami Parupu Gijutsu Taimusu **6734**
Japanese Journal of Pediatric Hematology *see* Nihon Shoni Ketsueki Gakkai Zasshi **5940**
Japanese Journal of Pediatric Medicine *see* Shoni Naika **6104**
Japanese Journal of Pediatric Surgery *see* Shoni Geka **6258**
Japanese Journal of Pediatrics *see* Shonika Rinsho **6104**
Japanese Journal of Personality *see* Pasonariti Kenkyuu **7389**
Japanese Journal of Pharmaceutical Health Care and Sciences *see* Iryo Yakugaku **6851**
The Japanese Journal of Pharmacology (Online Edition) *see* Journal of Pharmacological Sciences (Online Edition) **6855**
The Japanese Journal of Pharmacology (Print Edition) *see* Journal of Pharmacological Sciences (Print Edition) **6855**
• ➤ Japanese Journal of Phycology (Japanese Edition) (JPN) **795**
Japanese Journal of Physical Fitness and Sports Medicine *see* Tairyoku Kagaku **6998**
Japanese Journal of Physical Therapy *see* Rigaku Ryoho Janaru **6116**
Japanese Journal of Physiological Anthropology *see* Nihon Seiri Jinrui Gakkaishi **926**
Japanese Journal of Physiological Psychology and Psychophysiology *see* Seiri Shinrigaku to Seishin Seirigaku **7407**
▼ Japanese Journal of Plant Science (GBR ISSN 1750-2292) **795**
Japanese Journal of Plastic & Reconstructive Surgery/Keisei Geka (JPN ISSN 0021-5228) **6247**
• Japanese Journal of Political Science (GBR ISSN 1468-1099) **7145**
Japanese Journal of Polymer Science and Engineering *see* Kobunshi Ronbunshu **2126**
• Japanese Journal of Population (JPN ISSN 1348-7191) **7286**
Japanese Journal of Protozoology *see* Gensei Dobutsugaku Zasshi **944**
Japanese Journal of Psychiatric Research on Alcohol *see* Nihon Arukoru Seishin Igaku Zasshi **6170**
Japanese Journal of Psychiatric Treatment *see* Seishinka Chiryogaku **6184**
Japanese Journal of Psychology *see* Shinrigaku Kenkyu **7408**
Japanese Journal of Psychonomic Science *see* Kiso Shinrigaku Kenkyu **7382**
Japanese Journal of Psychopathology *see* Rinsho Seishin Byori **7405**
Japanese Journal of Psychopharmacology *see* Nihon Shinkei Seishin Yakurigaku Zasshi **6170**
Japanese Journal of Psychosomatic Medicine *see* Shinshin Igaku **6185**
Japanese Journal of Psychotherapy *see* Seishin Ryoho **6184**
Japanese Journal of Public Health *see* Nihon Koshu Eisei Zasshi **7533**
Japanese Journal of Radiation Safety Management *see* Nihon Houshasen Anzen Kanri Gakkaishi **7069**
Japanese Journal of Radiological Technology *see* Nippon Hoshasen Gijutsu Gakkai Zasshi **7069**
• ➤ Japanese Journal of Radiology (JPN ISSN 1867-1071) **6199**
Japanese Journal of Rehabilitation Medicine *see* Rihabiriteshon Igaku **6116**
• ➤ Japanese Journal of Religious Studies (JPN ISSN 0304-1042) **7737**
Japanese Journal of Rheumatism and Joint Surgery *see* Nihon Ryumachi Kansetsu Geka Gakkai Zasshi **6225**
Japanese Journal of Rural Economics (JPN) **125**
Japanese Journal of Sanitary Zoology *see* Eisei Dobutsu **941**
Japanese Journal of School Health *see* Gakkou Hoken Kenkyuu **7518**
Japanese Journal of Sexology *see* Nihon Sei Kagakkai Zasshi **5687**

Japanese Journal of Social Psychology *see* Shakai Shinrigaku Kenkyu **7408**
The Japanese Journal of Social Security Policy (JPN ISSN 1348-7183) **4510**
Japanese Journal of Soil Science and Plant Nutrition *see* Nippon Dojo Hiryogaku Zasshi **243**
Japanese Journal of Special Education *see* Tokushu Kyokugaku Kenkyu **3048**
Japanese Journal of Stroke *see* Nosotchu **6171**
Japanese Journal of Surgical Metabolism and Nutrition *see* Geka to Taisha Eiyo **6244**
Japanese Journal of Swine Science *see* Nihon Yoton Gakkaishi **295**
Japanese Journal of Systematic Entomology/Shikoku Konchu Gakkai Kaiho (JPN ISSN 1341-1160) **851**
Japanese Journal of Taste and Smell Research *see* Nihon Aji to Nioi Gakkaishi **926**
Japanese Journal of the History of Biology *see* Seibutsugakushi Kenkyu **703**
Japanese Journal of Therapeutic Drug Monitoring *see* T D M Kenkyu **6882**
The Japanese Journal of Thoracic and Cardiovascular Surgery *see* General Thoracic and Cardiovascular Surgery **6244**
Japanese Journal of Thoracic Surgery *see* Kyobu Geka **6251**
Japanese Journal of Tissue Culture Society for Dental Research *see* Koukou Soshiki Baiyou Gakkaishi **5659**
Japanese Journal of Tomography *see* Danso Eizo Kenkyukai Zasshi **6195**
Japanese Journal of Total Care *see* Gekkan Sogo Kea **5618**
Japanese Journal of Toxicology *see* Chudoku Kenkyu **3495**
Japanese Journal of Traffic Psychology *see* Kotsu Shinrigaku Kenkyu **8632**
Japanese Journal of Transfusion Medicine *see* Nippon Yuketsu Gakkai Zasshi **5940**
Japanese Journal of Transplantation *see* Nihon Ishoku Gakkai Zasshi **6253**
• ➤ Japanese Journal of Tribology (USA ISSN 1045-7828) **3384**
Japanese Journal of Tropical Agriculture *see* Nettai Nogyo **139**
Japanese Journal of Urological Surgery *see* Hinyoki Geka **6268**
The Japanese Journal of Urology *see* Nihon Hinyokika Gakkai Zasshi **6272**
Japanese Journal of Vascular Surgery *see* Nihon Kekkan Geka Gakkai Zasshi **6253**
Japanese Journal of Veterinary Anesthesia & Surgery *see* Jui Masui Gekagaku Zasshi **8802**
Japanese Journal of Veterinary Dermatology *see* Juui Rinshou Hifuka **8802**
➤ Japanese Journal of Veterinary Research (JPN ISSN 0047-1917) **8800**
Japanese Journal of Visual Science *see* Shikaku no Kagaku **6051**
Japanese Journal of Water Treatment Biology *see* Nihon Mizushori Seibutsu Gakkaishi **3509**
Japanese Journal of Zoo and Wildlife Medicine/Nihon Yasei Dobutsu Igakukaishi (JPN ISSN 1342-6133) **8800**
• ➤ Japanese Language and Literature (USA ISSN 1536-7827) **5131**
Japanese Lifestyle/U S A *see* LifeStyle - U S A **5075**
Japanese Literature *see* Nihon Bungaku **5341**
Japanese Literature Today (JPN ISSN 0385-1044) **5313**
Japanese Magazine of Mineralogical and Petrological Sciences *see* Ganseki Kobutsu Kagaku **2735**
Japanese Medical Industry Directory *see* Iryo Kiki Gyosha Nenkan **2009**
Japanese Medical Researchers Directory *see* Igaku Kenkyusha Meibo **5632**
Japanese Medical Society for Biological Interface. Journal *see* Nihon Kaimen Igakkai Zasshi **5823**
Japanese Midwives' Association. Journal *see* Josanshi **5994**
Japanese Military Aircraft Serials (JPN) **6455**
Japanese National Bibliography Weekly List *see* Nihon Zenkoku Shoshi **632**
Japanese Neurochemical Society. Bulletin *see* Shinkei Kagaku **6185**
† Japanese New Materials Yearbook (GBR ISSN 0954-3503) **8967**
Japanese Nursing Association Research Report (JPN ISSN 0911-0844) **5963**
Japanese Ophthalmological Society. Journal *see* Nippon Ganka Gakkai Zasshi **6046**
Japanese Organization for International Cooperation in Family Planning Inc. News *see* J O I C F P News **972**
Japanese Orthodontic Society. Annual Meeting (JPN) **5850**
Japanese Orthodontic Society. Journal *see* Orthodontic Waves **5860**
Japanese Orthopaedic Association. Journal *see* Nippon Seikei Geka Gakkai Zasshi **6068**
Japanese Orthoptic Journal *see* Nihon Shino Kunrenshi Kyokaishi **6046**
Japanese Paediatric Orthopaedic Association. Journal *see* Nihon Shoni Seikei Geka Gakkai Zasshi **6097**
Japanese Patent Office. Annual Report (JPN) **6753**
Japanese Patent Office Society. Journal *see* Tokugikon **6758**
Japanese Performance (GBR ISSN 1467-7792) **8587**
Japanese Periodical Index on CD *see* Kokuritsu Kokkai toshokan Zasshi Kiji Sakuin CD-ROM Karento-Ban **4485**
Japanese Pharmacology and Therapeutics *see* Yakuri to Chiryo **6886**
• The Japanese Pharmacopoeia (JPN) **6851**
The Japanese Pharmacopoeia. Supplement I *see* The Japanese Pharmacopoeia **6851**
The Japanese Pharmacopoeia. Supplement II *see* The Japanese Pharmacopoeia **6851**
Japanese Pharmacopoeial Forum *see* Nihon Yakkyokuho Foramu **6864**
Japanese Philately (USA ISSN 0146-0994) **6896**
• Japanese Physical Therapy Association. Journal (JPN ISSN 1344-1272) **6110**
The Japanese Press (Year) (JPN) **4577**
Japanese Progress in Climatology/Nippon no Kikogaku no Shinpo (JPN ISSN 0075-3467) **6358**
• ➤ Japanese Psychological Research (AUS ISSN 0021-5368) **7367**
Japanese Psychological Review *see* Shinrigaku Hyoron **7408**
Japanese Puzzles *see* Hanjie **8176**
Japanese Railway Engineering (JPN ISSN 0448-8938) **8619**
Japanese Religions (JPN ISSN 0448-8954) **7652**
Japanese Research in Business History (JPN ISSN 1349-807X) **1131**
Japanese Respiratory Society. Journal *see* Nihon Kokyuki Gakkai Zasshi **6217**
Japanese Review of Clinical Ophthalmology *see* Ganka Rinsho Iho **6042**
Japanese Scientific Monthly *see* Gakujutsu Geppo **7857**
Japanese Slavic & East European Studies (JPN ISSN 0389-1186) **7247**
Japanese Society for Animal Nutrition and Metabolism. Proceedings *see* Eiyo Seiri Kenkyukaiho **286**
Japanese Society for Artificial Intelligence. Journal *see* Jinko Chino Gakkaishi **2452**
Japanese Society for Artificial Intelligence. Transactions *see* Jinkou Chinou Gakkai Rombunshi **2452**
Japanese Society for Biomaterials. Journal *see* Baiomateriaru **655**
Japanese Society for Cataract Research. Journal *see* Nihon Hakunaisho Gakkaishi **6046**
Japanese Society for Clinical Biomechanics and Related Research. Proceedings of Annual Meeting *see* Nihon Rinsho Baiomekanikusu Gakkaishi **6067**
Japanese Society for Dental Materials and Devices. Journal *see* Shika Zairyo, Kikai **5865**
Japanese Society for Food Science and Technology. Journal *see* Nippon Shokuhin Kagaku Kogaku Kaishi **3658**
• ➤ Japanese Society for Horticultural Science. Journal (JPN ISSN 1882-3351) **3739**
• Japanese Society for Immunology. Newsletter (JPN) **5761**
➤ Japanese Society for Low-Vision Research and Rehabilitation. Journal (JPN) **6044**
Japanese Society for Lumbar Spine Disorders. Journal *see* Nihon Yotsu Gakkai Zasshi **6068**
Japanese Society for Magnesium Research. Journal *see* Maguneshumu **5897**
Japanese Society for Non-Destructive Inspection. Journal *see* Hi-hakai Kensa **3345**
Japanese Society for Ocular Pharmacology. Program and Abstracts of the Meeting *see* Nihon Gan Yakuri Gakkai Puroguramu Koen Yoshishu **5749**
Japanese Society for Parenteral and Enteral Nutrition. Journal *see* Jomyaku, Keicho Eiyo **6661**
Japanese Society for Plant Cell and Molecular Biology. Abstracts of the Meeting and Symposium *see* Shokubutsu Soshiki Saibou Bunshiseibutsu Gakkai Taikai Shinpojumu Koen Yoshishu **720**
Japanese Society for Plant Cell and Molecular Biology. Culture Colloquium *see* Nihon Shokubutsu Saibou Bunshiseibutu Gakkai Korokiamu **805**
Japanese Society for Public Administration. Annals *see* Nippon Gyosei Kenkyu Nenpo **7457**
Japanese Society for Skeletal Dysplasias. Proceedings of the Meeting *see* Kotsu Keito Shikkan Kenkyukai Shoroku **6066**
Japanese Society for Strength and Fracture of Materials. Journal *see* Nippon Zairyo Kyodo Gakkaishi **3355**
Japanese Society for Study of Bone and Joint Infections. Journal *see* Nihon Kotsu, Kansetsu Kansenshou Gakkai Zasshi **6067**
Japanese Society for Surgery of the Hand. Journal *see* Nihon Te no Geka Gakkai Zasshi **6068**
Japanese Society for Systematic Parasitology. Circular *see* Kiseichu Bunrui Keitai Danwakai Kaiho **5821**
Japanese Society for the History of Chemistry. Journal *see* Kagakushu Kenkyu (Tokyo, 1974) **2069**
• ➤ Japanese Society for Therapeutic Radiation and Oncology. Journal (JPN ISSN 1040-9564) **6199**
Japanese Society for Therapeutic Radiology and Oncology Newsletter *see* J A S T R O Newsletter **6199**
Japanese Society for Tissue Engineering. Annual Meeting *see* Nihon Soshiki Kogakkai Puroguramu Shorokushu **717**
Japanese Society for Vascular Surgery. Official Journal *see* Nihon Kekkan Geka Gakkai Zasshi **6253**
Japanese Society of Acupuncture. Journal *see* Keiraku Chiryo **312**
Japanese Society of Agricultural Machinery. Journal *see* Nogyo Kikai Gakkaishi **213**
Japanese Society of Animal Science. Annual Meeting (JPN) **949**
Japanese Society of Applied Entomology and Zoology. Chugoku Branch. Journal *see* Nihon Oyo Dobutsu Konchu Gakkai Chugoku Shibu Kaiho **856**
Japanese Society of Biorheology. Abstracts of the Annual Meeting *see* Nihon Baioreoroji Gakkai Nenkai Shorokushu **717**
Japanese Society of Bone Morphometry. Journal *see* Nihon Kotsu Keitai Keisoku Gakkai Zasshi **6067**
Japanese Society of Clinical Nutrition. Journal *see* Nihon Rinsho Eiyo Gakkai Zasshi **6664**
Japanese Society of Coleopterology. Special Bulletin/Nihon Shoshimoku Gakkai Tokubetsu Hokoku (JPN ISSN 1341-1128) **851**
➤ Japanese Society of Computational Statistics. Journal (JPN ISSN 0915-2350) **8382**
Japanese Society of Developmental Biologists. Proceedings of Annual Meeting/Nihon Hassei Seibutsu Gakkai Taikai Happyo Yoshishu (JPN) **680**
Japanese Society of Dialysis Therapy. Journal *see* Nihon Toseki Igakkai Zasshi **6273**
Japanese Society of Fisheries Oceanography. Bulletin *see* Suisan Kaiyo Kenkyu **3609**
Japanese Society of Gastric Secretion Research. Proceedings *see* I-bunpi Kenkyukaishi **5894**
Japanese Society of Hospital Pharmacists. Journal *see* Nihon Byoin Yakuzaishikai Zasshi **6864**
Japanese Society of Industrial and Technology Education. Journal (JPN) **3066**
Japanese Society of Internal Medicine. Journal *see* Nihon Naika Gakkai Zasshi **5948**
Japanese Society of Irrigation, Drainage and Reclamation Engineering. Transactions *see* Nogyo Doboku Gakkai Rombunshu **141**
Japanese Society of Irrigation, Drainage and Rural Engineering. Journal *see* Suido no Chi **159**
Japanese Society of Limnology. Abstracts of Meeting *see* Nihon Rikusui Gakkai Koen Yoshishu **2720**
Japanese Society of Lymphoreticular Tissue Research. Journal *see* Nihon Rimpa Monaikei Gakkai Kaishi **5687**
Japanese Society of Mechanical Engineers. Bioengineering Division Conference. Proceedings *see* Baioenjiniaringu Kouenkai Kouen Ronbunshuu **747**
Japanese Society of Microbial Ecology. Bulletin *see* Microbes and Environments **891**
Japanese Society of Nursing. Journal *see* Nihon Kango Gakkaishi **5971**
Japanese Society of Nutrition and Food Science. Journal *see* Nippon Eiyo Shokuryo Gakkaishi **6664**
Japanese Society of Ophthalmic Surgeons. Journal *see* Kikan Ganka Shujutsu **6045**
Japanese Society of Orthopedic Ultrasonics. Journal *see* Nihon Seikei Geka Choonpa Kenkyukai Kaishi **6067**
Japanese Society of Orthoptera. Bulletin *see* Battarigisu **840**
Japanese Society of Pathology. Proceedings *see* Nihon Byori Gakkai Kaishi **5686**
Japanese Society of Pediatric Radiology. Journal *see* Nihon Shoni Hoshasen Gakkai Zasshi **6204**
Japanese Society of Pediatric Surgeons. Journal *see* Nihon Shoni Geka Gakkai Zasshi **6097**
Japanese Society of People - Plant Relationships. Journal *see* Ningen Shokubutsu Kankei Gakkai Zasshi **805**
Japanese Society of Periodontology. Journal *see* Nihon Shishubyo Gakkai Kaishi **5857**
Japanese Society of Plant Physiologists. News/Nihon Shokubutsu Seiri Gakkai Tsushin (JPN) **795**
Japanese Society of Plant Physiologists Newsletter *see* J S P P Newsletter **795**
Japanese Society of Plant Physiologists. Proceedings of the Annual Meeting and Symposium *see* Nihon Shokubutsu Seiri Gakkai Nenkai Oyobi Shinpojumu Koeu Yoshishu **805**
Japanese Society of Prosthetics and Orthotics. Bulletin *see* Nihon Gishi Sogu Gakkaishi **5686**
Japanese Society of Reconstructive Microsurgery. Journal *see* Nihon Maikuro Sajari Gakkai Kaishi **6253**
Japanese Society of Revegetation Technology. Journal *see* Nihon Ryokka Kogakkaishi **140**
Japanese Society of Rheumatism and Joint Surgery. Congress *see* Nihon Ryumachi Kansetsu Geka Gekkai **6225**
Japanese Society of Scientific Fisheries. Bulletin *see* Nippon Suisan Gakkaishi **3603**
Japanese Society of Sexual Science News *see* Nihon Seikagaku Gakkai Nyusu **5687**
Japanese Society of Snow and Ice. Hokushin'etsu Branch. Journal *see* Seppyo Hokushin'etsu **6395**
Japanese Society of Snow and Ice. Hokushin'etsu Branch. Newsletter *see* Nyuzu Reta Seppyo Hokushin'etsu **6392**
Japanese Society of Snow and Ice. Journal *see* Seppyo **2716**
Japanese Society of Soil Mechanics and Foundation Engineering. Hokkaido Branch. Research Report *see* Doshitsu Kogakkai. Hokkaido Shibu. Gijutsu Hokokushu **3265**
Japanese Society of Steel Construction Bulletin *see* J S S C Bulletin **1017**
Japanese Society of Steel Construction Journal of Constructional Steel *see* J S S C Journal of Constructional Steel **1017**
Japanese Society of Steel Construction Tekunikaru Repoto *see* J S S C Tekunikaru Repoto **1017**
➤ Japanese Society of Sugar Beet Technologists. Proceedings (JPN) **238**
Japanese Society of Tribologists. Conference Proceedings *see* Toraiboroji Kaigi Yokoshu **3397**
Japanese Society of Tribologists. Journal *see* Toraiborojisuto **3397**
Japanese Society on Thrombosis and Hemostasis. Journal *see* Nihon Kessen Shiketsu Gakkaishi **5940**
Japanese Sociological Review/Shakaigaku Hyoron (JPN ISSN 0021-5414) **8111**
Japanese Stomatological Society. Journal *see* Nihon Kokuka Gakkai Zasshi **5857**
• ➤ Japanese Studies (AUS ISSN 1037-1397) **8111**
Japanese Studies *see* Riben Xuekan **1515**
Japanese Studies Forum *see* Ribenxue Luntan **7998**
Japanese Studies in German Language and Literature/Japanische Studien zur Deutschen Sprache und Literatur (CHE ISSN 0721-3719) **5313**
Japanese Study Group for the W C I P and W C A P Newsletter *see* Kiko Eikyo Riyo Kenkyukai Kaiho **6359**
Japanese Sword Society of the U S Bulletin (USA ISSN 1043-1640) **366**
Japanese Sword Society of the U S Newsletter (USA) **366**
Japanese Symposium on Plasma Chemistry. Abstract Papers/Purazuma Kagaku Godo Shinpojumu Abusutorak Utoshu (JPN ISSN 0915-0447) **2094**
Japanese Symposium on Plasma Chemistry. News/Purazuma Kagaku Godo Shinpojumu (JPN ISSN 0914-6415) **2066**
Japanese Telephone Directory and Guide of Southern California (USA) **2010**
Japanese Tissue Culture Association. News *see* Nihon Soshiki Baiyo Gakkai Kaiin Tsushin **835**
▼ Japanese Visual Culture (NLD) **552**
Japanese Yearbook on Business History *see* Japanese Research in Business History **1131**
Japanische Fachtexte (DEU ISSN 0934-9995) **552**
Japanische Studien zur Deutschen Sprache und Literatur *see* Japanese Studies in German Language and Literature **5313**
Japan's and I C H Guidelines for New Drug Registration (Year) (JPN) **6851**
Japan's Construction Today (JPN) **1017**
• Japanscan. Food Industry Bulletin (GBR ISSN 1755-5574) **3649**
Japanscan Food Industry Bulletin *see* Japanscan. Food Industry Bulletin **3649**
Japanstudien (DEU ISSN 0938-6491) **5131**
Japanu Miklas (LVA) **8182**
Japonica Humboldtiana (DEU ISSN 1433-3473) **552**
Japonica Neerlandica (NLD) **553**
J'Apprends a Dessiner (FRA ISSN 1257-9629) **2195**
J'Apprends l'Anglais (FRA ISSN 1950-3938) **2195**
Jara y Sedal (ESP) **8320**
El Jarchisi (KGZ) **3904**
Jardim Botanico do Rio de Janeiro. Arquivos (BRA ISSN 0103-2550) **795**
El Jardin (ARG ISSN 0329-322X) **3739**
Jardin Botanico de Cordoba. Monografias (ESP ISSN 1135-366X) **795**
• ➤ Jardin Botanico de Madrid. Anales (ESP ISSN 0211-1322) **796**
Jardin Botanico Nacional "Dr. Rafael M. Moscoso." Boletin (DOM ISSN 0254-6434) **796**
• Jardin Botanico Nacional. Revista (CUB ISSN 0253-5696) **796**
Jardin Botanique de Montreal. Legumes: Resultats des Cultures d'Essai (CAN) **3739**
• Le Jardin de Rachel (CAN ISSN 1712-5839) **2195**
El Jardin en la Argentina *see* El Jardin **3739**
Jardin Facile *see* Burda Jardin Facile **3726**
Jardin Familial *see* Gartenfreund **3733**
Jardin Familial (CHE) **3739**
Jardin Magazine (Paris, 2003) (FRA ISSN 1632-4161) **3739**
Jardin Romand (CHE ISSN 1423-5633) **3739**
† Jardinal (ESP) **8967**
Jardineries Vegetal (FRA ISSN 0151-4695) **3739**
Jardineros (ESP ISSN 1575-2232) **3739**
Le Jardinier d'Interieur *see* The Indoor Gardener Magazine **3738**
Jardins de France (FRA ISSN 0021-5481) **3739**
Les Jardins d'Eden/De Tuinen van Eden (BEL) **796**
Jardins Defis (FRA ISSN 1951-7793) **3739**
Jardins et Loisirs (BEL ISSN 1370-9968) **3739**
Jargalan/Happiness (MNG) **4361**
Jarida la Afya Morogoro (TZA ISSN 0856-9517) **7528**
Al-Jaridah ar-Rasmiyyah li-Dawlat al-Imarat al-Arabiyyah al-Muttahidah/United Arab Emirates. Official Gazette (UAE) **7447**
Jarlibro (NLD ISSN 0075-3491) **5131**

Title

Title

• Jiangsu Gongye Xueyuan Xuebao (Shehui Kexue Ban)/Jiangsu Polytechnic University. Journal (Social Sciences Edition) (CHN) **7977**
Jiangsu Health Care Management *see* Jiangsu Weisheng Shiye Guanli **6990**
Jiangsu Higher Education *see* Jiangsu Gaojiao **2988**
Jiangsu Huakan/Jiangsu Art Monthly Pictorial (CHN ISSN 1005-6890) **498**
Jiangsu Hygienic Undertakings and Management *see* Jiangsu Weisheng Shiye Guanli **6990**
Jiangsu Institute of Socialism. Journal *see* Jiangsu Sheng Shehui Zhuyi Xueyuan Xuebao **7977**
• Jiangsu Jishu Shifan Xueyuan Xuebao/Jiangsu Teachers University of Technology. Journal (CHN ISSN 1672-7401) **7977**
Jiangsu Jishu Shifan Xueyuan Xuebao (Ziran Kexue Ban)/Jiangsu Teachers University of Technology. Journal (Natural Science Edition) (CHN ISSN 1674-2222) **7870**
Jiangsu Journal of Agricultural Sciences *see* Jiangsu Nongye Xuebao **125**
Jiangsu Journal of Preventive Medicine *see* Jiangsu Yufang Yixue **5644**
† • Jiangsu Keji Chengguo Tongbao (CHN ISSN 1001-3687) **8968**
• Jiangsu Keji Daxue Xuebao (Shehui Kexue Ban)/Jiangsu University of Science and Technology. Journal (Social Science) (CHN ISSN 1673-0453) **7977**
• Jiangsu Keji Daxue Xuebao (Ziran Kexue Ban)/Jiangsu University of Science and Technology. Journal (Natural Science) (CHN ISSN 1673-4807) **7870**
• Jiangsu Keji Xinxi/Jiangsu Science & Technology Information (CHN ISSN 1004-7530) **8428**
Jiangsu Library Journal *see* Jiangsu Tushuguan Xuebao **5019**
Jiangsu Ligong Daxue Xuebao (Shehui Kexue Ban)/of Jiangsu University of Science and Technology. Journal (Social Sciences Edition) *see* Jiangsu Daxue Xuebao (Shehui Kexue Ban) **7976**
Jiangsu Ligong Daxue Xuebao (Ziran Kexue Ban)/of Jiangsu University of Science and Technology. Journal (Nature Science Edition) *see* Jiangsu Daxue Xuebao (Ziran Kexue Ban) **7870**
Jiangsu Linchuang Yixue Zazhi/Journal of Jiangsu Clinical Medicine *see* Shiyong Linchuang Yiyao Zazhi **5714**
• ➤ Jiangsu Linye Keji/Journal of Jisangsu Forestry Science & Technology (CHN ISSN 1001-7380) **3694**
Jiangsu Medical Journal *see* Jiangsu Yiyao **5643**
Jiangsu Music *see* Jiangsu Yinyue **6580**
• Jiangsu Nongye Kexue/Jiangsu Agricultural Sciences (CHN ISSN 1002-1302) **125**
• ➤ Jiangsu Nongye Xuebao/Jiangsu Journal of Agricultural Sciences (CHN ISSN 1000-4440) **125**
Jiangsu Nongye Yanjiu/Jiangsu Agricultural Research *see* Yangzhou Daxue Xuebao (Nongye yu Shengming Kexue Ban) **171**
Jiangsu Polytechnic University. Journal *see* Jiangsu Gongye Xueyuan Xuebao **6775**
Jiangsu Polytechnic University. Journal (Social Sciences Edition) *see* Jiangsu Gongye Xueyuan Xuebao (Shehui Kexue Ban) **7977**
Jiangsu Science & Technology Information *see* Jiangsu Keji Xinxi **8428**
• Jiangsu Sheng Shehui Zhuyi Xueyuan Xuebao/Jiangsu Institute of Socialism. Journal (CHN ISSN 1672-3163) **7977**
Jiangsu Ship *see* Jiangsu Chuanbo **8648**
Jiangsu Shiyou Huagong Xueyuan Xuebao/Jiangsu Institute of Petrochemical Technology. Journal *see* Jiangsu Gongye Xueyuan Xuebao **6775**
Jiangsu Teachers University of Technology. Journal *see* Jiangsu Jishu Shifan Xueyuan Xuebao **7977**
Jiangsu Teachers University of Technology. Journal (Natural Science Edition) *see* Jiangsu Jishu Shifan Xueyuan Xuebao (Ziran Kexue Ban) **7870**
Jiangsu Traditional Chinese Medicine *see* Jiangsu Zhongyiyao **311**
• Jiangsu Tushuguan Xuebao/Jiangsu Library Journal (CHN ISSN 1001-9618) **5019**
Jiangsu University. Journal (Higher Education Study Edition) *see* Jiangsu Daxue Xuebao (Gao-jiao Ban) **2988**
Jiangsu University. Journal (Medical Edition) *see* Jiangsu Daxue Xuebao (Yixue Ban) **5643**
Jiangsu University. Journal (Nature Science Edition) *see* Jiangsu Daxue Xuebao (Ziran Kexue Ban) **7870**
Jiangsu University. Journal (Social Science Edition) *see* Jiangsu Daxue Xuebao (Shehui Kexue Ban) **7976**
Jiangsu University of Science and Technology. Journal (Natural Science) *see* Jiangsu Keji Daxue Xuebao (Ziran Kexue Ban) **7870**
Jiangsu University of Science and Technology. Journal (Social Science) *see* Jiangsu Keji Daxue Xuebao (Shehui Kexue Ban) **7977**
• Jiangsu Weisheng Shiye Guanli/Jiangsu Health Care Management (CHN ISSN 1005-7803) **6990**
• Jiangsu Xingzheng Xueyuan Xuebao/Journal of Jiangsu Administration Institute (CHN ISSN 1009-8860) **7977**
Jiangsu Yinyue/Jiangsu Music (CHN) **6580**
• Jiangsu Yiyao/Jiangsu Medical Journal (CHN ISSN 0253-3685) **5643**
• Jiangsu Yufang Yixue/Jiangsu Journal of Preventive Medicine (CHN ISSN 1006-9070) **5644**
• Jiangsu Zhongyiyao/Jiangsu Traditional Chinese Medicine (CHN ISSN 1672-397X) **311**
Jiangxi Agricultural University. Journal (Social Sciences Edition) *see* Jiangxi Nongye Daxue Xuebao (Shehui Kexue Ban) **7977**
• Jiangxi Cai-Jing Daxue Xuebao/Jiangxi University of Finance and Economics. Journal (CHN ISSN 1008-2972) **1131**
Jiangxi Chengshi Jinrong/Jiangxi Urban Finance (CHN) **1359**
Jiangxi Communication Science & Technology *see* Jiangxi Tongxin Keji **2328**
Jiangxi Daily *see* Jiangxi Ribao **3825**
• Jiangxi Dizhi/Jiangxi Geology (CHN ISSN 1001-7356) **2749**
Jiangxi Food Industry *see* Jiangxi Shipin Gongye **3649**
Jiangxi Geology *see* Jiangxi Dizhi **2749**
Jiangxi Huabao/Jiangxi Pictorial (CHN ISSN 1006-7221) **3825**
Jiangxi Institute of Education. Journal *see* Jiangxi Jiaoyu Xueyuan Xuebao **2872**
• Jiangxi Jiaoyu Xueyuan Xuebao/Jiangxi Institute of Education. Journal (CHN ISSN 1005-3638) **2872**
Jiangxi Journal of Traditional Chinese Medicine *see* Jiangxi Zhongyiyao **5644**
• ➤ Jiangxi Kexue/Jiangxi Science (CHN ISSN 1001-3679) **7870**
Jiangxi Library Journal *see* Jiangxi Tushuguan Xuekan **5019**
• Jiangxi Ligong Daxue Xuebao/Jiangxi University of Science and Technology. Journal (CHN) **6318**
Jiangxi Medical Journal *see* Jiangxi Yiyao **5644**
• Jiangxi Nongye Daxue Xuebao/Acta Agriculturae Universitatis Jiangxiensis (Natural Sciences Edition) (CHN ISSN 1000-2286) **7870**
• Jiangxi Nongye Daxue Xuebao (Shehui Kexue Ban)/Jiangxi Agricultural University. Journal (Social Sciences Edition) (CHN ISSN 1671-6523) **7977**
• Jiangxi Nongye Xuebao/Acta Agriculturae Jiangxi (CHN ISSN 1001-8581) **125**
Jiangxi Normal University. Journal (Natural Science Edition) *see* Jiangxi Shifan Daxue Xuebao (Ziran Kexue Ban) **7870**
Jiangxi Normal University. Journal (Philosophy and Social Sciences Edition) *see* Jiangxi Shifan Daxue Xuebao (Zhexue Shehui Kexue Ban) **7977**
Jiangxi Pictorial *see* Jiangxi Huabao **3825**
Jiangxi Ribao/Jiangxi Daily (CHN) **3825**
Jiangxi Science *see* Jiangxi Kexue **7870**
• Jiangxi Shehui Kexue/Jiangxi Social Sciences (CHN ISSN 1004-518X) **7977**
• Jiangxi Shifan Daxue Xuebao (Zhexue Shehui Kexue Ban)/Jiangxi Normal University. Journal (Philosophy and Social Sciences Edition) (CHN ISSN 1000-579X) **7977**
• Jiangxi Shifan Daxue Xuebao (Ziran Kexue Ban)/Jiangxi Normal University. Journal (Natural Science Edition) (CHN ISSN 1000-5862) **7870**
• Jiangxi Shipin Gongye/Jiangxi Food Industry (CHN ISSN 1674-2435) **3649**
Jiangxi Social Sciences *see* Jiangxi Shehui Kexue **7977**
• Jiangxi Tongxin Keji/Jiangxi Communication Science & Technology (CHN ISSN 1009-0940) **2328**
Jiangxi Tushuguan Xuekan/Jiangxi Library Journal (CHN ISSN 1003-725X) **5019**
Jiangxi University of Finance and Economics. Journal *see* Jiangxi Cai-Jing Daxue Xuebao **1131**
Jiangxi University of Science and Technology. Journal *see* Jiangxi Ligong Daxue Xuebao **6318**
Jiangxi Urban Finance *see* Jiangxi Chengshi Jinrong **1359**
• Jiangxi Yixueyuan Xuebao/Acta Academiae Medicinae Jiangxi (CHN ISSN 1000-2294) **5644**
• Jiangxi Yiyao/Jiangxi Medical Journal (CHN ISSN 1006-2238) **5644**
• Jiangxi Zhongyiyao/Jiangxi Journal of Traditional Chinese Medicine (CHN ISSN 0411-9584) **5644**
Jiangyin Ribao (CHN) **3825**
Jianhong Zhengquan Touzi Yoekan/National Securities Investment Monthly *see* Yongfeng Touzi Yuekan **1660**
Jianhua Touzi Yuekan/SinoPac Monthly *see* Yongfeng Touzi Yuekan **1660**
• Jiankang/Health Magazine (CHN ISSN 1002-297X) **6990**
Jiankang Bao/Health Newspaper (CHN) **6990**
Jiankang Bolan/Health Review (CHN ISSN 1006-415X) **6990**
Jiankang Guwen/A Guide to Good Health *see* Xinli Yuekan **7415**
Jiankang Nuhai/Sunshine Girl (CHN ISSN 1009-9409) **6990**
• Jiankang Rensheng/Health Life (CHN ISSN 1671-0061) **7286**
Jiankang Shaonian Huabao/Healthy Children's Pictorial (CHN ISSN 1002-3089) **6990**
Jiankang Shijie/Health World (CHN ISSN 1005-4596) **6990**
Jiankang Tiandi/Health World (CHN ISSN 1002-431X) **6990**
Jiankang Wenzhai Bao/Digest of Health Newspaper (CHN) **7528**
Jiankang Xinlixue/Health Psychology Journal *see* Jiankang Xinlixue Zazhi **7367**
• Jiankang Xinlixue Zazhi/Health Psychology Journal (CHN) **7367**
• Jiankang zhi You/Women's Day (CHN ISSN 1002-8714) **8869**
Jiankang Zhinan (Zhong Lao Nan)/Guide to Health (CHN ISSN 1002-7270) **6990**
Jianmei Nuxing *see* Jiaren **8869**
• Jiansu Dizhi/Jiansu Geology (CHN ISSN 1003-6474) **2749**
Jiansu Geology *see* Jiansu Dizhi **2749**
• ➤ Jianyan Yixue yu Linchuang/Laboratory Medicine and Clinic (CHN ISSN 1672-9455) **5906**
• Jianzhu/Construction & Architecture (CHN ISSN 0577-7429) **446**
Jianzhu (Hong Kong) *see* B J. Building Journal **978**
• Jianzhu Anquan/Construction Safety (CHN ISSN 1004-552X) **1017**
• Jianzhu Cailiao Xuebao/Journal of Building Materials (CHN ISSN 1007-9629) **1017**
• Jianzhu Chuangzuo/Architectural Creation (CHN ISSN 1004-8537) **446**
Jianzhu Gongren/Construction Workers (CHN ISSN 1002-3232) **1017**
• Jianzhu Guanli Xiandaihua/Construction Management Modernization (CHN ISSN 1001-019X) **1017**
• Jianzhu Jiancai Zhuangshi/Building Materials, Architecture and Decoration (CHN ISSN 1674-3024) **1017**
▼ Jianzhu Jiandu Jiance yu Zaojia/Supervision Test and Cost of Construction (CHN ISSN 1674-2133) **1017**
• Jianzhu Jiegou/Building Structure (CHN ISSN 1002-848X) **3273**
• Jianzhu Jiegou Xuebao/Journal of Building Structures (CHN ISSN 1000-6869) **1017**
• Jianzhu Jingji (CHN ISSN 1002-851X) **1131**
• Jianzhu Jishu/Architectural Technology (CHN ISSN 1000-4726) **1017**
• Jianzhu Jishu Ji Sheji/Architecture Technology & Design (CHN ISSN 1006-2661) **446**
Jianzhu Jishu Kaifa/Building Technique Development (CHN ISSN 1001-523X) **1017**
• Jianzhu Jixie/Construction Machinery (CHN ISSN 1001-554X) **5453**
• Jianzhu Kexue/Building Science (CHN ISSN 1002-8528) **3273**
• Jianzhu Kexue yu Gongcheng Xuebao/Journal of Architecture and Civil Engineering (CHN ISSN 1673-2049) **446**
• Jianzhu Sheji Guanli/Architectural Design Management (CHN ISSN 1673-1093) **446**
Jianzhu Xibu/Architecture & Detail (CHN ISSN 1672-4518) **446**
Jianzhu Xuebao/Architectural Journal (CHN ISSN 0529-1399) **447**
• Jianzhu Zhishi/Architectural Knowledge (CHN ISSN 1002-8544) **447**
▼ • Jiaoke Shu Yanjiu/Journal of Textbook Research (TWN ISSN 1999-8856) **2872**
Jiaoshi/Teacher (CHN) **2872**
• Jiaoshi Jiaoyu Yanjiu/Teacher Education Research (CHN ISSN 1672-5905) **2873**
Jiaotong Anquan Zhoukan *see* Renmin Gongan Bao. Jiaotong Anquan Zhoukan **8634**
• Jiaotong Huanbao/Environmental Protection in Transportation (CHN) **3444**
Jiaotong Jianshe yu Guanli/Traffic Construction and Administration (CHN ISSN 1673-8098) **8632**
• Jiaotong Keji yu Jingji/Technology & Economy in Areas of Communications (CHN ISSN 1008-5696) **2328**
Jiaotong Laodong Weisheng Tongxun *see* Tiedao Laodong Anquan Weisheng yu Huan-bao **8626**
• Jiaotong Yunshu Gongcheng Xuebao/Journal of Traffic and Transportation Engineering (CHN ISSN 1671-1637) **3274**
Jiaotong Yunshu Jingji, Youdian Jingji/Economy in Communications and Transportation & in Post and Telecommunication (CHN ISSN 1001-9979) **8500**
• Jiaotong Yunshu Xitong Gongcheng yu Xinxi (CHN ISSN 1009-6744) **8632**
• Jiaotongbu Shanghai Chuanbo Yunshu Kexue Yanjiusuo Xuebao (CHN ISSN 1000-4696) **8648**
Jiaoxiang - Journal of Xi-an Conservatory of Music *see* Jiaoxiang - Xi'an Yinyue Xueyuan Xuebao **6580**
• Jiaoxiang - Xi'an Yinyue Xueyuan Xuebao/Jiaoxiang - Journal of Xi-an Conservatory of Music (CHN ISSN 1003-1499) **6580**
Jiaoxue Yanjiu/Research in Teaching (CHN) **3066**
Jiaoxue yu Keji *see* Shijiazhuang Tiedao Xueyuan Xuebao **8511**
• Jiaoxue yu Yanjiu/Teaching and Research (CHN ISSN 0257-2826) **3066**
▼ Jiaoyu Celiang yu Pingjia/Educational Measurement and Evaluation (CHN ISSN 1674-1536) **2873**
• Jiaoyu Daokan/Journal of Educational Development (CHN ISSN 1005-3476) **2873**
• ➤ Jiaoyu Fazhan Yanjiu/Exploring Education Development (CHN ISSN 1008-3855) **2988**
• Jiaoyu Kexue/Education Science (CHN ISSN 1002-8064) **2873**
• Jiaoyu Kexue Yanjiu/Journal of Educational Science Research (CHN ISSN 1009-718X) **2873**
• Jiaoyu Lilun yu Shijian (CHN ISSN 1004-633X) **2873**
• Jiaoyu Pinglun/Education Review (CHN ISSN 1004-1109) **2873**
Jiaoyu Wenhui (CHN ISSN 1009-8186) **5313**
• Jiaoyu Xinli Xuebao/Bulletin of Educational Psychology (TWN ISSN 1011-5714) **2873**
• Jiaoyu Xuebao/Journal of Educational Studies (CHN ISSN 1673-1298) **2873**
➤ Jiaoyu Xuebao/Education Journal (HKG ISSN 1025-1936) **2873**
• Jiaoyu Xueshu Uuekan/Education Research Monthly (CHN ISSN 1674-2311) **2873**
• ➤ Jiaoyu Yanjiu/Educational Research (CHN ISSN 1002-5731) **2873**
Jiaoyu Yanjiu Xuebao/Journal of Education Studies (TWN ISSN 1990-4428) **2873**
• Jiaoyu yu Shehui Yanjiu/Formosan Education and Society (TWN ISSN 1680-5550) **2873**
• Jiaoyu yu Xiandaihua/Education and Modernization (CHN ISSN 1007-3051) **2873**
• Jiaoyu yu Zhiye/Education and Occupation (CHN ISSN 1004-3985) **2943**
† Jiaoyu Zhanwang/Educational Prospects (CHN ISSN 0254-8682) **8968**
• ➤ Jiaoyu Ziliao yu Tushuguanxue/Journal of Educational Media and Library Sciences (TWN ISSN 1013-090X) **5019**
Jiaoyuxue (CHN ISSN 1001-2869) **3025**
Jiaoyuxue Wenzhai Ka/Pedagogics Abstracts on Cards (CHN) **2934**
• Jiaozuo Shifan Gaodeng Zhuanke Xuexiao Xuebao/Jiaozuo Teachers College. Journal (CHN ISSN 1672-3465) **4458**
Jiaozuo Teachers College. Journal *see* Jiaozuo Shifan Gaodeng Zhuanke Xuexiao Xuebao **4458**
• Jiaren/Marie Claire China (CHN ISSN 1672-4771) **8869**
Jiari/Holiday (NZL) **8725**
Jiari 100 Tian *see* Jiari Yibiatian **5074**
• Jiari Yibiatian/Holiday 100 (CHN) **5074**
• Jiashi Yuan/Driver's World (CHN ISSN 1561-2406) **8587**
Jiating *see* Family **5558**
Jiating Baishitong/Home Journal of Knowledge (CHN ISSN 1008-7532) **4361**
Jiating Baojianbao/Family Health Care Gazette (CHN) **3825**
• Jiating Dianzi/Family Electronics (CHN ISSN 1005-4669) **3106**
Jiating Hushi/Family Nurse (CHN ISSN 1672-1888) **5963**
Jiating Jiaoyu Daobao (CHN) **2873**
Jiating Jiaoyu Daodu/Guide to Family Education (CHN ISSN 1009-7481) **2873**
• Jiating Kexue (CHN) **8428**
• Jiating Shenghuo Bao (CHN) **3825**
Jiating Shenghuo Zhinan/Family Life Guide (CHN ISSN 1003-3335) **4361**
• Jiating Yishengbao/Family's Doctor Weekly (CHN) **5644**
• Jiating Yixue/Family Medicine (CHN ISSN 1001-0203) **5644**
Jiating yu Jiajiao (CHN ISSN 1671-1882) **4361**
Jiating - Yu'er (CHN) **7977**
Jiating Zhiyou/Family (CHN ISSN 1004-8472) **3825**
• Jiating Zhongyiyao/Family Traditional Chinese Medicine (CHN ISSN 1005-3743) **5644**
Jiaxing University. Journal *see* Jiaxing Xueyuan Xuebao **2873**
• Jiaxing Xueyuan Xuebao/Jiaxing University. Journal (CHN ISSN 1671-3079) **2873**
• Jiaying Daxue Xuebao/Jiaying University. Journal (CHN ISSN 1006-642X) **7977**
Jiaying University. Journal *see* Jiaying Daxue Xuebao **7977**
• Jiayong Dianqi/Household Appliance (CHN ISSN 1002-5626) **1890**
Jib (CAN ISSN 1910-2232) **8277**
Jib Gems *see* Jib **8277**
Jiban Kogakkai Ronbun Hokokushu/Japanese Geotechnical Society. Journal (JPN ISSN 1341-7452) **3274**
Jiban Kogaku Kenkyujo Hokoku/Geotechnical Research Institute. Technical Reports (JPN ISSN 0911-0143) **2749**
Jiban Shindo Shinpojumu/Symposium on Ground Vibrations (JPN) **2749**
Jiban Suiri Jikken Shisetsu Nenpo/Hydroscience and Geotechnology Laboratory. Annual Report (JPN ISSN 0385-308X) **3363**
Jiban to Kensetsu/Ground Engineering (JPN ISSN 0289-9418) **3274**
Jibek Jolu (KGZ) **3904**
Jibi Inkoka Rinsho/PracticaOto-Rhino-Laryngologica (JPN ISSN 0032-6313) **6081**
Jibi Inkoka Rinsho. Hosatsu *see* Practica Otologica Kyoto. Supplement **6084**
• Jibi Inkoka Tembo/Otorhinolaryngology Tokyo (JPN ISSN 0386-9687) **6081**
Jibi Inkoka, Tokeibu Geka *see* J O H N S: Journal of Otolaryngology, Head and Neck Surgery **6081**
• Jibi Inkoka, Tokeibu Geka/Otolaryngology - Head and Neck Surgery (JPN ISSN 0914-3491) **6081**
Jibi Inkouka Kyouto Rinshou *see* Jibi Inkoka Rinsho **6081**
• Jibing Jiance/Disease Surveillance (CHN ISSN 1003-9961) **5819**

Jibing Kongzhi Zazhi *see* Zhonghua Jibing Kongzhi Zazhi **5829**
JIBStrategy *see* Journal of International Business Strategy **1574**
Jicarilla Chieftain (USA ISSN 0021-695X) **3543**
Jicheng Dianlu Yingyong/Applications of I C (CHN ISSN 1674-2583) **2466**
• Jichu Yixue yu Linchuang/Basic & Clinical Medicine (CHN ISSN 1001-6325) **5644**
Jichu Zidonghua/Basic Automation *see* Kongzhi Gongcheng **3207**
• Jidi Yanjiu/Chinese Journal of Polar Research (CHN ISSN 1007-7073) **2711**
Jidian Chanpin Shichang/Machinery & Electronics Products Market (CHN ISSN 1672-3260) **5453**
• Jidian Jishu/Mechanical & Electrical Technology (CHN ISSN 1672-4801) **8428**
• Jidian Shebei/Mechanical and Electrical Equipment (CHN ISSN 1005-8354) **5453**
Jidian Xinxi *see* M M Xiandai Zhizao **1897**
Jidianqi/Relay *see* Dianli Xitong Baohu yu Kongzhi **3300**
Jidische Schtudies (DEU ISSN 0720-6666) **5132**
Jido Seinen Seishin Igaku to Sono Kinsetsu Ryoiki *see* Japanese Journal of Child & Adolescent Psychiatry **6149**
Jidosha Gijutsu/Society of Automotive Engineers of Japan. Journal (JPN ISSN 0385-7298) **8587**
Jidosha Gijutsukai Ronbunshu/Society of Automotive Engineers of Japan. Transactions (JPN ISSN 0287-8321) **8587**
Jidosha Hoyu Sharyosu (JPN ISSN 0910-9684) **8382**
Jidosha Kenkyu/Japan Automobile Research Institute. Journal (JPN ISSN 0387-3803) **8587**
Jidosha Kogaku/Automobile Engineering (JPN ISSN 0388-3841) **8587**
Jidosha Shogenhyo/Motor Vehicle Engineering Specifications - Japan (JPN ISSN 0919-1356) **8587**
Jidu Jiaosixiang Pinglun/Regent Review of Christian Thoughts (CAN) **7652**
• Jie Di Xuekan/Aletheia (TWN ISSN 1028-4583) **6927**
Jiefang Ribao/Liberation Daily (CHN) **3825**
Jiefang Ribao Hedingben/Liberation Daily Bound Index (CHN) **3825**
• Jiefangjun Bao/Liberation Army Daily (CHN) **6428**
Jiefangjun Huabao/P L A Pictorial (CHN ISSN 0009-3823) **6428**
• Jiefangjun Huli Zazhi/Nursing Journal of Chinese People's Liberation Army (CHN ISSN 1008-9993) **5963**
• Jiefangjun Jiankang/P L A Health (CHN ISSN 1000-9701) **6990**
• Jiefangjun Ligong Daxue Xuebao (Ziran Kexue Ban)/P L A University of Science and Technology (Natural Science Edition). Journal (CHN ISSN 1009-3443) **7870**
Jiefangjun Lilun Xuexi (CHN ISSN 1673-3347) **7145**
• Jiefangjun Shenghuo/P L A Life (CHN ISSN 1002-4654) **6429**
Jiefangjun Wenyi/Literature and Art of People's Liberation Army (CHN ISSN 0577-7410) **5313**
• Jiefangjun Yaoxue Xuebao/Pharmaceutical Journal of Chinese People's Liberation Army (CHN ISSN 1008-9926) **6851**
Jiefangjun Yixue Gaodeng Zhuanke Xuexiao Xuebao/P L A Junior Colleges of Medicine. Journal *see* Linchuang Junyi Zazhi **6431**
• Jiefangjun Yixue Zazhi/Medical Journal of Chinese People's Liberation Army (CHN ISSN 0577-7402) **5644**
• Jiefangjun Yiyuan Guanli Zazhi/Hospital Administration Journal of Chinese People's Liberation Army (CHN ISSN 1008-9985) **4103**
• Jiefangjun Yufang Yixue Zazhi/Journal of P L A Preventive Medicine (CHN ISSN 1001-5248) **5644**
• Jiegou Gongchengshi/Structural Engineers (CHN ISSN 1005-0159) **3274**
• ➤ Jiegou Huaxue/Chinese Journal of Structural Chemistry (CHN ISSN 0254-5861) **2066**
• Jiejingmei Jishu/Clean Coal Technology (CHN ISSN 1006-6772) **6467**
Jiemian Kexue Huizhi/Chinese Colloid and Interface Society. Journal (TWN ISSN 1026-325X) **3248**
• Jieneng Jishu/Energy Conservation Technology (CHN ISSN 1002-6339) **3140**
• Jieneng yu Huanbao/Energy Conservation and Environment Protection (CHN ISSN 1009-539X) **3140**
Jienisi Xiangqing Zazhi *see* Wink Up **3960**
• Jiepou Kexue Jinzhan/Progress of Anatomical Sciences (CHN ISSN 1006-2947) **923**
• Jiepou Xuebao/Acta Anatomica Sinica (CHN ISSN 0529-1356) **5644**
• Jiepouxue Yanjiu/Anatomy Research (CHN ISSN 1671-0770) **923**
• Jiepouxue Zazhi/Chinese Journal of Anatomy (CHN ISSN 1001-1633) **680**
• Jieru Fangshexue Zazhi/Journal of Interventional Radiology (CHN ISSN 1008-794X) **6200**
• Jieshui Guan'gai/Water Saving Irrigation (CHN ISSN 1007-4929) **8827**
• Jiguang Jishu/Laser Technology (CHN ISSN 1001-3806) **7077**
• Jiguang Shengwu Xuebao/Acta Laser Biology Sinica (CHN ISSN 1007-7146) **734**
• Jiguang yu Hongwai/Laser & Infrared (CHN ISSN 1001-5078) **7077**
• Jiguang Zazhi/Laser Journal (CHN ISSN 0253-2743) **7077**
Jihad (PAK) **3926**
Jihoceske Muzeum v Ceskych Budejovicich. Prirodni Vedy. Sbornik (CZE ISSN 0139-8172) **7870**
Jihocesky Sbornik Historicky (CZE ISSN 0323-004X) **4235**
JiiPee (FIN ISSN 1455-6189) **2195**
Jiji Bulletin *see* Jiji Sokuho **3900**
Jiji Sokuho/Jiji Bulletin (JPN) **3900**
Jijnasa (IND ISSN 0377-743X) **4184**
Jikeikai Medical Journal (JPN ISSN 0021-6968) **5644**
Jiki Kyomei Igakkai Puroguramu/Society of Magnetic Resonance in Medicine. Proceedings of Annual Conference (JPN) **6200**
Jikken Chiryo/Experimental Therapy (JPN ISSN 0910-7967) **5906**
Jikken Igaku/Experimental Medicine (JPN ISSN 0288-5514) **5906**
• Jikken Shakai Shinrigaku Kenkyu/Japanese Journal of Experimental Social Psychology (JPN ISSN 0387-7973) **7367**
Jikoketsu Yuketsu/Japanese Journal of Autologous Blood Transfusion (JPN ISSN 0915-0188) **5791**
• Jiliang Jishu/Measurement Technique (CHN ISSN 1000-0771) **6403**
• Jiliang Xuebao/Acta Metrologica Sinica (CHN ISSN 1000-1158) **6403**
Jilin Architectural and Civil Engineering Institute. Journal *see* Jilin Jianzhu Gongcheng Xueyuan Xuebao **447**
Jilin Daily *see* Jilin Ribao **3825**
Jilin Daxue Shehui Kexue Xuebao/Jilin University Journal (Social Science Edition) (CHN ISSN 0257-2834) **7977**
• Jilin Daxue Xuebao (Diqiu Kexue Ban)/Jilin Univeristy. Journal (Earth Science Edition) (CHN ISSN 1671-5888) **2749**
• Jilin Daxue Xuebao (Gongxue Ban) (CHN ISSN 1671-5497) **3204**
• Jilin Daxue Xuebao (Lixue Ban)/Jilin University. Journal (Science Edition) (CHN ISSN 1671-5489) **7870**
• Jilin Daxue Xuebao (Xinxi Kexue Ban)/Jilin University. Journal (Information Science Edition) (CHN ISSN 1671-5896) **2548**
• Jilin Daxue Xuebao (Yixue Ban)/Jilin University. Journal (Medicine Edition) (CHN ISSN 1671-587X) **5644**
Jilin Daxue Ziran Kexue Xuebao/Jilin University. Journal of Natural Science/Acta Scientiarum Naturalium Universitatis Jilinensis *see* Jilin Daxue Xuebao (Gongxue Ban) **3204**
Jilin Huabao/Jilin Pictorial (CHN) **3825**
• Jilin Jianzhu Gongcheng Xueyuan Xuebao/Jilin Architectural and Civil Engineering Institute. Journal (CHN ISSN 1009-0185) **447**
Jilin Journal of Traditional Chinese Medicine *see* Jilin Zhongyiyao **311**
Jilin Medical College. Journal *see* Jilin Yiyao Xueyuan Xuebao **5644**
Jilin Medical Journal *see* Jilin Yixue **5644**
• Jilin Nongye (CHN ISSN 1674-0432) **125**
• ➤ Jilin Nongye Daxue Xuebao/Jilin University of Agriculture. Journal (CHN ISSN 1000-5684) **125**
Jilin Pictorial *see* Jilin Huabao **3825**
Jilin Province Economic Management Cadre College. Journal *see* Jilin Sheng Jingji Guanli Ganbu Xueyuan Xuebao **1762**
Jilin Ribao/Jilin Daily (CHN) **3825**
Jilin Shanggaozhuan (CHN) **1131**
Jilin Shangye Gaodeng Zhuanke Xuexiao Xuebao/Jilin Commercial College. Journal *see* Jilin Shanggaozhuan **1131**
• Jilin Sheng Jingji Guanli Ganbu Xueyuan Xuebao/Jilin Province Economic Management Cadre College. Journal (CHN ISSN 1009-0657) **1762**
Jilin Teachers College. Journal *see* Beihua Daxue Xuebao (Shehui Kexue Ban) **7949**
Jilin Univeristy. Journal (Earth Science Edition) *see* Jilin Daxue Xuebao (Diqiu Kexue Ban) **2749**
Jilin University. Journal (Engineering and Technology Edition) *see* Jilin Daxue Xuebao (Gongxue Ban) **3204**
Jilin University. Journal (Information Science Edition) *see* Jilin Daxue Xuebao (Xinxi Kexue Ban) **2548**
Jilin University. Journal (Medicine Edition) *see* Jilin Daxue Xuebao (Yixue Ban) **5644**
Jilin University. Journal (Science Edition) *see* Jilin Daxue Xuebao (Lixue Ban) **7870**
Jilin University Journal (Social Science Edition) *see* Jilin Daxue Shehui Kexue Xuebao **7977**
Jilin University of Agriculture. Journal *see* Jilin Nongye Daxue Xuebao **125**
• Jilin Yixue/Jilin Medical Journal (CHN ISSN 1004-0412) **5644**
• Jilin Yiyao Xueyuan Xuebao/Jilin Medical College. Journal (CHN ISSN 1673-2995) **5644**
• Jilin Zhongyiyao/Jilin Journal of Traditional Chinese Medicine (CHN ISSN 1003-5699) **311**
Jill Oxton's Cross Stitch & Beading (AUS) **6639**
• Jim Rennie's Sports Letter (CAN ISSN 0712-2632) **8182**
• Jim Romenesko's Media News (USA) **4577**
Jimbun-Chiri *see* Human Geography **4014**
Jimbun Gakuho/Journal of Social Sciences and Humanities (JPN ISSN 0386-8729) **4458**
Jimbun Ronkyu/Humanities Review (JPN ISSN 0286-6773) **4458**
• Jimei Daxue Xuebao (Jiaoyu Kexue Ban) (CHN ISSN 1671-6493) **2873**
• Jimei Daxue Xuebao (Zhexue Shehui Kexue Ban)/Jimei University. Journal (Philosophy and Social Sciences) (CHN ISSN 1008-889X) **7977**
• Jimei Daxue Xuebao (Ziran Kexue Ban)/Jimei University. Journal (Natural Science) (CHN ISSN 1007-7405) **7871**
Jimei University. Journal (Natural Science) *see* Jimei Daxue Xuebao (Ziran Kexue Ban) **7871**
Jimei University. Journal (Philosophy and Social Sciences) *see* Jimei Daxue Xuebao (Zhexue Shehui Kexue Ban) **7977**
Jin Dun/Golden Shield (CHN) **4699**
Jin Ishoku Kekkan Geka/Renal Transplantation, Vascular Surgery (JPN ISSN 0915-9118) **6247**
Jin to Kotsu Taisha/Kidney and Metabolic Bone Diseases (JPN ISSN 0914-5265) **6270**
Jin to Toseki/Kidney and Dialysis (JPN ISSN 0385-2156) **5644**
Jin Yaoshi/Golden Key (CHN) **5313**
• Ji'nan Daxue Huawen Xueyuan Xuebao/Jinan University. College of Chinese Language and Culture. Journal (CHN ISSN 1671-5306) **4459**
• Ji'nan Daxue Xuebao (Shehui Kexue Ban)/Ji'nan University. Journal (Social Sciences Edition) (CHN ISSN 1671-3842) **7977**
• Ji'nan Daxue Xuebao (Ziran Kexue Ban)/Jinan University. Journal (Science and Technology Edition) (CHN ISSN 1671-3559) **1017**
• Jinan Daxue Xuebao (Ziran Kexue yu Yixue Ban)/Journal of Jinan University (Natural Science and Medicine Edition) (CHN ISSN 1000-9965) **7871**
Jinan University. College of Chinese Language and Culture. Journal *see* Ji'nan Daxue Huawen Xueyuan Xuebao **4459**
Jinan University. Journal (Philosophy & Social Sciences Edition) *see* Jinan Xuebao (Zhexue Shehui Kexue Ban) **6927**
Jinan University. Journal (Science and Technology Edition) *see* Ji'nan Daxue Xuebao (Ziran Kexue Ban) **1017**
Ji'nan University. Journal (Social Sciences Edition) *see* Ji'nan Daxue Xuebao (Shehui Kexue Ban) **7977**
Jinan Vocational College. Journal *see* Ji'nan Zheye Xueyuan Xuebao **6699**
• Jinan Xuebao (Zhexue Shehui Kexue Ban)/Jinan University. Journal (Philosophy & Social Sciences Edition) (CHN ISSN 1000-5072) **6927**
• Ji'nan Zheye Xueyuan Xuebao/Jinan Vocational College. Journal (CHN) **6699**
Jinbun Kagaku Kenkyu/Humanities: Christianity and Culture (JPN ISSN 0073-3938) **4459**
Jinbun Kenkyu *see* Journal of Humanities (Chiba) **4460**
Jinbun Shizen Kagaku Ronshu/Journal of Humanities and Natural Sciences (JPN ISSN 0495-8012) **4459**
• Jinchukou Jingliren/Imp - Exp Executive (CHN ISSN 1673-6532) **1573**
Jindai Zhongguo Funu Shi Yanjiu (TWN ISSN 1029-4759) **4184**
Jindai Zhongguo Shi Yanjiu Tongxun/Newsletter for Modern Chinese History (TWN ISSN 1016-0566) **4184**
• ➤ Jindaishi Yanjiu/Modern Chinese History Studies (CHN ISSN 1001-6708) **4184**
† Jinekoloji ve Obstetrik Bulteni (TUR ISSN 1300-0438) **8968**
Jinekoloji ve Obstetrik Dergisi/Journal of Gynecology and Obstetrics (TUR ISSN 1016-5126) **5994**
Jinfuzen o Ikiru/Dialysis and Transplant (JPN ISSN 0912-0319) **6270**
Jing Bao Journal (USA ISSN 1521-8708) **6429**
Jing Fang/China Police (CHN ISSN 1005-6556) **2656**
Jing Mao Shijie/World of Economy and Trade *see* Shangye Gushi **1173**
• Jin'gangshi yu Moliao Moju Gongcheng/Diamond & Abrasives Engineering (CHN ISSN 1006-852X) **3204**
• Jingcha Jishu/Police Technology (CHN ISSN 1009-9875) **2656**
Jingdezhen Ceramics *see* Jingdezhen Taoci **2043**
Jingdezhen Ceramics Institute. Journal *see* Jingdezhen Taoci Xueyuan Xuebao **2043**
• Jingdezhen Taoci/Jingdezhen Ceramics (CHN ISSN 1001-9545) **2043**
• Jingdezhen Taoci Xueyuan Xuebao/Jingdezhen Ceramics Institute. Journal (CHN ISSN 1000-2278) **2043**
Jinggangshan Medical College. Journal *see* Jinggangshan Yi-Zhuan Xuebao **5644**
• Jinggangshan Yi-Zhuan Xuebao/Jinggangshan Medical College. Journal (CHN ISSN 1008-2735) **5644**
Jinggu Chuanqi (Qihuan)/Stories & Anecdotes (Magic Fantasy) (CHN) **5444**
Jingguan Sheji/Landscape Design (CHN ISSN 1672-7460) **3740**
• Jingji/Economic Monthly (CHN ISSN 1672-8637) **1131**
• Jingji Cankao Bao/Economic Information Daily (CHN) **1131**
• Jingji Daobao (Jinan)/Economic Reporter (CHN) **1131**
Jingji Daobao (Wanchai)/Economic Reporter (HKG ISSN 0013-0265) **1494**
• Jingji Dili/Economic Geography (CHN ISSN 1000-8462) **4016**
• Jingji Dongwu Xuebao/Journal of Economic Animal (CHN ISSN 1007-7448) **4973**
Jingji Fazhi (CHN) **4872**
Jingji Gaige/Economic Reform *see* Xinxibu **1534**
Jingji Guanli/Economic Management (CHN ISSN 1002-5766) **1762**
Jingji Guanli Wenzhai/Economic Management Digest (CHN ISSN 1002-8668) **1763**
• Jingji Jingwei (CHN ISSN 1006-1096) **1131**
• Jingji Kexue/Economic Science (CHN ISSN 1002-5839) **1131**
Jingji Lilun yu Jingji Guanli/Economic Theory & Business Management (CHN ISSN 1000-596X) **1763**
• Jingji Luntan/Economic Tribune (CHN ISSN 1003-3580) **1131**
Jingji Lunwen. Zhongyang Yanjiuyuan Jingji Yanjiusuo *see* Academia Economic Papers **1056**
• Jingji Pinglun/Economic Review (CHN ISSN 1005-3425) **1131**
• Jingji Ribao/Economic Daily (CHN) **1131**
• Jingji Ribao/Economic Daily News (TWN ISSN 1607-9744) **1132**
• Jingji Shijie/Business World (CHN ISSN 1001-5310) **1132**
• Jingji Shuxue/Mathematics in Economics (CHN ISSN 1007-1660) **5499**
Jingji Tizhi Gaige/Reformation of Economic System (CHN) **1719**
• Jingji Wenti/On Economic Problems (CHN ISSN 1004-972X) **1132**
• Jingji Wenti Tansuo/Inquiry into Economic Problems (CHN ISSN 1006-2912) **1132**
• Jingji Yanjiu/Economic Research Journal (CHN ISSN 0577-9154) **1544**
Jingji yu Falu/Economy and Law (HKG ISSN 1011-9108) **1544**
• Jingji yu Guanli/Economics and Management (CHN ISSN 1003-3890) **1763**
• Jingji yu Guanli Yanjiu/Research on Economics and Management (CHN ISSN 1000-7636) **1763**
Jingji yu Jianmei/Athletics & Body Building (CHN ISSN 1004-2105) **8182**
• Jingji yu Shehui Fazhan (Nanning)/Economic and Social Development (CHN ISSN 1672-2728) **1494**
Jingji yu Shehui Fazhan (Taiyuan)/Economics and Social Development (CHN ISSN 1000-8330) **1132**
Jingji Yuce yu Xinxi/Economic Forecast and Information (CHN ISSN 1002-9818) **1132**
• Jingji Yuekan/Economic Monthly (CHN ISSN 1008-5130) **1132**
Jingji Zhengce Xinxi/Information on Economics Policy (CHN ISSN 1005-474X) **1132**
• Jingji Zongheng (CHN ISSN 1007-7685) **1132**
• Jingjiao Ribao/Beijing Suburbs Daily (CHN) **3825**
Jingjibu Zhongyang Diszhi Diaochasuo Huikan/Taiwan, Republic of China. Ministry of Economic Affairs. Central Geological Survey. Bulletin (TWN ISSN 1012-6821) **2749**
Jingjibu. Zhongyang Dizhi Diaochasuo. Nianbao/Taiwan, Republic of China. Ministry of Economic Affairs. Central Geological Survey. Annual Report (TWN ISSN 1019-8679) **2749**
Jingjibu. Zhongyang Dizhi Diaochasuo. Tekan/Taiwan, Republic of China. Ministry of Economic Affairs. Central Geological Survey. Special Publication (TWN ISSN 1016-3042) **2749**
Jingjifaxue, Laodongfaxue/Studies of Economic Law, Studies of Labor Law (CHN ISSN 1005-4251) **4872**
Jingjishi (Beijing)/Economics History (CHN ISSN 1001-3385) **1132**
• Jingjishi (Taiyuan)/China Economist (CHN ISSN 1004-4914) **1132**
Jingjixue Dongtai/Economic Perspectives (CHN ISSN 1002-8390) **1132**
• Jingjixue Jia/Economist (CHN ISSN 1003-5656) **1132**
Jingjixue Wenzhai Ka/Economics Abstracts on Cards (CHN ISSN 1009-7341) **1246**
Jingliren Wenzhai *see* World Executive's Digest - China Edition **1801**
Jingmen Technical College. Journal *see* Jingmen Zhiye Jishu Xueyuan Xuebao **7977**
• Jingmen Zhiye Jishu Xueyuan Xuebao/Jingmen Technical College. Journal (CHN ISSN 1008-4657) **7977**
Jingri Diannao/Computer Today (HKG ISSN 1023-5167) **2428**
Jingshen Wenming Daokan/Guide to Spiritual Civilization (CHN) **6927**
• Jingshui Chuli/Water Purification Technology (CHN ISSN 1009-0177) **8827**
Jingtan Fengyun (CHN ISSN 1001-0459) **5414**
Jingu Chuanqi/Stories & Anecdotes (CHN ISSN 1003-3327) **3619**
Jingu Chuanqi (Gushi Ban)/Legends Old & New: Short Stories (CHN ISSN 1009-7856) **5313**
Jingu Chuanqi (Wenzhai Ban) (CHN ISSN 1672-7959) **5313**
Jingu Chuanqi (Wuxia Ban)/Legends Old & New:Tales of Chivalry (CHN ISSN 1671-4601) **5313**
• Jingwu/Wushu Fineness (CHN ISSN 1002-6177) **8182**
• ➤ Jingxi Huagong/Fine Chemicals (CHN ISSN 1003-5214) **2066**

Title

10482 JINGXI HUAGONG ZHONGJIANTI ULRICH'S PERIODICALS

• Jingxi Huagong Zhongjianti/Fine Chemical Intermediates (CHN ISSN 1009-9212) **2066**
• Jingxi Shiyou Huagong/Specialty Petrochemicals (CHN ISSN 1003-9384) **6775**
Jingxi Shiyou Huagong Jinzhan/Advances in Fine Petrochemicals (CHN ISSN 1009-8348) **6775**
• Jingyaotong Zazhi/The Journal of Cervicodynia and Lumbodynia (CHN ISSN 1005-7234) **5644**
• Jingying Guanli Luncong/Operation Management Reviews (TWN ISSN 1816-5311) **1763**
Jingying Shenghuo *see* Elite **8783**
• Jingying yu Guanli (CHN ISSN 1003-3475) **1763**
Jinhua College of Profession and Technology. Journal *see* Jinhua Zhiye Jishu Xueyuan Xuebao **6699**
Jinhua Yuekan/Golden China Monthly (USA ISSN 1087-8157) **3543**
• Jinhua Zhiye Jishu Xueyuan Xuebao/Jinhua College of Profession and Technology. Journal (CHN ISSN 1671-3699) **6699**
Jining Shi-zhuan Xuebao *see* Jining Shifan Zhuanke Xuexiao Xuebao **2873**
• Jining Shifan Zhuanke Xuexiao Xuebao/Jining Teachers College. Journal (CHN) **2873**
Jining Teachers College. Journal *see* Jining Shifan Zhuanke Xuexiao Xuebao **2873**
• Jining Yixueyuan Xuebao (CHN ISSN 1000-9760) **5644**
Jinko Chino Gakkaishi/Japanese Society for Artificial Intelligence. Journal (JPN ISSN 0912-8085) **2452**
Jinko Kessho Kogakkai Tokubetsu Koenkai Koen Yoshishu/Association of Synthetic Crystal Science and Technology. Abstracts of the Special Meeting (JPN) **2094**
Jinko Ketsueki/Artificial Blood (JPN ISSN 1341-1594) **5939**
Jinko Mondai Kenkyu/Journal of Population Problems (JPN ISSN 0387-2793) **7286**
Jinko Zoki/Japanese Journal of Artificial Organs (JPN ISSN 0300-0818) **5644**
Jinkogaku Kenkyu/Journal of Population Studies (JPN ISSN 0386-8311) **7286**
• Jinkou Chinou Gakkai Rombunshi/Japanese Society for Artificial Intelligence. Transactions (JPN ISSN 1346-0714) **2452**
Jinling Institute of Technology. Journal (Natural Scienc Edition) *see* Jinling Keji Xueyuan Xuebao (Ziran Kexue Ban) **7871**
Jinling Institute of Technology. Journal (Social Science) *see* Jinling Keji Xueyuan Xuebao (Shehui Kexue Ban) **7977**
Jinling Keji Xueyuan Xuebao (Shehui Kexue Ban)/Jinling Institute of Technology. Journal (Social Science) (CHN ISSN 1673-131X) **7977**
• Jinling Keji Xueyuan Xuebao (Ziran Kexue Ban)/Jinling Institute of Technology. Journal (Natural Scienc Edition) (CHN ISSN 1672-755X) **7871**
Jinling Zhiye Daxue Xuebao/Nanjing Polytechnic College. Journal *see* Jinling Keji Xueyuan Xuebao (Shehui Kexue Ban) **7977**
Jinmin Chugoku/People's China (CHN ISSN 0449-0312) **3825**
Jinmin Netto (Nihongo-ban) *see* Renminwang **3827**
Jinri Dianzi/Electronic Products China (CHN ISSN 1004-9606) **3106**
• Jinri Gongcheng Jixie/Construction Macchinery Today (CHN ISSN 1671-9018) **5453**
Jinri Heku (TWN ISSN 1019-276X) **1359**
• Jinri Keji/Today Science and Technology (CHN ISSN 1003-7438) **7871**
† • Jinri Mingliu/Contemporary Celebrities (CHN ISSN 1005-3786) **8968**
• Jinri Nanguo/The South of China Today (CHN ISSN 1673-1190) **3826**
Jinri Shenghuo Huabao /Today's Life *see* Meishu Qimeng **8974**
Jinri Sichuan *see* Sichuan Today **8988**
• Jinri Yaoxue/Pharmacy Today (CHN ISSN 1674-229X) **6851**
▼ Jinri Yishu (CHN ISSN 1674-0777) **498**
• Jinri Zaobao/Today Morning Express (CHN) **3826**
• Jinri Zhongguo (CHN ISSN 1005-958X) **3826**
➤ Jinrong Luntan/Finance Forum (CHN ISSN 1009-9190) **1359**
• Jinrong Shibao/Financial News (CHN) **1360**
Jinrong Yanjiu/Banking and Finance Studies (CHN ISSN 0529-2794) **1360**
Jinrong yu Baoxian/Finance and Insurance (CHN ISSN 1005-4383) **1360**
Jinrong yu Fazhan *see* Finance and Development (Print) **1343**
Jinrong yu Fazhan *see* Finances et Developpement (Print) **1343**
• Jinrong yu Jingji/Finance and Economics (CHN ISSN 1006-169X) **1132**
Jinrong Zaobao/Financial Morning Post (CHN) **3826**
Jinrui Dotai Gakkai Kaiho/Human Ergology Society. Newsletter (JPN ISSN 0913-7785) **7019**
Jinrui Dotai Gakkai Purogouramu Yokoshu/Human Ergology Society. Program and Preprints of the Conference (JPN) **344**
Jinruigaku Shuho/Anthropological Reports (JPN ISSN 0289-5293) **344**
Jinshajiang Literature and Art *see* Jinshajiang Wenyi **5313**
Jinshajiang Wenyi/Jinshajiang Literature and Art (CHN ISSN 1003-904X) **5313**
Jinshan/Gold Mountain (CHN ISSN 1005-9407) **5313**
Jinshan Shibao/Chinese Times (USA ISSN 0746-5432) **3543**
• Jinshu Cailiao yu Yejin Gongcheng/Metal Materials and Metallurgy Engineering (CHN) **6318**
• Jinshu Jiagong. Lengjiagong/M W Metal Cutting (CHN ISSN 1674-1641) **6318**
• Jinshu Jiagong. Rejiagong/M W Metal Forming (CHN ISSN 1674-165X) **6318**
• Jinshu Kuangshan/Metal Mine (CHN ISSN 1001-1250) **6467**
• Jinshu Rechuli/Heat Treatment of Metals (CHN ISSN 0254-6051) **3348**
Jinshu Rechuli Xuebao/Transactions of Metal Heat Treatment *see* Cailiao Rechuli Xuebao **6307**
• ➤ Jinshu Xuebao/Acta Metallurgica Sinica (CHN ISSN 0412-1961) **6318**
J'Integre (FRA ISSN 0993-7064) **7871**
• Jintian/Today (CHN ISSN 1002-3917) **3826**
Jintian/Today Literary Magazine (USA ISSN 0803-0391) **5313**
• Jintu Xuekan/Shanxi Library Journal (CHN ISSN 1004-1680) **5020**
Jinwanbao/Tonight (CHN) **3826**
• Jinyang Xuekan/Academic Journal of Jinyang (CHN ISSN 1000-2987) **7977**
Jinzhan: Guoji Maoyi yu Keji Jiaoliu/Progress: International Exchange in Trade, Science and Technology (CHN ISSN 1002-1221) **1573**
Jinzhou Shi-yuan Xuebao (Zhexue Shehui Kexue Ban)/Jinzhou Teachers' College Journal (Philosophy and Social Science Edition) *see* Bohai Daxue Xuebao (Zhexue Shehui Kexue Ban) **7951**
Jinzhou Shifan Xueyuan Xuebao (Zike Ban) *see* Bohai Daxue Xuebao (Ziran Kexue Ban) **7841**
Jinzhou Yixueyuan Xuebao/Jinzhou Medical College. Journal *see* Liaoning Yixueyuan Xuebao **7879**
Jinzo/The Kidney (JPN ISSN 0911-9752) **6270**
➤ Jiosinsetikkusu Shinpojumu Happyo Ronbunshu/International Geosynthetics Society. Symposium Proceedings (JPN) **2749**
Jippo (Den Bosch, 2005) (NLD ISSN 1872-0293) **2195**
Jippo Zomerboek (NLD ISSN 1873-555X) **2195**
• Jiqiren/Robot (CHN ISSN 1002-0446) **2585**
Jiritsu Kunren Kenkyu/Japanese Journal of Autogenic Therapy (JPN ISSN 0913-4964) **7367**
• Jishengchong yu Yixue Kunchong Xuebao/Acta Parasitologica et Medica Entomologica Sinica (CHN ISSN 1005-0507) **851**
Jishin/Seismological Society of Japan. Journal (JPN ISSN 0037-1114) **2784**
Jishin Kansoku Hokoku/Matsushiro Seismological Observatory. Seismological Bulletin (JPN ISSN 0289-2723) **2784**
Jishin, Kazan Geppo. Bosai-hen/Monthly Report on Earthquakes and Volcanoes in Japan (JPN ISSN 1343-4977) **2784**
• Jishin, Kazan Geppo. Katarogu-hen (CD-ROM)/Seismological and Volcanological Bulletin of Japan (JPN ISSN 1349-8320) **2784**
Jishin, Kazan Geppo. Katarogu-hen (Print) *see* Jishin, Kazan Geppo. Katarogu-hen (CD-ROM) **2784**
Jishin Kogaku Bunken Mokuroku/Bibliography of Earthquake Engineering (JPN) **2720**
Jishin Kogaku Kenkyu Happyokai Koen Gaiyo/Japan Society of Civil Engineers. Earthquake Engineering Symposium. Proceedings (JPN) **2784**
Jishin Kogaku Shinkokai Nyusu/Japan Society for Earthquake Engineering Promotion News (JPN) **2784**
Jishin Saigai Yosoku no Kenkyu/Seismicity and Seismic Hazard (JPN) **2784**
Jishin Yochi Renrakukai Kaiho/Coordinating Committee for Earthquake Prediction. Report (JPN ISSN 0288-8408) **2227**
• Jishou Daxue Xuebao (Shehui Kexue Ban)/Jishou University. Journal (Social Sciences Edition) (CHN ISSN 1007-4074) **7977**
• Jishou Daxue Xuebao (Ziran Kexue Ban)/Jishou University. Journal (Natural Science Edition) (CHN ISSN 1007-2985) **7871**
Jishou University. Journal (Natural Science Edition) *see* Jishou Daxue Xuebao (Ziran Kexue Ban) **7871**
Jishou University. Journal (Social Sciences Edition) *see* Jishou Daxue Xuebao (Shehui Kexue Ban) **7977**
• Jishu Jingji yu Guanli Yanjiu/Technoeconomics and Management Research (CHN ISSN 1004-292X) **1763**
† ➤ Jishu Kaifa yu Yinjin/Technology Development and Introduction (CHN ISSN 1002-283X) **8968**
• Jishu yu Shichang/Technology and Market (CHN ISSN 1006-8554) **5020**
Jishu yu Xunlian/Technology & Training (TWN ISSN 0254-5888) **6318**
• ➤ Jishui Paishui/Water and Wastewater Engineering (CHN ISSN 1002-8471) **8827**
Jissen Kyoiku/Practical Technology Education (JPN ISSN 0912-9111) **2873**
Jissen Shogaiji Kyoiku/Practical Education for the Handicapped (JPN ISSN 0285-0788) **3042**
• Jisu Skee/Velocity Ski (CHN) **8320**
Jisu Sport - Squash/Velocity Sport - Squash (CHN) **8236**
➤ Jisuan Jiegou Lixue Jiqi Yingyong/Journal of Computational Structural Mechanics and Applications (CHN ISSN 1000-3401) **3384**
• Jisuan Lixue Xuebao/Chinese Journal of Computational Mechanics (CHN ISSN 1007-4708) **2428**
• ➤ Jisuan Shuxue/Mathematica Numerica Sinica (CHN ISSN 0254-7791) **5499**
• Jisuan Wuli/Chinese Journal of Computational Physics (CHN ISSN 1001-246X) **7019**
• Jisuanji Celiang yu Kongzhi/Measurement and Control (CHN ISSN 1671-4598) **6403**
• ➤ Jisuanji Fangzhen/Computer Simulation (CHN ISSN 1006-9348) **2517**
• ➤ Jisuanji Funzhu Sheji yu Tuxingxue Xuebao/Journal of Computer-Aided Design & Computer Graphics (CHN ISSN 1003-9767) **2487**
Jisuanji Fuzhu Gongcheng (CHN ISSN 1006-0871) **3292**
• Jisuanji Gongcheng/Computer Engineering (CHN ISSN 1000-3428) **2473**
• Jisuanji Gongcheng yu Kexue/Computer Engineering and Science (CHN ISSN 1007-130X) **2473**
Jisuanji Jiaoyu/Computer Education (CHN ISSN 1672-5913) **2873**
Jisuanji Jiaoyuxue/Computer Teaching and Learning *see* Jisuanji Jiaoyuxue - Xiandai Jiaoxue **2949**
Jisuanji Jiaoyuxue - Xiandai Jiaoxue/Computer Teaching and Learning (CHN) **2949**
• ➤ Jisuanji Jicheng Zhizao Xitong/Computer Integrated Manufacturing Systems (CHN ISSN 1006-5911) **5453**
• Jisuanji Kexue/Computer Science (CHN ISSN 1002-137X) **2428**
• Jisuanji Shidai/Computer Age (CHN ISSN 1006-8228) **2428**
• ➤ Jisuanji Xuebao/Chinese Journal of Computers (CHN ISSN 0254-4164) **2468**
• ➤ Jisuanji Yanjiu yu Fazhan/Computer Research and Development (CHN ISSN 1000-1239) **2473**
• Jisuanji Yingyong (CHN ISSN 1001-9081) **2428**
• Jisuanji Yingyong Yanjiu/Application Research of Computers (CHN ISSN 1001-3695) **2428**
• Jisuanji Yingyong yu Ruanjian/Computer Applications and Software (CHN ISSN 1000-386X) **2428**
Jisuanji yu Nongye/Computer and Agriculture *see* Nongye Wangluo Xinxi **215**
• Jisuanji yu Wangluo/China Computer & Network (CHN ISSN 1008-1739) **2359**
• ➤ Jisuanji yu Yingyong Huaxue/Computers and Applied Chemistry (CHN ISSN 1001-4160) **2108**
Jisuberi *see* Nihon Jisuberi Gakkaishi **2787**
Jisuberi Kyukeishachi no Chosa to Taisaku Koza/Investigation of Landslides and Their Control (JPN) **2784**
Jisuberi/Landslide *see* Nihon Jisuberi Gakkaishi **2787**
Jisunu (BOL) **344**
• Jitanjafora (USA ISSN 1537-5900) **5313**
Jitsu - Ten *see* Boira Kuren Yousetsu no Jitsu Ten **5450**
Jitsugyo no Burajiru *see* Selecoes Economicas **1605**
Jitsugyo no Nihon/Business of Japan (JPN ISSN 0446-8147) **1132**
Jitsumu Tembo *see* Boira Kuren Yousetsu no Jitsu Ten **5450**
• Jituan Jingji Yanjiu/Group Economics Research (CHN ISSN 1007-712X) **1132**
Jiu Shijie/Drink World (CHN ISSN 1673-0054) **605**
▼ • Jiudian yu Canyin Caigou Zhinan/Hotel and Catering Buyers' Guide (HKG) **4391**
Jiujiang Medical Sciences *see* Jiujiang Yixue **5644**
• Jiujiang Yixue/Jiujiang Medical Sciences (CHN ISSN 1006-3838) **5644**
• Jiuye Shichang Qingshi Yuebao (TWN ISSN 1029-8347) **1132**
➤ Jiuzhou Xuelin/Chinese Culture Quarterly (HKG ISSN 1729-9756) **4459**
Jive (USA) **3543**
Jiwan Dhara (IND ISSN 0021-6976) **4577**
➤ Jixiao yu Celue Yanjiu/Journal of Performance and Strategy Research (TWN ISSN 1815-1663) **1763**
• Jixie Chuandong/Mechanical Transmission (CHN ISSN 1004-2539) **5453**
• Jixie Gongcheng Cailiao/Materials for Mechanical Engineering (CHN ISSN 1000-3738) **3384**
• ➤ Jixie Gongcheng Xuebao (CHN ISSN 0577-6686) **3384**
Jixie Gongye Gao-jiao Yanjiu/Higher Education Research *see* Daxue Jiaoyu Kexue **2977**
• Jixie Kexue yu Jishu/Mechanical Science and Technology (CHN ISSN 1003-8728) **3384**
• Jixie Qiangdu/Journal of Mechanical Strength (CHN ISSN 1001-9669) **3204**
• Jixie Sheji yu Yanjiu/Machine Design and Research (CHN ISSN 1006-2343) **5453**
• Jixie Sheji yu Zhizao/Machinery Design & Manufacture (CHN ISSN 1001-3997) **5454**
• Jixie Zhizao (CHN ISSN 1000-4998) **5454**
Jixie Zhizao *see* Chinamac Journal **5450**
• Jixu Jiaoyu Yanjiu (CHN) **2873**
• Jiyeog Gyeongje/Regional Economic Trend (KOR ISSN 1738-8198) **1132**
• Jiyeog Sahoe Yeong-yang Hag-hoeji/Korean Journal of Community Nutrition (KOR ISSN 1226-0983) **6661**
Jiyou/Philately Magazine (CHN ISSN 0529-0325) **6896**
Jiyu to Seigi/Liberty and Justice (JPN ISSN 0447-7480) **4699**
• Jizhe Yaolan/Journalists Cradle (CHN) **4577**
• Jizhen Yixue/Journal of Emergency Medicine (CHN ISSN 1006-463X) **6062**
• Jizhu Waike Zazhi/Journal of Spine Surgery (CHN ISSN 1672-2957) **6247**
Jmag (AUS ISSN 1833-1440) **4978**
Jnanadhara (IND ISSN 0021-700X) **5313**
J'N'C Fashion Trend Magazine (DEU) **2257**
J'N'C News (DEU) **2257**
Jo (JOR) **3901**
• Jo-Ann etc. (USA) **536**
Jo Vicc (HUN ISSN 1418-2165) **4337**
➤ Joachim-Jungius-Gesellschaft der Wissenschaften, Hamburg. Berichte aus den Sitzungen (DEU ISSN 1435-960X) **7871**
➤ Joachim-Jungius-Gesellschaft der Wissenschaften, Hamburg. Veroeffentlichungen (DEU ISSN 1435-9596) **7871**
Joanna Briggs Institute Best Practice Technical Report *see* J B I Best Practice Technical Report **5643**
• Joannea Botanik (AUT ISSN 1562-9414) **796**
• Joannea Geologie und Palaeontologie (AUT ISSN 1562-9449) **2749**
Joannea Zoologie (AUT ISSN 1562-9430) **949**
Job & Future *see* V R - Future **1191**
Job Book *see* The Springboard Directory **6703**
• Job Choices (Year) (USA) **6699**
Job Choices. Diversity Edition (Year) (USA ISSN 1944-6918) **6699**
Job Choices in Business & Liberal Arts Students (Year) (USA ISSN 1946-9314) **6699**
Job Choices in Science, Engineering, and Technology (Year) (USA ISSN 1534-2301) **6699**
• Job Descriptions for Dealership Staff (USA) **8587**
• Job Futures (CAN ISSN 0833-7195) **1690**
Job Futures Companion *see* Job Futures **1690**
Job Guidelines (IND) **6699**
Job Hunters Guide (Central and South Edition) (GBR ISSN 1474-1164) **6699**
Job Hunters Guide (North and Central Edition) (GBR ISSN 1474-1156) **6699**
Job Hunter's Sourcebook (USA ISSN 1053-1874) **6699**
Job Interview Almanac *see* Adams Job Interview Almanac **6691**
Job Line and News from C P R S (California Park & Recreation Society Inc.) (USA ISSN 1084-8983) **4978**
Job Openings for Economists (USA ISSN 0196-1551) **6699**
Job Opportunities (GBR) **6699**
Job Opportunities Bulletin *see* J O B **7494**
The (Year) Job Outlook in Brief *see* Occupational Outlook Quarterly **6707**
Job Patterns for Minorities & Women in Private Industry *see* U.S. Equal Employment Opportunity Commission. Equal Opportunity Report. Job Patterns for Minorities and Women in Private Industry **6707**
Job Pratique Magazine *see* Le Nouvel Entrepreneur **1964**
Job Safety 21 (USA ISSN 1546-4679) **6679**
Job Safety and Health (USA) **6679**
The Job Search Handbook for Educators (USA) **1690**
• The Job Seeker (USA ISSN 1070-8952) **6699**
Job Service North Dakota. Annual Report (USA) **1690**
Job Service North Dakota. Biennial Report to the Governor (USA) **1690**
Job Service Openings and Starting Wages Reports (USA) **6699**
Job Shop Technology (USA ISSN 0746-8881) **1890**
Job Training and Placement Report (USA ISSN 1041-1488) **1763**
• Job uden Vold (DNK ISSN 1902-3294) **8048**
Job Watch (GBR ISSN 1472-0361) **1867**
• Jobber News (CAN ISSN 0021-7050) **8587**
Jobber News Annual Marketing Guide (CAN) **8587**
• Jobboom le Magazine (CAN ISSN 1492-9031) **6699**
jobboom mag *see* Jobboom le Magazine **6699**
Jobfit *see* Vigo! Jobfit Bleibgesund **6705**
Jobmag (DEU) **6699**
Jobmail (ZAF ISSN 1028-3307) **6699**
JobMart (USA ISSN 0826-788X) **6699**
Jobs Almanac *see* Adams Jobs Almanac **6691**
Jobs & Careers (Oxfordshire & Wiltshire Edition) (GBR ISSN 1479-0300) **6699**
Jobs & Careers Weekly (GBR) **6699**
• Jobs Clearinghouse Online (USA) **2873**
Jobs Direct (GBR) **6699**
Jobs for America *see* U.S. Economic Development Administration. Annual Report **1906**
Jobs for Philosophers (USA) **6699**
Jobs from Recyclables Possibility Newsletter (USA) **6699**
Jobs in Recessionary Times Possibility Newsletter (USA ISSN 1053-654X) **6700**
Jobs North West (GBR) **6700**
Jobs Only *see* The International Educator **3013**
Jobs South East (GBR ISSN 1354-6007) **3867**
Jobsearch U K (GBR ISSN 0962-9742) **6700**
Jobsite. Tools and Materials for the Floorcovering Professional *see* Jobsite. Tools & Materials for the Floorcovering Professional **4544**
Jobsite. Tools & Materials for the Floorcovering Professional (USA ISSN 1098-6871) **4544**
Jobsite. Tools & Materials for the Framing and Drywall Professional (USA) **1051**

DIRECTORY 2010 JOURNAL FOR THE HISTORY OF ASTRONOMY 10485

† Journal de Conchyliologie (AUS ISSN 0021-7719) **8968**

Journal de Droit Fiscal (BEL ISSN 0773-3453) **4699**

• Journal de Gynecologie Obstetrique et Biologie de la Reproduction (FRA ISSN 0368-2315) **5994**

Journal de la Broye (CHE) **3958**

Journal de la Construction de la Suisse Romande (CHE ISSN 0021-776X) **1018**

Journal de la Corse Agricole (FRA ISSN 0021-7778) **125**

Le Journal de la Culture *see* La Presse Litteraire **5354**

Le Journal de la Democratie Sanitaire *see* Le Journal du S I D A **5819**

Le Journal de la Maison (FRA ISSN 0750-3288) **4544**

Journal de la Marine Marchande (FRA ISSN 1633-7921) **8648**

Journal de la Marine Marchande et du Transport Multimodal *see* Journal de la Marine Marchande **8648**

Le Journal de la Paix (FRA ISSN 0021-7794) **7802**

Le Journal de la Production (FRA ISSN 1271-1276) **3348**

• Le Journal de la Renaissance (BEL ISSN 1630-4586) **4235**

• Journal de la Sante Autochtone (CAN ISSN 1710-0720) **6635**

▼ ➤ Journal de la Societe Francaise de Statistique & Revue de Statistique Appliquee (FRA ISSN 1962-5197) **8382**

Journal de la Vieille France (FRA ISSN 1254-5635) **4235**

Journal de l'Abolition (FRA ISSN 1958-1327) **7211**

Journal de l'Action Sociale (FRA ISSN 1268-4368) **1867**

Journal de l"Afrique en Expansion (FRA ISSN 1763-7570) **1494**

Le Journal de l'Agence Intergouvernementale de la Francophonie (FRA ISSN 1560-9790) **8111**

Journal de l'Amee du Salut *see* Heilsarmee Zeitung **7760**

† Journal de l'Annee (FRA ISSN 0449-4733) **8968**

Journal de l'Assurance (CAN ISSN 1198-4678) **4510**

Le Journal de l'Atelier *see* La Revue de l'Atelier **1432**

• Journal de l'Automobile (FRA ISSN 0242-0805) **8587**

Le Journal de l'Ecole Nationale Superieure d'Architecture Paris-Val-de-Seine *see* Ecole Nationale Superieure d'Architecture (Paris-Val-de-Seine). Journal **8952**

Journal de l'Electro *see* De Elektro Krant **3158**

Journal de l'Ile de la Reunion (REU ISSN 0395-8876) **3789**

Journal de l'imagerie Medicale et des Sciences de la Radiation *see* Journal of Medical Imaging and Radiation Sciences **6200**

Le Journal de l'Immersion/Immersion Journal (CAN ISSN 0833-1812) **3066**

Journal de Linguistique Arabe *see* Zeitschrift fuer Arabische Linguistik **5198**

Le Journal de l'Institut Curie *see* Institut Curie. Le Journal **6022**

Le Journal de l'Orthopedie (FRA ISSN 1621-7853) **6062**

• ➤ Journal de Mathematiques Pures et Appliquees (FRA ISSN 0021-7824) **5499**

† • Le Journal de Maths des Eleves (FRA) **8968**

Journal de Medecine Esthetique et de Chirurgie Dermatologique (FRA ISSN 0249-6380) **5878**

• Journal de Medecine Legale, Droit Medical, Victimologie, Dommage Corporel (FRA ISSN 0999-9809) **5914**

Journal de Medecine Traditionnelle Chinoise (FRA ISSN 1777-6457) **5645**

Journal de Mickey (FRA ISSN 0242-9225) **2195**

Journal de Monaco (MCO ISSN 1010-8742) **7448**

Journal de Morges (CHE) **3958**

• ➤ Journal de Mycologie Medicale/Journal of Medical Mycology (FRA ISSN 1156-5233) **5761**

Le Journal de Nervure *see* Nervure **6163**

Journal de Neuroradiologie *see* Journal of Neuroradiology **6201**

• Journal de Parodontologie et d'Implantologie Orale (FRA ISSN 1256-6128) **5850**

Journal de Pathologie Forestiere *see* Forest Pathology **3689**

• ➤ Journal de Pediatrie et de Puericulture (FRA ISSN 0987-7983) **5645**

• Journal de Pharmacie Clinique (FRA ISSN 0291-1981) **6852**

Journal de Pharmacie de Belgique (BEL ISSN 0047-2166) **6852**

Journal de Physique IV *see* The European Physical Journal. Special Topics **7012**

Journal de Physique IV. Proceedings *see* The European Physical Journal. Special Topics **7012**

• ➤ Journal de Radiologie (FRA ISSN 0221-0363) **6200**

• Journal de Readaptation Medicale (FRA ISSN 0242-648X) **6110**

Journal de Recherche Oceanographique (FRA ISSN 0397-5347) **2809**

Journal de Rosemont (CAN) **3811**

Journal de Tanger (MAR ISSN 0047-2174) **3913**

• ➤ Journal de Theorie des Nombres de Bordeaux (FRA ISSN 1246-7405) **5500**

• Journal de Therapie Comportamentale et Cognitive (FRA ISSN 1155-1704) **6149**

Le Journal de Toxicomanie et de Sante Mentale *see* CrossCurrents (Toronto) **2692**

• Journal de Traumatologie du Sport (FRA ISSN 0762-915X) **6230**

Journal d'Echographie en Radiologie (FRA ISSN 1771-4745) **6200**

Journal d'Echographie et de Medicine Ultrasonore *see* Journal de Radiologie **6200**

Journal d'Economie Medicale (FRA ISSN 0294-0736) **5645**

Journal Dentistry Indonesia/Jurnal Kedokteran Gigi Indonesia (IDN ISSN 1693-9697) **5850**

Journal der Deutschen Dermatologischen Gesellschaft (Print Edition) *see* J D D G (Print Edition) **5878**

Journal der Fachjournalisten *see* JOJO **4577**

• Journal des Africanistes (FRA ISSN 0399-0346) **344**

Journal des Anthropologues (FRA ISSN 1156-0428) **344**

Le Journal des Arts (FRA ISSN 1245-1495) **498**

Journal des Aspects Sociaux du VIH-SIDA *see* Sahara J **5826**

Journal des Cafetiers, Restaurateurs et Hoteliers (CHE) **4391**

Journal des Combattants (FRA ISSN 0021-8014) **6429**

Journal des Communes (FRA ISSN 0021-8030) **7494**

Journal des Comores *see* Al- Watwan **5245**

Journal des Debats (CAN ISSN 0709-3632) **7448**

Journal des Debats *see* British Columbia. Legislative Assembly. Debates (Hansard Sessional Edition) **7424**

Journal des Debats (Hansard) *see* Ontario Legislative Assembly. Select Committee on Electoral Reform. Official Report of Debates, Hansard **7458**

Journal des Diabetiques (CHE ISSN 0449-198X) **5895**

• ➤ Journal des Economistes et des Etudes Humaines (FRA ISSN 1145-6396) **4459**

Journal des Electriciens (FRA ISSN 0337-8500) **3322**

Le Journal des Enfants (FRA ISSN 0986-9050) **2195**

Le Journal des Entreprises (Loire) (FRA ISSN 1950-8581) **1763**

Journal des Entreprises de Saint-Denis (FRA ISSN 1246-8576) **1405**

Journal des Finances (FRA ISSN 0021-8049) **1360**

Journal des Fonctionnaires des P T T (CHE) **2369**

Le Journal des Grandes Ecoles (FRA ISSN 1278-5989) **2988**

Le Journal des Ingenieurs *see* Le Journal des Ingenieurs **3204**

Le Journal des Ingenieurs (BEL ISSN 1378-6652) **3204**

Journal des Instituteurs *see* J D I **2872**

Journal des Juges de Paix/Tijdschrift van de Vrederechters (BEL ISSN 1782-9747) **4699**

Journal des Juges de Paix et de Police *see* Journal des Juges de Paix **4699**

Journal des Juges de Paix et de Police *see* Journal des Juges de Police **4699**

Journal des Juges de Police/Tijdschrift van de Politierechters (BEL ISSN 1782-9755) **4699**

Journal des Juges Provinciaux *see* Provincial Judges Journal **4762**

Journal des Maires (FRA ISSN 0294-8095) **7494**

Journal des Maladies de la Fonction Sexuelle et de la Reproduction *see* Journal of Sexual and Reproductive Medicine **6270**

• ➤ Journal des Maladies Vasculaires (FRA ISSN 0398-0499) **5791**

Journal des Marques de Commerce *see* Trade Marks Journal **6758**

Journal des Mathematiques et de Physique Appliquees *see* Zeitschrift fuer Angewandte Mathematik und Physik **5547**

Journal des Medecins du Travail *see* Journal des Professionnels de la Sante au Travail **6679**

Journal des Menageres (FRA ISSN 0755-9895) **4361**

Journal des Orphelins de Guerre (FRA) **8048**

Le Journal des Parrains *see* Un Enfant par la Main. Le Magazine **2152**

Journal des Pays d'en Haut (CAN ISSN 0381-1263) **3811**

Journal des Plaies et des Cicatrisations (FRA ISSN 1268-8924) **5878**

Le Journal des Poetes (BEL ISSN 0774-4137) **5424**

Journal des Professionnels de la Sante au Travail (FRA ISSN 1775-0318) **6679**

Le Journal des Professionnels de l'Enfance (FRA ISSN 1297-5354) **6094**

Journal des Savants (FRA ISSN 0021-8103) **5314**

• ➤ Journal des Sciences et Techniques de la Tonnellerie/Journal of Cooperage Sciences and Techniques (FRA ISSN 1274-2244) **125**

Journal des Sciences Hydrologiques *see* Hydrological Sciences Journal **2794**

Journal des Sciences pour l'Ingenieur (SEN) **7871**

Le Journal des Telecoms (FRA ISSN 1628-1241) **2369**

➤ Journal des Tribunaux (BEL ISSN 0021-812X) **4699**

Journal des Tribunaux - Droit Europeen (BEL ISSN 0779-7656) **4699**

Journal des Tribunaux du Travail (BEL ISSN 0778-9009) **4699**

Journal d'Histoire de l'Imprimerie *see* Journal fuer Druckgeschichte **7324**

Journal d'Histoire Economique et Sociale de l'Orient *see* Journal of the Economic and Social History of the Orient **4322**

Journal d'Obstetrique et Gynecologie du Canada *see* Journal of Obstetrics and Gynaecology Canada **5996**

Journal d'Odonto-Stomatologie Pediatrique *see* Revue Francophone d'Odontologie Pediatrique **5864**

Journal du Barreau (CAN ISSN 0833-921X) **4699**

Journal du Bois (FRA ISSN 1154-6123) **3713**

Le Journal du Brasseur (BEL ISSN 1371-0052) **605**

Le Journal du C N R S *see* C N R S. Journal **7843**

Le Journal du Cancer *see* The Cancer Journal (Online Edition) **5592**

Journal du Chasseur (FRA ISSN 0755-7140) **8320**

Journal du Chauffage et du Sanitaire (FRA ISSN 1148-554X) **1018**

Journal du Controle Technique (FRA ISSN 0991-0298) **8587**

Le Journal du Dentiste (BEL ISSN 1370-2602) **5850**

Journal du Droit des Jeunes *see* La Revue d'Action Juridique et Sociale **4773**

Journal du Fermier et du Metayer (FRA ISSN 0446-9739) **125**

Le Journal du Medecin Coordonnateur et des Equipes Soignantes (FRA ISSN 1761-0095) **4048**

Journal du Mineur (FRA ISSN 0397-1511) **4596**

Le Journal du Multimedia et des Nouvelles Technologies (FRA ISSN 1263-5251) **2487**

Le Journal du Patissier *see* Le Journal du Patissier Confiseur Glacier Chocolatier Traiteur **3674**

Le Journal du Patissier Confiseur Glacier Chocolatier Traiteur (FRA ISSN 1279-3035) **3674**

Le Journal du S I D A (FRA) **5819**

▼ Journal du Technicien (CAN ISSN 1718-5661) **1763**

Le Journal du Telephone *see* Le Journal des Telecoms **2369**

Journal du Textile (FRA ISSN 0021-8197) **8454**

• Journal E (USA) **2711**

• ➤ Journ@l Electronique d'Histoire des Probabilites et de la Statistique/Electronic Journal for History of Probability and Statistics (FRA ISSN 1773-0074) **8382**

• Journal Europa (FRA ISSN 1778-171X) **2288**

Journal Europeen de Combinatoire *see* European Journal of Combinatorics **5487**

Journal Europeen de Droit International *see* European Journal of International Law **4925**

Journal Europeen de Psychologie de l'Education *see* European Journal of Psychology of Education **2855**

Journal Europeen de Recherche sur le Handicap *see* Alter **4063**

• Journal Europeen des Systemes Automatises (FRA ISSN 1269-6935) **2462**

• Journal Europeen des Urgences/European Journal of Emergencies (FRA ISSN 0993-9857) **6063**

Journal Europeen d'Hydrologie (FRA ISSN 1023-6368) **8827**

Journal Film (DEU ISSN 0724-7508) **6504**

➤ Journal for Academic Study of Magic (GBR ISSN 1479-0750) **6742**

• Journal for Advancement of Marketing Education (USA ISSN 1537-5137) **1823**

Journal for Anthroposophy (USA ISSN 0021-8235) **7737**

Journal for Applied Anthropology *see* Omertaa **351**

• ➤ Journal for Christian Theological Research (USA ISSN 1087-1624) **7653**

• Journal for Computing Teachers (USA ISSN 1943-9725) **2428**

Journal for Consumer Protection and Food Safety *see* Journal fuer Verbraucherschutz und Lebensmittelsicherheit **7528**

➤ Journal for Contemporary History/Joernaal vir Eietydse Geskiedenis (ZAF ISSN 0258-2422) **7247**

• ➤ Journal for Crime, Conflict and Media Culture (GBR ISSN 1741-1580) **4699**

• Journal for Critical Animal Studies (USA) **320**

• ➤ Journal for Critical Education Policy Studies (GBR ISSN 1740-2743) **2873**

• ➤ The Journal for Cultural and Religious Theory (USA ISSN 1530-5228) **7653**

• ➤ Journal for Cultural Research (GBR ISSN 1479-7585) **4459**

Journal for Deleuzian Studies *see* Actual Virtual **5249**

• Journal for Early Modern Cultural Studies (USA ISSN 1531-0485) **7977**

• ➤ Journal for East European Management Studies (DEU ISSN 0949-6181) **1763**

• The Journal for Education in the Built Environment (GBR ISSN 1747-4205) **447**

• Journal for Eighteenth-Century Studies (GBR ISSN 1754-0194) **4459**

• Journal for European Environmental & Planning Law (NLD ISSN 1613-7272) **4699**

Journal for Fluid Power and Automation *see* Ventil **7064**

• ➤ Journal for General Philosophy of Science/Zeitschrift fuer Allgemeine Wissenschaftstheorie (NLD ISSN 0925-4560) **7871**

• ➤ Journal for Geometry and Graphics (DEU ISSN 1433-8157) **5500**

▼ • ➤ Journal for Global Business Advancement (GBR ISSN 1746-966X) **1763**

Journal for Hawaiian and Pacific Agriculture (USA ISSN 1052-5394) **125**

The Journal for Healthcare Design & Development *see* H D: The Journal for Healthcare Design & Development **4094**

• ➤ Journal for Healthcare Quality (USA ISSN 1062-2551) **4103**

• ➤ Journal for Institutional Innovation, Development and Transition (SVN ISSN 1580-4615) **1494**

Journal for Intercultural History (USA) **8111**

• ➤ Journal for International Business and Entrepreneurship Development (GBR ISSN 1549-9324) **1573**

Journal for Islamic Studies *see* Tydskrif vir Islamkunde **7716**

• Journal for Juridical Science/Tydskrif vir Regswetenskap (ZAF ISSN 0258-252X) **4699**

Journal for Juvenile Justice and Detention Services *see* Journal for Juvenile Justice Services **2656**

• ➤ Journal for Juvenile Justice Services (USA ISSN 1932-5789) **2656**

Journal for Lacanian Studies (GBR ISSN 1477-3635) **7367**

▼ • The Journal for Late Antique Religion and Culture (GBR ISSN 1754-517X) **4235**

• Journal for Learning through the Arts (USA ISSN 1932-7528) **2873**

Journal for Legal Philosophy and Jurisprudence *see* Rechtsfilosofie en Rechtstheorie **4766**

Journal for Living (USA) **8111**

• ➤ Journal for Maritime Research (GBR ISSN 1469-1957) **8648**

➤ Journal for Meditation and Meditation Research (CHE ISSN 1617-528X) **7367**

• ➤ Journal for Millennial Studies (USA) **6645**

Journal for Minority Medical Students (USA ISSN 1074-5807) **5645**

• ➤ The Journal for MultiMedia History (USA ISSN 1528-3844) **2351**

• ➤ Journal for Nature Conservation (DEU ISSN 1617-1381) **3444**

Journal for New Generation Science (ZAF ISSN 1684-4998) **7871**

• Journal for Nurse Practitioners (USA ISSN 1555-4155) **5963**

• ➤ Journal for Nurses in Staff Development (USA ISSN 1098-7886) **5963**

Journal for Peace & Justice Studies (USA ISSN 1093-6831) **4459**

• Journal for Preachers (USA ISSN 1057-266X) **7762**

• ➤ Journal for Quality and Participation (USA ISSN 1040-9602) **1867**

• ➤ Journal for Research in Mathematics Education (USA ISSN 0021-8251) **3066**

• Journal for Research in Mathematics Education. Monograph (USA ISSN 0883-9530) **3067**

▼ • ➤ Journal for Research into Freemasonry and Fraternalism (GBR ISSN 1757-2460) **4235**

Journal for Respiratory Care & Sleep Medicine *see* FOCUS Journal for Respiratory Care & Sleep Medicine **6214**

Journal for S M E Development *see* Zhongxiao Qiye Fazhan Jikan **1198**

Journal for Sciene and Technology Studies *see* Vest **7928**

• ➤ Journal for Scientific Research. Medical Sciences/Magallat gami'at al-sultan qabus li-l-buhut al-'ilmiyyat. Al-'ulum al-tibbiyyat (OMN ISSN 1029-4066) **5645**

Journal for Semitics/Tydskrif vir Semitistiek (ZAF ISSN 1013-8471) **7724**

Journal for Social Work Education in Africa *see* A S W E A Journal for Social Work Education in Africa **8022**

Journal for Sociology of Education and Socialization *see* Zeitschrift fuer Soziologie der Erziehung und Sozialisation **8148**

• ➤ Journal for Specialists in Group Work (USA ISSN 0193-3922) **7367**

• ➤ Journal for Specialists in Pediatric Nursing (USA ISSN 1539-0136) **5963**

Journal for Stage Directors & Choreographers (USA ISSN 1078-4802) **8472**

Journal for Students of V C E International Studies (AUS) **7977**

Journal for Students of V C E Political Studies (AUS) **7146**

• ➤ Journal for Studies in Economics and Econometrics/Tydskrif vir Studies in Ekonomie en Ekonometrie (ZAF ISSN 0379-6205) **1544**

Journal for Technology of Plasticity (SRB ISSN 0354-3870) **3348**

▼ Journal for the Advancement of Performance Information and Value (USA ISSN 1941-191X) **1018**

• Journal for the Anthropological Study of Human Movement (Online) (USA) **344**

† • Journal for the Anthropological Study of Human Movement (Print) (USA ISSN 0891-7124) **8968**

Journal for the Aramaic Bible *see* Aramaic Studies **7622**

Journal for the Critical Study of Religion *see* Journal for the Scientific Examination of Religion **7653**

• ➤ Journal for the Education of the Gifted (USA ISSN 0162-3532) **3042**

Journal for the History of Arabic Science (SYR ISSN 0379-2927) **7871**

• ➤ Journal for the History of Astronomy (GBR ISSN 0021-8286) **576**

Title

▼ *new title* † *ceased* • *electronic media* ➤ *refereed*

Journal for the History of Modern Theology *see* Zeitschrift fuer Neuere Theologiegeschichte **7696**
Journal for the History of Physics *see* Butsurigakushi **7007**
Journal for the History of Technology *see* Polhem **8434**
➤ Journal for the Professional Counselor (USA ISSN 1080-6385) **2874**
• ➤ The Journal for the Public University (AUS ISSN 1449-5481) **2988**
• ➤ Journal for the Renewal of Religion and Theology (ZAF ISSN 1834-3627) **7653**
▼ • ➤ Journal for the School of Professional Counseling (USA ISSN 1940-624X) **7367**
Journal for the Scientific Examination of Religion (USA) **7653**
• ➤ Journal for the Scientific Study of Religion (USA ISSN 0021-8294) **7653**
➤ Journal for the Study of British Cultures (DEU ISSN 0944-9094) **4459**
Journal for the Study of Education and Development *see* Infancia y Aprendizaje **2866**
Journal for the Study of Food and Society *see* Food, Culture, and Society **4358**
• ➤ Journal for the Study of Judaism (NLD ISSN 0047-2212) **7725**
➤ Journal for the Study of Judaism. Supplement (NLD ISSN 1384-2161) **7725**
➤ Journal for the Study of Peace and Conflict (USA ISSN 1095-1962) **7247**
• Journal for the Study of Radicalism (USA ISSN 1930-1189) **7146**
• ➤ Journal for the Study of Religion (ZAF ISSN 1011-7601) **7653**
• Journal for the Study of Religion, Nature and Culture (GBR ISSN 1749-4907) **7653**
• ➤ Journal for the Study of Religious and Ideologies (ROM ISSN 1583-0039) **7653**
▼ • ➤ The Journal for the Study of Sephardic and Mizrahi Jewry (USA ISSN 1935-0643) **7725**
▼ • Journal for the Study of Sports and Athletes in Education (USA ISSN 1935-7397) **8182**
• ➤ Journal for the Study of the Historical Jesus (NLD ISSN 1476-8690) **7653**
• ➤ Journal for the Study of the New Testament (GBR ISSN 0142-064X) **7653**
Journal for the Study of the New Testament. Supplement Series (GBR ISSN 0143-5108) **7653**
• ➤ Journal for the Study of the Old Testament (GBR ISSN 0309-0892) **7653**
Journal for the Study of the Old Testament. Supplement Series (GBR ISSN 0309-0787) **7653**
• Journal for the Study of the Pseudepigrapha (GBR ISSN 0951-8207) **7653**
Journal for the Study of the Pseudepigrapha. Supplement Series *see* Library of Second Temple Studies **7660**
• ➤ Journal for the Theory of Social Behaviour (GBR ISSN 0021-8308) **7367**
Journal for Theory and Application in Foundry *see* Ljevarstvo **6321**
• The Journal for Transdisciplinary Environmental Studies (DNK ISSN 1602-2297) **3444**
The Journal for Transdisciplinary Research in Southern Africa (ZAF ISSN 1817-4434) **8111**
• Journal for Vascular Ultrasound (Online Edition) (USA ISSN 1544-3175) **5791**
• ➤ Journal for Vascular Ultrasound (Print Edition) (USA ISSN 1544-3167) **5791**
• ➤ Journal for Vocational Special Needs Education (Online Edition) (USA) **3042**
The Journal for Weavers, Spinners & Dyers (GBR ISSN 0267-7806) **8454**
Journal Forestier Suisse *see* Schweizerische Zeitschrift fuer Forstwesen **3701**
Journal Forestier Suisse. Supplement *see* Schweizerische Zeitschrift fuer Forstwesen. Beihefte **3701**
Journal Francais *see* France - Amerique **3534**
• Journal Francais de Psychiatrie (FRA ISSN 1260-5999) **6149**
• ➤ Journal Francais d'Ophtalmologie (FRA ISSN 0181-5512) **6044**
• Journal Francais d'Orthoptique (FRA ISSN 0240-7914) **6044**
Journal Frankfurt (DEU ISSN 0940-6530) **3850**
Journal from the Radical Reformation (USA ISSN 1058-3084) **7737**
➤ Journal fuer Anaesthesie und Intensivbehandlung (DEU ISSN 0941-4223) **5771**
Journal fuer Angewandte Sozialforschung *see* S W S - Rundschau **7999**
Journal fuer Begabtenfoerderung (AUT ISSN 1681-7001) **3042**
• ➤ Journal fuer Betriebswirtschaft (DEU ISSN 0344-9327) **1763**
➤ Journal fuer das Nephrologische Team (DEU ISSN 1433-5018) **6270**
Journal fuer die Apotheke (DEU) **8725**
• ➤ Journal fuer die Reine und Angewandte Mathematik (DEU ISSN 0075-4102) **5500**
Journal fuer Druckgeschichte/Journal d'Histoire de l'Imprimerie/Journal of Printing History (DEU ISSN 0932-4372) **7324**
Journal fuer Entwicklungspolitik (AUT ISSN 0258-2384) **1599**
• ➤ Journal fuer Ernaehrungsmedizin (AUT ISSN 1563-2873) **6661**
Journal fuer Fertiltaet und Reproduktion *see* Journal fuer Gynaekologische Endokrinologie (Print) **5994**
• Journal fuer Gastroenterologische und Hepatologische Erkrankungen (AUT ISSN 1728-6263) **5927**
Journal fuer Gynaekologische Endokrinologie (Online) *see* Journal fuer Gynaekologische Endokrinologie (Print) **5994**
▼ • ➤ Journal fuer Gynaekologische Endokrinologie (Print) (AUT ISSN 1997-6690) **5994**
Journal fuer Hotellerie, Gastronomie und Tourismus in Thueringen (DEU) **4391**
• Journal fuer Hypertonie (AUT ISSN 1028-2327) **5791**
▼ • Journal fuer Juristischen Zeitgeschichte (DEU ISSN 1863-9984) **4699**
• ➤ Journal fuer Kardiologie (AUT ISSN 1024-0098) **5791**
Das Journal fuer Kindergarten, Hort und Elternhaus (AUT) **2156**
▼ • Journal fuer Klinische Endokrinologie und Stoffwechsel (AUT) **5895**
Journal fuer Konflikt- und Gewaltforschung *see* International Journal of Conflict and Violence **7143**
• Journal fuer Kulturpflanzen (DEU ISSN 1867-0911) **238**
➤ Journal fuer Kunstgeschichte (DEU ISSN 1432-9506) **498**
Journal fuer Lehrerinnen- und Lehrerbildung (AUT ISSN 1681-7028) **3067**
• Journal fuer Mathematik-Didaktik (DEU ISSN 0173-5322) **5500**
Journal fuer Menopause *see* Journal fuer Gynaekologische Endokrinologie (Print) **5994**
• ➤ Journal fuer Mineralstoffwechsel (AUT ISSN 1023-7763) **734**
• ➤ Journal fuer Neurologie, Neurochirurgie und Psychiatrie (AUT ISSN 1608-1587) **6149**
Journal fuer Oberflaechentechnik *see* J O T **5453**
Journal fuer Ornithologie *see* Journal of Ornithology **909**
Journal fuer Perfektes Haushalten (DEU) **3850**
Journal fuer Pharmakologie und Therapie/Journal of Pharmacology and Therapy (DEU ISSN 1432-4334) **6852**
• ➤ Journal fuer Psychologie (DEU ISSN 0942-2285) **7368**
• ➤ Journal fuer Rechtspolitik (AUT ISSN 0943-4011) **4699**
• Journal fuer Reproduktionsmedizin und Endokrinologie (AUT ISSN 1810-2107) **5995**
Journal fuer Schulentwicklung (AUT ISSN 1029-2624) **3025**
Journal fuer U F O - Forschung (DEU ISSN 0723-7766) **63**
• ➤ Journal fuer Urologie und Urogynaekologie (AUT ISSN 1023-6090) **6270**
Journal fuer Urologie und Urogynaekologie. Ausgabe Schweiz *see* Journal fuer Urologie und Urogynaekologie **6270**
Journal fuer Vaskulaere Medizin (AUT ISSN 1992-674X) **5791**
• ➤ Journal fuer Verbraucherschutz und Lebensmittelsicherheit/Journal for Consumer Protection and Food Safety (CHE ISSN 1661-5751) **7528**
Journal Historique des Bernier (CAN ISSN 0021-8006) **3772**
Journal Holdings in the National Capital Area (USA ISSN 0893-5386) **5058**
• Journal in Computer Virology (FRA ISSN 1772-9890) **2515**
Journal Industriel du Quebec (CAN ISSN 0831-0122) **3369**
Journal International de Bioethique/International Journal of Bioethics (FRA ISSN 1287-7352) **6927**
Journal International de Psychologie *see* International Journal of Psychology **7365**
Journal International des Sciences de la Vigne et du Vin (FRA ISSN 1151-0285) **125**
Journal International du Cancer *see* International Journal of Cancer **6022**
➤ Journal International Medical Sciences Academy (IND ISSN 0971-071X) **5645**
Journal Ivoirien d'Oceanologie et de Limnologie (CIV ISSN 1018-0354) **2809**
Journal la Voix (CAN) **3811**
Journal l'Artisan (CAN) **3811**
Journal Le Plateau (CAN) **3811**
Journal Med (DEU ISSN 1616-220X) **5645**
Journal Medical Libanais *see* Lebanese Medical Journal **5660**
Journal: News of the Blood Programme in Canada (CAN ISSN 0715-8602) **5939**
• The Journal of 21st Century Accounting (USA) **1293**
Journal of A A P O S *see* American Association for Pediatric Ophthalmology and Strabismus. Journal **6038**
▼ The Journal of a Musician (USA ISSN 1937-6804) **6580**
Journal of A S T M International *see* A S T M International. Journal **3179**
Journal of Abdominal Emergency Medicine *see* Nihon Fukubu Kyukyu Igakkai Zasshi **6253**
Journal of Abdominal Surgery *see* Fubu Waike **6244**
• ➤ Journal of Abnormal Child Psychology (USA ISSN 0091-0627) **7368**
• ➤ Journal of Abnormal Psychology (USA ISSN 0021-843X) **7368**
• ➤ Journal of Aboriginal Economic Development (CAN ISSN 1481-9112) **1132**
• ➤ Journal of Aboriginal Health (CAN ISSN 1710-0712) **6635**
The Journal of Academic Administration in Higher Education (USA ISSN 1936-3478) **2989**
▼ • Journal of Academic and Business Ethics (USA ISSN 1941-336X) **6927**
• ➤ Journal of Academic Ethics (NLD ISSN 1570-1727) **2989**
• The Journal of Academic Legal Studies (DEU ISSN 1862-0280) **4700**
• ➤ The Journal of Academic Librarianship (GBR ISSN 0099-1333) **5020**
Journal of Academic Libraries *see* Daxue Tushuguan Xuebao **5005**
Journal of Academic Library and Information Science *see* Daxue Tushu Qingbao Xuekan **5005**
➤ Journal of Acarology (IND) **851**
The Journal of Accelerated Learning and Teaching (USA ISSN 1534-6536) **2874**
• Journal of Access Policy & Practice (GBR ISSN 1740-1348) **2943**
• ➤ Journal of Access Services (USA ISSN 1536-7967) **5062**
• Journal of Accord Integrative Medicine (USA ISSN 1932-4642) **311**
Journal of Account and Finance Development *see* Kuaiji yu Caijin Yanjiu Qikan **1296**
• Journal of Accountancy (USA ISSN 0021-8448) **1293**
• ➤ Journal of Accounting and Economics (NLD ISSN 0165-4101) **1293**
• Journal of Accounting and Finance Research (USA ISSN 1093-5770) **1293**
• ➤ Journal of Accounting & Organizational Change (GBR ISSN 1832-5912) **1293**
• ➤ Journal of Accounting and Public Policy (USA ISSN 0278-4254) **1293**
Journal of Accounting Auditing and Finance *see* J A A F **1293**
➤ Journal of Accounting, Business and Management (IDN ISSN 0216-423X) **1293**
➤ The Journal of Accounting Case Research (CAN ISSN 1192-2621) **1133**
• ➤ Journal of Accounting Education (GBR ISSN 0748-5751) **1293**
Journal of Accounting, Ethics & Public Policy (USA ISSN 1089-652X) **1293**
➤ Journal of Accounting, Finance & Management Strategy (TWN ISSN 1556-5793) **1294**
• ➤ Journal of Accounting Literature (USA ISSN 0737-4607) **1294**
• ➤ Journal of Accounting Research (USA ISSN 0021-8456) **1294**
• ➤ Journal of Achievements in Materials and Manufacturing Engineering (POL ISSN 1734-8412) **3204**
Journal of Acquired Immune Deficiency Syndromes *see* J A I D S **5819**
• ➤ Journal of Active and Passive Electronic Devices (USA ISSN 1555-0281) **3106**
➤ Journal of Actuarial Practice (USA ISSN 1064-6647) **4510**
▼ • ➤ Journal of Acupuncture and Meridian Studies (KOR ISSN 2005-2901) **311**
• ➤ Journal of Acupuncture and Tuina Science (DEU ISSN 1672-3597) **311**
▼ • ➤ Journal of Adaptation in Film and Performance (GBR ISSN 1753-6421) **8472**
The Journal of Addiction and Mental Health *see* CrossCurrents (Toronto) **2692**
▼ • Journal of Addiction Medicine (USA ISSN 1932-0620) **2695**
• ➤ Journal of Addiction Science & Clinical Practice (USA) **2695**
• ➤ Journal of Addictions & Offender Counseling (USA ISSN 1055-3835) **7368**
• ➤ Journal of Addictions Nursing (GBR ISSN 1088-4602) **5964**
• ➤ Journal of Addictive Diseases (USA ISSN 1055-0887) **2695**
• ➤ Journal of Adhesion (USA ISSN 0021-8464) **7019**
• ➤ Journal of Adhesion Science and Technology (NLD ISSN 0169-4243) **7093**
• ➤ The Journal of Adhesive Dentistry (GBR ISSN 1461-5185) **5850**
• ➤ Journal of Administration and Governance (AUS ISSN 1834-3511) **7448**
• ➤ Journal of Adolescence (GBR ISSN 0140-1971) **2156**
• ➤ Journal of Adolescent & Adult Literacy (USA ISSN 1081-3004) **3025**
• ➤ Journal of Adolescent Health (USA ISSN 1054-139X) **5645**
• ➤ Journal of Adolescent Research (USA ISSN 0743-5584) **7368**
• Journal of Adult & Continuing Education (GBR ISSN 1477-9714) **2943**
• ➤ Journal of Adult Development (USA ISSN 1068-0667) **7368**
Journal of Adult Diseases *see* Seijimbyou to Seikatsu Shuukambyou **5711**
Journal of Adult Education (TZA ISSN 0856-1109) **2943**
• ➤ Journal of Adult Education (USA ISSN 0090-4244) **2943**
➤ Journal of Adult Learning (NZL) **2943**
• The Journal of Adult Protection (GBR ISSN 1466-8203) **4700**
• ➤ Journal of Adult Theological Education (GBR ISSN 1740-7141) **7653**
Journal of Adults Education of Gansu Political Science and Law Institute *see* Gansu Zheng-Fa Chengren Jiaoyu Xueyuan Xuebao **7966**
• ➤ Journal of Advanced Academics (USA ISSN 1932-202X) **3042**
• ➤ Journal of Advanced Computational Intelligence and Intelligent Informatics (JPN ISSN 1343-0130) **2548**
• ➤ Journal of Advanced Concrete Technology (JPN ISSN 1346-8014) **1018**
Journal of Advanced Engineering *see* Xianjin Gongcheng Xuekan **3227**
• ➤ Journal of Advanced Manufacturing Systems (SGP ISSN 0219-6867) **1890**
• ➤ Journal of Advanced Materials (Commack) (GBR ISSN 0969-6849) **3348**
Journal of Advanced Materials (Covina) (USA ISSN 1070-9789) **3349**
• ➤ Journal of Advanced Nursing (GBR ISSN 0309-2402) **5964**
➤ Journal of Advanced Oxidation Technologies (CAN ISSN 1203-8407) **2136**
▼ • Journal of Advanced Practice Nursing (USA ISSN 1940-5626) **5964**
▼ • ➤ Journal of Advanced Researches on Bioinformatics (USA ISSN 1943-0213) **826**
▼ • ➤ Journal of Advanced Researches on Differential Equations (USA ISSN 1943-0248) **5500**
▼ • ➤ Journal of Advanced Researches on Dynamical and Control Systems (USA ISSN 1943-023X) **3384**
➤ Journal of Advanced Science (JPN ISSN 0915-5651) **7871**
• ➤ Journal of Advanced Transportation (CAN ISSN 0197-6729) **8500**
➤ Journal of Advanced Zoology (IND ISSN 0253-7214) **949**
Journal of Advances in Bioscience (IND) **680**
Journal of Advances in Chemical Physics (GBR ISSN 1479-4810) **7019**
• ➤ Journal of Advances in Management Research (GBR ISSN 0972-7981) **1763**
▼ • ➤ Journal of Advances in Modeling Earth Systems (USA ISSN 1942-2466) **6358**
Journal of Advances in Schizophrenia and Brain Research *see* Advances in Schizophrenia and Clinical Psychiatry **6120**
Journal of Adventist Education (USA ISSN 0021-8480) **7762**
• ➤ Journal of Adventure Education and Outdoor Learning (GBR ISSN 1472-9679) **8320**
• ➤ Journal of Advertising (USA ISSN 0091-3367) **27**
• Journal of Advertising Research (USA ISSN 0021-8499) **27**
Journal of Aeronautical Materials *see* Hangkong Cailiao Xuebao **57**
Journal of Aeronautics Astronautics and Aviation (TWN ISSN 1990-7710) **63**
Journal of Aeronautics Astronautics and Aviation. Series A *see* Journal of Aeronautics Astronautics and Aviation **63**
Journal of Aeronautics Astronautics and Aviation. Series B *see* Hangkong Taikong ji Minhang Xuekan **57**
Journal of Aerosol Medicine *see* Journal of Aerosol Medicine and Pulmonary Drug Delivery **6215**
• ➤ Journal of Aerosol Medicine and Pulmonary Drug Delivery (USA ISSN 1941-2703) **6215**
• ➤ Journal of Aerosol Science (GBR ISSN 0021-8502) **6711**
• Journal of Aerospace Computing, Information, and Communication (USA ISSN 1542-9423) **63**
Journal of Aerospace Engineering *see* Institution of Mechanical Engineers. Proceedings. Part G: Journal of Aerospace Engineering **60**
• ➤ Journal of Aerospace Engineering (USA ISSN 0893-1321) **3274**
Journal of Aerospace Power *see* Hangkong Dongli Xuebao **57**
Journal of Aerospace Science and Technology *see* J A S T **62**
Journal of Aerospace Sciences and Technologies (IND ISSN 0972-950X) **63**
• ➤ Journal of Aesthetic Education (USA ISSN 0021-8510) **2874**
• ➤ Journal of Aesthetics and Art Criticism (USA ISSN 0021-8529) **498**
• ➤ Journal of Affective Disorders (NLD ISSN 0165-0327) **6149**
Journal of Affordable Housing & Community Development Law *see* Journal of Affordable Housing and Community Development Law **4416**
Journal of Affordable Housing and Community Development Law (USA ISSN 1084-2268) **4416**
➤ The Journal of African American Children's Literature (USA ISSN 1557-2684) **5314**
• ➤ Journal of African American History (USA ISSN 1548-1867) **3544**
Journal of African American Men *see* Journal of African American Studies **6302**
Journal of African American Speeches *see* Vital Issues **7192**
• ➤ Journal of African American Studies (USA ISSN 1559-1646) **6302**

• ➤ Journal of African Archaeology (DEU ISSN 1612-1651) **400**
• ➤ Journal of African Business (USA ISSN 1522-8916) **1133**
Journal of African Children's and Youth Literature (USA ISSN 0795-4506) **2156**
Journal of African Christian Thought (GHA ISSN 0855-3262) **7653**
▼ • Journal of African Cinemas (GBR ISSN 1754-9221) **6505**
Journal of African Civilizations (USA ISSN 0270-2495) **344**
The Journal of African Communications (USA ISSN 1084-8142) **3544**
▼ Journal of African Conflicts and Peace Studies (RWA ISSN 1996-3157) **7247**
• ➤ Journal of African Cultural Studies (GBR ISSN 1369-6815) **4459**
Journal of African Cultures and Religion (KEN) **8111**
Journal of African Development (USA) **1133**
• ➤ Journal of African Earth Sciences (GBR ISSN 1464-343X) **2749**
• ➤ Journal of African Economies (GBR ISSN 0963-8024) **1494**
Journal of African Elections (ZAF ISSN 1609-4700) **7146**
• ➤ The Journal of African History (GBR ISSN 0021-8537) **4176**
• ➤ Journal of African Languages and Linguistics (DEU ISSN 0167-6164) **5132**
• Journal of African Law (GBR ISSN 0021-8553) **4700**
▼ • ➤ Journal of African Media Studies (GBR ISSN 1751-7974) **8111**
Journal of African Religion and Philosophy (UGA ISSN 1018-8592) **7654**
➤ Journal of African Studies/Afurika Kenkyu (JPN ISSN 0065-4140) **4176**
The Journal of African Traditional Studies (USA ISSN 1939-0661) **4176**
➤ Journal of African Travel-Writing (USA ISSN 1085-9527) **8725**
Journal of African Zoology (BEL ISSN 0776-7943) **949**
➤ Journal of Afro-Latin American Studies and Literatures (USA ISSN 1051-1865) **4459**
• Journal of Aggression, Maltreatment & Trauma (USA ISSN 1092-6771) **7368**
• ➤ Journal of Aging and Health (USA ISSN 0898-2643) **4048**
† • ➤ Journal of Aging & Pharmacotherapy (USA ISSN 1540-5303) **8968**
• ➤ Journal of Aging and Physical Activity (USA ISSN 1063-8652) **4048**
• ➤ Journal of Aging & Social Policy (USA ISSN 0895-9420) **4048**
▼ • Journal of Aging, Humanities, and the Arts (USA ISSN 1932-5614) **4048**
▼ • ➤ The Journal of Aging in Emerging Economies (USA ISSN 1944-009X) **4048**
• ➤ Journal of Aging Studies (GBR ISSN 0890-4065) **4048**
• ➤ Journal of Agrarian Change (GBR ISSN 1471-0358) **201**
Journal of Agribusiness (USA ISSN 0738-8950) **201**
• ➤ Journal of Agricultural and Applied Economics (USA ISSN 1074-0708) **201**
Journal of Agricultural and Environmental Engineering Technology *see* J A E E T **124**
• ➤ Journal of Agricultural and Environmental Ethics (NLD ISSN 1187-7863) **6927**
• ➤ Journal of Agricultural and Food Chemistry (USA ISSN 0021-8561) **238**
• ➤ Journal of Agricultural & Food Industrial Organization (USA ISSN 1542-0485) **201**
• ➤ Journal of Agricultural & Food Information (USA ISSN 1049-6505) **126**
• ➤ Journal of Agricultural & Resource Economics (USA ISSN 1068-5502) **201**
➤ Journal of Agricultural and Urban Entomology (USA ISSN 1523-5475) **851**
• ➤ Journal of Agricultural, Biological, and Environmental Statistics (USA ISSN 1085-7117) **716**
Journal of Agricultural Biotechnology *see* Nongye Shengwu Jishu Xuebao **141**
• ➤ Journal of Agricultural Economics (GBR ISSN 0021-857X) **202**
➤ Journal of Agricultural Education (USA ISSN 1042-0541) **2874**
• ➤ Journal of Agricultural Education and Extension (GBR ISSN 1389-224X) **126**
Journal of Agricultural Engineering (IND ISSN 0256-6524) **126**
▼ • Journal of Agricultural, Food, and Environmental Sciences (USA ISSN 1934-7235) **126**
• Journal of Agricultural Lending (USA ISSN 1542-5606) **1360**
Journal of Agricultural Research/Magallat al-Bihud al-Zira'iyyat Gaami'at Tantaa (EGY ISSN 1110-032X) **126**
• Journal of Agricultural Research (PAK ISSN 0368-1157) **126**
• ➤ Journal of Agricultural Safety and Health (USA ISSN 1074-7583) **126**
▼ • ➤ Journal of Agricultural Science (CAN ISSN 1916-9752) **126**
• ➤ The Journal of Agricultural Science (GBR ISSN 0021-8596) **126**
Journal of Agricultural Science and Technology (IRN ISSN 1680-7073) **126**
▼ • Journal of Agricultural Science and Technology (USA ISSN 1939-1250) **126**
Journal of Agricultural Sciences *see* Nongye Kexue Yanjiu **141**
Journal of Agricultural Sciences *see* Tarim Bilimleri Dergisi **160**
Journal of Agriculture and Environment for International Development (ITA ISSN 1590-7198) **126**
Journal of Agriculture & Forestry *see* Nonglin Xuebao **3698**
• ➤ Journal of Agriculture and Rural Development in the Tropics and Subtropics (DEU ISSN 1612-9830) **126**
• Journal of Agriculture and Social Research (NGA ISSN 1595-7470) **126**
• Journal of Agriculture, Science and Technology (KEN ISSN 1561-7645) **127**
Journal of Agro-Environment Science *see* Nongye Huanjing Kexue Xuebao **3457**
Journal of Agrobiology (CZE ISSN 1803-4403) **238**
• ➤ Journal of Agromedicine (USA ISSN 1059-924X) **6679**
Journal of Agrometeorology (IND ISSN 0972-1665) **127**
• ➤ Journal of Agronomy (PAK ISSN 1812-5379) **127**
• ➤ Journal of Agronomy and Crop Science/Zeitschrift fuer Acker- und Pflanzenbau (DEU ISSN 0931-2250) **239**
• ➤ Journal of Agronomy and Crop Science Online (DEU ISSN 1439-037X) **239**
Journal of Agrotechnical Economics *see* Nongye Jishu Jingji **204**
• ➤ Journal of AIDS/HIV (USA ISSN 1094-4958) **5819**
• ➤ Journal of Air Law and Commerce (USA ISSN 0021-8642) **4700**
Journal of Air Traffic Control (USA ISSN 0021-8650) **63**
• ➤ Journal of Air Transport Management (GBR ISSN 0969-6997) **1763**
• ➤ Journal of Air Transportation (USA ISSN 1544-6980) **8501**
Journal of Air Transportation World Wide *see* Journal of Air Transportation **8501**
• ➤ Journal of Aircraft (USA ISSN 0021-8669) **63**
• ➤ Journal of Airport Management (GBR ISSN 1750-1938) **8547**
• Journal of Alabama Archaeology (USA ISSN 0449-2153) **400**
Journal of Alaska Business and Commerce *see* Alaska Journal of Commerce **1425**
• ➤ Journal of Alcohol and Drug Education (USA ISSN 0090-1482) **2695**
• ➤ Journal of Algebra (USA ISSN 0021-8693) **5500**
• ➤ Journal of Algebra and its Applications (SGP ISSN 0219-4988) **5500**
• ➤ Journal of Algebraic Combinatorics (USA ISSN 0925-9899) **5500**
• ➤ Journal of Algebraic Geometry (USA ISSN 1056-3911) **5500**
• ➤ Journal of Algorithms (USA ISSN 0196-6774) **5553**
▼ • ➤ Journal of Algorithms & Computational Technology (GBR ISSN 1748-3018) **5500**
Journal of Algorithms in Cognition, Informatics and Logic *see* Journal of Algorithms **5553**
• ➤ Journal of Allergy and Clinical Immunology (USA ISSN 0091-6749) **5762**
• ➤ Journal of Allied Health (USA ISSN 0090-7421) **7528**
• ➤ Journal of Alloys and Compounds (NLD ISSN 0925-8388) **6319**
Journal of Alpine Research *see* La Revue de Geographie Alpine **4027**
• ➤ Journal of Alternative & Complementary Medicine (USA ISSN 1075-5535) **311**
† Journal of Alternative Dispute Resolution in Employment (USA ISSN 1525-7088) **8968**
Journal of Alternative Dispute Resolution, Mediation and Negotiation (GBR ISSN 1470-6717) **1690**
• The Journal of Alternative Investments (USA ISSN 1520-3255) **1634**
▼ ➤ Journal of Alternative Medicine Research (USA ISSN 1939-5868) **311**
▼ • ➤ Journal of Alternative Perspectives in the Social Sciences (USA ISSN 1944-1088) **7977**
• ➤ Journal of Alzheimer's Disease (NLD ISSN 1387-2877) **6149**
▼ Journal of Ambient Intelligence and Smart Environments (NLD ISSN 1876-1364) **2452**
• ➤ Journal of Ambulatory Care Management (USA ISSN 0148-9917) **4103**
Journal of American Academy of Business, Cambridge *see* American Academy of Business, Cambridge. Journal **1058**
➤ Journal of American and Canadian Studies (JPN ISSN 0914-8035) **4459**
Journal of American and Comparative Culture *see* Journal of American Culture **4459**
• The Journal of American Arbitration (USA ISSN 1535-4849) **4700**
• ➤ The Journal of American College Health (USA ISSN 0744-8481) **6990**
• ➤ Journal of American Culture (USA ISSN 1542-7331) **4459**
➤ Journal of American Drama and Theatre (USA ISSN 1044-937X) **8472**
• Journal of American - East Asian Relations (NLD ISSN 1058-3947) **7977**
• ➤ Journal of American Ethnic History (USA ISSN 0278-5927) **3544**
• ➤ Journal of American Folklore (USA ISSN 0021-8715) **3619**
➤ Journal of American Herbalists Guild (USA ISSN 1538-7496) **311**
• ➤ Journal of American History (USA ISSN 0021-8723) **4298**
• ➤ Journal of American Indian Education (USA ISSN 0021-8731) **6635**
Journal of American Indian Family Research (USA ISSN 0730-6148) **6635**
Journal of American Indian Family Research Monthly Newsletter (USA ISSN 1040-6581) **6635**
Journal of American Organbuilding (USA ISSN 1048-2482) **6580**
• ➤ Journal of American Physicians and Surgeons (USA ISSN 1543-4826) **5645**
The Journal of American Science (USA ISSN 1545-1003) **7871**
• ➤ Journal of American Studies (GBR ISSN 0021-8758) **4299**
Journal of American Studies of Turkey *see* J A S T **4298**
Journal of America's Military Past *see* J A M P **4298**
▼ • ➤ Journal of Amino Acids (USA ISSN 2090-0112) **734**
➤ Journal of Anaesthesia & Critical Care (PAK ISSN 1021-8009) **5771**
• Journal of Anaesthesiology - Clinical Pharmacology (IND ISSN 0970-9185) **5771**
Journal of Analysis (IND ISSN 0971-3611) **5500**
Journal of Analysis and Applications (IND ISSN 0972-5954) **5500**
Journal of Analysis and Computation (IND ISSN 0973-2861) **5500**
• ➤ Journal of Analytical and Applied Pyrolysis (NLD ISSN 0165-2370) **2066**
• ➤ Journal of Analytical Atomic Spectrometry (GBR ISSN 0267-9477) **2101**
Journal of Analytical Bio-Science *see* Seibutsu Shiryo Bunseki **703**
• ➤ Journal of Analytical Chemistry (RUS ISSN 1061-9348) **2101**
• ➤ Journal of Analytical Psychology (GBR ISSN 0021-8774) **7368**
Journal of Analytical Science *see* Fenxi Kexue Xuebao **7854**
• ➤ Journal of Analytical Toxicology (USA ISSN 0146-4760) **3498**
• ➤ Journal of Anatomy (GBR ISSN 0021-8782) **680**
Journal of Ancient and Medieval Studies (USA) **4148**
Journal of Ancient Books Collation and Studies *see* Guji Zhengli Yanjiu Xuekan **5011**
Journal of Ancient Christianity *see* Zeitschrift fuer Antikes Christentum **7696**
• Journal of Ancient Civilizations (CHN ISSN 1004-9371) **4149**
▼ • Journal of Ancient Egyptian Interconnections (USA ISSN 1944-2815) **400**
Journal of Ancient History *see* Vestnik Drevnei Istorii **4166**
• ➤ Journal of Ancient Near Eastern Religions (NLD ISSN 1569-2116) **7737**
Journal of Ancient Topography/Rivista di Topografia Antica (ITA ISSN 1121-5275) **2236**
Journal of Andrological Sciences (ITA ISSN 2035-3901) **5645**
• ➤ Journal of Andrology (USA ISSN 0196-3635) **5645**
▼ • Journal of Andrology, Sexual Medicine, Ageing and Gender (IND ISSN 0974-1224) **5645**
• ➤ Journal of Anesthesia (JPN ISSN 0913-8668) **5772**
• Journal of Anglican Studies (GBR ISSN 1740-3553) **7762**
Journal of Anglo-Italian Studies (MLT ISSN 1560-2168) **5314**
➤ Journal of Animal and Feed Sciences (POL ISSN 1230-1388) **290**
The Journal of Animal and Plant Sciences *see* The J A P S **949**
• Journal of Animal and Veterinary Advances (PAK ISSN 1680-5593) **8800**
• ➤ Journal of Animal Breeding and Genetics/Zeitschrift fuer Tierzuechtung und Zuechtungsbiologie (DEU ISSN 0931-2668) **291**
• Journal of Animal Breeding and Genetics Online (DEU ISSN 1439-0388) **291**
• ➤ Journal of Animal Ecology (GBR ISSN 0021-8790) **680**
• Journal of Animal Ethics (USA) **320**
Journal of Animal Genetics *see* Dobutsu Iden Ikushu Kenkyu **866**
• ➤ Journal of Animal Law (USA) **4700**
Journal of Animal Law and Ethics (USA) **4700**
Journal of Animal Morphology and Physiology (IND ISSN 0021-8804) **680**
• ➤ Journal of Animal Physiology and Animal Nutrition/Zeitschrift fuer Tierphysiologie und Tierernaehrung (DEU ISSN 0931-2439) **923**
• Journal of Animal Physiology and Animal Nutrition Online (DEU ISSN 1439-0396) **923**
Journal of Animal Production of the United Arab Republic *see* Egyptian Journal of Animal Production **285**
Journal of Animal Production Research *see* Nigeria. National Animal Production Research Institute. Journal **295**
• ➤ Journal of Animal Science (USA ISSN 0021-8812) **291**
Journal of Animal Science and Technology *see* Han'gug Dongmul Jawon Gwahag Hoeji **288**
➤ Journal of Animal Science. Supplement. Biennial Symposium on Animal Reproduction (USA ISSN 0890-0108) **923**
Journal of Ankem *see* Ankem Dergisi **5943**
• ➤ Journal of Anthropological Archaeology (USA ISSN 0278-4165) **344**
• ➤ Journal of Anthropological Research (USA ISSN 0091-7710) **344**
Journal of Anthropological Sciences (ITA ISSN 1827-4765) **344**
Journal of Anti-Aging Medicine *see* Rejuvenation Research **4054**
Journal of Antibacterial and Antifungal Agents *see* Bokin Bobai **882**
• ➤ Journal of Antibiotics (GBR ISSN 0021-8820) **5645**
• ➤ Journal of Antimicrobial Chemotherapy (GBR ISSN 0305-7453) **5819**
• ➤ Journal of Anxiety Disorders (GBR ISSN 0887-6185) **7368**
➤ Journal of Aphidology (IND ISSN 0970-3810) **851**
Journal of Apicultural Research *see* Journal of Apicultural Research & Bee World **127**
• ➤ Journal of Apicultural Research & Bee World (GBR ISSN 1751-2891) **127**
➤ Journal of Apicultural Science (POL ISSN 1643-4439) **127**
Journal of Apoplexy and Nervous Diseases *see* Zhongfeng yu Shenjing Jibing Zazhi **6191**
• ➤ Journal of Appalachian Studies (USA ISSN 1082-7161) **7977**
• Journal of Appellate Practice and Process (USA ISSN 1533-4724) **4700**
• ➤ Journal of Applied Accounting Research (GBR ISSN 0967-5426) **1294**
Journal of Applied Algebra and Discrete Structures (IND ISSN 0972-5946) **5500**
• ➤ Journal of Applied Analysis (DEU ISSN 1425-6908) **5500**
▼ • Journal of Applied and Industrial Mathematics (RUS ISSN 1990-4789) **5500**
• ➤ Journal of Applied Animal Research (IND ISSN 0971-2119) **949**
• ➤ Journal of Applied Animal Welfare Science (USA ISSN 1088-8705) **320**
• ➤ Journal of Applied Aquaculture (USA ISSN 1045-4438) **3599**
• ➤ Journal of Applied Behavior Analysis (USA ISSN 0021-8855) **7368**
• ➤ The Journal of Applied Behavioral Science (USA ISSN 0021-8863) **7368**
• ➤ Journal of Applied Biobehavioral Research (USA ISSN 1071-2089) **7369**
• Journal of Applied Biological Chemistry (KOR ISSN 1976-0442) **127**
▼ • Journal of Applied Biological Sciences (TUR ISSN 1307-1130) **680**
Journal of Applied Biology (IND ISSN 0971-4324) **680**
• Journal of Applied Biomaterials and Biomechanics (ITA ISSN 1722-6899) **766**
• ➤ Journal of Applied Biomechanics (USA ISSN 1065-8483) **923**
• ➤ Journal of Applied Biomedicine (CZE ISSN 1214-021X) **5645**
▼ • Journal of Applied Biosciences (KEN ISSN 1997-5902) **766**
• ➤ Journal of Applied Botany and Food Quality (DEU ISSN 1613-9216) **796**
➤ Journal of Applied Business and Economics (USA ISSN 1499-691X) **1133**
• ➤ Journal of Applied Business Research (USA ISSN 0892-7626) **1133**
Journal of Applied Chemistry & Biotechnology. Abstracts *see* Journal of Chemical Technology and Biotechnology **767**
➤ Journal of Applied Christian Leadership (USA ISSN 1933-3978) **7654**
• ➤ Journal of Applied Clinical Medical Physics (USA ISSN 1526-9914) **5906**
Journal of Applied Clinical Pediatrics *see* Shiyong Erke Linchuang Zazhi **6104**
• ➤ Journal of Applied Communication Research (USA ISSN 0090-9882) **2329**
➤ Journal of Applied Communications (USA ISSN 1051-0834) **127**
➤ Journal of Applied Computer Science (POL ISSN 1507-0360) **2428**
Journal of Applied Computer Science *see* Journal of Applied Computer Science & Mathematics **5500**
▼ • ➤ Journal of Applied Computer Science & Mathematics (ROM ISSN 2066-4273) **5500**
• ➤ Journal of Applied Corporate Finance (USA ISSN 1078-1196) **1360**
† Journal of Applied Cosmetology (ITA ISSN 0392-8543) **8968**
• ➤ Journal of Applied Crystallography (DNK ISSN 0021-8898) **2111**
• ➤ Journal of Applied Developmental Psychology (GBR ISSN 0193-3973) **7369**
• ➤ Journal of Applied Ecology (GBR ISSN 0021-8901) **680**
Journal of Applied Ecology. Supplement *see* Journal of Applied Ecology **680**
• ➤ Journal of Applied Econometrics (GBR ISSN 0883-7252) **1544**

Title

▼ *new title* † *ceased* • *electronic media* ➤ *refereed*

Title

DIRECTORY 2010 JOURNAL OF COMMUNITY INFORMATICS 10491

Journal of Chitin and Chitosan see Han'gug Kitin Kito'san Haghoeji **3244**
• Journal of Christian Apologetics (USA) **7762**
• ➤ Journal of Christian Education (AUS ISSN 0021-9657) **7654**
Journal of Christian Education (USA) **7762**
Journal of Christian Education of the African Methodist Episcopal Church see Journal of Christian Education **7762**
• The Journal of Christian Healing (USA ISSN 0738-2944) **7370**
• Journal of Christian Nursing (USA ISSN 0743-2550) **5964**
Journal of Christian Reconstruction (USA ISSN 0360-1420) **7654**
Journal of Christianity and Foreign Languages (USA ISSN 1538-439X) **5133**
• ➤ Journal of Chromatographic Science (USA ISSN 0021-9665) **2101**
• ➤ Journal of Chromatography A (NLD ISSN 0021-9673) **2101**
• ➤ Journal of Chromatography. B, Analytical Technologies in the Biomedical and Life Sciences (NLD ISSN 1570-0232) **2067**
Journal of Chromatography. Bibliography Section see Journal of Chromatography Library **2101**
Journal of Chromatography. Bibliography Section see Journal of Chromatography A **2101**
➤ Journal of Chromatography Library (NLD ISSN 0301-4770) **2101**
Journal of Chromatography. Supplementary Volume see Journal of Chromatography Library **2101**
Journal of Chromatography. Supplementary Volume see Journal of Chromatography A **2101**
† • ➤ Journal of Chronic Fatigue Syndrome (USA ISSN 1057-3321) **8968**
• ➤ Journal of Church and State (USA ISSN 0021-969X) **7654**
• ➤ Journal of Circadian Rhythms (GBR ISSN 1740-3391) **5646**
Journal of Circuits and Systems see Dianlu yu Xitong Xuebao **3092**
• ➤ Journal of Circuits, Systems and Computers (SGP ISSN 0218-1266) **2466**
Journal of Civil and Hydraulic Engineering (TWN ISSN 0253-3804) **3274**
Journal of Civil Defense (USA ISSN 0740-5537) **2227**
Journal of Civil Engineering see Journal of Civil Engineering Research and Practice **3274**
▼ • Journal of Civil Engineering and Architecture (USA ISSN 1934-7359) **3274**
➤ Journal of Civil Engineering and Management (LTU ISSN 1392-3730) **3274**
• ➤ Journal of Civil Engineering Research and Practice (KEN ISSN 1729-5769) **3274**
➤ Journal of Civil Liberties (GBR ISSN 1362-3451) **7211**
The Journal of Civil Litigation (USA) **4833**
Journal of Civil Practice and Procedure (IRL ISSN 1649-640X) **4833**
Journal of Civil Procedure/Minji Sosho Zasshi (JPN ISSN 0075-4188) **4833**
• Journal of Civil Society (GBR ISSN 1744-8689) **7146**
➤ The Journal of Civil War Medicine (USA ISSN 1545-4975) **5647**
Journal of Clan Ewing see Ewing Family Journal **3765**
• ➤ Journal of Classical Sociology (GBR ISSN 1468-795X) **8112**
Journal of Classical Studies see Seiyo Kotengaku Kenkyu **2240**
• ➤ Journal of Classification (USA ISSN 0176-4268) **5020**
• ➤ Journal of Classroom Interaction (USA ISSN 0749-4025) **2874**
▼ • Journal of Classroom Teaching & Learning (USA ISSN 1944-284X) **2874**
• ➤ Journal of Cleaner Production (NLD ISSN 0959-6526) **3369**
• ➤ Journal of Climate (USA ISSN 0894-8755) **6358**
Journal of Clinical Activities, Assignments & Handouts in Psychotherapy Practice see Journal of Creativity in Mental Health **7372**
▼ • ➤ The Journal of Clinical and Aesthetic Dermatology (USA ISSN 1941-2789) **5878**
▼ • Journal of Clinical and Diagnostic Research (IND ISSN 0973-709X) **5647**
• Journal of Clinical and Experimental Hematopathology (JPN ISSN 1346-4280) **5939**
Journal of Clinical and Experimental Medicine see Linchuang he Shiyan Yixue Zazhi **5909**
Journal of Clinical and Experimental Medicine see Igaku no Ayumi **5632**
Journal of Clinical and Experimental Neuropsychology see Neuropsychology, Development and Cognition. Section A: Journal of Clinical and Experimental Neuropsychology **7387**
Journal of Clinical and Experimental Pathology see Linchuang yu Shiyan Binglixue Zazhi **5662**
Journal of Clinical & Laboratory Immunology (GBR ISSN 0141-2760) **5762**
Journal of Clinical Anesthesia see Rinsho Masui **5774**
• ➤ Journal of Clinical Anesthesia (USA ISSN 0952-8180) **5772**
Journal of Clinical Anesthesiology see Linchuang Mazuixue Zazhi **5772**
• ➤ Journal of Clinical Apheresis (USA ISSN 0733-2459) **5939**
• ➤ Journal of Clinical Biochemical and Nutrition (JPN ISSN 0912-0009) **736**
Journal of Clinical Cardiology see Linchuang Xinxueguanbing Zazhi **5795**
• ➤ Journal of Clinical Child and Adolescent Psychology (USA ISSN 1537-4416) **7370**
➤ Journal of Clinical Chiropractic Pediatrics (USA) **5806**
• ➤ Journal of Clinical Densitometry (NLD ISSN 1094-6950) **5647**
➤ The Journal of Clinical Dentistry (USA ISSN 0895-8831) **5850**
Journal of Clinical Dermatology see Linchuang Pifuke Zazhi **5879**
Journal of Clinical Electroneurophysiology see Linchuang Shenjing Dianshenglixue Zazhi **6158**
† Journal of Clinical Electrophysiology (USA ISSN 0892-5070) **8968**
▼ • The Journal of Clinical Embryology (USA ISSN 1941-1901) **682**
Journal of Clinical Emergence Call see Linchuang Jizhen Zazhi **6066**
• ➤ Journal of Clinical Endocrinology and Metabolism (USA ISSN 0021-972X) **5895**
• ➤ Journal of Clinical Engineering (USA ISSN 0363-8855) **750**
• ➤ Journal of Clinical Epidemiology (USA ISSN 0895-4356) **5647**
• ➤ The Journal of Clinical Ethics (USA ISSN 1046-7890) **5647**
Journal of Clinical Excellence see Quality in Primary Care (Print) **5701**
• Journal of Clinical Forensic and Legal Medicine (GBR ISSN 1752-928X) **5914**
Journal of Clinical Forensic Medicine see Journal of Clinical Forensic and Legal Medicine **5914**
• ➤ Journal of Clinical Gastroenterology (USA ISSN 0192-0790) **5927**
Journal of Clinical Governance (Online) see Quality in Primary Care (Online) **5701**
Journal of Clinical Governance (Print) see Quality in Primary Care (Print) **5701**
• ➤ Journal of Clinical Hypertension (USA ISSN 1524-6175) **5793**
• ➤ Journal of Clinical Immunology (USA ISSN 0271-9142) **5762**
• ➤ Journal of Clinical Investigation (USA ISSN 0021-9738) **5647**
• ➤ Journal of Clinical Laboratory Analysis (USA ISSN 0887-8013) **5907**
Journal of Clinical Laboratory Science see Linchuang Jianyan Zazhi **5909**
Journal of Clinical Laser Medicine & Surgery see Photomedicine and Laser Surgery **6205**
• Journal of Clinical Ligand Assay (USA ISSN 1081-1672) **5762**
Journal of Clinical Ligand Assay (Italian Edition) (ITA ISSN 1124-8203) **5762**
▼ • ➤ Journal of Clinical Lipidology (USA ISSN 1933-2874) **5793**
Journal of Clinical Medicine see Linchuang Neike Zazhi **5661**
Journal of Clinical Medicine in Practice see Shiyong Linchuang Yiyao Zazhi **5714**
• ➤ Journal of Clinical Microbiology (USA ISSN 0095-1137) **5647**
• ➤ Journal of Clinical Monitoring and Computing (NLD ISSN 1387-1307) **5647**
Journal of Clinical Neurology see Linchuang Shenjingbingxue Zazhi **6158**
• Journal of Clinical Neuromuscular Disease (USA ISSN 1522-0443) **5647**
• ➤ Journal of Clinical Neurophysiology (USA ISSN 0736-0258) **6150**
• ➤ Journal of Clinical Neuroscience (GBR ISSN 0967-5868) **6150**
• ➤ Journal of Clinical Nursing (GBR ISSN 0962-1067) **5964**
• ➤ Journal of Clinical Oncology (USA ISSN 0732-183X) **6024**
Journal of Clinical Ophthalmology see Linchuang Yanke Zazhi **5661**
• ➤ Journal of Clinical Orthodontics (USA ISSN 0022-3875) **5850**
Journal of Clinical Otolaryngology see Linchuang Erbi Yanhouke Zazhi **6082**
• ➤ Journal of Clinical Outcomes Management (USA ISSN 1079-6533) **4103**
• ➤ Journal of Clinical Pathology (GBR ISSN 0021-9746) **5647**
• ➤ Journal of Clinical Pediatric Dentistry (USA ISSN 1053-4628) **5851**
Journal of Clinical Pediatrics see Linchuang Erke Zazhi **6096**
Journal of Clinical Pediatrics/Rinsho Shoni Igaku (JPN ISSN 0035-550X) **6094**
• ➤ Journal of Clinical Periodontology (DNK ISSN 0303-6979) **5851**
Journal of Clinical Periodontology. Supplement see Journal of Clinical Periodontology **5851**
• ➤ The Journal of Clinical Pharmacology (USA ISSN 0091-2700) **6852**
• ➤ Journal of Clinical Pharmacy and Therapeutics (GBR ISSN 0269-4727) **6852**
• ➤ Journal of Clinical Problem-Based Learning (USA ISSN 1522-7529) **2874**
• ➤ Journal of Clinical Psychiatry (USA ISSN 0160-6689) **6150**
Journal of Clinical Psychiatry (Audiograph Series) see Journal of Clinical Psychiatry **6150**
Journal of Clinical Psychiatry Monograph Series (USA ISSN 0742-1915) **6150**
➤ Journal of Clinical Psychoanalysis (USA ISSN 1076-044X) **7370**
Journal of Clinical Psychological Medicine see Linchuang Jingshen Yixue Zazhi **6158**
• ➤ Journal of Clinical Psychology (USA ISSN 0021-9762) **7370**
• ➤ Journal of Clinical Psychology in Medical Settings (USA ISSN 1068-9583) **7370**
• ➤ Journal of Clinical Psychopharmacology (USA ISSN 0271-0749) **6853**
Journal of Clinical Radiology see Linchuang Fangshexue Zazhi **6202**
Journal of Clinical Rehabilitation (JPN ISSN 0918-5259) **6111**
Journal of Clinical Rehabilitative Tissue Engineering Research see Zhongguo Zuzhi Gongcheng yu Linchuang Kangfu **6117**
Journal of Clinical Research see Yixue Linchuang Yanjiu **5733**
➤ Journal of Clinical Research (GBR ISSN 1369-5207) **6853**
• Journal of Clinical Research Best Practices (USA ISSN 1557-5101) **5907**
Journal of Clinical Research Practice see Research Practitioner **5910**
• ➤ Journal of Clinical Rheumatology (USA ISSN 1076-1608) **6224**
• The Journal of Clinical Sleep Medicine (USA ISSN 1550-9389) **6151**
▼ • ➤ Journal of Clinical Sport Psychology (USA ISSN 1932-9261) **7370**
Journal of Clinical Stomatology see Linchuang Kouqiang Yixue **5928**
Journal of Clinical Surgery see Linchuang Waike Zazhi **6251**
Journal of Clinical Surgery see Rinsho Geka **6257**
Journal of Clinical Transfusion and Laboratory Medicine see Linchuang Shuxue yu Jianyan **5909**
• Journal of Clinical Ultrasound (USA ISSN 0091-2751) **6200**
Journal of Clinical Urological Surgery see Linchuang Miniao Waike Zazhi **6271**
Journal of Clinical Veterinary Medicine see Rinsho Jui **8807**
• ➤ Journal of Clinical Virology (NLD ISSN 1386-6532) **5819**
• ➤ Journal of Cluster Science (USA ISSN 1040-7278) **2067**
• ➤ Journal of Co-operative Studies (GBR ISSN 0961-5784) **1424**
Journal of Co-ordination Chemistry see Journal of Coordination Chemistry **2068**
▼ • ➤ Journal of Coaching Education (USA ISSN 1938-7016) **8182**
• Journal of Coal Science & Engineering (CHN ISSN 1006-9097) **6467**
• ➤ Journal of Coastal Conservation (NLD ISSN 1400-0350) **2809**
• Journal of Coastal Development (IDN ISSN 1410-5217) **8827**
• ➤ Journal of Coastal Research (USA ISSN 0749-0208) **2809**
Journal of Coastal Research. Special Issue (USA) **2809**
▼ • ➤ Journal of Coatings Technology and Research (USA ISSN 1945-9645) **6718**
Journal of Coatings Technology CoatingsTech see J C T CoatingsTech **6718**
The Journal of Coelio-Surgery see Le Journal de Coelio-Chirurgie **6247**
Journal of Coffee Research (IND) **3649**
• ➤ Journal of Cognition and Culture (NLD ISSN 1567-7095) **7370**
• ➤ Journal of Cognition and Development (USA ISSN 1524-8372) **7370**
Journal of Cognitive and Behavioral Psychotherapies (ROM ISSN 1584-7101) **7371**
• ➤ Journal of Cognitive Education and Psychology (USA ISSN 1945-8959) **3067**
• Journal of Cognitive Engineering and Decision Making (USA ISSN 1555-3434) **7371**
Journal of Cognitive Liberties (USA ISSN 1527-3946) **7371**
• ➤ Journal of Cognitive Neuroscience (USA ISSN 0898-929X) **6151**
• ➤ Journal of Cognitive Psychotherapy (USA ISSN 0889-8391) **7371**
• Journal of Cognitive Rehabilitation (USA ISSN 1062-2969) **6111**
• ➤ Journal of Cold Regions Engineering (USA ISSN 0887-381X) **3274**
• ➤ Journal of Cold War Studies (USA ISSN 1520-3972) **7247**
▼ • ➤ Journal of Collective Bargaining in the Academy (USA ISSN 1941-8043) **2989**
• ➤ Journal of Collective Negotiations (USA) **4596**
• Journal of College Admission (USA ISSN 0734-6670) **2989**
• Journal of College and Character (USA ISSN 1940-1639) **2989**
• Journal of College and University Law (USA ISSN 0093-8688) **4700**
• ➤ Journal of College and University Student Housing (USA ISSN 0161-827X) **2989**
• ➤ Journal of College Counseling (USA ISSN 1099-0399) **2989**
➤ The Journal of College Literacy and Learning (USA) **2989**
Journal of College of Medicine see University of Nigeria. College of Medicine. Journal **5727**
Journal of College Radio (USA ISSN 0010-1133) **2359**
• ➤ Journal of College Reading and Learning (USA ISSN 1079-0195) **2989**
• ➤ Journal of College Science Teaching (USA ISSN 0047-231X) **7872**
• ➤ Journal of College Student Development (USA ISSN 0897-5264) **2989**
• ➤ Journal of College Student Psychotherapy (USA ISSN 8756-8225) **7371**
• ➤ Journal of College Student Retention: Research, Theory & Practice (USA ISSN 1521-0251) **2989**
➤ Journal of College Teaching and Learning (USA ISSN 1544-0389) **2989**
Journal of College Writing see Louisiana Association for College Composition Journal **5148**
• ➤ Journal of Colloid and Interface Science (USA ISSN 0021-9797) **2136**
• ➤ Journal of Colonialism & Colonial History (USA ISSN 1532-5768) **4149**
Journal of Coloproctological Surgery see Dachang-Gangmenbing Waike Zazhi **5603**
• ➤ Journal of Combinatorial Chemistry (USA ISSN 1520-4766) **2102**
• Journal of Combinatorial Designs (USA ISSN 1063-8539) **5501**
Journal of Combinatorial Mathematics and Combinatorial Computing see J C M C C **5499**
• ➤ Journal of Combinatorial Optimization (USA ISSN 1382-6905) **5553**
• ➤ Journal of Combinatorial Theory, Series A (USA ISSN 0097-3165) **5501**
• ➤ Journal of Combinatorial Theory. Series B (USA ISSN 0095-8956) **5501**
• ➤ The Journal of Combinatorics (USA ISSN 1097-1440) **5501**
▼ ➤ Journal of Combinatorics and Number Theory (USA ISSN 1942-5600) **5501**
Journal of Combustion Science and Technology see Ranshao Kexue yu Jishu **7056**
• Journal of Commerce (CAN ISSN 0709-1230) **1430**
• Journal of Commerce (THA ISSN 0125-0566) **1494**
• The Journal of Commerce (USA ISSN 1542-3867) **1430**
Journal of Commercial Banking and Finance see Academy of Banking Studies Journal **1305**
• ➤ Journal of Commercial Biotechnology (GBR ISSN 1462-8732) **767**
Journal of Commodity Science see Journal of Commodity Science, Technology and Quality **1430**
• Journal of Commodity Science, Technology and Quality (ITA ISSN 1971-4483) **1430**
• ➤ Journal of Common Market Studies (GBR ISSN 0021-9886) **7146**
➤ Journal of Commonwealth and Postcolonial Studies (USA ISSN 1073-1687) **5314**
• ➤ Journal of Commonwealth Law and Legal Education (GBR ISSN 1476-0401) **4700**
• ➤ Journal of Commonwealth Literature (GBR ISSN 0021-9894) **5314**
Journal of Communicable Diseases (IND ISSN 0019-5138) **5820**
• ➤ Journal of Communication (USA ISSN 0021-9916) **8112**
• Journal of Communication and Computer/Tongxun he Jisuanji (USA ISSN 1548-7709) **2351**
• The Journal of Communication and Religion (USA ISSN 0894-2838) **7654**
Journal of Communication between Rural Communities and Towns/Noson to Toshi o Musubu (JPN ISSN 0913-6134) **202**
• ➤ Journal of Communication Disorders (USA ISSN 0021-9924) **7371**
▼ • ➤ Journal of Communication in Healthcare (GBR ISSN 1753-8068) **5647**
• ➤ Journal of Communication Inquiry (USA ISSN 0196-8599) **8112**
• ➤ Journal of Communication Management (GBR ISSN 1363-254X) **1765**
Journal of Communication Studies (IND) **8112**
▼ • ➤ Journal of Communication Studies (USA ISSN 1940-9338) **8112**
• ➤ Journal of Communications (FIN ISSN 1796-2021) **2329**
• Journal of Communications and Networks (KOR ISSN 1229-2370) **2500**
▼ • Journal of Communications Research (USA ISSN 1935-3537) **8112**
• ➤ Journal of Communications Technology and Electronics (RUS ISSN 1064-2269) **2329**
• ➤ Journal of Communist Studies and Transition Politics (GBR ISSN 1352-3279) **7247**
• ➤ Journal of Community & Applied Social Psychology (GBR ISSN 1052-9284) **7371**
➤ The Journal of Community Association Law (USA ISSN 1096-2921) **4417**
Journal of Community Corrections see I C C A Journal on Community Corrections **2654**
▼ • Journal of Community Engagement and Higher Education (USA ISSN 1934-5283) **2989**
• ➤ Journal of Community Health (USA ISSN 0094-5145) **5647**
• ➤ Journal of Community Health Nursing (USA ISSN 0737-0016) **5964**
• ➤ Journal of Community Informatics (CAN ISSN 1712-4441) **2329**

Title

▼ *new title* † *ceased* • *electronic media* ➤ *refereed*

• ➤ Journal of Community Medicine and Primary Health Care (NGA ISSN 0794-7410) **5648**
• Journal of Community Nursing (GBR) **5964**
Journal of Community Nutrition *see* Nutrition Research and Practice **6666**
• ➤ Journal of Community Practice (USA ISSN 1070-5422) **8049**
• ➤ Journal of Community Psychology (USA ISSN 0090-4392) **7371**
The Journal of Community Work & Development (GBR ISSN 1475-9047) **8112**
▼ • Journal of Commutative Algebra (USA ISSN 1939-0807) **5501**
The Journal of Comparative Asian Development (USA ISSN 1533-9114) **1599**
• ➤ Journal of Comparative Economics (USA ISSN 0147-5967) **1134**
• ➤ Journal of Comparative Family Studies (CAN ISSN 0047-2328) **8112**
• ➤ The Journal of Comparative Germanic Linguistics (NLD ISSN 1383-4924) **5133**
• ➤ Journal of Comparative International Management (CAN ISSN 1481-0468) **1765**
Journal of Comparative Law *see* Bijiaofa Yanjiu **4630**
➤ Journal of Comparative Law (GBR ISSN 1477-0814) **4700**
➤ Journal of Comparative Literature and Aesthetics (IND ISSN 0252-8169) **5314**
• ➤ The Journal of Comparative Neurology (USA ISSN 0021-9967) **6151**
• ➤ Journal of Comparative Pathology (GBR ISSN 0021-9975) **682**
• ➤ Journal of Comparative Physiology A (DEU ISSN 0340-7594) **924**
• ➤ Journal of Comparative Physiology B (DEU ISSN 0174-1578) **924**
• Journal of Comparative Policy Analysis (GBR ISSN 1387-6988) **7448**
• ➤ Journal of Comparative Psychology (USA ISSN 0735-7036) **7371**
• ➤ Journal of Comparative Social Welfare (GBR ISSN 1748-6831) **8049**
• Journal of Compensation & Benefits (USA ISSN 0893-780X) **1868**
Journal of Compensation Medicine *see* Baisho Igaku **5583**
• ➤ Journal of Competition Law and Economics (GBR ISSN 1744-6414) **4700**
• ➤ Journal of Competitive Intelligence and Management (USA ISSN 1540-4242) **1765**
• ➤ Journal of Complementary & Integrative Medicine (USA ISSN 1553-3840) **311**
➤ The Journal of Complementary Medicine (AUS ISSN 1446-8263) **5648**
Journal of Complementary Medicine (GBR ISSN 0266-9072) **5648**
• ➤ Journal of Complexity (USA ISSN 0885-064X) **5553**
• ➤ Journal of Composite Materials (GBR ISSN 0021-9983) **3349**
• ➤ Journal of Composites for Construction (USA ISSN 1090-0268) **3274**
• ➤ Journal of Composition Theory (USA) **5314**
• ➤ Journal of Computational Acoustics (SGP ISSN 0218-396X) **7050**
• ➤ Journal of Computational Analysis and Applications (USA ISSN 1521-1398) **5501**
• ➤ Journal of Computational and Applied Mathematics (NLD ISSN 0377-0427) **5502**
• Journal of Computational and Applied Mechanics (HUN ISSN 1586-2070) **7059**
• ➤ Journal of Computational and Graphical Statistics (USA ISSN 1061-8600) **5502**
• ➤ Journal of Computational and Nonlinear Dynamics (USA ISSN 1555-1415) **3385**
• ➤ Journal of Computational and Theoretical Nanoscience (USA ISSN 1546-1955) **7019**
• ➤ Journal of Computational Biology (Online) (USA ISSN 1557-8666) **682**
† • ➤ Journal of Computational Biology (Print) (USA ISSN 1066-5277) **8968**
• ➤ Journal of Computational Chemistry (USA ISSN 0192-8651) **2068**
• ➤ Journal of Computational Electronics (USA ISSN 1569-8025) **2428**
The Journal of Computational Finance (GBR ISSN 1460-1559) **1419**
Journal of Computational Information Systems (USA ISSN 1553-9105) **2548**
▼ • ➤ Journal of Computational Intelligence in Bioinformatics (IND ISSN 0973-385X) **2453**
• ➤ Journal of Computational Mathematics (CHN ISSN 0254-9409) **5502**
• ➤ Journal of Computational Methods in Sciences and Engineering (NLD ISSN 1472-7978) **5502**
▼ • ➤ The Journal of Computational Multiphase Flows (GBR ISSN 1757-482X) **5553**
• ➤ Journal of Computational Neuroscience (USA ISSN 0929-5313) **6151**
▼ Journal of Computational Optimization in Economics and Finance (USA ISSN 1941-3971) **1393**
• ➤ Journal of Computational Physics (USA ISSN 0021-9991) **7050**
Journal of Computational Structural Mechanics and Applications *see* Jisuan Jiegou Lixue Jiqi Yingyong **3384**
• Journal of Computer Aided Chemistry (JPN ISSN 1345-8647) **2108**
Journal of Computer-Aided Design & Computer Graphics *see* Jisuanji Funzhu Sheji yu Tuxingxue Xuebao **2487**
• ➤ Journal of Computer - Aided Molecular Design (NLD ISSN 0920-654X) **2108**
Journal of Computer and Communication Applications *see* Diannao yu Tongxun Yingyong **2416**
• ➤ Journal of Computer and System Sciences (USA ISSN 0022-0000) **2523**
• ➤ Journal of Computer and System Sciences International (RUS ISSN 1064-2307) **2527**
Journal of Computer Applications *see* Jisuanji Yingyong **2428**
• ➤ Journal of Computer Assisted Learning (GBR ISSN 0266-4909) **2469**
• ➤ Journal of Computer Assisted Tomography (USA ISSN 0363-8715) **6200**
• Journal of Computer Chemistry, Japan (JPN ISSN 1347-1767) **2108**
• ➤ Journal of Computer Information Systems (USA ISSN 0887-4417) **2523**
• ➤ Journal of Computer-Mediated Communication (USA ISSN 1083-6101) **2351**
Journal of Computer Science (IND ISSN 0973-2926) **2428**
• ➤ Journal of Computer Science (USA ISSN 1549-3636) **2428**
▼ ➤ Journal of Computer Science and Control Systems (ROM ISSN 1844-6043) **2428**
▼ • Journal of Computer Science & Systems Biology (USA ISSN 0974-7230) **826**
• ➤ Journal of Computer Science and Technology (ARG ISSN 1666-6046) **2428**
• ➤ Journal of Computer Science and Technology (USA ISSN 1000-9000) **2468**
• ➤ Journal of Computer Security (NLD ISSN 0926-227X) **2515**
▼ • ➤ Journal of Computer Systems, Networks and Communications (USA ISSN 1687-7381) **2523**
• ➤ Journal of Computers (FIN ISSN 1796-203X) **2428**
• ➤ Journal of Computers in Mathematics and Science Teaching (USA ISSN 0731-9258) **5553**
▼ Journal of Computing and e-Systems (USA ISSN 1935-1534) **2523**
• ➤ Journal of Computing and Information Science in Engineering (USA ISSN 1530-9827) **3385**
• ➤ Journal of Computing in Civil Engineering (USA ISSN 0887-3801) **3292**
• ➤ Journal of Computing in Higher Education (USA ISSN 1042-1726) **2949**
➤ Journal of Computing in Teacher Education (USA ISSN 1040-2454) **2429**
▼ • ➤ Journal of Computing Science and Engineering (KOR ISSN 1976-4677) **2473**
• ➤ Journal of Computing Sciences in Colleges (USA ISSN 1937-4771) **2990**
• The Journal of Conceptual Modeling (USA ISSN 1533-3825) **2517**
➤ Journal of Conchology (GBR ISSN 0022-0019) **950**
• ➤ Journal of Concrete and Applicable Mathematics (USA ISSN 1548-5390) **5502**
➤ Journal of Confederate History (USA ISSN 0897-0475) **6429**
• ➤ Journal of Conflict and Security Law (GBR ISSN 1467-7954) **4933**
Journal of Conflict and Violence Research *see* International Journal of Conflict and Violence **7143**
† • Journal of Conflict Archaeology (NLD ISSN 1574-0773) **8968**
• ➤ Journal of Conflict Resolution (USA ISSN 0022-0027) **7978**
Journal of Conflict, Security and Development *see* Conflict, Security & Development **7227**
➤ Journal of Conflict Studies (CAN ISSN 1198-8614) **5221**
• The Journal of Conscious Evolution (USA ISSN 1555-9262) **7371**
• ➤ Journal of Consciousness Studies (GBR ISSN 1355-8250) **7371**
• Journal of Conservation & Museum Studies (GBR ISSN 1364-0429) **6526**
• ➤ Journal of Conservative Dentistry (IND ISSN 0972-0707) **5851**
Journal of Constitutional & Parliamentary Studies (IND ISSN 0022-0043) **7146**
Journal of Constitutional Law *see* University of Pennsylvania. Journal of Constitutional Law **4853**
Journal of Constitutional Law in Eastern and Central Europe (USA ISSN 0928-964X) **4850**
▼ Journal of Construction (ZAF ISSN 1994-7402) **1018**
• Journal of Construction Accounting and Taxation (USA ISSN 1054-3007) **1294**
• ➤ Journal of Construction Engineering and Management (USA ISSN 0733-9364) **3274**
➤ Journal of Construction Procurement (GBR ISSN 1358-9180) **3274**
• ➤ Journal of Construction Research (SGP ISSN 1609-9451) **1018**
• ➤ Journal of Constructional Steel Research (GBR ISSN 0143-974X) **3275**
• ➤ Journal of Constructivist Psychology (USA ISSN 1072-0537) **7371**
• ➤ Journal of Consulting and Clinical Psychology (USA ISSN 0022-006X) **7371**
• ➤ Journal of Consumer Affairs (USA ISSN 0022-0078) **2639**
• ➤ Journal of Consumer Behaviour (GBR ISSN 1472-0817) **2639**
• ➤ Journal of Consumer Culture (GBR ISSN 1469-5405) **2639**
• Journal of Consumer Health on the Internet (USA ISSN 1539-8285) **2562**
• ➤ Journal of Consumer Marketing (GBR ISSN 0736-3761) **1823**
• ➤ Journal of Consumer Policy (USA ISSN 0168-7034) **2639**
• ➤ Journal of Consumer Psychology (USA ISSN 1057-7408) **27**
• ➤ Journal of Consumer Research (USA ISSN 0093-5301) **1823**
• ➤ Journal of Consumer Satisfaction, Dissatisfaction and Complaining Behavior (USA ISSN 0899-8620) **1824**
• ➤ Journal of Contaminant Hydrology (NLD ISSN 0169-7722) **3488**
➤ Journal of Contemporary Accounting and Economics (HKG ISSN 1815-5669) **1294**
• ➤ Journal of Contemporary African Studies (GBR ISSN 0258-9001) **7978**
• ➤ Journal of Contemporary Asia (GBR ISSN 0047-2336) **4184**
▼ • Journal of Contemporary Asia & Europe (IND ISSN 0973-9297) **7146**
• Journal of Contemporary Athletics (USA ISSN 1554-9933) **8182**
➤ Journal of Contemporary Business Issues (USA ISSN 1553-5347) **1765**
• ➤ Journal of Contemporary China/Dangdai Zhongguo (GBR ISSN 1067-0564) **4184**
• ➤ Journal of Contemporary Criminal Justice (USA ISSN 1043-9862) **4892**
• ➤ Journal of Contemporary Dental Practice (USA ISSN 1526-3711) **5851**
• ➤ Journal of Contemporary Ethnography (USA ISSN 0891-2416) **8112**
• ➤ Journal of Contemporary European Research (GBR ISSN 1815-347X) **7247**
• Journal of Contemporary European Studies (Online Edition) (GBR ISSN 1478-2790) **7146**
• ➤ Journal of Contemporary European Studies (Print Edition) (GBR ISSN 1478-2804) **7146**
• ➤ The Journal of Contemporary Health Law and Policy (USA ISSN 0882-1046) **5648**
• ➤ Journal of Contemporary History (GBR ISSN 0022-0094) **4149**
Journal of Contemporary History *see* Casopis za Suvremenu Povijest **4209**
• ➤ Journal of Contemporary Issues in Business and Government (AUS ISSN 1323-6903) **1494**
• The Journal of Contemporary Legal Issues (USA ISSN 0896-5595) **4700**
• ➤ Journal of Contemporary Management (ZAF ISSN 1815-7440) **1765**
• ➤ Journal of Contemporary Mathematical Analysis (USA ISSN 1068-3623) **5502**
• ➤ Journal of Contemporary Physics (USA ISSN 1068-3372) **7020**
• ➤ Journal of Contemporary Politics (GBR ISSN 1750-0982) **7146**
• ➤ Journal of Contemporary Psychotherapy (USA ISSN 0022-0116) **7372**
• ➤ Journal of Contemporary Religion (GBR ISSN 1353-7903) **7654**
Journal of Contemporary Roman Dutch Law *see* Tydskrif vir Hedendaagse Romeins-Hollandse Reg **4799**
Journal of Contemporary Thought (IND) **7146**
Journal of Contemporary Tourism *see* Contemporary Tourism **8695**
• Journal of Contemporary Water Research & Education (USA ISSN 1936-7031) **8827**
➤ Journal of Content Area Reading (USA ISSN 1539-4220) **2874**
• ➤ Journal of Contingencies and Crisis Management (GBR ISSN 0966-0879) **1765**
• ➤ Journal of Continuing Education in Nursing (USA ISSN 0022-0124) **5964**
• ➤ Journal of Continuing Education in the Health Professions (USA ISSN 0894-1912) **5648**
➤ Journal of Continuing Education Topics & Issues (USA ISSN 1522-8606) **2874**
• ➤ Journal of Continuing Higher Education (USA ISSN 0737-7363) **2943**
• Journal of Contract Law (AUS ISSN 1030-7230) **4700**
Journal of Contract Management *see* Contract Management **1735**
• ➤ Journal of Control Science and Engineering (USA ISSN 1687-5249) **2473**
• Journal of Control Theory and Applications (CHN ISSN 1672-6340) **8429**
• ➤ Journal of Controlled Release (NLD ISSN 0168-3659) **6853**
† • Journal of Controversial Medical Claims (USA ISSN 1530-1060) **8968**
• Journal of Convention & Event Tourism (USA ISSN 1547-0148) **6280**
Journal of Convention & Exhibition Management *see* Journal of Convention & Event Tourism **6280**
• ➤ Journal of Convex Analysis (DEU ISSN 0944-6532) **5502**
Journal of Cooperage Sciences and Techniques *see* Journal des Sciences et Techniques de la Tonnellerie **125**
The Journal of Cooperation & Collaboration in College Teaching *see* The Journal of Student Centered Learning **3068**
• ➤ Journal of Cooperative Education and Internships (USA) **2874**
• ➤ Journal of Coordination Chemistry (GBR ISSN 0095-8972) **2068**
• ➤ Journal of Coptic Studies (BEL ISSN 1016-5584) **4322**
• Journal of Corporate Accounting and Finance (USA ISSN 1044-8136) **1294**
• ➤ The Journal of Corporate Citizenship (GBR ISSN 1470-5001) **1765**
• ➤ Journal of Corporate Finance (NLD ISSN 0929-1199) **1360**
• The Journal of Corporate Law Studies (GBR ISSN 1473-5970) **4872**
• ➤ Journal of Corporate Real Estate (GBR ISSN 1463-001X) **7596**
▼ • ➤ Journal of Corporate Treasury Management (GBR ISSN 1753-2574) **1360**
• ➤ The Journal of Corporation Law (USA ISSN 0360-795X) **4872**
• ➤ Journal of Correctional Education (USA ISSN 0740-2708) **2656**
• ➤ Journal of Correctional Health Care (USA ISSN 1078-3458) **5648**
• ➤ The Journal of Corrosion Science and Engineering (GBR ISSN 1466-8858) **6319**
• Journal of Cosmetic and Laser Therapy (Online) (GBR ISSN 1476-4180) **5878**
• ➤ Journal of Cosmetic and Laser Therapy (Print) (GBR ISSN 1476-4172) **5878**
Journal of Cosmetic and Laser Therapy. Supplement *see* Journal of Cosmetic and Laser Therapy (Print) **5878**
➤ The Journal of Cosmetic Dentistry (USA ISSN 1532-8910) **5851**
• ➤ Journal of Cosmetic Dermatology (GBR ISSN 1473-2130) **5878**
➤ Journal of Cosmetic Science (USA ISSN 1525-7886) **594**
• ➤ Journal of Cosmology and Astroparticle Physics (GBR ISSN 1475-7516) **7020**
➤ The Journal of Cost Analysis & Management (USA ISSN 1541-1656) **1294**
Journal of Cost Analysis and Parametrics (USA ISSN 1941-658X) **1294**
Journal of Cost Management *see* Cost Management **1087**
• ➤ Journal of Cotton Science (USA ISSN 1523-6919) **239**
• ➤ Journal of Counseling & Development (USA ISSN 0748-9633) **7372**
• ➤ Journal of Counseling Psychology (USA ISSN 0022-0167) **7372**
• Journal of Counterterrorism & Homeland Security International (USA ISSN 1552-5155) **2678**
Journal of Counterterrorism & Security International *see* Journal of Counterterrorism & Homeland Security International **2678**
Journal of Country Music (USA ISSN 0092-0517) **6580**
• ➤ Journal of Couple & Relationship Therapy (USA ISSN 1533-2691) **7372**
▼ • Journal of Court Innovation (USA) **4953**
• Journal of Court Reporting (USA ISSN 1057-5847) **4701**
• ➤ Journal of Cranio-Maxillofacial Surgery (GBR ISSN 1010-5182) **6247**
• ➤ Journal of Craniofacial Surgery (USA ISSN 1049-2275) **6247**
• Journal of Craniovertebral Junction and Spine (IND ISSN 0974-8237) **6063**
➤ Journal of Creation (AUS ISSN 1833-6213) **7654**
➤ The Journal of Creative Behavior (USA ISSN 0022-0175) **2875**
• Journal of Creative Communications (IND ISSN 0973-2586) **2329**
• Journal of Creativity in Mental Health (USA ISSN 1540-1383) **7372**
• Journal of Credibility Assessment and Witness Psychology (USA ISSN 1088-0755) **7372**
• ➤ Journal of Credit Control (GBR ISSN 1464-4665) **2639**
• ➤ The Journal of Credit Risk (GBR ISSN 1744-6619) **1360**
Journal of Critical Animal Studies *see* Journal for Critical Animal Studies **320**
➤ Journal of Crime & Justice (USA ISSN 0735-648X) **2656**
• ➤ Journal of Criminal Justice (GBR ISSN 0047-2352) **4892**
• ➤ Journal of Criminal Justice and Popular Culture (USA ISSN 1070-8286) **2656**
• ➤ Journal of Criminal Justice Education (GBR ISSN 1051-1253) **2656**
• ➤ The Journal of Criminal Law (GBR ISSN 0022-0183) **4892**
• Journal of Criminal Law/Keiho Zasshi (JPN ISSN 0022-0191) **4892**
• ➤ Journal of Criminal Law & Criminology (USA ISSN 0091-4169) **2657**
• ➤ Journal of Critical Care (USA ISSN 0883-9441) **6063**
➤ Journal of Critical Psychology, Counselling, and Psychotherapy (GBR ISSN 1471-7646) **8049**
• Journal of Critical Realism (GBR ISSN 1476-7430) **6928**
Journal of Croatian Studies (USA ISSN 0075-4218) **4235**

10494 JOURNAL OF EARLY SOUTHERN DECORATIVE ARTS ULRICH'S PERIODICALS

➤ Journal of Early Southern Decorative Arts (USA ISSN 0098-9266) **366**
Journal of Earth Sciences (JPN ISSN 0022-0442) **2711**
Journal of Earth Sciences and Environment *see* Diqiu Kexue yu Huanjing Xuebao **2705**
• ➤ Journal of Earth System Science (IND) **2711**
▼ • ➤ Journal of Earthquake and Tsunami (SGP ISSN 1793-4311) **2711**
• ➤ Journal of Earthquake Engineering (GBR ISSN 1363-2469) **3275**
Journal of Earthquake Prediction Research (CHN ISSN 1002-1604) **2785**
➤ Journal of East Africa Natural History (KEN ISSN 1026-1613) **682**
▼ ➤ Journal of East Asia and International Law (KOR ISSN 1976-9229) **4933**
➤ Journal of East Asian Affairs (KOR ISSN 1010-1608) **7248**
Journal of East Asian Cultural Interaction Studies *see* Higashiajia Bunka Koushou Kenkyuu. Bessatsu **7969**
Journal of East Asian Libraries (USA ISSN 1087-5093) **5020**
• ➤ Journal of East Asian Linguistics (NLD ISSN 0925-8558) **5133**
Journal of East Asian Social Thoughts *see* Dong'yang Sahoe Sa'sang **548**
• ➤ Journal of East Asian Studies (USA ISSN 1598-2408) **553**
Journal of East Asiatic Studies (PHL ISSN 0022-0450) **553**
The Journal of East European Law *see* Columbia Journal of East European Law **4645**
The Journal of East European Law *see* The Journal of Eurasian Law **4933**
Journal of East Tennessee History (USA ISSN 1058-2126) **4299**
• ➤ Journal of East - West Business (USA ISSN 1066-9868) **1544**
➤ Journal of Eastern African Research & Development (KEN ISSN 0251-0405) **7978**
▼ • Journal of Eastern African Studies (GBR ISSN 1753-1055) **7978**
• Journal of Eastern Caribbean Studies (BRB ISSN 1028-8813) **7978**
• ➤ The Journal of Eastern Christian Studies (BEL ISSN 1783-1555) **7737**
Journal of Eastern Religions *see* Toho Shukyo **7690**
• Journal of Eastern Townships Studies (CAN ISSN 1192-7062) **4299**
• ➤ Journal of Ecclesiastical History (GBR ISSN 0022-0469) **7654**
• ➤ Journal of Echocardiography (JPN ISSN 1349-0222) **5793**
➤ Journal of Ecobiology (IND ISSN 0970-9037) **682**
• Journal of Ecological Anthropology (USA ISSN 1528-6509) **344**
• ➤ Journal of Ecology (GBR ISSN 0022-0477) **682**
• Journal of Ecology and Field Biology (KOR ISSN 1975-020X) **682**
Journal of Ecology and Rural Environment *see* Shengtai yu Nongcun Huanjing Xuebao **3466**
• ➤ Journal of Econometrics (NLD ISSN 0304-4076) **1544**
Journal of Economic and Social Geography *see* Tijdschrift voor Economische en Sociale Geografie **4031**
• ➤ Journal of Economic and Social Measurement (NLD ISSN 0747-9662) **8382**
• ➤ Journal of Economic & Social Policy (AUS ISSN 1325-2224) **8049**
• Journal of Economic and Social Research (TUR ISSN 1302-1060) **1544**
Journal of Economic and Taxonomic Botany (IND ISSN 0250-9768) **796**
Journal of Economic Animal *see* Jingji Dongwu Xuebao **4973**
• ➤ Journal of Economic Behavior & Organization (NLD ISSN 0167-2681) **1134**
• Journal of Economic Cooperation and Development (TUR ISSN 1308-7800) **1134**
• Journal of Economic Crime Management (USA ISSN 1938-0925) **4892**
• Journal of Economic Development (KOR ISSN 0254-8372) **1600**
• ➤ Journal of Economic Dynamics and Control (NLD ISSN 0165-1889) **1544**
• ➤ The Journal of Economic Education (USA ISSN 0022-0485) **1134**
• ➤ Journal of Economic Entomology (USA ISSN 0022-0493) **851**
• ➤ Journal of Economic Geography (GBR ISSN 1468-2702) **1494**
Journal of Economic Geology (IND) **2749**
• ➤ Journal of Economic Growth (USA ISSN 1381-4338) **1544**
• ➤ The Journal of Economic History (GBR ISSN 0022-0507) **1544**
• The Journal of Economic Inequality (USA ISSN 1569-1721) **1494**
• ➤ Journal of Economic Integration (KOR ISSN 1225-651X) **1135**
• Journal of Economic Interaction and Coordination (DEU ISSN 1860-711X) **1135**
Journal of Economic Issues *see* J E I **1543**
• Journal of Economic Literature (USA ISSN 0022-0515) **1247**
Journal of Economic Maintenance Tribology *see* Junkatsu Keizai **3387**
• ➤ Journal of Economic Methodology (GBR ISSN 1350-178X) **1135**
• ➤ Journal of Economic Perspectives (USA ISSN 0895-3309) **1545**
• ➤ Journal of Economic Policy Reform (GBR ISSN 1748-7870) **1765**
• Journal of Economic Policy Reform (Online) (GBR ISSN 1748-7889) **1765**
• ➤ Journal of Economic Psychology (NLD ISSN 0167-4870) **1824**
Journal of Economic Research (KOR ISSN 1226-4261) **1135**
• ➤ Journal of Economic Studies (GBR ISSN 0144-3585) **1135**
• ➤ Journal of Economic Surveys (GBR ISSN 0950-0804) **1135**
• ➤ Journal of Economic Theory (USA ISSN 0022-0531) **1545**
Journal of Economic Theory and Econometrics (Online) (KOR) **1135**
• ➤ Journal of Economics/Zeitschrift fuer Nationaloekonomie (AUT ISSN 0931-8658) **1135**
Journal of Economics *see* Keizaigaku Ronshu **1140**
Journal of Economics *see* Keizai Kagaku Ronshu **1139**
Journal of Economics *see* Keizaigaku Ronsan **1140**
Journal of Economics *see* Ekonomicky Casopis **1103**
➤ Journal of Economics (Springfield) (USA ISSN 0361-6576) **1135**
• ➤ Journal of Economics and Business (USA ISSN 0148-6195) **1135**
Journal of Economics & Business Administration *see* Kokumin Keizai Zasshi **1141**
• Journal of Economics and Economic Education Research (USA ISSN 1533-3604) **1135**
• ➤ Journal of Economics and Finance (USA ISSN 1055-0925) **1135**
• Journal of Economics and Finance Education (USA ISSN 1543-0464) **1361**
• ➤ Journal of Economics & Management Strategy (USA ISSN 1058-6407) **1545**
Journal of Economics, Business and Law (JPN ISSN 1344-770X) **1135**
Journal of Economics, Niigata University *see* Niigata Daigaku Keizai Ronshu **1154**
➤ Journal of Economics. Supplement (AUT) **1135**
▼ • Journal of Economics Theory (PAK ISSN 1994-8212) **1545**
• Journal of Ecophysiology and Occupational Health (IND ISSN 0972-4397) **3444**
Journal of Ecotechnology Research *see* Ekotekunoroji Kenkyu **3419**
• ➤ Journal of Ecotourism (GBR ISSN 1472-4049) **8725**
➤ Journal of Ecotoxicology & Environmental Monitoring (IND ISSN 0971-0965) **3498**
• ➤ Journal of Ecumenical Studies (USA ISSN 0022-0558) **7655**
Journal of Education (CAN ISSN 0022-0566) **2875**
Journal of Education *see* Nastava i Vaspitanje **2889**
Journal of Education *see* Hacettepe Egitim Dergisi **2862**
• Journal of Education (USA ISSN 0022-0574) **2875**
• ➤ Journal of Education & Christian Belief (GBR ISSN 1366-5456) **7655**
▼ • Journal of Education and Ethics in Dentistry (IND ISSN 0974-7761) **5851**
▼ • Journal of Education & Human Development (USA ISSN 1934-7200) **2875**
➤ Journal of Education and Psychology (IND ISSN 0022-0590) **2875**
Journal of Education and Social Change (IND ISSN 0970-3500) **8113**
• ➤ Journal of Education and Work (GBR ISSN 1363-9080) **3067**
• ➤ Journal of Education Finance (USA ISSN 0098-9495) **3025**
• ➤ Journal of Education for Business (USA ISSN 0883-2323) **1136**
• ➤ Journal of Education for International Development (USA ISSN 1554-2262) **3013**
• ➤ Journal of Education for Library and Information Science (USA ISSN 0748-5786) **5020**
• ➤ Journal of Education for Students Placed at Risk (USA ISSN 1082-4669) **3067**
▼ • ➤ Journal of Education for Sustainable Development (IND ISSN 0973-4082) **3444**
• ➤ Journal of Education for Teaching (GBR ISSN 0260-7476) **2875**
Journal of Education in Museums (GBR ISSN 0260-9126) **6526**
▼ • ➤ Journal of Education, Informatics and Cybernetics (USA ISSN 1943-7978) **2875**
• ➤ Journal of Education Policy (GBR ISSN 0268-0939) **3026**
• ➤ Journal of Education Policy (USA) **3026**
▼ • Journal of Education Research (USA ISSN 1935-052X) **2875**
Journal of Education Resources in Computing *see* A C M Transactions on Computing Education **2822**
Journal of Education Studies *see* Jiaoyu Yanjiu Xuebao **2873**
• ➤ Journal of Educational Administration (GBR ISSN 0957-8234) **3026**
Journal of Educational Administration and Foundations *see* E A F Journal **3020**
• ➤ Journal of Educational Administration and History (GBR ISSN 0022-0620) **3026**
• ➤ Journal of Educational and Behavioral Statistics (USA ISSN 1076-9986) **2934**
• ➤ Journal of Educational and Psychological Consultation (USA ISSN 1047-4412) **2875**
Journal of Educational & Psychological Sciences (BHR) **7372**
• ➤ Journal of Educational Change (NLD ISSN 1389-2843) **2875**
• ➤ Journal of Educational Computing Research (USA ISSN 0735-6331) **2949**
▼ • Journal of Educational Concepts (USA ISSN 1940-4964) **3067**
• ➤ Journal of Educational Controversy (USA ISSN 1935-7699) **2875**
Journal of Educational Development *see* Jiaoyu Daokan **2873**
• The Journal of Educational Enquiry (AUS ISSN 1444-5530) **2875**
• ➤ Journal of Educational Evaluation for Health Professions (KOR ISSN 1975-5937) **5648**
The Journal of Educational Issues of Language Minority Students (USA ISSN 1077-0550) **2875**
Journal of Educational Measurement *see* J E M **2872**
Journal of Educational Media and Library Sciences *see* Jiaoyu Ziliao yu Tushuguanxue **5019**
• ➤ Journal of Educational Multimedia and Hypermedia (USA ISSN 1055-8896) **2469**
➤ Journal of Educational Planning and Administration (IND ISSN 0971-3859) **3026**
• ➤ Journal of Educational Psychology (USA ISSN 0022-0663) **2875**
Journal of Educational Research/Jurnal Pendidikan (MYS ISSN 0126-6020) **2990**
• ➤ Journal of Educational Research (PAK ISSN 1027-9776) **2876**
• ➤ The Journal of Educational Research (USA ISSN 0022-0671) **2875**
Journal of Educational Research and Extension (IND ISSN 0022-068X) **2876**
• Journal of Educational Research & Policy Studies (USA ISSN 1934-6875) **2876**
Journal of Educational Science of Hunan Normal University *see* Hunan Shifan Daxue. Jiaoyu Kexue Xuebao **2864**
Journal of Educational Sociology *see* Kyoiku Shakaigaku Kenkyu **2881**
Journal of Educational Studies *see* Jiaoyu Xuebao **2873**
▼ • ➤ Journal of Educational Technology Development and Exchange (USA ISSN 1941-8027) **8429**
• ➤ Journal of Educational Technology Systems (USA ISSN 0047-2395) **2949**
• The Journal of Educators Online (USA ISSN 1547-500X) **2876**
▼ • Journal of Effective Teaching (USA ISSN 1935-7869) **2990**
➤ Journal of Egyptian Archaeology (GBR ISSN 0307-5133) **400**
▼ • Journal of Egyptian History (NLD ISSN 1874-1657) **4176**
• ➤ Journal of Elasticity (NLD ISSN 0374-3535) **3349**
• ➤ Journal of Elastomers and Plastics (GBR ISSN 0095-2443) **7093**
• ➤ Journal of Elder Abuse & Neglect (USA ISSN 0894-6566) **4049**
Journal of Election Administration (USA) **7146**
• ➤ Journal of Elections, Public Opinion, and Parties (GBR ISSN 1745-7289) **7147**
Journal of Electric Power *see* Dianli Xuebao **3156**
Journal of Electric Power Science and Technology *see* Dianli Kexue yu Jishu Xuebao **7850**
▼ Journal of Electrical and Electronics Engineering (ROM ISSN 1844-6035) **3106**
Journal of Electrical Engineering (ROM ISSN 1582-4594) **3322**
• ➤ Journal of Electrical Engineering (SVK ISSN 1335-3632) **3322**
• Journal of Electrical Engineering & Technology (KOR ISSN 1975-0102) **3322**
Journal of Electrical - Machining Technology *see* Denki Kako Gijutsu **3299**
• ➤ Journal of Electrical Systems (FRA ISSN 1112-5209) **3322**
Journal of Electrical World *see* Jeon-gi Jeo-neol **3322**
† ➤ Journal of Electroacoustic Music (GBR ISSN 1355-7726) **8968**
• ➤ Journal of Electroanalytical Chemistry (CHE ISSN 1572-6657) **2102**
Journal of Electrocardiology *see* Xindianxue Zazhi **5802**
• ➤ Journal of Electrocardiology (USA ISSN 0022-0736) **5793**
• ➤ Journal of Electroceramics (USA ISSN 1385-3449) **3349**
• ➤ The Journal of Electroconvulsive Therapy (USA ISSN 1095-0680) **6151**
▼ Journal of Electromagnetic Analysis and Applications (USA ISSN 1942-0730) **7052**
• ➤ Journal of Electromagnetic Waves and Applications (NLD ISSN 0920-5071) **7020**
• ➤ Journal of Electromyography & Kinesiology (GBR ISSN 1050-6411) **754**
• ➤ Journal of Electron Microscopy (JPN ISSN 0022-0744) **899**
• ➤ Journal of Electron Spectroscopy and Related Phenomena (NLD ISSN 0368-2048) **7078**
• ➤ Journal of Electronic Commerce in Organizations (USA ISSN 1539-2937) **1419**
• ➤ Journal of Electronic Commerce Research (Online Edition) (USA ISSN 1526-6133) **3106**
Journal of Electronic Commerce Research (Print Edition) *see* Journal of Electronic Commerce Research (Online Edition) **3106**
Journal of Electronic Defense *see* eDefense **6420**
• ➤ Journal of Electronic Imaging (USA ISSN 1017-9909) **6970**
Journal of Electronic Industry *see* J E I T A Review **3105**
• ➤ Journal of Electronic Materials (USA ISSN 0361-5235) **3106**
Journal of Electronic Measurement and Instrument *see* Dianzi Celiang yu Yiqi Xuebao **6401**
• ➤ Journal of Electronic Packaging (USA ISSN 1043-7398) **3106**
• ➤ The Journal of Electronic Publishing (USA ISSN 1080-2711) **7580**
• ➤ Journal of Electronic Resources in Medical Libraries (USA ISSN 1542-4065) **5020**
• ➤ Journal of Electronic Resources Librarianship (USA ISSN 1941-126X) **5020**
• Journal of Electronic Science and Technology of China/Zhongguo Dianzi Keji (CHN ISSN 1672-6464) **3106**
• ➤ Journal of Electronic Testing (USA ISSN 0923-8174) **3322**
• ➤ Journal of Electronics (CHN ISSN 0217-9822) **3106**
Journal of Electronics Technology *see* Diangong Jishu Zazhi **3092**
• Journal of Electrophoresis (JPN ISSN 1349-9394) **3248**
Journal of Electrophysiological Technology *see* Association of Neurophysiological Scientists. Journal **920**
• ➤ Journal of Electrostatics (NLD ISSN 0304-3886) **3322**
➤ Journal of Electrotopography (USA) **7020**
Journal of Elementary Education *see* Revija za Elementarno Izobrazevanje **2905**
• ➤ Journal of Elementary Science Education (USA ISSN 1090-185X) **3067**
• Journal of Elementology (POL ISSN 1644-2296) **736**
• Journal of eLiteracy (GBR ISSN 1745-4360) **5020**
• Journal of Embedded Computing (NLD ISSN 1740-4460) **2429**
▼ • ➤ Journal of Emergencies, Trauma and Shock (IND ISSN 0974-2700) **6063**
Journal of Emergency in Traditional Chinese Medicine *see* Zhongguo Zhongyi Jizheng **6076**
➤ Journal of Emergency Management (USA ISSN 1543-5865) **7528**
Journal of Emergency Medical Services *see* J E M S **5643**
Journal of Emergency Medicine *see* Jizhen Yixue **6062**
• Journal of Emergency Medicine (Laguna Hills) (USA ISSN 1090-1280) **6063**
• ➤ The Journal of Emergency Medicine (New York) (USA ISSN 0736-4679) **6064**
Journal of Emergency Medicine Trauma & Acute Care *see* J E M T A C **5946**
• ➤ Journal of Emergency Nursing (USA ISSN 0099-1767) **5964**
• ➤ Journal of Emergency Primary Health Care (AUS ISSN 1447-4999) **5648**
• ➤ Journal of Emerging Market Finance (IND ISSN 0972-6527) **1635**
➤ Journal of Emerging Markets (USA ISSN 1083-9798) **1361**
• Journal of Emerging Technologies in Accounting (USA ISSN 1554-1908) **1294**
• ➤ Journal of Emotional and Behavioral Disorders (USA ISSN 1063-4266) **6151**
• ➤ Journal of Empirical Finance (NLD ISSN 0927-5398) **1361**
• ➤ Journal of Empirical Generalisations in Marketing Science (AUS ISSN 1326-4443) **1824**
• Journal of Empirical Legal Studies (USA ISSN 1740-1453) **4701**
• ➤ Journal of Empirical Research on Human Research Ethics (USA ISSN 1556-2646) **8113**
• ➤ Journal of Empirical Theology (NLD ISSN 0922-2936) **7655**
• Journal of Employee Assistance (USA ISSN 1544-0893) **6700**
Journal of Employee Communication Management (USA) **1765**
➤ Journal of Employee Ownership Law and Finance (USA ISSN 1046-7491) **4701**
• ➤ Journal of Employment Counseling (USA ISSN 0022-0787) **7372**
† Journal of Employment Discrimination Law (USA ISSN 1528-1337) **8968**
Journal of Emtional Abuse *see* Journal of Aggression, Maltreatment & Trauma **7368**
Journal of End User Computing *see* Journal of Organizational and End User Computing **2571**
▼ Journal of Endocardiology (USA ISSN 1939-5884) **5793**
• ➤ Journal of Endocrinological Investigation (ITA ISSN 0391-4097) **5896**
• ➤ Journal of Endocrinology (GBR ISSN 0022-0795) **5896**
Journal of Endocrinology and Reproduction (IND ISSN 0971-913X) **682**
The Journal of Endocrinology, Metabolism and Diabetes of South Africa (ZAF ISSN 1608-9677) **5896**

Link to your serials resources and content with ulrichsweb.com

● ➤ The Journal of Endodontics (USA ISSN 0099-2399) **5851**
▼ ● Journal of Endometriosis (ITA ISSN 2035-9969) **5995**
Journal of Endotoxin Research *see* Innate Immunity **5894**
● ➤ Journal of Endourology (USA ISSN 0892-7790) **6270**
● ➤ Journal of Endovascular Therapy (USA ISSN 1526-6028) **6247**
● ➤ Journal of Energetic Materials (USA ISSN 0737-0652) **7020**
➤ Journal of Energy and Development (USA ISSN 0361-4476) **3140**
● ➤ Journal of Energy and Natural Resources Law (GBR ISSN 0264-6811) **4701**
▼ ● Journal of Energy and Power Engineering (USA ISSN 1934-8975) **3140**
● ➤ Journal of Energy Engineering (USA ISSN 0733-9402) **3275**
➤ Journal of Energy, Heat and Mass Transfer (IND ISSN 0970-9991) **3140**
➤ Journal of Energy in Southern Africa (ZAF ISSN 1021-447X) **3140**
● The Journal of Energy Literature (GBR ISSN 1359-3714) **3153**
● ➤ Journal of Energy Resources Technology (USA ISSN 0195-0738) **3140**
▼ ● ➤ Journal of Energy Technology (SVN ISSN 1855-5748) **3140**
● Journal of Engineered Fabrics and Fibers (USA ISSN 1558-9250) **8454**
▼ ● Journal of Engineering (USA ISSN 1945-8711) **3385**
Journal of Engineering and Applied Science/Magallat al-Handasat wa al-'Lum al-Tatbiiqiyyat (EGY ISSN 1110-1903) **3204**
● Journal of Engineering & Applied Sciences (Faisalabad) (PAK ISSN 1816-949X) **3204**
● ➤ Journal of Engineering and Applied Sciences (Islamabad] (PAK ISSN 1819-6608) **3204**
➤ Journal of Engineering and Applied Sciences (Peshawar) (PAK ISSN 1023-862X) **3204**
● ➤ Journal of Engineering and Technology Management (NLD ISSN 0923-4748) **1765**
▼ ● Journal of Engineering, Computing & Architecture (USA ISSN 1934-7197) **3204**
Journal of Engineering Design *see* Gongcheng Sheji Xuebao **3194**
● ➤ Journal of Engineering Design (GBR ISSN 0954-4828) **3205**
● ➤ Journal of Engineering, Design and Technology (GBR ISSN 1726-0531) **3205**
● ➤ Journal of Engineering Education (USA ISSN 1069-4730) **3205**
● ➤ Journal of Engineering for Gas Turbines and Power (USA ISSN 0742-4795) **3385**
● Journal of Engineering for Sustainable Development (USA ISSN 1553-4677) **3205**
Journal of Engineering for the Maritime Environment *see* Institution of Mechanical Engineers. Proceedings. Part M: Journal of Engineering for the Maritime Environment **8646**
Journal of Engineering for Thermal Energy and Power *see* Reneng Dongli Gongcheng **3394**
Journal of Engineering Geology *see* Gongcheng Dizhi Xuebao **2745**
Journal of Engineering in Medicine *see* Institution of Mechanical Engineers. Proceedings. Part H: Journal of Engineering in Medicine **749**
Journal of Engineering, Islamic Republic of Iran - Majallah-i Muhandisi, Jumhuri Islami Iran *see* International Journal of Engineering. Transactions B: Applications **3201**
Journal of Engineering Manufacture *see* Institution of Mechanical Engineers. Proceedings. Part B: Journal of Engineering Manufacture **3380**
● ➤ Journal of Engineering Materials and Technology (USA ISSN 0094-4289) **3349**
● ➤ Journal of Engineering Mathematics (NLD ISSN 0022-0833) **3205**
● ➤ Journal of Engineering Mechanics (USA ISSN 0733-9399) **3275**
● Journal of Engineering Physics and Thermophysics (USA ISSN 1062-0125) **3205**
● The Journal of Engineering Research (OMN ISSN 1726-6009) **3322**
▼ ● ➤ Journal of Engineering Science and Technology Review (GRC ISSN 1791-2377) **3205**
Journal of Engineering Sciences (J E S)/Majallat al-'ulum al-Handasiyyat (EGY ISSN 1687-0530) **3205**
● ➤ Journal of Engineering Technology (USA ISSN 0747-9964) **3205**
Journal of Engineering Thermophysics *see* Gongcheng Rewuli Xuebao **7054**
● ➤ Journal of Engineering Thermophysics (RUS ISSN 1810-2328) **7020**
Journal of Engineering Tribology *see* Institution of Mechanical Engineers. Proceedings. Part J: Journal of Engineering Tribology **3381**
Journal of English and Foreign Languages (IND ISSN 0970-8332) **5133**
Journal of English and Germanic Philology *see* J E G P **5312**
● Journal of English for Academic Purposes (GBR ISSN 1475-1585) **3067**
Journal of English Language and Literature *see* Yeong'eo Yeongmunhag **5197**
● ➤ Journal of English Linguistics (USA ISSN 0075-4242) **5133**
● ➤ Journal of English Studies (ESP ISSN 1576-6357) **5133**
Journal of English Studies (NGA ISSN 0189-6652) **5133**
Journal of English Studies (PHL) **5133**
● ➤ Journal of Enhanced Heat Transfer (USA ISSN 1065-5131) **3385**
● Journal of Enterprise Architecture (USA) **447**
● ➤ Journal of Enterprise Information Management (GBR ISSN 1741-0398) **5021**
▼ ● ➤ Journal of Enterprising Communities (GBR ISSN 1750-6204) **1136**
● ➤ Journal of Enterprising Culture (SGP ISSN 0218-4958) **1136**
● Journal of Entomological Research (IND ISSN 0378-9519) **852**
● ➤ Journal of Entomological Science (USA ISSN 0749-8004) **852**
Journal of Entomological Society of Iran *see* Namah-yi Anjuman-i Hasharahshinasan-i Iran **855**
● ➤ Journal of Entomology (USA ISSN 1812-5670) **950**
Journal of Entomology in Tohoku District *see* Tohoku Konchu **860**
● ➤ Journal of Entrepreneurship (IND ISSN 0971-3557) **1765**
● ➤ Journal of Entrepreneurship Education (USA ISSN 1098-8394) **1765**
● Journal of Environment & Development (USA ISSN 1070-4965) **3444**
Journal of Environment and Health *see* Huanjing yu Jiankang Zazhi **3437**
Journal of Environment and Management *see* Huanjing yu Guanli Yanjiu **3437**
Journal of Environment and Pollution *see* Nature, Environment and Pollution Technology **3489**
➤ Journal of Environmental and Engineering Geophysics (FRA ISSN 1359-8155) **2785**
● ➤ Journal of Environmental & Engineering Geophysics (USA ISSN 1083-1363) **2785**
Journal of Environmental & Occupational Medicine *see* Huanjing yu Zhiye Yixue **5630**
▼ ● Journal of Environmental and Public Health (USA ISSN 1687-9805) **7528**
● ➤ Journal of Environmental Assessment Policy and Management (GBR ISSN 1464-3332) **3445**
➤ Journal of Environmental Biology (IND ISSN 0254-8704) **3445**
Journal of Environmental Chemistry *see* Huanjing Huaxue **2063**
Journal of Environmental Chemistry *see* Kankyo Kagaku **2069**
Journal of Environmental Dermatology *see* Journal of Environmental Dermatology and Cutaneous Allergology **5879**
▼ ● Journal of Environmental Dermatology and Cutaneous Allergology (JPN ISSN 1882-0123) **5879**
● ➤ Journal of Environmental Economics and Management (USA ISSN 0095-0696) **3445**
● ➤ The Journal of Environmental Education (USA ISSN 0095-8964) **3445**
● ➤ Journal of Environmental Engineering (USA ISSN 0733-9372) **3445**
➤ Journal of Environmental Engineering and Landscape Management/Environmental Engineering/Okhrana Okruzhaushchei Sredy (LTU ISSN 1648-6897) **3445**
➤ Journal of Environmental Engineering and Management (TWN) **3445**
● ➤ Journal of Environmental Engineering and Science (Online) (CAN ISSN 1496-256X) **3445**
† ● Journal of Environmental Engineering and Science (Print) (CAN ISSN 1496-2551) **8968**
Journal of Environmental Entomology *see* Huanjing Kunchong Xuebao **849**
● Journal of Environmental Extension (NGA ISSN 1595-5125) **3445**
● ➤ Journal of Environmental Health (USA ISSN 0022-0892) **3445**
● ➤ Journal of Environmental Health Research (GBR ISSN 1476-0932) **3445**
Journal of Environmental Health Sciences *see* Han'gug Hwan'gyeong Bo'geon Haghoeji **3436**
➤ Journal of Environmental Horticulture (USA ISSN 0738-2898) **3740**
● Journal of Environmental Hydrology (USA ISSN 1058-3912) **2796**
● ➤ Journal of Environmental Informatics (CAN ISSN 1726-2135) **3482**
● ➤ Journal of Environmental Law (GBR ISSN 0952-8873) **3445**
● Journal of Environmental Law and Litigation (USA ISSN 1049-0280) **3446**
Journal of Environmental Law and Policy *see* U C L A Journal of Environmental Law and Policy **3471**
● Journal of Environmental Law and Practice (CAN ISSN 1181-7534) **3446**
● ➤ Journal of Environmental Management (GBR ISSN 0301-4797) **3446**
● ➤ Journal of Environmental Monitoring (GBR ISSN 1464-0325) **2102**
Journal of Environmental Monitoring and Restoration (USA ISSN 1542-7102) **3446**
● ➤ Journal of Environmental Pathology, Toxicology and Oncology (USA ISSN 0731-8898) **3499**
● ➤ Journal of Environmental Planning and Management (GBR ISSN 0964-0568) **3446**
● ➤ Journal of Environmental Policy and Planning (GBR ISSN 1523-908X) **3446**
➤ Journal of Environmental Protection and Ecology (BGR ISSN 1311-5065) **3446**
● ➤ Journal of Environmental Psychology (GBR ISSN 0272-4944) **7373**
● ➤ Journal of Environmental Quality (USA ISSN 0047-2425) **3446**
● ➤ Journal of Environmental Radioactivity (GBR ISSN 0265-931X) **3446**
Journal of Environmental Research (IND ISSN 0971-2372) **3446**
Journal of Environmental Resources (IND) **3446**
Journal of Environmental Science (IND) **3446**
Journal of Environmental Science & Engineering (IND) **7528**
▼ ● Journal of Environmental Science and Engineering (USA ISSN 1934-8932) **3446**
● ➤ Journal of Environmental Science and Health. Part A: Toxic Hazardous Substances and Environmental Engineering (USA ISSN 1093-4529) **3499**
● ➤ Journal of Environmental Science and Health. Part B: Pesticides, Food Contaminants, and Agricultural Wastes (USA ISSN 0360-1234) **3447**
● ➤ Journal of Environmental Science and Health. Part C: Environmental Carcinogenesis & Ecotoxicology Reviews (USA ISSN 1059-0501) **3499**
▼ ● ➤ Journal of Environmental Science and Technology (PAK ISSN 1994-7887) **3447**
Journal of Environmental Science Laboratory *see* Kankyo Kagaku Kenkyujo Hokoku **3449**
Journal of Environmental Sciences (EGY ISSN 1110-192X) **3447**
● ➤ Journal of Environmental Sciences (NLD ISSN 1001-0742) **3447**
▼ ● Journal of Environmental Statistics (USA ISSN 1945-1296) **3480**
Journal of Environmental Studies *see* Muhit Shinasi **3454**
● Journal of Environmental Studies and Policy (IND ISSN 0972-0804) **3140**
● ➤ Journal of Environmental Systems (USA ISSN 0047-2433) **3447**
● ➤ Journal of Enzyme Inhibition and Medicinal Chemistry (GBR ISSN 1475-6366) **736**
● Journal of Epidemiology (JPN ISSN 0917-5040) **5648**
● ➤ Journal of Epidemiology & Community Health (GBR ISSN 0143-005X) **5648**
● ➤ Journal of Epilepsy and Clinical Neurophysiology (BRA ISSN 1676-2649) **6151**
● ➤ Journal of Epithelial Biology & Pharmacology (NLD ISSN 1875-0443) **6853**
● Journal of Equine Science (JPN ISSN 1340-3516) **8294**
● ➤ The Journal of Equine Veterinary Science (USA ISSN 0737-0806) **8800**
● ➤ The Journal of Equipment Lease Financing (USA ISSN 0740-008X) **1136**
Journal of Erie Studies (USA ISSN 0090-1938) **4299**
The Journal of Erotic Photography (GBR ISSN 1747-1192) **6293**
● Journal of Esoteric Psychology (USA ISSN 1048-8715) **6645**
● Journal of Essential Oil Research (USA ISSN 1041-2905) **595**
● ➤ Journal of Esthetic and Restorative Dentistry (GBR ISSN 1496-4155) **5852**
Journal of Estonian Archaelogy *see* Eesti Arheoloogia Ajakiri **391**
● ➤ The Journal of Ethics (NLD ISSN 1382-4554) **6928**
● ➤ Journal of Ethics & Social Philosophy (USA ISSN 1559-3061) **6928**
Journal of Ethics in Leadership (USA ISSN 1933-1185) **8113**
Journal of Ethiopian Law (ETH ISSN 0022-0914) **4701**
● Journal of Ethiopian Medical Practice (ETH ISSN 1562-0085) **5648**
Journal of Ethiopian Studies (ETH ISSN 0304-2243) **4176**
● ➤ Journal of Ethnic & Cultural Diversity in Social Work (USA ISSN 1531-3204) **8049**
● ➤ Journal of Ethnic and Migration Studies (GBR ISSN 1369-183X) **3544**
● Journal of Ethnicity in Criminal Justice (USA ISSN 1537-7938) **2657**
● ➤ Journal of Ethnicity in Substance Abuse (USA ISSN 1533-2640) **2696**
➤ Journal of Ethnobiology (USA ISSN 0278-0771) **345**
● Journal of Ethnobiology and Ethnomedicine (GBR ISSN 1746-4269) **5648**
▼ Journal of Ethnographic and Qualitative Research (USA ISSN 1935-3308) **3544**
Journal of Ethnography *see* Narodopisna Revue **349**
▼ Journal of Ethnology and Folkloristics (EST ISSN 1736-6518) **3619**
● ➤ Journal of Ethnopharmacology (IRL ISSN 0378-8741) **6853**
● ➤ Journal of Ethology (JPN ISSN 0289-0771) **950**
● ➤ The Journal of Eukaryotic Microbiology (USA ISSN 1066-5234) **889**
● The Journal of Eurasian Law (USA ISSN 1941-8930) **4933**
● ➤ Journal of Eurasian Research (USA ISSN 1538-0378) **4460**
Journal of Euro - Asian Management (THA ISSN 0859-449X) **1765**
● ➤ Journal of Euromarketing (USA ISSN 1049-6483) **1824**
➤ Journal of Euromed Pharmacy (MLT ISSN 1023-3857) **6853**
▼ ➤ Journal of European Competition Law & Practice (GBR ISSN 2041-7764) **4701**
● Journal of European Criminal Law (GBR ISSN 1750-7499) **2657**
Journal of European Ethnology *see* Ethnologia Europaea **337**
● ➤ Journal of European Industrial Training (GBR ISSN 0309-0590) **1765**
Journal of European Integration *see* Revue d'Integration Europeenne **7263**
Journal of European Integration History/Revue d'Histoire de l'Integration Europeenne/Zeitschrift fuer Geschichte der Europaeischen Integration (DEU ISSN 0947-9511) **7248**
Journal of European Psychoanalysis (ITA ISSN 1125-8217) **7373**
● ➤ Journal of European Public Policy (GBR ISSN 1350-1763) **7147**
▼ ● ➤ Journal of European Real Estate Research (GBR ISSN 1753-9269) **7596**
● ➤ Journal of European Social Policy (GBR ISSN 0958-9287) **7248**
Journal of European Society of Hypnosis in Psychotherapy and Psychosomatic Medicine *see* Hypnos **5943**
● Journal of European Studies (PAK ISSN 0258-9680) **4235**
● ➤ Journal of European Studies (Chalfont Saint Giles) (GBR ISSN 0047-2441) **4235**
▼ ● Journal of European Tort Law (DEU) **4833**
● ➤ Journal of Evaluation in Clinical Practice (GBR ISSN 1356-1294) **5648**
● ➤ Journal of Evaluation in Clinical Practice Online (GBR ISSN 1365-2753) **5649**
Journal of Evangelism and Missions (USA ISSN 1543-4680) **7655**
● ➤ Journal of Evidence-Based Dental Practice (USA ISSN 1532-3382) **5852**
▼ ● ➤ Journal of Evidence-Based Medicine (AUS ISSN 1756-5383) **5649**
The Journal of Evidence-Based Nursing *see* Shizheng Hulu Jikan **5981**
Journal of Evidence-Based Practices for Schools (USA ISSN 1948-7460) **2876**
● ➤ Journal of Evidence-Based Social Work (USA ISSN 1543-3714) **8049**
● ➤ Journal of Evolution and Technology (USA ISSN 1541-0099) **6928**
● ➤ Journal of Evolution Equations (CHE ISSN 1424-3199) **5503**
▼ ● Journal of Evolutionary and Historical Sciences (USA ISSN 1938-8128) **873**
● ➤ Journal of Evolutionary Biochemistry and Physiology (RUS ISSN 0022-0930) **736**
● ➤ Journal of Evolutionary Biology (GBR ISSN 1010-061X) **873**
● ➤ Journal of Evolutionary Economics (DEU ISSN 0936-9937) **1545**
● Journal of Evolutionary Psychology (HUN ISSN 1789-2082) **7373**
● ➤ Journal of Evolutionary Psychology (USA ISSN 0737-4828) **7373**
● Journal of Excellence (CAN ISSN 1496-9955) **7373**
● ➤ Journal of Exercise Physiology - Online (USA ISSN 1097-9751) **924**
➤ Journal of Exercise Science and Fitness (SGP ISSN 1728-869X) **6230**
Journal of Exercise Science and Physiotherapy (IND ISSN 0973-2020) **924**
● ➤ Journal of Exotic Pet Medicine (USA ISSN 1557-5063) **8800**
● ➤ Journal of Experiential Education (USA ISSN 1053-8259) **3067**
● ➤ Journal of Experimental Algorithmics (USA ISSN 1084-6654) **2508**
● ➤ Journal of Experimental and Clinical Anatomy (NGA ISSN 1596-2393) **924**
● ➤ Journal of Experimental & Clinical Assisted Reproduction (GBR ISSN 1743-1050) **5995**
● ➤ Journal of Experimental and Clinical Cancer Research (Online) (GBR ISSN 1756-9966) **6024**
Journal of Experimental and Clinical Cancer Research (Print) *see* Journal of Experimental and Clinical Cancer Research (Online) **6024**
● ➤ Journal of Experimental & Theoretical Artificial Intelligence (GBR ISSN 0952-813X) **2453**
● ➤ Journal of Experimental and Theoretical Physics (RUS ISSN 1063-7761) **7020**
● ➤ Journal of Experimental Animal Science (DEU ISSN 0939-8600) **5907**
● ➤ The Journal of Experimental Biology (GBR ISSN 0022-0949) **682**
● ➤ Journal of Experimental Botany (GBR ISSN 0022-0957) **796**
▼ ● Journal of Experimental Botany. Flowering Newsletter (GBR ISSN 1754-6613) **797**
● ➤ Journal of Experimental Child Psychology (USA ISSN 0022-0965) **7373**
● Journal of Experimental Criminology (NLD ISSN 1573-3750) **2657**
● ➤ The Journal of Experimental Education (USA ISSN 0022-0973) **3067**
Journal of Experimental Fiction (USA ISSN 1084-547X) **5314**
Journal of Experimental Hematology *see* Zhongguo Shiyan Xueyexue Zazhi **5942**

10496 JOURNAL OF EXPERIMENTAL MARINE BIOLOGY AND ECOLOGY ULRICH'S PERIODICALS

• ➤ Journal of Experimental Marine Biology and Ecology (NLD ISSN 0022-0981) **683**
• ➤ The Journal of Experimental Medicine (USA ISSN 0022-1007) **5762**
• Journal of Experimental Nanoscience (GBR ISSN 1745-8080) **2068**
• ➤ Journal of Experimental Psychology: Animal Behavior Processes (USA ISSN 0097-7403) **7373**
• ➤ Journal of Experimental Psychology: Applied (USA ISSN 1076-898X) **7373**
• ➤ Journal of Experimental Psychology: General (USA ISSN 0096-3445) **7373**
• ➤ Journal of Experimental Psychology: Human Perception and Performance (USA ISSN 0096-1523) **7373**
• ➤ Journal of Experimental Psychology: Learning, Memory, and Cognition (USA ISSN 0278-7393) **7373**
• ➤ Journal of Experimental Social Psychology (USA ISSN 0022-1031) **7373**
• ➤ Journal of Experimental Therapeutics and Oncology (USA ISSN 1359-4117) **6024**
• Journal of Experimental Therapeutics and Oncology Online (USA ISSN 1533-869X) **6024**
The Journal of Experimental Zoology *see* Journal of Experimental Zoology. Part B: Molecular and Developmental Evolution **951**
The Journal of Experimental Zoology *see* Journal of Experimental Zoology. Part A: Ecological Genetics and Physiology (Print Edition) **951**
Journal of Experimental Zoology India (IND ISSN 0972-0030) **950**
Journal of Experimental Zoology. Part A: Comparative Experimental Biology (Online Edition) *see* Journal of Experimental Zoology. Part A: Ecological Genetics and Physiology (Online Edition) **950**
Journal of Experimental Zoology. Part A: Comparative Experimental Biology (Print Edition) *see* Journal of Experimental Zoology. Part A: Ecological Genetics and Physiology (Print Edition) **951**
• Journal of Experimental Zoology. Part A: Ecological Genetics and Physiology (Online Edition) (USA ISSN 1932-5231) **950**
• ➤ Journal of Experimental Zoology. Part A: Ecological Genetics and Physiology (Print Edition) (USA ISSN 1932-5223) **951**
• Journal of Experimental Zoology. Part B: Molecular and Developmental Evolution (USA ISSN 1552-5007) **951**
➤ Journal of Experimental Zoology. Supplement (USA ISSN 1059-8324) **951**
Journal of Experiments in Fluid Mechanics *see* Shiyan Liuti Lixue **7063**
Journal of Explosives and Propellants, R.O.C. *see* Huoyao Jishu **3246**
Journal of Explosives Engineering (USA ISSN 0889-0668) **3248**
Journal of Exposure Analysis and Environmental Epidemiology *see* Journal of Exposure Science and Environmental Epidemiology **3447**
• ➤ Journal of Exposure Science and Environmental Epidemiology (GBR ISSN 1559-0631) **3447**
• ➤ Journal of Extension (Online) (USA ISSN 1077-5315) **2876**
Journal of Extra-Corporeal Technology *see* Taigai Junkan Gijutsu **5720**
Journal of Extra-Corporeal Technology (USA ISSN 0022-1058) **5649**
The Journal of Facial and Somato Prosthetics (USA ISSN 1082-1821) **6064**
• ➤ Journal of Facilities Management (GBR ISSN 1472-5967) **1766**
Journal of Facilities Management in Africa (ZAF) **1766**
➤ The Journal of Faculty Development (USA) **2990**
Journal of Faculty of Education *see* Magallat Kulliyyah al-Tarbiyah **2884**
Journal of Faculty of Fine Arts *see* Honar-ha-ye-ziba **493**
• ➤ Journal of Failure Analysis and Prevention (USA ISSN 1547-7029) **6319**
▼ Journal of Fair Trade Studies (USA ISSN 1945-4600) **1573**
▼ Journal of Faith and the Academy (USA ISSN 1949-2235) **7655**
Journal of Familial Tumor *see* Kazokusei Shuyo **6026**
• ➤ Journal of Family and Consumer Sciences (USA ISSN 1082-1651) **4361**
• ➤ Journal of Family and Consumer Sciences Education (USA ISSN 1938-5927) **4361**
• ➤ Journal of Family and Economic Issues (USA ISSN 1058-0476) **7373**
• Journal of Family Communication (USA ISSN 1526-7431) **8113**
• ➤ Journal of Family Ecology and Consumer Science (Online Edition)/Tydskrif vir Gesinekologie en Verbruikerswetenskappe (ZAF) **4361**
Journal of Family Ecology and Consumer Science (Print Edition) *see* Journal of Family Ecology and Consumer Science (Online Edition) **4361**
The Journal of Family Health Care (GBR ISSN 1474-9114) **5965**
• ➤ Journal of Family History (USA ISSN 0363-1990) **8113**
• ➤ Journal of Family Issues (USA ISSN 0192-513X) **8113**
▼ • ➤ Journal of Family Life (USA ISSN 1943-8338) **8113**
• Journal of Family Medicine (USA ISSN 1090-1205) **5649**
• ➤ Journal of Family Nursing (USA ISSN 1074-8407) **5965**
• ➤ Journal of Family Planning and Reproductive Health Care (GBR ISSN 1471-1893) **973**
• ➤ The Journal of Family Practice (USA ISSN 0094-3509) **5649**
• ➤ Journal of Family Psychology (USA ISSN 0893-3200) **7374**
• ➤ Journal of Family Psychotherapy (USA ISSN 0897-5353) **7374**
• ➤ Journal of Family Social Work (USA ISSN 1052-2158) **8049**
• ➤ Journal of Family Studies (AUS ISSN 1322-9400) **5559**
• ➤ Journal of Family Therapy (GBR ISSN 0163-4445) **6151**
• ➤ Journal of Family Violence (USA ISSN 0885-7482) **2657**
• Journal of Family Welfare (IND ISSN 0022-1074) **5995**
Journal of Farm Animal Science *see* Slovak Journal of Animal Science **300**
▼ • Journal of Farming (USA ISSN 1944-2343) **127**
• ➤ Journal of Fashion Marketing and Management (GBR ISSN 1361-2026) **1824**
• ➤ Journal of Feline Medicine and Surgery (GBR ISSN 1098-612X) **8800**
• ➤ Journal of Feminist Family Therapy (USA ISSN 0895-2833) **8899**
• ➤ Journal of Feminist Studies in Religion (USA ISSN 8755-4178) **7655**
Journal of Ferrocement (THA ISSN 0125-1759) **1047**
Journal of Fertility Counselling (GBR ISSN 1365-8913) **5649**
Journal of Fertilization and Implantation *see* Nihon Jusei Chakusho Gakkai Zasshi **5999**
▼ ➤ Journal of Fibre Bioengineering and Informatics (USA ISSN 1940-8676) **750**
• ➤ Journal of Field Archaeology (USA ISSN 0093-4690) **400**
• ➤ Journal of Field Ornithology (USA ISSN 0273-8570) **909**
• ➤ Journal of Field Robotics (USA ISSN 1556-4959) **2585**
• ➤ Journal of Film and Video (USA ISSN 0742-4671) **6505**
• ➤ The Journal of Film Music (GBR ISSN 1087-7142) **6580**
• Journal of Film Preservation (BEL ISSN 1609-2694) **6505**
Journal of Film Studies *see* P.o.v. **6509**
• ➤ The Journal of Finance (USA ISSN 0022-1082) **1361**
Journal of Finance and Management in Public Services (GBR ISSN 1475-1283) **1294**
Journal of Finance Case Research (USA ISSN 1527-5426) **1361**
Journal of Finance Literature (USA ISSN 1553-3778) **1136**
The Journal of Financial Advertising & Marketing (USA) **27**
➤ Journal of Financial and Economic Practice (USA ISSN 1937-6820) **1361**
• ➤ Journal of Financial and Quantitative Analysis (GBR ISSN 0022-1090) **1361**
• ➤ Journal of Financial Counseling and Planning (USA ISSN 1052-3073) **1361**
• ➤ Journal of Financial Crime (GBR ISSN 1359-0790) **4892**
• Journal of Financial Econometrics (GBR ISSN 1479-8409) **1361**
▼ • ➤ Journal of Financial Economic Policy (GBR ISSN 1757-6385) **1136**
• ➤ Journal of Financial Economics (NLD ISSN 0304-405X) **1136**
➤ Journal of Financial Education (USA ISSN 0093-3961) **2990**
• ➤ Journal of Financial Intermediation (USA ISSN 1042-9573) **1545**
• ➤ Journal of Financial Management and Analysis (IND ISSN 0970-4205) **1361**
• ➤ Journal of Financial Management of Property and Construction (GBR ISSN 1363-2175) **7596**
• ➤ Journal of Financial Markets (NLD ISSN 1386-4181) **1361**
• Journal of Financial Planning (USA ISSN 1040-3981) **1635**
• ➤ Journal of Financial Regulation and Compliance (GBR ISSN 1358-1988) **1361**
• ➤ Journal of Financial Reporting and Accounting (GBR ISSN 1985-2517) **1294**
• ➤ Journal of Financial Research (USA ISSN 0270-2592) **1136**
• ➤ Journal of Financial Service Professionals (USA ISSN 1537-1816) **1361**
• ➤ Journal of Financial Services Marketing (GBR ISSN 1363-0539) **1824**
• ➤ Journal of Financial Services Research (USA ISSN 0920-8550) **1361**
• ➤ Journal of Financial Stability (USA ISSN 1572-3089) **1136**
Journal of Financial Studies *see* Caiwu Jinrong Xuekan **1323**
Journal of Finnish Studies (CAN ISSN 1206-6516) **4235**
• ➤ Journal of Fire Protection Engineering (GBR ISSN 1042-3915) **3579**
• ➤ Journal of Fire Sciences (GBR ISSN 0734-9041) **3349**
• ➤ Journal of Fish Biology (GBR ISSN 0022-1112) **951**
• ➤ Journal of Fish Diseases (GBR ISSN 0140-7775) **3599**
• ➤ Journal of Fish Diseases Online (GBR ISSN 1365-2761) **3599**
• Journal of Fisheries and Aquatic Science (USA ISSN 1816-4927) **3599**
• Journal of Fisheries International (PAK ISSN 1817-3381) **3599**
• Journal of Fisheries Science and Technology (KOR ISSN 1226-9204) **3600**
▼ • ➤ Journal of FisheriesSciences.com (TUR ISSN 1307-234X) **3600**
Journal of Fishery Sciences of China *see* Zhongguo Shuichan Kexue **3612**
• The Journal of Fixed Income (USA ISSN 1059-8596) **1635**
▼ • ➤ Journal of Fixed Point Theory and Applications (CHE ISSN 1661-7738) **5503**
Journal of Flow Injection Analysis/F I A Kenkyu Kondankai Kaishi (JPN ISSN 0911-775X) **2102**
• ➤ Journal of Flow Visualization and Image Processing (USA ISSN 1065-3090) **3385**
• ➤ Journal of Fluency Disorders (USA ISSN 0094-730X) **7374**
• ➤ Journal of Fluid Mechanics (GBR ISSN 0022-1120) **3363**
Journal of Fluid Mechanics Digital Archive *see* Journal of Fluid Mechanics **3363**
• ➤ Journal of Fluids and Structures (GBR ISSN 0889-9746) **3205**
• ➤ Journal of Fluids Engineering (USA ISSN 0098-2202) **3363**
• ➤ Journal of Fluorescence (USA ISSN 1053-0509) **2117**
• ➤ Journal of Fluorine Chemistry (CHE ISSN 0022-1139) **2117**
• ➤ Journal of Folklore Research (USA ISSN 0737-7037) **3619**
• ➤ Journal of Food, Agriculture and Environment (FIN) **127**
➤ Journal of Food and Drug Analysis/Yaowu Shipin Fenxi (TWN ISSN 1021-9498) **3649**
• ➤ Journal of Food and Nutrition Research/Bulletin of Food Research (SVK ISSN 1336-8672) **6661**
• ➤ Journal of Food Biochemistry (USA ISSN 0145-8884) **3650**
• Journal of Food Composition and Analysis (USA ISSN 0889-1575) **3650**
• Journal of Food Distribution Research (USA ISSN 0047-245X) **3650**
• ➤ Journal of Food Engineering (GBR ISSN 0260-8774) **3650**
Journal of Food Investigations *see* Elelmiszervizsgalati Kozlemenyek **3634**
• Journal of Food Law & Policy (USA ISSN 1942-9762) **4701**
Journal of Food Legumes (IND) **239**
• ➤ Journal of Food Lipids (USA ISSN 1065-7258) **3650**
• ➤ Journal of Food Process Engineering (USA ISSN 0145-8876) **3650**
• Journal of Food Processing and Preservation (USA ISSN 0145-8892) **3650**
• ➤ Journal of Food Products Marketing (USA ISSN 1045-4446) **3650**
• ➤ Journal of Food Protection (USA ISSN 0362-028X) **3650**
• ➤ Journal of Food Quality (USA ISSN 0146-9428) **3651**
• Journal of Food Safety (USA ISSN 0149-6085) **3651**
• ➤ Journal of Food Science (USA ISSN 0022-1147) **3651**
Journal of Food Science and Nutrition *see* Rivista di Scienza dell'Alimentazione **3662**
• ➤ Journal of Food Science and Nutrition (KOR) **6661**
• ➤ Journal of Food Science and Technology (IND ISSN 0022-1155) **3651**
• Journal of Food Science Education (USA ISSN 1541-4329) **3651**
• Journal of Food Technology (PAK ISSN 1684-8462) **3651**
• The Journal of Food Technology in Africa (KEN ISSN 1028-6098) **3651**
• ➤ Journal of Foodservice (Online Edition) (USA ISSN 1748-0159) **3651**
• ➤ Journal of Foodservice (Print Edition) (USA ISSN 1748-0140) **3651**
• ➤ Journal of Foodservice Business Research (USA ISSN 1537-8020) **4392**
▼ • ➤ Journal of Foot and Ankle Research (GBR ISSN 1757-1146) **6064**
➤ Journal of Foot and Ankle Surgery (IND ISSN 0974-0341) **6248**
• ➤ The Journal of Foot & Ankle Surgery (USA ISSN 1067-2516) **6248**
The Journal of Foot Surgery *see* Journal of Foot and Ankle Surgery **6248**
• ➤ Journal of Foraminiferal Research (USA ISSN 0096-1191) **6725**
• ➤ Journal of Forecasting (GBR ISSN 0277-6693) **1766**
Journal of Foreign Economics and Trade *see* Duiwai Jingji Maoyi **1562**
Journal of Foreign Languages (Heilongjiang) *see* Waiyu Xuekan **5194**
Journal of Foreign Languages (Shanghai) *see* Waiguoyu **5194**
➤ Journal of Forensic Accounting (USA ISSN 1524-5586) **1295**
• Journal of Forensic Dental Sciences (IND ISSN 0974-2948) **5852**
• ➤ Journal of Forensic Economics (USA ISSN 0898-5510) **1545**
• ➤ Journal of Forensic Identification (USA ISSN 0895-173X) **5914**
Journal of Forensic Medicine *see* Fayixue Zazhi **5913**
Journal of Forensic Medicine *see* Adli Tip **5912**
• Journal of Forensic Medicine and Toxicology (IND ISSN 0971-1929) **5914**
† • ➤ Journal of Forensic Neuropsychology (USA ISSN 1521-1029) **8968**
• ➤ Journal of Forensic Nursing (USA ISSN 1556-3693) **5965**
• ➤ Journal of Forensic Odonto-Stomatology (Online) (NZL) **5915**
Journal of Forensic Odonto-Stomatology (Print) *see* Journal of Forensic Odonto-Stomatology (Online) **5915**
Journal of Forensic Psychiatry *see* Adli Psikiyatri Dergisi **5912**
• ➤ The Journal of Forensic Psychiatry & Psychology (Online) (GBR ISSN 1478-9957) **6151**
• ➤ The Journal of Forensic Psychiatry & Psychology (Print) (GBR ISSN 1478-9949) **6152**
• ➤ Journal of Forensic Psychology Practice (USA ISSN 1522-8932) **7374**
• ➤ Journal of Forensic Sciences (USA ISSN 0022-1198) **5915**
▼ • ➤ Journal of Forensic Social Work (USA ISSN 1936-928X) **8049**
Journal of Forensic Vocational Analysis (USA) **5915**
• ➤ Journal of Forest Economics (DEU ISSN 1104-6899) **3694**
Journal of Forest Policy (GBR ISSN 1475-5327) **3694**
• ➤ Journal of Forest Products Business Research (Online Edition) (USA) **3713**
Journal of Forest Products Business Research (Print Edition) *see* Journal of Forest Products Business Research (Online Edition) **3713**
• ➤ Journal of Forest Research (JPN ISSN 1341-6979) **3694**
➤ Journal of Forest Science (CZE ISSN 1212-4834) **3695**
• ➤ Journal of Forestry (USA ISSN 0022-1201) **3695**
• Journal of Forestry Research (CHN ISSN 1007-662X) **3695**
▼ • ➤ Journal of Formalized Reasoning (ITA ISSN 1972-5787) **5503**
Journal of Fossil Research *see* Kaseki Kenkyukai Kaishi **6726**
Journal of Foundry *see* Liteinoe Proizvodstvo **6321**
• ➤ Journal of Fourier Analysis and Applications (USA ISSN 1069-5869) **5503**
• ➤ Journal of French Language Studies (GBR ISSN 0959-2695) **5133**
➤ Journal of French Philosophy (USA ISSN 1936-6280) **6928**
➤ Journal of Freshwater Ecology (USA ISSN 0270-5060) **2796**
• ➤ Journal of Friction and Wear (USA ISSN 1068-3666) **3385**
➤ Journal of Fruit and Ornamental Plant Research (POL ISSN 1231-0948) **3740**
Journal of Fruit Science *see* Guoshu Xuebao **3735**
• ➤ Journal of Fuel Cell Science and Technology (USA ISSN 1550-624X) **3385**
Journal of Fuel Chemistry and Technology *see* Ranliao Huaxue Xuebao **3254**
Journal of Fujian Fisheries *see* Fujian Shuichan **3595**
Journal of Function Spaces and Applications (IND ISSN 0972-6802) **5503**
• ➤ Journal of Functional Analysis (USA ISSN 0022-1236) **5503**
• ➤ Journal of Functional and Logic Programming (USA ISSN 1080-5230) **2508**
▼ ➤ Journal of Functional Foods (NLD ISSN 1756-4646) **3651**
Journal of Functional Materials *see* Gongneng Cailiao **3345**
Journal of Functional Materials and Devices *see* Gongneng Cailiao yu Qijian Xuebao **6314**
Journal of Functional Polymers *see* Gongneng Gaofenzi Xuebao **3244**
• ➤ Journal of Functional Programming (GBR ISSN 0956-7968) **2508**
† Journal of Functional Syndromes (ITA ISSN 1591-0989) **8968**
Journal of Fungal Research *see* Junwu Yanjiu **685**
• ➤ Journal of Further and Higher Education (GBR ISSN 0309-877X) **2990**
• ➤ Journal of Fusion Energy (USA ISSN 0164-0313) **3170**
• ➤ The Journal of Futures Markets (USA ISSN 0270-7314) **1635**
▼ • ➤ Journal of G G T (Gokova Geometry Topology) (USA ISSN 1935-2565) **5503**
• ➤ Journal of G L B T Family Studies (Gay Lesbian Bisexual Transgender) (USA ISSN 1550-428X) **4375**

▼ Journal of G M P & Industrial Pharmacy (Good Manufacturing Practice) (IND) **6853**
• ➤ Journal of G X P Compliance (USA ISSN 1552-5791) **4701**
▼ • ➤ The Journal of Gambling Business and Economics (GBR ISSN 1751-7990) **1136**
• Journal of Gambling Issues (CAN ISSN 1910-7595) **5946**
• ➤ Journal of Gambling Studies (USA ISSN 1050-5350) **6152**
➤ Journal of Game Development (USA ISSN 1543-9399) **2478**
▼ • ➤ Journal of Gaming & Virtual Worlds (GBR ISSN 1757-191X) **8182**
Journal of Gandhian Studies (IND ISSN 0970-9908) **7147**
➤ Journal of Gang Research (USA ISSN 1079-3062) **2657**
Journal of Ganganatha Jha Research Institute *see* Ganganatha Jha Kendriya Sanskrit Vidyapeetha. Journal **549**
Journal of Gansu Science *see* Gansu Kexue Xuebao **7857**
Journal of Gastroenterological Imaging *see* Shokaki Gazo **6208**
Journal of Gastroenterological Mass Survey *see* Nihon Shokaki Shudan Kenshin Gakkai Zasshi **5929**
• ➤ Journal of Gastroenterology (JPN ISSN 0944-1174) **5927**
• ➤ Journal of Gastroenterology and Hepatology (AUS ISSN 0815-9319) **5928**
• ➤ Journal of Gastrointestinal Cancer (USA ISSN 1941-6628) **5896**
Journal of Gastrointestinal Research *see* G.I. Research **5923**
• ➤ Journal of Gastrointestinal Surgery (USA ISSN 1091-255X) **6248**
Journal of Gay & Lesbian Issues in Education *see* Journal of L G B T Youth **2876**
• ➤ Journal of Gay & Lesbian Mental Health (USA ISSN 1935-9705) **7374**
Journal of Gay & Lesbian Psychotherapy *see* Journal of Gay & Lesbian Mental Health **7374**
• ➤ Journal of Gay & Lesbian Social Services (USA ISSN 1053-8720) **8049**
Journal of Gem Industry (IND ISSN 0022-1244) **4567**
➤ The Journal of Gemmology (GBR ISSN 1355-4565) **4567**
Journal of Gems & Gemmology *see* Baoshi he Baoshixue Zazhi **4564**
• The Journal of Gender, Race & Justice (USA ISSN 1550-7815) **3544**
• ➤ Journal of Gender Studies (GBR ISSN 0958-9236) **8899**
• ➤ Journal of Gene Medicine (USA ISSN 1099-498X) **873**
Journal of Genealogy & Local History (USA ISSN 1542-1147) **3772**
• ➤ The Journal of General and Applied Microbiology (JPN ISSN 0022-1260) **889**
• ➤ Journal of General Education (USA ISSN 0021-3667) **2876**
• ➤ Journal of General Internal Medicine (USA ISSN 0884-8734) **5946**
• ➤ Journal of General Management (GBR ISSN 0306-3070) **1766**
• ➤ Journal of General Physiology (USA ISSN 0022-1295) **924**
• ➤ Journal of General Plant Pathology (JPN ISSN 1345-2630) **797**
• ➤ The Journal of General Psychology (USA ISSN 0022-1309) **7374**
• ➤ Journal of General Virology (GBR ISSN 0022-1317) **889**
▼ • Journal of Generalized Lie Theory and Applications (EST ISSN 1736-5279) **5503**
• ➤ Journal of Generic Medicines (GBR ISSN 1741-1343) **6853**
• ➤ Journal of Genetic Counseling (USA ISSN 1059-7700) **7374**
• The Journal of Genetic Genealogy (USA ISSN 1557-3796) **873**
• ➤ The Journal of Genetic Psychology (USA ISSN 0022-1325) **873**
• ➤ Journal of Genetics (IND ISSN 0022-1333) **873**
Journal of Genetics & Breeding (ITA ISSN 0394-9257) **874**
• ➤ Journal of Genetics and Genomics (NLD ISSN 1673-8527) **874**
• ➤ Journal of Genocide Research (GBR ISSN 1462-3528) **7147**
• Journal of Genome Science and Technology (Online Edition) (USA ISSN 1551-756X) **874**
• ➤ Journal of Genome Science and Technology (Print Edition) (USA ISSN 1551-7551) **874**
• ➤ Journal of Geochemical Exploration (NLD ISSN 0375-6742) **2711**
• ➤ Journal of Geodesy (DEU ISSN 0949-7714) **2785**
Journal of Geodesy and Geodynamics *see* Dadi Celiang yu Diqiu Donglixue **2779**
• ➤ Journal of Geodynamics (GBR ISSN 0264-3707) **2785**
Journal of Geographical Science *see* Dili Xuebao **4004**
• Journal of Geographical Sciences (CHN ISSN 1009-637X) **4017**
• ➤ Journal of Geographical Systems (DEU ISSN 1435-5930) **4037**
Journal of Geography *see* Chigaku Zasshi **2704**
• ➤ Journal of Geography (USA ISSN 0022-1341) **4017**
▼ • ➤ Journal of Geography and Geology (CAN ISSN 1916-9779) **2750**
• ➤ Journal of Geography in Higher Education (GBR ISSN 0309-8265) **4017**
Journal of Geography of Health *see* Cahiers de Geographie de la Sante **5591**
▼ • ➤ Journal of Geological Research (USA ISSN 1687-8833) **2750**
Journal of Geological Sciences: Anthropozoic *see* Sbornik Geologickych Ved: Antropozoikum **2766**
Journal of Geological Sciences: Geology *see* Sbornik Geologickych Ved: Geologie **2766**
Journal of Geological Sciences: Hydrogeology, Engineering Geology *see* Sbornik Geologickych Ved: Hydrogeologie, Inzenyrska Geologie **2798**
Journal of Geological Sciences: Paleontology *see* Sbornik Geologickych Ved: Paleontologie **6730**
• ➤ The Journal of Geology (USA ISSN 0022-1376) **2750**
Journal of Geomechanics *see* Dizhi Lixue Xuebao **2780**
• ➤ Journal of Geometric Analysis (USA ISSN 1050-6926) **5503**
▼ • ➤ Journal of Geometric Mechanics (USA ISSN 1941-4889) **5503**
• ➤ Journal of Geometry (CHE ISSN 0047-2468) **5503**
• ➤ Journal of Geometry and Physics (NLD ISSN 0393-0440) **5503**
➤ Journal of Geometry and Symmetry in Physics (BGR ISSN 1312-5192) **5503**
• ➤ Journal of Geophysical Research (USA ISSN 0148-0227) **2785**
Journal of Geophysical Research: Atmospheres *see* Journal of Geophysical Research: Solid Earth **2750**
Journal of Geophysical Research: Atmospheres *see* Journal of Geophysical Research **2785**
Journal of Geophysical Research: Biogeosciences *see* Journal of Geophysical Research **2785**
Journal of Geophysical Research: Biogeosciences *see* Journal of Geophysical Research: Solid Earth **2750**
Journal of Geophysical Research: Earth Surface *see* Journal of Geophysical Research: Solid Earth **2750**
Journal of Geophysical Research: Earth Surface *see* Journal of Geophysical Research **2785**
Journal of Geophysical Research: Oceans *see* Journal of Geophysical Research: Solid Earth **2750**
Journal of Geophysical Research: Oceans *see* Journal of Geophysical Research **2785**
Journal of Geophysical Research: Planets *see* Journal of Geophysical Research: Solid Earth **2750**
Journal of Geophysical Research: Planets *see* Journal of Geophysical Research **2785**
• ➤ Journal of Geophysical Research: Solid Earth (USA ISSN 1934-8843) **2750**
Journal of Geophysical Research: Space Physics *see* Journal of Geophysical Research: Solid Earth **2750**
Journal of Geophysical Research: Space Physics *see* Journal of Geophysical Research **2785**
Journal of Geophysics (EGY ISSN 1687-0999) **2785**
Journal of Geophysics *see* Geofizicheskii Zhurnal **2781**
• ➤ Journal of Geophysics and Engineering (GBR ISSN 1742-2132) **2785**
➤ Journal of Geoscience Education (USA ISSN 1089-9995) **2750**
• ➤ Journal of Geosciences/Ceska Geologicka Spolecnost. Casopis (CZE ISSN 1802-6222) **2750**
➤ Journal of Geosciences/Oosaka-shiritsu Daigaku Rigakubu Chikyugaku Kiyo (JPN ISSN 0449-2560) **2711**
➤ Journal of Geospatial Engineering (HKG ISSN 1563-3772) **3275**
• ➤ Journal of Geotechnical and Geoenvironmental Engineering (USA ISSN 1090-0241) **3275**
• Journal of Geriatric Cardiology (CHN ISSN 1671-5411) **5793**
• Journal of Geriatric Physical Therapy (USA ISSN 1539-8412) **4049**
• ➤ Journal of Geriatric Psychiatry and Neurology (USA ISSN 0891-9887) **4049**
• ➤ Journal of Germanic Linguistics (GBR ISSN 1470-5427) **5133**
• The Journal of Germanic Mythology and Folklore (USA ISSN 1555-6794) **7737**
Journal of Germfree Life and Gnotobiology *see* Mukin Seibutsu **690**
• Journal of Gerontological Nursing (USA ISSN 0098-9134) **4049**
• ➤ Journal of Gerontological Social Work (USA ISSN 0163-4372) **4049**
• The Journal of Gift Planning (USA ISSN 1096-5297) **8050**
• Journal of Ginseng Research (KOR ISSN 1226-8453) **6853**
• ➤ Journal of Glaciology (GBR ISSN 0022-1430) **2750**
Journal of Glaciology and Geocryology *see* Bingchuan Dongtu **2778**
➤ Journal of Glass Studies (USA ISSN 0075-4250) **536**
• ➤ Journal of Glaucoma (USA ISSN 1057-0829) **6044**
• Journal of Global Buddhism (USA ISSN 1527-6457) **7701**
➤ Journal of Global Business (USA ISSN 1053-7287) **1136**
Journal of Global Business And Technology (USA ISSN 1553-5495) **1573**
▼ ➤ Journal of Global Business Issues (USA ISSN 1931-311X) **1136**
• ➤ Journal of Global Business Management (USA ISSN 1817-3179) **1766**
▼ • Journal of Global Change and Governance (USA ISSN 1941-8760) **7248**
• The Journal of Global Drug Policy and Practice (USA ISSN 1934-4708) **2696**
Journal of Global Environment Engineering (JPN ISSN 1341-1268) **3447**
• ➤ Journal of Global Ethics (GBR ISSN 1744-9626) **7979**
• Journal of Global History (GBR ISSN 1740-0228) **4149**
• Journal of Global Infectious Diseases (IND ISSN 0974-777X) **5820**
• ➤ Journal of Global Information Management (USA ISSN 1062-7375) **1766**
• ➤ Journal of Global Information Technology Management (USA ISSN 1097-198X) **2429**
➤ Journal of Global Initiatives (USA ISSN 1930-3009) **7979**
▼ • ➤ Journal of Global Intelligence & Policy (USA ISSN 1942-8189) **7248**
• ➤ Journal of Global Marketing (USA ISSN 0891-1762) **1824**
▼ • ➤ Journal of Global Mass Communication (USA ISSN 1933-3218) **2329**
• ➤ Journal of Global Optimization (USA ISSN 0925-5001) **7940**
▼ • Journal of Global Responsibility (GBR ISSN 2041-2568) **1766**
▼ • ➤ Journal of Global Social Work Practice (USA ISSN 1944-6039) **8050**
▼ • ➤ Journal of Globalization and Development (USA ISSN 1948-1837) **1600**
Journal of Globalization, Competitiveness and Governability *see* Revista de Globalizacion, Competitividad y Gobernabilidad **1790**
➤ Journal of Government and Political Studies (IND ISSN 0251-3056) **7147**
• ➤ The Journal of Government Financial Management (USA ISSN 1533-1385) **1295**
Journal of Government Leasing (USA ISSN 1931-1974) **7596**
➤ The Journal of Graduate Teaching Assistant Development (USA ISSN 1068-6096) **2990**
• ➤ Journal of Graph Algorithms and Applications (USA ISSN 1526-1719) **2508**
• ➤ Journal of Graph Theory (USA ISSN 0364-9024) **5504**
Journal of Graphic Science of Japan *see* Zugaku Kenkyu **529**
• ➤ Journal of Graphic Technology (USA ISSN 1544-9599) **7324**
Journal of Graphics Tools (USA ISSN 1086-7651) **2487**
Journal of Graphoanalysis (USA ISSN 0022-1449) **7374**
➤ Journal of Gravitational Physiology (USA ISSN 1077-9248) **7020**
• ➤ Journal of Great Lakes Research (USA ISSN 0380-1330) **8827**
• Journal of Greek Linguistics (NLD ISSN 1566-5844) **5133**
• ➤ Journal of Green Building (USA ISSN 1552-6100) **1018**
➤ Journal of Grey System (GBR ISSN 0957-3720) **5504**
• Journal of Grid Computing (NLD ISSN 1570-7873) **2508**
Journal of Ground Water *see* Ground Water **2794**
Journal of Groundwater Hydrology *see* Chikasui Gakkaishi **2793**
• ➤ Journal of Group Psychotherapy, Psychodrama and Sociometry (USA ISSN 1545-3855) **7374**
• ➤ Journal of Group Theory (DEU ISSN 1433-5883) **5504**
• ➤ Journal of Groups in Addiction & Recovery (USA ISSN 1556-035X) **2696**
Journal of Growth *see* Seicho **703**
Journal of Guangxi Agriculture *see* Guangxi Nongxuebao **117**
Journal of Guangxi Meteorology *see* Guangxi Qixiang **6353**
• ➤ Journal of Guidance, Control, and Dynamics (USA ISSN 0731-5090) **63**
Journal of Gynaecology & Obstetrics *see* Acta Ginecologica **5985**
Journal of Gynecologic Oncology Nursing (USA ISSN 1536-9935) **6024**
• ➤ Journal of Gynecologic Surgery (USA ISSN 1042-4067) **5995**
• ➤ Journal of Gynecological Endoscopy and Surgery (IND ISSN 0974-1216) **5995**
Journal of Gynecology and Obstetrics *see* Jinekoloji ve Obstetrik Dergisi **5994**
Journal of Halacha and Contemporary Society (USA ISSN 0730-2614) **3544**
▼ • ➤ Journal of Hand and Microsurgery (IND ISSN 0974-3227) **6248**
• ➤ Journal of Hand Surgery (American Volume) (USA ISSN 0363-5023) **6248**
Journal of Hand Surgery (British Volume) *see* Journal of Hand Surgery (European Volume) **6248**
• ➤ Journal of Hand Surgery (European Volume) (GBR ISSN 1753-1934) **6248**
• ➤ Journal of Hand Therapy (USA ISSN 0894-1130) **6111**
• ➤ Journal of Happiness Studies (NLD ISSN 1389-4978) **7374**
• Journal of Hard Tissue Biology (JPN ISSN 1341-7649) **683**
• Journal of Hate Studies (USA ISSN 1540-2126) **7979**
• ➤ Journal of Hazardous Materials (NLD ISSN 0304-3894) **3508**
➤ Journal of Hazardous Substance Research (USA ISSN 1090-7025) **3499**
The Journal of HazMat Transportation (USA) **3508**
• ➤ Journal of Head Trauma Rehabilitation (USA ISSN 0885-9701) **6064**
• ➤ The Journal of Headache and Pain (ITA ISSN 1129-2369) **6152**
• ➤ The Journal of Headache and Pain Online (ITA ISSN 1129-2377) **6152**
➤ Journal of Health Administration Education (USA ISSN 0735-6722) **4103**
• Journal of Health Administration Ethics (USA ISSN 1559-0984) **4104**
• Journal of Health & Biomedical Law (USA ISSN 1556-052X) **750**
Journal of Health and Development (IND ISSN 0973-1814) **7529**
Journal of Health & Healing (USA ISSN 1044-2790) **6991**
• ➤ Journal of Health and Human Services Administration (USA ISSN 1079-3739) **4104**
• Journal of Health & Life Sciences Law (USA ISSN 1942-4736) **5649**
▼ • ➤ Journal of Health & Mass Communication (USA ISSN 1940-9354) **8113**
Journal of Health and Place *see* Health & Place **4014**
Journal of Health & Population in Developing Countries (USA ISSN 1095-8940) **7529**
• ➤ Journal of Health and Social Behavior (USA ISSN 0022-1465) **8113**
Journal of Health & Social Policy *see* Social Work in Public Health **8071**
• ➤ Journal of Health Care Chaplaincy (USA ISSN 0885-4726) **6991**
• Journal of Health Care Compliance (USA ISSN 1520-8303) **5649**
• Journal of Health Care Finance (USA ISSN 1078-6767) **4104**
• ➤ Journal of Health Care for the Poor and Underserved (USA ISSN 1049-2089) **5649**
• Journal of Health Care Law & Policy (USA ISSN 1097-4768) **4701**
• ➤ Journal of Health Communication (USA ISSN 1081-0730) **5649**
▼ • ➤ Journal of Health Disparities Research and Practice (USA) **5649**
• ➤ Journal of Health Economics (NLD ISSN 0167-6296) **4104**
Journal of Health Education *see* American Journal of Health Education **3050**
• ➤ The Journal of Health Informatics and Information Management Research (USA ISSN 1944-4907) **5649**
▼ • Journal of Health Informatics in Developing Countries (NZL ISSN 1178-4407) **5649**
Journal of Health Law *see* Journal of Health & Life Sciences Law **5649**
• ➤ Journal of Health Management (IND ISSN 0972-0634) **5649**
• ➤ Journal of Health, Organization and Management (GBR ISSN 1477-7266) **4104**
Journal of Health, Physical Education and Recreation *see* Taiiku no Kagaku **3083**
• ➤ Journal of Health Politics, Policy and Law (USA ISSN 0361-6878) **5649**
• ➤ Journal of Health Population and Nutrition (BGD ISSN 1606-0997) **5748**
Journal of Health Psychology *see* Revista de Psicologia de la Salud **7404**
• ➤ Journal of Health Psychology (GBR ISSN 1359-1053) **7374**
• ➤ Journal of Health Science/Eisei Kagaku (JPN ISSN 1344-9702) **3499**
Journal of Health Sciences Management and Public Health (GEO ISSN 1512-0651) **7529**
• Journal of Health Services Research & Policy (GBR ISSN 1355-8196) **5650**
Journal of Healthcare and Society *see* Iryo to Shakai **5642**
The Journal of Healthcare Contracting (USA ISSN 1548-4165) **4104**
▼ • ➤ Journal of Healthcare Engineering (GBR ISSN 2040-2295) **3385**
• ➤ Journal of Healthcare Information Management (USA ISSN 1099-811X) **4104**
• ➤ Journal of Healthcare Management (USA ISSN 1096-9012) **4104**
Journal of Healthcare Protection Management (USA ISSN 0891-7930) **4104**
Journal of Healthcare Risk Management (USA ISSN 1074-4797) **4104**
• ➤ The Journal of Heart and Lung Transplantation (USA ISSN 1053-2498) **6248**
• ➤ Journal of Heart-Centered Therapies (USA ISSN 1520-5495) **5650**

Title

10498 JOURNAL OF HEART FAILURE. SUPPLEMENT ULRICH'S PERIODICALS

Journal of Heart Failure. Supplement *see* European Journal of Heart Failure **5786**
• ➤ The Journal of Heart Valve Disease (GBR ISSN 0966-8519) **5793**
• ➤ Journal of Heat Transfer (USA ISSN 0022-1481) **3385**
Journal of Hebei Forestry Science and Technology *see* Hebei Linye Keji **3692**
Journal of Hebei Traditional Chinese Medicine and Pharmacology *see* Hebei Zhongyiyao Xuebao **5627**
• ➤ Journal of Hebrew Scriptures (CAN ISSN 1203-1542) **7725**
• ➤ Journal of Hellenic Religion (GBR ISSN 1748-7811) **2236**
• ➤ Journal of Hellenic Studies (GBR ISSN 0075-4269) **2236**
• ➤ Journal of Helminthology (GBR ISSN 0022-149X) **5820**
Journal of Hematological Research (PAK ISSN 1728-9475) **5939**
The Journal of Hematology and Hemoparasitic Diseases Research (PAK ISSN 1728-9483) **5939**
▼ • ➤ Journal of Hematology & Oncology (GBR ISSN 1756-8722) **5939**
▼ • ➤ Journal of Hematopathology (DEU ISSN 1865-5785) **5939**
Journal of Hematotherapy & Stem Cell Research *see* Stem Cells and Development **5941**
• ➤ Journal of Hepato - Biliary - Pancreatic Sciences (JPN) **6248**
Journal of Hepato - Biliary - Pancreatic Surgery *see* Journal of Hepato - Biliary - Pancreatic Sciences **6248**
Journal of Hepatobiliary Surgery *see* Gandan Waike Zazhi **5923**
• ➤ Journal of Hepatology (NLD ISSN 0168-8278) **5928**
➤ Journal of Hepatology, Gastroenterology, Infectious Diseases (EGY ISSN 1110-631X) **5820**
• Journal of Hepatology. Supplement (NLD ISSN 0169-5185) **5928**
Journal of Hepatopancreatobiliary Surgery *see* Gandanyi Waike Zazhi **5924**
Journal of Herbal Pharmacotherapy *see* Journal of Dietary Supplements **6853**
• ➤ Journal of Herbs, Spices & Medicinal Plants (USA ISSN 1049-6475) **3740**
• ➤ Journal of Heredity (GBR ISSN 0022-1503) **874**
• ➤ Journal of Heritage Tourism (GBR ISSN 1743-873X) **8725**
➤ Journal of Herpetological Medicine and Surgery (USA ISSN 1529-9651) **951**
• ➤ Journal of Herpetology (USA ISSN 0022-1511) **951**
• ➤ Journal of Heterocyclic Chemistry (USA ISSN 0022-152X) **2124**
• ➤ Journal of Heuristics (USA ISSN 1381-1231) **2453**
Journal of High Altitude Medicine *see* Gaoyuan Yixue Zazhi **5617**
• ➤ The Journal of High Energy Physics (Online) (GBR ISSN 1029-8479) **7020**
Journal of High Pressure Institute of Japan *see* Atsuryoku Gijutsu **3182**
• ➤ Journal of High Speed Networks (NLD ISSN 0926-6801) **2500**
• Journal of High Technology Law (USA ISSN 1536-7983) **4701**
• ➤ The Journal of High Technology Management Research (GBR ISSN 1047-8310) **1419**
Journal of Higher Correspondence Education (Natural Science Edition) *see* Gaodeng Hanshou Xuebao (Ziran Kexue Ban) **7857**
Journal of Higher Correspondence Education (Philosophy and Social Sciences Edition) *see* Gaodeng Hanshou Xuebao (Zhexue Shehui Kexue Ban) **7966**
• Journal of Higher Education (IND ISSN 0252-0397) **2990**
• ➤ Journal of Higher Education (USA ISSN 0022-1546) **2990**
• Journal of Higher Education Ethics (USA ISSN 1559-4440) **2990**
Journal of Higher Education in Africa (SEN ISSN 0851-7762) **2990**
Journal of Higher Education Outreach and Engagement (USA ISSN 1534-6102) **2990**
• ➤ Journal of Higher Education Policy and Management (AUS ISSN 1360-080X) **2990**
Journal of Highway and Transportation Research and Development *see* Gonglu Jiaotong Keji **8631**
Journal of Hill Research (IND ISSN 0970-7050) **2711**
➤ Journal of Himalayan Earth Sciences (PAK ISSN 1994-3237) **2750**
Journal of Himalayan Geology *see* Himalayan Geology **2746**
Journal of Himalayan Studies and Regional Development (IND ISSN 0250-8346) **3447**
Journal of Hindu - Christian Studies (USA) **7707**
▼ • ➤ The Journal of Hindu Studies (GBR ISSN 1756-4255) **7707**
• ➤ Journal of Hispanic Higher Education (USA ISSN 1538-1927) **2991**
† Journal of Hispanic - Latino Theology (USA ISSN 1077-7989) **8968**
Journal of Hispanic Philology (USA ISSN 0147-5460) **5315**
• ➤ Journal of Histochemistry and Cytochemistry (USA ISSN 0022-1554) **833**
Journal of Historic Madison, Inc. of Wisconsin *see* Historic Madison **4296**
• ➤ Journal of Historical Biography (CAN ISSN 1911-8538) **4149**
• ➤ Journal of Historical Geography (GBR ISSN 0305-7488) **4017**
• Journal of Historical Pragmatics (NLD ISSN 1566-5852) **5133**
Journal of Historical Research (IND ISSN 0022-1562) **4149**
▼ • ➤ Journal of Historical Research in Marketing (GBR ISSN 1755-750X) **1824**
➤ Journal of Historical Research in Music Education (USA ISSN 1536-6006) **6580**
Journal of Historical Researches *see* Majallat al-Buhuth al-Ta'rikhiyyah **4323**
Journal of Historical Review (USA ISSN 0195-6752) **4149**
Journal of Historical Science *see* Shixue Yuekan **4161**
• ➤ Journal of Historical Sociology (GBR ISSN 0952-1909) **8113**
Journal of Historical Studies *see* Seiji Keizai Shigaku **4160**
➤ Journal of Historical Studies (JPN ISSN 0386-9237) **4170**
Journal of Historiography *see* Shixueshi Yanjiu **4161**
Journal of History *see* Shirin **4188**
Journal of History (PHL ISSN 0115-2297) **4184**
Journal of History of Science *see* Kagakushi Kenkyu **7874**
➤ Journal of Histotechnology (USA ISSN 0147-8885) **834**
• ➤ Journal of HIV - AIDS & Social Services (USA ISSN 1538-1501) **8050**
Journal of HIV - AIDS Prevention & Education for Adolescents & Children *see* Journal of HIV - AIDS Prevention in Children & Youth **5820**
• ➤ Journal of HIV - AIDS Prevention in Children & Youth (USA ISSN 1553-8346) **5820**
• ➤ Journal of HIV Therapy (GBR ISSN 1462-0308) **5820**
Journal of Hokkaido Radiological Technology *see* Hokkaido Hoshasen Gijutsu Zasshi **6197**
• ➤ Journal of Holistic Nursing (USA ISSN 0898-0101) **5965**
The Journal of Holocaust Education *see* Holocaust Studies **4146**
• ➤ Journal of Holography and Speckle (USA ISSN 1546-900X) **7078**
Journal of Home Economics of Japan *see* Nihon Kasei Gakkaishi **4365**
Journal of Homeland Security (USA) **2678**
• ➤ Journal of Homeland Security and Emergency Management (USA ISSN 1547-7355) **2678**
• ➤ Journal of Homosexuality (USA ISSN 0091-8369) **4375**
▼ • ➤ Journal of Horror Studies (GBR ISSN 1751-939X) **5444**
• ➤ Journal of Horticultural Science and Biotechnology (GBR ISSN 1462-0316) **3740**
• ➤ Journal of Hospice and Palliative Nursing (USA ISSN 1522-2179) **5965**
▼ • Journal of Hospital Ethics (USA ISSN 1938-4920) **4104**
• ➤ Journal of Hospital Infection (GBR ISSN 0195-6701) **5820**
Journal of Hospital Infection. Supplement *see* Journal of Hospital Infection **5820**
• ➤ Journal of Hospital Librarianship (USA ISSN 1532-3269) **5021**
• ➤ Journal of Hospital Marketing & Public Relations (USA ISSN 1539-0942) **1824**
• ➤ Journal of Hospital Medicine (USA ISSN 1553-5592) **5650**
Journal of Hospitality & Leisure Marketing *see* Journal of Hospitality Marketing and Management **4392**
➤ Journal of Hospitality & Tourism Education (USA ISSN 1096-3758) **4392**
• ➤ Journal of Hospitality and Tourism Management (Online) (AUS) **8725**
• ➤ Journal of Hospitality & Tourism Research (USA ISSN 1096-3480) **4392**
▼ • Journal of Hospitality and Tourism Technology (GBR ISSN 1757-9880) **8726**
Journal of Hospitality Application and Research *see* J O H A R **4391**
The Journal of Hospitality Financial Management (USA ISSN 1091-3211) **4392**
• ➤ Journal of Hospitality, Leisure, Sports & Tourism Education (GBR ISSN 1473-8376) **8726**
• ➤ Journal of Hospitality Marketing and Management (USA ISSN 1936-8623) **4392**
• Journal of Housing and Community Development (USA ISSN 1534-648X) **4417**
• Journal of Housing and the Built Environment (NLD ISSN 1566-4910) **4417**
• ➤ Journal of Housing Economics (USA ISSN 1051-1377) **4417**
• ➤ Journal of Housing for the Elderly (USA ISSN 0276-3893) **4049**
The Journal of Housing Law (GBR ISSN 1368-6542) **4417**
• ➤ Journal of Housing Research (USA ISSN 1052-7001) **4417**
Journal of Huaihai Medicine *see* Huaihai Yiyao **5630**
• ➤ Journal of Human Behavior in the Social Environment (USA ISSN 1091-1359) **8050**
▼ • ➤ Journal of Human Capital (USA ISSN 1932-8575) **1136**
Journal of Human Development *see* Journal of Human Development and Capabilities **345**
• ➤ Journal of Human Development and Capabilities (GBR ISSN 1945-2829) **345**
• ➤ Journal of Human Ecology (IND ISSN 0970-9274) **3447**
➤ Journal of Human Ergology (JPN ISSN 0300-8134) **5650**
• ➤ Journal of Human Evolution (GBR ISSN 0047-2484) **874**
Journal of Human Factors and Aerospace Safety *see* Human Factors and Aerospace Safety **58**
• ➤ Journal of Human Genetics (GBR ISSN 1434-5161) **874**
• ➤ Journal of Human Hypertension (GBR ISSN 0950-9240) **5793**
Journal of Human Kinetics (POL ISSN 1640-5544) **6991**
• ➤ Journal of Human Lactation (USA ISSN 0890-3344) **5995**
➤ Journal of Human Movement Studies (GBR ISSN 0306-7297) **7375**
• ➤ Journal of Human Nutrition and Dietetics (GBR ISSN 0952-3871) **6661**
Journal of Human Nutrition and Dietetics (Supplement) *see* Journal of Human Nutrition and Dietetics **6661**
Journal of Human Relations *see* The International Journal of African Studies **3540**
▼ • ➤ Journal of Human Reproductive Sciences (IND ISSN 0974-1208) **5650**
• ➤ Journal of Human Resource Costing & Accounting (GBR ISSN 1401-338X) **1868**
• ➤ The Journal of Human Resources (USA ISSN 0022-166X) **1868**
• ➤ The Journal of Human Resources and Adult Learning (USA ISSN 1817-2105) **1868**
• Journal of Human Resources in Hospitality & Tourism (USA ISSN 1533-2845) **4392**
• ➤ Journal of Human Rights (GBR ISSN 1475-4835) **7211**
▼ • ➤ Journal of Human Rights Practice (GBR ISSN 1757-9619) **7211**
• ➤ Journal of Human Security (AUS ISSN 1835-3800) **7147**
Journal of Human Security and Development *see* Human Security & Development **3196**
• Journal of Human Sport and Exercise (ESP ISSN 1988-5202) **6230**
• Journal of Human Thermodynamics (USA ISSN 1559-386X) **3140**
• ➤ Journal of Human Values (IND ISSN 0971-6858) **1766**
Journal of Humanism & Ethical Religion (USA ISSN 0899-7691) **6928**
• ➤ Journal of Humanistic Counseling, Education and Development (USA ISSN 1931-0293) **7375**
• ➤ Journal of Humanistic Psychology (USA ISSN 0022-1678) **7375**
Journal of Humanities *see* Renwen Zazhi **4472**
Journal of Humanities *see* Inmun Gwahag **8964**
• Journal of Humanities (MWI ISSN 1016-0728) **4460**
Journal of Humanities (Chiba)/Jinbun Kenkyu (JPN ISSN 0386-2097) **4460**
Journal of Humanities and Natural Sciences *see* Jinbun Shizen Kagaku Ronshu **4459**
➤ The Journal of Humanities and Social Sciences (PAK ISSN 1024-0829) **4460**
Journal of Humanities and Social Sciences *see* Gami'at Qatar. Kulliyyat al-Insaniyyat Wa-al-'ulum al-Igtima'iyyat. Magallat **4453**
➤ Journal of Humanities and Social Sciences (UAE) **4460**
▼ • Journal of Humanities & Social Sciences (USA ISSN 1934-7227) **4460**
▼ • Journal of Humanoids (AUT ISSN 1996-7209) **2585**
Journal of Hungarian Radiology *see* Magyar Radiologia **6202**
Journal of Hungarian Terminology *see* Magyar Terminologia **5149**
• ➤ Journal of Hunger and Environmental Nutrition (USA ISSN 1932-0248) **6661**
Journal of Hybrid Rice *see* Zajiao Shuidao **260**
Journal of Hydraulic Engineering *see* Shuili Xuebao **3364**
• ➤ Journal of Hydraulic Engineering (New York) (USA ISSN 0733-9429) **3275**
• ➤ Journal of Hydraulic Research (ESP ISSN 0022-1686) **3363**
▼ • ➤ Journal of Hydro-Environment Research (NLD ISSN 1570-6443) **2796**
Journal of Hydrobiology (IND ISSN 0970-3594) **683**
• ➤ Journal of Hydrodynamics (NLD ISSN 1001-6058) **7020**
Journal of Hydroelectric Engineering *see* Shuili Fadian Xuebao **3163**
• ➤ Journal of Hydroinformatics (GBR ISSN 1464-7141) **3447**
• ➤ Journal of Hydrologic Engineering (USA ISSN 1084-0699) **3275**
Journal of Hydrological System *see* Mizu Junkan **8829**
• ➤ Journal of Hydrology (NLD ISSN 0022-1694) **2796**
Journal of Hydrology and Hydromechanics *see* Vodohospodarsky Casopis **2799**
➤ Journal of Hydrology. New Zealand (NZL ISSN 0022-1708) **2796**
• ➤ Journal of Hydrometeorology (USA ISSN 1525-755X) **2796**
➤ Journal of Hydroscience and Hydraulic Engineering (JPN ISSN 0912-2508) **3363**
Journal of Hygiene Research *see* Weisheng Yanjiu **7000**
Journal of Hygiene Research *see* Weisheng Dulixue Zazhi **5729**
Journal of Hymenoptera Research (USA ISSN 1070-9428) **852**
• ➤ Journal of Hyperbolic Differential Equations (SGP ISSN 0219-8916) **5504**
• ➤ Journal of Hypertension (GBR ISSN 0263-6352) **5793**
Journal of Hypertension. Supplement (GBR ISSN 0952-1178) **5793**
Journal of I M W M Observer *see* Instytut Meteorologii i Gospodarki Wodnej. Gazeta Obserwatora **6357**
Journal of I T Financial Management (USA) **2537**
➤ Journal of Iberian and Latin American Research (AUS) **4460**
Journal of Iberian and Latin American Studies *see* Journal of Iberian and Latin American Research **4460**
• Journal of Iberian and Latin American Studies (GBR ISSN 1470-1847) **4299**
Journal of Iberian Archaeology (PRT ISSN 0874-2677) **401**
• ➤ Journal of Iberian Geology (ESP ISSN 1698-6180) **2750**
• Journal of Ichthyology (RUS ISSN 0032-9452) **951**
▼ • Journal of Identity and Migration Studies (ROM ISSN 1843-5610) **7147**
➤ Journal of Illinois History (USA ISSN 1522-0532) **4299**
Journal of Image & Information Management *see* Gekkan I M **6969**
• ➤ Journal of Imagery Research in Sport and Physical Activity (USA ISSN 1932-0191) **7375**
• ➤ The Journal of Imaging Science and Technology (USA ISSN 1062-3701) **6970**
• The Journal of Imaging Services (USA) **2487**
Journal of Imagism (USA ISSN 1090-1558) **5315**
Journal of Imago Relationship Therapy (USA ISSN 1529-4129) **7375**
• ➤ Journal of Immigrant and Minority Health (USA ISSN 1557-1912) **5650**
Journal of Immigrant & Refugee Services (Print Edition) *see* Journal of Immigrant & Refugee Studies **7248**
• ➤ Journal of Immigrant & Refugee Studies (USA ISSN 1556-2948) **7248**
Journal of Immigrant & Refugee Studies (Online) *see* Journal of Immigrant & Refugee Studies **7248**
Journal of Immigrant Health *see* Journal of Immigrant and Minority Health **5650**
• ➤ Journal of Immune Based Therapies and Vaccines (GBR ISSN 1476-8518) **5762**
• Journal of Immunity (USA ISSN 1559-5803) **311**
• ➤ Journal of Immunoassay and Immunochemistry (USA ISSN 1532-1819) **2102**
• ➤ Journal of Immunological Methods (NLD ISSN 0022-1759) **5762**
Journal of Immunology *see* Mianyixue Zazhi **5679**
• ➤ Journal of Immunology (USA ISSN 0022-1767) **5762**
• Journal of Immunology and Immunopathology (IND ISSN 0972-0561) **5762**
• ➤ Journal of Immunotherapy (USA ISSN 1524-9557) **5763**
• ➤ Journal of Immunotoxicology (USA ISSN 1547-691X) **5763**
• ➤ The Journal of Imperial and Commonwealth History (GBR ISSN 0308-6534) **4149**
Journal of In-Service Education *see* Professional Development in Education **3077**
• ➤ Journal of Inclusion Phenomena and Macrocyclic Chemistry (NLD ISSN 1388-3127) **2136**
• Journal of Income & Wealth (IND ISSN 0974-0309) **1719**
• ➤ Journal of Income Distribution (USA ISSN 0926-6437) **1545**
Journal of Independent Studies and Research *see* J I S R Management and Social Sciences & Economics **1762**
Journal of Independent Studies and Research Management and Social Sciences & Economics *see* J I S R Management and Social Sciences & Economics **1762**
Journal of Independent Studies and Research on Computing *see* J I S R on Computing **2428**
• ➤ Journal of Index Derivatives (USA ISSN 1558-8254) **1362**
Journal of Indexing & Reference Work (IND) **5058**
▼ • Journal of India (USA ISSN 1944-1835) **127**
➤ Journal of Indian Academy of Mathematics (IND ISSN 0970-5120) **5504**
Journal of Indian and Buddhist Studies/Indogaku Bunkkyogaku Kenkyu (JPN ISSN 0019-4344) **7701**
▼ • ➤ Journal of Indian Business Research (GBR ISSN 1755-4195) **1136**
• Journal of Indian Education (IND ISSN 0377-0435) **2876**
Journal of Indian Folkloristics (IND) **3619**

10500 JOURNAL OF INTERNATIONAL BUSINESS LAW ULRICH'S PERIODICALS

Journal of International Business Law *see* University of Pennsylvania. Journal of International Law **4944**
▼ ➤ Journal of International Business Management & Research (USA ISSN 1940-185X) **1767**
• ➤ Journal of International Business Research (USA ISSN 1544-0222) **1574**
• ➤ Journal of International Business Strategy (USA ISSN 1552-2903) **1574**
• ➤ Journal of International Business Studies (GBR ISSN 0047-2506) **1137**
• ➤ Journal of International Commercial Law and Technology (DNK ISSN 1901-8401) **4872**
• ➤ Journal of International Communication (AUS ISSN 1321-6597) **8114**
• ➤ Journal of International Consumer Marketing (USA ISSN 0896-1530) **1825**
Journal of International Cooperation Studies *see* Kokusai Kyoryoku Ronshu **7250**
• Journal of International Criminal Justice (GBR ISSN 1478-1387) **2657**
• ➤ Journal of International Development (GBR ISSN 0954-1748) **1600**
▼ • Journal of International Dispute Settlement (GBR ISSN 2040-3585) **4933**
• ➤ Journal of International Economic Law (USA ISSN 1369-3034) **4933**
Journal of International Economic Studies (JPN ISSN 0911-1247) **1137**
• ➤ Journal of International Economics (NLD ISSN 0022-1996) **1137**
• Journal of International Entrepreneurship (USA ISSN 1570-7385) **1574**
➤ Journal of International Finance and Economics (USA ISSN 1555-6336) **1362**
• ➤ Journal of International Financial Management and Accounting (GBR ISSN 0954-1314) **1362**
• ➤ Journal of International Financial Markets, Institutions & Money (NLD ISSN 1042-4431) **1362**
• ➤ Journal of International Food & Agribusiness Marketing (USA ISSN 0897-4438) **202**
▼ The Journal of International Governmental Systems and Structures (USA ISSN 1947-5241) **7248**
Journal of International Information Management *see* Journal of International Technology and Information Management **1767**
Journal of International Law *see* Case Western Reserve Journal of International Law **4920**
Journal of International Law *see* Michigan State Journal of International Law **4935**
Journal of International Law *see* Southwestern Journal of International Law **4941**
Journal of International Law and Diplomacy *see* Kokusaiho Gaiko Zasshi **4934**
Journal of International Law and Foreign Affairs *see* U C L A Journal of International Law and Foreign Affairs **4943**
• Journal of International Law and International Relations (CAN) **4933**
Journal of International Law and Policy (USA ISSN 1080-6687) **4701**
Journal of International Law and Politics *see* New York University Journal of International Law and Politics **4936**
Journal of International Logistics and Trade (KOR ISSN 1738-2122) **1137**
• ➤ Journal of International Management (USA ISSN 1075-4253) **1767**
➤ Journal of International Management Studies (TWN ISSN 1993-1034) **1767**
➤ The Journal of International Maritime Law (GBR ISSN 1478-8586) **4970**
• ➤ Journal of International Marketing (USA ISSN 1069-031X) **1825**
• ➤ Journal of International Marketing and Exporting (AUS ISSN 1324-5864) **1825**
• Journal of International Media & Entertainment Law (USA ISSN 1556-875X) **4701**
• ➤ Journal of International Medical Research (GBR ISSN 0300-0605) **5650**
Journal of International Medical Research. Supplement *see* Journal of International Medical Research **5650**
Journal of International Medical Sciences Academy (IND) **5650**
• Journal of International Migration and Integration (GBR ISSN 1488-3473) **7286**
• ➤ Journal of International Money and Finance (GBR ISSN 0261-5606) **1362**
Journal of International Obstetrics and Gynecology *see* Guoji Fuchan Kexue Zazhi **5991**
Journal of International Oncology *see* Guoji Zhongliuxue Zazhi **6020**
Journal of International Pathology and Clinical Medicine *see* Guoji Bingli Kexue yu Linchuang Zazhi **5622**
Journal of International Peace Operations (USA ISSN 1933-8198) **7248**
• ➤ Journal of International Peacekeeping (NLD ISSN 1875-4104) **7248**
▼ • The Journal of International Policy Solutions (USA ISSN 1937-1284) **7248**
• ➤ Journal of International Political Theory (GBR ISSN 1755-0882) **7147**
➤ Journal of International Politics and Development (NGA ISSN 1597-3522) **7248**
Journal of International Relations *see* Uluslararasi Iliskiler **7270**
• ➤ Journal of International Relations and Development (GBR ISSN 1408-6980) **7248**
• Journal of International Research Publications: Economy & Business (BGR ISSN 1313-8006) **1137**
• Journal of International Research Publications: Materials, Methods & Technologies (BGR ISSN 1313-8014) **8429**
Journal of International Security *see* Kokusai Anzen Hosho **7149**
• The Journal of International Security Affairs (USA ISSN 1532-4060) **6429**
➤ Journal of International Selling & Sales Management (GBR ISSN 1356-0565) **1825**
▼ • ➤ Journal of International Social Research/Uluslararasi Sosyal Arastirmalar Dergisi (TUR ISSN 1307-9581) **7979**
• Journal of International Taxation (USA ISSN 1049-6378) **1931**
• ➤ Journal of International Technology and Information Management (USA ISSN 1543-5962) **1767**
• ➤ The Journal of International Trade and Economic Development (GBR ISSN 0963-8199) **1600**
• ➤ Journal of International Trade Law & Policy (GBR ISSN 1477-0024) **4933**
Journal of International Trust and Corporate Planning (GBR ISSN 1350-7605) **4872**
▼ • ➤ Journal of International Volunteer Tourism and Social Development (GBR ISSN 1754-6362) **8726**
• ➤ Journal of International Wildlife Law and Policy (USA ISSN 1388-0292) **3448**
• ➤ Journal of International Women's Studies (USA) **8899**
• Journal of Internet Banking and Commerce (CAN ISSN 1204-5357) **1362**
• ➤ Journal of Internet Business (AUS ISSN 1832-1151) **1137**
Journal of Internet Cataloging *see* Journal of Library Metadata **2563**
• ➤ Journal of Internet Commerce (USA ISSN 1533-2861) **1420**
• Journal of Internet Law (USA ISSN 1094-2904) **4701**
▼ • Journal of Internet Policy (USA ISSN 1944-2866) **2563**
• Journal of Internet Purchasing (CAN ISSN 1206-4890) **2563**
▼ • Journal of Internet Services and Applications (GBR ISSN 1867-4828) **2563**
• ➤ Journal of Internet Technology (TWN ISSN 1607-9264) **2563**
• ➤ Journal of Interpersonal Violence (USA ISSN 0886-2605) **2657**
➤ Journal of Interpretation (Rockville) (USA ISSN 0882-7893) **4075**
• ➤ Journal of Interpretation Research (USA ISSN 1092-5872) **3448**
• ➤ Journal of Interprofessional Care (GBR ISSN 1356-1820) **5650**
▼ • Journal of Intervention and Statebuilding (GBR ISSN 1750-2977) **7248**
• ➤ Journal of Interventional Cardiac Electrophysiology (USA ISSN 1383-875X) **5793**
• ➤ Journal of Interventional Cardiology (USA ISSN 0896-4327) **5793**
▼ • ➤ Journal of Interventional Oncology (CAN ISSN 1916-0518) **6024**
Journal of Interventional Radiology *see* Jieru Fangshexue Zazhi **6200**
Journal of Intestinal Microbiology *see* Chonai Saikingaku Zasshi **784**
Journal of Intravenous Therapy (USA ISSN 0194-1658) **5965**
• ➤ Journal of Invasive Cardiology (USA ISSN 1042-3931) **5793**
▼ ➤ The Journal of Invasive Fungal Infections (GBR ISSN 1753-3783) **5879**
• ➤ Journal of Inverse and Ill-Posed Problems (DEU ISSN 0928-0219) **5504**
• ➤ Journal of Invertebrate Pathology (USA ISSN 0022-2011) **951**
• ➤ Journal of Investigational Allergology and Clinical Immunology (ESP ISSN 1018-9068) **5763**
• ➤ The Journal of Investigative Dermatology (GBR ISSN 0022-202X) **5879**
• The Journal of Investigative Dermatology Symposium Proceedings (USA ISSN 1087-0024) **5879**
• ➤ Journal of Investigative Medicine (USA ISSN 1081-5589) **5915**
• Journal of Investigative Psychology and Offender Profiling (GBR ISSN 1544-4759) **7375**
Journal of Investigative Radiology *see* Investigative Radiology **6199**
• ➤ Journal of Investigative Surgery (GBR ISSN 0894-1939) **6248**
• The Journal of Investing (USA ISSN 1068-0896) **1635**
• Journal of Investment Compliance (GBR ISSN 1528-5812) **1635**
The Journal of Investment Consulting (USA ISSN 1524-6035) **1635**
• ➤ Journal of Investment Management (USA ISSN 1545-9144) **1362**
• ➤ Journal of Invitational Theory and Practice (USA ISSN 1060-6041) **2876**
Journal of Iranian Research and Analysis (USA ISSN 1525-9307) **7147**
▼ Journal of Irish and Scottish Studies (GBR ISSN 1753-2396) **4235**
Journal of Irish Archaeology (IRL ISSN 0268-537X) **401**
Journal of Irish Urban Studies (IRL ISSN 1649-1920) **5315**
• ➤ Journal of Iron and Steel Research International (CHN ISSN 1006-706X) **6319**
Journal of Irreproducible Results (USA ISSN 0022-2038) **7872**
Journal of Irrigation and Drainage *see* Guan'gai Paishui Xuebao **117**
• ➤ Journal of Irrigation and Drainage Engineering (USA ISSN 0733-9437) **3275**
▼ • ➤ Journal of Islamic Accounting and Business Research (GBR ISSN 1759-0817) **1295**
• ➤ Journal of Islamic Economics, Banking and Finance (BGD ISSN 2070-4658) **1362**
Journal of Islamic History/Majalla al-Tarikh al-Islami (IND) **7713**
• Journal of Islamic Law & Culture (USA ISSN 1528-817X) **7713**
▼ • ➤ Journal of Islamic Marketing (GBR ISSN 1759-0833) **1825**
• ➤ Journal of Islamic Philosophy (USA ISSN 1536-4569) **6928**
Journal of Islamic Science *see* M A A S Journal of Islamic Science **7713**
• ➤ Journal of Islamic State Practices in International Law (GBR ISSN 1742-4941) **4933**
• ➤ Journal of Islamic Studies (GBR ISSN 0955-2340) **7713**
• ➤ Journal of Island and Coastal Archaeology (USA ISSN 1556-4894) **401**
Journal of Island Studies (KOR ISSN 1226-881X) **7979**
Journal of Isotopes *see* Tongweisu **7072**
• ➤ The Journal of Israeli History (GBR ISSN 1353-1042) **4322**
Journal of Issues in Informing Science & Information Technology *see* Issues in Informing Science & Information Technology **8428**
Journal of Italian Translation (USA ISSN 1559-8470) **5134**
Journal of J A S T R O *see* Japanese Society for Therapeutic Radiation and Oncology. Journal **6199**
Journal of J.J. Group of Hospitals and Grant Medical College (IND ISSN 0022-2054) **5650**
Journal of J S N D I *see* Hi-hakai Kensa **3345**
Journal of Japan Clinical Dialysis *see* Nihon Toseki Ikai Zasshi **6273**
Journal of Japan Society of Dental Equipments *see* Nihon Iyou Shika Kiki Gakkaishi **5857**
Journal of Japanese Acupuncture & Moxibustion *see* Ido no Nippon **310**
▼ • ➤ Journal of Japanese & Korean Cinema (GBR ISSN 1756-4905) **6505**
Journal of Japanese Botany/Shokubutsu Kenkyu Zasshi (JPN ISSN 0022-2062) **797**
Journal of Japanese Grammar *see* Nihongo Bumpou **5155**
Journal of Japanese History *see* Nihonshi Kenkyu **4187**
Journal of Japanese Language Teaching *see* Nihongo Kyoiku **5155**
Journal of Japanese Language Teaching *see* Gengo to Kyoiku no Kenkyu **3062**
Journal of Japanese Linguistics (USA) **5134**
Journal of Japanese Linguistics and Education *see* Nihon Gogaku. Nihongo Kyoiku Ronshu **5155**
Journal of Japanese Scientists *see* Nihon no Kagakusha **7892**
Journal of Japanese Society of Shokuiku *see* Nihon Shokuiku Gakkaishi **6664**
Journal of Japanese Society of Stoma and Continence Rehabilitation *see* Nihon Sutoma Haisetsu Rihabiriteshon Gakkaishi **5929**
Journal of Japanese Studies *see* Riben Wenti Yanjiu **559**
• ➤ Journal of Japanese Studies (USA ISSN 0095-6848) **553**
Journal of Japanese Trade and Industry *see* Japan Spotlight: Economy, Culture & History **1131**
• ➤ Journal of Jewish Communal Service (USA ISSN 0022-2089) **7725**
• Journal of Jewish Education (USA ISSN 1524-4113) **2876**
▼ • ➤ Journal of Jewish Identities (USA ISSN 1939-7941) **3544**
• Journal of Jewish Music and Liturgy (USA ISSN 0197-0100) **6580**
• ➤ Journal of Jewish Studies (GBR ISSN 0022-2097) **7725**
▼ Journal of Jewish Though and Philosophy. Supplements (NLD ISSN 1873-9008) **7725**
• ➤ The Journal of Jewish Thought and Philosophy (NLD ISSN 1053-699X) **7725**
Journal of Jiangsu Administration Institute *see* Jiangsu Xingzheng Xueyuan Xuebao **7977**
Journal of Jinan University (Natural Science and Medicine Edition) *see* Jinan Daxue Xuebao (Ziran Kexue yu Yixue Ban) **7871**
Journal of Jisangsu Forestry Science & Technology *see* Jiangsu Linye Keji **3694**
Journal of Joint Surgery *see* Kansetsu Geka **6066**
• ➤ Journal of Judicial Administration (AUS ISSN 1036-7918) **4953**
Journal of Jungian Theory and Practice (USA ISSN 1530-5538) **7375**
The Journal of Juristic Papyrology (POL ISSN 0075-4277) **401**
Journal of Juvenile Law *see* University of La Verne Law Review **4915**
Journal of K I S S. Computer Systems and Theory *see* Jeongbo Gwahaghoe Nonmunji. Si'seu'tem Mich I'lon **2547**
Journal of K I S S. Computing Practices *see* Jeongbo Gwahaghoe Nonmunji. Keompyuting ui Silje **2547**
Journal of K I S S. Software and Applications *see* Jeongbo Gwahaghoe Nonmunji. So'peuteuweeo Mich Eung'yong **2547**
Journal of K K N N *see* Advances in Asian Environmental Engineering **3401**
▼ • Journal of K-Theory (GBR ISSN 1865-2433) **5504**
Journal of Kampo Medicine *see* Kanpo no Rinsho **312**
Journal of Kansai Physical Therapy *see* Kansai Rigaku Ryouhou **6112**
Journal of Kansas Herpetology (USA ISSN 1540-773X) **951**
Journal of Kansas Pharmacy (USA ISSN 0194-5106) **6854**
The Journal of Kentucky Studies (USA ISSN 8755-4208) **2876**
Journal of Kerala Studies (IND ISSN 0377-0443) **4184**
• ➤ Journal of Knee Surgery (USA ISSN 1538-8506) **6248**
• ➤ Journal of Knot Theory and Its Ramifications (SGP ISSN 0218-2165) **5504**
• Journal of Knowledge Advancement & Integration (NZL ISSN 1177-4576) **63**
Journal of Knowledge and Best Practices in Juvenile Justice & Psychology (USA ISSN 1937-1713) **2657**
▼ • Journal of Knowledge & Human Resource Management (USA ISSN 1945-5275) **1868**
▼ • ➤ Journal of Knowledge-Based Innovation in China (GBR ISSN 1756-1418) **1137**
▼ • ➤ Journal of Knowledge Globalization (USA ISSN 1938-7717) **1600**
• ➤ Journal of Knowledge Management (GBR ISSN 1367-3270) **1767**
• Journal of Knowledge Management Practice (CAN ISSN 1705-9232) **6928**
Journal of Kokugakuin University/Kokugakuin Zasshi (JPN ISSN 0288-2051) **6526**
Journal of KONBiN *see* Konferencja Bezpieczenstwa i Niezawodnosci. Journal **3207**
Journal of Korean History *see* Han'gugsa Yeon'gu **4182**
Journal of Korean Law (KOR ISSN 1598-1681) **4701**
• ➤ Journal of Korean Medical Science (KOR ISSN 1011-8934) **5650**
• Journal of Korean Pharmaceutical Sciences (KOR ISSN 0259-2347) **6854**
➤ Journal of Korean Studies (USA ISSN 0731-1613) **4184**
• The Journal of Kurdish Studies (BEL ISSN 1370-7205) **7979**
▼ • Journal of L G B T Health Research (Lesbian Gay Bisexual Transgender) (USA ISSN 1557-4091) **5651**
• ➤ Journal of L G B T Issues in Counseling (Lesbian Gay Bisexual Transgender) (USA ISSN 1553-8605) **7375**
• ➤ Journal of L G B T Youth (Lesbian, Gay, Bisexual, Transgender) (USA ISSN 1936-1653) **2876**
• ➤ Journal of Labelled Compounds and Radiopharmaceuticals (GBR ISSN 0362-4803) **2102**
Journal of Labor (USA ISSN 0745-4228) **4597**
• ➤ Journal of Labor Economics (USA ISSN 0734-306X) **1691**
Journal of Labor Hygiene in Iron and Steel Industry *see* Tekko Rodo Eisei **6334**
Journal of Labor Law *see* Rodo Ho **1706**
• ➤ Journal of Labor Research (USA ISSN 0195-3613) **1691**
Journal of Laboratory and Clinical Medicine *see* Translational Research **5911**
• Journal of Laboratory Physicians (IND ISSN 0974-2727) **5907**
Journal of Lake Sciences *see* Hupo Kexue **2709**
• Journal of Land, Resources, & Environmental Law (USA) **3140**
• Journal of Land Use & Environmental Law (USA ISSN 0892-4880) **3448**
• ➤ Journal of Land Use Science (GBR ISSN 1747-4248) **2711**
➤ Journal of Landscape Architecture (DEU ISSN 1862-6033) **447**
• ➤ Journal of Language and Learning (GBR ISSN 1740-4983) **2876**
Journal of Language and Linguistics *see* Lingua et Linguistica **5145**
• Journal of Language and Literacy Education (USA ISSN 1559-9035) **5134**
• ➤ Journal of Language and Literature (GBR ISSN 1478-9116) **5134**
• Journal of Language & Politics (NLD ISSN 1569-2159) **5134**
• ➤ Journal of Language and Social Psychology (USA ISSN 0261-927X) **7375**
• ➤ Journal of Language & Translation (KOR) **5134**
▼ • Journal of Language Contact (FRA ISSN 1955-2629) **5134**
• ➤ Journal of Language for International Business (USA ISSN 8755-0504) **5134**

Link to your serials resources and content with ulrichsweb.com

Title

10502 JOURNAL OF MARINE BIOLOGY ULRICH'S PERIODICALS

● ➤ Journal of Marine Biology (USA ISSN 1687-9481) **952**
● ➤ Journal of Marine Design and Operations (GBR ISSN 1476-1556) **8648**
● ➤ Journal of Marine Engineering and Technology (GBR ISSN 1476-1548) **8648**
● ➤ Journal of Marine Environmental Engineering (USA ISSN 1061-026X) **3448**
● ➤ Journal of Marine Research (USA ISSN 0022-2402) **2809**
● Journal of Marine Science and Application (CHN ISSN 1671-9433) **3206**
● ➤ Journal of Marine Science and Technology (JPN ISSN 0948-4280) **2809**
● Journal of Marine Science and Technology (TWN ISSN 1023-2796) **2809**
Journal of Marine Science & the Environment *see* Journal of Operational Oceanography **2809**
● ➤ Journal of Marine Systems (NLD ISSN 0924-7963) **2809**
● ➤ Journal of Marital and Family Therapy (USA ISSN 0194-472X) **7376**
● Journal of Maritime Archaeology (USA ISSN 1557-2285) **401**
● ➤ Journal of Maritime Law and Commerce (USA ISSN 0022-2410) **4970**
● ➤ Journal of Marketing (USA ISSN 0022-2429) **1825**
● ➤ Journal of Marketing Channels (USA ISSN 1046-669X) **1825**
● ➤ Journal of Marketing Communications (GBR ISSN 1352-7266) **1825**
● ➤ Journal of Marketing Education (USA ISSN 0273-4753) **1825**
● ➤ Journal of Marketing for Higher Education (USA ISSN 0884-1241) **2991**
● ➤ Journal of Marketing Management (GBR ISSN 0267-257X) **1825**
● ➤ Journal of Marketing Research (USA ISSN 0022-2437) **1825**
● ➤ Journal of Marketing Theory and Practice (USA ISSN 1069-6679) **1826**
● ➤ The Journal of Markets & Morality (USA ISSN 1098-1217) **1137**
➤ Journal of Maronite Studies (USA) **7802**
● ➤ Journal of Marriage and Family (USA ISSN 0022-2445) **8114**
Journal of Martial Arts & Healing (USA ISSN 1546-5381) **6991**
▼ ● Journal of Mass Communication at Francis Marion University (USA ISSN 1936-3648) **8114**
● ➤ Journal of Mass Media Ethics (USA ISSN 0890-0523) **8114**
● ➤ Journal of Mass Spectrometry (GBR ISSN 1076-5174) **2102**
● ➤ Journal of Material Culture (GBR ISSN 1359-1835) **8114**
● ➤ The Journal of Material Cycles and Waste Management (JPN ISSN 1438-4957) **3508**
Journal of Material Engineering *see* Cailiao Gongcheng **50**
Journal of Materials and Design *see* Materials & Design **3352**
Journal of Materials and Metallurgy *see* Cailiao yu Yejin Xuebao **6307**
● ➤ Journal of Materials Chemistry (GBR ISSN 0959-9428) **2068**
Journal of Materials: Design and Applications *see* Institution of Mechanical Engineers. Proceedings. Part L: Journal of Materials: Design and Applications **3381**
Journal of Materials Education (USA ISSN 0738-7989) **3206**
● ➤ Journal of Materials Engineering and Performance (USA ISSN 1059-9495) **3350**
● ➤ Journal of Materials in Civil Engineering (USA ISSN 0899-1561) **3276**
● ➤ Journal of Materials Processing Technology (CHE ISSN 0924-0136) **3386**
● ➤ Journal of Materials Research (USA ISSN 0884-2914) **3350**
● ➤ Journal of Materials Science (USA ISSN 0022-2461) **3350**
▼ ● Journal of Materials Science and Engineering (USA ISSN 1934-8959) **3350**
Journal of Materials Science and Technology (BGR ISSN 0861-9786) **3350**
● ➤ Journal of Materials Science & Technology (CHN ISSN 1005-0302) **6319**
● ➤ Journal of Materials Science: Materials in Electronics (USA ISSN 0957-4522) **3350**
● ➤ Journal of Materials Science: Materials in Medicine (USA ISSN 0957-4530) **3350**
● ➤ The Journal of Maternal - Fetal & Neonatal Medicine (GBR ISSN 1476-7058) **5995**
● ➤ Journal of Mathematical Analysis and Applications (USA ISSN 0022-247X) **5505**
Journal of Mathematical and Physical Sciences (IND ISSN 0047-2557) **5505**
● ➤ The Journal of Mathematical Behavior (GBR ISSN 0732-3123) **5505**
● ➤ Journal of Mathematical Biology (DEU ISSN 0303-6812) **683**
● ➤ Journal of Mathematical Chemistry (NLD ISSN 0259-9791) **5505**
▼ ● ➤ Journal of Mathematical Cryptology (DEU ISSN 1862-2976) **5505**
● ➤ Journal of Mathematical Economics (NLD ISSN 0304-4068) **1545**
● ➤ Journal of Mathematical Fluid Mechanics (CHE ISSN 1422-6928) **7021**
● ➤ Journal of Mathematical Imaging and Vision (USA ISSN 0924-9907) **5553**
● ➤ Journal of Mathematical Logic (SGP ISSN 0219-0613) **5505**
● Journal of Mathematical Modelling and Algorithms (NLD ISSN 1570-1166) **5505**
Journal of Mathematical Pharmacy *see* Shuli Yiyaoxue Zazhi **6881**
● ➤ Journal of Mathematical Physics (USA ISSN 0022-2488) **7021**
● ➤ Journal of Mathematical Psychology (USA ISSN 0022-2496) **7376**
Journal of Mathematical Research and Exposition *see* Shuxue Yanjiu yu Pinglun **5536**
● Journal of Mathematical Sciences (JPN ISSN 1340-5705) **5505**
● ➤ Journal of Mathematical Sciences (USA ISSN 1072-3374) **5505**
● ➤ Journal of Mathematical Sociology (USA ISSN 0022-250X) **8149**
Journal of Mathematical Study *see* Shuxue Yanjiu **5536**
Journal of Mathematics *see* Shuxue Zazhi **5536**
Journal of Mathematics *see* University of Tokushima. Journal of Mathematics **5545**
▼ ● Journal of Mathematics (USA ISSN 1945-8738) **5505**
Journal of Mathematics & Design (ARG ISSN 1515-7881) **5505**
▼ ● ➤ Journal of Mathematics and Music (GBR ISSN 1745-9737) **5505**
● ➤ Journal of Mathematics and Statistics/Hacettepe Bulletin on Natural Sciences and Engineering. Series B: Mathematics and Statistics (TUR ISSN 1303-5010) **5505**
● ➤ Journal of Mathematics and Statistics (USA ISSN 1549-3644) **5505**
▼ ● ➤ Journal of Mathematics and the Arts (GBR ISSN 1751-3472) **5505**
Journal of Mathematics Education *see* Shuxue Jiaoyu Xuebao **2912**
▼ ● Journal of Mathematics Education (USA ISSN 1945-7502) **5506**
▼ ● ➤ Journal of Mathematics Research (CAN ISSN 1916-9795) **5506**
● Journal of Mathematics Teacher Education (NLD ISSN 1386-4416) **5506**
➤ Journal of Mauritian Studies (MUS ISSN 1013-0152) **5315**
● ➤ Journal of Maxillofacial and Oral Surgery (IND ISSN 0972-8279) **6249**
The Journal of Maxillofacial Prosthetics and Technology (GBR ISSN 1366-4697) **5852**
➤ Journal of Mayan Linguistics (USA ISSN 0195-475X) **5134**
● ➤ Journal of Mechanical Design (USA ISSN 1050-0472) **3386**
Journal of Mechanical Engineering *see* Strojniski Vestnik **3396**
Journal of Mechanical Engineering Research and Developments (BGD ISSN 1024-1752) **3386**
Journal of Mechanical Engineering Science *see* Institution of Mechanical Engineers. Proceedings. Part C: Journal of Mechanical Engineering Science **3380**
● ➤ Journal of Mechanical Science and Technology (DEU ISSN 1738-494X) **3386**
Journal of Mechanical Strength *see* Jixie Qiangdu **3204**
● Journal of Mechanics (TWN ISSN 1727-7191) **3350**
● ➤ Journal of Mechanics in Medicine and Biology (SGP ISSN 0219-5194) **683**
● Journal of Mechanics of Materials and Structures (USA ISSN 1559-3959) **3206**
▼ ● Journal of Mechanisms and Robotics (USA ISSN 1942-4302) **3386**
● Journal of Media and Religion (USA ISSN 1534-8423) **2329**
➤ Journal of Media Business Studies (SWE ISSN 1652-2354) **8114**
● ➤ Journal of Media Economics (USA ISSN 0899-7764) **2329**
▼ ● ➤ The Journal of Media Law (GBR ISSN 1757-7632) **4703**
▼ ● ➤ Journal of Media Law & Ethics (USA ISSN 1940-9370) **4703**
The Journal of Media Literacy (USA ISSN 1944-4982) **8114**
● ➤ Journal of Media Practice (GBR ISSN 1468-2753) **2329**
● ➤ Journal of Media Psychology (DEU ISSN 1864-1105) **7376**
● ➤ Journal of Media Psychology (USA) **2329**
▼ ● ➤ Journal of Media Sociology (USA ISSN 1940-9397) **8114**
Journal of Media Studies (PAK ISSN 1812-7592) **8114**
● Journal of Medical Advances (USA ISSN 1541-6178) **5651**
Journal of Medical and Applied Malacology/Revista de Malacologia Medica y Aplicada (USA ISSN 1053-6388) **952**
Journal of Medical and Biological Engineering/Zhonghua Yixue Gongcheng Xuekan (TWN ISSN 1609-0985) **5651**
▼ ● Journal of Medical and Biological Sciences (USA ISSN 1934-7189) **5651**
➤ Journal of Medical and Dental Sciences (JPN ISSN 1342-8810) **5651**
● Journal of Medical and Pharmaceutical Marketing (NGA ISSN 0331-0124) **1826**
● ➤ Journal of Medical Biochemistry (POL ISSN 1452-8258) **736**
● ➤ Journal of Medical Biography (GBR ISSN 0967-7720) **643**
Journal of Medical Biomechanics *see* Yiyong Shengwu Lixue **5733**
▼ ● ➤ Journal of Medical Case Reports (GBR ISSN 1752-1947) **5651**
● ➤ The Journal of Medical Chemical Defense (USA ISSN 1540-6709) **5651**
● Journal of Medical Colleges of P L A (People's Liberation Army) (NLD ISSN 1000-1948) **5651**
▼ ● ➤ Journal of Medical Devices (USA ISSN 1932-6181) **4488**
● ➤ Journal of Medical Economics (GBR ISSN 1369-6998) **5651**
● ➤ Journal of Medical Engineering & Technology (GBR ISSN 0309-1902) **5651**
● ➤ Journal of Medical Entomology (USA ISSN 0022-2585) **852**
● ➤ Journal of Medical Entomology Online (USA) **852**
● ➤ Journal of Medical Ethics (GBR ISSN 0306-6800) **5651**
▼ ● ➤ Journal of Medical Ethics and History of Medicine (IRN ISSN 2008-0387) **5651**
Journal of Medical Ethics. Supplement *see* Journal of Medical Ethics **5651**
● ➤ Journal of Medical Genetics (GBR ISSN 0022-2593) **874**
● ➤ Journal of Medical Humanities (USA ISSN 1041-3545) **5651**
Journal of Medical Imaging *see* Yixue Yingxiangxue Zazhi **6210**
● ➤ Journal of Medical Imaging and Radiation Oncology (AUS ISSN 1754-9477) **6200**
➤ Journal of Medical Imaging and Radiation Sciences/Journal de l'imagerie Medicale et des Sciences de la Radiation (USA ISSN 1939-8654) **6200**
Journal of Medical Informatics *see* Yixue Xinxixue Zazhi **5832**
Journal of Medical Intelligence *see* Yixue Xinxixue Zazhi **5832**
● ➤ Journal of Medical Internet Research (CAN ISSN 1438-8871) **5832**
● ➤ Journal of Medical Investigation (JPN ISSN 1343-1420) **5907**
➤ Journal of Medical Investigation and Practice (NGA) **5652**
➤ Journal of Medical Laboratory Science (NGA ISSN 1116-1043) **5907**
● ➤ Journal of Medical Licensure and Discipline (USA ISSN 1547-481X) **5652**
● ➤ Journal of Medical Marketing (Online) (GBR ISSN 1745-7912) **6854**
● ➤ Journal of Medical Marketing (Print) (GBR ISSN 1745-7904) **6854**
● ➤ Journal of Medical Microbiology (GBR ISSN 0022-2615) **889**
Journal of Medical Mycology *see* Journal de Mycologie Medicale **5761**
● Journal of Medical Physics (IND ISSN 0971-6203) **7021**
➤ Journal of Medical Practice Management (USA ISSN 8755-0229) **5652**
● ➤ Journal of Medical Primatology (DNK ISSN 0047-2565) **952**
Journal of Medical Reference Services Quarterly. Monographic Supplement *see* Medical Reference Services Quarterly **5031**
Journal of Medical Science Yanbian University *see* Yanbian Daxue Yixue Xuebao **5733**
▼ ● Journal of Medical Sciences (NLD ISSN 1996-3262) **5652**
● ➤ Journal of Medical Sciences (PAK ISSN 1682-4474) **5652**
Journal of Medical Sciences *see* Yixue Yanjiu Zazhi **5733**
▼ ● ➤ Journal of Medical Sciences Research (USA ISSN 1938-5765) **5652**
● ➤ Journal of Medical Screening (GBR ISSN 0969-1413) **5820**
● ➤ Journal of Medical Speech - Language Pathology (USA ISSN 1065-1438) **6082**
● ➤ Journal of Medical Systems (USA ISSN 0148-5598) **5832**
Journal of Medical Technology *see* Rinsho Kensa **5910**
Journal of Medical Theory and Practice *see* Yixue Lilun yu Shijian **5733**
● ➤ Journal of Medical Toxicology (USA ISSN 1556-9039) **6854**
● Journal of Medical Ultrasonics (JPN ISSN 1346-4523) **7088**
Journal of Medical Ultrasound (HKG ISSN 0929-6441) **6201**
● ➤ Journal of Medical Virology (USA ISSN 0146-6615) **5652**
Journal of Medicinal and Aromatic Plant Sciences (IND) **797**
● ➤ Journal of Medicinal Chemistry (USA ISSN 0022-2623) **6854**
● ➤ Journal of Medicinal Food (USA ISSN 1096-620X) **5652**
▼ ● ➤ Journal of Medicinal Food Plants (USA ISSN 1947-3710) **5652**
▼ ● Journal of Medicinal Plant Research (NGA ISSN 1996-0875) **311**
Journal of Medicinal Plants *see* Faslnamah-i Giyahan-i Daruyi **309**
➤ Journal of Medicine (BGD ISSN 1997-9797) **5652**
● Journal of Medicine (USA ISSN 1090-1221) **5652**
▼ ● ➤ The Journal of Medicine (USA ISSN 1943-961X) **5652**
● ➤ Journal of Medicine and Biomedical Research (NGA ISSN 1596-6941) **5652**
● Journal of Medicine and Law (USA ISSN 1092-2083) **4704**
● Journal of Medicine and Medical Sciences (NGA ISSN 1119-3999) **5652**
Journal of Medicine and Pharmaceutical Science *see* Igaku to Yakugaku **6847**
Journal of Medicine & Pharmacy of Chinese Minorities *see* Zhongguo Minzu Yiyao Zazhi **5736**
● ➤ The Journal of Medicine and Philosophy (USA ISSN 0360-5310) **5652**
● ➤ Journal of Medicine and the Person (ITA ISSN 2035-9411) **5652**
➤ Journal of Medicine in the Tropics (NGA) **5652**
● ➤ Journal of Medieval and Early Modern Studies (USA ISSN 1082-9636) **4460**
● ➤ Journal of Medieval History (NLD ISSN 0304-4181) **4236**
▼ ● Journal of Medieval Iberian Studies (GBR ISSN 1754-6559) **4236**
Journal of Medieval Indian Literature (IND) **5315**
● ➤ The Journal of Medieval Latin (BEL ISSN 0778-9750) **5134**
● Journal of Mediterranean Archaeology (GBR ISSN 0952-7648) **401**
➤ Journal of Mediterranean Ecology (ITA ISSN 1388-7904) **3448**
➤ Journal of Mediterranean Studies (MLT ISSN 1016-3476) **4460**
● ➤ Journal of Membrane Biology (USA ISSN 0022-2631) **834**
● ➤ Journal of Membrane Science (NLD ISSN 0376-7388) **2137**
● ➤ Journal of Memetics - Evolutionary Models of Information Transmission (GBR ISSN 1366-4786) **6929**
● ➤ Journal of Memory and Language (USA ISSN 0749-596X) **5134**
▼ ● ➤ Journal of Men, Masculinities and Spirituality (NZL ISSN 1177-2484) **7655**
➤ Journal of Mennonite Studies (CAN ISSN 0824-5053) **7737**
● ➤ Journal of Men's Health (NLD ISSN 1875-6867) **6284**
The Journal of Men's Health & Gender *see* Journal of Men's Health **6284**
● ➤ Journal of Men's Studies (USA ISSN 1060-8265) **6302**
● ➤ Journal of Mental Health (GBR ISSN 0963-8237) **6152**
Journal of Mental Health *see* Seishin Hoken Kenkyu **6184**
Journal of Mental Health and Psychosomatics *see* Mentalhigiene es Pszichoszomatika **6160**
● ➤ Journal of Mental Health Counseling (USA ISSN 1040-2861) **7376**
● ➤ Journal of Mental Health Law (GBR ISSN 1466-2817) **6152**
Journal of Mental Health Policy and Economics (Online Edition) *see* Journal of Mental Health Policy and Economics (Print Edition) **7376**
● ➤ Journal of Mental Health Policy and Economics (Print Edition) (ITA ISSN 1091-4358) **7376**
Journal of Mental Health Promotion *see* Journal of Public Mental Health **7529**
▼ ● ➤ Journal of Mental Health Research in Intellectual Disabilities (USA ISSN 1931-5864) **6152**
● The Journal of Mental Health, Training, Education and Practice (GBR ISSN 1755-6228) **6152**
The Journal of Mental Health Workforce Development *see* The Journal of Mental Health, Training, Education and Practice **6152**
Journal of Mental Imagery (USA ISSN 0364-5541) **7376**
▼ ● ➤ Journal of Mentored Management Accounting Research (USA ISSN 1947-4482) **1295**
▼ ● Journal of Mesoamerican Languages and Linguistics (USA ISSN 1932-4413) **5134**
➤ Journal of Metabolism, Diabetes and Endocrinology in South Africa (ZAF) **5896**
● ➤ Journal of Metallurgy (USA ISSN 1687-9465) **6319**
● ➤ Journal of Metallurgy and Materials Science (IND ISSN 0972-4257) **6319**
Journal of Metallurgy, Part A & B *see* Jinshu Xuebao **6318**
Journal of Metals *see* J O M **6318**
● ➤ Journal of Metamorphic Geology (GBR ISSN 0263-4929) **2750**
Journal of Metastable and Nanocrystalline Materials *see* Materials Science Forum **7026**
Journal of Meteorological Research/Kishocho Kenkyu Jiho (JPN ISSN 0368-5942) **6358**
Journal of Meteorological Research of Tohoku District *see* Tohoku Chiho Kisho Kenkyukaishi **6396**
Journal of Meteorology *see* The International Journal of Meteorology **6358**
▼ ➤ Journal of Metropolitan Schooling (USA ISSN 1944-6861) **2877**
Journal of Mexican American Studies (USA ISSN 0022-2690) **3544**

DIRECTORY 2010 JOURNAL OF NEAR-DEATH STUDIES 10503

• Journal of Micro-Nano Mechatronics (DEU ISSN 1865-3928) **3386**
• ➤ Journal of Micro/Nanolithography, M E M S, and M O E M S (USA ISSN 1932-5150) **7078**
Journal of Micro/Nanolithography, Micro Electro Mechanical Systems, and Micro Optical Electro Mechanical System *see* Journal of Micro/Nanolithography, M E M S, and M O E M S **7078**
• ➤ Journal of Microbiological Methods (NLD ISSN 0167-7012) **889**
Journal of Microbiology *see* Weishengwuxue Zazhi **898**
• ➤ The Journal of Microbiology (KOR ISSN 1225-8873) **889**
• Journal of Microbiology and Biology Education (USA ISSN 1542-8818) **889**
• ➤ Journal of Microbiology and Biotechnology (KOR ISSN 1017-7825) **767**
Journal of Microbiology, Epidemiology and Immunobiology *see* Zhurnal Mikrobiologii, Epidemiologii i Immunobiologii **898**
• ➤ Journal of Microbiology, Immunology and Infection/Weimian yu Ganran Zazhi (HKG ISSN 1684-1182) **889**
• Journal of Microelectronics and Electronic Packaging (USA ISSN 1551-4897) **3106**
• ➤ Journal of Microencapsulation (GBR ISSN 0265-2048) **6854**
Journal of Microfinance *see* E S R Review **1336**
Journal of Microlithography, Microfabrication, and Microsystems *see* Journal of Micro/Nanolithography, M E M S, and M O E M S **7078**
• ➤ Journal of Micromechanics and Microengineering (GBR ISSN 0960-1317) **3386**
• ➤ Journal of Micromechatronics (NLD ISSN 1389-2258) **3322**
• ➤ Journal of Micropalaeontology (GBR ISSN 0262-821X) **6725**
• ➤ Journal of Microscopy (GBR ISSN 0022-2720) **899**
➤ Journal of Microwave Power and Electromagnetic Energy (USA ISSN 0832-7823) **3322**
Journal of Microwave Surgery (JPN ISSN 0917-7728) **6249**
Journal of Microwaves *see* Weibo Xuebao **3116**
• Journal of Microwaves and Optoelectronics (BRA ISSN 1516-7399) **3106**
Journal of Middle Atlantic Archaeology (USA ISSN 0883-9697) **401**
• ➤ Journal of Middle East Women's Studies (USA ISSN 1552-5864) **8900**
▼ Journal of Middle Eastern and Islamic Studies in Asia (USA ISSN 1937-0679) **553**
• ➤ Journal of Midwifery & Women's Health (USA ISSN 1526-9523) **5995**
• ➤ The Journal of Migration and Refugee Issues (AUS ISSN 1832-0643) **4850**
• ➤ Journal of Military and Strategic Studies (CAN ISSN 1488-559X) **6429**
• ➤ Journal of Military Ethics (NOR ISSN 1502-7570) **6429**
Journal of Military History *see* Sotahistoriallinen Aikakauskirja **6447**
• ➤ Journal of Military History (USA ISSN 0899-3718) **6429**
Journal of Military Nursing & Research *see* J M N R **5963**
➤ The Journal of Mind and Behavior (USA ISSN 0271-0137) **7376**
• Journal of Mine Action (USA ISSN 1533-9440) **8050**
• ➤ Journal of Mineralogical and Petrological Sciences (JPN ISSN 1345-6296) **2750**
Journal of Mineralogy and Petrology *see* Kuangwu Yanshi **2752**
Journal of Mines, Metals and Fuels (IND ISSN 0022-2755) **6467**
The Journal of Ming-Qing Fiction Studies *see* Mingqing Xiaoshuo Yanjiu **5334**
• ➤ Journal of Minimal Access Surgery (IND ISSN 0972-9941) **6249**
• ➤ Journal of Minimally Invasive Gynecology (USA ISSN 1553-4650) **5995**
• ➤ Journal of Mining and Geology (NGA ISSN 1116-2775) **6467**
Journal of Mining and Metallurgy. Section A: Mining (SRB ISSN 1450-5959) **6467**
➤ Journal of Mining and Metallurgy. Section B: Metallurgy (SRB ISSN 1450-5339) **6319**
Journal of Mining, Metallurgical, Materials, Geotechnical and Plant Engineering *see* B H M **6458**
Journal of Mining Research (IND ISSN 0971-1899) **6467**
• ➤ Journal of Mining Science (USA ISSN 1062-7391) **6467**
Journal of Ministry & Theology (USA ISSN 1092-9525) **7655**
➤ Journal of Mississippi History (USA ISSN 0022-2771) **4299**
▼ • ➤ Journal of Mixed Methods Research (USA ISSN 1558-6898) **7872**
▼ • Journal of Mobile Communication (PAK ISSN 1990-794X) **2369**
• ➤ Journal of Mobile Multimedia (USA ISSN 1550-4646) **2369**
• Journal of Modeling and Simulation of Microsystems (USA ISSN 1524-2021) **2517**
• Journal of Modeling, Design and Management of Engineering Systems (NGA ISSN 1596-3497) **3206**
• ➤ Journal of Modelling in Management (GBR ISSN 1746-5664) **1768**
• Journal of Modern Accounting and Auditing (USA ISSN 1548-6583) **1295**
• ➤ Journal of Modern African Studies (GBR ISSN 0022-278X) **7147**
• Journal of Modern Applied Statistical Methods (USA ISSN 1538-9472) **8383**
• ➤ Journal of Modern Business (USA) **1768**
▼ • ➤ Journal of Modern Chinese History (GBR ISSN 1753-5654) **4184**
▼ • ➤ The Journal of Modern Craft (GBR ISSN 1749-6772) **499**
• Journal of Modern Dentistry (SYR ISSN 1754-193X) **5852**
▼ • Journal of Modern Dynamics (USA ISSN 1930-5311) **5506**
Journal of Modern Educational League *see* Magallat Rabitat al-Tarbiyyat al-Hadithat **2884**
Journal of Modern Electrophysiology *see* Xiandai Dianshenglixue Zazhi **928**
• Journal of Modern European History/Revue d'Histoire Europeenne Contemporaine/Zeitschrift fuer Moderne Europaeische Geschichte (DEU ISSN 1611-8944) **4236**
• Journal of Modern Greek Studies (USA ISSN 0738-1727) **4236**
Journal of Modern Hellenism (USA ISSN 0743-7749) **3544**
• ➤ The Journal of Modern History (USA ISSN 0022-2801) **4149**
• ➤ Journal of Modern Italian Studies (GBR ISSN 1354-571X) **5315**
• ➤ Journal of Modern Jewish Studies (GBR ISSN 1472-5886) **4460**
The Journal of Modern Korean Studies/Kundae Han'guk Yon'gu (USA ISSN 8756-2235) **4185**
• ➤ Journal of Modern Literature (USA ISSN 0022-281X) **5315**
➤ Journal of Modern Literature in Chinese/Xiandai Zhongwen Wenxue Xuebao (USA ISSN 1026-5120) **5315**
▼ • Journal of Modern Mathematics and Statistics (PAK ISSN 1994-5388) **5506**
Journal of Modern Medical Inspection & Testing *see* Xiandai Jianyan Yixue Zazhi **5911**
Journal of Modern Oncology *see* Xiandai Zhongliu Yixue **6036**
• ➤ Journal of Modern Optics (GBR ISSN 0950-0340) **7078**
Journal of Modern Pharmacy (ZAF ISSN 1683-6707) **6854**
Journal of Modern Philology *see* Casopis pro Moderni Filologii **5105**
Journal of Modern Stomatology *see* Xiandai Kouqiang Yixue Zazhi **5932**
• Journal of Modern Turkish Studies/Modern Turkluk Arastirmalari Dergisi (TUR ISSN 1304-8015) **5134**
• ➤ Journal of Molecular and Cellular Cardiology (GBR ISSN 0022-2828) **5794**
• Journal of Molecular and Cellular Pathology/Revue Roumaine de Morphologie et Embryologie (ROM ISSN 1582-4918) **683**
• ➤ Journal of Molecular and Genetic Medicine (GBR ISSN 1747-0862) **5652**
• ➤ Journal of Molecular Biology (GBR ISSN 0022-2836) **736**
Journal of Molecular Catalysis *see* Fenzi Cuihua **7012**
• ➤ Journal of Molecular Catalysis A: Chemical (NLD ISSN 1381-1169) **2137**
• ➤ Journal of Molecular Catalysis B: Enzymatic (NLD ISSN 1381-1177) **736**
Journal of Molecular Cell Biology *see* Fenzi Xiabao Shengwu Xuebao **832**
▼ • ➤ Journal of Molecular Cell Biology (GBR ISSN 1674-2788) **683**
• ➤ The Journal of Molecular Diagnostics (USA ISSN 1525-1578) **5653**
• ➤ Journal of Molecular Endocrinology (GBR ISSN 0952-5041) **5896**
Journal of Molecular Epidemiology and Evolutionary Genetics and Infectious Diseases *see* Infection, Genetics and Evolution **5634**
• ➤ Journal of Molecular Evolution (USA ISSN 0022-2844) **874**
• ➤ Journal of Molecular Graphics and Modelling (USA ISSN 1093-3263) **2108**
• ➤ Journal of Molecular Histology (NLD ISSN 1567-2379) **834**
• ➤ Journal of Molecular Liquids (NLD ISSN 0167-7322) **2137**
• ➤ Journal of Molecular Medicine (DEU ISSN 0946-2716) **5653**
• ➤ Journal of Molecular Microbiology and Biotechnology (CHE ISSN 1464-1801) **890**
• ➤ Journal of Molecular Modeling (DEU ISSN 1610-2940) **2137**
• ➤ Journal of Molecular Neuroscience (USA ISSN 0895-8696) **6153**
• ➤ Journal of Molecular Recognition (GBR ISSN 0952-3499) **2124**
• Journal of Molecular Science (CHN ISSN 1000-9035) **2068**
• Journal of Molecular Signaling (GBR ISSN 1750-2187) **924**
• ➤ Journal of Molecular Spectroscopy (USA ISSN 0022-2852) **7078**
• ➤ Journal of Molecular Structure (NLD ISSN 0022-2860) **2068**
• ➤ Journal of Molecular Structure: THEOCHEM (NLD ISSN 0166-1280) **2068**
• ➤ Journal of Molluscan Studies (GBR ISSN 0260-1230) **952**
Journal of Molluscan Studies. Supplement *see* Journal of Molluscan Studies **952**
• ➤ Journal of Monetary Economics (NLD ISSN 0304-3932) **1362**
• ➤ Journal of Money, Credit & Banking (USA ISSN 0022-2879) **1362**
• ➤ Journal of Money Laundering Control (GBR ISSN 1368-5201) **1362**
• ➤ Journal of Moral Education (GBR ISSN 0305-7240) **2877**
• ➤ Journal of Moral Philosophy (NLD ISSN 1740-4681) **6929**
Journal of Moravian History (USA ISSN 1933-6632) **4299**
Journal of Maori and Pacific Development/Puna Korero (NZL ISSN 1175-3099) **1600**
• Journal of Mormon History (USA ISSN 0094-7342) **7737**
• ➤ Journal of Morphology (USA ISSN 0362-2525) **683**
• ➤ Journal of Motor Behavior (USA ISSN 0022-2895) **7376**
Journal of Motorcycle Technology *see* Motuoche Jishu **8594**
Journal of Mountain Agriculture and Biology *see* Shandi Nongye Shengwu Xuebao **155**
Journal of Mountain Agriculture in the Balkans (BGR ISSN 1311-0489) **128**
• ➤ Journal of Mountain Ecology (ITA ISSN 1590-3907) **3448**
• ➤ Journal of Mountain Science (CHN ISSN 1672-6316) **2750**
Journal of Movement Disorder and Disability *see* Undo Shogai **4070**
Journal of Multi-Body Dynamics *see* Institution of Mechanical Engineers. Proceedings. Part K: Journal of Multi-Body Dynamics **3381**
• Journal of Multi-Criteria Decision Analysis (GBR ISSN 1057-9214) **1769**
• ➤ Journal of Multicultural Counseling and Development (USA ISSN 0883-8534) **7376**
• ➤ Journal of Multicultural Discourses (GBR ISSN 1744-7143) **5134**
† • ➤ Journal of Multicultural Nursing and Health (USA ISSN 1526-8233) **8968**
▼ • Journal of Multicultural Research (USA ISSN 1947-4695) **4460**
• ➤ Journal of Multidisciplinary Evaluation (USA ISSN 1556-8180) **8115**
▼ • ➤ Journal of Multidisciplinary Healthcare (GBR ISSN 1178-2390) **5653**
▼ • ➤ Journal of Multidisciplinary Research (USA ISSN 1947-2900) **7979**
• ➤ Journal of Multilingual & Multicultural Development (GBR ISSN 0143-4632) **3013**
Journal of Multilingual Communication Disorders *see* Clinical Linguistics & Phonetics **6132**
• ➤ Journal of Multimedia (FIN ISSN 1796-2048) **2330**
• ➤ Journal of Multinational Financial Management (NLD ISSN 1042-444X) **1769**
• ➤ Journal of Multiple-Valued Logic and Soft Computing (USA ISSN 1542-3980) **5506**
▼ • ➤ Journal of Multiscale Modeling (SGP ISSN 1793-5237) **2429**
▼ • ➤ Journal of Multiscale Modelling (SGP ISSN 1756-9737) **7872**
• Journal of Multistate Taxation & Incentives (USA ISSN 1533-3124) **1931**
• ➤ Journal of Multivariate Analysis (USA ISSN 0047-259X) **5506**
• ➤ Journal of Muscle Foods (USA ISSN 1046-0756) **3651**
• ➤ Journal of Muscle Research and Cell Motility (NLD ISSN 0142-4319) **6064**
➤ Journal of Muscle Shoals History (USA ISSN 0094-8039) **4299**
• ➤ The Journal of Musculoskeletal and Neuronal Interactions (GRC) **6064**
• ➤ The Journal of Musculoskeletal Medicine (USA ISSN 0899-2517) **6064**
• ➤ Journal of Musculoskeletal Pain (USA ISSN 1058-2452) **6064**
Journal of Musculoskeletal Pain. Supplement *see* Journal of Musculoskeletal Pain **6064**
• ➤ Journal of Musculoskeletal Research (SGP ISSN 0218-9577) **6064**
Journal of Musculoskeletal System *see* Kotsu Kansetsu Jintai **6224**
Journal of Museum Education (USA ISSN 1059-8650) **6526**
➤ Journal of Museum Ethnography (GBR ISSN 0954-7169) **345**
Journal of Museums & Archaeology *see* Wen Bo **6540**
• ➤ The Journal of Music and Meaning (DNK ISSN 1603-7170) **6580**
• Journal of Music in China (USA ISSN 1092-1710) **6580**
Journal of Music in Ireland *see* The J M I **6578**
Journal of Music Scores *see* S C I Journal of Music Scores **6614**
• ➤ Journal of Music Teacher Education (Online) (USA ISSN 1945-0079) **6580**
▼ • ➤ Journal of Music, Technology and Education (GBR ISSN 1752-7066) **6580**
• ➤ Journal of Music Theory (USA ISSN 0022-2909) **6580**
➤ Journal of Music Theory Pedagogy (USA ISSN 0891-7639) **6581**
• ➤ Journal of Music Therapy (USA ISSN 0022-2917) **6111**
The Journal of Musical Instrument Technology (USA) **6581**
• ➤ Journal of Musicological Research (USA ISSN 0141-1896) **6581**
• ➤ Journal of Musicology (USA ISSN 0277-9269) **6581**
• Journal of Muslim Mental Health (USA ISSN 1556-4908) **7376**
• ➤ Journal of Muslim Minority Affairs (GBR ISSN 1360-2004) **7713**
➤ Journal of Mycopathological Research (IND ISSN 0971-3719) **890**
Journal of Mythic Arts *see* The Endicott Studio Journal of Mythic Arts **487**
The Journal of N A E T Energetics and Complementary Medicine (Nambudripad's Allergy Elimination Technique) (USA ISSN 1554-4168) **5763**
Journal of N P O Management *see* Feiyingli Zuzhi Guanli Xuekan **1745**
Journal of Nambudripad's Allergy Elimination Technique Energetics and Complementary Medicine *see* The Journal of N A E T Energetics and Complementary Medicine **5763**
Journal of Nannoplankton Research (GBR ISSN 1210-8049) **2809**
▼ • ➤ Journal of Nano Education (USA ISSN 1936-7449) **3206**
▼ • ➤ Journal of Nano Research (CHE ISSN 1662-5250) **7021**
• ➤ Journal of Nanobiotechnology (GBR ISSN 1477-3155) **767**
• ➤ Journal of Nanoelectronics and Optoelectronics (USA ISSN 1555-130X) **3106**
• ➤ Journal of Nanomaterials (USA ISSN 1687-4110) **7021**
▼ • ➤ Journal of Nanoneuroscience (USA ISSN 1939-0637) **6153**
• Journal of Nanoparticle Research (NLD ISSN 1388-0764) **7021**
▼ • ➤ Journal of Nanophotonics (USA ISSN 1934-2608) **7078**
• ➤ Journal of Nanoscience and Nanotechnology (USA ISSN 1533-4880) **7021**
Journal of Nanostructured Polymers and Nanocomposites (GRC) **3248**
• ➤ Journal of Nanotechnology (USA ISSN 1687-9503) **7021**
• ➤ Journal of Narrative Theory (USA ISSN 1549-0815) **5315**
➤ Journal of Natal and Zulu History (ZAF ISSN 0259-0123) **4176**
Journal of National Culture *see* San Yue San **5366**
Journal of National Development Studies *see* Guojia Fazheng Yanjiu **4683**
• ➤ Journal of National Security Law & Policy (USA ISSN 1553-3158) **2678**
• Journal of Native Aging & Health (USA ISSN 1559-8543) **4049**
➤ Journal of Natural & Physical Sciences (IND ISSN 0970-3799) **7872**
Journal of Natural Disasters *see* Ziran Zaihai Xuebao **2229**
• ➤ Journal of Natural Fibers (USA ISSN 1544-0478) **273**
• Journal of Natural Gas Chemistry (USA ISSN 1003-9953) **6775**
▼ • Journal of Natural Gas Science & Engineering (USA ISSN 1875-5100) **6775**
† ➤ Journal of Natural Geometry (GBR ISSN 0963-2654) **8968**
• ➤ Journal of Natural History (GBR ISSN 0022-2933) **684**
Journal of Natural History Museum *see* Tribhuvan University. Natural History Museum. Journal **820**
Journal of Natural Medicine (GBR ISSN 1368-3497) **312**
• Journal of Natural Medicines (JPN) **6854**
• ➤ Journal of Natural Products (USA ISSN 0163-3864) **6854**
Journal of Natural Remedies (IND ISSN 0972-5547) **312**
Journal of Natural Resources *see* Ziran Ziyuan Xuebao **2718**
• ➤ Journal of Natural Resources & Environmental Law (USA ISSN 1070-4833) **3448**
• ➤ Journal of Natural Resources and Life Sciences Education (USA ISSN 1059-9053) **684**
▼ • ➤ Journal of Natural Resources Policy Research (USA ISSN 1939-0459) **2616**
Journal of Natural Science (JPN ISSN 0075-4307) **7872**
Journal of Natural Sciences and Mathematics (PAK ISSN 0022-2941) **7872**
Journal of Nature Conservation (IND ISSN 0970-5945) **2616**
• Journal of Nature Science and Sustainable Technology (USA ISSN 1933-0324) **3140**
• Journal of Naval Architecture and Marine Engineering (BGD ISSN 1813-8535) **3386**
Journal of Naval Architecture and Ocean Engineering (JPN ISSN 0387-5504) **2809**
• ➤ Journal of Navigation (GBR ISSN 0373-4633) **8648**
• ➤ Journal of Near-Death Studies (USA ISSN 0891-4494) **6929**

Title

▼ *new title* † *ceased* • *electronic media* ➤ *refereed*

Title

• ➤ Journal of Practice Teaching in Health & Social Work (GBR ISSN 1460-6690) **8050**
• ➤ Journal of Pragmatics (NLD ISSN 0378-2166) **5203**
➤ Journal of Pre-Raphaelite Studies (CAN ISSN 1060-149X) **5316**
➤ Journal of Precision Teaching and Celeration (USA ISSN 1088-484X) **2877**
• The Journal of Prediction Markets (GBR ISSN 1750-6751) **1138**
Journal of Prehistoric Religion (SWE ISSN 0283-8486) **401**
➤ Journal of Prenatal & Perinatal Psychology & Health (USA ISSN 1097-8003) **5996**
▼ • Journal of Prenatal Medicine (ITA ISSN 1971-3282) **5997**
• ➤ Journal of Presbyterian History (USA ISSN 1521-9216) **7762**
• ➤ Journal of Pressure Vessel Technology (USA ISSN 0094-9930) **3386**
Journal of Prestressed Concrete *see* Puresutoresuto Konkurito **1030**
• ➤ Journal of Prevention and Intervention in the Community (USA ISSN 1085-2352) **7417**
Journal of Preventive and Social Medicine *see* J O P S O M **7528**
• Journal of Preventive Medicine (ROM ISSN 1582-5388) **5654**
Journal of Preventive Medicine and Hygiene (ITA ISSN 1121-2233) **5654**
Journal of Primary Care *see* Journal of Primary Care Medicine **5654**
▼ • Journal of Primary Care & Community Health (USA ISSN 2150-1319) **5654**
• Journal of Primary Care Medicine (USA) **5654**
• ➤ The Journal of Primary Prevention (USA ISSN 0278-095X) **7378**
• ➤ Journal of Primehe (GBR ISSN 1749-5482) **5654**
Journal of Printing History *see* Journal fuer Druckgeschichte **7324**
➤ Journal of Printing Science and Technology (JPN) **7324**
Journal of Prison Discipline and Philanthropy *see* The Prison Journal **2666**
• ➤ Journal of Prisoners on Prisons (CAN ISSN 0838-164X) **2657**
Journal of Private Enterprise (USA ISSN 0890-913X) **1138**
• The Journal of Private Equity (USA ISSN 1096-5572) **1635**
Journal of Private Equity and Venture Capital *see* Revista Espanola de Capital Riesgo **1648**
• ➤ Journal of Private International Law (GBR ISSN 1744-1048) **4933**
Journal of Probability and Statistical Science (TWN ISSN 1726-3328) **8383**
• ➤ Journal of Probability and Statistics (USA ISSN 1687-952X) **5506**
• The Journal of Problem Solving (USA ISSN 1932-6246) **7378**
• ➤ Journal of Process Control (GBR ISSN 0959-1524) **2537**
Journal of Process Mechanical Engineering *see* Institution of Mechanical Engineers. Proceedings. Part E: Journal of Process Mechanical Engineering **3380**
• ➤ Journal of Product and Brand Management (GBR ISSN 1061-0421) **1826**
• ➤ Journal of Product Innovation Management (USA ISSN 0737-6782) **1890**
• ➤ Journal of Productivity Analysis (USA ISSN 0895-562X) **1769**
Journal of Productivity and Development/Magallat al-Antaagiyyat wa al-Tanmiyyat (EGY ISSN 1110-2543) **1890**
• Journal of Professional Counseling, Practice, Theory & Research (USA ISSN 1556-6382) **2877**
• ➤ Journal of Professional Issues in Engineering Education and Practice (USA ISSN 1052-3928) **3276**
† ➤ Journal of Professional Legal Education (AUS ISSN 0810-9729) **8968**
• ➤ Journal of Professional Nursing (USA ISSN 8755-7223) **5967**
Journal of Professional Seamanship *see* Professional Mariner **8657**
Journal of Professional Studies *see* Policy and Practice in Education **2898**
• ➤ Journal of Progressive Human Services (USA ISSN 1042-8232) **8050**
• Journal of Progressive Judaism (GBR ISSN 1352-4178) **7725**
† Journal of Progressive Legal Thought (USA ISSN 1053-8445) **8968**
Journal of Project & Construction Management (AUS ISSN 1324-1605) **3206**
Journal of Projectiles, Rockets, Missiles and Guidance *see* Danjian yu Zhidao Xuebao **52**
▼ • Journal of Prolotherapy (USA ISSN 1944-0421) **6224**
• ➤ Journal of Promotion Management (USA ISSN 1049-6491) **27**
• ➤ Journal of Property Investment & Finance (GBR ISSN 1463-578X) **7596**
• Journal of Property Management (USA ISSN 0022-3905) **7596**
• ➤ Journal of Property Research (GBR ISSN 0959-9916) **4417**
• Journal of Property Tax Assessment and Administration (USA ISSN 1357-1419) **7597**
Journal of Property Tax Management *see* Journal of Property Valuation and Taxation **1931**
• Journal of Property Valuation and Taxation (USA ISSN 1538-2338) **1931**
• ➤ Journal of Propulsion and Power (USA ISSN 0748-4658) **63**
Journal of Propulsion Technology *see* Tuijin Jishu **73**
Journal of Prospective Research *see* Bohoth Mustaqbaliya **7951**
• ➤ Journal of Prosthetic Dentistry (USA ISSN 0022-3913) **5853**
• ➤ Journal of Prosthetics and Orthotics (USA ISSN 1040-8800) **6065**
➤ Journal of Prosthodontic Research/Japan Prosthodontic Society. Journal (JPN ISSN 1883-1958) **5853**
• ➤ Journal of Prosthodontics (USA ISSN 1059-941X) **5853**
• Journal of Protective Coatings & Linings (USA ISSN 8755-1985) **6718**
Journal of Protein Chemistry *see* The Protein Journal **743**
• ➤ Journal of Proteome Research (USA ISSN 1535-3893) **737**
• ➤ Journal of Proteomics (NLD ISSN 1874-3919) **737**
▼ • ➤ Journal of Proteomics & Bioinformatics (USA ISSN 0974-276X) **737**
Journal of Protozoology Research (JPN ISSN 0917-4427) **684**
Journal of Psaychological Trauma *see* Journal of Aggression, Maltreatment & Trauma **7368**
▼ • Journal of Pseudo-Differential Operators and Applications (CHE ISSN 1662-9981) **5506**
Journal of Psyche and Life *see* Al Nafs wa-al-Hayat **7386**
• ➤ Journal of Psychiatric and Mental Health Nursing (GBR ISSN 1351-0126) **6156**
• ➤ Journal of Psychiatric and Mental Health Nursing Online (GBR ISSN 1365-2850) **6156**
• Journal of Psychiatric Intensive Care (GBR ISSN 1742-6464) **6156**
• ➤ Journal of Psychiatric Practice (USA ISSN 1527-4160) **6156**
• ➤ Journal of Psychiatric Research (GBR ISSN 0022-3956) **6156**
Journal of Psychiatry *see* Shandong Jingshen Yixue **6185**
• Journal of Psychiatry (USA ISSN 1090-1248) **6156**
Journal of Psychiatry and Neurological Sciences *see* Dusunen Adam **8951**
• ➤ Journal of Psychiatry and Neuroscience/Revue de Psychiatrie and de Neuroscience (CAN ISSN 1180-4882) **6156**
• ➤ Journal of Psychoactive Drugs (USA ISSN 0279-1072) **2696**
• ➤ Journal of Psychoeducational Assessment (USA ISSN 0734-2829) **2877**
• ➤ Journal of Psychohistory (USA ISSN 0145-3378) **7378**
• ➤ Journal of Psycholinguistic Research (USA ISSN 0090-6905) **5135**
Journal of Psychological Practice (USA) **7378**
Journal of Psychological Researches (IND ISSN 0022-3972) **7378**
The Journal of Psychological Sciences *see* Majallat al-'ulum al-Nafsiyyat **7384**
• ➤ Journal of Psychological Type (USA ISSN 0895-8750) **7378**
Journal of Psychology *see* Giornale di Psicologia **7358**
• ➤ The Journal of Psychology (USA ISSN 0022-3980) **7378**
• ➤ Journal of Psychology and Christianity (USA ISSN 0733-4273) **7379**
Journal of Psychology and Financial Markets *see* The Journal of Behavioral Finance **7369**
Journal of Psychology & Human Sexuality *see* International Journal of Sexual Health **7366**
• ➤ Journal of Psychology and Theology (USA ISSN 0091-6471) **7379**
• Journal of Psychology in Africa (ZAF ISSN 1433-0237) **7379**
➤ Journal of Psychology in Chinese Societies (HKG ISSN 1563-3403) **7379**
▼ • ➤ Journal of Psychology of Science and Technology (USA ISSN 1939-7054) **7379**
• ➤ Journal of Psychopathology and Behavioral Assessment (USA ISSN 0882-2689) **7379**
• ➤ Journal of Psychopharmacology (GBR ISSN 0269-8811) **6856**
Journal of Psychopharmacology. Supplement *see* Journal of Psychopharmacology **6856**
• ➤ Journal of Psychophysiology (USA ISSN 0269-8803) **7379**
• ➤ Journal of Psychosocial Nursing and Mental Health Services (USA ISSN 0279-3695) **5967**
• ➤ Journal of Psychosocial Oncology (USA ISSN 0734-7332) **6025**
• ➤ Journal of Psychosomatic Obstetrics and Gynecology (GBR ISSN 0167-482X) **5997**
• ➤ Journal of Psychosomatic Research (USA ISSN 0022-3999) **6156**
Journal of Psychotherapy in Independent Practice *see* Journal of Creativity in Mental Health **7372**
• ➤ Journal of Psychotherapy Integration (USA ISSN 1053-0479) **6156**
Journal of Public Administration *see* Gonggong Xingzheng Pinglun **7439**
Journal of Public Administration *see* Revista de Administracion Publica **7466**
• ➤ Journal of Public Administration Research and Theory (GBR ISSN 1053-1858) **7448**
• ➤ Journal of Public Affairs (GBR ISSN 1472-3891) **7448**
• The Journal of Public Affairs (USA ISSN 1540-823X) **7448**
➤ Journal of Public Affairs and Issues (USA ISSN 1099-8721) **7448**
➤ Journal of Public Affairs Education (USA ISSN 1523-6803) **7448**
Journal of Public and International Affairs (Princeton) (USA ISSN 1070-521X) **1600**
• ➤ Journal of Public Budgeting, Accounting & Financial Management (USA ISSN 1096-3367) **7448**
▼ • ➤ Journal of Public Child Welfare (USA ISSN 1554-8732) **8050**
• ➤ Journal of Public Deliberation (USA ISSN 1937-2841) **7148**
• ➤ Journal of Public Economic Theory (USA ISSN 1097-3923) **1545**
• ➤ Journal of Public Economics (NLD ISSN 0047-2727) **1545**
Journal of Public Finance (ITA) **1546**
Journal of Public Health *see* Zeitschrift fuer Gesundheitswissenschaften **7546**
• ➤ Journal of Public Health (GBR ISSN 1741-3842) **7529**
Journal of Public Health *see* Warasan Satharanasuk Sat **7545**
• Journal of Public Health (Online) (GBR ISSN 1741-3850) **8050**
• ➤ Journal of Public Health Dentistry (USA ISSN 0022-4006) **5853**
▼ • ➤ Journal of Public Health Leadership (USA ISSN 1941-8337) **7529**
• ➤ Journal of Public Health Management and Practice (USA ISSN 1078-4659) **7529**
Journal of Public Health Medicine (Online Edition) *see* Journal of Public Health (Online) **8050**
• ➤ Journal of Public Health Policy (GBR ISSN 0197-5897) **7529**
Journal of Public Health Practice *see* Koshu Eisei **7530**
Journal of Public Management *see* Gonggong Guanli Xuebao **7439**
• ➤ Journal of Public Mental Health (GBR ISSN 1746-5729) **7529**
• ➤ Journal of Public Policy (GBR ISSN 0143-814X) **7979**
• ➤ Journal of Public Policy & Marketing (USA ISSN 0743-9156) **1826**
• ➤ Journal of Public Procurement (USA ISSN 1535-0118) **7449**
• ➤ Journal of Public Relations Research (USA ISSN 1062-726X) **27**
• Journal of Public Transportation (USA ISSN 1077-291X) **8501**
Journal of Public Utility Economics *see* Koeki Jigyo Kenkyu **3141**
▼ • Journal of Public Works & Infrastructure (GBR ISSN 1755-0955) **1769**
Journal of Publishing and Management *see* Chuban yu Guanli Yanjiu **7558**
• ➤ Journal of Pulp & Paper Science (CAN ISSN 0826-6220) **6734**
• Journal of Punjab Academy of Forensic Medicine & Toxicology (IND ISSN 0972-5687) **5915**
• ➤ Journal of Punjab Studies (USA) **7979**
• ➤ Journal of Purchasing & Supply Management (GBR ISSN 1478-4092) **1826**
• ➤ Journal of Pure and Applied Algebra (NLD ISSN 0022-4049) **5506**
▼ ➤ Journal of Pure and Applied Microbiology (IND ISSN 0973-7510) **890**
† Journal of Pure and Applied Sciences/Temel ve Uygulamali Bilmler Dergisi (TUR ISSN 0022-4057) **8968**
➤ Journal of Pure and Applied Ultrasonics (IND ISSN 0256-4637) **7088**
• ➤ Journal of Pyrotechnics (USA ISSN 1082-3999) **3249**
Journal of Qena Faculty of Arts *see* South Valley University. Faculty of Arts. Bulletin **5375**
➤ Journal of Quality and Technology Management (PAK ISSN 1816-2185) **1769**
• Journal of Quality Assurance in Hospitality & Tourism (USA ISSN 1528-008X) **4392**
• ➤ Journal of Quality in Maintenance Engineering (GBR ISSN 1355-2511) **3369**
• ➤ Journal of Quality Technology (USA ISSN 0022-4065) **3351**
• Journal of Quantitative Analysis in Sports (USA ISSN 1559-0410) **8182**
Journal of Quantitative & Technical Economics *see* Shuliang Jingji Jishu Jingji Yanjiu **1174**
• ➤ Journal of Quantitative Criminology (USA ISSN 0748-4518) **2658**
Journal of Quantitative Economics (IND ISSN 0971-1554) **1138**
• ➤ Journal of Quantitative Linguistics (GBR ISSN 0929-6174) **5203**
Journal of Quantitative Methods for Business and Administration *see* Revista de Metodos Cuantitativos para la Economia y la Empresa **1791**
• ➤ Journal of Quantitative Spectroscopy & Radiative Transfer (GBR ISSN 0022-4073) **7079**
▼ Journal of Quantum Electronics and Spintronics (USA) **7022**
• ➤ Journal of Quaternary Science (GBR ISSN 0267-8179) **2751**
Journal of Queer Studies in Finland *see* S Q S **8130**
➤ Journal of Questioned Document Examination (USA ISSN 1061-3455) **2658**
• ➤ Journal of Qur'anic Studies (GBR ISSN 1465-3591) **7713**
• ➤ Journal of R N A i and Gene Silencing (Ribonucleic Acid Interference) (USA ISSN 1747-0854) **874**
• The Journal of Race and Policy (USA ISSN 1540-8450) **7148**
Journal of Racial Affairs *see* Tydskrif vir Rasse-Aangeleenthede **3569**
• ➤ Journal of Radiation Research (JPN ISSN 0449-3060) **6201**
Journal of Radiation Research and Radiation Processing *see* Fushe Yanjiu yu Fushe Gongyi Xuebao **3167**
• Journal of Radio & Audio Media (USA ISSN 1937-6529) **2359**
Journal of Radio Studies *see* Journal of Radio & Audio Media **2359**
• ➤ Journal of Radioanalytical and Nuclear Chemistry (HUN ISSN 0236-5731) **2102**
Journal of Radioimmunology *see* Fangshe Mianyixue Zazhi **5758**
• Journal of Radiological Protection (GBR ISSN 0952-4746) **3170**
▼ • Journal of Radiology Case Reports (USA ISSN 1943-0922) **6201**
• ➤ Journal of Radiology Nursing (USA ISSN 1546-0843) **5967**
• ➤ Journal of Radiotherapy in Practice (GBR ISSN 1460-3969) **6201**
Journal of Rail and Rapid Transit *see* Institution of Mechanical Engineers. Proceedings. Part F: Journal of Rail and Rapid Transit **8619**
Journal of Rajasthan Academy of Physical Sciences (IND ISSN 0972-6306) **7872**
• ➤ Journal of Raman Spectroscopy (GBR ISSN 0377-0486) **2103**
• ➤ Journal of Rapid Methods and Automation in Microbiology (USA ISSN 1060-3999) **890**
➤ Journal of Raptor Research (USA ISSN 0892-1016) **909**
Journal of Rare and Uncommon Diseases *see* Hanshao Jibing Zazhi **5623**
† Journal of Rare Diseases (USA ISSN 1082-9695) **8968**
• ➤ Journal of Rare Earths (NLD ISSN 1002-0721) **6319**
• ➤ Journal of Rational - Emotive and Cognitive - Behavior Therapy (USA ISSN 0894-9085) **7379**
Journal of Rational Recovery (USA ISSN 1065-2019) **2696**
• ➤ Journal of Reading Education (USA ISSN 0886-5701) **2877**
➤ The Journal of Reading, Writing and Literacy (GBR ISSN 1743-0534) **2877**
➤ Journal of Real Estate and Construction (SGP) **7597**
• ➤ Journal of Real Estate Finance and Economics (USA ISSN 0895-5638) **7597**
• ➤ Journal of Real Estate Literature (USA ISSN 0927-7544) **7597**
• ➤ The Journal of Real Estate Portfolio Management (USA ISSN 1083-5567) **7597**
• Journal of Real Estate Practice and Education (USA ISSN 1521-4842) **7597**
• ➤ Journal of Real Estate Research (USA ISSN 0896-5803) **7597**
• ➤ Journal of Real-Time Image Processing (DEU ISSN 1861-8200) **3293**
Journal of Recent Advances in Applied Sciences (IND ISSN 0970-1990) **7872**
• ➤ Journal of Receptors and Signal Transduction (USA ISSN 1079-9893) **684**
• ➤ Journal of Reconstructive Microsurgery (USA ISSN 0743-684X) **6249**
• ➤ Journal of Recreational Mathematics (USA ISSN 0022-412X) **5507**
▼ • ➤ Journal of Reformed Theology (NLD ISSN 1872-5163) **7655**
• ➤ Journal of Refractive Surgery (USA ISSN 1081-597X) **6249**
• ➤ Journal of Refugee Studies (GBR ISSN 0951-6328) **7249**
• ➤ Journal of Regional Analysis & Policy (USA ISSN 1090-4999) **1138**
Journal of Regional Anatomy and Operative Surgery *see* Jujie Shushuxue Zazhi **6250**
Journal of Regional Criticism (USA) **499**
Journal of Regional Financial Research *see* Quyu Jinrong Yanjiu **1163**
Journal of Regional History (IND) **4185**
• ➤ Journal of Regional Science (USA ISSN 0022-4146) **4417**
• ➤ Journal of Registry Management (USA ISSN 1945-6123) **5748**
• ➤ Journal of Regression Therapy (USA ISSN 1054-0830) **7379**
Journal of Regulation Studies *see* Gyuje Wanhwa **1116**
• ➤ Journal of Regulatory Economics (USA ISSN 0922-680X) **1546**
• ➤ Journal of Rehabilitation (USA ISSN 0022-4154) **6111**
➤ Journal of Rehabilitation Administration (USA ISSN 0148-3846) **6111**

Title

Journal of Semitic Studies. Monograph *see* Journal of Semitic Studies **5135**
▼ • ➤ Journal of Sensors (USA ISSN 1687-725X) **2462**
• ➤ Journal of Sensory Studies (USA ISSN 0887-8250) **6157**
• ➤ Journal of Separation Science (DEU ISSN 1615-9306) **2103**
• ➤ Journal of Service Management (GBR ISSN 1757-5818) **1769**
• ➤ Journal of Service Research (USA ISSN 1094-6705) **1826**
• • ➤ Journal of Service Science (USA ISSN 1941-4722) **1138**
▼ • Journal of Service Science and Management (USA ISSN 1940-9893) **2548**
• ➤ Journal of Services Marketing (GBR ISSN 0887-6045) **1827**
• ➤ Journal of Services Research (IND ISSN 0972-4702) **1769**
• ➤ Journal of Seventeenth Century Music (USA ISSN 1089-747X) **6581**
• ➤ Journal of Sex & Marital Therapy (USA ISSN 0092-623X) **7380**
• ➤ Journal of Sex Research (USA ISSN 0022-4499) **7380**
• ➤ Journal of Sexual Aggression (GBR ISSN 1355-2600) **7380**
Journal of Sexual and Reproductive Medicine/Journal des Maladies de la Fonction Sexuelle et de la Reproduction (CAN ISSN 1488-5069) **6270**
Journal of Sexual Liberty (USA) **4833**
• ➤ Journal of Sexual Medicine (GBR ISSN 1743-6095) **5654**
• The Journal of Sexual Offender Civil Commitment, Science and the Law (USA ISSN 1556-8733) **2658**
• Journal of Shanxi Agricultural Science (CHN ISSN 1002-2481) **128**
Journal of Sharia & Law *see* Majallat al-Shari'ah wal-Qanun **4727**
• ➤ The Journal of Shellfish Research (USA ISSN 0730-8000) **952**
Journal of Ship Design *see* Chuanbo Sheji Tongxun **8641**
Journal of Ship Mechanics *see* Chuanbo Lixue **8641**
• ➤ Journal of Ship Production (USA ISSN 8756-1417) **8648**
• ➤ Journal of Ship Research (USA ISSN 0022-4502) **8649**
Journal of Ship Technology (IND ISSN 0973-1423) **8649**
The Journal of Short Film (USA ISSN 1558-9846) **6505**
Journal of Short Stories *see* Xiaoxiaoshuo Xuankan **5402**
• ➤ Journal of Shoulder and Elbow Surgery (USA ISSN 1058-2746) **6250**
Journal of Sichuan Traditional Chinese Medicine *see* Sichuan Zhongyi **315**
• Journal of Signal Processing/Shingo Shori (JPN ISSN 1342-6230) **2330**
• ➤ Journal of Signal Processing Systems (USA ISSN 1939-8018) **2534**
Journal of Sikh Studies (IND ISSN 0379-8194) **7737**
• ➤ Journal of Simulation (GBR ISSN 1747-7778) **2429**
• ➤ Journal of Singing (USA ISSN 1086-7732) **6581**
▼ • ➤ Journal of Sino-Western Communications (USA ISSN 1946-6188) **7656**
Journal of Sinological Studies/Shinagaku Kenkyu (JPN) **553**
• ➤ Journal of Slavic Linguistics (USA ISSN 1068-2090) **5135**
• ➤ The Journal of Slavic Military Studies (GBR ISSN 1351-8046) **6429**
• ➤ Journal of Sleep Research (GBR ISSN 0962-1105) **5654**
• Journal of Sleep Research Online (GBR ISSN 1365-2869) **5654**
• Journal of Sleep Research. Supplement (GBR ISSN 0966-6826) **5654**
• ➤ Journal of Small Animal Practice (GBR ISSN 0022-4510) **8801**
Journal of Small Animal Practice (Spanish Edition) *see* Journal of Small Animal Practice **8801**
• ➤ Journal of Small Business and Enterprise Development (GBR ISSN 1462-6004) **1962**
➤ Journal of Small Business and Entrepreneurship (CAN ISSN 0827-6331) **1962**
• ➤ Journal of Small Business Management (USA ISSN 0047-2778) **1962**
• ➤ Journal of Smoking Cessation (AUS ISSN 1834-2612) **6111**
• Journal of Smooth Muscle Research/Nihon Heikatsukin Gakkai Kikanshi (JPN ISSN 0916-8737) **5655**
Journal of Snake *see* Shezhi **5713**
Journal of Snow Engineering *see* Nihon Yuki Kogakkaishi **3212**
• ➤ Journal of Social Affairs/Shu'un Ijtima'iyyah (UAE ISSN 1025-059X) **4460**
• Journal of Social and Clinical Psychology (USA ISSN 0736-7236) **7380**
➤ Journal of Social and Ecological Boundaries (USA ISSN 1551-9880) **4461**
➤ Journal of Social and Economic Development (IND ISSN 0972-5792) **1600**
Journal of Social and Economic Policy (IND ISSN 0973-3426) **7148**

Journal of Social and Economic Studies (IND ISSN 0377-0508) **7980**
• ➤ Journal of Social and Personal Relationships (GBR ISSN 0265-4075) **7380**
• Journal of Social and Political Thought (CAN ISSN 1481-5842) **7148**
▼ • Journal of Social and Psychological Sciences (GBR ISSN 1756-7483) **7980**
Journal of Social Anthropology (IND ISSN 0973-3582) **345**
• ➤ Journal of Social Archaeology (GBR ISSN 1469-6053) **401**
Journal of Social Aspects of HIV-AIDS *see* Sahara J **5826**
† • ➤ Journal of Social Change and Critical Inquiry (AUS ISSN 1443-2161) **8968**
Journal of Social Development (BGD) **8051**
• ➤ Journal of Social Development in Africa (ZWE ISSN 1012-1080) **8051**
▼ • Journal of Social Entrepreneurship (GBR ISSN 1942-0676) **1769**
▼ • Journal of Social, Evolutionary & Cultural Psychology (USA ISSN 1933-5377) **7380**
• ➤ Journal of Social History (USA ISSN 0022-4529) **8115**
▼ • Journal of Social Intervention: Theory and Practice (NLD ISSN 1876-8830) **8115**
• ➤ Journal of Social Issues (USA ISSN 0022-4537) **7380**
• ➤ Journal of Social Philosophy (USA ISSN 0047-2786) **6929**
• ➤ Journal of Social Policy (GBR ISSN 0047-2794) **8051**
Journal of Social Policy Studies *see* Zhurnal Issledovanii Sotsial'noi Politiki **8019**
• ➤ Journal of Social, Political and Economic Studies (USA ISSN 0278-839X) **7148**
Journal of Social, Political and Economic Studies Monograph Series (USA ISSN 0895-724X) **7148**
• The Journal of Social Psychology (USA ISSN 0022-4545) **7380**
▼ • Journal of Social Science (ISL ISSN 1670-7788) **7980**
➤ Journal of Social Science (JPN ISSN 0454-2134) **7980**
Journal of Social Science of Jiamusi University *see* Jiamusi Daxue Shehui Kexue Xuebao **4458**
➤ Journal of Social Sciences (PAK ISSN 1812-0687) **7980**
Journal of Social Sciences *see* Sosyal Bilimler Dergisi **8006**
➤ Journal of Social Sciences (USA ISSN 1549-3652) **7980**
• ➤ Journal of Social Sciences (Agra) (IND ISSN 0449-3168) **7980**
• ➤ Journal of Social Sciences (Delhi) (IND ISSN 0971-8923) **7980**
Journal of Social Sciences and Humanities *see* Jimbun Gakuho **4458**
➤ Journal of Social Sciences and Humanities (PAK ISSN 1994-7046) **7980**
Journal of Social Sciences and Philosophy *see* Renwen ji Shehui Kexue Jikan **6947**
Journal of Social Sciences of the Turkish World *see* Bilig **7950**
Journal of Social Security Law (GBR ISSN 1354-7747) **4704**
• ➤ Journal of Social Service Research (USA ISSN 0148-8376) **8051**
• ➤ Journal of Social Structure (USA ISSN 1529-1227) **7980**
Journal of Social Studies (BGD ISSN 1012-7844) **7980**
Journal of Social Studies *see* Revista de Estudios Sociales **8129**
• ➤ Journal of Social Studies Research (USA ISSN 0885-985X) **7980**
Journal of Social Theory *see* Shehui Lilun Xuebao **8132**
• Journal of Social Theory in Art Education (USA ISSN 1057-0292) **499**
• The Journal of Social Welfare and Family Law (GBR ISSN 0964-9069) **4911**
• ➤ Journal of Social Work (GBR ISSN 1468-0173) **8051**
Journal of Social Work and Policy in Israel (ISR ISSN 0334-9977) **8051**
• ➤ Journal of Social Work Education (USA ISSN 1043-7797) **8051**
• Journal of Social Work in Disability & Rehabilitation (USA ISSN 1536-710X) **8051**
• ➤ Journal of Social Work in End-of-Life & Palliative Care (USA ISSN 1552-4256) **7380**
• ➤ Journal of Social Work Practice (GBR ISSN 0265-0533) **8051**
➤ Journal of Social Work Practice in the Addictions (USA ISSN 1533-256X) **8051**
• Journal of Social Work Values and Ethics (USA ISSN 1553-6947) **8052**
Journal of Social Work with Groups. Monographic Supplement *see* Social Work with Groups **8071**
• ➤ Journal of Socio-Economics (NLD ISSN 1053-5357) **1546**
• Journal of Sociolinguistics (GBR ISSN 1360-6441) **5135**
• ➤ Journal of Sociology (GBR ISSN 1440-7833) **8116**
Journal of Sociology *see* Shakaigaku Ronso **8132**
Journal of Sociology *see* Sosiologisk Tidsskrift **8139**
• ➤ Journal of Sociology and Social Welfare (USA ISSN 0191-5096) **8116**
Journal of Software *see* Ruanjian Xuebao **2596**

• Journal of Software (FIN ISSN 1796-217X) **2593**
Journal of Software Engineering (USA ISSN 1819-4311) **2593**
• ➤ Journal of Software Maintenance and Evolution (GBR ISSN 1532-060X) **2593**
Journal of Soil and Water Conservation *see* Shuitu Baochi Xuebao **252**
• ➤ Journal of Soil and Water Conservation (USA ISSN 0022-4561) **2616**
➤ Journal of Soil and Water Conservation in India (IND ISSN 0022-457X) **2616**
• ➤ Journal of Soil Biology and Ecology (IND ISSN 0970-1370) **684**
Journal of Soil Science and Plant Nutrition *see* Revista de la Ciencia del Suelo y Nutricion Vegetal **250**
• ➤ Journal of Soils and Sediments (DEU ISSN 1439-0108) **239**
• ➤ Journal of Sol-Gel Science and Technology (USA ISSN 0928-0707) **3351**
• ➤ Journal of Solar Energy Engineering (USA ISSN 0199-6231) **3176**
Journal of Solid Rocket Technology *see* Guti Huojian Jishu **57**
• ➤ Journal of Solid State Chemistry (USA ISSN 0022-4596) **2138**
• ➤ Journal of Solid-State Devices and Circuits (BRA ISSN 0104-9631) **3107**
• ➤ Journal of Solid State Electrochemistry (DEU ISSN 1432-8488) **2114**
➤ Journal of Solid Waste Technology and Management (USA ISSN 1088-1697) **3508**
Journal of Solidarity, Sustainability, and Nonviolence *see* The PelicanWeb Journal of Sustainable Development **3459**
• ➤ Journal of Solution Chemistry (USA ISSN 0095-9782) **2138**
▼ • ➤ Journal of Somaliland Studies (USA ISSN 2150-4628) **3545**
Journal of Sophia Asian Studies *see* Jochi Ajiagaku **553**
• Journal of Sound and Vibration (GBR ISSN 0022-460X) **7088**
Journal of South African Law *see* Tydskrif vir die Suid-Afrikaanse Reg **4799**
• ➤ Journal of South American Earth Sciences (GBR ISSN 0895-9811) **2711**
• ➤ Journal of South Asia Women Studies (USA ISSN 1085-7478) **8900**
Journal of South Asian and Middle Eastern Studies (USA ISSN 0149-1784) **4322**
• ➤ Journal of South Asian Development (IND ISSN 0973-1741) **1600**
▼ • Journal of South Asian Linguistics (USA ISSN 1947-8232) **5135**
Journal of South - East European Studies *see* Revue des Etudes Sud-Est Europeennes **4473**
• Journal of South Pacific Law (FJI ISSN 1684-5307) **4704**
Journal of South Texas History (USA ISSN 1099-9310) **4299**
Journal of Southeast Asian Education (THA ISSN 1513-4601) **2878**
• ➤ Journal of Southeast Asian Language Teaching (USA ISSN 1932-3611) **5136**
• ➤ Journal of Southeast Asian Studies (GBR ISSN 0022-4634) **4185**
Journal of Southeast Asian Studies Special Publication Series *see* J S E A S Special Publication Series **552**
• ➤ Journal of Southeast European and Black Sea Studies (GBR ISSN 1468-3857) **7249**
• ➤ Journal of Southern African Studies (GBR ISSN 0305-7070) **7980**
Journal of Southern Europe and the Balkans *see* Journal of Balkan and Near Eastern Studies **4235**
• ➤ Journal of Southern History (USA ISSN 0022-4642) **4300**
• The Journal of Southern Legal History (USA) **4704**
• ➤ Journal of Southern Religion (USA ISSN 1094-5253) **7656**
Journal of Southwest Georgia History (USA ISSN 0739-1943) **4300**
Journal of Southwestern Petroleum Institute *see* Xinan Shiyou Xueyuan Xuebao **6798**
• ➤ Journal of Space Commerce (USA ISSN 1529-353X) **63**
• Journal of Space Law (USA ISSN 0095-7577) **4933**
Journal of Space Technology and Science (JPN ISSN 0911-551X) **63**
• ➤ Journal of Spacecraft and Rockets (USA ISSN 0022-4650) **64**
Journal of Spacecraft Technology (IND ISSN 0971-1600) **64**
• ➤ Journal of Spanish Cultural Studies (GBR ISSN 1463-6204) **3545**
▼ • Journal of Spanish Language Media (USA ISSN 1940-0810) **2330**
▼ Journal of Spanish, Portuguese, and Italian Crypto Jews (USA ISSN 1943-8214) **7725**
• ➤ Journal of Spatial Hydrology (USA ISSN 1530-4736) **2712**
• ➤ Journal of Spatial Science (AUS ISSN 1449-8596) **4017**
• ➤ Journal of Special Education (USA ISSN 0022-4669) **3043**
➤ Journal of Special Education Leadership (USA ISSN 1525-1810) **3026**

➤ Journal of Special Education Technology (USA ISSN 0162-6434) **3043**
• ➤ Journal of Special Operations Medicine (USA ISSN 1553-9768) **6429**
• Journal of Specialised Translation (GBR ISSN 1740-357X) **5136**
• Journal of Speculative Philosophy (USA ISSN 0891-625X) **6930**
• ➤ The Journal of Speech and Language Pathology and Applied Behavior Analysis (USA ISSN 1932-4731) **7380**
• ➤ Journal of Speech, Language, and Hearing Research (USA ISSN 1092-4388) **4075**
Journal of Speech - Language Pathology and Audiology *see* Canadian Journal of Speech-Language Pathology and Audiology **3037**
• ➤ Journal of Spelean History (USA ISSN 0022-4693) **2751**
➤ Journal of Spices and Aromatic Crops (IND ISSN 0971-3328) **684**
➤ Journal of Spinal Cord Medicine (USA ISSN 1079-0268) **6111**
• Journal of Spinal Disorders & Techniques (Online) (USA ISSN 1539-2465) **6065**
• ➤ Journal of Spinal Disorders & Techniques (Print) (USA ISSN 1536-0652) **6065**
Journal of Spine Surgery *see* Jizhu Waike Zazhi **6247**
▼ • ➤ Journal of Spiritual Formation and Soul Care (USA ISSN 1939-7909) **7657**
• Journal of Spirituality and Paranormal Studies (USA ISSN 1932-5770) **6742**
• Journal of Spirituality in Mental Health (USA ISSN 1934-9637) **7381**
• ➤ Journal of Spirituality, Leadership and Management (AUS ISSN 1447-3771) **1769**
• Journal of Spirochetal and Tick-borne Diseases (USA ISSN 1060-0051) **5821**
▼ • ➤ Journal of Sponsorship (GBR ISSN 1754-1360) **28**
• ➤ Journal of Sport and Exercise Psychology (USA ISSN 0895-2779) **7381**
Journal of Sport and Recreation Research *see* Yundong yu Youqi Yanjiu **8217**
Journal of Sport and Science *see* Tiyu yu Kexue **8212**
• ➤ Journal of Sport and Social Issues (USA ISSN 0193-7235) **8182**
• ➤ Journal of Sport and Tourism (GBR) **4978**
• ➤ Journal of Sport Behavior (USA ISSN 0162-7341) **8182**
• ➤ Journal of Sport History (USA ISSN 0094-1700) **8182**
• ➤ Journal of Sport Management (USA ISSN 0888-4773) **8182**
• ➤ Journal of Sport Rehabilitation (USA ISSN 1056-6716) **6230**
Journal of Sport Tourism *see* Journal of Sport and Tourism **4978**
Journal of Sport Traumatology & Allied Sports Sciences (IND) **6231**
▼ • Journal of Sports and Entertainment Marketing (USA ISSN 1947-4180) **1827**
• ➤ Journal of Sports Economics (USA ISSN 1527-0025) **1138**
Journal of Sports, Engineering and Technology *see* Institution of Mechanical Engineers. Proceedings. Part P: Journal of Sports, Engineering and Technology **8180**
• ➤ Journal of Sports Law & Contemporary Problems (USA ISSN 1543-3927) **4704**
• Journal of Sports Media (USA ISSN 1558-4313) **8183**
• ➤ The Journal of Sports Medicine and Physical Fitness (ITA ISSN 0022-4707) **6231**
Journal of Sports Philately (USA ISSN 0447-953X) **6896**
➤ Journal of Sports Science and Medicine (TUR ISSN 1303-2968) **6231**
• ➤ Journal of Sports Sciences (GBR ISSN 0264-0414) **8183**
• Journal of Staff Development (USA ISSN 0276-928X) **1868**
Journal of State and Administration (IND) **7449**
• Journal of State Taxation (USA ISSN 0744-6713) **1932**
• ➤ Journal of Statistical Computation and Simulation (GBR ISSN 0094-9655) **2443**
• ➤ Journal of Statistical Mechanics: Theory and Experiment (GBR ISSN 1742-5468) **7060**
• ➤ Journal of Statistical Physics (USA ISSN 0022-4715) **7022**
• ➤ Journal of Statistical Planning and Inference (NLD ISSN 0378-3758) **8383**
➤ Journal of Statistical Research (BGD ISSN 0256-422X) **8383**
• ➤ Journal of Statistical Software (USA) **8383**
Journal of Statistical Studies (BGD ISSN 1022-4734) **8383**
➤ Journal of Statistical Theory and Applications (USA ISSN 1538-7887) **8383**
▼ • Journal of Statistical Theory and Practice (USA ISSN 1559-8608) **5507**
• Journal of Statistics and Applications (IND ISSN 0973-4600) **8383**
➤ Journal of Statistics and Management Systems (IND ISSN 0972-0510) **8383**
• ➤ Journal of Statistics Education (USA ISSN 1069-1898) **8383**
• Journal of Stem Cells (USA ISSN 1556-8539) **5907**

Title

▼ *new title*   † *ceased*   ● *electronic media*   ➤ *refereed*

Journal of the Worldwide Forum on Education and Culture *see* Worldwide Forum on Education and Culture. Journal **2926**
▼ • Journal of the Writing Research (BEL ISSN 2030-1006) **5316**
▼ Journal of Theological Interpretation (USA ISSN 1936-0843) **7657**
• ➤ Journal of Theological Studies (GBR ISSN 0022-5185) **7657**
Journal of Theology (USA ISSN 1551-367X) **7762**
• ➤ Journal of Theology for Southern Africa (ZAF ISSN 0047-2867) **7657**
The Journal of Theoretical Accounting Research (USA ISSN 1556-5106) **1295**
• Journal of Theoretical and Applied Electronic Research (CHL ISSN 0718-1876) **2473**
▼ • ➤ Journal of Theoretical and Applied Information Technology (PAK ISSN 1992-8645) **2430**
Journal of Theoretical and Applied Mechanics (BGR ISSN 0861-6663) **7060**
➤ Journal of Theoretical and Applied Mechanics (POL ISSN 1429-2955) **3351**
• ➤ Journal of Theoretical and Computational Chemistry (SGP ISSN 0219-6336) **2108**
Journal of Theoretical and Experimental Physics Letters *see* J E T P Letters **7019**
Journal of Theoretical & Philosophical Psychology (USA ISSN 1068-8471) **7381**
• ➤ Journal of Theoretical Biology (GBR ISSN 0022-5193) **685**
• ➤ Journal of Theoretical Politics (GBR ISSN 0951-6298) **7148**
• ➤ Journal of Theoretical Probability (USA ISSN 0894-9840) **5507**
Journal of Theory and Practice in Education *see* Egitimde Kuram ve Uygulama **2852**
• ➤ Journal of Theory Construction and Testing (USA ISSN 1086-4431) **5967**
➤ Journal of Therapeutic Horticulture (USA ISSN 1088-3487) **3740**
Journal of Therapy/Chiryo (JPN ISSN 0022-5207) **5655**
• ➤ Journal of Thermal Analysis and Calorimetry (HUN ISSN 1388-6150) **2138**
• ➤ Journal of Thermal Biology (GBR ISSN 0306-4565) **754**
• ➤ Journal of Thermal Science/Rekexue Xuebao (CHN ISSN 1003-2169) **7055**
▼ • ➤ Journal of Thermal Science and Engineering Applications (USA ISSN 1948-5085) **3206**
Journal of Thermal Science and Technology *see* Rekexue yu Jishu **7056**
• ➤ Journal of Thermal Spray Technology (USA ISSN 1059-9630) **7055**
• ➤ Journal of Thermal Stresses (USA ISSN 0149-5739) **3387**
▼ • ➤ Journal of Thermodynamics (USA ISSN 1687-9244) **7055**
Journal of Thermoelectricity (UKR ISSN 1607-8829) **3159**
• ➤ Journal of Thermophysics and Heat Transfer (USA ISSN 0887-8722) **7023**
• ➤ Journal of Thermoplastic Composite Materials (GBR ISSN 0892-7057) **7094**
• ➤ Journal of Third World Studies (USA ISSN 8755-3449) **4150**
• ➤ The Journal of Thoracic and Cardiovascular Surgery (USA ISSN 0022-5223) **6250**
• ➤ Journal of Thoracic Imaging (USA ISSN 0883-5993) **6201**
• Journal of Thoracic Oncology (USA ISSN 1556-0864) **6025**
• ➤ Journal of Thought (USA ISSN 0022-5231) **7980**
† • Journal of Threat Assessment (USA ISSN 1533-2608) **8968**
▼ • Journal of Threatened Taxa (IND ISSN 0974-7893) **952**
Journal of Three Dimensional Images *see* 3 D Eizo **2399**
• ➤ Journal of Thrombosis and Haemostasis (GBR ISSN 1538-7933) **5939**
• Journal of Thrombosis and Haemostasis. Supplement (GBR ISSN 1740-3332) **5939**
• ➤ Journal of Thrombosis and Thrombolysis (USA ISSN 0929-5305) **5794**
Journal of Tianzhong *see* Tianzhong Xuekan **8010**
Journal of Time and Frequency *see* Shijian Pinlu Xuebao **6406**
• ➤ Journal of Time Series Analysis (GBR ISSN 0143-9782) **8383**
▼ • Journal of Time Series Econometrics (USA ISSN 1941-1928) **1546**
• ➤ Journal of Time Series Finance (USA ISSN 1558-8246) **1363**
▼ • ➤ Journal of Tissue Engineering and Regenerative Medicine (USA ISSN 1932-6254) **750**
• ➤ Journal of Tissue Viability (GBR ISSN 0965-206X) **5879**
Journal of Tohkai Spinal Surgery *see* Tohkai Sekitsui Geka **6074**
Journal of Tokai Bone and Soft Tissue Tumors *see* Toukai Kotsu Nanbu Shuyou **6035**
▼ • ➤ Journal of Topology (GBR ISSN 1753-8416) **5507**
▼ • Journal of Topology and Analysis (SGP ISSN 1793-5253) **2330**
• Journal of Tort Law (USA ISSN 1932-9148) **4704**
Journal of Tourism *see* Luyou Xuekan **8731**
Journal of Tourism *see* Revista de Turism **8752**
• ➤ Journal of Tourism & Cultural Change (GBR ISSN 1476-6825) **8726**
Journal of Tourism and Travel Research *see* Guanguang Liuyou Yanjiu Xuekan **8715**
▼ • Journal of Tourism History (GBR ISSN 1755-182X) **8726**
† • ➤ The Journal of Tourism Studies (AUS ISSN 1035-4662) **8968**
• Journal of Toxicologic Pathology (JPN ISSN 0914-9198) **3499**
• Journal of Toxicological Sciences (JPN ISSN 0388-1350) **3499**
▼ • ➤ Journal of Toxicology (USA ISSN 1687-8191) **3499**
• ➤ Journal of Toxicology and Environmental Health. Part A (USA ISSN 1528-7394) **3499**
• ➤ Journal of Toxicology and Environmental Health. Part B: Critical Reviews (USA ISSN 1093-7404) **3499**
Journal of Toxicology and Environmental Health. Supplement *see* Journal of Toxicology and Environmental Health. Part B: Critical Reviews **3499**
Journal of Toxicology and Public Health *see* Toxicological Research **3470**
Journal of Toxicology. Clinical Toxicology *see* Clinical Toxicology **6829**
Journal of Toxicology. Cutaneous and Ocular Toxicology *see* Cutaneous and Ocular Toxicology **6832**
Journal of Toxicology. Toxin Reviews *see* Toxin Reviews **6883**
• ➤ Journal of Trace Elements in Medicine and Biology (DEU ISSN 0946-672X) **685**
• The Journal of Trading (USA ISSN 1559-3967) **1636**
Journal of Traditional Chinese Medical Culture *see* Zhongyiyao Wenhua **316**
Journal of Traditional Chinese Medicine *see* Zhongyi Zazhi **316**
Journal of Traditional Chinese Ophthalmology *see* Zhongguo Zhongyi Yanke Zazhi **6053**
Journal of Traditional Chinese Orthopedics and Traumatology *see* Zhongyi Zhenggu **6076**
• ➤ Journal of Traditional Medicines (JPN ISSN 1880-1447) **6856**
Journal of Traffic and Transportation Engineering *see* Jiaotong Yunshu Gongcheng Xuebao **3274**
• Journal of Traffic Safety Education (USA ISSN 0164-1344) **8587**
▼ • Journal of Trance Research (USA ISSN 1945-5445) **7657**
Journal of Trance Theory and Practice *see* Journal of Trance Research **7657**
• Journal of Transatlantic Studies (GBR ISSN 1479-4012) **7249**
• ➤ Journal of Transcultural Nursing (USA ISSN 1043-6596) **5967**
• ➤ Journal of Transformative Education (USA ISSN 1541-3446) **2879**
▼ • ➤ Journal of Transformative Studies (USA ISSN 1947-2668) **7381**
Journal of Transhumanism *see* Journal of Evolution and Technology **6928**
• ➤ Journal of Translation (USA ISSN 1558-7282) **5136**
Journal of Translation Studies *see* Fanyi Xuebao **5118**
Journal of Translation Studies *see* Ceviribilim Uygulamalari **5105**
• ➤ Journal of Translational Medicine (GBR ISSN 1479-5876) **5655**
▼ • ➤ Journal of Transnational American Studies (USA ISSN 1940-0764) **7980**
• Journal of Transnational Law & Policy (USA ISSN 1067-8182) **4934**
• ➤ Journal of Transnational Management (USA ISSN 1547-5778) **1574**
• Journal of Transpersonal Psychology (USA ISSN 0022-524X) **7381**
▼ • ➤ Journal of Transplantation (USA ISSN 2090-0007) **6250**
▼ • ➤ Journal of Transport and Land Use (USA ISSN 1938-7849) **4417**
▼ • Journal of Transport and Supply Chain Management (ZAF ISSN 1995-5235) **8501**
• ➤ Journal of Transport Economics and Policy (GBR ISSN 0022-5258) **8501**
• ➤ Journal of Transport Geography (GBR ISSN 0966-6923) **4017**
• ➤ The Journal of Transport History (GBR ISSN 0022-5266) **8501**
▼ • Journal of Transportation (USA ISSN 1944-1916) **8501**
• ➤ Journal of Transportation Engineering (USA ISSN 0733-947X) **8501**
• Journal of Transportation Law, Logistics and Policy (USA ISSN 1078-5906) **4704**
Journal of Transportation Medicine *see* Kotsu Igaku **6066**
▼ • ➤ Journal of Transportation Safety & Security (USA ISSN 1943-9962) **8501**
▼ • Journal of Transportation Security (USA ISSN 1938-7741) **8501**
Journal of Transportation Systems Engineering and Information Technology *see* Jiaotong Yunshu Xitong Gongcheng yu Xinxi **8632**
• ➤ Journal of Trauma (USA ISSN 0022-5282) **6066**
• ➤ Journal of Trauma and Dissociation (USA ISSN 1529-9732) **7381**
▼ • Journal of Trauma Management & Outcomes (GBR ISSN 1752-2897) **6066**
• ➤ Journal of Trauma Nursing (USA ISSN 1078-7496) **5967**
Journal of Trauma Practice *see* Journal of Aggression, Maltreatment & Trauma **7368**
• ➤ Journal of Traumatic Stress (USA ISSN 0894-9867) **7381**
Journal of Traumatic Surgery *see* Chuangshang Waike Zazhi **6239**
• ➤ Journal of Travel & Tourism Marketing (USA ISSN 1054-8408) **8726**
• ➤ Journal of Travel Medicine (USA ISSN 1195-1982) **5655**
• Journal of Travel Research (USA ISSN 0047-2875) **8726**
Journal of Tree Fruit Production *see* International Journal of Fruit Science **237**
• ➤ Journal of Tribology (USA ISSN 0742-4787) **6776**
Journal of Triticeae Crops *see* Mailei Zuowu Xuebao **242**
• ➤ Journal of Tropical Agriculture (IND ISSN 0971-636X) **128**
➤ Journal of Tropical Agriculture and Food Science (MYS ISSN 1394-9829) **128**
Journal of Tropical and Subtropical Botany *see* Redai Yaredai Zhiwu Xuebao **814**
Journal of Tropical Diseases and Parasitology *see* Redaibing yu Jishengchongxue **5702**
• ➤ Journal of Tropical Ecology (GBR ISSN 0266-4674) **3448**
• ➤ Journal of Tropical Forest Science (MYS ISSN 0128-1283) **3695**
Journal of Tropical Forestry (IND ISSN 0970-1494) **3695**
• ➤ Journal of Tropical Meteorology (CHN ISSN 1006-8775) **6359**
Journal of Tropical Microbiology *see* Journal of Tropical Microbiology and Biotechnology **890**
• ➤ Journal of Tropical Microbiology and Biotechnology (KEN ISSN 1814-7593) **890**
• ➤ Journal of Tropical Pediatrics (GBR ISSN 0142-6338) **6095**
Journal of Tsinghua University. Science and Technology *see* Qinghua Daxue Xuebao (Ziran Kexue Ban) **7900**
Journal of Tube Science *see* Guanzi Xuekan **4454**
➤ Journal of Tumor Marker Oncology (AUT ISSN 0886-3849) **6025**
• ➤ Journal of Turbomachinery (USA ISSN 0889-504X) **3387**
• ➤ Journal of Turbulence (GBR ISSN 1468-5248) **7023**
† • ➤ Journal of Turfgrass and Sports Surface Science (GBR ISSN 1478-548X) **8968**
Journal of Turfgrass Science *see* Journal of Turfgrass and Sports Surface Science **8968**
Journal of Turkish Administration *see* Turk Idare Dergisi **7472**
Journal of Turkish Cultural Studies *see* Turk Kulturu Incelemeleri Dergisi **358**
Journal of Turkish Literature (TUR ISSN 1302-1532) **5316**
• ➤ Journal of Turkish Science Education (TUR ISSN 1304-6020) **7873**
• Journal of Turkish Studies (TUR ISSN 1308-2140) **5136**
Journal of Turkish Studies/Turkluk Bilgisi Arastirmalari (USA ISSN 0743-0019) **4322**
Journal of U F O Research *see* Feidie Tansuo **55**
Journal of U F O Studies (USA ISSN 0730-5478) **64**
Journal of U O E H *see* Sangyo Ika Daigaku Zasshi **6686**
• Journal of U S-China Medical Science (USA ISSN 1548-6648) **5655**
Journal of U S-China Public Administration *see* Mei Zhong Gong Gong Guan Li **7452**
▼ • Journal of Ubiquitous Computing and Intelligence (USA ISSN 1555-1326) **2430**
• ➤ Journal of Ukrainian Studies (CAN ISSN 0228-1635) **5316**
• Journal of Ultrasound (ITA ISSN 1971-3495) **6201**
Journal of Ultrasound in Clinical Medicine *see* Linchuang Chaosheng Yixue Zazhi **6202**
• ➤ Journal of Ultrasound in Medicine (USA ISSN 0278-4297) **6201**
▼ • Journal of Uncertain Systems (GBR ISSN 1752-8909) **2454**
▼ • ➤ Journal of Unconventional Parks, Tourism & Recreation Research (USA ISSN 1942-6879) **4979**
Journal of Undergraduate Chemistry Research (USA ISSN 1541-6003) **2069**
• ➤ Journal of Undergraduate Kinesiology Research (USA ISSN 1936-7007) **6111**
Journal of Undergraduate Materials Research (USA ISSN 1934-7677) **3351**
➤ Journal of Undergraduate Mathematics (USA ISSN 0022-5339) **5507**
• ➤ Journal of Undergraduate Neuroscience Education (USA ISSN 1544-2896) **6157**
• Journal of Undergraduate Nursing Scholarship (USA ISSN 1522-8223) **5967**
• Journal of Undergraduate Research (USA ISSN 1547-9641) **2991**
➤ Journal of Undergraduate Research in Physics (USA ISSN 0731-3764) **7023**
Journal of Unification Studies (USA ISSN 1097-1769) **7738**
Journal of Union of Arab Biologists Cairo. A. Zoology (EGY ISSN 1110-5372) **952**
Journal of Union of Arab Biologists. Cytogenetics, Ecology and Toxonomy (EGY ISSN 1110-7456) **834**
Journal of Union of Arab Biologists. Microbiology and Viruses (EGY ISSN 1110-743X) **890**
Journal of Union of Arab Biologists. Physiology and Algae (EGY ISSN 1110-7448) **925**
• ➤ Journal of Unitarian Universalist History (USA ISSN 1550-0195) **7738**
• ➤ Journal of Universal Computer Science (AUT ISSN 0948-695X) **2430**
• ➤ Journal of Universal Knowledge Management (AUT ISSN 1991-0959) **1770**
Journal of Universal Language *see* Journal of Language & Translation **5134**
• ➤ Journal of Universal Science and Technology of Learning (AUT ISSN 1991-0940) **2950**
Journal of University of International Relations *see* Guoji Guanxi Xueyuan Xuebao **7239**
• ➤ Journal of University Teaching & Learning Practice (AUS ISSN 1449-9789) **2991**
▼ • Journal of Unschooling and Alternative Learning (CAN ISSN 1916-8128) **2879**
• ➤ Journal of Urban Affairs (USA ISSN 0735-2166) **4417**
Journal of Urban and Cultural Studies (USA ISSN 1054-1802) **8116**
• ➤ Journal of Urban Design (GBR ISSN 1357-4809) **4418**
• ➤ Journal of Urban Economics (USA ISSN 0094-1190) **1138**
Journal of Urban Education (USA ISSN 1546-3206) **2879**
• ➤ Journal of Urban Health (USA ISSN 1099-3460) **5655**
• ➤ Journal of Urban History (USA ISSN 0096-1442) **4150**
• ➤ Journal of Urban Planning and Development (USA ISSN 0733-9488) **4418**
▼ • ➤ Journal of Urban Regeneration and Renewal (GBR ISSN 1752-9638) **4418**
• ➤ Journal of Urban Technology (GBR ISSN 1063-0732) **8429**
▼ • Journal of Urbanism (GBR ISSN 1754-9175) **4418**
Journal of Urgent Care Medicine *see* J U C M **6062**
• ➤ The Journal of Urology (USA ISSN 0022-5347) **6270**
➤ The Journal of Urology (Italian Edition) (ITA ISSN 1828-6593) **6270**
• ➤ Journal of Usability Studies (USA ISSN 1931-3357) **3206**
Journal of V L S I Signal Processing Systems for Signal, Image, and Video Technology *see* Journal of Signal Processing Systems **2534**
• ➤ Journal of Vacation Marketing (GBR ISSN 1356-7667) **8726**
• ➤ Journal of Vacuum Science & Technology. A: International Journal Devoted to Vacuum, Surfaces, and Films (USA ISSN 1553-1813) **7023**
Journal of Vacuum Science and Technology. Part A. Vacuum, Surfaces and Films *see* Journal of Vacuum Science & Technology. A: International Journal Devoted to Vacuum, Surfaces, and Films **7023**
• ➤ Journal of Vacuum Science and Technology. Part B. Microelectronics and Nanometer Structures (USA ISSN 1071-1023) **7023**
• ➤ Journal of Validation Technology (USA ISSN 1079-6630) **4488**
• ➤ The Journal of Value Inquiry (NLD ISSN 0022-5363) **6930**
▼ • ➤ The Journal of Values Based Leadership (USA ISSN 1948-0733) **8116**
• ➤ The Journal of Vascular Access (ITA ISSN 1129-7298) **5794**
Journal of Vascular Access Devices *see* Association for Vascular Access. Journal **5778**
▼ Journal of Vascular and Interventional Neurology (USA ISSN 1941-5893) **6157**
• ➤ Journal of Vascular and Interventional Radiology (USA ISSN 1051-0443) **6201**
• ➤ Journal of Vascular Nursing (USA ISSN 1062-0303) **5967**
• ➤ Journal of Vascular Research (CHE ISSN 1018-1172) **5794**
• ➤ Journal of Vascular Surgery (USA ISSN 0741-5214) **6250**
Journal of Vascular Technology *see* Journal for Vascular Ultrasound (Print Edition) **5791**
The Journal of Vascular Technology (Online Edition) *see* Journal for Vascular Ultrasound (Online Edition) **5791**
• ➤ Journal of Vector Borne Diseases (IND ISSN 0972-9062) **5821**
• ➤ Journal of Vector Ecology (USA ISSN 1081-1710) **685**
• Journal of Vector Relativity (VEN ISSN 1856-6847) **7023**
Journal of Vegetable Science *see* International Journal of Vegetable Science **237**
• ➤ Journal of Vegetation Science (SWE ISSN 1100-9233) **799**
Journal of Venomous Animals and Toxins (Print Edition) *see* Journal of Venomous Animals and Toxins Including Tropical Diseases **952**
• ➤ Journal of Venomous Animals and Toxins Including Tropical Diseases (BRA ISSN 1678-9199) **952**
The Journal of Ventura County History (USA ISSN 1948-0970) **4300**

DIRECTORY 2010 JOURNAL SUISSE DE MEDECINE GLOBALE 10513

The Journal of Vermont Archaeology (USA ISSN 1559-8799) **401**
• ➤ Journal of Vertebral Subluxation Research (Online Edition) (USA ISSN 1536-2027) **5806**
Journal of Vertebral Subluxation Research (Print Edition) *see* Journal of Vertebral Subluxation Research (Online Edition) **5806**
• ➤ Journal of Vertebrate Paleontology (USA ISSN 0272-4634) **6726**
• ➤ Journal of Vestibular Research: Equilibrium and Orientation (NLD ISSN 0957-4271) **925**
➤ Journal of Veterinary and Animal Sciences (IND ISSN 0971-0701) **8801**
• ➤ Journal of Veterinary Behavior (USA ISSN 1558-7878) **8801**
• ➤ Journal of Veterinary Cardiology (NLD ISSN 1760-2734) **8801**
➤ Journal of Veterinary Dentistry (USA ISSN 0898-7564) **8801**
• ➤ Journal of Veterinary Diagnostic Investigation (USA ISSN 1040-6387) **8801**
• ➤ Journal of Veterinary Emergency and Critical Care (GBR ISSN 1479-3261) **8801**
Journal of Veterinary Epidemiology *see* Juiekigaku Zasshi **8802**
• ➤ Journal of Veterinary Internal Medicine (USA ISSN 0891-6640) **8801**
• ➤ Journal of Veterinary Medical Education (CAN ISSN 0748-321X) **8801**
Journal of Veterinary Medical Researches/Magallat Buhuth Al-'ulum Tibbiyyat al-Baytariyyat (EGY ISSN 1110-7219) **8801**
• ➤ Journal of Veterinary Medical Science (JPN ISSN 0916-7250) **8801**
Journal of Veterinary Medicine. Series A *see* Transboundary and Emerging Diseases **8809**
Journal of Veterinary Medicine. Series B *see* Zoonoses and Public Health **8816**
Journal of Veterinary Medicine. Series C *see* Anatomia, Histologia, Embryologia **8792**
• Journal of Veterinary Parasitology (IND ISSN 0971-1031) **8801**
• ➤ Journal of Veterinary Pharmacology and Therapeutics (GBR ISSN 0140-7783) **6857**
• ➤ Journal of Veterinary Pharmacology and Therapeutics Online (GBR ISSN 1365-2885) **6857**
Journal of Veterinary Pharmacology and Therapeutics. Supplement *see* Journal of Veterinary Pharmacology and Therapeutics **6857**
• Journal of Veterinary Science (KOR ISSN 1229-845X) **8801**
• ➤ Journal of Vibration and Acoustics (USA ISSN 1048-9002) **3387**
• ➤ Journal of Vibration and Control (GBR ISSN 1077-5463) **7088**
Journal of Vibration Engineering *see* Zhendong Gongcheng Xuebao **76**
• Journal of Victorian Culture (GBR ISSN 1355-5502) **4236**
Journal of Videology *see* Visual Impairment Research **4086**
• ➤ Journal of Vietnamese Studies (USA ISSN 1559-372X) **553**
• ➤ Journal of Vinyl & Additive Technology (USA ISSN 1083-5601) **7094**
➤ The Journal of Viral Entry (GBR ISSN 1748-0329) **5821**
• ➤ Journal of Viral Hepatitis (GBR ISSN 1352-0504) **5928**
Journal of Viral Hepatitis. Supplement *see* Journal of Viral Hepatitis **5928**
• ➤ Journal of Virological Methods (NLD ISSN 0166-0934) **890**
• ➤ Journal of Virology (USA ISSN 0022-538X) **890**
• ➤ The Journal of Virtual Environments (USA) **2430**
• ➤ Journal of Virtual Reality and Broadcasting (DEU ISSN 1860-2037) **2488**
▼ • ➤ Journal of Virtual Worlds Research (USA ISSN 1941-8477) **2330**
▼ • Journal of Virtues and Leadership (USA ISSN 1941-465X) **1770**
• ➤ Journal of Vision (USA ISSN 1534-7362) **6045**
• ➤ Journal of Visual Art Practice (GBR ISSN 1470-2029) **499**
• ➤ Journal of Visual Communication and Image Representation (USA ISSN 1047-3203) **2488**
• ➤ Journal of Visual Communication in Medicine (GBR ISSN 1745-3054) **5655**
• Journal of Visual Communication in Medicine (Online) (GBR ISSN 1745-3062) **5655**
• ➤ Journal of Visual Culture (GBR ISSN 1470-4129) **4461**
• ➤ Journal of Visual Impairment & Blindness (USA ISSN 0145-482X) **4082**
• ➤ Journal of Visual Languages and Computing (GBR ISSN 1045-926X) **5203**
• ➤ Journal of Visual Literacy (USA ISSN 1051-144X) **3068**
• ➤ Journal of Visualization (NLD ISSN 1343-8875) **7060**
• ➤ Journal of Visualized Experiments (USA ISSN 1940-087X) **685**
• ➤ Journal of Vocational Behavior (USA ISSN 0001-8791) **7381**
• ➤ Journal of Vocational Education and Training (GBR ISSN 1363-6820) **2943**
Journal of Vocational Education Research *see* Career and Technical Education Research **2834**
• ➤ Journal of Vocational Rehabilitation (NLD ISSN 1052-2263) **7381**
• ➤ The Journal of Voice (USA ISSN 0892-1997) **6082**
• ➤ Journal of Volcanology and Geothermal Research (NLD ISSN 0377-0273) **2785**
Journal of Volcanology & Seismology *see* Volcanology & Seismology **2791**
➤ Journal of Volunteer Administration (USA ISSN 0733-6535) **8052**
• ➤ Journal of W O C N (Wound, Ostomy, and Continence Nursing) (USA ISSN 1071-5754) **6250**
• ➤ Journal of W S C G (Winter School of Computer Graphics) (CZE ISSN 1213-6972) **2488**
▼ • Journal of War and Culture Studies (GBR ISSN 1752-6272) **8116**
▼ • ➤ Journal of Water and Climate (GBR ISSN 2040-2244) **6359**
• Journal of Water And Environment Technology (JPN ISSN 1348-2165) **8827**
Journal of Water and Environmental Issues *see* Mizu Shigen Kankyo Kenkyu **8829**
• ➤ Journal of Water and Health (GBR ISSN 1477-8920) **8827**
• ➤ Journal of Water and Land Development (POL ISSN 1429-7426) **240**
▼ • Journal of Water and Land Use Management (IND ISSN 0973-9300) **2616**
• ➤ Journal of Water Chemistry and Technology (USA ISSN 1063-455X) **8827**
• ➤ The Journal of Water Law (GBR ISSN 1478-5277) **8827**
Journal of Water Resources and Architectural Engineering *see* Shuili yu Jianzhu Gongcheng Xuebao **8832**
• ➤ Journal of Water Resources Planning and Management (USA ISSN 0733-9496) **8827**
• ➤ Journal of Water Supply: Research and Technology. AQUA (GBR ISSN 1606-9935) **8828**
Journal of Water Supply Research and Technology. Aqua Online *see* Journal of Water Supply: Research and Technology. AQUA **8828**
Journal of Water Works Association *see* Suido Kyokai Zasshi **8832**
• ➤ Journal of Waterway, Port, Coastal, and Ocean Engineering (USA ISSN 0733-950X) **8649**
▼ • ➤ Journal of Wavelet Theory and Applications (IND ISSN 0973-6336) **2351**
• The Journal of Wealth Management (USA ISSN 1534-7524) **1636**
Journal of Weather Modification (USA ISSN 0739-1781) **6359**
• ➤ Journal of Web Engineering (USA ISSN 1540-9589) **2473**
▼ • ➤ Journal of Web Librarianship (USA ISSN 1932-2909) **2563**
• Journal of Web Semantics (NLD ISSN 1570-8268) **2563**
† • Journal of Website Promotion (USA ISSN 1553-3611) **8968**
➤ Journal of Welsh Religious History (GBR ISSN 0967-3938) **7763**
Journal of West African Languages (CAN ISSN 0022-5401) **5136**
Journal of West China Forestry Science *see* Xibu Linye Kexue **3708**
• Journal of West Indian Literature (BRB ISSN 0258-8501) **5316**
Journal of Western Asiatic Studies *see* Al-Rafidan **323**
† • ➤ Journal of Whiplash & Related Disorders (USA ISSN 1533-2888) **8968**
• ➤ Journal of Wildlife Diseases (USA ISSN 0090-3558) **8802**
• ➤ The Journal of Wildlife Management (USA ISSN 0022-541X) **2616**
➤ Journal of Wildlife Rehabilitation (USA ISSN 1071-2232) **952**
Journal of Wilkinson County History (USA ISSN 1049-5932) **4150**
➤ The Journal of William Morris Studies (GBR ISSN 1756-1353) **644**
• ➤ Journal of Wind Engineering & Industrial Aerodynamics (NLD ISSN 0167-6105) **3387**
• Journal of Wine Economics (USA ISSN 1931-4361) **1138**
• ➤ Journal of Wine Research (GBR ISSN 0957-1264) **240**
• ➤ Journal of Women and Aging (USA ISSN 0895-2841) **8900**
• ➤ Journal of Women and Minorities in Science and Engineering (USA ISSN 1072-8325) **3206**
Journal of Women and the Law *see* William & Mary Journal of Women and the Law **8889**
➤ Journal of Women in Educational Leadership (USA ISSN 1541-6224) **2879**
• ➤ Journal of Women, Politics & Policy (USA ISSN 1554-477X) **7148**
Journal of Women's Cancer (USA ISSN 1529-0719) **6025**
• ➤ Journal of Women's Health (USA ISSN 1540-9996) **8846**
Journal of Women's Health and Gender-Based Medicine *see* Journal of Women's Health **8846**
Journal of Women's Health Physical Therapy (USA ISSN 1556-6803) **8846**
• ➤ Journal of Women's History (USA ISSN 1042-7961) **8900**
† • ➤ Journal of Women's Imaging (USA ISSN 1084-824X) **8969**
• ➤ Journal of Wood Chemistry and Technology (USA ISSN 0277-3813) **2069**
• ➤ Journal of Wood Science (JPN ISSN 1435-0211) **3713**
The Journal of Workers Compensation (USA ISSN 1059-4167) **4510**
The Journal of Workforce Development (USA ISSN 1556-1127) **1868**
• ➤ Journal of Workplace Behavioral Health (USA ISSN 1555-5240) **1868**
• ➤ Journal of Workplace Learning (GBR ISSN 1366-5626) **1868**
• ➤ Journal of Workplace Rights (USA ISSN 1938-4998) **1691**
Journal of World Affairs/Kaigai Jijo (JPN ISSN 0453-0950) **7249**
• ➤ Journal of World Business (GBR ISSN 1090-9516) **1574**
▼ ➤ Journal of World Christianity (Online) (DEU ISSN 1931-8235) **7657**
Journal of World Christianity (Print) *see* Journal of World Christianity (Online) **7657**
The Journal of World Economy *see* Shijie Jingji **1173**
Journal of World Education (DNK ISSN 0904-3063) **2879**
▼ • ➤ Journal of World Energy Law and Business (GBR ISSN 1754-9957) **3141**
• ➤ Journal of World History (USA ISSN 1045-6007) **4150**
• ➤ The Journal of World Intellectual Property (GBR ISSN 1422-2213) **6753**
The Journal of World Investment *see* The Journal of World Investment & Trade **1636**
The Journal of World Investment & Trade (CHE ISSN 1660-7112) **1636**
Journal of World of Turks *see* Zeitschrift fuer die Welt der Tuerken **4483**
• ➤ Journal of World Prehistory (USA ISSN 0892-7537) **401**
Journal of World Religions *see* Shijie Zongjiao Xuekan **7681**
• ➤ Journal of World-Systems Research (USA ISSN 1076-156X) **7980**
• ➤ Journal of World Trade (NLD ISSN 1011-6702) **4934**
Journal of Worry and Affective Experience *see* Psychology Journal **7399**
• ➤ Journal of Wound Care (GBR ISSN 0969-0700) **6066**
Journal of Writing Assessment (USA ISSN 1543-043X) **5316**
▼ • Journal of Writing in Creative Practice (GBR ISSN 1753-5190) **4577**
Journal of Wuhan Botanical Research *see* Wuhan Zhiwuxue Yanjiu **823**
• ➤ Journal of X-Ray Science and Technology (NLD ISSN 0895-3996) **7023**
Journal of Yangzhou University (Agricultural & Life Sciences Edition) *see* Yangzhou Daxue Xuebao (Nongye yu Shengming Kexue Ban) **171**
Journal of Yoga *see* J O Y **6645**
• ➤ Journal of Young Investigators (USA ISSN 1539-4026) **7873**
• Journal of Young Pharmacists (IND ISSN 0975-1483) **6857**
• ➤ Journal of Youth and Adolescence (USA ISSN 0047-2891) **2157**
• The Journal of Youth Ministry (USA ISSN 1541-0412) **7763**
• ➤ Journal of Youth Studies (GBR ISSN 1367-6261) **2157**
Journal of Zhejiang Agricultural Sciences *see* Zhejiang Nongye Kexue **172**
• ➤ Journal of Zoo and Wildlife Medicine (USA ISSN 1042-7260) **8802**
Journal of Zoological Research (IND ISSN 0253-7273) **952**
• ➤ Journal of Zoological Systematics and Evolutionary Research (DEU ISSN 0947-5745) **952**
• Journal of Zoological Systematics and Evolutionary Research Online (DEU ISSN 1439-0469) **953**
• ➤ Journal of Zoology (GBR ISSN 0952-8369) **953**
Journal Officiel de Guinee (GIN ISSN 0533-5701) **7449**
Journal Officiel de la Cote d'Ivoire (CIV) **7449**
Journal Officiel de la Republique de Djibouti (DJI) **7449**
Journal Officiel de la Republique Democratique de Madagascar *see* Gazetim-panjakan'ny Repoblika Demokratika Malagasy **7438**
Journal Officiel de la Republique du Cameroun/Official Gazette of the Republic of Cameroon (CMR) **7449**
Journal Officiel de la Republique du Niger (NER) **7449**
Journal Officiel de la Republique du Senegal (SEN) **7449**
Journal Officiel de la Republique Francaise. Debats Parlamentaires. Assemblee Nationale. Compte Rendu Integral (FRA ISSN 0242-6765) **7449**
• Journal Officiel de la Republique Francaise. Lois et Decrets (FRA ISSN 0373-0425) **4704**
Journal Officiel de la Republique Gabonaise (GAB) **7449**
Journal Officiel de la Republique Populaire du Benin (BEN) **7449**
Journal Officiel de la Republique Rwandaise (RWA) **7449**
Journal Officiel des Communautes Europeennes. Annexe. Debats *see* Diario Oficial de las Comunidades Europeas. Anexo Debates **4923**
Journal Officiel des Communautes Europeennes. C: Communications et Informations *see* Diario Oficial de las Comunidades Europeas. C: Comunicaciones e Informaciones **4923**
Journal Officiel des Communautes Europeennes. C: Communications et Informations *see* Official Journal of the European Union **7256**
Journal Officiel des Communautes Europeennes. L & C Serie: Legislation et Communications Informations *see* Official Journal of the European Union. L & C Series: Legislation and Information Notices (Quarterly Edition) **4937**
Journal Officiel des Communautes Europeennes. L: Legislation *see* Official Journal of the European Union. L Series: Legislation **7256**
Journal - Ohio School Boards Association *see* Ohio School Boards Association. Journal **3029**
Journal on African Philosophy *see* African Philosophy **4172**
Journal on Alternative Schooling (USA ISSN 1559-2766) **3069**
➤ Journal on Applied Information Technology (AUT ISSN 1683-1373) **2549**
• ➤ Journal on Chain and Network Science (NLD ISSN 1569-1829) **1138**
Journal on Communications, Computers, Convergence, Contents, Companies *see* Hiradastechnika **2322**
Journal on Composite Mechanics and Design (RUS ISSN 1682-3532) **7060**
Journal on Computing and Cultural Heritage *see* A C M Journal on Computing and Cultural Heritage **2405**
Journal on Developmental Disabilities/Le Journal sur les Handicaps du Developpement (CAN ISSN 1188-9136) **6157**
• ➤ Journal on Excellence in College Teaching (USA ISSN 1052-4800) **2991**
• Journal on Firearms and Public Policy (USA ISSN 1930-7616) **8183**
• ➤ The Journal on Information Technology in Healthcare (TWN ISSN 1479-649X) **5655**
▼ Journal on Jewish Aging (USA ISSN 1938-4904) **4050**
Journal on Media Management *see* J M M **2328**
▼ • Journal on Multimodal User Interfaces (DEU ISSN 1783-7677) **2549**
Journal on Numerical Methods and Computer Applications *see* Shuzhi Jisuan yu Jisuanji Yingyong **7940**
Journal on Special Topics in Mobile Networks & Applications *see* Mobile Networks and Applications **2501**
• Journal on Telecommunications & High Technology Law (USA ISSN 1543-8899) **4704**
Journal Onkologie (DEU ISSN 1618-7687) **6025**
• Journal Options HIV (USA) **5821**
Journal Philatelique de Berne *see* Berner Briefmarken-Zeitung **6892**
• The Journal Pioneer (CAN ISSN 0837-3337) **3811**
Journal Polique (FRA ISSN 1773-2719) **7148**
Journal pour le Transport International *see* International Transport Journal **8500**
Journal pour le Transport International *see* Internationale Transport Zeitschrift **8500**
Journal Quebec Quilles (CAN ISSN 0849-1623) **8236**
Journal. R I C S Arts Surveyor *see* The Arts Surveyor **475**
The Journal. R I C S Commercial Property *see* Royal Institution of Chartered Surveyors. Commercial Property Journal **7611**
The Journal. R I C S Land *see* Royal Institution of Chartered Surveyors. Land Journal **3464**
The Journal. R I C S Residential Property Journal *see* Royal Institution of Chartered Surveyors. Residential Property Journal **7611**
• Journal Record (Oklahoma City) (USA ISSN 0737-5468) **1138**
Journal Review Service *see* Access (Toorak) **5565**
The Journal. Royal Institution of Chartered Surveyors. Commercial Property *see* Royal Institution of Chartered Surveyors. Commercial Property Journal **7611**
The Journal. Royal Institution of Chartered Surveyors. Land *see* Royal Institution of Chartered Surveyors. Land Journal **3464**
The Journal. Royal Institution of Chartered Surveyors. Residential Property Journal *see* Royal Institution of Chartered Surveyors. Residential Property Journal **7611**
Journal S C E P *see* C E P Journal **6732**
Journal S O G C *see* Journal of Obstetrics and Gynaecology Canada **5996**
Journal - Saint Mary's University (CAN ISSN 0837-3760) **2288**
Journal Scientifique Libanais *see* Lebanese Science Journal **7879**
Journal: Section on Women's Health *see* Journal of Women's Health Physical Therapy **8846**
Journal Suisse d'Apiculture (CHE ISSN 0368-4040) **129**
Journal Suisse de Medecine Globale *see* Schweizerische Zeitschrift fuer Ganzheitsmedizin **314**

Title

10514 JOURNAL SUISSE DE MEDECINE HOLISTIQUE ULRICH'S PERIODICALS

Journal Suisse de Medecine Holistique *see* Schweizerische Zeitschrift fuer Ganzheitsmedizin **314**
Journal Suisse de Pharmacie *see* PharmaJournal **6874**
Journal Suisse des Entrepreneurs *see* Schweizer Bauwirtschaft **1035**
Journal Suisse des Maitres Ferblantiers et Appareilleurs *see* Schweizerische Spenglermeister- und Installateur-Zeitung **4126**
Journal Suisse d'Horlogerie (CHE ISSN 1422-9323) **4567**
Le Journal sur les Handicaps du Developpement *see* Journal on Developmental Disabilities **6157**
Journal Tekstylny (POL ISSN 1426-7411) **8454**
• Journal Tribuna da Imprensa (BRA) **3804**
Journal Trimestriel d'Agriculture Internationale *see* Quarterly Journal of International Agriculture **149**
• Journal Tunisien d'O R L, de Chirurgie Cervico - Faciale et d'Audiophonologie (Oto - Rhino - Laryngologie) (TUN ISSN 1737-7803) **6082**
Journal Vinicole Suisse *see* Schweizerische Weinzeitung **610**
Journal Watch *see* Journal Watch General Medicine **5748**
Journal Watch. Audio *see* Journal Watch General Medicine **5748**
• Journal Watch Cardiology (USA ISSN 1521-5822) **5748**
• Journal Watch Dermatology (USA ISSN 1521-3595) **5879**
Journal Watch Direct *see* Journal Watch General Medicine **5748**
• Journal Watch Emergency Medicine (USA ISSN 1521-6535) **6066**
• Journal Watch Gastroenterology (USA ISSN 1527-1579) **5748**
• Journal Watch General Medicine (USA) **5748**
• Journal Watch Infectious Diseases (USA ISSN 1521-3609) **5748**
• Journal Watch Neurology (USA ISSN 1524-0207) **5748**
• Journal Watch Oncology and Hematology (USA ISSN 1527-1560) **6025**
Journal Watch Online *see* Journal Watch General Medicine **5748**
• Journal Watch Pediatrics & Adolescent Medicine (USA ISSN 1538-3571) **6095**
• Journal Watch Psychiatry (USA ISSN 1521-3617) **5748**
• Journal Watch Women's Health (USA ISSN 1521-4710) **8850**
Journal Wirtschaftspraxis (DEU) **3069**
➤ Journal X (USA) **5316**
Journalen (DNK ISSN 0906-1614) **4236**
• Journalen (SWE) **5655**
• ➤ Journalism (GBR ISSN 1464-8849) **4577**
Journalism *see* Demosiografiki **4574**
Journalism and Communication *see* Xinwen yu Chuanbo Yanjiu **4586**
Journalism and Communication *see* Xinwen yu Chuanbo **4586**
• Journalism and Communication Monographs (USA ISSN 1522-6379) **4577**
Journalism and Mass Communication Abstracts (USA ISSN 1077-694X) **4587**
Journalism and Mass Communication Directory (USA ISSN 0895-6545) **4577**
• ➤ Journalism and Mass Communication Educator (USA ISSN 1077-6958) **4577**
• ➤ Journalism and Mass Communication Quarterly (USA ISSN 1077-6990) **4578**
(Year) Journalism Awards and Fellowships Directory (USA) **4578**
▼ • Journalism for Human Rights (USA ISSN 1946-5327) **7211**
• ➤ Journalism History (USA ISSN 0094-7679) **4578**
▼ • ➤ Journalism Practice (GBR ISSN 1751-2786) **4578**
• ➤ Journalism Studies (GBR ISSN 1461-670X) **4578**
Journalismus (DEU ISSN 0300-2004) **4578**
Journalismus und Geschichte (DEU ISSN 1437-5605) **4578**
Journalist (DEU ISSN 0022-5576) **4578**
• Journalist (GBR ISSN 0022-5541) **4578**
Journalist *see* Setguulch **4583**
De Journalist (NLD ISSN 0022-555X) **4578**
• The Journalist/Xin Xin Wen (TWN) **4578**
The Journalist (USA) **4578**
Journalist Front *see* Xinwen Zhanxian **4586**
• Journalisten (DNK ISSN 0447-9661) **4578**
Journalisten *see* Journalisti **4578**
• Journalisten (NOR ISSN 0332-7108) **4578**
• Journalisten (SWE ISSN 0022-5592) **4578**
Journalisten Jahrbuch (DEU ISSN 0176-9707) **4578**
• Journalisti/Journalisten (FIN ISSN 1236-3596) **4578**
Journalistic University *see* Xinwen Daxue **4586**
➤ Journalistica (DNK ISSN 1901-6220) **4578**
Journalistik (DEU ISSN 1617-447X) **4578**
Journalistik-Journal *see* Journalistik **4578**
Journalists *see* Xinwen Jizhe **4586**
Journalists Cradle *see* Jizhe Yaolan **4577**
• Journalist's Road to Success (USA) **4578**
• ➤ Journals of Cases on Information Technology (USA ISSN 1548-7717) **1770**
Journals of Dissent and Social Change (USA) **8149**
• ➤ Journals of Gerontology. Series A: Biological Sciences & Medical Sciences (USA ISSN 1079-5006) **4050**
• ➤ Journals of Gerontology. Series B: Psychological Sciences & Social Sciences (USA ISSN 1079-5014) **4050**
Journals of Intellectual Property Rights (IND) **6753**
• The Journals of Legal Scholarship (USA) **4704**
• The Journals of Legal Scholarship. Issues in Legal Scholarship (USA ISSN 1539-8323) **4704**
Journals of the Senate of Canada (CAN ISSN 0703-2579) **7449**
Journee dans la Vie de la Fonction Publique du Canada *see* A Day in the Life of the Public Service of Canada **7433**
Journee Nationale de la Guerison et de la Reconciliation *see* National Day of Healing and Reconciliation **7213**
• La Journee Vinicole (FRA ISSN 0151-4393) **605**
Journees Annuelles de Diabetologie de l'Hotel Dieu (FRA ISSN 0075-4439) **5896**
Journees Annuelles de Sante Publique (CAN ISSN 1910-6335) **7529**
Journees de la Recherche Porcine en France (FRA ISSN 0767-9874) **291**
Journees de Medecine Orthopedique et de Reeducation (FRA ISSN 1624-074X) **6111**
Journees Equations aux Derivees Partielles (FRA ISSN 0752-0360) **5507**
Journees Parisiennes de Pediatrie (FRA ISSN 0399-029X) **6095**
Les Journees Qui Ont Fait la France (FRA ISSN 1776-6400) **4236**
Journey (AUS ISSN 0817-4466) **7763**
Journey *see* C A A Magazine **8690**
The Journey (USA) **8869**
Journey (Antioch) (USA) **1138**
Journey: A Woman's Guide to Intimacy with God (USA ISSN 1073-4473) **7763**
Journey Prize Anthology *see* The Journey Prize Stories **5316**
The Journey Prize Stories (CAN ISSN 1707-9640) **5316**
Journey through the History of the English Language in England and America (DNK ISSN 1399-4409) **5136**
Journey to Glory *see* Liguorian **7804**
The Journeyman Roofer & Waterproofer (USA ISSN 0890-961X) **1018**
Journeymen (USA ISSN 1061-8538) **6293**
† Journeys (AUS ISSN 1449-0927) **8969**
• ➤ Journeys (GBR ISSN 1465-2609) **5222**
Journeys (Cincinnati) *see* Home & Away **8719**
Journeys (Kansas) *see* Home & Away **8719**
• Journeys (West Hartford) (USA) **8726**
• Journeywoman (Online Edition) (CAN) **8726**
Journeywoman (Print Edition) *see* Journeywoman (Online Edition) **8726**
Jours de Chasse (FRA ISSN 1622-8979) **8320**
Jousai Daigaku Yakugakubu Kiyou *see* Jousai Daigaku Yakugakubu Kyouiku Kenkyuu Gyousekishuu **6857**
Jousai Daigaku Yakugakubu Kyouiku Kenkyuu Gyousekishuu/Josai University. Pharmaceutical Bulletin (JPN) **6857**
Jovenes Agricultores (ESP) **129**
Jovenes Sonorenses (MEX) **2195**
Joy (CZE ISSN 1801-3279) **8869**
• Joy (DEU ISSN 1420-2255) **8869**
Joy (HRV ISSN 1845-7630) **8869**
Joy (HUN ISSN 1417-2518) **8869**
• Joy (ROM ISSN 1584-708X) **8869**
Joy (ZAF) **3949**
Joy Magazine *see* Christian Woman **7632**
Joy! Magazine (ZAF ISSN 1992-1993) **7657**
Joyasol (ESP) **4567**
• Joyce (DEU ISSN 1612-8168) **8869**
• Joyce Studies Annual (USA ISSN 1049-0809) **5316**
The Joyful Woman (USA ISSN 0164-4882) **7763**
Joyfull Noise (USA) **7802**
Joypad (FRA ISSN 1163-586X) **2478**
Joystick (FRA ISSN 1145-4806) **2478**
Jozo Kenkyujo Hokoku/Research Institute of Brewing. Report (JPN ISSN 1342-2510) **605**
• Jp Magazine (Jeep) (USA ISSN 1097-2730) **8587**
jtuner *see* J-tuner **8586**
Ju S *see* Juristische Schulung **4707**
• Juben/Play Monthly (CHN ISSN 0578-0659) **8472**
Jubilada *see* El Siglo **3927**
Jubilat (USA ISSN 1529-0999) **5424**
Jubilee (USA ISSN 0893-1607) **7763**
The Jubilee Series (GBR) **5316**
Juco Review (USA ISSN 0047-2956) **8183**
Judaica (CHE ISSN 0022-572X) **7725**
Judaica (ITA ISSN 1827-3262) **7725**
➤ Judaica Bohemiae (CZE ISSN 0022-5738) **7725**
Judaica Bulletin (NLD ISSN 1384-9050) **7725**
Judaica Iberoamericana (CHL ISSN 0716-6427) **3545**
• ➤ Judaica Librarianship (USA ISSN 0739-5086) **5022**
• Judaica Library Network of Metropolitan Chicago. Newsletter (USA) **5022**
• ➤ Judaism (USA ISSN 0022-5762) **7725**
Judaism in Context (USA ISSN 1935-6978) **7725**
Judaistische Texte und Studien (DEU ISSN 0175-9515) **7725**
Judentum - Christentum - Islam (DEU ISSN 1866-4873) **7657**
Judentum und Umwelt (DEU ISSN 0721-3131) **7725**
Judge (USA ISSN 0022-5789) **4704**
Judge Dredd - The Megazine (GBR ISSN 0960-1813) **2195**
➤ The Judges (NLD ISSN 0929-6301) **4934**
• The Judges' Journal (USA ISSN 0047-2972) **4953**
Judge's Retirement System. Annual Financial Report and Report of Operations (USA) **1495**
• Judgment and Decision Making (USA ISSN 1930-2975) **1138**
• Judgments of the Supreme Court of Canada (CAN ISSN 1719-9166) **4850**
• ➤ Judicature (USA ISSN 0022-5800) **4953**
Judicature of China *see* Zhongguo Sifa **4820**
• Judicial Business of the United States Courts: (Year) Report of the Director (USA) **4850**
• Judicial Commission of New South Wales. Monograph Series (AUS ISSN 1035-0896) **4953**
Judicial Conduct and Ethics (USA) **4953**
• Judicial Conduct Reporter (USA ISSN 0193-7367) **4953**
Judicial Council of California. Criminal Jury Instructions (USA ISSN 1932-314X) **4892**
Judicial Discipline *see* New Jersey Judicial Discipline **4957**
Judicial Division Record (USA ISSN 1528-7254) **4953**
Judicial Interim Release: Bail Manual (CAN) **4892**
Judicial - Legislative Watch Report (USA ISSN 1095-8371) **4704**
The Judicial Officer (ZAF ISSN 1029-6026) **4953**
Judicial Officers' Bulletin (AUS ISSN 1036-1294) **4953**
• ➤ The Judicial Review (AUS ISSN 1038-8559) **4953**
• Judicial Review (GBR ISSN 1085-4681) **4954**
• Judicial Staff Directory (USA ISSN 1091-3742) **4954**
Judicial Statistics *see* Michigan. State Court Administrator. Annual Report **4824**
Judicial Studies Board Journal *see* J S B Journal **4953**
Judicial Watch (USA) **4704**
• Judicial Yellow Book (USA ISSN 1082-3298) **4954**
Judisk Kroenika (SWE ISSN 0345-5580) **3545**
Judit *see* Gebruikabo Judit **4679**
Judo (FRA ISSN 1272-5161) **8183**
Judo (GBR ISSN 0022-5819) **8183**
Judo Journal (USA ISSN 1066-6257) **8183**
Judo Magazin (DEU ISSN 0179-3535) **8183**
Judo Ontario Newsletter (CAN ISSN 1193-7149) **8183**
Judo-Sport-Journal (DEU ISSN 1436-8781) **8183**
Judson Cameo (USA) **2288**
Judy (JPN) **8869**
Juece/Decision Making (CHN) **7449**
• Juece Tansuo/Policy Research (CHN ISSN 1003-5419) **7980**
Juece yu Xinxi/Decision & Information (CHN ISSN 1002-8129) **7149**
• Jueces para la Democracia (ESP ISSN 1133-0627) **4705**
Juedische Allgemeine (DEU ISSN 1618-9698) **3545**
Juedische Bildungsgeschichte in Deutschland (DEU ISSN 1616-0037) **2879**
Juedische Gemeindezeitung Frankfurt. Amtliches Organ (DEU) **3545**
Juedische Kultur (DEU ISSN 1431-6757) **4236**
Juedische Musik (DEU ISSN 1613-7493) **6581**
Juedische Zeitung (DEU ISSN 1861-4442) **3545**
Juedischer Almanach (DEU) **7725**
Juel *see* Berichte des Forschungszentrums Juelich **7065**
Juel-Berichte *see* Berichte des Forschungszentrums Juelich **7065**
Juelicher Geschichtsblaetter (DEU ISSN 0946-8749) **4236**
El Jueves (ESP ISSN 1695-4181) **5222**
Jueves de Excelsior (MEX ISSN 0185-6596) **3909**
Jugabheri (BGD) **3799**
• Ju'gan Han'gug (KOR ISSN 1599-9505) **3902**
• Ju'gan Jo'seon/Weekly Chosun (KOR ISSN 1228-2235) **3902**
Jugantar (IND) **3884**
Jugements de la Cour Supreme du Canada *see* Judgments of the Supreme Court of Canada **4850**
† Jugend Beruf Gesellschaft (DEU ISSN 0342-0175) **8969**
Jugend in Wien (AUT) **2195**
Jugend - Medien - Schutz - Report (DEU ISSN 0943-058X) **2157**
Jugend Musiziert (DEU ISSN 0939-883X) **2157**
Jugend - Religion - Unterricht (DEU ISSN 1430-2667) **7657**
Das Jugendamt (DEU ISSN 1867-6723) **4705**
Jugendbuecher zum Thema (DEU) **2195**
Jugendherbergen ... Auf Einen Blick (DEU) **4017**
Jugendherbergen in Deutschland *see* Jugendherbergen ... Auf Einen Blick **4017**
• Jugendhilfe (DEU ISSN 0022-5940) **8052**
➤ Jugendhilfe Aktuell (DEU ISSN 1614-3027) **8052**
Jugendhilfe-Info *see* Jugendhilfe Aktuell **8052**
• jugendhilfe-netz (DEU) **8052**
Jugendhilfe Report (DEU) **8052**
Jugendliteratur (CHE ISSN 0256-6532) **2157**
➤ Jugendnachrichten (DEU ISSN 1615-0228) **3014**
➤ Jugendpolitik (DEU ISSN 0939-8635) **5222**
† Jugendrotkreuz (DEU ISSN 1431-4800) **8969**
Juger (BEL) **4705**
Juggle (USA ISSN 1520-7471) **4337**
The Juggler (USA ISSN 0738-2669) **499**
Jugglezine *see* Juggle **4337**
Juggs (USA ISSN 0734-4309) **6293**
Jugon! (ESP ISSN 1885-1169) **8236**
Jugoslovenska Medicinska Biohemija *see* Journal of Medical Biochemistry **736**
Jugoslovenska Revija za Medjunarodno Pravo *see* Udruzenje za Medunarodno Pravo Srbije i Crne Gore. Godisnjak **4943**
Jugoslovenski Pregled *see* Pregled Srbija i Crna Gora **3945**
Jugoslovensko Bankarstvo *see* Bankarstvo **1316**
El Juguete Rabioso *see* Le Jouet Enrage **3802**
Juguetes (ARG) **4060**
Juguetes y Juegos de Espana (ESP ISSN 0022-6157) **4060**
Juguetes y Juegos de Espana Express (ESP ISSN 1575-1996) **4060**
• Jui Masui Gekagaku Zasshi/Japanese Journal of Veterinary Anesthesia & Surgery (JPN ISSN 0916-5908) **8802**
Jui Masui/Japanese Journal of Veterinary Anesthesiology *see* Jui Masui Gekagaku Zasshi **8802**
Juice (DEU ISSN 1614-9033) **6581**
Juice (NZL ISSN 1175-8953) **6224**
† Juiced (GBR) **8969**
Juicy (CZE ISSN 1214-4304) **8869**
• Juiekigaku Zasshi/Journal of Veterinary Epidemiology (JPN ISSN 1343-2583) **8802**
Juilliard Journal (USA ISSN 1064-1580) **6581**
• Jujie Shushuxue Zazhi/Journal of Regional Anatomy and Operative Surgery (CHN ISSN 1672-5042) **6250**
Jujuy al Dia (ARG) **3791**
Juke Blues (GBR ISSN 1351-5551) **6581**
Jukebox Collector (USA ISSN 1053-6884) **4337**
Jukebox Magazine (FRA ISSN 0296-6395) **6581**
Juki Magazine (JPN ISSN 0285-2217) **3387**
Jukic (BIH ISSN 0350-6398) **7657**
Jul i Frederikssund (DNK ISSN 0107-5446) **4236**
† Julehilsen (DNK ISSN 0107-8887) **8969**
Julemaerker Norden (DNK ISSN 1604-5599) **6896**
Jules Verne - Magasinet (SWE ISSN 0345-5599) **5444**
Juli-Magazin (DEU ISSN 1438-4701) **7211**
Julia (DEU ISSN 0949-5916) **5410**
Julia (DNK) **5410**
Julia (HUN ISSN 0864-9235) **5410**
Julia (ITA) **7941**
Julia (NOR ISSN 1502-6973) **2196**
Julia (PRI ISSN 1534-262X) **5425**
Julia (SWE ISSN 1404-918X) **2195**
Julia Exklusiv (DEU ISSN 0949-6483) **5410**
Julia Extra (DEU ISSN 0949-5924) **5410**
Julia Festival (DEU ISSN 1610-6059) **5410**
Julia Gold (DEU ISSN 1436-6460) **5410**
Julia Hochzeitsband (DEU ISSN 1862-9555) **5410**
Julia Kulonszam (HUN ISSN 1419-4414) **5410**
Julia Muttertagsband *see* Julia zum Muttertag **5411**
Julia Prestige (DEU ISSN 0949-6130) **5410**
Julia Saison (DEU ISSN 1435-3679) **5410**
† Julia Special (DEU ISSN 1435-3695) **8969**
Julia Valentinsband (DEU ISSN 1862-4421) **5411**
Julia zum Muttertag (DEU ISSN 0949-6890) **5411**
Julian J. Rothbaum Distinguished Lecture Series (USA) **7149**
Julie (FRA) **2196**
Juliet (JPN) **5411**
▼ Juliette & Victor (BEL ISSN 1784-844X) **3545**
Julio de Urquijo Euskal Filologiarako Mintegiaren Urtekaria *see* Seminario de Filologia Vasca Julio de Urquijo. Anuario **5173**
The Julio de Urquijo Seminar on Basque Philology. Journal *see* Seminario de Filologia Vasca Julio de Urquijo. Anuario **5173**
Julius-Hirschberg-Gesellschaft zur Geschichte der Augenheilkunde. Mitteilungen (DEU ISSN 1615-9241) **6045**
Julius Kuehn-Institut, Bundesforschungsinstitut fuer Kulturpflanzen. Jahresbericht (DEU) **129**
Julius Kuehn-Institut, Bundesforschungsinstitut fuer Kulturpflanzen. Mitteilungen (DEU ISSN 1867-1268) **129**
Juluka (USA ISSN 1526-5781) **8726**
Jumag (DEU) **4705**
• Jumbo (FRA ISSN 1958-1467) **1600**
Jumbo Flash Report (USA) **1636**
• Jumbo Rate News (USA ISSN 8756-2332) **1363**
Jump! (DEU) **8183**
Jump *see* Alive **5064**
• ➤ Jump Cut (USA) **6505**
Jump Start Your Garden (USA) **3740**
† Jumpin (DEU) **8969**
Jumu/Behold (USA ISSN 1535-2676) **7657**
Jun Ma/Steed (CHN) **5316**
Junction (USA) **5425**
• ➤ Junctures (NZL ISSN 1176-5119) **499**
Al-Jundi (UAE) **6430**
Jundui Dangde Shenghuo (CHN ISSN 1674-1528) **6430**
• Junee Area Landcare Network Newsletter (Print Edition) (AUS ISSN 1833-668X) **3448**
• ➤ Jung (USA ISSN 1715-7978) **7382**
• Jung History (USA ISSN 1945-5186) **6930**
• Jung Journal (USA ISSN 1934-2039) **7382**
Jung und Liberal (DEU) **7149**
Junge Familie (DEU ISSN 0179-3489) **6095**
Junge Freiheit (DEU ISSN 0932-660X) **5222**
Junge Gemeinde (AUT ISSN 0022-6289) **7763**
Junge Haeuser (DEU ISSN 1433-6316) **1018**
Junge Karriere *see* Karriere **6700**
• Junge Karriere Newsletter (DEU) **6700**
Junge Kirche (DEU ISSN 0022-6319) **7657**
Junge Kunst (DEU ISSN 0933-307X) **499**

Title

Jurisprudencia del Tribunal Supremo. Sala Segunda de lo Penal (ESP ISSN 0214-4158) **4892**
Jurisprudencia do Superior Tribunal Militar (BRA ISSN 0104-0952) **4971**
Jurisprudencia Tributaria *see* Jurisprudencia Tributaria (Bi-weekly Edition) **1932**
Jurisprudencia Tributaria (Bi-weekly Edition) (ESP ISSN 1132-8568) **1932**
• Jurisprudencija/Jurisprudence (LTU ISSN 1392-6195) **4707**
• Jurisprudentie Aansprakelijkheid (NLD ISSN 1574-132X) **4510**
Jurisprudentie. Ambtenarenrecht *see* European Court Reports. Reports of European Community Staff Cases **4669**
• Jurisprudentie Arbeidsrecht (NLD ISSN 0928-1886) **4707**
Jurisprudentie Arbeidsrecht Verklaard *see* J A R Verklaard **4698**
• Jurisprudentie Bestuursrecht (NLD ISSN 1380-7056) **4707**
Jurisprudentie Bestuursrecht Plus (NLD ISSN 1389-8396) **4707**
• Jurisprudentie Geneesmiddelenrecht (NLD ISSN 1567-8164) **4707**
Jurisprudentie Geneesmiddelenrecht Plus (NLD ISSN 1574-4140) **4707**
• Jurisprudentie in Nederland (NLD ISSN 1574-471X) **4707**
Jurisprudentie Nationaliteitsrecht (NLD ISSN 1873-9407) **4707**
Jurisprudentie Onderwijswetten *see* School en Wet **3031**
• Jurisprudentie Personen- en Familierecht (NLD ISSN 1574-1338) **4912**
Jurisprudentie Sociale Voorzieningen *see* Jurisprudentie Wet Werk en Bijstand (Print) **8969**
Jurisprudentie Strafrecht (NLD ISSN 1871-3629) **4892**
▼ Jurisprudentie Telecommunicatierecht (NLD ISSN 1876-4290) **2330**
Jurisprudentie van Het Hof van Justitie en van Het Gerecht van Eerste Aanleg *see* Recueil de la Jurisprudence de la Cour de Justice et du Tribunal de Premiere Instance. Partie 2, Tribunal de Premiere Instance **4938**
Jurisprudentie van Het Hof van Justitie en van Het Gerecht van Eerste Aanleg *see* Raccolta della Giurisprudenza della Corte e del Tribunale di Primo Grado. Parte 2. Tribunale di Primo Grado **4938**
Jurisprudentie van Het Hof van Justitie en van Het Gerecht van Eerste Aanleg *see* Court of Justice and the Court of First Instance. Reports of Cases before the Court **4922**
Jurisprudentie van Het Hof van Justitie en van Het Gerecht van Eerste Aanleg *see* Raccolta della Giurisprudenza della Corte e del Tribunale di Primo Grado. Parte 1. Corte di Giustizia **4938**
Jurisprudentie van Het Hof van Justitie en van Het Gerecht van Eerste Aanleg *see* Recueil de la Jurisprudence de la Cour de Justice et du Tribunal de Premiere Instance. Partie 1. Cour de Justice **4938**
Jurisprudentie Verhaal Bijstand *see* Jurisprudentie Wet Werk en Bijstand (Print) **8969**
Jurisprudentie voor Gemeenten (NLD ISSN 0924-4824) **4707**
Jurisprudentie Vreemdelingenrecht (NLD ISSN 1387-2346) **4850**
Jurisprudentie Wegenverkeersrecht (NLD ISSN 1574-1788) **4954**
• Jurisprudentie Wet Werk en Bijstand (Online) (NLD) **4510**
† • Jurisprudentie Wet Werk en Bijstand (Print) (NLD ISSN 1572-4336) **8969**
Jurist *see* Jurisuto **4707**
• ➤ Jurist (USA ISSN 0022-6858) **7802**
Juriste (CAN ISSN 0829-5476) **4707**
• ➤ Juristen (DNK ISSN 0107-699X) **4707**
Juristenvereniging voor Afgestudeerden in Tilburg Dag (NLD ISSN 1871-3475) **4707**
• Juristenzeitung (DEU ISSN 0022-6882) **4707**
Juristische Abhandlungen (DEU ISSN 0449-4342) **4707**
Juristische Ausbildung und Praxis Vorbereitung *see* J A P - Juristische Ausbildung und Praxis Vorbereitung **4698**
• ➤ Juristische Blaetter (AUT ISSN 0022-6912) **4707**
➤ Das Juristische Buero (DEU ISSN 0931-6000) **1890**
Juristische Gesellschaft Bremen. Jahrbuch (DEU) **4707**
• Juristische Rundschau (DEU ISSN 0022-6920) **4707**
Juristische Schriftenreihe (DEU ISSN 0935-6827) **4707**
• Juristische Schulung (DEU ISSN 0022-6939) **4707**
Juristische Studiengesellschaft Trier. Schriftenreihe (DEU ISSN 1610-028X) **4707**
Juristische Verlag Rechtsmarkt *see* J U V E Rechtsmarkt **4698**
• Juristkontakt (NOR ISSN 0332-7590) **4707**
Juristnytt *see* Lakimiesuutiset **4712**
Jurists Review *see* Faxuejia **4671**
Jurisuto/Jurist (JPN ISSN 0448-0791) **4707**
Jurnal Antropologi dan Sosiologi (MYS ISSN 0126-9518) **8116**
Jurnal Antropologi Indonesia (IDN ISSN 1693-167X) **345**
Jurnal Bihorean (ROM ISSN 1222-5940) **3933**
Jurnal Bihorean de Duminica *see* Jurnal Bihorean **3933**
• ➤ Jurnal Bioteknologi Pertanian (IDN ISSN 0853-8360) **129**
Jurnal Ekonomi Malaysia (MYS ISSN 0127-1962) **1495**
➤ Jurnal Fizik Malaysia (MYS ISSN 0128-0333) **7023**
Jurnal Institusi Jurutera Malaysia *see* Institution of Engineers, Malaysia. Journal **3199**
Jurnal Kedokteran Gigi Indonesia *see* Journal Dentistry Indonesia **5850**
Jurnal Pendidikan *see* Journal of Educational Research **2990**
➤ Jurnal Penelitian dan Pengembangan Pertanian (IDN ISSN 0216-4418) **129**
Jurnal Pengurusan (MYS ISSN 0127-2713) **1770**
Jurnal Perubatan U K M *see* Universiti Kebangsaan Malaysia. Jurnal Perubatan **5727**
Jurnal Psikologi Malaysia (MYS ISSN 0127-8029) **7382**
➤ Jurnal Riset Akuntansi Indonesia/Journal of the Educational Compartment of Accountants of The Indonesian Institute of Accountants (IDN ISSN 1410-6817) **1295**
Jurnal Sains Nuklear Malaysia/Nuclear Science Journal of Malaysia (MYS ISSN 0128-0155) **3170**
Jurnal Teknologi (MYS ISSN 0127-9696) **8429**
Jurnalul de Arges (ROM ISSN 1224-645X) **3933**
Jurnalul de Bacau (ROM ISSN 1224-9955) **3933**
Jurnalul de Botosani (ROM ISSN 1224-998X) **3933**
Jurnalul de Braila (ROM ISSN 1454-1599) **3933**
Jurnalul de Brasov (ROM ISSN 1224-9971) **3933**
Jurnalul de Calarasi (ROM ISSN 1224-0923) **3933**
• ➤ Jurnalul de Chirurgie/Journal de Chirurgie/Journal of Surgery (ROM ISSN 1584-9341) **6250**
Jurnalul de Dimineata (ROM ISSN 1222-5959) **3933**
Jurnalul de Dolj (ROM ISSN 1224-9998) **3933**
Jurnalul de Giurgiu (ROM ISSN 1453-3014) **3933**
Jurnalul de Mehedinti (ROM ISSN 1453-0007) **3933**
Jurnalul de Mures (ROM ISSN 1453-0015) **3933**
Jurnalul de Olt (ROM ISSN 1453-3022) **3933**
Jurnalul de Oltenita (ROM ISSN 1453-326X) **3933**
Jurnalul de Prahova (ROM ISSN 1453-0023) **3933**
Jurnalul de Romanati (ROM ISSN 1454-1602) **3933**
Jurnalul de Satu Mare (ROM ISSN 1454-1548) **3933**
Jurnalul de Sibiu (ROM ISSN 1453-0031) **3933**
Jurnalul de Sighet (ROM ISSN 1453-004X) **3933**
Jurnalul de Teleorman (ROM ISSN 1454-1556) **3933**
Jurnalul de Valcea (ROM ISSN 1453-0074) **3933**
Jurnalul de Vaslui (ROM ISSN 1453-0066) **3933**
Jurnalul de Vrancea (ROM ISSN 1453-0058) **3933**
• Jurnalul National (ROM ISSN 1221-7867) **3933**
• Jurnalul Pediatrului (ROM ISSN 2065-4855) **6095**
Jurutera (MYS) **3249**
The Jury (CAN) **4892**
Jury (SWE ISSN 0345-5734) **5414**
• The Jury Expert (USA ISSN 1943-2208) **4707**
Jury Instruction in Real Estate Litigation (USA) **4954**
• Jury Instructions for Personal Injury and Tort Cases (USA) **4954**
Jury Instructions in Automobile Actions (USA) **4954**
Jury Instructions in Automobile Negligence Actions *see* Jury Instructions in Automobile Actions **4954**
• Jury Instructions in Commercial Litigation (USA) **4954**
Jury Instructions on Damages in Tort Actions (USA) **4954**
Jury Instructions on Medical Issues (USA) **4954**
Jury Instructions on Products Liability (USA) **4954**
Jury Selection (USA) **4707**
Jury Trials & Tribulations (USA ISSN 0889-6003) **4707**
Jury Verdicts *see* West's Jury Verdicts. Louisiana Reports **4967**
Jury Verdicts *see* West's Jury Verdicts. Illinois Reports **4967**
Jury Verdicts *see* West's Jury Verdicts. Wisconsin Reports **4967**
Jury Verdicts *see* West's Jury Verdicts. Colorado Reports **4813**
Jury Verdicts Georgia Reports *see* West's Jury Verdicts. Georgia Reports **4813**
Jury Verdicts Indiana Reports *see* West's Jury Verdicts. Indiana Reports **4813**
Jury Verdicts Maryland Reports *see* West's Jury Verdicts. Maryland Reports **4813**
Jury Verdicts Missouri Reporter (USA ISSN 1932-2828) **4707**
Jury Verdicts Oklahoma Reports *see* West's Jury Verdicts. Oklahoma Reports **4813**
Jurysta (POL ISSN 1230-7114) **4707**
• Jus (ITA ISSN 0022-6955) **4708**
Jus (PER) **4707**
Jus & News (LIE ISSN 1028-6780) **4708**
Jus-Extra (AUT) **4850**
▼ Jus I T (AUT ISSN 1999-8228) **4708**
Jus Matrimoniale (POL ISSN 1429-3803) **7802**
Jushe/Residence (CHN ISSN 1674-1900) **4544**
JusIT *see* Jus I T **4708**
• Jussens Venner (NOR ISSN 0022-6971) **4708**
Just! (EST) **3836**
Just Add (FIN ISSN 1797-7738) **3249**
Just Another Name *see* J A N **3915**
• Just Between Us (USA ISSN 1069-3459) **7763**
Just Cards! (USA ISSN 1932-4294) **4337**
Just Change (NZL ISSN 1176-8185) **8052**
Just Criss-Cross (GBR ISSN 1362-8283) **4337**
• Just Cross Stitch (USA ISSN 0883-0797) **6639**
Just Crosswords (GBR) **4337**
Just Eat An Apple (USA) **6662**
Just for B C Doctors *see* Just for Canadian Doctors **5074**
Just for Black Men (USA ISSN 1090-0365) **6293**
Just for Canadian Doctors (CAN ISSN 1910-9040) **5074**
Just for Doctors *see* Just for Canadian Doctors **5074**
Just for Girls *see* Girls Only **2191**
Just Holdens Magazine (AUS ISSN 1833-2439) **8587**
Just Horses (USA) **8294**
Just Kick-It! (DEU) **2196**
Just Kids (USA) **2157**
• ➤ Just Labour (CAN ISSN 1705-1436) **7981**
Just Labs (USA ISSN 1534-0341) **6810**
† Just living (CAN ISSN 1715-0558) **8969**
Just Out (USA) **4375**
➤ Just Policy (AUS ISSN 1323-2266) **8052**
▼ Just Women (USA ISSN 1948-0431) **8870**
Justament (DEU ISSN 1615-4800) **4708**
▼ • Justcircuit.mag (USA ISSN 1944-6721) **4375**
JustCircuit.MAG *see* Justcircuit.mag **4375**
➤ Justica Penal (BRA) **4892**
Justice (FRA ISSN 0223-5536) **4708**
Justice (ISR ISSN 0793-176X) **4850**
Justice as Healing (CAN ISSN 1203-8393) **4708**
Justice - Bulletin (GBR ISSN 1467-4890) **7211**
• Justice Canada (CAN ISSN 1497-6595) **4708**
Justice Denied (USA ISSN 1937-2388) **2658**
Justice - Directory of Services/Justice - Repertoire des Services (CAN ISSN 0225-4115) **8052**
• Justice Expenditure and Employment in the United States (USA ISSN 1939-201X) **2674**
The Justice Express (USA ISSN 1541-6038) **2658**
Justice Institute of British Columbia. Annual Report (CAN) **2991**
Justice Journal (GBR ISSN 1743-2472) **7211**
† Justice Matters (NZL ISSN 1173-7573) **8969**
Justice News/Justisie Nuus (ZAF) **4708**
Justice of the Peace *see* Criminal Law & Justice Weekly **4887**
Justice of the Peace Reports (GBR ISSN 0264-3731) **4708**
• ➤ Justice Quarterly (GBR ISSN 0741-8825) **2658**
Justice - Repertoire des Services *see* Justice - Directory of Services **8052**
Justice Report/Actualites Justice (CAN ISSN 0823-9436) **2658**
➤ Justice Research and Policy (Online) (USA ISSN 1942-8022) **2658**
Justice Research and Policy (Print) *see* Justice Research and Policy (Online) **2658**
Justice Research and Statistics Association, Inc. Forum *see* J R S A Forum **2656**
Justice Research Notes (CAN ISSN 1181-9243) **2658**
• Justice Resource Update (USA) **4954**
• Justice Review (AUS ISSN 1449-0102) **4708**
The Justice Series - Putting Rights into Practice (GBR) **7211**
• ➤ Justice System Journal (USA ISSN 0098-261X) **4954**
Justice Trends (AUS ISSN 0157-6011) **7211**
Justices' Clerk (GBR) **4954**
• Justicia (ESP ISSN 0211-7754) **4708**
Justicia Administrativa (ESP ISSN 1139-4951) **4708**
Justicia Laboral *see* Revista de Justicia Laboral **1705**
Justicia Social (ARG ISSN 0327-1404) **1691**
• Justicia Uruguaya (URY ISSN 0797-2695) **4708**
La Justicia Uruguaya On Line *see* Justicia Uruguaya **4708**
† Justicni Praxe (CZE ISSN 1214-276X) **8969**
• Justidata (ESP ISSN 1132-6204) **4708**
† Justiforum (ESP ISSN 1134-3923) **8969**
Justine Magazine (USA ISSN 1548-8241) **2196**
Justinian (Online) (AUS ISSN 1442-6102) **4708**
• Justis CD-ROM Official Journal. C Series (GBR ISSN 1351-8518) **4934**
• Justis Celex (GBR ISSN 1351-1009) **4823**
Justis European Commentaries *see* European Update **1922**
Justis Family Law *see* Family Law Reports **4910**
Justis Industrial Cases *see* Industrial Cases Reports **4870**
JUSTIS Online *see* Weekly Law Reports **4811**
• Justis Parliament (GBR ISSN 1353-7814) **4823**
• Justis U K Statutes (GBR ISSN 1464-388X) **4954**
Justis U K Statutory Instruments *see* Great Britain. H.M.S.O. Statutory Instruments List **625**
JUSTIS Weekly Law Reports *see* Weekly Law Reports **4811**
Justisie Nuus *see* Justice News **4708**
➤ Justitia (DNK ISSN 0105-8908) **4708**
• Justitia (SWE ISSN 1651-1484) **1363**
Justitiele Verkenningen (NLD ISSN 0167-5850) **2674**
Die Justiz (DEU ISSN 0722-7612) **4954**
Justiz in Zahlen (DEU) **4823**
Justiz-Ministerial-Blatt fuer Hessen (DEU ISSN 0022-7064) **4708**
Justiz und NS-Verbrechen (NLD) **2658**
Justizforschung und Rechtssoziologie (DEU) **4708**
Justizvollzugsbediensteten Presse *see* J V B - Presse **7447**
JustNotes (USA) **2289**
• JustPeace (GBR ISSN 0306-7645) **7657**
Justuf (DEU ISSN 0941-6781) **4708**
Justus-Liebig-Universitaet Giessen-Lahn. Arbeitskreis Wildbiologie. Schriften (DEU ISSN 0947-2819) **685**
• Juta - State Library Index to the Government Gazette (ZAF) **7481**
• Jutaku/Housing (JPN ISSN 0449-4512) **4418**
Jutarnji List (HRV) **3831**
• Juta's Business Law (ZAF ISSN 1021-7061) **4873**
• Juta's Comprehensive G A A P (Generally Accepted Accounting Practices) (ZAF ISSN 1560-8468) **4873**
• Juta's Corporate Library (ZAF ISSN 1814-0629) **4873**
Juta's Current Unreported Judgments *see* Juta's Unreported Judgments **4954**
• Juta's Daily Law Reports (ZAF ISSN 1682-0657) **4708**
Juta's Digest of S A Law *see* Juta's Digest of South African Law **4954**
• Juta's Digest of South African Law (ZAF ISSN 1025-983X) **4954**
Juta's Eastern Cape Provincial Legislation Library *see* Eastern Cape Provincial Legislation Library **4663**
Juta's Free State Provincial Legislation Library *see* Free State Provincial Legislation Library **4677**
Juta's Gauteng Provincial Legislation Library *see* Gauteng Provincial Legislation Library **4679**
Juta's Income Tax (ZAF) **1932**
Juta's Insurance Law Bulletin (ZAF ISSN 1029-3302) **4873**
Juta's KwaZulu-Natal Provincial Legislation Library *see* KwaZulu-Natal Provincial Legislation Library **4710**
Juta's Mining Library *see* Jutastat Mining and Minerals Library **6467**
Juta's Mpumalanga Provincial Legislation Library *see* Mpumalanga Provincial Legislation Library **4736**
Juta's North West Provincial Legislation Library *see* North West Provincial Legislation Library **4748**
Juta's Northern Cape Provincial Legislation *see* Northern Cape Provincial Legislation Library **4748**
Juta's Occupational Health and Safety Library *see* Occupational Health and Safety Library **1701**
Juta's Quarterly Review of South African Law *see* Juta's Review of South African Law **4954**
▼ • Juta's Review of South African Law (ZAF ISSN 1997-6291) **4954**
Juta's Road Traffic and Transport Library *see* Road Traffic and Transport Library **8634**
• Juta's South African Regulations (ZAF ISSN 1682-5195) **4708**
Juta's Statutes *see* Juta's South African Regulations **4708**
Juta's Statutes of South Africa *see* Statutes of South Africa (Print) **4789**
Juta's Tax Law Report (ZAF ISSN 1028-3242) **1932**
• Juta's Tax Law Review (ZAF ISSN 1817-3535) **4708**
▼ • Juta's Unreported Judgments (ZAF ISSN 1997-048X) **4954**
• Juta's Weekly Statutes Bulletin (ZAF) **4708**
Juta's Western Cape Provincial Legislation Library *see* Western Cape Provincial Legislation Library **4812**
• Jutastat Mining and Minerals Library (ZAF ISSN 1562-3181) **6467**
• Jutastat's South African Statutes/Suid-Afrikaanse Wette (ZAF ISSN 1017-1185) **4708**
Jute and Jute Fabrics - Bangladesh (BGD ISSN 1010-3791) **8454**
Jutland Archaeological Society Publications *see* Jysk Arkaeologisk Selskab. Skrifter **4236**
Jutro (HRV ISSN 1331-4297) **3831**
Juu-san C Igaku *see* 13 C Igaku **5739**
• Juui Rinshou Hifuka/Japanese Journal of Veterinary Dermatology (JPN ISSN 1347-6416) **8802**
Juurikassarka (FIN ISSN 0789-2667) **129**
Juvenatrix (BRA) **5444**
• ➤ Juvenile and Family Court Journal (USA ISSN 0161-7109) **4912**
Juvenile and Family Justice Today (USA ISSN 1062-2926) **4912**
Juvenile and Family Law Digest (USA ISSN 0279-2257) **4912**
• Juvenile Court Statistics (USA ISSN 0091-3278) **4823**
Juvenile Court Trends *see* National Council on Crime and Delinquency. Juvenile Custody Trends **2661**
• Juvenile Justice (Online) (USA) **2157**
• Juvenile Justice Digest (USA ISSN 0094-2413) **2658**
• Juvenile Justice Series (AUS ISSN 1833-3230) **4954**
Juvenile Justice Update (USA ISSN 1080-0360) **2658**
Juvenile Literature *see* Shaonian Wenyi (Shanghai) **2212**
Juvenile Press *see* Shaonian Bao **2212**
Juvenile Scientific Pictorial *see* Shaonian Kexue Huabao **2212**
Juveniles Taken into Custody: Fiscal Year Report *see* National Council on Crime and Delinquency. Juveniles Taken into Custody: Fiscal Year Report **2661**
Juvenis *see* Iuvenis **5131**
Juventud del Mundo *see* World Youth **2222**

DIRECTORY 2010 K & K 10517

Juventud Panadera (ESP ISSN 0022-7218) **3674**
• Juventud Rebelde (CUB ISSN 0864-1412) **2157**
• Juventud Tecnica (CUB ISSN 0449-4555) **8429**
De Juwelier (NLD ISSN 1570-8284) **4567**
• Juxta (USA) **5316**
Juxtapoz (USA ISSN 1077-8411) **499**
• Juying Yuebao/Drama & Movies Monthly (CHN ISSN 1004-5864) **8472**
Juyo San'eob Donghyang Ji'pyo/Key Indicators of Major Industries (KOR ISSN 1739-662X) **1138**
Juzen Igakkai Zasshi/Juzen Medical Society. Journal (JPN ISSN 0022-7226) **5656**
Juzen Medical Society. Journal *see* Juzen Igakkai Zasshi **5656**
• Juzhi Gongye/Polyester Industry (CHN ISSN 1008-8261) **1139**
Juznoslovenski Filolog (SRB ISSN 0350-185X) **5136**
• Juzuojia/Playwright (CHN ISSN 1001-3768) **8472**
• JVibe (USA ISSN 1934-2675) **2196**
JWest Arizona (USA) **8784**
JWest Las Vegas (USA) **8784**
JydskeVestkysten (DNK ISSN 1398-5523) **3834**
• Jyllands-Posten (DNK ISSN 0109-1182) **3834**
Jyoti Chitra (IND) **3884**
Jyotsana (IND) **3884**
Jysk Arkaeologisk Selskab. Skrifter/Jutland Archaeological Society Publications/Publications de la Societe Archeologique du Jutland (DNK ISSN 0107-2854) **4236**
Jysk Selskab for Historie. Skrifter *see* Historie **4144**
• ➤ Den Jyske Historiker (DNK ISSN 0109-9280) **4236**
Jyvaeskylae Studies in Biological and Environmental Science (FIN ISSN 1456-9701) **685**
Jyvaskyla Cross - Language Studies (FIN ISSN 0358-6464) **5136**
Jyvaskyla Polytechnic. Reports *see* Jyvaskylan Ammattikorkeakoulu. Raportteja **2879**
Jyvaskyla Polytechnic. Reviews and Reflections *see* Jyvaskylan Ammattikorkeakoulu. Puheenvuoroja **2879**
Jyvaskyla Studies in Computer Science, Economics and Statistics (FIN ISSN 0357-9921) **2430**
• Jyvaskyla Studies in Education, Psychology and Social Research (FIN ISSN 0075-4625) **2879**
Jyvaskyla Studies in the Arts (FIN ISSN 0075-4633) **499**
Jyvaskyla University of Applied Sciences. Reports *see* Jyvaskylan Ammattikorkeakoulu. Julkaisuja **2879**
Jyvaskylan Ammattikorkeakoulu. Julkaisuja/Jyvaskyla University of Applied Sciences. Reports (FIN ISSN 1456-2332) **2879**
Jyvaskylan Ammattikorkeakoulu. Puheenvuoroja/Jyvaskyla Polytechnic. Reviews and Reflections (FIN ISSN 1796-010X) **2879**
• Jyvaskylan Ammattikorkeakoulu. Raportteja/Jyvaskyla Polytechnic. Reports (FIN ISSN 1795-3766) **2879**
Jyvaskylan Yliopisto. Bio- ja Ymparistotieteiden Laitos. Tiedonantoja/University of Jyvaskylan. Department of Biological and Environmental Sciences. Research Reports (FIN ISSN 1795-6900) **685**
Jyvaskylan Yliopisto. Biologian Laitos. Tiedonantoja *see* Jyvaskylan Yliopisto. Bio- ja Ymparistotieteiden Laitos. Tiedonantoja **685**
Jyvaskylan Yliopisto. Chydenius-Instituutti. Rapporter och Artiklar *see* Jyvaskylan Yliopisto. Chydenius-Instituutti. Selosteita ja Katsauksia **1139**
Jyvaskylan Yliopisto. Chydenius-Instituutti. Reports and Reviews *see* Jyvaskylan Yliopisto. Chydenius-Instituutti. Selosteita ja Katsauksia **1139**
Jyvaskylan Yliopisto. Chydenius-Instituutti. Selosteita ja Katsauksia/Jyvaskylan Yliopisto. Chydenius-Instituutti. Rapporter och Artiklar/Jyvaskylan Yliopisto. Chydenius-Instituutti. Reports and Reviews (FIN ISSN 1236-598X) **1139**
Jyvaskylan Yliopisto. Chydenius-Instituutti. Tutkimuksia (FIN ISSN 0789-0710) **1139**
Jyvaskylan Yliopisto. Matematiikan ja Tilastotieteen Laitos. Vaitokset/University of Jyvaskyla. Department of Mathematics and Statistics. Dissertations (FIN) **5507**
Jyvaskylan Yliopisto. Musiikin Laitos. Julkaisusarja. A, Tutkielmia ja Raportteja/University of Jyvaskyla. Department of Music. Research Reports (FIN ISSN 0359-629X) **6581**
Jyvaskylan Yliopisto. Perhetutkimuskeskus. Julkaisu (FIN ISSN 1796-105X) **8116**
Jyvaskylan Yliopiston. Perhetutkimusyksikon. Julkaisuja *see* Jyvaskylan Yliopisto. Perhetutkimuskeskus. Julkaisu **8116**
K (IRL ISSN 1649-8771) **4979**
• ➤ K A - Abwasser, Abfall (Korrespondenz Abwasser) (DEU ISSN 1866-0010) **3508**
K A B A M (Krant voor Aktieve Baanlozen in Amsterdam) (NLD) **1691**
K A B Impuls (Katholische Arbeitnehmer-Bewegung Deutschlands) (DEU ISSN 1434-4386) **7802**
K A - Betriebs-Info (Korrespondenz Abwasser) (DEU) **3508**
K A C B Auto Revue/Royal Auto (Koninklijke Automobiel Club van Belgie) (BEL ISSN 0022-7242) **8587**
K A C Research Series (Kampsville Archaeological Center) (USA ISSN 1047-742X) **401**
K A C Technical Reports (Kampsville Archaeological Center) (USA) **401**
K A E T Magazine *see* Ei8ht Magazine **2380**
K A F P Journal (Kentucky Academy of Family Physicians) (USA ISSN 0090-5089) **5656**
K A H P E R D Journal *see* Kentucky Association for Health, Physical Education, Recreation and Dance. Journal **2880**
K A I P *see* Koelner Arbeiten zur Internationalen Politik **7250**
K A K - Zhurnal dlya Dizainerov - Grafikov i Prosto Khudozhnikov (RUS) **499**
K A M E D O *see* K A M E D O - Report **8052**
• K A M E D O - Report (Katastorfmedicinska Organisationskommitten-Rapport) (SWE ISSN 1652-6775) **8052**
K A N Vastgoedrapportage (Knooppunt Arnhem-Nijmegen) (NLD ISSN 1573-9880) **4418**
K A P *see* Keep Up to Date on Accounts Payable **1295**
K A P T Union Pathrika (Kerala Aided Primary Teachers' Union) (IND) **2879**
K A R *see* Kent Archaeological Review **402**
• K A S - Taidetta (FIN ISSN 1459-9678) **6527**
K A T S Annual Report *see* Korean Agency forTechnology and Standards. Annual Report **8430**
K & H *see* Kran- und Hebetechnik **1020**
K & R *see* Keramische Rundschau Klima und Raum **536**
K & S Jounaal *see* Intech Klimaat en Sanitair **4121**
K B B Review (Kitchen, Bedroom and Bathroom) (GBR) **4559**
K B C Courrier Economique et Financier *see* K B C Economic and Financial Bulletin **1363**
K B C Economic and Financial Bulletin (BEL ISSN 1374-2124) **1363**
K B C Economisch Financiele Berichten *see* K B C Economic and Financial Bulletin **1363**
K B C Wirtschafts- und Finanzberichte *see* K B C Economic and Financial Bulletin **1363**
K + B Designer Magazine *see* Designer (Dartmouth) **4538**
• K B H (Koebenhavn) (DNK ISSN 1901-5038) **8726**
• K B Journal (Kenneth Burke) (USA ISSN 1930-0026) **5316**
K B L Nyt *see* H K Handelsbladet **4595**
K B M *see* Kantoor Business Magazine **1852**
• K B Ms Temaserie (Krisberedskapsmyndigheten) (SWE ISSN 1652-2915) **7529**
K B N Newsletter *see* Koori Business Network **1142**
• K B Nursing Connection (Kentucky Board) (USA) **5968**
• K B S Plastics (Knowledge Based Systems) (GBR) **7101**
• K B S Rubber (Knowledge Based Systems) (GBR) **7827**
† K B W (KOR ISSN 1225-0295) **8969**
K C Business (Kansas City) (USA ISSN 1931-8731) **1139**
† K C C I Business Journal (Korea Chamber of Commerce and Industry) (KOR) **8969**
K C D L *see* Krause Curriculum Development Library **3069**
K C Home Design *see* Home Design **4541**
K C K *see* Kampeer en Caravankampioen **8727**
K C M S Bulletin (Kings County Medical Society) (USA ISSN 0886-4772) **5656**
K C Magazine (Kansas City) (USA ISSN 1076-0938) **3979**
• K C Nyt (Foreningen af Kommunale Chefer) (DNK ISSN 0903-6237) **7494**
K C P T Magazine *see* K C Studio **6505**
K C Studio (Kansas City) (USA ISSN 1942-4132) **6505**
K C T S - Nine (USA ISSN 1050-513X) **2384**
K C Weddings (Kansas City) (USA) **5559**
K-Club (DEU ISSN 1860-0050) **2196**
K D A Communicator (Kansas Dietetic Association) (USA) **6662**
† K D B Economic & Industrial Focus (KOR) **8969**
K D C Cursor (Katholiek Documentatie Centrum) (NLD ISSN 1574-2296) **7802**
K D I Economic Outlook *see* K D I Gyeongje Jeonmang **1495**
• K D I Gyeongje Jeonmang/K D I Economic Outlook (Korea Development Institute) (KOR) **1495**
• K D I Jeongchaeg Yeon'gu/K D I Journal of Economic Policy (Korea Development Institute) (KOR) **1139**
• K D I Jiyeog Gyeongje/Monthly Economic Trends (KOR) **1495**
K D I Journal of Economic Policy *see* K D I Jeongchaeg Yeon'gu **1139**
K D I Monthly Economic Trends *see* K D I Jiyeog Gyeongje **1495**
K D I Quarterly Economic Outlook *see* K D I Gyeongje Jeonmang **1495**
K E A News (Kentucky Education Association) (USA ISSN 0164-3959) **2879**
K E A Research Publications (Kentucky Education Association) (USA) **2934**
K E B Operating Results for (Quarter) (Year) *see* Korea Exchange Bank. Quarterly Review **1364**
K E C Joho/Kansai Electronic Industry Development Center. Bulletin (JPN) **3107**
K E K High Energy Accelerator Research Organization. Annual Report (JPN ISSN 1344-1299) **7023**
K E K News/Koenerugiken Geppo (JPN) **7023**
K E K Preprint (JPN) **7023**
K E K Proceedings (JPN) **7023**
K E K Progress Report (JPN) **7024**
K E K Report (JPN) **7024**
K E M (Konstruktion, Elektronik Maschinenbau) (DEU ISSN 1612-7226) **3206**
K E M Sonderheft (Konstruktion, Elektronik Maschinenbau) (DEU ISSN 1614-2349) **3206**
K E N (Kent English News) (USA) **2289**
K E P Aktuell (Kurier Express Paketdienste) (DEU) **8501**
K E R & K E I *see* Kansas Economic Report & Kansas Economic Indicators **1495**
• K E R I Economic Bulletin (Korea Economic Research Institute) (KOR) **1495**
K E S (Kommunikations- und EDV Sicherheit) (DEU ISSN 0177-4565) **2515**
K E T C Guide (USA ISSN 1086-8828) **3979**
K F H Mainz. Schriftenreihe (Katholische Fachhochschule) (DEU) **7802**
K F O Zeitung (Kieferorthopaedie) (DEU) **5854**
K F R *see* Kommentierte Finanz Rechtsprechung **1364**
K F U *see* Kolloquium Fremdsprachenunterricht **5137**
• K F U M Idraet (DNK ISSN 0901-3334) **8183**
K f W - Gruendungsmonitor (Kreditanstalt fuer Wiederaufbau) (DEU ISSN 1864-0788) **1139**
K f W - Mittelstandspanel (Kreditanstalt fuer Wiederaufbau) (DEU ISSN 1864-2497) **1139**
K f W - Publikationen zu Gruendung und Mittelstand (Kreditanstalt fuer Wiederaufbau) (DEU ISSN 1613-0820) **1139**
K f W - Research. Mittelstands- und Strukturpolitik (Kreditanstalt fuer Wiederaufbau) (DEU ISSN 1618-8691) **1363**
K F Z Anzeiger (DEU ISSN 0341-9681) **8671**
K F Z Betrieb Aktuelle Wochenzeitung (Kraftfahrzeug) (DEU ISSN 0942-3613) **8587**
K F Z Boerse (Kraftfahrzeug) (DEU) **8587**
K F Z - Meisterservice (Kraftfahrzeug) (DEU ISSN 1436-8242) **8587**
K F Z Perfekt (AUT) **8587**
K F Z Wirtschaft (AUT) **8587**
K Forty-Eight *see* K48 **5222**
• K G B Report (Keving G. Barkes) (USA ISSN 1525-9366) **2563**
K G H. Klimatizacija, Grejanje, Hladenje (SRB ISSN 0350-1426) **4122**
• ➤ K G K. Kautschuk, Gummi, Kunststoffe (DEU ISSN 0948-3276) **7825**
• K G Report Berlin (DEU ISSN 0943-8106) **4708**
K-Geld (CHE) **1363**
K H Aktuell (Kreishandwerkerschaft) (DEU) **1691**
K I *see* Kuenstliche Intelligenz **2454**
K I D - KinderInformationsDienst (DEU ISSN 0946-4824) **2157**
K I E E International Transactions on Electrical Machinery and Energy Conversion Systems *see* Journal of Electrical Engineering & Technology **3322**
K I E E International Transactions on Electrophysics and Applications *see* Journal of Electrical Engineering & Technology **3322**
K I E E International Transactions on Power Engineering *see* Journal of Electrical Engineering & Technology **3322**
• K I E T Industrial Economic Review (KOR ISSN 1598-947X) **1139**
K I E T San'eob Gyeongje (Korea Institute for Industrial Economics and Trade) (KOR ISSN 1598-9461) **1139**
K I F O Perspektiv (Kirkeforskning) (NOR ISSN 0807-7525) **7657**
K I F O Rapport (Kirkeforskning) (NOR ISSN 0807-7517) **7657**
K I H (Krizanke Informacije Humor) (SVN ISSN 0353-3522) **4337**
K I H Jesen *see* K I H **4337**
K I H Poletje *see* K I H **4337**
K I H Pomlad *see* K I H **4337**
K I H Zima *see* K I H **4337**
K I K: Kunst in Koeln *see* Kunst in Koeln **6527**
K I - Kaelte Luft Klimatechnik (Klima und Kaelteingenieur) (DEU) **4122**
K I - Luft- und Kaeltetechnik *see* K I - Kaelte Luft Klimatechnik **4122**
K I M Keuken Adresgids (Keuken en Interieur Magazine) (NLD ISSN 1871-2339) **4559**
K I N D News Jr. (Kids in Nature's Defense) (USA ISSN 1050-821X) **320**
K I N D News Primary (Kids in Nature's Defense) (USA ISSN 1069-4544) **320**
K I N D News Sr. (Kids in Nature's Defense) (USA ISSN 1050-9542) **320**
K I P. Kunst in de Provincie (NLD ISSN 1871-1170) **499**
K I R D I Annual Report and Statement of Accounts (Kenya Industrial Research and Development Institute) (KEN) **1430**
K I Report *see* Korrosionsinstitutet Rapport **6320**
K I S R Technical Report (Kuwait Institute for Scientific Research) (KWT) **7873**
† K I T Newsletter (Koninklijk Instituut voor de Tropen) (NLD ISSN 1380-1643) **8969**
• K I T Newsletter (USA) **8116**
K I W A Nieuws *see* Kiwa Magazine **8828**
K Iv I Nieuws *see* De Ingenieur **3198**
K J B *see* Karlsruher Juristische Bibliographie **4823**
K J E S *see* Kakatiya Journal of English Studies **5316**
K J L & M (Kinder Jugend Literatur und Medien) (DEU) **2174**
K J L P P *see* Kansas Journal of Law & Public Policy **4709**
K J M *see* Kansas Journal of Medicine **5656**
K J R Burg Info (Kreisjugendring Muenchen-Land) (DEU) **8052**
K J S Series B: Biological Sciences *see* Kenya Journal of Sciences. Series B: Biological Sciences **685**
K J S Series: Humanities and Social Sciences *see* Kenya Journal of Sciences. Series C: Humanities and Social Sciences **4461**
K J S Series: Physical and Chemical Sciences *see* Kenya Journal of Sciences. Series A: Physical and Chemical Sciences **7875**
K J Z T News (Katolicka Jednota Zen Texaskych) (USA) **2267**
K K/Women & Clothes (Kvinner og Klaer) (NOR ISSN 0806-9034) **8870**
K K A *see* G V Kompakt **3644**
K K-Bladet (Kunskaps- och Kompetensutveckling) (SWE ISSN 1653-0047) **2879**
K K - die Kaelte und Klimatechnik (DEU ISSN 0343-2246) **4122**
K K H Journal *see* Aktiv (Munich) **6981**
K K H Nachrichten (Kaufmaennische Krankenkasse - Hauptverwaltung) (DEU) **4511**
K - Konstruktion Design Systeme (DEU) **462**
K. Krebs-Journal (DEU ISSN 1610-2657) **6025**
K L A G E (Koelner Linguistische Arbeiten - Germanistik) (DEU ISSN 0939-9275) **5136**
K L A Newsletter (Kansas Library Association) (USA) **5022**
K L G: Kritisches Lexikon zur Deutschsprachigen Gegenwartsliteratur (DEU) **5316**
K L J *see* Kentucky Law Journal **4709**
K L M Agent (Koninklijke Luchtvaart Maatschappij) (NLD ISSN 1872-3209) **8726**
K L M Amsterdam (NLD) **8784**
K L M Windmill (NLD) **8784**
K L R G - Kritisches Lexikon der Romanischen Gegenwartsliteraturen (DEU) **5316**
K L V Update (NLD) **129**
K M *see* Kaytannon Maamies **130**
K M 4 D *see* Knowledge Management for Development Journal **7981**
K M - Forum Weltkirche (DEU ISSN 1439-1694) **7802**
K M I *see* Kids' Ministry Ideas **7763**
K M I Buerowirtschaft - Lehre und Praxis (DEU ISSN 0178-594X) **1852**
† • K M News (Knowledge Management) (GBR) **8969**
K M P Pensioen Perspectief (Koster van Mil en Partners) (NLD ISSN 1572-5111) **4511**
K M R P *see* Knowledge Management Research & Practice **2430**
K M Review *see* Knowledge Management Review **1771**
K M T *see* Kyrkomusikernas Tidning **6584**
K M T: A Modern Journal of Ancient Egypt (USA ISSN 1053-0827) **402**
K M U Correspondence (Kilusang Mayo Uno, Philippines) (USA) **1691**
K M U Plus (Kleine und Mittlere Unternehmen) (DEU ISSN 1614-5593) **1420**
K M Vet (Kaytannon Maamies) (FIN ISSN 1239-0429) **129**
• K M World (Knowledge Management) (USA ISSN 1099-8284) **2537**
K M World & Intranets (Year) Conference Proceedings (Knowledge Management) (USA) **2538**
• K M World NewsLinks (Knowledge Management) (USA) **1770**
K Magazine *see* K **4979**
K Mitteilungen (DEU ISSN 0451-1646) **7094**
K N *see* Kieferorthopaedie Nachrichten **5854**
K N A A S News *see* Kenya National Academy for Advancement of Arts and Sciences. Newsletter **7875**
K N G M G *see* Geo.brief **2735**
K N G M G - A L W - K T F G Nieuwsbrief *see* Geo.brief **2735**
• K N K (Koks Nors Kelias) (LTU) **6582**
K N R *see* Kid's Nutrition Report **6662**
† K N V B Jaarboek (Koninklijke Nederlandse Voetbalbond) (NLD ISSN 1871-4978) **8969**
▼ K N W U Wieler Magazine (Koninklijke Nederlandsche Wielren Unie) (NLD ISSN 1875-2403) **8260**
K O (Knock Out) (USA ISSN 1048-1516) **8183**
K O A Directory (Kampgrounds of America) (USA) **2010**
➤ K O A L A S (Konzepte, Orientierungen, Abhandlungen, Lektueren, Australien Studien) (DEU ISSN 1434-0321) **4192**
K O B R A (Kommunale Branchenbuch) (DEU) **2010**
K O M B A Jahrbuch Nordrhein-Westfalen (Kommunalbeamten) (DEU) **7449**
K O M Magasinet (DNK ISSN 1604-0961) **4597**
K o R (Kapitalmarktorientierter Rechnungslegung) (DEU ISSN 1617-8084) **1363**
K O S *see* Kriminalwaard och Statistik **4823**
K O W A N I News (Kongres Wanita Indonesia) (IDN ISSN 0852-9744) **8870**
K Oe B *see* BiblioTheke **4996**
K OE F F - Bladet - I N *see* Koeffbladet - I N **1896**
K og K *see* K & K **8116**
K & K (Kultur og Klasse) (DNK ISSN 0905-6998) **8116**

Title

Kagoshima Daigaku Rigakubu Kiyo/Kagoshima University. Faculty of Science. Reports (JPN ISSN 1345-6938) **7874**
Kagoshima Daigaku Seibutsu Kenkyukai Kaishi *see* Leben **686**
Kagoshima Daigaku Shigakubu Kiyo/Kagoshima University Dental School. Annals (JPN ISSN 0389-7834) **5854**
Kagoshima Daigaku Sougou Kenkyuu Hakubutsukan Kenkyuu Houkoku (JPN) **6527**
Kagoshima Daigaku Sougou Kenkyuu Hakubutsukan Nempou/Kagoshima University Museum. Annual Report (JPN ISSN 1348-3471) **6527**
Kagoshima Daigaku Sougou Kenkyuu Hakubutsukan Newsletter *see* Kagoshima University Museum. Newsletter **6527**
Kagoshima Daigaku. Suisan Gakubu Kiyo/Kagoshima University. Faculty of Fisheries. Memoirs (JPN ISSN 0453-087X) **3600**
Kagoshima Entomological Society. Research Report *see* Satsuma **858**
Kagoshima Joshi Tanki Daigaku Kiyo/Kagoshima Women's Junior College. Bulletin (JPN ISSN 0286-8970) **4461**
Kagoshima-ken Rinsho Geka Gakkaishi/Kagoshima Society for Clinical Surgery. Journal (JPN ISSN 1346-0498) **6250**
Kagoshima-kenritsu Tanki Daigaku Kiyo. Shizen Kagaku Hen/Kagoshima Prefectural Junior College. Bulletin. Natural Sciences (JPN ISSN 0286-1208) **7874**
Kagoshima Nuclear Power News *see* Genshiryoku Dayori Kagoshima **3167**
Kagoshima Prefectural Junior College. Bulletin. Natural Sciences *see* Kagoshima-kenritsu Tanki Daigaku Kiyo. Shizen Kagaku Hen **7874**
Kagoshima Society for Clinical Surgery. Journal *see* Kagoshima-ken Rinsho Geka Gakkaishi **6250**
Kagoshima University Dental School. Annals *see* Kagoshima Daigaku Shigakubu Kiyo **5854**
Kagoshima University. Faculty of Agriculture. Bulletin *see* Kagoshima Daigaku Nogakubu Gakujutsu Hokoku **129**
Kagoshima University. Faculty of Agriculture. Memoirs/Kagoshima Daigaku Nogakubu Kiyo (JPN ISSN 0453-0853) **129**
Kagoshima University. Faculty of Education. Bulletin. Natural Science *see* Kagoshima Daigaku Kyoikugakubu Kenkyu Kiyo. Shizen Kagaku Hen **7874**
Kagoshima University. Faculty of Engineering. Research Reports. *see* Kagoshima Daigaku Kogakubu Kenkyu Hokoku **3206**
Kagoshima University. Faculty of Fisheries. Memoirs *see* Kagoshima Daigaku. Suisan Gakubu Kiyo **3600**
Kagoshima University. Faculty of Science. Reports *see* Kagoshima Daigaku Rigakubu Kiyo **7874**
Kagoshima University Museum. Annual Report *see* Kagoshima Daigaku Sougou Kenkyuu Hakubutsukan Nempou **6527**
Kagoshima University Museum Monographs (JPN ISSN 1347-2747) **6527**
• Kagoshima University Museum. Newsletter (JPN ISSN 1346-7220) **6527**
Kagoshima University. Research Center for the Pacific Islands. Occasional Papers (JPN ISSN 1345-0441) **7874**
Kagoshima Women's Junior College. Bulletin *see* Kagoshima Joshi Tanki Daigaku Kiyo **4461**
• Kahani (USA ISSN 1555-3787) **2196**
Kahrkivs'kyi Natsional'nyi Universytet. Visnyk (UKR ISSN 0453-8048) **2991**
Kahtou News (CAN ISSN 1193-3372) **6635**
Kahuna Magazine (NLD ISSN 1574-7581) **2430**
Kai Nakama/Hanshin Shell Club. Report (JPN ISSN 0912-2192) **953**
• ➤ Kai Tiaki: Nursing New Zealand (NZL ISSN 1173-2032) **5968**
Kaichu Koen Kenkyujo Kenkyu Hokoku *see* Marine Park Research Stations. Bulletin **7881**
• Kaifang Daobao/China Opening Herald (CHN ISSN 1004-6623) **3826**
Kaifang Xitong yu Wanglu/Open Systems & Network (TWN ISSN 1022-968X) **2500**
Kaifang Yuekan (CHN) **1139**
• Kaifeng Daxue Xuebao/Kaifeng University. Journal (CHN ISSN 1008-343X) **7981**
Kaifeng University. Journal *see* Kaifeng Daxue Xuebao **7981**
Kaifeng Yi-Zhuan Xuebao/Academic Journal of Kaifeng Medical College *see* Henan Daxue Xuebao (Yixue Kexue Ban) **5627**
Kaigai Denryoku/Japan Electric Power Information Center. Journal (JPN ISSN 0388-4015) **3323**
Kaigai Jijo *see* Journal of World Affairs **7249**
Kaigai Jijo Kenkyu/Foreign Affairs Studies (JPN ISSN 0287-0932) **7249**
Kaigai Rodo Jiho/International Labor Information (JPN ISSN 0285-3094) **1691**
Kaigai Sato Joho *see* World Sugar News **259**
Kaigai Shakai Hosho Joho/Overseas Social Security News *see* Kaigai Shakai Hosho Kenkyu **4511**
Kaigai Shakai Hosho Kenkyu/Review of Comparative Social Security Research (JPN ISSN 1344-3062) **4511**
Kaigaki Kagaku Gijutsu Joho Shiryo *see* Scientific and Technical Information in Foreign Countries **7912**
Kaigan/Sea Coast (JPN ISSN 0451-2219) **3276**
Kaigan Jitsumu Kogishu/Practical Lecture Notes on Sea Coast (JPN) **3276**
Kaigan Kogaku Ronbunshu/Proceedings of Coastal Engineering, JSCE (JPN ISSN 0916-7897) **3277**
Kaigan Shoko Kenchi Senta Choi Nenpo/Coast Rise and Fall Survey Center. Annual Tidal Observations (JPN) **2810**
Kaigo Bijon/Care Vision (JPN) **5968**
Kaigo no Gakkou (JPN) **5968**
Kaigo Shien Semmon'in/Care Manager (JPN ISSN 1344-8404) **5968**
Kaihatsu Doboku Kenkyujo Geppo *see* Hokkaidou Kaihatsu Doboku Kenkyuujo Geppou **3269**
Kaihatsu Doboku Kenkyujo Hokoku/Civil Engineering Research Institute. Report (JPN ISSN 0914-8167) **3277**
Kaihatsu Doboku Kenkyujo Koenkai Tokushu-go *see* Hokkaidou Kaihatsu Doboku Kenkyuujo Geppou **3269**
Kaihatsu Kin'yu Kenkyujoho/Research Institute for Development and Finance. Journal (JPN ISSN 1345-238X) **1600**
Kaihatsu Ronshu/Journal of Development Policy Studies (JPN ISSN 0288-089X) **1495**
Kaiji Kanren Gyosha Yoran/Maritime Directory in Japan (JPN) **8649**
Kaiji Sangyo Kenkyujoho/Japan Maritime Research Institute. Bulletin (JPN ISSN 0286-9152) **8649**
Kaijo Hoancho. Suirobu Kansoku Hokoku. Choryu Hen/Data Report of Hydrographic Observations. Series of Tidal Stream (JPN ISSN 0914-8272) **2796**
Kaijo Hoancho. Suirobu Kansoku Hokoku. Choseki Hen/Data Report of Hydrographic Observations. Series of Tide (JPN ISSN 0448-3308) **2796**
• Kaijo Hoancho. Suirobu Kansoku Hokoku. Eisei Sokuchi Hen/Data Report of Hydrographic Observations. Series of Satellite Geodesy (JPN ISSN 0914-5753) **2785**
Kaijo Hoancho. Suirobu Kansoku Hokoku. Hachijo Suiro Kansokujo Chijiki Kansoku Nenpo/Data Report of Hydrographic Observations. Hatizyo Hydrographic Observatory. Geomagnetic Observations (JPN ISSN 0910-9102) **2796**
Kaijo Hoancho. Suirobu Kansoku Hokoku. Haro Hen/Data Report of Hydrographic Observations. Wave Observations (JPN) **2796**
Kaijo Hoancho. Suirobu Kansoku Hokoku. Kaiyo Hen/Data Report of Hydrographic Observations. Series of Oceanography (JPN ISSN 0448-3316) **2796**
• Kaijo Hoancho. Suirobu Kansoku Hokoku. Tenmon Sokuchi Hen/Data Report of Hydrographic Observations. Series of Astronomy and Geodesy (JPN ISSN 0287-2633) **2785**
Kaijo Kisho Gaiho/Marine Meteorological Report (JPN) **6359**
Kaijou Gijutsu Anzen Kenkyuujo Houkoku/National Maritime Research Institute. Papers (JPN ISSN 1346-5066) **2810**
...Kaikille *see* Foer Alla **4066**
Kaikoura Star (NZL ISSN 1170-0580) **3917**
Kaikuja Hameesta (FIN) **4236**
Kailash (NPL ISSN 0377-7499) **4185**
Kaimana (USA ISSN 1089-8484) **5316**
Kainai News (CAN ISSN 0047-3081) **3545**
Kainji Lake Research Institute. Annual Report (NGA ISSN 0331-9296) **2796**
Kainuun Sanomat (FIN ISSN 0356-3502) **3838**
• Te Kairangahau (NZL ISSN 1178-3028) **8116**
➤ Kairaranga (NZL ISSN 1175-9232) **3043**
• Kairos (ARG ISSN 1514-9331) **7981**
➤ Kairos (FRA ISSN 1148-9227) **6930**
Kairos (GTM ISSN 1014-9341) **7657**
• ➤ Kairos (USA ISSN 1521-2300) **3069**
▼ Kairos (Weltrevreden Park) (ZAF ISSN 1999-2777) **1827**
Kaiser Karl Gebetsliga fuer den Voelkerfrieden. Journal (AUT) **7802**
▼ Kaiserin (FRA ISSN 1955-7167) **4375**
Kaiserswerther Mitteilungen (DEU ISSN 0022-779X) **7657**
Kaitse Kodu (EST) **6430**
Kaiun/Shipping (JPN ISSN 0022-7803) **8649**
➤ Kaiyo Chosa Gijutsu/Japan Society for Marine Surveys and Technology. Journal (JPN ISSN 0915-2997) **2810**
Kaiyo Chosa Gyogyo Shiken Yoho *see* Hokkaido University. Faculty of Fisheries. Data Record of Oceanographic Observations and Exploratory Fishing **2806**
Kaiyo Chosa Yoho/Data Record of Oceanographic Observations (JPN) **2810**
Kaiyo Enkaku Tansa. Kaiyo Rimoto Senshingu Gijutsu no Kenkyu. Kenkyu Seikashu/Report of Marine Remote Sensing Technique (JPN) **2810**
• Kaiyo Kagaku Gijutsu Senta Nenpo/Japan Marine Science and Technology Center. Annual Report (JPN) **2810**
Kaiyo Kagaku Gijutsu Senta Shiken Kenkyu Hokoku/Japan Marine Science and Technology Center. Report (JPN ISSN 0387-382X) **2810**
Kaiyo Kagaku Kenkyu/Research Institute of Oceanochemistry. Transactions (JPN ISSN 0912-4829) **2810**
Kaiyo Kaihatsu Ronbunshu/Ocean Development Symposium. Proceedings (JPN ISSN 0912-7348) **3277**
Kaiyo Kaihatsu Suishin Keikaku/Marine Science and Technology Development in Japan (JPN) **2810**
Kaiyo Kogaku Shinpojumu/Ocean Engineering Symposium (JPN) **2810**
Kaiyo Kyokaiho/Japan Ocean Development Construction Association. News (JPN ISSN 0910-5425) **2810**
Kaiyo Sangyo Kenkyu Shiryo/Research Materials on Ocean Economics (JPN ISSN 0912-8123) **1139**
Kaiyo Seibutsu Kankyo Kenkyujo Kenkyu Hokoku/Marine Ecology Research Institute. Report (JPN) **685**
Kaiyo to Seibutsu/Aquabiology (JPN ISSN 0285-4376) **2810**
Kaiyou Suisan Enjiniaringu/Fishing Boat and System Engineering Association of Japan. Journal (JPN ISSN 1346-9800) **3600**
Kaiyou - Toshi Kankyou Kaihatsu Jouhou (JPN) **2810**
➤ Kajian Malaysia (MYS ISSN 0127-4082) **8116**
Kajima Corporation. Kajima Technical Research Institute. Annual Report *see* Kajima Gijutsu Kenkyujo Nenpo **3277**
Kajima Gijutsu Kenkyujo Nenpo/Kajima Corporation. Kajima Technical Research Institute. Annual Report (JPN ISSN 0918-015X) **3277**
Kajima Kensetsu Gijutsu Kenkyujo Nenpo *see* Kajima Gijutsu Kenkyujo Nenpo **3277**
Kajitsu Kankei Tokei Shiryo (JPN) **605**
Kajitsu Nihon (JPN ISSN 0913-8242) **240**
Kajman (CZE ISSN 1211-5924) **8320**
Kaju Kenkyusho Kenkyu Hokoku/National Institute of Fruit Tree Service. Bulletin (JPN ISSN 1347-3549) **129**
Kaju Tokei *see* Nihon Engei Nogyo Kyodokumiai Rengokai. Kaju Tokei **184**
• Kak (RUS ISSN 1609-0284) **2488**
Kakatiya Journal of English Studies (IND ISSN 0971-8877) **5316**
Kaki Koza Atarashii Zozengaku/Summer Seminar on New Topics in Naval Architecture (JPN) **8649**
Kakioka Magnetic Observatory. Memoirs *see* Chijiki Kansokujo Yoho **2779**
Kakioka Magnetic Observatory. Report. Geoelectricity/Kishocho Chijiki Kansokujo Hokoku. Chikyu Denki (JPN) **2785**
Kakioka Magnetic Observatory. Report. Geomagnetism/Kishocho Chijiki Kansokujo Hokoku. Chikyu Jiki (JPN) **2785**
Kakioka Magnetic Observatory. Technical Report *see* Chijiki Kansokujo Gijutsu Hokoku **2779**
Kakkerlak (ZAF ISSN 1814-7801) **3949**
Kakocho/Nagoya Entomological Society. Journal (JPN ISSN 0287-6477) **853**
Kakovostna Starost (SVN ISSN 1408-869X) **4050**
Kaks'plus (FIN ISSN 0355-4252) **3838**
Kakteen und Andere Sukkulenten (DEU ISSN 0022-7846) **799**
Die Kaktusbluete (DEU) **2157**
Kaktusy (CZE ISSN 0862-4372) **3740**
Kaku Deta Nyusu/Nuclear Data News (JPN ISSN 0385-4876) **3170**
Kaku Igaku/Japanese Journal of Nuclear Medicine (JPN ISSN 0022-7854) **6202**
Kaku Igaku Gazo Shindan/Imaging Diagnosis in Nuclear Medicine (JPN ISSN 0912-4195) **6202**
Kaku Igaku Gijutsu/Japanese Journal of Nuclear Medicine Technology (JPN ISSN 0289-100X) **6202**
Kaku Igaku Shorei Kentokai Shoreishu/Meeting on Case of Nuclear Medicine. Proceedings (JPN ISSN 0910-2213) **6202**
Kaku Yugo Kenkyu Kaihatsu no Genjo/Status of Nuclear Fusion Research and Development (JPN) **7068**
Kaku Yugo Rengo Koenkai Yokoshu/Preprints of Joint Conference on Nuclear Fusion (JPN) **7068**
➤ Kaku Yuugou Kagaku Kenkyusho Nyusu/National Institute for Fusion Science. News (JPN ISSN 0915-6704) **7068**
Kakuriken Kenkyu Hokoku/Laboratory of Nuclear Science. Research Report (JPN ISSN 0385-2105) **7068**
Kakuro Classic (DEU) **8183**
• Kala- ja Riistaraportteja (FIN ISSN 1238-3325) **3600**
Kala Kaumudi (IND) **3884**
Kalaallit Nuaat *see* Greenland. Groenlands Statistik. Greenland (Year) - Statistical Yearbook **8375**
Kalaallit Nunaat *see* Greenland. Groenlands Statistik. Groenland (Year) - Statistisk Aarbog **8375**
Kalabash (NAM ISSN 1023-912X) **3913**
Kalai Magal (IND) **5316**
Kalaikathir (IND ISSN 0022-7870) **7874**
KalaiMagal Magazine *see* Kalai Magal **5316**
Kalakalpam (IND ISSN 0047-3103) **2686**
Kalakaumudi Daily (IND) **3884**
• Kalakorikos (ESP ISSN 1137-0572) **4236**
Kalamanakaranaya (LKA) **1770**
• ➤ Kalamazoo College Quarterly (USA ISSN 8750-5746) **2289**
Kalamazoo Valley Heritage (USA ISSN 1052-7672) **3772**
Kalami Rishate (IND) **5425**
Kalamunda Magazine *see* Swan Magazine **3796**
Kalantar (BGD) **3799**
Kalapaikat *see* Suomen Kalapaikkaopas **8336**
Kalaschnikow (DEU ISSN 1435-3121) **5222**
Kalastaja (FIN ISSN 0356-1585) **3600**
Kalastus Euroopassa *see* Fisheries and Aquaculture in Europe **3592**
Kalatalouden Keskusliiton Julkaisu (FIN ISSN 0783-3954) **3600**
Kalatdlit Nunane Inuit *see* Greenland. Groenlands Statistik. Groenlands Befolkning **7284**
Kalathos (ESP ISSN 0211-5840) **402**
Kalatutkimuksia/Vilt- och Fiskeriforskningsinstitutet. Fiskundersoekningar (FIN ISSN 0787-8478) **3600**
Kalava Ha Sahityaya (LKA) **5317**
➤ Kalbos Kultura (LTU ISSN 0130-2795) **5136**
Kalbotyra/Linguistics (LTU ISSN 1392-1517) **5136**
• ➤ Kalbu Studijos/Studies about Languages (LTU ISSN 1648-2824) **5136**
• Kaldron (USA) **5425**
Kale Memorial Lectures *see* R B R R Kale Memorial Lectures **7175**
• Kaleidoscope (FRA ISSN 1639-044X) **1247**
Kaleidoscope (POL) **8784**
Kaleidoscope (TWN ISSN 1016-4162) **5222**
Kaleidoscope (Akron) (USA ISSN 0748-8742) **4067**
Kaleidoscope (Birmingham) (USA) **2289**
Kaleidoscope (Columbia) (USA ISSN 1073-8479) **7763**
Kalejdoskop *see* Dziennik Zwiazkowy **3530**
Kalendar - Al'manakh Novoho Shliakhu/New Pathway Almanac (CAN ISSN 0832-5081) **3545**
Kalendar Liberecka (CZE ISSN 1212-8538) **3832**
† Kalendar Odborara (SVK) **8969**
Kalendar Znamennykh i Pam'yatnykh Dat/Calendar of Notable and Memorable Dates (UKR ISSN 0130-2043) **3120**
Kalendarz Lekarza Praktyka (POL ISSN 1231-8248) **5656**
Kalendarz Slowa Bozego (POL ISSN 0860-410X) **7802**
Kaleva (FIN ISSN 0356-1356) **3838**
Kalevalaseuran Vuosikirja (FIN ISSN 0355-0311) **3619**
kalgan.net *see* Marca **8186**
Kali Zoi *see* O Phileleftheros **3832**
† Kalias (ESP ISSN 0214-6762) **8969**
Kalibar (SRB ISSN 0354-513X) **8183**
Kalikkudukka (IND) **2196**
Al-Kalima (YEM) **5222**
Kaliningrad In Your Pocket (POL ISSN 1392-1193) **8726**
Kaliningradskaya Pravda (RUS) **3936**
Kalispell Livestock Weekly News *see* Cowboy's Digest **284**
Kalium (ESP ISSN 1132-8096) **3249**
Kalkandu (IND) **3884**
Kalkholm News (FIN ISSN 1795-4614) **8649**
Kalki (IND) **5317**
• Kalkulace Cen Stavebnich Praci a Materialu (CZE ISSN 1801-9897) **1019**
Kalle Anka & Co (SWE ISSN 0345-6048) **2196**
Kalle Ankas Pocket (SWE ISSN 0345-6056) **2196**
Kalligram (HUN) **5317**
➤ Kalliope (USA ISSN 0735-7885) **5425**
Kalmar Laen (SWE ISSN 0451-2715) **4236**
Kalmar Laens Museum. Rapport *see* Kalmar Laens Museums Arkeologiska Rapporter **402**
• Kalmar Laens Museums Arkeologiska Rapporter (SWE ISSN 1400-352X) **402**
Kalmar Studies in Archaeology (SWE ISSN 1653-431X) **402**
Kalmar Studies in Humanities and Social Sciences (SWE ISSN 1653-784X) **4461**
• Kalnirnay (IND) **566**
Kalokagathia (HUN ISSN 1218-1498) **8183**
Kalokerines Apodrasis *see* About Tessaloniki Kalokerines Apodrasis **8680**
Kalonikali Tonga *see* The Tonga Chronicle **3962**
Kalori (AUS ISSN 0047-312X) **499**
Kalt- und Warmmassivumformung *see* Informationsdienst F I Z Technik. Kalt- und Warmmassivumformung **6339**
• Kaltio (FIN ISSN 0355-4511) **5222**
Kalulu (MWI) **5317**
Kalundborg Folkeblad, Jyderup Folkeblad, Samsoe Folketidende *see* Folkebladet **3833**
Kalveproducenten (DNK ISSN 0109-3800) **291**
Kalyan (IND ISSN 0022-8028) **7657**
Kalyani (LKA) **4461**
Kaman Kalehoyok *see* Anatolian Archaeological Studies **373**
Kamar Dagang dan Industri di Jawa Barat. Daftar Anggota *see* Chamber of Commerce and Industry in West Java. Member List **1399**
Kamarat (SVK) **2196**
Kamen (ITA) **5425**
Kamer van Koophandel en Fabrieken voor Amsterdam. Jaarrede (NLD) **1406**
Kamer van Koophandel en Nijverheid van Antwerpen. Bulletin (BEL ISSN 0022-8087) **1406**
Kamer van Koophandel Limburg. Kamerkrant *see* Kamerkrant (Ed. Noord- en Midden-Limburg) **1719**
Kamer van Koophandel Limburg. Kamerkrant *see* Kamerkrant (Ed. Zuid-Limburg) **1719**
Kamer van Koophandel voor Veluwe en Twente. Kamerkrant (Veluwe/Stendriehoek Edition) *see* Kamerkrant voor Ondernemend Oost-Nederland (Ed. Regio Twente) **1720**
Kamer van Koophandel voor Zuid-Limburg. Kamerkrant *see* Kamerkrant (Ed. Zuid-Limburg) **1719**
Kamer van Koophandel voor Zuid-Limburg. Kamerkrant *see* Kamerkrant (Ed. Noord- en Midden-Limburg) **1719**
Kamera & Bild (SWE ISSN 1653-350X) **6970**
Kamerad Tier (AUT ISSN 0022-8117) **6810**
Kameraden (DEU ISSN 1434-4394) **6430**
Kameradschaft der Wiener Panzer-Division. Mitteilungsblatt (AUT ISSN 0029-974X) **6430**

• Kameralehti (FIN ISSN 0022-8133) **6970**
▼ Kamerkrant (Ed. Noord- en Midden-Limburg) (NLD ISSN 1876-3006) **1719**
▼ Kamerkrant (Ed. Zuid-Limburg) (NLD ISSN 1876-2980) **1719**
Kamerkrant (Landelijke Editie) (NLD) **1406**
Kamerkrant voor de Ondernemend Regio Rotterdam (NLD ISSN 1873-9288) **1720**
Kamerkrant voor de Ondernemende Regio Zwolle *see* Kamerkrant voor Ondernemend Oost Nederland (Ed. Regio Zwolle) **1720**
Kamerkrant voor Ondernemend Flevoland *see* Kamerkrant voor Ondernemend Gooi-, Eem- en Flevoland **1406**
▼ Kamerkrant voor Ondernemend Gooi-, Eem- en Flevoland (NLD ISSN 1877-3478) **1406**
Kamerkrant voor Ondernemend Gooi- en Eemland *see* Kamerkrant voor Ondernemend Gooi-, Eem- en Flevoland **1406**
Kamerkrant voor Ondernemend Limburg-Noord *see* Kamerkrant (Ed. Noord- en Midden-Limburg) **1719**
Kamerkrant voor Ondernemend Limburg-Noord *see* Kamerkrant (Ed. Zuid-Limburg) **1719**
Kamerkrant voor Ondernemend Oost-Nederland (Ed. Regio Twente) (NLD ISSN 1875-8002) **1720**
Kamerkrant voor Ondernemend Oost-Nederland (Ed. Regio Veluwe en Twente) *see* Kamerkrant voor Ondernemend Oost-Nederland (Ed. Regio Twente) **1720**
Kamerkrant voor Ondernemend Oost Nederland (Ed. Regio Zwolle) (NLD ISSN 1875-0001) **1720**
Kamerkrant voor Ondernemend Twente *see* Kamerkrant voor Ondernemend Oost-Nederland (Ed. Regio Twente) **1720**
Kamerkrant voor Ondernemend Veluwe en Twente *see* Kamerkrant voor Ondernemend Oost-Nederland (Ed. Regio Twente) **1720**
Kamerkrant voor Ondernemend Veluwe/ Stedendriehoek *see* Kamerkrant voor Ondernemend Oost-Nederland (Ed. Regio Twente) **1720**
Kamerton (POL ISSN 1233-8249) **6582**
Kami Insatsu Purasuchikku Gomu Seihin Toukei Geppou/Monthly Report of Paper, Printing, Plastics Products and Rubber Products Statistics (JPN ISSN 1349-4643) **6734**
Kami Pa Gikyoshi/Japan T A P P I Journal (JPN ISSN 0022-815X) **6734**
Kami Parupu Gijutsu Taimusu/Japanese Journal of Paper Technology (JPN ISSN 0453-1507) **6734**
Kami Parupu Tokei Nenpo/Yearbook of Pulp and Paper Statistics (JPN ISSN 0453-1515) **6734**
Kami Paupu Gijutsu Kyokai. Nenji Taikai. Kouen Yokoshu/Japan Technical Association of Pulp and Paper Industry. Annual Meeting. Proceedings (JPN) **6734**
Kamikadze Gazette (BGR) **3805**
Kamille (NOR ISSN 0809-6678) **8870**
Kamine und Kacheloefen (DEU) **4559**
Der Kaminfeger (DEU) **4122**
Kamishihoro-cho Higashi Taisetsu Hakubutsukan Kenkyu Hokoku/Higashi Taisetsu Museum of Natural History. Bulletin (JPN ISSN 0915-5074) **7874**
• Kamloops Daily News (CAN ISSN 1185-491X) **3812**
• Kamloops This Week (CAN ISSN 0841-2243) **3812**
Kammarmusik-Nytt *see* Musikant och Kammarmusik-Nytt **6596**
Die Kammer *see* I H K Magazin Krefeld, Moenchengladbach, Neuss und Viersen **1404**
Kammer Nachrichten (AUT ISSN 0022-8184) **1406**
KammerForum (DEU ISSN 1610-8140) **4708**
KammerMitteilungen Duesseldorf (DEU ISSN 1614-8843) **4708**
KAMnieuwsbrief *see* Kwaliteits-, Arbo- en Milieumanagementnieuwsbrief **1771**
▼ Kampala International University. Research Digest (UGA ISSN 1996-9023) **2879**
Kampanje! (NOR ISSN 0022-8214) **1827**
Kampeer en Caravankampioen (NLD ISSN 0165-4128) **8727**
Kampeertoerist (BEL ISSN 0775-8545) **8320**
Kamper Almanak (NLD ISSN 0923-8514) **4236**
Kampgrounds of America Directory *see* K O A Directory **2010**
Kampioen (NLD ISSN 0022-8265) **8727**
Kampos (GBR ISSN 1356-5109) **3545**
Kampsville Archaeological Center Research Series *see* K A C Research Series **401**
Kampsville Archaeological Center Technical Reports *see* K A C Technical Reports **401**
Kampsville Seminars in Archeology (USA) **402**
Kampsville Studies in Archeology and History (USA) **402**
Kamptal-Studien (AUT) **4236**
Kampuchea (SWE ISSN 0349-2850) **4185**
Kamratposten (SWE ISSN 0022-8273) **2196**
Kan Anders (NLD ISSN 0925-5893) **7249**
KAN in Ontwikkeling *see* Knooppunt Arnhem Nijmegen in Ontwikkeling **7495**
Kan, Tan, Sui, Japan (JPN ISSN 0389-4991) **5896**
• Kan Yisheng/See a Doctor (CHN ISSN 1672-1039) **5656**
Kana (HRV ISSN 0353-2828) **7802**
Kanada Kurier (CAN) **3545**
• Kanadai Magyar Hirlap/Canadian Hungarian Journal (CAN ISSN 1710-8837) **3545**
Kanadische Studien zur Deutschen Sprache und Literatur *see* Canadian Studies in German Language and Literature **5270**
Kanadske Listy/Canadian Pages (CAN ISSN 0449-7368) **3545**
Kanadski Srbobran/Canadian Serbian (CAN ISSN 0022-829X) **3545**
Kanadsky Slovak/Canadian Slovak (CAN ISSN 0047-3154) **3545**
Kanagawa Association of Psychiatry. Journal *see* Kanagawa-ken Seishin Igakkaishi **6157**
Kanagawa Chuho/Kanagawa Entomologist's Association. Journal (JPN ISSN 0288-3821) **853**
Kanagawa Daigaku Kogaku Kenkyujo Shoho/Kanagawa University. Research Institute for Engineering. Science Reports (JPN ISSN 0387-0324) **3206**
Kanagawa Dental College. Bulletin (JPN ISSN 0385-1443) **5854**
Kanagawa Entomologist's Association. Journal *see* Kanagawa Chuho **853**
Kanagawa Hogaku/Review of Law and Politics (JPN ISSN 0453-185X) **4708**
Kanagawa Hospital Pharmacists Association. Journal *see* Kanagawaken Byoin Yakuzaishikai Kaishi **6857**
Kanagawa Igakkai Zasshi/Kanagawa Prefecture Medical Association. Journal (JPN ISSN 0285-0680) **5656**
Kanagawa Institute of Technology. Research Reports. Part A, Humanities and Social Science *see* Kanagawa Koka Daigaku Kenkyu Hokoku. A, Jinbun Shakai Kagaku-hen **4461**
Kanagawa Institute of Technology. Research Reports. Part B. Science and Technology *see* Kanagawa Koka Daigaku Kenkyu Hokoku. B Rikogaku Hen **8430**
Kanagawa Journal of Orthopedics and Traumatology *see* Kanagawa Seikei Saigai Geka Kenkyuukai Zasshi **6066**
Kanagawa-ken Agricultural Research Institute of Kanagawa Prefecture. Bulletin *see* Kanagawa-ken Nogyo Sogo Kenkyujo Kenkyu Hokoku **130**
Kanagawa-ken Hakubutsukan Kyokai Kaiho/Kanagawa-ken Museum Gazette (JPN) **6527**
Kanagawa-ken Museum Gazette *see* Kanagawa-ken Hakubutsukan Kyokai Kaiho **6527**
Kanagawa-ken Nogyo Sogo Kenkyujo Kenkyu Hokoku/Kanagawa-ken Agricultural Research Institute of Kanagawa Prefecture. Bulletin (JPN ISSN 0388-8231) **130**
➤ Kanagawa-ken Seishin Igakkaishi/Kanagawa Association of Psychiatry. Journal (JPN ISSN 0288-9617) **6157**
Kanagawa-ken Suisan Sogo Kenkyujo. Kenkyu Hokoku/Kanagawa Prefectural Fisheries Research Institute. Bulletin (JPN ISSN 1342-176X) **3600**
Kanagawa-kenritsu Hakubutsukan Kenkyu Hokoku. Shizen Kagaku/Kanagawa Prefectural Museum of Natural History. Bulletin. Natural Science (JPN ISSN 0453-1906) **7874**
Kanagawa-kenritsu Hakubutsukan Shiryo Mokuroku. Shizen Kagaku/Kanagawa Prefectural Museum of Natural History. Catalogue of the Collection (JPN ISSN 1342-8993) **7874**
Kanagawa-kenritsu Shizen Hogo Senta Hokoku/Kanagawa Prefectural Nature Conservation Center. Bulletin (JPN ISSN 0914-8744) **2616**
Kanagawa Koka Daigaku Kenkyu Hokoku. A, Jinbun Shakai Kagaku-hen/Kanagawa Institute of Technology. Research Reports. Part A, Humanities and Social Science (JPN ISSN 0916-1899) **4461**
Kanagawa Koka Daigaku Kenkyu Hokoku. B Rikogaku Hen/Kanagawa Institute of Technology. Research Reports. Part B. Science and Technology (JPN ISSN 0916-1902) **8430**
Kanagawa Natural Preservation Society. Journal *see* Kanagawa Shizen Hozen Kenkyukai Hokokusho **2616**
Kanagawa Odontological Society. Journal *see* Kanagawa Shigaku **5854**
Kanagawa Physical Therapy Association. News *see* Kanagawaken Rigaku Ryohoshikai Nyusu **6111**
Kanagawa Prefectural Fisheries Research Institute. Bulletin *see* Kanagawa-ken Suisan Sogo Kenkyujo. Kenkyu Hokoku **3600**
Kanagawa Prefectural Museum of Natural History. Bulletin. Natural Science *see* Kanagawa-kenritsu Hakubutsukan Kenkyu Hokoku. Shizen Kagaku **7874**
Kanagawa Prefectural Museum of Natural History. Catalogue of the Collection *see* Kanagawa-kenritsu Hakubutsukan Shiryo Mokuroku. Shizen Kagaku **7874**
Kanagawa Prefectural Nature Conservation Center. Bulletin *see* Kanagawa-kenritsu Shizen Hogo Senta Hokoku **2616**
Kanagawa Prefecture Medical Association. Journal *see* Kanagawa Igakkai Zasshi **5656**
Kanagawa Prefecture. Monthly Report of Meteorology *see* Kanagawaken Kisho Geppo **6359**
Kanagawa Seikei Saigai Geka Ikai Zasshi *see* Kanagawa Seikei Saigai Geka Kenkyuukai Zasshi **6066**
Kanagawa Seikei Saigai Geka Kenkyuukai Zasshi/Kanagawa Journal of Orthopedics and Traumatology (JPN ISSN 1348-043X) **6066**
Kanagawa Shigaku/Kanagawa Odontological Society. Journal (JPN ISSN 0454-8302) **5854**
Kanagawa Shizen Hozen Kenkyukai Hokokusho/Kanagawa Natural Preservation Society. Journal (JPN) **2616**
Kanagawa Shizenshi Shiryo/Natural History Report of Kanagawa (JPN ISSN 0388-9009) **7874**
Kanagawa University. Institute for Humanities Research. Bulletin (JPN ISSN 0287-7082) **4461**
Kanagawa University. Research Institute for Engineering. Science Reports *see* Kanagawa Daigaku Kogaku Kenkyujo Shoho **3206**
Kanagawaken Byoin Yakuzaishikai Kaishi/Kanagawa Hospital Pharmacists Association. Journal (JPN ISSN 0285-4775) **6857**
Kanagawaken Kisho Geppo/Kanagawa Prefecture. Monthly Report of Meteorology (JPN ISSN 0449-7392) **6359**
Kanagawaken Rigaku Ryohoshikai Nyusu/Kanagawa Physical Therapy Association. News (JPN ISSN 0919-195X) **6111**
Kanak (BGD ISSN 0396-4965) **3799**
Kanalen (SWE) **5968**
Kan'aoi Kenkyu/Kanaoi Research (JPN) **799**
Kanaoi Research *see* Kan'aoi Kenkyu **799**
Kanara Chamber of Commerce & Industry Journal (IND ISSN 0300-4074) **1406**
Kanava (FIN ISSN 0355-0303) **5222**
Kanawa (CAN ISSN 1198-9580) **8277**
Kanawha Valley Genealogical Society. Journal (USA ISSN 0270-4064) **3772**
➤ Kanazawa Daigaku Igakubu Hoken Gakka Sagyo Ryohogaku Senko Sotsugyo Kenkyu Ronbunshu/Kanazawa University School of Health Sciences. Department of Occupational Therapy. Collection of Graduate Thesis (JPN ISSN 1345-9090) **5656**
Kanazawa Daigaku Kyoikugakubu Kiyo. Jinbun, Shakai Kyoiku Kagaku *see* Kanazawa University. Faculty of Education. Bulletin: Humanities, Social and Educational Sciences **2879**
Kanazawa Daigaku Kyoikugakubu Kiyo. Shizen Kagaku Hen/Kanazawa University. Faculty of Education. Bulletin. Natural Sciences (JPN ISSN 0387-0995) **7874**
Kanazawa Daigaku Kyoyobu Ronshu. Shizen Kagaku Hen/Kanazawa University. College of Liberal Arts. Annals of Science (JPN ISSN 0302-0479) **7874**
Kanazawa Daigaku Rigakubu Fuzoku Noto Rinkai Jikkenjo Kenkyu Gaiyo Nenji Hokoku/Kanazawa University. Noto Marine Laboratory. Annual Progress Reports (JPN) **2810**
Kanazawa Daigaku Rigakubu Ronbun Oyobi Chosho Mokuroku/Kanazawa University. Faculty of Science. List of Publications (JPN) **7937**
Kanazawa Daigaku Rika Hokoku *see* Kanazawa University. Science Reports **7874**
• Kanazawa Ika Daigaku Zasshi/Kanazawa Medical University. Journal (JPN ISSN 0385-5759) **5656**
Kanazawa Medical University. Journal *see* Kanazawa Ika Daigaku Zasshi **5656**
Kanazawa University. College of Liberal Arts. Annals of Science *see* Kanazawa Daigaku Kyoyobu Ronshu. Shizen Kagaku Hen **7874**
Kanazawa University. Faculty of Education. Bulletin: Humanities, Social and Educational Sciences/Kanazawa Daigaku Kyoikugakubu Kiyo. Jinbun, Shakai Kyoiku Kagaku (JPN) **2879**
Kanazawa University. Faculty of Education. Bulletin. Natural Sciences *see* Kanazawa Daigaku Kyoikugakubu Kiyo. Shizen Kagaku Hen **7874**
Kanazawa University. Faculty of Law and Literature. Studies and Essays (JPN ISSN 0453-1981) **5317**
Kanazawa University. Faculty of Science. List of Publications *see* Kanazawa Daigaku Rigakubu Ronbun Oyobi Chosho Mokuroku **7937**
Kanazawa University. Japan Sea Research Institute. Bulletin *see* Nihonkaiiki Kenkyujo Hokoku **2814**
Kanazawa University. Noto Marine Laboratory. Annual Progress Reports *see* Kanazawa Daigaku Rigakubu Fuzoku Noto Rinkai Jikkenjo Kenkyu Gaiyo Nenji Hokoku **2810**
Kanazawa University School of Health Sciences. Department of Occupational Therapy. Collection of Graduate Thesis *see* Kanazawa Daigaku Igakubu Hoken Gakka Sagyo Ryohogaku Senko Sotsugyo Kenkyu Ronbunshu **5656**
Kanazawa University. Science Reports/Kanazawa Daigaku Rika Hokoku (JPN ISSN 0022-8338) **7874**
† Kancelarska Abeceda (CZE ISSN 1801-8300) **8969**
Kanch (IND ISSN 0971-3751) **2043**
• Kancha Kexue Jishu/Site Investigation - Science and Technology (CHN ISSN 1001-3946) **6467**
• Kandokon/Japanese Journal of Environment, Entomology and Zoology (JPN ISSN 0915-4698) **853**
Kane and Levine's Civil Procedure in California State and Federal Supplemental Materials (USA) **4708**
Kane County Bar Association Bar Briefs (USA) **4709**
Kang Fu/Rehabilitation (CHN ISSN 1005-832X) **6112**
• Kang'ai/Anticancer (CHN ISSN 1008-3065) **6025**
† Kangaroo (AUS ISSN 1036-3262) **8969**
Kangaroo Valley Voice (AUS ISSN 1833-8402) **3795**
• Kangganran Yaoxue/Anti-Infection Pharmacy (CHN ISSN 1672-7878) **6857**
• Kangjian Zazhi/Common Health (TWN) **6991**
† Kangle Shijie/Health and Happiness (CHN ISSN 1005-314X) **8969**
Kango/Japanese Journal of Nursing (JPN ISSN 0022-8362) **5968**
Kango Gakusei/Nurse Student (JPN ISSN 0385-5988) **5968**
Kango Gijutsu/Japanese Journal of Nursing Arts (JPN ISSN 0449-752X) **5968**
Kango Kenkyu/Japanese Journal of Nursing Research (JPN ISSN 0022-8370) **5968**
Kango Kyoiku/Japanese Journal of Nursing Education (JPN ISSN 0047-1895) **5968**
Kango Tenbo/Japanese Journal of Nursing Science (JPN ISSN 0385-549X) **5968**
• Kangogaku Zasshi/Japanese Journal of Nursing (JPN ISSN 0386-9830) **5968**
• Kangri Zhanzheng Yanjiu/The Journal of Studies of China's Resistance War Against Japan (CHN ISSN 1002-9575) **4185**
Kanhistique (USA ISSN 0738-9736) **366**
• Kanina (CRI ISSN 0378-0473) **5317**
Kaninchen *see* Der Kleintierzuechter - Kaninchenzeitung **291**
Kanjo Shinrigaku Kenkyu (JPN) **7382**
Kankan (BGD) **3799**
Kankeigaku Kenkyu/Journal of the Science of Relationships (JPN ISSN 0286-7966) **4461**
Kankitsurui Hanbai Nenpo (JPN) **1139**
Kanko Bunka/Tourism & Culture (JPN ISSN 0385-5554) **8727**
Kankyo Business (JPN) **1139**
Kankyo Chishitsugaku Shinpojumu Koen Ronbunshu/Symposium on Geo-Environments. Proceedings (JPN ISSN 0917-7183) **3449**
Kankyo Eisei Kogaku Kenkyu/Environmental and Sanitary Engineering Research (JPN ISSN 0913-7025) **3449**
Kankyo Gijutsu/Environmental Conservation Engineering (JPN ISSN 0388-9459) **3449**
• Kankyo Joho Kagaku/Environmental Information Science (JPN ISSN 0389-6633) **3449**
Kankyo Kagakkaishi/Environmental Science (JPN ISSN 0915-0048) **3449**
Kankyo Kagaku/Journal of Environmental Chemistry (JPN ISSN 0917-2408) **2069**
➤ Kankyo Kagaku Kenkyujo Hokoku/Journal of Environmental Science Laboratory (JPN ISSN 1346-4736) **3449**
Kankyo Kaigi (JPN) **3449**
Kankyo Kenkyu/Environmental Research Quarterly (JPN ISSN 0285-9769) **3449**
Kankyo Marketing & Business *see* Kankyo Business **1139**
Kankyo Mondai Shinpojumu Koen Ronbunshu/Symposium on Environmental Problems. Proceedings (JPN ISSN 0913-4093) **3277**
Kankyo to Kogai (JPN ISSN 0918-7537) **3449**
Kankyou Jouka Gijutsu/Environmental Solution Technology (JPN ISSN 1347-9970) **3449**
• Kankyou Shigen Kougaku/Resources Processing (JPN ISSN 1348-6012) **6467**
Kankyougi/N I E S Research Booklet (JPN ISSN 1346-776X) **3449**
Kankyu Okoku (JPN ISSN 1345-6148) **8153**
• Kannada Prabha (IND) **3884**
Kannadamma (IND) **3884**
Kano (State). Directory of Industrial & Commercial Establishments (NGA) **1495**
Kano (State). Local Government Survey of Towns, Villages and Hamlets (NGA) **1247**
Kano (State) Manpower Statistics (NGA) **1247**
Kano (State). Market Calendar (NGA) **1430**
Kano (State). Motor Vehicle Statistics (NGA) **8527**
Kano (State). Prices of Selected Commodities in Some Towns in Kano State (NGA) **1247**
Kano (State). Public Finance Statistics of Kano State & Local Government Councils (NGA) **1247**
Kano (State). Statistical Year - Book (NGA) **1247**
Kano (State). Statistics Division. Area Codes (NGA) **8383**
Kano-Sport (NLD ISSN 0928-1495) **8277**
Kano State Courier (NGA) **3920**
• Kano State of Nigeria Gazette (NGA) **7449**
Kanon (AUT ISSN 0259-0727) **4709**
Kanonika (ITA) **7657**
Kanonistische Studien und Texte (DEU ISSN 0929-0680) **7658**
Kanot-Nytt *see* Paddling **8280**
Kanpo Igaku/Chinese Medicine (JPN ISSN 0288-2485) **312**
Kanpo Kenkyu/Study on Chinese Medicine (JPN ISSN 0385-6526) **312**
Kanpo no Rinsho/Journal of Kampo Medicine (JPN ISSN 0451-307X) **312**
Kanreichi Gijutsu Kenkyu Kaihatsu Senta Hokoku/Research Center for Gas Industry in Cold District. Technical Report (JPN ISSN 0914-496X) **6776**
Kanrin/Japan Society of Naval Architects and Ocean Engineers. Bulletin (JPN ISSN 1880-3725) **8649**
Kansai Branches Five Societies on Optics. Joint Convention Record *see* Kogaku Go Gakkai Kansai Shibu Rengo Koenkai Yokoshu **7079**
Kansai Byochugai Kenkyukaiho/Kansai Plant Protection Society. Proceedings (JPN ISSN 0387-1002) **240**

DIRECTORY 2010 KARNATAK UNIVERSITY, DHARWAD, INDIA. JOURNAL. SCIENCE 10521

Kansai Catalysis Research Group. Report of the Meeting see Shokubai Kenkyu Kondankai **2141**
Kansai College of Oriental Medicine. Bulletin see Kansai Shinkyuu Daigaku Kiyou **312**
Kansai Daigaku Keizai Ronshu see Kansai University Economic Review **1139**
Kansai Daigaku Kogaku Kenkyu Hokoku see Kansai University Technology Reports **8430**
Kansai Denryoku K.K. Soken Hokoku/Kansai Electric Power Co. Technical Research Center. Report (JPN ISSN 0285-6697) **3323**
Kansai Electric Power Co. Technical Research Center. Report see Kansai Denryoku K.K. Soken Hokoku **3323**
Kansai Electronic Industry Development Center. Bulletin see K E C Joho **3107**
Kansai Ika Daigaku. Zasshi/Kansai Medical University. Journal (JPN ISSN 0022-8400) **5656**
Kansai Isshukan (JPN) **3900**
Kansai Medical University. Journal see Kansai Ika Daigaku. Zasshi **5656**
Kansai Plant Protection Society. Proceedings see Kansai Byochugai Kenkyukaiho **240**
● Kansai Rigaku Ryouhou/Journal of Kansai Physical Therapy (JPN ISSN 1346-9606) **6112**
Kansai Shinkyuu Daigaku Kiyou/Kansai College of Oriental Medicine. Bulletin (JPN ISSN 1349-5739) **312**
Kansai Shizen Kagaku (JPN ISSN 0285-3205) **7874**
Kansai Society of Naval Architects. Preprints of Meeting see Kansai Zosen Kyokai Koen Ronbunshu **8649**
Kansai Tokkyu Joho Senta Shinkokai Nyusu/Association for Kansai Patent Information Center News (JPN) **6753**
Kansai University Economic Review/Kansai Daigaku Keizai Ronshu (JPN ISSN 0449-7554) **1139**
Kansai University Review of Business and Commerce (JPN ISSN 1344-8455) **1430**
Kansai University Review of Economics (JPN ISSN 1344-8463) **1495**
➤ Kansai University Review of Law and Politics (JPN ISSN 0388-886X) **4709**
Kansai University Technology Reports/Kansai Daigaku Kogaku Kenkyu Hokoku (JPN ISSN 0453-2198) **8430**
Kansai Zosen Kyokai Koen Ronbunshu/Kansai Society of Naval Architects. Preprints of Meeting (JPN ISSN 0919-7591) **8649**
Kansai Zousen Kyoukai Rombunshuu/Kansai Society of Naval Architects, Japan. Journal see Nihon Sempaku Kaiyou Kougakkai Rombunshuu **8655**
Kansalliskirjasto (FIN ISSN 1459-3467) **5022**
Kansan Tahto (FIN ISSN 0356-1380) **3838**
● Kansan Uutiset (FIN ISSN 0357-1521) **3838**
Kansanelaman Kuvauksia (FIN ISSN 0453-2201) **3619**
Kansanka Shishitsu Kenkyu/Lipid Peroxide and Research (JPN ISSN 0911-8691) **737**
Kansantaloudellinen Aikakauskirja/Finnish Economic Journal (FIN ISSN 0022-8427) **1139**
Kansantaloudellisia Tutkimuksia/Economic Studies (FIN ISSN 0355-7847) **1139**
Kansas! (USA ISSN 0022-8435) **3979**
Kansas 4-H Journal (USA) **130**
● ➤ Kansas Academy of Science. Transactions (Print) (USA ISSN 0022-8443) **7874**
Kansas Agricultural Experiment Station. Bulletin (USA ISSN 0097-0484) **130**
Kansas Agriculture Annual Report and Farm Facts (USA) **130**
Kansas: All-Industries see Harris Directory. Kansas All-Industries **2000**
● Kansas Alumni Magazine (USA ISSN 0745-3345) **2289**
Kansas Anthropological Association Newsletter (USA ISSN 1069-0360) **345**
The Kansas Anthropologist (USA ISSN 1069-0379) **345**
● The Kansas Banker (USA ISSN 0022-8478) **1363**
Kansas BankNews Bank Directory see BankNews Directory of Kansas Banks **1318**
● Kansas Bar Association. Journal (USA ISSN 0022-8486) **4709**
Kansas Beverage News (USA ISSN 0022-8494) **605**
➤ Kansas Biology Teacher (USA ISSN 1064-105X) **685**
● Kansas Business and Economic Review (USA) **1139**
● Kansas Business Directory (USA ISSN 1048-7271) **2010**
Kansas Citian (USA ISSN 0274-9912) **1406**
Kansas Cities and Counties Graphic Performance Analysis see Kansas Cities & Counties Graphic Performance Analysis **7481**
Kansas Cities & Counties Graphic Performance Analysis (USA ISSN 1935-6013) **7481**
Kansas City Board of Trade Review (USA) **273**
Kansas City Business see K C Business **1139**
● The Kansas City Business Journal (USA ISSN 0734-2748) **1495**
● Kansas City Call (USA) **3545**
The Kansas City Globe (USA) **3545**
Kansas City Home Design see Home Design **4541**
Kansas City Homes & Gardens (USA) **4362**
Kansas City Jewish Chronicle (USA ISSN 0022-8524) **3545**
Kansas City Magazine see K C Magazine **3979**
Kansas City Parent Magazine (USA) **2157**
● Kansas City Small Business Monthly (USA ISSN 1068-2422) **1963**
Kansas City Studio see K C Studio **6505**
Kansas City Voices (USA ISSN 1931-2776) **5317**
Kansas City Weddings see K C Weddings **5559**
Kansas Corn Performance Tests (USA) **273**
Kansas Country Living (USA ISSN 0091-9586) **130**
Kansas Court Rules and Procedure (USA ISSN 0748-5255) **4954**
● Kansas Crimes and Punishments, Criminal Procedure, Motor Vehicles and Related Statutes (USA) **4892**
Kansas Curiosities (USA ISSN 1932-7331) **8727**
● Kansas Dental Association. Journal (USA ISSN 0888-7063) **5854**
Kansas. Department of Health and Environment. Annual Summary of Vital Statistics (USA) **7286**
Kansas Dietetic Association Communicator see K D A Communicator **6662**
● ➤ Kansas Economic Report & Kansas Economic Indicators (USA) **1495**
● Kansas Employment Law Letter (USA ISSN 1074-0422) **4709**
Kansas Engineer (USA ISSN 0022-8559) **3207**
Kansas Engineer Magazine see Kansas Engineer **3207**
Kansas English (USA ISSN 0739-0157) **3069**
● ➤ Kansas Entomological Society. Journal (USA ISSN 0022-8567) **853**
Kansas Facts (USA ISSN 1051-7138) **3120**
● Kansas Family Physician (USA) **5656**
● Kansas Farmer (USA) **130**
Kansas Food News (USA) **3652**
● Kansas' Forest Resources in (Year) (USA ISSN 1931-0722) **3695**
● Kansas Geological Survey. Bulletin (USA ISSN 0097-4471) **2751**
Kansas Geological Survey. Educational Series (USA ISSN 0731-616X) **2751**
Kansas Government Journal (USA ISSN 0022-8613) **7495**
➤ Kansas Heritage (USA) **4300**
● ➤ Kansas History (USA ISSN 0149-9114) **4300**
Kansas Insurance Agent & Broker (USA ISSN 1069-1847) **4511**
Kansas Irrigation Water Use (USA) **8828**
Kansas Issues see Issues (Topeka) **2872**
● Kansas Journal of Law & Public Policy (USA ISSN 1055-8942) **4709**
▼ ● Kansas Journal of Medicine (USA ISSN 1948-2035) **5656**
Kansas Kin (USA ISSN 0451-4084) **3772**
Kansas Legislative Handbook (USA ISSN 1087-7207) **7495**
Kansas. Legislative Research Department. Report on Kansas Legislative Interim Studies (USA ISSN 0270-4331) **7149**
● Kansas Libraries (USA ISSN 0889-2709) **5022**
Kansas Library Association Newsletter see K L A Newsletter **5022**
Kansas Living (USA ISSN 1077-0453) **130**
● Kansas Manufacturers Directory (USA) **2010**
Kansas Municipal Water Use (USA) **8828**
Kansas Music Review (USA ISSN 0022-8702) **6582**
● ➤ Kansas Nurse (USA ISSN 0022-8710) **5968**
Kansas, Off the Beaten Path see Off the Beaten Path: Kansas **8743**
Kansas Oil Marketer (USA) **6776**
Kansas Optometric Journal (USA ISSN 1063-1623) **6045**
Kansas Ornithological Society. Bulletin (USA ISSN 0022-8729) **909**
Kansas Physician (USA) **5656**
Kansas Restaurant (USA ISSN 0022-8753) **4392**
Kansas Review (USA ISSN 1043-7657) **3772**
Kansas School Directory see M D R's School Directory. Kansas **2958**
Kansas School Naturalist (USA ISSN 0022-877X) **7874**
Kansas Sorghum Performance Tests. Grain & Forage (USA) **273**
† ● Kansas State Board of Nursing. Newsletter (USA) **8969**
Kansas State Collegian (USA) **2289**
Kansas State Engineer (USA ISSN 0047-3189) **3207**
Kansas State University. Food and Feed Grain Institute. Technical Assistance in Grain Storage, Processing and Marketing, and Agribusiness Development (USA) **273**
● Kansas Statistical Abstract (Online) (USA ISSN 1934-9319) **8384**
Kansas Statistical Abstract (Print) see Kansas Statistical Abstract (Online) **8384**
Kansas Stockman (USA ISSN 0022-8826) **291**
Kansas. Water Office. Fact Sheet (USA) **8828**
Kansas Water Plan (USA) **8828**
Kansas Wildflower Society Newsletter (USA) **3740**
Kansas Wildlife & Parks (USA ISSN 0898-6975) **2616**
Kansas Working Papers in Linguistics (USA ISSN 1043-3805) **5136**
Kansatieteellinen Arkisto (FIN ISSN 0355-1830) **345**
Kansen, Ensho, Men'eki/Infection, Inflammation & Immunity (JPN ISSN 0387-1010) **5821**
● Kansenshogaku Zasshi/Japanese Association for Infectious Diseases. Journal (JPN ISSN 0387-5911) **5821**
➤ Kansetsu Geka/Journal of Joint Surgery (JPN ISSN 0286-5394) **6066**
Kansetsu no Geka/Surgery of Joints (JPN ISSN 0285-6255) **6066**
Kansetsukyo/Arthroscopy (JPN ISSN 0910-223X) **6066**
● Kanshijie/World View (CHN ISSN 1006-0936) **3826**
KansRijk see A+O Fonds Rijk. Nieuwsbrief **1663**
● Kanssalainen (FIN ISSN 1795-4126) **7149**
● Kant e - Prints (BRA ISSN 1677-1621) **6930**
Kant-Forschungen (DEU) **6930**
● ➤ Kant Studien (DEU ISSN 0022-8877) **6930**
Kant-Studien see Kant Studien **6930**
▼ ➤ Kant Yearbook (DEU ISSN 1868-4599) **6930**
Kantaiheiyo Bijinesu Joho see Rim **1168**
● Kantian Review (GBR ISSN 1369-4154) **6930**
Kantieke Schoolmeester (BEL ISSN 0778-1806) **5317**
● Kantinen (DNK ISSN 0022-8885) **4597**
● Kantipur Daily (NPL) **3913**
● Kantipur Online (NPL ISSN 1563-9770) **3913**
De Kantlijn (NLD ISSN 1874-0235) **499**
Kanto Journal of Obstetrics and Gynecology see Nihon Sanka Fujinka Gakkai Kanto Rengo Chiho Bukai Kaiho **5999**
Kanto Journal of Orthopedics and Traumatology see Kanto Seikei Saigai Geka Gakkai Zasshi **6066**
Kanto Seikei Saigai Geka Gakkai Zasshi/Kanto Journal of Orthopedics and Traumatology (JPN ISSN 0389-7087) **6066**
Kanton Zuerich. Staatskalender (CHE) **7449**
Kantone und Staedte der Schweiz. Statistische Uebersichten/Cantons et Villes Suisses. Donnees Statistiques (CHE) **7481**
Kantoor Business Magazine (NLD ISSN 0929-7871) **1852**
Kantoor en Efficiency (NLD ISSN 0022-8893) **1852**
Kantoren in Cijfers (NLD ISSN 1874-0170) **7597**
Kantorenatlas Nederland see Kantoren in Cijfers **7597**
De Kantorenmarkt in Haaglanden see Monitor Kantorenmarkt Haaglanden **450**
Kantu Shuohua/Look and Say (CHN ISSN 1006-1614) **2196**
Kanu Culture (AUS ISSN 1328-1801) **8277**
Kanu Sport (DEU ISSN 0022-8923) **8277**
● Kanukoka. Nutaarsiassat (Kalaallit Nunaanni Kommuneqarfiit Kattuffiat) (GRL ISSN 1602-0286) **7449**
Kanumagazin (DEU ISSN 1436-7750) **8277**
➤ Kanunnah (AUS ISSN 1832-536X) **499**
Kanyaka (IND) **8870**
Kanzleien in Deutschland (GBR ISSN 1464-8865) **4709**
Kanzleifuehrung Professionell (DEU ISSN 1432-4903) **7449**
➤ Kanzo/Acta Hepatologica Japonica (JPN ISSN 0451-4203) **5928**
Kao Institute for Fundamental Research. Bulletin (JPN) **2069**
➤ Kaogu/Archaeology (CHN ISSN 0453-2899) **402**
➤ Kaogu Xuebao/Acta Archaeologica Sinica (CHN ISSN 0453-2902) **402**
● Kaogu yu Wenwu/Archaeology and Cultural Relics (CHN ISSN 1000-7830) **402**
● Kaohsiung Journal of Medical Sciences (TWN ISSN 1607-551X) **5656**
Kaoku Gaichu/House and Household Insect Pests (JPN ISSN 0912-974X) **240**
Kaoshi yu Zhaosheng/Examinations and Recruitment of Students (CHN ISSN 1674-1250) **2879**
Kapank (IRN) **5222**
Kapawa News (PHL ISSN 0116-2187) **3928**
Kapi-Mana News (NZL ISSN 1170-0599) **3917**
● Kapital/Capital (BGR) **1139**
† Kapital (DNK ISSN 1603-9947) **8969**
Kapital (HRV ISSN 1330-6537) **1363**
● Kapital (NOR ISSN 0332-5423) **1770**
Kapital (UKR) **1139**
● Kapital Nyt (DNK ISSN 1603-9955) **1363**
Kapitalmarknaden (SWE) **1363**
Kapitalmarktorientierter Rechnungslegung see K o R **1363**
Kapitalmarktrecht (DEU ISSN 0948-5163) **1636**
Kapiti Observer (NZL ISSN 1170-0602) **3917**
Kaplan L S A T see L S A T (Comprehensive Program) **4711**
Kaplan SAT Subject Test: Physics see SAT Subject Test. Physics **7039**
Kappa Alpha Psi Journal (USA) **2267**
Kappa Delta Epsilon Current (USA ISSN 0022-894X) **2289**
● ➤ Kappa Delta Pi Record (USA ISSN 0022-8958) **3069**
Kappa Gamma Pi News (USA) **2991**
Kappa Omicron Nu Dialogue (USA ISSN 1520-4855) **4362**
● ➤ Kappa Omicron Nu Forum (USA ISSN 1520-4820) **4362**
Kappa Pi International Honorary Art Fraternity. Sketch Book see Sketch Book **517**
The Kappa Profile (USA) **2991**
Kappa Tau Alpha. Newsletter (USA) **4578**
The Kappan see Phi Delta Kappan **2898**
De Kapper (NLD ISSN 1572-3208) **589**
Kapper en Kapsels (BEL ISSN 0775-8952) **589**
Kapriz (RUS) **4979**
Kaptein Sabeltann (NOR ISSN 1890-0631) **2196**
Kapuseru/Capsule (JPN ISSN 0287-2358) **6857**
Karaat (BEL ISSN 0777-642X) **5074**
Karaat Magazine (Roeselare Edition) see Karaat **5074**
Karachi. Chamber of Commerce and Industry (PAK ISSN 0047-3197) **1406**
Karachi. Chamber of Commerce and Industry. Annual Report (PAK ISSN 0075-5079) **1406**
Karachi. Chamber of Commerce and Industry. Guide for Industrial Investment in Pakistan (PAK) **1636**
Karachi. Chamber of Commerce and Industry. News Bulletin (PAK) **1406**
Karachi. Chamber of Commerce and Industry. Pattern of Foreign Trade of Pakistan (PAK) **1574**
Karachi Journal of Science (PAK ISSN 0250-5363) **7874**
Karachi Port Trust News Bulletin see K P T News Bulletin **8649**
Karachi Port Trust. Year Book of Information, Port of Karachi, Pakistan (PAK ISSN 0075-5109) **8501**
Karachi University Journal of Science see Karachi Journal of Science **7874**
● Te Karaka (NZL ISSN 1173-6011) **7149**
Karakul (NAM) **291**
Karala Sabdam (IND) **3884**
Karamu (USA ISSN 0022-8990) **5317**
Karapuz (RUS) **4461**
Karascio (ITA ISSN 1828-2245) **6505**
Karate, Bushido (FRA ISSN 1243-3853) **8183**
Karate - Kung Fu Illustrated see Black Belt Magazine **8161**
Karavan (KAZ) **3902**
Karavan (SWE ISSN 1404-3874) **5317**
Karavan Istorii (RUS ISSN 1560-4233) **4979**
● Karavan-ROS (RUS) **3936**
Karbo (POL) **6468**
▼ Karbone (FRA ISSN 1955-6497) **447**
▼ ● Kardiagram (USA ISSN 1937-1667) **7658**
● Kardiochirurgia i Torakochirurgia Polska (POL ISSN 1731-5530) **5794**
● Kardiolog.pl (POL ISSN 1732-6273) **5794**
● ➤ Der Kardiologe (Online) (DEU ISSN 1864-9718) **5794**
Der Kardiologe (Online) see Der Kardiologe **5794**
● ➤ Kardiologia/Cardiology (SVK ISSN 1210-0048) **5794**
● ➤ Kardiologia Polska/Polish Heart Journal (POL ISSN 0022-9032) **5794**
➤ Kardiologia pre Prax (SVK ISSN 1336-3433) **5794**
† Kardiologie Assistenz (DEU ISSN 0938-7293) **8969**
● Kardiologie up2date (DEU ISSN 1611-6534) **5794**
Kardiologie v Primarni Peci (CZE ISSN 1802-1379) **5794**
Kardiologija/Cardiology (SRB ISSN 0352-9320) **5794**
● ➤ Kardiologiya/Cardiology (RUS ISSN 0022-9040) **5794**
➤ Kardiotechnik (DEU ISSN 0941-2670) **5794**
● ➤ Kardiovaskulaere Medizin/Medecine Cardiovasculaire (CHE ISSN 1423-5528) **5795**
➤ Kardiovaskulyarnaya Terapiya i Profilaktika/Cardiovascular Therapy and Prevention (RUS ISSN 1728-8800) **5795**
Karei Igaku Kenkyusho Zasshi (JPN ISSN 1340-3397) **5821**
Kareliya (RUS) **3936**
Karen Brown's Tuscany & Umbria (USA ISSN 1557-3702) **8727**
Karen Brown's U.S.A.: Pacific Northwest (USA ISSN 1539-9915) **8727**
● Karen's Kuntry Khronicle (USA) **536**
Karento Aweanesu/Current Awareness (JPN ISSN 0387-8007) **5022**
● Karento Aweanesu - E/Current Awareness - E (JPN ISSN 1347-7315) **5022**
Karento Terapi/Current Therapy (JPN ISSN 0287-8445) **5656**
Kar'era (RUS) **6700**
Kar'era - Kapital (RUS) **6700**
Karg-Elert-Gesellschaft. Mitteilungen (DEU ISSN 0179-9894) **6582**
● Karger Gazette (CHE ISSN 0451-4475) **5656**
Karibu (KEN) **8727**
Kariera see O Phileleftheros **3832**
Karinca (TUR ISSN 1300-1450) **1424**
Kariwenhawi (USA) **5022**
Karjala (FIN ISSN 0782-8764) **4236**
● Karjalainen (FIN ISSN 0358-1705) **3838**
Karkonosze (POL ISSN 1232-3535) **8727**
† Karl-Marx-Universitaet Leipzig. Mathematisch-Naturwissenschaftliche Reihe. Wissenschaftliche Zeitschrift (DDR ISSN 0300-0540) **8969**
Karl-May-Gesellschaft. Jahrbuch (DEU ISSN 0300-1989) **5317**
Karlebynejden (FIN ISSN 0783-6864) **4236**
Karlovacki Tjednik (HRV ISSN 0022-9059) **5222**
Karlsbader Zeitung (DEU) **3545**
Karlsruhe Programm (DEU) **3851**
Karlsruher Greif (DEU) **4511**
Karlsruher Juristische Bibliographie (DEU ISSN 0453-3283) **4823**
Karlsruher Kind (DEU) **2157**
➤ Karlsruher Paedagogische Beitraege (DEU ISSN 0724-5688) **3069**
Karlsruher Reihe (DEU ISSN 0947-7497) **4511**
Karlstad University Studies (SWE ISSN 1403-8099) **3956**
Karmakshetra (IND ISSN 0971-7765) **1691**
Karmasangsthaan (IND) **3884**
➤ Al-Karmil (ISR ISSN 0334-8547) **5317**
Karmyug Prakash (IND) **3884**
Karnatak University. College of Education. Journal (IND ISSN 0022-4979) **2880**
Karnatak University, Dharwad, India. Journal. Humanities (IND ISSN 0075-515X) **4461**
Karnatak University, Dharwad, India. Journal. Science (IND ISSN 0075-5168) **7874**

Title

Karnatak University, Dharwad, India. Journal. Social Sciences (IND ISSN 0075-5176) 7981
Karnataka Consumer Voice (IND) 2639
Karnataka. Department of Tourism. Annual Report (IND) 8727
Karnataka. Finance Department. Annual Report (IND) 1932
Karnataka Law Journal (IND ISSN 0022-9091) 4709
Karnataka Law Journal - Tribunal Supplement Covering Commercial Taxes (IND) 4709
Karnataka Medical Journal (IND ISSN 0377-9378) 5656
➤ Karnataka State Dental Journal (IND ISSN 0973-3442) 5854
Karogs (LVA ISSN 0132-6295) 5317
Karolina (SWE ISSN 1104-4632) 5656
➤ Karolinska Forbundets Aarsbok (SWE ISSN 0348-9833) 4236
▼ • ➤ Karpa (USA ISSN 1937-8572) 8472
Karpaten Jahrbuch (DEU) 4236
Die Karpatenpost (DEU ISSN 0022-9105) 3545
Karpatenrundschau (ROM ISSN 1222-8354) 3545
• Karriere (DEU) 6700
• Karriere (NOR ISSN 1504-498X) 6700
Karrierefuehrer Bauingenieure (DEU ISSN 1435-327X) 6700
Karrierefuehrer Finanzdienstleistungen (DEU ISSN 1435-3261) 6700
Karrierefuehrer Hochschulen (DEU ISSN 1435-1978) 6700
Karrierefuehrer Informationstechnologie (DEU ISSN 1436-2139) 6700
Karrierefuehrer Life Sciences (DEU) 6700
Karrierefuehrer Recht (DEU) 6700
Karshakan (IND) 130
Karshakasree (IND) 130
Karst Chronicle (USA ISSN 1533-9882) 2751
• Karst Waters Institute. Special Publications (USA) 2751
➤ Karstenia (FIN ISSN 0453-3402) 799
➤ Karstologia (FRA ISSN 0751-7688) 2751
Karstological Review *see* Acta Carsologica 2701
Kart and Superkart Magazine (GBR ISSN 0956-411X) 8260
Kart Magazine (AUS) 8183
• Kart Marketing International (USA ISSN 1070-2059) 8183
Kart & Bildteknik (SWE ISSN 1651-8705) 4018
➤ Kart og Plan (NOR ISSN 0047-3278) 4018
Kart Racer (USA) 8587
Kart Sport (USA ISSN 0744-5962) 8587
Karta (POL ISSN 0867-3764) 4237
Kartbladet *see* Kart & Bildteknik 4018
Kartefakt (DEU) 4337
Karten/Cards/Cartes (DEU ISSN 0937-597X) 1363
Karter News (USA ISSN 0096-3216) 8587
• ➤ Karthago (BEL ISSN 0453-3429) 402
• Karting Magazine (GBR ISSN 0022-913X) 8587
Kartofel' i Ovoshchi (RUS ISSN 0022-9148) 240
Der Kartoffelbau (DEU ISSN 0022-9156) 240
• Kartoffelproduktion (DNK ISSN 0900-0461) 240
• Kartograficheskaya Letopis' (RUS ISSN 0130-2086) 4036
• Kartografija i Geoinformacije (HRV ISSN 1333-896X) 4018
Kartografisch Tijdschrift (NLD ISSN 0167-5788) 4018
Kartographische Nachrichten (DEU ISSN 0022-9164) 4018
Kartographisches Taschenbuch (DEU ISSN 0936-5745) 4018
KartRacing (GBR) 8588
➤ Karunungan (PHL ISSN 0116-7073) 6930
Karupoeg Puhh (EST ISSN 1406-8834) 2196
Karwei *see* Karwei Management 1827
Karwei Management (NLD ISSN 1571-4276) 1827
Karyl Bannister's Cook & Tell *see* Cook & Tell 4354
Karyoku Genshiryoku Hatsuden/Thermal and Nuclear Power (JPN ISSN 0387-1029) 3176
Karys (LTU ISSN 0022-9199) 6430
Kaseki/Fossils (JPN ISSN 0022-9202) 6726
➤ Kaseki Kenkyukai Kaishi/Journal of Fossil Research (JPN ISSN 0387-1924) 6726
Kaseki no Tomo/Tokai Fossil Society. Journal (JPN ISSN 0389-3847) 6726
Kasen/Rivers (JPN ISSN 0287-9859) 8828
Kasen Dento Koho (JPN ISSN 0914-0654) 8828
Kasen Joho Kenkyujo Hokoku/Institute of River and Basin Integrated Communications. Report (JPN ISSN 0914-7861) 8828
Kasen Rebyu/Rivers Review (JPN ISSN 0910-0938) 8828
Kasetsart Journal (THA ISSN 0075-5192) 130
Kasetsart University. Faculty of Fisheries. Notes (THA ISSN 0125-7978) 3600
Kasetsart University. Fishery Research Bulletin (THA ISSN 0125-796X) 3600
Kashgar Teachers College. Journal *see* Kashi Shifan Xueyuan Xuebao 7981
• Kashi Shifan Xueyuan Xuebao/Kashgar Teachers College. Journal (CHN ISSN 1006-432X) 7981
Kashika Joho Gakkaishi *see* Kashika Jouhou Gakkai Rombunshuu Gappon 7874
Kashika Jouhou Gakkai Rombunshuu *see* Kashika Jouhou Gakkai Rombunshuu Gappon 7874
• Kashika Jouhou Gakkai Rombunshuu Gappon/Visualization Society of Japan. Transactions (JPN ISSN 1346-5252) 7874
▼ • Kashmir Affairs (GBR ISSN 1754-8381) 7249
Kashmir Affairs (IND ISSN 0022-9210) 554
Kashmir Journal of Geology (PAK) 2751
➤ Kashmir Journal of Language Research (PAK ISSN 1028-6640) 5136
Kashmir Report (USA) 3546
• Kashmir Times (IND) 3884
Kashrus Faxletter (USA) 3652
• Kashrus Magazine (USA ISSN 1074-3502) 3652
Kashruth Directory (CAN ISSN 0843-3402) 3652
Kashshafat al-Imarat/Emirates Boy Scouts (UAE) 2267
Kasikorn (THA ISSN 0125-3697) 130
Kasino A 4 (FIN ISSN 1796-0614) 499
Kaskade (Bilingual Edition) (DEU ISSN 1432-9085) 8184
• ➤ Kasmera (VEN ISSN 0075-5222) 5656
• Kaspahraster (USA) 5222
Kaspiets (RUS) 6430
Kassei *see* Energetic Life 2941
Kasseler Beitraege zur Vor- und Fruehgeschichte (DEU ISSN 1610-4234) 402
Kasseler Schriften zur Musik (DEU) 6582
Kasseler Sonntagsblatt (DEU ISSN 0022-9245) 7658
Kasseler Statistik (DEU ISSN 0451-4874) 7481
Kassenaerztliche Vereinigung Blatt *see* K V Blatt 5656
Der Kassenarzt (DEU ISSN 0723-5380) 5657
Kassenarztrecht (DEU) 5657
Kassenzahnaerztliche Vereinigung Bayerns Express *see* K Z V B Express 5854
Kasteeljuweel (NLD ISSN 1871-7012) 5425
Kasten vol Verhalen *see* Flauwekul voor Kids 8956
Kastner & Oehler Firmen Zeitung (AUT ISSN 0022-9253) 1890
Kasturi (IND ISSN 0022-9261) 3884
➤ Kasvatus/Finnish Journal of Education (FIN ISSN 0022-927X) 2880
Kasvatus ja Koti (FIN ISSN 1796-2420) 2880
De Kat (ZAF ISSN 0257-3377) 3949
• Katab: Index Analytique Bibliographique (MAR ISSN 1113-531X) 1247
➤ Katachi no Kagakkaiho/Society for Science on Form. Bulletin (JPN ISSN 0915-6089) 7874
• Katakansetsu/Shoulder Joint (JPN ISSN 0910-4461) 6066
Katalíku Pasaulis (LTU ISSN 0235-8050) 7802
Kataliz i Neftekhimiya (UKR) 6776
Kataliz v Promyshlennosti (RUS ISSN 1816-0387) 3249
• Katalog (DNK ISSN 0904-2334) 6970
Katalog der Schweizer Presse. Publikumszeitschriften, Spezial- und Hobbyzeitschriften, Fachzeitschriften/Catalogue de la Presse Suisse. Periodiques s'adressant au Grand Public, Journaux Specialises Loisirs et Passe-temps, Journaux Professionnels (CHE ISSN 1424-4128) 7578
Katalog der Tibetischen und Mongolischen Sachkultur in Europaeischen Museen und Privatsammlungen (DEU) 554
Katalog Distributor (DEU ISSN 1435-4853) 2010
Katalog Fauny Pasozytniczej Polski (POL ISSN 0075-5230) 953
Katalog Fauny Polski/Catalogus Faunae Poloniae (POL ISSN 0453-3623) 953
† • Katalog for Skolebiblioteker. Eleverne (DNK ISSN 0904-1893) 8969
† • Katalog for Skolebiblioteker. Skolebibliotekaren (DNK ISSN 0904-1907) 8969
• Katalog Induk Majalart/Union Catalog of Serials (IDN ISSN 0854-6711) 10
Katalog Knjiga Jugoslovenskih Izdavaca (SRB) 628
• Katalog Mediow Polskich (POL ISSN 1426-1480) 628
Katalog Pendidikan Profesional Berkelanjutan/The Indonesian Institute of Accountants Catalog (IDN) 1295
Katalog Radiatsionnykh Dannykh/Catalogue of Solar Radiation Data (RUS) 6359
Katalog Zabytkow Sztuki w Polsce (POL ISSN 0075-5257) 499
Katalogaktuellt *see* Produktaktuellt 2024
Kataloge der Praehistorischen Staatssammlung (DEU ISSN 0343-5210) 4237
Kataloge des Oberoesterreichische Landesmuseums (AUT ISSN 1018-6077) 6541
Katapult (USA ISSN 0791-9441) 5136
Katastorfmedicinska Organisationskommitten-Rapport Report *see* K A M E D O - Report 8052
† Katastrophenmedizin (BRD ISSN 0455-0250) 8969
Katayama Giho/Katayama Technical Report (JPN) 6319
Katayama Technical Report *see* Katayama Giho 6319
Kate Sharpley Library *see* K S L 7149
Katechetische Blaetter (DEU ISSN 0342-5517) 7803
Katedra (POL ISSN 1641-7046) 8900
• Katedra (SVN ISSN 0022-9296) 2289
Katei-Gaho *see* Home Graphic 4360
Kateigaho (International Edition) (JPN ISSN 1349-8746) 499
Kateiyaku Kenkyu/Research on Home Medicines (JPN ISSN 0289-4750) 6857
Kateketnytt (SWE ISSN 0282-0234) 7803
Katera i Yakhty (RUS ISSN 0320-9199) 8277
Kateri (CAN ISSN 0315-8020) 7803
Kates Kin (USA ISSN 0741-2045) 3772
Katha-Sahitya (IND ISSN 0022-9318) 5317
▼ Kath'auton (ESP ISSN 1888-0592) 6930
Kathauton *see* Kath'auton 6930
Katherine Asher Engel Lectures (USA ISSN 0075-5265) 4461
Katherine Times (AUS ISSN 1833-7783) 3795
Katherine's of Broadway Market (USA) 3652
• Kathie's Herb Page (USA) 3740
Kathimerini (GRC) 3874
• The Kathmandu Post Review of Books (NPL) 5222
Kathmandu Summer School Lecture Notes (SGP) 7024
• ➤ Kathmandu University Medical Journal (NPL ISSN 1812-2027) 5657
Katholiek Documentatie Centrum. Bronnen en Studies (NLD ISSN 0924-0640) 5022
Katholiek Documentatie Centrum Cursor *see* K D C Cursor 7802
† Katholiek Documentatie Centrum. Jaarboek (NLD ISSN 0168-602X) 8969
Het Katholiek Nieuwsblad (NLD ISSN 0168-244X) 7803
Katholieke PlattelandsJongeren Limburg Magazine *see* Virus 2947
Katholieke Radio Omroep Extra *see* K R O Extra 2384
Katholieke Radio Omroep Magazine *see* K R O Magazine 2384
Katholieke Vrouwenorganisatie nu *see* K V O.nu 7802
Katholische Arbeitnehmer-Bewegung Deutschlands Impuls *see* K A B Impuls 7802
Katholische Bildung (DEU ISSN 0343-4605) 7803
Katholische Fachhochschule Mainz. Schriftenreihe *see* K F H Mainz. Schriftenreihe 7802
Katholische Frauenbewegung Oesterreichs. Fuehrungsblatt (AUT ISSN 0022-9377) 7803
Der Katholische Mesner (DEU) 7803
Katholische Oeffentliche Buecherei *see* BiblioTheke 4996
Katholische Sonntagszeitung fuer das Bistum Augsburg (DEU ISSN 0945-859X) 7803
Katholische Sonntagszeitung fuer Deutschland (DEU) 7803
Katholische Universitaet Eichstaett. Vorlesungsverzeichnis (DEU) 2957
Katholischen Militaerbischof fuer die Deutsche Bundeswehr. Verordnungsblatt (DEU) 7803
Katholischer Berufsverband fuer Pflegeberufe. Mitteilungsblatt (DEU) 5657
Katholischer Digest *see* Christlicher Digest 7633
Katholischer Schweizerbauer (CHE) 130
Katholisches Leben und Kirchenreform im Zeitalter der Glaubensspaltung (DEU ISSN 0170-7302) 7803
Katholisches Sonntagsblatt (DEU ISSN 0179-7395) 7803
Katikati Advertiser (NZL ISSN 1170-0610) 3917
Katilolehti/Tidskrift foer Barnmorskor (FIN ISSN 0022-9415) 5997
Katja (DEU) 6639
Katka (CZE ISSN 1211-1546) 8870
Katka Krizovky (CZE) 8184
Katka Special *see* Nas Utulny Byt 4561
Katka Ucesy (CZE) 589
Katolicka Jednota Zen Texaskych News *see* K J Z T News 2267
Katolicki Uniwersytet Lubelski. Wydzial Filozoficzny. Rozprawy (POL) 6930
Katolicki Uniwersytet Lubelski. Wydzial Historyczno-Filologiczny. Rozprawy (POL) 4150
Katolicki Uniwersytet Lubelski. Wydzial Nauk Spolecznych. Rozprawy (POL) 7981
Katolicki Uniwersytet Lubelski. Wydzial Teologiczno-Kanoniczny. Rozprawy (POL) 7803
Katolicki Uniwersytet Lubelski. Zeszyty Naukowe (POL ISSN 0044-4405) 7803
• Katolsk Orientering (DNK ISSN 0902-297X) 7803
Katolsk Ungdom *see* Q Katolsk Ungdom 7813
Katolski Posol (DEU ISSN 0138-2543) 7803
Katolskt Magasin (SWE ISSN 1402-3385) 7803
Katorikku Kenkyu (JPN ISSN 0387-3005) 7803
Katrien (NLD) 2196
Katsaus (FIN ISSN 1795-2131) 5222
Katso (FIN ISSN 0355-2969) 2384
Katsu/Japan Institute of Traditional Medicine. News (JPN ISSN 0912-0718) 312
Katte-Journalen *see* Hunde-Journalen - Katte-Journalen 6809
KattenManieren (NLD) 6810
Kattenwereld (NLD ISSN 1383-7451) 6810
Katzen Extra (DEU ISSN 0176-4853) 6810
Katzen Magazin (CHE ISSN 1423-6869) 6810
Katzenauge (CHE ISSN 1022-3770) 8260
Katzenschutz Korrespondenz (DEU) 320
Kauai, a Paradise Family Guide *see* Paradise Family Guides: Kauai 8746
Kauai Drive Guide *see* Oahu Drive Guide 8742
Kauai Drive Guide *see* Hawaii Drive Guide 8717
Kauai Update (USA ISSN 0898-1418) 8727
• Kauai Visitor (USA) 8727
• ➤ Kauchuk i Rezina (RUS ISSN 0022-9466) 7825
Kaufhaus und Warenhaus (DEU ISSN 0022-9474) 1430
Kaufmaennische Krankenkasse - Hauptverwaltung Nachrichten *see* K K H Nachrichten 4511
Kaufmaennische Schule (DEU ISSN 0724-7613) 2880
Kaukasienstudien/Caucasian Studies (DEU) 4237
• Kaukolampotilasto (FIN ISSN 0786-4809) 3153
Kaukomieli (FIN) 4237
Kaunas In Your Pocket (LTU ISSN 1392-0065) 8727
Kauneus ja Terveys (FIN ISSN 0047-3308) 589
Kaunseringu Kenkyu/Japanese Journal of Counseling Science (JPN ISSN 0914-8337) 7382
Kauperts Deutschland Reisefuehrer (DEU ISSN 0945-1498) 8727
➤ Kaupia (DEU ISSN 0941-8482) 7875
• Kauppalehti (FIN ISSN 0451-5560) 1139
Kauppalehti Optio *see* Kauppalehti Presso 1139
Kauppalehti Optio *see* Kauppalehti 1139
• Kauppalehti Presso (FIN ISSN 1795-3030) 1139
Kaupparekisterilehti/Handelsregistertidning (FIN ISSN 0789-4767) 6753
Kauppatieteiden Osaston Tutkimuksia/Studies in Business Administration (FIN ISSN 1457-1447) 1139
• Kaupunkilehti Ankkuri (FIN ISSN 1796-329X) 3838
Kauzar (IRN ISSN 1025-5346) 7713
Kav P'nim (ISR) 2289
Kavalan Journal of Medicine *see* Lanyang Yizhi 5660
Kavallo (CHE ISSN 1420-5696) 8294
Kaviamuthu (IND ISSN 0022-9539) 3884
Kavita (IND ISSN 0022-9547) 5425
Kavita Asia/Asian Identities (IND) 5425
Kavitha (USA) 5425
Kavkasioni (GEO) 3843
Kavkazskaya Khronika (RUS) 3936
➤ Kavkazskii Entomologicheskii Bulleten'/Caucasian Entomological Bulletin (RUS ISSN 1814-3326) 853
➤ Kavya Bharati (IND) 5425
Kawa to Hakimono/Leather & Footwears (JPN) 4973
Kawada Giho/Kawada Technical Report (JPN ISSN 0289-8705) 3369
Kawada Technical Report *see* Kawada Giho 3369
Kawaii (DEU) 499
• Kawaii (POL ISSN 1428-5894) 2478
• Kawakatsu & Sasaki's Webpages on Planarians, Sapporo and Tokyo (Online) (JPN ISSN 1348-3412) 685
Kawanku (IDN) 8870
Kawasaki Igakkai Shi (JPN ISSN 0386-5924) 5657
Kawasaki Juko Giho/Kawasaki Technical Review (JPN ISSN 0387-7906) 3369
Kawasaki Medical Journal (JPN ISSN 0385-0234) 5657
Kawasaki Municipal Hospital. Annual Report *see* Kawasaki Shiritsu Kawasaki Byoin Nenpo 4104
Kawasaki Municipal Ida Hospital. Annual Report *see* Kawasaki Shiritsu Ida Byoin Nenpo 4104
Kawasaki Shiritsu Ida Byoin Nenpo/Kawasaki Municipal Ida Hospital. Annual Report (JPN) 4104
Kawasaki Shiritsu Kawasaki Byoin Nenpo/Kawasaki Municipal Hospital. Annual Report (JPN) 4104
Kawasaki Steel Technical Report *see* J F E Technical Report 6318
Kawasaki Technical Review *see* Kawasaki Juko Giho 3369
Kayak (CAN ISSN 1712-3984) 2196
Kayak Magazine (USA ISSN 1527-4985) 8277
Kayak New Zealand (NZL) 8277
Kayak Touring *see* Complete Guide to Kayak Touring 8274
Kayaku Gakkaishi/Japan Explosives Society. Journal *see* Science and Technology of Energetic Materials 3255
Kayhan (IRN ISSN 0885-8179) 3891
Kayhan (Turkish Edition) (IRN) 3891
Kayhan al-Arabi (IRN ISSN 0885-8187) 3912
Kayhan Andisheh (IRN ISSN 1023-3687) 6930
Kayhan-e Bacheha/Children's World (IRN ISSN 1023-182X) 2196
Kayhan Elmi (IRN ISSN 1023-2079) 7875
Kayhan Farhangi (IRN ISSN 1023-0289) 5222
Kayhan-i Andishah *see* Kayhan Andisheh 6930
Kayhan-i Hava'i (IRN ISSN 1023-0815) 3891
Kayhan-i Hava'i (N. American edition) *see* Kayhan-i Hava'i 3891
Kayhan-i Sal/Kayhan Yearbook (IRN) 4322
Kayhan International (IRN ISSN 0885-8160) 3891
Kayhan Karikatur (IRN ISSN 1023-0270) 5222
Kayhan Urdu (IRN) 3891
Kayhan Varzeshi (IRN ISSN 1024-9842) 8184
Kayhan Yearbook *see* Kayhan-i Sal 4322
Kayikalokam (IND) 8184
• Kaytannon Laakari (FIN ISSN 0355-1075) 6857
Kaytannon Maamies (FIN ISSN 0022-9571) 130
Kaytannon Maamies Vet *see* K M Vet 129
Kazakh Adebieti (KAZ) 5317
Kazakhstan Aielderi (KAZ) 7981
• Kazakhstan Energy Monthly (GBR) 6776
• Kazakhstan Freight Transport Report (GBR ISSN 1752-7899) 8501
▼ • Kazakhstan Insurance Report (GBR ISSN 1752-8275) 4511
▼ • Kazakhstan Mining Report (GBR ISSN 1755-7836) 6468
Kazakhstan Respublikasy Gylym Zane Zogary Bilim Ministrliginin. Kazakhstan Respublikasy Ulttyk Gylym Akademiasynyn Khabarlary. Seriya Biologicheskaya i Meditsinskaya (KAZ ISSN 1682-4393) 685
Kazakhstan Sarbazy (KAZ) 6430
Kazakhstan Zhogary Mektebi (KAZ) 2880
• Kazakhstanskaya Pravda (KAZ ISSN 0233-3414) 3902
Kazakstan Geologiasy/Geology of Kazakhstan *see* Kazakstan Respublikasynyn Ulttyk Gylym Akademiasynyn Khabarlary. Geologialyk Seriasy 2751

Kazakstan Respublikasy Ulttyk Gylym Akademiasynyn Khabarlary. Seriya Khimicheskaya/Natsionalnaya Akademiya Nauk Respubliki Kazakhstan. Izvestiya. Seriya Khimicheskaya (KAZ ISSN 1025-9341) 2069
Kazakstan Respublikasyny Gylym Akademiasynyn Baandamalary/Republic of Kazakhstan. Ministry of Sciences and Higher Education. National Academy of Sciences. Reports (KAZ ISSN 1682-4296) 7875
Kazakstan Respublikasynyn Gylym Ministrligi. Gylym Akademiasynyn Khabarlary. Seriya Obshchestvennykh Nauk (KAZ ISSN 1029-8657) 7981
Kazakstan Respublikasynyn Ulttyk Gylym Akademiasynyn Khabarlary. Geologialyk Seriasy/National Academy of Sciences of the Republic of Kazakhstan. Geology Series (KAZ ISSN 1810-8776) 2751
Kazaliste (HRV) 8472
Kazan *see* Volcanological Society of Japan. Bulletin 2791
Kazan' (RUS ISSN 0869-6616) 4461
Kazan Funka Yochi Renrakukai Kaiho/Coordinating Committee for Prediction of Volcanic Eruption. Report (JPN ISSN 0389-9713) 2786
Kazan Hokoku/Japan Meteorological Agency (JPN ISSN 0447-3892) 2786
Kazan Medical Journal *see* Kazanskii Meditsinskii Zhurnal 5657
Kazan Utlary (RUS ISSN 0206-4189) 4461
Kazanskii Gosudarstvennyi Pedagogicheskii Institut. Voprosy Istorii, Teorii Muzyki i Muzykal'nogo Vospitaniya. Sbornik (RUS) 6582
Kazanskii Meditsinskii Zhurnal/Kazan Medical Journal (RUS ISSN 0368-4814) 5657
Kazanskii Universitet. Sbornik Aspirantskikh Rabot: Teoriya Plastin i Obolochek (RUS) 3207
Kaze ni Kansuru Shinpojumu Koen Yoshishu/Proceedings of the Wind Symposium (JPN) 6359
Kazi/Sail and Powerboat Magazine (JPN ISSN 0389-1771) 8277
Kazi Sonuclari Toplantisi (TUR ISSN 1017-7655) 402
Kazimierz (POL ISSN 1641-4608) 3930
Kazoku Shakaigaku Kenkyu/Japanese Journal of Family Sociology (JPN ISSN 0916-328X) 7981
Kazoku Shinrigaku Kenkyu/Japanese Journal of Family Psychology (JPN ISSN 0915-0625) 7382
• Kazokusei Shuyo (JPN ISSN 1346-1052) 6026
kbbreview *see* K B B Review 4559
Ke Xue (CHN ISSN 1002-1299) 7875
▼ Kea Conservation Trust. Newsletter (NZL ISSN 1177-8571) 2616
Keadaan Angakatan Kerja de Indonesia: Angka Sementara *see* Labour Force Situation in Indonesia: Preliminary Figures 1248
Keadilan (IDN ISSN 0215-4757) 4709
▼ The Kean Review (USA ISSN 1936-2021) 5317
Kearsarge Magazine (USA) 3979
• Keating on J C T Contracts (Joint Contracts Tribunal) (GBR) 1019
Keatinge and Conaway on Choice of Business Entity (USA ISSN 1941-8132) 1890
➤ Keats - Shelley Journal (USA ISSN 0453-4387) 5425
Keats - Shelley Review (GBR ISSN 0952-4142) 5317
Keche Jishu/Coach Technology (CHN ISSN 1006-6861) 8588
• ➤ Kecheng - Jiaocai - Jiaofa/Curriculum, Teaching Materials, and Method (CHN ISSN 1000-0186) 3069
Kecheng Luntan *see* Curriculum Forum 2976
➤ Keel ja Kirjandus (EST ISSN 0131-1441) 5136
Keele European Research Centre. Working Papers (GBR) 7249
Keele Papers in Geriatric Medicine and Gerontology (GBR ISSN 1365-9898) 4050
Keemat (IND) 2639
Keen Ager News (USA) 4050
Keeneland (USA) 8294
Keep Left! (ZAF) 7149
• Keep on Truckin' News (USA ISSN 1539-6142) 8671
• Keep On Truckin' Re-Visited (USA ISSN 1097-4156) 8116
Keep Tahoe Blue (USA) 3449
Keep Up to Date on Accounts Payable (USA ISSN 1098-0202) 1295
Keep Up to Date on Family Medicine Coding & Reimbursement (USA ISSN 1545-732X) 4511
Keep Up to Date on Internal Medicine Coding & Reimbursement (USA ISSN 1542-2488) 5947
Keep Up to Date on Payroll (USA ISSN 1076-3309) 1295
Keep Up to Date on Pediatric Coding & Reimbursement (USA ISSN 1540-6105) 4511
▼ • Keep Well (NZL ISSN 1177-5386) 8052
Keeper's Log (USA ISSN 0883-0061) 4150
• Keeping Good Companies (AUS ISSN 1444-7614) 1770
Keeping Place, Keeping Pace (USA) 6527
Keeping Track (CAN ISSN 0453-4441) 8619
Keeping Track (ZAF) 3449
Keepsake Calendar (USA) 6639
Keesing Journal of Documents & Identity (NLD ISSN 1871-272X) 2515
Keesing's Journal of Documents *see* Keesing Journal of Documents & Identity 2515
• Keesing's Record of World Events (USA ISSN 0950-6128) 7200
Keewatin Community College. Annual Report *see* University College of the North. Annual Report 3008
Keezette (USA) 6810
Kehilwenyane (ZAF ISSN 0022-9687) 7803
Kehittyvae Kauppa (FIN ISSN 0783-5167) 1827
▼ • Kehitysvammaliitto. Selvityksia (FIN ISSN 1797-0474) 6157
Kehitysvammaliitto. Tutkimuksia/Finnish Association on Intellectual and Developmental Disabilities. Studies (FIN ISSN 1797-0466) 8052
The Kehrer Report (USA) 1363
Kehuan Shijie/Science Fiction World (CHN ISSN 1003-7055) 5444
Kei Mercury (ZAF) 3949
Keichitsu (JPN ISSN 0913-9613) 853
Keidanren Clip (JPN) 1495
Keidanren Review (JPN ISSN 0022-9695) 1139
Keidanren Shiryo (JPN) 1495
Keiei Joho Kenkyu *see* Setsunan University. Journal of Business Administration and Information 1173
Keiei Shigaku/Japan Business History Review (JPN ISSN 0386-9113) 1139
Keieijoho Gakubu Ronshu *see* Chubu University. College of Business Administration and Information Science. Journal 1083
Keihatsu *see* Enlightenment 2941
Keiho Zasshi *see* Journal of Criminal Law 4892
• Keikinzoku (JPN ISSN 0451-5994) 6319
Keikinzoku Kogyo Tokei Nenpo/Light Metal Statistics in Japan (JPN ISSN 0451-6001) 6340
Keikinzoku Yosetsu/Journal of the Light Metal Welding & Construction (JPN ISSN 0368-5306) 6320
Keikotai Dogakkai Koen Yoko/Phosphor Research Society. Preprints of Meeting (JPN) 2111
Keikyu Aburatsubo Marin Paku Suizokukan Nenpo/Keikyu Aburatsubo Marine Park Aquarium. Annual Report (JPN) 3600
Keikyu Aburatsubo Marine Park Aquarium. Annual Report *see* Keikyu Aburatsubo Marin Paku Suizokukan Nenpo 3600
Keilor Messenger *see* Brimbank Leader 3793
Keilschrifttexte aus Boghazkoi (DEU) 402
Keio Business Review (JPN ISSN 0453-4557) 1139
Keio Communications Review (JPN ISSN 0388-7596) 7981
➤ Keio Economic Studies (JPN ISSN 0022-9709) 1139
Keio Gijuku Daigaku Hiyoshi Kiyo. Shizen Kagaku/Hiyoshi Review of Natural Science (JPN ISSN 0911-7237) 7875
Keio Gijuku Daigaku Rikogakubuho (JPN) 8430
Keio Igaku/Keio Medical Society. Journal *see* Keio Journal of Medicine 5657
• ➤ Keio Journal of Medicine (JPN ISSN 0022-9717) 5657
Keio Law Review (JPN ISSN 0389-116X) 4709
Keio Monographs of Business and Commerce (JPN ISSN 0075-5346) 1139
Keio University Bulletin (JPN ISSN 0910-1381) 2991
Keio University. Faculty of Science and Technology. Department of Mathematics. Research Report (JPN) 5507
Keio University. International Symposia for Life Sciences and Medicine (JPN) 5657
➤ Keiraku Chiryo/Japanese Society of Acupuncture. Journal (JPN) 312
Keiryo Kenkyusho Hokoku/National Research Laboratory of Metrology. Reports *see* Sansouken Keiryou Hyoujun Houkoku 6406
➤ Keiryo Kokugo Gaku/Mathematical Linguistics (JPN) 5136
Keisan Denki Denshi Kogaku Shinpojumu Ronbunshu/J S S T Symposium on Calculations in Electrical and Electronics Engineering. Proceedings (JPN) 3323
Keisan Kogaku (JPN ISSN 1341-7622) 3293
Keisan Kogaku Koenkai Ronbunshu/Conference on Computational Engineering and Science. Proceedings (JPN ISSN 1342-145X) 3293
Keisan Rikigaku Shinpojumu Hobunshu/Symposium on Computational Mechanics (JPN) 7060
Keisanki Tokeigaku/Bulletin of the Computational Statistics of Japan (JPN ISSN 0914-8930) 8384
Keisei Geka *see* Japanese Journal of Plastic & Reconstructive Surgery 6247
Keisha Kino Zairyo Shinpojumu Koenshu/Symposium of Functionally Gradient Materials Forum. Proceedings (JPN) 8430
Keiso/Instrumentation (Tokyo) (JPN ISSN 0368-5780) 4488
Keisoku Gijutsu/Instrumentation and Automation (JPN ISSN 0385-9886) 2462
Keisoku Jido Seigyo Gakkai Ronbunshu/Society of Instrument and Control Engineers. Transactions (JPN ISSN 0453-4654) 3207
Keisoku to Seigyo/Society of Instrument and Control Engineers. Journal (JPN ISSN 0453-4662) 6403
• Keith & Kin (USA ISSN 1946-0937) 3772
▼ Keith Martin's Corvette Market (USA ISSN 1939-6481) 8588
➤ Keizai Kagaku/Economic Science (JPN ISSN 0022-9725) 1139
Keizai Kagaku Ronshu/Shimane University. Faculty of Law and Literature. Memoirs (JPN ISSN 0387-7310) 1139
Keizai Kenkyu/Economic Review (Tokyo, 1950) (JPN ISSN 0022-9733) 1140
Keizai-Kyoryoku Series *see* Economic Cooperation Series 1595
Keizai Riron/Wakayama Economic Review (JPN ISSN 0451-6222) 1770
Keizai Ronso *see* Economic Review (Kyoto) 1100
Keizai Shirin/Hosei University Economic Review (JPN ISSN 0022-9741) 1140
Keizaigaku Kenkyu (Sapporo)/Economic Studies (JPN ISSN 0451-6265) 1140
Keizaigaku Kenkyu (Tokyo)/Journal of Political Economy (JPN ISSN 0022-975X) 1140
Keizaigaku Ronsan/Journal of Economics (JPN ISSN 0453-4778) 1140
Keizaigaku Ronshu/Journal of Economics (JPN ISSN 0022-9768) 1140
Keizaigakushi Gakkai Nenpo/Society for the History of Social and Economic Thought. Annual Bulletin (JPN ISSN 0453-4786) 1546
Keizaijin (JPN ISSN 0910-8858) 1140
Keizaikai (JPN) 1140
• Keji Chao/Science & Culture Science-Tech Waves (CHN ISSN 1004-8200) 7875
• Keji Daobao/Science and Technology Herald (CHN ISSN 1000-7857) 7875
➤ Keji Fazhan Biaogan/Benchmarking Sci-Tech Development (TWN ISSN 1680-2314) 7875
Keji Fazhan yu Gaige/Science and Technology Development and Reform *see* Keji Chao 7875
Keji Guanli/Management of Science and Technology (CHN ISSN 1000-1629) 1770
• ➤ Keji Guanli Yanjiu/Science and Technology Management Research (CHN ISSN 1000-7695) 7875
• ➤ Keji Jinbu yu Duice/Science & Technology Progress and Policy (CHN ISSN 1001-7348) 7875
Keji Qingbao Shichang/Information Market of Science and Technology (CHN) 5022
Keji Ribao/Science & Technology Daily (CHN) 7875
▼ Keji Shangpin/Premiere (CHN ISSN 1674-1064) 3107
• Keji Tongbao/Bulletin of Science and Technology (CHN ISSN 1000-7119) 7875
Keji, Yiliao yu Shehui/Taiwanese Journal of Studies for Science, Technology, and Medicine (TWN) 7875
• Keji Yingyu Xuexi/English of Science and Technology Learning (CHN ISSN 1006-5822) 5136
• Keji yu Chuban/Science Technology and Publication (CHN ISSN 1005-0590) 7564
• Keji yu Falu/Science, Technology and Law (CHN ISSN 1003-9945) 4709
• Keji yu Guanli/Science-Technology and Management (CHN ISSN 1008-7133) 1770
• Kejiao Wenhui (CHN ISSN 1672-7894) 2880
Kek Mama (NLD) 2157
Kekal Abadi (MYS ISSN 0127-2578) 5022
Kekkaku/Tuberculosis (JPN ISSN 0022-9776) 6215
Kekkan/Japanese Journal of Circulation Research (JPN ISSN 0911-4637) 5795
Kekkan Igaku/Vascular Biology & Medicine (JPN ISSN 1345-9031) 5795
Kekkan to Naihi/Blood Vessel & Endothelium *see* Kekkan Igaku 5795
• Kelan Sanomat (FIN) 4511
Keleti Tanulmanyok/Oriental Studies (HUN ISSN 0133-6193) 554
➤ Kelk - Mahnamah-i Farhangi va Hunari/Kelk - Review of Arts and Culture (IRN ISSN 1017-415X) 5222
Kelk - Review of Arts and Culture *see* Kelk - Mahnamah-i Farhangi va Hunari 5222
Kell-e-y Kinsfolk (USA) 3772
Keller's Compliance Focus (USA ISSN 1087-853X) 6680
Keller's Construction Regulatory Update (USA ISSN 1069-3297) 1019
Keller's Hazardous Materials Transportation Report (USA ISSN 1041-8296) 8672
Keller's Industrial Safety Report *see* Keller's Workplace Safety Advisor 6680
Keller's O S H A Safety Training Newsletter (Occupational Safety & Health Administration) (USA ISSN 1077-7008) 6680
Keller's Safety Management Today Newsletter (USA ISSN 1090-3445) 6680
Keller's Transportation Recruiting and Retention Insights (USA ISSN 1092-1788) 8672
Keller's Transportation Safety Training Newsletter (USA ISSN 1082-104X) 8501
• Keller's Workplace Safety Advisor (USA ISSN 1931-7638) 6680
Kelley Blue Book Auto Price Manual *see* Kelley Blue Book New Car Price Manual 8588
Kelley Blue Book Auto Residential Guide (USA ISSN 1932-6351) 8588
Kelley Blue Book New Car Price Manual (USA ISSN 0897-6171) 8588
Kelley Blue Book. Residual Value Guide *see* Kelley Blue Book Auto Residential Guide 8588
▼ Kello ja Koru Maailma (FIN ISSN 1797-3201) 4567
Kello & Kulta/Watch and Goldsmith Branch (FIN ISSN 1457-3768) 4567
Kellon - Haukiputaan Kotiseutujulkaisu (FIN ISSN 0786-8456) 4237
Kelly Observer *see* Kelly U S A Observer 6430
Kelly U S A Observer (USA) 6430
• Kelly's Industrial Directory (GBR ISSN 1467-1220) 2010
• Kelly's Industrial Pages (GBR ISSN 1467-1239) 2010
➤ Kelsey Review (USA ISSN 0451-6338) 5317
Kelso Courier (USA) 4300
Keltia (FRA ISSN 0022-9792) 6930
Keltic Fringe (USA ISSN 1057-7475) 3546
Keluarga (IDN) 4362
• Kelvin Magazine (USA) 5444
Kemerovo (RUS) 3936
• Kemia - Kemi/Finnish Chemical Journal (FIN ISSN 0355-1628) 2069
A Kemia Ujabb Eredmenyei (HUN ISSN 0075-5397) 2069
• ➤ Kemija u Industriji (HRV ISSN 0022-9830) 3249
Kemikalier (SWE) 2069
Kemira *see* Just Add 3249
Kemisk Tidskrift *see* Kemivaerlden, Biotech, Kemisk Tidskrift 2070
Kemisten *see* Luonnontieteiden Akateemiset 2072
Kemisti *see* Luonnontieteiden Akateemiset 2072
Kemistin Kalenteri (FIN ISSN 0356-7818) 2069
Kemivaerlden *see* Kemivaerlden, Biotech, Kemisk Tidskrift 2070
Kemivaerlden. Biotech *see* Kemivaerlden, Biotech, Kemisk Tidskrift 2070
• Kemivaerlden, Biotech, Kemisk Tidskrift (SWE ISSN 1653-5596) 2070
Kemp & Kemp: Personal Injury Law, Practice and Procedure *see* Personal Injury Law, Practice and Procedure 4840
Kemp & Kemp: The Quantum of Damages *see* Quantum of Damages 4841
Kemp News (GBR ISSN 1750-4317) 4834
Kemper Magazine (USA) 4511
† Kempe's Engineers Year-Book (GBR ISSN 0075-5400) 8969
• Kempffiana (BOL ISSN 1991-4652) 953
Kempinski Journal (DEU) 4392
Kemps Film, Television, Commercials (UK Edition) *see* Kemps Film, Television, Commercials Production Services Handbook (UK & Republic of Ireland Edition) 6505
Kemps Film, Television, Commercials Production Services Handbook (UK & Republic of Ireland Edition) (GBR ISSN 1754-8489) 6505
Kemps Film, TV & Video Handbook (UK Edition) *see* Kemps Film, Television, Commercials Production Services Handbook (UK & Republic of Ireland Edition) 6505
Kemps Licensed House Purchasing Guide (GBR ISSN 1460-048X) 7597
Kemps Local Authority and Public Service Buyers' Guide (GBR) 7495
• Ken Blanchard's Profiles of Success (USA ISSN 1085-0082) 8116
Ken Chun Ni (CHN) 5317
Ken Coleman's The Fed Tracker *see* The Fed Tracker 1109
Ken Ring's Predict Weather Almanac and Isobaric Maps (NZL ISSN 1177-651X) 6359
Ken Uzelve (NLD ISSN 1573-5699) 7658
Kena (MEX) 3909
Kenchiku Bunka/Architectural Culture (JPN ISSN 0003-8490) 447
Kenchiku Kenkyu Shiryo/Building Reserch Data (JPN ISSN 0286-4630) 1019
Kenchiku Kenkyujo Nenpo/Building Research Institute. Annual Report (JPN ISSN 0286-4622) 1019
Kenchiku no Gijutsu *see* Seko 1035
Kenchiku Setsubi to Haikan Koji/Heating Piping & Air Conditioning (JPN ISSN 0385-9851) 4122
Kenchiku Techo/Architect (JPN) 447
Kencho Kiroku/Tidal Record (JPN) 2810
Kenchreai. Eastern Port of Corinth (NLD ISSN 1874-5431) 402
Kendall Whaling Museum Newsletter *see* K W M Newsletter 6527
Kendo Nippon *see* Gekkan Kendo Nippon 8175
Kenko/Health (JPN) 6991
Kenko Shinrigaku Kenkyu/Japanese Journal of Health Psychology (JPN ISSN 0917-3323) 7382
Kenkou Sangyou Shinbun/The Health Industry News (JPN) 4104
• Kenkou Sangyou Sokuhou/Health Industry Flash News (JPN) 4104
Kenkyu Gijutsu Keikaku/Journal of Science Policy and Research Management (JPN ISSN 0914-7020) 1770
Kenkyu Happyokai Koen Ronbunshu - Energi, Shigen Kenkyukai/Japan Society of Energy and Resources. Proceedings of the Meeting (JPN ISSN 0914-112X) 3141
Kenkyu Jisshi Gaikyo Hokokusho/Summary Report of Fluid Power Technology (JPN) 3387
Kenkyu Josei Jigyo Josei Kenkyu Seika Hokoku Gaiyo/Sound Technology Promotion Foundation. Research Report (JPN) 7088
Kenkyu Kiyo. Jinbun Kagaku, Shizen Kagaku-hen *see* Kobe Shoin Joshi Gakuin Daigaku, Kobe Shoin Joshi Gakuin Tanki Daigaku. Gakujutsu Kenkyukai. Kenkyu Kiyo. Jinbun Kagaku, Shizen Kagaku-hen 4462
Kenkyu Shuroku (JPN) 2880
Kenkyu-Sosho *see* I D E Research Series 1120
Kenkyujoho (JPN ISSN 0917-818X) 7658
Kenkyujoho - Musashi Kogyo Daigaku Genshiryoku Kenkyujo *see* Musashi Kogyo Daigaku. Genshiryoku Kenkyujo. Kenkyujoho 3171

Title

10524 KENKYUKAI.KENKYU KIYO. IPPAN KYOIKU, GAIKOKUGO, HOKEN ULRICH'S PERIODICALS

Kenkyukai.Kenkyu Kiyo. Ippan Kyoiku, Gaikokugo, Hoken Taiiku *see* Nihon Daigaku. Keizaigaku Kenkyukai.Kenkyu Kiyo. Ippan Kyoiku, Gaikokugo, Hoken Taiiku **2892**
Kenkyukai Shiryo Shirizu/Japan Society for Software Science and Technology. Internet Conference. Proceedings. (JPN ISSN 1341-870X) **2593**
• Kenkyuu Chousa Houkokusho (CD-ROM)/Telecommunications Advancement Foundation. Research Report (JPN ISSN 1346-0404) **2330**
Kenkyuu Kyouiku Katsudou Houkoku *see* Tokei Suri Kenkyujo Kenkyuu Kyouiku Katsudou Houkoku **8409**
Kenmerken *see* Toets **7543**
• ➤ Kennedy Institute of Ethics Journal (USA ISSN 1054-6863) **5657**
Kennedy Institute of Ethics. Scope Note (USA) **5657**
• ➤ Kennedy School Review (USA ISSN 1535-0215) **7449**
Kennedy's Confection (GBR ISSN 1474-3841) **3674**
Kennedy's Confectionery Buyers' Guide (GBR ISSN 1746-1812) **3674**
Kennel and Cattery Management (GBR) **6810**
Kennel Club Yearbook (GBR ISSN 0305-442X) **6810**
Kennel Gazette (GBR ISSN 0022-9962) **6810**
Kennemer Kroniek *see* N H A Nieuws **407**
Kenneth Burke Journal *see* K B Journal **5316**
The Kenneth E Naylor Memorial Lecture Series in South Slavic Linguistics (USA ISSN 1933-6713) **5136**
Kennis! (NLD ISSN 1872-1869) **7875**
Kennis en Economie/The Knowledge-based Economy (NLD ISSN 1384-6973) **8430**
Kennis in Kaart *see* H O O P **2983**
Kenpo Nyusu (JPN ISSN 0022-989X) **4511**
Kenrail (KEN) **8619**
Kensa Gijutsu/Inspection Engineering (JPN ISSN 1342-9825) **3207**
Kensa to Gijutsu/Modern Medical Laboratory (JPN ISSN 0301-2611) **5907**
Kensetsu Gijutsu Shinbun/Construction Engineering News (JPN) **3277**
Kensetsu Gyokai *see* C E Kensetsu Gyoukai **3261**
Kensetsu Hakusho/White Paper of Construction Works (JPN) **1019**
Kensetsu Kikai/Construction Machinery and Equipment (JPN ISSN 0385-9878) **5454**
Kensetsu Kikai Doko Chosa Hokoku/Annual Report of Construction Machinery and Equipment (JPN) **1019**
Kensetsu Kikai Jouhou (JPN) **1019**
Kensetsu Kikaika Kenkyujo Nenpo/Construction Method and Machinery Research Institute. Annual Report (JPN ISSN 0388-4066) **1019**
Kensetsu Kikaikai Kenkyujo Seino Shiken Hokoku/Japanese Construction Method and Machinery Research Institute. Report of Performance Tests (JPN) **1019**
Kensetsu Kogaku Kenkyu Shinkokai Nenpo/Society for the Promotion of Construction Engineering. Annual Report (JPN ISSN 0288-9994) **3277**
Kensetsu Konsarutantsu Kyokai Kinki Shibu Gyomu Kenkyu Happyokai Ronshu/Japan Civil Engineering Consultants Association. Kinki Branch. Reports of the Annual Research Conference (JPN) **3277**
Kensetsu no Kikaika/Construction Mechanization (JPN ISSN 0285-5453) **5454**
Kensetsu Tokei Geppo/Monthly of Construction Statistics (JPN ISSN 0916-653X) **1047**
Kenshin Jiho/Quarterly Journal of Seismology (JPN ISSN 1342-5684) **2786**
Kent Alumni (USA) **2289**
Kent Archaeological Rescue Unit. Special Subject Series (GBR ISSN 1365-4055) **402**
Kent Archaeological Review (GBR ISSN 0023-0014) **402**
Kent Archaeological Society. Newsletter (GBR) **402**
Kent Business (GBR ISSN 0968-8684) **3867**
Kent Collector (USA ISSN 0163-1861) **500**
Kent English News *see* K E N **2289**
Kent Farmer (GBR ISSN 0023-0022) **130**
Kent Field Club. Bulletin (GBR ISSN 0140-9565) **2712**
Kent Field Club. Newsletter (GBR) **2712**
Kent Field Club. Transactions (GBR ISSN 0141-1225) **2712**
Kent History Project (GBR ISSN 1352-805X) **4237**
Kent Life (GBR ISSN 0023-0030) **3867**
Kent Messenger (GBR ISSN 0964-1351) **3867**
Kent Monograph Series (GBR ISSN 0141-2264) **402**
Kent Nature (GBR ISSN 1743-9256) **2616**
Kent Records (GBR ISSN 1357-3241) **402**
Kent State Research Papers in Archaeology (USA) **402**
Kent Today (GBR ISSN 1465-2390) **3867**
Kentalog (USA) **5022**
Kentaur (DNK ISSN 0023-0057) **6430**
Kentish Express (GBR ISSN 0964-1327) **3867**
Kentish Gazette Group (GBR ISSN 0964-1262) **3867**
Kentron Epistemonikon Ereunon. Epetirida/Cyprus Research Centre. Annual (CYP ISSN 1450-006X) **4237**
Kentuckiana Family (USA) **2157**
• Kentuckiana HealthFitness Magazine (USA) **6991**
Kentucky Academy of Family Physicians Journal *see* K A F P Journal **5656**
• ➤ Kentucky Academy of Science. Journal (USA ISSN 1098-7096) **7875**
Kentucky. Adjutant-General's Office. Report (USA) **6430**
Kentucky Afield (USA ISSN 1059-9177) **2616**
Kentucky Agricultural Statistics (USA) **183**
Kentucky: All-Industries *see* Harris Directory. Kentucky All-Industries **2000**
Kentucky Ancestors (USA ISSN 0023-0103) **3772**
Kentucky Annual Economic Report (Year) (USA) **1140**
Kentucky Annual Vital Statistics Report (USA) **7548**
Kentucky Appellate Reporter (USA ISSN 1075-7791) **4954**
The Kentucky Archivist (USA) **4300**
Kentucky Association for Health, Physical Education, Recreation and Dance. Journal (USA ISSN 1071-2577) **2880**
• Kentucky Attorney General Opinions (USA ISSN 0748-9080) **4954**
• Kentucky Banker (USA ISSN 0023-0111) **1363**
• Kentucky Banking and Related Laws and Rules Annotated (USA) **1363**
Kentucky Beverage Journal (USA ISSN 0023-0138) **605**
Kentucky Board Nursing Connection *see* K B Nursing Connection **5968**
• Kentucky Business Directory (USA ISSN 1048-728X) **2010**
• Kentucky Business Organizations Laws and Rules (USA ISSN 1538-1439) **4873**
Kentucky Checklist of State Publications (USA ISSN 1054-2841) **628**
Kentucky Cities and Counties Graphic Performance Analysis *see* Kentucky Cities & Counties Graphic Performance Analysis **7481**
Kentucky Cities & Counties Graphic Performance Analysis (USA ISSN 1935-6005) **7481**
Kentucky City Magazine (USA) **7495**
Kentucky Civil War Round Table. Bulletin (USA ISSN 0023-0146) **4300**
Kentucky College and University Degrees and other Formal Awards (Year) (USA) **2991**
Kentucky College and University Enrollments (Year) (USA) **2991**
• Kentucky Criminal Law and Procedure (USA ISSN 1529-904X) **4892**
Kentucky Curiosities (USA ISSN 1932-7358) **8727**
Kentucky. Department of Human Resources. Annual Report (USA) **8052**
Kentucky Directory of Black Elected Officials (USA) **7149**
Kentucky Education Association News *see* K E A News **2879**
Kentucky Education Association Research Publications *see* K E A Research Publications **2934**
• Kentucky Employment Law Letter (USA ISSN 1052-4371) **4709**
Kentucky Engineer (USA ISSN 0746-2255) **3207**
➤ Kentucky English Bulletin (USA ISSN 0023-0197) **5136**
• The Kentucky Evidence Law Handbook (USA) **4954**
Kentucky Explorer (USA ISSN 0890-8362) **4300**
Kentucky Facts (USA ISSN 1046-834X) **3120**
Kentucky Fish and Wildlife Statutes (USA) **2616**
Kentucky Game & Fish (USA ISSN 0889-3802) **8320**
Kentucky Gardener (USA ISSN 1541-8391) **3740**
Kentucky Geological Survey. Bulletin (USA ISSN 0075-5559) **2751**
Kentucky Geological Survey. County Report (USA ISSN 0075-5567) **2751**
Kentucky Geological Survey. Guidebook to Geological Field Trips (USA ISSN 0075-5575) **2751**
Kentucky Geological Survey. Information Circular (USA ISSN 0075-5583) **2751**
Kentucky Geological Survey. Map and Chart Series (USA ISSN 1522-0834) **2751**
Kentucky Geological Survey. Report of Investigations (USA ISSN 0075-5591) **2751**
Kentucky Geological Survey. Reprints (USA ISSN 0075-5605) **2751**
Kentucky Geological Survey. Special Publication (USA ISSN 0075-5613) **2752**
Kentucky Geological Survey. Thesis Series (USA ISSN 0075-5621) **2752**
➤ Kentucky Heritage (USA) **4300**
Kentucky Historical Society. Bulletin (USA) **4300**
Kentucky Historical Society. Register (USA ISSN 0023-0243) **4300**
Kentucky Jewish Post and Opinion (USA) **7726**
Kentucky Journal (USA ISSN 1063-9357) **7449**
Kentucky Journal of Commerce & Industry *see* Kentucky Journal of Manufacturing & Industry **1140**
➤ Kentucky Journal of Communication (USA ISSN 1533-3140) **2330**
Kentucky Journal of Communication Arts *see* Kentucky Journal of Communication **2330**
The Kentucky Journal of Economics and Business *see* Journal of Applied Economics and Policy **1133**
• ➤ Kentucky Journal of Excellence in College Teaching and Learning (USA) **3069**
Kentucky Journal of Manufacturing & Industry (USA ISSN 1931-9568) **1140**
Kentucky Kernel (USA) **2289**
• Kentucky Law Journal (USA ISSN 0023-026X) **4709**
• ➤ Kentucky Libraries (USA ISSN 0732-5452) **5022**
• Kentucky Living (USA ISSN 1043-853X) **3979**
Kentucky Local Debt Report (USA ISSN 0095-1498) **1932**
• The Kentucky Manufacturer (USA) **1140**
• Kentucky Manufacturers Register (USA ISSN 0741-9031) **2010**
Kentucky: Manufacturing *see* Harris Directory. Kentucky Manufacturing **2000**
➤ Kentucky Medical Association. Journal (USA ISSN 0023-0294) **5657**
Kentucky Medical News (USA) **5657**
• Kentucky Monthly (USA ISSN 1542-0507) **3979**
Kentucky Motions in Limine (USA ISSN 1945-4171) **4834**
Kentucky Motor Vehicle Insurance Law (USA ISSN 1930-8582) **4709**
• Kentucky Motor Vehicle Laws and Regulations Annotated (USA) **8501**
• Kentucky N R C S newsletter (National Resources Conservation Service) (USA ISSN 1939-5515) **202**
• Kentucky Nurse (USA ISSN 0742-8367) **5968**
• Kentucky Penal Code, Vehicles, Rules & Related Statutes (USA) **4892**
The Kentucky Pharmacist (USA ISSN 0194-567X) **6857**
Kentucky Philological Review (USA) **5317**
Kentucky Plumbing-Heating-Cooling Index (USA) **4128**
Kentucky Press (USA ISSN 0023-0324) **4578**
➤ Kentucky Review (USA ISSN 0191-1031) **4461**
Kentucky School Directory *see* M D R's School Directory. Kentucky **2959**
Kentucky School Laws *see* Kentucky School Laws Annotated **4709**
Kentucky School Laws Annotated (USA) **4709**
Kentucky Schools Directory (USA ISSN 0091-0775) **2957**
Kentucky State Agent Handbook (USA) **4511**
• Kentucky Teacher (USA ISSN 1526-3584) **2880**
Kentucky, Tennessee TourBook *see* TourBook: Kentucky, Tennessee **8762**
• Kentucky Travel Guide (USA ISSN 0453-5812) **8727**
Kentucky Unemployment Compensation Laws and Regulations (USA ISSN 1531-3581) **1691**
Kentucky Warbler (USA ISSN 0160-5070) **909**
Kentucky Wrongful Death Actions (USA ISSN 1931-9746) **4892**
Kenya *see* The P R S Group. Country Reports: Kenya **1507**
Kenya. Agricultural Census (Large Farm Areas) *see* Kenya. Central Bureau of Statistics. Agricultural Census (Large Farm Areas) **183**
Kenya Association of Manufacturers. Members List and International Standard Industrial Classification (KEN) **1890**
Kenya Birds (KEN ISSN 1023-3679) **909**
Kenya Business Spotlight (KEN) **1495**
Kenya. Central Bureau of Statistics. Agricultural Census (Large Farm Areas) (KEN ISSN 0300-2373) **183**
Kenya. Central Bureau of Statistics. Development Estimates (KEN) **1247**
Kenya. Central Bureau of Statistics. Directory of Industries (KEN ISSN 0376-8481) **2010**
Kenya. Central Bureau of Statistics. District Development Plan (KEN) **7449**
Kenya. Central Bureau of Statistics. Economic Survey (KEN ISSN 0075-5842) **1495**
Kenya. Central Bureau of Statistics. Employment and Earnings in the Modern Sector (KEN ISSN 0376-8864) **1247**
Kenya. Central Bureau of Statistics. Estimates of Recurrent Expenditures (KEN ISSN 0075-5834) **1247**
Kenya. Central Bureau of Statistics. Estimates of Revenue Expenditures (KEN) **1247**
Kenya. Central Bureau of Statistics. Kenya Consumer Price Index (KEN) **8384**
Kenya. Central Bureau of Statistics. Leading Economic Indicator (KEN) **1140**
Kenya. Central Bureau of Statistics. Migration and Tourism Statistics (KEN ISSN 0377-1385) **8779**
Kenya. Central Bureau of Statistics. Population Census (KEN) **7311**
Kenya. Central Bureau of Statistics. Populations and Housing Census (Year) (KEN) **8052**
Kenya. Central Bureau of Statistics. Register of Manufacturing Firms (KEN) **1247**
Kenya. Central Bureau of Statistics. Second Report on Poverty in Kenya. (KEN) **8052**
Kenya. Central Bureau of Statistics. Social Perspectives *see* Social Perspectives **8133**
Kenya. Central Bureau of Statistics. Surveys of Industrial Production (KEN) **1247**
Kenya Coffee (KEN ISSN 1010-3481) **3652**
Kenya Commercial Bank. Director's Report and Accounts and Executive Chairman's Statement (KEN) **1363**
Kenya. Commissioner of Customs and Excise. Annual Trade Report (KEN) **1574**
Kenya. Court of Appeal. Digest of Decisions of the Court (KEN) **4954**
Kenya Engineer (KEN) **3207**
Kenya Export Directory (KEN) **1574**
Kenya Farmer (KEN ISSN 0023-0421) **130**
Kenya Fisheries Reports (KEN) **3600**
Kenya Freight Transport Report (GBR ISSN 1752-5918) **8501**
Kenya Gazette (KEN) **7449**
Kenya Gazette Supplement (KEN) **7450**
Kenya. Government Printing and Stationery Department. Catalogue of Government Publications (KEN) **628**
Kenya Industrial Research and Development Institute Annual Report and Statement of Accounts *see* K I R D I Annual Report and Statement of Accounts **1430**
Kenya Journal of Sciences. Series A: Physical and Chemical Sciences (KEN) **7875**
Kenya Journal of Sciences. Series B: Biological Sciences (KEN) **685**
Kenya Journal of Sciences. Series C: Humanities and Social Sciences (KEN) **4461**
Kenya Leo (KEN) **3902**
Kenya Medical Research Institute. Annual Report (KEN ISSN 0076-5988) **5657**
Kenya Meteorological Department. Annual Report (KEN) **6359**
▼ Kenya Meteorological Society. Journal (KEN ISSN 1995-9834) **6359**
Kenya. Migration and Tourism Statistics *see* Kenya. Central Bureau of Statistics. Migration and Tourism Statistics **8779**
Kenya. Ministry of Agriculture. Development Planning Division. Yields, Costs, Prices (KEN) **202**
Kenya. Ministry of Cooperatives and Social Services. Sessional Papers (KEN ISSN 0378-8938) **7450**
Kenya. Ministry of Education. Annual Report (KEN ISSN 0075-5869) **2880**
Kenya. Ministry of Education. Newsletter (KEN) **2880**
Kenya. Ministry of Finance and Planning. Budget Speech by Minister for Finance and Planning (KEN) **7450**
Kenya. Ministry of Finance and Planning. National Development Plan (KEN) **7450**
Kenya. Ministry of Finance and Planning. Plan Implementation Report (KEN) **7450**
Kenya. Ministry of Foreign Affairs. Directory of Diplomatic Corps & International Organizations (KEN ISSN 0376-8465) **7249**
Kenya. Ministry of Housing. Annual Report (KEN) **4418**
Kenya. Ministry of Information and Broadcasting. Annual Report (KEN) **4176**
Kenya. Nafaka News (KEN) **240**
Kenya National Academy for Advancement of Arts and Sciences. Foundation Lectures (KEN) **4461**
Kenya National Academy for Advancement of Arts and Sciences. Newsletter (KEN) **7875**
Kenya National Academy for Advancement of Arts and Sciences. Proceedings (KEN) **4461**
Kenya National Academy for Advancement of Arts and Sciences. Research Information Circulars (KEN) **4176**
Kenya National Academy of Science. Research Papers (KEN) **7875**
Kenya National Chamber of Commerce and Industry. Trade and Industry Guide (KEN) **1406**
Kenya National Development Plan *see* Kenya. Ministry of Finance and Planning. National Development Plan **7450**
Kenya. National Housing Corporation. Annual Report (KEN) **4418**
Kenya. National Irrigation Board. Reports and Accounts (KEN ISSN 0075-5915) **240**
Kenya National Library Service Board. Annual and Audit Report (KEN ISSN 0075-5923) **5022**
Kenya National Library Services. Bibliography (KEN) **5058**
Kenya National Library Services. Classified Accession List of Books Added to Stock (KEN) **5058**
Kenya National Trading Corporation. Annual Report (KEN ISSN 0304-7202) **1430**
Kenya Newsletter (KEN ISSN 0454-949X) **3902**
Kenya Nursing Journal (KEN ISSN 0301-0333) **5968**
Kenya. Office of the District Commissioner. Annual Report (KEN) **7450**
Kenya Past and Present (KEN ISSN 0257-8301) **4176**
Kenya Police Review (KEN ISSN 0023-0448) **2658**
Kenya Population Census *see* Kenya. Central Bureau of Statistics. Population Census **7311**
Kenya. Public Accounts Committee. Annual Report (KEN ISSN 0075-5931) **1932**
Kenya. Public Service Commission. Annual Report (KEN ISSN 0075-594X) **8052**
Kenya Railways. Annual Report (KEN ISSN 1015-0986) **8501**
Kenya Record (KEN) **3902**
Kenya Society for the Blind. Annual Report and Accounts (KEN) **4082**
Kenya Stamp Bureau. Philatelic Bulletin (KEN) **6896**
Kenya Statistical Digest (KEN ISSN 0453-6002) **8384**
Kenya. Surveys of Industrial Production *see* Kenya. Central Bureau of Statistics. Surveys of Industrial Production **1247**
Kenya Tea Development Authority. Annual Report and Accounts (KEN) **3652**
Kenya: The Gateway to Africa (KEN) **1636**
Kenya Times (KEN) **3902**
Kenya Tourist Development Corporation. Report and Accounts (KEN) **8727**
Kenya Uhuru Factbook (KEN) **4176**
Kenya Veterinarian (KEN ISSN 0256-5161) **8802**
Kenya Yearbook (GBR) **1495**
Kenya Yetu (KEN) **3789**
Kenyan Periodicals Directory (KEN) **5058**
Kenyatta University College. Directory of Research (KEN) **2991**

Title

DIRECTORY 2010 KHELA 10527

Key Note Market Report: Mobile Phones (GBR) **2369**
• Key Note Market Report: Mobile Telecommunications (GBR) **2330**
Key Note Market Report. New Media Marketing (GBR ISSN 1468-1927) **2330**
• Key Note Market Report: Newspapers (GBR ISSN 1475-1712) **4579**
• Key Note Market Report: O T C Pharmaceuticals (Over The Counter) (GBR) **1895**
• Key Note Market Report: Office Furniture (GBR) **1852**
• Key Note Market Report: Ophthalmic Goods & Services (GBR) **1895**
• Key Note Market Report: Own Brands (GBR) **1895**
Key Note Market Report: Packaging (Food & Drink) *see* Packaging (Food & Drink) Industry **6712**
• Key Note Market Report: Packaging (Glass) (GBR) **6711**
• Key Note Market Report: Packaging (Metals & Aerosols) (GBR ISSN 1460-8200) **1895**
• Key Note Market Report: Packaging (Paper & Board) (GBR ISSN 1464-1186) **1895**
• Key Note Market Report: Packaging (Plastics) (GBR) **6711**
Key Note Market Report: Paper & Board Manufacturing (GBR ISSN 1368-1451) **1895**
Key Note Market Report: Pensions (GBR ISSN 1364-8004) **1895**
• Key Note Market Report: Personal Banking (GBR ISSN 1467-5684) **1364**
• Key Note Market Report: Pet Foods (GBR ISSN 1747-2148) **6810**
• Key Note Market Report: Photocopiers & Fax Machines (GBR ISSN 1367-4137) **1852**
• Key Note Market Report: Plant Hire (GBR ISSN 1747-2598) **1495**
• Key Note Market Report: Plastics Processing (GBR ISSN 1460-8294) **7094**
• Key Note Market Report Plus. Biscuits & Cakes (GBR ISSN 1740-4541) **3674**
• Key Note Market Report Plus. Premium Lagers, Beers & Ciders (GBR) **606**
Key Note Market Report: Poultry (GBR) **1895**
Key Note Market Report: Power Tools (GBR) **5454**
Key Note Market Report: Prescribed Pharmaceuticals *see* Key Note Market Review: The Pharmaceutical Industry **6857**
• Key Note Market Report: Printing (GBR) **7324**
• Key Note Market Report: Private Healthcare (GBR) **5657**
Key Note Market Report: Protective Clothing & Equipment (GBR ISSN 1460-7565) **1895**
Key Note Market Report: Rail Travel (GBR ISSN 1460-5961) **8619**
Key Note Market Report. Recruitment Agencies (Permanent) (GBR) **1868**
Key Note Market Report. Recruitment Agencies (Temporary and Contract) (GBR) **1868**
Key Note Market Report: Renewable Energy (GBR ISSN 1741-413X) **3141**
• Key Note Market Report: Retail Chemists & Drug Stores (GBR) **6857**
• Key Note Market Report: Road Haulage (GBR) **8672**
• Key Note Market Report: Rubber Manufacturing & Processing (GBR) **7825**
Key Note Market Report: Rugby Clubs & Finance (GBR ISSN 1468-1935) **8236**
Key Note Market Report: Scientific Instruments *see* Key Note Market Report: Laboratory Equipment **1894**
Key Note Market Report: Shopfitting (GBR) **1828**
Key Note Market Report: Short Break Holidays (GBR ISSN 1368-1532) **8727**
Key Note Market Report: Slimming Market *see* Key Note Market Assessment. The Slimming Market **1893**
• Key Note Market Report: Small Domestic Electrical Appliances (GBR ISSN 1473-818X) **4559**
Key Note Market Report: Soft Drinks (Carbonated & Concentrated) (GBR) **606**
Key Note Market Report. Soup Market (GBR) **3652**
• Key Note Market Report: Sports Clothing and Footwear (GBR ISSN 1368-5996) **2248**
• Key Note Market Report: Sports Equipment (GBR ISSN 1368-3713) **8184**
Key Note Market Report: Sports Sponsorhip (GBR) **8184**
• Key Note Market Report: Stationery (Personal & Office) (GBR ISSN 1363-0865) **1852**
• Key Note Market Report: Supermarkets & Superstores (GBR) **3680**
• Key Note Market Report: Telecommunications (GBR ISSN 1367-515X) **2330**
• Key Note Market Report: The Chemical Industry (GBR ISSN 1747-9924) **3249**
Key Note Market Report: The Film Industry (GBR) **6505**
Key Note Market Report: The Gas Industry (GBR ISSN 1474-2071) **1895**
Key Note Market Report: The Offshore Oil & Gas Industry (GBR ISSN 1475-0457) **6776**
• Key Note Market Report: The Take Home Trade (GBR ISSN 1366-6193) **1895**
Key Note Market Report: The Tire Industry *see* Key Note Market Report: The Tyre Industry **1895**
Key Note Market Report: The Tyre Industry (GBR ISSN 1476-0088) **1895**
Key Note Market Report: The Water Industry (GBR ISSN 1473-6667) **1895**
• Key Note Market Report: Timber & Joinery (GBR ISSN 1363-0954) **1895**
Key Note Market Report: Timber and Joinery (GBR) **3713**
• Key Note Market Report: Tourist Attractions (GBR ISSN 1367-4145) **8727**
• Key Note Market Report: Toys & Games (GBR ISSN 1366-5073) **1895**
• Key Note Market Report: Training (GBR ISSN 1368-5988) **1895**
• Key Note Market Report: Travel Agents & Overseas Tour Operators (GBR) **8727**
• Key Note Market Report: Vehicle Security (GBR) **8588**
• Key Note Market Report: Video & D V D Retail & Hire (GBR ISSN 1478-4270) **2402**
Key Note Market Report: Video Retail & Hire *see* Key Note Market Report: Video & D V D Retail & Hire **2402**
Key Note Market Report: Videoconferencing (GBR ISSN 1463-0397) **1896**
Key Note Market Report: Wallcoverings *see* Key Note Market Report: Wallcoverings and Ceramic Tiles **4544**
• Key Note Market Report: Wallcoverings and Ceramic Tiles (GBR) **4544**
• Key Note Market Report: Waste Management (GBR ISSN 1369-7668) **1896**
• Key Note Market Report: Water Utilities (GBR ISSN 1461-5304) **1896**
Key Note Market Report: White Spirits (GBR) **606**
• Key Note Market Report: Windows & Doors (GBR ISSN 1368-6321) **1896**
Key Note Market Report: Winter Holidays (GBR ISSN 1469-5200) **8727**
Key Note Market Review: Clothing & Footwear Industry *see* Clothing & Footwear Industry **2246**
Key Note Market Review: Construction Industry *see* Construction Industry **996**
Key Note Market Review: Contracted-Out Services (GBR ISSN 1476-5756) **1896**
Key Note Market Review: D I Y & Home Improvements Industry *see* D I Y & Home Improvements Industry **4536**
Key Note Market Review. Defence Industry *see* Defence Industry (Hampton) **6418**
Key Note Market Review: Distribution Industry *see* Distribution Industry **1884**
• Key Note Market Review: Drinks Market (GBR ISSN 1740-3286) **606**
Key Note Market Review: Film Market (GBR) **2384**
Key Note Market Review: Healthcare Market *see* Healthcare Market **5626**
• Key Note Market Review: Insurance Industry (GBR ISSN 1742-8548) **1896**
Key Note Market Review: Leisure & Recreation Market *see* Key Note Market Review. Leisure in the Home **1896**
Key Note Market Review: Leisure & Recreation Market *see* Key Note Market Review: Leisure Outside the Home **4979**
• Key Note Market Review. Leisure in the Home (GBR) **1896**
• Key Note Market Review: Leisure Outside the Home (GBR) **4979**
Key Note Market Review: Local Government Services (GBR) **1896**
• Key Note Market Review: Mechanical Handling (GBR) **1896**
• Key Note Market Review: Motor Industry (GBR) **1896**
Key Note Market Review: Motor Industry U K *see* Key Note Market Review: Motor Industry **1896**
Key Note Market Review: Multimedia in the U K *see* Key Note Market Report: Mobile Telecommunications **2330**
Key Note Market Review: Multimedia in the U K *see* Key Note Market Report: Telecommunications **2330**
Key Note Market Review: Music Industry (GBR) **6582**
Key Note Market Review: Packaging (Food & Drink) Industry *see* Packaging (Food & Drink) Industry **6712**
• Key Note Market Review: Passenger Travel in the U K (GBR ISSN 1356-7292) **1896**
Key Note Market Review: Personal Finance & Savings in the U.K. *see* Key Note Market Assessment. Personal Banking **1364**
Key Note Market Review: Personal Finance in the U K *see* Key Note Market Assessment. Personal Banking **1364**
• Key Note Market Review: Process Plant Industry (GBR) **1896**
Key Note Market Review: Railway Industry (GBR ISSN 1746-420X) **1896**
Key Note Market Review: The Catering Industry *see* Key Note Market Review: The Catering Market **4392**
• Key Note Market Review: The Catering Market (GBR ISSN 1743-047X) **4392**
Key Note Market Review. The Computer Market *see* The Computer Market **2491**
• Key Note Market Review: The Energy Industry (GBR ISSN 1477-7169) **3141**
Key Note Market Review: The Food Industry *see* The Food Industry (Hampton) **3639**
Key Note Market Review: The Office Equipment Industry *see* The Office Equipment Industry **1900**
• Key Note Market Review: The Pharmaceutical Industry (GBR) **6857**
Key Note Market Review: The Publishing Industry *see* The Publishing Industry **1902**
Key Note Market Review: The Security Industry *see* The Security Industry **1903**
Key Note Market Review: The Sports Market *see* The Sports Market **1904**
Key Note Market Review: Travel & Tourism Market *see* Travel & Tourism Market **1905**
Key Note Market Review. U K Catering Market *see* Key Note Market Review: Drinks Market **606**
Key Note Market Review: U K Clothing & Footwear *see* Clothing & Footwear Industry **2246**
Key Note Market Review: U K Computer Market *see* The Computer Market **2491**
Key Note Market Review: U K Construction Industry *see* Construction Industry **996**
Key Note Market Review: U K D I Y & Home Improvements *see* D I Y & Home Improvements Industry **4536**
Key Note Market Review: U K Defence Industry *see* Defence Industry (Hampton) **6418**
Key Note Market Review: U K Distribution *see* Distribution Industry **1884**
Key Note Market Review: U K Food Market *see* The Food Industry (Hampton) **3639**
Key Note Market Review: U K Healthcare *see* Healthcare Market **5626**
Key Note Market Review: U K Insurance Market *see* Key Note Market Review: Insurance Industry **1896**
Key Note Market Review: U K Leisure & Recreation *see* Key Note Market Review. Leisure in the Home **1896**
Key Note Market Review: U K Leisure & Recreation *see* Key Note Market Review: Leisure Outside the Home **4979**
Key Note Market Review: U K Motor Industry *see* Key Note Market Review: Motor Industry **1896**
Key Note Market Review: U K Office Equipment *see* The Office Equipment Industry **1900**
Key Note Market Review: U K Pharmaceutical Industry *see* Key Note Market Review: The Pharmaceutical Industry **6857**
Key Note Market Review: U K Security *see* The Security Industry **1903**
Key Note Market Review: U K Sports Market *see* The Sports Market **1904**
Key Note Market Review: U K Travel & Tourism *see* Travel & Tourism Market **1905**
Key Note Plus Market Report. Biscuits & Cakes *see* Key Note Market Report Plus. Biscuits & Cakes **3674**
• Key Note Plus Market Report. Canned Foods (GBR) **3652**
• Key Note Plus Market Report. Chilled Foods (GBR) **3653**
• Key Note Plus Market Report. China & Earthenware (GBR) **2044**
• Key Note Plus Market Report. Confectionery (GBR) **3674**
• Key Note Plus Market Report. Cosmetics & Fragrances (GBR) **1828**
Key Note Plus Market Report. Dark Spirits & Liqueurs (GBR ISSN 1461-5312) **1828**
• Key Note Plus Market Report. Ethnic Foods (GBR) **3653**
• Key Note Plus Market Report. Fast Food & Home Delivery Outlets (GBR) **3653**
• Key Note Plus Market Report. Footwear (GBR ISSN 1460-7662) **1896**
• Key Note Plus Market Report. Frozen Foods (GBR) **3653**
Key Note Plus Market Report. Greeting Cards *see* Greetings Cards **4060**
• Key Note Plus Market Report. Health Foods (GBR) **3653**
• Key Note Plus Market Report. Hotels (GBR) **4392**
Key Note Plus Market Report. Ice-Creams & Frozen Deserts *see* Key Note Plus Market Report. Ice-Creams & Frozen Desserts **3653**
• Key Note Plus Market Report. Ice-Creams & Frozen Desserts (GBR) **3653**
• Key Note Plus Market Report. Public Houses (GBR) **4392**
• Key Note Plus Market Report. Ready Meals (GBR) **3653**
• Key Note Plus Market Report. Restaurants (GBR) **4392**
• Key Note Plus Market Report. Sauces & Spreads (GBR) **3653**
• Key Note Plus Market Report. Snack Foods (GBR) **3653**
Key Note Plus Market Report. Soft Drinks *see* Key Note Market Report: Soft Drinks (Carbonated & Concentrated) **606**
• Key Note Plus Market Report. Toiletries (GBR ISSN 1367-2304) **1896**
Key Note Plus Market Report. White Spirits and Speciality Drinks *see* Key Note Market Report: White Spirits **606**
• Key Note Plus Market Report. Wine (GBR) **606**
Key Note Report: Insurance Brokers *see* Key Note Market Assessment: Independent Financial Advisers **4511**
Key Note Report. Paper & Board Manufacturers *see* Key Note Market Report: Paper & Board Manufacturing **1895**
Key Note Report: Prescribed Pharmaceuticals *see* Key Note Market Review: The Pharmaceutical Industry **6857**
Key of Kappa Kappa Gamma (USA ISSN 1063-4665) **2267**
• Key Rates and Data (GBR) **1140**
Key Readings in Social Psychology (GBR ISSN 1531-2569) **7382**
• The Key Reporter (USA ISSN 0023-0804) **2289**
Key Rubber Indicators (Year) (GBR) **7825**
▼ Key Sale (DEU) **6857**
• Key Scottish Environment Statistics (GBR) **3480**
• Key Skills Support Programme News (GBR ISSN 1748-9482) **3069**
• Key Small Business Financing Statistics (CAN ISSN 1911-6594) **1247**
• Key Small Business Financing Statistics (CAN ISSN 1911-6608) **1247**
• Key Small Business Statistics (Online) (CAN ISSN 1718-3456) **1963**
• Key Small Business Statistics (Print) (CAN ISSN 1718-3448) **1963**
Key Statistics of Thailand (Year) (THA) **1247**
Key Student Outcomes Indicators for B.C. College and Institutions. Analysis by Institution (CAN ISSN 1480-0551) **2934**
▼ ➤ Key Texts in Sports Studies (GBR ISSN 1745-7890) **8184**
Key to Cayman (CYM) **8727**
Key to Europe (BEL) **3014**
Key to Kingston (CAN ISSN 0710-9628) **8727**
Key to Rome (USA ISSN 1933-0960) **8727**
Key to the Church of Sweden *see* Nyckeln till Svenska Kyrkan **7667**
• Key to the Finnish Forest Industry (FIN ISSN 1238-4178) **3695**
➤ Key Topics in Brain Research (AUT ISSN 0934-1420) **6157**
• Key West Magazine (USA ISSN 1938-6532) **5074**
• Key Words (Port Aransas) (USA ISSN 1064-1211) **5058**
• Keyan Guanli/Science Research Management (CHN ISSN 1000-2995) **7876**
• Keyboard (USA ISSN 0730-0158) **6582**
Keyboard Companion *see* Clavier Companion **6557**
• Keyboard Player (GBR ISSN 0269-3836) **6582**
Keyboard Review (GBR ISSN 0962-2675) **6582**
Keyboard Teacher (USA ISSN 1083-835X) **6582**
Keyboards (DEU ISSN 0178-4641) **6582**
Keyboards Home Studio (FRA ISSN 1638-7155) **6582**
Keyboards Magazine *see* Keyboards Home Studio **6582**
Keyframe Magazine (USA ISSN 1536-3112) **2488**
▼ Keyhole (Nashville) (USA ISSN 1941-5362) **5222**
Keyhole (Washington) (USA) **3772**
Keying In (USA) **1140**
KeyNote (AUS) **1636**
Keynoter (USA) **2267**
Keynotes (GBR ISSN 0268-0467) **5317**
Keynotes (Dallas) (USA ISSN 0277-0792) **2679**
Keynotes (Manhattan) (USA) **4050**
Keynotes (Oak Brook) (USA) **1770**
• Keys (DEU ISSN 0938-3573) **6582**
Keys of Peter (GBR) **7803**
• Keys to Outsourcing and Offshoring (USA ISSN 1935-8385) **4934**
Keystone A A A Motorist *see* A A A World (York) **8553**
Keystone Builder (USA ISSN 0199-0411) **1019**
Keystone Connection (USA) **7450**
Keystone Conservationist *see* Keystone Outdoors **2616**
Keystone Motorcycle Press (USA ISSN 1092-4817) **8260**
• Keystone Outdoors (USA ISSN 1545-6102) **2616**
Keystoner (USA ISSN 0886-7666) **6045**
Keyways (GBR ISSN 0262-4478) **1054**
Keyword *see* Southern Communicator **2339**
Keyword Index to Serial Titles (GBR ISSN 0143-9553) **5058**
Keyword Index to Serial Titles Quarterly (GBR ISSN 0000-4995) **5058**
Keywords (Chicago) (USA ISSN 0197-7342) **2593**
• El Khabar (DZA) **3790**
Khabar (USA) **3546**
Khad Patrika (IND ISSN 0023-1010) **240**
Khadi and Village Industries Commission, Directorate of Publicity Annual Report *see* K V I C Annual Report **1963**
Khadi Gramodyog (IND ISSN 0023-1029) **202**
Khadya Vigyan (IND ISSN 0023-1037) **3653**
Khakasia (RUS) **3936**
Khaleej *see* Al- Khalij **3966**
• Khaleej Times (UAE) **3966**
Khalg Gazeti (AZE) **3799**
Al-Khalij (UAE) **3966**
Al-Khalij al-Jadid (QAT) **3912**
Khalk Ovozi (TJK) **3961**
Khalk Suzi (UZB) **3994**
Khanya (ZAF ISSN 1562-9627) **2880**
Khao Setthakit Kan-Kaset/Agricultural Economic News (THA ISSN 0023-1053) **266**
Khartoum Law Review (SDN) **4709**
Khartoum University Press. Classified List of Publications (SDN) **628**
Khatoon Mashriq (IND ISSN 0023-107X) **6639**
Khavaran (IRN) **5222**
Khawar (PAK) **3926**
➤ Khayaban (PAK ISSN 1993-9302) **5137**
Kheiat (AZE) **130**
Khel Bharati (IND) **8184**
Khel Halchal (IND) **8184**
Khel ki Dunya (PAK) **8184**
Khela (IND) **8184**

Title

10528 KHERADNAMEH-E SADRA ULRICH'S PERIODICALS

• Kheradnameh-e Sadra (IRN ISSN 1560-0874) 6930
Kheti (IND ISSN 0023-1088) 130
• Khil'a (BEL ISSN 1781-2534) 8454
Khimicheskaya Fizika (RUS ISSN 0207-401X) 2138
Khimicheskaya i Biologicheskaya Bezopasnost' (RUS) 2094
Khimicheskaya Promyshlennost' see Khimicheskaya Promyshlennost' Segodnia 3249
Khimicheskaya Promyshlennost' Segodnia (RUS) 3249
➤ Khimicheskaya Tekhnologiya/Chemical Technology (RUS) 2070
Khimicheskie Volokna (RUS ISSN 0023-1118) 3249
Khimicheskoe i Neftegazovoe Mashinostroenie/Chemical and Oil Industry (RUS ISSN 1029-8770) 3249
• Khimiko-Farmatsevticheskii Zhurnal/Journal of Pharmaceutical Chemistry (RUS ISSN 0023-1134) 6857
Khimiya (BGR ISSN 0861-9255) 2070
Khimiya dlya Shkol'nikov (RUS) 2070
➤ Khimiya Geterotsiklicheskikh Soedinenii (LVA ISSN 0132-6244) 2125
Khimiya i Biznes (RUS) 737
Khimiya i Industriya (BGR ISSN 1310-6716) 2070
Khimiya i Tekhnologiya Topliv i Masel (RUS ISSN 0023-1169) 6776
Khimiya i Tekhnolohiya Vody/Chemistry and Technology of Water (UKR ISSN 0204-3556) 2070
• Khimiya i Zhizn' - XXI Vek/Chemistry and Life - 21st Century (RUS) 2070
➤ Khimiya Prirodnykh Soedinenii (UZB ISSN 0023-1150) 2125
Khimiya Tverdogo Topliva (RUS ISSN 0023-1177) 3249
• Khimiya Ukrainy/Ukrainian Chemistry (UKR ISSN 1606-7304) 2070
Khimiya v Interesakh Ustoichivogo Razvitiya (RUS ISSN 0869-8538) 2070
Khimiya v Shkole (RUS ISSN 0368-5632) 2070
• Khimiya Vysokikh Energii (RUS ISSN 0023-1193) 2070
Khirurgia (BGR ISSN 0450-2167) 6251
• Khirurgiya. Zhurnal im. N.I. Pirogova/Surgery (RUS ISSN 0023-1207) 6251
Khlebopechenie Rossii/Baking in Russia (RUS) 3674
Khleboproducty (RUS ISSN 0235-2508) 274
Khlebosol (RUS) 4979
Khoa Hoc Ky Thuat Kinh Te The Gioi/World Science, Technology and Economy (VNM) 7876
Khoa Hoc va Doi Song/Science and Life (VNM ISSN 0866-7942) 7876
Khoj (DEU ISSN 0937-2105) 554
Khoj Darpan (IND ISSN 0972-3773) 3619
Khokkei (RUS) 8184
Kholodil'naya Tekhnika (RUS ISSN 0023-124X) 4123
Khorasan see Khurasan 3891
Khorhrdayin Karabakh see Azat Artsakh 3792
Khosana (USA ISSN 0898-1930) 8116
Khozyain (Minsk) (BLR) 130
Khozyain (Moscow) (RUS ISSN 0868-7188) 130
Khozyaistvo i Pravo (RUS ISSN 0134-2398) 4709
Khranenie i Pererabotka Sel'khozsyr'ya/Storage and Processing of Farm Products (RUS) 130
• Khreshchatyk (UKR) 3964
Khronika 2000 (UKR) 5222
Khronometr (Ivanovo) (RUS) 3936
Khronometr (Kostroma) (RUS) 3936
• Khronometr (Vladimir) (RUS) 3936
Khronometr (Vologda) (RUS) 3936
Khudozhestvennyi Sovet (RUS) 5317
Khudozhnik (RUS ISSN 0131-7555) 500
Khulumani see Speak Out 8903
Khurasan (IRN) 3891
Khvurjin (IRN) 3892
▼ Khyber Behavioural Studies (PAK ISSN 2075-6933) 7382
Ki-es-Ki see C E A Handbook 2833
Ki Kicsoda a Magyar Tavkozlesben see Budapest Business Journal's Who's Who in Hungarian Telecom 2314
Ki Kicsoda a Penzugyi Eletben see Budapest Business Journal's Who's Who in Finance 1321
Ki Kicsoda a Reklam es Media Vilagaban see Who's Who in Advertising and Media 37
Kia Ora (NZL ISSN 1177-7486) 8784
KiaOra see Kia Ora 8784
Kiasma (FIN ISSN 1455-173X) 6527
Kibaru (CAN ISSN 1914-9735) 3546
Kibaru (MLI) 3546
Kibbutz Journal (New York) (USA) 1424
† Kibbutz Trends (ISR ISSN 0792-7290) 8969
Kibernetika i Sistemnyi Analiz (UKR ISSN 1019-5262) 2527
Kibernetika i Vychislitel'naya Tekhnika (UKR ISSN 0454-9910) 2527
Kibi no Kusabana/Association of Wild Plant in Kurashiki. Journal (JPN) 3740
Kibris Arastirmalari Dergisi see Journal of Cyprus Studies 7978
Kibris - Northern Cyprus Monthly (TUR) 3962
Kibrisli Egitim Bilimleri Dergisi see Cypriot Journal of Educational Sciences 2840
Kick (London) (GBR ISSN 1749-8295) 2197
† Kick Club (DEU) 8969
Kick it Over (CAN ISSN 0823-6526) 7149
Kick Magazine (USA) 4375
Kick Off (CAN) 8236
Kick to Corruption (IND ISSN 0023-1282) 5222
• Kicker - Sportmagazin (DEU ISSN 0023-1290) 8184
Kicker - Sportmagazin. Sonderheft Bundesliga see Kicker - Sportmagazin 8184
Kickoff (USA) 8236
Kickoff (ZAF ISSN 1022-3819) 8236
• Kickoff (Nigeria Edition) (ZAF) 8236
Kicks (USA ISSN 0199-6657) 6582
• Kid (ITA) 5137
• Kid Klicks (USA) 2197
Kid Paddle Magazine (FRA ISSN 1633-5945) 2197
Kid Power! (USA ISSN 1533-8827) 2197
• Kid Pulse (CAN) 2197
Kid Zone (AUS) 7763
Kidaround Town (USA ISSN 1935-6889) 2158
KidNews Today (USA ISSN 1942-4167) 2158
The Kidney see Jinzo 6270
• Kidney (New York, 1992) (USA ISSN 0940-7936) 5748
• ➤ Kidney and Blood Pressure Research (CHE ISSN 1420-4096) 6270
Kidney and Dialysis see Jin to Toseki 5644
Kidney and Metabolic Bone Diseases see Jin to Kotsu Taisha 6270
• Kidney Cancer Journal (USA ISSN 1933-0863) 6026
• Kidney Disease Research Updates (USA ISSN 1934-8754) 6270
• ➤ Kidney Forum (GBR ISSN 1369-3050) 6270
• ➤ Kidney International (GBR ISSN 0085-2538) 6271
• Kidney International. Supplement (USA ISSN 0098-6577) 6271
• Kidney Research Journal (USA ISSN 1819-3374) 5896
Kidorui/Rare Earths (JPN ISSN 0910-2205) 6320
Kidpower see Kid Power! 2197
Kids' Acting for Brain Surgeons (USA ISSN 1549-814X) 2197
Kids Alive (GBR ISSN 1363-5662) 7763
Kids & Co. see Kids und Co. 2197
Kids + Parents (CAN ISSN 1912-2810) 2158
Kids Avenue (USA ISSN 1930-9996) 2197
• Kids Central Station (USA) 2197
Kids Company (SGP ISSN 0219-4848) 2197
Kids Copy (USA ISSN 1063-9659) 2197
• Kids Count Data Book (USA ISSN 1060-9814) 2158
• Kids Courier (USA) 2880
Kids Creations (CAN ISSN 1202-7588) 2248
• Kids Discover (USA ISSN 1054-2868) 2197
Kids Enabled (USA ISSN 1941-0557) 3043
• Kids Friendly New Zealand (NZL ISSN 1177-6080) 2158
▼ Kids Gamer (DEU) 2478
Kids' Guide (GBR ISSN 1740-0805) 2197
Kids' Guide (USA) 8728
The Kids Hall of Fame News (USA ISSN 1539-5472) 2197
Kids' Health (CAN ISSN 1493-7832) 6095
▼ Kids Health (IRL ISSN 1649-9417) 7529
• Kid's Health (USA) 6095
Kids' Health Matters (USA) 2158
Kids in Nature's Defense News Jr. see K I N D News Jr. 320
Kids in Nature's Defense News Primary see K I N D News Primary 320
Kids in Nature's Defense News Sr. see K I N D News Sr. 320
Kids Life see FitnessLife 6986
Kids Market (USA) 2010
• Kids Marketing Report (GBR ISSN 1464-8121) 1828
Kids' Ministry Ideas (USA) 7763
• Kid's Nutrition Report (GBR ISSN 1744-5450) 6662
Kids on Wheels (Kids' Edition) (USA ISSN 1934-9777) 2158
Kids on Wheels (Parents' Edition) (USA ISSN 1557-2218) 2158
Kids Ottawa & Gatineau (CAN ISSN 1715-5592) 2158
Kids Ottawa and Gatineau see Kids Ottawa & Gatineau 2158
Kids Out (GBR ISSN 1356-8272) 2197
Kids' Pages (USA ISSN 1547-5174) 2158
† Kids' Parties (USA ISSN 1938-4963) 8969
Kids plus Parents see Kids + Parents 2158
Kids Rhyme Newsletter (USA ISSN 0738-7431) 2197
Kids' Stuff see Take a Break's Kids' Stuff 8992
▼ Kids' Stuff (GBR ISSN 1757-6474) 2197
• Kids Today (USA) 2158
• Kid's Tracks (AUS ISSN 1832-4754) 2158
• Kids Tribute (CAN ISSN 0847-3935) 2158
Kids und Co. (DEU) 2197
Kids Vakantiegids (NLD ISSN 1872-1699) 2197
Kid's Wear (DEU ISSN 1614-0206) 2257
Kids Wear see Kid's Wear 2257
Kids With Food Allergies E-News (USA ISSN 1939-8166) 5763
Kid's World (USA) 2197
Kids World Magazine see Kidsworld 2197
Kids Zone (DEU ISSN 1615-5491) 2197
Kidsafe (AUS ISSN 1038-3409) 2158
• KidScreen (CAN ISSN 1205-7746) 1828
Kidscreen Retail see KidScreen 1828
KidsGo! (DEU) 2158
KidShop (DEU) 2158
† KidsLive! (NLD ISSN 1871-2622) 8969
KidsPower (DEU ISSN 1438-2210) 2197
▼ KidsSpirit Magazine (USA ISSN 1941-5222) 2197
Kidsville News (USA) 2197
KidsWeek (NLD ISSN 1571-3814) 2197
Kidsweek Junior (NLD ISSN 1574-213X) 2197
KidsWeek TVTips see KidsWeek 2197
• Kidsworld (CAN ISSN 1490-6341) 2197
• KidTECH News (USA ISSN 1079-3070) 2880
Kidz Chat (USA) 2197
Kidz Ch@t see Kidz Chat 2197
Kidz Magazine (USA) 2158
† KidZone (USA ISSN 1547-2019) 8969
KidZsay Magazine (AUS ISSN 1832-2395) 2197
Kieferorthopaedie (DEU ISSN 0945-7917) 5854
Kieferorthopaedie Journal (DEU ISSN 1438-0501) 5854
Kieferorthopaedie Nachrichten (DEU ISSN 1612-2577) 5854
Kieferorthopaedie Zeitung see K F O Zeitung 5854
Kiek Eben (DEU ISSN 0947-4080) 3851
Kiel (DEU ISSN 0936-6547) 3851
Kiel Discussion Papers see Kieler Diskussionsbeitraege 1495
Kiel Working Papers (Online) see Kieler Arbeitspapiere (Online) 1495
• ➤ Kieler Arbeitspapiere (Online)/Kiel Working Papers (Online) (DEU) 1495
Kieler Arbeitspapiere (Print) see Kieler Arbeitspapiere (Online) 1495
• ➤ Kieler Arbeitspapiere zur Landeskunde und Raumordnung (DEU ISSN 0940-0389) 4018
Kieler Beitraege zur Anglistik und Amerikanistik (DEU ISSN 0453-8463) 5317
Kieler Bibliographien zu Aktuellen Oekonomischen Themen (DEU ISSN 1433-8688) 1247
• ➤ Kieler Diskussionsbeitraege/Kiel Discussion Papers (DEU ISSN 0455-0420) 1495
➤ Kieler Geographische Schriften (DEU ISSN 0723-9874) 4018
Kieler Kurzberichte (DEU ISSN 0173-5241) 1495
Kieler Milchwirtschaftliche Forschungsberichte (DEU ISSN 0023-1347) 266
Kieler Nachrichten (DEU) 3851
Kieler Notizen zur Pflanzenkunde in Schleswig-Holstein und Hamburg (DEU ISSN 1615-3456) 799
Kieler Ostrechts-Notizen (DEU ISSN 1862-1589) 4954
Kieler Schriften zur Finanzwirtschaft (DEU ISSN 0932-206X) 1364
Kieler Schriften zur Musikwissenschaft (DEU) 6582
Kieler Studien (DEU ISSN 0340-6989) 1574
Kieler Studien zur Volkskunde und Kulturgeschichte (DEU ISSN 1616-8208) 8116
† ➤ Kieler Vortraege (DEU ISSN 0340-6970) 8969
Kieler Werkstuecke. Reihe A: Beitraege zur Schleswig-Holsteinischen und Skandinavischen Geschichte (DEU ISSN 0936-4005) 4237
Kieler Werkstuecke. Reihe B: Beitraege zur Nordischen und Baltischen Geschichte (DEU ISSN 0937-6275) 4237
Kieler Werkstuecke. Reihe C: Beitraege zur Europaeischen Geschichte des Fruehen und Hohen Mittelalters (DEU ISSN 0936-4935) 4237
Kieler Werkstuecke. Reihe D: Beitraege zur Europaeischen Geschichte des Spaeten Mittelalters (DEU ISSN 0936-4161) 4237
Kieler Werkstuecke. Reihe E: Beitraege zur Sozial- und Wirtschaftsgeschichte (DEU ISSN 1431-729X) 4237
Kieler Werkstuecke. Reihe F: Beitraege zur Osteuropaeischen Geschichte (DEU ISSN 0937-437X) 4237
Kieler Werkstuecke. Reihe G: Beitraege zur Fruehen Neuzeit (DEU ISSN 1431-7303) 4237
KielerLeben (DEU) 3851
Kielikello (FIN ISSN 0355-2675) 5317
• Kierkegaard Studies (DEU ISSN 1430-5372) 6930
➤ Kierkegaardiana (DNK ISSN 0075-6032) 6930
Kierkegaard's Writings (USA) 6931
Der Kieselstein (DEU ISSN 0174-3147) 3043
Kiev Business Directory see Kyivskii Dilovii Dovidnik 2012
• Kievskie Novosti (UKR) 3964
• Kievskie Vedomosti/Kyivski Vidomosti (UKR) 3964
Kievskie Vedomosti. Ponedel'nik (UKR) 3964
Kievskie Vedomosti. Pyatnitsa (UKR) 3964
Kievskii Politekhnicheskii Institut. Vestnik. Mashinostroenie see Natsional'nyi Tekhnichnyi Universytet Ukrainy "Kyivs'kyi Politekhnichnyi Instytut". Visnyk. Mashynobuduvannya 5457
Kiezen na de Basisschool (NLD ISSN 1871-8558) 2880
• Kig Ind (DNK ISSN 1398-2176) 3834
Kihara Institute for Biological Research. Report see Kihara Seibutsugaku Kenkyujo. Seiken Jiho 875
Kihara Seibutsugaku Kenkyujo. Seiken Jiho/Kihara Institute for Biological Research. Report (JPN ISSN 0080-8539) 875
Kiho Energi Sogo Kogaku see Enerugi Sogo Kogaku 7010
Kiho Kyosanken Mondai/Communist Bloc Problems see Roshia Kenkyu 7263
Kiho Soren Mondai/Soviet Problems see Roshia Kenkyu 7263
Kiinteisto ja Isannointi see Kiinteisto ja Isannoitsija 7597
Kiinteisto ja Isannoitsija (FIN ISSN 0782-7911) 7597
Kijk (NLD ISSN 0165-1390) 7876
Kijk op het Noorden/Outlook on the North (NLD ISSN 0023-1363) 1495
Kijk op het Westen (NLD ISSN 1574-6100) 1720
Kijk op Noord-Holland see Kijk op het Westen 1720
Kijk op Oost Nederland (NLD ISSN 0929-3116) 1140
Kijk op Zuid-Holland see Kijk op het Westen 1720
Kijkkez Techniek & Bouw (NLD ISSN 1873-8249) 3277
Kikai Gijutsu/Mechanical Engineering (JPN ISSN 0451-9396) 3387
Kikai Gijutsu Kenkyujo Hokoku/Mechanical Engineering Laboratory. Report (JPN ISSN 0286-2255) 3387
Kikai Gijutsu Kenkyujo. Kenkyu Koenkai Shiryo/Mechanical Engineering Laboratory. Proceedings of the Study Meeting (JPN) 3387
Kikai Gijutsu Kenkyujo Nenpo/Mechanical Engineering Laboratory. Annual Report (JPN) 3387
Kikai Gijutsu Kenkyujo Shiryo/Mechanical Engineering Laboratory. Technical Note (JPN ISSN 0286-2263) 3387
Kikai Gijutsu Kyokai Nyusu/Association of Mechanical Technology. News (JPN ISSN 0912-9626) 3387
Kikai Kogyo Keizai Kenkyu Hokokusho/Economic Research Reports on Machine Industry (JPN) 5454
Kikai no Kenkyu/Science of Machine (JPN ISSN 0368-5713) 5454
Kikai Sekkei see Machine Design 3388
Kikai Shinko/Promoting Machine Industry in Japan (JPN ISSN 0389-9500) 5454
Kikai Shinko Kaikan Bekkan. Shiken Kenkyu Hokokusho/Machine Tool Engineering Foundation. Research Report (JPN) 5454
Kikai Shinko Kyokai. Gijutsu Kenkyujo. Giken Nyusu/Japan Society for the Promotion of Machine Industry. Technical News (JPN ISSN 0385-8022) 5454
Kikai to Kogu/Tool Engineer (JPN ISSN 0387-1053) 3387
Kikai Tokei Geppo/Monthly Report of Machine Statistics (JPN ISSN 0916-4014) 5462
Kikai Tokei Nenpo/Yearbook of Machinery Statistics (JPN) 5462
Kikai Zairuo Zairuo Kako Gijutsu Koenkai Koen Ronbunshu see J S M E / A S M E International Conference on Materials and Processing (Year). Program and Abstract 3383
Kikaika Nogyo/Farming Mechanization (JPN ISSN 0023-1371) 212
Kikaiken Nyusu (JPN ISSN 0286-2271) 3387
Kikan Ganka Shujutsu/Japanese Society of Ophthalmic Surgeons. Journal (JPN ISSN 0914-6806) 6045
Kikan Kagaku Sosetsu/Survey of Chemistry. Quarterly (JPN) 2070
Kikan Keisei Kenkyukai Koen Yoshishu/Japanese Society for Basic and Applied Organ Research. Abstracts of the Meeting see Nihon Soshiki Kogakkai Puroguramu Shorokushu 717
Kikan Shakai Hosho Kenkyu/Quarterly of Social Security Research (JPN ISSN 0387-3064) 7286
• Kikan Shoshi Nabi/Books & Serials Navigator (JPN ISSN 1341-979X) 628
Kikan Togyo Shiho/Quarterly Information of Sugar Industry (JPN ISSN 0023-138X) 3653
Kikan Toyo Igaku/Oriental Medicine (JPN ISSN 1341-7460) 312
Kikanshi J E T O C (Japan Chemical Industry Ecology - Toxicology Information Center) (JPN ISSN 0914-4579) 3500
Kikanshigaku/Japan Society for Respiratory Endoscopy. Journal (JPN ISSN 0287-2137) 6215
Kikero see Lasten Oma Kirjakerho 2199
▼ Kiki (USA ISSN 1941-6350) 2197
Kikiriki (ESP ISSN 1133-0589) 2880
Kiko Eikyo Riyo Kenkyukai Kaiho/Japanese Study Group for the W C I P and W C A P Newsletter (JPN ISSN 0916-474X) 6359
Kikogaku Kishogaku Kenkyu Hokoku/Research Report of Meteorology and Climatology (JPN ISSN 0916-166X) 6359
Kikokei Kanshi Hokoku/Monthly Report on Climate System (JPN ISSN 0916-927X) 6359
Kilburn Times (GBR ISSN 0962-306X) 3867
Kildare Nationalist (IRL ISSN 1649-6469) 3893
Kilha see Khil'a 8454
Kilimo News (KEN) 130
Kilkenny People (IRL ISSN 1393-5232) 3893
The Kilkenny Voice (IRL ISSN 1649-7570) 3893
Killer App (USA) 2430
Killer Roads: From Crash to Verdict (USA) 4709
Killie Campbell Africana Library. Bibliographic Series (ZAF) 628
Kilpisjarvi Notes (FIN ISSN 0358-3279) 686
▼ • Kilter (USA ISSN 1945-3647) 500
Kilusang Mayo Uno, Philipppines Correspondence see K M U Correspondence 1691
Kim see Trefle 2218
Kim (SWE ISSN 1653-3348) 6582
▼ Kim Kolwiek (POL ISSN 1898-4991) 2197
Kimia Kini (MYS) 2070
➤ Kimika (PHL ISSN 0115-2130) 2070
Kimono see Utsukushii Kimono 2262
Kimya Muhendisligi (TUR ISSN 1301-3068) 3249
Kin (CAN ISSN 0023-1436) 2267
Kin Kollecting (USA ISSN 1069-207X) 3772
Kina-nytt (SWE ISSN 1100-4959) 1574
Kinaadman/Wisdom (PHL ISSN 0115-6012) 554
Kinabladet (DNK ISSN 1600-1273) 3826
Kinarapport (SWE ISSN 0345-5807) 3826

DIRECTORY 2010 KIRKJURITID 10529

† Kinbote (NLD ISSN 1871-3211) **8969**
Das Kind (DEU ISSN 0945-5582) **2158**
• Kind en Adolescent (NLD ISSN 0167-2436) **6096**
• Kind en Adolescent Praktijk (NLD ISSN 1571-4136) **6096**
Kind en Adolescent Review (NLD ISSN 1571-4969) **6096**
Kind en Ziekenhuis (NLD ISSN 0169-7072) **6096**
Kind - Jugend - Gesellschaft *see* Kinder- und Jugendschutz in Wissenschaft und Praxis **2158**
Kind op Zondag (NLD) **7658**
Kind & Gesundheit (DEU) **2158**
Kind und Vater (DEU ISSN 0176-8115) **2158**
Kindai (JPN ISSN 1342-4149) **6505**
Kindai Judo (JPN ISSN 0388-208X) **8184**
Kindai Kenchiku/Contemporary Architecture of the World (JPN ISSN 0023-1479) **447**
Kinder (DEU) **2158**
• Kinder (ITA ISSN 0766-0715) **5137**
Kinder Bastelspass (DEU) **2198**
Kinder Jugend Film Korrespondenz (DEU ISSN 0721-8486) **2198**
Kinder Jugend Literatur und Medien *see* K J L & M **2174**
kinder, kinder (DEU ISSN 1438-5066) **7529**
Kinder-Raetsel (DEU) **4337**
Kinder Raetsel Spass (DEU) **2198**
Kinder- und Jugendarzt (DEU ISSN 1436-9559) **5748**
Kinder- und Jugendkultur, -literatur und -medien (DEU ISSN 1435-4721) **5317**
Kinder- und Jugendliteraturforschung (DEU ISSN 1613-477X) **2158**
➤ Kinder- und Jugendmedizin (DEU ISSN 1617-0288) **6096**
➤ Kinder- und Jugendschutz in Wissenschaft und Praxis (DEU ISSN 1865-9330) **2158**
Kinderaerztliche Praxis (DEU ISSN 1432-3605) **6096**
Kinderanalyse (DEU ISSN 0942-6051) **7382**
Kinderen (NLD ISSN 0165-487X) **2158**
Kinderfysiotherapie *see* Nederlands Tijdschrift voor Kinderfysiotherapie **6113**
Kindergarten (ZAF) **7763**
Kindergarten connection learner guide *see* Bible Teaching for Kids: Kindergarten Connection Learner Guide **7626**
Kindergarten Heute (DEU ISSN 0344-3949) **2158**
Kindergarten Studies Weekly (USA ISSN 1550-3054) **2880**
Kindergarten Times *see* Pregnancy & Parenting **2166**
Kindergarten und Mission (DEU) **2158**
Die Kindergartenzeitschrift (DEU ISSN 1861-3101) **2880**
Der Kindergottesdienst (DEU) **7658**
Kinderhanden (NLD ISSN 1569-707X) **536**
KinderInformationsDienst *see* K I D - KinderInformationsDienst **2157**
Kinderkram (Kiel) (DEU) **2158**
Kinderkram Berlin (DEU ISSN 1433-0806) **2158**
Kinderkram Muenchen (DEU ISSN 1433-0865) **2158**
Kinderkrankenschwester (DEU ISSN 0723-2276) **5968**
Kinderleicht (DEU ISSN 0939-7817) **3069**
KinderMax (CHE ISSN 1660-2900) **2198**
▼ KinderMax Special (CHE ISSN 1661-8580) **2198**
KinderMode (NLD) **2257**
Kinderopvang (NLD ISSN 0926-0838) **2159**
KinderSpiel (AUT) **2159**
KinderTageseinrichtungen Spezial *see* KiTa Spezial **2159**
Kindertuin (ZAF) **7763**
Kinderzeit (DEU ISSN 0934-6570) **2880**
Kinderzeitung (DEU) **2159**
• Kindheit und Entwicklung (DEU ISSN 0942-5403) **6096**
Kindler (IND ISSN 0973-0486) **1770**
• Kindness Speaks All Languages (USA ISSN 1930-0689) **6810**
• Kindred Spirit (GBR ISSN 0955-7067) **6645**
• Kindred Spirits (CAN ISSN 0823-3837) **3772**
• Kindred Spirits (NAM ISSN 1816-9341) **4850**
Kindschaftsrechtliche Praxis *see* Zeitschrift fuer Kindschaftsrecht und Jugendhilfe **4915**
Kindschap Gods (NLD ISSN 1381-2327) **7803**
Kine Actualite (FRA ISSN 0766-2262) **6112**
Kine Point Presse (FRA ISSN 1772-8827) **6112**
• ➤ Kinema (CAN ISSN 1192-6252) **6505**
• ➤ Kinematics and Physics of Celestial Bodies (USA ISSN 0884-5913) **577**
Kinematika i Fizika Nebesnykh Tel *see* Kinematics and Physics of Celestial Bodies **577**
Kinematograph (DEU ISSN 0936-3777) **6505**
KineR (FRA ISSN 1958-4385) **6112**
Kinerea *see* KineR **6112**
• Kinesiologia (CHL ISSN 0716-4173) **8184**
➤ Kinesiologia Slovenica (SVN ISSN 1318-2269) **6991**
➤ Kinesiology (HRV ISSN 1331-1441) **6991**
• Kinesiology Abstracts (USA ISSN 1547-1284) **7001**
Kinesis (CAN ISSN 0317-9095) **8870**
Kinesis (Carbondale) (USA ISSN 0023-1568) **6931**
Kinesiterapia - Medicina Fisica *see* Encyclopedie Medico-Chirurgicale. Kinesiterapia - Medicina Fisica **6108**
• ➤ Kinesitherapie. La Revue (FRA ISSN 1779-0123) **6112**
Kinesitherapie. Les Annales *see* Kinesitherapie. La Revue **6112**
Kinesitherapie. Les Cahiers *see* Kinesitherapie. La Revue **6112**
Kinesitherapie, Medecine, Readaptation *see* Encyclopedie Medico-Chirurgicale. Kinesitherapie - Medecine Physique - Readaptation **6108**
• Kinesitherapie Scientifique (FRA ISSN 0023-1576) **6112**
▼ • Kinetic and Related Models (USA ISSN 1937-5093) **7024**
• Kinetic Art Words (USA ISSN 1935-0422) **500**
• ➤ Kinetics and Catalysis (RUS ISSN 0023-1584) **2138**
• ➤ Kinetika i Kataliz (RUS ISSN 0453-8811) **2138**
➤ Kinetoscopio (COL ISSN 0121-3776) **6505**
Kinfolk (USA ISSN 1083-1266) **3772**
King (DEU) **6582**
• King (USA ISSN 1536-531X) **6293**
• King Abdul Aziz Medical Journal (SAU ISSN 0254-413X) **5657**
King Abdul Aziz University. Faculty of Earth Sciences. Bulletin (SAU) **2712**
King Abdulaziz University. Faculty of Marine Science. Journal (SAU ISSN 1021-1802) **2810**
▼ King Air (USA ISSN 1938-9361) **64**
King County Medical Society. Bulletin (USA) **5657**
King Edward Medical College. Lahore. Annals (PAK ISSN 1684-6680) **5657**
King Faisal Center for Research and Islamic Studies. Manuscript Catalogue *see* Markaz al-Malik Faisal lil-Buhuth wal-Dirasat al-Islamiyyah. Fihris al-Makhtutat **564**
King Faisal Center for Research and Islamic Studies. Newsletter (SAU) **7713**
• King Guide to Parental Admixtures for Windows (CD-ROM Edition) (USA ISSN 1533-3671) **6857**
• King Guide to Parenteral Admixtures (Print Edition) (USA) **6857**
King James Version Standard Lesson Commentary *see* Standard Lesson Commentary King James Version **7683**
King-Mag.Com *see* King **6293**
• King of Pension Funds CD-ROM (USA) **1691**
King of Story Tellers *see* Gushi Dawang **5303**
King of the Road (NLD ISSN 1574-3322) **8502**
▼ King of the Street (USA) **8588**
King Pole Circus Magazine (GBR) **8472**
➤ King Saud University Journal. Administrative Sciences (SAU ISSN 1018-3582) **1140**
➤ King Saud University Journal. Agricultural Sciences (SAU ISSN 1018-3590) **130**
➤ King Saud University Journal. Architecture and Planning (SAU ISSN 1018-3604) **4418**
➤ King Saud University Journal. Arts (SAU ISSN 1018-3612) **500**
➤ King Saud University Journal. Computer and Information Sciences/Jami'at al-Malik Sa'ud. Majallah. Al-'Ulum al-Hasib wal-Ma'lumat (SAU ISSN 1319-1578) **2430**
➤ King Saud University Journal. Educational Sciences and Islamic Studies/Jami'at al-Malik Sa'ud. Majallah. Al-'Ulum al-Tarbawiyyah wal-Dirasat al-Islamiyyah (SAU) **7713**
➤ King Saud University Journal. Engineering Sciences (SAU ISSN 1018-3639) **3207**
➤ King Saud University Journal. Language and Translation (SAU ISSN 1319-6618) **5137**
➤ King Saud University Journal. Science (SAU ISSN 1018-3647) **7876**
King Township Sentinel (CAN) **3812**
Kingbird (USA ISSN 0023-1606) **909**
• The Kingdom (IRL) **3893**
Kingdom of the Stories *see* Gushi Daguan **8960**
Kingpin (GBR ISSN 0969-2150) **8184**
Kings Bay Periscope (USA) **6430**
King's Coal Export Report (USA ISSN 1047-4269) **6468**
King's Coalstats (USA) **6468**
King's College Law Journal *see* King's Law Journal **4709**
King's College London. Centre of Medical Law and Ethics. Dispatches (GBR ISSN 1358-0906) **5657**
Kings County Medical Society Bulletin *see* K C M S Bulletin **5656**
Kings County Memories (CAN ISSN 1494-9296) **3772**
King's Gazette (GBR ISSN 0085-2546) **5657**
King's Gulf Grain Guide (USA ISSN 0885-5811) **274**
King's International Coal Trade (USA ISSN 0749-9043) **6468**
• ➤ King's Law Journal (GBR) **4709**
Kings Mountain Herald (USA) **3546**
King's Northern Coal (USA ISSN 0749-1719) **6468**
Kings of Tomorrow Series (GBR ISSN 0075-6083) **644**
King's Southern Coal (USA ISSN 0749-1697) **6468**
King's Western Coal (USA ISSN 0749-1700) **6468**
Kingsbridge, Salcombe & South Hams Gazette (GBR ISSN 0963-7605) **3867**
• Kingsize (SWE ISSN 1502-7783) **6582**
• Kingsize (SWE ISSN 1652-8190) **6582**
The Kingsman (GBR ISSN 0140-0991) **6430**
• Kingston This Week (CAN ISSN 0712-9068) **3812**
• ➤ Kingston University Research & Innovation Reports (GBR ISSN 1749-5652) **2563**
• Kingston Whig-Standard (CAN ISSN 1197-4397) **3812**
• Kingswood Kranium (USA) **28**
Kinheart Connection (USA) **8870**
Kinisi *see* Motion **8785**
Kinjin Kenkyujo Kenkyu Hokoku/Tottori Mycological Institute. Reports (JPN ISSN 0388-8266) **799**
Kinjo Kokubun *see* Kinjou Nihongo Nihon Bunka **5137**
Kinjo Studies in Japanese Language, Literature and Culture *see* Kinjou Nihongo Nihon Bunka **5137**
Kinjou Nihongo Nihon Bunka/Kinjo Studies in Japanese Language, Literature and Culture (JPN ISSN 1348-4389) **5137**
Kinki Aruminyumu Hyomen Shori Kenkyukai Kaishi (JPN ISSN 0285-6689) **6320**
Kinki Bio-Industry Conference. Bio Industry (JPN) **767**
Kinki Botanical Society. News *see* Kinki Shokubutsu Dokokai Kaiho **799**
Kinki Chugoku Agricultural Research/Kinki Chugoku Nogyo Kenkyu (JPN ISSN 0385-311X) **130**
Kinki Chugoku Nogyo Kenkyu *see* Kinki Chugoku Agricultural Research **130**
• Kinki Chuugoku Shikoku Nougyou Kenkyuu Senta Kenkyuu Houkoku/National Agricultural Research Center for Western Region. Bulletin (JPN ISSN 1347-1244) **130**
Kinki Daigaku Genshiryoku Kenkyujo Nenpo/Kinki University. Atomic Energy Research Institute. Annual Report (JPN ISSN 0374-8715) **3170**
Kinki Daigaku Igaku Zasshi/Medical Journal of Kinki University (JPN ISSN 0385-8367) **5657**
Kinki Daigaku Kyushu Kogakubu Kenkyu Hokoku/Kinki University. Kyushu School of Engineering. Reports (JPN ISSN 1345-9430) **3207**
Kinki Daigaku. Nogakubu Kiyo/Kinki University. Faculty of Agriculture. Memoirs (JPN ISSN 0453-8889) **131**
Kinki Daigaku Raifu Saiensu Kenkyu Hokoku/Kinki University. Life Science Institute. Report of Studies (JPN) **686**
Kinki Daigaku Rikogakubu Kenkyu Hokoku/Kinki University. Faculty of Science and Technology. Journal (JPN ISSN 0386-4928) **7876**
Kinki Nogyo Josei Hokoku *see* Annual Review of Agriculture in Kinki District **92**
Kinki Shokubutsu Dokokai Kaiho/Kinki Botanical Society. News (JPN ISSN 0914-3823) **799**
Kinki University. Atomic Energy Research Institute. Annual Report *see* Kinki Daigaku Genshiryoku Kenkyujo Nenpo **3170**
Kinki University. Environmental Science Research Institute. Annals (JPN) **3449**
Kinki University. Faculty of Agriculture. Memoirs *see* Kinki Daigaku. Nogakubu Kiyo **131**
Kinki University. Faculty of Science and Technology. Journal *see* Kinki Daigaku Rikogakubu Kenkyu Hokoku **7876**
Kinki University. Kyushu School of Engineering. Reports *see* Kinki Daigaku Kyushu Kogakubu Kenkyu Hokoku **3207**
Kinki University. Life Science Institute. Report of Studies *see* Kinki Daigaku Raifu Saiensu Kenkyu Hokoku **686**
▼ Kinki University Series on Quantum Computing (SGP ISSN 1793-7299) **2430**
• Kinko's Impress (USA) **1140**
Kinky Fetishes (USA) **6293**
Kinnection (CAN ISSN 0823-0536) **5658**
• Kinnki: Dento Igaku Tsushin/Japan Kanpo Society Newsletter (JPN) **312**
Kino (BGR ISSN 0861-4393) **6506**
Kino *see* German Films Quarterly **6502**
Kino (IND) **6505**
Kino (POL ISSN 0023-1673) **6505**
• Kino Domowe (POL ISSN 1506-6428) **2402**
† Kino fuer Kinder (DDR ISSN 0233-2116) **8969**
• Kino - Glaz (RUS ISSN 0869-4370) **6506**
Kino Journal Frankfurt (DEU) **6506**
Kino-Teatr (UKR ISSN 1562-3238) **6506**
Kino Zairyo/Function & Materials (JPN ISSN 0286-4835) **3351**
Kino&Co. (DEU) **6506**
Kinohandbuch (DEU) **2010**
Kinokuni/Wakayama Insect Society. Bulletin (JPN ISSN 0913-5421) **853**
Kinomagazin (DEU) **6506**
Kinoshi Kenkyukaishi/High Performance Paper Society, Japan. Annals (JPN ISSN 0288-5867) **6735**
➤ Kinoteki No Shinkei Geka/Functional Neurosurgery (JPN) **6157**
kinowelt.de (DEU) **6506**
Kinship (USA ISSN 0023-1703) **8052**
Kinship Kronicle (USA ISSN 0882-9802) **3773**
Kintner's Federal Antitrust Law (USA) **4873**
KINtop (DEU ISSN 1024-1906) **6506**
Kintu (IND) **5222**
Kinyamateka (RWA) **1140**
Kinyu Kenkyu/Monetary and Economic Studies (JPN ISSN 0287-5306) **1364**
Kin'yu Zaisei Jijo/Financial Economist Weekly (JPN ISSN 1345-3033) **1364**
Kinzoku/Materials Science & Technology (JPN ISSN 0368-6337) **6320**
Kinzoku Hakubutsukan Kiyo/Metals Museum. Bulletin (JPN ISSN 0285-8452) **6320**
Kiongozi/Leader (TZA ISSN 0856-2563) **7803**
Kiosk *see* JOP Coach Magazine **2943**
Kiosk (Dutch Edition) *see* Kiosk (French Edition) **5074**
Kiosk (French Edition) (BEL ISSN 1378-6164) **5074**
Kioskinhaber (CHE) **1828**
Kiosko (ESP) **4579**
Kipalapala Leo (TZA) **7658**
• The Kipling Journal (GBR ISSN 0023-1738) **5317**
• Kiplinger Agriculture Letter (USA ISSN 0023-1746) **131**
• Kiplinger Business Forecasts (USA ISSN 1531-7692) **1495**
• Kiplinger California Letter (USA ISSN 0453-9249) **1636**
• The Kiplinger Letter (USA ISSN 1528-7130) **1636**
• Kiplinger Tax Letter (USA ISSN 0023-1762) **1932**
▼ • Kiplinger's Biofuels Market Alert (USA ISSN 1937-4615) **1636**
Kiplinger's New Car Buyer's Guide (Year) (USA) **8588**
• Kiplinger's Personal Finance (USA ISSN 1528-9729) **1364**
• Kiplinger's Personal Finance Mutual Funds (USA ISSN 1529-6245) **1636**
Kiplinger's Personal Finance New Cars and Trucks Buyer's Guide *see* Kiplinger's Personal Finance New Cars & Trucks Buyer's Guide **8588**
Kiplinger's Personal Finance New Cars & Trucks Buyer's Guide (USA ISSN 1529-8493) **8588**
• Kiplinger's Personal Finance Retirement Planning (USA ISSN 1528-9753) **1636**
Kiplinger's Retirement Planning (USA) **1636**
• Kiplinger's Retirement Report (USA ISSN 1075-6671) **1636**
Kippari (FIN ISSN 0780-5373) **8277**
Kipus (BOL) **8116**
➤ Kipus (ECU ISSN 1390-0102) **5222**
• Kipuviesti (FIN ISSN 1796-3141) **5658**
• Kirahviposti (FIN ISSN 1795-8032) **1600**
Kirajagat (BGD) **8184**
Die Kirche (DEU ISSN 0949-8672) **7763**
Kirche Heute (DEU ISSN 0946-5804) **7803**
Kirche im Laendlichen Raum (DEU ISSN 0173-4636) **7763**
➤ Kirche im Osten (DEU ISSN 0453-9273) **7763**
Kirche in Marburg (DEU) **7658**
➤ Kirche und Konfession (DEU ISSN 0453-929X) **7658**
Kirche und Leben (DEU) **7803**
Kirche und Recht (AUT ISSN 0259-0735) **4709**
Kirche und Recht (DEU ISSN 0947-8094) **4709**
Kirche und Schule (DEU) **7803**
Kirchenbote (DEU ISSN 1431-5637) **7803**
Kirchenmusikalische Mitteilungen der Dioezese Rottenburg-Stuttgart (DEU ISSN 1436-0276) **6582**
Kirchenmusikalische Nachrichten (DEU ISSN 0939-4761) **6582**
Kirchenmusikalisches Jahrbuch (DEU ISSN 0075-6199) **6582**
Kirchenzeitung fuer das Bistum Aachen (DEU ISSN 0936-9627) **7803**
Kirchenzeitung fuer das Bistum Eichstaett (DEU) **7803**
Kirchenzeitung fuer das Erzbistum Koeln (DEU) **7803**
KirchenZeitung Hildesheim (DEU) **7804**
➤ Kirchliche Zeitgeschichte (DEU ISSN 0932-9951) **4237**
Kirchlicher Dienst in der Arbeitswelt *see* Momente aus Kirche und Arbeitswelt **7768**
Kirchliches Amtsblatt fuer das Bistum Essen (DEU ISSN 0023-1827) **7658**
Kirchliches Amtsblatt fuer das Bistum Trier (DEU) **7658**
Kirchliches Buch- und Bibliothekswesen (DEU ISSN 1617-4674) **5023**
Kirchliches Jahrbuch fuer die Evangelische Kirche in Deutschland (DEU ISSN 0075-6210) **7763**
Kirikou (FRA ISSN 1952-9449) **2198**
Kirilo-Metodievski Studii/Cyrillo-Methodian Studies (BGR ISSN 0205-2253) **4237**
Kirin Brewery Company. Annual Report (JPN) **606**
Kirisutokyo Kagaku Sakigake *see* The Herald of Christian Science **8962**
Kirisutokyo Kagaku Sakigake *see* Le Heraut de la Christian Science **7736**
Kirisutokyo Ronso/Institute for Research of Christian Culture. Bulletin (JPN ISSN 0288-6138) **7658**
Kirjakauppalehti (FIN ISSN 0047-343X) **7564**
Kirjallisuudentutkimuksen Aikakauslehti Avain/Finnish Review of Literary Studies (FIN ISSN 1795-3790) **5317**
• Kirjastolehti/Finnish Library Journal (FIN ISSN 0023-1843) **5023**
Kirjeshakki (FIN ISSN 0358-1071) **8184**
• Kirke og Kultur (NOR ISSN 0023-186X) **7658**
Kirkebladet/Church Newsletter (CAN) **7763**
Kirkeforskning Perspektiv *see* K I F O Perspektiv **7657**
Kirkeforskning Rapport *see* K I F O Rapport **7657**
Kirkegaarden (DNK ISSN 1398-4586) **3720**
Kirkegaarden (NOR ISSN 1501-0406) **3740**
Kirkegaardskultur (DNK ISSN 0907-8541) **3720**
Kirkehistoriske Samlinger (DNK ISSN 0450-3171) **7658**
Kirkelig Forening for den Indre Mission i Danmark. Aarbog (DNK ISSN 0905-071X) **7763**
Kirken i Dag/News from Kirkefondet (DNK ISSN 1601-8230) **7658**
• Kirken Underviser (DNK ISSN 1602-2785) **7658**
• Kirkens Noedhjelp Magasinet (NOR ISSN 1503-9862) **8052**
Kirkens Noedhjelp Magasinet *see* Kirkens Noedhjelp Magasinet **8052**
Kirkia (ZWE ISSN 0451-9930) **799**
Kirkintilloch & Bishopbriggs Herald (GBR) **3867**
Kirkjuritid (ISL ISSN 1021-8351) **7763**

Title

• Kirkon Tutkimuskeskus. Julkaisuja (FIN ISSN 1459-2681) **7658**
Kirk's Current Veterinary Therapy (USA ISSN 1946-164X) **8802**
Kirk's Current Veterinary Therapy. Small Animal Practice *see* Kirk's Current Veterinary Therapy **8802**
• Kirkus Reviews (USA ISSN 1948-7428) **7564**
Kirovskaya Pravda (RUS) **3936**
KirRoyal (DEU) **6991**
Kirschner's Agent Source Book. Northern California (USA) **4511**
Kirschner's Agent Source Book. Southern California (USA) **4511**
Kirschner's Agent Source Book. West (USA) **4511**
Kirschner's Insurance Directories. Northern California *see* Kirschner's Agent Source Book. Northern California **4511**
Kirschner's Insurance Directories. Pacific Northwest *see* Kirschner's Agent Source Book. West **4511**
Kirschner's Insurance Directories. Southern California *see* Kirschner's Agent Source Book. Southern California **4511**
Kirsh's Construction Lien Case Finder (CAN) **4709**
Kirtlandia (USA ISSN 0075-6245) **7876**
• Kiruna Geophysical Data (SWE ISSN 0453-9478) **2786**
† Kiryat Sefer (ISR ISSN 0023-1851) **8969**
Kirykas/Herald (CYP) **4597**
Kis Epito (SVK) **2198**
Kisalfoeld (HUN ISSN 0133-1507) **3876**
Kisan World (IND) **131**
Kiseichu Bunrui Keitai Danwakai Kaiho/Japanese Society for Systematic Parasitology. Circular (JPN ISSN 0915-5007) **5821**
Kiselevskie Vesti (RUS) **3936**
Kishavaraz (IRN) **131**
Kishidaia/Tokyo Spider Study Group. Bulletin (JPN ISSN 0915-9754) **853**
Kishinevskie Novosti (MDA) **3913**
Kisho Eisei Senta Gijutsu Hokoku/Meteorological Satellite Center Technical Note (JPN ISSN 0388-9653) **6359**
Kisho Eisei Senta Nyusu/Meteorological Satellite Center News (JPN ISSN 0287-9247) **6359**
Kisho Gyomu Hokoku Chosa Shukeisho/Annual Report of Meteorological Service (JPN) **6359**
Kisho Kansokukyo Tetto Kansoku Shiryo/Report of Observation at the Meteorological Observation Tower (JPN) **6359**
Kisho Kenkyujo Gijutsu Hokoku/Meteorological Research Institute. Technical Reports (JPN ISSN 0386-4049) **6359**
Kisho Kenkyujo Nyusu/Meteorological Research Institute News (JPN) **6359**
Kisho Nenkan/Yearbook of Meteorology (JPN) **6359**
➤ Kisho Riyo Kenkyu/Applied Climate Resources Research (JPN ISSN 0917-494X) **6359**
Kisho Shushi *see* Meteorological Society of Japan. Journal **6391**
Kisho Yoran/Geophysical Review (JPN) **2786**
Kishocho Chijiki Kansokujo Hokoku. Chikyu Denki *see* Kakioka Magnetic Observatory. Report. Geoelectricity **2785**
Kishocho Chijiki Kansokujo Hokoku. Chikyu Jiki *see* Kakioka Magnetic Observatory. Report. Geomagnetism **2785**
Kishocho Geppo Zenkoku Kishohyo/Japan Meteorological Agency. Monthly Report. Meteorological Observations (JPN ISSN 0448-374X) **6359**
Kishocho Gijutsu Hokoku/Japan Meteorological Agency. Technical Report (JPN ISSN 0447-3868) **2786**
Kishocho Jishin Kansokujo Gijutsu Hokoku/Matsushiro Seismological Observatory. Technical Reports (JPN ISSN 0388-7359) **2786**
Kishocho Kaihyo Kansoku Shiryo/Results of Sea Ice Observations (JPN) **2810**
Kishocho Kaiyo Junpo/Ten-Day Marine Report (JPN) **6359**
Kishocho Kansoku Gijutsu Shiryo/Japan Meteorological Agency. Technical Data Series (JPN) **6359**
Kishocho Kenkyu Jiho *see* Journal of Meteorological Research **6358**
Kishocho Kisho Kenkyujo Kenkyu Hokokusho/Meteorological Research Institute. Annual Research Report (JPN) **6359**
Kishocho Nenpo Zenkoku Kishohyo *see* Japan Meteorological Agency. Annual Report **6358**
Kishocho Obun Kaiyo Hokoku *see* Oceanographical Magazine **2815**
Kishou Kenkyu Noto/Meteorological Study Note (JPN ISSN 0387-5369) **6359**
Kishu Biological News *see* Kishu Seibutsu **686**
Kishu Seibutsu/Kishu Biological News (JPN ISSN 0287-4970) **686**
Kisitsistigut Naatsorsueqqissaarneq Killiqarfeqanngitsumik *see* Statistics Across Borders **8990**
Kiskedyed (HUN ISSN 1215-7414) **8870**
Kiskedyed Konyhaja (HUN ISSN 1217-2227) **4362**
• Kismama (HUN ISSN 0865-1035) **8870**
Kiso Gijutsu Kenkyu Bukai Shiryo/Technical Report of Medical Ultrasound Engineering (JPN) **6202**
Kiso Kagaku Kenkyujo Koenkai Koenshu/Proceedings for the I F C Symposium (JPN ISSN 0916-4367) **2070**
Kiso Roka Gakkai Sakyura/Biomedical Gerontology Circular (JPN ISSN 0912-8948) **4050**
Kiso Roka Kenkyu/Biomedical Gerontology (JPN ISSN 0912-8921) **737**
Kiso Shinrigaku Kenkyu/Japanese Journal of Psychonomic Science (JPN ISSN 0287-7651) **7382**
Kisokan/Pneumatic Tube (JPN) **3170**
Kisoko/Foundation Engineering and Equipment (JPN ISSN 0285-5356) **3277**
Kiss (ITA ISSN 1125-6575) **5411**
Kiss (JPN) **8870**
Kiss Machine (CAN ISSN 1910-9644) **5317**
Kiss Machine Presents - Skim *see* Skim **518**
Kiss Machine Presents - Violet Miranda, Girl Pirate *see* Violet Miranda, Girl Pirate **2219**
Kissafani (FIN ISSN 1236-4525) **6810**
Kissan Bhaarti (IND) **131**
The Kist (GBR ISSN 0307-529X) **4237**
➤ Kiswahili (TZA ISSN 0856-048X) **5137**
Kit *see* Kit Flugzeug-Modell Journal **4337**
Kit *see* Kit Militaer-Modell Journal **4337**
Kit & Specialist Cars International (GBR ISSN 1467-3479) **8588**
Kit-Car (GBR ISSN 0955-4076) **8588**
Kit Cars International *see* Kit & Specialist Cars International **8588**
The Kit-Cat Review (USA ISSN 1099-3649) **5317**
Kit et + *see* Kit et Plus **2198**
Kit et Plus (FRA ISSN 1777-4934) **2198**
† Kit Figuren-Modell Journal (DEU ISSN 1619-5566) **8969**
Kit Flugzeug-Modell Journal (DEU ISSN 1619-5574) **4337**
Kit Militaer-Modell Journal (DEU ISSN 1619-5582) **4337**
Kita (DEU ISSN 0948-3314) **554**
KiTa KinderTageseinrichtungen Aktuell. Ausgabe Baden-Wuerttemberg (DEU ISSN 0943-0237) **2159**
KiTa KinderTageseinrichtungen Aktuell. Ausgabe Bayern (DEU ISSN 0936-5982) **2159**
KiTa KinderTageseinrichtungen Aktuell. Ausgabe Brandenburg, Mecklenburg-Vorpommern, Sachsen, Sachsen-Anhalt, Thueringen und Berlin (DEU ISSN 0941-4347) **2159**
KiTa KinderTageseinrichtungen Aktuell. Ausgabe Hessen, Rheinland-Pfalz, Saarland (DEU ISSN 1437-1790) **2159**
KiTa KinderTageseinrichtungen Aktuell. Ausgabe Niedersachsen, Schleswig-Holstein, Hamburg, Bremen (DEU ISSN 0944-4173) **2159**
KiTa Kindertageseinrichtungen Aktuell. Ausgabe Nordrhein-Westfalen (DEU ISSN 0942-2463) **2159**
Kita Nihon Byogaichu Kenkyukaiho/Society of Plant Protection of North Japan. Annual Report (JPN ISSN 0368-623X) **240**
Kita Nihon Kango Gakkaishi/North Japan Academy of Nursing Science. Journal (JPN ISSN 1344-168X) **5968**
KiTa Recht (DEU ISSN 1612-0809) **2159**
KiTa Spezial (DEU ISSN 1437-4013) **2159**
Kitab al-Hilal (EGY) **3836**
Kitab el Yawm (EGY) **3836**
Kitab-i Muqavamat (IRN) **6430**
Kitakami City Museum. Bulletin *see* Kitakami-shiritsu Hakubutsukan Kenkyu Hokoku **7876**
Kitakami-shiritsu Hakubutsukan Kenkyu Hokoku/Kitakami City Museum. Bulletin (JPN ISSN 0386-0655) **7876**
Kitakanto Igaku *see* Kitakanto Medical Journal **5658**
➤ Kitakanto Medical Journal (JPN ISSN 1343-2826) **5658**
Kitakyushu Botanical Association. Journal *see* Kitakyushu Shokubutsu Tomo no Kai Kaiho **799**
Kitakyushu Museum of Natural History and Human History. Bulletin. Series A, Natural History *see* Kitakyuushuu Shiritsu Shizenshi, Rekishi Hakubutsukan Kenkyuu Houkoku. Arui, Shizenshi **7876**
Kitakyushu Museum of Natural History and Human History. Bulletin. Series B, Human History *see* Kitakyuushuu Shiritsu Shizenshi, Rekishi Hakubutsukan Kenkyuu Houkoku. Brui, Rekishi **345**
Kitakyushu Shiritsu Shizenshi Hakubutsukan Kenkyu Hokoku/Kitakyushu Museum of Natural History. Bulletin *see* Kitakyuushuu Shiritsu Shizenshi, Rekishi Hakubutsukan Kenkyuu Houkoku. Brui, Rekishi **345**
Kitakyushu Shiritsu Shizenshi Hakubutsukan Kenkyu Hokoku/Kitakyushu Museum of Natural History. Bulletin *see* Kitakyuushuu Shiritsu Shizenshi, Rekishi Hakubutsukan Kenkyuu Houkoku. Arui, Shizenshi **7876**
Kitakyushu Shokubutsu Tomo no Kai Kaiho/Kitakyushu Botanical Association. Journal (JPN ISSN 0387-7361) **799**
Kitakyuushuu Shiritsu Shizenshi, Rekishi Hakubutsukan Kenkyuu Houkoku. Arui, Shizenshi/Kitakyushu Museum of Natural History and Human History. Bulletin. Series A, Natural History (JPN ISSN 1348-2653) **7876**
Kitakyuushuu Shiritsu Shizenshi, Rekishi Hakubutsukan Kenkyuu Houkoku. Brui, Rekishi/Kitakyushu Museum of Natural History and Human History. Bulletin. Series B, Human History (JPN ISSN 1349-323X) **345**
Kitami Institute of Technology. Memoirs *see* Kitami Kogyo Daigaku Kenkyu Hokoku **8430**
Kitami Kogyo Daigaku Kenkyu Hokoku/Kitami Institute of Technology. Memoirs (JPN ISSN 0387-7035) **8430**
➤ Kitano Hospital Journal of Medicine (JPN ISSN 0023-1916) **5658**
Kitap-lik (TUR ISSN 1300-0586) **5222**
KiTaRecht *see* KiTa Recht **2159**
Kitasato Daigaku Daigakuin Yakugaku Kenkyuka Rinsho Yakugaku Tokuron Kiyo/Kitasato University. Clinical Pharmacy Bulletin (JPN ISSN 0914-5079) **6857**
Kitasato Institute. Annual Report (JPN ISSN 0385-2024) **5658**
Kitasato University. Clinical Pharmacy Bulletin *see* Kitasato Daigaku Daigakuin Yakugaku Kenkyuka Rinsho Yakugaku Tokuron Kiyo **6857**
Kitbuilders Magazine (USA) **4338**
• Kitchen & Bath Business (USA ISSN 0730-2487) **1019**
• Kitchen & Bath Design News (USA ISSN 8750-345X) **4544**
Kitchen and Bath Emporium (USA ISSN 1935-231X) **4362**
Kitchen and Bath Ideas Products Guide (USA ISSN 1939-4764) **4560**
▼ Kitchen & Bath Ideas Under $100 (USA ISSN 1944-1983) **4544**
Kitchen & Bath Ideas Under One Hundred Dollars *see* Kitchen & Bath Ideas Under $100 **4544**
Kitchen & Bath Portfolio (USA) **1019**
The Kitchen & Bathroom Designer *see* Designer (Middle East Edition) **4538**
The Kitchen & Bathroom Designer *see* Designer (Dartmouth) **4538**
Kitchen & Bathroom Furniture & Fittings Industry *see* Business Ratio. The Kitchen and Bathroom Furniture and Fittings Industry **4534**
Kitchen & Cook (USA ISSN 1545-8105) **4362**
The Kitchen + Bath Designer (North America Edition) *see* Designer (U.S. Edition) **4538**
Kitchen Bath Specialist (USA) **1019**
Kitchen Bathroom Bedroom Business Monthly (GBR ISSN 0964-0347) **4560**
The Kitchen + Bathroom Designer (Middle East Edition) *see* Designer (Middle East Edition) **4538**
The Kitchen + Bathroom Designer (U K Edition) *see* Designer (Dartmouth) **4538**
Kitchen, Bedroom and Bathroom Review *see* K B B Review **4559**
Kitchen Cabinets and Countertops (USA ISSN 1940-5308) **1047**
The Kitchen Collection By Professional Designers (USA ISSN 1945-550X) **4544**
The Kitchen Designer *see* Designer (Dartmouth) **4538**
• The Kitchen Garden (GBR ISSN 1369-1821) **3740**
Kitchen Makeovers (USA ISSN 1547-5689) **4560**
Kitchen Planning Guide *see* Better Homes and Gardens Kitchen Planning Guide **4533**
Kitchen Sink (USA) **500**
† Kitchen Style & Storage (USA ISSN 1933-6241) **8969**
Kitchen Times (USA) **4362**
Kitchen Trends (NZL) **4544**
• Kitchener - Waterloo Record (CAN ISSN 0824-5150) **3812**
Kitchens & Bathrooms News (GBR ISSN 1757-5737) **4544**
Kitchens & Baths (New York) (USA ISSN 1550-6401) **4544**
Kitchens & Baths (Newtown) (USA) **1019**
Kitchens, Bedrooms & Bathrooms Magazine (GBR ISSN 0966-4114) **4560**
Kitchens By Professional Designers (USA) **4544**
Kitchenware *see* Key Note Market Report. Kitchenware **1894**
Kitchenware News (USA ISSN 1084-3027) **4560**
† Kite (NZL) **8969**
Kite & Friends (DEU ISSN 1615-1089) **4338**
Kite Boarding *see* Kiteboarding **8320**
Kite World *see* Kiteworld **8320**
Kiteboard (CAN) **8184**
Kiteboard Italia (ITA ISSN 1593-6392) **8277**
▼ Kiteboard Pro World Tour Mag (ZAF ISSN 1751-9624) **8184**
Kiteboarder (FRA ISSN 1624-8570) **8320**
• Kiteboarding (USA ISSN 1534-4282) **8320**
KiteLines (USA ISSN 0192-3439) **8320**
• Kiteworld (GBR ISSN 1477-1314) **8320**
Kition-Bamboula (FRA) **402**
Kitorogia *see* Cytologia **831**
• Kitplanes (USA ISSN 0891-1851) **64**
Kitsap Chronicle (USA) **3546**
Kitsap County Chronicle *see* Kitsap Chronicle **3546**
Kitsap County Dispatch (USA) **3546**
Kitte Shumi (JPN) **6896**
Kittens U S A (USA ISSN 1093-9415) **6810**
Kittseer Schriften zur Volkskunde (AUT) **3619**
Kitty Love (GBR) **6810**
▼ Kitu Kizuri (USA) **3546**
Kitz (DEU) **3851**
➤ Kiva (USA ISSN 0023-1940) **402**
Kivive *see* Xist in Christ **7695**
Kiwa Magazine (NLD ISSN 1574-7948) **8828**
• Kiwanis (USA ISSN 0162-5276) **2267**
The Kiwi (GBR ISSN 0964-7821) **6896**
• Kiwi (USA ISSN 1933-2920) **6662**
Kiwi Motorcycle Rider *see* Kiwi Rider **8260**
Kiwi Rider (NZL ISSN 1177-0023) **8260**
Kiwi Surf (AUS ISSN 1170-6139) **8320**
Kiwifruit (NZL ISSN 1175-9178) **240**
Kiwifruit Enthusiasts Journal (USA) **3741**
Kiwiphile File (USA) **3546**
† Kiyup Kyungyung/Business Management (KOR) **8969**
Kizili (RUS) **5317**
Kizito (UGA ISSN 0023-1975) **7804**
Kjedebutikken *see* Kjedemagasinet **1963**
Kjedemagasinet (NOR ISSN 1504-1271) **1963**
• Kjemi (NOR ISSN 0023-1983) **2070**
• Kjerteminde Avis (DNK) **3834**
Kjoekkenskriveren (NOR ISSN 0332-9046) **6662**
Kjoekkesjefen (NOR ISSN 0803-8562) **4392**
Kjoepmannen (NOR) **1829**
• Kjoettbransjen (NOR ISSN 0332-7078) **3680**
Kjoettsamvirket *see* Norturamagasinet **142**
Klachtenmanagement (NLD ISSN 1572-5219) **4709**
Kladblok (NLD ISSN 1574-6143) **4461**
Klaex (DEU ISSN 1612-8141) **2198**
Klagenfurt (AUT ISSN 0023-2017) **7495**
Klagenfurter Beitraege zur Philosophie (AUT ISSN 0259-0743) **6931**
Klagenfurter Beitraege zur Philosophie. Reihe: Diplomarbeiten & Dissertationen (AUT ISSN 0259-4943) **6931**
Klagenfurter Beitraege zur Philosophie. Reihe: Gruppendynamik & Organisationsentwicklung (AUT ISSN 0259-4951) **6931**
Klagenfurter Beitraege zur Philosophie. Reihe: Lehrmaterialen (AUT ISSN 0259-496X) **6931**
Klagenfurter Beitraege zur Philosophie. Reihe: Referate (AUT ISSN 0259-4978) **6931**
Klagenfurter Beitraege zur Sprachwissenschaft (AUT ISSN 1562-2878) **5137**
Klaipeda (LTU) **3905**
Klaipeda In Your Pocket (LTU ISSN 1392-0073) **8728**
Klang und Begriff (DEU) **6582**
Klang & Ton (DEU ISSN 0933-0097) **8153**
De Klank (NLD ISSN 1569-9420) **6582**
Klank en Show *see* Music and Show **6590**
Klank en Weerklank *see* De Klank **6582**
Klapalekiana (CZE ISSN 1210-6100) **853**
Klappe Auf (DEU) **3851**
• Klartekst (NOR ISSN 1503-0245) **7565**
Klartext (DEU) **2198**
Klasgids (ZAF ISSN 1010-3465) **5317**
• Klasifikacije/Classifications (SVN ISSN 1408-9114) **8384**
† Klask (FRA ISSN 1142-3056) **8969**
• Klasse (BEL ISSN 0777-5954) **3026**
Klasse! *see* Klasse Apart **2880**
Klasse Apart (NLD ISSN 1574-7816) **2880**
Klasse, die Evangelische Schule (DEU ISSN 1614-094X) **2880**
Klasse for Parents (BEL) **2880**
Klasse Musik (DEU ISSN 1618-4424) **6582**
Klasse voor Jongeren *see* Maks! **3027**
KlasseApart *see* Klasse Apart **2880**
• Klassekampen (NOR ISSN 0805-3839) **3923**
† Klassenziele (DEU) **8969**
Klassieke Zaken (NLD ISSN 1388-4581) **6583**
† De Klassieken Reeks (NLD ISSN 1574-2164) **8969**
• Klassik Heute (Online Edition) (DEU ISSN 1619-5663) **6583**
Klassik Motorrad (DEU) **8260**
Klassik Uhren (DEU ISSN 0947-9287) **4488**
Klassiker (SWE ISSN 1104-3180) **2236**
Klassiker der Luftfahrt (DEU ISSN 1860-0654) **64**
Klassische Moderne (DEU ISSN 1863-9585) **5317**
Klassische Philologie (DEU ISSN 1862-6041) **5317**
Klassische Texte des Romanischen Mittelalterszweisprachigen Ausgaben (DEU ISSN 0453-9834) **628**
Klassisk (DNK ISSN 1901-595X) **6583**
Klassisk Musikkmagasin (NOR ISSN 1502-0274) **6583**
Klasskampen (SWE ISSN 0345-6188) **7149**
Klassnyi Zhurnal (RUS ISSN 1562-3335) **2198**
Klasszikus Magyar Irok Keziratainak es Levelezesenek Katalogusa/Catalogue of Classical Hungarian Writer's Manuscripts (HUN ISSN 0865-5251) **5318**
Klaus Groth Gesellschaft. Jahresgaben (DEU ISSN 0453-9842) **5137**
▼ Klavernytt (SWE ISSN 1654-3734) **6583**
Der Klecks (DEU) **2880**
Kleeblatt (DEU) **3773**
➤ Klei. Germetiki. Tekhnologii (RUS ISSN 1813-7008) **3249**
Klei, Glas, Keramiek (NLD ISSN 0167-5001) **2044**
• ➤ Klein und Gross (DEU ISSN 0863-4386) **3069**
Kleinbrennerei (DEU ISSN 0341-2067) **767**
Kleindier Magazine Avicultura - Fokkersbelangen (NLD ISSN 1574-7751) **291**
De Kleine Aarde (NLD ISSN 0166-3704) **3741**
Kleine Aegyptische Texte (DEU ISSN 0343-1088) **554**
Kleine Bibliographische Reihe (DEU ISSN 0941-6617) **628**
Kleine Deutsche Prosadenkmaeler des Mittelalters (DEU ISSN 0075-6318) **5318**
Die Kleine Diana (DEU ISSN 0946-4395) **6639**
De Kleine Gids voor het Nederlandse Arbeidsrecht (NLD ISSN 1574-4566) **4873**
Kleine Hefte zur Stadtgeschichte (DEU) **4237**
Kleine Historische Reihe (DEU ISSN 0937-9835) **5023**
Der Kleine Raetselspass (DEU) **8184**
Kleine Schriften aus dem Stadtarchiv Muenster (DEU) **4237**
Kleine Schriften der Cusanus-Gesellschaft *see* Cusanus-Gesellschaft. Kleine Schriften **7794**

DIRECTORY 2010 KNOWN E-LEADER GUIDE 10531

Kleine Schriften der Gesellschaft fuer Theatergeschichte see Gesellschaft fuer Theatergeschichte. Kleine Schriften 8471
Kleine Schriften vn Z OE N K see Roskilde Universitetscenter. Center for Oestrigsk-Nordiske Kulturstudier. Smaaskrifter 4260
Kleine Schriften zur Celler Stadtgeschichte (DEU ISSN 1439-832X) 4237
Kleine Schriftenreihe des Stadtarchivs Konstanz see Stadtarchiv Konstanz. Kleine Schriftenreihe 4267
Kleine Senckenberg Reihe (DEU ISSN 0341-4086) 7877
Kleine Uelzener Kunstfuehrer (DEU ISSN 0948-8405) 4237
Kleine und Mittlere Unternehmen Plus see K M U Plus 1420
• Kleine Zeitung (AUT) 3797
Kleiner Roter Traktor (DEU) 2198
Der KleinGarten (DEU ISSN 0936-0638) 3741
• ➤ Kleinian Studies (CAN ISSN 1499-0970) 7382
• The Kleinman Report (USA) 2563
Kleinpferde & Ponys (DEU) 8294
Kleinrock Passive Activity Losses and At-Risk Rules see Passive Activity Losses and At-Risk Rules 1298
Kleinrock Plain-English Answers see Retirement Planning in Plain English 1165
Kleinrock Plain English Answers Tax Aspects of Owning a Home see Tax Aspects of Owning a Home 1947
• Kleintier Konkret (DEU ISSN 1434-9132) 8802
Kleintier-Praxis (DEU ISSN 0023-2076) 8802
Kleintiermedizin (DEU ISSN 1434-6400) 8802
Der Kleintierzuechter - Gefluegelzeitung (DEU ISSN 1613-6268) 291
Der Kleintierzuechter - Kaninchenzeitung (DEU ISSN 1613-6357) 291
Kleio (NLD ISSN 0165-6449) 4150
Kleio see African Historical Review 4129
Kleist-Jahrbuch (DEU ISSN 0722-8899) 5318
▼ Klempner Magazin (DEU ISSN 1863-4435) 4123
Klenkes (DEU) 3851
Klenoder/Treasures (SWE ISSN 1102-2329) 4237
† Kleopatra (CZE ISSN 1212-6586) 8969
Kleos (ITA ISSN 1127-008X) 2236
Klepa (RUS ISSN 0869-5814) 2198
De Klepel see Uniekum 3034
De Klepel (NLD ISSN 1872-5759) 4237
• Kleper Report on Digital Publishing (USA ISSN 0196-4127) 7580
Klepp Historie- og Aettesogelag. Aarsskrift see Klepp Historielag. Aarsskrift 4237
Klepp Historielag. Aarsskrift (NOR ISSN 0809-6414) 4237
• Klepsidra (BRA ISSN 1677-8944) 4150
Kleronomia (GRC ISSN 1105-2139) 7704
Klerusblatt (DEU ISSN 0948-6216) 7804
• klettern (DEU ISSN 1437-7462) 8320
Kleur (Utrecht) (NLD ISSN 1871-5931) 4067
• Kliatt (USA ISSN 1065-8602) 7565
Klick (DEU ISSN 0938-3026) 2198
Klik (GRC) 3874
• Klik (HRV ISSN 1333-2406) 6506
Klik (NLD ISSN 0166-5782) 8053
• Klima (NOR ISSN 1504-8136) 6359
Klima-, Reinraum-, Entstaubungs- und Trocknungstechnik, Kaelte- und Waermepumpentechnik see Informationsdienst F I Z Technik. Klima-, Reinraum-, Entstaubungs- und Trocknungstechnik, Kaelte- und Waermepumpentechnik 3479
Klima Technik (DEU) 4123
Klima und Kaelteingenieur Kaelte Luft Klimatechnik see K I - Kaelte Luft Klimatechnik 4122
Klimat i Gidrografiya Zabaikal'ya (RUS) 6359
Klimatechnik see Klima Technik 4123
Klinge (DEU) 8053
Klingenfuss (Year) Guide to Utility Radio Stations (DEU) 2360
Klinicheskaya Farmakologiya i Terapiya/Clinical Pharmacology and Therapy (RUS ISSN 0869-5490) 6857
➤ Klinicheskaya Fiziologiya Krovoobrashcheniya/Clinical Physiology of Circulation (RUS ISSN 1810-0686) 5795
➤ Klinicheskaya Gerontologiya (RUS ISSN 1607-2499) 4050
• Klinicheskaya Implantologiya i Stomatologiya (RUS) 5854
Klinicheskaya Laboratornaya Diagnostika/Clinical and Laboratory Diagnosis (RUS ISSN 0869-2084) 5907
Klinicheskaya Meditsina/Clinical Medicine (RUS ISSN 0023-2149) 5658
➤ Klinicheskaya Stomatologiya/Clinical Dentistry (RUS) 5854
• ➤ Klinichna Anatomiya ta Operatyvna Hhirurhiya/Clinical Anatomy and Operative Surgery (UKR ISSN 1727-0847) 6251
Klinichna Farmatsiya (UKR ISSN 1562-725X) 6857
➤ Klinichna i Transfuzionna Hematologiia/Clinical and Transfusion Haematology (BGR ISSN 0861-7880) 5939
➤ Klinichna Khirurhiya (UKR ISSN 0023-2130) 6251
† ➤ Klinicka Biochemie a Metabolismus (CZE ISSN 1210-7921) 8969
• ➤ Klinicka Farmakologie a Farmacie (CZE ISSN 1212-7973) 6857
Klinicka Imunologia a Alergologia (SVK ISSN 1335-0013) 5763
➤ Klinicka Mikrobiologie a Infekcni Lekarstvi/Clinical Microbiology and Infectious Diseases (CZE ISSN 1211-264X) 890
• ➤ Klinicka Onkologie (CZE ISSN 0862-495X) 6026
➤ Klinicka Urologia (SVK ISSN 1336-7579) 6271
Kliniczna Perinatologia i Ginekologia (POL ISSN 1230-6576) 5997
• ➤ Klinik & Forschung (DEU ISSN 0947-8736) 5658
• Klinik Gelisim (TUR ISSN 1300-0675) 5658
Klinik Pediatri see Klinik Pediatri Dergisi 6096
• ➤ Klinik Pediatri Dergisi (TUR) 6096
• ➤ Klinik Psikiyatri Dergisi (TUR ISSN 1302-0099) 6157
• ➤ Klinik Psikofarmakoloji Bulteni/Bulletin of Clinical Psychopharmacology (TUR ISSN 1017-7833) 6157
Klinik und Reha (DEU) 2010
Klinika Oczna (POL ISSN 0023-2157) 6045
Klinika Pediatryczna (POL ISSN 1230-7637) 6096
• ➤ Klinikarzt (DEU ISSN 0341-2350) 5658
• KlinikManagement Aktuell (DEU ISSN 1439-3514) 4105
Klinische Anaesthesiologie und Intensivtherapie (DEU ISSN 0341-5023) 5772
Klinische Chemie (DEU ISSN 0173-6647) 5658
▼ ➤ Klinische Diagnostik und Evaluation (DEU ISSN 1864-6050) 7382
Klinische Ernaehrung see Stoffwechselmanagement 6669
† Klinische Medizin (AUT ISSN 0368-6132) 8969
• ➤ Klinische Monatsblaetter fuer Augenheilkunde (DEU ISSN 0023-2165) 6045
• ➤ Klinische Neurophysiologie (DEU ISSN 1434-0275) 6158
Klinische Neuroradiologie see Clinical Neuroradiology 6194
• ➤ Klinische Paediatrie (DEU ISSN 0300-8630) 6096
➤ Klinische Pharmakologie (DEU ISSN 0939-5164) 6857
➤ Klinische und Experimentelle Notfallmedizin (DEU ISSN 0176-1765) 5658
➤ Klinische und Experimentelle Urologie (DEU ISSN 0174-2752) 6271
Klinisk biokemi i Norden see Klinisk Kemi i Norden 5658
Klinisk Kemi (SWE ISSN 0282-440X) 5658
Klinisk Kemi i Norden (SWE ISSN 1101-2013) 5658
Klinisk Patientnaera Forskning (SWE ISSN 1654-1421) 5658
Klinisk Sygepleje (DNK ISSN 0902-2767) 5968
Klinisk Sykepleie (NOR ISSN 1504-3576) 5968
† Kliniske Tandteknikere (DNK ISSN 0109-2294) 8969
† Klink (NLD ISSN 1872-0056) 8969
Klinkklaar (NLD) 4082
• ➤ Klio (DEU ISSN 0075-6334) 2236
➤ Klio (POL ISSN 1643-8191) 4237
• Klips (TUR ISSN 1300-5952) 3962
▼ Klipz (USA ISSN 1941-1316) 589
Kloaktuelt (DNK ISSN 0904-4787) 4123
Kloeckner Werke Heute (DEU ISSN 0948-0684) 6320
• Kloekt (NOR ISSN 1502-8313) 1770
Kloeverbladet (SWE ISSN 0281-1278) 2198
Klok en Klepel (NLD ISSN 0023-2181) 6583
• Klokhuis Magazine (NLD ISSN 1570-3258) 2570
Klokken-Koerier see Het Torenuurwerk 4569
KlostermannRoteReihe (DEU) 7981
KlostermannSeminar see KlostermannRoteReihe 7981
Klub (RUS ISSN 0235-5043) 4597
Klub dla Ciebie (POL ISSN 1641-2389) 4979
Klub Realisty (RUS) 7149
Klubb Nachrichten (DEU) 8184
• Klublife (CAN ISSN 1495-8503) 2686
Klublife Magazine see Klublife 2686
Klubs (LVA ISSN 1407-1649) 6583
Klubs Exclusive (LVA ISSN 1691-0257) 6583
Klucze do Oznaczania Owadow Polski (POL ISSN 0075-6350) 853
Kluwer Belastinggids (NLD ISSN 0923-5051) 1932
Kluwer International Handbooks of Education Series see Springer International Handbooks of Education Series 2914
Kluwer International Series in Electronic Materials: Science and Technology see Electronic Materials: Science and Technology 3095
Kluwer International Series in Engineering and Computer Science see Analog Circuits and Signal Processing Series 2406
➤ The Kluwer International Series in Software Engineering (NLD ISSN 1384-6469) 2593
Kluwer International Series on Advances in Database Systems see Advances in Database Systems 2529
The Kluwer International Series on Information Retrieval see The Springer International Series on Information Retrieval 2550
Kluwer Loonbelastinggids (NLD ISSN 0923-8468) 1932
Kluwer Sovac Series on Social Security (NLD) 1932
Kluwer Tarievenboek (NLD ISSN 1573-0182) 1932
Kluwer Tarievenboek. Tabellen see Kluwer Tarievenboek 1932
➤ Kluwer Texts in the Mathematical Sciences (NLD ISSN 0927-4529) 5507
Kluwers Agenda voor de Fiscale Praktijk (NLD ISSN 0923-0521) 4710
Kluwers Agenda voor de Rechtspraktijk (NLD ISSN 0922-9221) 4710
Kluwer's Handbook of Insurance (GBR) 4511
Kluwer's Regulation of Insurance see Regulation of Insurance in the U K, Ireland and E U 4520
Klynveld Peat Marwick Goerdeler Frettir see K P M G Frettir 1295
Kmart Diabetes Health (USA) 5896
Kmecki Glas (SVN ISSN 0023-2238) 131
• Kmubusiness Magazin (CHE) 1140
Knabenmusik der Stadt Zuerich. Mitteilungsblatt (CHE) 6583
• Knack (BEL ISSN 0772-3210) 3801
Knack Magazine see Knack 3801
Knanayamithram (IND ISSN 0254-6205) 2198
Knarr, Knerr, Knorr Family Newsletter (USA ISSN 1063-4142) 3773
Knasen (SWE ISSN 0345-620X) 2198
Knauber Magazin (DEU) 4544
• Knave (GBR ISSN 0265-1289) 6293
Knave Penpower (GBR ISSN 1365-0734) 6293
• ➤ The Knee (NLD ISSN 0968-0160) 925
• ➤ Knee Surgery, Sports Traumatology, Arthroscopy (DEU ISSN 0942-2056) 6231
Kneipp see Natuerlich Leben 6993
Kneipp Blaetter see Kneipp Journal 6991
Kneipp Journal (DEU) 6991
Kneipp Magazin see Kneipp Zeitschrift 6991
Kneipp Zeitschrift (AUT) 6991
† Knife Defense (USA) 8969
Knife World (USA ISSN 0276-9042) 4338
Kniga i Vremya (RUS) 4461
Kniga Issledovaniya (RUS ISSN 0134-837X) 7565
Knight see Vytis 2270
• Knight & Hale Ultimate Team Hunting (USA) 8320
Knight and Hale Ultimate Team Hunting see Knight & Hale Ultimate Team Hunting 8320
• Knight Examiner (USA) 2289
Knight Letter (USA ISSN 0454-8973) 3773
Knight's Guide to Best Value and Public Procurement (GBR) 4710
• Knights Inn. Directory (USA) 4392
The Knight's Page (USA) 2289
Knigi Belarusi/Byelorussian Books (BLR) 628
• Knigi Rossiskoi Federatsii (RUS ISSN 0201-6354) 628
• Knigi v Nalichii i Pechati/Russian Books in Print (RUS) 628
Knigoizdavane i Pechat (BGR) 8384
Knigotorgovyi Byulleten' (RUS) 3121
Knigovedenie see Knygotyra 5023
• Kniha Informatikov (SVK ISSN 1337-0367) 6700
• Knihovna (CZE ISSN 1801-3252) 5023
Knihovnicka Revue see Knihovna 5023
• Knihovnicky Zpravodaj Vysocina (CZE ISSN 1213-8231) 7565
• Knihy a Dejiny/Books and History (CZE ISSN 1210-8510) 7565
Knijevni Jivot (ROM ISSN 1222-8346) 5318
Knip Mode (NLD ISSN 0926-759X) 2257
Kniplebrevet (DNK ISSN 0900-8799) 6639
▼ Knippie (NLD) 2257
Knippie Idee see Knippie 2257
Knippie's Baby see Knippie 2257
Knipselkrant Biologische Landbouw (NLD) 240
Knit 1 (USA ISSN 1940-2058) 6639
Knit Americas (GBR ISSN 1476-1696) 8454
Knit Design (JPN) 8454
Knit It! (USA ISSN 1541-1990) 6639
Knit 'n Style (USA ISSN 1096-5408) 6639
Knit One see Knit 1 6639
Knit Simple (USA ISSN 1932-1325) 6639
• KnitNet (CAN) 6639
Knitscene (USA) 4338
Knitstats (GBR ISSN 0260-8855) 8464
Knitter's Magazine (USA ISSN 0747-9026) 6639
Knitting & Haberdashery: the Needlecrafts Review (GBR) 8454
Knitting International (GBR ISSN 0266-8394) 8454
Knitting Technology see Textile Network 8460
• Knitty (CAN) 2257
Knives (Year) (USA ISSN 0277-0725) 4338
Knives Illustrated (USA ISSN 0898-8943) 4338
• Knizhnaya Letopis' (RUS ISSN 0869-5962) 628
Knizhnaya Letopis'. Vspomogatel'nye Ukazateli (RUS) 7578
Knizhnaya Torgovlya. Nauchno-Tekhnicheskii Informatsionnyi Sbornik (RUS ISSN 0132-1897) 7565
Knizhnoe Delo (RUS ISSN 0869-6039) 7565
Knizhnoe Obozrenie (RUS ISSN 0023-2378) 7565
Knizhnyi Biznes (RUS) 7565
Knizhnyi Klub (RUS) 5318
• Knizna Revue (SVK ISSN 1210-1982) 7565
• Kniznica (SVK ISSN 1335-7026) 7565
Knjizevna Smotra (HRV ISSN 0455-0463) 5318
• Knjizhevna Novine (SRB ISSN 0023-2416) 7565
• ➤ Knjiznica (SVN ISSN 0023-2424) 5023
Knjiznica Annales/Library Annales (SVN ISSN 1408-1121) 5023
• Knjiznica Sigma (SVN ISSN 1408-1547) 7024
• Knjiznicarske Novice (SVN ISSN 0353-9237) 5023
Knock Out see K O 8183
Knooppunt Arnhem Nijmegen in Ontwikkeling (NLD ISSN 1872-4027) 7495
Knooppunt Arnhem-Nijmegen Vastgoedrapportage see K A N Vastgoedrapportage 4418
The Knot Wedding Gowns see The Knot Weddings Magazine 5559
The Knot Wedding Pages Central Florida (USA) 5559
The Knot Wedding Pages Colorado (USA) 5559
The Knot Wedding Pages Connecticut (USA) 5559
The Knot Wedding Pages Dallas Fort Worth (USA) 5559
The Knot Wedding Pages Georgia (USA) 5559
The Knot Wedding Pages Kansas City (USA) 5559
The Knot Wedding Pages New Jersey (USA) 5559
The Knot Wedding Pages Philadelphia (USA) 5559
The Knot Wedding Pages South Florida (USA) 5559
The Knot Wedding Pages West Coast Florida (USA) 5559
The Knot Weddings Magazine (USA) 5559
• Knotgrass (USA) 5318
Know (CAN ISSN 1715-751X) 2198
• Know (Menlo Park) (USA) 1829
Know (Tucker) (USA ISSN 1543-8724) 2880
Know Atlanta (USA) 3979
Know How (ANT) 1140
The Know-How Report, International Intellectual Property Licensing & Protection (GBR ISSN 1086-4458) 6754
Know More, Spend Less see A Native's Guide to Chicago 8740
▼ Know: The Magazine for Paralegals (USA) 6700
Know Your Medicine (IRL ISSN 1649-1254) 6858
† • Know Your World Extra (USA ISSN 0163-4844) 8969
• ➤ Knowgenesis (IND ISSN 0973-9408) 2430
• Knowit (AUS ISSN 1328-7176) 5023
• The Knowledge (GBR ISSN 0966-3371) 2384
Knowledge (GBR ISSN 1464-1453) 6583
• ➤ Knowledge and Information Systems (GBR ISSN 0219-1377) 2549
Knowledge and Life see Zhishi yu Shenghuo 3830
• ➤ Knowledge and Management of Aquatic Ecosystems (FRA ISSN 1961-9502) 2616
• Knowledge and Process Management (Online) (GBR ISSN 1099-1441) 1770
• ➤ Knowledge and Process Management (Print) (GBR ISSN 1092-4604) 1771
Knowledge and Society (GBR ISSN 0278-1557) 8116
• Knowledge Base Copyright Law (AUT ISSN 1990-987X) 6754
The Knowledge-based Economy see Kennis en Economie 8430
• ➤ Knowledge-Based Systems (NLD ISSN 0950-7051) 2454
Knowledge Based Systems Plastics see K B S Plastics 7101
Knowledge Based Systems Rubber see K B S Rubber 7827
• Knowledge Bridge/Zhishi Chuangxin (TWN ISSN 1606-9536) 7877
• Knowledge Discovery Nuggets News (USA) 2531
▼ • ➤ Knowledge Ecology Studies (USA ISSN 1936-2188) 7981
• ➤ Knowledge Engineering Review (GBR ISSN 0269-8889) 2454
▼ • Knowledge for Regional N R M Programme E-newsletter (Natural Resource Management) (AUS ISSN 1834-478X) 3449
Knowledge Hub (IND ISSN 0973-6425) 1771
▼ ➤ Knowledge Infrastructure and Knowledge Economy (NLD) 4462
Knowledge Is Power see Zhishi Jiushi Liliang 7934
• Knowledge Management (London) (GBR ISSN 1369-1368) 2531
• ➤ Knowledge Management for Development Journal (GBR ISSN 1947-4199) 7981
Knowledge Management Inpractice see Inpractice (Houston) 1124
Knowledge Management News see K M News 8969
• ➤ Knowledge Management Research & Practice (GBR ISSN 1477-8238) 2430
• Knowledge Management Review (GBR ISSN 1369-7633) 1771
Knowledge Management World see K M World 2537
Knowledge Management World & Intranets (Year) Conference Proceedings see K M World & Intranets (Year) Conference Proceedings 2538
Knowledge Management World NewsLinks see K M World NewsLinks 1770
The Knowledge of Japanese Language see Riyu Zhishi 5169
Knowledge of Library and Information Science see Tushu Qingbao Zhishi 5051
Knowledge of Literature and History see Wenshi Zhishi 8014
• ➤ Knowledge Organization (DEU ISSN 0943-7444) 5023
Knowledge Organization in Subject Areas (DEU ISSN 0946-9389) 5023
▼ • Knowledge Politics Quarterly (GBR ISSN 1757-7675) 7149
• ➤ Knowledge Quest (USA ISSN 1094-9046) 5023
• ➤ Knowledge, Technology and Policy (NLD ISSN 1946-4789) 7981
• ➤ The Knowledge Tree (AUS ISSN 1448-2673) 2880
Knowledge Window see Zhishi Chuang 7934
Knowledge, Work & Society/Savoir, Travail & Societe (FRA ISSN 1764-5476) 2881
• KnowledgeLink (USA) 686
• Knowledgespeak (IND) 7565
• Knowledge@Wharton (USA) 1771
• KnowMap (CAN ISSN 1499-1209) 7565
▼ • Known (USA ISSN 1939-0742) 7658
▼ • Known E-Leader Guide (USA ISSN 1943-6017) 7658

Title

▼ • Known Leader (USA ISSN 1939-0734) **7658**
▼ • Known Mid-Week Event (USA ISSN 1943-6033) **7658**
▼ • Known Quarterly Bundle (USA ISSN 1943-605X) **7658**
Knox Alumnus *see* Knox Magazine **2289**
Knox County Illinois Genealogical Society. Quarterly (USA ISSN 0741-7284) **3773**
Knox Historian (AUS ISSN 0810-9435) **4150**
Knox Magazine (USA) **2289**
Knoxville Automotive Report (USA ISSN 1054-254X) **8588**
• Knucklebones (USA ISSN 1554-3277) **8184**
Der Knuepfteppich (DEU ISSN 0936-5036) **4544**
Knutepunkt (NOR ISSN 1504-7601) **8649**
Knutsel Kids (NLD) **536**
• ➤ Knygotyra/Book Science/Knigovedenie (LTU ISSN 0204-2061) **5023**
Knyzhkova Palata Ukrainy. Visnyk (UKR) **7565**
Knyzhkovyi Klub (UKR) **3121**
Knyzhkovyi Kur'ier (UKR) **4462**
Ko e Kolonikali *see* The Tonga Chronicle **3962**
• Ko M C I Journal (KOR ISSN 1598-5245) **5748**
Ko Tane Mahuta Pupuke *see* New Zealand Journal of Outdoor Education **8324**
• Ko'aga Ron-e'eta (USA) **7211**
† Koala Brueder (DEU) **8969**
Koatsu Toronkai Koen Yoshishu/High Pressure Conference of Japan. Programme and Abstracts of Papers (JPN ISSN 0917-6373) **3207**
• Koatsuryoku no Kagaku to Gijutsu/Review of High Pressure Science and Technology (JPN ISSN 0917-639X) **3207**
Kobayashi Institute of Physical Research. Annual Report *see* Kobayasi Rigaku Kenkyujo Repoto **7024**
Kobayashi Institute of Physical Research. News *see* Kobayasi Riken Nyusu **7024**
Kobayasi Rigaku Kenkyujo Repoto/Kobayashi Institute of Physical Research. Annual Report (JPN) **7024**
Kobayasi Riken Nyusu/Kobayashi Institute of Physical Research. News (JPN) **7024**
Kobe College Studies *see* Kobe Jogakuin Daigaku Ronshu **2992**
Kobe Daigakuin Shizen Kagaku Kenkyuka Kiyo. A *see* Kobe University. Graduate School of Science and Technology. Memoirs. Series A **8430**
Kobe Daigakuin Shizen Kagaku Kenkyuka Kiyo B/Kobe University. Graduate School of Science and Technology. Memoirs. Series B (JPN ISSN 0287-6515) **7877**
➤ Kobe Daigaku Igakubu Kiyo/Kobe University. Medical Journal (JPN ISSN 0075-6431) **5658**
• Kobe Daigaku Nogakubu Gakujutsu Hokoku (CD-ROM)/Kobe University. Faculty of Agriculture. Science Reports (CD-ROM) (JPN ISSN 1349-4570) **131**
Kobe Daigaku Nogakubu Gakujutsu Hokoku (Print) *see* Kobe Daigaku Nogakubu Gakujutsu Hokoku (CD-ROM) **131**
Kobe Economic and Business Research Series (JPN ISSN 0075-6415) **1140**
Kobe Economic and Business Review (JPN ISSN 0075-6407) **1140**
Kobe Gakuin Daigaku Eiyogakubu Ronbunshu/Kobe Gakuin University. Faculty of Nutrition. Journal (JPN ISSN 0911-565X) **6662**
Kobe Gakuin Daigaku Yakugakkaishi/Kobe Gakuin University. Pharmaceutical Society. Annual Bulletin (JPN ISSN 0911-9191) **6858**
Kobe Gakuin Daigaku Yakugakubu Kiyo/Kobe Gakuin University. Faculty of Pharmaceutical Sciences. Memoirs (JPN ISSN 0911-9183) **6858**
Kobe Gakuin University. Faculty of Nutrition. Journal *see* Kobe Gakuin Daigaku Eiyogakubu Ronbunshu **6662**
Kobe Gakuin University. Faculty of Pharmaceutical Sciences. Memoirs *see* Kobe Gakuin Daigaku Yakugakubu Kiyo **6858**
Kobe Gakuin University. Pharmaceutical Society. Annual Bulletin *see* Kobe Gakuin Daigaku Yakugakkaishi **6858**
Kobe Jogakuin Daigaku Ronshu/Kobe College Studies (JPN ISSN 0389-1658) **2992**
Kobe Joshi Daigaku Bungakubu Kiyo *see* Kobe Women's University. Faculty of Literature. Bulletin **5318**
Kobe Joshi Daigaku Kasei Gakubu Kiyo *see* Kobe Women's University. Faculty of Home Economics. Bulletin **4362**
Kobe Journal of Mathematics (JPN ISSN 0289-9051) **5507**
• ➤ Kobe Journal of Medical Sciences (JPN ISSN 0023-2513) **5658**
➤ Kobe Kaiyo Kishodai. Iho/Kobe Marine Observatory. Bulletin (JPN ISSN 0368-5969) **2810**
Kobe Kaiyo Kishodai. Kaiyo Sokuho/Kobe Marine Observatory. Oceanographic Prompt Report (JPN) **2810**
Kobe Marine Observatory. Bulletin *see* Kobe Kaiyo Kishodai. Iho **2810**
Kobe Marine Observatory. Oceanographic Prompt Report *see* Kobe Kaiyo Kishodai. Kaiyo Sokuho **2810**
Kobe-shi Gaikokugo Daigaku Gaikokugaku Kenkyu *see* Nairiku Ajia Gengo no Kenkyu **557**
Kobe Shoin Joshi Gakuin Daigaku, Kobe Shoin Joshi Gakuin Tanki Daigaku. Gakujutsu Kenkyukai. Kenkyu Kiyo. Jinbun Kagaku, Shizen Kagaku-hen (JPN ISSN 1342-1689) **4462**
Kobe Steel Engineering Reports *see* R & D Kobe Seiko Giho **6330**
Kobe Tokiwa College. Bulletin *see* Kobe Tokiwa Tanki Daigaku Kiyo **7877**
Kobe Tokiwa Tanki Daigaku Kiyo/Kobe Tokiwa College. Bulletin (JPN ISSN 0389-9578) **7877**
➤ Kobe University Economic Review (JPN ISSN 0454-1111) **1140**
Kobe University. Faculty of Agriculture. Science Reports (CD-ROM) *see* Kobe Daigaku Nogakubu Gakujutsu Hokoku (CD-ROM) **131**
Kobe University. Faculty of Engineering. Memoirs (JPN ISSN 0368-9638) **3207**
Kobe University. Graduate School of Science and Technology. Memoirs. Series A/Kobe Daigaku Daigakuin Shizen Kagaku Kenkyuka Kiyo. A (JPN ISSN 0287-6507) **8430**
Kobe University. Graduate School of Science and Technology. Memoirs. Series B *see* Kobe Daigaku Daigakuin Shizen Kagaku Kenkyuka Kiyo B **7877**
Kobe University Law Review. International Edition (JPN ISSN 0075-6423) **4710**
Kobe University. Medical Journal *see* Kobe Daigaku Igakubu Kiyo **5658**
Kobe University of Commerce. Journal *see* Shodai Ronshu **1174**
Kobe University of Mercantile Marine. Review. Part 1. Studies in Humanities and Social Science (JPN ISSN 0285-7022) **4462**
Kobe University of Mercantile Marine. Review. Part 2. Maritime Studies, and Science and Engineering (JPN ISSN 0450-609X) **7877**
• Kobe University. Research Institute for Economics and Business Administration. Annals of Economics and Business (JPN) **1140**
• Kobe University. Research Institute for Economics and Business Administration. Business Machine Series (JPN) **1140**
Kobe University. Research Institute for Economics and Business Administration. Discussion Paper (English Edition) *see* Kobe University. Research Institute for Economics and Business Administration. Discussion Paper Series (English Edition) **1140**
Kobe University. Research Institute for Economics and Business Administration. Discussion Paper (Japanese Edition) *see* Kobe University. Research Institute for Economics and Business Administration. Discussion Paper Series (Japanese Edition) **1140**
• Kobe University. Research Institute for Economics and Business Administration. Discussion Paper Series (English Edition) (JPN ISSN 1345-2207) **1140**
• Kobe University. Research Institute for Economics and Business Administration. Discussion Paper Series (Japanese Edition) (JPN ISSN 1345-2215) **1140**
• Kobe University. Research Institute for Economics and Business Administration. Monetary Research Series (JPN) **1141**
Kobe University. School of Business Administration. Annals (JPN ISSN 0085-2570) **1771**
➤ Kobe Women's University. Faculty of Home Economics. Bulletin/Kobe Joshi Daigaku Kasei Gakubu Kiyo (JPN ISSN 1341-5905) **4362**
Kobe Women's University. Faculty of Literature. Bulletin/Kobe Joshi Daigaku Bungakubu Kiyo (JPN ISSN 1341-5913) **5318**
† Kobenhavns Statistiske Aarbog (DNK ISSN 1399-8870) **8969**
Kobie. Antropologia Cultural *see* Kobie, Revista de Bellas Artes y Ciencias: Serie Antropologia Cultural **345**
Kobie. Arte Ederrak *see* Kobie, Revista de Bellas Artes y Ciencias: Serie Bellas Artes **8969**
Kobie. Paleoantropologia *see* Kobie, Revista de Bellas Artes y Ciencias: Serie Paleoantropologia **346**
Kobie, Revista de Bellas Artes y Ciencias: Serie Antropologia Cultural (ESP ISSN 0214-7939) **345**
† Kobie, Revista de Bellas Artes y Ciencias: Serie Bellas Artes (ESP ISSN 0214-7955) **8969**
Kobie, Revista de Bellas Artes y Ciencias: Serie Paleoantropologia (ESP ISSN 0214-7971) **346**
➤ Kobieta i Biznes/Women & Business (POL ISSN 1230-9427) **1963**
Kobisena (IND) **5425**
Koblenzer Geographisches Kolloquium (DEU ISSN 1616-4784) **4018**
Kobunshi/High Polymers, Japan (JPN ISSN 0454-1138) **2125**
Kobunshi Kako *see* Polymer Application **3252**
➤ Kobunshi Ronbunshu/Japanese Journal of Polymer Science and Engineering (JPN ISSN 0386-2186) **2126**
Kobus (ZMB ISSN 1015-5546) **2616**
KoCa - Konditorei und Cafe (DEU ISSN 1612-6327) **3674**
Der Koch (DEU) **4392**
† Kochduell (DEU) **8969**
Kochen (CHE ISSN 1660-1262) **4362**
Kochen Leicht Gemacht (DEU) **3653**
Kochen und Geniessen (DEU ISSN 0933-9698) **3653**
• Kochen und Kueche (AUT) **4362**
Kocherburgbote (DEU) **3851**
The Kochi (JPN) **3900**
Kochi Daigaku Gakujutsu Kenkyu Hokoku. Jinbun Kagaku/Kochi University. Research Reports. Humanities (JPN ISSN 0389-0457) **4462**
Kochi Daigaku Gakujutsu Kenkyu Hokoku. Nogaku/Kochi University. Agricultural Science. Research Reports (JPN ISSN 0389-0473) **131**
Kochi Daigaku Gakujutsu Kenkyu Hokoku. Shizen Kagaku/Kochi University. Research Reports. Natural Science (JPN ISSN 0389-0244) **7877**
Kochi Daigaku Kyoikugakubu Kenkyu Hokoku. Dai-3-Bu/Kochi University. Faculty of Education. Bulletin. Series 3 (JPN ISSN 0389-0449) **2881**
Kochi Daigaku Rigakubu Kiyo. Kagaku *see* Kochi University. Faculty of Science. Memoirs. Series C, Chemistry **2070**
Kochi Daigaku Rigakubu Kiyo. Seibutsugaku *see* Kochi University. Faculty of Science. Memoirs. Series D, Biology **686**
Kochi Daigaku Rigakubu Kiyo. Sugaku *see* Kochi Journal of Mathematics **5507**
Kochi Iryo Gakuin Dosokaishi/Kochi School of Allied Health and Medical Professions. Alumni Association Journal (JPN ISSN 0914-4250) **5658**
Kochi Joshi Daigaku Kiyo. Shizen Kagaku Hen/Kochi Women's University. Bulletin. Series of Natural Sciences (JPN ISSN 0452-2486) **7877**
Kochi Journal of Mathematics/Kochi Daigaku Rigakubu Kiyo. Sugaku (JPN ISSN 1880-5515) **5507**
Kochi Prefecture. Monthly Report of Meteorology *see* Kochiken Kisho Geppo **6359**
Kochi Rehabilitation Institute. Department of Physical Therapy. Graduation theses *see* Kochi Rihabiriteshon Gakuin Rigaku Ryoho Gakka Sotsugyo Kenkyu Ronbunshu **6112**
Kochi Rihabiriteshon Gakuin Rigaku Ryoho Gakka Sotsugyo Kenkyu Ronbunshu/Kochi Rehabilitation Institute. Department of Physical Therapy. Graduation theses (JPN ISSN 1342-8551) **6112**
Kochi School of Allied Health and Medical Professions. Alumni Association Journal *see* Kochi Iryo Gakuin Dosokaishi **5658**
Kochi University. Agricultural Science. Research Reports *see* Kochi Daigaku Gakujutsu Kenkyu Hokoku. Nogaku **131**
Kochi University. Earthquake Observatory. Seismological Bulletin (JPN) **2786**
Kochi University. Faculty of Agriculture. Memoirs (JPN ISSN 0450-6219) **131**
Kochi University. Faculty of Education. Bulletin. Series 3 *see* Kochi Daigaku Kyoikugakubu Kenkyu Hokoku. Dai-3-Bu **2881**
Kochi University. Faculty of Science. Memoirs. Series B, Physics (JPN ISSN 0389-0260) **7024**
Kochi University. Faculty of Science. Memoirs. Series C, Chemistry/Kochi Daigaku Rigakubu Kiyo. Kagaku (JPN ISSN 0389-0279) **2070**
Kochi University. Faculty of Science. Memoirs. Series D, Biology/Kochi Daigaku Rigakubu Kiyo. Seibutsugaku (JPN ISSN 0389-0287) **686**
Kochi University. Faculty of Science. Memoirs. Series E, Geology (JPN ISSN 0389-0295) **2752**
Kochi University. Faculty of Science. Memoirs. Series F, Information Science (JPN ISSN 0919-2557) **5023**
Kochi University. Institute of the Kuroshio Sphere. Report *see* Kuroshio **2811**
Kochi University. Institute of the Kuroshio Sphere. Report. Special Series *see* Kuroshio. Tokubetsugo **2811**
Kochi University. Marine Sciences and Fisheries. Bulletin (JPN) **2810**
Kochi University. Research Reports. Humanities *see* Kochi Daigaku Gakujutsu Kenkyu Hokoku. Jinbun Kagaku **4462**
Kochi University. Research Reports. Natural Science *see* Kochi Daigaku Gakujutsu Kenkyu Hokoku. Shizen Kagaku **7877**
Kochi Women's University. Bulletin. Series of Natural Sciences *see* Kochi Joshi Daigaku Kiyo. Shizen Kagaku Hen **7877**
Kochiken Kisho Geppo/Kochi Prefecture. Monthly Report of Meteorology (JPN) **6359**
Kochkor (KGZ) **3904**
Kochu Nyusu/Coleopterists' News (JPN ISSN 0910-8785) **853**
Kociewski Magazyn Regionalny (POL ISSN 0860-1917) **5222**
Kodai/Archaeological Society of Waseda University. Journal (JPN ISSN 0452-2516) **402**
➤ Kodai Mathematical Journal (JPN ISSN 0386-5991) **5507**
Kodai Oriento Hakubutsukan Kiyo/Bulletin of the Ancient Orient Museum (JPN ISSN 0388-7219) **402**
Kodaikanal Observatory Bulletin. Series A (IND ISSN 0374-3632) **577**
Kodaikanal Observatory Bulletin. Series B (IND ISSN 0374-3667) **577**
• Kodak e-Magazine (USA) **6970**
Kodaly Envoy (USA ISSN 1084-1776) **6583**
Kodaly Society of Canada. Alla Breve (CAN ISSN 1180-1344) **6583**
Kodanseigaku Ronbunshu/Japan Society for Photoelasticity. Proceedings (JPN ISSN 0910-9854) **7079**
Kodeksy Ukrainy (UKR) **4710**
▼ • Kodex Bulletin (NLD ISSN 1873-3980) **8117**
Kodikas - Code - Ars Semeiotica (DEU ISSN 0171-0834) **8117**
Kodikas - Code Supplement (DEU ISSN 0941-0139) **8117**
Kodin Kuvalehti (FIN ISSN 0023-2610) **3838**
Kodin Pellervo (FIN ISSN 1456-7210) **131**
Kodintekniikka (FIN ISSN 0783-4632) **2360**
Kodix Nomikou Vematos (GRC ISSN 0302-1068) **4710**
Kodo Bunsekigaku Kenkyu/Japanese Journal of Behavior Analysis (JPN ISSN 0913-8013) **7382**
• ➤ Kodo Keiryogaku/Japanese Journal of Behaviormetrics (JPN ISSN 0385-5481) **8149**
➤ Kodo Ryoho Kenkyu/Japanese Journal of Behavior Therapy (JPN ISSN 0910-6529) **7382**
Kodo Seicho ki he no Shogen (JPN) **1141**
Kodomo No Kagaku (JPN ISSN 1345-8825) **2198**
Kodovi Slovenskih Kultura (SRB ISSN 0354-964X) **3619**
Kodry (MDA ISSN 1814-9383) **5318**
Kodukiri (EST ISSN 1406-2119) **3836**
Kodutokhter (EST) **5658**
Koebenhavn *see* K B H **8726**
Koebenhavnerstudier i Tosprogethed/Copenhagen Studies in Bilingualism (DNK ISSN 0901-9731) **3069**
† Koebenhavns Boligkommission. Aarsberetning (DNK ISSN 0573-9799) **8969**
† Koebenhavns Bymuseum (DNK ISSN 0105-936X) **8969**
Koebenhavns Bymuseum. Skrifter (DNK ISSN 1601-4235) **4237**
Koebenhavns Kommuneskole (DNK ISSN 0023-253X) **2881**
Koebenhavns Universitet. Datalogisk Institut. Rapport (DNK ISSN 0107-8283) **2430**
Koebenhavns Universitet. Geologisk Centralinstitut. Aarsberetning (DNK ISSN 0906-0294) **2752**
Koebenhavns Universitet. Institut for Almen og Anvendt Sprogvidenskab. Arbejdspapirer (DNK ISSN 0907-3388) **5137**
Koebenhavns Universitet. Oekonomisk Institut. Cykelafdelingen. Memo (DNK ISSN 0906-0669) **1141**
Koebenhavns Universitet. Oekonomisk Institut. Memo (DNK ISSN 0107-3664) **1141**
Koebenhavns Universitet. Oekonomisk Institut. Roed Serie (DNK ISSN 0108-2221) **1141**
† Koebenhavns Universitet. Oesteuropainstitut. Rapporter (DNK ISSN 0908-0627) **8969**
Koebenhavns Universitet. Retsvidenskabeligt Institut B. Studier (DNK ISSN 0108-9811) **4710**
Koebenhavns Universitet. Sociologisk Institut. Afhandling (DNK ISSN 0900-9922) **8117**
Koebenhavns Universitet. Sociologisk Institut. Rapportserie (DNK ISSN 0908-8687) **8117**
Koebrenhavns Universitet. Oekonomisk Institut. Blaat Memo *see* Koebenhavns Universitet. Oekonomisk Institut. Memo **1141**
Koedkvaeg (DNK ISSN 1901-3485) **291**
• ➤ Koedoe (ZAF ISSN 0075-6458) **953**
Koedoe. Monographs (ZAF ISSN 0075-6466) **2616**
Koeffbladet - I N (NOR) **1896**
Koege Museum (DNK ISSN 0107-931X) **4237**
Koehler Rundschau (DEU) **6735**
Koehlers Flotten-Kalender *see* Koehlers Flottenkalender **8649**
Koehlers Flottenkalender (DEU ISSN 0075-6474) **8649**
Koeki Jigyo Kenkyu/Journal of Public Utility Economics (JPN ISSN 0387-3099) **3141**
Koeln Erleben (DEU) **8728**
Koelner Arbeiten zum Bibliotheks- und Dokumentationswesen (DEU ISSN 0721-7587) **5058**
Koelner Arbeiten zur Internationalen Politik (DEU ISSN 0947-7993) **7250**
Koelner Beitraege zur Entwicklungslaenderforschung (DEU ISSN 0931-3729) **1600**
Koelner Beitraege zur Ethnopsychologie und Transkulturellen Psychologie (DEU ISSN 0949-1821) **7382**
Koelner Beitraege zur Musikforschung (DEU) **6583**
Koelner Beitraege zur Nationsforschung (DEU ISSN 0945-7763) **4237**
Koelner Ethnologische Mitteilungen (DEU ISSN 0075-6490) **346**
Koelner Forum fuer Geologie und Palaeontologie (DEU ISSN 1437-3246) **2752**
Koelner Germanistische Studien (AUT ISSN 0454-1308) **5137**
Koelner Illustrierte (DEU) **3851**
Koelner Informations Management (DEU ISSN 1432-1564) **2531**
Koelner Jahrbuch (DEU ISSN 0947-1553) **403**
Koelner Kongress Report (DEU) **6281**
Koelner Kriminalwissenschaftliche Schriften (DEU ISSN 0936-2711) **4892**
Koelner Linguistische Arbeiten - Germanistik *see* K L A G E **5136**
Koelner Medizinhistorische Beitraege (DEU ISSN 0172-7036) **5658**
Koelner Museums Bulletin (DEU ISSN 0933-257X) **6527**
Koelner Philharmoniepersoenlich (DEU) **6583**
Koelner Reihe (DEU ISSN 0522-6236) **4511**
Koelner Romanistische Arbeiten (CHE ISSN 0075-6520) **4462**
Koelner Schriften zur Politischen Wissenschaft (DEU ISSN 0075-6539) **7149**
Koelner Stadt-Anzeiger (DEU ISSN 1618-3061) **3851**

10534 KOMITET ROSSIISKOI FEDERATSII PO METALLURGII. VESTNIK ULRICH'S PERIODICALS

Komitet Rossiiskoi Federatsii po Metallurgii. Vestnik (RUS ISSN 0869-7531) **6320**
Komix (GRC ISSN 1105-1469) **2198**
Komm! (DEU ISSN 1611-325X) **7763**
Komma (SWE ISSN 1652-8883) **5318**
Kommentar Fertigpackungsrecht (DEU ISSN 0171-2713) **6711**
Kommentarii (UKR) **7149**
Kommentarii k Dokumentam dlya Bukhgaltera (RUS) **1295**
Kommentarii k Novym Dokumentam (RUS) **1295**
Kommentierte Finanz Rechtsprechung (DEU ISSN 0932-6782) **1364**
Kommercheskie Vesti (RUS) **1141**
• Kommersant (RUS ISSN 1561-347X) **1141**
Kommersant - Den'gi (RUS) **1141**
Kommersant Moldovy (MDA) **1141**
Kommersant S-Peterburg *see* Kommersant **1141**
Kommersant - Vlast' (RUS) **1141**
Kommision der Europaischen Gemeinschaften. Dokumente *see* Commission of the European Communities. Documents **7227**
Kommission fuer Archaeologische Landesforschung in Hessen. Berichte (DEU ISSN 0941-6013) **403**
Kommission fuer geschichtliche Landeskunde in Baden-Wuerttemberg. Veroeffentlichungen. Reihe A. Quellen (DEU ISSN 0067-2831) **4238**
Kommission fuer geschichtliche Landeskunde in Baden-Wuerttemberg. Veroeffentlichungen. Reihe B: Forschungen (DEU ISSN 0521-9884) **4238**
Kommission fuer Neuere Geschichte Oesterreichs. Veroeffentlichungen (AUT ISSN 1012-5744) **4238**
Kommission fuer Oekologie. Rundgespraeche (DEU ISSN 0938-5851) **3449**
Kommissionen for de Europaeiske Faelleskaber. Dokumenter *see* Commission of the European Communities. Documents **7227**
KommJur (DEU ISSN 1613-0235) **4710**
Kommun-Aktuellt *see* Dagens Samhaelle **7491**
• Kommunal Aarbog (DNK ISSN 0900-1484) **7495**
Kommunal Budgetredegoerelse *see* Budgetoversigt **7489**
Kommunal Butgetredegoerelse *see* Kommunernes Oekonomi **7495**
Kommunal Direkt (DEU) **7495**
Kommunal Ekonomi (SWE ISSN 0282-0099) **7495**
Kommunal Katalog (CHE) **1019**
Kommunalarbetaren (SWE ISSN 0345-6307) **1691**
Kommunalbeamten Jahrbuch Nordrhein-Westfalen *see* K O M B A Jahrbuch Nordrhein-Westfalen **7449**
Kommunalbladet *see* H K Kommunalbladet **4595**
Kommunale Branchenbuch *see* K O B R A **2010**
Kommunale Entsorgung (DEU ISSN 1431-8253) **7495**
Kommunale Fahrzeuge (DEU ISSN 1432-038X) **7495**
• Kommunale Noegletal om Udlaendinge (DNK ISSN 1603-6727) **7286**
Kommunale Noegletal om Udlaendinge *see* Kommunale Noegletal om Udlaendinge **7286**
Kommunale Steuer - Zeitschrift (DEU ISSN 0450-7126) **1932**
Kommunale Sundhedsordninger. Hjemmesygeplejen (DNK ISSN 1600-1621) **8053**
Kommunale Sundhedsordninger. Skolesundhedstjenesten (DNK ISSN 1395-6124) **2881**
▼ Kommunale Verwaltungssteuerung (DEU ISSN 1867-0822) **7450**
Kommunaler Beschaffungs-Dienst (DEU ISSN 0930-6439) **1424**
Kommunales Echo Rheinland-Pfalz (DEU) **8053**
Kommunaljurist *see* KommJur **4710**
Kommunalleasing Magazin (DEU) **7450**
Kommunalmagazin (CHE) **7495**
Kommunalpolitische Blaetter (DEU ISSN 0177-9184) **7149**
KommunalPraxis. Ausgabe Bayern (DEU ISSN 0171-7510) **7495**
† KommunalPraxis. Ausgabe Brandenburg, Mecklenburg-Vorpommern, Sachsen, Sachsen-Anhalt, Thueringen, Berlin (DEU ISSN 1437-2444) **8969**
KommunalPraxis Spezial (DEU ISSN 1617-3759) **7495**
KommunalTechnik (DEU ISSN 1615-4924) **7450**
• Kommunalteknikk (NOR ISSN 0452-389X) **3207**
Die Kommunalverwaltung Brandenburg (DEU ISSN 0942-5454) **7495**
Die Kommunalverwaltung Mecklenburg-Vorpommern (DEU ISSN 0949-0701) **7495**
Die Kommunalverwaltung Sachsen (DEU ISSN 0941-5815) **7495**
Die Kommunalverwaltung Sachsen-Anhalt (DEU ISSN 0949-0698) **7495**
Die Kommunalverwaltung Thueringen (DEU ISSN 0943-2434) **7495**
Kommunalwirtschaft (DEU ISSN 0450-7169) **3207**
Kommunalwissenschaftliche Dissertationen (DEU ISSN 0340-1170) **4418**
Kommunalwissenschaftliches Institut Arbeitshefte *see* K W I - Arbeitshefte **7449**
Kommunalwissenschaftliches Institut Gutachten *see* K W I - Gutachten **7449**
Kommunalwissenschaftliches Institut Info *see* K W I - Info **7449**
Kommunalwissenschaftliches Institut Projektberichte *see* K W I - Projektberichte **7449**
Kommune (DEU ISSN 0723-7669) **7149**
Kommunen (DNK ISSN 0903-0077) **7495**
▼ Kommuner och Landsting (SWE ISSN 1654-7373) **7450**
Kommunernas Ekonomiska Laege *see* Ekonomirapporten **1921**
† Kommunerne & Europa (DNK ISSN 1398-1420) **8969**
▼ Kommunernes Oekonomi (DNK ISSN 1903-072X) **7495**
Kommunikation (CHE) **2330**
Kommunikation Extra (DEU ISSN 1617-9056) **8117**
Kommunikation und Beratung (DEU ISSN 0947-0352) **7981**
Kommunikation und Institution (DEU ISSN 0939-9496) **5137**
Kommunikation und Recht (DEU ISSN 1434-6354) **2330**
• Kommunikation@gesellschaft (DEU ISSN 1616-2617) **7981**
Kommunikations- und EDV Sicherheit *see* K E S **2515**
Kommunikations-Wissenschaftliche Studien (DEU) **2331**
Kommunikationsforschung Aktuell (DEU ISSN 1615-9713) **8117**
Kommunikationsmanager (DEU ISSN 1613-5873) **28**
Kommunikationsstoerungen - Berichte aus Phoniatrie und Paedaudiologie (DEU ISSN 1436-1175) **6082**
Kommunikationswissenschaft (DEU ISSN 1860-8353) **7981**
▼ • Kommuninfo Obiz (SWE ISSN 1654-8361) **7450**
Kommunist (RUS) **7149**
Kommunisticheskaya Perspektiva (RUS) **7149**
Kommunteknik *see* Kuntatekniikka **4418**
Komondor Komments (USA) **6810**
Kompack (AUT) **6711**
Kompakt Dermatologie (DEU) **5879**
Kompakt Gastroenterologie (DEU) **5928**
Kompakt Onkologie *see* Haemato-Onkologische Nachrichten **5936**
Kompakt Pneumologie (DEU) **6216**
† Kompakt Rheumatologie und Osteoporose (DEU) **8969**
Kompanion (TJK) **1141**
Kompaniya (RUS) **1141**
• Komp&n'on (UKR) **1141**
Komparatistik (DEU ISSN 1432-5306) **5318**
Komparatistische Bibliothek/Bibliotheque d'Etudes Comparatives/Comparative Studies Series (DEU ISSN 0934-0858) **7981**
† Kompas voor Beleid. Horeca (NLD ISSN 1871-4951) **8969**
Kompass (DEU ISSN 0342-0809) **4511**
• Kompass (Online) (DNK ISSN 1902-7001) **2011**
Kompass (Print) *see* Kompass (Online) **2011**
Kompass Advertising Extracts (GBR) **2011**
• Kompass Australia (AUS ISSN 0075-6628) **2011**
• Kompass Belgium (BEL ISSN 0778-4147) **2011**
• Kompass. Company Information (GBR ISSN 1353-1069) **2011**
Kompass Danmark *see* Kompass (Online) **2011**
† • Kompass Deutschland. Band 1. Produkte/Service/Kompass Germany (DEU ISSN 0945-1900) **8969**
Kompass Directory (GBR) **7094**
• Kompass Finland/Handbok over Finlands Industri och Naeringsliv/Informationswerk fuer die Finnische Wirtschaft/Register of Finnish Industry and Commerce/Repertoire General de l'Economie Finlandaise (FIN ISSN 0786-7883) **1574**
Kompass France (FRA ISSN 0759-5689) **2011**
Kompass Germany *see* Kompass Deutschland. Band 1. Produkte/Service **8969**
† • Kompass Holland (NLD ISSN 0075-6660) **8969**
Kompass India (IND) **2011**
• Kompass. Industrial Trade Names (GBR ISSN 1353-1093) **2011**
• Kompass Ireland (Year) (IRL ISSN 1393-9289) **2011**
• Kompass Italia - Annuario Generale dell'Economia Italiana (ITA) **1247**
Kompass Maroc (MAR ISSN 0075-6695) **2011**
• Kompass Norge (NOR ISSN 0075-6709) **2011**
Kompass. Parents & Subsidiaries *see* Kompass. Parents and Subsidiaries **2011**
Kompass. Parents and Subsidiaries (GBR ISSN 1353-1085) **2011**
Kompass Philippines (PHL) **2011**
• Kompass Portugal (PRT ISSN 0872-0223) **2011**
Kompass Product Locator (GBR ISSN 1477-528X) **2011**
Kompass. Products & Services *see* Kompass. Products and Services **2011**
• Kompass. Products and Services (GBR ISSN 1353-1050) **2011**
Kompass Professionnel. Agriculture, Alimentation (FRA ISSN 0299-6154) **2011**
Kompass Professionnel. Batiment et Genie Civil, Manutention - Levage, Bois - Meubles (FRA ISSN 0299-6162) **2011**
Kompass Professionnel. Chimie, Plastiques, Caoutchouc, Produits Mineraux (FRA ISSN 0299-6111) **2011**
Kompass Professionnel. Distribution, Commerce de Gros (FRA ISSN 0990-8536) **2011**
Kompass Professionnel. Electricite, Electronique, Informatique (FRA ISSN 0299-612X) **2011**
Kompass Professionnel. Produits du Metal (FRA ISSN 0299-6138) **2011**
Kompass Professionnel. Services, Industries Graphiques (FRA ISSN 0299-609X) **2011**
Kompass Professionnel. Siderurgie, Metallurgie, Fonderie (FRA ISSN 0299-6170) **2012**
Kompass Professionnel. Techniques Hydrauliques et Pneumatiques, Climatisation (FRA ISSN 0299-6197) **2012**
Kompass Professionnel. Textile, Habillement, Cuirs et Peaux (FRA ISSN 0299-6146) **2012**
Kompass Professionnel. Transports, Moyens de Transports (FRA ISSN 0990-8552) **2012**
Kompass Professionnels (FRA) **2012**
Kompass Regional Economique et Industriel. Alsace (FRA ISSN 0295-7965) **1141**
Kompass Regional Economique et Industriel. Aquitaine (FRA ISSN 0295-7981) **1141**
Kompass Regional Economique et Industriel. Auvergne (FRA ISSN 0295-7957) **1141**
Kompass Regional Economique et Industriel. Bourgogne (FRA ISSN 0295-7922) **1141**
Kompass Regional Economique et Industriel. Bretagne (FRA ISSN 0759-3929) **1141**
Kompass Regional Economique et Industriel. Centre (FRA ISSN 0759-3910) **1141**
Kompass Regional Economique et Industriel. Champagne - Ardennes (FRA ISSN 0295-7930) **1141**
Kompass Regional Economique et Industriel. Franche-Comte (FRA ISSN 0295-7949) **1141**
Kompass Regional Economique et Industriel. Ile-de-France (FRA ISSN 0759-3813) **1141**
Kompass Regional Economique et Industriel. Languedoc - Roussillon (FRA ISSN 0295-7795) **1141**
Kompass Regional Economique et Industriel. Limousin, Poitou - Charentes (FRA ISSN 0759-4755) **1141**
Kompass Regional Economique et Industriel. Lorraine (FRA ISSN 0295-7914) **1141**
Kompass Regional Economique et Industriel. Midi-Pyrenees (FRA ISSN 0295-7787) **1141**
Kompass Regional Economique et Industriel. Nord, Pas-de-Calais (FRA ISSN 0295-7973) **1142**
Kompass Regional Economique et Industriel. Normandie (FRA ISSN 0752-9309) **1142**
Kompass Regional Economique et Industriel. Pays de la Loire *see* Kompass Regional. Pays de la Loire **1142**
Kompass Regional Economique et Industriel. Picardie (FRA ISSN 0759-5506) **1142**
Kompass Regional Economique et Industriel. Provence, Alpes, Cote-d'Azur, Corse (FRA ISSN 0759-3686) **1142**
Kompass Regional Economique et Industriel. Rhone - Alpes (FRA ISSN 0752-921X) **1142**
Kompass Regional. Pays de la Loire (FRA ISSN 1767-6509) **1142**
Kompass Regionaux (FRA) **1142**
Kompass Register C Ds *see* Kompass. Company Information **2011**
Kompass Schweiz - Liechtenstein (CHE ISSN 0075-6717) **2012**
Kompass Singapore (SGP ISSN 0217-0604) **2012**
• Kompass South Africa (ZAF ISSN 1022-3568) **2012**
Kompass Suomi *see* Kompass Finland **1574**
• Kompass Sverige (SWE ISSN 0075-6725) **2012**
Kompass Taiwan (TWN ISSN 0259-4021) **2012**
Kompendium Mediciny (SVK ISSN 1336-4871) **5658**
Kompetensutveckling med Tidningen Familjedaghem *see* Familjedaghem **2652**
Kompetenz (DEU) **1420**
Kompetenzentwicklung (DEU ISSN 1432-3257) **1868**
• Kompiuterija (LTU ISSN 1392-3498) **2430**
Kompleksnoe Ispol'zovanie Mineral'nogo Syr'ya/Complex Use of National Resources (KAZ ISSN 0202-1382) **6468**
➤ Komplementaere und Integrative Medizin (DEU ISSN 1863-8678) **312**
Komponisten der Gegenwart (DEU) **6583**
Komponisten Unserer Zeit (AUT) **6583**
Kompozyty/Composites (POL ISSN 1641-8611) **7094**
• Komputa Saiensu/Japanese Journal of Computer Science (JPN ISSN 1340-7732) **2430**
Komputek Computerworld Indonesia (IDN) **2430**
Komputer foer Alla *see* Bonnier PC-Tidningen **2408**
Komputer for Alle (DNK ISSN 1396-0342) **2574**
• Komputer Swiat (POL ISSN 1506-4026) **2430**
Komputer Swiat Biblioteczka (POL ISSN 1508-4280) **2430**
Komputer Swiat Ekspert (POL) **2430**
Komputer Swiat Extra (POL ISSN 1640-2332) **2430**
Komputer Swiat Film (POL) **2402**
Komputer w Firmie *see* Prawo Przedsiebiorcy **1161**
Komputer w Firmie *see* Gazeta Prawna **4679**
Komputerowa Gratka (POL ISSN 1643-8256) **2198**
Komputerowa Gratka. Wydanie Specjalne *see* Komputerowa Gratka **2198**
Komputery i Biuro (POL ISSN 1425-8250) **2430**
KompyuArt (RUS) **2488**
Komp'yuter Press (RUS ISSN 0868-6157) **2508**
Komp'yuter v Bukhgalterskom Uchete i Audite (RUS) **1420**
• Komp'yuternaya Gazeta/Computer News (BLR ISSN 1606-6464) **2430**
Komp'yuternaya Khronika - Itersotsioinform (RUS) **2508**
Komp'yuternaya Optika (RUS ISSN 0134-2452) **2473**
Komp'yuternoe Obozrenie/Computer Review (UKR) **2430**
• Komp'yuternye Instrumenty v Obrazovanii (RUS) **2473**
• Komp'yuternye Uchebnye Programmy i Innovatsii (RUS) **2508**
Komp'yuternyi Vestnik/Computer Bulletin (RUS) **2443**
• Komp'yuterra (RUS) **2473**
Komp'yutery + Programmy *see* P C World Ukraine **2582**
Komp'yutery v Obrazovanii (RUS) **2473**
Komp'yutery v Uchebnom Protsesse (RUS) **5023**
Komsomolets Kaspiya (RUS) **3936**
• Komsomol'skaya Pravda (RUS ISSN 0233-4194) **3936**
▼ Komunalne Financie (SVK ISSN 1337-2459) **1364**
▼ Komunalni Technika (CZE ISSN 1802-2391) **212**
Komunalni Vjesnik (HRV ISSN 1331-6303) **7450**
Komunikacie/Communications (SVK ISSN 1335-4205) **2331**
Komunikaty Mazursko-Warminskie/Masurisch-Ermlandische Mittelungen (POL ISSN 0023-3196) **4238**
Komunikaty Rybackie (POL ISSN 1230-641X) **3600**
The Kon-Lin Letter (USA) **1636**
Kon Polski (POL ISSN 0137-1487) **8294**
Kon-Tiki Museum. Occasional Papers (NOR ISSN 0802-6491) **346**
Konan Daigaku Kiyo. Rigaku Hen/Konan University. Memoirs. Science Series (JPN ISSN 0452-4160) **7877**
Konan University. Memoirs. Science Series *see* Konan Daigaku Kiyo. Rigaku Hen **7877**
Koncar Strucne Informacije (HRV ISSN 0350-5537) **3323**
Konchu. Nyu Shirizu *see* Japanese Journal of Entomology. New Series **851**
Konchu to Shizen/Nature and Insects (JPN ISSN 0023-3218) **853**
Konchugaku Hyoron/Entomological Review of Japan (JPN ISSN 0286-9810) **853**
Konchuk Munhwa *see* Geonchug Munhwa **443**
Koncize (NLD ISSN 0942-0568) **6281**
Kondinin Group Update (AUS) **131**
Konditerskoe Proizvodstvo/Confectionery Manufacture (RUS) **3674**
Konditor Nyt *see* Magasinet **3674**
Konditorei und Cafe *see* KoCa - Konditorei und Cafe **3674**
Koneko (DEU) **5074**
Koneviesti (FIN ISSN 0355-0729) **5454**
Konevodstvo i Konnyi Sport (RUS ISSN 0023-3285) **8294**
Konfeksiyon Teknik/Clothing Technology Magazine (TUR ISSN 1300-9974) **2248**
Konfer Normal *see* Konfernormal **8969**
• Konferencja Bezpieczenstwa i Niezawodnosci. Journal (POL ISSN 1895-8281) **3207**
Konferensie van Suid-Afrikaanse Opmeters. Verrigtinge *see* Conference of South African Surveyors. Proceedings **3263**
KonferensVaerlden (SWE ISSN 1100-4924) **1142**
† Konfernormal (DEU ISSN 1436-946X) **8969**
† Konfetti (DEU ISSN 0942-1343) **8970**
Konfirmandenunterricht Praxis *see* K U - Praxis **7657**
Konflikt, Verbrechen und Sanktion in der Gesellschaft Alteuropas, Symposien und Synthesen (AUT) **4238**
Konflikte und Kultur (DEU ISSN 1437-6083) **4238**
Kongelig Dansk Hof- og Statskalender (DNK ISSN 0085-2589) **7450**
• Det Kongelige Bibliotek. Aarsberetning (DNK ISSN 0909-9093) **5023**
Det Kongelige Bibliotek. Magasin (DNK ISSN 0905-5533) **5023**
Det Kongelige Bibliotek. Specialhjaelpemidler (DNK ISSN 0105-8215) **628**
† Det Kongelige Danske Videnskabernes Selskab. Biologiske Skrifter (DNK ISSN 0366-3612) **8970**
Kongelige Danske Videnskabernes Selskab. Historisk-Filosofiske Meddelelser (DNK ISSN 0106-0481) **4462**
Kongelige Danske Videnskabernes Selskab. Historisk - Filosofiske Skrifter (DNK ISSN 0023-3307) **4462**
Kongelige Danske Videnskabernes Selskab. Matematisk - Fysiske Meddelelser (DNK ISSN 0023-3323) **5508**
Kongelige Danske Videnskabernes Selskab. Oversigt over Selskabets Virksomhed (DNK ISSN 0368-7201) **7877**
Kongelige Norske Videnskabers Selskab. Aarbok for DKNVS Akademiet og DKNVS Stiftelsen (NOR ISSN 0803-1983) **7877**
Kongelige Norske Videnskabers Selskab. Forhandlinger *see* Kongelige Norske Videnskabers Selskab. Aarbok for DKNVS Akademiet og DKNVS Stiftelsen **7877**
➤ Kongelige Norske Videnskabers Selskab. Skrifter/Royal Norwegian Society of Sciences and Letters. Publications (NOR ISSN 0368-6310) **7877**
Det Kongelige Norske Videnskabers Selskab's Meddelelser *see* D K N V S 's Meddelelser **7849**
† Kongelige Veterinaer- og Landbohoejskole. De Studerendes Raad. Tvaerfagligt Rusudvalg. Brugsanvisning i KVL (DNK ISSN 1600-2490) **8970**

DIRECTORY 2010 KONYA POSTASI 10535

† Kongelige Veterinaer- og Landbohoejskole. Institut for Oekonomi, Skov og Landskab. Samfundsvidenskabelig Memo-Serie/Social Science Research Papers (DNK ISSN 0909-0703) **8970**
† Kongelige Veterinaer- og Landbohoejskole. Jordbrugsteknisk Institut. Rapport (DNK ISSN 0906-9550) **8970**
Kongetsu no Nogyo/Agricultural Chemicals Monthly (JPN ISSN 0912-1404) **240**
Kongetsu no Tenko to Norin Sagyo/Monthly News of Weather, Agriculture and Forestry (JPN) **6359**
Konggan *see* Gong'gan **443**
Kongjian/Space (TWN ISSN 1017-088X) **448**
• Kongjian Jiegou/Spatial Structures (CHN ISSN 1006-6578) **3277**
• ➤ Kongjian Kexue Xuebao/Chinese Journal of Space Science (CHN ISSN 0254-6124) **64**
• Kongjian Kongzhi Jishu yu Yingyong/Aerospace Control Application (CHN ISSN 1674-1579) **64**
• Kongjun Gongcheng Daxue Xuebao (Ziran Kexue Ban)/Air Force Engineering University. Journal (Natural Science Edition) (CHN ISSN 1009-3516) **7877**
• Kongjun Zongyiyuan Xuebao/People's Liberation Army. General Hospital of Air Force. Journal (CHN ISSN 1009-2811) **5658**
• ➤ Kongqi Donglixue Xuebao/Acta Aerodynamica Sinica (CHN ISSN 0258-1825) **7060**
Kongres for Svineproducenter (DNK ISSN 1603-8401) **291**
Kongres Wanita Indonesia News *see* K O W A N I News **8870**
Kongresa Libro (NLD ISSN 0083-3851) **6281**
Kongress Kalender Medizin (DEU) **6281**
Kongressbericht Bundesschulmusikwoche (DEU) **6583**
Kongyun Shangwu/Air Transport & Business (CHN ISSN 1671-3095) **8547**
• Kongzhi Gongcheng/Control Engineering of China (CHN ISSN 1671-7848) **3207**
• ➤ Kongzhi Lilun yu Yingyong/Control Theory & Applications (CHN ISSN 1000-8152) **3207**
• Kongzhi yu Juece/Control and Decision (CHN ISSN 1001-0920) **3207**
Kongzhong zhi Jia *see* Nihao **8785**
• Kongzi Yanjiu/Studies on Confucius (CHN ISSN 1002-2627) **7738**
• Konica Minolta Medical Network/Konica X-Ray Photographic Review (JPN) **6202**
Konica X-Ray Photographic Review *see* Konica Minolta Medical Network **6202**
Konigsberger Express (RUS) **3936**
Koningrijk der Nederlanden. Staatsblad (NLD ISSN 0920-2064) **7450**
Koninklijk Belgisch Instituut voor Natuurwetenschappen. Studiedocumenten/Institut Royal des Sciences Naturelles de Belgique. Documents de Travail (BEL ISSN 0777-0111) **686**
Koninklijk Instituut voor de Tropen. Critical Reviews and Annotated Bibliographies (NLD ISSN 1382-4686) **183**
Koninklijk Instituut voor de Tropen. Landenreeks (NLD ISSN 0922-4939) **4018**
Koninklijk Instituut voor de Tropen Newsletter *see* K I T Newsletter **8969**
• Koninklijk Instituut voor de Tropen. Survey of Activities (NLD) **4018**
Koninklijk Instituut voor het Kunstpatrimonium. Bulletin *see* Institut Royal du Patrimoine Artistique. Bulletin **496**
Koninklijk Instituut voor Taal-, Land- en Volkenkunde. Bibliographical Series (NLD ISSN 0074-0462) **362**
Koninklijk Instituut voor Taal-, Land- en Volkenkunde. Caribbean Series *see* Caribbean Series **332**
Koninklijk Instituut voor Taal-, Land- en Volkenkunde. Proceedings (NLD) **346**
Koninklijk Instituut voor Taal-, Land- en Volkenkunde. Translation Series (NLD ISSN 0074-0470) **346**
Koninklijk Instituut voor Taal-, Land- en Volkenkunde. Verhandelingen (NLD ISSN 1572-1892) **346**
† Koninklijk Instituut voor Taal-, Land- en Volkenkunde. Working Papers Series (NLD ISSN 0923-5418) **8970**
Koninklijk Kabinet van Schilderijen Mauritshuis. Jaarverslag (NLD ISSN 1574-4612) **500**
Koninklijk Meteorologisch Instituut van Belgie. Dageljks Weerbulletin *see* Institut Royal Meteorologique de Belgique. Bulletin Quotidien du Temps **6357**
Koninklijk Meteorologisch Instituut van Belgie. Jaarboek: Aardmagnetisme *see* Institut Royal Meteorologique de Belgique. Annuaire: Magnetisme Terrestre **2747**
Koninklijk Meteorologisch Instituut van Belgie. Maandbulletin. Geofysische Waarnemingen *see* Institut Royal Meteorologique de Belgique. Bulletin Mensuel: Observations Geophysiques **2783**
Koninklijk Meteorologisch Instituut van Belgie. Miscellanea. Serie A *see* Institut Royal Meteorologique de Belgique. Miscellanea. Serie A **6357**
Koninklijk Meteorologisch Instituut van Belgie. Publicaties. Reeks B *see* Institut Royal Meteorologique de Belgique. Publications. Serie B **6357**
Koninklijk Meteorologische Instituut van Belgie. Driemaandelijks Bulletin: Ozon Waarnemingen *see* Institut Royal Meteorologique de Belgique. Bulletin Trimestriel: Observations d'Ozone **6357**
Koninklijk Meteorologische Instituut van Belgie. Maandbulletin: Klimatologische Waarnemingen *see* Institut Royal Meteorologique de Belgique. Bulletin Mensuel: Observations Climatologiques **6357**
Koninklijk Meteorologische Instituut van Belgie. Maandbulletin: Waarnemingen van de Ionosfeer en de Kosmische Straling *see* Institut Royal Meteorologique de Belgique. Bulletin Mensuel: Observations Ionospheriques et du Rayonnement Cosmique **6357**
Koninklijk Museum voor Midden-Afrika. Annalen - Economische Wetenschappen. Reeks in 8 *see* Musee Royal de l'Afrique Centrale. Annales - Sciences Economiques. Serie in 8 **203**
Koninklijk Museum voor Midden-Afrika. Annalen - Geologische Wetenschappen. Reeks in 8 *see* Musee Royal de l'Afrique Centrale. Annales - Sciences Geologiques. Serie in 8 **2756**
Koninklijk Museum voor Midden-Afrika. Annalen - Historische Wetenschappen. Reeks in 8 *see* Musee Royal de l'Afrique Centrale. Annales - Sciences Historiques. Serie in 8 **4176**
Koninklijk Museum voor Midden-Afrika. Annalen - Menselijke Wetenschappen. Serie in 8 *see* Musee Royal de l'Afrique Centrale. Annales - Sciences Humaines. Serie in 8 **4465**
Koninklijk Museum voor Midden-Afrika. Annalen. Nieuwe Reeks in 4. Zoologische Wetenschappen *see* Studies in Afrotropical Zoology **964**
Koninklijk Museum voor Midden-Afrika. Annalen - Zoologische Wetenschappen. Reeks in 8 *see* Musee Royal de l'Afrique Centrale. Annales - Sciences Zoologiques. Serie in 8 **956**
Koninklijk Museum voor Midden-Afrika. Archief voor Antropologie *see* Musee Royal de l'Afrique Centrale. Archives d'Anthropologie **348**
Koninklijk Museum voor Midden-Afrika. Catalogus der Uitgaven *see* Musee Royal de l'Afrique Centrale. Catalogue des Editions **631**
Koninklijk Museum voor Midden-Afrika. Economische Documentatie *see* Musee Royal de l'Afrique Centrale. Documentation Economique **1151**
Koninklijk Museum voor Midden-Afrika. Zoologische Documentatie *see* Musee Royal de l'Afrique Centrale. Documentation Zoologique **956**
† ➤ Koninklijk Nederlands Geologisch Mijnbouwkundig Genootschap. Verhandelingen (NLD ISSN 0075-6741) **8970**
† Koninklijk Nederlands Historisch Genootschap. Kroniek (NLD ISSN 1386-8969) **8970**
Koninklijk Nederlands Meteorologisch Instituut. Technical Reports *see* Koninklijk Nederlands Meteorologisch Instituut. Technische Rapporten **6360**
Koninklijk Nederlands Meteorologisch Instituut. Technische Rapporten/Koninklijk Nederlands Meteorologisch Instituut. Technical Reports (NLD ISSN 0169-1708) **6360**
Koninklijk Nederlands Meteorologisch Instituut. Wetenschappelijke Rapporten (NLD ISSN 0169-1651) **6360**
Koninklijk Nederlandsch Genootschap voor Geslacht- en Wapenkunde. Werken Uitgegeven (NLD ISSN 0921-013X) **3773**
Koninklijk Verbond van Grafische Ondernemingen Kernnieuws *see* K V G O Kernnieuws **7324**
Koninklijke Academie voor Geneeskunde van Belgie. Verhandelingen (BEL ISSN 0302-6469) **5658**
Koninklijke Academie voor Nederlandse Taal- en Letterkunde. Jaarboek (BEL ISSN 0770-7762) **5137**
Koninklijke Academie voor Nederlandse Taal- en Letterkunde. Verslagen en Mededelingen (BEL ISSN 0770-786X) **5318**
Koninklijke Academie voor Overzeese Wetenschappen. Klasse voor Morele en Politieke Wetenschappen. Verhandelingen in 8 *see* Academie Royale des Sciences d'Outre-Mer. Classe des Sciences Morales et Politiques. Memoires in 8 **4440**
Koninklijke Academie voor Overzeese Wetenschappen. Klasse voor Natuur- en Geneeskundige Wetenschappen. Verzameling in 8 *see* Academie Royale des Sciences d'Outre-Mer. Classe des Sciences Naturelles et Medicales. Collection in 8 **7830**
Koninklijke Academie voor Overzeese Wetenschappen. Klasse voor Technische Wetenschappen. Verzameling in 8 *see* Academie Royale des Sciences d'Outre-Mer. Classe des Sciences Techniques. Collection in 8 **7830**
Koninklijke Academie voor Overzeese Wetenschappen. Mededelingen der Zittingen *see* Academie Royale des Sciences d'Outre-Mer. Bulletin des Seances **7830**
Koninklijke Automobiel Club van Belgie Auto Revue *see* K A C B Auto Revue **8587**
Koninklijke Belgische Duivenliefhebbersbond. Bondsblad *see* Royale Federation Colombophile Belge. Bulletin National **914**
Koninklijke Belgische Marine Academie. Mededelingen *see* Academie Royale de Marine de Belgique. Communications **8638**
Koninklijke Bibliotheek Albert 1. Driemaandelijks Informatie Bulletin *see* Bibliotheque Royal Albert 1er. Bulletin Trimestriel d'Information **4996**
Koninklijke Bibliotheek Albert I. Aangekondigde Publikaties *see* Bibliotheque Royale Albert 1er. Publications Annoncees **4997**
Koninklijke Bibliotheek Albert I. Jaarverslag (BEL ISSN 0770-447X) **5023**
Koninklijke Bibliotheek. Hoofdafdeling Research en Development. Jaaroverzicht (NLD ISSN 1567-293X) **5023**
Koninklijke Commissie voor de Uitgave der Oude Wetten en Verordeningen van Belgie. Handelingen *see* Commission Royale des Anciennes Lois et Ordonnances de Belgique. Bulletin **4136**
Koninklijke Commissie voor Toponymie en Dialectologie. Handelingen *see* Commission Royale de Toponymie et Dialectologie. Bulletin **5107**
Koninklijke Commissie voor Toponymie en Dialectologie. Werken *see* Commission Royale de Toponymie et Dialectologie. Memoires **5107**
Koninklijke Geneeskundige Kring van Antwerpen. Annales *see* Koninklijke Geneeskundige Kring van Antwerpen. Colmed Info **5658**
Koninklijke Geneeskundige Kring van Antwerpen. Colmed Info (BEL ISSN 1375-4505) **5658**
Koninklijke Kring voor Oudheidkunde Letteren en Kunst van Mechelen. Handelingen (BEL ISSN 0776-2976) **4238**
Koninklijke Luchtvaart Maatschappij Agent *see* K L M Agent **8726**
Koninklijke Musea voor Kunst en Geschiedenis. Bulletin *see* Musees Royaux d'Art et d'Histoire. Bulletin **4247**
Koninklijke Musea voor Schone Kunsten van Belgie. Bulletin *see* Musees Royaux des Beaux-Arts de Belgique. Bulletin **6530**
Koninklijke Nederlandsche Wielren Unie Wieler Magazine *see* K N W U Wieler Magazine **8260**
Koninklijke Nederlandse Akademie van Wetenschappen. Afdeling Letterkunde. Mededelingen. Nieuwe Reeks (NLD ISSN 0168-6968) **5318**
➤ Koninklijke Nederlandse Akademie van Wetenschappen. Afdeling Letterkunde. Verhandlingen. Nieuwe Reeks (NLD ISSN 0065-5511) **5137**
Koninklijke Nederlandse Oudheidkundige Bond. Bulletin (NLD ISSN 0166-0470) **403**
Koninklijke Nederlandse Voetbalbond Jaarboek *see* K N V B Jaarboek **8969**
Koninklijke Prijs voor Vrije Schilderkunst (NLD ISSN 1574-4361) **500**
Koninklijke Subsidie voor Vrije Schilderkunst Koninklijk Paleis Amsterdam *see* Koninklijke Prijs voor Vrije Schilderkunst **500**
• ➤ Koninklijke Vereniging voor Nederlandse Muziekgeschiedenis. Tijdschrift/Royal Society for Music History of The Netherlands. Review (NLD ISSN 1383-7079) **6583**
Konjunktur (DEU ISSN 1610-7586) **1495**
Konjunktur (DNK ISSN 1396-6030) **1142**
Konjunktur in Bayern (DEU) **1496**
• Konjunkturbarometern. Maanad (SWE ISSN 1650-9951) **1896**
Konjunkturberichte (HUN ISSN 1586-2534) **1142**
Konjunkturen (SWE ISSN 0282-9967) **1496**
Konjunkturinstitutet. K I Dokument *see* Konjunkturinstitutet. Specialstudier **1896**
Konjunkturinstitutet. Specialstudier (SWE ISSN 1650-996X) **1896**
• Konjunkturlaeget (SWE ISSN 0023-3463) **1896**
• Konjunkturstatistik (DNK ISSN 1901-8975) **1247**
• Konjunkturundersoegelse af Vognmandserhvervet i Danmark (DNK ISSN 1604-1720) **8672**
Konkret (DEU ISSN 0023-3528) **3851**
Konkreter Erfolg *see* Erfolg Konkret **587**
Konkurent (RUS) **3936**
➤ Konkurito Kogaku/Concrete Journal (JPN ISSN 0387-1061) **1019**
Konkurito Kogaku Ronbunshu/Concrete Research and Technology (JPN ISSN 1340-4733) **3277**
Konkurito Raiburari Intanashonaru *see* Concrete Library International (CD-ROM) **3263**
Konkursbuch (DEU) **6931**
The KonLin Letter (USA) **1636**
Konnichi no Chiryoyaku (JPN) **6858**
Konnichi no Ishoku/Transplantation Now (JPN ISSN 0916-0094) **6251**
Konnyaku News (JPN) **202**
Konoike Construction Co. Proceedings of Annual Meeting *see* Konoikegumi Gijutsu Kenkyu Happyokai Ronbunshu **1020**
Konoike Construction Co. Technical Research Reports *see* Konoikegumi Gijutsu Kenkyu Hokoku **1020**
Konoikegumi Gijutsu Kenkyu Happyokai Ronbunshu/Konoike Construction Co. Proceedings of Annual Meeting (JPN) **1020**
Konoikegumi Gijutsu Kenkyu Hokoku/Konoike Construction Co. Technical Research Reports (JPN ISSN 0914-6229) **1020**
Konpyuta Repoto *see* Computer Report **2412**
• Konpyuta Sofutowea/Computer Software (JPN ISSN 0289-6540) **2593**
Konpyuta Yuzakai Chousa Nenpo/Annual Survey of Computer Users (JPN) **2430**
Konrad (DNK ISSN 1902-4193) **7763**
Konradsblatt (DEU) **7804**
Konsainvalinen Soveltavan Estetiikan Instituutti. Raportteja (FIN ISSN 1239-1948) **500**
Konsequenz (ITA ISSN 1722-0270) **6583**
Konstanzer Dissertationen (DEU ISSN 0930-8105) **686**
Konstanzer Schriften aus Geld- und Aussenwirtschaft (DEU ISSN 0937-4760) **1142**
Konstanzer Schriften zum Verwaltungsrecht und zur Rechtstatsachenforschung (DEU ISSN 1431-7087) **4710**
Konstanzer Schriften zur Aussenwirtschaft (DEU ISSN 0935-8420) **1574**
Konstanzer Schriften zur Entwicklungspolitik (DEU ISSN 0944-6311) **7250**
Konstanzer Schriften zur Rechtswissenschaft (DEU ISSN 0934-7658) **4710**
Konstanzer Schriften zur Schoah und Judaica (DEU ISSN 0942-6043) **3546**
Konstanzer Schriften zur Sozialwissenschaft (DEU ISSN 0936-8868) **7981**
• ➤ Konsthistorisk Tidskrift/Journal of Art History (GBR ISSN 0023-3609) **500**
Konstitutsionnoe Pravo. Vostochnoevropeiskoe Obozrenie *see* Sravnitel'noe Konstitutsionnoe Obozrenie **4852**
Konstitutsionnyi Sud Rossiiskoi Federatsii. Vestnik (RUS ISSN 0869-5725) **4710**
• Konstkalendern (SWE) **6527**
Konstnaeren (SWE ISSN 0283-2887) **500**
Konstperspektiv (SWE ISSN 0347-4453) **500**
Konstruieren und Giessen (DEU ISSN 0341-6615) **3351**
Der Konstrukteur (DEU ISSN 0344-4570) **1020**
• Konstruktion (DEU ISSN 0720-5953) **5454**
Konstruktion & Entwicklung (DEU ISSN 1435-893X) **8430**
Konstruktion, Elektronik Maschinenbau *see* K E M **3206**
Konstruktion, Elektronik Maschinenbau Sonderheft *see* K E M Sonderheft **3206**
Konstruktion und Engineering (DEU ISSN 0947-9333) **1020**
Konstruktionspraxis (DEU ISSN 0937-4167) **3351**
• Konstrukto (AUS) **7149**
• Konstruktoeren (DNK ISSN 0907-3574) **1020**
Konsttidningen (SWE ISSN 1101-8623) **500**
Konstvaerlden & Disajn (SWE) **500**
Konstytutsiinyi Sud Ukrainy (UKR) **4710**
Konsul'tant/Consultant (RUS ISSN 0869-7272) **1932**
Konsul'tant Bukhgaltera (RUS) **1932**
Konsul'tant Direktora (RUS) **1932**
Konsultguiden (SWE ISSN 1403-0349) **1771**
Konsument (AUT) **2639**
De Konsument (LUX) **2639**
Konsumentinformation *see* Kuluttaja **2639**
Konsyliarz (POL ISSN 1732-0895) **6991**
▼ • Kontagious (USA ISSN 1945-0117) **7659**
Kontaks Philippines (Year) (PHL ISSN 0117-5718) **2012**
Kontakt (AUT) **2198**
Kontakt (DEU ISSN 0176-246X) **1691**
† • Kontakt (DNK ISSN 0105-0982) **8970**
Kontakt *see* Connect **3412**
Kontakt (Surgut) (RUS) **3141**
Kontakt Drei und Zwanzig (AUT ISSN 0023-3676) **7804**
Kontakt und Studium (DEU ISSN 0171-1938) **7877**
Kontaktblad *see* Dansk Fotografi **6966**
Kontaktblad Uitvaartbegeleiding *see* Contactblad Spreken bij Uitvaarten **6911**
Kontakte (CHE) **6158**
Kontakte (Tuebingen) (DEU ISSN 0949-7277) **7659**
• Kontakten/Contact (SWE ISSN 0345-6471) **2369**
Kontakten (Haarlem) (NLD ISSN 1872-3705) **577**
Der Kontakter (DEU ISSN 0721-975X) **28**
Kontaktkalender (DNK ISSN 0108-4291) **1574**
Die Kontaktlinse (DEU ISSN 0721-5096) **6045**
Kontakto (NLD ISSN 0023-3692) **2198**
Kontaktologia i Optyka Okulistyczna (POL ISSN 1509-4251) **6045**
Kontaktstencil (SWE ISSN 0345-6498) **403**
KontaktStudium *see* Kontakt und Studium **7877**
Konteksty. Polska Sztuka Ludowa (POL ISSN 1230-6142) **500**
Kontenrahmen fuer die Traeger der Gesetzlichen Krankenversicherung, Kontenrahmen fuer die Traeger der Sozialen Pflegeversicherung und den Ausgleichsfonds (DEU ISSN 0948-5228) **7530**
➤ Kontext (DEU ISSN 0720-1079) **7382**
Kontinent (RUS ISSN 0934-6317) **5222**
Kontinent (RUS ISSN 1563-227X) **3936**
Kontinent - Sibir (RUS) **1142**
Kontinenz Aktuell (DEU ISSN 1862-2887) **6271**
Kontor/papir (DNK ISSN 1603-8630) **1852**
Kontorsvaerlden/Traeffpunkten (SWE) **1852**
Kontrapunkte (DEU) **2198**
▼ • Kontrast (DNK ISSN 1902-2832) **7149**
Kontreinuus (ZAF ISSN 1814-599X) **3949**
Kontrol' Diagnostika (RUS ISSN 0201-7032) **3387**
Kontur (FIN ISSN 1235-2772) **5222**
Kontur *see* Negotia **4599**
• Kontur (Online) (DNK ISSN 1602-3595) **8117**
Kontura (HRV ISSN 1330-4976) **500**
Konturen (DEU ISSN 1437-6903) **2696**
• Konvergencias (ARG ISSN 1669-9092) **6931**
Konversiya/Conversion (RUS ISSN 0868-6378) **1142**
Konwersatorium im. Josepha von Eichendorffa. Zeszyty Edukacji Kulturalnej (POL ISSN 1232-5694) **5222**
Konya Postasi (TUR) **3962**

Title

Korean Journal of English Language and Linguistics see Yeong'eohag **5197**
Korean Journal of Food Science and Technology see Han'guk Sikp'um Kwahakhoe Chi **3645**
• ➤ Korean Journal of Gastroenterology (KOR ISSN 1598-9992) **5928**
Korean Journal of Genetics/Han'gug Yujeon Haghoeji see Genes and Genomics **867**
• Korean Journal of Hepatology (KOR ISSN 1738-222X) **5928**
Korean Journal of Horticultural Science and Technology see Weon'ye Gwahag Gi'sulji **822**
Korean Journal of International and Comparative Law (KOR) **4934**
Korean Journal of International Law see Korean Journal of International and Comparative Law **4934**
Korean Journal of International Relations see Gugje Jeongchi Nonchong **7239**
† Korean Journal of International Studies (KOR ISSN 0377-0451) **8970**
Korean Journal of Journalism and Communication Studies see Han'gug Eonlon Hagbo **2322**
Korean Journal of Latin American Studies see Asian Journal of Latin American Studies **3520**
Korean Journal of Materials Research see Han'gug Jaeryo Haghoeji **3345**
Korean Journal of Medical History see Yisahag **5733**
Korean Journal of Medical Mycology see Daehan'yi Jin'gyun Haghoeji **5603**
• ➤ The Korean Journal of Medicine (KOR ISSN 1738-9364) **5947**
Korean Journal of Microbiology and Biotechnology see Han'gug Mi'saengmul Saengmyeong Gong Haghoeji **886**
Korean Journal of Mycology see Hangug Gynnhaghoi Ji **792**
Korean Journal of Nuclear Medicine see Daehan Haeg Yihag Hoeji **6195**
• ➤ Korean Journal of Ophthalmology (KOR ISSN 1011-8942) **6045**
• ➤ Korean Journal of Parasitology (KOR ISSN 0023-4001) **5821**
Korean Journal of Pediatrics/Soa'gwa (KOR ISSN 1738-1061) **6096**
Korean Journal of Pharmacognosy see Sengyakhak-Hoeji **6880**
Korean Journal of Physical Anthropology see Cejil Inryu Haghoeji **332**
• ➤ Korean Journal of Physiology and Pharmacology (KOR ISSN 1226-4512) **6858**
Korean Journal of Plant Biotechnology see Sigmul Saengmyeong Gong Haghoeji **770**
Korean Journal of Plant Taxonomy see Sigmul Bunryu Hag-hoeji **817**
• ➤ Korean Journal of Policy Studies (KOR ISSN 1225-5017) **7450**
Korean Journal of Public Health see Bo'geonhag Nonjib **7510**
• Korean Journal of Radiology (KOR ISSN 1229-6929) **6202**
The Korean Journal of Sericultural Science (KOR ISSN 1010-1624) **853**
Korean Journal of Social and Personality Psychology see Han'gug Simlihag Hoeji. Sahoe mich Seong'gyeog **7359**
Korean Journal of Sociology see Hanguk Sahoehak **8105**
Korean Journal of Sport Psychology see Han'gug Seupoceu Simri Haghoeji **8176**
Korean Journal of Sport Science see Cheyug Gwahag Yeon'gu **8166**
The Korean Journal of Systematic Zoology see Han'gug Dongmul Bunryu Haghoeji **945**
Korean Journal of Thinking and Problem Solving see The International Journal of Creativity & Problem Solving **7364**
Korean Journal of Unification Studies see Tong'il Yeon'gu Noncong **562**
Korean Journal of Urology see Daihan Binyogigwa Haghoi Ji **6267**
Korean Library and Information Science Society. Journal see Han'gug Munheon Jeongbo Haghoeji **5011**
Korean Library Association. Bulletin see Doseo'gwan Munhwa **5007**
Korean Literature see Choson Munhak **5273**
• ➤ Korean Mathematical Society. Bulletin (KOR ISSN 1015-8634) **5508**
• ➤ Korean Mathematical Society. Communications/Daehan Suhaghoe Nonmunjib (KOR ISSN 1225-1763) **5508**
• ➤ Korean Mathematical Society. Journal (KOR ISSN 0304-9914) **5508**
Korean Mathematical Society. The Newsletter see Daehan Suhaghoe Sosig **5482**
Korean Medical Association. Journal see Taehan Uisa Hyophoe Chi **5720**
Korean Medical Citation Index Journal see Ko M C I Journal **5748**
Korean Neuropsychiatric Association. Journal see Taehan Sin'gyong Chongsin Uihak Hoeji **6187**
• Korean Neurosurgical Society. Journal/Daehan Sin'gyeong Oe'gwa Hag'hoeji (KOR ISSN 1225-8245) **6158**
Korean Nuclear Society. Journal see Nuclear Engineering and Technology **7069**
Korean Nurse see Taehan Kanho **5982**
Korean Ophthalmological Society. Journal see Daehan An'gwa Hag'hoeji **6041**
Korean Orthopedic Association. Journal see Taehan Chonghyong Oekwa Hakhoechi **6073**
Korean Philately (USA ISSN 1087-5107) **6896**
➤ Korean Physical Society. Journal (KOR ISSN 0374-4884) **7024**
Korean Public Health Research see Taehan Pogon Yongu **7543**
Korean Publications Yearbook see Hankuk Ch'ulpan Yongam **7562**
Korean Publishers Association. Directory of Members (KOR) **7565**
Korean Publishing Journal see Ch'ulpan Moonwha **7559**
Korean Quarterly (USA ISSN 1536-156X) **3546**
Korean Research Bulletin (USA) **7149**
Korean Review (USA ISSN 0163-0229) **7250**
Korean Review of Public Administration see International Review of Public Administration **7447**
Korean Scholarship Association in Japan. Science Report see Chosen Shogakkai Gakujutsu Ronbunshu **5478**
Korean Scientific Information see Chosen Gakujutsu Tsuho **8446**
➤ Korean Social Science Journal (KOR ISSN 1225-0368) **7981**
Korean Society for Aeronautical and Space Sciences International Journal see K S A S International Journal **64**
Korean Society for Applied Biological Chemistry. Journal see Han'gug Eung'yong Saengmyeong hwa Haghoeji **234**
Korean Society for Clinical Pharmacology and Therapeutics. Journal see Imsang Yagri Haghoeji **6847**
Korean Society for Food Science of Animal Resources. Journal see Han-gug Chugsan Sigpum Hag-hoeji **3645**
Korean Society for Microbiology. Journal see Journal of Bacteriology and Virology **888**
Korean Society for Nondestructive Testing. Journal see Bipa'goe Geomsa Haghoeji **3342**
Korean Society of Civil Engineers Journal of Civil Engineering see K S C E Journal of Civil Engineering **3276**
Korean Society of Emergency Medicine. Journal see Daehan Eung'geub Yihaghoeji **6058**
Korean Society of Food Science and Nutrition. Journal see Han'gug Sigpum Yeong'yang Gwahag Hoeji **6659**
Korean Society of Mechanical Engineers. Journal see Gigye Jeoneol **3378**
Korean Society of Mechanical Engineers. Transactions. A see Daehan Gigye Haghoe Nonmunjib. A **3376**
Korean Society of Mechanical Engineers. Transactions. B see Daehan Gigye Haghoe Nonmunjib. B **3376**
Korean Society of Mycology. Newsletter (KOR) **799**
Korean Society of Nursing Science. Journal see Daehan Ganho Haghoeji **5956**
Korean Society of Oceanography. Journal see Ocean Science Journal **2815**
Korean Society of Oceanography. Journal - Sea see Hangug Haeyang Haghoe Ji - Bada **2805**
Korean Society of Plastic and Reconstructive Surgery. Journal see Taehan Songhyong Oekwa Hakhoe Chi **6260**
Korean Society of Radiological Science. Journal see Daehan Bangsa'seon Gi'sul Haghoeji **6195**
Korean Society of Steel Construction. Journal see Han'gug Gang'gujo Haghoe Nonmunjib **1011**
Korean Society of Steel Construction. Magazine see Han'gug Gang'gujo Haghoeji **1011**
• Korean Statistical Society. Journal (NLD ISSN 1226-3192) **8384**
• ➤ Korean Studies (USA ISSN 0145-840X) **554**
Korean Studies in Canada (CAN ISSN 1195-8448) **554**
Korean Surgical Society. Journal see Oe Gwa Hag-hoeji **6254**
Korean Trade Directory (KOR) **2012**
Korean Vacuum Society. Journal see Han-gug Jin-gong Hag-hoeji **7014**
Korean Women's Health Nursing Academic Society. Journal see Yeoseong Geon-gang Ganho Hag-hoeji **5984**
Korean Youth and Students (PRK ISSN 0454-420X) **2159**
• Koreana (KOR ISSN 1016-0744) **554**
Korea's Economy (USA ISSN 0894-6302) **1142**
Korei Shakai Janaru/Aged Society Journal (JPN) **4050**
† He Korero Mahiri (NZL ISSN 1177-3111) **8970**
Korero Marautanga see Curriculum Update **8947**
Korespondence Pomembnih Slovencev (SVN ISSN 0353-2844) **5318**
Korfbal! (NLD ISSN 1871-6792) **8184**
De Korfbalster see Korfbal! **8184**
Korhaz/Hospital (HUN) **4105**
Korinf (RUS) **1142**
• Korkeakoulujen Arviointineuvosto. Julkaisuja/Finnish Higher Education Evaluation Council. Publications/Finskogo Attestacionnogo Soveta po Vysshemu Obrazovaniu. Publikacii/Raadet foer Utvaerdering av Hoegskolorna. Publikationer (FIN ISSN 1457-3121) **2992**
Kormoproizvodstvo (RUS) **274**
Kornyezetvedelmi Szakirodalmi Tajekoztato/ Environmental Control Abstracts (HUN ISSN 0231-0716) **3480**
Korosi Csoma Kiskonyvtar (HUN ISSN 0075-6911) **4185**
Korot see Qorot **5701**
➤ Koroze a Ochrana Materialu (CZE ISSN 0452-599X) **3250**
Korporativnye Sistemy (UKR ISSN 1605-5470) **1393**
Korporativnye Territoryal'nye Seti Svyazi (RUS) **3207**
Korporativnyi Vestnik (KGZ) **1142**
Korrespondent (UZB ISSN 0130-254X) **4579**
Korrespondenz (DEU) **2198**
Korrespondenz Abwasser Abwasser, Abfall see K A - Abwasser, Abfall **3508**
Korrespondenz Abwasser Betriebs-Info see K A - Betriebs-Info **3508**
Korrespondenzblatt (CHE) **7495**
Korrespondenzblatt - Nachrichten Evangelischer Schulen und Internate see Klasse, die Evangelische Schule **2880**
Korrespondenzen (DEU ISSN 0941-2107) **8472**
Korrosionsinstitutet Rapport (SWE ISSN 0348-7199) **6320**
Korrozios Figyelo/Corrosion Observer (HUN ISSN 0133-2546) **6718**
➤ Korroziya: Materialy, Zashchita (RUS ISSN 1813-7016) **6320**
Korrschack (SWE ISSN 1403-5057) **8184**
Korsets Evangelium see Domino **7735**
Kort Bestek (NLD ISSN 0168-9045) **7450**
Kort Geding see Nederlandse Jurisprudentie Feitenrechtspraak **4740**
Kort Relaes see Historisch Overijssel **4144**
Kortars (HUN ISSN 0023-415X) **5222**
Kortbegrip van Landboustatistieke see South Africa. Department of Agriculture. Directorate of Agricultural Statistics. Abstract of Agricultural Statistics **186**
Korunk (ROM ISSN 1222-8338) **3619**
Korurangi see Galaxy **8958**
Koruyucu Hekimlik Bilgisi see Turk Silahli Kuvvetler Koruyucu Hekimlik Bilgisi **5724**
Koryo (JPN ISSN 0368-6558) **595**
Korzar (SVK ISSN 1335-4566) **3946**
Kos (ESP) **2686**
Kos (ITA ISSN 0393-2095) **5659**
Kosaku Kikai/Machine Construction (JPN) **5454**
Kosaku Kikai Nyusu/Machine Tool News (JPN ISSN 0386-8192) **5454**
Kosaku Kikai Setsubito Tokei Chosa Hokokusho/Report of Survey on Machine Tools Installation (JPN) **5454**
• Kosarka (HRV ISSN 1330-4895) **8237**
Kosciol Wspolczesny, Alternatywa dla Chrzescijanstwa (POL ISSN 1233-9261) **7659**
The Kosciuszko Foundation. Annual Report (USA ISSN 1930-9988) **3546**
Kosciuszko Foundation Newsletter (USA ISSN 1081-2776) **3546**
Kosei Nenkin Byoin Nenpo/Kosei-Nenkin Hospitals. Annual Bulletin (JPN ISSN 0388-2314) **4105**
Kosei-Nenkin Hospitals. Annual Bulletin see Kosei Nenkin Byoin Nenpo **4105**
Kosher Directory (USA) **7726**
• Kosher Spirit (USA ISSN 1559-6265) **4362**
Koshien Daigaku Kiyo. A, Eiyogakubu Hen/Koshien University. Bulletin. A (JPN ISSN 0913-5537) **6662**
Koshien Daigaku Kiyo/Koshien University. Bulletin see Koshien Daigaku Kiyo. A, Eiyogakubu Hen **6662**
Koshien University. Bulletin. A see Koshien Daigaku Kiyo. A, Eiyogakubu Hen **6662**
Koshien University. College of Business Administration and Information Science. Bulletin (JPN ISSN 0913-5545) **1420**
Koshu Eisei/Journal of Public Health Practice (JPN ISSN 0368-5187) **7530**
Koshukai Shiryo Shirizu (JPN ISSN 1341-8718) **2594**
Koshunai Kiho/Koshunai Quarterly Report (JPN ISSN 0913-2430) **3695**
Koshunai Quarterly Report see Koshunai Kiho **3695**
Kosmas: Czechoslovak and Central European Journal (USA ISSN 1056-005X) **4238**
• Kosmetica (ITA ISSN 1590-1505) **595**
Kosmetiek (NLD ISSN 0165-2192) **595**
Kosmetiek Apropos see Beauty Xpert **8935**
Kosmetik (SWE ISSN 1403-0497) **595**
Kosmetik International (DEU ISSN 0342-2976) **595**
Kosmetikjahrbuch (DEU) **595**
➤ Kosmetische Medizin (DEU ISSN 1430-4031) **5659**
Kosmetische Praxis (DEU ISSN 1432-9018) **595**
• Kosmicheskie Issledovaniya (RUS ISSN 0023-4206) **64**
Kosmicheskii Vek (RUS) **7024**
Kosmon Unity (GBR) **7738**
Kosmon Voice (USA ISSN 0882-4606) **7738**
Kosmopolis (FIN ISSN 1236-1372) **7250**
Kosmopolitan (Jakarta) see Cosmopolitan (Indonesia) **8857**
Kosmopolitan (Tel Aviv) see Cosmopolitan (Israel) **8857**
Kosmorama (DNK ISSN 0023-4222) **6506**
Kosmos see Natur und Kosmos **3455**
➤ Kosmos (POL ISSN 0023-4249) **686**
Kosmos (SWE ISSN 0368-6213) **7024**
• Kosmos (Danish Edition) (DNK ISSN 0107-7902) **7659**
Kosmos. Series A. Biologia see Kosmos **686**
Kosmos tis Psychis/World of Soul (GRC ISSN 0023-4257) **6742**
Kosmoskyna/Cosmos Pen (FIN ISSN 0785-2517) **5444**
Kosmosophie (DEU ISSN 0454-448X) **6931**
Koso Geppo see Aerological Data of Japan **6346**
Koso Kishodai Iho/Aerological Observatory at Tateno. Journal (JPN ISSN 0373-5842) **6360**
Koso Kogaku Nyusu/Enzyme Engineering News (JPN ISSN 0911-9957) **737**
Kossetsu/Fracture (JPN ISSN 0287-2285) **6066**
Kostenerstattungsrechtliche Entscheidungen der Schieds- und Verwaltungsgerichte (DEU ISSN 1617-6804) **8053**
• Kostenkengetallen Bouwprojecten. Ramingsprogramma (NLD ISSN 1571-8530) **1295**
Koster (RUS ISSN 0130-2574) **2198**
Koster Service Schrift (NLD ISSN 1572-5103) **4511**
Koster van Mil en Partners Pensioen Perspectief see K M P Pensioen Perspectief **4511**
Kostnads- och Effektivitetsdata (SWE ISSN 1103-1905) **1247**
Kostprijsberekening Biologische Varkensbedrijven (NLD ISSN 1871-7373) **202**
Koszty (POL ISSN 1428-7382) **1142**
Kota Press Poetry Journal see KotaPress Journal **5425**
Kotai Butsuri/Solid State Physics (JPN ISSN 0454-4544) **7060**
Kotai no Hannosei Toronkai Koen Yokoshu/Abstracts of the Meeting on Solid Reactivity (JPN) **2094**
Kotaigun Seitaigaku no Kenkyu see Population Ecology **7290**
• KotaPress Journal (USA ISSN 1931-342X) **5425**
KotaPress Journals Online see KotaPress Journal **5425**
Kothari's Industrial Directory of India (IND) **2012**
Kothari's World of Reference Works (IND ISSN 0075-6970) **628**
Koti (FIN ISSN 0355-1555) **4362**
Koti Ja Keittio (FIN ISSN 1458-3755) **4560**
Kotilaakari (FIN ISSN 0787-9385) **6991**
Kotiliesi (FIN ISSN 0023-4281) **4362**
Kotimaa (FIN ISSN 0356-1135) **3839**
Kotimaisten Kielten Tutkimuskeskus. Skrifter (FIN ISSN 0355-7995) **5137**
Kotiristikko see Kotiristikko Extra **8184**
Kotiristikko Extra (FIN ISSN 1796-590X) **8184**
Kotiseutukuvauksia Lounais-Haemeestae (FIN) **4238**
Kotitalous (FIN ISSN 0047-3685) **4362**
Kotkansilma see Kaupunkilehti Ankkuri **3838**
Kotobuki/Longevity (JPN) **6991**
Kotona (FIN ISSN 1796-2439) **7597**
Kotonoura (JPN) **6527**
Kotsu Igaku/Journal of Transportation Medicine (JPN ISSN 0022-5274) **6066**
Kotsu Kansetsu Jintai/Journal of Musculoskeletal System (JPN ISSN 0915-1125) **6224**
Kotsu Keito Shikkan Kenkyukai Shoroku/Japanese Society for Skeletal Dysplasias. Proceedings of the Meeting (JPN) **6066**
➤ Kotsu Shinrigaku Kenkyu/Japanese Journal of Traffic Psychology (JPN ISSN 0910-9749) **8632**
Kotsuzai Shigen/Japan Institute of Aggregate Technology. Journal (JPN ISSN 0286-9179) **3277**
Kottke National End of Season Survey (USA ISSN 1079-5839) **8321**
Kotu-Raportteja (Print) see Kehitysvammaliitto. Selvityksia **6157**
Kotu-Tutkimuksia see Kehitysvammaliitto. Tutkimuksia **8052**
• ➤ Kotuitui (NZL ISSN 1177-083X) **7981**
Kotunet (Online) see Kehitysvammaliitto. Selvityksia **6157**
• The Kouch (AUS) **8154**
Koude en Luchtbehandeling see R C C Koude & Luchtbehandeling **4125**
Kouen Yokoushuu (Nihon Temmon Gakkai) see Nihon Tenmon Gakkai Koen Yokoshu **4036**
• Kouji Nou Kinou Kenkyuu/Higher Brain Function Research (JPN ISSN 1348-4818) **6158**
Koukou Soshiki Baiyou Gakkaishi/Japanese Journal of Tissue Culture Society for Dental Research (JPN ISSN 1347-6661) **5659**
Koululainen (FIN ISSN 0357-2714) **2881**
Kountry Korral Magazine (SWE ISSN 0349-7208) **6583**
Koupelna see Living Koupelna **4545**
• Kouqiang Cailiao Qixie Zazhi/Chinese Journal of Dental Materials and Devices (CHN ISSN 1004-7565) **5854**
• Kouqiang Hemian Waike Zazhi/Journal of Oral and Maxillofacial Surgery (CHN ISSN 1005-4979) **6251**
• Kouqiang Hemian Xiufuxue Zazhi/Chinese Journal of Prosthodontics (CHN ISSN 1009-3761) **5854**
• ➤ Kouqiang Yixue/Stomatology (CHN ISSN 1003-9872) **5854**
• Kouqiang Yixue Yanjiu/Journal of Oral Science Research (CHN ISSN 1671-7651) **5854**
Kouqiang Yixue Zongheng/Comprehensive Stomatology see Kouqiang Yixue Yanjiu **5854**
• Kouqiang Zhengjixue/Chinese Journal of Orthodontics (CHN ISSN 1005-0191) **5854**
Kousei Roudoushou. Kokumin Kenko - Eiyo Chosa Hokoku/Japan. Ministry of Health, Labour and Welfare. National Health and Nutrition Survey in Japan (JPN) **6662**

Title

10538 KOUSEIROUDOUSHOU. JINKO DOTAI SHAKAI KEIZAIMEN CHOSA ULRICH'S PERIODICALS

Kouseiroudoushou. Jinko Dotai Shakai Keizaimen Chosa Hokoku/Japan. Ministry of Health, Labour and Welfare. Report on Survey of Socio-Economic Aspects on Vital Events (JPN ISSN 0448-3960) **7311**
Kouseiroudoushou. Jinko Dotai Tokei/Japan. Ministry of Health, Labour and Welfare. Vital Statistics (JPN ISSN 0075-3270) **8384**
Kouseiroudoushou. Jinko Dotai Tokei Geppo, Gaisu/Japan. Ministry of Health, Labour and Welfare. Monthly Report on Vital Statistics (JPN ISSN 0385-969X) **8384**
Kouseiroudoushou. Jinkou Doutai Shokuguon. SangyouToukei: Jinkou Doutai Toukei Tokushu Houkoku/Japan. Ministry of Health, Labour and Welfare. Occupational and Industrial Aspects: Special Report of Vital Statistics in (Year) (JPN) **6706**
Kouseiroudoushou. Kosei Tokei Yoran/Japan. Ministry of Health, Labour and Welfare. Handbook of Health and Welfare Statistics (JPN ISSN 0911-8403) **7548**
Kouseiroudoushou. Seikatsu Hogo Dotai Chosa Hokoku/Japan. Ministry of Health, Labour and Welfare. Report on Survey of Public Assistance (JPN ISSN 0448-4002) **8083**
Kouseiroudoushou. Shakai Fukushi Gyosei Gyomu Hokoku/Japan. Ministry of Health, Labour and Welfare. Statistical Report on Social Welfare Administration and Services (JPN ISSN 0448-4010) **8083**
Kouseiroudoushou. Shakai Fukushi Shisetsu Tou Chosa Hokoku/Japan. Ministry of Health, Labour and Welfare. Report on Survey of Social Welfare Institutions (JPN ISSN 0448-4029) **8083**
Kouseiroudoushou. Shakai Iryo Shinryo Koibetsu Chosa Hokoku/Japan. Ministry of Health, Labour and Welfare. Report on Survey of National Medical Care Insurance Services (JPN ISSN 0911-8454) **4530**
Kouseiroudoushou. Shokuchudoku Tokei/Japan. Ministry of Health, Labour and Welfare. Statistical Report on Food Poisonings (JPN ISSN 0911-8497) **7548**
Kouvolan Sanomat (FIN) **3839**
Kovach Tire Report (USA) **8588**
Kovel's Antiques and Collectibles Price List (USA ISSN 0738-2405) **367**
Kovels' Bottle Price List (USA) **4338**
Kovels' Depression Glass & Dinnerware Price List (USA ISSN 1935-9101) **367**
Kovels' Depression Glass and Dinnerware Price List *see* Kovels' Depression Glass & Dinnerware Price List **367**
Kovels on Antiques and Collectibles (USA ISSN 0741-6091) **367**
➤ Kovove Materialy/Metal Materials (SVK ISSN 0023-432X) **6320**
Kowan/Port and Harbour (JPN ISSN 0287-4733) **3277**
Kowan Gijutsu Kenkyujo. Gaido/Port and Harbour Research Institute. Guide (JPN) **8649**
Kowan Gijutsu Kenkyujo Hokoku/Port and Harbour Research Institute. Report (JPN ISSN 0454-4641) **3277**
Kowan Gijutsu Kenkyujo Nenpo/Port and Harbour Research Institute. Annual Report (JPN) **3277**
Kowan Gijutsu Shinkokai. Koenkai Koen Gaiyo/Association for the Port and Harbour Engineering Promotion. Proceedings of the Meeting (JPN) **3277**
Kowan Gijutsu Shinkokai Shiryo/Materials for Port and Harbour Engineering Promotion (JPN) **3277**
Kowan Giken Shiryo/Port and Harbour Research Institute. Technical Note (JPN ISSN 0454-4668) **3277**
Kowan Koenkai Koenshu/Symposium on Port Science. Proceedings (JPN) **3277**
Koyo Engineering Journal (JPN ISSN 0911-145X) **3387**
Koyoju Kenkyu/Hardwood Research (JPN ISSN 0389-5505) **3695**
Kozarstvi/Leather Industry (CZE ISSN 0023-4338) **4973**
• ➤ Kozepiskolai Matematikai es Fizikai Lapok (HUN ISSN 1215-9247) **7024**
Kozgazdasagi Szemle/Economic Review (HUN ISSN 0023-4346) **1142**
Kozhevenno-Obuvnaya Promyshlennost' (RUS ISSN 0023-4354) **7941**
Kozhi i Obuvki (BGR ISSN 0861-2366) **4973**
• Kozlekedesi Ertesito (HUN ISSN 1588-7235) **1142**
Kozlekedestudomanyi Szemle/Scientific Review of Communications (HUN ISSN 0023-4362) **8502**
Kozmos (SVK ISSN 0323-049X) **577**
Kozo Kogaku Ronbunshu A/Journal of Structural Engineering A (JPN ISSN 0910-8009) **3277**
Kozo Kogaku Ronbunshu B/Journal of Structural Engineering B (JPN ISSN 0910-8033) **3277**
Kozo Kogaku Shirizu/Structural Engineering Series (JPN) **3277**
Kozoktatas (ROM ISSN 1221-5732) **2881**
Kozuti es Melyepitesi Szemle/Scientific Review of Civil Engineering (HUN ISSN 1419-0702) **3277**
Kozuti Kozlekedesi Szakirodalmi Tajekoztato/Road Transport Abstracts (HUN ISSN 0231-0724) **8527**
The Kpelle Messenger (LBR) **3789**
Kpodoga (GHA) **8053**
Kraemmerhuset *see* C B S Observer **1077**
Kraevye Zadachi dlya Differentsial'nykh Uravnenii (UZB) **5508**
Kraft *see* Vaar Energi **3162**
• Kraft Journalen (NOR ISSN 0807-2132) **3141**
Kraft Recovery Operations Short Course (USA ISSN 1059-2792) **6735**
Kraftfahrt-Bundesamt. Bestand an Kraftfahrzeugen und Kraftfahrzeuganhaengern (DEU ISSN 0943-1489) **8527**
Kraftfahrt-Bundesamt. Mitteilungen. Ergaenzungshefte (DEU ISSN 0943-7118) **8588**
Kraftfahrt-Bundesamt. Statistische Mitteilungen (DEU ISSN 0341-468X) **8588**
Kraftfahrzeug Betrieb Aktuelle Wochenzeitung *see* K F Z Betrieb Aktuelle Wochenzeitung **8587**
Kraftfahrzeug Boerse *see* K F Z Boerse **8587**
Kraftfahrzeug Meisterservice *see* K F Z - Meisterservice **8587**
Kraftfutter/Feed Magazine (DEU ISSN 0023-4427) **240**
Krafthand (DEU ISSN 0023-4435) **8430**
Kraftverkehrskontrolle (DEU) **8502**
† Kraftverkehrsrecht von A-Z (DEU ISSN 1437-5559) **8970**
Krageroe Blad (NOR) **3923**
➤ Kragujevac Journal of Mathematics (SRB ISSN 1450-9628) **5508**
▼ Kraina Zwierzat (POL ISSN 1898-4460) **2198**
Krainii Sever (RUS) **3936**
Krajske Nitrianske Noviny *see* Nitrianske Noviny **3946**
Krajske Nitrianske Noviny. Tyzden na Pohroni *see* Tyzden na Pohroni **3947**
Krakow In Your Pocket (POL ISSN 1508-2334) **8728**
Krakowskie Studia Malopolskie (POL ISSN 1643-6911) **4238**
Krakowskie Studia Prawnicze (POL ISSN 0023-4478) **4710**
Krakowsko-Wilenskie Studia Slawistyczne (POL ISSN 1734-042X) **5137**
Kraks Indkoebsboeger. Transport og Emballage *see* Kraks Transport og Emballage **8970**
† Kraks Transport og Emballage (DNK ISSN 1603-7812) **8970**
† Kraks Vejviser (DNK ISSN 0900-2243) **8970**
• Krakteknik (DNK ISSN 1603-7820) **5454**
Kran-Magazin *see* Kran und Schwertransport Magazin **1020**
Kran und Buehne (DEU ISSN 1436-7831) **1020**
Kran- und Hebetechnik (DEU ISSN 1614-1237) **1020**
Kran und Schwertransport Magazin (DEU ISSN 1861-1036) **1020**
Kranich (DEU) **2881**
Kranjcan (SVN ISSN 1318-0746) **7495**
Krankendienst (DEU ISSN 0023-4486) **4105**
Das Krankenhaus (DEU ISSN 0340-3602) **4105**
Krankenhaus-Finanzierungsrecht (DEU ISSN 0935-977X) **4105**
• Krankenhaus-Hygiene + Infektionsverhutung (DEU ISSN 0720-3373) **4105**
Krankenhaus-Rechtsprechung (DEU ISSN 0935-2112) **4105**
Krankenhaus Technik *see* Krankenhaus Technik und Management **4105**
Krankenhaus Technik und Management (DEU ISSN 1619-4772) **4105**
Krankenhaus Umschau (DEU ISSN 0023-4508) **4105**
Krankenhaus Umschau Gesundheitswelt *see* K U - Gesundheitswelt **4104**
Krankenhaus und Recht (DEU ISSN 1434-2618) **4105**
Die Krankenhaus-Zeitung *see* K U - Gesundheitswelt **4104**
Krankenhausapotheken-Register (DEU ISSN 0176-7186) **6858**
• Krankenhaushygiene up2date (DEU ISSN 1862-5797) **4105**
Krankenhauspharmazie (DEU ISSN 0173-7597) **6858**
• Krankenhauspsychiatrie (DEU ISSN 0937-289X) **7382**
• Krankenpflege Journal (Online) (DEU) **5968**
Krankenpflege Journal (Print) *see* Krankenpflege Journal (Online) **5968**
Krankentransport und Rettungswesen (DEU ISSN 0935-6223) **2696**
• Die Krankenversicherung (DEU ISSN 0301-4835) **4512**
Krankenversicherung der Rentner (DEU ISSN 0936-076X) **7530**
† Krankenversicherung und Unfallversicherung in Rechtsprechung und Schrifttum (DEU ISSN 0939-8104) **8970**
Krankenversicherungs- und Sozialrecht *see* Gesundheitspolitik, Management, Oekonomie **7519**
▼ De Krant van Ameland (NLD ISSN 1875-4481) **3915**
De Krant van de Aarde *see* De KrantvandeAarde **2616**
Krant voor Aktieve Baanlozen in Amsterdam *see* K A B A M **1691**
De KrantvandeAarde (NLD ISSN 1872-5104) **2616**
Kras i Speleologia *see* Uniwersytet Slaski w Katowicach. Prace Naukowe. Kras i Speleologia **2773**
Krasa Naseho Domova/Beauty of Our Homeland (CZE ISSN 1213-5488) **2616**
Krash (AUS ISSN 1448-7985) **2198**
• Krasnaya Zvezda (RUS ISSN 0023-4559) **6430**
Krasnoe Znamya (RUS) **3936**
• Krasnogruda (POL ISSN 1230-7645) **5223**
Krasnoyarskii Rabochii (RUS) **3936**
Krasnyi Krest Rossii (RUS ISSN 0869-7884) **4934**
Krasnyi Sever (RUS) **3936**
Krasnyi Voin (RUS) **6430**
Krasoslovni Zbornik *see* Acta Carsologica **2701**
Krasy Slovenska/Beauty of Slovakia (SVK ISSN 0323-0643) **3946**
Krater Quarterly (USA) **5318**
Kratki Stranitsi/Brief Pages (BGR) **8472**
Kratkie Soobshcheniya po Fizike *see* Lebedev Physics Institute. Bulletin **7024**
• Kratkosrochnye Ekonomicheskie Pokazateli Rossiiskoi Federatsii/Short-Term Indicators of the Russia's Economy (RUS) **1247**
➤ Kratylos (DEU ISSN 0023-4567) **5137**
• Krause Curriculum Development Library (USA) **3069**
• Kraut und Rueben (DEU ISSN 0178-0166) **3741**
Krave Magazine (USA ISSN 1933-0642) **3546**
Krcki Zbornik (HRV ISSN 0455-0609) **4238**
† KreaPlus (NLD ISSN 1382-368X) **8970**
Kreatif Jaarbook (BEL) **7565**
Kreativ (DEU) **536**
Kreativ (HUN ISSN 1218-9359) **28**
Kreativ: Basteln & Naehen *see* Kreativ: Dekorieren, Basteln & Naehen **8970**
† Kreativ: Dekorieren, Basteln & Naehen (DEU) **8970**
Kreativ Intern *see* Intern **1821**
Kreativ Journal (DEU ISSN 1434-3630) **536**
Kreativ Kueche *see* Lust auf Genuss **4363**
Kreativ Pedagogik (SWE ISSN 1100-9691) **2881**
▼ Kreativ Strik (DNK ISSN 1903-2099) **6639**
Kreativa Kvinnor *see* Kreative Kvinder **6639**
Kreative Kvinder (DNK ISSN 1902-2298) **6639**
Kreative Kvinner *see* Kreative Kvinder **6639**
Kreavak (NLD ISSN 0929-4627) **536**
Krebs-Journal *see* K. Krebs-Journal **6025**
Krebsforschung Heute (DEU ISSN 0177-0853) **6026**
Krebs:Hilfe! (AUT) **6026**
Krebsmedizin (DEU ISSN 0173-9395) **6026**
➤ Krebsnachsorge und Rehabilitation (DEU ISSN 0936-9236) **6026**
Kred (GBR) **2289**
• Kredit und Kapital (DEU ISSN 0023-4591) **1364**
Kredit und Rating Praxis (CHE) **1365**
Kreditanstalt fuer Wiederaufbau Gruendungsmonitor *see* K f W - Gruendungsmonitor **1139**
Kreditanstalt fuer Wiederaufbau Mittelstandspanel *see* K f W - Mittelstandspanel **1139**
Kreditanstalt fuer Wiederaufbau Publikationen zu Gruendung und Mittelstand *see* K f W - Publikationen zu Gruendung und Mittelstand **1139**
Kreditanstalt fuer Wiederaufbau Research. Mittelstands- und Strukturpolitik *see* K f W - Research. Mittelstands- und Strukturpolitik **1363**
Kreditguide (SWE ISSN 1103-0895) **1365**
Kreditwesengesetz (DEU ISSN 0939-3722) **1365**
Krefeld. Amt fuer Statistik und Stadtentwicklung. Statistisches Jahrbuch (DEU) **8384**
➤ Krefeld Historical Symposia Series (GBR ISSN 1354-5965) **4238**
Krefeld Immigrants and Their Descendants (USA ISSN 0883-7961) **3773**
Krefeld Life (DEU) **8728**
Krefelder Hefte zur Deutsch-Amerikanischen Geschichte (DEU ISSN 0943-1160) **4238**
• Kreftforeningen. Rapport (NOR ISSN 1504-2553) **6026**
Kreis der Freunde und Foerderer der Lutherischen Theologischen Hochschule in Oberursel. Mitteilungen (DEU) **7764**
Kreis Trebnitzer Heimatzeitung (DEU) **3851**
Kreis Wesel. Jahrbuch (DEU ISSN 0939-2041) **7450**
Kreisamtsblatt des Landkreises und Landratsamtes Kronach (DEU) **7495**
Kreisarchiv Guetersloh. Veroeffentlichungen (DEU ISSN 1615-0937) **4238**
• Kreisarchiv Soest. Schriften (DEU ISSN 0933-8217) **4238**
Kreisausschuss des Landkreises Kassel. Jahrbuch (DEU) **4238**
Kreishandwerkerschaft Aktuell *see* K H Aktuell **1691**
Kreishandwerkerschaft Moenchengladbach. Mitteilungsblatt (DEU) **1963**
Kreisjugendring Muenchen-Land Burg Info *see* K J R Burg Info **8052**
Kreispostille (DEU) **7495**
Kreisstandardzahlen Nordrhein-Westfalen (DEU) **8384**
Kreiszeitung (DEU) **3851**
Krejl (DNK ISSN 0107-6701) **4238**
Kremnicky Letopis (SVK ISSN 1337-0618) **4238**
Kremnicky Rumaj *see* Kremnicky Letopis **4238**
Kreo (BEL ISSN 0778-7871) **8728**
Kreolische Bibliothek (DEU ISSN 0720-9983) **5137**
Kresge Foundation. Annual Report (USA) **6527**
• Kress Report (DEU ISSN 1618-7202) **2331**
Krestanska Revue (CZE ISSN 0023-4613) **7659**
Krest'yanka (RUS ISSN 0130-2647) **8870**
Krest'yanskaya Gazeta (RUS) **131**
Krest'yanskie Vedomosti (RUS ISSN 1560-0947) **202**
Kresy (POL ISSN 0867-1125) **5318**
• Kretslopp (SWE ISSN 1102-5956) **3488**
Kreuz & Quer (DEU) **8321**
• Kreuzer (DEU ISSN 0943-0547) **3851**
Kreuzfahrten-Handbuch (CHE) **8728**
Kreuzstiche des Jahres *see* Aarets Korssting **6636**
Krew (ZAF ISSN 1990-942X) **6293**
Kridtstregen (DNK ISSN 0905-5320) **8237**
• Kriebel's Sat-Report (DEU ISSN 1436-6444) **2384**
Krieg und Literatur/War and Literature (DEU ISSN 0935-9060) **4238**
Der Kriegsblinde (DEU ISSN 0023-463X) **4082**
• Der Kriegsruf (DEU) **7764**
Krigshistorisk Tidsskrift (DNK ISSN 0454-5230) **6430**
Krigsvetenskapsakademiens Handlingar och Tidskrift *see* Militaerhistorisk Tidskrift **4245**
Kriittinen Katsaus *see* Katsaus **5222**
Krikos ton Vathmoforon (GRC ISSN 0023-4664) **2198**
Krimdok *see* Neue Kriminologische Literatur **2675**
Kriminal-Ekspress (RUS) **2658**
† Kriminalforsorgen (DNK ISSN 1397-355X) **8970**
Kriminalforsorgen. Statistik *see* Denmark. Kriminalforsorgen. Statistik **4822**
Kriminalforsorgens Aarsrapport *see* Denmark. Kriminalforsorgen. Aarsrapport **2650**
Der Kriminalist (DEU ISSN 0722-3501) **2659**
➤ Kriminalistik (DEU ISSN 0023-4699) **2659**
Kriminal'naya Khronika (RUS) **2659**
Die Kriminalpolizei (DEU ISSN 0938-9636) **2659**
Die Kriminalpraevention (DEU) **2659**
Kriminalstatistik *see* Norway. Statistisk Sentralbyraa. Kriminalstatistikk **2675**
Kriminalteknik (SWE ISSN 1653-6169) **2659**
▼ • Kriminalvaarden. Aarsbok (SWE ISSN 1654-871X) **8117**
• Kriminalvaarden. Kriminalvaardens Redovisning om Aaterfall (SWE ISSN 1653-1116) **4892**
• Kriminalvaarden. Rapport (SWE) **2659**
Kriminalvaardens Administrative Foereskrifter (SWE ISSN 1653-6657) **2659**
Kriminalvaardens Foerfattningssamling (SWE ISSN 1653-6665) **2659**
Kriminalvaardsstyrelsen. Rapport *see* Kriminalvaarden. Rapport **2659**
Kriminalvaardsverkets Administrative Foereskrifter *see* Kriminalvaardens Administrative Foereskrifter **2659**
Kriminalvaardsverkets Foerfattningssamling *see* Kriminalvaardens Foerfattningssamling **2659**
• Kriminalwaard och Statistik (SWE ISSN 1652-7690) **4823**
• Kriminalvaarden. Kriminalvaardens Redovisning om Drogsituationen (SWE ISSN 1403-5758) **2696**
Kriminalvaarden. Officiella Statistik *see* Kriminalwaard och Statistik **4823**
Kriminalwissenschaftliche Studien (DEU) **2659**
Kriminologi - Serien *see* Universitetet i Oslo. Institutt for Kriminologi og Rettssosiologi. Bokserien **2670**
Kriminologija & Socijalna Integracija (HRV ISSN 1330-2604) **2659**
Kriminologische und Sanktionenrechtliche Forschungen (DEU ISSN 0933-078X) **4892**
Kriminologisches Journal (DEU ISSN 0341-1966) **2659**
Kring Bibeln och Bekaennelsen *see* Kyrklig Samling Kring Bibeln och Bekaennelsen **7764**
De Kring van "Vrienden van de Hondsbossche". Uitgave (NLD ISSN 1572-3135) **4238**
Kriosfera Zemli (RUS ISSN 1560-7496) **2712**
Krisberedskap (SWE ISSN 1651-5420) **2227**
• Krisberedskapsmyndigheten. Aarsredovisning foer Budgetaaret (Year) (SWE ISSN 1652-3725) **2227**
Krisberedskapsmyndigheten Ms Temaserie *see* K B Ms Temaserie **7529**
• Krisen-, Sanierungs- und Insolvenzberatung (DEU ISSN 1861-0765) **1365**
Krishak Jagat (IND ISSN 0970-8650) **131**
Krishak Samachar (IND ISSN 0023-4710) **131**
Krishak Sandesh (IND) **131**
Krishanu (IND ISSN 0023-4737) **5318**
Krishi Chayanika (IND) **240**
Krishi Katha (BGD) **3800**
Krishi Sameeksha (IND) **1601**
▼ Krishna Institute Karad. Research Journal (IND ISSN 0973-9378) **5659**
Krishnachura (IND ISSN 0023-4745) **5318**
Krishnamurti Foundation. Bulletin (IND ISSN 0047-3693) **7738**
Krisis (DEU ISSN 0944-6575) **7149**
• ➤ Krisis (Online) (NLD ISSN 1875-7103) **6931**
† • Krisis (Print) (NLD ISSN 0168-275X) **8970**
Kriss Kross (GBR ISSN 0956-1641) **4338**
• KRISSaren (SWE) **7659**
• Kristallografiya (RUS ISSN 0023-4761) **2111**
• Kristdemokraten (SWE ISSN 0284-9941) **7211**
Kristdemokratisk Debatt *see* Civitas **7116**
Kristelig Fagbevaegelse Magasinet *see* K R I F A Magasinet **4597**
• Kristeligt Dagblad (DNK ISSN 0904-6054) **3834**
Kristen Vetenskaps Harold *see* The Herald of Christian Science **8962**
Kristen Vetenskaps Harold *see* Le Heraut de la Christian Science **7736**
Kristen Videnskabs Herold *see* Le Heraut de la Christian Science **7736**
Kristen Videnskabs Herold *see* The Herald of Christian Science **8962**
Kristen Vitenskaps Herold *see* The Herald of Christian Science **8962**
Kristen Vitenskaps Herold *see* Le Heraut de la Christian Science **7736**
Kristent Perspektiv (DNK ISSN 1901-7766) **7659**
• Kristianstadsbladet (SWE ISSN 1103-9523) **3956**

Link to your serials resources and content with ulrichsweb.com

Kristityn Vastuu (FIN ISSN 0356-3545) **3839**
Kristna Studentroerelsen i Sverige Skriftserie *see* K R I S S. Skriftserie **7657**
• Kristofer Lehmkuhl Forelesning (NOR ISSN 0452-7208) **1142**
KrisWorld (SGP) **8784**
Kriterii Sanitarno-Gigienicheskogo Sostoyaniya Okruzhayushchei Sredy *see* Environmental Health Criteria **3425**
➤ Kriterion (AUT ISSN 1019-8288) **6931**
• ➤ Kriterion (BRA ISSN 0100-512X) **6931**
Kritik (DNK ISSN 0454-5354) **5318**
Kritik (USA) **5318**
• ➤ Kritika (Bloomington) (USA ISSN 1531-023X) **4238**
Kritika a Kontext (SVK ISSN 1335-1710) **5223**
Kritika i Humanizm/Critique & Humanism (BGR ISSN 0861-1718) **4462**
• Kritika Kultura (PHL ISSN 1656-152X) **5137**
▼ • ➤ Kritike (PHL ISSN 1908-7330) **6931**
• ➤ Kritikon Litterarum (DEU ISSN 0340-9767) **5318**
• Kritikos (USA ISSN 1552-5112) **4462**
Kritisch Consumeren *see* Goede Waar **8960**
Kritische Berichte (DEU ISSN 0340-7403) **500**
Kritische Information (DEU ISSN 0178-1634) **4462**
Kritische Justiz (DEU ISSN 0023-4834) **7211**
➤ Kritische Studien zur Geschichtswissenschaft (DEU) **4150**
Kritische Theorie und Kulturforschung (DEU) **8117**
Kritische Vierteljahresschrift fuer Gesetzgebung und Rechtswissenschaft (DEU ISSN 0179-2830) **4710**
Kritisches Lexikon zur Fremdsprachigen Gegenwartsliteratur (DEU) **5407**
• Kritisk Forum for Praktisk Teologi (DNK ISSN 0106-6749) **7659**
➤ Kritisk Juss (NOR ISSN 0804-7375) **4710**
Kritisk Utbildningstidskrift *see* Krut **2881**
Kritiska EUfakta (SWE ISSN 1400-1489) **2012**
KritV *see* Kritische Vierteljahresschrift fuer Gesetzgebung und Rechtswissenschaft **4710**
Krizaljke & Rebusi (HRV ISSN 1332-6740) **8184**
Krizanke Informacije Humor *see* K I H **4337**
Krizovkarsky T V Magazin (CZE ISSN 1211-2755) **2384**
Krizovky *see* Katka Krizovky **8184**
Krizovy Manazment (SVK ISSN 1336-0019) **2679**
Krmiva (HRV ISSN 0023-4850) **274**
Krmivarstvi (CZE ISSN 1212-9992) **274**
➤ Kroeber Anthropological Society. Papers (USA ISSN 0023-4869) **346**
Kroedde (NLD ISSN 0168-180X) **5425**
Kroenika (SWE ISSN 1104-4969) **7659**
Kroenikan (SWE ISSN 1653-5952) **5024**
Kroger Diabetes Nutrition and Health *see* Kroger Diabetes Nutrition & Health **5896**
Kroger Diabetes Nutrition & Health (USA) **5896**
• Kroghs Lovinformation (DNK ISSN 0108-7878) **4710**
Krolikovodstvo i Zverovodstvo (RUS ISSN 0023-4885) **291**
Krompen *see* Fuglar i Hordaland **907**
Kronen Zeitung (AUT) **3797**
Kroniek Sint Aegten (NLD ISSN 1872-5260) **7659**
Kroniek Sint Agatha *see* Kroniek Sint Aegten **7659**
Kroniek van Het Rembrandthuis (NLD ISSN 0166-0381) **500**
Kroniek van het Strafrecht (NLD ISSN 0923-6775) **4892**
Kronika (ROM ISSN 1454-7821) **3933**
Kronika (SVN ISSN 0023-4923) **4238**
Kronika Miasta Poznania (POL ISSN 0137-3552) **4238**
Kronika Warszawy (POL ISSN 0137-3099) **4238**
Kronika Wielkopolski (POL ISSN 0137-3102) **4238**
Kronos (ESP ISSN 1579-5225) **6991**
• Kronos (ITA ISSN 1724-2541) **500**
➤ Kronos (ZAF ISSN 0259-0190) **4176**
• KronoScope (Online) (NLD ISSN 1568-5241) **577**
† • ➤ KronoScope (Print) (NLD ISSN 1567-715X) **8970**
Kroonika (EST ISSN 1406-0582) **3836**
Kroonika Ristsonad (EST) **8184**
Kroppsoeving (NOR ISSN 0333-0141) **2881**
Krotkofalowiec Polski (POL ISSN 1230-9990) **2360**
Krske Skofije. Zbornik *see* Dioezese Gurk. Jahrbuch **7795**
Krug/Circle (BGR ISSN 1311-1108) **2198**
Kruiz (KGZ) **3904**
Krung-govi Bod-rig-pa/China Tibetology (Tibetan Edition) (CHN ISSN 1002-9060) **554**
Krut (SWE ISSN 0347-5409) **2881**
Kruto (UKR) **2198**
Krygshistoriese Tydskrif *see* Military History Journal **6435**
• Kryl'ya Rodiny/Wings of the Motherland (RUS ISSN 0130-2701) **64**
Krymskaya Astrofizicheskaya Observatoriya. Izvestiya (UKR ISSN 0367-8466) **577**
• Krymskaya Pravda (UKR) **3964**
Krymskii Arkhiv (UKR) **4238**
Krynytsya (POL ISSN 1505-1951) **3546**
Kryssdax (SWE ISSN 0345-6609) **8184**
Krysset (SWE ISSN 0345-6617) **8184**
† Krystalinikum (CZE ISSN 0454-5524) **8970**
Krytyka Polityczna (POL ISSN 1644-0919) **5223**
Ksiazka w Dawnej Kulturze Polskiej (POL ISSN 0075-7179) **4462**
Ksiazki (POL ISSN 1425-4808) **7565**
Ksiaznica Slaska (POL ISSN 0208-5798) **5024**
Ksiezniczka (POL ISSN 1509-7935) **2198**
Ksiezniczka. Wydanie Specjalne *see* Ksiezniczka **2198**
Ktema (FRA ISSN 0221-5896) **4322**
➤ Ktemata (BEL) **5318**
Ku Nel *see* Ku:nel **3900**
▼ ➤ Kuaiji yu Caijin Yanjiu Qikan/Journal of Account and Finance Development (TWN ISSN 2070-1055) **1296**
Kuaile Yingyu (CHN ISSN 1673-7253) **5137**
Kuaile Zuowen/21st Century Elementary School Compositions (CHN ISSN 1673-0666) **2198**
Kuan Kuang Tzu Liao *see* Monthly Report on Tourism - Republic of China **8780**
Kuang Hua *see* Sinorama **3960**
Kuang Tien Medical Journal *see* Guangtian Yixue Zazhi **5621**
• Kuangchan Baohu yu Liyong/Conservation and Utilization of Mineral Resources (CHN ISSN 1001-0076) **2616**
• Kuangchan yu Dizhi/Minerals and Geology (CHN ISSN 1001-5663) **6320**
• Kuangchuang Dizhi/Mineral Deposits (CHN ISSN 0258-7106) **6468**
• ➤ Kuangshan Celiang/Mine Surveying (CHN ISSN 1001-358X) **6468**
Kuangshan Dizhi (CHN ISSN 1001-5892) **6468**
• Kuangshan Jixie/Mining & Processing Equipment (CHN ISSN 1001-3954) **6468**
• Kuangshan Yali yu Dingban Guanli/Ground Pressure and Strata Control (CHN ISSN 1003-5923) **6468**
• Kuangwu Xuebao/Acta Mineralogica Sinica (CHN ISSN 1000-4734) **6468**
• Kuangwu Yanshi/Journal of Mineralogy and Petrology (CHN ISSN 1001-6872) **2752**
• Kuangwu Yanshi Diqiu Huaxue Tongbao/Bulletin of Mineralogy, Petrology and Geochemistry (CHN ISSN 1007-2802) **2752**
• Kuangye Gongcheng/Mining and Metallurgical Engineering (CHN ISSN 0253-6099) **6468**
• Kuangye Kuaibao/Express Information of Mining Industry (CHN ISSN 1009-5683) **6468**
Kuangye Touzi Zhinan/Mining Investment Guide (CAN ISSN 1912-1326) **6468**
▼ Kuanle Shangqing Xiuxian Jikan/Taiwan Beer Life Magazine (TWN) **606**
Kuashiji/Across Centuries Men's World (CHN ISSN 1005-1074) **6293**
Kubaba *see* Cahiers Kubaba **4446**
Kubanskie Novosti (RUS) **7149**
Kubus Puchatek (POL ISSN 1429-6462) **2199**
Kubus Puchatek. Wydanie Specjalne (POL ISSN 1640-2286) **2199**
Kuchnia (POL ISSN 1233-2976) **4362**
Kuchyne pro Labuzniky *see* Living Kuchyne **4560**
• Kudos (FIN ISSN 1239-4505) **4462**
Kueche (DEU ISSN 0344-4376) **4393**
Kueche Bistro (DEU) **4545**
Kueche und Bad Forum (DEU) **4560**
Kuechen (CHE) **4560**
Kuechen News (DEU) **4362**
† Die Kuechen-Zeitung (DEU) **8970**
KuechenHandel (DEU) **4362**
Der Kuechenplaner (DEU ISSN 0722-9917) **4545**
Kuechenprofi (DEU ISSN 0948-3411) **4560**
† KuechenWelt (DEU ISSN 1435-103X) **8970**
Kuensel (Dzongkha Edition) (BTN) **3802**
• Kuensel (English Edition) (BTN ISSN 0259-1499) **3802**
Kuensel (Nepali Edition) (BTN) **3802**
Kuenstler - Kritisches Lexikon der Gegenwartskunst (DEU ISSN 0934-1730) **500**
Die Kuenstlergilde (DEU ISSN 0946-3100) **500**
Kuenstliche Intelligenz (DEU ISSN 0933-1875) **2454**
Kuerschners Deutscher Gelehrten-Kalender (DEU ISSN 1616-8399) **644**
Kuerschners Deutscher Literatur-Kalender (DEU ISSN 0343-0936) **628**
Kuerschners Deutscher Sachbuch-Kalender (DEU) **644**
Kuerschners Musiker-Handbuch (DEU) **644**
Die Kueste (DEU ISSN 0452-7739) **2811**
• Kuettner Personal - CD (DEU) **4823**
KuhFacto (NLD ISSN 1566-550X) **291**
Kuhinja (HRV ISSN 1331-789X) **4362**
Kuiper (NOR ISSN 0809-8212) **5318**
Kujira/West Japan Whales Society. News (JPN ISSN 0913-2244) **953**
• Kuka Kukin On/Who's Who in Finland (FIN ISSN 1237-7570) **644**
Kukhoe Tosogwanbo/National Assembly Library Review (KOR ISSN 0027-8572) **5024**
Kukhoebo/National Assembly Review (KOR) **7150**
Kuki Chowa Eisei Kogaku/Society of Heating, Air-Conditioning and Sanitary Engineering of Japan. Journal (JPN ISSN 0386-4081) **7530**
Kuki Seijo/Japan Air Cleaning Association. Journal (JPN ISSN 0023-5032) **3488**
➤ Kukila (IDN ISSN 0216-9223) **909**
Kukuruza i Sorgo (RUS ISSN 0233-7770) **240**
Kula/Tower (BGR ISSN 1310-6511) **500**
† Kulanu (ISR ISSN 0334-648X) **8970**
† Kulanu - Pilon (ISR ISSN 0792-8149) **8970**
Kulde (NOR ISSN 0801-7093) **4123**
Kulgazdasag (HUN ISSN 0324-4202) **1143**
▼ Kulinarische Reisen in Sachsen-Anhalt (DEU) **4393**
Kulinarske Tajne *see* Lisa. Kulinarske Tajne **4363**
Kulinarske Tajne Specijal *see* Lisa. Kulinarske Tajne Specijal **4363**
Kulisy (POL ISSN 0023-5083) **3930**
Kuljetusyrittaja (FIN ISSN 1236-066X) **8672**
• Kull Al-Arab (ISR ISSN 1606-3791) **3895**
Kullanu *see* Kulanu **8970**
Kullanu - Pilon *see* Kulanu - Pilon **8970**
Kulleraugen (DEU ISSN 0171-5208) **6506**
Kulleraugen - Materialsammlung (DEU ISSN 0174-2582) **6506**
Kulloja/Workers (PRK) **4597**
Kulon (POL ISSN 1427-3098) **7877**
Kult (CZE ISSN 1212-8120) **3832**
Kult (DEU) **3851**
Kult (Stockholm) (SWE ISSN 1103-8764) **4150**
Kult - Ali Agenda (DEU ISSN 0944-2162) **5223**
Kult am Pult (DEU) **1852**
Kultaneito (FIN ISSN 1239-3843) **3619**
† Kultaristikot (FIN ISSN 1459-1618) **8970**
Kultaristikot Extra (FIN ISSN 1459-1626) **8185**
Kultmag (NOR ISSN 1504-6591) **8117**
• Kulttuuripoliittisen Tutkimuksen Edistamissaatio. Cuporen Julkaisuja (FIN ISSN 1795-1739) **7450**
Kultur, Geschichte, Theorie (DEU ISSN 1863-9097) **8117**
Kultur - Herrschaft - Differenz (DEU ISSN 1862-2518) **4150**
Kultur Istatistikleri *see* Turkey. Turkiye Istatistik Kurumu. Kultur Istatistikleri (Year) **8410**
➤ Kultur-Kreise/Aires Culturelles (DEU ISSN 1434-0283) **4462**
Kultur Life (DEU) **6527**
Kultur News (DEU ISSN 1437-5958) **500**
Kultur og Klasse *see* K & K **8116**
Kultur, Recht und Politik in Muslimischen Gesellschaft (DEU ISSN 1863-9801) **7713**
Kultur Spiegel (DEU) **3851**
Kultur un Lebn (USA ISSN 0023-513X) **7726**
Kultur und Erkenntnis (DEU ISSN 0947-0298) **6931**
Kultur- und Stadtnachrichten aus Weitra (AUT) **4150**
Kultur und Technik (DEU ISSN 0344-5690) **6527**
• ➤ Kultur ve Iletisim/Culture & Communication (TUR ISSN 1301-7241) **8117**
Kultur, Wissenschaft, Literatur (DEU ISSN 1615-665X) **5319**
Kultura (BGR ISSN 0861-1408) **5319**
• Kultura (DEU ISSN 1867-0628) **7250**
Kultura (FRA ISSN 0023-5148) **5223**
Kul'tura (RUS) **5223**
Kultura (SRB ISSN 0023-5164) **4462**
Kultura *see* Biodynamisk Odling **96**
Kul'tura (Minsk) (BLR) **5223**
• Kultura-Extra (DEU) **500**
Kultura Fizyczna (POL ISSN 0137-7671) **6991**
▼ • ➤ Kultura. Historia. Globalizacja/Culture. History. Globalization (POL ISSN 1898-7265) **4462**
Kultura i Edukacja (POL ISSN 1230-266X) **2881**
Kultura i Spoleczenstwo (POL ISSN 0023-5172) **8117**
Kul'tura i Zhyttya (UKR ISSN 0023-5180) **5223**
Kultura i Zycie (POL ISSN 0860-6528) **5223**
• Kul'tura. Kul'turologiya. (RUS ISSN 0208-2039) **4485**
• ➤ Kul'tura Narodov Prichernomor'ya (UKR ISSN 1562-0808) **5223**
Kultura Popularna (POL) **5223**
Kultura Popullore (ALB ISSN 0257-6082) **3619**
Kultura Slova/Culture of the Word (SVK ISSN 0023-5202) **5137**
Kul'tura Slova (UKR ISSN 0201-419X) **5319**
Kul'tura v Sovremennom Mire: Opyt, Problemy, Resheniya (RUS ISSN 0206-5231) **7981**
Kultura Wspolczesna (POL ISSN 1230-4808) **4462**
Kulturanalysen (DEU ISSN 0936-4366) **7981**
• Kulturarv (SWE ISSN 1652-9138) **7982**
Kulturaustausch *see* Zeitschrift fuer KulturAustausch **7276**
Kulturberichte aus Tirol (AUT ISSN 0023-5210) **3797**
➤ Kulturella Perspektiv (SWE ISSN 1102-7908) **346**
Kulturelle und Sprachliche Kontakte (DEU ISSN 1864-0249) **7982**
Kultureller Wandel vom Mittelalter zur Fruehen Neuzeit *see* Medieval to Early Modern Culture **8120**
Kulturen Zivot/Cultural Life (MKD ISSN 0047-3731) **5223**
• Kulturens Vaerld (SWE ISSN 0282-5902) **501**
† Kulturgeografiske Haefter (DNK ISSN 0106-5866) **8970**
† Kulturgeografiske Haefters Skriftserie (DNK ISSN 0108-3945) **8970**
Kulturgeografiske Skrifter (DNK ISSN 0023-5245) **4018**
Kulturhistorisk Museums Skrifter (DNK ISSN 1601-6254) **6527**
KulturKommerz (DEU ISSN 0944-4351) **1771**
Kulturkontakte (DEU ISSN 1432-8194) **3014**
† • Kulturkontakten (DNK ISSN 0907-1156) **8970**
Kulturland Oldenburg (DEU ISSN 1430-4546) **4238**
Kulturlandschaft Schaumburg (DEU ISSN 1439-8338) **4238**
Kulturlandschaft Westfalen (DEU) **4239**
Kulturliv *see* Kultmag **8117**
† Kulturmagasinet Skopet (DNK ISSN 1901-144X) **8970**
• Kulturmiljoevaard Maelardalen. Rapport (SWE ISSN 1653-7408) **403**
Kulturna Bastina (HRV ISSN 0351-0557) **4150**
Kulturnews (Ausgabe Berlin) *see* Kulturnews (Ausgabe Hamburg) **3851**
Kulturnews (Ausgabe Duesseldorf) *see* Kulturnews (Ausgabe Hamburg) **3851**
Kulturnews (Ausgabe Frankfurt) *see* Kulturnews (Ausgabe Hamburg) **3851**
Kulturnews (Ausgabe Hamburg) (DEU ISSN 1860-2568) **3851**
Kulturnews (Ausgabe Hannover) *see* Kulturnews (Ausgabe Hamburg) **3851**
Kulturnews (Ausgabe Koeln) *see* Kulturnews (Ausgabe Hamburg) **3851**
Kulturnews (Ausgabe Muenchen) *see* Kulturnews (Ausgabe Hamburg) **3851**
Kulturnews (Ausgabe Ruhrgebiet) *see* Kulturnews (Ausgabe Hamburg) **3851**
Kulturnews (Ausgabe Stuttgart) *see* Kulturnews (Ausgabe Hamburg) **3851**
Kulturno Drustvo Primorska Srecanja (SVN) **5223**
Kul'turno-Prosvetitel'naya Rabota (RUS ISSN 0130-2833) **5223**
Kulturo (DNK ISSN 1395-4830) **5319**
Kul'turologiya 20-veka *see* Kul'turologiya: Daidzhest **8117**
Kul'turologiya: Daidzhest (RUS) **8117**
Kulturos Barai (LTU ISSN 0134-3106) **4462**
KulturPoetik (DEU ISSN 1616-1203) **5319**
Kulturpolitik (DEU ISSN 0941-4657) **5223**
Kulturrevolution (DEU ISSN 0723-8088) **7150**
Kultursmocken (SWE ISSN 1404-9341) **6583**
Kultursoziologie (DEU ISSN 0941-343X) **8117**
• Kulturstatistikk/Cultural Statistics (NOR ISSN 0800-2959) **8021**
• Kulturtidskriften (Year) (SWE ISSN 0280-0799) **628**
Kulturwissenschaften (DEU ISSN 1862-6092) **7982**
Kulturwissenschaftliche Japanstudien (DEU) **554**
Kulturwissenschaftliche Studien (DEU ISSN 1860-8809) **7982**
Kultus und Unterricht. Ausgabe A (DEU ISSN 0933-7776) **3026**
Kultuur ja Elu/Culture and Life (EST ISSN 0134-5605) **8117**
Kultuurleven (BEL ISSN 0023-5288) **8117**
Kulugyi Szemle/Foreign Affairs (HUN ISSN 1587-9089) **7250**
Kuluttaja (FIN ISSN 1236-0805) **2639**
Kuluttajansuoja *see* Ajankohtaista Kuluttajaoikeudesta **2634**
• Kuma (ITA ISSN 1724-9163) **8117**
Kuma Kange (EST) **8185**
Kumagai Gumi Gijyutsukenkyu Hokoku/Kumagai Technical Research Report (JPN ISSN 0919-8687) **3277**
Kumagai Technical Research Report *see* Kumagai Gumi Gijyutsukenkyu Hokoku **3277**
Kumake (EST) **8185**
Kumamoto Daigaku Eigo Eibungaku/Kumamoto Studies in English Language and Literature (JPN ISSN 0917-3528) **5319**
Kumamoto Daigaku Kogakubu Kenkyu Hokoku *see* Kumamoto University. Faculty of Engineering. Technical Reports **3208**
Kumamoto Daigaku Kogakubu Kiyo *see* Kumamoto University. Faculty of Engineering. Memoirs **3207**
Kumamoto Daigaku Kyoikugakubu Kiyo. Shizen Kagaku/Kumamoto University. Faculty of Education. Memoirs. Natural Science (JPN ISSN 0454-6148) **7877**
Kumamoto Daigaku Kyoyobu Kiyo. Shizen Kagaku Hen/Kumamoto University. Faculty of General Education. Memoirs. Natural Sciences (JPN ISSN 0286-5769) **7877**
Kumamoto Entomological Association. News *see* Kumamoto Konchu Dokokaiho **853**
Kumamoto Geographic Society. Journal *see* Kumatoto Chigakkaishi **4018**
Kumamoto Journal of Mathematics (JPN ISSN 0914-675X) **5508**
Kumamoto Konchu Dokokaiho/Kumamoto Entomological Association. News (JPN ISSN 0912-5957) **853**
Kumamoto National College of Technology. Research Reports *see* Kumamoto Denpa Kogyo Koto Senmon Gakko. Kenkyu Kiyo **3323**
Kumamoto Prefecture. Monthly Report (JPN) **6360**
Kumamoto Studies in English Language and Literature *see* Kumamoto Daigaku Eigo Eibungaku **5319**
Kumamoto University. Department of Geology. Journal (JPN) **2752**
Kumamoto University. Department of Physics. Physics Reports (JPN ISSN 0303-4070) **7024**
Kumamoto University. Faculty of Education. Memoirs. Natural Science *see* Kumamoto Daigaku Kyoikugakubu Kiyo. Shizen Kagaku **7877**
Kumamoto University. Faculty of Engineering. Memoirs/Kumamoto Daigaku Kogakubu Kiyo (JPN ISSN 0023-5334) **3207**
Kumamoto University. Faculty of Engineering. Technical Reports/Kumamoto Daigaku Kogakubu Kenkyu Hokoku (JPN ISSN 0023-5296) **3208**
Kumamoto University. Faculty of General Education. Memoirs. Natural Sciences *see* Kumamoto Daigaku Kyoyobu Kiyo. Shizen Kagaku Hen **7877**
Kumamoto Denpa Kogyo Koto Senmon Gakko. Kenkyu Kiyo/Kumamoto National College of Technology. Research Reports (JPN ISSN 0289-3886) **3323**
Kumar (IND ISSN 0023-5342) **501**
Kumatoto Chigakkaishi/Kumamoto Geographic Society. Journal (JPN ISSN 0389-1631) **4018**
Kumbez (KAZ ISSN 1028-9402) **448**
KuMi Magazine (USA) **3546**
Kumins (LVA) **8185**

Title

Kuml (DNK ISSN 0454-6245) **403**
Kumo/Chubu Spider Study Group. Report (JPN ISSN 0917-7906) **853**
Kumquat Meringue (USA ISSN 1063-5874) **5425**
• Kumudam (IND) **3884**
• Kumudam Bakthi Special (IND) **7707**
Kumudam.Com *see* Kumudam **3884**
• Kumudam Health (IND) **6991**
• Kumudam Jothidam (IND) **566**
• Kumudam Junction (IND) **3884**
• Kumudam Reporter (IND) **3884**
• Kumudam Snehidhi (IND) **8870**
• Kumudam Theeranadhi (IND) **5319**
➤ Kunapipi (AUS ISSN 0106-5734) **5319**
• Kunchong Fenlei Xuebao/Entomotaxonomia (CHN ISSN 1000-7482) **853**
Kunchong Tiandi/Natural Enemies of Insects *see* Huanjing Kunchong Xuebao **849**
• ➤ Kunchong Xuebao/Acta Entomologica Sinica (CHN ISSN 0454-6296) **853**
• Kunchong Zhishi/Entomological Knowledge (CHN ISSN 0452-8255) **854**
Kunchongxue Yanjiu Jikan/Contributions from Shanghai Institute of Entomology (CHN ISSN 1002-0926) **854**
Kundae Han'guk Yon'gu *see* The Journal of Modern Korean Studies **4185**
Kundalini (IND) **7659**
Die Kunde (DEU ISSN 0342-0736) **403**
Der Kunden-Manager (DEU ISSN 1615-1550) **1829**
Kundenbindung *see* Der Kunden-Manager **1829**
Kune (DEU ISSN 1615-0287) **5137**
Ku:nel (JPN) **3900**
Kung Kao Po/Catholic Chinese Weekly (HKG) **7804**
Kungliga Gustav Adolfs Akademien. Aarsbok *see* Saga och Sed. Kungliga Gustav Adolfs Akadeniens Aarsbok **3622**
Kungliga Humanistiska Vetenskapssamfundet i Lund. Aarsberattelse/Societe Royale de Lettres de Lund. Bulletin (SWE ISSN 0281-272X) **5319**
Kungliga Humanistiska Vetenskapssamfundet i Uppsala. Aarsbok/Societatis Litterarum Humaniorum Regiae Upsaliensis. Annales (SWE ISSN 0349-0416) **4185**
Kungliga Ingenjoersvetenskapsakademien aktuellt *see* I V A - aktuellt **3196**
➤ Kungliga Krigsvetenskapsakademien. Handlingar och Tidskrift/The Royal Swedish Academy of War Sciences. Proceedings and Journal (SWE ISSN 0023-5369) **6430**
Kungliga Musikaliska Akademien. Aarsskrift (SWE ISSN 1100-2751) **6583**
Kungliga Musikaliska Akademien. Skriftserie (SWE ISSN 0347-5158) **6583**
Kungliga Skog- och Lantbruksakademien. Skogs- och Lantbrukshistoriska Meddelanden (SWE ISSN 1402-0386) **131**
Kungliga Skogs- och Lantbruksakademien Nytt *see* K S L A Nytt **129**
Kungliga Skogs- och Lantbruksakademiens Tidskrift/Academie Royale d'Agriculture et de Sylviculture de Suede. Annales/Koenigliche Schwedische Akademie der Land- und Forstwirtschaft. Zeitschrift/Royal Swedish Academy of Agriculture and Forestry. Journal (SWE ISSN 0023-5350) **131**
Kungliga Skogs- och Lantbruksakademiens Tidskrift, Supplement *see* Kungliga Skogs- och Lantbruksakademiens Tidskrift **131**
Kungliga Skytteanska Samfundet. Handlingar (SWE ISSN 0560-2416) **4239**
Kungliga Tekniska Hoegskolan HochC O *see* K T HochC O **2991**
Kungliga Tekniska Hoegskolan. Institutionen foer Byggkonstruktion. Trita-B K N. Examensarbete/Royal Institute of Technology. Department of Structural Engineering. Trita-B K N. Diploma Work (SWE ISSN 1103-4297) **3277**
Kungliga Tekniska Hoegskolan. Institutionen foer Byggkonstruktion. Trita-B K N. Rapport/Royal Institute of Technology. Department of Structural Engineering. Trita-B K N. Report (SWE ISSN 1103-4289) **3277**
Kungliga Tekniska Hoegskolan. Institutionen foer Farkost och Flyg. Trita-A V E *see* Royal Institute of Technology. Department of Aeronautical and Vehicle Engineering. Transactions **69**
Kungliga Tekniska Hoegskolan. Institutionen foer Infrastruktut. Trita-I N F R A. EX *see* Royal Institute of Technology. Department of Infrastructure. Transactions **4027**
Kungliga Vetenskaps- och Vitterhets-Samhaellet i Goeteborg. Aarsbok (SWE ISSN 0436-113X) **4462**
Kungliga Vetenskapsakademien. Bidrag till Kungliga Vetenskapsakademiens Historia (SWE ISSN 0081-9956) **7877**
Kungliga Vetenskapssamhaellet i Uppsala. Aarsbok *see* Annales Academiae Regiae Scientiarum Upsaliensis **7835**
Kungliga Vitterhets Historie och Antikvitets Akademien. Aarsbok (SWE ISSN 0083-6796) **4239**
Kungliga Vitterhets Historie och Antikvitets Akademien. Antikvariskt Arkiv (SWE ISSN 0083-6737) **501**
Kungliga Vitterhets Historie och Antikvitets Akademien. Filologiskt Arkiv (SWE ISSN 0083-6745) **5137**
Kungliga Vitterhets Historie och Antikvitets Akademien. Handlingar. Antikvariska Serien/Royal Academy of Letters, History and Antiquities. Proceedings. Antiquarian Series (SWE ISSN 0083-6761) **501**
Kungliga Vitterhets Historie och Antikvitets Akademien. Handlingar. Filologisk-Filosofiska Serien/Royal Academy of Letters, History and Antiquities. Proceedings. Philological - Philosophical Series (SWE ISSN 0083-677X) **5138**
Kungliga Vitterhets Historie och Antikvitets Akademien. Handlingar. Historiska Serien/Royal Academy of Letters, History and Antiquities. Proceedings. Historical Series (SWE ISSN 0083-6788) **4239**
Kungliga Vitterhets Historie och Antikvitets Akademien. Historiskt Arkiv (SWE ISSN 0083-6753) **4239**
Kungliga Vitterhets Historie och Antikvitets Akademien. Konferenser (SWE ISSN 0348-1433) **6281**
Kunguman (IND) **3884**
Kungyeh Kungch'eng Hsuehk'an *see* Gongye Gongcheng Xuekan **3367**
Kuni no Shiken Kenkyu Gyomu Keikaku (JPN) **8447**
• Kunming Ligong Daxue Xuebao (Ligong Ban)/Kunming University of Science and Technology. Journal (Science and Technology) (CHN) **7877**
• Kunming Ligong Daxue Xuebao (Shehui Kexue Ban)/Kunming University of Science and Technology. Journal (Social Sciences) (CHN ISSN 1671-1254) **7982**
Kunming Metallurgy College. Journal *see* Kunming Yejin Gaodeng Zhuanke Xuexiao Xuebao **6320**
Kunming University of Science and Technology. Journal (Science and Technology) *see* Kunming Ligong Daxue Xuebao (Ligong Ban) **7877**
Kunming University of Science and Technology. Journal (Social Sciences) *see* Kunming Ligong Daxue Xuebao (Shehui Kexue Ban) **7982**
• Kunming Yejin Gaodeng Zhuanke Xuexiao Xuebao/Kunming Metallurgy College. Journal (CHN ISSN 1009-0479) **6320**
• Kunming Yixueyuan Xuebao/Academic Journal of Kunming Medical College (CHN ISSN 1003-4706) **5659**
Kunnskap om Idrett *see* Moving Bodies **6993**
Kunskaps- och Kompetensutveckling Bladet *see* K K-Bladet **2879**
• Kunskapslaeget paa Kaernavfallsomraadet (SWE ISSN 0284-6373) **3508**
Kunst 5 bis 10 (DEU ISSN 1861-7247) **501**
Das Kunst-Bulletin (CHE ISSN 1013-6940) **501**
Kunst en Recht (NLD ISSN 1571-7356) **4710**
Kunst en Wetenschap (NLD ISSN 0927-3506) **7877**
Kunst in Koeln (DEU ISSN 0937-9541) **6527**
Kunst-Katalog: Auktionen (AUT ISSN 0075-7241) **501**
Kunst, Literatur & Music *see* K U L I M U **5316**
Kunst-, Musik- und Theaterwissenschaft (DEU ISSN 1862-6114) **501**
• Kunst og Kultur (NOR ISSN 0023-5415) **501**
Kunst und Altertum am Rhein (DEU ISSN 0075-725X) **403**
Kunst und Architektur in der Schweiz/Art et Architecture en Suisse/Arte e Architettura in Svizzera (CHE ISSN 1421-086X) **448**
Kunst und Kirche (AUT ISSN 0023-5431) **501**
Kunst und Kultur (DEU ISSN 0946-5243) **501**
Kunst und Politik (DEU ISSN 1439-0205) **7250**
Kunst und Stadt (DEU) **448**
Kunst und Stein (CHE ISSN 0023-5458) **501**
Kunst und Therapie (DEU ISSN 0177-4352) **7382**
Kunst und Unterricht (DEU ISSN 0931-7112) **501**
Kunstagenda (NLD ISSN 1570-7202) **501**
• Kunstavisen (DNK ISSN 0107-6957) **501**
Kunstbeeld (NLD ISSN 0165-1129) **501**
Kunstblad *see* Origine **368**
Kunstchronik (DEU ISSN 0023-5474) **6527**
Kunstconnected (NLD ISSN 1871-5923) **2881**
De Kunstconnectie. Nieuwsbrief *see* Kunstconnected **2881**
Kunstforum International (DEU ISSN 0177-3674) **501**
Kunsthaandverk (NOR ISSN 0333-1059) **536**
Kunsthalle Basel (CHE ISSN 1421-1726) **501**
Der Kunsthandel (DEU ISSN 0023-5504) **501**
Kunsthandwerk und Design (DEU ISSN 0941-9179) **536**
• ➤ Kunsthistorische Sammlungen in Wien. Jahrbuch (AUT ISSN 0075-2312) **501**
Kunsthistorischen Institutes in Florenz. Mitteilungen (ITA ISSN 0342-1201) **4150**
Kunsthistorisches Jahrbuch Graz (AUT ISSN 1010-3856) **501**
Kunsthoegskolen i Oslo. Aarbok (NOR ISSN 1504-2774) **501**
➤ Kunstiteaduslikke Uurimusi/Studies on Art and Architecture (EST ISSN 1406-2860) **501**
Kunstjahr (DEU ISSN 1618-4106) **501**
Kunstjahrbuch der Stadt Linz (AUT ISSN 0454-6601) **501**
• Kunstkritikk.no (NOR ISSN 1504-0917) **501**
▼ Kunstmagasinet (NOR ISSN 1890-2251) **501**
Kunstmagasinet Janus (DNK ISSN 1901-418X) **501**
▼ Kunstmaterial (CHE ISSN 1661-8815) **501**
KunstPhilosophie (DEU) **502**
Kunstpublikaties van de Ledise Universiteetsbibliotheek *see* Leidse Universiteitsbibliotheek. Kunstpublikaties **5025**
Kunstquartal (DEU ISSN 1860-0530) **6527**
Kunstrecht und Urheberrecht (DEU ISSN 1437-2355) **6754**
Kunstschrift (NLD ISSN 0166-7297) **502**
Kunststof en Rubber (NLD ISSN 0167-9597) **7094**
Kunststof Magazine (NLD ISSN 1382-385X) **7094**
• Die Kunststoff-Industrie und Ihre Helfer (DEU ISSN 0075-7276) **7094**
Kunststoff-Magazin (DEU ISSN 1431-0554) **7094**
Kunststoff Trends (DEU ISSN 1618-7881) **7094**
Kunststoffberater (DEU ISSN 0172-6374) **7094**
• Kunststoffe (DEU ISSN 0023-5563) **7094**
Kunststoffe im Lebensmittelverkehr (DEU ISSN 0075-7292) **7094**
Kunststoffe International (DEU ISSN 1862-4243) **7094**
Kunststoffe, Kunststofftechnologien und Kunststoffverarbeitungsmaschinen *see* Informationsdienst F I Z Technik. Kunststoffe, Kunststofftechnologien und Kunststoffverarbeitungsmaschinen **3231**
Kunststoffe - Plast Europe *see* Kunststoffe International **7094**
Kunststoffe - Synthetics *see* SwissPlastics **7100**
Kunststoffrohrverband Nachrichten *see* K R V Nachrichten **3351**
Kunststoffverarbeitung Deutschland (DEU ISSN 0175-6753) **7094**
Kunststunde (DEU) **502**
• Kunsttexte.de (DEU ISSN 1618-8101) **502**
Kunstuff/Danish Crafts (DNK ISSN 1603-9092) **536**
Kunstzeitung (DEU ISSN 1431-2840) **502**
Kunstzone (NLD ISSN 1570-7989) **6583**
• Kuntalehti (FIN ISSN 1236-0066) **7495**
• Kuntatekniikka/Kommunteknik (FIN ISSN 1238-125X) **4418**
Kunterbunt (DEU) **2199**
Kuntien Tekniset *see* Uusi Insinoori **4604**
▼ Kuntsi (FIN ISSN 1796-9891) **502**
Kuntum (MYS ISSN 1511-0117) **2199**
Kuoli Taiwan Tahsueh Nunghsuehyuan Shihyen Linyenchiu Paokao/Experimental Forest of National Taiwan University. Journal (TWN ISSN 0255-6014) **3695**
Kuoli Taiwan Tahsueh Nunghsuehyuan Shihyen Linyenchiu Paokao *see* Kuoli Taiwan Tahsueh Nunghsuehyuan Shihyen Linyenchiu Paokao **3695**
Kuopia University. Occasional Papers. C, Natural and Environmental Sciences/Kuopion Yliopiston Selvityksiaa. C, Luonnontieteet ja Ympuristotieteet (FIN ISSN 1237-8186) **7877**
Kuopion Yliopiston Selvityksiaa. C, Luonnontieteet ja Ymparistotieteet *see* Kuopia University. Occasional Papers. C, Natural and Environmental Sciences **7877**
Kuoriti Manejimento/Quality Management (JPN ISSN 1347-0213) **1771**
Kupi - Prodai *see* Svobodnyi Kurs **3942**
• ➤ Te Kura Kete Aronui (NZL ISSN 1177-2700) **4462**
• Kuram ve Uygulamada Edytym Bylymlery/Educational Sciences: Theory & Practice (TUR ISSN 1303-0485) **2881**
Kurashi no Denka/Electrified Life (JPN) **3323**
Kurashi no Sekkei *see* Planning for Living **4365**
Kurashiki Central Hospital. Annals *see* Kurashiki Chuo Byoin Nempo **5659**
➤ Kurashiki Chuo Byoin Nempo/Kurashiki Central Hospital. Annals (JPN ISSN 0368-4954) **5659**
Kurashiki Museum of Natural History. Bulletin *see* Kurashiki-shiritsu Shizenshi Hakubutsukan Kenkyu Hokoku **7878**
Kurashiki-shiritsu Shizenshi Hakubutsukan Kenkyu Hokoku/Kurashiki Museum of Natural History. Bulletin (JPN ISSN 0913-1566) **7878**
Kurashiki-shiritsu Shizenshi Hakubutsukanpo (JPN ISSN 0913-1558) **6527**
Kuratorium fuer Technik und Bauwesen in der Landwirtschaft e.V. Arbeitsblaetter Bauwesen und Tierhaltung *see* K T B L Arbeitsblaetter Bauwesen und Tierhaltung **212**
Kuratorium fuer Technik und Bauwesen in der Landwirtschaft e.V. Arbeitsblaetter Gartenbau *see* K T B L Arbeitsblaetter Gartenbau **3740**
Kuratorium fuer Technik und Bauwesen in der Landwirtschaft e.V. Arbeitsblaetter Landtechnik und Pflanzenbau *see* K T B L Arbeitsblaetter Landtechnik und Pflanzenbau **212**
Kuratorium fuer Technik und Bauwesen in der Landwirtschaft e.V. Arbeitsblaetter Weinbau *see* K T B L Arbeitsblaetter Weinbau **240**
Kuratorium fuer Technik und Bauwesen in der Landwirtschaft e.V. Arbeitspapiere *see* K T B L Arbeitspapiere **129**
Kuratorium fuer Technik und Bauwesen in der Landwirtschaft e.V. Kalkulationsunterlagen *see* K T B L Kalkulationsunterlagen **202**
Kuratorium fuer Technik und Bauwesen in der Landwirtschaft e.V. Schriften *see* K T B L - Schriften **129**
Kuratorium fuer Technik und Bauwesen in der Landwirtschaft Sonderveroeffentlichungen *see* K T B L Sonderveroeffentlichungen **129**
Kuratorium fuer Verkehrssicherheit. Research Letter (AUT ISSN 1992-173X) **8632**
Les Kurdes (BEL ISSN 1783-8479) **346**
Les Kurdes dans l'Actualite *see* Les Kurdes **346**
• Kurdish Life (USA ISSN 1061-8457) **3912**
Kuren/Crane (JPN ISSN 0285-3892) **3387**
Kuren Nenkan/Yearbook of Crane and Similar Equipment (JPN) **3387**
Kur'er Tadzhikistana (TJK) **3961**
Kurganskii Vestnik (RUS) **3937**
• Kurier (AUT) **3797**
Kurier (Liesborn) (DEU) **7659**
Kurier am Sonntag (Bremen) (DEU) **3851**
Kurier am Sonntag (Kleve) (DEU) **3851**
Kurier Bayer (DEU ISSN 0948-762X) **241**
Kurier Dembudu (POL ISSN 1506-1426) **1424**
Kurier Express Paketdienste Aktuell *see* K E P Aktuell **8501**
Kurier Wilenski (LTU) **3546**
Kur'ier Yunesko (UKR ISSN 0236-3879) **7250**
Kurin Energuji/Clean Energy (JPN ISSN 0918-7510) **3141**
Kurin Tekunoroji/Clean Technology (JPN ISSN 0917-1819) **3449**
Kurinikaru Purakutisu/Clinical Practice (JPN ISSN 1349-4252) **5659**
Kurinikaru Sutadi/Clinical Study (JPN ISSN 0388-5585) **5968**
Kurinikku Magajin/Clinic Magazine (JPN ISSN 0389-7451) **5659**
Kurinishian *see* Clinician **5598**
Kuriren (FIN ISSN 0780-0126) **3839**
Kurkihirsi *see* Kotona **7597**
Kurortnaya Gazeta/Resort Newspaper (RUS) **4979**
Kurortnaya Nedelya/Resort Weekly (RUS) **3937**
Kurorty Mira (RUS) **4979**
Kuroshio/Kochi University. Institute of the Kuroshio Sphere. Report (JPN ISSN 0913-1302) **2811**
Kuroshio (Wakayamaken)/Nanki Biological Society. News (JPN ISSN 0287-5349) **686**
Kuroshio Exploitation Research and Utilization Report *see* Kuroshio no Kaihatsu Riyo Chosa Kenkyu Seika Hokokusho **2811**
Kuroshio no Kaihatsu Riyo Chosa Kenkyu Seika Hokokusho/Kuroshio Exploitation Research and Utilization Report (JPN) **2811**
Kuroshio. Tokubetsugo/Kochi University. Institute of the Kuroshio Sphere. Report. Special Series (JPN ISSN 0914-7225) **2811**
Kurowassan *see* Croissant **4355**
Kurs (DEU ISSN 1436-302X) **1365**
Kursblatt der Wiener Boerse (AUT) **1637**
Kursblatt der Wiener Wertpapierboerse *see* Kursblatt der Wiener Boerse **1637**
Kursbuch (DEU ISSN 0023-5652) **3851**
Kursbuch der Deutschen Museums - Eisenbahnen (DEU) **8619**
Kursbuch Kultur (AUT) **8472**
Kursiv (DEU ISSN 1433-2000) **3069**
Kurskaya Pravda (RUS) **3937**
Kurskii Gosudarstvennyi Tekhnicheskii Universitet. Isvestiya (RUS ISSN 1991-0754) **2289**
KursKontakte (DEU ISSN 1435-7518) **6645**
Kursliste for Danske Aktieselskaber og Anpartsselskaber samt Groenlandske Selskaber (DNK ISSN 0905-4472) **1143**
Kurt Weill Newsletter (USA ISSN 0899-6407) **6583**
Kurtrierisches Jahrbuch (DEU ISSN 0452-9081) **4239**
Kurtz Criminal Offenses and Defenses in Georgia (USA ISSN 1933-2157) **4893**
➤ Kurtziana (ARG ISSN 0075-7314) **799**
Kurukshetra (New Delhi) (IND ISSN 0023-5660) **7495**
Kurukshetra (Orissa) (IND) **3884**
Kurukshetra Law Journal (IND) **4710**
Kurume Igakkai Zasshi/Kurume Medical Association. Journal (JPN ISSN 0368-5810) **5659**
Kurume Institute of Technology. Bulletin *see* Kurume Kogyo Daigaku Kenkyu Hokoku **8430**
Kurume Kogyo Daigaku Kenkyu Hokoku/Kurume Institute of Technology. Bulletin (JPN ISSN 0389-6897) **8430**
Kurume Medical Association. Journal *see* Kurume Igakkai Zasshi **5659**
• ➤ Kurume Medical Journal (JPN ISSN 0023-5679) **5659**
Kurve (DEU) **8260**
• Kur'yer (UKR) **3964**
• Kur'yer Obrazovaniya/Courier of Education (RUS) **2881**
Kurzberichte aus der Bauforschung (DEU ISSN 0177-3550) **462**
Kurzeitung Bad Soden-Salmuenster (DEU) **3851**
Kusakli-Sarissa (DEU ISSN 1434-615X) **403**
➤ Kuschitische Sprachstudien/Cushitic Language Studies (DEU ISSN 0721-4340) **5138**
Kushiro City Museum. Memoirs *see* Kushiro-shiritsu Hakubutsukan Kiyo **7878**
Kushiro Kogyo Koto Senmon Gakko Kiyo/Kushiro National College of Technology. Research Reports (JPN ISSN 1598-7264) **8430**
Kushiro National College of Technology. Research Reports *see* Kushiro Kogyo Koto Senmon Gakko Kiyo **8430**
Kushiro-shiritsu Hakubutsukan Kiyo/Kushiro City Museum. Memoirs (JPN ISSN 0912-1897) **7878**
Kust en Zee Gids (NLD ISSN 1871-5117) **2617**
Kust&Zee Gids *see* Kust en Zee Gids **2617**
Kustbon (SWE ISSN 0345-6706) **3546**
Kustom (ITA) **8260**
Kusuri Hakubutsukan Dayori/Naito Museum. Semi-Annual Report (JPN) **6858**
Kutchmitra (IND) **3884**
Kutlwano/Mutual Understanding (BWA ISSN 0023-5733) **7150**
Kutsu no Igaku/Medical Footwear (JPN ISSN 0915-5015) **5659**
Kutter und Kueste (DEU ISSN 1431-9551) **8321**
Kuttikalude Deepika (IND) **2199**

Title

10542 KYODO KENKYU SEIKA HOKOKUSHO ULRICH'S PERIODICALS

Kyodo Kenkyu Seika Hokokusho/Annual Collaboration Report (JPN) **3170**
Kyodo to Hakubutsukan (JPN ISSN 0288-9102) **6527**
Kyodo to Kagaku/Nature and Science (JPN ISSN 0912-6449) **7878**
Kyoiku Hyoron/Educational Review (JPN ISSN 0023-5997) **2881**
Kyoiku Kenkyu/Educational Studies (JPN ISSN 0452-3318) **2881**
Kyoiku-No-Mori *see* Forest of Education **3689**
Kyoiku Ongaku, Chugaku Koko-ban/Educational Music, Junior High and High School (JPN ISSN 0388-7502) **6583**
Kyoiku Ongaku, Shogaku-ban/Educational Music, Elementary School (JPN ISSN 0388-7480) **6583**
➤ Kyoiku Shakaigaku Kenkyu/Journal of Educational Sociology (JPN ISSN 0387-3145) **2881**
➤ Kyoiku Shinrigaku Kenkyu/Japanese Journal of Educational Psychology (JPN ISSN 0021-5015) **7382**
Kyoiku Shinrigaku Nenpo/Annual Report of Educational Psychology in Japan (JPN ISSN 0452-9650) **2881**
Kyoikugaku Kenkyu/Japanese Journal of Educational Research (JPN ISSN 0387-3161) **2881**
Kyokai Ryoiki ni Okeru Denki Kagaku Semina/Seminar on Electrochemistry in Boundary Region. Proceedings (JPN) **2114**
Kyokuchi/Polar News (JPN ISSN 0023-6004) **7878**
Kyokuchiken Nyusu/National Institute of Polar Research. News (JPN ISSN 0911-0410) **2712**
Kyokuiki Seibutsu Shinpojumu Koen Yoshishu/Abstracts of the Symposium on Polar Biology (JPN) **717**
Kyongje Nonjip *see* Gyeongje Nonjib **1116**
Kyongyong Nonjip *see* Korean Business Journal **1771**
• ➤ Kyorin Igakkai Zasshi/Kyorin Medical Society. Journal (JPN ISSN 0368-5829) **5659**
Kyorin Medical Society. Journal *see* Kyorin Igakkai Zasshi **5659**
Kyoritsu Joshi Tanki Daigaku. Bunka. Kiyo/Kyoritsu Women's Educational Institution. Department of Language & Literature. Collected Essays (JPN ISSN 0388-3647) **5319**
Kyoritsu Joshi Tanki Daigaku Seikatsu Kagakuka Kiyo/Kyoritsu Women's Junior College. Department of the Science of Living. Annual Bulletin (JPN ISSN 0917-2300) **5074**
Kyoritsu University of Pharmacy. Journal *see* Kyouritsu Yakka Daigaku Zasshi **6858**
Kyoritsu Women's Educational Institution. Department of Language & Literature. Collected Essays *see* Kyoritsu Joshi Tanki Daigaku. Bunka. Kiyo **5319**
Kyoritsu Women's Junior College. Department of the Science of Living. Annual Bulletin *see* Kyoritsu Joshi Tanki Daigaku Seikatsu Kagakuka Kiyo **5074**
Kyoryo & Toshi Project/Bridge Engineering and Urban Project (JPN ISSN 1344-7084) **3277**
Kyoryo Nenkan/Steel Bridge Yearbook (JPN) **3278**
Kyoryo Shinbun/Bridge News (JPN) **3278**
Kyoryo to Kiso/Bridge and Foundation Engineering (JPN ISSN 0287-170X) **3278**
Kyosai Iho/Mutual Aid Association. Medical Journal (JPN ISSN 0454-7586) **5659**
Kyosan Circular *see* Kyosan Sakyura **3323**
Kyosan Sakyura/Kyosan Circular (JPN ISSN 0289-5676) **3323**
Kyoshin Kiroku *see* Strong-Motion Earthquake Records in Japan **2790**
Kyoto Botany *see* Kyoto Shokubutsu **799**
Kyoto Business Directory (JPN) **1406**
Kyoto Daigaku Abuyama Jishin Kansoku Hokoku *see* Kyoto University. Abuyama Seismological Observatory. Seismological Bulletin **2786**
Kyoto Daigaku Bosai Kenkyujo Nenpo/Disaster Prevention Research Institute Annuals (JPN ISSN 0386-412X) **7530**
Kyoto Daigaku Genshi Energi Kenkyujo Iho/Kyoto University. Institute of Atomic Energy. Bulletin (JPN ISSN 0368-5039) **3170**
Kyoto Daigaku Genshiro Jikkensho Gakujutsu Koenkai Houbunshu/Kyoto University. Research Reactor Institute. Proceedings of the Scientific Meeting (JPN ISSN 0917-1746) **7024**
Kyoto Daigaku Josanpu Dosokaishi *see* Kyouto Daigaku Josampu Dousoukaihou **5997**
Kyoto Daigaku Keizai Gakubu Kiyo *see* Kyoto Economic Review **1143**
Kyoto Daigaku Nogakubu Enshurin Hokoku/Kyoto University Forests. Bulletin *see* Shinrin Kenkyu **3702**
Kyoto Daigaku Nogakubu Kiyo *see* Kyoto University. College of Agriculture. Memoirs **131**
Kyoto Daigaku Ogata Keisanki Senta Eibun Repoto *see* Kyoto University. Data Processing Center. Report **2538**
Kyoto Daigaku. Reichorui Kenkyujo Nenpo/Kyoto University. Primate Research Institute. Annual Reports (JPN ISSN 0286-4568) **346**
Kyoto Daigaku Rigakubu Sugaku Kiyo *see* Kyoto University. Journal of Mathematics **5508**
Kyoto Daigaku Shokuryo Kagaku Kenkyusho Hokoku/Kyoto University. Research Institute for Food Science. Bulletin (JPN ISSN 0451-1476) **131**
Kyoto Daigaku. Suri Kaiseki Kenkyujo. Kokyuroku/Kyoto University. Research Institute for Mathematical Sciences. Proceedings (JPN) **5508**
Kyoto Daigaku Uirusu Kenkyujo Nenkan Kiyo *see* Kyoto University. Institute for Virus Research. Annual Report **890**
• Kyoto Economic Review/Kyoto Daigaku Keizai Gakubu Kiyo (JPN ISSN 1349-6786) **1143**
Kyoto Entomological Society. Journal *see* Akitu **838**
Kyoto Furitsu Daigaku Gakujutsu Hokoku. Jimbun Shakai/Kyoto Prefectural University. Scientific Reports: Humanities and Social Sciences (JPN ISSN 1343-3946) **4462**
Kyoto Furitsu Daigaku Gakujutsu Hokoku. Ningen Kankyogaku, Nogaku/Kyoto Prefectural University. Scientific Reports: Agriculture *see* Kyouto Furitsu Daigaku Gakujutsu Houkoku. Seimei Kankyougaku **3449**
Kyoto-Furitsu Daigaku Nogakubu Enshurin Hokoku/Kyoto Prefectural University Forests. Bulletin (JPN ISSN 0374-874X) **3695**
Kyoto-furitsu Ika Daigaku Zasshi *see* Kyoto Prefectural University of Medicine. Medical Society. Journal **5659**
Kyoto Furitsu Kaiyo Senta Jigyo Gaiyo/Kyoto Institute of Oceanic and Fishery Science. Report (JPN) **2811**
Kyoto Furitsu Kaiyo Senta Kenkyu Gyosekishu/Kyoto Institute of Oceanic and Fishery Science. Contributions (JPN ISSN 0289-9515) **2811**
Kyoto Furitsu Kaiyo Senta Kenkyu Hokoku/Kyoto Institute of Oceanic and Fishery Science. Bulletin (JPN ISSN 0386-5290) **2811**
Kyoto Furitsu Kaiyo Senta Kenkyu Ronbun/Kyoto Institute of Oceanic and Fishery Science. Special Report (JPN ISSN 0286-617X) **2811**
Kyoto Institute of Oceanic and Fishery Science. Bulletin *see* Kyoto Furitsu Kaiyo Senta Kenkyu Hokoku **2811**
Kyoto Institute of Oceanic and Fishery Science. Contributions *see* Kyoto Furitsu Kaiyo Senta Kenkyu Gyosekishu **2811**
Kyoto Institute of Oceanic and Fishery Science. Report *see* Kyoto Furitsu Kaiyo Senta Jigyo Gaiyo **2811**
Kyoto Institute of Oceanic and Fishery Science. Special Report *see* Kyoto Furitsu Kaiyo Senta Kenkyu Ronbun **2811**
Kyoto Institute of Technology. Faculty of Engineering and Design. Memoirs (JPN ISSN 0911-0305) **7878**
➤ Kyoto Journal (JPN ISSN 0913-5200) **554**
Kyoto Journal of Physical Therapy *see* Rigaku Ryouhou Kyouto **6116**
Kyoto Kyoiku Daigaku Kiyo. A: Jimbun, Shakai/Kyoto University of Education. Bulletin. Series A. Education, Social Sciences, Literature and Arts *see* Kyouto Kyouiku Daigaku Kiyou **7878**
Kyoto Kyoiku Daigaku Kiyo. B: Shizen Kagaku/Kyoto University of Education. Bulletin. Series B, Mathematics and Natural Science *see* Kyouto Kyouiku Daigaku Kiyou **7878**
Kyoto Prefectural University Forests. Bulletin *see* Kyoto-Furitsu Daigaku Nogakubu Enshurin Hokoku **3695**
➤ Kyoto Prefectural University of Medicine. Medical Society. Journal/Kyoto-furitsu Ika Daigaku Zasshi (JPN ISSN 0023-6012) **5659**
Kyoto Prefectural University. Scientific Reports: Humanities and Social Sciences *see* Kyoto Furitsu Daigaku Gakujutsu Hokoku. Jimbun Shakai **4462**
Kyoto Prefectural University. Scientific Reports. Life and Environmental Sciences *see* Kyouto Furitsu Daigaku Gakujutsu Houkoku. Seimei Kankyougaku **3449**
Kyoto Prefecture. Monthly Report of Meteorology *see* Kyotofu Kisho Geppo **6360**
• Kyoto Review of Southeast Asia (JPN) **4462**
Kyoto Rigaku Ryohoshikai Kaishi *see* Rigaku Ryouhou Kyouto **6116**
Kyoto Sangyo Daigaku Ronshu. Shizen Kagaku Keiretsu/Acta Humanistica et Scientifica Universitatis Sangio Kyotiensis. Natural Science Series (JPN ISSN 0287-7902) **7878**
Kyoto Sangyo University, Society of Economics and Business Administration Economic and Business Review *see* K S U Economic and Business Review **1139**
Kyoto Shobo/Fire Prevention (JPN ISSN 0023-6020) **3579**
Kyoto Shokubutsu/Kyoto Botany (JPN) **799**
Kyoto University. Abuyama Seismological Observatory. Seismological Bulletin/Kyoto Daigaku Abuyama Jishin Kansoku Hokoku (JPN ISSN 0454-7659) **2786**
➤ Kyoto University. Biological Laboratory. Contributions (JPN ISSN 0452-9987) **686**
• Kyoto University Bulletin (JPN) **2289**
Kyoto University. College of Agriculture. Memoirs/Kyoto Daigaku Nogakubu Kiyo (JPN ISSN 0388-2330) **131**
Kyoto University. Data Processing Center. Report/Kyoto Daigaku Ogata Keisanki Senta Eibun Repoto (JPN) **2538**
Kyoto University. Department of Astronomy. Contributions (JPN ISSN 0388-0230) **577**
Kyoto University. Faculty of Agriculture. Plant Germ-Plasm Institute. Report (JPN) **799**
Kyoto University. Faculty of Economics. Memoirs *see* Kyoto Economic Review **1143**
Kyoto University. Faculty of Engineering. Quantum Science and Engineering Center. Annual Report (JPN ISSN 1345-0700) **7024**
Kyoto University. Faculty of Science. Memoirs. Series of Biology (JPN ISSN 0454-7802) **686**
Kyoto University. Faculty of Science. Memoirs. Series of Geology and Mineralogy (JPN ISSN 0454-7810) **2752**
➤ Kyoto University. Faculty of Science. Memoirs. Series of Physics, Astrophysics, Geophysics and Chemistry (JPN ISSN 0368-9689) **7878**
Kyoto University. Institute for Virus Research. Annual Report/Kyoto Daigaku Uirusu Kenkyujo Nenkan Kiyo (JPN ISSN 0075-7357) **890**
Kyoto University. Institute of Atomic Energy. Bulletin *see* Kyoto Daigaku Genshi Energi Kenkyujo Iho **3170**
Kyoto University. Institute of Atomic Energy. Research Activities (JPN ISSN 0386-0752) **3170**
➤ Kyoto University. Journal of Mathematics/Kyoto Daigaku Rigakubu Sugaku Kiyo (JPN ISSN 0023-608X) **5508**
Kyoto University. Kwasan and Hida Observatories. Contributions (JPN ISSN 0388-2349) **577**
Kyoto University Linguistic Research *see* Kyouto Daigaku Gengogaku Kenkyuu **5138**
Kyoto University of Education. Bulletin *see* Kyouto Kyouiku Daigaku Kiyou **7878**
Kyoto University. Plasma Physics Laboratory. Annual Review (JPN) **7024**
Kyoto University. Plasma Physics Laboratory. Research Report (JPN) **7024**
Kyoto University. Primate Research Institute. Annual Reports *see* Kyoto Daigaku. Reichorui Kenkyujo Nenpo **346**
Kyoto University. Research Activities in Civil Engineering and Related Fields (JPN ISSN 0075-7365) **3278**
Kyoto University. Research Institute for Food Science. Bulletin *see* Kyoto Daigaku Shokuryo Kagaku Kenkyusho Hokoku **131**
Kyoto University. Research Institute for Mathematical Sciences. Proceedings *see* Kyoto Daigaku. Suri Kaiseki Kenkyujo. Kokyuroku **5508**
Kyoto University. Research Reactor Institute. Proceedings of the Scientific Meeting *see* Kyoto Daigaku Genshiro Jikkensho Gakujutsu Koenkai Houbunshu **7024**
Kyoto University Research Reactor Institute Progress Report Progress Report *see* K U R R I Progress Report **3170**
Kyoto University. Research Reactor Institute. Technical Report (JPN ISSN 0287-9808) **3170**
Kyotofu Kisho Geppo/Kyoto Prefecture. Monthly Report of Meteorology (JPN ISSN 0916-5169) **6360**
• Kyouritsu Yakka Daigaku Zasshi/Kyoritsu University of Pharmacy. Journal (JPN ISSN 1880-5116) **6858**
Kyouto Daigaku Gengogaku Kenkyuu/Kyoto University Linguistic Research (JPN ISSN 1349-7804) **5138**
Kyouto Daigaku Josampu Dousoukaihou/Midwives Association of Kyoto University. Annals (JPN ISSN 1348-334X) **5997**
Kyouto Furitsu Daigaku Gakujutsu Houkoku. Seimei Kankyougaku/Kyoto Prefectural University. Scientific Reports. Life and Environmental Sciences (JPN ISSN 1882-6946) **3449**
• Kyouto Kyouiku Daigaku Kiyou/Kyoto University of Education. Bulletin (JPN) **7878**
➤ Kyowa Engineering News/Kyowa Giho (JPN ISSN 0285-2969) **3208**
Kyowa Giho *see* Kyowa Engineering News **3208**
Kyowa Hakko Kogyo. Annual Report (JPN) **28**
Kyoyo Ronshu *see* Review on Liberal Arts **4472**
Kyoyudentai Oyo Kaigi Koen Yokoshu/Abstracts of the Meeting on Ferroelectric Materials and Their Applications (JPN) **7052**
▼ Kyperen (DNK ISSN 1903-945X) **606**
Kypria/Cypriot Woman (CYP) **8870**
Kypriakai Spoudai *see* Society of Cypriot Studies. Bulletin **4265**
Kypriakos Logos (CYP ISSN 0254-3184) **4239**
Kypros (CYP ISSN 0023-611X) **3832**
Kyrex (ZAF) **4050**
Kyrgyz Rukhu (KGZ) **3904**
Kyrgyz Tuusu (KGZ) **3904**
Kyrgyzstan Chronicle (KGZ) **3904**
Kyrgyzstan Review (KGZ) **3904**
Kyriatikis Ores/Sunday Hours (CYP) **3832**
Kyrka och Folk (SWE ISSN 0345-6757) **7764**
Kyrkans Tidning (SWE ISSN 1651-405X) **7659**
Kyrkfack (SWE ISSN 0283-7846) **7764**
Kyrklig Samling Kring Bibeln och Bekaennelsen (SWE ISSN 0345-682X) **7764**
Kyrkogaarden (SWE ISSN 0282-0595) **3720**
Kyrkohistorisk Aarsskrift (SWE ISSN 0085-2619) **7659**
Kyrkokoerjournalen (SWE ISSN 1101-9670) **6583**
Kyrkomusikernas Tidning (SWE ISSN 0281-286X) **6584**
Kysucke Noviny (SVK ISSN 1335-5651) **3946**
Kyuchaku Shinpojumu Abusutorakutoshu/Symposium on Adsorption. Abstracts (JPN) **2094**
Kyukyu Igaku/Japanese Journal of Acute Medicine (JPN ISSN 0385-8162) **5659**
• Kyungpook Mathematical Journal (KOR ISSN 1225-6951) **5508**
Kyushu American Literature (JPN ISSN 0454-8132) **5319**
Kyushu Chiiki Kazan Kido Kansoku Jisshi Hokoku/Report of Volcano Observation in Kyushu District (JPN ISSN 0285-0958) **2786**
Kyushu Daigaku Chuo Bunseki Senta Hokoku/Kyushu University. Center of Advanced Instrumental Analysis. Report (JPN ISSN 0916-0892) **4488**
Kyushu Daigaku Chuo Bunseki Senta Nyusu/Kyushu University. Center of Advanced Instrumental Analysis. News (JPN) **4488**
Kyushu Daigaku Daigakuin Hikaku Shakai Bunka Kenkyuka Kiyo *see* Hikaku Shakai Bunka **7969**
Kyushu Daigaku Daigakuin Shisutemu Joho Kagaku Kiyo *see* Research Reports on Information Science and Electrical Engineering **3329**
Kyushu Daigaku Daigakuin Sogo Rikogaku Kenkyuka Hokoku/Kyushu University. Engineering Sciences Reports (JPN ISSN 0388-1717) **3208**
Kyushu Daigaku Kogakubu Kiyo *see* Kyushu University. Faculty of Engineering. Memoirs **3208**
Kyushu Daigaku Kyoyobu Chigaku Kenkyu Hokoku/Kyushu University. College of General Education. Reports on Earth Science (JPN ISSN 0453-0276) **2712**
Kyushu Daigaku. Nogakubu. Fuzoku Suisan Jikkenjo Hokoku *see* Kyushu University. Fishery Research Laboratory. Report **3600**
Kyushu Daigaku Nogakubu Kiyo *see* Kyushu University. Faculty of Agriculture. Journal **132**
Kyushu Daigaku Nogakubu Suisangakka Gyosekishu/Kyushu University. Contributions from the Department of Fisheries and the Fishery Research Laboratory (JPN ISSN 0453-0314) **3600**
Kyushu Daigaku. Rigakubu Kenkyu Hokoku. Chikyu-Wakusei-Kagaku *see* Kyuushuu Daigaku. Daigakuin Rigaku Kenkyuuin Kenkyuu Houkoku. Chikyuu Wakusei Kagaku **2752**
Kyushu Daigaku Rigakubu Kiyo C. Kagaku *see* Kyushu University. Faculty of Science. Memoirs. Series C: Chemistry **2071**
Kyushu Daigaku Rigakubu Kiyo D. Chikyuwakusei Kagaku *see* Kyushu University. Faculty of Sciences. Memoirs. Series D: Earth and Planetary Sciences **2752**
Kyushu Daigaku Rigakubu Shimabara Jishin Kazan Kansokujo Kenkyu Hokoku/Kyushu University. Faculty of Science. Shimabara Earthquake and Volcano Observatory. Sciences Reports (JPN ISSN 0916-2259) **2786**
Kyushu Daigaku Shinri Rinsho Kenkyu/Kyushu University. Psychological Clinic. Archives (JPN ISSN 0285-4562) **7383**
Kyushu Denryoku K.K. Sogo Kenkyujo Kenkyu Kiho/Kyushu Electric Power Co. Research Department. Report (JPN ISSN 0287-9263) **3323**
Kyushu Dental Society. Journal *see* Kyushu Shika Gakkai Zasshi **5854**
Kyushu Electric Power Co. Research Department. Report *see* Kyushu Denryoku K.K. Sogo Kenkyujo Kenkyu Kiho **3323**
Kyushu Institute of Technology. Bulletin: Humanities, Social Sciences/Kyushu Kogyo Daigaku Kenkyu Hokoku: Jinbun-Shakai-Kagaku (JPN ISSN 0453-0349) **4462**
Kyushu Institute of Technology. Bulletin: Pure & Applied Mathematics (JPN ISSN 1343-8670) **5508**
Kyushu Institute of Technology. Bulletin: Science and Technology/Kyushu Kogyo Daigaku Kenkyu Hokoku: Kogaku (JPN ISSN 0453-0357) **8430**
• ➤ Kyushu Journal of Mathematics (JPN ISSN 1340-6116) **5508**
Kyushu Kogyo Daigaku Kenkyu Hokoku: Jinbun-Shakai-Kagaku *see* Kyushu Institute of Technology. Bulletin: Humanities, Social Sciences **4462**
Kyushu Kogyo Daigaku Kenkyu Hokoku: Kogaku *see* Kyushu Institute of Technology. Bulletin: Science and Technology **8430**
Kyushu Kogyo Gijutsu Shikenjo Nenpo/Government Industrial Research Institute, Kyushu. Annual Report (JPN) **1896**
Kyushu Neuro-Psychiatry/Kyushu Shinkei Seishin Igaku (JPN ISSN 0023-6144) **6158**
Kyushu no Kai/Shells of Kyushu (JPN ISSN 0911-985X) **953**
Kyushu Pharmaceutical Society. Journal *see* Kyushu Yakugakkai Kaiho **6858**
Kyushu Sangyo Daigaku Kokusai Bunka Gakubu Kiyo/Kyushu Sangyo University. Faculty of International Studies of Culture. Journal (JPN ISSN 1340-9425) **7250**
Kyushu Sangyo Daigaku Kyoyobu Kiyo/Kyushu Sangyo University. College of Liberal Arts. Bulletin *see* Kyushu Sangyo Daigaku Kokusai Bunka Gakubu Kiyo **7250**
Kyushu Sangyo University. Faculty of International Studies of Culture. Journal *see* Kyushu Sangyo Daigaku Kokusai Bunka Gakubu Kiyo **7250**
Kyushu Shika Gakkai Zasshi/Kyushu Dental Society. Journal (JPN ISSN 0368-6833) **5854**
Kyushu Shinkei Seishin Igaku *see* Kyushu Neuro-Psychiatry **6158**
Kyushu Tokai Daigaku Nogakubu Kiyo/Kyushu Tokai University. Faculty of Agriculture. Proceedings (JPN ISSN 0286-8180) **132**

Kyushu Tokai University. Faculty of Agriculture. Proceedings see Kyushu Tokai Daigaku Nogakubu Kiyo **132**
Kyushu Tokai University. School of Engineering. Bulletin see Kyuushuu Toukai Daigaku Kiyou. Ouyou Jouhou Gakubu. Kougakubu **3208**
Kyushu Tokai University. School of Information Science. Bulletin see Kyuushuu Toukai Daigaku Kiyou. Ouyou Jouhou Gakubu. Kougakubu **3208**
Kyushu University. Center of Advanced Instrumental Analysis. News see Kyushu Daigaku Chuo Bunseki Senta Nyusu **4488**
Kyushu University. Center of Advanced Instrumental Analysis. Report see Kyushu Daigaku Chuo Bunseki Senta Hokoku **4488**
Kyushu University. College of General Education. Reports on Earth Science see Kyushu Daigaku Kyoyobu Chigaku Kenkyu Hokoku **2712**
Kyushu University. Contributions from the Department of Fisheries and the Fishery Research Laboratory see Kyushu Daigaku Nogakubu Suisangakka Gyosekishu **3600**
Kyushu University. Department of Earth and Planetary Sciences. Science Reports see Kyuushuu Daigaku. Daigakuin Rigaku Kenkyuuin Kenkyuu Houkoku. Chikyuu Wakusei Kagaku **2752**
Kyushu University. Engineering Sciences Reports see Kyushu Daigaku Daigakuin Sogo Rikogaku Kenkyuka Hokoku **3208**
➤ Kyushu University. Faculty of Agriculture. Journal/Kyushu Daigaku Nogakubu Kiyo (JPN ISSN 0023-6152) **132**
Kyushu University. Faculty of Agriculture. Science Bulletin/Kyuushuu Daigaku Daigakuin Nougaku Kenkyuuin Kanzei Zasshi (JPN ISSN 1347-0159) **132**
Kyushu University. Faculty of Engineering. Memoirs/Kyushu Daigaku Kogakubu Kiyo (JPN ISSN 1345-868X) **3208**
Kyushu University. Faculty of Science. Memoirs. Series C: Chemistry/Kyushu Daigaku Rigakubu Kiyo C. Kagaku (JPN ISSN 0085-2635) **2071**
Kyushu University. Faculty of Science. Shimabara Earthquake and Volcano Observatory. Sciences Reports see Kyushu Daigaku Rigakubu Shimabara Jishin Kazan Kansokujo Kenkyu Hokoku **2786**
➤ Kyushu University. Faculty of Sciences. Memoirs. Series D: Earth and Planetary Sciences/Kyushu Daigaku Rigakubu Kiyo D. Chikyuwakusei Kagaku (JPN ISSN 0916-7390) **2752**
Kyushu University. Fishery Research Laboratory. Report/Kyushu Daigaku. Nogakubu. Fuzoku Suisan Jikkenjo Hokoku (JPN ISSN 0285-6921) **3600**
Kyushu University. Graduate School of Social and Cultural Studies. Bulletin see Hikaku Shakai Bunka **7969**
Kyushu University. Institute of Tropical Agriculture. Bulletin/Nettai Nogaku Kenkyu (JPN ISSN 0915-499X) **132**
Kyushu University. Psychological Clinic. Archives see Kyushu Daigaku Shinri Rinsho Kenkyu **7383**
Kyushu University. Research Institute for Applied Mechanics. Abstracts of Papers (JPN ISSN 0919-4673) **3232**
Kyushu University. Research Institute for Applied Mechanics. Reports (JPN ISSN 1345-5664) **3352**
Kyushu University. Tandem Accelerator Laboratory. Report (JPN) **7060**
Kyushu Yakugakkai Kaiho/Kyushu Pharmaceutical Society. Journal (JPN ISSN 0368-7279) **6858**
Kyuushuu Daigaku Daigakuin Nougaku Kenkyuuin Kanzei Zasshi see Kyushu University. Faculty of Agriculture. Science Bulletin **132**
➤ Kyuushuu Daigaku. Daigakuin Rigaku Kenkyuuin Kenkyuu Houkoku. Chikyuu Wakusei Kagaku/Kyushu University. Department of Earth and Planetary Sciences. Science Reports (JPN ISSN 1348-0545) **2752**
Kyuushuu Okinawa Nougyou Kenkyuu Senta Houkoku/National Agricultural Research Center for Kyushu Okinawa Region. Bulletin (JPN ISSN 1346-9177) **132**
Kyuushuu Toukai Daigaku Kiyou. Ouyou Jouhou Gakubu. Kougakubu/Kyushu Tokai University. School of Engineering. Bulletin/Kyushu Tokai University. School of Information Science. Bulletin (JPN ISSN 1346-7549) **3208**
Kyzyl-Tuu (KGZ) **3904**
▼ • L (USA ISSN 2150-6175) **5075**
L (New York) see L Magazine (New York) **4711**
L 3 3 T see GameAxis Unwired **2476**
L A see London Archaeologist **404**
L.A. see Linguistik Aktuell **5147**
L A A R see Latin American Arbitration Review **4934**
L A & I - Litere, Arte si Idei (ROM ISSN 1220-6938) **5223**
L A Architect see Form: Pioneering Design **442**
L A B A Newsnet (Leicestershire Asia Business Association) (GBR ISSN 1461-3697) **1771**
L A B I Enterprise (Louisiana Association of Business and Industry) (USA ISSN 1541-8197) **1430**
L A B - Laboratoria, Aparatura, Badania (POL ISSN 1427-5619) **5907**
L A B R see Latin American Business Review **1575**
L A Barhopper (Los Angeles) (USA) **4393**
L A C C Journal see Louisiana Association for College Composition Journal **5148**
L A C E S see Latin American and Caribbean Ethnic Studies **5320**
L A C I T O Documents Afrique (Laboratoire de Langues et Civilisations a Tradition Orale) (BEL ISSN 0754-2445) **5138**
➤ L A C I T O Documents Asie - Austronesie (Laboratoire de Langues et Civilisations a Tradition Orale) (BEL ISSN 0751-4875) **5138**
➤ L A C I T O Documents Eurasie (Laboratoire de Langues et Civilisations a Tradition Orale) (BEL ISSN 0751-4883) **5138**
L A C M A Physician see Southern California Physician **5717**
L A C M F see Literacy Across the CurriculuMedia Focus **5148**
➤ L A C U S Forum (Linguistic Association of Canada and the United States) (USA ISSN 0195-377X) **5138**
L.A. Commercial News see W C N Commercial News **1586**
L A E Journal (Lambda Alpha Epsilon) (USA ISSN 1094-8481) **4893**
L A E L see Labor and Employment Law **1692**
L A E News see L A E Voice **2881**
L A E Voice (Louisiana Association of Educators) (USA) **2881**
L A Family Magazine (Los Angeles) (USA) **2159**
L A I see Laser Applications International **3323**
L A I F S Journal (Los Angeles International Fern Society) (USA ISSN 0146-910X) **3741**
L A J A M see The Latin American Journal of Aquatic Mammals **953**
L A J C C Scene (Los Angeles Junior Chamber of Commerce) (USA) **1406**
L A J P E see Latin - American Journal of Physics Education **7024**
L A M R see Latin American Music Review **6584**
L A Multimedia (Lehrmittel Aktuell) (DEU ISSN 1432-8267) **3026**
L A N see LEAD Action News **7530**
• L A N (Local Area Network) (RUS ISSN 1027-0868) **2500**
† L A N A Nyt (Lokalhistoriske Arkiver i Nordjyllands Amt) (DNK ISSN 0108-7711) **8970**
L A N D Online see Landscape Architecture News Digest **448**
† L A N Internetworking Buyers Guide (Local Area Network) (NLD) **8970**
L A N Internetworking Product Guide see L A N Internetworking Buyers Guide **8970**
L A N Local Authority News see Local Authority News **7496**
• L A N Magazine (Local Area Network) (NLD ISSN 1574-115X) **2500**
L A N Management News and Analysis (Local Area Network) (USA) **2500**
L A N Newsletter see S A N / L A N **2503**
L A N/Premises Components Quarterly Reports (Local Area Networks) (USA) **2500**
• L A N Product News (Local Area Network) (USA) **2500**
L A N S A (Latin American Notaphilic Society) (USA ISSN 0308-8677) **6651**
L A P V. Local Authority Plant & Vehicles (GBR ISSN 1472-2607) **7495**
• L A Parent (Los Angeles) (USA ISSN 0740-3437) **2159**
L A R F Report. Annual (Latin American Reserve Fund) (COL) **1143**
• L A Ritmo.com (Latin American) (USA ISSN 1525-853X) **6584**
L A S see Library & Archival Security **5026**
L A S A Forum (Latin American Studies Association) (USA ISSN 0890-7218) **7982**
L A S News (London Ambulance Service) (GBR) **6066**
L A T see Legal Assistant Today **4719**
L A T A Directory (Local Access and Transport Area) (USA) **2369**
L A T E C. Document de Travail (Laboratoire d'Analyse et de Techniques Economiques) (FRA ISSN 1260-8556) **1496**
L A T H E see Learning and Teaching in Higher Education **2992**
L A T I S S see Learning and Teaching **7983**
▼ • L.A. Tails (Los Angeles) (USA ISSN 1940-5677) **6810**
L A VE. Liason des Amateurs de Volcanologie Europeenne (FRA ISSN 0982-9601) **2786**
L A W G Letter (Latin American Working Group) (CAN ISSN 0316-3393) **7250**
L A W R (Local Authority Waste & Recycling) (GBR ISSN 1750-9769) **3508**
• L A Y A! (Letter for American Young Adults) (USA) **2199**
L A Youth (Los Angeles) (USA) **2199**
L & B see Learning & Behavior **7383**
L & C P see Law and Contemporary Problems **4713**
• ➤ L & E Newsletter (Labor and Employment) (USA ISSN 1530-3950) **4710**
L and E Newsletter see L & E Newsletter **4710**
L & N W see Label & Narrow Web **2563**
L & S I see Lighting & Sound International **8473**
L & V see Lozarstvo i Vinarstvo **607**
L B I News (Leo Baeck Institute) (USA ISSN 0023-625X) **4150**
The L B J (little brown job) (USA ISSN 1942-4485) **5319**
• L B J Journal of Public Affairs (USA ISSN 1087-268X) **7982**
• L B L Currents Weekly Newsletter (Lawrence Berkeley Laboratory) (USA) **7878**
L B M Journal (Lumber Building Material) (USA ISSN 1930-5516) **1020**
• L B O Wire (Leverage Buyouts) (USA) **1637**
L B R see Luso - Brazilian Review **5225**
• L B S Journal of Management & Research (Lal Bahadur Shastri) (IND ISSN 0972-8031) **1771**
• L B S Management Review (Lagos Business School) (NGA ISSN 1118-3713) **1771**
L C a R see Listy Cukrovarnicke a Reparske **3654**
L C A T S see Library Collections, Acquisitions, and Technical Services **5027**
L C & R see Libraries & the Cultural Record **5026**
L C B O Annual Report see Liquor Control Board of Ontario. Annual Report **7451**
• L C Cataloging Newsline (Library of Congress) (USA ISSN 1066-8829) **5024**
L C D (Lowest Common Denominator) (USA) **2360**
L C D Bettles, Alaska. Monthly Summary see Local Climatological Data. Bettles, Alaska. Monthly Summary **6363**
L C D Big Delta, Alaska. Monthly Summary see Local Climatological Data. Big Delta, Alaska. Monthly Summary **6363**
L C D Kwajalein, Marshall Islands, Pacific. Annual Summary with Comparative Data see Local Climatological Data. Kwajalein, Marshall Islands, Pacific. Annual Summary with Comparative Data **6374**
L C D San Diego, California. Annual Summary with Comparative Data see Local Climatological Data. San Diego, California. Annual Summary with Comparative Data **6384**
• L C Folk Archive Finding Aid (Library of Congress) (USA ISSN 0736-4903) **5024**
L C G C Asia Pacific (Liquid Chromatography Gas Chromatography) (USA) **2103**
L C - G C Asia Pacific see L C G C Asia Pacific **2103**
• L C G C Europe (Liquid Chromatography Gas Chromatography) (GBR ISSN 1471-6577) **2103**
L C - G C Europe see L C G C Europe **2103**
• ➤ L C G C North America (Liquid Chromatography Gas Chromatography) (USA ISSN 1527-5949) **2103**
L C - G C North America see L C G C North America **2103**
L C H see Law, Culture & the Humanities **4714**
L C I see The Law of Commercial Insurance **4512**
L C I E Informations (Laboratoire Central des Industries Electriques) (FRA ISSN 0220-9535) **3323**
L C L R see Lewis & Clark Law Review **4723**
L C N Textile Care Yearbook (Laundry and Cleaning News) (GBR) **2243**
L C O M M News (Library Council of Metropolitan Milwaukee) (USA) **5024**
L C R I see U.S. Library of Congress. Rule Interpretations **5052**
• L C S: Guide to Hockey (Le Coq Sportif) (USA) **8237**
L C S H see U.S. Library of Congress. Subject Headings **5052**
L C Science Tracer Bullet (U.S. Library of Congress) (USA ISSN 0090-5232) **7937**
L C T see Liquid Crystals Today (Online) **2111**
L C T D see Luxury Car Tax Determination **1933**
L D+ see Jagt, Vildt & Vaaben **8319**
L D A Journal (Louisiana Dental Association) (USA ISSN 0092-4458) **5854**
L D A Newsbriefs (Learning Disabilities Association of America) (USA ISSN 0739-909X) **3043**
L D & A see Lighting Design + Application **3324**
L D B Interior Textiles (Linens, Domestics and Bath Products) (USA ISSN 0892-743X) **4560**
L D E I Quarterly see Les Dames d' Escoffier International Quarterly **3633**
L D Essentials (Learning Disabilities) (USA) **3043**
• L D I Issue Brief (Leonard Davis Institute of Health Economics) (USA ISSN 1553-0671) **7530**
• L D Online (Learning Disabilities) (USA) **4067**
L D R C Bulletin (Libel Defense Resource Center) (USA ISSN 0737-8130) **4834**
L D R C LibelLetter see L D R C MediaLawLetter **4710**
L D R C MediaLawLetter (Libel Defense Resource Center) (USA) **4710**
• The L D Reader (Learning Disabilities) (USA) **3043**
L D S Living (Latter Day Saints) (USA ISSN 1540-9678) **7738**
L D T Monographs (Landscape Design Trust) (GBR) **448**
L D V - Forum (Linguistische Datenverarbeitung) (DEU ISSN 0175-1336) **5203**
➤ L - Der Literatur Bote (DEU ISSN 1617-6871) **5319**
• L E A A (Lenguas en Aprendizaje Autodirigido) (MEX ISSN 1870-5820) **5138**
L E A D see Law, Environment & Development Journal **4714**
L E A F Lines (Legal Education and Action Fund) (CAN ISSN 1192-9359) **4710**
L E A Letterature d'Europa e d'America (Online Edition) see L E A Letterature d'Europa e d'America (Print) **5138**
• L E A Letterature d'Europa e d'America (Print) (ITA ISSN 1824-4920) **5138**
L E A. Libro Electronico Aranzadi. Formularios Aranzadi see Libro Electronico Aranzadi. Formularios Aranzadi **4723**
L E A P see Leeds East Asia Papers **7251**
L E A R N (Boulder) (Laboratory Experience in Atmospheric Research) (USA ISSN 1948-2582) **6360**
L E & W see Literature East and West **5326**
L E C I A Bulletin (Legon Centre for International Affairs) (GHA ISSN 0855-076X) **7250**
L E D see Legal Education Digest **2992**
• L E D Journal (Light Emitting Diodes) (USA ISSN 1930-7772) **3323**
• L E D Journal e-Report (Light Emitting Diodes) (USA ISSN 1938-081X) **3323**
L E D. Loisirs Electroniques d'Aujourd'hui see Electronique Pratique **3097**
• L E Ds Magazine (Light-Emitting Diode) (GBR) **3107**
L E Ds Suppliers Directory see L E Ds Magazine **3107**
• L E E M E. Revista Electronica (Lista Electronica Europea de Musica en la Educacion) (ESP ISSN 1575-9563) **6584**
L E I - Draad (Landbouw-Economisch Instituut) (NLD ISSN 0168-1850) **183**
L E I F Quaderni (Laboratorio di Etica e Informazione Filosofica) (ITA ISSN 1970-7401) **4462**
• L E I S A (Low External Input & Sustainable Agriculture) (NLD ISSN 1569-8424) **241**
L E L see Labor & Employment Law **1692**
L E M Collana (Laboratorio Educativo Meridionale) (ITA ISSN 1970-6200) **2943**
L E O S see I E E E L E O S **7076**
L E O S Newsletter see I E E E Photonics Society News **7076**
L E P see Library of Exact Philosophy **7880**
L E P N see Law Enforcement Product News **2659**
L E R A News (Labor and Employment Relations Association) (USA ISSN 1946-6978) **1691**
L E R A Newsletter see L E R A News **1691**
➤ L E R S Monograph Series (Laboratoires d'Etudes et de Recherches Synthelabo) (USA ISSN 0742-3896) **5659**
▼ • L E S C Ateliers (Laboratoire d'Ethnologie et de Sociologie Comparative) (FRA ISSN 1245-1436) **346**
L E S Nouvelles (Licensing Executives Society) (USA ISSN 0270-174X) **8430**
L E T see Law Enforcement Technology **2659**
L F C S Report Series (Laboratory for Foundations of Computer Science) (GBR ISSN 0952-3677) **2430**
L F I Food News (Leatherhead Food International Ltd.) (GBR ISSN 1755-1498) **3653**
L F I Newsletter (Labour Friends of Israel) (GBR) **7250**
L F L Reports (Libertarians for Life) (USA ISSN 0882-116X) **973**
L F N Bulletin (Libraries for Nursing) (GBR ISSN 1354-1412) **5968**
L F N V & A C see Journal of Low Frequency Noise Vibration and Active Control **7088**
L G A D Nachrichten (Landesverband Gross- und Aussenhandel, Vertrieb und Dienstleistungen Bayern e.V.) (DEU) **1430**
L G A Impulse (Landesgewerbeanstalt Bayern) (DEU ISSN 1611-8243) **1897**
L G A Reseach Report (Local Government Association) (GBR) **7450**
L G A Rundschau see L G A Impulse **1897**
L G A Yearbook see Local Government Association. Yearbook **7496**
• L G Argomenti (Letteratura Giovanile) (ITA) **5223**
L G B Telegram/Lehmann's Big Train Telegram (Lehmann Gross Bahn) (USA ISSN 1056-893X) **4338**
L G C Law and Administration see Local Government Chronicle **7496**
L G D see Law, Social Justice and Global Development **4716**
L G dos'e (Literaturnaa Gazeta) (RUS ISSN 1562-0395) **5223**
L G E R A see Local Government and Environmental Reports of Australia **7496**
L G I U Discussion Papers (Local Government Information Unit) (GBR) **7450**
L G I U Information Briefing (Local Government Information Unit) (GBR) **7495**
L G I U Policy Briefing (Local Government Information Unit) (GBR) **2881**
L G I U Special Briefings (Local Government Information Unit) (GBR) **7450**
L G L C Newsletter (Libertarians for Gay and Lesbian Concerns) (USA ISSN 1069-5966) **5319**
L G M see Local Government Manager **7497**
L G N Y (Lesbian and Gay New York) (USA ISSN 1088-1166) **4376**
L G N Y Latino (Lesbian and Gay New York) (USA) **4376**
L G R - Series (Laboratorium voor Geodetische Rekentechniek) (NLD ISSN 0928-2122) **2786**
L H see Leicestershire Historian **4151**
L H see Lodging Hospitality **4393**
L H (Year) Almanac (Lodging Hospitality) (USA) **4393**
L H & R B Newsletter (Legal History and Rare Books) (USA) **4710**
L H R see Law and History Review **4713**
L H R see Labour History Review **1694**

Title

DIRECTORY 2010 LABOUR FORCE SURVEY 10545

L Z Nonfood Trends (Lebensmittel Zeitung) (DEU) **3680**
L Z Rheinland (Landwirtschaftliche Zeitschrift) (DEU ISSN 0724-5580) **132**
L Z Spezial *see* Lebensmittel Zeitung Spezial **3654**
• L1 Educational Studies in Language and Literature (NLD ISSN 1567-6617) **2881**
L'A A R S E (Association des Auteurs Realisateurs du Sud Est) (FRA ISSN 1951-0705) **6506**
La Crosse Area Business and Economic Review (USA) **1496**
La Fayette (USA) **3773**
La Jolla Today (USA) **5075**
La Salle (USA) **2289**
• La Staa! (NOR ISSN 1501-8830) **4418**
• ➤ The La Trobe Journal (AUS ISSN 1441-3760) **5024**
Laagendalsposten (NOR) **3923**
Het Laatste Nieuws (BEL ISSN 1780-1273) **3801**
Lab Acta *see* Laborat-acta **5908**
Lab Africa (GBR ISSN 1365-7623) **2071**
Lab Africa. Annual Buyers Guide *see* Lab Africa **2071**
• ➤ Lab Animal (USA ISSN 0093-7355) **5907**
Lab Asia (GBR ISSN 1355-8625) **2071**
Lab Asia. Annual Buyers Guide *see* Lab Asia **2071**
• Lab Business Week (USA ISSN 1552-6461) **1143**
Lab Data (USA ISSN 0730-5672) **6403**
Lab Guide *see* LabGuide **2071**
Lab Instrumenten *see* Laboratorium Magazine **5908**
• Lab Law Weekly (USA ISSN 1551-5176) **5907**
Lab Lines (AUS ISSN 0819-0879) **3069**
Lab Magazine (GBR ISSN 1473-3374) **502**
➤ Lab Management Today (USA ISSN 1058-7845) **5854**
• Lab Manager (CAN ISSN 1931-3810) **1771**
• Lab Notes (USA) **3208**
• ➤ Lab On a Chip (GBR ISSN 1473-0197) **2071**
Lab Plus International (USA) **5908**
Lab South America (GBR ISSN 1463-080X) **5908**
Lab Talk (AUS ISSN 0159-2033) **3069**
Lab Times (DEU ISSN 1864-2381) **7878**
LabCompact Service - Produkte fuer das Labor (DEU) **5908**
Label & Logistik (DEU) **2354**
• Label & Narrow Web (USA ISSN 1095-3248) **2563**
Label Etiquettes Info *see* Label Pack **6711**
• Label France (FRA ISSN 1162-6208) **7250**
Label Letter (USA ISSN 0161-9365) **4597**
Label Magazine (NLD ISSN 1872-230X) **1829**
• The Label Newsletter (USA) **241**
Label Pack (FRA ISSN 1957-1828) **6711**
Label World (ITA) **6711**
Labeled Immunoassays and Clinical Medicine *see* Biaoji Mianyi Fenxi yu Linchuang **5755**
Labels and Labeling (GBR ISSN 1478-7520) **6711**
Labels & Labelling Annual Directory (GBR) **6711**
Labeo (ITA ISSN 0023-6462) **4711**
Laberinto Comunicacion (ESP ISSN 1699-0196) **2331**
LabFuture (DEU ISSN 1610-8256) **5908**
• LabGuide (USA ISSN 1520-4782) **2071**
Labirinti (Chieti) (ITA) **5319**
Labirinti (Rome) (ITA ISSN 1970-3813) **5411**
Labirinti (Trento) (ITA) **4463**
Labirinti del Fantastico (ITA ISSN 1971-5811) **5319**
Lablink *see* New Zealand Public Health Surveillance Report **7533**
➤ LabMedica International (USA ISSN 1068-1760) **5908**
Labmedicine *see* Laboratory Medicine **5908**
LabNotes *see* Big Picture On ... **5584**
Labo (DEU ISSN 0344-5208) **5908**
Labo Cards (DEU ISSN 0177-6509) **5908**
Labo Numerique (FRA ISSN 1773-6889) **6970**
Labolife *see* Pipette **5916**
† Labor (ITA ISSN 0023-6489) **8970**
Labor (Hanoi) *see* Lao Dong **1695**
Labor (Vientiane) *see* Lao Dong **4598**
Labor 2000 *see* LabFuture **5908**
Labor and Development (TGO) **1691**
Labor & Employment *see* Labour & Employment (Year) **1693**
• Labor and Employment Arbitration (USA) **4597**
Labor and Employment in California (USA) **1692**
• Labor and Employment in Connecticut (USA) **1692**
Labor and Employment in Georgia (USA) **1692**
Labor and Employment in Louisiana (USA) **1692**
• Labor and Employment in Massachusetts (USA) **1692**
Labor and Employment in Nebraska (USA) **1692**
Labor and Employment in New Hampshire (USA) **1692**
Labor and Employment in Rhode Island (USA) **1692**
Labor & Employment Law (USA ISSN 0193-5739) **1692**
Labor & Employment Law *see* Labor and Employment Law **1692**
• ➤ Labor and Employment Law (USA) **1692**
Labor and Employment Law Institute. Annual (USA) **4711**
• Labor and Employment Law Library (USA ISSN 1527-7356) **5024**
Labor and Employment Law Newsletter (USA ISSN 8756-792X) **1692**
Labor and Employment Newsletter *see* L & E Newsletter **4710**
Labor and Employment Relations Association. Annual Meeting. Proceedings (USA) **1692**
Labor and Employment Relations Association News *see* L E R A News **1691**
• Labor Arbitration Awards (USA ISSN 0023-6500) **4597**
Labor Arbitration Citations *see* Shepard's Labor Arbitration Citations **4961**
Labor Arbitration in Government (USA ISSN 0047-3839) **4597**
Labor Arbitration Information System (USA ISSN 0744-5253) **4873**
Labor Arbitration Reports *see* Labor Relations Reporter. Labor Arbitration and Dispute Settlements **1693**
Labor Cost Index *see* New Zealand. Statistics New Zealand. Labour Cost Index (All Labour Costs) **1700**
• Labor Council Of New South Wales. Annual Report (AUS) **1692**
Labor Dental Clinica (ESP ISSN 1888-4040) **5854**
Labor Dental Tecnica (ESP ISSN 1888-4253) **5854**
† • Labor Essays (AUS ISSN 0158-9245) **8970**
Labor Exchange *see* Birzha Truda **3935**
Labor Flash (CHE) **6680**
Labor Force and Employment in Washington State (USA) **1248**
Labor Force and Nonagricultural Employment Estimates (USA) **1248**
Labor Force in Idaho (USA) **1692**
† Labor Herald (AUS ISSN 1441-7707) **8970**
• ➤ Labor History (GBR ISSN 0023-656X) **1692**
Labor Interdisiplinaria de Labor Regional *see* L I D E R **7286**
Labor Law Institute (USA) **4711**
• Labor Law Journal (USA ISSN 0023-6586) **4711**
Labor Law Reports: Summary (USA) **1692**
Labor Law Symposium (USA ISSN 1559-5218) **1692**
• Labor Laws of Virginia (USA) **1692**
• Labor Lawyer (USA ISSN 8756-2995) **4711**
• Labor Leader (USA ISSN 0023-6594) **4597**
Labor Life (USA ISSN 1945-5216) **1692**
Labor Magazine (BEL ISSN 1562-5435) **4597**
Labor-Management Relations *see* Annual Editions: Labor-Management Relations **1663**
Labor Market Information Directory (USA ISSN 0732-6084) **629**
Labor Market Information Review *see* L M I Review **1691**
Labor Market Statistics *see* Vinnumarkadur **1274**
Labor News (New York) (USA ISSN 1053-7023) **4597**
Labor News, Inc. (USA) **1692**
• Labor Notes (USA ISSN 0275-4452) **1692**
The Labor Paper (Kenosha) (USA ISSN 1067-5019) **4597**
Labor Paper (Peoria) (USA ISSN 8750-2313) **4597**
Labor Party Press (USA ISSN 1529-563X) **7150**
• Labor Relations (Arlington) (USA ISSN 0149-2713) **1692**
• Labor Relations (Riverwoods) (USA) **4711**
Labor Relations Bulletin *see* Fair Employment Practices Guidelines **4670**
Labor Relations Circular (USA) **1693**
• Labor Relations Reference Manual (USA ISSN 1043-5506) **1693**
• Labor Relations Reporter (USA ISSN 0148-7981) **1693**
• Labor Relations Reporter. Fair Employment Practices (USA) **1693**
• Labor Relations Reporter. Labor Arbitration and Dispute Settlements (USA) **1693**
Labor Relations Reporter. State Labor Laws (USA) **1693**
• Labor Relations Reporter. Wage and Hour Cases (USA ISSN 1043-5689) **1693**
• Labor Relations Reporter. Wage and Hour Manual (USA) **1693**
• Labor Relations Week (USA ISSN 0891-4141) **1693**
Labor Research Association's Economic Notes *see* L R A's Economic Notes **1691**
Labor Review (AUS ISSN 1329-3745) **7150**
• ➤ Labor: Studies in Working-Class History of the Americas (USA ISSN 1547-6715) **1693**
• ➤ Labor Studies Journal (USA ISSN 0160-449X) **1693**
Labor Surplus Areas Zip *see* L S A - Zip **1691**
Labor Union Bimonthly *see* Gonghui Gongzuo **4595**
The Labor World (USA ISSN 0023-6667) **4597**
• Laborat-acta (MEX ISSN 0187-7607) **5908**
Laborativ Arkeologi *see* J O N A S **399**
Laboratoire Central des Industries Electriques Informations *see* L C I E Informations **3323**
Laboratoire d'Analyse et de Techniques Economiques Document de Travail *see* L A T E C. Document de Travail **1496**
Laboratoire d'Anthropologie, Prehistoire, Protohistoire et Quaternaire Armoricains. Travaux (FRA ISSN 0768-3685) **346**
Laboratoire de Cartographie du Department de Geographie. Rapports (GAB) **4018**
Laboratoire de Glaciologie et Geophysique de l'Environnement. Rapport d'Activite (FRA ISSN 0750-7151) **3449**
Laboratoire de Langues et Civilisations a Tradition Orale Documents Afrique *see* L A C I T O Documents Afrique **5138**
Laboratoire de Langues et Civilisations a Tradition Orale Documents Asie - Austronesie *see* L A C I T O Documents Asie - Austronesie **5138**
Laboratoire de Langues et Civilisations a Tradition Orale Documents Eurasie *see* L A C I T O Documents Eurasie **5138**
Laboratoire de Mecanique et d'Acoustique Publications *see* L M A. Publications **7565**
Laboratoire d'Ethnologie et de Sociologie Comparative Ateliers *see* L E S C Ateliers **346**
Laboratoire d'Informatique pour la Mecanique et les Sciences de l'Ingenieur. Rapport d'Activite (FRA ISSN 0765-0302) **3208**
Laboratoire d'Informatique pour la Mecanique et les Sciences de l'Ingenieur. Scientific Report (FRA ISSN 1260-433X) **3208**
Laboratoires de Geologie Lyon. Documents (FRA ISSN 0750-6635) **2752**
Laboratoires de Geologie Lyon. Documents. Hors Serie (FRA ISSN 0245-9825) **2752**
Laboratoires des Ponts et Chaussees. Bulletin *see* France. Laboratoires des Ponts et Chaussees. Bulletin **3267**
Laboratoires d'Etudes et de Recherches Synthelabo Monograph Series *see* L E R S Monograph Series **5659**
Laboratori Nazionali di Legnaro Annual Report *see* L N L Annual Report **7068**
Laboratoriet (SWE ISSN 0345-696X) **5908**
Laboratorio 2000 (ITA ISSN 1120-8376) **2103**
Laboratorio de Arte (ESP ISSN 1130-5762) **502**
Laboratorio di Etica e Informazione Filosofica Quaderni *see* L E I F Quaderni **4462**
Laboratorio di Storia (ITA ISSN 1724-1340) **4150**
Laboratorio Educativo Meridionale Collana *see* L E M Collana **2943**
Laboratorio EtnoAntropologico (ITA ISSN 1827-3173) **346**
Laboratorio Nacional de Engenharia Civil. Memoria (PRT ISSN 0369-1179) **3278**
Laboratorio Nacional de Investigacao Veterinaria. Repositorio de Trabalhos (PRT ISSN 0870-1067) **8802**
• Laboratorio sulle Varieta Romanze Antiche (ITA ISSN 1827-6091) **5138**
Laboratorio Xeoloxico de Laxe. Cadernos (ESP ISSN 0213-4497) **2752**
• Laboratorio y Analisis (USA) **7878**
Laboratorio y Clinica (ESP ISSN 1137-6619) **6931**
Laboratorium (POL ISSN 1643-7381) **5908**
Laboratorium Magazine (NLD ISSN 1567-1828) **5908**
Laboratorium voor Geodetische Rekentechniek Series *see* L G R - Series **2786**
• ➤ Laboratoriums-Medizin (DEU ISSN 0342-3026) **5908**
Laboratornaya Diagnostika Rossii (RUS) **5908**
Laboratory Accreditation Standards (USA ISSN 1939-0416) **5908**
Laboratory and Point-of-Care Testing Accreditation Standards *see* Laboratory Accreditation Standards **5908**
Laboratory Animal Handbooks (GBR ISSN 0458-5933) **5908**
Laboratory Animal Science & Management *see* Shiyan Dongwu Kexue yu Guanli **704**
Laboratory Animal Technology and Science *see* Anitekkusu **5902**
Laboratory Animal Welfare (USA ISSN 0898-3364) **320**
• ➤ Laboratory Animals (GBR ISSN 0023-6772) **953**
Laboratory Animals. Buyers Guide (GBR ISSN 0309-7382) **5908**
Laboratory Buyers Guide (CAN ISSN 0381-6729) **5908**
• Laboratory Compliance Insider (USA ISSN 1522-533X) **4105**
Laboratory Digest (USA ISSN 1091-5184) **5855**
Laboratory Equipment *see* Key Note Market Report: Laboratory Equipment **1894**
• Laboratory Equipment (USA ISSN 0023-6810) **5908**
Laboratory Equipment Buyers Guide *see* L M S - Laboratory Equipment Buyers Guide **5907**
Laboratory Experience in Atmospheric Research (Boulder) *see* L E A R N (Boulder) **6360**
• Laboratory Focus (CAN ISSN 1486-3197) **2071**
Laboratory Focus (Gazette Edition) (CAN ISSN 1495-5660) **2071**
Laboratory for Earthquake Chemistry. Bulletin *see* Tokyo Daigaku Rigakubu Chikaku Kagaku Jikken Shisetsu Iho **2717**
Laboratory for Foundations of Computer Science Report Series *see* L F C S Report Series **2430**
Laboratory Gazette *see* Laboratory Focus (Gazette Edition) **2071**
• Laboratory Hazards Bulletin (GBR ISSN 0261-2917) **6690**
• Laboratory Hematology (USA ISSN 1080-2924) **5939**
Laboratory I T User Service *see* L I T U S **5907**
• Laboratory Industry Report (USA ISSN 1060-5118) **7878**
• ➤ Laboratory Investigation (GBR ISSN 0023-6837) **5908**
Laboratory Marketing Spectrum *see* L M S **5907**
Laboratory Marketing Spectrum Laboratory Equipment Buyers Guide *see* L M S - Laboratory Equipment Buyers Guide **5907**
Laboratory Medicine *see* Shanghai Yixue Jianyan Zazhi **5911**
• ➤ Laboratory Medicine (USA ISSN 0007-5027) **5908**
Laboratory Medicine and Clinic *see* Jianyan Yixue yu Linchuang **5906**
Laboratory News (GBR ISSN 0266-7169) **5908**
Laboratory of Nuclear Science. Research Report *see* Kakuriken Kenkyu Hokoku **7068**
▼ • Laboratory Phonology (DEU ISSN 1868-6346) **5138**
• Laboratory Primate Newsletter (USA ISSN 0023-6861) **5909**
• Laboratory Product News (CAN ISSN 0047-3855) **5909**
Laboratory Products and Services Buyers' Guide *see* Inside Laboratory Management **2100**
Laboratory Safety & Environmental Management (USA ISSN 1079-784X) **7530**
• Laboratory Surveillance of Chlamydia and Gonorrhoea in New Zealand (NZL ISSN 1176-7316) **5821**
Laboratory Surveillance of Chlamydia and Gonorrhoea in the Auckland, Waikato and Bay of Plenty Regions *see* Laboratory Surveillance of Chlamydia and Gonorrhoea in New Zealand **5821**
• ➤ Laboratory Techniques in Biochemistry and Molecular Biology (NLD ISSN 0075-7535) **737**
Laboratory Yellow Pages (CAN) **2012**
• Laboreal (PRT ISSN 1646-5237) **7982**
Laboreo (ESP ISSN 0210-1718) **212**
• The Laborer (USA ISSN 0023-6888) **4597**
Labores *see* Vosotras **8888**
Labores Coleccion (ESP) **8871**
Labores del Hogar (ESP ISSN 0047-3863) **6640**
Labores del Hogar Colleccion *see* Labores del Hogar **6640**
Labores del Hogar Colleccion *see* Punto de Cruz **6641**
Laborjournal (DEU ISSN 1612-8354) **5909**
• LaborLetter (USA) **4597**
LaborManagement Aktuell *see* Trillium-Report **5724**
LaborPraxis (DEU ISSN 0344-1733) **5909**
† ➤ Labor's Heritage (USA ISSN 1041-5904) **8970**
Laborscope (CHE ISSN 1422-8165) **5909**
▼ • Laborstat Huelva (ESP ISSN 1988-7329) **1693**
Laborwatch (USA ISSN 1084-2160) **1693**
Laborwelt (DEU ISSN 1611-0854) **768**
▼ • Laboscope (FRA ISSN 1960-8454) **5659**
• ➤ Labour/Travail (CAN ISSN 0700-3862) **1693**
• ➤ Labour (GBR ISSN 1121-7081) **1693**
Labour and Development (IND ISSN 0973-0419) **1693**
• Labour & Employment (Year) (GBR ISSN 1750-9920) **1693**
• Labour and Employment Benefits (Year) (GBR ISSN 1744-6465) **1693**
Labour and Industrial Cases (IND) **1693**
Labour and Industrial Law Reporter (IND) **1693**
• ➤ Labour & Industry (AUS ISSN 1030-1763) **1694**
• ➤ Labour and Management in Development (AUS) **1694**
† Labour and Social Affairs and National Insurance/'Avoda Ur'waha Uvittu-ah L'ummi (ISR) **8970**
Labour and Social Security Law Department. Journal *see* Departamento do Direito do Trabalho e da Seguridade Social. Revista **1675**
Labour & Trade Union Review (GBR ISSN 0953-3494) **4597**
Labour Arbitration (CAN ISSN 0821-2635) **4711**
Labour Arbitration (CAN ISSN 1718-8253) **4711**
• Labour Arbitration Cases (CAN ISSN 0023-690X) **1694**
• Labour Arbitration Xpress (CAN ISSN 1717-4740) **1694**
Labour Arbitration Yearbook (CAN ISSN 1183-3068) **4834**
Labour Bulletin (IND) **1694**
• ➤ Labour, Capital and Society/Travail, Capital et Societe (CAN ISSN 0706-1706) **1601**
Labour Chronicle (IND) **1694**
Labour Code of Pakistan (PAK) **1694**
Labour Comment (Cork) (IRL ISSN 0790-1712) **7150**
Labour Cost Index *see* New Zealand. Statistics New Zealand. Labour Cost Index (All Labour Costs) **1700**
• ➤ Labour Economics (NLD ISSN 0927-5371) **1694**
Labour Economics and Labor Relations *see* Laodong Jingji yu Laodong Guanxi **1695**
Labour Education (CHE ISSN 0378-5467) **1694**
• Labour File (IND ISSN 0972-673X) **1694**
Labour Force and Migration Survey (CYP) **7311**
Labour Force, Australia *see* Australia. Bureau of Statistics. Labour Force, Australia (Online) **1207**
Labour Force, Australia - Seasonal Factors *see* Australia. Bureau of Statistics. Labour Force, Australia - Seasonal Factors **1207**
Labour Force Data, Historical, Revised Series (CAN ISSN 1719-8313) **1694**
• Labour Force Historical Review (CAN ISSN 1480-5502) **1694**
Labour Force Situation in Indonesia: Preliminary Figures/Keadaan Angakatan Kerja de Indonesia: Angka Sementara (IDN) **1248**
Labour Force Statistics *see* Saskatchewan Labour Force Statistics **1262**
• Labour Force Statistics (CAN ISSN 1184-9258) **1248**
Labour Force Statistics *see* O E C D Labour Force Statistics **1257**
• Labour Force Statistics. Aboriginal Population Off-Reserve Package (CAN ISSN 1910-2887) **6700**
Labour Force Survey (BLZ) **1248**

Title

▼ new title † ceased • electronic media ➤ refereed

Title

10548 LANDESVERBAND GROSS- UND AUSSENHANDEL, VERTRIEB UND ULRICH'S PERIODICALS

Landesverband Gross- und Aussenhandel, Vertrieb und Dienstleistungen Bayern e.V. Nachrichten *see* L G A D Nachrichten **1430**
Landesversicherungsanstalt Hessen. Nachrichten (DEU ISSN 0023-7922) **4512**
Landeswohlfahrtsverband Hessen Info *see* L W V Info **8053**
Landeszeitung (DEU) **3851**
Landeszentralbank in Hessen. Vierteljahresberichte (DEU) **1365**
• Landfall (NZL ISSN 0023-7930) **5223**
Landform Analysis *see* Uniwerstytet Slaski w Katowicach. Prace Naukowe. Landform Analysis **2799**
Die Landfrau (CHE ISSN 1421-170X) **8871**
Landfreund Plus (CHE) **133**
▼ Landgoed (NLD ISSN 1875-3752) **8728**
Landhaus Living (DEU ISSN 1614-8274) **5075**
Landing Zone (USA) **8784**
• Landings.com (USA) **64**
Landinspektoeren (DNK ISSN 0105-4570) **4018**
Landjugend (AUT ISSN 0023-7957) **2199**
Der Landkreis (DEU ISSN 0342-2259) **7451**
Der Landkreis (Bavarian State Edition) *see* Der Landkreis **7451**
Der Landkreis (Hessian State Edition) *see* Der Landkreis **7451**
Der Landkreis (Rheinland-Pfalz Edition) *see* Der Landkreis **7451**
Landkreises Birkenfeld. Heimatkalender (DEU ISSN 0174-4631) **4239**
Landline (AUS ISSN 0157-485X) **3450**
Landlines *see* Green Places News **443**
Landlines Tech (GBR ISSN 1470-3807) **3741**
Landlord *see* Landlord & Buy-to-Let Magazine **7598**
▼ • Landlord & Buy-to-Let Magazine (GBR ISSN 1757-7950) **7598**
Landlord & Tenant Factbook (GBR) **7598**
Landlord & Tenant Law Review (GBR ISSN 1365-8018) **7598**
Landlord & Tenant Reports (GBR ISSN 1463-4473) **7598**
Landlord & Tenant Review *see* Landlord & Tenant Law Review **7598**
• Landlord and Tenant Service (GBR) **7598**
• Landlord Law & Multi-Housing Report (USA ISSN 1934-5038) **4712**
• Landlord Tenant. California (USA ISSN 1932-975X) **7598**
• Landlord Tenant. Florida (USA ISSN 1933-0286) **7598**
• Landlord Tenant. Illinois (USA ISSN 1933-0308) **7598**
• Landlord Tenant Law Bulletin (USA ISSN 0271-5228) **7598**
Landlord - Tenant Monthly (USA) **7598**
• Landlord Tenant. New York (USA ISSN 1932-9776) **7598**
• Landlord Tenant. Ohio (USA ISSN 1932-9792) **7598**
• Landlord Tenant. Pennsylvania (USA ISSN 1932-9814) **7598**
• Landlord's 'Bottom Line' Bulletin (USA ISSN 1542-5010) **7598**
Landlust (DEU ISSN 1863-8074) **5075**
Landmacht (NLD ISSN 1572-1248) **6431**
Landman (USA ISSN 0457-088X) **6777**
▼ Landmandens Indkoebsbog (DNK ISSN 1902-844X) **133**
Landmark (Waukesha) (USA ISSN 0458-6972) **4301**
Landmark Briefs and Arguments of the Supreme Court of the United States: Constitutional Law (USA ISSN 0194-4010) **4850**
Landmark Decisions (USA ISSN 1933-5490) **4850**
Landmark Litigation Report (USA) **4712**
Landmarks Observer (USA ISSN 0272-1384) **4301**
Landmaschinen - Handwerk - Handel (AUT ISSN 0023-7973) **212**
Landoekonomisk Oversigt *see* Dansk Landbrug i Tal **179**
• Land&Liv (DNK ISSN 1901-9300) **133**
• Landolt-Boernstein: Numerical Data and Functional Relationships in Science and Technology. Group I, Elementary Particles, Nuclei and Atoms/Landolt-Boernstein Numerical Data and Functional Relationships in Science and Technology. New Series (USA ISSN 1615-1844) **7068**
• Landolt-Boernstein: Numerical Data and Functional Relationships in Science and Technology. Group II, Molecules and Radicals (USA ISSN 1615-1852) **7068**
• Landolt-Boernstein: Numerical Data and Functional Relationships in Science and Technology. Group III, Condensed Matter (USA ISSN 1615-1925) **7024**
• Landolt-Boernstein: Numerical Data and Functional Relationships in Science and Technology. Group IV, Physical Chemistry (USA ISSN 1615-2018) **8430**
Landolt-Boernstein Numerical Data and Functional Relationships in Science and Technology. New Series *see* Landolt-Boernstein: Numerical Data and Functional Relationships in Science and Technology. Group I, Elementary Particles, Nuclei and Atoms **7068**
Landowner (USA ISSN 0163-951X) **7598**
Die Landpost (DEU ISSN 0023-8007) **133**
Lands and People (CAN ISSN 1703-8553) **3450**
Lands and People Chronicle *see* Lands and People **3450**
Landsbygdens Folk (FIN ISSN 0023-8015) **133**
• Landsbynyt (DNK ISSN 0907-4791) **8118**
• Landscan (NZL ISSN 1174-2380) **2617**
Landscape (AUS ISSN 0815-4465) **2617**
• The Landscape (CAN ISSN 1912-2667) **3547**
Landscape (GBR ISSN 1742-2914) **448**
• Landscape and Ecological Engineering (JPN ISSN 1860-1871) **3450**
• Landscape & Hardscape Construction (USA ISSN 1945-0583) **3741**
• Landscape & Irrigation (USA ISSN 0745-3795) **241**
• ➤ Landscape and Urban Planning (NLD ISSN 0169-2046) **2617**
Landscape Architect & Specifier News (USA ISSN 1060-9962) **3741**
Landscape Architecture *see* Fengjing Yuanlin **3729**
Landscape Architecture (USA ISSN 0023-8031) **448**
Landscape Architecture and Town Planning in the Netherlands *see* Landschappsarchitectuur en Stedebouw in Nederland **448**
• Landscape Architecture Australia (AUS ISSN 1833-4814) **3741**
• Landscape Architecture News Digest (USA ISSN 0023-754X) **448**
Landscape Australia *see* Landscape Architecture Australia **3741**
Landscape Australia. Directory (Year) *see* Landscape Architecture Australia **3741**
Landscape Construction *see* Landscape & Hardscape Construction **3741**
Landscape Contractor (USA ISSN 0194-7257) **3741**
Landscape Contractor News (USA) **3741**
Landscape Design *see* Jingguan Sheji **3740**
Landscape Design *see* Green Places **443**
• Landscape Design / Build (USA ISSN 1544-872X) **3741**
Landscape Design Trust Monographs *see* L D T Monographs **448**
• ➤ Landscape Ecology (NLD ISSN 0921-2973) **3450**
➤ Landscape History (GBR ISSN 0143-3768) **4150**
➤ Landscape Issues (GBR ISSN 0265-9786) **448**
• ➤ Landscape Journal (USA ISSN 0277-2426) **448**
• Landscape Management (USA ISSN 0894-1254) **3741**
Landscape New Zealand (NZL ISSN 1173-7476) **3741**
▼ • ➤ Landscape Online (DEU ISSN 1865-1542) **3450**
• ➤ Landscape Research (GBR ISSN 0142-6397) **448**
Landscape Review (NZL ISSN 1173-3853) **3741**
Landscape SA (ZAF ISSN 1818-4715) **3741**
• Landscape Series (NLD ISSN 1572-7742) **3741**
Landscape Solutions *see* Better Homes and Gardens Landscape Solutions **3724**
Landscape South Africa *see* Landscape SA **3741**
Landscape Superintendent and Maintenance Professional (USA ISSN 1547-2396) **3741**
Landscape Systems *see* Indian Journal of Landscape Systems and Ecological Studies **3439**
• Landscape Today (SGP) **3741**
Landscape Trades (CAN ISSN 0225-6398) **3741**
Landscaper (USA) **4419**
Landscapes/Paysages (CAN ISSN 1492-9600) **448**
➤ Landscapes (GBR ISSN 1466-2035) **403**
Landscaping & Groundskeeping Journal (CAN ISSN 1492-3440) **448**
Landscaping Homes & Gardens (USA) **3742**
Landschaft Bauen und Gestalten (DEU ISSN 1432-7953) **3742**
Landschaften in Deutschland (AUT) **4018**
Landschaftsverband Rheinland. Beitraege zur Industrie- und Sozialgeschichte (DEU) **4239**
Landschaftsverband Rheinland Report *see* L V R - Report **3851**
Landschaftsverband Rheinland. Rheinisches Archiv- und Museumsamt. Archivhefte (DEU) **4239**
Landschaftsverband Westfalen-Lippe. Archivamt fuer Westfalen. Veroeffentlichungen (DEU ISSN 0942-6981) **4239**
Landschaftsverband Westfalen-Lippe. Mitteilungen des Landesjugendamtes *see* Jugendhilfe Aktuell **8052**
Landschap (NLD ISSN 0169-6300) **3450**
Landschappelijk (NLD ISSN 1871-3963) **2617**
Landschappsarchitectuur en Stedebouw in Nederland/Landscape Architecture and Town Planning in the Netherlands (NLD ISSN 1569-5689) **448**
Landscope *see* Landscape **2617**
Der Landser (DEU) **5411**
▼ Der Landser. Fliegergeschichten aus dem Zweiten Weltkrieg (DEU) **5411**
Der Landser Grossband (DEU) **5411**
Der Landser Praesentiert SOS Schiffsschicksale auf den Meeren der Welt (DEU) **5411**
▼ • ➤ Landshaft (USA ISSN 1940-0837) **6931**
Landshaftnyi Dizain (RUS) **4979**
• Landshagir/Statistical Yearbook of Iceland (ISL ISSN 1017-6683) **8385**
Landskab (DNK ISSN 0023-8066) **3742**
Landslaget for Norskundervisning. Skriftserie (NOR ISSN 0805-6048) **5138**
▼ Landslide (USA ISSN 1942-7239) **4712**
Landslide News *see* Kokusai Jisuberi Nyusu Reta **2786**
• ➤ Landslides (DEU ISSN 1612-510X) **2786**
Landsorganisationen i Danmark Dokumentation *see* L O-Dokumentation **4597**
Landsorganisationen i Danmark. Dokumentation *see* L O-Dokumentation **4597**
Landsorganisationen i Sverige Tidningen *see* L O-Tidningen **4597**
Landstingens Ekonomi *see* Ekonomirapporten **1921**
Landstingsvaerlden *see* Dagens Samhaelle **7491**
Landsudvalget for Svin. Aarsberetning/National Committee for Pig Breeding, Health and Production. Annual Report (DNK ISSN 0904-3640) **292**
• Landsudvalget for Svin. Afdelingen for Avl og Opformering. Aarsberetning (DNK ISSN 1395-3192) **292**
Landtechnik (Muenster) (DEU ISSN 0023-8082) **241**
Landtechnische Schriftenreihe (AUT) **133**
Landun/Blue Shield (CHN ISSN 1004-6828) **4712**
➤ Landwards (GBR ISSN 1363-8300) **133**
Landwehr's Who's Who in America's Restaurants *see* Who's Who in America's Restaurants **3122**
Landwerk (NLD ISSN 1567-1844) **241**
Die Landwirtschaft (AUT ISSN 0047-4010) **133**
Landwirtschaft Aktuell (LUX) **133**
Landwirtschaft ohne Pflug (DEU ISSN 1436-0306) **241**
Landwirtschaft und Umwelt (DEU ISSN 0176-7909) **133**
Landwirtschaftliche Blaetter (AUT) **133**
Landwirtschaftliche Mitteilungen (AUT ISSN 1010-1330) **133**
Landwirtschaftliche Zeitschrift Rheinland *see* L Z Rheinland **132**
Landwirtschaftliches Wochenblatt (DEU ISSN 0940-967X) **133**
Landwirtschaftliches Wochenblatt Westfalen-Lippe: Ausgabe A (DEU ISSN 0342-765X) **133**
Landwirtschafts Zeitung (AUT) **134**
Landwirtschaftsblatt Weser-Ems *see* Land und Forst. Ausgabe Weser-Ems **132**
Landworker (GBR) **4598**
Landworks Hot Line (USA) **3742**
• Lane County Labor Trends (USA) **1695**
• The Lane Report (USA ISSN 1063-925X) **1143**
Laneko Lesioen Estatistikak (Year)/Estadisticas de la Lesiones Profesionales (ESP) **6690**
Lang Classical Studies (USA ISSN 0891-4087) **2236**
Lang Van (CAN ISSN 0832-1922) **3547**
Le Langage et l'Homme (BEL ISSN 0458-7251) **5138**
Langage & Societe (FRA ISSN 0181-4095) **5139**
• ➤ Langages (FRA ISSN 0458-726X) **5139**
† Lange Smart Charts: Pathology (USA ISSN 1529-7780) **8970**
Lange Smart Charts: Pharmacology (USA ISSN 1542-6866) **6858**
Lange Smart Charts: Physiology (USA ISSN 1547-4100) **5660**
▼ • Lange U S M L E Road Map: Genetics (United States Medical Licensing Examination) (USA ISSN 1940-008X) **5660**
• ➤ Langenbecks Archives of Surgery (DEU ISSN 1435-2443) **6251**
• Lange's Handbook of Chemistry (USA ISSN 0748-4585) **2071**
• Langfang Shifan Xueyuan Xuebao (Shehui Kexue Ban)/Langfang Teachers College. Journal (Social Sciences Edition) (CHN ISSN 1674-3210) **7982**
• Langfang Shifan Xueyuan Xuebao (Ziran Kexue Ban)/Langfang Teachers College. Journal (Natural Science Edition) (CHN ISSN 1674-3229) **7982**
Langfang Shifan Xueyuan Xuebao/Langfang Teachers College. Journal *see* Langfang Shifan Xueyuan Xuebao (Shehui Kexue Ban) **7982**
Langfang Teachers College. Journal (Natural Science Edition) *see* Langfang Shifan Xueyuan Xuebao (Ziran Kexue Ban) **7982**
Langfang Teachers College. Journal (Social Sciences Edition) *see* Langfang Shifan Xueyuan Xuebao (Shehui Kexue Ban) **7982**
Der Langfristige Kredit *see* Immobilien und Finanzierung **1352**
Langgwij Matters (USA) **5203**
Langhaars-Nyt (DNK ISSN 0107-8585) **6810**
Langley Advance *see* AdvanceNews **3805**
• Langley Times (CAN ISSN 0711-7450) **3812**
• ➤ Langmuir (USA ISSN 0743-7463) **2138**
Langspielplatten Magazin *see* L P Magazin **6584**
• Langston Hughes Review (USA ISSN 0737-0555) **5320**
• ➤ Language (Washington) (USA ISSN 0097-8507) **5139**
• ➤ Language Acquisition (USA ISSN 1048-9223) **5139**
Language Acquisition and Language Disorders (NLD ISSN 0925-0123) **5139**
▼ • ➤ Language and Cognition (DEU ISSN 1866-9808) **5139**
• ➤ Language and Cognitive Processes (GBR ISSN 0169-0965) **5139**
• ➤ Language & Communication (GBR ISSN 0271-5309) **5139**
• Language and Computers (NLD ISSN 0921-5034) **5203**
Language and Cultural Contact *see* Sprog og Kulturmoede **5178**
Language and Culture *see* Gengo to Bunka (Nishinomiya) **5121**
Language and Culture *see* Gengo to Bunka **5121**
Language and Dialect Studies in East Africa (DEU ISSN 1438-485X) **5139**
• ➤ Language and Education (GBR ISSN 0950-0782) **5139**
• Language & Healthcare Newsletter (USA) **5139**
• ➤ Language and History (GBR ISSN 1759-7536) **5139**
Language and Ideology (USA) **7150**
• ➤ Language and Intercultural Communication (GBR ISSN 1470-8477) **5139**
Language and Learning Across the Disciplines *see* Across the Disciplines **5089**
Language and Learning for Human Service Professions Monograph Series (USA) **3069**
Language and Linguistics *see* Yuyan Ji Yuyangxue **5198**
▼ • ➤ Language and Linguistics Compass (GBR ISSN 1749-818X) **5139**
• Language & Literacy (CAN ISSN 1496-0974) **5320**
Language and Literacy Series (USA ISSN 1556-3073) **3069**
Language and Literature *see* Ezik i Literatura **5118**
• ➤ Language and Literature (GBR ISSN 0963-9470) **5139**
Language & literature Journal *see* L L Journal **5138**
Language and Literature Learning *see* Yuwen Xuexi **5197**
• ➤ Language and Speech (GBR ISSN 0023-8309) **5139**
Language and Style (USA ISSN 0023-8317) **5140**
• ➤ Language Arts (USA ISSN 0360-9170) **3070**
Language Arts Journal of Michigan (USA ISSN 1044-6702) **5140**
• ➤ Language Assessment Quarterly (USA ISSN 1543-4303) **5140**
• ➤ Language@Internet (DEU ISSN 1860-2029) **5140**
• ➤ Language at Work (DNK ISSN 1902-0465) **5140**
• ➤ Language Awareness (GBR ISSN 0965-8416) **5140**
Language Contact in Africa *see* Sprachkontakt in Afrika **8990**
Language, Context and Cognition (DEU ISSN 1866-8313) **5140**
Language, Culture and Cognition (GBR) **5140**
• ➤ Language, Culture and Curriculum (GBR ISSN 0790-8318) **5140**
• ➤ Language, Culture and Society (AUS ISSN 1327-774X) **5140**
• Language Design (ESP ISSN 1139-4218) **5140**
▼ • ➤ Language Documentation & Conservation (USA ISSN 1934-5275) **5140**
The Language Educator (USA ISSN 1558-6219) **5140**
▼ Language Faculty and Beyond (NLD ISSN 1877-6531) **5140**
Language for Special Purposes and Professional Communication *see* L S P and Professional Communication **5138**
Language for Special Purposes and Professional Communication *see* L S P and Professional Communication **5138**
➤ Language Forum (IND ISSN 0253-9071) **5140**
• Language in India (USA ISSN 1930-2940) **5140**
• Language in Performance (DEU ISSN 0939-9399) **5140**
Language in Social Life (GBR) **5140**
• ➤ Language in Society (GBR ISSN 0047-4045) **5140**
Language International World Directory (NLD ISSN 1383-7591) **5140**
Language Journal *see* Dil Dergisi **5112**
Language Learner *see* N A B E News **2888**
• ➤ Language Learning (USA ISSN 0023-8333) **5141**
• Language Learning and Development (USA ISSN 1547-5441) **5141**
Language Learning and Language Teaching (NLD ISSN 1569-9471) **5141**
• ➤ Language Learning & Technology (USA ISSN 1094-3501) **5203**
• ➤ Language Learning Journal (GBR ISSN 0957-1736) **5141**
Language, Literacy, and Learning (USA ISSN 1537-3703) **5141**
▼ • The Language Loofah (USA ISSN 1949-9027) **1852**
Language Magazine (USA ISSN 1542-5576) **5141**
• ➤ Language Matters (ZAF ISSN 1022-8195) **5141**
▼ • The Language of Science (ITA ISSN 1971-1352) **7878**
• Language Perils (USA ISSN 1533-8444) **4512**
• Language Policy (NLD ISSN 1568-4555) **5141**
Language, Power and Social Process (DEU ISSN 1861-4175) **8118**
• ➤ Language Problems and Language Planning (NLD ISSN 0272-2690) **5141**
• ➤ Language Research/Eohag Yeon'gu (KOR ISSN 0254-4474) **5141**
• ➤ Language Resources and Evaluation (NLD ISSN 1574-020X) **4485**
• Language Rights (CAN ISSN 1485-6212) **7451**
Language Rights. Annual Report (CAN ISSN 1719-7287) **4712**
• ➤ Language Sciences (GBR ISSN 0388-0001) **5141**
Language, Speech, and Communication (USA) **5141**
• ➤ Language, Speech and Hearing Services in Schools (USA ISSN 0161-1461) **6082**
Language Studies/Gengo Sentau Kouhou (JPN ISSN 0919-3006) **5141**

• The Language Teacher (JPN ISSN 0289-7938) **5141**
Language Teacher's Friend (Public Edition) *see* Yuwen Jiaoxue yu Yanjiu (Dazhong Ban) **5197**
Language Teacher's Friend (Student Edition) *see* Yuwen Jiaoxue yu Yanjiu (Xuesheng Ban) **5197**
Language Teacher's Friend (Teacher's Edition) *see* Yuwen Jiaoxue yu Yanjiu (Jiaoshi Ban) **5197**
• ➤ Language Teaching (GBR ISSN 0261-4448) **5201**
Language Teaching and Linguistic Studies *see* Yuyan Jiaoxue yu Yanjiu **5198**
Language Teaching at Berkeley *see* Berkeley Language Center Newsletter **5099**
• ➤ Language Teaching Research (GBR ISSN 1362-1688) **5141**
• ➤ Language Testing (GBR ISSN 0265-5322) **5141**
Language Testing and Evaluation (DEU ISSN 1612-815X) **5142**
Language Testing Update *see* L T U **8970**
• Language Today (GBR) **5142**
• Language Travel Magazine (GBR ISSN 1466-7428) **5142**
Language Update *see* L' Actualite Langagiere **5091**
• ➤ Language Variation and Change (GBR ISSN 0954-3945) **5142**
Language Workbook Series (GBR) **5142**
• Languages (AUS ISSN 1440-0529) **2882**
• Languages in Contrast (NLD ISSN 1387-6759) **5142**
Languages Learning Area Manual *see* Languages **2882**
Languages of the World (DEU ISSN 0940-0788) **5142**
➤ Languages Victoria (AUS ISSN 1328-7621) **5142**
Langue et Cultures (CHE ISSN 0085-2678) **5142**
• ➤ Langue Francaise (FRA ISSN 0023-8368) **5142**
Langue Francaise en Amerique du Nord *see* Collection Langue Francaise en Amerique du Nord **5002**
Langues Africaines *see* African Languages **5091**
Langues du Cameroun (CMR) **5142**
• Langues et Cite (FRA ISSN 1772-757X) **5142**
➤ Langues et Civilisations a Tradition Orale (BEL ISSN 0240-2041) **5142**
➤ Langues et Cultures Africaines (BEL ISSN 0755-9305) **5142**
➤ Langues et Cultures du Pacifique (BEL ISSN 0750-2036) **5142**
Langues et Langage (FRA ISSN 1158-629X) **5142**
Langues et Linguistique (CAN ISSN 0226-7144) **5142**
Langues et Litteratures (MAR ISSN 0851-0881) **5142**
➤ Langues et Societes d'Amerique Traditionnelle (BEL ISSN 1142-7019) **5142**
Langues Modernes (FRA ISSN 0023-8376) **5142**
Les Langues Neo-latines (FRA ISSN 0184-7570) **5142**
Lanioturdus (NAM ISSN 1023-8484) **909**
Lanius (DEU ISSN 0176-2532) **909**
Lanka Guardian (LKA) **5223**
Lankesteriana (CRI ISSN 1409-3871) **799**
LANline (DEU ISSN 0942-4172) **2500**
➤ Lannan Series (USA) **5320**
• Lanqiu/Basketball (CHN ISSN 1000-3460) **8237**
Lanqiu Julebu/Basketball Club (CHN ISSN 1673-1115) **8237**
Lansi - Savo (FIN ISSN 0356-1623) **3839**
Lansi - Suomi (FIN ISSN 0782-6419) **3839**
Lansing Labor News (USA ISSN 0023-8384) **4598**
Lansky: Bibliotheksrechtliche Vorschriften (DEU ISSN 0175-6524) **5024**
Lantbruksmagasinet (SWE ISSN 1402-0645) **134**
Lantbrukspraktika (SWE ISSN 0282-4132) **134**
• Lantern (ZAF ISSN 0023-8422) **2882**
Il Lanternino (ITA ISSN 0393-7445) **5660**
Lantliv (SWE ISSN 1404-4412) **5075**
Lantliv Sommarmat *see* Lantliv **5075**
Lantmaestaren (SWE ISSN 0023-8430) **134**
Lantmaetaren (SWE) **4018**
Lantmaetarnytt *see* Lantmaetaren **4018**
Lantmaeteritidskriften *see* Lantmaetaren **4018**
Lantmannen (SWE ISSN 0023-8449) **134**
Lanyang Yizhi/Kavalan Journal of Medicine (TWN ISSN 1819-8430) **5660**
Lanyungang Techincal College. Journal *see* Lianyungang Zhiye Jishu Xueyuan Xuebao **2883**
Lanzhou Commercial College. Journal *see* Lanzhou Shangxueyuan Xuebao **1143**
• Lanzhou Daxue Xuebao (Shehui Kexue Ban)/Lanzhou University. Journal (Social Sciences) (CHN ISSN 1000-2804) **7982**
• Lanzhou Daxue Xuebao (Ziran Kexue Ban)/Lanzhou University. Journal (Natural Sciences) (CHN ISSN 0455-2059) **7878**
• Lanzhou Gongye Gaodeng Zhuanke Xuexiao Xuebao/Lanzhou Polytechnic College. Journal (CHN ISSN 1009-2269) **7879**
Lanzhou Institute of Education. Journal *see* Lanzhou Jiaoyu Xueyuan Xuebao **2882**
• Lanzhou Jiaoyu Xueyuan Xuebao/Lanzhou Institute of Education. Journal (CHN ISSN 1008-5823) **2882**
• Lanzhou Ligong Daxue Xuebao/Lanzhou University of Technology. Journal (CHN ISSN 1673-5196) **7879**
Lanzhou Medical College. Journal *see* Lanzhou Yixueyuan Xuebao **5660**
Lanzhou Petrochemical College of Technology. Journal *see* Lanzhou Shihua Zhiye Jishu Xueyuan Xuebao **6777**
Lanzhou Polytechnic College. Journal *see* Lanzhou Gongye Gaodeng Zhuanke Xuexiao Xuebao **7879**
• Lanzhou Shangxueyuan Xuebao/Lanzhou Commercial College. Journal (CHN ISSN 1004-5465) **1143**
• Lanzhou Shihua Zhiye Jishu Xueyuan Xuebao/Lanzhou Petrochemical College of Technology. Journal (CHN ISSN 1671-4067) **6777**
Lanzhou University. Journal (Natural Sciences) *see* Lanzhou Daxue Xuebao (Ziran Kexue Ban) **7878**
Lanzhou University. Journal (Social Sciences) *see* Lanzhou Daxue Xuebao (Shehui Kexue Ban) **7982**
Lanzhou University of Technology. Journal *see* Lanzhou Ligong Daxue Xuebao **7879**
• Lanzhou Yixueyuan Xuebao/Lanzhou Medical College. Journal (CHN ISSN 1000-2812) **5660**
Lao Dong/Labor (Vientiane) (LAO) **4598**
• Lao Dong/Labor (Hanoi) (VNM ISSN 0866-7950) **1695**
Lao Youth *see* Noum Lao **2163**
Laodong Jingji yu Laodong Guanxi/Labour Economics and Labor Relations (CHN ISSN 1671-346X) **1695**
Laodong Yixue/Journal of Labour Medicine *see* Huanjing yu Zhiye Yixue **5630**
Laois Nationalist (IRL ISSN 1649-6477) **3893**
The Laois Voice (IRL ISSN 1649-8941) **3893**
Laonian Bolan/The Old Age Vision (CHN ISSN 1671-9328) **4050**
Laonian Jiaoyu/Education for the Elderly (CHN) **2943**
Laonian Shenghuo Bao (CHN) **4050**
• Laonianbao/Elderly Gazette (CHN) **4050**
• Laoren Bao (CHN) **4050**
• Laoren Shijie/World of the Elderly (CHN ISSN 1003-4846) **4050**
Laoren Tiandi/Elderly World (CHN ISSN 1002-4212) **4050**
Laos (LAO) **8728**
Laos Handbook (GBR ISSN 1363-7452) **8728**
Laotongzhi zhi You/Friend of Old Comrades (CHN ISSN 1002-8188) **4050**
Laparoscopy and S L S Report *see* Laparoscopy Today **6251**
Laparoscopy Today (USA ISSN 1553-7080) **6251**
Lapeer Legacy (USA ISSN 8756-7067) **3773**
▼ • ➤ Lapham's Quarterly (USA ISSN 1935-7494) **4151**
Lapidary Journal *see* Lapidary Journal Jewelry Artist **4568**
• Lapidary Journal Jewelry Artist (USA ISSN 1936-5942) **4568**
Lapin Kansa (FIN ISSN 0359-6753) **3839**
Lapin Yliopisto. Acta Universitatis Lapponiensis (FIN ISSN 0788-7604) **7879**
† Lapinpin (FRA ISSN 1956-2713) **8970**
• Lapis (Online Edition) (USA) **4463**
Lapiz (ESP ISSN 0212-1700) **502**
Lapologa (BWA ISSN 1812-8831) **3803**
Laporan Ketua Odit Negara. Kerajaan Persekutuan (MYS) **1496**
Laporan M A R D I *see* M A R D I Report **135**
Lappeenrannan Teknillinen Korkeakoulu. Asiantuntijaluettelo *see* Lappeenrannan Teknillinen Yliopisto. Asiantuntijaluettelo **2992**
Lappeenrannan Teknillinen Korkeakoulu. Energiatekniikan Osasto. D. Julkaisu *see* Lappeenrannan Teknillinen Yliopisto. Energia- ja Ymparistotekniikan Osasto. D. Julkaisu **3208**
Lappeenrannan Teknillinen Korkeakoulu. Koulutus- ja Kehittamiskeskus. Julkaisu *see* Lappeenrannan Teknillinen Yliopisto. Koulutus- ja Kehittamiskeskus. Julkaisu **2992**
Lappeenrannan Teknillinen Korkeakoulu. Sahkotekniikan Osasto. Opetusmoniste *see* Lappeenrannan Teknillinen Yliopisto. Sahkotekniikan Osasto. Opetusmoniste **3323**
Lappeenrannan Teknillinen Korkeakoulu. Tietotekniikan Osasto. Opetusmoniste *see* Lappeenranta University of Technology. Department of Information Technology. Lecture Notes **2473**
Lappeenrannan Teknillinen Korkeakoulu. Tietotekniikan Osasto. Tutkimusraportti *see* Lappeenranta University of Technology. Department of Information Technology. Research Report **2473**
Lappeenrannan Teknillinen Korkeakoulu. Tuotantotalouden Osasto. Selvitys *see* Lappeenranta University of Technology. Department of Industrial Engineering and Management. Report **3370**
Lappeenrannan Teknillinen Yliopisto. Asiantuntijaluettelo (FIN ISSN 1459-3203) **2992**
Lappeenrannan Teknillinen Yliopisto. Energia- ja Ymparistotekniikan Osasto. C. Opetusmoniste/Lappeenranta University of Technology. Department of Energy and Environmental Technology. C. Lecture Notes (FIN ISSN 1459-2649) **3208**
Lappeenrannan Teknillinen Yliopisto. Energia- ja Ymparistotekniikan Osasto. D. Julkaisu/Lappeenranta University of Technology. Department of Energy and Environmental Technology. D. Publication (FIN ISSN 1459-2657) **3208**
Lappeenrannan Teknillinen Yliopisto. Energia- ja Ymparistotekniikan Osasto. Tutkimusraportti A/Lappeenranta University of Technology. Department of Energy Technology. Research Report A (FIN ISSN 0785-823X) **3208**
Lappeenrannan Teknillinen Yliopisto. Energia- ja Ymparistotekniikan Osasto. Tutkimusraportti B/Lappeenranta University of Technology. Department of Energy and Environmental Technology. Research Report B (FIN ISSN 1459-2630) **3250**
Lappeenrannan Teknillinen Yliopisto. Kauppatieteiden Kandidaatin ja Maisterin Tutkinnot. Opinto-Opas (FIN ISSN 1795-8342) **2992**
Lappeenrannan Teknillinen Yliopisto. Kauppatieteiden Maisterin Tutkinto. Opinto-Opas *see* Lappeenrannan Teknillinen Yliopisto. Kauppatieteiden Kandidaatin ja Maisterin Tutkinnot. Opinto-Opas **2992**
Lappeenrannan Teknillinen Yliopisto. Kauppatieteiden Osasto. Opetusmoniste/ Lappeenranta University of Technology. Department of Business Administration. Lecture Notes (FIN ISSN 1459-2622) **1143**
Lappeenrannan Teknillinen Yliopisto. Kauppatieteiden Osasto. Raportti/Lappeenranta University of Technology. Department of Business Administration. Report (FIN ISSN 1459-2746) **1143**
Lappeenrannan Teknillinen Yliopisto. Kauppatieteiden Osasto. Tutkimusraportti/ Lappeenranta University of Technology. Department of Business Administration. Research Report (FIN ISSN 1459-286X) **1143**
Lappeenrannan Teknillinen Yliopisto. Kemiantekniikan Osasto. Julkaisu/Lappeenranta University of Technology. Department of Chemical Technology. Report (FIN ISSN 1459-2878) **2071**
Lappeenrannan Teknillinen Yliopisto. Kemiantekniikan Osasto. Opetusmoniste (FIN ISSN 1459-2886) **2071**
Lappeenrannan Teknillinen Yliopisto. Konetekniikan Osasto. Opetusmoniste/Lappeenranta University of Technology. Department of Mechanical Engineering. Lecture Notes (FIN ISSN 1459-2916) **2549**
Lappeenrannan Teknillinen Yliopisto. Konetekniikan Osasto. Raportti/Lappeenranta University of Technology. Department of Mechanical Engineering. Report (FIN ISSN 1459-2924) **3387**
Lappeenrannan Teknillinen Yliopisto. Konetekniikan Osasto. Tutkimusraportti/Lappeenranta University of Technology. Department of Mechanical Engineering. Research Report (FIN ISSN 1459-2932) **3387**
Lappeenrannan Teknillinen Yliopisto. Konetekniiken Osasto. Kasikirja/Lappeenranta University of Technology. Mechanical Engineering. Manual (FIN ISSN 1459-2908) **2549**
Lappeenrannan Teknillinen Yliopisto. Koulutus- ja Kehittamiskeskus. Julkaisu/Lappeenranta University of Technology. Centre for Training and Development. Publication (FIN ISSN 1459-3025) **2992**
Lappeenrannan Teknillinen Yliopisto. Sahkotekniikan Osasto. Opetusmoniste/Lappeenranta University of Technology. Department of Electrical Engineering. Lecture Notes (FIN ISSN 1459-3114) **3323**
Lappeenrannan Teknillinen Yliopisto. Sahkotekniikan Osasto. Tutkimusraportti/Lappeenranta University of Technology. Department of Electrical Engineering. Research Report (FIN ISSN 1459-3122) **3323**
Lappeenrannan Teknillinen Yliopisto. Tietotekniikan Osasto. Kasikirja/Lappeenranta University of Technology. Department of Information Technology. Manual (FIN ISSN 1459-3092) **2473**
Lappeenrannan Teknillinen Yliopisto. Tietotekniikan Osasto. Raportti (FIN ISSN 1459-3106) **2473**
Lappeenrannan Teknillinen Yliopisto. Tuotantotalouden Osasto. Opetusmoniste/ Lappeenranta University of Technology. Department of Industrial Engineering and Management Lecture Notes (FIN ISSN 1459-3157) **3369**
Lappeenrannan Teknillinen Yliopisto. Tuotantotalouden Osasto. Tutkimusraportti (FIN ISSN 1459-3173) **3370**
Lappeenranta University of Technology. Centre for Training and Development. Publication *see* Lappeenrannan Teknillinen Yliopisto. Koulutus- ja Kehittamiskeskus. Julkaisu **2992**
Lappeenranta University of Technology. Department of Business Administration. Lecture Notes *see* Lappeenrannan Teknillinen Yliopisto. Kauppatieteiden Osasto. Opetusmoniste **1143**
Lappeenranta University of Technology. Department of Business Administration. Report *see* Lappeenrannan Teknillinen Yliopisto. Kauppatieteiden Osasto. Raportti **1143**
Lappeenranta University of Technology. Department of Business Administration. Research Report *see* Lappeenrannan Teknillinen Yliopisto. Kauppatieteiden Osasto. Tutkimusraportti **1143**
Lappeenranta University of Technology. Department of Chemical Technology. Report *see* Lappeenrannan Teknillinen Yliopisto. Kemiantekniikan Osasto. Julkaisu **2071**
Lappeenranta University of Technology. Department of Electrical Engineering. Lecture Notes *see* Lappeenrannan Teknillinen Yliopisto. Sahkotekniikan Osasto. Opetusmoniste **3323**
Lappeenranta University of Technology. Department of Electrical Engineering. Research Report *see* Lappeenrannan Teknillinen Yliopisto. Sahkotekniikan Osasto. Tutkimusraportti **3323**
Lappeenranta University of Technology. Department of Energy and Environmental Technology. C. Lecture Notes *see* Lappeenrannan Teknillinen Yliopisto. Energia- ja Ymparistotekniikan Osasto. C. Opetusmoniste **3208**
Lappeenranta University of Technology. Department of Energy and Environmental Technology. D. Publication *see* Lappeenrannan Teknillinen Yliopisto. Energia- ja Ymparistotekniikan Osasto. D. Julkaisu **3208**
Lappeenranta University of Technology. Department of Energy and Environmental Technology. Research Report B *see* Lappeenrannan Teknillinen Yliopisto. Energia- ja Ymparistotekniikan Osasto. Tutkimusraportti B **3250**
Lappeenranta University of Technology. Department of Energy Technology. Research Report A *see* Lappeenrannan Teknillinen Yliopisto. Energia- ja Ymparistotekniikan Osasto. Tutkimusraportti A **3208**
Lappeenranta University of Technology. Department of Industrial Engineering and Management Lecture Notes *see* Lappeenrannan Teknillinen Yliopisto. Tuotantotalouden Osasto. Opetusmoniste **3369**
Lappeenranta University of Technology. Department of Industrial Engineering and Management. Report/Lappeenrannan Teknillinen Korkeakoulu. Tuotantotalouden Osasto. Selvitys (FIN ISSN 0784-7696) **3370**
Lappeenranta University of Technology. Department of Information Technology. Lecture Notes/Lappeenrannan Teknillinen Korkeakoulu. Tietotekniikan Osasto. Opetusmoniste (FIN ISSN 0783-8670) **2473**
Lappeenranta University of Technology. Department of Information Technology. Manual *see* Lappeenrannan Teknillinen Yliopisto. Tietotekniikan Osasto. Kasikirja **2473**
Lappeenranta University of Technology. Department of Information Technology. Research Report/Lappeenrannan Teknillinen Korkeakoulu. Tietotekniikan Osasto. Tutkimusraportti (FIN ISSN 0783-8069) **2473**
Lappeenranta University of Technology. Department of Mechanical Engineering. Lecture Notes *see* Lappeenrannan Teknillinen Yliopisto. Konetekniikan Osasto. Opetusmoniste **2549**
Lappeenranta University of Technology. Department of Mechanical Engineering. Report *see* Lappeenrannan Teknillinen Yliopisto. Konetekniikan Osasto. Raportti **3387**
Lappeenranta University of Technology. Department of Mechanical Engineering. Research Report *see* Lappeenrannan Teknillinen Yliopisto. Konetekniikan Osasto. Tutkimusraportti **3387**
Lappeenranta University of Technology. Mechanical Engineering. Manual *see* Lappeenrannan Teknillinen Yliopisto. Konetekniiken Osasto. Kasikirja **2549**
• Lappeenranta University of Technology. Northern Dimension Research Centre. Publication (FIN ISSN 1459-6679) **1143**
Lapphunden (SWE ISSN 0283-8958) **6810**
• Lapsen Elatus ja Huolto/Child Maintenance and Custody/Underhaall och Vaardnad av Barn (FIN ISSN 0789-8525) **8053**
Lapsen Maailma/Child's World (FIN ISSN 0786-0188) **8053**
• Laptop (USA ISSN 1535-4857) **2576**
• Laptop Newsletter (USA) **2576**
Lapuran Tahunan *see* Jabatan Mineral dan Geosains Malaysia. Lapuran Tahunan **2749**
Lara Croft Tomb Raider (GBR ISSN 1473-3625) **502**
Larcier Cassation (BEL ISSN 0778-8983) **4954**
The Larcom Review (USA ISSN 1523-0880) **5223**
• Lares (ITA ISSN 0023-8503) **3619**
Lares. Biblioteca (ITA ISSN 0409-6231) **3619**
• Large and Medium Scale Manufacturing and Electricity Industry Survey (ETH) **1248**
• ➤ Large Animal Veterinary Rounds (CAN) **8802**
• Large Display Report (USA ISSN 1937-9870) **2384**
Large Electric Machine and Hydraulic Turbine *see* Da Dianji Jishu **3376**
Large Encounters Singles (USA) **7943**
Large Format (DEU) **7329**
Large Marine Ecosystems (GBR ISSN 1570-0461) **2811**
• Large Scale Model Railroads (USA) **4338**
▼ Large-Scale Railroading (USA ISSN 1945-5461) **4338**
• Large-Volume Grower (USA) **292**
Larger Homes Collection (USA) **1020**

Title

DIRECTORY 2010 LAW REPORTS: APPEAL CASES 10551

El Latino San Diego (USA) 3547
• ➤ Latino Studies (GBR ISSN 1476-3435) 8118
Latino Stuff Review see L S R 5425
Latino Suave (USA ISSN 1941-6903) 3547
Latino University (USA) 3547
➤ Latino(a) Research Review (USA) 7982
Latinoamerica (MEX) 7982
Latinoamerican Rice Forum: F L A R Newsletter (COL) 241
† Latinoamericanistas en Europa (Year) (NLD ISSN 1384-5799) 8970
• LatinoLA (Los Angeles) (USA) 3547
Latinomineria (CHL ISSN 0717-0580) 6468
• Latinos On Wheels (USA) 3547
• LatinPetroleum Magazine (VEN) 6777
• Latinskaya Amerika (RUS ISSN 0044-748X) 4301
• LatinWorld (USA) 8728
Latissimus (GBR ISSN 0966-2235) 854
▼ Latitude Nord (FRA ISSN 1961-4128) 3841
• Latitudes (IDN ISSN 1411-7959) 8649
• Latitudes (Los Angeles) (USA ISSN 1544-743X) 5024
Latitudes & Attitudes (USA ISSN 1094-4435) 8277
Latitudes South see American Eagle Latitudes South 8782
Latium (ITA ISSN 0393-6813) 4239
Latium Vetus (ITA ISSN 1824-0577) 4151
Lato (ROM ISSN 1220-5982) 5320
➤ Latomus (BEL ISSN 0023-8856) 2237
Lattara (FRA ISSN 0996-6900) 403
• Il Latte (ITA ISSN 0392-6060) 266
Latter Day Saints Living see L D S Living 7738
LatterDayBride (USA ISSN 1936-1726) 5559
The Lattice see Elements (Ottawa) 6461
• Lattoneria (ITA) 1020
Latu ja Polku (FIN ISSN 0356-2395) 8321
• Latvia Food & Drink Report (GBR ISSN 1749-2807) 1144
Latvia Freight Transport Report (GBR ISSN 1752-5934) 8502
Latvian Academy of Sciences. Section A. Human and Social Sciences. Proceedings see Latvijas Zinatnu Akademijas Vetis. A Dala. Humanitaras Zinatnes 4463
• ➤ Latvian Academy of Sciences. Section B. Natural Sciences. Proceedings/Latvijas Zinatnu Akademijas Vetis. B Dala. Dabaszinatnes (POL ISSN 1407-009X) 7879
Latvian Collector (USA) 6896
Latvian Dimensions (USA ISSN 1062-9505) 3547
Latvian Journal of Chemistry see Latvijas Kimijas Zurnals 2071
Latvian Journal of Physics and Technical Sciences see Latvijas Fizikas un Tehnisko Zinatnu Zurnals 7024
Latvian News see Laiks 3547
Latviias Vestnesis (LVA ISSN 1407-0391) 3904
Latvija Amerika (CAN ISSN 0023-8902) 3547
Latvijas Arsts (LVA ISSN 1019-5068) 5660
• Latvijas Avize/The Rural Newspaper (LVA) 3904
Latvijas Ekonomist (LVA ISSN 1407-1010) 1144
• ➤ Latvijas Fizikas un Tehnisko Zinatnu Zurnals/Latvian Journal of Physics and Technical Sciences (POL ISSN 0868-8257) 7024
➤ Latvijas Kimijas Zurnals/Latvian Journal of Chemistry (LVA ISSN 0868-8249) 2071
Latvijas Prese (Year) (LVA ISSN 1407-0049) 629
Latvijas Preses Hronika (LVA ISSN 1017-7604) 629
➤ Latvijas Zinatnu Akademijas Vetis. A Dala. Humanitaras Zinatnes/Latvian Academy of Sciences. Section A. Human and Social Sciences. Proceedings (LVA ISSN 1407-0081) 4463
Latvijas Zinatnu Akademijas Vetis. B Dala. Dabaszinatnes see Latvian Academy of Sciences. Section B. Natural Sciences. Proceedings 7879
Latvju Maksla (USA ISSN 0362-7047) 502
Latvju Muzika (USA) 6584
Laubach Literacy International. Annual Report see ProLiteracy Worldwide. Annual Report 2945
Laubach LitScape (USA ISSN 1092-8367) 2943
Laubaner Tageblatt (DEU) 3851
Laudem (CAN ISSN 1914-4199) 6584
Laudem. Bulletin see Laudem 6584
Lauffener Bote (DEU) 3851
Lauffeuer (DEU ISSN 0179-2547) 3579
• Laufzeit (DEU ISSN 0863-3371) 6991
Laugh Factory (USA ISSN 0748-3090) 5224
Laugh-Makers (USA) 4338
Laugh While You Wait (AUS ISSN 1832-2999) 7383
Laughing Matters (USA ISSN 0731-1788) 7383
Lauku Avize see Latvijas Avize 3904
• Launch (USA) 6584
Launch Magazine (USA ISSN 1933-4087) 64
Launch Pad (USA) 28
• Launchspace (USA) 64
Laundry and Cleaning News (GBR ISSN 0142-9442) 2243
Laundry & Cleaning News International (GBR ISSN 0261-4421) 2243
Laundry and Cleaning News Textile Care Yearbook see L C N Textile Care Yearbook 2243
Launiana Minora (NLD ISSN 1875-449X) 6931
Laura (DEU ISSN 0948-8642) 8871
Laura Wohnen Kreativ (DEU ISSN 1862-0396) 4545
Laurel Messenger (USA ISSN 0023-8988) 3773
The Laurel of Phi Kappa Tau (USA ISSN 0023-8996) 2289
➤ The Laurel Review (USA ISSN 0023-9003) 5320
Laurence Reid Gas Conditioning Conference. Proceedings (USA ISSN 0887-6746) 6777
Laurentian University Magazine (CAN ISSN 1912-8177) 2289
The Laurentians (CAN) 8728
Laurentienne see Laurentian University Magazine 2289
Laurentius Flugschriften (DEU ISSN 0948-6550) 5024
Laurentius Sonderhefte (DEU ISSN 0930-9950) 5024
Laurier Campus (CAN ISSN 0700-5105) 2289
Laurier Centre for Military, Strategic and Disarmament Studies. Program Notes (CAN ISSN 1910-7587) 6431
Lauriston S. Taylor Lecture Series (USA ISSN 0277-9196) 7530
• Lauro (ESP ISSN 1133-0600) 6527
Laurus (VEN ISSN 1315-883X) 2882
Lausanne - Cites (CHE) 3958
Lausitzer Rundschau (DEU) 3851
Lausuntoja ja Selvityksia/Utlaatanden och Utredningar (FIN ISSN 1458-7149) 4713
➤ Lauterbornia (DEU ISSN 0935-333X) 686
Lava (NLD ISSN 1389-1847) 7150
Lava Literair Tijdschrift (NLD ISSN 0929-5968) 5224
Lavaggio Industriale (ITA ISSN 0393-4365) 2243
Laval Administration (CAN ISSN 0023-9038) 1772
➤ Laval Theologique et Philosophique (CAN ISSN 0023-9054) 6931
Lavender (USA) 4376
Lavender Godzilla (USA) 4376
Lavender Line (USA) 3773
Laverna (DEU ISSN 0938-5835) 2237
Laverock (GBR ISSN 1358-3972) 5320
• L'Avise (FRA ISSN 1776-0771) 7982
Il Lavoratore Elettrico (ITA) 3141
I Lavori di Beatrice (ITA ISSN 1828-6097) 6640
I Lavori di Carolina (ITA ISSN 1828-6089) 6640
Lavori Pubblici (ITA ISSN 1122-2506) 1020
† Il Lavoro (ITA) 8970
Il Lavoro see Consulenza Lavoro 4862
• Lavoro e Diritto (ITA ISSN 1120-947X) 4598
Lavoro e Finanza (ITA ISSN 1592-7555) 1695
Lavoro e Previdenza Oggi (ITA ISSN 0390-251X) 4713
• Lavoro e Sindacato (Online) (ITA ISSN 1826-2422) 1695
Lavoro e Sindacato (Print) see Lavoro e Sindacato (Online) 1695
Lavoro e Transporti (CHE) 4598
• Il Lavoro nella Giurisprudenza (ITA ISSN 1591-4178) 1695
• Il Lavoro nelle Pubbliche Amministrazioni (ITA ISSN 1591-7681) 4713
† Lavoro Sicuro (ITA ISSN 0390-2528) 8970
Lavoro Sociale (ITA ISSN 1721-4149) 8053
Lavoura (BRA ISSN 0023-9135) 134
Lavoura Arrozeira (BRA ISSN 0023-9143) 274
Lavra & Oficina (AGO ISSN 1017-5504) 4463
Lavrador (PRT) 134
Law see Integrated Bar of the Philippines. Journal 4693
Law Abstracts on Cards see Faxue Wenzhai Ka 4822
▼ Law Actuality Magazine (FRA ISSN 1958-7074) 4713
Law & Anthropology (NLD ISSN 0259-0816) 4713
• Law & Business Directory of Corporate Counsel (USA) 4874
• Law & Business Review of the Americas (USA ISSN 1571-9537) 4934
• Law and Contemporary Problems (USA ISSN 0023-9186) 4713
• ➤ Law and Critique (NLD ISSN 0957-8536) 4713
▼ • Law and Development Review (USA ISSN 1943-3867) 4713
Law and Economic Review see Al- Magallat al-Qanuniyyat al-Iqtisadiyyat 4726
Law and Economics see Al Qanun Wa-al Iqtisad 1162
Law and Electronic Commerce (NLD ISSN 1385-1888) 4713
▼ • Law & Ethics of Human Rights (USA ISSN 1938-2545) 7211
Law and Ethics Series (USA) 4713
▼ • Law and Financial Markets Review (GBR ISSN 1752-1440) 4874
• Law & Health Weekly (USA ISSN 1551-5354) 4713
Law and Health Weekly see Law & Health Weekly 4713
• ➤ Law and History Review (GBR ISSN 0738-2480) 4713
Law & Housing Journal (USA ISSN 0193-8290) 4713
• ➤ Law and Human Behavior (USA ISSN 0147-7307) 4713
▼ • ➤ Law and Humanities (GBR ISSN 1752-1483) 4713
• ➤ Law & Inequality (USA ISSN 0737-089X) 4713
Law and International Affairs (BGD) 4713
• Law & Justice (GBR ISSN 0269-817X) 4713
Law and Legal Information Directory (USA ISSN 0740-090X) 4713
Law & Life see Falu yu Shenghuo 4671
• ➤ Law and Literature (USA ISSN 1535-685X) 4713
Law and Mental Disability (USA) 4713
Law & Mortar (USA) 4713
Law and News see Fazhi yu Xinwen 4671
• Law and Order Magazine (USA ISSN 0023-9194) 2659
• ➤ Law and Philosophy (NLD ISSN 0167-5249) 4713
➤ Law and Philosophy Library (NLD ISSN 1572-4395) 4714
• ➤ Law & Policy (GBR ISSN 0265-8240) 4714
Law and Policy Journal see Article 13 8931
• Law and Politics Book Review (USA ISSN 1062-7421) 4714
• The Law and Practice of International Courts and Tribunals (NLD ISSN 1569-1853) 4934
Law & Practice of Registered Conveyancing (GBR) 4714
• ➤ Law and Psychology Review (USA ISSN 0098-5961) 4714
The Law and Regulation of International Finance (GBR) 1365
• Law & Sexuality (USA ISSN 1062-0680) 7211
• ➤ Law and Social Inquiry (USA ISSN 0897-6546) 4714
Law & Society Newsletter (USA ISSN 8755-7088) 4714
• ➤ Law & Society Review (USA ISSN 0023-9216) 4714
• Law and Society Review at the University of California, Santa Barbara (USA ISSN 1544-8746) 4714
Law and the Human Genome Review see Revista de Derecho y Genoma Humano 4771
Law and You (BRA) 1406
• Law Association for Asia and the Pacific. Legal Education Standing Committee. Newsletter (AUS ISSN 1320-9272) 2992
Law Association Journal (ZMB) 4714
• Law@Stanford (USA) 2289
• Law Books and Serials in Print (USA ISSN 0000-0752) 4823
Law Books in Print (USA ISSN 1094-9119) 4823
Law Books Published (USA ISSN 0023-9240) 4823
Law Commission Consultation Paper see Great Britain. Law Commission. Consultation Paper 4682
• Law Commission of Canada. Annual Report (CAN ISSN 1493-4086) 4714
• Law, Culture & the Humanities (GBR ISSN 1743-8721) 4714
Law Day see San Diego Daily Transcript 4778
Law. Democracy and Development (ZAF) 4714
Law Development Commission. Annual Report (ZMB) 4714
Law Diary (NZL ISSN 1175-0855) 4714
• Law Enforcement (Controlled Operations) Act. Annual Report (Year) (AUS ISSN 1832-1712) 2659
Law Enforcement Employment Bulletin (Online) see Law Enforcement Employment Bulletin (Print) 2659
• Law Enforcement Employment Bulletin (Print) (USA ISSN 1933-9143) 2659
Law Enforcement Legal Reporter (USA ISSN 0195-0290) 4714
Law Enforcement Legal Review (USA ISSN 1070-9967) 2659
• Law Enforcement Liability Reporter (USA) 4834
• Law Enforcement Management and Administrative Statistics (Year) (USA) 2674
• Law Enforcement Officers Killed and Assaulted (USA ISSN 0747-7961) 2659
• Law Enforcement Product News (USA ISSN 1060-5126) 2659
• Law Enforcement Technology (USA ISSN 0747-3680) 2659
† Law Enforcement Volunteers (USA) 8970
• ➤ Law, Environment & Development Journal (IND ISSN 1746-5893) 4714
• Law Firm Inc. (USA ISSN 1546-3974) 4874
• Law Firm Partnership and Benefits Report (USA ISSN 1091-6237) 4714
• Law Firms Yellow Book (USA ISSN 1054-4054) 4715
Law for Business (GBR ISSN 0954-2809) 4874
• ➤ The Law Handbook (AUS ISSN 1031-8569) 2639
Law in Africa see Recht in Afrika 4766
Law in Context (AUS ISSN 0811-5796) 4715
➤ Law in Eastern Europe (NLD ISSN 0075-823X) 4934
Law in Japan (USA ISSN 0458-8584) 4715
Law in Society (NGA ISSN 0458-8592) 4715
• Law Institute Journal (AUS ISSN 0023-9267) 4715
Law Journal (GBR ISSN 1758-2512) 4715
Law Journal Newsletters's Equipment Leasing Newsletter see L J N's Equipment Leasing Newsletter 4710
Law Journal Newsletters's Franchising Business & Law Alert see L J N's Franchising Business & Law Alert 4834
Law Journal Newsletters's Legal Tech Newsletter see L J N's Legal Tech Newsletter 4710
Law Journal Newsletters's Product Liability Law and Strategy see L J N's Product Liability Law and Strategy 1897
Law Letter see The Uniform Commercial Code Law Letter 1434
Law Librarian's Bulletin Board (USA ISSN 1090-3984) 4715
Law Library Association of Maryland News (USA) 5024
Law Library Benchmarks (USA ISSN 1559-1824) 5024
Law Library Information Reports (USA ISSN 0268-8336) 4715
• ➤ Law Library Journal (USA ISSN 0023-9283) 5024
Law Library Lights (USA ISSN 0457-2483) 5025
Law Life see Fazhi Rensheng 4671
Law Lines (USA ISSN 0148-0553) 5025
Law Marketing Exchange (USA ISSN 1064-8194) 4715
Law Matters (CAN ISSN 1704-9377) 4715
Law Matters (USA ISSN 1083-6225) 4968
• The Law of Advertising (USA) 4715
Law of Associations: An Operating Legal Manual for Executives and Counsel (USA) 4715
• Law of Bank Deposits, Collections and Credit Cards (USA) 1365
Law of Chemical Regulation and Hazardous Waste (USA) 3508
• The Law of Commercial Insurance (USA) 4512
• The Law of Commercial Trucking (USA) 8672
Law of Costs (CAN) 4715
The Law of Damages (CAN) 4834
Law of Defamation (USA) 4715
• The Law of Electronic Funds Transfer (USA) 1393
• The Law of Evidence in Virginia (USA) 4955
• The Law of Evidence in Washington (USA) 4955
Law of Federal Oil and Gas Leases (USA) 6777
• The Law of Hazardous Waste: Management, Cleanup, Liability, and Litigation (USA) 4715
Law of Historic Preservation (USA ISSN 1559-8551) 4715
Law of Internet Security and Privacy (USA ISSN 1542-2208) 4715
• The Law of Liability Insurance (USA) 4512
• The Law of Life and Health Insurance (USA) 4512
Law of Loans & Borrowing (GBR) 1365
Law of Macao Statistical Information System see Legislacao do Sistema de Informacao Estatistica de Macau 8385
The Law of Municipal Liability in Canada (CAN) 7496
• The Law of Negligence in Arizona (USA) 4715
The Law of Oil and Gas Leases (USA) 6777
The Law of Pooling and Unitization (USA) 4715
The Law of Probation and Parole (USA) 4893
Law of Products Liability (USA) 2639
Law of Professional and Amateur Sports (USA) 4715
Law of Publication Bans, Private Hearings and Sealing Orders (CAN ISSN 1719-9778) 4715
Law of Real Property (CAN ISSN 1719-9484) 4874
Law of Stamp Duties see Monroe & Nock on the Law of Stamp Duties 1368
The Law of the European Community see Smit & Herzog on the Law of the European Union 4941
Law of the European Union see Smit & Herzog on the Law of the European Union 4941
• Law of the Sea Bulletin/Droit de la Mer (USA ISSN 1015-1885) 4970
Law of the Sea Institute. Occasional Paper (USA ISSN 0080-2808) 4970
• Law of the Sea Institute. Proceedings of the Annual Conference (USA ISSN 0557-8620) 4970
Law of Toxic Torts (USA) 3500
Law of Wetlands Regulation (USA) 3450
Law Office Administrator (USA ISSN 1071-7242) 1772
Law Office Guide to Purchasing Legal Malpractice Insurance see Legal Malpractice 4834
Law Office Management and Administration Report see Law Office Management & Administration Report 4715
• Law Office Management & Administration Report (USA ISSN 0735-4843) 4715
Law Office Management and Administration Yearbook see Law Office Management & Administration Yearbook 4715
• Law Office Management & Administration Yearbook (USA) 4715
Law Officer (USA ISSN 1553-9555) 2659
• Law Officers' Bulletin (USA ISSN 0145-6571) 2659
Law Officer's Pocket Manual (USA ISSN 0271-7182) 2659
• Law Practice (USA ISSN 1547-9102) 4716
Law Practice Management see Law Practice 4716
Law Practice News (USA) 1852
• Law, Probability and Risk (GBR ISSN 1470-8396) 4716
• Law Quadrangle Notes (USA ISSN 0458-8665) 2290
Law Quarterly (IRN) 4716
Law Quarterly (PAK) 4716
• The Law Quarterly Review (GBR ISSN 0023-933X) 4716
Law Reform Commission of Nova Scotia. Annual Report (CAN ISSN 1189-6205) 4716
Law Reform Commission of Saskatchewan. Annual Report (CAN ISSN 1184-9878) 4955
Law Reform Commission of Western Australia. Reports. Annual Reports and Discussion Papers (AUS) 4716
Law-Related CD-ROM Update (USA ISSN 1065-9285) 4845
• The Law Relating to Banker and Customer in Australia (AUS) 4716
• Law Reporter (USA ISSN 1052-4649) 4716
Law Reporter (Alexandria) see Community Association Law Reporter 4407
• Law Reports: Appeal Cases (GBR ISSN 0265-122X) 4716

Title

▼ *new title* † *ceased* • *electronic media* ➤ *refereed*

10552 LAW REPORTS. APPEAL CASES BEFORE THE HOUSE OF LORDS ULRICH'S PERIODICALS

Law Reports. Appeal Cases Before the House of Lords see Law Reports: House of Lords **4716**
• Law Reports: Chancery and Family Division (GBR ISSN 0265-1211) **4912**
Law Reports: Chancery Division (GBR ISSN 0264-1097) **4912**
Law Reports. Family Division (GBR ISSN 0264-1119) **4912**
• Law Reports: House of Lords (GBR ISSN 0264-1135) **4716**
Law Reports. Index (GBR ISSN 0265-1238) **4716**
Law Reports of Tanzania (TZA ISSN 0377-0885) **4955**
Law Reports of the Commonwealth. Commercial Law Reports (GBR ISSN 0952-1046) **4874**
Law Reports of the Commonwealth. Constitutional and Administrative Law Reports (GBR ISSN 0951-0699) **4850**
Law Reports of the Commonwealth. Criminal Law Reports (GBR ISSN 0952-1038) **4893**
• Law Reports: Queen's Bench Division (GBR ISSN 0264-1127) **4716**
Law Reprints: Trade Regulation Series (USA) **1575**
Law Research see Fazhi Yanjiu **4671**
• Law Research Newsletter (USA) **4716**
Law Review see Faxue Pinlun **4671**
Law Review see Universite Nationale du Rwanda. Revue Scientifique du Droit **4803**
Law Review see Pravny Obzor **4760**
Law Review see Washington University. Law Review **4811**
Law Review Journal (USA ISSN 0734-1938) **4716**
• Law Scene (NZL ISSN 1172-2584) **4716**
Law School Administrator's Journal (USA ISSN 0741-1170) **4716**
Law School Admission Test see L S A T **4711**
Law School Admission Test Lesson Book see L S A T Lesson Book **4711**
Law School Admission Test Workout see L S A T Workout **2992**
Law School Admissions Test (Comprehensive Program) see L S A T (Comprehensive Program) **4711**
Law School Admissions Test (Premier Program) see L S A T (Premier Program) **4711**
Law School Journal (USA ISSN 0737-2590) **4716**
† • Law School Record (USA ISSN 0529-097X) **8970**
Law School Summer School Programs at Home and Abroad (USA) **4716**
➤ Law, Science and Policy (GBR ISSN 1475-5335) **686**
Law Science Magazine see Faxue Zazhi **4671**
Law Sciences Review see Jogtudomanyi Kozlony **4699**
Law Services Report (USA) **4716**
• Law, Social Justice and Global Development (GBR ISSN 1467-0437) **4716**
Law, Society, and Culture in China (USA) **4185**
➤ Law, Society and Policy (USA) **4716**
Law Society Digest (KEN) **4716**
Law Society. Gazette (GBR ISSN 1355-7971) **4716**
• Law Society Journal (AUS) **4716**
Law Society of Alberta. Newsletter see Law Matters **4715**
Law Society of Hong Kong Gazette (HKG ISSN 1015-5570) **4716**
Law Society of Hong Kong. New Gazette see Hong Kong Lawyer **4688**
Law Society of Ireland. Gazette (IRL ISSN 1393-6956) **4716**
The Law Society of Kenya. Journal (KEN ISSN 1992-1381) **4716**
The Law Society of Manitoba (Year) Annual Report (CAN) **4717**
• Law Society of Scotland. Journal (Year) (GBR ISSN 0458-8711) **4717**
Law Society of South Australia. Bulletin (AUS ISSN 1038-6777) **4717**
• Law Society of Upper Canada (CAN ISSN 0023-9364) **4717**
Law Society. Research & Policy Planning Unit. Annual Research Conference. Proceedings (GBR) **4717**
Law Society. Research and Policy Planning Unit. Annual Statistical Report (GBR) **4823**
Law Society's Conveyancing Handbook (Year) (GBR ISSN 1350-1852) **4717**
Law Society's Directory of Solicitors and Barristers (GBR ISSN 1358-8842) **4717**
Law Society's Guardian Gazette (GBR) **4717**
Law Students Competitions see Australian Law Students' Competitions Handbook **4624**
Law Studies (USA ISSN 0160-0265) **4717**
• ➤ The Law Teacher (GBR ISSN 0306-9400) **4717**
• The Law Teacher (Online) (USA) **4717**
The Law Teacher (Print) see The Law Teacher (Online) **4717**
Law Teacher's Journal (USA ISSN 0741-1197) **4717**
Law Tech Advisor see Databased Advisor Magazine **2554**
• Law - Technology (USA) **4845**
• Law Technology News (USA ISSN 1527-3520) **4717**
Law/Text/Culture see Law Text Culture **4717**
• ➤ Law Text Culture (AUS ISSN 1322-9060) **4717**
Law Thesaurus (IND ISSN 0023-9399) **4717**
Law Times (CAN ISSN 0847-5083) **4717**
Law Tools, Materials, Contacts (USA ISSN 0897-7585) **4717**
Law Weekly (IND) **4717**
Lawasia Journal (AUS ISSN 1441-3698) **4717**
Lawful Reservoir Market Demand for Prorated Gas Fields (USA) **6777**
† Lawn & Garden Equipment (GBR) **8970**
Lawn & Garden Trade (CAN ISSN 0705-212X) **1829**
Lawn and Gardern Retailer see Lawn & Gardern Retailer **3742**
• Lawn & Garden Retailer (USA ISSN 1540-9023) **3742**
• Lawn & Landscape (USA) **3742**
Lawn Tennis Association Handbook see L T A Handbook **8237**
• LawNow (CAN ISSN 0841-2626) **4717**
Lawrence Berkeley Laboratory Currents Weekly Newsletter see L B L Currents Weekly Newsletter **7878**
Lawrence Berkeley National Laboratory. Report (USA) **3170**
Lawrence Livermore National Laboratory. Report (USA) **7879**
D H Lawrence Society. Journal see D H Lawrence Society. Journal **5282**
Lawrence Technological University Magazine (USA) **2290**
Lawrence Technological University Web Design see L T U Web Design **2563**
Lawrentian (USA) **2290**
• Laws Affecting Children with Special Needs (USA) **4717**
Laws and Regulations and Legal Decisions Involving Food Stuffs see European Food Research and Technology **3669**
Laws and Regulations of the State of Maryland Relating to Alcoholic Beverages and Tobacco Tax. (Year) Cumulative Supplement (USA) **606**
• The Laws of Australia (AUS) **4717**
Laws of International Trade (USA) **4874**
Laws of Kenya. Supplement (KEN) **4955**
Laws of Maryland Relating to Public Libraries (USA) **5025**
Laws of South Africa see Current Law Service **4653**
Laws of Virginia Related to Financial Institutions (USA ISSN 1547-9587) **4874**
Laws of Virginia Relating to Adult Corrections (USA) **4893**
Laws of Virginia Relating to Game, Fish, and Dogs see Virginia Game, Inland Fish and Boat Laws **2631**
Laws Quarterly (USA ISSN 0738-2049) **4717**
• Lawsuit Abuse Fortnightly (USA) **4717**
• LawTalk (NZL ISSN 0114-989X) **4717**
• The Lawyer (GBR ISSN 0953-7902) **4717**
Lawyer (IND) **4717**
The Lawyer 200 see The Lawyer **4717**
▼ Lawyer and Judicial Ethics (USA ISSN 1944-4915) **4718**
† Lawyer Hiring & Training Report (USA ISSN 0739-1706) **8970**
Lawyer - Pilots Bar Association Journal (USA ISSN 0274-9319) **64**
• Lawyer Referral Directory (USA ISSN 1530-9207) **4718**
Lawyer Referral Network (USA ISSN 0887-7777) **4718**
The lawyer. The hot 100 see The Lawyer **4717**
Lawyering Skills Bulletin (USA ISSN 1055-4076) **4718**
Lawyering Skills News (USA ISSN 0736-4938) **4718**
Lawyers' Admission Handbook (AUS ISSN 1324-1427) **4718**
• Lawyers Alliance for New York. Newsletter (USA) **4718**
The Lawyer's Almanac (USA ISSN 0277-9544) **4718**
Lawyers' Committee on Nuclear Policy. Newsletter (USA ISSN 1059-6585) **4971**
Lawyers Competitive Edge (USA ISSN 1522-5054) **4845**
Lawyers Factbook (GBR) **4718**
Lawyers Guide to Medical Proof (USA) **4718**
• Lawyer's Guide to the Texas Deceptive Trade Practices Act (USA) **4834**
Lawyers' Handbook (USA) **4718**
• Lawyers Job E-Bulletin Board (USA) **4718**
Lawyers Journal (USA ISSN 1538-2869) **4718**
• Lawyers' Liability Review (USA ISSN 0896-7075) **4718**
Lawyers' Manual on Professional Conduct Current Reports see A B A / B N A Lawyers' Manual on Professional Conduct Current Reports **4606**
Lawyers' Medical Cyclopedia (USA) **4718**
• Lawyers' Micro Users Group Newsletter (USA) **4845**
Lawyer's P C (USA ISSN 0740-0942) **4845**
• Lawyers Practice Manual N S W (AUS) **4718**
Lawyers Practice Manual New South Wales see Lawyers Practice Manual N S W **4718**
Lawyers Practice Manual Q L D see Lawyers Practice Manual Queensland **4718**
• Lawyers Practice Manual Queensland (AUS) **4718**
• Lawyers Practice Manual Victoria (AUS) **4718**
Lawyers Professional Liability Update (USA) **4718**
Lawyer's Register International by Specialties and Fields of Law Including a Directory of Corporate Counsel (USA ISSN 1061-7272) **4718**
Lawyer's Remembrancer (GBR ISSN 0142-7490) **4718**
• Lawyers' Title Guaranty Funds Newsletter (USA ISSN 0361-3763) **4718**
Lawyers U S A see LawyersU S A **4718**
The Lawyers Weekly (CAN ISSN 0830-0151) **4718**
Lawyer's Weekly U S A see LawyersU S A **4718**
• LawyersU S A (USA ISSN 1931-9584) **4718**
Laxton's Building Price Book (Year) (GBR ISSN 0960-6823) **1020**
Lay Witness (USA ISSN 1541-602X) **7804**
Laya (PHL ISSN 0117-4134) **8871**
• Layers (USA ISSN 1554-415X) **2488**
• Lazaroa (ESP ISSN 0210-9778) **799**
Lazarus (AUT ISSN 1024-6908) **5969**
Lazarus (DEU ISSN 0174-6995) **7738**
▼ Lazer (GBR ISSN 1753-1608) **2199**
Lazernye Novosti/Laser News (RUS) **7080**
Lazio Ieri e Oggi (ITA ISSN 0047-4231) **502**
Il Lazio Paese per Paese (ITA ISSN 1824-4025) **8728**
Lazol (MUS) **2659**
Lazos (URY ISSN 1510-1835) **2290**
Lazur' (RUS) **5320**
Lazy Town (DEU) **2199**
Lazydays R V Living see Lazydays R V Showcase **8321**
Lazydays R V Showcase (Recreational Vehicle) (USA) **8321**
• L'Chaim (USA ISSN 1050-0480) **7726**
L'dor V'dor/From Generation to Generation (USA ISSN 1938-8616) **3547**
Le Coq Sportif Guide to Hockey see L C S: Guide to Hockey **8237**
• Le Fanu Studies (USA ISSN 1932-9598) **5414**
Lea (DEU ISSN 1614-8681) **8871**
Lea (SVN ISSN 1854-4258) **8871**
Lea - Backen (DEU) **4362**
Lea - Einfach Koestlich (DEU) **4362**
Lea - Frisuren (DEU) **589**
Lea - Grillen & Party see Grillen & Party **4359**
Lea - Kind & Kegel (DEU) **2159**
Lea - Kochen im Fruehling (DEU) **4362**
Lea - Raetselspass (DEU) **8185**
Lea - Schoen & Schlank (DEU) **8846**
Lea Wohnen (DEU ISSN 1863-6314) **4545**
An Leabharlann/Irish Library (IRL ISSN 0023-9542) **5025**
† Lead (NZL ISSN 1176-8487) **8970**
Lead (USA ISSN 1942-4221) **7764**
• LEAD Action News (AUS ISSN 1324-6011) **7530**
Lead and Zinc see Namari to Aen **6327**
• Lead and Zinc Statistics (PRT ISSN 0023-9577) **6340**
Lead Belly Letter (USA ISSN 1056-5329) **6584**
Leaded (AUS ISSN 1833-1122) **8589**
• The Leader (AUS) **3795**
The Leader (CAN ISSN 0711-5377) **2159**
The Leader (NGA ISSN 0331-5193) **7804**
Leader see Kiongozi **7803**
Leader see Girl Scout Leader **2153**
The Leader see C C U M C Leader **2970**
Leader (Morrisburg) (CAN ISSN 0834-6666) **3812**
The Leader (Nelson City Edition) (NZL ISSN 1172-7322) **3917**
The Leader (Norwich) (GBR) **4393**
The Leader (Richmond-Waimea Edition) see The Leader (Nelson City Edition) **3917**
• The Leader (Surrey) (CAN ISSN 1490-7526) **3812**
Leader Board (USA) **8237**
Leader for Chemist (ITA ISSN 1122-4967) **2071**
Leader for Chemist Health Strategy see Leader for Chemist **2071**
• Leader Guide Magazine (USA) **3979**
† Leader in Christian Education Ministries (USA ISSN 1931-8200) **8970**
Leader in the Church School Today see Leader in Christian Education Ministries **8970**
Leader Magazine (USA) **2159**
Leader News (CAN) **3812**
• Leader-Post (CAN ISSN 0839-2870) **3812**
• Leader to Leader (USA ISSN 1087-8149) **1772**
Leaders (USA ISSN 0194-3510) **1575**
Leaders see Market Watch (New York) **607**
† Leaders (Auckland) (NZL ISSN 1173-5058) **8970**
Leader's Edge (USA ISSN 1550-2937) **4512**
Leaders' Edge (USA) **1296**
Leader's Guide see YouthWalk **7696**
Leader's Magazin see Yritystalous **1802**
• ➤ Leadership (GBR ISSN 1742-7150) **4463**
Leadership (NLD ISSN 1872-4639) **1772**
Leadership (UGA ISSN 0047-424X) **7659**
Leadership see Academic Leadership (Mesa) **2965**
• Leadership (Carol Stream) (USA ISSN 0199-7661) **7659**
Leadership (Fairfield) (USA ISSN 1057-4816) **1772**
• Leadership (Sacramento) (USA ISSN 1531-3174) **2882**
Leadership (Washington, 1980) (USA ISSN 0195-9204) **1772**
▼ Leadership (Westchester) (USA ISSN 1948-089X) **7530**
† The Leadership Advantage (USA ISSN 1073-5631) **8970**
Leadership and Management Directions (USA ISSN 1055-4041) **4718**
• Leadership and Management in Engineering (USA ISSN 1532-6748) **3278**
• Leadership and Management Studies in Sub-Sahara Africa. Conference Proceedings (NZL ISSN 1177-3294) **8118**
• ➤ Leadership & Organization Development Journal (GBR ISSN 0143-7739) **1772**
▼ ➤ Leadership & Organizational Management Journal (USA) **1772**
• Leadership and Policy in Schools (USA ISSN 1570-0763) **3026**
Leadership Compass (USA ISSN 1546-0169) **3026**
• Leadership Excellence (USA) **1869**
• Leadership Exchange (USA ISSN 1941-4005) **7383**
• Leadership for the Front Lines (USA ISSN 1080-1863) **1772**
• Leadership in Action (USA ISSN 1093-6092) **1772**
• Leadership in Health Services (GBR ISSN 1751-1879) **4105**
Leadership in HIV/AIDS (ZAF ISSN 1992-0148) **5821**
Leadership in Project Management Annual (USA ISSN 1930-8639) **1772**
• The Leadership Letter (AUS) **1772**
• The Leadership Library (USA) **2012**
• Leadership Magazine (ZAF) **5224**
Leadership Magazine Online see Leadership Magazine **5224**
• Leadership Medica (ITA ISSN 1122-4959) **5660**
Leadership Montreal (CAN ISSN 1480-4638) **1406**
Leadership + (IRL ISSN 1649-5888) **2882**
• ➤ The Leadership Quarterly (GBR ISSN 1048-9843) **1772**
Leadership Strategies (USA ISSN 1526-0151) **1772**
• ➤ Leading and Managing (AUS ISSN 1329-4539) **2882**
Leading Architecture and Design (ZAF) **448**
• ➤ Leading Brands (ZAF ISSN 1818-975X) **1829**
Leading Business (CAN) **1144**
Leading Chain Tenants see Directory of Leading Chain Tenants **1987**
Leading Constitutional Cases on Criminal Justice (USA ISSN 0272-2151) **4850**
Leading Edge (AUS) **134**
• Leading Edge (Ojai) (USA) **64**
• The Leading Edge (Tulsa) (USA ISSN 1070-485X) **2786**
Leading Edge (Wright-Patterson Air Force Base) (USA) **6431**
• Leading Edge Living (USA ISSN 1930-0778) **6645**
Leading Edge Magazine (USA) **5444**
• Leading Ideas (Online) (USA) **6700**
Leading Light (NZL ISSN 1170-4918) **6527**
• Leading Minds (AUS ISSN 1834-4933) **8118**
• Leading Opinions. Gynaekologie (AUT ISSN 1991-9220) **5997**
• Leading Opinions. Haematologie und Onkologie (AUT ISSN 1991-2838) **5939**
• Leading Opinions. Kardiologie und Gefaessmedizin (AUT ISSN 1991-2803) **5795**
Leading Opinions. Kardiology see Leading Opinions. Kardiologie und Gefaessmedizin **5795**
Leading Opinions Medizin fuer die Frau (AUT ISSN 1997-7980) **8846**
• Leading Opinions. Neurologie und Psychiatrie (AUT ISSN 1608-8964) **6158**
Leading Opinions. Orthopaedie (AUT ISSN 1991-279X) **6066**
Leading Systematic School Improvement (USA) **3026**
Leading the Way (AUS ISSN 1448-1537) **1869**
Leads (CAN ISSN 0834-3586) **1497**
• Leads from L A M A (Online) (USA ISSN 1076-1926) **5025**
Leads in Life Sciences (NLD ISSN 1566-4600) **6663**
Leaf Bulletin see T M A Leaf Bulletin **8487**
Leaf of the Branch (CAN ISSN 1186-687X) **3773**
The Leaf Review (GBR ISSN 1747-3764) **448**
Leaf Venation Patterns (DEU) **800**
▼ • Leaflet (USA ISSN 2150-5233) **5425**
➤ Leaflet (Assonet) (USA ISSN 0023-964X) **5142**
Leaflet (Boston) (USA) **3742**
Leaflet Missal (USA ISSN 1072-7930) **7804**
Leaflets (USA) **800**
League see Sandara **3562**
League Cricket Review (GBR ISSN 1368-9029) **8237**
League of American Bicyclists Magazine (USA) **8260**
• League of Canadian Poets. Annual Report (CAN ISSN 1714-1524) **5425**
• League of Women Voters of Georgia. Legislative Newsletter (USA) **4718**
• League Sentinel (GBR ISSN 1461-5010) **5224**
League Week see Rugby League Week **8244**
League's Electronic Newsletter see St@nz@ **5435**
• ➤ Lean Construction Journal (USA ISSN 1555-1369) **1020**
Lean Trimmings (USA) **292**
Leaping (AUS ISSN 0726-626X) **7738**
Leap's Pond (USA ISSN 1540-3521) **2199**
Learn and Study see Xuexi yu Yanjiu **7197**
• Learn English in Britain with A R E L S (Association of Recognised English Language Services) (GBR) **5143**
• Learn It on the Web (USA) **2563**
• ➤ Learned Publishing (GBR ISSN 0953-1513) **7565**
• LearnFree Living (USA) **6810**
Learning About Indonesia see Inside Indonesia (Print) **8964**
Learning about Lupus see L S M B Newsletter **5659**
• ➤ Learning & Behavior (USA ISSN 1543-4494) **7383**
Learning & Development see Human Resources **1864**
• Learning and Development (GBR ISSN 1752-2765) **6700**
• ➤ Learning and Individual Differences (GBR ISSN 1041-6080) **2882**
• ➤ Learning and Instruction (GBR ISSN 0959-4752) **2882**
• Learning and Leading with Technology (USA ISSN 1082-5754) **2950**

▼ *new title*   † *ceased*   ● *electronic media*   ► *refereed*

Title

10556 LEO BAECK INSTITUTE LONDON. ANNUAL REPORT OF ACTIVITIES ULRICH'S PERIODICALS

Leo Baeck Institute London. Annual Report of Activities *see* Leo Baeck Institute London. Report of Activities **4240**
Leo Baeck Institute London. Report of Activities (GBR ISSN 1746-8663) **4240**
Leo Baeck Institute News *see* L B I News **4150**
• ➤ Leo Baeck Institute. Year Book (GBR ISSN 0075-8744) **4151**
Leo Baeck Institute. Yearbook. (Year) Bibliography *see* Leo Baeck Institute. Year Book **4151**
Leo Cteni (CZE ISSN 1211-4537) **6294**
Leo Leo (ESP ISSN 0214-2627) **2199**
Leo Leo. Extra (ESP ISSN 1575-3956) **2199**
Leo Special (CZE ISSN 1213-3167) **6294**
Leobener Gruene Hefte. Neue Folge (AUT ISSN 0259-0751) **6468**
† Leodiensian (GBR ISSN 0024-0923) **8971**
Leodium (BEL) **4240**
Leon. Boletin de Informacion Municipal (ESP) **7496**
Leonard Davis Institute of Health Economics Issue Brief *see* L D I Issue Brief **7530**
Leonard Maltin's Movie and Video Guide *see* Leonard Maltin's Movie Guide **6506**
Leonard Maltin's Movie Crazy (USA ISSN 1938-4505) **6506**
Leonard Maltin's Movie Guide (USA ISSN 1555-7235) **6506**
Leonardo (CHE) **8502**
• ➤ Leonardo: Art Science and Technology (USA ISSN 0024-094X) **502**
• Leonardo da Vinci Society Newsletter (GBR) **502**
• Leonardo Electronic Almanac (USA ISSN 1071-4391) **530**
• Leonardo Journal of Practices and Technology (ROM ISSN 1583-1078) **8431**
• Leonardo Journal of Sciences (ROM ISSN 1583-0233) **7879**
• ➤ Leonardo Music Journal (USA ISSN 0961-1215) **6584**
• Leonardo Reviews (USA ISSN 1559-0429) **4485**
Leonardo Supplemental Issue *see* Leonardo: Art Science and Technology **502**
Leonardo Supplemental Issue *see* Leonardo Music Journal **6584**
Leonard's Annual Price Index of Art Auctions (USA ISSN 0747-6566) **502**
Leonard's Guide. National Contract Carriers Directory (USA ISSN 1068-686X) **2013**
Leonard's Guide. National Third Party Logistics Directory (USA) **2013**
Leonard's Guide. National Warehouse and Distribution Directory (USA) **2013**
Leonard's Price Index of Latin American Art at Auction (USA) **502**
Leonce (DEU) **3852**
Il Leone (USA ISSN 0024-0958) **2267**
Leopard (GBR) **3548**
Leopoldianum (BRA ISSN 0101-9635) **2992**
Lepa & Zdrava (SVN) **8871**
Lepidoptera (DNK ISSN 0075-8787) **854**
Lepidoptera News (USA ISSN 1062-6581) **854**
➤ Die Lepidopterenfauna der Rheinlande und Westfalens (DEU ISSN 0941-3189) **854**
➤ Lepidopterists' Society. Journal (USA ISSN 0024-0966) **854**
Lepidopterists' Society. Memoirs (USA ISSN 0075-8795) **854**
Lepidopterists's Society. News (USA ISSN 0091-1348) **854**
Lepidopterological Society of Japan. Journal *see* Yadoriga **861**
Lepidopterological Society of Japan. Transactions *see* Cho to ga **842**
Lepidoptersites Parisiens. Bulletin (FRA ISSN 1635-2513) **854**
Leppis (FIN ISSN 0784-2546) **2199**
Leprazending *see* Leprazending Nieuws **5821**
Leprazending Nieuws (NLD ISSN 1873-9121) **5821**
• Leprosy Mission. Annual Report (GBR ISSN 0075-8809) **5822**
• ➤ Leprosy Review (GBR ISSN 0305-7518) **5822**
Leqach (DEU) **7726**
➤ Ler Historia (PRT ISSN 0870-6182) **4240**
Lern- und Lehr-Forschungs Berichte *see* L L F - Berichte **3069**
Lernchancen (DEU ISSN 1434-9817) **3070**
Lernen Foerdern (DEU ISSN 0720-8316) **3044**
Lernen fuer Europa (DEU ISSN 1430-2675) **2883**
Lernen Konkret (DEU ISSN 0722-1843) **3044**
Lernen, Organisiert und Selbstgesteuert (DEU ISSN 1434-3770) **2883**
Lernende Schule (DEU) **3070**
Lernhilfen fuer den Textilunterricht *see* Textil und Unterricht **8459**
Lernort Gemeinde (DEU ISSN 0931-6191) **7764**
LernSprache Deutsch (AUT ISSN 1028-1487) **5143**
Lernwelten (DEU) **3027**
Les. *see* Les Slovenske Lesokruhy **3703**
Les (SVN ISSN 0024-1067) **3713**
Les Nouvelles *see* L E S Nouvelles **8430**
Lesapp (ARG ISSN 0328-0586) **4850**
Lesbia Magazine (FRA ISSN 0754-944X) **4376**
Lesbian and Gay Archivist (CAN) **4376**
Lesbian and Gay New York *see* L G N Y **4376**
Lesbian and Gay New York Latino *see* L G N Y Latino **4376**
Lesbian Connection (USA ISSN 1081-3217) **4376**
• Lesbian - Gay Law Notes (USA ISSN 8755-9021) **4722**
Lesbian Herstory Archives Newsletter (USA ISSN 1064-0819) **4376**
• Lesbian News (USA ISSN 0739-1803) **4376**
Lesbians on the Loose *see* L O T L **8870**
Lesbisch Archivaria (NLD) **8893**
Lesbok Morgunbladsins *see* Morgunbladid **3877**
Leseli Ka Sepolesa (LSO) **3905**
Leselinyana la Lesotho/Lesotho Christian Newspaper (LSO) **7659**
Die Lesepredigt (DEU ISSN 0173-4199) **7764**
▼ Leserabe (DEU) **2199**
Lesesaal (DEU) **629**
• Leshan Shifan Xueyuan Xuebao (CHN ISSN 1009-8666) **7983**
Leshonenu (ISR ISSN 0334-3626) **5143**
Leshonenu La'am (ISR ISSN 0024-1091) **5143**
Lesley University Series in Art and Education (USA) **502**
Leslie and Britts: Motor Vehicle Law in N S W (New South Wales) *see* Motor Vehicle Law N S W **4736**
Leslie Harris Centre of Regional Policy and Development. Annual Report (CAN ISSN 1910-6890) **7451**
Leslie L. Schaffer Lectureship in Forest Science (CAN ISSN 0836-0618) **3695**
Lesnaya Gazeta (RUS) **134**
Lesnaya Nov' (RUS ISSN 0132-828X) **3695**
Lesnaya Promyshlennost' (RUS ISSN 0368-7619) **3713**
Lesne Prace Badawcze (POL ISSN 1732-9442) **3695**
• Lesnicka Prace (CZE ISSN 0322-9254) **3696**
Lesnicky Casopis/Forestry Journal (SVK ISSN 0323-1046) **3696**
Lesnoe Khozyaistvo (RUS ISSN 0024-1113) **3696**
Lesotho Bank. Annual Report (LSO) **1365**
Lesotho Business Directory (ZAF ISSN 1016-3999) **2013**
Lesotho Catholic Directory (LSO) **7804**
Lesotho Christian Newspaper *see* Leselinyana la Lesotho **7659**
Lesotho. Department of Water Affairs. Hydrological Yearbook *see* Lesotho. Ministry of Natural Resources. Hydrological Yearbook **2796**
Lesotho Environment and Environment Law (LSO) **3450**
Lesotho Government Telephone Directory (ZAF) **2013**
Lesotho Law Journal (LSO ISSN 0255-6472) **4722**
Lesotho. Ministry of Education, Sports and Culture. Annual Report of the Permanent Secretary (LSO) **2883**
Lesotho. Ministry of Foreign Affairs. Diplomatic and Consular List (LSO ISSN 0460-2099) **7251**
Lesotho. Ministry of Natural Resources. Hydrological Yearbook (LSO) **2796**
Lesotho National Development Corporation. Newsletter (LSO) **1497**
Lesotho. Treasury. Report on the Finances and Accounts (LSO ISSN 0075-8817) **1933**
• Lesovedenie (RUS ISSN 0024-1148) **3696**
• lespress (DEU ISSN 1616-2099) **4376**
Lessen (NLD ISSN 1872-3659) **6528**
Lessici (ITA ISSN 1828-6860) **4463**
Lessico dell'Estetica (ITA) **4463**
Lessico Intellettuale Europeo (ITA ISSN 0075-8825) **5143**
Lessing Yearbook (DEU ISSN 0075-8833) **5321**
• Lessons in Conservation (USA ISSN 1938-7024) **2617**
Lessons Learned/Lecons Apprises (CAN ISSN 1702-8957) **7451**
Lessons of Yellow Pages Competition (USA) **2013**
Lest We Forget (USA ISSN 0887-2856) **3773**
Let the Conquest Begin *see* Conquest **5068**
Let Them Eat Cake (GBR) **2257**
Letapis Druku Belarusi. Knizhny Letapis (BLR) **629**
Letapis Druku Belarusi. Letapis Chasopisnykh Artykulau (BLR ISSN 1561-3496) **629**
Letapis Druku Belarusi. Letapis Gazetnykh Artykulau (BLR ISSN 1561-350X) **629**
Letectvi a Kosmonautika (CZE ISSN 0024-1156) **65**
Leterary Supplement *see* Sanchar **3888**
• ➤ Lethaia (GBR ISSN 0024-1164) **6726**
Lethbridge Daily Herald *see* Lethbridge Herald **3812**
• Lethbridge Herald (CAN ISSN 0839-4938) **3812**
Lethbridge Historical Society Newsletter (CAN ISSN 0838-7249) **4301**
Lethbridge Living (CAN ISSN 1202-7480) **5075**
Letitia Baldrige's Executive Advantage *see* Executive Advantage **1743**
Letizia (ITA ISSN 1125-6613) **5411**
Letopis (DEU ISSN 0943-2787) **4240**
• Letopis' Avtoreferatov Dissertatsii (RUS ISSN 0869-5954) **629**
• Letopis' Gazetnykh Statei (RUS ISSN 0024-1172) **629**
• Letopis' Izoizdanii (RUS ISSN 0134-8388) **629**
• ➤ Letopis Matice Srpske (SRB ISSN 0025-5939) **5321**
• Letopis na Statiite ot Bulgarskite Spisaniia i Sbornitsi/Articles from Bulgarian Journals and Collections (BGR ISSN 0324-0398) **629**
• Letopis na Statiite ot Bulgarskite Vestnitsi/Articles from Bulgarian Newspapers (BGR ISSN 0324-0347) **629**
• Letopis' Periodicheskikh i Prodolzhayushchikhsya Izdanii (RUS ISSN 0201-6265) **629**
• Letopis' Retsenzii (RUS ISSN 0130-9242) **629**
• Letopis' Zhurnal'nykh Statei (RUS ISSN 0024-1202) **629**
Letra Grande, Arte y Literatura (DOM) **502**
Letra Internacional (ESP ISSN 0213-4721) **5224**
• Letra Magna.com (BRA ISSN 1807-5193) **5143**
▼ • Letraceluloide (ARG ISSN 1851-4855) **5321**
➤ Letras (BRA ISSN 0102-0250) **5321**
Letras (CRI ISSN 1409-424X) **5321**
Letras (PER ISSN 0378-4878) **4463**
Letras (Caracas) (VEN ISSN 0459-1283) **5143**
• Letras de Buenos Aires (ARG ISSN 0326-2928) **5321**
➤ Letras de Deusto (ESP ISSN 0210-3516) **4463**
• Letras de Hoje (BRA ISSN 0101-3335) **5143**
Letras del Ecuador (ECU) **5321**
Letras e Artes (BRA) **5321**
Letras & Letras (BRA ISSN 0102-3527) **5143**
Letras Femeninas (USA ISSN 0277-4356) **5321**
• ➤ Letras Hispanas (USA ISSN 1548-5633) **5321**
Letras Hispanas (Edinburg) (USA ISSN 1074-794X) **5144**
• Letras Libres (ESP ISSN 1578-4312) **5321**
• Letras Libres (MEX ISSN 1606-5913) **5224**
Letras Peninsulares (USA ISSN 0897-7542) **5321**
Letras Potosinas (MEX ISSN 0024-1245) **5321**
Letras Traduzidas (BRA ISSN 0104-2289) **6584**
Der Letroner (DEU) **1695**
Letr@s Hispanas *see* Letras Hispanas **5321**
Let's Dance (USA ISSN 0024-1253) **2686**
Let's Find Out (AUS ISSN 1835-5218) **3070**
Let's Find Out (English Edition) *see* Scholastic Let's Find Out **3080**
• Let's Find Out (Spanish Edition) (USA ISSN 1076-6766) **3070**
▼ Let's Get Crafting (GBR ISSN 1754-8470) **537**
Let's Go: Alaska (Year) (USA ISSN 1549-926X) **8728**
Let's Go: Alaska & Pacific Northwest *see* Let's Go: Pacific Northwest (Year) **8730**
Let's Go Amsterdam *see* Let's Go: Amsterdam **8729**
Let's Go: Amsterdam (USA ISSN 1542-5150) **8729**
Let's Go Australia *see* Let's Go: Australia (Year) **8729**
Let's Go: Australia (Year) (USA ISSN 1098-8114) **8729**
Let's Go: Austria & Switzerland (Year) (USA) **8729**
Let's Go: Barcelona (USA ISSN 1550-0047) **8729**
Let's Go: Boston (USA ISSN 1536-3414) **8729**
Let's Go: Brazil (USA ISSN 1549-5930) **8729**
Let's Go Britain *see* Let's Go: Britain **8729**
Let's Go: Britain (USA) **8729**
Let's Go: California (Year) (USA ISSN 1546-6876) **8729**
Let's Go: Central America (Year) (USA ISSN 1546-4032) **8729**
Let's Go: Chile (Year) (USA ISSN 1543-4982) **8729**
Let's Go: China (USA ISSN 1530-5333) **8729**
Let's Go: Costa Rica (USA ISSN 1543-4974) **8729**
Let's Go Costa Rica *see* Let's Go: Costa Rica **8729**
Let's Go Eastern Europe *see* Let's Go: Eastern Europe (Year) **8729**
Let's Go: Eastern Europe (Year) (USA ISSN 1530-826X) **8729**
Let's Go: Ecuador, Including the Galapogos Islands (Year) (USA ISSN 1558-7479) **8729**
Let's Go: Egypt (USA ISSN 1541-7549) **8729**
Let's Go Europe *see* Let's Go: Europe (Year) **8729**
Let's Go: Europe (Year) (USA ISSN 1530-8251) **8729**
Let's Go France *see* Let's Go: France (Year) **8729**
Let's Go: France (Year) (USA ISSN 1098-9366) **8729**
Let's Go Germany *see* Let's Go: Germany (Year) **8729**
Let's Go: Germany (Year) (USA ISSN 1530-8405) **8729**
Let's Go Greece *see* Let's Go: Greece (Year) **8729**
Let's Go: Greece (Year) (USA ISSN 1524-086X) **8729**
Let's Go: Hawaii (USA ISSN 1543-4966) **8729**
Let's Go Hawaii *see* Let's Go: Hawaii **8729**
Let's Go: India and Nepal *see* Let's Go: India & Nepal (Year) **8729**
Let's Go: India & Nepal (Year) (USA ISSN 1546-6868) **8729**
Let's Go Ireland *see* Let's Go: Ireland (Year) **8729**
Let's Go: Ireland (Year) (USA ISSN 1530-8235) **8729**
Let's Go: Israel (USA) **8729**
Let's Go Italy *see* Let's Go: Italy (Year) **8729**
Let's Go: Italy (Year) (USA ISSN 1540-7470) **8729**
Let's Go: Japan (USA ISSN 1549-9154) **8729**
Let's Go London *see* Let's Go: London (Year) **8730**
Let's Go: London (Year) (USA ISSN 1535-4903) **8730**
Let's Go Mexico *see* Let's Go: Mexico (Year) **8730**
Let's Go: Mexico (Year) (USA ISSN 1530-1702) **8730**
Let's Go: Middle East (USA ISSN 1531-6289) **8730**
Let's Go New York City *see* Let's Go: New York City (Year) **8730**
Let's Go: New York City (Year) (USA ISSN 1533-7553) **8730**
Let's Go New Zealand *see* Let's Go: New Zealand **8730**
Let's Go: New Zealand (USA ISSN 1930-7497) **8730**
Let's Go: New Zealand, Including Fiji (Year) *see* Let's Go: New Zealand **8730**
Let's Go: Pacific Northwest (Year) (USA ISSN 1549-5949) **8730**
Let's Go Paris *see* Let's Go: Paris (Year) **8730**
Let's Go: Paris (Year) (USA ISSN 1530-8413) **8730**
Let's Go: Peru (USA ISSN 1930-7500) **8730**
Let's Go: Puerto Rico (USA ISSN 1549-8476) **8730**
Let's Go Puerto Rico *see* Let's Go: Puerto Rico **8730**
Let's Go Roadtripping U S A *see* Let's Go: Roadtripping U S A **8730**
Let's Go: Roadtripping U S A (USA ISSN 1556-4258) **8730**
Let's Go: Rome (Year) (USA ISSN 1534-7184) **8730**
Let's Go: San Francisco (Year) (USA ISSN 1541-7182) **8730**
Let's Go: South Africa (Year) (USA ISSN 1528-9850) **8730**
† Let's Go: Southeast Asia (Year) (USA ISSN 1530-8278) **8971**
Let's Go: Southwest U S A (USA ISSN 1543-5695) **8730**
Let's Go Spain & Portugal *see* Let's Go: Spain & Portugal (Year) **8730**
Let's Go: Spain and Portugal *see* Let's Go: Spain & Portugal (Year) **8730**
Let's Go: Spain & Portugal (Year) (USA) **8730**
Let's Go: Thailand (USA ISSN 1544-5496) **8730**
Let's Go - The Budget Guide to Rome *see* Let's Go: Rome (Year) **8730**
Let's Go - The Budget Guide to Southeast Asia *see* Let's Go: Southeast Asia (Year) **8971**
Let's Go: Turkey (Year) (USA ISSN 1524-0851) **8730**
Let's Go U S A *see* Let's Go: U S A (Year) **8730**
Let's Go: U S A (Year) (USA ISSN 1534-4800) **8730**
Let's Go Vietnam *see* Let's Go: Vietnam **8730**
Let's Go: Vietnam (USA ISSN 1556-1917) **8730**
Let's Go: Washington, D.C. (Year) (USA ISSN 1536-3465) **8730**
Let's Go: Western Europe (USA ISSN 1540-1456) **8730**
Let's Go Western Europe *see* Let's Go: Western Europe **8730**
Let's Grow Dynamic Business *see* Dynamic Business **1959**
▼ Let's Grow Veg (GBR ISSN 1753-822X) **3742**
▼ Let's Knit (GBR ISSN 1753-4895) **6640**
† • Let's Live (USA ISSN 0024-1288) **8971**
Let's Love Oita (JPN) **3900**
Let's Make Cards (GBR ISSN 1750-9343) **537**
Let's Make It Official (USA) **8185**
• Let's Play Hockey (USA ISSN 0889-4795) **8185**
Let's Play Softball (USA ISSN 0892-9440) **8237**
Let's Prepare for the Grade Eight Intermediate Social Studies Test *see* New York State Grade 8 Intermediate Social Studies Test **2891**
Let's Review: Biology, the Living Environment (USA ISSN 1945-1768) **686**
Let's Square Dance (GBR ISSN 0301-8881) **2686**
• Let's Start! (ITA ISSN 0996-4959) **5144**
Let's Talk (GBR) **4050**
Let's Talk Entertainment (ZAF) **4980**
Let's Talk Families! (CAN) **8053**
Letter & Spirit (USA ISSN 1555-4147) **7804**
• Letter Arts Review (USA ISSN 1076-7339) **502**
Letter for American Young Adults *see* L A Y A! **2199**
A Letter from Minnesota (USA ISSN 1098-5638) **3980**
Letter from Plymouth Rock (USA) **7659**
Letter from Taize *see* Lettre de Taize **7804**
Letter of Credit Update *see* Documentary Credit World **1092**
The Letter of the College de France *see* College de France. The Letter **4447**
Letter of the L A A *see* Library Association of Alberta. Letter **5027**
Letter of the L A A. Newsletter (CAN) **5025**
The Letter Parade (USA) **5321**
Letter to Friends Around the World *see* Lettre aux Amis du Monde **8053**
• Letter to Libraries Online (USA ISSN 1059-3195) **5062**
Lettera agli Amici (ITA ISSN 1827-3246) **7804**
Lettera Clinica (ITA ISSN 1970-1071) **5661**
Lettera da Taize *see* Lettre de Taize **7804**
Lettera di Urologia (ITA ISSN 1120-3471) **6271**
• La Lettera Finanziaria (ITA ISSN 0391-7711) **1365**
• Lettera Internazionale (ITA ISSN 1592-2898) **8118**
• ➤ Lettera Matematica Pristem (ITA ISSN 1593-5884) **5509**
Letterato (ITA ISSN 0024-130X) **5224**
• Letteratura & Arte (ITA ISSN 1724-613X) **5321**
Letteratura e Dintorni (ITA ISSN 1828-6852) **5321**
▼ • Letteratura e Letterature (ITA ISSN 1971-906X) **5321**
Letteratura & Societa (ITA ISSN 1722-5531) **5321**
Letteratura Giovanile Argomenti *see* L G Argomenti **5223**
• Letteratura Italiana. Aggiornamento Bibliografico (ITA ISSN 1121-0753) **629**
• Letteratura Italiana Antica (ITA ISSN 1129-4981) **5321**
Letterature d'America (ITA ISSN 1125-1743) **5321**
† Lettere Filosofiche (ITA ISSN 1970-6197) **8971**
• Lettere Italiane (ITA ISSN 0024-1334) **5321**
Lettere Italiane. Biblioteca (ITA ISSN 0075-8892) **5321**
Lettere Italiane. Saggi (ITA ISSN 1122-0724) **5322**
Letterhead (USA) **503**
Letterheads (USA) **503**
Letterhoeke (NLD ISSN 1871-966X) **5025**
Letterlik *see* Op Ruwe Planken **5346**
• ➤ Letters in Applied Microbiology (GBR ISSN 0266-8254) **890**
Letters in Biotechnology *see* Shengwu Jishu Tongxun **770**
• Letters in Drug Design & Discovery (NLD ISSN 1570-1808) **6858**
• ➤ Letters in Mathematical Physics (NLD ISSN 0377-9017) **7025**

Title

The Lhasa Apso Reporter (USA ISSN 0273-8333) **6811**
Lhasa Bulletin (USA) **6811**
Li B e R *see* Libri per Bambini e Ragazzi **7566**
Li Jiang/Li River (CHN) **5322**
Li River *see* Li Jiang **5322**
• Liability & Insurance Week (USA) **4512**
Liability of Attorneys and Accountants for Securities Transactions (USA ISSN 1069-2312) **1637**
• Liability of Corporate Officers and Directors (USA) **4874**
Liability Prevention Series. State and Local Government Employment Liability (USA) **3450**
Liability Prevention Series. State & Local Government Environmental Liability (USA) **3451**
Liability Risk & Insurance (GBR ISSN 0960-099X) **4512**
• Liaison (Hamilton) (CAN ISSN 0831-5604) **6680**
• Liaison (Vanier) (CAN ISSN 0227-227X) **503**
Liaison Energie - Francophonie (CAN ISSN 0840-7827) **3141**
Liaison for Civil-Military Humanitarian Relief Collaborations (USA ISSN 1527-7208) **8053**
Liaisons Scientifiques (FRA ISSN 0290-6465) **3070**
Liaisons Sociales. Bref Social *see* Liaisons Sociales Quotidien **1695**
• Liaisons Sociales Europe (FRA ISSN 1621-2282) **8053**
Liaisons Sociales Magazine *see* Liaisons Sociales Quotidien **1695**
Liaisons Sociales Quotidien (FRA ISSN 1955-5024) **1695**
Liaisons Transports Equipement (FRA ISSN 0180-7811) **8502**
Liames (BRA ISSN 1678-0531) **5144**
➤ Al Liamm (FRA ISSN 0024-1733) **5322**
• Lianes (FRA ISSN 1776-3150) **8118**
• Liang-you Jiagong yu Shipin Jixie (CHN ISSN 1009-1807) **3654**
• Liang'an Guanxi/Relations Across Taiwan Straits (CHN ISSN 1006-5679) **7251**
• Liangshi Chucang/Grain Storage (CHN ISSN 1000-6958) **3654**
• ➤ Liangshi Wenti Yanjiu/Grain Issues Research (CHN ISSN 1003-2576) **3654**
• Liangshi yu Siliao Gongye/Cereal & Feed Industry (CHN ISSN 1003-6202) **241**
• Liangyou Cangchu Keji Tongxun (CHN ISSN 1674-1943) **3654**
Liangyou Zhiyin Wenzhai (CHN) **3826**
• Liangzi Dianzi Xuebao/Chinese Journal of Quantum Electronics (CHN ISSN 1007-5461) **7025**
• Liangzi Guangxue Xuebao/Acta Sinica Quantum Optica (CHN ISSN 1007-6654) **7025**
• Lianhe Bao/United Daily News (TWN ISSN 1607-9701) **3960**
Lianhe Shibao/United Times (CHN) **3826**
Lianhe Wanbao (SGP) **3945**
Lianhe Wanbao/United Evening News (TWN ISSN 1607-9760) **3960**
Lianhe Zaobao (SGP) **3945**
Lianhegui Guoji Maoyifa Weiyuanhui Huiyi Gongzuo Baogao (AUT ISSN 0251-916X) **4935**
Lianheguo. Anquan Lishihui. Zhengshi Jilu *see* United Nations. Security Council. Official Records **7271**
Lianheguo Jishi/United Nations Chronicle (CHN ISSN 1003-2282) **7251**
Lianheguo Liangshi ji Nongye Zuzhi. Dayanghou Quyu Huiyi Baogao. Liangnong Zuzhi *see* F A O Regional Conference for Asia and the Pacific. Report **109**
Lianheguo Liangshi ji Nongye Zuzhi. Dayanghou Quyu Huiyi Baogao. Liangnong Zuzhi *see* Conference Regionale de la F A O pour l'Asie et le Pacifique. Rapport **102**
Lianhuan Huabao (CHN ISSN 0457-8090) **3826**
• Liansuo yu Texu - Guanli Gongchengshi (CHN) **1144**
• Liantie/Ironmaking (CHN ISSN 1001-1471) **6320**
Lianyou Huagong Zidonghua/Automation in Refined and Chemical Industry *see* Shiyou Huagong Zidonghua **6792**
• ➤ Lianyou Sheji/Petroleum Refinery Engineering (CHN ISSN 1002-106X) **6777**
• Lianyou yu Huagong/Refining and Chemicals (CHN ISSN 1671-4962) **6777**
Lianyungang Huagong Gaodeng Zhuanke Xuexiao Xuebao/Lianyungang College of Chemical Technology. Journal *see* Huaihai Gongxueyuan Xuebao (Ziran Kexue Ban) **7862**
• Lianyungang Zhiye Jishu Xueyuan Xuebao/Lanyungang Techincal College. Journal (CHN ISSN 1009-4318) **2883**
• Liaocheng Daxue Xuebao (Shehui Kexue Ban)/Liaocheng University. Journal (Social Sciences Edition) (CHN ISSN 1672-1217) **7983**
• Liaocheng Daxue Xuebao (Ziran Kexue Ban)/Liaocheng University. Journal (Natural Science Edition) (CHN ISSN 1672-6634) **7879**
Liaocheng University. Journal (Natural Science Edition) *see* Liaocheng Daxue Xuebao (Ziran Kexue Ban) **7879**
Liaocheng University. Journal (Social Sciences Edition) *see* Liaocheng Daxue Xuebao (Shehui Kexue Ban) **7983**
• Liaodong Xueyuan Xuebao (Shehui Kexue Ban)/Eastern Liaodong University. Journal (Social Sciences) (CHN ISSN 1672-8572) **7983**
• Liaodong Xueyuan Xuebao (Ziran Kexue Ban)/Eastern Liaodong University. Journal (Natural Science Edition) (CHN ISSN 1008-2174) **7879**
Liaoning Cai-Zhuan Xuebao *see* Liaodong Xueyuan Xuebao (Shehui Kexue Ban) **7983**
Liaoning Cai-Zhuan Xuebao/Liaoning Financial College Journal *see* Liaodong Xueyuan Xuebao (Ziran Kexue Ban) **7879**
Liaoning Chaoxianwen Bao/Liaoning Gazette in Korean (CHN) **3826**
Liaoning Chemical Industry *see* Liaoning Huagong **3250**
Liaoning Daily *see* Liaoning Ribao **3826**
• Liaoning Daxue Xuebao (Zhexue Shehui Kexue Ban)/Liaoning University. Journal (Philosophy and Social Sciences Edition) (CHN ISSN 1002-3291) **7983**
• Liaoning Daxue Xuebao (Ziran Kexue Ban)/Liaoning University. Journal (Natural Sciences Edition) (CHN ISSN 1000-5846) **7879**
† Liaoning Dizhi/Liaoning Geology (CHN ISSN 1000-6273) **8971**
Liaoning Economic Daily *see* Liaoning Jingji Ribao **1497**
Liaoning Economics *see* Liaoning Jingji **1144**
Liaoning Education *see* Liaoning Jiaoyu **2883**
Liaoning Forestry Technology *see* Liaoning Linye Keji **3696**
• Liaoning Gaozhi Xuebao/Liaoning Higher Vocational Technical Institute Journal (CHN ISSN 1009-7600) **2992**
Liaoning Gazette in Korean *see* Liaoning Chaoxianwen Bao **3826**
Liaoning Geology *see* Liaoning Dizhi **8971**
• Liaoning Gongcheng Jishu Daxue Xuebao (Shehui Kexue Ban)/Liaoning Technical University. Journal (Social Science Edition) (CHN ISSN 1008-391X) **7983**
• Liaoning Gongcheng Jishu Daxue Xuebao (Ziran Kexue Ban)/Liaoning Technical University. Journal (Natural Science Edition) (CHN ISSN 1008-0562) **7879**
Liaoning Gongxueyuan Xuebao (Shehui Kexue Ban)/Liaoning Institute of Technology. Journal (Social Science Edition) *see* Liaoning Gongye Daxue Xuebao (Shehui Kexue Ban) **7983**
• Liaoning Gongye Daxue Xuebao (Shehui Kexue Ban)/Liaoning University of Technology. Journal (Social Science Edition) (CHN ISSN 1674-327X) **7983**
• Liaoning Gongye Daxue Xuebao (Ziran Kexue Ban)/Liaoning University of Technology. Journal (Natural Science Edition) (CHN ISSN 1674-3261) **7879**
Liaoning Gongye Daxue Xuebao/Liaoning Institute of Technology. Journal *see* Liaoning Gongye Daxue Xuebao (Ziran Kexue Ban) **7879**
Liaoning Higher Vocational Technical Institute Journal *see* Liaoning Gaozhi Xuebao **2992**
† Liaoning Huabao/Liaoning Pictorial (CHN ISSN 0457-6306) **8971**
• ➤ Liaoning Huagong/Liaoning Chemical Industry (CHN ISSN 1004-0935) **3250**
Liaoning Institute of Science and Technology. Journal *see* Liaoning Keji Xueyuan Xuebao **7879**
• Liaoning Jiaoyu/Liaoning Education (CHN ISSN 1002-8196) **2883**
• Liaoning Jing-Zhuan Xuebao/Liaoning Police Academy. Journal (CHN ISSN 1008-5378) **4893**
• Liaoning Jingji/Liaoning Economics (CHN ISSN 1003-4617) **1144**
Liaoning Jingji Ribao/Liaoning Economic Daily (CHN) **1497**
Liaoning Journal of Medicine and Clinic *see* Shiyong Yaowu yu Linchuang **5714**
Liaoning Journal of Traditional Chinese Medicine *see* Liaoning Zhongyi Zazhi **312**
• ➤ Liaoning Keji Daxue Xuebao/Liaoning University of Science and Technology. Journal (CHN ISSN 1674-1048) **6320**
• Liaoning Keji Xueyuan Xuebao/Liaoning Institute of Science and Technology. Journal (CHN) **7879**
• Liaoning Linye Keji/Liaoning Forestry Technology (CHN ISSN 1001-1714) **3696**
Liaoning Medical University. Journal *see* Liaoning Yixueyuan Xuebao **7879**
Liaoning Medical University. Journal (Social Sciednce Edition) *see* Liaoning Yixueyuan Xuebao (Shehui Kexue Ban) **7983**
• Liaoning Nongmin Bao (CHN) **3826**
Liaoning Normal University. Journal (Natural Science Edition) *see* Liaoning Shifan Daxue Xuebao (Ziran Kexue Ban) **7879**
Liaoning Normal University. Journal (Social Sciences Edition) *see* Liaoning Shifan Daxue Xuebao (Shehui Kexue Ban) **7983**
Liaoning Pictorial *see* Liaoning Huabao **8971**
Liaoning Police Academy. Journal *see* Liaoning Jing-Zhuan Xuebao **4893**
Liaoning Provincial College of Communications. Journal *see* Liaoning Sheng Jiaotong Gaodeng Zhuanke Xuexiao Xuebao **2331**
Liaoning Qingnian/Liaoning Youth (CHN ISSN 1002-1922) **2199**
Liaoning Ribao/Liaoning Daily (CHN) **3826**
Liaoning Ribao (Haiweiban) *see* Liaoning Ribao **3826**
• Liaoning Sheng Jiaotong Gaodeng Zhuanke Xuexiao Xuebao/Liaoning Provincial College of Communications. Journal (CHN ISSN 1008-3812) **2331**
• Liaoning Shi-Zhuang Xuebao (Ziran Kexue Ban)/Liaoning Teachers College. Journal (Natural Science Edition) (CHN ISSN 1008-5688) **7879**
• Liaoning Shifan Daxue Xuebao (Shehui Kexue Ban)/Liaoning Normal University. Journal (Social Sciences Edition) (CHN ISSN 1000-1751) **7983**
• Liaoning Shifan Daxue Xuebao (Ziran Kexue Ban)/Liaoning Normal University. Journal (Natural Science Edition) (CHN ISSN 1000-1735) **7879**
• Liaoning Shiyou Huagong Daxue Xuebao/Liaoning University of Petroleum & Chemical Technology. Journal (CHN ISSN 1672-6952) **6777**
• Liaoning Shuiwu Gaodeng Zhuanke Xuexiao Xuebao/Liaoning Taxation College Journal (CHN ISSN 1008-2859) **1933**
Liaoning Taxation College Journal *see* Liaoning Shuiwu Gaodeng Zhuanke Xuexiao Xuebao **1933**
Liaoning Teachers College. Journal (Natural Science Edition) *see* Liaoning Shi-Zhuang Xuebao (Ziran Kexue Ban) **7879**
Liaoning Technical University. Journal (Natural Science Edition) *see* Liaoning Gongcheng Jishu Daxue Xuebao (Ziran Kexue Ban) **7879**
Liaoning Technical University. Journal (Social Science Edition) *see* Liaoning Gongcheng Jishu Daxue Xuebao (Shehui Kexue Ban) **7983**
Liaoning University. Journal (Natural Sciences Edition) *see* Liaoning Daxue Xuebao (Ziran Kexue Ban) **7879**
Liaoning University. Journal (Philosophy and Social Sciences Edition) *see* Liaoning Daxue Xuebao (Zhexue Shehui Kexue Ban) **7983**
Liaoning University of Petroleum & Chemical Technology. Journal *see* Liaoning Shiyou Huagong Daxue Xuebao **6777**
Liaoning University of Science and Technology. Journal *see* Liaoning Keji Daxue Xuebao **6320**
Liaoning University of Technology. Journal (Natural Science Edition) *see* Liaoning Gongye Daxue Xuebao (Ziran Kexue Ban) **7879**
Liaoning University of Technology. Journal (Social Science Edition) *see* Liaoning Gongye Daxue Xuebao (Shehui Kexue Ban) **7983**
Liaoning Universtity of Traditional Chinese Medicine. Journal *see* Liaoning Zhongyiyao Daxue Xuebao **5661**
Liaoning Yaowu yu Linchuang *see* Shiyong Yaowu yu Linchuang **5714**
• Liaoning Yixue Zazhi/Medical Journal of Liaoning (CHN ISSN 1001-1722) **5661**
• Liaoning Yixueyuan Xuebao/Liaoning Medical University. Journal (CHN ISSN 1674-0424) **7879**
• Liaoning Yixueyuan Xuebao (Shehui Kexue Ban)/Liaoning Medical University. Journal (Social Sciednce Edition) (CHN ISSN 1674-0416) **7983**
Liaoning Youth *see* Liaoning Qingnian **2199**
Liaoning Zhongyi Xueyuan Xuebao/Liaoning College of Traditional Chinese Medicine. Journal *see* Liaoning Zhongyiyao Daxue Xuebao **5661**
• Liaoning Zhongyi Zazhi/Liaoning Journal of Traditional Chinese Medicine (CHN ISSN 1000-1719) **312**
• Liaoning Zhongyiyao Daxue Xuebao/Liaoning Universtity of Traditional Chinese Medicine. Journal (CHN ISSN 1673-842X) **5661**
• Liaoshen Wanbao (CHN) **3826**
• Liaowang/Outlook Weekly (CHN ISSN 1002-5723) **3826**
Liason Cells for University - Industry Interaction (Year) (IND) **2992**
Liat Islander (ATG) **8784**
Liaudies Kultura (LTU ISSN 0236-0551) **346**
Lib Ed (GBR ISSN 0267-8500) **2883**
Libas International (GBR ISSN 0954-1411) **8871**
Libel Defense Resource Center Bulletin *see* L D R C Bulletin **4834**
Libel Defense Resource Center MediaLawLetter *see* L D R C MediaLawLetter **4710**
Libelle (BEL ISSN 0024-175X) **8871**
• Libelle (NLD ISSN 0165-4926) **8871**
Libelle. Balance (NLD ISSN 1871-3831) **8871**
Libelle Bookazine (NLD ISSN 1874-0405) **5322**
Libelles (FRA ISSN 1767-2163) **6932**
➤ Libellula (DEU ISSN 0723-6514) **854**
Libellus (DEU) **7566**
Liber *see* Arts and Minds **2967**
Liber (NLD ISSN 1872-0862) **7151**
• ➤ Liber (ROM ISSN 1454-265X) **2883**
† Liber Academiae Kierkegaardiensis (DNK ISSN 0109-5978) **8971**
• Liber Annuus (BEL ISSN 0081-8933) **403**
Liber: Revista de Bibliotecologia (MEX) **5025**
Liberaal Reveil (NLD ISSN 0167-0883) **5224**
• Liberabit (PER ISSN 1729-4827) **7383**
• El Liberal (COL ISSN 0121-9022) **3830**
Liberal (DEU ISSN 0459-1992) **7151**
Liberal *see* Liberalt Overblik **7151**
• Liberal (NOR ISSN 1504-7431) **7151**
Liberal Aerogramme *see* Liberal Matters **7151**
Liberal Arts Fans *see* Wenke Aihaozhe **4482**
Liberal Catholic (GBR ISSN 0024-1792) **7764**
Liberal Debatt (SWE ISSN 0024-1814) **7151**
• Liberal Democracy Nepal Bulletin (USA ISSN 1940-283X) **4185**
Liberal Democrat News (GBR ISSN 0954-5735) **7151**
Liberal Digest (IND ISSN 0973-0273) **7151**
• El Liberal Digital (ARG) **3791**
• Liberal Education (USA ISSN 0024-1822) **2992**
Liberal Matters (GBR ISSN 1754-1964) **7151**
Liberal.no *see* Liberal **7151**
Liberal Ungdom (SWE ISSN 0024-1857) **7151**
De Liberale Vrouw (NLD) **8871**
• Liberalt Overblik (DNK ISSN 1602-1878) **7151**
Liberation (CAN ISSN 0829-0954) **7764**
• Liberation (FRA ISSN 0335-1793) **3841**
Liberation (GBR ISSN 0024-1873) **7212**
Liberation (IND ISSN 0024-1881) **7151**
Liberation Army Daily *see* Jiefangjun Bao **6428**
Liberation Daily *see* Jiefang Ribao **3825**
Liberation Daily Bound Index *see* Jiefang Ribao Hedingben **3825**
▼ Liberation. Next (FRA ISSN 1958-1440) **5075**
Liberation Path *see* Vyzvol'nyi Shlyakh **5244**
Liberation War (IND ISSN 0047-4495) **5224**
• The Liberator (Cartersville) (USA ISSN 1046-5065) **7151**
The Liberator (Forest Lake) (USA ISSN 1040-3760) **6302**
LiberEta (ITA) **4051**
Liberia. Ministry of Lands, Mines and Energy. Annual Report (LBR) **3278**
Liberia. Office of Fiscal Policy and Planning. Finance Bulletin *see* Finance Bulletin **1487**
Liberian Philatelic Society Journal (USA) **6896**
Liberian Shipping Journal (GBR) **8649**
Liberian Star (LBR) **3789**
➤ Liberian Studies Journal (USA ISSN 0024-1989) **7983**
Liberian Studies Monograph Series (USA) **7983**
Liberian Studies Research Working Papers (USA) **7983**
Liberian Trade Topics and Newsletter and Forecasts (LBR) **1406**
Liberpolis (PRT) **5025**
LIBERQuarterly *see* L I B E R Quarterly (Online) **5024**
• La Liberta (ITA ISSN 0024-1997) **7804**
Liberta di Educazione (ITA) **2883**
Libertad (CRI) **7151**
Libertad de Expresion (PAN) **8118**
Libertarian Alliance. Atheist Notes (GBR ISSN 0953-7791) **7151**
Libertarian Alliance. Background Briefings (GBR ISSN 0267-7121) **7151**
Libertarian Alliance. Cultural Notes (GBR ISSN 0267-677X) **7151**
Libertarian Alliance. Economic Notes (GBR ISSN 0267-7164) **1497**
Libertarian Alliance. Educational Notes (GBR ISSN 0953-7775) **2883**
Libertarian Alliance. Foreign Policy Perspectives (GBR ISSN 0267-6761) **7251**
Libertarian Alliance. Historical Notes (GBR ISSN 0267-7105) **4240**
Libertarian Alliance. Legal Notes (GBR ISSN 0267-7083) **4723**
Libertarian Alliance. Pamphlets (GBR ISSN 0953-7783) **7151**
Libertarian Alliance. Personal Perspectives (GBR ISSN 0267-7156) **7151**
Libertarian Alliance. Philosophical Notes (GBR ISSN 0267-7091) **6932**
Libertarian Alliance. Political Notes (GBR ISSN 0267-7059) **7151**
• Libertarian Alliance. Psychological Notes (GBR ISSN 0267-7172) **7383**
Libertarian Alliance. Religious Notes (GBR ISSN 0953-7805) **7660**
Libertarian Alliance. Scientific Notes (GBR ISSN 0267-7067) **7151**
Libertarian Alliance. Sociological Notes (GBR ISSN 0267-7113) **8118**
Libertarian Alliance. Study Guides (GBR ISSN 0267-7180) **7151**
Libertarian Alliance. Tactical Notes (GBR ISSN 0268-2923) **7151**
Libertarian Alliance. World Reports (GBR) **7151**
Libertarian Heritage (GBR ISSN 0959-566X) **7151**
Libertarian Heritage Reprints (GBR ISSN 0959-5678) **7151**
Libertarian News (GBR ISSN 0267-6788) **7151**
• ➤ Libertarian Papers (USA ISSN 1947-6949) **7151**
Libertarian Party News (USA ISSN 8755-139X) **7151**
Libertarian Reprints (GBR ISSN 0267-6796) **7151**
Libertarian Student (GBR ISSN 0267-7199) **7151**
Libertarians for Gay and Lesbian Concerns Newsletter *see* L G L C Newsletter **5319**
Libertarians for Life Reports *see* L F L Reports **973**
• Libertas (MEX) **2992**
Libertas (SWE ISSN 1100-3693) **2290**
Libertas (USA) **7151**
➤ Libertas Mathematica (USA ISSN 0278-5307) **5509**
Libertas Optima Rerum (DEU ISSN 0944-8039) **7251**
• Libertatea (ROM ISSN 1220-8019) **3933**
➤ Liberte (CAN ISSN 0024-2020) **5425**
Liberte (DZA) **3790**
Liberte de Circulation et d'Etablissement, Charte des Droits et Libertes *see* Mobility Rights and the Charter of Rights and Freedoms **4851**
Liberte de l'Est (FRA ISSN 0990-5200) **3841**
Liberty *see* Svoboda **3567**

Title

Libya Past and Present Series (GBR) 8730
Libya Petrochemicals Report (GBR ISSN 1749-2327) 6777
Libyan Journal of Agriculture (LBY ISSN 1010-3740) 134
• ➤ Libyan Journal of Medicine (LBY ISSN 1993-2820) 5661
Libyan Journal of Sciences (LBY ISSN 0368-7481) 7880
➤ Libyan Studies (GBR ISSN 0263-7189) 403
Licai Zhoubao/Money Week (CHN) 1144
Licencias Actualidad (ESP ISSN 1139-7152) 6754
License! see License! Global 1829
License! Europe (GBR) 1829
• License! Global (USA ISSN 1936-4989) 1829
Licensed and Catering News (GBR) 606
Licensed Fuel Facility Status Report (USA) 3170
Licensed Practical Nurse (Year) see L P N (Year) 5968
Licensee Contractor and Vendor Inspection Status Report (USA ISSN 1056-9049) 3171
Licensee Event Report Compilation (USA ISSN 1056-9057) 3171
Licensee Name Index to Non-Government Master Frequency Data Base (USA) 2348
Licensing (DEU) 6754
• Licensing and Gaming Laws New South Wales (AUS) 4723
Licensing & Merchandising (DEU) 28
• Licensing and Surplus Lines Laws (USA) 4512
The Licensing Book (USA ISSN 0741-0107) 6754
Licensing Business Yearbook see The Licensing Letter 6754
Licensing Business Yearbook Combined with the Licensing Letter see The Licensing Letter 6754
Licensing Economics Review (USA) 4874
Licensing Executives Society Nouvelles see L E S Nouvelles 8430
• The Licensing Journal (USA ISSN 1040-4023) 6754
Licensing Law Handbook (USA ISSN 0731-5783) 4723
Licensing Law Reports (GBR ISSN 1473-706X) 6754
• The Licensing Letter (USA ISSN 8755-6235) 6754
Licensing Procedures and Precedents (GBR) 4723
Licensing Reporter Europe (GBR) 6754
Licensing Review (GBR ISSN 0959-8421) 4723
Licensing World (IRL ISSN 1393-0826) 606
LicensingWeek (USA) 2478
Licensure Exchange (USA ISSN 1093-541X) 3208
Liceo Classico G Garibaldi di Palermo. Annali (ITA ISSN 1128-210X) 2883
Liceo Franciscano (ESP ISSN 0211-4011) 7660
▼ Lichaamstaal (NLD ISSN 1876-1895) 5661
Lichamelijke Opvoeding (NLD ISSN 0024-2810) 3070
Lichen (FRA ISSN 1953-7603) 7152
Lichen see Raiken 814
• ➤ The Lichenologist (GBR ISSN 0024-2829) 800
➤ Lichens (VEN ISSN 1316-4899) 800
Lichnost', Kultura, Obshchestvo/Personality, Culture, Society (RUS ISSN 1606-951X) 7983
Licht (DEU ISSN 0171-5496) 3323
Licht (NLD ISSN 0929-2160) 3323
Licht Architektur Technik (DEU) 4560
Licht des Lebens (USA) 7660
Licht im Osten (DEU ISSN 0945-4179) 7660
Licht und Leben (DEU ISSN 0047-4584) 7764
Lichtbogen (DEU ISSN 0024-2845) 2071
Lichtenberg-Jahrbuch (DEU ISSN 0936-4242) 644
Lichtenrader Rundschau (DEU ISSN 0932-318X) 3852
Lichtentaler Pfarrnachrichten (AUT) 7804
Lichtfokus (DEU) 6646
Der Lichtgang (DEU) 3620
Lichtleiter und Glasfaserkabel see Informationsdienst F I Z Technik. Lichtleiter und Glasfaserkabel 2347
F.O. Licht's Buyer's Guide for the Sugar and Allied Industries (Year) see Buyer's Guide for the Sugar and Allied Industries (Year) 3629
F.O. Licht's International Coffee and Tea Directory (Year) see World Coffee and Tea Yearbook (Year) 3668
F.O. Licht's World Sugar and Sweetener Yearbook (Year) see World Sugar Yearbook (Year) 3668
Lichtstrahlen (DEU) 7764
Lichtungen (AUT ISSN 1012-4705) 5322
• Licitationen (DNK ISSN 0024-287X) 1020
Lickety Split (CAN ISSN 1715-2089) 5322
Licking Lantern (USA ISSN 0748-1012) 3773
➤ The Licking River Review (USA ISSN 1087-7509) 5322
Licni Dohoci (SRB ISSN 0300-2535) 1249
La Licorne (FRA ISSN 0398-9992) 5322
Lide a Zeme/People and Countries (CZE ISSN 0024-2896) 4018
Lider (POL ISSN 0867-7697) 2883
Lidia (As) (NOR ISSN 0801-1524) 134
• Lidove Noviny (CZE ISSN 0862-5921) 3832
Das Liebhaberorcheste (DEU ISSN 0460-0932) 6584
Liechtenstein. Botanisch-Zoologische Gesellschaft Liechtenstein Sargans-Werdenberg. Bericht (LIE ISSN 0302-119X) 686
Liechtenstein - Fuerstentum im Herzen Europas see Liechtenstein - Principality in the Heart of Europe 4240
• Liechtenstein News (LIE ISSN 1563-6003) 3905
Liechtenstein Politische Schriften (LIE ISSN 0259-4137) 7152
Liechtenstein - Principality in the Heart of Europe (LIE) 4240
Liechtenstein - Principaute au Coeur de L'Europe see Liechtenstein - Principality in the Heart of Europe 4240
Liechtensteiner Bau- und Hauszeitung (LIE) 1020
• Liechtensteiner Vaterland (LIE ISSN 1818-9202) 3905
• Liechtensteiner Volksblatt (LIE) 3905
Liechtensteinische Industrie- und Handelskammer. Annual Report (LIE) 1406
Liechtensteinische Industrie- und Handelskammer. Bulletin (LIE) 1406
Liecive Rastliny/Medicinal Herbs (SVK ISSN 1335-9878) 800
• Lied und Populaere Kultur/Song and Popular Culture (DEU ISSN 1619-0548) 6584
Liegenschaft Aktuell (DEU) 1144
Liehuvan Varit (FIN ISSN 0357-1432) 3773
Liekki (SWE ISSN 0347-3597) 5322
Lielas Rutis (LVA) 8185
Le Lien (FRA ISSN 1766-9634) 7804
Le Lien (SYR) 7804
Lien des Fournisseurs de la Defense Nationale (FRA ISSN 0290-9464) 2227
Le Lien des Freres Mennonites (CAN ISSN 0840-5972) 7738
Le Lien entre les Parents de Pretres, Religieux et Religieuses see Le Lien 7804
Lien Ho Wen Hsueh see Unitas 5243
Lien Horticole (FRA ISSN 0293-6852) 3742
Lien Informatique (FRA ISSN 0180-0957) 5030
Le Lien Israel-Diaspora.info (FRA ISSN 1772-0664) 3548
Le Lien Social (FRA ISSN 1285-3097) 8118
• Lien Social (Toulouse) (FRA ISSN 0994-1819) 8053
Lien Social et Politiques - R I A C (CAN ISSN 1204-3206) 8054
Lienzo (PER ISSN 1025-9902) 2290
• ➤ Lier en Boog (NLD ISSN 0925-8191) 503
Liesma (LVA ISSN 0132-6449) 3904
Lietuva Pristato (LTU ISSN 1822-1009) 3905
Lietuvis (IRL ISSN 1649-5594) 3548
Lietuviu Dienos/Lithuanian Days (USA ISSN 0024-2950) 3548
Lietuvos Aidas (LTU) 3905
Lietuvos Archeologija (LTU ISSN 0207-8694) 404
• Lietuvos Bankas. Banku Statistikos Metrastis (LTU ISSN 1392-687X) 1365
• Lietuvos Bankas. Finansinio Stabilumo Apzvalga (LTU ISSN 1822-5063) 1365
• Lietuvos Bankas. Menesinis Biuletenis/Bank of Lithuania. Monthly Bulletin (LTU ISSN 1392-0413) 1365
• Lietuvos Bankas. Metu Ataskaita (LTU ISSN 1392-4699) 1365
• ➤ Lietuvos Chirurgija (LTU ISSN 1392-0995) 6251
➤ Lietuvos Etnologija (LTU ISSN 1392-4028) 346
Lietuvos Istorijos Metrastis/Ezhegodnik Istorii Litovy/Jahrbuch fuer Litauische Geschichte/Yearbook of Lithuanian History (LTU ISSN 0202-3342) 4240
Lietuvos Istorijos Studijos/Studies of Lithuanian History (LTU ISSN 1392-0448) 4240
➤ Lietuvos Matematikos Rinkinys (LTU ISSN 0132-2818) 5509
Lietuvos Metine Strategine Apzvalga (LTU ISSN 1648-8016) 6431
Lietuvos Metine Strategine Apzvalga see Lithuanian Annual Strategic Review 6431
Lietuvos Mokslas/Science and Arts of Lithuania (LTU ISSN 1392-4044) 4463
➤ Lietuvos Mokslu Akademija. Chemija/Lithuanian Academy of Sciences. Chemistry (LTU ISSN 0235-7216) 2071
• Lietuvos Mokslu Akademija. Energetika/Power Engineering (LTU ISSN 0235-7208) 3141
Lietuvos Muziejai/Lithuanian Museums (LTU ISSN 1648-7109) 6528
Lietuvos Muzikologija/Lithuanian Musicology (LTU ISSN 1392-9313) 6584
Lietuvos Oftalmologija (LTU ISSN 1648-5289) 6046
• Lietuvos Respublikos Mokejimu Balansas (LTU ISSN 1392-3161) 1365
• Lietuvos Respublikos Mokejimu Balansas (Annual)/Balance of Payments of the Republic of Lithuania (Annual) (LTU ISSN 1822-3788) 1365
• Lietuvos Rytas (LTU ISSN 1392-2351) 3905
Lietuvos Sportas (LTU) 8185
Lietuvos T.S.R. Mokslu Akademijos Darbai. B Serija. Chemija, Technika, Fizine Geografija / Akademiya Nauk Litovskoi S.S.R. Trudy. Seriya B. Khimiya, Tekhnika, Fizicheskaya Geografiya see Lietuvos Mokslu Akademija. Energetika 3141
Lietuvos Trombozes Hemostazes Zurnalas (LTU ISSN 1648-4517) 5795
Lietuvos Ukis (LTU) 3905
Lieux d'Utopies (FRA ISSN 1772-5003) 6932
Liezhiwen Shi Bao (CAN ISSN 1202-9459) 3548
Life see Ren Sheng 973
Life! (DEU) 8871
Life see Official N A I C Quarterly Statement Blank. Life 4517
The Life see La Vida 5086
Life and Companions see Rensheng yu Banlu 7995
Life and Environment see Vie et Milieu 710
Life and Environment see Seikatsu to Kankyo 3465
Life and Films of Michelle Pfeiffer (GBR) 6506
Life & Health see Shenghuo yu Jiankang 6996
Life & Health Advisor / Mid Atlantic see Life&Health Advisor / Mid Atlantic 4513
Life & Health Advisor / New England see Life&Health Advisor / New England 4513
Life & Health Advisor / Southeast see Life&Health Advisor / Southeast 4513
Life and Learning (USA ISSN 1097-0878) 6932
Life and Literature see Elet es Irodalom 5215
• Life & Pensions (GBR ISSN 1748-9024) 1637
Life and School see Zivot i Skola 2929
Life and Science (DEU ISSN 1612-927X) 6700
Life & Style (GRC) 3874
Life & Style see Life&Style Weekly 3980
▼ Life & Style Weekly (DEU ISSN 1866-7759) 5075
Life and Style Weekly see Life&Style Weekly 3980
Life & Style Weekly see Life&Style Weekly 3980
Life and Taxes (USA) 1933
Life and Thought see Zycie i Mysl 6962
• Life & Work (GBR ISSN 0024-306X) 7764
Life At Ken-Caryl (USA ISSN 0899-6318) 3980
Life at Work (USA ISSN 1099-2650) 7660
Life Communications see Communique 23
Life Concepts (USA ISSN 1939-7690) 4512
Life - Creation see Shenghuo Chuangzao 3828
Life Daily see Shenghuo Ribao 3828
Life etc (AUS ISSN 1833-0266) 5075
• Life Extension (USA ISSN 1524-198X) 312
Life Guardian (CAN) 8054
▼ Life Images (USA ISSN 1940-5782) 6970
Life Imitating Art see L I A: Life Imitating Art 502
Life in Action Magazine (USA) 6932
• Life in New Zealand (NZL ISSN 1177-5637) 1696
• A Life in the Day (GBR ISSN 1366-6282) 8054
• Life Insurance Business in Japan (JPN) 4512
Life Insurance Business in Taiwan (Year) (TWN) 4512
Life Insurance Companies, Property and Casualty Insurance Companies. Summary Financial Data (CAN ISSN 1209-5478) 4512
• Life Insurance International (GBR ISSN 0956-327X) 4512
Life Insurance Marketing and Research Association International Learning Institute. Newsletter see L I M R A International Learning Institute. Newsletter 4512
Life Insurance Marketing and Research Association's MarketFacts Quarterly see L I M R A's MarketFacts Quarterly 4512
Life Insurance Marketing and Research Association's Vision see L I M R A's Vision 8970
Life Insurance Policy Comparisons and Underwriting (USA ISSN 1939-8220) 4512
Life Insurance Selling (USA ISSN 0024-3140) 4513
Life Insurers Fact Book (USA ISSN 1553-8443) 4513
Life is Better Outdoors see Downhome 5069
Life Is Local see The Irish View 4233
Life Learning (CAN ISSN 1499-7533) 2883
Life-Line (USA ISSN 1059-6593) 6158
Life Lines (USA) 4513
Life News see Shenghuobao 3828
Life Office Management Association, Inc. Resource see L O M A Resource 4512
Life Overseas/Hua Jen (HKG) 3875
Life Renewed see Obnovljeni Zivot 7810
• Life Safety Code Handbook (Year) (USA ISSN 0192-1002) 3580
Life Science Foundation of Japan. Annuals see Raifu Saiensu Shinko Zaidan Nenpo 699
Life Science Instruments see Shengming Kexue Yiqi 704
• Life Science Journal (CHN ISSN 1097-8135) 5661
Life Science Law Review (HKG) 4723
Life Science News (SWE) 7880
• Life Science Quarterly (USA) 686
Life Science Research see Shengming Kexue Yanjiu 704
• Life Science Today (GBR ISSN 1470-4560) 6858
• Life Science Weekly (USA ISSN 1552-2466) 686
Life Sciences (NLD ISSN 1574-6895) 2071
• ➤ Life Sciences (USA ISSN 0024-3205) 7880
Life Sciences Education see C B E Life Sciences Education 828
Life Sciences: Law and Business see Bio-Science Law Review 4858
Life Sciences Law & Business (GBR ISSN 1743-5951) 4724
▼ • Life Sciences Law and Industry Report (USA ISSN 1935-7257) 5661
Life Sector Earnings Recap (CAN ISSN 1719-3680) 1637
Life Span and Disability see Ciclo Evolutivo e Disabilita 6131
Life Story (USA ISSN 1938-582X) 644
Life Sucks Die (USA) 6584
Life Support and Biosphere Science see Habitation 3645
• Life Tables, Canada, Provinces and Territories (CAN ISSN 1910-3484) 8385
Life Tables for Korea see Saengmyeong Pyo 7314
Life Video (POL ISSN 1230-8188) 3107
• Life Words: K J V Leader Guide (King James Version) (USA ISSN 1557-4865) 7764
• Life Words: K J V Leader Guide (Large Print Edition) (King James Version) (USA ISSN 1557-4873) 7764
Life Words K J V Learner Guide see Life Words: K J V Leader Guide (Large Print Edition) 7764
Life Words: King James Version Leader Guide see Life Words: K J V Leader Guide 7764
Life World see Shengming Shijie 817
• Life Writing (GBR ISSN 1448-4528) 5322
Life Writing (NZL ISSN 1177-1704) 5323
Life&Health Advisor / Mid Atlantic (USA) 4513
Life&Health Advisor / New England (USA) 4513
Life&Health Advisor / Southeast (USA) 4513
Life&Style Weekly see Life & Style Weekly 5075
Life&Style Weekly (USA ISSN 1550-6274) 3980
Lifeboat (GBR ISSN 0024-3086) 8277
Lifeboat International (GBR ISSN 0308-7441) 8649
Lifecycle Solutions see Adelphi Lifecycle Solutions 6818
• LifeDate (USA ISSN 1098-5859) 7764
• LifeExcellence Newsletter (USA ISSN 2150-1971) 7383
• Lifeglow (USA) 7660
Lifeline (GBR ISSN 0308-3624) 7660
Lifeline (IND) 8620
Lifeline (Syracuse) (USA ISSN 1528-6479) 3773
Lifelineletter (USA) 6663
Lifeliner (Riverside) (USA ISSN 0047-4630) 3773
• Lifelines (USA ISSN 1047-8655) 3773
Lifelines (Saskatoon) (CAN ISSN 1182-0489) 6992
Lifelines (Toronto) (CAN ISSN 0834-3543) 6663
Lifelong (USA) 4051
Lifelong Education Bibliography (DEU) 2943
Lifelong Learning Book Series (NLD ISSN 1871-322X) 2943
➤ Lifelong Learning in Europe (FIN ISSN 1239-6826) 2944
Lifelong Learning Institute Review see The L L I Review 2881
Lifelong Learning Trends (USA ISSN 1553-1619) 2944
Lifescapes see Art Ltd. 470
LifeStory (USA ISSN 1067-9243) 5323
LifeStyle (ITA) 5075
Lifestyle (Blackburn) (GBR ISSN 1749-1916) 5075
LifeStyle (Bury St. Edmunds) (GBR) 3867
Lifestyle (Devizes) (GBR ISSN 1744-9685) 5075
Lifestyle (Stockholm) (SWE ISSN 1650-0873) 5075
Lifestyle & Specialist Magazines Market Assessment see Key Note Market Assessment. Lifestyle & Specialist Magazines 1892
Lifestyle and Travel for Physicians (USA) 5075
Lifestyle and Wellness (CAN) 312
Lifestyle Asia (PHL ISSN 0116-6395) 5075
• Lifestyle Farmer (NZL ISSN 1175-3390) 134
Lifestyle Issue see Inside Out 4543
Lifestyle Market Analyst see S R D S Lifestyle Market Analyst (Online) 1261
Lifestyle Media Relations Reporter (USA) 28
Lifestyle Pocket Book (GBR ISSN 0967-0041) 28
Lifestyle Southern California (USA) 7943
LifeStyle - U S A (USA) 5075
• lifestylemagazin (DEU) 5075
Lifestyles (New York) (USA) 3980
Lifestyles (Winnetka) (USA) 5075
Lifestyles (Year) (USA) 5559
Lifetime (Kansas City) (USA) 4513
Lifetime, an Adoption Magazine see Lifetime for Women Considering Adoption 2159
• ➤ Lifetime Data Analysis (USA ISSN 1380-7870) 8385
Lifetime for Women Considering Adoption (USA ISSN 1937-9889) 2159
▼ LifeWalk (USA ISSN 1939-0831) 7660
Lifewatch (GBR) 2617
Life@Work see Life at Work 7660
The Lifewriter's Digest (USA) 3773
Lifewriting Annual (USA ISSN 1559-2898) 5323
The Lifewriting Professional (USA) 3773
Liffey Champion (IRL) 3893
• Lift and Access (USA) 5454
▼ Lift & Crane Applications and Equipment (USA ISSN 1945-9629) 5454
Lift Applications & Equipment see Lift & Crane Applications and Equipment 5454
Lift-Journal (DEU ISSN 1614-6654) 1020
Lift Magazine (USA) 5323
Lift Report see Lift-Report 5454
Lift-Report (DEU ISSN 0341-3721) 5454
• Lift Stuttgart (DEU ISSN 1615-6463) 3852
Lift Uni-Tip (DEU) 2992
Liftbouw (NLD ISSN 1872-650X) 3388
• Lifted Magazine (USA ISSN 1932-9326) 7660
Lifting & Transportation International (USA ISSN 1045-442X) 8672
Lifting & Transportation International. Buyer's Guide see Lifting & Transportation International 8672
Liftinstituut Magazine (NLD ISSN 1873-9105) 3388
Liftinstituut. Mededeling see Liftinstituut Magazine 3388
▼ • Liftoff (DNK ISSN 1902-4827) 1772
Liftouts (USA) 7566
Lig see L I G 7764
Liga (AUT) 7212
Liga (PRT ISSN 0873-6243) 6158
Ligand Assay (ITA) 5909
Ligdraer (ZAF) 7764
• Lige Nu! (DNK ISSN 1602-9585) 5030
Ligeia (FRA ISSN 0989-6023) 503
Ligestilling Mellem Maend og Kvinder i den Europaiske Union see Equal Opportunities for Women and Men in the European Union 1680
• Lighedstegn (DNK ISSN 1395-8054) 4067
Light see Svitlo 7819
Light see Goleuad 7759
Light see Light on a New World 7660
The Light (GBR) 4082

Light see Cucina Light **4355**
Light (NLD ISSN 1872-5228) **6992**
• Light (USA ISSN 1064-8186) **5323**
Light see The Utility Worker **4604**
The Light (Arlington) (USA) **8620**
➤ Light (London, 1881) (GBR ISSN 0047-4649) **6742**
Light (London, 1994) (GBR ISSN 1353-6095) **3160**
Light (Wheaton) (USA) **4082**
Light Aircraft Manufacturers Association. Newsletter (USA) **8547**
Light Among the Least Reached (USA) **7764**
Light & Easy (GBR ISSN 1745-5405) **4363**
Light and Life (USA ISSN 0024-3299) **7764**
Light & Lighting see Deng yu Zhaoming **3298**
• Light and Medium Truck (USA ISSN 1091-9651) **8672**
Light and Shade (USA) **6971**
Light and Shadow see Guang yu Ying **492**
Light & Textile Industries of Fujian see Fujian Qingfang **7965**
Light: Annual Report (USA) **4082**
Light Design and Technology see Watt Elettrofornitture **3334**
Light-Emitting Diode Ds Magazine see L E Ds Magazine **3107**
Light Emitting Diodes Journal see L E D Journal **3323**
Light Emitting Diodes Journal e-Report see L E D Journal e-Report **3323**
Light For Our Path (GBR ISSN 0140-8267) **7765**
• Light for the Last Days (GBR) **7765**
Light Industry Machinery see Qinggong Jixie **5459**
• Light - Lines (USA) **6742**
Light List (USA ISSN 0565-1557) **8649**
• Light Metal Age (USA ISSN 0024-3345) **6320**
Light Metal Statistics in Japan see Keikinzoku Kogyo Tokei Nenpo **6340**
Light Metal Statistics in Japan. Annual Report see Keikinzoku Kogyo Tokei Nenpo **6340**
Light Metals (Year) (CAN) **6320**
• Light Metals (Year) (USA ISSN 0147-0809) **6320**
Light Music see Qing Yinyue **6608**
Light of Consciousness (USA ISSN 1040-7448) **6646**
Light of Home see Ie-no-Hikari **120**
Light of Life (USA) **7660**
Light of the Moon (GBR ISSN 0024-3361) **4082**
Light of the Word see Svjetlo Rijeci **7819**
• Light on a New World (GBR ISSN 0047-4657) **7660**
Light on my Path see Lumiere sur mon Sentier **7765**
The Light Papers see Light Reading's White Paper **2331**
Light Plane Maintenance (USA ISSN 0278-8950) **65**
Light Quarterly see Light **5323**
Light Rail Transit News (Online Edition) see L R T News (Online Edition) **8502**
• Light Railways (AUS ISSN 0727-8101) **8620**
• Light Reading Asia (USA) **2331**
• Light Reading Case Studies Monthly (USA) **2500**
• Light Reading Daily (USA) **2331**
Light Reading Europe (USA) **2331**
• Light Reading Insider (USA) **2331**
• The Light Reading Service Provider E-Newsletter (USA) **2331**
• Light Reading Weekly (USA) **2331**
• Light Reading's Ethernet Update (USA) **2500**
• Light Reading's I P Update (Internet Protocols) (USA) **2500**
• Light Reading's Metro Update (USA) **2501**
• Light Reading's Multiservice Update (USA) **2501**
• Light Reading's Testing Update (USA) **2431**
• Light Reading's White Paper (USA) **2331**
• Light Truck and S U V (Sports Utility Vehicle) (USA) **1829**
Light Truck and S U V Accessory Business & Product News see Light Truck and S U V **1829**
• Light Up Your Kitchen and Bath (USA) **4545**
Light Up Your Landscape (USA) **3742**
The Light Within (CAN) **7738**
Light Years (GBR ISSN 1743-2324) **7660**
Lightbox (GBR) **6971**
The Lightbulb - Invent! (USA) **8431**
• Lighthouse (USA ISSN 1536-173X) **7152**
Lighthouse Digest (USA ISSN 1066-0038) **448**
Lighthouse International Annual Report (USA) **8054**
• Lighting (AUS ISSN 1320-8403) **3324**
• Lighting (CAN ISSN 1493-6151) **4560**
Lighting (GBR) **4560**
Lighting (USA ISSN 1941-3459) **4545**
• Lighting & Sound International (GBR ISSN 0268-7429) **8473**
Lighting Answers (USA ISSN 1069-0050) **1020**
• Lighting Design + Application (USA ISSN 0360-6325) **3324**
Lighting Dimensions see Live Design **8473**
Lighting Equipment see Key Note Market Report: Lighting Equipment **1894**
Lighting Equipment Industry see Business Ratio. The Lighting Equipment Industry **4534**
Lighting Equipment Industry see Financial Survey. The Lighting Equipment Industry **1994**
Lighting Equipment News see Lighting **4560**
➤ Lighting Journal (GBR ISSN 0950-4559) **3324**
Lighting Management and Maintenance see L M & M: Lighting Management & Maintenance **3159**
Lighting Online see Lighting **4560**
• ➤ Lighting Research and Technology (GBR ISSN 1477-1535) **3324**
• Lighting Today (SGP) **4545**
Lighting Your Life (USA) **4545**
The Lightnin' Ridge Outdoor Journal (USA) **8321**
Lightning Bug (USA ISSN 1540-1081) **2199**
Lightning Protection for Engineers (USA) **3324**
Lightning Strikes (USA ISSN 1068-8404) **6584**
† Light's List of Literary Magazines (GBR ISSN 1741-7880) **8971**
Lights of the Homeland see Teviskes Ziburiai **3568**
Lightspeed (GBR) **4980**
• Lightwave (USA ISSN 0741-5834) **2331**
• Lightwave Buyers Guide (USA) **2331**
• Lightwave Europe (USA) **2331**
Lightwave Fiber Exchange see Lightwave **2331**
Lightweight Concrete Information Sheets (USA ISSN 0075-9457) **1020**
Lightweight Design see Lightweightdesign **1020**
▼ Lightweightdesign (DEU ISSN 1865-4819) **1020**
➤ Lightworks (USA ISSN 0161-4223) **503**
Ligne de Front (FRA ISSN 1953-0544) **6431**
Lignes (FRA ISSN 0988-5226) **3841**
Lignes d'Art (FRA ISSN 1778-4867) **503**
Lignes Directrices Concernant la Subvention de Soutien au Cours d'Anglais Langue Additionnelle (Year) (CAN ISSN 1912-0001) **2883**
• Lignes Directrices pour les Essais de Produits Chimiques (FRA ISSN 1607-3088) **3500**
• Ligong Gaojiao Yanjiu/Journal of Technology College Education (CHN ISSN 1671-606X) **2883**
Ligong Yanjiu Xuebao/Journal of Scientific and Technological Studies (TWN ISSN 1990-4401) **7880**
▼ Ligorodo (FRA ISSN 1959-1195) **3548**
Ligue des Bibliotheques Europeennes de Recherche Quarterly (Online) see L I B E R Quarterly (Online) **5024**
Ligue pour l'Adaptation du Diminue Physique au Travail. Cahiers (FRA ISSN 0182-5437) **3044**
Ligue Suisse de Litterature pour la Jeunesse. Rapport Annuel see Schweizerischer Bund fuer Jugendliteratur. Jahresbericht **2211**
Ligue Urbaine et Rurale. Cahiers see Patrimoine et Cadre de Vie **3459**
Liguori Editore. Testi (ITA) **5323**
• Liguorian (USA ISSN 0024-3450) **7804**
Ligures (ITA ISSN 1824-7776) **404**
† Liguria (ITA) **8971**
Liguria Tre (ITA) **1406**
• Lihatalous (FIN ISSN 1236-1895) **292**
• Lihua Jianyan (Huaxue Fence) (CHN ISSN 1001-4020) **3250**
• Lihua Jianyan (Wuli Fence)/Physical Testing and Chemical Analysis Part A: Physical Testing (CHN ISSN 1001-4012) **6403**
Lihyot Mishpacha see Lihyot Mishpaha **8118**
• Lihyot Mishpaha/Etre Parents (ISR) **8118**
• Liikennetuva. Reports (FIN ISSN 0355-6654) **7530**
• Liikennetuva. Tutkimuksia (FIN ISSN 0782-2421) **7530**
➤ Liiketaloudellinen Aikakauskirja/Finnish Journal of Business Economics (FIN ISSN 0024-3469) **1144**
Liiketalous (FIN ISSN 1239-6044) **1144**
Liikunnan ja Kansanterveyden Edistamissaatio. Julkaisuja/Likes Research Reports on Sport and Health/Research Reports on Sport and Health (FIN ISSN 0357-2498) **6231**
Liikunta & Tiede (FIN ISSN 0358-7010) **8185**
Liikuntatieteellisen Seura. Julkaisuja/Finnish Society for Research in Sport and Physical Education. Publication (FIN ISSN 0356-746X) **8185**
Liikuntatieteellisen Seuran Impulssisarja (FIN ISSN 1237-0576) **8185**
➤ Lijecnicki Vjesnik (HRV ISSN 0024-3477) **5661**
Lijecnicki Vjesnik. Supplement see Lijecnicki Vjesnik **5661**
Lijfblad (NLD ISSN 1381-3145) **6858**
Lijst van Lopende Seriele Publikaties - List of Current Serial Publications see Technische Universiteit te Delft. Bibliotheek. Lijst van Lopende Seriele Publikaties **636**
Lik (BGR) **503**
Lika Mojligheter for Kvinnor och Man i Euopeiska Unionen see Equal Opportunities for Women and Men in the European Union **1680**
Likarska Sprava/Vrachebnoe Delo (UKR ISSN 1019-5297) **5661**
Like Aihaozhe/Science Fans (CHN ISSN 1671-8437) **7880**
† Like, Art Magazine (AUS ISSN 1327-5445) **8971**
Likembe (COD) **6584**
Likereke Ntlafatsong (LSO) **3905**
Likes Research Reports on Sport and Health see Liikunnan ja Kansanterveyden Edistamissaatio. Julkaisuja **6231**
Likha (PHL ISSN 0115-6144) **5323**
Likundoli. Archives et Documents (COD) **4176**
Likundoli. Enquete d'Histoire Zairoise (COD) **4176**
Likundoli, Histoire et Devenir (COD) **4176**
Likutim (USA ISSN 0792-0873) **4082**
Lilac Hinge (USA) **6896**
Lilacs Quarterly Journal (USA ISSN 1046-9761) **3742**
LiLi see Zeitschrift fuer Literaturwissenschaft und Linguistik **5199**
Lilies & Cannonballs Review (USA ISSN 1548-8365) **5323**
Lilipoh (USA) **312**
• ➤ Lilith (AUS ISSN 0813-8990) **8900**
• Lilith (USA ISSN 0146-2334) **7726**
Lillbladet see S V R Medlemsblad **4601**
Lillebi (DEU) **2199**
Lillesands-Posten (NOR) **3923**
† • Lilleskolen (DNK ISSN 1902-6501) **8971**
Lilleskolenyt see Lilleskolen **8971**
Lilliput Review (USA) **5323**
Lilloa (ARG ISSN 0075-9481) **800**
Lilun Jingjixue/Theoretical Economics (CHN ISSN 1005-4286) **1546**
• Lilun Qianyan/Theory Front (CHN ISSN 1007-1962) **7152**
• Lilun Tantao/Theoretical Investigation (CHN ISSN 1000-8594) **7983**
Lilun Wuli see Communications in Theoretical Physics **7008**
• Lilun yu Xiandaihua/Theory and Modernization (CHN ISSN 1003-1502) **7983**
Lily of the Mohawks (USA) **7804**
Lima (DEU) **2290**
Lima - Callao Compendio Estadistico (PER) **8385**
Lima Times (PER) **3927**
Limba Romana/Romanian Language (ROM ISSN 0024-3523) **5144**
➤ Limba si Literatura (ROM ISSN 0583-8045) **5144**
The Limbaugh Letter (USA ISSN 1065-0377) **7152**
Limbo see Teorema **6956**
Limbs and Needles (USA ISSN 1520-7145) **3696**
Limburg in Beeld see Limburg in Cijfers **8118**
Limburg in Cijfers (NLD ISSN 1574-3845) **8118**
Limburg Nu see Limburg in Cijfers **8118**
Limburgs Geschied- en Oudheidkundig Genootschap. Jaarboek see Societe Historique et Archeologique dans le Limbourg. Publications **4265**
Limburgs Landschap (NLD ISSN 1382-8088) **2617**
➤ Limburgs Tijdschrift voor Genealogie (NLD ISSN 0169-5177) **3773**
Lime (SGP) **2199**
Limelight Casting Directory see Casting Directory **8467**
Limelight Contacts see Contacts **8468**
Limelight Rolverdelingsgids see Casting Directory **8467**
Limerick Chronicle (IRL ISSN 1649-8968) **3894**
The Limerick Leader (City Edition) (IRL ISSN 1649-8992) **3894**
The Limerick Leader (County Edition) (IRL ISSN 1649-8984) **3894**
The Limerick Leader (Midweek Edition) (IRL ISSN 1649-8976) **3894**
▼ Limerick Now (IRL ISSN 1649-9751) **3894**
Limerick Papers in Criminal Justice (IRL ISSN 1393-581X) **4893**
Limerick's Motor Trader (IRL ISSN 1649-6922) **8589**
Limes (CHL ISSN 0716-5919) **2883**
Limesmuseum Aalen. Schriften (DEU) **2237**
• ➤ Limina (AUS ISSN 1324-4558) **4193**
Liminaires (CHE ISSN 1660-1505) **5323**
Liminar (MEX ISSN 1665-8027) **4301**
† De Limit (NLD ISSN 1574-0943) **8971**
Limit (USA) **7152**
• Limite (CHL ISSN 0718-1361) **6932**
Limited Edition (Oxford) (GBR) **3867**
Limited Edition (Worcester) (GBR ISSN 1754-081X) **3967**
• Limited Liability Companies: Tax & Business Law (USA) **1933**
The Limited Liability Company (USA) **4875**
• Limited Liability Entities (USA ISSN 1932-2186) **4875**
Limited Offering Exemptions: Regulation D (USA ISSN 0739-1889) **4875**
• Limited Partnership Investment Review (USA ISSN 0892-516X) **1933**
Limited Skateboarding Magazine (DEU) **8186**
▼ Limitless Impact Magazine (USA ISSN 1947-1572) **1773**
• Limits in the Seas (USA ISSN 0092-6426) **4970**
Limn (USA ISSN 1528-6193) **503**
• ➤ Limnetica (ESP ISSN 0213-8409) **2796**
• ➤ Limnologica (DEU ISSN 0075-9511) **2796**
Limnological Society of Koshin'etsu District. Bulletin see Nihon Rikusui Gakkai Koshin'etsu Shibukai Kaiho **2797**
Limnologie Aktuell (DEU ISSN 0937-2881) **2797**
• ➤ Limnology (JPN ISSN 1439-8621) **2797**
• ➤ Limnology and Oceanography (USA ISSN 0024-3590) **2797**
• Limnology and Oceanography Bulletin (USA ISSN 1539-607X) **2811**
• ➤ Limnology and Oceanography: Methods (USA ISSN 1541-5856) **2811**
• Limon (KGZ) **3904**
Limonka (RUS) **5224**
➤ Limosa (NLD ISSN 0024-3620) **910**
Limousin Leader (CAN ISSN 0381-5552) **292**
Limousin World (USA ISSN 8750-2127) **292**
• Limousine & Chauffeured Transportation (USA ISSN 1097-4814) **8589**
Limousine Digest (USA) **8589**
Limousine Nyt (DNK ISSN 0900-050X) **292**
• Limpieza Inform (ESP ISSN 1135-0733) **2243**
▼ Limpopo Business (ZAF ISSN 1993-0119) **2013**
LIMRA's Recruit! see Recruit! **4520**
Linacre Lectures (GBR ISSN 1366-2694) **8632**
Linacre Quarterly (USA ISSN 0024-3639) **5661**
Linchan Gongye/Forest Products Industries (TWN ISSN 0254-6523) **3696**
• Linchan Huaxue yu Gongye/Chemistry and Industry of Forest Products (CHN ISSN 0253-2417) **2071**
• Linchuang Chaosheng Yixue Zazhi/Journal of Ultrasound in Clinical Medicine (CHN ISSN 1008-6978) **6202**
• Linchuang Erbi Yanhouke Zazhi/Journal of Clinical Otolaryngology (CHN ISSN 1001-1781) **6082**
• Linchuang Erke Zazhi/Journal of Clinical Pediatrics (CHN ISSN 1000-3606) **6096**
• Linchuang Fangshexue Zazhi/Journal of Clinical Radiology (CHN ISSN 1001-9324) **6202**
• Linchuang Gandanbing Zazhi/Chinese Journal of Clinical Hepatology (CHN ISSN 1001-5256) **5928**
• Linchuang Guke Zazhi (CHN ISSN 1008-0287) **6066**
• Linchuang he Shiyan Yixue Zazhi/Journal of Clinical and Experimental Medicine (CHN ISSN 1671-4695) **5909**
• ➤ Linchuang Huicui/Clinical Focus (CHN ISSN 1004-583X) **5661**
• Linchuang Jianyan Zazhi/Journal of Clinical Laboratory Science (CHN ISSN 1001-764X) **5909**
• Linchuang Jingshen Yixue Zazhi/Journal of Clinical Psychological Medicine (CHN ISSN 1005-3220) **6158**
Linchuang Jizhen Zazhi/Journal of Clinical Emergence Call (CHN ISSN 1009-5918) **6066**
• Linchuang Junyi Zazhi/Clinical Journal of Medical Officer (CHN ISSN 1671-3826) **6431**
• Linchuang Kouqiang Yixue/Journal of Clinical Stomatology (CHN ISSN 1003-1634) **5928**
• Linchuang Mazuixue Zazhi/Journal of Clinical Anesthesiology (CHN ISSN 1004-5805) **5772**
• Linchuang Miniao Waike Zazhi/Journal of Clinical Urological Surgery (CHN ISSN 1001-1420) **6271**
Linchuang Naodianxue Zazhi/Journal of Clinical Electroencephalogy see Linchuang Shenjing Dianshenglixue Zazhi **6158**
• Linchuang Neike Zazhi/Journal of Clinical Medicine (CHN ISSN 1001-9057) **5661**
• Linchuang Pifuke Zazhi/Journal of Clinical Dermatology (CHN ISSN 1000-4963) **5879**
• Linchuang Shenjing Dianshenglixue Zazhi/Journal of Clinical Electroneurophysiology (CHN ISSN 1009-5934) **6158**
• Linchuang Shenjingbingxue Zazhi/Journal of Clinical Neurology (CHN ISSN 1004-1648) **6158**
• Linchuang Shuxue yu Jianyan/Journal of Clinical Transfusion and Laboratory Medicine (CHN ISSN 1671-2587) **5909**
• Linchuang Waike Zazhi/Journal of Clinical Surgery (CHN ISSN 1005-6483) **6251**
• Linchuang Wuzhen Wuzhi/Clinical Misdiagnosis & Mistherapy (CHN ISSN 1002-3429) **5661**
• Linchuang Xiaohuabing Zazhi/Clinical Digestion (CHN ISSN 1005-541X) **5928**
• Linchuang Xindianxue Zazhi/Clinical Cardiology (CHN ISSN 1005-0272) **5795**
• Linchuang Xinxueguanbing Zazhi/Clinical Cardio-Disease (CHN ISSN 1001-1439) **5795**
• Linchuang Xueyexue Zazhi/Clinical Hematology (CHN ISSN 1004-2806) **5940**
• Linchuang Yanke Zazhi/Journal of Clinical Ophthalmology (CHN ISSN 1006-8422) **5661**
• Linchuang Yaowu Zhiliao Zazhi/Clinical Medication Journal (CHN ISSN 1672-3384) **5661**
• Linchuang Yixue (Zhengzhou) (CHN ISSN 1003-3548) **5662**
• Linchuang Yiyao Shijian/Proceeding of Clinical Medicine (CHN ISSN 1671-8631) **5662**
• Linchuang yu Shiyan Binglixue Zazhi/Journal of Clinical and Experimental Pathology (CHN ISSN 1001-7399) **5662**
• Linchuang Zhongliuxue Zazhi/Chinese Clinical Oncology (CHN ISSN 1009-0460) **6026**
Lincoln Archaeological Studies (GBR ISSN 1754-7768) **404**
Lincoln Archaeology Studies see Lincoln Archaeological Studies **404**
Lincoln Center Calendar (USA) **8473**
• Lincoln Center Theater Review (USA ISSN 1524-0940) **8473**
• Lincoln Editor (USA ISSN 1537-2278) **4301**
Lincoln Herald (USA ISSN 0024-3671) **4301**
Lincoln Heritage Trail Foundation (USA) **8321**
• Lincoln Laboratory Journal (USA ISSN 0896-4130) **3108**
• Lincoln Law Review (USA ISSN 0024-368X) **4724**
Lincoln Library Bulletin (USA ISSN 0024-3698) **5030**
Lincoln Longwool Sheep Breeders' Association. Annual Flock Book (GBR) **292**
Lincoln Lore (USA ISSN 0162-8615) **4301**
Lincoln Memorial Association Newsletter (USA) **4301**
Lincoln Record Society. Publications (USA ISSN 0267-2634) **5323**
Lincoln Red Cattle Society Annual Herd Book (GBR) **292**
Lincoln Review. Letter (USA ISSN 1521-8848) **3548**
Lincoln Road Magazine (USA ISSN 1540-8213) **3980**
Lincoln Smitweld Reportage (NLD ISSN 0927-751X) **6343**
Lincoln Studies in Religion and Society (GBR) **7660**
† Lincoln University. Agribusiness and Economics Research Unit. Discussion Paper (NZL ISSN 1170-7607) **8971**
• Lincoln University. Agribusiness and Economics Research Unit. Research Report (NZL ISSN 1170-7682) **202**

Title

Lincoln University. Research Profile (NZL ISSN 1178-0843) **7880**
The Lincolnator (USA) **4301**
Lincoln's Premier Lifestyle Magazine *see* L **5075**
Lincolnshire Bird Report (GBR ISSN 0261-5525) **910**
The Lincolnshire Family History Society. Journal (GBR ISSN 1749-0685) **3773**
Lincolnshire Family History Society. Newsletter *see* The Lincolnshire Family History Society. Journal **3773**
Lincolnshire Farmer (GBR ISSN 0955-6893) **134**
Lincolnshire History and Archaeology (GBR ISSN 0459-4487) **4240**
Lincolnshire Information. Employment (GBR ISSN 0262-1452) **1696**
Lincolnshire Life (GBR ISSN 0024-371X) **3867**
Lincolnshire Methodist History Society. Journal (GBR ISSN 0265-2226) **7765**
Lincolnshire Naturalist (GBR ISSN 1756-1884) **953**
Lincolnshire Past and Present (GBR ISSN 0960-9555) **4240**
Lincolnshire Rare & Scarce Bird Report (GBR ISSN 1756-1949) **910**
Lincom Studies in Afroasiatic Linguistics (DEU) **5144**
Lincom Studies in Asian Linguistics (DEU) **5144**
Lincom Studies in Language Typology (DEU) **5144**
Linda (NLD ISSN 1572-4166) **3915**
Lindbergia (SWE ISSN 0105-0761) **800**
Die Linde (DEU) **4240**
Linde Technology *see* Linde Technology (German Edition) **7880**
Linde Technology (German Edition) (DEU ISSN 1612-2224) **7880**
Lindeblad (NLD ISSN 1871-9775) **5662**
Lindenmaier - Moehring Nachschlagewerk des Bundesgerichtshofs (DEU ISSN 0949-3476) **4835**
Linder Quarterly (USA) **3773**
Lindesnes (NOR) **3923**
Lindey and Parley on Separation Agreements and Antenuptial Contracts (USA) **4912**
Lindey on Entertainment, Publishing and the Arts (USA) **4724**
Lindey's Sports Annual *see* Lindy's Baseball Scouting Report (Year) **8237**
Lindley Lecture (USA ISSN 0075-9554) **6932**
Lindleyana (USA ISSN 0889-258X) **3742**
Lindner Early Childhood Training Institute Newsletter (USA) **2159**
Lindquist - Lepic Market Letter (USA) **1637**
• Lindsay Daily Post (CAN ISSN 0839-2730) **3812**
• Lindsay this Week (CAN ISSN 1483-3727) **3812**
The Lindsborg News-Record (USA) **3980**
L'Industrie en France (FRA ISSN 1771-2521) **1497**
l'Industrie Minerale Environnement *see* I M Environnement **6464**
Lindy's A C C Football Annual (Atlantic Coast Conference) (USA) **8237**
Lindy's Baseball (USA) **8237**
Lindy's Baseball Scouting Report (Year) (USA ISSN 1546-6795) **8237**
Lindy's Big 10 Football Annual (USA) **8237**
Lindy's Big 12 Football Annual (USA ISSN 1523-1852) **8237**
Lindy's Big Ten Football Annual *see* Lindy's Big 10 Football Annual **8237**
Lindy's Big Twelve Football Annual *see* Lindy's Big 12 Football Annual **8237**
Lindy's College Basketball Annual (USA) **8237**
▼ Lindy's Draft Guide (USA) **8237**
Lindy's Fantasy Baseball (USA ISSN 1554-3765) **8237**
Lindy's Football Annuals *see* Lindy's National College Football Annual **8237**
Lindy's National College Football Annual (USA ISSN 1542-5940) **8237**
Lindy's Pac 10 Football Annual (USA) **8237**
Lindy's Pac Ten Football Annual *see* Lindy's Pac 10 Football Annual **8237**
Lindy's Pro Basketball (USA ISSN 1077-9612) **8237**
Lindy's Pro Edition Football Annual (USA ISSN 1062-4198) **8237**
Lindy's Pro Fantasy Football (USA) **8237**
Lindy's Scouting Report *see* Lindy's Baseball Scouting Report (Year) **8237**
Lindy's Southeastern Football (USA) **8237**
• Lindy's Sports Annuals (USA) **8186**
Line of Departure (USA) **8186**
Line Rider (USA) **292**
• Line56.com (USA) **2563**
• Line56 E-Business Journal (USA) **2563**
Linea (New York) (USA ISSN 1544-4716) **503**
• En Linea at 2 (MEX) **2431**
Linea Directa Con Israel y Medio Oriente (ISR) **3895**
Linea E D P (Entry Data Products) (ITA ISSN 0392-9027) **2538**
Linea Intima (ITA ISSN 0394-8048) **2248**
La Linea Veneta nella Cultura Contemporanea (ITA ISSN 1122-0813) **4463**
Linea Verde (ITA ISSN 0394-3704) **3742**
† Lineagrafica/International Review of Graphic Design and Visual Communications (ITA ISSN 0024-3744) **8971**
Lineaires (FRA ISSN 0981-4183) **292**
• ➤ Linear Algebra and Its Applications (USA ISSN 0024-3795) **5509**
• ➤ Linear and Multilinear Algebra (GBR ISSN 0308-1087) **5509**
Linear Motion *see* Motion System Design **3390**
Lineaverde *see* Linea Verde **3742**
† Lineaverde (ITA) **8971**
Linedancer (GBR ISSN 1366-6509) **2686**
Linens, Domestics and Bath - Interior Textile Annual Buyer's Guide *see* Linens, Domestics & Bath - Interior Textile Annual Buyer's Guide **4560**
Linens, Domestics & Bath - Interior Textile Annual Buyer's Guide (USA) **4560**
Linens, Domestics and Bath Products Interior Textiles *see* L D B Interior Textiles **4560**
Liner Register *see* The Containership Register (London, 2002) **8641**
Lines *see* St. Lawrence District News **7741**
Lines and Cables for Power Transmission Series (GBR) **3324**
• Lines Available Bulletin (USA) **3324**
Lines Available Bulletin (Print) *see* Lines Available Bulletin **3324**
• Linfei yu Fufei/Phosphate & Compound Fertilizer (CHN ISSN 1007-6220) **241**
Linfield Review (USA) **2290**
L'Infirmiere en Geriatrie *see* Reperes en Geriatrie **4054**
L'Info F I Q (Federation de l'Informatique du Quebec) (CAN ISSN 1714-4000) **2431**
L'Informatore Sportivo (ITA ISSN 1824-4130) **8186**
Ling Shui (CHN) **5323**
Ling yu Yi Byte Keji Zazhi *see* 0 yu 1 Byte Keji Zazhi **2494**
Ling yu Yi Keji Zashi/0 & 1 Technology Byte (Chinese Edition) (TWN) **2468**
Lingdale Papers (GBR ISSN 1369-8095) **7660**
L'Ingegnere Edilizia Ambiente Territorio (ITA ISSN 1826-0535) **1020**
Linger Longer (USA) **8730**
Lingerie Buyer (GBR ISSN 1472-7609) **2248**
• Lingnan Pifu-xingbingke Zazhi/Southern China Journal of Dermato-Venereology (CHN ISSN 1009-8968) **5880**
Lingnan Xinxueguanbing Zazhi (CHN ISSN 1007-9688) **5795**
Lingnan Yinyue/Music of South Mountain (CHN ISSN 1671-413X) **6584**
Lingo (USA ISSN 1081-1419) **5425**
Le Lingot (CAN ISSN 0707-8013) **6320**
• ➤ Lingua (NLD ISSN 0024-3841) **5144**
Lingua (Hamburg) (DEU ISSN 1614-5550) **5144**
➤ Lingua Aegyptia (DEU ISSN 0942-5659) **5144**
Lingua Aegyptia. Studia Monographica (DEU ISSN 0946-8641) **5144**
Lingua Americana (VEN ISSN 1316-6689) **5144**
Lingua e Cultura (PRT ISSN 0047-4703) **5144**
Lingua e Literatura (BRA ISSN 0101-4862) **5145**
• Lingua e Stile (ITA ISSN 0024-385X) **5145**
Lingua e Vita (GBR) **5145**
• ➤ Lingua et Linguistica (GBR) **5145**
Lingua et Traditio (DEU ISSN 0342-3581) **5145**
• La Lingua Italiana (ITA ISSN 1724-9074) **5145**
• Lingua Italiana d'Oggi (ITA ISSN 1825-8298) **5145**
Lingua Nostra (ITA ISSN 0024-3868) **5145**
Lingua Portuguesa (BRA ISSN 1808-3498) **5145**
➤ Lingua Posnaniensis (POL ISSN 0079-4740) **5145**
• Lingua Quiltra (CHL ISSN 0718-4484) **5425**
• Lingua Romana (USA ISSN 1551-4730) **4463**
• Linguae & (ITA ISSN 1724-8698) **5145**
• ➤ Linguagem & Ensino (BRA ISSN 1415-1928) **5145**
• Linguagem em (Dis)curso (BRA ISSN 1518-7632) **5145**
Linguaggio Astrale (ITA) **566**
Linguaggio dell'Architettura Romana (ITA ISSN 1122-0805) **449**
▼ LinguaLauxa (ESP ISSN 1888-0657) **5145**
Lingue e Iscrizioni dell'Italia Antica (ITA ISSN 1122-0791) **5145**
• Lingue e Linguaggio (ITA ISSN 1720-9331) **5145**
Linguist (GBR ISSN 0268-5965) **5145**
Linguiste/Taalkundige (BEL ISSN 0776-9989) **5145**
• ➤ Linguistic Analysis (USA ISSN 0098-9053) **5145**
Linguistic and Oriental Studies from Poznan (POL ISSN 1230-6029) **5145**
Linguistic Approaches to Literature (NLD ISSN 1569-3112) **5145**
Linguistic Association of Canada and the United States Forum *see* L A C U S Forum **5138**
Linguistic Association of Finland. Journal *see* SKY Journal of Linguistics **5174**
• Linguistic Bibliography/Bibliographie Linguistique (NLD ISSN 0378-4592) **5201**
Linguistic Circle of Manitoba and North Dakota. Proceedings (USA ISSN 0075-9597) **5323**
• ➤ Linguistic Discovery (USA ISSN 1537-0852) **5145**
• ➤ Linguistic Inquiry (USA ISSN 0024-3892) **5145**
Linguistic Insights (CHE ISSN 1424-8689) **5145**
▼ • Linguistic Issues in Language Technology (USA ISSN 1945-3590) **5203**
➤ Linguistic Notes from La Jolla (USA ISSN 0737-4720) **5145**
• ➤ The Linguistic Review (DEU ISSN 0167-6318) **5146**
Linguistic Society of America Bulletin (Online) *see* L S A Bulletin (Online) **5138**
Linguistic Society of America. Meeting Handbooks (USA ISSN 0075-9600) **5146**
Linguistic Society of India. Bulletin (IND ISSN 0075-9627) **5146**
➤ Linguistic Society of Japan. Journal/Gengo Kenkyu (JPN ISSN 0024-3914) **5146**
Linguistic Society of Korea. Journal *see* Han'gug Eon'eo Haghoe. Eon'eohag **5124**
Linguistic Studies *see* Nyelvtudomanyi Kozlemenyek **5157**
• ➤ Linguistic Typology (DEU ISSN 1430-0532) **5146**
• ➤ Linguistic Variations Yearbook (NLD ISSN 1568-1483) **5146**
Linguistica (ESP ISSN 1132-0214) **5146**
➤ Linguistica (SVN ISSN 0024-3922) **5146**
Linguistica Antverpiensia *see* Linguistica Antverpiensia. New Series **5146**
Linguistica Antverpiensia. New Series (BEL) **5146**
➤ Linguistica Atlantica (CAN ISSN 1188-9322) **5146**
Linguistica Baltica (LTU ISSN 1230-3984) **5146**
† • Linguistica Computazionale (ITA ISSN 0392-6907) **8971**
† Linguistica e Dialetti (ITA) **8971**
Linguistica e Filologia (ITA ISSN 1594-6517) **5146**
• Linguistica e Letteratura (ITA ISSN 0392-6915) **5146**
• Linguistica en la Red (ESP ISSN 1697-0780) **5146**
• Linguistica Espanola Actual (ESP ISSN 0210-6345) **5146**
Linguistica et Philologica (SVN) **5146**
Linguistica Iberoamericana (DEU ISSN 1610-3386) **5146**
• ➤ Linguistica Occitana (FRA ISSN 1773-0538) **5146**
• ➤ Linguistica Online (CZE ISSN 1801-5336) **5146**
• ➤ Linguistica Pragensia (POL ISSN 0862-8432) **5146**
Linguistica Septentrionalia (DEU ISSN 1438-4140) **5146**
➤ Linguistica Silesiana (POL ISSN 0208-4228) **5146**
• ➤ Linguistica Uralica (EST ISSN 0868-4731) **5146**
Linguistica y Literatura (COL ISSN 0120-5587) **5146**
Linguisticae Investigationes *see* Lingvisticae Investigationes **5147**
• ➤ Linguistics (DEU ISSN 0024-3949) **5147**
Linguistics *see* Kalbotyra **5136**
• Linguistics Abstracts (GBR ISSN 0267-5498) **5201**
• Linguistics Abstracts Online (GBR ISSN 1368-5295) **5201**
• ➤ Linguistics and Education (GBR ISSN 0898-5898) **5147**
• Linguistics and Language Behavior Abstracts (USA ISSN 0888-8027) **5201**
Linguistics and Philology *see* Yuyan Wenzixue **5198**
• ➤ Linguistics and Philosophy (NLD ISSN 0165-0157) **5147**
• Linguistics & Science Fiction (E-mail Edition) (USA) **5147**
• Linguistics and the Human Sciences (GBR ISSN 1742-2906) **4463**
• Linguistics in Potsdam (DEU ISSN 1616-7392) **5147**
• Linguistics in the Netherlands (Algemene Vereniging voor Taalwetenschap) (NLD ISSN 0929-7332) **5147**
• The Linguistics Journal (VGB ISSN 1718-2301) **5147**
• ➤ Linguistics of the Tibeto-Burman Area (AUS ISSN 0731-3500) **5147**
Linguistics Today *see* Linguistik Aktuell **5147**
Linguistik (DEU ISSN 1613-4532) **5203**
Linguistik Aktuell/Linguistics Today (NLD ISSN 0166-0829) **5147**
Linguistik - Impulse und Tendenzen (DEU ISSN 1612-8702) **5147**
• ➤ Linguistik Online (DEU ISSN 1615-3014) **5147**
La Linguistique (FRA ISSN 0075-966X) **5147**
Linguistique et Enseignement (MDG) **5147**
➤ Linguistique Generale (BEL ISSN 0298-461X) **5147**
Linguistique Institut Nanterre Paris X *see* L I N X **5138**
Linguistische Arbeiten (DEU ISSN 0344-6727) **5147**
➤ Linguistische Berichte (DEU ISSN 0024-3930) **5147**
Linguistische Berichte. Sonderheft *see* Linguistische Berichte **5147**
Linguistische Datenverarbeitung Forum *see* L D V - Forum **5203**
Linguodidactica (POL ISSN 1731-6332) **5147**
• ➤ Lingvisticae Investigationes (NLD ISSN 0378-4169) **5147**
Lingvisticae Investigationes: Supplementa (NLD ISSN 0165-7569) **5147**
Linhas (BRA ISSN 1518-367X) **2883**
• Linhas Criticas (BRA ISSN 1516-4896) **2883**
Die Linie (Cologne) *see* Linie International **2257**
Linie International (DEU ISSN 1862-5649) **2257**
Linington Lineup (USA ISSN 8756-5609) **5323**
The Link (AUS ISSN 0812-6240) **7738**
Link (AUS ISSN 1447-2023) **4067**
➤ The Link (CAN ISSN 1701-2473) **5928**
The Link (CAN ISSN 1719-9611) **2992**
Link (IND) **7152**
† Link (ISR ISSN 0792-9765) **8971**
Link (MEX) **2563**
Link (ZAF) **241**
The Link (Albuquerque) *see* The New Mexico Jewish Link **7727**
• Link (Baltimore) (USA ISSN 1097-9700) **503**
Link (Burnaby) (CAN) **2883**
Link (Conway) (USA) **2883**
Link (London, 1966) (GBR ISSN 1360-323X) **4067**
Link (Manchester) (GBR ISSN 1741-6140) **6584**
Link (Market Harborough) (GBR) **4082**
The Link (Montreal) (CAN ISSN 0841-2758) **2290**
Link (Montreal) (CAN) **5224**
Link (New York, 1967) (USA ISSN 0024-4007) **7251**
Link (New York, 1995) (USA ISSN 1071-5487) **2290**
Link (San Antonio) (USA) **3654**
Link (Sevenoaks) (GBR) **8871**
Link (Troy) (USA ISSN 1045-9723) **28**
The Link (Vancouver) (CAN ISSN 0380-299X) **3548**
Link (Victoria) (CAN ISSN 0827-6978) **4018**
Link A W S *see* Link (Sevenoaks) **8871**
Link & Visitor (CAN ISSN 0380-4100) **7765**
Link for McMaster Part-time Students *see* The Link **2992**
Link in (to Gender and Development) (GBR) **8118**
Link Indian News Magazine (IND) **3884**
Link International (USA ISSN 1681-9594) **7805**
Link International: Educational Newsletter (GBR ISSN 0268-8352) **7713**
Link-up (GBR ISSN 1748-6947) **5969**
Linkage (Baltimore) (USA) **6159**
LinkAge (Phoenix) (USA) **2462**
Linkage Newsletter (USA) **875**
• Linkages Update (CAN) **3451**
Linking Libraries (USA) **5030**
• Linking Ring (USA ISSN 0024-4023) **4338**
Linkoeping Studies in Arts and Science (SWE ISSN 0282-9800) **4463**
Linkoeping Studies in Science and Technology (SWE ISSN 0345-7524) **7880**
Linkoeping Universitet. Department of Water and Environmental Studies. Tema V Report (SWE ISSN 0281-966X) **8828**
Linkoeping Universitet. Medical Dissertations (SWE ISSN 0345-0082) **5662**
Linkoepings Universitet. Institutionen foer Beteendevetenskap (SWE ISSN 1650-3643) **7383**
Linkoepings Universitet. Tema Kultur och Samhaelle. Skriftserie (SWE ISSN 1653-0373) **4151**
Links (CAN ISSN 1910-2453) **2883**
Links (GBR ISSN 1478-484X) **8431**
• Links (ITA ISSN 1594-5359) **5323**
Links *see* Ecosphere **3418**
• Links (Hilton Head Island) (USA ISSN 1554-9151) **8237**
Links (Nashville) (USA) **7765**
• Links (Online) (AUS) **7152**
Links and Letters (ESP ISSN 1133-7397) **5147**
Links und Rechts der Autobahn (DEU ISSN 0343-4192) **4393**
Linlithgowshire Journal and Gazette (GBR ISSN 0964-3540) **3867**
Linmine News (GUY) **6468**
• The Linnean (GBR ISSN 0950-1096) **687**
• ➤ Linnean Society. Biological Journal (GBR ISSN 0024-4066) **687**
• ➤ Linnean Society. Botanical Journal (GBR ISSN 0024-4074) **800**
Linnean Society. Occasional Publications (GBR) **2617**
➤ Linnean Society of New South Wales. Proceedings (AUS ISSN 0370-047X) **953**
Linnean Society. Symposia Series (USA ISSN 0161-6366) **687**
• ➤ Linnean Society. Zoological Journal (GBR ISSN 0024-4082) **953**
Linneana Belgica/European Entomology Journal (BEL ISSN 0024-4090) **854**
Linneavhandlingar i Nytryck (SWE ISSN 1651-2731) **800**
• Linn's Stamp News (USA ISSN 0161-6234) **6896**
Lino: Revista de Arte (ESP ISSN 0211-2574) **503**
L'Inoui (FRA ISSN 1772-2470) **6584**
LinRed *see* Linguistica en la Red **5146**
Linschoten-Vereeniging. Werken (NLD ISSN 0168-7107) **4240**
• Linscott's Directory of Immunological and Biological Reagents (USA ISSN 0740-7394) **737**
Linus (ITA ISSN 1120-4419) **5224**
Linux Developer's Journal (POL ISSN 1896-6314) **2594**
Linux Enterprise (DEU ISSN 1619-7968) **2594**
• Linux Format (GBR ISSN 1470-4234) **2594**
• ➤ Linux Gazette (USA ISSN 1934-371X) **2594**
Linux Gram *see* LinuxGram **2594**
Linux Intern (DEU) **2594**
• Linux Journal (USA ISSN 1075-3583) **2594**
Linux Journal Buyer's Guide (USA) **2594**
Linux-Magazin (DEU ISSN 1432-640X) **2594**
Linux Magazin (ROM ISSN 1583-9656) **2594**
• Linux Magazine (ESP ISSN 1576-4079) **2508**
Linux Magazine (GBR ISSN 1471-5678) **2594**
Linux Magazine (ITA ISSN 1592-8152) **2594**
Linux Magazine (NLD ISSN 1567-6056) **2594**
• Linux Magazine (USA ISSN 1536-4674) **2508**
Linux Magazine (Brazilian Edition) (BRA) **2594**
Linux Magazine (Edycja Polska) (POL) **2594**
• Linux + (POL ISSN 1427-5562) **2594**
Linux Plus DVD *see* Linux + **2594**
Linux Plus Extra! *see* Linux + **2594**
Linux Pro (ITA ISSN 1722-6163) **2594**
• Linux Resources (USA) **2594**
Linux Server Computing (USA ISSN 1533-4139) **2523**
• Linux Today (USA) **2594**
Linux User (DEU ISSN 1615-4444) **2594**
• LinuxGram (USA) **2594**
• LinuxWorld (Online) (USA ISSN 1522-2217) **2431**
† • LinuxWorld (Print) (USA ISSN 1544-4511) **8971**
LinuxWorld Magazine *see* LinuxWorld (Print) **8971**

DIRECTORY 2010 LLOYD'S MARITIME DIRECTORY (YEAR) 10565

Liturgiewissenschaftliche Quellen und Forschungen (DEU ISSN 0076-0048) **7660**
Liturgisches Jahrbuch (DEU ISSN 0024-5100) **7660**
• ➤ Liturgy (USA ISSN 0458-063X) **7660**
Liturgy News (AUS ISSN 1039-0464) **7805**
Liturgy of the Word (USA ISSN 1084-0842) **7660**
Litva Predstavlyaet (LTU ISSN 1822-1017) **3906**
• Liu Institute Newsletter (CAN ISSN 1910-2895) **7152**
Liubopitko/Curious Kid (BGR ISSN 1310-8972) **2200**
• Liusuan Gongye (CHN ISSN 1002-1507) **3250**
• Liuti Jixie/Fluid Machinery (CHN ISSN 1005-0329) **5454**
Liuti Lixue Shiyan yu Celiang/Experiments and Measurements in Fluid Mechanics *see* Shiyan Liuti Lixue **7063**
Liuxing Kubao *see* Cool **3960**
Liuxing Tongxun *see* Call **2366**
Liuxuesheng/Student Studying Abroad (CHN ISSN 1671-8739) **2884**
Liuzhou Vocational & Technical College. Journal *see* Liuzhou Zhiye Jishu Xueyuan Xuebao **7983**
• Liuzhou Zhiye Jishu Xueyuan Xuebao/Liuzhou Vocational & Technical College. Journal (CHN ISSN 1671-1084) **7983**
• Liv (GBR) **3868**
Livability (USA ISSN 1062-2497) **4419**
Livable City (USA ISSN 0885-4394) **4464**
Livable Communities @ Work (USA ISSN 1936-0134) **8118**
Livarski Vestnik (SVN ISSN 0024-5135) **6321**
Live *see* Ziva **712**
Live (JPN) **2944**
• Live (San Francisco) (USA ISSN 1944-4346) **6528**
Live (Springfield) (USA ISSN 0190-3845) **7738**
Live 24 Seven (GBR ISSN 1752-4687) **5075**
• Live & Learn (USA ISSN 1542-1813) **4051**
Live and Let Live (USA) **320**
Live Animals Regulations (CAN ISSN 0256-4742) **8547**
• Live Design (USA ISSN 1559-2359) **8473**
▼ • Live Fit E-Zine (USA ISSN 1946-1690) **6992**
Live Hudong Yingyu *see* Live Interactive English Magazine **5148**
Live in Concert (DEU) **6585**
Live Interactive English Magazine/Live Hudong Yingyu (TWN ISSN 1609-4867) **5148**
Live It! *see* Metroland Live It! **6992**
Live It Your Way Weekend *see* Weekend **8773**
Live je Lijf *see* D A Leve je Lijf Blad **6832**
Live Letters (USA ISSN 1062-0087) **5327**
Live Magazin (DEU) **6585**
Live Magazin (Baden-Baden) (DEU ISSN 1863-3137) **3852**
Live Magazin Saar (DEU ISSN 0944-453X) **5225**
▼ Live Pain Free (USA ISSN 1947-4814) **5806**
Live Rail (GBR ISSN 0142-7326) **8620**
Live Reef Fish (NCL ISSN 1026-2040) **3601**
• Live Sound! International (USA ISSN 1079-0888) **8154**
Live Steam & Outdoor Railroading (USA ISSN 1554-8090) **4338**
Live To Ride (AUS ISSN 1320-1220) **8260**
Live Twenty-Four Seven *see* Live 24 Seven **5075**
Live Well with Cancer (USA) **6026**
Live Wire (USA) **2200**
Live Wires (USA) **3160**
Live Young Girls (USA ISSN 1094-0456) **6294**
Lived Values, Valued Lives (NLD) **6932**
• ➤ Liver International (DNK ISSN 1478-3223) **5928**
Liver. Supplement *see* Liver International **5928**
• ➤ Liver Transplantation (USA ISSN 1527-6465) **5929**
Liverpool Catholic Directory (GBR) **7805**
Liverpool Classical Monthly (GBR ISSN 0309-3700) **2237**
Liverpool Classical Papers (GBR ISSN 0966-9000) **6585**
Liverpool Cotton Association. Raw Cotton Report and Value Differences for Shipment Circular (GBR) **1430**
Liverpool English Texts and Studies (GBR) **5327**
Liverpool F C Official Magazine (Football Club) (GBR ISSN 1356-2231) **8237**
Liverpool Family Historian (GBR ISSN 0260-759X) **3773**
Liverpool Historical Studies (GBR ISSN 0954-3066) **4151**
• Liverpool Investment Letter (GBR ISSN 0951-9262) **1637**
Liverpool Latin American Studies (GBR) **7983**
• ➤ Liverpool Law Review (NLD ISSN 0144-932X) **4724**
Liverpool Link (GBR ISSN 0266-8750) **8054**
Liverpool Monographs in Archaeology and Oriental Studies (GBR) **404**
Liverpool Monthly (GBR ISSN 1356-854X) **8238**
Liverpool Newsletter (GBR ISSN 0047-4827) **7152**
Liverpool Science Fiction Texts and Studies (GBR) **5444**
Liverpool Studies in European Population (GBR) **7286**
Liverpool Studies in European Regional Cultures (GBR ISSN 1367-5133) **346**
Lives in Music (USA) **6585**
Lives of Real Estate (USA) **7599**
Livestock and Meat Monthly (GBR ISSN 1356-9139) **292**
Livestock Crop Pocket Book (GBR) **292**
Livestock, Cultivation & Industry *see* Daam, Kesht Va San'at **3891**
Livestock, Dairy and Poultry *see* Situation & Outlook Report. Livestock, Dairy and Poultry **300**
• Livestock Horizons (AUS ISSN 1832-3677) **292**
Livestock Market Digest (USA ISSN 0024-5208) **292**
Livestock, Meat and Wool Market News (USA) **292**
Livestock Production Science *see* Livestock Science **292**
• ➤ Livestock Research for Rural Development (Online Edition) (COL) **292**
Livestock Roundup (USA) **292**
• ➤ Livestock Science (NLD ISSN 1871-1413) **292**
Livestock Slaughter *see* U.S. Department of Agriculture. National Agricultural Statistics Service. Livestock Slaughter **188**
• Livestock Update (USA) **292**
Livestock Weekly (USA ISSN 0162-5047) **292**
Living (ARG ISSN 1514-6073) **4545**
Living (AUS) **5896**
Living (CZE ISSN 1214-1976) **4545**
Living (NLD ISSN 1387-5906) **4980**
Living (Grottoes) (USA) **8118**
Living (Nevada) (USA ISSN 1098-5840) **7765**
Living Aboard (USA ISSN 0897-2656) **8277**
Living Abroad in Guatemala *see* Moon Living Abroad in Guatemala **8738**
Living Abroad in Ireland (USA ISSN 1555-9750) **8731**
Living Africa (ZAF ISSN 1026-0447) **3949**
Living & Learning (USA ISSN 1534-7508) **7383**
Living and Loving (ZAF ISSN 0256-0496) **8872**
Living Architecture (DNK ISSN 0108-4135) **449**
Living at Home (DEU ISSN 1617-3589) **4545**
† Living at Home (ESP) **8971**
Living Better (USA ISSN 1059-2539) **4363**
Living Bird (USA ISSN 1059-521X) **910**
Living Blues (USA ISSN 0024-5232) **6585**
Living Blues Blues Directory (USA ISSN 1044-1026) **6585**
Living Bluesletter *see* Living Blues **6585**
Living Buddhism (USA ISSN 1093-5169) **7701**
Living Church (USA ISSN 0024-5240) **7765**
Living City (USA ISSN 0193-5968) **7661**
Living Common Law (CAN ISSN 1712-9354) **4912**
Living Costs Abroad, Quarters Allowances, and Hardship Differentials *see* U.S. Department of State. Quarterly Report **1523**
▼ Living Crafts (USA ISSN 1942-6046) **537**
Living Earth (GBR ISSN 1360-1741) **241**
Living Especial *see* Living **4545**
Living Etc. (GBR ISSN 1461-9180) **4363**
Living Ethics (AUS ISSN 1444-6545) **6932**
• Living Faith (USA ISSN 1055-5463) **7805**
Living Fit (USA ISSN 1091-8671) **8846**
Living Forge (USA ISSN 1545-7176) **5327**
Living France (GBR ISSN 0960-5444) **8731**
Living Free (USA) **7152**
Living Gardens (DEU) **3742**
Living Healthy (USA) **6992**
Living Historical Farms Bulletin (USA ISSN 0047-4851) **6528**
Living History (GBR ISSN 1750-5887) **8731**
Living History (USA) **4302**
Living History Association Quarterly (USA) **4151**
• Living Home (USA) **4545**
Living in Ecuador (ECU) **1406**
▼ Living in Gauteng (ZAF ISSN 1994-2192) **5075**
Living in Japan (JPN ISSN 0913-8102) **3900**
Living in Milano *see* Vivere a Milano **8773**
Living in New Kinds of Situations *see* L I N K S **3043**
Living in South Carolina (USA ISSN 0047-486X) **3980**
Living in Stamford (USA) **3980**
Living in Style *see* Plaisirs de Vivre **4549**
Living in Thailand (THA ISSN 0125-1953) **3961**
▼ Living in the Cape (ZAF ISSN 1994-2265) **5076**
Living in the Spectrum: Autism & Asperger's (USA) **7383**
Living in Venezuela (VEN) **8731**
Living It (IRL ISSN 1649-606X) **3894**
Living Koupelna (CZE ISSN 1214-682X) **4545**
Living Kuchyne (CZE ISSN 1214-6838) **4560**
The Living Light (USA) **7738**
Living Light News (CAN ISSN 1487-9557) **7661**
The Living Light Philosophy *see* The Living Light **7738**
▼ Living Liturgy for Cantors (USA ISSN 1947-2862) **7805**
▼ Living Liturgy Sunday Missal (USA ISSN 1949-1166) **7805**
• Living M S Magazine (Multiple Sclerosis) (USA) **6159**
Living Marxism *see* L M **7150**
The Living Museum (USA ISSN 0024-5283) **503**
Living Music (USA) **6585**
Living Options in Practice Project Paper (GBR) **4067**
Living Orthodoxy (USA ISSN 0279-8433) **7705**
Living Planet (USA ISSN 1444-4046) **2617**
• ➤ Living Poets (GBR) **5426**
• The Living Pulpit (USA ISSN 1059-2733) **7661**
• The Living Resources Newsletter (USA ISSN 1947-7422) **3980**
• ➤ Living Reviews in European Governance (AUT ISSN 1813-856X) **7251**
▼ • ➤ Living Reviews in Landscape Research (DEU ISSN 1863-7329) **134**
• ➤ Living Reviews in Relativity (DEU ISSN 1433-8351) **7025**
• ➤ Living Reviews in Solar Physics (DEU ISSN 1614-4961) **577**
Living Safety (CAN ISSN 0714-5896) **7530**
Living Southern Style (USA ISSN 1539-3208) **7599**
Living Space (IRL ISSN 1393-5283) **4545**
Living Standards Measurement Study Working Paper *see* L S M S Working Paper **1601**
• Living Sustainably (AUS ISSN 1833-2153) **3451**
Living the Word (USA) **7805**
Living the Word, Not Only on Sunday *see* Living the Word **7805**
• The Living Tradition (GBR ISSN 1351-4105) **6585**
Living Trusts: Forms and Practice (USA) **4903**
Living & More (DEU) **3742**
Living Water (PHL) **7805**
Living Well *see* Learning Disability Today **4067**
Living Well (JOR) **5076**
• Living Well (USA ISSN 1556-9780) **4051**
Living With Antiques *see* The New England Antiques Journal **367**
Living with Christ Complete - American Edition (CAN ISSN 1481-9244) **7805**
Living with Christ - Complete Edition (CAN ISSN 0703-6752) **6585**
Living with Christ - Large Print Edition (CAN) **7805**
Living with Christ - Sunday Edition (CAN ISSN 0703-6760) **6585**
• Living with Crystals (USA ISSN 1521-1924) **6646**
Living with Loss Magazine (USA ISSN 1935-701X) **7383**
• Living with Moshiach (USA) **7726**
Living with Teenagers (USA ISSN 0162-4261) **7765**
Living Without (USA ISSN 1941-2770) **5076**
Living without Cruelty Diary (Year) (GBR) **320**
Living World (TTO ISSN 1029-3299) **687**
➤ Living World (USA ISSN 0896-2154) **8054**
Livingetc *see* Living Etc. **4363**
Livingston County Agricultural News (USA ISSN 0024-5313) **134**
Livingston County Genealogical Society - Newsletter (USA ISSN 1047-8647) **3773**
Livingston Survey (USA) **1145**
Livingstone Museum. Research Notes (ZMB) **4176**
Livius (ESP ISSN 1132-3191) **5327**
• Livornocronaca il Vernacoliere (ITA ISSN 1721-7741) **5225**
• Livraisons d'Histoire de l'Architecture (FRA ISSN 1627-4970) **449**
Livraria Figueirinhas Catalogo (PRT) **7566**
Le Livre Citoyen (FRA ISSN 1951-5774) **7152**
Livre du Congres l'A F T P V (FRA) **503**
Le Livre et l'Estampe (BEL ISSN 0024-533X) **7566**
Livre Suisse *see* Schweizer Buch **7573**
Livres Africains Disponibles *see* African Books in Print **615**
Livres Canadiens Courants *see* Current Canadian Books **7559**
Livres de France (FRA ISSN 0294-0019) **7566**
• Livres Disponibles (FRA ISSN 0240-6608) **630**
Les Livres du Mois (FRA ISSN 0294-0027) **7566**
▼ Livres en Vie (FRA ISSN 1957-1410) **7566**
Livres & Manuscrits (FRA ISSN 1951-4387) **5327**
Livres et Revues d'Italie *see* Libri e Riviste d'Italia **7566**
Livres Hebdo (FRA ISSN 0294-0000) **7578**
Livres Jeunes Aujourd'hui (FRA ISSN 0223-4289) **5327**
Livres Quebecois a Paraitre (CAN ISSN 1716-7477) **630**
Les Livres qui Soignent (FRA ISSN 1776-6443) **5662**
Livret de la Quatrieme Section, Ecole des Hautes Etudes *see* Ecole Pratiques des Hautes Etudes. Section des Sciences Historiques et Philologiques. Livret - Annuaire **4138**
Livret de Reference du Conseiller Financier (CAN ISSN 1912-3140) **1366**
Livret des Reglements de la Federation Canadienne des Archers *see* Federation of Canadian Archers. Rules Book **8173**
Livret Trimestriel de la Christian Science. Lecons Bibliques *see* Christian Science Quarterly. Bible Lessons (English Citation Edition) **7734**
Livrete Trimestral da Christian Science. Licoes Biblicas *see* Christian Science Quarterly. Bible Lessons (English Citation Edition) **7734**
Livro d'Ouro do Carro Usado (PRT) **8589**
Livros de Portugal (PRT ISSN 0870-5259) **7566**
Livros Disponiveis (Year) (PRT ISSN 0870-6093) **630**
Livrustkammaren (SWE ISSN 0024-5372) **4240**
Livsglede *see* Armer & Bein **4077**
Livsmedel i Fokus (SWE) **3654**
Livsmedelsteknik *see* Livsmedel i Fokus **3654**
Al-Liwa' al-Islami/The Islamic Banner/Islamic Standard (EGY) **7713**
• ➤ Lixue Jinzhan/Advances in Mechanics (CHN ISSN 1000-0992) **7060**
• ➤ Lixue Xuebao/Acta Mechanica Sinica (CHN ISSN 0459-1879) **7060**
• ➤ Lixue yu Shijian/Mechanics and Practice (CHN ISSN 1000-0879) **3388**
Liza (RUS ISSN 1560-5434) **4980**
Liza (UKR ISSN 1681-3162) **8872**
Liza. Dobrye Sovety (RUS ISSN 1728-7928) **8872**
Liza. Dobrye Sovety (UKR ISSN 1682-9743) **8872**
Liza. Dobrye Sovety. Luchshie Retsepty (UKR) **4363**
Liza. Goroskop (RUS ISSN 1606-8726) **566**
Liza. Goroskop (UKR) **566**
Liza. Krossvordy (RUS ISSN 1606-8769) **8186**
Liza. Krossvordy (UKR) **8186**
Liza. Modnye Pricheski (RUS ISSN 1681-3464) **589**
Liza. Moi Liubimye Zhivotnye (RUS ISSN 1726-0868) **6811**
Liza. Moi Rebenok (RUS ISSN 1606-8734) **2160**
Liza. Moi Rebenok (UKR) **2160**
Liza. Priyatnogo Appetita! (Kiev) (UKR) **4363**
Liza. Priyatnogo Appetita! (Moscow) (RUS ISSN 1560-5442) **4363**
Liza. Priyatnogo Appetita! Specials (RUS) **4363**
Liza. Tsvety v Dome (RUS ISSN 1606-9609) **3742**
Liza. Tsvety v Dome (UKR) **3742**
• ➤ Lizi Jiaohuan yu Xifu/Ion Exchange and Adsorption (CHN ISSN 1001-5493) **2072**
• Lizing Reviu/Leasing Review (RUS) **7599**
Lizzengreasy (JPN) **3900**
• ➤ Ljekarska Komora Zenicko-Dobojskog Kantona. Medicinski Glasnik (BIH ISSN 1840-0132) **5662**
• Ljetopis Socijalnog Rada (HRV ISSN 1846-5412) **2659**
Ljetopis Srpskog Kulturnog Drustva Prosvjeta *see* Srpsko Kulturno Drustvo Prosvjeta. Ljetopis **4267**
Ljetopis Studijskog Centra Socijalnog Rada *see* Ljetopis Socijalnog Rada **2659**
• Ljevarstvo/Journal for Theory and Application in Foundry (HRV ISSN 1330-2132) **6321**
Ljosmaedrabladid (ISL ISSN 1670-2670) **5997**
Ljubljanski Zurnal *see* Zurnal **3947**
• Ljud & Bild i Elektronikvaerlden (SWE ISSN 1653-9907) **2332**
Ljud och Bild *see* Ljud & Bild i Elektronikvaerlden **2332**
Ljuskultur (SWE ISSN 0024-5429) **3324**
Llafar Gwlad (GBR ISSN 1356-3777) **4240**
Llafur (GBR ISSN 0306-0837) **1696**
Llais (GBR) **2290**
Llandaff Diocesan Directory (GBR) **7765**
Llanelli Star (GBR ISSN 0961-432X) **3868**
Llanelli Star (Bont and Estuary Edition) *see* Llanelli Star **3868**
Llanelli Star (Gwendraeth Edition) *see* Llanelli Star **3868**
Llawlyfr Cyllido Cymru - Diweddariad *see* Wales Funding Handbook **8077**
La Llei de Catalunya/La Ley de Cataluna (ESP ISSN 1139-8531) **4724**
• Llen Cymru (GBR ISSN 0076-0188) **5327**
• Llengua i Us (ESP ISSN 1134-7724) **5148**
➤ Llenyddiaeth Mewn Theori (GBR ISSN 1747-7476) **5327**
† Lletra de Canvi (ESP ISSN 0213-9936) **8971**
• Lletres Asturianes (ESP ISSN 0212-0534) **5148**
Lleuve Tlaloc (USA) **5327**
▼ Llewellyn's (Year) Green Living Guide (USA ISSN 1945-0044) **3451**
Llewellyn's New Worlds of Mind & Spirit (USA) **6646**
Llewellyn's Starview Almanac (USA ISSN 1554-6373) **566**
Llewellyn's Sun Sign Book *see* Sun Sign Book **567**
@lliance *see* Alliance **4916**
Lligall (ESP ISSN 1130-5398) **5030**
LLinE *see* Lifelong Learning in Europe **2944**
De Lloyd (Dutch Edition) (BEL) **8650**
Le Lloyd (French Edition) (BEL) **8650**
Lloyd: Information Technology Law (GBR) **4724**
Lloydminster Meridian Booster (CAN) **3812**
Lloydminster Sask/Alta Meridian Booster *see* Lloydminster Meridian Booster **3812**
▼ • Lloyd's Asbestos Litigation Reporter (USA ISSN 1945-4694) **4724**
Lloyd's Casualty Week (GBR ISSN 0966-761X) **4513**
Lloyd's Confidential Index of Steam and Motor Vessels (GBR) **4513**
Lloyd's Cruise International (GBR ISSN 1363-2043) **8731**
Lloyd's Electronic Law Reports *see* Lloyd's Law Reports **4724**
• Lloyd's Electronic Law Reports on CD-ROM (GBR) **4724**
Lloyd's Electronic Maritime Directory *see* Lloyd's Maritime Directory (Year) **8650**
Lloyd's Freight Transport Buyer (GBR) **8502**
Lloyd's Freight Transport Buyer Asia (GBR ISSN 1561-7823) **8502**
• Lloyd's Law Reports (GBR ISSN 0024-5488) **4724**
Lloyd's Law Reports Citator *see* Lloyd's Law Reports **4724**
Lloyd's Law Reports: Insurance & Reinsurance (GBR ISSN 1744-5434) **4513**
• Lloyds Law Reports. Medical (GBR ISSN 1461-8540) **5662**
• Lloyd's List (GBR ISSN 0144-820X) **8650**
Lloyd's List D C N *see* Lloyd's List Daily Commercial News **8650**
• Lloyd's List Daily Commercial News (AUS) **8650**
Lloyd's List Directory of Shipping Agents (GBR) **8650**
▼ Lloyd's List Maritime Americas (GBR) **8650**
Lloyd's List Maritime Asia (HKG) **8650**
Lloyd's List Ports of the World (Year) (GBR ISSN 1478-4696) **8650**
Lloyd's Loading List (GBR ISSN 0144-6681) **8650**
Lloyd's Marine Equipment Buyers' Guide *see* Lloyd's Marine Equipment Guide **8650**
Lloyd's Marine Equipment Guide (GBR) **8650**
• Lloyd's Maritime & Commercial Law Quarterly (GBR ISSN 0306-2945) **4970**
Lloyd's Maritime Atlas (GBR ISSN 0076-020X) **8650**
• Lloyd's Maritime Directory (Year) (GBR ISSN 0268-327X) **8650**

Title

▼ *new title* † *ceased* • *electronic media* ➤ *refereed*

DIRECTORY 2010 LOCOMOTIVE ENGINEERS AND TRAINMEN NEWS 10569

- • Local Climatological Data. South Bend, Indiana. Monthly Summary (USA ISSN 0198-2028) **6385**
- • Local Climatological Data. Spokane, Washington. Annual Summary with Comparative Data (USA ISSN 0198-5485) **6385**
- • Local Climatological Data. Spokane, Washington. Monthly Summary (USA ISSN 0198-5493) **6385**
- • Local Climatological Data. Springfield, Illinois. Annual Summary with Comparative Data (USA ISSN 0198-1927) **6385**
- • Local Climatological Data. Springfield, Illinois. Monthly Summary (USA ISSN 0198-1935) **6385**
- • Local Climatological Data. Springfield, Missouri. Annual Summary with Comparative Data (USA ISSN 0198-2923) **6386**
- • Local Climatological Data. Springfield, Missouri. Monthly Summary (USA ISSN 0198-2931) **6386**
- • Local Climatological Data. St. Louis, Missouri. Annual Summary with Comparative Data (USA ISSN 0198-2907) **6386**
- • Local Climatological Data. St. Louis, Missouri. Monthly Summary (USA ISSN 0198-2915) **6386**
- • Local Climatological Data. St. Paul Island, Alaska. Annual Summary with Comparative Data (USA ISSN 0198-0513) **6386**
- • Local Climatological Data. St. Paul Island, Alaska. Monthly Summary (USA ISSN 0198-0416) **6386**
- • Local Climatological Data. Stampede Pass, Washington. Annual Summary with Comparative Data (USA ISSN 0198-5507) **6386**
- • Local Climatological Data. Stockton, California. Annual Summary with Comparative Data (USA ISSN 0198-1013) **6386**
- • Local Climatological Data. Stockton, California. Monthly Summary (USA ISSN 0198-0858) **6386**
- • Local Climatological Data. Syracuse, New York. Annual Summary with Comparative Data (USA ISSN 0198-3679) **6386**
- • Local Climatological Data. Syracuse, New York. Monthly Summary (USA ISSN 0198-3687) **6386**
- • Local Climatological Data. Talkeetna, Alaska. Annual Summary with Comparative Data (USA ISSN 0198-0521) **6386**
- • Local Climatological Data. Talkeetna, Alaska. Monthly Summary (USA ISSN 0198-0424) **6386**
- • Local Climatological Data. Tallahassee, Florida. Annual Summary with Comparative Data (USA ISSN 0198-1293) **6386**
- • Local Climatological Data. Tallahassee, Florida. Monthly Summary (USA ISSN 0198-1412) **6386**
- • Local Climatological Data. Tampa, Florida. Annual Summary with Comparative Data (USA ISSN 0198-1307) **6386**
- • Local Climatological Data. Tampa, Florida. Monthly Summary (USA ISSN 0198-1420) **6386**
- • Local Climatological Data. Toledo, Ohio. Annual Summary with Comparative Data (USA ISSN 0198-4012) **6387**
- • Local Climatological Data. Toledo, Ohio. Monthly Summary (USA ISSN 0198-4020) **6387**
- • Local Climatological Data. Topeka, Kansas. Annual Summary with Comparative Data (USA ISSN 0198-2192) **6387**
- • Local Climatological Data. Topeka, Kansas. Monthly Summary (USA ISSN 0198-2206) **6387**
- • Local Climatological Data. Truk Caroline Island Pacific. Monthly Summary (USA ISSN 0198-4403) **6387**
- • Local Climatological Data. Truk, Eastern Caroline Island, Pacific. Annual Summary with Comparative Data (USA ISSN 0198-439X) **6387**
- • Local Climatological Data. Tucson, Arizona. Annual Summary with Comparative Data (USA ISSN 0198-0580) **6387**
- • Local Climatological Data. Tucson, Arizona. Monthly Summary (USA ISSN 0198-0483) **6387**
- • Local Climatological Data. Tulsa, Oklahoma. Annual Summary with Comparative Data (USA ISSN 0198-4071) **6387**
- • Local Climatological Data. Tulsa, Oklahoma. Monthly Summary (USA ISSN 0198-408X) **6387**
- • Local Climatological Data. Tupelo, Mississippi. Annual Summary with Comparative Data (USA ISSN 0742-8782) **6387**
- • Local Climatological Data. Tupelo, Missouri. Monthly Summary (USA ISSN 0739-7259) **6387**
- • Local Climatological Data. Unalakleet, Alaska. Annual Summary with Comparative Data (USA ISSN 0198-053X) **6387**
- • Local Climatological Data. Unalakleet, Alaska. Monthly Summary (USA ISSN 0198-0432) **6387**
- • Local Climatological Data. Valdez, Alaska. Annual Summary with Comparative Data (USA ISSN 0198-0548) **6387**
- • Local Climatological Data. Valdez, Alaska. Monthly Summary (USA ISSN 0198-0440) **6387**
- • Local Climatological Data. Valentine, Nebraska. Annual Summary with Comparative Data (USA ISSN 0198-3237) **6387**
- • Local Climatological Data. Valentine, Nebraska. Monthly Summary (USA ISSN 0198-3245) **6387**
- • Local Climatological Data. Vero Beach, Florida. Annual Summary with Comparative Data (USA ISSN 0742-8758) **6388**
- • Local Climatological Data. Vero Beach, Florida Municipal Airport. Monthly Summary (USA ISSN 0742-874X) **6388**
- • Local Climatological Data. Victoria, Texas. Annual Summary with Comparative Data (USA ISSN 0198-5205) **6388**
- • Local Climatological Data. Victoria, Texas. Monthly Summary (USA ISSN 0198-5213) **6388**
- • Local Climatological Data. Waco, Texas. Annual Summary with Comparative Data (USA ISSN 0198-5221) **6388**
- • Local Climatological Data. Waco, Texas. Monthly Summary (USA ISSN 0198-523X) **6388**
- • Local Climatological Data. Wake Island, Pacific. Annual Summary with Comparative Data (USA ISSN 0198-4411) **6388**
- • Local Climatological Data. Wake Island, Pacific. Monthly Summary (USA ISSN 0198-442X) **6388**
- • Local Climatological Data. Walla Walla, Washington. Annual Summary with Comparative Data (USA ISSN 0198-5523) **6388**
- • Local Climatological Data. Wallops Island, Virginia. Monthly Summary (USA ISSN 0198-7658) **6388**
- • Local Climatological Data. Washington, D.C. Dulles International Airport. Annual Summary with Comparative Data (USA ISSN 0198-120X) **6388**
- • Local Climatological Data. Washington D.C. Dulles International Airport. Monthly Summary (USA ISSN 0198-1323) **6388**
- • Local Climatological Data. Washington, D.C. National Airport. Annual Summary with Comparative Data (USA ISSN 0198-1196) **6388**
- • Local Climatological Data. Washington D.C. National Airport. Monthly Summary (USA ISSN 0198-1188) **6388**
- • Local Climatological Data. Waterloo, Iowa. Annual Summary with Comparative Data (USA ISSN 0198-2117) **6388**
- • Local Climatological Data. Waterloo, Iowa. Monthly Summary (USA ISSN 0198-2125) **6388**
- • Local Climatological Data. West Palm Beach, Florida. Annual Summary with Comparative Data (USA ISSN 0198-1315) **6388**
- • Local Climatological Data. West Palm Beach, Florida. Monthly Summary (USA ISSN 0198-1439) **6388**
- • Local Climatological Data. Wichita Falls, Texas. Annual Summary with Comparative Data (USA ISSN 0198-5248) **6389**
- • Local Climatological Data. Wichita Falls, Texas. Monthly Summary (USA ISSN 0198-5256) **6389**
- • Local Climatological Data. Wichita, Kansas. Annual Summary with Comparative Data (USA ISSN 0198-2214) **6389**
- • Local Climatological Data. Wichita, Kansas. Monthly Summary (USA ISSN 0198-2222) **6389**
- • Local Climatological Data. Williamsport, Pennsylvania. Annual Summary with Comparative Data (USA ISSN 0198-4551) **6389**
- • Local Climatological Data. Williamsport, Pennsylvania. Monthly Summary (USA ISSN 0198-456X) **6389**
- • Local Climatological Data. Williston, North Dakota. Annual Summary with Comparative Data (USA ISSN 0198-3857) **6389**
- • Local Climatological Data. Williston, North Dakota. Monthly Summary (USA ISSN 0198-3865) **6389**
- • Local Climatological Data. Wilmington, Delaware. Annual Summary with Comparative Data (USA ISSN 0198-1145) **6389**
- • Local Climatological Data. Wilmington, Delaware. Monthly Summary (USA ISSN 0198-117X) **6389**
- • Local Climatological Data. Wilmington, North Carolina. Annual Summary with Comparative Data (USA ISSN 0198-3792) **6389**
- • Local Climatological Data. Wilmington, North Carolina. Monthly Summary (USA ISSN 0198-3806) **6389**
- • Local Climatological Data. Winnemucca, Nevada. Annual Summary with Comparative Data (USA ISSN 0198-3342) **6389**
- • Local Climatological Data. Winnemucca, Nevada. Monthly Summary (USA ISSN 0198-3350) **6389**
- • Local Climatological Data. Winslow, Arizona. Annual Summary with Comparative Data (USA ISSN 0198-0599) **6389**
- • Local Climatological Data. Winslow, Arizona. Monthly Summary (USA ISSN 0198-0491) **6389**
- • Local Climatological Data. Worcester, Massachusetts. Annual Summary with Comparative Data (USA ISSN 0198-2451) **6389**
- • Local Climatological Data. Worcester, Massachusetts. Monthly Summary (USA ISSN 0198-246X) **6390**
- • Local Climatological Data. Yakima, Washington. Monthly Summary (USA ISSN 0198-5558) **6390**
- • Local Climatological Data. Yakutat, Alaska. Annual Summary with Comparative Data (USA ISSN 0198-0556) **6390**
- • Local Climatological Data. Yakutat, Alaska. Monthly Summary (USA ISSN 0198-0459) **6390**
- • Local Climatological Data. Yap Island, Pacific. Annual Summary with Comparative Data (USA ISSN 0198-4438) **6390**
- • Local Climatological Data. Yap Island, Pacific. Monthly Summary (USA ISSN 0198-4446) **6390**
- • Local Climatological Data. Youngstown, Ohio. Annual Summary with Comparative Data (USA ISSN 0198-4039) **6390**
- • Local Climatological Data. Youngstown, Ohio. Monthly Summary (USA ISSN 0198-4047) **6390**
- • Local Climatological Data. Yuma, Arizona. Annual Summary with Comparative Data (USA ISSN 0198-0653) **6390**
- • Local Climatological Data. Yuma, Arizona. Monthly Summary (USA ISSN 0198-0602) **6390**
- Local Climatological Summary, with Comparative Data. Dayton, Ohio *see* Local Climatological Data. Dayton, Ohio. Annual Summary with Comparative Data **6367**
- Local Colour: A Literary Monthly *see* Xiangtu **3829**
- † • Local Competition Report (USA ISSN 1087-8998) **8971**
- • Local Connections (AUS ISSN 1834-3961) **3451**
- • Local Content and Diversity (NZL ISSN 1177-7028) **2360**
- Local Council Review (GBR ISSN 0308-3594) **7496**
- • Local Courts Civil Procedure New South Wales (AUS) **4835**
- Local Development Social Inclusion Programme. Newsletter *see* Inclusion Through Local Development **8107**
- • ➤ Local Economy (GBR ISSN 0269-0942) **1145**
- • ➤ Local Environment (GBR ISSN 1354-9839) **4419**
- Local Europe (GBR ISSN 0964-4148) **7451**
- Local Focus (USA) **4725**
- • ➤ Local Global (AUS ISSN 1832-6919) **7983**
- Local Governance *see* Critical Policy Studies **7127**
- Local Government (PAK) **7496**
- • Local Government and Environmental Law Library (AUS ISSN 1443-8631) **7496**
- • Local Government and Environmental Reports of Australia (AUS ISSN 1039-7213) **7496**
- Local Government and Law (GBR ISSN 0968-2430) **7496**
- Local Government and Planning Law Guide (AUS ISSN 1326-9739) **7496**
- • Local Government Association. Circular Checklists (GBR) **7496**
- Local Government Association. Housing Finance Survey (Year) (GBR) **4419**
- Local Government Association Reseach Report *see* L G A Reseach Report **7450**
- Local Government Association. Yearbook (GBR ISSN 1369-8532) **7496**
- Local Government Bulletin (PHL ISSN 0024-5526) **7496**
- • Local Government Chronicle (GBR ISSN 0024-5534) **7496**
- Local Government Companion (GBR ISSN 0305-0130) **7496**
- Local Government Directory (Year) (GBR) **7496**
- Local Government Elections *see* Sveitarstjornarkosningar **7187**
- Local Government Employment and Payroll Data *see* U.S. Bureau of the Census. Governments Division. Local Government Employment and Payroll Data **1271**
- Local Government Executive (GBR ISSN 1472-3484) **7496**
- Local Government Finance *see* Sveitarsjodareikningar **1269**
- Local Government Finance: Law & Practice (GBR) **1366**
- Local Government Finances in Maryland (USA ISSN 0085-2821) **1933**
- Local Government First (GBR ISSN 1468-3024) **7496**
- • Local Government Focus (Green Edition) (AUS ISSN 0819-470X) **7496**
- Local Government I T in Use (Information Technology) (GBR ISSN 1368-2660) **2549**
- Local Government in Mauritius *see* Association of Urban Authorities. Annual Bulletin **7488**
- Local Government in Victoria (Year) (AUS ISSN 1832-4169) **7451**
- Local Government Index New South Wales (AUS ISSN 0727-7989) **7481**
- Local Government Information Unit Discussion Papers *see* L G I U Discussion Papers **7450**
- Local Government Information Unit Information Briefing *see* L G I U Information Briefing **7495**
- Local Government Information Unit Policy Briefing *see* L G I U Policy Briefing **2881**
- Local Government Information Unit Special Briefings *see* L G I U Special Briefings **7450**
- Local Government Law *see* Cross on Local Government Law **7490**
- Local Government Law and Practice New South Wales *see* Local Government Law & Practice New South Wales **7496**
- • Local Government Law & Practice New South Wales (AUS ISSN 0727-7830) **7496**
- • Local Government Law Bulletin (USA ISSN 0362-5729) **7496**
- Local Government Law Journal (AUS ISSN 1324-1265) **4725**
- Local Government Library Bulletin (ZAF) **7496**
- Local Government Manager (AUS ISSN 1445-4335) **7497**
- Local Government News (GBR ISSN 0261-5185) **7497**
- Local Government Planning and Environment N S W *see* Local Government Planning & Environment N S W **7497**
- • Local Government Planning & Environment N S W (New South Wales) (AUS) **7497**
- Local Government Postal Elections Report (AUS ISSN 1832-9187) **7451**
- Local Government Precedents and Procedures (GBR) **7497**
- Local Government Queensland (AUS) **7497**
- • Local Government Regulations N S W (New South Wales) (AUS) **7497**
- Local Government Regulations Services New South Wales *see* Local Government Regulations N S W **7497**
- Local Government Service Victoria (AUS) **7497**
- • ➤ Local Government Studies (GBR ISSN 0300-3930) **7497**
- † Local Governmental Accounting Trends and Techniques (USA ISSN 1042-0231) **8971**
- Local Hammersmith & Fulham Independent (GBR ISSN 1471-289X) **3868**
- • Local Health Area Population Estimates and Projections (Online Edition) (CAN) **7311**
- Local Health Area Population Estimates and Projections (Print Edition) *see* Local Health Area Population Estimates and Projections (Online Edition) **7311**
- ➤ The Local Historian (GBR ISSN 0024-5585) **4240**
- The Local Historian (USA ISSN 0893-3340) **4302**
- • Local History & Genealogy Librarian (USA) **5030**
- • Local History & Genealogy Librarian Online (USA) **5030**
- Local History Magazine (GBR ISSN 0266-2698) **4240**
- • Local History News (AUS ISSN 1833-8828) **4193**
- Local History News (GBR ISSN 0969-3521) **4240**
- Local Kensington & Chelsea Independent (GBR ISSN 1471-2903) **3868**
- ➤ Local-Link (AUS ISSN 1329-8356) **5030**
- Local Management and Finance (GBR ISSN 1356-9805) **1933**
- • Local Media Journal (USA) **1829**
- Local News (USA) **4598**
- Local Notting Hill & Bayswater Independent (GBR ISSN 1471-2911) **3868**
- Local Paralegal Club Directory (USA) **4725**
- The Local Planet (IRL ISSN 1649-6221) **2617**
- Local Planet Visibility Report (Year) (USA ISSN 0889-9622) **577**
- ➤ Local Population Studies (GBR ISSN 0143-2974) **7286**
- Local Population Studies. Supplement (GBR ISSN 0143-2982) **7286**
- Local Preachers Magazine (GBR ISSN 0024-5607) **7765**
- ▼ Local Real Estate Deals Magazine (USA ISSN 1943-4510) **7599**
- • Local Rules of the District Courts in Texas (USA) **4955**
- Local/State Funding Report (USA ISSN 0741-3173) **1933**
- Local Studies Librarian (GBR ISSN 0263-0273) **5030**
- ▼ • Local Table (USA ISSN 1941-5370) **3742**
- • Local Transport Today (GBR ISSN 0962-6220) **8502**
- Local Westminster Independent (GBR ISSN 1471-292X) **3868**
- • Local Work (GBR ISSN 0950-3080) **1696**
- Locali Top (ITA) **4393**
- ➤ Localisation Focus (IRL ISSN 1649-2358) **2352**
- ▼ Localisation Research Centre. Annual Conference Proceedings (IRL ISSN 2009-0331) **2352**
- Locating Gold, Gems, & Minerals (USA ISSN 1544-7774) **6468**
- Location Canada *see* Area Development Site & Facility Planning **4403**
- Location Guides for Family and Local Historians (GBR) **3774**
- • Location Identifiers (USA ISSN 0364-5282) **65**
- Location Update *see* Production Update **6510**
- Locational Characteristics of Housing Land Supply in Kent (Year) (GBR) **4419**
- LocationReport (DEU ISSN 1611-8316) **1829**
- Locations (USA) **6506**
- Locations of Industries in Gujarat State (IND ISSN 0076-0269) **1897**
- Locations Vacances *see* Bertrand Vacances **7583**
- The Locator (USA) **2013**
- Locator of Used Machinery, Equipment & Plant Services (USA) **5454**
- • Locator Upfront Magazine (USA) **8589**
- ▼ • ➤ Loci (USA ISSN 1941-9198) **5509**
- Locke Newsletter *see* Locke Studies **6932**
- Locke Sickle & Sword (USA ISSN 1078-7720) **3774**
- ➤ Locke Studies (GBR ISSN 1476-0290) **6932**
- • Lockergnome's Free Windows 95 - N T E-Zine (USA ISSN 1095-3965) **2594**
- Lockert Library of Poetry in Translation (USA) **5426**
- Lockheed M S C Star (Missiles and Space Company) (USA) **77**
- Locksmith Gazette (USA ISSN 0193-3191) **1054**
- • Locksmith Ledger International (USA ISSN 1050-2254) **1054**
- Locksmith Ledger - International Directory (USA) **2679**
- Lockwood Post Pulp & Paper Directory *see* Lockwood - Post's Directory American Traveler's Edition **2013**
- • Lockwood - Post's Directory American Traveler's Edition (USA) **2013**
- Lockwood - Post's Directory Asian Traveler's Edition (Online) (USA) **6735**
- • Lockwood - Post's Directory European Traveler's Edition (Online) (USA) **6735**
- • Lockwood - Post's Directory Global Edition (USA) **2013**
- Loco Revue (FRA ISSN 0024-5739) **4338**
- Locomotion Papers (GBR ISSN 0305-5493) **8502**
- Locomotive (USA ISSN 0741-8760) **5455**
- Locomotive Engineer Newsletter *see* Locomotive Engineers and Trainmen News **8620**
- • Locomotive Engineers and Trainmen News (USA ISSN 1549-6422) **8620**

Title

Title

10572 LOS CABOS & BAJA ULRICH'S PERIODICALS

Los Cabos & Baja *see* Frommer's Los Cabos & Baja **8711**
Los/Solitarios y Sus Amigos (ESP ISSN 1699-0382) **5328**
Losange (FRA ISSN 0755-4680) **8486**
• Losers Magazine (USA) **3980**
Loss, Grief & Care *see* Journal of Social Work in End-of-Life & Palliative Care **7380**
Loss Minimizer *see* Medical Liability Monitor **4514**
Loss Prevention (New York) (USA ISSN 0097-2312) **3250**
• ➤ Loss Prevention Bulletin (GBR ISSN 0260-9576) **3250**
• Loss Prevention Letter for Supermarket Executives (USA) **3680**
Lost (GBR ISSN 1747-8162) **2384**
• Lost Armadillos in Heat (USA) **5225**
Lost Birds (USA) **65**
Lost Generation Journal (USA ISSN 0091-2948) **5328**
Lost Time & Fatal Injuries Queensland Mines and Quarries Statistical Report *see* Queensland Mines and Quarries Safety Performance and Health Report **6477**
Lost-time Claims *see* Lost-time Claims. Young Workers **7548**
Lost-time Claims and Claim Rates *see* Alberta Construction Safety Association Industries **7506**
Lost-time Claims. Young Workers (CAN ISSN 1912-5879) **7548**
Lost Treasure (USA ISSN 0195-2692) **4338**
Lost Worlds (USA ISSN 1087-2027) **5444**
Lotharingia (FRA ISSN 1161-2045) **4241**
Lothian & Edinburgh Labour Market Assessment (GBR) **1696**
Lothian Bird Report (GBR ISSN 0265-6213) **910**
Lothian Foundation. Annals (GBR) **4241**
Lotnictwo (POL ISSN 1732-5323) **65**
Lotnictwo Wojskowe *see* Lotnictwo **65**
Loto - Quebec. Annual Report *see* Loto - Quebec. Rapport Annuel **1933**
Loto - Quebec. Rapport Annuel (CAN ISSN 0709-5724) **1933**
Lott Lineages (USA ISSN 1081-2350) **3774**
Lotta Comunista (ITA ISSN 1970-6278) **7152**
Lottebladet (NOR) **6431**
Lottery Cash for Schools *see* School Financial Management **3031**
Lottery Monitor *see* External Funding Bulletin **8039**
• Lottery, Parimutuel & Casino Regulation - State Capitals (USA) **4725**
Lottery Winning Guide (USA) **8186**
Lottoroscopo (ITA ISSN 0024-6662) **8186**
Lotus (JPN ISSN 0288-3929) **6933**
Lotus Advisor *see* Databased Advisor Magazine **2554**
➤ Lotus Bleu (FRA ISSN 0024-6670) **6933**
Lotus International (ITA ISSN 1124-9064) **449**
Lotus Lantern International Buddhist Center. Newsletter (KOR) **7701**
Lotus Leaves (USA ISSN 1933-0111) **503**
The Lou Dobbs Money Letter (USA ISSN 1545-1135) **1637**
Lou Lou (English Edition) (CAN ISSN 1710-2987) **8872**
Lou Lou (French Edition) *see* Lou Lou (English Edition) **8872**
LOUD (USA) **2200**
Loud Fast Rules! (USA) **6585**
Loughborough Students' Union. Newspaper (GBR) **2290**
Loughborough University Banking Centre. Research Paper Series (GBR ISSN 0958-0654) **1366**
• Loughborough University. Department of Economics. Discission Paper Series (GBR ISSN 1750-4171) **1145**
Loughborough University. Department of Economics. Economic Research Paper (GBR) **1145**
Loughborough University. Department of Economics. Economic Research Papers *see* Loughborough University. Department of Economics. Economic Research Paper **1145**
Loughborough University. Department of Geography. Occasional Paper (GBR) **4018**
Loughton Review (GBR ISSN 0305-1765) **28**
Louis Navellier's Blue Chip Growth Letter (USA ISSN 1096-1461) **1637**
• Louis Rukeyser's Mutual Funds (USA) **1637**
• Louis Rukeyser's Wall Street (USA ISSN 1060-9903) **1637**
The Louise Lindsey Merrick Natural Environment Series (USA) **3451**
• ➤ Louisiana Academy of Sciences. Proceedings (USA ISSN 0096-9192) **7880**
Louisiana Administrative Code (USA) **7451**
Louisiana Agricultural Experiment Station. Report of Projects (USA ISSN 0456-5959) **134**
➤ Louisiana Agriculture (USA ISSN 0024-6735) **134**
Louisiana Almanac (USA ISSN 0896-6206) **8731**
Louisiana Archaeology (USA) **404**
• Louisiana Archives and Manuscripts Association. Newsletter (USA ISSN 1073-1008) **5030**
➤ Louisiana Association for College Composition Journal (USA ISSN 1077-5056) **5148**
Louisiana Association of Business and Industry Enterprise *see* L A B I Enterprise **1430**
Louisiana Association of Educators Voice *see* L A E Voice **2881**
Louisiana Banker (USA ISSN 1050-379X) **1366**
Louisiana Baptist Builder (USA ISSN 0024-6743) **7765**
• Louisiana Bar Journal (USA ISSN 0459-8881) **4725**
Louisiana Beverage Journal (USA) **607**
Louisiana Builder (USA ISSN 1552-8731) **1021**
• Louisiana Business Credit Directory (USA) **2013**
• Louisiana Business Directory (USA ISSN 1048-7298) **2013**
Louisiana Cattleman (USA) **292**
Louisiana Cities & Counties Graphic Performance Analysis (USA ISSN 1935-5998) **7481**
Louisiana Cities and Counties Graphic Performance Analysis *see* Louisiana Cities & Counties Graphic Performance Analysis **7481**
▼ Louisiana Civil Jury Instruction Companion Handbook (USA ISSN 1942-8685) **4725**
Louisiana Coastal Law (USA) **4725**
Louisiana Conservationist (USA ISSN 0024-6778) **2617**
Louisiana Contractor *see* South Central Construction **1036**
Louisiana Cookin' (USA) **4363**
Louisiana Country (USA) **3324**
Louisiana Criminal Law and Motor Vehicle Handbook *see* Louisiana Criminal Law and Motor Vehicle Handbook with Legal Guidelines **4893**
Louisiana Criminal Law & Motor Vehicle Handbook *see* Louisiana Criminal Law and Motor Vehicle Handbook with Legal Guidelines **4893**
• Louisiana Criminal Law and Motor Vehicle Handbook (USA) **4893**
• Louisiana Criminal Law and Motor Vehicle Handbook with Legal Guidelines (USA ISSN 1933-2769) **4893**
Louisiana Cultural Vistas (USA ISSN 1082-4553) **4302**
Louisiana Dental Association Journal *see* L D A Journal **5854**
Louisiana. Department of Justice. Report and Opinions of the Attorney General *see* Opinions of the Attorney General of the State of Louisiana from (Year-Year) **4753**
Louisiana. Department of Public Safety. Summary of Motor Vehicle Traffic Accidents. Kenner (USA ISSN 0741-4439) **8385**
Louisiana. Department of Public Safety. Summary of Motor Vehicle Traffic Accidents. Rural (USA ISSN 0741-434X) **8385**
Louisiana. Department of Public Safety. Summary of Motor Vehicle Traffic Accidents. Shreveport (USA ISSN 0741-4382) **8385**
Louisiana. Department of Public Safety. Summary of Motor Vehicle Traffic Accidents. Statewide (USA ISSN 0741-4358) **8386**
• Louisiana Employment Law Letter (USA ISSN 1059-5058) **4725**
Louisiana Engineer & Surveyor Journal (USA ISSN 1527-5965) **3208**
➤ Louisiana English Journal (USA ISSN 0456-7463) **5328**
Louisiana Estate Planning, Will Drafting and Estate Administration with Forms (USA) **4903**
• Louisiana Folklore Miscellany (USA ISSN 0090-9769) **3620**
Louisiana Game & Fish (USA ISSN 0744-3692) **8321**
Louisiana Genealogical Register (USA ISSN 0148-7655) **3774**
Louisiana Geological Survey. Anthropological Studies Series (USA) **346**
Louisiana Geological Survey. Clay Resources Bulletin (USA ISSN 0069-4592) **6469**
Louisiana Geological Survey. Educational Series (USA) **2753**
Louisiana Geological Survey. Folio Series (USA ISSN 0458-3329) **2753**
Louisiana Geological Survey. Geological Bulletin (USA ISSN 0096-3720) **2753**
Louisiana Geological Survey. Geological Pamphlets (USA) **2753**
Louisiana Geological Survey. Guidebook Series (USA ISSN 1047-739X) **2753**
Louisiana Geological Survey. Mineral Resources Bulletin (USA ISSN 0160-8517) **2753**
Louisiana Geological Survey. Public Information Series (USA) **2753**
Louisiana Geological Survey. Resources Information Series (USA ISSN 0278-4777) **2753**
Louisiana Geological Survey. Water Resources Bulletin (USA ISSN 0459-8474) **2753**
Louisiana Geological Survey. Water Resources Pamphlet (USA) **8828**
Louisiana Geological Survey. Water Resources Series (USA) **8828**
Louisiana History (USA ISSN 0024-6816) **4302**
Louisiana History Newsletter (USA ISSN 1946-9950) **4302**
Louisiana History Quarterly Newsletter (USA) **4302**
Louisiana Holiday & Travel Guide (GBR) **8731**
Louisiana Industry Environmental Alert (USA ISSN 1055-257X) **3451**
Louisiana Labor Market Information (USA) **1696**
• ➤ Louisiana Law Review (USA ISSN 0024-6859) **4725**
Louisiana Levant Magazine (USA ISSN 1554-3315) **3451**
• Louisiana Libraries (USA ISSN 1535-2102) **5030**
• Louisiana Life (USA ISSN 1042-9980) **3980**
➤ Louisiana Literature (USA ISSN 0890-0477) **5328**
Louisiana Magasin (DNK ISSN 1601-1724) **6528**
• Louisiana Manufacturers Register (USA ISSN 1053-8992) **2013**
Louisiana: Manufacturing *see* Harris Directory. Louisiana Manufacturing **2000**
Louisiana Market Bulletin (USA ISSN 0279-8824) **134**
Louisiana - Mississippi State Agent Handbook (USA) **4513**
Louisiana Municipal Review (USA ISSN 0164-3622) **7497**
• Louisiana Music Directory (USA ISSN 1072-4427) **6585**
▼ • Louisiana N R C S Conservation Update (Natural Resources Conservation Service) (USA ISSN 1943-2119) **2618**
Louisiana Personal Injury (USA ISSN 1559-9094) **4835**
Louisiana Pharmacist (USA ISSN 0192-3838) **6859**
Louisiana Political Fax Weekly (USA) **5225**
Louisiana Practice Series. Louisiana Construction Law (USA ISSN 1942-0196) **4725**
Louisiana Register (USA ISSN 0098-8545) **7451**
Louisiana Reports *see* West's Jury Verdicts. Louisiana Reports **4967**
Louisiana Revy (DNK ISSN 0024-6891) **503**
Louisiana Roots (USA) **3774**
Louisiana School Directory *see* M D R's Louisiana School Directory **2957**
Louisiana Social Studies Journal (USA ISSN 1040-2748) **2884**
Louisiana Society of Association Executives Resource *see* L S A E Resource **1143**
Louisiana State Bar Association. Bar Briefs (USA) **4725**
• Louisiana State Board of Nursing. Annual Report to the Governor of the State of Louisiana (USA) **5969**
➤ Louisiana State Medical Society. Journal (USA ISSN 0024-6921) **5662**
Louisiana State University Engineering News *see* L S U Engineering News **2289**
Louisiana State University Forestry Notes *see* L S U Forestry Notes **3695**
Louisiana State University. Library Lectures (USA ISSN 0085-2759) **5030**
Louisiana State University Magazine *see* L S U Magazine **2289**
Louisiana State University, Rice Research Station. Annual Research Report (USA ISSN 1054-8300) **134**
Louisiana State University. School of Forestry, Wildlife and Fisheries. Research Reports (USA) **3696**
• Louisiana Statutes Annotated (Premise CD-ROM Edition) (USA) **4725**
Louisiana Super Lawyers (USA ISSN 1939-5191) **4725**
Louisiana Surplus Line Reporter (USA) **4513**
Louisiana Tort Law (USA) **4835**
Louisiana Water Resources Research Institute. Annual Report (USA) **8828**
Louisiana Weekly (USA) **3548**
Louisville Business First *see* Business First (Louisville) **1072**
Louisville Defender (USA) **3548**
Louisville Eccentric Observer (USA) **3980**
• Louisville Magazine (USA) **3980**
Louisville Medicine Magazine (USA) **4513**
The Louisville Review (USA ISSN 0148-3250) **5328**
Lounais-Haemeen Kotiseutu- ja Museoyhdistys. Vuosikirja (FIN ISSN 0359-1832) **4241**
Lounais-Hameen Luonto (FIN ISSN 0355-3728) **7880**
Lounge (USA) **5076**
• Lounge Los Angeles (USA) **4393**
Lourdes-Rosen (DEU) **7805**
Lourens J.C. (Groot Den Haag Edition) *see* Lourens J.C. (Zuid-Holland Edition) **3915**
Lourens J.C. (Groot-Kennemerland Edition) *see* Lourens J.C. (Noord-Holland Edition) **3915**
Lourens J.C. (Groot Kennemerland/Noord-Holland Noord Edition) *see* Lourens J.C. (Noord-Holland Edition) **3915**
Lourens J.C. (Groot Rotterdam Edition) *see* Lourens J.C. (Zuid-Holland Edition) **3915**
Lourens J.C. (Noord-Holland Edition) *see* Lourens J.C. (Noord-Holland Edition) **3915**
Lourens J.C. (Noord-Holland Edition) (NLD ISSN 1875-1830) **3915**
Lourens J. C. (Noord-Nederland Edition) (NLD ISSN 1872-1443) **3915**
Lourens J. C. (Oost-Nederland Edition) (NLD ISSN 1871-9562) **3915**
▼ Lourens J.C. (Zuid-Holland Edition) (NLD ISSN 1875-0575) **3915**
Lourens Jan Coster (Groot Kennemerland/Noord-Holland Noord Edition) *see* Lourens J.C. (Noord-Holland Edition) **3915**
Lourens Jan Coster (Noord-Nederland Edition) *see* Lourens J. C. (Noord-Nederland Edition) **3915**
Lourens Jan Coster (Oost-Nederland Edition) *see* Lourens J. C. (Oost-Nederland Edition) **3915**
Loutkar/Puppeteer (CZE ISSN 1211-4065) **8473**
Louvain Chinese Studies (BEL) **555**
Louvain Economic Studies *see* Recherches Economiques de Louvain **1164**
Louvain Medical (BEL ISSN 0024-6956) **5662**
Louvain Philosophical Studies (BEL) **6933**
• ➤ Louvain Studies (BEL ISSN 0024-6964) **7805**
• ➤ Louvain Theological and Pastoral Monographs (BEL) **7661**
† Louveteau (FRA ISSN 0751-5685) **8972**
Lov i Ribolov (BGR ISSN 0324-0541) **8321**
• Lov & Data (NOR ISSN 0800-7853) **4725**
• Lov og Rett (NOR ISSN 0024-6980) **4725**
Lovacki Vjesnik (HRV ISSN 0024-6999) **8186**
Lovatt's Colossus Crosswords (GBR ISSN 0956-4861) **4338**
Love (USA) **6646**
Love and Marriage (IRL ISSN 2009-0757) **5559**
Love Letters (USA ISSN 1068-8439) **3774**
Love Marriage and Family *see* Aiqing Hunyin Jiating (Sifang Xinqing) **4351**
Love, Marriage and Family *see* Aiqing Hunyin Jiating (Shenghuo Jishi) **4351**
Love of Quilting *see* Fons and Porter's Love of Quilting **6639**
Love og Bekendtgoerelser m.v. (DNK ISSN 0108-9102) **4725**
Love People *see* Airen **8024**
Love Pouting (GBR ISSN 1751-097X) **2257**
Love Story (ITA ISSN 1122-0317) **5411**
• Lovec (SVN ISSN 0024-7014) **8321**
▼ Lovecraft Annual (USA ISSN 1935-6102) **5328**
Lovecraft Studies (USA ISSN 0899-8361) **5444**
Loveland: Constitutional Law - A Critical Introduction (GBR) **4850**
Lovely Daze (USA) **5328**
Lover (NLD ISSN 0165-8042) **8900**
LoveStar (CZE ISSN 1802-8977) **8872**
Lovin' Life After 50 - Arizona (USA) **4051**
Lovin' Life After 50 - Nevada (USA) **4051**
Loving Alternatives Magazine (USA) **7943**
Loving Life After 50 - Nevada *see* Lovin' Life After 50 - Nevada **4051**
Loving More Magazine (USA ISSN 1523-5858) **5076**
Lovnoeglen (DNK ISSN 0108-6847) **4725**
• Lovregister for Faeroerne (FRO ISSN 0907-3728) **4725**
† • Lovtidende for Kongeriget Danmark. Afdeling A (DNK ISSN 0106-8458) **8972**
Lovtidende for Kongeriget Danmark. Afdeling A (Print) *see* Denmark. Civilstyrelsen. Lovtidende, A **4656**
Lovtidende for Kongeriget Danmark. Afdeling B (Print) *see* Denmark. Civilstyrelsen. Lovtidende, B **4656**
† • Lovtidende for Kongeriget Danmark. Afdeling C (DNK ISSN 0106-8474) **8972**
Low Back Pain (USA) **5662**
Low Back Pain and Osteoporosis *see* Back Pain and Osteoporosis **6056**
Low Bidder (USA ISSN 0024-7030) **8632**
Low Carb Living *see* LowCarb Living **6663**
Low Carb Recipes (USA) **6663**
Low Cost Airline Business *see* Low Cost & Regional Airline Business **8547**
Low Cost & Regional Airline Business (GBR ISSN 1755-1242) **8547**
The Low Countries (BEL ISSN 0779-5815) **4464**
Low Countries Historical Review *see* Bijdragen en Mededelingen Betreffende de Geschiedenis der Nederlanden **4205**
Low Country Courier (USA) **3774**
Low External Input & Sustainable Agriculture *see* L E I S A **241**
Low-Fare & Regional Airlines (GBR ISSN 1753-0598) **8547**
Low-Fare and Regional Aviation (GBR ISSN 1753-1845) **8548**
Low Frequency Noise Vibration and Active Control *see* Journal of Low Frequency Noise Vibration and Active Control **7088**
Low-Income Housing Tax Credit Handbook (USA) **1933**
Low-Income Housing Tax Credit Property Management *see* L I H T C Property Management **7597**
Low Priced Stock Survey (USA ISSN 0273-7752) **1638**
Low Rider *see* Lowrider **8589**
Low Temperature Medicine *see* Teion Igaku **5720**
• ➤ Low Temperature Physics (USA ISSN 1063-777X) **7055**
Low Temperature Science. Series A. Data Report (JPN ISSN 0385-3683) **7056**
Low Voltage Appartus *see* Diya Dianqi **3300**
• The Lowbrow Lowdown (USA) **28**
The Lowbrow Reader (USA ISSN 1940-1922) **5328**
LowCarb Living (USA ISSN 1549-991X) **6663**
LowCarbiz (USA) **3654**
Lowcountry Sun (USA) **3980**
The Lowdown (USA) **2360**
Lowdown Magazine (AUS ISSN 0158-099X) **2200**
Lowell Wakefield Fisheries Symposium Series (USA) **3601**
Lower Basin Links (AUS) **2797**
Lower Cape Fear Historical Society, Inc. Newsletter (USA) **4302**
➤ Lower Extremity (USA ISSN 1068-6991) **5662**
Lower Thames Valley Conservation Foundation. Annual Report (CAN ISSN 1719-4210) **3451**
Lowest Common Denominator *see* L C D **2360**
Lowland Technology International (JPN ISSN 1344-9656) **2753**
• Lowrider (USA ISSN 0199-9362) **8589**
• Lowrider Arte (USA ISSN 1527-4209) **503**
Lowry Airman *see* Mile High Guardian **6434**
Lowveld Research Stations. Annual Report (ZWE) **134**
• Loxias (Online Edition) (FRA ISSN 1765-3096) **5328**
Loxias (Print Edition) *see* Loxias (Online Edition) **5328**
Loxton News (AUS) **3795**
Loyal (DEU ISSN 0343-0103) **6431**

DIRECTORY 2010 THE LUTHERAN WITNESS 10573

Loyal (USA) **503**
Loyal Legion Historical Journal (USA) **4302**
Loyal Soldier Magazine *see* Chizi **7954**
• Loyalist Gazette (CAN ISSN 0047-5149) **4302**
• Loyalty Magazine (GBR ISSN 1354-5868) **1829**
➤ Loyola (USA ISSN 1054-7614) **2290**
Loyola College Berlin Seminar (USA ISSN 1091-8582) **5328**
• Loyola Consumer Law Review (USA ISSN 1530-5449) **4726**
Loyola Journal of Public Interest Law (USA ISSN 1536-5778) **7451**
➤ Loyola Journal of Social Sciences (IND ISSN 0971-4960) **7984**
Loyola Law and Technology Annual (USA ISSN 1930-9422) **8431**
• Loyola Law Review (USA ISSN 0192-9720) **4726**
Loyola Maritime Law Journal (USA ISSN 1545-2506) **4970**
Loyola Medicine *see* Stritch Medicine **2302**
• Loyola of Los Angeles Entertainment Law Review (USA ISSN 1536-5751) **4726**
• ➤ Loyola of Los Angeles International and Comparative Law Review (USA ISSN 1533-5860) **4726**
• Loyola of Los Angeles Law Review (USA ISSN 0147-9857) **4726**
Loyola Poverty Law Journal *see* Loyola Journal of Public Interest Law **7451**
• The Loyola University Chicago International Law Review (USA ISSN 1558-9226) **4935**
• ➤ Loyola University Chicago Law Journal (USA ISSN 0024-7081) **4726**
Loyola University New Orleans School of Law Intellectual Property & High Technology Journal *see* Loyola Law and Technology Annual **8431**
Loyola University New Orleans School of Law: Law & Technology Annual *see* Loyola Law and Technology Annual **8431**
Lozania (COL ISSN 0085-2899) **954**
Lozarstvo i Vinarstvo (BGR ISSN 0458-4244) **607**
Lpf Nyt om Ledelse *see* M P P Leads **1774**
Lraber Hasarakakan Gitut'yunneri/Herald of Social Sciences/Vestnik Obshchestvennykh Nauk (ARM ISSN 0320-8117) **4464**
Lu Hsing Tsa Chih *see* Travelling Magazine **8768**
Lu Ming (MNG ISSN 1008-0732) **5328**
Lu Xun Academy of Fine Art. Journal *see* Meiyuan **505**
Lu Xun Meishu Xueyuan Xuebao *see* Meiyuan **505**
• ➤ Lu Xun Yanjiu Yuekan/Luxun Studies Monthly (CHN ISSN 1003-0638) **644**
• Lua Nova (BRA ISSN 0102-6445) **7152**
Lu'ah ha-Hodesh - Yad La'achim *see* Yad L'achim Wall Calendar **8999**
Lubavitch International Update (USA ISSN 1931-9649) **3548**
Lubbock Illustrated (USA) **3980**
Lubelski Osrodek Samopomocy *see* L O S **8053**
Lubelskie Towarzystwo Naukowe. Wydzial Humanistyczny. Prace. Monografie (POL ISSN 0208-4996) **4464**
Lubelskie Wiadomosci Numizmatyczne (POL ISSN 1233-9695) **6651**
Lubes 'n' Greases (USA ISSN 1080-9449) **6777**
Lubes 'n' Greases (Europe - Middle East - Africa) *see* Lubes 'n' Greases **6777**
Lubie Gotowac (POL ISSN 1429-2866) **4363**
Lubrication (USA ISSN 0024-7146) **6777**
Lubrication & Fluid Power *see* Lubrication Management & Technology **3352**
Lubrication Engineering *see* Runhua yu Mifeng **3395**
Lubrication Engineering *see* Tribology & Lubrication Technology **3398**
Lubrication Management & Technology (USA ISSN 1941-4447) **3352**
• ➤ Lubrication Science (GBR ISSN 0954-0075) **6777**
Luca (MNE ISSN 0352-4973) **8119**
Lucan Echo (IRL ISSN 1649-9638) **3894**
• Il Lucano Magazine (ITA ISSN 1827-3637) **3897**
Lucanor (ESP ISSN 0214-4581) **5328**
Lucas Mallada (ESP ISSN 0214-8315) **687**
• Luce e Design (ITA ISSN 1722-7402) **3324**
† Luce International (ITA ISSN 1720-8017) **8972**
Luceafarul (ROM ISSN 1220-627X) **5328**
Lucentum (ESP ISSN 0213-2338) **404**
Lucero (USA ISSN 1098-2892) **5328**
Luchshie Meditsinskie Tsentry Moskvy (RUS) **5662**
Luchtvaart *see* Piloot en Vliegtuig **68**
Luchtvaart Bulletin *see* Journaal Luchtrecht **63**
Luchtvaartkennis (NLD ISSN 1381-9100) **65**
Luchtvaartwereld (Maarssen) *see* Piloot en Vliegtuig **68**
Luchtvracht (NLD ISSN 1381-7078) **8548**
Luchtwijzer (NLD ISSN 1574-1893) **6216**
Luciernaga (COL) **5328**
Lucina (ITA ISSN 1590-6353) **5997**
• Lucire (NZL ISSN 1176-8169) **2257**
Lucknow City Magazine (IND) **3884**
Lucknow Law Times (IND ISSN 0459-9756) **4726**
• ➤ Lucknow Librarian (IND ISSN 0024-7219) **5030**
† Lucky (DEU ISSN 1862-460X) **8972**
Lucky (GRC) **8872**
• Lucky (USA ISSN 1531-4294) **8872**
Lucky Dog (USA) **6811**
Lucky Mee Family Association Newsletter (USA) **3774**
Lucky Mee Family Association. Yearbook (USA) **3774**
LuckyStar *see* LoveStar **8872**
Lucrari de Muzicologie (ROM ISSN 1222-894X) **6585**
Lucratief (NLD ISSN 1871-8698) **1773**
Lucre-Hatif (BEL) **5328**
Lucru de Mana (ROM ISSN 1841-5296) **6640**
▼ Lucullus Succulus (FRA ISSN 1963-2223) **2200**
Lucus Lingua (ESP ISSN 1698-0433) **5148**
Lud (POL ISSN 0076-1435) **8119**
Ludica (MEX) **2488**
➤ Ludica Pedagogica (COL ISSN 0121-4128) **3071**
• Ludong Daxue Xuebao (Zheshe Ban)/Ludong University Journal (Philosophy and Social Sciences Edition) (CHN ISSN 1673-8039) **7984**
• Ludong Daxue Xuebao (Ziran Kexue Ban)/Ludong University Journal (Natural Science Edition) (CHN ISSN 1673-8020) **7880**
Ludong University Journal (Natural Science Edition) *see* Ludong Daxue Xuebao (Ziran Kexue Ban) **7880**
Ludong University Journal (Philosophy and Social Sciences Edition) *see* Ludong Daxue Xuebao (Zheshe Ban) **7984**
Ludovico Maximilianea Forschungen (DEU ISSN 0720-7662) **2992**
Ludovico Maximilianea Quellen (DEU ISSN 0720-7670) **2992**
• ➤ Ludus (NLD ISSN 1385-0393) **8473**
Ludus Vitalis (MEX ISSN 1133-5165) **6933**
Ludwig (DEU) **3852**
Ludwig Boltzmann-Institut fuer Europarecht. Schriftenreihe (AUT) **4726**
Ludwig Boltzmann-Institut fuer Gesetzgebungspraxis und Rechtsanwendung. Veroeffentlichungen (AUT) **4726**
Ludwig Boltzmann-Institut fuer Rechtsvorsorge und Urkundenwesen. Veroeffentlichungen (AUT) **4726**
Ludwig Boltzmann-Institut fuer Umweltwissenschaften und Naturschutz. Mitteilungen (AUT) **3451**
Ludwig Feuerbach: Gesammelte Werke (DEU) **6933**
Ludwig-Maximilians-Universitaet. Institut fuer Phonetik und Sprachliche Kommunikation. Forschungsberichte (DEU ISSN 0342-782X) **5148**
Ludwig-Maximilians-Universitaet Muenchen. Personal- und Vorlesungsverzeichnis (DEU) **2957**
Ludwig-Uhland-Instituts der Universitaet Tuebingen. Untersuchungen (DEU) **4152**
Ludwigsburger Geschichtsblaetter (DEU ISSN 0179-1842) **4241**
Ludwigsburger Kreiszeitung (DEU) **3852**
Ludwigsteiner Blaetter (DEU) **3852**
Luebecker Nachrichten (DEU) **3852**
Luebecker Wochenspiegel (DEU) **5225**
Luebeckische Blaetter (DEU ISSN 0344-5216) **1145**
LueftungsKomfort (DEU) **4123**
▼ • Luel (KOR ISSN 1975-9649) **6294**
Luft- und Raumfahrt (DEU ISSN 0173-6264) **65**
Luftballon (DEU) **2160**
Luftfahrt Journal (DEU) **8548**
• Luftfart/Civil Aviation (SWE ISSN 1402-1919) **8527**
Lufthansa Magazin (DEU) **8784**
Lufthansa Woman's World (DEU) **8872**
Lufthanseat (DEU ISSN 0949-5487) **8548**
Lufthygienischer Monatsbericht (DEU ISSN 0172-1127) **3488**
Lufthygienisches Ueberwachungssystem Niedersachsen (DEU ISSN 0940-1776) **3488**
Luftqualitaet in Nordrhein-Westfalen. Mobile Immissionsmessung (DEU ISSN 0946-9079) **3488**
Luftsport (DEU) **65**
Lufttransport Unternehmen Exklusiv *see* L T U Exklusiv **8784**
Lufttransport Unternehmen Magazin *see* L T U Magazin **8784**
Luftverunreinigung (DEU ISSN 0460-2374) **3488**
Lugano Theological Review *see* Rivista Teologica di Lugano **7815**
Luganskaya Pravda (UKR) **3965**
Lugares (ARG ISSN 0329-4633) **8731**
• Lugares Divinos (ESP) **4393**
Lugares Especial *see* Lugares **8731**
Lugha Yetu (TZA ISSN 0047-5165) **5148**
• Luhua yu Shenghuo (CHN ISSN 1002-1973) **3696**
Luis Palau Letter (USA) **7661**
Luisa la Santa (ITA) **7805**
• Luister (NLD ISSN 0024-7286) **6585**
Lujiang Zhiye Daxue Xuebao/Lujiang University. Journal *see* Xiamen Ligong Xueyuan Xuebao **7930**
Lukanga News (ZMB) **3995**
Lukoil - Beopetrol (SRB ISSN 1452-2012) **6777**
Lukufiilis (FIN ISSN 0784-8641) **5328**
Lukullus (DEU ISSN 0941-5734) **3852**
• Luliang Gaodeng Zhuanke Xuexiao Xuebao/Luliang Higher College. Journal (CHN ISSN 1008-7834) **7984**
Luliang Higher College. Journal *see* Luliang Gaodeng Zhuanke Xuexiao Xuebao **7984**
Lullwater Review (USA ISSN 1051-5968) **5426**
Lumber Building Material Journal *see* L B M Journal **1020**
Lumber Co-Operator (USA ISSN 0024-7294) **3713**
• Lumber Price Index. P N W Coast Index (USA ISSN 0735-066X) **3709**
• Lumber Track (USA ISSN 1535-7023) **3713**
Lumberjack (USA) **2290**
Lumbermens Red Book (USA) **3713**
▼ The Lumberyard Magazine (USA) **5426**
Lumea Femeilor (ROM ISSN 1223-1479) **8872**
• Lumen (AUS ISSN 0310-3315) **2290**
➤ Lumen (CAN ISSN 1209-3696) **4152**
Lumen Vitae (BEL ISSN 0024-7324) **7805**
• Lumi Virtuale (ROM) **5444**
• Lumiere (GBR) **2257**
Lumiere Classique (FRA ISSN 1250-6060) **5328**
Lumiere et Vie (FRA ISSN 0024-7359) **7661**
Lumiere sur mon Sentier/Light on my Path (CAN ISSN 1718-2263) **7765**
Lumina (SRB ISSN 0350-4174) **3548**
† Luminaire (FRA ISSN 1251-4012) **8972**
• ➤ Luminescence (GBR ISSN 1522-7235) **2138**
• Luminus (CAN) **2884**
Lummox Journal (USA ISSN 1525-2140) **5426**
Lumo (CAN ISSN 0827-3154) **5148**
• Lumpen Magazine (USA ISSN 1092-3667) **7152**
Lumpsum Nieuwsbrief (NLD ISSN 1873-9385) **2884**
Lun Wen (DEU) **555**
• Luna (ARG ISSN 0328-9885) **8872**
Luna (DEU) **2160**
Luna (ITA ISSN 1594-6738) **8872**
Luna Azul (COL ISSN 1909-2474) **3451**
Luna Cornea (MEX ISSN 0188-8005) **6971**
Luna de Madrid (ESP) **2200**
Luna Negra (USA) **5328**
▼ • Luna Park (USA) **5225**
• Lunar and Planetary Information Bulletin (USA ISSN 1534-6587) **577**
Lunar and Planetary Institute Contribution *see* L P I Contribution **577**
➤ Lunar Calendar (Year) (USA) **566**
▼ Lunar Jim (GBR ISSN 1752-9441) **2200**
Lunarietto Giuliano (ITA ISSN 1827-3947) **4152**
Lunch (USA) **5328**
Lunch (Charlottesville) (USA ISSN 1931-7786) **449**
Lund Archaeological Review (SWE ISSN 1401-2189) **404**
Lund Dissertations in Sociology (SWE ISSN 1102-4712) **8119**
Lund Middle Eastern and North African Studies (SWE ISSN 1400-0237) **4323**
Lund Monographs in Social Anthropology (SWE ISSN 1101-9948) **7984**
Lund Publications in Geology *see* Litholund Theses **2752**
Lund Studies in Economic History (SWE ISSN 1400-4860) **1546**
Lund Studies in Economics and Management (SWE ISSN 0284-5075) **1546**
Lund Studies in Education (SWE) **2884**
Lund Studies in English (SWE ISSN 0076-1451) **5148**
Lund Studies in Ethics and Theology (SWE ISSN 1102-769X) **7661**
Lund Studies in European Ethnology (SWE ISSN 1401-3371) **3548**
Lund Studies in Geography (SWE ISSN 1400-1144) **4019**
Lund Studies in Historical Archaeology (SWE ISSN 1653-1183) **404**
Lund Studies in Law and Society (SWE ISSN 1100-1100) **4726**
Lund Studies in Legal History (SWE ISSN 1101-2005) **4726**
Lund Studies in Medieval Archaeology *see* Lund Studies in Historical Archaeology **404**
Lund Studies in Psychology of Religion (SWE ISSN 1103-5757) **7661**
Lund University. Department of Linguistics. Working Papers: General Linguistics, Phonetics (SWE ISSN 0280-526X) **5148**
Lundagaard (SWE ISSN 0345-7338) **2267**
Lundastudier i Nordisk Spraakvetenskap. Serie A (SWE ISSN 0347-8971) **5148**
Lundberg Letter (USA ISSN 0195-4563) **6800**
Lundellia (USA ISSN 1097-993X) **800**
• Lundero (PER ISSN 1605-3567) **3927**
Le Lundi (CAN ISSN 1491-1221) **8872**
Lundian (SWE) **3956**
Lundiana (BRA ISSN 1676-6180) **687**
Lundqua Thesis (SWE ISSN 0281-3033) **2753**
Lunds Universitet, Department of Linguistics and Phonetics. Travaux (SWE ISSN 0347-2558) **5148**
Lunds Universitet Meddelar *see* Lunds Universitets Magasin **2992**
Lunds Universitets Historiska Museum. Papers (SWE ISSN 1653-3917) **4241**
Lunds Universitets Magasin (SWE ISSN 1653-2295) **2992**
Lundy Collectors Club Philatelic Quarterly (USA) **6896**
• Lundy Field Society. Annual Report (GBR ISSN 0143-8026) **2618**
Il Lunedi della Repubblica *see* La Repubblica **3898**
• ➤ Lung (USA ISSN 0341-2040) **6216**
➤ Lung Biology in Health and Disease (USA ISSN 0362-3181) **925**
• ➤ Lung Cancer (IRL ISSN 0169-5002) **6026**
Lung Cancer in Practice (GBR ISSN 1743-8047) **6026**
• Lung Cancer Update (USA ISSN 1559-9701) **6026**
Lung Disorders (USA ISSN 1542-1961) **6216**
• ➤ Lung India (IND ISSN 0970-2113) **6216**
The Lung Perspectives (JPN ISSN 0919-5742) **6216**
Lungfull Magazine (USA) **5328**
Lunlixue/Ethics (CHN ISSN 1001-2737) **6933**
Lunlixue Wenzhai Ka/Ethics Abstracts on Cards (CHN) **6933**
Lunlixue Yanjiu/Studies in Ethics (CHN ISSN 1671-9115) **6933**
• Luntai Gongye/Tire Industry (CHN ISSN 1006-8171) **3250**
• Luobo Baogao/Robb Report (Beijing) (CHN) **5076**
Luoji/Logic (CHN ISSN 1001-2524) **6933**
Luonnon Tutkija/The Naturalist (FIN ISSN 0024-7383) **687**
Luonnontieteiden Akateemiset/Kemisten (FIN ISSN 1457-9936) **2072**
Luontaisterveys (FIN ISSN 1456-7792) **312**
• Luoyang Gongye Gaodeng Zhuanke Xuexiao Xuebao/Luoyang Technology College. Journal (CHN ISSN 1008-8814) **7984**
• Luoyang Shifan Xueyuan Xuebao (CHN ISSN 1009-4970) **2884**
Luoyang Technology College. Journal *see* Luoyang Gongye Gaodeng Zhuanke Xuexiao Xuebao **7984**
Luoyang University. Journal *see* Luoyang University. Journal **7984**
• Luoyang University. Journal/Luoyang University. Journal (CHN ISSN 1007-113X) **7984**
• ➤ Lupus (GBR ISSN 0961-2033) **6224**
Lupus Beacon (USA) **6224**
Lupus Link Notes (CAN ISSN 1910-6165) **5947**
Lupus Links (AUS) **6224**
Lupus News (USA ISSN 0732-0280) **6224**
Lupus Now (USA ISSN 1547-1780) **6224**
Lupus Society of Manitoba Newsletter *see* L S M B Newsletter **5659**
Luqman (IRN ISSN 0259-904X) **7713**
Luratha (BOL) **362**
Lurralde (ESP ISSN 0211-5891) **4019**
Lurzer's International Archive (USA ISSN 0893-0260) **28**
Lusaka City Library. Annual Report (ZMB) **5030**
Luscinia (DEU ISSN 0024-7391) **910**
Luse Shiye/Green Vision (CHN ISSN 1673-0267) **3451**
▼ Lush for Life (USA ISSN 1938-8519) **5225**
• Lushi Shijie (CHN ISSN 1004-0064) **4726**
Lushi yu Fazhi/Lawyer and Legality *see* Fazhi Yanjiu **4671**
➤ Lusitania Sacra (PRT ISSN 0076-1508) **7661**
Lusko Libro (HRV ISSN 1330-6561) **4241**
Luso - Americano (USA ISSN 0898-9052) **3548**
• ➤ Luso - Brazilian Review (USA ISSN 0024-7413) **5225**
➤ Lusorama (DEU ISSN 0931-9484) **5149**
lusotopie *see* Collection Lusotopie **4447**
† • Lusotopie (NLD ISSN 1257-0273) **8972**
Lust auf Genuss (DEU) **4363**
Lustiges Taschenbuch *see* Walt Disney's Lustiges Taschenbuch **2221**
LUSTLine (USA) **3451**
Lustracje Dobr Krolewskich XVI-XVIII Wieku (POL ISSN 0076-1516) **4241**
• Lustre (USA ISSN 1098-5697) **1021**
Lustre Lookbook *see* Lustre **1021**
➤ Lustrum (DEU ISSN 0024-7421) **2237**
Lusty Letters (USA) **6294**
➤ The Lute (GBR ISSN 0952-0759) **6585**
Lute Society of America. Journal (USA ISSN 0076-1524) **6585**
Lute Society of America. Quarterly (USA ISSN 1547-982X) **6585**
Luther (DEU ISSN 0340-6210) **7765**
Luther Alumni Magazine (USA) **2290**
Luther Family Newsletter (USA ISSN 0896-4602) **3774**
Die Luther-Kirche (AUT) **7765**
• The Lutheran (USA ISSN 0024-743X) **7765**
The Lutheran Annual (USA) **7765**
Lutheran Church of Australia. Yearbook (AUS ISSN 0726-4305) **7765**
Lutheran Church of Central Africa. Statistical Report (ZMB) **7698**
Lutheran Churches in Canada. Directory (CAN ISSN 0316-800X) **7765**
➤ Lutheran Digest (USA ISSN 0458-497X) **7765**
Lutheran Digest (Large Print Edition) (USA) **4082**
• Lutheran Education (USA ISSN 0024-7448) **7765**
Lutheran Forum (USA ISSN 0024-7456) **7765**
Lutheran Forum. Forum Letter (USA ISSN 0046-4732) **7765**
Lutheran Historical Conference. Essays and Reports (USA ISSN 0090-3817) **7765**
• Lutheran Historical Conference. Newsletter (USA ISSN 0460-0274) **7765**
Lutheran Historical Society of Eastern Pennsylvania. Periodical (USA ISSN 1070-5252) **7766**
† • Lutheran Hour Messages (USA) **8972**
Lutheran Immigration and Refugee Service Bulletin *see* L I R S Bulletin **7764**
Lutheran Journal (USA ISSN 0360-6945) **7766**
Lutheran Layman (USA ISSN 0024-7464) **7766**
Lutheran Libraries (USA ISSN 0024-7472) **5030**
Lutheran Messenger for the Blind (USA ISSN 0024-7480) **4083**
Lutheran Partners (USA ISSN 0885-9922) **7766**
Lutheran Quarterly (USA) **7766**
Lutheran Sentinel (USA ISSN 0024-7510) **7766**
• Lutheran Spokesman (USA ISSN 0024-7537) **7766**
• Lutheran Theological Journal (AUS ISSN 0024-7553) **7766**
• Lutheran Theological Seminary Bulletin (USA ISSN 0362-0581) **7766**
Lutheran Theological Seminary Bulletin *see* Seminary Ridge Review **7774**
The Lutheran Witness (USA ISSN 0024-757X) **7766**

Title

10574 LUTHERAN WITNESS (LARGE PRINT EDITION) ULRICH'S PERIODICALS

Lutheran Witness (Large Print Edition) (USA) **7766**
Lutheran Woman Today (USA ISSN 0896-209X) **7766**
Lutheran Woman's Quarterly (USA) **7766**
Lutheran World Federation Documentation *see* L W F Documentation **7764**
Lutheran World Federation Studies *see* L W F Studies **7764**
Lutherische Beitraege (DEU ISSN 0949-880X) **7766**
Lutherische Rundschau *see* L W F Documentation **7764**
Lutherische Theologie und Kirche (DEU ISSN 0170-3846) **7766**
➤ Lutherjahrbuch (DEU ISSN 0342-0914) **7766**
Die Lutherkirche (AUT ISSN 0024-7626) **7766**
Luton - Dunstable on Sunday (GBR) **3868**
➤ Lutra (NLD ISSN 0024-7634) **954**
Lutte (SEN) **7152**
Lutte de Classe (FRA ISSN 0295-5385) **7251**
Lutte Ouvriere (FRA ISSN 0024-7650) **7152**
Lutteur Canadien *see* Canadian Wrestler Newsletter **8164**
Luup (EST ISSN 1406-0612) **3836**
Luvah (FRA ISSN 0754-927X) **5328**
Luventicus Academy Reports *see* Academia Luventicus Reportes **6902**
Luventicus Academy. Transactions *see* Actas de la Academia Luventicus **7832**
Lux (DEU) **3852**
Lux (FRA ISSN 0024-7669) **3324**
Lux Biblica (ITA) **7661**
Lux Vera (FRA ISSN 0024-7685) **4083**
LuxDesign *see* LuxDesign Twin Cities **5076**
LuxDesign Twin Cities (USA ISSN 1945-1245) **5076**
Luxe (USA) **449**
Le Luxembourg en Chiffres (Year) (LUX ISSN 1019-6471) **7311**
Luxembourg in Figures *see* Le Luxembourg en Chiffres (Year) **7311**
Luxembourg. Inspection Generale de la Securite Sociale. Apercu sur la Legislation de la Securite Sociale au Grand-Duche de Luxembourg (LUX) **4513**
Luxembourg. Inspection Generale de la Securite Sociale. Bulletin Luxembourgeois sur les Questions Sociales (LUX) **4513**
Luxembourg. Inspection Generale de la Securite Sociale. Rapport General sur la Securite Sociale au Grand-Duche de Luxembourg (LUX ISSN 0259-8108) **4513**
Luxembourg. Inspection Generale de la Securite Sociale. Recueil des Lois et Reglements de la Securite Sociale (LUX) **4513**
Luxembourg Institute for European and International Studies (NLD) **7251**
▼ Luxembourg Journal of Law, Economics and Finance/Revue de Droit, Economie et Finance (LUX ISSN 1993-7962) **4726**
Luxembourg. Ministere des Finances. Budget de l'Etat (LUX ISSN 0076-1559) **1933**
Luxembourg. Ministere des Finances. Projet de Loi Concernant le Budget des Recettes et des Depenses de l'Etat (LUX) **1933**
Luxembourg. Ministere d'Etat. Bulletin d'Information et de Documentation (LUX ISSN 1021-058X) **7451**
Luxembourg. Service Central de la Statistique et des Etudes Economiques. Annuaire Statistique (LUX ISSN 0076-1575) **1249**
Luxembourg. Service Central de la Statistique et des Etudes Economiques. Bulletin du STATEC (LUX ISSN 0076-1583) **1249**
Luxembourg. Service Central de la Statistique et des Etudes Economiques. Cahiers Economiques (LUX ISSN 0076-1605) **1249**
Luxembourg. Service Central de la Statistique et des Etudes Economiques. Collection RP: Recensement de la Population et Mouvement de la Population (LUX) **7311**
Luxembourg. Service Central de la Statistique et des Etudes Economiques. Conjoncture Actuelle (LUX) **1249**
Luxembourg. Service Central de la Statistique et des Etudes Economiques. Indicateurs Rapides. Serie A1: Indices des Prix a la Comsommation (LUX ISSN 1012-6619) **1249**
Luxembourg. Service Central de la Statistique et des Etudes Economiques. Indicateurs Rapides. Serie A2: Indices des Prix de la Construction (LUX ISSN 1012-6597) **1047**
Luxembourg. Service Central de la Statistique et des Etudes Economiques. Indicateurs Rapides. Serie A3: Indices des Prix a la Production des Produits Industriels (LUX ISSN 1012-6589) **1249**
Luxembourg. Service Central de la Statistique et des Etudes Economiques. Indicateurs Rapides. Serie B1: Indices de l'Activite Industrielle (LUX ISSN 0019-6916) **1249**
Luxembourg. Service Central de la Statistique et des Etudes Economiques. Indicateurs Rapides. Serie B2: Indices de l'Activite dans la Construction (LUX) **1047**
Luxembourg. Service Central de la Statistique et des Etudes Economiques. Indicateurs Rapides. Serie C: Emploi et Chomage - Siderurgie - Finances- Transport et Commerce (LUX ISSN 1012-6627) **1249**
Luxembourg. Service Central de la Statistique et des Etudes Economiques. Indicateurs Rapides. Serie D. Immatriculations de Vehicules Automoteurs (LUX ISSN 1012-6635) **8527**
Luxembourg. Service Central de la Statistique et des Etudes Economiques. Indicateurs Rapides. Serie E: Naissances, Mariages, Divorces, Deces (LUX ISSN 1012-6643) **7311**
Luxembourg. Service Central de la Statistique et des Etudes Economiques. Indicateurs Rapides. Serie G: Autorisations de Batir - Batiments, Logements et Volume Bati (LUX ISSN 1012-666X) **1047**
Luxembourg. Service Central de la Statistique et des Etudes Economiques. Indicateurs Rapides. Serie H: Commerce Exterieur du Luxembourg (LUX ISSN 1012-6678) **1249**
Luxembourg. Service Central de la Statistique et des Etudes Economiques. Indicateurs Rapides. Serie J: Resultats de l'Enquete de Conjoncture (LUX) **7311**
Luxembourg. Service Central de la Statistique et des Etudes Economiques. Indicateurs Rapides. Serie M: Meteorologie (LUX) **6400**
Luxembourg. Service Central de la Statistique et des Etudes Economiques. Note de Conjoncture (LUX ISSN 1019-6463) **1249**
Luxembourg. Service Central de la Statistique et des Etudes Economiques. Statistiques Historiques (LUX) **1249**
Luxembourg Stock Exchange. Annual Report *see* Societe de la Bourse de Luxembourg. Rapport Annuel **1651**
Luxembourg Stock Exchange. Facts and Figures *see* Societe de la Bourse de Luxembourg. Faits et Chiffres **1263**
Luxembourg Stock Exchange. Official Price List *see* Societe de la Bourse de Luxembourg. Cote Officielle de la Bourse de Luxembourg (Daily) **1651**
Luxembourg Stock Exchange. Official Price List *see* Societe de la Bourse de Luxembourg. Cote Officielle de la Bourse de Luxembourg (Monthly) **1651**
Luxembourg Stock Exchange. Official Price List *see* Societe de la Bourse de Luxembourg. Cote Officielle de la Bourse de Luxembourg (Weekly) **1651**
Luxembourg Stock Exchange. Official Price List *see* Societe de la Bourse de Luxembourg. Cote Officielle de la Bourse de Luxembourg (Bi-monthly) **1651**
Luxemburg in Cijfers *see* Le Luxembourg en Chiffres (Year) **7311**
Luxemburg in Zahlen *see* Le Luxembourg en Chiffres (Year) **7311**
Luxun Studies Monthly *see* Lu Xun Yanjiu Yuekan **644**
● Luxury Briefing (GBR) **2248**
Luxury Business (USA ISSN 1542-5266) **1829**
● Luxury Car Tax Determination (AUS ISSN 1448-4919) **1933**
▼ Luxury Dream's (FRA ISSN 1963-2290) **3841**
Luxury Files (ITA) **4568**
Luxury Golf & Spa (USA) **5076**
Luxury Golf & Travel *see* Golf Connoisseur **8231**
Luxury Home & Renovation *see* LuxDesign Twin Cities **5076**
● Luxury Home Builder (USA) **1021**
Luxury Home Design (AUS ISSN 1327-3930) **4545**
▼ Luxury Hotelier (USA) **4393**
Luxury House *see* Casa Lux **4535**
▼ ● ➤ Luxury Intelligence (GBR ISSN 2041-3831) **1145**
● Luxury Living (Columbus) (USA) **5076**
Luxury Living (Park City) (USA) **4545**
Luxury Log & Timber Homes *see* Custom Wood Homes **1001**
Luxury Log Homes & Timber Frame *see* Custom Wood Homes **1001**
Luxury Pools (USA) **4980**
Luxury Properties *see* L P Luxury Properties **7597**
▼ ● Luxury Renovation (USA ISSN 1937-2299) **4545**
Luxury Resorts *see* Robb Report Luxury Resorts **4397**
Luxury Spa Finder *see* Luxury SpaFinder Magazine **6992**
Luxury SpaFinder Magazine (USA ISSN 1553-0698) **6992**
● Luxury Travel Advisor (USA) **8731**
▼ Luxveria (USA) **5076**
Luxx (SGP) **4568**
Luyebao/T T G China (SGP) **8731**
● Luyou/Tourist (CHN ISSN 1000-7253) **8731**
Luyou Daobao/Guide to Tourism (CHN) **8731**
Luyou Guangli/Management of Tourism (CHN ISSN 1009-1637) **8731**
● Luyou Guanli Yanjiu (TWN ISSN 1682-5098) **8731**
Luyou Tiandi/Travelling Scope (CHN ISSN 1005-7730) **8731**
● Luyou Xuekan/Journal of Tourism (CHN ISSN 1002-5006) **8731**
Luz (ARG ISSN 0024-7693) **7726**
Luz (USA ISSN 0271-0846) **3548**
La Luz (USA) **3548**
Luz de la Vida (USA) **7661**
Luzerner Historische Veroeffentlichungen (CHE) **4241**
Luzerner Kantonsblatt (CHE) **7497**
Luzerner Saengerblatt (CHE) **6585**
Luzes de Galiza (ESP) **4464**
● Luzhong Chenbao (CHN) **3826**
Luzhou Medical College. Journal *see* Luzhou Yixueyuan Xuebao **5662**
● Luzhou Yixueyuan Xuebao/Luzhou Medical College. Journal (CHN ISSN 1000-2669) **5662**
Luzifer-Amor (DEU ISSN 0933-3347) **7383**
Lybarger Linkages (USA ISSN 0887-9354) **3774**
Lyboen (DNK ISSN 0107-1238) **4241**
● Lyceum (USA ISSN 1934-242X) **6933**
Lyceum of Natural History of New York. Annals *see* New York Academy of Sciences. Annals **7892**
➤ Lychnos (SWE ISSN 0076-1648) **7880**
Lycoming County Historical Society Journal (USA ISSN 0887-543X) **4302**
Lydia (DEU ISSN 0939-138X) **8872**
Lydskrift (NOR ISSN 1502-8860) **6585**
Lyell Lectures in Bibliography (GBR) **5328**
Lykia (TUR ISSN 1300-6444) **404**
Lymfo (NLD ISSN 1871-7314) **5896**
● ➤ Lymphatic Research and Biology (USA ISSN 1539-6851) **6026**
Lymphologie in Forschung und Praxis (DEU ISSN 1433-5255) **5896**
➤ Lymphology (USA ISSN 0024-7766) **5896**
▼ ● Lymphoma / Leukaemia Review (NZL ISSN 1170-3105) **5940**
Lymphoma Leukaemia Review *see* Lymphoma / Leukaemia Review **5940**
Lynch Municipal Bond Advisory (USA) **1638**
Lynch's Ferry (USA ISSN 1949-2146) **4152**
Lyngby-Bogen (DNK ISSN 0107-7848) **4241**
Lynn - Linn Lineage Quarterly (USA ISSN 0892-418X) **3774**
Lynx (CZE ISSN 0024-7774) **954**
Lynx (ESP ISSN 0214-4611) **5149**
➤ Lynx (USA ISSN 1049-4502) **5426**
Lyon Decouverte (FRA ISSN 1953-6224) **8732**
Lyon Mag (FRA ISSN 1254-2717) **4579**
● Lyonpeople.com (FRA ISSN 1952-7772) **5076**
Lyra (Long Island City) (USA ISSN 1538-8700) **6585**
The Lyre (GBR) **5444**
Lyric (USA ISSN 0024-7820) **5426**
Lyric (Houston) (USA ISSN 1533-1776) **5426**
Lyric Opera News (USA ISSN 0024-7839) **6585**
† Lyrica (ITA ISSN 1124-7355) **8972**
Lyrical Iowa (USA ISSN 0076-1699) **5426**
Lyrik im Hoelderlinturm (DEU) **5426**
Lyrikvaennen (SWE ISSN 0460-0762) **5426**
● Lys (DNK ISSN 0904-7824) **3324**
Lys Rouge (FRA ISSN 0150-4428) **7152**
● Lyublyu! (LVA ISSN 1407-2629) **8872**
● Lyudi Dela (RUS) **1145**
Lyudyna i Pratsya (UKR) **4726**
Lyudyna i Svit (UKR ISSN 0132-084X) **3965**
Lyukasora (HUN ISSN 1216-4399) **5328**
▼ ● Lyztran (SWE ISSN 1654-1618) **6646**
M (CHE ISSN 1423-6664) **7567**
M! (DNK ISSN 1397-6257) **6294**
M: (USA) **3071**
M (Englewood Cliffs) (USA) **6585**
● M (Lebanon) (USA ISSN 1559-0186) **3071**
M (San Diego) (USA) **5076**
M (The Colony) (USA ISSN 1555-6875) **6294**
M 2 M (USA) **2332**
M 8 (GBR ISSN 0954-6898) **6294**
M A *see* Materials Australia **6321**
M A A Focus *see* Focus (Washington, D.C. 1981) **5488**
M A A Notes (Mathematical Association of America) (USA ISSN 1556-6447) **5510**
M A A Open Entry (Michigan Archival Association) (USA) **5030**
M A A S Journal of Islamic Science (Muslim Association for the Advancement of Science) (IND ISSN 0970-1672) **7713**
M A A S Newsletter (Muslim Association for the Advancement of Science) (IND) **7713**
M A A Studies in Mathematics *see* Studies in Mathematics (Washington) **5539**
M A B Report Series (Man and the Biosphere) (FRA ISSN 0252-0206) **3451**
m A b s *see* mAbs **5763**
M A C (Materiali Accessori Componenti) (ITA) **4560**
M A C International *see* Casarredo & Design **4535**
● M A C L A S Latin American Essays (Middle Atlantic Council of Latin American Studies) (USA ISSN 1525-125X) **5328**
M A C News (Mid-Atlantic Council of Shopping Center Managers) (USA) **1773**
M A C Newsletter *see* Elements (Ottawa) **6461**
M A C Newsletter (Midwest Archives Conference) (USA ISSN 0741-0379) **5030**
M A C S Action! *see* Action Magazine **4116**
M A C S Service Reports (Mobile Air Conditioning Society Worldwide) (USA) **4123**
M A C T. Journal *see* M A N I T. Journal **3208**
➤ M A D E (Materials Architecture Design Environment) (GBR ISSN 1742-416X) **449**
▼ M A D E (Materials and Design Exchange) (GBR ISSN 1753-2973) **3352**
M A D E at W S A *see* M A D E **449**
M A E *see* Military Advanced Education **6435**
● M A E S (Society of Mexican American Engineers & Scientists) (USA ISSN 1552-9711) **3208**
M A E S National Magazine *see* M A E S **3208**
● M A F E S Research Highlights (Mississippi Agricultural and Forestry Experiment Station) (USA ISSN 0091-4460) **134**
M A F Policy News *see* New Zealand. Ministry of Agriculture and Forestry. Policy News **7456**
M A F R I Report *see* Victoria. Department of Natural Resources and Environment. Marine and Freshwater Resources Institute. Report **710**
M A F R M Update (Online) *see* New Zealand. Ministry of Agriculture and Forestry. Policy News **7456**
M A G *see* Music Australia Guide **6590**
M A G *see* Modern African Generation **3551**
M A G A Zine (Los Angeles) (Mexican American Grocers Association) (USA ISSN 0894-8097) **3680**
● M A G A Zine (Phoenix) (Maricopa Association of Governments) (USA) **7497**
▼ ➤ M A I M T Journal of I T & Management (Maharaja Agrasen Institute of Management and Technology) (IND ISSN 0974-066X) **2431**
M A I N (Media Arts Information Network) (USA) **8119**
M A I Strategic Market Report. Internet Advertising (Market Assessment International) *see* Key Note Market Assessment. Internet Advertising **1892**
M A I Strategic Market Report. Marketing to Children 4-11 *see* Key Note Market Assessment. Marketing to Children 4-11 **1892**
M A J *see* Melbourne Art Journal **505**
M A J *see* Managerial Auditing Journal **1778**
M A K (Mladosc, Aktivnosc, Kreativnocs) (SRB ISSN 0350-8080) **2200**
The M A K - Collection for Occupational Health and Safety (Maximale Arbeitsplatzkonzentrationen) (DEU ISSN 1860-496X) **6680**
The M A K - Collection for Occupational Health and Safety (DEU ISSN 1860-4994) **3500**
M A L A Bulletin (Malawi Library Association) (MWI) **5030**
M A L D E F Newsletter (Mexican American Legal Defense and Educational Fund) (USA) **3548**
M A L I A Newsletter (Malta Library and Information Association) (MLT) **5030**
M A L R *see* Mergers & Acquistions Law Report **4876**
M A L T Newsletter (Manitoba Association of Library Technicians) (CAN ISSN 0710-3417) **5030**
M A M *see* Museums Australia Magazine **6532**
M A M A (Magasin foer Modern Arkitektur) (SWE) **3956**
M A M News (Miami Art Museum) (USA) **6528**
M A M S *see* Maritime Archaeology Monograph Series **405**
● M + A - Messeplaner International (DEU ISSN 0932-3317) **2013**
M A N *see* Modern Applications News **6326**
M A N *see* Medicare Advantage News **4514**
M A N A (Mexican American National Association) (USA) **3548**
M A N C E P T Working Paper Series (University of Manchester, Manchester Centre for Political Thought) (GBR ISSN 1367-2010) **7152**
† M A N Forschen, Planen, Bauen (DEU ISSN 0173-9646) **8972**
M A N I P *see* Manipulacion de Materiales en la Industria **1022**
M A N I T. Journal (Maulana Azad National Institute of Technology) (IND) **3208**
† M A N Roland Revue (DEU) **8972**
M A P (Mentis Anthologien Philosophie) (DEU) **6933**
M A P *see* Muslim & Arab Perspectives **3552**
M A P *see* I O M A's Report on Managing Accounts Payable **1290**
M A P A Annual Report (Omaha - Council Bluffs Metropolitan Area Planning Agency) (USA) **7451**
M A P A Community Assistance Report (Omaha - Council Bluffs Metropolitan Area Planning Agency) (USA) **7452**
M A P A LOG Magazine (Mooney Aircraft Pilots Association) (USA ISSN 0199-5243) **65**
M A P A Regional Directory of Public Officials (Omaha - Council Bluffs Metropolitan Area Planning Agency) (USA) **7497**
M A P Actualite (Maghreb Arabe Presse) (MAR ISSN 0851-0229) **7152**
M A P News (Medical Aid for Palestine) (CAN) **8054**
M A P S (Media, Advertising, Promotions & Sponsorship) (IRL ISSN 0790-2751) **28**
M A P S (Minutes and Appendices) (NLD ISSN 1574-4620) **2431**
M A P S Data Base (Mid-Atlantic Preservation Service) (USA) **2348**
M A P Technical Reports Series (United Nations Environment Programme, Mediterranean Action Plan) (GRC ISSN 1011-7148) **2811**
M A R *see* Management Accounting Research **1296**
M A R *see* M A R Hedge **1638**
M.A.R. (Mid-Atlantic Riviera) (USA) **5076**
M A R A D (Year) (U.S. Maritime Administration) (USA ISSN 0882-9004) **8651**
M A R B E F Newsletter (Marine Biodiversity and Ecosystem Functioning) (IRL ISSN 1649-5519) **687**
M A R C E T Red Guides. Series 1: Placements (Materials and Resources Centre for Enterprising Teaching) (GBR) **3071**
M A R C E T Red Guides. Series 10: Flexible Learning (Materials and Resources Centre for Enterprising Teaching) (GBR ISSN 1366-6452) **3071**
M A R C E T Red Guides. Series 11: Guides for Staff (Northumbria University, Materials and Resources Centre for Education and Technology) (GBR ISSN 1366-6460) **3071**
M A R C E T Red Guides. Series 12: The Use of Technology in Teaching and Learning (Northumbria University, Materials and Resources Centre for Education and Technology) (GBR) **3071**

Link to your serials resources and content with ulrichsweb.com

DIRECTORY 2010 M D R'S SCHOOL DIRECTORY. NEW YORK 10575

M A R C E T Red Guides. Series 2: Portfolios, Profiles, Records of Achievement (Northumbria University, Materials and Resources Centre for Education and Technology) (GBR) **3071**
M A R C E T Red Guides. Series 3: Guides for Students (Northumbria University, Materials and Resources Centre for Education and Technology) (GBR ISSN 1367-529X) **3071**
M A R C E T Red Guides. Series 4: Partnership (Northumbria University, Materials and Resources Centre for Education and Technology) (GBR) **3071**
M A R C E T Red Guides. Series 5: Competence, NVQs, Learning Outcomes (Northumbria University, Materials and Resources Centre for Education and Technology) (GBR ISSN 1367-5303) **3071**
M A R C E T Red Guides. Series 6: Implications of Gender for Skills Development (Materials and Resources Centre for Enterprising Teaching) (GBR) **3071**
M A R C E T Red Guides. Series 7: The Student Perspective (Northumbria University, Materials and Resources Centre for Education and Technology) (GBR) **3071**
M A R C E T Red Guides. Series 8: Skills Development (Northumbria University, Materials and Resources Centre for Education and Technology) (GBR ISSN 1367-5311) **3071**
M A R C E T Red Guides. Series 9: Experiential Learning (Northumbria University, Materials and Resources Centre for Education and Technology) (GBR ISSN 1366-6444) **3071**
M A R C Newsletter (Mission Advanced Research & Communication Center) (USA ISSN 0740-6460) **7661**
M A R D I Report/Laporan M A R D I (Malaysian Agricultural Research & Development Institute) (MYS ISSN 0127-4007) **135**
• M A R G I N (Monash Australian Research Group Informal Notes) (AUS ISSN 0314-6782) **5328**
M A R Gospel Ministries Newsletter (Middle Atlantic Regional) (USA ISSN 1049-152X) **7661**
• M A R Hedge (Managed Account Reports) (USA ISSN 1558-8645) **1638**
M A R I (Magazine of the Americas Revista Interamericana) (COL ISSN 0121-6554) **6711**
M A R I - Board Converting News Espanol (USA) **6711**
M A R I N T E K. Aarsberetning (Norwegian Marine Technology Research Institute) (NOR ISSN 0802-6211) **8651**
M A R I N T E K. Annual Report *see* M A R I N T E K. Aarsberetning **8651**
M A R T A Magazine (Metropolitan Atlanta Rapid Transit Authority, Department of Marketing and Communications) (USA) **3980**
M A R T A Rider's Digest (Metropolitan Atlanta Rapid Transit Authority, Department of Marketing and Communications) (USA) **3980**
M + A Report (DEU ISSN 0723-3361) **28**
The M A Report (Mothers of Asthmatics) (USA ISSN 1042-4075) **5763**
M A S *see* Mathematical Models and Methods in Applied Sciences **5513**
The M A S A Fortnighter *see* The M A S A Leader **3027**
• The M A S A Leader (Michigan Association of School Administrators) (USA) **3027**
M A S B Journal (Michigan Association of School Boards, Inc.) (USA ISSN 1052-2824) **3027**
M A S C Journal (Massachusetts Association of School Committees) (USA) **3027**
M A S K C Komondor News (Middle Atlantic States Komondor Club, Inc.) (USA ISSN 0146-9436) **292**
M A S Newsletter (Maine Archaeological Society, Inc.) (USA ISSN 1062-1504) **404**
M A S Report Series: Modelling, Analysis and Simulation *see* Modelling, Analysis and Simulation **5554**
M A S T. Maritime Studies (NLD ISSN 1872-7859) **3451**
• M A S Ultra - School Edition (USA) **10**
M A Scotland *see* On Trade Scotland **609**
M A T H D I - M A T H E D U C *see* Z D M **5547**
M A T S O L Currents (Massachusetts Association of Teachers of English to Speakers of Other Languages) (USA) **5149**
M A Training (Martial Arts) (USA ISSN 0898-4786) **8186**
M A V *see* Maschinen Anlagen Verfahren **1779**
• M A V I S (Online) (Medicines Act Veterinary Information Service) (GBR ISSN 1755-134X) **8802**
M A V I S (Print) *see* M A V I S (Online) **8802**
M A W A Review (Middle-Atlantic Writers Association) (USA ISSN 0742-9738) **5328**
M & A *see* Mergers and Acquisitions in Canada **1148**
M & A (Mergers and Acquisitions) (GBR ISSN 1478-4742) **1145**
† M & A (Meccanica e Automazione) (ITA ISSN 1126-4284) **8972**
• M & A Asia (HKG ISSN 1817-1656) **1366**
• M & A E-News (USA) **2563**
• The M & A Lawyer (USA ISSN 1093-3255) **2564**
The M and A Lawyer *see* The M & A Lawyer **2564**
• M & A Review (Mergers & Acquisitions) (DEU ISSN 0941-1089) **1366**
• The M & A Tax Report (Mergers & Acquisitions) (USA ISSN 1085-3693) **1933**
The M & A Weekly *see* The Health Care M & A Monthly **1117**
M & C *see* Meetings and Conventions **6281**
M & C *see* Memory and Cognition **7384**
M & C. Meeting e Congressi *see* M C Meeting e Congress **6281**
M & C Publishing (Media et Communicatie) (BEL ISSN 1378-8957) **7580**
M & E *see* Maquinas y Equipos, Herramientas e Insumos Industriales **5456**
M & E Design (GBR ISSN 1366-8730) **3324**
M & F Hers *see* Hers **6988**
M & M *see* Markt & Mededinging **1834**
M & M A *see* Macchine e Motori Agricoli **212**
M & O H *see* Management & Organizational History **1775**
A M & P *see* Advanced Materials & Processes **3335**
M & P (Year) *see* J S M E / A S M E International Conference on Materials and Processing (Year). Program and Abstract **3383**
M & S Magazine *see* Your M & S **3873**
M & S O M *see* Manufacturing and Service Operations Management **1778**
M & T *see* Mentoring & Tutoring **3072**
M & T *see* Metaal & Techniek **6322**
M & T - Metallhandwerk (DEU ISSN 1436-0446) **1021**
M & W *see* Mieten und Wohnen **7599**
M B *see* Alberi e Territorio **3683**
M B *see* Molecular Biotechnology **768**
M B A *see* Mountain Bike Action (Tel Aviv) **8265**
M B A A Communicator *see* Master Brewers Association of the Americas. Communicator **607**
▼ M B A Banking (Michigan Bankers Association) (USA ISSN 1934-6492) **1366**
M B A Guide *see* The Hobsons M B A Guide **2956**
• M B A Jungle (Masters in Business Administration) (USA ISSN 1541-3284) **1145**
M B A Review (Masters in Business Administration) (IND ISSN 0972-6764) **1773**
Das M B A Studium (Masters in Business Administration) (DEU) **2992**
M B & R *see* Multiple Buyer and Retailer **3680**
M B B *see* Maandblad Belasting Beschouwingen **1934**
M B C B *see* Medecine Buccale Chirurgie Buccale **5855**
M B Dossier *see* P T Industrieel Management **3214**
M B E *see* Measuring Business Excellence **1779**
M B E *see* Molecular Biology and Evolution **689**
M B E *see* Mathematical Biosciences and Engineering **5512**
M B E Questions *see* Multistate Bar Examination Questions **4737**
M B H Newsletter (USA) **1638**
M B H Weekly Futures Trading Letter (USA) **1638**
M B I *see* Music Business International **6590**
M B I *see* Minorities in Business Insider **1149**
† • M B I Asian Report (Music Business International) (GBR) **8972**
• M B I Eastern European Report (Music Business International) (GBR) **1575**
• M B I Latin American Report (Music Business International) (GBR) **1575**
• M B I World Report (Music Business International) (GBR ISSN 1361-746X) **1575**
M B I's Indian Industries Annual (IND ISSN 0541-5357) **1897**
M B K - Mission Aktuell (DEU) **7766**
▼ • M B M (San Francisco) (Mind - Body Management) (USA ISSN 1947-1068) **6231**
M B News (Monument Builders of North America) (USA ISSN 0192-2491) **503**
M B O Magazine (Middelbaar Beroepsonderwijs) (NLD ISSN 1872-6798) **2944**
M B O T Magazine *see* Mississauga Board of Trade **1431**
M B P *see* I O M A's Report on Managing Benefits Plans **1865**
M B Q *see* Montana Business Quarterly **1150**
M B R *see* Multiple Buyer and Retailer **3680**
M B R *see* Multinational Business Review **1578**
M B S Informer (Malawi Bureau of Standards) (MWI) **6403**
M B S News (Malawi Bureau of Standards) (MWI) **6403**
M B T *see* Manufacturing Business Technology **1898**
M B Z - Modellbahnzeitschrift (DEU ISSN 0722-9879) **4339**
† M-Business (USA ISSN 1532-3137) **8972**
M C *see* Messaggero Cappuccino **7806**
M C *see* Mission Critical **2432**
M C 2 (Bremerton) (Mini Classic Mini Cooper) (USA ISSN 1557-2617) **8186**
† M C 2 (San Mateo) (Music Computer Culture) (USA ISSN 1533-3019) **8972**
M C 2 Magazine *see* M C 2 (Bremerton) **8186**
M C 2 R *see* Mobile Computing and Communications Review **2333**
M C A A Info (Mason Contractors Association of America) (USA) **1021**
M C A Business Plan *see* M H R A Business Plan **5663**
M C A D (Mechanical Computer-Aided Design) (USA ISSN 1471-5082) **3388**
M C A Guidance Note (Medicines Control Agency) (GBR) **6859**
M C A T Comprehensive Review (Medical College Admissions Test) (USA ISSN 1090-901X) **2993**
▼ M C A T Workout (Medical College Admission Test) (USA ISSN 1937-6375) **5662**
M C & B *see* Michigan Contractor & Builder **1024**
M C B *see* Molecular & Cellular Biomechanics **750**
M C B A Newsletter *see* Monterey County Bar Association Newsletter **4736**
M C C *see* Journal of Integrated Care **8050**
M C C *see* The Metropolitan Corporate Counsel **4733**
M C C Annual Report (Mennonite Central Committee) (USA) **7738**
The M C C Connection (Manhattan Christian College) (USA) **2290**
M C C Mensa Canada Communications (CAN ISSN 0820-4217) **2267**
M C C Post (Mott Community College) (USA) **2290**
M C C Resource Update (Mennonite Central Committee) (USA) **8054**
• M C D A Magazine (Manitoba Conservation Districts Association) (CAN ISSN 1719-4326) **3451**
M C E E R Bulletin *see* Multidisciplinary Center for Earthquake Engineering Research Bulletin **2787**
• M C E E R Information Service News (Multidisciplinary Center for Earthquake Engineering Research) (USA ISSN 1520-2941) **3208**
➤ M C E E R Technical Report Series (Multidisciplinary Center for Earthquake Engineering Research) (USA ISSN 1520-295X) **2786**
M C - Folket (SWE ISSN 0281-7403) **8260**
M C G Today (Medical College of Georgia Foundation, Inc.) (USA ISSN 0047-6471) **5662**
M C Gill Doorway Magazine (USA) **7094**
M C H *see* Military Club & Hospitality **3656**
M C I *see* Management Consultant International **1775**
M C J A *see* Midcontinental Journal of Archaeology **406**
• ➤ M - C Journal (Media and Culture) (AUS ISSN 1441-2616) **8119**
▼ M C L A (Men's Collegiate Lacrosse Association) (USA ISSN 1940-3178) **8238**
M C M *see* Manualita Creativita Maestria **537**
• M C M (Motorcykelmagasinet) (SWE ISSN 0282-9134) **8260**
M C M D S *see* Mathematical and Computer Modelling of Dynamical Systems **5554**
• M C Magazine (USA ISSN 1932-9962) **1021**
M C Meeting e Congress (ITA ISSN 0390-2692) **6281**
† M C - Microcomputer Software (ITA ISSN 1123-2722) **8972**
M C N *see* Motorcycle News **8263**
M C N *see* Multichannel News **2385**
M C N *see* Molecular and Cellular Neuroscience **6161**
M C N *see* Motorcycle Consumer News **8263**
• M C N: American Journal of Maternal Child Nursing (USA ISSN 0361-929X) **5969**
M C - Nytt (SWE ISSN 0024-7995) **8260**
M C P *see* Molecular and Cellular Proteomics **739**
M C R C *see* I O M A's Report on Managing Credit, Receivables and Collections **1352**
M C Revyen (Motorcykel) (DNK ISSN 0107-0606) **8260**
M C S *see* Media, Culture & Society **8120**
M C S *see* Motor City Sports **8188**
M C S C C On Cover (Motor City Stamp and Cover Club) (USA) **6896**
M C S Newsletter (SLB) **3601**
M C S S *see* Mathematics of Control, Signals and Systems **3370**
M C Squared *see* M C 2 (San Mateo) **8972**
M C Squared *see* M C 2 (Bremerton) **8186**
M C T *see* Metal Casting Technologies **6323**
M C T - Multicultural Teaching *see* Race Equality Teaching **3015**
M C V (GBR ISSN 1469-4832) **2478**
M C W Alumni News (Medical College of Wisconsin) (USA) **2290**
▼ M Comme Maison (FRA ISSN 1957-4061) **4545**
m-Commerce World (GBR) **2564**
➤ M Computing (USA ISSN 1072-3226) **2508**
M D *see* Modern Drama **5335**
M D (Moebel Interior Design) (DEU ISSN 0343-0642) **4545**
M D *see* Revista Andaluza de Medicina del Deporte **6232**
M D *see* Management Decision **1775**
M D *see* Monthly Digest of Statistics **8389**
M D *see* Tidskriften Opera **6623**
M D (Materials Division) (USA ISSN 1071-6939) **3388**
M D A *see* Marina Dock Age **8277**
The M D A / A L S Newsletter (Amyotrophic Lateral Sclerosis) (USA) **6159**
M D & D I *see* Medical Device & Diagnostic Industry **4489**
M.D. Anderson Breast Medical Oncology (USA ISSN 1940-1329) **6026**
▼ M.D. Anderson Clinical Perspectives. Lymphoma & Myeloma (USA ISSN 1940-7319) **6027**
M D B L *see* Mine Development Business Leads (MDBL) **6470**
The M D B Magazine Directory (GBR) **7567**
M D C Business Journal (Management Development Centre) (TTO) **1145**
M D Design-Jahrbuch *see* M D **4545**
M D Dialogue (CAN ISSN 1715-8966) **5662**
M D E *see* Managerial and Decision Economics **1777**
M D L R *see* Maryland Law Review **4728**
M D - Marketing Digest (DEU) **1829**
M D N A News (Machinery Dealers National Association) (USA) **5455**
• M D N G Endocrinology (Medical Doctor Net Guide) (USA) **5897**
† • M D N G eNewsletter (Medical Doctor Net Guide) (USA) **8972**
▼ • M D N G Hospitalist (Medical Doctor Net Guide) (USA) **4105**
• M D N G Multicultural Healthcare (Medical Doctor Net Guide) (USA) **5662**
• M D N G Neurology (Medical Doctor Net Guide) (USA) **6159**
• M D N G Primary Care (Medical Doctor Net Guide) (USA) **5662**
• M D N G Psychiatry (Medical Doctor Net Guide) (USA) **5662**
M D News (Medical Doctor) (USA) **5662**
M D R *see* Meat & Deli Retailer **3655**
M D R T Annual Meeting. Proceedings (Million Dollar Round Table) (USA) **4513**
• M D R's Louisiana School Directory (Market Data Retrieval) (USA) **2957**
• M D R's New Mexico School Directory (Market Data Retrieval) (USA ISSN 1540-2274) **2957**
• M D R's Oregon School Directory (Market Data Retrieval) (USA ISSN 1540-2282) **2957**
• M D R's Rhode Island School Directory (Market Data Retrieval) (USA ISSN 1540-2290) **2957**
• M D R's School Directories (National Set) (Market Data Retrieval) (USA) **2957**
• M D R's School Directories. Mid-Atlantic (Regional Set) (USA) **2957**
• M D R's School Directories. Midwest (Regional Set) (USA) **2957**
• M D R's School Directories. Mountain / Plains (Regional Set) (USA) **2957**
• M D R's School Directories. New England (Regional Set) (USA) **2957**
• M D R's School Directories. Southeast (Regional Set) (USA) **2957**
• M D R's School Directories. Southwest (Regional Set) (USA) **2957**
• M D R's School Directories. West (Regional Set) (USA) **2958**
M D R's School Directory *see* M D R's School Directories (National Set) **2957**
• M D R's School Directory. Alabama (Market Data Retrieval) (USA ISSN 1077-7393) **2958**
• M D R's School Directory. Alaska (Market Data Retrieval) (USA ISSN 1077-7407) **2958**
• M D R's School Directory. Arizona (Market Data Retrieval) (USA ISSN 1077-7415) **2958**
• M D R's School Directory. Arkansas (Market Data Retrieval) (USA ISSN 1077-7423) **2958**
• M D R's School Directory. California (Market Data Retrieval) (USA ISSN 1077-7431) **2958**
• M D R's School Directory. Colorado (Market Data Retrieval) (USA ISSN 1077-744X) **2958**
• M D R's School Directory. Connecticut (Market Data Retrieval) (USA ISSN 1077-7458) **2958**
• M D R's School Directory. Delaware (Market Data Retrieval) (USA ISSN 1077-7466) **2958**
• M D R's School Directory. District of Columbia (Market Data Retrieval) (USA ISSN 1077-7474) **2958**
• M D R's School Directory. Florida (Market Data Retrieval) (USA ISSN 1077-7482) **2958**
• M D R's School Directory. Georgia (Market Data Retrieval) (USA ISSN 1077-7490) **2958**
• M D R's School Directory. Hawaii (Market Data Retrieval) (USA ISSN 1077-7504) **2958**
• M D R's School Directory. Idaho (Market Data Retrieval) (USA ISSN 1077-7512) **2958**
• M D R's School Directory. Illinois (Market Data Retrieval) (USA ISSN 1077-7520) **2958**
• M D R's School Directory. Indiana (Market Data Retrieval) (USA ISSN 1077-7539) **2958**
• M D R's School Directory. Iowa (Market Data Retrieval) (USA ISSN 1077-7547) **2958**
• M D R's School Directory. Kansas (Market Data Retrieval) (USA ISSN 1077-7555) **2958**
• M D R's School Directory. Kentucky (Market Data Retrieval) (USA ISSN 1077-7563) **2959**
• M D R's School Directory. Maine (Market Data Retrieval) (USA ISSN 1077-758X) **2959**
• M D R's School Directory. Maryland (Market Data Retrieval) (USA ISSN 1077-7598) **2959**
• M D R's School Directory. Massachusetts (Market Data Retrieval) (USA ISSN 1077-7601) **2959**
• M D R's School Directory. Michigan (Market Data Retrieval) (USA ISSN 1077-761X) **2959**
• M D R's School Directory. Minnesota (Market Data Retrieval) (USA ISSN 1077-7628) **2959**
• M D R's School Directory. Mississippi (Market Data Retrieval) (USA ISSN 1077-7636) **2959**
• M D R's School Directory. Missouri (Market Data Retrieval) (USA ISSN 1077-7644) **2959**
• M D R's School Directory. Montana (Market Data Retrieval) (USA ISSN 1077-7652) **2959**
• M D R's School Directory. Nebraska (Market Data Retrieval) (USA ISSN 1077-7660) **2959**
• M D R's School Directory. Nevada (Market Data Retrieval) (USA ISSN 1077-7679) **2959**
• M D R's School Directory. New Hampshire (Market Data Retrieval) (USA ISSN 1077-7687) **2959**
• M D R's School Directory. New Jersey (Market Data Retrieval) (USA ISSN 1077-7695) **2959**
• M D R's School Directory. New York (Market Data Retrieval) (USA ISSN 1077-7717) **2959**

Title

10576 M D R'S SCHOOL DIRECTORY. NORTH CAROLINA ULRICH'S PERIODICALS

• M D R's School Directory. North Carolina (Market Data Retrieval) (USA ISSN 1077-7725) **2959**
• M D R's School Directory. North Dakota (Market Data Retrieval) (USA ISSN 1077-7733) **2959**
• M D R's School Directory. Ohio (Market Data Retrieval) (USA ISSN 1077-7741) **2959**
• M D R's School Directory. Oklahoma (Market Data Retrieval) (USA ISSN 1077-775X) **2959**
• M D R's School Directory. Pennsylvania (Market Data Retrieval) (USA ISSN 1077-7776) **2960**
• M D R's School Directory. South Dakota (Market Data Retrieval) (USA ISSN 1077-7806) **2960**
• M D R's School Directory. Utah (Market Data Retrieval) (USA ISSN 1077-7830) **2960**
• M D R's School Directory. Vermont (Market Data Retrieval) (USA ISSN 1077-7849) **2960**
• M D R's School Directory. Washington (Market Data Retrieval) (USA ISSN 1077-7865) **2960**
• M D R's School Directory. West Virginia (Market Data Retrieval) (USA ISSN 1077-7873) **2960**
• M D R's School Directory. Wisconsin (Market Data Retrieval) (USA ISSN 1077-7881) **2960**
• M D R's School Directory. Wyoming (Market Data Retrieval) (USA ISSN 1077-789X) **2960**
• M D R's South Carolina School Directory (Market Data Retrieval) (USA ISSN 1540-2304) **2960**
• M D R's Tennessee School Directory (Market Data Retrieval) (USA ISSN 1540-2312) **2960**
• M D R's Texas School Directory (Market Data Retrieval) (USA) **2960**
• M D R's Virginia School Directory (Market Data Retrieval) (USA ISSN 1540-2320) **2960**
M D S (Misce, Da, Signa) (FIN ISSN 0024-8045) **6859**
▼ • M D S 3.0 Update (Minimum Data Set) (USA ISSN 1947-8887) **4105**
M D S News (Massachusetts Dental Society) (USA ISSN 0738-4556) **5855**
M D T (Motorsport Dealer & Trade) (CAN) **8260**
M D T *see* Medical Device Technology **5668**
M D T *see* Medical Design Technology (Print) **8973**
M D T R S *see* Department of Mathematics. Technical Report **5482**
M D T V Retailer *see* H D T V Retailer **2382**
• M D Week (USA ISSN 1552-8812) **5662**
M E *see* Minerals & Energy **1601**
M E *see* La Medicina Estetica **5673**
M E *see* Materiali Edili **1022**
M E *see* Materials Evaluation **3353**
M E *see* Minority Engineer **3210**
M E *see* Your New Pryor Report - Managers Edge **1802**
M E A *see* Municipal Engineering in Australia **3278**
M E A J O *see* Middle East African Journal of Ophtalmology **6046**
M E A - M F T Today (Montana Education Association - Montana Federation of Teachers) (USA) **2884**
M E A Voice *see* M E A Voice of Action **2884**
M E A Voice of Action (Michigan Education Association) (USA) **2884**
M E C D *see* Measurement and Evaluation in Counseling and Development **2886**
M E C E S U P. Boletin (Mejoramiento de la Calidad y Equidad en la Educacion Superior) (CHL ISSN 0717-7186) **2884**
M E C Ortofrutticolo (ITA ISSN 1826-2236) **241**
M E D A N Z News (Middle Eastern Dance Association of New Zealand) (NZL ISSN 1177-2808) **2686**
• M E D I C C Review (Medical Education Cooperation with Cuba) (USA ISSN 1527-3172) **5662**
† M E D I C. Metodologia e Didattica Clinica/Clinical Methodology and Didactics (ITA ISSN 1122-1909) **8972**
M E D L I P *see* Medical Literature Indexing Services in Pakistan **5749**
M E E *see* Middle East Expatriate **3912**
M E E D *see* Middle East Economic Digest **1499**
• M E E D Plus (GBR) **1497**
M E E M *see* I E E E Multidisciplinary Engineering Education Magazine **3313**
M E E N Imaging Technology News (Medical Electronics and Equipment News) (USA) **6202**
M E E S *see* Middle East Economic Survey **6778**
M E H B *see* Maryland Essays in Human Biodiversity **347**
M E H D *see* Tradeshow Week's Major Exhibit Hall Directory **36**
➤ M E I E A Journal (Music & Entertainment Industry Educators Association) (USA ISSN 1559-7334) **4980**
M E J A *see* Middle East Journal of Anesthesiology **5772**
M E L *see* Maritime Economics & Logistics **8652**
M E L A Notes (Middle East Librarians Association) (USA ISSN 0364-2410) **5030**
M E L E C O N *see* Mediterranean Electrotechnical Conference **3325**
• M.E.L.O.N. (Multimedia & Entertainment Law Online News) (USA) **4726**
M E L P R *see* Missouri Environmental Law and Policy Review **4735**
• ➤ M E L U S (Multi-Ethnic Literature of the United States) (USA ISSN 0163-755X) **5328**
M E M *see* Managing Education Matters **3027**
M E M *see* Medical Electronics Manufacturing **3108**
M E M *see* Marketing to the Emerging Majorities **1833**
M E M A Market Analysis (Motor & Equipment Manufacturers Association) (USA) **1897**
M E M C O News (Miller Electric Manufacturing Co.) (USA) **6343**
M E M D *see* Microinfo Electronic Media Directory **2494**
M E M E S *see* Milteon Gwa Geunse Yeongmunhag **5334**
• M E M I (Magazin fuer Elektronische Musik im Internet) (DEU) **6586**
M e M o *see* Mechatronik Mobil **3209**
M E M O (SWE ISSN 1400-3414) **5030**
M E M S *see* M E M S: Micro-Electromechanical Systems **8431**
• M E M S: Micro-Electromechanical Systems (USA ISSN 1555-5135) **8431**
M E M S: Micro-Electromechanical Systems to Two Thousand and Eight *see* M E M S: Micro-Electromechanical Systems **8431**
M E N *see* Motor Equipment News **8592**
M E N *see* Motor Equipment News **8592**
M E N *see* Metalworking Equipment News **6326**
M E N A Petroleum Bulletin (Middle East & North Africa) (GBR ISSN 1466-1683) **6777**
M E N Z A Magazine *see* Sound Arts **6618**
M E O (Muelheim Essen Oberhausen) (DEU) **1406**
M E P. Annual Report (Music Entrepreneur Program) (CAN ISSN 1910-9512) **8054**
• M E P S Chartbook (Medical Expenditure Panel Survey) (USA ISSN 1531-5649) **7530**
M E Q *see* Management of Environmental Quality **3451**
M E R *see* M E R. Marine Engineers Review **3208**
• ➤ M E R G A. Annual Conference Proceedings (AUS) **2884**
M E R G A. Membership Directory (Mathematics Education Research Group of Australasia) (AUS) **2884**
M E R I A (French Edition) *see* M E R I A Journal **555**
• ➤ M E R I A Journal (Middle East Review of International Affairs) (ISR ISSN 1565-8996) **555**
M E R I T Annual Report (Magistrates Early Referral into Treatment) (AUS ISSN 1449-1672) **2660**
M E R I's Monthly Circular (Mitsubishi Economic Research Institute) (JPN ISSN 0026-6809) **1497**
M E R J *see* Mathematics Education Research Journal **3072**
M E R K U R - Schriften zum Innovativen Marketing-Management (DEU) **1773**
M E R. Marine Engineers Review (GBR ISSN 0047-5955) **3208**
• M E S A Journal (Mines and Energy South Australia) (AUS ISSN 1326-3544) **6469**
M E S - M S C Steel Construction Group Technical Review *see* Mitsui Zosen Tekko Kensetsu Kouji Gurupu Giho **3278**
M E T E M. Hirek *see* M E T E M - International Society of Toronto for Hungarian Church History. Newsletter **4241**
M E T E M - International Society of Toronto for Hungarian Church History. Newsletter/M E T E M. Hirek (Magyar Egyhaztorteneti Enciklopedia Munkakozossege) (CAN) **4241**
M E T - Network Working Paper Series *see* Managing Economic Transition Network. Working Paper Series **1146**
M E T U Journal of Pure and Applied Sciences *see* Journal of Pure and Applied Sciences **8968**
M E T U Studies in Development *see* O D T U Gelisme Dergisi **1547**
• M E - Tidningen (Maskinentreprenoerna) (SWE ISSN 1400-4968) **3388**
M E U *see* Medical Environment Update **4106**
M E W Technical Report *see* Matsushita Denko Giho **3325**
M E X - Musenalp Express (CHE) **2200**
M & C Grafiek (BEL ISSN 1371-6085) **7324**
• M & O (NLD ISSN 0165-1722) **1773**
M & C Graphique *see* M & C Grafiek **7324**
M & T 2 (FRA ISSN 1637-8962) **2248**
M F *see* Managerial Finance **1778**
M F *see* Milano Finanza **1639**
M F *see* Men's Fitness **6284**
M F A T Businesslink *see* Business Link **1554**
• M F Bladet (Menighedsfakultetet) (DNK ISSN 1604-911X) **7661**
M F E Collector's Bookline (Modern First Editions) (USA ISSN 1073-3027) **5328**
M F I (Modellflug International) (DEU ISSN 1431-3995) **4339**
M F J *see* Multinational Finance Journal **1393**
M F J *see* Municipal Finance Journal **1935**
M F L *see* Matematicko Fizicki List **5511**
M F Plus (Mlada Fronta) (CZE ISSN 1214-4746) **5225**
M F R *see* Marriage & Family Review **8119**
M F S *see* M F S Modern Fiction Studies **5335**
M F S Perspective (USA) **1638**
M G A Focus (Maine Grocers Association) (USA) **3654**
M G B *see* Marron Growers Bulletin **3601**
M.G. Business (Mercantile Gazette) (NZL) **1430**
M G Enthusiast Magazine (GBR ISSN 0950-3307) **8589**
M G G *see* Molecular Genetics and Genomics **875**
M G I Magazine (Mahatma Gandhi Institute) (MUS) **4176**
• M G M A Connexion (Medical Group Management Association) (USA ISSN 1537-0240) **5663**
M G P Record (Museum of the Great Plains) (USA) **6528**
M G S Q *see* Montgomery Genealogical Society Quarterly **3775**
• ➤ M G V (Maandblad Geestelijke Volksgezondheid) (NLD ISSN 0024-8576) **6159**
M G W Newspaper *see* Mom Guess What Newspaper **4376**
M! Games (DEU) **2478**
M Guide *see* Marketing News **1832**
M H *see* Medical Humanities **5669**
M H (Missionary Herald) (GBR) **7766**
M H A *see* Microbiologie Hygiene Alimentaire **891**
M H D Supply Chain Solutions (Materials Handling and Distribution) (AUS ISSN 1445-0801) **1773**
M H F A Update (Massachusetts Housing Finance Agency) (USA) **4419**
M H H - Info (Medizinische Hochschule Hannover) (DEU ISSN 1619-201X) **2290**
M H J *see* Melbourne Historical Journal **4193**
M H J *see* Minnesota Hockey Journal **8187**
M H L A News (Manitoba Health Libraries Association) (CAN ISSN 0848-9009) **5030**
M H N *see* Materials Handling News **5457**
M H N *see* Multi-Housing News **1025**
M H N Directory (Materials Handling News) (GBR) **2013**
• M H Online (Medical Humanities) (GBR ISSN 1473-4265) **5663**
• M H Q (Military History Quarterly) (USA ISSN 1040-5992) **4302**
M H R *see* Molecular Human Reproduction **5999**
M H R A Business Plan (Medicines and Healthcare Products Regulatory Agency) (GBR) **5663**
M H R A Critical Texts (GBR ISSN 1746-1642) **5149**
M H R I Report *see* Mizuho Economic Outlook & Analysis **1499**
M H S *see* Marketing Health Services **1832**
M H S Keywords *see* Time Lines **4315**
M H S L A News (Michigan Health Sciences Libraries Association) (USA ISSN 1543-0359) **5030**
M H S Miscellany. N (Massachusetts Historical Society) (USA ISSN 0024-8185) **4302**
M H S News (Maryland Historical Society) (USA) **4302**
• M I (Montajes e Instalaciones) (ESP ISSN 0210-184X) **4123**
M I *see* Microelectronics International **3109**
M I *see* Molecular Interventions **6862**
M I A C P *see* Media International Australia Incorporating Culture and Policy **8120**
M I & T *see* Management Issues & Trends **7599**
M I B A - Die Eisenbahn im Modell (Miniaturbahnen) (DEU ISSN 1430-886X) **4339**
M I B A Messe (Miniaturbahnen) (DEU) **4339**
M I B A Spezial (Miniaturbahnen) (DEU ISSN 0938-1775) **4339**
M I C (Meetings, Incentives and Conventions) (CHE) **8732**
M I C *see* Modeling, Identification and Control (Online) **2463**
➤ M I C A Communications Review (Mudra Institute of Communications, Ahmedabad) (IND ISSN 0973-015X) **1829**
M I C C I Bulletin (Malaysian International Chamber of Commerce and Industry) (MYS) **1406**
• M I C E (Meetings Incentives Conferences Events) (ITA) **6281**
M I C E Guide (Year) *see* M I C E **6281**
M I C E. Meetings Incentives Congressen Exhibitions *see* Holland in Congres **6280**
M I C I Digest *see* Maladies Inflammatoires Chroniques de l'Intestin Digest **5929**
M I C - Minimal Invasive Chirurgie (DEU ISSN 0941-455X) **6251**
M I C Mission News (Missionary Sisters of the Immaculate Conception) (CAN ISSN 0315-9655) **8054**
M I D *see* Managing Information and Documents **5031**
M I D E O *see* Institut Dominicain d'Etudes Orientales du Caire. Melanges **4321**
• M I D I R S Midwifery Digest (Midwives Information and Resource Service) (GBR ISSN 0961-5555) **5997**
M I D S Newsletter (Miscarriage, Infant Death, and Stillbirth) (USA) **5997**
M I E *see* Management in Education **3027**
M I E A Notes *see* Music and Entertainment Industry Educators' Notes **6589**
M I E C Servico de Documentacion (Movimiento Internacional de Estudiantes Catolicos, Centro de Documentacion) (PER) **2993**
M I F A O *see* Institut Francais d'Archeologie Orientale du Caire. Memoires **398**
M I F L C Review (Mountain Interstate Foreign Language Conference) (USA ISSN 1079-7866) **5149**
M I G A Annual Report (Multilateral Investment Guarantee Agency) (USA ISSN 1014-823X) **1601**
• M I G A News (Multilateral Investment Guarantee Agency) (USA ISSN 1564-5533) **1601**
M I G Risk Update *see* Risk Update (London, 1997) **1581**
M I H M I *see* Majalah Ilmiah Himpunan Matematika Indonesia **5510**
M I J N S R *see* M R S Internet Journal of Nitride Semiconductor Research **3352**
M I L C O M *see* I E E E Military Communications Conference. Conference Record **3313**
M I L U S *see* Stockholms Universitet. Institutionen foer Linguistics. Monographs **5178**
M.I.M Europe (Marking Industry Magazine) (USA) **1852**
M I M - Medien Insight Multimedia (DEU) **2332**
M I M S (Monthly Index of Medical Specialties) (GBR ISSN 0957-9095) **6859**
M I M S Africa (GBR ISSN 0140-4415) **6859**
• M I M S Annual (Monthly Index of Medical Specialties) (AUS ISSN 0725-4709) **6859**
• M I M S Bi-Monthly (Monthly Index of Medical Specialties) (AUS ISSN 1035-5723) **6859**
• M I M S C D (Monthly Index of Medical Specialties) (AUS) **5663**
M I M S Cardiovascular (Monthly Index of Medical Specialties) (GBR) **5795**
M I M S Caribbean (Monthly Index of Medical Specialties) (GBR) **6859**
M I M S Colour Index (Monthly Index of Medical Specialties) (GBR ISSN 0957-9109) **6859**
• M I M S Companion (CD-ROM) (Monthly Index of Medical Specialties) (AUS) **5663**
M I M S Companion (Print) *see* M I M S Companion (CD-ROM) **5663**
M I M S Dermatology (Monthly Index of Medical Specialties) (GBR) **5880**
M I M S Desk Reference (Monthly Index of Medical Specialties) (ZAF ISSN 0076-8847) **6859**
M I M S for Nurses (Monthly Index of Medical Specialties) (GBR) **5969**
M I M S Hospital Equipment & Supplies Directory (Monthly Index of Medical Specialties) (AUS ISSN 1444-5344) **4105**
➤ M I M S Ireland (Monthly Index of Medical Specialties) (IRL ISSN 0300-8223) **5663**
• M I M S Medical Specialities (Monthly Index of Medical Specialties) (ZAF ISSN 0580-6755) **5748**
M I M S Middle East (Monthly Index of Medical Specialties) (GBR ISSN 0302-4172) **6859**
M I M S New Ethicals (Monthly Index of Medical Specialties) (NZL ISSN 1176-5844) **6859**
M I M S Women's Health (Monthly Index of Medical Specialties) (GBR) **8846**
M.I. Montajes e Instalaciones *see* M I **4123**
M I N *see* Media Industry Newsletter **29**
• M I N E X (Mineral Exploration Newsletter) (DNK ISSN 1602-2475) **6469**
• M I N Magazine (Media Industry Newsletter) (USA ISSN 1537-8462) **7567**
m i n: Media Industry Newsletter *see* Media Industry Newsletter **29**
• m i n's b2b (Media Industry Newsletter) (USA ISSN 1520-9830) **7567**
m i n's blob *see* m i n's b2b **7567**
m i n's New Media Report *see* Media Industry Newsletter **29**
m i n's New Media Report *see* m i n's b2b **7567**
• M I O S H A News (Michigan Occupational Safety and Health Act) (USA) **6681**
M I O S Journal *see* McAllen International Orchid Society Journal **800**
M I P *see* Marketing Intelligence & Planning **1832**
M I P D O C Preview Magazine *see* Marche International des Programmes Documentaires. Preview Magazine **2384**
▼ M I P T V Preview Magazine (Marche International des Programmes de Television) (FRA ISSN 1963-2258) **2384**
M I Pro (Musical Instrument) (GBR ISSN 1750-4198) **6586**
M I R *see* Musical Interpretation Research **6593**
M I R *see* Metalworking Insiders' Report **5457**
• M I R A Automotive Business News (Motor Industry Research Association) (GBR) **1249**
• M I R A Virtual Automotive Information Centre (Motor Industry Research Association) (GBR) **8527**
† M I R I N Z (Meat Industry Research Institute of New Zealand) (NZL ISSN 0465-4390) **8972**
M I R L Reports (Mineral Industry Research Laboratory) (USA) **6469**
• ➤ M I R: Management International Review (DEU ISSN 0938-8249) **1773**
M I R S Legislative Report (Michigan Information and Research Service, Inc.) (USA) **7152**
M I R T Projectenboek (Meerjarenprogramma Infrastructuur, Ruimte en Transport) (NLD) **7452**
M I S *see* Minerals Industry Survey Report (Online) **6471**
M I S (Asia Edition) *see* M I S (Australian Edition) **1773**
• M I S (Australian Edition) (Managing Information Strategies) (AUS ISSN 1445-5382) **1773**
M I S (UK Edition) *see* M I S (Australian Edition) **1773**
M I S 100 (Managing Information Strategies) (NZL ISSN 1177-9233) **2531**
• M I S Information (USA) **2431**
M I S New Zealand *see* C I O New Zealand **1415**
M I S New Zealand. New Zealand's 100 Biggest I T Users *see* M I S 100 **2531**
• ➤ M I S Quarterly (Management Information Systems) (USA ISSN 0276-7783) **2523**
• ➤ M I S Quarterly Executive (Management Information Systems) (USA ISSN 1540-1960) **1145**
M I S Strategic 100 *see* Strategic 100 **1795**
M I T *see* Military Information Technology **6435**
M I T- C T L Supply Chain Strategy *see* Supply Chain Strategy **1796**
M I T Mittelstandsmagazin (DEU ISSN 0932-3325) **3852**
M I T Occasional Papers in Linguistics (Massachusetts Institute of Technology) (USA) **5149**

Link to your serials resources and content with ulrichsweb.com

The M I T Press Eurasian Population and Family History Series *see* Eurasian Population and Family History **7283**
M I T Press Series in Computer Systems *see* Computer Systems Series **2519**
M I T Press Series in Information Systems (Massachusetts Institute of Technology) (USA ISSN 0891-4702) **2431**
M I T/S N I P-Projectenboek *see* M I R T Projectenboek **7452**
• ➤ M I T Sloan Management Review (USA ISSN 1532-9194) **1773**
M I T Working Papers in Linguistics (Massachusetts Institute of Technology) (USA ISSN 1049-1058) **5149**
M I U S A's Global Impact (Mobility International U S A) (USA) **3014**
M I V: Museerne i Viborg Amt (DNK ISSN 0107-9328) **4241**
M I W A *see* Major Indian Works Annual **630**
M I Z - Materialien und Informationen zur Zeit (DEU ISSN 0170-6748) **5225**
M J *see* Municipal Journal **7498**
M J A *see* Medical Journal of Australia **5669**
M J C R *see* Monographs of the Journal of Consumer Research **1150**
M J C S L *see* Michigan Journal of Community Service Learning **2994**
M J E C T *see* Midwest Journal for Educational Communications and Technology **2950**
M J G L *see* Michigan Journal of Gender & Law **4733**
M J H S S *see* Micronesian Journal of the Humanities and Social Sciences **4465**
M J I L *see* Michigan Journal of International Law **4935**
M J I L *see* Minnesota Journal of International Law **1578**
M J L S T *see* Minnesota Journal of Law, Science & Technology **4734**
M J M *see* McGill Journal of Medicine **5665**
M J Musen to Jikken/Audio Technology (JPN ISSN 1345-8817) **8154**
M J P *see* Melbourne Journal of Politics **7154**
M J R L *see* Michigan Journal of Race & Law **3550**
• M J S A Journal (Manufacturing Jewelers and Suppliers of America) (USA ISSN 1941-6539) **4568**
M ja M *see* Markkinointi & Mainonta **29**
• M jak Mieszkanie (POL ISSN 1508-2083) **4545**
M K *see* Moskovskii Komsomolets **3937**
M K *see* Milliyet Kardes **2202**
M K B-Nederland - N I P O Ondernemerspanel *see* Ondernemerspanel M K B-Nederland - T N S N I P O **1720**
• M K Bul'var (Moskovskii Komsomolets) (RUS ISSN 1682-6930) **3937**
▼ • Der M K G - Chirurg (Mund Kiefer Gesichts) (DEU ISSN 1865-9659) **6251**
• M K G Rapport (Miljoeorganisationernas Kaernavfallsgranskning) (SWE ISSN 1653-6800) **3508**
M K-Lehti (Moottorikelkka) (FIN ISSN 0788-3749) **8321**
M - K M G *see* Mitteilungen der Karl-May-Gesellschaft **5335**
• M K Marketing y Ventas para Directivos (ESP ISSN 1130-8761) **1829**
• M K Voskresen'ye (Moskovskii Komsomolets) (RUS ISSN 1682-6876) **3937**
• M K - Z W O (DEU) **6586**
• M K Zdorov'ye (Moskovskii Komsomolets) (RUS ISSN 1682-7090) **6992**
M Kmobil' (RUS ISSN 1682-7201) **2332**
M L *see* Ministry & Liturgy **7663**
† • ➤ M L A A N Z Journal (Maritime Law Association of Australia and New Zealand) (AUS ISSN 0811-4293) **8972**
M L A A N Z Journal (Online) *see* Australian and New Zealand Maritime Law Journal **4969**
• M L A Annual Report (Meat and Livestock Australia) (AUS ISSN 1444-3171) **292**
M L A Bibliography *see* M L A International Bibliography **5407**
• M L A Directory of Periodicals (Modern Language Association of America) (USA ISSN 0197-0380) **5407**
M L A Directory of Scholarly Presses in Language and Literature (Modern Language Association of America) (USA ISSN 1057-2899) **2993**
• M L A Forum (Michigan Library Association) (USA ISSN 1539-4123) **5030**
M L A Index and Bibliography Series *see* Music Library Association. Index and Bibliography Series **6632**
• M L A International Bibliography (Modern Language Association of America) (USA) **5407**
M L A Job Information Lists (Modern Language Association of America) (USA) **6700**
• M L A News (Chicago) (Medical Library Association) (USA ISSN 0541-5489) **5663**
M L A News (Raleigh) (Multi-Housing Laundry Association) (USA) **2243**
M L A Newsletter *see* Music Library Association. Newsletter **6591**
M L A Newsletter (Minneapolis) (Minnesota Library Association) (USA ISSN 0748-9285) **5030**
M L A Newsletter (New York) (Modern Language Association of America) (USA ISSN 0160-5720) **2993**
M L A Northwest. Annual Reports and Accounts *see* Museums Libraries and Archives North West. Annual Report and Accounts **6532**
M L A's Feedback *see* Feedback (North Sydney) **286**
M L B D Newsletter (Motilal Banarsidass (Delhi)) (IND ISSN 0970-1435) **7698**
▼ M L B Insiders Club Magazine (Major League Baseball) (USA ISSN 1941-5060) **8238**
M L C U K Market Survey (Meat and Livestock Commission United Kingdom) (GBR ISSN 0969-9791) **292**
M L D S Newz *see* Vitalia **5932**
M L D S Report *see* Vitalia **5932**
M L M Australia & New Zealand (Multi-Level Marketing) (AUS ISSN 1832-1739) **1830**
• M L M Insider (Multi-Level Marketing) (USA) **1830**
M L M Magazine Australia & New Zealand *see* M L M Australia & New Zealand **1830**
• M L M Woman Newsletter (Multi-Level Marketing) (USA) **1830**
• ➤ M L N (Modern Language Notes) (USA ISSN 0026-7910) **5149**
M L O *see* Medical Laboratory Observer **5909**
M L Q *see* Mathematical Logic Quarterly **5513**
M L Q *see* Modern Language Quarterly **5335**
M L R *see* The Modern Law Review **4735**
M L R *see* Michigan Law Review **4733**
M L R *see* Montana Law Review **4736**
M L R *see* Municipal Litigation Reporter **7498**
M L S *see* M L S: Marketing Library Services **5030**
M L S: Marketing Library Services (USA ISSN 0896-3908) **5030**
M L Seidman Memorial Town Hall Lecture Series (USA ISSN 0076-1729) **7152**
• m.logistics (GBR ISSN 1474-8193) **2369**
M M *see* Maquinas & Metais **5456**
M M *see* Moving Manchester **3968**
M - M *see* Mind - Magic **6742**
M M A Authority Magazine *see* Mixed Martial Arts Authority Magazine **8187**
M M A C Milwaukee Commerce Hot-Line Annual Report (Metropolitan Milwaukee Association of Commerce) (USA) **1430**
▼ M M A Cage (Mixed Martial Arts) (USA ISSN 1947-539X) **8186**
▼ M M A Worldwide (Mixed Martial Arts) (USA ISSN 1937-1071) **8186**
M M & D *see* Materials Management & Distribution **8503**
M M & M *see* Medical Marketing & Media **6860**
M M & M Healthcare Advertising Goldbook *see* Medical Marketing & Media **6860**
M M Branchen Handbuch (Musik Markt) (DEU ISSN 0722-9119) **6586**
M M C *see* Museum Management and Curatorship **6531**
M M C A News (Montana Motor Carriers Association, Inc.) (USA) **8672**
M M D B *see* A C M International Workshop on Multimedia Databases. Proceedings **2528**
M M - das aktuelle MonatsMagazin (DEU) **3852**
M M E *see* Money Management Executive **1640**
M M E E M *see* Minnesota Mediterranean and East European Monographs **3550**
M M H *see* Modern Materials Handling **5457**
M M I Bulletin (Medicaid Management Institute) (USA) **8054**
• M M I Interaktiv (Mensch Maschine Interaktion) (DEU ISSN 1439-7854) **2454**
M M I J International Conferences. Proceedings (Mining and Materials Processing Institute of Japan) (JPN) **6321**
M M I P *see* Music Management & International Promotion **6591**
M M I R *see* Military Miniatures in Review **4340**
• M M I S Xtra (MultiMedia & Internet@School) (USA) **2950**
M M J *see* Makerere Medical Journal **5664**
M M L *see* Managing the Modern Laboratory **2072**
The M M L Series *see* Microspheres, Microcapsules & Liposomes **6861**
M M Logistik (Maschinenmarkt) (DEU) **5455**
M M M *see* Motorcaravan & Motorhome Monthly **8323**
M M M *see* Many Mountains Moving **5330**
M M Magazyn Przemyslowy (Maschinen Markt) (POL ISSN 0945-5485) **5455**
▼ M M Maintenance and Facility Management (ITA ISSN 1971-1735) **1897**
• M M Makina Magazin (TUR ISSN 1301-0425) **5455**
M M - Maschinenmarkt (DEU ISSN 0341-5775) **5455**
M M Money & Technologies (Maschinen Markt) (UKR) **5455**
M M Muszaki Magazin (HUN ISSN 1417-0132) **5455**
M M News (Manhattan Medical) (USA) **5663**
M M Nieuws (Marketing Management) (NLD ISSN 1566-6247) **503**
M M P *see* Molecular Plant Pathology **802**
M M Prumyslove Spektrum (Maschinen Markt) (CZE ISSN 1212-2572) **5455**
M M R *see* Multimedia und Recht **2488**
M M R *see* Musical Merchandise Review **6593**
• M M R (Mass Market Retailers) (USA ISSN 1080-0794) **1774**
M M S *see* Mathematics and Mechanics of Solids **7026**
M M S *see* Modern Machine Shop **5457**
M M S *see* Multiscale Modeling & Simulation: a S I A M Interdisciplinary Journal **5519**
M M S *see* The Money for Main Street Monitor **1150**
M M S A *see* Mortgage Market Statistical Annual **2017**
M M S Mag (Mining and Manufacturing Systems) (ZAF ISSN 1818-2380) **6469**
• M M S Offshore Stats (Minerals Management Service) (USA) **6800**
M M T *see* Military Medical/C B R N Technology **5679**
M M T C News (Minerals and Metals Trading Corp. of India Ltd.) (IND ISSN 0377-1482) **6469**
M M - The Industrial Magazine (Maschine Market) (THA ISSN 1686-6525) **5455**
M M - The Industry Magazine (IND) **1146**
M M U - E R I Journal for Deleuzian Studies *see* Actual Virtual **5249**
➤ M M W - Fortschritte der Medizin (Muenchener Medizinische Wochenschrift) (DEU ISSN 1438-3276) **5663**
M M W - Fortschritte der Medizin. Beilage *see* M M W - Fortschritte der Medizin **5663**
M M W - Fortschritte der Medizin. Extrablatt *see* M M W - Fortschritte der Medizin **5663**
• M M W R (Morbidity and Mortality Weekly Report) (USA ISSN 0149-2195) **7530**
M M W R. C D C Surveillance Summaries *see* M M W R. Surveillance Summaries **5663**
• M M W R. Surveillance Summaries (Morbidity and Mortality Weekly Report) (USA ISSN 1546-0738) **5663**
• M M Xiandai Zhizao (Modern Manufacturing) (CHN ISSN 1671-9395) **1897**
M M Zulieferer (Maschinenmarkt) (DEU ISSN 1865-5823) **5455**
M Magazine (GBR ISSN 1461-8990) **2160**
• M Magazine (USA ISSN 1533-9149) **2200**
M - Menschen, Machen, Medien (DEU ISSN 0946-1132) **4579**
M - Moderne Metalltechnik *see* Moderne Metalltechnik und Kunststofftechnik **6326**
M Museos de Mexico y del Mundo (MEX) **6528**
M. Muzykal'nyi Zhurnal *see* Metal Music Magazine **6587**
M N *see* Molecular Neurobiology **739**
M N A Accent *see* Minnesota Nursing Accent **5970**
M N A S S A *see* Astronomical Society of Southern Africa. Monthly Notes **570**
M N C H *see* The Men's Book Chicago **6295**
M N R Nuus *see* M R C News **5663**
M O (Mandarin Oriental) (GBR) **8784**
• M O C I (Moniteur du Commerce International) (FRA ISSN 0026-9719) **1575**
M O C I. Hors Serie (Moniteur du Commerce International) (FRA ISSN 1253-0808) **1575**
M O D Contracts Bulletin *see* United Kingdom. Ministry of Defence. Contracts Bulletin **6451**
M O D Defence Contracts Bulletin *see* United Kingdom. Ministry of Defence. Defence Contracts Bulletin **6451**
M O D - Music, Opera, Dance & Drama in Asia, the Pacific and North America *see* Performing Arts Yearbook **8476**
M O D News *see* United Kingdom. Ministry of Defence. News **1186**
M O E - Wirtschaft in Mittel- und Osteuropa (DEU ISSN 1864-1822) **1497**
M O I *see* Men of Integrity **7662**
M O M A (Museum of Modern Art) (USA ISSN 0893-0279) **6528**
M O - Metalloberflaeche (DEU ISSN 0026-0797) **6321**
M O N E T *see* Mobile Networks and Applications **2501**
M O P S A Newsletter (Missouri Political Science Association) (USA ISSN 0464-1973) **7152**
M O S (Memoires Optiques et Systemes) (FRA ISSN 1761-9955) **7080**
M O S T Journal on Multicultural Societies *see* International Journal on Multicultural Societies **8110**
M O T C's Notebook (National Organization of Mothers of Twins Clubs, Inc.) (USA ISSN 8756-9965) **8872**
• M O T S (Mots, Ordinateurs, Textes, Societes) (FRA ISSN 0243-6450) **7152**
M P *see* Modern Philology **5152**
M P *see* Music Perception **6591**
M P A Bulletin (Maine Press Association) (USA) **4579**
M P A E A Newsletter (Mountain Plains Adult Education Association) (USA) **2944**
M P A - Messen, Pruefen, Automatisieren (DEU ISSN 0945-7143) **6403**
M P A: Sales Edge (Magazine Publishers of America) (USA) **28**
M P & T *see* Marketers, Purchasers and Trading Companies **6778**
M P C World (Mail and Parcel Centers) (USA ISSN 1081-9347) **2354**
M P E J *see* Mathematical Physics Electronic Journal **5514**
M P E R *see* Michigan Public Employee Reporter **4733**
• M P Exposure Magazine (USA) **6971**
M P I Series in Biological Cybernetics (Max-Planck-Institut) (DEU ISSN 1618-3037) **768**
M P J *see* Medizinprodukte Journal **5677**
M P L A Newsletter (Mountain Plains Library Association) (USA ISSN 0145-6180) **5030**
M P L now (Muncie Public Library) (USA) **5031**
M P M I *see* Molecular Plant - Microbe Interactions **740**
M P M - Mexican Advertising Agencies Directory *see* Directorio M P M - Agencias y Anunciantes **24**
M P M - Mexican Audiovisual Media Rates & Data *see* Directorio M P M - Medios Audio-visuales **38**
M P M - Mexican Print Media Rates & Data *see* Directorio M P M - Medios Impresos **38**
M P M N *see* Medical Product Manufacturing News **4489**
M.P. Medical Practice *see* Medical Practice **5670**
M P N *see* Motorcycle Product News **8263**
M P O B Technology (Malaysian Palm Oil Board) (MYS) **135**
• M P P Leads (Management, Politics and Philosophy) (DNK) **1774**
M P P Working Paper *see* Copenhagen Business School. Department of Management, Politics and Philosophy. Wp **1086**
M P R *see* MedizinProdukte Recht **5909**
M P R *see* Monthly Prescribing Reference **6862**
▼ M P R (Hematology/Oncology Edition) (Monthly Prescribing Reference) (USA) **6859**
• M P R (Long Term Care Edition) (Monthly Prescribing Reference) (USA ISSN 1938-9531) **6859**
• M P R (Obstetrician & Gynecologist Edition) (Monthly Prescribing Reference) (USA) **6859**
• M P R (Pediatricians' Edition) (Monthly Prescribing Reference) (USA) **6859**
▼ M P R (Pharmacists' Edition) (Monthly Prescribing Reference) (USA ISSN 1938-9523) **6859**
M P R (Residents' Edition) (Monthly Prescribing Reference) (USA) **6859**
• M P R (Urologists Edition) (Monthly Prescribing Reference) (USA ISSN 1938-9515) **6859**
M P R C Report on Finance, Commerce, Industry: Indonesia (MYS) **1497**
M P R C Report on Finance, Commerce, Industry: Indonesia. Supplement (MYS) **1497**
M P R C Report on Finance, Commerce, Industry: Singapore (MYS) **1497**
M P R C Report on Finance, Commerce, Industry: South East Asia (MYS) **1497**
M P R C Report on Finance, Commerce, Industry: Thailand (MYS) **1497**
M P R Research File *see* E C R Research File **1676**
• M P S Casebook (Medical Protection Society) (GBR ISSN 1366-4409) **5663**
➤ M P S - S I A M Series on Optimization (Mathematical Programming Society - Society for Industrial and Applied Mathematics) (USA ISSN 1549-2540) **5510**
M P T. Metallurgical Plant and Technology International (DEU ISSN 0935-7254) **6321**
M P T. Metallurgicheskoe Proizvodstvo i Tekhnologiya Metallurgicheskih Protsessov (RUS ISSN 0934-8077) **6321**
• M P T Review (Modern Portfolio Theory) (USA) **1638**
M P T V *see* Moving Pictures Television **6508**
M P W *see* Modern Plastics Worldwide **7095**
• M P Z Info (Museums-Paedagogisches Zentrum) (DEU) **6528**
• M P Z Museumsdienst (Museums-Paedagogisches Zentrum) (DEU) **6528**
• M P Z Programm (Museums-Paedagogisches Zentrum) (DEU) **6528**
• M P Z Publik (Museums-Paedagogisches Zentrum) (DEU) **6541**
M Ph *see* Medizin und Philosophie **6934**
M-plus *see* Miljoeaktuellt Plus **3453**
M Q *see* The Musical Quarterly **6594**
M Q R. Mining Quarrying & Recycling *see* Mining Quarrying & Recycling **6473**
• M R (Medicina Riabilitativa) (ITA ISSN 1827-1995) **6112**
A M R *see* Academy of Management Review **1723**
M @ R *see* Marketing @ Retail **1831**
M R (Norwalk) (Menswear Retailing) (USA ISSN 1049-6726) **2248**
M R A *see* Le Modele Reduit d'Avion **4341**
M R A A Newsletter (Marine Retailers Association of America) (USA) **8277**
M R A Blue Book Research Services Directory (Marketing Research Association, Inc.) (USA) **1830**
M R C News (Medical Research Council) (GBR ISSN 0143-0130) **5663**
M R C News/M N R Nuus (Medical Research Council) (ZAF ISSN 1017-611X) **5663**
M R C Strategic Plan (Medical Research Council) (GBR) **5663**
M R C Technical Paper (Mekong River Commission) (KHM ISSN 1683-1489) **3601**
M R D D Express *see* D D D Express **3038**
M R D S *see* Mineral Resources Data System **6470**
M R E Action (Manitoba Real Estate Association) (CAN) **7599**
M R H R *see* Manchester Region History Review **4242**
M R I *see* Materials Research Innovations **7881**
M R I Bankers' Guide to Foreign Currency (Monetary Research Institute) (USA ISSN 1055-3851) **1366**

Title

M R I Clinics see Magnetic Resonance Imaging Clinics of North America 6202
M R L see Mathematical Research Letters 5514
M R N see Management Research Review 1776
M R O Management (Maintenance, Repair and Overhaul) (GBR ISSN 1466-6448) 8548
M R O News Focus (Maintenance, Repair and Overhaul) (GBR) 8548
M R O Today (Maintenance, Repair & Operations) (USA ISSN 1091-0638) 1146
M R Personal Health & Wealth (Main Report) (NZL ISSN 1177-6846) 2639
M R R see Maximum Rock 'n' Roll 6586
• ➤ M R S Bulletin (Materials Research Society) (USA ISSN 0883-7694) 3352
• ➤ M R S Internet Journal of Nitride Semiconductor Research (Materials Research Society) (USA ISSN 1092-5783) 3352
M R S Q see Medical Reference Services Quarterly 5031
M R Series see Monash University Accident Research Centre. Minor Reports Series 8632
M R W see Materials Recycling Week 6322
M R W see Magic, Ritual, and Witchcraft 6742
M R W Handbook (Materials Recycling Week) (GBR) 3508
M S see Medecine Sciences 5666
• M S A Link (Muslim Students' Association) (USA ISSN 1943-8400) 7713
M S A N see Marlowe Society of America Newsletter 5331
M S A News Journal (Motor Schools Association of G.B.) (GBR) 8589
M S A Newslink (Motor Schools Association of Great Britain) (GBR) 8260
M S & T see Modern Simulation and Training 6437
M S B Credentialing see Medical Staff Briefing 4107
M S Bladet see Action Magazine 7219
M S C Buyer's Reference (USA) 5455
• M S Canada (Multiple Sclerosis) (CAN ISSN 0315-1131) 6159
† M S Coder (Microsoft) (POL ISSN 1896-4745) 8972
➤ M S D A Journal (USA) 5855
M S D D Digest (PHL) 8054
• M S D N Magazine (Microsoft Development Network) (USA ISSN 1528-4859) 2508
M S D N Magazine. Australia - New Zealand Edition (Microsoft Development Network) (SGP) 2594
M S D N Magazine Europe (Microsoft Developers Network) (DEU) 2508
M S D N Magazine. India Edition (Microsoft Development Network) (SGP) 2594
M S D N Magazine. Southeast Asia Edition (Microsoft Development Network) (SGP) 2594
M S D S see Material Safety Data Sheets 6681
M S D S + CHEMINFO see Material Safety Data Sheets 6681
M S D S Software Report (Materials Safety Data Sheets) (USA ISSN 1074-1984) 3482
M S Exchange (Multiple Sclerosis) (USA) 6159
M S F at Work (Manufacturing, Science and Finance Union) (GBR) 4598
M S G Bulletins see Mesemb Study Group. Bulletin 801
M S H D A Review (State Housing Development Authority) (USA) 4419
M S I Newsletter see Marketing Science Institute. Newsletter 1833
• M S in Focus (Multiple Sclerosis) (GBR ISSN 1478-467X) 6159
M S J see Mayan Studies Journal 5150
➤ M S L A Journal (Manitoba School Library Association) (CAN ISSN 1189-7163) 3071
M S L Law Review see M S L Review 4726
M S L Review (Massachusetts School of Law at Andover) (USA ISSN 1530-3217) 4726
M S M (Marche Suisse des Machines) (CHE ISSN 1422-8823) 5455
• M S M C e-News (Medical Society of Milwaukee County) (USA) 5663
M S M C Happenings (Mount Saint Mary College) (USA) 2290
M S N see Mortgage Servicing News 1369
M S N Z Information Series see Multiple Sclerosis Society of New Zealand Information Series 6162
• M S O R Connections (Maths, Stats & Operational Research) (GBR ISSN 1473-4869) 5510
• M S Ontario (Multiple Sclerosis) (CAN ISSN 0707-0934) 6159
M S P B Digest Service see Merit Systems Protection Board Service 1697
M S Q see Managing Service Quality 1778
M S Q R see M S Quarterly Report 6159
M S Quarterly Report (USA ISSN 0738-3967) 6159
• M S R B Manual (Municipal Security Rulemaking Board) (USA) 1146
• M S R Belgian (MailServeR) (BEL) 3549
▼ M S R I Mathematical Circles Library (Mathematical Sciences Research Institute) (USA ISSN 1944-8074) 5510
M S R Magazin (Messen Steuern Regeln) (DEU ISSN 0936-692X) 3324
† M S R Youth (Middle School Review) (NZL ISSN 1178-5454) 8972
M S Reality Bytes see Living M S Magazine 6159
M S S see Medieval Sermon Studies 5332
M S S P see Mechanical Systems and Signal Processing 3389
M S T A Action Line see Action Line (Annapolis) 2965
M S T English Quarterly (D C S Manila Teachers of Secondary English) (PHL ISSN 0047-5289) 3071
M S T News (Microsystems Technology) (DEU ISSN 0948-3128) 2473
• M S U Alumni Magazine (Michigan State University) (USA ISSN 0273-6977) 2290
M S U - D O E Plant Research Laboratory. Annual Report (Michigan State University - Department of Energy) (USA ISSN 0893-1674) 3141
M S U Exponent see Exponent 2283
➤ M S U Professional Papers (Mindanao State University) (PHL) 7984
M S U R J see McGill Science Undergraduate Research Journal 7882
M S U U Newsletter: Gleanings (Ministerial Sisterhood Unitarian Universalist) (USA) 7738
M S W Management (Municipal Solid Waste) (USA ISSN 1053-7899) 3508
M S W Solutions (Municipal Solid Waste) (USA ISSN 1087-5743) 3509
M Six Cine Video see M6 Cine Video 2402
M Six Kid see M6 Kid 2200
M Six Multimedia see M6 Multimedia 2576
M Six Tomb Raider see M6 Tomb Raider 2478
M Six Turbo see M6 Turbo 8589
• The M Street Journal (USA ISSN 1052-7109) 2360
The M Street Radio Directory (USA ISSN 1052-7117) 2360
M T see Management Today 1777
M T see Mathematics Teaching 5516
M T see Musical Times 6594
M T (GBR ISSN 1350-4312) 6586
M T see Marinarkeologisk Tidsskrift 405
M T see Mass Transit 8503
M T see Mortgage Technology 7600
M T see Microscopy Today 900
• M T A Dialog (Medizinisch Technische Assistenten) (DEU ISSN 1439-071X) 5663
M T A Pediatria (Metodos Terapeutico-diagnosticos de Actualidad) (ESP ISSN 0210-8135) 6096
The (Year) M T A S Salary and Fringe Benefit Survey (University of Tennessee at Knoxville, Municipal Technical Advisory Service) (USA) 1696
M T A Today (Massachusetts Teachers Association) (USA ISSN 0898-2481) 2884
M T & M (Manufacturing Technology & Management) (IND) 5455
M T C see More than Classic 367
M T Cardio see Medecine Therapeutique Cardio 5795
M T D see Modern Tire Dealer 7825
M T D - Medizin-Technischer Dialog und Der Sanitaetsfachhandel (DEU ISSN 0935-137X) 5663
M T E see Medecine Therapeutique Medecine de la Reproduction 5897
M T E see Micro Technology Europe 2524
M T E D see Mathematics Teacher Education and Development 2885
M T Europe see Manufacturing Today Europe 1898
M T F-Nyt see Hoerelsen 4074
• M T I A C Current Awareness Bulletin (U.S. Department of Defense, Manufacturing Technology Information Analysis Center) (USA) 3388
• M T I Econews (Eco) (HUN) 1431
M T I Reporter see Solidarity Newsletter 4602
M T International see Material & Technik Moebel 4560
M T Logistica (Motor Transport) (GBR ISSN 1356-9104) 8672
M T Medecine de la Reproduction see Medecine Therapeutique Medecine de la Reproduction 5897
M T - Medizintechnik (DEU) 5663
M T. Mejeritidskrift foer Finlands Svenskbygd (FIN ISSN 0782-2383) 266
M T N Week see EuroWeek 1340
M T P. Medecine Therapeutique Pediatrie see Medecine Therapeutique Pediatrie 6096
M T S see Music Theory Spectrum 6592
M T S Echo (Manitoba Telephone System) (CAN ISSN 0849-6501) 2369
M T S Journal see Memphis Theological Seminary Journal 7767
M T S Testing News (USA) 6321
M T T E L O (Maa- ja Elintarviketalouden Tutkimuskeskus) (FIN ISSN 1797-7312) 135
M T T L R see Michigan Telecommunications & Technology Law Review 4734
M T V Ireland (Music Television) (USA ISSN 1939-5639) 8732
M T V Magazine (Music Television) (USA) 6586
M T Vs S N (Music Television's Spankin New) (USA) 6586
M T W see Marketing to Women 1833
M T Yellow Pages see Mauritius Telecom Yellow Pages 2016
• M T Z (Motortechnische Zeitschrift) (DEU ISSN 0024-8525) 8589
M TelePal (JPN) 6506
M the Lifestyle Magazine of MGM Mirage see M (San Diego) 5076
M - the Magazine for Britannia Members (GBR) 7599
† M U C G - Raker (Macquarie University, Caving Group) (AUS ISSN 1035-4697) 8972
M U D O T see Mudot 4419
• M U F A C E (Mutualidad General de Funcionarios Civiles del Estado) (ESP ISSN 1695-2995) 7497
M U F O N - International U F O Symposium Proceedings (Mutual U F O Network, Inc.) (USA) 65
M U F O N U F O Journal (Mutual U F O Network, Inc.) (USA ISSN 0270-6822) 65
M U L P see Monash University. Linguistics Papers 5152
M U M see Melbourne University Magazine 2291
M U M (Magic, Unity, Might) (USA ISSN 0047-5300) 4339
M U S E (Mainz University Studies in English) (DEU) 5329
• M U S E, MUsic SEarch (USA ISSN 1054-2639) 6631
M U T C D see Manual on Uniform Traffic Control Devices 8503
M V A Viewpoints (Minnesota Vocational Association) (USA ISSN 0464-2082) 2884
M V M see Mobility and Vehicles Mechanics 8591
▼ M V P (Most Valuable Players) (NZL ISSN 1177-6757) 8589
M V P Magazine see IceBerg Magazine 3538
M V R see Motor Vehicle Reports 4824
• M V R Book (Motor Vehicle Report) (USA ISSN 1052-4568) 8589
M W A Annual see Mystery Writers' Annual 5414
M W Golf see Mountain West Golf 8239
M W J see Maritime Workers' Journal 8653
M W L see Midwest Living 3981
M W Metal Cutting see Jinshu Jiagong. Lengjiagong 6318
M W Metal Forming see Jinshu Jiagong. Rejiagong 6318
M W P see Metalworking Production 6326
M W R Today (Morale, Welfare, and Recreation) (USA ISSN 1089-7054) 6431
M W V Jahresbericht (Mineraloelwirtschafts Verband e.V.) (DEU ISSN 0076-891X) 2126
M W - Zeitschrift fuer Medienwirtschaft und Medienmanagement see MedienWirtschaft 2360
• M Web Magazine (MLT ISSN 1093-5193) 2508
• The M Word (USA) 4980
M World see MWorld 1780
M X see Weekly Book Newlsetter Media Extra 8998
M X see Media Extra 7567
M X (AUS) 3795
M X (DEU) 8186
• M X (USA) 1146
M X Machine Magazine (USA ISSN 1538-313X) 8260
M X Magazine (FRA ISSN 1285-8374) 8186
† M X Racer (Motocross) (USA ISSN 1531-1198) 8972
M X U K (Motor Cross United Kingdom) (GBR) 8260
M Y M see Marketing y Medios 29
† M-Zone (DEU) 8972
M2 (NZL ISSN 1176-9777) 3795
M2 Nordic Business Report see Nordic Business Report 1154
M2M see M 2 M 2332
• M3 (SWE ISSN 1650-5786) 2572
M3 Hemmabio (SWE) 2402
M6 Cine Video (FRA ISSN 1269-0015) 2402
M6 Dance (FRA ISSN 1265-356X) 6586
M6 Fantastique (FRA ISSN 1275-8345) 6506
M6 Kid (FRA ISSN 1253-5532) 2200
M6 Multimedia (FRA ISSN 1287-6364) 2576
M6 Tomb Raider (FRA ISSN 1628-3414) 2478
M6 Turbo (FRA ISSN 1278-6691) 8589
M8 see M 8 6294
Ma Cuisine (FRA ISSN 1954-8281) 4363
MA F L A Newsletter (Massachusetts Foreign Language Association) (USA) 5149
† Ma K'dai (ISR ISSN 0334-0902) 8972
Ma Maison A des Idees (FRA ISSN 1960-7911) 4545
▼ Ma Maison A des Idees. Design (FRA ISSN 1959-7649) 4545
Ma Part de Verite (FRA ISSN 1633-8901) 7984
Ma Petite Entreprise.net (FRA ISSN 1779-031X) 2564
Ma Tsui Hsueh Tsa Chi see Acta Anaesthesiologica Taiwanica 5768
Maa Bra (SWE ISSN 0346-6280) 6992
Maa- ja Elintarviketalouden Tutkimuskeskus E L O see M T T E L O 135
Maadini (COD ISSN 0250-538X) 2753
Maag Lever Darm Stichting. Nieuws see Vitalia 5932
Maagilised Ruudud (EST) 8186
Maajan - Die Quelle (CHE ISSN 1011-4009) 7726
Maakodu (EST ISSN 0235-6899) 135
Maal & Medel (SWE ISSN 0345-7702) 3654
Maal & Maele (DNK ISSN 0106-567X) 5149
• ➤ Maal og Minne (NOR ISSN 0024-855X) 5149
Maalai Malar (IND) 3884
Maalardalen - Bergslagens Affaerer (SWE) 1774
Maalarilehti see Vaeri ja Pinta 6721
Maalarmaestaren (SWE ISSN 0280-8226) 6718
Maalarnas Facktidning (SWE ISSN 0345-7710) 6718
Maaleht (EST ISSN 1406-2984) 3836
Maaltidskunskap (SWE ISSN 1652-2656) 3654
Maamajandus (EST ISSN 1406-6238) 135
Maanadens Affaerer see Veckans Affaerer 1191
Maanadsrapport oever Anmaelningspliktiga Djursjukdomar see Monthly Report on Notifiable Diseases of Animals 8803
Maandblad Aktiviteitensektor see A S 8022
Maandblad Belasting Beschouwingen (NLD ISSN 0005-8335) 1934
Maandblad Geestelijke Volksgezondheid see M G V 6159
Maandblad voor Ondewijs in Vlaanderen see Klasse 3026
Maandblad voor Vermogensrecht (NLD ISSN 1574-5767) 4835
Maandschrift Economie see Kwartaalschrift Economie 1143
Maandschrift voor het Gevangeniswezen see Balans 2645
Maanedsmagasinet Erhverv/Vest see Erhverv/Vest 1742
Maanedsmagasinet IN see IN 8868
• Maanedsskrift for Praktisk Laegegerning (DNK ISSN 0373-2746) 5663
† Ma'anit (ISR) 8972
Maankaytto (FIN ISSN 0782-8438) 3278
Maanmittaus/Surveying (FIN ISSN 0047-5319) 3278
Maanpuolustuskorkeakoulu. Johtamisen Laitos. Julkaisusarja 1: Tutkimuksia/National Defence University. Department of Leadership and Management Studies. Publication Series 1. Research Reports (FIN ISSN 1455-7495) 6431
Maanpuolustuskorkeakoulu. Johtamisen Laitos. Julkaisusarja 2: Artikkelikokoelmat/National Defence University. Department of Leadership and Management Studies. Publication Series 2. Article Collection (FIN ISSN 1456-7377) 6431
Maanpuolustuskorkeakoulu. Johtamisen Laitos. Julkaisusarja 3: Tyopapereita (FIN ISSN 1456-7385) 6431
• Maanpuolustuskorkeakoulu. Strategian Laitos. Julkaisusarja 1: Strategian Tutkimuksia/National Defence University. Department of Strategic Studies. Series 1, Strategic Research (FIN ISSN 1236-4959) 6431
• Maanpuolustuskorkeakoulu. Strategian Laitos. Julkaisusarja 2: Strategian Tutkimusselosteita/ National Defence University. Department of Strategic Studies. Series 2, Research Reports (FIN ISSN 1455-2108) 6431
• Maanpuolustuskorkeakoulu. Strategian Laitos. Julkaisusarja 3: Strategian Asiatietoa (FIN ISSN 1236-4975) 6432
• Maanpuolustuskorkeakoulu. Strategian Laitos. Julkaisusarja 4: Strategian Tyopapereita/National Defence College. Department of Strategic and Defence Studies. Series 4, Working Papers (FIN ISSN 1236-4983) 6432
Maansiirto see Infrarakentaja 3270
Ha-Maapil (USA ISSN 0017-6850) 7153
Ma'arakhot (ISR ISSN 0464-2147) 6432
Maarav (USA ISSN 0149-5712) 5149
Ma'arif (IRN ISSN 1015-2822) 7713
Al-Ma'arif (PAK ISSN 0002-4015) 7713
• Ma'ariv (ISR) 3895
Ma'ariv Lano'ar (ISR ISSN 0333-5461) 2200
† Ma'aseh Hoshev (ISR ISSN 0303-142X) 8972
• Maaseudun Tulevaisuus (FIN ISSN 0355-3787) 135
De Maasgouw (NLD ISSN 1380-4170) 4241
Maastricht Journal of European and Comparative Law (CHE ISSN 1023-263X) 4726
Maastrichtse Fiscale Symposia (NLD) 1934
Maataloustilastollinen Kuukausikatsaus see Finland. Maa- ja Metsatalousministerio. Tietopalvelukeskus Tietokappa (Online) 180
Maatgevend see Zorgbelang 4070
Maatschappij & Politiek (NLD ISSN 1566-1555) 2884
Maatschappij en Politiek see Maatschappij & Politiek 2884
Maatschappijbelangen (NLD ISSN 0024-8843) 1897
Maatskaplike Werk see Social Work 8070
• Maatwerk (NLD ISSN 1567-6587) 8054
M@+abs see m@bs 1249
• m@bs (DEU ISSN 1434-7490) 1249
▼ • ➤ mAbs (Monoclonal Antibodies) (USA ISSN 1942-0862) 5763
• Mabuhay (PHL ISSN 0217-6998) 8784
Mac+ (BRA ISSN 1809-676X) 2576
Mac Addict see Macfe 2576
Mac and Co Magazine see Mac & Co 8972
Mac Design see Layers 2488
† Mac & Co (FRA ISSN 1950-1773) 8972
Mac Journal (GBR ISSN 1355-3046) 449
• Mac Life (DEU ISSN 1860-9988) 2576
Mac / Life see Macfe 2576
• Macfe (USA ISSN 1935-4010) 2576
• Mac Net Journal (USA) 2564
Mac People see MacPeople 2523
Mac Power (JPN) 2577
▼ • Macabre Cadaver (USA ISSN 1943-9296) 5444
MacAddict see Macfe 2576
▼ Macalester Civic Forum (USA ISSN 1941-3742) 8119
Macalester Today (USA) 2290
Macao. Census and Statistics Department. Activities Plan see Macao. Direccao dos Servicos de Estatistica e Censos. Plano de Actividades 8386
Macao. Census and Statistics Department. Activities Report see Macao. Direccao dos Servicos de Estatistica e Censos. Relatorio de Actividades 8386

• Macquarie University Annual Report (AUS ISSN 0815-578X) **2993**
• Macquarie University Calendar of Governance, Legislation & Rules (AUS ISSN 1446-4691) **6281**
Macquarie University, Caving Group Raker *see* M U C G - Raker **8972**
• Macquarie University Handbook of Postgraduate Studies (AUS ISSN 1446-4705) **2993**
• Macquarie University. Handbook of Undergraduate Studies (AUS ISSN 1446-4713) **2993**
† • Macquarie University News (AUS ISSN 1327-7774) **8972**
Macquarie University Research Report (AUS ISSN 0159-2165) **2993**
• MacRae's Blue Book (CAN ISSN 0886-9189) **2013**
Macrame (ITA ISSN 1594-9060) **537**
▼ • Macrame (Florence) (ITA ISSN 1971-6249) **4419**
Macro Economische Verkenning (NLD ISSN 0920-6183) **1720**
Macrobiotics Today (USA) **6663**
• Macroeconomia (MEX) **1720**
• ➤ Macroeconomic Dynamics (GBR ISSN 1365-1005) **1720**
Macroeconomics *see* American Economic Journal. Macroeconomics **1717**
▼ • Macroeconomics and Finance in Emerging Market Economies (GBR ISSN 1752-0843) **1720**
• ➤ Macroeconomics Annual (USA ISSN 0889-3365) **1720**
▼ Macrolinguistics (USA ISSN 1934-5755) **5149**
Macromedia User Journal (Gualala) (USA ISSN 1065-3929) **2572**
• ➤ Macromolecular Bioscience (DEU ISSN 1616-5187) **738**
• ➤ Macromolecular Chemistry and Physics (DEU ISSN 1022-1352) **2126**
• ➤ Macromolecular Materials & Engineering (DEU ISSN 1438-7492) **2126**
• ➤ Macromolecular Rapid Communications (DEU ISSN 1022-1336) **2126**
▼ • ➤ Macromolecular Reaction Engineering (DEU ISSN 1862-832X) **3208**
➤ Macromolecular Research (KOR ISSN 1598-5032) **2126**
Macromolecular Structures (GBR ISSN 0963-6986) **2126**
• ➤ Macromolecular Symposia (DEU ISSN 1022-1360) **2126**
• ➤ Macromolecular Theory and Simulations (DEU ISSN 1022-1344) **2126**
• ➤ Macromolecules (USA ISSN 0024-9297) **2126**
• Macromolecules Containing Metal and Metal-Like Elements (USA ISSN 1545-438X) **2127**
• MacroPolitics de Mexico (MEX) **1497**
• MacroView (GBR) **6859**
• MacTech Magazine (USA ISSN 1067-8360) **2577**
▼ MacTribe (USA ISSN 1942-7298) **2577**
Macular Degeneration & Other Diseases of the Aging Eye (USA ISSN 1938-6672) **6046**
MACup (DEU ISSN 0935-6282) **2577**
MACup (RUS) **2577**
MACup Extra (DEU ISSN 0935-6290) **2577**
• MacUser (GBR ISSN 0269-3275) **2577**
MacUser's Mac Sources *see* MacUser **2577**
• Macwelt (DEU ISSN 0937-4906) **2577**
• Macworld (GBR ISSN 0957-2341) **2577**
• MacWorld (USA ISSN 0741-8647) **2577**
• Macworld Espana (ESP ISSN 1132-1156) **2577**
Macworld France *see* Univers Mac **8996**
• MacWorld Italia (ITA) **2577**
Macworld Korea (KOR) **2577**
• Macworld Sweden (SWE ISSN 0284-3005) **2577**
• Macworld Turkey (TUR ISSN 1300-6169) **2577**
Mad (DEU ISSN 0723-9289) **5226**
• Mad (USA ISSN 0024-9319) **5226**
† Mad About Dogs (GBR ISSN 1464-553X) **8972**
MAD Classics (AUS) **2200**
Mad Color Classics (USA ISSN 1550-4239) **5226**
Mad Guide *see* Madison Relocation Guide **8972**
Mad Kids (USA) **2200**
Mad Magazine Australia (AUS ISSN 0726-1810) **2200**
Mad Maths (GBR ISSN 1470-0158) **2200**
• Mad & Bolig Magasinet (DNK ISSN 0906-4060) **4545**
Mad Poets Review (USA) **5426**
Mad Rhythms (USA ISSN 1094-5555) **3980**
Mad XL (USA ISSN 1540-9775) **5226**
• ➤ Madagascar Conservation & Development (CHE ISSN 1662-2510) **3451**
Madagascar. Direction Generale de l'Institut National de la Statistique. Bulletin de Statistique Mensuelle (MDG) **1250**
Madagascar. Ministere de la Production Agricole et du Patrimoine Foncier. Statistiques Agricoles. Annuaire (MDG) **183**
Madagascar Primates *see* Lemur News **953**
Madagascar Renouveau (MDG) **3906**
Madagascar. Service Geologique. Rapport d'Activite: Geologie (MDG) **2753**
Madagascar Tribune (MDG ISSN 1025-3572) **3906**
• Madagaskar Forum (NOR ISSN 1504-4750) **4176**
Madam (GBR ISSN 0024-9351) **4083**
• Madame (CAN ISSN 1494-7684) **8872**
Madame (DEU ISSN 0024-936X) **8872**
Madame (FIN ISSN 1456-2456) **8872**
Madame au Foyer *see* Homemaker's **4360**
Madame Figaro (FRA ISSN 0246-5205) **8872**
Madame Figaro (ROM) **8872**
Madame Figaro (THA) **8872**
MadAminA! (USA ISSN 0740-5812) **6586**
Al Madan (PRT ISSN 0871-066X) **404**
Ma'dang: Journal of Contextual Theology in East Asia (KOR ISSN 1738-3196) **7661**
▼ • Madaplus (FRA ISSN 1959-4909) **3549**
Le Madawaska (CAN) **3812**
Chris Madden *see* At Home with Chris Madden **4532**
Madden Family Newsletter (USA ISSN 0883-556X) **3774**
Maddux Business Report (USA) **1146**
Maddux Report *see* Maddux Business Report **1146**
Maddvocate (USA) **8503**
Made *see* M A D E **3352**
• Made for Export & Electronic Commerce (CHE) **1575**
Made in (ITA) **1146**
Made in Alsace (FRA ISSN 1953-7840) **5076**
Made in Bergamo. Trimestrale di Economia (ITA) **1146**
Made in Biella (ITA ISSN 1123-8313) **2248**
Made in Brazil (BRA) **1575**
Made in Canada (CAN ISSN 0228-7749) **503**
Made in Europe. Hotel and Catering Supply Guide *see* Hotel and Catering Supply Guide **4389**
Made in Germany (DEU ISSN 0179-6291) **1575**
Made in Holland (English Edition) (NLD ISSN 1872-1613) **1575**
Made in Holland (French Edition) (NLD ISSN 1872-1621) **1576**
Made in Holland (German Edition) (NLD ISSN 1872-1664) **1576**
Made in Holland (Portuguese Edition) (NLD ISSN 1872-1672) **1576**
Made in Holland (Spanish Edition) (NLD ISSN 1872-1648) **1576**
Made in Holland. Agrarindustrie (NLD ISSN 1872-2695) **1576**
Made in Holland. Agro-Industria (NLD ISSN 1872-2709) **1576**
Made in Holland. Airport Technology (NLD ISSN 1872-2733) **1576**
Made in Holland. Assistencia Medica Sustentavel *see* Made in Holland. Sustainable Health Care **1576**
Made in Holland. Atencion Sanitaria Sostenible *see* Made in Holland. Sustainable Health Care **1576**
Made in Holland. Composites (NLD ISSN 1872-2563) **1576**
Made in Holland. Decoration Interieur (NLD ISSN 1872-2601) **1576**
Made in Holland. Industria Naval (NLD ISSN 1872-3039) **1576**
Made in Holland. Interior Design (English Edition) (NLD ISSN 1872-258X) **1576**
Made in Holland. Interior Design (German Edition) (NLD ISSN 1872-2652) **1576**
Made in Holland. Land + Water International (NLD ISSN 1872-2717) **1576**
Made in Holland. L'Industrie Agroalimentaire (NLD ISSN 1872-2687) **1576**
Made in Holland. L'Industrie de la Mode (NLD ISSN 1872-2989) **1576**
Made in Holland. Maritime Industry (NLD ISSN 1872-3063) **1576**
Made in Holland. Materiaux Composites (NLD ISSN 1872-2520) **1576**
Made in Holland. Medical Technology (NLD ISSN 1872-2954) **1576**
Made in Holland. Microtechnology (NLD ISSN 1872-2806) **1576**
Made in Holland. Mikrotechnologie (NLD ISSN 1872-2792) **1576**
Made in Holland. Oil & Gas Industry (NLD ISSN 1872-3020) **1576**
Made in Holland. Sector de Petroleo & Gas (NLD ISSN 1872-3004) **1576**
Made in Holland. Sustainable Health Care (NLD ISSN 1872-2776) **1576**
Made in Holland. Technologie Medicale (NLD ISSN 1872-2962) **1576**
Made in Holland. The Fashion Industry (English Edition) (NLD ISSN 1872-2997) **1576**
Made in Holland. The Fashion Industry (German Edition) (NLD ISSN 1872-2970) **1576**
Made in Holland. Verbundwerkstoffe (NLD ISSN 1872-2512) **1576**
▼ Made in Italy Magazine (USA ISSN 1941-0417) **2639**
Made in Sweden *see* Swedish Film **6515**
Made in the Arab World (BHR) **2013**
Made in Turkey (TUR) **1577**
• Made in U.S.A. (USA) **1897**
Made in Varese (ITA) **1431**
Made to Measure (USA) **2248**
Madeira. Direccao Regional de Estatistica. Anuario Estatistico da Madeira (PRT) **8386**
Maden Istatistikleri *see* Turkey. Turkiye Istatistik Kurumu. Maden Istatistikleri **8995**
• ➤ Madencilik (TUR ISSN 0024-9416) **6469**
La Madera (ESP ISSN 0211-8378) **3713**
• Madera y Bosques (MEX ISSN 1405-0471) **3713**
Madera y Carbon (ESP ISSN 0214-0233) **4123**
• Maderas (CHL ISSN 0717-3644) **3713**
Maderas Comerciales de Venezuela (VEN ISSN 0798-2100) **3696**
Madhuparka (NPL) **5329**
Madhuprapancha (IND ISSN 0970-0919) **135**
Madhur Kathayen (IND) **5411**
Madhuri (IND ISSN 0024-9432) **6506**
Madhya Pradesh Chronicle (IND) **3884**
Madhya Pradesh. Directorate of Agriculture. Agricultural Statistics (IND ISSN 0304-6184) **183**
Madhya Pradesh Law Journal (IND ISSN 0024-9459) **4726**
Madhya Pradesh State Agro-Industries Development Corporation Ltd. Annual Report (IND ISSN 0304-7245) **203**
Madhya Pradesh Vikas Varshiki (IND) **3885**
Madhya Pradesh Who's Who (IND) **644**
Madhyamam (IND ISSN 0971-7536) **3885**
Al-Madinah (SAU ISSN 1319-0237) **3944**
Madison (AUS ISSN 1832-4886) **8872**
Madison *see* Stella **3919**
• Madison Area's Gay - Lesbian Calendar and Guide (USA) **4376**
Madison County Genealogical Society Quarterly *see* Stalker **3784**
Madison County Heritage (USA ISSN 0197-498X) **4302**
Madison County Musings (USA ISSN 1071-1937) **3774**
Madison Magazine (USA ISSN 0192-7442) **3980**
† Madison Relocation Guide (USA) **8972**
Madison Review (Madison) (USA ISSN 1093-569X) **5426**
Madison Town Guide (USA) **1406**
Madison's Canadian Lumber Directory (CAN ISSN 0316-6414) **2013**
Madison's Canadian Lumber Reporter (CAN ISSN 0715-5468) **3714**
Madoc (NLD ISSN 0922-369X) **4241**
† Madonna (ITA ISSN 0391-7169) **8972**
La Madonna del Divino Amore (ITA) **7805**
Madoqua (NAM ISSN 1011-5498) **2618**
• ➤ The Madras Agricultural Journal (IND ISSN 0024-9602) **135**
Madras. Government Museum. Bulletin. New Series (IND ISSN 0085-2945) **7880**
Madras Law Journal (IND) **4835**
Madras Law Journal (Criminal) (IND) **4893**
Madras Musings (IND) **3885**
Madras University. Journal. Section A: Humanities (IND) **4464**
Madras University. Journal. Section B: Sciences (IND) **7880**
La Madre (ITA ISSN 1120-6101) **8873**
• Madre di Dio (ITA) **7805**
• Madre Speaks (USA ISSN 1946-9934) **8873**
Madre y Maestra (ESP) **7805**
Madres de Plaza de Mayo (ARG ISSN 0327-1129) **7153**
Madrid (ESP ISSN 1139-5362) **503**
Madrid Port (ESP) **8651**
Madrid, Revista de Arte, Geografia e Historia *see* Madrid **503**
Madrider Beitraege (DEU ISSN 0179-2873) **404**
➤ Madrider Forschungen (DEU ISSN 0418-9736) **404**
Madrider Mitteilungen (DEU ISSN 0418-9744) **404**
• ➤ Madrono (USA ISSN 0024-9637) **800**
• ➤ Madrygal (ESP ISSN 1138-9664) **5426**
Maeander. Beitraege zur Deutschen Literatur (DEU) **5329**
Maecenas (ITA ISSN 1724-6385) **2237**
• Maedchen (DEU ISSN 1420-2239) **2201**
▼ • ➤ Maejo International Journal of Science and Technology (THA ISSN 1905-7873) **7880**
Maelardalens Hoegskola. Ekonomihoegskolan. Forskningsrapport (SWE ISSN 1652-3512) **1146**
• Maelkeproducent Nyt (DNK ISSN 1604-1380) **266**
• Maelkeritidende (DNK ISSN 0024-9645) **266**
Maenner (DEU) **4376**
Maenner Aktuell *see* Maenner **4376**
Maenniskors Vaerde, Haelsa och Vitaliserande Processer (SWE ISSN 1651-0224) **8054**
Die Maerchen Zeitschrift (DEU) **5329**
Maerchenspiegel (DEU ISSN 0946-1140) **5329**
Der Maerker (DEU ISSN 0024-9661) **4241**
Maerkische Allgemeine (DEU) **3852**
Maerkische Oderzeitung (DEU) **3852**
Maerklin-Magazin (DEU ISSN 0024-9688) **4339**
• Maerkte der Welt (DEU ISSN 1614-6239) **1577**
Maerkte im Saarland (DEU ISSN 0177-7491) **1963**
• Maerlant Centrum Digitaal (BEL) **4152**
Maestarkryss (SWE ISSN 1403-1698) **4339**
I Maestri della Paura (ITA ISSN 1824-5889) **5444**
I Maestri dell'Arte Sarda (ITA ISSN 1824-3339) **503**
Il Maestro (ITA ISSN 0024-9696) **7805**
• ➤ Maetagused (EST ISSN 1406-992X) **3620**
† Maffra & District Historical Society. Bulletin (AUS ISSN 0811-1197) **8972**
Mafusailov Vek (RUS) **5664**
† The Mag (AUS ISSN 1449-9347) **8972**
[Mag] (NOR ISSN 1501-0058) **2201**
Le Mag de l'Autoreleve (CAN ISSN 1910-6157) **8589**
Mag het Wat Minder Zijn? (NLD ISSN 1574-1044) **2640**
Mag Weekly (PAK) **3926**
Mag1010 (NLD ISSN 1572-3305) **3324**
Maga Scene (USA) **7567**
Magalat al-sarq al-awsat (Guddat) *see* Majallat al-Sharq al-Awsat **3912**
Magalat al-Zaqaziq li-l-Sihhat wa-al-Salamat al-Mihaniyyat *see* Zagazig Journal of Occupational Health and Safety **6689**
Magalat Tilifizun al-Halig *see* Tilivisyon al-Khalij **2397**
➤ Al Magallah al-'arabiyyah li-l-adab/The Arab Journal for Arts (JOR ISSN 1818-9849) **4464**
Al Magallah Al-'arabiyyah Li-l-tibb Al-nafsi/The Arab Journal of Psychiatry (JOR ISSN 1016-8923) **6159**
Magallah al-Misriyah lil-Mikrubiyulugiya *see* Egyptian Journal of Microbiology **884**
• Magallania (CHL ISSN 0718-0209) **7984**
Magallat al-Azhar lil-Behuth al-Zira'iyyat *see* Al-Azhar Journal of Agricultural Sciences Sector Research **89**
Al Magallat al-Akadimiyyat al-Misriyyat li-l-'Ulum al-Bayulugiyyat *see* Egyptian Academic Journal of Biological Sciences **670**
Magallat al-Antaagiyyat wa al-Tanmiyyat *see* Journal of Productivity and Development **1890**
Al-Magallat Al-'arabiyyat li-l-Idhtrabat Al-Bawliyyat *see* Pan Arab Journal of Voiding Dysfunction **6273**
Magallat al-Basrat al-'ulum al-Handasiyyat *see* al Basrat al-'ulum al-Handasiyyat. Majalla **3183**
Magallat al-batrul wa-al-gaz al-'arabi *see* Arab Oil & Gas Magazine (Monthly) **6762**
Magallat al-Bihu? al-Ziraa'iyyat Koliyyat al-Ziraa'at al-Zaqaaziq *see* Zagazig Journal of Agricultural Research **171**
Magallat al-Bihud al-Ziraa'iyyat Gaami'at Tantaa *see* Journal of Agricultural Research **126**
Magallat al-Buhuth al-Idariyyat/Administrative Research Review (EGY ISSN 1110-225X) **7452**
Magallat al-Faisal (SAU ISSN 0258-1140) **5329**
Magallat al-Faysal *see* Magallat al-Faisal **5329**
Magallat al-Fayyum al-Bihuth wa-al-Tanmiyyat al-Zira'iyyat *see* Fayoum Journal of Agricultural Research and Development **112**
Magallat al-Gala' al-Tibbiyyat *see* Galaa Medical Journal **5617**
Magallat al-Gamieyat al-Missriyyat lil-Kimiyaa al-Hayaweyyat *see* The Egyptian Journal of Biochemistry **731**
Magallat al-Gami'iat al-Misriyyat lil-Adwiyyat wa-al-'ilag al-Tagribi *see* Egyptian Society of Pharmacology and Experimental Therapeutics. Journal **6837**
Magallat al-Gam'iyyat al-Misriyyat al-Almaaniyyat li-'lm al-Hayyawaan. al-Tasrih wa 'Ilm al-Aginat *see* Egyptian German Society for Zoology. Journal. B, Anatomy and Embryology **941**
Magallat al-Gam'iyyat al-Misriyyat al-Almaaniyyat li-'lm al-Hayyawaan. 'Ilm al-Fisyulugia al-Muqaran *see* Egyptian German Society for Zoology. Journal. A, Comparative Zoology **941**
Magallat al-Gam'iyyat al-Misriyyat al-Almaaniyyat li-'lm al-Hayyawaan. 'Ilm al-Hasharat *see* Egyptian German Society for Zoology. Journal. E, Entomology **941**
Magallat al-Gam'iyyat al-Misriyyat al-Almaaniyyat li-'lm al-Hayyawaan. 'Ilm al-Haywan al-Faqqary wa al-Tufayliat *see* Egyptian German Society for Zoology. Journal. D, Invertebrate Zoology and Parasitology **941**
Magallat al-Gam'iyyat al-Tibiyyat al-Baytariyyat al-Misriyyat *see* Egyptian Veterinary Medical Association. Journal **8797**
Magallat al-Giraahat al-Misriyyat *see* The Egyptian Journal of Surgery **6242**
Magallat al-Handasat wa al-'Lum al-Tatbiiqiyyat *see* Journal of Engineering and Applied Science **3204**
➤ Magallat al-Huquq/Journal of Law (KWT ISSN 1029-6069) **4726**
Al-Magallat al-'ilmiyyat li-l-Gam'iyyat al-Misriyyat li-Istshari al-Ridha'at al-Tabi'iyyat *see* E L C A Scientific Journal **5989**
• Al Magallat al-'ilmiyyat li-l-Tanmiyat/Scientific Magazine for Development (LBN ISSN 1818-9814) **1146**
Al-Magallat al-'Ilmiyyat li-l-'Ulum al-Tarbiyyat al-Badaniyyat wa-al-Riyyadiyyat/The Scientific Journal for Physical Education and Sports Sciences (EGY ISSN 1687-7292) **2993**
▼ Magallat al-Iqtisadiyyin al-Zira'iyyin al-'Arab (EGY ISSN 1687-7551) **203**
Magallat al-'lum al-Tibiyyat al-Shar'iyyat *see* The Journal of Legal Medicine Forensic Sciences **5915**
Magallat al-Mansour *see* Majallat al-Mansur **7881**
Magallat al-Minufiyyat lil-Bihuo al-Ziraa'iyyat *see* Minufiya Journal of Agricultural Research **137**
Al-Magallat al-Misriyyat li-l-Taghziyyat wa-al-Sihhat *see* Egyptian Journal of Nutrition and Health **6658**
Magallat al-Muhandisin/Engineers Journal (EGY ISSN 1110-2861) **3209**
Magallat al-Muhasabt wa-al-Idarat wa-al-Ta'min/Accounting, Management and Insurance Review (EGY ISSN 1110-628X) **1296**
Magallat al-Nafs al-Motma'enna *see* Mental Peace **6160**
Magallat al-Qalb al-Misriyyat *see* The Egyptian Heart Journal **5785**
➤ Al-Magallat al-Qanuniyyat al-Iqtisadiyyat/Law and Economic Review (EGY ISSN 1110-6964) **4726**
Magallat al-Shoruq li-l-'Ulum al-Tigariyyat *see* Magallat al-Shuruq li-l-'Ulum al-Tigariyyat **1146**
▼ Magallat al-Shuruq li-l-'Ulum al-Tigariyyat/El-Sharouk Journal for Commercial Studies (EGY ISSN 1687-8523) **1146**
➤ Magallat al-Tanmiyat wa-al-Siyasat al-Iqtisadiyyat/Journal of Development and Economic Policies (KWT ISSN 1561-0411) **1146**
Magallat al-Tefl al-'Arabi *see* Journal of Arab Child **6094**
Magallat al-Tibbiyat al-Lubnaniyyat *see* Lebanese Medical Journal **5660**

Title

Magistrates' Courts Practice (GBR ISSN 1361-5815) 4955
Magistrates Early Referral into Treatment Annual Report see M E R I T Annual Report 2660
La Magistratura (ITA ISSN 1971-5404) 4726
Magliazzurra (ITA) 8238
Maglieria Italiana (ITA ISSN 1127-0470) 2248
Magma see Magnetic Resonance Materials in Physics, Biology and Medicine 7068
• m@gm@ (ITA ISSN 1721-9809) 7984
▼ MagMa (NLD ISSN 1877-0711) 1021
• Magma (NOR ISSN 1500-0788) 1774
Magma Poetry Magazine (GBR ISSN 1352-9269) 5226
Magna (BRA ISSN 0104-6330) 5329
† Magna Graecia (ITA ISSN 0024-9955) 8972
• Magna's Campus Legal Monthly (USA ISSN 1932-5800) 2993
Magnes News (USA) 6528
Magnesium see Maguneshumu 5897
• Magnesium Monthly Review (USA ISSN 0047-5491) 6321
Magnesium Newsletter (USA ISSN 0891-6942) 6321
• ➤ Magnesium Research (FRA ISSN 0953-1424) 5664
Magnet (AUS ISSN 1832-3774) 3795
• Magnet (USA ISSN 1088-7806) 6586
• Magnet Leader Weekly (USA ISSN 1948-058X) 4106
Magnet Marketing & Sales (USA) 1830
• Magnet Online (USA) 6586
Magnet Status Advisor see H C Pro's Advisor to the A N C C Magnet Recognition Program 5959
Magnetic and Electrical Separation see Physical Separation in Science and Engineering 7032
• ➤ Magnetic Resonance Imaging (USA ISSN 0730-725X) 6202
• Magnetic Resonance Imaging Clinics of North America (USA ISSN 1064-9689) 6202
• ➤ Magnetic Resonance in Chemistry (GBR ISSN 0749-1581) 2103
• Magnetic Resonance in Medical Sciences (JPN ISSN 1347-3182) 6202
• ➤ Magnetic Resonance in Medicine (USA ISSN 0740-3194) 6202
• ➤ Magnetic Resonance in Solids (RUS) 7068
▼ • ➤ Magnetic Resonance Insights (NZL ISSN 1178-623X) 6202
• ➤ Magnetic Resonance Materials in Physics, Biology and Medicine (DEU ISSN 0968-5243) 7068
Magnetic Results Sodankyla (FIN ISSN 0781-9625) 2712
• Magnetics Business & Technology (USA ISSN 1535-1998) 2712
Magnetics Business and Technology see Magnetics Business & Technology 2712
• Magnetics Business & Technology e-Report (USA ISSN 1938-0828) 7025
Magnetics Japan see Magune 7025
• Magnetics Society of Japan. Journal/Nihon Oyo Jiki Gakkaishi (JPN ISSN 0285-0192) 7025
Magnetics Society of Japan. Journal. Supplement (JPN ISSN 1341-7290) 7025
Magnetics Society of Japan. Papers of Technical Meeting see Nihon Oyo Jiki Gakkai Kenkyukai Shiryo 7028
Magnetics Society of Japan. Transactions see Magnetics Society of Japan. Journal 7025
• ➤ Magnetohydrodynamics (LVA ISSN 0024-998X) 3324
Magnetwerkstoffe see Informationsdienst F I Z Technik. Magnetwerkstoffe 3231
Magnificant (PRT ISSN 0874-4998) 7661
Magnificat (CAN ISSN 0025-0007) 7805
Magnificat (DEU ISSN 1254-7697) 7661
Magnitnoimpul'snaya Obrabotka Metallov (UKR) 3324
Magnito-Poluprovodnikovye i Elektromashinnye Elementy Avtomatiki (RUS ISSN 0130-9323) 3324
• MagNNet (DEU) 3852
▼ Magno (CHL ISSN 0718-4549) 5664
Magnolia (Winston-Salem) (USA ISSN 1054-9153) 3742
Magnolia Magazine (USA) 3742
Magnolia Society. Journal (USA ISSN 0738-3053) 3742
Magnum see Man Magnum 8321
Magny Families Association Newsletter (USA) 3774
Magonia (GBR) 6742
• Magpies (AUS ISSN 0817-0088) 2160
Maguare (COL ISSN 0120-3045) 346
Magune/Magnetics Japan (JPN ISSN 1880-7208) 7025
Maguneshumu/Magnesium (JPN ISSN 0913-4867) 5897
➤ Magyar Allatorvosok Lapja/Hungarian Veterinary Journal (HUN ISSN 0025-004X) 8802
Magyar Baromfi (HUN ISSN 1219-0187) 293
Magyar Belorvosi Archivum (HUN ISSN 0133-5464) 5664
Magyar Egyhaztorteneti Enciklopedia Munkakozossege International Society of Toronto for Hungarian Church History. Newsletter see M E T E M - International Society of Toronto for Hungarian Church History. Newsletter 4241
➤ Magyar Egyhaztorteneti Vazlatok/Essays in Church History in Hungary (CAN ISSN 0865-5227) 4241
Magyar Elektronika/Hungarian Electronics (HUN ISSN 0236-6134) 3108
• Magyar Elektronikus Tozsde/Hungarian Electronic Exchange (HUN ISSN 1216-0229) 1638
A Magyar Elelmiszer-Gazdasag Evkonyve (HUN ISSN 1417-8346) 3655
Magyar Epitestechnika/Hungarian Building Technology (HUN ISSN 1216-6022) 1021
Magyar Epitoipar/Hungarian Building Industry (HUN ISSN 0025-0074) 1021
• Magyar Epuletgepeszet (HUN ISSN 1215-9913) 3388
Magyar Fangoria see Fangoria 5442
Magyar Filozofiai Szemle/Hungarian Philosophical Review (HUN ISSN 0025-0090) 6933
Magyar Fogorvos/Hungarian Dentist (HUN ISSN 1216-2213) 5855
Magyar Grafika/Hungarian Graphic Arts (HUN ISSN 0479-480X) 7324
Magyar Gyomkutatas es Technologia/Hungarian Weed Research and Technology (HUN ISSN 1586-894X) 241
• Magyar Hirlap (HUN ISSN 0133-1906) 3876
Magyar Holnap/Hungarian Tomorrow (USA) 3549
Magyar Immunologia/Hungarian Immunology (HUN ISSN 1588-3280) 5763
Magyar Installateur (HUN ISSN 0866-6024) 4123
Magyar Jog (HUN ISSN 0025-0147) 4727
Magyar Kemiai Folyoirat, Kemiai Kozlemenyek/Hungarian Journal of Chemistry, Chemical Communications (HUN ISSN 1418-9933) 2072
Magyar Kemikusok Lapja (HUN ISSN 0025-0163) 2072
• Magyar Konyveszet (HUN ISSN 1218-5604) 630
Magyar Konyvtari Szakirodalom Bibliografiaja/Bibliography on Hungarian Library Literature (HUN ISSN 0133-736X) 2444
Magyar Kozlony/Official Journal of Hungary (HUN ISSN 0076-2407) 4242
Magyar Kulpolitikai Evkonyv (HUN ISSN 0541-9220) 7251
Magyar Mezogazdasag/Hungarian Agriculture (HUN ISSN 0025-018X) 135
Magyar Mezogazdasagi Bibliografia (HUN ISSN 0025-0198) 183
Magyar Mezogazdasagi Muzeum Kozlemenyei/Hungarian Agricultural Museum. Proceedings (HUN ISSN 0521-4238) 135
Magyar Naplo (CAN ISSN 0836-6993) 3549
Magyar Nemzeti Bank. Havi Jelentes see National Bank of Hungary. Monthly Report 1500
• Magyar Nemzeti Bibliografia. Idoszaki Kiadvanyok Bibliografiaja (HUN ISSN 0231-4592) 630
Magyar Nemzeti Bibliografia. Idoszaki Kiadvanyok Repertoriuma (HUN ISSN 0133-6894) 8021
• Magyar Nemzeti Bibliografia. Konyvek/Hungarian National Bibliography. Books (HUN ISSN 1218-2192) 630
• Magyar Nemzeti Bibliografia. Konyvek Bibliografiaja (HUN ISSN 0133-6843) 630
• Magyar Nemzeti Bibliografia. Periodikumok/ Hungarian National Bibliography. Serials (HUN ISSN 1416-5414) 630
• Magyar Nemzeti Bibliografia. Sajtorepertorium/ Hungarian National Bibliography. Repertory of Serials (HUN ISSN 1419-1903) 630
Magyar Nemzeti Bibliografia. Uj Periodikumok (HUN ISSN 1219-6835) 630
Magyar Nemzeti Bibliografia. Zenemuvek Bibliografiaja (HUN ISSN 0133-5782) 6631
Magyar Nepmuveszet (HUN ISSN 1217-9833) 504
Magyar Neprajzi Bibliografia/Hungarian Folklore Bibliography (HUN ISSN 0865-1906) 3620
Magyar Noorvosok Lapja (HUN ISSN 0025-021X) 5997
Magyar Nyelv/Hungarian Language (HUN ISSN 0025-0228) 5149
Magyar Nyelvjarasok (HUN ISSN 0541-9298) 5149
• ➤ Magyar Nyelvor/Hungarian Language Guardian (HUN ISSN 0025-0236) 5149
Magyar Olajipari Muzeum. Evkonyv (HUN) 6777
• ➤ Magyar Onkologia/Hungarian Oncology (HUN ISSN 0025-0244) 6027
Magyar Orvos (HUN ISSN 1217-6052) 5664
➤ Magyar Pedagogia (HUN ISSN 0025-0260) 2884
• Magyar Pszichologiai Szemle/Hungarian Psychological Review (HUN ISSN 0025-0279) 7384
Magyar Radiologia/Journal of Hungarian Radiology (HUN ISSN 0025-0287) 6202
Magyar Reumatologia (HUN ISSN 0139-4495) 6224
• Magyar Sebeszet/Hungarian Journal of Surgery (HUN ISSN 0025-0295) 6251
• Magyar Statisztikai Evkonyv/Statistical Yearbook of Hungary (HUN ISSN 1215-7864) 8386
Magyar Statisztikai Zsebkonyv (HUN ISSN 0133-5847) 8386
Magyar Szemle/Hungarian Review (HUN ISSN 1216-6235) 5226
Magyar Szo Naptara (SRB ISSN 0541-9344) 3121
Magyar Szolo- es Borgazdasag/Hungarian Journal of Viticulture and Enology (HUN ISSN 0866-6083) 241
Magyar Termeszettudomanyi Muzeum. Evkonyve see Musei Nationalis Hungarici. Annales Historico-Naturales 7883
▼ • ➤ Magyar Terminologia/Journal of Hungarian Terminology (HUN ISSN 1789-9486) 5149
Magyar Textiltechnika (HUN ISSN 1788-1722) 8454
Magyar Tortenelmi Szemle/Hungarian Historical Review/Revista Historica Hungara (ARG ISSN 0300-3817) 4242
Magyar Traumatologia, Orthopedia, Kezsebeszet es Plasztikai Sebeszet (HUN ISSN 1217-3231) 6067
Magyar Tudomany/Hungarian Science (HUN ISSN 0025-0325) 7881
Magyar Tudomanyos Akademia Konvytaranak Kiadvanyai see Magyar Tudomanyos Akademia Konvytaranak Kozlemenyei 7938
Magyar Tudomanyos Akademia Konvytaranak Kozlemenyei/Publicationes Bibliothecae Academiae Scientiarum Hungaricae (HUN ISSN 0133-8862) 7938
Magyar Tudomanyos Akademia Konyvtara Kezirattaranak Katalogusai/Catalogi Collectionis Manuscriptorum Bibliothecae Academiae Scientiarum Hungaricae (HUN ISSN 0541-9492) 630
Magyar Tudomanyos Akademia. Kozponti Fizikai Kutato Intezet. Evkonyv see Hungarian Academy of Sciences. Central Research Institute for Physics. Yearbook 7015
Magyar Urologia (HUN ISSN 0864-8921) 6271
Magyar Villamos Muvek Rt. Kozlemenyei (HUN ISSN 1216-4992) 3160
Magyarok Vilaglapja/New Hungarian News (HUN ISSN 1216-4461) 3876
Magyarorszag (HUN ISSN 0230-5828) 8386
Magyarorszag Allatvilaga/Fauna Hungariae (HUN ISSN 0076-2474) 954
Magyarorszag Kulturfloraja (HUN ISSN 0076-2482) 800
Magyarorszag Nagy Vallalatai es Vallalkozasai see Grosse und Mittelstaendische Unternehmen in Ungarn 1887
† Magyarorszag Regeszeti Topografiaja/ Archeological Topography of Hungary (HUN ISSN 0076-2504) 8972
Maha Bodhi (IND ISSN 0025-0406) 7701
Maha Milan (IND) 5226
Mahajanmer Lagna (IND ISSN 0025-0414) 6933
Mahalli Idareler Secimi Sonuclari see Turkey. Turkiye Istatistik Kurumu. Mahalli Idareler Secimi 7485
• Mahanagar (NPL) 3913
Maharaja Agrasen Institute of Management and Technology Journal of I T & Management see M A I M T Journal of I T & Management 2431
Maharaja Sawai Man Singh II Memorial Series (IND) 6528
Maharaja Sayajirao University of Baroda. Department of Archaeology and Ancient History. Archaeology Series (IND ISSN 0076-2520) 404
Maharaja Sayajirao University of Baroda. Department of History Series (IND ISSN 0464-5030) 4152
Maharaja Sayajirao University of Baroda. Journal (IND ISSN 0025-0422) 7881
Maharashtra Bhugolshastra Sanshodhan Patrika (IND ISSN 0971-6785) 4019
Maharashtra Chamber Patrika (IND) 1407
The Maharashtra Co-Operative Quarterly (IND ISSN 0025-0430) 1424
Maharashtra Economic Development Council. Monthly Economic Digest for Business Executives (IND) 1497
Maharashtra Herald (IND) 3885
Maharashtra Law Journal (IND ISSN 0025-0465) 4727
Maharashtra Quarterly Bulletin of Economics and Statistics (IND ISSN 0025-0481) 1250
Maharashtra State Budget in Brief (IND ISSN 0076-2555) 1934
Maharashtra State Financial Corporation. Annual Report (IND ISSN 0076-2563) 1366
Maharashtra State Institute of Education. Research Bulletin (IND) 2884
Maharashtra Sugar see Bharatiya Sugar 221
Maharashtra Times (IND) 3885
Mahasagar (Goa) (IND ISSN 0542-0938) 2811
Mahasagar (Nagpur) (IND) 3885
Mahatma Gandhi Institute Magazine see M G I Magazine 4176
Mahenjodaro (IND ISSN 0025-049X) 5329
Mahi a Rehia no Aotearoa see Research in New Zealand Performing Arts 2687
Mahinda (LKA) 7702
Mahjubah (IRN ISSN 1019-0767) 7713
Mahkuzine (NLD ISSN 1872-4728) 504
Mahlzeit! (DEU) 8054
Die Mahnung (DEU ISSN 0025-0511) 7212
Mahogany (ZWE) 8873
Mahratta (IND ISSN 0076-2571) 4185
➤ Mahut (ISR ISSN 0792-4585) 3549
Mai Ez a Divat (HUN ISSN 1586-5908) 2258
Mai Piac (HUN ISSN 1218-1927) 2013
Mai Piac Tema see Tema 3666
• ➤ MAI Review (NZL ISSN 1177-5904) 8119
Maia (ITA ISSN 0025-0538) 2237
Maidstone K M Extra (GBR) 3868
Maidstone Mirror (CAN ISSN 0837-0028) 3813
Maidstone Star (GBR) 3868
Maihaugen (NOR ISSN 0333-0974) 4242
➤ Maikotokishin/Mycotoxins (JPN ISSN 0285-1466) 3500
Maikuromekatoronikusu/Micromechatronics (JPN ISSN 1343-8565) 2572
Mail Advertising Service Association International. Performance Profiles (USA) 28
Mail Advertising Service Association International. Postscripts (USA) 28
Mail Advertising Service Association International. Quarterly Business Outlook (USA) 28
Mail Advertising Service Association International. Wage and Salary, and Fringe Benefits Survey (USA) 38
• Mail & Guardian (ZAF) 3949
Mail and Parcel Centers World see M P C World 2354
Mail Bag (USA) 910
The Mail Coach (NZL ISSN 0542-0997) 6896
• Mail Marketing (ESP ISSN 1135-7029) 28
• The Mail on CD-ROM (USA) 3868
• The Mail on Sunday (GBR ISSN 0263-8878) 3868
Mail on Sunday see The Irish Mail on Sunday 3893
Mail Order and Catalogue Houses see Business Ratio. Mail Order & Catalogue Houses 1808
Mail Order Business Directory (USA ISSN 0085-2953) 2014
Mail Order Digest see N M O A - Mail Order Digest 1835
• Mail Order Europe Business Directory on CD-ROM (CAN) 1830
• The Mail Order Secrets Newsletter (USA) 1963
• Mail Order U S A Business Directory on CD-ROM (CAN) 1830
The Mail Research Society. Journal see The Armour Research Society. Journal 364
Mail: The Journal of Communication Distribution (USA ISSN 1053-0703) 2354
The Mailbox (USA ISSN 0199-6045) 3071
Mailbox Bookbag (USA ISSN 1088-6397) 3071
Mailbox Companion see The Mailbox 3071
The Mailbox. Grade 1 (USA ISSN 1948-688X) 3071
▼ The Mailbox. Grade 1 Yearbook (USA ISSN 1946-3367) 3071
The Mailbox. Grade One see The Mailbox. Grade 1 3071
The Mailbox. Grades 2-3 Yearbook (USA ISSN 1930-3580) 2201
The Mailbox. Grades Two-Three Yearbook see The Mailbox. Grades 2-3 Yearbook 2201
The Mailbox. Kindergarten (USA ISSN 1948-6863) 3071
The Mailbox. Kindergarten - Grade 1 see The Mailbox. Kindergarten 3071
Mailbox News (USA ISSN 0889-4884) 3674
Mailbox News for Cake Decorators see Mailbox News 3674
Mailbox. Primary Yearbook see The Mailbox. Grades 2-3 Yearbook 2201
• Mailei Zuowu Xuebao/Journal of Triticeae Crops (CHN ISSN 1009-1041) 242
▼ • The Mailer Review (USA ISSN 1936-4679) 5329
Mailing & Systems Technology see Mailing Systems Technology 2354
• Mailing Systems Technology (USA ISSN 1088-2677) 2354
Mailles (FRA ISSN 1962-4050) 6640
Mailout (GBR ISSN 0959-0013) 504
Mails Calientes (ARG ISSN 1850-146X) 566
MailServeR Belgian see M S R Belgian 3549
Maimonidean Studies (USA ISSN 1050-1630) 5031
• Main Board Listing Guide For Foreign Companies (KOR) 1638
† Main de Singe (FRA ISSN 1163-7307) 8972
Main-Echo (DEU) 3852
• Main Economic Indicators (Organisation for Economic Cooperation and Development) (FRA ISSN 1816-9007) 1250
Main Economic Indicators (NPL) 1497
Main Economic Indicators. O E C D Statistics see Main Economic Indicators 1250
Main Gazette (USA) 3774
• ➤ Main Group Chemistry (GBR ISSN 1024-1221) 2072
➤ Main Group Metal Chemistry (ISR ISSN 0792-1241) 6321
Main Indicators of Construction and Investment Activities in the Russian Federation see Osnovnye Pokazateli Investitsionnoi i Stroitel'noi Deyatel'nosti v Rossiiskoi Federatsii 1257
Main Indicators of Environmental Protection see Osnovnye Pokazateli Okhrany Okruzhayushchei Sredy 3480
The Main Ingredient (USA) 3655
Main Line (GBR ISSN 0264-7028) 8620
Main Line Today (USA ISSN 1086-6078) 5076
Main-Post (DEU) 3852
Main Report (Agriculture Edition) see Main Report's Profitable Agri-Business 135
Main Report Personal Health & Wealth see M R Personal Health & Wealth 2639
Main Report's Profitable Agri-Business (NZL ISSN 1177-939X) 135
Main Science and Technology Indicators see O E C D Science, Technology and R & D Statistics 3233
Main Street Low Ridaz (USA) 8260
Main Street Memorandum (USA) 3980
• Main Street Mom (USA) 2160
Mainake (ESP ISSN 0212-078X) 404
Mainau-Inselpost (DEU ISSN 1864-2365) 3742
MainCity Guide (DEU ISSN 1616-8933) 3852
Maine Agricultural and Forest Experiment Station. Bulletin (USA ISSN 1070-1494) 242
Maine Agricultural and Forest Experiment Station. Miscellaneous Report (USA ISSN 1070-1516) 135
Maine Agricultural and Forest Experiment Station. Technical Bulletin (USA ISSN 1070-1524) 135
Maine Antique Digest (USA ISSN 0147-0639) 367

Title

DIRECTORY 2010 MALAYSIA. JABATAN PERANGKAAN. PERANGKAAN TAHUNAN INDUSTRI 10585

Malawi. Ministry of Justice. Annual Report (MWI ISSN 0076-3160) **4955**
Malawi. Ministry of Justice. Laws Amendments (MWI) **4955**
Malawi. Ministry of Local Government. Annual Report (MWI ISSN 0076-3225) **7153**
• Malawi National Bibliography (MWI) **630**
Malawi. National Library Service Board. Annual Report (MWI) **5031**
Malawi. National Library Service Board. Bulletin (MWI) **5031**
Malawi. National Library Service Board. Staff Newsletter (MWI) **5031**
Malawi. National Statistical Office. Annual Statement of External Trade (MWI ISSN 0076-325X) **1250**
Malawi. National Statistical Office. Annual Survey of Economic Activities (MWI ISSN 0076-3241) **1250**
Malawi. National Statistical Office. Balance of Payments (MWI ISSN 0085-3003) **1250**
Malawi. National Statistical Office. Employment and Earnings: Annual Report (MWI) **1250**
Malawi. National Statistical Office. Family Formation Survey (Year) (MWI) **8149**
Malawi. National Statistical Office. Monthly Statistical Bulletin (MWI) **8387**
Malawi. National Statistical Office. National Accounts Report (MWI ISSN 0076-3284) **8387**
Malawi. National Statistical Office. National Sample Survey of Agriculture (MWI ISSN 0076-3292) **183**
Malawi. National Statistical Office. Population Census Final Report (MWI ISSN 0076-3306) **7312**
Malawi. National Statistical Office. Survey of Handicapped Persons (MWI) **4071**
Malawi. National Statistical Office. Transport Statistics (MWI) **8527**
Malawi. National Statistical Office. Urban Household Expenditure Survey (MWI) **7312**
Malawi. National Statistical Office. Urban Housing Survey (MWI) **4436**
Malawi News (MWI) **3906**
Malawi. Office of the Auditor General. Report (MWI ISSN 0076-3314) **1934**
Malawi Patent Journal and Trade Marks Journal (MWI ISSN 0025-1267) **6754**
Malawi. Police Force. Annual Report (MWI ISSN 0076-308X) **2660**
Malawi. Post Office Savings Bank. Annual Report (MWI ISSN 0076-3322) **1366**
Malawi Products Handbook (Year) (MWI) **1577**
Malawi Railways. Annual Reports and Accounts (MWI ISSN 0076-3330) **8620**
Malawi Railways. Directors' Reports and Accounts *see* Malawi Railways. Annual Reports and Accounts **8620**
Malawi. Registrar of Insurance. Report (MWI ISSN 0076-3349) **4513**
Malawi Statistical Yearbook (MWI) **8387**
Malawi Tourism Report (MWI) **8779**
Malawi Treaty Series (MWI ISSN 0076-3357) **4935**
Malawian (MWI) **3906**
Malawian Geographer (MWI ISSN 1010-5549) **4019**
➤ Malay (PHL ISSN 0115-6195) **4464**
Malay Literature (MYS ISSN 0128-1186) **5329**
Malaya Buhgalteriya (RUS) **1296**
Malayala Manorama (IND) **3885**
➤ Malayalam Literary Survey (IND) **5226**
• Malayalam Varika (IND) **3885**
• Malayan Law Journal (MYS ISSN 0025-1283) **4727**
Malaysia *see* The P R S Group. Country Reports: Malaysia **1508**
Malaysia and Singapore Handbook (GBR ISSN 1363-7363) **8732**
Malaysia Automotive Directory (MYS) **2015**
Malaysia Builders Directory (MYS) **1022**
• The Malaysia Business Forecast Report (GBR ISSN 1744-8794) **1497**
• Malaysia Chemicals Report (GBR ISSN 1749-205X) **2072**
Malaysia Convention & Exhibition Directory (MYS) **2015**
• Malaysia Defence & Security Report (GBR ISSN 1749-1525) **6432**
Malaysia. Department of Inland Revenue. Annual Report/Malaysia. Jabatan Hasil Dalam Negeri. Lapuran Tahunan (MYS) **1431**
Malaysia. Department of Mines. Statistics Relating to the Mining Industry of Malaysia (MYS ISSN 0126-818X) **6486**
Malaysia. Department of Statistics. Annual Censuses of Mining and Stone Quarrying, Malaysia/Malaysia. Jabatan Perangkaan. Banci Industri Perlombongan dan Penggalian Batu Tahunan, Malaysia (MYS) **6486**
Malaysia. Department of Statistics. Annual Censuses of Mining and Stone Quarrying, Malaysia - Additional Tables/Malaysia. Jabatan Perangkaan. Banci Tahunan Perlombongan dan Penggalian Batu, Malaysia - Jadual Tambahan (MYS) **6486**
Malaysia. Department of Statistics. Annual Censuses of Mining and Stone Quarrying, Malaysia - Principal Statistics/Malaysia. Jabatan Perangkaan. Banci Tahunan Perlombongan dan Penggalian Batu, Malaysia - Perangkaan Utama (MYS ISSN 0128-9918) **6486**
Malaysia. Department of Statistics. Annual Statistics of Manufacturing Industries, Malaysia - Part A/Malaysia. Jabatan Perangkaan. Perangkaan Tahunan Industri Pembusatan, Malaysia - Bahagian A (MYS ISSN 1394-4924) **1250**
Malaysia. Department of Statistics. Annual Statistics of Manufacturing Industries, Malaysia - Part B/Malaysia. Jabatan Perangkaan. Perangkaan Tahunan Industri Pembuatan, Malaysia - Bahagian B (MYS ISSN 1394-6048) **1250**
Malaysia. Department of Statistics. Annual Survey of Manufacturing Industries, Malaysia/Malaysia. Jabatan Pergangkaan. Penyiasatan Tahunan Industri Pembuatan, Malaysia (MYS ISSN 0128-973X) **1250**
Malaysia. Department of Statistics. Balance of Payments Report, Malaysia/Malaysia. Jabatan Perangkaan. Laporan Imbangan Pembayaran, Malaysia. (MYS ISSN 0127-8541) **1250**
Malaysia. Department of Statistics. Business Expectations Survey of Limited Companies Malaysia/Malaysia. Jabatan Perangkaan. Penyiasatan Jangkaan Perniagaan Bagi Syarikat-Syarikat Berhad Malaysia (MYS) **1146**
Malaysia. Department of Statistics. Census of Professional and Institutional Establishments - Private Sector/Malaysia. Jabatan Perangkaan. Banci Pertubuhan Profesional dan Institusi - Sektor Swasta (MYS ISSN 0126-6837) **1250**
Malaysia. Department of Statistics. Census of Selected Service Industries, Malaysia/Malaysia. Jabatan Perangkaan. Perangkaan Akaun Negara, Malaysia (MYS ISSN 0127-8363) **1250**
Malaysia. Department of Statistics. Cocoa, Coconut and Tea Statistics Handbook, Malaysia/Malaysia. Jabatan Perangkaan. Buku Maklumat Perangkaan Koko, Kelapa dan Teh, Malaysia (MYS) **183**
Malaysia. Department of Statistics. Compendium of Environment Statistics, Malaysia/Malaysia. Jabatan Perangkaan. Laporan Perangkaan Alam Kekitar, Malaysia (MYS ISSN 1511-3396) **3480**
Malaysia. Department of Statistics. External Trade Statistics, Malaysia/Malaysia. Jabatan Perangkaan. Perangkaan Perdagangan Luar Negeri, Malaysia (MYS ISSN 0127-8533) **1250**
Malaysia. Department of Statistics. External Trade Statistics, Sabah/Malaysia. Jabatan Perangkaan. Perangkaan Perdangangan Luar Negeri. Sabah (MYS) **1250**
Malaysia. Department of Statistics. External Trade Summary Malaysia (MYS ISSN 0127-9637) **1250**
Malaysia. Department of Statistics. Framework for the Development of Environment Statistics (F D E S) in Malaysia (MYS ISSN 1511-3388) **3480**
Malaysia. Department of Statistics. Index of Industrial Production, Malaysia/Malaysia. Jabatan Perangkaan. Indeks Pengeluaran Peridustrian, Malaysia (MYS) **1250**
Malaysia. Department of Statistics. Industrial Surveys, Malaysia/Malaysia. Jabatan Perangkaan. Penyiasatan - Penyiasatan Perindustrian, Malaysia (MYS ISSN 0126-6993) **1250**
Malaysia. Department of Statistics. Labour Force Survey Report, Malaysia/Malaysia. Jabatan Perangkaan. Laporan Penyiasatan Tenaga Buruh, Malaysia (MYS ISSN 0128-0503) **7312**
Malaysia. Department of Statistics. Malaysian Economy in Brief/Malaysia. Jabatan Perangkaan. Ekonomi Malaysia Sepintas Lalu (MYS ISSN 1394-0546) **1250**
Malaysia. Department of Statistics. Migration Survey Report, Malaysia/Malaysia. Jabatan Perangkaan. Laporan Penyiasatan Migrasi, Malaysia (MYS) **7312**
Malaysia. Department of Statistics. Monthly Bulletin of Statistics, Sabah/Malaysia. Jabatan Perangkaan. Siaran Perangkaan Bulanan, Sabah (MYS) **8387**
Malaysia. Department of Statistics. Monthly Consumer Price Index, Malaysia/Malaysia. Jabatan Perangkaan. Indeks Harga Pengguna, Malaysia (MYS) **8387**
Malaysia. Department of Statistics. Monthly External Trade Statistics, Malaysia/Malaysia. Jabatan Perangkann. Perangkaan Perdagangan Luar Negeri Bulanan, Malaysia (MYS) **1250**
Malaysia. Department of Statistics. Monthly Manufacturing Statistics, Malaysia (MYS ISSN 0128-3499) **1250**
Malaysia. Department of Statistics. Monthly Rubber Statistics, Malaysia/Malaysia. Jabatan Perangkaan. Perangkaan Getah Bulanan, Malaysia (MYS ISSN 0127-6778) **7828**
Malaysia. Department of Statistics. Monthly Statistical Bulletin, Malaysia/Siaran Perangkaan Bulanan Semenanjung Malaysia (MYS) **8387**
Malaysia. Department of Statistics. Monthly Statistical Bulletin, Sarawak/Malaysia. Jabatan Perangkaan. Siaran Perangkaan Bulanan, Sarawak (MYS ISSN 0127-9238) **8387**
Malaysia. Department of Statistics. National Accounts Statistics, Malaysia/Malaysia. Jabatan Perangkaan. Perangkaan Akaun Negara, Malaysia (MYS ISSN 0126-7086) **8387**
Malaysia. Department of Statistics. Quarterly Balance of Payments Report, Malaysia/Malaysia. Jabatan Perangkaan. Laporan Imbangan Pembayaran Suku Tahunan, Malaysia (MYS) **1250**
Malaysia. Department of Statistics. Quarterly Review of Malaysian Population Statistics/Malaysia. Jabatan Perangkaan. Saran Perangkaan Penduduk Suku Tahunan, Malaysia (MYS ISSN 0127-8312) **7312**
Malaysia. Department of Statistics. Report of the Financial Survey of Limited Companies, Malaysia/Malaysia. Jabatan Perangkaan. Laporan Penyiasatan Kewangan Syarikat - Syarikat Bhd., Malaysia (MYS) **1250**
Malaysia. Department of Statistics. Report of the Paddy Yield Survey, Malaysia/Malaysia. Jabatan Perangkaan. Laporan Penyiasatan Hasil Padi, Malaysia (MYS) **183**
Malaysia. Department of Statistics. Rubber Statistics Handbook, Malaysia/Malaysia. Jabatan Perangkaan. Buku Maklumat Perangkaan Getah, Malaysia (MYS ISSN 0127-8509) **7828**
Malaysia. Department of Statistics. Social Statistics Bulletin, Malaysia/Malaysia. Jabatan Perangkaan. Buletin Perangkaan Sosial, Malaysia (MYS ISSN 0127-4686) **8083**
Malaysia. Department of Statistics. Special Release 1 - For Civil Engineering Works, Malaysia/Malaysia. Jabatan Perangkaan. Siaran Khas 1 - Untuk Kerja-kerja Kej. Awam, Malaysia (MYS ISSN 0127-8568) **3232**
Malaysia. Department of Statistics. Special Release 1 - For Civil Engineering Works, Sabah/Malaysia. Jabatan Perangkaan. Siaran Khas 1 - Untuk Kerja-kerja Kej. Awam, Sabah (MYS) **3232**
Malaysia. Department of Statistics. Special Release 1 - For Civil Engineering Works, Sarawak/Malaysia. Jabatan Perangkaan. Siaran Khas 1 - Untuk Kerja-kerja Kej. Awam, Sarawak (MYS) **3232**
Malaysia. Department of Statistics. Special Release 2 - For Building Works, Peninsular Malaysia/Malaysia. Jabatan Perangkaan. Siaran Khas 2 - Untuk Kerja-kerja Pembinaan, Sem. Malaysia (MYS ISSN 0127-8576) **1047**
Malaysia. Department of Statistics. Special Release 2 - For Building Works, Sabah/Malaysia. Jabatan Perangkaan. Siaran Khas 2 - Untuk Kerja-kerja Pembinaan, Sabah (MYS) **1047**
Malaysia. Department of Statistics. Special Release 2 - For Building Works, Sarawak/Malaysia. Jabatan Perangkaan. Siaran Khas 2 - Untuk Kerja-kerja Pembinaan, Sarawak (MYS) **1047**
Malaysia. Department of Statistics. State - District Data Bank, Malaysia/Malaysia. Jabatan Perangkaan. Bank Data Negeri - Daerah, Malaysia (MYS) **1250**
Malaysia. Department of Statistics. Statistics of External Trade. Sarawak/Malaysia. Jabatan Perangkaan. Perangkaan Perdagangan Luar Negeri. Sarawak (MYS ISSN 0127-0451) **1251**
Malaysia. Department of Statistics. Vital Statistics, Malaysia (Year)/Malaysia. Jabatan Perangkaan. Perangkaan Penting, Malaysia. (MYS) **7312**
Malaysia. Department of Statistics. Yearbook of Statistics/Malaysia. Jabatan Perangkaan. Buku Tahnan Perangkaan, Malaysia (MYS) **8387**
Malaysia. Department of Statistics. Yearbook of Statistics, Sabah/Malaysia. Jabatan Perangkaan. Buku Tahunan Perangkaan, Sabah (MYS) **1251**
Malaysia. Department of Statistics. Yearbook of Statistics, Sarawak/Malaysia. Jabatan Perangkaan. Buku Tahunan Perangkaan, Sarawak (MYS) **1251**
Malaysia Food Business Directory (MYS) **1146**
Malaysia Freight Transport Report (GBR ISSN 1752-5950) **8503**
Malaysia in Brief (MYS ISSN 0301-7095) **4185**
Malaysia Information Technology Report *see* Business Monitor International. Information Technology Country Reports **2491**
Malaysia. Jabatan Hasil Dalam Negeri. Lapuran Tahunan *see* Malaysia. Department of Inland Revenue. Annual Report **1431**
Malaysia. Jabatan Perangkaan. Banci Industri Perlombongan dan Penggalian Batu Tahunan, Malaysia *see* Malaysia. Department of Statistics. Annual Censuses of Mining and Stone Quarrying, Malaysia **6486**
Malaysia. Jabatan Perangkaan. Banci Pertubuhan Profesional dan Institusi - Sektor Swasta *see* Malaysia. Department of Statistics. Census of Professional and Institutional Establishments - Private Sector **1250**
Malaysia. Jabatan Perangkaan. Banci Tahunan Perlombongan dan Penggalian Batu, Malaysia - Jadual Tambahan *see* Malaysia. Department of Statistics. Annual Censuses of Mining and Stone Quarrying, Malaysia - Additional Tables **6486**
Malaysia. Jabatan Perangkaan. Banci Tahunan Perlombongan dan Penggalian Batu, Malaysia - Perangkaan Utama *see* Malaysia. Department of Statistics. Annual Censuses of Mining and Stone Quarrying, Malaysia - Principal Statistics **6486**
Malaysia. Jabatan Perangkaan. Bank Data Negeri - Daerah, Malaysia *see* Malaysia. Department of Statistics. State - District Data Bank, Malaysia **1250**
Malaysia. Jabatan Perangkaan. Buku Maklumat Perangkaan Getah, Malaysia *see* Malaysia. Department of Statistics. Rubber Statistics Handbook, Malaysia **7828**
Malaysia. Jabatan Perangkaan. Buku Maklumat Perangkaan Koko, Kelapa dan Teh, Malaysia *see* Malaysia. Department of Statistics. Cocoa, Coconut and Tea Statistics Handbook, Malaysia **183**
Malaysia. Jabatan Perangkaan. Buku Tahnan Perangkaan, Malaysia *see* Malaysia. Department of Statistics. Yearbook of Statistics **8387**
Malaysia. Jabatan Perangkaan. Buku Tahunan Perangkaan, Sabah *see* Malaysia. Department of Statistics. Yearbook of Statistics, Sabah **1251**
Malaysia. Jabatan Perangkaan. Buku Tahunan Perangkaan, Sarawak *see* Malaysia. Department of Statistics. Yearbook of Statistics, Sarawak **1251**
Malaysia. Jabatan Perangkaan. Buletin Perangkaan Sosial, Malaysia *see* Malaysia. Department of Statistics. Social Statistics Bulletin, Malaysia **8083**
Malaysia. Jabatan Perangkaan. Direktori Sumber Data Sektor Awam, Malaysia (MYS ISSN 0128-990X) **8843**
Malaysia. Jabatan Perangkaan. Ekonomi Malaysia Sepintas Lalu *see* Malaysia. Department of Statistics. Malaysian Economy in Brief **1250**
Malaysia. Jabatan Perangkaan. Indeks Harga Pengguna, Malaysia *see* Malaysia. Department of Statistics. Monthly Consumer Price Index, Malaysia **8387**
Malaysia. Jabatan Perangkaan. Indeks Pengeluaran Peridustrian, Malaysia *see* Malaysia. Department of Statistics. Index of Industrial Production, Malaysia **1250**
Malaysia. Jabatan Perangkaan. Laporan Imbangan Pembayaran, Malaysia. *see* Malaysia. Department of Statistics. Balance of Payments Report, Malaysia **1250**
Malaysia. Jabatan Perangkaan. Laporan Imbangan Pembayaran Suku Tahunan, Malaysia *see* Malaysia. Department of Statistics. Quarterly Balance of Payments Report, Malaysia **1250**
Malaysia. Jabatan Perangkaan. Laporan Penyiasatan Hasil Padi, Malaysia *see* Malaysia. Department of Statistics. Report of the Paddy Yield Survey, Malaysia **183**
Malaysia. Jabatan Perangkaan. Laporan Penyiasatan Kewangan Syarikat - Syarikat Bhd., Malaysia *see* Malaysia. Department of Statistics. Report of the Financial Survey of Limited Companies, Malaysia **1250**
Malaysia. Jabatan Perangkaan. Laporan Penyiasatan Migrasi, Malaysia *see* Malaysia. Department of Statistics. Migration Survey Report, Malaysia **7312**
Malaysia. Jabatan Perangkaan. Laporan Penyiasatan Tenaga Buruh, Malaysia *see* Malaysia. Department of Statistics. Labour Force Survey Report, Malaysia **7312**
Malaysia. Jabatan Perangkaan. Laporan Perangkaan Alam Kekitar, Malaysia *see* Malaysia. Department of Statistics. Compendium of Environment Statistics, Malaysia **3480**
Malaysia. Jabatan Perangkaan. Penyiasatan Jangkaan Perniagaan Bagi Syarikat-Syarikat Berhad Malaysia *see* Malaysia. Department of Statistics. Business Expectations Survey of Limited Companies Malaysia **1146**
Malaysia. Jabatan Perangkaan. Penyiasatan - Penyiasatan Perindustrian, Malaysia *see* Malaysia. Department of Statistics. Industrial Surveys, Malaysia **1250**
Malaysia. Jabatan Perangkaan. Perangkaan Akaun Negara, Malaysia *see* Malaysia. Department of Statistics. National Accounts Statistics, Malaysia **8387**
Malaysia. Jabatan Perangkaan. Perangkaan Akaun Negara, Malaysia *see* Malaysia. Department of Statistics. Census of Selected Service Industries, Malaysia **1250**
Malaysia. Jabatan Perangkaan. Perangkaan Getah Bulanan, Malaysia *see* Malaysia. Department of Statistics. Monthly Rubber Statistics, Malaysia **7828**
Malaysia. Jabatan Perangkaan. Perangkaan Penting, Malaysia. *see* Malaysia. Department of Statistics. Vital Statistics, Malaysia (Year) **7312**
Malaysia. Jabatan Perangkaan. Perangkaan Perdagangan Luar Negeri, Malaysia *see* Malaysia. Department of Statistics. External Trade Statistics, Malaysia **1250**
Malaysia. Jabatan Perangkaan. Perangkaan Perdagangan Luar Negeri. Sarawak *see* Malaysia. Department of Statistics. Statistics of External Trade. Sarawak **1251**
Malaysia. Jabatan Perangkaan. Perangkaan Perdangangan Luar Negeri. Sabah *see* Malaysia. Department of Statistics. External Trade Statistics, Sabah **1250**
Malaysia. Jabatan Perangkaan. Perangkaan Tahunan Industri Pembuatan, Malaysia - Bahagian B *see* Malaysia. Department of Statistics. Annual Statistics of Manufacturing Industries, Malaysia - Part B **1250**
Malaysia. Jabatan Perangkaan. Perangkaan Tahunan Industri Pembusatan, Malaysia - Bahagian A *see* Malaysia. Department of Statistics. Annual Statistics of Manufacturing Industries, Malaysia - Part A **1250**

Title

10586 MALAYSIA. JABATAN PERANGKAAN. SARAN PERANGKAAN PENDUDUK ULRICH'S PERIODICALS

Malaysia. Jabatan Perangkaan. Saran Perangkaan Penduduk Suku Tahunan, Malaysia *see* Malaysia. Department of Statistics. Quarterly Review of Malaysian Population Statistics **7312**
Malaysia. Jabatan Perangkaan. Siaran Khas 1 - Untuk Kerja-kerja Kej. Awam, Malaysia *see* Malaysia. Department of Statistics. Special Release 1 - For Civil Engineering Works, Malaysia **3232**
Malaysia. Jabatan Perangkaan. Siaran Khas 1 - Untuk Kerja-kerja Kej. Awam, Sabah *see* Malaysia. Department of Statistics. Special Release 1 - For Civil Engineering Works, Sabah **3232**
Malaysia. Jabatan Perangkaan. Siaran Khas 1 - Untuk Kerja-kerja Kej. Awam, Sarawak *see* Malaysia. Department of Statistics. Special Release 1 - For Civil Engineering Works, Sarawak **3232**
Malaysia. Jabatan Perangkaan. Siaran Khas 2 - Untuk Kerja-kerja Pembinaan, Sabah *see* Malaysia. Department of Statistics. Special Release 2 - For Building Works, Sabah **1047**
Malaysia. Jabatan Perangkaan. Siaran Khas 2 - Untuk Kerja-kerja Pembinaan, Sarawak *see* Malaysia. Department of Statistics. Special Release 2 - For Building Works, Sarawak **1047**
Malaysia. Jabatan Perangkaan. Siaran Khas 2 - Untuk Kerja-kerja Pembinaan, Sem. Malaysia *see* Malaysia. Department of Statistics. Special Release 2 - For Building Works, Peninsular Malaysia **1047**
Malaysia. Jabatan Perangkaan. Siaran Perangkaan Bulanan, Sabah *see* Malaysia. Department of Statistics. Monthly Bulletin of Statistics, Sabah **8387**
Malaysia. Jabatan Perangkaan. Siaran Perangkaan Bulanan, Sarawak *see* Malaysia. Department of Statistics. Monthly Statistical Bulletin, Sarawak **8387**
Malaysia. Jabatan Perangkann. Perangkaan Perdagangan Luar Negeri Bulanan, Malaysia *see* Malaysia. Department of Statistics. Monthly External Trade Statistics, Malaysia **1250**
Malaysia. Jabatan Pergangkaan. Penyiasatan Tahunan Industri Pembuatan, Malaysia *see* Malaysia. Department of Statistics. Annual Survey of Manufacturing Industries, Malaysia **1250**
Malaysia. Kementerian Kewangan. Economic Report *see* Malaysia. Ministry of Finance. Economic Report **1497**
Malaysia. Kementerian Pertanian. Bahagian Perikanan. Perangkaan Tahunan Perikanan *see* Malaysia. Ministry of Agriculture. Fisheries Division. Annual Fisheries Statistics **3601**
Malaysia Logistics Directory (MYS) **8503**
Malaysia. Minerals and Geoscience Department Malaysia. Annual Report *see* Jabatan Mineral dan Geosains Malaysia. Lapuran Tahunan **2749**
▼ • Malaysia Mining Report (GBR ISSN 1755-7992) **6469**
Malaysia. Ministry of Agriculture. Fisheries Division. Annual Fisheries Statistics/Malaysia. Kementerian Pertanian. Bahagian Perikanan. Perangkaan Tahunan Perikanan (MYS ISSN 0126-8856) **3601**
Malaysia. Ministry of Agriculture. Technical and General Bulletins (MYS) **135**
• Malaysia. Ministry of Finance. Economic Report (MYS ISSN 0126-8171) **1497**
Malaysia Official Year Book (MYS ISSN 0126-6098) **4185**
Malaysia Petrochemicals Report (GBR ISSN 1749-2335) **6777**
Malaysia Printing and Supporting Industries Directory (MYS) **2015**
Malaysia Quarterly Forecast Report *see* The Malaysia Business Forecast Report **1497**
Malaysia Source Book for Architects and Designers (Year) *see* Malaysia Source Book for Architects, Designers & Building Contractors **2015**
Malaysia Source Book for Architects, Designers & Building Contractors (MYS) **2015**
Malaysia Sports and Fitness Directory (MYS) **2015**
Malaysia Tatler (HKG ISSN 1394-7354) **3907**
Malaysia Times Guide to Computers (MYS) **2494**
▼ Malaysia Tourism Report (GBR ISSN 1747-8944) **8732**
➤ Malaysian Accounting Review (MYS ISSN 1675-4077) **1296**
Malaysian Agricultural Journal (MYS ISSN 0025-1321) **135**
Malaysian Agricultural Research & Development Institute Report *see* M A R D I Report **135**
➤ Malaysian Applied Biology/Biologi Gunaan Malaysia (MYS ISSN 0126-8643) **135**
• Malaysian Business (MYS ISSN 0126-5504) **1146**
Malaysian Chamber of Mines. Council Report (MYS) **6469**
Malaysian Chamber of Mines. Yearbook (MYS) **6469**
Malaysian Chinese Association. Annual Report (MYS ISSN 0542-397X) **4185**
Malaysian Digest (MYS ISSN 0047-5629) **7153**
Malaysian Employers Federation Annual Report (MYS) **1696**
• Malaysian Family Physician (MYS ISSN 1985-207X) **5664**
Malaysian Forester (MYS ISSN 0302-2935) **3696**
Malaysian International Chamber of Commerce and Industry Bulletin *see* M I C C I Bulletin **1406**
• ➤ Malaysian Journal of Computer Science (MYS ISSN 0127-9084) **2549**
Malaysian Journal of Economic Studies (MYS ISSN 0126-5350) **1146**
Malaysian Journal of Family Studies (MYS ISSN 0128-1232) **7286**
• ➤ Malaysian Journal of Library and Information Science (MYS ISSN 1394-6234) **5031**
• Malaysian Journal of Medical Science (MYS ISSN 1394-195X) **5664**
➤ Malaysian Journal of Pathology (MYS ISSN 0126-8635) **5664**
➤ Malaysian Journal of Science. Series A: Life Sciences (MYS ISSN 1394-1712) **687**
Malaysian Journal of Science. Series B: Physical & Earth Sciences (MYS ISSN 1394-3065) **7025**
Malaysian Management Review (MYS ISSN 0025-1348) **1774**
Malaysian Mathematical Society. Bulletin (MYS ISSN 0126-6705) **5510**
Malaysian Medical Association Newsletter *see* Berita M M A **5584**
Malaysian Meteorological Service. Annual Summary of Meteorological Observations *see* Ringkasan Tahunan Pemerhatian Kajicuaca **6394**
Malaysian Minerals Yearbook (MYS ISSN 1394-5076) **6469**
Malaysian Mining Industry (MYS) **6469**
• Malaysian National Bibliography (CD-ROM Edition) (MYS ISSN 1394-5602) **630**
• Malaysian National Bibliography (Online Edition) (MYS) **631**
Malaysian Naturalist (MYS ISSN 1511-970X) **2618**
Malaysian Oil Palm Statistics (Year) (MYS) **3153**
Malaysian Palm Oil Board Technology *see* M P O B Technology **135**
• Malaysian Palm Oil Fortune (MYS) **3655**
Malaysian Palm Oil Update (MYS) **3141**
Malaysian Panorama (MYS ISSN 0126-527X) **3907**
Malaysian Philatelist *see* Pemungut Setem Malaysia **6897**
Malaysian Pineapple (MYS ISSN 0126-5601) **135**
Malaysian Rubber Board. Planters Bulletin (MYS ISSN 0032-096X) **7825**
Malaysian Rubber Board. Rubber Growers' Conference - Proceedings (MYS ISSN 0127-9785) **7825**
Malaysian Rubber Producers' Council. Annual Report/Majlis Pengeluar-Pengeluar Getah Malaysia. Lapuran Tahunan (MYS ISSN 0126-8309) **7825**
Malaysian Rubber Producers' Council. Monthly Bulletin (MYS) **7825**
➤ The Malaysian Surveyor (MYS) **2753**
Malaysian Technologist (MYS ISSN 0127-6441) **8431**
The Malaysian Women's Weekly (MYS) **8873**
Malaysia's Best Restaurants (MYS ISSN 1394-7338) **4393**
Malcolm Millar Lecture in Psychotherapy (GBR ISSN 0955-386X) **7384**
Male Kobietki (POL ISSN 0947-4609) **2258**
Male Monografie Muzyczne (POL) **6586**
Male View Magazine *see* ManKind Magazine **6294**
Maledicta (USA ISSN 0363-3659) **5149**
Maledicta Press Publications (USA ISSN 0363-9037) **5150**
Malegleder *see* Decor-Magasinet **534**
Maler Praxis (DEU ISSN 0943-3872) **6718**
Maler und Lackierer (DEU ISSN 1614-6158) **6718**
Der Maler und Lackierermeister (DEU ISSN 0947-7489) **6719**
Malerblatt (DEU ISSN 1434-1360) **6719**
• Maleren (NOR ISSN 0333-3531) **6719**
Malfregnir (ISL ISSN 1011-5889) **5150**
• Mali Food Security Update (USA ISSN 1948-738X) **1601**
Ma'li Kkeulle'leu *see* Marie Claire **8873**
Mali Monthly Food Security Update *see* Mali Food Security Update **1601**
Mali. Service de la Statistique Generale, de la Comptabilite Nationale et de la Mecanographie. Bulletin Mensuel de Statistique (MLI) **8387**
• Malibu Magazine (USA ISSN 1938-9272) **5076**
Malibu Mirage (USA ISSN 1543-8805) **65**
Malibu Mirage Owners and Pilots Association Newsletter *see* Malibu Mirage **65**
• ➤ Malignant Hyperthermia (AUT ISSN 1609-7041) **6027**
Malingshu Zazhi/Journal of Potatoes *see* Zhongguo Malingshu **260**
Mallal's Monthly Digest (MYS ISSN 0961-5563) **4727**
Mallas ja Olut (FIN ISSN 0356-3014) **607**
• Malleable Jangle (AUS ISSN 1832-4126) **5426**
• Mallee Catchment Management Authority. Annual Report (AUS ISSN 1833-0924) **8828**
Mallige (IND ISSN 0025-1399) **3885**
• Mallorca Directions (USA ISSN 1559-4289) **8732**
Mallorn (GBR ISSN 0308-6674) **5444**
• Malmoe Hoegskola. Konst, Kultur och Kommunikation. Dissertations in Arts and Communication (SWE ISSN 1653-6606) **8119**
Malmoe Hoegskola. Konst, Kultur och Kommunikation. Studies in Arts and Communications (SWE ISSN 1652-0343) **8119**
• Malmoe Hoegskola. Laerarutbildningen. Rapporter om Utbildning (SWE ISSN 1101-7643) **2885**
Malmoe Hoegskola. Laerarutbildningen. Saertryck och Smaatryck fraan Forskarutbildning i Pedagogik/Malmoe University. School of Teacher Education. Reprints and Miniprints from Department of Educational Research (SWE ISSN 1652-053X) **2885**
Malmoe Hoegskola. Odontologiska Fakulteten. Odontological Dissertations (SWE ISSN 1650-6065) **5855**
Malmoe Kulturmiljoe. Rapport (SWE ISSN 1650-8122) **4242**
• Malmoe Museer. E-Skrifter (SWE ISSN 1651-9795) **6528**
Malmoe Museer. Skriftserie (SWE ISSN 1650-9811) **6528**
Malmoe Studies in Sport Sciences (SWE ISSN 1652-3180) **8186**
Malmoe University. Faculty of Odontology. Annual Publications (SWE ISSN 1651-2936) **5855**
Malmoe University. School of Teacher Education. Reprints and Miniprints from Department of Educational Research *see* Malmoe Hoegskola. Laerarutbildningen. Saertryck och Smaatryck fraan Forskarutbildning i Pedagogik **2885**
Malmoeya (SWE ISSN 0349-697X) **404**
• Maloe Predprinimatel'stvo v Rossii (Year) (RUS) **1251**
Malone Society Reprints (GBR ISSN 0265-4032) **5329**
Malot's Guide to the Session of the Legislative Assembly for the Australian Capital Territory *see* Proceedings of the Legislative Assembly for the Australian Capital Territory. Digest **7460**
Malovane Obrazky *see* Diana - Malovane Obrazky **534**
Malspass Kinderleicht (DEU) **2201**
• Malt Advocate (USA ISSN 1086-4199) **607**
Malta. Central Office of Statistics. Annual Abstract of Statistics (MLT ISSN 0256-8047) **8387**
Malta. Central Office of Statistics. Demographic Review of the Maltese Islands (MLT ISSN 0076-3470) **7312**
Malta. Central Office of Statistics. Education Statistics (MLT ISSN 0076-3489) **2934**
Malta. Central Office of Statistics. Industry Statistics (MLT ISSN 1027-4960) **1251**
Malta. Central Office of Statistics. Quarterly Digest of Statistics (MLT ISSN 0025-1437) **8387**
Malta. Central Office of Statistics. Shipping and Aviation Statistics (MLT ISSN 0377-791X) **8527**
Malta. Central Office of Statistics. Trade Statistics (MLT ISSN 0580-5260) **1577**
Malta. Department of Information. Reports on the Working of Government Departments (MLT ISSN 0377-4503) **7481**
Malta Library and Information Association Newsletter *see* M A L I A Newsletter **5030**
• Malta Medical Journal (MLT ISSN 1813-3339) **5664**
Malta. Ministry of Finance and Commerce. Economic Survey (MLT) **1498**
Malta National Bibliography/Bibliografija Nazzjonalita Malta (MLT ISSN 0258-669X) **631**
Malta Trade Directory (Year) (MLT) **2015**
Malta Yearbook (GBR ISSN 0542-4550) **7153**
Malta's Economic Indicators (MLT) **1251**
Maltese Herald (AUS) **3549**
Maltese Magazine (USA ISSN 8750-5487) **6811**
Maltese Medical Journal *see* Malta Medical Journal **5664**
Maltese Narrazioni (ITA ISSN 1825-6430) **5329**
Malteser-Magazin (DEU ISSN 1436-641X) **8055**
Maltose Falcons Brews & News *see* Brews & News **601**
• Maltrattamento e Abuso all'Infanzia (ITA ISSN 1591-4267) **2160**
Malus (USA) **3742**
The Malvern Examiner (USA) **4513**
Malvern Physics Series (GBR ISSN 0953-3206) **7025**
Malyatko (UKR ISSN 0025-1453) **2201**
Malyi Biznes Rossii (RUS) **1146**
Malzenstwo i Rodzina (POL ISSN 1643-7489) **8119**
Mama *see* Foraeldre & Boern **2153**
Mama Bears News and Notes (USA) **8873**
• Mama Lianyihui Jianxun (USA) **2160**
• Mama, Papa, Ya (RUS) **6096**
Mamalicious (USA) **8873**
• MaMaMedia (USA ISSN 1090-5529) **2201**
Mamamia (DEU ISSN 0945-2400) **2201**
Maman! (FRA ISSN 1634-5398) **8873**
Mamane (IND) **2885**
Mami (ROM ISSN 1224-6492) **5997**
Mami Baobei/Mum & Baby (CHN ISSN 1671-2137) **8873**
Mamimiling Pindy *see* Filipino Consumer **2638**
Mamina (SVK ISSN 1336-7269) **2160**
Maminka (CZE ISSN 1213-5100) **2160**
➤ Mamluk Studies Review (USA ISSN 1086-170X) **555**
Mamm (USA ISSN 1099-5633) **8846**
Mamma (NOR ISSN 1503-1519) **2160**
• ➤ Mammal Review (GBR ISSN 0305-1838) **954**
• ➤ Mammal Review Online (GBR ISSN 1365-2907) **954**
Mammal Society. Occasional Publication (GBR ISSN 0141-3392) **954**
• Mammal Study (JPN ISSN 1343-4152) **954**
• ➤ Mammalia (DEU ISSN 0025-1461) **954**
• ➤ Mammalian Biology (DEU ISSN 1616-5047) **954**
Mammalian Biology. Sonderheft *see* Mammalian Biology **954**
• ➤ Mammalian Genome (USA ISSN 0938-8990) **875**
Mammalian Science *see* Honyurui Kagaku **946**
• ➤ Mammalian Species (Online) (USA ISSN 1545-1410) **955**
† • ➤ Mammalian Species (Print) (USA ISSN 0076-3519) **8972**
• Mammalogy Abstracts (USA) **717**
Mammals' Newsletter in Homeland Gifu *see* Gifu Furusato to Dobutsu Tsushin **944**
➤ Mammillaria (DEU ISSN 1613-9941) **800**
Mammillaria Journal *see* Mammillaria Society. Journal **3742**
Mammillaria Society. Journal (GBR ISSN 0464-8072) **3742**
Mammography Centers Directory (USA ISSN 1559-4645) **4106**
• Mammography Regulation and Reimbursement (USA ISSN 1554-3285) **4106**
Mammography Regulation Report *see* Mammography Regulation and Reimbursement **4106**
Mammologiya (RUS ISSN 0130-1667) **955**
The Mammoth Book of Best New Horror (GBR) **5444**
Mammoth Monthly (USA ISSN 1541-5600) **3981**
Mammoth Trumpet (USA ISSN 8755-6898) **404**
I Mammut (ITA ISSN 1970-3805) **955**
Mamo to Ja (POL ISSN 1233-7366) **2160**
Mampa (DEU) **5076**
† Man (NLD ISSN 0165-4578) **8972**
Man & Environment (IND ISSN 0258-0446) **346**
➤ Man and Life (IND ISSN 0972-4109) **346**
Man and Society *see* Meddelelser om Groenland. Man & Society **347**
Man and Society *see* Manusia dan Masyarakat **347**
Man and the Biosphere *see* Ren yu Shengwuquan **700**
Man and the Biosphere Report Series *see* M A B Report Series **3451**
Man and the Biosphere Series (FRA ISSN 1020-2714) **3451**
Man at Arms (USA ISSN 0191-3522) **367**
Man Bag Magazine (USA) **6294**
Man - Environment Systems (USA ISSN 0025-1550) **3451**
Man from Mainz and His Descendants (USA ISSN 0890-8192) **3774**
Man from U N C L E Fan Club Newsletter (USA) **2384**
➤ Man in India (IND ISSN 0025-1569) **347**
Man in the Gulf (UAE) **6294**
Man-Made Fiber Year Book (DEU ISSN 0932-5522) **8454**
Man-Made Fibre Statistics (Year) (IND) **8464**
➤ Man-Made Textiles in India (IND ISSN 0377-7537) **8454**
Man Magnum (ZAF) **8321**
Man to Machine *see* M 2 M **2332**
• ➤ Mana (BRA ISSN 0104-9313) **347**
Mana (FJI ISSN 0379-5268) **5329**
Mana (NZL ISSN 1172-0425) **3549**
Manaar al-Islam (UAE) **7714**
Manab Mon (IND ISSN 0025-1615) **7384**
Man!ac *see* M! Games **2478**
ManACE Journal (CAN ISSN 1199-0767) **3071**
• Manage (Online) (USA ISSN 1552-3748) **1774**
Managed Account Reports *see* M A R Hedge **1638**
Managed Account Reports Hedge *see* M A R Hedge **1638**
Managed Account Reports Hedge *see* M A R Hedge **1638**
Managed Care *see* Care Management **5592**
• Managed Care (USA ISSN 1062-3388) **4513**
• The Managed Care Acquisition Report (USA ISSN 1525-9706) **1146**
➤ Managed Care & Cancer (USA ISSN 1522-6395) **6027**
Managed Care and Medical Cost Containment in Worker's Compensation (USA ISSN 1523-2433) **4513**
• Managed Care Business Week (USA ISSN 1552-5678) **1146**
Managed Care Consultant - First Report (USA) **5664**
• Managed Care Contracting & Reimbursement Advisor (USA ISSN 1533-5453) **4106**
Managed Care Europe (GBR ISSN 1366-9613) **6860**
▼ Managed Care First Report (USA ISSN 2150-1696) **4106**
➤ Managed Care Interface (USA ISSN 1096-5645) **4106**
Managed Care Law Strategist (USA ISSN 1529-4161) **4727**
• Managed Care Law Weekly (USA ISSN 1551-5052) **4727**
Managed Care Litigation Reporter *see* Andrews Managed Care Litigation Reporter **4617**
• Managed Care Outlook (USA ISSN 0896-6567) **4513**
Managed Care Pharmacy Update (USA ISSN 1540-2355) **6860**
Managed Care Quarterly *see* Managed Care Outlook **4513**
Managed Care Report *see* Medicine & Health's Managed Care Report **4515**
Managed Care Week *see* Health Plan Week **4505**
• Managed Care Weekly Digest (USA ISSN 1543-6365) **5664**

Link to your serials resources and content with ulrichsweb.com

DIRECTORY 2010 MANCHESTER UNITED MAGAZINE 10587

• Managed Dental Care (USA ISSN 1083-3641) **4106**
• Managed Healthcare Executive (USA ISSN 1533-9300) **4106**
Managed Medicare & Medicaid News *see* Part B News **4518**
† Managed Pharmaceutical Report (USA ISSN 1075-2358) **8972**
• ➤ M@n@gement (FRA ISSN 1286-4692) **1774**
• Management (FRA ISSN 1627-4792) **1774**
Management (HRV ISSN 1331-0194) **1774**
Management (POL ISSN 1429-9321) **1774**
Management (SRB ISSN 0354-8635) **1774**
• Management (SVN ISSN 1854-4223) **1774**
Management *see* Management Journal **1776**
Management (Washington) (USA ISSN 0198-8557) **1774**
The Management Accountant (IND ISSN 0025-1674) **1296**
Management Accountant (PAK) **1296**
The Management Accountants Compartment of the Indonesian Institute of Accountants Bulletin *see* Buletin Akuntan Manajemen **1282**
• ➤ Management Accounting Quarterly (Online Edition) (USA) **1296**
• ➤ Management Accounting Research (GBR ISSN 1044-5005) **1296**
Management Agenda (GBR) **1774**
Management and Administration in Rural Economy *see* Nongye Hezuo Jingji Jingying Guanli **204**
Management and Benefit *see* Guanli yu Xiaoyi **1749**
• Management & Change (IND ISSN 0972-2149) **1774**
Management and Development (IRN) **1774**
† Management and Industrial Relations Series (GBR) **8972**
▼ ➤ Management & Informatics (USA ISSN 1939-4187) **2431**
Management & Information *see* Guanli yu Xinxi **8960**
Management & Krankenhaus *see* Management und Krankenhaus **4106**
➤ Management and Labour Studies (IND ISSN 0258-042X) **1696**
Management and Leadership in Education Series (GBR) **3027**
• Management and Marketing (ROM ISSN 1841-2416) **1774**
• Management and Marketing Abstracts (GBR ISSN 0308-2172) **1251**
• ➤ Management & Organization Review (AUS ISSN 1740-8776) **1775**
• ➤ Management & Organizational History (GBR ISSN 1744-9359) **1775**
Management and Supervision of Law Enforcement Personnel (USA) **1775**
Management & Supervision of Law Enforcement Personnel *see* Management and Supervision of Law Enforcement Personnel **1775**
Management Assistant *see* Management Support Magazine **1852**
Management Berater (DEU ISSN 1433-9862) **1775**
Management Briefing (USA) **6403**
Management Buy-Outs (GBR ISSN 1353-8950) **1775**
• ➤ Management Communication Quarterly (USA ISSN 0893-3189) **1775**
Management Compensation Survey (USA ISSN 1076-1594) **5664**
Management Consultancies *see* Business Ratio Report. Management Consultancies (Year) **1730**
• Management Consultancy (GBR ISSN 1351-0924) **1775**
Management Consultant *see* Management en Consulting **1775**
• Management Consultant International (USA ISSN 0956-3253) **1775**
Management Consultants *see* Key Note Market Report: Management Consultants **1894**
Management Consultants News (GBR ISSN 1351-0894) **1775**
Management Control en Accounting (NLD ISSN 1386-3452) **1296**
Management dan Usahawan Indonesia (IDN ISSN 0302-9859) **1775**
Management Data List (ML): ML - Marine Corps (USA) **6455**
Management Data List (ML): ML - Navy (USA) **6432**
Management de Projet. Methodes et Outils (FRA ISSN 1957-6552) **1775**
• ➤ Management Decision (GBR ISSN 0025-1747) **1775**
Management Development Centre Business Journal *see* M D C Business Journal **1145**
Management Development Series (CHE ISSN 0074-6703) **1775**
Management Diary *see* Management Today **1777**
Management Digest (IND) **1869**
Management Dynamics *see* Bestuursdinamika **1728**
Management en Consulting (NLD ISSN 1871-2797) **1775**
Management et Gestion des Ressources Humaines (FRA ISSN 1957-648X) **1869**
Management et Gestion des Ressources Humaines en Etablissement Sanitaire, Social et Medico-Social *see* Management et Gestion des Ressources Humaines **1869**
Management & Sciences Sociales (FRA ISSN 1952-3262) **1775**
Management et Secteur Public *see* Public Sector Management **7463**
• Management Executive (NLD ISSN 1571-862X) **1775**
Management for Strategic Business Ideas *see* C M A Management **1283**
Management - Forschung und Praxis (DEU ISSN 1615-2107) **1775**
Management Forum (USA) **1775**
Management Ideas (IND ISSN 0025-1771) **1775**
• ➤ Management in Education (GBR ISSN 0892-0206) **3027**
Management in Government (GBR ISSN 0263-4678) **1775**
Management in Government (IND ISSN 0047-570X) **7452**
➤ Management in Nigeria (NGA ISSN 0025-178X) **1775**
Management in Practice (GBR ISSN 1747-9304) **4106**
Management in Practice (USA ISSN 1067-9391) **1775**
Management in Practice (Corpus Christi) (USA ISSN 1945-5623) **1776**
Management Information Service (IND ISSN 0300-2667) **1776**
Management Information Systems (GBR ISSN 1470-6326) **2549**
Management Information Systems Quarterly *see* M I S Quarterly **2523**
Management Information Systems Quarterly Executive *see* M I S Quarterly Executive **1145**
Management Insight (IND ISSN 0973-936X) **1776**
• ➤ Management International (CAN ISSN 1206-1697) **1776**
Management Issues & Trends (USA) **7599**
Management Issues in Social Care (GBR ISSN 1360-936X) **7531**
† Management Jakosti s Podporou Norem ISO 9000:2000 (CZE ISSN 1801-7738) **8972**
Management Journal (UGA ISSN 0300-2144) **1776**
Management Kinderopvang (NLD ISSN 1382-4406) **2160**
• ➤ Management Learning (GBR ISSN 1350-5076) **1776**
Management. Les Guides (FRA ISSN 1771-9895) **1776**
Management Magazine (TWN ISSN 1011-7792) **1776**
• Management Matters (CAN ISSN 1201-7817) **1776**
Management O H S & E *see* EurOhs **6676**
Management of Agriculture Science and Technology *see* Nongye Keji Guanli **141**
Management of Commercial Enterprise *see* Shangye Qiye Guanli **1793**
• ➤ Management of Environmental Quality (GBR ISSN 1477-7835) **3451**
Management of National Economy *see* Guomin Jingji Guanli **1116**
Management of Science and Technology *see* Keji Guanli **1770**
• The Management of Security Assistance (USA ISSN 1532-0359) **7251**
▼ Management of Technology (SGP) **8431**
Management of Technology (SWE ISSN 1102-5581) **1776**
The Management of the Menopause: Annual Review (GBR ISSN 1460-1397) **5997**
Management of Tourism *see* Luyou Guangli **8731**
Management of Voluntary Organisations (GBR ISSN 0968-6630) **8055**
The Management of Water Resources (GBR) **8828**
Management Pay Review *see* I D S Executive Compensation Review **1686**
▼ Management Perspectives (ZAF ISSN 1996-7187) **1776**
Management, Politics and Philosophy Leads *see* M P P Leads **1774**
Management Portfolio *see* Printing Industries of America: The Magazine **1786**
Management Professionals Association. Events Diary (IND) **1776**
Management Professionals Association. Journal (IND ISSN 0970-0447) **1776**
• Management Quarterly (USA ISSN 0025-1860) **1776**
Management, Rechnungslegung und Unternehmensbesteuerung (DEU ISSN 0948-7026) **1934**
Management Rendement (NLD ISSN 1569-3694) **1776**
• Management Report (Online Edition) (USA ISSN 1530-8286) **1696**
• Management Research (USA ISSN 1536-5433) **1776**
Management Research News *see* Management Research Review **1776**
• ➤ Management Research Review (GBR ISSN 0140-9174) **1776**
• Management Review (USA ISSN 0025-1895) **1776**
• Management Revue (DEU ISSN 0935-9915) **1776**
Management Rewards (GBR ISSN 1475-8156) **1696**
Management Science *see* Guanli Kexue **1748**
• ➤ Management Science (USA ISSN 0025-1909) **1776**
• Management Sciences for Health. Occasional Papers (USA ISSN 1930-0298) **7531**
Management Sciences Research *see* Guanli Kexue Yanjiu **1748**
Management Scope (NLD ISSN 1387-5183) **1776**
Management Select *see* Management Executive **1775**
• Management Services (GBR ISSN 0307-6768) **1777**
Management Services Department Legal Reporting Service *see* N R E C A - A P P A Legal Reporting Service **4737**
Management Social *see* Collection Management Social **1734**
The Management Specialist (GBR ISSN 0307-3041) **1777**
Management Support Magazine (NLD ISSN 1382-3590) **1852**
Management Team (NLD ISSN 0166-1256) **1777**
• Management Today (AUS ISSN 1440-5636) **1777**
• Management Today (GBR ISSN 0025-1925) **1777**
Management Today (IND ISSN 0973-5550) **1777**
• Management Today (MEX ISSN 0186-5609) **1777**
• Management Today (ZAF ISSN 1027-4324) **1777**
Management Today's Guide to Britain's Best Factories *see* Management Today **1777**
Management Training and Research Centres in India. Directory (IND) **1777**
Management.travel (USA) **8732**
Management Trends (IND ISSN 0973-9203) **1869**
Management Trends (NLD ISSN 1567-2883) **1869**
Management Trends, Tools en Visies *see* Management Trends **1869**
Management und Krankenhaus (DEU ISSN 0176-053X) **4106**
Management und Qualitaet (CHE ISSN 1422-6634) **6403**
Management und Qualitaet (DEU ISSN 1862-2623) **1777**
Management und Wirtschaft Studien (DEU ISSN 1861-1745) **1777**
Management World *see* Guanli Shijie **1749**
Managementblad Rijksdienst (NLD ISSN 1381-0928) **7452**
Managementforschung (DEU ISSN 1615-6005) **1777**
ManagementReport Health (DEU ISSN 1863-1479) **4106**
Management's Discussion and Analysis (CAN ISSN 1719-9700) **1296**
• The Manager (AUS) **1777**
• Manager (GBR ISSN 1746-1278) **1777**
Manager (POL ISSN 1426-0204) **1777**
Manager (SDN) **1777**
• The Manager (USA) **4106**
The Manager as... (USA ISSN 1555-7480) **1777**
Manager Magazin (DEU ISSN 0341-4418) **1777**
Manager Magazin (Edycja Polska) (POL ISSN 1733-4292) **1777**
Manager Update *see* Finance & Management **1745**
• ➤ Managerial and Decision Economics (GBR ISSN 0143-6570) **1777**
• ➤ Managerial Auditing Journal (GBR ISSN 0268-6902) **1778**
• ➤ Managerial Finance (GBR ISSN 0307-4358) **1778**
Managerial Law *see* International Journal of Law and Management **1689**
Manager's Business Report (USA) **2360**
Manager's Digest (IND) **1778**
Managers Guide to the Americans with Disabilities Act (USA) **1696**
The Manager's Intelligence Report (USA ISSN 1099-7261) **1778**
Manager's Legal Bulletin (USA ISSN 0889-4493) **1778**
Manager's Report *see* Florida Community Association Journal **7591**
Manager's Security Alert (USA ISSN 1541-7379) **1778**
ManagerSeminare (DEU ISSN 0938-6211) **1778**
• Managing 24/7 (USA) **1778**
Managing 401k Plans *see* I O M A's Report on Managing 401k Plans **1865**
• Managing 401k Plans Yearbook (USA) **1869**
Managing Accounts Payable *see* I O M A's Report on Managing Accounts Payable **1290**
• Managing Accounts Payable Yearbook (USA) **1296**
• Managing Automation (USA ISSN 0895-3805) **2462**
Managing Benefits Plans *see* I O M A's Report on Managing Benefits Plans **1865**
• Managing Benefits Plans Yearbook (USA) **1869**
Managing Best Practice (GBR ISSN 1355-1515) **1869**
Managing Clinically Important Drug Interactions (USA ISSN 1931-146X) **6860**
Managing Credit, Receivables and Collections *see* I O M A's Report on Managing Credit, Receivables and Collections **1352**
• Managing Credit, Receivables & Collections Yearbook (USA) **1366**
Managing Credit, Receivables and Collections Yearbook *see* Managing Credit, Receivables & Collections Yearbook **1366**
Managing Diabetes *see* Safeway Managing Diabetes **5900**
Managing Economic Transition Network. Working Paper Series (GBR ISSN 1471-9894) **1146**
• Managing Education Matters (CYP ISSN 1463-7081) **3027**
Managing Employees Under F M L A and A D A (Federal Family & Medical Leave Act and Americans with Disabilities Act) (USA ISSN 1521-5326) **1869**
Managing Employees Under F M L A & A D A *see* Managing Employees Under F M L A and A D A **1869**
Managing Exports & Imports *see* I O M A's Report on Managing Exports & Imports **1568**
Managing Forest Ecosystems (NLD ISSN 1568-1319) **3451**
• Managing Global Transitions (SVN ISSN 1581-6311) **1778**
• Managing High Blood Pressure (Online Edition) (USA) **5664**
Managing in Today's Government (USA ISSN 1551-2819) **7452**
Managing Infection Control (USA ISSN 1535-3575) **5822**
• Managing Information (GBR ISSN 1352-0229) **5031**
Managing Information and Documents (GBR) **5031**
Managing Information Strategies (Australian Edition) *see* M I S (Australian Edition) **1773**
Managing Information Strategies 100 *see* M I S 100 **2531**
• Managing Intellectual Property (GBR ISSN 0960-5002) **6754**
Managing Intellectual Property Assets Worldwide *see* Global Intellectual Property Asset Management Report **6750**
Managing Intellectual Property World I P Contacts Handbook *see* World I P Contacts Handbook (Year) **6760**
• ➤ Managing Leisure (GBR ISSN 1360-6719) **4980**
Managing Menopause (USA ISSN 1091-5680) **5997**
Managing Object Technology Series *see* S I G S: Managing Object Technology Series **8437**
• Managing Partner (GBR ISSN 1462-5571) **1147**
Managing Partner (USA) **1778**
• Managing People at Work (USA ISSN 1525-8181) **1869**
• Managing School Business (USA ISSN 1092-2229) **3027**
Managing Schools Today *see* School Leadership **2909**
• ➤ Managing Service Quality (GBR ISSN 0960-4529) **1778**
Managing Technology (USA ISSN 1062-1709) **1366**
• Managing the Border: Immigration Compliance (AUS ISSN 1449-6461) **7286**
• Managing the Florida Condominium (USA) **4727**
Managing the Margin (USA ISSN 1544-2632) **4106**
➤ Managing the Modern Laboratory (USA ISSN 1082-5878) **2072**
Managing the Nation's Public Lands (USA) **7452**
• Managing Today's Federal Employees (USA ISSN 1526-0739) **1869**
Managing Training & Development *see* I O M A's Report on Managing Training & Development **1865**
Managing Training and Development Yearbook *see* Managing Training & Development Yearbook **1869**
• Managing Training & Development Yearbook (USA) **1869**
Managing Twenty-Four/Seven *see* Managing 24/7 **1778**
Managing Your Career (USA) **6701**
Managing Your Regional Council: Techniques for the Director (USA) **7452**
Manak (IND) **3885**
Manana (Mexico, D.F.) (MEX ISSN 0034-9844) **3909**
• El Manana (Nuevo Laredo) (MEX) **3909**
• Manana (Reynosa) (MEX) **3909**
El Manana Daily (USA) **3549**
Mananam Publication Series (USA ISSN 0276-0444) **7707**
Manar al-Huda (USA) **7714**
Manasseh/Menasheh (USA) **3549**
Manatee (USA) **3981**
• Manawatu Standard (NZL ISSN 1176-3558) **3917**
Manay Inder/Our Platform (MNG) **7153**
Manazment Podnikania a Veci Verejnych (SVK ISSN 1337-0510) **1778**
Manazment Skoly v Praxi (SVK ISSN 1336-9849) **3027**
Manchester (IND) **8454**
Manchester (USA ISSN 1046-1280) **3981**
Manchester Business School Review (GBR ISSN 0308-5244) **1147**
Manchester Chamber of Commerce. Record (GBR ISSN 0025-1992) **1407**
• ➤ Manchester Journal of International Economic Law (GBR ISSN 1742-3945) **1577**
Manchester Metropolitan University. Department of Economics. Discussion Papers (GBR ISSN 1460-4906) **1546**
Manchester Metropolitan University. Department of Library and Information Studies. Occasional Papers (GBR) **5031**
• Manchester Papers in Economic and Social History (GBR ISSN 1753-7762) **7984**
Manchester Papers in Social Anthropology (GBR ISSN 1362-3559) **347**
• Manchester Region History Review (GBR ISSN 0952-4320) **4242**
• ➤ The Manchester School (GBR ISSN 1463-6786) **1546**
➤ Manchester Sociology Occasional Papers (GBR ISSN 1366-2554) **8119**
➤ Manchester Sociology Working Papers (GBR) **8119**
Manchester Training Handbooks (GBR ISSN 0260-4388) **7452**
Manchester United Magazine *see* Inside United **8236**

Title

10588 MANCHESTER UNITED SUPERREDS ULRICH'S PERIODICALS

Manchester United SuperReds (GBR ISSN 1353-9124) 8238
Manchete (BRA) 3804
Manchete (PRT ISSN 0872-3303) 5226
Manchete Rural (BRA ISSN 0102-8901) 135
Manchu Literature *see* Manzu Wenxue 5330
Manchu Studies *see* Manzu Yanjiu 3549
Mandacaruzinho (NLD ISSN 1572-3356) 8055
Mandaeistische Forschungen (DEU) 5329
Mandag Morgen (DNK ISSN 0905-4332) 4242
Mandag Morgen Norge (NOR ISSN 1503-7096) 1778
Mandag Morgen Norge. Rapporter *see* Mandag Morgen Norge 1778
• Mandala (USA ISSN 1075-4113) 7702
Mandanten-Information fuer Aerzte und Zahnaerzte (DEU) 5664
Mandanten-Information fuer das Bau- und Baunebengewerbe (DEU) 1022
Mandanten-Information fuer das Hotel- und Gaststaetten-Gewerbe (DEU) 4393
Mandanten-Information fuer das Kfz-Gewerbe (DEU) 8589
Mandanten-Information fuer das Personalbuero (DEU) 1869
Mandanten-Information fuer den GmbH-Geschaeftsfuehrer (DEU) 1778
Mandanten-Information fuer Haus- und Grundbesitzer (DEU) 7599
Mandanten-Information fuer Vereine (DEU) 2267
Mandarin Children Monthly *see* Guoyu Youer 5124
Mandarin Oriental *see* M O 8784
Mandarin Teenager Monthly *see* Guoyu Qingshaonan 5124
Mandarin Weekly *see* Guoyu Zhoukan 5124
Mandate (CAN ISSN 0225-7068) 7661
† Mandate (USA ISSN 0360-1005) 8972
• Mandate News (IRL) 1830
Mandatory Aircraft Modifications and Inspections Summary (GBR) 8548
➤ Mande Studies (USA ISSN 1536-5506) 5330
• Mandenkan (FRA ISSN 0752-5443) 5150
Mandeville's Used Book Price Guide (USA ISSN 1045-5388) 7567
Mandolin Quarterly (USA ISSN 1081-3918) 6586
➤ Mandorla (USA ISSN 1550-7432) 5226
• MandoZine (USA) 6586
Mandragora (BRA) 8900
Mandragora (POL ISSN 1429-9496) 5226
Mandurah Coastal Times (AUS) 3795
MANE *see* Monographs on the Ancient Near East 4323
The Maneater Newspaper (USA) 2291
➤ Manejo Integrado de Plagas (CRI ISSN 1016-0469) 768
Maneo (ZAF) 1296
• Manequim (BRA ISSN 0025-2077) 2258
Manequim. Faca e Venda (BRA ISSN 1415-8582) 2258
Manequim Ponto Cruz (BRA ISSN 1414-4972) 6640
Mang Zhong (Grain in Beard) Literature *see* Mangzhong 5330
Manga Force (GBR ISSN 1469-459X) 4339
Manga Max (GBR ISSN 1470-8817) 504
Mangai (IND) 3885
Mangalam Weekly (IND) 8873
Mangalore Sociology Association. Journal *see* Samaja Shodhana 8131
Mangayar Malar (IND) 3885
I Mangiari (ITA ISSN 1970-3503) 4363
Mangkai *see* Mangai 3885
Manglar (PER ISSN 1816-7667) 4464
Mangle (IDN ISSN 0852-8217) 3891
Mango (Year) (ZAF ISSN 1814-2575) 242
• Mangren Yuekan/Blind Monthly (CHN ISSN 1003-1103) 4083
• Mangrove (AUS ISSN 1441-9289) 5330
Mangrove (USA) 5226
The Mangrove Review (USA) 5226
Mangyuan (CHN ISSN 1003-2746) 504
Mangzhong/Mang Zhong (Grain in Beard) Literature (CHN ISSN 1003-9309) 5330
Al-Manhal (SAU ISSN 1319-0342) 5226
Al-Manhal/Fountain (UAE) 2201
▼ Manhattan (New York) (USA) 5076
Manhattan (Riverdale) (USA) 2291
Manhattan Arts International (USA ISSN 1524-4180) 504
Manhattan Bride (USA) 5559
Manhattan Catalogue (USA ISSN 0193-3116) 28
Manhattan Christian College Connection *see* The M C C Connection 2290
Manhattan: Compass American Guides *see* Compass American Guides: Manhattan 8694
Manhattan Jewish Sentinel (USA) 7726
Manhattan Literary Review (USA ISSN 1541-4248) 5226
Manhattan Living (USA) 5076
Manhattan Medical News *see* M M News 5663
Manhattan Poetry Review (USA ISSN 0885-9205) 5426
Manhattan Review (USA ISSN 0275-6889) 5426
Manhua Party *see* Xuesheng Guangjiao 2222
Manhua Yuekan/Cartoon (CHN ISSN 1003-7128) 2201
Mani di Fata (ITA ISSN 0025-2131) 4363
† Mani-festa (ITA) 8972
Mani Tese *see* ManiTese 8055
Mania (AUS ISSN 1445-0682) 3795
Mania (ESP ISSN 1576-5113) 6933
Maniac *see* M! Games 2478
Manica Post (ZWE ISSN 1996-4382) 3996
Manichaean Studies (BEL) 7738
Manicomic (ESP ISSN 1575-474X) 504
Maniere de Voir (FRA ISSN 1241-6290) 7153
• Manifest (AUS ISSN 1329-7961) 2660
• Il Manifesto (ITA ISSN 0025-2158) 3897
Manifesto. Quaderno *see* Il Manifesto 3897
El Manifiesto *see* El Manifiesto contra la Muerte del Espiritu de la Tierra 5226
• El Manifiesto contra la Muerte del Espiritu de la Tierra (ESP ISSN 1698-4676) 5226
Manifold (GBR ISSN 0025-2166) 5426
• Manila Bulletin (PHL) 3928
➤ Manila Journal of Science (PHL) 7881
• Manila Standard (PHL ISSN 0116-5054) 3928
• The Manila Times (PHL) 3928
Manip (FRA ISSN 1772-2950) 8473
▼ Manip Info (FRA ISSN 1960-1824) 6202
Manipulacion de Materiales en la Industria (ESP ISSN 0210-1513) 1022
Manipulateurs Info *see* Manip Info 6202
Manipulating Pig Production (AUS ISSN 1324-9177) 293
Manipur Express (IND) 3885
Manipur State Kala Akademi. Quarterly Journal (IND) 5330
Manipur State Museum. Bulletin (IND) 6528
ManiTese (ITA ISSN 1594-7920) 8055
Manitoba (Year) Events Guide *see* Events Guide 8702
Manitoba Accommodation and Campground Guide *see* Accommodation and Campground Guide 8680
Manitoba Agricultural Financial Statistics (CAN ISSN 1912-8533) 183
Manitoba Agricultural Profile (CAN ISSN 1912-8452) 135
Manitoba Agriculture Yearbook (CAN ISSN 0084-3865) 136
• Manitoba and Saskatchewan Tax Reporter (CAN) 1934
• Manitoba and Saskatchewan Tax Reporter Newsletter (CAN) 1934
Manitoba Archaeological Journal (CAN ISSN 1188-5424) 404
Manitoba Archaeological Newsletter *see* Manitoba Archaeological Journal 404
Manitoba Association for Schooling at Home Newsletter (CAN) 2885
Manitoba Association of Library Technicians Newsletter *see* M A L T Newsletter 5030
Manitoba Beekeeper (CAN ISSN 0708-3483) 136
The Manitoba Broker (CAN) 4513
Manitoba Budget Address (CAN ISSN 0380-4488) 1934
Manitoba Building and Construction Trades Council Yearbook *see* Manitoba Building Trades Yearbook 1022
Manitoba Building Trades Yearbook (CAN ISSN 1912-3272) 1022
• Manitoba Business Directory (USA ISSN 1203-522X) 2015
• Manitoba Business Magazine (CAN ISSN 0709-2423) 1498
Manitoba. Co-Operative Loans and Loans Guarantee Board. Annual Report (CAN ISSN 0848-5542) 1366
• Manitoba Co-operator (CAN ISSN 0025-2239) 136
Manitoba Conference on Numerical Mathematics. Proceedings (CAN ISSN 0384-997X) 5510
Manitoba Conservation. Annual Report (CAN ISSN 1497-9012) 2618
Manitoba Conservation Districts Association Magazine *see* M C D A Magazine 3451
Manitoba Council for Exceptional Children (CAN ISSN 0844-0441) 2160
Manitoba Crop Insurance Corporation. Annual Report (CAN ISSN 0542-5395) 4513
Manitoba Dental Association. Bulletin (CAN ISSN 0701-1717) 5855
Manitoba Dentist (CAN ISSN 1209-5176) 5855
Manitoba Explorer's Guide *see* Manitoba Vacation Guide 8732
Manitoba. Fishing & Hunting Adventures (CAN ISSN 1704-6718) 8732
Manitoba Fishing & Hunting Guide *see* Manitoba. Fishing & Hunting Adventures 8732
Manitoba Gardener *see* Manitoba Gardener Living 3742
Manitoba Gardener Living (CAN ISSN 1914-5519) 3742
Manitoba Gazette (CAN ISSN 0706-3350) 4727
Manitoba Health Libraries Association News *see* M H L A News 5030
Manitoba Historical Society Newsletter *see* Time Lines 4315
• ➤ Manitoba History (CAN ISSN 0226-5044) 4302
Manitoba. Horse Racing Commission. Annual Report (CAN ISSN 0317-7262) 8294
Manitoba. Human Rights Commission. Annual Report (CAN ISSN 0383-5588) 7212
Manitoba Industry, Trade and Mines. Aggragate Report Series (CAN) 2753
Manitoba Industry, Trade and Mines. Annual Report Series (CAN) 6469
Manitoba Industry, Trade and Mines. Canadian Geoscience Publications Directory (CAN) 2753
Manitoba Industry, Trade and Mines. Economic Geology Paper Series (CAN ISSN 0826-8916) 2753
Manitoba Industry, Trade and Mines. Economic Geology Report Series (CAN ISSN 0228-8311) 2753
Manitoba Industry, Trade and Mines. Educational Series (CAN) 2753
Manitoba Industry, Trade and Mines. Federal - Provincial Annual Progress Reports (CAN) 6469
Manitoba Industry, Trade and Mines. Geological Paper Series (CAN) 2753
Manitoba Industry, Trade and Mines. Geological Report Series (CAN) 2754
Manitoba Industry, Trade and Mines. Mineral Deposit Report Series (CAN) 2754
Manitoba Industry, Trade and Mines. Mineral Education Series (CAN) 6469
Manitoba Industry, Trade and Mines. Miscellaneous Publication Series (CAN) 6469
Manitoba Industry, Trade and Mines. Open File Report Series (CAN) 2754
Manitoba Industry, Trade and Mines. Publications Series (CAN) 2754
Manitoba Industry, Trade and Mines. Report of Activities Series (CAN) 2754
Manitoba Journal of Counselling (CAN ISSN 0831-3245) 2885
Manitoba Labour - Management Review Committee. Annual Report (CAN ISSN 0076-3853) 1696
Manitoba Law Foundation. Annual Report *see* The Law Society of Manitoba (Year) Annual Report 4717
• Manitoba Law Journal (CAN ISSN 0076-3861) 4727
Manitoba Law Reform Commission. Annual Report (CAN ISSN 0701-7081) 4727
Manitoba Library Association. Newsline (CAN ISSN 0700-3684) 5031
Manitoba Lotteries Corporation. Annual Report (CAN) 8186
Manitoba Magic, Provincial Parks Guide *see* Manitoba Parks Guide 8732
Manitoba. Municipal Employees Benefits Board. Annual Report (CAN ISSN 0706-3792) 1696
Manitoba Museum of Man and Nature. Annual Report (CAN ISSN 0715-0105) 6528
Manitoba Museum of Man and Nature. Happenings (CAN ISSN 0843-9133) 6528
Manitoba Naturalists Society Bulletin (CAN ISSN 0823-2911) 7881
Manitoba. Office of the Auditor General. Operations of the Office (CAN ISSN 1706-2675) 7452
Manitoba. Ombudsman Manitoba. Annual Report (CAN ISSN 1493-7220) 7452
Manitoba Parks Guide (CAN ISSN 1910-6939) 8732
Manitoba Physical Education Teachers' Association. Journal (CAN ISSN 1206-0011) 6992
Manitoba. Provincial Auditor. Operations of the Office *see* Manitoba. Office of the Auditor General. Operations of the Office 7452
Manitoba, Provincial Parks Guide *see* Manitoba Parks Guide 8732
Manitoba Public Library Statistics (CAN ISSN 0707-0438) 5059
Manitoba. Public Utilities Board. Annual Report (CAN ISSN 0464-8625) 7452
Manitoba Queen's Bench Act and Rules, Annotated (CAN ISSN 0846-0345) 4727
Manitoba Real Estate Association Action *see* M R E Action 7599
Manitoba Record Society. Publications (CAN ISSN 0076-3896) 4302
• Manitoba Reports (CAN ISSN 0713-7109) 4727
Manitoba School Library Association Journal *see* M S L A Journal 3071
Manitoba Science Teacher (CAN ISSN 0315-9159) 7881
Manitoba Social Science Teacher (CAN) 3071
Manitoba Social Worker (CAN ISSN 0715-3481) 8055
Manitoba Spectra *see* E B I T Journal 3058
Manitoba Statistical Review (CAN ISSN 0700-2971) 8387
Manitoba Teacher (CAN ISSN 0025-228X) 2885
Manitoba Telephone System Echo *see* M T S Echo 2369
Manitoba Theatre Centre. Ovation House Programme (CAN) 8473
Manitoba Vacation Guide (CAN ISSN 1702-0042) 8732
Manitoba. Water Services Board. Annual Report (CAN ISSN 0318-3912) 8828
Manitoban (CAN ISSN 0025-2298) 2291
Manitoba's Northern Experience, Canada *see* Northern Experience Magazine 8742
Manitowoc County Historical Society. Monographs (USA) 4302
Manja (SGP) 3945
Mankato Poetry Review (USA ISSN 0894-2242) 5426
• ManKind Magazine (GBR ISSN 1745-9257) 6294
• ➤ Mankind Quarterly (USA ISSN 0025-2344) 347
Mankind Quarterly Monograph Series (USA ISSN 0076-4116) 347
Manley Family Newsletter (USA ISSN 0883-7805) 3774
Mann (NOR ISSN 0807-0164) 6294
Mann Report (USA) 7599
Manna (GBR ISSN 0266-4003) 7726
Manna (ZAF ISSN 1817-4108) 7661
Mannekragopname Beroepsgegewens *see* South Africa. Statistics South Africa. Manpower Survey (Occupational Information) 1265
Mannenmode (NLD ISSN 0168-7883) 2258
The Mannequin (ZAF ISSN 1684-8349) 2258
Mannesmann Magazin (DEU ISSN 0946-9214) 1431
Mannheimer Beitraege zum Oeffentlichen Recht und Steuerrecht (DEU) 1934
Mannheimer Beitraege zur Oekonomischen Oekologie (DEU ISSN 0934-5620) 2618
Mannheimer Beitraege zur Slavischen Philologie (DEU ISSN 0175-2987) 5150
Mannheimer Beitraege zur Sprach- und Literaturwissenschaft (DEU ISSN 0175-3169) 5150
Mannheimer Geschichtsblaetter. Neue Folge (DEU ISSN 0948-2784) 4242
Mannheimer Hefte fuer Schriftvergleichung (DEU ISSN 0172-8563) 2660
Mannheimer Liedertafel. Mitteilungen (DEU) 2267
Mannheimer Morgen (DEU) 3852
Mannheimer Reihe (DEU ISSN 0170-2254) 4513
Mannheimer Schriften zur Politik und Zeitgeschichte (DEU ISSN 0933-1042) 4242
Mannheimer Studien zur Literatur- und Kulturwissenschaft (DEU) 5330
Mannheimer Universitaets-Reden (DEU ISSN 0935-3348) 2291
Mannheimer Vortraege zur Versicherungswissenschaft (DEU ISSN 0171-466X) 4514
Mannlicher Collector (USA ISSN 0883-6949) 367
Mannlif (ISL ISSN 1017-3587) 3877
La Mano (ARG) 5330
• ➤ Manoa (USA ISSN 1045-7909) 5330
Manohar Kahaniyan (IND) 3885
Manohara (IND) 3885
Manorama (IND) 3885
Manorama Bengali Year Book (IND) 5226
Manorama English Year Book (IND) 5226
Manorama Hindi Year Book (IND) 5226
Manorama Malayalam Year Book (IND) 5226
Manorama Tamil Year Book (IND) 5226
Manorama Weekly (IND) 5226
Manos Unidas (ESP ISSN 0214-5979) 8055
Manpower Demonstration Research Corporation. Annual Report (USA ISSN 0749-7903) 1696
• Manpower Employment Outlook Survey. New Zealand (NZL ISSN 1176-905X) 6701
• ➤ Manpower Journal (IND ISSN 0542-5808) 1696
• Manpower. Melbourne Institute Employment Report (AUS ISSN 1834-1365) 1147
Manpower Review (PAK) 1696
Manresa (ESP ISSN 0214-2457) 7661
Mans Mazais (LVA ISSN 1407-1614) 2161
Le Mans Racing (FRA ISSN 1630-4969) 8186
Man's World (IND) 6294
Mansfield Historical Society's Magazine (AUS ISSN 0814-5296) 4193
Mansfield Stock Chart Service (USA) 1638
➤ Mansholt Publication Series (NLD ISSN 1871-9309) 8119
• Mansholt Studies (Online Edition) (NLD ISSN 1383-6803) 1147
Mansholt Studies (Print Edition) *see* Mansholt Studies (Online Edition) 1147
• Mansholt Working Papers (NLD) 1147
Manshots (USA) 2402
Al Mansour Journal *see* Majallat al-Mansur 7881
Mansoura Engineering Journal/Al-Magallat al-'ilmiyyat li-Kolliyyat al-Handasa (EGY ISSN 1110-0141) 3209
Mansoura Journal of Biology/Nashrat Koliyyat al-'lum B Baiulugi (EGY ISSN 1687-5087) 687
Mansoura Journal of Chemistry/Nashrat Koliyyat al-'lum A Kimyyaa (EGY ISSN 1687-5060) 2072
Mansoura Journal of Geology and Geophysics (EGY ISSN 1687-5109) 7881
Mansoura Journal of Mathematics (EGY ISSN 1687-5079) 5510
Mansoura Journal of Physics/Nashrat Koliyyat al-'lum G 'lum Tabi'yyat (EGY ISSN 1687-5095) 7881
Mansoura Science Bulletin *see* Mansoura Journal of Geology and Geophysics 7881
Mansoura Science Bulletin. A, Chemistry *see* Mansoura Journal of Chemistry 2072
Mansoura Science Bulletin. B, Biology *see* Mansoura Journal of Biology 687
Mansoura Science Bulletin. C, Natural Sciences *see* Mansoura Journal of Physics 7881
Mansoura University. Faculty of Engineering. Bulletin *see* Mansoura Engineering Journal 3209
Mansoura University Journal of Agricultural Sciences (EGY ISSN 1110-0346) 136
Mantenimiento (ESP ISSN 0214-4344) 5456
• Mantex Newsletter (GBR ISSN 1470-1863) 2469
Manthan (IND) 7984
Mantooth Report (USA) 7153
Mantram (USA ISSN 1534-4878) 1147
† • Manu Matauranga (NZL ISSN 1176-3590) 8972
Manu Rere *see* Vista 8077
Manu Sprint (ITA ISSN 1827-8086) 2201
Manual del Instrumentista (CUB) 3209
• The Manual for Florida Legal Secretaries (USA) 4727
Manual for Police in the State of New York (USA ISSN 1931-9738) 2660
Manual of Air Force Law - Amendments (GBR) 4971
Manual of Air Traffic Services - Part 1 (GBR) 8548
Manual of Biological Markers of Disease (NLD) 5763
Manual of Credit and Commercial Laws (USA ISSN 1524-5853) 1366

DIRECTORY 2010 MARCO POLO 10589

• ➤ Manual of Environmental Policy: The E U and Britain (GBR ISSN 1467-0445) **3451**
Manual of Foreign Investment in the United States (USA) **1638**
Manual of Military Law - Amendments (GBR) **4971**
Manual of Model Criminal Jury Instructions (USA ISSN 1092-0005) **4893**
Manual of Motorcycle Sport (AUS ISSN 1833-2609) **8260**
Manual of Patent Examining Procedure *see* U.S. Patent and Trademark Office. Manual of Patent Examining Procedure **6759**
The Manual of Procedure for New York Courts *see* New York Courts Manual of Procedure **4957**
• Manual of Regulations & Procedures for Federal Radio Frequency Management (USA) **2360**
Manual of Rules, Classifications and Interpretations for Workers Compensation Insurance (USA) **4514**
• Manual on Uniform Traffic Control Devices (USA) **8503**
Manual para el Lider *see* Estudios Biblicos LifeWay para Adultos. Manual para el Lider **7756**
Manual-State of Maryland *see* Maryland Manual **7452**
• ➤ Manual Therapy (GBR ISSN 1356-689X) **6112**
Manuali d'Arte (ITA ISSN 1593-4101) **537**
I Manuali della Biblioteca (ITA ISSN 1827-3211) **631**
Manuali. Linguistica (ITA ISSN 1970-2019) **5150**
Manuali Universitari (ITA ISSN 1971-226X) **7567**
Manualita Creativita Maestria (ITA ISSN 0393-8190) **537**
Manuals in Biomedical Research (SGP ISSN 1793-1894) **687**
• Manuel d'Application des Taxes sur les Produits et Services (CAN ISSN 1912-8169) **1934**
Manuel d'Application des Taxes sur les Produits et Services PLUS *see* Manuel d'Application des Taxes sur les Produits et Services **1934**
Manuel de Billeterie *see* I A T A Ticketing Handbook **8544**
Manuel de Comptabilite de l'I C C A pour le Secteur Public *see* C I C A Public Sector Accounting Handbook **1283**
Manuel de Droit Fiscal *see* Handboek voor Fiscaal Recht **1927**
Manuel de Saisie de l'Information *see* Discharge Abstract Database Abstracting Manual **5744**
Manuel de Statistiques de la C N U C E D *see* U N C T A D Handbook of Statistics **1271**
Manuel des Corporations du Quebec (CAN) **4875**
Manuel des Usines Europeennes de la Siderurgie *see* Handbuch der Europaeischen Eisen- und Stahlwerke **6314**
Manuel d'Impot des Societes (CAN ISSN 1912-1539) **1934**
Manuel d'Instructions, Patients en Traitement pour l'Insuffisance Renale Chronique *see* Instruction Manual. Chronic Renal Failure Patients on Renal Replacement Therapy (Print) **6269**
Manuel d'Instructions, Patients en Traitement pour l'Insuffisance Renale Chronique *see* Instruction Manual. Chronic Renal Failure Patients on Renal Replacement Therapy (Online) **6269**
Manuel d'Orientation pour les Membres du Bureau *see* Orientation Manual for Board Members **8060**
Manuel General de la Peinture et de la Decoration (FRA ISSN 0755-1533) **6719**
Manuel International de Caoutchouc *see* Handbuch der Internationalen Kautschukindustrie **7824**
Manuel International des Plastiques *see* Handbuch der Internationalen Kunststoffindustrie **7092**
Manuel U N I M A R C *see* U N I M A R C Manual - Bibliographic Format **5052**
• ➤ Manuelle Medizin (DEU ISSN 0025-2514) **6112**
• ➤ Manuelle Therapie (DEU ISSN 1433-2671) **6112**
Manuels du Traducteur (FRA ISSN 1952-2339) **7661**
• Manufactura (MEX ISSN 1405-1559) **1898**
Manufacture of Alcohol Liqueur and Vodka Products *see* Proizvodstvo Spirta i Likero-Vodochnykh Izdelii **609**
Manufacture of Narcotic Drugs and Psychotropic Substances under International Control (USA ISSN 1010-9595) **2697**
▼ Manufactured Home Living (USA ISSN 1938-6818) **7599**
• Manufactured Home Merchandiser (USA ISSN 1047-2967) **4419**
Manufactured Housing Institute. Quarterly Economic Report (USA) **4419**
Manufacturer (GBR ISSN 1477-3201) **1898**
• Manufacturer of Michigan (USA) **1898**
Manufacturers and Suppliers Directory (Year) *see* Australasian Bus and Coach **8490**
Manufacturers Forum (DEU ISSN 1614-1598) **6046**
• Manufacturers' Mart (USA ISSN 0191-7234) **1898**
• Manufacturers' Monthly (AUS ISSN 0025-2530) **1898**
Manufacturers' Monthly's Pulse Report *see* Manufacturers' Monthly **1898**
• Manufacturers' Tax Alert (USA) **1934**
ManufacturersLink (SGP ISSN 0218-1983) **2015**
Manufacturing (GBR ISSN 0141-450X) **1778**
Manufacturing *see* Multistate Guide to Sales and Use Tax. Manufacturing **1935**
Manufacturing & Distribution U S A (USA ISSN 1529-7659) **1898**
• Manufacturing and Logistics I T (GBR ISSN 1467-1271) **2431**
Manufacturing and Logistics Information Technology *see* Manufacturing and Logistics I T **2431**
• ➤ Manufacturing and Service Operations Management (USA ISSN 1523-4614) **1778**
• Manufacturing and Technology News (USA) **1898**
Manufacturing Automation (CAN ISSN 1480-2996) **3370**
Manufacturing Automation *see* Zhizaoye Zidonghua **1909**
• Manufacturing Business Technology (USA ISSN 1554-3404) **1898**
• Manufacturing Chemist (GBR ISSN 0262-4230) **3250**
• Manufacturing Computer Solutions (GBR ISSN 1358-1066) **3293**
The Manufacturing Confectioner (USA ISSN 0163-4364) **3674**
Manufacturing Engineer *see* Engineering & Technology **3189**
Manufacturing Engineering *see* Vyrobne Inzinierstvo **3372**
• Manufacturing Engineering (USA ISSN 0361-0853) **3209**
Manufacturing Engineering and Materials Processing Series (USA) **1898**
Manufacturing I T (USA ISSN 1534-6803) **2524**
Manufacturing I T (Carol Stream) (Information Technology) (USA ISSN 1547-6731) **2549**
Manufacturing Industry, Western Australia (Online) *see* Australia. Bureau of Statistics. Western Australian Office. Manufacturing Industry, Western Australia (Online) **1211**
Manufacturing Information Engineering of China *see* Zhongguo Zhizaoye Xinxihua **5462**
Manufacturing Intelligence (GBR ISSN 0963-7176) **1147**
Manufacturing Ireland (IRL) **1898**
Manufacturing Jewelers and Suppliers of America Journal *see* M J S A Journal **4568**
Manufacturing Management (Kenilworth) (GBR ISSN 0141-4518) **1778**
Manufacturing News *see* Manufacturing and Technology News **1898**
• ➤ Manufacturing Research and Technology (NLD ISSN 1572-4417) **1898**
Manufacturing Science and Engineering (USA ISSN 1096-6668) **1898**
Manufacturing, Science and Finance Union at Work *see* M S F at Work **4598**
• Manufacturing Survey (USA) **1898**
Manufacturing Technology & Machine Tool *see* Zhizao Jishu yu Jichuang **5461**
Manufacturing Technology and Management *see* International Journal of Manufacturing Technology and Management **3382**
Manufacturing Technology & Management *see* M T & M **5455**
• Manufacturing Today (USA ISSN 1930-1359) **1778**
Manufacturing Today Europe (GBR) **1898**
Manukau Courier (NZL ISSN 1170-0696) **3917**
• Manukau Matters (NZL ISSN 1177-5211) **5076**
Manure Manager (CAN) **242**
Manure Matters (USA) **293**
† Manurenboek Burgerwerk (NLD ISSN 1872-1052) **8972**
† Manurenboek Woning- en Utiliteitsbouw (NLD ISSN 1872-1044) **8972**
Manurewa Week *see* The Aucklander Manukau City **3916**
➤ Manusaya: Journal of Humanities (THA ISSN 0859-9920) **4464**
ManuScript (GBR ISSN 1360-3140) **5330**
The Manuscript Society News (USA ISSN 0195-7813) **5031**
Manuscript Studies (USA ISSN 0267-2510) **5330**
• Manuscripta (BEL ISSN 0025-2603) **5330**
Manuscripta Indonesica (NLD ISSN 0929-6484) **4185**
• ➤ Manuscripta Mathematica (DEU ISSN 0025-2611) **5510**
Manuscripta Orientalia (RUS ISSN 1238-5018) **555**
Manuscripts (USA ISSN 0025-262X) **7567**
Manuscripts in Miniature (BEL) **5330**
Manuscripts of the Middle East (NLD ISSN 0920-0401) **4323**
Manuscriptum (ROM ISSN 1010-5492) **5330**
➤ Manuscrito (BRA ISSN 0100-6045) **6933**
• Manuscrits (ESP ISSN 0213-2397) **4152**
Manuscrits (FRA ISSN 1243-0617) **5330**
Manuscrits du C.E.D.R.E. *see* Cercle d'Etudes des Dynasties Royales Europeennes. Manuscrits **4210**
Manuscrits Medievaux en Caracteres Hebraiques (FRA ISSN 0295-7108) **5330**
Manuscrits Medievaux en Caracteres Hebraiques Portant des Indications de Date Jusqu'en 1540 *see* Manuscrits Medievaux en Caracteres Hebraiques **5330**
Manuscrits Musicaux Apres 1600 *see* Music Manuscripts After 1600 **6632**
† Manuscrt.cao (ESP ISSN 1136-3703) **8972**
• Manushi (IND ISSN 0257-7305) **8900**
➤ Manusia dan Masyarakat/Man and Society (MYS ISSN 0126-8678) **347**
Manuskripte (AUT ISSN 0025-2638) **5330**
Manutencion y Almacenaje (ESP ISSN 0025-2646) **8503**
Manutention et Systemes (FRA ISSN 1291-696X) **8431**
Manutention et Systemes Special VRAC *see* Manutention et Systemes **8431**
Manwees (ZAF ISSN 1990-7222) **6294**
The Manx Law Reports (GBR ISSN 0267-534X) **4955**
Manx Life (GBR ISSN 0308-0978) **3968**
Manx Lifestyle (GBR) **5076**
The Manx Line (USA) **6811**
Manx Star (GBR ISSN 0047-5823) **3968**
Manx Tails (GBR) **8732**
▼ • Many Good Turns (USA ISSN 1946-5793) **1051**
Many Hands (USA ISSN 1069-1057) **6646**
• Many Happy Returns (USA ISSN 1524-2943) **8186**
➤ Many Mountains Moving (USA ISSN 1080-6474) **5330**
Many Voices: Ethnic Literatures of the Americas (USA ISSN 1077-0216) **5330**
• ➤ Manyu Yanjiu/Journal of Manchu Studies (CHN ISSN 1000-7873) **555**
• Manzu Wenxue/Manchu Literature (CHN ISSN 1003-7012) **5330**
• Manzu Yanjiu/Manchu Studies (CHN ISSN 1006-365X) **3549**
Mao yu Dun *see* Defence Asia - Pacific **6417**
• Mao Zedong Deng Xiaoping Lilun Yanjiu/Studies on Mao Zedong and Deng Xiaoping Theories (CHN ISSN 1005-8273) **7153**
Mao Zedong Sixiang/Mao Zedong Thoughts (CHN ISSN 1009-7570) **7153**
Mao Zedong Sixiang (Nian Kan)/Mao Zedong Thought (Annual Edition) (CHN) **7153**
• Mao Zedong Sixiang Yanjiu/Study of Mao Zedong Thought (CHN ISSN 1001-8999) **7153**
Mao Zedong Thought (Annual Edition) *see* Mao Zedong Sixiang (Nian Kan) **7153**
Mao Zedong Thoughts *see* Mao Zedong Sixiang **7153**
• Maofang Keji/Wool Textile Journal (CHN ISSN 1003-1456) **8454**
Maoming College. Journal *see* Maoming Xueyuan Xuebao **7984**
• Maoming Xueyuan Xuebao/Maoming College. Journal (CHN ISSN 1671-6590) **7984**
Maori Education Trust. Annual Report (NZL) **2885**
▼ • Maori Health Review (NZL ISSN 1178-6191) **7531**
Maori Law Review (NZL ISSN 1172-8434) **4727**
Maoyi Jingji/Commercial and Trading Economics (CHN ISSN 1009-752X) **1431**
Maozedong Sixiang Yanjiu *see* Mao Zedong Sixiang **7153**
Map (GBR ISSN 1745-4484) **504**
Map *see* Chizu **4002**
▼ Map (USA) **6586**
Map and Landscape *see* Chizu no Tomo **4002**
• Map - Lexter (ESP ISSN 1133-4398) **4955**
The Map Report (USA ISSN 1065-6324) **4019**
• Mapan (IND ISSN 0970-3950) **6403**
• Mapas Geologicos (CHL ISSN 0717-2532) **2754**
Mapenzi ya Mungu (KEN) **7714**
Mapfre Medicina *see* Trauma **6188**
Mapfre Medicina. Suplemento *see* Trauma **6188**
Mapfre Seguridad *see* Seguridad y Medio Ambiente **6687**
• Mapfte'ah L'khit've 'Et B'ivrit/Index to Hebrew Periodicals (ISR ISSN 0334-2921) **10**
• Maple Leaf (CAN ISSN 1480-4336) **6432**
The Maple Leaf (CAN ISSN 1718-5440) **3774**
Maple Leaves (GBR ISSN 0951-5283) **6897**
The Maple News (USA ISSN 1930-2258) **242**
• Maple Orchard (CAN ISSN 0827-1755) **2577**
• Maple Ridge News (CAN ISSN 0839-4733) **3813**
• Maple Ridge, Pitt Meadows Times (CAN ISSN 1202-9408) **3813**
▼ Maple Street Press (Year) Red Sox Annual (USA ISSN 1942-2016) **8238**
▼ Maple Street Press Cardinals Annual (USA ISSN 1944-3889) **8238**
▼ Maple Street Press Indians Annual (USA ISSN 1944-3897) **8238**
▼ Maple Street Press Phillies Annual (USA ISSN 1944-3870) **8238**
Maple Syrup Digest (USA ISSN 0886-6376) **3655**
Mapline (USA ISSN 0196-0881) **4019**
Maplines (GBR) **4019**
Mappa dei Fornitori (ITA ISSN 1121-7456) **1022**
Die Mappe (DEU ISSN 0025-2697) **6719**
• M@ppemonde (Online Edition) (FRA ISSN 1769-7298) **4019**
• Mapping (ESP ISSN 1131-9100) **2712**
Mapping and Image Science *see* Kart & Bildteknik **4018**
Mapping Sciences & Remote Sensing *see* GIScience and Remote Sensing **4013**
Maps on File (USA ISSN 0275-8083) **4019**
• Maquetren (ESP ISSN 1132-2063) **4339**
Maquettes Militaires Magazine (FRA ISSN 1956-3833) **4339**
Maquiladora Industry (USA ISSN 1549-7720) **1898**
Maquiladora Monthly Monitor *see* Maquiladora Industry **1898**
Maquillaje Paso a Paso (ESP ISSN 1696-4241) **589**
La Maquina Contemporanea (ESP ISSN 1697-476X) **4464**
Maquinaria y Equipo (ESP) **5456**
Maquinas & Metais (BRA ISSN 0025-2700) **5456**
Maquinas e Metais (PRT) **5456**
Maquinas y Equipos, Herramientas e Insumos Industriales (ARG ISSN 0328-7769) **5456**
Mar (CHL ISSN 0047-5866) **8651**
Mar (Lisboa) (PRT ISSN 0874-5846) **8651**
Mar (Madrid, 1965) (ESP ISSN 1131-9240) **2811**
Mar de Cortes (MEX) **8732**
Il Mar Nero (ITA ISSN 1125-3878) **404**
Mar Oceana (ESP ISSN 1134-7627) **4152**
Mar y Pesca (CUB ISSN 0025-2735) **3601**
Al-Mar'a Magazine (LBN) **8873**
• Marabo (DEU) **3852**
Marabout d'Nature (FRA ISSN 1951-7920) **800**
Maraicher Nantais (FRA ISSN 0295-7841) **136**
Maranatha (NLD ISSN 1573-997X) **7661**
Maranatha (ZAF ISSN 1019-5092) **7766**
• Maranatha Christian Journal (USA) **7766**
Maranatha Kalender *see* Maranatha **7661**
➤ Marang (BWA ISSN 1816-7659) **5330**
Marathon Aktuell (DEU ISSN 0179-5597) **8321**
Marathon & Beyond (USA ISSN 1088-6672) **8186**
Marathon-Journal (DEU) **8321**
Marathonloeparen (SWE ISSN 0283-1015) **8186**
Marathwada (IND) **3885**
Marbacher Magazin (DEU) **5330**
Marble Mart Newsletter (USA) **4339**
Marblehead Magazine (USA ISSN 0274-6115) **3981**
• Marburg Journal of Religion (DEU ISSN 1612-2941) **7661**
Marburger Abhandlungen zur Geschichte und Kultur Osteuropas (DEU ISSN 0474-8328) **4242**
Marburger Beitraege zur Musikwissenschaft (DEU) **6586**
Marburger Bibliothek (DEU ISSN 1615-6234) **4242**
Marburger Buecherlisten (DEU) **4083**
Marburger Bund Zeitung (DEU) **5665**
Marburger Gelehrten Gesellschaft. Abhandlungen (DEU ISSN 0178-1804) **2885**
Marburger Geographische Gesellschaft. Jahrbuch (DEU ISSN 0931-6272) **4019**
Marburger Geographische Schriften (DEU ISSN 0341-9290) **4019**
• Marburger Index (DEU) **530**
• Marburger Jahrbuch fuer Kunstwissenschaft (DEU ISSN 0342-121X) **504**
Marburger Literatur-Almanach (DEU ISSN 1431-5548) **5330**
Marburger Personalschriften-Forschungen (DEU ISSN 1610-0409) **4242**
Marburger Schriften zur Medizingeschichte (DEU ISSN 0721-3859) **5665**
Marburger Studien zur Kunst- und Kulturgeschichte (DEU) **504**
Marburger Studien zur Vor- und Fruehgeschichte (DEU ISSN 0724-4304) **4242**
Marburger Theologische Studien (DEU ISSN 0542-657X) **7661**
• Marca (ESP) **8186**
marca.com *see* Marca **8186**
Marcan Handbook of Arts Organisations (GBR) **504**
Marcato (USA ISSN 1543-0235) **5031**
Marcel Magazine *see* Marcel Paris **4376**
• Marcel Paris (FRA ISSN 1769-809X) **4376**
➤ Marcel Proust Aujourd'hui (NLD ISSN 1571-5647) **5330**
Marcellino's Restaurant Report Deutschalnd (DEU) **4393**
• March Magazine (USA ISSN 1543-1258) **5330**
March of Karnataka (IND) **1898**
Marchand Forain (FRA ISSN 0183-3308) **1830**
Le Marche (Monthly) *see* Gastromania **4386**
Le Marche (Weekly) *see* Gastromania **4386**
† Le Marche Archeologia, Storia, Territorio (ITA) **8972**
† Marche Contemporanee (ITA ISSN 1126-9022) **8972**
Marche de l'Habitation *see* Intentions d'Achat ou de Renovation des Consommateurs. Halifax **1430**
Marche de l'Habitation *see* Intentions d'Achat ou de Renovation des Consommateurs. Calgary **1430**
Marche de l'Habitation *see* Intentions d'Achat ou de Renovation des Consommateurs. Vancouver **1430**
Marche de l'Habitation *see* Intentions d'Achat ou de Renovation des Consommateurs. Toronto **1430**
Marche di Orologi in Italia (ITA ISSN 1128-5338) **4568**
• Le Marche du Travail et l'Emploi Sectoriel au Quebec (CAN ISSN 1719-9069) **1696**
Marche & Organisations (FRA ISSN 1953-6119) **1898**
Le Marche Euro-Obligataire en E C U - Statistiques Mensuelles/Eurobond Market in E C U - Monthly Statistics (European Currency Unit) (LUX) **1251**
Marche International des Programmes de Television Preview Magazine *see* M I P T V Preview Magazine **2384**
Marche International des Programmes Documentaires. Preview Magazine (FRA ISSN 1963-2266) **2384**
Le Marche Locatif. R M R de Quebec. Rapport *see* Rapport sur le Marche Locatif. Quebec **7607**
Marche Romane (BEL ISSN 0542-6669) **5150**
Marche Suisse des Machines *see* M S M **5455**
Les Marches (FRA ISSN 0988-324X) **136**
• Marches Africains (FRA ISSN 0984-9521) **1577**
Marches Agricoles. Prix *see* Mercados Agrarios. Precios **136**
Marches Arabes (FRA ISSN 1147-7717) **1577**
Marches de la Mer (FRA ISSN 1161-7462) **3601**
Marches Internationaux de la Viande *see* International Markets for Meat **290**
• Marches Latino-Americains (FRA ISSN 0989-8131) **1577**
• Marches Tropicaux et Mediterraneens (FRA ISSN 0025-2859) **1577**
Marchigiana News (USA) **293**
Marco Polo (USA) **8732**

Title

Title

DIRECTORY 2010 MASSACHUSETTS ASSOCIATION OF SCHOOL COMMITTEES JOURNAL 10593

Martindale-Hubbell Bar Register *see* Martindale-Hubbell Bar Register of Preeminent Lawyers **4728**
Martindale-Hubbell Bar Register of Preeminent Lawyers (USA ISSN 1051-5518) **4728**
Martindale-Hubbell Buyer's Guide *see* Martindale-Hubbell Directory of Experts & Legal Services **4728**
Martindale-Hubbell Canadian Law Directory (USA ISSN 1083-7558) **4728**
† • Martindale-Hubbell Corporate Law Directory (USA ISSN 1099-7881) **8972**
Martindale-Hubbell Directory of Experts & Legal Services (USA ISSN 1559-548X) **4728**
• Martindale-Hubbell International Dispute Resolution Directory (USA) **4728**
Martindale-Hubbell International Dispute Resolution Directory (Year) (GBR) **4728**
Martindale-Hubbell International Law Digest (USA ISSN 1088-9779) **4728**
Martindale-Hubbell International Law Directory (Year) (USA) **4728**
† • Martindale-Hubbell Law Directory on CD-ROM (USA ISSN 1071-7455) **8972**
Martindale-Hubbell Premier Account News (USA) **644**
• Martindale: the Complete Drug Reference (GBR) **6860**
Martinique. Institut National de la Statistique et des Etudes Economiques. Bulletin de Statistique (FRA ISSN 0399-242X) **8388**
Martinique Tourisme (MTQ ISSN 1953-5902) **8732**
Martin's Annual Criminal Code (CAN ISSN 0527-7892) **4893**
Martin's Related Criminal Statutes (CAN ISSN 0710-1805) **4893**
Martinus Nijhoff Philosophy Texts (NLD ISSN 0924-4948) **6933**
Martlet (CAN) **2291**
Martor (ROM ISSN 1224-6271) **347**
The Martyr *see* Al- Shahid **4325**
➤ Martyrdom and Resistance (USA ISSN 0892-1571) **7726**
Martyrs' Shrine Message (CAN) **7806**
Maruee (IND ISSN 0025-4096) **3885**
Marulic (HRV ISSN 0350-4220) **5226**
Marvel (BRA ISSN 1415-1359) **2201**
Marvel (KWT ISSN 1819-4621) **2201**
Marvel Heroes Reborn (GBR ISSN 1368-8111) **2201**
• ➤ Marvels & Tales (USA ISSN 1521-4281) **3620**
Marvels of Krakow *see* Cracoviana **3928**
Marvil *see* Marvel **2201**
Marx Memorial Library. Bulletin (GBR ISSN 0969-1154) **7153**
Marx Zhuyi, Liening Zhuyi Yanjiu *see* Makesi Zhuyi, Liening Zhuyi Yanjiu **7153**
Marx Zhuyi Yanjiu *see* Makesi Zhuyi Yanjiu **7153**
Marx Zhuyi yu Xianshi *see* Makesi Zhuyi yu Xianshi **7153**
Marxism & Reality *see* Makesi Zhuyi yu Xianshi **7153**
Marxism-Leninism Research *see* Makesi Zhuyi, Liening Zhuyi Yanjiu **7153**
Le Marxisme Aujourd'hui (FRA ISSN 1157-7762) **7153**
Marxismo Oggi (ITA) **7153**
Marxist Criticism *see* Critica Marxista **7126**
Marxist Veekshanam (IND ISSN 0025-4134) **7153**
Marxistische Blaetter (DEU ISSN 0542-7770) **7153**
Mary Dee's Quick and Tasty Recipes (USA ISSN 1523-4045) **4363**
Mary Engelbreit's Home Companion (USA ISSN 1096-5289) **537**
Mary Jane's Farm *see* MaryJanesFarm **136**
Mary Janes Farm *see* MaryJanesFarm **136**
Mary Seacole Research Center. Research Papers (GBR ISSN 1472-782X) **5969**
• ➤ Mary Slessor Journal of Medicine (NGA ISSN 1119-409X) **5822**
MaryJanesFarm (USA ISSN 1547-7592) **136**
Maryknoll Magazine (USA ISSN 0025-4142) **7806**
• Maryknoll Study Guide (USA) **7806**
Maryland Air and Radiation Management Administration. Data Report (USA) **3488**
Maryland Air Quality Data Report *see* Maryland Air and Radiation Management Administration. Data Report **3488**
Maryland and Delaware, Off the Beaten Path *see* Off the Beaten Path: Maryland and Delaware **8743**
Maryland and Mid-Atlantic Nutrition Conference for Feed Manufacturers. Proceedings (USA) **274**
Maryland & the District of Columbia Laws Governing Business Entities (USA ISSN 1933-1088) **4875**
Maryland Archeology (USA ISSN 0148-6012) **405**
• Maryland Bar Journal (USA ISSN 0025-4177) **4728**
Maryland Beverage Journal (USA ISSN 1058-935X) **607**
➤ Maryland Birdlife (USA ISSN 0147-9725) **910**
Maryland Bride *see* Modern Bride Maryland **5560**
Maryland Builder (USA) **4419**
• Maryland Business Credit Directory (USA) **2015**
• Maryland Business Directory (USA ISSN 1048-7123) **2015**
• Maryland Civil Procedure Forms (USA) **4835**
Maryland Cracker Barrel (USA) **4303**
• Maryland Criminal Jury Instructions and Commentary (USA) **4893**
• Maryland Criminal Law and Motor Vehicle Handbook (USA ISSN 1933-3617) **4893**
• Maryland Criminal Laws Annotated (USA) **4893**
• Maryland - D.C. Manufacturers Directory (USA ISSN 1065-2507) **2015**
Maryland - Delaware Directory of Manufacturers (USA) **2015**
Maryland. Department of Natural Resources. Annual Activities Report (USA) **2618**
• Maryland Department of Natural Resources Laws (USA) **2618**
Maryland. Department of Public Safety & Correctional Services. Division of Correction. Report (USA ISSN 0362-9198) **2660**
Maryland Documents (USA ISSN 0195-3443) **7481**
• Maryland Domestic Relations Forms (USA) **4912**
• Maryland Employment Law (USA) **4728**
• Maryland Employment Law Letter (USA ISSN 1049-9377) **4728**
• Maryland Essays in Human Biodiversity (USA ISSN 1546-7805) **347**
• Maryland Estate Planning, Will Drafting and Estate Administration Forms (USA) **4904**
• Maryland Evidence Handbook (USA) **4955**
• The Maryland Family Doctor (USA) **5665**
• Maryland Family Law (USA) **4912**
Maryland Fruit Grower (USA ISSN 0025-4223) **3742**
Maryland Genealogical Society Bulletin *see* Maryland Genealogical Society. Journal **3774**
Maryland Genealogical Society. Journal (USA ISSN 1948-0962) **3774**
Maryland Genealogical Society Newsletter (USA) **3774**
Maryland. General Assembly. Subject Index to Bills Introduced in the Session (USA) **7153**
Maryland. Geological Survey. Bulletin (USA ISSN 0076-4779) **2754**
Maryland. Geological Survey. Educational Series (USA ISSN 0076-4787) **2754**
Maryland. Geological Survey. Information Circular (USA ISSN 0076-4795) **2754**
Maryland. Geological Survey. Report of Investigations (USA ISSN 0076-4809) **2754**
Maryland. Geological Survey. Water Resources Basic Data Report (USA ISSN 0076-4817) **8828**
The Maryland Grapevine (USA ISSN 1052-6161) **3743**
Maryland Herpetological Society. Bulletin (USA ISSN 0025-4231) **955**
➤ Maryland Historian (USA ISSN 0025-424X) **4152**
Maryland Historical Magazine (USA ISSN 0025-4258) **4303**
Maryland Historical Society News *see* M H S News **4302**
The Maryland Horse (USA ISSN 0025-4274) **8294**
Maryland. House of Delegates. Journal of Proceedings. Regular Session (USA) **7154**
Maryland Landlord - Tenant Law: Practice and Procedure (USA) **7599**
• ➤ Maryland Law Review (USA ISSN 0025-4282) **4728**
Maryland Lawyer's Manual (USA ISSN 0542-836X) **4728**
Maryland Lawyers' Rules of Professional Conduct and Attorney Trust Accounts (USA ISSN 1543-2343) **4728**
Maryland Life (USA ISSN 1553-3166) **3981**
Maryland Manual (USA ISSN 0094-4491) **7452**
Maryland: Manufacturing *see* Harris Directory. Maryland Manufacturing **2000**
➤ Maryland Medicine (USA ISSN 1538-2656) **5665**
Maryland Monthly Labor Review (USA) **1696**
▼ Maryland Motions in Limine (USA ISSN 1944-0715) **4955**
Maryland Motor Truck (USA) **8672**
• Maryland Motor Vehicle Insurance (USA) **4514**
Maryland Motor Vehicle Laws Annotated (USA) **8503**
Maryland Motorist (USA ISSN 1062-516X) **8732**
Maryland Music Educator (USA ISSN 0025-4312) **6586**
➤ Maryland Naturalist (USA ISSN 0096-4158) **7881**
• ➤ Maryland Nurse (USA) **5969**
Maryland Nutrition Conference for Feed Manufacturers. Proceedings *see* Maryland and Mid-Atlantic Nutrition Conference for Feed Manufacturers. Proceedings **274**
Maryland Orchardist *see* Maryland Fruit Grower **3742**
Maryland P H C C Contractor Magazine (Plumbing Heating Cooling Contractor) (USA) **4123**
Maryland P T A Bulletin (USA ISSN 0025-4339) **2885**
Maryland Pharmacist (USA ISSN 0025-4347) **6860**
➤ Maryland Poetry Review (USA ISSN 0892-807X) **5426**
• Maryland Real Estate Forms (USA) **7599**
Maryland Register (USA ISSN 0360-2834) **7452**
Maryland Registration and Election Laws *see* Registration and Election Laws of Maryland **7176**
The Maryland Report (USA ISSN 1042-1564) **7452**
Maryland Report's Guidebook to Maryland Legislators (USA) **7452**
• Maryland Rules Commentary (USA) **4728**
Maryland School Directory *see* M D R's School Directory. Maryland **2959**
Maryland School Law Deskbook (USA ISSN 1942-2849) **4728**
Maryland. Senate. Journal of Proceedings. Regular Session (USA) **7154**
Maryland Series in Contemporary Asian Studies (USA) **4728**
Maryland Sports, Health & Fitness Magazine (USA ISSN 1090-7122) **6992**
Maryland State Bar Association. Bar Bulletin (USA) **4728**
Maryland State Dental Association. Journal *see* M S D A Journal **5855**
Maryland. State Department of Legislative Reference. Synopsis of Laws Enacted by the State of Maryland (USA ISSN 0093-0520) **4955**
Maryland. State Highway Administration. Traffic Trends (USA ISSN 0094-6265) **8632**
Maryland Tax Court Service (USA) **1934**
• Maryland Tort Law Handbook (USA) **4835**
• The Maryland Vehicle Law (USA) **8503**
Maryland Workers' Compensation Handbook (USA) **4514**
Maryland Workers' Compensation Law (USA) **1696**
Marynka: Mercados de Mexico en Accion (MEX) **1431**
Mas (ESP) **4598**
Mas Alla del Derecho *see* Beyond Law **4629**
Mas Caminos (MEX) **8503**
Mas de las Matas (ESP ISSN 0212-5749) **4152**
• Uno Mas Magazine (USA) **5226**
Masa Acher *see* Massa Aher **8732**
Masala! (UAE ISSN 1729-9713) **3967**
Masalah Pendidikan (MYS ISSN 0126-5024) **2885**
• ➤ Al-Masaq (GBR ISSN 0950-3110) **7714**
† Masaryk University. Faculty of Sciences. Scripta Biology/Scripta Facultatis Scientiarum Naturalium Universitatis Masarykianae Brunensis. Biology (CZE ISSN 1211-2836) **8972**
† Masaryk University. Faculty of Sciences. Scripta Chemia/Scripta Facultatis Scientiarum Naturalium Universitatis Masarykianae Brunensis. Chemia (CZE ISSN 1211-2828) **8972**
† Masaryk University. Faculty of Sciences. Scripta Computer Science and Applied Mathematics/Scripta Facultatis Scientiarum Naturalium Universitatis Masarykianae Brunensis. Mathematica (CZE ISSN 1211-4723) **8973**
† Masaryk University. Faculty of Sciences. Scripta Geography/Scripta Facultatis Scientiarum Naturalium Universitatis Masarykianae Brunensis. Geographia (CZE ISSN 1211-2844) **8973**
Masaryk University. Faculty of Sciences. Scripta Geology/Facultatis Scientiarum Naturalium Universitatis Masarykianae Brunensis. Geology (CZE ISSN 1211-281X) **2754**
▼ • ➤ Masaryk University Journal of Law and Technology (CZE ISSN 1802-5943) **4728**
➤ Masarykova Univerzita. Filozoficka Fakulta. Sbornik Praci. A: Rada Jazykovedna (CZE) **5150**
Masarykova Univerzita. Filozoficka Fakulta. Sbornik Praci. B: Rada Filozoficka (CZE) **6933**
➤ Masarykova Univerzita. Filozoficka Fakulta. Sbornik Praci. C: Rada Historicka (CZE) **4242**
Masarykova Univerzita. Filozoficka Fakulta. Sbornik Praci. F: Rada Umenovedna (CZE ISSN 1211-7390) **504**
➤ Masarykova Univerzita. Filozoficka Fakulta. Sbornik Praci. L: Rada Romanisticka (CZE ISSN 0531-1985) **5150**
➤ Masarykova Univerzita. Filozoficka Fakulta. Sbornik Praci. M: Rada Archeologicka (CZE ISSN 1211-6327) **405**
➤ Masarykova Univerzita. Filozoficka Fakulta. Sbornik Praci. N: Rada Klasicka (CZE ISSN 1211-6335) **2237**
Masarykova Univerzita. Filozoficka Fakulta. Sbornik Praci. O: Rada Filmologicka (CZE ISSN 1214-0414) **6507**
† Masarykova Univerzita. Filozoficka Fakulta. Sbornik Praci. P: Rada Psychologicka (CZE ISSN 1211-3522) **8973**
➤ Masarykova Univerzita. Filozoficka Fakulta. Sbornik Praci. Q: Rada Teatrologicka (CZE ISSN 1214-0406) **8473**
➤ Masarykova Univerzita. Filozoficka Fakulta. Sbornik Praci. R: Rada Germanisticka/Bruenner Beitraege zur Germanistik und Nordistik (CZE ISSN 1211-4979) **5150**
➤ Masarykova Univerzita. Filozoficka Fakulta. Sbornik Praci. S: Rada Anglisticka/Brno Studies in English (CZE ISSN 1211-1791) **5150**
† Masarykova Univerzita. Filozoficka Fakulta. Sbornik Praci. T: Rada Politologicka (CZE ISSN 1211-7013) **8973**
➤ Masarykova Univerzita. Filozoficka Fakulta. Sbornik Praci. U: Rada Pedagogicka (CZE ISSN 1211-6971) **2885**
Masarykova Univerzita. Filozoficka Fakulta. Spisy/Opera Universitatis Masarykianae Brunensis. Facultas Philosophica (CZE ISSN 1211-3034) **6933**
Maschen-Industrie *see* Textile Network **8460**
Maschere dell'Immaginario (ITA ISSN 1970-3511) **8473**
Die Maschine (DEU ISSN 0340-5737) **5456**
Maschine Market The Industrial Magazine *see* M M - The Industrial Magazine **5455**
Maschine und Werkzeug (DEU ISSN 0343-3471) **5456**
Maschinen Anlagen Verfahren (DEU ISSN 0343-043X) **1779**
Maschinen im Modellbau (DEU ISSN 0947-6598) **4339**
Maschinen Markt Magazyn Przemyslowy *see* M M Magazyn Przemyslowy **5455**
Maschinen Markt Money & Technologies *see* M M Money & Technologies **5455**
Maschinen Markt Prumyslove Spektrum *see* M M Prumyslove Spektrum **5455**
Maschinenbau (CHE) **5456**
Maschinenbau (DEU ISSN 1438-6704) **3388**
Maschinenbau und Metallbearbeitung Deutschland (DEU) **2015**
Die Maschinenbauindustrie (DEU) **5456**
Maschinenmarkt Logistik *see* M M Logistik **5455**
Maschinenmarkt Zulieferer *see* M M Zulieferer **5455**
Maschinenring Aktuell (DEU) **212**
➤ Mash'abei Enosh/Human Resources (ISR ISSN 0792-0970) **1870**
Al-Masha'il (QAT) **2201**
Mashal (PAK) **3926**
Al-Mash'al/Torch (QAT) **6778**
➤ Mashhad University. Faculty of Letters and Humanities. Journal (IRN) **5331**
Mashin/Machine (JPN ISSN 0910-8106) **5456**
Mashinostroitel' (RUS ISSN 0025-4568) **5456**
• Mashinostroyeniye Ukrainy (UKR) **3388**
Mashonaland Chamber of Industries. Annual Report (ZWE) **1407**
Mashriq (GBR ISSN 0025-4584) **3549**
Mashriq (USA) **3549**
Masihi Avaza (IND ISSN 0376-6608) **7662**
Masihi Sevak (IND) **7662**
• The Masik (USA ISSN 1946-4657) **8278**
▼ Masinka Tomas (CZE ISSN 1802-9914) **2201**
Masinstvo (SRB ISSN 0461-2531) **5456**
Al-Masirah (BHR) **5226**
Mask (AUS ISSN 0726-9072) **3072**
Maskan (UZB ISSN 1026-3551) **1022**
Maskayu (MYS ISSN 0126-771X) **3714**
Maske und Kothurn (AUT ISSN 0025-4606) **8473**
Maskin (SWE ISSN 1652-8506) **212**
• Maskin - Aktuelt (DNK ISSN 0905-2151) **6321**
• Maskinbladet (DNK ISSN 1395-8526) **136**
Maskinentreprenoerna Tidningen *see* M E - Tidningen **3388**
MaskinKontakt (SWE ISSN 0345-7788) **5456**
• Maskinmesteren (DNK ISSN 0047-6102) **4598**
Maskinstationen og Landbrugslederen (DNK ISSN 0109-0291) **212**
Maslozhirovaya Promyshlennost'/Fat and Oil Processing Industry (RUS ISSN 0025-4649) **3655**
Maso (CZE ISSN 1210-4086) **3655**
Mason Contractors Association of America Info *see* M C A A Info **1021**
Mason-Dixon Arrive (USA) **3981**
• Masonic Homes. Annual Report (AUS ISSN 1449-9401) **4051**
Masonry (USA ISSN 0025-4681) **1022**
• Masonry Construction (USA) **1022**
➤ Masonry International (GBR ISSN 0950-2289) **449**
➤ The Masonry Society Journal (USA ISSN 0741-1294) **1022**
Mass A B D A Newsletter *see* Massachusetts American Ballroom Dance Association Newsletter **2686**
Mass Appeal (USA ISSN 1532-1649) **6586**
Mass Appeal Queens (USA) **3981**
Mass Builder *see* MassBuilder **1022**
Mass Com Periodical Literature Index (SGP ISSN 0217-1287) **8149**
• ➤ Mass Communication and Society (USA ISSN 1520-5436) **8119**
• ➤ Mass Communicator (IND ISSN 0973-9688) **2332**
Mass Communicator: A Journal of Communication Studies *see* Mass Communicator **2332**
Mass Cyclist (USA) **8260**
• Mass High Tech (USA ISSN 8750-2100) **8431**
Mass Jazz (ESP ISSN 1138-5405) **6586**
Mass Market Retailers *see* M M R **1774**
The Mass Media (USA) **5331**
Mass Media Articles Index *see* Communication and Mass Media Complete **2347**
Mass Media in India (IND) **8119**
Mass Spectrometry Bulletin (GBR ISSN 0025-4738) **2094**
• ➤ Mass Spectrometry Reviews (USA ISSN 0277-7037) **7080**
• Mass Spectrometry Society of Japan. Journal/Mass Spectroscopy (JPN ISSN 1340-8097) **2103**
Mass Spectroscopy *see* Mass Spectrometry Society of Japan. Journal **2103**
• Mass Storage News (USA) **2540**
• Mass Transit (USA ISSN 0364-3484) **8503**
Massa' 'Aher *see* Massa Aher **8732**
• Massa Aher (ISR ISSN 0792-0571) **8732**
• Massa Yisre'eli (ISR) **8732**
Massa' Yisr'eli *see* Massa Yisre'eli **8732**
Massachusettes General Hospital Mind, Mood & Memory *see* Mind, Mood & Memory **7385**
Massachusetts American Ballroom Dance Association Newsletter (USA) **2686**
Massachusetts Appellate Tax Board Reporter (USA ISSN 0732-0825) **1934**
Massachusetts Archaeological Society. Bulletin (USA ISSN 0148-1886) **405**
Massachusetts Archaeological Society. Newsletter (USA) **405**
Massachusetts Association of School Committees. Bulletin (USA) **3027**
Massachusetts Association of School Committees Journal *see* M A S C Journal **3027**

Title

▼ new title *† ceased* *• electronic media* *➤ refereed*

Massachusetts Association of Teachers of English to Speakers of Other Languages Currents *see* M A T S O L Currents **5149**

Massachusetts Attorney Discipline Reports (USA) **4728**

Massachusetts Banker (USA) **1366**

Massachusetts Bar Association Lawyers Journal (USA ISSN 1524-1823) **4728**

Massachusetts Beverage Business (USA ISSN 1090-9214) **607**

● Massachusetts Business Credit Directory (USA) **2015**

● Massachusetts Business Directory (USA ISSN 1048-7131) **2015**

Massachusetts Cities & Counties Graphic Performance Analysis (USA ISSN 1935-598X) **7481**

Massachusetts Cities and Counties Graphic Performance Analysis *see* Massachusetts Cities & Counties Graphic Performance Analysis **7481**

Massachusetts Civil Service Reporter (USA ISSN 1522-6689) **4728**

● Massachusetts College of Pharmacy. Bulletin (USA ISSN 0025-4789) **6860**

Massachusetts Condominium Law (USA) **4835**

● Massachusetts Corporate Forms (USA) **4875**

● Massachusetts Criminal Law and Motor Vehicle Handbook (USA ISSN 1930-1774) **4893**

● Massachusetts Criminal Law and Procedure (USA) **4729**

Massachusetts Curiosities (USA ISSN 1550-6932) **8732**

● The Massachusetts Daily Collegian (USA ISSN 0890-0434) **2291**

Massachusetts Dental Society. Journal (USA ISSN 0025-4800) **5855**

Massachusetts Dental Society News *see* M D S News **5855**

Massachusetts. Department of Employment and Training. Employment and Wages State Summary (USA) **1251**

Massachusetts Directory of Manufacturers (USA ISSN 0195-5810) **2015**

Massachusetts Directory of Technology Companies (USA) **2016**

Massachusetts Discrimination Law Reporter (USA ISSN 0199-5235) **4729**

Massachusetts. Division of Fisheries and Wildlife. Annual Report (USA) **2618**

Massachusetts Division of Marine Fisheries. Completion Report (USA) **3601**

Massachusetts Domestic Relations (USA) **4912**

Massachusetts Employment Law (USA ISSN 1945-0249) **1697**

● Massachusetts Employment Law Letter (USA ISSN 1049-2062) **4729**

● Massachusetts Environmental Compliance Update (USA ISSN 1064-2374) **4729**

Massachusetts Environmental Law Handbook (USA) **4729**

Massachusetts Estate Planning, Will Drafting and Estate Administration Forms (USA) **4904**

Massachusetts Facts (USA ISSN 0894-3427) **3121**

† Massachusetts Family Law Guidebook (USA) **8973**

Massachusetts Family Law Journal (USA) **4912**

Massachusetts Foreign Language Association Newsletter *see* MA F L A Newsletter **5149**

Massachusetts Getaway Guide (USA) **8732**

Massachusetts Golfer *see* MassGolfer **8238**

Massachusetts Historical Review (USA ISSN 1526-3894) **4303**

Massachusetts Historical Society Miscellany. N *see* M H S Miscellany. N **4302**

Massachusetts Horse (USA ISSN 1945-1393) **8294**

Massachusetts Housing Finance Agency. Annual Report (USA ISSN 0076-499X) **4419**

Massachusetts Housing Finance Agency Update *see* M H F A Update **4419**

Massachusetts Institute of Technology. Department of Earth, Atmospheric and Planetary Sciences. Report (USA) **2712**

Massachusetts Institute of Technology. Flight Transportation Laboratory. F T L Reports and Memoranda (USA) **65**

Massachusetts Institute of Technology Occasional Papers in Linguistics *see* M I T Occasional Papers in Linguistics **5149**

Massachusetts Institute of Technology Press Series in Information Systems *see* M I T Press Series in Information Systems **2431**

Massachusetts Institute of Technology. Research Laboratory of Electronics. R L E Progress Report (USA ISSN 0163-9218) **3324**

Massachusetts Institute of Technology Working Papers in Linguistics *see* M I T Working Papers in Linguistics **5149**

● Massachusetts Jury Instruction - Criminal (USA) **4893**

Massachusetts Labor Cases (USA ISSN 1051-6123) **1697**

Massachusetts Labor Leader (USA) **4598**

Massachusetts Labor Relations Reporter (USA ISSN 1522-6670) **1697**

The Massachusetts Law Reporter (USA ISSN 1080-1464) **4729**

● Massachusetts Law Review (USA ISSN 0163-1411) **4729**

● Massachusetts Lawyers Weekly (USA ISSN 0196-7509) **4729**

Massachusetts Legal History (USA ISSN 1092-5880) **4729**

● Massachusetts Manufacturers Register (USA) **2016**

Massachusetts: Manufacturing *see* Harris Directory. Massachusetts Manufacturing **2000**

● Massachusetts Motor Vehicle and Traffic Laws (USA) **4729**

Massachusetts Municipal Association Directory (USA ISSN 0361-2090) **7497**

Massachusetts Music News (USA ISSN 0147-2550) **6586**

Massachusetts Nurse *see* The Massachusetts Nurse Advocate **5969**

● The Massachusetts Nurse Advocate (USA ISSN 1941-367X) **5969**

Massachusetts Off the Beaten Path *see* Off the Beaten Path, Massachusetts **8743**

● Massachusetts Pleading and Practice: Forms and Commentary (USA) **4729**

Massachusetts Practice Series (USA) **4729**

Massachusetts Practice Series. Administrative Law and Practice (USA) **4729**

Massachusetts Practice Series. Appellate Procedure (USA) **4729**

Massachusetts Practice Series. Business Corporations *see* Massachusetts Practice Series. Business Corporations with Forms **4875**

Massachusetts Practice Series. Business Corporations with Forms (USA ISSN 1550-4573) **4875**

Massachusetts Practice Series. Civil Practice (USA) **4835**

Massachusetts Practice Series. Collection Law (USA) **4729**

Massachusetts Practice Series. Criminal Defense Motions (USA) **4893**

Massachusetts Practice Series. Criminal Law (USA) **4893**

Massachusetts Practice Series. Criminal Practice and Procedure (USA) **4894**

Massachusetts Practice Series. Employment Law (USA) **4875**

Massachusetts Practice Series. Equitable Remedies (USA) **4875**

Massachusetts Practice Series. Estate Planning with Forms on Disk (USA) **4904**

Massachusetts Practice Series. Evidence (USA) **4729**

Massachusetts Practice Series. Family Law and Practice with Forms (USA) **4912**

Massachusetts Practice Series. Federal Civil Practice (USA) **4835**

Massachusetts Practice Series. Juvenile Law (USA) **4729**

Massachusetts Practice Series. Landlord and Tenant Law with Forms (USA) **4729**

Massachusetts Practice Series. Legal Forms (USA) **4729**

Massachusetts Practice Series. Manual on Uniform Commercial Code (USA) **4875**

Massachusetts Practice Series. Massachusetts Rules of Civil Procedure (USA) **4835**

Massachusetts Practice Series. Mediation & Arbitration Practice (USA) **4729**

Massachusetts Practice Series. Methods of Practice (USA) **4729**

Massachusetts Practice Series. Motor Vehicle Law and Practice with Forms (USA) **4729**

Massachusetts Practice Series. Municipal Law and Practice (USA) **4730**

Massachusetts Practice Series. Prima Facie Case/Proof and Defense (USA) **4730**

Massachusetts Practice Series. Probate Law and Practice (USA) **4730**

Massachusetts Practice Series. Procedural Forms Annotated (USA) **4835**

Massachusetts Practice Series. Real Estate Law with Forms (USA) **7599**

Massachusetts Practice Series. Summary of Basic Law (USA) **4730**

Massachusetts Practice Series. Taxation (USA) **1934**

Massachusetts Practice Series. Tort Law (USA) **4730**

Massachusetts Practice Series. Trial Practice (USA) **4730**

Massachusetts Practice Series. Uniform Commercial Code Forms Annotated (USA) **4875**

Massachusetts Practice Series. Workmen's Compensation (USA) **1697**

● Massachusetts Professional Responsibility (USA) **4730**

● Massachusetts Psychologist (USA) **7384**

Massachusetts Reports *see* West's Jury Verdicts. Massachusetts Reports **4967**

● ➤ Massachusetts Review (USA ISSN 0025-4878) **5227**

Massachusetts Rules of Criminal Court Handbook (USA ISSN 1938-7784) **4894**

Massachusetts School Directory *see* M D R's School Directory. Massachusetts **2959**

Massachusetts School of Law at Andover Review *see* M S L Review **4726**

Massachusetts Sierran (USA ISSN 1071-9229) **2618**

Massachusetts Spy (USA) **6897**

Massachusetts State Labor Council A F L - C I O Newsletter (USA ISSN 0025-4894) **4598**

Massachusetts Studies in Early Modern Culture (USA) **4242**

Massachusetts Super Lawyers (USA ISSN 1556-8016) **4730**

Massachusetts Taxpayers Foundation. State Budget Trends (USA) **7481**

Massachusetts Teachers Association Today *see* M T A Today **2884**

Massachusetts Telephone Tickler for Insurance Men & Women (USA) **4514**

● Massachusetts Tort Damages (USA) **4835**

† Massachusetts Tort Law (USA) **8973**

Massachusetts Travel & Holiday Guide (GBR) **8732**

Massachusetts Voter (USA ISSN 1057-4549) **7154**

Massachusetts Wildlife (USA ISSN 0025-4924) **2618**

Massachusetts Workers' Compensation Reports (USA) **4514**

● Massachusetts Zoning and Land Use Law (USA) **4730**

● Massage (USA ISSN 1057-378X) **6112**

● Massage and Bodywork (USA ISSN 1544-8827) **6992**

Massage and Health Review (GBR ISSN 1749-1924) **312**

● Massage Australia (AUS ISSN 1328-8431) **6112**

Massage Therapists *see* Australian Association of Massage Therapists. Journal **6107**

Massage Therapy Canada (CAN ISSN 1499-8084) **6112**

Massage Therapy Journal (USA ISSN 0895-0814) **312**

▼ Massage Therapy Today (CAN ISSN 1911-8813) **6112**

● Massage Today (USA ISSN 1531-8079) **6112**

Al-Massaiyah (SAU ISSN 1319-0261) **3944**

Al-Massar (GBR) **7154**

● MassBuilder (USA) **1022**

Masscitizen (USA ISSN 8750-8516) **3452**

Massenet Society. Newsletter (GBR) **6586**

Massey Collectors News - Wild Harvest (USA ISSN 0897-215X) **367**

● Massey Magazine (NZL) **2291**

● Massey Research (NZL ISSN 1177-2247) **2291**

Massey University. Centre for Applied Economics and Policy Studies. Agricultural Policy Discussion Paper (NZL ISSN 0112-0603) **203**

† Massey University. Centre for Applied Economics and Policy Studies. Agricultural Policy Paper (NZL ISSN 0110-5558) **8973**

† Massey University. Centre for Applied Economics and Policy Studies. Agricultural Policy Proceedings (NZL ISSN 0111-6339) **8973**

Massey University. Centre for Applied Economics and Policy Studies. Discussion Paper in Natural Resource and Environmental Economics (NZL ISSN 1174-474X) **1498**

● Massey University. Centre for Public Health Research. Monitoring Report (NZL ISSN 1173-6437) **7531**

Massey University. Centre for Public Health Research. Quarterly Monitoring Report *see* Massey University. Centre for Public Health Research. Monitoring Report **7531**

● Massey University. Department of Applied and International Economics. Discussion Paper (NZL ISSN 1174-2542) **1147**

† Massey University. Department of Information Systems. Technical Report (NZL ISSN 1175-1738) **8973**

Massey University. Geography Programme. Occasional Paper (NZL ISSN 1176-953X) **4019**

Massey University. School of Accountancy. Discussion Paper Series (NZL ISSN 1175-2874) **1296**

Massey University. Veterinary Continuing Education. Publication *see* VetLearn Foundation. Publication **8814**

MassGolfer (USA) **8238**

Massif Central (FRA ISSN 1265-5651) **4019**

Massif Central. Hors Serie *see* Massif Central **4019**

Massif Central. Hors Serie Balades *see* Massif Central **4019**

Massif Central. Hors Serie Gourmand *see* Massif Central **4019**

● Massilia (ESP ISSN 1695-3576) **449**

Massimario del Foro Italiano (ITA ISSN 0025-4932) **4730**

● Massimario della Giurisprudenza Italiana (ITA ISSN 0025-4940) **4730**

Massimario di Giurisprudenza del Lavoro (ITA ISSN 0025-4959) **1697**

Massis (LBN ISSN 0025-4975) **7705**

Massive (London) (GBR) **2291**

● Massmedia (SWE ISSN 0280-2147) **8119**

Masson Newsletter de Ginecologia (ESP ISSN 1138-8196) **5997**

Masson Newsletter de Internet Medicina (ESP ISSN 1138-6215) **5832**

Massorot (ISR ISSN 0334-1674) **7726**

Massu'a (ISR ISSN 0542-9943) **3549**

Massuah *see* Massu'a **3549**

The Mast *see* The Mooring Mast **2292**

● ➤ Mast Cells (AUT ISSN 1609-5510) **834**

Mastatstva' (BLR) **5331**

Master (RUS) **4464**

Master A P U.S. Government & Politics *see* Peterson's Master A P U.S. Government & Politics **7165**

Master and the Multitude (GBR) **7662**

Master Brewers Association of America. Communications *see* Master Brewers Association of the Americas. Communicator **607**

Master Brewers Association of the Americas. Communicator (USA) **607**

Master Brewers Association of the Americas. Technical Quarterly *see* Technical Quarterly & the M B A A Communicator **611**

Master Builder (AUS ISSN 1443-9638) **1022**

● Master Builder (Melbourne) (AUS ISSN 1323-0514) **1022**

● Master Builders' Journal (GBR ISSN 0025-4991) **1022**

Master Choice Magazine (USA) **3655**

Master Collector (USA) **4339**

▼ Master Crucigramas (ARG ISSN 1851-3891) **8187**

Master Detective (GBR ISSN 0262-4141) **2660**

Master Directory *see* Mix Annual Directory of Recording Industry Facilities and Services **2017**

● ➤ Master Drawings (USA ISSN 0025-5025) **504**

Master Frequency Data Base (Frequency Sequence) (USA) **2348**

Master Frequency Data Base (Service Group Code Sequence) (USA) **2348**

Master Funds *see* Investor Weekly **1633**

Master Guide (CAN) **6971**

Master, Mate & Pilot (USA ISSN 0025-5033) **4598**

Master na Vse Ruki (RUS) **4438**

● Master of Public Health Essay (SWE ISSN 1104-5701) **7531**

Master Performers (RUS) **6586**

The Master Photographer (GBR ISSN 0047-6196) **6971**

Master Piece (GBR) **6971**

Master Plan for Professional Home Remodeling (USA) **1022**

Master Salesmanship (USA ISSN 0199-3887) **1834**

The Master Teacher (USA ISSN 0889-6259) **2885**

Master the A P Government & Politics Tests *see* Peterson's Master A P U.S. Government & Politics **7165**

Master the Civil Service Exams (USA ISSN 1557-2706) **2944**

Master the Corrections Officer Exam (USA ISSN 1933-1940) **2660**

● Master the G M A T (Graduate Management Admission Test) (USA ISSN 1939-6198) **2993**

Master the P C A T (Pharmacy College Admission Test) (USA ISSN 1931-5481) **6860**

Master the Police Officer Exam (USA ISSN 1939-6988) **6701**

Master the Postal Exams (USA ISSN 1930-4803) **6701**

Master the State Trooper Exams (USA ISSN 1930-6512) **6701**

Master Theses in the Pure and Applied Sciences *see* Masters Theses in the Pure and Applied Sciences Accepted by Colleges and Universities of the United States and Canada **2934**

● Master Type Locator (USA ISSN 1080-983X) **3108**

Masterfiles (NLD) **2332**

▼ MasterGardener (USA ISSN 1936-7058) **3743**

Masterilka (RUS) **2201**

● Mastering Life (USA) **7662**

Mastering Written Discovery (USA) **4730**

Masterlink (CAN) **8260**

Masterlist of Major International Companies *see* Hoover's Masterlist of Major International Companies (Year) **2004**

MasterList of U S Companies *see* Hoover's MasterList of U S Companies (Year) **2004**

Masterpieces in the National Gallery of Canada/Chefs-d'Oeuvre de la Galerie Nationale du Canada (CAN ISSN 0383-5391) **504**

Masterrind (DEU ISSN 1867-2809) **293**

Masters *see* Dajia **5282**

● Masters Abstracts International (USA ISSN 0898-9095) **2934**

Masters Annual (USA ISSN 1933-3234) **8238**

Masters in Business Administration Jungle *see* M B A Jungle **1145**

Masters in Business Administration Review *see* M B A Review **1773**

Masters in Business Administration Studium *see* Das M B A Studium **2992**

Masters Magazine *see* Martial Arts Masters Magazine **8187**

The Masters of Golf (JPN) **8238**

Masters of Role Playing (USA) **8187**

Masters of the Fighting Arts (USA) **8187**

Masters Pelle (ITA) **4974**

● Master's Seminary Journal (USA ISSN 1066-3959) **7766**

Masters Theses in the Pure and Applied Sciences Accepted by Colleges and Universities of the United States and Canada (USA ISSN 0736-7910) **2934**

Masterwork Studies (USA) **5331**

● Masterworks for Learning: A College Catalogue (USA) **6528**

Masterworks in the Western Tradition (USA ISSN 1086-539X) **5331**

† ● Masthead (CAN ISSN 0832-512X) **8973**

● The Masthead (Harrisburg) (USA ISSN 0025-5122) **4579**

The Masthead (Philadelphia) (USA) **6528**

Mastiff Club of America. Journal (USA) **6811**

Mastika (MYS ISSN 0126-5598) **3907**

● Mastozoologia Neotropical (ARG ISSN 0327-9383) **955**

Mastozoologia Neotropical. Publicaciones Especiales (ARG ISSN 0329-1006) **955**

Masui/Japanese Journal of Anesthesiology (JPN ISSN 0021-4892) **5772**

Masui to Sosei/Anesthesia and Resuscitation (JPN ISSN 0385-1664) **5772**

Masurari si Automatizari (ROM ISSN 1582-2834) **6403**

Masurisch-Ermlandische Mittelungen *see* Komunikaty Mazursko-Warminskie **4238**
Masvingo Diary (ZWE) **8733**
Masyarakat Indonesia: Majalah Ilmu - Ilmu Sosial Indonesia (IDN ISSN 0125-9989) **7984**
Maszyny Elektryczne (POL ISSN 0239-3646) **3325**
Maszyny Przeplywowe (POL ISSN 0860-3324) **3209**
Maszyny, Technologie, Materialy (POL ISSN 1505-7038) **3209**
Mat & Pack *see* Emballering **6709**
▼ Mat Environnement (FRA ISSN 1959-2590) **1022**
Mat og Industri (NOR ISSN 1502-1491) **3655**
† Matador (DEU ISSN 1862-0876) **8973**
Matador (ESP ISSN 1135-1772) **5227**
▼ Matalana (FRA ISSN 1960-2359) **3549**
Matamata Chronicle (NZL ISSN 1170-0718) **3917**
Matancer Libre (USA) **3549**
El Matancero Libre *see* Libre **3548**
Matangi Tonga (TON ISSN 0113-0374) **3962**
Matapli (FRA ISSN 0762-5707) **5510**
Matar Abu Dhabi al-Dawli/Shoptalk - Abu Dhabi Duty Free Guide (UAE) **8784**
Matar Dubai al-Dawli/Dubai International Airport (UAE) **8733**
• ➤ Matatu (NLD ISSN 0932-9714) **5331**
Matavimai/Measurements (LTU ISSN 1392-1223) **6403**
Matbaa & Teknik (TUR) **7324**
Match (GBR ISSN 0955-4947) **8238**
➤ Match (SRB ISSN 0340-6253) **2072**
The Match (USA) **7154**
Match Angling Plus (GBR) **8321**
• Match News (CAN ISSN 0836-7515) **8874**
Match of the Day (GBR ISSN 1364-4521) **8238**
Match Show Bulletin (USA) **6811**
Mate *see* Banlu **8853**
Mate Amargo (URY) **7154**
Mate Postal (ESP) **8187**
Matemarica Fisica (BRA ISSN 0102-3896) **7881**
Matematica Aplicada e Computacional *see* Computational and Applied Mathematics **5551**
• ➤ Matematica Contemporanea (BRA ISSN 0103-9059) **5510**
Matematica e Dintorni (ITA ISSN 1970-3678) **5510**
Matematica e Fisica *see* Serie di Matematica e Fisica **5534**
➤ La Matematica e la sua Didattica (ITA ISSN 1120-9968) **5510**
La Matematica nella Societa e nella Cultura (ITA ISSN 1972-7356) **5510**
• Matematicalia (ESP ISSN 1699-7700) **5510**
• Matematicas (COL ISSN 0120-6788) **5510**
Matematicas en Breve (ESP ISSN 1578-6099) **5510**
Le Matematiche (ITA ISSN 0373-3505) **5510**
Matematicheskaya Fizika, Analiz, Geometriya *see* Zhurnal Matematicheskoi Fiziki, Analiza, Geometrii **5548**
Matematicheskaya Fizika i Nelineinaya Mekhanika (UKR ISSN 0233-7568) **5510**
Matematicheskie Trudy (RUS ISSN 1560-750X) **5511**
Matematicheskie Zametki (RUS ISSN 0025-567X) **5511**
Matematicheskii Institut im. V.A. Steklova. Trudy (RUS ISSN 0371-9685) **5511**
➤ Matematicheskii Sbornik (RUS ISSN 0368-8666) **5511**
Matematicheskoe Modelirovanie (RUS ISSN 0234-0879) **5511**
➤ Matematicki Bilten (MKD ISSN 0351-336X) **5511**
Matematicki List (SRB ISSN 0352-714X) **5511**
Matematicki List za Ucenike Osnovne Skole *see* Matematicki List **5511**
• ➤ Matematicki Vesnik (SRB ISSN 0025-5165) **5511**
Matematicko Fizicki List (HRV ISSN 1332-1552) **5511**
• Matematika (MYS ISSN 0127-8274) **5511**
Matematika Crne Gore *see* Mathematica Montisnigri **5512**
Matematika dlya Shkol'nikov (RUS) **5511**
Matematika, Fyzika, Informatika (CZE ISSN 1210-1761) **2885**
Matematika i Informatika (BGR ISSN 1310-2230) **5511**
Matematika v Shkole (RUS ISSN 0130-9358) **5511**
Matematika v Vysshem Obrazovanii/Mathematics in Higher Education (RUS ISSN 1729-5440) **5511**
➤ Matematikai Lapok/Mathematical Papers (HUN ISSN 0025-519X) **5511**
➤ Matematychni Mashyny i Systemy (UKR ISSN 1028-9763) **2462**
➤ Matematychni Studii (UKR ISSN 1027-4634) **5511**
Matematyka (Poznan) (POL ISSN 0551-6625) **5511**
➤ Matematyka (Warsaw) (POL ISSN 0137-8848) **5511**
➤ Matematyka Stosowana (POL ISSN 1730-2668) **5511**
• Materia/Bergshanteringen (FIN ISSN 1459-9694) **6469**
Materia (ITA ISSN 1121-0516) **449**
Materia/Japan Institute of Metals. Bulletin (JPN ISSN 1340-2625) **6321**
Materia (Barcelona) (ESP ISSN 1579-2641) **504**
• Materia (Rio de Janeiro) (BRA ISSN 1517-7076) **3352**
• Materia Socio Medica (BIH ISSN 1512-7680) **5665**
Material & Technik Moebel (DEU) **4560**
† Material Culture Directories (USA ISSN 0743-7528) **8973**
➤ Material Culture Review/Revue d'Histoire de la Culture Materielle (CAN ISSN 1718-1259) **4152**
Material Engineering Series (USA) **3389**
Material Flow (JPN ISSN 1342-4599) **5456**
Material Handling Equipment & Systems (USA ISSN 1940-7270) **3389**
• Material Handling Management (USA ISSN 1529-4897) **5456**
• Material Handling Management Directory (Online) (USA) **2016**
Material Handling Network (USA) **8503**
• Material Handling Product News (USA ISSN 0195-2366) **2462**
Material Handling Wholesaler (USA) **1022**
Material History Review *see* Material Culture Review **4152**
Material Management (DEU ISSN 1436-8331) **1898**
Material Management Magazin (DEU ISSN 0932-6243) **1898**
• ➤ Material Religion (GBR ISSN 1743-2200) **7662**
• Material Safety Data Sheets (CAN ISSN 1912-3000) **6681**
Material Science and Engineering *see* Cailiao Kexue yu Gongcheng Xuebao **3342**
Material Science and Technology *see* Cailiao Kexue yu Gongyi **6307**
Material Science Study *see* Bussei Kenkyu **7007**
Materialdienst (DEU ISSN 0721-2402) **7662**
Materialdienst des Konfessionskundlichen Instituts (DEU ISSN 0934-8522) **7806**
➤ Materiale Plastice (ROM ISSN 0025-5289) **7095**
Materiale si Cercetari Arheologice (ROM ISSN 1220-5222) **405**
Materialen zum Sumerischen Lexikon/Materials for the Sumerian Lexicon (ITA) **5150**
Materialen zur Altlasten-Sanierung und zum Bodenschutz (DEU ISSN 1432-3575) **3489**
Materialen zur Bodendenkmalpflege im Rheinland (DEU) **4242**
Materialen zur Marktberichterstattung (DEU) **136**
Materialen zur Regionalgeschichte (DEU ISSN 1439-8583) **4242**
• Materiales (USA) **3072**
• Materiales de Construccion (ESP ISSN 0465-2746) **1022**
Materialfluss (DEU ISSN 0170-334X) **8503**
Materialfluss. Markt (DEU ISSN 1613-8279) **8431**
Materialhefte zur Archaeologie des Mittelalters und der Neuzeit (DEU ISSN 0948-6976) **405**
Materialhefte zur Archaeologie in Baden-Wuerttemberg (DEU ISSN 1430-3442) **405**
Materialhefte zur Bayerischen Vorgeschichte (DEU) **405**
Materialhefte zur Ur- und Fruehgeschichte Niedersachsens (DEU ISSN 0465-2770) **4242**
Materiali Accessori Componenti *see* M A C **4560**
Materiali di Storia Urbana (ITA) **4152**
• Materiali e Discussioni per l'Analisi dei Testi Classici (ITA ISSN 0392-6338) **2237**
Materiali e Documenti Ticinesi (CHE ISSN 0088-7714) **4242**
Materiali e Strutture (ITA ISSN 1121-2373) **2618**
Materiali Edili (ITA ISSN 1126-3946) **1022**
• ➤ Materiali in Tehnologije/Materials and Technology (SVN ISSN 1580-2949) **3352**
† Materiali per il Vocabolario Neosumerico (ITA) **8973**
• Materiali per una Storia della Cultura Giuridica (ITA ISSN 1120-9607) **4955**
Materiali per una Storia delle Istituzioni Giuridiche e Politiche Medievali Moderne e Contemporanee. Atti (ITA ISSN 1970-2078) **4956**
Materiali per una Storia delle Istituzioni Giuridiche e Politiche Medievali Moderne e Contemporanee. Quaderni (ITA ISSN 1970-206X) **4956**
Materiali per una Storia delle Istituzioni Giuridiche e Politiche Medievali Moderne e Contemporanee. Strumenti (ITA ISSN 1970-2051) **4956**
Materiali per una Storia delle Istituzioni Giuridiche e Politiche Medievali Moderne e Contemporanee. Studi (ITA ISSN 1970-2043) **4956**
Materialien aus der Bildungsforschung (DEU ISSN 0173-3842) **2885**
Materialien aus der Forschung (DEU ISSN 0937-7379) **7984**
Materialien fuer die Betriebliche Praxis (DEU ISSN 1436-8463) **1367**
Materialien und Studien zur Ostmitteleuropa (DEU) **4242**
Materialien zum Suedosteuropasprachatlas (DEU) **5150**
Materialien zur Berufs- und Arbeitspaedagogik (DEU ISSN 0177-4018) **2885**
Materialien zur Bevoelkerungswissenschaft (DEU ISSN 0178-918X) **7287**
Materialien zur Geschichte der Sprachwissenschaft und der Semiotik (DEU ISSN 0721-6920) **5150**
Materialien zur Information und Dokumentation (DEU) **2332**
Materialien zur Mittelstandsoekonomie (DEU ISSN 1436-977X) **1147**
Materialien zur Raumordnung (DEU) **4019**
Materialien zur Roemisch-Germanischen Keramik (DEU ISSN 0076-5171) **2044**
➤ Materializing Culture (GBR ISSN 1460-3349) **8119**
• Materially Speaking (USA) **3352**
Materialovedenie (RUS ISSN 0130-3678) **7025**
➤ Materialovedenie (RUS ISSN 1684-579X) **3370**
Materialoznanie i Tekhnologiia (BGR ISSN 0204-7535) **3352**
Materialpruefung *see* Materials Testing **3354**
▼ • Materials (CHE ISSN 1996-1944) **3278**
Materials and Components in Fossil Energy Applications (USA) **3141**
• ➤ Materials and Corrosion (DEU ISSN 0947-5117) **6321**
• Materials & Design (GBR ISSN 0264-1275) **3352**
Materials and Design Exchange *see* M A D E **3352**
Materials and Geoenvironment *see* R M Z - Materials and Geoenvironment **6477**
• ➤ Materials & Manufacturing Processes (USA ISSN 1042-6914) **3389**
Materials and Plant Protection (USA) **7048**
Materials and Resources Centre for Enterprising Teaching Red Guides. Series 1: Placements *see* M A R C E T Red Guides. Series 1: Placements **3071**
Materials and Resources Centre for Enterprising Teaching Red Guides. Series 10: Flexible Learning *see* M A R C E T Red Guides. Series 10: Flexible Learning **3071**
Materials and Resources Centre for Enterprising Teaching Red Guides. Series 6: Implications of Gender for Skills Development *see* M A R C E T Red Guides. Series 6: Implications of Gender for Skills Development **3071**
• ➤ Materials and Structures/Materiaux et Constructions (NLD ISSN 1359-5997) **1022**
Materials and Studies for Kassite History (USA ISSN 0146-6798) **4323**
Materials and Technology *see* Materiali in Tehnologije **3352**
Materials Architecture Design Environment *see* M A D E **449**
• ➤ Materials at High Temperatures (GBR ISSN 0960-3409) **3352**
Materials Australia (AUS ISSN 1037-7107) **6321**
• Materials Business File (USA ISSN 1555-8444) **6340**
• ➤ Materials Characterization (USA ISSN 1044-5803) **6322**
• ➤ Materials Chemistry and Physics (CHE ISSN 0254-0584) **3352**
Materials Division *see* M D **3388**
Materials Education Yearbook for the United States and Abroad *see* Metallurgy - Materials Education Yearbook **6325**
Materials Engineering (USA ISSN 1075-8577) **3352**
Materials Engineering News (USA ISSN 1556-1798) **3352**
• Materials Engineering News e-Report (USA ISSN 1938-0836) **3209**
• ➤ Materials Evaluation (USA ISSN 0025-5327) **3353**
▼ Materials for Engineering (SGP) **3353**
Materials for Mechanical Engineering *see* Jixie Gongcheng Cailiao **3384**
Materials for Port and Harbour Engineering Promotion *see* Kowan Gijutsu Shinkokai Shiryo **3277**
Materials for Resource Recovery and Transport (CAN) **6322**
Materials for the Sumerian Lexicon *see* Materialen zum Sumerischen Lexikon **5150**
• Materials Forum (CD-ROM) (AUS ISSN 1447-6738) **6322**
Materials Handling and Distribution Supply Chain Solutions *see* M H D Supply Chain Solutions **1773**
Materials Handling & Logistics Today *see* Supply Chain Today **5460**
Materials Handling & Logistics Today *see* Bulk Handling Today **5450**
Materials Handling News (GBR ISSN 0025-5351) **5457**
Materials Handling News Directory *see* M H N Directory **2013**
• Materials Handling Solutions (USA) **5457**
• Materials Issues in Art and Archaeology (USA ISSN 1095-1318) **504**
Materials K T N Focus (Knowledge Trasnfer Network) (GBR ISSN 1752-7473) **7095**
• ➤ Materials Letters (NLD ISSN 0167-577X) **7025**
Materials Life Society. Journal *see* Materiaru Raifu Gakkaishi **3370**
• Materials Management & Distribution (CAN ISSN 0025-5343) **8503**
• Materials Management in Health Care (USA ISSN 1059-4531) **4106**
Materials Management Journal of India (IND ISSN 0543-0313) **1834**
Materials Modelling Series (GBR ISSN 1352-9692) **3353**
Materials Monthly (USA ISSN 1939-4993) **1022**
Materials on Antitrust Compliance (USA) **4875**
Materials on Canadian Income Tax (CAN ISSN 0844-5648) **4730**
† Materials on Corporate Political Activity (USA) **8973**
Materials on International & E C Tax Law *see* Materials on International and European Community Tax Law **1934**
Materials on International and European Community Tax Law (NLD ISSN 1574-4086) **1934**
• Materials Performance (USA ISSN 0094-1492) **3353**
• Materials Physics and Mechanics (RUS ISSN 1605-2730) **3353**
† Materials Processing News (GBR ISSN 1462-0138) **8973**
Materials Protection *see* Cailiao Baohu **3342**
Materials Protection *see* Zastita Materijala **6721**
• Materials Recycling and Processing in the United States (USA) **3509**
Materials Recycling Week (GBR ISSN 1354-8522) **6322**
Materials Recycling Week Handbook *see* M R W Handbook **3508**
• ➤ Materials Research (BRA ISSN 1516-1439) **3353**
• ➤ Materials Research Bulletin (GBR ISSN 0025-5408) **2111**
• ➤ Materials Research Innovations (GBR ISSN 1432-8917) **7881**
Materials Research Laboratories. Bulletin of Research and Development (TWN ISSN 1010-2744) **8431**
Materials Research Society Bulletin *see* M R S Bulletin **3352**
Materials Research Society Internet Journal of Nitride Semiconductor Research *see* M R S Internet Journal of Nitride Semiconductor Research **3352**
➤ Materials Research Society of Japan. Transactions (JPN ISSN 1382-3469) **3353**
• Materials Research Society Symposium Proceedings (USA ISSN 0272-9172) **7025**
Materials Safety Data Sheets Software Report *see* M S D S Software Report **3482**
Materials Science *see* Medziagotyra **3354**
• Materials Science (POL ISSN 0137-1339) **3389**
• ➤ Materials Science (USA ISSN 1068-820X) **3353**
• ➤ Materials Science and Engineering A: Structural Materials: Properties, Microstructures and Processing (CHE ISSN 0921-5093) **3353**
• ➤ Materials Science and Engineering B: Advanced Functional Solid-state Materials (CHE) **3353**
Materials Science and Engineering B: Solid-State Materials for Advanced Technology *see* Materials Science and Engineering B: Advanced Functional Solid-state Materials **3353**
Materials Science and Engineering C: Biomimetic Materials, Sensors and Systems *see* Materials Science and Engineering C: Materials for Biological Applications **3353**
• ➤ Materials Science and Engineering C: Materials for Biological Applications (CHE) **3353**
• ➤ Materials Science and Engineering R: Reports (CHE ISSN 0927-796X) **3353**
Materials Science and Engineering Technology *see* Materialwissenschaft und Werkstofftechnik **6322**
• ➤ Materials Science and Technology (GBR ISSN 0267-0836) **3353**
Materials Science & Technology *see* Kinzoku **6320**
Materials Science and Technology *see* Zairyou no Kagaku to Kougaku **3360**
• Materials Science and Technology (SVK ISSN 1335-9053) **3389**
• ➤ Materials Science and Technology (VEN ISSN 1316-2012) **3354**
• Materials Science Citation Index (USA) **3232**
➤ Materials Science Forum (CHE ISSN 0255-5476) **7026**
• ➤ Materials Science Foundations (CHE ISSN 1422-3597) **3354**
• ➤ Materials Science in Semiconductor Processing (GBR ISSN 1369-8001) **3108**
• ➤ Materials Science Monographs (NLD ISSN 0166-6010) **3209**
➤ Materials Science of Minerals and Rocks (NLD ISSN 0924-4972) **2754**
Materials Science Quarterly *see* Cailiao Kexue **6307**
Materials Science Research India (IND ISSN 0973-3469) **3354**
▼ • Materials Science Research Journal (USA ISSN 1935-2441) **7881**
Materials Solutions for Environmental Problems (CAN) **6322**
• ➤ Materials Structure in Chemistry, Biology, Physics and Technology (CZE ISSN 1211-5894) **7026**
Materials System *see* Zairyo Shisutemu **3228**
Materials, Technologies, Tools *see* Materialy, Tekhnologii, Instrumenty **8431**
• ➤ Materials Technology (GBR ISSN 1066-7857) **6322**
Materials Technology Series (NLD ISSN 1389-2126) **3354**
Materials Testing (DEU) **3354**
• Materials Today (NLD ISSN 1369-7021) **2072**
• ➤ Materials Transactions (JPN ISSN 1345-9678) **6322**
• Materials World (GBR ISSN 0967-8638) **6322**
Materialwirtschaft und Logistik im Unternehmen (DEU ISSN 0937-4183) **1779**
• ➤ Materialwissenschaft und Werkstofftechnik/ Materials Science and Engineering Technology (DEU ISSN 0933-5137) **6322**
Materialy Archeologiczne Muzeum Archeologicznego w Krakowie *see* Muzeum Archeologiczne, Krakow. Materialy Archeologiczne **407**
Materialy Archeologiczne Nowej Huty *see* Muzeum Archeologiczne, Krakow. Oddzial w Nowej Hucie. Materialy Archeologiczne Nowej Huty **407**
Materialy Budowlane (POL ISSN 0137-2971) **1022**
Materialy Ceramiczne (POL ISSN 1644-3470) **2044**
Materialy Elektroniczne (POL ISSN 0209-0058) **3108**
Materialy Elektronnoi Tekhniki. Izvestiya Vuzov (RUS ISSN 1609-3577) **3108**

Title

DIRECTORY 2010 MAZUIPIN GONGBAO 10597

Matica Hrvatska Slavonski Brod. Godisnjak *see* Ogranak Matice Hrvatske Slavonski Brod. Godisnjak **4251**

Matica Srpska Review of Stage Art and Music *see* Zbornik Matice Srpske za Scenske Umetnosti i Muziku **8485**

Matices (DEU ISSN 0948-7557) **7252**

Maticne Citanie. Narodny Kalendar (SVK) **3946**

Matieland (ZAF ISSN 0025-5947) **2291**

Matieres a Creer (FRA ISSN 1771-9607) **537**

▼ Matieres a Profits (FRA ISSN 1956-2527) **1638**

† Matilda Magazine: Literary and Art Magazine (AUS ISSN 0810-2740) **8973**

▼ Matilde Salvador (ESP ISSN 1888-3699) **2885**

Matimyas Matematika (PHL ISSN 0115-6926) **5517**

Le Matin (CHE ISSN 1018-3736) **3958**

Le Matin Bleu (CHE) **3958**

Le Matin Dimanche (CHE) **3958**

• Le Matinal (BEN ISSN 1563-5848) **3802**

• Matindustrien (NOR ISSN 0809-8042) **3655**

Matka (HRV ISSN 1330-1047) **5517**

Matkailu/Tourism (FIN ISSN 0789-1393) **8733**

Matkaopas (FIN ISSN 1456-419X) **8733**

Matmagasinet (SWE ISSN 1402-974X) **4363**

Matra (IDN ISSN 0215-1715) **6294**

Matriart (CAN ISSN 1182-6169) **8901**

Matribhoomi/Nepali Weekly (NPL) **3914**

• Le Matricule des Anges (FRA ISSN 1241-7696) **5331**

Matrimonial Advertisements International (IRL) **5560**

Matrimonial Decisions for G B & I (Great Britain & Ireland) (GBR) **4912**

Matrimonial Law Reporter (IND) **4912**

• Matrimonial Strategist (USA ISSN 0736-4881) **4912**

Matrix (CAN ISSN 0318-3610) **504**

➤ Matrix (DNK ISSN 0109-646X) **7384**

Matrix (GBR ISSN 0307-3335) **5444**

Matrix (Herefordshire) (GBR ISSN 0261-3093) **7567**

Matrix (Urbana) (USA ISSN 8755-7266) **5426**

• ➤ Matrix Biology (NLD ISSN 0945-053X) **5665**

• Matrix Maps Quarterly (USA ISSN 1073-0958) **2501**

• Matrix.Net White Papers (USA) **2564**

• Matrix News (USA ISSN 1059-0749) **2564**

▼ • Matrizes (BRA ISSN 1982-2073) **2332**

The Matron (GBR ISSN 1745-3518) **2161**

Matronas Profesion (ESP ISSN 1578-0740) **5998**

Matrubhasa (IND) **3885**

Matschalla (DEU) **3852**

Matsumoto Dental University Society. Journal *see* Matsumoto Shigaku **688**

• ➤ Matsumoto Shigaku/Matsumoto Dental University Society. Journal (JPN ISSN 0385-1613) **688**

Matsushiro Gunpatsu Jishin Shiryo Hokoku/Bulletin of Data and Information on the Matsushiro Earthquake Swarm (JPN ISSN 0385-2016) **2786**

Matsushiro Seismological Observatory. Seismological Bulletin *see* Jishin Kansoku Hokoku **2784**

Matsushiro Seismological Observatory. Technical Reports *see* Kishocho Jishin Kansokujo Gijutsu Hokoku **2786**

Matsushita Denko Giho/M E W Technical Report (JPN ISSN 0285-5054) **3325**

Matsushita Medical Journal *see* Shojinkai Igakushi **5714**

➤ Matsushita Technical Journal (JPN ISSN 1343-9529) **3325**

Matsuyama Red Cross Hospital Journal of Medicine *see* Matsuyama Sekijuji Byoin Igaku Zasshi **5665**

Matsuyama Sekijuji Byoin Igaku Zasshi/Matsuyama Red Cross Hospital Journal of Medicine (JPN ISSN 0389-3888) **5665**

Mattanawcook Observer (USA) **3774**

▼ Matten (NLD ISSN 1873-9210) **8187**

Matter (Fort Collins) (USA ISSN 1548-8411) **5331**

• A Matter of Fact: Statements Containing Statistics on Current Social, Economic and Political Issues (USA ISSN 0897-3954) **4152**

A Matter of Wit (USA) **5331**

Matterzine *see* Matter (Fort Collins) **5331**

The Matthay News (USA ISSN 0360-8484) **6586**

Il Mattino (ITA ISSN 1592-3908) **3897**

Il Mattino Illustrato *see* Il Mattino **3897**

➤ Mattoid (AUS ISSN 0314-5913) **5331**

Maturango Museum Newsletter (USA) **6529**

Mature Lifestyles (Franklin Sq.) (USA) **4051**

Mature Lifestyles (Madison) (USA) **4051**

Mature Living (USA ISSN 0162-427X) **7766**

Mature Living Choices (USA) **4051**

The Mature Traveler (USA ISSN 1532-9526) **8733**

• Mature Years (USA ISSN 0025-6021) **7766**

• ➤ Maturitas (IRL ISSN 0378-5122) **5998**

Matze (DEU) **8589**

• Maudsley Monographs (GBR ISSN 0076-5465) **6159**

Der Maueranker (DEU ISSN 0176-3539) **449**

• Das Mauerwerk (DEU ISSN 1432-3427) **1023**

Mauerwerk-Kalender (DEU ISSN 0170-4958) **1023**

Maui, a Paradise Family Guide *see* Paradise Family Guides: Maui **8746**

Maui Drive Guide *see* Oahu Drive Guide **8742**

Maui Drive Guide *see* Hawaii Drive Guide **8717**

Maui Revealed (USA ISSN 1937-9447) **8733**

Maui Update (USA ISSN 0895-9390) **8733**

• Maui Visitor (USA) **8733**

• The Maui Windsurfing Report (USA) **8321**

Maukef al-Riadi (SYR) **8187**

Maulana Azad National Institute of Technology Journal *see* M A N I T. Journal **3208**

Maurice Ewing Series (USA ISSN 0197-6346) **2786**

Maurice Falk Institute for Economic Research in Israel. Report and Discussion Paper Series (ISR ISSN 0333-7839) **1147**

• Le Mauricien (MUS ISSN 1025-3718) **3907**

Mauritania. Direction de la Statistique et des Etudes Economiques. Bulletin Mensuel Statistique (MRT ISSN 0543-1433) **8388**

• Mauritania Food Security Update (USA ISSN 1947-7015) **1601**

Mauritania Monthly Food Security Update *see* Mauritania Food Security Update **1601**

Mauritania. Office National de la Statistique. Bulletin Statistique et Economique (MRT) **8388**

Mauritian Abroad (GBR ISSN 1359-3781) **3549**

† Mauritian International (GBR ISSN 0265-444X) **8973**

Mauritiana (NLD ISSN 1574-3187) **555**

Mauritiana (Altenburg) (DEU ISSN 0233-173X) **7881**

Mauritius. Archives Department. Annual Report (MUS ISSN 0076-5481) **5031**

Mauritius. Central Electricity Board. Annual Report (MUS) **3325**

Mauritius. Central Statistical Office. Annual Digest of Statistics (MUS ISSN 1013-6061) **1251**

Mauritius. Central Statistical Office. Business Activity Statistics (MUS) **1251**

Mauritius. Central Statistical Office. Digest of Agricultural Statistics (MUS) **183**

Mauritius. Central Statistical Office. Digest of Demographic Statistics (MUS) **7312**

Mauritius. Central Statistical Office. Digest of Educational Statistics (MUS) **2934**

Mauritius. Central Statistical Office. Digest of External Trade Statistics (MUS) **1251**

Mauritius. Central Statistical Office. Digest of Industrial Statistics (MUS) **1251**

Mauritius. Central Statistical Office. Digest of International Travel and Tourism Statistics (MUS) **8779**

Mauritius. Central Statistical Office. Digest of Labour Statistics (MUS) **1251**

Mauritius. Central Statistical Office. Digest of Productivity and Competitiveness Statistics (MUS) **1251**

Mauritius. Central Statistical Office. Digest of Public Finance Statistics (MUS) **1251**

Mauritius. Central Statistical Office. Digest of Road Transport & Road Accidents Statistics (MUS) **8527**

Mauritius. Central Statistical Office. Household Budget Survey (MUS) **4370**

Mauritius. Central Statistical Office. Housing and Population Census (Year). Results (MUS) **4436**

Mauritius. Central Statistical Office. Housing and Population Census. Analysis Reports (MUS) **4436**

Mauritius. Central Statistical Office. Housing and Population Census. Census of Economic Activities (Year) (MUS) **1251**

Mauritius. Central Statistical Office. National Accounts of Mauritius (MUS) **1251**

Mauritius. Central Statistical Office. Statistics on Rodrigues (MUS) **1251**

Mauritius. Central Statistics Office. Labour Force Sample Survey (Year) (MUS) **8388**

Mauritius Chamber of Agriculture. Annual Report (MUS ISSN 1694-0091) **136**

Mauritius Chamber of Commerce and Industry. Annual Report (MUS) **1407**

Mauritius. Director of Audit. Report (MUS ISSN 0543-1565) **1934**

Mauritius. Fire Services. Report (MUS) **3580**

Mauritius. Forestry Service. Annual Report (MUS) **3696**

Mauritius Housing Corporation. Report and Accounts (MUS) **4419**

Mauritius Institute Bulletin (MUS ISSN 1694-0016) **7881**

Mauritius Institute of Education. Annual Report (MUS) **2885**

Mauritius Institute of Education. Journal (MUS) **2885**

Mauritius. Judicial Department. Annual Report (MUS) **4956**

Mauritius. Ministry of Agriculture, Food Technology and Natural Resources. Annual Report (MUS) **136**

Mauritius. Ministry of Agriculture, Food Technology and Natural Resources. Technical Bulletin (MUS) **136**

Mauritius. Ministry of Co-operatives and Co-operative Development. Annual Report (MUS) **1424**

Mauritius. Ministry of Environment and National Developing Unit. Factsheets (MUS ISSN 1694-0520) **3452**

Mauritius. Ministry of Finance. Insurance Unit. Controller of Insurance. Report (MUS) **4514**

Mauritius. Ministry of Finance. Unified Revenue Board. Report (MUS) **1934**

Mauritius. Ministry of Social Security. National Solidarity and Reform Institutions (MUS) **8055**

Mauritius. Ombudsman. Annual Report (MUS) **7452**

Mauritius Police Force. Annual Report (MUS) **2660**

Mauritius Police Magazine (MUS) **2660**

• Mauritius Post Office Savings Bank. Annual Report (MUS) **1367**

Mauritius. Posts & Telegraphs. Annual Report (MUS) **2354**

Mauritius. Public Accounts Committee. Report (MUS ISSN 0076-5562) **1934**

Mauritius. Public Service Commission. Annual Report (MUS) **7452**

Mauritius, Reunion & Seychelles Directory (ZAF) **2016**

Mauritius Standards Bureau. Annual Report (MUS) **6403**

Mauritius Sugar Industry Research Institute. Advisory Bulletin (MUS) **3655**

Mauritius Sugar Industry Research Institute. Annual Report (MUS ISSN 0369-2043) **3655**

Mauritius Sugar Industry Research Institute. Occasional Paper (MUS ISSN 0369-2035) **3655**

Mauritius Telecom Yellow Pages (MUS ISSN 1694-0156) **2016**

Mauritius. Telecommunications Department. Annual Report (MUS) **2369**

Mauritius Times (MUS ISSN 0025-6064) **3789**

Mauritius. Tobacco Board. Annual Report *see* Mauritius. Tobacco Board. Annual Report and Accounts **8486**

Mauritius. Tobacco Board. Annual Report and Accounts (MUS ISSN 1694-0318) **8486**

Maurizio (DEU) **6897**

† Die Maus (Berlin) (DEU) **8973**

Mausam (IND ISSN 0252-9416) **6390**

MausKlick (DEU) **2201**

Mausolee *see* Pierre Actual **6476**

Mavbima (LKA) **7154**

Maverick (ZAF ISSN 1817-1966) **1147**

Mavin (USA ISSN 1534-9829) **3981**

MAVIS *see* M A V I S (Online) **8802**

Mavors. Roman Army Researches (DEU ISSN 0927-1759) **4152**

Mavrica/Rainbow (SVN) **7806**

Mavrik Magazine (USA ISSN 1559-6508) **6586**

Mawakef Weekly Magazine *see* Al- Mawaqif **3799**

Al-Mawaqif/Mawakef Weekly Magazine (BHR) **3799**

Mawqif al-Adabi (SYR ISSN 0258-3992) **5331**

† Max (DEU ISSN 1617-5530) **8973**

• Max (ITA ISSN 1120-4435) **3897**

Max (MEX) **6294**

Max (USA ISSN 8756-7644) **6294**

Max Euwe-Centrum. Nieuwsbrief (NLD ISSN 0927-9768) **8187**

Max Freiherr von Oppenheim-Stiftung. Schriften (DEU ISSN 0543-1719) **555**

Max Planck Commentaries on World Trade Law (NLD ISSN 1574-907X) **4935**

➤ Max-Planck-Gesellschaft. Jahrbuch (DEU ISSN 0341-0218) **7881**

Max-Planck-Institut fuer Europaeische Rechtsgeschichte. Veroeffentlichungen. Ius Commune. Sonderhefte (DEU ISSN 0175-6532) **4935**

➤ Max-Planck-Institut fuer Geschichte. Veroeffentlichungen (DEU) **4152**

† Max-Planck-Institut fuer Metallforschung. Mitteilungen (DEU ISSN 0585-783X) **8973**

Max-Planck-Institut fuer Meteorologie. Examensarbeit (DEU ISSN 0938-5177) **6390**

Max-Planck-Institut fuer Meteorologie. Report (DEU ISSN 0937-1060) **6390**

Max-Planck-Institut fuer Physik. Werner-Heisenberg-Institut. Jahresbericht (DEU ISSN 0943-2930) **577**

Max-Planck-Institut fuer Stroemungsforschung. Bericht (DEU ISSN 0436-1199) **7060**

Max-Planck-Institut Series in Biological Cybernetics *see* M P I Series in Biological Cybernetics **768**

Max-Planck-Instituts fuer Europaeische Rechtsgeschichte. Rechtsgeschichte (DEU ISSN 1619-4993) **4730**

• Max Planck Yearbook of United Nations Law (NLD ISSN 1389-4633) **4935**

Max Plank Series on Asian Intellectual Property Law (NLD ISSN 1567-8318) **6754**

Max Power (GBR ISSN 0968-8714) **8590**

Max Power (ZAF ISSN 1990-4568) **8590**

• Max Weber Studies (GBR ISSN 1470-8078) **7984**

Maxi (DEU ISSN 0930-1224) **8874**

Maxi (FRA ISSN 0981-6836) **8874**

• Maxi (USA) **8874**

Maxi Astro (FRA ISSN 1280-4371) **566**

Maxi Cuisine (FRA ISSN 1287-4035) **4364**

Maxi Moto *see* Maximoto **8260**

Maxi Tuning (CZE ISSN 1801-1594) **8590**

Maxi Tuning (ESP) **8590**

Maxi Tuning *see* MegaTuning **8187**

Maxi Tunning (PRT) **8590**

• Maxillo Ondontostomatologia (ITA ISSN 1824-1603) **5855**

Maxim (BGR) **6294**

Maxim (CZE ISSN 1214-1569) **6294**

• Maxim (DEU) **6294**

Maxim (ESP) **6294**

• Maxim (GBR ISSN 1357-0862) **6294**

† • Maxim (ITA ISSN 1127-1108) **8973**

Maxim (POL ISSN 1641-9162) **6294**

Maxim (RUS ISSN 1682-8976) **6294**

Maxim (SRB ISSN 1820-5151) **6294**

Maxim (Chinese Mainland Edition) (HKG) **6295**

Maxim (Hong Kong Edition) (HKG) **6295**

• Maxim (Print) (USA ISSN 1092-9789) **6295**

Maxim en Espanol (USA ISSN 1657-9119) **6295**

Maxim Goes to the Movies *see* Maxim Movies **6507**

Maxim Movies (USA ISSN 1543-7582) **6507**

• Maxim Online (USA) **6295**

† Maxim Singapore (SGP) **8973**

Maxim Your Life *see* Fengdu **6290**

Maximale Arbeitsplatzkonzentrationen Collection for Occupational Health and Safety *see* The M A K - Collection for Occupational Health and Safety **6680**

† maximize (DEU) **8973**

Maximoto (FRA ISSN 1628-2124) **8260**

Maximum (BGR) **3805**

Maximum Concentrations at the Workplace and Biological Tolerance Values for Working Materials *see* Deutsche Forschungsgemeinschaft. Commission for the Investigation of Health Hazards of Chemical Compounds in the Work Area. Report **6675**

Maximum Fitness (USA) **6992**

Maximum Fitness for Men (CAN ISSN 1911-6225) **6992**

† Maximum Guitar (USA) **8973**

† Maximum Mountain Bike (GBR ISSN 1461-1619) **8973**

† Maximum P C (ITA ISSN 1824-5706) **8973**

• Maximum P C (Personal Computer) (USA ISSN 1522-4279) **2577**

Maximum PC *see* Maximum P C **2577**

Maximum Rock and Roll *see* Maximum Rock 'n' Roll **6586**

Maximum Rock 'n' Roll (USA ISSN 0743-3530) **6586**

Maximum Rocknroll *see* Maximum Rock 'n' Roll **6586**

• Maximum Travel Per Diem Allowances for Foreign Areas (Email) (USA ISSN 1943-1309) **4730**

MaxPlanckForschung (DEU ISSN 1616-4172) **7881**

MaxPlanckResearch *see* MaxPlanckForschung **7881**

Maxwell Papers (USA) **6434**

Maxwell Review (USA ISSN 0025-6110) **2885**

Maxwell, Williams, Martin and Kramer's the Law of Oil and Gas (USA) **6778**

MaxxTuner (CHE ISSN 1661-657X) **8590**

Maxy's Journal (USA) **5331**

May Day Bulletin (ITA ISSN 1826-1140) **1697**

• The May Report (USA) **3981**

May Trends (USA ISSN 0025-6137) **1963**

Maya (IND) **3885**

Maya World *see* Mundo Maya **348**

Mayab (ESP ISSN 1130-6157) **347**

▼ • Mayan Studies Journal (USA ISSN 2150-3273) **5150**

† Ma'yanot (ISR ISSN 0543-1786) **8973**

Ma'yanot *see* Wellsprings **7731**

Mayapur Journal (CHE ISSN 1019-9969) **7707**

Mayapuri (IND) **6507**

▼ • The Maybala Review (USA ISSN 1934-399X) **5331**

Maybe *see* Mozhet Byt **3937**

Maydaon *see* Meda'on **2431**

Maydica (ITA ISSN 0025-6153) **242**

† Maydorn-Report (DEU ISSN 1611-1400) **8973**

Mayer (FRA ISSN 1422-8122) **504**

Mayfair (GBR ISSN 0025-6161) **6295**

Mayfair (USA) **6295**

Mayfair Specials (USA ISSN 0966-5374) **6295**

Mayfair Summer Special (Year) (GBR ISSN 1748-7420) **6295**

Mayflower Descendant (USA ISSN 8756-3959) **3774**

Mayflower Quarterly (USA ISSN 0148-5032) **3775**

Mayfly (USA) **5427**

• Mayibuye (ZAF ISSN 0025-6188) **7212**

Mayim ve-Hashkaya (ISR ISSN 0333-8835) **8829**

Mayim ve-Hashqaya *see* Mayim ve-Hashkaya **8829**

➤ Maynooth Occasional Papers (IRL ISSN 0791-2145) **4019**

Mayo Agricola (MEX) **136**

Mayo Alumni (USA) **5665**

• Mayo Clinic Gesundheits-Brief (DEU ISSN 0946-3704) **5665**

• Mayo Clinic Health Letter (USA ISSN 0741-6245) **5665**

Mayo Clinic Health Letter Supplement *see* Mayo Clinic Health Letter **5665**

• ➤ Mayo Clinic Proceedings (USA ISSN 0025-6196) **5665**

• Mayo Clinic Women's HealthSource (USA ISSN 1091-0220) **8846**

• Mayo Clinical Update (USA ISSN 0882-6617) **5665**

The Mayo News (IRL ISSN 1393-9130) **3894**

Mayoreo y Distribucion (MEX) **3680**

Mayors' Newsletter (IND) **7497**

The Mayors of America's Principal Cities (USA) **7497**

Mayura (IND) **3885**

Mayuri Sachitra Vara Patrika (IND) **3885**

Mazal U'Bracha Diamonds *see* I D E X Magazine **1120**

Mazama (USA ISSN 0275-6226) **4980**

Mazandaran University of Medical Sciences. Journal *see* Majallah-i Danishgah-ulum-i Pizishki-i Mazandaran **5664**

Al-Mazari' (OMN) **136**

MazdaSport (USA) **8590**

Mazdoor News (IND) **8620**

• Mazengarb's Employment Law (NZL) **4730**

Mazina'igan (USA) **6635**

Mazoji Lietuva (LTU) **3906**

Mazon *see* Mazon Plus **3655**

Mazon Plus/Food (ISR) **3655**

➤ Mazowieckie Studia Humanistyczne (POL ISSN 1234-5075) **4464**

Mazui yu Zhentong (CHN ISSN 1673-3134) **5772**

Mazuipin Gongbao *see* United Nations. Bulletin on Narcotics **2700**

Title

Mazuixue Zazhi/Anaesthesiologica Sinica *see* Acta Anaesthesiologica Taiwanica **5768**
• MBAJungle.com (USA) **1147**
MBeat (DEU) **6586**
▼ • ➤ mBio (USA) **891**
Mbioni (TZA ISSN 0025-6234) **7984**
† M'Bolo (FRA ISSN 0754-4766) **8973**
Mbya Guarani (PRY ISSN 1017-2793) **3549**
Mc Sister *see* McSister **2201**
MC2R *see* Mobile Computing and Communications Review **2333**
MCAD *see* M C A D **3388**
McAllen International Orchid Society Journal (USA ISSN 1934-4880) **800**
McAlvany Intelligence Advisor (USA) **1638**
• McArthur Business Systems Developer Newsletter (USA) **2508**
McBroom's Camera Bluebook (USA ISSN 1092-7816) **6971**
McCall's Quick Quilts *see* Quick Quilts **6641**
McCall's Quick Quilts (USA ISSN 1549-7631) **6640**
McCall's Quilting (USA ISSN 1072-8295) **6640**
McCance and Widdowson's The Composition of Foods *see* The Composition of Foods **6656**
McCarthy on Trademarks and Unfair Competition (USA) **6754**
• McCarthy Tetrault on Tax Disputes (CAN ISSN 1496-581X) **1934**
McClain County Oklahoma Historical and Genealogical Society. Quarterly (USA ISSN 1066-8446) **3775**
McClain's Inland SoCal (USA) **3981**
McClain's Inland Southern California *see* McClain's Inland SoCal **3981**
McClain's Orange County (USA) **3981**
McCutcheon's Emulsifiers and Detergents (North American Edition) (USA ISSN 0145-7055) **2072**
McCutcheon's Functional Materials (International Edition) (USA ISSN 1058-9937) **2127**
McCutcheon's Functional Materials (North American Edition) (USA ISSN 0734-0559) **2127**
McCutcheon's Volume 1: Emulsifiers and Detergents (International Edition) (USA ISSN 1550-1639) **2072**
McDermott's Handbook of Ohio Real Estate Law (USA) **7599**
McDonald, Henry and Meek: Australian Bankruptcy Law and Practice *see* McDonald, Henry & Meek: Australian Bankruptcy Law & Practice **4835**
• McDonald, Henry & Meek: Australian Bankruptcy Law & Practice (AUS) **4835**
McDonald Institute Monographs (GBR ISSN 1363-1349) **405**
McDonald's Licensing and Gaming Laws of N S W *see* Licensing and Gaming Laws New South Wales **4723**
• McEwan & Paton on Damages for Personal Injuries in Scotland (GBR) **4730**
McFadden American Financial Directory *see* American Financial Directory **1307**
McFadden Southwestern Financial Directory *see* Southwestern Financial Directory **1384**
McFarland Literary Companions (USA ISSN 1933-5458) **5331**
• McGeorge Law Review (USA ISSN 1520-9245) **4730**
McGill Daily (CAN ISSN 1192-4608) **2291**
McGill European Studies (USA ISSN 1089-4934) **4242**
➤ McGill International Journal of Sustainable Development Law and Policy/Revue Internationale de Droit et Politique du Developpement Durable de McGill (CAN ISSN 1712-9664) **4730**
• ➤ McGill Journal of Education/Revue des Sciences de l'Education de McGill (CAN ISSN 0024-9033) **2885**
• ➤ McGill Journal of Medicine (CAN ISSN 1201-026X) **5665**
• ➤ McGill Law Journal/Revue de Droit de McGill (CAN ISSN 0024-9041) **4730**
McGill News (CAN ISSN 0024-9068) **2291**
McGill-Queen's Studies in the History of Ideas (CAN ISSN 0711-0995) **6933**
• McGill Reporter (CAN ISSN 0848-8436) **2291**
• ➤ McGill Science Undergraduate Research Journal (CAN ISSN 1718-0775) **7882**
McGill Tribune (CAN ISSN 1199-2816) **3813**
McGill University Graduate School of Library and Information Studies Newsletter (CAN ISSN 0843-0217) **2291**
McGill University Monographs in Classical Archaeology and History (NLD ISSN 0926-4639) **405**
McGill University, Montreal. Mechanical Engineering Research Laboratories. Report (CAN ISSN 0076-1966) **3389**
McGill University, Montreal. Mechanical Engineering Research Laboratories. Technical Note (CAN ISSN 0076-1974) **3389**
McGill University. Register (CAN ISSN 0226-7586) **4152**
McGill Working Papers in Linguistics/Cahiers Linguistiques de McGill (CAN ISSN 0824-5282) **5150**
McGill's Life Insurance (USA ISSN 1945-2462) **4514**
McGoldrick's Canadian Customs Guide "Harmonized System" (CAN ISSN 1183-3246) **1577**
McGraw Hill Construction Dodge Construction News Weekly Covering North and South Dakota *see* Construction News Weekly Covering North and South Dakota **997**
McGraw Hill Construction Dodge Construction News Weekly Covering the State of Nebraska *see* Construction News Weekly Covering the State of Nebraska **998**
McGraw-Hill Series in Developmental Psychology (USA ISSN 1556-665X) **7384**
McGraw-Hill Series in Electrical Engineering (USA ISSN 0736-6973) **3325**
Mcgraw Hill Series in Management Information Systems *see* McGraw-Hill Series in Management Information Systems **2531**
McGraw-Hill Series in Management Information Systems (USA ISSN 0891-4699) **2531**
McGraw-Hill Yearbook of Science and Technology (USA ISSN 0076-2016) **7882**
▼ McGraw-Hill's A C T (American College Tests) (USA ISSN 1943-4987) **2993**
▼ McGraw-Hill's A C T (with CD-ROM) (American College Tests) (USA ISSN 1943-4995) **2993**
McGraw-Hill's A S V A B (Armed Services Vocational Aptitude Battery) (USA ISSN 1934-2241) **6434**
• McGraw-Hill's A S V A B Basic Training for the A F Q T (Armed Services Vocational Aptitude Battery / Armed Forces Qualifying Test) (USA ISSN 1933-4397) **6434**
McGraw-Hill's L S A T (Law School Admission Test) (USA ISSN 1943-4960) **4730**
McGraw-Hill's L S A T (with CD-ROM) (Law School Admission Test) (USA ISSN 1943-4979) **4730**
McGraw-Hill's National Electrical Code Handbook (USA ISSN 0277-6758) **3325**
• McGraw-Hill's Power Markets Week (USA ISSN 1078-9820) **3160**
McGraw-Hill's S A T Subject Test. U.S. History (USA ISSN 1935-6080) **4303**
McGregor's Who Owns Whom (ZAF ISSN 1350-1143) **2016**
The McGruffletter (National Edition) (USA ISSN 1074-8083) **2660**
• McGuire's Home Business Newsletter (AUS) **2564**
➤ McIlvainea (USA ISSN 0099-8400) **800**
† McK Wissen (DEU ISSN 1619-9138) **8973**
McKinney's New York Court Rules, State & Federal Pamphlet *see* Court Rules Pamphlet(s). McKinney's New York Rules of Court, State & Federal **4949**
McKinney's New York Rules of Court *see* Court Rules Pamphlet(s). McKinney's New York Rules of Court, State & Federal **4949**
• The McKinsey Quarterly (USA ISSN 0047-5394) **1779**
• McKnight's Long-Term Care News (USA ISSN 1048-3314) **4051**
• The McMaster Journal of Theology and Ministry (Online) (CAN ISSN 1481-0794) **7662**
McMaster School for Advancing Humanity. Journal (USA ISSN 1931-5457) **8055**
• McMaster University. Centre for Health Economics and Policy Analysis. Annual Report (CAN ISSN 1912-1865) **1148**
McMichael Canadian Art Collection. Annual Report (CAN ISSN 1208-0721) **6529**
McMullen - Business Transfers and Employee Rights (GBR) **4875**
• McNair Papers (USA ISSN 1071-7552) **6434**
➤ McNair Research Journal (USA) **7882**
McNaughton Papers (CAN) **7252**
McNeese Review (USA ISSN 0885-467X) **5331**
McQuillin Municipal Law Report (USA ISSN 1530-1389) **4730**
McSister (JPN) **2201**
McSweeney's (USA) **5227**
• McTrans: Center for Microcomputers in Transportation. Newsletter (USA) **8504**
MCVGamesmarkt *see* GamesMarkt **2477**
➤ M'dina VaHevra/State and Society (ISR) **7154**
Me (FIN ISSN 0025-6269) **1424**
Me (USA ISSN 0272-5657) **504**
Me Magazine (USA ISSN 1551-2045) **504**
Me Naiset (FIN ISSN 0025-6277) **8874**
Me'a *see* Mea (Print) **3601**
Mea (Online) *see* Mea (Print) **3601**
• Mea (Print) (NOR ISSN 1504-7466) **3601**
Mea Nytt (Print) *see* Mea (Print) **3601**
Meade County Historian (USA) **4303**
• The Meadow (USA ISSN 0886-8654) **5331**
➤ Meadowlark (USA ISSN 1065-2043) **910**
• Mealey's Asbestos Bankruptcy Report (USA ISSN 1537-2065) **4835**
Mealey's Business Interruption Insurance *see* Mealey's Litigation Report: Catastrophic Loss **4836**
• Mealey's California Section 17200 Report (USA ISSN 1543-2106) **4875**
• Mealey's Daubert Report (USA ISSN 1092-7565) **4836**
▼ Mealey's Diabetes Drugs Report (USA ISSN 1941-1332) **4730**
▼ Mealey's Diet Drugs Report (USA ISSN 1940-9001) **4731**
• Mealey's Emerging Drugs & Devices (USA ISSN 1524-9573) **4875**
Mealey's Emerging Drugs and Devices *see* Mealey's Emerging Drugs & Devices **4875**
• Mealey's Emerging Insurance Disputes (USA ISSN 1087-139X) **4514**
• Mealey's Emerging Securities Litigation (USA ISSN 1541-2512) **4731**
• Mealey's Emerging Toxic Torts (USA ISSN 1089-0882) **3509**
• Mealey's Insurance Pleadings (USA ISSN 1538-9898) **4836**
• Mealey's Insurance Regulatory Compliance Report (USA ISSN 1934-9718) **4514**
• Mealey's International Arbitration Quarterly Law Review (USA ISSN 1530-7484) **4956**
• Mealey's International Arbitration Report (USA ISSN 1089-2397) **4935**
• Mealey's International Asbestos Liability Report (USA ISSN 1544-9270) **4836**
Mealey's Litigation Report: Americans with Disabilities Act *see* Mealey's Litigation Report: Employment Law **4956**
• Mealey's Litigation Report: Antidepressant Drugs (USA ISSN 1554-2785) **4731**
• Mealey's Litigation Report: Arthritis Drugs (USA ISSN 1552-8510) **4836**
• Mealey's Litigation Report: Asbestos (USA ISSN 0742-4647) **4836**
Mealey's Litigation Report: Automotive Product Liability *see* Mealey's Product Liability & Risk **4837**
Mealey's Litigation Report: Baycol *see* Mealey's Litigation Report: Heart Drugs & Devices **4731**
• Mealey's Litigation Report: Benzene (USA ISSN 1932-8907) **4836**
• Mealey's Litigation Report: California Insurance (USA ISSN 1536-5522) **4836**
• Mealey's Litigation Report: Catastrophic Loss (USA ISSN 1559-9221) **4836**
• Mealey's Litigation Report: Class Actions (USA ISSN 1535-234X) **4836**
• Mealey's Litigation Report: Construction Defects (USA ISSN 1529-644X) **4836**
• Mealey's Litigation Report: Construction Defects Insurance (USA ISSN 1550-2910) **4514**
Mealey's Litigation Report: Copyright (USA ISSN 1539-6177) **6754**
• Mealey's Litigation Report: Cyber Tech & E-Commerce (USA ISSN 1535-718X) **4875**
Mealey's Litigation Report: Cyber Tech and E-Commerce *see* Mealey's Litigation Report: Cyber Tech & E-Commerce **4875**
▼ Mealey's Litigation Report: Data and Identity Security (USA ISSN 1942-7387) **4731**
• Mealey's Litigation Report: Disability Insurance (USA ISSN 1532-7523) **4836**
• Mealey's Litigation Report: Discovery (USA ISSN 1548-6834) **4731**
• Mealey's Litigation Report: E R I S A (Employee Retirement Income Security Act) (USA ISSN 1540-3629) **4836**
Mealey's Litigation Report: Employment Law (USA ISSN 1553-2410) **4956**
† Mealey's Litigation Report: Ephedra & P P A (USA ISSN 1543-2149) **8973**
• Mealey's Litigation Report: Fen-Phen - Redux (USA ISSN 1097-5497) **6860**
▼ • Mealey's Litigation Report: Food Liability (USA ISSN 1939-2664) **3655**
Mealey's Litigation Report: Heart Drugs and Devices *see* Mealey's Litigation Report: Heart Drugs & Devices **4731**
• Mealey's Litigation Report: Heart Drugs & Devices (USA ISSN 1936-7422) **4731**
• Mealey's Litigation Report: Hormone Replacement Therapy (USA ISSN 1553-2429) **4731**
• Mealey's Litigation Report: Insurance (USA ISSN 8755-9005) **4836**
• Mealey's Litigation Report: Insurance Bad Faith (USA ISSN 1526-0267) **4836**
• Mealey's Litigation Report: Insurance Broker Liability (USA ISSN 1555-6816) **4875**
• Mealey's Litigation Report: Insurance Fraud (USA ISSN 1075-380X) **4836**
• Mealey's Litigation Report: Insurance Insolvency (USA ISSN 1043-8416) **4836**
• Mealey's Litigation Report: Intellectual Property (USA ISSN 1065-9390) **6754**
• Mealey's Litigation Report: Lead (USA ISSN 1059-4116) **4836**
• Mealey's Litigation Report: Mold (USA ISSN 1533-8460) **4836**
▼ Mealey's Litigation Report: Mortgage Lending (USA ISSN 1941-1324) **4731**
Mealey's Litigation Report: Nursing Home Liability (USA ISSN 1534-8199) **4837**
• Mealey's Litigation Report: Patents (USA ISSN 1070-4043) **6754**
• Mealey's Litigation Report: Reinsurance (USA ISSN 1049-5347) **4837**
• Mealey's Litigation Report: Silica (USA ISSN 1543-2122) **4731**
Mealey's Litigation Report: Thimerosal and Vaccines *see* Mealey's Litigation Report: Thimerosal & Vaccines **6860**
• Mealey's Litigation Report: Thimerosal & Vaccines (USA ISSN 1541-2814) **6860**
• Mealey's Litigation Report: Tobacco (USA ISSN 0886-0122) **4837**
• Mealey's Litigation Report: Trademarks (USA ISSN 1528-2422) **4875**
• Mealey's Litigation Report: Welding Rods (USA ISSN 1551-8884) **4837**
• Mealey's Managed Care Liability Report (USA ISSN 1098-173X) **4731**
• Mealey's Mass Tort Pleadings (Online) (USA) **4731**
Mealey's Mass Tort Pleadings (Print) *see* Mealey's Mass Tort Pleadings (Online) **4731**
• Mealey's Personal Injury Report (USA ISSN 1553-2364) **4837**
• Mealey's Pollution Liability Report (USA ISSN 1528-5383) **4837**
Mealey's Privacy Report (USA ISSN 1553-5908) **4837**
• Mealey's Product Liability & Risk (USA ISSN 1537-8748) **4837**
Mealey's Product Liability and Risk *see* Mealey's Product Liability & Risk **4837**
• Mealey's Tort Reform Update (USA ISSN 1547-3759) **4731**
• Mealey's Year 2000 Report (USA ISSN 1098-5786) **4845**
Mean Machines Sega (GBR ISSN 0967-9014) **2478**
† Mean Streets (AUS ISSN 1035-9761) **8973**
Meander (POL ISSN 0025-6285) **2237**
➤ Meander (Kampen) (NLD) **7806**
Meander Berichten (NLD ISSN 1871-6024) **7212**
Meander Magazine *see* Meander Berichten **7212**
Meanderings (USA) **8829**
• Meanjin (AUS ISSN 0815-953X) **5227**
Means Assemblies Cost Data (Year) (USA ISSN 0894-4342) **1023**
Means Concrete and Masonry Cost Data (USA ISSN 1075-0274) **1023**
Means Construction Cost Indexes (USA ISSN 0361-9591) **1048**
• Means CostWorks Building Construction Cost Data (USA) **1023**
Means Electrical Cost Data (Year) (USA ISSN 0748-7002) **3209**
Means Facilities Construction Cost Data (USA ISSN 1075-0789) **1023**
Means Heavy Construction Cost Data (USA ISSN 0893-5602) **1023**
Means Interior Cost Data (Year) (USA) **1023**
Means Labor Rates for the Construction Industry (USA ISSN 1529-6164) **1023**
Means Light Commercial Cost Data (Year) (USA ISSN 0896-7601) **1023**
Means Mechanical Cost Data (Year) (USA) **1023**
Means Open Shop Building Construction Cost Data (Year) (USA) **1023**
Means Plumbing Cost Data (USA ISSN 1042-3850) **4128**
Means Repair and Remodeling Cost Data (Year) (USA ISSN 0898-5006) **1023**
Means Site Work and Landscape Cost Data (year) (USA ISSN 1064-5128) **1023**
Measles Surveillance Report (USA ISSN 0198-6899) **5822**
Measles Weekly Bulletin *see* Pan American Health Organization. Expanded Program on Immunization. Measles Surveillance in the Americas. Bulletin **5824**
Measure (Evansville) (USA ISSN 1555-4791) **5427**
• ➤ Measurement (NLD ISSN 0263-2241) **6403**
• ➤ Measurement (USA ISSN 1536-6367) **5517**
Measurement and Control *see* Jisuanji Celiang yu Kongzhi **6403**
• ➤ Measurement + Control (GBR ISSN 0020-2940) **4488**
Measurement & Control News (USA ISSN 0194-1461) **4488**
Measurement & Control Technology *see* Cekong Jishu **51**
• ➤ Measurement and Evaluation in Counseling and Development (USA ISSN 0748-1756) **2886**
Measurement + Control *see* Measurement + Control **4488**
Measurement Good Practice Guide (GBR ISSN 1368-6550) **7026**
• ➤ Measurement in Physical Education and Exercise Science (USA ISSN 1091-367X) **6992**
Measurement Methods in the Social Sciences Series (USA) **6404**
• ➤ Measurement Science and Technology (GBR ISSN 0957-0233) **4489**
Measurement Science and Technology Series (USA) **6404**
• Measurement Science Review (POL ISSN 1335-8871) **5517**
Measurement Technique *see* Jiliang Jishu **6403**
• ➤ Measurement Techniques (USA ISSN 0543-1972) **6404**
Measurements *see* Matavimai **6403**
• ➤ Measuring Business Excellence (GBR ISSN 1368-3047) **1779**
• Measuring Council Performance in Tasmania (AUS ISSN 1833-7546) **7497**
Measuring Globalisation Statistics *see* Source O E C D. Measuring Globalisation Statistics **1263**
Measuring Ireland's Progress (IRL ISSN 1649-6728) **4171**
The Meat *see* A Hus **3646**
Meat and Deli Retailer *see* Meat & Deli Retailer **3655**
• Meat & Deli Retailer (USA ISSN 1555-8339) **3655**
Meat and Livestock Australia Annual Report *see* M L A Annual Report **292**
Meat and Livestock Commission. Economics Services. Meat Demand Trends (GBR ISSN 0140-6388) **293**
Meat and Livestock Commission. International Meat Market Review (GBR ISSN 0263-2217) **293**
Meat and Livestock Commission United Kingdom Market Survey *see* M L C U K Market Survey **292**
• Meat & Livestock Weekly (AUS ISSN 1448-0387) **293**

DIRECTORY 2010 MEDIA DIRECTORY BOTSWANA (YEAR) 10599

Meat & Meat Products *see* Key Note Market Report: Meat & Meat Products **1895**
• Meat & Poultry (USA ISSN 0892-6077) **3655**
Meat and Poultry *see* Meat & Poultry **3655**
Meat & Poultry Directory *see* Urner Barry's Meat & Poultry Directory **303**
Meat & Poultry News (GBR ISSN 0961-8139) **3655**
Meat & Seafood Merchandising (USA ISSN 1096-9365) **3655**
† Meat and Wool Boards' Economic Service. Annual Review of the New Zealand Sheep & Beef Industry (NZL ISSN 0112-739X) **8973**
Meat and Wool Boards' Economic Service. Autumn Farm Revenue and Production Report (NZL) **203**
Meat and Wool Boards' Economic Service. Domestic Meat Consumption Calendar Year (NZL) **203**
Meat and Wool Boards' Economic Service. Lamb Crop (NZL) **293**
• Meat and Wool Boards' Economic Service. Movements in Sheep & Beef Input Prices (NZL) **203**
• Meat and Wool Boards' Economic Service. N Z Sheep and Beef Farm Survey (New Zealand) (NZL) **203**
Meat and Wool Boards' Economic Service. One Off General Papers (NZL) **203**
Meat and Wool Boards' Economic Service. Sheep and Beef Industry Mid-season Review (NZL) **203**
• Meat and Wool Boards' Economic Service. Stock Number Survey as at 30 June (NZL) **203**
Meat and Wool Economic Service of New Zealand. Publication *see* Meat and Wool New Zealand. Economic Service. Paper **203**
Meat and Wool Innovation. Economic Service. Publication *see* Meat and Wool New Zealand. Economic Service. Paper **203**
• Meat and Wool New Zealand. Economic Service. Paper (NZL ISSN 1176-824X) **203**
Meat Animals: Production, Disposition and Income *see* U.S. Department of Agriculture. National Agricultural Statistics Service. Meat Animals: Production, Disposition and Income **188**
Meat Demand Trends *see* Meat and Livestock Commission. Economics Services. Meat Demand Trends **293**
Meat&Meal Management (NLD ISSN 1572-073X) **3656**
Meat Goat Monthly News (USA ISSN 1940-6495) **293**
Meat Hygiene *see* Roupin Weisheng **7540**
Meat Industry Research Institute of New Zealand *see* M I R I N Z **8972**
Meat International (NLD ISSN 0924-7068) **293**
Meat Marketing & Technology *see* Meatingplace **1834**
Meat Paper *see* Meatpaper **3656**
Meat, Poultry and Egg Product Inspection Directory (USA) **3656**
Meat Processing *see* Meat & Poultry **3655**
Meat Processing Global *see* Meat & Poultry **3655**
Meat Processors *see* Business Ratio. Meat Processors **282**
Meat Research *see* Roulei Yanjiu **3662**
Meat Science (JPN ISSN 0289-0542) **3656**
• ➤ Meat Science (NLD ISSN 0309-1740) **3656**
Meat Science Institute. Proceedings (USA ISSN 0090-5631) **3656**
Meat Sheet (USA ISSN 0889-3608) **293**
Meat Technology *see* Tehnologija Mesa **302**
• Meat Trades Journal (GBR ISSN 0025-6412) **3656**
Meat Trades Journal Directory (Year) (GBR ISSN 1750-1288) **3656**
Meat Wholesalers *see* Business Ratio. Meat Wholesalers **282**
† MeatBusiness (NLD ISSN 1572-0748) **8973**
• Meatec Nachrichten (LIE ISSN 1818-9628) **293**
Meath Chronicle (IRL ISSN 0791-8399) **3894**
▼ Meath Post (IRL ISSN 2009-0412) **3894**
Meatingplace (USA ISSN 1931-7816) **1834**
▼ Meatpaper (USA ISSN 1937-5085) **3656**
Mebio (JPN ISSN 0910-0474) **5795**
Mebio Oncology (JPN ISSN 1349-2179) **6027**
Meble (POL ISSN 1642-8412) **5227**
Mecanica Popular (ARG) **8431**
Mecanica Popular *see* Popular Mechanics en Espanol **8435**
Mecanipel (ESP ISSN 0211-299X) **4974**
• Mecanique & Industries (FRA ISSN 1296-2139) **3389**
• ➤ Meccanica (NLD ISSN 0025-6455) **7060**
Meccanica e Automazione *see* M & A **8972**
Meccanismi Sociali (ITA) **8119**
• Mech (USA ISSN 1093-8753) **6434**
• Mechademia (USA ISSN 1934-2489) **505**
• Mechaid (GBR) **1023**
Mechanical and Electrical Design *see* M & E Design **3324**
Mechanical and Electrical Equipment *see* Jidian Shebei **5453**
Mechanical & Electrical Technique of Hydropower Station *see* Shuidianzhan Jidian Jishu **3163**
Mechanical & Electrical Technology *see* Jidian Jishu **8428**
Mechanical & Transportation Engineering Abstracts *see* C S A Mechanical & Transportation Engineering Abstracts **3229**
▼ Mechanical Business (CAN ISSN 1916-0674) **4123**
Mechanical Computer-Aided Design *see* M C A D **3388**
Mechanical Engineering *see* Kikai Gijutsu **3387**
• ➤ Mechanical Engineering (USA ISSN 0025-6501) **3389**
• Mechanical Engineering Abstracts from C S A (USA ISSN 1063-7311) **3232**
Mechanical Engineering & Machine Tool Abstracts *see* Gepgyartastechnologiai es Szerszamgepipari Szakirodalmi Tajekoztato **3230**
Mechanical Engineering Applications *see* Oyo Kikai Kogaku **5458**
Mechanical Engineering Bulletin (IND ISSN 0379-5527) **3389**
Mechanical Engineering Laboratory. Annual Report *see* Kikai Gijutsu Kenkyujo Nenpo **3387**
Mechanical Engineering Laboratory. Bulletin (JPN ISSN 0374-2725) **3389**
Mechanical Engineering Laboratory. Proceedings of the Study Meeting *see* Kikai Gijutsu Kenkyujo. Kenkyu Koenkai Shiryo **3387**
Mechanical Engineering Laboratory. Report *see* Kikai Gijutsu Kenkyujo Hokoku **3387**
Mechanical Engineering Laboratory. Technical Note *see* Kikai Gijutsu Kenkyujo Shiryo **3387**
Mechanical Engineering Magazine *see* Strojnicky Casopis **3396**
➤ Mechanical Engineering Series (USA ISSN 0899-3858) **3389**
Mechanical Handling Market Review *see* Key Note Market Review: Mechanical Handling **1896**
Mechanical Science and Technology *see* Jixie Kexue yu Jishu **3384**
• ➤ Mechanical Systems and Signal Processing (GBR ISSN 0888-3270) **3389**
† Mechanical Translation and Computational Linguistics (USA ISSN 0543-2073) **8973**
Mechanical Transmission *see* Jixie Chuandong **5453**
➤ Mechanics (POL ISSN 1734-8927) **3389**
Mechanics (USA ISSN 0076-5783) **7061**
Mechanics & Chemistry of Biosystems *see* Molecular & Cellular Biomechanics **750**
➤ Mechanics and Mathematical Methods - Series of Handbooks (NLD) **5517**
➤ Mechanics and Physics of Discrete Systems (NLD ISSN 0926-9282) **3389**
Mechanics and Practice *see* Lixue yu Shijian **3388**
• ➤ Mechanics Based Design of Structures and Machines (USA ISSN 1539-7734) **3389**
• ➤ Mechanics of Advanced Materials and Structures (USA ISSN 1537-6494) **3354**
• ➤ Mechanics of Composite Materials (USA ISSN 0191-5665) **3250**
† Mechanics of Creep Brittle Materials (GBR ISSN 0959-5864) **8973**
Mechanics of Machines *see* Mekhanika na Mashinite **3390**
• ➤ Mechanics of Materials (NLD ISSN 0167-6636) **3354**
Mechanics of Rigid Bodies (USA ISSN 0886-2443) **7061**
• ➤ Mechanics of Solids/Mekhanika Tverdogo Tela (USA ISSN 0025-6544) **7061**
• ➤ Mechanics of Time Dependent Materials (NLD ISSN 1385-2000) **7061**
• ➤ Mechanics Research Communications (GBR ISSN 0093-6413) **3354**
Mechanik (POL ISSN 0025-6552) **3389**
➤ Mechanika (LTU ISSN 1392-1207) **7061**
Das Mechanische Musikinstrument (DEU ISSN 0721-6092) **6586**
Mechanische Verbindungstechnik *see* Informationsdienst F I Z Technik. Mechanische Verbindungstechnik **3231**
• ➤ Mechanism and Machine Theory (GBR ISSN 0094-114X) **3389**
• ➤ Mechanisms of Ageing and Development (IRL ISSN 0047-6374) **4051**
Mechanisms of B Cell Neoplasia (DEU ISSN 1018-7243) **925**
• ➤ Mechanisms of Development (IRL ISSN 0925-4773) **834**
Mechanizace Zemedelstvi (CZE ISSN 0373-6776) **212**
• ➤ Mechatronics (GBR ISSN 0957-4158) **3390**
Mechatronik (DEU ISSN 1867-2590) **3209**
▼ Mechatronik Mobil (DEU ISSN 1867-7371) **3209**
Mecklenburg Medicine (USA) **5665**
The Mecklenburg Times (USA ISSN 1933-7345) **1148**
Mecklenburger Pferde (DEU) **8294**
Mecklenburger Pferde Journal *see* Mecklenburger Pferde **8294**
Mectronic Buyers Directory (Northern California Edition) *see* Mectronic Buyers Directory (Online) **2016**
• Mectronic Buyers Directory (Online) (USA) **2016**
Mectronic Buyers Directory (Print) *see* Mectronic Buyers Directory (Online) **2016**
Mectronic Buyers Directory (Southern California Edition) *see* Mectronic Buyers Directory (Online) **2016**
Med. (ESP ISSN 1697-8897) **7252**
MED (Year) *see* Mediterranean Conference on Control and Automation. Proceedings **2463**
• Med Ad News (USA ISSN 1067-733X) **1834**
Med Bil i Europa *see* N A F Guide Europe **8739**
Med.-dent.-Magazin *see* Medizin Dental Magazin **5855**
Med Evangeliet til Asiens Millioner *see* Asias Millioner **7746**
Med in Germany (DEU ISSN 0942-1998) **5665**
Med-Online (DEU ISSN 1434-2243) **5665**
• Med-Report (DEU ISSN 0934-3148) **5665**
Med-Report Austria (AUT) **5665**
• Med Review (DEU ISSN 1615-777X) **5666**
Med Review Online *see* Med Review **5666**
Med-Surg Matters *see* A M S N News **5949**
▼ Med-Tech Precision (USA ISSN 1938-0445) **4489**
Meda (ESP ISSN 1579-4539) **3452**
Meda' 'al Shivyon *see* Israel Equality Monitor **7210**
Meda' Shnati 'al Hatta'agidim Habbanqa'iyyim *see* Bank of Israel. Annual Information on the Banking Corporations **1213**
Meda'at/Reader's Aid (ISR ISSN 1565-544X) **5031**
Medailles (FRA ISSN 0025-6625) **4339**
Les Medailles d'Or *see* Centre National de la Recherche Scientifique. Les Medailles d'Or **7844**
Les Medailles du C N R S *see* Centre National de la Recherche Scientifique. Cristal **7844**
Les Medailles du C N R S *see* Centre National de la Recherche Scientifique. Les Medailles d'Or **7844**
➤ The Medal (GBR ISSN 0263-7707) **6651**
Medal News (GBR ISSN 0958-4986) **4339**
Medallion (USA ISSN 0890-7595) **4152**
MedAmbiente (DEU ISSN 1437-1065) **4106**
• Meda'on (ISR ISSN 0333-7685) **2431**
Medarbeideren *see* Hoeyremagasinet **7140**
Medborgaren (SWE ISSN 0025-665X) **7154**
MedChi Physician (USA) **5666**
Meddelande fraan Kvismare Faagelstation (SWE ISSN 0454-7217) **910**
Meddelande fraan Lunds Universitet Historiska Museum *see* University of Lund. Archeological Institute. Papers. Yearbook **422**
Meddelande fraan S O F (Svensk Onkologisk Foerening) (SWE ISSN 1400-7347) **6027**
Meddelanden *see* V T T Tiedotteita **8444**
Meddelanden fraan Lunds Universitets Geografiska Institute. Avhandlingar (SWE ISSN 0346-6787) **4019**
• Meddelanden fraan Parasitologen (SWE ISSN 1402-5787) **8803**
• ➤ Meddelelser om Groenland. Bioscience/Monographs on Greenland, Bioscience (DNK ISSN 0106-1054) **689**
• ➤ Meddelelser om Groenland. Geoscience/Monographs on Greenland, Geoscience (DNK ISSN 0106-1046) **2754**
• ➤ Meddelelser om Groenland. Man & Society/Monographs on Greenland, Man and Society (DNK ISSN 0106-1062) **347**
Meddelelser om Konservering (SWE ISSN 0106-469X) **2618**
Meddelelser til Medlemmerne *see* Vaapenbrevet **3786**
Medecin de Famille Canadien *see* Canadian Family Physician **5591**
• Medecin de France (FRA ISSN 0399-385X) **5666**
➤ Le Medecin du Quebec (CAN ISSN 0025-6692) **5666**
Le Medecin Generaliste (FRA ISSN 1286-1197) **5666**
Medecin Veterinaire du Quebec (CAN ISSN 0225-9591) **8803**
• Medecine (FRA ISSN 1777-2044) **5666**
Medecine a Travers les Siecles (FRA ISSN 1953-910X) **5666**
Medecine Aeronautique et Spatiale (FRA ISSN 0294-0817) **5666**
Medecine au Feminin (FRA) **5666**
• Medecine Buccale Chirurgie Buccale (FRA ISSN 1273-2761) **5855**
Medecine Cardiovasculaire *see* Kardiovaskulaere Medizin **5795**
Medecine Clinique Endocrinologie & Diabete (FRA ISSN 1639-6685) **5897**
Medecine Clinique et Experimentale *see* Clinical and Investigative Medicine (Print) **8941**
† Medecine Clinique pour les Pediatres (FRA ISSN 1639-6758) **8973**
Medecine d'Afrique Noire (FRA ISSN 0047-6404) **5666**
▼ • Medecine des Maladies Metaboliques (FRA ISSN 1957-2557) **5897**
Medecine d'Urgence (Societe Francaise d'Editions Medicales) (FRA ISSN 1148-8115) **6067**
Medecine et Armees (FRA ISSN 0300-4937) **5666**
• ➤ Medecine et Chirurgie du Pied (FRA ISSN 0759-2280) **6252**
Medecine & Culture (FRA ISSN 1772-0966) **5666**
• ➤ Medecine et Droit (FRA ISSN 1246-7391) **5915**
• ➤ Medecine et Enfance (FRA ISSN 0291-0233) **6096**
Medecine et Enfance Actualites *see* Medecine et Enfance **6096**
Medecine et Hygiene *see* Revue Medicale Suisse **5706**
▼ Medecine et Longevite (FRA ISSN 1875-7170) **5666**
• ➤ Medecine et Maladies Infectieuses (FRA ISSN 0399-077X) **5822**
Medecine et Maladies Infectieuses. Supplement *see* Medecine et Maladies Infectieuses **5822**
Medecine et Nutrition (FRA ISSN 0398-7604) **6663**
Medecine & Sciences Humaines (FRA ISSN 1768-5109) **5666**
Medecine et Societe (FRA ISSN 1778-3232) **5666**
Medecine et Travail *see* Journal des Professionnels de la Sante au Travail **6679**
• ➤ Medecine Nucleaire (FRA ISSN 0928-1258) **6202**
• Medecine Palliative (FRA ISSN 1636-6522) **5666**
• ➤ Medecine Sciences (FRA ISSN 0767-0974) **5666**
Medecine Sociale et Preventive *see* International Journal of Public Health **5639**
• ➤ Medecine Therapeutique (FRA ISSN 1264-6520) **5666**
• Medecine Therapeutique Cardio (FRA ISSN 1774-8747) **5795**
Medecine Therapeutique - Cardiologie *see* Medecine Therapeutique Cardio **5795**
Medecine Therapeutique - Endocrinologie & Reproduction *see* Medecine Therapeutique Medecine de la Reproduction **5897**
• Medecine Therapeutique Medecine de la Reproduction (FRA ISSN 1774-640X) **5897**
• Medecine Therapeutique Pediatrie (FRA ISSN 1286-5494) **6096**
Medecine Tropicale (FRA ISSN 0025-682X) **5822**
Medecines d'Asie. Savoirs et Pratiques (FRA ISSN 1952-1529) **5666**
Medecines du Monde (FRA ISSN 1269-8555) **5666**
Medecines Nouvelles (FRA ISSN 0760-811X) **312**
Medecins du Sport (FRA ISSN 1279-1334) **6231**
† Medecins du Val-de-Marne (FRA ISSN 0183-5734) **8973**
• Medeconomics (GBR ISSN 0144-4271) **5666**
Mededelingen van het Rijksmuseum voor Volkenkunde (Leiden) (NLD ISSN 0169-9156) **347**
Mededelingen voor de Kapitein *see* Notice to Master Mariners **8655**
Mededelingenblad (NLD ISSN 1383-1992) **2267**
Mededelingenblad / Club van Ankervrienden *see* Mededelingenblad **2267**
• Mededingingsrecht (NLD ISSN 1573-9848) **4875**
Medelhavsmuseet. Bulletin (SWE ISSN 0585-3214) **405**
Medellin (COL ISSN 0121-4977) **7806**
Mederic Infos Sante (FRA ISSN 1779-9171) **4514**
Medesthetics (USA ISSN 1937-2140) **5880**
MedFAX *see* HealthFax **4098**
• Medfax (USA) **4106**
MedGenMed *see* Medscape Journal of Medicine **5677**
• Medi Ciego (CUB ISSN 1029-3035) **5666**
• Medi-k (PER ISSN 1609-9516) **5666**
Medi-Planner (IRL) **5666**
Medi Theme (GBR ISSN 0967-2281) **6897**
• Media (CAN ISSN 1198-2209) **4579**
Media *see* Chuanmei **2315**
• Media (HKG ISSN 1562-1138) **29**
Media (USA ISSN 1533-9475) **4579**
Media (French Edition) (LUX ISSN 1023-4349) **2332**
Media: A Directory (ZAF) **4579**
Media, Advertising, Promotions & Sponsorship *see* M A P S **28**
Media Akuntansi (IDN ISSN 1410-0886) **1296**
• ➤ Media and Arts Law Review (AUS ISSN 1325-1570) **4731**
▼ • Media & Communications Report (USA ISSN 1932-9431) **2332**
Media and Cultural Memory/Medien und Kulturelle Erinnerung (DEU ISSN 1613-8961) **7985**
Media and Culture (USA ISSN 1098-4208) **2332**
Media and Culture Journal *see* M - C Journal **8119**
Media & Entertainment Employers *see* Vault Guide to the Top Media & Entertainment Employers **1713**
• Media and Gender Monitor (GBR) **2332**
Media & Marketing (BEL ISSN 0777-0812) **29**
Media & Marketing Polska (POL ISSN 1507-174X) **2332**
† • Media & Methods (USA ISSN 0025-6897) **8973**
Media and Society Series (USA ISSN 0890-7161) **8119**
Media Arts Information Network *see* M A I N **8119**
• Media Asia (SGP ISSN 0129-6612) **7567**
Media Asia-Pacific Agency Directory *see* Asia-Pacific Agency Directory **1973**
• Media Biz (AUT ISSN 1605-4598) **6507**
• Media Biz Branchenfuehrer (AUT) **2016**
Media Calendar Directory *see* Bacon's Media Calendar Directory **1974**
Media Communications *see* MediaKommunikacio **2886**
• Media Computing (USA ISSN 1090-4255) **2564**
• Media Comunicacion (MEX) **8120**
• Media Contact Directory (USA ISSN 1931-468X) **2332**
• ➤ Media, Culture & Society (GBR ISSN 0163-4437) **8120**
Media Culture Review (USA ISSN 1072-3552) **8120**
Media-Daten (Zurich) *see* Schweizer Media-Daten **39**
Media-Daten: Deutschland Ost (DEU ISSN 0943-1764) **2016**
Media-Daten: Fachzeitschriften (DEU ISSN 0170-4192) **4587**
Media-Daten: Radio - T V (DEU ISSN 1610-0840) **2360**
Media-Daten: Zeitschriften (DEU ISSN 0170-4176) **4587**
Media-Daten: Zeitungen - Anzeigenblaetter (DEU ISSN 0931-3265) **38**
• Media Detail (NLD ISSN 1385-9005) **3108**
• ➤ Media Development (GBR ISSN 0143-5558) **2332**
Media Directory (NZL ISSN 0113-2202) **29**
Media Directory Botswana (Year) (BWA) **2332**

Title

▼ *new title* † *ceased* • *electronic media* ➤ *refereed*

● ➤ Medical Imaging Technology (JPN ISSN 0288-450X) **6203**
● Medical Imaging Week (USA ISSN 1552-9355) **6203**
● ➤ Medical Immunology (GBR ISSN 1476-9433) **5763**
Medical Immunology (USA ISSN 1095-5992) **5763**
● Medical Industry Conference Calendar Newsletter (USA) **2016**
● Medical Industry E-Mail News Service (USA) **5669**
● Medical Industry Week (GBR) **4489**
Medical Informatics and the Internet in Medicine *see* Informatics for Health and Social Care **5831**
● Medical Informatics Newsletter (CAN) **5832**
Medical Information Express *see* Gekkan Mikusu **5618**
† The Medical Information Technology Law Report (USA ISSN 1532-9224) **8973**
▼ ● Medical Innovation & Business (USA ISSN 1943-0701) **5669**
Medical Instrument News *see* Hoken Sangyo Jiho **5628**
● ➤ Medical Journal Armed Forces India (IND ISSN 0377-1237) **5669**
Medical Journal for Enterprises *see* Gongqi Yikan **5620**
● ➤ Medical Journal of Australia (AUS ISSN 0025-729X) **5669**
Medical Journal of Bakirkoy *see* Bakirkoy Tip Dergisi **5583**
Medical Journal of Chinese People Health *see* Zhongguo Minkang Yixue **7547**
Medical Journal of Chinese People's Liberation Army *see* Jiefangjun Yixue Zazhi **5644**
Medical Journal of Industrial Enterprise *see* Gongqi Yikan **5620**
Medical Journal of Inner Mongolia *see* Neimenggu Yixue Zazhi **5684**
Medical Journal of Kagoshima University *see* Kagoshima Daigaku Igaku Zasshi **5656**
Medical Journal of Kinki University *see* Kinki Daigaku Igaku Zasshi **5657**
Medical Journal of Kobe University *see* Kobe Daigaku Igakubu Kiyo **5658**
Medical Journal of Liaoning *see* Liaoning Yixue Zazhi **5661**
Medical Journal of Malaysia (MYS ISSN 0300-5283) **5669**
Medical Journal of Minami Osaka Hospital *see* Minami Oosaka Byoin Igaku Zasshi **5679**
Medical Journal of National Defending Forces in Northwest China *see* Xibei Guofang Yixue Zazhi **5732**
Medical Journal of Qilu *see* Qilu Yixue Zazhi **5701**
Medical Journal of South Taiwan (TWN ISSN 1991-4784) **5669**
The Medical Journal of Teaching Hospitals & Institutes (EGY ISSN 1110-2039) **4106**
Medical Journal of the Chinese People's Armed Police Forces *see* Wujing Yixue **5732**
● ➤ Medical Journal of the Islamic Republic of Iran (IRN ISSN 1016-1430) **5669**
Medical Journal of Uzbekistan *see* Meditsinskii Zhurnal Uzbekistana **5676**
Medical Journal - University of Toronto *see* University of Toronto. Medical Journal **5727**
● Medical Laboratory Observer (USA ISSN 0580-7247) **5909**
Medical Laboratory World (GBR ISSN 0140-3028) **5909**
● Medical Laser Application (DEU ISSN 1615-1615) **5909**
● Medical Law Cases for Doctors (IND ISSN 0974-1232) **5669**
➤ Medical Law International (GBR ISSN 0968-5332) **4731**
● Medical Law Monitor (GBR ISSN 1351-6345) **4731**
Medical Law Reports *see* Lloyds Law Reports. Medical **5662**
● ➤ Medical Law Review (GBR ISSN 0967-0742) **4731**
● Medical Law's Regan Report (USA ISSN 1528-8471) **5669**
▼ The Medical-Legal News (USA ISSN 1936-1254) **4732**
The Medical Letter *see* The Medical Letter on Drugs and Therapeutics (Italian Edition) **6860**
➤ The Medical Letter Handbook of Adverse Drug Interaction (USA ISSN 0897-5418) **6860**
● ➤ The Medical Letter on Drugs and Therapeutics (English Edition) (USA ISSN 0025-732X) **6860**
The Medical Letter on Drugs and Therapeutics (French Edition) (CHE ISSN 0253-8512) **6860**
The Medical Letter on Drugs and Therapeutics (Italian Edition) (ITA ISSN 0393-9391) **6860**
The Medical Letter on Drugs and Therapeutics (Spanish Edition) (USA ISSN 0214-3178) **6860**
● Medical Letter on the C D C & F D A (Centers for Disease Control and Food and Drug Administration) (USA) **4106**
Medical Liability Alert (USA) **4732**
Medical Liability Monitor (USA ISSN 0732-9636) **4514**
Medical Library *see* Igaku Toshokan **5014**
● ➤ Medical Library Association. Journal (USA ISSN 1536-5050) **5669**
Medical Library Association News (Chicago) *see* M L A News (Chicago) **5663**
Medical Literature Indexing Services in Pakistan (PAK) **5749**
Medical Litigation (GBR ISSN 1461-5738) **4732**
● Medical Malpractice (Albany) (USA) **4837**
● Medical Malpractice (Charlottesville) (USA) **4837**
● Medical Malpractice: Checklists and Discoveries (USA) **5670**
Medical Malpractice: Guide to Medical Issues (USA) **4732**
Medical Malpractice Information Center in Japan. Newsletter *see* Iryo Jiko Joho Senta. Senta Nyusu **4833**
● Medical Malpractice Law & Strategy (USA ISSN 0747-8925) **4837**
Medical Malpractice Reports (USA ISSN 1045-960X) **4837**
Medical Malpractice Verdicts, Settlements & Experts (USA ISSN 0888-658X) **4837**
Medical Management Information *see* Iryo Keiei Joho **4102**
● Medical Marketing & Media (USA ISSN 0025-7354) **6860**
Medical Marketing and Media *see* Medical Marketing & Media **6860**
● Medical Masterclass (GBR ISSN 1740-2441) **5670**
● Medical Meetings (USA ISSN 0093-1314) **6281**
● ➤ Medical Microbiology and Immunology (DEU ISSN 0300-8584) **5763**
Medical Mission News (USA) **7806**
Medical Mission Sisters News (USA) **8846**
● ➤ Medical Molecular Morphology (JPN ISSN 1860-1480) **899**
Medical Monitor (GBR) **5670**
● ➤ Medical Mycology (GBR ISSN 1369-3786) **5822**
Medical Mycology *see* Mikologia Lekarska **5823**
Medical News *see* Meditsiiniuudised **5676**
Medical News of the Month *see* Gekkan Iryo Joho **5618**
Medical News Report (USA ISSN 1054-3066) **1834**
● Medical Newswire (USA) **5670**
Medical Nutrition (JPN) **5670**
● Medical Office Billing and Collections Alert (USA ISSN 1536-3244) **4514**
● Medical Office Front Desk Pro (USA ISSN 1947-2064) **1852**
† ● Medical Office H I P A A Alert (Health Insurance Portability and Accountability Act) (USA ISSN 1558-6391) **8973**
Medical Office Manager (USA ISSN 1052-4894) **1779**
† ● Medical Office Nurse (USA ISSN 1553-4383) **8973**
Medical Office Report (USA ISSN 0895-4313) **5670**
Medical Office Staff Management Strategies (USA) **4106**
Medical Officer of Health Public Health Advice *see* Public Health Advice **7537**
● ➤ Medical Oncology (USA ISSN 1357-0560) **6027**
Medical Parasitology and Parasitic Diseases *see* Meditsinskaya Parazitologiya i Parazitarnye Bolezni **5822**
● Medical Patent Business Week (USA ISSN 1552-5597) **6754**
● Medical Patent Law Weekly (USA ISSN 1551-5230) **6754**
● Medical Patent Week (USA ISSN 1552-5619) **6755**
Medical Pharmacy (JPN ISSN 0025-7427) **6860**
● ➤ Medical Physics (USA ISSN 0094-2405) **5670**
Medical Physiology *see* Review of Medical Physiology **927**
▼ ● The Medical Pipeline (USA ISSN 1947-4830) **5670**
● The Medical Post (CAN ISSN 0025-7435) **5670**
Medical Practice (JPN ISSN 0910-1551) **5670**
Medical Practice (SVK ISSN 1336-8109) **5670**
● Medical Practice Communicator (USA ISSN 1074-1321) **5670**
Medical Practices Committee. Recruitment Survey (Year) (GBR) **5670**
● ➤ Medical Principles and Practice (CHE ISSN 1011-7571) **5670**
● ➤ Medical Problems of Performing Artists (USA ISSN 0885-1158) **5670**
● Medical Product Manufacturing News (USA ISSN 0893-6250) **4489**
● Medical Product Outsourcing (USA ISSN 1935-0805) **1148**
Medical Products of Japan (JPN ISSN 1341-6146) **5670**
➤ Medical Progress (Hong Kong Edition) (HKG ISSN 0377-9963) **5670**
➤ Medical Progress (Indonesia Edition) (SGP ISSN 1015-4256) **5670**
➤ Medical Progress (Korea Edition) (SGP) **5670**
➤ Medical Progress (Malaysia Edition) (SGP ISSN 1015-4272) **5671**
➤ Medical Progress (Pakistan Edition) (SGP ISSN 1015-4280) **5671**
➤ Medical Progress (Philippines Edition) (SGP ISSN 1015-4299) **5671**
➤ Medical Progress (Singapore Edition) (SGP ISSN 1015-4302) **5671**
➤ Medical Progress (Taiwan Edition) (SGP ISSN 1015-4310) **5671**
➤ Medical Progress (Thailand Edition) (SGP ISSN 1015-4329) **5671**
Medical Protection Society Casebook *see* M P S Casebook **5663**
Medical Protection Society. Reports and Accounts (Year) (GBR) **5671**
Medical Psychology *see* Meditsinskaya Psikhologiya **7384**
Medical Radiology (USA ISSN 0942-5373) **6203**
● Medical Records Briefing (USA ISSN 1052-4924) **4106**
● ➤ Medical Reference Services Quarterly (USA ISSN 0276-3869) **5031**
Medical Reform (CAN) **5671**
Medical Rehabilitation, Balneology, Physiotherapy *see* Meditsinskaya Reabilitatsiya, Kurortologiya, Fizioterapiya **6112**
● Medical Reporter (USA) **5671**
Medical Research Centres in Ghana: Current Research Projects (GHA) **5671**
Medical Research Council News *see* M R C News **5663**
Medical Research Council News *see* M R C News **5663**
● Medical Research Council of Canada. Grants and Awards Guide/Guide de Subventions et Bourses (CAN ISSN 0839-8283) **5671**
Medical Research Council of Canada. Report of the President (CAN ISSN 0384-2029) **5671**
Medical Research Council of New Zealand, Newsletter *see* H R C News **7520**
Medical Research Council. Performance Report *see* Canadian Institutes of Health Research. Performance Report **7428**
Medical Research Council Strategic Plan *see* M R C Strategic Plan **5663**
● Medical Research Funding Bulletin (USA) **5671**
The Medical Research Institute. Journal (EGY ISSN 1110-0133) **5671**
● Medical Research Law and Policy Report (USA ISSN 1539-1035) **5671**
Medical Review. Acupuncture *see* Meditsinski Pregled. Akupunktura **312**
Medical Review. Allergology and Immunology *see* Meditsinski Pregled. Alergologiia i Klinichna Imunologiia **5764**
Medical Review. Children's Diseases *see* Meditsinski Pregled. Detski Bolesti **6096**
Medical Review. Clinical Oncology *see* Meditsinski Pregled. Onkologiia i Radiologiia **6027**
Medical School Admissions Adviser *see* Get into Medical School **2982**
Medical Science *see* Seitai no Kagaku **704**
Medical Science & Practice *see* Medicinsk Vetenskap & Praxis **5675**
Medical Science Digest (JPN ISSN 1347-4340) **5671**
● ➤ Medical Science Monitor (POL ISSN 1234-1010) **5671**
Medical Science Series (GBR) **5671**
➤ Medical Science Symposia Series (NLD ISSN 0928-9550) **5671**
Medical Sciences and Society *see* Yixue yu Shehui **5733**
Medical Sciences for Land Reclamation *see* Nongken Yixue **5687**
Medical Scientific Update *see* MedSci Update **6216**
The Medical Sentinel *see* Journal of American Physicians and Surgeons **5645**
Medical Service and Facility *see* Iryo to Shisetsu **5642**
(Year) Medical Services Directory (USA) **5671**
Medical Society. Journal (IND ISSN 0972-4958) **5671**
Medical Society of London. Transactions (GBR ISSN 0076-6011) **5671**
Medical Society of Milwaukee County News *see* M S M C e-News **5663**
Medical Society of the County of Queens and the Academy of Medicine of Queens. Bulletin (USA) **5671**
Medical Software Reviews *see* Medical Computing Review **5832**
Medical Solutions (DEU ISSN 1614-5569) **5671**
● Medical Spa Report (USA) **589**
Medical Special (DEU ISSN 1435-9405) **5671**
Medical Specialists Directory. Queensland (NZL ISSN 1176-483X) **5672**
Medical Specialists Referral Directory. Queensland *see* Medical Specialists Directory. Queensland **5672**
● Medical Staff Affairs Monthly (USA ISSN 1947-8879) **4107**
● Medical Staff Briefing (USA ISSN 1076-6022) **4107**
● Medical Staff Leader Connection (USA ISSN 1947-9549) **4107**
● Medical Staff Leader Handbook Online Resource (USA) **4837**
Medical Student International (FRA ISSN 1026-5538) **5672**
Medical Subject Headings (USA ISSN 0565-811X) **5672**
● ➤ Medical Teacher (GBR ISSN 0142-159X) **5672**
Medical Technology/Rinsho Kensagaku Zasshi (JPN ISSN 0389-1887) **5672**
The Medical Technology Acquisition Record (USA ISSN 1541-8073) **1367**
● Medical Technology & Devices Week (USA ISSN 1935-696X) **5672**
● ➤ Medical Technology S A (ZAF ISSN 1011-5528) **5909**
● Medical Technology Stock Letter (USA ISSN 1065-996X) **1638**
Medical Tests & Signs *see* Medical Tests and Signs **4514**
Medical Tests and Signs (USA ISSN 1940-5561) **4514**
Medical Tests Sourcebook (USA) **6203**
● Medical Textiles (GBR ISSN 0266-2078) **5672**
▼ ● Medical Tourism (USA ISSN 1937-8769) **5672**
● Medical Trial Technique Quarterly (USA ISSN 0025-7591) **4837**
Medical Tribune (AUT ISSN 0344-8304) **5672**
● Medical Tribune (CHE ISSN 0170-1894) **5672**
Medical Tribune (CZE ISSN 1214-8911) **5672**
Medical Tribune (DEU ISSN 0543-2936) **5672**
Medical Tribune (HKG) **5672**
Medical Tribune Klinik (DEU ISSN 1612-460X) **5672**
Medical Tribune Kolloquium (CHE ISSN 1420-6862) **5672**
Medical Tribune Kolloquium (DEU) **5672**
▼ Medical Tribune Neurologie - Psychiatrie (DEU) **6159**
▼ Medical Tribune Onkologie - Haematologie (DEU) **6027**
● Medical Tribune Online (CHE) **5672**
Medical Tribune. Von Aerzten fuer Sie (DEU ISSN 1863-8902) **5672**
Medical Ultrasonography (ROM ISSN 1844-4172) **6203**
Medical University, Bialystok. Annals *see* Advances in Medical Sciences **5568**
● Medical Update (BRA ISSN 1678-6300) **5672**
Medical Update *see* V I C Medical Update **6670**
● Medical Update (Chicago) (USA ISSN 0732-0183) **5672**
Medical Verdicts and Law Weekly *see* Medical Verdicts & Law Weekly **4732**
● Medical Verdicts & Law Weekly (USA ISSN 1551-5559) **4732**
➤ Medical Veritas (USA ISSN 1549-1404) **5672**
Medicalife (USA) **5672**
MedicalSpas (USA) **6992**
Medicamento, Historia e Sociedade (PRT ISSN 0872-2331) **6860**
● ➤ Medicamundi (NLD ISSN 0025-7664) **6203**
● Medicare Advantage News (USA) **4514**
Medicare Advisor (USA ISSN 0897-9634) **4514**
Medicare and Medicaid Fraud and Abuse (USA ISSN 1554-5350) **2660**
● Medicare and Medicaid Guide (USA ISSN 0162-1254) **4514**
▼ Medicare and Medicaid Reimbursement Update (USA ISSN 1947-4504) **4732**
● Medicare & Reimbursement Advisor Weekly (USA ISSN 1556-1100) **4107**
Medicare Compliance Alert (USA ISSN 1047-1863) **4514**
Medicare Coverage Issues Manual *see* U.S. Health Care Financing Administration. Medicare Coverage Issues Manual **4526**
† ● Medicare Drug Focus (USA ISSN 1559-8160) **8973**
† ● Medicare Drug Reimbursement Guide (USA ISSN 1558-5530) **8973**
● Medicare Drug Watch (USA ISSN 1552-6011) **4107**
Medicare Explained (USA ISSN 0733-4672) **8055**
Medicare Home Health Agency Manual *see* U.S. Health Care Financing Administration. Medicare Home Health Agency Manual **4526**
Medicare Hospital Manual *see* U.S. Health Care Financing Administration. Medicare Hospital Manual **4526**
Medicare Legislation & Regulation (USA ISSN 1548-9876) **4514**
Medicare Manager (USA ISSN 1068-2465) **4514**
Medicare. Part A. Intermediary Manual. Part 3. Claims Process (USA) **4515**
Medicare. Part B. Carrier Manual. Part 3. Claims Process (USA) **4515**
● Medicare Part D Compliance News (USA ISSN 1937-6642) **4515**
Medicare Patient Management (USA ISSN 1558-9072) **4515**
Medicare Provider Reimbursement Manual *see* U.S. Health Care Financing Administration. Medicare Provider Reimbursement Manual **4526**
Medicare Review (USA ISSN 0885-0925) **4515**
Medicare Skilled Nursing Facility Manual *see* U.S. Health Care Financing Administration. Medicare Skilled Nursing Facility Manual **4526**
▼ Medicare Update for Physician Services (USA ISSN 1947-8933) **4107**
● ➤ Medicas U I S (Universidad Industrial de Santander) (COL ISSN 0121-0319) **5672**
Medications and Mothers' Milk (USA ISSN 1934-2187) **6860**
Medici Oggi (ITA ISSN 1721-0208) **5672**
Medici Oggi - O T O D I Educational *see* Medici Oggi **5672**
● Medicin.dk (DNK ISSN 1902-1453) **6860**
Medicin.dk, Kittelbogen (DNK ISSN 1902-1461) **6860**
● ➤ Medicina (ARG ISSN 0025-7680) **5673**
➤ Medicina (BRA ISSN 0076-6046) **5673**
➤ Medicina (COL ISSN 0120-5498) **5673**
Medicina (ECU ISSN 1390-0218) **5673**
● Medicina (HRV ISSN 0025-7729) **5673**
Medicina (JPN ISSN 0025-7699) **5947**
● ➤ Medicina (LTU ISSN 1010-660X) **5672**
† ● Medicina Aerospacial y Ambiental (ESP ISSN 1134-9913) **8973**
● Medicina Antropologica (ARG ISSN 1666-3659) **5673**
● La Medicina Biologica (ITA ISSN 1125-6834) **5673**
● ➤ Medicina Clinica (ESP ISSN 0025-7753) **5673**
Medicina Cutanea *see* Medicina Cutanea Ibero-Latino-Americana **5880**

Title

➤ Mediterranean Archaeology (AUS ISSN 1030-8482) **405**
• Mediterranean Archaeology and Archaeometry (GRC ISSN 1108-961X) **405**
Mediterranean Archaeology. Supplement *see* Mediterranean Archaeology **405**
Mediterranean Conference on Control and Automation. Proceedings (USA ISSN 1934-1776) **2463**
• ➤ Mediterranean Council for Burns and Fire Disasters. Annals (ITA ISSN 1592-9558) **6067**
• Mediterranean Electrotechnical Conference (USA) **3325**
• ➤ Mediterranean Historical Review (GBR ISSN 0951-8967) **4323**
➤ The Mediterranean Journal of Computers & Networks (GBR ISSN 1744-2397) **2431**
• ➤ Mediterranean Journal of Educational Studies (MLT ISSN 1024-5375) **2886**
➤ The Mediterranean Journal of Electronics & Communications (GBR ISSN 1744-2400) **3108**
➤ Mediterranean Journal of Human Rights (MLT ISSN 1027-4375) **7212**
• ➤ Mediterranean Journal of Mathematics (CHE ISSN 1660-5446) **5517**
The Mediterranean Journal of Measurement & Control (GBR ISSN 1743-9310) **3210**
▼ • ➤ Mediterranean Journal of Nutrition and Metabolism (ITA ISSN 1973-798X) **6663**
➤ Mediterranean Journal of Pacing and Electrophysiology (ITA ISSN 1128-4293) **5795**
Mediterranean Language and Culture Monograph Series (DEU ISSN 0179-1621) **555**
Mediterranean Language Review (DEU ISSN 0724-7567) **555**
• Mediterranean Marine Science (GRC ISSN 1108-393X) **2812**
• ➤ Mediterranean Politics (GBR ISSN 1362-9395) **7252**
• ➤ Mediterranean Quarterly (USA ISSN 1047-4552) **7252**
Mediterranean Shipping Directory (GBR ISSN 0957-5855) **8653**
• ➤ Mediterranean Studies (GBR ISSN 1074-164X) **4323**
Mediterraneans Mediterraneennes (FRA) **5227**
Mediterranee (Aix-en-Provence) (FRA ISSN 0025-8296) **4019**
Mediterranee (Paris, 1994) (FRA ISSN 1263-8978) **3841**
Mediterranees (FRA ISSN 1263-8935) **8120**
• Mediterraneo Antico (ITA ISSN 1127-6061) **4244**
▼ Meditsiiniuudised/Medical News (EST) **5676**
Meditsina (KAZ) **7531**
Meditsina Kriticheskikh Sostoyanii (RUS) **5676**
➤ Meditsina Neotlozhnykh Sostoyanii (UKR) **6067**
➤ Meditsina Truda i Promyshlennaya Ekologiya (RUS ISSN 1026-9428) **6681**
Meditsinska Praksa (SRB ISSN 0350-2945) **5676**
Meditsinskaya Gazeta (RUS ISSN 0025-8318) **5676**
Meditsinskaya Nauka Armenii *see* Hayastani Bzhshkagitutyun **5905**
Meditsinskaya Parazitologiya i Parazitarnye Bolezni/Medical Parasitology and Parasitic Diseases (RUS ISSN 0025-8326) **5822**
Meditsinskaya Pomoshch/Medical Care (RUS ISSN 0869-7760) **5969**
➤ Meditsinskaya Psikhologiya/Medical Psychology (UKR) **7384**
Meditsinskaya Radiologiya i Radiatsionnaya Bezopasnost' (RUS ISSN 1024-6177) **6203**
Meditsinskaya Reabilitatsiya, Kurortologiya, Fizioterapiya/Medical Rehabilitation, Balneology, Physiotherapy (UKR) **6112**
Meditsinskaya Sestra (RUS) **5969**
Meditsinskaya Tekhnika/Medical Engineering (RUS ISSN 0025-8075) **5676**
Meditsinski Daidzhest/Medical Digest (BGR) **5676**
➤ Meditsinski Pregled (BGR ISSN 1312-2193) **5749**
Meditsinski Pregled. Akupunktura/Medical Review. Acupuncture (BGR ISSN 1311-2759) **312**
➤ Meditsinski Pregled. Akusherstvo i Ginekologiia (BGR ISSN 0204-0956) **5998**
Meditsinski Pregled. Alergologiia i Klinichna Imunologiia/Medical Review. Allergology and Immunology (BGR ISSN 0204-9724) **5764**
➤ Meditsinski Pregled. Detski Bolesti/Medical Review. Children's Diseases (BGR ISSN 0324-1122) **6096**
➤ Meditsinski Pregled. Endokrinni Zaboliavaniia (BGR ISSN 0324-1475) **5897**
➤ Meditsinski Pregled. Gastroenterologiia (BGR ISSN 1311-5030) **5929**
Meditsinski Pregled. Infektsiozni Zaboliavaniia (BGR ISSN 0324-1432) **5822**
➤ Meditsinski Pregled. Khirurgichni Zaboliavaniia (BGR ISSN 0204-5389) **6252**
➤ Meditsinski Pregled. Klinichna Laboratoriia (BGR ISSN 0204-9716) **738**
Meditsinski Pregled. Klinichna Onkologiia *see* Meditsinski Pregled. Onkologiia i Radiologiia **6027**
Meditsinski Pregled. Klinika i Predklinika *see* Meditsinski Pregled **5749**
➤ Meditsinski Pregled. Meditsinski Menidzhment i Zdravna Politika (BGR ISSN 1312-0336) **7548**
➤ Meditsinski Pregled. Nevrologiia i Psikhiatriia (BGR ISSN 1311-6584) **6159**
➤ Meditsinski Pregled. Onkologiia i Radiologiia/Medical Review. Clinical Oncology (BGR ISSN 1312-1111) **6027**
➤ Meditsinski Pregled. Prakticheska Meditsina (BGR ISSN 1311-6770) **7531**
➤ Meditsinski Pregled. Sardechno-Sadovi Zaboliavaniia (BGR ISSN 0204-6865) **5795**
Meditsinski Pregled. Savremenna Stomatologia (BGR ISSN 1310-8999) **5855**
➤ Meditsinski Pregled. Sestrinsko Delo (BGR ISSN 1310-7496) **5969**
Meditsinskie Nauki (RUS) **5676**
Meditsinskie Novosti (BLR) **5676**
Meditsinskii Biznes (RUS) **4489**
Meditsinskii Obzor *see* Synopsis Medicinalis **5719**
Meditsinskii Vestnik (RUS) **5676**
Meditsinskii Zhurnal Uzbekistana/Medical Journal of Uzbekistan/O'zbekiston Tibbiyot Jurnali (UZB ISSN 0025-830X) **5676**
• The Medium (CAN ISSN 0025-8377) **5032**
Medium (CZE ISSN 1212-1738) **6646**
• Medium (FRA ISSN 1771-3757) **7985**
The Medium (New Brunswick) (USA) **2291**
• ➤ Medium Aevum (GBR ISSN 0025-8385) **5332**
Medium Aevum Quotidianum (AUT ISSN 1029-0737) **4244**
Medium and Small Scale River in Hokkaido *see* Hokkaido no Chusho Kasen **8824**
• Medium/Small Hydro Power & Equipment (CHN ISSN 1007-4740) **3325**
Medium - Term Programme (Years) (NLD) **5032**
MediumMagazin (AUT ISSN 0178-8558) **4580**
• Mediuutiset (FIN ISSN 1456-1484) **4107**
Medizin 2000 plus (DEU ISSN 1435-8581) **5676**
Medizin - Bibliothek - Information *see* G M S Medizin - Bibliothek - Information **5617**
Medizin Dental Magazin (DEU ISSN 0940-2500) **5855**
Medizin fuer die Frau *see* Leading Opinions Medizin fuer die Frau **8846**
Medizin fuer Manager (DEU ISSN 1861-3888) **1870**
➤ Medizin, Gesellschaft und Geschichte (DEU ISSN 0939-351X) **5676**
Medizin, Gesellschaft und Geschichte. Beihefte (DEU ISSN 0941-5033) **5676**
† Medizin Heute (DEU ISSN 0179-0404) **8973**
Medizin Historisches Journal *see* Medizinhistorisches Journal **5677**
Medizin in Entwicklungslaendern (DEU ISSN 0721-3247) **5676**
Medizin ohne Nebenwirkungen (DEU ISSN 0939-6292) **6861**
• Medizin Online (DEU ISSN 1610-9287) **5676**
Medizin Populaer (AUT) **5676**
Medizin, Technik und Gesellschaft/Medicine, Technology and Society (DEU ISSN 0943-5131) **5676**
Medizin und Ethik (AUT ISSN 0948-065X) **5676**
Medizin und Philosophie (DEU) **6934**
Medizin und Technik (DEU ISSN 1863-7604) **5676**
Medizin Zweitausend plus *see* Medizin 2000 plus **5676**
• MediZine (USA) **5676**
• MediZine.com (USA) **5676**
Medizine's Healthy Living (USA) **5676**
Medizingeschichte im Kontext (DEU) **5677**
• ➤ Medizinhistorisches Journal (DEU ISSN 0025-8431) **5677**
Medizini (DEU) **2201**
† Medizinisch Juristische Nachrichten (DEU) **8973**
Medizinisch-Orthopaedische Technik (DEU ISSN 0340-5508) **6067**
Medizinisch-Pharmakologisches Kompendium (DEU ISSN 0934-9170) **6861**
Medizinisch Technische Assistenten Dialog *see* M T A Dialog **5663**
Medizinische Ausbildung *see* G M S Zeitschrift fuer Medizinische Ausbildung **5617**
Medizinische Ethik im 21. Jahrhundert (DEU) **5677**
Die Medizinische Fachangestellte (DEU ISSN 1864-1938) **5969**
Medizinische Forschung (CHE ISSN 0933-9051) **5677**
• ➤ Medizinische Genetik (DEU ISSN 0936-5931) **875**
Medizinische Hochschule Hannover Info *see* M H H - Info **2290**
• ➤ Medizinische Klinik (DEU ISSN 0723-5003) **5677**
Medizinische Klinik. Supplement (DEU ISSN 0931-2595) **5677**
Medizinische Kongresse (DEU ISSN 0175-3053) **6281**
Medizinische Monatsschrift fuer Pharmazeuten (DEU ISSN 0342-9601) **5677**
Der Medizinische Sachverstaendige (DEU ISSN 0025-8490) **5677**
Medizinische Technik *see* Informationsdienst F I Z Technik. Medizinische Technik **5747**
Medizinische Universitat Luebeck. Focus *see* Focus M U L **5614**
➤ Die Medizinische Welt (DEU ISSN 0025-8512) **5677**
† Medizinischer Literatur Anzeiger (DEU) **8973**
Medizinprodukte Journal (DEU ISSN 0944-6885) **5677**
MedizinProdukte Recht (DEU ISSN 1618-9027) **5909**
• ➤ Medizinrecht (DEU ISSN 0723-8886) **5915**
Medizinrecht in Forschung und Praxis (DEU ISSN 1861-1508) **5916**
Medizinsoziologie (DEU) **7985**
Medjimurje (HRV ISSN 0025-8229) **5227**
Medjunarodna Politika (SRB ISSN 0543-3657) **7252**
• Medjunarodni Problemi/International Problems (SRB ISSN 0025-8555) **7252**
Medkalender (CHE ISSN 1422-4720) **5677**
Medlemsnytt *see* Skogsliv **3702**
• MEDLINE (USA) **5749**
Medline C D *see* MEDLINE **5749**
• Medmaensklighet (SWE ISSN 1653-932X) **1601**
Medmenneske *see* Kirkens Noedhjelp Magasinet **8052**
MedNet (NLD ISSN 1568-7716) **5677**
▼ MedNet Jaarboek (NLD ISSN 1876-2697) **5677**
MedR *see* Medizinrecht **5915**
Medscape Gastroenterology (USA ISSN 1532-0413) **5929**
• Medscape Hematology-Oncology (USA ISSN 1535-6701) **5940**
Medscape HIV/AIDS (USA ISSN 1532-0448) **5822**
• Medscape Journal of Medicine (USA ISSN 1934-1997) **5677**
• ➤ Medscape Mental Health (USA ISSN 1532-043X) **6159**
• ➤ Medscape Orthopedics & Sports Medicine (USA ISSN 1532-0421) **6067**
• ➤ Medscape Respiratory Care (USA) **6216**
• ➤ Medscape Women's Health (USA ISSN 1521-2076) **8847**
• MedSci Update (USA) **6216**
Medspeak (NZL ISSN 1177-0570) **5677**
MEDSUBHYP International (FRA ISSN 1244-7730) **5677**
• ➤ MedSurg Nursing (USA ISSN 1092-0811) **6252**
• Medtech Insight (USA) **5677**
• Meducator (CAN ISSN 0972-267X) **5677**
▼ Medugorje Tribune (IRL ISSN 1649-8674) **4244**
• ➤ MedULA (VEN ISSN 0798-3166) **5677**
• MedUNAB (Medicina Universidad Autonoma de Bucaramanga) (COL ISSN 0123-7047) **5677**
Medusa (SWE ISSN 0349-456X) **405**
Medusa-Medias (DEU ISSN 1437-3033) **5332**
Medved' (RUS) **6295**
MedVep. Revista Cientifica de Medicina Veterinaria. Pequenos Animais e Animais de Estimacao (BRA ISSN 1678-1430) **8803**
Medvidek Pu (CZE ISSN 1212-1118) **2201**
• Medvind (SWE ISSN 1652-9464) **2886**
Medvjedic Winnie Pooh (HRV ISSN 1331-7717) **2201**
Medway K M Extra (GBR) **3868**
➤ Medychna Khimiya/Medical Chemistry (UKR ISSN 1681-2557) **2072**
Medycyna Doswiadczalna i Mikrobiologia (POL ISSN 0025-8601) **891**
Medycyna Dydaktyka Wychowanie (POL ISSN 0137-6543) **5678**
Medycyna Intensywna i Ratunkowa/Intensive Care & Emergency Medicine (POL ISSN 1506-4077) **6067**
Medycyna Metaboliczna (POL ISSN 1428-1430) **5897**
➤ Medycyna Nowozytna/Modern Medicine (POL ISSN 1231-1960) **5678**
Medycyna Ogolna/Rural Medicine (POL) **5678**
• ➤ Medycyna Paliatywna w Praktyce/Advances in Palliative Medicine (POL ISSN 1898-0678) **5678**
• ➤ Medycyna Pracy (POL ISSN 0465-5893) **5678**
Medycyna Praktyczna (POL ISSN 0867-499X) **5678**
Medycyna Praktyczna. Chirurgia (POL ISSN 1428-2712) **6252**
Medycyna Praktyczna. Ginekologia i Poloznictwo (POL) **5998**
Medycyna Praktyczna. Pediatria (POL) **6096**
Medycyna Praktyczna. Ultrasonografia (POL ISSN 1429-4966) **6203**
• Medycyna Rodzinna (POL ISSN 1505-3768) **5678**
Medycyna Sportowa (POL ISSN 1232-406X) **6231**
➤ Medycyna Weterynaryjna (POL ISSN 0025-8628) **8803**
Medycyna Wiejska *see* Medycyna Ogolna **5678**
Medycyna Wieku Rozwojowego (POL ISSN 1428-345X) **6096**
Medyk/Physician (POL ISSN 0867-3055) **5678**
• Medytsyna Svitu (UKR) **5678**
➤ Medziagotyra/Materials Science (LTU ISSN 1392-1320) **3354**
Medzinarodne Otazky *see* International Issues & Slovak Foreign Policy Affairs **7243**
Mee (NLD ISSN 1875-0516) **4067**
MEEdelen *see* Mee **4067**
MEEdelen (Middelburg) (NLD ISSN 1573-4145) **8055**
Meedoen! (NLD ISSN 1874-6985) **4067**
MEEDplus *see* M E E D Plus **1497**
Meeleven (NLD ISSN 1384-0606) **2697**
Meena (USA ISSN 1556-2786) **5332**
Meer & Yachten (DEU ISSN 1158-0437) **8278**
Meer und Museum (DEU ISSN 0863-1131) **2812**
† Meereskundliche Beobachtungen und Ergebnisse (DEU ISSN 0433-7670) **8973**
Meereswissenschaftliche Berichte (DEU ISSN 0939-396X) **2812**
Meerjarenafspraken Energie Efficiency (NLD ISSN 1874-7892) **3141**
Meerjarenprogramma Infrastructuur, Ruimte en Transport Projectenboek *see* M I R T Projectenboek **7452**
Meerjarenprogramma Verkeer, Vervoer en Infrastructuur (NLD ISSN 1871-5796) **8504**
Meertens Ethnology Cahiers (NLD ISSN 1872-0986) **347**
Meerut Samachar (IND) **3885**
Meerut University Sanskrit Research Journal (IND) **7985**
Meespierson International Commodities Handbook (Year) (GBR) **1638**
▼ Meet the Mets (USA ISSN 1942-0560) **8238**
Meet the Press (USA ISSN 0543-3754) **4580**
Meeting and Incentive Travel (GBR ISSN 0953-2803) **6281**
Meeting Ground (USA) **6635**
• Meeting News (USA ISSN 0145-630X) **6281**
Meeting of Coconut Products Exporters (Year). Proceedings (IDN) **242**
Meeting on Case of Nuclear Medicine. Proceedings *see* Kaku Igaku Shorei Kentokai Shoreishu **6202**
Meeting on Cryogenics and Superconductivity. Prceedings *see* Teion Kogaku Chodendo Gakkai Koen Gaiyoshu **7056**
The Meeting Professional *see* One+ **6282**
Meeting Professional European Digest *see* One+ Europe, Middle East, and Africa **6282**
Meeting Skill Needs *see* Quarterly Regional Labour Market Update **1704**
Meeting Special Education Needs (GBR ISSN 1367-3947) **3044**
• Meetings and Conventions (USA ISSN 0025-8652) **6281**
Meetings and Conventions Asia Pacific (SGP) **6281**
Meetings and Conventions Gavel (USA) **6281**
Meetings & Expositions (USA) **1779**
• Meetings & Incentive Travel (CAN ISSN 0225-8285) **6281**
Meetings East (USA) **8733**
Meetings in the West *see* Meetings West **8733**
Meetings, Incentives and Conventions *see* M I C **8732**
Meetings Incentives Conferences Events *see* M I C E **6281**
Meetings Market Trends Survey *see* Meetings MidAmerica **8733**
Meetings Market Trends Survey *see* Meetings East **8733**
Meetings MidAmerica (USA) **8733**
Meetings Monthly, News Bulletin (CAN ISSN 0841-9663) **6281**
▼ • ➤ Meetings on Acoustics. Proceedings (USA ISSN 1939-800X) **7088**
• Meetings on Atomic Energy (AUT ISSN 0047-6641) **6281**
Meetings South (USA) **8733**
Meetings West (USA ISSN 1089-5930) **8733**
Meetnet Amfibieen Mededelingen (NLD ISSN 1875-2853) **955**
Meetnet Reptielen (NLD ISSN 1871-8221) **955**
Meetnet Weidevogels Zuid-Holland (NLD ISSN 1871-6555) **910**
• Mega (PHL ISSN 0117-5823) **2248**
Mega Bikes (GBR ISSN 1469-4581) **4339**
Mega Boobs (GBR ISSN 1354-8905) **6295**
Mega Dream Homes International (USA ISSN 1931-8332) **7599**
Mega Hiro (DEU) **2201**
Mega Hiro (ESP ISSN 1886-2934) **2201**
Mega Hiro Card Master *see* Card Master **2181**
Mega Hiro Raetsel Master (DEU) **2202**
Megadim (ISR ISSN 0334-8814) **7662**
➤ Megadrilogica (CAN ISSN 0380-9633) **955**
• El Megafono (ARG) **5332**
MegaLife (ZAF) **8187**
Megalink (CHE ISSN 1662-9558) **2352**
Megalink Precision *see* Megalink **2352**
Megalithic Magazine (GBR) **405**
Megalon (BRA) **5444**
† • ➤ Megamot (ISR ISSN 0025-8679) **8973**
Meganeura (FRA ISSN 1561-0799) **6726**
• Megaphon (AUT) **3797**
† Megaphon (DEU) **8973**
Megaphone (Canton) (USA ISSN 0025-8687) **2291**
Megaphone (Georgetown) (USA ISSN 0025-8709) **2291**
Megapolis Ekspress (RUS) **3549**
† Megasex (CZE ISSN 1213-7642) **8973**
• MegaStar (GBR) **5227**
• MegaTech (AUT) **1898**
Megatech (GBR ISSN 0964-5764) **2478**
Megator (SWE) **5332**
MegaTuning (ITA) **8187**
Megavatios (ARG ISSN 0325-352X) **3325**
• Megawatt (DNK ISSN 1902-6765) **3178**
• Megawatt Daily (USA ISSN 1088-4319) **3160**
Megawatt Markets (USA ISSN 1087-2140) **3160**
• Megawatt Week (USA ISSN 1091-4250) **3160**
Megazin (DEU) **3852**
Meghalaya Guardian (IND) **3885**
Meghalaya Industrial Development Corporation. Annual Report (IND ISSN 0376-5423) **1148**
Megiddo Message (USA ISSN 0194-7826) **7662**
Meglepetes (HUN ISSN 1218-6848) **8874**
† Meglio (ITA ISSN 0025-8717) **8973**
† Il Meglio del Cane (ITA ISSN 1825-3008) **8973**
† Il Meglio di Fantasia in Cucina (ITA ISSN 1825-3016) **8973**
Il Meglio di Harmony (ITA ISSN 1122-5432) **5411**
Il Meglio di Sale e Pepe (ITA ISSN 1122-9144) **4364**
▼ • Il Meglio E Possibile (ITA) **449**
Megliopossibile *see* Il Meglio E Possibile **449**
Mehanizacija Sumarstva *see* Nova Mehanizacija Sumarstva **3699**
Mehanizacija Sumarstva *see* Croatian Journal of Forest Engineering **3687**
Mehfil (CAN ISSN 1483-4367) **3549**
Mehilainen (FIN ISSN 0783-3377) **136**

Title

† Mehkarim Bageografiya Shel Eretz Yisrael/Studies in the Geography of Israel (ISR ISSN 0081-8585) **8973**
Mehk're Mishpat *see* Mehq're Mishpat **4732**
Mehq're Mishpat/Bar-Ilan Law Studies (ISR ISSN 0334-0716) **4732**
Mehq're Yerushalayim B'Mahshevet Yisra'el/Jerusalem Studies in Jewish Thought (ISR ISSN 0333-7081) **7726**
The Mehram (IND) **3885**
Mehran University Research Journal of Engineering and Technology (PAK ISSN 0254-7821) **3210**
Mehrsprachigkeit (DEU ISSN 1433-0792) **5150**
Mehrsprachigkeit in Schule und Unterricht (DEU) **5150**
• Mei Huagong/Coal Chemical Industry (CHN ISSN 1005-9598) **3250**
Mei Obstetrics and Gynecology. Annual Bulletin *see* Mie-ken Sanfujinka Iho **5998**
Mei yu Shidai (Shishang Ban)/Beauty & Times (Fashion Edition) (CHN) **6934**
Mei yu Shidai (Xueshu Ban)/Beauty & Times (Academics Edition) (CHN) **7882**
• Mei Zhong Fa Lu Ping Lun/U S - China Law Review (USA ISSN 1548-6605) **4732**
• Mei Zhong Gong Gong Guan Li/Journal of U S-China Public Administration (USA ISSN 1548-6591) **7452**
Mei Zhong Guo ji Chuang Shang za Zhi/U.S. Chinese International Journal of Traumatology (USA ISSN 1538-814X) **6067**
Meidaat *see* Meda'at **5031**
➤ Meidai Uchusan Kenkyushitsu Kiji/Nagoya University. Solar-Terrestrial Environment Laboratory. Cosmic Ray Section. Proceedings (JPN ISSN 0910-0717) **7026**
Meidan Mokki (FIN ISSN 1456-6257) **1023**
Meidan Perhe (FIN ISSN 1459-9929) **2161**
Meidan Sauna/Finnish Sauna (FIN ISSN 1459-5311) **6992**
Meidan Talo (FIN ISSN 1455-2825) **1023**
Meiden Magazine (NLD ISSN 1872-129X) **2202**
MeidenMagazine *see* Meiden Magazine **2202**
Meie Elu/Our Life (CAN ISSN 0047-665X) **3549**
Meie Meel (EST) **3836**
Meier (DEU) **5076**
Meier - Uni Extra (DEU) **5076**
Meieriposten (NOR ISSN 0025-8776) **267**
• ➤ Meiguo Yanjiu/American Studies Quarterly (CHN ISSN 1002-8986) **7985**
Meiguo Yanjiu *see* Oumei Yanjiu **4307**
† • Meiguo Yixuehui Yanke Zazhi (Zhongwen Ban)/Archives of Ophthalmology (Chinese Edition) (CHN ISSN 1000-0348) **8973**
Meiguo Yixuehui Zazhi (Chinese Edition)/J A M A: The Journal of the American Medical Association (Chinese Edition) (CHN ISSN 1000-842X) **5678**
Meiguo Zhonghua Yixue Jinzhan yu Linchuang Zazhi/U.S. Chinese Journal of Medical Progress and Clinical Medicine (USA ISSN 1539-0624) **5678**
Meihao Jiaju *see* Home Journal **4541**
Meijerbergs Arkiv for Svensk Ordforskning (SWE ISSN 0348-7741) **5150**
Meijers-reeks *see* Meijersreeks **4732**
Meijersreeks (NLD ISSN 1875-3345) **4732**
Meiji Daigaku Kagaku Gijutsu Kenkyujo Hokoku. Sogo Kenkyu/Meiji University. Institute of Science and Technology. Report. Special Project (JPN ISSN 0285-8258) **8431**
Meiji Daigaku Kagaku Gijutsu Kenkyujo Kiyo/Meiji University. Institute of Science and Technology. Memoirs (JPN ISSN 0386-4944) **8431**
Meiji Daigaku Kagaku Gijutsu Kenkyujo Nenpo/Meiji University. Institute of Science and Technology. Annual Report (JPN ISSN 0543-3916) **8432**
Meiji Daigaku Riko Gakubu Kenkyu Hokoku/Meiji University. School of Science and Technology. Research Reports (JPN ISSN 0916-4944) **7882**
Meiji Pharmaceutical University. Bulletin *see* Meiji Yakka Daigaku Kenkyu Kiyo **6861**
➤ Meiji Shinkyu Igaku/Meiji University of Oriental Medicine. Bulletin (JPN ISSN 0912-2419) **313**
Meiji University. Institute of Science and Technology. Annual Report *see* Meiji Daigaku Kagaku Gijutsu Kenkyujo Nenpo **8432**
Meiji University. Institute of Science and Technology. Memoirs *see* Meiji Daigaku Kagaku Gijutsu Kenkyujo Kiyo **8431**
Meiji University. Institute of Science and Technology. Report. Special Project *see* Meiji Daigaku Kagaku Gijutsu Kenkyujo Hokoku. Sogo Kenkyu **8431**
Meiji University of Oriental Medicine. Bulletin *see* Meiji Shinkyu Igaku **313**
Meiji University. School of Science and Technology. Research Reports *see* Meiji Daigaku Riko Gakubu Kenkyu Hokoku **7882**
Meiji Yakka Daigaku Kenkyu Kiyo/Meiji Pharmaceutical University. Bulletin (JPN ISSN 0543-3975) **6861**
Meijo Daigaku Nogakubu Gakujutsu Hokoku/Meijo University. Faculty of Agriculture. Scientific Reports (JPN ISSN 0910-3376) **136**
➤ Meijo Daigaku Rikogakubu Kenkyu Hokoku/Meijo University. Faculty of Science and Technology. Research Reports (JPN ISSN 0386-4952) **8432**
Meijo University. Faculty of Agriculture. Scientific Reports *see* Meijo Daigaku Nogakubu Gakujutsu Hokoku **136**
Meijo University. Faculty of Science and Technology. Research Reports *see* Meijo Daigaku Rikogakubu Kenkyu Hokoku **8432**
➤ Meikai Daigaku Shigaku Zasshi/Meikai University Dental Journal/Meikai University School of Dentistry. Journal (JPN ISSN 0916-0701) **5855**
Meikai Nihongo (JPN ISSN 1341-2582) **5150**
Meikai University Dental Journal *see* Meikai Daigaku Shigaku Zasshi **5855**
Meikai University School of Dentistry. Journal *see* Meikai Daigaku Shigaku Zasshi **5855**
Meiken Kisho Geppo/Mie Prefecture. Monthly Report of Meteorology (JPN) **6390**
Meikuang Huanjing Baohu/Coal Mine Environmental Protection (CHN ISSN 1006-8759) **3452**
Meili Jiaren/Marie Claire (TWN ISSN 1023-4551) **8874**
Mein Eigenheim (DEU ISSN 0025-8792) **1367**
Mein Erlebnis (DEU ISSN 0179-8596) **8874**
Mein Freund, der Rassehund (DEU ISSN 1860-7071) **6811**
Mein Geheimnis (DEU ISSN 1430-9351) **8874**
Mein Geld (DEU ISSN 0947-4102) **1638**
† Mein Gestaendnis (DEU) **8973**
Mein Glueck (DEU) **8874**
Mein Holzhaus (DEU) **1023**
Mein Horoskop (DEU) **566**
Mein Kind (DEU) **2161**
† Mein Kleines Pony (DEU) **8974**
Mein Kreativ-Atelier (DEU) **537**
Mein Leben (DEU ISSN 1619-6899) **8874**
Mein Neues Bad *see* Bad Pool Sauna **4554**
Mein Paradies (DEU) **3743**
Mein Paradies Extra (DEU) **3743**
Mein Pferd (DEU ISSN 1861-4205) **8294**
Mein Schicksal (DEU ISSN 1437-7217) **8874**
• Mein Schoener Garten (DEU ISSN 0178-1308) **3743**
Mein Schoener Garten Classic (DEU) **3743**
Mein Schoener Garten Spezial (DEU) **3743**
Mein Schoenes zu Hause (DEU) **4546**
† Mein Tier und Ich (DEU) **8974**
Meine Apotheke (DEU) **6861**
† Meine Bunte Woche (DEU) **8974**
• Meine Familie und Ich (DEU ISSN 0933-081X) **3852**
Meine Familie und Ich Kreativ Kueche *see* Lust auf Genuss **4363**
• Meine Familie und Ich Online (DEU) **3852**
Meine Gefuehle (DEU) **5411**
Meine Geschichte (DEU ISSN 0935-8005) **8874**
Meine Gesundheit (DEU) **8733**
Meine Katze (DEU) **6811**
Meine Kueche (DEU) **4560**
Meine Lebensluege (DEU) **5411**
† Meine Leidenschaft (DEU) **8974**
Meine Liebesbeichte (DEU) **5411**
Meine Melodie (DEU) **6587**
Meine Schicksals-Story (DEU) **8874**
Meine Schuld (DEU) **5411**
▼ Meine Sprechstunde (DEU) **5411**
Meine Sternstunden *see* Das Grosse Horoskop - Meine Sternstunden **566**
† Meine Versuchung (DEU) **8974**
Meine Wahrheit (DEU ISSN 1616-9115) **5411**
Meine Welt (DEU) **7662**
Meininger Magazin (DEU ISSN 0937-3918) **607**
Meininger Tageblatt (DEU) **3852**
Meio Ambiente (BRA ISSN 0103-913X) **3452**
➤ Meiofauna Marina (DEU ISSN 1611-7557) **689**
• Meios (PRT) **30**
• Meiqi yu Reli/Gas and Heat (CHN ISSN 1000-4416) **3325**
Meira (BGD) **5427**
• Meiri Xinbao (CHN) **3826**
Meirong Huazhuang Zaoxing (CHN ISSN 1671-1378) **8874**
Meisei Daigaku Kenkyu Kiyo. Rikogakubu/Meisei University. Research Bulletin. Physical Sciences and Engineering (JPN ISSN 0388-130X) **3210**
Meisei University. Research Bulletin. Physical Sciences and Engineering *see* Meisei Daigaku Kenkyu Kiyo. Rikogakubu **3210**
Meishi Daobao/Gourmand Herald (CHN) **4393**
• Meishi yu Meijiu/Food & Wine (CHN ISSN 1673-6745) **3656**
• Meishu/Art (CHN ISSN 1003-1774) **505**
Meishu Bao/China Art Weekly (CHN) **505**
Meishu Daguan/Art Panorama (CHN) **505**
• Meishu Guancha/Art Observation (CHN ISSN 1006-8899) **505**
Meishu Jie/Air Circle (CHN) **505**
† Meishu Qimeng (CHN ISSN 1007-4805) **8974**
Meishu Shilun *see* Meishu Guancha **505**
• Meishu Xiangdao/A Guide to Art (CHN ISSN 1003-0441) **505**
• Meishu Xuebao/Art Journal (CHN ISSN 1004-1060) **505**
• Meishu Yanjiu/Art Research (CHN ISSN 0461-6855) **505**
• Meishu zhi You/Friend of Fine Arts (CHN ISSN 1003-045X) **505**
Meissner Tageblatt (DEU ISSN 0940-0516) **3853**
Meister-Brief (DEU) **1697**
Der Meisterbrief fuer den Betriebsleiter (DEU ISSN 0941-8342) **1779**
Meistermagazin (DEU) **4393**
Meistertipp (DEU) **1023**
Meisterwerke der Kunst (DEU ISSN 0171-3973) **505**
Meistriristik (EST) **8187**
• Meitan Gongcheng/Coal Engineering (CHN ISSN 1671-0959) **6469**
• Meitan Jingji Yanjiu/Coal Economics Study (CHN ISSN 1002-9605) **1148**
• Meitan Jishu/Coal Technology (CHN ISSN 1008-8725) **3142**
• Meitan Kexue Jishu/Coal Science and Technology (CHN ISSN 0253-2336) **3250**
• Meitan Qiye Guanli/Coal Industry Management (CHN ISSN 1002-8315) **1779**
Meitan Xinxi (CHN) **6470**
• Meitan Xuebao/China Coal Society. Journal (CHN ISSN 0253-9993) **6470**
• Meitan Zhuanhua/Coal Conversion (CHN ISSN 1004-4248) **6470**
• Meitian Dizhi yu Kantan/Coal Geology and Prospecting (CHN ISSN 1001-1986) **2754**
Meiwen (Chengren Ban) (CHN) **5332**
• Meiwen (Shaonian Ban) (CHN ISSN 1004-8855) **5332**
Meixue/Aesthetics (CHN ISSN 1001-2567) **6934**
Meiyu Tiandi/The World of English (TWN) **5150**
• ➤ Meiyuan/Lu Xun Academy of Fine Art. Journal (CHN ISSN 1003-5605) **505**
Meizhong Jingji Pinglun *see* China - USA Business Review **1555**
• Meizhou Wenzhai (CHN) **3826**
• Mejeri (DNK ISSN 1604-1259) **267**
• Mejeristen (DNK ISSN 0107-7635) **4598**
Mejong (Han'gugpan) *see* Maison Marie Claire **4546**
Mejong Ma'li Kkeulle'leu Han'gugpan *see* Maison Marie Claire **4546**
• Mejoramiento de la Calidad de la Educacion. Documento de Trabajo (PER ISSN 1682-4962) **2886**
Mejoramiento de la Calidad y Equidad en la Educacion Superior Boletin *see* M E C E S U P. Boletin **2884**
Los Mejores Automoviles del Mundo (ARG ISSN 0329-3343) **8590**
Los Mejores Automoviles del Mundo (ESP) **8590**
Los Mejores Automoviles del Mundo (MEX) **8590**
• Mejores Datos (CHL) **1148**
Mekanisten (SWE ISSN 0284-9763) **3210**
• Mekeel's and Stamps Magazine (USA ISSN 1095-0443) **6897**
Mekeel's Stamp News *see* Mekeel's and Stamps Magazine **6897**
Mekevot *see* Sources of Contemporary Jewish Thought **8989**
➤ Mekhanika Kompozitnykh Materialov (LVA ISSN 0203-1272) **7061**
Mekhanika Kompozitsionnykh Materialov i Konstruktsii (RUS ISSN 1029-6670) **7061**
Mekhanika na Mashinite/Mechanics of Machines (BGR ISSN 0861-9727) **3390**
➤ Mekhanika Tverdogo Tela/Solid State Mechanics (UKR ISSN 0321-1975) **7061**
Mekhanika Tverdogo Tela *see* Mechanics of Solids **7061**
Mekhanizatsia na Zemedelieto (BGR) **203**
Mekhanizatsiya i Elektrifikatsiya Sel'skogo Khozyaistva (RUS ISSN 0206-572X) **212**
Mekhanizatsiya Stroitel'stva (RUS ISSN 0025-8903) **3278**
Mekong Development Series (KHM ISSN 1680-4023) **8829**
Mekong Fish Catch and Culture (KHM ISSN 0859-290X) **3601**
Mekong News (KHM ISSN 1014-0360) **8829**
Mekong River Commission Technical Paper *see* M R C Technical Paper **3601**
Melanargia (DEU ISSN 0941-3170) **854**
Melanesia News (GBR) **7662**
Melanesian Journal of Theology (PNG ISSN 0256-856X) **7662**
• Melanesian Law Journal (PNG ISSN 0254-0657) **4732**
Melanges C R A P E L *see* Universite de Nancy II. Centre de Recherches et d'Applications Pedagogiques en Langues. Melanges **3086**
➤ Melanges Chinois et Bouddhiques. Nouvelle Serie (BEL) **555**
Les Melanges de la Casa de Velazquez/Casa de Velasquez, Madrid. Miscellanies (FRA ISSN 0076-230X) **505**
• Melanges de l'Ecole Francaise de Rome. Moyen Age (FRA ISSN 1123-9883) **4244**
Melanges de l'Institut Dominicain d'Etudes Orientales du Caire *see* Institut Dominicain d'Etudes Orientales du Caire. Melanges **4321**
➤ Melanges de Science Religieuse (FRA ISSN 0025-8911) **7806**
Melanges d'Histoire de l'Architecture (BEL) **449**
Melanin (USA) **8874**
Melanoma Letter (USA) **5880**
• ➤ Melanoma Research (USA ISSN 0960-8931) **6027**
• Melanoma Research Today (AUS ISSN 1833-0592) **5880**
Melbourne (AUS ISSN 0156-2312) **3795**
Melbourne 2030 Email Bulletin *see* Melbourne 2030 Email Update **1148**
• Melbourne 2030 Email Update (AUS ISSN 1834-3856) **1148**
• Melbourne 2030. Implementation Bulletin (AUS ISSN 1833-5373) **8120**
Melbourne Anglican (AUS ISSN 1324-5724) **7767**
• ➤ Melbourne Art Journal (AUS ISSN 1329-9441) **505**
Melbourne Bride (AUS ISSN 0818-8173) **5560**
• Melbourne Citymission. Annual Report (AUS ISSN 0728-1897) **8055**
• Melbourne Cityscope (AUS) **7618**
• Melbourne Cityscope Unit Report (AUS) **7618**
Melbourne Cup Carnival (AUS ISSN 1449-8731) **8294**
Melbourne Formal and Debutante Guide (AUS ISSN 1449-7662) **5076**
➤ Melbourne Historical Journal (AUS ISSN 0076-6232) **4193**
Melbourne in Fact - Census Statistics for Melbourne's New Local Government Areas *see* Australia. Bureau of Statistics. Victorian Office. Melbourne in Fact - (Year) Census Statistics for Melbourne's New Local Government Areas **7302**
• Melbourne Institute Report (AUS ISSN 1832-6250) **1148**
• ➤ Melbourne Journal of International Law (AUS ISSN 1444-8602) **4935**
• ➤ Melbourne Journal of Politics (AUS ISSN 0085-3224) **7154**
Melbourne Land & Homes (AUS ISSN 1832-4967) **7599**
• Melbourne Papers in Language Testing (Online) (AUS) **5150**
Melbourne Port & Shipping Handbook (Year) (AUS) **2016**
• The Melbourne Review (AUS ISSN 1833-6353) **1148**
Melbourne Sheep and Wool (AUS) **537**
Melbourne Studies in Education *see* Critical Studies in Education **2840**
• ➤ Melbourne University Law Review (AUS ISSN 0025-8938) **4732**
• Melbourne University Magazine (AUS ISSN 1442-1348) **2291**
• Melbourne's Child (AUS ISSN 1320-6176) **2161**
Os Melhores Automoveis do Mundo (PRT) **8590**
Melhores e Maiores (BRA ISSN 0104-3234) **1898**
Melhores Receitas da Culinaria Passe Bem (BRA ISSN 1678-2836) **4364**
Melhores Trabalhos da Casa Facil Artesanato (BRA ISSN 1678-2828) **537**
Melhores Trabalhos da Casa Facil Bordados (BRA ISSN 1678-281X) **2258**
Melhusbyggen (NOR ISSN 1503-7991) **4244**
Melibea (PER) **5332**
Melilla Hoy (ESP) **3952**
Melioratsiya i Vodnoe Khozyaistvo (RUS ISSN 0235-2524) **8829**
Meliorist (CAN) **2291**
Melita Theologica (MLT ISSN 1012-9588) **7662**
➤ Melita Theologica Supplementary Series (MLT) **7662**
Melk (NOR ISSN 1890-114X) **4364**
Melksham Independent News (GBR) **3868**
Melkvee Magazine (NLD ISSN 1571-4640) **267**
Melkveebedrijf (BEL ISSN 1376-7232) **267**
Melland Schill Studies in International Law (GBR) **4935**
Mellemoestinformation (DNK ISSN 0904-9789) **4323**
Mellen Bibliographies for Biblical Research. New Testament Series (USA) **7698**
Mellen Bibliographies for Biblical Research. Old Testament Series (USA) **7698**
Mellen Bibliographies for Biblical Research. Periodic Literature for the Study of the New Testament (USA) **7699**
Mellen Bibliographies for Biblical Research. Periodic Literature for the Study of the Old Testament (USA) **7699**
Mellen Bibliographies for Biblical Research. Supplemental Series (USA) **7699**
Mellen Opera Reference Index (USA) **6631**
Mellen Poetry Press (USA) **5427**
Mellen Studies in Geography (USA ISSN 1933-5482) **4019**
Mellen Studies in Literature: Elizabethan and Renaissance Studies (USA) **5332**
Mellen Studies in Literature: English and American Studies (USA) **5332**
Mellen Studies in Literature: Jacobean Drama (USA) **5332**
Mellen Studies in Literature: Poetic Drama and Poetic Theory (USA) **5332**
Mellen Studies in Literature: Romantic Reassessment (USA) **5332**
Melliand - China *see* Guoji Fangzhi Daobao **8451**
Melliand International (DEU ISSN 0947-9163) **8455**
Melliand Textilberichte/International Textile Reports (DEU ISSN 0341-0781) **8455**
• ➤ Mellifera/Journal of Beekeeping in Turkey (TUR ISSN 1302-5821) **136**
Mellitus Lauf (DEU ISSN 0940-0109) **8187**
Melodiva (DEU) **6587**
Melodiya (RUS ISSN 0206-8052) **6587**
Il Melograno (ITA) **3897**
Melomano (ESP ISSN 1136-4939) **6587**
Melos (SWE ISSN 1103-0968) **6587**
Meloussa (ESP ISSN 0214-2600) **347**
Melting Pot (CHE ISSN 1423-9787) **5227**
Melton Center for Jewish Studies. Annual Newsletter (USA ISSN 1931-406X) **3549**
Melton Center Newsletter *see* Melton Center for Jewish Studies. Annual Newsletter **3549**
• Melty (USA) **3981**
Melville: Forms and Agreements on Intellectual Property and International Licensing (GBR) **4732**
• ➤ Melville Society Extracts (USA ISSN 0193-8991) **5332**

Title

10606 MEN'S HEALTH WATCH ULRICH'S PERIODICALS

Men's Health Watch *see* Harvard Men's Health Watch **6284**
Mens. Intellectual History Review of French America *see* Mens. Revue d'Histoire Intellectuelle de l'Amerique Francaise **4303**
• Men's Journal (USA ISSN 1063-4657) **6295**
† Men's Magazine (DEU) **8974**
➤ Mens. Revue d'Histoire Intellectuelle de l'Amerique Francaise/Mens. Intellectual History Review of French America (CAN ISSN 1492-8647) **4303**
• ➤ Mens Sana Monographs (IND ISSN 0973-1229) **6160**
Men's Style (USA ISSN 1079-6207) **6295**
Men's Style Australia (AUS ISSN 1449-6704) **6295**
Men's Vogue (USA ISSN 1556-4096) **6295**
• Men's Voices (USA ISSN 1520-247X) **6303**
Men's Workout (USA ISSN 1058-3041) **6285**
Men's World (GBR ISSN 0955-5552) **6295**
• Mensa Bulletin (USA ISSN 0025-9543) **2268**
Mensa Magazine (GBR ISSN 0958-0638) **2268**
Mensa Quest (GBR) **8187**
Mensa Research Journal (USA ISSN 0025-9551) **3044**
Mensa Spezial (DEU) **2291**
El Mensage de Az-Zaqalain (IRN) **7714**
Mensageiro do Coracao de Jesus (PRT ISSN 0874-4955) **7662**
Mensagem Economica/Economic Message (BRA) **1367**
Mensagens de Amor (BRA ISSN 1806-3489) **5411**
• Mensaje (CHL ISSN 0716-0062) **7806**
Mensaje (URY) **7726**
Mensaje (USA) **7154**
Mensaje News *see* Mensaje **7154**
Mensajero *see* The Messenger **577**
• Mensajero (ESP ISSN 0211-6561) **7662**
• El Mensajero (USA ISSN 1040-5712) **3549**
Mensajero de San Antonio *see* Messaggero di Sant' Antonio **7806**
Mensans (FRA ISSN 1771-8813) **7384**
▼ Mensbook Journal (USA ISSN 1944-5482) **6295**
Der Mensch als Soziales und Personales Wesen (DEU ISSN 0543-4726) **8121**
Mensch Maschine Interaktion Interaktiv *see* M M I Interaktiv **2454**
Mensch - Taetigkeit - Entwicklung (DEU ISSN 1615-732X) **8121**
Mensch und Arbeit (AUT) **1697**
Mensch und Buero (DEU ISSN 0933-8241) **1852**
Mensch und Gesellschaft (DEU ISSN 0930-939X) **7985**
Mensch und Pferd (AUT) **8294**
Mensch und Recht (CHE ISSN 1420-1038) **4935**
Mensch und Tier (AUT) **6811**
Mensch und Umwelt (AUT) **3452**
Mensch und Umwelt (DEU ISSN 0949-0671) **3452**
• Menschen Brauchen Menschen...und Informationen (AUT ISSN 1023-8220) **8055**
Menschen im Blickpunkt (DEU) **8055**
Menschen und Strukturen (DEU ISSN 0179-3705) **7985**
▼ Menschen - Wissen - Medien (DEU ISSN 1610-076X) **7985**
Das Menschenrecht *see* Liga **7212**
Menschenrechte (DEU ISSN 0171-5976) **7212**
MenschenRechtsMagazin (DEU ISSN 1434-2820) **7212**
Mense (ZAF ISSN 1819-205X) **3949**
Mensen in Nood Nieuws (NLD ISSN 1568-3478) **1601**
Mensen Werken (NLD ISSN 1874-9739) **1697**
MensenWerk *see* Personeelbeleid **1872**
• Menstuff (USA) **6303**
Menstyle (LIE) **6295**
Mensuel Culturel du Centre-du-Quebec *see* Quoi? Magazine **5081**
Mensuel des Maisons de Retraites (FRA ISSN 1769-9460) **4051**
Menswear in Ireland (IRL) **2248**
Menswear Retailing (Norwalk) *see* M R (Norwalk) **2248**
• Mental (USA ISSN 1679-4427) **7384**
The Mental and Cultural World of Tudor and Stuart England (CAN) **5332**
Mental and Physical Disability Law Reporter *see* Joint Commission Advisor for Behavioral Health **4833**
Mental Disability Law: Civil and Criminal (USA) **4732**
The Mental Edge (USA) **7384**
➤ Mental Fitness (USA) **8847**
Mental Floss (USA ISSN 1543-4702) **3981**
Mental Health *see* Mielenterveys **6160**
Mental Health *see* Psykisk Haelsa **7401**
Mental Health (Farmington Hills) *see* Information Plus Reference Series. Mental Health **8964**
• Mental Health Act Commission. Biennial Report (GBR ISSN 1463-9610) **8055**
Mental Health & Aging (USA ISSN 1931-4205) **4051**
• Mental Health and Learning Disabilities Research and Practice (GBR ISSN 1743-6885) **6160**
▼ • ➤ Mental Health and Physical Activity (NLD ISSN 1755-2966) **7384**
Mental Health and Social Work Career Directory (USA ISSN 1070-7298) **7531**
Mental Health and Specialist Care Services (GBR) **1898**
▼ • ➤ Mental Health and Substance Use (GBR ISSN 1752-3281) **2697**
➤ Mental Health Aspects of Developmental Disabilities (USA ISSN 1557-5187) **6160**
• Mental Health Business Week (USA ISSN 1552-9096) **6160**
Mental Health Data *see* New Zealand Health Information Service. Mental Health **5749**
Mental Health Directorate Newsletter *see* Mental Health Newsletter **6160**
Mental Health Disorders Sourcebook (USA) **7384**
Mental Health in Children (USA) **7384**
• ➤ Mental Health in Family Medicine (GBR) **6160**
• Mental Health Law Bulletin (USA) **4837**
Mental Health Law News (USA ISSN 0889-017X) **6160**
Mental Health Law Reporter *see* Joint Commission Advisor for Behavioral Health **4833**
• Mental Health Law Weekly (USA ISSN 1551-5133) **6160**
Mental Health Library Series (USA) **7384**
Mental Health Matters (AUS) **6160**
Mental Health Matters (CAN ISSN 1196-5304) **7385**
• Mental Health Newsletter (NZL ISSN 1178-4997) **6160**
• ➤ Mental Health Nursing Journal (GBR ISSN 1353-0283) **6160**
Mental Health Occupational Therapy (GBR ISSN 1363-4682) **7385**
• Mental Health Practice (GBR ISSN 1465-8720) **6160**
Mental Health Reforms (NLD ISSN 1385-4933) **6160**
• ➤ Mental Health, Religion & Culture (GBR ISSN 1367-4676) **7385**
• Mental Health Research Review (Online) (GBR) **7385**
• The Mental Health Review (GBR ISSN 1361-9322) **6160**
Mental Health Review Tribunals for England and Wales. Annual Report (GBR) **7531**
Mental Health Services Research *see* Administration and Policy in Mental Health and Mental Health Services Research **5567**
Mental Health Special Interest Section Quarterly (USA ISSN 1093-7226) **7385**
• Mental Health Today (GBR ISSN 1474-5186) **6160**
Mental Health: United States (USA ISSN 0892-0664) **8055**
• Mental Health Weekly (USA ISSN 1058-1103) **7385**
• Mental Health Weekly Digest (USA ISSN 1543-6616) **6160**
• Mental Illness Foundation. Activity Report (CAN ISSN 1910-3255) **6160**
Mental Illness Foundation. Bulletin *see* Fondation des Maladies Mentales. Bulletin **6141**
• The Mental Lexicon (NLD ISSN 1871-1340) **5151**
• Mental Measurements Yearbook (USA ISSN 0076-6461) **7385**
Mental Peace/Magallat al-Nafs al-Motma'enna (EGY ISSN 1110-1334) **6160**
Mental Retardation *see* Intellectual and Developmental Disabilities **3041**
• Mentalhigiene es Pszichoszomatika/Journal of Mental Health and Psychosomatics (HUN ISSN 1419-8126) **6160**
Mentalites *see* Mentalities **4153**
➤ Mentalities/Mentalites (CAN ISSN 0111-8854) **4153**
Mente Sana (ESP ISSN 1699-0579) **7385**
Mente Social (BRA ISSN 1414-1868) **7385**
Mente y Cerebro (ESP ISSN 1695-0887) **7385**
▼ MenteCorpo (ITA ISSN 1971-8888) **6992**
Mentis Anthologien Philosophie *see* M A P **6933**
Mentis Vita (USA ISSN 1932-5762) **4464**
Mentor (CAN) **2886**
O Mentor (GRC ISSN 1105-7181) **405**
The Mentor (Fayetteville) (USA ISSN 1530-8219) **2993**
• The Mentor (University Park) (USA ISSN 1521-2211) **2993**
The Mentor Management Digest (GBR ISSN 0963-6404) **1779**
• ➤ Mentoring & Tutoring (GBR ISSN 1361-1267) **3072**
† Menu (ITA ISSN 1127-0489) **8974**
Menu (New York) (USA) **4393**
Menuiserie (BEL) **1051**
• Menz Magazine (CAN ISSN 1202-7472) **6295**
Menzelia (USA) **3743**
➤ La Mer/Umi (JPN ISSN 0503-1540) **689**
Mer & Bateaux (FRA ISSN 0999-7148) **8278**
Mer et Littoral (FRA ISSN 1266-2585) **3489**
La Mer Gelee (FRA ISSN 1772-0613) **5333**
Il Meraviglioso Mondo delle Bambole di Pezza (ITA ISSN 1825-4527) **4339**
Merbein Historian (AUS) **4193**
Mercadieta *see* Horticultura **3737**
• Mercado/Business (ARG ISSN 0325-0687) **1498**
Mercado (URY ISSN 0797-2733) **1407**
Mercado Ambiental/Environmental Market (ESP ISSN 1133-8989) **3452**
Mercado Comun Internacional. Noticiario Z (ESP) **1577**
Mercado de Deuda Publica (ESP ISSN 1697-8609) **1934**
Mercado de las Franquicias en Chile (CHL ISSN 0718-3909) **1431**
Mercado de Suelo (CHL ISSN 0716-775X) **449**
• Mercado de Valores (MEX ISSN 0185-1268) **1638**
Mercado de Valores (English Edition) (MEX) **1638**
▼ • Mercado Energetico (CHL ISSN 0718-4840) **3142**
Mercado Mundial/World Market (ESP ISSN 0539-3728) **1577**
Mercado Previsor (ESP) **4515**
† Mercadocontinuo (ESP ISSN 1137-7615) **8974**
Mercados Agrarios. Precios/Agrarmarkte. Preise/Agricultural Markets. Prices/Landbrugsmarkeder. Priser/Marches Agricoles. Prix/Mercados Agricolas. Precos/Mercati Agricoli. Prezzi (LUX ISSN 1014-8159) **136**
Mercados Agricolas. Precos *see* Mercados Agrarios. Precios **136**
Mercados Internacionales de la Carne *see* International Markets for Meat **290**
Mercancia de Taiwan *see* Taiwan Merchandise **1583**
Mercantile Gazette Business *see* M.G. Business **1430**
Mercati Agricoli. Prezzi *see* Mercados Agrarios. Precios **136**
• Mercati e Competitivita (ITA ISSN 1826-7386) **1834**
• Mercato Concorrenza Regole (ITA ISSN 1590-5128) **1148**
Mercato Metalsiderurgico (ITA ISSN 0025-9829) **6322**
† Mercato Nautico (ITA ISSN 1123-9867) **8974**
▼ • Mercator (DNK ISSN 1902-164X) **8653**
• Mercator Media Forum (GBR ISSN 1357-7220) **2385**
• Mercatus Policy Series: Country Brief (USA ISSN 1943-6777) **7154**
• Mercatus Policy Series: Policy Comment (USA ISSN 1944-4591) **7154**
• Mercatus Policy Series: Policy Primer (USA ISSN 1943-6793) **7154**
• Mercatus Policy Series: Policy Resource (USA ISSN 1943-6750) **7154**
Mercedes (ZAF ISSN 1811-9069) **8590**
Mercedes-Benz Classic (DEU ISSN 1610-8043) **8590**
Mercedes-Benz Star *see* The Star (Lakewood) **8605**
Mercedes Enthusiast (GBR ISSN 1474-7030) **8590**
Mercedes Magazine *see* Mercedes **8590**
Mercedesmagazin (DEU) **3853**
Mercer Bulletin (CAN ISSN 0714-6914) **4515**
• Mercer Business Magazine (USA ISSN 0194-9101) **1407**
Mercer Cluster (USA ISSN 0025-9853) **2291**
Mercer County Board of Realtors. Newsline (USA ISSN 0891-7698) **7599**
Mercer County Heritage (USA) **4303**
Mercer County Law Journal (USA ISSN 0539-385X) **4732**
Mercer County Tourism Guide *see* Mercer Business Magazine **1407**
• ➤ Mercer Law Review (USA ISSN 0025-987X) **4732**
Mercer Pension Manual (CAN) **1697**
Merceria Actualidad (ESP) **2248**
Merchandise Imports America Directory (CAN) **1577**
Merchandise Mart Resource Guide (USA) **1834**
Merchant and Gould Computer Law Newsletter (USA) **4732**
Merchant Explorer (USA ISSN 0543-5056) **4244**
Merchant Magazine (USA ISSN 0739-9723) **3714**
• Merchants News (USA) **1834**
Merchantville Stamp Club. Monthly Bulletin (USA) **6897**
Merchistonian (GBR) **2291**
➤ Mercian Geologist (GBR ISSN 0025-990X) **2755**
• The Merck Index: An Encyclopedia of Chemicals and Drugs (USA ISSN 0076-6518) **6890**
• The Merck Manual of Diagnosis and Therapy (USA ISSN 0076-6526) **5678**
The Merck Manual of Geriatrics (USA ISSN 1527-6708) **4051**
The Merck Manual of Medical Information - Home (USA) **5678**
The Merck Veterinary Manual (USA ISSN 0076-6542) **8803**
I Mercoledi dell'Accademia (ITA ISSN 1971-5439) **7882**
Mercosul: Sinopse Estatistica/Mercosur: Sinopsis Estadistica (BRA ISSN 1021-7398) **1251**
• Mercosur (ARG) **1252**
Mercosur Agropecuario (ARG ISSN 0328-2708) **136**
Mercosur: Sinopsis Estadistica *see* Mercosul: Sinopse Estatistica **1251**
Mercur (AUT ISSN 0025-9926) **1638**
Mercure 10 (FRA ISSN 0765-4448) **1431**
• El Mercurio (CHL) **3822**
Mercurio (ESP ISSN 1138-1140) **1148**
Mercurio *see* El Mercurio de Tamaulipas **3909**
Mercurio (Sevilla) (ESP ISSN 1139-7705) **631**
• El Mercurio de Tamaulipas (MEX ISSN 1605-0495) **3909**
• El Mercurio de Valparaiso (CHL) **3822**
• The Mercury (AUS ISSN 1039-9992) **3795**
The Mercury (CAN ISSN 0841-3223) **3813**
Mercury (GBR) **3757**
The Mercury (ZAF) **3949**
Mercury (Glenville) (USA) **2291**
Mercury (Los Angeles) (USA ISSN 0025-9969) **2268**
Mercury (Online) (USA ISSN 0047-6773) **577**
Mercury (Print) *see* Mercury (Online) **577**
• Mercury Messenger (USA) **577**
• Merdeka & Oesttimor Information (SWE ISSN 1402-2559) **4185**
Mere Nouvelle *see* New Mother **2162**
MeReC Briefing (GBR) **5678**
• MeReC Bulletin (GBR ISSN 1465-5659) **5678**
MeReC Extra (GBR) **5678**
Meredith Specials Holiday Cooking with America's Top Chefs *see* Holiday Cooking with America's Top Chefs **4360**
• Merenkulkulaitos. Julkaisuja/Finnish Maritime Administration. Publications (FIN ISSN 1456-7814) **8653**
• Merenkulkulaitos. Tiedotuslehti/Finnish Maritime Administration. Bulletin (FIN ISSN 1455-9048) **4970**
• Merentutkimuslaitos. Vuosikertomus/Finnish Institute of Marine Research. Annual Report/Havsforskningsinstitutet. Aarsberaettelse (FIN ISSN 1237-3982) **2813**
Mergaite (LTU ISSN 1648-276X) **2202**
▼ Merge Magazine (USA ISSN 1937-4879) **5076**
Mergent Annual Bond Record (USA) **1639**
Mergent Bank and Finance Manual (USA ISSN 1539-6444) **1367**
Mergent Bond Record (USA ISSN 1532-5997) **1639**
Mergent ... Company Archives Supplement (USA) **1296**
Mergent Company Data *see* Company Data **1415**
• Mergent Complete Corporate Index (USA) **1252**
Mergent Industrial Manual and News Reports (USA ISSN 0545-0217) **1639**
Mergent International Manual and News Reports (USA ISSN 0278-3509) **1639**
Mergent Municipal and Government Manual (USA ISSN 1539-6355) **1639**
Mergent O T C Industrial Manual and News Reports (Over-the-Counter) (USA ISSN 1539-6843) **1639**
Mergent O T C Unlisted Manual (Over-the-Counter) (USA ISSN 1546-6159) **1639**
• Mergent O T C Unlisted News Reports (Over the Counter) (USA) **1639**
Mergent Over the Counter Unlisted News Reports *see* Mergent O T C Unlisted News Reports **1639**
• Mergent Public Utility & Transportation Manual (USA ISSN 1930-1588) **7453**
Mergent Unit Investment Trusts (USA ISSN 1527-4675) **1639**
Mergent's Annual Bond Record *see* Mergent Annual Bond Record **1639**
• Mergent's Dividend Achievers (USA ISSN 1547-8335) **1639**
• Mergent's Handbook of Common Stocks (USA ISSN 1547-8343) **1639**
• Mergent's Handbook of N A S D A Q Stocks (National Association of Securities Dealers Automated Quotations) (USA ISSN 1542-9326) **1639**
Mergent's Industry Review (USA ISSN 1527-4683) **1252**
• Merger and Acquisition Sourcebook (Year) (USA ISSN 0742-602X) **1148**
† The Merger Yearbook (USA ISSN 1076-3600) **8974**
Mergers & Acquisitions (CAN ISSN 1717-6468) **4876**
Mergers and Acquisitions *see* M & A **1145**
• Mergers and Acquisitions (NLD) **1934**
Mergers & Acquisitions *see* Telecommunications Mergers and Acquisitions Newsletter **2372**
• Mergers & Acquisitions (New York, 1965) (USA ISSN 0026-0010) **1148**
Mergers & Acquisitions (Year) (GBR ISSN 1471-1230) **4733**
Mergers & Acquisitions Asia *see* M & A Asia **1366**
• Mergers & Acquisitions - Asia Pacific (USA ISSN 1532-4745) **1148**
▼ • Mergers & Acquisitions Business (USA ISSN 1945-600X) **1779**
• Mergers and Acquisitions in Canada (CAN ISSN 0843-5421) **1148**
Mergers and Acquisitions Journal *see* Mergers & Acquisitions (New York, 1965) **1148**
Mergers & Acquisitions News *see* Mergers&Acquisitions News **1898**
• Mergers & Acquisitions Report (USA ISSN 1099-3428) **1148**
Mergers and Acquisitions Report *see* Mergers & Acquisitions Report **1148**
Mergers & Acquisitions Review *see* M & A Review **1366**
Mergers & Acquisitions Tax Report *see* The M & A Tax Report **1933**
Mergers & Acquisitions: The (Year) Yearbook *see* The Guide to Mergers and Acquisitions (Year) **4869**
▼ • Mergers & Acquisitions Week (USA ISSN 1945-6026) **1779**
Mergers and Acquisitions Worldwide (GBR) **3656**
Mergers and Acquistions Law Report *see* Mergers & Acquistions Law Report **4876**
• Mergers & Acquistions Law Report (USA ISSN 1098-4720) **4876**
Mergers&Acquisitions News (POL) **1898**
• Mergerstat Review (USA ISSN 1071-4065) **1639**
• Merginet News (USA) **4107**
Meri-Lappi Institute. Reports *see* Meri-Lappi Instituutti. Tiedotteita **3452**
Meri-Lappi Instituutti. Tiedotteita/Meri-Lappi Institute. Reports (FIN ISSN 1456-5145) **3452**
Meri - Report Series of the Finnish Institute of Marine Research (FIN ISSN 1238-5328) **2813**
Meri Saheli (IND) **3885**
Merian (DEU ISSN 0026-0029) **3853**
Merida Ciudad y Patrimonio (ESP ISSN 1577-2845) **4153**
➤ Meridian (AUS ISSN 0728-5914) **5333**

Meridian (DEU ISSN 0177-3852) 6646
Meridian see Meridian Travel 8733
Meridian (Charlottesville) (USA ISSN 1527-3555) 5333
Meridian (Incline Valley) (USA) 5077
• Meridian (Raleigh) (USA ISSN 1097-9778) 2950
Meridian: Crossing Aesthetics (USA ISSN 1543-7442) 6934
▼ Meridian Travel (NLD) 8733
• Meridiana (ITA ISSN 0394-4115) 4153
Meridiani (ITA ISSN 1120-804X) 8733
Meridiani. Le Grandi Vie (ITA ISSN 1824-2723) 8733
Meridiani Montagne (ITA ISSN 1721-5072) 8321
Meridiani Montagne. Gli Speciali (ITA ISSN 1825-5175) 8733
Meridiani Montagne. Rifugi e Bivacchi (ITA ISSN 1824-2731) 8322
Meridiani. Viaggi del Gusto see I Viaggi del Gusto 8771
Meridiano (VEN) 8187
• Meridiano 47 (BRA ISSN 1518-1219) 7252
Meridiano C E R I (Centro Espanol de Relaciones Internacionales) (ESP ISSN 1135-710X) 7252
Meridiano Quarenta e Sete see Meridiano 47 7252
• ➤ Meridians (USA ISSN 1536-6936) 8901
Meridijani (HRV ISSN 1333-7289) 4019
Meridione, Sud e Nord nel Mondo (ITA ISSN 1594-5472) 7154
➤ Il-Merill (MLT ISSN 1013-3933) 910
Merisotakoulu. Julkaisusarja. A, Tutkimuksia (FIN ISSN 1796-0800) 6434
Merisotakoulu. Julkaisusarja. B, Asiatietoja (FIN ISSN 1796-1076) 6434
Merit Systems Protection Board Service (USA) 1697
• Merivayla (FIN ISSN 1455-7525) 8653
Meriya Moskvy. Vestnik (RUS) 7453
Merk en Reputatie (NLD) 1148
Merkblaetter fuer die Wasser-, Abwasser- und Schlammuntersuchung (DEU ISSN 0940-0494) 3489
Merkblaetter Gefaehrliche Arbeitsstoffe (DEU ISSN 0936-1197) 6681
Merkblatt fuer die Praxis (CHE ISSN 1422-2876) 2618
Merkels' Builders' Pricing and Management Manual (ZAF) 1023
Merkenregister see Markassiet 6754
• ➤ Merkourios (NLD ISSN 0927-460X) 4935
Merkur (DEU ISSN 0026-0096) 5227
Merkurius-Kirjakerho (FIN ISSN 1238-5980) 2202
Der Merkurstab (DEU ISSN 0935-798X) 7739
Merleg (HUN ISSN 0026-0126) 7662
• Merle's Mission (USA) 2564
Meroitica (DEU ISSN 0138-3663) 555
Merredin-Wheatbelt Mercury (AUS ISSN 1321-537X) 3795
† Merrick - Washington Magazine for the Blind (USA) 8974
Merrill Lynch Market Letter (USA) 1639
• ➤ Merrill - Palmer Quarterly (USA ISSN 0272-930X) 7385
• Merrill's EDGAR Advisor (USA) 2524
Merritt Insurance Report (USA) 4515
Merritt Risk Management News (USA ISSN 0742-3446) 4515
Merry-Go-Roundup (USA) 367
Merseburger Schriften zur Unternehmensfuehrung (DEU) 1779
Merseyside Archaeological Society. Journal (GBR ISSN 0140-4032) 406
Merseyside Business Prospect (GBR ISSN 1368-1427) 1498
Mersmak (SWE ISSN 1102-2930) 2640
Mertens Current Tax Highlights (USA ISSN 0279-9286) 1935
Mertens Federal Tax Regulations (USA) 4733
Mertens Law of Federal Income Taxation (USA ISSN 0164-4041) 4733
Mertens Rulings (USA) 4733
Mertens Treatise on the Law of Federal Income Taxation (USA) 4733
Mertensiella (DEU ISSN 0934-6643) 955
• Merton Annual: Studies in Thomas Merton, Religion, Culture, Literature, and Social Concerns (USA ISSN 0894-4857) 5333
Merton Messenger (GBR) 3868
The Merton Seasonal (USA ISSN 0899-4927) 7663
Meru (JPN) 4364
Mervyn Peake Review (GBR ISSN 0309-1309) 5444
Mes Consultations Psy (FRA ISSN 1951-7572) 7385
Mes Droits (FRA ISSN 1776-5722) 4733
† Mes Premieres Grilles (FRA ISSN 0396-4914) 8974
Mes Premiers J'aime Lire (FRA ISSN 1297-8671) 2202
Mes P'tits Bobos (FRA ISSN 1779-7594) 2202
Mes Tissages (FRA ISSN 1770-6025) 8121
Mesa Legend (USA) 2292
Meschede (DEU) 3853
Il Mese di Caccia (ITA ISSN 0392-3665) 8322
Il Mese di Modena (ITA ISSN 1827-5958) 3897
Il Mese di Reggio Emilia (ITA ISSN 1827-5966) 3897
Il Mese Magazine (ITA ISSN 1592-6230) 3897
Mesechabe: The Journal of Surregionalism (USA) 5333
Mesecni Statisticni Pregled Republike Slovenije see Pomembnejsi Statisticni Podatki o Sloveniji 8394
• Mesemb Study Group. Bulletin (GBR ISSN 0955-8276) 801
Mesgil Unu (Jalal-Abad) (KGZ) 3904
Mesgil Unu (Kara-Kulja) (KGZ) 3904
• The Mesh (USA) 2564
• Mesh (Online) (AUS ISSN 1447-4646) 505
Meshcherskaya Storona (RUS) 3937
Mesias (MEX ISSN 0026-0185) 7767
Mesilot (ISR ISSN 0333-9726) 7726
Mesilot see Religious Zionism in Action - Essays 8985
Meso (HRV ISSN 1332-0025) 3656
Meso Magazine (NLD ISSN 0924-8250) 3027
Mesoamerica (CRI ISSN 0254-170X) 3830
➤ Mesoamerica (GTM ISSN 0252-9963) 7985
Mesoamerican Archaeological Research Laboratory. Journal see Mono y Conejo 406
Mesogeios (GRC ISSN 1284-1935) 4244
Mesopotamia (ITA ISSN 0076-6615) 406
Mesovita Gradja/Miscellanea (SRB ISSN 0350-5650) 4244
Mess und Regeltechnik (CHE) 2463
Message (DEU ISSN 1438-499X) 4580
The Message (GBR) 7714
Message (JPN ISSN 0911-5234) 8653
The Message (Evansville) (USA) 7806
Message (Hagerstown) (USA ISSN 0026-0231) 7663
The Message (Jamaica) (USA ISSN 1071-5215) 7714
Message (New Cumberland) (USA ISSN 0271-5732) 7767
The Message (Northborough) (USA ISSN 0896-3290) 8322
• The Message (Spokane) (USA) 5678
Le Message de l'Ahmadiyyat (MUS) 7714
Le Message de l'Islam (IRN ISSN 1012-0734) 7714
Message d'Extreme-Orient (BEL) 4185
A Message from the Middle (CAN ISSN 1719-4334) 2886
Message Line see Headlines on the Path to Progress 6021
The Message of Fatima Today see Soul (Washington, New Jersey) 7817
Message of Thaqalayn (IRN) 7714
Message of the Cross (USA ISSN 0746-0635) 7663
Message of the Library/Risalat al-Maktaba (JOR ISSN 0257-7739) 5032
Message of the Open Bible (USA ISSN 0889-4159) 7663
➤ Message of the Teacher/Risalat al-Mu'allim (JOR ISSN 0040-0505) 2993
Messager (CMR) 3805
Messager (FRA ISSN 0026-024X) 3841
Messager (Strasbourg) (FRA ISSN 1632-6768) 7767
• Le Messager (Verdun) (FRA ISSN 1762-0112) 5764
Messager de la Haute Savoie (FRA ISSN 0026-0258) 3841
Messager du Nord-Ouest (HTI) 3874
Messager Evangelique see Messager (Strasbourg) 7767
Le Messager Lachine (CAN) 3813
Le Messager Lasalle (CAN) 3813
Messager Regional de Comte (CAN ISSN 1718-5726) 7453
Le Messager Verdun (CAN) 3813
Messages see Sans Frontieres 5709
Messages (USA ISSN 0895-5719) 505
Messages du Secours Catholique (FRA ISSN 0026-0290) 7806
• Messages From the Future (USA) 2564
• Il Messaggero (ITA ISSN 1126-8352) 3898
• Il Messaggero Avventista (ITA ISSN 0392-6346) 7767
Messaggero Cappuccino (ITA ISSN 1972-8239) 7806
Messaggero dei Ragazzi (ITA ISSN 0026-0304) 2202
Messaggero di Sant' Antonio (ITA ISSN 0026-0312) 7806
Messaggi Carismatici Cattolici (ITA) 7806
Il Messaggio della Santa Casa (ITA ISSN 0036-116X) 7806
• Messaging News (USA) 2564
† Messana (ITA ISSN 0461-9080) 8974
Messe Digest see Digest 2040
Messe & Event (AUT) 6281
Le Messeger de Saint Antoine see Messaggero di Sant' Antonio 7806
Messen Steuern Regeln Magazin see M S R Magazin 3324
Messen und Pruefen Elektrischer und Magnetischer Groessen see Informationsdienst F I Z Technik. Messen und Pruefen Elektrischer und Magnetischer Groessen 3231
The Messenger (AUS) 7767
Messenger (AUS) 3795
Messenger (CAN ISSN 0228-2828) 3549
• The Messenger/Mensajero (DEU ISSN 0722-6691) 577
Messenger (SGP ISSN 0026-0371) 7767
The Messenger (Belleville) (USA ISSN 0279-3911) 7806
Messenger (Covington) (USA) 7807
The Messenger (Coxsackie) (USA ISSN 1946-9403) 537
Messenger (Dunn) (USA) 7767
Messenger (Elgin) (USA ISSN 0026-0355) 7767
Messenger (Grantham) (GBR ISSN 0309-3654) 7767
The Messenger (Hewitt) (USA) 3452
The Messenger (Julian) (USA) 7739
The Messenger (Lambertville) (USA) 4123
The Messenger (Omaha) (USA) 7767
Messenger (Worcester) (USA ISSN 0893-0872) 7705
Messenger Line (USA) 6529
The Messenger Magazine see Take Pride! Community Magazine 3567
Messenger of Saint Anthony see Messaggero di Sant' Antonio 7806
The Messenger of the Chesterfield Historical Society of Virginia (USA ISSN 0731-3012) 4303
Messenger of Truth (USA) 7767
Messenger Reporter (USA) 4515
Messergebnisse des Zentralen Immissionsmessnetzes. Monatsbericht (DEU ISSN 0720-3934) 3452
Messianic Jewish Life (USA) 7739
Messianic Testimony (GBR) 7739
† Messidor (FRA ISSN 0026-0401) 8974
Messimvrini (GRC) 3874
Messing about in Boats (USA) 8278
MessTec & Automation (DEU) 3370
MessTec Jahrbuch (DEU ISSN 0947-9805) 3370
Messung von Gefahrstoffen (DEU ISSN 0936-4544) 3500
Mester (USA ISSN 0160-2764) 5333
• Mester Tidende (DNK ISSN 0904-1559) 1023
Mestertidende see Mester Tidende 1023
• Il Mestiere di Storico (ITA ISSN 1594-3836) 4153
➤ Mestizo Spaces/Espaces Mestisses (USA) 8121
Mestni Organi na Upravlenie (BGR ISSN 1311-2325) 8388
Mestnoe Vremya (Ioshkar-Ola) (RUS) 3937
Mestnoe Vremya (Perm) (RUS) 3937
Mesuesi/Instituteur (ALB) 2886
Mesure et Evaluation en Education (CAN ISSN 0823-3993) 2886
Mesures (FRA ISSN 0755-219X) 2463
Met-Aviisi (SWE ISSN 1104-0939) 3549
Met Golfer (USA ISSN 1042-7678) 8238
Met Mar (FRA ISSN 0222-5123) 2755
• Meta (CAN ISSN 0026-0452) 5151
• Meta (NOR ISSN 1890-1956) 2501
Meta (SWE ISSN 0348-7903) 406
La Meta Rugby (ITA ISSN 1724-6792) 8238
Metaal en Kunststof see Metaal Magazine 5457
Metaal & Techniek (NLD ISSN 0026-0479) 6322
† Metaal Krant (NLD ISSN 1873-9466) 8974
Metaal Magazine (NLD ISSN 1574-9533) 5457
Metaalbewerking see P T Industrieel Management 3214
De Metaalkrant see Vraag & Aanbod 1908
MetaalPunt (NLD ISSN 1872-1397) 6322
• ➤ Metabolic Brain Disease (USA ISSN 0885-7490) 5678
• ➤ Metabolic Engineering (USA ISSN 1096-7176) 750
➤ Metabolic, Pediatric and Systemic Ophthalmology (USA ISSN 0882-889X) 6046
• ➤ Metabolic Syndrome and Related Disorders (USA ISSN 1540-4196) 5897
• ➤ Metabolism (USA ISSN 0026-0495) 5897
Metabolismes, Hormones, Diabetes et Nutrition see Correspondances en M H N D 5885
▼ Metabolismo Oseo (ESP ISSN 1888-2552) 5897
• Metabolomics (USA ISSN 1573-3882) 925
• ➤ Metacognition and Learning (USA ISSN 1556-1623) 2886
Metafora (POL ISSN 0867-0544) 5333
Metai (LTU ISSN 0134-3211) 5333
• Metal (DNK ISSN 0026-0517) 4598
• Metal & Steel Traders of the World (Year) (GBR ISSN 1755-5604) 2016
Metal Architecture (USA ISSN 0885-5781) 449
Metal Asia (IND ISSN 0972-2238) 6322
• ➤ Metal-Based Drugs (USA ISSN 0793-0291) 2103
Metal Building Developer (USA ISSN 1941-3815) 1023
Metal Building Today see A B C Today 974
• Metal Bulletin (GBR ISSN 0026-0533) 6322
• Metal Bulletin Monthly (GBR ISSN 0373-4064) 6323
Metal Bulletin Prices & Data Book on Disk (GBR) 6323
Metal Bulletin Weekly see Metal Bulletin 6322
The Metal Business see Metall Ukrainy 6324
• Metal Casting Technologies (AUS) 6323
• Metal Center News (USA ISSN 0539-4511) 6323
Metal Center News Buyers Guide see Metal Distribution 6323
Metal Construction News (USA ISSN 8756-2014) 1023
• Metal Curse (USA) 6587
Metal Distribution (USA ISSN 0098-2210) 6323
• Metal Edge (USA ISSN 1068-2872) 6587
Metal Finishers' Association of India. Transactions see India Surface Finishing 6315
• Metal Finishing (USA ISSN 0026-0576) 6323
Metal Forming see Obrobka Plastyczna Metali 6328
Metal Hammer (DEU) 6587
• Metal Hammer (GBR ISSN 0955-1190) 6587
• Metal Hammer & Heavy Metal (GRC ISSN 1108-5045) 6587
Metal Head (BRA ISSN 1413-6163) 6587
Metal Home Digest see Metal Building Developer 1023
• Metal Industry Indicators (USA) 6470
➤ Metal Ions in Biological Systems (USA ISSN 0161-5149) 2117
Metal Ions in Life Sciences (USA ISSN 1559-0836) 2127
† • Metal Maniacs (USA ISSN 1559-4297) 8974
† Metal Marketplace (USA) 8974
Metal Materials see Kovove Materialy 6320
Metal Materials and Metallurgy Engineering see Jinshu Cailiao yu Yejin Gongcheng 6318
Metal Mine see Jinshu Kuangshan 6467
Metal Mining Agency of Japan. Close Examination Report see Seimitsu Chosa Hokokusho 6479
• Metal Music Magazine (BLR) 6587
• Metal Powder Report (GBR ISSN 0026-0657) 6340
• Metal Producers of the World Directory (Year) (GBR ISSN 1741-6167) 6323
• Metal Producing & Processing (USA ISSN 1547-1411) 6323
Metal Recycling see Key Note Market Report: Metal Recycling 1895
Metal Revolution (USA ISSN 1056-2826) 6587
• Metal Roofing (USA ISSN 1533-8711) 1023
• ➤ Metal Science and Heat Treatment (USA ISSN 0026-0673) 6323
Metal Soefart see C O Soefart 4591
Metal Stockholders see Business Ratio. Metal Stockholders 6307
Metal Technology see Tekhnologiya Metallov 6334
Metal Traders of the World (GBR ISSN 0143-7607) 6323
Metal Working Metal Cutting see Jinshu Jiagong. Lengjiagong 6318
Metal Working Metal Forming see Jinshu Jiagong. Rejiagong 6318
Metal World (CHN ISSN 1000-6826) 6323
Metalektro Profiel (NLD ISSN 0167-9511) 5457
Metaleptea (USA) 854
• Metales y Metalurgia (ESP ISSN 1697-3119) 6323
Metaletter (USA ISSN 0047-6870) 4598
MetalForming (USA ISSN 1040-967X) 6323
Metalforming Mexico (USA) 6323
MetalHead see Metal Head 6587
Metalinguistica (DEU ISSN 0946-4174) 5151
Metall (AUT) 6324
Metall (CHE) 6324
Metall (DEU ISSN 0026-0746) 6323
Metall Aktuell (DEU) 6324
Metall Byulleten'. Ukraina (UKR) 6324
Metall i Lit'e Ukrainy (UKR) 6324
• Metall Ukrainy (UKR ISSN 1606-6294) 6324
Metallbau und Aluminium - Kurier (DEU ISSN 0947-9430) 1023
Metalleiologika-Metallourgika Hronika/Mining and Metallurgical Annals (GRC ISSN 1105-2430) 6324
Metallerie (Dutch Edition) see Metallerie (French Edition) 6324
Metallerie (French Edition) (BEL) 6324
† Metallgesellschaft Aktiengesellschaft. Review of the Activities (DEU ISSN 0369-2345) 8974
Metalli (ITA ISSN 1122-1410) 6324
Metallic Materials (GBR ISSN 0264-7303) 3354
• Metallitekniikka (FIN ISSN 1237-6663) 6324
➤ Metallized Plastics (USA ISSN 1068-7440) 2114
• Metallofizika i Noveishie Tekhnologii (UKR ISSN 1024-1809) 6324
▼ • ➤ Metallomics (GBR ISSN 1756-5901) 738
Metallosnabzhenie i Sbyt (RUS) 6324
Metallovedenie i Termicheskaya Obrabotka Metallov (RUS ISSN 0026-0819) 6324
Metallurg (RUS ISSN 0026-0827) 6324
Metallurgia see Furnaces International 6313
La Metallurgia Italiana (ITA ISSN 0026-0843) 6324
Metallurgical Analysis see Yejin Fenxi 6337
• ➤ Metallurgical and Materials Transactions A - Physical Metallurgy and Materials Science (USA ISSN 1073-5623) 6324
• ➤ Metallurgical and Materials Transactions B - Process Metallurgy and Materials Processing Science (USA ISSN 1073-5615) 6324
Metallurgical and Mining Industry see Metallurgicheskaya i Gornorudnaya Promyshlennost' 6325
Metallurgical Equipment see Yejin Shebei 6337
Metallurgical Industry Automation see Yejin Zidonghua 6337
Metallurgical Journal (GBR ISSN 0951-0869) 6324
Metallurgical Plantmakers of the World (GBR ISSN 0308-7794) 6324
Metallurgical Review of M M I J see Mining and Materials Processing Institute of Japan. Metallurgical Review 6326
Metallurgical Science & Technology (ITA ISSN 0393-6074) 6325
Metallurgical Works in Canada, Primary Iron and Steel (Year)/Activite Metallurgique au Canada. Fer et Acier de Premiere Fusion (CAN ISSN 0828-0835) 6470
• ➤ Metallurgicheskaya i Gornorudnaya Promyshlennost'/Metallurgical and Mining Industry (UKR ISSN 0543-5749) 6325
Metallurgicheskoe Proizvodstvo i Tekhnologiya Metallurgicheskikh Protsessov see M P T. Metallurgicheskoe Proizvodstvo i Tekhnologiya Metallurgicheskikh Protsessov 6321
• ➤ Metallurgist (USA ISSN 0026-0894) 6325
Metallurgiya Mashinostroeniya (RUS) 6325
Metallurgy see Metalurgija 6325
Metallurgy and Foundry Abstracts see Kohaszati es Onteszeti Szakirodalmi Tajekoztato 6340
➤ Metallurgy and Foundry Engineering (POL ISSN 1230-2325) 6325
Metallurgy - Materials Education Yearbook (USA ISSN 0094-5447) 6325
• ➤ Metally (RUS ISSN 0869-5733) 6325
Metally Evrazii (RUS) 6325

▼ *new title* † *ceased* • *electronic media* ➤ *refereed*

• Metalmag (USA ISSN 1542-295X) **6325**
• Metalmecanica (USA) **6325**
Metalocus (ESP ISSN 1139-6415) **449**
• Metals Abstracts (USA ISSN 0026-0924) **6340**
• Metals Abstracts Index (USA ISSN 0026-0932) **6341**
• ➤ Metals and Materials International (KOR ISSN 1598-9623) **6325**
Metals & Minerals Annual Review (GBR) **6325**
Metals and Minerals Review (IND ISSN 0026-0959) **6470**
Metals Bulletin (HKG ISSN 1024-4654) **6325**
The Metals Directory (USA ISSN 1559-3320) **2117**
Metals Economics Group Strategic Report (CAN) **6470**
Metals, Materials and Minerals Bulletin *see* Warasan Loha, Watsadu lae Lae **6336**
➤ Metals Materials and Processes (IND ISSN 0970-423X) **6325**
Metals Museum. Bulletin *see* Kinzoku Hakubutsukan Kiyo **6320**
Metals Sourcing Guide (USA) **6325**
• Metals Watch (USA) **6325**
• Metalsmith (USA ISSN 0270-1146) **537**
Metalurgia (Bucharest) (ROM ISSN 0461-9579) **6325**
Metalurgia y Electricidad (ESP ISSN 0026-0991) **6325**
• ➤ Metalurgija/Metallurgy (HRV ISSN 0543-5846) **6325**
• Metalurji (TUR ISSN 1300-4824) **6325**
Metalworking Abstracts (IND ISSN 0970-7034) **5462**
Metalworking Digest Literature Review *see* Industrial Digest **6315**
Metalworking Equipment News (USA) **6326**
• Metalworking Insiders' Report (USA ISSN 1069-9643) **5457**
• Metalworking Production (GBR ISSN 0026-1033) **6326**
• Metalworking Production & Purchasing (CAN ISSN 0383-090X) **6326**
• Metalworking Technology Updates (USA) **6326**
▼ • ➤ Metamaterials (NLD ISSN 1873-1988) **7061**
• MetaMoreTalk (NZL ISSN 1177-9624) **6646**
Metamorfos (SWE ISSN 0347-0024) **5333**
• Metamorfosi (ITA ISSN 0394-6835) **450**
• Metamorphic Association Programme (GBR) **6742**
▼ Metamorphose (DEU) **450**
• Metamorphoses (USA ISSN 1068-7831) **5151**
Metamorphoses (Ridgecrest) (USA ISSN 1931-1982) **5333**
Metamorphosis (GBR) **6742**
➤ Metamorphosis (ZAF ISSN 1018-6409) **854**
Metanica (CUB ISSN 1026-048X) **7061**
• ➤ Metaphilosophy (GBR ISSN 0026-1068) **6934**
mETAphor (AUS ISSN 1440-0022) **3072**
• ➤ Metaphor and Symbol (USA ISSN 1092-6488) **5151**
• Metaphoria (USA) **6934**
• metaphorik.de (DEU ISSN 1618-2006) **5151**
• Metaphysica (NLD ISSN 1437-2053) **6934**
• The Metaphysical Review (AUS ISSN 0814-8805) **5227**
• ➤ Metapolitica (MEX ISSN 1405-4558) **7154**
Metapsichica (ITA ISSN 0026-1076) **6742**
• Metapsychology Online Reviews (USA ISSN 1931-5716) **7385**
• Metas de Enfermeria (ESP ISSN 1138-7262) **5970**
Metas de Enfermeria. Suplemento *see* Metas de Enfermeria **5970**
• Metascience (NLD ISSN 0815-0796) **7882**
Metascience Annual (USA) **6742**
† Metaux Deformation (FRA ISSN 0153-9035) **8974**
Metaylim *see* Metayyelim **8733**
• Metayyelim (ISR) **8733**
MeteoMonde *see* MeteoWorld **6391**
• Meteor (USA) **3981**
• Meteor - Berichte (DEU ISSN 0936-8957) **2813**
Meteor News (USA ISSN 0146-9959) **577**
Meteorite! (USA ISSN 1173-2245) **577**
Meteorites News (JPN) **2712**
• ➤ Meteoritics and Planetary Science (USA ISSN 1086-9379) **578**
Meteorologia b'Yisra'el *see* Israel Meteorological Society **6358**
Meteorologia Colombiana (COL ISSN 0124-6984) **6390**
Meteorologica (ARG ISSN 0325-187X) **6390**
• Meteorological and Geoastrophysical Abstracts (USA ISSN 0026-1130) **6400**
• Meteorological Applications (GBR ISSN 1350-4827) **6390**
Meteorological Data of Hokkaido/Hokkaido no Kisho (JPN ISSN 0018-3423) **6391**
Meteorological Disaster in Saitama Prefecture *see* Saitama-ken no Kisho Saigai **6394**
Meteorological Monthly *see* Qixiang **6393**
Meteorological Research Institute. Annual Research Report *see* Kishocho Kisho Kenkyujo Kenkyu Hokokusho **6359**
Meteorological Research Institute News *see* Kisho Kenkyujo Nyusu **6359**
Meteorological Research Institute. Technical Reports *see* Kisho Kenkyujo Gijutsu Hokoku **6359**
• Meteorological Satellite Center. Monthly Report (JPN ISSN 0387-4028) **6391**
Meteorological Satellite Center News *see* Kisho Eisei Senta Nyusu **6359**
Meteorological Satellite Center Technical Note *see* Kisho Eisei Senta Gijutsu Hokoku **6359**
Meteorological Science and Technology *see* Qixiang Keji **6393**
• Meteorological Service of Canada. Annual Report (CAN ISSN 1704-1244) **7453**
• ➤ Meteorological Society of Japan. Journal/Kisho Shushi (JPN ISSN 0026-1165) **6391**
Meteorological Society of Japan. Preprints of Meeting/Nihon Kisho Gakkai Taikai Koen Yokoshu (JPN) **6391**
Meteorological Society of Japan. Weather *see* Tenki **6396**
Meteorological Society of New Zealand. Newsletter (NZL ISSN 0111-1736) **6391**
Meteorological Study Note *see* Kishou Kenkyu Noto **6359**
➤ Meteorologicke Zpravy (CZE ISSN 0026-1173) **6391**
Meteorologische Abhandlungen. Serie A, Monographien (DEU ISSN 0342-4324) **6391**
† Meteorologische Abhandlungen. Serie B, Grundlagenmaterial (DEU ISSN 0342-4332) **8974**
• ➤ Meteorologische Zeitschrift (DEU ISSN 0941-2948) **6391**
• Meteorologisk Institutt. Met.no-Report, Klima/Norwegian Meteorological Institute. Climate Report (NOR ISSN 1504-1549) **6391**
Meteorologiske Annaler (NOR ISSN 0373-4463) **6391**
Meteorologiya i Gidrologiya (RUS ISSN 0130-2906) **6391**
• ➤ Meteorology and Atmospheric Physics (AUT ISSN 0177-7971) **6391**
Meteorology Journal of Hubei *see* Hubei Qixiang **6356**
• MeteoWorld (CHE ISSN 1818-7137) **6391**
The Meter (USA) **2292**
Metering International (ZAF ISSN 1025-8248) **3325**
Methane Recovery from Landfill Yearbook (USA ISSN 1043-013X) **3509**
Methexis (DEU ISSN 0327-0289) **6934**
• ➤ Method & Theory in the Study of Religion (NLD ISSN 0943-3058) **7663**
➤ Method: Journal of Lonergan Studies (USA ISSN 0736-7392) **6934**
Methode (FRA ISSN 1285-9915) **5333**
Methodensammlung der Elektronenmikroskopie/Methods of Electron Microscopy (DEU ISSN 0076-6771) **899**
Methodes et Outils Qualite (FRA ISSN 1953-4701) **5457**
Methodiek Schoolverlatersinformatiesysteem (NLD ISSN 1871-7136) **3027**
Methodist Church Music Society. Notes (GBR) **6587**
Methodist College Today (USA) **2292**
Methodist Conference. Minutes and Yearbook (GBR) **7767**
• ➤ Methodist DeBakey Cardiovascular Journal (USA ISSN 1947-6094) **5795**
Methodist Diaries (GBR) **7767**
➤ Methodist History (USA ISSN 0026-1238) **7767**
Methodist Recorder (GBR ISSN 0026-1262) **7767**
▼ • ➤ Methodist Review (USA ISSN 1946-5254) **7767**
Methodix (FRA ISSN 1951-3658) **3072**
Methodmag (Print) (AUT) **8322**
Methodmag (Video) (AUT) **8322**
• Methodologia (ITA ISSN 1120-3854) **5151**
• ➤ Methodological Innovations Online (GBR ISSN 1748-0612) **7985**
Methodological Material *see* Metodolosko Gradivo **8388**
• ➤ Methodology (USA ISSN 1614-1881) **7385**
• Methodology and Computing in Applied Probability (USA ISSN 1387-5841) **5517**
Methodology and History in Anthropology (GBR) **347**
Methodology Explanation of Trade Price and Quantity Indexes *see* Turkey. Turkish Statistical Institute. Methodology Explanation of Trade Price and Quantity Indexes **1270**
Methodology in the Social Sciences (USA) **8021**
Methodology of Music Research (DEU) **6587**
Methodology of Short-Term Business Statistics (LUX ISSN 1725-0099) **1498**
• Methodology Reports (USA ISSN 1531-5673) **7531**
• Methodos (Online) (FRA ISSN 1769-7379) **6934**
• ➤ Methods (USA ISSN 1046-2023) **738**
• Methods and Applications of Analysis (USA ISSN 1073-2772) **5517**
• ➤ Methods and Findings in Experimental and Clinical Pharmacology (ESP ISSN 0379-0355) **6861**
† ➤ Methods and Phenomena (NLD ISSN 0377-9025) **8974**
Methods and Principles in Medicinal Chemistry (DEU ISSN 1432-4636) **5678**
• Methods & Tools (CHE ISSN 1023-4918) **2594**
Methods and Tools in Biosciences and Medicine (CHE) **689**
• ➤ Methods in Biotechnology (USA ISSN 1940-6061) **768**
• ➤ Methods in Cell Biology (USA ISSN 0091-679X) **834**
Methods in Cell Science *see* Cytotechnology **832**
Methods in Chromatography (SGP ISSN 1793-1371) **2073**
➤ Methods in Computational Chemistry (USA ISSN 1059-7530) **2108**
• ➤ Methods in Enzymology (USA ISSN 0076-6879) **738**
• ➤ Methods in Geochemistry and Geophysics (NLD ISSN 0076-6895) **2713**
• Methods in Materials Research (USA) **3354**
• ➤ Methods in Microbiology (USA ISSN 0580-9517) **891**
• Methods in Molecular Biology (USA ISSN 1064-3745) **689**
• ➤ Methods in Molecular Medicine (USA ISSN 1543-1894) **5947**
• Methods in Neurosciences (USA ISSN 1043-9471) **6160**
• Methods in Organic Synthesis (GBR ISSN 0265-4245) **2095**
• ➤ Methods in Pharmacology and Toxicology (USA ISSN 1557-2153) **6861**
➤ Methods in Physiology Series (USA ISSN 1521-4605) **925**
• The Methods of Attacking Scientific Evidence (USA) **4956**
• ➤ Methods of Biochemical Analysis (USA ISSN 0076-6941) **738**
Methods of Electron Microscopy *see* Methodensammlung der Elektronenmikroskopie **899**
➤ Methods of Functional Analysis and Topology (UKR ISSN 1029-3531) **5517**
• ➤ Methods of Information in Medicine (DEU ISSN 0026-1270) **5678**
➤ Methods of Surface Characterization (USA ISSN 1063-8814) **2114**
Methodus (BRA ISSN 1516-3407) **4464**
Methodus (CHL ISSN 0718-2775) **6934**
• Methyl Bromides Alternatives Newsletter (USA) **242**
• Metiers de la Petite Enfance (FRA ISSN 1258-780X) **2161**
Metiers Reussite 01 *see* Entreprise et Metiers **1402**
† Metis (DEU ISSN 0939-5970) **8974**
Metis (FRA ISSN 0995-3310) **2237**
• Metis (San Francisco) (USA ISSN 1087-5433) **8874**
Metis: Historia e Cultura (BRA ISSN 1677-0706) **4153**
Metis Voyageur (CAN ISSN 1910-4499) **3549**
Ha-Metivta (USA ISSN 0094-9701) **4733**
• Metlan Tyoraportteja/Finnish Forest Research Institute. Working Papers (FIN ISSN 1795-150X) **3696**
➤ Metmenys (USA ISSN 0543-615X) **5333**
Metode (ESP ISSN 1133-3987) **7882**
• Metode & Data (DNK ISSN 1902-1534) **8121**
Metoder foer Foeraendring (SWE ISSN 1653-2449) **1779**
Metodicke Listy pro Predskolni Vzdelavani (CZE ISSN 1802-3452) **3072**
• ➤ Metodicki Ogledi (HRV ISSN 0353-765X) **2886**
Metodistkyrkans i Sverige Aarsbok (SWE ISSN 0543-6206) **7767**
† Metodologia delle Scienze e Filosofia del Linguaggio (ITA) **8974**
Metodologia e Didattica Clinica *see* M E D I C. Metodologia e Didattica Clinica **8972**
• Metodologicheskie Polozheniya po Statistike (RUS) **8388**
Metodoloski Zvezki (SVN ISSN 1854-0031) **8021**
• Metodolosko Gradivo/Methodological Material (SVN ISSN 1408-1482) **8388**
† • Metodos de Informacion (ESP ISSN 1134-2838) **8974**
• Metodos en Ecologia y Sistematica (CRI ISSN 1659-2182) **689**
Metodos Terapeutico-diagnosticos de Actualidad Pediatria *see* M T A Pediatria **6096**
• Metody Menedzhmenta Kachestva (RUS) **6404**
Metre (Dublin) (IRL ISSN 1393-4414) **5427**
Metric Fact Sheets (CAN ISSN 0383-9184) **6404**
Metric Fastener Standards (USA) **3354**
Metric Reporter (USA) **6404**
Metric Today (USA ISSN 1050-5628) **6404**
• ➤ Metrika (DEU ISSN 0026-1335) **8388**
• Metro (AUS ISSN 0312-2654) **6507**
• Metro (CAN ISSN 1488-7037) **5227**
Metro (GRC ISSN 1108-8095) **5227**
• Metro (NZL ISSN 0113-0668) **3918**
Metro (Budapest) (HUN ISSN 1419-0230) **3876**
Metro (Dutch Edition) (BEL ISSN 1376-6651) **3801**
Metro (French Edition) (BEL ISSN 1376-6643) **3801**
Metro (Goeteborg) (SWE ISSN 1403-3569) **3956**
Metro (Helsinki) (FIN) **3839**
Metro (Minneapolis) (USA ISSN 1934-4961) **8733**
Metro (Netherlands) (NLD) **3915**
Metro (Prague) (CZE ISSN 1211-7811) **3832**
Metro (Santiago) (CHL) **3822**
Metro (Scottsdale) (USA ISSN 1543-8902) **8733**
• Metro (Silicon Valley) (USA) **3981**
Metro (Skaane) (SWE ISSN 1404-5699) **3834**
Metro (Stockholm) (SWE ISSN 1402-7852) **3834**
Metro (Torrance) *see* Metro Magazine **8504**
Metro California Media (USA ISSN 0889-2776) **30**
Metro Chicago Office Guide (USA) **1852**
Metro Chicago Real Estate (USA ISSN 0893-0775) **7599**
Metro-Chicago Retail Space Guide (USA) **7599**
• Metro Cigar News (USA) **8486**
Metro Courier (USA) **3549**
Metro Detroit Labor News (USA ISSN 1072-1525) **4598**
Metro Doctors *see* MetroDoctors **5678**
Metro Eireann (IRL) **3550**
Metro. Gazeta (RUS) **8504**
Metro Golf (USA ISSN 1063-2425) **8238**
Metro Inc. Annual Report (CAN ISSN 1498-3680) **3680**
Metro Jewish News (USA) **7726**
• Metro Magazine (USA) **8504**
Metro Miscellaneous Publication *see* METRO: New York Metropolitan Reference and Research Library Agency. Miscellaneous Publications Series **5032**
Metro Monthly (USA) **3981**
Metro New York Directory of Manufacturers (USA ISSN 0317-252X) **2016**
METRO: New York Metropolitan Reference and Research Library Agency. Miscellaneous Publications Series (USA ISSN 0732-801X) **5032**
Metro News (USA) **4339**
• Metro Nyt (DNK ISSN 1603-7383) **8620**
• Metro Parent (Southfield) (USA) **2161**
Metro.pop (USA ISSN 1537-3118) **5077**
Metro Report (GBR) **8620**
• Metro Reporter (USA ISSN 0890-3522) **3550**
Metro Source (USA ISSN 1529-935X) **4376**
Metro Source N Y *see* Metro Source **4376**
Metro Tramway Magazine (FRA ISSN 1955-9003) **8504**
Metro-Urban Newsletter (USA ISSN 0580-5902) **4419**
Metro Voice (USA) **2333**
Metro Weekly Telecaster (CAN ISSN 1191-7962) **2385**
• Metro Woman Directory (USA) **8874**
Metro Woman Directory - Houston (USA) **8874**
Metrociencia (ECU ISSN 1390-2989) **5678**
MetroDoctors (USA ISSN 1526-4262) **5678**
• ➤ Metroeconomica (GBR ISSN 0026-1386) **1149**
Metroguide *see* Baltimore Magazine **5065**
MetroHOUSE (USA) **7599**
• MetroKids (USA ISSN 1094-8503) **2161**
Metroland Live It! (CAN ISSN 1718-3758) **6992**
Metrolina Golf Magazine (USA ISSN 1080-3874) **8238**
Metroline (USA) **4376**
Metrolink Impact Study. Working Paper (GBR) **8504**
• ➤ Metrologia (GBR ISSN 0026-1394) **6404**
Metrologia i Systemy Pomiarowe/Metrology and Measuring Systems (POL ISSN 0860-8229) **6404**
Metrologie (ROM) **6404**
▼ • Metrologist (USA ISSN 1940-2988) **6404**
Metrologiya (RUS ISSN 0132-4713) **6404**
Metrology and Measuring Systems *see* Metrologia i Systemy Pomiarowe **6404**
Metrology Society of India. Journal *see* Mapan **6403**
▼ Metromom's Direct Connect (USA ISSN 1941-6857) **8875**
➤ Metron (ITA ISSN 0026-1424) **8388**
Metronome Magazine (USA) **6587**
• Metronomie (ITA ISSN 1123-4679) **4419**
Metronyt *see* Metro Nyt **8620**
Metroparent (Wauwatosa) (USA ISSN 1524-1467) **2161**
Metropol (CHE) **3958**
• Metropola (HRV ISSN 1845-9978) **3831**
▼ Metropoles (FRA ISSN 1957-7788) **450**
Metropolis *see* Dushi - Fanyue Rili **3824**
Metropolis *see* Dadushi (Nanshi Ban) **6288**
• Metropolis (USA ISSN 0279-4977) **450**
Metropolis B I B A *see* Dadushi **8858**
Metropolis M (NLD ISSN 0168-9053) **505**
Metropolist (GBR) **8733**
Metropolitan (USA) **2292**
Metropolitan Archivist (USA ISSN 1546-3125) **5032**
Metropolitan Area Wage Analysis (USA) **8672**
Metropolitan Atlanta Rapid Transit Authority, Department of Marketing and Communications Magazine *see* M A R T A Magazine **3980**
Metropolitan Atlanta Rapid Transit Authority, Department of Marketing and Communications Rider's Digest *see* M A R T A Rider's Digest **3980**
Metropolitan Beaumont (USA ISSN 0746-2786) **3981**
Metropolitan Chamber of Commerce and Industry, Dhaka. Chamber News (BGD) **1407**
The Metropolitan Complex (IRL ISSN 2009-0455) **505**
The Metropolitan Corporate Counsel (USA ISSN 1073-3000) **4733**
Metropolitan Domiciliary Care. Annual Report (AUS ISSN 1833-1963) **4107**
• The Metropolitan Economy (CAN ISSN 1708-5500) **7497**
Metropolitan Historic Structures Association. News (USA) **450**
• Metropolitan Home (USA ISSN 0273-2858) **4546**
Metropolitan Living (USA) **5077**
† Metropolitan Market Series (ITA) **8974**
Metropolitan Milwaukee Association of Commerce. Membership Directory & Buyers' Guide (Year) (USA) **2016**
Metropolitan Milwaukee Association of Commerce Milwaukee Commerce Hot-Line Annual Report *see* M M A C Milwaukee Commerce Hot-Line Annual Report **1430**
Metropolitan Milwaukee Economic Fact Book (USA) **1498**
• ➤ Metropolitan Museum Journal (BEL ISSN 0077-8958) **6529**
• Metropolitan Museum of Art. Board of Trustees. Annual Report of the Trustees (USA) **505**
• Metropolitan Museum of Art Bulletin (USA ISSN 0026-1521) **6529**

† The Metropolitan New York JobBank (USA ISSN 1098-979X) **8974**
• Metropolitan News - Enterprise (USA ISSN 0897-2281) **4876**
• Metropolitan Universities (USA ISSN 1047-8485) **2993**
Metropolitan Washington D.C. Area Labor Summary (USA) **1697**
Metropolregion Hamburg *see* Magazin der Metropolregion Hamburg **1830**
Metropoolregio Amsterdam in Beeld (NLD ISSN 1876-9675) **7287**
• Metro's Plus Business (USA) **30**
▼ • Metrosenses (USA ISSN 1937-5301) **3656**
MetroSports Boston (USA) **8187**
MetroSports New York (USA) **8187**
MetroSports Washington (USA) **8187**
MetroTrends (CAN) **7599**
MetroWest Jewish News *see* New Jersey Jewish News, United Jewish Communities of MetroWest NJ Edition **7727**
MetroWest Jewish Reporter (USA) **7726**
• ➤ Metsanduslikud Uurimused/Forestry Studies (EST ISSN 1406-9954) **3696**
• Metsanhoitaja (FIN ISSN 0355-7596) **3697**
• Metsantutkimus (FIN ISSN 1455-0393) **3697**
• Metsantutkimuslaitos. Tiedonanto/Finnish Forest Research Institute. Research Papers (FIN ISSN 0358-4283) **3697**
• Metsastaja (FIN ISSN 0047-6986) **2618**
Metsastys ja Kalastus (FIN ISSN 0026-1629) **8322**
• Metsatilastollinen Vuosikirja/Finnish Forest Research Institute. Yearbook of Forest Statistics/Skogsforskningsinstitutet. Skogsstatistisk Aarsbok (FIN ISSN 0359-968X) **3709**
• Metsatilastotiedote (Online) (FIN ISSN 1797-3074) **3709**
Metsatilastotiedote (Print) *see* Metsatilastotiedote (Online) **3709**
MetSoc International Symposium on Metals and the Environment. Proceedings Volume (CAN) **6326**
• ➤ Metstieteen Aikakauskirja (FIN ISSN 1455-2515) **3697**
Metta (USA) **7702**
Mettler-Toledo Magazin (DEU) **1898**
Metzger und Wurster/Boucher - Charcutier/Macellaio - Salumiere (CHE ISSN 0026-1645) **3656**
Der Metzgermeister (DEU ISSN 0005-7088) **3656**
Meu Dinheiro (BRA) **1639**
Meubel (NLD ISSN 0165-4543) **4560**
Le Meunier (CAN ISSN 0831-9421) **274**
• Meuse Economique (FRA ISSN 0755-7078) **1407**
Mex (CHE) **3958**
El Mexicalo (USA) **3550**
Mexican (USA ISSN 1934-5968) **4364**
Mexican Advertising Agencies Directory *see* Directorio M P M - Agencias y Anunciantes **24**
Mexican American Educators Association. Journal (USA) **3550**
Mexican American Grocers Association Zine (Los Angeles) *see* M A G A Zine (Los Angeles) **3680**
Mexican American Legal Defense and Educational Fund Newsletter *see* M A L D E F Newsletter **3548**
Mexican American National Association *see* M A N A **3548**
Mexican American Studies Series (USA) **3550**
Mexican American Sun (USA ISSN 0888-7764) **3550**
Mexican Audiovisual Media Rates & Data *see* Directorio M P M - Medios Audio-visuales **38**
Mexican Audiovisual Media Rates & Data *see* S R D S Mexican Audiovisual Media Rates & Data **39**
Mexican Chemical Industry Guide *see* Guia de la Industria Quimica **3244**
Mexican Chemical Production *see* Produccion Quimica Mexicana **3254**
Mexican Economy (MEX) **1498**
Mexican Electricity Review *see* I E E E. Revista Mexicana de Electricidad **3313**
Mexican Food & Feed Industry Guide *see* Guia de la Industria Alimentaria **3645**
Mexican Forecast (MEX) **1149**
Mexican Journal of Behavior Analysis *see* Revista Mexicana de Analisis de la Conducta **7404**
Mexican Journal of Educational Research *see* Revista Mexicana de Investigacion Educativa **2907**
Mexican Journal of Psychology *see* Revista Mexicana de Psicologia **7405**
➤ Mexican Law Review (MEX) **4733**
Mexican Print Media Rates & Data *see* Directorio M P M - Medios Impresos **38**
Mexican Print Media Rates & Data *see* S R D S Mexican Print Media Rates & Data **39**
Mexican Product Guide (USA ISSN 1055-9124) **2016**
Mexican Society for Soil Mechanics Meeting. Proceedings (MEX ISSN 0185-402X) **3278**
Mexican Stock Exchange. Annual Financial Facts and Figures (Year) *see* Bolsa Mexicana de Valores. Anuario Financiero (Year) **1215**
Mexican Stock Exchange. Capital Market Bulletin *see* Bolsa Mexicana de Valores. Boletin Bursatil Capitales **1613**
Mexican Stock Exchange. Facts and Figures *see* Indicadores Bursatiles **1242**
Mexican Stock Exchange. Financial Facts and Figures *see* Bolsa Mexicana de Valores. Indicadores Financieros **1215**
Mexican Stock Exchange. General Stockholders' Meetings Information *see* Bolsa Mexicana de Valores. Informacion Financiera Anual sobre Asambleas **1613**
Mexican Stock Exchange. Money & Metal Market Bulletin *see* Bolsa Mexicana de Valores. Boletin Bursatil Dinero y Metales **1613**
Mexican Stock Exchange. Monthly Financial Information *see* Bolsa Mexicana de Valores. Informacion Financiera Mensual **1613**
Mexican Stock Exchange. Quarterly Financial Information (MEX) **1639**
Mexican Stock Exchange. Statistics Summary *see* Bolsa Mexicana de Valores. Resumen Bursatil **1215**
• ➤ Mexican Studies/Estudios Mexicanos (USA ISSN 0742-9797) **4464**
Mexican War Journal (USA) **4303**
Mexicana Linda (MEX) **8875**
El Mexicano (USA) **3550**
Mexico *see* The P R S Group. Country Reports: Mexico **1508**
Mexico (Year) (USA ISSN 0884-1209) **8733**
• Mexico Alternativo (MEX ISSN 1563-7581) **3909**
Mexico and Central America Handbook (Year) (GBR ISSN 0965-5492) **8733**
• Mexico & N A F T A Report (North American Free Trade Agreement) (GBR ISSN 0968-2724) **1498**
Mexico. Archivo General de la Nacion. Boletin (MEX ISSN 0185-1926) **4303**
Mexico Banco de Datos *see* Mexico Data Bank **1252**
• Mexico Business Forecast Report (GBR ISSN 1744-8891) **1498**
Mexico C E O Total Compensation Report *see* Chief Executive Officers' Total Compensation Report - Mexico **1858**
Mexico. Centro de Informacion Tecnica y Documentacion. Indice Bibliografico (MEX) **631**
Mexico. Centro de Informacion Tecnica y Documentacion. Indice de Peliculas (MEX) **6518**
Mexico. Centro de Informacion Tecnica y Documentacion. Indice de Revistas. Seccion de Educacion y Comunicacion (MEX) **2934**
Mexico Chemicals Report (GBR ISSN 1749-2068) **6778**
Mexico City Daily Bulletin (MEX) **8733**
Mexico. Comision Nacional Bancaria. Boletin Estadistico (MEX ISSN 0185-1675) **1367**
Mexico. Comision Nacional de Seguros y Fianzas. Anuario Estadistico de Seguros (MEX ISSN 0303-4763) **4530**
Mexico Company Handbook (BRA) **1498**
• Mexico Consensus Economic Forecast/Consenso de Pronosticos Economicos (USA ISSN 1068-8307) **1498**
† Mexico Country Report (USA) **8974**
Mexico Data Bank/Mexico Banco de Datos (MEX) **1252**
• Mexico Defence & Security Report (GBR ISSN 1749-1533) **6434**
Mexico. Departamento de Investigacion de las Tradiciones Populares. Boletin (MEX) **347**
• Mexico Desconocido (MEX ISSN 0187-1560) **8733**
Mexico Freight Transport Report (GBR ISSN 1752-5969) **8504**
Mexico Holstein (MEX) **267**
• Mexico Hoy (MEX ISSN 1563-7018) **3909**
Mexico: Informacion Economica y Social (MEX ISSN 0188-8714) **1499**
Mexico Insight (MEX) **3909**
Mexico. Instituto Nacional de Estadistica, Geografia e Informatica. Encuesta Industrial Mensual (MEX ISSN 0186-0488) **1252**
Mexico. Instituto Nacional de Estadistica, Geografia e Informatica. Encuesta Nacional de Educacion Capacitacion y Empleo (MEX) **2934**
Mexico. Instituto Nacional de Estadistica, Geografia e Informatica. Estadisticas del Medio Ambiente (MEX) **3480**
Mexico. Instituto Nacional de Estadistica, Geografia e Informatica. Revista de Estadistica (MEX ISSN 0186-2707) **8388**
• Mexico Meeting and Incentive Planner (USA) **8733**
▼ • Mexico Mining Report (GBR ISSN 1755-8506) **6470**
The Mexico News (MEX ISSN 0462-1069) **8733**
Mexico NewsPak (USA ISSN 1068-2074) **1407**
Mexico Petrochemicals Report (GBR ISSN 1749-2343) **6778**
Mexico Quarterly Forecast Report *see* Mexico Business Forecast Report **1498**
Mexico. Secretaria de Educacion Publica. Informe de Labores (MEX ISSN 0188-0446) **2886**
• Mexico Service (USA ISSN 1044-6303) **1639**
Mexico Traveler (USA) **8733**
Mexico Vogue (MEX) **2258**
Mexicon (DEU ISSN 0720-5988) **348**
Meyers Modeblatt (CHE ISSN 0026-1866) **2258**
Meyibo (MEX ISSN 0187-702X) **348**
Meying Lao (LAO) **8875**
† Meyler and Peck's Drug-Induced Diseases (NLD ISSN 0167-5885) **8974**
• Meyler's Side Effects of Drugs (NLD ISSN 0376-7396) **6861**
➤ Meyniana (DEU ISSN 0076-7689) **2755**
Mezdunarodnoe Agentstvo po Atomnoj Energii Bulleten' *see* I A E A Bulletin **3168**
Mezdunarodnoe Agentstvo po Atomnoj Energii. Doklady po Bezopasnosti *see* International Atomic Energy Agency. Safety Reports Series **3169**
Mezdunarodnoe Migracionnoe Pravo *see* International Migration Law **4932**
Mezdunarodnyi Komitet po Kontrolu nad Narkotikami. Doklad za (God) *see* International Narcotics Control Board. Report for (Year) **6850**
Mezdunarodnyj Valutnyj Fond. Voprosy Ekonomiki *see* International Monetary Fund. Economic Issues **1571**
Mezhdu Koshkoi i Sobakoi (RUS) **4980**
Mezhdunarodanaya Organizatsiya Grazhdanskoi Aviatsii. Assambleya. Doklady i Protokoly Ispolnitel'nogo Komiteta *see* International Civil Aviation Organization. Assembly. Reports and Minutes of the Executive Committee **8545**
Mezhdunarodnaya Akademiya Kholoda. Vestnik (RUS ISSN 1606-4313) **4123**
Mezhdunarodnaya Evreiskaya Gazeta (RUS) **3550**
Mezhdunarodnaya Organizatsiya Grazhdanskoi Aviatsii. Assambleya. Doklady i Protokoly Administrativnoi Komissii *see* International Civil Aviation Organization. Assembly. Report and Minutes of the Administrative Commission **8545**
Mezhdunarodnaya Organizatsiya Grazhdanskoi Aviatsii. Assambleya. Doklady i Protokoly Tekhnicheskoi Komissii *see* International Civil Aviation Organization. Assembly. Report of the Technical Commission **60**
Mezhdunarodnaya Organizatsiya Grazhdanskoi Aviatsii. Assambleya. Doklady i Protokoly Yuridicheskoi Komissii *see* International Civil Aviation Organization. Assembly. Report and Minutes of the Legal Commission **8545**
Mezhdunarodnaya Organizatsiya Grazhdanskoi Aviatsii. Assambleya. Rezolyutsii i Protokoly Plenarnogo Zasedaniya *see* International Civil Aviation Organization. Assembly. Minutes of the Plenary Meetings **8545**
Mezhdunarodnaya Organizatsiya Grazhdanskoi Aviatsii. Statisticheskii Sbornik. Seriya AF. Aeroportnoe i Marshrutnoe Oborudovanie. Finansovye Izlozheniya Dannykh po Perevozkam *see* International Civil Aviation Organization. Digests of Statistics. Series AF. Airport and Route Facilities. Financial Data and Summary Traffic Data **8526**
Mezhdunarodnaya Organizatsiya Grazhdanskoi Aviatsii. Statisticheskii Sbornik. Seriya OFOD. Nachalnyi i Konechnyi Punkty Poleta *see* International Civil Aviation Organization. Digests of Statistics. Series OFOD. On-Flight Origin and Destination **8526**
• Mezhdunarodnaya Zhizn' (RUS ISSN 0130-9625) **7252**
Mezhdunarodni Otnosheniia (BGR ISSN 0324-1092) **4244**
Mezhdunarodnyi Agropromyshlennyi Zhurnal (RUS ISSN 0235-7801) **136**
Mezhdunarodnyi Forum po Informatsii/International Forum on Information and Documentation (RUS ISSN 0203-6460) **5032**
Mezhdunarodnyi Spravochnyi Registr Istochnikov Informatsii. Infoterra *see* International Directory of Sources. Infoterra **3441**
Mezhdunarodnyi Zhurnal Radiatsionnoi Meditsiny (UKR) **6203**
Mezhotraslevaya Informatsionnaya Sluzhba (RUS) **3210**
Mezinarodni Politika (CZE ISSN 0543-7962) **7252**
➤ Mezinarodni Vztahy (CZE ISSN 0323-1844) **7252**
Mezlim (USA) **6742**
Mezogazdasagi Technika (HUN ISSN 0026-1890) **212**
Mezpravitel'stvennaja Okeanograficeskaja Komissija. Mehaniceskaja Serija *see* Intergovernmental Oceanographic Commission. Technical Series **2808**
Mezzi Corazzati (ITA ISSN 1128-6806) **6434**
Mezzocielo (ITA ISSN 1720-2892) **7985**
Mfanyakazi/Worker (TZA ISSN 0856-390X) **3961**
MGZN (NLD ISSN 1874-0499) **1407**
MHNH (ESP ISSN 1578-4517) **566**
• MHSalud (CRI ISSN 1659-097X) **6231**
Mi (HRV ISSN 1331-8837) **7807**
▼ Mi Bebe (ARG ISSN 1851-6335) **2161**
Mi Bebe y Yo (ESP ISSN 1135-450X) **2161**
Mi Biblioteca (ESP ISSN 1699-3411) **631**
Mi Cartera de Inversion (ESP ISSN 1698-1952) **1639**
Mi Casa (ESP ISSN 1139-7616) **4546**
Mi Casa Extra (ESP ISSN 1139-7624) **4546**
Mi Doctor (USA) **5679**
Mi Gente (CAN ISSN 1481-1804) **3550**
Mi Gente (USA) **3550**
Mi Jardin (ESP ISSN 1133-9632) **3743**
Mi Jardin Extra (ESP ISSN 1575-2607) **3743**
Mi-Mizrah Umi-Ma'arav (ISR) **7726**
➤ Mi Mladi (HRV ISSN 0026-1939) **2202**
Mi Na Shishang (Guoji Zhongwen Ban) *see* Mina **8875**
• Mi2N (USA ISSN 1526-2324) **6587**
• Mia (ARG ISSN 0328-4239) **8875**
Mia (ESP) **8875**
La Mia 4 x 4 (ITA ISSN 1721-3932) **8590**
La Mia Auto (ITA ISSN 1128-3653) **8590**
La Mia Barca (ITA ISSN 1723-3658) **8278**
Mia Belleza (ESP) **8875**
La Mia Boutique (ITA ISSN 1121-1741) **2258**
La Mia Casa (ITA ISSN 1123-3508) **4546**
† La Mia Casa (Formello) (ITA ISSN 1970-9455) **8974**
Mia Cocina *see* Mia Extra **4364**
Mia Cocina (ESP) **4364**
Mia Decoracion (ESP) **4546**
Mia Extra (ARG ISSN 0328-4549) **4364**
La Mia Piscina (ITA ISSN 1825-4195) **1024**
La Mia Quattro per Quattro *see* La Mia 4 x 4 **8590**
Miami! (FRA ISSN 1951-3496) **4364**
Miami (Miami, 1994) (USA) **3981**
▼ • Miami (Miami, 2007) (USA) **5077**
Miami Art Museum News *see* M A M News **6528**
Miami Business *see* SouthFloridaC E O Magazine **1178**
• Miami Daily Business Review (USA ISSN 1070-6437) **1149**
Miami Design and Architectural Review *see* Miami Design & Architectural Review **4546**
Miami Design & Architectural Review (USA) **4546**
Miami Hurricane (USA ISSN 1064-6442) **2292**
Miami Living (USA ISSN 1547-1756) **8734**
Miami Meanderings (USA ISSN 0889-3640) **3775**
Miami Mensual/Miami Monthly *see* Miami Monthly **3981**
Miami Metro *see* Miami Metro City Guide **3981**
Miami Metro City Guide (USA ISSN 1538-229X) **3981**
Miami Model Agency Directory (USA) **2258**
Miami Monthly (USA) **3981**
Miami Skyline (USA) **7599**
The Miami Student (USA) **2292**
• Miami Times (USA ISSN 0739-0319) **3550**
Miami Today (USA ISSN 0889-2296) **3981**
Miamian (USA) **2292**
• Mian Fangzhi Jishu/Cotton Textile Technology (CHN ISSN 1000-7415) **8455**
• Mianyixue Zazhi/Journal of Immunology (CHN ISSN 1000-8861) **5679**
Miata *see* MazdaSport **8590**
MiBiz (USA ISSN 1933-0618) **1149**
MiBiz Southwest *see* MiBiz **1149**
MiBiz West *see* MiBiz **1149**
M!CE Travel! (NLD ISSN 1574-9487) **6281**
Michael (CAN ISSN 0317-8498) **7807**
Michael (ISR ISSN 0334-4150) **3550**
• Michael Gray C P A's Option Alert (Certified Public Accountant) (USA ISSN 1931-2768) **1639**
• Michael Gray C P A's Real Estate Tax Letter (Certified Public Accountant) (USA ISSN 1930-0387) **1296**
• Michael Gray C P A's Tax & Business Insight (Certified Public Accountant) (USA ISSN 1930-9023) **1935**
Michael Murphy's Technology Investing *see* Technology Investing **1655**
Michael Shapiro's Internet Travel Planner *see* Internet Travel Planner **8724**
Michel-Briefmarken-Kataloge (DEU ISSN 0076-7727) **6897**
Michel-Rundschau (DEU ISSN 0026-198X) **6897**
Michelin Green Guide Series: Alpes du Nord (FRA) **8734**
Michelin Green Guide Series: Alpes du Sud (FRA) **8734**
Michelin Green Guide Series: Alps (of France) (FRA) **8734**
Michelin Green Guide Series: Alsace et Lorraine (FRA) **8734**
Michelin Green Guide Series: Alsace Lorraine Champagne (FRA) **8734**
Michelin Green Guide Series: Antilles: Guadeloupe - Martinique (FRA) **8734**
Michelin Green Guide Series: Atlantic Coast (FRA) **8734**
Michelin Green Guide Series: Austria (FRA) **8734**
Michelin Green Guide Series: Auvergne (FRA) **8734**
Michelin Green Guide Series: Auvergne - The Rhone Valley (FRA) **8734**
Michelin Green Guide Series: Belgium (FRA) **8734**
Michelin Green Guide Series: Berlin (FRA) **8734**
Michelin Green Guide Series: Berry-Limousin (FRA) **8734**
Michelin Green Guide Series: Bourgogne (FRA) **8734**
Michelin Green Guide Series: Brittany (FRA) **8734**
Michelin Green Guide Series: Brussels (FRA) **8734**
Michelin Green Guide Series: Burgundy - Jura (FRA) **8734**
Michelin Green Guide Series: California (FRA) **8734**
Michelin Green Guide Series: Canada (FRA) **8734**
Michelin Green Guide Series: Catalogne (FRA) **8734**
Michelin Green Guide Series: Cataluna (FRA) **8734**
Michelin Green Guide Series: Champagne-Ardennes (FRA) **8734**
Michelin Green Guide Series: Chateaux of the Loire (FRA) **8734**
Michelin Green Guide Series: Chicago (FRA) **8734**
Michelin Green Guide Series: Corse (FRA) **8734**
Michelin Green Guide Series: Cote d'Azur (FRA) **8734**
Michelin Green Guide Series: Disneyland Paris (FRA) **8734**
Michelin Green Guide Series: Dordogne Berry Limousin (FRA) **8734**
Michelin Green Guide Series: Europe (FRA) **8734**
Michelin Green Guide Series: Flandres, Artois, Picardie (FRA) **8734**
Michelin Green Guide Series: Florence et Toscane (FRA) **8734**
Michelin Green Guide Series: Florida (FRA) **8734**
Michelin Green Guide Series: France (FRA) **8734**

Title

Michelin Green Guide Series: French Riviera (FRA) **8734**
Michelin Green Guide Series: Germany (FRA) **8734**
Michelin Green Guide Series: Gorges du Tarn (FRA) **8734**
Michelin Green Guide Series: Great Britain (FRA) **8734**
Michelin Green Guide Series: Greece (FRA) **8734**
Michelin Green Guide Series: Hollande (FRA) **8734**
Michelin Green Guide Series: Ile-de-France (FRA) **8734**
Michelin Green Guide Series: Ireland (FRA) **8734**
Michelin Green Guide Series: Italia (FRA) **8734**
Michelin Green Guide Series: Italy (FRA) **8734**
Michelin Green Guide Series: Jura - Franche Comte (FRA) **8734**
Michelin Green Guide Series: London (FRA) **8734**
Michelin Green Guide Series: Maroc (FRA) **8735**
Michelin Green Guide Series: Mexico, Guatemala, Belize (FRA) **8735**
Michelin Green Guide Series: Netherlands (FRA) **8735**
Michelin Green Guide Series: New England (FRA) **8735**
Michelin Green Guide Series: New York (City) (FRA) **8735**
Michelin Green Guide Series: New York, New Jersey, Pennsylvania (FRA) **8735**
Michelin Green Guide Series: Normandie, Contentin (FRA) **8735**
Michelin Green Guide Series: Normandie, Vallee de la Seine (FRA) **8735**
Michelin Green Guide Series: Normandy (FRA) **8735**
Michelin Green Guide Series: Northern France and Paris Region (FRA) **8735**
Michelin Green Guide Series: Paris (FRA) **8735**
Michelin Green Guide Series: Perigord-Quercy (FRA) **8735**
Michelin Green Guide Series: Poitou-Vendee-Charentes (FRA) **8735**
Michelin Green Guide Series: Portugal (FRA) **8735**
Michelin Green Guide Series: Provence (FRA) **8735**
Michelin Green Guide Series: Pyrenees Aquitaine (FRA) **8735**
Michelin Green Guide Series: Pyrenees Roussillon (FRA) **8735**
Michelin Green Guide Series: Quebec (FRA) **8735**
Michelin Green Guide Series: Rome (FRA) **8735**
Michelin Green Guide Series: San Francisco (FRA) **8735**
Michelin Green Guide Series: Scandinavia - Finland (FRA) **8735**
Michelin Green Guide Series: Scotland (FRA) **8735**
Michelin Green Guide Series: Sicily (FRA) **8735**
Michelin Green Guide Series: Spain (FRA) **8735**
Michelin Green Guide Series: Switzerland (FRA) **8735**
Michelin Green Guide Series: Thailand (FRA) **8735**
Michelin Green Guide Series: Tuscany (FRA) **8735**
Michelin Green Guide Series: Vallee du Rhone (FRA) **8735**
Michelin Green Guide Series: Venice (FRA) **8735**
Michelin Green Guide Series: Vienna (FRA) **8735**
Michelin Green Guide Series: Wales (FRA) **8735**
Michelin Green Guide Series: Washington, D.C. (FRA) **8735**
Michelin Green Guide Series: West Country of England - Channel Islands (FRA) **8735**
Michelin in Your Pocket Series: Algarve, Portugal (FRA) **8735**
Michelin in Your Pocket Series: Amsterdam (FRA) **8735**
Michelin in Your Pocket Series: Barcelona (FRA) **8735**
Michelin in Your Pocket Series: Berlin (FRA) **8735**
Michelin in Your Pocket Series: Brittany (FRA) **8735**
Michelin in Your Pocket Series: Budapest, Hungary (FRA) **8735**
Michelin in Your Pocket Series: Florida (FRA) **8735**
Michelin in Your Pocket Series: Greek Islands of the Aegean (FRA) **8735**
Michelin in Your Pocket Series: Istanbul, Turkey (FRA) **8735**
Michelin in Your Pocket Series: Italy Lake District (FRA) **8735**
Michelin in Your Pocket Series: Lisbon (FRA) **8735**
Michelin in Your Pocket Series: Loire Valley (FRA) **8735**
Michelin in Your Pocket Series: London (FRA) **8735**
Michelin in Your Pocket Series: Madrid (FRA) **8735**
Michelin in Your Pocket Series: Morocco (FRA) **8736**
Michelin in Your Pocket Series: New Orleans (FRA) **8736**
Michelin in Your Pocket Series: New York (FRA) **8736**
Michelin in Your Pocket Series: Paris (FRA) **8736**
Michelin in Your Pocket Series: Prague (FRA) **8736**
Michelin in Your Pocket Series: Rome (FRA) **8736**
Michelin in Your Pocket Series: Sicily (FRA) **8736**
Michelin in Your Pocket Series: South of France - Riviera (FRA) **8736**
Michelin in Your Pocket Series: Southern Spain (FRA) **8736**
Michelin in Your Pocket Series: Thailand (FRA) **8736**
Michelin in Your Pocket Series: Tuscany (FRA) **8736**
Michelin in Your Pocket Series: Venice (FRA) **8736**
Michelin in Your Pocket Series: Vienna (FRA) **8736**
Michelin Red Guide Series: Benelux (FRA) **8736**
Michelin Red Guide Series: Camping, Caravaning in France (FRA) **8736**
Michelin Red Guide Series: Deutschland (FRA) **8736**
Michelin Red Guide Series: Espana & Portugal (FRA) **8736**
Michelin Red Guide Series: Europe (Main Cities) (FRA) **8736**
Michelin Red Guide Series: France (FRA) **8736**
Michelin Red Guide Series: Great Britain and Ireland (FRA) **8736**
Michelin Red Guide Series: Ireland (FRA) **8736**
Michelin Red Guide Series: Italia (FRA) **8736**
Michelin Red Guide Series: London (FRA) **8736**
Michelin Red Guide Series: Paris et Environs (FRA) **8736**
Michelin Red Guide Series: Portugal (FRA) **8736**
Michelin Red Guide Series: Switzerland (FRA) **8736**
Michelin Voyager Pratique (FRA ISSN 1772-5100) **8736**
• Michie on Banks and Banking (USA) **1367**
• Michie's Alabama Criminal Code Annotated (USA) **4894**
• Michie's Alabama Motor Vehicle Laws Annotated with Commentaries (USA ISSN 1536-5786) **8504**
Michie's Annotated Rules of New Mexico (USA ISSN 1931-0447) **4733**
• Michie's Jurisprudence of Virginia and West Virginia (USA) **4733**
Michigan 4-H Today (USA ISSN 1049-0175) **136**
• ➤ Michigan Academician (USA ISSN 0026-2005) **4465**
• Michigan Academy of Science, Arts, and Letters. Academy Letter (USA ISSN 0047-7052) **2993**
Michigan Academy of Science, Arts, and Letters. Papers *see* Michigan Academician **4465**
Michigan Airport Directory (USA) **8548**
Michigan: All-Industries *see* Harris Directory. Michigan All-Industries **2000**
Michigan Alumnus (USA ISSN 0746-2565) **2292**
Michigan Appeals Reports *see* Michigan Court of Appeals. Court Opinions **4733**
Michigan Apple Report (USA) **203**
➤ Michigan Archaeologist (USA ISSN 0543-9728) **406**
Michigan Archival Association Open Entry *see* M A A Open Entry **5030**
Michigan Association of School Administrators Leader *see* The M A S A Leader **3027**
Michigan Association of School Boards, Inc. Journal *see* M A S B Journal **3027**
• Michigan Association of Secondary School Principals' Bulletin (USA ISSN 0026-2013) **2886**
➤ Michigan Association of Speech Communication Journal (USA ISSN 1081-4086) **2886**
▼ Michigan Ave. (USA) **5077**
Michigan Aviation (USA ISSN 0539-8703) **65**
• Michigan Banker (USA ISSN 1044-1948) **1499**
Michigan Bankers Association Banking *see* M B A Banking **1366**
• Michigan Bar Journal (USA ISSN 0164-3576) **4733**
Michigan Beverage Journal *see* The Beverage Journal **599**
➤ Michigan Botanist (USA ISSN 0026-203X) **801**
Michigan Builder (USA) **1024**
• Michigan Business Credit Directory (USA) **2016**
• Michigan Business Directory (USA ISSN 1047-1790) **2016**
• The Michigan Business Law Journal (USA ISSN 0899-9651) **4733**
Michigan Catholic (USA) **7807**
Michigan Chess (USA) **8187**
Michigan Christian Advocate (USA ISSN 0026-2072) **7767**
Michigan Christmas Tree Journal (USA) **3697**
Michigan Cities & Counties Graphic Performance Analysis (USA ISSN 1935-5947) **7481**
Michigan Cities and Counties Graphic Performance Analysis *see* Michigan Cities & Counties Graphic Performance Analysis **7481**
• Michigan Citizen (USA ISSN 1072-2041) **3550**
Michigan Civil Procedure (USA ISSN 1931-2725) **4837**
Michigan. Civil Rights Commission. Annual Report (USA) **7212**
Michigan Civil Rights Commission Newsletter (USA ISSN 0047-7087) **7212**
Michigan. Civil Service Department. Annual Work Force Report (USA) **1697**
Michigan Construction Liens (USA) **1024**
• Michigan Construction News Weekly, Covering the Southern Peninsula Beyond Detroit (USA ISSN 1087-092X) **1024**
• Michigan Constructor (USA) **1024**
Michigan Contractor and Builder *see* Michigan Contractor & Builder **1024**
• Michigan Contractor & Builder (USA ISSN 1553-3816) **1024**
• Michigan Corporate Forms (USA) **4876**
Michigan Corporation Law with Federal Tax Analysis (USA) **4876**
Michigan Country Lines (USA) **3981**
• Michigan Court of Appeals. Court Opinions (USA) **4733**
Michigan Court of Appeals. Michigan Appeals Reports *see* Michigan Court of Appeals. Court Opinions **4733**
Michigan Court Rules Annotated (USA ISSN 1533-726X) **4956**
• The Michigan Daily (USA ISSN 0745-967X) **2292**
Michigan Dairy Line (USA) **267**
Michigan Deer & Turkey Show Preview (USA) **8322**
Michigan Dental Association. Journal (USA ISSN 0026-2102) **5855**
Michigan Dental Hygienists' Association. Bulletin (USA ISSN 0746-5564) **5855**
Michigan. Department of Social Services. Assistance Payments Statistics (USA) **8055**
Michigan. Department of Social Services. Program Statistics (USA ISSN 0093-7835) **8083**
• Michigan. Department of State Police. Annual Report (USA) **2660**
• ➤ Michigan Discussions in Anthropology (USA ISSN 0193-7804) **348**
Michigan Education Association Voice of Action *see* M E A Voice of Action **2884**
▼ • Michigan Employment Law (USA ISSN 1934-158X) **1697**
• Michigan Employment Law Letter (USA ISSN 1046-9109) **4733**
Michigan. Employment Security Commission. Annual Planning Report (USA) **1697**
Michigan Entomological Society. Newsletter (USA ISSN 1554-2092) **854**
Michigan Environmental Report (USA ISSN 0747-735X) **3452**
• Michigan Estate Planning, Will Drafting and Estate Administration Forms (USA) **4904**
Michigan Facts (USA ISSN 1051-7146) **3121**
• ➤ Michigan Family Review (USA ISSN 1094-0952) **8121**
Michigan Farm News (USA ISSN 1063-598X) **136**
Michigan Farm News Rural Living *see* Benefits Advisor **95**
• Michigan Farmer (USA ISSN 0026-2153) **136**
• ➤ Michigan Feminist Studies (USA ISSN 1055-856X) **8875**
Michigan Florist (USA ISSN 0026-217X) **3757**
Michigan Food News (USA ISSN 0047-7117) **3656**
The Michigan Front Page (USA ISSN 1546-4466) **3550**
Michigan Fruit & Vegetable Report (USA) **203**
Michigan. Geological Survey Division. Bulletin (USA) **2755**
Michigan. Geological Survey Division. Report of Investigation (USA ISSN 0543-8497) **2755**
Michigan Golfer (USA ISSN 1071-2313) **8238**
Michigan Health Sciences Libraries Association News *see* M H S L A News **5030**
• ➤ Michigan Historical Review (Mt. Pleasant) (USA ISSN 0890-1686) **4303**
• Michigan History for Kids (USA ISSN 1550-6053) **2202**
Michigan History Magazine (USA) **4303**
The Michigan Independent (USA) **2292**
Michigan Information and Research Service, Inc. Legislative Report *see* M I R S Legislative Report **7152**
▼ • Michigan Journal of Business (USA ISSN 1941-5745) **1149**
• ➤ Michigan Journal of Community Service Learning (USA ISSN 1076-0180) **2994**
• Michigan Journal of Counseling (USA ISSN 1944-821X) **2886**
Michigan Journal of Economics (USA ISSN 1090-8919) **1149**
• Michigan Journal of Gender & Law (USA ISSN 1095-8835) **4733**
• Michigan Journal of International Law (USA ISSN 1052-2867) **4935**
• Michigan Journal of Political Science (USA ISSN 0733-4486) **7154**
• Michigan Journal of Public Health (USA ISSN 1937-2515) **7531**
• Michigan Journal of Race & Law (USA ISSN 1095-2721) **3550**
Michigan Labor Market News (USA) **1697**
• ➤ Michigan Law Review (USA ISSN 0026-2234) **4733**
• Michigan Lawyers Weekly (USA ISSN 0897-618X) **4733**
Michigan Librarian (USA ISSN 0884-9919) **5032**
Michigan Library Association Forum *see* M L A Forum **5030**
Michigan Links Magazine (USA ISSN 1531-1732) **8238**
Michigan Lutheran (USA) **7767**
Michigan Magazine (USA ISSN 1081-8502) **4303**
Michigan Manual (USA ISSN 0091-1933) **7453**
• Michigan Manufacturers Directory (USA ISSN 0736-2889) **2017**
Michigan: Manufacturing *see* Harris Directory. Michigan Manufacturing **2000**
Michigan Manufacturing Insight (USA ISSN 1936-8860) **1898**
Michigan Master Plumber & Mechanical Contractor (USA) **4123**
• ➤ Michigan Mathematical Journal (USA ISSN 0026-2285) **5517**
Michigan Medical Law Report (USA) **4733**
• ➤ Michigan Medicine (USA ISSN 0026-2293) **5679**
▼ Michigan Meetings + Events (USA) **6281**
▼ Michigan Merit (USA ISSN 1938-9051) **1024**
Michigan Milk Messenger (USA ISSN 0026-2315) **267**
➤ Michigan Monographs in Chinese Studies (USA ISSN 1081-9053) **4185**
Michigan Monographs in Japanese Studies (USA ISSN 1557-430X) **5333**
• Michigan Motor Vehicle Laws (USA) **4733**
▼ • Michigan Movie Magazine (USA ISSN 1949-4122) **6507**
Michigan Municipal League. Municipal Legal Briefs (USA ISSN 0076-8014) **7497**
Michigan Municipal Review *see* Review (Ann Arbor) **7501**
Michigan Natural Resources Magazine (USA ISSN 0275-8180) **2619**
▼ Michigan Nonstandard Jury Instructions. Civil (USA ISSN 1942-0277) **4733**
▼ • Michigan Nonstandard Jury Instructions. Criminal (USA ISSN 1942-0285) **4894**
Michigan Notary Law Primer (USA) **4733**
Michigan Nurse (USA ISSN 0026-2366) **5970**
Michigan Occupational Safety and Health Act News *see* M I O S H A News **6681**
Michigan Oil & Gas News (USA) **6778**
The Michigan Optometrist (USA ISSN 1071-1627) **6046**
Michigan Out-of-Doors (USA ISSN 0026-2382) **2619**
• Michigan Outdoor News (USA ISSN 1529-5486) **8322**
Michigan Overseas Veteran (USA ISSN 1067-0661) **6434**
Michigan Papers in Japanese Studies (USA ISSN 0894-7112) **4186**
Michigan Papers on South and Southeast Asia (USA ISSN 0160-354X) **4186**
Michigan Penal Code (USA) **4894**
Michigan Pharmacist (USA ISSN 1081-6089) **6861**
Michigan Plumbing & Mechanical Contractor (USA) **4123**
Michigan Police Chiefs Newsletter (USA) **2660**
Michigan Postsecondary Admissions & Financial Assistance Handbook (USA ISSN 0363-7433) **2960**
Michigan Probate Code (USA) **4904**
Michigan Probate Laws and Rules (USA ISSN 1931-1044) **4904**
• Michigan Public Employee Reporter (USA) **4733**
Michigan Public Employment Library on CD-ROM *see* Michigan Public Employee Reporter **4733**
Michigan Quarter Horse Journal (USA) **8294**
• ➤ Michigan Quarterly Review (USA ISSN 0026-2420) **5227**
➤ Michigan Reading Journal (USA ISSN 0047-7125) **5201**
• Michigan Real Estate Forms (USA) **7599**
Michigan Reports *see* West's Jury Verdicts. Michigan Reports **4969**
• Michigan Restaurateur (USA ISSN 0892-8231) **4394**
Michigan Review (USA) **2292**
Michigan Roads and Construction (USA) **3278**
Michigan Runner (USA ISSN 0279-1773) **8322**
Michigan School Directory *see* M D R's School Directory. Michigan **2959**
Michigan Sea Grant College Program. Technical Report (USA) **689**
Michigan Sentencing Guidelines Manual (USA ISSN 1535-5160) **4956**
Michigan Series in English for Academic & Professional Purposes (USA) **5151**
Michigan Slavic Contributions (USA ISSN 0076-8103) **5333**
Michigan Slavic Materials (USA ISSN 0543-9930) **5333**
Michigan Slavic Translations (USA) **5333**
Michigan Snowmobile News (USA ISSN 0193-2632) **8322**
Michigan Snowmobiler (USA ISSN 0746-2298) **8322**
Michigan Sociological Review (USA ISSN 1934-7111) **8121**
Michigan Sportsman (USA ISSN 0539-8908) **8322**
Michigan. State Court Administrator. Annual Report (USA ISSN 0098-7875) **4824**
Michigan State Employees' Retirement System (USA ISSN 0092-9212) **1697**
Michigan State Housing Development Authority. Annual Report (USA) **4419**
Michigan State Journal of International Law (USA ISSN 1556-6374) **4935**
• ➤ Michigan State Law Review (USA) **4733**
Michigan State University. Agricultural Economics Report (USA ISSN 0065-4442) **203**
Michigan State University. Agricultural Experiment Station. Research Report (USA ISSN 0543-8233) **136**
Michigan State University Alumni Magazine *see* M S U Alumni Magazine **2290**
Michigan State University. Asian Studies Center. Occasional Papers: South Asia Series (USA ISSN 0076-8138) **4186**
Michigan State University - Department of Energy Plant Research Laboratory. Annual Report *see* M S U - D O E Plant Research Laboratory. Annual Report **3141**
Michigan State University. Institute of Water Research. Annual Report (USA ISSN 0271-9606) **8829**
Michigan State University. Institute of Water Research. Technical Reports (USA ISSN 0580-9746) **8829**
Michigan State University Journal of Medicine and Law *see* Journal of Medicine and Law **4704**
Michigan State University. Latin American Studies Center. Monograph Series (USA ISSN 0076-8189) **4303**
Michigan State University. Latin American Studies Center. Research Reports (USA ISSN 0076-8200) **4303**

DIRECTORY 2010 MID-MONTH GLOBAL FINANCIAL REPORT 10611

➤ Michigan State University. Museum Publications. Anthropological Series. (USA) **348**
Michigan State University. Museum Publications. Cultural Series (USA ISSN 0076-8235) **6529**
Michigan State University. Museum Publications. Folk Art Series (USA) **505**
Michigan State University. Museum Publications. Paleontological Series (USA ISSN 0198-8565) **6726**
Michigan State University. National Superconducting Cyclotron Laboratory (Publication) (USA) **7068**
Michigan State University. School of Labor and Industrial Relations. Newsletter (USA ISSN 0036-6706) **1697**
Michigan Studies in the Humanities (USA) **5333**
Michigan Super Lawyers (USA ISSN 1939-6945) **4733**
• Michigan Tails (USA ISSN 1945-6719) **6811**
Michigan Tax Lawyer (USA ISSN 0899-2460) **4734**
Michigan Teacher (USA) **3073**
Michigan Tech Alumnus (USA) **2292**
• ➤ Michigan Telecommunications & Technology Law Review (USA ISSN 1528-8625) **4734**
Michigan Times (USA) **2292**
• Michigan Today (USA ISSN 0041-9850) **2292**
Michigan Township News (USA ISSN 1542-0957) **7497**
Michigan Trucking Today (USA) **8672**
• Michigan War Studies Review (USA ISSN 1930-045X) **6434**
Michigan Water Environment Matters (USA) **8829**
• Michigan Web Journal (USA) **1149**
Michigan, Wisconsin TourBook *see* TourBook: Michigan, Wisconsin **8762**
Michigan Workers' Comp Reporter (USA) **4515**
Michigan Workers' Compensation Law Reporter (USA ISSN 0899-9090) **4515**
Michigan's Most Eligible Bachelors and Bachelorettes (USA) **7943**
Michigan's Oil and Gas Fields: Annual Statistical Summary (USA ISSN 0085-3429) **6800**
Michiru Sun (MWI) **3906**
Michmanim (ISR ISSN 0334-7311) **406**
• Michnet News (USA) **2501**
Micimacko Magazin (HUN ISSN 1418-141X) **2202**
Mickey (BRA ISSN 0104-2114) **2202**
Mickey *see* Miki **2202**
Mickey Max! (CZE ISSN 1801-6308) **2202**
• Mickey News (USA ISSN 1932-5665) **4980**
Mickey Parade *see* Mickey Parade Geant **2202**
Mickey Parade Geant (FRA ISSN 1631-5227) **2202**
Micky Maus *see* Walt Disney's Micky Maus **2221**
Micmac Maliseet Nation News *see* Micmac-Maliseet Nations News **3550**
Micmac-Maliseet Nations News (CAN ISSN 1184-6402) **3550**
Mico (TUR) **2202**
• ➤ Micologia Aplicada International (USA ISSN 1534-2581) **801**
Micologia e Vegetazione Mediterranea (ITA ISSN 0394-2597) **801**
Micologia Italiana (ITA ISSN 0390-0460) **801**
Micomlife (JPN ISSN 0285-6425) **2431**
• Micro (CAN ISSN 1198-3558) **1149**
Micro Actuel (FRA ISSN 1773-6064) **2431**
• Micro & Macro Marketing (ITA ISSN 1121-4228) **1835**
• ➤ Micro and Nano Letters (GBR ISSN 1750-0443) **3210**
▼ • ➤ Micro and Nanosystems (NLD ISSN 1876-4029) **2454**
Micro-Cap Reporter (CAN ISSN 1712-7513) **1639**
Micro-Capitalization Reporter *see* Micro-Cap Reporter **1639**
Micro Computer Mart (GBR ISSN 0956-3881) **2572**
Micro Control Journal (CAN ISSN 0849-8180) **2540**
Micro Dingo (FRA ISSN 1628-1632) **2578**
Micro Electro Mechanical Systems Conference. Proceedings (USA) **2466**
Micro Electronics *see* Xing Dianzi Keji **3116**
Micro Hebdo (FRA ISSN 1276-549X) **2578**
Micro O L M (Occupations in the Labor Market) (USA) **1697**
† Micro P C (FRA ISSN 0765-2887) **8974**
Micro Photo Video (FRA ISSN 1771-4036) **6971**
Micro-Portable Etudiant (FRA ISSN 1778-1515) **2431**
Micro Portable Magazine (FRA ISSN 1775-8602) **2578**
Micro Pratique (FRA ISSN 1253-1022) **2431**
Micro Simulateur (FRA ISSN 1163-4561) **2431**
Micro Stars Magazine *see* MicroStars Magazine **2202**
Micro Systemes (FRA ISSN 0183-5084) **2572**
• Micro Technology Europe (GBR ISSN 1352-7312) **2524**
Micro Technology Europe: Media Pack (Year) *see* Micro Technology Europe **2524**
• Microbanker Banking Technology Strategies Newsletter (USA) **1393**
• The Microbanking Bulletin (USA ISSN 1934-3884) **1367**
• Microbe (USA ISSN 1558-7452) **891**
Microbe Magic (IRL ISSN 1649-6000) **5679**
• Microbes and Environments/Japanese Society of Microbial Ecology. Bulletin (JPN ISSN 1342-6311) **891**
• ➤ Microbes and Infection (FRA ISSN 1286-4579) **891**
▼ • ➤ Microbial Biotechnology (GBR) **768**
• ➤ Microbial Cell Factories (GBR ISSN 1475-2859) **834**
• ➤ Microbial Drug Resistance (USA ISSN 1076-6294) **5679**
Microbial Ecology *see* Biseibutsu no Seitai **882**
• ➤ Microbial Ecology (USA ISSN 0095-3628) **891**
• ➤ Microbial Ecology in Health & Disease (GBR ISSN 0891-060X) **5822**
• ➤ Microbial Pathogenesis (GBR ISSN 0882-4010) **5823**
• Microbial Update International (USA ISSN 1082-9296) **3656**
Microbial Utilization of Renewable Resources (JPN) **768**
Microbiologia Medica (ITA ISSN 1120-0146) **5679**
Microbiological Publications *see* Mikrobiologian Julkaisuja **892**
• ➤ Microbiological Research (DEU ISSN 0944-5013) **891**
The Microbiological Update (USA ISSN 0889-3381) **891**
Microbiologie Hygiene Alimentaire (TUN ISSN 0330-8030) **891**
• Microbiology (AUS) **5855**
Microbiology *see* Weishengwuxue Tongbao **898**
• ➤ Microbiology (GBR ISSN 1350-0872) **892**
• ➤ Microbiology (RUS ISSN 0026-2617) **891**
• Microbiology Abstracts: Section A. Industrial & Applied Microbiology (USA ISSN 0300-838X) **717**
• Microbiology Abstracts: Section B. Bacteriology (USA ISSN 0300-8398) **717**
• Microbiology Abstracts: Section C. Algology, Mycology and Protozoology (USA ISSN 0301-2328) **717**
• ➤ Microbiology and Immunology (AUS ISSN 0385-5600) **892**
• ➤ Microbiology and Molecular Biology Reviews (USA ISSN 1092-2172) **892**
➤ Microbiology Australia (AUS ISSN 1324-4272) **892**
Microbiology Education *see* Journal of Microbiology and Biology Education **889**
▼ • ➤ Microbiology Insights (NZL ISSN 1178-6361) **892**
Microbiology Newsletter (GBR ISSN 1360-4511) **892**
• Microbiology Today (GBR ISSN 1464-0570) **892**
Microcap (CAN ISSN 1718-584X) **1639**
• MicroCapital Monitor (USA ISSN 1935-505X) **1367**
• ➤ Microchemical Journal (USA ISSN 0026-265X) **899**
• ➤ Microchimica Acta (AUT ISSN 0026-3672) **2103**
Microchip Report *see* Dow Jones Microchip Report **3093**
• ➤ Microcirculation (GBR ISSN 1073-9688) **5679**
➤ Microcirculation Review (NLD ISSN 0168-1745) **925**
• Microcirugia Ocular (ESP ISSN 1134-654X) **6046**
Microcomputer (THA ISSN 0857-0140) **2572**
Microcomputer Applications *see* Weijisuanji Yingyong **2573**
MicroComputer Investor (USA) **1420**
MicroComputer Journal (USA ISSN 1076-8289) **2572**
Microcomputer Magazine *see* Microcomputer **2572**
Microcomputer Market Place (Year) (USA ISSN 1066-1824) **2572**
Microcomputer Systems *see* Xiaoxing Weixing Jisuanji Xitong **2574**
The Microcomputer Trainer (USA ISSN 1055-3258) **2572**
Microcomputer User (THA) **2572**
Microcontrolles & Embedded Systems *see* Danpianji yu Qianrushi Xitong Yingyong **2416**
• Micrococsm - I I I (Institute of Infection and Immunity) (CAN ISSN 1703-907X) **5823**
Microcosm, Institute of Infection and Immunity *see* Microcosm - I I I **5823**
Microcosm - Lyrical Ways (USA ISSN 0747-8216) **5227**
Microcosme - I M I I *see* Microcosm - I I I **5823**
Microdatorn *see* Techworld **2504**
• ➤ Microelectronic Engineering (NLD ISSN 0167-9317) **3108**
Microelectronics *see* Weidianzixue **2466**
Microelectronics and Reliability *see* Microelectronics Reliability **3109**
Microelectronics and Signal Processing (USA ISSN 0736-6914) **3108**
• Microelectronics International (GBR ISSN 1356-5362) **3109**
• ➤ Microelectronics Journal (GBR ISSN 0959-8324) **3109**
• ➤ Microelectronics Reliability (GBR ISSN 0026-2714) **3109**
• Microelectronics Technology Alert (USA ISSN 1084-4546) **3109**
† Microelettronica e Imprese (ITA ISSN 0394-1361) **8974**
Microengineering and Nanotechnology News *see* Nanoparticle Technology News **3212**
• The Microenterprise Journal (USA ISSN 1541-3268) **1963**
Microfabrication Technology *see* Weixi Jiagong Jishu **3116**
Microfilmed Newspapers of Finland *see* Suomen Sanomalehtien Mikrofilmit **4588**
• ➤ Microfluidics and Nanofluidics (DEU ISSN 1613-4982) **3390**
• Microform and Imaging Review (DEU ISSN 0949-5770) **5032**
Micrographics and Optical Storage Buyer's Guide (GBR) **6971**
• ➤ Microgravity - Science and Technology (NLD ISSN 0938-0108) **65**
Microinfo Electronic Media Directory (GBR) **2494**
Microlepidoptera of Europe (DNK ISSN 1395-9506) **854**
Microlight Flying (GBR ISSN 0968-3100) **65**
• Microlithography World (USA ISSN 1074-407X) **3109**
Micrologus (BEL) **4244**
Micromania (ESP) **2578**
▼ • MICROmanufacturing (USA) **3390**
Micromaterials and Nanomaterials (DEU ISSN 1619-2486) **3354**
Micromechatronics *see* Maikuromekatoronikusu **2572**
▼ MicroMineral Magazine (FRA ISSN 1957-4290) **6470**
Micromotors *see* Weidianji **3226**
• ➤ Micron (GBR ISSN 0968-4328) **899**
Micronanoelectronic Technology *see* Wei-Na Dianzi Jishu **3116**
• ➤ Micronesian Editor (GUM) **2886**
➤ Micronesian Educator (GUM ISSN 1061-088X) **2886**
• ➤ Micronesian Journal of the Humanities and Social Sciences (AUS ISSN 1449-7336) **4465**
➤ Micronesica (GUM ISSN 0026-279X) **348**
• ➤ Micropaleontology (USA ISSN 0026-2803) **6726**
Micropaleontology Special Papers (USA ISSN 0160-2071) **6726**
• ➤ Microporous and Mesoporous Materials (NLD ISSN 1387-1811) **2138**
Microprocess Conference. Digest of Papers (JPN) **7026**
➤ Microprocessor-Based and Intelligent Systems Engineering (NLD) **3210**
• Microprocessor I C's D.A.T.A. Digest (Integrated Circuits) (USA ISSN 1049-2445) **2572**
• Microprocessor Report (USA ISSN 0899-9341) **2468**
• ➤ Microprocessors and Microsystems (NLD ISSN 0141-9331) **2572**
• Microscope (GBR ISSN 0269-5766) **2572**
➤ Microscope (USA ISSN 0026-282X) **2104**
Microscope Book (USA ISSN 1051-404X) **899**
The Microscope Journal *see* Microscope **2104**
Microscopical Society of Canada. Bulletin (CAN ISSN 0383-1825) **899**
Microscopical Society of Canada. Proceedings (CAN ISSN 0381-1751) **899**
Microscopy and Analysis (Asia / Pacific Edition) *see* Microscopy and Analysis (U K Edition) **900**
Microscopy and Analysis (European Edition) *see* Microscopy and Analysis (U K Edition) **900**
Microscopy and Analysis (The Americas Edition) *see* Microscopy and Analysis (U K Edition) **900**
Microscopy and Analysis (U K Edition) (GBR ISSN 0958-1952) **900**
• ➤ Microscopy and Microanalysis (GBR ISSN 1431-9276) **900**
• Microscopy in Focus (Online) (NZL ISSN 1178-282X) **900**
Microscopy in Focus (Print) *see* Microscopy in Focus (Online) **900**
• ➤ Microscopy Research and Technique (USA ISSN 1059-910X) **900**
• Microscopy Society of America. Directory (USA) **7080**
Microscopy Society of Southern Africa. Proceedings/Mikroskopievereniging van Suidelike Afrika. Verrigtings (ZAF ISSN 1028-3455) **900**
• ➤ Microscopy Today (USA ISSN 1551-9295) **900**
• Microsemanario (ARG) **689**
The Microsoft Architecture Journal *see* The Architecture Journal **2407**
Microsoft Business Journal (BRA) **2594**
Microsoft Certified Professional Magazine *see* Redmond **2503**
Microsoft Coder *see* M S Coder **8972**
Microsoft Developers Network Magazine Europe *see* M S D N Magazine Europe **2508**
Microsoft Development Network Magazine *see* M S D N Magazine **2508**
Microsoft Development Network Magazine. Australia - New Zealand Edition *see* M S D N Magazine. Australia - New Zealand Edition **2594**
Microsoft Development Network Magazine. India Edition *see* M S D N Magazine. India Edition **2594**
Microsoft Development Network Magazine. Southeast Asia Edition *see* M S D N Magazine. Southeast Asia Edition **2594**
Microsoft.NET Magazine (NLD ISSN 1574-0382) **2431**
Microsoft Office Solutions *see* Smart Solutions **8988**
Microsoft Office X P Quick Reference Card (USA ISSN 1542-278X) **2594**
Microsoft Office X P Quick Reference Guide (USA ISSN 1542-2798) **2595**
Microsoft TechNet *see* TechNet Magazine **2439**
Microsoft Tracker (USA) **2595**
† Microsoft Visual J++ Informant (USA) **8974**
• Microsoft Windows Server 2003 Solutions (USA ISSN 1547-8165) **2508**
Microsoft Windows X P le Magazine Officiel *see* Le Magazine Officiel Windows X P **2594**
Microsoft Windows X P: The Official Magazine (GBR ISSN 1745-1299) **2595**
Microsoft Windows XP *see* Windows XP **2600**
Microsoft Windows XP (CD Edition) (GBR ISSN 1474-2799) **2595**
➤ Microspheres, Microcapsules & Liposomes (GBR ISSN 1461-1732) **6861**
MicroStars Magazine (GBR ISSN 1743-6079) **2202**
Microstate Studies (VIR ISSN 0147-7935) **7985**
• MicroStation World (USA ISSN 1083-396X) **2493**
Microstructure of High Temperature Materials (GBR ISSN 1366-5510) **6326**
• ➤ Microsurgery (USA ISSN 0738-1085) **6252**
• ➤ Microsystem Technologies (DEU ISSN 0946-7076) **2473**
Microsystems (USA ISSN 1389-2134) **2572**
Microsystems Handbook (USA ISSN 1063-1488) **2572**
Microsystems Technology News *see* M S T News **2473**
• Microtechnologies and Microsystems Series (GBR) **3210**
• ➤ Microvascular Research (USA ISSN 0026-2862) **5795**
▼ • ➤ Microvascular Reviews and Communications (JPN ISSN 1880-5906) **5796**
Microview (CAN ISSN 0836-5482) **2572**
• ➤ Microwave & Optical Technology Letters (USA ISSN 0895-2477) **7080**
• Microwave Engineering (GBR ISSN 1474-9203) **3109**
Microwave Engineering Europe *see* Microwave Engineering **3109**
Microwave Heating Symposium. Proceedings (USA) **3325**
Microwave Journal (Euro-Global Edition) *see* Microwave Journal (International Edition) **3325**
• Microwave Journal (International Edition) (USA ISSN 0192-6225) **3325**
Microwave Licenses Issued (USA) **2360**
Microwave Licenses Issued Report *see* Microwave Licenses Issued **2360**
Microwave News (USA ISSN 0275-6595) **7531**
Microwave Power Symposium. Proceedings *see* Microwave Heating Symposium. Proceedings **3325**
Microwave Product Digest (USA ISSN 1061-754X) **3325**
Microwave Science Series Report (GBR) **3109**
Microwave Update (USA) **2360**
Microwave World (USA ISSN 0276-7961) **3656**
• Microwaves & R F (USA ISSN 0745-2993) **3325**
Microwaves & R F Online Product Data Directory *see* Microwaves & R F Product Data Directory **3325**
• Microwaves & R F Product Data Directory (USA) **3325**
Microwaves, Antennas & Propagation *see* I E T Microwaves Antennas & Propagation **3317**
Mid-Am Antique Appraisers Association. Newsletter (USA) **367**
• Mid-America Commerce & Industry (USA ISSN 0193-2047) **1499**
Mid-America Farmer Grower *see* MidAmerica Farmer Grower **137**
Mid-America Folklore *see* Overland Review **3621**
Mid-America Journal of Theology (USA ISSN 0887-1760) **7663**
▼ Mid-America Lifestyle (USA) **5077**
Mid-America Theological Journal (USA ISSN 0734-9882) **7663**
Mid-American Journal of Business *see* American Journal of Business **1059**
➤ Mid-American Review (USA ISSN 0747-8895) **5227**
The Mid-Atlantic Almanack (USA ISSN 1063-1763) **8121**
Mid-Atlantic Archivist (USA ISSN 0738-9396) **5032**
Mid-Atlantic Beef & Dairy *see* Delmarva Farmer **104**
Mid-Atlantic Brewing News (USA) **607**
Mid Atlantic Bulletin of Korean Studies (USA ISSN 1050-3935) **555**
• Mid-Atlantic Construction (USA ISSN 1548-6567) **1024**
Mid-Atlantic Council of Shopping Center Managers News *see* M A C News **1773**
Mid-Atlantic - Delaware, District of Columbia, Maryland, Virginia, West Virginia TourBook *see* TourBook: Mid-Atlantic **8762**
Mid-Atlantic Executive Legal Adviser (USA ISSN 1932-7269) **4876**
Mid-Atlantic Executive Legal Advisor (USA) **4876**
Mid-Atlantic Game & Fish (USA ISSN 1055-6540) **8322**
Mid-Atlantic Poultry Farmer *see* Delmarva Farmer **104**
Mid-Atlantic Preservation Service Data Base *see* M A P S Data Base **2348**
Mid Atlantic Real Estate Journal (USA ISSN 1945-8053) **7599**
Mid-Atlantic Riviera *see* M.A.R. **5076**
Mid-Atlantic Thoroughbred (USA ISSN 1056-3245) **8294**
The Mid-Atlantic's Best Bed and Breakfasts *see* The Mid-Atlantic's Best Bed & Breakfasts **8736**
The Mid-Atlantic's Best Bed & Breakfasts (USA ISSN 1099-4203) **8736**
• Mid Columbia Labor Trends (USA) **1697**
Mid-Columbian (USA ISSN 1552-9568) **5077**
Mid Devon Gazette (GBR ISSN 1353-7695) **3868**
Mid Essex Express (GBR) **3868**
Mid-Missouri Business Journal (USA) **1963**
Mid-Month Global Financial Report *see* F X 4casts **1485**

Title

▼ *new title* † *ceased* • *electronic media* ➤ *refereed*

10612 MID-NORTH MONITOR ULRICH'S PERIODICALS

Mid-North Monitor (CAN ISSN 0227-3853) **3813**
Mid - Ocean News (BMU) **3802**
Mid-Ohio Golfer (USA ISSN 1058-8590) **8238**
Mid South Coast Mail (ZAF) **3949**
Mid South Family (USA) **2161**
• Mid-South Farmer (USA ISSN 1074-357X) **203**
Mid-South Horse Review (USA) **8294**
Mid-South Hunting & Fishing News (USA ISSN 0894-7767) **8322**
Mid-South Trucking News (USA) **8672**
Mid-Stream *see* Call to Unity **7629**
Mid-Taiwan Journal of Medicine *see* Zhong-Taiwan Yixue Kexue Zazahi **5735**
Mid-Term Forecast of Japanese Economy (JPN) **1499**
Mid Wales & Borders Living (GBR ISSN 1754-4572) **5077**
Mid Week Magazine (PAK) **3926**
Mid-Week Petroleum Argus (GBR ISSN 0268-7852) **6778**
Mid-West Farmer (GBR) **136**
Mid-Western 4-Wheeler (USA) **8590**
Mid-Western Educational Researcher (USA ISSN 1056-3997) **2886**
MidAmerica (USA ISSN 0190-2911) **5333**
MidAmerica Farmer Grower (USA) **137**
Midas Touch *see* Beef Review **261**
Midatlantic Antiques Magazine (USA ISSN 1042-2501) **367**
MidCoaster (USA ISSN 0892-970X) **5333**
Midcon Conference Record (USA) **2473**
Midcontinent Petroleum Industry (USA) **6778**
• ➤ Midcontinental Journal of Archaeology (USA ISSN 0146-1109) **406**
Midde Hodesh B'Hod'sho *see* Middei Chodesh Bechodsho **3073**
• Middei Chodesh Bechodsho (ISR) **3073**
Middelaar Tussen de Genealogische Navorsers *see* Intermediaire des Genealogistes **3771**
Middelbaar Beroepsonderwijs Magazine *see* M B O Magazine **2944**
Middeleeuwse Studies en Bronnen (NLD ISSN 0929-9726) **4244**
Middeleeuwse Verzamelhandschriften uit de Nederlanden (NLD ISSN 0929-9866) **5333**
Middelnederlandse Tekstedities (NLD ISSN 0929-9734) **5333**
The Midden (CAN ISSN 0047-7222) **406**
Middernachtsroep (NLD ISSN 0165-3121) **7663**
The Middle-Aged *see* Zhongnian Zuzhe **3830**
Middle and Junior High Core Collection *see* Middle and Junior High School Library Catalog **5032**
• Middle and Junior High School Library Catalog (USA) **5032**
Middle and Primary School Education *see* Zhongxiaoxue Jiaoyu **2929**
Middle Atlantic Council of Latin American Studies Latin American Essays *see* M A C L A S Latin American Essays **5328**
Middle Atlantic Perspective (USA) **5679**
Middle Atlantic Regional Gospel Ministries Newsletter *see* M A R Gospel Ministries Newsletter **7661**
Middle Atlantic States Komondor Club, Inc. Komondor News *see* M A S K C Komondor News **292**
Middle-Atlantic Writers Association Review *see* M A W A Review **5328**
• The Middle East (GBR ISSN 0305-0734) **5227**
▼ • ➤ Middle East African Journal of Ophtalmology (IND ISSN 0974-9233) **6046**
• Middle East & Africa Financial Alert (GBR ISSN 1475-5211) **1499**
Middle East and Africa Survey (GBR) **4394**
• Middle East and Africa Wireless Analyst (GBR ISSN 1741-8658) **2333**
Middle East and Indian Ocean *see* Moyen Orient et Ocean Indien **4186**
Middle East and North Africa (Year) (GBR ISSN 0076-8502) **7154**
Middle East & North Africa Petroleum Bulletin *see* M E N A Petroleum Bulletin **6777**
The Middle East and South Asia Folklore Bulletin (USA ISSN 1074-0244) **3620**
Middle East and World Construction Directory (LBN) **1024**
Middle East and World Food Directory (LBN) **3656**
Middle East and World Water Directory (LBN ISSN 0255-8564) **8829**
Middle East Appropriate Technology News *see* Al-Tiknulujia al-Mula'imah **8443**
The Middle East Book Review (GBR) **3912**
Middle East Broadcast and Satellite (GBR ISSN 0968-4344) **2385**
➤ Middle East Business and Economic Review (AUS ISSN 1035-3704) **1149**
• Middle East Business Intelligence (USA ISSN 0731-6305) **1577**
Middle East Business Law Series (NLD ISSN 0141-6650) **4936**
Middle East Business Review (GBR ISSN 1363-3740) **1499**
• Middle East Business Strategies (USA) **1577**
Middle East Cardio (GBR) **5796**
† ➤ Middle East Commercial Law Review (GBR ISSN 1357-0005) **8974**
Middle East Communications (SGP) **2333**
• Middle East Contemporary Survey (USA ISSN 0163-5476) **4323**
• ➤ Middle East Critique (GBR ISSN 1943-6149) **555**
Middle East Cultures Series (GBR ISSN 0962-0087) **4323**
Middle East Directory *see* Polymers Paint Color Year Book (Year) **6720**
Middle East Directory *see* P P C J **6719**
Middle East Directory *see* European Adhesives and Sealants **6311**
• Middle East Economic Digest (GBR ISSN 0047-7230) **1499**
• Middle East Economic Survey (CYP ISSN 0544-0424) **6778**
Middle East Education & Training Buyers Guide (GBR) **2886**
Middle East Electricity *see* Power (Houston) **3393**
Middle East Electricity Buyers Guide (GBR ISSN 1740-9071) **3160**
Middle East Energy *see* African Energy **3123**
• Middle East Executive Reports (USA ISSN 0271-0498) **1577**
Middle East Expatriate (BHR ISSN 0266-5697) **3912**
• ➤ Middle East Fertility Society Journal (EGY ISSN 1110-5690) **5998**
Middle East Food (Online) *see* Ma'kulat al-Sharq al-Awsat **3655**
Middle East Food International *see* Ma'kulat al-Sharq al-Awsat **3655**
➤ Middle East Forum (GRC) **7252**
Middle East Golfer (UAE ISSN 1816-1146) **8238**
Middle East Grocer/Al-Baqqa lah fi al-Sharq al Awsat (GBR ISSN 1368-5929) **3680**
Middle East Health (UAE ISSN 1475-0805) **7531**
Middle East Institute Newsletter (USA) **7252**
• Middle East Intelligence Bulletin (USA) **7252**
• Middle East International (GBR ISSN 0047-7249) **7154**
• ➤ Middle East Journal (USA ISSN 0026-3141) **7252**
Middle East Journal of Anesthesiology (LBN ISSN 0544-0440) **5772**
▼ • Middle East Journal of Culture and Communication (NLD ISSN 1873-9857) **555**
Middle East Journal of Emergency Medicine *see* J E M T A C **5946**
▼ • ➤ Middle East Law and Governance (NLD ISSN 1876-3367) **555**
Middle East Librarians Association Notes *see* M E L A Notes **5030**
• Middle East Media Research Institute (USA) **7252**
Middle East Military Balance (Year) (USA ISSN 1099-5552) **6434**
Middle East Monitor (USA ISSN 0026-315X) **7252**
• Middle East Monitor. East Med (GBR ISSN 1469-526X) **1499**
• Middle East Monitor. The Gulf (GBR ISSN 1469-5251) **1499**
Middle East Paediatrics *see* Paediatrics.me **6098**
Middle East Pharmacy (GBR ISSN 1368-5945) **6861**
• ➤ Middle East Policy (USA ISSN 1061-1924) **7252**
Middle East Policy Survey (USA ISSN 0276-5632) **7253**
• Middle East Quarterly (USA ISSN 1073-9467) **7253**
† Middle East Record (ISR ISSN 0076-8529) **8974**
• ➤ Middle East Report (USA ISSN 0899-2851) **4323**
• Middle East Review (GBR ISSN 1351-4717) **1499**
Middle East Review of International Affairs Journal *see* M E R I A Journal **555**
Middle East Science Policy Series (GBR ISSN 0956-1021) **7882**
Middle East Studies Association Bulletin (USA ISSN 0026-3184) **7985**
• Middle East - Taxation & Investment (NLD) **1935**
Middle East Technical University. Faculty of Architecture. Journal *see* Orta Dogu Teknik Universitesi. Mimarlik Fakultesi. Dergisi **452**
Middle East Technical University. Journal of the Faculty of Architecture *see* Orta Dogu Teknik Universitesi. Mimarlik Fakultesi. Dergisi **452**
• Middle East Times Egypt (EGY) **3912**
Middle East Trade/Tijjarat ash-Sharq al-'Awssat (GBR ISSN 0026-3192) **1578**
Middle East Travel (LBN ISSN 1991-2412) **8736**
Middle East Travel (UAE ISSN 0140-8321) **8736**
• The Middle East Women's Studies Review (USA ISSN 1097-0525) **8901**
▼ Middle Eastern and Russian Journal of Plant Science and Biotechnology (GBR ISSN 1752-3907) **801**
Middle Eastern Dance Association of New Zealand News *see* M E D A N Z News **2686**
Middle Eastern Dancer Magazine (USA ISSN 1041-7591) **2686**
• Middle Eastern Lectures (Online) (ISR) **4323**
• Middle Eastern Literatures (Online) (GBR ISSN 1475-2638) **5333**
• ➤ Middle Eastern Literatures (Print) (GBR ISSN 1475-262X) **5333**
▼ Middle Eastern Outlook (USA ISSN 1937-9242) **7253**
• ➤ Middle Eastern Studies (GBR ISSN 0026-3206) **4323**
Middle English Texts (DEU) **5333**
Middle English Texts Series (USA) **5333**
• ➤ Middle Grades Research Journal (USA ISSN 1937-0814) **2886**
The Middle Magazine (USA ISSN 1933-2254) **2202**
Middle Management and Clerical Compensation Report - Mexico (USA) **1779**
Middle Management Compensation - Regression Analysis Report (USA) **1779**
Middle Management Compensation Survey (Year) (CAN ISSN 1197-5857) **6707**
Middle Management Hi - Comp Report (USA) **1779**
Middle School *see* Helping Students Learn (Middle School English Edition) **2863**
Middle School Biology *see* Zhongxue Shengwuxue **2929**
➤ Middle School Journal (USA ISSN 0094-0771) **3073**
Middle School Math *see* Zhongxuesheng Shuxue **5548**
Middle School Review Youth *see* M S R Youth **8972**
Middle School Science & Technology *see* Zhongxue Keji **2929**
Middle School Student *see* Zhongxuesheng **2929**
Middle School Student Science Education *see* Zhongxuesheng Kexue Jiaoyu **2929**
Middle School Teachers Guide to Free Curriculum Materials (USA) **3073**
Middle School Times *see* Zhongxue Shishi Bao **2224**
Middle Schooling Review *see* M S R Youth **8972**
➤ Middle States Council for the Social Studies. Journal (USA ISSN 0739-8069) **7985**
Middle Tennessee State University. Business and Economic Research Center. Conference Paper (USA) **1499**
• The Middle Way (GBR ISSN 0026-3214) **7702**
Middlebury Campus (USA) **2292**
Middlebury College Magazine (USA ISSN 0745-2454) **2292**
Middlebury Studies in Russian Language and Literature (USA ISSN 0888-8752) **5151**
Middlesex Genealogical Society Newsletter (USA ISSN 1936-3494) **3775**
Middlesex Health and Life *see* Middlesex Health & Life **5077**
▼ Middlesex Health & Life (USA) **5077**
Middlesex, We're on the Way! (CAN ISSN 1719-4512) **8736**
Middleton Area Historical Society. Newsletter (USA) **4303**
Middleveld Indaba (ZAF) **3949**
• Middlewich Guardian (GBR ISSN 1478-7415) **3968**
• Mideast Mirror (GBR ISSN 0544-0556) **3868**
• Mideast Monitor (USA) **7253**
Mideast Security and Policy Studies/Diyyunim Bevitahon Le'umi (ISR ISSN 0793-1050) **7253**
Midei Chodesh Bechodsho *see* Middei Chodesh Bechodsho **3073**
† Midi (NLD ISSN 1566-6891) **8974**
• Midi Madagaskara (MDG ISSN 1025-3556) **3906**
Midi Media (FRA ISSN 0295-3943) **1835**
• Midi Olympique (FRA ISSN 0994-6187) **8238**
Midi Olympique - Rugbyrama (FRA) **8238**
• Midi-Pyrenees Info (FRA ISSN 1955-0146) **7497**
Midi-Pyrenees Notre Region *see* Midi-Pyrenees Info **7497**
Midia (BRA) **30**
Midland Auto Trader (GBR ISSN 0958-5893) **8590**
Midland Bonsai Society Journal (GBR ISSN 0144-6916) **3743**
➤ Midland Catholic History (GBR) **7807**
Midland Genealogical Society. Newsletter (USA) **3775**
Midland Group News (GBR) **1367**
• ➤ Midland History (GBR ISSN 0047-729X) **4244**
Midland News (ZAF ISSN 0048-119X) **3949**
• Midland Penetanguishene Mirror (CAN ISSN 1191-4114) **3813**
➤ Midland Review (USA ISSN 0886-7976) **5333**
Midland Tribune (IRL) **3894**
The Midlander (USA ISSN 1082-5584) **8620**
Midlands & Eastern Instructor (GBR) **8590**
Midlands Business Insider *see* Insider. Midlands Business Insider **1753**
Midlands Business Journal (USA ISSN 0194-4525) **1149**
Midlands Corporate Finance Directory *see* Insider Dealmakers Guides. Midlands **1354**
• MidLink Magazine (USA) **2202**
Midnight Engineering (USA ISSN 1050-0324) **3210**
Midnight Graffiti (USA) **5445**
Midnight Marquee (USA ISSN 0886-8719) **6507**
Midnight Shambler (USA) **5445**
Midol Mag (FRA ISSN 1274-5707) **8238**
Midrange Developer (USA) **2595**
Midrange Magazin (DEU ISSN 0946-2880) **1420**
MidSouth Living Home & Garden Magazine (USA) **4546**
Midsouthwest Restaurant (USA) **4394**
MidState Economic Indicators (USA) **1499**
Midstream (IND) **8829**
• Midstream (USA ISSN 0026-332X) **7727**
• Midtjyllands Avis (DNK) **3834**
Midtjyske Fortaellinger (DNK ISSN 1901-2144) **6529**
Midweek (GBR) **3868**
• The Midweek Mercury (GBR) **3868**
Midweek Sun (BWA) **3803**
Midwest *see* My Midwest **8785**
Midwest Airlines *see* My Midwest **8785**
Midwest Archives Conference Newsletter *see* M A C Newsletter **5030**
Midwest Art Fairs (USA) **506**
Midwest Beat Magazine (USA) **6587**
Midwest Bowhunter (USA) **8322**
Midwest Bulletin (NGA) **3920**
Midwest Bullseye (USA) **137**
Midwest Clearing Corporation and Midwest Securities Trust Company. Directory of Participants (USA) **2017**
• Midwest Construction (USA ISSN 1522-7294) **1024**
• Midwest Contractor Magazine (USA ISSN 0026-3044) **1024**
Midwest Dairybusiness (USA ISSN 1087-7096) **267**
Midwest Engineer (USA ISSN 0026-3370) **3210**
Midwest Express Magazine *see* My Midwest **8785**
Midwest Flyer Magazine (USA ISSN 0194-5068) **8548**
Midwest Food Service (USA) **4394**
Midwest Galloway News (USA) **293**
Midwest Gardening (USA ISSN 1555-0214) **3743**
Midwest Golf News (USA) **8238**
Midwest Historical and Genealogical Register. Quarterly (USA ISSN 0271-8685) **3775**
Midwest Home (USA ISSN 1947-0142) **4560**
Midwest In-House (USA) **4734**
▼ ➤ Midwest Journal for Educational Communications and Technology (USA ISSN 1938-7709) **2950**
Midwest Law Review (USA ISSN 0885-2650) **4734**
• Midwest Living (USA ISSN 0889-8138) **3981**
Midwest Living Best of the Midwest *see* Best of the Midwest **8687**
Midwest Living Best Vacations *see* Best of the Midwest **8687**
Midwest Manufacturers & Industrial Classified Directory & Buyers Guide (USA) **2017**
Midwest Messenger (Iowa Edition) *see* Midwest Messenger (North Edition) **137**
Midwest Messenger (North Edition) (USA) **137**
Midwest Messenger (South Edition) *see* Midwest Messenger (North Edition) **137**
Midwest Messenger (West Edition) *see* Midwest Messenger (North Edition) **137**
• ➤ Midwest Modern Language Association. Journal (USA ISSN 0742-5562) **5334**
Midwest Museum Bulletin (USA) **506**
Midwest Musicians Hotline (USA) **6587**
• Midwest Note-Book (Online) (USA) **5032**
MidWest Outdoors (USA ISSN 0747-3648) **8322**
Midwest Players (USA ISSN 1071-4081) **8187**
Midwest Poetry Review (USA ISSN 0745-8738) **5427**
Midwest Political Consultant (USA) **7154**
• ➤ Midwest Quarterly (USA ISSN 0026-3451) **4465**
Midwest Racing News (USA ISSN 0047-732X) **8187**
• Midwest Real Estate News (USA ISSN 0893-2719) **7599**
Midwest Research Institute. Annual Report (USA) **7882**
Midwest Retailer (USA) **1835**
• Midwest Studies in Philosophy (USA ISSN 0363-6550) **6934**
• Midwest Symposium on Circuits and Systems. Conference Proceedings (USA ISSN 1548-3746) **2466**
• Midwest Today (USA) **3981**
• Midwest Transaction Guide (USA) **4734**
Midwest Traveler (USA ISSN 1524-5268) **8590**
▼ Midwest Wealth Management Business (USA ISSN 1945-0486) **1639**
Midwestern Association of Graduate Schools. Proceedings of the Annual Meeting (USA) **2994**
Midwestern Dentist (USA ISSN 0026-3478) **5856**
• Midwestern Epigraphic Newsletter (USA ISSN 1932-5711) **5151**
Midwestern Folklore (USA ISSN 0894-4059) **3620**
Midwestern Journal of Theology (USA ISSN 1543-6977) **7767**
Midwestern Miscellany (USA ISSN 0885-4742) **5334**
Midwife *see* Jordemodern **5994**
• ➤ Midwifery (GBR ISSN 0266-6138) **5998**
• Midwifery Matters (GBR ISSN 0961-1479) **5970**
• Midwifery Today (USA ISSN 1551-8892) **5998**
Midwives Association of Kyoto University. Annals *see* Kyouto Daigaku Josampu Dousoukaihou **5997**
Midwives Information and Resource Service Midwifery Digest *see* M I D I R S Midwifery Digest **5997**
Mie Biological Society. Journal *see* Mie Seibutsu **689**
† Le Mie Canzoni (ITA ISSN 1826-4174) **8974**
Mie Daigaku Kogakubu Kenkyu Hokoku/Mie University. Faculty of Engineering. Research Reports (JPN ISSN 0385-6208) **3210**
Mie Daigaku Kyoiku Gakubu Kenkyu Kiyo. Jimbun Kagaku/Mie University. Faculty of Education. Bulletin. Humanities *see* Mie Daigaku Kyouiku Gakubu Kenkyuu Kiyou **2886**
Mie Daigaku Kyoiku Gakubu Kenkyu Kiyo. Kyoiku Kagaku/Mie University. Faculty of Education. Bulletin. Educational Science *see* Mie Daigaku Kyouiku Gakubu Kenkyuu Kiyou **2886**
Mie Daigaku Kyoiku Gakubu Kenkyu Kiyo. Shizen Kagaku/Mie University. Faculty of Education. Bulletin. Natural Science *see* Mie Daigaku Kyouiku Gakubu Kenkyuu Kiyou **2886**
Mie Daigaku Kyouiku Gakubu Kenkyuu Kiyou/Mie University. Faculty of Education. Bulletin (JPN ISSN 1880-2419) **2886**
Mie Daigaku Sebutsu Shigen Gakubu Enshurin Hokoku/Mie University Forests. Bulletin (JPN ISSN 0916-8974) **3697**
Mie Daigaku Seibutsu Shigen Gakubu Kiyo/Mie University. Faculty of Bioresources. Bulletin (JPN ISSN 0915-0471) **3697**
Mie Daigaku Suisan Kenkyujo Hokoku *see* Mie University. Fisheries Research Laboratory. Report **955**

Link to your serials resources and content with ulrichsweb.com

Title

Title

DIRECTORY 2010 MISSOURI BOTANICAL GARDEN. MONOGRAPHS IN SYSTEMATIC 10617

Il Mio Cavallo (ITA ISSN 1121-3183) **8294**
Il Mio Computer (ITA ISSN 1124-0415) **2431**
Il Mio Giardino (ITA ISSN 1125-4866) **3743**
† Il Mio Orto (ITA ISSN 1825-4144) **8974**
Il Mio Palmare (ITA ISSN 1723-0683) **2572**
Il Mio Portatile *see* Portatile & Wireless **8982**
Il Mio Prato (ITA ISSN 1824-1298) **3743**
† Il Mio Terrazzo (ITA ISSN 1824-2227) **8974**
Miombo (TZA ISSN 0856-2806) **2619**
Mipel Magazine (ITA) **4974**
MIPTV Preview Magazine *see* M I P T V Preview Magazine **2384**
MIR *see* M I R: Management International Review **1773**
▼ Mir (FRA ISSN 1958-3710) **5334**
Mir Bezopasnosti (RUS) **2660**
Mir Biblii/World of the Bible (RUS ISSN 1562-1413) **7663**
Mir Bibliotek Segodnya (RUS) **5032**
Mir Deneg (UKR) **1149**
Mir i Dom (RUS) **7600**
Mir I N Gumileva (RUS) **5334**
Mir Internet (RUS) **2564**
• Mir Istorii (RUS ISSN 1561-8463) **4245**
Mir Izmerenii (RUS) **6404**
➤ Mir Kamnya/World of Stones (RUS) **6473**
Mir Komp'yuternoi Avtomatizatsii/The World of Computer-Aided Automation (RUS) **2463**
Mir Lyudei (RUS) **3937**
Mir Muzeya (RUS ISSN 0869-8171) **6529**
Mir Novostei (RUS) **4580**
Mir Obrazovaniya (RUS) **2887**
• Mir P K (RUS ISSN 0235-3520) **2432**
Mir Piva *see* Brauwelt International **600**
Mir Razvlechenii (RUS ISSN 1680-5968) **6295**
Mir Rossii (RUS) **3551**
Mir Sporta (RUS) **8187**
Mir Tsen (RUS) **1367**
Mir Zhenshchiny (RUS ISSN 0869-494X) **8875**
Mira (IND ISSN 0026-5780) **5227**
MiRA (NOR ISSN 0805-357X) **7212**
Mira! (USA ISSN 1529-9090) **3982**
MiRA-Senteret. Temahefte (NOR ISSN 1503-5662) **8875**
Miracles Magazine (USA) **6646**
Miracles Now (USA) **7767**
Miraculous Medal (USA ISSN 0026-5802) **7663**
La Mirada (ESP ISSN 1576-3048) **3952**
La Mirada del Fin de Semana *see* La Mirada **3952**
La Mirada Limpia (ESP ISSN 1695-8993) **7155**
▼ • Miradas de UNdeC (Universidad Nacional de Chilecito) (ARG ISSN 1851-3670) **2994**
Mirage (USA) **506**
• Mirage Magazine (USA) **2292**
Miramichi City & Area Directory *see* Miramichi Leader **3813**
• Miramichi Leader (CAN ISSN 1493-6208) **3813**
• Miranda Literary Magazine (USA ISSN 1936-0932) **5334**
Miras-e Farhangi (IRN) **406**
Miras I Iran *see* Persian Heritage **3557**
Mirase Iran *see* Persian Heritage **3557**
Mirasi Iran *see* Persian Heritage **3557**
Mir'at al-Manatiq al-Sina'iyyat *see* P E I E Mirror **1900**
Mirat al-Tahqiq *see* Ayeneh-e Pazhoohesh **7709**
• ➤ Mirator (FIN ISSN 1457-2362) **4245**
• Mires and Peat (GBR ISSN 1819-754X) **689**
Miriam (ESP ISSN 0214-3879) **7807**
Mirjam (CHE) **7807**
Miro (DEU ISSN 1861-9894) **1024**
Le Miroir des Humanistes (FRA ISSN 1764-4283) **4465**
Miroir du Moyen Age (BEL ISSN 1251-5906) **4245**
Miroir et Image (DEU ISSN 0944-2405) **6935**
Miroirs du Monde *see* Collection Miroirs du Monde **7955**
Miromente (AUT ISSN 1816-711X) **5334**
Miron *see* Gazer **8713**
• Mirovaya Ekonomika i Mezhdunarodnye Otnosheniya (RUS ISSN 0026-5829) **1149**
Mirovoe Mashinostroenie i Avtomatizaciya. Pokazateli i Perspektivy Gody *see* World Engineering Industries and Automation **3359**
• Mirror (DEU ISSN 0252-2535) **7807**
• The Mirror (GBR ISSN 1462-995X) **3869**
Mirror (GHA ISSN 0855-1537) **3861**
Mirror (GUY) **3874**
The Mirror/Ching Pao (HKG) **3875**
Mirror (IND ISSN 0026-5845) **3885**
Mirror (LBR) **3789**
The Mirror (LSO) **3905**
Mirror (MWI) **3906**
Mirror *see* Y Drych **3530**
The Mirror (Central Otago Edition) *see* The Mirror (Queenstown-Lakes Edition) **3918**
Mirror (Lancaster) (USA ISSN 0738-7237) **4303**
The Mirror (Mayport) (USA) **6437**
• Mirror (Montreal) (CAN ISSN 1182-5812) **3813**
The Mirror (Queenstown-Lakes Edition) (NZL) **3918**
Mirror (Somerset) (USA) **2292**
The Mirror (Springfield) (USA) **7807**
Mirror & Sunday Mirror *see* Sunday Mirror **3871**
• Mirror Magazine (USA) **506**
Mirror News (USA) **2292**
Mirror of Opinion (SGP ISSN 0544-4055) **3945**
Mirror of Research *see* Ayeneh-e Pazhoohesh **7709**
Mirror on the Urban Scene (CAN) **7453**
Miruku Saiensu/Milk Science (JPN ISSN 1343-0289) **267**
Mis *see* Sweden. Statistiska Centralbyraan. Meddelanden i Samordningsfraagor **8408**
Mis Primeros Cuentos *see* Popi **2208**
Misca, Da, Signa *see* M D S **6859**
Miscarriage, Infant Death, and Stillbirth Newsletter *see* M I D S Newsletter **5997**
Misce, Da, Signa *see* M D S **6859**
Miscel.lania Cerverina (ESP ISSN 0213-2451) **7498**
† Miscel.lania de Textos Medievals (ESP ISSN 0213-2257) **8974**
Miscel.lania d'Estudis Bagencs (ESP ISSN 0212-2812) **4153**
Miscel.lania Liturgica Catalana (ESP ISSN 0213-0742) **7807**
Miscelanea Antropologica Ecuatoriana (ECU ISSN 0254-7678) **348**
Miscelanea Comillas (ESP ISSN 0210-9522) **7663**
Miscelanea de Estudios Arabes y Hebraicos. Seccion Arabe-Islam (ESP ISSN 1696-5868) **556**
Miscelanea de Estudios Arabes y Hebraicos. Seccion Hebreo (ESP ISSN 1696-585X) **556**
• Miscelanea de la Fisica (MEX) **7026**
• Miscelanea Matematica (MEX) **5518**
• Miscelanea Poliana (ESP ISSN 1699-2849) **6935**
Miscellanea *see* Mesovita Gradja **4244**
Miscellanea Byzantina Monacensia (DEU ISSN 0076-9347) **4245**
Miscellanea di Studi Storici (ITA ISSN 0581-1643) **4153**
Miscellanea Faunistica Helvetiae (CHE ISSN 1421-5616) **854**
Miscellanea Francescana (ITA ISSN 0026-587X) **7807**
Miscellanea Historiae Pontificiae (ITA ISSN 0080-3979) **7807**
Miscellanea Historico-Iuridica (POL ISSN 1732-9132) **4734**
Miscellanea Malacologica (NLD ISSN 1573-9953) **955**
➤ Miscellanea Mediaevalia (DEU ISSN 0544-4128) **6935**
➤ Miscellanea Musicologica (CZE ISSN 0544-4136) **6588**
➤ Miscellanea Neerlandica (BEL) **4465**
Miscellanea Storica della Valdelsa (ITA ISSN 0026-5888) **4245**
Miscellaneous Report - State of Ohio, Department of Natural Resources, Division of Geological Survey *see* Ohio. Division of Geological Survey. Miscellaneous Report **2760**
Miscellany (IND ISSN 0026-5896) **5334**
Miscellany Magazine (USA) **2292**
• ➤ Miscolc Mathematical Notes (HUN ISSN 1787-2405) **5518**
• Mise a Jour des Etudes Analytiques (CAN ISSN 1708-0932) **8388**
• Mise a Jour sur les Pesticides a Risque Reduit au Canada (CAN ISSN 1715-1813) **7531**
† Mise aux Normes et Securite des Batiments (FRA ISSN 1951-8641) **8974**
Mise en Marche du Bois de la Foret Privee du Quebec (CAN ISSN 1910-9768) **3697**
Misereor Aktuell (DEU ISSN 0942-2269) **1601**
• The Miser's Gazette (CAN ISSN 1203-3154) **4364**
† Mises au Point de Biochimie Pharmacologique (FRA ISSN 0294-0671) **8974**
• Mises Review (USA ISSN 1537-4564) **1546**
Misesu *see* Mrs **4364**
Misha/Teddy Bear (RUS ISSN 0208-1563) **2202**
Misha dlya Roditelei (RUS) **2161**
Mishigan Daigaku Nihon Kenkyu Ronshu *see* Michigan Papers in Japanese Studies **4186**
† Mishkafayim (ISR ISSN 0334-9810) **8974**
• ➤ Mishkan (USA ISSN 0792-0474) **7663**
Mishkat (IRN) **7714**
Mishpacha Tova *see* Mishpaha Tova **8121**
• Mishpaha Tova (ISR) **8121**
Mishpatim (ISR ISSN 0581-1651) **4734**
• Mishu (CHN ISSN 1674-2354) **7155**
• Mishu Gongzuo/Secretary Work (CHN ISSN 1003-9740) **1852**
• Mishu Zhi You/Secretary's Companion (CHN ISSN 1004-3071) **1852**
Misioneros Javerianos (ESP) **7663**
Misjonshoegskolen. Dissertation Series/School of Mission and Theology. Dissertation Series (NOR ISSN 0809-8999) **7663**
Misjonshoegskolen. Ressursserie (NOR ISSN 1504-1204) **7663**
• Misjonstidende (NOR ISSN 0800-5346) **7767**
Misjonstidende (CD-ROM) *see* Misjonstidende **7767**
Miskolci Egyetem. Kozlemenyei. 3 Sorozat, Gepeszet (HUN ISSN 1215-0851) **8432**
Miskolci Egyetem Kozlemenyei. Bolcsesz- es Tarsadalomtudomanyi Kozlemenyek *see* Publicationes Universitatis Miskolciensis. Sectio Philosophica **4471**
Miskotte Nieuwsbrief (NLD ISSN 1574-9754) **7663**
Misli/Thoughts (AUS ISSN 1443-8364) **7807**
Miss (AUT) **3797**
Miss Beauty (HUN) **2202**
Miss Information's Automotive Calendar of Events (USA ISSN 1074-3510) **367**
Al-Missa (EGY) **3836**
Missbehave Magazine (USA ISSN 1932-8044) **8875**
Misset Cafe (NLD ISSN 1574-342X) **4394**
Misset Catering (NLD ISSN 1872-2814) **4394**
Misset Hotel (NLD ISSN 1574-3411) **4394**
Misset Restaurant (NLD ISSN 1574-3403) **4394**
• Missets Horeca (NLD ISSN 0929-3515) **4394**
† Misset's Milieuhandboek (NLD ISSN 1380-2070) **8974**
Missieinteractie *see* Missio Wereldwijd **7663**
Missile Forecast *see* Market Intelligence Reports: Missile Forecast **6433**
Missiles and Rockets *see* Jane's Missiles and Rockets **6427**
Missiles and Space Vehicles *see* Daodan yu Hangtian Yunzai Jishu **52**
• Missim (ISR ISSN 0334-9853) **1935**
Missio Aktuell (DEU ISSN 0945-3407) **7807**
Missio Wereldwijd (NLD ISSN 1874-5873) **7663**
• ➤ Missiology (USA ISSN 0091-8296) **7739**
Mission (CAN ISSN 1198-0400) **7664**
mission (DEU) **7663**
† Mission (DNK ISSN 0106-5610) **8974**
Mission (USA) **7663**
Mission (Uppsala) *see* Kyrkans Tidning **7659**
• Mission Action (NZL) **7767**
Mission Advanced Research & Communication Center Newsletter *see* M A R C Newsletter **7661**
• Mission Australia. Annual Review (AUS ISSN 1834-2523) **8055**
▼ • Mission Critical (USA ISSN 1947-1521) **2432**
Mission Critical Communications *see* MissionCritical Communications **2360**
Mission de l'Eglise (FRA ISSN 0755-138X) **7807**
Mission Frontiers (USA ISSN 0889-9436) **7664**
Mission Handbook. U.S. and Canadian Protestant Ministries Overseas (USA) **7767**
Mission Hill Gazette (USA) **3551**
• Mission i Stockholm (SWE ISSN 1403-1248) **8055**
Mission Nature (BEL) **955**
Mission Outlook (GBR ISSN 0962-8142) **7807**
Mission Partners *see* Uniting World **7691**
• ➤ Mission Studies (NLD ISSN 0168-9789) **7664**
Mission to Military Garrisons News (GBR) **6437**
• Mission Today (GBR ISSN 0967-8379) **7807**
• Mission Update (USA ISSN 1542-6130) **7807**
Mission Weltweit (DEU ISSN 1430-9092) **7767**
Missionalia (ZAF ISSN 0256-9507) **7699**
Missionari del P I M E (Pontificio Istituto Missioni Estere) (ITA) **7807**
Missionaries of the Sacred Heart. Annals Australasia (AUS ISSN 1444-4178) **7807**
Missionary Herald *see* M H **7766**
Missionary Herald (USA) **7767**
Missionary Monthly (USA ISSN 0161-7133) **7664**
Missionary Reporter (USA) **7767**
Missionary Sisters of the Immaculate Conception Mission News *see* M I C Mission News **8054**
MissionCritical Communications (USA ISSN 1544-9556) **2360**
Missione Salute (ITA) **6992**
Missionhurst (USA ISSN 0026-6086) **7807**
▼ Missionnaires Serviteurs des Pauvres du Tiers-Monde (FRA ISSN 1957-3928) **7807**
Missions (USA) **7767**
Missions des Franciscains (CAN ISSN 0700-4192) **7807**
Missions-Etrangeres (CAN ISSN 0026-6116) **7664**
• Missions Leader (USA) **7768**
Missions Leader - Associational Edition (USA) **7768**
• Missions Mosaic (USA ISSN 1083-3293) **7768**
Missions Permanentes aupres de l'Organisation des Nations Unies *see* Permanent Missions to the United Nations **7259**
Missions to Seafarers Annual Report (GBR) **7768**
Missionsblaetter (DEU ISSN 0179-0102) **7807**
Missionsgeschichtliches Archiv (DEU ISSN 1430-1016) **4245**
Missionskalender - Jahrbuch St. Ottilien (DEU) **7807**
Missionszentrale der Franziskaner. Berichte, Dokumente, Kommentare (DEU ISSN 1618-9264) **7807**
Missisquoi Historical Society Reports (CAN) **3775**
Mississauga Board of Trade (CAN ISSN 1912-7731) **1431**
Mississauga Business Times (CAN ISSN 1185-2186) **1431**
• Mississauga News (CAN ISSN 0834-6585) **3813**
• Mississippi (USA ISSN 0747-1602) **3982**
• Mississippi Academy of Science. Journal (USA ISSN 0076-9436) **7882**
Mississippi Agricultural and Forestry Experiment Station. Bulletin (USA ISSN 0898-0497) **137**
Mississippi Agricultural and Forestry Experiment Station Research Highlights *see* M A F E S Research Highlights **134**
Mississippi Agricultural & Forestry Experiment Station. Research Report (USA ISSN 0147-2186) **137**
Mississippi-Alabama Sea Grant Consortium. Report (USA) **2813**
Mississippi Archaeology (USA ISSN 0738-775X) **406**
Mississippi Banker (USA ISSN 0026-6159) **1367**
Mississippi Builder (USA ISSN 1552-8723) **1024**
• Mississippi Business Directory (USA ISSN 1046-056X) **2017**
• Mississippi Business Journal (USA ISSN 0195-0002) **1964**
Mississippi Cities and Counties Graphic Performance Analysis *see* Mississippi Cities & Counties Graphic Performance Analysis **7482**
Mississippi Cities & Counties Graphic Performance Analysis (USA ISSN 1935-6056) **7482**
• ➤ Mississippi College Law Review (USA ISSN 0277-1152) **4735**
Mississippi Congress of Parents and Teachers. Yearbook (USA ISSN 0076-9479) **2887**
• Mississippi Crimes, Vehicles, Traffic Regulations and Related Statutes (USA) **4735**
Mississippi. Department of Wildlife Conservation. Annual Report (USA ISSN 0733-2017) **3601**
Mississippi Economics Review & Outlook (USA ISSN 1530-5546) **1499**
Mississippi Educator (USA ISSN 0164-8683) **2887**
• Mississippi Employment Law Letter (USA ISSN 1074-0430) **4735**
Mississippi Entomological Museum Series (USA ISSN 1051-3108) **854**
The Mississippi Episcopalian (USA ISSN 1942-8154) **7768**
Mississippi Farm Bureau Country *see* Mississippi Farm Country **137**
• Mississippi Farm Country (USA ISSN 1529-9600) **137**
Mississippi Folklife (USA) **3620**
Mississippi Game & Fish (USA ISSN 0744-4192) **8322**
Mississippi Geology (USA ISSN 0275-8555) **2755**
Mississippi Government Register (USA ISSN 1094-0685) **7453**
Mississippi History Newsletter (USA) **4304**
Mississippi Holiday Guide (GBR) **8736**
Mississippi Homes & Gardens *see* Mississippi **3982**
➤ Mississippi Kite (USA ISSN 0737-0393) **910**
Mississippi Language Crusader (USA ISSN 0026-6272) **5151**
• Mississippi Law Journal (USA ISSN 0026-6280) **4735**
The Mississippi Lawyer (USA ISSN 0462-8551) **4735**
Mississippi Legion-Aire (USA ISSN 0026-6299) **2268**
• Mississippi Libraries (USA ISSN 0194-388X) **5032**
• Mississippi Manufacturers Register (USA ISSN 1078-2249) **2017**
Mississippi Manufacturers Register for Windows 95/98, Windows N T *see* Mississippi Manufacturers Register **2017**
Mississippi: Manufacturing *see* Harris Directory. Mississippi Manufacturing **2000**
• Mississippi Matters (USA) **2887**
Mississippi Municipalities (USA ISSN 0026-6337) **7498**
Mississippi Music Educator (USA) **6588**
Mississippi Music Educator Journal *see* Mississippi Music Educator **6588**
Mississippi Native Plants (USA) **3743**
Mississippi Outdoors (USA ISSN 1041-9306) **2619**
Mississippi Pharmacist (USA ISSN 0161-3189) **6861**
Mississippi Philological Association. Publications (USA ISSN 0740-9478) **5334**
• ➤ The Mississippi Quarterly (USA ISSN 0026-637X) **5227**
• Mississippi R N (Registered Nurse) (USA ISSN 0026-6388) **5970**
The Mississippi Rag (USA ISSN 0742-4612) **6588**
Mississippi Research & Development Center *see* Mississippi Economics Review & Outlook **1499**
• ➤ Mississippi Review (USA ISSN 0047-7559) **5334**
Mississippi School Directory *see* M D R's School Directory. Mississippi **2959**
Mississippi. State Board of Architecture. Annual Report (USA) **450**
➤ Mississippi State Medical Association. Journal (USA ISSN 0026-6396) **5680**
Mississippi State University Alumnus (USA) **2292**
Mississippi State University. Extension Service. Publication (USA) **137**
Mississippi State University. Forest Products Laboratory. Information Series (USA) **3714**
Mississippi State University. Forest Products Laboratory. Research Report (USA) **3714**
Mississippi State University. Social Research Report Series (USA) **8121**
Mississippi Times (USA) **3453**
Mississippi United Methodist Advocate (USA) **7768**
Mississippi Valley Review (USA ISSN 0270-3521) **5334**
Missives *see* Societe Litteraire de la Poste et de France Telecom. Missives **5239**
Missouri Academy of Science. Bulletin (USA) **7882**
Missouri Academy of Science. Occasional Paper (USA ISSN 0148-0944) **7882**
• ➤ Missouri Academy of Science. Transactions (USA ISSN 0544-540X) **7882**
Missouri: All-Industries *see* Harris Directory. Missouri All-Industries **2000**
Missouri & Kansas Super Lawyers *see* K C Magazine **3979**
Missouri Annual Campaign Finance Report (USA) **7155**
Missouri Archaeological Society. Quarterly (USA ISSN 0743-7641) **406**
Missouri Archaeologist (USA ISSN 0076-9576) **406**
Missouri Area Labor Trends (USA ISSN 0148-4214) **1697**
Missouri BankNews Bank Directory *see* BankNews Directory of Missouri Banks **1318**
Missouri Bar. Family Law Section. Newsletter (USA) **4913**
• Missouri Bar. Journal (USA ISSN 0026-6485) **4735**
Missouri Bar. Legislative Digest (USA) **4735**
Missouri Beef Cattleman (USA ISSN 0192-3056) **293**
Missouri Beverage Journal (USA ISSN 0191-4685) **607**
• ➤ Missouri Botanical Garden. Annals (USA ISSN 0026-6493) **801**
• Missouri Botanical Garden. Annual Report (USA ISSN 1060-7854) **801**
Missouri Botanical Garden. Monographs in Systematic Botany (USA ISSN 0161-1542) **801**

Title

10618 MISSOURI BUSINESS ULRICH'S PERIODICALS

Missouri Business (USA ISSN 0540-4428) **1407**
• Missouri Business Credit Directory (USA) **2017**
• Missouri Business Directory (USA ISSN 1048-7301) **2017**
Missouri Cities & Counties Graphic Performance Analysis (USA ISSN 1935-5963) **7482**
Missouri Cities and Counties Graphic Performance Analysis *see* Missouri Cities & Counties Graphic Performance Analysis **7482**
Missouri Civil Procedure Forms (USA) **4838**
• Missouri Conservationist (USA ISSN 0026-6515) **2619**
Missouri Corporate Forms (USA) **4876**
Missouri Court Rules (USA ISSN 1093-6467) **4956**
• Missouri Crime and Punishment, Vehicles & Related Statutes (USA) **4735**
• Missouri D W I Handbook (Driving While Intoxicated) (USA ISSN 1932-1562) **4894**
Missouri. Department of Agriculture. Weekly Market Summary (USA ISSN 0279-2346) **137**
Missouri. Department of Insurance. Annual Report and Statistical Data (USA) **4530**
Missouri. Department of Revenue. Comprehensive Annual Financial Report (USA) **1935**
Missouri. Division of Geological Survey and Water Resources. Engineering Geology Series (USA ISSN 0076-9606) **3278**
Missouri. Division of Geological Survey and Water Resources. Water Resources Report (USA ISSN 0076-9614) **8829**
Missouri. Division of Geology and Land Survey. Special Publication (USA ISSN 1046-0594) **2755**
Missouri. Division of Youth Services. Annual Report (USA) **8055**
Missouri Domestic Relations Forms (USA) **4913**
Missouri Economic Indicators (USA ISSN 0195-6159) **1499**
• Missouri. Emergency Management Agency. Newsletter (USA ISSN 0197-6672) **2227**
• Missouri Employment Law Letter (USA ISSN 1054-6375) **4735**
Missouri Engineer (USA ISSN 0026-6558) **3210**
Missouri English Bulletin (USA) **5151**
Missouri Environmental Law and Policy Review (USA ISSN 1072-7396) **4735**
• Missouri Estate Planning, Will Drafting and Estate Administration Forms (USA) **4904**
Missouri Evidentiary Foundations (USA) **4956**
Missouri Facts (USA ISSN 1056-9596) **3121**
Missouri Farmer Today (USA ISSN 1937-0105) **137**
➤ Missouri Folklore Society. Journal (USA ISSN 0731-2946) **3620**
Missouri Game & Fish (USA ISSN 0889-3799) **8322**
Missouri Grocer (USA ISSN 1522-1008) **3680**
➤ Missouri Historical Review (USA ISSN 0026-6582) **4304**
Missouri Journal of Health, Physical Education, Recreation and Dance (USA ISSN 1058-6288) **6992**
• Missouri Journal of Mathematical Sciences (USA ISSN 0899-6180) **5518**
➤ Missouri Journal of Research in Music Education (USA ISSN 0085-350X) **6588**
• ➤ Missouri Law Review (USA ISSN 0026-6604) **4735**
• Missouri Lawyers Weekly (USA ISSN 0899-5907) **4735**
Missouri Lawyers Weekly Directory of In-House Counsel (USA ISSN 1549-2516) **4735**
• Missouri Life (USA ISSN 1525-0814) **3982**
• Missouri Manufacturers Register (USA ISSN 0893-2816) **2017**
Missouri: Manufacturing *see* Harris Directory. Missouri Manufacturing **2000**
Missouri Medical Law Report (USA) **5680**
Missouri Medicine (USA ISSN 0026-6620) **5680**
Missouri Monthly Vital Statistics (USA) **7312**
Missouri Municipal Review (USA ISSN 0026-6647) **7498**
Missouri Notary Law Primer (USA ISSN 1930-7055) **4735**
Missouri Nurse (USA ISSN 0026-6655) **5970**
Missouri Pharmacist (USA ISSN 0026-6663) **6861**
Missouri Philological Association. Publications (USA ISSN 0194-035X) **5335**
Missouri Political Science Association Newsletter *see* M O P S A Newsletter **7152**
Missouri Population Estimates (USA ISSN 0734-032X) **7287**
Missouri Practice Series. Landlord-Tenant Handbook (USA ISSN 1930-3408) **4735**
Missouri Press News (USA ISSN 0026-6671) **4580**
Missouri Realtor (USA ISSN 1087-1128) **7600**
• Missouri Record (USA ISSN 1059-7506) **4075**
• The Missouri Review (USA ISSN 0191-1961) **5335**
• Missouri Ruralist (USA ISSN 0026-668X) **137**
Missouri School Board (USA ISSN 0026-6698) **3027**
Missouri School Directory *see* M D R's School Directory. Missouri **2959**
† Missouri Sources, Queries and Reviews (USA ISSN 1075-6191) **8974**
Missouri Speech & Theatre Journal (USA) **8474**
Missouri Speleology (USA ISSN 0026-671X) **2756**
• Missouri State Board of Nursing. Newsletter (USA) **5970**
Missouri State Genealogical Association Journal (USA ISSN 0747-5667) **3775**
• Missouri State Government Publications (USA) **7482**
Missouri State Library. Newsline *see* Newsline (Jefferson City) **5036**
Missouri Teamster (USA ISSN 0026-6728) **4599**
• Missouri Travel Guide (USA) **8736**
Missouri Trial Objections (USA) **4956**
Missouri Vital Statistics (USA ISSN 0098-1974) **7312**
Missouri Wildlife (USA ISSN 1082-8591) **2619**
• Missouri's Forest Resources in (Year) (USA ISSN 1931-0730) **3697**
Missouri's New and Expanding Industry (USA ISSN 0540-4193) **1899**
Mistelbach in Vergangenheit und Gegenwart (AUT) **4245**
Mister Motley (NLD ISSN 1574-2938) **506**
Mister Pulo *see* Mr. Pulo **3960**
Mister Writer's Expressions Magazine *see* MisterWriter's Expressions Magazine **5228**
▼ • MisterWriter's Expressions Magazine (USA ISSN 1947-6000) **5228**
Mistletoe Leaves (USA ISSN 1932-0108) **4304**
• Mistni Kultura (Online) (CZE ISSN 1803-2818) **8474**
Mistni Kultura (Print) *see* Mistni Kultura (Online) **8474**
• Misuljaryo/National Museum Journal of Arts (KOR ISSN 0540-4568) **506**
Misur Jaryo *see* Misuljaryo **506**
Misure Critiche (ITA ISSN 0392-6397) **5335**
Misyjne Drogi (POL ISSN 0209-1348) **7807**
▼ Mit Liebe (DEU) **4364**
➤ Mita Gakkai Zasshi/Mita Journal of Economics (JPN ISSN 0026-6760) **1149**
Mita Journal of Economics *see* Mita Gakkai Zasshi **1149**
Mitamaki/Sagami Shell Club. News (JPN ISSN 0912-1390) **955**
Die Mitarbeiterin (DEU ISSN 0342-9962) **8875**
mitbestimmung (AUT ISSN 1561-2341) **1697**
• Die Mitbestimmung (DEU ISSN 0723-5984) **4735**
Mitchell Air Bag Service & Repair Manual. Reference Information (USA ISSN 1930-8493) **8591**
Mitchell Collision Estimating & Reference Guide. Medium Duty Trucks & Commercial Vehicles (USA ISSN 1930-4293) **8591**
• Mitchell Imported Cars, Light Trucks & Vans Service & Repair (USA ISSN 1080-9392) **8591**
Mitchell, Taylor and Talbot on Confiscation and the Proceeds of Crime (GBR) **4894**
Miteinander (Wuerzburg) (DEU ISSN 1612-9873) **5680**
Miteinander Gott Entdecken (DEU) **2887**
Miteinander Leben Lernen (DEU ISSN 0342-3174) **7386**
Miteinander Unterwegs (DEU) **7768**
• Mithani - Directors' Disqualification (GBR) **4876**
• ➤ Mitigation and Adaptation Strategies for Global Change (NLD ISSN 1381-2386) **3453**
Mito Kagaku Gijutsu/Society of Non-Traditional Technology. Journal (JPN ISSN 0914-627X) **8432**
• ➤ Mitochondrial D N A (Deoxyribonucleic Acid) (GBR ISSN 1940-1736) **738**
• ➤ Mitochondrion (NLD ISSN 1567-7249) **893**
• Mitologicas (ARG ISSN 0326-5676) **348**
• MitoMatters (USA ISSN 1542-5355) **834**
Mitomycin-C Kyowa Update (GBR) **6027**
Mitrania (SWE ISSN 1651-3053) **5445**
Mitre (CAN) **5228**
Mitsubachi Kagaku/Honeybee Science (JPN ISSN 0388-2217) **855**
Mitsubishi Cable Industries Review *see* Mitsubishi Densen Kogyo Jiho **3325**
Mitsubishi Denki Giho/Mitsubishi Denki Technical Review (JPN ISSN 0369-2302) **3325**
Mitsubishi Denki Technical Review *see* Mitsubishi Denki Giho **3325**
Mitsubishi Densen Kogyo Jiho/Mitsubishi Cable Industries Review (JPN ISSN 0913-0101) **3325**
Mitsubishi Economic Research Institute's Monthly Circular *see* M E R I's Monthly Circular **1497**
• Mitsubishi Electric Advance (JPN ISSN 0386-5096) **3325**
• Mitsubishi Heavy Industries Technical Review (Online) (JPN) **8432**
Mitsubishi Juko Giho (JPN ISSN 0387-2432) **8432**
➤ Mitsubishi Kagaku Institute of Life Sciences. Annual Report (JPN) **689**
Mitsui Kensetsu Gijutsu Kenkyu Hokoku *see* Mitsui Sumitomo Kensetsu Gijutsu Kenkyuujo Houkoku **1024**
• Mitsui Sumitomo Kensetsu Gijutsu Kenkyuujo Houkoku/Sumitomo Mitsui Construction Co., Ltd. Technical Research Institute. Reports (JPN ISSN 1348-8627) **1024**
Mitsui Zosen Giho *see* Mitsui Zosen Technical Review **8653**
Mitsui Zosen Technical Review/Mitsui Zosen Giho (JPN ISSN 0026-6825) **8653**
Mitsui Zosen Tekko Kensetsu Kouji Gurupu Giho/M E S - M S C Steel Construction Group Technical Review (JPN) **3278**
Mitteilen (DEU ISSN 1436-9397) **7768**
Mitteilungen *see* Naukove Tovarystvo Imeni Shevchenka. Zapysky **3553**
Mitteilungen aus Baltischem Leben (DEU ISSN 0026-6833) **5228**
Mitteilungen aus dem Brenner-Archiv (AUT ISSN 1027-5649) **4465**
Mitteilungen aus dem Institut fuer Nachrichtentechnik der Technischen Universitaet Braunschweig *see* Technische Universitaet Braunschweig. Institut fuer Nachrichtentechnik. Mitteilungen **2340**
• ➤ Mitteilungen aus dem Museum fuer Naturkunde in Berlin - Deutsche Entomologische Zeitschrift (DEU ISSN 1435-1951) **855**
• ➤ Mitteilungen aus dem Museum fuer Naturkunde in Berlin - Geowissenschaftliche Reihe (DEU ISSN 1435-1943) **2713**
Mitteilungen aus dem Museum fuer Naturkunde in Berlin - Zoologische Reihe *see* Zoosystematics and Evolution **971**
Mitteilungen aus dem Storm-Haus (DEU ISSN 0938-3751) **5335**
Mitteilungen aus der Arbeitsmarkt- und Berufsforschung *see* Zeitschrift fuer Arbeitsmarktforschung **1717**
Mitteilungen aus der F f H Berlin (Forschungsstelle fuer den Handel Berlin e.V.) (DEU ISSN 0931-5934) **1431**
Mitteilungen aus Lebensmitteluntersuchung und Hygiene/Travaux de Chimie Alimentaire et d'Hygiene (CHE ISSN 1424-1307) **6663**
Mitteilungen "Berufsbildung" (DEU) **1407**
Mitteilungen der Aerztekammer fuer Wien - Wiener Arzt *see* DoktorinWien **5606**
Mitteilungen der Anthropologischen Gesellschaft in Wien *see* Anthropologische Gesellschaft in Wien. Mitteilungen **326**
Mitteilungen der Deutschen Gesellschaft fuer Allgemeine und Angewandte Entomologie *see* Deutsche Gesellschaft fuer Allgemeine und Angewandte Entomologie. Mitteilungen **843**
Mitteilungen der Deutschen Malakozoologischen Gesellschaf *see* Deutsche Malakozoologische Gesellschaft. Mitteilungen **940**
Mitteilungen der Deutschen Patentanwaelte (DEU ISSN 0026-6884) **6755**
† Mitteilungen der Deutschen und der Oesterrichischen Gesellschaft fuer Internistische Intensivmedizin (BRD ISSN 0172-4258) **8974**
• Mitteilungen der Fachgruppe Umweltchemie und Okotoxikologie, Gesellschaft Deutscher Chemiker (DEU ISSN 1617-5301) **2073**
Mitteilungen der Internationalen Joseph Martin Kraus-Gesellschaft *see* International Joseph Martin Kraus-Gesellschaft. Mitteilungen **6576**
• Mitteilungen der Karl-May-Gesellschaft (DEU ISSN 0941-7842) **5335**
➤ Mitteilungen der Naturforschenden Gesellschaften beider Basel (CHE ISSN 1420-4606) **7882**
Mitteilungen der Oesterreichischen Gesellschaft fuer Tropenmedizin und Parasitologie *see* Oesterreichische Gesellschaft fuer Tropenmedizin und Parasitologie. Mitteilungen **5823**
Mitteilungen der Universitaet Hamburg (DEU ISSN 0438-4717) **2994**
• Mitteilungen des Bayerischen Notarvereins, der Notarkasse und der Landesnotarkammer Bayern (DEU ISSN 0941-4193) **4735**
Mitteilungen des Deutschen Archaeologischen Instituts Roemische Abteilung *see* Deutsches Archaeologisches Institut. Roemische Abteilung. Mitteilungen **390**
Mitteilungen des Instituts fuer Oesterreichische Geschichtsforschung *see* Institut fuer Oesterreichische Geschichtsforschung. Mitteilungen **4232**
Mitteilungen des Obstbauversuchsringes des Alten Landes *see* Obstbauversuchsring des Altes Landes. Mitteilungen **244**
Mitteilungen des Oesterreichischen Staatsarchivs (AUT ISSN 0259-4153) **4245**
➤ Mitteilungen fuer Anthropologie und Religionsgeschichte (DEU ISSN 0939-9186) **7664**
Mitteilungen fuer Dolmetscher und Uebersetzer (DEU ISSN 1618-5595) **5151**
• Mitteilungen fuer Wissenschaft und Technik (DEU ISSN 0340-5117) **7081**
Mitteilungen und Forschungsbeitraege der Cusanus-Gesellschaft *see* Cusanus-Gesellschaft. Mitteilungen und Forschungsbeitraege **7794**
Mitteilungen und Materialen *see* Zeitschrift fuer Museum und Bildung **6540**
† • Mitteilungen zur Astronomiegeschichte (DEU ISSN 0944-1999) **8974**
• Mitteilungen zur Christlichen Archaeologie (AUT ISSN 1025-6555) **506**
Mitteilungen zur Fischerei/Informations Concernant la Peche (CHE) **3601**
† Mitteilungen zur Geschichte der Medizin der Naturwissenschaften und Technik (DDR ISSN 0368-9913) **8974**
Mitteilungen zur Sozial- und Kulturgeschichte der Islamischen Welt (DEU ISSN 1436-8080) **7714**
Mitteilungen zur Spaetantiken Archaeologie und Byzantinischen Kunstgeschichte (DEU ISSN 1434-7091) **406**
Mitteilungsblatt Berliner Zahnaerzte (DEU ISSN 0343-0162) **5856**
Mitteilungsblatt der Arbeitsgemeinschaft Verkehrsrecht *see* Der Verkehrsanwalt **4807**
Mitteilungsblatt der Deutschen China Gesellschaft *see* Deutsche China Gesellschaft. Mitteilungsblatt **547**
Mitteilungsblatt der Stadt Villach (AUT) **7498**
Mitteilungsblatt des Zivilschutzes *see* Feuille Officielle de la Protection Civile **2226**
Mitteilungsblatt - Gesellschaft Deutscher Chemiker, Fachgruppe Analytische Chemie *see* Analytical and Bioanalytical Chemistry **2097**
Mitteilungsblatt - Gesellschaft Deutscher Chemiker, Fachgruppe Umweltchemie und Okotoxikologie *see* Mitteilungen der Fachgruppe Umweltchemie und Okotoxikologie, Gesellschaft Deutscher Chemiker **2073**
Mittel- und Osteuropa Perspektiven Jahrbuch (DEU) **1499**
• ➤ Das Mittelalter (DEU ISSN 0949-0345) **4245**
Mittelalter (Basel)/Medioevo/Moyen Age/Temp Medieval (CHE ISSN 1420-6994) **7600**
Mittelbayerische Zeitung (DEU) **3853**
Mitteldeutsche Studien zu Ostasien (DEU ISSN 1436-9591) **556**
Mitteldeutsche Wirtschaft (DEU) **1407**
Mitteldeutsche Zeitung (DEU) **3853**
➤ Mitteldeutsches Jahrbuch fuer Kultur und Geschichte (DEU ISSN 0946-3119) **4245**
Mitteleuropa - Osteuropa. Oldenburger Beitraege zur Kultur und Geschichte Ostmitteleuropas (DEU) **4245**
➤ Mittellateinische Studien und Texte (NLD ISSN 0076-9754) **4245**
➤ Mittellateinisches Jahrbuch (DEU ISSN 0076-9762) **4245**
• Mittelstaendische Unternehmen (DEU ISSN 0930-3618) **1899**
Der Mittelstand (DEU) **1149**
Mittelweg 36 (DEU ISSN 0941-6382) **5228**
Mittendrin (Detmold) (DEU) **8736**
Mittendrin (Dillenburg) (DEU) **7768**
† Mitternachts-Roman (DEU) **8974**
Mittex: Mitteilungen ueber Textilindustrie (CHE ISSN 1015-5910) **8455**
Der Mittler-Brief (DEU ISSN 0936-4013) **6437**
Mittlere Deutsche Literatur in Neu- und Nachdrucken (CHE ISSN 0172-1763) **5335**
Mittuniversitetet. Avdelingen foer Medie- och Kommunikationsvetenskap. Communique (SWE ISSN 1653-2082) **8121**
• Mivhar ha-Peninim (USA ISSN 1930-0581) **3551**
Mivnim (ISR ISSN 0333-7502) **1024**
Mivo + 16 *see* AanZet **7743**
• Mix (CAN ISSN 1204-5349) **506**
Mix (DEU) **3853**
Mix (FIN ISSN 1458-3763) **6588**
• The Mix (GBR ISSN 1354-4284) **6588**
Mix *see* Vakblad Mix **4439**
Mix (SRB ISSN 1451-9836) **8187**
▼ Mix (USA) **3551**
Mix Annual Directory of Recording Industry Facilities and Services (USA) **2017**
Mix Annual Recording Industry Directory *see* Mix Annual Directory of Recording Industry Facilities and Services **2017**
Mix Fashion *see* Mix Fashion. Future Womenswear **2258**
Mix Fashion *see* Mix Fashion. Future Menswear **2258**
Mix Fashion. Future Menswear (GBR ISSN 1751-0430) **2258**
Mix Fashion. Future Womenswear (GBR ISSN 1751-0422) **2258**
• Mix Magazine (USA ISSN 0164-9957) **8154**
Mixage (DEU) **6971**
† Mixart News (ITA) **8974**
Mixdown Monthly (AUS ISSN 1441-1822) **8154**
▼ Mixed Martial Arts Authority Magazine (USA ISSN 1939-5787) **8187**
Mixed Martial Arts Cage *see* M M A Cage **8186**
Mixed Martial Arts Worldwide *see* M M A Worldwide **8186**
Mixed Media (USA) **506**
• Mixed Messages (USA) **3509**
† Mixer (ITA) **8974**
Mixer (USA) **6588**
Mixi (EST) **8187**
Mixin' (USA) **607**
Mixmag (GBR ISSN 0957-6622) **6588**
Mixman (FRA ISSN 1957-522X) **2203**
Mixtape (USA) **6588**
Mixte (FRA ISSN 1299-9180) **8875**
▼ Mixte 100% Homme (FRA ISSN 1961-6759) **2258**
Mixte Cent pour Cent Homme *see* Mixte 100% Homme **2258**
Mixtura (ISL ISSN 1021-0075) **6861**
Mixtures (CAN ISSN 1201-5741) **6588**
Miyabea/Illustrated Flora of Hokkaido (JPN ISSN 0917-043X) **801**
Miyagi Daigaku Shokusangyou Gakubu Kiyou/Miyagi University. School of Food, Agricultural and Environmental Sciences. Journal (JPN ISSN 1880-6589) **137**
Miyagi-ken Genshiryoku Senta Nenpo/Environmental Radioactivity Research Institute of Miyagi. Annual Report (JPN ISSN 0912-3490) **3171**
Miyagi-ken Yakuji Joho/Miyagi Prefecture Drug Information (JPN ISSN 0913-2147) **6861**
Miyagi Kogyo Koto Senmon Gakko Kenkyu Kiyo/Miyagi National College of Technology. Research Reports (JPN ISSN 0286-3707) **8432**
Miyagi National College of Technology. Research Reports *see* Miyagi Kogyo Koto Senmon Gakko Kenkyu Kiyo **8432**
Miyagi Nuclear Power News *see* Genshiryoku Dayori Miyagi **3167**
Miyagi Prefectural Report of Fisheries Science *see* Miyagiken Suisan Kenkyuu Houkoku **3601**

Title

Modellbauer-Handwerk (DEU) **3370**
† ModellCollector (DEU ISSN 1862-7498) **8974**
Modellfan *see* Modell Fan **4341**
Modellflieger (DEU ISSN 0720-9215) **4341**
Modellflug International *see* M F I **4339**
Modellflygnytt (SWE ISSN 0345-813X) **8187**
Modelli Auto (ITA ISSN 1124-4240) **4341**
† Modellina (ITA ISSN 1121-8290) **8974**
Modelling (GRC) **4342**
Modelling, Analysis and Simulation (NLD ISSN 1386-3703) **5554**
Modelling and Simulation (CAN ISSN 1021-8181) **5554**
• ➤ Modelling and Simulation in Engineering (USA ISSN 1687-5591) **3109**
• ➤ Modelling and Simulation in Materials Science and Engineering (GBR ISSN 0965-0393) **7026**
Modelling, Identification, and Control (CAN ISSN 1025-8973) **2432**
➤ Modelling, Measurement and Control (FRA) **5554**
➤ Modelling, Measurement & Control. A: General Physics, Electronics, Electrical Engineering (FRA ISSN 1259-5985) **5554**
➤ Modelling, Measurement & Control. B: Solid & Fluid Mechanics & Thermics, Mechanical Systems (FRA ISSN 1259-5969) **5554**
➤ Modelling, Measurement & Control. C: Energetics, Chemistry, Earth, Environmental & Biomedical Problems (FRA ISSN 1259-5977) **5554**
➤ Modelling, Measurement & Control. D: Manufacturing, Management, Human and Socio-Economic Problems (FRA ISSN 1240-4551) **5555**
Modelling of Mechanical Systems (GBR ISSN 1874-7051) **3390**
† Modell's Drugs in Current Use and New Drugs (USA ISSN 1044-0704) **8974**
Modelltaag (SWE ISSN 1101-0207) **4342**
Modellvision (SWE ISSN 1653-6215) **2259**
Modellwerft (DEU ISSN 0170-1819) **4342**
Models and Modeling in Science Education (NLD ISSN 1871-2983) **2994**
Models & Talent Contracts (USA) **8474**
Models of Care (USA ISSN 1097-069X) **4107**
ModelSPORT Magazine (USA) **4342**
† Modeltoget (DNK ISSN 0107-6310) **8974**
Modem Notes (USA ISSN 0741-580X) **2564**
• Modem User News (USA) **2501**
Modemagasinet IN *see* IN **8868**
Modena Economica (ITA ISSN 0391-6626) **1407**
Modena Mondo *see* Emme Modena Mondo **1427**
▼ • Modeng Shenshi/Mr. Modern (CHN ISSN 1674-5299) **6295**
Moderat Debatt (SWE) **7155**
Moderator (USA) **2292**
Moderen Clinical Medical Bioengineering *see* Xiandai Linchuang Yixue Shengwu Gongchengxue Zazhi **751**
• Modern Accounting and Auditing Checklists (USA ISSN 1076-660X) **1297**
Modern African Generation (GBR ISSN 1747-7212) **3551**
• Modern Age (USA ISSN 0026-7457) **5228**
• ➤ Modern Aging Research (USA ISSN 0275-360X) **4051**
Modern American History: the United States Since 1865 (USA ISSN 1085-066X) **4304**
Modern American Literature (USA ISSN 1078-0521) **5335**
➤ Modern Analytical Chemistry (USA ISSN 1573-4501) **2104**
Modern and Ancient Legends *see* Jingu Chuanqi **3619**
• ➤ Modern and Contemporary France (GBR ISSN 0963-9489) **4245**
Modern and Contemporary Poetics (USA) **5427**
Modern & Mature (GBR ISSN 1747-5309) **5077**
• Modern Applications News (USA ISSN 0277-9951) **6326**
▼ • ➤ Modern Applied Science (CAN ISSN 1913-1844) **7883**
➤ Modern Approaches in Geophysics (NLD ISSN 0924-6096) **2786**
Modern Arabian Horse (USA ISSN 1942-4183) **8294**
Modern Architectural Research Group *see* Marg (Mumbai) **449**
• ➤ Modern Asian Studies (GBR ISSN 0026-749X) **556**
➤ Modern Aspects of Electrochemistry (USA ISSN 0076-9924) **2114**
Modern Astronomer (GBR ISSN 1368-0919) **578**
Modern Athlete and Coach *see* Modern Athlete & Coach **8322**
Modern Athlete & Coach (AUS ISSN 0047-7672) **8322**
• ➤ Modern Austrian Literature (USA ISSN 0026-7503) **5335**
• Modern Baking (USA ISSN 0897-6201) **3675**
Modern Banking (SWE ISSN 1100-4738) **1367**
Modern Believing (GBR ISSN 1353-1425) **7664**
• ➤ Modern Biology Series (USA ISSN 1549-1692) **689**
Modern Boating (AUS ISSN 1443-2838) **8278**
• Modern Brewery Age (USA ISSN 0026-7538) **607**
Modern Brewery Age Blue Book (USA ISSN 0076-9932) **607**
Modern Brewery Age: Tabloid Edition (USA) **607**
• Modern Bride (USA ISSN 0026-7546) **5560**
Modern Bride Atlanta (USA) **5560**
Modern Bride Boston (USA) **5560**
Modern Bride Chicago (USA) **5560**
Modern Bride Colorado (USA) **5560**
Modern Bride Connecticut (USA) **5560**
Modern Bride Florida (USA) **5560**
Modern Bride Houston (USA) **5560**
Modern Bride Maryland (USA) **5560**
Modern Bride Michigan (USA) **5560**
Modern Bride New Jersey (USA) **5560**
Modern Bride New York (USA) **5560**
Modern Bride Northern California (USA) **5560**
Modern Bride Philadelphia (USA) **5560**
Modern Bride South Jersey (USA) **8875**
Modern Bride Southern California (USA) **5560**
Modern Bride Washington (USA) **5560**
Modern Bulk Transporter *see* Bulk Transporter **8669**
Modern Business Trade Industry *see* Xiandai Shangmao Gongye **1196**
Modern Car *see* Dangdai Qiche **8577**
• Modern Car Care (USA) **8591**
Modern Cartography (NLD ISSN 1363-0814) **4037**
• Modern Casting (USA ISSN 0026-7562) **6326**
• Modern Chemical Industry (CHN ISSN 0253-4320) **3251**
• Modern Child Custody Practice (USA) **4913**
Modern China/Chin Tai Chung-kuo (TWN ISSN 1015-843X) **5228**
• ➤ Modern China (USA ISSN 0097-7004) **4186**
Modern Chinese (Education Research) *see* Xiandai Yuwen (Jiaoyu Yanjiu) **5196**
Modern Chinese (Linguistics Research) *see* Xiandai Yuwen (Yuyan Yanjiu) **5196**
Modern Chinese (Literarary Research) *see* Xiandai Yuwen (Wenxue Yanjiu) **5196**
Modern Chinese History Studies *see* Jindaishi Yanjiu **4184**
Modern Chinese Literature (USA ISSN 0190-2369) **5335**
Modern Chinese Literature and Culture (USA ISSN 1520-9857) **348**
Modern Chlor-Alkali Technology (GBR ISSN 0747-7406) **2073**
Modern Churchpeople's Union. Occasional Papers (GBR) **7664**
Modern Clinical Nursing *see* Xiandai Linchuang Huli **5984**
Modern Communication *see* Xiandai Chuanbo **2345**
Modern Computer (Professional Edition) *see* Xiandai Jisuanji (Zhuanye Ban) **2441**
Modern Computer (Regular Edition) *see* Xiandai Jisuanji (Puji Ban) **2441**
Modern Contractor S.O.L.U.T.I.O.N.S. *see* Modern Contractor Solutions **1024**
▼ Modern Contractor Solutions (USA) **1024**
Modern Corporation Checklists (USA) **1899**
Modern Courts (USA) **4956**
Modern Decoration *see* Xiandai Zhuangshi **4553**
Modern Defence Technology *see* Xiandai Fangyu Jishu **6454**
Modern Diabetes Management (GBR ISSN 1469-3895) **5897**
Modern Diagnosis & Treatment *see* Xiandai Zhenduan yu Zhiliao **5732**
Modern Distance Education Study *see* Xiandai Yuancheng Jiaoyu Yanjiu **2399**
Modern Distribution Management (USA ISSN 0544-6538) **1835**
Modern Dog (CAN ISSN 1703-812X) **6811**
• Modern Drafting Practices and Standards Manual (USA) **8432**
• ➤ Modern Drama (CAN ISSN 0026-7694) **5335**
• Modern Drummer (USA ISSN 0194-4533) **6588**
• Modern Drunkard (USA) **5077**
Modern Economic Research *see* Xiandai Jingji Tantao **1551**
Modern Education *see* Shidai Jiaoyu **2912**
Modern Educational Technology *see* Xiandai Jiaoyu Jishu **2927**
Modern Electric Power *see* Xiandai Dianli **3162**
Modern Elegance *see* Shidai Fengcai **3828**
Modern English Digest (GBR ISSN 1478-9019) **5151**
• Modern English Professional (GBR ISSN 1362-5276) **3073**
• Modern English Tanka (USA ISSN 1930-8132) **5335**
• Modern English Teacher (GBR ISSN 0308-0587) **3073**
Modern Enterprise *see* Xiandai Qiye **1196**
Modern Enterprise Culture *see* Xiandai Qiye Wenhua **1196**
Modern Enterprise World *see* Dangdai Qiye Shijie **1090**
• The Modern Estate (USA) **450**
• Modern Estate Planning (USA) **1367**
• ➤ Modern European Research (GBR ISSN 1361-2689) **7155**
Modern Family *see* Xiandai Jiating **4369**
Modern Farming *see* Ukulima wa Kisasa **164**
• Modern Federal Jury Instructions (USA) **4735**
• ➤ M F S Modern Fiction Studies (USA ISSN 0026-7724) **5335**
▼ Modern Filmmakers (USA ISSN 1943-183X) **6507**
Modern Filologiai Fuzetek (HUN ISSN 0076-9967) **5151**
Modern First Editions Collector's Bookline *see* M F E Collector's Bookline **5328**
▼ Modern First Nations Legislation Annotated (CAN ISSN 1914-9069) **4735**
Modern Fisheries Information *see* Xiandai Yuye Xinxi **3612**
Modern Fishing (AUS ISSN 0026-7732) **3602**
Modern Food Manufacturing and Marketing (USA) **3657**
Modern Food Science & Technology *see* Xiandai Shipin Keji **3668**
Modern Food Service (USA ISSN 1086-0460) **3657**
Modern Foreign Languages *see* Xiandai Waiyu **5196**
Modern French Identities (GBR ISSN 1422-9005) **5335**
† Modern German Studies (GBR ISSN 0268-5930) **8975**
Modern German Studies (USA) **8121**
Modern Government *see* Moderngov **1780**
Modern Greek Society: A Social Science Newsletter (USA ISSN 0147-0779) **4245**
Modern Greek Studies (Australia and New Zealand) (AUS ISSN 1039-2831) **4245**
Modern Greek Studies Association Bulletin (USA ISSN 0047-7702) **4245**
Modern Grocer Industry Directory (USA) **2017**
Modern Guns (USA ISSN 1550-8188) **367**
▼ Modern Haiga (USA ISSN 1941-4986) **5335**
Modern Haiku (USA ISSN 0026-7821) **5427**
Modern Hair + Beauty (AUS ISSN 1448-2649) **8875**
Modern Hair and Beauty Magazine *see* Modern Hair + Beauty **8875**
Modern Hair Plus Beauty *see* Modern Hair + Beauty **8875**
• Modern Healthcare (USA ISSN 0160-7480) **4107**
Modern Hebrew Literature (USA ISSN 0334-4266) **5335**
Modern History *see* Moderni Dejiny **4245**
Modern History of China *see* Zhongguo Jindaishi **4191**
Modern History Review *see* 20th Century History Review **4168**
Modern Homes (USA ISSN 1539-5650) **1024**
Modern Hospital Management *see* Xiandai Yiyuan Guanli **4113**
Modern Hotel (HUN ISSN 1785-9174) **4394**
Modern Household Appliances *see* Xiandai Jiadian **3116**
Modern Humanities Research Association. Publications (GBR ISSN 0581-0280) **4465**
Modern Humanities Research Association. Texts and Dissertations (GBR ISSN 0957-0322) **4465**
• Modern Hygienist (USA ISSN 1558-9242) **5856**
Modern Hypertension Management (GBR ISSN 1465-5691) **5796**
➤ Modern Inorganic Chemistry (USA ISSN 0891-4540) **2117**
Modern Intellectual and Political History in the Middle East (USA ISSN 1556-6641) **4323**
• Modern Intellectual History (GBR ISSN 1479-2443) **5228**
• ➤ Modern Italy (GBR ISSN 1353-2944) **4245**
• Modern Jeweler (USA ISSN 0744-2513) **4568**
Modern Jewish Masters (USA ISSN 1048-1575) **3551**
Modern Jewish Studies Annual (USA ISSN 0270-9406) **7727**
▼ • Modern Journal of Applied Linguistics (IND ISSN 0974-8741) **5151**
Modern Journal of Integrated Chinese Traditional and Western Medicine *see* Xiandai Zhongxiyijiehe Zazhi **5732**
Modern Journalism *see* Savremenna Zhurnalistika **4583**
• ➤ Modern Judaism (GBR ISSN 0276-1114) **3551**
The Modern Kheti (IND) **137**
Modern Klassiek (NLD ISSN 1574-3047) **5335**
Modern Klassiki (RUS) **506**
Modern Language Association of America Directory of Periodicals *see* M L A Directory of Periodicals **5407**
Modern Language Association of America Directory of Scholarly Presses in Language and Literature *see* M L A Directory of Scholarly Presses in Language and Literature **2993**
Modern Language Association of America International Bibliography *see* M L A International Bibliography **5407**
Modern Language Association of America Job Information Lists *see* M L A Job Information Lists **6700**
Modern Language Association of America Newsletter (New York) *see* M L A Newsletter (New York) **2993**
• Modern Language Association of America. Proceedings (USA) **2994**
Modern Language Association of Northern Ireland *see* N I M L A **5153**
• ➤ Modern Language Journal (USA ISSN 0026-7902) **5151**
Modern Language Linguistics *see* Web Journal of Modern Language Linguistics **5194**
Modern Language Notes *see* M L N **5149**
• ➤ Modern Language Quarterly (USA ISSN 0026-7929) **5335**
• ➤ Modern Language Review (GBR ISSN 0026-7937) **5335**
Modern Language Society of Helsinki. Bulletin *see* Neuphilologischer Verein in Helsinki. Mitteilungen **5155**
• Modern Language Studies (USA ISSN 0047-7729) **5336**
• ➤ The Modern Law Review (GBR ISSN 0026-7961) **4735**
Modern Law Science *see* Xiandai Faxue **4816**
Modern Leadership *see* Xiandai Lingdao **7197**
Modern Literary Magazine *see* Dangdai Wentan **5282**
Modern Literary World *see* Dangdai Wentan **5282**
• Modern Living (DEU ISSN 1439-0752) **5077**
Modern Living (JPN) **4364**
Modern Locomotive Handbook (USA) **8620**
Modern Logic *see* Review of Modern Logic **5529**
Modern Lounge (USA) **8875**
• Modern Luxury Dallas (USA) **3982**
▼ • Modern Luxury Dallas Brides (USA) **5560**
▼ • Modern Luxury Dallas Interiors (USA) **5077**
• Modern Luxury Hawai'i (USA) **8785**
Modern Luxury Hawaii *see* Modern Luxury Hawai'i **8785**
• Modern Machine Shop (USA ISSN 0026-8003) **5457**
Modern Machinery *see* Xiandai Jixie **5461**
Modern Manufacturing (THA) **3370**
Modern Manufacturing Xiandai Zhizao *see* M M Xiandai Zhizao **1897**
• Modern Maryland Civil Procedure (USA) **4838**
Modern Master Series (USA ISSN 0738-0429) **506**
Modern Materials (CAN) **7095**
• Modern Materials Handling (USA ISSN 0026-8038) **5457**
Modern Materials Handling Casebook Directory (USA) **5457**
Modern Materials Handling Planning Guidebook (USA) **5457**
• Modern Media (JPN ISSN 0026-8054) **893**
Modern Medical Imagelogy *see* Xiandai Yiyong Yingxiangxue **6210**
Modern Medical Journal *see* Xiandai Yixue **5732**
Modern Medical Laboratory *see* Kensa to Gijutsu **5907**
Modern Medicine *see* Suvremenna Medicina **5719**
Modern Medicine *see* Medycyna Nowozytna **5678**
Modern Medicine & Health *see* Xiandai Yiyao Weisheng **5732**
Modern Medicine of Ireland (IRL ISSN 0306-6657) **5680**
Modern Medicine of South Africa (ZAF ISSN 0259-9333) **5680**
• Modern Metals (USA ISSN 0026-8127) **6326**
Modern Metals. Directory of Metalworking Equipment, Materials & Services *see* The Metals Directory **2117**
➤ Modern Methods in Pharmacology (USA ISSN 0732-7218) **6861**
Modern Middle East Literature in Translation (USA) **5336**
Modern Middle East Series (USA ISSN 0077-0027) **4186**
Modern Military Tradition (USA ISSN 1553-7196) **4304**
Modern Miner *see* Dangdai Kuanggong **6461**
The Modern Navy *see* Dangdai Haijun **6417**
Modern Nomad *see* Places (Carrboro) **5080**
Modern Novelists *see* Palgrave Modern Novelists Series **5348**
Modern Nursing *see* Xiandai Huli **5984**
Modern Paint and Coatings Paint Red Book *see* Modern Paint & Coatings Paint Red Book **6719**
Modern Paint & Coatings Paint Red Book (USA ISSN 0090-5402) **6719**
• Modern Painters (USA ISSN 0953-6698) **506**
Modern Party Member *see* Dangdai Dangyuan **7128**
• ➤ Modern Pathology (GBR ISSN 0893-3952) **5680**
Modern Perfuming *see* Perfumeria Moderna **596**
▼ ➤ Modern Pharmaceutical Research (USA ISSN 1940-9257) **6861**
Modern Pharmacy *see* Journal of Modern Pharmacy **6854**
• ➤ Modern Philology (USA ISSN 0026-8232) **5152**
Modern Philosophy *see* Xiandai Zhexue **6961**
• Modern Physician (USA ISSN 1098-1845) **5680**
Modern Physics *see* Xiandai Wuli Zhishi **7047**
• ➤ Modern Physics Letters A (SGP ISSN 0217-7323) **7068**
• ➤ Modern Physics Letters B (SGP ISSN 0217-9849) **7068**
† Modern Phytotherapist (AUS ISSN 1322-2775) **8975**
Modern Pictorial *see* Xiandai Huabao **3829**
Modern Plastics - Rubber Technology (IND) **7095**
• Modern Plastics Worldwide (USA ISSN 1554-8589) **7095**
Modern Plastics Worldwide World Encyclopedia, with Buyer's Guide (USA) **7095**
Modern Poetry (GBR ISSN 1661-2744) **5427**
➤ Modern Poetry in Translation (GBR ISSN 0969-3572) **5427**
Modern Portfolio Theory Review *see* M P T Review **1638**
• Modern Power Systems (GBR ISSN 0260-7840) **3142**
Modern Practical Medicine *see* Xiandai Shiyong Yixue **5732**
Modern Preventive Medicine *see* Xiandai Yufang Yixue **5732**
Modern Primary and Secondary Education *see* Xiandai Zhong-xiaoxue Jiaoyu **2927**
Modern Probability and Statistics (NLD) **5518**
➤ Modern Problems in Condensed Matter Sciences (NLD ISSN 0167-7837) **7026**
Modern Problems of Pharmacopsychiatry *see* Modern Trends in Pharmacopsychiatry **6161**
• ➤ Modern Psychoanalysis (USA ISSN 0361-5227) **7386**
Modern Publishing - 21 Century Journalism & Communication Studies *see* Xiandai Chuban Xue - 21 Shiji Xinwen yu Chuanboxue Xilie Jiaocai **7576**

Modern Quaternary Research in Southeast Asia (NLD ISSN 0168-6151) **2756**
Modern Radar *see* Xiandai Leida **7073**
Modern Railways (GBR ISSN 0026-8356) **8620**
Modern Reformation (USA ISSN 1076-7169) **7768**
Modern Reprographics *see* The Wide - Format Imaging **7329**
▼ • Modern Republic (USA ISSN 1941-9732) **7155**
The Modern Review (CAN ISSN 1557-265X) **5336**
• ➤ Modern Rheumatology (JPN ISSN 1439-7595) **6225**
Modern Rural News *see* Xiandai Nongcunbao **3829**
• Modern Salon Magazine (USA ISSN 0148-4001) **589**
➤ Modern Schoolman (USA ISSN 0026-8402) **6935**
Modern Scientific Evidence. Forensics (USA ISSN 1942-938X) **2660**
▼ • Modern Seamster (USA ISSN 1946-5629) **6640**
• Modern Securities Transfers (USA ISSN 0734-3957) **1639**
Modern Simulation and Training (GBR ISSN 1471-1052) **6437**
Modern Sisters *see* Shidai Jiemei **8883**
Modern Song Circles *see* Dangdai Getan **6561**
Modern Spiritual Masters (USA) **7807**
Modern Sports *see* Dangdai Tiyu **8168**
Modern Sri Lanka Studies (LKA) **7986**
• Modern Steel Construction (USA ISSN 0026-8445) **1024**
Modern Studies in European Law (GBR) **4735**
Modern Studies in Property Law (GBR ISSN 1757-8116) **7600**
Modern Suzhou *see* Xiandai Suzhou **3829**
Modern: the Elite of our Generation *see* Fengliu Yidai **2255**
• ➤ Modern Theology (GBR ISSN 0266-7177) **7664**
• Modern Tire Dealer (USA ISSN 0026-8496) **7825**
† Modern Trends in Pharmacology and Therapeutics (GBR ISSN 0544-6910) **8975**
• ➤ Modern Trends in Pharmacopsychiatry (CHE ISSN 1662-2685) **6161**
Modern Trends in Plant Sciences (IND ISSN 0971-7269) **801**
Modern Tunnelling Technology *see* Xiandai Suidao Jishu **1043**
Modern Turkluk Arastirmalari Dergisi *see* Journal of Modern Turkish Studies **5134**
Modern U C C Litigation Forum (Uniform Commercial Code) (USA) **4736**
Modern Underwear *see* Shishang Neiyi **8457**
† • Modern Uniforms (USA ISSN 1548-3258) **8975**
Modern Urban Transit *see* Xiandai Chengshi Guidao Jiaotong **8628**
Modern Utility Management (GBR ISSN 1479-1129) **4419**
Modern Weaponry *see* Xiandai Bingqi **6454**
Modern Wedding (AUS ISSN 1441-256X) **5560**
Modern Wedding Hair and Beauty Magazine *see* Modern Hair + Beauty **8875**
▼ Modern Witch (USA ISSN 1941-3319) **6646**
Modern Witch Magazine *see* Modern Witch **6646**
Modern Woman (IRL ISSN 0790-3855) **8875**
Modern Woman (NGA ISSN 0047-7761) **8875**
Modern Women *see* Xiandai Funu **8892**
Modern Woodmen Magazine (USA ISSN 1539-3089) **2268**
• Modern Woodworking (USA ISSN 1055-4440) **4560**
Modern Words (USA ISSN 1079-7777) **5336**
Modern Workers Compensation (USA) **4876**
Modern Writers *see* Dangdai Zuojia **8948**
Modern Youth *see* Dangdai Qingnian **2185**
• Moderna (ITA ISSN 1128-6326) **5336**
• Moderna Laekare (SWE ISSN 1403-5502) **4599**
Moderna Spraak (SWE ISSN 0026-8577) **5152**
• Moderna Vremena (HRV ISSN 1330-7630) **5228**
Moderna Zena (SVK ISSN 1336-9911) **8875**
Moderne Energie und Wohnen (DEU) **3142**
Moderne Gebaeudetechnik (DEU ISSN 1436-686X) **4123**
Moderne Geschichte und Politik (DEU ISSN 0170-9127) **4245**
Moderne Informationstechnik *see* I T **2421**
Moderne Kaarten *see* Nederlandse Freecard Catalogus **4342**
Moderne - Kulturen - Relationen (CHE ISSN 1619-358X) **7986**
Moderne Metalltechnik und Kunststofftechnik (DEU ISSN 1864-3515) **6326**
Moderne Produksjon (NOR ISSN 0803-0502) **1780**
Moderne Sprachen (AUT ISSN 0026-8666) **5152**
Moderne Transport (NOR ISSN 0802-5193) **8504**
Moderne Transport Inside *see* Transport Inside **8515**
Moderne Unfallverhuetung (DEU ISSN 0544-7119) **7531**
Modernes Geschaeftsreise Management (DEU) **8737**
Modernes Office Management (DEU) **1852**
Moderngov (GBR ISSN 1755-9464) **1780**
Moderni Byt (CZE ISSN 1211-6637) **4547**
Moderni Dejiny/Modern History (CZE ISSN 1210-6860) **4245**
Moderni e Antichi (ITA ISSN 1825-3547) **2237**
Moderni Obchod (CZE ISSN 1210-4094) **1780**
Moderni Obec (CZE ISSN 1211-0507) **1149**
Moderni Rizeni (CZE ISSN 0026-8720) **1780**
Modernisation du Systeme de Classification. Rapport Annuel *see* Modernizing the Classification System. Annual Report **1870**
Modernisierungs-Magazin (DEU ISSN 0943-528X) **1024**
• The Modernism Magazine (USA ISSN 1547-3775) **450**
• ➤ Modernism/Modernity (USA ISSN 1071-6068) **4153**
• Modernist Cultures (GBR ISSN 2041-1022) **8121**
The Modernist Revolution in World Literature (USA ISSN 1528-9672) **5336**
Modernista (USA ISSN 1556-5912) **4547**
Modernizing Agriculture *see* Xiandaihua Nongye **171**
Modernizing the Classification System. Annual Report/Modernisation du Systeme de Classification. Rapport Annuel (CAN ISSN 1719-3966) **1870**
Modersmaal Selskabet. Aarbog (DNK ISSN 0107-2390) **5152**
† Modes et Techniques (FRA ISSN 0248-0034) **8975**
Modes et Techniques Deux *see* M & T 2 **2248**
Modes et Travaux (FRA ISSN 0026-8739) **2259**
• Modest Proposals (IRL) **2385**
Modified Luxury & Exotics (CAN) **8591**
• Modified Magazine (CAN) **8591**
Modified Mustangs (CAN ISSN 1715-4448) **8591**
Modified Mustangs and Fords *see* Modified Mustangs & Fords **367**
Modified Mustangs & Fords (USA ISSN 1944-9887) **367**
Modin (FIN ISSN 1457-554X) **8455**
Modis (BEL ISSN 0773-4468) **8455**
Modna Jana (SVN ISSN 1318-4636) **2259**
Modnye Pricheski *see* Liza. Modnye Pricheski **589**
Mod's Hair (DEU) **589**
Modular Machine Tool & Automatic Manufacturing Technique *see* Zuhe Jichuang yu Zidonghua Jiagong Jishu **5462**
Modular Power Magazine (USA ISSN 1939-5728) **8187**
• Modulo (ITA ISSN 0390-1025) **1025**
Modulus (USA ISSN 0191-4022) **450**
Modus (DNK ISSN 0902-6711) **6588**
Modus *see* D A T A Practice **3057**
Modus *see* Blauw **4630**
Modus (POL ISSN 1641-9715) **506**
Modus (PRT) **6588**
Modus (RUS) **1149**
Modus Statistisch Magazine (ANT) **1252**
Modus Vivendi (ITA ISSN 1591-5204) **3453**
• Die Moebel-Industrie und Ihre Helfer (DEU ISSN 0077-0205) **4560**
Moebel Interior Design *see* M D **4545**
Moebel-Kultur (DEU ISSN 0047-7796) **4560**
Moebel & Interioer (NOR ISSN 1504-4858) **4560**
Moebel + Interioer Branchebladet (DNK) **4561**
Moebel plus Interioer Branchebladet *see* Moebel + Interioer Branchebladet **4561**
Moebel Raum Design (AUT) **4547**
Moebelfertigung (DEU ISSN 0948-891X) **4561**
Moebelhandleren *see* Moebel & Interioer **4560**
Moebelmarkt (DEU ISSN 0949-6521) **4561**
Moebelmarkt Bambini (DEU) **4561**
Der Moebelspediteur (DEU ISSN 0047-780X) **8504**
Moebler & Miljoe (SWE ISSN 0345-7737) **4561**
Moebler och Miljoe *see* Moebler & Miljoe **4561**
Moeglich (DEU) **2493**
Moeldrup Kommunes Lokalhistoriske Arkiv. Aarsskrift *see* Foreningsaarsskrift **4220**
Moeletsi oa Basotho/Counsellor of Basotho (LSO) **7808**
Moellen (DNK ISSN 0026-8852) **274**
Moelposen (DNK ISSN 0106-1917) **4245**
Moenchengladbacher Schriften zur Wirtschaftswissenschaftlichen Praxis (DEU ISSN 1615-9160) **1149**
• ➤ Moenia (ESP ISSN 1137-2346) **5152**
Moenster Raetts Tidning *see* Finland. Patentti- ja Rekisterihallitus. Mallioikeuslehti **6750**
Moenter fra Norden samt de Baltiske Lande (DNK) **6651**
Moentsamleren (DNK ISSN 0900-1409) **6651**
Moere-Nytt (NOR) **3923**
• Moessbauer Effect Reference and Data Journal (USA ISSN 0163-9587) **7081**
• Moessbauer Effect Reference and Data Journal. Index (USA) **11**
Moesson (NLD ISSN 0165-6546) **7253**
Moestuin (NLD ISSN 1381-740X) **3743**
Moet je Horen (NLD) **4083**
➤ Moeteplass Middelalder (NOR ISSN 0809-8646) **4246**
Moethaukpan/Aurora (MMR) **3966**
▼ • ➤ Mofa (ISR ISSN 1565-8473) **8474**
Moftul Roman (ROM ISSN 1018-0419) **5228**
Mogjae Gonghag/Journal of the Korean Wood Science and Technology (KOR ISSN 1017-0715) **3714**
Mogucnosti (HRV ISSN 0544-7267) **4465**
The Mohawk (USA ISSN 0740-9699) **3775**
Mohawk Valley History (USA ISSN 1547-9072) **3775**
Mohlanka (LSO) **3905**
Mohr Kurier (DEU) **7568**
Mohr Stadtillu Bamberg (DEU) **3853**
Mohr Stadtillu Bayreuth (DEU) **3853**
Mohr Stadtillu Coburg (DEU) **3853**
Mohr Stadtillu Kulmbach (DEU) **3853**
• Mohu Xitong yu Shuxue/Fuzzy Systems and Mathematics (CHN ISSN 1001-7402) **5518**
Moi Je Lis (FRA ISSN 1625-4759) **2203**
Moi Krokha i Ya (RUS ISSN 1560-2648) **2161**
Moi Liubimye Zhivotnye *see* Liza. Moi Liubimye Zhivotnye **6811**
Moi Prekrasnyi Sad (RUS ISSN 1560-5426) **3743**
Moi Prekrasnyi Sad (UKR) **3743**
Moi Prekrasnyi Sad. Specials (RUS) **3743**
Moi Rebenok *see* Liza. Moi Rebenok **2160**
Moi Rebenok *see* Liza. Moi Rebenok **2160**
Moi Uiutnyi Dom (RUS ISSN 1560-5418) **4547**
Moi Uiutnyi Dom (UKR) **4547**
Moisture Manager (GBR) **3453**
The Moisture Seekers (USA) **5764**
Moj Dom (SVK ISSN 1335-5902) **4547**
Moj Dom *see* Dnevnik **3947**
Moj Hobi (SVN ISSN 1408-0133) **4438**
• Moj Interier (SVK ISSN 1337-012X) **4547**
Moj Kucyk Pony/My Little Pony (POL ISSN 1734-2228) **2203**
Moj Lepi Vrt (SVN ISSN 1581-5897) **3743**
Moj Lijepi Vrt (HRV ISSN 1334-1448) **3743**
Moj Lijepi Vrt. Specijalno Izdanje *see* Moj Lijepi Vrt **3743**
Moj Mali Svet (SVN ISSN 0580-8197) **137**
• Moj Mikro (SVN ISSN 0352-4833) **2432**
• Moj Moby (HRV ISSN 1332-3423) **2334**
Moj Pas (HRV ISSN 0026-8895) **6507**
• Moj Pes (SVN ISSN 1318-296X) **6811**
Moj Piekny Ogrod (POL ISSN 1426-6334) **3743**
Moj Piekny Ogrod Extra (POL ISSN 1509-7021) **3743**
Moj Piekny Ogrod. Specjalne (POL) **3743**
Moj Pies (POL ISSN 0867-2822) **6811**
Moj Stan (HRV ISSN 1334-7144) **4547**
Moj Stan (SRB ISSN 1451-5237) **4547**
• Moja Kariera (SVK ISSN 1336-9687) **6701**
Moja Kuhinja (HRV ISSN 0354-0073) **4364**
Moja Lepa Basta (SRB ISSN 1451-5229) **3743**
Moja Rodzina (POL ISSN 1230-9435) **3930**
Moja Romanca (HRV ISSN 1331-159X) **8875**
Moja Sudbina (HRV ISSN 1330-8262) **8875**
Moja Tajna (HRV ISSN 1330-8270) **8875**
Moje Dete *see* Lisa. Moje Dete **2159**
Moje Dete *see* Lisa. Moje Dete **2159**
Moje Gotowanie (POL ISSN 1233-4847) **4364**
Moje Mieszkanie (POL ISSN 0945-5310) **4547**
Moje Psychologie (CZE ISSN 1802-2073) **7386**
Moje Stanovanje *see* Lisa. Moje Stanovanje **4545**
Moje Zdravi (CZE ISSN 1214-3871) **6992**
Moje Zdravje *see* Dnevnik **3947**
Moje Zdrowie (POL ISSN 1231-3203) **7531**
Mojo (GBR ISSN 1351-0193) **6588**
• Moju Gongye/Mould & Die Industry (CHN ISSN 1001-2168) **3210**
• Moju Jishu/Die and Mould Technology (CHN ISSN 1001-4934) **6343**
Mokchae Konghak *see* Mogjae Gonghag **3714**
Mokhtarein va Mobtakerin (IRN) **8432**
Moko (IND) **5336**
Moko (NZL ISSN 1177-0082) **955**
• ➤ Moksha Journal (USA ISSN 1051-127X) **6935**
Mokushitsu Tanka Gakkaishi/Wood Carbonization Research (JPN ISSN 1349-3418) **3714**
• ➤ Mokuzai Gakkaishi (Japanese Edition)/Japan Wood Research Society. Journal (JPN) **3714**
Mokuzai Kogyo *see* Wood Industry **3718**
Molaetsa-Molaetsa (ZAF ISSN 0378-410X) **7768**
Molasses Market News (USA ISSN 0145-0662) **3657**
• Molbank (CHE ISSN 1422-8599) **2073**
Mold Reporter (USA ISSN 1535-3729) **7531**
Molde e Cia (BRA ISSN 1415-0654) **2259**
Moldes (ESP ISSN 1132-0354) **6326**
Moldes Manequim *see* Manequim **2258**
Moldova i Mir *see* Moldova si Lumea **3913**
Moldova si Lumea/Moldova i Mir (MDA) **3913**
Moldova Suverana (MDA) **3913**
• ➤ Molecular and Biochemical Parasitology (NLD ISSN 0166-6851) **738**
• ➤ Molecular and Cellular Biochemistry (USA ISSN 0300-8177) **738**
• ➤ Molecular and Cellular Biology (USA ISSN 0270-7306) **739**
• Molecular & Cellular Biomechanics (USA ISSN 1556-5297) **750**
• ➤ Molecular and Cellular Endocrinology (IRL ISSN 0303-7207) **5897**
• ➤ Molecular and Cellular Neuroscience (USA ISSN 1044-7431) **6161**
▼ • ➤ Molecular and Cellular Pharmacology (USA ISSN 1938-1247) **6861**
• ➤ Molecular and Cellular Probes (GBR ISSN 0890-8508) **5909**
• ➤ Molecular and Cellular Proteomics (USA ISSN 1535-9476) **739**
• Molecular and Cellular Toxicology (KOR ISSN 1738-642X) **834**
Molecular and Developmental Evolution *see* Journal of Experimental Zoology. Part B: Molecular and Developmental Evolution **951**
▼ • ➤ Molecular and Supramolecular Materials (USA ISSN 1687-5656) **2127**
Molecular and Translational Cancer Epidemiology *see* Journal of Cancer Epidemiology **6024**
Molecular Aspects of Fish & Marine Biology (SGP ISSN 0219-9777) **689**
• ➤ Molecular Aspects of Medicine (GBR ISSN 0098-2997) **5680**
▼ • ➤ Molecular Autism (GBR) **6161**
• ➤ Molecular Biology (RUS ISSN 0026-8933) **739**
• ➤ Molecular Biology and Evolution (USA ISSN 0737-4038) **689**
• Molecular Biology Notebook (GBR ISSN 1468-4624) **689**
• ➤ Molecular Biology of the Cell (USA ISSN 1059-1524) **834**
• ➤ Molecular Biology Reports (NLD ISSN 0301-4851) **739**
• Molecular BioSystems (GBR ISSN 1742-206X) **689**
• ➤ Molecular Biotechnology (USA ISSN 1073-6085) **768**
▼ • ➤ Molecular Brain (GBR ISSN 1756-6606) **6161**
Molecular Brain Research *see* Brain Research **6128**
• ➤ Molecular Breeding (NLD ISSN 1380-3743) **801**
• ➤ Molecular Cancer (GBR ISSN 1476-4598) **6027**
• ➤ Molecular Cancer Research (USA ISSN 1541-7786) **6027**
• ➤ Molecular Cancer Therapeutics (USA ISSN 1535-7163) **6027**
• ➤ Molecular Carcinogenesis (USA ISSN 0899-1987) **6028**
Molecular Cardiology of China *see* Zhongguo Fenzi Xinzangbingxue Zazhi **5802**
• ➤ Molecular Cell (USA ISSN 1097-2765) **835**
• ➤ Molecular Crystals and Liquid Crystals (USA ISSN 1542-1406) **2111**
Molecular Crystals and Liquid Crystals Science and Technology. Section A. Molecular Crystals and Liquid Crystals *see* Molecular Crystals and Liquid Crystals **2111**
Molecular Crystals and Liquid Crystals Science and Technology. Section C. Molecular Materials *see* Molecular Crystals and Liquid Crystals **2111**
▼ • Molecular Cytogenetics (GBR ISSN 1755-8166) **875**
Molecular Diagnosis *see* Molecular Diagnosis and Therapy **5680**
• Molecular Diagnosis and Therapy (NZL ISSN 1177-1062) **5680**
• ➤ Molecular Diversity (NLD ISSN 1381-1991) **7068**
• ➤ Molecular Ecology (GBR ISSN 0962-1083) **893**
Molecular Ecology Notes *see* Molecular Ecology Resources **893**
• ➤ Molecular Ecology Resources (GBR ISSN 1755-098X) **893**
Molecular Ecology. Supplement *see* Molecular Ecology **893**
• ➤ Molecular Endocrinology (USA ISSN 0888-8809) **5897**
• ➤ Molecular Genetics and Genomics (DEU ISSN 1617-4615) **875**
• ➤ Molecular Genetics and Metabolism (USA ISSN 1096-7192) **739**
• ➤ Molecular Genetics, Microbiology and Virology (USA ISSN 0891-4168) **893**
Molecular Genetics, Microbiology and Virusology *see* Molekulyarnaya Genetika, Mikrobiologiya i Virusologiya **893**
• ➤ Molecular Human Reproduction (GBR ISSN 1360-9947) **5999**
• ➤ Molecular Imaging (CAN ISSN 1535-3508) **835**
• ➤ Molecular Imaging and Biology (USA ISSN 1536-1632) **6203**
▼ • Molecular Imaging Insight (USA ISSN 1941-0549) **6203**
• ➤ Molecular Immunology (GBR ISSN 0161-5890) **739**
• Molecular Interventions (USA ISSN 1534-0384) **6862**
Molecular Medicine (JPN ISSN 0918-6557) **5897**
Molecular Medicine *see* Molekulyarnaya Meditsina **740**
• ➤ Molecular Medicine (USA ISSN 1076-1551) **6862**
Molecular Medicine Advance Sciences *see* International Journal Molecular Medicine Advance Sciences **5637**
▼ • ➤ Molecular Medicine Reports (GRC ISSN 1791-2997) **5680**
• ➤ Molecular Membrane Biology (GBR ISSN 0968-7688) **739**
Molecular Methods of Plant Analysis (USA ISSN 1619-5221) **801**
Molecular Microbial Ecology Manual (NLD) **893**
• ➤ Molecular Microbiology (GBR ISSN 0950-382X) **893**
Molecular Modeling Annual *see* Journal of Molecular Modeling **2137**
• ➤ Molecular Neurobiology (USA ISSN 0893-7648) **739**
• ➤ Molecular Neurodegeneration (GBR ISSN 1750-1326) **6161**
• ➤ Molecular Nutrition & Food Research (DEU ISSN 1613-4125) **6663**
• ➤ Molecular Nutrition & Food Research (Online) (DEU ISSN 1613-4133) **6663**
▼ • Molecular Oncology (NLD ISSN 1574-7891) **6028**
• Molecular Pain (GBR ISSN 1744-8069) **5680**
Molecular Pathology *see* Journal of Clinical Pathology **5647**
• Molecular Pharmaceutics (USA ISSN 1543-8384) **2073**
• ➤ Molecular Pharmacology (USA ISSN 0026-895X) **6862**
• ➤ Molecular Phylogenetics and Evolution (USA ISSN 1055-7903) **875**
• ➤ Molecular Physics (GBR ISSN 0026-8976) **2138**
Molecular Physics Reports (POL ISSN 1505-1250) **7068**

• ➤ Molecular Plant/Journal of Plant Physiology and Molecular Biology (GBR ISSN 1674-2052) 801
• ➤ Molecular Plant - Microbe Interactions (USA ISSN 0894-0282) 740
• Molecular Plant Pathology (GBR ISSN 1464-6722) 802
• ➤ Molecular Psychiatry (GBR ISSN 1359-4184) 6161
Molecular Psychiatry (Online) *see* Molecular Psychiatry 6161
• ➤ Molecular Reproduction and Development (USA ISSN 1040-452X) 740
• Molecular Sieves - Science and Technology (USA ISSN 1436-8269) 2073
• ➤ Molecular Simulation (GBR ISSN 0892-7022) 2073
➤ Molecular Structures and Dimensions. Bibliography (NLD ISSN 0377-2012) 2111
▼ • Molecular Syndromology (CHE ISSN 1661-8769) 875
• ➤ Molecular Systems Biology (GBR ISSN 1744-4292) 690
• Molecular Therapy (GBR ISSN 1525-0016) 6028
• ➤ Molecular Vision (USA ISSN 1090-0535) 740
• ➤ Molecules (CHE ISSN 1420-3049) 2127
Molecules (Print Archive Edition) (CHE ISSN 1431-5157) 690
• ➤ Molecules and Cells (KOR ISSN 1016-8478) 690
• Molekulyarnaya Biologiya (RUS ISSN 0026-8984) 740
Molekulyarnaya Genetika, Mikrobiologiya i Virusologiya/Molecular Genetics, Microbiology and Virusology (RUS ISSN 0208-0613) 893
Molekulyarnaya Meditsina/Molecular Medicine (RUS ISSN 1728-2918) 740
De Molenaar (NLD ISSN 0165-4284) 274
Molens (NLD ISSN 0169-6459) 2619
• Molineria y Panaderia (ESP ISSN 0026-900X) 3675
Molini d'Italia (ITA ISSN 0026-9018) 274
Die Molkerei-Zeitung Welt der Milch (DEU ISSN 0043-2512) 267
Moll Monografies Cientifiques (ESP) 7883
Moll Monografies d'Historia Local (ESP) 4246
▼ The Molloy Literary Journal (USA ISSN 1940-4255) 5336
Mollusc World (GBR) 955
• ➤ Molluscan Research (NZL ISSN 1323-5818) 955
Molnarok Lapja/Miller's Journal (HUN ISSN 1416-2792) 274
➤ Molochnaya Promyshlennost' (RUS ISSN 1019-8946) 267
Molochno-m'yasne Skotarstvo *see* Natsional'na Akademiya Nauk Ukrainy. Instytut Tvarynnytstva. Naukovo-Tekhnichnyi Biuleten' 268
Molochnoe i Myasnoe Skotovodstvo (RUS ISSN 0026-9034) 293
Molod' Ukrainy (UKR) 3965
• Molodaya Gvardiya (RUS ISSN 0131-2251) 5228
Molodaya i Privlekatel'naya (RUS) 2259
Molodezh' Altaya (RUS) 3937
Molodezh' Estonii (EST) 2203
Molodezh' Moldovy (MDA) 2203
Molodezh' Uzbekistana (UZB) 2203
Molodezhnaya Estrada (RUS ISSN 0132-8816) 2203
Molodezhnaya Gazeta (RUS) 3937
Molodoi Dal'nevostochnik (RUS) 3937
Molodost' Sibiri (RUS) 3937
Molossi (ITA ISSN 1591-0261) 6811
Molossi & Guardiani (ITA ISSN 1593-9804) 6811
Molot (RUS) 3937
Molt *see* Musik & LjudTeknik 6595
Molten Salt Forum (CHE ISSN 1021-6138) 3251
Molten Salts *see* Yoyuen Oyobi Koon Kagaku 2119
Molva (RUS) 3937
Molva (Vladimir) (RUS) 3937
• Moly Review (GBR) 6326
• Mom Guess What Newspaper (USA ISSN 1093-5908) 4376
Momberger Airport Information (Online) (DEU) 8548
Momberger Airport Information (Print) *see* Momberger Airport Information (Online) 8548
• Mome (ITA ISSN 0997-0312) 5152
Mome (USA ISSN 1933-5652) 5445
• Moment (USA ISSN 0099-0280) 3551
Momente (DEU ISSN 1619-1609) 4246
Momente aus Kirche und Arbeitswelt (DEU ISSN 1614-4589) 7768
Momento (MEX) 3909
Momento (VEN ISSN 0026-9131) 3994
El Momento Catolico (USA) 7808
• Momento do Professor (BRA ISSN 1807-4723) 3073
• Momento Economico (MEX ISSN 0186-2901) 1149
Momento Economico. Boletin Electronico *see* Momento Economico 1149
Moments (IRL) 4394
Moments (NLD ISSN 1873-6637) 607
moMentum *see* Jord og Viden 125
▼ • Momentum (FRA) 1639
† Momentum (GBR) 8975
Momentum (Calgary) (CAN ISSN 1709-870X) 8620
• Momentum (Little Rock) (USA) 5970
• Momentum (New York) (USA ISSN 1940-3410) 6161
• Momentum (Rochester) (USA) 5856
• Momentum (Washington) (USA ISSN 0026-914X) 2887
Momentumnytt *see* Armer & Bein 4077
Momjian & Momjian Pennsylvania Family Law Annotated *see* Pennsylvania Family Law Annotated 4914
Momoyama Gakuin Daigaku Sogo Kenkyujo Kiyo/St. Andrew's University.Research Institute. Bulletin (JPN ISSN 1346-048X) 7883
• Mom's Old-Fashioned Internet Gazette (USA) 2564
Momsareew (SEN) 7155
MOMsense (USA ISSN 1559-2537) 2161
Mon Bebe (CAN ISSN 0384-0816) 2161
Mon Chalet (CAN ISSN 1710-7423) 4547
Mon Enfant *see* Today's Parent, Baby & Toddler 2169
Mon Jardin, Ma Maison (FRA ISSN 0026-9166) 3743
▼ Mon Journal Sarah Kay (FRA ISSN 1964-941X) 2203
Mon Juridic (ESP ISSN 1135-9196) 4736
Mon Look a Moi (FRA ISSN 1951-7246) 4547
† Mon Premier Aquarium (FRA ISSN 1771-3129) 8975
Mon Quotidien (FRA ISSN 1258-6447) 2203
➤ Monaldi Archives for Chest Disease (ITA ISSN 1122-0643) 6216
Monarchist Book Review (GBR ISSN 0077-0280) 4171
Monarchist League of New Zealand. Newsletter *see* Monarchy New Zealand 7453
Monarchist Press Association. Historical Series (GBR ISSN 0077-0299) 4246
Monarchy (GBR) 7155
Monarchy Canada (CAN ISSN 0319-4019) 7155
• Monarchy New Zealand (NZL ISSN 1174-8435) 7453
Monash Asia Institute. Japanese Studies Centre. Working Papers (AUS ISSN 1441-4120) 4186
Monash Asia Institute. Occasional Papers of the Japanese Studies Centre (AUS) 4186
Monash Australian Research Group Informal Notes *see* M A R G I N 5328
• Monash Bioethics Review (AUS ISSN 1321-2753) 6935
† • ➤ Monash Business Review (AUS ISSN 1832-8490) 8975
• Monash Magazine (AUS ISSN 1447-1302) 1150
† Monash Publications in Geography and Environmental Science (AUS) 8975
• Monash University Accident Research Centre. Consultants' Reports Series (AUS) 8632
• Monash University Accident Research Centre. Minor Reports Series (AUS) 8632
• Monash University Accident Research Centre. Other Reports Series (AUS) 8632
• Monash University. Centre for Health Economics. Research Paper (AUS ISSN 1833-1173) 1150
Monash University. Centre of Southeast Asian Studies. Annual Indonesian Lecture Series (AUS ISSN 0729-3623) 4186
Monash University. Centre of Southeast Asian Studies. Monash Papers on Southeast Asia (AUS ISSN 0727-6680) 4186
Monash University. Centre of Southeast Asian Studies. Working Papers (AUS ISSN 0314-6804) 4186
• ➤ Monash University. Department of Civil Engineering. Civil Engineering Research Report (AUS ISSN 0155-6282) 3278
• Monash University. Department of Economics. Discussion Papers (AUS ISSN 1441-5429) 1150
† Monash University. Development Studies Centre. Occasional Papers (AUS ISSN 1323-2649) 8975
• Monash University. Faculty of Business and Economics. Faculty Newsletter (AUS) 1150
• ➤ Monash University Law Review (AUS ISSN 0311-3140) 4736
➤ Monash University. Linguistics Papers (AUS) 5152
Monash University Magazine *see* Monash Magazine 1150
Monastic Research Bulletin (GBR ISSN 1361-3022) 4246
† Monastica (ITA) 8975
Monasticon Italiae (ITA) 7808
Monat - Sozialpolitische Rundschau (AUT) 4068
Monatliches Panorama Europaeischer Unternehmen *see* Monthly Panorama of European Business 1578
Monatsgruss (DEU) 7768
• ➤ Monatshefte (USA ISSN 0026-9271) 5152
• ➤ Monatshefte fuer Chemie/Chemical Monthly (AUT ISSN 0026-9247) 2073
➤ Monatshefte fuer Chemie. Supplementum (AUT ISSN 0935-8439) 2073
Monatshefte fuer Evangelische Kirchengeschichte des Rheinlandes (DEU ISSN 0540-6226) 7768
• ➤ Monatshefte fuer Mathematik (AUT ISSN 0026-9255) 5518
Monatshefte Occasional Volumes *see* Monatshefte 5152
• ➤ Monatsschrift fuer Brauwissenschaft (Online) (DEU ISSN 1613-2041) 614
• Monatsschrift fuer Deutsches Recht (DEU ISSN 0340-1812) 4736
Monatsschrift fuer Kriminologie und Strafrechtsreform (DEU ISSN 0026-9301) 2660
• ➤ Monatsschrift Kinderheilkunde (DEU ISSN 0026-9298) 6097
Monatsschrift Magazin fuer den Gartenbauprofi (DEU ISSN 1435-5396) 3743
Monatsspiegel (DEU) 3853
Moncada (CUB) 3831
Monday Developments (USA ISSN 1043-8157) 8055
Monday Magazine (CAN ISSN 0832-4719) 3813
• Monday Magazine (IND) 3982
• Monday Morning (LBN ISSN 0301-3529) 3905
Monday Morning Report (USA ISSN 0891-8651) 2697
• Monday Phenomenon (ZAF) 3551
• Monday Report on Retailers (CAN ISSN 0700-3528) 1835
• The Monday Review (USA) 2994
Der Mondbaer (DEU) 2203
• Le Monde (FRA ISSN 0395-2037) 3841
Monde *see* Collection Monde 7955
Le Monde Alimentaire (CAN ISSN 1206-4025) 3657
† ➤ Monde Alpin et Rhodanien (FRA ISSN 0758-4431) 8975
Monde Arabe *see* Maghreb - Machrek 7153
Monde Arabe Maghreb - Machrek *see* Maghreb - Machrek 7153
Le Monde Byzantin (FRA ISSN 0544-7704) 4323
Le Monde de la Bible (FRA ISSN 0154-9049) 406
Le Monde de la Musique (FRA ISSN 0181-7949) 6588
Monde de la Technologie (FRA) 3210
Le Monde de l'Art Tribal *see* Tribal Art 6538
Le Monde de l'Assurances *see* De Verzekeringswereld 4527
Le Monde de l'Auto (CAN ISSN 0831-2958) 8591
Le Monde de l'Education (FRA ISSN 1297-2185) 2887
Monde de l'Electricite (CAN ISSN 0026-9379) 3325
▼ Le Monde de l'Enfance (FRA ISSN 1959-6219) 2161
Le Monde de l'Intelligence (FRA ISSN 1778-7890) 7386
Monde Dentaire/Tandartsen Wereld (BEL) 5856
Le Monde des Ados (FRA ISSN 1773-3014) 2203
Le Monde des Cartes (FRA ISSN 1634-3522) 4019
Monde des Femmes *see* Women's World 8892
Le Monde des Religions (FRA ISSN 1763-3346) 7808
• Le Monde Diplomatique (CHL ISSN 0718-4344) 7253
Le Monde Diplomatique *see* Le Monde Diplomatique en Espanol 7253
• Le Monde Diplomatique (FRA ISSN 0026-9395) 7253
Le Monde Diplomatique en Espanol (ESP ISSN 1888-6434) 7253
Le Monde. Dossiers et Documents (FRA ISSN 0153-419X) 3841
Le Monde du Camping Car (FRA ISSN 0993-1996) 8737
▼ Le Monde du Droit (FRA ISSN 1960-8985) 4736
Le Monde du Muscle *see* Le Monde du Muscle du Fitness 6993
Le Monde du Muscle du Fitness (FRA ISSN 1772-192X) 6993
Le Monde du Plein Air (FRA ISSN 1638-3494) 8322
Le Monde du Surgele (FRA ISSN 1249-2159) 3657
Monde Imparfait (FRA ISSN 1775-7266) 7155
Monde Indien. Sciences Sociales, 15e - 20e Siecle (FRA ISSN 1621-2843) 7986
• Le Monde Informatique (Online) (FRA) 2432
Le Monde Informatique (Print) *see* Le Monde Informatique (Online) 2432
Le Monde Informatique. NP Journal *see* Le Monde Informatique (Online) 2432
Le Monde Libertaire (FRA ISSN 0026-9433) 7155
Le Monde. Selection Hebdomadaire (FRA ISSN 0026-9360) 3841
Monden Institute of Management and Accounting: Japanese Management and International Comparative Studies *see* Monden Institute of Management and Accounting: Japanese Management and International Comparative Studies 1297
Monden Institute of Management and Accounting: Japanese Management and International Comparative Studies (SGP ISSN 1793-2874) 1297
Les Mondes Antiques (FRA ISSN 1955-5628) 4154
Mondes Contemporains (FRA ISSN 1777-4977) 7986
• Mondes en Developpement/Spreading Worlds (BEL ISSN 0302-3052) 1601
Mondes et Cultures (FRA ISSN 0221-0436) 7883
Mondes et Nations (FRA ISSN 1961-1331) 7986
Mondes Hispanophones (FRA ISSN 1768-2436) 5336
Mondes Mysterieux (FRA ISSN 1778-5936) 5411
Mondhygienisten Vademecum (NLD ISSN 1571-053X) 5856
Mondi *see* Mondi Personal 1639
Mondi Personal (NLD ISSN 1574-9371) 1639
Mondial/Federaliste Mondial du Canada (CAN ISSN 1488-612X) 4936
• Il Mondo (ITA ISSN 0391-6855) 1150
• Mondo Agricolo (ITA ISSN 0026-9484) 137
Mondo Baby (ITA ISSN 1970-9331) 2161
† Mondo Bancario (ITA ISSN 0026-9506) 8975
Mondo Barca (ITA ISSN 1826-1914) 8278
† Mondo C A D (Computer-Aided Design) (ITA) 8975
† Mondo Cinese (ITA ISSN 0390-2811) 8975
• Mondo Contemporaneo (ITA ISSN 1825-8905) 4154
Il Mondo del Ciclismo (ITA ISSN 1593-0769) 8261
Il Mondo del Golf (ITA ISSN 1128-0352) 8239
Il Mondo del Latte, il Latte nel Mondo (ITA ISSN 0368-9123) 267
• Mondo del Nuoto (ITA ISSN 1125-1786) 8187
Il Mondo del Vino (ITA ISSN 1828-3209) 607
Il Mondo della Bibbia (ITA ISSN 1120-7353) 7808
Il Mondo della Birra (ITA ISSN 1121-1598) 607
† Mondo della Calzatura: Tecnologie e Materie (ITA) 8975
Il Mondo della Musica (ITA ISSN 0544-7763) 6588
† Il Mondo della Pelletteria (ITA ISSN 1127-1876) 8975
Mondo Digitale (ITA ISSN 1720-898X) 2432
• Mondo e Missione (ITA ISSN 0026-6094) 7808
Mondo Erre (ITA ISSN 0391-5484) 2203
Il Mondo Giudiziario (ITA ISSN 1971-5005) 4956
Mondo Latte Latte Mondo *see* Il Mondo del Latte, il Latte nel Mondo 267
Mondo Lavoro (ITA ISSN 1723-137X) 1698
Mondo Legno (ITA ISSN 0392-6443) 3714
Mondo Online *see* Il Mondo 1150
Mondo Ortodontico (ITA ISSN 0391-2000) 5856
† • Mondo Padano (ITA) 8975
† Mondo Popolare (ITA) 8975
• Mondo Sanitario (ITA ISSN 0544-7771) 4107
Mondo Sommerso (ITA ISSN 0026-9573) 2813
Mondo Sports *see* MondoSports 8239
MondoLegno *see* Mondo Legno 3714
Mondomix (FRA ISSN 1772-8916) 6588
Mondomix Papier *see* Mondomix 6588
MondOperaio (ITA ISSN 0392-1115) 7155
▼ MondoSports (FRA ISSN 1959-0164) 8239
Moneda (PRI) 1367
Moneda y Credito (ESP ISSN 0026-959X) 1367
Moneda y Finanzas del Cono Sur. Cuadernos (ARG) 1367
Moneta e Credito (ITA ISSN 0026-9611) 1367
Moneta International (VGB ISSN 0958-1545) 6651
Monetaire Monografieen *see* De Nederlandsche Bank. Occasional Studies 1936
• Monetaria (MEX ISSN 0185-1136) 1367
• Monetary and Economic Review (USA) 1150
Monetary and Economic Studies *see* Kinyu Kenkyu 1364
Monetary and Economic Studies (JPN ISSN 1348-7787) 1367
Monetary Digest (USA) 1640
Monetary Monographs *see* De Nederlandsche Bank. Occasional Studies 1936
Monetary Policy and Reserve Requirements Handbook (USA) 1367
• Monetary Policy Report/Rapport sur la Politique Monetaire (CAN ISSN 1201-8783) 1499
Monetary Policy Review (ZAF ISSN 1609-3194) 1368
Monetary Policy Statement *see* Reserve Bank of New Zealand. Monetary Policy Statement 1514
Monetary Research Institute Bankers' Guide to Foreign Currency *see* M R I Bankers' Guide to Foreign Currency 1366
Monetary Research Series (Kobe) *see* Kobe University. Research Institute for Economics and Business Administration. Monetary Research Series 1141
Monetary Studies *see* Pinigu Studijos 1375
Monete Storiche da Collezione (ITA ISSN 1824-1468) 6651
Money *see* Money Magazine 1368
† Money (NLD ISSN 0925-4129) 8975
Money (UAE ISSN 1819-611X) 1368
• Money (New York) (USA ISSN 0149-4953) 1368
• Money Affairs (MEX ISSN 0187-7615) 1368
Money and Capital Market *see* Denmark. Danmarks Statistik. Penge- og Kapitalmarked (Online) 1224
Money & Finance (IND) 1368
Money & Jobs *see* Irish Examiner 3893
Money and Politics Report *see* Money & Politics Report 7453
• Money & Politics Report (USA ISSN 1523-570X) 7453
Money China *see* Caijing Jie 1079
• Money Digest (CAN) 1640
▼ • The Money for Main Street Monitor (USA ISSN 2150-0835) 1150
Money - Forecast Letter (USA) 1640
• Money Fund Intelligence (USA ISSN 1931-3497) 1640
• Money Fund Report (USA ISSN 1931-9118) 1640
Money Japan (JPN ISSN 0911-9353) 1368
• Money Laundering Alert (USA ISSN 1046-3070) 2660
Money Laundering Bulletin (GBR ISSN 1462-141X) 2660
Money Laundering Law Report (USA ISSN 1050-4826) 4876
Money Lines Magazine (USA) 1368
• Money Magazine (AUS ISSN 1444-6219) 1368
Money Maker's Monthly (USA ISSN 1050-5652) 1964
Money Making Opportunities (USA ISSN 0192-9399) 1964
• Money Management (AUS ISSN 1322-7254) 1368
• Money Management (GBR ISSN 1463-1911) 1368
Money Management *see* Money Management Letter 1640
• Money Management Executive (USA ISSN 1549-9111) 1640
• Money Management Letter (USA ISSN 1529-2347) 1640
Money Market Capital *see* Trziste, Novac, Kapital 1846

Title

10624 MONOGRAPHS ON GREENLAND, GEOSCIENCE ULRICH'S PERIODICALS

Monographs on Greenland, Geoscience *see* Meddelelser om Groenland. Geoscience **2754**
Monographs on Greenland, Man and Society *see* Meddelelser om Groenland. Man & Society **347**
➤ Monographs on Invertebrate Taxonomy (AUS ISSN 1326-5725) **956**
Monographs on Journal of Research in Teacher Education (SWE ISSN 1651-0127) **2887**
† ➤ Monographs on Numerical Analysis (GBR) **8975**
Monographs on Oceanographic Methodology Series (FRA ISSN 0077-104X) **2813**
Monographs on South-East Asian Politics and International Relations (GBR) **7253**
Monographs on Teacher Education and Research *see* Monographs on Journal of Research in Teacher Education **2887**
Monographs on the Ancient Near East (USA ISSN 0732-6491) **4323**
Monographs on the Fine Arts (USA ISSN 1053-976X) **506**
➤ Monographs on the Physics and Chemistry of Materials (GBR ISSN 0969-3386) **7026**
Monolithographien (DEU) **6588**
Monopol (DEU ISSN 1614-5445) **506**
Monosson Report on D E C and I B M (Digital Equipment Corporation and International Business Machines) (USA ISSN 1040-0966) **2541**
Monozine (USA) **5228**
Monroe & Nock on the Law of Stamp Duties (GBR) **1368**
Monroe County Genealogical Society News (USA ISSN 0893-5718) **3775**
Monroe County Medical Society. Bulletin (USA) **5680**
Monroe Dispatch (USA) **3551**
The Monroe Institute Focus *see* T M I Focus **3004**
† Monsalvat (ESP ISSN 0210-4083) **8975**
Monsieur (FRA ISSN 1265-0080) **6296**
Monsieur Chat (FRA ISSN 0760-3290) **2203**
Monsieur. Hors-Serie (FRA ISSN 1950-3466) **6296**
▼ Monsta (USA) **6588**
Monster *see* Norway Rock Magazine **6600**
Monster Truck Special *see* Radio Control Car Action Monster Trucks **4345**
Monster Trucks *see* Radio Control Car Action Monster Trucks **4345**
MonsterFun *see* Kawaii **499**
MonsterScene (USA ISSN 1082-930X) **6507**
• MonsterZine (USA ISSN 1530-9436) **6507**
Montachusett Messenger (USA ISSN 1930-6415) **2203**
The Montachusett Scout *see* Montachusett Messenger **2203**
Montage (CAN ISSN 1488-2531) **6507**
Montage (USA ISSN 1556-584X) **589**
The Montage (USA) **2292**
Montage AV (DEU) **6507**
Montage H F M *see* Montage **589**
Montage Magazine (USA) **4981**
▼ MONTAGEtechnik (DEU ISSN 1868-9957) **3370**
Montagna (CHE ISSN 1420-0422) **1407**
La Montagne (FRA ISSN 0767-4007) **3841**
La Montagne et l'Alpinisme (FRA ISSN 0047-7923) **8322**
Montagnes Magazine (FRA ISSN 0184-2595) **8322**
Montagnes Mediterraneennes (FRA ISSN 1268-6603) **4019**
• Montague Institute Review (USA ISSN 1554-303X) **5032**
Montaigne Studies (USA ISSN 1049-2917) **5336**
Montajes e Instalaciones *see* M I **4123**
• ➤ Montalban (VEN ISSN 0252-9076) **4465**
Montan Aktuell *see* Dow Jones Montan Aktuell **1621**
Montana (ROM ISSN 1221-0684) **8737**
➤ Montana (USA ISSN 0026-9891) **4304**
Montana: All-Industries *see* Harris Directory. Montana All-Industries **2000**
Montana and the Sky (USA) **8548**
Montana. Bureau of Mines and Geology. Biennial Report (USA) **6473**
Montana. Bureau of Mines and Geology. Bulletin (USA ISSN 0077-1090) **2756**
Montana. Bureau of Mines and Geology. Memoir (USA ISSN 0077-1120) **2756**
Montana. Bureau of Mines and Geology. Montana Mining Directory (USA ISSN 0077-1104) **6474**
Montana. Bureau of Mines and Geology. Special Publications (USA ISSN 0077-1139) **2756**
• Montana Business Directory (USA ISSN 1048-731X) **2017**
• Montana Business Quarterly (USA ISSN 0026-9921) **1150**
Montana Catholic (USA ISSN 0883-7899) **7808**
Montana Chamber of Commerce. Legislative Bulletin (USA) **4876**
• Montana Code Annotated (USA) **4736**
• Montana Crimes, Criminal Procedure, Motor Vehicles & Related Statutes (USA) **4894**
Montana. Department of Commerce. Professional and Occupational Licensing Bureau. Public Safety Division. Biennial Report (USA) **7453**
Montana. Department of Fish and Game. Job Progress Report *see* Montana. Department of Fish, Wildlife and Parks. Job Progress Report **2619**
Montana. Department of Fish, Wildlife and Parks. Job Progress Report (USA) **2619**
Montana. Department of Social and Rehabilitation Services. Statistical Report (USA ISSN 0091-1143) **8083**
Montana Education Association - Montana Federation of Teachers Today *see* M E A - M F T Today **2884**
Montana Education Association - Montana Federation of Teachers Today *see* M E A - M F T Today **2884**
• Montana Employment Law Letter (USA ISSN 1085-9136) **4736**
Montana Farm Bureau Federation News Brief (USA ISSN 1940-123X) **137**
Montana Farm Bureau Spokesman (USA ISSN 0886-3075) **137**
Montana Food Distributor (USA ISSN 0047-7931) **3657**
Montana Heritage Bulletin *see* Heritage Education **4294**
Montana Kaimin (USA) **2292**
Montana Land Magazine (USA ISSN 1052-469X) **7600**
• Montana Law Review (USA ISSN 0026-9972) **4736**
• Montana Lawyer (USA ISSN 0276-3788) **4736**
Montana League of Cities & Towns. Newsletter (USA ISSN 0026-9980) **7498**
Montana Legionnaire (USA ISSN 0026-9999) **2268**
• Montana Library Directory (USA) **5032**
Montana Living (USA ISSN 1094-6187) **3982**
Montana Magazine (USA ISSN 0274-9955) **3982**
The Montana Magazine of History *see* Montana **4304**
• Montana Manufacturers Directory (USA ISSN 1057-6681) **2017**
• ➤ The Montana Math Enthusiast (USA ISSN 1551-3440) **5518**
Montana Motor Carriers Association, Inc. News *see* M M C A News **8672**
Montana Newsletter *see* Montana League of Cities & Towns. Newsletter **7498**
Montana Nutrition Conference. Proceedings (USA) **293**
Montana. Office of the Legislative Auditor. State of Montana Board of Investments. Report on Examination of Financial Statements (USA ISSN 0090-9912) **7453**
Montana Outdoors (USA ISSN 0027-0016) **8323**
Montana Post (USA ISSN 0047-7958) **4304**
Montana Public Library. Annual Report of Statistics (USA) **5059**
Montana Rules of Court *see* Court Rules Pamphlet(s). Montana Rules of Court, State and Federal **4652**
Montana Stockgrower (USA ISSN 0047-7990) **293**
Montana Vital Statistics (USA ISSN 0077-1198) **7312**
Montana Water Center. Technical Reports (USA) **8829**
Montana Water Resources Center. Annual Report (USA) **8829**
Montana Wildlife (USA ISSN 0746-9896) **2619**
Montana Wool Grower (USA ISSN 0027-0024) **293**
➤ Montanan (USA) **2292**
Montaneros de Aragon. Boletin (ESP ISSN 1698-2150) **8187**
Montazhnye i Spetsial'nye Raboty v Stroitel'stve (RUS ISSN 0027-0040) **1025**
Montclair Art Museum. Bulletin (USA) **6529**
Monte Carlo Cote d'Azur (MCO) **3841**
• ➤ Monte Carlo Methods and Applications (DEU ISSN 0929-9629) **5555**
Montearabi (ESP ISSN 1133-4886) **5336**
Montebello Comet (USA) **3551**
• Montebianco (ITA ISSN 1128-0204) **8323**
• Montenegro Economic Trends (MNE ISSN 1451-3617) **1499**
Monterey County Bar Association Newsletter (USA) **4736**
• Monterey County Coast Weekly (USA) **3982**
Monterey Museum of Art News (USA) **506**
Montes (ESP ISSN 0027-0105) **3697**
Montessori International (GBR ISSN 1470-8647) **3073**
• Montessori Life (USA ISSN 1054-0040) **3073**
Montessori News (USA ISSN 0889-6720) **3073**
Montessori Observer (USA ISSN 0889-5643) **3073**
Monteur Electricien (CHE) **3325**
Montfort (AUT ISSN 0027-0148) **4246**
Montgomery - Bucks Dental Society. Bulletin (USA ISSN 0027-0156) **5856**
Montgomery County Insight (USA ISSN 1936-3524) **5077**
Montgomery County Town & Country Living (USA ISSN 1934-5356) **5077**
Montgomery Genealogical Society Quarterly (USA ISSN 1949-470X) **3775**
MontGuide (USA) **4364**
Month in Review *see* United States Government Accountability Office. Month in Review **7474**
• The Monthly (AUS ISSN 1832-3421) **3795**
Monthly Abstract of Meteorological Observations of Malaysia *see* Ringkasan Bulanan Pemerhatian Kajicuaca **6400**
Monthly & Quarterly Reports *see* Manufactured Housing Institute. Quarterly Economic Report **4419**
Monthly Art/Gekkan Bijutsu (JPN ISSN 0910-4364) **506**
Monthly Asahi *see* Gekkan Asahi **3900**
The Monthly Atrocity Review (USA) **5228**
• Monthly Banking Statistics (AUS ISSN 1449-9371) **1368**
Monthly Book Derma *see* Derma **5874**
Monthly Book Entoni *see* Entoni **6079**
Monthly Book Medical Rehabilitation (JPN ISSN 1346-0773) **6112**
Monthly Book Orthopaedics (JPN ISSN 0914-8124) **6067**
Monthly Boy's Champion/Gekkan Shonen-Champion (JPN) **2203**
Monthly Broadcasting Journal *see* Gekkan Hoso Janaru **2381**
Monthly Bulletin of Agricultural Statistics and Research *see* Norin Tokei Chosa **184**
Monthly Bulletin of External Trade *see* Norway. Statistisk Sentralbyraa. Maanedsstatistikk over Utenrikshandelen (Online) **1256**
Monthly Bulletin of Lake Levels for the Great Lakes (USA) **3363**
Monthly Bulletin of the Petroleum and Natural Gas Industry of Indonesia (IDN) **6778**
Monthly Business Starts (USA) **1500**
• Monthly Catalog of United States Government Publications (USA ISSN 0362-6830) **7482**
Monthly Catalog of United States Government Publications: Serials Supplement *see* Monthly Catalog of United States Government Publications **7482**
• Monthly Climatic Data for the World (USA ISSN 0027-0296) **6391**
Monthly Commentary on Indian Economic Conditions (IND ISSN 0027-030X) **1500**
Monthly Commodity Price Bulletin (CHE ISSN 0251-6438) **1252**
Monthly Commodity Price News Service *see* Chonghap Mulka Chongbo **1327**
Monthly Community Medicine *see* Gekkan Chiiki Igaku **5618**
Monthly Completion Report *see* American Petroleum Institute. Monthly Completion Report **6799**
Monthly Cotton Linters Review (USA ISSN 0027-0318) **203**
Monthly Crude Oil Production (USA) **6778**
The Monthly D O S E (Development through Organization and Solidarity towards Excellence) (PHL) **4107**
Monthly Daegu - Gyeongbook Economic Trend *see* Wolgan Daegu Gyeongbuk Gyeongje Donghyang **1413**
• ➤ Monthly Digest of Statistics (GBR ISSN 0308-6666) **8389**
Monthly Digest of Swedish Statistics *see* Sweden. Statistiska Centralbyraan. Allmaen Maanadsstatistik **8408**
Monthly Digest of Tax Articles (USA ISSN 0027-0385) **1935**
Monthly Economic Indicators of Puerto Rico *see* Indicadores Economicos Mensuales de Puerto Rico **1490**
Monthly Economic Review (CAN ISSN 0712-4791) **1720**
• Monthly Economic Review (NZL ISSN 1176-5860) **1500**
Monthly Economic Review (SLE) **1500**
Monthly Economic Trends *see* K D I Jiyeog Gyeongje **1495**
Monthly Education Journal/Gekkan Kyoiku Journal (JPN) **2887**
Monthly Engineering Horizons (PAK ISSN 1017-8260) **3211**
Monthly Fern Lesson (USA) **3743**
Monthly Field & Production Report *see* Petroleum Services Group. Monthly Field & Production Report **6787**
Monthly Finance Review (JPN ISSN 0388-0605) **1368**
Monthly Gas Station *see* Gekkan Gasorin Stutando **6771**
Monthly Guide to Childrens Activity in London *see* Kids Out **2197**
Monthly Highlights of I C E S Research Findings for Stakeholders *see* At a Glance **5580**
Monthly Import Detention List (USA) **1578**
Monthly Independent Tribune Times Journal Post Gazette News Chronicle Bulletin (USA) **3982**
Monthly Index of Medical Specialities Africa *see* M I M S Africa **6859**
Monthly Index of Medical Specialities Caribbean *see* M I M S Caribbean **6859**
Monthly Index of Medical Specialities Middle East *see* M I M S Middle East **6859**
Monthly Index of Medical Specialties *see* M I M S C D **5663**
Monthly Index of Medical Specialties *see* M I M S **6859**
Monthly Index of Medical Specialties Annual *see* M I M S Annual **6859**
Monthly Index of Medical Specialties Bi-Monthly *see* M I M S Bi-Monthly **6859**
Monthly Index of Medical Specialties Cardiovascular *see* M I M S Cardiovascular **5795**
Monthly Index of Medical Specialties Caribbean *see* M I M S Caribbean **6859**
Monthly Index of Medical Specialties Colour Index *see* M I M S Colour Index **6859**
Monthly Index of Medical Specialties Companion (CD-ROM) *see* M I M S Companion (CD-ROM) **5663**
Monthly Index of Medical Specialties Dermatology *see* M I M S Dermatology **5880**
Monthly Index of Medical Specialties Desk Reference *see* M I M S Desk Reference **6859**
Monthly Index of Medical Specialties for Nurses *see* M I M S for Nurses **5969**
Monthly Index of Medical Specialties Hospital Equipment & Supplies Directory *see* M I M S Hospital Equipment & Supplies Directory **4105**
Monthly Index of Medical Specialties Ireland *see* M I M S Ireland **5663**
Monthly Index of Medical Specialties Medical Specialities *see* M I M S Medical Specialities **5748**
Monthly Index of Medical Specialties Middle East *see* M I M S Middle East **6859**
Monthly Index of Medical Specialties New Ethicals *see* M I M S New Ethicals **6859**
Monthly Index of Medical Specialties Women's Health *see* M I M S Women's Health **8846**
Monthly Index to The Financial Times *see* Financial Times Index (Monthly) **1231**
Monthly Indicators of Current Economic Situation of Bangladesh (BGD) **1252**
Monthly Industrial Product Statistics *see* San'eob Saengsan Tong'gye **1261**
Monthly Japanese Fencing *see* Gekkan Kendo Nippon **8175**
Monthly Job Service Statistics *see* Washington (State). Employment Security Department. Monthly Job Service Statistics **6707**
Monthly Journal of Entomology *see* Mushi **855**
Monthly Journal of Gasoline Service Stations/Gekkan Kyuyusho Nihon (JPN ISSN 0016-5964) **6778**
Monthly Journal of Imaging and Information Technology *see* Eizo Joho Industrial **6195**
Monthly Journal of Medical Imaging and Information *see* Eizo Joho Medical **6195**
Monthly Journal of Taipower's Engineering *see* Taidian Gongcheng Yuekan **3161**
Monthly Key Investment *see* Money Reporter **1640**
Monthly Law Digest (PAK) **4956**
Monthly Legislation Status Report *see* European Environment Law for Industry **3430**
Monthly Life (NGA) **3920**
Monthly Market Bulletin (KEN) **1500**
Monthly Media Data *see* Gekkan Media Deeta **1997**
Monthly Meteorological Bulletin *see* Miniaio Klimatologiko Deltio **6391**
Monthly Mini-Lessons in Care of the Aging (USA ISSN 0889-4744) **4051**
Monthly News of Weather, Agriculture and Forestry *see* Kongetsu no Tenko to Norin Sagyo **6359**
Monthly News on Radio *see* Gekkan Musen Shuchi **2358**
Monthly Notices of the Royal Astronomical Society *see* Royal Astronomical Society. Monthly Notices **580**
Monthly of Construction Statistics *see* Kensetsu Tokei Geppo **1047**
Monthly of Essays *see* Zawen Yuekan **5246**
Monthly Outlook. Asia and Oceania *see* Monthly Outlook. Asia Pacific **1150**
Monthly Outlook. Asia Pacific (USA ISSN 1553-7048) **1150**
Monthly Outlook. Non-Eurozone Europe (USA ISSN 1553-4324) **1150**
Monthly Outlook. North America and Western Europe *see* Monthly Outlook. United States, Canada, and Eurozone **1150**
Monthly Outlook. United States, Canada, and Eurozone (USA ISSN 1553-4332) **1150**
Monthly Panorama of European Business (LUX ISSN 1561-6177) **1578**
Monthly Pratirodha (BGD) **7453**
Monthly Precipitation Report in Shikoku District *see* Shikoku Uryo Geppo **6395**
• Monthly Prescribing Reference (USA ISSN 0883-0266) **6862**
Monthly Prescribing Reference (Hematology/Oncology Edition) *see* M P R (Hematology/Oncology Edition) **6859**
Monthly Prescribing Reference (Long Term Care Edition) *see* M P R (Long Term Care Edition) **6859**
Monthly Prescribing Reference (Obstetrician & Gynecologist Edition) *see* M P R (Obstetrician & Gynecologist Edition) **6859**
Monthly Prescribing Reference (Pediatricians' Edition) *see* M P R (Pediatricians' Edition) **6859**
Monthly Prescribing Reference (Pharmacists' Edition) *see* M P R (Pharmacists' Edition) **6859**
Monthly Prescribing Reference (Residents' Edition) *see* M P R (Residents' Edition) **6859**
Monthly Prescribing Reference (Urologists Edition) *see* M P R (Urologists Edition) **6859**
• Monthly Price Review (USA ISSN 0566-3628) **3657**
Monthly Product Announcement (Print) *see* Census Product Update **1081**
Monthly Railway Statistics (IND ISSN 0027-0504) **8527**
Monthly Record for the Events of the United Arab Emirates *see* As- Sijil ash-Shahri li-Ahdath Dawlat al-Imarat al-Arabiyyah al-Muttahidah **7468**
Monthly Record of World Events *see* Al- Sijil al-Shahri li-Ahdath al-Alam **7265**
Monthly Report (Human Rights Commission) *see* South African Human Rights Commission. Monthly Report **7215**
Monthly Report of Agricultural Meteorology *see* Oshima-Hiyama Chiho Nogyo Kisho Sokuho **6393**
Monthly Report of Invention *see* Geppo Hatsumei **6750**

Link to your serials resources and content with ulrichsweb.com

Title

DIRECTORY 2010 MOTORCYKELMAGASINET 10627

The Most Beautiful Swiss Books *see* Die Schoensten Schweizer Buecher **7573**
● Most Fuel-efficient Vehicles (CAN ISSN 1719-6442) **8591**
Most Valuable Players *see* M V P **8589**
Most Wired Magazine *see* Health Care's Most Wired Magazine **4114**
➤ Mostovi (SRB ISSN 0350-6525) **5152**
† Mostre e Musei (ITA) **8975**
Mostviertler (AUT) **607**
Mosty (DEU ISSN 1613-1770) **5228**
➤ Mosul University. College of Medicine. Annals (IRQ ISSN 0027-1446) **5681**
† Mot (DEU ISSN 0027-1462) **8975**
Mot-Auto-Journal *see* Mot **8975**
Mot-Auto-Kritik *see* Mot **8975**
Mot - Bau (DEU ISSN 0027-1470) **3278**
The Motability First Class Supplier Directory (GBR) **4068**
Motability Lifestyle (GBR) **5077**
Motadit (CAN) **2293**
Motdrag (SWE ISSN 0280-3348) **2697**
● Motel Magazine (USA) **8739**
Moteris (LTU) **8876**
Moteur Boat Magazine (FRA ISSN 0994-964X) **8278**
Moteurs Loisirs et Paysages (FRA ISSN 1245-3609) **3744**
Mother & Baby (AUS ISSN 1031-4830) **4364**
Mother & Baby (GBR ISSN 0047-8172) **2161**
Mother & Baby (SGP) **4364**
Mother Earth (GBR ISSN 1358-0604) **3454**
Mother Earth International Journal (USA) **5228**
● Mother Earth News (USA ISSN 0027-1535) **3982**
Mother India (IND ISSN 0027-1543) **6935**
● Mother Jones (USA ISSN 0362-8841) **5228**
Mother of the Bride (USA) **8876**
Mother Tongue Education Research Series (DEU) **5152**
● Motherhood (SGP ISSN 0129-1823) **4364**
● Mothering (USA ISSN 0733-3013) **8847**
MotherJones.com *see* Mother Jones **5228**
Motherland (BGD) **3800**
● Mother's Day Report (USA) **4051**
Mothers of Asthmatics Report *see* The M A Report **5763**
Mothertown (USA) **3982**
▼ ● Motherwords (USA ISSN 1941-5907) **2161**
Motilal Banarsidass (Delhi) Newsletter *see* M L B D Newsletter **7698**
● Motion (FIN ISSN 0788-0332) **8187**
Motion/Kinisi (GRC) **8785**
Motion *see* Motion Windsurfing Magazine **8188**
Motion (USA ISSN 0889-3934) **7061**
Motion Control (Dutch Edition) *see* Motion Control (French Edition) **2463**
Motion Control (French Edition) (BEL ISSN 1379-0641) **2463**
Motion Picture and Television Technology *see* Tekhnika Kino i Televideniya **2395**
● Motion Picture Editors Guild Magazine (USA ISSN 1541-2679) **6507**
Motion Picture Editors Guild Magazine & Directory Articles *see* Motion Picture Editors Guild Magazine **6507**
● Motion Picture Investor (Online) (USA) **6507**
Motion Picture Investor (Print) *see* Motion Picture Investor (Online) **6507**
Motion Picture, T V & Theatre Directory (USA ISSN 0580-0412) **2017**
Motion Pictures Technical Bulletin (IND ISSN 0027-1632) **6507**
Motion Surfing Magazine *see* Motion Windsurfing Magazine **8188**
● Motion System Design (USA ISSN 1537-1794) **3390**
Motion System Hydraulics & Pneumatics *see* Hydraulics & Pneumatics **3361**
Motion Windsurfing Magazine (NLD ISSN 1874-3463) **8188**
Motions in Federal Court (USA) **4838**
▼ Motions in Limine (USA ISSN 1942-0323) **4956**
● Motions- og Ernaeringsraadet. Nyhedsbrev (DNK ISSN 1901-2470) **6663**
Motionsgang (DNK ISSN 0107-8976) **8188**
Motitalia (ITA ISSN 0392-3681) **8261**
● Motivate (NZL ISSN 1177-1569) **8504**
● ➤ Motivation and Emotion (USA ISSN 0146-7239) **7386**
Motivation Strategies (USA ISSN 1557-5152) **30**
● Motivational Manager (USA ISSN 1099-7229) **2334**
● Motley Fool Champion Funds (USA ISSN 1550-7955) **1641**
● Motley Fool Global Gains (USA ISSN 1935-0368) **1641**
● Motley Fool Hidden Gems (USA ISSN 1545-3286) **1641**
● Motley Fool Income Investor (USA ISSN 1546-5047) **1641**
● Motley Fool Inside Value (USA ISSN 1551-9902) **1641**
● Motley Fool Rule Breakers (USA ISSN 1553-7625) **1641**
● Motley Fool Rule Your Retirement (USA ISSN 1552-8073) **1641**
● Motmaele (NOR ISSN 0809-2109) **5153**
La Moto (ESP) **8261**
† La Moto (ITA ISSN 0390-0304) **8975**
● Moto (RUS) **8261**
Moto 73 (NLD ISSN 0165-8859) **8261**
Moto 80 (BEL) **8261**
Moto Accessories (GRC ISSN 1108-7846) **8261**
Moto Conso (FRA ISSN 1950-8506) **8261**
Moto Crampons (FRA ISSN 0766-0847) **8261**
Moto Crampons Enduro (FRA) **8261**
Moto Crampons Guide d'Achat (FRA) **8261**
Moto Crampons Motocross (FRA) **8261**
Moto Crampons Posters (FRA) **8261**
Moto Crampons Special Images (FRA) **8261**
Le Moto del Campione (ITA ISSN 1826-316X) **8261**
Moto Design (ITA ISSN 1828-1141) **8591**
Moto Flash (FRA ISSN 0336-6596) **8591**
Moto G P Collection (ITA ISSN 1825-0270) **8261**
Moto Journal (CAN ISSN 0319-2865) **8261**
Moto Journal (FRA ISSN 0751-591X) **8261**
Moto Journal 125 (FRA) **8261**
Moto Journal Accessoires (FRA) **8261**
Moto Journal Compilations (FRA) **8261**
Moto Journal Essais (FRA) **8261**
Moto Journal Grands Prix (FRA) **8261**
Moto Journal Harley (FRA) **8261**
Moto Journal Sportives (FRA) **8261**
Moto Journal Toutes les Motos (FRA) **8261**
† La Moto Junior (ITA ISSN 1121-6263) **8975**
Moto Katalog *see* Avto Magazin. Moto Katalog **8254**
Moto Kids (FRA ISSN 1766-9553) **8261**
Moto Kids (USA ISSN 1933-9712) **8261**
Moto Legende (FRA ISSN 1155-2069) **8261**
Moto Magazine (ZWE) **3996**
Moto Magazyn *see* MotoMagazyn **8591**
† Moto Manual (AUS ISSN 1449-0684) **8975**
Moto Puls (HRV ISSN 1331-3266) **8591**
Moto Revue (FRA ISSN 0047-8180) **8261**
Moto Revue Classic (FRA ISSN 1633-2776) **8261**
Moto Sport Schweiz (CHE ISSN 1420-0457) **8261**
Moto Sport Suisse (CHE ISSN 1420-0465) **8261**
Moto Storiche & d'Epoca (ITA ISSN 1125-6400) **8261**
Moto Triti (GRC ISSN 1108-7854) **8261**
Moto Triti On-Off (GRC) **8261**
Moto Triti Scooter (GRC) **8262**
Moto Triti Test Book (GRC) **8262**
Moto Verde (ESP) **8262**
Moto Verte (FRA) **8262**
● Moto X (DEU) **8262**
Motocasion (ESP) **8262**
Motociclette da Leggenda *see* Legend Bike **8260**
Motociclismo (ESP ISSN 1579-203X) **8262**
● Motociclismo (ITA ISSN 0027-1691) **8262**
● Motociclismo (PRT) **8262**
Motociclismo Catalogo (ESP ISSN 1131-785X) **8262**
Motociclismo Catalogo (Cruz Quebrada) (PRT) **8262**
● Motociclismo d'Epoca (ITA ISSN 1123-4571) **8262**
Motociclismo Especial Pruebas (ESP) **8262**
Motociclismo Fuori Strada *see* Motociclismo Fuoristrada **8262**
● Motociclismo Fuoristrada (ITA ISSN 1722-3083) **8262**
Motociclismo Grandes Premios (ESP) **8262**
Motociclismo Magazine (BRA ISSN 1415-1863) **8262**
Motociclismo Motocatalogo *see* Motociclismo Catalogo (Cruz Quebrada) **8262**
Motociclismo Pruebas (ESP) **8262**
Motocourse (GBR ISSN 0309-4642) **8262**
Motocross (ITA) **8262**
Motocross Action (USA ISSN 0146-3292) **8262**
Motocross Enduro (DEU ISSN 1611-1184) **8262**
Motocross Enduro Aktuell *see* Motocross Enduro **8262**
Motocross Journal (USA ISSN 1082-5029) **8262**
Motocross Racer *see* M X Racer **8972**
Motocykl (CZE ISSN 1210-1419) **8262**
Motocykl (POL ISSN 1426-2932) **8262**
Motocykl Katalog *see* Motocykl Pruvodce **8262**
Motocykl Pruvodce (CZE ISSN 1214-6137) **8262**
Motocykle Katalog (POL ISSN 1426-2622) **8262**
Motohouse (CZE ISSN 1213-3086) **8591**
Motohouse Katalog (CZE ISSN 1212-3412) **8591**
● MotoMagazyn (POL ISSN 1230-5251) **8591**
MotoMama (USA) **8262**
Motomax (BRA ISSN 1809-3825) **8262**
Motomondiale Collection (ITA ISSN 1824-7695) **8262**
● Motonautica (ITA ISSN 1825-988X) **8278**
MotoPlus (NLD ISSN 1872-6410) **8591**
● Motor (DNK ISSN 0047-8199) **8592**
● Motor (IND ISSN 0027-1713) **8591**
Motor (ITA ISSN 1591-240X) **8548**
Motor (KEN ISSN 1991-0991) **8592**
● Motor (NLD ISSN 0027-1721) **8262**
● Motor (NOR ISSN 0027-173X) **8592**
● Motor (RUS ISSN 1028-8910) **8591**
● Motor (SWE ISSN 0027-1764) **8591**
● MOTOR (USA ISSN 0027-1748) **8591**
● Motor (Sydney) (AUS) **8592**
● Motor a Diesel (MEX) **3390**
● Motor Age (USA ISSN 1520-9385) **8592**
Motor & Equipment Manufacturers Association Market Analysis *see* M E M A Market Analysis **1897**
● Motor and Traffic Law New South Wales (AUS) **4838**
● Motor & Traffic Law - Victoria (AUS) **4838**
Motor and Traffic Law - Victoria *see* Motor & Traffic Law - Victoria **4838**
Motor Auto Repair Manual (USA ISSN 0098-1745) **8592**
● Motor Boat & Yachting (GBR ISSN 0027-1780) **8278**
● Motor Boating (USA ISSN 1531-2623) **8278**
Motor Boats Monthly (GBR ISSN 0958-1898) **8278**
† ● Motor Business Asia Pacific (USA ISSN 1359-4532) **8975**
● Motor Business Japan (USA ISSN 1359-4524) **8592**
Motor Caravan (GBR ISSN 0268-6120) **8323**
Motor Caravanner (GBR) **8323**
Motor Carrier Annual Reports (USA) **8527**
Motor Carrier - Freight Forwarder Service (USA) **8673**
Motor Carrier Permit and Tax Bulletin *see* Motor Carrier Permit & Tax Bulletin **8673**
Motor Carrier Permit & Tax Bulletin (USA ISSN 1537-8349) **8673**
● Motor Carrier Safety Report (USA ISSN 1092-3101) **8504**
Motor City Sports (USA) **8188**
Motor City Stamp and Cover Club On Cover *see* M C S C C On Cover **6896**
Motor Clasico (ESP) **8592**
Motor Coach Age (USA ISSN 0739-117X) **8504**
Motor Component & Accessory Manufacturers *see* Business Ratio Report. Motor Component & Accessory Manufacturers (Year) **5450**
● ➤ Motor Control (USA ISSN 1087-1640) **6113**
Motor Cross United Kingdom *see* M X U K **8260**
Motor Detroit *see* Motor Detroit Magazine **6589**
▼ ● Motor Detroit Magazine (USA ISSN 1948-9242) **6589**
Motor Domestic Car Crash Estimating Guide (USA) **8592**
Motor - E - Motion *see* Motor Emotion **8592**
Motor Early Model Crash Estimating Guide (USA ISSN 0160-1644) **8592**
Motor Emotion (NLD ISSN 1566-1598) **8592**
Motor Engine Control Module, Wiring Diagrams & P I N Identification, includes Light Trucks, Vans & SUV's *see* Engine Control Module Wiring Diagrams & P I N Identification **8579**
Motor Equipment News (AUS ISSN 0129-1483) **8592**
Motor Equipment News (NZL ISSN 1175-1908) **8592**
Motor Fleet Supervision (USA) **1870**
Motor Freight Controller (USA ISSN 0886-8778) **8673**
Motor Freight Directory (USA) **2017**
Motor Home *see* MotorHome **8323**
Motor Imported Car Crash Estimating Guide (USA ISSN 0164-6346) **8592**
● Motor Industry Bargaining Council Consolidated Agreements (ZAF ISSN 1682-1068) **4736**
Motor Industry in Figures (Year) *see* Automobile in Cifre (Year) **8522**
Motor Industry Management (GBR ISSN 0265-0843) **8592**
Motor Industry of Great Britain (Year) World Automotive Statistics (GBR) **8592**
Motor Industry Research Association Automotive Business News *see* M I R A Automotive Business News **1249**
Motor Industry Research Association Virtual Automotive Information Centre *see* M I R A Virtual Automotive Information Centre **8527**
Motor Industry U K *see* Key Note Market Review: Motor Industry **1896**
† Motor Italia. Euromotor (ITA ISSN 0391-6456) **8975**
Motor Journal (CHE) **8592**
Motor Journal (CZE ISSN 1213-2527) **8592**
Motor Katalogus (HUN ISSN 0865-7165) **8262**
Motor Klassik (DEU ISSN 0177-8862) **8592**
Motor Light Truck Tune Up and Repair Manual *see* Motor Light Truck Tune Up & Repair Manual **8592**
Motor Light Truck Tune Up & Repair Manual (USA) **8592**
● Motor-Magasinet (DNK ISSN 0109-7490) **8592**
Motor-Magasinet *see* Det Svenska Motor-Magasinet **8606**
Motor - Nachrichten *see* Notiziario Motoristico **8596**
Motor News (AUS ISSN 0818-5549) **8592**
Motor News *see* Notiziario Motoristico **8596**
Motor News (UKR) **8592**
Motor News *see* S J First **8754**
Motor O B D I I Drive Cycle Guide *see* O B D I I Drive Cycle Guide: Domestic & Import Cars, Light Trucks, Vans & SUVs **3213**
Motor Parts and Labor Guide (USA) **8592**
Motor Racing Australia (AUS ISSN 1039-4516) **8188**
† ● Motor Report International (GBR ISSN 0306-6274) **8975**
Motor Revue (HUN ISSN 0865-4131) **8262**
Motor Revue Belgium *see* Auto Loisirs Motor Revue **8558**
Motor Roller Katalog (DEU) **8263**
Motor Schools Association of G.B. News Journal *see* M S A News Journal **8589**
Motor Schools Association of Great Britain Newslink *see* M S A Newslink **8260**
● Motor Ship (GBR ISSN 0027-2000) **8654**
Motor Ship Directory (GBR ISSN 0963-8466) **8654**
Motor Ship Directory of Shipowners & Shipbuilding *see* Motor Ship Directory **8654**
Motor Sport (GBR ISSN 0027-2019) **8592**
Motor Sport (ROM ISSN 1453-9608) **8188**
Motor Sport Aktuell Rennterminkalender (CHE) **8188**
Motor Sports Year Book (GBR) **8188**
Motor Super Market (ITA ISSN 1128-6210) **8263**
Motor Times *see* Waikato Times **3919**
Motor Trade Journal (AUS ISSN 0027-2035) **8593**
Motor Trader (AUS) **8593**
Motor Trader (GBR ISSN 0027-2043) **8593**
The Motor-Trader *see* Ireland's Motor Trader **8586**
Motor Trader and Fleet Operator (ZWE ISSN 0027-2051) **8593**
Motor Traders Association Journal (AUS) **8593**
Motor Traffic in Sweden (SWE ISSN 0077-1619) **8593**
● Motor Transport (GBR ISSN 0027-206X) **8673**
Motor Transport Logistica *see* M T Logistica **8672**
Motor Trend *see* Qiche Zu **8600**
● Motor Trend (USA ISSN 0027-2094) **8593**
Motor Trend Sport Utility, Truck & Van Buyer's Guide (USA) **8593**
Motor Trend's New Car Buyers' Guide (USA ISSN 0160-8886) **8593**
● Motor Trend's Truck Trend (USA ISSN 1094-4370) **8593**
● Motor Truck (CAN ISSN 0027-2108) **8673**
Motor Tuning Car (BRA ISSN 1806-3705) **8593**
Motor und Reisen (DEU ISSN 0176-3792) **8593**
● Motor Vehicle Accident Reconstruction and Cause Analysis (USA) **8504**
Motor Vehicle and Traffic Laws of Massachusetts *see* Massachusetts Motor Vehicle and Traffic Laws **4729**
Motor Vehicle and Traffic Laws of New Jersey *see* New Jersey Motor Vehicle and Traffic Laws **4743**
Motor Vehicle Collision Information (CAN ISSN 1719-5918) **7532**
● Motor Vehicle Crashes in New Zealand (NZL ISSN 1176-3949) **8527**
Motor Vehicle Data Book (CAN ISSN 0316-6198) **8593**
Motor Vehicle Engineering Specifications - Japan *see* Jidosha Shogenhyo **8587**
● Motor Vehicle Law N S W (New South Wales) (AUS) **4736**
● Motor Vehicle Law. Queensland (AUS ISSN 0728-5981) **4736**
Motor Vehicle Law South Australia (AUS) **4838**
● Motor Vehicle Laws of North Carolina (USA ISSN 1537-1549) **8504**
● Motor Vehicle Laws of Vermont (USA ISSN 1549-019X) **4736**
● Motor Vehicle Regulation - State Capitals (USA) **8593**
● Motor Vehicle Repair Industry Authority. Annual Report (AUS ISSN 1833-0347) **8504**
Motor Vehicle Report Book *see* M V R Book **8589**
● Motor Vehicle Reports (AUS ISSN 0813-782X) **4824**
Motor Vehicle Reports (4th Series) (CAN ISSN 0709-5341) **8504**
Motor Vehicle Safety Defect Recall Campaigns (USA ISSN 0565-7717) **8593**
Motor Vehicle Statistics of Japan (JPN ISSN 0463-6635) **8593**
Motor Vikatan (IND) **8593**
Motor W A (Western Australia) (AUS ISSN 1442-8148) **8593**
Motor Xtrem (ROM ISSN 1582-8107) **8188**
Motoracing (ESP) **8593**
MotoRacing (USA ISSN 1080-9929) **8593**
Motoraver Magazine (DEU) **8593**
MotorBladet (DNK ISSN 0107-7554) **8263**
Motorboot (NLD ISSN 1381-8708) **8278**
● Motorbooty (USA ISSN 1089-8522) **6589**
Motorbranschen (SWE ISSN 0027-2140) **8593**
● Motorbransjen (NOR ISSN 0332-8864) **8593**
Motorcaravan & Motorhome Monthly (GBR ISSN 0141-9269) **8323**
▼ Motorclassic (DNK ISSN 1902-4908) **8593**
Motorcoach Marketer (USA) **8504**
Motorcycle *see* Motuo Che **8265**
Motorcycle Blue Book (USA ISSN 0091-3774) **8263**
Motorcycle Classics (GBR ISSN 1361-8997) **8263**
Motorcycle Classics (USA ISSN 1556-0880) **8263**
● Motorcycle Consumer News (USA ISSN 1073-9408) **8263**
Motorcycle Cruiser (USA ISSN 1525-772X) **8263**
Motorcycle Dealer (GBR) **8263**
Motorcycle Dealers' Guide (ZAF ISSN 0258-5073) **8263**
Motorcycle Enthusiast *see* Enthusiast **8258**
Motorcycle Events Magazine (USA ISSN 1099-0100) **8263**
Motorcycle Fashion (GBR ISSN 1476-8747) **8263**
Motorcycle Guide (AUS) **8504**
Motorcycle Industry Magazine (USA ISSN 0884-626X) **8263**
Motorcycle Japan (JPN) **8504**
Motorcycle Magazine (THA ISSN 0125-1732) **8593**
Motorcycle Monthly (GBR ISSN 1754-6478) **8263**
Motorcycle News (GBR ISSN 0027-1853) **8263**
● Motorcycle Online (USA) **8263**
Motorcycle Product News (USA ISSN 0164-8349) **8263**
● Motorcycle Product News Trade Directory (USA) **2017**
Motorcycle Safety Foundation (USA) **8263**
● Motorcycle Shopper (USA ISSN 1075-2447) **8263**
Motorcycle Sport & Leisure (GBR) **8263**
Motorcycle Trader & News (NZL ISSN 1174-2747) **8263**
Motorcycle World (GRC) **8263**
Motorcycle Xpress *see* Black Book. Motorcycle Xpress **1975**
● Motorcycles, Parts & Accessories Buyers' Guide (TWN ISSN 1029-8711) **2017**
● Motorcyclist (USA ISSN 0027-2205) **8263**
▼ Motorcyclist Retro (USA ISSN 1946-9780) **8263**
Motorcyclist's Post (USA ISSN 0164-9256) **8263**
Motorcykel Revyen *see* M C Revyen **8260**
Motorcykelmagasinet *see* M C M **8260**

Title

10628 MOTORCYLE TRAVEL & ADVENTURE ULRICH'S PERIODICALS

Motorcyle Travel & Adventure *see* Cycle World's Motorcycle Travel & Adventure 8257
Motoretta (DEU ISSN 1610-5125) 8263
Motorfahrzeuge in der Schweiz. Bestand am 30. September (Year)/Vehicules a Moteur en Suisse. Effectif au 30 Septembre (Year) (CHE) 8527
Motorfahrzeuge in der Schweiz. Eingefuehrte Motorfahrzeuge/Vehicules a Moteur en Suisse. Vehicules a Moteur Importes (CHE ISSN 1422-5107) 8527
Motorfoeraren (SWE ISSN 0463-6678) 8593
Motorfoereren (NOR ISSN 0027-2213) 8593
• MotorHome (USA ISSN 0744-074X) 8323
Motorhome Monthly (GBR ISSN 1363-8971) 8505
Motorhome World (AUS) 8594
† Motori (ITA ISSN 0393-7666) 8975
Motorik (DEU ISSN 0170-5792) 6993
Motorindia (IND ISSN 0027-223X) 8594
Motoring (IND ISSN 0027-2248) 8594
Motoring (SGP ISSN 0217-393X) 8594
Motoring & Home - Life (GBR) 3869
Motoring & Leisure (GBR) 8594
Motoring Annual (SGP) 8594
• Motoring Directions (AUS ISSN 1323-4595) 8505
Motoring Life (IRL ISSN 0027-2256) 8594
Motorist (DEU ISSN 0932-5395) 8432
The Motorist *see* EnCompass 8701
Motorist's Advocate (CAN) 8594
• La Motorizzazione (ITA ISSN 1120-415X) 8505
▼ Motorjacht (NLD ISSN 1875-5062) 8278
Der Motorjournalist (DEU ISSN 0342-9954) 4580
Motorlu Kara Tasitlari Istatistikleri *see* Turkey. Turkiye Istatistik Kurumu. Motorlu Kara Tasitlari Istatistikleri (Year) 8532
Motorola Technical Developments (USA ISSN 0887-5286) 2370
MotoRoute *see* Motorrad und Reisen 8264
MotoRoute Magazin (CZE ISSN 1801-0997) 8263
Motorrad (CHE) 8264
Das Motorrad (DEU ISSN 0027-237X) 8263
Motorrad Abenteuer (DEU ISSN 1619-4462) 8264
Motorrad Adressbuch (DEU) 2018
Motorrad Boerse (DEU) 8264
Motorrad Classic (DEU ISSN 0937-9495) 8264
Motorrad Haendler (AUT) 8264
Motorrad Handel (DEU) 8264
Motorrad Katalog (DEU ISSN 0949-0892) 8264
Motorrad Kontakte (DEU) 8264
Motorrad Magazin M O (DEU ISSN 0723-2616) 8264
Motorrad Markt (DEU) 8264
Motorrad News (DEU) 8264
Motorrad Oldtimer Katalog (DEU) 8264
Motorrad Spiegel (DEU) 8264
Motorrad Szene (DEU) 8264
Motorrad Test (Year) (DEU) 8264
Motorrad Treff (DEU) 8264
Motorrad und Reisen (DEU) 8264
Motorradfahrer (DEU ISSN 0935-7645) 8264
Motorradmagazin (AUT) 8264
• Motorradmagazin (DEU) 8264
Motorradszene Bayern (DEU) 8264
Motorradtreff Spinner (DEU) 8264
Motorraeder (DEU) 8264
Motorraeder aus Italien (DEU) 8264
† Motors (DEU ISSN 1861-6143) 8975
Motorscot (GBR) 8188
Motorsport Aktuell (CHE ISSN 1421-8488) 8264
Motorsport America (USA) 8188
motorsport + business (DEU) 8188
Motorsport Dealer and Trade *see* Canadian Powersport Trade 8256
Motorsport Dealer & Trade *see* M D T 8260
Motorsport News (GBR) 8264
Motorsport - S.A. News Bulletin (ZAF) 8594
Motorsports (USA ISSN 1057-0691) 8188
Motorsports Now! (GBR) 8188
Motorsports Sponsorship Marketing News (USA) 8264
Motortechnische Zeitschrift *see* M T Z 8589
• MotorWatch (USA) 8594
Motosprint (ITA ISSN 1122-1739) 8264
MotoSuperMarket *see* Motor Super Market 8263
Mototaller (ESP) 8505
Mototech de Motociclismo (ESP) 8264
MotoTecnica (ITA) 8264
• Mototurismo (ITA ISSN 1128-3947) 8264
Motricidad (ESP ISSN 0214-0071) 6993
Motricidad y Persona (CHL ISSN 0718-3151) 2887
Motricidade Humana (PRT) 5681
• Motricite Cerebrale (FRA ISSN 0245-5919) 6161
• Motriz. Revista de Educacao Fisica (BRA ISSN 1980-6574) 8188
Mots a Mots (FRA ISSN 1770-2224) 644
Mots en Fleches (MUS ISSN 1694-0075) 3907
Mots et Images (FRA ISSN 1771-611X) 506
Mots, Ordinateurs, Textes, Societes *see* M O T S 7152
• Mots Palabras Words (ITA ISSN 1720-3708) 5153
Les Mots qui Rient (FRA ISSN 1951-5898) 2203
Les Mots-Sesames (FRA ISSN 1952-1413) 2203
Mott Community College Post *see* M C C Post 2290
Motto (USA) 1150
• Motu Moments (NZL ISSN 1177-1208) 2619
• Motu Working Paper (NZL ISSN 1176-2667) 1150
Motueka - Golden Bay News (NZL) 3918
• Motuo Che/Motorcycle (CHN ISSN 1002-6754) 8265
Motuoche Jishu/Journal of Motorcycle Technology (CHN ISSN 1001-7666) 8594
Motus Corporis (BRA ISSN 1413-9111) 5681
Al-Moubawab *see* An- Nahar 3905
El Moudjahid (DZA ISSN 1111-0287) 3790
Al-Mouhandis Al-Arabi (SYR) 3211
Mould & Die Industry *see* Moju Gongye 3210
Mould Engineering (JPN) 3211
Moultrie County Heritage *see* Moultrie County, Illinois Heritage Journal 3775
Moultrie County, Illinois Heritage Journal (USA ISSN 1942-7824) 3775
Mount Allison Record (CAN ISSN 0027-2485) 2293
Mount Buller News (AUS) 8739
Mount Carmel (GBR ISSN 0307-5958) 7808
• Mount Desert Island Biological Laboratory. Bulletin (USA ISSN 0097-0883) 690
Mount Holyoke Alumnae Quarterly (USA ISSN 0027-2493) 2293
Mount Magazine (USA) 2293
➤ Mount Olive Review (USA ISSN 0893-8288) 5336
Mount Rainier National Park *see* Hiking Mount Rainier National Park 8718
Mount Saint Mary College Happenings *see* M S M C Happenings 2290
• ➤ Mount Sinai Journal of Medicine (USA ISSN 0027-2507) 5681
Mountain and Museum *see* Yama to Hakubutsukan 6540
Mountain and Valley *see* The-Yama-to-Keikoku 8337
• The Mountain Astrologer (USA ISSN 1079-1345) 566
Mountain Athletics (USA) 8323
• Mountain Bike (DEU ISSN 0946-2996) 8265
• Mountain Bike (USA ISSN 0897-5213) 8265
Mountain Bike Action (ITA ISSN 1970-027X) 8265
Mountain Bike Action (USA ISSN 0895-8467) 8265
• Mountain Bike Action (Tel Aviv) (ISR) 8265
Mountain Bike Rider (GBR ISSN 1367-0824) 8265
Mountain Bike Test-Special (DEU ISSN 1860-1650) 8265
Mountain Bike Touren-Special (DEU ISSN 1860-1715) 8265
• Mountain Bike World (ITA) 8265
Mountain Biking (USA ISSN 1062-2918) 8265
Mountain Biking U K (GBR ISSN 0954-8696) 8265
Mountain Biking World (GBR ISSN 1744-7267) 8265
Mountain Blossoms (Guizhou) *see* Shanhua 5371
Mountain Club of South Africa. Journal (ZAF ISSN 0258-0101) 8323
Mountain Diggings (USA ISSN 0146-8855) 4304
Mountain Empire Genealogical Quarterly (USA ISSN 0882-4266) 3775
Mountain Gazette (USA ISSN 0160-726X) 8323
➤ Mountain Geologist (USA ISSN 0027-254X) 2756
• Mountain Ideals (USA) 3982
Mountain Interstate Foreign Language Conference Review *see* M I F L C Review 5149
Mountain Life (CAN) 8323
Mountain Light (USA) 4304
• Mountain Living (USA ISSN 1088-6451) 4981
Mountain Manager (DEU ISSN 1618-3622) 8739
• Mountain Online (GBR) 8188
Mountain Path (IND ISSN 0027-2574) 6935
Mountain Pilot (USA) 8548
Mountain Pine Beetle Action Plan (CAN ISSN 1912-4627) 3697
Mountain Plains Adult Education Association Newsletter *see* M P A E A Newsletter 2944
• ➤ Mountain Plains Journal of Business and Economics (USA ISSN 1932-2070) 1151
Mountain Plains Library Association Newsletter *see* M P L A Newsletter 5030
Mountain Record (USA ISSN 0896-8942) 7702
• ➤ Mountain Research and Development (CHE ISSN 0276-4741) 2713
Mountain Resort Magazine (USA) 4394
Mountain-Skiing *see* Gornye Lyzhi 8316
Mountain Spirit (USA) 8055
Mountain States BankNews Bank Directory *see* BankNews Mountain States Bank Directory 1318
Mountain Trails (USA) 4020
Mountain Travel - Sobek, The Adventure Company (USA) 8739
• Mountain West Golf (USA) 8239
Mountain Wutai Researches *see* Wutaishan Yanjiu 4167
Mountainbike Rider (DEU) 8265
Mountaineer (CAN ISSN 1181-2257) 3813
Mountaineer (Colorado Springs) (USA) 6437
Mountaineer (Seattle) (USA ISSN 0027-2620) 8323
• Mountainfreak (USA ISSN 1524-2579) 8323
• ➤ MountainRise (USA ISSN 1555-7200) 2887
Mountains and Sea *see* Serra e Mar 8332
Mourne Observer & County Down News (IRL ISSN 1366-3372) 3894
• ➤ Mousaion (ZAF ISSN 0027-2639) 5032
Mouse (CHL) 2432
† Mousebit (NLD) 8975
➤ Mouseion/Revue de la Societe Canadienne des Etudes Classiques (CAN ISSN 1496-9343) 2237
Mousiki (GRC) 6633
Moussons (FRA ISSN 1620-3224) 7986
Mouth (Chicago) (USA ISSN 1529-5044) 5856
Mouth (Topeka) (USA ISSN 1071-5657) 4068
Mouthpiece (Redwood City) (USA) 5856
➤ Mouton Grammar Library (DEU ISSN 0933-7636) 5153
Mouvement Anti-Utilitariste dans les Science Sociales. Revue Semestrielle (FRA ISSN 1247-4819) 8121
Mouvement Communal (BEL) 7498
Mouvement de la Population en Suisse *see* Bevoelkerungsbewegung in der Schweiz 7278
Mouvement des Entreprises de France. Annuaire Officiel *see* Mouvement des Entreprises de France. L'Annuaire 2018
Mouvement des Entreprises de France. L'Annuaire (FRA ISSN 1950-9405) 2018
Le Mouvement Hotelier et Touristique (FRA ISSN 1169-8217) 4394
Mouvement Naturel de la Population de la Grece (GRC ISSN 0077-6114) 7312
Le Mouvement Psychanalitique *see* Le Mouvement Psychanalitique. Collection 6162
Le Mouvement Psychanalitique. Collection (FRA ISSN 1963-1596) 6162
• ➤ Le Mouvement Social (FRA ISSN 0027-2671) 4154
• Mouvements (FRA ISSN 1291-6412) 7986
Move (AUT) 6778
Move (BGR) 8188
Move! (ZAF ISSN 1813-5749) 3551
Move Magazine (USA) 8505
➤ Moveast (HUN ISSN 1215-234X) 6507
The Movement (USA) 3982
Movement and Dance Quarterly (GBR) 2686
▼ • Movement and Rhythm (USA ISSN 2150-4970) 2887
• ➤ Movement Disorders (USA ISSN 0885-3185) 6162
Movement Research Performance Journal (USA ISSN 1077-0933) 2687
Movement Theatre Quarterly (USA ISSN 1065-1519) 8474
Movements in Sheep & Beef Input Prices *see* Meat and Wool Boards' Economic Service. Movements in Sheep & Beef Input Prices 203
Movements in the Arts (USA ISSN 8756-890X) 506
Movers News (USA ISSN 8750-1155) 8673
Movicarga (ESP) 1899
† Movie (AUS ISSN 0314-0326) 8975
† Movie (GBR ISSN 0027-268X) 8975
Movie (IND ISSN 0971-3182) 6507
Movie & D V D (Digital Video Disc) (ZAF ISSN 1817-0331) 6507
Movie & DVD *see* Movie & D V D 6507
• Movie Collector's World (USA ISSN 8750-5401) 2402
Movie Entertainment (CAN) 6507
Movie F X Video Magazine (USA) 2402
Movie Idols (GBR ISSN 1367-0670) 6507
Movie - Kino Kultur Aachen (DEU) 6507
Movie Mag International (GBR) 6508
Movie Mirror (USA ISSN 0027-271X) 6508
• Movie Review Query Engine (USA) 6508
Movie Scope *see* MovieScope 6508
The Movie Show *see* Dianying Shijie 6496
Movie - T V Marketing (JPN ISSN 0047-8288) 6508
Movie - T V Marketing Annual Worldwide Television Survey (JPN) 2385
Movie - T V Marketing Global Motion Picture Year Book (JPN ISSN 0085-3577) 6508
Movie Weekly (USA) 6508
Movieline's Hollywood Life *see* Hollywood Life 6502
Moviemaker (USA) 6508
Movies Plus (IRL) 6508
• MovieScope (GBR ISSN 1751-1356) 6508
Moviestar (DEU) 6508
Movimento (Porto Alegre) (BRA ISSN 0104-754X) 8188
• Movimento e Percepcao (Centro Regional Universitario Espirito Santo do Pinhal) (BRA ISSN 1677-7360) 6231
• Movimiento Actual (MEX) 3909
Movimiento de Rock (ESP) 6589
Movimiento Internacional de Estudiantes Catolicos, Centro de Documentacion Servico de Documentacion *see* M I E C Servico de Documentacion 2993
Movimiento Sindical de America Latina y el Caribe (CUB) 4599
Movin' (CAN ISSN 0704-1500) 8620
• Movin' Out (USA) 8673
• Moving Ahead (CAN ISSN 1484-2246) 8055
Moving & Relocation Directory (USA ISSN 1930-3173) 7600
Moving and Relocation Directory *see* Moving & Relocation Directory 7600
Moving Bodies/Menneske i Bevegelse (NOR ISSN 1503-6065) 6993
Moving Home (USA) 4364
➤ The Moving Image (AUS ISSN 1320-4181) 6508
• The Moving Image (USA ISSN 1532-3978) 6508
Moving In (IRL ISSN 1393-7359) 4547
The Moving Industry Professional Sourcebook (USA) 8673
Moving Industry Transportation Statistics (Year) (USA) 8527
A Moving Journal (USA ISSN 1088-8195) 5336
Moving Manchester (GBR ISSN 1751-1003) 3968
Moving Matters (CAN ISSN 1490-618X) 3073
Moving Pictures' European Film Reviews (GBR ISSN 1358-1996) 6508
Moving Pictures International (GBR ISSN 0959-6992) 6508
Moving Pictures Television (GBR ISSN 1360-1083) 6508
Moving Through History (USA ISSN 1932-4766) 8505
Moving to Alberta (CAN ISSN 1495-9542) 7600
Moving to Montreal/Emmenager a Montreal (CAN ISSN 1485-8304) 7600
Moving to Montreal Metropolitain *see* Moving to Montreal 7600
Moving to Ottawa/Emmenager a Ottawa - Hull (CAN ISSN 1709-4321) 7600
Moving to Saskatchewan (CAN ISSN 1496-5437) 7600
Moving to Southwestern Ontario (CAN ISSN 1495-995X) 7600
Moving to Toronto (CAN ISSN 1496-5445) 7600
Moving to Vancouver & British Columbia (CAN ISSN 1495-9569) 7601
Moving to Winnipeg & Manitoba (CAN ISSN 1496-5453) 7601
† The Moving World (USA ISSN 1064-4253) 8975
➤ Moving Worlds (GBR ISSN 1474-4600) 5336
• Movium Bulletin (SWE ISSN 1103-0836) 4419
• Movium Rapport (SWE ISSN 1651-3401) 4419
Moviumsrapport *see* Movium Rapport 4419
Movmnt (USA) 2687
Movoznavstvo (UKR ISSN 0027-2833) 5153
The Mower's Tree (USA ISSN 1547-9307) 5336
Mowia Wieki (POL ISSN 1230-4018) 4246
Mox (DEU) 3853
• MoXie (Berkeley) (USA) 8876
• Moya Hazeta (UKR) 3965
Moya Moskva (RUS) 3937
Moya Stolitsa (KGZ) 3904
• ➤ Le Moyen Age (BEL ISSN 0027-2841) 4246
Moyen Age *see* Mittelalter (Basel) 7600
Moyen Age (FRA ISSN 1276-4159) 4246
Moyen Age Europeen (FRA ISSN 1270-9794) 4246
• Le Moyen Francais (BEL ISSN 0226-0174) 5153
Moyen-Orient (FRA ISSN 1621-2509) 4324
Moyen Orient et Ocean Indien/Middle East and Indian Ocean (FRA ISSN 0764-5562) 4186
Moyo (MWI ISSN 0378-4703) 3906
Moyo Delo (RUS) 3657
Moys Classification and Thesaurus for Legal Materials (DEU) 5032
Mozambique. Direccao Nacional de Geologia. Boletim Geomagnetico Preliminar (MOZ) 2787
Mozambique. Dirrecao Nacional de Geologia. Boletim Seismique (MOZ) 2787
Mozambique File (MOZ) 3913
Mozambique. Instituto Nacional de Estatistica. Estatisticas do Comercio Externo (MOZ) 1252
Mozambique. Instituto Nacional de Estatistica. Estatisticas do Turismo (MOZ) 8780
Mozambique. Instituto Nacional de Estatistica. Estatisticas Industriais (MOZ) 1252
Mozambique. Instituto Nacional de Estatistica. Indice de PrePrecos ao Consumidor (MOZ) 1252
Mozambique. Instituto Nacional de Meteorologia. Boletim Meteorologico para Agricultura (MOZ) 6391
Mozambique. Instituto Nacional de Meteorologia. Informacoes de Caracter Astronomico (Astronomical Information) (MOZ) 2787
▼ • Mozambique Mining Report (GBR ISSN 1755-8956) 6474
Mozambique News Agency Reports *see* A I M Reports 1589
Mozambique Statistical Yearbook/Anuario Estatistico de Mocambique (MOZ) 8389
Mozart Society of America. Newsletter (USA ISSN 1527-3733) 6589
Mozhet Byt/Maybe (RUS) 3937
Moznayim (ISR ISSN 0027-2892) 5336
MP3 Magazine (BRA) 6633
MPLA Newsletter *see* M P L A Newsletter 5030
• Mpls. - Saint Paul Magazine (USA ISSN 0162-6655) 3982
Mpls. - St. Paul Magazine *see* Mpls. - Saint Paul Magazine 3982
Mpls. - St.Paul Wedding Guide *see* Mpls. - Saint Paul Magazine 3982
▼ Mpower Plus (USA ISSN 1936-8607) 6296
Mprove (USA ISSN 1091-3963) 3551
MPuls (DEU ISSN 1862-9725) 8188
Mpumalanga Directory (ZAF) 2018
• Mpumalanga Provincial Legislation Library (ZAF ISSN 1683-2647) 4736
The Mputa (UGA) 3602
MqJICEL *see* Macquarie Journal of International and Comparative Environmental Law 4935
† • Mr. Cheap's Chicago (USA) 8975
† • Mr. Cheap's New York (USA ISSN 1529-1170) 8975
† Mr. Cheap's Washington D.C. (USA) 8975
Mr. Landlord (USA) 7601
MR Magazine (NLD ISSN 1872-6569) 6701
Mr. Modern *see* Modeng Shenshi 6295
▼ Mr. No-No Says, "Don't Touch, Stay Away" (USA) 2161
Mr. Pulo (TWN) 3960
Mr. Writer's Expressions Magazine *see* MisterWriter's Expressions Magazine 5228
• Mrez@ (HRV ISSN 1331-2839) 2352
Mrs/Misesu (JPN) 4364
Mrs. Eagle (USA ISSN 0889-4760) 2268
• Ms. (USA ISSN 0047-8318) 8901
Ms. Fitness (USA ISSN 1078-0661) 6993
Ms. Magazine *see* Ms. 8901
MS Reality Bytes *see* Living M S Magazine 6159
Msafiri (KEN ISSN 0251-0340) 8739
MSC Ph.D.-Thesis Series (NLD ISSN 1570-1530) 5519
MSCoder *see* M S Coder 8972
MSCommunique (CAN ISSN 1209-2053) 7532
MSDN Magazine. Australia - New Zealand Edition *see* M S D N Magazine. Australia - New Zealand Edition 2594

Title

10630 MULTINATIONAL P R REPORT ULRICH'S PERIODICALS

Multinational P R Report (USA ISSN 0743-0795) **30**
• Multinational Pharmaceutical Companies (GBR ISSN 1469-3828) **1601**
• Multinational Telecommunications Companies (GBR ISSN 1469-3836) **1578**
• Multinational Transport (GBR) **1578**
• ➤ Multiphase Science and Technology (USA) **3211**
Multiple Buyer and Retailer (GBR ISSN 1462-6527) **3680**
Multiple Europes (BEL ISSN 1376-0912) **7253**
➤ Multiple Linear Regression Viewpoints (USA ISSN 0195-7171) **2888**
• ➤ Multiple Sclerosis (GBR ISSN 1352-4585) **6162**
Multiple Sclerosis Canada *see* M S Canada **6159**
Multiple Sclerosis Exchange *see* M S Exchange **6159**
Multiple Sclerosis in Focus *see* M S in Focus **6159**
Multiple Sclerosis Ontario *see* M S Ontario **6159**
Multiple Sclerosis Quarterly Report *see* M S Quarterly Report **6159**
Multiple Sclerosis Society of Canada. Alberta Division. Consolidated Annual Report (CAN ISSN 1719-699X) **6162**
• Multiple Sclerosis Society of New Zealand Information Series (NZL ISSN 1176-4473) **6162**
Multiple Sclerosis. Supplement *see* Multiple Sclerosis **6162**
▼ Multiples (USA ISSN 1936-2986) **2161**
▼ Multiscale Modeling (SGP) **3211**
• ➤ Multiscale Modeling & Simulation: a S I A M Interdisciplinary Journal (Society for Industrial and Applied Mathematics) (USA ISSN 1540-3459) **5519**
Multisensor Fusion and Integration for Intelligent Systems (USA) **2455**
• The MultiSimplex Newsletter (SWE) **2595**
MultiSpecialty Coding Pro (USA ISSN 1941-9058) **4515**
Multisport, Triathlete *see* Triathlete **8213**
Multistate Bar Examination Questions (USA ISSN 1072-3102) **4737**
Multistate Corporate Income Tax Guide *see* (Year) U.S. Multistate Corporate Tax Guide **1953**
• (Year) Multistate Corporate Tax Guide (USA ISSN 1051-1555) **1935**
Multistate Corporate Tax Guide Mid-Year Supplement *see* (Year) Multistate Corporate Tax Guide **1935**
Multistate Guide to Regulation and Taxation of Nonprofits (USA ISSN 1931-163X) **1935**
Multistate Guide to Sales and Use Tax. Manufacturing (USA ISSN 1936-9514) **1935**
Multistate Payroll Guide (USA ISSN 1932-524X) **1698**
Multistate Sales Tax Review (USA ISSN 1094-9666) **1935**
Multistate Tax Commission Review (USA) **1935**
• Multitemas (BRA ISSN 1414-512X) **2994**
• Multitudes (FRA ISSN 0292-0107) **6935**
▼ Multitudes-Idees (FRA ISSN 1958-9743) **7156**
• ➤ Multivariate Behavioral Research (USA ISSN 0027-3171) **7386**
Multivariate Experimental Clinical Research *see* Applied Multivariate Research **7335**
• Multiworld (USA) **3982**
Multunk (HUN ISSN 0864-960X) **4154**
Mum & Baby *see* Mami Baobei **8873**
Mum & Dad (KEN ISSN 1991-0983) **2161**
Mumbai Tarun Bharat (IND) **3885**
• Il-Ument (MLT ISSN 1017-2092) **3907**
Munazzamat al-Sihhah al-'Alamiyyah. Silsilat al-Taqarir al-Fanniyyah (CHE ISSN 0251-0111) **5681**
Munazzamat al-Sihhiyyah al-'Alamiyyah. Dalil Qararat Jam'iyyah al-Sihhiyyah wal-Majlis al-Tanfidhi *see* World Health Organization. Handbook of Resolutions and Decisions of the World Health Assembly and the Executive Board. **7545**
Munazzamat al-Sihhiyyah al-'Alamiyyah. Nashrah *see* World Health Organization. Bulletin **5731**
Muncie Public Library now *see* M P L now **5031**
Muncie Times (USA) **3551**
Mund Kiefer Gesichts Chirurg *see* Der M K G - Chirurg **6251**
Mund-, Kiefer- und Gesichtschirurgie *see* Oral and Maxillofacial Surgery **6083**
Mundaiz (ESP ISSN 0213-3040) **5337**
Mundaring Magazine *see* Swan Magazine **3796**
Mundartfreunde Oesterreichs. Mitteilungen (AUT ISSN 0027-3228) **5153**
The Mundi Club. Special Publications (GBR ISSN 1360-8347) **3454**
Mundi Medicina (USA ISSN 1524-251X) **7664**
• El Mundo (BOL ISSN 1563-809X) **3802**
• El Mundo (COL) **3830**
Mundo (DEU ISSN 1612-9393) **7883**
• El Mundo (ESP ISSN 1134-4261) **3953**
El Mundo (Boston) (USA) **3551**
El Mundo (Las Vegas) (USA) **3551**
El Mundo (Oakland) (USA) **3551**
• Mundo Agrario (ARG ISSN 1515-5994) **137**
El Mundo al Vuelo - Inflight Notes (COL) **8785**
• El Mundo Andalucia (ESP ISSN 1576-6977) **3953**
• El Mundo. Anuario (ESP ISSN 1137-1404) **3953**
Mundo Ceramico (BRA) **2044**
Mundo Ceramico. Buyers Guide *see* Mundo Ceramico **2044**
Mundo Cooperativo (ESP) **3160**
Mundo Cristiano (ESP ISSN 0027-3252) **3953**
• Mundo da Optica (BRA ISSN 1678-1139) **6046**
Mundo da Optica News (BRA ISSN 1981-3368) **6046**
O Mundo da Usinagem (BRA ISSN 1518-6091) **1054**
Mundo de la Optica (ESP) **6046**
El Mundo de los Astros (ESP ISSN 1577-9084) **566**
El Mundo de Tu Bebe (ESP ISSN 1132-7731) **2203**
El Mundo del Gato (ESP ISSN 1133-0007) **6811**
Mundo del Mayorista Electrico (ESP) **3109**
Mundo del Perro (ESP ISSN 0212-4947) **6811**
El Mundo del Siglo Veintiuno *see* El Mundo **3953**
• El Mundo del Siglo Veintiuno, El Dia de Baleares (ESP ISSN 1576-6888) **3953**
Mundo Deportivo (ESP) **8188**
Mundo Deportivo (USA) **8188**
• Mundo Ejecutivo (MEX) **1151**
Mundo, El Dia de Baleares *see* El Mundo del Siglo Veintiuno, El Dia de Baleares **3953**
• Mundo Electronico (ESP ISSN 0300-3787) **3109**
Mundo Eletronico (BRA) **3109**
Mundo Eslavo (ESP ISSN 1579-8372) **4154**
El Mundo Financiero (ESP ISSN 0300-3884) **1369**
Mundo Ganadero (ESP ISSN 0214-9192) **293**
• Mundo Hispanico (USA ISSN 1051-4147) **3551**
Mundo Hispanico Yellow Pages (USA) **3552**
Mundo Hostelero (ESP) **4394**
Mundo Indigena *see* Indigenous World **342**
• El Mundo Indigena (DNK ISSN 1024-4573) **348**
Mundo Industrial (ESP) **1899**
Mundo Israelita (ARG ISSN 0327-5930) **7727**
Mundo Justicialista (ARG) **4737**
Mundo Linux (ESP ISSN 1577-6883) **2432**
• Mundo Maya/Maya World (MEX) **348**
Mundo Minero en Linea *see* Revista Mundo Minero **6477**
Mundo Negro (ESP ISSN 1134-7074) **7664**
Mundo Nuevo (VEN ISSN 0379-6922) **3950**
Mundo Plast (ESP ISSN 1887-8067) **7095**
Mundo Precolombino (CHL ISSN 0717-1056) **507**
Mundo Recambio y Taller (ESP ISSN 1139-8647) **8594**
Mundo T & L (ESP) **2243**
Mundo Textil Argentino (ARG ISSN 0027-3376) **8455**
Mundo Universitario (COL ISSN 0120-3460) **2293**
Mundo Vending - Tecnicas y Servicios (ESP) **4394**
Mundos Subterraneos (MEX ISSN 0188-8102) **2756**
Mundus Arabicus (USA ISSN 8755-4925) **5337**
Munger Map Book (USA) **6778**
Munhwao Haksup/Study of Korean Language (PRK ISSN 1728-0311) **5153**
Munibe Antropologia - Arkeologia (ESP ISSN 1132-2217) **348**
Munibe Ciencias Naturales (ESP ISSN 0214-7688) **7883**
Munich and Bavaria *see* Munich & Bavaria **8739**
Munich & Bavaria (USA ISSN 1939-991X) **8739**
Municipal Act and Index to Local Government Legislation Manual (CAN) **7482**
Municipal Administration & Techology *see* Chengshi Guanli yu Keji **7489**
Municipal Advocate (USA ISSN 1046-2422) **7498**
Municipal and Government Manual *see* Mergent Municipal and Government Manual **1639**
Municipal and Planning Law Reports (3rd Series) (CAN ISSN 0702-7206) **4420**
Municipal Association of Victoria. Minutes of Proceedings of Annual Session (AUS ISSN 0077-2143) **7498**
The Municipal Board. Annual Report (CAN ISSN 0464-8617) **7454**
Municipal Bulletin (USA) **7498**
Municipal Cable TV & Telecommunications News (USA) **2385**
▼ Municipal Connection (USA) **1899**
Municipal Engineer *see* Teknik & Miljoe **3222**
Municipal Engineering in Australia (AUS ISSN 0311-354X) **3278**
Municipal Engineers Journal (USA ISSN 0027-3465) **3279**
• Municipal Finance Journal (USA) **1935**
Municipal Financial Information (CAN ISSN 1180-5994) **7498**
Municipal Issuers Registry (USA ISSN 1076-8491) **1641**
Municipal Journal (GBR ISSN 0143-4187) **7498**
Municipal Law Report *see* McQuillin Municipal Law Report **4730**
• ➤ Municipal Lawyer (Albany) (USA ISSN 1530-3969) **4737**
Municipal Lawyer (Bethesda) (USA) **4737**
Municipal Leader (CAN) **7498**
• Municipal Liability Risk Management (CAN) **4737**
• Municipal Litigation Reporter (USA ISSN 0278-1301) **7498**
Municipal Marketplace *see* The Bond Buyer's Municipal Marketplace **1976**
Municipal Maryland (USA ISSN 0196-9986) **7498**
• Municipal Open Line (CAN) **7454**
Municipal Pension Plan Annual Report (CAN ISSN 1201-4184) **1641**
Municipal Pension Plan. Pension News (CAN ISSN 1912-4007) **1698**
• Municipal Planning - Land Use Bulletin (USA ISSN 1545-9500) **7498**
Municipal Problems *see* Toshi Mondai **7504**
Municipal Redbook (British Columbia & Alberta) (CAN) **7498**
Municipal Redbook (British Columbia) (CAN ISSN 1489-6168) **7498**
Municipal Security Rulemaking Board Manual *see* M S R B Manual **1146**
▼ Municipal Sewer & Water (USA) **8829**
Municipal Solid Waste Management *see* M S W Management **3508**
Municipal Solid Waste Solutions *see* M S W Solutions **3509**
Municipal Statistics. Annual Report (CAN ISSN 0319-4183) **7454**
• Municipal World (CAN ISSN 0027-3589) **7498**
Municipal Year Book (GBR ISSN 0305-5906) **7498**
• Municipal Year Book (USA ISSN 0077-2186) **7498**
Municipal Yearbook *see* Municipal Year Book **7498**
• Municipal Yellow Book (USA ISSN 1054-4062) **7498**
Municipalia (ESP) **7498**
Municipalite (CAN ISSN 0713-4800) **7454**
Municipalities and Corporation Cases (IND ISSN 0377-757X) **4737**
The Municipality (USA ISSN 0027-3597) **7498**
• Munis Entomology & Zoology (TUR ISSN 1306-3022) **855**
Munitsipal'naya Vlast' (RUS) **7156**
MuniWireless Magazine (USA ISSN 1930-1081) **2564**
Munno (UGA) **7664**
• Munnpleien (NOR ISSN 0047-8377) **5856**
Munro Eagle (USA) **3775**
Munsif (IND) **3885**
Munskaenken med Vinjournalen (SWE ISSN 0345-8202) **607**
Munson-Williams-Proctor Institute. Bulletin (USA ISSN 0027-3627) **6529**
Munster Express (Early Edition) (IRL ISSN 1649-6612) **3894**
Munster Express (Weekender Edition) (IRL ISSN 1649-6620) **3894**
Munster Interiors (IRL ISSN 1649-6434) **4547**
Al-Muntada (UAE) **5337**
Muntada as-Salaam *see* Workshop of Peace **3016**
Muntada Hawla al-Garimat wa-al-Mugtama' *see* Forum on Crime and Society **2653**
Al-Muntijun (LBY) **8432**
Muntjac (GBR) **690**
Muntkoerier (NLD ISSN 0165-5442) **6651**
Muntpers (NLD ISSN 0924-0039) **6651**
Muntpers Internationaal (NLD) **6651**
Muovi - Plast (FIN ISSN 0788-8430) **7095**
• ➤ Muqarnas (NLD ISSN 0732-2992) **507**
➤ Muqarnas, Supplements (NLD ISSN 0921-0326) **507**
Mur *see* Mur + Betong **450**
Mur og Betong *see* Mur + Betong **450**
➤ Mur + Betong (NOR ISSN 1504-7903) **450**
• Mural (MEX ISSN 1563-7751) **3909**
mural.com *see* Mural **3909**
Murasoli (IND) **3885**
Muratho (ZAF ISSN 1680-1938) **5153**
• Murator (POL ISSN 0239-6866) **450**
Murator Dolnoslaski *see* Murator **450**
Murator Lodzki *see* Murator **450**
Murator Malopolski *see* Murator **450**
Murator Mazowiecki *see* Murator **450**
Murator Numer Specjalny *see* Murator **450**
Murator Pomorski *see* Murator **450**
Murator Slaski *see* Murator **450**
Murator Wielkopolski *see* Murator **450**
Muraveinik (RUS) **2203**
Murder Can Be Fun (USA) **5414**
• Murder Dog (USA ISSN 1542-4405) **6589**
Murder in Mind (GBR ISSN 1364-5803) **2660**
Murder is Academic (USA ISSN 1076-9471) **5414**
Murder Most Foul (GBR ISSN 0963-0473) **5414**
Murderous Intent (USA) **5414**
Murdoch University. Asia Research Centre. Working Paper (AUS ISSN 1444-6855) **556**
• Murdoch University. Department of Economics. Working Paper Series (AUS ISSN 1440-5059) **1151**
Murdoch University Electronic Journal of Law *see* eLaw Journal **4663**
Murerhaandbog (DNK ISSN 0108-8602) **1025**
Murgetana (ESP ISSN 0213-0939) **4465**
The Muriel Spark Society Newsletter (GBR ISSN 1752-9328) **5337**
Murmanskii Vestnik (RUS) **3937**
Murmesteren (NOR ISSN 0027-3678) **1025**
Murphy Mates (USA ISSN 1059-3713) **3775**
• Murphy's Will Clauses: Annotations and Forms with Tax Effects (USA) **4904**
Murray Bridge Business and Community Services Guide *see* Murray Bridge Business & Community Services Guide **1151**
Murray Bridge Business & Community Services Guide (AUS) **1151**
Murray - Darling Basin Program Working Paper (AUS ISSN 1832-4266) **1151**
Murray Hill News (USA ISSN 0027-3686) **3982**
• The Murray Pioneer (AUS) **5228**
Murray Region Tourist News (AUS) **8739**
Al-Murshid/Guide (BHR) **3799**
Al-Murshid/Guide (QAT) **8739**
Der Murtenbieter (CHE ISSN 1661-4615) **3958**
Murumiwa (ZAF ISSN 0378-4126) **7768**
Murzilka (RUS ISSN 0132-1943) **2203**
Al-Musafir al-Arabi/Arab Traveller (BHR) **8739**
Musashi Institute of Technology. Atomic Energy Research Laboratory. Bulletin *see* Musashi Kogyo Daigaku. Genshiryoku Kenkyujo. Kenkyujoho **3171**
Musashi Kogyo Daigaku. Genshiryoku Kenkyujo. Kenkyujoho/Musashi Institute of Technology. Atomic Energy Research Laboratory. Bulletin (JPN ISSN 0285-0354) **3171**
Musashino Art University. Bulletin (JPN ISSN 0288-6030) **507**
Musashino Junior College. Bulletin *see* Musashino Tanki Daigaku Kenkyu Kiyo **2888**
Musashino Tanki Daigaku Kenkyu Kiyo/Musashino Junior College. Bulletin (JPN ISSN 0288-8025) **2888**
Al-Musawwar (EGY) **3836**
Muscle and Fitness (GBR ISSN 0955-1387) **6993**
• Muscle & Fitness (USA ISSN 0744-5105) **6993**
Muscle and Fitness *see* Muscle & Fitness **6993**
• ➤ Muscle & Nerve (USA ISSN 0148-639X) **5681**
Muscle Car Review (USA ISSN 0891-4796) **8594**
Muscle Elegance (USA) **6285**
Muscle Evolution (ZAF ISSN 1728-9130) **6993**
Muscle Evolution Fitness *see* Fitness **8845**
Muscle Mag International (CAN ISSN 0317-087X) **8188**
• Muscle Media (USA ISSN 1079-2465) **6993**
• Muscle Mustangs & Fast Fords (USA ISSN 1054-8912) **8594**
Muscle Mustangs and Fast Fords *see* Muscle Mustangs & Fast Fords **8594**
Musclecar Enthusiast (USA ISSN 1546-2811) **8188**
MuscleMag International (GBR ISSN 0955-906X) **8188**
• MuscleZine (USA) **6993**
Musconetcong River News (USA) **2619**
• Muscular Development (USA) **6993**
Muscular Development (Moscow) (RUS) **6993**
Muscular Development Magazine *see* Muscular Development **6993**
Muscular Dystrophy Campaign *see* Campaign (London) **4077**
• Musculoskeletal Care (GBR ISSN 1478-2189) **6225**
Musculoskeletal Medicine *see* Today in Medicine. Musculoskeletal Medicine **6227**
• ➤ Musculoskeletal Surgery (ITA ISSN 2035-5106) **6252**
Muse *see* Explore **7854**
Muse (AUS ISSN 1832-0139) **2994**
• The Muse (CAN ISSN 1912-1717) **2888**
Muse *see* A-Muse **3036**
Muse (NGA ISSN 0331-3468) **5337**
• Muse (Chicago) (USA ISSN 1090-0381) **2203**
Muse (Cleveland) (USA ISSN 1942-275X) **5337**
Muse (Columbia) (USA ISSN 0077-2194) **507**
➤ Muse (Ottawa) (CAN ISSN 0820-0165) **6529**
Muse (St. John's) (CAN ISSN 0820-5299) **2293**
Muse 2 *see* Muse Squared **5427**
• The Muse Journal (Online) (CAN) **5427**
MUSE, MUsic SEarch *see* M U S E, MUsic SEarch **6631**
Muse - Pie (USA) **5427**
• Muse Squared (USA ISSN 1547-2868) **5427**
• Musea (USA ISSN 1086-301X) **507**
Musea Nostra (BEL ISSN 0778-1350) **6529**
Museaal & Historisch Perspectief Noord-Holland. Nieuws (NLD ISSN 1874-5059) **6529**
Musealverein Wels. Jahrbuch (AUT) **4246**
Musee Canadien des Civilisations. Collection Mercure *see* Canadian Museum of Civilization. Mercury Series **6522**
Musee Canadien des Civilisations. Collection Mercure. Centre Canadien d'Etudes sur la Culture Traditionnelle. Dossier *see* Canadian Museum of Civilization. Mercury Series. Canadian Centre for Folk Culture Studies. Paper (No.) **332**
Musee Canadien des Civilisations. Collection Mercure. Commission Archaeologique du Canada. Dossier *see* Canadian Museum of Civilization. Mercury Series. Archaeological Survey of Canada. Paper (No.) **386**
Musee Canadien des Civilisations. Collection Mercure. Division de l'Histoire. Dossier *see* Canadian Museum of Civilization. Mercury Series. History Division. Paper (No.) **4134**
Musee Canadien des Civilisations. Collection Mercure. Service Canadien d'Ethnologie. Dossier *see* Canadian Museum of Civilization. Mercury Series. Ethnology Paper **332**
Musee d'Alta. Brochures *see* Alta Museum. Smaaskrifter **4197**
Musee d'Anthropologie Prehistorique de Monaco. Bulletin (MCO ISSN 0544-7631) **348**
Musee des Beaux-Arts de Lyon. Cahiers (FRA ISSN 1765-2480) **6529**
Musee des Beaux-Arts du Canada. Catalogue. Art Canadien *see* National Gallery of Canada Catalogue. Canadian Art **6534**
Musee des Beaux-Arts du Canada. Rapport Annuel *see* National Gallery of Canada. Annual Report **508**
Musee Ingres. Bulletin (FRA ISSN 1141-4782) **507**
Musee National d'Art Moderne. Cahiers (FRA ISSN 0181-1525) **6529**
➤ Musee National de Varsovie. Bulletin (POL ISSN 0027-3791) **6529**
Musee National des Sciences et de la Technologie. Rapport Annuel *see* National Museum of Science and Technology. Annual Report **6534**
Musee National d'Histoire et d'Art. Collections (LUX ISSN 1991-5926) **407**

Musee Royal de l'Afrique Centrale. Annales - Sciences Economiques. Serie in 8/Koninklijk Museum voor Midden-Afrika. Annalen - Economische Wetenschappen. Reeks in 8 (BEL ISSN 0773-4123) **203**
Musee Royal de l'Afrique Centrale. Annales - Sciences Geologiques. Serie in 8/Koninklijk Museum voor Midden-Afrika. Annalen - Geologische Wetenschappen. Reeks in 8 (BEL ISSN 0368-489X) **2756**
Musee Royal de l'Afrique Centrale. Annales - Sciences Historiques. Serie in 8/Koninklijk Museum voor Midden-Afrika. Annalen - Historische Wetenschappen. Reeks in 8 (BEL ISSN 0773-5006) **4176**
Musee Royal de l'Afrique Centrale. Annales - Sciences Humaines. Serie in 8/Koninklijk Museum voor Midden-Afrika. Annalen - Menselijke Wetenschappen. Serie in 8 (BEL ISSN 0065-4124) **4465**
Musee Royal de l'Afrique Centrale. Annales - Sciences Zoologiques. Serie in 8/Koninklijk Museum voor Midden-Afrika. Annalen - Zoologische Wetenschappen. Reeks in 8 (BEL ISSN 0379-1785) **956**
Musee Royal de l'Afrique Centrale. Archives d'Anthropologie/Koninklijk Museum voor Midden-Afrika. Archief voor Antropologie (BEL) **348**
Musee Royal de l'Afrique Centrale. Catalogue des Editions/Koninklijk Museum voor Midden-Afrika. Catalogus der Uitgaven (BEL ISSN 0773-8560) **631**
Musee Royal de l'Afrique Centrale. Departement de Geologie et de Mineralogie. Rapport Annuel (BEL ISSN 0378-0953) **2756**
Musee Royal de l'Afrique Centrale. Documentation Economique/Koninklijk Museum voor Midden-Afrika. Economische Documentatie (BEL) **1151**
Musee Royal de l'Afrique Centrale. Documentation Zoologique/Koninklijk Museum voor Midden-Afrika. Zoologische Documentatie (BEL ISSN 0778-466X) **956**
Museerne i Viborg Amt *see* M I V: Museerne i Viborg Amt **4241**
Musees (CAN ISSN 0706-098X) **6530**
Musees de Macon. Les Cahiers d'Inventaire (FRA ISSN 1775-6472) **507**
Musees du Manitoba (Year) *see* Museums in Manitoba (Year) **6532**
Musees et Collections Publiques de France (FRA ISSN 0027-383X) **6530**
Musees et Monuments *see* Museums and Monuments Series **6532**
Musees et Monuments Lyonnais. Bulletin *see* Musee des Beaux-Arts de Lyon. Cahiers **6529**
Musees Royaux d'Art et d'Histoire. Bulletin/Koninklijke Musea voor Kunst en Geschiedenis. Bulletin (BEL ISSN 0776-1414) **4247**
Musees Royaux des Beaux-Arts de Belgique. Bulletin/Koninklijke Musea voor Schone Kunsten van Belgie. Bulletin (BEL ISSN 0027-3856) **6530**
Museet for Fotokunst. Katalog *see* Katalog **6970**
Museet for Holbaek og Omegn. Aarsberetning (DNK ISSN 0108-917X) **6530**
Musei Civici Veneziani. Bollettino (ITA) **6530**
Musei Comunali di Roma. Bollettino (ITA ISSN 0523-9346) **6530**
Musei de Iano Pannonio Nominati. Annales *see* Janus Pannonius Muzeum. Evkonyve **6526**
Musei d'Italia (ITA ISSN 1827-4226) **8739**
Musei e Collezioni d'Etruria (ITA ISSN 1824-0593) **6530**
Musei Nationalis Hungarici. Annales Historico-Naturales/Magyar Termeszettudomanyi Muzeum. Evkonyve (HUN ISSN 0521-4726) **7883**
Musei Nationalis Pragae. Acta Entomologica (CZE ISSN 0374-1036) **855**
Musei Nationalis Pragae. Acta Entomologica. Supplementum *see* Musei Nationalis Pragae. Acta Entomologica **855**
Museiarkeologi (SWE ISSN 0284-9976) **4154**
Museion (AUT ISSN 0077-2208) **5033**
Museion (CHE ISSN 1661-7924) **4247**
Museion 2000 *see* Museion **4247**
Museletter (CAN ISSN 1198-3183) **5427**
Museletter (USA ISSN 1523-8083) **4154**
Museo (ESP ISSN 1136-601X) **6530**
Museo Archeologico di Tarquinia. Materiali (ITA ISSN 0391-9293) **6530**
Museo Argentino de Ciencias Naturales "Bernardino Rivadavia". Extra (ARG) **6530**
Museo Argentino de Ciencias Naturales Bernardino Rivadavia. Monografias (ARG ISSN 1515-7652) **6530**
Museo Argentino de Ciencias Naturales. Revista. Nueva Serie (ARG ISSN 1514-5158) **7883**
Museo Arqueologico de la Serena. Boletin (CHL ISSN 0582-7124) **407**
Museo Arqueologico Nacional. Boletin/Bulletin of the National Archaeological Museum (ESP ISSN 0212-5544) **407**
Museo Arqueologico Nacional. Catalogos Cientificos (ESP) **407**
Museo Bodoniano di Parma. Bollettino (ITA ISSN 0392-2413) **6530**
Museo Chileno de Arte Precolombino. Boletin (CHL ISSN 0716-1530) **507**
Museo Civico di Padova. Bollettino (ITA ISSN 0393-0750) **4465**
Museo Civico di Scienze Naturali "E.Caffi". Rivista (ITA ISSN 0393-8700) **7883**
➤ Museo Civico di Storia Naturale di Ferrara. Annali (ITA ISSN 1127-4476) **2756**
➤ Museo Civico di Storia Naturale di Ferrara. Stazione di Ecologia. Quaderni (ITA ISSN 0394-5782) **855**
Museo Civico di Storia Naturale di Morbegno. Atti *see* Il Naturalista Valtellinese **692**
Museo Civico di Storia Naturale di Trieste. Cataloghi (ITA ISSN 1123-4806) **7883**
Museo Civico di Storia Naturale di Venezia. Bollettino (ITA ISSN 0505-205X) **690**
Museo Civico di Storia Naturale di Venezia. Quaderni (ITA ISSN 1120-9216) **690**
Museo Civico di Storia Naturale di Verona. Bollettino *see* Museo Civico di Storia Naturale di Verona. Bollettino. Geologia Paleontologia Preistoria **2756**
Museo Civico di Storia Naturale di Verona. Bollettino *see* Museo Civico di Storia Naturale di Verona. Bollettino. Botanica Zoologia **802**
Museo Civico di Storia Naturale di Verona. Bollettino. Botanica Zoologia (ITA ISSN 1590-8399) **802**
Museo Civico di Storia Naturale di Verona. Bollettino. Geologia Paleontologia Preistoria (ITA ISSN 1590-8402) **2756**
Museo Civico di Storia Naturale di Verona. Memorie. Serie 2, Sezione A: Scienze della Vita (ITA ISSN 0392-0097) **691**
Museo Civico di Storia Naturale di Verona. Memorie. Serie 2, Sezione B: Scienze della Terra (ITA ISSN 0392-0089) **2713**
Museo Civico di Storia Naturale di Verona. Memorie. Serie 2, Sezione C: Scienze dell'Uomo (ITA ISSN 0392-0070) **7883**
Museo Civico di Storia Naturale "Giacomo Doria", Genoa. Annali (ITA ISSN 0365-4389) **7883**
Museo de America. Anales (ESP ISSN 1133-8741) **6530**
Museo de Arte Colonial de Bogota. Boletin Informativo (COL) **6530**
➤ Museo de Ciencias Naturales de Alava. Estudios (ESP ISSN 0214-915X) **7883**
Museo de Geologia de Extremadura. Publicaciones (ESP ISSN 1134-0207) **2756**
Museo de Historia Natural de Montevideo. Comunicaciones Paleontologicas (URY ISSN 0374-7123) **6727**
➤ Museo de Historia Natural de Valparaiso. Anales (CHL ISSN 0716-0178) **7883**
Museo de la Plata. Notas (ARG ISSN 0326-7202) **6530**
Museo de la Plata. Notas. Antropologia (ARG ISSN 0375-4634) **348**
Museo de la Plata. Notas. Botanica (ARG ISSN 0372-4557) **802**
Museo de la Plata. Notas. Geologia (ARG ISSN 0372-4530) **2756**
Museo de la Plata. Notas. Paleontologia (ARG ISSN 0325-2256) **6727**
Museo de la Plata. Notas. Zoologia (ARG ISSN 0372-4549) **956**
Museo de La Plata. Revista. Seccion Antropologia (ARG ISSN 0376-2149) **348**
Museo de La Plata. Revista. Seccion Botanica (ARG ISSN 0372-4611) **802**
Museo de La Plata. Revista. Seccion Geologia (ARG ISSN 0372-462X) **2756**
Museo de La Plata. Revista. Seccion Paleontologia (ARG ISSN 0373-3823) **6727**
Museo de La Plata. Revista. Seccion Zoologia (ARG ISSN 0372-4638) **956**
Museo de Pontevedra (ESP ISSN 0210-7791) **6530**
Museo de Zaragoza. Boletin (ESP ISSN 0212-548X) **6530**
Museo de Zoologia. Publicaciones Especiales (MEX ISSN 0188-7394) **956**
Museo degli Strumenti Musicali. Rassegna di Studi e Notizie (ITA ISSN 0394-4808) **6589**
Museo del Hombre Dominicano. Boletin (DOM ISSN 0252-8614) **348**
Museo del Hombre Dominicano. Papeles Ocasionales (DOM) **348**
Museo del Hombre Dominicano. Serie Catalogos y Memorias (DOM) **6530**
Museo del Hombre Dominicano. Serie Conferencias Pensamiento Dominicano (DOM) **6935**
Museo del Hombre Dominicano. Serie Conferencias sobre el Pensamiento de Pedro Henriquez Urena (DOM) **6935**
Museo del Hombre Dominicano. Serie Investigaciones Antropologicas (DOM) **348**
Museo del Hombre Dominicano. Serie Mesa Redonda Conferencias (DOM) **6530**
Museo del Oro. Boletin (COL ISSN 0120-7296) **348**
Museo del Prado. Boletin (ESP ISSN 0210-8143) **6530**
Museo di Alta. Opuscoli *see* Alta Museum. Smaaskrifter **4197**
Museo di Storia Naturale della Maremma. Atti (ITA ISSN 1126-0882) **691**
Museo di Storia Naturale di Livorno. Quaderni (ITA ISSN 0393-3377) **7883**
Museo di Storia Naturale di Livorno. Quaderni. Serie Atti *see* Museo di Storia Naturale di Livorno. Quaderni **7883**
Museo di Storia Naturale di Livorno. Quaderni. Supplemento *see* Museo di Storia Naturale di Livorno. Quaderni **7883**
Museo e Instituto Camon Aznar. Boletin (ESP ISSN 0211-3171) **6530**
Museo Friulano di Storia Naturale. Pubblicazione (ITA ISSN 1121-9548) **7883**
Museo Municipal de Historia Natural de San Rafael. Revista (ARG ISSN 0375-1155) **7883**
Museo Nacional de Antropologia. Anales (ESP ISSN 1135-1853) **348**
Museo Nacional de Antropologia y Arqueologia. Serie: Antropologia Fisica (PER) **348**
Museo Nacional de Historia Natural. Boletin (CHL ISSN 0027-3910) **7884**
Museo Nacional de Historia Natural de Montevideo. Anales (URY ISSN 0797-6828) **6727**
Museo Nacional de Historia Natural. Noticiario Mensual (CHL ISSN 0376-2041) **7884**
Museo Nacional de Historia Natural. Publicacion Ocasional *see* Museo Nacional de Historia Natural. Publicaciones Ocasionales **6530**
Museo Nacional de Historia Natural. Publicaciones Ocasionales (CHL ISSN 0716-0224) **6530**
➤ Museo Nacional de Historia Natural y Antropologia. Publicacion Extra (URY ISSN 1510-7353) **6530**
† Museo Nazionale d'Arte Orientale. Schede (ITA) **8975**
Museo Provincial de Lugo. Boletin (ESP ISSN 0212-8438) **6530**
Museo Regionale di Scienze Naturali. Bollettino (ITA ISSN 0392-758X) **691**
Museo Regionale di Scienze Naturali Torino. Cataloghi (ITA ISSN 1121-7553) **7884**
Museo Regionale di Scienze Naturali Torino. Guide (ITA ISSN 1590-6388) **7884**
Museo Regionale di Scienze Naturali Torino. Monografie (ITA ISSN 1121-7545) **7884**
Museo Risorgimento. Bollettino (ITA ISSN 0523-9478) **4247**
Museo Sefardi. Noticias (ESP ISSN 0214-6975) **7727**
Museo Stibbert Firenze (ITA ISSN 1723-9400) **6530**
Museo Tridentino di Scienze Naturali. Monografie (ITA ISSN 1970-2094) **2713**
Museo y Monumento Nacional "Justo Jose de Urquiza". Serie 3 (ARG) **6530**
Museogramme (CAN ISSN 0380-4623) **6530**
▼ • ➤ Museologia e Patrimonio (BRA ISSN 1984-3917) **6530**
➤ Museologia Scientifica (ITA ISSN 1123-265X) **6530**
Museologia Scientifica. Memorie *see* Museologia Scientifica **6530**
Museological Review (GBR ISSN 1354-5825) **6530**
Museologies (CAN ISSN 1718-5181) **6531**
Museologies (FRA ISSN 1951-3283) **6531**
† Museology (USA ISSN 0196-0237) **8975**
• ➤ Le Museon (BEL ISSN 0771-6494) **556**
Museoscienza (ITA ISSN 0541-377X) **6531**
• Muse's News (USA) **6589**
Museu Arxiu de Santa Maria. Fulls (ESP ISSN 0212-9248) **4247**
➤ Museu Bocage. Arquivos (PRT ISSN 0871-4843) **956**
Museu Bocage. Publicacoes Avulsas (PRT ISSN 0874-4416) **7884**
Museu Botanico Municipal. Boletim (BRA ISSN 0100-008X) **802**
➤ Museu de Arqueologia e Etnologia. Revista (BRA ISSN 0103-9709) **407**
Museu de Biologia Mello Leitao. Boletim (BRA ISSN 0103-9121) **691**
➤ Museu de Ciences Naturals. Monografies (ESP ISSN 1695-8950) **956**
Museu de Ciencias da P U C R G S. Comunicacoes. Serie Botanica *see* Pontificia Universidade Catolica do Rio Grande do Sul. Museu de Ciencias e Tecnologia. Comunicacoes. Serie Botanica **813**
Museu de Ciencias e Tecnologia da P U C R G S. Comunicacoes. Serie Ciencias da Terra *see* Pontificia Universidade Catolica do Rio Grande do Sul. Museu de Ciencias e Tecnologia. Comunicacoes. Serie Ciencias da Terra **2762**
Museu de Ciencias e Tecnologia da P U C R G S. Comunicacoes. Serie Zoologia *see* Pontificia Universidade Catolica do Rio Grande do Sul. Museu de Ciencias e Tecnologia. Comunicacoes. Serie Zoologia **960**
Museu de Ciencias e Tecnologia. Divulgacoes (BRA ISSN 0104-6969) **7884**
Museu de Geologia de Barcelona. Treballs (ESP ISSN 1130-4995) **2713**
Museu de Historia Natural. Arquivos (BRA ISSN 0102-4272) **7884**
Museu Municipal do Funchal. Boletim (PRT ISSN 0870-3876) **956**
Museu Municipal do Funchal. Boletim. Suplemento *see* Museu Municipal do Funchal. Boletim **956**
Museu Nacional. Arquivos (BRA ISSN 0365-4508) **7884**
Museu Nacional. Boletim. Antropologia (BRA ISSN 0080-3189) **349**
Museu Nacional. Boletim. Botanica (BRA ISSN 0080-3197) **802**
Museu Nacional. Boletim. Geologia (BRA ISSN 0080-3200) **2756**
Museu Nacional. Boletim. Zoologia (BRA ISSN 0080-312X) **956**
Museu Nacional d'Art de Cataluyna. Butlleti (ESP ISSN 1133-6455) **507**
Museu Nacional. Publicacoes Avulsas (BRA ISSN 0100-6304) **7884**
Museu Nacional. Relatorio Anual (BRA ISSN 0557-0689) **7884**
Museu Nacional. Serie Livros (BRA) **7884**
Museu Paraense Emilio Goeldi. Boletim. Nova Serie Antropologia (BRA) **349**
Museu Paraense Emilio Goeldi. Boletim. Nova Serie Botanica (BRA) **802**
Museu Paraense Emilio Goeldi. Boletim. Nova Serie Geologia (BRA) **2713**
Museu Paraense Emilio Goeldi. Boletim. Nova Serie Zoologia (BRA) **956**
• Museum (USA ISSN 1938-3940) **6531**
• ➤ Museum & Society (GBR ISSN 1479-8360) **6531**
• ➤ Museum Anthropology (USA ISSN 0892-8339) **349**
The Museum Archaeologist (GBR) **407**
Museum Boymans-van Beuningen. Agenda/Museum Boymans-van Beuningen. Diary (NLD ISSN 0077-2275) **6531**
Museum Boymans-van Beuningen. Diary *see* Museum Boymans-van Beuningen. Agenda **6531**
† Museum Catharijneconvent Magazine (NLD ISSN 1872-3160) **8975**
† Museum Criticum (ITA ISSN 0392-6931) **8975**
Museum Currents (USA) **6531**
Museum de Fundatie. Bulletin (NLD ISSN 1871-9015) **6531**
➤ Museum Ethnographers Group. Occasional Paper (GBR ISSN 0264-1704) **349**
Museum fuer Naturkunde Chemnitz. Veroeffentlichungen (DEU ISSN 1432-1696) **691**
Museum fuer Voelkerkunde, Berlin. Veroeffentlichungen. Neue Folge. Abteilung: Afrika (DEU ISSN 0067-5962) **349**
Museum fuer Voelkerkunde, Berlin. Veroeffentlichungen. Neue Folge. Abteilung: Amerikanische Archaeologie (DEU) **407**
Museum fuer Voelkerkunde, Berlin. Veroeffentlichungen. Neue Folge. Abteilung: Amerikanische Naturvoelker (DEU) **349**
Museum fuer Voelkerkunde, Berlin. Veroeffentlichungen. Neue Folge. Abteilung: Musikethnologie (DEU) **6589**
Museum fuer Voelkerkunde, Berlin. Veroeffentlichungen. Neue Folge. Abteilung: Suedsee (DEU ISSN 0067-5989) **349**
Museum fuer Voelkerkunde Dresden. Staatliche Ethnographische Sammlungen. Abhandlungen und Berichte (DEU ISSN 1865-4355) **6531**
Museum fuer Voelkerkunde Dresden. Staatliche Ethnographische Sammlungen. Jahrbuch (DEU ISSN 1865-4347) **6531**
Museum fuer Voelkerkunde Hamburg. Mitteilungen (DEU ISSN 0072-9469) **349**
Museum fuer Voelkerkunde, Leipzig. Jahrbuch *see* Museum fuer Voelkerkunde Dresden. Staatliche Ethnographische Sammlungen. Jahrbuch **6531**
Museum Genius Loci *see* Chiesa Oggi **437**
Museum Heineanum. Abhandlungen und Berichte (DEU ISSN 0947-1057) **802**
Museum Heineanum. Ornithologische Jahresberichte (DEU ISSN 0947-1065) **910**
Museum Helveticum (CHE ISSN 0027-4054) **2238**
Museum Highlights (USA) **6531**
▼ • ➤ Museum History Journal (USA ISSN 1936-9816) **6531**
• ➤ Museum International (English Edition) (GBR ISSN 1350-0775) **6531**
Museum International (French Edition) *see* Museum International (English Edition) **6531**
• ➤ Museum Management and Curatorship (GBR ISSN 0964-7775) **6531**
Museum Matters (AUS ISSN 1320-2677) **6531**
➤ Museum National d'Histoire Naturelle. Archives - Nouvelle Serie (FRA ISSN 1281-7139) **7884**
• ➤ Museum National d'Histoire Naturelle. Geodiversitas (FRA ISSN 1280-9659) **2756**
➤ Museum National d'Histoire Naturelle "Grigore Antipa". Travaux/Muzeul National de Istorie Naturala "Grigore Antipa". Travaux (ROM ISSN 1223-2254) **691**
➤ Museum National d'Histoire Naturelle. Memoires (FRA ISSN 1243-4442) **7884**
Museum National d'Histoire Naturelle. Patrimoines Naturels (FRA ISSN 1158-422X) **7884**
• ➤ Museum National d'Histoire Naturelle. Zoosystema (FRA ISSN 1280-9551) **956**
Museum News *see* Museum **6531**
Museum News *see* Toledo Museum of Art Members Newsletter **6538**
Museum News Magazine *see* Muzejski Vjesnik **407**
Museum Notes (Providence) (USA ISSN 0027-4097) **507**
Museum Notes (Spokane) (USA) **6531**
Museum of African-American History. Newsletter (USA) **3552**
• Museum of Comparative Zoology. Bulletin (USA ISSN 0027-4100) **956**
➤ Museum of Far Eastern Antiquities. Bulletin (SWE ISSN 0081-5691) **6531**
Museum of Flight News (USA ISSN 1077-9647) **66**
Museum of Life Sciences. Bulletin (USA ISSN 0883-9484) **691**
Museum of Modern Art *see* M O M A **6528**
Museum of National Antiguities. Monographs (SWE ISSN 1101-9301) **6531**

Title

Title

Title

10636 N A T O NYT (ONLINE) ULRICH'S PERIODICALS

N A T O Nyt (Online) *see* N A T O Review (Online) **7156**
N A T O Nytt (Online) *see* N A T O Review (Online) **7156**
N A T O Pregled *see* N A T O Review (Online) **7156**
N A T O Review (Czech Edition) (Online) *see* N A T O Review (Online) **7156**
• N A T O Review (Online) (North Atlantic Treaty Organization) (BEL ISSN 1608-7569) **7156**
N A T O Revu *see* N A T O Review (Online) **7156**
N A T O Science and Society Newsletter *see* Science, Society Security News **7911**
N A T O Science for Peace and Security Series. A: Chemistry and Biology (North Atlantic Treaty Organization) (NLD ISSN 1874-6489) **2073**
N A T O Science for Peace and Security Series. B: Physics and Biophysics (North Atlantic Treaty Organization) (NLD) **7027**
• N A T O Science for Peace and Security Series. C: Environmental Security (North Atlantic Treaty Organization) (NLD) **3454**
N A T O Science for Peace and Security Series. D: Information and Communication Security (North Atlantic Treaty Organization) (NLD ISSN 1874-6268) **7253**
N A T O Science for Peace and Security Series. E: Human and Societal Dynamics (North Atlantic Treaty Organization) (NLD ISSN 1874-6276) **7254**
N A T O Science Series. Series 1: Life and Behavioural Sciences (North Atlantic Treaty Organization) (NLD ISSN 1566-7693) **4465**
N A T O Science Series. Series II: Mathematics, Physics and Chemistry (North Atlantic Treaty Organization) (USA ISSN 1568-2609) **5519**
• ➤ N A T O Science Series. Series III: Computer and Systems Sciences (North Atlantic Treaty Organization) (NLD ISSN 1387-6694) **2524**
N A T O Science Series. Series IV: Earth and Environmental Sciences (North Atlantic Treaty Organization) (USA ISSN 1568-1238) **2713**
N A T O Science Series. Series V: Science and Technology Policy (North Atlantic Treaty Organization) (NLD ISSN 1873-0337) **7884**
N A T O Science Series. Series Five: Science and Technology Policy *see* N A T O Science Series. Series V: Science and Technology Policy **7884**
N A T O Science Series. Series Four: Earth and Environmental Sciences *see* N A T O Science Series. Series IV: Earth and Environmental Sciences **2713**
N A T O Science Series. Series I: Life and Behavioural Sciences *see* N A T O Science Series. Series 1: Life and Behavioural Sciences **4465**
N A T O Science Series. Series One: Life and Behavioural Sciences *see* N A T O Science Series. Series 1: Life and Behavioural Sciences **4465**
N A T O Science Series. Series Three: Computer and Systems Sciences *see* N A T O Science Series. Series III: Computer and Systems Sciences **2524**
N A T O Science Series. Series Two: Mathematics, Physics and Chemistry *see* N A T O Science Series. Series II: Mathematics, Physics and Chemistry **5519**
• N A T O Scientific Publications. Newsletter (North Atlantic Treaty Organization) (BEL ISSN 0255-7134) **7885**
N A T O Security Through Science Series. A: Chemistry and Biology *see* N A T O Science for Peace and Security Series. A: Chemistry and Biology **2073**
N A T O Security Through Science Series. B: Physics and Biophysics *see* N A T O Science for Peace and Security Series. B: Physics and Biophysics **7027**
N A T O Security Through Science Series. C: Environmental Security (Print Edition) *see* N A T O Science for Peace and Security Series. C: Environmental Security **3454**
N A T O Security Through Science Series. D: Information and Communication Security *see* N A T O Science for Peace and Security Series. D: Information and Communication Security **7253**
N A T O Security Through Science Series. E: Human and Societal Dynamics *see* N A T O Science for Peace and Security Series. E: Human and Societal Dynamics **7254**
N A T O Teataja *see* N A T O Review (Online) **7156**
N A T O Tukor (Online) *see* N A T O Review (Online) **7156**
N A T O Vestnesis *see* N A T O Review (Online) **7156**
N A T O Vestnik (Online) *see* N A T O Review (Online) **7156**
• N A T O's Nations and Partners for Peace (North Atlantic Treaty Organization) (DEU ISSN 1566-9009) **7254**
N A T P E Monthly (National Association of Television Program Executives) (USA) **2386**
N A T S Current News (North American Truffling Society, Inc.) (USA) **803**
N A T S O Truckers News *see* Truckers News **8678**
N A U M D News (National Association of Uniform Manufacturers and Distributors) (USA) **2248**
N A U M D Office Reports (National Association of Uniform Manufacturers and Distributors) (USA) **2248**
N A U M D Postal Update (National Association of Uniform Manufacturers and Distributors) (USA) **2248**
N A U N L U (Natal Agricultural Union) (ZAF ISSN 0028-128X) **138**
N A V A News (North American Vexillological Association) (USA ISSN 1053-3338) **3775**
N A V A S *see* N O A Magazine **1025**
N A V B Info (Nationaal Actiecomite voor Veiligheid en Hygiene in het Bouwbedrijf) (BEL ISSN 1780-7875) **7532**
N A V C Clinician's Brief (North American Veterinary Conference) (USA ISSN 1542-4014) **8803**
• N A V H Update (National Association for Visually Handicapped) (USA) **4083**
N A V O Kroniek (Online) *see* N A T O Review (Online) **7156**
N A V S Animal Action Report (National Anti-Vivisection Society) (USA) **320**
N A W C C Mart (National Association of Watch and Clock Collectors, Inc.) (USA) **4568**
The N A W I C Image (National Association of Women in Construction) (USA ISSN 1081-6569) **1025**
N A W J Counterbalance (National Association of Women Judges) (USA) **4956**
N A W Report (National Association of Wholesaler - Distributors) (USA) **1780**
The N A W W Writer's Guide (National Association of Women Writers) (USA ISSN 1534-0414) **5337**
• The N A Way Magazine (Narcotics Anonymous) (USA ISSN 1046-5421) **2697**
N A Y S I Resource List (North American Youth Sport Institute) (USA) **8189**
• N & C - Networks und Communications (DEU ISSN 0946-7513) **2501**
N & K Plus *see* Techworld **2504**
N & R *see* Netzwirtschaften und Recht **4740**
N B (Naerbutikken) (DNK ISSN 1395-1831) **1835**
N B *see* New Builder **1026**
N B (New Beacon) (GBR) **4083**
N B *see* Il Nuovo Bagno **1027**
N B (Braille Edition) (New Beacon) (GBR) **4083**
N B A A Digest (National Business Aviation Association) (USA ISSN 1091-1553) **66**
N B A Annual Report *see* National Blood Authority. Annual Report **5940**
• N B A F Magazine (National Bodybuilding and Fitness) (USA) **6993**
† • N B A Inside Stuff (National Basketball Association) (USA ISSN 1067-5159) **8975**
N B A Magazine (National Bar Association) (USA ISSN 0741-0115) **4737**
N B A Register *see* The Sporting News Official N B A Register **8246**
N B C C News Notes *see* National Certified Counselor **8056**
N B D BouwPraktijk *see* N B D Magazine **1025**
N B D C S News (National Book Development Council of Singapore) (SGP ISSN 0129-9239) **7568**
N B D Magazine (Nederlandse Bouw Documentatie) (NLD ISSN 1877-2684) **1025**
• N B E B Magazin (Online) (Niedersaechsischer Bund fuer Freie Erwachsenenbildung) (DEU ISSN 1611-6585) **2944**
• The N B E R Digest (Online) (National Bureau of Economic Research) (USA) **1151**
• The N B E R Digest (Print) (National Bureau of Economic Research) (USA ISSN 0888-949X) **1151**
N B E R - Frontiers in Health Policy *see* Frontiers in Health Policy Research (Print) **8958**
N B E R Innovation Policy and the Economy *see* Innovation Policy and the Economy **1124**
• N B E R International Seminar on Macroeconomics (National Bureau of Economic Research) (USA ISSN 1932-8796) **1720**
N B E R Macroeconomics Annual *see* Macroeconomics Annual **1720**
• N B E R Reporter (National Bureau of Economic Research) (USA ISSN 0276-119X) **1546**
N B E R Reporter OnLine *see* N B E R Reporter **1546**
N B E R Tax Policy and the Economy *see* Tax Policy and the Economy **1949**
• N B E R Technical Working Paper Series (National Bureau of Economic Research) (USA ISSN 1073-2489) **1151**
N B F - Nytt *see* Paidos **6099**
N B I A Newsletter (New Brunswick Institute of Agrologists) (CAN ISSN 0848-8851) **138**
N B I A Review (National Business Incubation Association) (USA ISSN 1073-5534) **1500**
N B K Economic & Financial Quarterly *see* Economic & Financial Quarterly **1479**
N B L J *see* The National Black Law Journal **4738**
N B L Review (National Bank of Liberia) (LBR) **1369**
N B M G. Open-File Report (Nevada Bureau of Mines and Geology) (USA ISSN 0749-937X) **2757**
N B N *see* Nation's Building News **1026**
N B Naturalist/Naturaliste du N B (New Brunswick) (CAN ISSN 0047-9551) **7885**
N B O Abstracts (National Buildings Organisation) (IND ISSN 0027-6138) **1048**
N B P W Journaal (Nederlandse Bond van Poeliers en Wildhandelaren) (NLD ISSN 1574-1710) **294**
N B R *see* The Nonprofit Board Report **1154**
• N B R Analysis (National Bureau of Asian Research) (USA ISSN 1052-164X) **7254**
• N B R Special Report (National Bureau of Asian Research) (USA) **7254**
N B S Fish & Hunt *see* Nation's Best Sports **8324**
N B T A News (New Brunswick Teachers' Association) (CAN ISSN 0317-5227) **2888**
N B T Magazine (Nederlandse Bakkerij Techniek) (NLD ISSN 1567-0392) **3657**
N B T V (Narrow Bandwidth Television Association) (GBR) **4342**
N B W A Handbook (National Beer Wholesalers Association) (USA) **607**
N B W A Legislative and Regulatory Issues Alert (National Beer Wholesalers Association) (USA) **607**
N-Bahn Magazin (DEU ISSN 0937-7220) **4342**
N C *see* Neues Curriculum **4466**
N C 1 (Now Culture) (USA ISSN 1539-3194) **5337**
• N C A A Baseball Rules (National Collegiate Athletic Association) (USA ISSN 0736-5209) **8239**
N C A A Basketball. Official (Year) Men's Basketball Records Book (National Collegiate Athletic Association (N C A A)) (USA) **8239**
▼ • N C A A Champion (National Collegiate Athletic Association (N C A A)) (USA ISSN 1937-9064) **8189**
N C A A Convention Proceedings (National Collegiate Athletic Association) (USA) **8189**
• N C A A Directory (National Collegiate Athletic Association) (USA ISSN 0162-1467) **8189**
N C A A Division I Manual (National Collegiate Athletic Association) (USA ISSN 1093-3174) **8189**
N C A A Drug Testing Program (National Collegiate Athletic Association) (USA) **8189**
N C A A Football Records (National Collegiate Athletic Association (N C A A)) (USA ISSN 0738-1611) **8239**
• N C A A Football Rules and Interpretations (National Collegiate Athletic Association) (USA ISSN 0736-5160) **8239**
• N C A A Men's and Women's Basketball Rules and Interpretations (National Collegiate Athletic Association) (USA ISSN 1042-3877) **8239**
• N C A A Men's and Women's Cross Country and Track & Field Rules (National Collegiate Athletic Association) (USA ISSN 0736-7783) **8323**
• N C A A Men's and Women's Ice Hockey Rules and Interpretations (National Collegiate Athletic Association) (USA) **8189**
• N C A A Men's and Women's Illustrated Basketball Rules (National Collegiate Athletic Association) (USA ISSN 1042-3869) **8239**
• N C A A Men's and Women's Lacrosse Records Book. Official Records (National Collegiate Athletic Association (N C A A)) (USA ISSN 1555-3531) **8189**
• N C A A Men's and Women's Rifle Rules (National Collegiate Athletic Association) (USA) **8189**
• N C A A Men's and Women's Skiing Rules (National Collegiate Athletic Association) (USA ISSN 0741-9279) **8323**
• N C A A Men's and Women's Soccer Rules and Interpretations (National Collegiate Athletic Association) (USA) **8239**
• N C A A Men's and Women's Swimming and Diving Rules and Interpretations (National Collegiate Athletic Association) (USA) **8189**
• N C A A Men's and Women's Water Polo Rules and Interpretations (National Collegiate Athletic Association) (USA) **8189**
N C A A Men's Basketball (National Collegiate Athletic Association (N C A A)) (USA) **8239**
• N C A A Men's Lacrosse Rules (National Collegiate Athletic Association) (USA ISSN 0736-7775) **8239**
• The N C A A News (National Collegiate Athletic Association (N C A A)) (USA ISSN 0027-6170) **8189**
• N C A A Sports Medicine Handbook (National Collegiate Athletic Association (N C A A)) (USA ISSN 1079-5022) **6231**
N C A A Women's Basketball (National Collegiate Athletic Association (N C A A)) (USA) **8239**
• N C A A Wrestling Rules and Interpretations (National Collegiate Athletic Association) (USA) **8189**
N C A C Newsletter (National Council of Acoustical Consultants) (USA) **7088**
N C A C S News *see* National Coalition News **2889**
N C A Cave Talk (National Caves Association) (USA) **8739**
N C A E News Bulletin (North Carolina Association of Educators) (USA ISSN 0027-6189) **2888**
• N C A H F Newsletter (National Council Against Health Fraud) (USA ISSN 0890-3417) **7532**
N C A M P's Technical Report (National Coalition against the Misuse of Pesticides) (USA) **3454**
N C A News (National Campaign for the Arts) (GBR) **507**
• N C A R Scientific Reports (National Center for Atmospheric Research) (USA) **6391**
N C A R Technical Notes (National Center for Atmospheric Research) (USA) **6391**
N C A S I Technical Bulletin *see* National Council of the Paper Industry for Air and Stream Improvement. Technical Bulletin **3489**
N C B A Cooperative Business Journal (National Cooperative Business Association) (USA ISSN 1065-7207) **1424**
N C B A Reports (National Commodity & Barter Association) (USA) **1935**
N C B Abstracts (National Council for Cement and Building Materials) (IND ISSN 0972-3420) **1048**
N C B Current Contents (National Council for Cement and Building Materials) (IND ISSN 0972-3439) **1048**
• N C B I News (National Council for the Blind of Ireland) (IRL) **4083**
• N C B I News (U.S. National Center for Biotechnology Information) (USA ISSN 1060-8788) **876**
N C B Newsletter (National Council for Cement and Building Materials) (IND) **1025**
N C B P Best Projects (National Conference of Bar Presidents) (USA) **4737**
† N C Boating Lifestyle (North Carolina) (USA ISSN 1545-8733) **8975**
N C C L S Document *see* Clinical and Laboratory Standards Institute Document **5596**
• N C C Occasional Series (National Competition Council) (AUS ISSN 1834-5409) **1151**
N C Criminal and Vehicle Handbook *see* North Carolina Criminal Law and Motor Vehicle Handbook **4895**
▼ • N C D B E-News (National Consortium on Deaf-Blindness) (USA ISSN 1946-8911) **4083**
• N C D Bulletin (National Council on Disability) (USA) **4068**
N C D C Bulletin (National Cooperative Development Corporation) (IND ISSN 0027-6278) **1424**
N C E *see* New Civil Engineer **3279**
N C E A Notes (National Catholic Educational Association) (USA ISSN 1060-8575) **2888**
N C E C A Journal (National Council on Education for the Ceramic Arts) (USA ISSN 0739-1544) **537**
N C E C A News (National Council on Education for the Ceramic Arts) (USA) **537**
N C E I *see* N C E International **3279**
N C E International (New Civil Engineer) (GBR ISSN 1469-7076) **3279**
N C E R T Newsletter (National Council of Educational Research and Training) (IND ISSN 0302-508X) **2888**
N C E Road Rail and Transport Directory (New Civil Engineer) (GBR) **3279**
N C E Water Directory (New Civil Engineer) (GBR) **3279**
† N C F International (Notiziario Chimico Farmaceutico) (ITA ISSN 1592-2286) **8975**
• N C F. Notiziario Chimico e Farmaceutico (ITA ISSN 0393-3733) **6862**
N C F P *see* North Carolina Family Physician **5688**
▼ N C F R P Report (National Cooperative Freight Research Program) (USA ISSN 1947-5659) **8620**
N C F R Report *see* National Council on Family Relations. Report **8122**
N C F S *see* Nineteenth Century French Studies **5342**
N C Family Physician *see* North Carolina Family Physician **5688**
• N C Fertigung (Numeric Control) (DEU ISSN 0174-4534) **6326**
N C G A Golf (Northern California Golf Association) (USA ISSN 1524-4385) **8189**
N C G S News *see* North Carolina Genealogical Society Newsletter **3777**
N C G S Open-File Report (North Carolina Geological Survey) (USA) **2757**
▼ • N C H S Data Brief (National Center for Health Statistics) (USA ISSN 1941-4927) **7548**
N C I *see* Chemie Magazine **3240**
N C I A News (National Correctional Industries Association) (USA) **2661**
• N C I Cancer Bulletin (National Cancer Institute) (USA) **6028**
N C I Fact Book (National Cancer Institute) (USA ISSN 0270-7950) **6028**
N C I Foundation. News (National Caption Institute) (USA) **2386**
N C I L News (Niagara Centre for Independent Living) (CAN ISSN 1718-9675) **8056**
N C I S A Annual Review (National Council of Independent Schools' Associations) (AUS) **2888**
• N C I V Network News (National Council for International Visitors) (USA) **3014**
N C J *see* National Contest Journal **2360**
N C J O L T *see* North Carolina Journal of Law & Technology **4748**
• N C J R S Abstracts Database (National Criminal Justice Reference Service) (USA) **4824**
N C J R S Catalog (National Criminal Justice Reference Service) (USA) **2661**
• N C J W Journal (National Council of Jewish Women) (USA) **7727**
N C L *see* Nature, Culture and Literature **5338**
N C L B Advisor *see* Thompson's N C L B Advisor **3034**
N C L C Energy & Utility Update (National Consumer Law Center) (USA ISSN 1070-9312) **4737**
N C L C Reports: Bankruptcy & Foreclosures (National Consumer Law Center) (USA ISSN 1054-3775) **4737**
N C L C Reports: Consumer Credit & Usury (National Consumer Law Center) (USA ISSN 0890-2615) **4737**
N C L C Reports: Debt Collection & Repossessions (National Consumer Law Center) (USA ISSN 0890-2607) **4737**

Link to your serials resources and content with ulrichsweb.com

Title

10638 N G K REVIEW. OVERSEAS EDITION ULRICH'S PERIODICALS

N G K Review. Overseas Edition (Nippon Gaishi K.K.) (JPN ISSN 0386-5843) **7052**
N G K Technical Report on Nuclear Engineering *see* N G K Genshiryoku Giho **3171**
N G Kids Magazine *see* National Geographic Kids **4021**
• N G M A eBulletin (National Grants Management Association) (USA) **1151**
N G M A News Brief (National Grants Management Association) (USA) **1151**
N G Magazine *see* Gas Daily's N G **6770**
• N G Regiony (Nezavisimaya Gazeta) (RUS) **5228**
• N G Religii (Nezavisimaya Gazeta) (RUS ISSN 1810-1623) **7664**
N G S News Magazine (National Genealogical Society) (USA ISSN 1529-4323) **3775**
N G U Rapport (Norges Geologiske Undersoekelse) (NOR ISSN 0800-3416) **2713**
N G U Special Publication (Norges Geologiske Undersoekelse) (NOR ISSN 0801-5961) **2757**
† N G V Worldwide (Natural Gas Vehicles) (NZL ISSN 1175-2807) **8976**
N G Z - Der Hotelier *see* Der Hotelier **4390**
N Gamer *see* NGamer **2478**
N Gamer (NLD ISSN 1872-2342) **2478**
N H *see* Nisse Hult **7159**
N H A Annual Report (National Housing Authority) (PHL) **4420**
N H A Benefits Guide (National Homeless Alliance) (GBR) **8056**
N H A Nieuws (Noord-Hollands Archief) (NLD ISSN 1871-6326) **407**
N H Arts News (New Hampshire) (USA) **507**
N H Business Law Handbook *see* Business N H Magazine **1426**
N H C at Work (National Housing Conference) (USA) **4420**
N H Commercial Real Estate & Lending Guide *see* Business N H Magazine **1426**
N H D S Newsletter (New Hampshire Dental Society) (USA ISSN 0027-6545) **5856**
N H F Directory of Members *see* National Housing Federation Directory of Members **8057**
• N H F Head Lines (National Headache Foundation) (USA ISSN 1521-2106) **6162**
N H G-Standaarden voor de Huisarts (Nederlands Huisartsen Genootschap) (NLD ISSN 1872-3772) **5682**
N H H Spraak *see* Synaps **5184**
N H Health Care Guide *see* Business N H Magazine **1426**
N H Human Resources Guide *see* Business N H Magazine **1426**
N H I M V 2 *see* National Health Information Model. Version 2 (Online) **7548**
N H K Broadcast Museum News *see* N H K Hoso Hakubutsukan Dayori **2386**
N H K Giken R & D/Japan Broadcasting Corporation Science & Technical Research Laboratories R & D (Nippon Hoso Kyokai) (JPN ISSN 0914-7535) **2386**
N H K Hoso Hakubutsukan Dayori/N H K Broadcast Museum News (Nippon Hoso Kyokai) (JPN) **2386**
N H K Laboratories Note (Nippon Hoso Kyokai) (JPN ISSN 0027-657X) **2386**
N H K - No Okasanto Issho (JPN) **2204**
N H K Science and Technical Research Laboratories. Annual Report *see* Nippon Hoso Kyokai Hoso Gijutsu Kenkyujo Kenkyu Nenpo **2386**
N H K Science & Technical Research Laboratories. News *see* Giken Dayori **2381**
N H L A Newsletter (New Hampshire Library Association) (USA ISSN 0028-5269) **5033**
N H L A Newsletter (National Hardwood Lumber Association) (USA) **3714**
N H L Home Ice (National Hockey League) (USA) **8239**
N H L S Annual Report *see* National Health Laboratory Service. Annual Report **7533**
N H M R C Enews *see* National Health and Medical Research Council. Enews **5683**
• N H N E News Brief (New Heaven New Earth) (USA) **6646**
N H O *see* Navajo Hopi Observer **3553**
N H O Newsline (National Hospice Organization) (USA ISSN 1081-5678) **313**
N H P Rapport (Nordisk Hydrologisk Program) (DNK ISSN 0900-0267) **2797**
N H R C Report (U.S. Naval Health Research Center) (USA ISSN 0161-1607) **6162**
N H Resource Directory *see* Business N H Magazine **1426**
• N H S A Dialog (National Head Start Association) (USA ISSN 1524-0754) **3044**
• N H S Breast Screening Programme (National Health Service) (GBR) **8847**
• N H S Cervical Screening Programme (Year) (National Health Service) (GBR) **8847**
N H S D A Report *see* The N S D U H Report **2697**
N H S Information Authority. Occasional Paper (National Health Service) (GBR) **4107**
N H S Magazine (National Health Service) (GBR ISSN 1359-4443) **7532**
N H S News (National Health Service) (GBR ISSN 1354-2362) **7532**
N H S Occupational Therapy Services. England (National Health Service) (GBR) **6113**
N H Small Business Finance Guide *see* Business N H Magazine **1426**
N H U Journal of Applied Art and Design *see* Yingyong Yishu yu Sheji Xuebao **527**
N H V-Report *see* Nordiska Hoegskolan foer Folkhaelsovetenskap. N H V-Rapport **7534**
N H Writer (New Hampshire) (USA ISSN 1932-8206) **7568**
N H Z (Neue Hanauer Zeitung) (DEU ISSN 0949-3182) **5228**
N H's Meeting & Convention Resource Directory *see* Business N H Magazine **1426**
N I A A A - R U C A S Alcoholism Treatment Series (National Institute on Alcohol Abuse and Alcoholism - Rutgers University Center of Alcohol Studies) (USA ISSN 0147-0515) **2697**
N I A B Descriptive List of Grasses and Herbage Legumes *see* Grasses and Herbage Legumes Variety Leaflet **273**
The N I A F News (National Italian - American Foundation) (USA ISSN 1092-1893) **3552**
N I A I D Council News *see* N I A I D Funding News **5682**
• N I A I D Funding News (National Institute of Allergy and Infectious Diseases) (USA ISSN 1932-1333) **5682**
• N I A Informerar (Naemnd foer Internationella Adoptionsfraagor) (SWE) **8056**
• N I A S Nytt/Nordic Newsletter of Asian Studies (Nordisk Institut for Asienstudier) (DNK ISSN 0904-4337) **556**
N I B A Convention Review *see* Insurance & Risk Professional **4506**
N I B E S A News (National Independent Bank Equipment & Systems Association) (USA) **1369**
• N I B R-Notat (Online) (Norsk Institutt for By- og Regionforskning) (NOR ISSN 0809-6929) **4420**
N I B R-Rapport (Norsk Institutt for By- og Regionforskning) (NOR ISSN 1502-9794) **4420**
N I C Bulletin (National - Interstate Council of State Boards of Cosmetology) (USA) **595**
The N I C E C Journal *see* Career Research & Development **6695**
N I C H D Annual Report *see* Division of Intramural Research Annual Report **7514**
N I C Sentinel (North Idaho College) (USA) **2293**
N I C T News/Japan. Ministry of Posts and Telecommunications. Communications Research Laboratory. News (National Institute of Information and Communications Technology) (JPN) **2334**
N I D A Bulletin (National Institute of Development Administration) (THA ISSN 0125-5606) **5033**
• N I D A Notes (National Institute on Drug Abuse) (USA ISSN 1535-7325) **2697**
N I D A Research Monograph (National Institute on Drug Abuse) (USA ISSN 1046-9516) **2697**
N I D I Rapport *see* Nederlands Interdisciplinair Demografisch Instituut. Rapport - Report - Bericht - Rapporto **7288**
N I E R Occasional Paper (National Institute for Educational Research) (JPN) **2888**
• N I E S Annual Report (National Institute for Environmental Studies) (JPN ISSN 1341-6936) **3454**
N I E S Research Booklet *see* Kankyougi **3449**
N I F Notes (North American Interfraternal Foundation) (USA) **2293**
N I F S - P R O C Series *see* National Institute for Fusion Science. Research Report. P R O C Series **7027**
N I F S Series. Research Report (National Institute for Fusion Science) (JPN ISSN 0915-633X) **7069**
N I F U S T E P. Arbeidsnotat *see* N I F U S T E P. Rapport **4465**
• N I F U S T E P. Rapport (Norsk Institutt for Studier av Forskning og Utdanning, Senter for Innovasjonsforskning) (NOR ISSN 1504-1824) **4465**
• N I H Almanac (National Institutes of Health) (USA ISSN 8756-601X) **7532**
• N I H Consensus and State-of-the-Science Statements (National Institutes of Health) (USA ISSN 1553-0957) **5682**
N I H F W Technical Reports (National Institute of Health and Family Welfare) (IND ISSN 0253-6757) **8056**
• N I H Guide for Grants and Contracts (Online) (National Institutes of Health) (USA ISSN 1551-8965) **8056**
• N I H Medline Plus (National Institutes of Health Medline Plus) (USA ISSN 1935-956X) **5682**
• The N I H News in Health (National Institutes of Health) (USA ISSN 1556-3898) **5682**
N I H Publications List (National Institutes of Health Publications List) (USA ISSN 0027-6650) **5682**
• N I H Record (National Institutes of Health) (USA ISSN 1057-5871) **5682**
• N I H Senior Health (National Institutes of Health) (USA) **4052**
N I H Word on Health *see* The N I H News in Health **5682**
N I I Journal *see* Progress in Informatics **2435**
N.I.I. Sotsyal'noi Gigieny i Upravleniya Zdravookhraneniem. Byulleten' (RUS) **5682**
N I J O S. Rapport *see* Viten fra Skog og Landskap **3707**
N I J O S-Ressursoversikt *see* Ressursoversikt fra Skog og Landskap **3700**
† • N I J Research Review (National Institute of Justice) (USA ISSN 1555-2179) **8976**
N I K (Nachrichten und Informationen zur Kultur) (DEU ISSN 1615-2468) **7986**
N I K H E F Annual Report (Nationaal Instituut voor Kernfysica en Hoge-Energiefysica) (NLD) **7027**
• N I K K Magasin (Nordisk Institut for Kvinde- og Koensforskning) (NOR ISSN 1502-1521) **8901**
• N I L F - Rapport (Norsk Institutt for Landbruksoekonomisk Forskning) (NOR ISSN 0805-7028) **138**
N I L R *see* Netherlands International Law Review **4936**
➤ N I M H A N S Journal (National Institute of Mental Health & Neuro Sciences) (IND ISSN 0254-0886) **6162**
N I M H A N S Newsletter (National Institute of Mental Health & Neuro Sciences) (IND) **6162**
N I M L A (Modern Language Association of Northern Ireland) (GBR ISSN 0143-859X) **5153**
N I M S Corrosion Data Sheets/Busshitsu Zairyou Kenkyuu Kikou Fushoku Deta Shito (National Institute for Materials Science) (JPN ISSN 1348-141X) **6327**
N I M S Creep Data Sheet (National Institute for Materials Science) (JPN ISSN 1346-7514) **3160**
N I M S Fatigue Data Sheet/Busshitsu Zairyou Kenkyuu Kikou Hirou Deta Shito (National Institute for Materials Science) (JPN ISSN 1347-3093) **6327**
N I M S now *see* N I M S NOW International **7885**
• N I M S NOW International (National Institute for Materials Science) (JPN) **7885**
N I M S Space Use Materials Strength Data Sheet/Busshitsu Zairyou Kenkyuu Kikou Uchuu Kanren Zairyou Kyoudo Deta Shito (JPN ISSN 1348-1428) **6327**
N I N (Nedeljne Informativne Novine) (SRB ISSN 0027-6685) **3945**
N I N A. Fagrapport (Norsk Institutt for Naturforskning) (NOR ISSN 0805-469X) **2619**
• N I N A Fakta (Norsk Institutt for Naturforskning) (NOR ISSN 1503-5158) **2619**
N I N A - N I K U. Project Report *see* Stiftelsen for Naturforskning og Kulturminneforskning. Project Report **3468**
N I N A. Oppdragsmelding (NOR ISSN 0802-4103) **2619**
• N I N A Temahefte (Norsk Institutt for Naturforskning) (NOR ISSN 0804-421X) **3454**
N I News (Nihon Inter Electronics Corp.) (JPN ISSN 0916-0345) **3109**
• N I O S H Current Intelligence Bulletin (National Institute for Occupational Safety and Health) (USA ISSN 0893-4940) **7532**
N I O S H Manual of Analytical Methods (U.S. National Institute for Occupational Safety and Health) (USA) **6681**
• N I O S H Pocket Guide to Chemical Hazards (National Institute for Occupational Safety and Health) (USA) **6681**
† N I O S H Publications Catalog (National Institute for Occupational Safety and Health) (USA ISSN 1041-5327) **8976**
• N I O S H T I C (U.S. National Institute for Occupational Safety and Health) (USA) **6681**
• N I P R Arctic Data Reports (National Institute of Polar Research) (JPN ISSN 1342-4033) **2713**
N I R *see* National Intelligence Report **7454**
N I R A's World Directory of Think Tanks (National Institute for Research Advancement) (JPN) **7885**
N I R E. Bulletin (National Institute for Rural Engineering) (JPN) **213**
• N I R News (Near Infrared) (GBR ISSN 0960-3360) **2104**
• ➤ N I R. Nordiskt Immateriellt Raettsskydd/Nordic Intellectual Property Law Review (SWE ISSN 0027-6723) **6755**
N I R S A Journal *see* Recreational Sports Journal **2962**
N I R S A Journal (National Intramural - Recreational Sports Association Foundation) (USA) **8189**
N I R S A. Working Paper Series (National Institute for Regional and Spatial Analysis) (IRL) **7986**
N I R S Symposium. Proceedings *see* Hoiken Shinpojumu Shirizu **6197**
N I S E R Occasional Papers (Nigerian Institute of Social and Economic Research) (NGA) **7986**
• N I S O Newsline (National Information Standards Organization) (USA ISSN 1559-2774) **5033**
N I S S A T Newsletter (National Information System for Science and Technology, Society for Information Science) (IND ISSN 0970-0188) **7885**
† N I S Studi Superiori (Nuova Italia Scientifica) (ITA ISSN 1970-5484) **8976**
N I S T Building Science Series (National Institute of Standards and Technology) (USA ISSN 1049-7579) **1025**
N I S T Handbook (National Institute of Standards and Technology) (USA) **6404**
N I S T Monograph (National Institute of Standards and Technology) (USA) **6404**
N I S T Special Publication (National Institute of Standards and Technology) (USA ISSN 1048-776X) **2432**
N I S T Technical Notes (National Institute of Standards and Technology) (USA ISSN 1054-013X) **6404**
N I T *see* National Indigenous Times **3552**
• N I T O Refleks (Norges Ingenioerorganisasjon) (NOR ISSN 0803-320X) **4599**
N I V A. Aarsberetning (Norsk Institutt for Vannforskning) (NOR ISSN 0801-955X) **8829**
• N I V A-Rapport/N I V A-Report (Norsk Institutt for Vannforskning) (NOR ISSN 0803-625X) **3489**
N I V A-Report *see* N I V A-Rapport **3489**
N I W A. Annual Report (National Institute of Water and Atmospheric) (NZL ISSN 1172-8450) **3454**
➤ N I W A Biodiversity Memoir (National Institute of Water and Atmospheric Research Ltd.) (NZL ISSN 1174-0043) **691**
➤ N I W A Technical Report (National Institute of Water and Atmospheric Research Ltd.) (NZL ISSN 1174-2631) **3602**
N J (New Jersey) (USA) **3982**
N J A NewsLetter (Nepal Journalists Association) (NPL) **3914**
N J A S *see* N J A S Wageningen Journal of Life Sciences **138**
N J A S C D's Focus on Education *see* New Jersey Journal of Supervision and Curriculum Development **3074**
➤ N J A S Wageningen Journal of Life Sciences (Netherlands Journal of Agricultural Science) (NLD ISSN 1573-5214) **138**
N J Association of Osteopathic Physicians and Surgeons. Journal (USA ISSN 0892-0249) **5806**
N J Audubon (New Jersey) (USA ISSN 0886-6619) **2619**
N J Banker *see* New Jersey Banker **1371**
• N J Biz (USA ISSN 1540-4161) **1151**
▼ N J C E O (New Jersey Chief Executive Officer) (USA) **1151**
N J C L *see* Nordic Journal of Commercial Law **4877**
N J C M Bulletin (Nederlands Juristen Comite voor de Mensenrechten) (NLD ISSN 0167-8434) **4936**
N J C T A (New Jersey Cable Television Association) (USA) **2386**
N J Drama Australia Journal (AUS ISSN 1445-2294) **8474**
N J E A Reporter (New Jersey Education Association) (USA ISSN 0027-674X) **3028**
N J E A Review (New Jersey Education Association) (USA ISSN 0027-6758) **2888**
• ➤ N J E S (Online) (Nordic Journal of English Studies) (SWE ISSN 1654-6970) **5153**
N J E S (Print) *see* N J E S (Online) **5153**
N J F *see* Nederlandse Jurisprudentie Feitenrechtspraak **4740**
• N J H A Newsletter (Online) (National Junior Horticultural Association) (USA) **3744**
N J I A *see* Nigerian Journal of International Affairs **7255**
N J I L B *see* Northwestern Journal of International Law & Business **4937**
N J L *see* Nordic Journal of Linguistics **5155**
N J L J *see* New Jersey Law Journal **4743**
• N J L L A In-Site (New Jersey Law Librarians Association) (USA ISSN 1542-5673) **4737**
N J L S P *see* Northwestern Journal of Law and Social Policy **4749**
N. J. Lawcast *see* New Jersey Lawcast **4743**
N J N Guide (New Jersey Network) (USA) **2386**
N J P *see* New Journal of Physics **7028**
N J P A Real Estate Journal *see* Mid Atlantic Real Estate Journal **7599**
N J P H (New Jersey Postal History Society Inc.) (USA ISSN 1078-1625) **2354**
N J R Annual Report *see* National Joint Registry for England and Wales. Annual Report **4107**
N J R S *see* Nordic Journal of Religion and Society **7666**
N J T *see* Nordisk Jaernbanetidskrift **8621**
N J W *see* Neue Juristische Wochenschrift **4740**
N J W Cassetten *see* Neue Juristische Wochenschrift **4740**
N J W - D V D *see* Neue Juristische Wochenschrift **4740**
N J W - R R *see* N J W - Rechtsprechungs-Report Zivilrecht **4838**
• N J W - Rechtsprechungs-Report Zivilrecht (Neue Juristische Wochenschrift) (DEU ISSN 0179-4043) **4838**
N J W Volltext CD-ROM *see* Neue Juristische Wochenschrift **4740**
N K B A's Puget Sound Kitchen & Bath (The National Kitchen & Bath Association (N K B A)) (USA) **4547**
N.K. Bose Memorial Foundation. Newsletter (IND) **7986**
N K H Nagaoka-shiritsu Kagaku Hakubutsukanpo (JPN) **6533**
N K-Info *see* Innsikt **6146**
N K K News (Nippon Kokan K.K.) (JPN ISSN 0388-600X) **3390**
N K K Technical Review *see* J F E Technical Report **6318**
N K W - Partner (Nutzkraftwagen) (DEU ISSN 1437-6229) **8673**
N L A D A Cornerstone (National Legal Aid and Defender Association) (USA ISSN 0739-9111) **4968**
N L C H S Newsletter (New London County Historical Society) (USA ISSN 1940-2074) **3775**
N L Communicator (Nebraska Library) (USA ISSN 0895-0806) **5033**
N L E *see* Natural Language Engineering **2509**
N L G I Spokesman (National Lubricating Grease Institute) (USA ISSN 0027-6782) **6778**
N L J *see* The National Law Journal **4739**
N L K Monitor. Market Pulp (GBR ISSN 1474-7138) **1899**

Link to your serials resources and content with ulrichsweb.com

DIRECTORY 2010 N R I A G JOURNAL OF GEOPHYSICS 10639

• N L M Newsline (National Library of Medicine) (USA ISSN 1094-5970) 5033
• N L M Technical Bulletin (U.S. National Library of Medicine) (USA ISSN 0146-3055) 5033
N L P see Natural Language Processing 5154
N L R B Advice Memorandum Reporter (National Labor Relations Board) (USA ISSN 0194-8784) 4737
• N L R B Case Handling Manual (U.S. National Labor Relations Board) (USA) 4737
• N L R B Election Report. Cases Closed (U.S. National Labor Relations Board) (USA ISSN 0270-9732) 1698
N L R B Election Statistics (National Labor Relations Board) (USA ISSN 1932-5347) 1698
N L R B Representation and Decertification Elections see N L R B Election Statistics 1698
N L R R see Nursing Law's Regan Report 5974
N L R Report (Nationaal Lucht -en Ruimtevaartlaboratorium) (NLD ISSN 0369-478X) 66
• N L S Handbook (National Longitudinal Surveys) (USA ISSN 1060-4979) 1870
N L T A Bulletin see Newfoundland and Labrador Teachers' Association. Bulletin 2891
N L T P Fact Sheet see New Zealand Transport Agency. Factsheet 8506
N L W see New Library World 5035
N. London, Herts & Beds Auto Trader see London, Herts, Beds & Essex Auto Trader 8589
N M A HealthyLiving (National Medical Association) (USA) 5682
N M A M see N I O S H Manual of Analytical Methods 6681
N M A Online see New Media Age 2335
• N M B Update (Nurses and Midwives Board) (AUS ISSN 1832-4800) 5970
N M C D see Nutrition, Metabolism & Cardiovascular Diseases 6666
N M C J see Nepal Medical College Journal 5685
• N M C News (Nursing and Midwifery Council) (GBR) 5970
N M E see New Musical Express 6599
N M L R see New Mexico Law Review 4744
N M M A Certification Handbook (National Marine Manufacturers Association) (USA) 8278
N M - Nordelbische Mission (DEU) 7768
• N M O A - Mail Order Digest (National Mail Order Association) (USA) 1835
N M R see Neumaticos & Mecanica Rapida 8595
N M R Igaku/Journal of Nuclear Magnetic Resonance Medicine see Nihon Jiki Kyomei Igakkai Zasshi 6204
• ➤ N M R in Biomedicine (Nuclear Magnetic Resonance) (GBR ISSN 0952-3480) 6203
N M R T Footnotes see New Member Round Table Footnotes 5035
N M T B. Lung Cancer see New Medical Therapies Briefs. Lung Cancer 6029
N M T B. Type 2 Diabetes Mellitus see New Medical Therapies Briefs. Type 2 Diabetes Mellitus 5898
N M T Briefs. Addiction see New Medical Therapies Briefs. Addiction 2697
N M T Briefs. Alzheimer's Disease see New Medical Therapies Briefs. Alzheimer's Disease 6170
N M T Briefs. Breast Cancer see New Medical Therapies Briefs. Breast Cancer 6029
N M T Briefs. C O P D see New Medical Therapies Briefs. Chronic Obstructive Pulmonary Disease 6216
N M T Briefs. Chronic Obstructive Pulmonary Disease see New Medical Therapies Briefs. Chronic Obstructive Pulmonary Disease 6216
N M T Briefs. Crohn's Disease see New Medical Therapies Briefs. Crohn's Disease 6272
N M T Briefs. Depression see New Medical Therapies Briefs. Depression 6170
N M T Briefs. Head and Neck Cancer see New Medical Therapies Briefs. Head and Neck Cancer 6029
N M T Briefs. Hepatitis see New Medical Therapies Briefs. Hepatitis 5823
N M T Briefs. HIV / AIDS see New Medical Therapies Briefs. HIV / AIDS 5823
N M T Briefs. Hyperlipidemia see New Medical Therapies Briefs. Hyperlipidemia 5796
N M T Briefs. Kidney Cancer see New Medical Therapies Briefs. Kidney Cancer 6029
N M T Briefs. Obesity see New Medical Therapies Briefs. Obesity 5685
N M T Briefs. Osteoporosis see New Medical Therapies Briefs. Osteoporosis 5948
N M T C Monthly Report see Novogradac New Markets Tax Credit Report 1937
N Magazine (Nygard International) (CAN) 2259
N N B see New Nutrition Business 6664
N N B - Numismatisches Nachrichtenblatt (DEU ISSN 0937-6488) 6651
N N C R K. Bulletin see Natsional'nyi Yadernyi Tsentr Respubliki Kazakhstan. Vestnik 7069
N N D C Newsletter (New Nigeria Development Company Ltd.) (NGA) 1899
N N F A Today (National Nutritional Foods Association) (USA) 3657
• N N I Journal (Nevada Neuroscience Institute) (USA ISSN 1933-9607) 6162
N N O Magazine (Noord - Nederlands Orkest) (NLD ISSN 0926-0692) 6598
N N P C News (Nigerian National Petroleum Corporation) (NGA ISSN 0189-0069) 6778
N Noticias (USA) 4580
N O A (Norsk som Andrespraak) (NOR ISSN 0801-3284) 5153
N O A A Business Report see U.S. National Oceanic and Atmospheric Administration. Business Report 2819
• N O A A Coastal Ocean Program Project News Update (National Oceanic and Atmospheric Administration) (USA) 2619
N O A A Data Report. E R L-G L E R L see National Oceanic and Atmospheric Administration. Environmental Research Laboratories. Great Lakes Environmental Research Laboratory. Data Report 2797
N O A A Data Report. E R L-P M E L see National Oceanic and Atmospheric Administration. Environmental Research Laboratories. Pacific Marine Environmental Laboratory. Data Report 2797
N O A A Professional Paper N M F S see U.S. National Oceanic and Atmospheric Administration. National Marine Fisheries Service. Professional Paper 3610
N O A C A News (Northeast Ohio Areawide Coordinating Agency) (USA) 8505
N O A Magazine (Nederlandse Onderneming voor Afbouwbedrijven) (NLD ISSN 1569-0520) 1025
N O A Newsletter (National Opera Association, Inc.) (USA ISSN 0749-9345) 6598
• N O B C Ch E News Online (National Organization for Black Chemists and Chemical Engineers) (USA ISSN 1932-8141) 3251
N O B C Ch E. Proceedings (National Organization for the Professional Advancement of Black Chemists and Chemical Engineers) (USA ISSN 0896-2367) 2074
N O B S Newsletter (Northern Ohio Bibliophilic Society) (USA ISSN 1524-119X) 4342
• N O C I R C Annual Newsletter (National Organization of Circumcision Information Resource Centers) (USA) 6097
N O D A National News (National Operatic and Dramatic Association) (GBR ISSN 1475-3812) 8474
N O F A - N J's Organic News see Organic News 144
N O F Forum see N OE F Info 2661
N O H see News of Hymnody 6599
N O H A News (Nutrition for Optimal Health Association) (USA) 6664
N O H S A C Technical Report (National Occupational Health and Safety Advisory Commission) (NZL ISSN 1177-2239) 6681
N O M E S C O Publications see Helsestatistik for de Nordiske Lande 5747
N O M M A Newsletter (National Ornamental & Miscellaneous Metals Association) (USA) 6327
N O Oe Journal (USA ISSN 1939-4802) 5228
N O P A Membership Directory and Buyer's Guide (Year) (National Office Products Association) (USA ISSN 0196-3287) 1852
N O P E F Aktuelt see Industri Energi 4596
N O R see New Oxford Review 7809
• N O R C Update (National Opinion Research Center) (USA ISSN 1937-2469) 7986
• N O R D I C O M - Information (Nordic Information Centre for Media and Communication Research) (SWE ISSN 0349-5949) 8122
• ➤ N O R D I C O M Review (Nordic Information Centre for Media and Communication Research) (SWE ISSN 1403-1108) 8122
N O R I S S. Fagnotat (Norsk Institutt for Strategiske Studier) (NOR ISSN 1890-0534) 8122
N O R M Report (Naturally Occurring Radioactive Material) (USA ISSN 1085-5386) 2757
• N O S (Noviny Odboroveho Svazu Statnich Organu a Organizaci) (CZE ISSN 0862-9633) 1780
N O S A Fashion Bulletin (National Outerwear and Sportswear Association) (USA) 2248
N O S A News (National Outerwear and Sportswear Association) (USA) 2248
N O S A. Production Bulletin (National Outerwear and Sportswear Association) (USA) 2248
N O S A Update (National Office Systems Association) (USA) 1297
• N O S P Adresseliste til Nordiske Bibliothek (Nordisk Samkatalog for Periodika) (NOR ISSN 0805-7575) 631
• N O S P on Web (Nordisk Samkatalog for Periodika) (NOR) 631
N O T E see Notes on Teaching English 5156
• N O V A. Rapport (Norsk Institutt for Forskning om Opvekst, Velferd og Aldring) (NOR ISSN 0808-5013) 8056
N O V A. Skriftserie (Norsk Institutt for Forskning om Opvekst, Velferd og Aldring) (NOR ISSN 0808-9183) 8056
N O V A. Temahefte (Norsk Institutt for Forskning om Opvekst, Velferd og Aldring) (NOR ISSN 1500-3183) 8056
N O W E L E (North-Western European Language Evolution) (DNK ISSN 0108-8416) 5153
N O W E L E. Supplement (North-Western European Language Evolution) (DNK ISSN 0900-8675) 5153
N O W San Diego News (National Organization for Women) (USA) 8876
• N OE F Info (Norsk Oeko-Forum) (NOR ISSN 1504-1441) 2661
N P see National Parks Journal 2620
• N P A (National Public Accountant) (USA) 1297
N P A Annual Report (Nigerian Ports Authority) (NGA) 8654
N P A Bulletin (Nigerian Ports Authority) (NGA ISSN 0794-3008) 8654
N.P.A. Journal (National Pawnbrokers Association (Inc.)) (GBR ISSN 0047-9020) 4568
N P A News (Institute of Transport, Nigerian Ports Authority) (NGA ISSN 0547-0730) 8654
N P A Supplement (National Pharmaceutical Association) (GBR) 6862
N P & P see Northamptonshire Past and Present 4249
N P C see Natural Product Communications 2074
N P C A (Years) Report to Members (National Paint and Coatings Association) (USA) 6719
N P C Annual Report (National Prescribing Centre) (GBR) 5682
N P C C Newsletter (National Productivity and Competitiveness Council) (MUS ISSN 1694-0229) 1780
N P C H N Journal see Neonatal, Paediatric and Child Health Nursing 5970
• N P E Advisor (USA) 7095
N P E R see National Public Employment Reporter 1699
• N P E R C I Informa (Non-Profit Evaluation & Resource Center Inc.) (PRI ISSN 1554-6357) 1780
N P G see N I O S H Pocket Guide to Chemical Hazards 6681
• N P G A Reports (National Propane Gas Association) (USA ISSN 1040-0354) 6778
• N P G - Neurologie Psychiatrie Gerontologie (FRA ISSN 1627-4830) 6162
N P G Review (National Portrait Gallery) (GBR) 507
• N P I Daily (CAN) 6664
• N P I Watch (CAN) 6664
N P L Annual Review (National Physical Laboratory) (GBR) 7027
N P L D see National Property Law Digests 4739
N P L Report C I R M (National Physical Laboratory) (GBR ISSN 1369-6793) 7027
N P L Report C I S E (National Physical Laboratory) (GBR) 2534
N P L Report C M M T (A) (National Physical Laboratory) (GBR ISSN 1361-4061) 3355
N P L Report C Q M (National Physical Laboratory) (GBR) 6404
N P L Report COAM (National Physical Laboratory, Centre for Optical and Analytical Measurement) (GBR ISSN 1475-6684) 7081
N P L Report M O M (National Physical Laboratory) (GBR ISSN 0309-3069) 6404
N P L Report on D Q L - O R (National Physical Laboratory) (GBR ISSN 1744-0610) 7027
N P L Technical Bulletin (National Physical Laboratory) (IND ISSN 0027-6898) 7027
N P N see National Petroleum News 6779
† • N P N International (National Petroleum News) (USA ISSN 1090-1906) 8976
N P. Nationellt Pistolskytte (SWE ISSN 1404-8647) 8189
N P O - Forum (Non Profit Organisation) (AUT) 8056
• N P O Journal (National Preservation Office) (GBR ISSN 1461-4154) 2619
N P P R see Nurse Practitioners' Prescribing Reference 6864
N P Q see New Perspectives Quarterly 7158
N P R A Annual Meeting. Conference Papers (National Petrochemical & Refiners Association) (USA) 6779
• N P R A Annual Meeting. Conference Papers. Multi-Year CD-ROM (National Petroleum Refiners Association) (USA) 6779
N P R A Computer Conference. Proceedings (National Petroleum Refiners Association) (USA) 6802
N P R A Cracker Seminar Transcripts (National Petroleum Refiners Association) (USA) 6779
N P R A Environmental Conference. Proceedings (National Petrochemical & Refiners Association) (USA) 6779
N P R A Legislative Update see Weekly Legislative Update 6797
N P R A National Lubricants & Waxes Meeting. Proceedings (National Petroleum & Refiners Association) (USA) 6779
N P R A National Safety Conference. Proceedings (National Petrochemical & Refiners Association) (USA) 6779
• N P R A Question & Answer Session on Refining and Petrochemical Technology Transcripts (CD-ROM Edition) (National Petroleum Refiners Association) (USA) 6779
N P R A Question & Answer Session on Refining and Petrochemical Technology Transcripts (Print Edition) see N P R A Question & Answer Session on Refining and Petrochemical Technology Transcripts (CD-ROM Edition) 6779
N P R A Question & Answer Session on Refining and Petrochemical Technology Transcripts. 5-Year Volume see N P R A Question & Answer Session on Refining and Petrochemical Technology Transcripts (CD-ROM Edition) 6779
N P R A Refinery and Petrochemical Plant Maintenance Conference (National Petroleum Refiners Association) (USA) 6779
N P R A Refinery and Petrochemical Plant Maintenance Conference. Technical Transcripts (National Petroleum Refiners Association) (USA) 6779
N P R A Statistical Report. Annual Survey of Occupational Injuries & Injuries (National Petrochemical & Refiners Association) (USA) 6690
N P R A Statistical Report. Lubricating Oil and Wax Capacity (National Petrochemical & Refiners Association) (USA) 6800
N P R A Statistical Report. U S Lubricating Oil & Wax Sales (National Petrochemical & Refiners Association) (USA) 6800
N P R A Statistical Report. U S Lubricating Oil Sales see N P R A Statistical Report. U S Lubricating Oil & Wax Sales 6800
• ➤ N P R A Statistical Report. U S Refining Capacity (National Petrochemical & Refiners Association) (USA) 6800
N P R A Washington Bulletin see Washington Bulletin 6796
N P R A Weekly Regulatory Update see Weekly Regulatory Update 6797
The N P R Interviews (National Public Radio) (USA ISSN 1078-0211) 4580
N P S Newsletter (Nonpoint Source Pollution) (USA) 3489
N P S R see National Political Science Review 7156
• ➤ N P S R A D A R (National Prescribing Service Rational Assessment of Drugs and Research) (AUS ISSN 1832-3596) 6862
N P S Rational Assessment of Drugs and Research see N P S R A D A R 6862
N P T Procestechnologie (Nederlandse Proces Technologen) (NLD ISSN 1380-3638) 3370
• N P W H Newsletter: The Monthly Cycle (Nurse Practitioners in Women's Health) (USA) 8847
• ➤ n.paradoxa (GBR ISSN 1461-0434) 507
N Plus One see n+1 5337
N+1 (USA) 5229
N Q Industry Advocate see The Mining Advocate 6472
N R see Naturwissenschaftliche Rundschau 7890
N R see National Review 7156
N R see Nova Religio 7739
N R A Annual R & D Review (National Rivers Authority) (GBR ISSN 1358-3263) 8829
N R A Annual Report (National Rivers Authority) (GBR) 8829
N R A C Inventories (Nederlands-Russisch Archiefcentrum) (NLD ISSN 1873-0590) 4247
N R A Corporate Plan (National Rivers Authority) (GBR) 8829
N R A Fisheries Statistics (National Rivers Authority) (GBR ISSN 1358-3298) 3613
N R A Journal (National Rifle Association) (GBR ISSN 0028-0070) 8323
N R A Newsletter see Contemporary Rehab 6108
• N R A O Newsletter (National Radio Astronomy Observatory) (USA ISSN 0894-5985) 578
▼ N R A Scheme Monographs (National Roads Authority) (IRL ISSN 2009-0471) 4247
N R A Water Quality Series (National Rivers Authority) (GBR) 8829
N R & E see Natural Resources & Environment 3455
• N R B Magazine (National Religious Broadcasters) (USA ISSN 1521-1754) 2386
N R C A Membership Directory (National Roofing Contractors Association) (USA ISSN 1053-8305) 2018
N R C Docket Microfiche (Nuclear Regulatory Commission) (USA) 7048
• N R C - Handelsblad (NLD ISSN 0002-5259) 3915
N R C Regulatory Agenda (Nuclear Regulatory Commission) (USA ISSN 0742-2652) 8432
N R C Regulatory Guides. Occupational Health (Division 8) (Nuclear Regulatory Commission) (USA) 6690
N R C S A Directory of Educational Programs (National Registration Center for Study Abroad) (USA ISSN 0275-9357) 2888
• N R C S A Program Directory. Europe (Online) (National Registration Center for Study Abroad) (USA) 3014
N R C T L D Direct Radiation Monitoring Network (USA ISSN 0883-3311) 7069
N R C Yearbook (National Reading Conference) (USA ISSN 0547-8375) 3074
N R E A News see National Rural Education News 2890
N R E C A - A P P A Legal Reporting Service (Management Services Department) (USA ISSN 0362-8833) 4737
• N R E L Technical Reports (Online) (National Renewable Energy Laboratory) (USA) 3142
N R F-Nytt see Avfallnorge 3504
N R F Publikaties (Nederlandse Federatie van Reclasseringsinstellingen) (NLD) 4894
N R G (USA) 5427
N R G Ma'ariv see Ma'ariv 3895
• N R H A E News (National Rural Health Association) (USA) 7532
• N R H A Reiner (National Reining Horse Association) (USA ISSN 0199-6762) 8295
N R H S Bulletin (National Railway Historical Society) (USA ISSN 1940-3615) 8621
N R I A G Journal of Geophysics see Journal of Geophysics 2785

Title

▼ *new title* † *ceased* • *electronic media* ➤ *refereed*

N R I Bibliographies (National Research Institute) (PNG) **631**
N R I Discussion Papers (National Research Institute) (PNG) **7986**
N R I Monographs (National Research Institute) (PNG) **7986**
N R I Special Publications (National Research Institute) (PNG) **7986**
N R L News *see* National Right to Life News **8057**
N R L Review (Naval Research Laboratory) (USA ISSN 1062-130X) **8432**
N R M A Drive Travel Tourist Parks Guide (AUS) **2018**
N R M C A Publication (National Ready Mixed Concrete Association) (USA ISSN 0077-5355) **1025**
N R O Gijutsu Hokoku/N R O Technical Report (Nobeyama Radio Observatory) (JPN) **578**
N R O Report (National Astronomical Observatory, Nobeyama Radio Observatory) (JPN ISSN 0911-5501) **578**
N R O Technical Report *see* N R O Gijutsu Hokoku **578**
N R O Yuzazu Mitingu (Nobeyama Radio Observatory) (JPN) **578**
N R P A Bulletin *see* Straaleverninfo **7542**
N R P A Report *see* Straalevernrapport **7543**
N R P Lettres Lycee (Nouvelle Revue Pedagogique) (FRA ISSN 1636-3566) **2889**
• N R P News (Norwich Research Park) (GBR) **876**
• N R R A News (Online) (National Risk Retention Association) (USA) **4516**
N R R I Now (Natural Resources Research Institute) (USA) **2713**
N R T E E Newsletter *see* National Round Table on the Environment and the Economy. Review (Print) **3454**
N R U *see* Nintendo **2478**
N R W Magazin (Nordrhein-Westfalen) (DEU ISSN 1860-6695) **7499**
n - Revolution (Nintendo) (GBR ISSN 1751-4584) **8189**
N S *see* Natural Science **7888**
N S A C I News (Northwest & Schaumburg Association of Commerce and Industry) (USA) **1151**
The N S A Practitioner (USA ISSN 1091-1596) **1297**
N S B E Bridge (National Society of Black Engineers) (USA ISSN 1060-3115) **3211**
N S B E Magazine (National Society of Black Engineers) (USA ISSN 1060-3123) **3211**
N S C A Bulletin *see* National Strength & Conditioning Association Bulletin **6993**
N S C A News (National Society for Clean Air) (GBR ISSN 0265-9379) **3489**
N S C A Pollution Handbook *see* Pollution Control Handbook (Year) **3490**
N S C A R Magazine (National Society of the Children of the American Revolution) (USA) **2268**
N S C Alliance Newsletter *see* Alliance Gazette **6518**
N S C Revue (Narodne Sportove Centrum) (SVK ISSN 1336-9903) **8189**
N S D C A Times (National Square Dance Campers Association) (USA ISSN 0195-0150) **2687**
• The N S D U H Report (National Survey on Drug Use and Health) (USA ISSN 1559-4386) **2697**
N S E (National Student Extra) (GBR) **2994**
N S E E Quarterly (National Society for Experiential Education) (USA ISSN 1093-5738) **6701**
N S E News Letter (Nigerian Society of Engineers) (NGA) **3211**
N S E R C Annual Report *see* Natural Sciences and Engineering Research Council of Canada. Annual Report **7888**
• N S E R C Award Holder's Guide for Postgraduate Scholarship (PGS) Holders at Canadian Universities (Natural Sciences and Engineering Research Council of Canada) (CAN ISSN 1493-1850) **7885**
N S E Technical Transactions (Nigerian Society of Engineers) (NGA) **3211**
• N S F Current (National Science Foundation) (USA ISSN 1946-2638) **7885**
N S F E-Bulletin *see* National Science Foundation. E-Bulletin **7887**
N S F Engineering News *see* National Science Foundation. Directorate for Engineering. Engineering News **3212**
• N S G A Sporting Goods Buying Guide (National Sporting Goods Association) (USA) **8189**
N S I Advisory (National Security Institute) (USA ISSN 0882-9667) **2679**
• N S I D C Annual Report (National Snow and Ice Data Center) (USA) **2757**
• N S I D C Notes (National Snow and Ice Data Center) (USA) **2757**
• N S I D C Special Reports (National Snow and Ice Data Center) (USA) **2757**
N S K News Bulletin (Nihon Shinbun Kyokai) (JPN ISSN 0916-295X) **4580**
N S K Technical Journal (Nippon Seiko K.K.) (JPN ISSN 0911-4920) **3211**
N S L *see* North Sea Letter **6781**
N S M F News (New Superconducting Materials Forum) (JPN) **8432**
N S Man (SGP ISSN 0218-690X) **6437**
N S N *see* Nuclear Standards News **3172**
• N S Newsbreak (USA) **8621**
N S O Monthly Bulletin of Statistics (National Statistics Office) (PHL ISSN 0115-2092) **8389**
N S P A Washington Reporter (National Society of Public Accountants) (USA ISSN 0469-3922) **1297**
N S P C C News (National Society for the Prevention of Cruelty to Children) (GBR ISSN 1351-864X) **8056**
The N S P I Business Owners (National Spa & Pool Institute) (USA) **6993**
N S P News (Northern States Power Company) (USA) **3142**
N S S B A Matters! (Nova Scotia School Boards Association) (CAN ISSN 1207-5272) **3028**
• N S S D C News (National Space Science Data Center) (USA) **66**
• N S S E A Membership Directory (National School Supply & Equipment Association) (USA ISSN 1045-0033) **3028**
N S S E A Membership Directory & Buyer's Guide *see* N S S E A Membership Directory **3028**
N S S L H A Clinical Series (National Student Speech Language Hearing Association) (USA ISSN 0887-6584) **6083**
N S S News (National Speleological Society, Inc.) (USA ISSN 0027-7010) **2757**
N S S News Bulletin (National Sculpture Society) (USA ISSN 1081-1478) **507**
N S S R A Cost of Doing Business Survey (National Ski & Snowboard Retailers Association) (USA) **8219**
N S S R A Newsletter (National Ski & Snowboard Retailers Association) (USA) **1835**
N S T A Reports (National Science Teachers Association) (USA) **2889**
N S T - N (Niedersaechsischer Staedtetag - Nachrichten) (DEU ISSN 1615-0511) **7499**
N S U *see* No Solo Usabilidad Journal **2433**
N S W Administrative Law *see* New South Wales Administrative Law **7455**
N S W Agriculture Today (New South Wales) (AUS ISSN 1038-8613) **138**
N S W Civil Practice & Procedure (New South Wales) (AUS) **4838**
N S W Department of Primary Industries. Fisheries Final Report Series (New South Wales) (AUS ISSN 1449-9967) **3602**
N S W Department of Primary Industries. Fisheries Resource Assessment Series (New South Wales) (AUS ISSN 1449-9940) **3602**
➤ N S W Department of Primary Industries. Science and Research Division. Forest Resources Research. Research Papers (New South Wales) (AUS ISSN 1833-0517) **3697**
➤ N S W Department of Primary Industries. Science and Research Division. Forest Resources Research. Technical Papers (New South Wales) (AUS) **3697**
• N S W Department of Primary Industries. Science and Research Division. Forests N S W. Research and Development Annual Report (New South Wales) (AUS ISSN 1834-5557) **3697**
N S W in Focus *see* N S W State and Regional Indicators **7288**
N S W L R *see* New South Wales Law Reports **4957**
N S W Master Plumber (New South Wales) (AUS ISSN 0819-1824) **4123**
N S W Police. Annual Report *see* New South Wales. Police Force. Annual Report **4895**
• ➤ N S W Public Health Bulletin (New South Wales) (AUS ISSN 1034-7674) **7532**
N S W Public Health Bulletin. Supplement *see* N S W Public Health Bulletin **7532**
• N S W State and Regional Indicators (New South Wales) (AUS) **7288**
• N S W Women (New South Wales) (AUS ISSN 1832-2530) **8876**
N-Scale (USA ISSN 1045-5140) **4342**
N St Z *see* Neue Zeitschrift fuer Strafrecht **4894**
N St Z - R R *see* Neue Zeitschrift fuer Strafrecht Rechtsprechungs Report Strafrecht **4894**
N St Z Rechtsprechungs Report Strafrecht *see* Neue Zeitschrift fuer Strafrecht Rechtsprechungs Report Strafrecht **4894**
N St Z Volltext CD-ROM *see* Neue Zeitschrift fuer Strafrecht **4894**
N T *see* Nano Today **750**
N T *see* Nuclear Technology **7070**
† N T A Forum (National Tax Association) (USA) **8976**
N T Administrator (DEU) **2501**
N T B Magazin (Niedersaechsischer Turner-Bund e.V.) (DEU) **8189**
N T B R *see* Nederlands Tijdschrift voor Burgerlijk Recht **4838**
N.T.C.I. Current Affairs Update (Northern Transvaal Chamber of Industries) (ZAF) **1407**
N T D B *see* National Trade Data Bank **1407**
N T E A Technical Report (National Truck Equipment Association) (USA) **8673**
• N T E A Washington Update (National Truck Equipment Association) (USA) **8673**
N T E U Advocate *see* Advocate **2965**
N T E U Bulletin (National Treasury Employees Union) (USA ISSN 0279-540X) **4599**
• ➤ N T E U Express (National Tertiary Education Union) (AUS) **2994**
• N T E U Frontline (National Tertiary Education Union) (AUS ISSN 1322-2945) **2994**
N T F R *see* Nederlands Tijdschrift voor Fiscaal Recht **1936**
N T F R Beschouwingen *see* Nederlands Tijdschrift voor Fiscaal Recht Beschouwingen **1936**
• N T I A C Newsletter (Nondestructive Testing Information Analysis Center) (USA ISSN 0730-8086) **3355**
N T I Bulletin (National Tuberculosis Institute) (IND) **6216**
N T I - Neue Thueringer Illustrierte (DEU) **3853**
N T I S Alerts: Agriculture & Food (National Technical Information Service) (USA) **183**
N T I S Alerts: Biomedical Technology & Human Factors Engineering (National Technical Information Service) (USA) **5749**
N T I S Alerts: Building Industry Technology (National Technical Information Service) (USA) **1048**
N T I S Alerts: Business & Economics (National Technical Information Service) (USA ISSN 1074-1674) **1252**
N T I S Alerts: Civil Engineering (National Technical Information Service) (USA) **3232**
N T I S Alerts: Communication (National Technical Information Service) (USA) **2348**
N T I S Alerts: Computers, Control & Information Theory (National Technical Information Service) (USA) **2444**
N T I S Alerts: Electrotechnology (National Technical Information Service) (USA) **3109**
N T I S Alerts: Energy (National Technical Information Service) (USA) **3153**
N T I S Alerts: Environmental Pollution & Control (National Technical Information Service) (USA) **3480**
N T I S Alerts: Government Inventions for Licensing (National Technical Information Service) (USA) **8447**
N T I S Alerts: Health Care (National Technical Information Service) (USA) **7002**
N T I S Alerts: Manufacturing Technology (National Technical Information Service) (USA ISSN 1043-9897) **8447**
N T I S Alerts: Materials Sciences (National Technical Information Service) (USA) **3232**
N T I S Alerts: Ocean Sciences & Engineering (National Technical Information Service) (USA) **2720**
N T I S Alerts: Transportation (National Technical Information Service) (USA) **8527**
• N T I S Bibliographic Database (National Technical Information Service) (USA ISSN 1064-0479) **7938**
N T I S Title Index (U.S. Department of Commerce, National Technical Information Service) (USA) **7200**
N T J *see* National Tax Journal **1936**
N T L News (National Transient Lodge) (USA) **4599**
N T M *see* Norsk Tidsskrift for Migrasjonsforskning **7288**
N T M A Record *see* The Record **5459**
N T M International Journal of History and Ethics of Natural Sciences, Technology and Medicine *see* N T M Journal of History of Sciences, Technology, and Medicine **7885**
• ➤ N T M Journal of History of Sciences, Technology, and Medicine/N T M Zeitschrift fuer Geschichte der Wissenschaften, Technik und Medizin (Natural Sciences, Technology & Medicine) (CHE) **7885**
N T M Zeitschrift fuer Geschichte der Wissenschaften, Technik und Medizin *see* N T M Journal of History of Sciences, Technology, and Medicine **7885**
N T N Technical Review (JPN ISSN 0915-0528) **3211**
N T N U Samfunnsforskning AS. Studio Apertura. Work Report (Norges Teknisk-Naturvitenskapelige Universitet) (NOR ISSN 1890-2022) **8122**
N T O R *see* Nederlands Tijdschrift voor Onderwijsrecht **4740**
N T P A Directory *see* National Trade and Professional Associations of the United States **2019**
N T P C E R H R M O N *see* National Toxicology Programme, Center for the Evaluation of Risks to Human Reproduction MON **3500**
• N T Q. New Theatre Quarterly (GBR ISSN 0266-464X) **8474**
N T R *see* New Theology Review **7809**
N T R S *see* N A S A Technical Reports Server **66**
N T S A Reporter (National Technical Services Association) (USA) **1698**
N T S B Reporter (National Transportation Safety Board) (USA ISSN 0745-9874) **8548**
N T T Do Co Mo Technical Journal (Nippon Telegraph and Telephone) (JPN) **2334**
N T T Gijutsu Janaru/N T T Technical Journal (Nippon Telegraph and Telephone) (JPN ISSN 0915-2318) **2370**
N T T International Researcher's Newsletter *see* Global News **2368**
N T T Kenkyujo Kono Ichinen/N T T Telecommunications Laboratories. Annual Report (JPN) **2370**
N T T: Nordisk Traeteknik *see* N T T Saag & Trae **3714**
N T T R & D (Nippon Telegraph and Telephone Research and Development) (JPN ISSN 0915-2326) **2370**
N T T Research & Development *see* N T T R & D **2370**
• N T T Saag & Trae (SWE ISSN 1651-6818) **3714**
N T T Technical Journal *see* N T T Gijutsu Janaru **2370**
N T T Technical Review (Nippon Telegraph and Telephone) (JPN ISSN 1348-3447) **2334**
N T T Telecommunications Laboratories. Annual Report *see* N T T Kenkyujo Kono Ichinen **2370**
N T U Bulletin (Newark Teachers Union) (USA) **4599**
N T U C Lifestyle (SGP ISSN 0129-1467) **5077**
N T U Library Bulletin (Nanyang Technological University) (SGP ISSN 0218-5008) **5033**
† N T Update (USA) **8976**
N T V Mag (TUR) **3962**
N T Z (Nachrichtentechnische Zeitschrift) (DEU ISSN 0948-728X) **2334**
N T Z *see* Nederlands Tijdschrift voor de Zorg aan Mensen met Veerstandelijke Beperkingen **4068**
• N-Touch (GBR) **2259**
N U C Annual Report *see* Nigeria. National Universities Commission. Annual Report **2996**
• N U C O S on Disk (AUS) **631**
N U C Project News (World Bank Implementation Unit) (NGA) **2994**
N U C Statistical Digest *see* Nigeria. National Universities Commission. Statistical Digest **2934**
N U C University System News *see* Nigeria. National Universities Commission. University System News **2996**
N U E Comment (National Union of Educators) (ZAF) **2889**
N U J Freelance Directory (National Union of Journalists) (GBR) **4580**
N U K T A (COD) **138**
N U L R *see* Northwestern University Law Review **4749**
N U M O G *see* Numerical Models in Geomechanics **2787**
• N U P I Notat (Online)/N U P I Working Paper (Norsk Utenrikspolitisk Institutt) (NOR ISSN 0809-7445) **7254**
N U P I Rapport/N U P I Report (Norsk Utenrikspolitisk Institutt) (NOR ISSN 0804-7235) **7254**
N U P I Report *see* N U P I Rapport **7254**
N U P I Working Paper *see* N U P I Notat (Online) **7254**
N U S Economic Journal (National University of Singapore) (SGP ISSN 0218-3269) **1151**
N U T Education Review *see* Education Review **2979**
N V Amateurtheater *see* De Theater N V **8482**
N V B *see* Noise & Vibration Bulletin **7088**
N V B B Magazine - Brand- en Diefstalbeveiliging *see* A N P I Magazine (Dutch Edition) **3575**
▼ N V B Krant (Nederlandse Vereniging voor Beroepsbeoefenaren in de Bibliotheek-, Informatie- en Kennissector) (NLD ISSN 1875-2586) **5033**
N V B. Noise & Vibration Bulletin *see* Noise & Vibration Bulletin **7088**
N V Bulletin *see* Bank Wereld **1316**
N V C Actueel (Nederlands Verpakkingscentrum) (NLD ISSN 1873-9334) **6712**
N V D A Nieuws *see* De Doktersassistent **5606**
N V G N Magazine Geestelijke Genezer (Nederlandse Vereniging voor Geestelijke- en Natuurgeneeswijzen) (NLD ISSN 1871-7241) **6113**
N V I *see* Noise & Vibration in Industry **7088**
N V K Publikatiereeks (Nederlandse Vereniging voor Kartografie) (NLD ISSN 0926-5007) **4020**
N V Magazine (New Vision) (USA) **3552**
N V Naamloze Vennootschappen *see* Samsom Naamloze Vennootschappen **1170**
N V - Neue Verpackung (DEU ISSN 0341-0390) **6712**
N V O *see* La Nouvelle Vie Ouvriere **4600**
N V O Espace Elus (Nouvelle Vie Ouvriere) (FRA ISSN 1633-3284) **1698**
N V O N Maandblad (Nederlandse Vereniging voor het Onderwijs in de Natuurwetenschappen) (NLD ISSN 0921-1713) **7885**
N V P Private Equity Gids (Nederlandse Vereniging van Participatiemaatschappijen) (NLD ISSN 1871-8566) **1369**
N V R Reports (National Video Resources) (USA) **2402**
N V S - N V L Actueel (Nederlandse Vereniging van Schooldekanen) (NLD ISSN 1574-972X) **3028**
N V V K Info (Nederlandse Vereniging voor Veiligheidskunde) (NLD ISSN 0928-4923) **6681**
N Vw Z *see* Neue Zeitschrift fuer Verwaltungsrecht **4957**
N Vw Z - R R *see* N Vw Z Rechtsprechungs Report Verwaltungsrecht **4737**
• N Vw Z Rechtsprechungs Report Verwaltungsrecht (Neue Zeitschrift fuer Verwaltungsrecht) (DEU ISSN 0934-8603) **4737**
• N W (News Weekly) (AUS) **8876**
N W *see* Northern Woman **8878**
N W B *see* Neue Wirtschafts-Briefe **1936**
N W B - Dokumentation Steuerrecht (Neue Wirtschafts-Briefe) (DEU ISSN 0171-8185) **1935**
N W Europe Petroleum Database (GBR) **6779**
• N W Fishletter (Northwest) (USA) **3602**
N W Florida's Business Climate (Northwest) (USA) **1151**
N W G H & G S Quarterly (Northwest Georgia Historical and Genealogical Society) (USA ISSN 1541-8650) **3776**
• N W H P Network (National Women's History Project) (USA) **8901**
N W I G (New West Indian Guide) (NLD ISSN 1382-2373) **7986**

DIRECTORY 2010 NAGALAND TIMES 10641

N W O Jaaroverzicht *see* Synthese (The Hague) 7921
N W O Reeks Sociale Cohesie *see* Sociale Cohesie in Nederland 8134
N W O-Spinozapremies (Nederlandse Organisatie voor Wetenschappelijk Onderzoek) (NLD ISSN 1874-8546) 7885
N W O Synthese *see* Synthese (The Hague) 7921
N W Palate Magazine (USA) 8739
N W Posthumus Reeks (NLD ISSN 0929-9742) 4247
● N W Q E P Notes (National Water Quality Evaluation Project) (USA) 8829
● N W R A Daily (National Water Resources Association) (USA) 8829
● ➤ N W S A Journal (National Women's Studies Association) (USA ISSN 1040-0656) 8901
N W S Action (National Women's Studies Association) (USA) 8901
N W S Magazin (Neckarwerke Stuttgart AG) (DEU) 3326
N W T Airport Statistics Report (Northwest Territories) (CAN ISSN 1719-3656) 8548
N W T Arts Strategy Progress Report (Northwest Territories) (CAN ISSN 1912-7030) 507
N W T Labour Force Survey (Year) (Northwest Territories) (CAN ISSN 0830-1611) 1698
N W T Traffic Accident Facts *see* N W T Traffic Collision Facts 8632
N W T Traffic Collision Facts (Northwest Territories) (CAN ISSN 1719-3842) 8632
N X T G (NLD ISSN 1574-7980) 2204
N Y A R S Reports *see* National Youth Affairs Research Scheme Reports 2162
N Y Arts (New York) (USA) 507
N Y Auction Advertiser (New York) (USA) 1835
N Y C *see* New Youth Connections 2205
N Y C - On Stage (New York City) (USA) 8474
N Y C Parents - F L A G Newsletter (New York City - Friends of Lesbians and Gays) (USA) 4377
● N Y C Plus (New York City) (USA) 4052
N Y C R R *see* New York Codes, Rules and Regulations 4744
N Y C V E (New York City Venice) (ITA) 3898
N.Y. Civil Liberties (USA ISSN 0746-0201) 7213
N Y Civil Service Law (New York) (USA) 4838
The N Y Connection *see* The New York Connection 4124
● N.Y. County Lawyer (USA ISSN 1558-5786) 4737
N Y Defender Digest (New York) (USA) 4876
N.Y. Defense of Justification (USA) 2661
The N Y G & B Newsletter *see* The New York Researcher 3776
N Y Gold (New York) (USA ISSN 0893-3170) 6971
N Y Gold's Tilt (New York) (USA) 6971
● N Y L A Bulletin (New York Library Association) (USA ISSN 0027-7134) 5033
N Y L I C Review (New York Life Insurance Co.) (USA ISSN 0027-7142) 4516
N Y L J *see* New York Law Journal 4745
N Y Law Digest *see* New York State Law Digest 4745
N Y Litigator *see* New York Litigator 4895
N Y Mortgage Report (New York) (USA ISSN 1529-8485) 1369
N Y P I R G Agenda (New York Public Interest Research Group, Inc.) (USA ISSN 1044-3134) 2640
N Y Q *see* New York Quarterly 5428
● N Y R A Freedom (National Youth Rights Association) (USA ISSN 1933-5229) 2162
● N.Y. Real Property Law Journal (USA ISSN 1530-3918) 7601
N Y Real Property Law Journal *see* N Y Real Property Law Section Journal 4738
N Y Real Property Law Section Journal (New York) (USA) 4738
● N Y Rock (New York) (USA) 6598
N Y S D Focus *see* Focus (Washington, D.C. 1976) 2284
N Y S E Magazine (New York Stock Exchange) (USA) 1642
N Y S E Weekly Stock Buys *see* Elton Stephens - Investment Advisor 1621
N Y S P A Notebook (New York State Psychological Association) (USA ISSN 1048-6925) 7386
● ➤ N Y S Psychologist (New York State) (USA ISSN 0028-7687) 7386
N Y S Register *see* New York State Register 7499
N Y S S A Sphere (New York State Society of Anesthesiologists, Inc.) (USA ISSN 0095-2273) 5772
N Y Search and Seizure (New York) (USA) 4894
N Y T T S Newsnotes (New York Turtle and Tortoise Society) (USA) 321
N Y U Alumni Magazine (New York University) (USA ISSN 1938-4823) 2293
● ➤ N Y U Hospital for Joint Diseases. Bulletin (New York University) (USA ISSN 1936-9719) 6067
N Y U Journal of Law and Business (New York University) (USA ISSN 1558-5778) 4876
● N Y U Journal of Law & Liberty (New York University) (USA ISSN 1930-5044) 4738
N Y U Physician (New York University School of Medicine) (USA ISSN 0277-9749) 2293
N Y U Physician's Directory (New York University) (USA ISSN 1930-2215) 5682
N Y U Today (New York University) (USA) 2293
N Z A *see* Neue Zeitschrift fuer Arbeitsrecht 4740
N.Z.A.A.C.A Newsletter (N.Z. Amateur Aircraft Constructors Association) *see* Sport Flying 72
● N Z A I Bulletin (New Zealand Asia Institute) (NZL ISSN 1178-1122) 556
N Z A I M S Newsletter *see* M S R Youth 8972
● N Z A I Regional Analysis (New Zealand Asia Institute) (NZL ISSN 1177-8628) 7254
N Z A M I News (New Zealand Association for Migration & Investment, Inc.) (NZL ISSN 1177-2328) 7288
N Z A - R R *see* N Z A Rechtsprechungs Report Arbeitsrecht 1698
N Z A Rechtsprechungs Report Arbeitsrecht (Neue Zeitschrift fuer Arbeitsrecht) (DEU ISSN 0949-7137) 1698
N Z A Volltext CD-ROM *see* Neue Zeitschrift fuer Arbeitsrecht 4740
● N Z Army News (New Zealand) (NZL ISSN 1170-8859) 6437
N Z B i P *see* New Zealand Books in Print 632
N.Z. Beekeeper *see* New Zealand Beekeeper 856
N Z Bioscience (New Zealand) (NZL ISSN 1172-7101) 740
● N Z Business (New Zealand) (NZL ISSN 0113-4957) 1151
N Z C E R Researched News *see* Insight (Wellington, 1965) 2867
N Z Catholic (New Zealand) (NZL ISSN 1174-0086) 7808
N Z Dog World (NZL) 6811
● N Z E I Rourou (New Zealand Educational Institute) (NZL ISSN 0114-8206) 2889
N Z Education Review Postgraduate Report *see* Higher Ground 2985
● N Z F S A Background Paper (New Zealand Food Safety Authority) (NZL ISSN 1177-7109) 7532
N Z F S A Food Focus *see* Food Focus 3638
N Z Farmers Weekly *see* New Zealand Farmers Weekly 140
N Z Film *see* New Zealand Film 6508
N Z Fishing Guide Book *see* Spot X 8336
N Z G *see* Neue Zeitschrift fuer Gesellschaftsrecht 4741
N Z Hearing Review *see* Hearing Review 6080
N Z Hepatitis Research Review *see* Hepatitis Research Review 5926
N Z Herefords Upfront *see* Red Rag 298
● N Z Holiday Hotspots (New Zealand) (NZL ISSN 1177-312X) 8739
N Z House and Garden (New Zealand) (NZL) 3744
N Z I *see* Neue Zeitschrift fuer das Recht der Insolvenz und Sanierung 4740
N Z IMAges (NZL ISSN 1177-4819) 5519
N Z Inflammatory Bowel Disease Research Review *see* I B D Research Review 5926
N Z InfoTech *see* The Dominion Post 3917
N Z Life & Leisure (New Zealand) (NZL ISSN 1176-8894) 5077
N Z Listener *see* Listener 3917
N Z Logger *see* New Zealand Logger Magazine 3714
N Z Lymphoma / Leukaemia Review *see* Lymphoma / Leukaemia Review 5940
N Z M *see* Neue Zeitschrift fuer Miet- und Wohnungsrecht 4741
▼ N Z M J Digest (New Zealand Medical Journal) (NZL ISSN 1177-7990) 5682
● N Z Marketing Magazine (New Zealand) (NZL) 1835
N Z Micro *see* New Zealand Computer Club. Newsletter 2572
N Z Motorhomes, Caravans & Destinations *see* New Zealand Motorhomes, Caravans & Destinations 8595
N Z Oral Health Research Review *see* Oral Health Research Review 5859
N Z Outdoor Power Equipment (New Zealand) (NZL ISSN 1177-4215) 5457
N Z Outside. Coastal Life (New Zealand) (NZL ISSN 1177-5580) 450
N Z P *see* New Zealand Printer 7325
N Z Performance Car *see* New Zealand Performance Car 8595
N Z Poets Online *see* Blackmail Press 5418
N Z Purchase & Supply Directory *see* N Z Purchase and Supply Directory for Government Departments and Local Authorities 1835
N Z Purchase and Supply Directory for Government Departments and Local Authorities (New Zealand) (NZL ISSN 1177-326X) 1835
N Z R A Newsletter (Online) (New Zealand Rafting Association) (NZL) 8278
N Z Radiator Magazine (New Zealand) (NZL ISSN 1174-5428) 8594
N Z Rehabilitation Research Review *see* Rehabilitation Research Review 6115
N Z Rosarian *see* New Zealand Rosarian 3745
● N Z Rugby World (New Zealand) (NZL ISSN 1175-1088) 8239
N Z Runner *see* New Zealand Runner 8977
N Z S *see* Neue Zeitschrift fuer Sozialrecht 4741
N Z Sheep and Beef Farm Survey *see* Meat and Wool Boards' Economic Service. N Z Sheep and Beef Farm Survey 203
N Z Today (New Zealand) (NZL ISSN 1176-3051) 8739
N Z Turf Digest *see* Turf Digest 8299
N Z U G R *see* NZUniGradReport 1701
N Z U G S *see* NZUniGradStats 1701
N Z U P G R *see* NZUniPostgradReport 1701
N Z Uni Grad Report *see* NZUniGradReport 1701
N Z V *see* Neue Zeitschrift fuer Verkehrsrecht 8506
N Z V8 (New Zealand) (NZL ISSN 1176-9920) 8594
N Z W W A Journal (New Zealand Water and Wastes Association) (NZL ISSN 1177-1313) 8829
N Z Woodturner *see* Creative Wood New Zealand 4555
N Z Z am Sonntag (Neue Zuercher Zeitung) (CHE ISSN 1660-0851) 3958
N-Zone (DEU ISSN 1433-8424) 2478
n+1 (USA ISSN 1549-0033) 5337
● N3: Nebraska Library Commission Network Services News (USA ISSN 1082-4383) 5034
Na Boevom Postu/At the Beat (RUS ISSN 0869-6403) 6437
Na Okika O Hawaii/Hawaii Orchid Journal (USA ISSN 0099-8745) 803
Na Przykład (POL ISSN 1231-0530) 5229
Na Rublevke (RUS) 3937
Na Smenu! (RUS) 3937
Na Strazhe (BLR) 6437
Na Strazhe Rodiny (RUS) 6437
Na Strazhe Zapolyarya (RUS) 6437
Na Szlaku (POL ISSN 1230-9931) 8739
Na Watykanie *see* Vatican-Magazin 7821
Na Watykanie *see* Inside the Vatican 7801
Na Zywo (POL ISSN 1234-2491) 8877
Naa (NOR) 3924
Na'amat Woman (USA ISSN 0888-191X) 7727
● Naamkunde (BEL ISSN 0167-5257) 5154
Naamkundevereniging van Suider-Afrika. Nuusbrief *see* Names Society of Southern Africa. Newsletter 5154
Naamkundevereniging van Suider-Afrika. Tydskrif *see* Names Society of Southern Africa. Journal 5154
Naamlijsten voor de Statistiek van de Buitenlandse Handel *see* Goederennaamlijst 8960
De Naamlooze Vennootschap *see* Ondernemingsrecht 4752
Naamloze Vennootschappen *see* Samsom Naamloze Vennootschappen 1170
Nabakallol (IND) 3885
● ➤ Nabokov Studies (USA ISSN 1080-1219) 5337
Nabokovian (USA ISSN 0894-7120) 5337
Nabor Carrillo Lecture Series. Proceedings (MEX ISSN 0185-4011) 3279
Nach der Arbeit (AUT ISSN 0027-7363) 2944
Nach Feierabend (CHE) 7987
Nachal'naya Shkola (Moscow, 1933) (RUS ISSN 0027-7371) 2889
Nachal'naya Shkola (Moscow, 1993) (RUS) 2889
Nachalno Obrazovanie (BGR) 2889
Nachbar G K N (DEU) 3171
Nachbarsprache Niederlaendisch (DEU ISSN 0936-5761) 5154
Nachdruck (DEU) 7324
† ● Nachgefragt (DEU ISSN 1864-5151) 8976
Nachhaltiges Niedersachsen (DEU ISSN 0949-8265) 2619
Nachrichten aus dem Karten- und Vermessungswesen. Reihe I: Originalbeitraege (DEU ISSN 0469-4236) 4020
Nachrichten aus dem Karten- und Vermessungswesen. Reihe II: Uebersetzungen (DEU ISSN 0469-4244) 4020
Nachrichten aus dem Martin-von-Wagner-Museum (DEU ISSN 1432-0282) 407
Nachrichten aus den Staatlichen Archiven Bayerns (DEU ISSN 0721-9733) 4247
† Nachrichten aus der Basler Mission (DEU) 8976
● ➤ Nachrichten aus der Chemie (DEU ISSN 1439-9598) 2074
● Nachrichten aus der Evidenzbasierten Medizinischen Diagnostik (AUT ISSN 1991-5020) 5682
Nachrichten aus Niedersachsens Urgeschichte (DEU ISSN 0342-1406) 407
Nachrichten aus Niedersachsens Urgeschichte. Beiheft *see* Nachrichten aus Niedersachsens Urgeschichte 407
Nachrichten der Stadtgemeinde Liezen (AUT) 7499
Nachrichten des Entomologischen Vereins Apollo *see* Entomologischer Verein Apollo. Nachrichten 846
Nachrichten des Entomologischen Vereins Apollo. Supplementum *see* Entomologischer Verein Apollo. Nachrichten 846
Nachrichten - Elektronik - Telematik Zeitschrift fuer Kommunikationsmanagement *see* N E T - Zeitschrift fuer Kommunikationsmanagement 2386
Nachrichten fuer Aussenhandel (DEU ISSN 0027-741X) 1642
Nachrichten fuer Aussenhandel Geschaeftswuensche *see* N f A - Geschaeftswuensche 1578
Nachrichten fuer Aussenhandel Projektfruehinformationen und Auslandsausschreibungen *see* N f A - Projektfruehinformationen und Auslandsausschreibungen 1578
Nachrichten fuer Seefahrer (DEU ISSN 0027-7444) 8654
Nachrichten - Paritaet *see* Der Paritaetische 8061
Nachrichten und Informationen zur Kultur *see* N I K 7986
● Nachrichten zur Mahler Forschung (AUT ISSN 1608-8956) 6598
Nachrichtenblatt der Bayerischen Entomologen (DEU ISSN 0027-7452) 855
Nachrichtenblatt der Gemeinde Bisingen (DEU) 3853
Nachrichtenblatt der Gemeinde Grosselfingen (DEU) 3853
Nachrichtenblatt des Deutschen Pflanzenschutzdienstes *see* Journal fuer Kulturpflanzen 238
Nachrichtenblatt Deutscher Jagdterrierclub *see* Deutscher Jagdterrierclub. Nachrichtenblatt 6806
Nachrichtenblatt fuer das Untere Haertsfeld (DEU) 7499
Nachrichtenblatt fuer die Gemeinden Sinzheim und Hugelsheim (DEU) 3853
Nachrichtenleitungen und Antennen *see* Informationsdienst F I Z Technik. Nachrichtenleitungen und Antennen 2348
Nachrichtentechnische Zeitschrift *see* N T Z 2334
Nachrichtenuebertragung, Verfahren, Geraete und Systeme *see* Informationsdienst F I Z Technik. Nachrichtenuebertragung, Verfahren, Geraete und Systeme 2348
Nachrichtenvermittlung, Netze, Teilnehmereinrichtungen *see* Informationsdienst F I Z Technik. Nachrichtenvermittlung, Netze, Teilnehmereinrichtungen 2348
● Nachschlagewerk des Bundesarbeitsgerichts - Arbeitsrechtliche Praxis (DEU ISSN 0469-4333) 1698
Nachschlagewerke Handbuch der Grossunternehmen *see* Firmendatenbank Ostdeutschland 1885
Nachtflug (DEU) 4394
Nachtlichter (DEU) 4394
● La Nacion (ARG ISSN 0325-0946) 3791
● La Nacion (COL) 3830
● Nacion (MEX ISSN 0027-7509) 7156
● La Nacion (PRY ISSN 1606-0512) 3927
● Nacion.com (CRI) 3821
Nacion Cubana (CUB) 3831
La Nacion U S A (USA) 3552
● El Nacional (DOM ISSN 1605-3699) 3835
● Nacional (HRV ISSN 1330-9048) 5229
● EL Nacional (VEN) 3994
Nacional Financiera. Annual Report (MEX ISSN 0185-4968) 1369
El Nacional News (USA) 3552
Naciones Unidas Anuario Juridico *see* United Nations Juridical Yearbook 4943
Naciones Unidas. Anuario sobre Desarme *see* United Nations Disarmament Yearbook 7270
Naciones Unidas. Comision Economica para America Latina y el Caribe. Boletin de Planificacion (CHL ISSN 0252-2209) 1547
Naciones Unidas. Consejo de Seguridad. Documentos Oficiales *see* United Nations. Security Council. Official Records 7271
Naciones Unidas. Consejo de Seguridad. Documentos Oficiales. Suplemento *see* United Nations. Security Council. Official Records. Supplement 7271
Naciones Unidas. Origenes, Organizacion, Actividades *see* Everyone's United Nations 8955
Naczelna Izba Aptekarska. Biuletyn (POL ISSN 1426-0514) 6862
● Nad Buhom i Narwoyu (POL ISSN 1230-2759) 3552
● ➤ Nadcisnienie Tetnicze/Arterial Hypertension (POL ISSN 1428-5851) 5796
Nadezhda (RUS) 2889
An-Nadi (SAU) 8189
Nadi Abu Dhabi al-Siyahi/Abu Dhabi Tourist Club (UAE) 2268
Nadi al-Wasl (UAE) 2268
Al-Nadwah (SAU ISSN 1319-0229) 3944
Nadyezhnost': Voprosy Teorii i Praktiki *see* Reliability: Theory & Applications 3217
Nadzvychaina Sytuatsiya (UKR) 3965
Naedal (EST ISSN 1406-1015) 8877
Naemnaren (SWE ISSN 0348-2723) 5519
Naemnd foer Internationella Adoptionsfraagor Informerar *see* N I A Informerar 8056
Naemndemannen (SWE ISSN 0348-4351) 4738
Naer och Fjaerran (SWE ISSN 1652-764X) 8739
Naerbutikken *see* N B 1835
Naeringseiendom (NOR ISSN 0805-9837) 7601
Naeringsmiddelindustrien *see* Matindustrien 3655
Naeringsvaert (SWE ISSN 1653-8137) 6664
Naestved Tidende - Sjaellands Tidende (DNK) 3834
Naetmagazin med Saekerhet *see* Datormagazin 2416
● Naettidningen Roetter (SWE ISSN 1402-9596) 3776
Naetverk och Kommunikation *see* Techworld 2504
Nafarroako Aldizkari *see* Boletin Oficial de Navarra 8937
Nafarroako Aldizkari Ofiziala *see* Boletin Oficial de Navarra 8937
NaFo - Nytt *see* Naturviteren 4599
Al Nafs wa-al-Hayat/Journal of Psyche and Life (IRQ ISSN 1815-6762) 7386
➤ Nafta (HRV ISSN 0027-755X) 6779
Nafta & Gaz Biznes (POL ISSN 1428-6564) 6779
Nafta - Gaz (POL ISSN 0867-8871) 6779
Naftika Chronika (GRC ISSN 0047-861X) 8654
Naftiliaki (GRC) 8654
Naftoprodukty (UKR) 6779
Naftova i Hazova Promyslovist' (UKR ISSN 0548-1414) 8432
➤ Nag Hammadi and Manichaean Studies (NLD ISSN 0929-2470) 7705
● Naga (MYS ISSN 0116-290X) 957
Nagaland Times (IND) 3885

Title

▼ *new title* † *ceased* ● *electronic media* ➤ *refereed*

Nagano Association of Occupational Therapists. Journal *see* Naganoken Sagyo Ryohoshikai Gakujutsushi **6681**
Nagano-ken Toseki Kenkyukaishi/Nagano Prefectural Society of Dialysis Therapy. Journal (JPN ISSN 1346-0005) **6271**
Nagano Prefectural Society of Dialysis Therapy. Journal *see* Nagano-ken Toseki Kenkyukaishi **6271**
Nagano Prefecture. Monthly Report Meteorology *see* Naganoken Kisho Geppo **6391**
Naganoken Kisho Geppo/Nagano Prefecture. Monthly Report Meteorology (JPN ISSN 0916-5185) **6391**
Naganoken Sagyo Ryohoshikai Gakujutsushi/ Nagano Association of Occupational Therapists. Journal (JPN ISSN 0917-3617) **6681**
Naganoken Sanka Fujinka Ikaiho/Gynecological Society of Nagano. Bulletin (JPN) **5999**
Naganoken Shokubutsu Kenkyukaishi/Botanical Society of Nagano. Bulletin (JPN ISSN 0385-9916) **803**
Nagaoka College of Technology. Research Reports/Nagaoka Kogyo Koto Senmon Gakko Kenkyu Kiyo (JPN ISSN 0027-7568) **3211**
Nagaoka Kogyo Koto Senmon Gakko Kenkyu Kiyo *see* Nagaoka College of Technology. Research Reports **3211**
Nagaoka Municipal Science Museum. Bulletin *see* Nagaoka-shiritsu Kagaku Hakubutsukan Kenkyu Hokoku **7885**
Nagaoka-shiritsu Kagaku Hakubutsukan Kenkyu Hokoku/Nagaoka Municipal Science Museum. Bulletin (JPN ISSN 0285-6085) **7885**
Nagar Tarun Bharat (IND) **3885**
Nagare/Japan Society of Fluid Mechanics. Journal (JPN ISSN 0286-3154) **3363**
Nagare no Keisoku/Association for the Study of Flow Measurements of Japan. Journal (JPN ISSN 0916-1546) **6404**
Nagare no Keisoku Oosaka Shinpojumu Koen Yoshishu/Proceedings of the Osaka Symposium on Flow Measuring Techniques (JPN) **6404**
Nagarlok (IND ISSN 0027-7584) **7499**
Nagasaki Biological Society. Transactions *see* Nagasakiken Seibutsu Gakkaishi **691**
Nagasaki Daigaku Kogakubu Kenkyu Hokoku/Nagasaki University. Faculty of Engineering. Reports (JPN ISSN 0286-0902) **3211**
Nagasaki Daigaku Kyoiku Gakubu Kiyo. Shizen Kagaku/Nagasaki University. Faculty of Education. Bulletin: Natural Science. (JPN ISSN 1345-1359) **7885**
Nagasaki Daigaku Kyoyobu Kiyo. Shizen Kagaku Hen/Nagasaki University. Faculty of Liberal Arts. Bulletin (JPN ISSN 0287-1319) **7885**
Nagasaki Daigaku Suisangakubu. Kenkyu Hokoku/Nagasaki University. Faculty of Fisheries. Bulletin (JPN ISSN 0547-1427) **691**
Nagasaki Earth Science Association. Journal *see* Nagasakiken Chigakkaishi **2713**
➤ Nagasaki Igakkai Zasshi/Nagasaki Medical Journal (JPN ISSN 0369-3228) **5682**
Nagasaki Kaiyo Kishodai. Kaiyo Sokuho/Nagasaki Marine Observatory. Oceanographic Prompt Report (JPN) **2813**
Nagasaki-ken Suisan Shikenjo. Kenkyu Hokoku/Nagasaki Prefectural Institute of Fisheries. Bulletin (JPN ISSN 0388-8401) **3602**
Nagasaki Marine Observatory. Oceanographic Prompt Report *see* Nagasaki Kaiyo Kishodai. Kaiyo Sokuho **2813**
Nagasaki Medical Journal *see* Nagasaki Igakkai Zasshi **5682**
Nagasaki Prefectural Institute of Fisheries. Bulletin *see* Nagasaki-ken Suisan Shikenjo. Kenkyu Hokoku **3602**
Nagasaki Prefecture. Monthly Report of Meteorology *see* Nagasakiken Kisho Geppo **6392**
Nagasaki University. Faculty of Education. Bulletin: Natural Science. *see* Nagasaki Daigaku Kyoiku Gakubu Kiyo. Shizen Kagaku **7885**
Nagasaki University. Faculty of Engineering. Reports *see* Nagasaki Daigaku Kogakubu Kenkyu Hokoku **3211**
Nagasaki University. Faculty of Fisheries. Bulletin *see* Nagasaki Daigaku Suisangakubu. Kenkyu Hokoku **691**
Nagasaki University. Faculty of Liberal Arts. Bulletin *see* Nagasaki Daigaku Kyoyobu Kiyo. Shizen Kagaku Hen **7885**
Nagasakiken Chigakkaishi/Nagasaki Earth Science Association. Journal (JPN ISSN 0386-8559) **2713**
Nagasakiken Kisho Geppo/Nagasaki Prefecture. Monthly Report of Meteorology (JPN ISSN 0916-5312) **6392**
Nagasakiken Seibutsu Gakkaishi/Nagasaki Biological Society. Transactions (JPN ISSN 0387-4249) **691**
Nagelmanns Blaetter zum Lernen (DEU ISSN 1614-6972) **4738**
Nager Sauver (FRA ISSN 1141-1872) **8189**
Nagoya City Environmental Science Research Institute. Annual Report *see* Nagoyashi Kankyo Kagaku Kenkyujoho **3454**
Nagoya City University. Institute of Natural Sciences. Annual Review (Year) (JPN ISSN 1342-9329) **7885**
Nagoya City University. Medical Association. Journal *see* Nagoya Shiritsu Daigaku Igakkai Zasshi **5682**
Nagoya Daigaku Bungakubu Kenkyu Ronshu/Nagoya University. Faculty of Literature. Journal (History)/Nagoya University. Faculty of Literature. Journal (Literature)/Nagoya University. Faculty of Literature. Journal (Philosophy) (JPN ISSN 0469-4716) **5337**
Nagoya Daigaku Denshi Kogaku Kenkyu no Ayumi/Progress in Electron Optics Research (JPN) **7081**
Nagoya Daigaku Hakubusukan Hokoku/Nagoya University Museum. Bulletin (JPN) **6533**
Nagoya Daigaku Kankyo Igaku Kenkyujo Nenpo/Nagoya University. Research Institute of Environmental Medicine. Annual Report (JPN ISSN 0369-3570) **5682**
Nagoya Daigaku Kogakubu Kiyo *see* Nagoya University. School of Engineering. Memoirs **3211**
Nagoya Daigaku Suiken Kagaku Kenkyujo Nenpo/Nagoya University. Water Research Institute. Annual Report (JPN) **8829**
Nagoya Daigaku Uchusan Kenkyushitsu Kiji *see* Meidai Uchusan Kenkyushitsu Kiji **7026**
Nagoya Data of Aeronautical Meteorology *see* Nagoya Koku Kishohyo **6392**
Nagoya Economics University and Ichimura Gakuen Junior College. Natural Scientific Society. Journal *see* Nagoya Keizai Daigaku, Ichimura Gakuen Tanki Daigaku Shizen Kagaku Kenkyukai Kaishi **7885**
Nagoya Entomological Society. Journal *see* Kakocho **853**
Nagoya Institute of Technology. Bulletin *see* Nagoya Kogyo Daigaku Kiyo **3211**
Nagoya Joshi Daigaku Kiyo. Jinbun, Shakai-hen/Nagoya Women's University. Journal. Humanities, Social Science (JPN ISSN 0915-2261) **4465**
Nagoya Joshi Daigaku Kiyo. Kasei, Shizen-hen/Nagoya Women's University. Journal. Home Economics, Natural Science (JPN ISSN 0915-3098) **4364**
Nagoya Journal of Medical Science (JPN ISSN 0027-7622) **5682**
Nagoya Keizai Daigaku, Ichimura Gakuen Tanki Daigaku Shizen Kagaku Kenkyukai Kaishi/Nagoya Economics University and Ichimura Gakuen Junior College. Natural Scientific Society. Journal (JPN ISSN 0285-4538) **7885**
Nagoya Kogyo Daigaku Kiyo/Nagoya Institute of Technology. Bulletin (JPN ISSN 0918-595X) **3211**
Nagoya Kogyo Gijutsu Kenkyujo Hokoku/National Industrial Research Institute of Nagoya. Reports (JPN ISSN 1340-3729) **8432**
Nagoya Koku Kishohyo/Nagoya Data of Aeronautical Meteorology (JPN) **6392**
Nagoya Konchu Dokokai Renraku Geppo/N A P I News (JPN) **855**
● ➤ Nagoya Mathematical Journal/Nagoya Sugaku Zasshi (JPN ISSN 0027-7630) **5519**
➤ Nagoya Medical Journal (JPN ISSN 0027-7649) **5682**
Nagoya Port Statistics Annual/Nagoyako Tokei Nenpo (JPN ISSN 0469-4783) **8527**
Nagoya Port Statistics Monthly *see* Nagoyako Tokei Sokuho **8527**
➤ Nagoya Shiritsu Daigaku Igakkai Zasshi/Nagoya City University. Medical Association. Journal (JPN ISSN 0027-7606) **5682**
Nagoya Sugaku Zasshi *see* Nagoya Mathematical Journal **5519**
Nagoya University. Faculty of Literature. Journal (History) *see* Nagoya Daigaku Bungakubu Kenkyu Ronshu **5337**
Nagoya University. Faculty of Literature. Journal (Literature) *see* Nagoya Daigaku Bungakubu Kenkyu Ronshu **5337**
Nagoya University. Faculty of Literature. Journal (Philosophy) *see* Nagoya Daigaku Bungakubu Kenkyu Ronshu **5337**
Nagoya University. Journal of Earth and Planetary Sciences (JPN ISSN 0919-875X) **578**
Nagoya University Museum. Bulletin *see* Nagoya Daigaku Hakubusukan Hokoku **6533**
Nagoya University. Research Institute of Environmental Medicine. Annual Report *see* Nagoya Daigaku Kankyo Igaku Kenkyujo Nenpo **5682**
Nagoya University. School of Engineering. Memoirs/Nagoya Daigaku Kogakubu Kiyo (JPN ISSN 0919-0805) **3211**
Nagoya University. Solar-Terrestrial Environment Laboratory. Cosmic Ray Section. Proceedings *see* Meidai Uchusan Kenkyushitsu Kiji **7026**
Nagoya University. Water Research Institute. Annual Report *see* Nagoya Daigaku Suiken Kagaku Kenkyujo Nenpo **8829**
Nagoya University. Water Research Institute. Publication List (JPN) **2813**
Nagoya Women's University. Journal. Home Economics, Natural Science *see* Nagoya Joshi Daigaku Kiyo. Kasei, Shizen-hen **4364**
Nagoya Women's University. Journal. Humanities, Social Science *see* Nagoya Joshi Daigaku Kiyo. Jinbun, Shakai-hen **4465**
Nagoyako Tokei Nenpo *see* Nagoya Port Statistics Annual **8527**
Nagoyako Tokei Sokuho/Nagoya Port Statistics Monthly (JPN) **8527**
Nagoyashi Kankyo Kagaku Kenkyujoho/Nagoya City Environmental Science Research Institute. Annual Report (JPN ISSN 0919-8032) **3454**
Nagyvilag (HUN ISSN 0547-1613) **5337**
Nah und Frisch (AUT) **3657**
● An-Nahar (LBN ISSN 0378-8253) **3905**
Nahar al Chabab *see* An- Nahar **3905**
Nahar al-Shabab *see* An- Nahar **3905**
▼ ● ➤ Naharaim (DEU ISSN 1862-9148) **5338**
Nahost Jahrbuch (DEU ISSN 0935-1051) **557**
● Die Nahrungs- und Genussmittel-Industrie und Ihre Helfer/Food and Beverage Industry and Its Suppliers (DEU) **3657**
Nahrungsmittel & Getraenke (AUT) **3657**
● The Nahua Newsletter (USA ISSN 1066-0089) **6635**
Der Nahverkehr (DEU ISSN 0722-8287) **8505**
Nahverkehrs Nachrichten (DEU ISSN 0179-504X) **8505**
Nahverkehrs-Praxis (DEU ISSN 0342-9849) **8505**
Nahverkehrs-Taschenbuch. Berater, Industrie, Lieferanten (DEU ISSN 1436-3739) **8505**
Nahverkehrs-Taschenbuch. Verkehrsunternehmen, Verkehrsorganisation, Verbaende, Behoerden, Wissenschaft (DEU ISSN 1436-3720) **8505**
Nahverkehrs-Taschenbuch. Wer, Was, Wo im Nahverkehr (DEU ISSN 1436-3747) **8505**
➤ Naibunpi Geka/Endocrine Surgery (JPN ISSN 0914-9953) **5898**
Naibunpi, Tonyobyoka (JPN ISSN 1341-3724) **5898**
Naidunia (IND) **3886**
Naidunia Daily (Indore) (IND) **3886**
● Naihuo Cailiao (CHN ISSN 1001-1935) **6327**
Naika/Internal Medicine (Tokyo, 1958) (JPN ISSN 0022-1961) **5947**
Naiko Senpaku Meisaisho/Register of Ships (in Japanese Coastal Shipping Service) (JPN) **8654**
Nail News (GBR ISSN 1352-2639) **595**
Nail und Body Professionell (DEU ISSN 1613-6551) **590**
Nailing the New S A T (Scholastic Assessment Test) (USA ISSN 1933-6489) **2889**
Nailm News *see* N A I L M News **2243**
Nailpro (HUN ISSN 1788-1927) **595**
Nailpro (POL ISSN 1734-9664) **595**
Nailpro (USA ISSN 1049-4553) **595**
Nailpro Europe *see* Beauty Forum Nailpro **593**
● Nails (USA ISSN 0896-193X) **590**
Naimusho Doboku Shikenjo Hokoku *see* Doboku Kenkyujo Hokoku **3265**
Nainen Kikan/Internal Combustion Engine (JPN ISSN 0387-1142) **3390**
Nainen Kikan Godo Shinpojumu Koen Ronbunshu/Internal Combustion Engine Symposium. Proceedings (JPN) **3390**
Nairiku Ajia Gengo no Kenkyu/Studies on the Inner Asian Languages (JPN ISSN 1341-5670) **557**
The Nairobi Journal of Literature (KEN ISSN 1814-1706) **5338**
● ➤ Nairobi Law Monthly (KEN) **4738**
Naisten ja Miesten Yhtalaiset Mahdollisuuet Euroopan Unionissa *see* Equal Opportunities for Women and Men in the European Union **1680**
Naistutkimus/Kvinnoforskning (FIN ISSN 0784-3844) **8901**
Naito Museum. Semi-Annual Report *see* Kusuri Hakubutsukan Dayori **6858**
Naito Zaidan Jiho (JPN ISSN 0911-971X) **7885**
● Naj (POL ISSN 1232-7654) **8877**
Naj Poleca *see* Naj **8877**
Najaarsnota Financiele Ontwikkeling LISV-Fondsen *see* Oktobernota Financiele Ontwikkeling UWV-Fondsen **4517**
Najda Newsletter (USA) **8877**
Najlepsia Gazdinka (SVK ISSN 1336-9164) **4364**
Nakanune/On the Eve (RUS) **5338**
Nakayoshi *see* Nakayosi **2204**
Nakayosi (JPN) **2204**
Naked Magazine (USA) **4377**
● The Naked P C Newsletter (USA) **2578**
Naked! Screaming! Terror! (USA) **6508**
● NakedPoetry.com (USA) **5427**
Nakeeran *see* Nakkeeran **3886**
Nakkeeran (IND) **3886**
● Naku (NZL ISSN 1174-5703) **2661**
Nalk Report (JPN) **6327**
Nalle Puh (FIN ISSN 0359-1174) **2204**
Nalle Puh Magasinet *see* Disney's Nalle Puh Magasinet **2186**
Nalogi (RUS) **1935**
● Nalogi i Biznes (RUS ISSN 1606-1462) **1935**
Nalogi i Ekonomika (RUS) **1935**
Nalogovaya Politsiya (RUS) **1936**
Nalogovoe Planirovanie (RUS) **1936**
Nalogovye Izvestiya Moskovskogo Regiona (RUS) **1936**
● Nalogovyi i Bukhgalterskii Uchet (RUS) **1297**
● Nalogovyi Vestnik (RUS) **1936**
Nalu Underground (USA ISSN 1557-7953) **8323**
Namah-'i Utaq-i Bazargani (IRN ISSN 1024-3011) **1407**
➤ Namah-yi Anjuman-i Hasharahshinasan-i Iran/Journal of Entomological Society of Iran (IRN ISSN 0259-9996) **855**
Namah-yi Anjuman-i Hasharahshinasan-i Iran. Shumarah Fawq al-Adah *see* Namah-yi Anjuman-i Hasharahshinasan-i Iran **855**
Namari to Aen/Lead and Zinc (JPN ISSN 0027-772X) **6327**
● Namarupa (USA ISSN 1559-9817) **6935**
Namaskaar (IND) **8785**
Namaste *see* Yoga - Nytt **6648**
Namaste *see* Odyssey (Tokai) **6937**
Namdal Arbeiderblad (NOR) **3924**
Nameh-e Anjoman-e Hasharehshenasi-e Iran *see* Namah-yi Anjuman-i Hasharahshinasan-i Iran **855**
Nameh Sanaat-e-Naft *see* Iran Oil Journal **6775**
➤ Namenkundliche Informationen (DEU ISSN 0943-0849) **5154**
N'Amerind Friendship Centre. Newsletter (CAN ISSN 0845-8073) **3552**
● ➤ Names (GBR ISSN 0027-7738) **5154**
Names and Denominations *see* Namn og Nemne **5154**
Names of Persons (DEU) **5034**
Names Society of Southern Africa. Journal/Naamkundevereniging van Suider-Afrika. Tydskrif (ZAF) **5154**
Names Society of Southern Africa. Newsletter/Naamkundevereniging van Suider-Afrika. Nuusbrief (ZAF) **5154**
Nameste (GBR) **4465**
● Nami Jishu yu Jingmi Gongcheng/Nanotechnology and Precision Engineering (CHN ISSN 1672-6030) **3211**
Nami to Nagisa/Journal of Disaster Prevention of Harbours (JPN ISSN 0919-4304) **2227**
Namib Bulletin (NAM ISSN 0255-9544) **3454**
Namib Times (NAM ISSN 0027-7746) **3913**
Namibia Brief (NAM ISSN 1012-2818) **1601**
Namibia Business Climate Survey (NAM ISSN 1680-6603) **1500**
Namibia Development Briefing (NAM ISSN 0963-8229) **1601**
● Namibia Development Journal (NAM ISSN 1995-4735) **1500**
● Namibia Economist (NAM ISSN 1028-9143) **1151**
Namibia Handbook (GBR ISSN 1363-7495) **8739**
● Namibia Holiday and Travel (NAM ISSN 1028-0820) **8740**
▼ ● Namibia Mining Report (GBR ISSN 1755-7852) **6474**
Namibia Scientific Society. Journal (NAM ISSN 1018-7677) **7885**
Namibia Scientific Society. Newsletter/Namibia Wissenschaftliche Gesellschaft. Mitteilungen (NAM ISSN 1018-7685) **7885**
● Namibia Trade Directory (NAM ISSN 1028-0839) **2018**
Namibia Wissenschaftliche Gesellschaft. Mitteilungen *see* Namibia Scientific Society. Newsletter **7885**
● The Namibian (NAM ISSN 1560-6023) **3913**
● Namibian Law Reports (ZAF ISSN 1024-6991) **4738**
Namibian Top Companies (ZAF ISSN 1998-7153) **2018**
Namibiana (NAM ISSN 0259-2010) **4176**
Namn och Bygd (SWE ISSN 0077-2704) **5154**
Namn og Nemne/Names and Denominations (NOR ISSN 0800-4684) **5154**
NAMNEWS *see* N A M News **3680**
Namo Buddha Newsletter (USA) **7702**
Namoi C M A Annual Report (Catchment Management Authority) (AUS ISSN 1833-1084) **3454**
Namoi Catchment Management Authority Annual Report *see* Namoi C M A Annual Report **3454**
Nan Daxue Bao (Jiaoyu Lei)/National University Tainan. Journal (Education) *see* Jiaoyu Yanjiu Xuebao **2873**
Nan Daxue Bao (Renwen yu Shehui Lei)/National University Tainan. Journal (Humanities & Social Science) *see* Renwen Yanjiu Xuebao **4472**
Nan Daxue Bao (Shuli yu Kexue Lei)/National University Tainan. Journal (Mathematics, Science & Technology) *see* Ligong Yanjiu Xuebao **7880**
● Nan Feng Chuang/South Wind Through Window (CHN ISSN 1004-0641) **7254**
● ➤ Nan Nu (NLD ISSN 1387-6805) **557**
Nan Pei Chi *see* The Perspective **3875**
Nan-Shi Xuebao (Jiaoyu Lei)/National Tainan Teachers College. Journal (Education) *see* Jiaoyu Yanjiu Xuebao **2873**
Nan-Shi Xuebao (Renwen yu Shehui Lei)/National Tainan Teachers College. Journal (Humanities & Social Science) *see* Renwen Yanjiu Xuebao **4472**
Nan-Shi Xuebao (Shuli yu Kexue Lei)/National Tainan Teachers College. Journal (Mathematics, Science & Technology) *see* Ligong Yanjiu Xuebao **7880**
NaNa *see* Nahverkehrs Nachrichten **8505**
Nana Film Weekly (IND) **6508**
Nanaimo Daily Free Press *see* Daily News (Nanaimo) **3808**
Nanak Prakash Patrika (IND ISSN 0027-7770) **7707**
Nanayam Vikatan (IND) **1151**
Nanchang College of Education. Journal *see* Nanchang Jiaoyu Xueyuan Xuebao **2889**
Nanchang College of Water Conservancy and Hydroelectric Power *see* Nanchang Shuizhan Xuebao **3163**
● ➤ Nanchang Daxue Xuebao (Gongke Ban)/Nanchang University. Journal (Engineering Technology) (CHN ISSN 1006-0456) **8432**
● Nanchang Daxue Xuebao (Like Ban)/Nanchang University. Journal (Natural Sciences Edition) (CHN ISSN 1006-0464) **7885**

• Nanchang Daxue Xuebao (Shehui Kexue Ban)/Nanchang University. Journal (Humanities and Social Sciences) (CHN ISSN 1006-0448) **4465**
• Nanchang Gao-Zhuan Xuebao/Nanchang Junior College. Journal (CHN ISSN 1008-7354) **2889**
Nanchang Hangkong Gongye Xueyuan Xuebao *see* Nanchang Hangkong Gongye Xueyuan Xuebao (Ziran Kexue Ban) **7885**
• Nanchang Hangkong Gongye Xueyuan Xuebao (Shehui Kexue Ban)/Nanchang Institute of Aeronautical Technology. Journal (Social Science Edition) (CHN ISSN 1009-1912) **7987**
• Nanchang Hangkong Gongye Xueyuan Xuebao (Ziran Kexue Ban)/Nanchang Institute of Aeronautical Technology. Journal (Natural Sciences) (CHN) **7885**
Nanchang Institute of Aeronautical Technology. Journal (Natural Sciences) *see* Nanchang Hangkong Gongye Xueyuan Xuebao (Ziran Kexue Ban) **7885**
Nanchang Institute of Aeronautical Technology. Journal (Social Science Edition) *see* Nanchang Hangkong Gongye Xueyuan Xuebao (Shehui Kexue Ban) **7987**
• Nanchang Jiaoyu Xueyuan Xuebao/Nanchang College of Education. Journal (CHN ISSN 1008-6757) **2889**
Nanchang Junior College. Journal *see* Nanchang Gao-Zhuan Xuebao **2889**
• Nanchang Shuizhan Xuebao/Nanchang College of Water Conservancy and Hydroelectric Power (CHN ISSN 1006-4869) **3163**
Nanchang University. Journal (Engineering Technology) *see* Nanchang Daxue Xuebao (Gongke Ban) **8432**
Nanchang University. Journal (Humanities and Social Sciences) *see* Nanchang Daxue Xuebao (Shehui Kexue Ban) **4465**
Nanchang University. Journal (Natural Sciences Edition) *see* Nanchang Daxue Xuebao (Like Ban) **7885**
Nanchang Zhiye Daxue Xuebao *see* Nanchang Gao-Zhuan Xuebao **2889**
Nancy's Magazine (USA ISSN 0895-7576) **4466**
Nandan (IND) **2162**
Nandan Kanan (IND) **7707**
Nande Reko (PRY ISSN 1012-5507) **5338**
Nandu Xuetan (CHN ISSN 1002-6320) **4466**
▼ Nanfang Dianwang Jishu/Southern Power System Technology (CHN ISSN 1674-0629) **3160**
Nanfang Gangtie *see* Nanfang Jinshu **6327**
• Nanfang Guotu Ziyuan/Guangxi Geology (CHN ISSN 1672-321X) **2757**
• Nanfang Hangkong/Gateway (HKG ISSN 1004-7441) **8785**
Nanfang Huli Xuebao/Nanfang Journal of Nursing *see* Huli Xuebao **5960**
• Nanfang Jianzhu/South-China Architecture (CHN ISSN 1000-0232) **450**
• Nanfang Jinrong/South China Finance (CHN) **1369**
• Nanfang Jinshu/Southern Metals (CHN ISSN 1009-9700) **6327**
Nanfang Ribao/Southern Daily (CHN) **3826**
Nanfang Weekend Edition *see* Nanfang Zhoumo **3826**
• Nanfang Wentan/Southern Cultural Forum (CHN ISSN 1003-7772) **5338**
Nanfang Wenxue/South Literature (CHN ISSN 1002-3968) **5338**
Nanfang Zhoumo/Nanfang Weekend Edition (CHN) **3826**
Nanfeng/South Wind (CHN ISSN 0257-2885) **5338**
Nanhai Haiyang Kexue Jikan/Nanhai Studia Marina Sinica (CHN ISSN 1000-8624) **2813**
Nanhai Studia Marina Sinica *see* Nanhai Haiyang Kexue Jikan **2813**
Nanhua Daxue Xuebao (Ligongban)/Nanhua University. Journal (Science & Engineering Edition) *see* Nanhua Daxue Xuebao (Ziran Kexue Ban) **7885**
• Nanhua Daxue Xuebao (Shehui Kexue Ban)/Nanhua University. Social Journal (Social Science Edition) (CHN ISSN 1673-0755) **7987**
• Nanhua Daxue Xuebao (Yixue Ban)/Nanhua University. Journal (Medical Edition) (CHN ISSN 1672-7444) **5682**
• Nanhua Daxue Xuebao (Ziran Kexue Ban)/Nanhua University. Journal (Science & Technology) (CHN ISSN 1673-0062) **7885**
Nanhua General Education Research *see* Nanhua Tongshi Jiaoyu Yanjiu **2889**
• Nanhua Tongshi Jiaoyu Yanjiu/Nanhua General Education Research (TWN ISSN 1812-4356) **2889**
Nanhua University. Journal (Medical Edition) *see* Nanhua Daxue Xuebao (Yixue Ban) **5682**
Nanhua University. Journal (Science & Technology) *see* Nanhua Daxue Xuebao (Ziran Kexue Ban) **7885**
Nanhua University. Social Journal (Social Science Edition) *see* Nanhua Daxue Xuebao (Shehui Kexue Ban) **7987**
Nanji Yanjiu/South Pole Research (CHN ISSN 1000-4947) **2713**
Nanjing Agricultural University. Journal *see* Nanjing Nongye Daxue Xuebao **138**
Nanjing Agricultural University. Journal *see* Nanjing Nongye Daxue Xuebao (Shehui Kexue Ban) **7987**
Nanjing Architectural and Civil Engineering Institute. Journal *see* Nanjing Jianzhu Gongcheng Xueyuan Xuebao **450**
Nanjing Cai-Jing Daxue Xuebao/Nanjing University of Finance and Economics. Journal (CHN ISSN 1672-6049) **1151**
Nanjing College for Population Programme Management. Journal *see* Nanjing Renkou Guanli Ganbu Xueyuan Xuebao **7288**
• Nanjing Daxue Xuebao (Shuxue Banniankan) (CHN ISSN 1004-258X) **5519**
• ➤ Nanjing Daxue Xuebao (Zhexue Renwen Shehui Kexue)/Nanjing University. Journal (Philosophy, Humanities and Social Sciences) (CHN ISSN 1007-7278) **7885**
Nanjing Daxue Xuebao (Zhexue Shehui Kexue Ban) *see* Nanjing Daxue Xuebao (Zhexue Renwen Shehui Kexue) **7885**
Nanjing Daxue Xuebao (Ziran Kexue Ban)/Nanjing University. Journal (Natural Sciences) (CHN ISSN 0469-5097) **7886**
Nanjing Forestry University. Journal (Humanities and Social Sciences Edition) *see* Nanjing Linye Daxue Xuebao (Renwen Shehui Kexue Ban) **7987**
Nanjing Forestry University. Journal (Natural Science Edition) *see* Nanjing Linye Daxue Xuebao (Ziran Kexue Ban) **3697**
Nanjing Gongcheng Xueyuan Xuebao (Shehui Kexue Ban)/Nanjing Institute of Technology. Journal (Social Science Edition) (CHN) **7987**
• Nanjing Gongcheng Xueyuan Xuebao (Ziran Kexue Ban) (CHN ISSN 1672-2558) **7886**
Nanjing Gongye Daxue Xuebao (Shehui Kexue Ban)/Nanjing University of Technology. Journal (Social Science Edition) (CHN ISSN 1671-7287) **7987**
• Nanjing Gongye Daxue Xuebao (Ziran Kexue Ban)/Nanjing University of Technology. Journal (Natural Science Edition) (CHN ISSN 1671-7627) **3251**
• Nanjing Gongye Zhiye Jishu Xueyuan Xuebao/Nanjing Institute of Industry Technology. Journal (CHN ISSN 1671-4644) **7987**
• Nanjing Guangbo Dianshi Daxue Xuebao/Nanjing Radio & Television University. Journal (CHN ISSN 1009-1459) **2360**
• Nanjing Hangkong Hangtian Daxue Xuebao/Nanjing University of Aeronautics and Astronautics. Journal (CHN ISSN 1005-2615) **66**
Nanjing Huagong Daxue Xuebao/Nanjing University of Chemical Technology. Journal *see* Nanjing Gongye Daxue Xuebao (Ziran Kexue Ban) **3251**
Nanjing Institute of Industry Technology. Journal *see* Nanjing Gongye Zhiye Jishu Xueyuan Xuebao **7987**
Nanjing Institute of Technology. Journal (Social Science Edition) *see* Nanjing Gongcheng Xueyuan Xuebao (Shehui Kexue Ban) **7987**
Nanjing Institute of Traditional Chinese Medicine. Journal *see* Nanjing Zhongyi Xueyuan Xuebao **5682**
• Nanjing Jianzhu Gongcheng Xueyuan Xuebao/Nanjing Architectural and Civil Engineering Institute. Journal (CHN ISSN 1003-711X) **450**
• Nanjing Junyi Xueyuan Xuebao (CHN ISSN 1009-1874) **5682**
• Nanjing Ligong Daxue Xuebao/Nanjing University of Science and Technology. Journal (CHN ISSN 1005-9830) **3211**
Nanjing Ligong Daxue Xuebao (Shehui Kexue Ban)/Nanjing University of Science and Technology. Journal (Social Sciences Edition) (CHN ISSN 1008-2646) **7987**
Nanjing Linye Daxue Xuebao *see* Nanjing Linye Daxue Xuebao (Ziran Kexue Ban) **3697**
• Nanjing Linye Daxue Xuebao (Renwen Shehui Kexue Ban)/Nanjing Forestry University. Journal (Humanities and Social Sciences Edition) (CHN ISSN 1671-1165) **7987**
• Nanjing Linye Daxue Xuebao (Ziran Kexue Ban)/Nanjing Forestry University. Journal (Natural Science Edition) (CHN) **3697**
• Nanjing Medical University. Journal/Nanjing Yike Daxue Xuebao (Yinwen Ban) (CHN ISSN 1007-4376) **5682**
Nanjing Nong-Zhuan Xuebao/Nanjing Agricultural Technology College. Journal *see* Jinling Keji Xueyuan Xuebao (Shehui Kexue Ban) **7977**
• ➤ Nanjing Nongye Daxue Xuebao/Nanjing Agricultural University. Journal (CHN ISSN 1000-2030) **138**
• Nanjing Nongye Daxue Xuebao (Shehui Kexue Ban)/Nanjing Agricultural University. Journal (CHN ISSN 1671-7465) **7987**
Nanjing Normal University. Journal (Engineering and Technology) *see* Nanjing Shifan Daxue Xuebao (Gongcheng Jishu Ban) **3211**
Nanjing Normal University. Journal (Natural Science Edition) *see* Nanjing Shi-Daxue Bao (Ziran Kexue Ban) **7886**
Nanjing Normal University. Journal (Social Science Edition) *see* Nanjing Shi-Daxue Bao (Shehui Kexue Ban) **7987**
Nanjing Qixiang Xueyuan Xuebao/Nanjing Institute of Meteorology. Journal *see* Nanjing Xinxi Gongcheng Daxue Xuebao **6392**
Nanjing Radio & Television University. Journal *see* Nanjing Guangbo Dianshi Daxue Xuebao **2360**
• Nanjing Renkou Guanli Ganbu Xueyuan Xuebao/Nanjing College for Population Programme Management. Journal (CHN ISSN 1007-032X) **7288**
• Nanjing Shehui Kexue/Social Sciences in Nanjing (CHN ISSN 1001-8263) **7987**
• Nanjing Shi-Daxue Bao (Shehui Kexue Ban)/Nanjing Normal University. Journal (Social Science Edition) (CHN ISSN 1001-4608) **7987**
• Nanjing Shi-Daxue Bao (Ziran Kexue Ban)/Nanjing Normal University. Journal (Natural Science Edition) (CHN ISSN 1001-4616) **7886**
• Nanjing Shifan Daxue Xuebao (Gongcheng Jishu Ban)/Nanjing Normal University. Journal (Engineering and Technology) (CHN ISSN 1672-1292) **3211**
Nanjing Tiedao Yixueyuan Xuebao *see* Dongnan Daxue Xuebao (Yixue Ban) **5606**
Nanjing University. Journal (Natural Sciences) *see* Nanjing Daxue Xuebao (Ziran Kexue Ban) **7886**
Nanjing University. Journal (Philosophy, Humanities and Social Sciences) *see* Nanjing Daxue Xuebao (Zhexue Renwen Shehui Kexue) **7885**
Nanjing University. Journal. Mathematical Biquarterly *see* Nanjing Daxue Xuebao (Shuxue Banniankan) **5519**
Nanjing University of Aeronautics and Astronautics. Journal *see* Nanjing Hangkong Hangtian Daxue Xuebao **66**
Nanjing University of Aeronautics and Astronautics. Transactions (CHN ISSN 1005-1120) **66**
Nanjing University of Finance and Economics. Journal *see* Nanjing Cai-Jing Daxue Xuebao **1151**
Nanjing University of Information Science & Technology. Journal *see* Nanjing Xinxi Gongcheng Daxue Xuebao **6392**
Nanjing University of Posts and Telecommunications. Journal (Natural Science) *see* Nanjing Youdian Daxue Xuebao (Ziran Kexue Ban) **7886**
Nanjing University of Posts and Telecommunications. Journal (Social Science) *see* Nanjing Youdian Daxue Xuebao (Shehui Kexue Ban) **2334**
Nanjing University of Science and Technology. Journal *see* Nanjing Ligong Daxue Xuebao **3211**
Nanjing University of Science and Technology. Journal (Social Sciences Edition) *see* Nanjing Ligong Daxue Xuebao (Shehui Kexue Ban) **7987**
Nanjing University of Technology. Journal (Natural Science Edition) *see* Nanjing Gongye Daxue Xuebao (Ziran Kexue Ban) **3251**
Nanjing University of Technology. Journal (Social Science Edition) *see* Nanjing Gongye Daxue Xuebao (Shehui Kexue Ban) **7987**
Nanjing University of Traditional Chinese Medicine. Journal (Social Science) *see* Nanjing Zhongyiyao Daxue Xuebao (Shehui Kexue Ban) **7987**
• Nanjing Xinxi Gongcheng Daxue Xuebao/Nanjing University of Information Science & Technology. Journal (CHN) **6392**
• Nanjing Yike Daxue Xuebao (Shehui Kexue Ban)/Acta Universitatis Medicinalis Nanjing (Social Science) (CHN ISSN 1671-0479) **7987**
Nanjing Yike Daxue Xuebao (Yinwen Ban) *see* Nanjing Medical University. Journal **5682**
• Nanjing Yike Daxue Xuebao (Ziran Kexue Ban)/Acta Universitatis Medicinalis Nanjing (CHN ISSN 1007-4368) **5682**
• Nanjing Youdian Daxue Xuebao (Shehui Kexue Ban)/Nanjing University of Posts and Telecommunications. Journal (Social Science) (CHN ISSN 1673-5420) **2334**
• Nanjing Youdian Daxue Xuebao (Ziran Kexue Ban)/Nanjing University of Posts and Telecommunications. Journal (Natural Science) (CHN ISSN 1673-5439) **7886**
Nanjing Youdian Xueyuan Xuebao (Shehui Kexue Ban) *see* Nanjing Youdian Daxue Xuebao (Shehui Kexue Ban) **2334**
Nanjing Youdian Xueyuan Xuebao (Ziran Kexue Ban) *see* Nanjing Youdian Daxue Xuebao (Ziran Kexue Ban) **7886**
• ➤ Nanjing Zhongyi Xueyuan Xuebao/Nanjing Institute of Traditional Chinese Medicine. Journal (CHN ISSN 1000-5005) **5682**
• Nanjing Zhongyiyao Daxue Xuebao (Shehui Kexue Ban)/Nanjing University of Traditional Chinese Medicine. Journal (Social Science) (CHN ISSN 1009-3222) **7987**
▼ • ➤ Nankai Business Review International (GBR ISSN 2040-8749) **1780**
• Nankai Daxue Xuebao/Acta Scientiarum Naturalium Universitatis Nankaiensis (Natural Science Edition) (CHN ISSN 0465-7942) **7886**
Nankai Economic Studies *see* Nankai Jingji Yanjiu **1152**
• Nankai Jingji Yanjiu/Nankai Economic Studies (CHN ISSN 1001-4691) **1152**
Nankai Lectures on Mathematical Physics (SGP) **5519**
Nankai Series in Pure, Applied Mathematics and Theoretical Physics (SGP) **5519**
Nankai Tracts in Mathematics (SGP ISSN 1793-1118) **5519**
Nankai University. Journal. Philosophy and Social Sciences Edition *see* Nankai Xuebao. Zhexue Shehui Kexue Ban **7987**
• Nankai Xuebao. Zhexue Shehui Kexue Ban/Nankai University. Journal. Philosophy and Social Sciences Edition (CHN ISSN 1001-4667) **7987**
Nanke Xuebao/Acta Andrologica Sinica *see* Zhonghua Nankexue **6285**
Nanki Biological Society. News *see* Kuroshio (Wakayamaken) **686**
Nanki Seibutsu (JPN ISSN 0389-7842) **691**
Nanki Seibutsukaiho/Nanki Biological Society. News *see* Kuroshio (Wakayamaken) **686**
➤ Nankyoku Shiryo/Antarctic Record (JPN ISSN 0085-7289) **4020**
Nanmin Zazhi (CHE ISSN 1014-5389) **7254**
Nanning Polytechnic. Journal *see* Nanning Zhiye Jishu Xueyuan Xuebao **7987**
• Nanning Shifan Gaodeng Zhuanke Xuexiao Xuebao/Nanning Teachers College. Journal (CHN ISSN 1008-696X) **2889**
Nanning Teachers College. Journal *see* Nanning Shifan Gaodeng Zhuanke Xuexiao Xuebao **2889**
• Nanning Zhiye Jishu Xueyuan Xuebao/Nanning Polytechnic. Journal (CHN ISSN 1009-3621) **7987**
Nanny Fanny (USA ISSN 1529-434X) **5427**
▼ • Nano (GBR ISSN 1757-2517) **3211**
• ➤ Nano (SGP ISSN 1793-2920) **3211**
• ➤ Nano-Express (USA) **7027**
• ➤ Nano Letters (USA ISSN 1530-6984) **3355**
▼ • ➤ Nano Research (CHN ISSN 1998-0124) **768**
• ➤ Nano Today (GBR ISSN 1748-0132) **750**
• ➤ NanoBioTechnology (USA ISSN 1551-1286) **768**
Nanoelektronik (DEU ISSN 1616-5802) **3326**
▼ • ➤ NanoEthics (NLD ISSN 1871-4757) **8432**
▼ • Nanograms (USA ISSN 1941-2576) **5940**
• Nanomaterials News (GBR) **6712**
Nanomechanics Science and Technology *see* International Journal of Nanomechanics Science and Technology **3202**
• ➤ Nanomedicine (GBR ISSN 1743-5889) **5683**
• ➤ Nanomedicine: Nanotechnology, Biology and Medicine (USA ISSN 1549-9634) **5683**
Nanonow *see* Nano **3211**
• ➤ Nanopages (HUN ISSN 1787-4033) **7027**
• Nanoparticle News (USA ISSN 1528-8528) **7027**
• Nanoparticle Technology News (USA) **3212**
• nanoRISK (USA ISSN 1931-6941) **8432**
• NanoS (DEU ISSN 1614-7847) **7027**
▼ • ➤ Nanoscale (GBR ISSN 2040-3364) **2074**
• Nanoscale & Microscale Thermophysical Engineering (Online) (USA ISSN 1556-7273) **7056**
• ➤ Nanoscale & Microscale Thermophysical Engineering (Print) (USA ISSN 1556-7265) **7056**
• Nanoscale Research Letters (USA ISSN 1931-7573) **2074**
• Nanoscience (USA ISSN 1555-4880) **8433**
▼ • Nanoscience and Applications (USA ISSN 1935-7532) **3212**
▼ • ➤ Nanoscience and Nanotechnology Letters (USA ISSN 1941-4900) **3326**
➤ Nanosystemy, Nanomaterialy, Nanotekhnolohii (UKR ISSN 1816-5230) **7027**
• Nanotech Alert (USA ISSN 1524-3613) **8433**
• Nanotech Business Update (USA ISSN 1541-7611) **1780**
† Nanotech-Report (DEU ISSN 1611-7611) **8976**
• Nanotechnologies in Russia (RUS ISSN 1995-0780) **7027**
• ➤ Nanotechnology (GBR ISSN 0957-4484) **7027**
Nanotechnology & MEMS Industry Almanac *see* Plunkett's Nanotechnology & M E M S Industry Almanac **3327**
Nanotechnology and Precision Engineering *see* Nami Jishu yu Jingmi Gongcheng **3211**
▼ • Nanotechnology Business Journal (USA ISSN 1945-8231) **7027**
• Nanotechnology in Paper & Packaging News (GBR) **6712**
• Nanotechnology Law & Business (USA ISSN 1546-203X) **4738**
Nanotechnology Perceptions (CHE ISSN 1660-6795) **7027**
▼ • Nanotechnology Research Journal (USA ISSN 1935-2484) **7027**
▼ • ➤ Nanotechnology, Science and Applications (GBR ISSN 1177-8903) **7027**
▼ • Nanotechnology Weekly (USA ISSN 1944-2483) **768**
• Nanotoxicology (GBR ISSN 1743-5404) **6203**
• Nanping Shi-Zhuan Xuebao/Nanping Teachers College. Journal (CHN ISSN 1008-5963) **2889**
Nanping Teachers College. Journal *see* Nanping Shi-Zhuan Xuebao **2889**
• Nanrenzhuang/F H M (Beijing) (CHN ISSN 1672-8378) **6296**
• Nansen News (NOR) **7254**
Nansen Remote Sensing Center. Technical Report/Nansen Senter for Miljoe og Fjernmaaling. Teknisk Rapport (NOR ISSN 0802-9601) **2713**
Nansen Senter for Miljoe og Fjernmaaling. Teknisk Rapport *see* Nansen Remote Sensing Center. Technical Report **2713**
Nansenskolen. Skriftserie (NOR ISSN 1502-3524) **3924**
Nantahala *see* Nantahala Review **5338**
• Nantahala Review (USA) **5338**

Title

10644 NANTO BUKKYO ULRICH'S PERIODICALS

Nanto Bukkyo/Nanto Society for Buddhist Studies (JPN ISSN 0547-2032) **7702**
Nanto Society for Buddhist Studies *see* Nanto Bukkyo **7702**
• Nantong Daxue Xuebao (Jiaoyu Kexue Ban)/Nantong University. Journal (Education Sciences Edition) (CHN) **2889**
• Nantong Daxue Xuebao (Shehui Kexue Ban)/Nantong University. Journal (Social Science Edition) (CHN ISSN 1673-2359) **7987**
• Nantong Daxue Xuebao (Yixue Ban)/Nantong University. Journal (Medical Sciences) (CHN) **5683**
• Nantong Daxue Xuebao (Ziran Kexue Ban) (CHN ISSN 1673-2340) **7886**
• Nantong Fangzhi Zhiye Jishu Xueyuan Xuebao/Nantong Textile Vocational Technology College. Journal (CHN ISSN 1671-6191) **7987**
Nantong Gongxueyuan Xuebao (Ziran Kexue Ban)/Nantong Institute of Technology. Journal (Natural Science) *see* Nantong Daxue Xuebao (Ziran Kexue Ban) **7886**
Nantong Gongxueyuan Xuebao/Nantong Institute of Technology. Journal *see* Nantong Daxue Xuebao (Jiaoyu Kexue Ban) **2889**
Nantong Textile Vocational Technology College. Journal *see* Nantong Fangzhi Zhiye Jishu Xueyuan Xuebao **7987**
Nantong University. Journal (Education Sciences Edition) *see* Nantong Daxue Xuebao (Jiaoyu Kexue Ban) **2889**
Nantong University. Journal (Medical Sciences) *see* Nantong Daxue Xuebao (Yixue Ban) **5683**
Nantong University. Journal (Social Science Edition) *see* Nantong Daxue Xuebao (Shehui Kexue Ban) **7987**
Nantong Vocational College. Journal *see* Nantong Zhiye Daxue Xuebao **6701**
Nantong Zhiye Daxue Xuebao/Nantong Vocational College. Journal (CHN ISSN 1008-5327) **6701**
▼ Nantucket Island Living (USA) **7601**
• Nanya Yanjiu Jikan/South Asian Studies Quarterly (CHN ISSN 1004-1508) **557**
Nanyang Business News *see* Nanyang Siang Pau **3907**
Nanyang Shifan Xueyuan Xuebao (CHN ISSN 1671-6132) **7886**
• Nanyang Siang Pau/Nanyang Business News (MYS) **3907**
Nanyang Technological University Library Bulletin *see* N T U Library Bulletin **5033**
• Nanyang Wenti Yanjiu/Southeast Asian Studies (CHN ISSN 1003-9856) **557**
• Nanyang Ziliao Yicong/Southeast Asian Translation Data (CHN) **557**
Nan'yo Biological Society. Reports *see* Nan'yo Seibutsu **691**
Nan'yo Seibutsu/Nan'yo Biological Society. Reports (JPN ISSN 0912-0114) **691**
Nanzan Anthropological Institute Newsletter (JPN) **349**
Nanzan Daigaku Nihon Bunka Gakka Ronshuu/Nanzan Studies on Japanese Language and Culture (JPN ISSN 1346-387X) **5338**
Nanzan Institute for Religion and Culture. Bulletin (JPN ISSN 0386-720X) **7664**
Nanzan Institute for Social Ethics Monograph Series (JPN) **6935**
Nanzan Journal of Economic Studies *see* Nanzan Keizai Kenkyu **1152**
Nanzan Journal of Theological Studies (JPN ISSN 0387-3730) **7665**
Nanzan Keiei Kenkyu/Nanzan Management Review (JPN ISSN 0912-6147) **1780**
Nanzan Keizai Kenkyu/Nanzan Journal of Economic Studies (JPN ISSN 0912-6139) **1152**
Nanzan Kokubun Ronshu *see* Nanzan Daigaku Nihon Bunka Gakka Ronshuu **5338**
Nanzan Law Review (JPN ISSN 0387-1592) **4738**
• Nanzan Linguistics (JPN) **5154**
Nanzan Management Review *see* Nanzan Keiei Kenkyu **1780**
Nanzan Review of American Studies (JPN ISSN 0288-3872) **4304**
Nanzan Shukyo Bunka Kenkyujo Kenkyujoho *see* Kenkyujoho **7658**
Nanzan Studies on Japanese Language and Culture *see* Nanzan Daigaku Nihon Bunka Gakka Ronshuu **5338**
Nanzan University. Centre for Australian Studies. Newsletter (JPN) **4193**
Nanzan University. Centre for Australian Studies. Reference Paper (JPN) **4193**
Nanzan University. Centre for Australian Studies. Working Paper (JPN) **4193**
Nanzan University. Centre for Latin American Studies. Working Paper (JPN) **4304**
• Nao yu Shenjing Jibing Zazhi/Journal of Brain and Nervous Disease (CHN ISSN 1006-351X) **6162**
▼ Naober (NLD ISSN 1874-6837) **3915**
Napa Sonoma (USA) **5077**
Napa Valley (USA ISSN 1541-3160) **4304**
The Naperville Glancer (USA ISSN 1937-5808) **5077**
NAPETCOR (NGA ISSN 0189-0050) **6779**
Napier University Business School. Working Paper Series (GBR ISSN 1460-0838) **1152**
▼ Napisane Zivotom (SVK ISSN 1803-3776) **4364**
Naples & Southern Italy *see* National Geographic Traveler. Naples & Southern Italy **8740**
Naples Dog (USA) **6811**
• Naples Guide (USA) **8740**
Naples Illustrated (USA ISSN 1099-6303) **3982**
Naplo (HUN ISSN 0133-2104) **3876**
• ➤ Napoleon (GBR ISSN 0027-7827) **4247**
Napoleon (USA) **4247**
Napoleon.org La Lettre *see* Napoleon.org The Bulletin **4247**
• Napoleon.org The Bulletin (FRA) **4247**
Napoleonic Society of America. Member's Bulletin (USA) **4342**
▼ • Napoleonica La Revue (FRA) **4247**
Napoli Nobilissima (ITA ISSN 0027-7835) **508**
NaPRA ReView *see* N A P R A ReView **6646**
Napravi Pauzu (SRB) **5077**
Napred (SRB ISSN 0027-7843) **3945**
Napredak (HRV ISSN 1330-0059) **2889**
➤ Naprstek Museum. Annals (CZE ISSN 0231-844X) **349**
Napsano Zivotem (CZE ISSN 1211-6505) **8877**
Naptural Roots (USA ISSN 1556-6714) **590**
Naqd (DNK ISSN 1399-8811) **5338**
Naqib-i Millat (PAK) **7156**
Nar & Fjarran *see* Naer och Fjaerran **8739**
Nar Nari (IND) **3886**
Nara Botany *see* Nara Shokubutsu Kenkyu **803**
Nara-e-Haq (PAK) **3926**
Nara Joshi Daigaku Hoken Kanri Senta Nenpo/Nara Women's University. Health Administration Center. Archives of Health Care (JPN ISSN 0287-9549) **7532**
Nara Kogyo Koto Senmon Gakko Kenkyu Kiyo/Nara National College of Technology. Research Reports (JPN ISSN 0387-1150) **8433**
Nara Kyoiku Daigaku Kiyo. Shizen Kagaku/Nara University of Education. Bulletin. Natural Science (JPN ISSN 0547-2407) **7886**
➤ Nara Medical Association. Journal (JPN ISSN 1345-0069) **5683**
Nara National College of Technology. Research Reports *see* Nara Kogyo Koto Senmon Gakko Kenkyu Kiyo **8433**
Nara Prefecture. Monthly Report of Meteorology *see* Naraken Kisho Geppo **6392**
Nara Sangyo Daigaku Sangyo to Keizai/Journal of Industrial Economics, Nara Sangyo University (JPN ISSN 0915-9789) **1152**
Nara Sangyo University. Journal of Industrial Economics *see* Nara Sangyo Daigaku Sangyo to Keizai **1152**
Nara Shokubutsu Kenkyu/Nara Botany (JPN ISSN 0386-7080) **803**
Nara University of Education. Bulletin. Natural Science *see* Nara Kyoiku Daigaku Kiyo. Shizen Kagaku **7886**
Nara Women's University. Health Administration Center. Archives of Health Care *see* Nara Joshi Daigaku Hoken Kanri Senta Nenpo **7532**
The Naracoorte Herald (AUS) **3795**
Naraken Kisho Geppo/Nara Prefecture. Monthly Report of Meteorology (JPN) **6392**
Nar'ana Vynder (RUS) **3938**
Narc Officer (USA ISSN 0889-7794) **4738**
Narcomafie (ITA ISSN 1127-9117) **2661**
• Narcotic Drugs: Estimated World Requirements for (Year) (USA ISSN 1013-3453) **6890**
Narcotics and Drug Abuse A to Z (USA ISSN 0094-3991) **2697**
Narcotics Anonymous Way Magazine *see* The N A Way Magazine **2697**
• Narcotics Enforcement & Prevention Digest (USA ISSN 1079-1582) **2661**
Narcotics Enforcement and Prevention Digest *see* Narcotics Enforcement & Prevention Digest **2661**
• Narcotics Law Bulletin (USA ISSN 8755-8289) **2661**
Nargun (AUS ISSN 1037-4361) **2757**
Narinkka (FIN ISSN 0355-9106) **4247**
Ta Narkotika sto Proskenio *see* Drugs in Focus **2693**
Narkotikafraagan (SWE ISSN 0347-4836) **2697**
Narod (HRV ISSN 1330-7223) **7288**
Narod Polski/Polish Nation (USA ISSN 0027-7894) **3552**
Narodna Armiya (UKR) **6438**
• Narodna Banka Srbije. Godisnji Izvestaj (SRB) **1500**
• Narodna Banka Srbije. Statisticki Bilten (SRB) **1252**
• Narodna Hazeta (UKR) **3965**
Narodna in Univerzitetna Knjiznica. Zbornik (SVN ISSN 0350-3569) **5034**
† • Narodna Obroda (SVK ISSN 1335-4671) **8976**
Narodna Tvorchist' ta Etnografiya (UKR ISSN 0130-6936) **349**
• ➤ Narodna Umjetnost/Croatian Journal of Ethnology and Folklore Research (HRV ISSN 0547-2504) **3620**
Narodna Volya/People's Will (USA) **3552**
Narodnaya Gazeta (BLR) **3800**
Narodnaya Gazeta (TJK) **3961**
Narodnaya Gazeta (Ul'yanovsk) (RUS) **3938**
Narodnaya Volya (BLR) **3800**
Narodne Novine (HRV ISSN 0027-7932) **5229**
• Narodne Novine (SRB ISSN 0350-7572) **3945**
Narodne Sportove Centrum Revue *see* N S C Revue **8189**
▼ Narodni 3 (CZE ISSN 1802-9884) **4466**
† • Narodni Bibliografie Ceske Republiky. Mapy (CD-ROM Edition) (CZE) **8976**
Narodni Knihovna *see* Knihovna **5023**
Narodni List (HRV ISSN 0027-7975) **5229**
Narodni Muzeum. Rada Historicka. Casopis (CZE ISSN 1214-0627) **6533**
Narodni Muzeum. Rada Prirodovedna. Casopis (CZE ISSN 1214-0635) **6533**
➤ Narodni Muzeum v Praze. Sbornik. Rada A: Historie/Acta Musei Nationalis Pragae. Series A: Historia (CZE ISSN 0036-5335) **6533**
➤ Narodni Muzeum v Praze. Sbornik. Rada B: Prirodni Vedy/Acta Musei Nationalis Pragae. Series B: Historia Naturalis (CZE ISSN 0036-5343) **6533**
➤ Narodni Muzeum v Praze. Sbornik. Rada C: Literarni Historie/Acta Musei Nationalis Pragae. Series C: Historia Litterarum (CZE ISSN 0036-5351) **6533**
† Narodni Technicke Muzeum. Bibliografie a Prameny (CZE) **8976**
Narodni Technicke Muzeum. Katalog (CZE) **6533**
Narodni Zdravstveni List (HRV ISSN 0351-9384) **7533**
Narodnoe Khozyaistvo Altaiskogo Kraya (RUS) **8389**
Narodnoe Obrazovanie (RUS ISSN 0027-8033) **2889**
Narodnoe Slovo (UZB) **3994**
Narodnoe Tvorchestvo (RUS ISSN 0235-5051) **537**
Narodnostopanski Arkhiv/Archives of National Economy (BGR ISSN 0323-9004) **1152**
➤ Narodopisna Revue/Journal of Ethnography (CZE ISSN 0862-8351) **349**
Narodovlastie (RUS) **3938**
Narodowy Bank Polski. Biuletyn Informacyjny (Monthly) (POL ISSN 1230-0020) **1369**
Narodowy Bank Polski. Dziennik Urzedowy (POL ISSN 0239-7013) **1369**
Narodowy Bank Polski. Informacja Wstepna (POL) **1369**
Narodowy Bank Polski. Raport Roczny (POL ISSN 1427-0277) **1369**
Narr Studienbuecher (DEU ISSN 0941-8105) **5154**
• Narrabeen Chamber News (AUS) **1407**
Narradores de Arca (URY ISSN 0077-2801) **5338**
Narratio (CHE ISSN 0935-2872) **5154**
Narrativa (FRA ISSN 1166-3243) **5338**
Narrativa Latinoamericana (URY ISSN 0077-2844) **4304**
Narrativas Historicas (ARG ISSN 1851-586X) **4304**
• ➤ Narrative (USA ISSN 1063-3685) **5338**
Narrative Architecture Today *see* N A T O **450**
• ➤ Narrative Inquiry (NLD ISSN 1387-6740) **5338**
Narratologia (DEU ISSN 1612-8427) **5338**
Narrazioni (ITA ISSN 1826-8986) **4466**
Narria (ESP ISSN 0210-9441) **6533**
Narrow Bandwidth Television Association *see* N B T V **4342**
The Narrow Gauge (GBR ISSN 0142-5587) **8621**
Narrow Gauge and Short Line Gazette (USA ISSN 0148-2122) **4342**
Narrow Gauge Annual (USA ISSN 1940-2120) **4342**
Narrow Gauge Inform *see* Smalspaarsinform **8625**
Narrow Gauge News (GBR ISSN 0142-5595) **8621**
Narrow Way (USA) **7739**
NarroWebTech (DEU ISSN 1617-206X) **7324**
Narthex (NLD ISSN 1569-3015) **2889**
Naruzhnaya Reklama Rossii (RUS) **30**
Nas Chov (CZE ISSN 0027-8068) **294**
Nas Jezik (SRB ISSN 0027-8084) **5154**
Nas Utulny Byt (CZE ISSN 1212-4788) **4561**
Nasa Nada/Our Hope (USA ISSN 0164-470X) **7808**
Nasa Orava (SVK ISSN 1336-0051) **3946**
Nasa Rec (SRB ISSN 0027-8122) **3945**
Nasa Slovenija (SVN ISSN 0353-5347) **7213**
• Nasa Zena (SVN ISSN 0350-9737) **8877**
Nasaba Magazine (USA ISSN 1536-4550) **3552**
• Nascer e Crescer (PRT ISSN 0872-0754) **6097**
Nase Doba *see* Aetas Nostra **2175**
Nase Doba Senioru *see* Doba Senioru **4043**
• ➤ Nase Gospodarstvo/Our Economy: Review of Current Problems in Economics (SVN ISSN 0547-3101) **1152**
Nase Gradevinarstvo (SRB ISSN 0350-2619) **1025**
Nase Krasna Zahrada (CZE ISSN 1211-4995) **3744**
Nase Krasna Zahrada. Special (CZE) **3744**
• Nase More (HRV ISSN 0469-6255) **3454**
Nase Nebo (SVN ISSN 1318-0614) **578**
Nase Novosti (SVK) **3946**
Nase Obcestvo (SVN) **7808**
➤ Nase Rec/Our Language (CZE ISSN 0027-8203) **5154**
Nase Rodina (USA ISSN 1045-8190) **3776**
Naselenie/Population (BGR ISSN 0205-0617) **7288**
Naselenie i Demografski Protsesi (BGR ISSN 1311-2341) **8389**
• Nash & Cibinic Report (USA ISSN 0891-9291) **4738**
Nash Belgorod (RUS) **3938**
Nash Gorod (RUS) **3938**
Nash Malysh (RUS) **2162**
Nash Notations (USA ISSN 8756-4718) **3776**
• Nash Sovremennik (RUS ISSN 0027-8238) **5229**
Nash Times (USA) **8595**
Nash Variant (RUS) **3938**
Nasha Gazeta (Bishkek) (KGZ) **3904**
Nasha Gazeta (Kemerovo) (RUS) **3938**
Nasha Gil'diya (RUS) **3938**
Nasha Niva (BLR) **3800**
Nasha Obshchina (USA) **3552**
• Nasha Sprava (UKR ISSN 1681-6102) **1642**
• Nasha Svaboda (BLR) **3800**
Nasha Ukraina (UKR) **3965**
Nasha Zhizn': Ploskopechatnyi Shrift (RUS ISSN 0131-5803) **4083**
• Nasha Zhizn': Rel'efnotochechnyi Shrift (RUS ISSN 0321-0626) **4083**
Nashe Nasledie (RUS ISSN 0234-1395) **5229**
Nashe Slovo (POL ISSN 0027-8254) **3552**
Nashe Zdorov'e (AZE) **5683**
Nashe Zhittya (UKR) **3965**
Nashik Tarun Bharat (IND) **3886**
• ➤ Nashim (ISR ISSN 0793-8934) **8901**
Nashingu Bijinesu *see* Nursing Business **5973**
Nashr-i Danish (IRN ISSN 0259-9090) **4466**
Nashr-i Riyazy/Mathematics Journal (IRN ISSN 1015-2857) **5519**
Nashrat al-'lum al-Saydaliyyat Gami't Asiut *see* Bulletin of Pharmaceutical Sciences **6827**
Nashrat al-Mukhaddirat *see* United Nations. Bulletin on Narcotics **2700**
Nashrat Buhuth al-Iqtisad al-Manzili/Research Bulletin for Home Economics (EGY ISSN 1110-2578) **4364**
Nashrat Koliyyat al-'lum A Kimyyaa *see* Mansoura Journal of Chemistry **2072**
Nashrat Koliyyat al-'lum B Baiulugi *see* Mansoura Journal of Biology **687**
Nashrat Koliyyat al-'lum G 'lum Tabi'yyat *see* Mansoura Journal of Physics **7881**
Nashrat Koliyyat al-'ulum Gami'at al-Qahirat *see* Cairo University. Faculty of Science. Bulletin **7843**
Nashriyyah-i 'ilmi Sazman-i Inirzhi-i Atumi-i Iran/Atomic Energy Organization of Iran. Scientific Bulletin *see* Majallah-i 'ulum va Funun-i Hastah-i **7068**
Nashriyyah-i Inirzhi-i Iran/Iranian Journal of Energy (IRN ISSN 1028-3706) **3142**
Nashriyyah-i Shimi va-Muhandisi-i Shimi-i Iran *see* Iranian Journal of Chemistry and Chemical Engineering (International English Edition) **2066**
Nashua (USA) **3982**
Nashui Ren (CHN) **1936**
Nashville Automotive Report (USA ISSN 1042-0282) **8595**
• Nashville Business and Lifestyles (USA ISSN 1052-4215) **1152**
• Nashville Business Journal (USA ISSN 0889-2873) **1152**
Nashville Lifestyles (USA) **3982**
Nashville Lifestyles (Year) Menu Guide (USA) **4394**
Nashville Parent Magazine (USA) **2162**
Nashville Scene (USA) **6598**
➤ Nasi Zbori (SVN ISSN 0027-8270) **6598**
Nasinec (USA ISSN 0744-6594) **3552**
Nasionale Afrikaanse Letterkundige-museum en Navorsingsentrum Nuusbrief *see* N A L N Nuusbrief **6533**
Nasionale Biblioteek van Suid Afrika. Kwartaalblad *see* National Library of South Africa. Quarterly Bulletin **5034**
Nasionale Kultuurhistoriese Museum. Navorsing *see* National Cultural History Museum. Research Journal **6533**
➤ Nasionale Museum, Bloemfontein. Navorsinge/National Museum, Bloemfontein. Researches (ZAF ISSN 0067-9208) **691**
Nasionale Veiligheid *see* National Safety & Occupational Hygiene **7533**
Nasjonalregnskapsstatistikk *see* Norway. Statistisk Sentralbyraa. Nasjonalregnskapsstatistikk. Institusjonelt Sektorregnskap **1256**
Nasjonalt Formidlingssenter i Geriatri. Geritri Norge. Rapport (NOR ISSN 1502-9247) **4052**
Nasjonalt Formidlingssenter i Geriatri. Nasjonalt Geriatriprogram. Rapport *see* Nasjonalt Formidlingssenter i Geriatri. Geritri Norge. Rapport **4052**
Nasjonalt Formidlingssenter i Geriatri. Nasjonalt Geriatriprogram. Skriftserie (NOR ISSN 1502-2277) **4052**
Nasjonalt Formidlingssenter i Geriatri. Undervisningssykehjem. Rapport (NOR ISSN 1502-9085) **4052**
Nasjonalt Forskningssenter innen Komplementaere og Alternativ Medisin Skriftserie *see* N A F K A M. Skriftserie **313**
• Nasjonalt Kunnskapssenter for Helsetjenesten. Rapport (NOR ISSN 1503-9544) **4107**
NaSPA Technical Support *see* National Systems Programmers Association Technical Support **2508**
Al-Nasr (UAE) **2268**
Nasra Uquq al-Mu'allif *see* Copyright Bulletin (Online) **4650**
Nasrat al-Ihsa'at al Hayawiyyat f Mintaqat al-Lagnat al-Iqtisadiyyat wa-al-Iqtima'iyyat li-Garbi Asiya *see* Bulletin on Vital Statistics in the E S C W A Region **7304**
Nasrat al-Ihsa'iyyat al-Sanawiyyat li-i-Magrib (MAR ISSN 0851-0903) **8389**
Nasrat al-Tigarat al-Harigiyyat li-Mintaqat al-Lagnat al-Iqtisadiyyat li-Garbi Asiya *see* Nasrat al-Tigarat al-Harigiyyat li-Mintaquat al-Lagnat al-Iqtisadiyyat wa-al-Iqtima'iyyat li-Garbi Asiya **1578**
Nasrat al-Tigarat al-Harigiyyat li-Mintaqat al-Lagnat al-Iqtisadiyyat wa-al-Iqtima'iyyat li-Garbi Asiya/External Trade Bulletin of the ESCWA Region (LBN ISSN 1564-7617) **1578**
Nasrat Aswan lil-A!lum wa al-Tiknulugyyaa *see* Aswan Science and Technology Bulletin **7837**
➤ Nassarre (ESP ISSN 0213-7305) **6598**
Nassau County Dental Society. Newsletter (USA) **5856**
Nassau Lawyer (USA ISSN 0047-8695) **4738**

➤ Nassau Review (USA ISSN 0077-2879) **5338**
Nassau Weekly (USA ISSN 1075-5004) **2293**
Nassauer Gespraeche der Freiherr-vom-Stein-Gesellschaft (DEU ISSN 0176-6023) **7987**
➤ Nassauische Annalen (DEU ISSN 0077-2887) **4247**
Nassauischer Verein fuer Naturkunde. Jahrbuecher (DEU ISSN 0368-1254) **7886**
Nassauischer Verein fuer Naturkunde. Mitteilungen (DEU ISSN 0946-9427) **7886**
Nastava i Vaspitanje/Journal of Education (SRB ISSN 0547-3330) **2889**
Nastava Matematike/L' Enseignement Mathematique (SRB ISSN 0351-4463) **5519**
Nastava Matematike i Fizike *see* Nastava Matematike **5519**
Nasty Letters (USA) **6296**
Nasty Photos (USA) **6296**
Nasu Binzu *see* Nasu Binzu Smart Nurse **5970**
Nasu Binzu Smart Nurse (JPN) **5970**
• Nasza Politechnika (POL ISSN 1428-295X) **3028**
➤ Nasza Przeszlosc (POL ISSN 0137-3218) **7808**
Nasze Drzewa Lesne. Monografie Popularno Naukowe (POL) **3697**
NaTaBu - Berater, Industrie, Lieferanten *see* Nahverkehrs-Taschenbuch. Berater, Industrie, Lieferanten **8505**
NaTaBu - Verkehrsunternehmen, Verkehrsorganisation, Verbaende, Behoerden, Wissenschaft *see* Nahverkehrs-Taschenbuch. Verkehrsunternehmen, Verkehrsorganisation, Verbaende, Behoerden, Wissenschaft **8505**
NaTaBu - Wer, Was, Wo im Nahverkehr *see* Nahverkehrs-Taschenbuch. Wer, Was, Wo im Nahverkehr **8505**
Natagora (BEL ISSN 1780-3756) **910**
Natal Agricultural Union *see* N A U N L U **138**
Natal Creative Homes & Gardens (ZAF) **4547**
Natal Museum Journal of Humanities *see* Southern African Humanities **418**
Natal Witness (ZAF) **3949**
Natali (UKR) **8877**
Natalia (ZAF ISSN 0085-3674) **4177**
Natation (FRA ISSN 1169-8152) **8189**
Natation Magazine (FRA ISSN 1268-631X) **8323**
Natchez Holiday & Travel Guide (GBR ISSN 1360-7197) **8740**
Natchez Trace Traveler (USA ISSN 0738-985X) **3776**
• ➤ Nathaniel Hawthorne Review (USA ISSN 0890-4197) **5338**
• The Nation (CAN ISSN 1206-2642) **3552**
• The Nation (GMB ISSN 0796-000X) **3843**
The Nation (MWI) **3906**
• The Nation (USA ISSN 0027-8378) **5229**
Nation and the World (IND) **7156**
La Nation Djibouti (DJI ISSN 0255-9617) **3789**
Nation Economic Report *see* Daily Nation **3902**
Nation Europa (DEU ISSN 0027-8408) **5229**
• Nation Junior (THA ISSN 1513-2110) **2204**
Nationaal Actiecomite voor Veiligheid en Hygiene in het Bouwbedrijf Info *see* N A V B Info **7532**
Nationaal Fonds Ouderenhulp. Info Nieuwsbrief (NLD ISSN 1875-2225) **4052**
Nationaal Fonds voor de Geestelijke Volksgezondheid. Nieuwsbrief *see* Fonds Psychische Gezondheid. Nieuwsbrief **6141**
Nationaal Instituut voor de Statistiek. Aantal Vergunningen voor Autoradio's en Televisietoestellen *see* Belgium. Nationaal Instituut voor de Statistiek. Media. Aantal Vergunningen voor Autoradio's en Televisietoestellen **1214**
Nationaal Instituut voor de Statistiek. Binnenscheepvaart *see* Belgium. Nationaal Instituut voor de Statistiek. Vervoer. Binnenscheepvaart (Jaar) **8522**
Nationaal Instituut voor de Statistiek. Economische Nieuws *see* Belgium. Nationaal Instituut voor de Statistiek. Economische Nieuws **1214**
Nationaal Instituut voor de Statistiek. Industriele Statistieken *see* Belgium. Nationaal Instituut voor de Statistiek. Industrie en Bouwnijverheid **1214**
Nationaal Instituut voor de Statistiek. Landbouwstatistieken *see* Belgium. Nationaal Instituut voor de Statistiek. Landbouw. Landbouwstatistieken **176**
Nationaal Instituut voor de Statistiek. Motorvoertuigenpark *see* Belgium. Nationaal Instituut voor de Statistiek. Vervoerstatistieken. Motorvoertuigenpark op (Year) **8522**
Nationaal Instituut voor de Statistiek. Nieuwe to het Verkeer Toegelaten Motorvoergtuigen *see* Belgium. Nationaal Instituut voor de Statistiek. Vervoer. In het Verkeer Gebrachte Nieuwe en Tweedehands Motorvoertuigen in (Year) **8522**
Nationaal Instituut voor de Statistiek. Regionaal Statistisch Jaarboek *see* Belgium. Nationaal Instituut voor de Statistiek. Regionaal Statistisch Jaarboek **1214**
Nationaal Instituut voor de Statistiek. Sociale Statistieken *see* Belgium. Nationaal Instituut voor de Statistiek. Sociale Statistieken **8081**
Nationaal Instituut voor de Statistiek. Sociale Statistieken: Enquete naar de Beroepsbevolking *see* Belgium. Nationaal Instituut voor de Statistiek. Werkgelegenheid en Werkloosheid. Enquete naar de Arbeidskrachten (Year) **1214**
Nationaal Instituut voor de Statistiek. Statistiek over de Internationale Trafiek (B.L.E.U.) in de Havens *see* Belgium. Nationaal Instituut voor de Statistiek. Statistiek over de Internationale Trafiek (B.L.E.U.) in de Havens **8522**
Nationaal Instituut voor de Statistiek. Statistiek van het Toerisme en het Hotelwezen *see* Belgium. Nationaal Instituut voor de Statistiek. Statistiek van het Toerisme en het Hotelwezen **8778**
Nationaal Instituut voor de Statistiek. Statistisch Tijdschrift *see* Belgium. Nationaal Instituut voor de Statistiek. Statistisch Tijdschrift **1214**
Nationaal Instituut voor de Statistiek. Statistisch Zakjaarboek *see* Belgium. Nationaal Instituut voor de Statistiek. Statistisch Zakjaarboek **1214**
Nationaal Instituut voor de Statistiek. Weekbericht *see* Belgium. Nationaal Instituut voor de Statistiek. Weekbericht **1214**
Nationaal Instituut voor Kernfysica en Hoge-Energiefysica Annual Report *see* N I K H E F Annual Report **7027**
Nationaal Lucht -en Ruimtevaartlaboratorium Report *see* N L R Report **66**
Nationaal Natuurhistorisch Museum. Zoologische Bijdragen (NLD ISSN 0459-1801) **957**
• Nationaal Natuurhistorisch Museum. Zoologische Mededelingen (NLD ISSN 0024-0672) **957**
Nationaal Sport Magazine *see* Sport Bestuur & Management **8203**
Le National (CHE) **7454**
• The National (PNG) **3927**
National (ROM ISSN 1220-7799) **3933**
National (Ottawa, 1970) (CAN ISSN 0709-1370) **3044**
National (Ottawa, 1974) (CAN ISSN 0315-2286) **4738**
• National Aboriginal Health Organization. Annual Report (CAN ISSN 1703-7697) **7533**
National Academic Advising Association Journal *see* N A C A D A Journal **2994**
• ➤ The National Academies In Focus (USA ISSN 1534-8334) **7886**
• National Academy of Arbitrators. Annual Meeting. Proceedings (USA ISSN 0148-4176) **4599**
National Academy of Design. Annual Exhibition Catalogue (USA ISSN 0191-0825) **508**
National Academy of Elder Law Attorneys Journal *see* N A E L A Journal **4851**
National Academy of Elder Law Attorneys Student Journal *see* N A E L A Student Journal **4851**
National Academy of Indian Medicine. Annals (IND) **5683**
National Academy of Mathematics. India. Journal (IND ISSN 0970-5228) **5519**
National Academy of Medical Sciences. Annals (IND ISSN 0379-038X) **5683**
National Academy of Recording Arts and Sciences Journal *see* N A R A S Journal **8154**
National Academy of Sciences. Biographical Memoirs (USA ISSN 0077-2933) **644**
National Academy of Sciences, India. Proceedings. Section A. Physical Sciences (IND ISSN 0369-8203) **7886**
National Academy of Sciences, India. Proceedings. Section B. Biological Sciences (IND ISSN 0369-8211) **691**
National Academy of Sciences, India. Science Letters (IND ISSN 0250-541X) **7886**
National Academy of Sciences of Belarus. Annual Report *see* Natsiyanal'naya Akademiya Navuk Belarusi. Spravazdacha ab Dzeinastsi **7887**
National Academy of Sciences of Belarus. Institute of Forest. Proceedings *see* Natsiyanal'naya Akademiya Navuk Belarusi. Instytut Lesu. Trudy **3697**
National Academy of Sciences of Belarus. Institute of History. The Annual Collection *see* Natsiyanal'naya Akademiya Navuk Belarusi. Instytut Gistoryi. Shtogodnik **4154**
National Academy of Sciences of Belarus. Institute of Mathematics. Proceedings *see* Natsiyanal'naya Akademiya Navuk Belarusi. Instytut Matematyki. Trudy **5519**
National Academy of Sciences of Belarus. Papers *see* Natsiyanal'naya Akademiya Navuk Belarusi. Doklady **7887**
National Academy of Sciences of Belarus. Proceedings. Series of Biological Sciences *see* Natsiyanal'naya Akademiya Navuk Belarusi. Vestsi. Seryya Biyalagichnykh Navuk **692**
National Academy of Sciences of Belarus. Proceedings. Series of Chemical Sciences *see* Natsiyanal'naya Akademiya Navuk Belarusi. Vestsi. Seryya Khimichnykh Navuk **2074**
National Academy of Sciences of Belarus. Proceedings. Series of Humanitarian Sciences *see* Natsiyanal'naya Akademiya Navuk Belarusi. Vestsi. Seryya Gumanitarnykh Navuk **7987**
National Academy of Sciences of Belarus. Proceedings. Series of Medical-Biological Sciences *see* Natsiyanal'naya Akademiya Navuk Belarusi. Vestsi. Seryya Medyka-Biyalagichnykh Navuk **5684**
National Academy of Sciences of Belarus. Proceedings. Series of Physico-Mathematical Sciences *see* Natsiyanal'naya Akademiya Navuk Belarusi. Vestsi. Seryya Fizika-Matematychnykh Navuk **7028**
National Academy of Sciences of Belarus. Proceedings. Series of Physico-Technical Sciences *see* Natsiyanal'naya Akademiya Navuk Belarusi. Vestsi. Seryya Fizika-Technichnykh Navuk **7028**
National Academy of Sciences of the Republic of Kazakhstan. Geology Series *see* Kazakstan Respublikasynyn Ulttyk Gylym Akademiasynyn Khabarlary. Geologialyk Seriasy **2751**
National Academy of Sciences of the Republic of Kazakhstan. Proceedings. Physics and Mathematics Series *see* Natsional'naya Akademiya Nauk Respubliki Kazakhstan. Izvestiya. Seriya Fiziko-Matematicheskaya **7028**
• ➤ National Academy of Sciences. Proceedings (USA ISSN 0027-8424) **7886**
National Accident Sampling System *see* National Automotive Sampling System **8527**
National Accommodation Guide (AUS ISSN 1328-7214) **8740**
National Accommodation Guide (ZAF) **8740**
National Account Managers News *see* N A M News **3680**
National Accountant (AUS ISSN 1039-608X) **1297**
National Accounts & Historical Statistics *see* Source O E C D. National Accounts & Historical Statistics **1263**
National Accounts. Detailed Tables. O E C D Department of Economics and Statistics *see* National Accounts of O E C D Countries. Volume 2 Detailed Tables **1252**
National Accounts E S A - Aggregates (Years) (LUX ISSN 0256-7601) **1152**
National Accounts: Main Aggregates and Detailed Tables *see* Source O E C D. National Accounts Statistics **1264**
National Accounts. Main Aggregates. O E C D Department of Economics and Statistics *see* National Accounts of O E C D Countries. Volume 1 Main Aggregates **1252**
National Accounts Occasional Paper *see* Centraal Bureau voor de Statistiek. Occasional Paper. National Accounts **8940**
• National Accounts of Botswana (BWA ISSN 0302-2056) **1720**
National Accounts of Mauritius *see* Mauritius. Central Statistical Office. National Accounts of Mauritius **1251**
National Accounts of O E C D Countries *see* Source O E C D. National Accounts Statistics **1264**
• National Accounts of O E C D Countries. Volume 1 Main Aggregates/Comptes Nationaux des pays de l'O C D E. Volume I (FRA ISSN 0256-758X) **1252**
• National Accounts of O E C D Countries. Volume 2 Detailed Tables (FRA ISSN 0256-7571) **1252**
National Accounts of O E C D Countries. Volume 3, Financial Accounts/Comptes Nationaux des pays de l'O C D E. Volume III - Comptes Financiers (Organization for Economic Cooperation and Development) (FRA) **1369**
National Accounts of O E C D Countries. Volume 4, General Government Accounts/Comptes Nationaux des pays de l'O C D E. Volume IV, Comptes des Administrations Publiques (Organization for Economic Cooperation and Development) (FRA) **1936**
National Accounts of the Maltese Islands (MLT ISSN 0077-295X) **1253**
National Accounts Statistics *see* Norway. Statistisk Sentralbyraa. Nasjonalregnskapsstatistikk. Institusjonelt Sektorregnskap **1256**
National Accrediting Agency for Clinical Laboratory Sciences News *see* N A A C L S News **5681**
National Accrediting Commission of Cosmetology Arts & Sciences Review *see* N A C C A S Review **589**
National Acquisitions Group News *see* N A G News **5033**
National Active and Retired Federal Employees Association Magazine *see* N A R F E Magazine **4051**
• National Adoption Report (USA ISSN 1046-5103) **8056**
National Adult Cardiac Surgical Database Report (Year) (GBR) **5796**
National Advertising Division Case Report (USA) **30**
National Advertising Division - Children's Advertising Review Unit / C A R U Case Reports *see* N A D / C A R U Case Reports **30**
• National Advisory Dental and Craniofacial Research Council. Minutes of Meeting (USA ISSN 1944-3064) **5856**
The National Advocate (CAN ISSN 1194-5958) **2994**
National Advocate (USA) **8056**
National Advocates Society. Bulletin (USA) **4738**
National Aeronatics and Space Administration Thesaurus (Online) *see* N A S A Thesaurus (Online) **66**
National Aeronautical and Space Administration Tech Briefs *see* N A S A Tech Briefs **66**
National Aeronautics (USA) **66**
National Aeronautics and Space Administration Conference Publication *see* N A S A. Conference Publication **66**
National Aeronautics and Space Administration Contractor Report *see* N A S A. Contractor Report **7884**
National Aeronautics and Space Administration Reference Publication *see* N A S A Reference Publication **66**
National Aeronautics and Space Administration Special Publication National Aeronautics and Space Administration. Scientific and Technical Information Office. N A S A S P *see* U.S. National Aeronautics and Space Administration. Scientific and Technical Information Office. N A S A S P **73**
National Aeronautics and Space Administration Technical Paper *see* N A S A. Technical Paper **66**
National Aeronautics and Space Administration Technical Reports Server *see* N A S A Technical Reports Server **66**
National Aeronautics and Space Administration Technology Innovation *see* N A S A Technology Innovation **8432**
National Aeronautics and Space Administration - U.S. Department of Defense Conference on Evolvable Hardware. Proceedings *see* N A S A - D O D Conference on Evolvable Hardware. Proceedings **2468**
National Aerospace Laboratories. Annual Report (IND ISSN 0077-2976) **66**
National Aerospace Laboratories. Combined Aerospace Book Additions (IND) **76**
National Aerospace Laboratories. Combined Aerospace Reports Additions (IND) **66**
National Aerospace Laboratory News *see* N A L News **66**
National Aerospace Laboratory. Special Publication *see* Koku Uchu Gijutsu Kenkyujo Tokubetsu Shiryo **64**
National Aerospace Laboratory. Technical Report *see* Koku Uchu Gijutsu Kenkyujo Hokoku **64**
National Agency of Industry and Trade. Annual Reports (Year)/Aarsberetninger (DNK) **1899**
National Aging Information Center Online Newsletter *see* N A I C Online Newsletter **4051**
National Agri-Marketing Association News (USA) **138**
National Agricultural Aviation Association Newsletter *see* N A A A Newsletter **66**
National Agricultural Biotechnology Council Report *see* N A B C Report **138**
National Agricultural Cooperative Federation News *see* N A C F News **203**
National Agricultural Cooperative Marketing Federation of India Ltd. Marketing Review *see* N A F E D Marketing Review **1835**
National Agricultural Marketing Council. Annual Report (ZAF ISSN 1684-2596) **203**
National Agricultural Plastics Congress. Proceedings (USA ISSN 1073-1768) **7095**
National Agricultural Research and Extension Users Advisory Board. Report to the President and Congress - United States (USA ISSN 1045-1579) **138**
National Agricultural Research Center for Hokkaido Region. Annual Reports *see* Hokkaido Nogyo Shikenjo Nenpo **119**
National Agricultural Research Center for Hokkaido Region. Miscellaneous Publication *see* Hokkaido Nogyo Shikenjo Kenkyu Shiryo **118**
National Agricultural Research Center for Hokkaido Region. Research Bulletin *see* Hokkaido Nogyo Shikenjo Kenkyu Hokoku **118**
National Agricultural Research Center for Kyushu Okinawa Region. Bulletin *see* Kyuushuu Okinawa Nougyou Kenkyuu Senta Houkoku **132**
National Agricultural Research Center for Western Region. Bulletin *see* Kinki Chuugoku Shikoku Nougyou Kenkyuu Senta Kenkyuu Houkoku **130**
National Agricultural Society of Sri Lanka. Journal (LKA) **138**
National Aids Treatment Advocacy Project Reports *see* N A T A P Reports **5823**
National Air Pollution Surveillance *see* Canada. Environment Canada. Conservation and Protection Service. Annual Summary: National Air Pollution Surveillance **3408**
National Air Quality and Emissions Trends Report (USA ISSN 0885-2448) **3489**
National Air Traffic Controllers Association Voice *see* N A T C A Voice **8548**
National Air Transportation Association. Annual Report (USA) **8548**
National Air Transportation Association. Industry Compensation Guide (USA) **8549**
National Alliance (Washington) (USA ISSN 0027-8513) **4599**
National Alliance for the Mentally Ill Advocate *see* N A M I Advocate **6162**
National Alliance for the Mentally Ill California. Journal *see* N A M I California. Journal **6162**
National Alliance of Breast Cancer Organizations Breast Cancer Resource List *see* N A B C O Breast Cancer Resource List **6028**
National Alliance of Breast Cancer Organizations News *see* N A B C O News **6028**
National Alopecia Areata Foundation Newsletter (USA ISSN 0894-1769) **5880**
• National Alternative Dispute Resolution Advisory Council. Annual Report (AUS ISSN 1832-0821) **4738**
National Amateur (USA ISSN 0027-8521) **4580**
National Amputee Golf Association Newsletter *see* N A G A Newsletter **8239**
National Amusement Park Historical Association News *see* N A P A A News **8739**
National AMVET (USA ISSN 0027-853X) **6438**
National and Folk Music *see* Minzu Minjian Yinyue **6587**

Title

10646 NATIONAL ANIMAL CONTROL ASSOCIATION NEWS ULRICH'S PERIODICALS

National Animal Control Association News see N A C A News 6811
• National Animal Welfare Advisory Committee. Code of Welfare (NZL ISSN 1176-2942) 321
National Anti-Poverty Organization News see N A P O News 8056
National Anti-Vivisection Society Animal Action Report see N A V S Animal Action Report 320
National Apostolate for Inclusion Ministry Newsletter see N A F I M Newsletter 3044
National Aquatic Resources Research and Development Agency. Journal (LKA ISSN 1391-6246) 2619
National Arborist Association Reporter see N A A Reporter 3697
National Archives & Records Administration. Annual Report (USA) 5034
National Archives Microfilm Publications. Catalog (USA ISSN 0094-629X) 5034
• National Archives of Canada. Annual Review (CAN ISSN 0848-7308) 5034
• National Archives of Canada. Performance Report (CAN ISSN 1483-8532) 5034
National Archives of Malaysia. Annual Report/Arkib Negara Malaysia. Laporan Tahunan (MYS ISSN 0076-3381) 4186
National Archives of Scotland. Newsletter (GBR ISSN 1466-1934) 5034
National Archives of Zambia. Annual Report (ZMB ISSN 0084-4942) 5034
National Archives of Zambia. Calendars of the District Notebooks (ZMB) 7454
National Archives of Zambia. Information (ZMB) 4177
National Archives of Zambia. National Archives Occasional Paper (ZMB) 4177
National Art Education Association News see N A E A News 507
National Art Materials Trade Association News & Views see N A M T A News & Views 507
National Arts Centre. Annual Report (CAN ISSN 0382-1455) 508
National Asian Pacific American Legal Consortium Review see The N A P A L C Review 3552
• National Assembly for Wales. Planning Division. Planning Policy Wales. Technical Advice Note (GBR) 7454
The National Assembly for Wales Statistical Directorate. Statistical Report (GBR) 7288
National Assembly Library Review see Kukhoe Tosogwanbo 5024
National Assembly Review see Kukhoebo 7150
National Association for Bilingual Education News see N A B E News 2888
National Association for Business Economics Industry Survey see N A B E Industry Survey 1500
National Association for Business Economics News (Online) see N A B E News (Online) 1500
National Association for Business Economics Outlook & Policy Survey see N A B E Outlook & Policy Survey 1500
National Association for Business Economics. Salary Survey see Salary Survey (Washington) 1516
National Association for Business Teacher Education Review see N A B T E Review 1151
National Association for Colitis and Crohn's Disease News see N A C C News 5929
National Association for College Admission Counseling Bulletin see N A C A C Bulletin 2994
National Association for College Admission Counseling. Membership Directory (USA) 2994
National Association for Drama in Education Research Monograph Series see N A D I E Research Monograph Series 2888
National Association for Female Executives Magazine see N A F E Magazine 8876
National Association for Foreign Student Affairs Directory of Institutions and Individuals in International Educational Exchange (Online) see N A F S A Directory of Institutions and Individuals in International Educational Exchange (Online) 3014
National Association for Gifted Children. Communique see Compass Points (Washington) 3038
National Association for Girls and Women in Sport Research Reports see N A G W S Research Reports 8188
National Association for Home Care Report see N A H C Report 5681
National Association for Law Placement Bulletin see N A L P Bulletin 4737
National Association for Law Placement Directory of Legal Employers see N A L P Directory of Legal Employers 4737
National Association for Olmsted Parks. Field Notes (USA) 2619
National Association for Printing Leadership Economic Edge see N A P L Economic Edge 7324
National Association for Special Educational Needs. Publications (GBR) 3044
National Association for Stock Car Auto Racing Illustrated see N A S C A R Illustrated 8188
National Association for Stock Car Auto Racing NEXTEL Cup Series see N A S C A R NEXTEL Cup Series 8594
National Association for Stock Car Auto Racing Performance see N A S C A R Performance 8594
National Association for Stock Car Auto Racing Scene see N A S C A R Scene 8188
National Association for the Advancement of Colored People Annual Report see N A A C P Annual Report 3552
National Association for the Blind, India. Annual Report (IND) 4083
National Association for the Care and Resettlement of Offenders Annual Review see N A C R O Annual Review 2660
National Association for the Care and Resettlement of Offenders Race Unit Newsletter see N A C R O Race Unit Newsletter 2660
National Association for the Care and Resettlement of Offenders Youth Crime Section see N A C R O Youth Crime Section 2161
National Association for the Exchange of Industrial Resources Advantage see N A E I R Advantage 8056
National Association for the Practice of Anthropology Bulletin see N A P A Bulletin 349
National Association for the Teaching of English Classroom see N A T E Classroom 5153
National Association for the Teaching of English. Newsletter (GBR ISSN 0143-4136) 3074
National Association for Visually Handicapped Update see N A V H Update 4083
National Association of Academies of Science. Directory, Proceedings and Handbook (USA ISSN 1071-8966) 7886
National Association of Administrative Law Judges. Journal see National Association of Administrative Law Judiciary. Journal 4738
• National Association of Administrative Law Judiciary. Journal (USA) 4738
National Association of Agricultural Contractors Newsletter see N A A C Newsletter 138
National Association of Aluminum Distributors. Topics (USA) 6327
National Association of Animal Breeders. Annual Proceedings (USA ISSN 0077-3255) 267
National Association of Anorexia Nervosa and Associated Disorders Working Together see A N A D: Working Together 7330
National Association of Attorneys General Bulletin see A G Bulletin 4607
National Association of Bankruptcy Trustees Talk see N A B Talk 1369
National Association of Bench and Bar Spouses. Newsletter (USA) 4738
National Association of Beverage Retailers. News and Views (USA) 607
• National Association of Biology Teachers. News and Views (Email) (USA) 691
National Association of Black Accountants. Chapter to Chapter (USA) 1297
National Association of Black Accountants. News Plus (USA) 1297
National Association of Black Journalists Journal see N A B J Journal 3552
National Association of Blacks Within Government. Newsletter (USA) 3552
National Association of Boards of Pharmacy Newsletter see N A B P Newsletter 6862
National Association of Broadcast Employees and Technicians - Communications Workers of America, A F News see N A B E T - C W A News 4599
National Association of Career & Guidance Teachers. Journal (GBR ISSN 0954-3732) 2944
National Association of Catalog Showroom Merchandisers. Census of All Catalog Showrooms (USA) 2018
National Association of Chain Drug Stores Chain Pharmacist Practice Memo see N A C D S Chain Pharmacist Practice Memo 6862
National Association of Chain Drug Stores. Executive Newsletter (USA ISSN 1079-1116) 1780
National Association of Chain Drug Stores Federal Report see N A C D S Federal Report 6862
National Association of Chain Drug Stores Sourcebook Online see N A C D S Sourcebook Online 6862
National Association of Chain Drug Stores Works see N A C D S Works 1899
National Association of College & University Food Services. Journal (USA ISSN 1535-489X) 3657
National Association of College Wind & Percussion Instructors Journal see N A C W P I Journal 6598
National Association of Colleges and Employers Journal see N A C E Journal 1698
National Association of Colleges and Employers National Directory see N A C E National Directory 6701
National Association of Colleges and Employers. Salary Survey (USA ISSN 1520-8648) 1698
National Association of Colleges and Teachers of Agriculture Journal see N A C T A Journal 138
National Association of Conservation Districts. Tuesday Letter (USA ISSN 0047-8733) 2620
National Association of Consumer Agency Administrators News see N A C A A News 2640
National Association of Convenience Stores see N A C S 1431
National Association of County Recorders, Election Officials, and Clerks Bulletin see N A C R C Bulletin 7454
National Association of Development Organizations News see N A D O News 1500
National Association of Development Organizations Special Report see N A D O Special Report 1500
National Association of Disability Examiners Advocate see N A D E Advocate 8056
National Association of Document Examiners. Communique (USA) 2661
National Association of Document Examiners. Journal (USA ISSN 8755-1020) 2661
▼ • National Association of Eco-Friendly Salons & Spas. Newsletter (USA ISSN 1949-3312) 3454
National Association of Educational Buyers, Inc. Bulletin see N A E B Bulletin 2994
National Association of Educational Office Professionals Connector see N E S Connector 3028
National Association of Elder Law Attorneys Student Journal see N A E L A Student Journal 4851
National Association of Elementary School Principals. Professional Resources Catalog (USA) 3028
National Association of Emergency Medical Technicians News see N A E M T News 5681
National Association of Energy Service Companies Newsletter see N A E S C O Newsletter 3142
National Association of Federal Credit Unions's Credit Union Regulatory Compliance Report see N A F C U's Credit Union Regulatory Compliance Report 4876
National Association of Field Study Officers Journal see N A F S O Journal 3454
National Association of Fire Officers Yearbook see N A F O Yearbook 3580
National Association of Fleet Administrators, Inc. Annual Reference Book see N A F A Annual Reference Book 8594
National Association of Fleet Administrators, Inc. Fleet Executive see N A F A Fleet Executive 8505
National Association of Fleet Administrators, Inc. FleetFocus see N A F A FleetFocus 8505
National Association of Fleet Resale Dealers Inside Tracks see N A F R D Inside Tracks 8594
National Association of Foreign Student Advisers Adviser's Manual see The N A F S A Adviser's Manual 4737
National Association of Government Archives and Records Administration Clearinghouse see N A G A R A Clearinghouse 5033
National Association of Health Authorities and Trusts Research Paper see N A H A T Research Paper 8056
National Association of Home and Workshop Writers Newsletter (USA) 4580
National Association of Home Builders Remodelor see N A H B Remodelor 1025
National Association of Housing and Redevelopment Officials Agency Awards of Merit in Housing and Community Development see N A H R O Agency Awards of Merit in Housing and Community Development 4420
National Association of Housing and Redevelopment Officials Monitor see N A H R O Monitor 4420
National Association of Independent Fee Appraisers Convention. Proceedings see N A I F A Convention. Proceedings 7601
National Association of Independent Insurers Reporter see N A I C Reporter 4515
National Association of Independent Schools. Annual Report (Print Edition) see National Association of Independent Schools. Stats Online 2889
• National Association of Independent Schools. Stats Online (USA) 2889
National Association of Institutional Linen Management News see N A I L M News 2243
National Association of Insurance Commissioners. Compilation of Minutes (USA) 4516
National Association of Insurance Commissioners. Emerging Accounting Issues Working Group. Minutes (USA) 4516
National Association of Insurance Commissioners. Issues (USA) 4516
National Association of Insurance Commissioners. Life and Health Actuarial Report (USA) 4516
National Association of Insurance Commissioners. Listing of Companies (USA) 4516
National Association of Insurance Commissioners News see N A I C News 4515
• National Association of Insurance Commissioners. Proceedings (USA ISSN 0363-0358) 4516
National Association of Insurance Commissioners. Progess Report on the Implementation of 24 Hour Coverage (USA) 4516
National Association of Insurance Commissioners Report on Receiverships see N A I C Report on Receiverships 4515
National Association of Insurance Commissioners. Synopsis (USA) 4516
National Association of Intercollegiate Athletics Handbook see N A I A Handbook 8188
National Association of Intercollegiate Athletics News Weekly Edition see N A I A News Weekly Edition 8188
National Association of Intercollegiate Athletics Official Championship Summaries see N A I A Official Championship Summaries 8188
National Association of Judiciary Interpreters and Translators News see N A J I T News 4956
National Association of Juvenile Correction Agencies. Proceedings (USA) 2661
National Association of Laboratory Schools Journal see N A L S Journal 2888
National Association of Men's Sportswear Buyers, Inc. News see N A M S B News 2248
National Association of Milliners, Dressmakers and Tailors Newsletter see N A M D T Newsletter 2248
National Association of Music Merchants. Cost of Doing Business Survey see Cost of Doing Business Report: Operating Performance Comparisons for Music Product Dealers 6631
National Association of Neighborhoods Bulletin see N A N Bulletin 4420
National Association of Neonatal Nurses Central see N A N N Central 5970
National Association of Neonatal Nurses. Position Statement (USA) 5970
National Association of Pension Funds. Annual Survey (GBR) 1253
National Association of Pension Funds. Annual Survey of Occupational Pension Schemes see National Association of Pension Funds. Annual Survey 1253
National Association of Pension Funds Pensions Legislation Service see N A P F Pensions Legislation Service 4515
• National Association of Pension Funds. Year Book (GBR ISSN 0144-2589) 1253
National Association of Performing Arts Managers and Agents News see N A P A M A News 8474
National Association of Photo Equipment Technicians News see N A P E T News 6971
National Association of Printers and Lithographers. Special Reports (USA ISSN 0893-4975) 7324
National Association of Prison Visitors Newsletter see N A P V Newsletter 2661
National Association of Private Schools for Exceptional Children Membership Directory see N A P S E C Membership Directory 3044
National Association of Private Schools for Exceptional Children News see N A P S E C News 3044
National Association of Probation Officers News see N A P O News 2660
National Association of Probation Officers Probation Directory see N A P O Probation Directory 2661
National Association of Public Child Welfare Administrators Network see N A P C W A Network 8056
National Association of Public Insurance Adjusters Bulletin see N A P I A Bulletin 4515
National Association of Publishers' Representatives Bulletin see N A P R Bulletin 30
National Association of Pupil Services Administration News see N A P S A News 3044
National Association of Railroad Passengers News (USA ISSN 0739-3490) 8621
National Association of Real Estate Editors News see N A R E E News 7601
National Association of Real Estate Investment Trusts, Inc. Handbook see N A R E I T Handbook 7601
National Association of Recording Merchandisers Sounding Board see N A R M Sounding Board 6598
National Association of Regional Councils. Regional Reporter (USA ISSN 1060-5029) 7499
National Association of Regional Councils. Special Report (USA) 7454
National Association of Regional Media Centers Highlights see N A R M C Highlights 5033
National Association of Regulatory Utility Commissioners. Bulletin (USA ISSN 0027-8645) 7454
National Association of Regulatory Utility Commissioners. Proceedings (USA ISSN 0077-3387) 7454
National Association of Residents and Interns Stethoscope see N A R I Stethoscope 1642
National Association of School Nurses Inc. School Nurse see N A S N School Nurse 5970
National Association of Schools of Music. Directory (USA ISSN 0547-4175) 6598
National Association of Schools of Music. Handbook (USA ISSN 0164-2847) 6598
National Association of Schools of Music. Proceedings of the Annual Meeting (USA ISSN 0190-6615) 6598
National Association of Science Writers. Newsletter (USA ISSN 1949-9736) 4580
National Association of Secondary School Principals Bulletin see N A S S P Bulletin 3027
National Association of Secondary School Principals Leadership for Student Activities see N A S S P Leadership for Student Activities 3027
National Association of Secondary School Principals Legal Memorandum see N A S S P Legal Memorandum 3027
National Association of Secondary School Principals Newsleader see N A S S P Newsleader 3028
National Association of Securities Dealers Automated Quotations - American Stock Exchange Market Group. Annual Report see N A S D A Q - A M E X Market Group. Annual Report 1642
National Association of Securities Dealers Automated Quotations - American Stock Exchange Market Group. Fact Book see N A S D A Q - A M E X Market Group. Fact Book 1642
National Association of Securities Dealers Automated Quotations Fact Book see N A S D A Q Fact Book 1642
National Association of Securities Dealers Automated Quotations Subscriber Bulletin see N A S D A Q Subscriber Bulletin 1642

DIRECTORY 2010 NATIONAL CHILD BENEFIT PROGRESS REPORT 10647

National Association of Securities Dealers, Inc. Annual Report see N A S D Annual Report **1642**
National Association of Securities Dealers, Inc. Notices to Members see N A S D Notices to Members **1642**
National Association of Securities Dealers, Inc. Regulatory and Compliance Alert see N A S D Regulatory and Compliance Alert **1642**
National Association of Small Business Investment Companies News see N A S B I C News **1642**
National Association of Social Workers News see N A S W News **8056**
National Association of Social Workers Register of Clinical Social Workers see N A S W Register of Clinical Social Workers **8056**
National Association of State Aviation Officials Newsletter see N A S A O Newsletter **66**
National Association of State Boards of Accountancy. State Board Report (USA ISSN 0889-3500) **1297**
National Association of State Development Agencies Directory of Development Agencies and Officials see N A S D A Directory of Development Agencies and Officials **1500**
National Association of State Development Agencies Letter see N A S D A Letter **1500**
National Association of State Development Agencies State Economic Development Expenditures and Salary Survey see N A S D A State Economic Development Expenditures and Salary Survey **7454**
National Association of State Development Agencies State Enterprise Zone Roundup see N A S D A State Enterprise Zone Roundup **1500**
National Association of State Park Directors. Annual Information Exchange (USA) **2620**
➤ National Association of Student Affairs Professionals Journal (USA ISSN 1094-6624) **3028**
● National Association of Student Anthropologists. Bulletin (USA ISSN 1556-3618) **349**
National Association of Student Financial Aid Administrators Newsletter see N A S F A A Newsletter **2994**
National Association of Student Personnel Administrators Forum see N A S P A Forum **1870**
National Association of Student Personnel Administrators Journal (Online) see N A S P A Journal (Online) **2994**
National Association of Television Program Executives Guide to North American Media see N A P T E Guide to North American Media **2385**
National Association of Television Program Executives Monthly see N A T P E Monthly **2386**
National Association of Temple Educators News see N A T E News **7727**
National Association of Testing Authorities Annual Directory see N A T A Annual Directory **3354**
National Association of Testing Authorities News see N A T A News **7884**
National Association of the Deaf Mag see N A D Mag **4075**
National Association of the Remodeling Industry Remodeler's Journal see N A R I Remodeler's Journal **1025**
National Association of Uniform Manufacturers and Distributors News see N A U M D News **2248**
National Association of Uniform Manufacturers and Distributors Office Reports see N A U M D Office Reports **2248**
National Association of Uniform Manufacturers and Distributors Postal Update see N A U M D Postal Update **2248**
National Association of Watch and Clock Collectors. Bulletin (USA ISSN 0027-8688) **4568**
National Association of Watch and Clock Collectors, Inc. Mart see N A W C C Mart **4568**
National Association of Wholesaler - Distributors Report see N A W Report **1780**
National Association of Women Artists. Annual Exhibition Catalog (USA) **508**
National Association of Women in Construction Image see The N A W I C Image **1025**
National Association of Women Judges Counterbalance see N A W J Counterbalance **4956**
National Association of Women Writers Writer's Guide see The N A W W Writer's Guide **5337**
National Association to Advance Fat Acceptance, Inc. Newsletter see N A A F A Newsletter **6663**
National Astronomical Observatory. Mizusawa Astrogeodynamics Observatory. Mizusawa Kansoku Center. Technical Report (JPN ISSN 0915-3780) **578**
National Astronomical Observatory, Nobeyama Radio Observatory Report see N R O Report **578**
National Astronomical Observatory. Publications/Kokuritsu Tenmondai Obun Hokoku (JPN ISSN 0915-3640) **578**
National Astronomical Observatory. Report see Kokuritsu Tenmondaiho **577**
National Astronomical Observatory. Reprint (JPN ISSN 0915-0021) **578**
National Auction Bulletin (USA ISSN 0739-327X) **1835**
National Auricula & Primula Society (Northern) Year Book (GBR ISSN 0027-8726) **3744**
National Automobile Dealers Association Classic Collectible and Special Interest Car Appraisal Guide see N A D A Classic Collectible and Special Interest Car Appraisal Guide **8594**
National Automobile Dealers Association Manufactured Housing Appraisal Guide see N A D A Manufactured Housing Appraisal Guide **1025**
National Automobile Dealers Association Marine Appraisal Guide see N A D A Marine Appraisal Guide **8278**
National Automobile Dealers Association Motorcycle - Snowmobile - A T V - Personal Watercraft Appraisal Guide see N A D A Motorcycle - Snowmobile - A T V - Personal Watercraft Appraisal Guide **8265**
National Automobile Dealers Association Official Heavy Duty Truck Guide see N A D A Official Heavy Duty Truck Guide **8673**
National Automobile Dealers Association Official Used Car Guide see N A D A Official Used Car Guide **8594**
National Automobile Dealers Association Older Used Car Guide see N A D A Older Used Car Guide **8594**
National Automobile Dealers Association Recreation Vehicle Appraisal Guide see N A D A Recreation Vehicle Appraisal Guide **8594**
National Automobile Dealers Association, Used Car Guide Co. Auctionnet Auction Guide see N A D A Auctionnet Auction Guide **8594**
National Automobile Dealers Association's Automotive Executive see N A D A's Automotive Executive **8594**
National Automotive Parts Association. Outlook (USA) **8595**
National Automotive Radiator Service Association Service Report see N A R S A Service Report **3211**
National Automotive Sampling System (USA) **8527**
National Balance Sheet Accounts (CAN ISSN 0825-9216) **1253**
National Bank of Belgium. Financial Stability Review (BEL ISSN 1378-4633) **1500**
National Bank of Commerce. Annual Report and Accounts (TZA) **1369**
National Bank of Egypt. Economic Bulletin (EGY ISSN 0304-274X) **1500**
National Bank of Ethiopia. Annual Report (ETH ISSN 1015-2717) **1370**
National Bank of Ethiopia. Quarterly Bulletin (ETH ISSN 0027-8750) **1370**
National Bank of Greece. Annual Report/Ethnike Trapeza tes Hellados. Apologismos (GRC ISSN 0077-3514) **1370**
National Bank of Hungary. Monthly Report (HUN ISSN 1216-4879) **1500**
National Bank of Kuwait. Annual Report of the Board of Directors and Accounts (KWT) **1370**
National Bank of Liberia. Annual Report (LBR) **1370**
National Bank of Liberia. Quarterly Statistical Bulletin (LBR) **1370**
National Bank of Liberia Review see N B L Review **1369**
● National Bank of New Zealand. Business Outlook (Online) (NZL ISSN 1177-8466) **1152**
National Bank of New Zealand. Business Outlook (Print) see National Bank of New Zealand. Business Outlook (Online) **1152**
National Bank of Pakistan. Annual Report (PAK) **1370**
National Bank of Pakistan. Monthly Economic Letter (PAK) **1370**
National Bank of Pakistan. Report and Statement of Accounts (PAK ISSN 0077-3522) **1370**
National Bank of Poland. Annual Report (POL ISSN 1427-0285) **1370**
National Bank of Poland. Inflation Report (POL ISSN 1640-0755) **1370**
National Bank of Poland. Information Bulletin see Narodowy Bank Polski. Biuletyn Informacyjny (Monthly) **1369**
● National Bank of Serbia. Annual Report (SRB) **1500**
● National Bank of Serbia. Statistical Bulletin (SRB ISSN 1451-6349) **1253**
● National Banking Law Review (CAN ISSN 0822-1081) **1370**
National Bar Association Magazine see N B A Magazine **4737**
National Bark & Soil Producers Association. Special Regional Releases (USA) **3697**
● National Baseball Hall of Fame & Museum Yearbook (USA ISSN 0278-1867) **8239**
National Basketball Association Inside Stuff see N B A Inside Stuff **8975**
National Beauty News see State of the Art **596**
National Beer Wholesalers Association. Beer Perspectives Newsletter (USA ISSN 1062-0990) **607**
National Beer Wholesalers Association. Distributor Productivity Report (USA) **607**
National Beer Wholesalers Association Handbook see N B W A Handbook **607**
National Beer Wholesalers Association Legislative and Regulatory Issues Alert see N B W A Legislative and Regulatory Issues Alert **607**
National Belgian Newsletter see The Belgian Sheepdog **6804**
The (Year) National Benchmarking Report (USA ISSN 1942-3632) **1297**
National Bible Society of Scotland. Annual Report (GBR ISSN 0077-3557) **7768**
● National Bibliography of Barbados (BRB ISSN 0256-7709) **631**
National Bibliography of Botswana (BWA ISSN 0027-8777) **7578**
National Bibliography of Nigeria (NGA ISSN 0331-0019) **631**
National Bibliography of Zambia (ZMB ISSN 0377-1636) **631**
National Billiard News (USA ISSN 0747-3265) **8239**
National Biodynamics Laboratory. Report (USA) **750**
National Biotech Register (USA ISSN 1074-9942) **768**
● The National Black Law Journal (USA ISSN 0896-0194) **4738**
➤ National Black Nurses' Association. Journal (USA ISSN 0885-6028) **5970**
National Black - Police Association. Newsletter (USA) **2661**
● National Blood Authority. Annual Report (AUS ISSN 1832-1909) **5940**
● National Board Bulletin (USA ISSN 0894-9611) **3390**
National Board of Medical Examiners. Annual Report (USA ISSN 0146-1524) **5683**
National Bodybuilding and Fitness Magazine see N B A F Magazine **6993**
National Book Development Council of Singapore News see N B D C S News **7568**
➤ National Botanic Gardens. Occasional Papers (IRL ISSN 0790-0422) **803**
➤ National Botanic Research Institute, Lucknow. Progress Report (IND) **804**
National Botanical Institute. Annual Review (ZAF ISSN 1021-7460) **804**
National Botanical Society. Journal (IND ISSN 0971-2976) **804**
National Braille Association. Bulletin (USA ISSN 0550-5666) **4083**
National Braille Association. General Interest Catalog (USA) **4083**
National Braille Association. Music Catalog (USA) **4083**
National Braille Association. Textbook Catalog (USA) **4083**
National Braille Press Release (USA) **4083**
National Buckskin Society. Newsletter (AUS ISSN 0726-1799) **8295**
National Building (IND) **1025**
National Building Code of Canada (CAN ISSN 0700-1207) **4738**
● National Building Service (AUS) **4738**
National Buildings Construction Corporation. Bulletin (IND ISSN 0255-8165) **1025**
National Buildings Organisation Abstracts see N B O Abstracts **1048**
National Buildings Organisation. Journal (IND ISSN 0027-8815) **1025**
The National Bulletin of Good Practice in Adult Community Education see The Bulletin of Good Practice in Popular Education **2833**
● National Bulletin on Domestic Violence Prevention (USA ISSN 1083-7310) **7533**
National Bulletin on Liturgy see Canadian Conference of Catholic Bishops. National Bulletin on Liturgy **7787**
National Bureau of Asian Research Analysis see N B R Analysis **7254**
National Bureau of Asian Research Special Report see N B R Special Report **7254**
National Bureau of Economic Research Digest (Online) see The N B E R Digest (Online) **1151**
National Bureau of Economic Research Digest (Print) see The N B E R Digest (Print) **1151**
National Bureau of Economic Research International Seminar on Macroeconomics see N B E R International Seminar on Macroeconomics **1720**
National Bureau of Economic Research Reporter see N B E R Reporter **1546**
National Bureau of Economic Research Technical Working Paper Series see N B E R Technical Working Paper Series **1151**
● National Bureau of Economic Research. Working Paper Series (USA ISSN 0898-2937) **1152**
National Bureau of Economic Research. Working Paper Series on Historical Factors in Long Run Growth (USA ISSN 1058-8450) **1547**
National Bureau of Fish Genetic Resources. Annual Report (IND ISSN 0970-6135) **876**
National Bus Trader (USA ISSN 0194-939X) **8505**
National Business Aircraft Association. Maintenance and Operations Bulletin (USA) **8549**
National Business Aviation Association Digest see N B A A Digest **66**
† ● National Business Bulletin (AUS ISSN 1036-4145) **8976**
National Business Education Association Yearbook (USA ISSN 1553-1600) **1780**
National Business Education Yearbook see National Business Education Association Yearbook **1780**
National Business Incubation Association Review see N B I A Review **1500**
● National Business Review (NZL ISSN 0110-6813) **1500**
† National Business Review Desk Companion (NZL ISSN 1176-2977) **8976**
National Button Bulletin (USA ISSN 0027-884X) **4342**
National Campaign for the Arts News see N C A News **507**
National Cancer Institute Cancer Bulletin see N C I Cancer Bulletin **6028**
National Cancer Institute Fact Book see N C I Fact Book **6028**
● National Cancer Institute. Journal (Online) (GBR ISSN 1460-2105) **6028**
● ➤ National Cancer Institute. Journal (Print) (GBR ISSN 0027-8874) **6028**
● ➤ National Cancer Institute. Journal. Monographs (USA ISSN 1052-6773) **6028**
National Cancer Institute of Canada. Annual Report (CAN ISSN 0834-8855) **6028**
National Cancer Institute of Canada. Report see National Cancer Institute of Canada. Annual Report **6028**
● National Capital Scan (CAN ISSN 1910-992X) **1152**
National Caption Institute Foundation. News see N C I Foundation. News **2386**
National Carer (GBR) **8056**
National Carlot Meat Report (USA) **294**
National Casting Guide see Screen & Stage Directory **8478**
National Cat (AUS ISSN 1035-6398) **6811**
● The National Catholic Bioethics Quarterly (USA ISSN 1532-5490) **6935**
National Catholic Educational Association Notes see N C E A Notes **2888**
● National Catholic Register (USA ISSN 0027-8920) **7808**
● National Catholic Reporter (USA ISSN 0027-8939) **7808**
National Cattlemen (USA ISSN 0885-7679) **294**
National Caves Association Cave Talk see N C A Cave Talk **8739**
National Center for Agricultural Utilization Research Publications and Patents (USA ISSN 1066-257X) **183**
National Center for Atmospheric Research. Annual Report (USA) **6392**
National Center for Atmospheric Research. Climate and Global Dynamics. News (USA ISSN 1949-4319) **2757**
National Center for Atmospheric Research Scientific Reports see N C A R Scientific Reports **6391**
National Center for Atmospheric Research Technical Notes see N C A R Technical Notes **6391**
National Center for Health Statistics Data Brief see N C H S Data Brief **7548**
National Center for Juvenile Justice. Juvenile Court Statistics see Juvenile Court Statistics **4823**
National Center for Manufacturing Sciences at a Glance see N C M S at a Glance **3354**
National Center for Research on Earthquake Engineering Newsletter see N C R E E Newsletter **3279**
National Center for Research Resources Reporter see N C R R Reporter **5682**
➤ National Center for Science Education. Reports (USA) **7886**
● National Center for State Courts. Caseload Highlights (USA ISSN 1934-0095) **2661**
National Center for State Courts. Publications Catalog (USA ISSN 0271-0676) **4956**
National Center for the Study of Collective Bargaining in Higher Education and the Professions. Annual Conference Proceedings (USA ISSN 0742-3667) **2994**
● National Center for Toxicological Research. Research Accomplishments and Plans (USA) **3500**
National Central Library Bulletin see Guojia Tushuguan Guankan **5011**
National Central Library Newsletter (TWN ISSN 0034-5016) **5034**
National Centre for Documentation Publication see NRCd Publication **6972**
National Centre for English Cultural Tradition Bibliographical and Special Series see N A T C E C T Bibliographical and Special Series **7986**
National Centre for English Cultural Tradition Conference Papers Series see N A T C E C T Conference Papers Series **5153**
National Centre for English Cultural Tradition Occasional Publications see N A T C E C T Occasional Publications **7986**
National Centre for English Language Teaching and Research. Research Series (AUS ISSN 1035-6487) **5154**
National Centre for Occupational Health. Annual Report (ZAF ISSN 0374-9800) **6681**
National Centre for Research in Children's Literature. Papers (GBR) **5338**
National Centre for Research on Europe Online Papers see N C R E Online Papers **4247**
National Centre for Research on Europe Working Paper see N C R E Working Paper **7254**
National Centre for Vocational Education Research Monograph Series see N C V E R Monograph Series **2944**
National Ceramics Quarterly (ZAF ISSN 1015-2369) **537**
National Certified Counselor (USA) **8056**
National Character Laboratory Newsletter (USA ISSN 1067-1161) **7386**
● National Chemical Inventories (USA ISSN 1089-6279) **2095**
National Ch'eng Kung University. Department of History. Bulletin see Guoli Chengda Lishi Xuebao **4182**
● National Child Benefit Progress Report (CAN ISSN 1498-9220) **8056**

Title

Title

DIRECTORY 2010 NATIONAL MIRROR 10651

National Institute for Regional and Spatial Analysis Working Paper Series see N I R S A. Working Paper Series **7986**
National Institute for Research Advancement's World Directory of Think Tanks see N I R A's World Directory of Think Tanks **7885**
National Institute for Resources and Environment. Journal see Shigen to Kankyo **3466**
National Institute for Rural Engineering Bulletin see N I R E. Bulletin **213**
National Institute of Agricultural Botany. Annual Report and Accounts (GBR) **242**
National Institute of Agro-Environmental Sciences. Annual Report see National Institute for Agro-Environmental Sciences. Annual Report **138**
National Institute of Agrobiological Resources. Annual Report see Nogyo Seibutsu Shigen Kenkyujo Nenpo **694**
National Institute of Agrobiological Resources. Annual Report (JPN ISSN 0912-1315) **691**
National Institute of Agrobiological Resources. Miscellaneous Publication see Nogyo Seibutsu Shigen Kenkyujo Kenkyu Shiryo **694**
National Institute of Agrobiological Resources. News see Nogyo Seibutsu Shigen Kenkyujo Nyusu **694**
National Institute of Allergy and Infectious Diseases Funding News see N I A I D Funding News **5682**
National Institute of Animal Agriculture. Annual Meeting Proceedings (USA) **294**
National Institute of Building Sciences. Annual Report to the President (USA) **1026**
National Institute of Child Health and Human Development. Center for Population Research. Progress Report (USA ISSN 0895-0466) **5683**
National Institute of Crop Science. Bulletin see Sakumotsu Kenkyuujo Kenkyu Houkoku **251**
National Institute of Development Administration Bulletin see N I D A Bulletin **5033**
National Institute of Economic and Social Research, London. Annual Report (GBR ISSN 0077-491X) **7987**
National Institute of Economic and Social Research, London. Economic and Social Studies (GBR ISSN 0070-8453) **1152**
† National Institute of Economic and Social Research, London. Occasional Papers (GBR ISSN 0077-4928) **8976**
National Institute of Fruit Tree Service. Bulletin see Kaju Kenkyusho Kenkyu Hokoku **129**
• National Institute of Genetics. Annual Report (JPN ISSN 0077-4995) **876**
National Institute of Health and Family Welfare Technical Reports see N I H F W Technical Reports **8056**
National Institute of Health and Nutrition. Annual Report see Kokuritsu Kenko, Eiyo Kenkyujo Kenkyu Hokoku **6662**
National Institute of Health Sciences. Bulletin see Kokuritsu Iyakuhin Shokuhin Eisei Kenkyujo Hokoku **7530**
• National Institute of Health Sciences. Research Bulletin (IRL ISSN 1649-0681) **5683**
National Institute of Industrial Safety. Research Report see Sangyo Anzen Kenkyujo Kenkyu Hokoku **6686**
National Institute of Information and Communications Technology. Journal/Tsushin Kenkyuu Kikou Eibun Rombunshuu. Jouhou (JPN ISSN 1349-3205) **2386**
National Institute of Information and Communications Technology News see N I C T News **2334**
National Institute of Information and Communications Technology. Review see Jouhou Tsuushin Kenkyuu Kikou Kihou **2383**
National Institute of Japanese Literature. Bulletin see Kokubungaku Kenkyuu Shiryoukan Kiyou. Bungaku Kenkyuu Hen **5318**
• National Institute of Justice Journal (USA ISSN 1067-7453) **2661**
National Institute of Justice Research Review see N I J Research Review **8976**
National Institute of Justice. Sponsored Research Programs (USA) **2661**
National Institute of Mental Health & Neuro Sciences Journal see N I M H A N S Journal **6162**
National Institute of Mental Health & Neuro Sciences Newsletter see N I M H A N S Newsletter **6162**
National Institute of Nutrition. Annual Report (IND ISSN 0377-3744) **6664**
National Institute of Occupational Safety and Health. Technical Recommendation see Roudou Anzen Eisei Sougou Kenkyujo Gijutsu Shishin **6685**
National Institute of Oceanography. Annual Report (IND ISSN 0547-7530) **2813**
National Institute of Oceanography. Technical Report (IND) **2813**
National Institute of Polar Research. Annual Report see Kokuritsu Kyokuchi Kenkyujo Nenpo **2712**
National Institute of Polar Research Arctic Data Reports see N I P R Arctic Data Reports **2713**
National Institute of Polar Research. Joint Research Report see Kokuritsu Kyokuchi Kenkyujo Kyodo Kenkyu Hokokusho **2712**
➤ National Institute of Polar Research. Memoirs. Series A: Upper Atmosphere Physics (JPN) **6392**
➤ National Institute of Polar Research. Memoirs. Series B: Meteorology (JPN ISSN 0386-5525) **6392**
➤ National Institute of Polar Research. Memoirs. Series C: Earth Sciences (JPN ISSN 0386-5533) **2713**
➤ National Institute of Polar Research. Memoirs. Series D: Oceanography (JPN) **2813**
➤ National Institute of Polar Research. Memoirs. Series E: Biology and Medical Science (JPN ISSN 0386-5541) **691**
➤ National Institute of Polar Research. Memoirs. Series F: Logistics (JPN ISSN 0386-555X) **7887**
➤ National Institute of Polar Research. Memoirs. Special Issue (JPN ISSN 0386-0744) **2713**
National Institute of Polar Research. News see Kyokuchiken Nyusu **2712**
National Institute of Population and Social Security Research see Kokuritsu Shakai Hosho, Jinko Mondai Kenkyujo Nenpo **7286**
National Institute of Public Health. Journal (JPN) **7533**
National Institute of Radiological Sciences. Annual Report see Hoshasen Igaku Sogo Kenkyujo Nenpo **6197**
National Institute of Radiological Sciences. Survey Report see Hoshano Chosa Kenkyu Hokokusho **6197**
National Institute of Sericultural and Entomological Science. Miscellaneous Publication see Sanshi. Konchu Nogyo Gijutsu Kenkyusho Shiryo **858**
National Institute of Special Education. Bulletin/Kokuritsu Tokushu Kyoiku Sogo Kenkyujo Kenkyu Kiyo (JPN ISSN 0387-3528) **3044**
National Institute of Special Education. Newsletter (JPN) **3044**
National Institute of Special Education Seminar. Final Report (JPN) **3044**
National Institute of Standards and Technology. Annual Report (USA) **6405**
National Institute of Standards and Technology Building Science Series see N I S T Building Science Series **1025**
National Institute of Standards and Technology Handbook see N I S T Handbook **6404**
• National Institute of Standards and Technology. Journal of Research (USA ISSN 1044-677X) **6405**
National Institute of Standards and Technology Monograph see N I S T Monograph **6404**
National Institute of Standards and Technology Special Publication see N I S T Special Publication **2432**
National Institute of Standards and Technology Technical Notes see N I S T Technical Notes **6404**
National Institute of Virology, Pune. Brief Annual Reports (IND) **5823**
National Institute of Water and Atmospheric Annual Report see N I W A. Annual Report **3454**
National Institute of Water and Atmospheric Research Ltd. Biodiversity Memoir see N I W A Biodiversity Memoir **691**
National Institute of Water and Atmospheric Research Ltd. Technical Report see N I W A Technical Report **3602**
National Institute on Alcohol Abuse and Alcoholism - Rutgers University Center of Alcohol Studies Alcoholism Treatment Series see N I A A A - R U C A S Alcoholism Treatment Series **2697**
National Institute on Drug Abuse Notes see N I D A Notes **2697**
National Institute on Drug Abuse Research Monograph see N I D A Research Monograph **2697**
National Institutes of Health Almanac see N I H Almanac **7532**
National Institutes of Health Annual Report of International Activities (USA ISSN 0146-6690) **5683**
National Institutes of Health Consensus and State-of-the-Science Statements see N I H Consensus and State-of-the-Science Statements **5682**
National Institutes of Health Guide for Grants and Contracts (Online) see N I H Guide for Grants and Contracts (Online) **8056**
National Institutes of Health Medline Plus Medline Plus see N I H Medline Plus **5682**
National Institutes of Health News in Health see The N I H News in Health **5682**
National Institutes of Health Organization Handbook (USA ISSN 0502-2975) **5683**
National Institutes of Health. Program in Biomedical and Behavioral Nutrition Research and Training. Annual Report (USA ISSN 0732-7013) **6664**
National Institutes of Health Publications List Publications List see N I H Publications List **5682**
National Institutes of Health Record see N I H Record **5682**
National Institutes of Health Senior Health see N I H Senior Health **4052**
National Insurance Corporation of Tanzania. Annual Report and Accounts (TZA) **4516**
National Insurance Institute, Jerusalem. Annual Survey/S'qira Sh'natit (ISR ISSN 0333-8649) **4516**
† National Insurance Institute, Jerusalem. Full Actuarial Report (ISR) **8976**
National Insurance Law Review (USA ISSN 0743-7927) **4739**
National Intelligence Journal (USA ISSN 1940-4042) **7254**
• National Intelligence Report (USA ISSN 0270-6768) **7454**
• The National Interest (USA ISSN 0884-9382) **7254**
National - Interstate Council of State Boards of Cosmetology Bulletin see N I C Bulletin **595**
National Intramural - Recreational Sports Association Foundation Journal see N I R S A Journal **8189**
• National Inventory Report (CAN ISSN 1910-7048) **3454**
National Inventory Report see New Zealand's Greenhouse Gas Inventory (Online) **3489**
National Investor Relations Institute. Annual Report (USA) **1642**
National Italian - American Foundation News see The N I A F News **3552**
National Jail and Adult Detention Directory (USA ISSN 0192-8228) **2661**
• National Jeweler (USA ISSN 0027-9544) **4568**
National Jewish News (USA ISSN 1043-2795) **7727**
The National Jewish Post & Opinion (USA ISSN 0888-0379) **7727**
• The National JobBank (USA ISSN 1051-4872) **6701**
• National Joint Registry for England and Wales. Annual Report (GBR ISSN 1745-1450) **4107**
• National Journal (USA ISSN 0360-4217) **7156**
National Journal of Andrology see Zhonghua Nankexue **6285**
• National Journal of Constitutional Law/Revue Nationale de Droit Constitutionnel (CAN ISSN 1181-9340) **4851**
• National Journal of Sexual Orientation Law (USA ISSN 1552-8901) **4377**
National Journal of Sociology (USA ISSN 0892-4287) **8122**
National Journal's Congress Daily see Congress Daily **7118**
National Journal's Technology Daily see Technology Daily **8992**
National Judges College Law Journal see Falu Shiyong **4671**
National Judicial Reporting Program (USA) **2674**
National Junior Horticultural Association Newsletter (Online) see N J H A Newsletter (Online) **3744**
The National Jurist (USA ISSN 1094-866X) **4739**
National Jury Verdict Review and Analysis (USA ISSN 0887-2899) **4739**
National Juvenile Detention Directory (USA) **2674**
• National Kart News (USA) **8190**
National Kidney Foundation. Annual Report (USA ISSN 0077-5096) **6271**
National Kidney Foundation. Proceedings Book (USA) **6271**
National Kidney Foundation. Research Program (USA) **6271**
The National Kitchen & Bath Association (N K B A)'s Puget Sound Kitchen & Bath see N K B A's Puget Sound Kitchen & Bath **4547**
• National Labor Relations Act: Law and Practice (USA) **1699**
National Labor Relations Board Advice Memorandum Reporter see N L R B Advice Memorandum Reporter **4737**
National Labor Relations Board Election Statistics see N L R B Election Statistics **1698**
• National Laboratory for Applied Network Research Packets (USA) **2501**
National Lamb Summary see U.S.D.A. National Lamb Market Summary **302**
• National Land Transport Programme (NZL ISSN 1176-1024) **8632**
• National Law Enforcement and Corrections Technology News Summary (USA) **2661**
• The National Law Journal (USA ISSN 0162-7325) **4739**
National Laws and Regulations Relating to the Control of Narcotic Drugs. Cumulative Index (Years) (USA ISSN 0077-510X) **4894**
National Laws on Dangerous Substances and Preparations see National Laws on the Marketing and Use of Dangerous Substances and Preparations **3509**
National Laws on the Marketing and Use of Dangerous Substances and Preparations (GBR ISSN 1357-4450) **3509**
National Lawyers Guild Disorientation Handbook (USA) **4739**
• National Lawyers Guild. Guild Notes (USA ISSN 0148-0588) **4851**
National Lawyers Guild Practitioner see The Guild Practitioner **4832**
National Lawyers Guild Referral Directory (USA) **4739**
National Leader (AUS) **7156**
• National League of Families of American Prisoners and Missing in Action in Southeast Asia Newsletter (USA) **8057**
National Leased Housing Association. Bulletin (USA) **4420**
National Legal Aid and Defender Association Cornerstone see N L A D A Cornerstone **4968**
National Library and Documentation Service. Annual Report (ZWE) **5034**
• The National Library Magazine (AUS ISSN 1836-6147) **5034**
• National Library of Australia. Annual Report (AUS ISSN 0313-1971) **5034**
• National Library of Australia Gateways (Online) (AUS ISSN 1443-0568) **5034**
† • National Library of Australia Gateways (Print) (AUS ISSN 1039-3498) **8976**
National Library of Australia News (Print) see The National Library Magazine **5034**
• National Library of Canada. Bulletin/Bibliotheque Nationale. Bulletin (CAN ISSN 1492-4668) **5034**
National Library of Canada. National Core Library Statistics Program. Statistical Report (CAN ISSN 1206-727X) **5034**
• National Library of Canada. Performance Report (CAN ISSN 1483-6769) **5034**
National Library of China. Journal see Guojia Tushuguan Xuekan **5011**
National Library of Ireland. Council of Trustees. Annual Report see National Library of Ireland. Report of the Board **5034**
National Library of Ireland. Report of the Board (IRL ISSN 2009-020X) **5034**
National Library of Medicine Classification (USA) **5034**
National Library of Medicine. Current Bibliographies in Medicine (USA ISSN 1052-9063) **5749**
National Library of Medicine Newsline see N L M Newsline **5033**
National Library of Medicine Programs and Services (USA ISSN 0163-4569) **5034**
National Library of New Zealand. Departmental Forecast Report see National Library of New Zealand. Statement of Intent **5034**
• National Library of New Zealand. Statement of Intent/Tauaki Whakamaunga Atu (NZL ISSN 1176-2306) **5034**
National Library of Nigeria. Annual Report (NGA ISSN 0075-7624) **5034**
National Library of Nigeria. National Library Occasional Publication (NGA ISSN 0075-7632) **5034**
• National Library of South Africa. Annual Report (ZAF ISSN 1681-2743) **5034**
• National Library of South Africa. Quarterly Bulletin/Nasionale Biblioteek van Suid Afrika. Kwartaalblad (ZAF ISSN 1562-9392) **5034**
National Library of Wales. Annual Report see Llyfrgell Genedlaethol Cymru. Adroddiad Blynyddol **5030**
National Library of Wales Journal see Cylchgrawn Llyfrgell Genedlaethol Cymru **5004**
• National Library Service for the Blind and Physically Handicapped (USA) **4083**
• National Library Service. Newsletter Series. News (USA) **4083**
• National Library Service. Newsletter Series. Updates (USA) **4083**
• National Library Service. Reference Circulars (USA) **4083**
National Library, Singapore. Annual Report (SGP ISSN 0217-1546) **5035**
National Library Year-Book see Biblioteka Narodowa. Rocznik **4995**
National Lighting Product Information Program. Specifier Reports see Specifier Reports **1037**
National Liquor News (AUS ISSN 0816-0430) **608**
National List of Advertisers (CAN ISSN 0077-5177) **30**
National Locksmith (USA ISSN 0364-3719) **2679**
National Longitudinal Surveys Handbook see N L S Handbook **1870**
The National Lottery Yearbook (GBR) **8190**
National Lubricating Grease Institute Spokesman see N L G I Spokesman **6778**
National Mail Order Association Mail Order Digest see N M O A - Mail Order Digest **1835**
National Manufacturing Week. Proceedings (USA) **2463**
National Marine Bankers Association. Summary Annual Report (USA) **1370**
National Marine Business Journal see Marine Business Journal **8277**
National Marine Manufacturers Association Certification Handbook see N M M A Certification Handbook **8278**
National Maritime Research Institute. Papers see Kaijou Gijutsu Anzen Kenkyuujo Houkoku **2810**
National Masters News (USA ISSN 0744-2416) **8323**
National Mastitis Council. Annual Meeting Proceedings (USA ISSN 0271-9967) **267**
• National Mastitis Council. Regional Meeting Proceedings (USA) **268**
National Medical and Dental Association. Bulletin (USA ISSN 0027-9676) **5683**
National Medical Association HealthyLiving see N M A HealthyLiving **5682**
• ➤ National Medical Association. Journal (USA ISSN 0027-9684) **5683**
National Medical Fellowships (USA) **5683**
National Medical Journal of China see Zhonghua Yixue Zazhi **5738**
➤ National Medical Journal of India (IND ISSN 0970-258X) **5683**
National Medical-Legal Journal see Legal Nurse Consulting Ezine **5915**
National Mining Association. Weekly Statistical Summary (USA) **6486**
National Minorities Digest (Chinese Edition) (CHN) **3553**
National Minorities Quarterly (Tibetan edition) (CHN) **3553**
National Minorities Quarterly (Yi edition) (CHN) **3553**
National Minority and Women-Owned Business Directory (USA ISSN 1553-6025) **2018**
National Minority Literature see Minzu Wenxue **5334**
National Mirror (ZMB ISSN 1010-8394) **2334**

Title

▼ *new title* † *ceased* • *electronic media* ➤ *refereed*

10652 NATIONAL MISSING PERSONS REPORT ULRICH'S PERIODICALS

National Missing Persons Report (USA ISSN 1041-3022) **2661**
National Model Railroad Association. Bulletin *see* Scale Rails **4346**
National Monuments Record. Newsletter *see* The Record **413**
National Mortgage Broker (USA ISSN 1086-475X) **7601**
• National Mortgage News (USA ISSN 1050-3331) **1370**
National Mortgage News Daily *see* National Mortgage News **1370**
National Motor Museum Pictorial Guide (GBR) **8595**
National Museum, Bloemfontein. Annual Report (ZAF) **6534**
National Museum, Bloemfontein. Researches *see* Nasionale Museum, Bloemfontein. Navorsinge **691**
National Museum. Bulletin *see* Raffles Bulletin of Zoology **961**
National Museum in Cracow. Catalogues of the Collections *see* Muzeum Narodowe w Krakowie. Katalogi Zbiorow **6533**
National Museum Journal of Arts *see* Misuljaryo **506**
National Museum of Ethnology. Bulletin *see* Kokuritsu Minzokugaku Hakubutsukan Kenkyu Hokoku **346**
National Museum of Ireland. Medieval Dublin Excavations. Series A (IRL) **407**
National Museum of Ireland. Medieval Dublin Excavations. Series B (IRL) **407**
National Museum of Ireland. Medieval Dublin Excavations. Series C (IRL) **407**
National Museum of Modern Art, Tokyo. Annual Report (JPN) **6534**
National Museum of Modern Art, Tokyo. Bulletin (JPN ISSN 0914-7489) **508**
National Museum of Natural History. Arctic Studies Center. Newsletter (USA ISSN 1931-8782) **6534**
National Museum of Natural History Quest (USA ISSN 1059-4566) **7887**
National Museum of Science and Technology. Annual Report (CAN ISSN 1187-3728) **6534**
National Museum of Tanzania. Annual Report (TZA ISSN 0082-1675) **6534**
National Museum of the Philippines. Annual Report (PHL ISSN 0076-3756) **6534**
National Museums & Galleries of Wales. Annual Report/Amgueddfeydd ac Orielau Cenedlaethol Cymru. Adroddiad Blynyddol (GBR ISSN 1368-1583) **6534**
National Museums & Galleries of Wales. Geological Series (GBR ISSN 0962-0575) **2757**
National Museums of Sri Lanka. Bulletin *see* Spolia Zeylanica **7920**
National Music Publishers' Association. News & Views (USA) **6598**
• National N O W Times (USA ISSN 0149-4740) **8877**
• National Neighborhood News (USA) **3982**
National Network (USA ISSN 1075-3753) **5035**
National New Books List *see* Quanguo Xinshumu **7579**
National News (USA) **2386**
• National Newsagent (AUS) **4580**
• National Newspaper Index (USA) **4587**
The National Notary (USA ISSN 0894-7872) **4739**
National Notary Yearbook (USA) **4739**
National Nutritional Foods Association. Newsletter *see* Natural Products Association. Newsletter **3657**
National Nutritional Foods Association Today *see* N N F A Today **3657**
• National Observer (AUS) **7254**
National Occupational Health and Safety Advisory Commission Technical Report *see* N O H S A C Technical Report **6681**
National Oceanic and Atmospheric Administration Coastal Ocean Program Project News Update *see* N O A A Coastal Ocean Program Project News Update **2619**
National Oceanic and Atmospheric Administration. Environmental Research Laboratories. Great Lakes Environmental Research Laboratory. Data Report (USA ISSN 0733-4044) **2797**
National Oceanic and Atmospheric Administration. Environmental Research Laboratories. Pacific Marine Environmental Laboratory. Data Report (USA ISSN 1060-1929) **2797**
National Oceanic and Atmospheric Administration. Great Lakes Environmental Research Laboratory. Annual Report (USA) **3454**
National Oceanic and Atmospheric Administration. Special Report (USA) **2813**
National Oceanographic Program of Japan *see* Kokunai Kaiyo Chosa Hokoku Ichiran **2810**
National Office for the Information Economy. Annual Report *see* Australian Government Information Management Office. Annual Report **8933**
National Office Products Association Membership Directory and Buyer's Guide (Year) *see* N O P A Membership Directory and Buyer's Guide (Year) **1852**
National Office Systems Association Update *see* N O S A Update **1297**
National Oil Company Statutes *see* World National Oil Company Statutes **4945**
National Oilseed Processors Association. Yearbook and Trading Rules (USA) **274**
• National On-Campus Report (USA ISSN 0300-6646) **2293**
National Opera Association, Inc. Newsletter *see* N O A Newsletter **6598**
National Operatic and Dramatic Association National News *see* N O D A National News **8474**
National Opinion Research Center Update *see* N O R C Update **7986**
National Organic Directory (USA ISSN 1073-0540) **139**
National Organization for Black Chemists and Chemical Engineers Ch E News Online *see* N O B C Ch E News Online **3251**
National Organization for the Professional Advancement of Black Chemists and Chemical Engineers Ch E. Proceedings *see* N O B C Ch E. Proceedings **2074**
National Organization for Victim Assistance Newsletter (USA) **8057**
National Organization for Women San Diego News *see* N O W San Diego News **8876**
National Organization of Circumcision Information Resource Centers Annual Newsletter *see* N O C I R C Annual Newsletter **6097**
National Organization of Mothers of Twins Clubs, Inc.'s Notebook *see* M O T C's Notebook **8872**
National Ornamental & Miscellaneous Metals Association Newsletter *see* N O M M A Newsletter **6327**
National Outerwear and Sportswear Association Fashion Bulletin *see* N O S A Fashion Bulletin **2248**
National Outerwear and Sportswear Association News *see* N O S A News **2248**
National Outerwear and Sportswear Association Production Bulletin *see* N O S A. Production Bulletin **2248**
• National P A L E-News (Police Athletic Leagues) (USA) **2204**
The National P R Pitch Book. Business and Consumer Edition *see* The National P R Pitch Book. Business & Consumer Edition **2019**
The National P R Pitch Book. Business & Consumer Edition (USA) **2019**
The National P R Pitch Book. Computers & Technology Edition (USA) **2019**
The National P R Pitch Book. Computers and Technology Edition *see* The National P R Pitch Book. Computers & Technology Edition **2019**
The National P R Pitch Book. Health, Fitness and Medicine Edition *see* The National P R Pitch Book. Health, Fitness & Medicine Edition **2019**
The National P R Pitch Book. Health, Fitness & Medicine Edition (USA) **2019**
The National P R Pitch Book. Investment, Banking and Financial Services Edition *see* The National P R Pitch Book. Investment, Banking & Financial Services Edition **2019**
The National P R Pitch Book. Investment, Banking & Financial Services Edition (USA) **2019**
The National P R Pitch Book. Issues, Policy and Politics Edition *see* The National P R Pitch Book. Issues, Policy & Politics Edition **2019**
The National P R Pitch Book. Issues, Policy & Politics Edition (USA) **2019**
The National P R Pitch Book. Travel, Hospitality & Destinations Edition (USA) **2019**
National Packing News (USA ISSN 1073-6948) **3657**
National Paint and Coatings Association (Years) Report to Members *see* N P C A (Years) Report to Members **6719**
National Palace Museum Bulletin/Gugong Tongxun Yingwen Shuangyuekan (TWN ISSN 1011-906X) **6534**
National Palace Museum. Monthly of Chinese Art *see* Gugong Wenwu Yuekan **6524**
National Palace Museum. Newsletter (TWN ISSN 1011-9086) **6534**
National Palace Museum. Newsletter & Gallery Guide *see* National Palace Museum. Newsletter **6534**
National Palace Museum Research Quarterly *see* Gugong Xueshu Jikan **6524**
National Paralegal Employment & Salary Survey (USA) **4739**
National Paralegal Reporter (USA ISSN 1058-482X) **4739**
National Park *see* Hiking Mount Rainier National Park **8718**
† National Park and Wildlife Journal (AUS ISSN 1442-5505) **8976**
• National Parks (USA ISSN 0276-8186) **4981**
• National Parks Advisory Council. Annual Report (AUS ISSN 1834-1217) **3454**
National Parks Journal (AUS ISSN 0047-9012) **2620**
National Parks of the American West For Dummies (USA ISSN 1930-8558) **8740**
National Parks Today (GBR ISSN 0265-0460) **2620**
• The National Parks Traveler (USA ISSN 1548-3452) **8740**
National Parks with Kids *see* Frommer's National Parks with Kids **8711**
National Partnership News (USA) **4739**
• National Pastime (USA ISSN 0734-6905) **8239**
• National Patterns of R & D Resources (USA ISSN 1057-6886) **7887**
National Pawnbrokers Association (Inc.) Journal *see* N.P.A. Journal **4568**
National Pensioners and Senior Citizens Federation. National News (CAN ISSN 0849-2115) **4052**
National Perinatal Association. Bulletin (USA) **5999**
National Petrochemical & Refiners Association Annual Meeting. Conference Papers *see* N P R A Annual Meeting. Conference Papers **6779**
National Petrochemical & Refiners Association Environmental Conference. Proceedings *see* N P R A Environmental Conference. Proceedings **6779**
National Petrochemical & Refiners Association National Safety Conference. Proceedings *see* N P R A National Safety Conference. Proceedings **6779**
National Petrochemical & Refiners Association Statistical Report. Annual Survey of Occupational Injuries & Injuries *see* N P R A Statistical Report. Annual Survey of Occupational Injuries & Injuries **6690**
National Petrochemical & Refiners Association Statistical Report. Lubricating Oil and Wax Capacity *see* N P R A Statistical Report. Lubricating Oil and Wax Capacity **6800**
National Petrochemical & Refiners Association Statistical Report. U S Lubricating Oil & Wax Sales *see* N P R A Statistical Report. U S Lubricating Oil & Wax Sales **6800**
National Petrochemical & Refiners Association Statistical Report. U S Refining Capacity *see* N P R A Statistical Report. U S Refining Capacity **6800**
National Petroleum & Refiners Association National Lubricants & Waxes Meeting. Proceedings *see* N P R A National Lubricants & Waxes Meeting. Proceedings **6779**
• National Petroleum News (USA ISSN 0149-5267) **6779**
National Petroleum News Buyers's Guide (USA) **6779**
National Petroleum News International *see* N P N International **8976**
• National Petroleum News Market Facts (USA) **6779**
National Petroleum Refiners Association Annual Meeting. Conference Papers. Multi-Year CD-ROM *see* N P R A Annual Meeting. Conference Papers. Multi-Year CD-ROM **6779**
National Petroleum Refiners Association Computer Conference. Proceedings *see* N P R A Computer Conference. Proceedings **6802**
National Petroleum Refiners Association Cracker Seminar Transcripts *see* N P R A Cracker Seminar Transcripts **6779**
National Petroleum Refiners Association Question & Answer Session on Refining and Petrochemical Technology Transcripts (CD-ROM Edition) *see* N P R A Question & Answer Session on Refining and Petrochemical Technology Transcripts (CD-ROM Edition) **6779**
National Petroleum Refiners Association Refinery and Petrochemical Plant Maintenance Conference *see* N P R A Refinery and Petrochemical Plant Maintenance Conference **6779**
National Petroleum Refiners Association Refinery and Petrochemical Plant Maintenance Conference. Technical Transcripts *see* N P R A Refinery and Petrochemical Plant Maintenance Conference. Technical Transcripts **6779**
National Pharmaceutical Association Supplement *see* N P A Supplement **6862**
National Pharmacists Select Pinpointer *see* Scott's Canadian Pharmacists Directory **2027**
National Pharmacists Select Profiler *see* Scott's Canadian Pharmacists Directory **2027**
National Pharmacists Select Prospector *see* Scott's Canadian Pharmacists Directory **2027**
National Physical Laboratory Annual Review *see* N P L Annual Review **7027**
National Physical Laboratory, Centre for Optical and Analytical Measurement Report COAM *see* N P L Report COAM **7081**
National Physical Laboratory Report C I R M *see* N P L Report C I R M **7027**
National Physical Laboratory Report C I S E *see* N P L Report C I S E **2534**
National Physical Laboratory Report C M M T (A) *see* N P L Report C M M T (A) **3355**
National Physical Laboratory Report C Q M *see* N P L Report C Q M **6404**
National Physical Laboratory Report Center for Material Measurement and Technology *see* N P L Report C M M T (A) **3355**
National Physical Laboratory Report Centre for Ionising Radiation Metrology *see* N P L Report C I R M **7027**
National Physical Laboratory Report M O M *see* N P L Report M O M **6404**
National Physical Laboratory Report on D Q L - O R *see* N P L Report on D Q L - O R **7027**
National Physical Laboratory Technical Bulletin *see* N P L Technical Bulletin **7027**
National Physician Database *see* Physician Services Benefit Rates Report. Canada **1703**
National Planning and Research Program. Brochures *see* U.S. Federal Transit Administration. National Transit Planning and Research Program. Project Directory **8636**
National Planning and Research Program. Technical Assistance Briefs. *see* U.S. Federal Transit Administration. National Planning and Research Program. Technical Assistance Briefs **8636**
National Plumbing Code of Canada (CAN ISSN 1207-652X) **1026**
The National Poetry Review (USA ISSN 1543-3455) **5427**
National Police Review (USA ISSN 1072-6551) **2661**
National Policy Association Reports (USA) **1500**
• ➤ National Political Science Review (USA ISSN 0896-629X) **7156**
National Pollutant Release Inventory. Summary Report *see* Environment Canada. National Pollutant Release Inventory. National Overview **3478**
National Portrait Gallery (NLD) **508**
National Portrait Gallery. Report (GBR) **508**
National Portrait Gallery Review *see* N P G Review **507**
• National Post (Toronto) (CAN ISSN 1486-8008) **3813**
• National Post (Vancouver) (CAN ISSN 1493-4779) **5229**
• National Post Business (CAN ISSN 1494-1988) **1370**
National Postsecondary Student Aid Study (USA ISSN 1077-8365) **3074**
National Potato Council. Potato Statistical Yearbook (USA) **242**
National Poultry News (USA) **294**
National Power Environmental Performance Review (Year) (GBR) **3326**
National Power. Report and Accounts (GBR) **3326**
National Precast Concrete Association. Membership Directory & Buyer's Guide (USA) **1026**
• National Precaster (AUS ISSN 1037-9908) **1026**
National Prescribing Centre Annual Report *see* N P C Annual Report **5682**
National Prescribing Service Rational Assessment of Drugs and Research R A D A R *see* N P S R A D A R **6862**
National Preservation Office Journal *see* N P O Journal **2619**
National Press Club Record (USA ISSN 0027-9927) **4580**
National Prison Project Journal (USA ISSN 1076-769X) **2661**
National Productivity and Competitiveness Council. Annual Report (MUS ISSN 1694-0245) **1780**
National Productivity and Competitiveness Council Newsletter *see* N P C C Newsletter **1780**
National Productivity Corporation, Malaysia. Annual Report/Perbadanan Produktiviti Negara. Lapuran Tahunan (MYS) **1780**
National Products Liability Database Report (USA) **4739**
National Products News (IND) **1899**
(Year) National Profile Directory of Independent Agents and Brokers (CAN) **1370**
National Profile of Community Colleges: Trends & Statistics (USA) **2960**
National Propane Gas Association Reports *see* N P G A Reports **6778**
• National Property Law Digests (USA ISSN 0363-8340) **4739**
The National Provisioner *see* Independent Provisioner **3646**
The National Provisioner's Meat & Deli Retailer *see* Meat & Deli Retailer **3655**
• National Psoriasis Foundation. Annual Report (USA ISSN 8756-2243) **5880**
National Psychological Association for Psychoanalysis. Bulletin (USA ISSN 0077-5339) **7386**
National Psychological Association for Psychoanalysis. News and Reviews (USA) **7386**
National Public Accountant *see* N P A **1297**
• National Public Employment Reporter (USA ISSN 1094-4079) **1699**
National Public Radio Interviews *see* The N P R Interviews **4580**
National Quality Engineering Industry Review *see* Global Engineering Review **3367**
National Radio Astronomy Observatory Newsletter *see* N R A O Newsletter **578**
† • National Radio Science Conference. Proceedings/Al-Mu'tamar al-Qawmi li-'ilm al-Radyu (EGY ISSN 1110-6972) **8976**
National Radiological Protection Board. Report (GBR ISSN 0308-5430) **7069**
National Railway Bulletin *see* N R H S Bulletin **8621**
National Railway Historical Society Bulletin *see* N R H S Bulletin **8621**
National Railways of Zimbabwe. Annual Report (ZWE) **8621**
National Reading Conference Yearbook *see* N R C Yearbook **3074**
National Ready Mixed Concrete Association Publication *see* N R M C A Publication **1025**
• National Real Estate Investor (USA ISSN 0027-9994) **7601**
National Reconnaissance (USA ISSN 1557-0304) **6438**
• National Referral Roster (USA ISSN 1075-1084) **7601**
National Register of Health Service Providers in Psychology (USA ISSN 0099-2151) **7386**
National Register of Independent Schools of Australia (AUS ISSN 1444-0288) **2960**
National Register of Prominent Americans and International Notables (USA ISSN 0077-5371) **644**
National Registration Center for Study Abroad Directory of Educational Programs *see* N R C S A Directory of Educational Programs **2888**

DIRECTORY 2010 NATIONAL TERRITORY OF TIERRA DEL FUEGO, ANTARCTICA 10653

National Registration Center for Study Abroad Program Directory. Europe (Online) *see* N R C S A Program Directory. Europe (Online) **3014**
National Rehabilitation Association Newsletter *see* Contemporary Rehab **6108**
National Rehabilitation Center for Persons with Disabilities. Research Bulletin *see* Kokuritsu Shintai Shogaisha Rihabiriteshon Senta Kenkyu Kiyo **4067**
▼ National Rehabilitation Compensation Study (USA ISSN 1941-1774) **4107**
National Reining Horse Association Reiner *see* N R H A Reiner **8295**
National Relay Conference. Proceedings (USA ISSN 0077-5401) **3326**
• National Relay Service Performance Report (AUS ISSN 1833-0754) **2370**
National Relay Service Provider Performance Report *see* National Relay Service Performance Report **2370**
National Religious Broadcasters Magazine *see* N R B Magazine **2386**
National Relocation & Real Estate (USA ISSN 1073-2047) **1870**
• National Renderers Association. Bulletin (USA ISSN 0968-3240) **3657**
National Renewable Energy Laboratory. Technical Paper (USA) **3142**
National Renewable Energy Laboratory Technical Reports (Online) *see* N R E L Technical Reports (Online) **3142**
• National Renewal (PHL) **7665**
National Report of Space Research in Poland (POL) **66**
• National Reporter (CAN ISSN 0317-641X) **4739**
National Reporter on Legal Ethics and Professional Responsibility (USA) **4739**
• National Reporter System. Federal Rules Decisions (USA) **4739**
• National Research Center on the Gifted and Talented Newsletter (USA) **3044**
➤ National Research Centre. Bulletin (EGY ISSN 1110-0591) **7887**
National Research Council Canada. Aeronautical Notes (CAN ISSN 0823-048X) **66**
• National Research Council Canada. Performance Report (CAN ISSN 1483-7463) **7454**
National Research Council of Canada. N R C Annual Report - Rapport Annuel du C N R C (CAN ISSN 0842-6066) **7887**
➤ National Research Council of Thailand. Journal (THA ISSN 0028-0011) **7887**
National Research Council. Transit Cooperative Research Program. Annual Report (USA ISSN 1073-4872) **8505**
National Research Council. Transportation Research Board. Bibliography (USA ISSN 0148-849X) **8528**
National Research Council. Transportation Research Board. Conference Proceedings (USA ISSN 1073-1652) **8506**
National Research Council. Transportation Research Board. Millennium Papers (USA) **8506**
National Research Council. Transportation Research Board. Policy Study Reports (USA) **8506**
National Research Council. Transportation Research Board. Practical Papers (USA) **8506**
• National Research Council. Transportation Research Board. Publications Index (USA) **8528**
National Research Council. Transportation Research Board. Research Pays Off (USA) **8506**
National Research Council. Transportation Research Board. Special Report (USA ISSN 0360-859X) **8632**
National Research Institute Bibliographies *see* N R I Bibliographies **631**
National Research Institute Discussion Papers *see* N R I Discussion Papers **7986**
National Research Institute. Division of Educational Research. Occasional Papers (PNG) **2890**
National Research Institute. Division of Educational Research. Research Papers (PNG) **2890**
National Research Institute. Division of Educational Research. Special Report (PNG) **2890**
National Research Institute. Division of Educational Research. Working Papers (PNG) **2890**
National Research Institute for Earth Science and Disaster Prevention. Annual Report *see* Bosai Kagaku Gijutsu Kenkyujo Nenpo **2702**
National Research Institute for Earth Science and Disaster Prevention. Technical Note *see* Bosai Kagaku Gijutsu Kenkyujo Kenkyu Shiryo **2702**
National Research Institute Monographs *see* N R I Monographs **7986**
National Research Institute of Agricultural Economics. Annual Report *see* Nogyo Sogo Kenkyujo Nenpo **141**
National Research Institute of Aquaculture. Bulletin/Tansui-ku Suisan Kenkyujo Kenkyu Hokoku (JPN ISSN 0389-5858) **3602**
National Research Institute of Far Seas Fisheries. Bulletin (JPN) **3602**
National Research Institute of Fire and Disaster. Report *see* Shobo Kenkyujo Hokoku **3581**
National Research Institute of Fisheries Engineering. Bulletin *see* Suisan Kogaku Kenkyujo Kenkyu Hokoku **3609**
National Research Institute of Fisheries Engineering. Technical Report *see* Suisan Kogaku Kenkyujo Giho **3609**
National Research Institute of Legal Policy Research. Report *see* Oikeuspoliittinen Tutkimuslaitos. Tutkimus **4752**
National Research Institute of Police Science. Annual Report *see* Kagaku Keisatsu Kenkyujo Nenpo **2658**
National Research Institute of Police Science. Reports *see* Kagaku Keisatsu Kenkyuujo Houkoku **2658**
National Research Institute Special Publications *see* N R I Special Publications **7986**
National Research Laboratory of Metrology. Bulletin (JPN ISSN 0451-6109) **6405**
National Retirement Quarterly (GBR ISSN 1353-3185) **3869**
• National Review (USA ISSN 0028-0038) **7156**
National Review of Medicine (CAN) **5684**
National Review of Real Estate Markets (USA ISSN 1079-0292) **7601**
National Rifle Association Journal *see* N R A Journal **8323**
• National Right to Life News (USA ISSN 0164-7415) **8057**
National Right to Work Newsletter (USA ISSN 0197-7032) **1699**
National Risk Retention Association News (Online) *see* N R R A News (Online) **4516**
National Rivers Authority Annual R & D Review *see* N R A Annual R & D Review **8829**
National Rivers Authority Annual Report *see* N R A Annual Report **8829**
National Rivers Authority Corporate Plan *see* N R A Corporate Plan **8829**
National Rivers Authority Fisheries Statistics *see* N R A Fisheries Statistics **3613**
National Rivers Authority Water Quality Series *see* N R A Water Quality Series **8829**
National Rivers Hall of Fame Newsletter (USA) **2620**
National Roading Program *see* National Land Transport Programme **8632**
National Roads Authority Scheme Monographs *see* N R A Scheme Monographs **4247**
National Roofing Contractors Association Membership Directory *see* N R C A Membership Directory **2018**
• National Round Table on the Environment and the Economy. Annual Report (CAN ISSN 1482-6852) **2620**
• National Round Table on the Environment and the Economy. Performance Report (CAN ISSN 1483-8834) **7454**
• National Round Table on the Environment and the Economy. Review (Online) (CAN ISSN 1910-8419) **3454**
• National Round Table on the Environment and the Economy. Review (Print) (CAN ISSN 1200-0442) **3454**
National Rugby Post (CAN) **8239**
• National Rural Education News (USA ISSN 0036-0023) **2890**
National Rural Health Association News *see* N R H A E News **7532**
The National Rural Letter Carrier (USA ISSN 0028-0089) **2354**
▼ • ➤ National Rural School Leadership Journal (USA ISSN 1948-9463) **2890**
National Safety (AUS ISSN 1445-9922) **7533**
National Safety *see* National Safety & Occupational Hygiene **7533**
National Safety & Occupational Hygiene/Nasionale Veiligheid (ZAF) **7533**
National Safety Council of Australia. Annual Report (AUS ISSN 0813-1694) **6681**
National Salmon Resources Center. Bulletin *see* Sake, Masu Shigen Kanri Senta Kenkyu Hokoku **3607**
National Sash and Door Jobbers Association. Bulletin (USA) **1026**
National Sash and Door Jobbers Association. Newsletter (USA) **1026**
National School Supply & Equipment Association Membership Directory *see* N S S E A Membership Directory **3028**
• National Science Council Review (TWN) **7887**
National Science Foundation Current *see* N S F Current **7885**
• National Science Foundation Custom News Service (USA) **7887**
• National Science Foundation. Directorate for Engineering. Engineering News (USA) **3212**
• National Science Foundation. E-Bulletin (USA) **7887**
National Science Foundation of Sri Lanka. Journal (LKA ISSN 1391-4588) **7887**
National Science Museum. Bulletin. Series A: Zoology/Kokuritsu Kagaku Hakubutsukan Kenkyu Hokoku. A Rui: Dobutsugaku (JPN ISSN 0385-2423) **957**
National Science Museum. Bulletin. Series B: Botany/Kokuritsu Kagaku Hakubutsukan Kenkyu Hokoku. B Rui: Shokubutsugaku (JPN ISSN 0385-2431) **804**
National Science Museum. Bulletin. Series C: Geology & Paleontology (JPN ISSN 0385-244X) **2757**
National Science Museum. Bulletin. Series D: Anthropology/Kokuritsu Kagaku Hakubutsukan Kenkyu Hokoku. D Rui: Jinruigaku (JPN ISSN 0385-3039) **349**
National Science Museum. Bulletin. Series E: Physical Sciences and Engineering/Kokuritsu Kagaku Hakubutsukan Kenkyu Hokoku. E Rui, Rikogaku (JPN ISSN 0387-8511) **3212**
National Science Museum. Memoirs *see* Kokuritsu Kagaku Hakubutsukan Senpo **7877**
National Science Museum Monographs (JPN ISSN 1342-9574) **7887**
National Science Teachers Association Reports *see* N S T A Reports **2889**
National Science Teachers Association. Yearbook (USA) **2890**
National Sculpture Society News Bulletin *see* N S S News Bulletin **507**
National Secular Society. Annual Report (GBR) **6935**
National Security (Farmington Hills) *see* Information Plus Reference Series. National Security **2677**
National Security Institute Advisory *see* N S I Advisory **2679**
National Security Law Report (USA) **4739**
➤ National Security Review (PHL ISSN 0115-5113) **6438**
National Senior Citizens Law Center Washington Weekly (USA) **4739**
• National Seniors Productive Ageing Centre. Research Bulletin (AUS ISSN 1834-2108) **8057**
National Service News (USA) **8057**
• National Shellfisheries Association. Quarterly Newsletter (USA) **957**
National Shipping Corporation. Report and Accounts (PAK) **8654**
National Shorthand Reporters Association. Membership Directory and Registry of Professional Reporters *see* National Court Reporters Association. Membership Directory and Registry of Professional Reporters **4957**
National Skeet Shooting Association. Records Annual (USA ISSN 0077-5738) **8323**
National Ski & Snowboard Retailers Association Cost of Doing Business Survey *see* N S S R A Cost of Doing Business Survey **8219**
National Ski & Snowboard Retailers Association Newsletter *see* N S S R A Newsletter **1835**
National Slovak Society of the United States of America. National News (USA ISSN 1534-1925) **3553**
National Snow and Ice Data Center Annual Report *see* N S I D C Annual Report **2757**
National Snow and Ice Data Center New Accessions List *see* World Data Center A for Glaciology (Snow and Ice). New Accessions List **2721**
National Snow and Ice Data Center Notes *see* N S I D C Notes **2757**
National Snow and Ice Data Center Special Reports *see* N S I D C Special Reports **2757**
National Social Science Documentation Centre Research Information Series. Bibliographic Reprints *see* N A S S D O C Research Information Series. Bibliographic Reprints **631**
National Social Science Documentation Centre Research Information Series. Conference Alert *see* N A S S D O C Research Information Series. Conference Alert **6282**
National Society for Clean Air News *see* N S C A News **3489**
National Society for Experiential Education Quarterly *see* N S E E Quarterly **6701**
National Society for the Preservation of Covered Bridges Newsletter (USA) **4304**
National Society for the Prevention of Cruelty to Children. Annual Report (GBR ISSN 0077-5754) **8057**
National Society for the Prevention of Cruelty to Children News *see* N S P C C News **8056**
• National Society for the Study of Education. Yearbook (USA ISSN 0077-5762) **2890**
• ➤ National Society of Allied Health. Journal (USA ISSN 1945-3361) **7533**
National Society of Black Engineers Bridge *see* N S B E Bridge **3211**
National Society of Black Engineers Magazine *see* N S B E Magazine **3211**
National Society of Mural Painters. Newsletter (USA) **508**
National Society of Public Accountants Washington Reporter *see* N S P A Washington Reporter **1297**
National Society of the Children of the American Revolution Magazine *see* N S C A R Magazine **2268**
National Society of United States Daughters of 1812. News-Letter (USA) **3776**
National Son (USA) **2268**
National Spa & Pool Institute Business Owners *see* The N S P I Business Owners **6993**
National Space Science Data Center News *see* N S S D C News **66**
National Speed Sport News (USA ISSN 0028-0208) **8190**
National Speedway Directory (USA) **8190**
National Speleological Society, Inc. News *see* N S S News **2757**
National Spiritualist (USA ISSN 0882-1275) **7665**
National Sporting Goods Association Buying Guide *see* N S G A Sporting Goods Buying Guide **8189**
National Sporting Goods Association Sporting Goods Buying Guide *see* N S G A Sporting Goods Buying Guide **8189**
National Square Dance Campers Association Times *see* N S D C A Times **2687**
National Squares (USA ISSN 0746-3685) **2687**
National Statistics Office Monthly Bulletin of Statistics *see* N S O Monthly Bulletin of Statistics **8389**
National Stock Dog (USA ISSN 0028-0267) **6811**
National Storytelling Directory (Online) (USA) **5035**
• National Strength & Conditioning Association Bulletin (USA) **6993**
National Student Extra *see* N S E **2994**
National Student Speech Language Hearing Association Clinical Series *see* N S S L H A Clinical Series **6083**
National Summary of Domestic Trade Receivables (USA) **1152**
National Survey of State Laws (USA ISSN 1078-2095) **4851**
National Survey on Drug Use and Health Report *see* The N S D U H Report **2697**
National Survey on Drug Use & Health. Results (USA ISSN 1559-4688) **7533**
National Sweet Pea Society. Annual (GBR ISSN 0269-6304) **3744**
National Sweet Pea Society. Bulletin (GBR) **3744**
National Symposium on Atomic Energy. Proceedings *see* Genshiryoku Sogo Shinpojiumu Yokoshu **3168**
National Systems Programmers Association Technical Support (USA ISSN 1079-3135) **2508**
National Taiwan Museum. Journal *see* Guoli Taiwan Bowuguan Xuekan **340**
National Taiwan Museum Special Publication Series (TWN ISSN 1607-5722) **7887**
National Taiwan University. College of Agriculture. Annual Report (TWN) **139**
National Taiwan University. College of Law. Journal of Social Science (TWN ISSN 0077-5835) **7987**
National Taiwan University. Department of Anthropology. Bulletin (TWN) **349**
National Taiwan University. Institute of Fishery Biology. Report (TWN) **3602**
National Taiwan University Journal of Sociology (TWN ISSN 0077-5851) **8122**
National Tank Truck Carrier Directory (USA ISSN 0077-586X) **8673**
National Tax Association Forum *see* N T A Forum **8976**
• National Tax Association. Proceedings of the Annual Conference on Taxation and Minutes of the Annual Meeting (USA ISSN 0069-8687) **1936**
• ➤ National Tax Journal (USA ISSN 0028-0283) **1936**
National Teaching & Learning Forum (USA ISSN 1057-2880) **2995**
National Technical Information Service Alerts: Agriculture & Food *see* N T I S Alerts: Agriculture & Food **183**
National Technical Information Service Alerts: Biomedical Technology & Human Factors Engineering *see* N T I S Alerts: Biomedical Technology & Human Factors Engineering **5749**
National Technical Information Service Alerts: Building Industry Technology *see* N T I S Alerts: Building Industry Technology **1048**
National Technical Information Service Alerts: Business & Economics *see* N T I S Alerts: Business & Economics **1252**
National Technical Information Service Alerts: Civil Engineering *see* N T I S Alerts: Civil Engineering **3232**
National Technical Information Service Alerts: Communication *see* N T I S Alerts: Communication **2348**
National Technical Information Service Alerts: Computers, Control & Information Theory *see* N T I S Alerts: Computers, Control & Information Theory **2444**
National Technical Information Service Alerts: Electrotechnology *see* N T I S Alerts: Electrotechnology **3109**
National Technical Information Service Alerts: Energy *see* N T I S Alerts: Energy **3153**
National Technical Information Service Alerts: Environmental Pollution & Control *see* N T I S Alerts: Environmental Pollution & Control **3480**
National Technical Information Service Alerts: Government Inventions for Licensing *see* N T I S Alerts: Government Inventions for Licensing **8447**
National Technical Information Service Alerts: Health Care *see* N T I S Alerts: Health Care **7002**
National Technical Information Service Alerts: Manufacturing Technology *see* N T I S Alerts: Manufacturing Technology **8447**
National Technical Information Service Alerts: Materials Sciences *see* N T I S Alerts: Materials Sciences **3232**
National Technical Information Service Alerts: Ocean Sciences & Engineering *see* N T I S Alerts: Ocean Sciences & Engineering **2720**
National Technical Information Service Alerts: Transportation *see* N T I S Alerts: Transportation **8527**
National Technical Information Service Bibliographic Database *see* N T I S Bibliographic Database **7938**
National Technical Services Association Reporter *see* N T S A Reporter **1698**
National Territory of Tierra del Fuego, Antarctica and Islands of the South Atlantic. Ministerio de Economia y Hacienda. Anuario Estadistico (ARG) **8389**

Title

▼ *new title* † *ceased* • *electronic media* ➤ *refereed*

10654 NATIONAL TERTIARY EDUCATION UNION EXPRESS ULRICH'S PERIODICALS

National Tertiary Education Union Express *see* N T E U Express **2994**
National Tertiary Education Union Frontline *see* N T E U Frontline **2994**
National Textile Center - Research Briefs (USA) **8455**
National Theatre of Japan (JPN ISSN 0388-0648) **8474**
National Tooling and Machining Association. Buyers Guide (USA) **5457**
National Tooling and Machining Association. Record *see* The Record **5459**
National Tourist Park Guide (AUS) **8740**
National Towing News (USA) **8595**
National Toxicology Program Technical Report Series (USA ISSN 0888-8051) **3455**
National Toxicology Programme, Center for the Evaluation of Risks to Human Reproduction MON (USA ISSN 1556-2271) **3500**
National Trade and Professional Associations of the United States (USA ISSN 0734-354X) **2019**
National Trade and Tariff Service (CAN) **1936**
• National Trade Data Bank (USA ISSN 1064-9913) **1407**
National Trade Estimate, Report on Foreign Trade Barriers (USA ISSN 0898-3887) **1578**
National Transient Lodge News *see* N T L News **4599**
National Transportation Agency of Canada. Annual Review *see* Canadian Transportation Agency. Annual Report **8493**
National Transportation Brokers Directory *see* Leonard's Guide. National Third Party Logistics Directory **2013**
National Transportation Safety Board Decisions (USA ISSN 0094-761X) **8506**
National Transportation Safety Board Digest Service (USA) **8549**
National Transportation Safety Board. Report (USA) **8506**
National Transportation Safety Board Reporter *see* N T S B Reporter **8548**
• National Trauma Registry Provincial Report. Alberta: Hospital Injury Admissions (CAN ISSN 1910-832X) **4107**
• National Trauma Registry Provincial Report. British Columbia: Hospital Injury Admissions (CAN ISSN 1910-7757) **4107**
• National Trauma Registry Provincial Report. Manitoba Hospital Injury Admissions (CAN ISSN 1910-8206) **4107**
• National Trauma Registry Provincial Report. New Brunswick Hospital Injury Admissions (CAN ISSN 1910-7714) **4107**
• National Trauma Registry Provincial Report. Newfoundland and Labrador: Hospital Injury Admissions (CAN ISSN 1910-8222) **4108**
National Trauma Registry Provincial Report. Nova Scotia: Hospital Injury Admissions *see* National Trauma Registry Provincial Report. Newfoundland and Labrador: Hospital Injury Admissions **4108**
National Trauma Registry Provincial Report. Prince Edward Island: Hospital Injury Admissions *see* National Trauma Registry Provincial Report. Newfoundland and Labrador: Hospital Injury Admissions **4108**
National Trauma Registry Provincial Report. Quebec: Hospital Injury Admissions *see* National Trauma Registry Provincial Report. Newfoundland and Labrador: Hospital Injury Admissions **4108**
National Trauma Registry Provincial Report. Saskatchewan: Hospital Injury Admissions *see* National Trauma Registry Provincial Report. Newfoundland and Labrador: Hospital Injury Admissions **4108**
• National Trauma Registry Report: Hospital Injury Admissions (CAN ISSN 1486-1453) **5684**
National Trauma Registry Report. Injury Hospitalizations *see* National Trauma Registry Report: Hospital Injury Admissions **5684**
National Trauma Registry Territorial Report. Northwest Territories: Hospital Injury Admissions *see* National Trauma Registry Provincial Report. Newfoundland and Labrador: Hospital Injury Admissions **4108**
National Trauma Registry Territorial Report. Nunavut: Hospital Injury Admissions *see* National Trauma Registry Provincial Report. Newfoundland and Labrador: Hospital Injury Admissions **4108**
National Trauma Registry Territorial Report. Yukon Territory: Hospital Injury Admissions *see* National Trauma Registry Provincial Report. Newfoundland and Labrador: Hospital Injury Admissions **4108**
National Treasury Employees Union Bulletin *see* N T E U Bulletin **4599**
National Truck Equipment Association Annual Report (USA) **8673**
National Truck Equipment Association Technical Report *see* N T E A Technical Report **8673**
National Truck Equipment Association Washington Update *see* N T E A Washington Update **8673**
• The National Trust (GBR ISSN 0266-8068) **2620**
National Trust for Historic Preservation. Annual Report (USA ISSN 0091-5467) **4304**
National Trust for Historic Preservation in the United States. Preservation Books (USA) **450**
• The National Trust for Scotland Guide (Year) (GBR) **2620**
• National Trust Magazine (AUS ISSN 1834-7320) **2620**
The National Trust Magazine *see* The National Trust **2620**
• National Trust of Australia (W.A.) Annual Report (AUS ISSN 1034-1102) **4193**
National Tuberculosis Institute Bulletin *see* N T I Bulletin **6216**
National Undersea Research Program. Research Report (USA ISSN 1054-240X) **2813**
• National Underwriter. Life & Health (USA ISSN 1940-1345) **4516**
• National Underwriter. P & C (Property & Casualty) (USA ISSN 1940-1353) **4516**
National Underwriter. Property & Casualty - Risk & Benefits Management Edition *see* National Underwriter. P & C **4516**
National Unification and North Korean Social Culture (KOR) **557**
National Union of Educators Comment *see* N U E Comment **2889**
National Union of Journalists Freelance Directory *see* N U J Freelance Directory **4580**
National Union of Teachers. Annual Report (GBR ISSN 0077-5940) **2890**
National Unionist *see* Al Watani Al Ittihadi **3790**
National University of Defense Technology. Journal *see* Guofang Keji Daxue Xuebao **6423**
National University of Ireland. Economics Department. Working Papers Series (IRL) **1152**
National University of Ireland, Galway. Social Sciences Research Centre. Occasional Paper (IRL) **7987**
National University of Singapore. Department of Sociology. Working Paper Series (SGP) **8122**
National University of Singapore Economic Journal *see* N U S Economic Journal **1151**
➤ National University of Singapore. Faculty of Business Administration. Research Paper Series (SGP) **1780**
National University of Singapore. Institute for Mathematical Sciences. Lecture Notes Series (SGP ISSN 1793-0758) **5519**
National Urban League Annual Report (USA) **4420**
National Utility Contractor (USA ISSN 0192-0359) **3279**
National Valentine Collectors Bulletin (USA ISSN 1044-8896) **4342**
National Vanguard (USA) **7156**
National Veal Summary *see* U S D A Weekly Veal Market Summary **207**
National Vegetable Society. Newsletter (GBR) **3744**
National Video Resources Reports *see* N V R Reports **2402**
National Vital Statistics Reports *see* U.S. Department of Health and Human Services. National Center for Health Statistics. National Vital Statistics Reports **7317**
• National Voter (USA ISSN 0028-0372) **7156**
National Warehouse and Distribution Directory *see* Leonard's Guide. National Warehouse and Distribution Directory **2013**
National Water Industry Handbook *see* The Global Environment **8824**
† National Water Polo News (AUS ISSN 1323-1197) **8976**
National Water Quality Evaluation Project Notes *see* N W Q E P Notes **8829**
National Water Resources Association Daily *see* N W R A Daily **8829**
• National Water Rights Digest (USA) **8830**
• National Weather Association Newsletter (USA ISSN 0271-1044) **6392**
• National Weather Digest (USA ISSN 0271-1052) **6392**
• National Weekly Cattle and Beef Summary (USA ISSN 1931-4469) **294**
National Wetlands Newsletter (USA ISSN 0164-0712) **3455**
National Wheelchair Basketball Association. Directory (USA) **8240**
National Wheelchair Basketball Association. Newsletter (USA) **8240**
• National Wildlife (USA ISSN 0028-0402) **2620**
• National Wildlife (World Edition) (USA ISSN 1545-5157) **2620**
• National Winter Storms Operations Plan (USA ISSN 0742-4043) **2227**
National Women's Health Network (USA) **8847**
• National Women's Health Report (USA ISSN 0741-9147) **8847**
National Women's History Project Network *see* N W H P Network **8901**
National Women's Studies Association Action *see* N W S Action **8901**
National Women's Studies Association Journal *see* N W S A Journal **8901**
National Woodlands Magazine (USA ISSN 0279-9812) **3714**
National Wool Market Review (USA ISSN 1066-0593) **294**
• National Writing Project. Quarterly (Online) (USA) **3074**
• The National Yellow Book of Funeral Directors (USA ISSN 1054-8238) **2019**
• National Youth Affairs Research Scheme Reports (AUS) **2162**
National Youth Rights Association Freedom *see* N Y R A Freedom **2162**
• National-Zeitung (DEU) **3853**
• Nationalbibliografin - Boecker/Swedish National Bibliography (SWE) **631**
Nationale Bank van Belgie. Statistisch Tijdschrift *see* Banque Nationale de Belgique. Bulletin Statistique **1320**
De Nationale Botenbank (NLD) **8278**
Nationale Enquete Arbeidsomstandigheden (NLD ISSN 1875-385X) **1699**
Nationale Genossenschaft fuer die Lagerung Radioaktiver Abfaelle Bulletin *see* N A G R A Bulletin **3509**
Nationale Genossenschaft fuer die Lagerung Radioaktiver Abfaelle Technischer Bericht *see* N A G R A Technischer Bericht **3509**
Nationale Havenraad. Jaarverslag (Year) (NLD) **8654**
Nationale Maatschappij van Belgische Spoorwegen. Informatie en Aanwinsten (BEL ISSN 0777-4931) **8528**
De Nationale MolenGids (NLD ISSN 1871-7098) **451**
Nationale Monitor Geestelijke Gezondheid (NLD ISSN 1573-8140) **6162**
Nationale Plantentuin van Belgie. Bulletin *see* Systematics and Geography of Plants **819**
Nationale Raad voor Landbouwkundig Onderzoek. Jaarverslag/National Council for Agricultural Research. Annual Report (NLD ISSN 0169-1449) **139**
† • Nationaleinkommen und Einkommenskreislauf (DEU) **8976**
• ➤ Nationalism & Ethnic Politics (GBR ISSN 1353-7113) **7254**
The Nationalist (IRL ISSN 1649-6485) **3894**
The Nationalist & Leinster Times *see* The Nationalist **3894**
Nationalist and Munster Advertiser (IRL ISSN 1393-9076) **3894**
The Nationalist Clonmel (IRL) **3894**
The Nationalist Observer (USA) **7213**
Nationalities *see* Minzu **3550**
Nationalities Education of China *see* Zhongguo Minzu Jiaoyu **2928**
Nationalities Forum *see* Minzu Luntan **7155**
• ➤ Nationalities Papers (GBR ISSN 0090-5992) **7987**
Nationality Pictorial *see* Minzu Huabao **3550**
Nationally Coordinated Program of Highway Research, Development, and Technology (USA) **8632**
➤ Nationaloekonomisk Tidsskrift (DNK ISSN 0028-0453) **7987**
Nationalpark (DEU ISSN 0342-9806) **2620**
Nationalpark Bayerischer Wald (DEU ISSN 0937-0048) **2620**
Nationalpark Berchtesgaden. Forschungsberichte (DEU ISSN 0172-0023) **2620**
Nationalpark-Forschung in der Schweiz (CHE ISSN 1022-9493) **2620**
Nationalpark Schleswig-Holsteinisches Wattenmeer. Schriftenreihe (DEU ISSN 0946-7645) **2620**
Nationalratswahlen (Year)/Elections au Conseil National (Year) (CHE ISSN 1012-6325) **7482**
Nationalsozialistische Besatzungspolitik in Europa 1939-1945 (DEU) **4247**
Nationellt Pistolskytte *see* N P. Nationellt Pistolskytte **8189**
• Nationen (NOR ISSN 0805-3782) **3924**
• ➤ Nations and Nationalism (GBR ISSN 1354-5078) **7157**
• Nation's Best Sports (USA ISSN 1931-6267) **8324**
Nation's Best Sports Fish & Hunt *see* Nation's Best Sports **8324**
• Nation's Building News (USA ISSN 8750-6580) **1026**
• Nations Building News Online (USA) **1026**
• Nation's Cities Weekly (USA ISSN 0164-5935) **7499**
• The Nation's Health (USA ISSN 0028-0496) **7533**
Nations in Transit (Year) (USA ISSN 1538-6309) **8122**
• Nation's Restaurant News (USA ISSN 0028-0518) **4394**
Nation's Restaurant News Daily NewsFax *see* Daily NewsFax **4384**
Nations Unies Annuaire de Desarmement *see* United Nations Disarmament Yearbook **7270**
Nations Unies Annuaire Juridique *see* United Nations Juridical Yearbook **4943**
Nations Unies. Assemblee Generale. Index des Actes *see* United Nations. General Assembly. Index to Proceedings **7201**
Nations Unies. Commission Economique et Sociale pour l'Asie et le Pacifique. Rapport Annuel *see* Economic and Social Commission for Asia and the Pacific. Annual Report **1595**
Nations Unies. Commission Economique pour l'Europe. Rapport Annuel *see* Economic Commission for Europe. Annual Report **1099**
Nations Unies. Commission Economique pour l'Europe. Serie sur l'Energie *see* United Nations. Economic Commission for Europe. Energy Series **3149**
Nations Unies. Conseil de Securite. Documents Officials. Supplement *see* United Nations. Security Council. Official Records. Supplement **7271**
Nations Unies. Conseil de Securite. Documents Officiels *see* United Nations. Security Council. Official Records **7271**
Nations Unies. Recueil des Sentences Arbitrales *see* United Nations. Reports of International Arbitral Awards **4801**
Nations Unies. Recueil des Traites. Index Cumulatif *see* United Nations. Treaty Series. Cumulative Index **4825**
Nations Unies. Releve des Traites et Accords Internationaux *see* United Nations. Statement of Treaties and International Agreements **7271**
Nations Unies. Traites Multinationaux Deposes aupres du Secretaire General *see* United Nations. Multilateral Treaties Deposited with the Secretary - General **4943**
Nationwide Directory of Corporate Meeting Planners (USA ISSN 0735-4444) **6282**
Nationwide Directory of Gift, Housewares & Home Textile Buyers (USA) **4061**
Nationwide Directory of Men's and Boys' Wear Buyers (USA ISSN 0077-5983) **2248**
Nationwide Directory of Sporting Goods Buyers (USA ISSN 0739-6074) **8190**
Nationwide Directory of Women's and Children's Wear Buyers (USA ISSN 0077-5991) **2248**
Nationwide Major Mass Market Merchandisers (USA ISSN 0077-6009) **2249**
Nationwide Overnight Stabling Directory *see* Nationwide Overnight Stabling Directory & Equestrian Vacation Guide **8295**
Nationwide Overnight Stabling Directory & Equestrian Vacation Guide (USA ISSN 0886-5647) **8295**
Nationwide Properties (GBR ISSN 0950-3382) **7601**
Native *see* Alaska Native Business & Resource Directory **1971**
Native America Yesterday and Today (USA ISSN 1552-8022) **4304**
Native American Bibliography Series (USA ISSN 1040-9629) **3574**
• Native American Connections (USA ISSN 1070-0587) **4304**
▼ Native American Journal (USA) **3553**
Native American Journalists Association News *see* N A J A News **4580**
Native American Law Digest (USA ISSN 1067-019X) **6635**
Native American News *see* Wotanging Ikche **6636**
Native American Rights Fund. Annual Report (USA ISSN 1556-682X) **6635**
Native American Rights Fund Legal Review *see* N A R F Legal Review **6635**
Native American Times (USA ISSN 1542-4928) **6635**
† Native Americans Information Directory (USA ISSN 1063-9632) **8976**
Native Americans of the Northeast (USA ISSN 1555-7073) **6635**
• Native Americas (USA ISSN 1092-3527) **6635**
• Native Forest Network. Eastern North American Resource Center. Bulletin (USA) **3697**
Native Journal (CAN ISSN 1198-8762) **3553**
Native Language *see* Rodna Rech **2210**
Native North American Almanac (USA ISSN 1070-8014) **6635**
• Native Peoples (USA ISSN 0895-7606) **6635**
Native Plant Society of New Mexico. Newsletter (USA) **804**
Native Plants *see* Wildflower **822**
• ➤ Native Plants Journal (USA ISSN 1522-8339) **804**
• Native Realities (USA) **6635**
Native Social Work Journal (CAN ISSN 1206-5323) **8057**
▼ ➤ Native South (USA ISSN 1943-2569) **6635**
• ➤ Native Studies Review (CAN ISSN 0831-585X) **6636**
Native Title *see* Native Title Service **4739**
Native Title News (AUS ISSN 1321-8301) **4739**
• Native Title Service (AUS) **4739**
Native Voice (CAN ISSN 0028-0542) **3602**
A Native's Guide to Chicago (USA ISSN 1933-4451) **8740**
Natnet Lanka (LKA ISSN 1391-2658) **5035**
NATO *see* N A T O **450**
NatoData *see* N A T O Data **6437**
Natotawin (CAN ISSN 0703-4733) **3553**
Natsionalen Voennoistoricheski Muzei, Sofia. Izvestiya (BGR ISSN 0324-0835) **6438**
Natsional'na Akademiya Nauk Ukrainy. Dopovidi (UKR ISSN 1025-6415) **7027**
➤ Natsional'na Akademiya Nauk Ukrainy. Instytut Tvarynnytstva. Naukovo-Tekhnichnyi Biuleten' (UKR) **268**
➤ Natsional'naya Akademiya Nauk Armenii. Izvestiya. Seriya Mekhanika/Hayastani Hanrapetutian Gitutsunneri Azgain Academiay Tegekagir Mechanics (ARM) **3390**
Natsional'naya Akademiya Nauk Respubliki Kazahstan. Izvestiya. Seriya Fiziko-Matematicheskaya/National Academy of Sciences of the Republic of Kazakhstan. Proceedings. Physics and Mathematics Series (KAZ ISSN 1991-346X) **7028**
Natsionalnaya Akademiya Nauk Respubliki Kazakhstan. Izvestiya. Seriya Biologicheskaya (KAZ) **691**
Natsionalnaya Akademiya Nauk Respubliki Kazakhstan. Izvestiya. Seriya Filologicheskaya (KAZ) **2238**
Natsionalnaya Akademiya Nauk Respubliki Kazakhstan. Izvestiya. Seriya Khimicheskaya *see* Kazakstan Respublikasy Ulttyk Gylym Akademiasynyn Khabarlary. Seriya Khimicheskaya **2069**

Link to your serials resources and content with ulrichsweb.com

Natsionalnaya Akademiya Nauk Respubliki Kazakhstan. Izvestiya. Seriya Obshchestvennykh Nauk (KAZ) **7987**
Natsionalnaya Ekonomicheskaya Gazeta (BLR) **1152**
Natsional'naya Gazeta (RUS) **3938**
• Natsional'nye Scheta Rossii (RUS) **1254**
Natsional'nyi Tekhnichnyi Universytet Ukrainy "Kyivs'kyi Politekhnichnyi Instytut". Visnyk. Mashynobuduvannya (UKR) **5457**
• Natsional'nyi Yadernyi Tsentr Respubliki Kazakhstan. Vestnik/N N C R K. Bulletin (KAZ ISSN 1729-7516) **7069**
➤ Natsiyanal'naya Akademiya Navuk Belarusi. Doklady/National Academy of Sciences of Belarus. Papers (BLR ISSN 1561-8323) **7887**
Natsiyanal'naya Akademiya Navuk Belarusi. Instytut Gistoryi. Shtogodnik/National Academy of Sciences of Belarus. Institute of History. The Annual Collection (BLR) **4154**
➤ Natsiyanal'naya Akademiya Navuk Belarusi. Instytut Lesu. Trudy/National Academy of Sciences of Belarus. Institute of Forest. Proceedings (BLR) **3697**
➤ Natsiyanal'naya Akademiya Navuk Belarusi. Instytut Matematyki. Trudy/National Academy of Sciences of Belarus. Institute of Mathematics. Proceedings (BLR) **5519**
Natsiyanal'naya Akademiya Navuk Belarusi. Naviny (BLR) **2995**
Natsiyanal'naya Akademiya Navuk Belarusi. Spravazdacha ab Dzeinastsi/National Academy of Sciences of Belarus. Annual Report (BLR) **7887**
➤ Natsiyanal'naya Akademiya Navuk Belarusi. Vestsi. Seryya Biyalagichnykh Navuk/National Academy of Sciences of Belarus. Proceedings. Series of Biological Sciences (BLR ISSN 1029-8940) **692**
➤ Natsiyanal'naya Akademiya Navuk Belarusi. Vestsi. Seryya Fizika-Matematychnykh Navuk/National Academy of Sciences of Belarus. Proceedings. Series of Physico-Mathematical Sciences (BLR ISSN 1561-2430) **7028**
➤ Natsiyanal'naya Akademiya Navuk Belarusi. Vestsi. Seryya Fizika-Technichnykh Navuk/National Academy of Sciences of Belarus. Proceedings. Series of Physico-Technical Sciences (BLR ISSN 1561-8358) **7028**
➤ Natsiyanal'naya Akademiya Navuk Belarusi. Vestsi. Seryya Gumanitarnykh Navuk/National Academy of Sciences of Belarus. Proceedings. Series of Humanitarian Sciences (BLR) **7987**
Natsiyanal'naya Akademiya Navuk Belarusi. Vestsi. Seryya Khimichnykh Navuk/National Academy of Sciences of Belarus. Proceedings. Series of Chemical Sciences (BLR ISSN 1561-8331) **2074**
➤ Natsiyanal'naya Akademiya Navuk Belarusi. Vestsi. Seryya Medyka-Biyalagichnykh Navuk/National Academy of Sciences of Belarus. Proceedings. Series of Medical-Biological Sciences (BLR ISSN 1680-6387) **5684**
• NatStat (USA) **8455**
Natsushima/Japan Marine Science and Technology Center News (JPN) **2813**
• Nattereria (BRA ISSN 1517-5359) **910**
Natturufraedingurinn (ISL ISSN 0028-0550) **7887**
Natturufraedistofnun Islands. Fjoelrit (ISL ISSN 1027-832X) **7887**
Natuerlich (CHE ISSN 1423-5129) **8324**
Natuerlich Gaertnern (DEU ISSN 0944-4564) **3744**
Natuerlich Leben (CHE ISSN 1660-8976) **6993**
Natuerlich Natur (DEU) **6993**
Natuerlich Vegetarisch (DEU ISSN 1437-0735) **6664**
• Natun Bangla (BGD) **3800**
Natun Dainik (IND) **3886**
Natun Katha (BGD) **3800**
Natun Thikana (IND ISSN 0300-3809) **5229**
Natur & Lifestyle (DEU) **5077**
Natur Erleben (DEU ISSN 1619-0319) **5077**
Natur i Norr (SWE ISSN 0280-5618) **855**
Natur-Museum Luzern. Veroeffentlichungen (CHE ISSN 1018-2462) **7887**
Natur og Mijoe Bulletin *see* Miljoejournalen **3453**
Natur og Miljoe (NOR ISSN 0807-9234) **3455**
Natur og Miljoe (Copenhagen) (DNK ISSN 0107-1653) **3455**
Natur og Miljoe, Illustreret Sammenfatning (DNK ISSN 1901-3027) **3455**
• Natur og Miljoe, Paavirkninger og Tilstand (Roskilde) (DNK ISSN 1601-9830) **3455**
Natur og Museum (DNK ISSN 0028-0585) **7887**
• Natur og Samfunn (NOR ISSN 0332-7469) **3455**
Natur-Raum-Gesellschaft (DEU) **4021**
Natur-Spiegel (DEU) **2620**
Natur und Artenschutz (DEU ISSN 1618-7490) **692**
• Natur und Gesundheit (DEU ISSN 1433-9935) **313**
Natur und Heilen (DEU ISSN 0932-3503) **6664**
Natur und Heimat (DEU ISSN 0028-0593) **7887**
• Natur und Kosmos (DEU ISSN 1615-3928) **3455**
Natur und Land (AUT ISSN 0028-0607) **7887**
Natur- und Landeskunde (DEU ISSN 1611-3829) **4247**
Natur und Landschaft (DEU ISSN 0028-0615) **2620**
Natur und Mensch (DEU ISSN 0077-6025) **692**
Natur und Museum (DEU ISSN 0028-1301) **7887**
• ➤ Natur und Recht (DEU ISSN 0172-1631) **4739**
Natur und Tierschutz Kalender des Deutschen Tierschutzbundes (DEU) **957**
Natura (ESP) **692**
Natura (ITA ISSN 0369-6243) **7887**
Natura (NLD ISSN 0028-0631) **7888**
Natura (VEN ISSN 0028-064X) **7888**
Natura Alpina (ITA ISSN 0392-4149) **2713**
Natura & Montagna (ITA ISSN 0028-0658) **692**
Natura Bresciana (ITA ISSN 0391-156X) **7888**
Natura Carpatica (SVK ISSN 1335-3535) **2713**
Natura Croatica (HRV ISSN 1330-0520) **7888**
Natura Croatica. Supplementum (HRV ISSN 1330-3430) **692**
Natura e Societa (ITA ISSN 0393-8875) **3455**
Natura Jutlandica. Occasional Papers (DNK ISSN 1399-6010) **692**
Natura Modenese (ITA ISSN 1127-2716) **7888**
Natura Mosana (BEL ISSN 0028-0666) **855**
Natura Nascosta (ITA ISSN 1590-9522) **2713**
➤ Natura Neotropicalis (ARG ISSN 0329-2177) **7888**
Natura Segreta (ITA ISSN 1826-3933) **7888**
• ➤ Natura Sloveniae (SVN ISSN 1580-0814) **692**
Natura Somogyiensis (HUN ISSN 1587-1908) **692**
Natural Animal Connections *see* Natural Living for Animals **6811**
➤ Natural Areas Journal (USA ISSN 0885-8608) **3455**
Natural Areas News (USA ISSN 1094-9860) **3455**
Natural Bodybuilding and Fitness (USA ISSN 1071-555X) **6993**
• Natural Bridge (USA ISSN 1525-9897) **5338**
Natural Business L O H A S Journal *see* L O H A S Journal **1143**
Natural Cat (USA ISSN 1523-5092) **6811**
• Natural Computing (NLD ISSN 1567-7818) **2432**
Natural Cures Newsletter (USA ISSN 1932-1619) **313**
Natural Disaster Reduction in China *see* Zhongguo Jianzai **2228**
Natural Environment Research Council. Centre for Ecology and Hydrology. Report (GBR) **2797**
Natural Environment Research Council. Institute of Terrestrial Ecology. Scientific Report (GBR) **692**
Natural Environment Research Council. Proudman Oceanographic Laboratory. Cruise Report (GBR) **2813**
Natural Environment Research Council. Proudman Oceanographic Laboratory. Report (GBR) **2813**
Natural Environment Research Council. Report (GBR ISSN 0072-7008) **3455**
Natural Environment Research Council. Sea Mammal Research Unit. Scientific Report (GBR) **957**
➤ Natural Fibres/Wlokna Naturalne (POL ISSN 1230-4476) **8455**
• Natural Food Network (USA ISSN 1937-7126) **3657**
• Natural Foods Merchandiser (USA ISSN 0164-338X) **1835**
• Natural Forces School Leadership Journal (USA ISSN 1930-2487) **2890**
Natural Gas (GBR ISSN 0140-3222) **6779**
• Natural Gas & Electricity (USA ISSN 1545-7893) **6779**
Natural Gas Chemical Industry *see* Tianranqi Huagong **6795**
Natural Gas Directory *see* Annuario del Metano **8930**
Natural Gas Exports *see* Exportations de Gaz Naturel **6768**
Natural Gas Fuels (USA) **8506**
Natural Gas Geoscience *see* Tianranqi Diqiou Kexue **6795**
Natural Gas Hedger *see* The Natural Gas Lookout **6780**
Natural Gas Imports *see* Importations de Gaz Naturel **6773**
Natural Gas Industry *see* Tianranqi Gongye **6795**
Natural Gas Industry's Daily Gas Price Index *see* N G I's Daily Gas Price Index **6778**
Natural Gas Industry's Weekly Gas Price Index *see* N G I's Weekly Gas Price Index **6778**
• Natural Gas Information (FRA ISSN 1995-3933) **6779**
• Natural Gas Intelligence (USA ISSN 0739-1811) **6779**
• The Natural Gas Lookout (CAN ISSN 1491-2279) **6780**
Natural Gas Market Report *see* Canadian Natural Gas Market Report **6765**
Natural Gas Monthly *see* U.S. Department of Energy. Energy Information Administration. Natural Gas Monthly (Online) **6796**
Natural Gas Resources *see* Tennen Gasu Kankei Shiryo **6794**
• Natural Gas Transportation and Distribution/Canada. Statistique Canada. Services de Gaz (CAN ISSN 1481-4234) **6800**
Natural Gas Utility Directory (CAN) **6780**
Natural Gas Vehicles Worldwide *see* N G V Worldwide **8976**
• Natural Gas Week (USA ISSN 8756-3037) **6780**
Natural Glow (USA) **8847**
Natural Golfer (USA ISSN 1525-1268) **8240**
• ➤ Natural Hazards (NLD ISSN 0921-030X) **2713**
• ➤ Natural Hazards and Earth System Sciences (DEU ISSN 1561-8633) **2787**
• Natural Hazards Center. Quick Response Reports (USA) **7988**
Natural Hazards Center. Special Publications (USA) **7988**
• Natural Hazards Center. Topical Bibliographies (USA) **2229**
• Natural Hazards Observer (USA ISSN 0193-8355) **2227**
• Natural Hazards Research Working Papers (USA ISSN 0082-5166) **7988**
• ➤ Natural Hazards Review (USA ISSN 1527-6988) **3455**
Natural Healing with Dr. Mark Stengler *see* Bottom Line / Natural Healing **307**
Natural Health (GBR) **313**
• Natural Health (USA ISSN 1067-9588) **313**
Natural Health & Beauty (GBR ISSN 1748-0833) **6993**
• Natural Health and Vegetarian Life (AUS) **6664**
Natural Health Products *see* Tianran Baojian Pin **8993**
Natural Health Products, Canada (CAN ISSN 1912-0192) **2019**
Natural Health Products Canada B2B Industry Guide *see* Natural Health Products, Canada **2019**
Natural Health Products Canada Guide *see* Natural Health Products, Canada **2019**
Natural Health Products, Canada, Industry Guide *see* Natural Health Products, Canada **2019**
Natural Health Retailer (USA ISSN 1554-1282) **1835**
† Natural Health Review (AUS) **8976**
• Natural Health Review (NZL ISSN 1177-570X) **313**
• Natural Heritage (AUS ISSN 1440-7256) **2620**
Natural Heritage (ZMB) **2620**
Natural History *see* Watashitachi no Shizenshi **7928**
• Natural History (USA ISSN 0028-0712) **7888**
Natural History Bulletin of Ibaraki University *see* Ibaraki University. Natural History Bulletin **7864**
Natural History Contributions (CAN ISSN 0707-3887) **692**
Natural History Inventory of Colorado (USA ISSN 0890-6882) **957**
Natural History Journal of Chulalongkorn University *see* Chulalongkorn University. Natural History Journal **4135**
Natural History Museum and Institute, Chiba. Annual Report (JPN ISSN 0917-8902) **6534**
➤ Natural History Museum and Institute, Chiba. Bulletin. Humanities (JPN ISSN 0915-9126) **4186**
➤ Natural History Museum and Institute, Chiba. Journal (JPN ISSN 0915-9452) **7888**
➤ Natural History Museum and Institute, Chiba. Journal. Special Issue (JPN ISSN 1340-2684) **692**
• Natural History Museum. Annual Review (GBR ISSN 1746-1022) **7888**
➤ Natural History Museum in Belgrade. Bulletin (SRB) **2757**
➤ Natural History Museum of Los Angeles County. Science Series (USA ISSN 0076-0943) **7888**
Natural History Occasional Paper (CAN ISSN 0838-5971) **7888**
Natural History of the National Parks of Hungary (HUN) **2620**
Natural History Report of Kanagawa *see* Kanagawa Shizenshi Shiryo **7874**
➤ Natural History Research (JPN ISSN 0915-9444) **7888**
➤ Natural History Research. Special Issue (JPN ISSN 1340-2692) **692**
➤ Natural History Society of Northumbria. Transactions (GBR ISSN 0144-221X) **7888**
Natural Home (USA ISSN 1933-1134) **4364**
Natural Home and Garden *see* Natural Home **4364**
• Natural Horse (USA ISSN 1522-8436) **321**
• ➤ Natural Language and Linguistic Theory (NLD ISSN 0167-806X) **5154**
• ➤ Natural Language Engineering (GBR ISSN 1351-3249) **2509**
Natural Language Processing (NLD ISSN 1567-8202) **5154**
• ➤ Natural Language Semantics (NLD ISSN 0925-854X) **5154**
Natural Law Studies *see* Studies in Jurisprudence **4790**
• Natural Life (CAN ISSN 0701-8002) **3813**
Natural Lifestyle (GBR) **5078**
• Natural Living for Animals (USA ISSN 1933-9291) **6811**
▼ • Natural Living Magazine (USA ISSN 1939-6562) **5078**
Natural Living Today (USA ISSN 1087-5050) **5078**
Natural Medicine Law (USA ISSN 1095-6336) **4739**
Natural Medicine Law Newsletter *see* Natural Medicine Law **4739**
Natural Muscle Magazine (USA) **6993**
Natural New England (USA ISSN 1527-5736) **2620**
• Natural Outlook (USA) **2620**
Natural Outlook Monthly Update *see* Natural Outlook **2620**
• Natural Parent (GBR ISSN 1369-9911) **2162**
Natural Philosophy Alliance. Proceedings (USA ISSN 1555-4775) **6935**
• ➤ Natural Product Communications (USA ISSN 1934-578X) **2074**
• ➤ Natural Product Reports (GBR ISSN 0265-0568) **2127**
• ➤ Natural Product Research (GBR ISSN 1478-6419) **2074**
Natural Product Research and Development *see* Tianran Chanwu Yanjiu yu Kaifa **2082**
Natural Product Sciences (KOR ISSN 1226-3907) **6862**
• Natural Product Updates (GBR ISSN 0950-1711) **2095**
Natural Products (Year) *see* Grocers' Review **3679**
Natural Products Alert *see* N A P R A L E R T **6862**
Natural Products Association. Newsletter (USA) **3657**
• Natural Products Industry Insider (USA ISSN 1525-5301) **6664**
• Natural Products Marketplace (USA) **6664**
Natural Products News (GBR) **2127**
Natural Resource *see* Ziran Ziyuan **2634**
➤ Natural Resource Management and Policy (NLD ISSN 0929-127X) **3455**
• Natural Resource Modeling (USA ISSN 0890-8575) **5520**
• Natural Resource Perspectives (GBR ISSN 1356-9228) **1601**
• Natural Resource Year in Review (USA ISSN 1544-5429) **2621**
Natural Resources *see* Prirodnye Resursy **3461**
• Natural Resources & Environment (USA ISSN 0882-3812) **3455**
Natural Resources and Environment *see* Natural Resources & Environment **3455**
Natural Resources and Environmental Issues (USA ISSN 1069-5370) **3455**
• Natural Resources Canada. Office of Energy Efficiency. Report to Parliament under the Energy Efficiency Act (CAN ISSN 1491-0624) **3142**
• ➤ Natural Resources Forum (GBR ISSN 0165-0203) **4021**
• ➤ The Natural Resources Journal (USA ISSN 0028-0739) **2621**
• ➤ Natural Resources Research (USA ISSN 1520-7439) **6474**
Natural Resources Research Institute Now *see* N R R I Now **2713**
Natural Rubber & Rubber Products Exporters in India. Directory (IND) **7825**
• ➤ Natural Rubber Research (IND) **7825**
▼ • Natural Science (USA ISSN 2150-4091) **7888**
Natural Science Journal of Hainan University *see* Hainan Daxue Xuebao (Ziran Kexue Ban) **7859**
Natural Science Journal of Xiangtan University *see* Xiangtan Daxue Ziran Kexue Xuebao **7931**
Natural Science Series *see* Acta Jutlandica. Naturvidenskabelig Serie **7832**
Natural Sciences *see* Polish Journal of Natural Sciences **7898**
The Natural Sciences (Yokohama, 1998) *see* Yokohama Kokuritsu Daigaku Kyoiku Ningen Kagakubu Kiyo. IV, Shizen Kagaku **7932**
Natural Sciences and Engineering Research Council of Canada. Annual Report (CAN ISSN 1702-1359) **7888**
Natural Sciences and Engineering Research Council of Canada Award Holder's Guide for Postgraduate Scholarship (PGS) Holders at Canadian Universities *see* N S E R C Award Holder's Guide for Postgraduate Scholarship (PGS) Holders at Canadian Universities **7885**
• Natural Sciences and Engineering Research Council of Canada. Contact (Online) (CAN ISSN 1910-460X) **7888**
• Natural Sciences and Engineering Research Council of Canada. Contact (Print)/Conseil de Recherches en Sciences Naturelles et en Genie du Canada. Contact (CAN ISSN 1714-7425) **7888**
• Natural Sciences and Engineering Research Council of Canada. List of Scholarships and Grants in Aid of Research/Conseil de Recherches en Sciences Naturelles et en Genie du Canada. Liste des Bourses et Subventions de Recherche (CAN) **2995**
• Natural Sciences and Engineering Research Council of Canada. Performance Report (CAN ISSN 1483-9350) **7454**
Natural Sciences and Engineering Research Council of Canada. Program Guide for Students and Fellows (CAN ISSN 1707-3022) **2995**
Natural Sciences Journal of Harbin University *see* Harbin Shifan Daxue Ziran Kexue Xuebao **7860**
Natural Sciences Journal of Hunan Normal University *see* Hunan Shifan Daxue. Ziran Kexue Xuebao **7863**
Natural Sciences, Technology & Medicine Journal of History of Sciences, Technology, and Medicine *see* N T M Journal of History of Sciences, Technology, and Medicine **7885**
• Natural Solutions (USA ISSN 1940-8153) **313**
Natural State Magazine (AUS ISSN 1834-3112) **3455**
Natural Stone Directory (GBR ISSN 1362-6299) **1054**
Natural Stone in the World *see* Roc Maquina (Spanish Edition) **6478**
Natural Stone Specialist (GBR ISSN 1356-5443) **1026**
Natural Style (ITA ISSN 1723-2724) **8877**
Natural Traveler (USA) **8740**
Naturaleza Aragonesa (ESP ISSN 1138-8013) **6727**
Naturaleza y Gracia (ESP ISSN 0470-3790) **7665**
➤ Naturalia (BRA ISSN 0101-1944) **692**
Naturalia Family Life (ITA ISSN 1828-1559) **5078**
➤ Naturalia Patagonica. Serie Ciencias Biologicas (ARG ISSN 0327-8050) **692**
➤ Naturalia Patagonica. Serie Ciencias de la Tierra (ARG ISSN 0327-5272) **2757**
Naturalia Patagonica. Serie Reportes Tecnicos (ARG ISSN 0327-9510) **692**

Title

The Naturalist see Luonnon Tutkija 687
➤ The Naturalist (GBR ISSN 0028-0771) 692
Naturalist (TTO) 7888
The Naturalist News (AUS ISSN 1448-238X) 7888
Il Naturalista Siciliano (ITA ISSN 0394-0063) 7888
➤ Il Naturalista Valtellinese (ITA ISSN 1120-6519) 692
Naturaliste du N B see N B Naturalist 7885
Les Naturalistes Belges (BEL ISSN 0028-0801) 692
Naturalists (JPN ISSN 0914-028X) 7888
The Naturalists' Directory and Almanac International (USA ISSN 0277-609X) 692
Naturalist's Handbooks see Looduseuurija Kasiraamatud 7880
Naturalists' Handbooks (GBR ISSN 0962-6360) 7889
Naturally (USA ISSN 1076-3295) 5078
▼ • Naturally Good Magazine (USA ISSN 1944-7434) 5684
Naturally Northumbria (GBR ISSN 1460-6119) 2621
Naturally Occurring Radioactive Material Report see N O R M Report 2757
Naturally Speaking (GBR ISSN 1360-3728) 2621
† Naturalmente (ITA ISSN 1128-6334) 8976
Naturamed (DEU ISSN 0931-1513) 5684
Der Naturarzt (DEU ISSN 0720-826X) 313
Nature see Priroda 7899
Nature see Daziran 7849
• ➤ Nature (GBR ISSN 0028-0836) 7889
Nature see Shizen 8438
Nature see Watakushitachi no Shizen 916
Nature Alberta (CAN ISSN 1713-8639) 2621
• ➤ Nature and Culture (USA ISSN 1558-6073) 692
Nature and Environment Series (FRA ISSN 0252-0575) 2621
Nature & Health (AUS ISSN 0815-7006) 313
Nature and Human Activities (JPN ISSN 1342-0054) 349
Nature and Insects see Konchu to Shizen 853
Nature and Man see Ziran yu Ren 4168
Nature and Science see Kyodo to Kagaku 7878
Nature and Science (USA ISSN 1545-0740) 7889
Nature Australia see Explore 7854
• ➤ Nature Biotechnology (USA ISSN 1087-0156) 768
Nature Biotechnology Directory (Year) (GBR) 2019
• Nature Canada (CAN ISSN 0374-9894) 2621
• ➤ Nature Cell Biology (GBR ISSN 1465-7392) 835
• ➤ Nature Chemical Biology (GBR ISSN 1552-4450) 2074
▼ Nature Chemistry (GBR ISSN 1755-4330) 2074
▼ • Nature China (GBR ISSN 1751-5793) 7889
▼ • Nature Climate Change (GBR) 6392
• ➤ Nature Clinical Practice Cardiovascular Medicine (GBR ISSN 1743-4297) 5796
• ➤ Nature Clinical Practice Endocrinology & Metabolism (GBR ISSN 1745-8366) 5898
• ➤ Nature Clinical Practice Gastroenterology & Hepatology (GBR ISSN 1743-4378) 5929
• Nature Clinical Practice Nephrology (GBR ISSN 1745-8323) 6271
• Nature Clinical Practice Neurology (GBR ISSN 1745-834X) 6162
• ➤ Nature Clinical Practice Oncology (GBR ISSN 1743-4254) 6028
• Nature Clinical Practice Rheumatology (GBR ISSN 1745-8382) 6225
Nature Clinical Practice Urology see Nature Reviews. Urology 6271
• Nature Conservancy (USA ISSN 1540-2428) 2621
The Nature Conservation see Shizen Hogo 2627
➤ Nature Conservation (POL ISSN 1643-9252) 2621
Nature Conservation see Varstvo Narave 2630
Nature Conservation Society of Japan. Reports see Nihon Shizen Hogo Kyokai Hokoku 2622
Nature, Culture and Literature (NLD ISSN 1572-4344) 5338
• Nature Digest (JPN ISSN 1880-0556) 7889
Nature, Environment and Pollution Technology (IND ISSN 0972-6268) 3489
Nature et Faune (GHA) 2621
La Nature & l'Homme (FRA ISSN 1637-2425) 313
Nature et Progres (FRA) 139
Nature Ethique (BEL ISSN 1379-2652) 8324
Nature Fitness (DEU) 6993
Nature Friend (USA ISSN 0888-4862) 2204
Nature Friend Magazine see Nature Friend 2204
Nature Gekkan Daijesuto see Nature Digest 7889
• ➤ Nature Genetics (USA ISSN 1061-4036) 876
▼ • Nature Geoscience (GBR ISSN 1752-0894) 2757
Nature Gourmande (FRA ISSN 1952-577X) 6664
• Nature Immunology (USA ISSN 1529-2908) 5764
• ➤ Nature in Avon (GBR) 7889
Nature in Cambridgeshire (GBR ISSN 0466-6046) 2621
Nature in Hokkaido see Hokkaido no Shizen 2613
Nature in Okayama see Okayama no Shizen 2623
▼ • Nature India (GBR ISSN 1755-3180) 7889
Nature Journal see Ziran Zazhi 7935
Nature Kids N B (New Brunswick) (CAN ISSN 1912-2861) 692
Nature Labscene (GBR ISSN 1479-0734) 740
Nature Management see Prirodopol'zovaniye 3461
• ➤ Nature Materials (GBR ISSN 1476-1122) 3355
• Nature Matters (CAN ISSN 1491-2139) 2621
Nature Matters (USA ISSN 1938-9795) 2621
• ➤ Nature Medicine (USA ISSN 1078-8956) 5684
• Nature Methods (GBR ISSN 1548-7091) 7889
• ➤ Nature Nanotechnology (GBR ISSN 1748-3387) 7028
• ➤ Nature Neuroscience (USA ISSN 1097-6256) 6162
• Nature North Zine (CAN) 2621
Nature of Enshu see Enshu no Shizen 7853
Nature of Irrigation Pond see Tameike no Shizen 255
Nature of Kagoshima see Shizen Aigo 2627
Nature of Tohoku see Tohoku no Shizen 7923
• Nature Pages (USA) 2621
Nature Photographer (USA ISSN 1049-6602) 6971
▼ • ➤ Nature Photonics (GBR ISSN 1749-4885) 7081
• ➤ Nature Physics (GBR ISSN 1745-2473) 7028
• Nature Precedings (GBR ISSN 1756-0357) 5684
• ➤ Nature Protocols (Online) (GBR ISSN 1750-2799) 692
• ➤ Nature Protocols (Print) (GBR ISSN 1754-2189) 693
▼ • Nature Reports. Climate Change (GBR ISSN 1753-9315) 6392
▼ • Nature Reports. Stem Cells (GBR ISSN 1754-8705) 876
• ➤ Nature Reviews. Cancer (GBR ISSN 1474-175X) 6028
Nature Reviews Cancer see Nature Reviews. Cancer 6028
Nature Reviews Drug Discovery see Nature Reviews. Drug Discovery 6863
• Nature Reviews. Drug Discovery (GBR ISSN 1474-1776) 6863
Nature Reviews Genetics see Nature Reviews. Genetics 876
• ➤ Nature Reviews. Genetics (GBR ISSN 1471-0056) 876
• ➤ Nature Reviews. Immunology (GBR ISSN 1474-1733) 5764
Nature Reviews Immunology see Nature Reviews. Immunology 5764
• ➤ Nature Reviews. Microbiology (GBR ISSN 1740-1526) 893
Nature Reviews Microbiology see Nature Reviews. Microbiology 893
• ➤ Nature Reviews. Molecular Cell Biology (GBR ISSN 1471-0072) 893
Nature Reviews Molecular Cell Biology see Nature Reviews. Molecular Cell Biology 893
Nature Reviews Neuroscience see Nature Reviews. Neuroscience 6162
• ➤ Nature Reviews. Neuroscience (GBR ISSN 1471-003X) 6162
• ➤ Nature Reviews. Urology (GBR ISSN 1759-4812) 6271
• ➤ Nature, Society, and Thought (USA ISSN 0890-6130) 7157
Nature Society News (USA ISSN 0890-3735) 7889
• ➤ Nature Structural and Molecular Biology (USA ISSN 1545-9993) 693
Nature Structural Biology see Nature Structural and Molecular Biology 693
Nature Study see Neicha Sutadi 7891
Nature Study (USA ISSN 0028-0860) 3455
Nature Views (CAN) 7889
NatureChina see Nature China 7889
➤ Naturellement (FRA ISSN 0754-8826) 3455
• Naturen (NOR ISSN 0028-0887) 7889
➤ Naturens Verden (DNK ISSN 0028-0895) 7889
Nature's Best Photography (USA) 2621
Nature's Corner (USA ISSN 1559-9175) 6811
▼ Nature's Garden (USA ISSN 1934-9807) 3744
Nature's Place (GBR ISSN 0969-2215) 2621
Nature's Resources (CAN ISSN 1480-1167) 2621
• ➤ Natures - Sciences - Societes (FRA ISSN 1240-1307) 2714
Natureza (BRA ISSN 0104-3609) 3744
Natureza & Conservacao (BRA ISSN 1679-0073) 3455
• Naturfag (NOR ISSN 1504-4564) 3074
➤ Naturforschende Gesellschaft der Oberlausitz. Berichte (DEU ISSN 0941-0627) 804
Naturforschende Gesellschaft des Kantons Solothurn. Mitteilungen (CHE ISSN 1421-5551) 7889
Naturforschende Gesellschaft Graubuenden. Jahresbericht (CHE ISSN 0373-384X) 7889
Naturforschende Gesellschaft in Bern. Mitteilungen (CHE ISSN 0077-6130) 7889
Naturforschende Gesellschaft Schaffhausen. Mitteilungen (CHE ISSN 0373-3092) 7889
Naturforschende Gesellschaft zu Freiburg. Berichte (DEU ISSN 0028-0917) 7889
• Naturforvaltning (DNK ISSN 0908-8245) 2621
NaturFoto (DEU ISSN 1615-3545) 6971
Naturfotografen (NOR ISSN 0803-0987) 6971
Naturfreund/Ami de la Nature (CHE ISSN 0028-0925) 8740
NaturfreundIn (DEU) 8324
Die Naturheilkunde (DEU ISSN 1613-3943) 6993
➤ Naturheilpraxis mit Naturmedizin (DEU ISSN 0177-6754) 313
Naturhistorische Gesellschaft Hannover. Beihefte zu den Berichten (DEU ISSN 0374-6054) 693
Naturhistorische Gesellschaft Hannover. Berichte (DEU ISSN 0365-9844) 2714
Naturhistorische Gesellschaft Nuernberg. Abhandlungen (DEU ISSN 0077-6149) 407
Naturhistorischer Verein der Rheinlande und Westfalens. Arbeitsgemeinschaft Rheinischer Koleopterologen. Mitteilungen (DEU ISSN 0939-7736) 957
Naturhistorisches Museum Basel. Veroeffentlichungen (CHE) 7889
Naturhistorisches Museum Bern. Jahrbuch (CHE ISSN 0253-4401) 7889
➤ Naturhistorisches Museum in Wien. Annalen. Serie A, Mineralogie und Petrographie, Geologie und Palaeontologie, Anthropologie und Praehistorie (AUT ISSN 0255-0091) 7889
➤ Naturhistorisches Museum in Wien. Annalen. Serie B: Botanik und Zoologie (AUT ISSN 0255-0105) 957
Naturhistorisches Museum in Wien. Kataloge der Wissenschaftlichen Sammlungen (AUT) 7889
Naturhistorisches Museum in Wien. Monatsprogramm (AUT ISSN 0028-095X) 6534
Naturhistorisches Museum in Wien. Veroeffentlichungen. Neue Folge (AUT ISSN 0378-8202) 7890
Naturhistorisches Museum Schloss Bertholdsburg Schleusingen. Veroeffentlichungen (DEU ISSN 0863-6338) 2757
Naturhistoriska Riksmuseet. Ringmaerkningscentralen. Report of Swedish Bird Ringing (SWE ISSN 0282-390X) 910
Naturism (BEL) 8740
Naturisme see Uit! 6999
† Naturismo (ITA ISSN 0392-4173) 8976
Der Naturist (DEU) 5078
Naturist Life International (USA ISSN 0895-0911) 6993
Naturkundemuseum Erfurt. Veroeffentlichungen (DEU ISSN 0232-9565) 693
Naturkundemuseum Leipzig. Veroeffentlichungen (DEU ISSN 1438-440X) 6534
Naturkundemuseums Goerlitz. Abhandlungen und Berichte (DEU ISSN 0373-7586) 804
Naturkundlche Beitraege des D J N see Deutscher Jugendbund fuer Naturbeobachtung. Naturkundliche Beitraege 2608
• Naturkundliches Jahrbuch der Stadt Linz (AUT ISSN 0470-3901) 7890
Naturlaekemedel (SWE ISSN 1650-0172) 6863
Naturli (DNK ISSN 1602-0219) 6993
Naturlig Energi (DNK ISSN 0106-1127) 3390
Naturligvis (DNK ISSN 0109-2995) 7890
Naturmedicinaren see Svenska Homeopaters Tidskrift 5807
Naturo (FRA ISSN 1777-814X) 313
Naturopa see Futuropa 2612
• Naturopathy Digest (Online) (USA ISSN 1559-0402) 313
† • Naturopathy Digest (Print) (USA ISSN 1559-0399) 8976
Naturschutz Heute (DEU ISSN 0934-8883) 2621
Naturschutz im Land Sachsen-Anhalt (DEU ISSN 0940-6638) 2621
Naturschutz, Landschaftspflege, Jagd- und Forstrecht (DEU ISSN 0936-6954) 2621
Naturschutz-Spectrum (DEU ISSN 1437-0115) 2621
Naturschutz und Biologische Vielfalt (DEU) 804
Naturschutz und Landschaftspflege in Niedersachsen (DEU ISSN 0933-1247) 2621
Naturschutz und Landschaftsplanung (DEU ISSN 0940-6808) 451
➤ Naturschutzblaetter (DEU ISSN 1615-5726) 693
Naturstein (DEU ISSN 0028-1026) 1026
Naturvaardsverket. Handbok (SWE ISSN 1650-2361) 3455
• Naturvaardsverkets Foerfattningssamling (SWE ISSN 1403-8234) 2622
Naturvetaren (SWE ISSN 0345-8296) 7890
Naturvidenskabelig Serie see Acta Jutlandica. Naturvidenskabelig Serie 7832
• Naturviteren (NOR ISSN 0809-8921) 4599
• ➤ Naturwissenschaften (DEU ISSN 0028-1042) 7890
➤ Naturwissenschaftlich - Medizinischen Vereins in Innsbruck. Berichte (AUT ISSN 0379-1416) 693
Naturwissenschaftlich - Medizinischen Vereins in Innsbruck. Berichte. Supplementum see Naturwissenschaftlich - Medizinischen Vereins in Innsbruck. Berichte 693
Naturwissenschaftliche Beitraege des Museums Dessau (DEU ISSN 0138-1636) 7890
Naturwissenschaftliche Beitraege des Museums Dessau. Sonderheft see Naturwissenschaftliche Beitraege des Museums Dessau 7890
Naturwissenschaftliche Forschungsergebnisse (DEU ISSN 1435-6511) 7890
➤ Naturwissenschaftliche Rundschau (DEU ISSN 0028-1050) 7890
Naturwissenschaftliche Zeitschrift fuer Niederbayern (DEU ISSN 0932-9447) 693
Naturwissenschaftlicher Arbeitskreis Kempten-Allgaeu. Mitteilungen (DEU ISSN 0344-5054) 2714
Naturwissenschaftlicher und Historischer Verein fuer das Land Lippe. Sonderveroeffentlichungen (DEU ISSN 0466-6224) 4247
Naturwissenschaftlicher Verein Darmstadt. Bericht (DEU ISSN 0470-3979) 693
Naturwissenschaftlicher Verein fuer Bielefeld und Umgegend. Bericht (DEU ISSN 0340-3831) 693
Naturwissenschaftlicher Verein fuer Bielefeld und Umgegend. Bericht Sonderheft (DEU ISSN 0931-5225) 693
➤ Naturwissenschaftlicher Verein fuer Schleswig-Holstein. Schriften (DEU ISSN 0077-6165) 7890
Naturwissenschaftlicher Verein fuer Schwaben. Berichte (DEU ISSN 0720-3705) 693
➤ Naturwissenschaftlicher Verein fuer Steiermark. Mitteilungen (AUT ISSN 0369-1136) 7890
➤ Naturwissenschaftlicher Verein in Hamburg. Abhandlungen (DEU ISSN 0173-7481) 957
➤ Naturwissenschaftlicher Verein in Hamburg. Verhandlungen (DEU ISSN 0173-749X) 957
➤ Naturwissenschaftlicher Verein Wuerzburg. Abhandlungen (DEU ISSN 0547-9770) 693
Naturwissenschaftlicher Verein Wuppertal. Jahresberichte (DEU ISSN 0547-9789) 804
➤ Naturwissenschaftlicher Verein zu Bremen. Abhandlungen (DEU ISSN 0340-3718) 693
Naturzale (ESP ISSN 1137-8603) 693
Natuschutz und Landschaftspflege Baden-Wuerttemberg (DEU ISSN 1437-0093) 2622
Natuur. Blad (BEL ISSN 1377-7297) 804
Natuur en Milieu see Terra (Utrecht) 2629
Natuur en Techniek see Natuurwetenschap & Techniek 7890
Natuur.Oriolus (BEL ISSN 1379-8863) 911
Natuurbehoud (NLD ISSN 0166-2627) 2714
Natuurhistorisch Genootschap in Limburg. Publicaties (NLD ISSN 0374-955X) 693
Natuurhistorisch Maandblad (NLD ISSN 0028-1107) 7890
NatuurMuseumJannink see Typisch Twente 7925
Natuurplanbureau. Vestiging Wageningen. Planbureaurapporten see Wettelijke Onderzoekstaken Natuur en Milieu. Rapporten 3474
Natuurspoor see Natuurbehoud 2714
Natuursteen (NLD ISSN 0165-6368) 1026
Natuurwetenschap & Techniek (NLD ISSN 1573-6083) 7890
NatWest Quarterly Survey of Small Business in Britain see NatWest / S E R Team Quarterly Survey of Small Business in Britain 1964
NatWest S B R T Quarterly Survey of Small Business in Britain see NatWest / S E R Team Quarterly Survey of Small Business in Britain 1964
NatWest / S E R Team Quarterly Survey of Small Business in Britain (Small Enterprise Research Team) (GBR) 1964
Nauchnaya Mysl' Kavkaza (RUS) 7988
Nauchno-Issledovatel'skii Institut Prikladnoi Geodezii. Trudy (RUS) 2757
Nauchno-Issledovatel'skii Institut Transportnogo Stroitel'stva. Trudy (RUS) 8506
Nauchno-Tekhnicheskaya Informatsiya. Seriya 1. Organizatsiya i Metodika Informatsionnoi Raboty (RUS ISSN 0548-0019) 5035
Nauchno-Tekhnicheskaya Informatsiya. Seriya 2. Informatsionnye Protsessy i Sistemy (RUS ISSN 0548-0027) 5035
Nauchno-Tekhnicheskie Dostizheniya i Peredovoi Opyt v Oblasti Geologii i Razvedki Nader (RUS ISSN 0868-4502) 6474
Nauchnye i Tekhnicheskie Biblioteki (RUS ISSN 0130-9765) 5035
Nauchnye Tsentry Chernomorskogo Ekonomicheskogo Sotrudnichestva. Ekologicheskii Vestnik/Research Centers of the Black Sea Economic Cooperation. Ecological Bulletin (RUS ISSN 1729-5459) 3456
Nauchnye Zapiski Tsentra Politicheskikh Issledovanii v Rossii (RUS) 6438
Naucno-Tehnicki Pregled see Scientific-Technical Review 3219
Naucnyi Komitet po Sohraneniyu Morskikh Zhivykh Resursov Antarktiki. Otchet Soveshchaniya Nauchnogo Komiteta see Commission for the Conservation of Antarctic Marine Living Resources. Report of the Meeting of the Scientific Committee 2802
▼ • Naugatuck River Review (USA ISSN 1944-0952) 5338
Naughty Baby see Wanpi Wawa 2221
Naughty Neighbors (USA ISSN 1092-728X) 6296
Naujasis Zidinys - Aidai (LTU) 3906
Nauka (BGR) 7890
Nauka (POL ISSN 1231-8515) 7890
Nauka dla Wszystkich/Science for Everyone (POL ISSN 0077-6181) 7890
Nauka Fantastika (UKR ISSN 0130-1632) 4466
Nauka i Oborona (UKR) 6438
Nauka i Religiya (RUS ISSN 0028-1239) 7665
Nauka i Suspil'stvo/Science and Society (UKR ISSN 0130-7037) 7988
Nauka i Tekhnika v Dorozhnoi Otrasli (RUS) 8506
• ➤ Nauka i Zhizn' (RUS ISSN 0028-1263) 7890
• Nauka v Rossii (RUS ISSN 0869-706X) 7890
Nauka v Sibiri (RUS) 7890
Nauka v Sibiri i Na Dal'nem Vostoke (RUS) 7938
Nauka za Gorata (BGR ISSN 0861-007X) 3697
Nauki Ekonomiczne (POL ISSN 0137-1428) 1152
Nauki Polityczne (POL ISSN 0137-141X) 7157
Naukoemkie Tekhnologii/High Technologies (RUS) 8433
Naukove Tovarystvo Imeni Shevchenka. Biblioteka Ukrainoznavstva/Library of Ukrainian Studies (USA) 4247
Naukove Tovarystvo Imeni Shevchenka. Proceedings of the Section of Chemistry, Biology and Medicine (USA ISSN 0195-7198) 2074
Naukove Tovarystvo Imeni Shevchenka. Proceedings of the Section of Mathematics and Physics (USA) 7890
Naukove Tovarystvo Imeni Shevchenka. Ukrainska Literaturna Biblioteka/Ukrainian Literary Library (USA) 5338

DIRECTORY 2010 NEDERLAND'S PATRICIAAT 10657

Naukove Tovarystvo Imeni Shevchenka. Ukrains'kyi Arkhiv/Ukrainian Archives (USA) **3553**
Naukove Tovarystvo Imeni Shevchenka. Zapysky/Mitteilungen/Shevchenko Scientific Society. Memoirs (USA) **3553**
➤ Naukovi Visti (UKR) **7890**
Naumann - Museum. Beitraege zur Gefiederkunde und Morphologie der Voegel (DEU ISSN 0949-9512) **911**
• Naumann - Museum. Blaetter (DEU ISSN 0233-0415) **911**
• ➤ Naunyn-Schmiedeberg's Archives of Pharmacology (DEU ISSN 0028-1298) **6863**
Nauplius (BRA ISSN 0104-6497) **6029**
Nauta/Cattle (FIN ISSN 1238-268X) **294**
Nautic Press see Port Nautic Press **8280**
• Nautic Service (ITA) **8654**
Nautica (ESP ISSN 0214-6983) **8279**
Nautica (GRC ISSN 1108-2712) **8279**
• Nautica (ITA ISSN 0392-369X) **8279**
Nautica Magazine (BRA ISSN 1413-1412) **8279**
The Nautical Almanac (USA ISSN 0077-619X) **8654**
Nautical Magazine (GBR ISSN 0028-1336) **8654**
Nautical Research Journal (USA ISSN 0738-7245) **8654**
† • Nautical World (USA ISSN 1094-0170) **8976**
Nautilus (DEU ISSN 0946-3534) **5445**
† • Nautilus (ITA) **8976**
Nautilus (Dublin) (USA) **2352**
➤ Nautilus (Sanibel) (USA ISSN 0028-1344) **957**
Nautilus Maritiem Magazine (NLD ISSN 1873-9067) **8654**
Nautiocasion (ESP) **8279**
Nautique (NLD ISSN 1383-8067) **8279**
Nautisches Jahrbuch (DEU ISSN 1614-0788) **578**
Nautisk Tidskrift (SWE ISSN 0028-1379) **8654**
Nautologia (POL ISSN 0548-0523) **2813**
Nav Karmyug Prakashan (IND) **3886**
Nava Bharat (IND) **3886**
Nava Sama Samaja Bulletine (LKA) **7157**
Nava Yugaya (LKA) **5338**
Navaho (USA) **3553**
Navajo Hopi Observer (USA) **3553**
Navajo Times (USA) **3553**
Navakal (IND) **3886**
Naval Affairs (USA ISSN 0028-1409) **6438**
• Naval & Military Press. Booklist (GBR) **7568**
• ➤ The Naval Architect (GBR ISSN 0306-0209) **8654**
Naval Architects and Marine Engineers, Republic of China. Society see Zhongguo Zaochuan ji Lunji Gongcheng Xuekan **8666**
Naval Astronomical Yearbook see Morskoi Astronomicheskii Ezhegodnik **578**
• Naval Aviation News (USA ISSN 0028-1417) **67**
Naval Command, Control and Ocean Surveillance Center. Naval Research and Development Division. Technical Document see Space and Naval Warfare Systems Center San Diego. Technical Document **6447**
Naval Command, Control and Ocean Surveillance Center. Naval Research and Development Division. Technical Report see Space and Naval Warfare Systems Center San Diego. Technical Report **6447**
Naval Construction and Retrofit Markets see Jane's Naval Construction and Retrofit Markets **1017**
Naval Digest (ZAF ISSN 1561-9060) **6438**
• ➤ Naval Engineers Journal (USA ISSN 0028-1425) **3212**
• Naval Forces (DEU ISSN 0722-8880) **6438**
Naval Historical Review (AUS ISSN 0158-5738) **6438**
• Naval History (USA ISSN 1042-1920) **6438**
• Naval Institute Guide to Combat Fleets of the World (USA ISSN 1057-4581) **6438**
Naval Institute Guide to Ships and Aircraft of the United States Fleet see Ships and Aircraft of the United States Fleet **6446**
Naval Institute Guide to World Military Aviation see World Military Aviation (Year) **75**
Naval Institute Guide to World Naval Weapons Systems see World Naval Weapons Systems **6454**
• Naval Law Review (USA ISSN 1049-0272) **4972**
Naval Policy and History (GBR ISSN 1366-9478) **4154**
Naval Research Laboratory Review see N R L Review **8432**
• ➤ Naval Research Logistics (USA ISSN 0894-069X) **6438**
Naval Reservist News (USA) **6438**
Naval Submarine Medical Research Laboratory. Report (USA ISSN 0363-0765) **5684**
Naval University of Engineering. Journal see Haijun Gongcheng Daxue Xuebao **3194**
• Naval War College Review (USA ISSN 0028-1484) **6438**
Naval Wargaming Review (USA) **8190**
Navarra Agraria (ESP ISSN 0214-6401) **294**
Navarra Forestal (ESP ISSN 1579-8771) **3698**
Navarro Leaves and Branches (USA ISSN 1558-495X) **3776**
Navasart Monthly (USA) **3553**
• Navbharat Times (IND ISSN 0028-1506) **3886**
Navbharat Times (Sunday Edition) see Navbharat Times **3886**
Nave Parva (IND) **8740**
• The Nave Weekly (USA ISSN 1932-4618) **2995**
Naveen Dunia (IND) **3886**
Naveena Velaanmai (IND) **139**
• El Navegante (PER ISSN 1606-1055) **3928**
Navegar (ESP) **8654**
Navenant (NLD ISSN 1572-7939) **8740**
Navhind Times (IND) **3886**
Navi (JPN ISSN 0289-6079) **8595**
Navi-Magazin (DEU ISSN 1863-4540) **8614**
Navi Parbhat (IND) **3886**
Navicula (DEU) **6897**
Navigating the Federal Trial (USA ISSN 1942-2911) **4957**
• Navigating Trademark Practice Before the P T O (Patent and Trademark Office) (USA ISSN 1930-3106) **4739**
Navigation (FRA ISSN 0028-1530) **8654**
Navigation/Kokai Gakkaishi (JPN ISSN 0919-9985) **8654**
Navigation (Washington) (USA ISSN 0028-1522) **67**
Navigation Douce (FRA ISSN 1957-584X) **8740**
Navigation Law of New York see New York Navigation Laws **4970**
Navigation News (GBR ISSN 0268-6317) **8654**
Navigation, Ports and Industries see Navigation Ports et Industries **8654**
Navigation Ports et Industries (FRA ISSN 1769-8588) **8654**
Navigational Radio Aids (JPN) **2360**
Navigatoer see Soefartens Ledere **8662**
Navigator (FIN ISSN 0355-7871) **8654**
The Navigator (Bridgewater) (USA) **631**
The Navigator (Nanaimo) (CAN ISSN 1193-6312) **2293**
• The Navigator (Online) (USA) **7890**
The Navigator (St John's) (CAN ISSN 1719-2323) **3602**
Navigator Nederland see Navigator NL **8655**
Navigator NL (NLD ISSN 1872-6550) **8655**
Navigators Daily Walk (USA) **7768**
† Navigazione Interna (ITA ISSN 0390-2927) **8976**
Navigazione. Monografie (ITA) **8506**
Navigo (USA) **2890**
Navin Weekly (GBR ISSN 0307-0832) **7157**
† Navint (GBR ISSN 0955-7261) **8976**
Navioneers (USA ISSN 0028-1581) **67**
Navires & Histoire (FRA ISSN 1280-4290) **6438**
Navis (SWE ISSN 0028-1603) **8279**
Navneet Hindi (IND) **7707**
Navnirman (IND ISSN 0028-162X) **3212**
Navorsinge van die Nasionale Museum see Nasionale Museum, Bloemfontein. Navorsinge **691**
Navorsingshoogtepunte (ZAF ISSN 1021-1063) **3602**
Navshakti (IND) **3886**
Navtex Manual (GBR) **2334**
• Navy Annual (AUS ISSN 1035-6088) **6438**
Navy Army & Air Force Institutes News see N A A F I News **6437**
Navy Chaplain (USA) **6438**
Navy Civil Engineer (USA ISSN 0096-9419) **6439**
The Navy Compass see Today's Vintage Magazine **369**
Navy Experimental Diving Unit. Report (USA) **6439**
Navy Guide see What's Up? Annapolis **5086**
Navy Journal see Mornaricki Glasnik **6437**
Navy List of Retired Officers (GBR) **6439**
• Navy Medicine (USA ISSN 0895-8211) **5684**
Navy News (GBR ISSN 0028-1670) **6439**
• Navy News. Sea Cadet Edition (GBR) **2204**
• Navy Supply Corps Newsletter (USA ISSN 0360-716X) **6439**
• Navy Times (USA ISSN 0028-1697) **6439**
NavyTimes.com see Navy Times **6439**
▼ ➤ Nawa (NAM ISSN 1993-3835) **5154**
Nawpa Pacha (USA ISSN 0077-6297) **407**
▼ The Nay Sprayer (USA ISSN 1937-6545) **3500**
Naya Padkar (IND) **3886**
Nayade (ESP ISSN 1579-282X) **4466**
➤ Nazan Studies in Religion & Culture (USA) **6935**
La Nazione (ITA ISSN 0391-6863) **3898**
In-Nazzjon Taghna (MLT ISSN 1017-2106) **3907**
nb!ict see Nordic and Baltic Journal of Information and Communications Technologies **2335**
NCBoatingLifestyle see N C Boating Lifestyle **8975**
NCFRP Report see N C F R P Report **8620**
Nchi Yetu/Our Country (TZA ISSN 0856-0188) **3961**
• NCNatural Digest (USA) **8740**
Ndertuesi/Constructeur (ALB ISSN 1010-4003) **1026**
N'Digo Profiles (USA) **3553**
▼ Ndivhuwo (ZAF ISSN 1996-8701) **5229**
N'djamena Hebdo (TCD) **3821**
• Ta Nea (GRC) **3874**
Nea Agrotiki Epitheoresis (GRC ISSN 0028-1727) **139**
Nea Dimossiotis (GRC) **30**
Nea Elladas/Greek Times (AUS) **3553**
Nea Epochi/New Epoch (CYP ISSN 0470-522X) **5229**
Nea Hestia (GRC ISSN 0028-1735) **5338**
NEA News (Nederlandse Editie) see NEA Nieuws **8506**
NEA Nieuws (NLD ISSN 1875-421X) **8506**
Nea Oikologia (GRC ISSN 1105-9664) **3456**
Nea Poreia (GRC ISSN 0470-5238) **5338**
Nea Rhome see Nea Romi. Rivista di Ricerche Bizantinistiche **2238**
Nea Romi. Rivista di Ricerche Bizantinistiche (ITA ISSN 1970-2345) **2238**
Neafon (DEU) **8741**
Neale Sourna's North Coast Academies Diary (USA ISSN 1553-8656) **5338**
Near and Middle East Monographs (DEU ISSN 0932-2728) **557**
The Near East Archaeological Society. Bulletin (USA ISSN 0739-0068) **407**
Near East Foundation. Annual Report (USA) **1602**
• Near East Quarterly (USA ISSN 1931-9541) **7254**
• Near East Report (Online) (USA ISSN 1947-4458) **3553**
† • Near East Report (Print) (USA ISSN 0028-176X) **8976**
Near East School of Theology. Quarterly see Theological Review **7689**
• ➤ Near Eastern Archaeology (USA ISSN 1094-2076) **407**
Near Infrared News see N I R News **2104**
• Near Surface Geophysics (NLD ISSN 1569-4445) **2787**
▼ Near Us Digest (USA ISSN 1946-0589) **5078**
Near West Gazette (USA ISSN 1069-8213) **4981**
N'East Magazine (USA) **8324**
Nebelspalter (CHE ISSN 0028-1786) **5229**
Nebenwerte-Journal (DEU ISSN 1439-5819) **1642**
Nebenwerte-Journal Express see Nebenwerte-Journal **1642**
➤ Nebo (USA ISSN 0741-1316) **5338**
Nebraska see Off the Beaten Path: Nebraska **8743**
Nebraska (USA) **2293**
• ➤ Nebraska Academy of Sciences and Affiliated Societies. Transactions (USA ISSN 0163-9013) **7891**
Nebraska Academy of Sciences. Program and Proceedings (USA) **7891**
Nebraska Agri-Business Digest (USA ISSN 1536-8815) **242**
• Nebraska Agri-facts (USA ISSN 0744-7523) **183**
Nebraska: All-Industries see Harris Directory. Nebraska All-Industries **2000**
Nebraska Ancestree (USA) **3776**
Nebraska BankNews Bank Directory see BankNews Directory of Nebraska Banks **1318**
Nebraska Beverage Analyst (USA ISSN 0028-1808) **608**
The Nebraska Bird Review (USA ISSN 0028-1816) **911**
Nebraska Blueprint (USA) **3212**
• Nebraska Business Directory (USA ISSN 1048-7328) **2019**
Nebraska Cattleman (USA ISSN 1062-8274) **294**
Nebraska Chamber of Commerce & Industry. Legislative Report (USA) **4740**
Nebraska Cities and Counties Graphic Performance Analysis see Nebraska Cities & Counties Graphic Performance Analysis **7482**
Nebraska Cities & Counties Graphic Performance Analysis (USA ISSN 1935-6048) **7482**
Nebraska Crimes and Punishments, Criminal Procedure, Motor Vehicles & Related Statutes (USA) **4894**
• Nebraska Criminal and Traffic Law Manual (USA ISSN 1524-0916) **4894**
Nebraska. Department of Roads. Nebraska Selected Transportation Statistics (USA) **8528**
Nebraska. Department of Roads. Traffic Analysis Unit. Continuous Traffic Count Data and Traffic Characteristics on Nebraska Streets and Highways (USA ISSN 0091-844X) **8633**
Nebraska. Department of Social Services. Annual Report (USA) **8057**
Nebraska Department of Water Resources. Biennial Report (USA ISSN 0466-6992) **8830**
Nebraska Development News (USA ISSN 0890-6092) **1500**
• Nebraska Employment Law Letter (USA ISSN 1085-3332) **4740**
Nebraska Farm Bureau News (USA ISSN 0745-6522) **139**
• Nebraska Farmer (USA ISSN 1049-1880) **139**
Nebraska Fence Post (USA) **139**
Nebraska. Fisheries Division. Annual Report (USA ISSN 0092-1696) **3602**
Nebraska Golf (USA) **8240**
Nebraska Highway Program (USA) **8633**
Nebraska History (USA ISSN 0028-1859) **4304**
• ➤ Nebraska Law Review (USA ISSN 0047-9209) **4740**
• The Nebraska Lawyer Magazine (USA ISSN 1095-905X) **4740**
Nebraska Legal Forms: Bankruptcy (USA) **4876**
Nebraska Legal Forms: Commercial Real Estate (USA) **4740**
Nebraska Legal Forms: Creditors' Remedies (USA) **4876**
Nebraska Legal Forms: Criminal Law (USA) **4894**
Nebraska Legal Forms: Personal Injury (USA) **4838**
Nebraska Legal Forms: Residential Real Estate (USA) **7601**
Nebraska Legal Forms: Workers' Compensation (USA) **1699**
Nebraska Legionnaire (USA ISSN 0028-1875) **2268**
• Nebraska Libraries: A Directory (USA ISSN 1043-8807) **5035**
• ➤ Nebraska Library Association. Quarterly (USA ISSN 0028-1883) **5035**
Nebraska Library Communicator see N L Communicator **5033**
• Nebraska Life (USA ISSN 1091-2886) **3982**
Nebraska Livestock Brand Book (USA) **294**
• Nebraska Manufacturers Register (USA ISSN 1059-7727) **2019**
Nebraska Mortar and Pestle (USA ISSN 0028-1891) **6863**
Nebraska Municipal Review (USA ISSN 0028-1905) **7499**
Nebraska. Natural Resources Commission. State Water Planning and Review Process (USA) **8830**
• Nebraska Nurse (USA ISSN 0028-1921) **5970**
Nebraska Petroleum and Convenience Store Marketer (USA) **6780**
Nebraska Resources (USA ISSN 0047-9217) **2622**
The Nebraska Review (USA ISSN 8755-514X) **5339**
The Nebraska School Directory see M D R's School Directory. Nebraska **2959**
Nebraska Selected Transportation Statistics see Nebraska. Department of Roads. Nebraska Selected Transportation Statistics **8528**
Nebraska Smoke-Eater (USA) **3580**
Nebraska State Bar News see The Nebraska Lawyer Magazine **4740**
Nebraska State Historical Society. Historical Newsletter (USA ISSN 0199-9664) **4304**
Nebraska. State Patrol. Annual Report (USA ISSN 0094-1247) **2674**
Nebraska Statistical Report of Abortions (USA ISSN 0095-3105) **973**
Nebraska Symposium on Motivation (USA ISSN 0146-7875) **7386**
Nebraska Tractor Test (USA ISSN 0093-1489) **213**
• Nebraska Transcript (USA) **4740**
Nebraska Trucker (USA) **8673**
Nebraska Union Farmer (USA) **139**
Nebraskaland Magazine (USA ISSN 0028-1964) **2622**
• Nebula (AUS ISSN 1449-7751) **4466**
Nebula Awards Showcase (USA) **5445**
Necessary Elements of Common Legal Actions (USA) **4838**
Neck Pain (USA) **5684**
Neckarsulm News (USA) **8595**
Neckartal Anzeiger (DEU) **3853**
Neckarwerke Stuttgart AG Magazin see N W S Magazin **3326**
Neckarwestheimer Gemeindeblatt (DEU) **3853**
Neckwear Industry Directory (USA) **2249**
Necrofile (USA ISSN 1077-8187) **5445**
▼ Nectar (USA ISSN 1942-3373) **5078**
Nedcor Economic Profile (ZAF) **1501**
Nedcor Ekonomiese Profiel see Nedcor Economic Profile **1501**
Nedcor Gids tot die Ekonomie see Nedcor Guide to the Economy **1501**
Nedcor Guide to the Economy/Nedcor Gids tot die Ekonomie (ZAF ISSN 1023-7097) **1501**
Nedeljna Dalmacija (HRV ISSN 0351-6792) **3831**
Nedeljne Informativne Novine see N I N **3945**
Nedeljne Novine (SRB ISSN 0028-1980) **3945**
• Nedeljski Dnevnik (SVN ISSN 1318-0339) **3947**
Nedelni Blesk (CZE ISSN 1210-8774) **3832**
Nedelni Hlasatel Newspaper see Denni Hlasatel **3529**
Nedelni Sport (CZE ISSN 1801-383X) **8190**
Nedelya (RUS) **1152**
Nedelya (Baku) (AZE) **3799**
Nedelya Udmurtii (RUS) **3938**
Nederduitse Gereformeerde Kerk van Natal Gemeente Vryheid. Maandbrief (ZAF ISSN 0024-8665) **7768**
• ➤ Nederduitse Gereformeerde Teologiese Tydskrif (ZAF ISSN 0378-9888) **7768**
Nederland en Bouwen aan de Toekomst (NLD) **451**
Nederland Maritiem Land/Dutch Maritime Network (NLD) **8655**
Nederland Museumland (NLD ISSN 1875-2489) **6534**
Nederland onder de Loep (DEU) **6897**
• Nederlands A B C (NLD) **2019**
Nederland's Adelsboek (NLD ISSN 0921-9021) **3776**
Nederlands Elektronica- en Radiogenootschap see N E R G **2334**
Nederlands Fotoarchief. Jaarverslag (NLD) **6971**
Nederlands Historisch-Archaeologisch Instituut te Istanbul. Uitgaven see Institut Historique Archeologique Neerlandais de Stamboul. Publications **4321**
Nederlands Huisartsen Genootschap Standaarden voor de Huisarts see N H G-Standaarden voor de Huisarts **5682**
Nederlands Instituut te Rome. Mededelingen see Fragmenta **4453**
Nederlands Instituut voor Oorlogsdocumentatie. Jaarboek (NLD ISSN 1569-3724) **6439**
Nederlands Interdisciplinair Demografisch Instituut. Rapport - Report - Bericht - Rapporto (NLD ISSN 0922-7210) **7288**
Nederlands Internationaal Privaatrecht (NLD ISSN 0167-7594) **4936**
Nederlands Jazz Archief Bulletin see Jazz Bulletin **6578**
Nederlands Juristen Comite voor de Mensenrechten Bulletin see N J C M Bulletin **4936**
Nederlands Juristenblad (NLD ISSN 0165-0483) **4740**
Nederlands Korfbalblad see Korfbal! **8184**
Nederlands Kunsthistorisch Jaarboek (NLD ISSN 0169-6726) **508**
• ➤ Nederlands Militair Geneeskundig Tijdschrift (NLD ISSN 0028-2103) **5684**
Nederlands Normalisatie-instituut BouwNieuws (NLD ISSN 1871-6199) **1026**
Nederlands Omroep Handboek (NLD ISSN 0925-6261) **2386**
Nederlands op de Werkvloer Nieuws see Taal en Arbeidsmarkt **8992**
Nederland's Patriciaat (NLD ISSN 0928-0979) **3776**

Title

Nederlands-Russisch Archiefcentrum Inventories *see* N R A C Inventories **4247**
Nederlands Stripmuseum Groningen. Vriendenblad (NLD ISSN 1875-3779) **6534**
Nederlands Tandartsenblad (NLD ISSN 0028-2111) **5856**
Nederlands Textielmuseum. Museumkrant *see* Textuur **6538**
Nederlands Theaterboek *see* Nederlands Theaterjaarboek **8474**
Nederlands Theaterjaarboek (NLD ISSN 0929-2640) **8474**
Nederlands Theologisch Tijdschrift (NLD ISSN 0028-212X) **7665**
Nederlands Tijdschrift tegen de Kwakzalverij (NLD ISSN 1571-5469) **5684**
➤ Nederlands Tijdschrift voor Allergie/The Dutch Journal of Allergology (NLD ISSN 1568-2498) **5764**
Nederlands Tijdschrift voor Allergie. Huisartseneditie/The Dutch Journal of Allergology. General Practitioner's Edition (NLD ISSN 1872-7670) **5764**
Nederlands Tijdschrift voor Anesthesiemedewerkers (NLD ISSN 0169-2178) **5772**
➤ Nederlands Tijdschrift voor Anesthesiologie (NLD ISSN 0921-8769) **5772**
• Nederlands Tijdschrift voor Bestuursrecht (NLD ISSN 0921-3554) **4740**
• Nederlands Tijdschrift voor Burgerlijk Recht (NLD ISSN 0927-2747) **4838**
Nederlands Tijdschrift voor Chiropodie *see* Podopost **2260**
Nederlands Tijdschrift voor Coaching *see* Tijdschrift voor Coaching **1798**
Nederlands Tijdschrift voor de Psychologie en haar Grensgebieden *see* Netherlands Journal of Psychology **7386**
➤ Nederlands Tijdschrift voor de Zorg aan Mensen met Verstandelijke Beperkingen (NLD) **4068**
Nederlands Tijdschrift voor de Zorg aan Verstandelijk Gehandicapten *see* Nederlands Tijdschrift voor de Zorg aan Mensen met Verstandelijke Beperkingen **4068**
• Nederlands Tijdschrift voor Dermatologie en Venereologie (NLD ISSN 0925-8604) **5880**
➤ Nederlands Tijdschrift voor Diabetologie (NLD ISSN 1567-2743) **5898**
Nederlands Tijdschrift voor Dietisten (NLD ISSN 0166-7203) **6664**
Nederlands Tijdschrift voor E H B O en Reddingwezen (NLD ISSN 0925-6040) **7533**
Nederlands Tijdschrift voor Ergotherapie (NLD ISSN 0166-4751) **6113**
Nederlands Tijdschrift voor Europees Recht (NLD ISSN 1382-4120) **4740**
• Nederlands Tijdschrift voor Evidence Based Practice (NLD ISSN 1572-2082) **5684**
• Nederlands Tijdschrift voor Fiscaal Recht (NLD ISSN 1389-6423) **1936**
▼ Nederlands Tijdschrift voor Fiscaal Recht Beschouwingen (NLD ISSN 1874-1703) **1936**
Nederlands Tijdschrift voor Fotonica *see* Fotonica Magazine **6968**
Nederlands Tijdschrift voor Fysioterapie *see* Dutch Journal of Physical Therapy **6108**
• Nederlands Tijdschrift voor Geneeskunde (NLD ISSN 0028-2162) **5684**
• Nederlands Tijdschrift voor Handelsrecht (NLD ISSN 1572-7807) **4740**
Nederlands Tijdschrift voor Heelkunde (NLD ISSN 0926-7522) **5684**
➤ Nederlands Tijdschrift voor Hematologie/The Dutch Journal of Hematology (NLD ISSN 1572-1590) **5940**
Nederlands Tijdschrift voor Jeugdzorg *see* Tijdschrift Jeugdbeleid **2169**
Het Nederlands Tijdschrift voor Keel- Neus- Oorheelkunde (NLD ISSN 1381-6683) **5856**
Nederlands Tijdschrift voor Kinderfysiotherapie (NLD ISSN 1874-2726) **6113**
Nederlands Tijdschrift voor Klinische Chemie *see* Nederlands Tijdschrift voor Klinische Chemie en Laboratoriumgeneeskunde **2074**
Nederlands Tijdschrift voor Klinische Chemie en Laboratoriumgeneeskunde (NLD ISSN 1570-8306) **2074**
➤ Nederlands Tijdschrift voor Medische Microbiologie (NLD ISSN 0929-0176) **5684**
Nederlands Tijdschrift voor Mondhygiene (NLD ISSN 1384-3966) **5856**
Nederlands Tijdschrift voor Natuurkunde (NLD ISSN 0926-4264) **7891**
Nederlands Tijdschrift voor Obstetrie & Gynaecologie (NLD ISSN 0921-4011) **5999**
Nederlands Tijdschrift voor Oefentherapie-Mensendieck *see* Beweegreden **6107**
➤ Nederlands Tijdschrift voor Oncologie/The Dutch Journal of Oncology (NLD ISSN 1572-1604) **6029**
Nederlands Tijdschrift voor Onderwijsrecht (NLD ISSN 0923-4640) **4740**
Nederlands Tijdschrift voor Onderwijsrecht en Onderwijsbeleid *see* Nederlands Tijdschrift voor Onderwijsrecht **4740**
Nederlands Tijdschrift voor Osteoporose en Andere Botziekten (NLD ISSN 1386-1565) **5684**
Nederlands Tijdschrift voor Rechtsfilosofie en Rechtstheorie *see* Rechtsfilosofie en Rechtstheorie **4766**
Nederlands Tijdschrift voor Reumatologie (NLD ISSN 1572-1698) **6225**
• Nederlands Tijdschrift voor Tandheelkunde/Dutch Journal of Dentistry (NLD ISSN 0028-2200) **5856**
Nederlands Tijdschrift voor Traumatologie (NLD ISSN 0929-8622) **6067**
➤ Nederlands Tijdschrift voor Urologie (NLD ISSN 0929-0184) **6271**
Nederlands Verpakkingscentrum Actueel *see* N V C Actueel **6712**
Nederlands Vervoer (NLD ISSN 0924-6584) **8506**
Nederlands-Vlaams Tijdschrift voor Mediation en Conflictmanagement (NLD) **4957**
Nederlands-Vlaamse Kring van Diatomisten. Diatomededelingen (NLD ISSN 1872-9673) **804**
Nederlandsch Archief voor Kerkgeschiedenis *see* Church History and Religious Culture **7633**
• De Nederlandsche Bank N.V. Annual Report (NLD ISSN 0169-0922) **1370**
Nederlandsche Bank N.V. Kwartaalbericht *see* De Nederlandsche Bank N.V. Quarterly Bulletin **1370**
De Nederlandsche Bank N.V. Quarterly Bulletin/Dutch Central Bank. Quarterly Bulletin (NLD ISSN 0922-6184) **1370**
De Nederlandsche Bank. Occasional Studies (NLD ISSN 1570-9159) **1936**
Nederlandsche Commissie voor Internationale Natuurbescherming. Mededelingen (NLD ISSN 0165-0912) **3456**
De Nederlandsche Leeuw (NLD ISSN 0028-226X) **3776**
Nederlandse Bakkerij Techniek Magazine *see* N B T Magazine **3657**
Nederlandse Begripsgeschiedenis (NLD) **4247**
† Het Nederlandse Boek (NLD ISSN 0166-0586) **8976**
Nederlandse Bond van Plattelandsvrouwen *see* Vrouwen van Nu **8888**
Nederlandse Bond van Poeliers en Wildhandelaren Journaal *see* N B P W Journaal **294**
Nederlandse Bouw Documentatie Magazine *see* N B D Magazine **1025**
Nederlandse Christelijke Radio Vereniging Magazine *see* N C R V Magazine **2360**
Nederlandse Commissie voor Geodesie. Publications on Geodesy (NLD) **2714**
Nederlandse Courant (CAN ISSN 0316-9782) **3553**
Nederlandse Cystic Fibrosis Stichting. C F Nieuws (NLD ISSN 0925-1944) **6216**
De Nederlandse Dagbladpers. Jaarverslag (NLD ISSN 1874-8007) **4580**
Nederlandse Entomologische Vereniging. Monographs (NLD ISSN 0548-1163) **855**
Nederlandse Fauna (NLD ISSN 1386-3762) **855**
Nederlandse Faunistische Mededelingen (NLD ISSN 0169-2453) **957**
Nederlandse Federatie van Reclasseringsinstellingen Publikaties *see* N R F Publikaties **4894**
Nederlandse Freecard Catalogus (NLD ISSN 1872-4469) **4342**
Nederlandse Genealogieen (NLD ISSN 1574-3233) **3776**
Nederlandse Genealogische Vereniging. Afdeling Kempen- en Peelland. Mededelingenblad (NLD ISSN 1566-0052) **3776**
Nederlandse Geografische Studies/Netherlands Geographical Studies (NLD ISSN 0169-4839) **4021**
Nederlandse Historien (NLD ISSN 0166-3801) **4247**
† Nederlandse Historische Bronnen (NLD ISSN 0920-4032) **8976**
Nederlandse Investeringsbank voor Ontwikkelingslanden. Verslag *see* Netherlands Investment Bank for Developing Countries. Report **1371**
De Nederlandse Jager (NLD ISSN 0166-0004) **8324**
Nederlandse Jezuieten *see* Jezuieten **7802**
• Nederlandse Jurisprudentie (NLD ISSN 0165-0637) **4740**
• Nederlandse Jurisprudentie Feitenrechtspraak (NLD ISSN 1567-2298) **4740**
• Nederlandse Jurisprudentie Feitenrechtspraak Strafzaken (NLD ISSN 1871-3335) **4740**
† Nederlandse Jurisprudentie Inzake Internationaal Belastingrecht (NLD) **8976**
Nederlandse Jurisprudentie Kort *see* Nederlandse Jurisprudentie Feitenrechtspraak **4740**
Nederlandse Kattenfokkers Vereniging. Jaarboek (NLD ISSN 1383-746X) **6812**
Nederlandse Letterkunde (NLD ISSN 1384-5829) **5339**
Nederlandse Malacologische Vereniging. Correspondentieblad *see* Spirula **964**
Nederlandse Onderneming voor Afbouwbedrijven Magazine *see* N O A Magazine **1025**
Het Nederlandse Ondernemingsklimaat in Cijfers (NLD ISSN 1872-325X) **1254**
Nederlandse Orde van Accountants - Administratieconsultenten. Leden - Info (NLD) **1297**
Nederlandse Organisatie voor Toegepast Natuurwetenschappelijk Onderzoek. Jaarverslag (NLD ISSN 0925-5621) **7891**
Nederlandse Organisatie voor Wetenschappelijk Onderzoek Spinozapremies *see* N W O-Spinozapremies **7885**
Nederlandse Organisatie voor Zuiver-Wetenschappelijk Onderzoek. Jaarboek/Netherlands Organisation for the Advancement of Pure Research. Yearbook (NLD ISSN 0167-6792) **7891**
Nederlandse Oudheden (NLD ISSN 0167-9783) **408**
Nederlandse Politie Academie Onderzoeksreeks *see* Politieacademie Onderzoeksreeks **4759**
Nederlandse Proces Technologen Procestechnologie *see* N P T Procestechnologie **3370**
Nederlandse Sportalmanak (NLD ISSN 1873-9091) **8190**
Nederlandse Taalkunde (NLD ISSN 1384-5845) **5154**
Nederlandse TentoonstellingsAgenda *see* Tentoonstellingsboekje **6538**
Nederlandse Vacuumvereniging Blad *see* N E V A C Blad **7027**
Nederlandse Verantwoordelijkheidstekens vanaf 1797 (NLD ISSN 1875-208X) **6327**
Nederlandse Vereniging "de Rijwiel- en Automobiel Industrie" Voorrang *see* R A I Voorrang **8600**
Nederlandse Vereniging van Blinden en Slechtzienden. Donateursbrief (NLD ISSN 1574-9622) **4083**
Nederlandse Vereniging van Participatiemaatschappijen Private Equity Gids *see* N V P Private Equity Gids **1369**
Nederlandse Vereniging van Schooldekanen. Actueel *see* N V S - N V L Actueel **3028**
Nederlandse Vereniging van Schooldekanen Actueel *see* N V S - N V L Actueel **3028**
Nederlandse Vereniging voor Beroepsbeoefenaren in de Bibliotheek-, Informatie- en Kennissector Krant *see* N V B Krant **5033**
Nederlandse Vereniging voor Geestelijke- en Natuurgeneeswijzen Magazine Geestelijke Genezer *see* N V G N Magazine Geestelijke Genezer **6113**
Nederlandse Vereniging voor Hepatologie. Nieuwsbrief *see* Lever **5928**
Nederlandse Vereniging voor het Onderwijs in de Natuurwetenschappen Maandblad *see* N V O N Maandblad **7885**
Nederlandse Vereniging voor Internationaal Recht. Mededelingen (NLD ISSN 0077-6440) **4936**
Nederlandse Vereniging voor Kartografie Publikatiereeks *see* N V K Publikatiereeks **4020**
Nederlandse Vereniging voor Klinische Chemie. Almanak (NLD) **5909**
Nederlandse Vereniging voor Veiligheidskunde Info *see* N V V K Info **6681**
De Nederlandse Vliegvisser (NLD ISSN 1384-8054) **8324**
Nederlandse Werkgemeenschap voor Individualpsychologie. Nieuwsbrief (NLD ISSN 1574-602X) **7386**
Nedge (USA) **5339**
NedKAD/Silhouet *see* Silhouet **6185**
Nedorosl' (RUS) **2204**
➤ Nedslag i Boernelitteraturforskningen (DNK ISSN 1600-9843) **5339**
Nedvizhimost' za Rubezhom (RUS) **7601**
Need (USA ISSN 1934-5593) **8057**
Need a Lift? (USA ISSN 0548-1384) **3028**
Need to Know (GBR) **2432**
Needle Arts (USA ISSN 0047-925X) **6640**
A Needle Pulling Thread (CAN ISSN 1715-4650) **6640**
• Needle Tips (USA ISSN 1944-2009) **5823**
Needle Tips and the Hepatitis B Coalition News *see* Needle Tips **5823**
Needlecraft (GBR ISSN 0961-4540) **6640**
Needlecraft Magic (GBR ISSN 1368-8081) **6640**
Needlepoint Bulletin (USA) **6640**
Needlepunch Conference Papers (USA) **8455**
The Needle's Eye (USA) **3074**
Needle's Eye Worldwide (USA ISSN 8750-7366) **2249**
Needlework (GBR ISSN 0966-6729) **6640**
Needlework Retailer (USA) **6640**
Needs (JPN ISSN 0287-3052) **7891**
Needs & Seeds *see* Taiyo Yuden Giho **3332**
Neeleshwari (IND) **7708**
Neerlandia (NLD ISSN 0028-2383) **5229**
• ➤ Neerlandistiek (NLD ISSN 1567-6633) **5154**
Neerlands Postduiven Orgaan (NLD ISSN 0028-2391) **8190**
Neerslag (NLD ISSN 1389-8329) **8830**
Neetee (IND) **3886**
Neeuropa (LUX) **508**
• ➤ Nefrologia (ESP ISSN 0211-6995) **6271**
Nefrologia i Nadcisnienie Tetnicze (POL ISSN 1644-485X) **6271**
• Nefrologia Mexicana (MEX ISSN 0187-7801) **6271**
Nefrologia. Suplemento *see* Nefrologia **6271**
Nefrologiia, Hemodializa i Transplantatsiia/Nephrology, Hemodialysis and Transplantation (BGR ISSN 0204-6105) **6272**
Neft', Gaz i Biznes (RUS) **6780**
Neft' i Kapital (RUS) **2622**
Neft' Priob'ya (RUS ISSN 1607-5242) **6780**
Neft' Rossii (RUS ISSN 1028-9976) **2622**
• Nefte Compass (USA ISSN 0968-6452) **6780**
• Nefte Compass (Online) (USA ISSN 1742-4372) **6780**
Neftegazonosnye i Perspektivnye Kompleksy Tsentral'nykh i Vostochnykh Oblastei Russkoi Platformy (RUS) **6780**
Neftegazovaya Vertikal' (RUS) **6780**
• Neftegazovoe Delo (RUS ISSN 1813-503X) **6780**
Neftegazovye Tekhnologii/Oil and Gas Technologies (RUS) **6780**
• Neftekhimiya (RUS ISSN 0028-2421) **6780**
Neftepanorama (GBR ISSN 1463-4295) **6780**
Neftepererabotka i Neftekhimiya. Nauchno-Tekhnicheskie Dostizheniya i Peredovoi Opyt (RUS ISSN 0233-5727) **6780**
Nefteprodukty *see* Naftoprodukty **6779**
Neftepromyslovoe Delo/Oilfield Engineering (RUS ISSN 0207-2351) **6780**
Neftyanik (Moscow, 1974) (RUS) **6800**
Neftyanik Orenburzh'ya (RUS) **6780**
Neftyanoe Khozyaistvo/Oil Industry (RUS ISSN 0028-2448) **6780**
Nefuroroji Furontia *see* Nephrology Frontier **5898**
• Negations (USA ISSN 1949-3371) **8122**
Negen Maanden Magazine (NLD) **5999**
➤ Negentiende Eeuw (NLD ISSN 1381-8546) **4247**
Negobancos *see* Negocios y Bancos **1370**
Negoce Agriculture (FRA ISSN 0753-2415) **204**
• Negociations (BEL ISSN 1780-9231) **7988**
Negocios (ARG ISSN 0328-8579) **1152**
• Negocios (Veracruz) (MEX ISSN 1606-819X) **1152**
Negocios al Dia (GBR ISSN 0960-8710) **1578**
• Negocios Globales (CHL ISSN 0718-3488) **1578**
• Negocios y Bancos (MEX ISSN 0028-2456) **1370**
Negocis *see* Regio 7 **3953**
• Negotia (NOR) **4599**
Negotiability Determinations by the Federal Labor Relations Authority *see* U.S. Office of Personnel Management. Negotiability Determinations by the Federal Labor Relations Authority **1712**
Negotiating International Joint Venture Agreements (GBR) **4876**
Negotiating International Software Licence and Data Transfer Agreements (GBR) **5063**
• Negotiation (USA ISSN 1546-9522) **1780**
▼ • Negotiation and Conflict Management Research (GBR ISSN 1750-4708) **8122**
• ➤ Negotiation Journal (USA ISSN 0748-4526) **7254**
Negotiator (GBR) **7601**
• The Negotiator Magazine (USA ISSN 1559-9116) **4740**
• ➤ Negotium (VEN ISSN 1856-1810) **1781**
† Negozio Moderno (ITA) **8976**
• ➤ Negro Educational Review (USA ISSN 0548-1457) **2890**
The Negro Spiritual (USA ISSN 1546-6078) **6598**
• Nehnutel'nosti a Byvanie (SVK ISSN 1336-9431) **1026**
• Nei Menggu Daxue Xuebao (Renwen - Shehui Kexue Ban)/Inner Mongolia University. Journal (Humanities & Social Sciences Edition) (CHN) **7988**
Nei Menggu Daxue Xuebao (Shehui Kexue Ban)/Inner Mongolian University. Journal (Social Science Edition) *see* Nei Menggu Daxue Xuebao (Renwen - Shehui Kexue Ban) **7988**
• Nei Menggu Daxue Xuebao (Ziran Kexue Ban)/Acta Scientiarum Naturalium Universitatis Neimongol (CHN ISSN 1000-1638) **7891**
Nei Menggu Funu/Inner Mongolian Women (CHN) **8877**
• Nei Menggu Shehui Kexue/Inner Mongolian Social Sciences (CHN) **7988**
• Nei Menggu Shifan Daxue Xuebao (Jiaoyu Kexue Ban)/Inner Mongolia Normal University. Journal (Education Science Edition) (MNG ISSN 1671-0916) **2890**
• Nei Menggu Shifan Daxue Xuebao (Zhexue Shehui Kexue Hanwen Ban)/Inner Mongolia Normal University. Journal (Philosophy & Social Science Chinese Edition) (MNG ISSN 1001-7623) **6935**
• Nei Menggu Shifan Daxue Xuebao (Ziran Kexue Ban)/Inner Mongolia Normal University. Journal (Natural Science Edition) (MNG ISSN 1001-8735) **7891**
Nei til E U. Skriftserie *see* Vett **4944**
Nei til EU. Aarbok (NOR ISSN 1890-5668) **4936**
Neicha Sutadi/Nature Study (JPN ISSN 0466-6089) **7891**
Neige et Avalanches (FRA ISSN 1247-5327) **6392**
Neighborhood *see* Neighbourhood **4420**
Neighborhood Builder (USA) **1026**
Neighborhood Reinvestment Corporation. Annual Report (USA) **4420**
Neighboring Property Owners (USA) **4838**
Neighborline (USA) **8057**
Neighbors (USA ISSN 0162-3974) **139**
NeighborWorks Bright Ideas *see* Bright Ideas (Washington, D.C.) **4405**
NeighborWorks Journal (USA ISSN 1096-7117) **4420**
▼ • Neighbourhood (GBR ISSN 1756-8676) **4420**
Neihardt Foundation Newsletter (USA) **5229**
Neijiang Shifan Xueyuan Xuebao/Neijiang Teachers College. Journal (CHN ISSN 1671-1785) **2890**
Neijiang Teachers College. Journal *see* Neijiang Shifan Xueyuan Xuebao **2890**
• Neike Jiwei Zhongzheng Zazhi/Journal of Internal Intensive Medicine (CHN ISSN 1007-1024) **5947**
Neike Xuezhi/Journal of Internal Medicine R O C (TWN ISSN 1016-7390) **5947**
Neil Muscott's Success Newsletter (CAN ISSN 1188-2921) **5078**
Neil Sperry's Gardens (USA ISSN 1061-3994) **3744**
Neil Squire Society Annual Report (CAN ISSN 1912-2764) **8057**
Neilreichia (AUT ISSN 1681-5947) **804**
• Neimenggu Caijing Xueyuan Xuebao/Inner Mongolia Finance and Economics College. Journal (CHN ISSN 1004-5295) **1152**

Title

10660 NETHERLANDS. CENTRAAL BUREAU VOOR DE STATISTIEK. SOCIAAL-ECONOMISCHE ULRICH'S PERIODICALS

Netherlands. Centraal Bureau voor de Statistiek. Sociaal-Economische Trends (NLD ISSN 1573-2215) **8083**
Netherlands. Centraal Bureau voor de Statistiek. Statistiek Financien van Ondernemingen (NLD ISSN 0921-5999) **1254**
Netherlands. Centraal Bureau voor de Statistiek. Statistisch Bulletin (NLD ISSN 0166-9680) **1254**
• Netherlands. Centraal Bureau voor de Statistiek. Statistisch Jaarboek/Netherlands. Central Bureau of Statistics. Pocket Yearbook (NLD ISSN 0924-2686) **7312**
Netherlands. Centraal Bureau voor de Statistiek. Toerisme in Nederland/Netherlands. Central Bureau for Statistics. Tourism in the Netherlands (NLD ISSN 1383-7214) **8780**
Netherlands. Centraal Bureau voor de Statistiek. Verkeersongevallen *see* Netherlands. Ministerie van Verkeer en Waterstaat. Directoraat-Generaal Rijkswaterstaat. Adviesdienst Verkeer en Vervoer. Verkeersongevallen in Nederland **8528**
Netherlands. Centraal Planbureau. Centraal Economisch Plan (NLD ISSN 0166-9478) **1899**
Netherlands. Central Bureau for Statistics. Tourism in the Netherlands *see* Netherlands. Centraal Bureau voor de Statistiek. Toerisme in Nederland **8780**
Netherlands. Central Bureau of Statistics. National Accounts *see* Netherlands. Centraal Bureau voor de Statistiek. Nationale Rekeningen **1254**
Netherlands. Central Bureau of Statistics. Pocket Yearbook *see* Netherlands. Centraal Bureau voor de Statistiek. Statistisch Jaarboek **7312**
Netherlands. Central Bureau of Statistics. Statistics of Road-Traffic Accidents *see* Netherlands. Ministerie van Verkeer en Waterstaat. Directoraat-Generaal Rijkswaterstaat. Adviesdienst Verkeer en Vervoer. Verkeersongevallen in Nederland **8528**
Netherlands. Centrale Commissie voor de Statistiek. Jaarverslag (NLD ISSN 0922-5897) **8390**
Netherlands Energy Research Foundation. Annual Report *see* Energieonderzoek Centrum Nederland. Jaarverslag **3129**
Netherlands Entomological Society Meeting. Proceedings (NLD ISSN 1874-9542) **855**
The Netherlands Financial Analysis Service (GBR) **6780**
Netherlands Geographical Studies *see* Nederlandse Geografische Studies **4021**
• Netherlands Heart Journal (NLD ISSN 1568-5888) **5796**
➤ Netherlands Institute at Athens. Publications (NLD) **408**
Netherlands Institute for Sea Research. Annual Report (NLD ISSN 0165-9162) **2813**
Netherlands Institute for the Law of the Sea. Annual Report (NLD) **4970**
† ➤ Netherlands Institute of Archaeology and Arabic Studies in Cairo. Publications (NLD ISSN 0922-5234) **8976**
• ➤ Netherlands International Law Review (NLD ISSN 0165-070X) **4936**
Netherlands Investment Bank for Developing Countries. Report/Nederlandse Investeringsbank voor Ontwikkelingslanden. Verslag (NLD) **1371**
Netherlands Journal of Agricultural Science Wageningen Journal of Life Science *see* N J A S Wageningen Journal of Life Sciences **138**
Netherlands Journal of Agricultural Sciences Wageningen Journal of Life Sciences *see* N J A S Wageningen Journal of Life Sciences **138**
• ➤ Netherlands Journal of Geosciences/Geology and Mining (NLD) **2757**
• ➤ Netherlands Journal of Medicine (NLD ISSN 0300-2977) **5947**
Netherlands Journal of Psychology (NLD ISSN 1872-552X) **7386**
† The Netherlands Journal of Social Sciences (NLD ISSN 0924-1477) **8976**
Netherlands Journal of Veterinary Science *see* Tijdschrift voor Diergeneeskunde **8808**
Netherlands Journal of Zoology *see* Animal Biology **932**
Netherlands Military Medical Review *see* Nederlands Militair Geneeskundig Tijdschrift **5684**
Netherlands. Ministerie van Algemene Zaken. Beleidsprogramma (NLD ISSN 1872-2458) **7454**
Netherlands. Ministerie van Binnenlandse Zaken en Koninkrijksrelaties. Periodiek Onderhoudsrapport Gemeentefonds (NLD ISSN 1872-3594) **7499**
Netherlands. Ministerie van Binnenlandse Zaken en Koninkrijksrelaties. Salarisniveaus Overheidspersoneel (NLD ISSN 1872-0463) **1699**
Netherlands. Ministerie van Binnenlandsezaken en Koninkrijksrelaties. Circulaire Gemeentefonds (NLD ISSN 1871-6520) **7499**
Netherlands. Ministerie van Onderwijs, Cultuur en Wetenschap. Actieplan Cultuurbereik (NLD ISSN 1874-8104) **7454**
Netherlands. Ministerie van Sociale Zaken en Werkgelegenheid. Nationaal Actieplan ter Bestrijding van Armoede en Sociale Uitsluiting (NLD ISSN 1872-0471) **8057**
Netherlands. Ministerie van Verkeer en Waterstaat. Directoraat-Generaal Rijkswaterstaat. Adviesdienst Verkeer en Vervoer. Verkeersongevallen in Nederland/Netherlands. Central Bureau of Statistics. Statistics of Road-Traffic Accidents (NLD ISSN 1574-5473) **8528**
Netherlands. Ministerie van Verkeer en Waterstaat, Rijkswaterstaat. Adviesdienst Verkeer en Vervoer. Kerncijfers Infrastructuur (NLD ISSN 1573-9511) **8506**
† Netherlands Official Statistics (NLD ISSN 0920-2048) **8976**
Netherlands Offshore Catalogue *see* Netherlands Oil & Gas Catalogue **6780**
Netherlands Oil & Gas Catalogue (NLD ISSN 1573-3033) **6780**
Netherlands Organisation for the Advancement of Pure Research. Yearbook *see* Nederlandse Organisatie voor Zuiver-Wetenschappelijk Onderzoek. Jaarboek **7891**
Netherlands Organization for Applied Scientific Research. Annual Review *see* Nederlandse Organisatie voor Toegepast Natuurwetenschappelijk Onderzoek. Jaarverslag **7891**
Netherlands Petrochemicals Report (GBR ISSN 1749-2351) **6780**
Netherlands Philately Journal (USA) **6897**
• ➤ Netherlands Quarterly of Human Rights (BEL ISSN 0924-0519) **4838**
Netherlands. Rijksdienst voor de Monumentenzorg. Jaarverslag (NLD) **451**
Netherlands. Rijksinstituut voor Oorlogsdocumentatie. Documenten (NLD ISSN 0066-1287) **4248**
Netherlands. Rijksinstituut voor Oorlogsdocumentatie. Progress Report (NLD) **4248**
Netherlands. Sociaal en Cultureel Planbureau. Cahiers (NLD ISSN 0927-0833) **8122**
• Netherlands. Sociaal en Cultureel Planbureau. Rapportage Gehandicapten (NLD ISSN 1385-0458) **4068**
• Netherlands. Sociaal en Cultureel Planbureau. Rapportage Ouderen (NLD ISSN 1381-3048) **4052**
• Netherlands. Sociaal en Cultureel Planbureau. Sociale en Cultureel Rapport (NLD ISSN 0922-8772) **8122**
Netherlands. Sociaal en Cultureel Planbureau. Studies (NLD) **8122**
• Netherlands Yearbook of International Law (NLD ISSN 0167-6768) **4936**
Nethra (LKA ISSN 1391-2380) **7157**
Netiva (DEU ISSN 1437-8965) **4248**
Netiverk (NOR) **4599**
• NetMag (PAK ISSN 1561-3550) **2501**
• ➤ Netnomics (USA ISSN 1385-9587) **2501**
Neto Plus (ISR ISSN 0334-6234) **1870**
NetOpus (NLD ISSN 1573-577X) **2565**
NetPEM Newsletter (IND ISSN 0973-4198) **3456**
Netpreneur *see* Entrepreneur's Netpreneur **2556**
• NetProfessional (USA) **2565**
• Netscapepress.com (USA) **2565**
NetSci *see* Network Science **7891**
Netsec News *see* Network Security **2501**
• Netsources (FRA ISSN 1270-0193) **5063**
Netspar News *see* N E T S P A R News **1698**
† netspotting (DEU) **8976**
➤ Netsu Bussei/Japan Journal of Thermophysical Properties (JPN ISSN 0913-946X) **7056**
Netsu Kogaku Sukuringu & Wakushoppu Shiryo/Schooling & Workshop (JPN) **3391**
Netsu Shori/Japan Society for Heat Treatment. Journal (JPN ISSN 0288-0490) **6327**
Netsu Sokutei/Calorimetry and Thermal Analysis (JPN ISSN 0386-2615) **7056**
Netsu Sokutei Toronkai Koen Yoshishu/Abstracts of Japanese Calorimetry Conference (JPN) **7048**
• Netsuds (FRA ISSN 1763-7864) **2335**
• Netsurfer Digest (USA) **2565**
• Netsurfer Science (USA) **7891**
Nettai Doshokubutsu Tomo no Kai Kaiho/News of the Tropical Plants and Animals (JPN) **804**
Nettai Igaku *see* Tropical Medicine **5827**
Nettai Kenkyu *see* Tropics **708**
Nettai Nogaku Kenkyu *see* Kyushu University. Institute of Tropical Agriculture. Bulletin **132**
Nettai Nogyo/Japanese Journal of Tropical Agriculture (JPN ISSN 0021-5260) **139**
Nettai Shokubutsu Chosa Kenkyu Nenpo/Annual Bulletin of Tropical Arboretum (JPN) **804**
• Nettverk (NOR ISSN 1501-5882) **4599**
• Nettverk & Kommunikasjon (NOR ISSN 1501-0333) **2501**
Netvaerket *see* Sundhed, Teknologi, Informatik **5718**
NetWare Advisor (USA ISSN 1040-5747) **2501**
• Netwatcher (Online) (USA) **2335**
• NetWatchers Cyberzine (USA) **2565**
Network *see* Australian Music Therapy Association. Network **6546**
Network (CAN ISSN 0830-1417) **3720**
Network *see* Reseaux V R D **1032**
Network *see* Instrument Pilot **8545**
• The Network (GBR ISSN 1750-1733) **8506**
The Network (USA) **8295**
Network (Atlanta) (USA) **7665**
• Network (Auckland) (NZL ISSN 1178-3583) **2293**
† • Network (Durham) (USA ISSN 0270-3637) **8976**
Network (Edinburgh) (GBR ISSN 1361-6005) **2890**
• Network (Exhall) (GBR) **2890**
• ➤ Network (London, 1990) (GBR ISSN 0954-898X) **6163**
Network (New York) (USA ISSN 1044-1476) **4580**
Network (Rockville) (USA ISSN 1076-254X) **30**
Network (Salt Lake City) (USA ISSN 0890-3530) **8877**
Network (The Hague) *see* Network Newsletter **7533**
• Network (Winnipeg) (CAN ISSN 1480-0039) **8847**
• Network (Year) (USA ISSN 1093-7951) **2565**
• Network 21 (GBR) **2622**
Network 2d (USA ISSN 1063-9829) **4740**
Network & Telecom (BEL ISSN 1374-8114) **2501**
• Network Audio Bits (USA) **6598**
• Network Briefing (GBR ISSN 1360-1369) **2370**
▼ • Network Business Weekly (USA ISSN 1945-8258) **2501**
Network Cabling (CAN ISSN 1711-4632) **2386**
▼ Network Centric Security (USA ISSN 1944-6845) **2515**
• Network Chicago Guide (USA ISSN 1543-9585) **2386**
Network China Business Directory/Xinjiapo Zhongguo Gongshang Lianhui Shangye Zhinan (SGP) **2019**
Network Computing (DEU ISSN 1435-2524) **2501**
Network Computing (GBR) **2501**
Network Computing *see* Information Week (US Edition) **2531**
Network Computing India (IND) **2501**
Network Connection (USA ISSN 1061-9615) **7808**
Network Contracts Report (USA) **2495**
• Network E-News (AUS) **6993**
Network for Studies on Pensions, Aging and Retirement News *see* N E T S P A R News **1698**
Network Futures & ProLog (USA) **2386**
Network India Business Directory (SGP) **2019**
• The Network Journal (USA ISSN 1094-1908) **3553**
• Network Magazine (AUS ISSN 1832-5548) **6231**
Network Magazine *see* NetMag **2501**
Network Marketing Lifestyles (USA ISSN 1528-0799) **1371**
NetWork Marketing Today (USA) **1836**
• Network News (AUS ISSN 0158-9539) **2162**
• Network News (GBR ISSN 1361-892X) **2501**
• Network News (NZL ISSN 1177-9543) **8057**
• Network News (Bluffton) (USA ISSN 0745-418X) **7768**
Network News (Madison) (USA) **8057**
• Network News (Montreal) (CAN ISSN 1488-1004) **8057**
Network News (Ottawa) (CAN ISSN 1481-0999) **6029**
Network News (Sherman) (USA) **7213**
Network News (Washington, 1975) *see* The Women's Health Activist **8849**
Network News (Washington) (USA) **4052**
Network Newsletter (NLD) **7533**
• Network Newsletter (Boulder) (USA) **6392**
† • Network Newsletter and E N S O Signal (Environmental Societal Impacts Group) (USA ISSN 1948-2558) **8976**
Network Nottinghamshire (GBR) **1407**
Network of African Countries on Cost-Effective Building Technologies (KEN) **1026**
Network of Aquaculture Centres in Asia-Pacific. Newsletter (THA ISSN 0115-8503) **958**
Network of Care *see* Release **2667**
Network Operations and Management Symposium *see* I E E E - I F I P Network Operations and Management Symposium **2520**
▼ • ➤ Network Protocols and Algorithms (USA ISSN 1943-3581) **2501**
• Network Science (USA ISSN 1092-7360) **7891**
• Network Security (GBR ISSN 1353-4858) **2501**
• Network Solutions (GBR ISSN 1367-9678) **2501**
Network Support (USA ISSN 1554-3730) **2501**
• Network Technology Report (Asynchronous Transfer Mode and Internet Protocol Report) (USA ISSN 1542-6009) **2567**
Network Wales/Rhwydwaith Cymru (GBR ISSN 0265-783X) **8057**
▼ • Network Weekly News (USA ISSN 1944-253X) **2502**
Network Work News (NAM) **4580**
Network World *see* Seti **2503**
• Network World (USA ISSN 0887-7661) **2502**
Network World Argentina *see* NetworkWorld Argentina **2502**
• Network World Canada (CAN ISSN 1187-2985) **2352**
• Network World Italia (ITA) **2502**
Network World Middle East (UAE) **2502**
Network World Portugal (PRT) **2502**
Network World Romania *see* NetworkWorld Romania **2502**
Network World S A (ZAF) **2502**
• Networked Cultural Heritage Newsletter (USA) **3776**
The Networker (New York, 1955) (USA) **4377**
• ➤ netWorker (USA ISSN 1091-3556) **2502**
• The Networker (Windsor) (USA) **3456**
Networking Alternatives for Publishers, Retailers, and Artists, Inc. ReView *see* N A P R A ReView **6646**
Networking and Information Systems *see* Ingenierie des Systemes d'Information **2521**
† Networking for Women (ISR) **8976**
Networking in New Jersey (USA ISSN 1093-3859) **2019**
• Networking Magazine (USA) **8877**
• Networking Times (USA ISSN 1539-3151) **1836**
• Networkletter (CAN ISSN 1497-1518) **2370**
▼ • Networks (AUS) **2661**
• ➤ Networks (New York) (USA ISSN 0028-3045) **5555**
• Networks (Washington, D.C.) (USA) **8057**
• ➤ Networks: An On-line Journal for Teacher Research (CAN) **3074**
• Networks and Heterogeneous Media (USA ISSN 1556-1801) **5520**
• Networks and Spatial Economics (USA ISSN 1566-113X) **2518**
Networks Magazine (GBR ISSN 1752-8186) **8240**
• Networks of Centres of Excellence. Annual Report (CAN ISSN 1489-2707) **7454**
• Networks Update (USA) **2502**
Networkworld *see* Network World Italia **2502**
NetworkWorld *see* L A N Magazine **2500**
NetworkWorld Argentina (ARG) **2502**
NetworkWorld Bulgaria (BGR ISSN 1311-3151) **2502**
NetworkWorld Portugal *see* Network World Portugal **2502**
• NetworkWorld Romania (ROM ISSN 1454-4997) **2502**
• NetWorld (POL ISSN 1232-8723) **2565**
Netz (DEU ISSN 1619-6570) **8057**
Netz Werk Magazin (DEU) **8633**
Netzpraxis (DEU ISSN 1611-0412) **3326**
Der Netzwerkadministrator (DEU ISSN 1863-7973) **2502**
Netzwirtschaften und Recht (DEU ISSN 1612-9245) **4740**
NEU (ITA ISSN 1723-2538) **5971**
▼ • NEU Magazine (USA ISSN 1936-9263) **5078**
† Neucleus (AUS ISSN 1036-4587) **8976**
Neudin (Year) (FRA) **4342**
Neudrucke Deutscher Literaturwerke (DEU ISSN 0077-7668) **5339**
Das Neue (DEU ISSN 0939-852X) **3853**
Neue Alternative (AUT ISSN 0028-3061) **7157**
Neue Apotheken Illustrierte (DEU ISSN 0047-9381) **6863**
Der Neue Apotheker (DEU ISSN 1862-8907) **6863**
Neue Arbeitsrecht von A-Z fuer den Geschaeftsfuehrer (DEU) **1870**
Neue Argumente (AUT ISSN 1027-8303) **3456**
Neue Arzneimittel (DEU ISSN 0724-567X) **6863**
Das Neue Automobil. Testjahrbuch *see* Automobil Jahrbuch **8563**
Neue Bahn (AUT) **8621**
Neue Beitraege zur George-Forschung (DEU ISSN 0342-9547) **5427**
Neue Beitraege zur Juelicher Geschichte (DEU ISSN 0939-2904) **4248**
Neue Betriebs Sicherheit *see* Sicherheitsmagazin **6687**
Neue Bienenzucht (DEU) **139**
Das Neue Bilanz-Handbuch (DEU) **1297**
Neue Bildpost (DEU ISSN 1611-891X) **3853**
Das Neue Blatt (DEU ISSN 0939-8538) **3853**
Neue Caritas (DEU ISSN 1438-7832) **8057**
Neue Caritas Jahrbuch (DEU) **8057**
Das Neue China (DEU ISSN 0172-4878) **3553**
Neue Chorzeit (DEU) **6598**
† Die Neue D L (DEU ISSN 0937-9851) **8976**
Neue Denkschriften des Naturhistorischen Museums in Wien (AUT ISSN 1016-605X) **7988**
Neue Deutsche-Amerikanische Studien *see* New German-American Studies **4466**
Neue Deutsche Schule *see* N D S **2888**
Neue Energie (DEU ISSN 0949-8656) **3178**
Neue Entomologische Nachrichten (DEU ISSN 0722-3773) **856**
• Neue Entwicklungen im Financial Planning (LIE ISSN 1818-5444) **1371**
Die Neue Esotera (DEU ISSN 1617-8769) **6646**
Neue Fertigungsverfahren *see* Informationsdienst F I Z Technik. Neue Fertigungsverfahren **6339**
Die Neue Frau (DEU ISSN 1614-8673) **8877**
Die Neue Frau - Astro *see* Astro **565**
Die Neue Frau - Die Besten Obstkuchen *see* Die Besten Obstkuchen **4352**
Die Neue Frau - Frisuren (DEU) **590**
Die Neue Frau - Ostern (DEU) **4364**
Neue Freie Zeitung *see* N F Z - Neue Freie Zeitung **7156**
• Neue Gegenwart (DEU) **5078**
Die Neue Gesellschaft - Frankfurter Hefte (DEU ISSN 0177-6738) **7157**
Neue Gespraeche (DEU ISSN 0930-1143) **7809**
† Neue Gesundheit (DEU ISSN 1436-915X) **8976**
Der Neue GmbH-Berater von A-Z (DEU) **1781**
Neue Hanauer Zeitung *see* N H Z **5228**
Neue Heidelberger Studien zur Musikwissenschaft (DEU ISSN 0550-6212) **6598**
Neue Heimat (DEU ISSN 0548-2801) **7255**
Neue Helvetische Gesellschaft. Mitteilungen (CHE ISSN 0257-3830) **2268**
• Neue Juristische Wochenschrift (DEU ISSN 0341-1915) **4740**
Neue Juristische Wochenschrift Rechtsprechungs-Report Zivilrecht *see* N J W - Rechtsprechungs-Report Zivilrecht **4838**
Neue Justiz (DEU ISSN 0028-3231) **4740**
Der Neue Kaemmerer (DEU ISSN 1860-7292) **1153**
Neue Keramik/New Ceramics (DEU ISSN 0933-2367) **2044**
Das Neue Kontierungs-Praxis-abc (DEU) **1297**
Neue Kriminalpolitik (DEU ISSN 0934-9200) **7157**
• Neue Kriminologische Literatur/New Criminological Literature/Nouvelle Litterature Criminologique/Nueva Literatura Criminologica (DEU) **2675**
Neue Kriminologische Schriftenreihe (DEU) **2662**
Neue Kronen Zeitung *see* Kronen Zeitung **3797**
Neue Kronstaedter Zeitung (DEU ISSN 0934-4713) **3853**

▼ *new title*   † *ceased*   ● *electronic media*   ➤ *refereed*

DIRECTORY 2010 NEW HAMPSHIRE FOR-PROFIT AND NON-PROFIT BUSINESS LAWS 10663

New Contents Slavistics (DEU ISSN 0173-6388) **632**
New Contrast (ZAF ISSN 1017-5415) **5340**
➤ New Contree (ZAF) **4177**
New Conversations (USA ISSN 0360-0181) **7665**
New Country (AUS) **3553**
New Countryside Commerce *see* Xinnongcun Shangbao **1196**
New Creation Connection *see* Global Chinese Times **3535**
• ➤ New Criminal Law Review (USA ISSN 1933-4192) **4894**
New Criminological Literature *see* Neue Kriminologische Literatur **2675**
New Crisis *see* The Crisis **3528**
• New Criterion (USA ISSN 0734-0222) **5229**
• The New Critic (AUS ISSN 1833-7597) **7988**
The New Critical Idiom (GBR) **5155**
New Crucible (USA) **7387**
New Crystal Palace Matters (GBR ISSN 0964-8011) **4248**
New Cultural Studies (USA ISSN 1545-0384) **8122**
New Culture (NGA ISSN 0331-7080) **508**
• The New D A W N Report (Drug Abuse Warning Network) (USA) **2697**
New Daily Cardinal *see* Daily Cardinal **2280**
• The New Dawn (AUS ISSN 1036-8035) **6646**
• ➤ New Dawn (CAN ISSN 1715-4081) **3553**
New Dawn *see* Fajr al-Jadid **8862**
New Day (GBR) **7665**
New Day Herald (USA ISSN 1040-2047) **6646**
New Day Publications (USA) **5427**
• New Deal (USA) **4305**
New Deal Handbook (GBR) **8058**
New Delhi (IND) **3886**
➤ The New Delta Review (USA ISSN 1050-415X) **5340**
New Departures (GBR) **5340**
New Design (GBR ISSN 1472-2674) **8433**
• New Developments in Cardiovascular Diseases (USA ISSN 1550-6231) **5796**
• New Developments in Rheumatic Diseases (USA ISSN 1543-4516) **6225**
• New Dialogue (Online) (NZL ISSN 1177-0813) **8058**
• New Dialogue (Wellington, 2007. Print) (NZL ISSN 1178-3753) **8058**
New Dialogue Mini *see* New Dialogue (Wellington, 2007. Print) **8058**
New Diamond *see* Nyu Daiyamondo **2112**
➤ New Diamond and Frontier Carbon Technology (JPN ISSN 1344-9931) **3391**
New Diet Therapy *see* Nyu Daietto Serapi **6667**
New Digest (GBR ISSN 1476-4806) **5999**
New Dimension Chorus *see* New Dimension Notes **6599**
• New Dimension Notes (USA ISSN 1949-0801) **6599**
• New Dimensions Journal (USA) **2361**
New Direction (GBR) **6296**
New Direction (USA ISSN 1059-5902) **4377**
† New Directions (Chicago) (USA) **8976**
• New Directions (Denver) (USA) **6216**
• New Directions for Adult and Continuing Education (USA ISSN 1052-2891) **2944**
• New Directions for Child and Adolescent Development (USA ISSN 1520-3247) **7387**
• ➤ New Directions for Community Colleges (USA ISSN 0194-3081) **2995**
• New Directions for Evaluation (USA ISSN 1097-6736) **7988**
• New Directions for Higher Education (USA ISSN 0271-0560) **2995**
• New Directions for Institutional Research (USA ISSN 0271-0579) **2995**
• New Directions for Student Services (USA ISSN 0164-7970) **2995**
• New Directions for Teaching and Learning (USA ISSN 0271-0633) **2995**
• New Directions for Youth Development (USA ISSN 1533-8916) **2162**
▼ New Directions in Aesthetics (USA) **6936**
New Directions in Cognitive Science (GBR) **7387**
➤ New Directions in Cultural Analysis (USA) **4466**
▼ ➤ New Directions in Diplomatic History (NLD) **7157**
• New Directions in Folklore (USA) **3621**
• New Directions in Information Management (USA ISSN 0887-3844) **5035**
▼ New Directions in Media (USA ISSN 1939-2494) **8122**
• New Directions in Psychoanalytic Writing (USA ISSN 1932-5649) **7387**
New Directions in Public Administration Research (USA) **7455**
New Directions Journal *see* New Directions in Psychoanalytic Writing **7387**
• New Disease Reports (GBR) **804**
• New Doctor (AUS ISSN 0313-2153) **5685**
New Documents Illustrating Early Christianity (USA ISSN 0812-9576) **7665**
New Drug Approval Pipeline *see* The N D A Pipeline **8975**
New Drugs (DEU) **6863**
New Drugs in Japan *see* Saikin no Shinyaku **6879**
New Earnings Survey. Part A: Report and Key Results (GBR ISSN 0262-0502) **1699**
New Earnings Survey. Part B: Analyses by Agreement (GBR ISSN 0262-0510) **1254**
New Earnings Survey. Part C: Analyses by Industry (GBR ISSN 0262-0529) **1699**
New Earnings Survey. Part D: Analyses by Occupation (GBR ISSN 0262-0537) **1254**
New Earnings Survey. Part E: Analyses by Region and Age Group (GBR ISSN 0262-0545) **1254**
New Earnings Survey. Part F: Hours, Earnings and Hours of Part-Time Women Workers (GBR ISSN 0262-0553) **1254**
• New Earth (USA ISSN 1067-6406) **7809**
The New Earth Reader (USA) **6936**
New East *see* Ham-mizrah He-Hadash **550**
New East Asia *see* Shin Dong-A **4583**
New Economic Policy Era *see* The N E P Era **4247**
New Economy Weekly *see* Xinjinji Daokan **1802**
The New Educational Review (POL ISSN 1732-6729) **2890**
• ➤ The New Educator (USA ISSN 1547-688X) **2890**
• New Egyptian Journal of Medicine/Al-Majallat al-Tibiyyat al-Misriyyat al-Jadidat (EGY ISSN 1110-1946) **5685**
• New Electronic Products Japan (JPN ISSN 0286-5122) **3326**
New Electronics (GBR ISSN 0047-9624) **3109**
New Energy (DEU ISSN 1619-6228) **3178**
New Energy Economy (USA ISSN 1535-0037) **3142**
New Energy Finance Briefing *see* New Energy Finance Weekly Briefing **3142**
New Energy Finance Briefing *see* New Energy Finance Monthly Briefing **3142**
• New Energy Finance Monthly Briefing (GBR ISSN 1754-6516) **3142**
• New Energy Finance Weekly Briefing (GBR ISSN 1754-6508) **3142**
• New Energy News (USA ISSN 1075-0045) **3142**
New Engineer Journal (AUS) **1899**
New England (USA ISSN 1934-6530) **8741**
New England: All-Industries *see* Harris Directory. New England All-Industries **2001**
New England Ancestors (New England Historic Genealogical Society) (USA ISSN 1527-9405) **3776**
New England Anti-Vivisection Society Update *see* N E A V S Update **320**
• The New England Antiques Journal (USA ISSN 0897-5795) **367**
➤ New England Antiquities Research Association Journal (USA ISSN 0149-2551) **408**
New England Antiquities Research Association Transit Newsletter *see* N E A R A Transit Newsletter **407**
New England Archivists of Religious Institutions Newsletter *see* N E A R I Newsletter **5033**
New England Association of Chemistry Teachers Newsletter *see* The N E A C T Newsletter **2888**
New England Association of ChemistryTeachers Journal *see* The N E A C T Journal **2888**
New England Association of Teachers of English Newsletter *see* N E A T E Newsletter **5153**
New England Beauty Journal (USA) **590**
New England Bed and Breakfast and Inn Directory *see* Yankee Magazine's New England Bed & Breakfast and Inn Directory **4400**
New England Board of Higher Education. New England Regional Student Program: Enrollment Report (USA) **2995**
• New England Board of Higher Education. New England Regional Student Program: Undergraduate and Graduate Catalog (USA) **2995**
New England Classical Journal (USA) **2238**
New England Coalition on Nuclear Pollution, Inc. Newsletter *see* N E C N P Newsletter **3142**
• New England Condominium (USA ISSN 1550-946X) **1424**
• New England Construction (USA ISSN 0028-470X) **1026**
The New England Doll Collector (USA) **4342**
• New England Economic Indicators (USA ISSN 0548-4448) **1501**
New England Engineering Journal (USA ISSN 0274-6484) **3212**
New England Entertainment Digest (USA ISSN 0896-1506) **4981**
• New England Environmental Directory (USA ISSN 1078-4616) **2622**
New England Farm Bulletin and Garden Gazette (USA) **139**
New England Financial Directory (USA) **1371**
• New England Fiscal Facts (USA) **1371**
New England Food Service (USA) **3680**
New England Fruit Meetings (USA ISSN 0099-426X) **243**
New England Game & Fish (USA ISSN 0897-8972) **8324**
New England Garden History Society. Journal (USA ISSN 1053-2617) **3744**
New England Golf Magazine (USA) **8240**
• New England Historical and Genealogical Register (USA ISSN 0028-4785) **3776**
New England Home (USA ISSN 1936-6051) **4547**
New England In-House (USA) **4741**
New England Interstate Water Pollution Control Commission Annual Report *see* N E I W P C C Annual Report **3489**
New England Interstate Water Pollution Control Commission Water Connection *see* N E I W P C C Water Connection **3489**
• The New England Journal of Higher Education (USA ISSN 1938-5978) **2995**
➤ New England Journal of History (USA) **4305**
New England Journal of Homeopathy (USA) **5806**
• New England Journal of International and Comparative Law (USA ISSN 1936-279X) **4741**
• ➤ New England Journal of Medicine (USA ISSN 0028-4793) **5685**
• New England Journal of Medicine (International Edition) (USA) **5685**
• ➤ The New England Journal of Political Science (USA ISSN 1550-1604) **7158**
• New England Journal of Public Policy (USA ISSN 0749-016X) **7499**
• New England Journal of Traditional Chinese Medicine/Xinyinggelan Zhongyi Zazhi (USA ISSN 1536-8017) **313**
• New England Journal on Criminal and Civil Confinement (USA ISSN 0740-8994) **4741**
New England Jury Verdict Review & Analysis (USA ISSN 0886-2540) **4741**
• New England Law Review (USA ISSN 0028-4823) **4741**
New England Legal Foundation. Docket (USA) **4741**
New England Libraries (USA ISSN 1063-5408) **5035**
New England: Manufacturing *see* Harris Directory. New England Manufacturing **2001**
New England Printer and Publisher (USA ISSN 0162-8771) **7325**
New England Progress (USA) **4123**
New England Purchaser (USA) **1836**
• ➤ The New England Quarterly (USA ISSN 0028-4866) **5340**
• ➤ New England Reading Association. Journal (USA ISSN 0028-4882) **2890**
New England Real Estate Journal (USA ISSN 0028-4890) **7601**
New England Region'estah *see* N E R'estah **5682**
• New England Review (USA ISSN 1053-1297) **5340**
New England Runner (USA ISSN 1041-4800) **8324**
New England Science Fiction Association Inc. Index to Short Science Fiction *see* The N E S F A Index to Short Science Fiction **5408**
• ➤ New England Theatre Journal (USA ISSN 1050-9720) **8474**
New England Travel & Life (USA ISSN 1528-7335) **5078**
New England War Tax Resistance. Annual Report (USA) **1936**
New England Water And Wastewater News (USA) **8830**
New England Water Environment Association. Journal (USA ISSN 1077-3002) **3489**
• New England Water Works Association. Journal (USA ISSN 0028-4939) **8830**
New England Watershed Magazine (USA ISSN 1557-3095) **3553**
• New England Wedding Guide (USA ISSN 1539-2120) **5560**
New England Wild Flower *see* New England Wild Flower Conservation News **3744**
New England Wild Flower Conservation News (USA) **3744**
New England Wild Flower Conservation Notes (USA) **804**
New England Wild Flower Garden, Farm, and Sanctuary News (USA) **3744**
New England Wild Flower Journal & Programs / Events Catalog (USA) **3744**
New England Windsurfing Journal (USA) **8324**
New England World of Sanyo (USA) **2578**
† New England's Best Bed and Breakfasts (USA ISSN 1099-4114) **8976**
New English Art Club (GBR) **508**
New Entomologist/Nyu Entomorojisuto (JPN ISSN 0028-4955) **856**
New Environment Bulletin (USA) **6646**
New Epoch *see* Nea Epochi **5229**
• New Equipment Digest (USA ISSN 0028-4963) **8433**
New Equipment News (ZAF ISSN 0028-498X) **8433**
New Equipment News. Natal Supplement *see* New Equipment News **8433**
New Equipment News Western Cape *see* New Equipment News **8433**
New Era (NAM) **3913**
New Era (Ely)/Nova Doba (USA ISSN 0028-5021) **2268**
• New Era (Salt Lake City) (USA ISSN 0164-5285) **7739**
➤ New Era in Education (GBR ISSN 0957-0942) **2891**
New Era Magazine (USA ISSN 1068-7076) **2244**
New Era of Telecommunications in Japan (JPN ISSN 0912-0076) **2335**
New Era of Telecommunications in Japan (Nihongo-ban) *see* New Era of Telecommunications in Japan **2335**
New Ethicals Catalogue *see* M I M S New Ethicals **6859**
New Ethicals Journal *see* M I M S New Ethicals **6859**
New Ethnicities Newsletter (GBR) **7988**
• New Europe (GRC ISSN 1106-8299) **1501**
New Europe (LUX) **5428**
New Express *see* Xinkuaibao **3829**
New Expression *see* Novi Izraz **5344**
New Expression (USA ISSN 1520-734X) **2204**
New Family (Milford) (USA) **2162**
New Family Life (USA ISSN 0889-7875) **4364**
New Farmer (ZWE ISSN 1996-3866) **139**
New Fashion *see* Thoi Trang Tre **8886**
New Federalist (USA ISSN 1043-2264) **1501**
New Films *see* Dianying Xinzuo **6496**
New Finance *see* Xin Jinrong **1391**
• New Food (GBR ISSN 1461-4642) **608**
• New Food Products in Japan (JPN) **3680**
New Food Products Worldwide (GBR) **3657**
New Foods *see* NewFoods **3658**
New Forest Post (GBR) **3869**
The New Forester (DMA) **3698**
• ➤ New Forests (NLD ISSN 0169-4286) **3698**
• ➤ New Formations (GBR ISSN 0950-2378) **5229**
New Fortune *see* Xin Caifu **1196**
➤ New Forum Books (USA) **7158**
New Freeman (CAN ISSN 0838-0341) **7809**
➤ New French Thought Series (USA) **6936**
New from C O P A F S *see* Council of Professional Association on Federal Statistics. News **8365**
• New from I C T P (International Centre for Theoretical Physics) (ITA) **7028**
• New Frontier (USA ISSN 0886-4616) **6646**
New Frontiers *see* Frontier **1112**
New Frontiers (ZAF ISSN 1814-2621) **7158**
New Frontiers in Education (IND ISSN 0047-9705) **2996**
▼ New Frontiers in Robotics (SGP) **2586**
New Gandy Dancer (GBR ISSN 0260-3330) **6599**
New Generating Plants *see* Power Engineering **3328**
New Generation (GBR ISSN 0263-5429) **5999**
• ➤ New Generation Computing (JPN ISSN 0288-3635) **2572**
• ➤ New Genetics and Society (GBR ISSN 1463-6778) **876**
New German-American Studies/Neue Deutsche-Amerikanische Studien (GBR ISSN 1043-5808) **4466**
• New German Critique (USA ISSN 0094-033X) **4466**
• ➤ New German Review (USA ISSN 0889-0145) **5340**
New Glass *see* Neues Glas **537**
New Glass Review (USA ISSN 0275-469X) **537**
New Glimpses in Plant Research (IND) **804**
▼ • New Global Studies (USA ISSN 1940-0004) **8122**
The New Globe (SLE) **3945**
New Ground (GBR ISSN 0266-7835) **7158**
New Ground (USA) **7158**
New Gun Week (USA ISSN 0195-1599) **8190**
New Hamburg Independent (CAN ISSN 0834-6992) **3813**
New Hampshire (Woodstock) (USA ISSN 1538-8409) **8741**
† New Hampshire Actions and Proceedings (Year) (USA) **8976**
➤ New Hampshire. Agricultural Experiment Station, Durham. Research Reports (USA ISSN 0077-832X) **139**
New Hampshire. Agricultural Experiment Station, Durham. Station Bulletins (USA ISSN 0077-8338) **139**
New Hampshire: All-Industries *see* Harris Directory. New Hampshire All-Industries **2001**
New Hampshire Antiques Monthly (USA) **367**
New Hampshire Archeological Society Newsletter (USA ISSN 0545-1604) **408**
New Hampshire Archeologist (USA ISSN 0077-8346) **408**
New Hampshire Arts News *see* N H Arts News **507**
New Hampshire Audubon (USA ISSN 0162-5284) **2622**
• New Hampshire Bar Journal (USA ISSN 0548-4928) **4741**
New Hampshire Bar News (USA ISSN 1051-4023) **4741**
New Hampshire Bird Records (USA) **911**
• New Hampshire Business Directory (USA ISSN 1048-714X) **2020**
New Hampshire Business Education Association. Newsletter (USA) **1153**
• New Hampshire Business Review (USA ISSN 0164-8152) **1431**
• New Hampshire Civil Jury Instructions (USA) **4838**
New Hampshire Committee for the Promotion of History. Bulletin (USA) **4305**
New Hampshire Corporations, Partnerships and Associations *see* New Hampshire For-Profit and Non-Profit Business Laws Annotated with Forms **4877**
New Hampshire Court Rules Annotated (USA ISSN 1539-655X) **4957**
• New Hampshire Criminal Code (USA ISSN 1540-8345) **4894**
New Hampshire Dental Society Newsletter *see* N H D S Newsletter **5856**
New Hampshire Directory of Foundations (USA ISSN 1947-1300) **8058**
• New Hampshire Education Laws Annotated (USA) **4741**
• New Hampshire Employment Law Letter (USA ISSN 1086-7589) **4741**
New Hampshire Environmental Monitor (USA) **3456**
• New Hampshire Evidence Manual (USA) **4957**
New Hampshire Facts (USA ISSN 0895-8114) **3121**
New Hampshire. Fish and Game Department. Biennial Report (USA ISSN 0077-8362) **2622**
New Hampshire Fish and Game Laws Annotated (USA) **4957**
New Hampshire For-Profit and Non-Profit Business Laws Annotated with Forms (USA ISSN 1539-6207) **4877**

Title

DIRECTORY 2010 NEW ORLEANS HOMES & LIFESTYLES 10665

New Jersey League News (USA) **1371**
• New Jersey Legal Professional's Handbook (USA) **4743**
New Jersey. Legalized Games of Chance Control Commission. Report (USA ISSN 0467-3530) **4981**
New Jersey Library for the Blind and Handicapped Newsletter (USA) **5035**
New Jersey Life (USA) **3982**
New Jersey Manufacturers Directory *see* Harris Directory. New Jersey Manufacturing **2001**
• New Jersey Manufacturers Register (USA ISSN 1094-1010) **2020**
New Jersey Media Guide (USA ISSN 1054-5190) **2020**
• New Jersey Monthly (USA ISSN 0273-270X) **3983**
New Jersey Mosquito Control Association. Proceedings (USA ISSN 0198-7267) **243**
New Jersey Mosquito Control Association. Proceedings. Supplement (USA ISSN 0190-9614) **243**
New Jersey Motions in Limine *see* Motions in Limine **4956**
New Jersey Motor Truck Association. Bulletin (USA ISSN 1554-2610) **8673**
• New Jersey Motor Vehicle and Traffic Laws (USA) **4743**
New Jersey Municipalities (USA ISSN 0028-5846) **7499**
New Jersey Nets Official Yearbook (USA) **8240**
New Jersey Network Guide *see* N J N Guide **2386**
New Jersey Notary Law Primer (USA ISSN 1098-6502) **4743**
New Jersey Numismatic Journal (USA) **6651**
• New Jersey Nurse (USA ISSN 0196-4895) **5971**
New Jersey Parent Teacher (USA ISSN 0028-5897) **2891**
New Jersey Postal History Society Inc. *see* N J P H **2354**
New Jersey Practice Series. Local Government Law (USA) **7499**
• New Jersey Public Employee Reporter (USA) **4743**
New Jersey Public Employment Library on CD-ROM *see* New Jersey Public Employee Reporter **4743**
New Jersey Public Library Statistics For (Year) (USA) **5059**
• New Jersey Real Estate Forms (USA) **7602**
New Jersey Realtor (USA ISSN 0028-5919) **7602**
New Jersey Reporter (USA ISSN 0195-3192) **3983**
New Jersey Savvy Living (USA ISSN 1092-2040) **5078**
New Jersey School Boards Association. School Board Notes (USA ISSN 0039-0070) **3028**
New Jersey School Boards Association. School Leader (USA) **3028**
New Jersey School Directory *see* M D R's School Directory. New Jersey **2959**
New Jersey Service Directory *see* New Jersey Home & Design **4547**
New Jersey Shore Builders Association Bulletin Board (USA) **1026**
New Jersey Staff Directory (USA ISSN 1934-502X) **7455**
New Jersey State Agent Handbook (USA) **4516**
New Jersey State Bar Association. Banking Law Section. Newsletter (USA) **1371**
New Jersey State Bar Association. Casino Law Section. Newsletter (USA) **4743**
New Jersey State Bar Association. Certified Trial Attorneys Section. Newsletter (USA) **4957**
New Jersey State Bar Association. Civil Trial Bar Section. Newsletter (USA) **4839**
New Jersey State Bar Association. Corporate and Business Law Section. Newsletter (USA) **4877**
New Jersey State Bar Association. Creditor and Debtor Relations Section. Newsletter (USA) **1371**
New Jersey State Bar Association. Criminal Law Section. Newsletter (USA) **4895**
New Jersey State Bar Association. Environmental Law Section. Newsletter (USA) **3456**
New Jersey State Bar Association. Health and Hospital Law Section. Newsletter (USA) **4108**
New Jersey State Bar Association. International Law and Organizations Section. Newsletter (USA) **4936**
New Jersey State Bar Association. Land Use Law Section. Newsletter (USA) **4904**
New Jersey State Bar Association. Real Property, Probate and Trust Law Section. Newsletter (USA) **7602**
New Jersey State Fire Code (USA) **3580**
New Jersey State Legistature, Office of Legislative Services Staff Directory *see* New Jersey Staff Directory **7455**
New Jersey State Tax News (USA ISSN 1073-6808) **1936**
New Jersey Suburban Parent Magazine (USA) **2162**
New Jersey Super Lawyers (USA ISSN 1930-5435) **4743**
New Jersey Tax Court Reports (USA ISSN 0279-6481) **1936**
New Jersey Telephone Tickler for Insurance Men & Women (USA) **4516**
• New Jersey Transaction Guide (USA) **4743**
New Jersey Trial Objections (USA) **4957**
New Jersey. Victims of Crimes Compensation Board. Annual Report (USA) **8058**
New Jersey Woman Magazine (USA) **8877**
New Journal (USA ISSN 0028-6001) **2293**
The New Journal & Guide (USA) **3554**
New Journal News (GBR ISSN 1368-5015) **7568**
• ➤ New Journal of Chemistry (GBR ISSN 1144-0546) **2074**
• ➤ New Journal of Physics (GBR ISSN 1367-2630) **7028**
New Journal of Student Research Abstracts (USA ISSN 1558-7932) **11**
New Journal of Traditional Chinese Medicine *see* Xinzhongyi **315**
New Korea (USA ISSN 1054-5891) **3554**
New Korea Times (CAN ISSN 0845-5503) **3554**
• ➤ New Labor Forum (USA ISSN 1095-7960) **4599**
New Labor Review (USA) **1699**
➤ New Laurel Review (USA ISSN 0145-8388) **5340**
• New Law Journal (GBR ISSN 0306-6479) **4744**
New Law Journal. Charities Appeals Supplement *see* New Law Journal **4744**
The New Law of Negotiable Instruments (USA) **4744**
• New Lebanese American Journal (USA ISSN 0884-3201) **4154**
• ➤ New Left Review (GBR ISSN 0028-6060) **5229**
• New Left Review (Spanish Edition) (ESP ISSN 1575-9776) **5230**
New Leisure Markets (GBR ISSN 0968-9400) **1836**
New Letters *see* Nuove Lettere **5344**
New Letters (USA ISSN 0146-4930) **5340**
The New Liberator (AUS) **6936**
The New Liberian (LBR) **3789**
New Libertarian (USA) **7158**
The New Library Scene *see* Shelflife (Jupiter) **5047**
• ➤ New Library World (GBR ISSN 0307-4803) **5035**
• New Life (AUS ISSN 1033-7903) **7768**
• New Life (USA ISSN 1088-1441) **6646**
New Life (London, 1971) (GBR ISSN 0260-2792) **7665**
New Life Post (MYS) **3907**
• The New Light of Myanmar (MMR ISSN 1025-854X) **3966**
New Literacies and Digital Epistemologies (USA ISSN 1523-9543) **2891**
• ➤ New Literary History (USA ISSN 0028-6087) **5340**
New Literature on Old Age (GBR ISSN 0140-2447) **4058**
New Literature on Visual Impairment (GBR) **4071**
New Literature on Women *see* Ny Litteratur om Kvinnor **8906**
➤ New Literature Review (AUS ISSN 0314-7495) **5340**
New Living (USA) **6994**
New Local Government Area Monitor (GBR ISSN 1363-1462) **7312**
New London County Historical Society Newsletter *see* N L C H S Newsletter **3775**
The New Look (USA ISSN 1931-0110) **2249**
▼ • The New Look Magazine (USA ISSN 1946-956X) **4394**
The New Look Pattern Catalog *see* The New Look **2249**
▼ New Love Stories Magazine (USA ISSN 1937-7932) **5411**
The New Lovecraft Collector (USA) **5445**
New Machine Tools/Nyu Mashin Tsuru (JPN ISSN 0914-5249) **5457**
New Madrid (USA ISSN 1935-3936) **5340**
• New Magazine (MDG) **3906**
New Magic Lantern Journal (GBR ISSN 0143-036X) **6971**
• New Man (Online) (USA) **7665**
New Man (Print) *see* New Man (Online) **7665**
New Management *see* I O New Management **1751**
New Management (GBR ISSN 0548-5924) **2354**
New Markets Tax Credit Report *see* Novogradac New Markets Tax Credit Report **1937**
New Massachusetts Universalist Convention. Newsletter (USA ISSN 1933-8732) **7739**
• New Materials Asia (GBR ISSN 1749-1126) **3355**
New Materials Developed in Japan (Year) (JPN) **7095**
New Materials International (GBR ISSN 0954-3538) **1899**
New Materials Japan *see* New Materials Asia **3355**
• New Mathematics and Natural Computation (SGP ISSN 1793-0057) **5520**
• New Media Age (GBR ISSN 1364-7776) **2335**
• ➤ New Media & Society (GBR ISSN 1461-4448) **8123**
• New Media Creative (GBR ISSN 1471-4329) **2335**
New Media Information (JPN ISSN 0289-1115) **2335**
• New Media Investor (GBR ISSN 1462-8856) **1642**
• New Media Markets (GBR ISSN 1753-8998) **2386**
• New Medical Therapies Briefs. Addiction (USA) **2697**
• New Medical Therapies Briefs. Alzheimer's Disease (USA) **6170**
• New Medical Therapies Briefs. Breast Cancer (USA) **6029**
• New Medical Therapies Briefs. Chronic Obstructive Pulmonary Disease (USA) **6216**
• New Medical Therapies Briefs. Crohn's Disease (USA) **6272**
• New Medical Therapies Briefs. Depression (USA) **6170**
• New Medical Therapies Briefs. Head and Neck Cancer (USA) **6029**
• New Medical Therapies Briefs. Hepatitis (USA) **5823**
• New Medical Therapies Briefs. HIV / AIDS (USA) **5823**
• New Medical Therapies Briefs. Hyperlipidemia (USA) **5796**
• New Medical Therapies Briefs. Kidney Cancer (USA) **6029**
• New Medical Therapies Briefs. Lung Cancer (USA) **6029**
• New Medical Therapies Briefs. Obesity (USA) **5685**
• New Medical Therapies Briefs. Osteoporosis (USA) **5948**
• New Medical Therapies Briefs. Parkinson's Disease (USA) **6170**
• New Medical Therapies Briefs. Sexual Dysfunction (USA) **5948**
• New Medical Therapies Briefs. Type 2 Diabetes Mellitus (USA) **5898**
New Medical Therapies Briefs. Type Two Diabetes Mellitus *see* New Medical Therapies Briefs. Type 2 Diabetes Mellitus **5898**
New Medical Treatment *see* Gekkan Shin Iryo **5618**
New Medical World Weekly *see* Shukan Igakkai Shinbun **5714**
• ➤ New Medicine (POL ISSN 1427-0994) **5685**
• New Medicine (USA ISSN 1089-2524) **5685**
• New Medieval Literatures (BEL ISSN 1465-3737) **5340**
New Medit (ITA ISSN 1594-5685) **140**
• New Member Round Table Footnotes (USA ISSN 1076-9722) **5035**
The New Mercersburg Review (USA ISSN 0895-7460) **7665**
• The New Message (USA) **6170**
New Metro News (USA) **3554**
New Metropolitan Daily *see* Xin Dushi Bao **3829**
New Mexico Agricultural Statistics (USA ISSN 0077-8540) **184**
New Mexico: All-Industries *see* Harris Directory. New Mexico All-Industries **2001**
New Mexico Almanac (USA) **3983**
New Mexico Appellate Manual (USA) **4957**
New Mexico Beverage Analyst (USA ISSN 0194-813X) **608**
New Mexico. Bureau of Geology and Mineral Resources. Annual Report (USA) **6474**
New Mexico. Bureau of Geology and Mineral Resources. Bulletin (USA ISSN 0096-4581) **6474**
New Mexico. Bureau of Geology and Mineral Resources. Circular (USA) **6474**
New Mexico. Bureau of Geology and Mineral Resources. Memoir (USA ISSN 0548-5975) **6474**
New Mexico. Bureau of Geology and Mineral Resources. Scenic Trips to the Geologic Past (USA) **2758**
New Mexico Business, Current Economic Report (USA ISSN 0889-5937) **1153**
• New Mexico Business Directory (USA ISSN 1048-7344) **2020**
▼ New Mexico Business Magazine (USA ISSN 1942-0064) **1153**
• New Mexico Business Weekly (USA ISSN 1524-248X) **1153**
New Mexico Citations *see* Shepard's New Mexico Citations **4962**
† New Mexico Creditor - Debtor Law, Revised Edition (USA) **8976**
• New Mexico Criminal and Traffic Law Manual (USA) **4895**
• New Mexico Criminal, Vehicles and Related Statutes (USA) **4744**
• New Mexico Daily Lobo (USA) **2293**
New Mexico Dental Journal (USA ISSN 0028-6176) **5856**
New Mexico. Department of Labor. Covered Employment and Wages. Quarterly Report (USA) **1699**
• New Mexico Employment Law Letter (USA ISSN 1079-6363) **4744**
New Mexico Farm & Ranch (USA ISSN 0028-6192) **140**
New Mexico Farm, Ranch and Rural Living *see* New Mexico Farm & Ranch **140**
New Mexico Genealogist (USA ISSN 0545-3186) **3776**
➤ New Mexico Geological Society. Guidebook, Field Conference (USA ISSN 0077-8567) **2758**
New Mexico Geological Survey. Special Publication (USA ISSN 0548-6327) **2758**
➤ New Mexico Geology (USA ISSN 0196-948X) **2758**
➤ The New Mexico Historical Review (USA ISSN 0028-6206) **4305**
The New Mexico Jewish Link (USA ISSN 1559-8098) **7727**
New Mexico Journey (USA ISSN 1092-6186) **8595**
New Mexico Labor Market Review (USA) **1699**
• ➤ New Mexico Law Review (USA ISSN 0028-6214) **4744**
New Mexico Library Association Newsletter (USA ISSN 0893-2956) **5035**
New Mexico Magazine (USA ISSN 0028-6249) **8741**
New Mexico Manufacturers Directory (USA) **2020**
• New Mexico Manufacturers Register (USA ISSN 1088-7601) **2020**
New Mexico: Manufacturing *see* Harris Directory. New Mexico Manufacturing **2001**
New Mexico Municipal League. Municipal Reporter (USA ISSN 0028-6257) **7499**
New Mexico Museum of Natural History and Science. Bulletin (USA ISSN 1524-4156) **6727**
New Mexico Musician (USA ISSN 0028-6265) **6599**
† New Mexico Probate Manual (USA) **8976**
New Mexico Progress (USA ISSN 0896-6478) **4075**
• New Mexico Reports and West's New Mexico Statutes (Premise CD-ROM) (USA) **4744**
New Mexico Rules Annotated *see* Michie's Annotated Rules of New Mexico **4733**
† New Mexico Rules of Evidence (USA) **8976**
New Mexico School Directory *see* M D R's New Mexico School Directory **2957**
New Mexico State Bar Bulletin & Advance Opinions *see* State Bar of New Mexico. Bar Bulletin **4788**
New Mexico State University. Agricultural Experiment Station. Bulletin (USA) **204**
New Mexico State University. Agricultural Experiment Station. Research Report (USA ISSN 0548-5967) **140**
New Mexico State University. Cooperative Extension Service. Circular (USA ISSN 0891-6691) **140**
New Mexico State University. Cooperative Extension Service. Guide C (USA ISSN 1062-9882) **4365**
New Mexico State University. Cooperative Extension Service. Guide D (USA ISSN 1062-9807) **294**
New Mexico State University. Cooperative Extension Service. Guide E (USA ISSN 1062-9858) **4365**
New Mexico State University. Cooperative Extension Service. Guide F (USA ISSN 1062-9831) **4365**
New Mexico State University. Cooperative Extension Service. Guide G (USA ISSN 1062-9823) **4365**
New Mexico State University. Cooperative Extension Service. Guide H (USA ISSN 1062-9890) **3745**
New Mexico State University. Cooperative Extension Service. Guide Z (USA ISSN 1062-9866) **204**
New Mexico State University. Water Resources Research Institute. Report (USA ISSN 0375-7145) **8830**
New Mexico Stockman (USA) **294**
• New Mexico Travel Newsletter (USA) **8741**
New Mexico. Veterans' Service Commission. Report (USA ISSN 0094-7326) **6439**
New Mexico Water Resources Research Institute Report *see* W R R I Report **8835**
New Mexico Water Resources Research Institute. Technical Completion Report *see* W R R I Report **8835**
New Mexico Wildlife (USA ISSN 0028-6338) **2622**
• New Mexico Woman (USA ISSN 1098-7223) **8877**
➤ The New Microbiologica (ITA ISSN 1121-7138) **894**
The New Middle Ages (GBR) **4248**
• New Millennium Writings (USA ISSN 1086-7678) **5230**
• The New Minerva Report (GBR) **1642**
• New Mobility (USA ISSN 1086-4741) **4068**
New Moon *see* New Moon Girls **2204**
• New Moon Girls (USA ISSN 1943-488X) **2204**
New Moon Rising (USA) **6742**
New Mormon Studies *see* Dialogue (Salt Lake City) **7734**
New Mother (CAN ISSN 1193-9397) **2162**
New Muse of Contempt (CAN ISSN 0840-4747) **5340**
New Museum Members' Bulletin (USA) **6534**
New Museum Paper (USA) **6534**
New Music Connoisseur (USA) **6599**
New Music News (IRL ISSN 0791-5268) **6599**
• New Musical Express (GBR ISSN 0028-6362) **6599**
• New N A R U Discussion Paper Series (Online) (North Australian Research Unit) (AUS ISSN 1447-235X) **7988**
New Nation (GUY) **3874**
The New Nation (NGA) **3920**
New Nation (London) (GBR ISSN 1365-7496) **4580**
New Netherland Connections (USA ISSN 1087-4542) **3776**
New Nietzsche Studies (USA ISSN 1091-0239) **6936**
New Nigeria Development Company Limited. Annual Report and Accounts (NGA ISSN 0189-1316) **1899**
New Nigeria Development Company Ltd. Newsletter *see* N N D C Newsletter **1899**
New Nigerian (NGA ISSN 0331-2755) **3920**
The New Nonprofit Almanac and Desk Reference (USA) **1781**
The New Nonwovens World (USA ISSN 1065-5247) **8455**
New Novel Review (NZL ISSN 1177-763X) **5230**
➤ New Novel Review (USA ISSN 1070-8499) **5340**
The New Now Now New Millennium Turn-on Anthology 2001 to 3000 & Beyond *see* The Berkeley Review of Books **7552**
• New Nutrition Business (GBR ISSN 1464-3308) **6664**
New Observations (USA ISSN 0737-5387) **508**
▼ New Ohio Review (USA ISSN 1935-357X) **5340**
New Old House *see* Old-House Journal's New Old House **1028**
New on the Charts (USA ISSN 0276-7031) **6599**
New Orient *see* Novy Orient **557**
➤ New Orleans Academy of Ophthalmology. Transactions (NLD ISSN 0077-8605) **6046**
• New Orleans CityBusiness (USA ISSN 0279-4527) **1964**
• New Orleans Homes & Lifestyles (USA ISSN 1933-771X) **4547**

Title

▼ new title † ceased • electronic media ➤ refereed

10666 NEW ORLEANS MAGAZINE ULRICH'S PERIODICALS

• New Orleans Magazine (USA ISSN 0897-8174) **3983**
New Orleans Meetings Planners Guide (USA) **6282**
New Orleans Official Visitors Guide (USA) **8741**
New Orleans Preservation in Print (USA ISSN 0734-4481) **451**
➤ New Orleans Review (USA ISSN 0028-6400) **5340**
New Orleans Times - Picayune Index (USA ISSN 0893-2484) **4587**
New Orleans Travel Planners Guide (USA) **8741**
• New Orleans Tribune (USA) **3554**
New Outlook *see* New Outlook Tanzania **7158**
New Outlook Tanzania (TZA) **7158**
New Oxford History of Music (GBR) **6599**
• New Oxford Review (USA ISSN 0149-4244) **7809**
• New Pages (USA ISSN 0271-8197) **7568**
The New Paper (SGP) **3945**
New Paradigms Newsletter (GBR ISSN 0951-6026) **7891**
New Parent (USA ISSN 1936-1203) **2162**
New Parent en Espanol (USA ISSN 1936-1211) **2162**
• New Parks North (CAN ISSN 1189-4512) **2622**
New Party (USA) **7213**
New Pathway *see* Novy Shliakh **3555**
New Pathway Almanac *see* Kalendar - Al'manakh Novoho Shliakhu **3545**
New Pedagogical Review *see* Uj Pedagogiai Szemle **2921**
New Perspectives in Criminology and Criminal Justice (USA ISSN 1555-3418) **2662**
New Perspectives in Philosophical Scholarship: Texts and Issues (USA ISSN 1045-4500) **6936**
New Perspectives in Powder Metallurgy (USA ISSN 0146-9711) **6327**
• ➤ New Perspectives on Political Economy (CZE ISSN 1801-0938) **7158**
New Perspectives on the South (USA) **4305**
➤ New Perspectives on Turkey (TUR ISSN 0896-6346) **4186**
• ➤ New Perspectives Quarterly (USA ISSN 0893-7850) **7158**
The New Philosophy (USA ISSN 0028-6443) **6936**
The New Physician (USA ISSN 0028-6451) **5685**
New Physics *see* Sae Mulli **7039**
• ➤ New Phytologist (GBR ISSN 0028-646X) **804**
• New Pittsburgh Courier (USA ISSN 1047-8051) **3554**
New Plains Review (USA) **5340**
• New Plant Report (USA) **1027**
➤ The New Plantsman (GBR ISSN 1352-4186) **3745**
• ➤ New Political Economy (GBR ISSN 1356-3467) **1547**
• ➤ New Political Science (GBR ISSN 0739-3148) **7158**
New Politics (ITA ISSN 1825-7445) **7158**
• New Politics (USA ISSN 0028-6494) **7158**
• The New Presence (CZE ISSN 1211-8303) **7158**
New Product Development News (GBR) **1836**
• New Product Focus (GBR) **6863**
New Product Newsletter (GBR) **1899**
• New Products Magazine (USA ISSN 1545-9705) **3657**
• New Products Online (USA) **3658**
▼ • ➤ New Proposals: Journal of Marxism and Interdisciplinary Inquiry (CAN ISSN 1715-6718) **7158**
New Puppy Handbook (USA) **6812**
The New Quarterly (CAN ISSN 0227-0455) **5340**
New Race (USA) **3776**
New Rain (USA) **5340**
The New Rambler (GBR ISSN 0028-6540) **5340**
New, Rare and Unusual Plants *see* Dirk van der Werff's Plants **3728**
• New Readings (Online) (GBR) **4248**
New Real Estate *see* Xin Zhiye **7616**
➤ New Redland Papers (GBR ISSN 1754-1204) **2891**
New Reference Books *see* Sifre Ya'ats Hadashim **635**
New Registrations (SWE) **8528**
The New Renaissance (USA ISSN 0028-6575) **5340**
New Reportable Occurrences *see* Great Britain. Civil Aviation Authority. New Reportable Occurrences **8543**
• The New Republic (USA ISSN 0028-6583) **5230**
New Research *see* The Family in America **8102**
New Research Centers (USA ISSN 0028-6591) **7891**
• New Residential Construction (USA) **1048**
New Resources (USA) **7482**
New Review *see* Novyi Zhurnal **3555**
New Review (London, 1979) (GBR ISSN 1360-4384) **3142**
New Review (London, 1989) (GBR ISSN 0960-5231) **8058**
• ➤ The New Review of Academic Librarianship (GBR ISSN 1361-4533) **5035**
• ➤ The New Review of Children's Literature and Librarianship (GBR ISSN 1361-4541) **5341**
New Review of Document and Text Management (GBR ISSN 1361-4584) **2531**
• ➤ The New Review of Film and Television Studies (GBR ISSN 1740-0309) **2386**
• ➤ New Review of Hypermedia and Multimedia (GBR) **2488**
• ➤ The New Review of Information Networking (GBR ISSN 1361-4576) **2502**
The New Review of Literature (USA) **5341**
New Rhythm (BGR ISSN 1310-9626) **6599**
• New River Journal (USA) **5341**
New River News (USA ISSN 0548-6599) **4305**
New Ross Standard (IRL ISSN 0791-7082) **3894**
New Routes (SWE ISSN 1403-3755) **7255**
• New Sabah Times (MYS) **3907**
The New SAT Math Workbook (USA) **5520**
New Scholars, New Visions in Canadian Studies (USA ISSN 1087-9293) **7158**
New School Observer (USA ISSN 0883-6248) **2293**
• The New School Psychology Bulletin (USA ISSN 1931-793X) **7387**
• New Scientist (GBR ISSN 0262-4079) **7891**
• New Scientist (Chatswood) (AUS ISSN 1032-1233) **7892**
• New Scientist on CD-ROM (GBR ISSN 1356-1766) **7892**
New Scientist: Planet Science *see* New Scientist **7891**
New Scientist: Planet Science *see* New Scientist on CD-ROM **7892**
New Scouting News (NZL ISSN 1177-8911) **2204**
The New Searchlight (CAN ISSN 1718-5203) **3776**
New Sense (USA) **5230**
New Setsubi Shizai Joho/Information on New Equipments (JPN ISSN 0917-0782) **1027**
New Settler Interview (USA) **3983**
The New Shaft (SLE) **3945**
The New Shetlander (GBR ISSN 0047-987X) **3968**
• New Single Copy (USA ISSN 1521-1169) **7568**
† • New Slant (NZL ISSN 1171-591X) **8976**
† New Small Homes (USA) **8976**
▼ • The New Social Europe (BEL ISSN 1783-8940) **7158**
• The New Social Worker (USA ISSN 1073-7871) **7988**
• New Socialist (CAN) **7158**
▼ New Society (Cambridge) (USA ISSN 1945-9971) **7255**
The New Society of Letters at Lund. Publications *see* Vetenskapssocieteten in Lund. Skrifter **4481**
New Society of Letters at Lund. Yearbook *see* Vetenskapssocieteten i Lund. Aarsbok **4481**
• ➤ New Solutions (USA ISSN 1048-2911) **6681**
New Sound (SRB ISSN 0354-818X) **6599**
New South African Outlook (ZAF ISSN 0038-2523) **7665**
New South Wales Administrative Law (AUS) **7455**
New South Wales Agriculture Today *see* N S W Agriculture Today **138**
New South Wales & Australian Capital Territory Retail Directory (AUS ISSN 0817-024X) **2020**
† New South Wales. Attorney General's Department. Bureau of Crime Statistics and Research. Research Study (AUS) **8976**
New South Wales, Australia. Department of Environment and Conservation. Annual Report *see* New South Wales. Department of Environment and Climate Change. Annual Report **7455**
New South Wales - Australian Capital Territory Nursery Register (AUS) **3745**
New South Wales Bar Association. Annual Report (AUS) **4744**
New South Wales Civil Practice & Procedure *see* N S W Civil Practice & Procedure **4838**
New South Wales Civil Practice & Procedure *see* N S W Civil Practice & Procedure **4838**
† New South Wales Coal Statistics (AUS) **8977**
• New South Wales Criminal Courts Statistics (AUS ISSN 1038-6998) **4895**
• New South Wales. Department of Ageing, Disability and Home Care. Annual Report (AUS ISSN 1447-4565) **8058**
New South Wales. Department of Agriculture. Commodity Bulletin (AUS ISSN 0310-186X) **204**
New South Wales. Department of Agriculture. Science Bulletin (AUS ISSN 0369-5867) **140**
• New South Wales, Department of Commerce. Annual Report (AUS ISSN 1832-1232) **1431**
New South Wales. Department of Energy, Utilities and Sustainability. Annual Report *see* New South Wales. Department of Water and Energy. Annual Report **3142**
New South Wales. Department of Environment and Climate Change. Annual Report (AUS ISSN 1835-3606) **7455**
• New South Wales. Department of Housing. Annual Report (AUS ISSN 0819-6028) **4420**
• New South Wales. Department of Lands. Annual Report (AUS ISSN 1833-8801) **7455**
New South Wales. Department of Natural Resources. Annual Report *see* New South Wales. Department of Water and Energy. Annual Report **3142**
• New South Wales. Department of Primary Industries. Annual Report (AUS ISSN 1833-2080) **140**
New South Wales Department of Primary Industries. Fisheries Final Report Series *see* N S W Department of Primary Industries. Fisheries Final Report Series **3602**
New South Wales Department of Primary Industries. Fisheries Resource Assessment Series *see* N S W Department of Primary Industries. Fisheries Resource Assessment Series **3602**
New South Wales Department of Primary Industries. Science and Research Division. Forest Resources Research. Research Papers *see* N S W Department of Primary Industries. Science and Research Division. Forest Resources Research. Research Papers **3697**
New South Wales Department of Primary Industries. Science and Research Division. Forest Resources Research. Technical Papers *see* N S W Department of Primary Industries. Science and Research Division. Forest Resources Research. Technical Papers **3697**
New South Wales Department of Primary Industries. Science and Research Division. Forests N S W. Research and Development Annual Report *see* N S W Department of Primary Industries. Science and Research Division. Forests N S W. Research and Development Annual Report **3697**
New South Wales. Department of Primary Industries. Technical Bulletin (AUS) **140**
• New South Wales. Department of Water and Energy. Annual Report (AUS) **3142**
• New South Wales. Geological Survey. Bulletin (AUS ISSN 0155-5561) **2758**
New South Wales. Geological Survey. Memoirs: Palaeontology (AUS ISSN 0077-8699) **6727**
New South Wales. Geological Survey. Metallogenic Study and Mineral Deposit Data Sheets (AUS) **2758**
New South Wales. Geological Survey. Mineral Industry of New South Wales (AUS ISSN 0077-8729) **6474**
• New South Wales. Geological Survey. Mineral Resources Series (AUS ISSN 0077-8737) **6474**
New South Wales. Geological Survey. Quarterly Notes (AUS ISSN 0155-3410) **2758**
New South Wales. Geological Survey. Records (AUS ISSN 0155-3372) **2758**
New South Wales in Focus (Print) *see* N S W State and Regional Indicators **7288**
• New South Wales Industrial Gazette (AUS ISSN 0028-677X) **1699**
• New South Wales Law Reform Commission. Annual Report (AUS ISSN 0816-4525) **4744**
New South Wales. Law Reform Commission. Reports (AUS ISSN 1030-0244) **4744**
• New South Wales Law Reports (AUS ISSN 0312-1674) **4957**
New South Wales Master Plumber *see* N S W Master Plumber **4123**
• New South Wales. Police Force. Annual Report (AUS) **4895**
• New South Wales. Premier's Department. Strategic Management Calendar (AUS ISSN 1833-8348) **7455**
• New South Wales Premier's Literary Awards (AUS ISSN 1832-6110) **5341**
New South Wales. Public Employment Office. Occasional Paper (AUS ISSN 1832-2700) **1699**
New South Wales Public Health Bulletin *see* N S W Public Health Bulletin **7532**
• New South Wales Recorded Crime Statistics (AUS ISSN 1035-9044) **4895**
New South Wales. Rental Bond Board. Annual Report (AUS ISSN 1832-1585) **4420**
New South Wales State and Regional Indicators *see* N S W State and Regional Indicators **7288**
• New South Wales State Emergency Services. Annual Report (AUS ISSN 1322-7610) **2227**
New South Wales Statutes Annotation and References (AUS ISSN 0729-5987) **4744**
• New South Wales Statutes Annotations (AUS ISSN 1031-7872) **4824**
New South Wales Women *see* N S W Women **8876**
The New Southern Presbyterian Review (USA) **7768**
• New Southerner (USA ISSN 1934-5879) **5078**
New Spirit (USA) **2662**
New Spirit Journal (USA ISSN 1930-370X) **6646**
New Sports *see* Xintiyu **8217**
New Stamps Gazette (USA ISSN 1073-0222) **6897**
New Standpoints (FRA ISSN 1292-8976) **3074**
• New Start (London) (GBR ISSN 1465-573X) **8123**
New Start News *see* New Start (London) **8123**
• New Statesman (GBR ISSN 1364-7431) **5230**
• New Steel Construction (GBR ISSN 0968-0098) **1027**
New Stitches (GBR ISSN 0967-5884) **6640**
New Stone Circle (USA) **5341**
New Studies in Aesthetics (USA ISSN 0893-6005) **6936**
† New Studies in Archaeology (GBR) **8977**
New Studies in Athletics (DEU ISSN 0961-933X) **8190**
New Studies in Christian Ethics (GBR) **7665**
New Studies in European Cinema (GBR ISSN 1661-0261) **6508**
New Studies in Social Policy (USA) **7158**
New Studies on the Left (USA ISSN 0886-0629) **5230**
New Superconducting Materials Forum News *see* N S M F News **8432**
New Surveys in the Classics (GBR ISSN 0533-2451) **2238**
➤ New Synthese Historical Library (NLD) **6936**
New T C S & D (GBR ISSN 1365-1773) **3658**
• New T V Strategies (GBR ISSN 1466-3988) **2386**
New Taiwan Weekly *see* Xin Taiwan **7197**
New Talent DVD (GBR ISSN 1741-9638) **6296**
New Talent Video Special (GBR ISSN 1368-8030) **6296**
New Teacher (PAK ISSN 0077-8826) **2891**
New Teacher Advocate (USA ISSN 1070-7379) **2891**
New Tech Times (USA) **2293**
New Technical Books (USA ISSN 0028-6869) **7938**
New Techniques *see* Neue Technik **2432**
➤ New Technologies / New Cultures (GBR ISSN 1472-2895) **7989**
New Technologies - the Future Today? (GBR) **3658**
New Technology-Based Firms in the New Millennium (GBR ISSN 1876-0228) **1153**
† ➤ New Technology in the Human Services (GBR ISSN 0959-0684) **8977**
New Technology Magazine *see* Nickle's New Technology Magazine **6780**
New Technology of Library and Information Service *see* Xiandai Tushu Qingbao Jishu **5064**
• ➤ New Technology, Work & Employment (GBR ISSN 0268-1072) **1699**
• New Telephony (USA) **2370**
• New Testament Abstracts (USA ISSN 0028-6877) **7699**
The New Testament in the Greek Fathers (NLD ISSN 1570-5994) **7739**
• ➤ New Testament Studies (GBR ISSN 0028-6885) **7666**
New Testament Studies in Contextual Exegesis/Neutestamentliche Studien zur Kontextuellen Exegese (DEU ISSN 1616-816X) **7666**
New Testament Tools and Studies *see* New Testament Tools, Studies and Documents **7666**
▼ New Testament Tools, Studies and Documents (NLD) **7666**
New Theology Review (USA ISSN 0896-4297) **7809**
New Thinking *see* Xinsilu **8016**
New Thought (USA ISSN 0146-7832) **7739**
• New Threads (USA) **3826**
• New Times (AUS ISSN 0726-2612) **7768**
New Times (GBR) **7158**
New Times *see* Novoe Vremya **3938**
The New Times *see* Evergreen Monthly **6645**
New Times and New Horizons *see* Business Development Bank of Canada. Annual Report **1322**
New Titles in Bioethics (USA ISSN 0361-6347) **5749**
New Trail (CAN ISSN 0028-6907) **2293**
• New Trend (USA) **7715**
New Trends in Philosophy (NLD) **6936**
New Trends in Probability and Statistics (NLD ISSN 0928-1614) **5520**
New Trends in Synthetic Medicinal Chemistry (DEU) **5685**
• New Unesco Documents and Publications (FRA) **2934**
New Unionist (USA ISSN 1070-7727) **4599**
• New University (USA) **2293**
New Urban Features (GBR ISSN 1479-1528) **8633**
New Urban News (USA ISSN 1096-1844) **4420**
New Uses Industry Guide (Year) *see* BioProducts Canada **1974**
• ➤ New Vico Studies (USA ISSN 0733-9542) **6936**
➤ New Views (USA) **5685**
New Virginia Review (USA ISSN 0163-2299) **5341**
New Vision *see* Xinguangjiao **3829**
New Vision (GBR ISSN 1460-2660) **7666**
• The New Vision (UGA) **3963**
New Vision (ZAF) **3949**
New Vision Magazine *see* N V Magazine **3552**
• New Visions Magazine (USA) **313**
New Visions of Aztlan (USA) **5341**
The New Voice (MWI) **3906**
The New Voices (TTO ISSN 0254-9549) **5341**
• New Voices (Hanover) (USA ISSN 1543-3323) **3554**
New Voices (Minneapolis) (USA) **6636**
• New Voices in Classical Reception Studies (GBR ISSN 1750-6581) **8474**
➤ New Voices in Psychology (ZAF ISSN 1812-6731) **7388**
▼ • New Voices in Public Policy (USA ISSN 1947-2633) **7158**
• ➤ New Voices in Translation Studies (KOR ISSN 1819-5644) **5155**
The New Walford Guide to Reference Resources *see* Walford's Guide to Reference Material **638**
New Wave (IND ISSN 0047-9969) **3886**
New Wave Wrestling (USA ISSN 1060-5908) **8190**
• New Waves (College Station) (USA ISSN 0897-5094) **8830**
New Weekly (NZL) **8877**
New Weekly Magazine (CAN ISSN 0835-9423) **3813**
New Well Authorizations (CAN) **6800**
New Welsh Review (GBR ISSN 0954-2116) **5230**
New West *see* Xinxibu **1534**
New West Indian Guide *see* N W I G **7986**
New West Notes (USA ISSN 0895-8505) **7158**
• New Wineskins (USA ISSN 1941-9562) **7809**
† • New Woman (GBR ISSN 0955-6907) **8977**
New Woman Instant Beauty (AUS) **595**
New Women, New Church (USA ISSN 1043-2221) **7666**
New Working Paper Series *see* L S E Gender Institute. New Working Paper Series **8900**
New Works in Accounting History (USA) **1297**
† New World (DEU ISSN 1435-1730) **8977**
• New World (GBR ISSN 0028-6990) **7255**
New World (GUY ISSN 0028-7008) **7158**
New World Archaeological Foundation. Papers (USA ISSN 0077-8915) **408**
• New World Arts Magazine (USA) **508**
New World Journal (New York) (USA) **3456**
New World - New Worlds *see* Nuevo Mundo - Mundos Nuevos **4306**
New World Outlook (USA ISSN 0043-8812) **7666**
New World Studies (USA) **4305**

Link to your serials resources and content with ulrichsweb.com

Title

10668 NEW YORK PUBLIC LIBRARY LECTURES IN HUMANITIES ULRICH'S PERIODICALS

New York Public Library Lectures in Humanities (USA) **4466**
New York Public Library News (USA ISSN 1060-8176) **5035**
New York Quarterly (USA ISSN 0028-7482) **5428**
New York Rangers Yearbook (USA) **8190**
New York Real Estate Journal (USA ISSN 1057-2104) **7602**
• New York Real Estate Law Reporter (USA ISSN 0894-4903) **4745**
• New York Real Property (USA) **7602**
• New York Real Property Law Handbook (USA ISSN 1942-8669) **4745**
New York Real Property Law Section Journal *see* N Y Real Property Law Section Journal **4738**
New York Red Book (USA ISSN 0196-4623) **7158**
New York Report *see* New York State Realtor **7602**
The New York Researcher (USA ISSN 1548-8284) **3776**
• New York Review of Books (USA ISSN 0028-7504) **7568**
• New York Review of Magazines (USA) **4580**
• New York Review of Science Fiction (USA ISSN 1052-9438) **5445**
New York Rock *see* N Y Rock **6598**
New York Runner (USA ISSN 1096-9209) **8190**
New York School Boards (USA ISSN 1080-7152) **3028**
New York School Directory *see* M D R's School Directory. New York **2959**
New York Screenwriter Monthly (USA) **6508**
New York Sea Grant Institute. Annual Report (USA) **7455**
New York Sea Grant Institute. Report Series (USA) **693**
New York Search and Seizure *see* N Y Search and Seizure **4894**
New York Search and Seizure for Law Enforcement Officers (USA) **4745**
New York Security Officer Training Manual (USA) **2679**
New York Skirt and Sportswear Association. Bulletin (USA) **2249**
New York Small Claims Guide (USA ISSN 1559-9205) **4745**
New York Snowmobile News (USA) **8324**
New York Spaces (New Jersey Edition) (USA ISSN 1555-3922) **4547**
New York Sportscene (USA ISSN 1081-6461) **8240**
New York Staff Directory (USA ISSN 1933-6578) **7455**
• New York Standard Civil Practice Service Desk Book (USA ISSN 1079-4921) **4839**
New York Standard Civil Practice Service Desk Book on CD-ROM *see* New York Standard Civil Practice Service Desk Book **4839**
New York State Agent Handbook (USA) **4516**
New York State Agricultural Experiment Station. Special Report (USA ISSN 0886-7623) **140**
New York State Archaeological Association. Bulletin (USA ISSN 1046-2368) **408**
New York State Association of School Nurses Communicator (USA) **5971**
• New York State Bar Association. Antitrust Law Section Symposium (USA ISSN 1056-4136) **4745**
New York State Bar Association. Business Law Section. Newsletter (USA ISSN 1054-0326) **4877**
New York State Bar Association. Business Law Section. Proceedings of the Annual Meeting (USA ISSN 1060-4081) **4877**
• New York State Bar Association. Journal (USA ISSN 1529-3769) **4745**
• New York State Bar Journal (USA ISSN 1934-2020) **4745**
New York State Bar News *see* State Bar News (Albany) **4788**
New York State Committee on Open Government. Annual Report (USA) **4745**
• The New York State Conservationist (USA) **2622**
New York State Criminal Law Review (USA ISSN 0271-6283) **4895**
New York State Dairy Statistics (USA ISSN 0732-9121) **268**
• ➤ The New York State Dental Journal (USA ISSN 0028-7571) **5857**
New York State Directory (USA ISSN 0737-1314) **7499**
New York State. Education Department. College and University Enrollment (USA) **2996**
New York State English Council. Monograph Series (USA ISSN 0548-9040) **5341**
New York State Fair Magazine (USA) **8741**
New York State Geological Associaction. Guidebook Meeting (USA ISSN 1061-8724) **2758**
▼ New York State Grade 3 Elementary-Level English Language Arts Test (USA ISSN 1942-0145) **2891**
▼ New York State Grade 3 Elementary-Level Math Test (USA ISSN 1942-0137) **2891**
New York State Grade 8 Intermediate Social Studies Test (USA ISSN 1930-3610) **2891**
New York State Grade Eight Intermediate Social Studies Test *see* New York State Grade 8 Intermediate Social Studies Test **2891**
New York State Grade Three Elementary-Level English Language Arts Test *see* New York State Grade 3 Elementary-Level English Language Arts Test **2891**
New York State Grade Three Elementary-Level Math Test *see* New York State Grade 3 Elementary-Level Math Test **2891**
New York State Jury Verdict Review & Analysis (USA ISSN 8750-8044) **4745**
• New York State Law Digest (USA ISSN 0028-7636) **4745**
New York State Legislative Annual (USA ISSN 0197-3983) **4745**
New York State Library, Albany. Library Development. Excerpts from New York State Education Law, Rules of the Board of Regents, and Regulations of the Commissioner of Education Pertaining to Public and Free Association Libraries, Library Systems, Trustees and Librarians (USA ISSN 0077-930X) **5035**
New York State Library, Albany. Library Development. Public and Association Libraries Statistics (USA ISSN 0077-9326) **5059**
New York State Mathematics Teachers' Journal (USA) **2891**
New York State Municipal Bulletin (USA) **7499**
New York State Museum. Biennial Report (USA ISSN 0883-1548) **6534**
New York State Museum. Bulletin (USA ISSN 0278-3355) **7892**
New York State Museum. Circular (USA ISSN 1052-2018) **7892**
New York State Museum. Educational Leaflet Series (USA ISSN 0735-4401) **7892**
New York State Museum. Map and Chart Series (USA ISSN 0097-3793) **2758**
New York State Museum. Memoir (USA ISSN 0749-1158) **7892**
➤ New York State Nurses Association. Journal (USA ISSN 0028-7644) **5971**
New York State Nurses Association. Report (USA ISSN 0028-7652) **5971**
New York State Outdoor Education Association's Pathways to Outdoor Communication *see* Pathways to Outdoor Communication **2625**
New York State Pharmacist - Century II (USA ISSN 0739-7062) **6863**
New York State Pharmacist - Century Two *see* New York State Pharmacist - Century II **6863**
New York State Psychological Association Notebook *see* N Y S P A Notebook **7386**
New York State Psychologist *see* N Y S Psychologist **7386**
New York State Public Employees Federation. Communicator *see* The Communicator (Albany) **1671**
• New York State Realtor (USA ISSN 1555-9343) **7602**
New York State Register (USA ISSN 0197-2472) **7499**
New York State Report (USA) **7455**
New York State School Boards Association. On Board *see* New York School Boards **3028**
➤ New York State School Counseling Journal (USA ISSN 1555-8924) **7388**
New York State School of Industrial and Labor Relations. Bulletin (USA ISSN 0070-0134) **1699**
New York State Society of Anesthesiologists, Inc. Sphere *see* N Y S S A Sphere **5772**
New York State Statistical Yearbook (USA ISSN 0077-9334) **8390**
The New York State Trooper (USA) **2662**
New York Statutes Citations *see* Shepard's New York Statute Citations **4963**
New York Stock Exchange. Fact Book *see* New York Stock Exchange. Fact Book Online **1642**
• New York Stock Exchange. Fact Book Online (USA) **1642**
• New York Stock Exchange Guide (USA ISSN 0271-0714) **1642**
New York Stock Exchange Magazine *see* N Y S E Magazine **1642**
New York Stories (USA ISSN 1096-2956) **5341**
• The New York Sun (USA ISSN 1542-5762) **3983**
New York Super Lawyers (USA ISSN 1937-139X) **4745**
New York Supervisor (USA) **3028**
New York Supplement Citations *see* Shepard's New York Supplement Citations **4963**
New York Suppression Manual: Arrest, Search and Seizure, Confession, and Identification (USA) **4895**
New York Supreme Court Appellate Division Case Names Citator *see* Shepard's New York Supreme Court Appellate Division Case Names Citator **4963**
New York Surrogate's Court Procedure Act (USA) **4958**
New York Tails (USA ISSN 1544-8789) **6812**
• New York Teacher (USA ISSN 0195-1521) **4599**
New York Teacher (City Edition) (USA ISSN 1074-0503) **2891**
New York Telephone Tickler for Insurance Men and Women (USA) **4516**
• New York Theatre Guide (USA) **8474**
New York Thoroughbred Life (USA) **8295**
New York Times - Acapulco *see* Diario 17 **3908**
The New York Times Almanac (USA ISSN 1523-7079) **3121**
• New York Times Book Review (USA ISSN 0028-7806) **7568**
The New York Times Book Review (Microform) (USA) **7568**
The New York Times Current Events Edition (USA ISSN 0190-1990) **4154**
† New York Times Film Reviews (USA ISSN 0362-3688) **8977**
• The New York Times Index (USA ISSN 0147-538X) **4587**
The New York Times Index Highlights (USA) **7200**
• New York Times Magazine (USA ISSN 0028-7822) **3983**
The New York Times Magazine (Microform) (USA) **3983**
The New York Times School Microfilm Collection Index (USA) **632**
• The New York Times Upfront (Student Edition) (USA ISSN 1525-1292) **2205**
The New York Times Upfront (Teachers' Edition) *see* The New York Times Upfront (Student Edition) **2205**
New York Tort Citator (USA) **4839**
New York TourBook *see* TourBook: New York **8762**
New York Town Law (USA) **4746**
New York Trial Guide (USA) **4958**
New York Turtle and Tortoise Society Newsnotes *see* N Y T T S Newsnotes **321**
New York Typographical Union Number Six. Bulletin (USA ISSN 0049-4968) **4599**
• New York: Understanding the Penal Law (USA) **4895**
New York University Alumni Magazine *see* N Y U Alumni Magazine **2293**
New York University Annual Conference on Tax Planning for 501(c)(3) Organizations (USA) **1936**
• New York University. Annual Institute on Federal Taxation. Proceedings (USA ISSN 0886-3679) **1937**
• New York University Annual Survey of American Law (USA) **4746**
New York University Biomedical Engineering Series (USA) **750**
New York University Business Magazine Publishing Series (USA) **7568**
• ➤ New York University Environmental Law Journal (USA ISSN 1061-8651) **3456**
New York University Hospital for Joint Diseases. Bulletin *see* N Y U Hospital for Joint Diseases. Bulletin **6067**
• ➤ New York University Journal of International Law and Politics (USA ISSN 0028-7873) **4936**
New York University Journal of Law and Business *see* N Y U Journal of Law and Business **4876**
New York University Journal of Law & Liberty *see* N Y U Journal of Law & Liberty **4738**
• New York University Journal of Legislation and Public Policy (USA ISSN 1094-513X) **7455**
• ➤ New York University Law Review (New York, 1950) (USA ISSN 0028-7881) **4746**
New York University Physician's Directory *see* N Y U Physician's Directory **5682**
New York University Review of Law & Social Change *see* Review of Law & Social Change **4769**
New York University. Salomon Center. Newsletter (USA) **1371**
New York University. Salomon Center. Occasional Papers (USA) **1371**
New York University. Salomon Center. Occasional Papers in Business and Finance (USA ISSN 0884-318X) **1371**
New York University. Salomon Center. Series on Financial Markets and Institutions (USA ISSN 1387-6899) **1371**
New York University. Salomon Center. Working Papers Series (USA) **1371**
New York University School of Medicine Physician *see* N Y U Physician **2293**
New York University Studies in French Culture and Civilization (USA) **4248**
New York University. Studies in Near Eastern Civilization (USA ISSN 0081-8291) **557**
New York University Today *see* N Y U Today **2293**
New York Upstate Folio Physician Directory *see* Folio Physician Directory with Healthcare Facilities. New York Upstate **5615**
New York Village Law (USA) **4746**
▼ New York Visitor's Guide (USA ISSN 1935-5122) **8741**
New York Voice (USA ISSN 1074-0465) **3554**
New York Voice / Harlem U S A *see* New York Voice **3554**
New York Workers' Compensation Handbook *see* New York Workers' Compensation Law Handbook **4746**
• New York Workers' Compensation Law Handbook (USA) **4746**
New York Workers' Compensation Law Reporter (USA) **4517**
New York Yankees *see* Yankees Magazine **8252**
• The New Yorker (USA ISSN 0028-792X) **5230**
New Yorker Beitraege zur Literaturwissenschaft (DEU ISSN 1435-0939) **5341**
New Yorker Staats-Zeitung (USA ISSN 1061-7604) **3554**
New Yorker Studien zur Neueren Deutschen Literaturgeschichte (DEU ISSN 0721-4030) **5341**
New York's Finest (USA) **2662**
New York's Nightlife (USA) **8741**
New Youth *see* Xin Qingnian **2172**
New Youth Connections (USA ISSN 0737-285X) **2205**
New Zealan Institute of Chemistry. Education Group. Newsletter *see* Chem N Z **2053**
New Zealand 4 W D Magazine (NZL ISSN 1175-1827) **8506**
▼ • New Zealand A M (Asian Magazine) (NZL ISSN 1177-6919) **3554**
New Zealand Aberdeen Angus Herd Book *see* Angus Herd Book of New Zealand **278**
• New Zealand Administrative Reports (NZL ISSN 0110-1277) **4746**
• New Zealand Agency for International Development. Annual Review (NZL) **1602**
New Zealand Agrichemical Manual *see* New Zealand Novachem Agrichemical Manual **243**
New Zealand Agrichemical Manual (NZL) **243**
New Zealand Alpine Journal (NZL ISSN 0110-1080) **8324**
The New Zealand Angus Cattleman (NZL ISSN 1170-2915) **294**
New Zealand Angus Review *see* The New Zealand Angus Cattleman **294**
New Zealand Animal Advisory Committee. Code of Animal Welfare *see* National Animal Welfare Advisory Committee. Code of Welfare **321**
➤ New Zealand Annual Review of Education (NZL ISSN 1171-3283) **2891**
New Zealand Antique and Historical Arms Association. Gazette (NZL ISSN 1177-1984) **367**
New Zealand Antique Arms Gazette *see* New Zealand Antique and Historical Arms Association. Gazette **367**
• New Zealand Aquaculture (NZL ISSN 1176-5402) **3603**
New Zealand Aquatic Environment and Biodiversity Report (NZL ISSN 1176-9440) **3456**
• New Zealand Archaeological Association Monograph (NZL ISSN 0111-5715) **408**
• ➤ New Zealand Armed Forces Law Review (NZL ISSN 1175-6136) **4972**
New Zealand Army News *see* N Z Army News **6437**
New Zealand Asia Institute Bulletin *see* N Z A I Bulletin **556**
New Zealand Asia Institute Regional Analysis *see* N Z A I Regional Analysis **7254**
New Zealand Association for Migration & Investment, Inc. News *see* N Z A M I News **7288**
• New Zealand Association for Research in Education National Conference. Conference Papers & Presentations (NZL ISSN 1176-4902) **2891**
• New Zealand Association of Resource Management. Broadsheet (NZL ISSN 1172-9139) **2622**
• New Zealand Autocar (NZL ISSN 1174-1600) **8595**
• New Zealand Aviation News (NZL ISSN 1172-0522) **8549**
The New Zealand Baptist *see* Baptist **7747**
New Zealand Beekeeper (NZL ISSN 0110-6325) **856**
New Zealand Bioethics Journal *see* Journal of Bioethical Inquiry **4460**
New Zealand Bioscience *see* N Z Bioscience **740**
† New Zealand Bloodhorse (NZL ISSN 0113-7859) **8977**
New Zealand Books in Print (AUS ISSN 0549-0170) **632**
New Zealand Books in Print Update *see* New Zealand Books in Print **632**
New Zealand Building Economist (NZL) **451**
New Zealand Business *see* N Z Business **1151**
New Zealand Business Law Quarterly (NZL ISSN 1173-311X) **4877**
New Zealand Business Roundtable. Occasional Paper (NZL ISSN 1176-8819) **1153**
• New Zealand Business Roundtable. Working Paper (NZL ISSN 1177-2565) **1501**
• New Zealand Business Who's Who (NZL ISSN 0077-9571) **2020**
New Zealand Camellia Bulletin (NZL ISSN 0028-7989) **3745**
New Zealand Camera (NZL ISSN 1177-2417) **6971**
† New Zealand Cartography and Geographic Information Systems (NZL ISSN 1171-1337) **8977**
New Zealand Catholic *see* N Z Catholic **7808**
New Zealand Census of Population and Dwellings. Unpaid Work *see* New Zealand. Statistics New Zealand. Census Reports. Unpaid Work **7313**
• New Zealand Chart Catalogue (NZL ISSN 0113-5597) **8655**
New Zealand Chess (NZL) **8190**
New Zealand Childcare Association. Newsletter *see* Te Tari Puna Ora O Aotearoa. Iti Rearea **2917**
New Zealand Childcare Association. Report to Annual Conference (NZL) **2891**
New Zealand Classic Car (NZL ISSN 1170-9332) **8595**
New Zealand Collection (NZL ISSN 1177-2271) **6897**
• New Zealand College of Midwives. Journal (NZL ISSN 0114-7870) **5999**
New Zealand. Commerce Commission. Annual Plan *see* New Zealand. Commerce Commission. Statement of Intent **7455**
• New Zealand. Commerce Commission. Decision (NZL ISSN 0114-2720) **4877**
New Zealand. Commerce Commission. Statement of Intent (NZL ISSN 1177-0368) **7455**
• New Zealand Company and Commercial Law Reports (NZL ISSN 1747-5821) **4877**
New Zealand Company Vehicle and Executive Cars (NZL) **8595**

Link to your serials resources and content with ulrichsweb.com

Title

NICE Management College. Journal *see* NICE Journal of Business **1781**
Nice Matin (FRA ISSN 0224-5477) **3841**
• Nice Matin Magazine (FRA ISSN 0224-5469) **3841**
Nice Week *see* Dazhoumo **3824**
Niche (Baltimore) (USA) **1836**
Niche (Idyllwild) (USA) **5341**
▼ • Niche Commercial Finance (GBR ISSN 1754-1042) **1371**
Nichibei Josei Journal/US - Japan Women's Journal (JPN ISSN 0898-8900) **8901**
Nichibei Kyoryo Wakushoppu Ronbunshu/Japan - U.S. Bridge Engineering Workshop. Proceedings (JPN) **3279**
Nichibunken (JPN ISSN 0915-0889) **557**
➤ Nichibunken Japan Review (JPN ISSN 0915-0986) **557**
Nichibunken Newsletter/Nihon Bunka (JPN ISSN 0914-6482) **557**
➤ Nichidai Igaku Zasshi/Nihon University Medical Association. Journal (JPN ISSN 0029-0424) **5686**
➤ Nichidai Koku Kagaku/Nihon University. Journal of Oral Science (JPN ISSN 0385-0145) **5857**
➤ Nichidai Shigaku/Nihon University Dental Journal (JPN ISSN 0385-0102) **5857**
Nichifutsu Seibutsu Gakkaishi *see* Societe Franco-Japonaise de Biologie. Bulletin **705**
Nichii Seibutsugaku Kyokai Kaiho/Associazione Biologica Italo-Giapponese Bollettino (JPN) **694**
Nichinairen Joho/Japan Internal Combustion Engine Federation. Information (JPN ISSN 0287-122X) **3391**
Nichiyu Nyusu/Nippon Yusoki Company. News (JPN) **3391**
Nicholas Copernicus Observatory and Planetarium in Brno. Contributions *see* Hvezdarna a Planetarium Mikulase Kopernika v Brne. Prace **8962**
The Nicholls Worth (USA) **2293**
Nichols News (USA) **2294**
Nichols Nostalgia (USA ISSN 1043-027X) **3777**
• Nichols on Eminent Domain (USA) **4747**
Nicht-Markt-Oekonomik (DEU ISSN 0720-6968) **8058**
Nichteisenmetalle und Ihre Legierungen *see* Informationsdienst F I Z Technik. Nichteisenmetalle und Ihre Legierungen **3231**
Nichtlineare und Stochastische Physik (DEU ISSN 1435-7151) **7028**
Nick Jr. *see* Nick Jr. Family **8977**
† Nick Jr. Family (USA ISSN 1540-9333) **8977**
▼ Nick Jr. Magazine (USA) **2205**
Nickel, Chrome, Molybdenum Monitor *see* C R U Metal Monitor Annual **6307**
Nickel - Cobalt (Year): Volume III: Pyrometallurgical Operations, Environment, Vessel Integrity (CAN) **6327**
Nickel Odeon (ESP ISSN 1135-7681) **6508**
Nickelodeon Magazine (NLD ISSN 1872-2318) **2205**
† Nickelodeon Magazine (USA ISSN 1073-7510) **8977**
† Nicki (DEU) **8977**
Nicklaus (USA ISSN 1549-8379) **5078**
Nickle's Canadian Oil Register *see* Canadian Oil Register **6765**
• Nickle's Daily Oil Bulletin (CAN ISSN 0709-681X) **6780**
Nickle's Daily Oil Bulletin. Weekly Drilling Report *see* Nickle's Weekly Drilling Reports **6781**
• Nickle's Daily Well Licences (CAN) **6780**
• Nickle's New Technology Magazine (CAN ISSN 1480-2147) **6780**
• Nickle's Petroleum Explorer (CAN ISSN 1204-2951) **6780**
• Nickle's Weekly Drilling Reports (CAN ISSN 1189-2927) **6781**
Nico *see* Nico International **508**
Nico International (LUX ISSN 1992-4267) **508**
Nicolaus (VAT ISSN 0390-2935) **7809**
Nicolaus Copernicus University. Limnological Papers *see* Acta Universitatis Nicolai Copernici. Prace Limnologiczne **2792**
➤ Nicolaus. Studi Storici (ITA ISSN 1121-323X) **4248**
Nicolay (NOR ISSN 0332-8937) **408**
Nicosia this Month (CYP) **3832**
• ➤ Nicotine & Tobacco Research (GBR ISSN 1462-2203) **8486**
➤ Nidan (ZAF ISSN 1016-5320) **7708**
• Nida'ul Islam (AUS) **7715**
NiDi Rapport *see* Nederlands Interdisciplinair Demografisch Instituut. Rapport - Report - Bericht - Rapporto **7288**
Il Nido d'Aquila *see* R Ni d'Aigura **350**
Nie (POL ISSN 0867-2237) **5230**
Niederbayerische Wirtschaft (DEU) **1407**
Niederbayerischer Archaeologentag. Vortraege (DEU) **408**
Niederdeutsche Beitraege zur Kunstgeschichte (DEU ISSN 0078-0537) **508**
Niederdeutsches Jahrbuch *see* Jahrbuch des Vereins fuer Niederdeutsche Sprachforschung **5131**
Niederdeutsches Wort (DEU ISSN 0078-0545) **5155**
Niederdruckanschlussverordnung - Gasgrundversorgungsverordnung (DEU) **6781**
Der Niedergelassene Arzt (DEU ISSN 0468-1746) **5686**
Der Niedergelassene Chirurg *see* Ambulante Chirurgie **6235**
➤ Niederlande-Studien (DEU ISSN 1436-3836) **4248**
Niederlande-Studien. Beiheft *see* Niederlande-Studien **4248**
Niederlande-Studien. Kleinere Schriften *see* Niederlande-Studien **4248**
Niederoesterreich-Perspektiven (AUT) **3797**
Niederoesterreichische Landes-Landwirtschaftskammer. Amtlicher Marktbericht (AUT ISSN 0028-9744) **184**
Der Niederrhein (DEU ISSN 0342-5673) **3854**
Niederrhein Tennis (DEU) **8240**
Niedersachsen Magazin (DEU) **7500**
Niedersachsen-Tennis (DEU ISSN 0948-2962) **8191**
Niedersachsenturner *see* N T B Magazin **8189**
➤ Niedersaechsische Archivverwaltung. Veroeffentlichungen (DEU) **4154**
Niedersaechsische Bibliographie (DEU ISSN 0342-1449) **632**
Niedersaechsische Gemeinde (DEU ISSN 0028-9779) **7500**
Niedersaechsische Landesbibliothek. Kleine Schriften. Neue Folge *see* Gottfried Wilhelm Leibniz Bibliothek. Kleine Schriften **625**
Niedersaechsische Landesmedienanstalt. Schriftenreihe (DEU) **8123**
Niedersaechsische Rechtspflege (DEU) **4824**
Niedersaechsische Rundschau (DEU) **8058**
Niedersaechsische Verwaltungsblaetter (DEU ISSN 0946-7971) **7500**
Niedersaechsische Wirtschaft (DEU ISSN 0341-1982) **1501**
Niedersaechsischer Bund fuer Freie Erwachsenenbildung Magazin (Online) *see* N B E B Magazin (Online) **2944**
Niedersaechsischer Jaeger (DEU ISSN 0048-0339) **8325**
Niedersaechsischer Staatsanzeiger (DEU ISSN 0028-9787) **4747**
Niedersaechsischer Staedte- und Gemeindebund. Schriftenreihe (DEU) **7500**
Niedersaechsischer Staedtetag - Nachrichten *see* N S T - N **7499**
Niedersaechsischer Turner-Bund e.V. Magazin *see* N T B Magazin **8189**
Niedersaechsisches Aerzteblatt (DEU ISSN 0028-9795) **5686**
Niedersaechsisches Gesetz- und Verordnungsblatt (DEU ISSN 0341-3497) **7457**
Niedersaechsisches Jahrbuch (DEU) **4248**
Niedersaechsisches Ministerialblatt (DEU ISSN 0341-3500) **7457**
Niedersaechsisches Zahnaerzteblatt *see* Zahnaerzteblatt Niedersachsen **5870**
Niekas (USA ISSN 0028-9809) **5445**
➤ Niels Bohr - Collected Works (NLD) **7028**
† Nielsen Marketing Research. News (DNK ISSN 0902-8242) **8977**
Nielsen Report on Television (USA) **2386**
• Nieman Reports (USA ISSN 0028-9817) **4581**
Nienhua Yishu/Art of New Year Picture (CHN) **509**
Niepodleglosc/Independence (USA ISSN 0272-0280) **4248**
➤ Nieren- und Hochdruckkrankheiten (DEU ISSN 0300-5224) **5796**
Nieruchomosci (POL ISSN 1506-2899) **7602**
Nieruchomosci Stoleczne (POL ISSN 1506-5855) **7602**
• Nietzsche-Studien (DEU ISSN 0342-1422) **6936**
Nietzscheana (ITA ISSN 1970-6138) **6936**
Nietzscheana Saggi *see* Nietzscheana **6936**
Nietzscheforschung (DEU) **6936**
Nieuw Archief voor Wiskunde (NLD ISSN 0028-9825) **5520**
Nieuw Commercieel Vastgoed in Nederland (NLD ISSN 1871-0549) **1371**
Nieuw Computer Tijdschrift *see* N C T **4083**
Nieuw Erfrecht *see* Tijdschrift Erfrecht **4905**
Nieuw Klimaat (BEL) **7457**
Nieuw Leven (NLD ISSN 0167-3602) **7769**
Nieuw - Neuf (BEL) **451**
Nieuw Rotterdam (NLD ISSN 1873-3638) **3915**
Nieuw Vuur *see* Lopend Vuur **7738**
Nieuwe Blotto (NLD ISSN 1871-6970) **6508**
Nieuwe Drogist (NLD ISSN 0927-0574) **6863**
Nieuwe Groene Carriere *see* Carriere+ **100**
➤ Nieuwe Nederlandse Bijdragen tot de Geschiedenis der Geneeskunde en der Natuurwetenschappen (NLD ISSN 0168-9827) **5686**
Nieuwe Oogst (Noord Edition) (NLD ISSN 1871-0875) **243**
Nieuwe Oogst (Oost Edition) (NLD ISSN 1871-0891) **243**
Nieuwe Oogst (West Edition) (NLD ISSN 1871-0883) **243**
Nieuwe Oogst (Zuid Edition) (NLD ISSN 1871-0905) **243**
Nieuwe Oogst. Gewas (NLD ISSN 1871-093X) **243**
Nieuwe Oogst. Tuinbouw (NLD ISSN 1871-0921) **243**
Nieuwe Oogst. Veehouderij (NLD ISSN 1871-0948) **295**
Nieuwe Revu (NLD ISSN 0165-4411) **3801**
• ➤ De Nieuwe Sekstant (NLD ISSN 1380-8656) **6296**
➤ Nieuwe Wiskrant (NLD ISSN 0928-7167) **5520**
Nieuwe Woordenkalender (NLD ISSN 1874-8848) **5155**
Nieuwe Zelfwichter (NLD ISSN 1386-4920) **2622**
† Nieuws Berichten Informatie (NLD ISSN 0920-1319) **8977**
Nieuwsblad Stromen *see* Energiegids.nl **3129**
Nieuwsblad Transport (NLD ISSN 0921-4593) **8506**
Nieuwsblad voor Wereldouders *see* WereldOuders. Nieuwsbrief **4944**
Nieuwsbrief Absent! (NLD ISSN 0929-7774) **1781**
Nieuwsbrief Administratie *see* Tijdschrift Administratie **1798**
Nieuwsbrief Ambacht en Gereedschap (NLD ISSN 1875-4309) **1054**
Nieuwsbrief Ambtenarenrecht (NLD ISSN 0922-7644) **4747**
Nieuwsbrief Arbeidsveiligheid (BEL ISSN 1378-8450) **6681**
Nieuwsbrief Bedrijfsjuridische Berichten *see* Bedrijfsjuridische Berichten **4628**
Nieuwsbrief Beenprothesegebruikers *see* Landelijke Vereniging van Geamputeerden Nieuwsbrief **6066**
Nieuwsbrief Bodem (NLD ISSN 0929-1954) **3456**
Nieuwsbrief Burgerlijk Wetboek *see* Maandblad voor Vermogensrecht **4835**
Nieuwsbrief Clienten Participatie *see* Klachtenmanagement **4709**
Nieuwsbrief Crisisbeheersing (NLD ISSN 1871-2843) **7457**
Nieuwsbrief Cultureel Erfgoed *see* Historisch Overijssel **4144**
Nieuwsbrief Cultureel Erfgoed Groningen *see* Groningen (Groningen) **4225**
Nieuwsbrief Direkt Marketing en Verkoop (BEL) **1836**
Nieuwsbrief Douane (BEL) **1579**
Nieuwsbrief Finaciering in de Zog *see* Zorg & Financiering **4529**
Nieuwsbrief GD Uiergezondheidscoach *see* Nieuwsbrief Gezondheidsdienst voor Dieren Uiergezondheidscoach **8977**
Nieuwsbrief Gemeentelijke Activering (NLD ISSN 1572-4964) **8058**
Nieuwsbrief Gemeenteraadsleden (NLD ISSN 0928-0723) **7500**
Nieuwsbrief Gender (NLD ISSN 1871-1367) **7159**
† Nieuwsbrief Gezondheidsdienst voor Dieren Uiergezondheidscoach (NLD ISSN 1872-3586) **8977**
Nieuwsbrief Grondzaken *see* Grondzaken in de Praktijk **4683**
Nieuwsbrief Hanzelijn *see* Bouwkrant Hanzelijn **8615**
Nieuwsbrief Jongeren *see* Nieuwsbrief Tiener- en Jongerenwerk **8058**
Nieuwsbrief Lokale Heffingen (NLD ISSN 1574-7875) **1937**
Nieuwsbrief M N G M (Meldpuntennetwerk Gezondheid en Milieu) (NLD ISSN 1873-9547) **7533**
Nieuwsbrief Milieunormalisatie *see* MilieuNieuws **3452**
Nieuwsbrief Milieuvergunningen *see* Milieuvergunningen **3452**
Nieuwsbrief N V C Actueel *see* N V C Actueel **6712**
Nieuwsbrief N Z G (Nederlandse Zeevogelgroep) (NLD ISSN 1566-6778) **911**
Nieuwsbrief Nederlands Fotoarchief (NLD ISSN 0927-8311) **6971**
Nieuwsbrief Nederlandse Muziek (NLD ISSN 1574-7662) **6599**
Nieuwsbrief Notariaat (BEL ISSN 1377-4387) **4747**
Nieuwsbrief Notariaat Fiscaal *see* Nieuwsbrief Notariaat **4747**
Nieuwsbrief O P C *see* O P C Nieuws **8507**
† Nieuwsbrief Onderbouw (NLD ISSN 1574-3594) **8977**
Nieuwsbrief Oud Deventer (NLD ISSN 1872-7735) **4248**
Nieuwsbrief Politie (NLD ISSN 0925-2711) **2662**
Nieuwsbrief Ruimtelijke Ordening *see* Bulletin R O Totaal **4405**
Nieuwsbrief S S N R *see* Documentatieblad Nadere Reformatie **7754**
Nieuwsbrief Sociale Vernieuwing (NLD ISSN 0928-8090) **8058**
Nieuwsbrief Sportsecretariaat *see* Samsom Sportsecretaris **8199**
Nieuwsbrief StAB *see* StAB **4427**
Nieuwsbrief Telematica *see* Telecom Review **2341**
Nieuwsbrief Thuis in Zorgvernieuwing *see* Thuis in Zorgvernieuwing **8074**
Nieuwsbrief Tiener- en Jongerenwerk (NLD ISSN 1871-5966) **8058**
Nieuwsbrief Transport (BEL) **1579**
Nieuwsbrief TV-Geweld (NLD ISSN 1574-664X) **2386**
Nieuwsbrief Universiteitsgeschiedenis *see* Studium **3003**
Nieuwsbrief van de Werkgroep Monitoring Stichting RAVON *see* Meetnet Reptielen **955**
Nieuwsbrief Verkeerspecialist (BEL) **8633**
Nieuwsbrief Volkshuisvesting (NLD ISSN 0927-4936) **4421**
Nieuwsbrief voor Donateurs van de Nederlandse Vereniging van Blinden en Slechtzienden *see* Nederlandse Vereniging van Blinden en Slechtzienden. Donateursbrief **4083**
Nieuwsbrief W V G *see* Meedoen! **4067**
Nieuwsbrief Werk (NLD ISSN 0923-8646) **1700**
Nieuwsbrief "Werk in Uitvoering" *see* Lumpsum Nieuwsbrief **2884**
Nieuwsbrief West Sociale Werkvoorziening/Wet Inschakeling Werkzoekenden *see* Nieuwsbrief Gemeentelijke Activering **8058**
• Nieuwsbrief Wft (Wet op het Financieel Toezicht) (NLD ISSN 1874-706X) **1371**
Nieuwsbrief ZorgVisie (NLD ISSN 1384-4202) **4108**
Nieuwspoort Forum (NLD ISSN 1873-8990) **4581**
Nieuwspoort Nieuws *see* Nieuwspoort Forum **4581**
Nigdy Wiecej/Never Again (POL ISSN 1428-0884) **7213**
Nigelnagelneu (DEU) **7569**
Niger. Direction de la Statistique et des Comptes Nationaux. Bulletin Trimestriel de Statistique (NER) **8390**
Niger: Fraternite - Travail - Progres (NER ISSN 0545-9532) **7159**
Niger. Office des Postes et Telecommunications. Annuaire Officiel des Telephones (NER) **2370**
Nigerama (NER) **3789**
Nigeria *see* The P R S Group. Country Reports: Nigeria **1508**
Nigeria Banking, Finance & Commerce (NGA ISSN 0794-6430) **1371**
Nigeria Bulletin on Foreign Affairs (NGA ISSN 0331-2151) **7255**
Nigeria Business Guide Annual (NGA ISSN 0794-2877) **1153**
Nigeria Educational Forum. Journal (NGA ISSN 0189-2916) **2892**
Nigeria Engineer (NGA ISSN 0331-5967) **3212**
Nigeria. Federal Department of Forest Research. Research Paper (NGA ISSN 0300-2403) **3698**
Nigeria. Federal Ministry of Labour and Productivity. Annual Report (NGA) **1700**
Nigeria. Federal Ministry of Labour and Productivity. Quarterly Bulletin of Labour Statistics (NGA) **1255**
Nigeria. Federal Office of Statistics. Annual Abstract of Statistics (NGA ISSN 0078-0626) **8391**
Nigeria. Federal Office of Statistics. Review of External Trade (NGA ISSN 0078-0634) **1255**
Nigeria Finance Yearbook (NGA) **1371**
• Nigeria Focus (GBR ISSN 1477-2426) **1501**
▼ • Nigeria Food Security Update (USA ISSN 1947-7023) **1602**
Nigeria Freight Transport Report (GBR ISSN 1752-5977) **8506**
Nigeria Industrial Directory (NGA ISSN 1116-1027) **2021**
▼ • Nigeria Insurance Report (GBR ISSN 1752-8313) **4517**
• Nigeria Journal of Pure and Applied Physics (NGA ISSN 1596-0862) **7028**
Nigeria Magazine (NGA ISSN 0029-0033) **3920**
Nigeria. Meteorological Service. Agrometeorological Bulletin (NGA ISSN 0545-9923) **6392**
Nigeria. National Animal Production Research Institute. Journal (NGA ISSN 0189-0514) **295**
Nigeria. National Integrated Survey of Households. Building and Construction Survey (NGA) **1027**
Nigeria. National Integrated Survey of Households. Industrial Survey (NGA ISSN 0331-1570) **1255**
Nigeria. National Integrated Survey of Households. Report on General Consumer Survey (NGA) **1255**
Nigeria. National Integrated Survey of Households. Report on General Household (NGA) **1255**
Nigeria. National Integrated Survey of Households. Report on General Household Survey (NGA ISSN 0794-4055) **4436**
Nigeria. National Integrated Survey of Households. Report on National Consumer Survey (NGA ISSN 0189-336X) **1255**
Nigeria. National Integrated Survey of Households. Report on Urban Household Survey (NGA) **4436**
Nigeria. National Manpower Board. Manpower Studies (NGA) **1700**
Nigeria. National Universities Commission. Annual Report (NGA ISSN 1117-062X) **2996**
Nigeria. National Universities Commission. Convocation Speeches of Nigerian Universities (NGA ISSN 1117-0611) **2996**
Nigeria. National Universities Commission. Research Bulletin (NGA ISSN 1117-0638) **2996**
Nigeria. National Universities Commission. Statistical Digest (NGA ISSN 1117-0603) **2934**
Nigeria. National Universities Commission. University System News (NGA ISSN 0795-9931) **2996**
Nigeria Periodicals Review (NGA ISSN 0794-3865) **5036**
Nigeria Petrochemicals Report (GBR ISSN 1749-236X) **6781**
➤ Nigeria Society of Physiotherapy. Journal (NGA ISSN 0331-3735) **6113**
Nigeria Tourism Development Corporation. Official Tourist Guide (NGA) **8741**
Nigeria Trade Journal (NGA ISSN 0029-0041) **1579**
Nigeria Trade Summary (NGA ISSN 0078-0650) **1579**
• Nigeria Veterinary Journal (NGA ISSN 0331-3026) **8803**
Nigeria. Work in Progress (NGA) **5230**
Nigeria Year Book (NGA ISSN 0078-0685) **7255**
• Nigerian Agricultural Journal (NGA ISSN 0300-368X) **140**
Nigerian Books in Print (NGA ISSN 0078-0693) **632**
Nigerian Business Journal (NGA ISSN 0189-5036) **1407**
Nigerian Businessman's Magazine (NGA) **1501**
Nigerian Christian (NGA ISSN 0029-005X) **7666**
Nigerian Current Law Review (NGA ISSN 0189-207X) **4747**

Title

Nihon Hoken Igakkai Shi/Association of Life Insurance Medicine of Japan. Journal (JPN ISSN 0301-262X) **5686**

Nihon Horei Sakuin/Index to Japanese Laws & Regulations in Force (JPN ISSN 0286-3502) **4824**

Nihon Hosenkin Gakkaishi/Actinomycetologica (JPN ISSN 0914-5818) **894**

Nihon Hoso Gakkaishi/Journal of Packaging Science & Technology, Japan (JPN ISSN 0918-5283) **6712**

Nihon Hotetsu Shika Gakkai Zasshi *see* Journal of Prosthodontic Research **5853**

Nihon Hou Kagaku Gijutsu Gakkaishi/Japanese Journal of Forensic Science and Technology (JPN ISSN 1880-1323) **5916**

• Nihon Houshasen Anzen Kanri Gakkaishi/Japanese Journal of Radiation Safety Management (JPN ISSN 1347-1503) **7069**

Nihon Hozon Shikagaku Zasshi *see* Nihon Shika Hozongaku Zasshi **5857**

Nihon Iden Gakkai Taikai Puroguramu Yokoshu *see* Genetics Society of Japan. Abstracts of the Annual Meeting **716**

Nihon Igaku Butsuri Gakkai Kikanshi *see* Igaku Butsuri **6198**

Nihon Iji Shinpo/Japan Medical Journal (JPN ISSN 0385-9215) **5686**

• Nihon Ika Daigaku Igakkai Zasshi (JPN ISSN 1349-8975) **5686**

Nihon Insatsu Nenkan/Japan Printing Art Annual (JPN ISSN 0546-0719) **7325**

Nihon Inter Electronics Corp. News *see* N I News **3109**

Nihon Ion Kokan Gakkaishi/Japan Association of Ion Exchange. Journal (JPN ISSN 0915-860X) **2075**

Nihon Ishigaku Zasshi/Japan Society of Medical History. Journal (JPN ISSN 0549-3323) **5687**

Nihon Ishikai Zasshi/Japan Medical Association. Journal (JPN ISSN 0021-4493) **5687**

Nihon Ishinkin Gakkai Zasshi *see* Nippon Ishinkin Gakkai Zasshi **894**

➤ Nihon Ishoku Gakkai Zasshi/Japanese Journal of Transplantation (JPN ISSN 0578-7947) **6253**

Nihon Iyaku Bunken Shorokushu/Japan Pharmaceutical Abstracts (JPN ISSN 0915-1621) **6890**

Nihon Iyou Shika Kiki Gakkaishi/Journal of Japan Society of Dental Equipments (JPN ISSN 1881-7734) **5857**

Nihon Jakushi Shashi Gakkai Zasshi/Japanese Association of Strabismus and Amblyopia. Journal (JPN ISSN 0289-3843) **6046**

Nihon Jakushi Shashi Gakkaiho/Japanese Association of Strabismus and Amblyopia. Bulletin (JPN ISSN 0386-4200) **6046**

Nihon Jibi Inkoka Gakkai Kaiho *see* Journal of Otolaryngology of Japan **6082**

Nihon Jibi Inkoka Kansensho Kenkyukai Kaishi/Japan Society for Infectious Diseases in Otolaryngology. Journal (JPN ISSN 0913-3976) **6083**

• Nihon Jiki Kyomei Igakkai Zasshi (JPN ISSN 0914-9457) **6204**

Nihon Jikken Dobutsu Gakkai Sokai Koen Yoshishu/Japanese Association for Laboratory Animal Science. Abstracts of General Meeting (JPN) **717**

Nihon Jinrui Iden Gakkai Taikai Shorokushu/Japan Society of Human Genetics. Abstracts of the Annual Meeting (JPN) **717**

Nihon Jinzo Gakkaishi/Japanese Journal of Nephrology (JPN ISSN 0385-2385) **6273**

Nihon Jishin Gakkai Nyusu Reta/Seismological Society of Japan. Newsletter (JPN ISSN 0919-5319) **2787**

Nihon Jishin Kogaku Shinpojumu Koenshu/Japan Earthquake Engineering Symposium. Proceedings (JPN) **2787**

Nihon Jisuberi Gakkaishi/Japan Landslide Society. Journal (JPN ISSN 1348-3986) **2787**

Nihon Jomyaku Keicho Eiyo Kenkyukaishi *see* Jomyaku, Keicho Eiyo **6661**

Nihon Josan Gakkaishi/Japan Academy of Midwifery. Journal (JPN ISSN 0917-6357) **5999**

Nihon Josei Kagakusha no Kai Nyusu/Society of Japanese Women Scientists. News (JPN ISSN 1346-9827) **8877**

Nihon Joshi Daigaku Daigakuin Bungaku Kenkyuka Kiyo/Japan Women's University. Graduate School of Humanities. Journal (JPN ISSN 1341-2361) **4466**

Nihon Joshi Daigaku Ei-Bei Bungaku Kenkyu/Studies in English and American Literature (JPN ISSN 0288-3015) **5341**

Nihon Joshi Daigaku Kiyo. Bungakubu/Japan Women's University. Faculty of Humanities. Journal (JPN ISSN 0288-3031) **4466**

Nihon Joshi Daigaku Kiyo. Rigakubu/Japan Women's University. Faculty of Science. Journal (JPN ISSN 0919-1593) **7892**

Nihon Jusei Chakusho Gakkai Zasshi/Journal of Fertilization and Implantation (JPN ISSN 0914-6776) **5999**

Nihon Kabutogani o Mamoru Kai Kaiho/Horseshoe Crab (JPN) **958**

Nihon Kafun Gakkai Kaishi/Japanese Journal of Palynology (JPN ISSN 0387-1851) **6727**

• Nihon Kagaku Gijutsu Kankei Chikuji Kankobutsu Soran (Online)/Directory of Japanese Scientific Periodicals (Online) (JPN) **7578**

➤ Nihon Kagaku Ryoho Gakkai Zasshi/Japanese Journal of Chemotherapy (JPN ISSN 1340-7007) **6864**

Nihon Kagakushi Gakkai Nenkai Kenkyu Happyo Koen Yoshishu (JPN) **7892**

Nihon Kaiji Shimbun/Japan Maritime Daily (JPN) **8655**

Nihon Kaimen Igakkai Zasshi/Japanese Medical Society for Biological Interface. Journal (JPN ISSN 0288-8262) **5823**

Nihon Kaisui Gakkai Kenkyu Gijutsu Happyokai Koen Yoshishu/Society of Sea Water Science, Japan. Abstracts of Meeting (JPN) **2720**

Nihon Kaisui Gakkaishi/Society of Sea Water Science, Japan. Bulletin (JPN ISSN 0369-4550) **2814**

Nihon Kaiyo Gakkai Kikanshi *see* Umi no Kenkyu **2819**

Nihon Kaiyo Gakkai Taikai Koen Yoshishu *see* Oceanographical Society of Japan. Abstracts on the Conference **2720**

Nihon Kaku Igakkai Kikanshi *see* Kaku Igaku **6202**

Nihon Kan Shikkan Gakkai Zasshi/Japanese Coronary Association. Journal (JPN ISSN 1341-7703) **5796**

Nihon Kango Gakkaishi/Japanese Society of Nursing. Journal (JPN ISSN 0917-513X) **5971**

Nihon Kango Kagakkaishi/Japan Academy of Nursing Science. Journal (JPN ISSN 0287-5330) **5971**

Nihon Kansensho Gakkai Higashi Nihon Chihokai Sokai Nihon Kagaku Ryoho Gakkai Higashi Nihon Shibu Sokai Godo Gakkai Puroguramu Koen Shoroku (JPN) **5823**

Nihon Kaoku Gaichu Gakkai Taikai Kenkyu Happyo Yoshishu/House and Household Insect Pests Society of Japan. Abstracts of Meeting (JPN) **717**

Nihon Kasei Gakkaishi/Journal of Home Economics of Japan (JPN ISSN 0913-5227) **4365**

• Nihon Kaze Kougakkai Rombunshuu (JPN ISSN 1349-3507) **3178**

Nihon Keiei Kogakukai Rombunshi/Japan Industrial Management Association. Communications (JPN) **1781**

Nihon Keikei Kogakkaishi/Japan Industrial Management Association. Journal (JPN ISSN 0386-4812) **1781**

Nihon Keisei Geka Gakkai Gakujutsu Shukai/Japan Society of Plastic and Reconstructive Surgery. Annual Meeting (JPN) **6253**

Nihon Keisei Geka Gakkai Kaishi/Japan Society of Plastic and Reconstructive Surgery. Journal (JPN ISSN 0389-4703) **6253**

Nihon Keizai o Chushin Tosuru Kokusai Hikaku Tokei *see* Comparative Economic and Financial Statistics - Japan and Other Major Countries **1222**

Nihon Kekkan Geka Gakkai Zasshi (JPN ISSN 0918-6778) **6253**

Nihon Kenchiku Gakkai Keikaku-Kei Ronbunshu/Journal of Architecture, Planning and Environmental Engineering (JPN ISSN 1340-4210) **451**

Nihon Kenchiku Gakkai Kozo-Kei Ronbunshu/Journal of Structural and Construction Engineering (JPN ISSN 1340-4202) **451**

Nihon Kenkyu (Hiroshima)/Review of Japanese Studies (JPN ISSN 0911-3401) **4186**

Nihon Kenkyu (Kyoto)/International Research Center for Japanese Studies. Bulletin (JPN ISSN 0915-0900) **4186**

Nihon Kessen Shiketsu Gakkaishi/Japanese Society on Thrombosis and Hemostasis. Journal (JPN ISSN 0915-7441) **5940**

Nihon Kessho Gakkaishi/Crystallographic Society of Japan. Journal (JPN ISSN 0369-4585) **2111**

Nihon Kessho Seicho Gakkaishi/Japanese Association of Crystal Growth. Journal (JPN ISSN 0385-6275) **2111**

Nihon Kikai Gakkai. Koenkai Koen Ronbunshu/Japan Society of Mechanical Engineers. Preprints of the Meeting (JPN) **3391**

• Nihon Kikai Gakkai Ronbunshu. A Hen/Japan Society of Mechanical Engineers. Transactions. Series A (JPN ISSN 0387-5008) **3391**

• Nihon Kikai Gakkai Ronbunshu. B Hen/Japan Society of Mechanical Engineers. Transactions. Series B (JPN ISSN 0387-5016) **3391**

• Nihon Kikai Gakkai Ronbunshu. C Hen/Japan Society of Mechanical Engineers. Transactions. Series C (JPN ISSN 0387-5024) **3391**

Nihon Kikai Gakkaishi *see* Japan Society of Mechanical Engineers. Journal **3384**

Nihon Kikai Kogyo Rengokai. Jigyo Hokoku/Japan Machinery Federation. Report (JPN) **5457**

• ➤ Nihon Kikan Shokudoka Gakkai Kaiho/Japan Broncho-Esophagological Society. Journal (JPN ISSN 0029-0645) **6216**

Nihon Kiko Shinbun/Japan Machinery Journal (JPN) **5457**

Nihon Kisho Gakkai Taikai Koen Yokoshu *see* Meteorological Society of Japan. Preprints of Meeting **6391**

Nihon Kobutsu Gakkai Nenkai Koen Yoshishu *see* Mineralogical Society of Japan. Annual Meeting Abstracts **2720**

Nihon Kodansei Gakkai Kaiho/Japan Society for Photoelasticity. Journal (JPN) **7081**

Nihon Kodansei Gakkai Kenkyu Happyo Koenkai Koen Ronbunshu/Proceedings of the Symposium on Photoelasticity (JPN ISSN 0910-9862) **7081**

Nihon Kodo Keiryo Gakkai Taikai Happyo Ronbun Shorokushu (JPN) **8149**

Nihon Kodo Ryoho Gakkai Nyuzu Reta/Japanese Association of Behavior Therapy. Newsletter (JPN) **7388**

Nihon Kokai Gakkai Ronbunshu/Japan Institute of Navigation. Journal (JPN ISSN 0388-7405) **8655**

Nihon Kokogaku/Japanese Archaeological Association. Journal (JPN ISSN 1340-8488) **408**

➤ Nihon Kokogaku Nenpo/Archaeologia Japonica/Japanese Archaeologists Association. Annual Report (JPN ISSN 0402-852X) **408**

Nihon Koku Shuyo Gakkaishi/Japan Society for Oral Tumors. Journal (JPN ISSN 0915-5988) **6029**

• Nihon Koku Uchu Gakkai Rombunshu/Japan Society for Aeronautical and Space Sciences (JPN ISSN 1344-6460) **67**

Nihon Kokuka Gakkai Zasshi/Japanese Stomatological Society. Journal (JPN ISSN 0029-0297) **5857**

• Nihon Kokusai Igaku Kyoukaishi/International Medical News (JPN ISSN 0535-1405) **5687**

• Nihon Kokyuki Gakkai Zasshi/Japanese Respiratory Society. Journal (JPN ISSN 1343-3490) **6217**

Nihon Kokyuki Geka Gakkai Zasshi/Japanese Association for Chest Surgery. Journal (JPN ISSN 0919-0945) **6253**

• Nihon Konchu Gakkai Taikai Koen Yoshi/Entomological Society of Japan. Abstracts of Annual Meeting (JPN) **717**

• Nihon Konchu Kyokai Nyusu Reta/Japan Insect Association. Newsletter (JPN ISSN 0917-9895) **856**

Nihon Kontakuto Renzu Gakkai Kaishi *see* Nihon Contact Lens Gakkaishi **6046**

Nihon Koseibutsu Gakkai Nenkai Koen Yokoshu/Palaeontological Society of Japan. Abstracts of the Annual Meeting (JPN) **6731**

Nihon Koshu Eisei Zasshi/Japanese Journal of Public Health (JPN ISSN 0546-1766) **7533**

➤ Nihon Kotsu, Kansetsu Kansenshou Gakkai Zasshi/Japanese Society for Study of Bone and Joint Infections. Journal (JPN ISSN 1881-9893) **6067**

Nihon Kotsu Keitai Keisoku Gakkai Zasshi/Japanese Society of Bone Morphometry. Journal (JPN ISSN 0917-4648) **6067**

Nihon Koukarei Igakkai Zasshi *see* Anti-Aging Medicine **5576**

Nihon Kyobu Rinsho/Japanese Journal of Chest Diseases (JPN ISSN 0385-3667) **5796**

Nihon Kyoikuho Gakkai Nenpo (JPN) **4747**

Nihon Kyuchaku Gakkai Kenkyu Happyokai Koen Yoshishu/Japan Society on Adsorption. Abstracts of the Meeting (JPN) **2095**

Nihon Kyukyu Igakkai Zasshi/Japanese Association for Acute Medicine. Journal (JPN ISSN 0915-924X) **5948**

Nihon Kyumei Iryo Gakkai Zasshi/Japanese Association for Critical Care Medicine. Journal (JPN) **5687**

Nihon Kyumei Iryo Kenkyukai Zasshi *see* Nihon Kyumei Iryo Gakkai Zasshi **5687**

Nihon Kyuukyuu Kango Gakkai Zasshi (JPN ISSN 1348-0928) **6067**

Nihon Maikuro Sajari Gakkai Kaishi/Japanese Society of Reconstructive Microsurgery. Journal (JPN ISSN 0916-4936) **6253**

• Nihon Maketto Shea Jiten (Japanese Edition)/Market Share in Japan (Japanese Edition) (JPN) **1154**

Nihon Maku Gakkai Nenkai Koen Yoshishu/Membrane Society of Japan. Abstracts of Annual Meeting (JPN) **2095**

Nihon Mizushori Seibutsu Gakkaishi/Japanese Journal of Water Treatment Biology (JPN ISSN 0910-6758) **3509**

Nihon Monki Senta Nenpo/Japan Monkey Centre. Annual Report (JPN) **958**

Nihon Mukin Seibutsu Noto Baioroji Gakkai Sokai Nittei to Shoroku/Japanese Association of Germfree Life and Gnotobiology. Abstracts of Meeting (JPN) **717**

Nihon Musen Giho/J R C Review (JPN ISSN 0287-1564) **2361**

Nihon N P O Gakkai Kikanshi *see* Nonpurofitto Rebyu **8059**

Nihon Naibunpi Gakkai Zasshi/Folia Endocrinologica Japonica (JPN ISSN 0029-0661) **5898**

• Nihon Naika Gakkai Zasshi/Japanese Society of Internal Medicine. Journal (JPN ISSN 0021-5384) **5948**

Nihon Naishikyo Geka Gakkai Zasshi/Japan Society for Endoscopic Surgery. Journal (JPN ISSN 1344-6703) **6253**

Nihon Neji Kenkyu Kyokaishi/Japan Research Institute for Screw Threads and Fasteners. Journal (JPN ISSN 0287-8313) **3391**

Nihon Netsu Bussei Shinpojiumu Koen Ronbunshu *see* Thermophysical Properties **7057**

Nihon Netsu Ryutai Kogakkai Ronbunshu/Japan Society of Heat and Fluid Engineering. Transactions (JPN ISSN 1340-3354) **7056**

Nihon Nettai Igakkai Zasshi/Japanese Journal of Tropical Medicine and Hygiene *see* Tropical Medicine and Health **5827**

Nihon Ninchi Gengo Gakkai Rombunshuu/Japanese Cognitive Linguistics Association. Annual Meetings. Proceedings (JPN ISSN 1346-7964) **5155**

Nihon no Bijutsu/Visual Art in Japan (JPN ISSN 0549-401X) **509**

Nihon no Denki Jigyo *see* Electric Power Industry in Japan **3302**

Nihon no Ganka/Japan Ophthalmologists Association. Journal (JPN ISSN 0285-1326) **6046**

Nihon no Kagakusha/Journal of Japanese Scientists (JPN ISSN 0029-0335) **7892**

Nihon no Kawa/Rivers in Japan (JPN ISSN 0288-9455) **8830**

Nihon no Toshokan *see* Statistics on Libraries in Japan **5060**

• Nihon Noson Igakkai Zasshi/Japanese Association of Rural Medicine. Journal (JPN ISSN 0468-2513) **5687**

Nihon Nou Shinkei Geka Gakkai Soukai Shourokushuu (CD-ROM)/Japan Neurosurgical Society. Abstracts of the Annual Meeting (CD-ROM) (JPN ISSN 1347-9040) **5749**

Nihon Ongakushi Kenkyu/Ueno Gakuen University. Research Archives for Japanese Music. Bulletin (JPN ISSN 1342-2308) **6599**

Nihon Onkyo Gakkai Kenkyu Happyokai Koen Ronbunshu/Acoustical Society of Japan. Proceedings of the Annual Meetings (JPN ISSN 1340-3168) **7088**

• ➤ Nihon Onkyo Gakkaishi/Acoustical Society of Japan. Journal (JPN ISSN 0369-4232) **7088**

Nihon Onsen Kiko Butsuri Igakkai Zasshi/Japanese Association of Physical Medicine, Balneology, and Climatology. Journal (JPN ISSN 0029-0343) **5687**

Nihon Opereshonzu Risachi Gakkai Ronbunshi *see* Operations Research Society of Japan. Journal **1783**

Nihon Oyo Chishitsu Gakkai Kenkyu Happyokai Koen Ronbunshu/Japan Society of Engineering Geology. Proceedings of Meeting (JPN) **2759**

Nihon Oyo Chishitsu Gakkai Kyushu Shibu Kaiho/Japan Society of Engineering Geology. Kyushu Branch Report (JPN ISSN 0917-2289) **2759**

➤ Nihon Oyo Dobutsu Konchu Gakkai Chugoku Shibu Kaiho/Japanese Society of Applied Entomology and Zoology. Chugoku Branch. Journal (JPN ISSN 0387-9003) **856**

Nihon Oyo Dobutsu Konchu Gakkai Kyushu Shibu Kaiho/Delphax (JPN) **958**

• ➤ Nihon Oyo Dobutsu Konchu Gakkaishi/Japanese Journal of Applied Entomology and Zoology (JPN ISSN 0021-4914) **856**

Nihon Oyo Jiki Gakkai Gakujutsu Koen Gaiyoshu/Annual Conference on Magnetics in Japan. Digests (JPN ISSN 1340-8100) **7028**

Nihon Oyo Jiki Gakkai Kenkyukai Shiryo/Magnetics Society of Japan. Papers of Technical Meeting (JPN ISSN 1340-7562) **7028**

Nihon Oyo Jiki Gakkaishi *see* Magnetics Society of Japan. Journal **7025**

Nihon Oyo Koso Kyokaishi/Japan Foundation for Applied Enzymology. Journal (JPN ISSN 0913-3348) **740**

Nihon Oyo Suri Gakkai Ronbunshi/Japan Society for Industrial and Applied Mathematics. Transactions (JPN ISSN 0917-2246) **5520**

Nihon P D A Gakujutsushi GMP to Barideshon (Personal Digital Assistant) (JPN ISSN 1344-4891) **6864**

Nihon Parapurejia Igakkai Zasshi *see* Nihon Sekizui Shougai Igakkai Zasshi **6068**

Nihon Pein Kurinikku Gakkaishi *see* Japan Society of Pain Clinics. Journal **4103**

Nihon Purankuton Gakkaiho/The Plankton Society of Japan. Bulletin (JPN ISSN 0387-8961) **694**

Nihon Raigakkai Zasshi/Japanese Journal of Leprosy *see* Nihon Hansenbyo Gakkai Zasshi **5823**

Nihon Rajio Shinbun/Japan Radio News (JPN) **2361**

Nihon Reichorui Gakkai Taikai Yokoshu/Primate Society of Japan. Preprints of the Annual Meeting (JPN) **958**

➤ Nihon Reito Kucho Gakkai Rombunshu/Japan Society of Refrigeration and Air Conditioning Engineers. Transactions (JPN ISSN 1344-4905) **4124**

➤ Nihon Reito Kuchou Gakkai Gakujutsu Koenkai Koen Ronbunshu/Japan Society of Refrigeration and Air Conditioning Engineers. Proceedings of Annual Conference (JPN) **4124**

Nihon Reito Reibo Shinbun/Japan Refrigeration and Air Conditioning News (JPN ISSN 0029-036X) **4124**

Nihon Rekishi (JPN ISSN 0386-9164) **4187**

Nihon Reoroji Gakkai Nenkai Koen Yokoshu/Abstracts of Annual Meeting on Rheology (JPN) **7048**

• ➤ Nihon Reoroji Gakkaishi/Society of Rheology, Japan. Journal (JPN ISSN 0387-1533) **7061**

Nihon Rikagaku Kyokai. Kenkyu Kiyo (JPN ISSN 0287-864X) **7028**

Nihon Rikusui Gakkai Koen Yoshishu/Japanese Society of Limnology. Abstracts of Meeting (JPN) **2720**

Nihon Rikusui Gakkai Koshin'etsu Shibukai Kaiho/Limnological Society of Koshin'etsu District. Bulletin (JPN ISSN 0913-4859) **2797**

Title

10676 NIHON RIMOTO SENSHINGU GAKKAISHI ULRICH'S PERIODICALS

Nihon Rimoto Senshingu Gakkaishi/Remote Sensing Society of Japan. Journal (JPN ISSN 0289-7911) **4022**

• Nihon Rimpa Monaikei Gakkai Kaishi/Japanese Society of Lymphoreticular Tissue Research. Journal (JPN ISSN 1342-9248) **5687**

Nihon Rinsho Baiomekanikusu Gakkaishi/Japanese Society for Clinical Biomechanics and Related Research. Proceedings of Annual Meeting (JPN ISSN 1340-9018) **6067**

➤ Nihon Rinsho Eiyo Gakkai Zasshi/Japanese Society of Clinical Nutrition. Journal (JPN ISSN 0286-8202) **6664**

Nihon Rinsho Geka Gakkai Zasshi/Japan Surgical Association. Journal (JPN ISSN 1345-2843) **6253**

• Nihon Rinsho Masui Gakkaishi/Japan Society for Clinical Anesthesia. Journal (JPN ISSN 0285-4945) **5772**

• Nihon Rinsho Men'eki Gakkai Kaishi/Japanese Journal of Clinical Immunology (JPN ISSN 0911-4300) **5764**

Nihon Rinsho Seikei Gekaikai Kaishi/Japanese Clinical Orthopaedic Association. Journal (JPN ISSN 0912-0580) **6067**

Nihon Rinsho Seiri Gakkai Zasshi/Japanese Journal of Clinical Physiology (JPN ISSN 0286-7052) **5687**

Nihon Rodo Kenkyu Kiko Kenkyu Kiyo/Japan Institute of Labour. Studies (JPN ISSN 0917-1843) **1700**

Nihon Rodo Kenkyu Zasshi/Japan Institute of Labour. Journal (JPN ISSN 0916-3808) **1700**

Nihon Ronen Igakkai Zasshi/Japanese Journal of Geriatrics (JPN ISSN 0300-9173) **4052**

Nihon Ryokka Kogakkaishi/Japanese Society of Revegetation Technology. Journal (JPN ISSN 0916-7439) **140**

Nihon Ryumachi Kansetsu Geka Gakkai Zasshi/Japanese Journal of Rheumatism and Joint Surgery (JPN ISSN 0287-3214) **6225**

Nihon Ryumachi Kansetsu Geka Gekkai/Japanese Society of Rheumatism and Joint Surgery. Congress (JPN) **6225**

Nihon S I D S Gakkai Zasshi/Japan S I D S Research Society. Journal (Sudden Infant Death Syndrome) (JPN ISSN 1346-1680) **6097**

Nihon Saibo Seibutsu Gakkai Taikai Koen Yoshishu/Japan Society for Cell Biology. Abstracts of the Meeting (JPN) **717**

• Nihon Saikingaku Zasshi/Japanese Journal of Bacteriology (JPN ISSN 0021-4930) **5823**

Nihon Saisei Iryou Gakkai Zasshi/Japanese Society for Regenerative Medicine. Journal *see* Saisei Iryou **5708**

• ➤ Nihon Saisei Shikaigakkai Zasshi/Japanese Association of Regenerative Dentistry. Journal (JPN ISSN 1348-9615) **5857**

Nihon Saiseki Shinbun/Japan Crushed Stone News (JPN) **1027**

• ➤ Nihon Sakumotsu Gakkai Kiji/Crop Science Society of Japan. Proceedings/Japanese Journal of Crop Science (JPN ISSN 0011-1848) **243**

Nihon Sakyu Gakkaishi/Sand Dune Research (JPN ISSN 0918-5623) **2759**

Nihon Sanfujinka Kansensho Kenkyukai Gakujutsu Koenkai Kirokushu/Conference on Obstetrical and Gynecological Infection. Proceedings (JPN ISSN 0918-4031) **5999**

➤ Nihon Sanfujinka Shinseiji Ketsueki Gakkaishi/Japanese Journal of Obstetrical, Gynecological and Neonatal Hematology (JPN ISSN 0916-8796) **5999**

Nihon Sanfujinkai Kaihou/J A O G News (JPN ISSN 1348-5938) **5999**

Nihon Sangyo Gijutsushi Gakkai Nenkai Koen Gaiyoshu/Japan Society for the History of Industrial Technology. Annual Conference. Proceedings (JPN) **8447**

Nihon Sanka Fujinka Gakkai Akita Chihobu Kaishi/Akita Society of Obstetrics and Gynecology. Journal (JPN ISSN 1341-8165) **5999**

Nihon Sanka Fujinka Gakkai Chugoku Shinkoku Godo Chiho Bukai Zasshi/Japan Society of Obstetrics and Gynecology. Chugoku and Shikoku Districts Journal (JPN ISSN 0546-1790) **5999**

Nihon Sanka Fujinka Gakkai Kanagawa Chiho Bukai Kaishi/Japan Society of Obstetrics and Gynecology. Kanagawa District Journal (JPN ISSN 0910-2485) **5999**

• Nihon Sanka Fujinka Gakkai Kanto Rengo Chiho Bukai Kaiho/Kanto Journal of Obstetrics and Gynecology (JPN ISSN 0285-8096) **5999**

Nihon Sanka Fujinka Gakkai Kumamoto Chiho Bukai Zasshi/Japan Society of Obstetrics and Gynecology. Kumamoto District Journal (JPN ISSN 1341-5050) **6000**

Nihon Sanka Fujinka Gakkai Kyushu Rengo Chiho Bukai Zasshi/Japan Society of Obstetrics and Gynecology. Kyushu District Journal (JPN ISSN 0913-2368) **6000**

Nihon Sanka Fujinka Gakkai Niigata Chiho Bukai Kaisshi/Japan Society of Obstetrics and Gynecology. Niigata Districts Journal (JPN ISSN 0285-3485) **6000**

Nihon Sanka Fujinka Gakkai Saitama Chiho Bukai Kaishi/Japan Society of Obstetrics and Gynecology. Saitama District Journal (JPN ISSN 0911-6281) **6000**

Nihon Sanka Fujinka Gakkai Tohoku Rengo Chiho Bukai Kaishi/Tohoku Journal of Obstetrics and Gynecology (JPN) **6000**

Nihon Sanka Fujinka Gakkai Tokyo Chiho Bukai Kaishi/Tokyo Journal of Obstetrics and Gynecology (JPN ISSN 0288-5751) **6000**

Nihon Sanka Fujinka Gakkai Zasshi/Acta Obstetrica et Gynaecologica Japonica (JPN ISSN 0300-9165) **6000**

Nihon Sanka Fujinka Naishikyo Gakkai Zasshi/Japanese Journal of Gynecologic and Obstetric Endoscopy (JPN) **6000**

Nihon Sanshigaku Zasshi/Journal of Sericultural Science of Japan *see* Sanshi Konchuu Baiotekku **858**

Nihon Sei Kagakkai Zasshi/Japanese Journal of Sexology (JPN ISSN 1349-6654) **5687**

Nihon Sei Kino Gakkai Zasshi/Japanese Journal of Impotence Research (JPN ISSN 1345-8361) **6273**

Nihon Seibutsu Chiri Gakkai Kaiho/Biogeographical Society of Japan. Bulletin (JPN ISSN 0067-8716) **694**

Nihon Seikagakkai Kinki Shibu Reikai Yoshishu/Japanese Biochemical Society. Kinki Branch Office. Abstracts of Meeting (JPN) **3613**

Nihon Seikagaku Gakkai Nyusu/Japanese Society of Sexual Science News (JPN) **5687**

➤ Nihon Seikei Geka Choonpa Kenkyukai Kaishi/Japanese Society of Orthopedic Ultrasonics. Journal (JPN ISSN 0915-7107) **6067**

Nihon Seikei Geka Supotsu Igakkaishi/Japanese Journal of Orthopedic Sports Medicine (JPN ISSN 0916-1643) **6067**

• Nihon Seikisho Gakkai Zasshi/Japanese Journal of Biometeorology (JPN ISSN 0389-1313) **6392**

Nihon Seikosho Giho/Japan Steel Works Technical Review (JPN ISSN 0546-126X) **6327**

➤ Nihon Seiri Jinrui Gakkaishi/Japanese Journal of Physiological Anthropology (JPN ISSN 1342-3215) **926**

Nihon Seirigaku Zasshi/Physiological Society of Japan. Journal (JPN ISSN 0031-9341) **926**

Nihon Seishoku Geka Gakkai Zasshi/Japan Society of Reproductive Surgery. Journal (JPN) **6000**

Nihon Seitai Gakkai Kanto Chikukai Kaiho/Ecological Society of Japan. Kanto Branch. News (JPN ISSN 0289-2421) **694**

Nihon Seitai Gakkai Kyushu Chikukai Kaiho/Ecological Society of Japan. Kyushu Branch. Bulletin (JPN) **694**

Nihon Seitai Gakkai Tohoku Chikukai Kaiho/Ecological Society of Japan. Tohoku Branch. News (JPN) **694**

Nihon Seitai Jiki Gakkaishi/Japan Biomagnetism and Bioelectromagnetics Society. Journal (JPN ISSN 0915-0374) **754**

➤ Nihon Sekigaisen Gakkaishi/Japan Society of Infrared Science and Technology. Journal (JPN ISSN 0916-7900) **7056**

Nihon Sekitsui Sekizuibyou Gakkai Zasshi/Japan Spine Research Society. Journal (JPN ISSN 1346-4876) **6068**

Nihon Sekizui Shougai Igakkai Zasshi/Japan Medical Society of Paraplegia. Journal (JPN ISSN 1348-3242) **6068**

Nihon Semi no Kai Kaiho/Cicada (JPN ISSN 0915-2067) **856**

Nihon Sempaku Kaiyou Kougakkai Rombunshuu/Japan Society of Naval Architects and Ocean Engineers. Journal (JPN ISSN 1880-3717) **8655**

Nihon Sempaku Kaiyou Kougakkaishi *see* Kanrin **8649**

Nihon Senchu Gakkai Nyusu/Japan Nematology News (JPN ISSN 0919-343X) **958**

Nihon Senchu Gakkaishi/Japanese Journal of Nematology (JPN ISSN 0919-6765) **958**

Nihon Senpaku Meisaisho I/Japan Register of Ships I (JPN) **8655**

Nihon Senpaku Meisaisho II/Japan Register of Ships II (of Japanese flag, under 100 GT) (JPN) **8655**

Nihon Senshokutai Idenshi Kensa Gakkai Shorokushu/Japanese Association for Chromosome and Gene Analaysis. Abstract of Annual Meeting (JPN) **717**

Nihon Senshokutai Idenshi Kensa Gakkai Zasshi/Japanese Association for Chromosome and Gene Analaysis. Official Journal (JPN) **740**

Nihon Setchaku Gakkaishi/Journal of Adhesion (JPN ISSN 0916-4812) **7095**

Nihon Shakai Jigyo Daigaku Kenkyu Kiyo/Japan College of Social Work. Study Report (JPN ISSN 0916-765X) **8059**

Nihon Shashin Gakkaishi/Society of Photographic Science and Technology of Japan. Journal (JPN ISSN 0369-5662) **6972**

Nihon Shashin Sokuryo Gakkai. Gakujutsu Koenkai Happyo Ronbunshu (JPN) **4022**

Nihon Shika Hozongaku Zasshi/Japanese Journal of Conservative Dentistry (JPN ISSN 0387-2343) **5857**

Nihon Shika Ishikai Zasshi/Japan Dental Association. Journal (JPN ISSN 0047-1763) **5857**

• ➤ Nihon Shika Masui Gakkai Zasshi/Japanese Dental Society of Anesthesiology. Journal (JPN ISSN 0386-5835) **5772**

Nihon Shika Rikou Gakkai Gakujutsu Kouenkai Kouenshuu *see* Shika Zairyo, Kikai **5865**

Nihon Shikisai Gakkai Nyuzu/C S A J News (JPN) **7081**

Nihon Shikisai Gakkaishi/Color Science Association of Japan. Journal (JPN ISSN 0389-9357) **7081**

Nihon Shikkan Moderu Dobutsu Kenkyukai Kiroku *see* Nihon Shikkan Moderu Gakkai Kiroku **926**

Nihon Shikkan Moderu Gakkai Kiroku/Japanese Association of Animal Models for Human Diseases. Proceedings (JPN ISSN 0918-8991) **926**

Nihon Shinbun Kyokai News Bulletin *see* N S K News Bulletin **4580**

Nihon Shinkei Gaisho Gakkai Koenshu *see* Shinkei Gaisho **6185**

Nihon Shinkei Seishin Yakurigaku Zasshi/Japanese Journal of Psychopharmacology (JPN ISSN 1340-2544) **6170**

Nihon Shino Kunrenshi Kyokaishi/Japanese Orthoptic Journal (JPN ISSN 0387-5172) **6046**

Nihon Shinrin Gakkaishi/Japanese Forest Society. Journal (JPN ISSN 1349-8509) **3698**

Nihon Shinseiji Gakkai Zasshi/Acta Neonatologica Japonica *see* Nihon Shuusanki Shinseiji Igakkai Zasshi **6097**

➤ Nihon Shinzo Kekkan Geka Gakkai Zasshi/Japanese Journal of Cardiovascular Surgery (JPN ISSN 0285-1474) **6253**

• Nihon Shiruku Gakkaishi (JPN ISSN 1880-8204) **8455**

• ➤ Nihon Shishubyo Gakkai Kaishi/Japanese Society of Periodontology. Journal (JPN ISSN 0385-0110) **5857**

Nihon Shizen Hogo Kyokai Hokoku/Nature Conservation Society of Japan. Reports (JPN) **2622**

• Nihon Shokaki Geka Gakkai Zasshi/Japanese Journal of Gastroenterological Surgery (JPN ISSN 0386-9768) **5929**

Nihon Shokaki Naishikyo Gakkai Koshin'etsu Chihokai Zasshi/Endoscopic Forum for Digestive Disease (JPN ISSN 0912-0505) **5929**

Nihon Shokaki Shudan Kenshin Gakkai Zasshi/Journal of Gastroenterological Mass Survey (JPN ISSN 1345-4110) **5929**

• Nihon Shokakibyo Gakkai Zasshi/Japanese Journal of Gastroenterology (JPN ISSN 0446-6586) **5929**

Nihon Shokubutsu Bunrui Gakkai (JPN) **805**

Nihon Shokubutsu Bunrui Gakkai Kaiho (JPN) **805**

Nihon Shokubutsu Bunrui Gakkai Taikai Happyo Yoshishu/Japan Society of Plant Taxonomists. Proceeding of the Annual Meeting (JPN) **805**

Nihon Shokubutsu Byori Gakkai Baiokontororu Kenkyukai Koen Yoshi/Phytopathological Society of Japan. Abstracts of the Meeting of Biocontrol (JPN ISSN 0916-958X) **694**

Nihon Shokubutsu Byori Gakkai Shokubutsu Kansen Seiri Danwakai/Symposium on Physiological Plant Pathology in Japan. Proceedings (JPN) **805**

Nihon Shokubutsu Byori Gakkaiho *see* Phytopathological Society of Japan. Annals **809**

Nihon Shokubutsu Gakkai Taikai Kenkyu Happyo Kiroku/Botanical Society of Japan. Proceedings of the Annual Meeting (JPN) **805**

Nihon Shokubutsu Saibou Bunshiseibutu Gakkai Korokiamu/Japanese Society for Plant Cell and Molecular Biology. Culture Colloquium (JPN) **805**

Nihon Shokubutsu Seiri Gakkai Nenkai Oyobi Shinpojumu Koeu Yoshishu/Japanese Society of Plant Physiologists. Proceedings of the Annual Meeting and Symposium (JPN) **805**

Nihon Shokubutsu Seiri Gakkai Tsushin *see* Japanese Society of Plant Physiologists. News **795**

Nihon Shokubutsuen Kyokaishi/Japan Association of Botanical Gardens. Bulletin (JPN ISSN 0389-5246) **805**

Nihon Shokuhin Biseibutsu Gakkai Zasshi/Japanese Journal of Food Microbiology (JPN ISSN 1340-8267) **894**

Nihon Shokuhin Kagaku Gakkaishi/Japanese Journal of Food Chemistry (JPN ISSN 1341-2094) **3658**

Nihon Shokuhin Shinsozai Kenkyukaishi/Japanese Council for Advanced Food Ingredients Research. Journal (JPN ISSN 1344-8935) **3658**

▼ Nihon Shokuiku Gakkaishi/Journal of Japanese Society of Shokuiku (JPN ISSN 1882-4773) **6664**

Nihon Shoni Geka Gakkai Zasshi/Japanese Society of Pediatric Surgeons. Journal (JPN ISSN 0288-609X) **6097**

Nihon Shoni Hoshasen Gakkai Zasshi/Japanese Society of Pediatric Radiology. Journal (JPN ISSN 0918-8487) **6204**

• Nihon Shoni Ketsueki Gakkai Zasshi/Japanese Journal of Pediatric Hematology (JPN ISSN 0913-8706) **5940**

Nihon Shoni Rinsho Yakuri Gakkai Zasshi/Japanese Journal of Developmental and Therapeutic Pharmacology (JPN ISSN 1342-6753) **6864**

Nihon Shoni Seikei Geka Gakkai Zasshi/Japanese Paediatric Orthopaedic Association. Journal (JPN ISSN 0917-6950) **6097**

Nihon Shosen Senpuku Tokei (JPN) **8528**

Nihon Shoshimoku Gakkai Tokubetsu Hokoku *see* Japanese Society of Coleopterology. Special Bulletin **851**

➤ Nihon Shujutsu Igakkaishi/Japanese Association for Operative Medicine. Journal (JPN ISSN 1340-8593) **6253**

Nihon Shutei Kogyokaiho/Japan Boating Industry Association. News (JPN) **8279**

➤ Nihon Shuusanki Shinseiji Igakkai Zasshi/Japan Society of Perinatal and Neonatal Medicine. Journal (JPN ISSN 1348-964X) **6097**

Nihon Sogai Kotei, Kotsu Encho Gakkai Zasshi/Japanese Association of External Fixation and Limb Lengthening. Journal (JPN ISSN 1342-3495) **6068**

Nihon Soshiki Baiyo Gakkai Kaiin Tsushin/Japanese Tissue Culture Association. News (JPN) **835**

Nihon Soshiki Kogakkai Puroguramu Shorokushu/Japanese Society for Tissue Engineering. Annual Meeting (JPN) **717**

Nihon Spindle Technical Report *see* Nihon Supindoru Giho **3391**

Nihon Suimon Kagaku Kaishi/Japanese Association of Hydrological Sciences. Journal (JPN ISSN 1342-9612) **2797**

Nihon Supindoru Giho/Nihon Spindle Technical Report (JPN ISSN 0385-2911) **3391**

Nihon Sutoma Haisetsu Rihabiriteshon Gakkaishi/Journal of Japanese Society of Stoma and Continence Rehabilitation (JPN ISSN 1882-0115) **5929**

Nihon Sutoma Rihabiriteshon Gakkaishi *see* Nihon Sutoma Haisetsu Rihabiriteshon Gakkaishi **5929**

Nihon Taipogurafi Nenkan *see* Japan Typography Annual **7324**

Nihon Taishitsu Igakkai Zasshi/Japanese Journal of Constitutional Medicine (JPN ISSN 1347-7137) **926**

Nihon Taishitsugaku Zasshi *see* Nihon Taishitsu Igakkai Zasshi **926**

Nihon Tanpaku Kogakkai Nenkai Puroguramu Yoshishu/Protein Engineering Society of Japan. Abstracts of the Meeting (JPN) **3613**

Nihon Te no Geka Gakkai Zasshi/Japanese Society for Surgery of the Hand. Journal (JPN ISSN 0910-5700) **6068**

Nihon Tenmon Gakkai Koen Yokoshu (JPN ISSN 1347-0639) **4036**

Nihon Tenmon Gakkai Obun Kenkyu Hokoku *see* Publications of Astronomical Society of Japan **580**

Nihon Tenmon Kenkyukai Kansoku Geppo/Japan Astronomical Study Association. Monthly Bulletin (JPN) **578**

Nihon Togai Gaku Ganmen Geka Gakkaishi/Japan Society of Cranio-Maxillo-Facial Surgery. Journal (JPN ISSN 0914-594X) **6253**

Nihon Tokei Gakkaishi (Tokyo, 1957)/Horological Institute of Japan. Journal (Tokyo, 1957) *see* Maikuromekatoronikusu **2572**

• Nihon Tokei Gakkaishi (Tokyo, 1971)/Japan Statistical Society. Journal (JPN ISSN 0389-5602) **1255**

Nihon Tokei Kyokai. Chochiku Doko Chosa Hokoku *see* Japan. Statistics Bureau. Management and Coordination Agency. Family Savings Survey (Year) **1246**

Nihon Tokei Kyokai. Jumin Kihon Daicho Jinko Ido Hokoku Kiho *see* Japan. Statistics Bureau. Management and Coordination Agency. Quarterly Report on the Internal Migration in Japan Derived from the Basic Resident Registers **7311**

Nihon Tokei Kyokai. Jumin Kihon Daicho Jinko Ido Hokoku Nenpo *see* Japan. Statistics Bureau. Management and Coordination Agency. Annual Report on the Internal Migration in Japan Derived from the Basic Resident Registers (Year) **7311**

Nihon Tokei Kyokai. Kagaku Gijutsu Kenkyu Chosa Hokoku *see* Japan. Statistics Bureau. Management and Coordination Agency. Report on the Survey of Research and Development (Year) **8428**

Nihon Tokei Kyokai. Kakei Chosa Hokoku *see* Japan. Statistics Bureau. Management and Coordination Agency. Monthly Report on the Family Income and Expenditure Survey **1246**

Nihon Tokei Kyokai. Kakei Chosa Nenpo *see* Japan. Statistics Bureau. Management and Coordination Agency. Annual Report on Family Income and Expenditure Survey (Year) **4370**

Nihon Tokei Kyokai. Kojin Kigyo Keizai Chosa Kiho *see* Japan. Statistics Bureau. Management and Coordination Agency. Quarterly Report on the Unincorporated Enterprise Survey **1246**

Nihon Tokei Kyokai. Kojin Kigyo Keizai Chosa Nenpo *see* Japan. Statistics Bureau. Management and Coordination Agency. Annual Report on the Unincorporated Enterprise Survey (Year) **1246**

Nihon Tokei Kyokai. Kouri Bukka Tokei Chosa Hokoku *see* Japan. Statistics Bureau. Management and Coordination Agency. Monthly Report of Retail Prices Survey **1246**

Nihon Tokei Kyokai. Kouri Bukka Tokei Chosa Nenpo *see* Japan. Statistics Bureau. Management and Coordination Agency. Annual Report on the Retail Price Survey **1246**

Nihon Tokei Kyokai. Nihon No Tokei (Year)/Japan Statistical Association. Statistics of Japan (Year) (JPN ISSN 0286-1402) **8391**

Nihon Tokei Kyokai. Nihon Tokei Geppo *see* Japan. Statistics Bureau. Management and Coordination Agency. Monthly Statistics of Japan **8382**

Nihon Tokei Kyokai. Rodoryoku Chosa Nenpo *see* Japan. Statistics Bureau. Management and Coordination Agency. Annual Report on the Labour Force Survey **1246**

DIRECTORY 2010 NINGBO GUANGBO DIANSHI DAXUE XUEBAO 10677

Nihon Tokei Kyokai. Rodoryoku Chosa Tokubetsu Chosa Hokoku *see* Japan. Statistics Bureau. Management and Coordination Agency. Report on the Special Survey of the Labour Force Survey (Year) **1246**
Nihon Tokei Kyokai. Sekai No Tokei (Year) (JPN ISSN 1344-0446) **8391**
Nihon Tokei Kyokai. Shohisha Bukka Shisu Geppo *see* Japan. Statistics Bureau. Management and Coordination Agency. Monthly Report on the Consumer Price Index **2642**
Nihon Tokei Kyokai. Shohisha Bukka Shisu Nenpo *see* Japan. Statistics Bureau. Management and Coordination Agency. Annual Report on the Consumer Price Index (Year) **2642**
Nihon Tokei Kyokai. Tokei de Miru Ken No Sugata (Year) (JPN ISSN 0289-131X) **8391**
Nihon Tokei Kyokai. Tokei de Miru Nippon (Year)/Japan Statistical Association. Facts and Findings About Japan by Statistical Data (Year) (JPN) **8391**
• Nihon Tokei Kyokai. Tokei Joho Indekkusu (Year)/Japan Statistical Association. Index to Statistical Data Sources (Year) (JPN) **8391**
Nihon Tokei Nenkan *see* Japan. Statistics Bureau. Management and Coordination Agency. Japan Statistical Yearbook **8382**
Nihon. Tokeikyoku Kenkyu Iho *see* Japan. Bureau of Statistics. Research Memoir **8382**
Nihon Toseki Igakkai Zasshi/Japanese Society of Dialysis Therapy. Journal (JPN ISSN 1340-3451) **6273**
Nihon Toseki Ikai Zasshi/Journal of Japan Clinical Dialysis (JPN ISSN 0914-7136) **6273**
Nihon Uirusu Gakkai Sokai Enzetsu Shoroku/Society of Japanese Virologists. Proceedings of the Annual Meeting (JPN) **894**
Nihon University. Atomic Energy Research Institute. Annual Report (JPN ISSN 0285-1989) **3171**
Nihon University. Atomic Energy Research Institute. Annual Report. Japanese Edition *see* Nihon Daigaku Genshiryoku Kenkyujo Hokoku **3171**
Nihon University. College of Industrial Technology. Journal. A *see* Nihon Daigaku Seisan Kogakubu Kenkyu Hokoku. A, Rikokei **8433**
Nihon University. College of Industrial Technology. Journal. B *see* Nihon Daigaku Seisan Kogakubu Kenkyu Hokoku. B, Bunkei **8433**
Nihon University Comparative Law (JPN ISSN 0289-8101) **4936**
Nihon University Dental Journal *see* Nichidai Shigaku **5857**
Nihon University. Economic and Commercial Research Society. Research Bulletin. Liberal Arts *see* Nihon Daigaku. Keizaigaku Kenkyukai.Kenkyu Kiyo. Ippan Kyoiku, Gaikokugo, Hoken Taiiku **2892**
Nihon University. Institute of Natural Sciences. Proceedings *see* Nihon Daigaku Bunrigakubu Shizen Kagaku Kenkyujo Kenkyu Kiyo **7892**
Nihon University. Institute of Natural Sciences. Proceedings. Geosystem Sciences *see* Nihon Daigaku Bunrigakubu Shizen Kagaku Kenkyujo Kenkyu Kiyo. Chikyu System Kagaku **2714**
Nihon University Journal of Business *see* Shogaku Shushi **1174**
Nihon University Journal of Medicine (JPN ISSN 0546-0352) **5687**
Nihon University. Journal of Oral Science *see* Nichidai Koku Kagaku **5857**
Nihon University Medical Association. Journal *see* Nichidai Igaku Zasshi **5686**
Nihon University. Research Institute of Science and Technology. Journal *see* Nihon Daigaku Rikogaku Kenkyujo Shoho **8433**
Nihon University. Research Institute of Science and Technology. Proceedings of Meeting *see* Nihon Daigaku Rikogakubu Gakujutsu Koenkai Koen Ronbunshu **8433**
Nihon University. Research Institute of Science and Technology. Report (JPN ISSN 0370-7024) **7892**
Nihon University. Research Institute of Technology. Report *see* Nihon University. Research Institute of Science and Technology. Report **7892**
Nihon Yacho no Kai Kenkyu Hokoku *see* Strix **915**
Nihon Yakkyokuho Foramu/Japanese Pharmacopoeial Forum (JPN ISSN 1344-6541) **6864**
Nihon Yasei Dobutsu Igakukaishi *see* Japanese Journal of Zoo and Wildlife Medicine **8800**
Nihon Yoton Gakkaishi/Japanese Journal of Swine Science (JPN ISSN 0913-882X) **295**
• Nihon Yotsu Gakkai Zasshi/Japanese Society for Lumbar Spine Disorders. Journal (JPN ISSN 1345-9074) **6068**
Nihon Yougo Kyouyu Kyouiku Gakkaishi/Japanese Association of Yogo Teacher Education. Journal (JPN ISSN 1343-9693) **3044**
Nihon Yuki Kogakkai Taikai Ronbun Hokokushu (JPN ISSN 0916-6750) **3212**
Nihon Yuki Kogakkaishi/Journal of Snow Engineering (JPN ISSN 0913-3526) **3212**
Nihon Zairyou Kagakkaishi *see* Zairyou no Kagaku to Kougaku **3360**
Nihon Zaitaku Igakkai Zasshi/Japanese Academy of Home Care Physicians. Journal (JPN ISSN 1345-3777) **5687**
• Nihon Zenkoku Shoshi/Japanese National Bibliography Weekly List (JPN ISSN 0389-4002) **632**
Nihon Zosen Gakkai Ronbunshu/Society of Naval Architects of Japan. Journal *see* Nihon Sempaku Kaiyou Kougakkai Rombunshuu **8655**
Nihongo (JPN ISSN 0916-0574) **5155**
Nihongo Bumpou/Journal of Japanese Grammar (JPN ISSN 1346-8057) **5155**
• Nihongo Journal (JPN ISSN 0912-5361) **5155**
Nihongo Kyoiku/Journal of Japanese Language Teaching (JPN ISSN 0389-4037) **5155**
Nihongogaku (JPN ISSN 0288-0822) **5155**
Nihonkai Chiiki no Shizen to Kankyo/Fukui University. Research and Education Center for Regional Environment. Memoirs (JPN ISSN 1343-084X) **3456**
➤ Nihonkai Mathematical Journal (JPN ISSN 1341-9951) **5520**
Nihonkaiiki Kenkyujo Hokoku/Kanazawa University. Japan Sea Research Institute. Bulletin (JPN ISSN 0287-623X) **2814**
Nihonshi Kenkyu/Journal of Japanese History (JPN ISSN 0386-8850) **4187**
Nihul (ISR ISSN 0333-5658) **1781**
Niigata Airglow Observatory. Bulletin (JPN ISSN 0388-0125) **7028**
Niigata College of Pharmacy and Applied Life Sciences. Bulletin *see* Niigata Yakka Daigaku Kenkyu Hokoku **6864**
Niigata Daigaku Keizai Ronshu/Journal of Economics, Niigata University (JPN ISSN 0286-1569) **1154**
Niigata Daigaku Kogakubu Kenkyu Hokoku/Niigata University. Faculty of Engineering. Research Report (JPN ISSN 0374-4345) **3212**
Niigata Daigaku Kyoikugakubu Kiyo. Shizen Kagaku Hen/Niigata University. Faculty of Education. Memoirs. Natural Sciences (JPN ISSN 0288-3422) **7893**
Niigata Daigaku Nogakubu Kenkyu Hokoku/Niigata University. Faculty of Agriculture. Bulletin (JPN ISSN 0385-8634) **140**
• ➤ Niigata Daigaku Rigakubu Fuzoku Sado Rinkai Jikkenjo Kenkyu Hokoku/Niigata University. Sado Marine Biological Station. Annual Activity Report (JPN ISSN 1343-1633) **694**
Niigata Daigaku Rigakubu Kenkyu Hokoku. E-rui, Chishitsu Kobutsugaku *see* Niigata University. Faculty of Science. Science Reports. Series E: Geology and Mineralogy **2759**
Niigata Igakkai Zasshi/Niigata Medical Journal (JPN ISSN 0029-0440) **5687**
Niigata Investigation and Design Office. News *see* Chosetsu Koho Niigata **3360**
Niigata Kogyo Tanki Daigaku Kenkyu Kiyo/Niigata Technical Junior College. Journal (JPN ISSN 0913-7912) **8433**
Niigata Medical Journal *see* Niigata Igakkai Zasshi **5687**
Niigata Prefectural Biological Society for Education. Bulletin *see* Niigataken Seibutsu Kyoiku Kenkyukaishi **694**
Niigata Prefecture. Monthly Report of Meteorology *see* Niigataken Kisho Geppo **6392**
Niigata Rikagaku/Journal of Physics and Chemistry of Niigata (JPN ISSN 0286-7125) **7028**
Niigata Seikei Geka Kenkyukai Kaishi/Niigata Society for Orthopaedic Surgery. Archives (JPN ISSN 0914-6636) **6068**
Niigata Shell Club. Report *see* Shibukitsubo **963**
Niigata Society for Orthopaedic Surgery. Archives *see* Niigata Seikei Geka Kenkyukai Kaishi **6068**
Niigata Technical Junior College. Journal *see* Niigata Kogyo Tanki Daigaku Kenkyu Kiyo **8433**
Niigata University. Faculty of Agriculture. Bulletin *see* Niigata Daigaku Nogakubu Kenkyu Hokoku **140**
Niigata University. Faculty of Education. Memoirs. Natural Sciences *see* Niigata Daigaku Kyoikugakubu Kiyo. Shizen Kagaku Hen **7893**
Niigata University. Faculty of Engineering. Research Report *see* Niigata Daigaku Kogakubu Kenkyu Hokoku **3212**
Niigata University. Faculty of Science. Science Reports. Series B: Physics (JPN ISSN 0371-2699) **7028**
Niigata University. Faculty of Science. Science Reports. Series C: Chemistry (JPN ISSN 0369-4356) **2075**
Niigata University. Faculty of Science. Science Reports. Series E: Geology and Mineralogy/Niigata Daigaku Rigakubu Kenkyu Hokoku. E-rui, Chishitsu Kobutsugaku (JPN ISSN 0369-5638) **2759**
Niigata University. Sado Marine Biological Station. Annual Activity Report *see* Niigata Daigaku Rigakubu Fuzoku Sado Rinkai Jikkenjo Kenkyu Hokoku **694**
Niigata University. Sado Marine Biological Station. Report *see* Niigata Daigaku Rigakubu Fuzoku Sado Rinkai Jikkenjo Kenkyu Hokoku **694**
Niigata Yakka Daigaku Kenkyu Hokoku/Niigata College of Pharmacy and Applied Life Sciences. Bulletin (JPN ISSN 0285-3663) **6864**
Niigataken Kisho Geppo/Niigata Prefecture. Monthly Report of Meteorology (JPN) **6392**
Niigataken Seibutsu Kyoiku Kenkyukaishi/Niigata Prefectural Biological Society for Education. Bulletin (JPN ISSN 0388-7154) **694**
Niihama Kogyo Koto Senmon Gakko Kiyo. Rikogaku Hen/Niihama National College of Technology. Memoirs. Science and Engineering (JPN ISSN 0286-2743) **8433**
Niihama National College of Technology. Memoirs. Science and Engineering *see* Niihama Kogyo Koto Senmon Gakko Kiyo. Rikogaku Hen **8433**
Nijgh Assu Disc *see* Vademecum voor het Verzekeringswezen **4526**
Nijgh Catalogus Bouwwereld *see* Arko Catalogus Bouwwereld **976**
Nijgh Hout in de Bouw (NLD ISSN 1567-8237) **3714**
Nijgh Media Disc *see* Handboek van de Nederlandse Pers en Publiciteit **626**
➤ Nijhoff International Philosophy Series (NLD ISSN 0924-4530) **6936**
➤ Nijhoff Law Specials (NLD ISSN 0924-4549) **4747**
Nijmeegs Katern (NLD ISSN 0927-4642) **4248**
• Nijmegen C N S (NLD ISSN 1872-1427) **6171**
Nijmegen Studies in Development and Cultural Change (DEU) **8123**
Nijsblad veur t Grunneger Pladdelaand (NLD ISSN 1874-060X) **4421**
† Nika (CZE ISSN 0862-514X) **8977**
Nikephoros (DEU ISSN 0934-8913) **4154**
Nikephoros-Beihefte (DEU ISSN 0944-4327) **4154**
Niki (AUT) **8785**
Nikkakyo Geppo/Japan Chemical Industry Association Monthly (JPN ISSN 0029-0483) **3251**
Nikkan Denki Tsushin/Daily Electricity News (JPN) **3326**
Nikkan Kogyo Shimbun/Business & Technology Daily News (JPN) **1154**
Nikkan Koku Tsushin/Aviation Daily Japan (JPN) **1154**
Nikkei. Annual Corporation Reports (Listed Companies) (JPN) **1371**
Nikkei. Annual Corporation Reports (Unlisted Companies) (JPN) **1371**
Nikkei Annual Financial Report (JPN) **1371**
Nikkei. Annual Foreign Corporation Reports (JPN) **1154**
Nikkei Architecture (JPN ISSN 0385-0870) **451**
Nikkei Baioteku *see* Nikkei Biotechnology **769**
Nikkei Best P C (JPN ISSN 1341-9919) **2578**
• Nikkei Bijinesu/Nikkei Business (JPN ISSN 0029-0491) **1501**
Nikkei Biotechnology/Nikkei Baioteku (JPN ISSN 0285-4600) **769**
Nikkei Board Guide (JPN) **3109**
Nikkei Business *see* Nikkei Bijinesu **1501**
Nikkei Byte (JPN ISSN 0289-6508) **2578**
Nikkei C G *see* Nikkei Computer Graphics **2489**
Nikkei Click (JPN ISSN 1340-8372) **2578**
Nikkei Communications (JPN ISSN 0910-7215) **2335**
Nikkei Computer (JPN ISSN 0285-4619) **2433**
Nikkei Computer Graphics (JPN ISSN 0912-1609) **2489**
Nikkei Construction (JPN ISSN 0915-3470) **3279**
Nikkei Corporate Guide (JPN) **2021**
Nikkei Corporate Who's Who (Year) (JPN) **1154**
Nikkei Design (JPN ISSN 0913-3429) **1781**
Nikkei Digital Engineering (JPN) **3293**
Nikkei Digital Kensetsu (JPN) **462**
Nikki Drug Information (JPN) **6864**
Nikkei Ecology (JPN ISSN 1344-9001) **3456**
Nikkei Electronics (JPN ISSN 0385-1680) **3110**
Nikkei Electronics Asia (HKG ISSN 0917-429X) **3110**
Nikkei Electronics China *see* Electronic Design & Application World - Nikkei Electronics **3095**
Nikkei Entertainment! (JPN) **2565**
Nikkei Financial Analysis (Listed Companies) (JPN) **1371**
Nikkei Financial Analysis (Unlisted Companies) (JPN) **1371**
Nikkei Financial Daily *see* Nikkei Kinyu Shimbun **1371**
Nikkei Health (JPN) **6994**
Nikkei Healthcare (JPN ISSN 0915-4191) **4108**
Nikkei Home Builder (JPN ISSN 1344-901X) **1027**
Nikkei Image Climate Forecast (JPN) **30**
Nikkei Industrial Daily *see* Nikkei Sangyo Shimbun **1900**
Nikkei Information Strategy/Nikkei Joho Sutorateji (JPN ISSN 0917-5342) **2524**
Nikkei Internet Technology (JPN) **2565**
Nikkei Joho Sutorateji *see* Nikkei Information Strategy **2524**
Nikkei Kinyu Shimbun/Nikkei Financial Daily (JPN) **1371**
Nikkei Linux/Nikkei Rinakkusu (JPN ISSN 1345-0182) **2433**
Nikkei Mac (JPN ISSN 0918-8894) **2578**
Nikkei Manee (JPN) **1372**
Nikkei Marketing Journal *see* Nikkei Ryutsu Shimbun **30**
Nikkei Mechanical (JPN ISSN 0386-3638) **3391**
Nikkei Medical/Nikkei Medikaru (JPN ISSN 0385-1699) **5687**
Nikkei Medikaru *see* Nikkei Medical **5687**
Nikkei Microdevices (JPN ISSN 0910-7207) **2433**
Nikkei Mobile Computing (JPN) **2335**
• Nikkei Net Business (JPN) **5063**
Nikkei Net Interactive *see* The Nikkei Weekly **1154**
Nikkei Net Trading (JPN) **1420**
Nikkei Netnavigator (JPN ISSN 1342-0100) **2565**
Nikkei Network (JPN) **2433**
Nikkei Open Systems (JPN ISSN 0918-581X) **2573**
Nikkei P C 21 (JPN ISSN 1341-9900) **2578**
Nikkei P C Beginners 21 (JPN) **2578**
Nikkei Personal Computing (JPN ISSN 0287-9506) **2578**
Nikkei Placement Guide (JPN) **6701**
Nikkei Quarterly Newsletter on Commodities (JPN) **1836**
Nikkei Regional Economic Report (JPN ISSN 0912-3881) **1154**
Nikkei Restaurants (JPN ISSN 0914-7845) **4394**
Nikkei Rinakkusu *see* Nikkei Linux **2433**
Nikkei Ryutsu Shimbun/Nikkei Marketing Journal (JPN) **30**
Nikkei Saiensu (JPN ISSN 0917-009X) **7893**
Nikkei Sangyo Shimbun/Nikkei Industrial Daily (JPN) **1900**
Nikkei Software (JPN) **2509**
Nikkei System Provider (JPN) **2493**
Nikkei Techno Frontier (JPN) **8433**
Nikkei Trendy (JPN) **1900**
Nikkei Venture (JPN ISSN 0289-6516) **1964**
Nikkei Venture Business Almanac (JPN) **1154**
• The Nikkei Weekly (JPN ISSN 0918-5348) **1154**
Nikkei Weekly Newsletter on Commodities (JPN) **1836**
Nikkei Windows N T (JPN) **2595**
Nikkei WinPC (JPN ISSN 1341-1497) **2578**
Nikkei Woman (JPN) **8877**
• Nikki Style (USA) **5078**
Nikkiren Geppo/Japan Machinery Federation. Monthly (JPN ISSN 0912-0866) **5457**
Nikko Foramu/Nikko Producer - Goods Forum (JPN ISSN 0388-709X) **1900**
Nikko Forum (JPN) **1154**
Nikko Producer - Goods Forum *see* Nikko Foramu **1900**
Nikkyoso Kyoiku Shinbun (JPN ISSN 0029-0505) **2892**
Nikol'skoe Kol'tso (RUS) **3938**
Nikon Pro (GBR ISSN 1365-6821) **6972**
Nile Mirror (SDN) **3954**
The Nilson Report (USA ISSN 1087-8718) **1372**
Nilus (ESP ISSN 1133-5343) **4177**
Nimbus (ESP ISSN 1139-7136) **4022**
Nimbus (ITA ISSN 1122-4339) **6392**
Nimitz Lectures (USA) **7255**
• Nimmer on Copyright (USA) **6755**
➤ Nimrod International Journal (USA ISSN 1931-1214) **5341**
Nina (BEL) **8877**
Ninad (IND ISSN 0973-3787) **6599**
Ninad Highlights *see* Ninad **6599**
• Ninchi Kagaku/Cognitive Studies (JPN ISSN 1341-7924) **6171**
• ➤ Nine (USA ISSN 1188-9330) **8240**
Nine Five One Plus *see* 951+ **3993**
Nine Five One Southwest *see* 951 S.W. **3993**
Nine Four Four *see* 944 **8777**
Nine Hundred Four *see* 904 **1199**
Nine Magazine *see* 9 Magazine **8614**
Nine N - Two N - Eight N - NAA Newsletter *see* 9N - 2N - 8N - NAA Newsletter **215**
• Nine O'Clock (ROM ISSN 1220-9376) **3933**
Nine One One and Porsche World *see* 911 and Porsche World **8614**
Nine-One-One Magazine *see* 9-1-1 Magazine **2346**
Nine to Five National Association of Working Women *see* 9 to 5 National Association of Working Women **1717**
Nineteen *see* 19 (London, 2005) **5405**
Nineteen Thirty Two Buick Registry *see* 1932 Buick Registry **369**
• ➤ Nineteenth-Century Art Worldwide (USA ISSN 1543-1002) **509**
• Nineteenth Century Bibliographic Records (USA ISSN 1353-1980) **632**
• ➤ Nineteenth-Century Contexts (GBR ISSN 0890-5495) **5341**
• ➤ Nineteenth Century French Studies (USA ISSN 0146-7891) **5342**
• Nineteenth Century Gender Studies (USA ISSN 1556-7524) **8901**
• ➤ Nineteenth-Century Literature (Berkeley) (USA ISSN 0891-9356) **5342**
• Nineteenth-Century Literature Criticism (USA ISSN 0732-1864) **5342**
Nineteenth Century Literature in English *see* 19 Se'gi Yeong'eo'gwon Munhag **5405**
• ➤ Nineteenth Century Music (USA ISSN 0148-2076) **6599**
➤ Nineteenth-Century Music Review (GBR ISSN 1479-4098) **6599**
➤ Nineteenth-Century Prose (USA ISSN 1052-0406) **5342**
The Nineteenth Century Series (GBR) **5342**
➤ Nineteenth-Century Studies (USA ISSN 0893-7931) **5342**
• Nineteenth Century Theatre and Film (GBR ISSN 1748-3727) **8474**
Ninety-five per Cent *see* 95 Per Cent **2224**
Ninety Minutes *see* 90 Minutes **8252**
Ninety-Nine News (USA ISSN 0273-608X) **67**
Ninety-six Inc *see* 96 Inc **5406**
Nineveh (USA ISSN 0749-5919) **4324**
• Ningbo Daxue Xuebao (Ligong Ban)/Ningbo University. Journal (Natural Science and Engineering Edition) (CHN ISSN 1001-5132) **7893**
• Ningbo Daxue Xuebao (Renwen Kexue Ban)/Ningbo University. Journal (Liberal Arts Edition) (CHN ISSN 1001-5124) **7989**
• Ningbo Gongcheng Xueyuan Xuebao/Ningbo University of Technology. Journal (CHN) **8433**
• Ningbo Guangbo Dianshi Daxue Xuebao/Ningbo Radio & TV University. Journal (CHN) **2361**

Title

10678 NINGBO INSTITUTE OF EDUCATION. JOURNAL ULRICH'S PERIODICALS

Ningbo Institute of Education. Journal *see* Ningbo Jiaoyu Xueyuan Xuebao **7989**
• Ningbo Jiaoyu Xueyuan Xuebao/Ningbo Institute of Education. Journal (CHN ISSN 1009-2560) **7989**
Ningbo Polytechnic. Journal *see* Ningbo Zhiye Jishu Xueyuan Xuebao **7989**
Ningbo Radio & TV University. Journal *see* Ningbo Guangbo Dianshi Daxue Xuebao **2361**
Ningbo University. Journal (Liberal Arts Edition) *see* Ningbo Daxue Xuebao (Renwen Kexue Ban) **7989**
Ningbo University. Journal (Natural Science and Engineering Edition) *see* Ningbo Daxue Xuebao (Ligong Ban) **7893**
Ningbo University of Technology. Journal *see* Ningbo Gongcheng Xueyuan Xuebao **8433**
• Ningbo Zhiye Jishu Xueyuan Xuebao/Ningbo Polytechnic. Journal (CHN ISSN 1671-2153) **7989**
Ningde Shi-Zhuan Xuebao (Ziran Kexueban)/Ningde Teachers College. Journal (Natural Science) (CHN ISSN 1004-2911) **7893**
Ningde Teachers College. Journal (Natural Science) *see* Ningde Shi-Zhuan Xuebao (Ziran Kexueban) **7893**
Ningen Bunka Kenkyu/Hiroshima University. Faculty of Integrated Arts and Science. Bulletin (JPN ISSN 0918-7782) **4466**
Ningen Bunka Kenkyu Nempo (JPN ISSN 0911-5250) **4466**
Ningen Bunka Ronso/Ochanomizu University. Graduate School of Humanities and Sciences. Journal (JPN ISSN 1344-8013) **4467**
Ningen Bunkakei Sizen Kagakukei Bumon Kiyou/Dokkyo University School of Medicine. Bulletin of Humanities and Natural Sciences (JPN ISSN 1348-9917) **4467**
Ningen Igaku/Human Medicine (JPN ISSN 0029-0572) **6664**
Ningen Kagaku Kenkyu/Studies in Human Sciences (JPN ISSN 1345-2975) **7893**
Ningen Kagaku Kenkyu/Wasada Journal of Human Sciences (JPN ISSN 1880-0270) **350**
Ningen Kaigi (JPN) **7989**
Ningen Kogaku/Japanese Journal of Ergonomics (JPN ISSN 0549-4974) **1700**
Ningen Shokubutsu Kankei Gakkai Zasshi/Japanese Society of People - Plant Relationships. Journal (JPN ISSN 1346-7336) **805**
• ➤ Ningxia Daxue Xuebao (Shehui Kexue Ban)/Ningxia University Journal (Philosophy and Social Science Edition) (CHN ISSN 1001-5744) **7989**
• ➤ Ningxia Daxue Xuebao. (Ziran Kexue Ban)/Ningxia University. Journal (Natural Science Edition) (CHN ISSN 0253-2328) **7893**
Ningxia Engineering Technology *see* Ningxia Gongcheng Jishu **3212**
• Ningxia Gongcheng Jishu/Ningxia Engineering Technology (CHN ISSN 1671-7244) **3212**
Ningxia Gongxueyuan Xuebao/Ningxia Institute of Technology. Journal *see* Ningxia Daxue Xuebao. (Ziran Kexue Ban) **7893**
Ningxia Medical College. Journal *see* Ningxia Yixueyuan Xuebao **5687**
Ningxia Medical Journal *see* Ningxia Yixue Zazhi **5687**
Ningxia Nongxueyuan Xuebao/Ningxia Agricultural College. Journal *see* Nongye Kexue Yanjiu **141**
• Ningxia Shehui Kexue/Social Science in Ningxia (CHN ISSN 1002-0292) **7989**
• Ningxia Shifan Xueyuan Xuebao/Ningxia Teachers University. Journal (CHN ISSN 1674-1331) **7989**
Ningxia Teachers University. Journal *see* Ningxia Shifan Xueyuan Xuebao **7989**
Ningxia University. Journal (Natural Science Edition) *see* Ningxia Daxue Xuebao. (Ziran Kexue Ban) **7893**
Ningxia University Journal (Philosophy and Social Science Edition) *see* Ningxia Daxue Xuebao (Shehui Kexue Ban) **7989**
• Ningxia Yixue Zazhi/Ningxia Medical Journal (CHN ISSN 1001-5949) **5687**
• Ningxia Yixueyuan Xuebao/Ningxia Medical College. Journal (CHN ISSN 1005-8486) **5687**
Ninnau (USA ISSN 0890-0485) **3554**
El Nino (ESP ISSN 1135-6901) **7388**
• El Nino Southern Oscillation Diagnostic Advisory (USA) **2622**
• Nino Update (CHE) **6392**
Ninsmoda (ESP ISSN 1136-3630) **2259**
Nintendo (ITA ISSN 1594-9389) **2478**
Nintendo 64 Magazine (GBR ISSN 1366-6266) **2479**
Nintendo Accion (ESP) **2479**
Nintendo Magazine (FRA ISSN 1633-0684) **2479**
Nintendo Official Magazine *see* Official Nintendo **2479**
Nintendo Power (USA ISSN 1041-9551) **2479**
Nintendo Revolution *see* n - Revolution **8189**
Ninth Circuit Manual of Model Jury Instructions: Criminal *see* Manual of Model Criminal Jury Instructions **4893**
Ninth District Dental Association. Bulletin (USA) **5857**
Ninth District Dental Society. Bulletin *see* Ninth District Dental Association. Bulletin **5857**
Ninth Letter (USA ISSN 1547-8440) **5342**
Ninth Street Center Journal (USA ISSN 0895-5239) **4377**
Niobium Update (USA) **6327**
• Nioi Kaori Kankyou Gakkaishi/Japan Association on Odor Environment. Journal (JPN ISSN 1348-2904) **7893**
Nipmuc Indian Association of Connecticut. Historical Series (USA) **6636**
• Nipperdey Plus Arbeitsrecht (DEU) **4824**
Nippon Acta Radiologica *see* Nippon Igaku Hoshasen Gakkai Zasshi **6204**
Nippon Biseibutsu Kabu Hozon Renmei Kaishi/Japan Federation for Culture Collections. Bulletin (JPN ISSN 0911-6788) **694**
Nippon Biyo Geka Gakkaishi/Japan Society of Aesthetic Surgery. Journal (JPN ISSN 0387-9194) **6253**
Nippon Chugoku Gakkaiho/Bulletin of the Sinological Society of Japan (JPN ISSN 0387-3196) **4187**
Nippon Daicho Komonbyo Gakkai Zasshi/Japan Society of Colo-Proctology. Journal (JPN ISSN 0047-1801) **5930**
Nippon Dobutsu Kodo Gakkai Taikai Happyo Yoshishu/Japan Ethological Society. Abstracts of Meeting (JPN ISSN 0917-5725) **717**
Nippon Dojo Hiryogaku Zasshi/Japanese Journal of Soil Science and Plant Nutrition (JPN ISSN 0029-0610) **243**
Nippon Eiyo Shokuryo Gakkaishi/Japanese Society of Nutrition and Food Science. Journal (JPN ISSN 0287-3516) **6664**
Nippon Electric Company Giho *see* N E C Giho **3326**
Nippon Electric Company News *see* N E C News **2432**
Nippon Electric Company Research and Development *see* N E C Research and Development **8975**
Nippon Electric Company Technical Journal *see* N E C Technical Journal **8432**
Nippon Electric Company Update *see* N E C Update **3326**
Nippon Eya Bureki K.K. Giho *see* N A B U K O Giho **3390**
Nippon Fernist Club. Journal *see* Nippon Shida no Kai Kaiho **805**
Nippon Gaishi K.K. Genshiryoku Giho *see* N G K Genshiryoku Giho **3171**
Nippon Gaishi K.K. Rebyu *see* N G K Rebyu **7052**
Nippon Gaishi K.K. Review. Overseas Edition *see* N G K Review. Overseas Edition **7052**
Nippon Gakushiin Kiyo/Japan Academy. Transactions (JPN ISSN 0388-0036) **7989**
Nippon Gakushiin Kiyo A *see* Japan Academy. Proceedings. Series A: Mathematical Sciences **5499**
Nippon Gakushiin Kiyo B *see* Japan Academy. Proceedings. Series B: Physical and Biological Sciences **7870**
➤ Nippon Ganka Gakkai Zasshi/Japanese Ophthalmological Society. Journal (JPN ISSN 0029-0203) **6046**
Nippon Ganka Kiyo/Folia Ophthalmologica Japonica *see* Japanese Society for Low-Vision Research and Rehabilitation. Journal **6044**
Nippon Geijutsu Ryoho Gakkaishi/Japanese Bulletin of Arts Therapy (JPN ISSN 0916-6688) **509**
Nippon Geka Gakkai Zasshi/Japan Surgical Society. Journal (JPN ISSN 0301-4894) **6253**
Nippon Genshiryoku Gakkaishi/Atomic Energy Society of Japan. Journal *see* Atomos **3165**
Nippon Genshiryoku Kenkyusho Kenkyu Hokoku/J A E R I Research Report *see* J A E A - Research **3169**
Nippon Ginko Chosa Geppo/Bank of Japan Monthly Bulletin (JPN) **1372**
Nippon Ginko Seisaku Iinkai Geppo/Bank of Japan. Policy Board. Monthly Report (JPN) **1372**
Nippon Gyosei Kenkyu Nenpo/Japanese Society for Public Administration. Annals (JPN ISSN 0548-1570) **7457**
Nippon Herpetological Journal *see* Ryosei Hachurui Kenkyukaishi **962**
Nippon Hoigaku Zasshi (JPN ISSN 0047-1887) **5916**
• Nippon Hoshasen Gijutsu Gakkai Zasshi/Japanese Journal of Radiological Technology (JPN ISSN 0369-4305) **7069**
Nippon Hoso Kyokai Giken R & D *see* N H K Giken R & D **2386**
Nippon Hoso Kyokai Hoso Gijutsu Kenkyujo Kenkyu Nenpo/N H K Science and Technical Research Laboratories. Annual Report (JPN) **2386**
Nippon Hoso Kyokai Hoso Hakubutsukan Dayori *see* N H K Hoso Hakubutsukan Dayori **2386**
Nippon Hoso Kyokai Laboratories Note *see* N H K Laboratories Note **2386**
Nippon Ibaraki Chikusan Shikenjo. Chikusan Shikenjo Kenkyu Hokoku *see* Japan. Ibaraki National Institute of Animal Industry. Bulletin **290**
Nippon Ibaraki Chikusan Shikenjo Nenpo *see* Japan. Ibaraki National Institute of Animal Industry. Annual Report **290**
• Nippon Igaku Hoshasen Gakkai Zasshi/Nippon Acta Radiologica (JPN ISSN 0048-0428) **6204**
Nippon Insatsu Shinbun/Japan Printing News (JPN) **7325**
Nippon Institute for Biological Science. Newsletter *see* Nisseiken Tayori **694**
Nippon Institute of Technology. Report of Researches *see* Nippon Kogyo Daigaku Knkyu Hokoku **7893**
• Nippon Ishinkin Gakkai Zasshi/Japanese Journal of Medical Mycology (JPN ISSN 0916-4804) **894**
Nippon Jinrui Gakkai Kineshioroji Bunkakai Nyusureta/Anthropological Society of Nippon. Division of Kinesiology. Newsletter (JPN) **350**
Nippon Jozo Kyokaishi/Brewing Society of Japan. Journal (JPN ISSN 0914-7314) **608**
Nippon Kagakkai Koen Yokoshu/Chemical Society of Japan. Preprints of the Conference (JPN ISSN 0285-7626) **2075**
Nippon Kakin Gakkaishi *see* Journal of Poultry Science **291**
Nippon Kayaku. Annual Report (JPN) **6864**
Nippon Kayaku Research Laboratories. Annual Report *see* Nippon Kayaku Sogo Kenkyujo Nenpo **6864**
Nippon Kayaku Sogo Kenkyujo Nenpo/Nippon Kayaku Research Laboratories. Annual Report (JPN) **6864**
Nippon Kikinzoku Tokei Shinbun/Japan Precious Metals and Watch News (JPN ISSN 0029-0653) **4568**
Nippon Kin Gakkai Nyusu/Mycological Society of Japan. News (JPN ISSN 0913-7955) **805**
• ➤ Nippon Kinzoku Gakkaishi/Japan Institute of Metals. Journal (JPN ISSN 0021-4876) **6327**
Nippon Kitte Nyt (SWE ISSN 1603-2985) **6897**
Nippon Kogyo Daigaku Knkyu Hokoku/Nippon Institute of Technology. Report of Researches (JPN ISSN 0389-2514) **7893**
Nippon Kokan K.K. News *see* N K K News **3390**
Nippon Koku Geka Gakkai Zasshi/Japanese Journal of Oral and Maxillofacial Surgery (JPN ISSN 0021-5163) **5857**
Nippon Koku Shimbun/Japan Aviation News (JPN) **8549**
• Nippon Laser Igakkaishi/Japan Society for Laser Medicine. Journal (JPN ISSN 0288-6200) **5687**
• ➤ Nippon Medical School. Journal (JPN ISSN 1345-4676) **5687**
Nippon no Kikogaku no Shinpo *see* Japanese Progress in Climatology **6358**
Nippon Nogeikagaku Kaishi/Agricultural Chemical Society of Japan. Journal *see* Kagaku to Seibutsu **737**
Nippon Noyaku Gakkaishi *see* Journal of Pesticide Science **3248**
Nippon Rinsho/Japanese Journal of Clinical Medicine (JPN ISSN 0047-1852) **5687**
• Nippon Rinsho Saibo Gakkai Zasshi (JPN ISSN 0387-1193) **5687**
• Nippon Seikei Geka Gakkai Zasshi/Japanese Orthopaedic Association. Journal (JPN ISSN 0021-5325) **6068**
Nippon Seiko K.K. Technical Journal *see* N S K Technical Journal **3211**
Nippon Seisaku Toshi Ginko. Chosabu. Chosa/Development Bank of Japan. Research Report (JPN ISSN 1345-1308) **1372**
• Nippon Seitai Gakkaishi/Japanese Journal of Ecology (JPN ISSN 0021-5007) **3456**
Nippon Seramikkusu Kyokai Gakujutsu Ronbunshi *see* Ceramic Society of Japan. Journal **2039**
Nippon Sharyo Technical Review *see* Nissha Giho **8595**
Nippon Shida no Kai Kaiho/Nippon Fernist Club. Journal (JPN ISSN 0287-3257) **805**
Nippon Shingo Giho/Nippon Signal Technical Journal (JPN ISSN 0387-0235) **2335**
➤ Nippon Shokuhin Kagaku Kogaku Kaishi/Japanese Society for Food Science and Technology. Journal (JPN ISSN 1341-027X) **3658**
Nippon Shonika Gakkai Zasshi *see* Pediatrics International **6102**
Nippon Signal Technical Journal *see* Nippon Shingo Giho **2335**
Nippon Sochi Gakkai-shi *see* Grassland Science **233**
Nippon Steel Forum (JPN) **6327**
Nippon Steel News (JPN ISSN 0048-0452) **6327**
Nippon Steel Report (JPN) **6327**
Nippon Steel Technical Report (JPN ISSN 0300-306X) **6327**
• ➤ Nippon Suisan Gakkaishi/Japanese Society of Scientific Fisheries. Bulletin (JPN ISSN 0021-5392) **3603**
Nippon Tekko Kyokai International *see* I S I J International **6315**
Nippon Telegraph and Telephone Do Co Mo Technical Journal *see* N T T Do Co Mo Technical Journal **2334**
Nippon Telegraph and Telephone Gijutsu Janaru *see* N T T Gijutsu Janaru **2370**
Nippon Telegraph and Telephone Research and Development *see* N T T R & D **2370**
Nippon Telegraph and Telephone Technical Review *see* N T T Technical Review **2334**
Nippon Thompson Company. Annual Report (JPN) **5458**
• ➤ Nippon Toshokan Joho Gakkai-shi/Japan Society of Library and Information Science. Journal (JPN ISSN 1344-8668) **5036**
Nippon Tungsten Review (JPN ISSN 0388-0664) **2117**
• Nippon Valqua Industries, Ltd. Annual Report (JPN) **1154**
• ➤ Nippon Veterinary and Life Science University. Bulletin (JPN) **8803**
Nippon Veterinary and Zootechnical College. Bulletin *see* Nippon Veterinary and Life Science University. Bulletin **8803**
Nippon Yakurigaku Zasshi *see* Folia Pharmacologica Japonica (Kyoto, 1944) **6842**
Nippon Yakuzaishikai Zasshi/Japan Pharmaceutical Association. Journal (JPN ISSN 0369-674X) **6864**
Nippon Yuketsu Gakkai Zasshi/Japan Society of Blood Transfusion. Journal (JPN ISSN 0546-1448) **5940**
Nippon Yusen. Annual Report (JPN) **8655**
Nippon Yusoki Company. News *see* Nichiyu Nyusu **3391**
Nippon Zairyo Kyodo Gakkaishi/Japanese Society for Strength and Fracture of Materials. Journal (JPN ISSN 0286-4010) **3355**
• Nipponia (JPN ISSN 1343-1196) **3900**
Nipponia, Discovering Japan *see* Nipponia **3900**
Nips (GBR ISSN 1365-8875) **6812**
Nipun (BGD) **3800**
Nir Va-Telem (ISR) **243**
Niranjan (IND ISSN 0029-0688) **3886**
Nirvana Woman (USA ISSN 1942-132X) **8877**
† Nisaba (NLD ISSN 0169-930X) **8977**
Nisf al-Dunya/Half the World (EGY) **3836**
• Nisha Yanjiu/Journal of Sediment Research (CHN ISSN 0468-155X) **2714**
Nishi Nihon Hinyokika/Nishinihon Journal of Urology (JPN ISSN 0029-0726) **6273**
Nishinhon Kaikyo Junpo/Ten-Day Marine Report of the East China Sea (JPN) **6392**
Nishinihon Ganban Kogaku Shinpojumu Ronbunshu/Proceedings of West Japan Symposium on Rock Engineering (JPN ISSN 0917-2580) **3279**
• Nishinihon Hifuka/Nishinihon Journal of Dermatology (JPN ISSN 0386-9784) **5880**
Nishinihon Journal of Dermatology *see* Nishinihon Hifuka **5880**
Nishinihon Journal of Urology *see* Nishi Nihon Hinyokika **6273**
Nishinihon Sekitsui Kenkyukaishi/Western Japanese Research Society for Spine. Journal (JPN ISSN 0287-1092) **6068**
Nishinippon Institute of Technology. Memoirs. Science and Technology *see* Nishinippon Kogyo Daigaku Kiyo. Rikogaku Hen **8433**
Nishinippon Kogyo Daigaku Kiyo. Rikogaku Hen/Nishinippon Institute of Technology. Memoirs. Science and Technology (JPN ISSN 0910-6227) **8433**
Nishinomiya Municipal Central Hospital. Bulletin *see* Nishinomiya Shiritsu Chuo Byoin Kiyo **4108**
Nishinomiya Shiritsu Chuo Byoin Kiyo/Nishinomiya Municipal Central Hospital. Bulletin (JPN ISSN 0914-8574) **4108**
Nishishiba Denki/Nishishiba Review (JPN) **3326**
Nishishiba Review *see* Nishishiba Denki **3326**
Nispaksh Bharat Doot (IND) **3886**
Nissan Aktuell (AUT) **8595**
Nissan Construction. Technical Department. Technical Report *see* Nissan Kensetsu. Gijutsu Honbu. Gijutsu Repoto **3279**
Nissan Construction. Technological Report *see* Nissan Kensetsu. Gijutsu Honbu. Tekunikaru Repoto **1027**
Nissan Diesel Technical Review (JPN ISSN 0029-0734) **8595**
Nissan Kagaku Shinko Zaidan Jigyo Hokokusho/Nissan Science Foundation. Annual Report (JPN ISSN 0914-1340) **7893**
Nissan Kagaku Shinko Zaidan Kenkyu Hokokusho/Nissan Science Foundation. Research Projects in Review (JPN ISSN 0911-4572) **7893**
Nissan Kensetsu. Gijutsu Honbu. Gijutsu Repoto/Nissan Construction. Technical Department. Technical Report (JPN) **3279**
Nissan Kensetsu. Gijutsu Honbu. Tekunikaru Repoto/Nissan Construction. Technological Report (JPN) **1027**
Nissan Science Foundation. Annual Report *see* Nissan Kagaku Shinko Zaidan Jigyo Hokokusho **7893**
Nissan Science Foundation. Research Projects in Review *see* Nissan Kagaku Shinko Zaidan Kenkyu Hokokusho **7893**
Nissan Sport (USA ISSN 1934-3949) **8595**
Nisse Hult (SWE ISSN 1100-763X) **7159**
Nissei Byoin Igaku Zasshi/Nissei Hospital. Journal (JPN ISSN 0301-2581) **4108**
Nissei Hospital. Journal *see* Nissei Byoin Igaku Zasshi **4108**
Nisseiken Tayori/Nippon Institute for Biological Science. Newsletter (JPN ISSN 0029-0750) **694**
Nisseki Mitsubishi Rebyu/Nisseki Mitsubishi Technical Review (Year) (JPN ISSN 1344-5871) **6781**
Nisseki Mitsubishi Technical Review (Year) *see* Nisseki Mitsubishi Rebyu **6781**
Nissha Giho/Nippon Sharyo Technical Review (JPN) **8595**
Nisshin (JPN) **6327**
Nisshin Denki Giho/Nisshin Electric Review (JPN ISSN 0549-5377) **3326**
Nisshin Electric Review *see* Nisshin Denki Giho **3326**
Nisshin Steel. Annual Report (JPN) **6327**
Nisuco Chronicle (NGA) **3658**
N!te (DEU) **2205**

Title

DIRECTORY 2010 NORIN SUISAN TOSHO SHIRYO GEPPO 10681

• ➤ The Nordic Textile Journal (SWE ISSN 1404-2487) **8456**
Nordic Theatre Studies (NOR ISSN 0904-6380) **8474**
Nordic Value Studies (NLD) **6936**
† Nordic Walker (DEU ISSN 1860-5966) **8977**
Nordica (DNK ISSN 0109-3967) **5230**
➤ Nordica Bergensia (NOR ISSN 0804-5372) **5155**
Nordicana *see* Collection Nordicana **333**
• ➤ Nordicum - Mediterraneum (ISL ISSN 1670-6242) **4467**
NordicWalker *see* Nordic Walker **8977**
➤ NorDiNa (NOR ISSN 1504-4556) **7893**
Nordis (DEU ISSN 0946-1116) **8742**
† Nordisk Administrativt Tidsskrift (DNK ISSN 0029-1285) **8977**
• ➤ Nordisk Alkohol- & Narkotikatidskrift/Nordic Studies on Alcohol and Drugs (FIN ISSN 1455-0725) **2697**
Nordisk Arkitekturforskning/Nordic Journal of Architectural Research (SWE ISSN 1102-5824) **451**
Nordisk Arkivnyt (FIN ISSN 0546-2851) **4248**
▼ • Nordisk Barnehageforskning/Early Childhood Education and Care (NOR ISSN 1890-9167) **2892**
Nordisk Domssamling *see* Tidsskrift for Rettsvitenskap **4796**
Nordisk Energi (SWE ISSN 1654-0328) **3143**
Nordisk Estetisk Tidskrift (SWE ISSN 0284-7698) **6936**
Nordisk Exlibris Tidsskrift (DNK ISSN 1604-8202) **7569**
Nordisk Filateli (SWE ISSN 0029-134X) **6897**
Nordisk Filatelistisk Tidsskrift (DNK ISSN 0903-3440) **6897**
Nordisk Filologi *see* Arkiv foer Nordisk Filologi **5096**
Nordisk Flagkontakt (NOR ISSN 0109-7539) **3777**
Nordisk Forsikringstidsskrift *see* N F T **4515**
Nordisk Genbank Husdyr Genviten *see* N G H-Genviten **294**
Nordisk Genbank Husdyr Nytt *see* N G H - Nytt **294**
Nordisk Geomatik (SWE ISSN 1653-2376) **4022**
Nordisk Geriatrik (SWE ISSN 1403-2082) **4052**
• Nordisk Haelsa (SWE) **7533**
Nordisk Herpetologisk Forening (DNK ISSN 0900-484X) **958**
Nordisk Hydrologisk Program Rapport *see* N H P Rapport **2797**
Nordisk Industri (SWE ISSN 1654-398X) **3213**
Nordisk Infrastruktur (SWE ISSN 1401-8772) **8506**
Nordisk Infrastruktur *see* Nordisk Geomatik **4022**
Nordisk Institut for Asienstudier Nytt *see* N I A S Nytt **556**
Nordisk Institut for Kvinde- og Koensforskning Magasin *see* N I K K Magasin **8901**
Nordisk Interioer (SWE ISSN 1404-2959) **4547**
Nordisk Jaernbanetidskrift (SWE ISSN 0029-1382) **8621**
Nordisk Jordbruksforskning (DNK ISSN 0048-0495) **142**
Nordisk Julemaerke Katalog (DNK ISSN 0105-9106) **6897**
Nordisk Kamp (SWE ISSN 0345-8512) **7159**
• Nordisk Kriminologi (SWE ISSN 0805-5033) **2662**
➤ Nordisk Kulturpolitisk Tidskrift (SWE ISSN 1403-3216) **4467**
Nordisk Litteratur/Nordic Literature (NOR ISSN 0908-049X) **5342**
Nordisk Makrofokus *see* Nordisk Oekonomi **1154**
➤ Nordisk Museologi (DNK ISSN 1103-8152) **6534**
Nordisk Musikkpedagogisk Forskning/Nordic Research in Music Education (NOR ISSN 1504-5021) **6600**
Nordisk Numismatisk Aarsskrift (DNK ISSN 0078-107X) **6652**
Nordisk Numismatisk Unions Medlemsblad (DNK ISSN 0025-8539) **6652**
▼ Nordisk Nutrition (SWE) **6664**
• Nordisk Oekonomi (DNK ISSN 1902-3685) **1154**
➤ Nordisk Oestforum (NOR ISSN 0801-7220) **4249**
• Nordisk Oestmission (SWE ISSN 0345-8571) **7769**
Nordisk Ostforum *see* Nordisk Oestforum **4249**
Nordisk Papper & Massa (SWE ISSN 1651-2995) **6735**
Nordisk Papperskalender *see* Nordic Paper & Pulp Makers' Directory **6735**
• Nordisk Papperstidning/Nordic Paper Journal (SWE ISSN 1651-9515) **6735**
• ➤ Nordisk Pedagogik/Pohjoismainen Pedagogiikka (NOR ISSN 0901-8050) **2892**
Nordisk Rettsmedisin *see* Scandinavian Journal of Forensic Science **5916**
Nordisk Samkatalog for Periodika Adresseliste til Nordiske Bibliothek *see* N O S P Adresseliste til Nordiske Bibliothek **631**
Nordisk Samkatalog for Periodika on Web *see* N O S P on Web **631**
Nordisk Socialstatistisk Komite (DNK ISSN 1395-7562) **8059**
• Nordisk Sosialt Arbeid (NOR ISSN 0333-1342) **8059**
Nordisk Statistisk Aarsbok *see* Nordic Statistical Yearbook **8391**
• ➤ Nordisk Teologi (DNK ISSN 1901-2888) **7666**
Nordisk Tidende *see* Norway Times **3555**
Nordisk Tidskrift foer Beteendeterapi *see* Cognitive Behaviour Therapy **7346**
Nordisk Tidskrift foer Bok- och Bibliotekshistoria/Scandinavian Journal of Libraries (SWE ISSN 1601-3875) **5036**
➤ Nordisk Tidskrift for Vetenskap, Konst och Industri (SWE ISSN 0029-1501) **5230**
Nordisk Tidsskrift for Kriminalvidenskab/Scandinavian Journal of Criminal Law and Criminology (DNK ISSN 0029-1528) **4747**
• Nordisk Tidsskrift for Menneskerettigheter (NOR ISSN 1503-6480) **7213**
Nordisk Tidsskrift for Musikketerapi *see* Nordic Journal of Music Therapy **6113**
• ➤ Nordisk Tidsskrift for Selskabsret (DNK ISSN 1399-140X) **1154**
• Nordisk Uddannelsescenter for Doevblindepersonale. Nyhedsbrev (DNK ISSN 0902-7890) **8059**
Nordisk Uddannelsescenter for Doevblindepersonale. Nyhedsbrevet *see* Nordisk Uddannelsescenter for Doevblindepersonale. Nyhedsbrev **8059**
Nordisk Uddannelsescenter for Doevblindepersonle. Arbeidstekst *see* Nordisk Uddannelsescenter for Doevblindepersonle. Arbejdstekst **8059**
• Nordisk Uddannelsescenter for Doevblindepersonle. Arbejdstekst/Nordisk Uddannelsescenter for Doevblindepersonle. Arbeidstekst/Nordisk Uddannelsescenter for Doevblindepersonle. Arbetstext/Nordisk Uddannelsescenter for Doevblindepersonle. Publication (DNK ISSN 1398-3237) **8059**
Nordisk Uddannelsescenter for Doevblindepersonle. Arbetstext *see* Nordisk Uddannelsescenter for Doevblindepersonle. Arbejdstekst **8059**
Nordisk Uddannelsescenter for Doevblindepersonle. Publication *see* Nordisk Uddannelsescenter for Doevblindepersonle. Arbejdstekst **8059**
• ➤ Nordiska Afrikainstitutet - Annual Report (SWE ISSN 1104-5256) **4177**
• ➤ Nordiska Afrikainstitutet. Discussion Papers (SWE ISSN 1104-8417) **1602**
• ➤ Nordiska Afrikainstitutet. Research Report (SWE ISSN 1104-8425) **4177**
Nordiska Genbanken. Skrifter (SWE ISSN 1100-3456) **876**
• Nordiska Hoegskolan foer Folkhaelsovetenskap. N H V-Rapport/N H V-Report (SWE ISSN 0283-1961) **7534**
Nordiska Hoegskolan foer Folkhaelsovetenskap. Thesis (SWE ISSN 1404-904X) **7534**
Nordiska Industriprojekt *see* Nordisk Industri **3213**
Nordiska Medieforskare Reflekterar (SWE ISSN 1650-5131) **2335**
Nordiska Museets och Skansens Aarsbok Fataburen *see* Fataburen **3617**
Nordiska Naemnden foer Alkohol- och Drogforskning Publikation *see* N A D - Publikation **2697**
Nordiska Rikspartiet (SWE ISSN 0345-858X) **7159**
Nordiska Samarbetsorgan (DNK ISSN 0347-9315) **7255**
• Nordiske Domme i Sjoefartsanliggender (NOR ISSN 0085-4220) **4971**
• Nordiske GENressurser (DNK ISSN 1603-3914) **876**
Nordiske Organisasjonsstudier (NOS) (NOR ISSN 1501-8237) **8123**
• Det Nordiske Samarbejde i EU (DNK ISSN 1604-4509) **4249**
➤ Nordiske Udkast (DNK ISSN 1396-3953) **8123**
Nordiskt Samarbete i Europa *see* Det Nordiske Samarbejde i EU **4249**
Nordistica Gothoburgensia (SWE ISSN 0078-1134) **5155**
• Nordjyske Stiftstidende (DNK ISSN 1399-865X) **3834**
Nordkurier (DEU) **3854**
Nordlands-doktor'n *see* Doktor i Nord **4593**
Nordlands Framtid (NOR) **3924**
Nordlandsforskning Rapport *see* N F - Rapport **7986**
Nordlandsposten (NOR) **3924**
• Nordlit (NOR ISSN 0809-1668) **5342**
Nordlund (SWE ISSN 0281-5427) **5156**
• Nordlyd (NOR ISSN 0332-7531) **5156**
Nordlys (NOR) **3924**
Nordmahrisches Heimatbuch (DEU ISSN 0546-305X) **3555**
Nordnorsk Magasin (NOR ISSN 0332-6004) **5342**
Nordo News (USA ISSN 1930-0131) **67**
Nordost-Archiv (DEU ISSN 0029-1595) **4249**
Nordost-Institut. Veroeffentlichungen (DEU) **4249**
Nordostafrikanisch - Westasiatische Studien (DEU ISSN 0946-9184) **4177**
Nordrhein Verkehr (DEU ISSN 0171-2012) **8621**
Nordrhein-Westfaelische Akademie der Wissenschaften. Abhandlungen. Sonderreihe Papyrologica Coloniensia (DEU ISSN 0944-8837) **4249**
Nordrhein-Westfaelische Akademie der Wissenschaften. Geisteswissenschaften Vortraege (DEU ISSN 0944-8810) **6937**
Nordrhein-Westfaelische Akademie der Wissenschaften. Jahrbuch (DEU ISSN 0944-8446) **2294**
Nordrhein-Westfaelische Akademie der Wissenschaften. Vortraege Natur-, Ingenieur- und Wirtschaftswissenschaften (DEU ISSN 0944-8799) **7893**
Nordrhein-Westfaelische Verwaltungsblaetter (DEU ISSN 0932-710X) **4747**
Nordrhein-Westfalen. Finanzministerium. Finanz Report (DEU) **7457**
Nordrhein-Westfalen. Justizministerialblatt (DEU ISSN 0721-8311) **4747**
Nordrhein-Westfalen Magazin *see* N R W Magazin **7499**
Nordrhein-Westfalen. Ministerium fuer Schule und Weiterbildung. Wissenschaft und Forschung. Teil 1: Schule und Weiterbildung. Amtsblatt (DEU ISSN 1615-309X) **3028**
Nordrhein-Westfalen. Statistisches Jahrbuch (DEU ISSN 0468-656X) **8391**
• Nordrug 2000 (Online) (SWE) **2701**
• Nordschleswiger (DNK ISSN 0905-8567) **3834**
† Nordsee (ITA) **8977**
Nordsee-Zeitung (DEU) **3854**
Nordslesvigske Museer (DNK ISSN 0107-9336) **4249**
Nordstjernan (USA ISSN 1059-7670) **3555**
Nordstrand - Oestre Aker Blad (NOR) **3924**
• Nordtest Method. NT Mech (Online) (NOR ISSN 1459-2827) **3391**
• Nordtest. N T Techn Report (NOR ISSN 0283-7234) **3213**
Nordtroenderen og Namdalen (NOR) **3924**
Nordverkehr (DEU) **8633**
Nordwest-Zeitung (DEU) **3854**
Nor'Easter (Duluth) (USA ISSN 1552-6194) **4305**
Nor'easter Leadership News (USA) **7769**
Norev Mag *see* Nos Reves d'Automobile **4342**
Norevmag *see* Nos Reves d'Automobile **4342**
Norfolk & Norwich Archaeology Society. Original Papers *see* Norfolk Archaeology **408**
Norfolk and Norwich Naturalists' Society. Occasional Publication (GBR ISSN 0962-435X) **2622**
Norfolk and Norwich Naturalists' Society. Transactions (GBR ISSN 0375-7226) **2622**
Norfolk Archaeology (GBR ISSN 0142-7962) **408**
Norfolk Farmer (GBR ISSN 0955-0208) **142**
Norfolk Island Government Gazette (NFK) **7457**
• Norfolk Journal (GBR ISSN 1751-3278) **4981**
Norfolk Journal & East Anglian Life *see* Norfolk Journal **4981**
Norfolk Record Society. Publications (GBR ISSN 0078-1169) **4249**
Norfolk Wildlife Trust. Annual Review (GBR) **2622**
Norfolklore (CAN) **3777**
Norge-Amerika Foreningen. Yearbook (NOR ISSN 0803-8201) **3014**
• Norges Apotekerforenings Tidsskrift (NOR ISSN 0802-8400) **6864**
Norges Automobil Forbund Guide Europe *see* N A F Guide Europe **8739**
Norges Bank. Annual Report *see* Norges Bank. Report and Accounts **1372**
Norges Bank. Arbeidsnotat *see* Norges Bank. Working Papers **1372**
• Norges Bank. Beretning og Regnskap (NOR ISSN 0800-8507) **1372**
• Norges Bank. Doctoral Dissertations in Economics (NOR ISSN 1503-0741) **1372**
• Norges Bank. Economic Bulletin/Penger og Kreditt (NOR ISSN 0029-1676) **1501**
• Norges Bank. Financial Stability (NOR ISSN 1502-2749) **1372**
Norges Bank. Finansiell Stabilitet *see* Norges Bank. Financial Stability **1372**
Norges Bank. Forvaltning av Statens Petroleumsfond. Aarsrapport *see* Norges Bank Investment Management. Aarsrapport **1502**
Norges Bank. Government Petroleum Fund. Annual Report *see* Norges Bank Investment Management. Aarsrapport **1502**
• Norges Bank. Inflasjonsrapport (NOR ISSN 0807-8521) **1501**
Norges Bank. Inflation Report *see* Norges Bank. Monetary Policy Report **1502**
• Norges Bank Investment Management. Aarsrapport/Norges Bank. Government Petroleum Fund. Annual Report (NOR ISSN 1890-3517) **1502**
• Norges Bank Investment Management. Annual Report (NOR ISSN 1890-3541) **1372**
• Norges Bank. Monetary Policy Report (NOR ISSN 1504-8470) **1502**
Norges Bank. Occasional Papers *see* Norges Bank. Skriftserie **1502**
• Norges Bank. Report and Accounts (NOR ISSN 0078-1185) **1372**
Norges Bank. Reprints (NOR ISSN 0802-8079) **1154**
• Norges Bank. Skriftserie/Norges Bank. Occasional Papers (NOR ISSN 0802-7188) **1502**
• Norges Bank. Staff Memo (NOR ISSN 1503-9714) **1372**
• Norges Bank. Working Papers (NOR ISSN 1502-5780) **1372**
Norges Byggforskningsinstitutt. Prosjektrapport *see* S I N T E F Byggforsk. Prosjektrapport **1034**
Norges Forskningsraad. HOEYKOM-Rapport (NOR ISSN 1504-5048) **2502**
Norges Forsvar (NOR ISSN 0029-1692) **6439**
Norges Geologiske Undersoekelse Rapport *see* N G U Rapport **2713**
Norges Geologiske Undersoekelse Special Publication *see* N G U Special Publication **2757**
Norges Geotekniske Institutt. Publikasjon/Norwegian Geotechnical Institute. Publications (NOR ISSN 0078-1193) **3279**
Norges Handelhoegskole. Senter for Fiskerioekonomi. Rapport/Centre for Fisheries Economics. Report (NOR ISSN 0805-3669) **3603**
• Norges Handelshoeyskole. Institutt for Foretaksoekonomi. Discussion Paper (NOR ISSN 1500-4066) **1781**
• Norges Handelshoeyskole. Institutt for Samfunnsoekonomi. Discussion Paper (NOR ISSN 0804-6824) **1154**
Norges Handelshoeyskole. Institutt for Samfunnsoekonomi. Saertrykkserie/Norwegian School of Economics and Business Administration. Department of Economics. Reprint Series (NOR ISSN 0801-9215) **1154**
• Norges Handelshoeyskole. Institutt for Strategi og Ledelse. Discussion Paper/Norwegian School of Economics and Business Administration. Department of Strategy and Management. Discussion Paper (NOR ISSN 1503-5093) **1782**
Norges Handelshoeyskole. Senter for Fiskerioekonomi. Discussion Paper Series (NOR) **1900**
Norges Handelshoeyskole. Senter for Fiskerioekonomi. Monografiserie (NOR ISSN 0804-0575) **1154**
Norges Handikapforbund. Akershus. Fylkesnytt *see* Regionsnytt (Ski) **8064**
Norges Handikapforbund. Buskerud. Medlemsnytt *see* Norges Handikapforbund. Oslofjord Vest. Regionsnytt **8059**
Norges Handikapforbund. Oslofjord Vest.Medlemsnytt *see* Norges Handikapforbund. Oslofjord Vest. Regionsnytt **8059**
Norges Handikapforbund. Oslofjord Vest. Regionsnytt (NOR ISSN 0809-6457) **8059**
Norges Ingenioerorganisasjon Refleks *see* N I T O Refleks **4599**
Norges Kjoebmannsblad (NOR ISSN 0332-8074) **3680**
Norges Landbrukshoegskole. Institutt for Jord- og Vannfag. Rapport *see* Universitetet for Miljoe- og BioVitenskap. Institutt for Plante- og Miljoevitenskap. Rapport **256**
Norges Landbrukshoegskole. Institutt for Landskapsplanlegging. Melding/Agricultural University of Norway. Department of Land Use Planning. Serie (NOR ISSN 0809-4551) **204**
Norges Landbrukshoegskole. Institutt for Tekniske Fag. I M T - Rapport *see* Universitetet for Miljoe- og BioVitenskap. Institutt for Matematiske Realfag og Teknologi. I M T- Rapport **7926**
Norges Landbrukshoegskole. Institutt for Tekniske Fag. I T F Rapport *see* Universitetet for Miljoe- og BioVitenskap. Institutt for Matematiske Realfag og Teknologi. I M T- Rapport **7926**
Norges Musikkhoegskole. N M H Publikasjoner (NOR ISSN 0333-3760) **6600**
Norges Naturvernforbund. Rapport (NOR ISSN 0807-0946) **2623**
• Norges Offentlige Utredninger (NOR ISSN 0333-2306) **3924**
Norges Offisielle Statistikk/Official Statistics of Norway (NOR ISSN 0300-5585) **1255**
Norges Teknisk-Naturvitenskapelige Universitet. Vitenskapsmuseeet. Seksjon for Naturhistorie. Zoologisk Notat (NOR ISSN 1504-503X) **958**
Norges Teknisk-Naturvitenskapelige Universitet. Fakultet for Arkitektur og Billedkunst. Aarbok (NOR ISSN 1890-1379) **451**
• Norges Teknisk-Naturvitenskapelige Universitet. Institutt for Bygg, Anlegg og Transport. Concept Rapport (NOR ISSN 0803-9763) **1154**
• Norges Teknisk- Naturvitenskapelige Universitet. Institutt for Datateknikk og Informasjonsvitenskap. I D I - Rapport/Norwegian University of Science and Technology. Department of Computer and Information Science. I D I Report (NOR ISSN 1503-416X) **2433**
Norges Teknisk-Naturvitenskapelige Universitet. Institutt for Historie og Klassiske Fag. Forum for Kunnskapshistorie. Publikasjon (NOR ISSN 1504-0828) **7893**
Norges Teknisk-Naturvitenskapelige Universitet. Institutt for Socialt Arbeid og Helsevitenskap. Rapportserie (NOR ISSN 1504-1840) **8059**
Norges Teknisk-Naturvitenskapelige Universitet. Institutt for Socialt Arbeid og Helsevitenskap. Social Arbeids Rapportserie *see* Norges Teknisk-Naturvitenskapelige Universitet. Institutt for Socialt Arbeid og Helsevitenskap. Rapportserie **8059**
Norges Teknisk-Naturvitenskapelige Universitet Samfunnsforskning AS. Studio Apertura. Work Report *see* N T N U Samfunnsforskning AS. Studio Apertura. Work Report **8122**
Norges Teknisk-Naturvitenskapelige Universitet. Senter for Oekonomisk Forskning. Rapport *see* S OE F Rapport **1170**
• Norges Teknisk-Naturvitenskapelige Universitet. Vitenskapsmuseet. Seksjon for Naturhistorie. Botanisk Notat (NOR ISSN 0804-0079) **805**
• Norges Teknisk-Naturvitenskapelige Universitet. Vitenskapsmuseet. Seksjon for Naturhistorie. Rapport. Botanisk Serie (NOR ISSN 0802-2992) **805**
• Norges Teknisk-Naturvitenskapelige Universitet. Vitenskapsmuseet. Seksjon for Naturhistorie. Rapport. Zoologisk Serie (NOR ISSN 0802-0833) **959**
Norim Suisan Seisaku Kemkyu (JPN) **204**
Norin Suisan Tokei Geppo/Monthly Statistics on Agriculture, Forestry and Fisheries (JPN ISSN 0029-1757) **184**
Norin Suisan Tosho Shiryo Geppo (JPN ISSN 0388-5976) **184**

Title

▼ *new title* † *ceased* • *electronic media* ➤ *refereed*

10682 NORIN SUISANSHO KACHIKU EISEI SHIKENJO KENKYU HOKOKU/JAPAN. ULRICH'S PERIODICALS

Norin Suisansho Kachiku Eisei Shikenjo Kenkyu Hokoku/Japan. National Institute of Animal Health. Bulletin *see* Doubutsu Eisei Kenkyuujo Kenkyuu Houkoku **8796**
Norin Tokei Chosa/Monthly Bulletin of Agricultural Statistics and Research (JPN ISSN 1342-5757) **184**
Norinsho Koho/Agriculture, Forestry, Fishery (JPN ISSN 0387-1452) **142**
Nork (ARM ISSN 0235-6848) **5342**
Nork Quarterly (GBR ISSN 1749-4702) **7457**
Norm Report *see* N O R M Report **2757**
Norm und Struktur (AUT) **4249**
• ➤ Norma (NOR ISSN 1890-2138) **8123**
▼ The Normal School (USA ISSN 1943-0760) **5342**
• Normalisatie-Nieuws (NLD ISSN 0929-2985) **6405**
Normalizacja (POL ISSN 0029-179X) **3213**
Norman Kaplan's Clinical Hypertension (USA ISSN 1044-4645) **5796**
Norman Paterson School of International Affairs. Bibliography Series (CAN ISSN 0383-2848) **7200**
Normande (FRA ISSN 1621-7500) **295**
Normanton Advertiser (GBR) **3869**
Normas Legales (PER ISSN 1025-5524) **4747**
➤ Normat/Nordic Studies in Mathematics Education (SWE ISSN 0801-3500) **5521**
Normativa Contable (ESP ISSN 1138-8846) **1297**
Normativni Aktove (BGR) **4851**
Normativnye Akty dlya Bukhgaltera (RUS) **1372**
Normativnye Dokumenty po Finansam, Nalogam, Bukhgalterskomy Uchetu (BLR) **1372**
Normatyvni Akty z Finansiv, Podatkiv, Strakhuvannya ta Bukhalters'koho Obliku (UKR) **1372**
Normer i den Offentliga Sektion *see* F A Rs Normsamling foer den Offentliga Sektion **1288**
Normtal for Sportsbranchen i Danmark (DNK ISSN 1602-7574) **8191**
• Normtallsundersoekelsen (NOR ISSN 1504-4203) **7578**
Norna - Rapporter (SWE ISSN 0346-6728) **5156**
Noro Psikiyatri Arsivi *see* Noropsikiyatri Arsivi **6171**
• Noroeste (MEX ISSN 1605-0312) **3910**
• Noroeste. Culiacan (MEX) **3910**
• ➤ Noroeste de Mexico (MEX) **350**
• Noroeste. Mazatlan (MEX) **3910**
Noroil Contacts - Offshore Directory (NOR ISSN 0964-4636) **6781**
Noroil Newswire (NOR) **6781**
• ➤ Norois (FRA ISSN 0029-182X) **4022**
Norolojik Bilimler Dergisi *see* Journal of Neurological Sciences (Print) **8968**
• ➤ Noropsikiyatri Arsivi/Archives of Neuropsychiatry (TUR ISSN 1300-0667) **6171**
Norr (DEU) **8325**
Norra Skogsmagasinet (SWE ISSN 1653-5154) **3698**
Norrlaendsk Tidskrift (SWE ISSN 0029-1838) **1154**
Norrlaendska Socialdemokraten (SWE) **3956**
Norseman (NOR ISSN 0029-1846) **5230**
• Norsk Antropologisk Tidsskrift (NOR ISSN 0802-7285) **350**
Norsk Araberhest (NOR ISSN 0809-8697) **8295**
Norsk Artilleri-Tidsskrift (NOR ISSN 0029-1854) **6439**
Norsk Bokfortegnelse. Nyhetsliste (Online)/Norwegian National Bibliography. List of New Books (NOR ISSN 1502-7384) **632**
Norsk Bufe. Aarsskrift (NOR ISSN 1504-4920) **295**
• Norsk Designtidende (NOR ISSN 1503-5808) **6755**
Norsk Elghund Quarterly (USA) **6812**
• Norsk Energi (NOR ISSN 0800-7896) **3143**
• Norsk Epidemiologi/Norwegian Journal of Epidemiology (NOR ISSN 0803-2491) **7534**
Norsk Farmaceutisk Tidsskrift (NOR ISSN 0029-1935) **6864**
Norsk Filatelistisk Tidsskrift (NOR ISSN 0332-8848) **6897**
Norsk Filminstitutt. Skriftsserie (NOR ISSN 0807-9862) **6509**
Norsk Filosofisk Tidsskrift/Norwegian Journal of Philosophy (NOR ISSN 0029-1943) **6937**
Norsk Fiskaralmanakk (NOR ISSN 0804-1202) **3603**
• Norsk Fiskeoppdrett (NOR ISSN 0332-7132) **3603**
Norsk Foerskolelaererblad *see* Utdanning **2924**
Norsk Folkemusikklag. Skrifter (NOR ISSN 0800-3734) **6600**
Norsk Fotografisk Tidsskrift (NOR ISSN 0332-8597) **6972**
• ➤ Norsk Geografisk Tidsskrift/Norwegian Journal of Geography (GBR ISSN 0029-1951) **4022**
• ➤ Norsk Geologisk Tidsskrift/Norwegian Journal of Geology (NOR ISSN 0029-196X) **2759**
Norsk Geologisk Tidsskrift. Supplement *see* Norsk Geologisk Tidsskrift **2759**
Norsk Hagetidend (NOR ISSN 0029-1986) **3745**
Norsk Husflid (NOR ISSN 0048-0592) **537**
Norsk Institutt for By- og Regionforskning Notat (Online) *see* N I B R-Notat (Online) **4420**
Norsk Institutt for By- og Regionforskning Rapport *see* N I B R-Rapport **4420**
Norsk Institutt for Forskning om Opvekst, Velferd og Aldring Rapport *see* N O V A. Rapport **8056**
Norsk Institutt for Forskning om Opvekst, Velferd og Aldring Skriftserie *see* N O V A. Skriftserie **8056**
Norsk Institutt for Forskning om Opvekst, Velferd og Aldring Temahefte *see* N O V A. Temahefte **8056**
• Norsk Institutt for Landbruksoekonomisk Forskning. Notat (NOR ISSN 0805-9691) **142**
Norsk Institutt for Landbruksoekonomisk Forskning Rapport *see* N I L F - Rapport **138**
Norsk Institutt for Naturforskning Fagrapport *see* N I N A. Fagrapport **2619**
Norsk Institutt for Naturforskning Fakta *see* N I N A Fakta **2619**
Norsk Institutt for Naturforskning Temahefte *see* N I N A Temahefte **3454**
Norsk Institutt for Strategiske Studier Fagnotat *see* N O R I S S. Fagnotat **8122**
Norsk Institutt for Studier av Forskning og Utdanning. Rapport *see* N I F U S T E P. Rapport **4465**
Norsk Institutt for Studier av Forskning og Utdanning, Senter for Innovasjonsforskning S T E P. Rapport *see* N I F U S T E P. Rapport **4465**
Norsk Institutt for Vannforskning Aarsberetning *see* N I V A. Aarsberetning **8829**
Norsk Institutt for Vannforskning Rapport *see* N I V A-Rapport **3489**
Norsk Kirkemusikk (NOR ISSN 0333-0176) **6600**
• Norsk Kirkesang (NOR ISSN 0807-6685) **6600**
Norsk Laererlag. Hefte *see* Utdanningsforbundet. Hefteserie **2924**
Norsk Landbruk (NOR ISSN 0332-5474) **142**
➤ Norsk Lingvistisk Tidsskrift (NOR ISSN 0800-3076) **5156**
Norsk Litteraer Aarbok (NOR ISSN 0078-1266) **5342**
• Norsk Litteraturvitenskapelig Tidsskrift (NOR ISSN 0809-2044) **5342**
• Norsk Lovtidend. Avd. I Lover og Sentrale Forskrifter m.v. (NOR ISSN 0333-0753) **4851**
• Norsk Lovtidend. Avd. II Regionale og Lokale Forskrifter m.v. (NOR ISSN 0333-0761) **4851**
Norsk Lovtidende *see* Norsk Lovtidend. Avd. I Lover og Sentrale Forskrifter m.v. **4851**
Norsk Lovtidende *see* Norsk Lovtidend. Avd. II Regionale og Lokale Forskrifter m.v. **4851**
Norsk Lovtidende. 2den afdeling. Samling af Love, Resolutioner m.m. *see* Norsk Lovtidend. Avd. II Regionale og Lokale Forskrifter m.v. **4851**
Norsk Luftfatshistorisk Magasin (NOR ISSN 0809-8409) **8549**
Norsk Maskin Tidende *see* Maritim Logg **8652**
• ➤ Norsk Medietidsskrift (NOR ISSN 0804-8452) **8123**
Norsk Militaert Tidsskrift/Norwegian Military Journal (NOR ISSN 0029-2028) **6439**
Norsk Motorveteran (NOR ISSN 0803-5172) **8595**
• Norsk Musikkfortegnelse. Lydfestinger/Norwegian National Discography (NOR) **6632**
• Norsk Musikkfortegnelse. Notetrykk/Norwegian National Bibliography of Printed Music (NOR) **6632**
Norsk Naturforvalterforbund Nytt *see* Naturviteren **4599**
• Norsk Oekonomisk Tidsskrift (Online) (NOR ISSN 1890-0658) **1154**
Norsk Ornitologisk Forening. N O F Rapportserie (NOR ISSN 0805-4932) **911**
• Norsk Patenttidende (Online) (NOR ISSN 1503-4933) **6755**
• Norsk Pedagogisk Tidsskrift/Norwegian Journal of Education (NOR ISSN 0029-2052) **2892**
Norsk Pelsdyrblad (NOR ISSN 0369-5255) **4974**
• Norsk Periodikafortegnelse/Norwegian List of Serials (NOR) **632**
• Norsk Polarinstitutt. Aarsmelding (NOR ISSN 0804-9505) **2759**
Norsk Polarinstitutt. Polarhaandbok (NOR ISSN 0474-8042) **2759**
Norsk Polarinstitutt. Rapportserie (NOR ISSN 0803-0421) **2714**
• Norsk Polarinstitutt. Temakart/Thematic Maps (NOR ISSN 0801-8588) **4022**
➤ Norsk Psykologforening. Tidsskrift/The Norwegian Psychological Association. Journal (NOR ISSN 0332-6470) **7388**
Norsk Retstidende (NOR ISSN 0029-2060) **4747**
Norsk Revmatikerforbund. Temahefte (NOR ISSN 1503-3791) **8059**
Norsk Shakespeare og Teater-Tidsskrift (NOR ISSN 1503-2310) **5342**
Norsk Sjakkblad (NOR ISSN 0332-9771) **8191**
Norsk Sjoefartsmuseum. Aarbok (NOR ISSN 1502-170X) **4249**
Norsk Sjoefartsmuseum. Skrift (NOR ISSN 0801-6593) **8655**
Norsk Sjoemat (NOR ISSN 0807-1551) **3603**
Norsk Skattelovsamling *see* Jaroey Skattelovsamling **1931**
Norsk Skogbruk (NOR ISSN 0029-2087) **3698**
Norsk Skogbruksmuseum. Aarbok (NOR ISSN 0549-6896) **3698**
Norsk Skogmuseum. Skrifter (NOR ISSN 0809-8603) **3698**
Norsk Skoleblad *see* Utdanning **2924**
Norsk Skyttertidende (NOR ISSN 0333-4538) **8191**
Norsk Slektshistorisk Tidsskrift (NOR ISSN 0029-2141) **3777**
• Norsk Sokkel (NOR ISSN 1504-1468) **6781**
Norsk som Andrespraak *see* N O A **5153**
• Norsk Statsvitenskapelig Tidsskrift/Norwegian Political Science Journal (NOR ISSN 0801-1745) **7159**
Norsk-Svensk Traverstambok for Kaldblodshester (NOR ISSN 1504-4351) **8295**
Norsk Svoemming (NOR ISSN 0333-452X) **8191**
Norsk Teknisk Museum. Yearbook *see* Volund **8445**
• Norsk Teologisk Tidsskrift/Norwegian Theological Journal (NOR ISSN 0029-2176) **7666**
• Norsk Tidend (NOR ISSN 0801-8774) **5156**
Norsk Tidsskrift for Ernaering (NOR ISSN 1503-5034) **6664**
Norsk Tidsskrift for Migrasjonsforskning/Norwegian Journal of Migration Research (NOR ISSN 1502-4008) **7288**
Norsk Tidsskrift for Misjon *see* Norsk Tidsskrift for Misjonsvitenskap **7666**
➤ Norsk Tidsskrift for Misjonsvitenskap/Norwegian Journal of Mission and Missionary Questions (NOR ISSN 1504-6605) **7666**
Norsk Tidsskrift for Sjovesen (NOR ISSN 0029-2222) **6439**
Norsk Traverstambok for Kaldblodshester *see* Norsk-Svensk Traverstambok for Kaldblodshester **8295**
Norsk Treteknisk Institutt. Meddelelse (NOR ISSN 0546-3637) **3714**
Norsk Treteknisk Institutt. Rapport (NOR ISSN 0333-2020) **3714**
Norsk Treteknisk Institutt. Teknisk Smaaskrift (NOR ISSN 0468-4168) **3714**
Norsk Ukeblad (NOR ISSN 0029-2257) **3924**
Norsk Utemiljoe (NOR ISSN 1503-0814) **3745**
Norsk Utenrikspolitisk Institutt Notat (Online) *see* N U P I Notat (Online) **7254**
Norsk Utenrikspolitisk Institutt Rapport *see* N U P I Rapport **7254**
• Norsk V V S (NOR ISSN 0029-2265) **4124**
• Norsk Varemerketidende (Online) (NOR ISSN 1503-4925) **6755**
➤ Norsk Veterinaer-Tidsskrift/Norwegian Veterinary Medical Journal (NOR ISSN 0332-5741) **8803**
Norsk Zoologisk Forening. Rapport (NOR ISSN 0806-7813) **959**
Den Norske Advokatforening. Temahefte (NOR ISSN 1890-0984) **4747**
Norske Arkitektkonkurranser (NOR ISSN 0332-6578) **451**
• Den Norske Atlanterhavskomite. Internett Tekster (NOR ISSN 1502-5373) **7255**
• Norske Boligbyggelags Landsforbund. Aarsstatistik (Year) (NOR ISSN 1504-4157) **4436**
• Det Norske Forsknings- og Innovasjonssystemet - Statistikk og Indikatorer (NOR ISSN 1500-0869) **8391**
Norske Insekttabeller (NOR ISSN 1503-2108) **856**
Den Norske Kirke i Tall (Year) (NOR ISSN 1501-2573) **7699**
Den Norske Kreftforening. D N K-Rapport *see* Kreftforeningen. Rapport **6026**
• Den Norske Laegeforening. Tidsskrift/Norwegian Medical Association. Journal (NOR ISSN 0029-2001) **5688**
Det Norske Meteorologiske Institutt. D N M I-Rapport, Klima *see* Meteorologisk Institutt. Met.no-Report, Klima **6391**
Norske Moebler (NOR ISSN 1504-2022) **4561**
• ➤ Den Norske Tannlegeforenings Tidende/The Norwegian Dental Journal (NOR ISSN 0029-2303) **5857**
• Norske Tidsskriftartikler (Online)/Norwegian Index to Periodical Articles (NOR) **12**
Det Norske Veritas. Aarsberetning *see* Det Norske Veritas. Annual Report **8655**
• Det Norske Veritas. Annual Report (NOR ISSN 0804-2462) **8655**
Det Norske Videnskaps-Akademi. I. Mat.-Naturv. Klasse. Ny Serie. Avhandlinger *see* Det Norske Videnskaps-Akademi. I. Mat.-Naturv. Klasse. Skrifter og Avhandlinger **7893**
Det Norske Videnskaps-Akademi. I. Mat.-Naturv. Klasse. Skrifter og Avhandlinger (NOR ISSN 1890-3533) **7893**
Det Norske Videnskaps-Akademi. II. Hist.-Filos. Klasse. Skrifter og Avhandlinger (NOR ISSN 1502-9727) **4467**
• Det Norske Videnskaps-Akademi. Senter for Grunnforskning. Informasjonsblad (NOR ISSN 1503-4224) **4467**
• Det Norske Videnskaps-Akademi. Senter for Grunnforskning. Newsletter (NOR ISSN 1503-4232) **4467**
Det Norske Videnskaps-Akademi. Senter for Hoejere Studier. Informasjonsblad *see* Det Norske Videnskaps-Akademi. Senter for Grunnforskning. Informasjonsblad **4467**
Det Norske Videnskaps-Akademi. Senter for Hoejere Studier. Newsletter *see* Det Norske Videnskaps-Akademi. Senter for Grunnforskning. Newsletter **4467**
Norsklaereren (NOR ISSN 0332-7264) **5156**
Norskrift (NOR ISSN 0800-7764) **5156**
• El Norte (MEX ISSN 1563-7867) **3910**
• El Norte (USA ISSN 1523-6986) **3555**
• Norte (Chaco) (ARG) **3791**
Norte (Mexico City) (MEX ISSN 0188-2848) **5343**
• El Norte de Castilla (ESP) **3953**
The North (GBR ISSN 0269-9885) **5428**
• The North Africa Journal (USA ISSN 1097-8844) **1154**
North Africa Monitor *see* Africa Monitor. North Africa **1435**
North African Historical Review *see* Revue d'Histoire Maghrebine **4177**
North America Executive Flight Guide *see* O A G Pocket Flight Guide. North America Edition **8549**
North America Fairs, Festivals and Expositions *see* Directory of North American Fairs, Festivals and Expositions **8950**
• ➤ North American Actuarial Journal (USA ISSN 1092-0277) **4517**
North American Aluminum Industry Plant Directory (USA) **6328**
• ➤ North American Archaeologist (USA ISSN 0197-6931) **408**
North American Association for Environmental Education Communicator *see* N A A E E Communicator **3454**
• North American Association for Environmental Education. Conference Proceedings (USA) **3457**
North American Association of Education Negotiators Bulletin *see* N A E N Bulletin **3027**
North American Association of Food Equipment Manufacturers in Print *see* N A F E M in Print **3657**
North American Association of Summer Sessions. Annual Conference. Proceedings (USA) **3028**
North American Association of Summer Sessions. Newsletter (USA) **3028**
North American Association of Wardens and Superintendents Grapevine Newsletter *see* N A A W S Grapevine Newsletter **2660**
North American Benthological Society. Bulletin (CAN) **694**
• ➤ North American Benthological Society. Journal (CAN ISSN 0887-3593) **694**
North American Biotechnology Directory (USA ISSN 1937-0989) **769**
North American Bird Bander (USA ISSN 0363-8979) **911**
• North American Birds (USA ISSN 1525-3708) **911**
North American Brewers Resource Directory (USA) **2021**
North American Building Material Distribution Association. Channels (USA) **1027**
North American Cement Directory (USA ISSN 1048-3853) **1027**
North American Classic M G Magazine (USA ISSN 1533-421X) **8595**
▼ North American Clean Energy (CAN) **3143**
North American Coins & Prices (USA ISSN 1935-0562) **6652**
North American Congress on Latin America, Inc. Report on the Americas *see* N A C L A Report on the Americas **7253**
North American Country Inns (CAN) **4394**
• North American Crude Wire (USA ISSN 1931-2210) **6781**
• North American Design (USA) **4561**
• North American Dialogue (USA ISSN 1539-2546) **350**
North American Die Casting Association International Die Casting Congress. Transactions *see* N A D C A International Die Casting Congress. Transactions **3354**
North American Electric Reliability Council. Annual Report (USA ISSN 1048-4744) **3160**
North American Environmental Law and Policy (CAN ISSN 1491-1728) **4747**
North American Equipment Dealers Association Equipment Dealer *see* N A E D A Equipment Dealer **212**
North American Exploration and Production Industry (USA) **6781**
• ➤ North American Fauna (USA ISSN 0078-1304) **959**
North American Financial Institutions Directory (USA ISSN 1529-1367) **2021**
• North American Fisherman (USA ISSN 1043-2450) **8325**
➤ North American Flora (USA ISSN 0078-1312) **805**
North American Food Report (GBR) **3658**
North American Free Trade Agreement Law and Policy Series *see* N A F T A Law and Policy Series **4936**
North American Free Trade Agreement Register *see* The N A F T A Register **2018**
North American Free Trade Agreement Report *see* N A F T A Report **2018**
• North American Free Trade & Investment Report (USA ISSN 1556-0376) **1579**
North American Free Trade and Investment Report *see* North American Free Trade & Investment Report **1579**
• ➤ North American Fungi (USA ISSN 1937-786X) **805**
North American Fuzzy Information Processing Society. Annual Meeting (USA) **2455**
North American Gladiolus Council Bulletin (USA ISSN 0029-2370) **3745**
North American Guide to Nude Recreation (USA) **8742**
North American Hunter (USA ISSN 0194-4320) **8325**
North American Interfraternal Foundation Notes *see* N I F Notes **2293**
• ➤ North American Journal of Aquaculture (USA ISSN 1522-2055) **3603**
• ➤ The North American Journal of Economics and Finance (NLD ISSN 1062-9408) **1502**
▼ • ➤ North American Journal of Finance and Banking Research (USA ISSN 1933-3447) **1372**
• ➤ North American Journal of Fisheries Management (USA ISSN 0275-5947) **3603**
• ➤ North American Journal of Psychology (USA ISSN 1527-7143) **7388**
• ➤ North American Journal of Sports Physical Therapy (USA ISSN 1558-6162) **6113**
• The North American Journal of Welsh Studies (USA ISSN 1554-8112) **4249**

North American Lily Society. Quarterly Bulletin (USA) **3745**
North American Lily Society. Yearbook (USA ISSN 0741-9910) **3745**
North American Man - Boy Love Association Bulletin *see* N A M B L A Bulletin **4377**
North American Man - Boy Love Association Topics *see* N A M B L A Topics **4377**
North American Masonry Conference. Proceedings (USA ISSN 1053-2366) **1027**
North American Meat Processors Association. Newsfax (USA) **3658**
North American Menopause Society. Annual Meeting Proceedings (USA) **8847**
North American Minerals News (GBR ISSN 1358-3344) **6475**
North American Missions (USA) **7769**
North American Montessori Teacher's Association Journal *see* The N A M T A Journal **2888**
• North American Post/Hokubei Hochi (USA ISSN 8756-6451) **3555**
North American Potato Variety Inventory (USA) **244**
North American Power Symposium (Year) Proceedings *see* N A P S (Year) Proceedings **3326**
North American Pylon (USA ISSN 1053-4881) **8595**
North American Quarry News *see* N A Q N **6474**
North American Repeater Atlas (USA) **2361**
North American Retail Dealers Association Independent Retailer *see* N A R D A Independent Retailer **1780**
North American Retail Dealers Association's Cost of Doing Business Survey *see* N A R D A's Cost of Doing Business Survey **1964**
• ➤ The North American Review (USA ISSN 0029-2397) **5230**
North American Riding for the Handicapped Association, Inc. News *see* N A R H A News **8294**
North American Riding for the Handicapped Association, Inc. Strides *see* N A R H A Strides **8295**
• The North American Scrap Metals Directory (CD-ROM) (USA) **3509**
• The North American Scrap Metals Directory (Print) (USA) **3509**
North American Serials Interest Group. Conference Proceedings (USA) **5036**
North American Serials Interest Group Membership Directory *see* N A S I G Membership Directory **5033**
North American Serials Interest Group Newsletter (Online) *see* N A S I G Newsletter (Online) **5033**
North American Ski Journalists Association Newsletter (USA) **4581**
• North American Skies (USA) **578**
North American Society for Oceanic History. Newsletter (USA) **4305**
North American Society for Sport History. Newsletter (USA) **8191**
North American Society for Sport History. Proceedings (USA ISSN 0093-6235) **8191**
North American Society of Adlerian Psychology. Newsletter (USA ISSN 0889-9428) **7388**
North American Sport Library Network *see* N A S L I N E **8188**
North American Students of Cooperation Guide to Campus Co-Ops *see* N A S C O Guide to Campus Co-Ops **8056**
North American Studies in Nineteenth-Century German Literature (GBR ISSN 0891-4095) **5343**
North American Supply, Distribution, Manufacturing and Service (USA) **6781**
North American Swans (USA ISSN 1094-6144) **911**
▼ • North American Tax Handbook (USA ISSN 1876-0481) **1937**
North American Telecom NewsWatch *see* The Telecom Manager's Voice Report **2372**
North American Trade Guide (USA ISSN 1071-958X) **1579**
North American Truffling Society, Inc. Current News *see* N A T S Current News **803**
North American Tunneling (USA ISSN 1574-5716) **3279**
North American Veterinary Conference Clinician's Brief *see* N A V C Clinician's Brief **8803**
• The North American Veterinary Conference. Proceedings (USA) **8803**
North American Vexillological Association News *see* N A V A News **3775**
North American Wetlands Conservation Act Progress Report (CAN ISSN 1098-1942) **2623**
North American Whitetail (USA ISSN 0746-6250) **8325**
• North American Wildlife & Natural Resources Abstracts (USA) **717**
North American Wildlife and Natural Resources Conference. Transactions (USA ISSN 0078-1355) **2623**
• North American Windpower (USA ISSN 1939-0947) **3178**
North American Youth Sport Institute Resource List *see* N A Y S I Resource List **8189**
• North & South (NZL ISSN 0112-9023) **3918**
North & South (USA ISSN 1522-9742) **4305**
North & West London Journal of General Practice (GBR ISSN 1475-1763) **5688**
North Atlanta Home (USA) **4547**
North Atlantic Free Trade Agreement Canadian Section. Performance Report *see* N A F T A. Canadian Section. Performance Report **7454**
North Atlantic Marine Mammal Commission Annual Report *see* N A M M C O. Annual Report **957**
North Atlantic Marine Mammal Commission Scientific Publications *see* N A M M C O. Scientific Publications **957**
North Atlantic Review (USA ISSN 1040-7324) **5343**
North Atlantic Treaty Organization (NATO) Data *see* N A T O Data **6437**
North Atlantic Treaty Organization Advanced Science Institutes Series G: Ecological Sciences *see* N A T O Advanced Science Institutes Series G: Ecological Sciences **3454**
North Atlantic Treaty Organization Advanced Science Institutes Series H: Cell Biology *see* N A T O Advanced Science Institutes Series H: Cell Biology **835**
North Atlantic Treaty Organization Advanced Science Institutes Series. Partnership Sub-Series 4: Science and Technology Policy *see* N A T O Advanced Science Institutes Series. Partnership Sub-Series 4: Science and Technology Policy **7884**
North Atlantic Treaty Organization Annual Economic Colloquia. Proceedings *see* N A T O Annual Economic Colloquia. Proceedings **1578**
North Atlantic Treaty Organization Challenges of Modern Society *see* N A T O Challenges of Modern Society **7884**
North Atlantic Treaty Organization. Expert Panel on Air Pollution Modeling. Proceedings (BEL ISSN 0377-7669) **3490**
North Atlantic Treaty Organization Final Communiques *see* N A T O Final Communiques **7253**
North Atlantic Treaty Organization Handbogen *see* N A T O Handbogen **7253**
North Atlantic Treaty Organization Handbook *see* N A T O Handbook **7253**
North Atlantic Treaty Organization Review (Online) *see* N A T O Review (Online) **7156**
North Atlantic Treaty Organization Science for Peace and Security Series. A: Chemistry and Biology *see* N A T O Science for Peace and Security Series. A: Chemistry and Biology **2073**
North Atlantic Treaty Organization Science for Peace and Security Series. B: Physics and Biophysics *see* N A T O Science for Peace and Security Series. B: Physics and Biophysics **7027**
North Atlantic Treaty Organization Science for Peace and Security Series. C: Environmental Security *see* N A T O Science for Peace and Security Series. C: Environmental Security **3454**
North Atlantic Treaty Organization Science for Peace and Security Series. D: Information and Communication Security *see* N A T O Science for Peace and Security Series. D: Information and Communication Security **7253**
North Atlantic Treaty Organization Science for Peace and Security Series. E: Human and Societal Dynamics *see* N A T O Science for Peace and Security Series. E: Human and Societal Dynamics **7254**
North Atlantic Treaty Organization Science Series. Series 1: Life and Behavioural Sciences *see* N A T O Science Series. Series 1: Life and Behavioural Sciences **4465**
North Atlantic Treaty Organization Science Series. Series II: Mathematics, Physics and Chemistry *see* N A T O Science Series. Series II: Mathematics, Physics and Chemistry **5519**
North Atlantic Treaty Organization Science Series. Series III: Computer and Systems Sciences *see* N A T O Science Series. Series III: Computer and Systems Sciences **2524**
North Atlantic Treaty Organization Science Series. Series IV: Earth and Environmental Sciences *see* N A T O Science Series. Series IV: Earth and Environmental Sciences **2713**
North Atlantic Treaty Organization Science Series. Series V: Science and Technology Policy *see* N A T O Science Series. Series V: Science and Technology Policy **7884**
North Atlantic Treaty Organization Scientific Publications. Newsletter *see* N A T O Scientific Publications. Newsletter **7885**
North Atlantic Treaty Organization's Nations and Partners for Peace *see* N A T O's Nations and Partners for Peace **7254**
North Bay Business Journal (Napa, Sonoma and Marin Counties) (USA) **1155**
North Bay Living (USA) **4548**
• North Bay Nugget (North Bay, 1989) (CAN) **3814**
• North Bi Northwest (USA ISSN 1050-4680) **4377**
North Canterbury News (NZL) **3918**
➤ North Carolina Academy of Science. Journal (USA) **7893**
North Carolina Agricultural Chemicals Manual (USA ISSN 0065-4418) **244**
North Carolina Agricultural Research Service. Technical Bulletin (USA ISSN 0747-8194) **142**
North Carolina: All-Industries *see* Harris Directory. North Carolina All-Industries **2001**
North Carolina American Legion News (USA) **2268**
North Carolina Archaeological Society. Newsletter (USA) **408**
North Carolina Archaeology (USA ISSN 1546-797X) **408**
North Carolina Architecture (USA ISSN 1045-3253) **451**
North Carolina Archivist (USA) **5036**
North Carolina Association of Educators News Bulletin *see* N C A E News Bulletin **2888**
North Carolina Association of Historians. Journal (USA ISSN 1078-4330) **4305**
• North Carolina Attorney General Reports (USA ISSN 0364-362X) **4747**
North Carolina Banking Institute *see* University of North Carolina School of Law Banking Institute **4804**
North Carolina Beverage Journal (USA ISSN 1054-657X) **608**
North Carolina Boating Lifestyle *see* N C Boating Lifestyle **8975**
North Carolina Botanical Garden Newsletter (USA) **805**
North Carolina Builder (USA ISSN 1552-8685) **1027**
• North Carolina Business Credit Directory (USA) **2021**
• North Carolina Business Directory (USA ISSN 1046-9060) **2021**
North Carolina Catholic (USA) **7809**
• North Carolina Central Law Journal (USA ISSN 0549-7434) **4748**
North Carolina Christian Advocate *see* North Carolina Conference Christian Advocate **7769**
North Carolina Citations *see* Shepard's North Carolina Citations **4963**
• North Carolina Civil Procedure (USA) **4839**
North Carolina Conference Christian Advocate (USA ISSN 1933-0626) **7769**
▼ • North Carolina Conversations (USA ISSN 1941-3165) **4467**
• North Carolina Corporations, Partnerships and Securities Laws Annotated (USA ISSN 1546-914X) **4877**
• North Carolina. Court of Appeals. Reports (USA ISSN 0549-7450) **4958**
• North Carolina Criminal and Traffic Law Manual (USA ISSN 1534-3383) **4895**
• North Carolina Criminal Law and Motor Vehicle Handbook (USA ISSN 1931-4604) **4895**
North Carolina Curiosities (USA ISSN 1934-581X) **8742**
North Carolina Dairy Extension Newsletter (USA ISSN 0468-5822) **268**
North Carolina Dental Review (USA) **5857**
North Carolina. Department of Agriculture. Agricultural Review (USA ISSN 0744-5466) **142**
North Carolina Department of Environment and Natural Resources. Division of Marine Fisheries. Completion Report (USA) **3603**
North Carolina. Department of Environment, Health, and Natural Resources. Division of Land Resources. Bulletin (USA) **2759**
North Carolina. Department of Environment, Health, and Natural Resources. Division of Land Resources. Information Circular (USA) **2759**
North Carolina. Department of Revenue. Franchise Tax and Corporate Income Tax Rules and Bulletins (USA) **1937**
North Carolina Directory of Trade and Professional Associations (USA) **2021**
▼ • North Carolina Employment Law (USA ISSN 1937-8432) **1700**
• North Carolina Employment Law Letter (USA ISSN 1054-6359) **4748**
➤ North Carolina English Teacher (USA ISSN 0887-5596) **5156**
North Carolina Facts (USA ISSN 0895-8106) **3121**
• North Carolina Family and Related Laws Annotated (USA ISSN 1549-3156) **4913**
North Carolina Family Law Statutes (USA ISSN 1942-0226) **4913**
• North Carolina Family Physician (USA) **5688**
North Carolina Farm Bureau Magazine (USA) **142**
➤ North Carolina Folklore Journal (USA ISSN 0090-5844) **3621**
North Carolina Folklore Society. Newsletter *see* Folklore in the Carolinas **3618**
North Carolina Game & Fish (USA ISSN 0897-8816) **8325**
North Carolina Genealogical Society Journal (USA ISSN 0360-1056) **3777**
North Carolina Genealogical Society Newsletter (USA) **3777**
North Carolina Geological Survey Open-File Report *see* N C G S Open-File Report **2757**
• ➤ North Carolina Historical Review (USA ISSN 0029-2494) **4305**
North Carolina Holiday & Visitors Guide (GBR ISSN 1360-7243) **8742**
North Carolina Insight (USA) **7159**
• North Carolina Journal of International Law and Commercial Regulation (USA ISSN 0743-1759) **4937**
• North Carolina Journal of Law & Technology (USA ISSN 1542-5177) **4748**
North Carolina Juvenile Code: Practice and Procedure (USA ISSN 1932-2089) **4748**
• North Carolina Law of Torts (USA) **4877**
• ➤ North Carolina Law Review (USA ISSN 0029-2524) **4748**
North Carolina Laws Animal Investigators Field Reference Pocket Guide *see* North Carolina Laws for Animal Control, Animal Protection, Public Health **4748**
▼ North Carolina Laws for Animal Control, Animal Protection, Public Health (USA ISSN 1947-4490) **4748**
North Carolina Lawyer (USA) **4748**
• North Carolina Lawyers Weekly (USA ISSN 1041-1747) **4748**
• ➤ North Carolina Libraries (USA ISSN 0029-2540) **5036**
North Carolina Literary Review (USA ISSN 1063-0724) **5231**
• North Carolina Magazine (USA ISSN 1063-2875) **1431**
North Carolina Manual (USA) **7457**
• North Carolina Manufacturers Register (USA ISSN 1073-2128) **2021**
North Carolina: Manufacturing *see* Harris Directory. North Carolina Manufacturing **2001**
• ➤ North Carolina Medical Journal (USA ISSN 0029-2559) **5688**
North Carolina Mental Health, Developmental Disabilities and Substance Abuse Laws (USA ISSN 1536-4771) **6171**
(Year) North Carolina Metal Processors Directory (USA) **5458**
North Carolina Motions in Limine (USA ISSN 1942-0358) **4958**
North Carolina Naturalist (USA ISSN 1070-468X) **6534**
North Carolina Notary Law Primer (USA ISSN 1933-1029) **4748**
North Carolina Office of Archives and History. Biennial Report (USA) **4305**
North Carolina Pharmacist (USA ISSN 1529-918X) **6864**
North Carolina Plumbing, Heating & Cooling Forum (USA ISSN 0739-3830) **4124**
North Carolina Preservation (USA) **4305**
North Carolina Propane Gas News (USA) **6781**
North Carolina Reported Pregnancies (USA) **7288**
North Carolina Revised Rules of Professional Conduct (USA ISSN 1548-9507) **4748**
North Carolina Rules of Court - Desk Copy *see* Court Rules Pamphlet(s). North Carolina Rules of Court, State & Federal **4949**
North Carolina Rules of Court with Amendments Received *see* Court Rules Pamphlet(s). North Carolina Rules of Court, State & Federal **4949**
North Carolina School Directory *see* M D R's School Directory. North Carolina **2959**
North Carolina. Secretary of State. Directory of State and County Officials (USA) **7457**
North Carolina Seed Law (USA) **142**
▼ North Carolina Signature (USA ISSN 1935-7109) **5078**
North Carolina State Bar Journal (USA ISSN 1092-8626) **4748**
North Carolina State Economist *see* N C State Economist **203**
North Carolina State University. Chancellor's Report (USA) **2996**
North Carolina State University. College of Forest Resources. Technical Report (USA) **3698**
North Carolina State University Libraries Focus *see* N C S U Libraries Focus **5033**
North Carolina State University. School of Design. (Student Publication Magazine) (USA ISSN 0078-1444) **451**
North Carolina Studies in the Romance Languages and Literatures (USA ISSN 0885-6001) **5343**
North Carolina Super Lawyers (USA ISSN 1933-1819) **4748**
North Carolina Tobacco Report (USA) **8486**
North Carolina Trial Practice (USA) **4958**
North Carolina Turfgrass (USA) **244**
• North Carolina Unfair Business Practice (USA) **4877**
North Carolina Vital Statistics (USA ISSN 0078-1371) **7313**
North Carolina Wild Flower Preservation Society. Newsletter (USA ISSN 1048-4582) **3745**
• North Carolina Workers' Compensation Law Annotated (USA) **1700**
North Castle History (USA) **4305**
North-Caucasus Scientific Center of High School. Natural Sciences. News *see* Izvestiya Vysshikh Uchebnykh Zavedenii. Severo-Kavkazskii Region. Estestvennye Nauki **5499**
North-Caucasus Scientific Center of High School. Social Science. News *see* Severo-Kavkazskii Nauchnyi Tsentr Vysshei Shkoly. Obshchestvennye Nauki. Izvestiya **4263**
North-Caucasus Scientific Center of High School. Technical Science. News *see* Severo-Kavkazskii Nauchnyi Tsentr Vysshei Shkoly. Tekhnicheskie Nauki. Izvestiya **8438**
North Central Florida Senior Voice *see* Seniors Voice **4056**
North Central North Dakota Genealogical Record (USA ISSN 0736-5667) **3777**
North Central TourBook - Iowa, Minnesota, Nebraska, North Dakota, South Dakota *see* TourBook: North Central **8762**
North Central Weed Science Society. Research Report (USA ISSN 1062-421X) **244**
North Cheshire Family Historian (GBR ISSN 0306-9206) **3777**
North China Agriculture Journal *see* Huabei Nongxue Bao **119**
North China Coal Medical College. Journal *see* Huabei Meitan Yixueyuan Xuebao **5629**
North China Earthquake Sciences *see* Huabei Dizhen Kexue **2783**
North China Electric Power University. Journal *see* Huabei Dianli Daxue Xuebao **3158**
North China Electric Power University. Journal (Social Sciences) *see* Huabei Dianli Daxue Xuebao (Shehui Kexue Ban) **7969**
North China Institute of Astronautic Engineering. Journal *see* Huabei Hangtian Gongye Xueyuan Xuebao **7862**

Title

10684 NORTH CHINA INSTITUTE OF SCIENCE AND TECHNOLOGY. JOURNAL ULRICH'S PERIODICALS

North China Institute of Science and Technology. Journal *see* Huabei Keji Xueyuan Xuebao **7862**
North China Institute of Water Conservancy and Hydroelectric Power. Journal *see* Huabei Shuili Shuidian Xueyuan Xuebao **8825**
North China Institute of Water Conservancy and Hydroelectric Power. Journal (Social Science) *see* Huabei Shuili Shuidian Xueyuan Xuebao (She-ke Ban) **7969**
North China University of Technology. Journal *see* Beifang Gongye Daxue Xuebao **7839**
North Circular (GBR) **2294**
North Coast and Zululand Directory *see* Braby's North Coast and Zululand Directory **1976**
North Coast Co-Op Newsletter (USA) **3658**
North Coast Labor Trends *see* Northwest Oregon Labor Trends **1700**
North Coast Literary Review (USA ISSN 1930-5559) **5428**
North Coast Review (USA ISSN 1073-7553) **5428**
North Coast Review *see* North Coast Literary Review **5428**
North Country Catholic (USA) **7809**
North Country Cheviot Sheep Society. Flock Book (GBR) **295**
North Country Music (GBR) **6600**
➤ North Country Naturalist (USA ISSN 1056-8360) **7893**
North Country Notes (USA) **4306**
• ➤ North Dakota Academy of Science. Proceedings (USA ISSN 0096-9214) **7893**
• North Dakota Agricultural Research (USA) **142**
North Dakota Agricultural Statistics (USA ISSN 0737-1624) **184**
North Dakota: All-Industries *see* Harris Directory. North Dakota All-Industries **2001**
North Dakota Banner *see* N D Banner **4075**
• North Dakota Business Directory (USA ISSN 1046-8129) **2021**
North Dakota Century Code Annotated Court Rules *see* North Dakota Court Rules Annotated **4958**
• North Dakota Century School Code (USA) **2892**
North Dakota Citations *see* Shepard's North Dakota Citations **4963**
North Dakota Cities and Counties Graphic Performance Analysis *see* North Dakota Cities & Counties Graphic Performance Analysis **7482**
North Dakota Cities & Counties Graphic Performance Analysis (USA ISSN 1935-6021) **7482**
North Dakota Court Rules *see* Court Rules Pamphlet(s). North Dakota Court Rules, State and Federal **4949**
North Dakota Court Rules Annotated (USA ISSN 1059-9584) **4958**
• North Dakota Criminal and Traffic Law Manual (USA ISSN 1529-8701) **4896**
North Dakota. Department of Agriculture. Biennial Report of the Commissioner of Agriculture (USA ISSN 1550-5618) **142**
North Dakota. Department of Public Instruction. Biennial Report of the Superintendent of Public Instruction (USA) **2934**
North Dakota Education News (USA ISSN 0048-0681) **2892**
• North Dakota Employment Law Letter (USA ISSN 1086-2641) **4748**
North Dakota. Geological Survey. Educational Series (USA ISSN 0091-9004) **2759**
North Dakota. Geological Survey. Field Study (USA ISSN 1070-2873) **2759**
North Dakota. Geological Survey. Miscellaneous Series (USA ISSN 0078-1576) **2759**
North Dakota. Geological Survey. Newsletter (USA ISSN 0889-3594) **2759**
North Dakota. Geological Survey. Report of Investigations (USA ISSN 0099-4227) **2759**
North Dakota Grain and Oilseed Transportation Statistics (USA) **184**
➤ North Dakota History (USA ISSN 0029-2710) **4306**
North Dakota Horizons (USA ISSN 1078-1331) **8742**
• ➤ North Dakota Journal of Speech and Theatre (USA ISSN 1081-8057) **8474**
North Dakota. Judicial System. Annual Report (USA) **4824**
• ➤ North Dakota Law Review (USA ISSN 0029-2745) **4748**
North Dakota Library Statistics (USA) **5059**
• North Dakota Manufacturers Register (USA ISSN 1087-8343) **2021**
North Dakota Manufacturers Register for Windows 95 & Up, Windows N T *see* North Dakota Manufacturers Register **2021**
North Dakota: Manufacturing *see* Harris Directory. North Dakota Manufacturing **2001**
North Dakota Medicine (USA ISSN 1933-0596) **5688**
North Dakota. Milk Stabilization Board. Annual Report of Administrative Activities (USA ISSN 0091-9446) **268**
North Dakota Music Educator (USA ISSN 0029-2753) **6600**
• North Dakota Outdoors (USA ISSN 0029-2761) **2623**
➤ North Dakota Quarterly (USA ISSN 0029-277X) **4467**
• North Dakota R E C Magazine (USA ISSN 0885-2499) **3983**
North Dakota Research Report (USA ISSN 0748-4372) **142**
North Dakota School Directory *see* M D R's School Directory. North Dakota **2959**
North Dakota Securities Bulletin (USA ISSN 0549-8333) **1643**
North Dakota Society of Medical Technologists. Newsletter (USA ISSN 0048-069X) **5910**
North Dakota. State Board of Law Examiners. Directory of Lawyers and Judges (USA ISSN 1075-2390) **4748**
The North Dakota Stockman (USA ISSN 1062-4287) **295**
North Dakota Workers' Compensation Law (USA) **1700**
North Dakota's Highway Safety Plan (USA) **8633**
North Devon Journal (Barnstaple) (GBR ISSN 0962-3418) **3869**
North Devon Journal (Bideford Edition) (GBR ISSN 1750-8940) **3968**
North Devon Journal (Torridge Edition) *see* North Devon Journal (Bideford Edition) **3968**
North East & Goulburn Murray Farmer (AUS) **3795**
North East Angler (AUS ISSN 1325-3204) **8325**
North East Auto Trader (GBR ISSN 0958-3335) **8595**
North East Corporate Finance Directory *see* Insider Dealmakers Guides. North East **1354**
North East Farmer (GBR) **142**
North East Food Service Buyer's Guide (USA) **4395**
➤ North East History (GBR ISSN 1474-3248) **4249**
North-East India Council for Social Science Research. Journal (IND ISSN 0970-7913) **7159**
➤ North East India Studies (IND ISSN 0973-1180) **7989**
➤ North East Journal of Legal Studies (USA ISSN 1545-0597) **4748**
North East Linguistic Society. Proceedings (USA ISSN 0883-5500) **5156**
North East Midlands Salary Survey (GBR) **1700**
The North East Times (IND) **3886**
▼ North East Weddings (IRL ISSN 1649-931X) **5560**
North-Eastern Affairs (IND ISSN 0301-6404) **7159**
North Eastern Geographer (IND ISSN 0973-0915) **4022**
North European and Baltic Sea Integration Yearbook (Year) *see* The N E B I Yearbook (Year) **7254**
North Georgia Journal *see* Georgia Backroads **8713**
North Harbour News (NZL ISSN 1172-1057) **3918**
➤ North-Holland Delta Series (NLD ISSN 0927-5029) **7028**
➤ North-Holland Linguistic Series (NLD ISSN 0078-1592) **5156**
• ➤ North-Holland Mathematical Library (NLD ISSN 0924-6509) **5521**
• ➤ North-Holland Mathematics Studies (NLD ISSN 0304-0208) **5521**
➤ North-Holland Personal Library (NLD ISSN 0925-5818) **7029**
• ➤ North-Holland Series in Applied Mathematics and Mechanics (NLD ISSN 0167-5931) **5521**
➤ North-Holland Studies in Telecommunication (NLD ISSN 0923-0068) **2335**
North Idaho College Sentinel *see* N I C Sentinel **2293**
The North India Church Review (IND) **7666**
North Iowa Farmer (USA) **142**
• North Island Gazette (CAN ISSN 1181-4128) **3814**
North Island Televiewer (CAN) **2387**
• North Island Weekender (CAN ISSN 1482-3659) **3814**
North Japan Academy of Nursing Science. Journal *see* Kita Nihon Kango Gakkaishi **5968**
North Jersey Highlander (USA ISSN 0029-2850) **4306**
• North Korea Defence & Security Report (GBR ISSN 1749-1541) **6439**
North Korea Directory (Year) (JPN) **7457**
• ➤ North Korean Review (USA ISSN 1551-2789) **4187**
North Korean Studies Review *see* Hyeondae Bughan Yeon'gu **7141**
North London Auto Trader *see* London, Herts, Beds & Essex Auto Trader **8589**
North Louisiana Genealogical Society Journal (USA) **3777**
North Louisiana History (USA) **4306**
North, Mid Wales & Borders Living *see* Mid Wales & Borders Living **5077**
North Mississippi All Sports Review (USA) **8191**
North of England Museums Service Annual Report *see* N E M S Annual Report **6533**
North of England Weddings (GBR ISSN 1478-6060) **5560**
North Pacific Anadromous Fish Commission. Annual Report (CAN ISSN 1022-9078) **3603**
North Pacific Anadromous Fish Commission. Bulletin (CAN ISSN 1028-9127) **959**
North Pacific Anadromous Fish Commission. Newsletter (CAN ISSN 1028-0227) **3603**
North Pacific Anadromous Fish Commission. Statistical Yearbook (CAN ISSN 1028-0235) **3613**
North Pacific Marine Science Organization. Annual Report (CAN ISSN 1192-7771) **2814**
North Queensland Industry Advocate *see* The Mining Advocate **6472**
North Queensland Register (AUS ISSN 1321-1668) **3795**
North Rice *see* Beifang Shuidao **270**
North Riding and Durham Farmer. Whole Edition (GBR ISSN 0306-0675) **142**
• North Ryde Cityscope (AUS) **7618**
North San Diego Living (USA) **4548**
North Sea and Europe Offshore Yearbook and Buyers' Guide *see* Walter Skinner's North Sea and Europe Offshore Yearbook and Buyers' Guide **8998**
North Sea Facts (GBR) **6781**
• North Sea Letter (GBR ISSN 0950-1037) **6781**
North Sea Observer *see* Offshore og Energi **6782**
• North Sea Rig Forecast (GBR ISSN 1351-802X) **3143**
• North Sea Rig Report (USA ISSN 1369-1171) **6781**
North Sea Study Occasional Papers (GBR ISSN 0143-022X) **1155**
North Sea Supply Vessel Forecast (USA) **6781**
North Shore (USA ISSN 0195-1653) **3983**
The North Shore Aucklander *see* The Aucklander North Shore **3916**
North Shore Homes (USA) **7602**
• North Shore News (CAN ISSN 0712-5348) **3814**
• North Shore Outlook (CAN ISSN 1495-7612) **3814**
North Shore Times (NZL) **3918**
North Shore Times Advertiser *see* North Shore Times **3918**
North Shore Woman's Newspaper (USA) **8878**
North Somerset Council. Local Transport Plan (GBR) **8507**
North - South Carolina State Agent Handbook (USA) **4517**
North-South Institute. Annual Report (CAN ISSN 0825-5814) **1602**
North South Trader's Civil War (USA ISSN 1053-0010) **4306**
North Star (Grand Rapids) (USA) **8325**
• ➤ The North Star (Rochester) (USA ISSN 1094-902X) **3555**
North Star (Stevens Point) *see* Gwiazda Polarna **3536**
▼ • North Star Family Matters (USA ISSN 1937-8483) **4365**
• ➤ The North Stone Review (USA ISSN 1046-9389) **5343**
North Suburban Genealogical Society. Newsletter (USA ISSN 0743-1341) **3777**
North Suburban Living (USA) **4548**
• North Sydney Cityscope (AUS) **7618**
North Tahoe - Truckee This Week *see* The Weekly **3992**
North Taranaki Midweek (NZL ISSN 1170-151X) **3918**
North Texas Automotive Report (USA) **8596**
North Texas Catholic (USA ISSN 0899-7020) **7809**
North Texas Daily (USA) **2294**
North Texas Golfer (USA ISSN 0889-2377) **8240**
North Texas P C News (USA) **2573**
North Texas Teens (USA) **2163**
North Texas World Literatures Review *see* Etc... (Denton) **5291**
• North Thompson Star / Journal (CAN) **3814**
North Thompson Times (CAN) **3814**
North University of China. Journal (Natural Science Edition) *see* Zhongbei Daxue Xuebao (Ziran Kexue Ban) **8446**
North University of China. Journal (Social Science edition) *see* Zhongbei Daxue Xuebao (Shehui Kexue Ban) **8018**
North Waikato News (NZL) **3918**
North Wales Living (GBR ISSN 1747-714X) **5078**
North West Auto Trader (GBR ISSN 0958-4277) **8596**
North West Business (GBR ISSN 0306-5650) **1431**
North West Business Insider *see* Insider. North West Business Insider **1124**
• North West Commodity Corner (USA) **142**
North West Corporate Finance Directory *see* Insider Dealmakers Guides. North West **1354**
North West England Directory of Industry & Commerce (GBR) **2021**
North West Ethno-National Studies *see* Xibei Minzu Yanjiu **563**
North West Europe Company Report (GBR) **6781**
North West Express (AUS ISSN 0729-4026) **5036**
• ➤ The North West Geographer (Online) (GBR ISSN 1476-1580) **4022**
North West Kent Family History (GBR ISSN 0263-6506) **3777**
North West Labour History (GBR ISSN 1362-6302) **4249**
North West Magazine (AUS) **8191**
North West Nature (GBR ISSN 1365-9146) **2623**
North - West Passage (ITA ISSN 1826-641X) **6509**
North West plc. (GBR ISSN 1748-1473) **2021**
• North West Provincial Legislation Library (ZAF ISSN 1683-2698) **4748**
North West Rugby (GBR) **8240**
North West Salary Survey (GBR) **1700**
North West Telegraph (AUS ISSN 1446-9960) **3795**
North-Western European Language Evolution *see* N O W E L E **5153**
North-Western European Language Evolution Supplement *see* N O W E L E. Supplement **5153**
• North - Western Journal of Zoology (ROM ISSN 1584-9074) **959**
• ➤ North Wind (GBR ISSN 0265-7295) **5231**
• North Wind (USA) **2294**
North Woods Call (USA ISSN 0029-2958) **2623**
• The North York Mirror (CAN ISSN 1204-4369) **3814**
Northampton Business Directory *see* Commerce Business Directories. Northampton **1980**
† Northamptoniana (GBR ISSN 0309-8486) **8977**
Northamptonshire Archaeology (GBR ISSN 0305-4659) **408**
➤ Northamptonshire Bird Report (GBR ISSN 1363-4844) **911**
Northamptonshire Image (GBR ISSN 0960-9512) **3869**
Northamptonshire Natural History Society and Field Club Journal (GBR ISSN 0144-0586) **7893**
Northamptonshire Past and Present (GBR ISSN 0140-9131) **4249**
NorthBay Biz (USA ISSN 1542-3549) **1155**
• Northbound (USA ISSN 1070-812X) **3457**
Northcoast Sports Pro Football Preview (USA) **8240**
Northcon Conference Record (USA) **3391**
Northeast (La Crosse) (USA ISSN 0549-8880) **5343**
The Northeast (Portland) (USA) **7769**
Northeast African Monograph Series (USA) **3555**
• Northeast African Studies (USA ISSN 0740-9133) **3555**
Northeast Agricultural University. Journal *see* Dongbei Nongye Daxue Xuebao **105**
• Northeast Agricultural University. Journal (CHN ISSN 1006-8104) **142**
➤ Northeast Anthropology (USA ISSN 1068-9982) **350**
• Northeast Bioengineering Conference. Proceedings (USA ISSN 0277-1063) **750**
Northeast Boating (USA ISSN 1938-6354) **8279**
• Northeast Business and Economics Association. Annual Meeting. Proceedings (USA ISSN 1936-203X) **1155**
† Northeast C-Store Journal (USA) **8977**
Northeast Canine Companion (USA ISSN 1041-1496) **6812**
Northeast China Institute of Electric Power Engineering. Journal *see* Dongbei Dianli Xueyuan Xuebao **3156**
Northeast Cities and Counties Graphic Performance Analysis *see* Northeast Cities & Counties Graphic Performance Analysis **7482**
Northeast Cities & Counties Graphic Performance Analysis (USA ISSN 1935-5750) **7482**
Northeast Conference on the Teaching of Foreign Languages. Newsletter *see* N E C T F L Review **5153**
Northeast Conference on the Teaching of Foreign Languages Review *see* N E C T F L Review **5153**
Northeast Convenience Store Journal *see* Northeast C-Store Journal **8977**
Northeast Corridor (USA ISSN 1085-0449) **5231**
Northeast Dairy Business (USA) **268**
Northeast Export Magazine (USA ISSN 1092-6682) **1579**
➤ Northeast Florida Medicine (USA) **5688**
Northeast Folklore (USA ISSN 0078-1681) **3621**
Northeast Forestry University. Journal *see* Dongbei Linye Daxue Xuebao **3687**
Northeast Historical Archaeology (USA ISSN 0048-0738) **408**
Northeast - Journal of Antiques & Art (USA) **368**
Northeast Magazine (USA) **3983**
Northeast Magazine *see* N'East Magazine **8324**
Northeast Mississippi Historical and Genealogical Society Quarterly (USA ISSN 1060-5568) **4306**
Northeast Modern Language Association Italian Studies *see* N E M L A Italian Studies **5337**
Northeast Normal University. Journal (Natural Science Edition) *see* Dongbei Shi-Daxuebao (Ziran Kexue Ban) **7851**
Northeast Normal University. Journal (Philosophy, Social Sciences Edition) *see* Dongbei Shi-Daxuebao (Zhexue Shehui Kexue Ban) **7960**
Northeast Ohio Areawide Coordinating Agency News *see* N O A C A News **8505**
• Northeast Ohio Journal of History (USA ISSN 1552-2059) **4306**
• Northeast Pennsylvania Business Journal (USA ISSN 1078-5698) **1155**
Northeast Real Estate Business (USA ISSN 1554-0847) **7602**
Northeast Region Report (USA) **3457**
• Northeast Regional Employment Law Institute. Annual (USA ISSN 1931-230X) **4748**
The Northeast Square Dancer Magazine (USA ISSN 1044-2928) **2687**
Northeast States Petroleum Industry (USA) **6781**
Northeast Sun (CAN ISSN 1912-1415) **3814**
Northeast Sun (Greenfield) (USA) **3143**
Northeast Sun (Los Angeles) (USA) **3555**
▼ • Northeast Wealth Management Business (USA ISSN 1942-5015) **1372**
• Northeast Woods & Waters (USA) **8325**
NorthEastArts Magazine (USA) **5428**
Northeastern *see* CampBook: Northeastern **8690**
▼ The Northeastern Geographer (USA ISSN 1948-5417) **4022**
➤ Northeastern Geology and Environmental Sciences (USA ISSN 1933-2742) **2759**
Northeastern Illinois University. Working Papers in Linguistics (USA) **5156**
• Northeastern Mathematical Journal (CHN) **5521**
• ➤ Northeastern Naturalist (USA ISSN 1092-6194) **805**
➤ Northeastern Nevada Historical Society Quarterly (USA ISSN 0160-9602) **4306**
• Northeastern News (USA ISSN 0029-3032) **2294**
Northeastern Reporter Citations *see* Shepard's Northeastern Reporter Citations **4963**
Northeastern University Alumni Magazine (USA ISSN 1938-5951) **2294**

Title

DIRECTORY 2010 NUCLEAR ALMANAC 10689

Nova Scotia. Apprenticeship Training and Skill Development. Annual Report (CAN ISSN 1914-1394) **6701**
Nova Scotia Archaeology Society. Curatorial Report (CAN) **409**
Nova Scotia Association of Architects. Newsletter (CAN ISSN 0834-7816) **451**
● Nova Scotia Barristers' Society. Annual Report (CAN ISSN 0704-8394) **4749**
Nova Scotia Birds (CAN) **911**
Nova Scotia Business Journal (CAN ISSN 0820-2737) **1964**
Nova Scotia Civil Procedure Rules (CAN) **4839**
● Nova Scotia Craft News (CAN ISSN 1193-011X) **538**
● Nova Scotia Current Law (Online) (CAN) **4824**
Nova Scotia Dentist (CAN) **5857**
Nova Scotia Department of Community Services (Year) (CAN ISSN 0844-7535) **8059**
Nova Scotia. Department of Economic Development and Tourism. Annual Report (CAN) **7457**
Nova Scotia. Department of Education. Apprenticeship Training Division. Annual Report *see* Nova Scotia. Apprenticeship Training and Skill Development. Annual Report **6701**
Nova Scotia. Department of Health. Vital Statistics. Annual Report (CAN ISSN 0837-2462) **7288**
Nova Scotia. Department of Labour. Annual Report (CAN ISSN 0380-5689) **1700**
Nova Scotia. Department of Labour. Compendium of Grievance Arbitration Decisions (CAN) **4600**
Nova Scotia. Department of Transportation and Communications. Annual Report *see* Nova Scotia. Department of Transportation and Public Works. Accountability Report **7457**
Nova Scotia. Department of Transportation and Public Works. Accountability Report (CAN ISSN 1910-4243) **7457**
Nova Scotia Employment Program for Students Job Catalogue *see* Student Career Skills Development Program. Job Catalogue **6704**
Nova Scotia. Fire Marshal. Annual Report (CAN ISSN 0085-4395) **3580**
Nova Scotia Fruit Growers Association. Annual Report and Proceedings (CAN ISSN 0078-2386) **244**
Nova Scotia Genealogist (CAN ISSN 0714-3672) **3777**
Nova Scotia Institute of Agrologists Newsletter (CAN ISSN 0833-8485) **142**
Nova Scotia Labour Market *see* Labour Market Monthly **6700**
Nova Scotia Law News (CAN ISSN 0316-6325) **4749**
Nova Scotia Manufacturing Profile (CAN ISSN 1718-1488) **1900**
Nova Scotia. Office of the Ombudsman. Annual Report (CAN ISSN 0380-5670) **7457**
Nova Scotia Open to the World (CAN ISSN 1208-8676) **1155**
Nova Scotia Power Inc. Annual Report (CAN ISSN 0703-0789) **3143**
Nova Scotia Public Service Superannuation Plan (CAN ISSN 1910-6882) **1700**
Nova Scotia Real Property Practice Manual (CAN) **7602**
● Nova Scotia Reports (CAN ISSN 0048-0983) **4749**
Nova Scotia School Boards Association Matters! *see* N S S B A Matters! **3028**
Nova Scotia Trappers Newsletter (CAN ISSN 0705-4831) **4974**
➤ Nova Scotian Institute of Science. Proceedings (CAN ISSN 0078-2521) **7894**
Nova Scotian Surveyor (CAN ISSN 0380-9242) **3279**
● Nova Supplementa Entomologica (DEU ISSN 0948-6038) **856**
● Nova Tellus (MEX ISSN 0185-3058) **4467**
† Nova Thalassia (ITA ISSN 0369-5271) **8978**
Nova Trgovina (SRB ISSN 0469-0281) **1431**
Nova24 Review (ITA ISSN 1970-4089) **4877**
Novachem Manual *see* New Zealand Novachem Agrichemical Manual **243**
Novaensia *see* Novensia **409**
Novaesium (DEU ISSN 1860-6091) **4250**
Novalis (CHE ISSN 1420-3235) **5231**
Novantanove Idee Casa *see* 99 Idee Casa **462**
Novantanove Idee Tech *see* 99 Idee Tech **462**
† Novantiqua (ITA) **8978**
Novarien (ITA ISSN 0078-253X) **7810**
● Novartis Foundation Symposium (GBR ISSN 1528-2511) **7894**
Novartis Oncology News (CZE ISSN 1801-870X) **6029**
Novas de Alegria (PRT ISSN 0029-5116) **7739**
Novascope (USA ISSN 0892-5003) **3984**
● Novatica (ESP ISSN 0211-2124) **2433**
● ➤ NOVAtions (USA) **2892**
● Novaya Buhgalteriya (RUS) **1298**
Novaya Delovaya Kniga (RUS) **3121**
Novaya Gazeta (RUS ISSN 1682-7384) **3938**
● Novaya i Noveishaya Istoriya (RUS ISSN 0029-5124) **4154**
Novaya Igrushechka (RUS) **4981**
Novaya Kamchatskaya Pravda (RUS) **3938**
Novaya Khronika (RUS) **3938**
▼ ● Novaya Kozha (USA ISSN 1939-0645) **5343**
Novaya Literatura po Sotsial'nym i Gumanitarnym Naukam. Ekonomika (RUS) **1256**
Novaya Literatura po Sotsial'nym i Gumanitarnym Naukam. Filosofiya i Sotsiologiya (RUS) **6962**
Novaya Literatura po Sotsial'nym i Gumanitarnym Naukam. Istoriya. Arkheologiya. Etnologiya (RUS) **362**
Novaya Literatura po Sotsial'nym i Gumanitarnym Naukam. Literaturovedenie (RUS) **5408**
Novaya Literatura po Sotsial'nym i Gumanitarnym Naukam. Naukovedenie (RUS) **7938**
Novaya Literatura po Sotsial'nym i Gumanitarnym Naukam. Pravovedenie. Politoligiya (RUS) **4824**
Novaya Literatura po Sotsial'nym i Gumanitarnym Naukam. Religiovedenie (RUS) **7699**
Novaya Literatura po Sotsial'nym i Gumanitarnym Naukam. Yazykoznanie (RUS ISSN 1561-2716) **5201**
Novaya Molodezhnaya Gazeta (RUS) **3938**
● Novaya Nikolayevskaya Gazeta (UKR) **3965**
Novaya Poligrafiya (RUS) **31**
Novaya Rossiya (RUS) **3938**
● Novaya Sibir' (RUS) **3938**
● Novaya Yunost' (RUS ISSN 0869-7361) **509**
Nove Ilhas (CAN) **3815**
Novecento *see* Cahiers d'Etudes Italiennes **5268**
Novecento Europeo (ITA ISSN 1971-2294) **4250**
Novecento Teologico (ITA ISSN 1827-6784) **7666**
Novedades (ESP) **632**
● Novedades (MEX ISSN 0188-2856) **3910**
Novedades (USA) **3555**
● Novedades Acapulco (English Edition) (Online) (MEX ISSN 1605-4172) **3910**
● Novedades Acapulco (Spanish Edition) (Online) (MEX ISSN 1605-4180) **3910**
● Novedades Acapulco (Spanish Edition) (Print) (MEX) **3910**
Novedades Bibliograficas (ARG ISSN 0327-9979) **632**
● Novedades de Tabasco (MEX ISSN 1605-5543) **3910**
† Novedades Electronicas (ESP ISSN 1138-1477) **8978**
Novedades Legislativas (ARG) **4851**
● Novedades Quintana Roo (MEX) **3910**
● Novedades Quintana Roo (Online) (MEX ISSN 1605-4164) **3910**
Novedades y Perspectivas Terapeuticas *see* Drug News & Perspectives **6836**
● ➤ Novel: A Forum on Fiction (USA ISSN 0029-5132) **5344**
Novel & Short Story Writer's Market (USA ISSN 0897-9812) **5344**
Novel and Short Story Writer's Market *see* Novel & Short Story Writer's Market **5344**
Novel Methods for Integrated Risk Assessment of Cumulative Stressors in Europe *see* NoMiracle Newsletter **3500**
Novela Historica (ESP ISSN 2013-0007) **5344**
● NovelAdvice Cyber Journal (USA) **5344**
Noveldiana (ESP ISSN 1136-8489) **5344**
Novelette *see* Zhongpian Xiaoshuo **5405**
● Novell Connection (USA ISSN 1533-7960) **2502**
Novella 2000 (ITA ISSN 1120-4443) **3898**
● Novelleregister (Online) (DNK) **5344**
I Novellieri Italiani (ITA ISSN 1970-397X) **5344**
● Novels for Students (USA ISSN 1094-3552) **5344**
● November Spawned (Science Ficition) (GBR ISSN 1746-6024) **5445**
Novemberakademie (DEU ISSN 1612-2194) **8124**
Noveno Conferencia de las Naciones Unidas Sobre la Normalizacion de los Nombres Geograficos *see* United Nations Conference on the Standardization of Geographical Names. Report **4031**
Novensia (POL ISSN 0860-5777) **409**
● ➤ Novenytermeles/Crop Production (HUN ISSN 0546-8191) **244**
Novenyvedelem/Plant Protection (HUN ISSN 0133-0829) **244**
➤ Nover (HUN ISSN 0864-7003) **5971**
Novgorodskie Vedomosti (RUS) **3938**
Novi Izraz/New Expression (BIH ISSN 1512-5335) **5344**
Novi Knigi/New Books (BGR) **7569**
Novi List (HRV ISSN 0350-4301) **3831**
➤ Novi Materijali (SRB ISSN 0354-2300) **3213**
● Novi Sad Journal of Mathematics (SRB ISSN 1450-5444) **5521**
Novi Vydannya Ukrainy (UKR ISSN 0136-0922) **7578**
● Novi Zvuk (SRB ISSN 0354-4362) **6600**
Novias Sposabella *see* Sposabella Novias **2261**
Novinar (HRV ISSN 1330-1543) **4581**
Novinar (SVN ISSN 0469-0729) **4581**
Novinky (SVK ISSN 1337-0634) **6097**
Novinky Detskej Fakultnej Nemocnice s Poliklinikou Banska Bystrica *see* Novinky **6097**
† Novinky Literatury. Zdravotnictvi-Prirustky Fondu Narodni Lekarske Knihovny (CZE ISSN 1212-3862) **8978**
Noviny Odboroveho Svazu Statnich Organu a Organizaci *see* N O S **1780**
Novitaet (DEU) **7569**
Novitas (RUS ISSN 0868-4928) **7894**
▼ ● ➤ Novitas - R O Y A L (Research on Youth and Language) (TUR ISSN 1307-4733) **5156**
Novitas-ROYAL *see* Novitas - R O Y A L **5156**
Novo Jornal Cabo Verde (CPV) **3821**
Novo Mundo - Mundos Novos *see* Nuevo Mundo - Mundos Nuevos **4306**
● Novoe Literaturnoe Obozrenie (RUS ISSN 0869-6365) **5231**
Novoe Meditsinskoe Oborudovanie *see* Novye Meditsinskie Tekhnologii **5910**
● Novoe Omskoe Slovo (RUS) **3938**
Novoe Pokolenie (KAZ) **2205**
Novoe Sel'skoe Khozyaistvo (RUS) **142**
Novoe v Bukhgalterskom Uchete i Otchetnosti v Rossiiskoi Federatsii (RUS ISSN 1028-7442) **1298**
➤ Novoe v Oftal'mologii (RUS) **6046**
Novoe Vremya (ARM) **3792**
● Novoe Vremya (RUS ISSN 0137-0723) **3938**
● Novogradac New Markets Tax Credit Report (USA ISSN 1941-482X) **1937**
Novogradac Property Compliance Report *see* Property Compliance Report **1940**
Novogradiski Glasnik (HRV ISSN 0353-7838) **142**
Novogradiski Zbornik (HRV ISSN 0352-7417) **4467**
Novohradske Noviny (SVK ISSN 1210-0641) **3946**
Novokuznetskii Rabochii (RUS) **3938**
➤ Novon (USA ISSN 1055-3177) **806**
Novos Estudos C E B R A P *see* Centro Brasileiro de Analise e Planejamento. Novos Estudos **7953**
● ➤ Novos Estudos Juridicos (BRA ISSN 1413-2117) **4749**
Novosibirskie Novosti (RUS) **3938**
Novosti (AUS) **3555**
● Novosti e-Kommertsii (RUS ISSN 1606-156X) **1420**
Novosti Energetiki (AZE) **3143**
Novosti Enigma (SRB ISSN 0352-7123) **5078**
Novosti Iskustvennogo Intellekta/A I News (RUS ISSN 1682-8917) **2455**
Novosti Kosmonavtiki (RUS ISSN 1561-1078) **67**
● Novosti Malogo Biznesa (RUS ISSN 1606-1535) **1964**
Novosti Oglasi (SRB ISSN 1450-8273) **31**
Novosti Poligrafii (RUS) **7325**
Novosti Pskova (RUS) **3938**
Novosti Razvedki i Kontrazvedki (RUS ISSN 1028-9674) **6439**
● Novosti Sistemy M M Ts (Mezhregional'nyi Marketingovyi Tsentr) (RUS ISSN 1606-1519) **1836**
Novosti Turkmenistana (TKM) **3963**
Novosti Yugry (RUS) **3938**
Novoto Danuchno Zakonodatelstvo (BGR) **1937**
Novoye Russkoye Slovo (USA ISSN 0730-8949) **3555**
Novum (DEU ISSN 1438-1753) **31**
➤ Novum Commentarium Lovaniense in Codicem Iuris Canonici (BEL) **7810**
Novum Glossarium Mediae Latinitatis (CHE ISSN 1376-7461) **5156**
● ➤ Novum Testamentum (NLD ISSN 0048-1009) **7666**
Novum Testamentum et Orbis Antiquus (CHE ISSN 1420-4592) **7666**
➤ Novum Testamentum. Supplements (NLD ISSN 0167-9732) **7667**
● Novy Cas (SVK ISSN 1335-4655) **3946**
Novy Cas Byvanie (SVK ISSN 1336-8842) **8878**
† Novy Cas L'udia (SVK ISSN 1336-7781) **8978**
Novy Cas Nedel'a (SVK ISSN 1336-7463) **3946**
● Novy Cas pre Zeny (SVK ISSN 1336-3654) **8878**
Novy Cas Special. Krizovky (SVK ISSN 1336-7587) **8191**
Novy Domov/New Homeland (CAN ISSN 0839-2668) **3555**
Novy Orient/New Orient (CZE ISSN 0029-5302) **557**
Novy Shliakh/New Pathway/Nouveau Chemin (CAN ISSN 0029-5310) **3555**
Novy Vpred Zurnal (SVK ISSN 1336-006X) **3946**
● Novy Zakonik Prace v Praxi (CZE ISSN 1802-1360) **1700**
Novy Zivot Turca (SVK ISSN 0139-6374) **3946**
Novye Issledovaniya v Gornoi Elektromekhanike (RUS) **3110**
Novye Issledovaniya v Khimii, Metallurgii i Obogashchenii (RUS) **6328**
Novye Izvestiya (RUS) **3938**
● Novye Knigi Rossii (RUS) **632**
Novye Meditsinskie Tekhnologii (RUS) **5910**
Novye Promyshlennye Katalogi. Elektrotekhnika. Radiotekhnika. Svyaz'. Energetika i Yadernaya Tekhnika. Energeticheskoe Oborudovanie (RUS) **3110**
Novye Promyshlennye Katalogi. Gorno-Shakhtnoe i Metallurgicheskoe Oborudovanie (RUS ISSN 0208-1008) **6328**
Novye Promyshlennye Katalogi. Mashiny i Oborudovanie dlya Legkoi, Pishchevoi Promyshlennosti, Sel'skogo i Lesnogo Khozyaistva (RUS) **3699**
Novye Promyshlennye Katalogi. Mashiny i Oborudovanie dlya Torgovli i Obshchestvennogo Pitaniya. Bytovye Mashiny i Pribory (RUS) **3658**
Novye Promyshlennye Katalogi. Meditsinskaya Tekhnika. Tekhnika Bezopasnosti. Veterinarnoe Oborudovanie/New Industrial Catalogs. Medical Equipment. Safety Techniques.Veterinary Equipment (RUS ISSN 0208-1857) **2021**
Novye Promyshlennye Katalogi. Oborudovanie dlya Khimicheskoi, Neftyanoi, Tsellyulozno-Bumazhnoi Promyshlennosti i dlya Lesozagotovok i Lesosplava (RUS) **3699**
Novye Promyshlennye Katalogi. Oborudovanie dlya Obrabotki i Otdelki Metalla i Drevesiny. Detali Mashin. Robototekhnika (RUS) **6328**
Novye Promyshlennye Katalogi. Oborudovanie dlya Poligraficheskoi Promyshlennosti. Fotokinotekhnika. Sredstva Orgtekhniki (RUS) **6509**
Novye Promyshlennye Katalogi. Pribory. Avtomatika. Telemekhanika i Vychislitel'naya Tekhnika (RUS) **7061**
Novye Promyshlennye Katalogi. Stroitel'nye, Dorozhnye i Kommunal'nye Mashiny i Oborudovanie. Stroitel'nye Materialy (RUS) **1027**
Novye Promyshlennye Katalogi. Transport. Pod'emno-Transportnoe i Skladskoe Oborudovanie (RUS) **8507**
● Novye Tekhnologii (RUS ISSN 1606-1470) **8433**
Novye Vekhi (RUS) **5231**
● Novyi Den' (UKR) **3965**
● Novyi Gorod (RUS) **3938**
Novyi Krokodil (RUS ISSN 1680-9521) **5231**
Novyi Kurdistan (USA) **3938**
● ➤ Novyi Mir (RUS ISSN 0130-7673) **5231**
● Novyi Mir Iskusstva (RUS ISSN 1560-8697) **509**
Novyi Sadovod i Fermer (RUS) **3745**
Novyi Zemlevladelets (RUS) **142**
Novyi Zhurnal/New Review (USA ISSN 0029-5337) **3555**
Now (CAN ISSN 0712-1326) **3815**
Now (GBR ISSN 1365-6864) **8878**
Now (IND ISSN 0029-5345) **3886**
Now (Bloemfontein) (ZAF) **3949**
Now (Longview) (USA ISSN 1066-3347) **2294**
● Now and Then (AUS ISSN 1442-3030) **7457**
Now & Then (Johnson City) (USA ISSN 0896-2693) **5344**
Now and Then (Muncy) (USA ISSN 0029-5361) **4306**
Now Australia (AUS ISSN 1833-8682) **4581**
Now Culture 1 *see* N C 1 **5337**
Now Hear This - U S S Callaway Newsletter (USA ISSN 1083-2246) **6440**
Now Hiring (USA ISSN 1059-6445) **6701**
Now Playing Magazine (USA) **8742**
Nowa Fantastyka (POL ISSN 0867-132X) **5445**
Nowa Klinika (POL ISSN 1231-3025) **6217**
Nowa Krytyka (POL ISSN 0867-647X) **5231**
● ➤ Nowa Medycyna (POL ISSN 1233-5991) **5688**
Nowa Miss *see* Boutique **8854**
Nowa Okolica Poetow (POL ISSN 1506-3682) **5428**
● ➤ Nowa Pediatria (POL ISSN 1428-1848) **6097**
● Nowa Stomatologia (POL ISSN 1426-6911) **5857**
Nowa Szkola (POL ISSN 0029-537X) **2892**
Nowa Technika Wojskowa (POL ISSN 1230-1655) **6440**
Nowa Trybuna Opolska (POL ISSN 1230-6134) **3930**
Nowa Wies Europejska (POL ISSN 1644-3381) **143**
Nowe Ksiazki (POL ISSN 0137-8562) **7569**
Nowe Powisle Dabrowskie (POL ISSN 1429-1096) **5231**
Nowe Ubezpieczenia (POL ISSN 1428-8060) **4517**
Nowiny Lekarskie (POL ISSN 0860-7397) **5688**
➤ Nowiny Psychologiczne (POL ISSN 0867-7980) **7388**
Nowoczesny Technik Dentystyczny (POL) **5857**
Nowosci Ginekologiczne *see* Ob/Gyn Clinical Alert **6000**
Nowosci Neurologiczne *see* Neurology Alert **6166**
Nowosci w Chorobach Infekcyjnych *see* Infectious Disease Alert **5817**
➤ Nowotwory (POL ISSN 0029-540X) **6029**
Nowy Casnik (DEU ISSN 0029-5418) **3555**
● Nowy Dziennik/Polish Daily News (USA ISSN 1064-8402) **3555**
Nowy Filomata (POL ISSN 1428-6327) **2238**
Nowy Kurier *see* Polish Canadian Courier **3558**
Nowy Swiat Ciszy *see* Swiat Ciszy **4076**
Nox (ESP ISSN 1576-6136) **6296**
Nox (JOR ISSN 1999-6675) **6296**
Noyaku Jidai *see* Ag-Chem Age **80**
Noyaku Kensasho Hokoku/Agricultural Chemicals Inspection Station. Bulletin (JPN ISSN 0369-4658) **244**
Noyan Tapan Highlights (ARM) **3792**
Noyce Publishing. Religion and Development Series. (AUS) **7667**
Nozzle (USA ISSN 0029-5434) **8596**
The Nozzle & Wrench (USA) **8596**
Nozzle Chatter (USA) **3391**
N'quda *see* Nekuda **3896**
NRC.next (NLD ISSN 1574-6054) **3915**
NRCd Publication (National Centre for Documentation) (GBR ISSN 0307-9384) **6972**
nRevolution *see* n - Revolution **8189**
NRUe *see* Nomos Rechtsprechungsuebersicht **4747**
NSMan *see* N S Man **6437**
Nsukka Journal of Linguistics and African Languages (NGA ISSN 0794-6961) **5156**
Nsukka Library Notes (NGA ISSN 0331-1481) **5037**
Ntieyong Business Review (NGA ISSN 0331-4464) **1155**
NTT DoCoMo Technical Journal *see* N T T Do Co Mo Technical Journal **2334**
NTT R&D *see* N T T R & D **2370**
Nu (SWE ISSN 0281-4285) **7160**
Nu *see* Tempo (Stockholm) **1797**
▼ ● Nu Delta Alpha. Journal (USA ISSN 1934-7626) **2687**
Nu-Power (IND ISSN 0971-9911) **3171**
● Nua Internet Surveys (IRL) **2565**
● Nua Making It Work (IRL) **1420**
● Nua New Thinking (IRL) **6937**
● Nuantong Kongtiao/Heating, Ventilation and Air Conditioning (CHN ISSN 1002-8501) **4124**
➤ Nubia (POL ISSN 0860-7923) **409**
Nuclear Almanac *see* Genshiryoku Nenkan **3167**

Title

▼ *new title* † *ceased* ● *electronic media* ➤ *refereed*

DIRECTORY 2010 NUTRITIONAL PERSPECTIVES 10691

Nuntiaturberichte aus Deutschland nebst Ergaenzenden Aktenstuecken (DEU ISSN 0078-2742) 4154
Nuori Voima (FIN ISSN 0785-6776) 5344
Nuorisotutkimus (FIN ISSN 0780-0886) 2163
Nuorten Sarka *see* 4 H Pilke 173
Nuova Antologia (ITA ISSN 0029-6147) 5231
Nuova Biblioteca di Scienze Religiose (ITA) 7667
La Nuova Citta (ITA ISSN 1128-1790) 3898
Nuova Civilta delle Macchine (ITA) 6937
• ➤ Nuova Corrente (ITA ISSN 0029-6155) 5344
Nuova Cronaca Vera (ITA ISSN 1125-5536) 3898
La Nuova Ecologia (ITA ISSN 1592-5048) 3457
Nuova Elettrauto (ITA) 3326
Nuova Elettronica (ITA ISSN 1124-5174) 3110
• La Nuova Europa (ITA ISSN 1127-8722) 7667
Nuova Finestra (ITA ISSN 0394-3216) 1055
• La Nuova Giurisprudenza Civile Commentata (ITA ISSN 1593-7305) 4839
• Nuova Informazione Bibliografica (ITA ISSN 1824-0771) 632
Nuova Italia Scientifica Studi Superiori *see* N I S Studi Superiori 8976
Nuova Narrativa Newton (ITA ISSN 1970-3848) 5344
• La Nuova Provincia (ITA) 3898
Nuova Puglia Emigrazione (ITA) 7288
Nuova Rassegna (ITA ISSN 0029-6201) 5231
• Nuova Rassegna di Legislazione, Dottrina e Giurisprudenza (ITA ISSN 0392-7059) 4750
† Nuova Rassegna di Studi Musicali (ITA ISSN 0391-3724) 8978
• La Nuova Ricerca (ITA ISSN 1593-7577) 5157
Nuova Rivista di Letteratura Italiana (ITA ISSN 1590-7929) 5344
† Nuova Rivista di Neurologia (ITA ISSN 1122-035X) 8978
Nuova Rivista GeoActa *see* GeoActa 2707
Nuova Rivista Musicale Italiana (ITA ISSN 0029-6228) 6600
Nuova Rivista Storica (ITA ISSN 0029-6236) 4154
Nuova Secondaria (ITA ISSN 1828-4582) 2892
Nuova Stoa (ITA ISSN 0390-3036) 6937
Nuova Storia Contemporanea (ITA ISSN 1126-098X) 4155
Nuova Umanita (ITA) 7810
Nuova Universale Studium (ITA ISSN 0391-8548) 5344
Le Nuove Leggi Civili Commentate (ITA ISSN 0391-3740) 4839
• ➤ Nuove Lettere/New Letters (ITA ISSN 1126-2559) 5344
† Nuove Ricerche Metodologiche (ITA ISSN 1121-774X) 8978
Nuove Tecnologie in Medicina (ITA ISSN 1593-1994) 5910
Nuove Tendenze della Psicologia *see* Psicologia dell'Educazione 2900
• Nuovi Annali della Scuola Speciale per Archivisti e Bibliotecari (ITA ISSN 1122-0775) 5037
Nuovi Argomenti (ITA ISSN 0029-6295) 5344
I Nuovi Bestsellers (ITA ISSN 1122-5483) 5411
I Nuovi Bestsellers Special (ITA ISSN 1124-3538) 5411
Nuovi Quaderni di Vita Notarile *see* Vita Notarile 4882
Nuovi Saggi (ITA ISSN 0078-2769) 4467
Nuovi Studi Storici *see* Istituto Storico Italiano per il Medio Evo. Nuovi Studi Storici 4233
Il Nuovo Anestesista Rianimatore (ITA) 5772
† Nuovo Archivio Trimestrale (ITA ISSN 1122-6900) 8978
Il Nuovo Bagno (ITA ISSN 1592-1387) 1027
Nuovo Bullettino Archeologico Sardo (ITA ISSN 1722-5183) 409
Il Nuovo Calcio (ITA ISSN 1121-3256) 8240
• Il Nuovo Cantiere (ITA ISSN 0029-6325) 1027
Nuovo Cimento B *see* Societa Italiana di Fisica. Nuovo Cimento B. Basic Topics in Physics 7040
Il Nuovo Club (ITA ISSN 1120-4931) 6994
• Nuovo Collegamento (ITA) 6864
Il Nuovo Diritto (ITA ISSN 0029-6368) 4750
Nuovo Diritto Agrario *see* Economia e Diritto Agroalimentare 106
† Nuovo Giornale dei Distillatori (ITA ISSN 0017-0119) 8978
• Il Nuovo Giornale dei Militari (ITA) 6440
† Il Nuovo Management (ITA) 8978
Nuovo Medioevo (ITA ISSN 0391-6049) 4250
† Nuovo Mezzogiorno (ITA ISSN 0029-6376) 8978
Il Nuovo Mondo (CAN ISSN 0821-6525) 3556
Nuovo Orione (ITA ISSN 1122-7869) 578
Nuovo Repertorio di Giurisprudenza del Lavoro (ITA ISSN 1826-6681) 4750
• Il Nuovo Riformista (ITA ISSN 1723-0047) 3898
• Il Nuovo Saggiatore (ITA ISSN 0393-4578) 7029
• Nuovo Totoguida Sport (ITA ISSN 1590-0908) 8191
Nur al-Hikma (DEU ISSN 1860-9775) 7715
Nur Premiere (DEU) 2387
Nur T V (DEU) 2387
† Nur - The Light (TUR) 8978
Le Nurb (GBR ISSN 0307-9244) 2294
• Nure Investigacion (ESP ISSN 1697-218X) 5971
• ➤ Nuritinga (AUS ISSN 1440-1541) 5971
Nurscene (CAN ISSN 0382-8476) 5971
Nurse 2 Nurse (GBR ISSN 1473-2114) 5971
Nurse Aide - V I P (USA ISSN 1524-2900) 4052
• Nurse Author and Editor (Online) (GBR ISSN 1750-4910) 4581
• ➤ Nurse Education in Practice (GBR ISSN 1471-5953) 5971
• ➤ Nurse Education Today (GBR ISSN 0260-6917) 5971
• ➤ Nurse Educator (USA ISSN 0363-3624) 5972
• Nurse Leader (USA ISSN 1541-4612) 5972
• Nurse Manager Weekly (USA ISSN 1543-7353) 5972
• ➤ The Nurse Practitioner (USA ISSN 0361-1817) 5972
Nurse Practitioner World News (USA ISSN 1520-8737) 5972
Nurse Practitioners in Women's Health Newsletter: The Monthly Cycle *see* N P W H Newsletter: The Monthly Cycle 8847
• Nurse Practitioners' Prescribing Reference (USA ISSN 1074-3871) 6864
† • ➤ Nurse Prescriber (GBR ISSN 1467-1158) 8978
• ➤ Nurse Researcher (GBR ISSN 1351-5578) 5972
Nurse Student *see* Kango Gakusei 5968
Nurse to Nurse *see* Nurse 2 Nurse 5971
• Nurse-Zine (USA) 5972
• Nurseline (USA ISSN 1557-3184) 5972
• Nurselinx (USA) 5972
• Nursery & Childcare Market News (GBR ISSN 1747-5147) 1900
The Nursery Book (USA) 3757
Nursery Education (GBR) 3075
Nursery Industry (GBR ISSN 0967-4535) 4561
Nursery Management & Production (USA ISSN 1080-6695) 3745
Nursery Management Today (GBR) 6097
Nursery Market News *see* Nursery & Childcare Market News 1900
• Nursery News (USA) 3745
Nursery Retailer (USA ISSN 1073-9432) 3745
Nursery Today (GBR) 2163
Nursery World (GBR ISSN 0029-6422) 2163
Nurses and Midwives Board Update *see* N M B Update 5970
• Nurses-Digest (USA ISSN 1548-5269) 5972
Nurses' Drug Alert (USA ISSN 0191-2291) 5972
• Nurses Paycheck (AUS ISSN 1832-5025) 1700
Nurse's Pocket Drug Guide (Year) (USA ISSN 1550-2554) 6864
Nurses World (USA) 5972
Nurseweek *see* Nurseweek California 5972
NurseWeek (Great Lakes Edition) *see* Nurseweek California 5972
NurseWeek (Midwest Edition) *see* Nurseweek California 5972
NurseWeek (Mountain West Edition) *see* Nurseweek California 5972
NurseWeek (South Central Edition) *see* Nurseweek California 5972
• Nurseweek California (USA ISSN 1534-2204) 5972
• Nursing (BRA) 5972
Nursing (NLD ISSN 1381-5911) 5972
• Nursing (PRT ISSN 0871-6196) 5972
• Nursing (Spanish Edition) (ESP ISSN 0212-5382) 5972
• Nursing (Year) (USA ISSN 0360-4039) 5972
Nursing (Year): A N S *see* American Nursing Student 5951
Nursing (Year) Career Directory (USA ISSN 0192-2394) 5972
• Nursing (Year) Critical Care (USA ISSN 1558-447X) 5972
Nursing (Year) Drug Handbook (USA ISSN 0273-320X) 5972
Nursing (Year) Student Drug Handbook (USA ISSN 1941-739X) 6864
• ➤ Nursing Administration Quarterly (USA ISSN 0363-9568) 5973
Nursing & Care Home Business (GBR) 5973
➤ Nursing and Health Science Education (AUS ISSN 1033-6303) 5973
• ➤ Nursing and Health Sciences (AUS ISSN 1441-0745) 5973
Nursing and Healthcare *see* Nursing Education Perspectives 5973
Nursing and Midwifery Council News *see* N M C News 5970
Nursing and Midwifery Newsletter *see* C T I Centre for Nursing and Midwifery. Newsletter 5954
Nursing and Rehabilitation Journal *see* Huli yu Kangfu 5960
• ➤ Nursing & Residential Care (GBR ISSN 1465-9301) 5973
• Nursing Assistant Monthly (USA ISSN 1542-2178) 5973
• Nursing B C (British Columbia) (CAN ISSN 1185-3638) 5973
• Nursing Bulletin (USA) 5973
▼ Nursing Business/Nashingu Bijinesu (JPN ISSN 1881-5766) 5973
• Nursing Clinics of North America (USA ISSN 0029-6465) 5973
Nursing Drug Guide *see* Lippincott's Nursing Drug Guide 6859
Nursing Economic$ *see* Nursing Economics 5973
• ➤ Nursing Economics (USA ISSN 0746-1739) 5973
• ➤ Nursing Education Perspectives (USA ISSN 1536-5026) 5973
Nursing Electronic Newsletter *see* Nurse-Zine 5972
• ➤ Nursing Ethics (GBR ISSN 0969-7330) 5973
• ➤ Nursing for Women's Health (USA ISSN 1751-4851) 8847
• ➤ Nursing Forum (USA ISSN 0029-6473) 5973
• ➤ Nursing History Review (USA ISSN 1062-8061) 5973
• Nursing Home & Elder Business Week (USA ISSN 1552-2563) 5974
Nursing Home and Elder Business Week *see* Nursing Home & Elder Business Week 5974
Nursing Home Legal Insider (USA ISSN 1527-716X) 4750
Nursing Home Statistical Yearbook (USA ISSN 1085-0309) 5974
Nursing Homes *see* Long-Term Living 5969
• ➤ Nursing in Critical Care (GBR ISSN 1362-1017) 5974
Nursing in Focus (CAN ISSN 1492-2878) 5974
Nursing in Practice (GBR ISSN 1473-9445) 5974
Nursing in the Community (IRL ISSN 1649-0657) 5974
• ➤ Nursing Inquiry (GBR ISSN 1320-7881) 5974
Nursing IV Drug Handbook (USA ISSN 1040-2373) 5974
Nursing Journal of Chinese People's Liberation Army *see* Jiefangjun Huli Zazhi 5963
• ➤ Nursing Journal of India (IND ISSN 0029-6503) 5974
• Nursing Law's Regan Report (USA ISSN 1528-848X) 5974
• ➤ Nursing Leadership (CAN ISSN 1910-622X) 5974
† • ➤ Nursing Leadership Forum (USA ISSN 1076-1632) 8978
• Nursing Made Incredibly Easy! (USA ISSN 1544-5186) 5974
• Nursing Management (GBR ISSN 1354-5760) 5974
• Nursing Management (USA ISSN 0744-6314) 5974
• Nursing News (Concord) (USA ISSN 0029-6538) 5974
Nursing News (Floral Park) (USA ISSN 0029-6546) 5974
• Nursing Older People (GBR ISSN 1472-0795) 4052
Nursing Opportunities (USA) 5974
• ➤ Nursing Outlook (USA ISSN 0029-6554) 5974
• ➤ Nursing Philosophy (GBR ISSN 1466-7681) 5975
• ➤ Nursing Praxis in New Zealand (NZL ISSN 0112-7438) 5975
Nursing Programs (USA ISSN 1552-7743) 5975
Nursing Progress (USA) 5975
• ➤ Nursing Research (USA ISSN 0029-6562) 5975
Nursing Review (AUS ISSN 1326-0472) 5975
Nursing Science *see* Hoitotiede 5960
Nursing Science and Research in the Nordic Countries *see* Vaard i Norden 5983
• ➤ Nursing Science Quarterly (USA ISSN 0894-3184) 5975
▼ • Nursing Shortage Update (USA ISSN 1940-6983) 5975
Nursing Spectrum - D.C. - Maryland - Virginia Edition (USA ISSN 1559-4653) 5975
Nursing Spectrum Drug Handbook (USA ISSN 1550-0543) 6864
• Nursing Spectrum - Florida Edition (USA ISSN 1077-7946) 5975
• The Nursing Spectrum - Greater Chicago Edition (USA) 5975
• The Nursing Spectrum - Greater New York/New Jersey Metro Edition (USA ISSN 1081-3101) 5975
Nursing Spectrum - Greater Philadelphia - Tri-State Edition (USA ISSN 1074-858X) 5975
Nursing Spectrum - New England Edition (USA) 5975
• Nursing Standard (GBR ISSN 0029-6570) 5975
Nursing Standard. Special Supplement *see* Nursing Standard 5975
Nursing Technology (IND) 5975
• Nursing Times (GBR ISSN 0954-7762) 5975
▼ • Nursing Today (USA ISSN 1940-6975) 5975
➤ Nursing Update (ZAF) 5975
• Nursingmatters: Wisconsin Edition (USA) 5976
Nursing's Social Policy Statement (USA) 5976
Nurture (AUS ISSN 1443-7368) 2892
Nurture (GBR ISSN 1746-4366) 7894
• Nurungi (AUS ISSN 0311-1016) 4193
Nusa (IDN ISSN 0126-2874) 5157
Nushi/Ladies (CHN) 8878
Nusleca (GBR) 4124
• Nustrale.com (FRA ISSN 1777-6333) 3658
The Nut Kernel (USA ISSN 0738-596X) 3745
Nutan Kahaniyan (IND) 3886
Nuthouse (USA) 5232
• Nutida Musik/Contemporary Music (SWE ISSN 1652-6082) 6600
• The Nutmeg Point District Mail (USA ISSN 1089-764X) 5445
Nutraceutical Science and Technology (USA) 769
Nutraceutical Weekly Bulletin *see* F D A News Nutraceutical Weekly Bulletin 6840
• Nutraceuticals International (GBR ISSN 1362-5411) 6864
Nutraceuticals Now (GBR ISSN 1478-6605) 6664
• Nutraceuticals World (USA ISSN 1531-0671) 6664
• NutraCos (ITA ISSN 1720-4011) 3658
Nutrafoods (ITA ISSN 1827-8590) 6664
NutraNews *see* Bio-Bulletin 96
➤ Nutricia Symposia (NLD ISSN 0167-4587) 6664
Nutricion Clinica (MEX ISSN 1665-5125) 5948
• Nutricion Hospitalaria (ESP ISSN 0212-1611) 4108
• Nutridate (Online) (AUS) 6665
Nutridate (Print) *see* Nutridate (Online) 6665
• ➤ Nutrient Cycling in Agroecosystems (NLD ISSN 1385-1314) 244
Nutriform' Magazine (FRA ISSN 1772-7553) 6864
Nutrition *see* Ernaehrung 3634
Nutrition (IND ISSN 0550-404X) 6665
• ➤ Nutrition (USA ISSN 0899-9007) 6665
• Nutrition Abstracts and Reviews. Series A: Human and Experimental (GBR ISSN 0309-1295) 6671
• Nutrition Abstracts and Reviews. Series B: Livestock Feeds and Feeding (GBR ISSN 0309-135X) 184
• Nutrition Action Health Letter (USA ISSN 0885-7792) 6665
Nutrition Action Healthletter *see* Nutrition Action Health Letter 6665
Nutrition, Aliments Fonctionnels, Aliments Sante *see* N A F A S 5681
• ➤ Nutrition and Cancer (USA ISSN 0163-5581) 6665
• ➤ Nutrition and Dietetics (AUS ISSN 1446-6368) 6665
• Nutrition & Food Science (GBR ISSN 0034-6659) 6665
➤ Nutrition and Health (GBR ISSN 0260-1060) 6665
Nutrition & Health *see* Kroger Diabetes Nutrition & Health 5896
➤ Nutrition and Health (USA) 6665
Nutrition & Mental Health (CAN ISSN 1199-7699) 6171
Nutrition and Metabolic Disorders in HIV Infection (ESP ISSN 1579-7376) 5823
Nutrition & Metabolic Therapy *see* Leczenie Zywieniowe i Metaboliczne 6663
• ➤ Nutrition & Metabolism (GBR ISSN 1743-7075) 5688
Nutrition & the M.D. *see* Clinical Nutrition Insight 6656
Nutrition and Your Health: Dietary Guidelines for Americans (USA) 6665
• ➤ Nutrition Bulletin (GBR ISSN 1471-9827) 6665
• Nutrition Business Journal (USA ISSN 1548-6168) 6665
• Nutrition Bytes (USA ISSN 1548-4327) 6665
• ➤ Nutrition Clinique et Metabolisme (FRA ISSN 0985-0562) 5898
Nutrition en Oceanie *see* Pacific Islands Nutrition 6668
Nutrition Factor (CAN ISSN 1491-8536) 6665
Nutrition Focus (USA ISSN 1094-8309) 2163
Nutrition for Optimal Health Association News *see* N O H A News 6664
• Nutrition Forum/Forum de Nutrition (CAN ISSN 0318-4501) 6665
• Nutrition Forum (USA ISSN 1093-4545) 6665
Nutrition Foundation of India Bulletin *see* N F I Bulletin 6663
• The Nutrition Funding Report (USA ISSN 0892-1474) 6666
• Nutrition Health Review (USA ISSN 0164-7202) 6666
• ➤ Nutrition in Clinical Practice (USA ISSN 0884-5336) 6666
• Nutrition in Practice (GBR ISSN 1470-4730) 6666
Nutrition Industry Executive (USA) 6666
† The Nutrition Institute of the Arab Republic of Egypt. Bulletin (EGY ISSN 1110-0974) 8978
• ➤ Nutrition Journal (GBR ISSN 1475-2891) 6666
• Nutrition Legislation and Regulatory News (USA) 6666
• ➤ Nutrition, Metabolism & Cardiovascular Diseases (GBR ISSN 0939-4753) 6666
Nutrition News (IND) 6666
• Nutrition News (Riverside) (USA ISSN 8756-5919) 6666
• Nutrition News Focus (USA) 6666
Nutrition News in Zambia (ZMB ISSN 0078-284X) 3658
• Nutrition Notes (USA) 6666
• Nutrition Noteworthy (USA ISSN 1556-1895) 6666
• Nutrition Nuggets (USA ISSN 1935-4630) 6666
Nutrition of Japan *see* Eiyo Nippon 6658
Nutrition Post *see* Nutrition Factor 6665
• ➤ Nutrition Research (USA ISSN 0271-5317) 6666
▼ • Nutrition Research and Practice (KOR ISSN 1976-1457) 6666
• Nutrition Research Newsletter (USA ISSN 0736-0037) 6666
• ➤ Nutrition Research Reviews (GBR ISSN 0954-4224) 6666
• Nutrition Resources Bulletin (CAN) 6666
• ➤ Nutrition Reviews (USA ISSN 0029-6643) 6666
Nutrition Sciences (NLD ISSN 0924-4557) 6667
Nutrition Society of India. Proceedings (IND ISSN 0253-7567) 6667
• ➤ Nutrition Society. Proceedings (GBR ISSN 0029-6651) 6667
• ➤ Nutrition Today (USA ISSN 0029-666X) 6667
Nutrition Update (USA ISSN 0735-4762) 6667
Nutrition Week (USA ISSN 0736-0096) 6667
Nutritional Genomics & Functional Foods (USA ISSN 1542-1821) 6667
Nutritional Menuing *see* FoodService Director 3643
• Nutritional Neuroscience (Online) (GBR ISSN 1476-8305) 6171
• Nutritional Outlook (USA ISSN 1098-1179) 6667
Nutritional Perspectives (USA ISSN 0160-3922) 6667

▼ *new title* † *ceased* • *electronic media* ➤ *refereed*

Title

Nutritional Science of Soy Protein, Japan *see* Daizu Tampakushitsu Kenkyu **6657**
• Nutritional Sciences (KOR ISSN 1229-232X) **6667**
• Nutritional Therapy & Metabolism (ITA ISSN 1828-6232) **6667**
• Nutritional Wellness (USA ISSN 1559-8705) **6667**
Nutritions *see* Nutritions & Endocrinologie **5898**
Nutritions & Endocrinologie (FRA ISSN 1953-695X) **5898**
Nutritions et Facteurs de Risque *see* Nutritions & Endocrinologie **5898**
Nuts (GBR ISSN 1742-8858) **6296**
• Nuts & Volts (USA ISSN 1528-9885) **3110**
Nuts & Volts Magazine *see* Nuts & Volts **3110**
Nutshell (Etters) (USA ISSN 1093-376X) **3745**
Nuttall Ornithological Club. Memoirs (USA) **911**
➤ Nuttall Ornithological Club. Publications (USA ISSN 0550-4082) **911**
Nutz & Boltz Newsletter *see* MotorWatch **8594**
Nutzfahrzeug Katalog (DEU ISSN 1436-994X) **8674**
Nutzfahrzeug Werkstatt *see* N f Z Werkstatt **8673**
Nutzfahrzeuge-Management (DEU ISSN 1614-1229) **8674**
Nutzkraftwagen Partner *see* N K W - Partner **8673**
Nutzverkehr Magazin T I R (CHE) **8507**
Nuusbrief - Suid-Afrikaanse Vereniging vir Taalonderrig *see* Tydskrif vir Taalonderrig **5189**
Nuveau Monde - Mondes Nuveaux *see* Nuevo Mundo - Mundos Nuevos **4306**
† Nuvole (ITA ISSN 1592-2308) **8978**
Nuwe Voertuie Geregistreer *see* South Africa. Statistics South Africa. New Vehicles Registered **8530**
Nux (ZAF ISSN 0029-6716) **2294**
• Nuxue Xuezhi (TWN ISSN 1683-4852) **8902**
Nuyou/Woman Friend (CHN ISSN 1001-4209) **8878**
NuYou (MYS ISSN 1511-564X) **8878**
Nuyou (SGP) **8878**
NuYou Time (SGP) **4568**
• ➤ Nuytsia (AUS ISSN 0085-4417) **806**
Nuzi Shijie/Women's World (CHN) **8878**
Nuzi Wenxue/Women's Literature (CHN) **5344**
▼ Nvision (USA ISSN 1948-9412) **2489**
Nvmisma (ESP ISSN 0029-6015) **6652**
▼ • [nxtlvl] Magazine (USA ISSN 1947-590X) **7769**
nxtlvlmag.com *see* [nxtlvl] Magazine **7769**
NY Arts *see* N Y Arts **507**
Ny Carlsberg Glyptotek. Meddelelser (DNK ISSN 0085-3208) **409**
Ny Dag (NOR ISSN 0804-1997) **2205**
Ny Framtid *see* Kristdemokraten **7211**
NY Gold's Tilt *see* N Y Gold's Tilt **6971**
• Ny Litteratur om Kvinnor/New Literature on Women (SWE ISSN 0348-7962) **8906**
Ny Litteratur om Kvinnor. Supplement (SWE ISSN 0280-5774) **8906**
Ny Livsstil (SWE ISSN 0347-5395) **8124**
† Ny Medicin (DNK ISSN 1901-6360) **8978**
Det Ny Reception *see* Reception **5358**
NY Seach and Seizure *see* N Y Search and Seizure **4894**
Ny Sociallovgivning *see* Sociallovgivning **4969**
Ny Solidaritet (SWE ISSN 0345-8350) **3956**
• Ny Teknik (SWE ISSN 0550-8754) **3213**
Ny Teknik Med Teknisk Tidskrift *see* Ny Teknik **3213**
Ny Teknikk (NOR ISSN 0801-6844) **3213**
Ny Tid (FIN ISSN 1456-0518) **3839**
Ny Tid *see* Ukeavisa Ny Tid **3925**
Den Ny Verden (DNK ISSN 0029-6775) **1602**
• Ny Viden (DNK ISSN 1399-0772) **2996**
Ny Viden fra Miljoestyrelsen *see* Miljoenyt.dk **7882**
Nya Aaka Skidor *see* Aaka Skidor **8301**
Nya Arbetartidningen (SWE ISSN 1402-0637) **7160**
Nya Argus (FIN ISSN 0027-7126) **5232**
Nya Broderskap *see* Broderskap **7111**
Nya Byggregler (SWE ISSN 0281-7276) **1048**
Nya Cykeltidningen (SWE ISSN 1102-8629) **8265**
Nya Cyklisten (SWE ISSN 0048-1211) **8265**
• Nya Dagen (SWE ISSN 1404-8051) **3956**
Nya Elektroniktidningen *see* Elektroniktidningen **3098**
Nya Faaglar i Blekinge *see* Faaglar i Blekinge **906**
Nya Fiskejournalen *see* Fiskejournalen **8313**
Nya Flygposten *see* Flygposten **8541**
Nya Foersvarstjaenstemannen *see* Foersvarstjaenstemannen **1682**
• Nya Gamla Stan (SWE ISSN 1653-2813) **3956**
Nya High Fidelity *see* High Fidelity (Swedish Edition) **8153**
Nya Judisk Kroenika *see* Judisk Kroenika **3545**
Nya Kraftsport *see* Tynglyftaren **8213**
Nya Lantmaetaren *see* Lantmaetaren **4018**
Nya LoA *see* L o A **132**
Nya Miljoeaktuellt *see* Miljoeaktuellt **3453**
Nya Motor *see* Motor **8591**
Nya Soendagsnisse Strix (SWE ISSN 1652-1862) **5232**
Nya Svenska Filmvaagen (SWE ISSN 1650-8882) **6509**
Nya Svenska Pressen *see* Swedish Press **3567**
Nya Tillsynsnytt *see* Tillsynsnytt (2000) **3470**
Nya Veckorevyn *see* Vecko-Revyn **2219**
Nya Vi Bilaegare *see* Vi Bilaegare **8610**
Nyala (MWI ISSN 0251-1924) **959**
Nyam News (JAM ISSN 0255-8203) **6667**
Nyame Akuma (USA ISSN 0713-5815) **409**
Nyando Roots (USA) **3777**
• Nyans (SWE ISSN 1403-1094) **3956**
• Nyanya (RUS) **2163**
Nyaya (IND) **3886**
Nyckeln till Svenska Kyrkan/Key to the Church of Sweden (SWE ISSN 1651-0755) **7667**
The NYConnection *see* The New York Connection **4124**
Nydanske Sprogstudier *see* NyS **5157**
Nydanske Studier og Almen Kommunikationsteori *see* NyS **5157**
• Det Nye (NOR ISSN 0048-122X) **8878**
• Den Nye Dialog (DNK ISSN 0900-1441) **6937**
Nye Family Newsletter (USA) **3777**
Nye Film i Skolekataloget *see* Film i Skolen **6499**
Nye Huse *see* Bedre Bolig **8935**
Det Nye MakeUp (NOR) **595**
Det Nye MakeUp og Har *see* Det Nye MakeUp **595**
Nye Publikationer om den Europaeiske Union Modtaget af Biblioteket *see* Recent Publications on the European Union Received by the Library **7200**
Det Nye Shape-Up *see* Shape-Up **6996**
• Nye Tal fra Sundhedsstyrelsen (Online Edition) (DNK ISSN 1397-4114) **5688**
Nye Troms (NOR) **3924**
• ➤ Nyelv- es Irodalomtudomanyi Kozlemenyek/Journal of Linguistics and Literature/Studii si Cercetari de Llingvistica si Istorie Lliterara (ROM ISSN 0567-6223) **5157**
Nyelvtudomany/Acta Universitatis Szegediensis. Sectio Linguistica (HUN ISSN 1786-7428) **5157**
Nyelvtudomanyi Ertekezesek/Philological Papers (HUN ISSN 0078-2866) **5157**
Nyelvtudomanyi Kozlemenyek/Linguistic Studies (HUN ISSN 0029-6791) **5157**
Nyenrode Now (NLD ISSN 1574-6631) **2294**
Nyensubrim Nyengu Bogo: Seoul Daihaggyo Nongkwa Daihag *see* Seoul National University Forests. Research Bulletin **3702**
Nyfoeretagaren *see* Eget Foeretag **1740**
• Nygard.com (CAN) **2259**
• Nyheder fra uvm.dk (DNK) **2892**
Nyhedsbrev *see* Dansk Kvaeg Nyt **285**
Nyhedsbrev Oeresundsbron *see* Fokus Oeresund **1487**
Nyhedsbrev om Islam og Kristendom *see* Tidsskrift om Islam & Kristendom **7690**
• Nyhedsbrev om Ulykkesforskning & Forebyggelse (DNK ISSN 1600-3373) **7534**
• Nyhedsinformation for Social- og Sundhedssektor (DNK ISSN 1397-1867) **4052**
• Nyhedsmagasinet Danske Kommuner (DNK ISSN 1398-0440) **7500**
Nyhedsmagasinet Elektronik & Data (DNK ISSN 0906-4052) **3110**
Nyhedsmagasinet om Energi *see* Om Energi **3326**
Nyhedsmagasinet Raeson *see* Raeson **5236**
Nyhedsorientering *see* Thomson H R **1797**
Nyheter Fraan Nicaragua (SWE ISSN 0281-7632) **4306**
• Nyheter & Debatt (SWE ISSN 1651-3363) **2996**
Nyhetsbladet fraan Eldrimner *see* Eldrimner. Nyhetsblad **3634**
Nyhetsbrev. S A F Tidningen Naeringsliv *see* Entreprenoer **1960**
Nykyaika (FIN ISSN 0355-3280) **7769**
Nykyposti (FIN ISSN 0355-9637) **3839**
Nyliberalen (SWE ISSN 1100-6447) **7160**
• Nylink Connection (USA ISSN 1525-0741) **5037**
NYLitigator *see* New York Litigator **4895**
Nylon (USA ISSN 1524-1750) **8878**
Nylon Guys (New York) (USA ISSN 1931-2784) **6296**
▼ Nymphos Libertines (FRA ISSN 1959-5425) **6296**
▼ Nynade (NLD ISSN 1876-2271) **5428**
Nyre Nyt *see* Nyrenyt **6273**
• Nyrenyt (DNK ISSN 0108-2388) **6273**
NyS (Nydanske Sprogstudier) (DNK ISSN 0106-8040) **5157**
Nysvensk Tidende (SWE ISSN 1404-7853) **7160**
Nyt (FIN ISSN 1238-9838) **3839**
Nyt Aspekt (DNK ISSN 0108-3503) **6646**
• Nyt for Bogvenner/News for Booklovers (DNK ISSN 0109-0208) **7569**
• Nyt fra Ankestyrelsen (DNK ISSN 0907-9300) **8059**
• Nyt fra Bibelselskabet (DNK ISSN 1902-4746) **7667**
• Nyt fra Bibliotek og Medier (DNK ISSN 1903-0819) **5037**
Nyt fra Biblioteksstyrelsen *see* Nyt fra Bibliotek og Medier **5037**
• Nyt fra Danmark (DNK ISSN 0107-4687) **3834**
• Nyt fra Danmarks Statistik (DNK ISSN 0106-9799) **8392**
• Nyt fra Danske Soemands- og Udlandskirker (DNK ISSN 1603-6689) **7667**
Nyt fra det Dansk Bibelselskab *see* Nyt fra Bibelselskabet **7667**
Nyt fra Europa (LUX ISSN 0255-6499) **4937**
Nyt fra Historien (DNK ISSN 0029-6848) **4155**
Nyt fra Island (DNK ISSN 0469-2985) **3878**
• Nyt fra Kriminalforsorgen (DNK ISSN 0904-3179) **4896**
Nyt fra Nationalmuseet (DNK ISSN 0105-8819) **350**
Nyt fra Nyhavn *see* Nyt fra Bibliotek og Medier **5037**
• Nyt fra Sprognaevnet (DNK ISSN 0550-7332) **5157**
Nyt om Arbejdermuseet (DNK ISSN 0907-0753) **350**
† Nyt om Biler (DNK ISSN 1603-3744) **8978**
Nyt om Excellence *see* Excellence **1743**
• ➤ Nyt om Mikrobiologi (DNK ISSN 1397-4858) **894**
† • Nyt Syn paa Europa (DNK ISSN 1397-4289) **8978**
• Nytt fra Eureka (NOR ISSN 1504-8276) **8433**
Nytt fra Eureka *see* Nytt fra Eureka **8433**
• Nytt fra F U G E (Funksjonall Genomforskning) (NOR ISSN 1504-8241) **741**
Nytt fra U K F *see* Afrodite **8024**
• Nytt fraan Revisorn (SWE ISSN 1104-2982) **1298**
• Nytt fraan Socialstyrelsen (SWE ISSN 1401-7172) **8059**
Nytt i Ekspropriasjonsretten *see* Tidsskrift for Eiendomsrett **4905**
Nytt i Privatretten (NOR ISSN 1501-9594) **4913**
• Nytt i Sexualpolitiken (SWE ISSN 1401-9639) **4377**
Nytt i Strafferetten *see* Tidsskrift for Strafferett **4899**
• Nytt Juridiskt Arkiv. Avd. 1 - Raettsfall fraan Hoegsta Domstolen (SWE ISSN 0282-9525) **4750**
• Nytt Juridiskt Arkiv. Avd. 2 - Tidskrift foer Lagstiftning m.m. (SWE ISSN 0345-8792) **4750**
Nytt Lif (ISL ISSN 1017-3595) **8878**
Nytt Norsk Kirkeblad (NOR ISSN 0802-9504) **7667**
• Nytt Norsk Tidsskrift (NOR ISSN 0800-336X) **7160**
Nytt om 9000 & 14000 (SWE) **6405**
• Nytt om E U-Forskningen (NOR ISSN 1504-6915) **4467**
Nytt om Niotusen *see* Nytt om 9000 & 14000 **6405**
Nytt om Niotusen och Fjortontusen *see* Nytt om 9000 & 14000 **6405**
• Nytt om Runer (NOR ISSN 0801-3756) **5157**
Nytt Paradigme (NOR ISSN 1504-436X) **7160**
Nyu Daietto Serapi/New Diet Therapy (JPN ISSN 0910-7258) **6667**
Nyu Daiyamondo/New Diamond (JPN) **2112**
Nyu Entomorojisuto *see* New Entomologist **856**
Nyu Kolia Taims *see* New Korea Times **3554**
Nyu Mashin Tsuru *see* New Machine Tools **5457**
Nyu Media Hakusho/White Paper on New Medium (JPN) **2335**
Nyugan no Rinsho/Japanese Journal of Breast Cancer (JPN ISSN 0911-2251) **6029**
Nyugikyo Shiryo/Japan Dairy Technical Association. Bulletin (JPN ISSN 0910-7878) **268**
Nyuton *see* Newton **7892**
Nyuuyouji Igaku, Shinrigaku Kenkyuu/Japanese Journal of Medical and Psychological Study of Infants (JPN ISSN 0918-7065) **7388**
Nyuzu Reta Seppyo Hokushin'etsu/Japanese Society of Snow and Ice. Hokushin'etsu Branch. Newsletter (JPN) **6392**
† Nyx (FRA ISSN 0982-4677) **8978**
NZ Angus Herd Book *see* Angus Herd Book of New Zealand **278**
NZ House and Garden *see* N Z House and Garden **3744**
NZ Outside. Coastal Life *see* N Z Outside. Coastal Life **450**
NZ Rugby World *see* N Z Rugby World **8239**
NZBau *see* Neue Zeitschrift fuer Baurecht und Vergaberecht **1026**
• NZBio Report (NZL ISSN 1177-1607) **769**
• nzgirl (NZL) **5079**
NZIMA Images *see* N Z IMAges **5519**
• Nzine (NZL) **3918**
NZRA Newsletter *see* N Z R A Newsletter (Online) **8278**
NZUniGradReport (NZL ISSN 1177-3782) **1701**
NZUniGradStats (NZL ISSN 1177-2220) **1701**
NZUniPostgradReport (NZL ISSN 1177-4045) **1701**
O (DEU) **6296**
O *see* The Observer **3869**
O (NLD ISSN 1573-4668) **7457**
O A B - R J. Revista (Ordem dos Advogados do Brasil - Rio de Janeiro) (BRA) **4750**
• O A G Air Cargo Guide with Rates (Official Airline Guide) (GBR ISSN 1365-9774) **8549**
• O A G Air Cargo Rules (Official Airline Guide) (GBR ISSN 1367-9414) **8549**
O A G Air CargoDisk *see* O A G Air Cargo Guide with Rates **8549**
• O A G Cargo Guide Worldwide (Official Airline Guide) (USA ISSN 0191-152X) **8549**
O A G Executive Flight Guide. Asia Pacific *see* O A G Pocket Flight Guide. Asia Pacific **8549**
O A G Executive Flight Guide. Europe, Africa, Middle East *see* O A G Pocket Flight Guide. Europe, Africa, Middle East **8549**
O A G Executive Flight Guide. Latin American - Caribbean (Official Airline Guide) (USA ISSN 1541-373X) **8549**
O A G Executive Flight Planner: Asia, Pacific (Official Airline Guide) (GBR ISSN 1365-9782) **8549**
O A G Flight Atlas. Worldwide (Official Airline Guide) (GBR ISSN 1471-2989) **8742**
O A G Flight Guide. North America (Official Airline Guide) (USA ISSN 1528-7556) **8549**
O A G Flight Guide - Worldwide (Official Airline Guide) (GBR ISSN 1466-8718) **8549**
• O A G FlightDisk (GBR) **8549**
O A G North American Pocket Flight Guide *see* O A G Pocket Flight Guide. North America Edition **8549**
O A G Official Traveler. Travel Guide (Official Airline Guide) (USA ISSN 1073-0338) **8742**
O A G Pocket Flight Guide. Asia Pacific (Official Airline Guide) (USA) **8549**
O A G Pocket Flight Guide. Europe, Africa, Middle East (Official Airline Guide) (USA) **8549**
O A G Pocket Flight Guide. Latin American - Caribbean *see* O A G Executive Flight Guide. Latin American - Caribbean **8549**
O A G Pocket Flight Guide. North America Edition (Official Airline Guide) (USA) **8549**
O A G Pocket Travel Planner (Official Airline Guides) (USA ISSN 0199-5162) **8742**
O A G Rail Guide (Official Airline Guide) (GBR ISSN 1365-6112) **8621**
O A H Council of Chairs Newsletter (Organization of American Historians) (USA ISSN 1071-5622) **4306**
O A H Magazine of History *see* Magazine of History **4152**
• O A H Newsletter (Organization of American Historians) (USA ISSN 1059-1125) **4306**
O A L A Membership Directory *see* Ontario Association of Landscape Architects. Resource Guide **452**
O A Lifeline (Overeaters Anonymous) (USA) **6994**
O A N Digger *see* Digger **3728**
O A N Directory & Buyer's Guide (Oregon Association of Nurseries) (USA) **2022**
O A P E C Energy Resources Monitor (Organization of Arab Petroleum Exporting Countries) (KWT) **6781**
O A P E C Monthly Bulletin (Library & Information Department) (KWT ISSN 1018-595X) **6781**
O A S D I Beneficiaries by State and County (Old Age, Survivors, Disability Insurance) (USA ISSN 1073-1482) **4517**
O A S. General Secretariat. Annual Report (Organization of American States) (USA ISSN 0078-6403) **4306**
O A S I S *see* Observatorio de Analisis de los Sistemas Internacionales **7256**
O A S W Newsmagazine *see* Ontario Association of Social Workers. Newsmagazine **8060**
• O A U G Conference Proceedings (Oracle Applications User Group) (USA) **2531**
• O A U G Forum (Oracle Applications User Group) (USA) **2531**
• O A U G Insight (Oracle Applications User Group) (USA) **2531**
O A U Review/Revue de l'O U A (Organization of African Unity) (ETH ISSN 0078-6306) **4177**
O and A Marketing News (Oil and Automotive) (USA ISSN 0192-009X) **6782**
O & D V *see* Obiettivi e Documenti Veterinari **8804**
O & F *see* Onderneming en Financiering **4752**
O & P Almanac (Orthotics and Prosthetics) (USA ISSN 1061-4621) **6068**
• O & P Business News (Orthotics & Prosthetics) (USA ISSN 1060-3220) **6068**
O & P - Oelhydraulik und Pneumatik (DEU ISSN 0341-2660) **3392**
O & S N *see* Office and Stationery News **1853**
† O at Home (USA ISSN 1549-1994) **8978**
O B D I I Drive Cycle Guide: Domestic & Import Cars, Light Trucks, Vans & SUVs (On Board Diagnostics) (USA ISSN 1930-2029) **3213**
O B D I I Drive Cycle Guide: Domestic and Import Cars, Light Trucks, Vans & SUVs *see* O B D I I Drive Cycle Guide: Domestic & Import Cars, Light Trucks, Vans & SUVs **3213**
• O B G Management (Obstetrics and Gynecology) (USA ISSN 1044-307X) **6000**
• O B G Y N & Reproduction Week (USA ISSN 1543-6691) **6000**
O B G Y N and Reproduction Week *see* O B G Y N & Reproduction Week **6000**
O B M *see* Official Board Markets **6712**
• O B O S - Bladet (Oslo Bolig og Sparelag) (NOR ISSN 0807-9323) **4421**
O B R A S (CUB ISSN 1028-2149) **1027**
O B S Info (Ornithologische Beobachterring Saar) (DEU) **911**
O B S T. Osnabruecker Beitraege zur Sprachtheorie (DEU ISSN 0936-0271) **5157**
O C A Image (Organization of Chinese Americans) (USA) **3556**
O C A News (Organization of the Cooperatives of America) (COL) **1424**
O C C Annual Report *see* U.S. Office of the Comptroller of the Currency. Annual Report **1953**
• O C C Bulletins (Office of the Comptroller of the Currency) (USA) **1937**
O C D Diamond (Organic Chemical Division) (USA) **8433**
O C D E. Estudios Economicos *see* O E C D Economic Surveys **1502**
O C D E. Estudios Economicos *see* O C D E. Etudes Economiques **1502**
• O C D E. Etudes Economiques (Organisation de Cooperation et de Developpement Economiques) (FRA ISSN 0304-3363) **1502**
O C D E Perspectives Agricoles *see* O E C D Agricultural Outlook **143**
O C D E Perspectives de l'Emploi *see* O E C D Employment Outlook **1504**
O C D E Principaux Indicateurs de la Science et de la Technologie *see* O E C D Main Science and Technology Indicators **8433**
O C D E Principaux Indicateurs Economiques *see* O E C D Main Economic Indicators **1504**
O C D E Statistiques de la Population Active *see* O E C D Labour Force Statistics **1257**
O C D E Statistiques Trimestrielles de la Population Active *see* Quarterly Labour Force Statistics **8983**
O C D E Statistiques Trimestrielles. Electricite, Charbon, Gaz & Petrole *see* Oil, Gas, Coal & Electricity Quarterly Statistics **6801**

O C E A News/Nouvelles de l'Association de l'Education Cooperative de l'Ontario (Ontario Co-operative Education Association) (CAN ISSN 1718-942X) **2893**
O C Family (Orange County) (USA) **2640**
O C H A News (United Nations, Office for the Coordination of Humanitarian Affairs) (CHE) **4937**
O C L *see* Oleagineux Corps Gras Lipides (Print) **8978**
O C L A E Revista (Organizacion Continental Latino Americana de Estudiantes) (CUB ISSN 0029-6961) **5232**
• O C L C Abstracts Electronic Newsletter (Online Computer Library Center) (USA ISSN 1932-4847) **5037**
• O C L C Annual Report (Online Computer Library Center) (USA ISSN 1044-3800) **5037**
O C L C Newsletter *see* NextSpace **5036**
O C L C Participating Institutions. Arranged by Institution Name (Online Computer Library Center) (USA ISSN 1043-3384) **5037**
O C L C Reference & Resource Sharing News (Online Computer Library Center) (USA) **5037**
• O C L C Reports (Online Computer Library Center) (USA ISSN 1545-8628) **5037**
O C L C Selected Titles for University and Research Libraries (Online Computer Library Center) (USA ISSN 1060-6033) **5037**
• ➤ O C L C Systems & Services (Online Computer Library Center) (GBR ISSN 1065-075X) **5037**
• O C Menus (Orange Country) (USA) **4395**
• O C Metro (Orange County) (USA) **1502**
O C News (Orchestras Canada) (CAN) **6600**
O C S News (USA) **3556**
O C S Nouvelles (Office des Communications Sociales) (CAN ISSN 0381-8632) **2335**
O C S Report *see* U.S. Department of the Interior. Minerals Management Service. Alaska Outer Continental Shelf Region. Report **3471**
O C S S Review *see* The Review (Columbus) **3078**
O C T M Newsletter (Ohio Council of Teachers of Mathematics) (USA) **5522**
• O D (Overheidsdocumentatie) (NLD ISSN 0923-6600) **5037**
O D *see* Overdrive Motoring.com **8597**
• ➤ O D A Journal (Oklahoma Dental Association) (USA ISSN 0164-9442) **5857**
O D A Loan Report (JPN) **1602**
O D A N *see* Opus Dei Awareness Network **7668**
O D A Today (Ohio Dental Association) (USA ISSN 1536-1683) **5857**
O D Debate (Organisations and Development) (ZAF ISSN 1025-1073) **1782**
O D E O N *see* Observatorio de Economia y Operaciones Numericas **1156**
O D I Briefing Paper *see* Overseas Development Institute. Briefing Paper **1602**
O D I N AFRICA Annual Report (Ocean Data and Information Network for Africa) (KEN) **2814**
➤ O D I Poverty Briefings (Overseas Development Institute) (GBR ISSN 1465-2617) **1602**
O D L Record (Oklahoma Department of Libraries) (USA) **5037**
O D P Newsletter *see* O D P Nyusu Reta **2814**
O D P Nyusu Reta/O D P Newsletter (Ocean Drilling Program) (JPN ISSN 0289-9078) **2814**
• O D Practitioner (Organization Development) (USA ISSN 1086-2609) **1782**
• ➤ O D T U Gelisme Dergisi/M E T U Studies in Development (Orta Dogu Teknik Universitesi) (TUR ISSN 1010-9935) **1547**
▼ O E (FRA ISSN 1959-4720) **6972**
O E *see* The Organized Executive **1784**
O E C D Agricultural Outlook (Organisation for Economic Cooperation and Development) (FRA ISSN 1563-0447) **143**
O E C D Agricultural Policies, Markets and Trade. Monitoring and Outlook *see* Agricultural Policies in O E C D Countries: Monitoring and Evaluation **1909**
• O E C D Agriculture Statistics (Organisation for Economic Cooperation and Development) (FRA ISSN 1816-7586) **184**
• O E C D Banking Statistics/Source O C D E Rentabilite des Banques (Organisation for Economic Cooperation and Development) (FRA ISSN 1816-7594) **1256**
• O E C D Development Co-operation (Organisation for Economic Cooperation and Development) (FRA ISSN 0474-5663) **1602**
• O E C D Economic Outlook (Organisation for Economic Cooperation and Development) (FRA ISSN 0474-5574) **1502**
O E C D Economic Outlook Statistics and Projections *see* O E C D Economic Outlook: Statistics and Projections **1256**
• O E C D Economic Outlook: Statistics and Projections/Source O C D E Statistiques des Perspectives Economiques de l'O C D E (Organisation for Economic Cooperation and Development) (FRA ISSN 1816-9031) **1256**
O E C D Economic Studies *see* O E C D Journal **1155**
• O E C D Economic Surveys (Organisation for Economic Cooperation and Development) (FRA ISSN 0376-6438) **1502**
• O E C D Economic Surveys: Austria (Organisation for Economic Cooperation and Development) (FRA ISSN 1995-3127) **1503**
• O E C D Economic Surveys: Belgium (Organisation for Economic Cooperation and Development) (FRA ISSN 1995-3704) **1503**
• O E C D Economic Surveys: Brazil (Organisation for Economic Cooperation and Development) (FRA ISSN 1995-3763) **1503**
• O E C D Economic Surveys: Denmark (Organisation for Economic Cooperation and Development) (FRA ISSN 1995-3151) **1503**
• O E C D Economic Surveys: Euro Area (Organisation for Economic Cooperation and Development) (FRA ISSN 1995-3747) **1503**
• O E C D Economic Surveys: Finland (Organisation for Economic Cooperation and Development) (FRA ISSN 1995-3488) **1503**
• O E C D Economic Surveys: France (Organisation for Economic Cooperation and Development) (FRA ISSN 1995-3178) **1503**
• O E C D Economic Surveys: Germany (Organisation for Economic Cooperation and Development) (FRA ISSN 1995-3194) **1503**
• O E C D Economic Surveys: Greece (Organisation for Economic Cooperation and Development) (FRA ISSN 1995-3224) **1503**
• O E C D Economic Surveys: Hungary (Organisation for Economic Cooperation and Development) (FRA ISSN 1995-3461) **1503**
• O E C D Economic Surveys: Iceland (Organisation for Economic Cooperation and Development) (FRA ISSN 1995-3240) **1503**
• O E C D Economic Surveys: Ireland (Organisation for Economic Cooperation and Development) (FRA ISSN 1995-3267) **1503**
• O E C D Economic Surveys: Italy (Organisation for Economic Cooperation and Development) (FRA ISSN 1995-3283) **1503**
• O E C D Economic Surveys: Korea (Organisation for Economic Co-operation and Development) (FRA ISSN 1995-364X) **1155**
• O E C D Economic Surveys: Luxembourg (Organisation for Economic Cooperation and Development) (FRA ISSN 1995-3720) **1503**
• O E C D Economic Surveys: Mexico (Organisation for Economic Cooperation and Development) (FRA ISSN 1995-3666) **1503**
• O E C D Economic Surveys: Netherlands (Organisation for Economic Cooperation and Development) (FRA ISSN 1995-3305) **1503**
• O E C D Economic Surveys: New Zealand (Organisation for Economic Co-operation and Development) (FRA ISSN 1995-3100) **1503**
• O E C D Economic Surveys: Norway (Organisation for Economic Cooperation and Development) (FRA ISSN 1995-3321) **1504**
• O E C D Economic Surveys: Poland (Organisation for Economic Cooperation and Development) (FRA ISSN 1995-3542) **1504**
• O E C D Economic Surveys: Russian Federation (Organisation for Economic Cooperation and Development) (FRA ISSN 1995-3607) **1155**
• O E C D Economic Surveys: Slovak Republic (Organisation for Economic Cooperation and Development) (FRA ISSN 1995-3526) **1504**
• O E C D Economic Surveys: Spain (Organisation for Economic Cooperation and Development) (FRA ISSN 1995-3364) **1504**
• O E C D Economic Surveys: Sweden (Organisation for Economic Cooperation and Development) (FRA ISSN 1995-3380) **1504**
• O E C D Economic Surveys: Switzerland (Organisation for Economic Cooperation and Development) (FRA ISSN 1995-3402) **1504**
• O E C D Economic Surveys: The Baltic States (Organisation for Economic Cooperation and Development) (FRA ISSN 1995-3682) **1504**
• O E C D Economic Surveys: The Czech Republic (Organisation for Economic Cooperation and Development) (FRA ISSN 1995-350X) **1504**
• O E C D Economic Surveys: Turkey (Organisation for Economic Cooperation and Development) (FRA ISSN 1995-3429) **1504**
▼ • O E C D Economic Surveys. Ukraine (Organisation for Economic Cooperation and Development) (FRA) **1155**
• O E C D Economic Surveys: United Kingdom (Organisation for Economic Cooperation and Development) (FRA ISSN 1995-3445) **1504**
• O E C D Economic Surveys: United States (Organisation for Economic Cooperation and Development) (FRA ISSN 1995-3046) **1504**
• O E C D Education Statistics/Source O C D E Statistiques de l'Education (Organisation for Economic Cooperation and Development (O E C D)) (FRA ISSN 1816-7578) **2935**
• O E C D Employment and Labour Market Statistics/Statistiques de l'O C D E sur l'Emploi et le Marche du Travail (Organisation for Economic Cooperation and Development (O E C D)) (FRA ISSN 1816-7616) **1256**
• O E C D Employment Outlook (Organisation for Economic Cooperation and Development) (FRA ISSN 1013-0241) **1504**
• O E C D Environmental Data: Compendium/Organisation de Cooperation et de Developpement Economiques (Organisation for Economic Cooperation and Development) (FRA ISSN 1015-0293) **3457**
• O E C D Guidelines for the Testing of Chemicals (Online) (Organisation for Economic Cooperation and Development) (FRA ISSN 1607-310X) **3500**
• O E C D Health Working Papers (Organization for Economic Cooperation and Development) (FRA) **5688**
† • O E C D Historical Statistics (Print) (Organisation for Economic Cooperation and Development) (FRA ISSN 1026-1877) **8978**
• O E C D Information Technology Outlook/Perspectives des Technologies de l'Information (Organisation for Economic Cooperation and Development) (FRA ISSN 1996-3475) **5063**
• O E C D International Development Statistics (CD-ROM) (Organisation for Economic Cooperation and Development) (FRA) **1256**
• O E C D International Development Statistics (Online)/Statistiques de l'O C D E sur le Developpement International (Organisation for Economic Cooperation and Development) (FRA ISSN 1816-7624) **1256**
• O E C D International Direct Investment Statistics (CD-ROM) (Organisation for Economic Cooperation and Development) (FRA) **1256**
• O E C D International Direct Investment Statistics (Online) (Organisation for Economic Cooperation and Development) (FRA ISSN 1816-8973) **1256**
• O E C D International Migration Statistics/Source O C D E Statistiques des Migrations Internationales (Organisation for Economic Cooperation and Development) (FRA ISSN 1816-8981) **1256**
• O E C D International Trade by Commodities Statistics/O E C D Statistiques du Commerce International par Produits (Organisation for Economic Cooperation and Development) (FRA) **1257**
▼ • O E C D Journal (Organisation for Economic Cooperation and Development) (FRA ISSN 1995-2805) **1155**
O E C D Journal. General Papers *see* O E C D Journal General Papers **1155**
O E C D Journal General Papers (Organisation for Economic Cooperation and Development) (FRA ISSN 1995-2821) **1155**
O E C D Journal of Business Cycle Measurement and Analysis *see* O E C D Journal **1155**
O E C D Journal of Competition Law and Policy *see* O E C D Journal **1155**
O E C D Journal on Budgeting *see* O E C D Journal **1155**
• O E C D Journal on Development (Organization for Economic Co-operation and Development) (FRA ISSN 1816-8124) **1602**
O E C D Kornyezeti Adattar *see* O E C D Environmental Data: Compendium **3457**
• O E C D Labour Force Statistics/O C D E Statistiques de la Population Active (Organisation for Economic Cooperation and Development) (FRA ISSN 0474-5515) **1257**
• O E C D Main Economic Indicators/O C D E Principaux Indicateurs Economiques (Organisation for Economic Cooperation and Development) (FRA ISSN 0474-5523) **1504**
• O E C D Main Science and Technology Indicators/O C D E Principaux Indicateurs de la Science et de la Technologie (Organisation for Economic Cooperation and Development) (FRA ISSN 1011-792X) **8433**
O E C D Non-Members Labour Market Database *see* O E C D Employment and Labour Market Statistics **1256**
• O E C D Nuclear Energy Agency. Annual Report (Year) (Organisation for Economic Cooperation and Development) (FRA) **3173**
• O E C D Nuclear Energy Agency. Nuclear Energy Data (Organisation for Economic Cooperation and Development) (FRA ISSN 1017-9402) **3173**
• O E C D Observer (Organisation for Economic Cooperation and Development) (FRA ISSN 0029-7054) **1504**
O E C D Papers *see* O E C D Journal **1155**
• O E C D Science, Technology and R & D Statistics/Statistiques de l'O C D E de la Science et Technologie et de la R - D (Organisation for Economic Cooperation and Development) (FRA ISSN 1816-904X) **3233**
• O E C D Social, Employment and Migration Working Papers (Organisation for Economic Cooperation and Development) (FRA) **8060**
• O E C D Social Expenditure Statistics/Statistiques de l'O C D E sur les Depenses Sociales (Organisation for Economic Cooperation and Development) (FRA ISSN 1816-9066) **1257**
• O E C D Statistics on International Trade in Services/Source O C D E Statistiques des Services (Organisation for Economic Cooperation and Development) (FRA ISSN 1816-9058) **1257**
O E C D Statistiques du Commerce International par Produits *see* O E C D International Trade by Commodities Statistics **1257**
• O E C D Telecommunications and Internet Statistics/Source O C D E Base de Donnees des Telecommunications de l'O C D E (Organisation for Economic Cooperation and Development) (FRA ISSN 1816-9147) **2348**
O E C D. Wirtschaftsberichte *see* O C D E. Etudes Economiques **1502**
O E C D. Wirtschaftsberichte *see* O E C D Economic Surveys **1502**
O E C S Annual Digest of Statistics (Organisation of Eastern Caribbean States) (ATG ISSN 1021-7274) **8393**
O E C S Current Awareness Bulletin (Organisation of Eastern Caribbean States) (ATG ISSN 1021-7312) **1505**
O E C S Digest of External Trade Statistics (Organisation of Eastern Caribbean States) (ATG ISSN 1021-7320) **1257**
O E C S Energy Review (Organisation of Eastern Caribbean States) (ATG ISSN 1021-7347) **3153**
O E C S National Accounts Digest (Organisation of Eastern Caribbean States) (ATG ISSN 1021-7339) **8393**
O E C S Select Bibliography (Organisation of Eastern Caribbean States) (ATG ISSN 1021-7304) **1505**
O E C S Statistical Pocket Digest (Organisation of Eastern Caribbean States) (ATG ISSN 1021-7290) **8393**
O E D A Newsletter (Occupational and Environmental Diseases Association) (GBR) **6681**
O E E News (Office of Energy Efficiency News) (CAN ISSN 1481-5567) **3143**
O E G A I Journal (Oesterreichische Gesellschaft fuer Artificial Intelligence) (AUT ISSN 0254-4326) **2455**
O E M *see* O E M Off-Highway **213**
† • O E M Magazine (Original Equipment Manufacturer) (USA ISSN 1071-8990) **8978**
O E M News (GBR) **213**
• O E M Off-Highway (Original Equipment Manufacturer) (USA ISSN 1048-3039) **213**
O E M Online *see* Occupational and Environmental Medicine **6682**
The O E M Report (Occupational and Environmental Medicine) (USA ISSN 0894-2811) **6681**
O E M Worldwide (Original Equipment Manufacturer) (USA ISSN 1523-049X) **213**
O E N *see* Office Equipment News **1853**
O E N Dealer *see* Channelinfo **4555**
O E Report and Fibre News (Open End) (GBR ISSN 1351-3176) **8456**
O E T *see* Oil and Energy Trends **3143**
O en C *see* Oppervlaktetechnieken **6328**
O Estado de Sao Paulo (BRA ISSN 1516-2931) **3804**
O F I Occasional Papers (Oxford Forestry Institute) (GBR ISSN 0269-5790) **3699**
O F S A *see* Safe Magasinet **4601**
O F S Philatelic Magazine (Orange Free State Philatelic Society) (ZAF ISSN 1016-6734) **6897**
O F W I M Newsletter (Organization of Fish and Wildlife Information Managers) (USA) **2623**
O G *see* Organic Gardening **3746**
O G B - L'Actualites *see* O G B - L'Aktuell **4600**
O G B - L'Aktuell/O G B - L'Actualites (Onofhaengege Gewerkschaftsbond Leetzebuerg) (LUX) **4600**
O G: Oriental Guys (USA ISSN 0818-6065) **4377**
O G S *see* Oxford German Studies **5347**
O G S Genealogy News (Ohio Genealogical Society) (USA) **3777**
O G Y I Kozlemenyek *see* Gyogyszereink, O G Y I Kozlemenyek **6845**
• O Gauge Railroading (USA ISSN 1062-1482) **4342**
O H & S *see* Occupational Health & Safety **6682**
O H & S Current Contents *see* Occupational Health & Safety Current Contents **6691**
O H I *see* Open House International **4421**
O H L A Newsline (Ontario Hospital Libraries Association) (CAN ISSN 0843-5901) **5037**
O H L News *see* Prospects **8194**
O H R *see* Occupational Health Review **6683**
• O H S Bulletin (Occupational Health and Safety) (AUS ISSN 1443-9832) **6682**
O H S Bulletin (Ontario Historical Society) (CAN ISSN 0714-6736) **4306**
• O H S Canada Magazine (Occupational Health & Safety) (CAN ISSN 0827-4576) **6682**
• O H S Compliance.ca (Occupational Health and Safety) (CAN ISSN 1910-7994) **6682**
O H S N *see* Occupational Health and Safety Law New South Wales **4750**
O H S U Views *see* New Views **5685**
O H T A News (Organ Historical Trust of Australia) (AUS ISSN 0314-4623) **6600**
• O-Hayo Sensei (USA ISSN 1077-0313) **3014**
➤ The O. Henry Prize Stories (USA ISSN 1555-7847) **5344**
O I A Z *see* Oesterreichische Ingenieur und Architekten Zeitschrift **3213**
O I Archive *see* Offshore Investment **1373**
O I D F A Bulletin (Organisation Internationale de la Dentelle au Fuseau et a l'Aiguille) (FRA ISSN 0771-7571) **6641**
O I E Boletin (French Edition) *see* O I E Bulletin (English Edition) **8803**
O I E Boletin (Spanish Edition) *see* O I E Bulletin (English Edition) **8803**
O I E Bulletin (English Edition) (Office International des Epizooties) (FRA ISSN 1684-3770) **8803**
O I E C Bulletin (Office International de l'Enseignement Catholique) (BEL ISSN 0770-1683) **2893**
O I E Revista Cientifica y Tecnica *see* O I E Revue Scientifique et Technique **8803**
• ➤ O I E Revue Scientifique et Technique/O I E Revista Cientifica y Tecnica/O I E Scientific and Technical Review (Office International des Epizooties) (FRA ISSN 0253-1933) **8803**
O I E S Papers. Electricity (Oxford Institute for Energy Studies) (GBR) **3160**

Title

10694 O I E S PAPERS. ENERGY & THE ENVIRONMENT ULRICH'S PERIODICALS

O I E S Papers. Energy & the Environment (Oxford Institute for Energy Studies) (GBR) **3143**
O I E S Papers. Energy Economics (Oxford Institute for Energy Studies) (GBR) **3143**
O I E S Papers. Finance (Oxford Institute for Energy Studies) (GBR) **1372**
O I E S Papers. Natural Gas (Oxford Institute for Energy Studies) (GBR) **6782**
O I E S Papers. World Petroleum Market (Oxford Institute for Energy Studies) (GBR) **6782**
O I E Scientific and Technical Review *see* O I E Revue Scientifique et Technique **8803**
O I Internews *see* Orphans International Worldwide Internews **8061**
O I M L. Bulletin *see* Organisation Internationale de Metrologie Legale. Bulletin **6405**
O I O C Newsletter (Oriental and India Office Collections) (GBR ISSN 0960-7935) **557**
O I O News (Oklahomans for Indian Opportunity) (USA) **3556**
O I R *see* Online Information Review **5038**
O I R C A A *see* Organisations, Institutes and Research Centres, Asia-Australasia **2023**
O I S Newsletter *see* United States. General Services Administration. Office of Intergovernmental Solutions. Newsletter **7473**
O I Society of Australia Newsletter *see* Osteogenesis Imperfecta (Brittle Bones) Society of Australia. Newsletter **5691**
O I T Comision de Empleados y de Trabajadores Intelectuales. Informe *see* I L O Committee on Salaried Employees and Professional Workers. Report **1686**
O I T Comision de Industrias Mecanicas. Informe *see* I L O Metal Trades Committee. Report **1686**
O I T Comision Paritaria del Servicio Publico. Informe *see* I L O Joint Committee on the Public Service. Report **1686**
O I T News (Office of Industrial Technologies) (USA) **3143**
O I T Programa de Empresas Multinacionales. Documentos de Trabajo *see* I L O Multinational Enterprises Programme. Working Paper **1490**
The O I V Newsletter *see* Office International de la Vigne et du Vin. La Lettre **606**
O I W Communique (Order of the Indian Wars) (USA) **6440**
O J (Om Jazz) (SWE ISSN 1102-7428) **6600**
O J B *see* Online Journal of Bioinformatics **826**
O J C D (Official Journal of the European Communities) (NLD ISSN 1381-4400) **7256**
• ➤ O J H A S (Online Journal of Health and Allied Sciences) (IND ISSN 0972-5997) **5688**
O J I M *see* Online Journal of Immunology **5764**
O J Index (Official Journal) (USA) **7256**
O J N I *see* Online Journal of Nursing Informatics **5977**
O J P *see* Online Journal of Physiology **5690**
O J P H I *see* Online Journal of Public Health Informatics **5823**
O J P K *see* Online Journal of Pharmacokinetics **6865**
O J V R *see* Online Journal of Veterinary Research **8804**
O Jornal (USA) **3556**
O K! *see* Weekly Australian OK! **8888**
O.K. *see* Ohlasene Knihy **633**
▼ O K! (DEU ISSN 1866-1246) **5079**
O K! (GBR ISSN 1742-4119) **8878**
O K! (HRV ISSN 1330-7983) **2205**
O K! (PHL) **5079**
O K! (USA ISSN 1556-8172) **5079**
O K C Business (Oklahoma City) (USA) **1155**
O K J O L T *see* Oklahoma Journal of Law and Technology **4752**
O K la Salute Prima di Tutto (ITA ISSN 1825-9375) **6994**
† O K! Podium (FRA ISSN 1248-0452) **8978**
O K V Tento (Openbaar Kunstbezit in Vlaanderen) (BEL ISSN 1379-7271) **509**
O Katanalotis/The Consumer (CYP ISSN 0255-8408) **2640**
O! Kay! (DEU) **2205**
O L *see* Oceanic Linguistics **5157**
O L *see* Optics Letters **7083**
O L A C Newsletter (Online Audiovisual Catalogers, Inc.) (USA ISSN 0739-1153) **5037**
• O L A Quarterly (Oregon Library Association) (USA ISSN 1093-7374) **5037**
O L E *see* Optics & Laser Europe **7082**
O L G - N L *see* O L G - Rechtsprechung Neue Laender **8978**
† O L G - Rechtsprechung Neue Laender (Oberlandesgerichte) (DEU ISSN 0945-2176) **8978**
O L G Report BayObLG, Muenchen, Bamberg, Nuernberg *see* O L G Report Muenchen, Stuttgart, Karlsruhe, Nuernberg, Bamberg, BayObLG **4750**
• O L G Report Brandenburg - Dresden - Jena - Naumburg - Rostock (Oberlandesgericht) (DEU ISSN 0947-5885) **4750**
O L G Report Bremen, Hamburg, Schleswig *see* O L G Report Celle, Hamburg, Schleswig, Oldenburg, Braunschweig, Bremen **4750**
O L G Report Celle, Braunschweig, Oldenburg *see* O L G Report Celle, Hamburg, Schleswig, Oldenburg, Braunschweig, Bremen **4750**
O L G Report Celle, Hamburg, Schleswig, Oldenburg, Braunschweig, Bremen (Oberlandesgericht) (DEU ISSN 1860-5435) **4750**
O L G Report Frankfurt *see* O L G Report Frankfurt, Koblenz, Zweibruecken, Saarbruecken **4750**
O L G Report Frankfurt, Koblenz, Zweibruecken, Saarbruecken (DEU ISSN 1860-5346) **4750**
O L G Report Hamm, Duesseldorf, Koeln (Oberlandesgericht) (DEU ISSN 1860-532X) **4750**
O L G Report Karlsruhe, Stuttgart *see* O L G Report Muenchen, Stuttgart, Karlsruhe, Nuernberg, Bamberg, BayObLG **4750**
O L G Report Koblenz, Saarbruecken, Zweibruecken *see* O L G Report Frankfurt, Koblenz, Zweibruecken, Saarbruecken **4750**
O L G Report Muenchen, Stuttgart, Karlsruhe, Nuernberg, Bamberg, BayObLG (Oberlandesgericht) (DEU ISSN 1860-5419) **4750**
O L L I Journal *see* Northwestern University School of Continuing Studies. Osher Lifelong Learning Institute. Journal **5343**
O L M S Occasional Paper (Office of Leadership and Management Services) (USA) **5063**
O L O *see* On Line Opinion **7161**
O L O *see* Our Living Oceans **959**
O L O G O S (Orthodox Lore of the Gospel of Our Savior Mission) (USA ISSN 0029-7143) **7705**
O L R *see* Oceanographic Literature Review **2720**
O L R *see* Oregon Law Review **4754**
• O Laske (SVK ISSN 1336-9989) **8878**
• ➤ O M (Orthomolekulare Medizin) (DEU ISSN 1611-5562) **6667**
O M (RUS ISSN 1680-5976) **6296**
O M *see* Operations Management **1643**
O M B Watcher (Office of Management and Budget) (USA) **7458**
O M C A Resource Guide (Ontario Motor Coach Association) (CAN ISSN 1187-4198) **8742**
• O M D Actualites (Organisation Mondiale des Douanes) (BEL ISSN 1782-1843) **7458**
O M F G *see* Official Meeting Facilities Guide **6282**
• O M G in Motion (Object Management Group) (USA) **2509**
O M G News (Object Management Group) (USA) **2509**
O M I *see* Oil Market Intelligence **6801**
• ➤ O M I C S: A Journal of Integrative Biology (USA ISSN 1536-2310) **876**
O M J *see* Organization Management Journal **1784**
O M P O. Newsletter (Oiseaux Migrateurs du Paleoarctique Occidental) (HUN) **2623**
O M R F Findings *see* Oklahoma Medical Research Foundation. Findings **5689**
• O M T. Barometro del Turismo Mundial (Organizacion Mundial de Turismo) (ESP ISSN 1728-9254) **8780**
O M V Annual Report (Year) (AUT) **6782**
O Magazine (GBR) **6296**
• O Mundo da Saude (BRA ISSN 0104-7809) **5688**
O N E R A. Activites Scientifiques et Techniques (Office National d'Etudes et de Recherches Aerospatiales) (FRA ISSN 1770-4448) **67**
• O N S A. Bulletin (Organisation Nationale de la Sante Autochtone) (CAN ISSN 1703-0102) **3556**
• O N S Connect (Oncology Nursing Society) (USA ISSN 1935-1623) **6029**
O N S Foundation News (Oncology Nursing Society) (USA ISSN 1931-6321) **5976**
O N S News *see* O N S Connect **6029**
O N S Omnibus Survey (Social Survey Division) (GBR) **7288**
† • O N - W I J S (Online Onderwijs) (NLD ISSN 1567-5599) **8978**
† O O A - Saertryk (Organisationen til Oplysning om Atomkraft) (DNK ISSN 0105-4899) **8978**
• O O B R (Off-Off-Broadway Review) (USA) **8475**
O O H *see* Occupational Outlook Handbook **6707**
➤ O O H N A Journal (Ontario Occupational Health Nurses Association) (CAN ISSN 0828-542X) **5976**
O O Q *see* Occupational Outlook Quarterly **6707**
O O S H Update (Outside of School Hours) (AUS ISSN 1034-7232) **8060**
O P *see* Centre for Independent Studies. Occasional Papers **1537**
O P A *see* Office Products Analyst **1853**
• ➤ O P A L Journal (Oriental Philatelic Association of London) (GBR ISSN 0267-8071) **6897**
O P A L Supplement *see* O P A L Journal **6897**
O P A Newsgram (Oregon Psychological Association) (USA) **7388**
O P A Pratique (O R L, Pneumo, Allergo) (FRA ISSN 0983-8201) **6083**
O P A S T C O Roundtable (Organization for the Promotion and Advancement of Small Telecommunications Companies) (USA ISSN 1043-6073) **2370**
O P B Member Guide *see* O P B Primetime **2387**
• O P B Primetime (Oregon Public Broadcasting) (USA ISSN 1949-3827) **2387**
O P C Bulletin *see* Overseas Press Club Bulletin **4581**
O P C Nieuws (NLD ISSN 1872-6674) **8507**
O P C S Monitor. DH3: Sudden Infant Death Syndrome (Office of Population Censuses and Surveys) (GBR ISSN 0953-4415) **7288**
† O P C S Monitor. PP3 (Office of Population Censuses and Surveys) (GBR ISSN 0953-3435) **8978**
† O P C S Monitor. Weekly Return (Office of Population Censuses and Surveys) (GBR ISSN 0951-4287) **8978**
• O P C W Annual Report (Organisation for the Prohibition of Chemical Weapons) (NLD ISSN 1607-503X) **7160**
O P D Chemical Buyers Directory (Oil Paint Drug) (USA ISSN 0276-539X) **2022**
O P D Reference Book & Buyers Guide (Office Products Dealer) (GBR ISSN 1742-531X) **1853**
O P D Restauro (Opificio delle Pietre Dure) (ITA ISSN 1120-2513) **509**
O P E *see* Outdoor Power Equipment **3746**
O P E C Annual Report (Organization of the Petroleum Exporting Countries) (AUT ISSN 0257-1617) **6782**
• O P E C Annual Statistical Bulletin (Organization of the Petroleum Exporting Countries) (AUT ISSN 0475-0608) **6782**
• O P E C Bulletin (Organization of the Petroleum Exporting Countries, PR and Information Department) (AUT ISSN 0474-6279) **6782**
• ➤ O P E C Energy Review (Organization of the Petroleum Exporting Countries) (GBR ISSN 1753-0229) **6782**
• O P E C Monthly Oil Market Report (Organization of the Petroleum Exporting Countries) (AUT) **6782**
† O P E C Papers (Organization of the Petroleum Exporting Countries) (AUT ISSN 1015-6224) **8978**
O P E C Review *see* O P E C Energy Review **6782**
O P E Nursing/Ope Nashingu (Operating Room) (JPN ISSN 0913-5014) **5976**
O P E R *see* Ohio Public Employee Reporter **4752**
O P I *see* Office Products International **1853**
• O P I Issues Notes (Oxford Policy Institute) (GBR ISSN 1748-8311) **8060**
• O P I Policy Briefs (Oxford Policy Institute) (GBR ISSN 1748-8303) **8060**
O P I S Fuel Ethanol Report *see* Fuel Ethanol Report **6769**
O P I S Newsletter *see* Oil Price Information Service Newsletter **6785**
O P I S Retail Fuel Watch *see* Retail Fuel Watch **6790**
O P, Ingenieria y Territorio *see* Ingenieria y Territorio **3270**
• O P Journal (Operations) (DEU ISSN 0178-1715) **6254**
O P M *see* Ogolnopolski Przeglad Medyczny **5689**
O P M A Overseas Media Guide (Overseas Press and Media Association) (GBR) **2022**
O P Magazine *see* Fine Books & Collections **7561**
O P N *see* Optics & Photonics News **7083**
O P N Trends *see* Optics & Photonics News **7083**
O P O *see* Ophthalmic and Physiological Optics **6047**
O P / Position (CAN ISSN 1910-1112) **7160**
O P R *see* Offender Programs Report **2662**
O P R Extra *see* Platt's Oilgram Price Report (Online) **6789**
O P T *see* Optimizing Process and Technology **1784**
O P T I M A Newsletter/Informateur O P T I M A (Organization for the Phyto-Taxonomic Investigation of the Mediterranean Area) (ESP ISSN 0376-5016) **806**
O P T: One Parent Times (GBR ISSN 0143-0211) **2163**
O Papel (BRA ISSN 0031-1057) **6735**
O plus E (JPN ISSN 0911-5943) **3110**
O plus M *see* Oplagstal og Markedstal **4581**
O Praktikos Odegos Tou Taxidiote *see* Traveler National Geographic **8768**
O Q E *see* Optical and Quantum Electronics **7081**
O R A C L E Newsletter (USA) **6646**
O R A Newsletter (Oklahoma Reading Association) (USA) **2893**
O R C A (Organisation Cetacea) (GBR ISSN 1477-1217) **2623**
O R E R *see* Official Railway Equipment Register **8621**
O R E S Working Paper Series (Office of Research, Evaluation and Statistics) (USA) **8060**
O R I L *see* Oregon Review of International Law **4937**
† O R in de Overheid (Ondernemingsraad) (NLD ISSN 1874-4052) **8978**
O R Informatie (Ondernemingsraad) (NLD ISSN 0165-0823) **1701**
• ➤ O R Insight (Operational Research) (GBR ISSN 0953-5543) **1782**
• ➤ O R L (Oto Rhino Laryngology) (CHE ISSN 0301-1569) **6083**
O R L - Aktuell (Otorhinolaryngologie) (CHE) **6083**
O.R.L. Aragon (Otorrinolaringologia Aragon) (ESP ISSN 1576-9127) **6083**
O.R.L. Dips (ESP ISSN 0210-7309) **6083**
➤ O R L - Head and Neck Nursing (Otorhinolaryngology) (USA ISSN 1064-3842) **6083**
O R L Highlights *see* O R L - Praxis **6083**
O R L, Pneumo, Allergo Pratique *see* O P A Pratique **6083**
O R L - Praxis (Oto Rhino Laryngologie) (CHE) **6083**
• ➤ O R - M S Today (Operations Research - Management Science) (USA ISSN 1085-1038) **7894**
• O R Manager (Operating Room) (USA ISSN 8756-8047) **4108**
O R N L (Oak Ridge National Laboratory) (USA ISSN 0735-9861) **3143**
▼ • ➤ O R Nurse (Operating Room) (USA ISSN 1933-3145) **5976**
O R-Praktijk. Basiskennis (Ondernemingsraad) (NLD ISSN 1571-8891) **1701**
O R R M *see* Operating Room Risk Management **6254**
• O R Reports (Operating Room) (USA ISSN 1065-8173) **4114**
O R S T O M. Resumes des Travaux Oceanographie *see* Office de la Recherche Scientifique et Technique Outre-Mer. Resumes des Travaux. Oceanographie **2816**
O R Series *see* Monash University Accident Research Centre. Other Reports Series **8632**
• ➤ O R Spectrum (Operations Research) (DEU) **2433**
O R T Bulletin (American Organization for Rehabilitation Through Training) (USA) **3556**
➤ O R T E S O L Journal (Oregon Teachers of English to Speakers of Other Languages) (USA ISSN 0192-401X) **5157**
O R T Reporter *see* The Reporter (New York, 1966) **7728**
O R Today (Operating Room) (USA) **6254**
A O S *see* Actualites Odonto-Stomatologiques **5833**
O S *see* Organization Studies **7990**
• O S/2 e-Zine! (CAN ISSN 1203-5696) **2595**
† O S A Internationalia (ITA) **8978**
O S A Messenger (Orthodox Society of America) (USA) **7705**
O S A Proceeding Series (Optical Society of America) (USA ISSN 1053-8526) **7081**
O S A Trends in Optics and Photonics *see* Trends in Optics and Photonics Series **7085**
O S & H Bulletin (Occupational Safety and Health) (GBR ISSN 1462-4958) **6682**
O S B Today (Ondernemersorganisatie Schoonmaak- en Bedrijfsdiensten) (NLD ISSN 1875-7685) **6682**
O S C A Reports *see* O S C A Today **2893**
O S C A Today (Ontario School Counsellors' Association) (CAN ISSN 1711-3865) **2893**
O S C O News (Old South Community Organization) (CAN ISSN 1912-3086) **3457**
† O S E A P Centre Update (Organisation for Scientific Evaluation of Aerial Phenomena) (GBR ISSN 0262-7795) **8978**
† O S E A P Journal (Organisation for Scientific Evaluation of Aerial Phenomena) (GBR ISSN 0262-5954) **8978**
• O S F I Annual Report (Office of the Superintendent of Financial Institutions) (CAN ISSN 1701-0802) **7458**
O S H A *see* Occupational Safety and Health Act **6683**
• O S H A Compliance Advisor (Occupational Safety and Health Administration) (USA ISSN 0896-9949) **3457**
▼ • O S H A Compliance Manual (Occupational Safety and Health Administration) (USA ISSN 1948-7924) **6682**
O S H A Construction Industry Regulations *see* 29 C F R 1926 O S H A Construction Industry Regulations **6689**
O S H A Environmental Compliance Handbook (Occupational Safety and Health Administration) (USA ISSN 1537-1999) **3457**
O S H A General Industry Regulations *see* 20 C F R 1910 O S H A General Industry Regulations Book **6689**
• O S H A Healthcare Connection (Occupational Safety and Health Administration) (USA) **4108**
O S H A News (Occupational Safety and Health Administration) (USA ISSN 0740-1418) **6682**
• O S H A Regulations, Documents, and Technical Information on CD-ROM (Occupational Safety and Health Administration) (USA ISSN 1065-9277) **6682**
O S H A Required Training for Supervisors (Occupational Safety and Health Administration) (USA ISSN 1093-5045) **3457**
O S H A Safety Training Newsletter *see* Keller's O S H A Safety Training Newsletter **6680**
• O S H A Up To Date Newsletter (Occupational Safety & Health Administration) (USA) **6682**
• O S H A Watch (Occupational Safety and Health Administration) (USA ISSN 1944-6772) **6682**
O S H A Week (Occupational Safety and Health Administration) (USA ISSN 1529-9791) **6682**
• O S H Briefing (Online) (Occupational Safety and Health) (GBR) **6682**
O S I R *see* Oil Spill Intelligence Report **3490**
O S J. Offshore Support Journal (GBR ISSN 1463-581X) **8655**
• O S K a (Osrodek Informacji Srodowisk Kobiecych) (POL ISSN 1429-7027) **8878**
O S M T Advocate (Ontario Society of Medical Technologists) (CAN ISSN 1200-751X) **5910**
• O S Magasinet (Olympiska Spelen) (SWE ISSN 1654-4625) **8191**
O S Magazine *see* Office Secretary **1870**
O S N *see* Office and Stationery News **1853**
O S N I E *see* Ocular Surgery News (Europe / Asia-Pacific Edition) **6254**

Title

Observatorio del Ebro. Boletin, Ionsofera (ESP ISSN 0211-5166) **2787**
Observatorio del Ebro. Magnetismo. Boletin (ESP ISSN 1139-5745) **2759**
Observatorio del Ebro. Publicaciones. Memoria (ESP ISSN 0212-9760) **2787**
Observatorio del Ebro. Publicaciones. Miscelanea (ESP ISSN 0211-4534) **2787**
• ➤ Observatorio Medioambiental (ESP ISSN 1139-1987) **3457**
Observatorio Nacional Rio de Janeiro. Efemerides Astronomicas (BRA) **579**
Observatorio Nacional Rio de Janeiro. Publicacoes (BRA) **579**
Observatorio Sismologico y Vulcanologico de Arenal y Miravalles. Boletin (CRI) **2787**
• Observatorio Social de America Latina (ARG ISSN 1515-3282) **8124**
Observatorio Vasco de Drogodependencia. Informe (ESP) **2698**
➤ The Observatory (GBR ISSN 0029-7704) **579**
Observed Minima Timings of Eclipsing Binaries (USA) **579**
• Observer (CAN ISSN 0839-1270) **3815**
• The Observer (GBR ISSN 0029-7712) **3869**
The Observer (NZL) **3918**
Observer (Anchorage) (USA) **3490**
Observer (Aptos) (USA) **1853**
Observer (Ellensburg) (USA) **2294**
Observer (Ft. Lauderdale) (USA) **2294**
The Observer (Monterey) (USA ISSN 0745-9491) **7810**
Observer (Nashville) (USA ISSN 8750-5290) **7727**
The Observer (New York, 1981) (USA) **2294**
• Observer (Notre Dame) (USA) **2294**
Observer (Rock Island) (USA ISSN 1063-1631) **2294**
The Observer (Rockford) (USA ISSN 0029-7739) **7810**
Obshchaya i Regional'naya Geologiya, Geologiya Morei i Okeanov, Geologicheskoe Kartorovanie (RUS) **2759**
Obshchaya Programa po Informatsii - Byulleten' J U N I S I S T (FRA ISSN 0379-2234) **5037**
• Obshchestvennye Nauki i Sovremennost' (RUS ISSN 0869-0499) **7990**
Obshchestvennye Nauki v Uzbekistane (UZB ISSN 0029-7763) **7990**
Obshchestvennye Rating (KGZ) **3904**
• Obshchestvo i Ekonomika (RUS ISSN 0207-3676) **1156**
Obshta Meditsina/General Medicine (BGR ISSN 1311-1817) **5689**
Obsidian 3: Literature in the African Diaspora *see* Obsidian III: Literature in the African Diaspora **5345**
• ➤ Obsidian III: Literature in the African Diaspora (USA) **5345**
Obsidian Three: Literature in the African Diaspora *see* Obsidian III: Literature in the African Diaspora **5345**
• Obsledovanie Naseleniya po Problemam Zanyatosti/Survey on Employment of Population (RUS) **1257**
Obst und Garten (DEU ISSN 0029-7798) **3745**
Obst und Gemuese *see* T A S P O Obst und Gemuese **3751**
Obst- und Weinbau (CHE ISSN 1023-2958) **608**
Obst - Wein - Garten (AUT) **3745**
Obsta Medicina (SRB) **5689**
Obstbau (DEU ISSN 0179-7077) **143**
Obstbauversuchsring des Altes Landes. Mitteilungen (DEU ISSN 0178-2916) **244**
• ➤ Obstetric Anesthesia Digest (USA ISSN 0275-665X) **5772**
▼ • ➤ Obstetric Medicine (GBR ISSN 1753-495X) **6000**
† Obstetric Ultrasound (GBR ISSN 1362-6337) **8978**
Obstetrica si Ginecologie (ROM ISSN 1220-5532) **6000**
Obstetrical and Gynecological Practice *see* Sanfujinka no Jissai **6004**
• Obstetrical & Gynecological Survey (USA ISSN 0029-7828) **6000**
Obstetrical and Gynecological Therapy *see* Sanfujinka Chiryo **6004**
• ➤ The Obstetrician & Gynaecologist (GBR ISSN 1467-2561) **6001**
Obstetricians and Gynecologists / GYN Reimbursement & Compliance Report *see* OB / GYN Reimbursement & Compliance Report **4108**
• Obstetrics & Gynaecology Forum (ZAF ISSN 1029-1962) **6001**
Obstetrics and Gynaecology Today (GBR ISSN 1352-3759) **6001**
Obstetrics and Gynaecology Today *see* Obs. & Gynae. Today **6000**
Obstetrics and Gynecology *see* Akusherstvo i Ginekologiya **5985**
• ➤ Obstetrics and Gynecology (USA ISSN 0029-7844) **6001**
Obstetrics and Gynecology *see* Today in Medicine. Obstetrics & Gynecology **6005**
• ➤ Obstetrics and Gynecology Clinics of North America (USA ISSN 0889-8545) **6001**
• ➤ Obstetrics and Gynecology International (USA ISSN 1687-9589) **6001**
Obstetrics and Gynecology Management *see* O B G Management **6000**
• Obstetrics, Gynecology and Reproductive Medicine (GBR ISSN 1751-7214) **6001**
Obstetrics - Gynecology Clinical Alert *see* Ob/Gyn Clinical Alert **6000**
Obstetrics - Gynecology Malpractice Prevention *see* OB-GYN Malpractice Prevention **8978**
Obstetrics - Gynecology News *see* Ob-Gyn News **6000**
Obstetrics - Gynecology Practice Advisor *see* Ob-Gyn Practice Advisor **4108**
Obstetrics - Gynecology Special Edition *see* OB-GYN Special Edition **6000**
Obuchenieto po Geografia (BGR) **4022**
• Obucheniye za Rubezhom/Study and Training Abroad (RUS) **3014**
Obvestila (SVN) **509**
Obwaldner Bauernblatt (CHE) **143**
Obwaldner Geschichtsblaetter (CHE) **4250**
Obyczaje (POL ISSN 1506-8331) **3930**
Obyvatel' (RUS) **4981**
Obywatel (POL ISSN 1641-1021) **3930**
• Obzine (DNK) **3834**
Obzor (SVK ISSN 0231-861X) **3946**
Obzor A B B *see* A B B Review **3293**
Obzor Morskogo Transporta *see* Review of Maritime Transport **8658**
Obzornaya Informatsiya. Ekologicheskaya Ekspertiza (RUS ISSN 0869-1010) **3480**
Obzornaya Informatsiya. Ekonomika Prirodopol'zovaniya (RUS) **3480**
Obzornaya Informatsiya. Geologiya, Metody Poiskov, Razvedki i Otsenki Mestorozhdenii Toplivnoenergeticheskogo Syr'ia (RUS ISSN 0235-554X) **2760**
Obzornaya Informatsiya. Geologiya, Metody Poiskov, Razvedki i Otsenki Mestorozhdenii Tverdykh Poleznykh Iskopaemykh (RUS ISSN 0235-5531) **2760**
Obzornaya Informatsiya. Laboratornye i Tekhnologicheskie Issledovaniya Mineral'nogo Syr'ya (RUS) **2623**
Obzornaya Informatsiya. Nauchnye i Tekhnicheskie Aspekty Okhrany Okruzhayushchei Sredy (RUS ISSN 0869-1002) **3480**
Obzornaya Informatsiya. Problemy Bezopasnosti i Chrezvychainykh Situatsii (RUS) **2229**
Obzornaya Informatsiya. Problemy Bezopasnosti Poletov (RUS ISSN 0235-5000) **76**
Obzornaya Informatsiya. Problemy Bezopasnosti pri Chrezvychainykh Situatsiyakh *see* Obzornaya Informatsiya. Problemy Bezopasnosti i Chrezvychainykh Situatsii **2229**
Obzornaya Informatsiya. Problemy Okruzhayushchei Sredy i Prirodnykh Resursov (RUS ISSN 0235-5019) **3480**
Obzornaya Informatsiya. Razvedochnaya Geofizika (RUS) **2787**
Obzornaya Informatsiya. Transport: Nauka, Tekhnika, Upravlenie (RUS ISSN 0236-1914) **8528**
• ➤ Obzornik za Matematiko in Fiziko (SVN ISSN 0473-7466) **5522**
➤ Obzornik Zdravstvene in Babiske Nege (SVN ISSN 1854-4754) **5976**
Obzornik Zdravstvene Nege *see* Obzornik Zdravstvene in Babiske Nege **5976**
Ocarina (IND) **5428**
Occasional A U R A Publication (Australian Rock Art Research Association) (AUS ISSN 1834-4488) **409**
Occasional Bulletin of Nungalinya College, Darwin (AUS) **3556**
Occasional Paper Series. Friends of the Greenbelt Foundation *see* Friends of the Greenbelt Foundation. Occasional Paper Series **114**
Occasional Papers and Monographs - Centre of Asian Studies *see* University of Hong Kong. Centre of Asian Studies. Occasional Papers and Monographs **563**
➤ Occasional Papers in Anthropology (USA ISSN 0078-3005) **350**
➤ Occasional Papers in Entomology (USA ISSN 0362-2622) **856**
Occasional Papers in German Studies (Coventry) (GBR ISSN 0307-7497) **5345**
Occasional Papers in Irish Science and Technology (IRL ISSN 0791-461X) **7894**
• Occasional Papers in Open and Distance Learning (AUS ISSN 1038-8958) **2944**
Occasional Papers in Politics and International Relations (GBR ISSN 0968-4476) **7160**
Occasional Papers in Slavic Languages and Literature (USA ISSN 0739-8972) **5345**
Occasional Papers in Swiss Studies (GBR ISSN 1423-9825) **5157**
Occasional Papers in Work-Based Learning *see* University of London. Institute of Education. Occasional Papers in Work-Based Learning **2923**
Occasional Papers of the Museum of Zoology, University of Michigan *see* University of Michigan. Museum of Zoology. Occasional Papers **966**
➤ Occasional Papers on Islands and Small States (MLT ISSN 1024-6282) **7256**
Occasional Papers on Systematic Entomology (GBR ISSN 0962-5275) **856**
Occasional Papers on the Near East (USA ISSN 0732-6475) **4324**
• ➤ Occasional Series in Criminal Justice and International Studies (AUS) **4750**
Occasional Working Papers in Literary & Cultural Studies (GBR) **5345**
Occasions Mag (FRA ISSN 1763-7155) **8596**
Occhio Clinico. Pediatria *see* Il Pediatra **6099**
Occident & Orient (JOR ISSN 1818-7854) **409**
Occult Publications Directory (USA) **6744**
• Occultation Newsletter (USA ISSN 0737-6766) **579**
Occupation and Health *see* Zhiye yu Jiankang **7546**
Occupational and Environmental Dermatology *see* Dermatologie in Beruf und Umwelt **5875**
Occupational and Environmental Diseases Association Newsletter *see* O E D A Newsletter **6681**
• ➤ Occupational and Environmental Medicine (GBR ISSN 1351-0711) **6682**
Occupational and Environmental Medicine Report *see* The O E M Report **6681**
Occupational and Technical Education *see* Zhiye Jishu Jiaoyu **3088**
Occupational Compensation Summaries (USA) **1257**
† Occupational Compensation Surveys (USA) **8978**
• ➤ Occupational Ergonomics (NLD ISSN 1359-9364) **6682**
Occupational Hazards *see* E H S Today **6676**
• ➤ Occupational Health (GBR ISSN 0029-7917) **5976**
• Occupational Health & Safety (USA ISSN 0362-4064) **6682**
Occupational Health and Safety Act *see* Occupational Health and Safety Library **1701**
Occupational Health and Safety Bulletin *see* O H S Bulletin **6682**
Occupational Health & Safety Canada Magazine *see* O H S Canada Magazine **6682**
Occupational Health and Safety Compliance.ca *see* O H S Compliance.ca **6682**
Occupational Health & Safety Current Contents (AUS ISSN 1324-8715) **6691**
Occupational Health & Safety Health Facilities Report (USA ISSN 1075-6973) **4108**
Occupational Health and Safety in Educational Establishments. Newsletter *see* Al- Sihhat al-Mihaniyyat wa-al-Salamat fi al-Munsha'at al-Ta'limiyyat **6116**
Occupational Health and Safety in Ontario Education (CAN) **6682**
Occupational Health and Safety in Ontario Health Care (CAN ISSN 1719-9522) **6683**
Occupational Health and Safety Law (CAN ISSN 0706-5019) **4750**
• Occupational Health and Safety Law New South Wales (AUS) **4750**
• Occupational Health and Safety Library (ZAF ISSN 1682-0738) **1701**
Occupational Health & Safety News (USA ISSN 0896-3835) **6683**
Occupational Health [at Work] (GBR) **6683**
• Occupational Health Management (USA ISSN 1082-5339) **6683**
• Occupational Health News (AUS ISSN 1441-144X) **6683**
Occupational Health Review (GBR ISSN 0951-4600) **6683**
Occupational Illness Litigation (GBR) **6683**
Occupational Injuries and Diseases of Young Workers *see* Lost-time Claims. Young Workers **7548**
• Occupational Injuries and Illnesses (USA) **6683**
Occupational Injuries & Illnesses in Maine (USA ISSN 0198-7771) **6683**
• Occupational Injury & Illness Information (USA ISSN 1063-3820) **6691**
• ➤ Occupational Medicine (GBR ISSN 0962-7480) **6683**
Occupational Medicine *see* Clinics in Occupational and Environmental Medicine **5598**
• Occupational Outlook Handbook (USA ISSN 0082-9072) **6707**
• Occupational Outlook Quarterly (USA ISSN 0199-4786) **6707**
Occupational Pensions (GBR ISSN 0952-231X) **4517**
Occupational Pensions Law Reports (GBR ISSN 0967-8115) **4517**
Occupational Profiles *see* Washington (State). Employment Security Department. Occupational Profiles **6707**
Occupational Programs in California Public Community Colleges (USA ISSN 0731-8650) **2961**
Occupational Projections and Training Data *see* Occupational Outlook Handbook **6707**
Occupational Radiation Exposure, Annual Report *see* U.S. Nuclear Regulatory Commission. Occupational Radiation at Commercial Nuclear Power Reactors and Other Facilities. Annual Report **6688**
Occupational Safety & Health (JPN ISSN 1345-2649) **6683**
• Occupational Safety and Health Act (USA) **6683**
Occupational Safety and Health Administration Compliance Advisor *see* O S H A Compliance Advisor **3457**
Occupational Safety and Health Administration Compliance Manual *see* O S H A Compliance Manual **6682**
Occupational Safety and Health Administration Environmental Compliance Handbook *see* O S H A Environmental Compliance Handbook **3457**
Occupational Safety and Health Administration Healthcare Connection *see* O S H A Healthcare Connection **4108**
Occupational Safety and Health Administration News *see* O S H A News **6682**
Occupational Safety and Health Administration Regulations, Documents, and Technical Information on CD-ROM *see* O S H A Regulations, Documents, and Technical Information on CD-ROM **6682**
Occupational Safety and Health Administration Required Training for Supervisors *see* O S H A Required Training for Supervisors **3457**
Occupational Safety & Health Administration Up To Date Newsletter *see* O S H A Up To Date Newsletter **6682**
Occupational Safety and Health Administration Watch *see* O S H A Watch **6682**
Occupational Safety and Health Administration Week *see* O S H A Week **6682**
Occupational Safety and Health Briefing (Online) *see* O S H Briefing (Online) **6682**
Occupational Safety and Health Bulletin *see* O S & H Bulletin **6682**
Occupational Safety and Health Cases (USA ISSN 0095-5515) **6683**
• Occupational Safety & Health Daily (USA ISSN 1535-1602) **6683**
Occupational Safety and Health Daily *see* Occupational Safety & Health Daily **6683**
Occupational Safety and Health Handbook (AUS) **6683**
• Occupational Safety and Health Handbook (USA) **6683**
Occupational Safety & Health Procedures Manual *see* Occupational Safety and Health Procedures Manual **6683**
• Occupational Safety and Health Procedures Manual (AUS) **6683**
• Occupational Safety & Health Reporter (USA ISSN 0095-3237) **6683**
Occupational Safety and Health Reporter *see* Occupational Safety & Health Reporter **6683**
Occupational Safety and Health Series (CHE ISSN 0078-3129) **6683**
Occupational Safety and Health Statistics of the Federal Government (USA ISSN 0092-8712) **6691**
• ➤ Occupational Therapy in Health Care (USA ISSN 0738-0577) **5689**
• ➤ Occupational Therapy in Mental Health (USA ISSN 0164-212X) **6171**
• ➤ Occupational Therapy International (GBR ISSN 0966-7903) **6683**
Occupational Therapy Journal of Research Occupation, Participation and Health *see* O T J R: Occupation, Participation and Health **5688**
Occupational Therapy News (GBR ISSN 0969-5095) **6113**
• Occupational Therapy Now (CAN ISSN 1481-5532) **6113**
Occupational Therapy Practice *see* O T Practice **6682**
Occupational Therapy Services *see* N H S Occupational Therapy Services. England **6113**
Occupational Toxicants *see* The M A K - Collection for Occupational Health and Safety **6680**
Occurrence Digest *see* Great Britain. Civil Aviation Authority. Occurrence Digest **8543**
Ocean (CZE ISSN 1213-1857) **2814**
Ocean (Corona Del Mar) (USA ISSN 1556-9829) **2259**
Ocean (Rodanthe) (USA) **2814**
Ocean Alert (USA) **321**
The Ocean and Coastal Conservation Guide (USA ISSN 1554-3137) **3457**
• Ocean & Coastal Law Journal (USA ISSN 1073-8843) **4750**
• ➤ Ocean & Coastal Management (GBR ISSN 0964-5691) **2814**
Ocean & Cruise News (USA) **8655**
• Ocean and Polar Research (KOR ISSN 1598-141X) **2814**
Ocean Biocoenosis Series (USA) **2814**
Ocean Challenge (GBR ISSN 0959-0161) **2814**
Ocean Data and Information Network for Africa AFRICA Annual Report *see* O D I N AFRICA Annual Report **2814**
• ➤ Ocean Development and International Law (USA ISSN 0090-8320) **2814**
Ocean Development and Management *see* Haiyang Kaifa yu Guanli **2805**
Ocean Development Symposium. Proceedings *see* Kaiyo Kaihatsu Ronbunshu **3277**
Ocean Drilling Program Nyusu Reta *see* O D P Nyusu Reta **2814**
Ocean Drilling Program. Proceedings. Initial Reports *see* Integrated Ocean Drilling Program. Proceedings. Expedition Reports **2807**
• ➤ Ocean Drilling Program. Scientific Results. Proceedings. Scientific Results (USA ISSN 0884-5891) **2814**
Ocean Drive (USA ISSN 1092-7530) **5079**
Ocean Drive en Espanol (USA) **5079**
• ➤ Ocean Dynamics/German Journal of Hydrography (DEU ISSN 1616-7341) **2814**
Ocean Engineering *see* Haiyang Gongcheng **3194**
• ➤ Ocean Engineering (GBR ISSN 0029-8018) **2814**
Ocean Engineering Symposium *see* Kaiyo Kogaku Shinpojumu **2810**
Ocean Freight Rates *see* International Grains Council. Ocean Freight Rates **8647**
• Ocean Home (USA) **7602**
Ocean Indien Actuel (MDG) **3906**
• ➤ Ocean Modelling (USA ISSN 1463-5003) **2814**
• Ocean Navigator (USA ISSN 0886-0149) **8279**

Title

Title

Ogrody, Ogrodki, Zielence (POL ISSN 1507-4161) **3746**
The Oguaa Educator (GHA ISSN 0855-0913) **2996**
Oh (CAN ISSN 1192-4047) **8879**
Oh Calcutta (IND ISSN 0377-7596) **3886**
• Ohemaa (USA ISSN 1930-7896) **8879**
Ohinemuri Regional History Journal (NZL ISSN 0472-6480) **4193**
• Ohio (USA ISSN 0279-3504) **3984**
Ohio A F L - C I O Working Papers (USA) **4600**
Ohio Administrative Code *see* Ohio Monthly Record **7458**
Ohio Agent (USA) **4517**
Ohio Agricultural Research and Development Center, Wooster. Research Bulletin (USA ISSN 0078-3951) **143**
Ohio Agricultural Research and Development Center, Wooster. Research Circular (USA ISSN 0078-396X) **143**
Ohio: All-Indsutries *see* Harris Directory. Ohio All-Indsutries **2001**
Ohio & Northern Kentucky Gasoline Dealers & Garage News (USA) **8596**
Ohio Annotated Commercial Law Handbook *see* Anderson's Ohio Annotated Commercial Law Handbook **4615**
Ohio Annotated Workers' Compensation Law Handbook *see* Anderson's Ohio Annotated Workers' Compensation Law Handbook (Years) **1663**
Ohio Archaeologist (USA ISSN 0048-153X) **409**
Ohio Archivist (Online) (USA ISSN 1047-5400) **5037**
Ohio Arts Council. Biennial Report (USA ISSN 0731-3284) **510**
• Ohio Attorney General Opinions (USA ISSN 0748-6170) **4958**
Ohio Banker *see* Ohio Record **1373**
Ohio Bankruptcy Handbook *see* Anderson's (Year) Ohio Bankruptcy Handbook **4854**
Ohio Beverage Journal (USA ISSN 0740-1361) **608**
➤ Ohio Biological Survey. Bulletin. New Series (USA ISSN 0078-3994) **695**
➤ Ohio Biological Survey. Miscellaneous Contributions (USA ISSN 1074-9233) **695**
➤ Ohio Biological Survey Notes (USA ISSN 1097-1904) **695**
Ohio Builder (USA ISSN 1552-8707) **1028**
• Ohio Business Credit Directory (USA) **2022**
• Ohio Business Directory (USA ISSN 1048-7360) **2022**
Ohio Business Entities (USA) **4878**
Ohio Business Entities *see* Anderson's (Year) Ohio Business Entities Handbook **4854**
Ohio Business Entities Handbook *see* Anderson's (Year) Ohio Business Entities Handbook **4854**
Ohio Business Law Journal (USA ISSN 1931-0013) **4878**
Ohio Case Locator *see* Anderson's Ohio Case Locator **4615**
Ohio Chess Bulletin (USA ISSN 0885-6583) **8191**
Ohio Citations *see* Shepard's Ohio Citations **4963**
Ohio Cities and Counties Graphic Performance Analysis *see* Ohio Cities & Counties Graphic Performance Analysis **7482**
Ohio Cities & Counties Graphic Performance Analysis (USA ISSN 1935-553X) **7482**
Ohio Cities and Villages *see* Cities and Villages **4407**
Ohio Civil Practice with Forms *see* Anderson's Ohio Civil Practice with Forms **4826**
Ohio Civil War Genealogy Journal (USA ISSN 1095-273X) **3777**
Ohio Commercial Law Handbook *see* Anderson's (Year) Ohio Commercial Law Handbook **8930**
Ohio Commercial Law Handbook *see* Anderson's (Year) Ohio Commercial Law Handbook **8930**
Ohio Construction and Code Journal (USA ISSN 1932-099X) **1028**
Ohio Contractor (USA ISSN 0030-0861) **8633**
Ohio Corporation Law (USA) **4878**
Ohio Corporation Law with Federal Tax Analysis *see* Ohio Business Entities **4878**
Ohio Council for the Social Studies. Review *see* The Review (Columbus) **3078**
Ohio Council of Teachers of Mathematics Newsletter *see* O C T M Newsletter **5522**
Ohio Courtroom Evidence (USA) **4958**
Ohio Courts (USA) **4958**
• Ohio Criminal Code (USA) **4896**
Ohio Criminal Code Handbook (Year) *see* Anderson's Ohio Criminal Code Handbook (Year) **4884**
• Ohio Criminal Law and Motor Vehicle Handbook (USA) **4751**
• Ohio Criminal Law Handbook (USA) **2662**
Ohio Criminal Law Handbook (Year) *see* Anderson's Ohio Criminal Law Handbook (Year) **4884**
Ohio Criminal Practice and Procedure *see* Anderson's Ohio Criminal Practice and Procedure **4884**
▼ Ohio Curiosities (USA ISSN 1934-5836) **8745**
Ohio Deer & Turkey Show Preview (USA) **8325**
Ohio Dental Association Today *see* O D A Today **5857**
• Ohio Department of Aging. Annual Report (USA) **4052**
Ohio. Department of Human Services. Child Welfare Statistics (USA) **8083**
Ohio District Court Review (USA ISSN 0274-7294) **4958**
Ohio. Division of Geological Survey. Bulletin (USA ISSN 0097-5478) **2760**
Ohio. Division of Geological Survey. Educational Leaflet (USA ISSN 0472-6685) **2760**
Ohio. Division of Geological Survey. Geological Note (USA) **2760**
Ohio. Division of Geological Survey. Guidebook (USA ISSN 0097-9473) **2760**
Ohio. Division of Geological Survey. Information Circular (USA ISSN 0097-5605) **2760**
Ohio. Division of Geological Survey. Miscellaneous Report (USA ISSN 0361-0519) **2760**
Ohio. Division of State Personnel. Annual Report (USA ISSN 0078-4001) **1870**
Ohio Documents (USA ISSN 0147-2542) **633**
• The Ohio e-C P A Weekly (USA) **1298**
Ohio Ecological Food and Farm Association News (USA ISSN 1087-6626) **244**
• Ohio Education Laws (USA ISSN 1932-0507) **2893**
▼ • Ohio Employment Law (USA ISSN 1934-1571) **1701**
Ohio Employment Law Handbook *see* Anderson's Ohio Employment Law Handbook **1663**
• Ohio Employment Law Letter (USA ISSN 1046-9206) **4751**
Ohio Engineer (USA ISSN 0194-9276) **3213**
• Ohio Entrepreneur (USA) **1156**
Ohio Facts (USA ISSN 1040-4872) **3121**
The Ohio Family Physician (USA ISSN 1536-0474) **5689**
• Ohio Farmer (USA ISSN 0030-0896) **143**
Ohio Fish and Wildlife Report (USA ISSN 0085-4468) **959**
Ohio Fishwrapper (USA) **8325**
• Ohio Forms of Pleading and Practice (USA) **4751**
Ohio Forms on Disc *see* Anderson's Ohio Forms on Disc **4615**
Ohio Game & Fish (USA ISSN 0897-9170) **8326**
Ohio Genealogical Society Genealogy News *see* O G S Genealogy News **3777**
Ohio Genealogical Society. Newsletter *see* O G S Genealogy News **3777**
Ohio Genealogical Society. Quarterly (USA ISSN 1546-1408) **3777**
Ohio Genealogical Society. Report *see* Ohio Genealogical Society. Quarterly **3777**
Ohio Genealogical Society. Wood County Chapter. Newsletter (USA ISSN 0893-1593) **3777**
• Ohio Geological Society Newsletter (USA) **2760**
Ohio Geological Society. Publications (USA) **2760**
Ohio Geology (USA) **2760**
Ohio Government Directory *see* News Briefs (Columbus) **8673**
Ohio Government Directory - Ohio Trucking Times (USA) **8674**
Ohio Granger (USA ISSN 0749-4009) **143**
Ohio Higher Education. Basic Data Series (USA ISSN 0094-6109) **2935**
• ➤ Ohio History (Online) (USA ISSN 1934-6042) **4306**
Ohio in Perspective (USA ISSN 1065-5638) **5079**
Ohio Insurance Law Handbook *see* Anderson's (Year) Ohio Insurance Law Handbook **4492**
Ohio Jersey News (USA ISSN 0048-1556) **295**
Ohio Jewish Chronicle (USA ISSN 0030-0942) **7727**
† • The Ohio JobBank (USA ISSN 1099-0186) **8978**
Ohio Journal of School Mathematics (USA) **5523**
• ➤ The Ohio Journal of Science (USA ISSN 0030-0950) **7895**
Ohio Journal of the English Language Arts (USA ISSN 1085-2492) **5157**
The Ohio Labor Citizen (USA ISSN 1063-9853) **1701**
Ohio Labor Market Information: Labor Market Review (USA) **1701**
Ohio Law on Disc, Anderson's Ohio law on CD-ROM *see* Anderson's Ohio Law on Disc **8930**
Ohio Lawyer (USA ISSN 1097-6493) **4751**
Ohio Legal Rights Service. Annual Report (USA) **4968**
Ohio Legion News (USA) **6440**
Ohio Legislative Service *see* Baldwin's Ohio Legislative Service **4625**
The Ohio Lepidopterist (USA ISSN 0884-5956) **959**
• Ohio Libraries (USA ISSN 1046-4336) **5038**
Ohio Libraries (Columbus) (USA ISSN 0360-8069) **5038**
• Ohio Manufacturer (USA) **1900**
• Ohio Manufacturers Directory (USA ISSN 0737-7495) **2022**
Ohio: Manufacturing *see* Harris Directory. Ohio Manufacturing **2001**
Ohio Matters (USA) **1408**
Ohio Monthly Record (USA ISSN 0163-0008) **7458**
Ohio Motions in Limine (USA ISSN 1942-0331) **4958**
• Ohio Motor Vehicle Laws (USA) **4751**
The Ohio Motorist (USA ISSN 0030-0985) **8745**
Ohio News (USA ISSN 0899-4862) **268**
• Ohio Northern University Law Review (USA ISSN 0094-534X) **4752**
Ohio Nurses Review (USA ISSN 0030-0993) **5976**
• Ohio Outdoor News (USA ISSN 1935-0392) **8326**
• Ohio Outdoors (USA) **8326**
Ohio P H C Contractor (USA) **4124**
Ohio P T A News (Parent Teacher Association) (USA ISSN 0199-0918) **2893**
Ohio Pharmacist (USA ISSN 1072-2424) **6865**
Ohio Probate Law Handbook *see* Anderson's Ohio Probate Law Handbook **4900**
Ohio Probate Practice and Procedure *see* Anderson's Ohio Probate Practice and Procedure **4900**
The Ohio Psychologist (USA ISSN 0472-7290) **7388**
• Ohio Public Employee Reporter (USA) **4752**
Ohio Public Employment Library on CD-ROM *see* Ohio Public Employee Reporter **4752**
• ➤ Ohio Reading Teacher (USA ISSN 0030-1035) **3075**
Ohio Real Estate Law Handbook *see* Anderson's Ohio Real Estate Law Handbook **7581**
• Ohio Real Property, Law and Practice (USA) **7603**
Ohio Realtor (USA ISSN 1042-8119) **7603**
• Ohio Record (USA) **1373**
Ohio Records & Pioneer Families (USA ISSN 1063-4649) **3777**
Ohio Register of Manufacturers (USA ISSN 0884-173X) **2022**
• Ohio Report (USA ISSN 1063-990X) **7458**
Ohio Reports *see* West's Jury Verdicts. Ohio Reports **4967**
Ohio Residential Real Estate Manual (USA ISSN 1931-521X) **7603**
Ohio School Boards Association. Journal (USA ISSN 0893-5289) **3029**
Ohio School Directory *see* M D R's School Directory. Ohio **2959**
Ohio School Law Guide *see* Anderson's Ohio School Law Guide **3017**
Ohio Schools (USA ISSN 0030-1086) **2893**
Ohio Sea Grant College Program. Guide Series (USA) **4023**
Ohio Sea Grant College Program. Technical Summary (USA) **3604**
Ohio Search Warrant Manual *see* Anderson's Ohio Search Warrant Manual **4616**
Ohio Securities Law Handbook *see* Anderson's Ohio Securities Law Handbook **1307**
Ohio Slavic and East European Newsletter (USA ISSN 1048-6615) **4251**
Ohio Southland (USA) **4306**
Ohio Speech Journal (USA ISSN 0078-4052) **5157**
Ohio State Alumni Magazine (USA ISSN 1072-3234) **2294**
Ohio State Bar Association Report (USA ISSN 0744-8376) **4752**
Ohio State Engineer (USA) **3213**
• ➤ Ohio State Journal of Criminal Law (USA ISSN 1546-7619) **4896**
• Ohio State Journal on Dispute Resolution (USA ISSN 1046-4344) **4752**
• Ohio State Lantern (USA ISSN 0030-1116) **2294**
• Ohio State Law Journal (USA ISSN 0048-1572) **4752**
Ohio. State Library. Annual Report (USA ISSN 0164-1794) **5038**
Ohio State University. Agricultural Research and Development Center, Wooster. Special Circular (USA ISSN 0736-8003) **143**
Ohio State University. Byrd Polar Research Center. Miscellaneous Series (USA) **7895**
Ohio State University. Byrd Polar Research Center. Report Series (USA ISSN 0896-2472) **7895**
➤ Ohio State University Mathematical Research Institute Publications (DEU ISSN 0942-0363) **5523**
➤ Ohio State University. Working Papers in Linguistics (Online) (USA) **5157**
Ohio Tavern News (USA ISSN 0030-1183) **608**
Ohio Thoroughbred (USA) **8295**
• Ohio Traffic Law Handbook (USA ISSN 1551-3424) **8507**
Ohio United Way. Administrative Report (USA) **7458**
➤ Ohio University Press. Eastern Africa Series (USA) **4177**
➤ Ohio University Press. Series in Continental Thought (USA) **6937**
Ohio Unreported Appellate Citations *see* Shepard's Ohio Unreported Appellate Citations **4963**
➤ Ohio Valley History (USA ISSN 1544-4058) **4307**
• Ohio Valley Tails (USA ISSN 1945-6735) **6812**
Ohio Veterinary Medical Association Newsline *see* O V M A Newsline **8804**
Ohio Wesleyan Magazine (USA ISSN 0030-1221) **2294**
Ohio Woodland Journal (USA) **3699**
Ohio Worker's Compensation *see* Ohio Workers' Compensation Law **1701**
Ohio Workers' Compensation Law (USA ISSN 1931-1990) **1701**
Ohio Workers' Compensation Law. Companion Laws and Rules (USA ISSN 1931-2008) **1701**
Ohio Writer *see* Muse (Cleveland) **5337**
Ohioana Quarterly (USA ISSN 0030-1248) **5345**
Ohio's Country Journal (USA ISSN 1082-7854) **143**
Ohio's Heritage (USA) **4052**
Ohio's Last Frontier (USA ISSN 1090-851X) **3778**
• Ohio's Worker's Comp Advisor (USA ISSN 1527-1463) **4517**
• Ohlasene Knihy (CZE ISSN 1210-4566) **633**
Ohm (JPN ISSN 0386-5576) **3326**
† Ohnicek (CZE ISSN 0030-1272) **8978**
Ohnik (SVK ISSN 0139-8911) **2205**
Oho! (FIN ISSN 1458-9931) **3839**
• Ohoi (FIN ISSN 0357-1084) **7458**
OhsCompliance Newsletter (Occupational Health & Safety) (CAN) **6684**
Ohta General Hospital. Annals *see* Ota Sogo Byoin Gakujutsu Nenpo **5691**
Ohu Daigaku Shigakushi/Ohu University Dental Journal (JPN ISSN 0916-2313) **5858**
Ohu University Dental Journal *see* Ohu Daigaku Shigakushi **5858**
• Oideas (IRL ISSN 0475-0047) **2893**
Oideion (NLD) **510**
Oifig Naisiunta Leanai. Tuarascail Bhliantuil *see* National Children's Office. Annual Report **8056**
Oifig um Rialu Tobac. Tuarascail Bhliantuil *see* Office of Tobacco Control. Annual Report **7534**
Oihenart (ESP ISSN 1137-4454) **5345**
Oikeusministerion Toiminta ja Hallinto/Operations and Administartion/Verksamhet och Foervaltning (FIN ISSN 1458-6436) **4752**
Oikeuspoliittinen Tutkimuslaitos. Tutkimus/National Research Institute of Legal Policy Research. Report (FIN ISSN 1797-562X) **4752**
Oikeuspoliittisen Tutkimuslaitos. Julkaisu *see* Oikeuspoliittinen Tutkimuslaitos. Tutkimus **4752**
Oikeustiede-Jurisprudentia (FIN ISSN 0355-8215) **4752**
Oikogeneia kai Skoleio/Family and School (CYP ISSN 0253-0910) **2163**
• Oikonomia (VAT ISSN 1720-1691) **7990**
Oikonomike Biomehanike Epitheorese (GRC ISSN 1109-1584) **1900**
Oikonomiki Viomichaniki Epitheorissi *see* Oikonomike Biomehanike Epitheorese **1900**
Oikonomikos Tahudromos (GRC ISSN 1106-1936) **1156**
• Oikos (CHL ISSN 0717-327X) **1782**
Oikos (COL ISSN 0121-070X) **1505**
• ➤ Oikos (GBR ISSN 0030-1299) **3458**
Oikos (USA) **5428**
Oil Activity Review (CAN ISSN 0848-2780) **6783**
Oil: An Integrated Industry (USA) **6783**
Oil and Arab Cooperation (KWT ISSN 0251-415X) **6783**
Oil & Chemical Worker (IND ISSN 0030-1329) **4600**
Oil & Energy (USA) **6783**
• Oil and Energy Trends (GBR ISSN 0950-1045) **3143**
• Oil and Energy Trends: Annual Statistical Review (GBR ISSN 0953-1033) **3153**
• Oil and Gas (USA ISSN 0747-5306) **6783**
Oil & Gas (London) (GBR ISSN 1742-7606) **6783**
Oil and Gas Business Journal *see* Neftegazovoe Delo **6780**
Oil and Gas Developments in Pennsylvania (USA) **6783**
Oil and Gas Directory *see* Oil & Gas Directory **6783**
Oil & Gas Directory (USA ISSN 0471-380X) **6783**
Oil & Gas Eurasia (RUS ISSN 1812-2086) **6783**
Oil & Gas Executive (USA ISSN 1522-516X) **1782**
Oil and Gas Field Designations (CAN) **2760**
Oil and Gas Field Names *see* Texas. Railroad Commission. Oil and Gas Division. Oil and Gas Field Names **6794**
• Oil & Gas Financial Journal (USA ISSN 1555-4082) **6783**
• Oil & Gas Gazette (AUS ISSN 1038-1317) **6783**
Oil and Gas Geology *see* Shiyou yu Tianranqi Dizhi **2767**
Oil and Gas Investigations *see* Oregon. Department of Geology and Mineral Industries. Oil and Gas Investigations **6785**
• Oil and Gas Investor (USA ISSN 0744-5881) **6783**
Oil & Gas Investor *see* Oil and Gas Investor **6783**
• Oil and Gas Investor This Week (USA ISSN 1940-5189) **6783**
• Oil and Gas Investor's A & D Watch (Acquisitions & Divestitures) (USA ISSN 1940-8471) **6783**
Oil and Gas Investor's Petroleum Finance Week *see* Oil and Gas Investor This Week **6783**
Oil and Gas Journal *see* Oil & Gas Journal **6783**
• Oil & Gas Journal (USA ISSN 0030-1388) **6783**
Oil & Gas Journal Data Book *see* Oil & Gas Journal **6783**
Oil & Gas Journal Latinoamerica (USA) **6784**
Oil & Gas Journal Petroleum Software & Technology Guide *see* Oil & Gas Journal **6783**
• Oil and Gas Law (USA) **6784**
Oil and Gas Lease Equipment and Operating Costs (USA) **1900**
• Oil and Gas News (BHR ISSN 0217-6602) **6784**
Oil and Gas Pool Descriptions (CAN) **2760**
Oil & Gas Product News (CAN ISSN 1482-468X) **3144**
Oil and Gas Production in Denmark *see* Denmark's Oil and Gas Production **6766**
Oil and Gas Production Report (CAN ISSN 0702-8202) **6784**
• Oil and Gas Radar (AUS) **6784**
Oil and Gas Reporter (USA ISSN 0472-7630) **6784**
† Oil and Gas Resources of Australia (AUS ISSN 1038-118X) **8978**
The Oil & Gas Review *see* Exploration & Production. The Oil and Gas Review **6768**
• Oil & Gas Science & Technology (FRA ISSN 1294-4475) **6784**
Oil and Gas Statistics Report (CAN) **6800**
Oil and Gas Technologies *see* Neftegazovye Tekhnologii **6780**
Oil and Natural Gas Commission. Bulletin (IND ISSN 0537-0094) **6784**
Oil & Natural Gas Producing Industry in Your State (USA) **6800**
Oil and Tanker Market (NOR) **8656**
Oil & Tanker Trades Outlook (GBR ISSN 1363-9617) **8656**
Oil Asia (IND ISSN 0970-1214) **6784**
• The Oil Can (USA) **6784**

Title

DIRECTORY 2010 OMAN FREIGHT TRANSPORT REPORT 10703

• Oklahoma City University Law Review (USA ISSN 0364-9458) **4752**
• Oklahoma Civil Procedure Forms (USA) **4839**
Oklahoma. Commission on Consumer Credit. Annual Report (USA) **2640**
Oklahoma. Conservation Commission. Biennial Report (USA ISSN 0095-442X) **2623**
The Oklahoma Constitution (USA ISSN 0890-1007) **7458**
▼ Oklahoma Construction Law (USA ISSN 1944-0693) **4752**
Oklahoma Cooperative Extension Service. Circular (USA) **143**
Oklahoma Corporate Forms (USA) **4878**
Oklahoma Council on Economic Education Newsletter (USA) **1156**
Oklahoma Country (USA ISSN 1544-6476) **144**
Oklahoma Court Rules and Procedure *see* Court Rules Pamphlet(s). Oklahoma Court Rules and Procedure **4949**
Oklahoma Cowman (USA ISSN 0030-1698) **295**
• Oklahoma Crimes and Punishments, Vehicles and Related Statutes (USA) **4896**
Oklahoma Criminal Justice Research Consortium. Journal (USA ISSN 1096-8504) **2662**
▼ Oklahoma Curiosities (USA ISSN 1935-6463) **8745**
• Oklahoma Daily (USA ISSN 0030-171X) **2294**
Oklahoma Dental Association Journal *see* O D A Journal **5857**
Oklahoma. Department of Human Services. Annual Report (USA ISSN 0277-8289) **8060**
Oklahoma Department of Libraries Record *see* O D L Record **5037**
Oklahoma. Department of Mental Health and Substance Abuse Services. Annual Report (USA) **7388**
Oklahoma. Department of Transportation. Sufficiency Rating Report and Needs Study: Oklahoma State Transportation (USA) **8633**
Oklahoma Directory of Manufacturers and Processors (USA ISSN 1051-919X) **2022**
† Oklahoma Discovery Practice Manual (USA) **8978**
▼ Oklahoma Edge (USA ISSN 1937-7541) **3984**
Oklahoma Electric Co-op News (USA) **3326**
• Oklahoma Employment Law Letter (USA ISSN 1066-1123) **4752**
Oklahoma. Employment Security Commission. Research Division. Annual Report to the Governor (USA) **1701**
Oklahoma. Employment Security Commission. Research Division. County Employment and Wage Data (USA) **1257**
• Oklahoma Estate Planning, Will Drafting and Estate Administration Forms (USA) **4904**
Oklahoma Farm Bureau Journal *see* Oklahoma Country **144**
Oklahoma Game & Fish (USA ISSN 0746-6013) **8326**
Oklahoma Gardener (USA ISSN 1541-8413) **3746**
Oklahoma Genealogical Society Quarterly (USA ISSN 0474-0742) **3778**
Oklahoma Geological Survey. Bulletin (USA ISSN 0078-4389) **2760**
Oklahoma Geological Survey. Circular (USA ISSN 0078-4397) **2760**
Oklahoma Geological Survey. Educational Publication (USA ISSN 0160-8746) **2760**
Oklahoma Geological Survey. Guidebook (USA ISSN 0078-4400) **2760**
➤ Oklahoma Geological Survey. Special Publication Series (USA ISSN 0275-0929) **2760**
Oklahoma Geology Notes (USA ISSN 0030-1736) **2760**
Oklahoma. Grand River Dam Authority. Annual Report (USA ISSN 0078-4508) **3363**
Oklahoma Grocers Journal (USA ISSN 1042-8976) **3680**
Oklahoma Health Statistics (USA ISSN 0098-5651) **7548**
Oklahoma Insurance Report (USA) **4517**
• Oklahoma Journal of Law and Technology (USA) **4752**
• ➤ Oklahoma Law Review (USA ISSN 0030-1752) **4752**
Oklahoma Legionnaire (USA) **2268**
Oklahoma Librarian (USA ISSN 0030-1760) **5038**
• Oklahoma Living (USA ISSN 1064-8968) **3984**
Oklahoma Magazine (USA) **3984**
• Oklahoma Manufacturers Register (USA ISSN 1059-4523) **2022**
Oklahoma: Manufacturing *see* Harris Directory. Oklahoma Manufacturing **2002**
Oklahoma Mason (USA ISSN 0030-1779) **2268**
Oklahoma Medical Research Foundation. Findings (USA) **5689**
Oklahoma Motor Carrier (USA) **8674**
Oklahoma Museum of Natural History. Newsletter (USA) **7895**
Oklahoma Museum of Natural History. Scientific Publication (USA) **7895**
Oklahoma Music Magazine (USA ISSN 1543-0197) **6601**
Oklahoma Native Plant Record (USA ISSN 1536-7738) **806**
• Oklahoma Nurse (USA ISSN 0030-1787) **5976**
Oklahoma Observer (USA ISSN 0030-1795) **7161**
Oklahoma Odd Fellow (USA ISSN 0030-1809) **2268**
Oklahoma Ornithological Society. Bulletin (USA ISSN 0474-0750) **911**
Oklahoma P T A (Parent Teacher Association) (USA) **2893**
Oklahoma Pontotoc County Quarterly (USA ISSN 0091-1054) **4307**
Oklahoma Population Estimates (USA) **7313**
Oklahoma Professional Engineer (USA) **3213**
Oklahoma Project for Discourse and Theory (USA) **5345**
Oklahoma. Public Employees Retirement System. Annual Report (USA) **1870**
Oklahoma Publisher (USA ISSN 1526-811X) **7569**
Oklahoma Reader (USA ISSN 0030-1833) **3075**
Oklahoma Reading Association Newsletter *see* O R A Newsletter **2893**
• Oklahoma Real Estate Forms (USA) **7603**
Oklahoma Register (Oklahoma City) (USA ISSN 0030-1728) **4958**
Oklahoma Report (USA) **3144**
Oklahoma Retailer (USA ISSN 0030-1841) **1836**
▼ Oklahoma Revelator (USA) **5232**
Oklahoma School Board Journal (USA ISSN 0030-185X) **3029**
Oklahoma School Directory *see* M D R's School Directory. Oklahoma **2959**
Oklahoma Series in Classical Culture (USA) **2238**
Oklahoma State Agencies, Boards, Commissions, Courts, Institutions, Legislature and Officers (USA) **7161**
Oklahoma State Medical Association. Journal (USA ISSN 0030-1876) **5689**
Oklahoma State University. College of Business Administration. Working Papers (USA) **1156**
Oklahoma State University. Cooperative Extension Service. Forestry Extension Report (USA ISSN 1059-2547) **3699**
Oklahoma State University Current Reports *see* O S U Current Reports **143**
Oklahoma State University Extension Facts *see* O S U Extension Facts **143**
• Oklahoma Today (USA ISSN 0030-1892) **3984**
Oklahoma Turnpike Authority. Annual Report to the Governor (USA) **8633**
Oklahoma Turnpike Authority. Report to Bondholders (USA) **8633**
Oklahoma Water Resources Research Institute. Annual Report (USA ISSN 0092-2528) **8830**
Oklahoma Western Biographies (USA) **645**
Oklahoma Wills and Intestate Succession (USA) **4904**
Oklahomans for Indian Opportunity News *see* O I O News **3556**
Oko (TJK) **3961**
Oko Cyklopa (POL) **3930**
Okochi Memorial Foundation. Journal *see* Gocho **7858**
Okolis (HRV ISSN 1330-6154) **2623**
Okolna Sreda/Environment (BGR ISSN 1311-2368) **8393**
Okregowa Izba Lekarska w Koszalinie. Biuletyn (POL ISSN 1233-5037) **5689**
Okrety Wojenne (POL ISSN 1231-014X) **8656**
• Okruzni Sud u Beogradu. Bilten (SRB ISSN 0351-0247) **4958**
Oktobernota Financiele Ontwikkeling UWV-Fondsen (Uitvoering Werknemersverzekeringen) (NLD ISSN 1571-7682) **4517**
• Oktyabr' (RUS ISSN 0132-0637) **5232**
Okulistyka (POL ISSN 1505-2753) **6047**
Okumura Technical Research Report *see* Okumuragumi Gijutsu Kenkyu Nenpo **1028**
Okumuragumi Gijutsu Kenkyu Nenpo/Okumura Technical Research Report (JPN ISSN 0285-3469) **1028**
La Ola (USA) **3556**
Olaj, Szappan, Kozmetika/Journal of Oil, Soap, Cosmetics (HUN ISSN 0472-8602) **595**
Olam HaOmanut *see* World of Art **8999**
Old Abe's News (USA ISSN 0896-4955) **213**
† Old Age: a Register of Social Research (GBR ISSN 1367-1065) **8978**
Old Age Psychiatrist (GBR ISSN 1463-6662) **6171**
Old Age Security, Child Tax Benefit, Children's Special Allowances and Canada Pension Plan. Report (CAN ISSN 1200-5533) **8060**
Old Age, Survivors, Disability Insurance Beneficiaries by State and County *see* O A S D I Beneficiaries by State and County **4517**
The Old Age Vision *see* Laonian Bolan **4050**
Old Allis News (USA ISSN 0897-2540) **213**
• The Old and New Concepts of Physics (POL ISSN 1733-8026) **7029**
Old Autos (CAN ISSN 0841-775X) **8596**
Old Ben News (GBR) **1431**
Old Bike Australasia (AUS ISSN 1833-3249) **8265**
Old Bradfieldian (GBR) **2295**
Old Bulgarian Literature *see* Starobulgarska Literatura **5377**
Old Car Market Guide *see* Black Book. Official Old Car Market Guide **1975**
Old Car Trader (USA) **8596**
• Old Cars (USA ISSN 0048-1637) **8596**
Old Cars Especial (BRA ISSN 1806-7484) **8596**
Old Cars Price Guide (USA ISSN 0194-6404) **368**
Old Cars Weekly *see* Old Cars **8596**
Old Cornwall (GBR ISSN 1741-0932) **4251**
Old Crow Review (USA ISSN 1085-6323) **5428**
Old English Newsletter (USA ISSN 0030-1973) **5345**
Old English Newsletter. Subsidia (USA ISSN 0739-8549) **5345**
Old English Times (USA) **6812**
• The Old Farmer's Almanac (USA ISSN 0078-4516) **3121**
The Old Farmer's Almanac All-Seasons Garden Guide (USA) **3746**
The Old Farmer's Almanac Gardener's Companion *see* The Old Farmer's Almanac All-Seasons Garden Guide **3746**
The Old Farmer's Almanac Guide to Summer Recipes (USA) **4365**
The Old Fart (CAN ISSN 1192-6562) **5232**
Old Fishing Lures & Tackle (USA ISSN 1935-0856) **8326**
Old Fort Genealogical Society. Quarterly (USA) **3778**
Old Fort Log (USA ISSN 0098-4760) **3778**
Old Fort News (USA ISSN 0196-7045) **4307**
Old Garden Rose & Shrub Gazette (USA) **3746**
Old Glory Magazine (GBR ISSN 0956-5922) **8507**
Old Gold and Black (USA) **2295**
Old Herborn University Seminar Monograph (DEU ISSN 1431-6579) **5930**
▼ Old Home Renovation (USA ISSN 1934-7804) **1028**
• Old-House Interiors (USA ISSN 1079-3941) **4548**
Old-House Interiors Design Center Sourcebook (USA ISSN 1539-8269) **4561**
• Old-House Journal (USA ISSN 0094-0178) **1028**
Old House Journal *see* Old-House Journal **1028**
Old-House Journal Restoration Directory (USA ISSN 1077-2332) **1028**
Old-House Journal's New Old House (USA ISSN 1941-7721) **1028**
The Old Lady (GBR ISSN 0030-199X) **3869**
Old Man (CHE ISSN 0030-2007) **2387**
Old Mill News (USA ISSN 0276-3338) **4307**
Old Moore's Almanac (IRL ISSN 0791-7716) **3121**
Old News (USA ISSN 1047-3068) **4155**
Old Red Kimono (USA) **5345**
Old South Community Organization News *see* O S C O News **3457**
Old Sturbridge Visitor (USA ISSN 0485-6724) **4307**
• Old Testament Abstracts (USA ISSN 0364-8591) **7699**
• ➤ Old Testament Essays (ZAF ISSN 1010-9919) **7667**
Old-Time Herald (USA ISSN 1040-3582) **6601**
Old-Time New England (USA ISSN 0030-2031) **368**
Old Time Radio Digest (USA ISSN 1083-8376) **2361**
Old Time Western Film Club Newsletter (USA) **6509**
Old Timers' Bulletin *see* The A W A Journal **4326**
Old Toy Soldier (USA ISSN 1064-4164) **368**
Old Tractor (GBR ISSN 1740-9802) **213**
Old Trout (USA) **7161**
Old Westmoreland (USA) **3778**
Old York Road Historical Society Bulletin (USA ISSN 1072-5822) **4307**
Olde Mecklenburg Genealogical Society Quarterly (USA ISSN 0740-8951) **3778**
Oldenburger Beitraege zur Geschlechterforschung (DEU ISSN 1614-5577) **8902**
Oldenburger Forschungen. Neue Folge (DEU) **4251**
Oldenburger Jahrbuch (DEU ISSN 0340-4447) **4251**
Oldenburger Studien (DEU) **4251**
Oldenburgische Familienkunde (DEU ISSN 0030-2074) **3778**
Oldenburgische Volkszeitung (DEU) **3854**
Oldenburgische Wirtschaft (DEU ISSN 0936-3599) **1408**
The Older American (USA ISSN 0738-9639) **4052**
• Older Americans (Year) (USA ISSN 1939-0297) **4052**
• Older Americans Report (USA ISSN 0146-3640) **8060**
Older and Bolder (Auckland Edition) (NZL ISSN 1177-5602) **4052**
Older and Bolder (Christchurch Edition) (NZL ISSN 1174-6998) **4052**
Older and Bolder (Wellington Edition) (NZL ISSN 1177-5114) **4053**
Older Car Blue Book (USA) **8674**
† Older Car Price Guide (GBR ISSN 1361-3766) **8978**
Older Cars and Commercial Guide *see* Older Cars & Commercial Guide **8596**
Older Cars & Commercial Guide (AUS) **8596**
• The Older Population in the United States (USA) **7313**
Older Truck Blue Book (USA ISSN 1041-9756) **8674**
Older Vehicle Data Digest (Cars, Ldv's pre - 1977) (ZAF) **8596**
Older Women's League Observer *see* O W L Observer **4052**
Oldham Evening Chronicle (GBR) **3869**
The Oldie (GBR ISSN 0965-2507) **3869**
Oldie - Markt (DEU) **6601**
Oldies (CZE ISSN 1801-0776) **6296**
Olds Gazette (CAN) **3815**
Oldtimer Adressen Lexikon (DEU ISSN 0932-0075) **8596**
Oldtimer Anzeiger (DEU) **31**
Oldtimer Boerse (DEU) **8596**
† Oldtimer Catalogus (NLD ISSN 1871-4986) **8978**
Oldtimer Handel (DEU) **8596**
▼ Oldtimer Hockey (SWE ISSN 1654-8345) **8191**
Oldtimer Inserat (DEU) **31**
Oldtimer Katalog (DEU) **8596**
Oldtimer-Markt (DEU ISSN 0943-7320) **8597**
Oldtimer Motorrad Markt (DEU) **8265**
Oldtimer Praxis (DEU ISSN 0937-6291) **8597**
Oldtimer-Traktor (DEU ISSN 1862-1716) **213**
• Ole (ARG) **8191**
Ole Brumm og Dyrene i Hundremeterskogen (NOR ISSN 1500-841X) **2205**
Ole Brumm og Vennene Hans (NOR ISSN 1500-7316) **2205**
Ole Miss Alumni Review (USA) **2295**
Ole Miss Engineer (USA) **3213**
• Oleagineaux Corps Gras Lipides (Online) (FRA ISSN 1950-697X) **2127**
† • ➤ Oleagineux Corps Gras Lipides (Print) (FRA ISSN 1258-8210) **8978**
Oleander Games and Pastimes Series (GBR) **8191**
Oleander Travel Books Series (GBR) **8745**
Oleandry (POL) **4251**
Oleo *see* Semanal Oleo **3663**
• Oleo (ESP ISSN 1695-0089) **3659**
Oleo. Guia de la Industria y Comercio de Aceites y Grasas (ESP ISSN 1696-8301) **3659**
• Oleodinamica Pneumatica Lubrificazione (ITA ISSN 0391-8645) **3392**
Olhar de Profesor (BRA ISSN 1518-5648) **3075**
Olieberetning (DNK ISSN 0109-3916) **6785**
• ➤ Olifant (USA ISSN 0381-9132) **5428**
• ➤ Oligonucleotides (USA ISSN 1545-4576) **877**
Olimp (RUS ISSN 0201-4785) **8191**
Olimpiiskaya Panorama (RUS ISSN 0204-2177) **8191**
Olimpionik *see* Pionerskaya Pravda **2207**
Oliphant Washington Service. Energy Summary (USA ISSN 0733-0219) **3144**
Olivae (ESP ISSN 0255-996X) **244**
Olivar (ARG ISSN 1515-1115) **5345**
Olive (GBR) **4395**
Oliver Chronicle (CAN ISSN 1195-5996) **3815**
Olivia (DNK ISSN 1604-8504) **2206**
Olivia (POL ISSN 1429-6950) **8879**
Olivia (ROM ISSN 1454-721X) **8879**
El Olivo (ESP ISSN 0211-5514) **7667**
Olivo e Olio (ITA ISSN 1127-0713) **244**
† Oljyhuolto (FIN ISSN 1237-5608) **8978**
Ollantay Theater Magazine (USA ISSN 1065-805X) **8475**
Olli und Molli (DEU ISSN 0948-4949) **2206**
Olms-Forum *see* Olms Forum **6601**
Olms Forum (DEU ISSN 1612-4162) **6601**
O'Lochlainns Irish Family Journal (USA ISSN 1056-0378) **3778**
O'Lochlainns Personal Journal of Irish Families *see* O'Lochlainns Irish Family Journal **3778**
Olomeinu/Our World (USA ISSN 0030-2139) **7727**
Olomoucky Archivni Sbornik (CZE ISSN 1214-4711) **4251**
Oltner Tagblatt (CHE ISSN 1422-6820) **3958**
† • Oltre (ITA ISSN 1124-3708) **8978**
† Oltre ... (ITA) **8978**
Oluja (CAN) **3556**
Olum Istatistikleri *see* Turkey. Turkiye Istatistik Kurumu. Olum Istatistikleri; Il ve Ilce Merkezlerinde (Year) **7317**
Olympe (CHE) **8902**
▼ Olympia (DNK ISSN 1902-7885) **8326**
Olympia Aktuell (AUT) **8191**
Olympia Genealogical Society. Quarterly (USA) **3778**
Olympian's News (ITA ISSN 1126-0874) **8191**
Olympic *see* Wuhuan Mingxing **8216**
Olympic Collectors Newsletter *see* Bill Nelson Newsletter **4330**
Olympic Health News (BEL) **6232**
Olympic Message (CHE ISSN 1025-5737) **8191**
Olympic Panorama *see* Olimpiiskaya Panorama **8191**
Olympic Review (Year) (CHE ISSN 0377-192X) **8191**
Olympics News (BEL ISSN 0772-2095) **8191**
➤ Olympika (CAN ISSN 1188-5963) **8191**
➤ Olympische Forschungen (DEU ISSN 0474-1242) **409**
Olympisches Feuer (DEU ISSN 0471-5640) **8192**
Olympisches Panorama *see* Olimpiiskaya Panorama **8191**
Olympiska Spelen Magasinet *see* O S Magasinet **8191**
• OM (USA) **3556**
• Om Energi (DNK ISSN 1901-1989) **3326**
Om Jazz *see* O J **6600**
OM-online *see* OM **3556**
Om Sakhti (IND) **3886**
Om Vaerlden *see* OmVaerlden **1602**
▼ Oma Koti Kullan Kallis (FIN ISSN 1796-8992) **4561**
Omaha (New York) (USA) **5411**
Omaha - Council Bluffs Metropolitan Area Planning Agency Annual Report *see* M A P A Annual Report **7451**
Omaha - Council Bluffs Metropolitan Area Planning Agency Community Assistance Report *see* M A P A Community Assistance Report **7452**
Omaha - Council Bluffs Metropolitan Area Planning Agency. Population, Household and Housing Unit Estimates (USA) **7313**
Omaha - Council Bluffs Metropolitan Area Planning Agency Regional Directory of Public Officials *see* M A P A Regional Directory of Public Officials **7497**
Omaha Magazine (USA) **3984**
Omaha Weekly Reader (USA) **3984**
• Omaid Weekly (USA ISSN 1098-8777) **3556**
Omalovanky Moudre Sovy (CZE) **2206**
Omaly sy Anio/Hier et Aujourd'hui (MDG ISSN 0255-0385) **4177**
Oman *see* The P R S Group. Country Reports: Oman **1508**
Oman Commerce *see* Al-Ghurfa **1394**
• Oman Daily Observer (OMN) **3926**
▼ Oman Freight Transport Report (GBR ISSN 1752-7902) **8507**

Title

Oman Information Technology Report *see* Business Monitor International. Information Technology Country Reports **2491**
▼ Oman Infrastructure Report (GBR ISSN 1752-7856) **1156**
▼ • Oman Journal of Ophtalmology (IND ISSN 0974-620X) **6047**
Oman Today (OMN) **3926**
The Omaniyyah (OMN) **8879**
Omas Herzhafte Kueche (DEU) **4365**
L'Ombra (ITA ISSN 1126-0653) **7388**
• Ombudsman Manitoba. Annual Reports and Other Publications (CAN ISSN 1912-7723) **7458**
Ombudsman's Report on Inspection of the Australian Crime Commission's Surveillance Device Records *see* Commonwealth Ombudsman's Report on Inspection of the Australian Crime Commission's Surveillance Device Records **2647**
Omega (CAN) **2295**
• ➤ Omega (GBR ISSN 0305-0483) **1782**
Omega (Amityville) *see* Omega: Journal of Death and Dying **7388**
Omega (Milton Keynes) (GBR ISSN 0964-4237) **2996**
• ➤ Omega: Journal of Death and Dying (USA ISSN 0030-2228) **7388**
Omega New Age Directory (USA) **7739**
• The Omega Report: North Sea Supply Vessels (USA ISSN 1469-378X) **6785**
Omens (GBR ISSN 0308-4752) **5428**
Omero (ITA ISSN 1123-3311) **5345**
▼ Omertaa (BEL ISSN 1784-3308) **351**
➤ Ometeca (USA ISSN 1041-3650) **4467**
Omhoog (SUR) **7810**
Ominia (VEN ISSN 1315-8856) **2893**
Omkring et Kunstvaerk (DNK ISSN 0108-3511) **510**
Omnia (MEX ISSN 0186-4742) **2996**
Omnibus (London) (GBR ISSN 0261-507X) **2238**
Omnibus Magazine (GBR ISSN 0305-9243) **8507**
Omnibus-Revue (DEU ISSN 1436-9974) **8597**
Omnibusnachrichten (DEU ISSN 1432-3923) **8507**
Omnibusrevue Aktuell (DEU ISSN 1865-4657) **8597**
Omnibusspiegel (DEU ISSN 0724-7664) **8507**
Omnific (USA) **5428**
OmniFile Full Text Mega Edition *see* Wilson OmniFile Full Text Mega Edition **18**
Omnigraphics Health Reference Series (USA) **5689**
Omnigraphics' Security Reference Series (USA) **2679**
Omnigraphics' Teen Health Series (USA) **5689**
OMOlogie (NLD ISSN 0166-6223) **2893**
Omring Plus (NLD ISSN 1871-7896) **7534**
Omron Technics (JPN ISSN 0474-1315) **3327**
Omsk University. Communications *see* Omskii Universitet. Vestnik **7895**
Omskaya Pravda (RUS) **3939**
• Omskii Universitet. Vestnik/Omsk University. Communications (RUS) **7895**
Omsorg (NOR ISSN 0800-7489) **8060**
• Omusubi (Email) (AUS ISSN 1832-0341) **3556**
Omusubi (Print) *see* Omusubi (Email) **3556**
• Omvaardaren (SWE ISSN 0280-4123) **8060**
Omvaardnadsmagasinet (SWE ISSN 1652-0858) **5976**
• OmVaerlden (SWE ISSN 1400-4569) **1602**
On (SWE ISSN 1404-4595) **2370**
• On... (USA) **6601**
• On (Hopkinton) (USA) **2549**
• On-Air Job Tipsheet (USA) **6702**
On and Off Off Broadway (USA) **8475**
On Balance (USA) **1298**
† • On Board (ITA ISSN 1124-5514) **8978**
On Board Diagnostics Drive Cycle Guide: Domestic & Import Cars, Light Trucks, Vans & SUVs *see* O B D I I Drive Cycle Guide: Domestic & Import Cars, Light Trucks, Vans & SUVs **3213**
On Buying or Selling a Business (USA) **1964**
On Campus *see* Around the Ridges **2273**
On-Campus Hospitality (USA ISSN 1087-3163) **2295**
• On Campus with Women (USA ISSN 0734-0141) **2996**
On Collecting Photographs (USA) **6972**
On Course/Association Internationale de Navigation. Bulletin (BEL) **8656**
On Course (GBR ISSN 1363-1411) **8879**
On Court (CAN ISSN 0824-6629) **8241**
On Demand (USA ISSN 1076-0334) **2387**
On Demand (Malmoe) *see* Aktuell Grafisk Information **7318**
• On Design (USA ISSN 1092-7794) **4548**
On Digital (GBR) **2387**
On Directv *see* Access Directv **2374**
• On Diseno (ESP ISSN 1695-2308) **452**
On Dit (AUS ISSN 0030-2333) **2295**
• On-E Magazine (USA ISSN 1934-8274) **6972**
On Economic Problems *see* Jingji Wenti **1132**
• On Edge (DNK ISSN 1603-2551) **2549**
On Guard (USA ISSN 1064-007X) **6440**
On Ice (CAN) **8192**
On Indian Land (USA) **6636**
▼ • On Korea (USA ISSN 1937-9196) **1156**
On-Line (Durham) (USA ISSN 0731-8367) **2502**
On Line (Sunbury-on-Thames) (GBR ISSN 0263-2187) **2549**
▼ On-line Journal of Modern Biology (IND ISSN 0973-9394) **695**
• On Line Opinion (AUS ISSN 1442-8458) **7161**
On-line Undergrunt *see* Undergrunt **5243**
• On-math (USA ISSN 1534-6749) **5523**
On Message *see* The Business Communicator **1071**
On Mission (USA) **7667**
ON Nature (CAN ISSN 1711-9138) **2623**
On Off (ESP ISSN 1575-1686) **3110**
On Off Extra *see* On Off **3110**
On Off Guia *see* On Off **3110**
• On/Off News (DNK ISSN 1901-7782) **6785**
• On/Off Yearbook (DNK ISSN 1901-7774) **6785**
• On Office (GBR ISSN 1752-6264) **1156**
On One Wheel (USA ISSN 0893-4606) **8265**
▼ • On Patrol (USA ISSN 1947-4997) **6440**
On Point: The Journal of Army History (USA) **6440**
On Pointe (USA ISSN 1060-3972) **2687**
On Premise (USA ISSN 1051-4562) **609**
• On Scene (Groton) (USA ISSN 0093-2124) **8656**
On Scene (Lakewood) (USA ISSN 1556-956X) **7534**
▼ On se Bouge (FRA ISSN 1960-2995) **7895**
On Show (NZL ISSN 1177-4614) **6535**
• On-site (CAN ISSN 1910-118X) **1028**
on site review (CAN ISSN 1481-8280) **452**
On Spec (CAN ISSN 0843-476X) **5445**
➤ On-Stage Studies (USA ISSN 0749-1549) **8475**
† • On Station (NLD ISSN 1562-8019) **8978**
On Tap (Alexandria) (USA ISSN 1534-3030) **5079**
On Tap (Boston) (USA) **7161**
• On Tap (Morgantown) (USA ISSN 1061-9291) **8830**
On Target (GBR ISSN 0308-1230) **7161**
On Target (NLD) **2361**
• On the Access to Information Act and the Privacy Act. Annual Report (CAN ISSN 1910-3506) **7534**
• On the Administration and Enforcement of the Fish Habitat Protection and Pollution Prevention Provisions of the Fisheries Act. Annual Report to Parliament (CAN ISSN 1910-2356) **3604**
On the Administration of the Access to Information Act and the Privacy Act. Annual Reports *see* Loi sur l'Acces a l'Information et la Loi sur la Protection des Renseignements Personnels (Annee). Rapport Annuel **7530**
On the Administration of the Access to Information Act and the Privacy Act. Annual Reports (Print) *see* On the Access to Information Act and the Privacy Act. Annual Report **7534**
On the Ball (GBR ISSN 1365-4039) **8241**
On the Beam (USA ISSN 0740-218X) **5689**
➤ On the Boundary of Two Worlds (NLD ISSN 1570-7121) **7990**
On the Brain (USA ISSN 1077-0747) **6171**
On the Bus *see* Onthebus **5428**
• On the Case (GBR ISSN 1746-8930) **1701**
On The Cutting Edge *see* Diabetes Care and Education Newsletter **5887**
On the Edge (Madison) (USA) **2295**
On the Edge Magazine (GBR ISSN 1352-0571) **8326**
On the Eve *see* Nakanune **5338**
On the Fringe (USA ISSN 8756-6087) **3746**
On the Go (USA ISSN 1083-2203) **3984**
On the Green (USA) **2295**
On the Homefront (CAN) **8879**
• ➤ On the Horizon (GBR ISSN 1074-8121) **2996**
On the Implementation of the European Commission's External Assistance (Year). Annual Report (LUX ISSN 1683-3457) **1602**
• On the Learning Edge (USA) **1782**
On the Level (CAN) **1028**
On the Line (JPN) **2335**
On the Line (Laurel) (USA ISSN 0190-2571) **2662**
On the Line (New York) (USA) **1701**
On the Line (Pensacola) (USA) **4981**
• On The Line (Washington, D.C.) (USA ISSN 1526-2863) **4600**
On the Loose in Eastern Europe (USA) **8745**
On the Making of Europe (BEL) **6937**
On the March! (CAN) **7739**
On the Mark (USA ISSN 1087-6391) **1782**
• On the Mhove (USA) **5458**
On the Move (AUS) **6225**
On the Move (CAN ISSN 1180-7563) **3075**
On the Move (GBR) **8507**
• On the Page Magazine (USA ISSN 1556-701X) **5345**
On the Ramage Trail (USA ISSN 1066-5382) **3778**
On the Risk (USA ISSN 0885-4416) **4517**
On the Road (Cape Town) (ZAF ISSN 0030-2368) **1836**
• On the Safety Performance of the Canadian Nuclear Power Industry. Annual C N S C Staff Report for (Year) (Canadian Nuclear Safety Commission) (CAN ISSN 1912-6840) **3173**
On the Spot (CAN ISSN 1492-6849) **2387**
On the State of the Public Health *see* Great Britain. Department of Health. On the State of the Public Health **7519**
• On the Subject (USA) **4752**
On the Town (USA) **3984**
On the Trail (USA) **8326**
On the Trails with S A M (Snowmobile Association of Massachusetts) (USA) **8326**
On the Use of Electronic Surveillance, as Required under Subsection 1951 of the Criminal Code. Annual Report *see* Use of Electronic Surveillance. Annual Report **2681**
On the Water (USA ISSN 1090-963X) **8326**
On the Waterfront (NLD ISSN 1574-2156) **8124**
On the Way with American Baptist Women *see* Vital Woman Magazine **7779**
On the Wild Side (USA) **3458**
† On the Wire (AUS) **8978**
On Top (DEU) **1373**
On Tour (DEU) **8597**
On Tour (GBR) **8475**
On Track (IRL) **8621**
• On Track (Charlotte) (USA ISSN 0279-2737) **8597**
On Track (Washington) (USA) **8621**
On Track Online *see* On Track (Charlotte) **8597**
On Trade Scotland (GBR ISSN 1749-3838) **609**
† On Two Wheels (GBR ISSN 0309-5584) **8978**
On va de l'Avant *see* Moving Ahead **8055**
On Video (CAN ISSN 1194-3130) **2402**
• On Wall Street (USA ISSN 1092-1370) **1643**
On Watch (AUS ISSN 0030-2392) **3392**
On Watch (USA ISSN 1047-1731) **6440**
On Wax (USA ISSN 1933-2351) **6601**
On Wings (USA) **8879**
On Wisconsin Magazine (USA) **2295**
On Your Bike (GBR) **8265**
Onafhankelijk Museumtijdschrift *see* Museumtijdschrift **6533**
Onagawa Genshiryoku Hatsudenjo Kankyo Hoshano Oyobi Onhaisui Chosa Kekka/Monitoring Report of Environmental Radioactivity and Warm Waste Water around Onagawa Nuclear Power Station (JPN ISSN 0910-7193) **3509**
Onati International Series in Law and Society (GBR) **4752**
Onboard Hospitality (GBR) **4395**
• OnCampus (CAN) **2295**
Once Upon A Time (USA ISSN 1071-2526) **7569**
Onchikai Kaiho/News of Onchikai (JPN ISSN 1341-4100) **6001**
• ➤ Oncogene (GBR ISSN 0950-9232) **6029**
Oncogenes and Growth Factors Abstracts *see* C S A Oncogenes and Growth Factors Abstracts **5742**
• ➤ Oncologia (ECU ISSN 1390-0110) **6030**
Oncologica (NLD ISSN 0929-8703) **6030**
• ➤ Oncologie (FRA ISSN 1292-3818) **6030**
Oncologie Magazine (NLD ISSN 1874-1827) **6030**
Oncologie Vademecum (NLD ISSN 1574-2377) **6030**
Oncologisch (NLD ISSN 1874-7140) **6030**
Oncologische Heelkunde *see* Surgical Oncology **6035**
• ➤ The Oncologist (USA ISSN 1083-7159) **6030**
• ➤ Oncology (CHE ISSN 0030-2414) **6030**
• ➤ Oncology (USA ISSN 0890-9091) **6030**
• Oncology & Biotechnology News (USA) **6030**
• Oncology & Hematology Coding Alert (USA ISSN 1941-3262) **4517**
Oncology and Hematology Coding Alert *see* Oncology & Hematology Coding Alert **4517**
• Oncology Business Week (USA ISSN 1552-5635) **6030**
➤ Oncology Exchange (CAN ISSN 1705-2394) **6030**
Oncology Forum (HKG ISSN 1027-779X) **6030**
• Oncology Issues (USA ISSN 1046-3356) **6030**
• Oncology Net Guide (USA) **6030**
• Oncology Net Guide eNewsletter (USA) **6030**
▼ Oncology News International (NLD ISSN 1875-3795) **6030**
• Oncology News International (USA ISSN 1065-2957) **6030**
(Year) Oncology Nursing Drug Handbook (USA ISSN 1536-0024) **5976**
• ➤ Oncology Nursing Forum (USA ISSN 0190-535X) **5976**
▼ Oncology Nursing News (USA ISSN 1936-4385) **5976**
Oncology Nursing Society Connect *see* O N S Connect **6029**
Oncology Nursing Society Foundation News *see* O N S Foundation News **5976**
Oncology Nutrition Connection (USA ISSN 1545-9896) **6030**
▼ • The Oncology Pharmacist (USA ISSN 1944-9607) **6865**
The Oncology Report (USA ISSN 1548-5323) **6030**
▼ Oncology Reporter (Macclesfield) (GBR ISSN 1753-8769) **6030**
• ➤ Oncology Reports (GRC ISSN 1021-335X) **6030**
• ➤ Oncology Research (USA ISSN 0965-0407) **6031**
▼ • Oncology Reviews (ITA ISSN 1970-5557) **6031**
Oncology Special Edition (USA) **6031**
• Oncology Times (USA ISSN 0276-2234) **6031**
Oncology Times (U.K. Edition) (GBR ISSN 1742-8009) **6031**
▼ • ➤ OncoMagazine (FRA ISSN 1950-2184) **6031**
▼ • ➤ OncoTargets and Therapy (GBR ISSN 1178-6930) **6031**
OnCue (USA ISSN 1041-6234) **3075**
† Onda Quadra (ITA ISSN 0390-3087) **8978**
Onda T V Magazine *see* Onda Tivu **2387**
Onda Tivu (ITA ISSN 0393-814X) **2387**
• Ondare (ESP ISSN 1137-4403) **510**
Ondas (PER ISSN 0472-948X) **5232**
• Ondasalud.com (ESP) **5689**
Ondaverde (ITA ISSN 1120-6276) **8633**
• Onder Stoom (NLD ISSN 1382-2349) **3213**
Onderbouw *see* Nieuwsbrief Onderbouw **8977**
Onderbouw Magazine (NLD ISSN 1871-9449) **2893**
Ondernemen! (NLD ISSN 1383-3391) **1900**
Ondernemen in de Detailhandel *see* Ondernemen in de Sectoren **1782**
Ondernemen in de Diensten *see* Ondernemen in de Sectoren **1782**
Ondernemen in de Financiele Dienstverlening (NLD ISSN 1389-5079) **1782**
Ondernemen in de Groothandel *see* Ondernemen in de Sectoren **1782**
Ondernemen in de Industrie *see* Ondernemen in de Sectoren **1782**
Ondernemen in de Sectoren (NLD ISSN 1872-1168) **1782**
Ondernemen in het Ambacht *see* Ondernemen in de Sectoren **1782**
Ondernemen in Innovatie (NLD ISSN 1871-9716) **244**
Ondernemend Limburg (NLD) **1431**
De Ondernemer (BEL ISSN 1372-357X) **1156**
De Ondernemer (NLD ISSN 1574-8634) **1782**
▼ De Ondernemer (Ed. Achterhoek) (NLD ISSN 1875-2969) **1782**
De Ondernemer (Ed. Groot Rotterdam) (NLD ISSN 1874-5091) **1424**
De Ondernemer (Ed. Midden-Nederland) (NLD ISSN 1574-6283) **1782**
De Ondernemer (West-Brabant Edition) (NLD ISSN 1871-6768) **1836**
De Ondernemer (Zeeland Edition) (NLD ISSN 1871-6776) **1836**
Ondernemers Tips & Signalen (NLD ISSN 1574-7743) **1782**
Het Ondernemersbelang Drenthe (NLD ISSN 1871-2568) **1782**
Het Ondernemersbelang Fryslan (NLD ISSN 1871-2886) **1782**
Het Ondernemersbelang Groningen (NLD ISSN 1871-2614) **1782**
Het Ondernemersbelang Het Groene Hart (NLD) **1782**
Het Ondernemersbelang Noord-Holland Noord (NLD ISSN 1872-5937) **1782**
Het Ondernemersbelang Noordwest Veluwe en Eemland (NLD ISSN 1873-7366) **1782**
Het Ondernemersbelang Rivierenland (NLD ISSN 1872-6038) **1782**
Het Ondernemersbelang Salland (NLD ISSN 1874-7108) **1782**
Het Ondernemersbelang van Amsterdam (NLD ISSN 1873-7439) **1783**
Het Ondernemersbelang van De Graafschap-Liemers (NLD ISSN 1873-7269) **1783**
Het Ondernemersbelang van De Kempen (NLD ISSN 1873-6718) **1783**
Het Ondernemersbelang van Drechtsteden (NLD ISSN 1873-7099) **1783**
Het Ondernemersbelang van Haaglanden (NLD ISSN 1873-7102) **1783**
Het Ondernemersbelang van Haarlemmermeerlanden (NLD ISSN 1873-6661) **1783**
Het Ondernemersbelang van IJmond (NLD ISSN 1873-7501) **1783**
Het Ondernemersbelang van Leiden (NLD ISSN 1873-7420) **1783**
▼ Het Ondernemersbelang van Limburg Zuid (NLD ISSN 1875-3841) **1783**
Het Ondernemersbelang van Nijmegen e.o. (NLD ISSN 1875-4252) **1783**
Het Ondernemersbelang van Noord-Brabant (NLD ISSN 1872-6046) **1783**
Het Ondernemersbelang van Peelland (NLD ISSN 1875-3825) **1783**
Het Ondernemersbelang van Revuss (NLD ISSN 1873-6688) **1783**
Het Ondernemersbelang van Rijn en Gouwe *see* Het Ondernemersbelang Het Groene Hart **1782**
Het Ondernemersbelang van Rotterdam (NLD ISSN 1875-4260) **1783**
Het Ondernemersbelang van 't Gooi (NLD ISSN 1873-7242) **1783**
Het Ondernemersbelang van Twente (NLD ISSN 1873-667X) **1783**
Het Ondernemersbelang van Utrecht (NLD ISSN 1873-7498) **1783**
Het Ondernemersbelang van Waalboss (NLD ISSN 1873-7471) **1783**
Het Ondernemersbelang van West-Friesland (NLD ISSN 1875-3833) **1783**
Het Ondernemersbelang van Zeeland (NLD ISSN 1873-7110) **1783**
Het Ondernemersbelang van Zwolle e.o (NLD ISSN 1874-5466) **1783**
Het Ondernemersbelang Wageningen, Ede, Rhenen en Veenendaal (NLD ISSN 1872-5570) **1783**
Het Ondernemersbelang Westerkwartier (NLD ISSN 1873-7412) **1783**
Ondernemersorganisatie Schoonmaak- en Bedrijfsdiensten Today *see* O S B Today **6682**
Ondernemerspanel M K B-Nederland - T N S N I P O (NLD ISSN 1872-9258) **1720**
OndernemersZaken Signaal *see* Ondernemers Tips & Signalen **1782**
De Onderneming *see* L' Entreprise **4118**
Onderneming en Financiering (NLD ISSN 1570-1247) **4752**
† Ondernemingsanalyses. Trends bij Banken (NLD ISSN 1381-4427) **8979**
† Ondernemingsanalyses. Trends bij Verzekeringsmaatschappijen (NLD ISSN 1381-4435) **8979**
† Ondernemingsanalyses. Trends in de Chemie (NLD ISSN 1381-4478) **8979**
† Ondernemingsanalyses. Trends in de Metaal- en Elektro-industrie (NLD ISSN 1381-4443) **8979**
† Ondernemingsanalyses. Trends in de Voedings- en Genotmiddelenindustrie (NLD ISSN 1381-446X) **8979**
† Ondernemingsanalyses. Trends in Transport (NLD ISSN 1381-4486) **8979**

DIRECTORY 2010 ONTARIO CRAFT 10705

OndernemingsRaad (NLD ISSN 1387-4276) 1156
Ondernemingsraad in de Overheid see O R in de Overheid 8978
Ondernemingsraad Informatie see O R Informatie 1701
Ondernemingsraad Praktijk see O R-Praktijk. Basiskennis 1701
Ondernemingsraad Praktijk. Basiskennis see O R-Praktijk. Basiskennis 1701
OndernemingsRaad Rendement see OR Rendement 6702
● Ondernemingsrecht (NLD ISSN 1389-1456) 4752
● ➤ Onderstepoort Journal of Veterinary Research (ZAF ISSN 0030-2465) 8804
Onderwatersport (NLD ISSN 0048-1696) 8326
● Onderwijs en Gezondheidszorg (NLD ISSN 0920-8100) 5690
Het Onderwijs in West-Friesland. Schooljaar (NLD ISSN 1874-8589) 2893
Het Onderwijsblad (NLD ISSN 1386-3827) 2893
Onderwijsdeelname 1990-2020 (NLD ISSN 1874-639X) 3029
De Onderwijskalender (NLD ISSN 1874-5571) 3029
Onderwijsprofiel van Nederland (NLD ISSN 1872-0544) 2893
Het Onderwijssysteem in Nederland (NLD ISSN 1574-5864) 2893
Onderzoek en Beleid (NLD ISSN 0923-6414) 4896
Onderzoek en Kennisverspreiding (NLD ISSN 1872-3373) 3280
Onderzoek en Netwerkinformatie see Koninklijke Bibliotheek. Hoofdafdeling Research en Development. Jaaroverzicht 5023
Onderzoek van Onderwijs (NLD ISSN 0920-0665) 2996
Onderzoeksinstituut Technische Bestuurskunde Bouwstenen see O T Bouwstenen 1027
Onderzoeksinstituut Technische Bestuurskunde Werkdocument see O T B Werkdocument 7458
Onderzoeksinstituut Technische Bestuurskunde Working Paper see O T B Working Paper 7894
OnDigital see On Digital 2387
OnDirectv see Access Directv 2374
➤ Ondokuz Mayis Universitesi Tip Dergisi/University of Ondokuz Mayis Journal of Medicine (TUR ISSN 1300-2996) 5690
One + see One+ 6282
● One+ (USA ISSN 1943-1864) 6282
One (New York) (USA ISSN 1552-2016) 7810
One (San Diego) (USA) 8326
one. a magazine (USA) 31
One A: the Picks of the Week! see 1A: the Picks of the Week! 3802
One Black World (NGA) 3556
● One Country (USA ISSN 1018-9300) 3458
One+ E M E A see One+ Europe, Middle East, and Africa 6282
● One Earth (Hong Kong) (HKG) 3458
▼ ● One+ Europe, Middle East, and Africa (USA ISSN 1947-4733) 6282
One Family Matters (IRL ISSN 1649-4857) 8124
▼ ● One Green Thing (USA ISSN 1949-4211) 3458
One Hundred Arrows see 100 Arrows 4351
One Hundred Best Books see 100 Best Books 7577
One Hundred Best U.S. Wedding Destinations see 100 Best U.S. Wedding Destinations 8777
● One Hundred Books (and Videos Too) in Pre- and Perinatal Psychology and Health (USA) 7389
One Hundred Crosswords see 100 Crosswords 4351
One Hundred Decorating Ideas Under One Hundred Dollars see 100 Decorating Ideas Under $100 4553
One Hundred Eight see 108 8252
One Hundred Mile House Free Press see 100 Mile House Free Press 3821
The One Hundred Percent Unofficial Windows X P Handbook see The 100% Unofficial Windows X P Handbook 2600
$100,000 Quilting Challenge (USA ISSN 1557-2676) 6641
One Hundred Winners for (Year) see 100 Winners for (Year) 8300
One Hundred Wordsearch see 100 Wordsearch 4351
One I G L A Bulletin (International Gay & Lesbian Archives) (USA) 4377
One in Christ (GBR ISSN 0030-252X) 7810
One in Seven (GBR ISSN 1460-0811) 4075
One-in-Ten (USA ISSN 0258-610X) 4068
One Institute - I G L A Bulletin (USA) 5038
One Less (USA ISSN 1555-4627) 5346
One Life (USA) 3556
OnE Magazine see On-E Magazine 6972
One Magazine see 1 MagDenver 5087
The One Magazine see TheOne Magazine 5084
One Magazine (Antioch) (USA ISSN 1554-3323) 7769
One MagDenver see 1 MagDenver 5087
One Meadway (USA ISSN 1055-5609) 5232
One More Kiss (JPN) 5411
One off General Papers see Meat and Wool Boards' Economic Service. One Off General Papers 203
● ➤ One on One (Albany) (USA ISSN 0733-639X) 4753
One - One Journal see 1/1 6630
One People Newsletter (CAN ISSN 1486-2174) 7213
● The One-Person Library (USA ISSN 0748-8831) 5038
One plus see One+ 6282
One plus Europe, Middle East, and Africa see One+ Europe, Middle East, and Africa 6282
One Purpose Magazine see Empowered 7735
One Seventy News see The 170 News 2271
One Show (USA ISSN 0273-2033) 31
One Small Seed (ZAF ISSN 1816-8965) 510
One Thousand Fourteen G R E Practice Questions see 1,014 G R E Practice Questions 3011
One Thousand Leaders of Scientific Influence see 1000 World Leaders of Scientific Influence 648
One Thousand Six Hundred and Eleven see 1611 5200
One Thousand Ten Magazine see 1010 Magazine 5088
One Thousand Twelve GMAT Practice Questions see 1,012 G M A T Practice Questions 3011
One Thousand Two Hundred Ninety Six A C T Practice Questions see 1,296 A C T Practice Questions 3011
One to One (DEU) 1836
● One-to-One (Colorado Springs) (USA) 7667
● One to One (Fresno) (USA ISSN 0739-5442) 2361
● One to One (London, 1985) (GBR ISSN 0268-8786) 8154
One to One (Stamford) (USA ISSN 1540-5249) 1836
One Trenchless Technology Research Supplement see Tunnelling and Underground Space Technology 3224
One Trick Pony (USA ISSN 1524-1394) 5428
● One Up (GBR ISSN 1360-3051) 7667
One Voice see ONEvoice (Anderson) 7739
One Voice (Birmingham) (USA) 7810
One Voice (Des Moines) (USA) 2893
One Way (USA ISSN 1542-3018) 6601
One World (JPN) 3901
One World Archaeology (USA) 409
One2One Living (USA ISSN 1541-3136) 7943
● OnEarth (USA ISSN 1537-4246) 3458
Onesti (ROM) 5232
OneStop (GBR ISSN 1363-7576) 7325
● Onestopenglish (GBR) 3075
ONEvoice (Anderson) (USA ISSN 1549-5388) 7739
● OneWorld Magazine (USA) 3458
● Onfilm (NZL ISSN 0112-2789) 6509
Ongaku Bunken Mokuroku (JPN) 6632
Ongaku Kenkyu see Music Research 6591
Ongaku no Tomo/Friends of Music (JPN ISSN 0289-3606) 6601
Ongaku Onkyo Kenkyukai Shiryo/Acoustical Society of Japan. Technical Committees. Transactions (JPN ISSN 0912-7283) 7089
● ➤ Ongakugaku/Musicology (JPN ISSN 0030-2597) 6601
➤ Ongangan (PHL) 5346
Ongelooflijk! see Leven.nu 7659
● ➤ Online Journal of Analytic Combinatorics (USA ISSN 1931-3365) 5523
The Onion (USA ISSN 1534-6978) 5232
Onion Head see Onionhead 5232
Onion River Review (USA) 5232
Onion World (USA ISSN 0892-578X) 244
Onionhead (USA ISSN 1051-3612) 5232
Oniota (USA) 4307
● ➤ Der Onkologe (DEU ISSN 0947-8965) 6031
➤ Onkologia (SVK ISSN 1336-8176) 6031
Onkologia Polska (POL ISSN 1505-6732) 6031
● ➤ Onkologia w Praktyce Klinicznej (POL ISSN 1734-3542) 6031
● ➤ Onkologie (CHE ISSN 0378-584X) 6031
▼ ● ➤ Onkologie (CZE ISSN 1802-4475) 6031
➤ Onkologie Heute (AUT ISSN 1436-1280) 6031
Onkologie in der Praxis (AUT) 6031
Onkologie-Service Aktuell (DEU ISSN 0949-3441) 6031
● Onkologija (SVN ISSN 1408-1741) 6031
➤ Onkologische Seminare Lokoregionaler Therapie (DEU) 6031
➤ Onkologische Welt (DEU ISSN 1869-0874) 5948
● Onkologiya (UKR ISSN 1562-1774) 6031
▼ ● ➤ Onkopipeline (DEU ISSN 1866-5861) 6031
● Onkruid (NLD ISSN 0165-5027) 6646
● Online (USA ISSN 0146-5422) 2565
● ➤ Online Academic Journal (USA ISSN 1559-9388) 4467
Online Audiovisual Catalogers, Inc. Newsletter see O L A C Newsletter 5037
Online Banking Report (USA ISSN 1095-2829) 1373
● ➤ Online Brazilian Journal of Nursing (BRA ISSN 1676-4285) 5976
● Online Buffalo (USA) 8745
● Online Business Analyst (IRL) 2565
Online Business Sourcebook (DEU ISSN 1614-1148) 2022
● Online-C T O (USA ISSN 1930-0417) 2335
● Online Chronicle of Distance Education and Communication (USA) 3075
● Online Cl@ssroom (USA ISSN 1546-2625) 2950
Online Computer Library Center Abstracts Electronic Newsletter see O C L C Abstracts Electronic Newsletter 5037
Online Computer Library Center Annual Report see O C L C Annual Report 5037
Online Computer Library Center Participating Institutions. Arranged by Institution Name see O C L C Participating Institutions. Arranged by Institution Name 5037
Online Computer Library Center Reference & Resource Sharing News see O C L C Reference & Resource Sharing News 5037
Online Computer Library Center Reports see O C L C Reports 5037
Online Computer Library Center Selected Titles for University and Research Libraries see O C L C Selected Titles for University and Research Libraries 5037
Online Computer Library Center Systems & Services see O C L C Systems & Services 5037
Online Connection see N A T P E Monthly 2386
● Online Courses Newsletter (URY) 2950
● Online Currents (AUS ISSN 0816-956X) 2531
Online Degrees Magazine (USA) 2997
Online Files: Comparative Cost Analysis (GBR ISSN 0967-6090) 5063
Online Gamer (FRA ISSN 1628-8556) 2479
● Online Golf Solutions Newsletter (USA) 8241
● Online Help Journal (USA) 2509
● Online Hotline News Service - Archive Edition (USA ISSN 1040-6646) 2565
● Online Information. Conference Proceedings and Event Guide (GBR ISSN 1465-4202) 6282
● ➤ Online Information Review (GBR ISSN 1468-4527) 5038
● Online Insider (USA) 2565
Online International Command Chart (USA ISSN 0882-8040) 2433
● The Online Inventor (USA) 1836
● Online Investor (USA ISSN 1070-1117) 1643
Online J Vet Res see Online Journal of Veterinary Research 8804
● Online Journal for Global Engineering Education (USA ISSN 1933-1703) 3213
● ➤ The Online Journal of Bass Research (USA ISSN 1552-9657) 6601
● ➤ Online Journal of Bioinformatics (AUS ISSN 1443-2250) 826
● Online Journal of Biological Sciences (USA ISSN 1608-4217) 695
● Online Journal of Clinical Innovations (USA ISSN 1521-219X) 5976
● The Online Journal of Dentistry and Oral Medicine (BRA) 5858
● Online Journal of Distance Learning Administration (USA ISSN 1556-3847) 3029
▼ ● Online Journal of Earth Sciences (PAK ISSN 1991-7708) 2714
Online Journal of Health and Allied Sciences see O J H A S 5688
● Online Journal of Health Ethics (USA ISSN 1551-4218) 5690
● ➤ Online Journal of Immunology (AUS ISSN 1443-265X) 5764
● Online Journal of International Case Analysis (USA ISSN 1548-5137) 1156
● ➤ Online Journal of Issues in Nursing (USA ISSN 1091-3734) 5976
● ➤ Online Journal of Justice Studies (USA) 8124
● Online Journal of Knowledge Synthesis for Nursing (USA ISSN 1072-7639) 5976
● ➤ Online Journal of Nursing Informatics (USA ISSN 1089-9758) 5977
● The Online Journal of Peace and Conflict Resolution (USA ISSN 1522-211X) 7256
● ➤ Online Journal of Pharmacokinetics (AUS ISSN 1443-2285) 6865
● ➤ Online Journal of Physiology (AUS ISSN 1443-2374) 5690
▼ ● ➤ Online Journal of Public Health Informatics (USA ISSN 1947-2579) 5823
● ➤ Online Journal of Rural Nursing and Health Care (USA ISSN 1539-3399) 5977
● ➤ Online Journal of Rural Research and Policy (USA ISSN 1936-0487) 8124
● Online Journal of Space Communication (USA ISSN 1542-0639) 2335
● ➤ Online Journal of Veterinary Research (AUS ISSN 1328-925X) 8804
● Online Journalism Review (USA ISSN 1522-6883) 4581
● Online Libraries and Microcomputers (USA) 5063
● Online Logistics Bibliography (USA) 1257
▼ Online Marketing Monthly (USA) 1836
● Online Marketplace (USA) 2565
● Online Modern History Review (CAN) 4307
● Online Newsletter (USA) 2565
● Online Noetic Network (USA) 6647
Online Onderwijs see O N - W I J S 8978
● Online PC (CHE) 2578
● Online PC Zeitung (CHE) 2578
➤ Online Planning Journal (GBR ISSN 1471-3128) 4421
● Online Product News (USA) 2565
● Online Publishers Digest (USA) 7569
● Online Publishing (USA ISSN 1559-3134) 7569
● ➤ Online Publishing in Medicine (AUT ISSN 1609-2775) 7580
● ➤ Online Refereed Articles (AUS ISSN 1447-5111) 2997
● ➤ Online Trombone Journal (USA) 6601
Online Werbeplanung (DEU ISSN 1863-8147) 1836
● Online World Monitor Newsletter (NOR ISSN 0805-6315) 2565
Onlinegaming (ITA ISSN 1724-5311) 2479
Onlinewerbeplanung.de see Online Werbeplanung 1836
Onlooker (IND ISSN 0030-2619) 3886
Only 18 see 18up DVD 6302
Only You (NLD ISSN 1573-6326) 2259
▼ OnlyBike Magazine (FRA ISSN 1961-3830) 8265
OnMovies (USA) 6509
Onoda Cement Company. Journal of Research see Chichibu Onoda Kenkyu Hokoku 991
Onoffice Info see On Office 1156
Onofhaengege Gewerkschaftsbond Leetzebuerg/Aktuell see O G B - L'Aktuell 4600
● ➤ Onoma (BEL ISSN 0078-463X) 5157
● ➤ Onomasiology Online (DEU ISSN 1616-9484) 5158
➤ Onomastica (POL ISSN 0078-4648) 5158
➤ Onomastica Canadiana (CAN ISSN 0078-4656) 5158
Onomastica Slavogermanica (POL ISSN 0474-1471) 5158
Onomata/Revue Onomastique (GRC) 4023
● ➤ Onomazein (CHL ISSN 0717-1285) 5158
OnOn see Onomasiology Online 5158
Onpa no Bussei to Kagaku Toronkai Koen Ronbunshu see Chemical Society of Japan. Symposium on Physical and Chemical Aspects of Ultrasound. Proceedings 2055
● OnPolitics (USA) 7161
Ons Amsterdam (NLD ISSN 0166-1809) 4251
Ons Burgerschap see HandSchrift 7140
Ons Eie (ZAF ISSN 0259-9341) 144
● Ons Erfdeel (BEL ISSN 0030-2651) 3801
Ons Erfgoed see Ons Genealogisch Erfgoed 3778
● ➤ Ons Geestelijk Erf (BEL ISSN 0774-2827) 7667
Ons Genealogisch Erfgoed (NLD) 3778
OnSat (USA ISSN 0747-4059) 2387
OnScreen see RealTime 8477
Onsei Gengo Igaku/Japan Journal of Logopedics and Phoniatrics (JPN ISSN 0030-2813) 6083
Onsei Kagaku Kenkyu see Studia Phonologica 5180
● ➤ Onsei Kenkyu/Phonetic Society of Japan. Journal (JPN ISSN 1342-8675) 5158
Onsen Kagaku/Balneological Society of Japan. Journal (JPN ISSN 0030-2821) 2760
Onsen Kogakkaishi/Society of Engineers for Mineral Springs. Journal (JPN ISSN 0369-7665) 2760
▼ ● OnSite (USA ISSN 1946-8857) 1373
Onsite Fitness (USA ISSN 1932-8788) 6994
Onsite Installer (USA) 3509
● OnSite Ireland (IRL) 452
OnSite Restaurants see Nation's Restaurant News 4394
● Onsite Water Treatment (USA ISSN 1934-8304) 3509
Onslow Historian (NZL ISSN 0110-4896) 4193
Our Ontario (CAN) 1701
● Ontario Accident Benefit Case Summaries (CAN ISSN 1910-1600) 4517
Ontario Advisory Council on Senior Citizens. Annual Report (CAN ISSN 0704-2663) 7458
Ontario Advisory Council on Women's Issues. Annual Report (CAN ISSN 0830-9442) 8879
Ontario Agri-food Exporter see Exporter (Guelph) 109
Ontario All Select see Ontario Business Directory 2022
The Ontario Alternative Budget (CAN ISSN 1910-7765) 1938
Ontario Annotated Family Law Service (CAN) 4913
Ontario Annual Practice (CAN ISSN 0318-3556) 4753
● Ontario Appeal Cases (CAN ISSN 0827-3308) 4753
Ontario Archaeological Society. Arch Notes (CAN ISSN 0048-1742) 409
➤ Ontario Archaeology (CAN ISSN 0078-4672) 409
Ontario Arts Council. Annual Report/Conseil des Arts de l'Ontario. Rapport Annuel (CAN ISSN 0701-5429) 510
Ontario Association for Geographical & Environmental Education. Monograph (CAN) 4023
Ontario Association of Children's Aid Societies. Journal (CAN ISSN 0030-283X) 8060
Ontario Association of Landscape Architects. Membership Resource Guide see Ontario Association of Landscape Architects. Resource Guide 452
Ontario Association of Landscape Architects. Resource Guide (CAN ISSN 1912-0214) 452
Ontario Association of Social Workers. Newsmagazine (CAN ISSN 1203-3421) 8060
Ontario Badminton Today (CAN) 8192
Ontario Beef (CAN) 295
Ontario Beef Farmer Magazine (CAN ISSN 1195-5457) 295
Ontario Birchbark (CAN ISSN 1702-9295) 3556
➤ Ontario Birds (CAN ISSN 0822-3890) 911
Ontario Board of Parole. Annual Report (CAN ISSN 0847-1746) 7500
Ontario Budget. Budget Papers (CAN ISSN 1483-2623) 7458
● Ontario Business Directory (CAN ISSN 1717-1415) 2022
● Ontario Business Directory (USA ISSN 1203-5246) 2022
Ontario Casino Corporation. Annual Report see Ontario Lottery and Gaming Corporation. Annual Report 7458
Ontario Civil Practice (CAN ISSN 1184-7433) 4839
Ontario Co-operative Education Association News see O C E A News 2893
Ontario College of Family Physicians. Chapter (CAN ISSN 0843-9575) 5690
Ontario. Commission on Conflict of Interest. Annual Report see Ontario. Office of the Integrity Commissioner. Annual Report 4753
Ontario Corn Producer (CAN ISSN 0008-7297) 244
● Ontario Corporations Law Guide (CAN) 4878
Ontario Craft (CAN ISSN 0229-1320) 538

Title

▼ new title † ceased ● electronic media ➤ refereed

Title

Title

10710 ORANGE ULRICH'S PERIODICALS

Orange (DEU ISSN 1862-4642) **7896**
Orange (TWN) **8879**
Orange & Blue (USA) **2295**
Orange Book *see* Approved Drug Products with Therapeutic Equivalence Evaluations **6822**
• Orange Coast Magazine (USA ISSN 0279-0483) **3984**
▼ Orange Coast Weddings (USA) **5560**
Orange Country Menus *see* O C Menus **4395**
• Orange County Business Journal (USA ISSN 1051-7480) **1505**
Orange County California Genealogical Society Journal (USA) **3778**
Orange County Coast Kids *see* Coast Kids **2149**
Orange County Family *see* O C Family **2640**
Orange County Home (USA) **4548**
Orange County Jewish Heritage (USA ISSN 0030-4298) **3556**
Orange County Lawyer (USA ISSN 0897-5698) **4753**
Orange County Living (North Edition) (USA) **4548**
Orange County Living (South Edition) (USA) **4548**
Orange County Metro *see* O C Metro **1502**
• The Orange County Real Estate Report (USA) **7603**
Orange County Realtor (USA ISSN 1945-2179) **7603**
Orange County Report *see* Martin Brower's Orange County Report **1431**
Orange County Service Directory *see* Orange County Living (North Edition) **4548**
Orange County Woman (USA) **8879**
Orange Empire Railway Museum Gazette (USA) **6535**
Orange Free State Philatelic Society Philatelic Magazine *see* O F S Philatelic Magazine **6897**
Orange Free State. Provincial Gazette *see* Oranje-Vrystaat. Provinsiale Koerant **7458**
The Orange Guide *see* Rules and Guidance for Pharmaceutical Manufacturers and Distributors **6879**
Orange Journal *see* International Journal of Geriatric Psychiatry **4048**
Orange Magazine *see* O Magazine **6296**
Orange Seed Technical Bulletin (USA) **5038**
Orangeburg Black Voice (USA) **3556**
Orangeburgh German-Swiss Newsletter (USA ISSN 1059-0064) **3778**
Orangeville Banner *see* The Banner **3806**
Oranje Fonds Bericht (NLD ISSN 1872-1818) **8060**
Oranje-Nassau Museum. Jaarboek (NLD ISSN 0922-775X) **6535**
Oranje - Schakel (NLD) **4251**
Oranje-Vrystaat. Provinsiale Koerant/Orange Free State. Provincial Gazette (ZAF) **7458**
Oratoire (CAN ISSN 0701-4090) **7810**
Oratoire Saint Joseph. Cahiers (CAN ISSN 1206-050X) **7810**
† Gli Oratori del Giorno (ITA ISSN 0393-4012) **8979**
The Oratory (CAN ISSN 0384-1871) **7810**
Oratory School Magazine (GBR) **5346**
• El Orbe (MEX ISSN 1605-0347) **3910**
• ➤ Orbis (BEL ISSN 0030-4379) **5158**
Orbis (DEU ISSN 1435-6562) **8124**
• ➤ Orbis (VEN ISSN 1856-1594) **2894**
• ➤ Orbis (Kidlington) (GBR ISSN 0030-4387) **7256**
• Orbis (Nuneaton) (GBR ISSN 0030-4425) **5428**
Orbis Antiquus (DEU ISSN 0078-5555) **2238**
Orbis Biblicus et Orientalis (CHE ISSN 1015-1850) **2238**
Orbis Biblicus et Orientalis. Series Archaeologica (CHE ISSN 1422-4399) **409**
• ➤ Orbis Litterarum (DNK ISSN 0105-7510) **5346**
† ➤ Orbis Musicae (ISR ISSN 0303-3937) **8979**
Orbis Phaenomenologicus (DEU) **6937**
➤ Orbis Supplementa (BEL ISSN 1375-5153) **5158**
➤ Orbis Terrarum (DEU ISSN 1385-285X) **4023**
Orbis Tertius (ARG ISSN 0328-8188) **5346**
Orbit *see* School Magazine. Orbit **2211**
• Orbit (CAN ISSN 0030-4433) **2894**
• ➤ Orbit (GBR ISSN 0167-6830) **6050**
Orbit (Royal Oak) *see* Orbit Magazine **4981**
Orbit "Education for All" Magazine (ZMB) **2206**
Orbit Magazine (USA ISSN 1079-0454) **4981**
Orbita Cientifica (CUB ISSN 1027-4472) **5523**
▼ • Orbital (BRA ISSN 1984-6428) **2075**
Orbiter (USA) **2387**
The Orcadian (GBR ISSN 1355-3143) **3869**
The Orchadian (AUS ISSN 0474-3342) **3746**
➤ The Orchard (USA ISSN 1067-3784) **7727**
• The Orchardist (NZL ISSN 1173-3802) **244**
Das Orchester (DEU ISSN 0030-4468) **6602**
Orchestral Outlook (AUS ISSN 1832-4533) **6602**
Orchestras Canada. Membership Directory/Annuaire Canadien des Orchestres et Ensembles Musicaux (CAN ISSN 1705-2807) **6602**
Orchestras Canada News *see* O C News **6600**
Orchid Advocate (USA ISSN 0097-9546) **3746**
Orchid Digest (USA ISSN 0199-9559) **3746**
• Orchid Research Newsletter (GBR ISSN 1359-5199) **806**
The Orchid Review (GBR ISSN 0030-4476) **3746**
▼ Orchid Science and Biotechnology (GBR ISSN 1752-3443) **806**
Orchid Society of India. Journal (IND ISSN 0971-5371) **806**
Die Orchidee (DEU ISSN 0473-1425) **3746**
Orchideeen (NLD ISSN 0030-4484) **806**
Orchids (USA ISSN 1087-1950) **3746**
• Ord & Bild/Words and Pictures (SWE ISSN 0030-4492) **5232**
• Ord & Sag (DNK ISSN 0108-8025) **5158**
† Ord & Tekst (DNK ISSN 0908-715X) **8979**
Ord og Tunga (ISL ISSN 1022-4610) **5158**
• Ordained Servant (USA ISSN 1525-3503) **7769**
Ordem dos Advogados do Brasil - Rio de Janeiro Revista *see* O A B - R J. Revista **4750**
Ordem dos Advogados. Revista (PRT ISSN 0870-8118) **4753**
• Ordem dos Farmaceuticos. Revista (PRT ISSN 0872-7554) **6865**
Orden pour le Merite fuer Wissenschaften und Kuenste. Reden und Gedenkworte (DEU ISSN 0473-145X) **4468**
Ordenador Personal (ESP ISSN 0211-9579) **2578**
• ➤ Order (NLD ISSN 0167-8094) **5523**
Order in Council and Ministerial Order Resume (CAN ISSN 0844-7071) **4753**
Order of Buddhist Contemplatives. Journal (USA ISSN 0891-1177) **7702**
Order of Ontario/Ordre de l'Ontario (CAN ISSN 0845-9304) **3778**
Order of the Indian Wars Communique *see* O I W Communique **6440**
Orderly Payment of Debts Regulations *see* The (Year) Annotated Bankruptcy and Insolvency Act **4617**
Orders and Medals Society of America. Journal (USA ISSN 1067-1609) **4342**
Orders Guam (GUM) **6440**
Ordet (DNK ISSN 1602-5334) **6509**
• Ordet (NOR ISSN 0803-379X) **5158**
Ordfront Magasin (SWE) **3956**
Ordia Prima (ARG ISSN 1666-7743) **4468**
▼ Ordinace Dr. Norden (CZE ISSN 1802-8624) **5411**
L'Ordinaire Latinoamericain (FRA ISSN 1262-1692) **7161**
Ordinary Lives (GBR) **5346**
Ordinateur Individuel (FRA ISSN 0183-570X) **2578**
• Ordine Degli Ingegneri della Provincia di Palermo. Bollettino (ITA) **1028**
Ordine dei Servi di Maria. Studi Storici (ITA ISSN 0039-3045) **7810**
• Ordine di Malta. Newsletter (ITA) **6440**
Ordine Provinciale dei Medici Chirurghi e degli Odontoiatri. Notiziario (ITA) **6255**
Ordines Militares (POL ISSN 0867-2008) **4155**
Ordnance and Technology *see* Heiki to Gijutsu **6423**
Ordnance Industry Automation *see* Binggong Zidonghua **6413**
Ordnance Knowledge *see* Bingqi Zhishi **6413**
Ordnance Material Science and Engineering *see* Bingqi Cailiao Kexue yu Gongcheng **6413**
Ordnance Society. Journal (GBR ISSN 0957-1698) **6440**
Ordo (CAN ISSN 1912-0680) **7810**
➤ Ordo (DEU ISSN 0048-2129) **1784**
Ordo (Bishkek) (KGZ) **3904**
Ordo Politicus (DEU ISSN 0474-3385) **7458**
Ordre de l'Ontario *see* Order of Ontario **3778**
Ordre des Comptables Agrees du Quebec. Bilan (CAN) **1298**
Ordre des Experts-Comptables Bourgogne - Franche-Comte. Annuaire *see* Les Experts-Comptables de Bourgogne-France-Comte **1288**
Ordre des Geometres-Experts. Annuaire (FRA ISSN 0078-5601) **7896**
• Ordre des Medecins. Bulletin (FRA ISSN 0030-4565) **5690**
Ordre Professionnel des Travailleurs Sociaux du Quebec. Bulletin (CAN ISSN 1716-3706) **8060**
Ordre Professionnel des Travailleurs Sociaux du Quebec. Bulletin de Nouvelles *see* Ordre Professionnel des Travailleurs Sociaux du Quebec. Bulletin **8060**
Ordres des Comptables Agrees du Canada et des Bermudes. Annales de l'Examen Final Uniforme (CAN ISSN 0820-0386) **1298**
Ore & Alloys for the Global Steel Industry *see* Ferro-Alloy Directory **6311**
Ore & Alloys for the Global Steel Industry *see* Metal Producers of the World Directory (Year) **6323**
• ➤ Ore Geology Reviews (NLD ISSN 0169-1368) **2761**
Ore Horizons *see* Newfoundland. Department of Mines and Energy. Geological Survey Branch. Ore Horizons **6474**
Oregon: All-Industries *see* Harris Directory. Oregon All-Industries **2002**
Oregon Association of Nurseries Directory & Buyer's Guide *see* O A N Directory & Buyer's Guide **2022**
Oregon Bankruptcy (USA) **4878**
Oregon Beef Producer (USA) **295**
Oregon Blue Book (USA ISSN 0196-4577) **7459**
Oregon Builder (USA ISSN 1552-874X) **1028**
• Oregon Bulletin (USA) **7459**
• Oregon Business Directory (USA ISSN 1047-8809) **2022**
• Oregon Business Magazine (USA ISSN 0279-8190) **1157**
Oregon Business Network News (USA) **1157**
Oregon Camping *see* Moon Outdoors: Oregon Camping **8738**
Oregon Coast (USA ISSN 0744-8317) **3984**
Oregon Coast *see* Northwest Travel **8742**
Oregon Coast *see* Insider's Guide Oregon Coast **8721**
• Oregon Crimes and Punishments, Vehicles & Related Statutes (USA) **2662**
Oregon Crimes and Punishments, Vehicles and Related Statutes *see* Oregon Crimes and Punishments, Vehicles & Related Statutes **2662**
Oregon Criminal Practice (USA) **4896**
▼ Oregon Curiosities (USA ISSN 1935-1135) **8745**
Oregon Daily Emerald (USA ISSN 0030-4662) **2295**
Oregon. Department of Geology and Mineral Industries. Bulletin (USA ISSN 0078-5709) **2761**
Oregon. Department of Geology and Mineral Industries. Coastal Hazard Publication (USA) **2761**
Oregon. Department of Geology and Mineral Industries. Earthquake Hazard Publication (USA) **2761**
Oregon. Department of Geology and Mineral Industries. Oil and Gas Investigations (USA ISSN 0078-5741) **6785**
Oregon. Department of Geology and Mineral Industries. Open File Reports (USA) **2761**
Oregon. Department of Geology and Mineral Industries. Special Papers (USA ISSN 0278-3703) **2761**
Oregon. Department of Revenue. Income, Inheritance and Gift Tax Law Book (USA) **1938**
Oregon. Department of Revenue. Income Tax and Property Tax Laws and Administrative Rules (USA) **1938**
Oregon. Department of Revenue. Property Assessment and Taxation Administrative Rule Book (USA) **1938**
Oregon. Department of Revenue. Summary of Oregon Taxes (USA) **1938**
Oregon Distance Runner (USA) **8192**
• Oregon Employment Law Letter (USA ISSN 1077-2081) **4754**
Oregon English Journal (USA ISSN 1934-5674) **2894**
Oregon Episcopal Church News (USA ISSN 1068-8811) **7769**
• Oregon Evidence (USA) **4958**
Oregon Farm Bureau News (USA ISSN 0162-5179) **144**
Oregon Genealogical Society Quarterly (USA ISSN 0738-1891) **3778**
➤ Oregon Geology (USA ISSN 0164-3304) **2761**
• Oregon Grange Bulletin (USA ISSN 0030-4697) **144**
Oregon Grocery Line (USA) **3680**
Oregon Health *see* New Views **5685**
Oregon Health Division, Vital Statistics Annual Report *see* Oregon Vital Statistics Annual Report **7548**
• ➤ Oregon Historical Quarterly (USA ISSN 0030-4727) **4307**
Oregon Home (USA ISSN 1536-3201) **3984**
Oregon Insider (USA ISSN 1043-7142) **3458**
Oregon Labor Market Information Directory *see* Labor Market Information Directory **629**
• Oregon Labor Trends (USA) **1701**
• Oregon Law Review (USA ISSN 0196-2043) **4754**
Oregon Legislation Highlights (USA ISSN 1931-2377) **4754**
Oregon Library Association Quarterly *see* O L A Quarterly **5037**
• Oregon Literary Review (USA ISSN 1556-0325) **5232**
• Oregon Manufacturers Directory (USA ISSN 1525-4097) **1900**
Oregon: Manufacturing *see* Harris Directory. Oregon Manufacturing **2002**
Oregon Notary Law Primer (USA ISSN 1098-6529) **4754**
• Oregon Nurse (USA ISSN 0030-4751) **5977**
The Oregon Outlook (USA ISSN 0277-8785) **4075**
Oregon Outside (USA ISSN 1083-9348) **8326**
Oregon PeaceWorker (USA) **7256**
Oregon Personal Income Tax Statistics (USA) **1257**
Oregon Property Tax Statistics (USA ISSN 0145-4269) **1257**
Oregon Psychological Association Newsgram *see* O P A Newsgram **7388**
Oregon Public Broadcasting Primetime *see* O P B Primetime **2387**
Oregon. Public Utility Commissioner. Oregon Utility Statistics (USA) **7482**
Oregon Publisher (USA ISSN 0745-6379) **7569**
Oregon Quarterly (USA) **2295**
Oregon Review of International Law (USA ISSN 1543-9860) **4937**
Oregon School Directory (USA ISSN 0078-5679) **2961**
Oregon School Directory *see* M D R's Oregon School Directory **2957**
Oregon Science Teacher (USA ISSN 0030-4794) **7896**
• Oregon. Secretary of State. Administrative Rules Compilation (USA) **7459**
Oregon Snowsports Guide (USA) **8326**
• Oregon State Bar Bulletin (USA ISSN 0030-4816) **4754**
• Oregon State University. Forest Research Laboratory. Biennial Report (USA ISSN 0889-7298) **3699**
• ➤ Oregon State University. Forest Research Laboratory. Research Contribution (USA) **3699**
Oregon State University. Sea Grant College Program. Publications (USA) **3604**
The Oregon Stater (USA ISSN 0885-3258) **2295**
Oregon Teachers of English to Speakers of Other Languages Journal *see* O R T E S O L Journal **5157**
Oregon Teamster (USA ISSN 0030-4840) **4600**
† Oregon Trail Sources, Queries and Reviews (USA ISSN 1069-7454) **8979**
Oregon Vital Statistics *see* Oregon Vital Statistics Annual Report **7548**
Oregon Vital Statistics Annual Report (USA ISSN 1524-377X) **7548**
Oregon Vital Statistics County Data (USA ISSN 1524-3796) **7549**
Oregon, Washington TourBook *see* TourBook: Oregon, Washington **8762**
Oregon Wheat (USA ISSN 0897-5051) **274**
Oregon's Agricultural Progress (USA ISSN 0474-4721) **144**
O'Reilly Make *see* Make **6294**
Oremus (POL ISSN 1234-1762) **7810**
Orenburgskaya Nedelya (RUS) **3939**
Orenburgskie Vedomosti (RUS) **3939**
Orenburzh'e (RUS) **3939**
Ores and Metals *see* Rudy i Metally **6478**
Orfey/Orpheus (BGR ISSN 0861-4334) **510**
➤ The Orff Echo (USA ISSN 0095-2613) **6602**
Organ (DEU ISSN 1435-7941) **6602**
• The Organ (GBR ISSN 0030-4883) **6602**
Organ Australia (AUS ISSN 1832-8725) **6602**
Organ Canada (CAN ISSN 1486-2492) **6603**
Organ Club Journal (GBR ISSN 0306-0357) **6603**
Organ Handbook *see* Annual Organ Handbook **6545**
Organ Historical Trust of Australia News *see* O H T A News **6600**
The Organ Portfolio (USA ISSN 0193-6670) **6603**
L'Organe *see* Concordian **2279**
Organe du Syndicat du Batiment et du Bois (CHE) **1028**
L'Organe International de Controle des Stupefiants pour (Year). Rapport *see* International Narcotics Control Board. Report for (Year) **6850**
Organes Directeurs et des Principaux Organes Subsidiaires. Rapport *see* Intergovernmental Oceanographic Commission. Reports of Governing and Major Subsidiary Bodies **1126**
• Organet (NOR ISSN 0804-1253) **8060**
• Organi di Trasmissione (ITA ISSN 0030-4905) **3214**
• Organic AlterNETive (BRA) **4981**
• ➤ Organic & Biomolecular Chemistry (GBR ISSN 1477-0520) **2127**
Organic & Natural Business (GBR ISSN 1743-0429) **3681**
• The Organic & Non-G M O Report (Genetically Modified) (USA) **244**
Organic and Organometallic Crystal Structures; Bibliography (NLD) **633**
▼ • Organic & Printed Electronics (USA ISSN 1937-1195) **3110**
Organic and Printed Electronics *see* Organic & Printed Electronics **3110**
• Organic & Printed Electronics e-Report (USA ISSN 1938-0844) **3327**
▼ Organic Beauty (USA) **590**
Organic Business News (USA) **3659**
Organic Chemical Division Diamond *see* O C D Diamond **8433**
➤ Organic Chemistry (USA ISSN 0078-611X) **2127**
▼ • Organic Communications (TUR ISSN 1307-6175) **2127**
Organic Directory (Santa Cruz) *see* Organic Directory & Resource Guide **244**
Organic Directory & Resource Guide (USA ISSN 1942-4264) **244**
➤ Organic Electronic Spectral Data (USA ISSN 0078-6136) **2104**
• ➤ Organic Electronics (NLD ISSN 1566-1199) **3327**
The Organic Equine *see* New Zealand Natural Equine **294**
Organic Farming (GBR ISSN 1464-1224) **144**
Organic Foods Market Assessment *see* Key Note Market Assessment. Organic Foods **1892**
Organic Gardening (GBR ISSN 0953-7465) **3746**
• Organic Gardening (USA) **3746**
• ➤ Organic Geochemistry (GBR ISSN 0146-6380) **2128**
† Organic Growing (Ulverstone) (AUS ISSN 0816-6668) **8979**
Organic Guide (CAN ISSN 1910-6238) **4518**
• ➤ Organic Letters (USA ISSN 1523-7060) **2128**
Organic Life (GBR ISSN 1473-8392) **144**
• Organic Living (CAN) **6668**
▼ The Organic Mom (USA ISSN 1933-7876) **4365**
Organic N Z (NZL ISSN 1175-5970) **245**
Organic News (USA) **144**
• Organic Pages (USA ISSN 1523-0325) **3659**
• Organic Perspectives (USA) **144**
• ➤ Organic Preparations and Procedures International (USA ISSN 0030-4948) **2128**
• ➤ Organic Process Research and Development (USA ISSN 1083-6160) **2128**
• Organic Processing (USA ISSN 1936-6698) **3659**
Organic Producer (USA ISSN 1556-1739) **144**
Organic Products Retailer (USA) **3659**
• Organic Reaction Mechanisms (GBR ISSN 0474-4772) **2128**
➤ Organic Reaction Mechanisms. Annual Survey (USA ISSN 0078-6160) **2128**
➤ Organic Reactions (USA ISSN 0078-6179) **2128**
The Organic Report (USA) **3659**
• Organic Research Database (GBR) **184**
• Organic Spa Magazine (USA ISSN 1944-5644) **590**
➤ Organic Syntheses (USA ISSN 0078-6209) **2128**
Organic Syntheses - Collective Volumes (USA ISSN 0078-6217) **2128**

Link to your serials resources and content with ulrichsweb.com

Title

10712 ORGANISMO INTERNACIONAL DE ENERGIA ATOMICA. COLECCION ULRICH'S PERIODICALS

Organismo Internacional de Energia Atomica. Coleccion de Informes de Seguridad *see* International Atomic Energy Agency. Safety Reports Series **3169**
• ➤ Organisms Diversity & Evolution (DEU ISSN 1439-6092) **696**
The Organist (USA ISSN 1931-6178) **6603**
Organist en Erediienst *see* Muziek en Liturgie **6597**
Organistica (ITA) **6603**
Organists' Benevolent League. Annual Report (GBR) **6603**
• ➤ Organists' Review (GBR ISSN 0048-2161) **6603**
• ➤ Organizacija (POL ISSN 1318-5454) **1870**
Organizacion Continental Latino Americana de Estudiantes Revista *see* O C L A E Revista **5232**
Organizacion de Aviacion Civil Internacional. Asamblea. Actas de las Sesiones Plenarias *see* International Civil Aviation Organization. Assembly. Minutes of the Plenary Meetings **8545**
Organizacion de Aviacion Civil Internacional. Asamblea. Informe y Actas de la Comision Administrativa *see* International Civil Aviation Organization. Assembly. Report and Minutes of the Administrative Commission **8545**
Organizacion de Aviacion Civil Internacional. Asamblea. Informe y Actas de la Comision Juridica *see* International Civil Aviation Organization. Assembly. Report and Minutes of the Legal Commission **8545**
Organizacion de Aviacion Civil Internacional. Asamblea. Informe y Actas de la Comision Tecnica *see* International Civil Aviation Organization. Assembly. Report of the Technical Commission **60**
Organizacion de Aviacion Civil Internacional. Compendio Estadistico. Serie AF. Instalaciones y Servicios de Aeropuerto y en Ruta. Datos Financieros y Resumen de Datos de Trafico *see* International Civil Aviation Organization. Digests of Statistics. Series AF. Airport and Route Facilities. Financial Data and Summary Traffic Data **8526**
Organizacion de Aviacion Civil Internacional. Compendio Estadistico. Serie OFOD. Origen y Destino por Vuelo *see* International Civil Aviation Organization. Digests of Statistics. Series OFOD. On-Flight Origin and Destination **8526**
Organizacion Meteorologica Mundial. Asociacion Regional III (America del Sur). Informe Final Abreviado de la (No.) Reunion *see* World Meteorological Organization. Regional Association III (South America). Abridged Final Report of the (No.) Session **6399**
Organizacion Meteorologica Mundial. Asociacion Regional IV (America del Norte y America Central). Informe Final Abreviado de la (No.) Reunion *see* World Meteorological Organization. Regional Association IV (North America and Central America). Abridged Final Report of the (No.) Session **6399**
Organizacion Meteorologica Mundial. Comision de Hidrologia. Informe Final Abrevido de la (No) Reunion *see* World Meteorological Organization. Commission for Hydrology. Abridged Final Report of the (No.) Session **6399**
Organizacion Meteorologica Mundial. Comision de Instrumentos y Metodos de Observacion. Informe Final Abrevido de la (No) Reunion *see* World Meteorological Organization. Commission for Instruments and Methods of Observation. Abridged Final Report of the (No.) Session **6399**
Organizacion Meteorologica Mundial. Comision de Meteorologia Aeronautica. Informe Final Abrevido de la (No) Reunion *see* World Meteorological Organization. Commission for Aeronautical Meteorology. Abridged Final Report of the (No.) Session **6398**
Organizacion Meteorologica Mundial. Comision de Meteorologia Agricola. Informe Final Abrevido de la (No) Reunion *see* World Meteorological Organization. Commission for Agricultural Meteorology. Abridged Final Report of the (No.) Session **6398**
Organizacion Meteorologica Mundial. Comision de Meteorologia Marina. Informe Final Abrevido de la (No) Reunion *see* World Meteorological Organization. Commission for Marine Meteorology. Abridged Final Report of the (No.) Session **6399**
Organizacion Meteorologica Mundial. Comision de Sistemas Basicos. Informe Final Abrevido de la (No) Reunion *see* World Meteorological Organization. Commission for Basic Systems. Abridged Final Report of the (No.) Session **6398**
Organizacion Meteorologica Mundial. Congreso. Informe Abrevido y Resoluciones *see* World Meteorological Organization. Congress. Abridged Report with Resolutions **6399**
Organizacion Meteorologica Mundial. Reunion del Consejo Ejecutivo. Informe Abreviado y Resoluciones (CHE ISSN 1011-3576) **6393**
Organizacion Meteorologico Mundial. Comision de Ciencias Atmosfericas. Informe Final Abrevido de la (No) Reunion *see* World Meteorological Organization. Commission for Atmospheric Sciences. Abridged Final Report of the (No.) Session **6398**
Organizacion Mundial de la Salud. Serie de Informes Tecnicos (CHE ISSN 0509-2507) **5690**
Organizacion Mundial de Turismo Barometro del Turismo Mundial *see* O M T. Barometro del Turismo Mundial **8780**
Organizacion Mundial del Comercio, Informe Anual *see* W T O Annual Report **1586**
Organizacion Mundial del Turismo. Documentos Basicos *see* World Tourism Organization. Basic Documents **8776**
Organizacion Mundial del Turismo. Noticias *see* W T O News **8773**
Organizacion Regional Interamericana de Trabajadores Inter-American Labor News *see* I C F T U - O R I T Inter-American Labor News **4595**
Organizacion y Gestion Educativa (ESP ISSN 1134-0312) **3029**
Organizacja i Kierowanie/Organization and Management (POL ISSN 0137-5466) **1784**
Organizacja i Zarzadzanie w Regionie Nadmorskim (POL ISSN 1641-8077) **1431**
• ➤ Organizacoes & Sociedade (BRA ISSN 1413-585X) **4468**
Organizacoes e Trabalho (PRT ISSN 0871-4835) **8124**
Organizate (ESP) **1784**
• ➤ Organization (GBR ISSN 1350-5084) **1784**
• ➤ Organization & Environment (USA ISSN 1086-0266) **6684**
Organization and Management *see* Organizacja i Kierowanie **1784**
• Organization Development Journal (USA ISSN 0889-6402) **1784**
Organization Development Practitioner *see* O D Practitioner **1782**
The Organization Dimensions of Global Environmental Change *see* Organization & Environment **6684**
Organization for Economic Co-operation and Development Journal on Development *see* O E C D Journal on Development **1602**
Organization for Economic Cooperation and Development Health Working Papers *see* O E C D Health Working Papers **5688**
Organization for the Phyto-Taxonomic Investigation of the Mediterranean Area Newsletter *see* O P T I M A Newsletter **806**
Organization for the Promotion and Advancement of Small Telecommunications Companies Roundtable *see* O P A S T C O Roundtable **2370**
Organization for Tropical Studies Liana *see* O T S Liana **2623**
• ➤ Organization Management Journal (USA ISSN 1541-6518) **1784**
Organization of African Unity Review *see* O A U Review **4177**
Organization of African Unity. Scientific Technical and Research Commission. Publication (NGA ISSN 0474-6171) **7896**
Organization of American Historians Council of Chairs Newsletter *see* O A H Council of Chairs Newsletter **4306**
Organization of American Historians Newsletter *see* O A H Newsletter **4306**
Organization of American Historians. Program of the Annual Meeting (USA ISSN 0197-9884) **4307**
• Organization of American States. Directory (Online) (USA) **7256**
Organization of American States. General Assembly. Actas y Documentos (USA) **7257**
Organization of American States General Secretariat. Annual Report *see* O A S. General Secretariat. Annual Report **4306**
Organization of American States. Official Records. Indice y Lista General (USA ISSN 0078-642X) **4307**
Organization of Arab Petroleum Exporting Countries Energy Resources Monitor *see* O A P E C Energy Resources Monitor **6781**
Organization of Arab Petroleum Exporting Countries. Secretary General's Annual Report (KWT) **6785**
Organization of Black Airline Pilots. Convention Journal (USA) **67**
Organization of Black Airline Pilots. Newsletter (USA) **67**
Organization of Chinese Americans Image *see* O C A Image **3556**
Organization of Fish and Wildlife Information Managers Newsletter *see* O F W I M Newsletter **2623**
Organization of the Cooperatives of America News *see* O C A News **1424**
Organization of the Petroleum Exporting Countries Annual Report *see* O P E C Annual Report **6782**
Organization of the Petroleum Exporting Countries Annual Statistical Bulletin *see* O P E C Annual Statistical Bulletin **6782**
Organization of the Petroleum Exporting Countries Energy Review *see* O P E C Energy Review **6782**
Organization of the Petroleum Exporting Countries Monthly Oil Market Report *see* O P E C Monthly Oil Market Report **6782**
Organization of the Petroleum Exporting Countries Papers *see* O P E C Papers **8978**
Organization of the Petroleum Exporting Countries, PR and Information Department Bulletin *see* O P E C Bulletin **6782**
• ➤ Organization Science (USA ISSN 1047-7039) **1784**
• ➤ Organization Studies (GBR ISSN 0170-8406) **7990**
• ➤ Organizational Behavior and Human Decision Processes (USA ISSN 0749-5978) **1784**
• Organizational Dynamics (GBR ISSN 0090-2616) **1784**
➤ Organizational Intersections in Healthcare, Business and Policy (USA ISSN 1541-1036) **5691**
• ➤ Organizational Research Methods (USA ISSN 1094-4281) **1784**
Organizational Science *see* Soshiki Kagaku **1794**
Organizational Systems Research Association. Conference Proceedings (USA) **2434**
Organizations and Change (USA) **1870**
Organizatsiya Ob'edinennykh Natsii. Evropeiskaya Ekonomicheskaya Komissiya. Godovoi Doklad *see* Economic Commission for Europe. Annual Report **1099**
Organizatsiya Ob'edinennykh Natsii. Evropeiskaya Ekonomicheskaya Komissiya. Seriya po Energetike *see* United Nations. Economic Commission for Europe. Energy Series **3149**
Organizatsiya Ob'edinennykh Natsii. Sovet Bezopasnosti. Ofitsial'nye Otchety. Dopolnenie *see* United Nations. Security Council. Official Records. Supplement **7271**
Organizatsiya Ob'edinennykh Natsii. Sovet Bezopasnosti. Ofitsial'nyi Otchet *see* United Nations. Security Council. Official Records **7271**
Organizatsiya Ob'edinennykh Natsii. Yuridicheskiy Ezhegodnik *see* United Nations Juridical Yearbook **4943**
Organizatsiya Upravleniya (RUS) **1784**
Organize (CAN) **4600**
▼ Organize (USA ISSN 1936-6566) **4365**
Organize Your Luck! (USA ISSN 0734-1776) **6702**
• The Organized Approach Digest (USA ISSN 1943-460X) **4365**
• Organized Crime Digest (USA ISSN 1521-7310) **2662**
The Organized Executive (USA ISSN 1556-8997) **1784**
➤ Organizing (USA ISSN 1063-9403) **8060**
Organizing Corporate and Other Business Enterprises (USA) **4878**
† Organizzarsi (ITA ISSN 0474-635X) **8979**
• Organizzazione Sanitaria (ITA ISSN 0394-283X) **4108**
L'Organo (ITA ISSN 0474-6376) **6603**
Organo Informativo de la Escuela Nacional Preparatoria *see* E N P Gaceta **2978**
Organo Informativo de la Facultad de Medicina *see* Universidad Nacional Autonoma de Mexico. Facultad de Medicina. Gaceta **5726**
L'Organo nella Liturgia (ITA) **6603**
Organo Oficial del Grupo Angeles, Servicios de Salud *see* Acta Medica Grupo Angeles **5566**
Organo Oficial del Instituto de Investigaciones Economicas *see* Problemas del Desarrollo **1603**
• ➤ Organogenesis (USA ISSN 1547-6278) **926**
Organometallic Chemistry (GBR ISSN 0301-0074) **2128**
Organometallic News (JPN ISSN 0917-1274) **2128**
• ➤ Organometallics (USA ISSN 0276-7333) **2128**
Organon (POL ISSN 0078-6500) **7896**
Organon F (SVK ISSN 1335-0668) **6937**
Organophosphorus Chemistry (GBR ISSN 0306-0713) **2128**
Organs and Tissues *see* Organs, Tissues and Cells **6255**
Organs, Tissues and Cells (ITA ISSN 1828-0595) **6255**
• ➤ Het Orgel (NLD ISSN 0166-0101) **6603**
Orgelforum (SWE ISSN 0280-0047) **6603**
De Orgelkrant *see* NotaBene **6600**
De Orgelvriend (NLD ISSN 1386-1417) **6603**
Orglet (DNK ISSN 0106-1011) **6603**
Orgonomic Functionalism (USA ISSN 1054-075X) **6172**
L'Orgue (FRA ISSN 0030-5170) **6603**
L'Orgue Dossier (FRA ISSN 1149-6851) **6603**
L'Orgue Francophone (FRA ISSN 0985-3642) **6603**
Oriel Stringer (GBR) **7569**
• ➤ Oriens (NLD ISSN 0078-6527) **557**
Oriens Christianus (DEU ISSN 0340-6407) **7668**
Oriens et Occidens (DEU ISSN 1615-4517) **4324**
Oriens Extremus (DEU ISSN 0030-5197) **558**
Oriens Graecolatinus (ITA) **2238**
Oriens - Occidens (FRA ISSN 1284-2060) **5523**
Orient (CAN ISSN 0472-0490) **7810**
Orient *see* Dongfang **5214**
Orient *see* Dongfang Wenhua Zhoukan **486**
Orient (DEU ISSN 0030-5227) **558**
Orient (JPN ISSN 0473-3851) **558**
Orient-Archaeologie (DEU ISSN 1434-162X) **409**
Orient Beauty/Furong Yajie (HKG ISSN 1023-7593) **2259**
Orient Express (Newport) (GBR) **6509**
Orient-Express Magazine *see* Sphere **8757**
Orient Journal (DEU ISSN 1617-4488) **558**
Orient Journal of Medicine (NGA ISSN 1115-0521) **5691**
Orientacao (BRA ISSN 0103-3220) **4023**
Orientacion (SLV) **7810**
Orientacion Economica y Financiera (ESP ISSN 0212-7385) **1408**
Orientacion y Sociedad (ARG ISSN 1515-6877) **7389**
Oriental and India Office Collections Newsletter *see* O I O C Newsletter **557**
The Oriental Anthropologists (IND ISSN 0972-558X) **351**
Oriental Archives *see* Archiv Orientalni **543**
Oriental Art *see* Dongfang Yishu **487**
Oriental Art (SGP ISSN 0030-5278) **558**
Oriental Ceramic Society of Hong Kong. Bulletin (HKG) **2044**
The Oriental Ceramic Society. Transactions (GBR ISSN 0306-0926) **2044**
• Oriental College Magazine/Majallah al-Kulliyah al-Sharqiyyah (PAK) **5346**
Oriental Consultants Co., Ltd. Technical Report *see* Orientaru Konsarutantsu Gijutsuho **3280**
Oriental Culture *see* Dongfang Wenhua **4450**
Oriental Daily News *see* Dongfang Ribao **3875**
Oriental Diet, Therapy & Healthcare *see* Dongfang Shiliao yu Baojian **6657**
Oriental Dolls (USA) **6296**
Oriental Dolls Presents: Asian Hotties (USA ISSN 1083-768X) **6296**
Oriental Forum *see* Dongfang Luntan **548**
Oriental Geographer (BGD ISSN 0030-5308) **4023**
➤ Oriental Insects (USA ISSN 0030-5316) **857**
Oriental Institute Communications (USA ISSN 0146-678X) **409**
Oriental Institute. Journal (IND ISSN 0030-5324) **558**
Oriental Institute Museum Publications (USA) **6535**
Oriental Institute Nubian Expedition (USA) **409**
Oriental Institute Publications *see* University of Chicago Oriental Institute. Publications **4326**
Oriental Journal of Chemistry (IND ISSN 0970-020X) **2075**
Oriental Legal Magazine *see* Dongfang Fazhi Daokan **4660**
Oriental Library. Research Department. Memoirs/Zaidan Hojin Toyo Bunko (JPN ISSN 0082-562X) **4187**
Oriental Medicine *see* Kikan Toyo Igaku **312**
Oriental Philatelic Association of London Journal *see* O P A L Journal **6897**
Oriental Qigong *see* Dongfang Qigong **6984**
• Oriental Rug Review (Online Edition) (USA) **4561**
Oriental Sports Daily *see* Tonfan Tiyu Ribao **8212**
Oriental Studies *see* Keleti Tanulmanyok **554**
Oriental Studies (USA ISSN 0078-6551) **510**
Oriental Sunday *see* Dongfang Xindi **3875**
Oriental Sword *see* Dongfang Jian **5409**
The Oriental Times *see* Donglushibao **3824**
Oriental Women *see* Dongfang Nuxing **8859**
Orientalia (ITA ISSN 0030-5367) **558**
Orientalia Biblica et Christiana (DEU ISSN 0946-5065) **7810**
Orientalia Christiana Analecta (ITA ISSN 1590-7449) **558**
Orientalia Christiana Periodica (ITA ISSN 0030-5375) **7739**
Orientalia Gothoburgensia (SWE ISSN 0078-656X) **558**
The Orientalia Journal (USA ISSN 0164-3398) **368**
Orientalia Judaica Christiana *see* Scrinium **7706**
▼ Orientalia, Judaica, Christiana (USA ISSN 1942-1281) **7668**
➤ Orientalia Lovaniensia Analecta (BEL ISSN 0777-978X) **558**
• Orientalia Lovaniensia Periodica (BEL ISSN 0085-4522) **558**
Orientalia Monspeliensia (NLD ISSN 0169-9458) **4324**
➤ Orientalia Rheno-Traiectina (NLD ISSN 0169-9504) **558**
➤ Orientalia Suecana (SWE ISSN 0078-6578) **558**
Orientalisches Muenzkabinett Jena (DEU ISSN 1613-9682) **6652**
Orientaliska Studier (SWE ISSN 0345-8997) **558**
Orientalistik Bibliographien und Dokumentationen (DEU) **558**
• ➤ Orientalistische Literaturzeitung (DEU ISSN 0030-5383) **558**
Orientamenti Linguistici (ITA) **5158**
Orientamenti Pastorali (ITA ISSN 0472-0784) **7810**
➤ Orientamenti Pedagogici (ITA ISSN 0030-5391) **2894**
† Orientamento Scolastico Professionale (ITA) **8979**
Orientaru Konsarutantsu Gijutsuho/Oriental Consultants Co., Ltd. Technical Report (JPN ISSN 0914-3904) **3280**
Orientatie *see* Orientations **1870**
Orientatie op Planologische en Juridische Geodesie (NLD) **2787**
L'Orientation (CAN ISSN 0833-0530) **6702**
Orientation Manual for Board Members/Manuel d'Orientation pour les Membres du Bureau (CAN ISSN 1719-427X) **8060**
➤ Orientation Scolaire et Professionnelle (FRA ISSN 0249-6739) **7389**
Orientations (BEL ISSN 0030-543X) **1870**
Orientations (HKG ISSN 0030-5448) **510**
Les Orientations de la Politique de l'Immigration (FRA ISSN 1957-5750) **7459**
† Oriente e Occidente (ITA) **8979**
Oriente Moderno (ITA ISSN 0030-5472) **558**
Orienteering Canada (CAN ISSN 0227-6658) **8326**
Orienteering North America (USA ISSN 0886-1080) **8326**
Orienteering World (FIN ISSN 1015-4965) **8326**
• Orientering (DNK ISSN 1903-2498) **8393**
• Orientering.dk (DNK ISSN 1901-3825) **8192**
Orientering fra Koebenhavns Kommune, Statistisk Kontor (Print) *see* Orientering **8393**

▼ *new title*   † *ceased*   ● *electronic media*   ➤ *refereed*

Otolaryngological Society of the Republic of China. Journal *see* Zhonghua Minguo Erbihouke Yixuehui Zazhi **6086**
● Otolaryngology Coding Alert (USA ISSN 1526-064X) **4518**
Otolaryngology - Head and Neck Surgery *see* Jibi Inkoka, Tokeibu Geka **6081**
● ➤ Otolaryngology - Head and Neck Surgery (USA ISSN 0194-5998) **6083**
● Otoliths (AUS ISSN 1833-6221) **5346**
➤ Otologia Fukuoka - Jibi to Rinsho (JPN) **6084**
● ➤ Otology & Neurotology (USA ISSN 1531-7129) **6084**
Otology Japan (JPN ISSN 0917-2025) **6084**
Otomasyon/Automation (TUR) **1157**
Otomodachi (JPN) **2206**
Otomotif (IDN) **8507**
Otomotiv Endustrisi/Automotive Industry (TUR) **8597**
Otomotivde Servis, Ekipman ve Yedekparca (TUR) **8597**
Otorhinolaryngologica Hungarica *see* Ful-, Orr-, Gegegyogyaszat **6080**
Otorhinolaryngologie Aktuell *see* O R L - Aktuell **6083**
● ➤ The Otorhinolaryngologist (GBR ISSN 1752-9360) **6084**
Otorhinolaryngology and Phoniatrics *see* Otorinolaryngologie a Foniatrie **6084**
Otorhinolaryngology Head and Neck Nursing *see* O R L - Head and Neck Nursing **6083**
Otorhinolaryngology Tokyo *see* Jibi Inkoka Tembo **6081**
● ➤ Otorinolaringologia (ITA ISSN 0392-6621) **6084**
➤ Otorinolaryngologia a Chirurgia Hlavy a Krku (SVK ISSN 1337-2181) **6084**
➤ Otorinolaryngologie a Foniatrie/ Otorhinolaryngology and Phoniatrics (CZE ISSN 1210-7867) **6084**
Otorrinolaringologia Aragon Aragon *see* O.R.L. Aragon **6083**
Otosport (IDN) **8507**
Otrante (FRA ISSN 1148-0904) **5446**
Otraparte (COL) **4468**
Otro Derecho (COL ISSN 0122-2252) **4754**
El Otro Lado-Ensayo (ARG ISSN 1851-2259) **5346**
Otrok in Druzina (SVN ISSN 0030-6681) **2894**
➤ Otrok in Knjiga (SVN ISSN 0351-5141) **2163**
Otrosi (ESP) **4754**
Otsuchi Marine Research Center Report *see* Coastal Marine Science **2802**
Otsuka Pharmaceutical Factory. Journal *see* Otsuka Yakuho **6865**
Otsuka Yakuho/Otsuka Pharmaceutical Factory. Journal (JPN ISSN 0030-669X) **6865**
Ottagono (ITA ISSN 0391-7487) **4548**
Ottar (NOR ISSN 0030-6703) **6535**
Ottar (Stockholm, 2001) (SWE ISSN 1650-8017) **8124**
Ottawa (CAN ISSN 1717-5763) **4307**
Ottawa 24 Hours (CAN ISSN 1912-2586) **3815**
Ottawa Archaeologist (CAN ISSN 0702-7974) **409**
● Ottawa Business Journal (CAN ISSN 1207-8166) **1157**
Ottawa Campus (CAN) **2295**
● Ottawa Citizen (CAN ISSN 0839-3222) **3815**
Ottawa City *see* Ottawa **4307**
Ottawa City Interiors (CAN) **4548**
Ottawa City Woman (CAN) **8847**
Ottawa - Gatineau 24 Heures (CAN ISSN 1912-2594) **3815**
Ottawa - Gatineau Vingtquatre Heures *see* Ottawa - Gatineau 24 Heures **3815**
Ottawa Hispanic Studies (CAN) **5346**
Ottawa Jewish Bulletin (CAN ISSN 1196-1929) **7727**
● ➤ Ottawa Law Review (CAN ISSN 0048-2331) **4754**
● Ottawa Letter (CAN ISSN 0702-8210) **7459**
Ottawa R & D Report (CAN ISSN 0380-6251) **3214**
Ottawa Rushhour (CAN ISSN 1912-2659) **3815**
● Ottawa Sun (CAN ISSN 0843-2570) **3815**
Ottawa Twentyfour Hours *see* Ottawa 24 Hours **3815**
● Ottawa Update (CAN) **7459**
● Ottawa X Press (CAN) **6603**
Ottawa's Vital Signs (CAN ISSN 1912-6050) **8124**
Ottawa's Vital Signs Report *see* Ottawa's Vital Signs **8124**
Otter Raft (USA) **2623**
Otterbein Miscellany (USA) **5232**
Otthon (HUN ISSN 0865-2007) **4548**
Ottico (ITA) **6050**
Ottilianer Reihe (DEU) **7811**
Otto Graf Journal (DEU ISSN 0938-409X) **3356**
Otto - Novecento Ritrovato (ITA) **5346**
● Otto Scott's Compass (USA ISSN 1074-584X) **3984**
OTTO Work Force (NLD) **6702**
➤ The Ottoman Empire and its Heritage (NLD ISSN 1380-6076) **4324**
Otwarta Szkola (POL ISSN 1230-2899) **3075**
Ou-Hua-Wen-Ts'ung *see* Euro-Sinica **5292**
Ou Pais Mentounasc (FRA ISSN 1142-155X) **4252**
● Oud - Holland (NLD ISSN 0030-672X) **510**
Oud Holland *see* Oud - Holland **510**
Oud Meppel (NLD ISSN 1384-0886) **4252**
Oud - Utrecht (NLD ISSN 1380-7137) **4252**
Oud - Utrecht. Jaarboek (NLD) **4252**
Oud Wageningen (NLD ISSN 1384-7678) **4252**
Oude Paden (NLD ISSN 0030-6746) **7668**
Ouder en Wijzer *see* Ouderenwijzer **1701**
Ouderenwijzer (NLD ISSN 1873-9938) **1701**
Ouderenzorg *see* ZorgVisie **4113**
Ouderlingenblad (NLD ISSN 0166-2392) **7668**
Ouders van Nu (NLD ISSN 0165-6414) **2163**
Oudheidkundig Cultuurhistorisch Genootschap Landgraaf. Jaarboek (NLD ISSN 1872-017X) **4155**
Oudheidkundig Genootschap Niftarlake. Jaarboekje (NLD) **410**
➤ Oudtestamentische Studien (NLD ISSN 0169-7226) **7727**
Ouest Echos (CMR) **3805**
● Ouest France (FRA ISSN 0999-2138) **3841**
L'Ouest Saharien/The Western Sahara (FRA ISSN 1292-136X) **4468**
Oughtred Society. Journal (USA ISSN 1061-6292) **5523**
Oui Magazine (FRA ISSN 1964-9169) **8879**
Oulu Port Handbook *see* Port of Oulu Handbook **8657**
Oulun Sukututkija (FIN ISSN 0784-6037) **4252**
● Oulun Yliopiston Kirjaston Julkaisuja/Publications of Oulu University Library (FIN ISSN 0357-1440) **5038**
Oulun Ylipiston. Sodankylan Geofysiikan Observatorio. Publications (FIN ISSN 1456-3673) **2787**
Al-Oum *see* Al- Umm **8886**
Oumei Yanjiu/EurAmerica (TWN ISSN 1021-3058) **4307**
Oumia/Lake Biwa Environmental Research Institute. News (JPN) **2797**
Our Afghans (USA ISSN 1084-1822) **6812**
Our Animals (USA ISSN 0030-6789) **321**
Our Bible Matters (CAN ISSN 1486-5327) **7668**
Our Business (USA) **2295**
Our Canada (CAN ISSN 1708-749X) **3815**
● Our Cats (DEU ISSN 0944-6192) **6812**
Our Cats (GBR ISSN 1468-5787) **6812**
● Our Changing Environment (NZL ISSN 1177-7540) **3458**
● Our Changing Planet (USA) **3458**
● Our Children (USA ISSN 1083-3080) **2163**
Our Choice (CAN ISSN 1192-2125) **7569**
Our Country *see* Nchi Yetu **3961**
● Our Daily Bread (USA) **4084**
Our Daily Manna (NGA ISSN 1597-376X) **7668**
Our Diverse Cities *see* Nos Diverses Cites **8123**
● Our Dogs (GBR ISSN 0955-9469) **6812**
Our Dwelling *see* Hem & Hyra **4412**
Our Economy: Review of Current Problems in Economics *see* Nase Gospodarstvo **1152**
Our Faith *see* Vor Tru **7743**
Our Family (CAN ISSN 0030-6843) **7811**
Our Family (DEU ISSN 0946-3933) **7739**
Our Forest (CAN ISSN 1912-2942) **3699**
Our Fourfooted Friends (USA ISSN 0030-6851) **321**
Our Gifted Children (USA ISSN 1055-1336) **2163**
Our Havanese (USA ISSN 1934-5666) **6812**
Our Haven *see* Musu Pastoge **3552**
Our Health (CAN ISSN 1715-9040) **7534**
Our Heritage (IND ISSN 0474-9030) **558**
Our Heritage (USA ISSN 0733-4559) **3778**
Our Hope *see* Nasa Nada **7808**
▼ Our Iowa (USA ISSN 1942-3586) **3984**
Our Islam (USA) **7715**
Our Kids Atlanta (USA) **2163**
Our Kids Austin (USA) **2163**
● Our Kids San Antonio (USA ISSN 1933-9801) **2163**
Our Kingdom Ministry (USA ISSN 1067-7259) **7739**
Our Lady of Holy Cross College. Journal (USA) **2295**
Our Lady's Rosary Makers of Australia. Annual Report (AUS ISSN 1833-0126) **7811**
Our Language *see* Nase Rec **5154**
Our Languages are the Voice of the Land (AUS ISSN 1834-4216) **5158**
Our Life *see* Meie Elu **3549**
Our Life (USA ISSN 0740-0225) **3556**
● Our Living Oceans (USA ISSN 1559-8446) **959**
Our Magazine (CHE) **510**
Our Missing Links (USA) **3778**
† ● Our Munich (DEU) **8979**
● Our Nature (NPL ISSN 1991-2951) **696**
Our Northland Diocese (USA ISSN 0030-6924) **7811**
Our P C Magazine *see* OurPC Magazine **2434**
Our Place (USA) **7603**
● Our Planet (KEN ISSN 1013-7394) **3458**
Our Platform *see* Manay Inder **7153**
Our Programme for the Countryside (GBR ISSN 0265-2129) **2623**
Our Quarterly (USA ISSN 1529-7071) **4377**
Our Region (NZL ISSN 1178-8429) **8745**
Our Review *see* Basiman Shelanu **4072**
Our Roots *see* Nos Racines **3777**
Our Roots *see* Nuestras Raices **3777**
Our Schools (CAN ISSN 0384-6636) **2894**
● Our Schools, Our Selves (CAN ISSN 0840-7339) **2894**
Our Special (USA ISSN 0030-6959) **4084**
Our State (USA ISSN 1092-0838) **3984**
Our Stories (USA ISSN 1053-296X) **4377**
Our Struggle/Nuestra Lucha (USA) **7213**
● Our Sunday Visitor (USA ISSN 0030-6967) **7811**
Our Sunday Visitor's Catholic Almanac (USA) **7811**
† ● Our Sunday Visitor's New Covenant (USA) **8979**
Our Texas (USA ISSN 1074-0732) **3984**
● Our Times Magazine (CAN ISSN 0822-6377) **4600**
Our Town Papakura *see* The Aucklander Manukau City **3916**
● Our Toxic Times (USA) **5764**
Our Union Voice (CAN ISSN 1718-8652) **4600**
Our Voice (CAN ISSN 1486-2018) **6273**
Our Voice (Cleveland) (USA) **4518**
Our Voices (DEU) **7770**
Our Wedding (Illawarra Edition) (AUS ISSN 1833-5322) **5560**
Our Wedding Illawarra *see* Our Wedding (Illawarra Edition) **5560**
Our Weekly (USA) **3556**
Our World *see* Olomeinu **7727**
● Our World (USA ISSN 1044-6699) **4377**
Our World 50 Plus (CAN) **5079**
● OurPC Magazine (USA ISSN 1544-6093) **2434**
● Ourtheory Magazine (USA) **5079**
Al-Ousbou' al-Arabi (LBN ISSN 0002-3965) **5232**
† Out! (NZL ISSN 0110-4454) **8979**
● Out (USA ISSN 1062-7928) **4377**
Out & About (USA ISSN 1066-7776) **8745**
Out & About with Kids (AUS ISSN 1832-3316) **2163**
▼ Out of Egypt Magazine (USA ISSN 1942-2598) **2662**
Out of Home Advertising Source *see* S R D S Out-of-Home Advertising Source **39**
Out Traveler (USA ISSN 1548-5684) **8746**
Out West (USA ISSN 0899-1413) **8746**
Out Your Backdoor (USA ISSN 1079-6304) **4981**
OUT&About with Kids *see* Out & About with Kids **2163**
● Outback (AUS ISSN 1441-1776) **3795**
Outback Travel Guide (Year) *see* Outback **3795**
Outback Utes Annual (AUS ISSN 1833-0916) **3795**
Outbound (CAN ISSN 0843-1566) **67**
Outburn (USA ISSN 1542-1309) **6603**
Outcomes in Community Care Practice (GBR ISSN 1365-9839) **8061**
Outcomes Management *see* Quality Management in Health Care **4110**
Outcomes Management for Nursing Practice *see* Quality Management in Health Care **4110**
● Outcry Magazine (USA) **7569**
Outdoor (DEU ISSN 0935-3356) **8326**
Outdoor Advertising (IND) **31**
Outdoor Advertising Expenditure Report (USA) **31**
Outdoor Alabama (USA ISSN 1085-6153) **2624**
Outdoor America (USA ISSN 0021-3314) **2624**
● Outdoor Australia (AUS ISSN 1324-5643) **8326**
Outdoor Business (USA) **8192**
Outdoor California (USA ISSN 0030-7025) **3459**
● Outdoor Canada (CAN ISSN 0315-0542) **8327**
Outdoor Crest (CAN ISSN 0700-9909) **8327**
Outdoor Delaware (USA ISSN 1068-3240) **2624**
Outdoor Edge (CAN ISSN 1186-8023) **8327**
Outdoor Education and Recreation Law Quarterly (USA ISSN 1545-0716) **4878**
Outdoor Enthusiast (GBR ISSN 1744-9898) **8327**
An Outdoor Family Guide to Yellowstone & Grand Teton National Parks (USA ISSN 1933-3013) **8746**
Outdoor Gears *see* Huwai Zhuangbei **8318**
Outdoor Guide (CAN) **8192**
● Outdoor Guides News (USA) **8327**
Outdoor Illinois (USA ISSN 1072-7175) **2624**
● Outdoor Indiana (USA ISSN 0030-7068) **2624**
▼ Outdoor Kids Club Magazine (USA ISSN 1941-2762) **2206**
● Outdoor Life (USA ISSN 0030-7076) **8327**
Outdoor Living *see* HomePlanners Outdoor Living **3736**
▼ Outdoor.markt (DEU ISSN 1865-1216) **8327**
Outdoor News (USA ISSN 0279-9065) **2624**
Outdoor News *see* Minnesota Outdoor News **8322**
Outdoor News Bulletin (USA ISSN 0030-7092) **2624**
Outdoor Oklahoma (USA ISSN 0030-7106) **2624**
Outdoor Photographer (USA ISSN 0890-5304) **6972**
● Outdoor Power Equipment (USA ISSN 0192-7558) **3746**
● Outdoor Power Equipment Official Guide (USA ISSN 0735-6676) **213**
Outdoor Power Guide (USA ISSN 1541-0013) **213**
Outdoor Report (CAN ISSN 0826-3019) **4981**
Outdoor Rooms (USA ISSN 1936-3176) **452**
Outdoor Showman (AUS ISSN 1440-3900) **8327**
● Outdoor Singles Network (USA) **7943**
● The Outdoor Source Book (Year) (GBR) **8327**
Outdoor - Special (NLD) **8327**
Outdoor Today *see* Outdoor Advertising **31**
Outdoor Trade and Industry (GBR) **8327**
▼ Outdoor Woman Magazine (USA ISSN 1936-3796) **8327**
Outdoor Writers Association of America. Directory (USA ISSN 0195-6124) **4581**
Outdoors Magazine (USA ISSN 1931-8294) **8327**
● Outdoors Network (USA) **8327**
● Outdoors OnLine (USA) **8327**
Outdoors Unlimited (USA ISSN 0030-7181) **2624**
Outdoors West (USA) **2624**
The Outdoorsmen (USA) **8327**
Outdoorsmen Newspaper *see* The Outdoorsmen **8327**
Outerbridge (USA ISSN 0739-4969) **5346**
Outerwear (USA ISSN 1066-3991) **2249**
● Outland Ezine (USA) **5446**
Outlander (USA) **6938**
Outlaw Biker (USA ISSN 0885-2030) **8265**
Outlet (ATG) **7161**
Outlet (GBR) **6603**
Outlets for Specialist New Books in the U K (GBR) **7569**
Outline of Japanese Tax (JPN ISSN 0078-7094) **1938**
An Outline of Statistical Development *see* Hong Kong Special Administrative Region of China. Census and Statistics Department. An Outline of Statistical Development **7308**
● An Outline of the History of Economic Thought (USA) **1157**
Outlines (DNK ISSN 1399-5510) **8124**
Outlook *see* Retail & Consumer Outlook **1165**
● Outlook (CAN ISSN 0834-0242) **4754**
● Outlook (IND) **3886**
Outlook *see* Chamber News (Tucson) **1399**
● Outlook (Auckland) (NZL ISSN 1177-052X) **4084**
Outlook (Colchester) (GBR ISSN 0969-1049) **7739**
● The Outlook (New York) (USA ISSN 0030-7246) **1643**
Outlook (Pembroke) (CAN ISSN 1499-3627) **5977**
Outlook (Seattle) (USA ISSN 0737-3732) **7534**
Outlook (Wake Forest) (USA ISSN 0030-7238) **7770**
Outlook (Year) Proceedings *see* Agricultural Outlook Forum. Proceedings **192**
▼ ● Outlook by the Bay (USA ISSN 1948-044X) **6994**
Outlook for Elastomers (Year) (GBR ISSN 1356-2584) **7826**
Outlook for Global Recovered Paper Markets (USA) **6735**
Outlook for International Travel to and from the United States (USA) **8746**
Outlook for the World Tissue Business (USA) **6735**
Outlook for U.S. Agricultural Trade *see* Situation & Outlook Report. Outlook for U.S. Agricultural Trade **206**
● Outlook Money (IND) **1373**
● ➤ Outlook on Agriculture (GBR ISSN 0030-7270) **145**
Outlook on Global Science, Technology and Economy *see* Quanqiu Keji Jingji Liaowang **7901**
● Outlook on Science Policy (GBR ISSN 0165-0262) **7896**
Outlook on the North *see* Kijk op het Noorden **1495**
Outlook Weekly *see* Liaowang **3826**
● Outlookpower Magazine (USA ISSN 1554-5679) **2595**
● Outlooks on Pest Management (Online) (GBR ISSN 1743-1034) **245**
● Outlooks on Pest Management (Print) (GBR ISSN 1743-1026) **245**
Outpatient Benchmarks (USA ISSN 1087-0350) **5691**
Outpatient Care Technology (USA) **4108**
Outpatient Department E M T A L A Handbook (Emergency Medical Treatment and Active Labor Act) (USA ISSN 1545-9136) **6070**
Outpost (USA) **7257**
Outpost (ZWE ISSN 0030-7289) **2662**
Outpost (Toronto) (CAN ISSN 1203-7125) **8746**
Outpost Exchange (USA ISSN 0748-8394) **6668**
Outposts Poetry Quarterly (GBR ISSN 0950-7264) **5428**
Output (NLD ISSN 1871-4730) **4421**
● Output (Online) (CAN) **3075**
Outre (Evanston) (USA ISSN 0895-0393) **6509**
➤ Outre-Mers. Revue d'Histoire (FRA ISSN 1631-0438) **4155**
● Outre - Terre (FRA ISSN 1636-3671) **7257**
● Outreach (CAN) **6032**
Outreach (USA ISSN 1537-2758) **7770**
Outreach (Athens) (USA ISSN 1935-0198) **2997**
Outreach (College Park) (USA) **7500**
Outreach (New York) (USA ISSN 1064-3087) **7705**
● Outreach (San Francisco) (USA) **5823**
Outrider (AUS ISSN 0813-5886) **5347**
Outrider (USA ISSN 0030-7319) **5038**
Outsell Now *see* OutsellNow **1157**
● OutsellNow (USA) **1157**
Outside (SWE ISSN 1652-4624) **8327**
● Outside (Santa Fe) (USA ISSN 0278-1433) **8327**
Outside Buyer's Guide (USA ISSN 1079-6258) **8327**
Outside Counsel (USA) **4878**
Outside Magazine's Urban Adventure: Seattle (USA ISSN 1930-9309) **8746**
Outside of School Hours Update *see* O O S H Update **8060**
Outside Plant Magazine (USA ISSN 0747-8763) **2370**
Outside Travel Guide *see* Outside Traveler **8327**
Outside Traveler (USA ISSN 1933-5628) **8327**
Outsider (GBR ISSN 0260-6402) **7213**
The Outsider (USA) **510**
Outsider Magazin (DNK ISSN 1901-3132) **3837**
Outsideren (DNK ISSN 1397-0577) **6172**
▼ Outside's Go (USA ISSN 1934-6271) **6296**
Outside's Guide to Family Vacations (USA ISSN 1092-6674) **8327**
● ➤ Outskirts (Online) (AUS ISSN 1445-0445) **5232**
Outsmart (USA) **4377**
Outsource Magazine (NLD ISSN 1872-0692) **1784**
● Outsourced Logistics (USA) **8507**
Outsourcing and Offshoring *see* Keys to Outsourcing and Offshoring **4934**
Outsourcing & Offshoring Industry Almanac *see* Plunkett's Outsourcing & Offshoring Industry Almanac **1901**
● Outsourcing Center (USA) **2434**
The Outsourcing Revolution *see* Keys to Outsourcing and Offshoring **4934**
Outsourcing Transactions (CAN ISSN 1717-998X) **4878**
Outspokin' (USA) **8266**
Outstanding Dissertations in Linguistics (USA) **5158**

Title

10716 OUTSTANDING SCIENCE TRADE BOOKS FOR CHILDREN ULRICH'S PERIODICALS

Outstanding Science Trade Books for Children *see* Outstanding Science Trade Books for Students K-12 **2174**
Outstanding Science Trade Books for Students K-12 (USA) **2174**
• Outstate Business (USA ISSN 1064-3621) **1505**
➤ Outubro (BRA ISSN 1516-6333) **7161**
• OutWord Online (USA ISSN 1545-4681) **4053**
Outwords (CAN) **7213**
OutYouth (USA ISSN 1099-2065) **4377**
Ouzhou/Europe *see* Ouzhou Yanjiu **7990**
• Ouzhou Guoji Pinglun/European Journal of International Review (TWN) **7257**
• Ouzhou Yanjiu/Chinese Journal of European Studies (CHN) **7990**
Ovadan (TKM) **4468**
Ovako Steel A B. Technical Report (SWE ISSN 0284-3366) **6328**
▼ • Ovarian Diseases (NLD ISSN 1873-894X) **6001**
Over 40 (USA) **6296**
Over-40s Consumer Market Assessment *see* Key Note Market Assessment. Over-40s Consumer **1892**
Over 50 (USA) **6296**
† Over Broen (DNK ISSN 0904-3853) **8979**
Over Multatuli (NLD ISSN 0166-2058) **5347**
Over My Dead Body! (USA ISSN 1067-2540) **5414**
Over Onderwijs (The Hague) (NLD ISSN 1389-0638) **2894**
Over Soe og Land *see* Refleks **8984**
Over Taal (BEL ISSN 1373-5470) **5158**
• Over the Airwaves (USA ISSN 1937-3848) **67**
Over the Back Fence (USA ISSN 1546-0630) **3984**
Over the Counter (GBR ISSN 0957-7831) **6865**
Over the Counter Bulletin *see* O T C Bulletin **6864**
Over the Counter Growth Stock Watch *see* O T C Growth Stock Watch **1643**
Over the Counter LatinA *see* O T C LatinA **6865**
Over the Counter News and Market Report *see* O T C News and Market Report **6865**
Over-The-Counter Stock Review *see* O T C Stock Review **1643**
Over The Counter Update *see* O T C Update **6865**
Over the Counter Yearbook *see* O T C Yearbook **6865**
Over the Edge (CAN) **2295**
Over the Road (USA) **8674**
Over.Werk (BEL ISSN 1379-7034) **1701**
Over Zorg Gesproken *see* SeniorProof **7541**
Overbacher Bruecke (DEU) **2206**
Overcrowded Times (USA ISSN 1077-8209) **2662**
Overdrive (IND) **8597**
• Overdrive (USA ISSN 0030-7394) **8674**
• Overdrive Motoring.com (ZAF ISSN 1991-4962) **8597**
Overdrive Truck Stop and Travel Guide (USA) **8674**
Overeaters Anonymous Lifeline *see* O A Lifeline **6994**
• Overenskomster med Fremmede Stater (NOR ISSN 1501-5734) **4937**
Overflate Teknikk (NOR ISSN 0801-9606) **6328**
Overhaul and Maintenance *see* Overhaul & Maintenance **67**
• Overhaul & Maintenance (USA ISSN 1086-0983) **67**
Overheid en Overleg *see* O R in de Overheid **8978**
Overheid en Personeel *see* Tijdschrift Overheid en Personeel **4796**
Overheid Facilitair *see* Weekblad Facilitair & Gebouwbeheer **1801**
Overheidsdocumentatie *see* O D **5037**
Overheidsmanagement (NLD ISSN 0928-8503) **1373**
OverHolland (NLD ISSN 1574-3160) **452**
Overholser Family Association. Bulletin (USA ISSN 0742-8472) **3778**
Overijssels Erfgoed (NLD ISSN 1574-5600) **410**
• Overland (AUS ISSN 0030-7416) **5232**
Overland (IND) **3886**
Overland Express *see* Overland **5232**
Overland Journal (Indepedence) (USA ISSN 0738-1093) **4307**
▼ Overland Journal (Prescott) (USA) **8327**
➤ Overland Review (USA) **3621**
Overlander 4WD Touring Guide (AUS ISSN 1030-9896) **8597**
• Overlook View (USA) **4109**
Overpriced Stock Service (USA) **1643**
Overseas (GBR ISSN 0030-7424) **8746**
Overseas Academic Opportunities (USA ISSN 0889-8839) **3014**
Overseas Advertising (GBR ISSN 0048-251X) **31**
Overseas Aid News *see* Uniting World **7691**
Overseas Books (GBR ISSN 0048-2528) **7569**
Overseas Business Contacts (IND) **1579**
Overseas Campus *see* Haiwai Xiaoyuan **7646**
Overseas Chinese News of Fujian *see* Fujian Qiao Bao **3534**
Overseas Chinese News of Hainan *see* Hainan Qiaobao **3536**
Overseas Conference Visitors to the U K (Year) (GBR) **8780**
Overseas Development Council. Annual Report (USA ISSN 0092-7643) **1602**
Overseas Development Group. Humanitarian Practice Network Papers (GBR) **7161**
Overseas Development Institute. Annual Report (GBR ISSN 0260-860X) **1602**
• Overseas Development Institute. Briefing Paper (GBR ISSN 0140-8682) **1602**
Overseas Development Institute Poverty Briefings *see* O D I Poverty Briefings **1602**
Overseas Diplomat (GBR ISSN 1477-1969) **7257**
Overseas Directories, Who's Who, Press Guides, Year Books and Overseas Periodical Subscriptions (GBR ISSN 0078-7124) **633**
Overseas English *see* Haiwai Yingyu **5124**
Overseas Exporters (CAN) **1579**
Overseas Geology and Mineral Resources *see* Great Britain. Natural Environment Research Council. British Geological Survey. Overseas Geology and Mineral Resources **2745**
Overseas Jobs Express (GBR ISSN 0966-7660) **1870**
Overseas Newspapers and Periodicals (GBR ISSN 0078-7159) **7569**
Overseas Non-scheduled Flight Clearances Guide (GBR) **8549**
Overseas Outlook (Large Print Edition) (USA ISSN 0161-1828) **5038**
Overseas Press and Media Association Overseas Media Guide *see* O P M A Overseas Media Guide **2022**
Overseas Press Club Bulletin (USA ISSN 0738-7202) **4581**
Overseas Road Note (GBR ISSN 0951-8797) **8633**
Overseas Summer Jobs *see* Directory of Overseas Summer Jobs **1988**
• Overseas Trade (GBR ISSN 0268-1684) **1580**
Overseas Trade (Plymouth) *see* Montserrat. Statistics Office. Overseas Trade Report **2017**
Overseas Trade Directories (GBR) **2023**
Overseas Trade Fair - Exhibition Visitors to the U K (Year) (GBR) **8780**
Overseas Trade Indexes (Prices) *see* New Zealand. Statistics New Zealand. Overseas Trade in Services Price Index **1579**
Overseas Trade Price Indexes - Services *see* New Zealand. Statistics New Zealand. Overseas Trade in Services Price Index **1579**
Overseas Trade Statistics *see* Guide to the Classification of Overseas Trade Statistics **1236**
Overseas Trade Statistics of the United Kingdom (Annual Revision) *see* Overseas Trade Statistics. United Kingdom Trade with the European Community and the World **1257**
Overseas Trade Statistics of the United Kingdom (Quarterly Revision) *see* Business Monitor: Overseas Trade Statistics of the United Kingdom (Quarterly Revision) **1216**
Overseas Trade Statistics. United Kingdom Trade with the European Community and the World (GBR ISSN 1465-671X) **1257**
Overseas Transactions *see* Business Monitor: Overseas Direct Investment **1216**
Oversight (USA) **5232**
• Oversigt over Landsforsoegene (DNK ISSN 0900-5293) **245**
• Oversigt over Norske Fag- og Forskningsbibliotek (Online Edition) (NOR) **5038**
Overspray (USA) **5347**
Overthrow (USA ISSN 0886-9030) **5232**
OverTime (USA ISSN 1553-1910) **8192**
OverTime Magazine *see* OverTime **8192**
Overtone Series (USA) **5232**
Overture (CAN) **6603**
Overture (Baltimore) (USA ISSN 0885-3347) **6603**
Overture (Los Angeles) (USA ISSN 0030-7556) **6603**
Overture (New York) (USA) **8475**
Overtures (GBR) **8475**
Overview (CAN ISSN 0700-3617) **1505**
Overview (Chicago) (USA ISSN 0030-7564) **7811**
Overview of Disaster Prevention *see* Fangzai Bolan **7517**
• Overview of Korea's Industries. Promising Investment Opportunities (KOR) **1580**
Overview of the F A A Engineering & Development Programs (U.S. Federal Aviation Administration) (USA ISSN 0092-3591) **67**
Overzicht van de Werkgelegenheid op de Luchthaven Schiphol (NLD ISSN 1872-4167) **1701**
The Ovid Observer (USA) **7580**
Ovidius University. Annals. Series Physical Education and Sport *see* Universitatea "Ovidius" Constanta. Analele. Serie Educatie Fizica si Sport **8214**
• Ovis (ESP ISSN 1130-4863) **295**
• Ovi's World of the Bizarre (USA) **3984**
• ovivo (DEU) **3855**
Ovodai Jogfutar (HUN ISSN 1787-3517) **3029**
Ovtsy, Kozy, Sherstyanoe Delo (RUS) **295**
Ovulation Method Research and Reference Centre of Australia. Bulletin (AUS ISSN 1323-675X) **973**
• Owen H. Wangensteen Surgical Forum (USA) **6255**
Owen Wister Review (USA ISSN 1069-2215) **5347**
• Owl (CAN ISSN 0382-6627) **2206**
Owl Observer *see* O W L Observer **4052**
➤ Owl of Minerva (USA ISSN 0030-7580) **6938**
▼ Own (NZL ISSN 1177-7265) **7603**
Own Brands *see* Key Note Market Report: Own Brands **1895**
• Owner Builder Magazine (AUS ISSN 0728-7275) **1028**
Owner - Driver (AUS ISSN 1321-6279) **8674**
Owner Operator *see* Overdrive **8674**
• Owner Operator / Company Driver (USA) **8674**
† Owners Own (AUS ISSN 1449-6526) **8979**
Owoce Warzywa Kwiaty (POL ISSN 0137-673X) **3746**
Ox Fanzine (DEU) **6603**
Oxbow Book News (GBR ISSN 0269-2147) **7569**
Oxbow Lecture Series (GBR) **410**
• Oxbridge Directory of Newsletters (USA ISSN 0163-7010) **633**
The Oxcart (USA ISSN 0737-0954) **6897**
Oxebo! (FRA ISSN 1281-2072) **2206**
Oxfam Canada. Annual Report (CAN ISSN 1494-0825) **8061**
• Oxfam Exchange (USA) **1602**
Oxfam GB (GBR ISSN 0965-433X) **1603**
• Oxfam International. Policy Papers (GBR) **1603**
• Oxfam News (AUS) **1603**
Oxfam News (GBR ISSN 0262-3803) **1603**
Oxford (GBR ISSN 0030-7645) **5232**
The Oxford American (USA ISSN 1074-4525) **5347**
Oxford Applied Mathematics and Computing Series (GBR ISSN 0953-3044) **5523**
Oxford Archaeological Guides (GBR ISSN 1754-7857) **410**
• ➤ Oxford Art Journal (GBR ISSN 0142-6540) **510**
➤ Oxford Biogeography Series (GBR ISSN 1363-0946) **696**
• ➤ Oxford Bulletin of Economics and Statistics (GBR ISSN 0305-9049) **1157**
Oxford Business Directory *see* Commerce Business Directories. Oxford **1980**
Oxford Chemistry Primers (GBR ISSN 1367-109X) **2075**
† Oxford Chemistry Series (GBR ISSN 0302-4199) **8979**
Oxford Commentaries on the G A T T / W T O Agreements (General Agreement on Tariffs and Trade / World Trade Organization) (GBR ISSN 1754-5455) **1580**
• ➤ Oxford Development Studies (GBR ISSN 1360-0818) **1603**
The Oxford Diocesan Year Book (GBR) **7668**
Oxford Down Sheep Breeder's Association Magazine (GBR) **295**
• ➤ Oxford Economic Papers (GBR ISSN 0030-7653) **1158**
Oxford Editions of Cuneiform Texts (GBR ISSN 0309-0701) **410**
Oxford Energy Forum (GBR ISSN 0959-7727) **3144**
Oxford Engineering Science Series (GBR ISSN 0953-3222) **3214**
Oxford English Monographs (GBR) **5347**
Oxford English Texts (GBR) **5347**
Oxford Finance Series (GBR) **1373**
Oxford Forestry Institute Occasional Papers *see* O F I Occasional Papers **3699**
• ➤ Oxford German Studies (GBR ISSN 0078-7191) **5347**
Oxford Graduate Texts in Mathematics (GBR) **5523**
Oxford Handbooks in Emergency Medicine (GBR ISSN 1363-0938) **6070**
Oxford Hispanic Studies (GBR) **3556**
Oxford Historical Monographs (GBR) **4252**
Oxford India Paperbacks (GBR) **559**
Oxford Institute for Energy Studies Papers. Electricity *see* O I E S Papers. Electricity **3160**
Oxford Institute for Energy Studies Papers. Energy & the Environment *see* O I E S Papers. Energy & the Environment **3143**
Oxford Institute for Energy Studies Papers. Energy Economics *see* O I E S Papers. Energy Economics **3143**
Oxford Institute for Energy Studies Papers. Finance *see* O I E S Papers. Finance **1372**
Oxford Institute for Energy Studies Papers. Natural Gas *see* O I E S Papers. Natural Gas **6782**
Oxford Institute for Energy Studies Papers. World Petroleum Market *see* O I E S Papers. World Petroleum Market **6782**
Oxford Institute of European and Comparative Law. Studies (GBR) **4754**
Oxford Institute of Retail Management. Research Papers. Retail Development, Planning and Policy (GBR) **1784**
Oxford Introduction to Language Study (GBR ISSN 1754-7865) **5158**
• ➤ Oxford Journal of Archaeology (GBR ISSN 0262-5253) **410**
• ➤ Oxford Journal of Legal Studies (GBR ISSN 0143-6503) **4754**
Oxford Lecture Series in Mathematics and Its Applications (GBR) **5523**
• ➤ Oxford Literary Review (GBR ISSN 0305-1498) **5347**
Oxford Magazine (USA) **5347**
➤ Oxford Mathematical Monographs (GBR ISSN 0964-9174) **5523**
Oxford Medical School Gazette *see* Oxford University Medical School Gazette **5691**
Oxford Medieval Texts (GBR) **5347**
Oxford Mission News (GBR) **7668**
Oxford Modern Languages and Literature Monographs (GBR) **5347**
Oxford Monographs on Classical Archaeology (GBR) **410**
➤ Oxford Monographs on Geology and Geophysics (GBR ISSN 0952-7028) **2761**
➤ Oxford Monographs on Medical Genetics (GBR ISSN 1352-240X) **877**
Oxford Monographs on Music (GBR) **6603**
Oxford Oriental Institute Monographs (GBR) **559**
Oxford Ornithology Series (GBR ISSN 1363-3201) **913**
Oxford Philosophical Monographs (GBR ISSN 1754-5463) **6938**
• Oxford Poetry (GBR ISSN 1465-6213) **5428**
Oxford Policy Institute Issues Notes *see* O P I Issues Notes **8060**
Oxford Policy Institute Issues Notes *see* O P I Issues Notes **8060**
Oxford Policy Institute Policy Briefs *see* O P I Policy Briefs **8060**
† Oxford Psychiatry Series (GBR ISSN 1362-9980) **8979**
Oxford Readings in Feminism (GBR) **8902**
• ➤ Oxford Review of Economic Policy (GBR ISSN 0266-903X) **1158**
• ➤ Oxford Review of Education (GBR ISSN 0305-4985) **2894**
Oxford Series in Ecology and Evolution (GBR) **696**
Oxford Series on Neutron Scattering in Condensed Matter (GBR ISSN 0956-9545) **7070**
Oxford Series on Synchrotron Radiation (GBR) **7070**
Oxford Statistical Science Series (GBR ISSN 0952-9942) **8393**
➤ Oxford Studies in Ancient Philosophy (GBR ISSN 0265-7651) **6938**
Oxford Studies in Anthropological Linguistics (GBR) **351**
➤ Oxford Studies in Comparative Education (GBR ISSN 0961-2149) **2894**
Oxford Studies in Early Modern Philosophy (GBR ISSN 1754-7873) **6938**
Oxford Studies in Lexicography and Lexicology (GBR) **5159**
Oxford Studies in Sociolinguistics (USA) **8124**
Oxford Studies of Composers (GBR ISSN 0078-7264) **6603**
† Oxford Surveys in Evolutionary Biology (GBR ISSN 0265-072X) **8979**
Oxford Television Studies (GBR) **2387**
Oxford Texts in Applied and Engineering Mathematics (GBR) **3214**
Oxford Theatre Texts (GBR ISSN 0141-1152) **8475**
Oxford Theological Monographs (GBR ISSN 0078-7272) **7668**
• Oxford Today (GBR ISSN 0954-1306) **2295**
Oxford Tracer (CAN) **3778**
• ➤ Oxford University Commonwealth Law Journal (GBR ISSN 1472-9342) **4754**
• ➤ Oxford University History Society. Journal (GBR ISSN 1742-917X) **4252**
Oxford University Medical School Gazette (GBR) **5691**
Oxford University Museum Publications (GBR ISSN 0962-5305) **7896**
➤ Oxford University. School of Archaeology. Monograph (GBR) **410**
Oxford University. Working Papers in Linguistics, Philology & Phoenetics (GBR ISSN 1473-9356) **5159**
Oxford-Warburg Studies (GBR ISSN 1754-7881) **4468**
• ➤ The Oxfordian (USA ISSN 1521-3641) **5428**
Oxfordshire Commercial & Industrial Directory (GBR) **1408**
The Oxfordshire Family Historian (GBR ISSN 0309-2275) **3778**
Oxfordshire Life (GBR) **3869**
Oxfordshire Local History (GBR ISSN 0260-7565) **4252**
Oxfordshire Museums. Occasional Paper (GBR ISSN 0962-5313) **7896**
Oxfordshire Record Society (GBR) **4252**
➤ Oxidation Communications (BGR ISSN 0209-4541) **2128**
• ➤ Oxidation of Metals (USA ISSN 0030-770X) **2139**
▼ • ➤ Oxidative Medicine and Cellular Longevity (USA ISSN 1942-0900) **5691**
• Oxmox (DEU) **3855**
Oxoniensia (GBR ISSN 0308-5562) **410**
• Oxonomics (GBR ISSN 1752-5195) **1158**
Oxy-Fuel News *see* Ethanol & Biodiesel News **3134**
OxyChem Newsbriefs (USA) **7095**
Oxygen (CAN ISSN 1095-7073) **8847**
Oxygen (USA ISSN 1056-2613) **5347**
• Oxygene Familles et Sante Mentale (CAN ISSN 1914-8291) **6172**
• Oxyjen Magazine (MTQ ISSN 1768-4455) **3907**
• Oxymag (FRA ISSN 0990-1310) **5773**
Oxymura (ESP ISSN 0212-9221) **6393**
Oye! *see* Que Tal **5164**
Oye (USA) **3557**
Oyen Echo (CAN) **3815**
Oyez (CAN ISSN 0475-1671) **4754**
Oyez Review (USA ISSN 1933-6705) **5347**
Oyfn Shvel (USA ISSN 1058-1111) **5159**
Oyo Butsuri *see* Oyo Buturi **7029**
Oyo Butsuri Gakkai Gakujutsu Koenkai ko en Yokoshu/Japan Society of Applied Physics. Autumn Meeting. Extended Abstracts (JPN) **7029**
Oyo Buturi/Journal of Applied Physics (JPN ISSN 0369-8009) **7029**
Oyo Chishitsu/Applied Geology (JPN ISSN 0286-7737) **2761**
Oyo Chishitsu Nenpo/Oyo Technical Report (JPN ISSN 0912-6325) **2761**
Oyo Denshi Bussei Bunkakai Kenkyu Hokoku/Japan Society of Applied Physics. Solid State Physics and Application Division. Bulletin (JPN) **7029**
Oyo Hoshasen Kagaku Shinpojumu Koen Yoshishu/Proceedings of Applied Radiation Chemistry Symposium (JPN) **2139**

Title

10718 P C MAGAZINE (ISRAELI EDITION) ULRICH'S PERIODICALS

• P C Magazine (Israeli Edition) (ISR ISSN 0792-9285) 2573
• P C Magazine (Online) (USA) 2434
P C Magazine (Portuguese Edition) (PRT ISSN 0871-6625) 2580
† • P C Magazine (Print) (USA ISSN 0888-8507) 8979
P C Magazine (Russian Edition) (RUS ISSN 0869-4257) 2580
P C Magazine Australia *see* Technology & Business 8992
P C Magazine Belgie (BEL ISSN 1377-0586) 2434
P C Magazine. Edicion Argentina *see* P C Magazine 2434
P C Magazine en Espanol *see* P C Magazine (Print) 8979
P C Magazine Latin America (USA) 2503
• P C Magazine Romania (ROM ISSN 1454-220X) 2434
P C Magazine Turkiye (TUR ISSN 1300-8064) 2434
P C Management (GBR ISSN 0269-0640) 1420
P C Mania *see* Personal Computer & Internet 2582
† P C Market (ITA ISSN 1126-5132) 8979
P C Marketplace (GBR ISSN 0969-1839) 2573
P C Markt (AUT) 2580
P C Mart (GBR ISSN 0968-607X) 2434
P C Master (BRA ISSN 1414-3828) 2580
P C Master (GRC ISSN 1105-5472) 2580
P C Max (Personal Computer) (BRA ISSN 1677-4493) 2580
P C Max. Hors-Serie (FRA ISSN 1290-3159) 2580
P C Media (MEX) 2580
P C Mix (Personal Computer) (BRA ISSN 1808-9682) 2489
P C Mundo Especial (Personal Computer) (BRA ISSN 1678-2712) 2580
P C N Network News *see* N D T News 3355
P C N Network News *see* Insight (Northampton) 3345
P C N Network News *see* NewsLink 3355
P C N Y State Report (Police Conference of New York, Inc.) (USA) 2662
• P C Net (TUR ISSN 1301-4773) 2434
• P C NetGuide (USA) 2503
P C NetGuide On-Line *see* P C NetGuide 2503
• P C News (AUT ISSN 1022-1611) 2434
P C News Sedu *see* P C News 2434
• P C News Weekly (USA) 2434
• P C O S Today Magazine (Polycystic Ovarian Syndrome) (USA ISSN 1933-6187) 8847
P C Open (ITA ISSN 1123-7600) 2580
P C Oplossingen (NLD ISSN 1871-1308) 2580
P C Opportunities (USA) 2580
P C P *see* Plant and Cell Physiology 835
P C P A *see* Popular Culture and Politics in Asia Pacific 7172
P C P C I Membership Directory and Product Listing (Power Conversion Products Council International) (USA) 3327
P C Photo (ITA ISSN 1594-9184) 6972
P C Photo *see* Digital Photo 6979
P C Piu Facile Mese (Personal Computer) (ITA ISSN 1591-7010) 2580
• P C Planet (DNK ISSN 1600-9185) 2434
• P C Plus (GBR ISSN 0952-2565) 2580
P C Plus (Haarlem) (Personal Computer) (NLD ISSN 1570-4173) 2580
P C PowerPlay (AUS ISSN 1326-5644) 2479
† P C PowerPlay (Personal Computer) (DEU) 8979
† P C Pratico Magazine (ITA ISSN 1826-5375) 8979
• P C Praxis (Personal Computer) (DEU ISSN 0940-6743) 2580
P C Praxis MyJob *see* MyJob 8975
P C Praxis Open Source (Personal Computer) (DEU) 2595
P C Praxis Selber Planen *see* Selber Planen 8987
• P C Pro (GBR ISSN 1355-4603) 2580
P C Professionale (ITA ISSN 1121-3337) 2580
• P C Quest (IND ISSN 0971-216X) 2580
P C R *see* Production and Casting Report 6510
P C R (Psychological Cinema Register) (USA ISSN 0272-0582) 7417
P C Regional (COL) 2580
P C Report (ZAF) 2580
• P C Retail (GBR ISSN 1742-8440) 2493
• P C Review (London) (GBR ISSN 0964-4547) 2573
• P C Revue (Personal Computer) (SVK ISSN 1335-0226) 2580
P C S Advisor (Progressive Computer Software) (USA) 2580
P C S Focus (Personal Communications Service) (GBR ISSN 1462-0820) 2335
P C S I R Annual Report *see* Pakistan Council of Scientific and Industrial Research. Annual Report 7897
P C S View *see* View (London) 7476
P C S W Annual Report (Permanent Commission on the Status of Women) (USA) 8879
P C Security (Personal Computer) (DEU) 2515
• P C Semanal (MEX) 2580
P C Shareware *see* P C Format 2579
† P C Soluzioni (ITA ISSN 1720-7649) 8979
• P C Space (SVK ISSN 1335-8049) 2434
P C Support Expert (USA ISSN 1081-7026) 2580
P C T *see* Pest Control Technology 3252
P C T A Action *see* Action (Clearwater) 3050
P C T E Journal of Business Management (Punjab College of Technical Education) (IND ISSN 0973-4066) 1784
P C T E Journal of Computer Sciences (Punjab College of Technical Education) (IND ISSN 0973-4058) 2434
• P C T Gazette (Bilingual Edition) (Patent Cooperation Treaty) (CHE ISSN 1020-6264) 6755
P C T Newsletter (Patent Cooperation Treaty) (CHE ISSN 1020-072X) 6755
P.C. Talk (CAN) 7161
† P C Team (FRA ISSN 1264-935X) 8979
• P C Tip (Personal Computer) (CHE ISSN 1422-4704) 2580
P C Today (Personal Computer) (ESP) 2580
P C Today (GBR ISSN 0960-0124) 2581
• P C Today (USA ISSN 1040-6484) 2581
P C Tools (GBR) 2434
P C T's Ultimate Industry Resource Book (Pest Control Technology) (USA) 2023
P C Ultra (ITA ISSN 1127-6916) 2479
P C und Co (Personal Computer) (AUT) 7580
P C und Industrie (Personal Computer) (DEU ISSN 1614-743X) 1420
• P C Update (AUS ISSN 1031-8208) 2581
P C Upgrade *see* Computer Upgrade 2413
P C Upgrade's Learning Series *see* Learning Series 2431
P C User *see* Australian P C User 2574
P C Utilities (FRA ISSN 1628-3376) 2581
P C Utilities (GBR ISSN 1469-042X) 2434
• P C Video (Personal Computer) (DEU ISSN 1430-5704) 2402
P C Videolog (USA) 2352
P C W Plus (GBR ISSN 0964-8836) 2509
• P C Week (ESP ISSN 1136-4769) 2581
P C Week (GBR ISSN 0269-3011) 2581
• P C Week (Russian Edition) (RUS ISSN 1560-6929) 2581
• P C Welt (Personal Computer) (DEU ISSN 0175-0496) 2581
P C Welt Linux (Personal Computer) (DEU ISSN 1860-7926) 2595
† P C Windows (ITA) 8979
• P C Works - News (USA) 2581
† • P C World (Personal Computer) (DNK ISSN 1600-2822) 8979
P C World (EST ISSN 1736-2474) 2581
• P C World (Personal Computer) (USA ISSN 0737-8939) 2581
• P C World (Online) (Personal Computer) (CZE ISSN 1212-6829) 2581
† • P C World (Print) (Personal Computer) (CZE ISSN 1210-1079) 8979
P C World Argentina (ARG ISSN 0328-4255) 2503
P C World Bangladesh (Personal Computer) (BGD) 2581
• P C World Belarus (BLR) 2581
P C World Belgium (Personal Computer) (BEL ISSN 1373-668X) 2581
• P C World Brazil (Personal Computer) (BRA ISSN 1413-9367) 2581
P C World Bulgaria (Personal Computer) (BGR ISSN 1311-3127) 2581
P C World Centro America (CRI) 2503
• P C World Chile (CHL) 2503
P C World China *see* Weidiannao Shijie 2441
P C World Colombia (COL ISSN 0122-3135) 2503
P C World Diannao Yingyong *see* @live 3089
P C World East Africa (KEN) 2581
P C World Ecuador (ECU) 2503
• P C World Espana (ESP ISSN 0213-1307) 2581
P C World Hong Kong (HKG ISSN 1023-4942) 2581
• P C World Hungary (HUN ISSN 1215-5055) 2581
P C World India (IND) 2503
P C World Island *see* Tolvuheimur 2583
• P C World Italia (ITA ISSN 1120-8066) 2581
• P C World Japan/Gekkan Pishi Warudo Japan (JPN ISSN 1344-4751) 2581
• P C World Komputer (POL ISSN 1232-3004) 2581
P C World Komputer Extra *see* P C World Komputer 2581
P C World Komputer na Gwiazdke *see* P C World Komputer 2581
P C World Komputer Special *see* P C World Komputer 2581
P C World Korea (KOR) 2581
P C World Latvia *see* e-Pasaule 2417
P C World Lithuania *see* Kompiuterija 2430
• P C World Malaysia (MYS ISSN 1511-404X) 2581
• P C World Malta (MLT) 2581
• P C World Mexico (MEX ISSN 0188-932X) 2503
P C World Myanmar (MMR) 2493
• P C World New Zealand (NZL ISSN 0114-7285) 2582
• P C World Norge (NOR ISSN 0801-5236) 2493
P C World Norge Ekspress *see* P C World Norge Ekstra 2493
• P C World Norge Ekstra (NOR ISSN 1503-8408) 2493
P C World Norge ProduktGuide (NOR) 2582
P C World Pakistan (PAK) 2582
• P C World Panama (Personal Computer) (PAN) 2582
P C World Peru (Personal Computer) (PER) 2503
• P C World Philippines (PHL ISSN 0118-1882) 2582
• P C World Portugal (PRT ISSN 0870-161X) 2434
P C World Professional (Personal Computer) (PER) 2503
• P C World Romania (Personal Computer) (ROM) 2582
P C World Russia *see* Mir P K 2432
P C World Security *see* Security World 2516
• P C World Singapore (SGP) 2582
P C World Turkey (TUR ISSN 1300-6150) 2582
P C World Ukraine (UKR) 2582
P C World Venezuela (VEN) 2503
P C World Vietnam (VNM) 2582
P C World West Africa (NGA) 2582
• P C World Zimbabwe (ZWE) 2582
P C Year Book. Hardware Volume (GBR) 2573
P C Year Book. Software Volume (GBR) 2573
• P C Zone (GBR ISSN 0967-8220) 2480
A P Computer Science *see* Barron's A P Computer Science. Levels A and AB 2408
P Cs for Dummies Quick Reference (Personal Computer) (USA ISSN 1930-8523) 2582
P D *see* Professional Distributor 3393
P D A & Smartphones Magazine (Personal Digital Assistant) (FRA ISSN 1775-0733) 2434
P D A Essentials *see* P D A Essentials and G P S Advisor 2582
P D A Essentials and G P S Advisor (GBR ISSN 1754-2693) 2582
P D A et Smartphones Magazine *see* P D A & Smartphones Magazine 2434
P D A Journal of G M P and Validation in Japan *see* Nihon P D A Gakujutsushi GMP to Barideshon 6864
• ➤ P D A Journal of Pharmaceutical Science and Technology (Parenteral Drug Association) (USA ISSN 1079-7440) 6866
P D A Letter (Parenteral Drug Association) (USA) 6866
P D A Magazine *see* P D A & Smartphones Magazine 2434
P D A Technical Reports (Parenteral Drug Association) (USA) 6866
P D A Today (Pennsylvania Department of Agriculture) (USA) 145
P D A User (Personal Digital Assistant) (HKG ISSN 1729-8156) 2582
P D & D *see* Product Design and Development 3216
P D B *see* Pontoon & Deck Boat 8280
• P D C (Participatory Design Conference) (USA ISSN 2150-5896) 2434
P D C N Advocate *see* P D C N Live! 8061
• P D C N Live! (Physical Disability Council of New South Wales) (AUS ISSN 1446-9154) 8061
P D. European Journal of Pediatric Dermatology (English Edition) *see* European Journal of Pediatric Dermatology (English Edition) 5876
P D. European Journal of Pediatric Dermatology (Italian Edition) *see* European Journal of Pediatric Dermatology (Italian Edition) 5876
P D F Newsletter (Parkinson's Disease Foundation) (USA) 6172
P.D. Gune Memorial Lecture Series (IND) 5159
P D N *see* Photo District News 6973
• P D N - PIX (Photo District News) (USA) 6972
P D R *see* Physicians' Desk Reference 5696
P D R Companion Guide *see* P D R Guide to Drug Interactions, Side Effects, and Indications 5691
P D R Drug Guide for Mental Health Professionals (Physicians' Desk Reference) (USA ISSN 1546-3443) 6172
• P D R Electronic Library on CD-ROM (Physicians' Desk Reference) (USA ISSN 1094-4095) 5691
• P D R Family Guide to Prescription Drugs (Physicians' Desk Reference) (USA ISSN 1523-9411) 6866
P D R for Herbal Medicines (Physicians' Desk Reference) (USA ISSN 1099-9566) 313
P D R for Nonprescription Drugs and Dietary Supplements *see* P D R for Nonprescription Drugs, Dietary Supplements, and Herbs 5691
• P D R for Nonprescription Drugs, Dietary Supplements, and Herbs (USA ISSN 1943-6955) 5691
P D R for Nutritional Supplements (Physicians' Desk Reference) (USA ISSN 1534-3642) 6668
P D R Guide to Biological and Chemical Warfare Response (Physicians' Desk Reference) (USA ISSN 1540-6156) 6866
P D R Guide to Drug Interactions, Side Effects, and Indications (Physicians' Desk Reference) (USA ISSN 1933-706X) 5691
† P D R Monthly Prescribing Guide (Physicians' Desk Reference) (USA ISSN 1537-9892) 8979
P D R Nurse's Drug Handbook *see* Delmar Nurse's Drug Handbook 5957
P D R Ophthalmic Medicines *see* Physicians' Desk Reference for Ophthalmic Medicines 6050
P D R Pharmacopoeia Pocket Dosing Guide (Physician's Desk Reference) (USA ISSN 1558-5107) 5692
P D S Report (Parallel and Distributed Systems) (NLD ISSN 1387-2109) 5524
P D T R T *see* Personality Disorders 7390
P D T U Revue Annuelle *see* Programme de Demonstration en Transport Urbain. Revue Annuelle 8508
P D U F A Financial Reports *see* U.S. Department of Health and Human Services. Food and Drug Administration. Prescription Drug User Fee Act. Financial Report to Congress 7472
† P D X Magazine (USA) 8979
• P E (Professional Engineer) (USA ISSN 1930-5745) 3214
P E A *see* Power Equipment Australasia 213
P E & R S *see* Photogrammetric Engineering and Remote Sensing 4023
• P E & Sport Today (Physical Education) (GBR ISSN 1470-6121) 3075
P E B *see* T E S O L Placement E-Bulletin 5185
P E C L *see* Principles of European Contract Law 4938
P E D C Newsletter (Plymouth Engineering Design Centre) (GBR) 2473
P E D Kenkyukai/Research Group of Passive Electrochemical Devices. Proceedings (JPN) 2114
P E D S *see* Protein Engineering Design and Selection 743
P E D S *see* Protein Engineering Design and Selection (Online) 743
P E E R Reports (Pacific Earthquake Engineering Center) (USA) 3280
The P E E R Review (Pacific Earthquake Engineering Center) (USA) 2787
P E F O *see* Australia. Department of the Treasury. Pre-election Economic and Fiscal Outlook 1211
The P E File (Physical Education) (GBR ISSN 1748-6327) 3075
The P E G G (Professional Engineer, Geologist, Geophysicist) (CAN ISSN 0823-1745) 3214
P E I *see* Produits Equipements Industriels 3356
P E I *see* Photo Electronic Imaging 6973
P E I Asia (Private Equity International) (GBR ISSN 1751-2948) 1373
P E I E Mirror/Mir'at al-Manatiq al-Sina'iyyat (Public Establishment for Industrial Estates) (OMN ISSN 1815-7548) 1900
▼ • The P E I Journal (Petroleum Equipment Institute) (USA ISSN 1936-0355) 6786
P E I Manager (Private Equity International) (GBR) 1373
P E I Online *see* Difficolta di Apprendimento 4064
P E I T F Newsletter (Prince Edward Island Teachers Federation) (CAN ISSN 0383-199X) 2894
P E L Occasional Papers on Business, Economy and Society (Polytechnic of East London) (GBR ISSN 0963-8563) 1158
P E L: Panorama Economico Latinoamericano (CUB ISSN 0030-7920) 1505
• P E L Plastics Update (USA ISSN 1094-656X) 7095
P E L R *see* Pace Environmental Law Review 4755
P E M *see* Probabilistic Engineering Mechanics 3393
P E M *see* Port Engineering Management 8656
• P E M: Industrial Sourcebook (CAN ISSN 1487-475X) 1785
• P E M: Plant Engineering and Maintenance (CAN ISSN 0710-362X) 1785
The P E N (Poetry Explosion Newsletter) (USA ISSN 1542-1570) 5428
P E N America (USA ISSN 1536-0261) 5347
P E N International. Bulletin of Selected Books (GBR ISSN 1010-4534) 5347
P E Newsletter (USA) 5347
P E O (DNK ISSN 0901-9235) 5347
P E P (Pflegekompetenz Ethik Persoenlichkeit) (DEU ISSN 1436-8013) 5977
P E P *see* Public Employee Press 7462
P E P A R S (Perspective Essential Plastic Aesthetic Reconstructive Surgery) (JPN ISSN 1349-645X) 6255
P E P A R S *see* P E P A R S 6255
P E R *see* Pacific Economic Review 1510
P E R *see* Professional Ethics Report 6945
P E R *see* Potchefstroom Electronic Law Journal 4759
P E R B News (Public Employment Relations Board) (USA ISSN 0732-1988) 7459
P E R E *see* Private Equity Real Estate 7604
The P E R E Year Book (Year) (Private Equity Real Estate) (GBR) 7603
† • The P E R M Quarterly (USA ISSN 1559-2073) 8979
P E S *see* Pediatric Exercise Science 6100
P E S A Journal (Petroleum Exploration Society of Australia) (AUS ISSN 0729-4069) 6786
P E S C Record *see* I E E E Power Electronics Specialists Conference. Proceedings 59
P E T *see* Power Equipment Trade 5458
P E T A's Animal Times (English Edition) (People for the Ethical Treatment of Animals, Inc.) (USA) 321
P E T A's Animal Times (German Edition) (People for the Ethical Treatment of Animals Inc.) (DEU ISSN 0947-8507) 321
• P E T Clinics (Positron Emission Tomography) (USA ISSN 1556-8598) 6205
P E T Clinics: Continuing Medical Education Supplement *see* P E T Clinics 6205
P E T Europe *see* Global P E T Report 6771
P E V *see* Planning and Environment Victoria 3460
P E W *see* Philosophy East and West 6943
▼ P E - W O W (Press - Enterprise Wheels - Offroad - Waves) (USA) 8327
P E X: Australia's Petroleum Exploration Newsletter *see* Pex Monthly 6788
P E X News und Trends (Praxiswissen fuer Export-Profis) (DEU ISSN 1860-3858) 1580
P F *see* Pacific Flyer 67
P - F (Professionele Fotografie) (NLD ISSN 0168-9991) 6972
P F *see* Products Finishing 6720
P F A D (DEU ISSN 1613-1460) 2163
P F A Schriftenreihe (Polizei-Fuehrungsakademie) (DEU ISSN 0720-6283) 2662

Title

• The P R S Group. Country Reports: Philippines (Political Risk Services) (USA ISSN 1054-6065) **1508**
• The P R S Group. Country Reports: Poland (Political Risk Services) (USA ISSN 1054-6073) **1508**
• The P R S Group. Country Reports: Portugal (Political Risk Services) (USA) **1508**
• The P R S Group. Country Reports: Puerto Rico (Political Risk Services) (USA) **1508**
• The P R S Group. Country Reports: Qatar (Political Risk Services) (USA) **1508**
• The P R S Group. Country Reports: Romania (Political Risk Services) (USA ISSN 1054-6103) **1508**
• The P R S Group. Country Reports: Russia (Political Risk Services) (USA ISSN 1060-8753) **1508**
• The P R S Group. Country Reports: Saudi Arabia (Political Risk Services) (USA ISSN 1054-6111) **1508**
• The P R S Group. Country Reports: Singapore (Political Risk Services) (USA ISSN 1054-612X) **1508**
• The P R S Group. Country Reports: Slovak Republic (Political Risk Services) (USA ISSN 1531-4707) **1509**
• The P R S Group. Country Reports: South Africa (Political Risk Services) (USA ISSN 1054-6138) **1509**
• The P R S Group. Country Reports: South Korea (Political Risk Services) (USA ISSN 1054-6146) **1509**
• The P R S Group. Country Reports: Spain (Political Risk Services) (USA) **1509**
• The P R S Group. Country Reports: Sri Lanka (Political Risk Services) (USA ISSN 1054-6162) **1509**
• The P R S Group. Country Reports: Sudan (Political Risk Services) (USA ISSN 1054-6170) **1509**
• The P R S Group. Country Reports: Suriname (Political Risk Services) (USA) **1509**
• The P R S Group. Country Reports: Sweden (Political Risk Services) (USA) **1509**
• The P R S Group. Country Reports: Switzerland (Political Risk Services) (USA) **1509**
• The P R S Group. Country Reports: Syria (Political Risk Services) (USA ISSN 1054-6197) **1509**
• The P R S Group. Country Reports: Taiwan (Political Risk Services) (USA ISSN 1054-6200) **1509**
• The P R S Group. Country Reports: Thailand (Political Risk Services) (USA ISSN 1054-6219) **1509**
• The P R S Group. Country Reports: Trinidad & Tobago (Political Risk Services) (USA) **1509**
• The P R S Group. Country Reports: Tunisia (Political Risk Services) (USA ISSN 1054-6227) **1509**
• The P R S Group. Country Reports: Turkey (Political Risk Services) (USA ISSN 1054-6235) **1509**
• The P R S Group. Country Reports: Turkmenistan (Political Risk Services) (USA ISSN 1099-2308) **1509**
• The P R S Group. Country Reports: Ukraine (Political Risk Services) (USA ISSN 1061-1304) **1509**
• The P R S Group. Country Reports: United Arab Emirates (Political Risk Services) (USA ISSN 1054-6251) **1509**
• The P R S Group. Country Reports: United Kingdom (Political Risk Services) (USA) **1509**
• The P R S Group. Country Reports: United States (Political Risk Services) (USA) **1509**
• The P R S Group. Country Reports: Uruguay (Political Risk Services) (USA ISSN 1054-6286) **1509**
• The P R S Group. Country Reports: Uzbekistan (Political Risk Services) (USA ISSN 1099-226X) **1509**
• The P R S Group. Country Reports: Venezuela (Political Risk Services) (USA ISSN 1054-6294) **1509**
• The P R S Group. Country Reports: Vietnam (Political Risk Services) (USA ISSN 1058-3831) **1510**
• The P R S Group. Country Reports: World Service (Political Risk Services) (USA) **1510**
• The P R S Group. Country Reports: Yemen (Political Risk Services) (USA) **1510**
• The P R S Group. Country Reports: Zambia (Political Risk Services) (USA ISSN 1054-6324) **1510**
• The P R S Group. Country Reports: Zimbabwe (Political Risk Services) (USA ISSN 1054-6332) **1510**
The P R S - L T S N Journal *see* Discourse (Heslington) **7638**
P R S M *see* Professional Retail Store Maintenance **1965**
P R S Members Handbook (Performing Right Society Ltd.) (GBR ISSN 0964-9875) **6604**
P R S News (Performing Right Society Ltd.) (GBR) **6604**
P R T *see* Pigment & Resin Technology **6720**
P R W *see* Plastics & Rubber Weekly **7096**
P R Watch (USA ISSN 1091-5583) **32**
P R Week (Asia-Pacific Edition) (HKG) **32**
• P R Week (UK Edition) (Public Relations) (GBR ISSN 0267-6087) **32**
• P R Week (US Edition) (Public Relations) (USA ISSN 1524-1696) **32**
P S *see* Post Script **6875**
P.S. (Post Scriptum) (BGR) **8879**
P S (DEU ISSN 0938-6645) **8597**
P S *see* P S Documenta **4518**
P S *see* Professioneel Schoonmaken **6684**
P S! (SWE ISSN 1651-8845) **5692**
P S *see* Pacific Science **7896**
• P S (USA ISSN 0475-2953) **5458**
P S *see* Produtos e Servicos **2024**
† P S 2 (PlayStation) (ITA ISSN 1591-3775) **8979**
P S 2 Evolution (PlayStation) (BRA ISSN 1807-6904) **2480**
P S 2 Magazine (PlayStation) (GRC) **2480**
P S A (USA ISSN 1042-4822) **5347**
P S A (Public Service Advertising) (USA) **32**
P S A *see* Plastics Southern Africa **7098**
P S A and B I S A Directory (GBR) **7162**
P S A C Union Update (Public Service Alliance of Canada) (CAN ISSN 0849-0287) **4600**
P S A Journal *see* Public Service Association Journal **7463**
• P S A Journal (Photographic Society of America, Inc.) (USA ISSN 0030-8277) **6972**
The P S A Media Register of Experts (Political Studies Association) (GBR) **7162**
P S A News (Political Studies Association) (GBR ISSN 0955-6281) **7163**
• P S A Population Report and Price Guide (Professional Sports Authenticator) (USA) **4343**
P S A Vintage Population Report (Professional Sports Authenticator) (USA) **4343**
P S Actua (Periodiek voor Sociale Verzekering) (NLD ISSN 1388-2708) **4518**
P S B A Bulletin (Pennsylvania School Boards Association) (USA ISSN 0162-3559) **3029**
† P S B Bulletin (Public Service Board) (AUS ISSN 0157-6178) **8979**
P S B Bulletin *see* P S B Bulletin **8979**
• P S B M B Newsletter (Philippine Society for Biochemistry and Molecular Biology) (PHL) **741**
P S C Clarion (Professional Staff Congress) (USA) **2997**
P S C Discussion Papers *see* University of Waikato. Population Studies Centre. Discussion Papers **7295**
P S C P Newsletter (Philadelphia Society of Clinical Psychologists) (USA) **7389**
P S Documenta (Periodiek voor Sociale Verzekering) (NLD ISSN 1388-2694) **4518**
P S E 2 (USA) **8192**
P S E Economic Analyst (IND) **1547**
P S E L R *see* Penn State Environmental Law Review **4756**
P S Extreme (PlayStation) (USA) **2480**
P S G (GBR) **2480**
• p.s. Grants (USA) **8061**
P S H E & Citizenship Update (Personal, Social and Health Education) *see* Learning for Life **2882**
P S I Bericht (Paul Scherrer Institut) (CHE ISSN 1019-0643) **3173**
P S I Discussion Papers (Policy Studies Institute) (GBR ISSN 0954-3694) **7990**
P S I Jahresbericht (Paul Scherrer Institut) (CHE) **3173**
P S I Journal (Praesent Service Institut) (DEU ISSN 1436-6193) **32**
P S I L R *see* Penn State International Law Review **4937**
P S I Proceedings (Paul Scherrer Institut) (CHE ISSN 1019-6447) **3173**
P S I: Report Series (Policy Studies Institute) (GBR) **7163**
P S J Soilborne Disease Workshop Report *see* Dojo Densenbyo Danwakai Repoto **228**
P S L G (Public Service & Local Government) (GBR ISSN 0144-4212) **7459**
† P S M (Play Station Magazine) (ITA ISSN 1126-490X) **8979**
P S M *see* PlayStation **2480**
P S M. 100% Independent P S 2 & PlayStation Magazine *see* PlayStation **2480**
P S M 2 (FRA ISSN 1624-4710) **2480**
P S M 3 (GBR) **2480**
P S Mania 2.0 *see* P S Mania 3.0 **2480**
P S Mania 3.0 (PlayStation) (ITA ISSN 1828-0277) **2480**
P S N *see* Psychiatrie, Sciences Humaines, Neurosciences **6177**
P S N *see* Prorodeo Sports News **8194**
P S O - Aktuellt *see* Psoriasistidningen **5881**
P S P (PlayStation Portable) (HKG ISSN 1815-8544) **2480**
• P S P Bulletin (Professional Scholarly Publishing) (USA) **7569**
P S P I *see* Psychological Science in the Public Interest **7397**
▼ P S P Magazine Ufficiale (PlayStation Portable) (ITA ISSN 1971-7431) **2480**
P S P Review (PlayStation Portable) (ITA ISSN 1827-5869) **2480**
• ➤ P S: Political Science & Politics (GBR ISSN 1049-0965) **7163**
P S Q *see* Public Services Quarterly **5041**
P S R *see* Portuguese Studies Review **4469**
P S R *see* Political Studies Review **7169**
• P S R Monitor (Online) (Physicians for Social Responsibility) (USA) **7534**
P S R Reports (Physicians for Social Responsibility) (USA ISSN 0894-6264) **7534**
P S S C Social Science Information (Philippine Social Science Council) (PHL ISSN 0115-1169) **7990**
• P S S R U Bulletin (Personal Social Services Research Unit) (GBR ISSN 1350-4703) **8061**
P S S T *see* Plasma Sources Science and Technology **7035**
P S Special (Periodiek voor Sociale Verzekeringen) (NLD ISSN 1573-3807) **4518**
P S V *see* Public Sector Voice **4601**
P S V Flits (Philips Sport Vereniging) (NLD) **8242**
P S V Inside (Philips Sport Vereniging) (NLD) **8242**
P S V Inzake (Philips Sport Vereniging) (NLD) **8242**
P S V PhoxyNieuws (Philips Sport Vereniging) (NLD) **8242**
P S W (PlayStation World) (GBR ISSN 1468-7240) **2480**
P S W *see* Psychoanalytic Social Work **8063**
P S World (BRA ISSN 1679-5008) **2480**
† P S X (HRV ISSN 1331-7849) **8979**
P T *see* Zeitschrift fuer Physiotherapeuten **6117**
P T *see* The Plain Truth **6944**
P T *see* Plastics Technology **7098**
P T *see* Photo Techniques **6973**
P T A Dialog (Pharmazeutisch - Technische Assistentin) (DEU) **6866**
P T A Forum (DEU) **6866**
P T A Fundraising Essentials (Parent Teacher Association) (USA ISSN 1548-2936) **3029**
P T A Heute (DEU ISSN 0302-167X) **6866**
Die P T A in der Apotheke (DEU ISSN 0722-1029) **6866**
P T A in Pennsylvania (USA ISSN 1072-3242) **3029**
▼ Das P T A Magazin (Pharmazeutisch Technischen Assistentin) (DEU ISSN 1864-2756) **6866**
P T A Perspectives (Parent-Teacher Association) (USA) **2894**
P T A - Repetitorium (DEU ISSN 0342-8397) **6866**
P T B *see* Potsdamer Textbuecher **7260**
P T B *see* Photonics Tech Briefs **7084**
P T B-Bericht. MA *see* P T B-Bericht. Mechanik und Akustik **7062**
P T B-Bericht. Mechanik und Akustik (Physikalisch-Technische Bundesanstalt) (DEU ISSN 0179-0595) **7062**
P T B-Bericht. N *see* P T B Berichte. Neutronenphysik **8434**
P T B-Bericht. Radioaktivitaet (Physikalisch-Technische Bundesanstalt) (DEU ISSN 0341-6747) **7070**
P T B - Bericht. Thermodynamik (Physikalisch-Technische Bundesanstalt) (DEU ISSN 1614-9327) **3144**
P T B Berichte. Neutronenphysik (Physikalisch-Technische Bundesanstalt) (DEU ISSN 0936-0492) **8434**
P T B - Mitteilungen Forschen und Pruefen (Physikalisch-Technische Bundesanstalt) (DEU) **6405**
P T B-W *see* P T B - Bericht. Thermodynamik **3144**
P T C *see* Physiotherapy Canada **6114**
• P T C (Year) Proceedings (Pacific Telecommunications Council) (USA) **2370**
P.T.D. Annual Tax Digest (Pakistan Tax Decisions) (PAK) **1938**
P T E N *see* Professional Tool and Equipment News **8599**
P T Embedded Systems (PolyTechnisch Tijdschrift) *see* Elektronica Plus Embedded Systems **3097**
P T I Journal (Phoenix) (Post Tensioning Institute) (USA ISSN 1544-2314) **3356**
P T I Newsletter (Post-Tensioning Institute) (USA) **452**
P T Industrieel Management (Polytechnisch Tijdschrift) (NLD ISSN 1571-9405) **3214**
P T J *see* Physical Therapy **6113**
P T L *see* The Practical Tax Lawyer **1939**
P.T. Magazin (DEU) **1158**
• P T - Magazine of Physical Therapy (USA ISSN 1065-5077) **6113**
P T N Americas *see* Travel News Americas **8767**
P T N Asia - Pacific *see* Pata Travel News Asia - Pacific **8747**
P T O Today (Parent Teacher Organization) (USA) **3029**
P T R *see* Physical Therapy Reviews **6114**
P T R *see* Pacific Telecommunications Review **2370**
P T R C Perspectives (Planning and Transport Research and Computation) (GBR ISSN 0960-9938) **8633**
P T R C Summer Annual Meeting. Proceedings (Planning and Transport Research and Computation) (GBR) **8614**
P T R C Traffex Conference Reports (Planning and Transport Research and Computation) (GBR) **8633**
P T S *see* Practical Tax Strategies **1939**
• P T S D Research Quarterly (USA ISSN 1050-1835) **6172**
P T S News (GBR) **6897**
P T - Sports Science (IND) **8192**
P T T *see* Persoenlichkeitsstoerungen - Theorie und Therapie **6173**
P T T Revue (Postes Telephones et Telegraphes Suisses) (CHE) **2370**
P T T Syndicaliste (FRA ISSN 0475-302X) **2335**
P T T und Zollbeamte (Postes Telephones et Telegraphes Suisses) (CHE) **2370**
• P T U Nyt (Polio-, Trafik- of Ulykkesskadede) (DNK ISSN 0901-7798) **6172**
P U C - Campinas. Revista de Educacao (Pontificia Universidade Catolica) (BRA ISSN 1519-3993) **2894**
P U Magazin (Polyurethan) (DEU ISSN 1618-0674) **3251**
P U R Utility Weekly (Public Utilities Reports) (USA) **3144**
P U S *see* Public Understanding of Science **7900**
P.U.S.H. *see* People United to Save Humanity. P.U.S.H.-Operation Push **5233**
P U T A J *see* Peshawar University Teachers' Association. Journal **7992**
P und A Kompendium (Prozesstechnik und Automation) (DEU) **2463**
P und G (Porzellan und Glas) (DEU ISSN 1616-5691) **2044**
P V D (Publicacion del Distribuidor de Informatica) (ESP) **2493**
P V Info (Personalverrechnung) (AUT ISSN 1816-9783) **1298**
P V News (Photo Voltaic) (USA ISSN 0739-4829) **3177**
P V P (Plant Variety Protection) (USA) **245**
P V P - P B (USA ISSN 0197-8608) **3392**
▼ • P V R I Review (Pulmonary Vascular Research Institute) (IND ISSN 0974-6013) **5797**
P V - Report (Professionelle Verpflegung) (DEU ISSN 1431-9136) **4395**
P V S *see* Politische Vierteljahresschrift **7171**
P V Working with Industry (Photovoltaics) (USA) **3160**
P W *see* Praxis der Werbung **32**
P W *see* IntermediairPW **1866**
P W *see* Publishers Weekly **7571**
P W *see* Panel World **3715**
• P W (Production Weekly) (USA) **2387**
P W A C Contact (Periodical Writers Association of Canada) (CAN ISSN 0845-8499) **3815**
P W Booklife (Publishers Weekly) (USA ISSN 1559-1468) **7569**
P W C *see* Painting and Wallcovering Contractor **6719**
• P W Daily for Booksellers (Publishers Weekly) (USA) **7569**
P W I *see* Pro Wrestling Illustrated **8194**
P W I *see* Plastics World Insight **7098**
• P W Newsline (Publishers Weekly) (USA) **7569**
P W P Newsletter (Professional Women Photographers) (USA) **6972**
• P W Religion BookLine (Publishers Weekly) (USA ISSN 0000-1694) **7569**
P W Rights Alert *see* Publishers Weekly Rights Alert **7571**
P W T *see* Practical Welding Today **6329**
P W V. Provincial Gazette *see* P W V. Provinsiale Koerant **7459**
P W V. Provinsiale Koerant/P W V. Provincial Gazette (Pretoria Witwatersrand Vaal) (ZAF) **7459**
P W Wetenschappelijk Platform *see* Pharmaceutische Weekblad Wetenschappelijk Platform **6871**
• P W World (Paula Walla Imports, Inc.) (USA) **3984**
† P Wie Papi (DEU) **8979**
• P X I Test & Technology (USA) **2574**
P Z *see* Pharmazeutische Zeitung **6875**
P Z Prisma (Pharmazeutische Zeitung) (DEU ISSN 0945-5566) **6866**
P Z Schriftenreihe (Pharmazeutische Zeitung) (DEU ISSN 0936-658X) **6866**
Pa Harakeke (NZL ISSN 1176-5917) **8124**
Pa L A Bulletin (Pennsylvania Library Association) (USA ISSN 1522-5852) **5038**
Pa M Y E *see* The Primary and Middle Years Educator **2899**
▼ Pa T V (NOR ISSN 1890-3983) **2387**
Pa TV *see* Pa T V **2387**
pA2 *see* P A 2 **6865**
• Paa Flukt Aktuelt (NOR ISSN 1504-1166) **7289**
Paa Flukt. Magasin *see* Paa Flukt Aktuelt **7289**
• Paa Flukt - Web (NOR ISSN 1501-9942) **7257**
Paa Hjul (NOR ISSN 0801-0986) **8266**
Paa Kryss (SWE ISSN 1404-9597) **8279**
Paa Kryss Till Rors *see* Paa Kryss **8279**
Paa Sekundet (NOR ISSN 0803-8309) **4568**
Paa Skogssidan *see* Vi Skogsaegare **3707**
Paa T V (SWE ISSN 1100-3138) **2387**
• Paallystolehti (FIN ISSN 0788-8554) **6441**
Paar Sammukest (EST ISSN 1406-5428) **5347**
Paard en Sport (NLD ISSN 1388-0047) **8295**
Paarden & Cap *see* Hoefslag **8292**
Paarden & Cap *see* Paard en Sport **8295**
Paardesport *see* Draf en Rensport **8290**
Paardesport en Fokkerij *see* Draf en Rensport **8290**
Paardesport in Ren en Draf *see* Draf en Rensport **8290**
Paarl Post (ZAF ISSN 0030-8447) **3949**
▼ • Paattajien Metsaakateria (FIN ISSN 1797-3341) **3699**
Pablisiti (RUS) **32**
• Pablo Journal (DEU ISSN 1437-1367) **510**
Pablo Lennis (USA) **5446**
Pace, Diritti dell'Uomo, Diritti dei Popoli (ITA ISSN 0394-7440) **7213**
Pace Diritti Umani/Peace Human Rights (ITA ISSN 1827-4056) **7213**
† Pace e Bene, Assisi (ITA) **8979**
• ➤ Pace Environmental Law Review (USA ISSN 0738-6206) **4755**

Title

10722 PACE INTERNATIONAL LAW REVIEW ULRICH'S PERIODICALS

Pace International Law Review (USA ISSN 1553-7897) **4937**
• ➤ Pace Law Review (USA ISSN 0272-2410) **4755**
Pace Magazine (USA) **2295**
Pace Press (USA) **2295**
Pacer (USA) **2295**
Pacer Times (USA) **2295**
The Pacesetter *see* U S W@Work **4604**
Pacesetter (USA) **2295**
• PACEsetterS (AUS ISSN 1449-7700) **5692**
Pachim Bangla (IND) **3887**
Pachyderm (CHE ISSN 1026-2881) **959**
• ➤ Pacific Accounting Review (GBR ISSN 0114-0582) **1373**
• ➤ Pacific Affairs (CAN ISSN 0030-851X) **7257**
Pacific AIDS Alert Bulletin (NCL ISSN 1018-2152) **5824**
• ➤ Pacific and Asian Journal of Energy (IND ISSN 0970-3888) **3144**
• Pacific & Southwest Arabian (USA) **8295**
Pacific Anthropological Records (USA ISSN 0078-740X) **351**
Pacific Area Travel Association Factfinder *see* P A T A Factfinder **8979**
Pacific Arts (USA ISSN 1018-4252) **510**
▼ • Pacific Asia Journal of the Association for Information Systems (USA ISSN 1943-7536) **2524**
Pacific Asia Travel Association. Annual Statistical Report (USA) **8780**
Pacific Asia Travel Association. Quarterly Statistical Report (USA ISSN 1066-0356) **8780**
Pacific Asia Travel Association Task Force Reports *see* P A T A Task Force Reports **8746**
Pacific Bakers News (USA ISSN 0030-8528) **3675**
• ➤ Pacific-Basin Finance Journal (NLD ISSN 0927-538X) **1373**
Pacific Beach Life Magazine *see* P B Life Magazine **5079**
Pacific Boating Almanac. Northern California (USA) **8279**
Pacific Boating Almanac. Pacific Northwest (USA) **8279**
Pacific Boating Almanac. Southern California (USA) **8279**
• Pacific Builder and Engineer (USA ISSN 0030-8544) **1029**
• Pacific Business News (USA ISSN 0030-8552) **1158**
Pacific Christian College Bulletin (USA) **7668**
Pacific Citizen (USA ISSN 0030-8579) **3557**
Pacific Coast Archaeological Society, Inc. Newsletter (Costa Mesa) *see* P C A S Newsletter (Costa Mesa) **410**
Pacific Coast Archaeological Society Quarterly (USA ISSN 0552-7252) **410**
Pacific Coast Business Times (USA ISSN 1543-6195) **1510**
Pacific Coast Highway *see* Road Trip U S A: Pacific Coast Highway **8752**
Pacific Coast Journal (Carlsbad) (USA ISSN 1065-1594) **5429**
Pacific Coast Journal (Temecula) (USA ISSN 0894-4458) **8295**
Pacific Coast Nurseryman and Garden Supply Dealer (USA ISSN 0192-7159) **3746**
Pacific Coast Paleogeography Symposium (USA ISSN 0275-5521) **2761**
• ➤ Pacific Coast Philology (USA ISSN 0078-7469) **5347**
Pacific Coast Sportfishing (USA ISSN 1544-7480) **8327**
• Pacific Conference on Computer Graphics and Applications. Proceedings (USA ISSN 1550-4085) **2489**
➤ Pacific Conservation Biology (AUS ISSN 1038-2097) **2624**
Pacific Cultural Foundation. Annual Report (TWN) **559**
• Pacific Daily News (GUM ISSN 0196-2485) **3874**
Pacific Diet Advisory Leaflet (NCL ISSN 1023-9197) **6668**
Pacific Earthquake Engineering Center Reports *see* P E E R Reports **3280**
Pacific Earthquake Engineering Center Review *see* The P E E R Review **2787**
Pacific Echo (USA) **2268**
• ➤ Pacific Economic Bulletin (AUS ISSN 0817-8038) **1510**
Pacific Economic Outlook (AUS ISSN 1715-3549) **1510**
• Pacific Economic Outlook (CAN) **1158**
Pacific Economic Papers *see* Asia Pacific Economic Papers **1552**
• ➤ Pacific Economic Review (AUS ISSN 1361-374X) **1510**
• Pacific Fisherman (USA ISSN 1069-0689) **8327**
Pacific Fishing (USA ISSN 0195-6515) **3604**
Pacific Flyer (AUS ISSN 1441-1121) **67**
Pacific Flyer (USA) **8550**
• ➤ Pacific Focus (AUS ISSN 1225-4657) **7257**
Pacific Folkore Studies (CAN ISSN 1719-797X) **3621**
• Pacific Forestry Centre. Forest Pest Leaflet (CAN) **3699**
Pacific Forestry Centre. Information Report (CAN ISSN 0830-0453) **3699**
Pacific Forestry Centre. Pest Report (CAN ISSN 0837-6549) **3699**
Pacific Forestry Centre. Technology Transfer Note (CAN ISSN 1209-6571) **3699**
Pacific Golf (CAN) **8242**
Pacific Halibut Fishery Regulations (USA ISSN 1019-0384) **3604**
➤ Pacific Health Dialog (COK ISSN 1015-7867) **7534**
▼ • Pacific Health Review (NZL ISSN 1178-6167) **7534**
Pacific High School Science Symposium. Proceedings (USA) **7896**
• ➤ Pacific Historical Review (USA ISSN 0030-8684) **4307**
Pacific Horticulture (USA ISSN 0163-7843) **3747**
Pacific Hosteller (CAN ISSN 0030-8692) **8746**
▼ • Pacific Human Rights Issues Series (NZL ISSN 1178-1912) **7213**
Pacific Information Centre Newsletter *see* P I C Newsletter **5038**
• Pacific Island Focus (Online) (USA ISSN 1936-6043) **4193**
Pacific Islands Books News Letters (IND) **633**
Pacific Islands Communication Journal (FJI ISSN 1605-6728) **2335**
Pacific Islands Heartbeat. Newsletter *see* Tala Lelei **7543**
Pacific Islands Monthly (FJI ISSN 0030-8722) **8746**
Pacific Islands Nutrition (NCL ISSN 1022-2782) **6668**
• Pacific Islands Policy (USA ISSN 1933-1223) **7163**
Pacific Islands Year Book (FJI ISSN 0078-7523) **4193**
▼ Pacific Journal of Applied Mathematics (USA ISSN 1941-3963) **5524**
Pacific Journal of Baptist Research (NZL ISSN 1177-0228) **7770**
• ➤ Pacific Journal of Mathematics (USA ISSN 0030-8730) **5524**
• Pacific Journal of Optimization (JPN ISSN 1348-9151) **5524**
Pacific Journal of Science and Technology (Catarman) (PHL ISSN 0117-522X) **145**
• ➤ Pacific Journal of Science and Technology (Hilo) (USA ISSN 1551-7624) **7896**
Pacific Journal of Theology (FJI ISSN 1027-037X) **7668**
• Pacific Journalism Review (NZL ISSN 1023-9499) **4581**
Pacific Linguistics (AUS ISSN 1448-8310) **5159**
Pacific Lutheran University Scene *see* Scene (Tacoma) **2300**
Pacific Magazine (USA ISSN 0744-1754) **1580**
Pacific Manuscripts Bureau *see* Pambu **4193**
Pacific Manuscripts Bureau. Manuscript Series (AUS) **4193**
Pacific Manuscripts Bureau. Printed Document Series (AUS) **4193**
Pacific Maritime Association Update *see* P M A Update **8656**
Pacific Maritime Magazine (USA ISSN 0741-7586) **8656**
• Pacific McGeorge Global Business & Development Law Journal (USA ISSN 1936-3931) **4937**
Pacific Medical Technology Symposium Transcending Time, Distance and Structural Barriers. Postproceedings (USA) **2474**
Pacific MotorYacht (NZL ISSN 1175-4370) **8279**
Pacific - Mountain Oil Directory (USA ISSN 1042-4865) **2023**
Pacific - Mountain Oil Directory. Buyer's Guide *see* Pacific - Mountain Oil Directory **2023**
• Pacific News Service (USA) **3984**
Pacific North West *see* P N W **145**
Pacific Northwest Animal Nutrition Conference. Proceedings (USA ISSN 1098-8483) **295**
Pacific Northwest: Compass Americn Guides *see* Compass American Guides: Pacific Northwest **8694**
• Pacific Northwest Environmental Directory (USA ISSN 1091-0301) **2624**
• Pacific Northwest Feed Market News (USA ISSN 0889-0447) **295**
Pacific Northwest Forest and Range Experiment Station. Research Notes (USA ISSN 0097-2398) **3699**
Pacific Northwest Fungi *see* North American Fungi **805**
Pacific Northwest Golfer (USA ISSN 1087-7045) **8242**
Pacific Northwest Grain Market News (USA) **274**
• Pacific Northwest Inlander (USA) **3985**
Pacific Northwest Library Association Quarterly *see* P N L A Quarterly **5038**
Pacific Northwest Lily Society. Newsletter (USA) **3747**
Pacific Northwest National Laboratory. Technical Paper (USA) **3144**
Pacific Northwest National Laboratory. Technical Report (USA) **3144**
➤ Pacific Northwest Quarterly (USA ISSN 0030-8803) **4307**
Pacific Northwest Software Quality Conference Proceedings (USA) **2595**
Pacific Northwest Weed Control Handbook *see* Pacific Northwest Weed Management Handbook **245**
Pacific Northwest Weed Management Handbook (USA) **245**
Pacific Northwesterner (USA ISSN 0030-882X) **4307**
The Pacific Northwest's Best Bed & Breakfasts (USA) **8746**
Pacific Outlook (AUS ISSN 1834-5077) **1580**
Pacific P O P I N Directory (FJI ISSN 1022-4289) **7289**
Pacific Perspective (FJI ISSN 0379-525X) **7990**
• Pacific Pest Info (FJI ISSN 1728-5291) **245**
• ➤ Pacific Philosophical Quarterly (GBR ISSN 0279-0750) **6938**
Pacific - Prairie Restaurant News (CAN ISSN 1702-3483) **4395**
Pacific Reader *see* International Examiner **3540**
Pacific Reporter Citations *see* Shepard's Pacific Reporter Citations **4783**
• ➤ The Pacific Review (GBR ISSN 0951-2748) **7257**
Pacific Review (San Bernardino) (USA ISSN 1043-5050) **5232**
Pacific Review (San Diego) (USA ISSN 0739-8360) **4468**
Pacific Review (Stockton) (USA ISSN 0164-9426) **2295**
Pacific Review of Ethnomusicology (USA ISSN 1096-1291) **6604**
• Pacific Rim Law & Policy Journal (USA ISSN 1066-8632) **4755**
The Pacific Rim Review of Books (CAN ISSN 1715-3700) **633**
▼ • Pacific Rim Studies (USA ISSN 1935-6145) **4193**
Pacific Russia Oil and Gas Report (USA ISSN 1098-1152) **6786**
• Pacific Salmon Commission. Annual Report (CAN ISSN 0842-2702) **3604**
• ➤ Pacific Science (USA ISSN 0030-8870) **7896**
Pacific Science Association. Congress and Inter-Congress Proceedings (USA) **7897**
Pacific Seabird Group. Technical Publication (USA ISSN 1521-3366) **913**
Pacific Seabirds (USA ISSN 1089-6317) **913**
• Pacific Shipper (USA ISSN 0030-8900) **8656**
Pacific Shipper's Transportation Services Shipper *see* Pacific Shipper **8656**
➤ Pacific Society. Journal/Taiheiyo Gakkai Shi (JPN ISSN 0387-4745) **351**
Pacific South West Forest Service. Pacific Southwest Forest and Range Experiment Station. Research Note P S W *see* U.S. Forest Service. Pacific Southwest Forest and Range Experiment Station. Research Note P S W **3706**
Pacific Southwest Directory (USA ISSN 0555-8581) **2023**
Pacific Stars & Stripes (JPN) **6441**
Pacific States Marine Fisheries Commission. Annual Report (USA ISSN 1057-2538) **3604**
Pacific Stock Exchange. Annual Report (USA) **1643**
• Pacific Stock Exchange Guide (USA) **1643**
➤ Pacific Strategic Papers (SGP ISSN 0218-1924) **7257**
• ➤ Pacific Studies (USA ISSN 0275-3596) **7990**
Pacific Symposium on Biocomputing. Proceedings *see* Biocomputing (Year) **824**
Pacific Telecommunications Council (Year) Proceedings *see* P T C (Year) Proceedings **2370**
Pacific Telecommunications Review (USA ISSN 1066-3894) **2370**
Pacific Tourism Review *see* Tourism Review International **8764**
Pacific Trade and Development Conference Series (GBR ISSN 1754-789X) **1580**
† Pacific Travel Directory (AUS ISSN 0311-0826) **8979**
• Pacific Union Recorder (USA ISSN 0744-6381) **7739**
Pacific Voices Talk Story (USA ISSN 1537-0992) **8124**
Pacific Wings (NZL ISSN 1174-8052) **67**
• ➤ Pacific World (USA) **7702**
Pacific Yachting (CAN ISSN 0030-8986) **8279**
† Pacific Yachting (NZL ISSN 1175-7213) **8979**
• ➤ Pacifica (AUS ISSN 1030-570X) **7668**
Pacifica (GBR ISSN 0306-0896) **6897**
• Pacifican (USA ISSN 0030-8994) **2295**
Pacifico Sur (ECU ISSN 0255-4925) **696**
• ➤ Pacing and Clinical Electrophysiology (USA ISSN 0147-8389) **5797**
† Pack (ITA ISSN 1123-3273) **8979**
Pack Aktuell (CHE) **6712**
Pack News & Mechanical Handling News/Pack News & Verpakkingsgids (BEL ISSN 1370-2491) **6712**
Pack News & Verpakkingsgids *see* Pack News & Mechanical Handling News **6712**
• Pack-o-Fun (USA ISSN 0030-901X) **538**
• Pack + Plast (DNK ISSN 1602-1436) **6712**
Pack of Apples and Apple Products (CAN ISSN 1180-5986) **3659**
Pack plus Plast *see* Pack + Plast **6712**
Package Design Magazine (USA ISSN 1554-6772) **6712**
Package Printing *see* PackagePrinting **7325**
Package Ten *see* Package X **1938**
Package X (USA ISSN 0160-9912) **1938**
• PackagePrinting (USA ISSN 1536-1039) **7325**
Packaging (AUS ISSN 1328-3847) **6712**
Packaging (Food & Drink) Industry (GBR ISSN 1743-4882) **6712**
Packaging (Glass) *see* Key Note Market Report: Packaging (Glass) **6711**
Packaging (Metals & Aerosols) *see* Key Note Market Report: Packaging (Metals & Aerosols) **1895**
Packaging (Paper & Board) *see* Key Note Market Report: Packaging (Paper & Board) **1895**
Packaging (Plastics) *see* Key Note Market Report: Packaging (Plastics) **6711**
Packaging: A World Survey (GBR) **6712**
Packaging and Bottling International *see* Italian Food Materials and Machinery **6711**
Packaging & Converting Intelligence (GBR) **6712**
Packaging and Converting Technology Series (USA) **6712**
The Packaging and Design Directory (ISR) **2023**
Packaging and Food Machinery *see* Baozhuang yu Shipin Jixie **6708**
• Packaging Business (GBR ISSN 1360-8282) **6712**
• Packaging Digest (USA ISSN 0030-9117) **6713**
Packaging Digest Edicion Latino Americana (USA) **6713**
Packaging Digest Machinery - Materials Guide (USA) **6713**
Packaging Directory *see* Pakkaus **6714**
Packaging Focus (GBR ISSN 1361-1720) **6713**
Packaging, Handling, Logistics Bulletin *see* P H L Bulletin **6712**
• Packaging Hotline (USA) **6713**
Packaging India (IND ISSN 0030-9125) **6713**
Packaging Japan (JPN ISSN 0288-3864) **6713**
Packaging Journal (DEU) **6713**
Packaging Machinery Directory *see* Packaging Machinery Manufacturers Institute. Official Packaging Machinery Directory (CD-ROM) **6713**
• Packaging Machinery Manufacturers Institute. Official Packaging Machinery Directory (CD-ROM) (USA) **6713**
Packaging Machinery Manufacturers Institute. Official Packaging Machinery Directory (Print) *see* Packaging Machinery Manufacturers Institute. Official Packaging Machinery Directory (CD-ROM) **6713**
Packaging Machinery News *see* Hoso Kikai Shinbun **6710**
• Packaging Machinery Technology (USA ISSN 1556-1658) **6713**
• Packaging Month (GBR ISSN 1475-598X) **6715**
• Packaging News (GBR ISSN 0030-9133) **6713**
Packaging Pro (HKG) **6713**
• The Packaging Professional (GBR ISSN 1477-8467) **6713**
Packaging Report *see* Motion System Design **3390**
Packaging Review South Africa (ZAF ISSN 1014-8280) **6713**
Packaging Scotland (GBR ISSN 0952-4495) **6713**
• (Year) Packaging Sourcebook (International Edition) (USA) **6713**
• (Year) Packaging Sourcebook (North American Edition) (USA ISSN 1076-1659) **6713**
• Packaging Strategies (USA ISSN 8755-6189) **6713**
• Packaging Technology and Engineering (Online) (USA) **6713**
• Packaging Technology and Science (GBR ISSN 0894-3214) **6713**
Packaging Today (AUS ISSN 0159-1843) **6714**
• Packaging Today (GBR ISSN 1747-7468) **6714**
Packaging Today International *see* Packaging Today **6714**
• ➤ Packaging, Transport, Storage & Security of Radioactive Material (GBR ISSN 1746-5095) **8508**
Packaging World *see* Baozhuang Shijie **6708**
• Packaging World (USA ISSN 1073-7367) **6714**
Packard Cormorant (USA ISSN 0362-9368) **368**
• The Packer (USA ISSN 0030-9168) **3659**
• The Packer. Guide (USA ISSN 1548-2871) **3659**
• Packer Plus (USA ISSN 1064-4296) **8242**
• Packer Report (USA ISSN 1081-9851) **8242**
• The Packet (USA ISSN 0195-9646) **5038**
Packet (USA) **2565**
• Packet & Times (CAN ISSN 0837-1989) **3815**
▼ Packingtown Review (USA ISSN 1946-0570) **5347**
• Packmarkedet (DNK ISSN 1395-4652) **6714**
• Packmarknaden Nordica (SWE ISSN 1404-8477) **6714**
• PackMittel (DEU ISSN 1864-1482) **6735**
PackPlas International (GBR) **6714**
PackReport (DEU ISSN 0342-3743) **1837**
Pacs & Networking News, Telemedicine Business Newsletter *see* Health Networking News **8961**
• ➤ Pact/Reseau Europeen de Sciences et Techniques Appliquees au Patrimoine Culturel. Revue (BEL ISSN 0257-8727) **410**
Pactnieuws *see* Informatiebulletin SamenWerkend Limburg **4596**
Pada *see* Hangug Haeyang Haghoe Ji - Bada **2805**
† Padania (Milan) (ITA) **8979**
Paddestoelen (NLD ISSN 1380-359X) **3747**
Paddington Times (GBR ISSN 0962-3078) **3869**
Paddle Dealer (USA) **8279**
Paddle News (CAN) **8242**
Paddle Wheels (GBR) **8656**
† • Paddler (AUS) **8979**
Paddler (USA ISSN 1058-5710) **8280**
Paddler Pasifika *see* New Zealand Paddler Pasifika **8279**
Paddler's Print *see* Paddlesports Pro **8280**
Paddles (GBR ISSN 1364-0259) **8280**
Paddlesports Business (USA) **8192**
Paddlesports Pro (USA) **8280**
Paddling (SWE ISSN 1653-2503) **8280**
▼ Paddling Life (USA ISSN 1934-8347) **8280**
Paddock (CAN ISSN 1911-0049) **8192**
▼ The Paddock (GBR) **8192**
Paddock Revue (CZE ISSN 1801-6812) **8295**

Link to your serials resources and content with ulrichsweb.com

• ➤ Paddy and Water Environment (DEU ISSN 1611-2490) **245**
Paderborn Journal (DEU) **8746**
Paderborner Beitraege zur Geschichte (DEU ISSN 0944-8365) **4252**
Paderborner Historische Forschungen (DEU ISSN 0937-3721) **4252**
Paderborner Universitaets Zeitschrift (DEU) **2296**
Padiham Express (GBR) **3869**
Padova e il Suo Territorio (ITA ISSN 1120-9755) **510**
Padre Santo (ITA ISSN 0030-9214) **7668**
• Padres (PER ISSN 1605-3206) **4365**
• Los Padres aun Hacen la Diferencia! (Escuela Secundaria) (USA ISSN 1523-2417) **2894**
• Los Padres aun Hacen la Diferencial (Escuela Intermedia) (USA ISSN 1523-2387) **2895**
Padres Caracola *see* Caracola **2181**
Padres de Sesame Street (USA) **2164**
• Padres e Hijos (MEX ISSN 0188-0667) **2164**
• Los Padres Hacen la Diferencia! (USA ISSN 1523-2360) **2895**
• Los Padres Hacen la Diferencia! (Elementary Edition) (USA ISSN 1523-2379) **2895**
➤ Padres y Maestros (ESP ISSN 0210-4679) **2895**
PADUA *see* P A D U A **3075**
• Padua Working Papers in Linguistics (ITA ISSN 1827-0522) **5159**
• Padusa (ITA ISSN 0393-0149) **410**
Paed (DEU ISSN 0949-7641) **6098**
PAeD-Forum: Unterrichten Erziehen (DEU ISSN 1611-406X) **3075**
• ➤ Paedagogica Historica (GBR ISSN 0030-9230) **2895**
Paedagogik (Berlin) (DEU ISSN 1862-6122) **2895**
➤ Paedagogik (Weinheim) (DEU ISSN 0933-422X) **2895**
▼ Paedagogik und Ethik (DEU) **8124**
▼ Paedagogik und Philosophie (DEU) **2895**
Paedagogische Akademie des Bundes in Oberoesterreich. Schriften (AUT ISSN 1999-9275) **3075**
Paedagogische Arbeitsstelle fuer Erwachsenenbildung. Schriften (DEU ISSN 0723-7197) **2945**
Der Paedagogische Blick (DEU ISSN 0943-5484) **2895**
➤ Paedagogische Fuehrung (DEU ISSN 0939-0413) **3029**
➤ Paedagogische Fuehrung. Ausgabe Bayern (DEU ISSN 0939-1045) **3029**
➤ Paedagogische Fuehrung. Ausgabe Berlin, Brandenburg, Mecklenburg-Vorpommern, Sachsen, Sachsen-Anhalt, Thueringen (DEU ISSN 0939-1053) **3029**
Paedagogische Fuehrung. Ausgabe Neue Laender *see* Paedagogische Fuehrung. Ausgabe Berlin, Brandenburg, Mecklenburg-Vorpommern, Sachsen, Sachsen-Anhalt, Thueringen **3029**
➤ Paedagogische Fuehrung. Ausgabe Rheinland-Pfalz/Saarland (DEU ISSN 0939-1037) **3029**
➤ Paedagogische Fuehrung. Hessen (DEU ISSN 0944-2901) **3029**
➤ Paedagogische Fuehrung. Nordrhein-Westfalen (DEU ISSN 0948-0552) **3029**
Paedagogische Hochschule Freiburg *see* P H - F R **2945**
Paedagogische Psychologie und Entwicklungspsychologie (DEU ISSN 1430-2977) **2895**
Paedagogische Rundschau (DEU ISSN 0030-9273) **2895**
Paedagogische Umschau *see* Rassegna di Pedagogia **2903**
Paedagogisches Institut der Stadt Wien. Mitteilungen (AUT ISSN 0030-9281) **2895**
• ➤ Paedagogisk Psykologisk Tidsskrift/Journal of School Psychology (DNK ISSN 1903-0002) **7389**
• ➤ Paediatria Croatica (HRV ISSN 1330-1403) **6098**
• ➤ Paediatric Anaesthesia (GBR ISSN 1155-5645) **5773**
• ➤ Paediatric Anaesthesia Online (GBR ISSN 1460-9592) **5773**
Paediatric and Perinatal Drug Therapy *see* Archives of Disease in Childhood **6088**
• ➤ Paediatric and Perinatal Epidemiology (Online) (GBR ISSN 1365-3016) **6098**
• ➤ Paediatric and Perinatal Epidemiology (Print) (GBR ISSN 0269-5022) **6098**
Paediatric and Perinatal Epidemiology. Supplement *see* Paediatric and Perinatal Epidemiology (Print) **6098**
The Paediatric Asthma Virtual Journal *see* The Pediatric Asthma Virtual Journal **8980**
• ➤ Paediatric Drugs (NZL ISSN 1174-5878) **6866**
• Paediatric Nursing (GBR ISSN 0962-9513) **5977**
• Paediatric Respiratory Reviews (GBR ISSN 1526-0542) **6217**
• ➤ Paediatrica (PER ISSN 1728-239X) **6098**
• Paediatrica Indonesiana (IDN ISSN 0030-9311) **6098**
• ➤ Paediatrics and Child Health (CAN ISSN 1205-7088) **6098**
• Paediatrics and Child Health (GBR ISSN 1751-7222) **6098**
Paediatrics.me (GBR ISSN 1755-3172) **6098**
Paediatrics Middle East *see* Paediatrics.me **6098**
Paediatrics Today (IND ISSN 0972-0537) **6098**
Paediatrics Today (NZL ISSN 1174-5894) **6098**
➤ Paediatrie Aktuell (DEU ISSN 0937-096X) **6098**
Paediatrie Hautnah (DEU ISSN 1437-1782) **6098**
• ➤ Paediatrie und Paedologie (AUT ISSN 0030-9338) **6098**
▼ • Paediatrie up2date (DEU ISSN 1611-6445) **6098**
Paediatrische Allergologie in Klinik und Praxis (DEU ISSN 1435-4233) **5764**
† Paediatrische Nachrichten (DEU ISSN 1439-488X) **8979**
Paediatrische Praxis (DEU ISSN 0030-9346) **6098**
Paediatrische Zeitung (DEU) **6099**
Paediki Chara/Children's Joy (CYP) **2895**
Paediki Hara (CYP ISSN 1022-9582) **2206**
Paepste und Papsttum (DEU ISSN 0340-7993) **7811**
Paesaggio Urbano (ITA ISSN 1120-3544) **4422**
Paese Nostro (ITA) **3898**
Pagan America (GBR ISSN 1354-1056) **5429**
Pagan Dawn (GBR ISSN 1357-5147) **7739**
Pagans for Peace (CAN ISSN 0838-1550) **7740**
A Page *see* Stranitsa **5378**
• Page (DEU ISSN 0935-6274) **2582**
The Page (IND) **3887**
Page & Panel Journal *see* American Society for Philatelic Pages and Panels. Page & Panel Journal **6891**
Page des Libraires (FRA ISSN 1145-6094) **5039**
• The Page of the Immortals (USA) **5348**
The Page Review (AUS ISSN 1832-3952) **7163**
Pageantry (USA ISSN 1075-3133) **2259**
PAGEOPH *see* Pure and Applied Geophysics **2788**
Pages *see* The Global Educator **7238**
• Pages (Marion) (USA ISSN 0883-6752) **4581**
Pages (San Diego) (USA) **5232**
Pages d'Archeologie Medievale en Rhone - Alpes (FRA ISSN 1265-9983) **410**
Pages d'Archives (FRA ISSN 1270-962X) **4252**
Pages: Theology, Culture, Education *see* Stranitsy. Bogoslovie, Kul'tura, Obrazovanie **7818**
Pages Web Pratiques (FRA ISSN 1628-8971) **2565**
La Pagina (ESP ISSN 0214-8390) **5348**
Pagina Abierta (ESP ISSN 1132-8886) **8124**
Paginas (CUB) **559**
Paginas (PER ISSN 1022-7873) **5232**
Paginas (VEN) **8879**
Paginas Amarillas *see* Hispanic Yellow Pages (Fairfax) **2004**
Paginas Amarillas Hispanas *see* Hispanic Yellow Pages (Atlanta) **2004**
• Paginas de Actualizacion en Oftalmologia (ARG ISSN 1515-7202) **6050**
Paginas para los Padres y Madres (USA ISSN 1091-3181) **2164**
▼ • Paginasenferurg.com (ESP ISSN 1989-2829) **5977**
Pagine della Dante (ITA ISSN 1972-9456) **5233**
Pagine Giovani (ITA) **7570**
Pagine Web Facile (ITA ISSN 1591-2515) **2565**
• Pagonya (BLR) **3800**
• Paideia (BRA ISSN 0103-863X) **7389**
Paideia (ITA ISSN 0030-9435) **5159**
Paideia (POL ISSN 0137-3943) **2945**
Paideia (Madrid) (ESP ISSN 0214-7300) **6938**
Paideuma (DEU ISSN 0078-7809) **351**
➤ Paideuma (USA ISSN 0090-5674) **5348**
• ➤ Paideusis (Online) (CAN ISSN 1916-0348) **2895**
Paidi kai Nei Gonis (GRC ISSN 1105-9893) **2164**
To Paidi Mou Kai Ego (GRC ISSN 1108-622X) **2164**
Paidiatrike Boreiou Ellados (GRC ISSN 1105-2325) **6099**
Paidika (NLD ISSN 0167-5907) **8124**
Paidonomia (ZAF ISSN 0377-8576) **6232**
• Paidos (NOR ISSN 1503-5360) **6099**
Paiedia (CHL ISSN 0716-4815) **2895**
Paihdetilastollinen Vuosikirja/Rusmedelsstatistisk Aarsbok. Alcohol och Narkotika/Yearbook of Alcohol and Drug Statistics (FIN ISSN 1455-7444) **2701**
Pailiomtolojiya Indika *see* Palaeontologia Indica **6728**
• ➤ Pain (NLD ISSN 0304-3959) **6172**
• Pain & Central Nervous System Week (USA ISSN 1531-6394) **6172**
• ➤ Pain and Headache (CHE ISSN 0255-3910) **6172**
Pain: Cause, Effect, Evaluation (USA) **5692**
• ➤ The Pain Clinic (GBR ISSN 0169-1112) **5773**
➤ The Pain Clinic: A Multidisciplinary Approach to Acute and Chronic Pain Management (USA ISSN 1525-576X) **6070**
† The Pain Clinic. Proceedings (ITA) **8979**
Pain. Clinical Updates (USA ISSN 1083-0707) **6172**
Pain Control in Dentistry *see* American Society for the Advancement of Anesthesia in Dentistry. Proceedings **5834**
Pain & Patisserie (BEL ISSN 1372-2042) **3675**
Pain Forum *see* The Journal of Pain **6155**
▼ • Pain Management (GBR ISSN 1758-1869) **5692**
† • Pain Management Coding Alert (USA ISSN 1536-8270) **8979**
• Pain Management Coding & Billing Answer Book (USA ISSN 1942-2296) **4518**
• ➤ Pain Management Nursing (USA ISSN 1524-9042) **5773**
• Pain Medicine (AUT ISSN 1681-1232) **6172**
Pain Medicine *see* Current Medical Literature. Pain Medicine **6058**
• Pain Medicine (USA ISSN 1526-2375) **6172**
• Pain Medicine News (USA ISSN 1942-1419) **5692**
• ➤ Pain Physician (USA ISSN 1533-3159) **5773**
• Pain Practice (USA ISSN 1530-7085) **6173**
The Pain Practitioner (USA) **5692**
➤ Pain Research and Clinical Management (NLD ISSN 0921-3287) **5692**
• ➤ Pain Research & Management (CAN ISSN 1203-6765) **6173**
• ➤ Pain Reviews (GBR ISSN 0968-1302) **5692**
The Pain Series (USA) **5692**
▼ • Pain Solutions (USA ISSN 1948-5522) **5692**
Pain. Supplement *see* Pain **6172**
Paine Webber Euromoney Directory *see* Fincareer Euromoney Capital Markets Directory (Year) **1995**
Painomaailma (FIN ISSN 1235-905X) **7325**
Paint and Coatings 2000: Review and Forecast (USA) **6719**
Paint & Coatings Industry *see* Tuliao Gongye **6721**
Paint and Coatings Industry *see* Paint & Coatings Industry **6719**
• Paint & Coatings Industry (USA ISSN 0884-3848) **6719**
Paint & Decorating Retailer (USA ISSN 1096-6927) **4548**
Paint & Decorating Retailer's Decorating Registry (USA) **4548**
Paint & Decorating Retailer's Directory of the Wallcovering Industry (USA) **4548**
Paint & Printing Ink Manufacturers *see* Business Ratio Report. Paint & Printing Ink Manufacturers (Year) **6716**
• Paint and Resin Times (GBR ISSN 1476-0274) **6719**
Paint Consumer Research Program (USA) **6719**
▼ The Paint Contractor (USA) **6719**
The Paint Dealer (USA ISSN 1067-1110) **6719**
Paint Decor (USA ISSN 1536-7002) **4548**
Paint Horse Journal (USA ISSN 0164-5706) **8295**
Paint Rag (USA) **510**
• Paint Titles (GBR ISSN 0144-4425) **6722**
Paint Works (USA ISSN 1077-5404) **538**
Paintball Adventures (GBR ISSN 0955-9124) **8327**
Paintball Games International (GBR ISSN 1465-3532) **8192**
Paintball Sports (USA ISSN 1932-5355) **8192**
Paintbrush (USA ISSN 0094-1964) **5348**
Painted Bride Quarterly (USA ISSN 0362-7969) **5429**
Painter & Allied Trades Journal (USA ISSN 0030-9532) **4600**
Paintindia (IND ISSN 0556-4409) **6719**
• Painting (USA ISSN 1079-6819) **538**
Painting & Calligraphy Arts *see* Shuhua Yishu **517**
Painting and Decorating Association. Members Reference Handbook (GBR) **6719**
• Painting and Wallcovering Contractor (USA ISSN 0735-9713) **6719**
Paintworks *see* Paint Works **538**
Pairotto (JPN ISSN 0912-490X) **67**
• El Pais (COL) **3830**
El Pais (URY) **3994**
• El Pais (Andalucia Edition) (ESP ISSN 1698-5044) **3953**
El Pais (Barcelona Edition) (ESP ISSN 1576-3765) **3953**
• El Pais (Comunidad Valenciana Edition) (ESP ISSN 1697-9680) **3953**
El Pais (Galicia Edition) (ESP ISSN 1697-9389) **3953**
• El Pais (Madrid Edition) (ESP ISSN 1134-6582) **3953**
El Pais (National Edition) (ESP ISSN 1697-9397) **3953**
• El Pais (Pais Vasco Edition) (ESP ISSN 1697-9435) **3953**
• Pais & Filhos (PRT) **2164**
• El Pais. Anuario (ESP ISSN 0211-9366) **3953**
El Pais Digital *see* El Pais (Madrid Edition) **3953**
• El Pais Digital (URY) **3994**
• El Pais Semanal (ESP ISSN 1134-6590) **3953**
El Paisano (USA) **3459**
Paises del I C E (Informacion Comercial Espanola) (ESP ISSN 1134-2145) **1580**
Pak & Papir (DNK) **6972**
Pak Jamhuriat (PAK ISSN 0030-9591) **3926**
The Pak-Scout (PAK ISSN 0030-9605) **2164**
Pakblad (NLD ISSN 1389-7381) **6714**
Pakeeza International (CAN ISSN 0711-4222) **3557**
Pakenham Gazette (AUS) **3795**
Pakha Sanjam (IND ISSN 0556-4417) **5159**
➤ Pakistan (PAK ISSN 1990-6579) **7990**
Pakistan *see* The P R S Group. Country Reports: Pakistan **1508**
Pakistan (USA ISSN 1061-6101) **4187**
➤ Pakistan Academy of Sciences. Proceedings (PAK ISSN 0377-2969) **7897**
• Pakistan and Gulf Economist (PAK ISSN 0253-1941) **1158**
Pakistan Annual Law Digest (PAK ISSN 0078-785X) **4755**
Pakistan Archaeology (PAK ISSN 0078-7868) **410**
• Pakistan Armed Forces Medical Journal (PAK ISSN 0030-9648) **5692**
Pakistan Army Journal (PAK ISSN 0030-9656) **6441**
Pakistan Association for the Advancement of Science. Annual Report (PAK) **7897**
➤ Pakistan Association of Dermatologists. Journal (PAK ISSN 1560-9014) **5880**
Pakistan Basic Facts (PAK ISSN 0078-7892) **1938**
Pakistan Book of Cricket (PAK) **8242**
Pakistan. Central Bureau of Education. Educational Statistics Bulletin Series (PAK ISSN 0078-7914) **2935**
Pakistan Central Cotton Committee. Agricultural Survey Report (PAK ISSN 0078-7930) **245**
Pakistan Central Cotton Committee. Monthly Cotton Review (PAK ISSN 0027-0334) **245**
Pakistan Central Cotton Committee. Technological Bulletin. Series A (PAK ISSN 0078-7949) **245**
Pakistan Central Cotton Committee. Technological Bulletin. Series B (PAK ISSN 0078-7957) **245**
Pakistan Chess Magazine (PAK) **8192**
➤ Pakistan Congress of Zoology. Proceedings (PAK ISSN 1013-3461) **959**
Pakistan Cottons (PAK ISSN 0030-9699) **145**
Pakistan Council of Scientific and Industrial Research. Annual Report (PAK ISSN 0078-804X) **7897**
Pakistan Criminal Law Journal (PAK) **4896**
• Pakistan Customs Tariff (PAK ISSN 0078-8058) **1580**
• Pakistan Defence & Security Report (GBR ISSN 1749-155X) **6441**
Pakistan Defense & Security Report *see* Pakistan Defence & Security Report **6441**
➤ Pakistan Development Review (PAK ISSN 0030-9729) **7990**
Pakistan Digest (PAK ISSN 0377-256X) **3926**
Pakistan. Directorate of Livestock Farms. Report (PAK ISSN 0083-8292) **295**
Pakistan Directory of Trade and Industry (PAK) **1408**
➤ Pakistan Economic and Social Review (PAK ISSN 1011-002X) **1603**
Pakistan Economic Journal (PAK) **1158**
Pakistan Economic Survey (PAK ISSN 0078-8082) **1510**
Pakistan Entomologist (PAK ISSN 1017-1827) **857**
Pakistan Exports (PAK ISSN 0030-977X) **1580**
Pakistan. Finance Division. Annual Budget Statement (Final) (PAK ISSN 0304-6478) **1938**
Pakistan. Finance Division. Budget in Brief (PAK) **1938**
Pakistan. Finance Division. Economic Analysis of the Budget (PAK ISSN 0376-9208) **1938**
Pakistan. Finance Division. Estimates of Foreign Assistance (PAK ISSN 0376-9011) **1938**
Pakistan. Finance Division. Public Finance Statistics (PAK) **1257**
Pakistan. Finance Division. Supplementary Demands for Grants and Appropriations (PAK) **1938**
Pakistan. Food and Agriculture Division. Agricultural Statistics of Pakistan (PAK) **184**
Pakistan Forest Institute, Peshawar. Annual Progress Report (PAK ISSN 0078-8147) **3699**
Pakistan Forest Institute, Peshawar. Progress Report *see* Pakistan Forest Institute, Peshawar. Annual Progress Report **3699**
▼ Pakistan Freight Transport Report (GBR ISSN 1752-606X) **8508**
Pakistan. Geological Survey. Memoirs; Paleontologia Pakistanica (PAK ISSN 0078-8155) **6727**
Pakistan. Geological Survey. Records (PAK ISSN 0078-8163) **2761**
Pakistan Handbook (GBR ISSN 1363-7991) **8746**
Pakistan Heart Journal (PAK ISSN 0048-2706) **5797**
Pakistan Historical Society. Journal (PAK ISSN 0030-9796) **4155**
Pakistan Historical Society. Memoir (PAK ISSN 0078-8171) **4187**
Pakistan Historical Society. Proceedings of the Pakistan History Conference (PAK ISSN 0078-818X) **4187**
Pakistan Horizon (PAK ISSN 0030-980X) **7257**
Pakistan Hotel and Restaurant Guide (PAK ISSN 0250-4359) **4395**
Pakistan Hotel Guide (PAK ISSN 0250-3654) **4395**
Pakistan Hotels & Tourism (PAK) **8746**
Pakistan Industrial Credit and Investment Corporation Ltd., Economic and Research Department Annual Report *see* P I C I C Annual Report **1643**
Pakistan Industrial Credit and Investment Corporation Ltd., Economic and Research Department News *see* P I C I C News **1643**
Pakistan Industrial Development Corporation. Report (PAK ISSN 0078-8201) **1900**
Pakistan Institute of Development Economics. Statistical Papers Series (PAK) **1257**
▼ Pakistan Insurance Report (GBR ISSN 1752-833X) **4518**
• Pakistan Journal of Agricultural Research (PAK ISSN 0251-0480) **145**
Pakistan Journal of Agricultural Sciences (PAK ISSN 0552-9034) **145**
Pakistan Journal of Agriculture, Agricultural Engineering and Veterinary Sciences (PAK ISSN 1023-1072) **145**
Pakistan Journal of Agronomy *see* Journal of Agronomy **127**
➤ Pakistan Journal of Applied Economics (PAK ISSN 0254-9204) **1510**
Pakistan Journal of Applied Sciences *see* Journal of Applied Sciences **7871**
• Pakistan Journal of Biochemistry and Molecular Biology (PAK ISSN 1681-4525) **741**
• ➤ Pakistan Journal of Biological Sciences (PAK ISSN 1028-8880) **696**
• ➤ Pakistan Journal of Botany (PAK ISSN 0556-3321) **807**
• ➤ Pakistan Journal of Clinical Psychology (PAK ISSN 1019-438X) **7389**
▼ • ➤ Pakistan Journal of Commerce and Social Sciences (PAK ISSN 1997-8553) **1158**

Title

➤ Pakistan Journal of Education (PAK ISSN 1818-3344) 2895
• ➤ Pakistan Journal of Engineering and Applied Sciences (PAK ISSN 1995-1302) 3214
➤ Pakistan Journal of Entomology (PAK ISSN 1018-1180) 857
Pakistan Journal of Forestry (PJF) (PAK ISSN 0030-9818) 3700
• Pakistan Journal of Health (PAK ISSN 0030-9834) 7534
Pakistan Journal of History & Culture (PAK ISSN 1012-7682) 4468
➤ Pakistan Journal of Hydrocarbon Research (PAK ISSN 1017-0626) 6786
Pakistan Journal of Information & Technology *see* Information Technology Journal 2423
➤ Pakistan Journal of Library and Information Science (PAK ISSN 1680-4465) 5039
Pakistan Journal of Marine Biology (PAK ISSN 1562-1286) 696
Pakistan Journal of Marine Sciences (PAK ISSN 1019-8415) 2816
▼ Pakistan Journal of Medical & Health Sciences (PAK ISSN 1996-7195) 5692
➤ Pakistan Journal of Medical Research (PAK ISSN 0030-9842) 5692
• ➤ Pakistan Journal of Medical Sciences (PAK ISSN 1682-024X) 5692
➤ Pakistan Journal of Nematology (PAK ISSN 0255-7576) 959
• ➤ Pakistan Journal of Nutrition (PAK ISSN 1680-5194) 6668
• Pakistan Journal of Otolaryngology (PAK ISSN 0257-4985) 6084
Pakistan Journal of Pathology (PAK ISSN 1024-6193) 5692
• ➤ Pakistan Journal of Pharmaceutical Sciences (PAK ISSN 1011-601X) 6866
Pakistan Journal of Pharmacology (PAK ISSN 0255-7088) 6866
Pakistan Journal of Phytopathology (PAK ISSN 1019-763X) 807
• ➤ Pakistan Journal of Psychology (PAK ISSN 0030-9869) 7389
Pakistan Journal of Radiology (PAK ISSN 1607-2006) 6205
Pakistan Journal of Science (PAK ISSN 0030-9877) 7897
➤ Pakistan Journal of Scientific and Industrial Research (PAK ISSN 0030-9885) 7897
Pakistan Journal of Scientific Research (PAK ISSN 0552-9050) 7897
Pakistan Journal of Social Science (PAK ISSN 1019-729X) 7257
▼ • Pakistan Journal of Social Sciences (Faisalabad) (PAK ISSN 1683-8831) 7991
➤ Pakistan Journal of Social Sciences (Multan) (PAK ISSN 2074-2061) 7991
➤ Pakistan Journal of Statistics (PAK ISSN 1012-9367) 5524
➤ Pakistan Journal of Statistics and Operation Research (PAK ISSN 1816-2711) 5524
➤ Pakistan Journal of Weed Science Research (PAK ISSN 1815-1094) 245
Pakistan Journal of Women's Studies *see* Alam-e-Niswan 8893
➤ Pakistan Journal of Zoology (PAK ISSN 0030-9923) 959
Pakistan Journal of Zoology. Supplementary Series *see* Pakistan Journal of Zoology 959
Pakistan Labour Cases (PAK ISSN 0030-994X) 4755
Pakistan Law Journal (PAK) 4755
Pakistan Leather Trade Journal (PAK) 4974
• ➤ Pakistan Library & Information Science Journal (PAK ISSN 1994-3059) 5039
Pakistan Library Association Newsletter *see* P L A Newsletter 5038
Pakistan Library Bulletin *see* Pakistan Library & Information Science Journal 5039
Pakistan Management Review (PAK ISSN 0969-8027) 1785
• Pakistan Medical Association. Journal (PAK ISSN 0030-9982) 5692
Pakistan. Ministry of Education. Yearbook (PAK ISSN 0078-8287) 2895
Pakistan. National Assembly. Debates. Official Report (PAK ISSN 0078-8333) 7459
Pakistan. Office of the Economic Adviser. Government Sponsored Corporations and Other Institutions (PAK ISSN 0078-8392) 1900
• Pakistan Pediatric Journal (PAK ISSN 0048-2722) 6099
Pakistan Petroleum Limited. Annual Report (PAK ISSN 0552-9115) 6786
Pakistan Philosophical Congress. Proceedings (PAK ISSN 0078-8406) 6938
Pakistan Philosophical Journal (PAK ISSN 0552-914X) 6938
Pakistan Pictorial (PAK ISSN 0377-2586) 3926
Pakistan. Planning and Development Division. Development Programme (PAK ISSN 0078-8414) 1900
• Pakistan Psychiatric Society. Journal (PAK ISSN 1726-8710) 6173
Pakistan Science Abstracts (PAK ISSN 0031-0085) 7938
Pakistan Science Conference. Proceedings (PAK ISSN 0078-8430) 7897
Pakistan Seafood Digest (PAK ISSN 1010-3562) 3604
Pakistan Statistical Association. Proceedings (PAK ISSN 0078-8473) 8393
Pakistan Studies (GBR ISSN 0262-3277) 4187
Pakistan Supreme Court Cases (PAK) 4958
Pakistan Tax Decisions (PAK ISSN 0031-0115) 1938
Pakistan Tax Decisions Annual Tax Digest *see* P.T.D. Annual Tax Digest 1938
Pakistan Textile (PAK) 8456
• Pakistan Textile Journal (PAK ISSN 0048-2757) 8456
Pakistan Tourism Newsletter (PAK) 8746
Pakistan Trade Directory - Exporters and Manufacturers (PAK) 2023
Pakistan Veterinarian (PAK) 8804
Pakistan Veterinary Index (PAK) 8816
• ➤ Pakistan Veterinary Journal (PAK ISSN 0253-8318) 8804
Pakistan. Water and Power Development Authority. Report (PAK ISSN 0083-8349) 3363
Pakistan Year Book (PAK ISSN 0552-9263) 3926
▼ • ➤ Pakistaniaat (USA ISSN 1948-6529) 4187
Pakistan's Balance of Payments (Annual) (PAK ISSN 0078-852X) 1938
Pakistan's Balance of Payments (Quarterly) (PAK) 1938
Pakistan's Books & Libraries (PAK) 7570
Pakkaus (FIN ISSN 0031-0131) 6714
• Pakn Treger/Book Peddler (USA ISSN 1093-1627) 7727
➤ Pakphyton (PAK ISSN 1016-0035) 807
The Pakshik Protirodh (BGD) 3800
La Palabra (ESP ISSN 1132-0591) 7811
La Palabra (USA ISSN 0277-1535) 5348
Palabra (Los Angeles) (USA ISSN 1932-7374) 5348
• Palabra (Saltillo) (MEX ISSN 1563-793X) 3910
Palabra Clave (ARG ISSN 1666-2938) 5039
• ➤ Palabra Clave (COL ISSN 0122-8285) 7991
palabra.com *see* Palabra (Saltillo) 3910
Palabra de Mujer (MEX) 8902
• La Palabra del Beni (BOL ISSN 1607-0062) 3802
La Palabra Diaria (USA ISSN 0475-4816) 7668
La Palabra entre Nosotros (USA ISSN 0896-1727) 7811
La Palabra: Revista de Literatura Chicana (USA) 5348
▼ Palabra, Vida y Fe (USA ISSN 1939-2990) 7811
La Palabra Viviente (CHL ISSN 0718-4417) 7770
➤ La Palabra y el Hombre (MEX ISSN 0185-5727) 4468
Palabras (ARG) 5348
Las Palabras (Taos) (USA) 6535
Palabras Pastorales (USA ISSN 1541-8138) 7668
Palace Hotel (ESP) 4395
Palace Museum. Journal *see* Gugong Bowuyuan Yuankan 4454
Palace Peeper (USA) 8475
El Palacio (USA ISSN 0031-0158) 4307
➤ Palacky University in Olomouc. Medical Faculty. Biomedical Papers (CZE ISSN 1213-8118) 5692
Paladin (USA) 2296
Palaeo Ichthyologica (DEU ISSN 0724-6331) 960
• ➤ Palaeobiodiversity and Palaeoenvironments (DEU ISSN 1867-1594) 6727
➤ Palaeobotanist (IND ISSN 0031-0174) 807
Palaeobulgarica (BGR ISSN 0204-4021) 4252
➤ Palaeodiversity (DEU ISSN 1867-6294) 2761
• ➤ Palaeogeography, Palaeoclimatology, Palaeoecology (NLD ISSN 0031-0182) 6727
➤ Palaeohispanica (ESP ISSN 1578-5386) 4252
Palaeohistoria (NLD ISSN 0552-9344) 410
• Palaeontographia Italica (ITA ISSN 0373-0972) 6727
➤ Palaeontographica. Abt. A: Palaeozoologie - Stratigraphie (DEU ISSN 0375-0442) 6727
➤ Palaeontographica. Abt. B: Palaeophytologie (DEU ISSN 0375-0299) 6728
➤ Palaeontographica Americana (USA ISSN 0078-8546) 6728
Palaeontographica Canadiana (CAN ISSN 0821-7556) 2761
➤ Palaeontographical Society. Monographs (London) (GBR ISSN 0269-3445) 2761
➤ Palaeontologia Africana (ZAF ISSN 0078-8554) 6728
➤ Palaeontologia Cathayana/Huaxia Gushengwu (CHN) 6728
• ➤ Palaeontologia Electronica (USA ISSN 1094-8074) 6728
Palaeontologia Indica/Pailiomtolojiya Indika (IND ISSN 0971-2844) 6728
Palaeontologia Polonica (POL ISSN 0078-8562) 6728
Palaeontological Abstracts *see* Gushengwuxue Wenzhai 6731
Palaeontological Society of India. Journal (IND ISSN 0552-9360) 6728
Palaeontological Society of Japan. Abstracts of the Annual Meeting *see* Nihon Koseibutsu Gakkai Nenkai Koen Yokoshu 6731
Palaeontological Society of Japan. Special Papers (JPN ISSN 0549-3927) 6728
• ➤ Palaeontologische Zeitschrift (DEU ISSN 0031-0220) 6728
• ➤ Palaeontology (GBR ISSN 0031-0239) 6728
• Palaeontology Newsletter (GBR ISSN 0954-9900) 6728
Palaeoslavica (USA ISSN 1070-5465) 5348
Palaeovertebrata (FRA ISSN 0031-0247) 6728
Palaeoworld (CHN ISSN 1671-2412) 6728
• ➤ Palaeoworld (NLD ISSN 1871-174X) 6728
➤ Palaestina Antiqua (BEL ISSN 0920-7422) 410
Palaestra (DEU ISSN 0303-4607) 5348
† • Palaestra (ITA ISSN 0031-0255) 8980
• Palaestra (USA ISSN 8756-5811) 3045
• ➤ Palaios (USA ISSN 0883-1351) 6728
Le Palais des Beaux-Arts (BEL) 510
Palante (CUB ISSN 0552-9395) 5233
Palatinate (GBR) 5348
Palatine Immigrant (USA ISSN 0884-5735) 3778
Palatine Patter (USA ISSN 8755-6014) 3778
Palaveri *see* Forma & Furniture 4540
➤ Paleoecology of Africa (NLD ISSN 0168-6208) 6728
Paleo (FRA ISSN 1145-3370) 410
Paleo-aktueel (NLD ISSN 1572-6622) 6728
• ➤ Paleobiology (USA ISSN 0094-8373) 6728
➤ PaleoBios (USA ISSN 0031-0298) 6729
• ➤ Paleoceanography (USA ISSN 0883-8305) 2816
The Paleoclimate Data Record (USA) 6729
Paleoclimate Publications Series (USA) 6729
Paleoetnologica (ARG ISSN 0326-5668) 351
• PaleoNet Forum (GBR) 6729
Paleontologia i Evolucio (ESP ISSN 0211-609X) 6729
Paleontologia Lombarda (ITA ISSN 1121-3361) 6729
Paleontologia Mexicana (MEX ISSN 0543-7652) 6729
• ➤ Paleontological Journal (RUS ISSN 0031-0301) 6729
• ➤ Paleontological Research (JPN ISSN 1342-8144) 6729
• Paleontological Society. Memoir (USA ISSN 0078-8597) 6729
Paleontological Society of Korea. Journal *see* Go'saengmul Haghoeji 6725
The Paleontological Society. Papers (USA ISSN 1089-3326) 6729
➤ Paleontologicheskii Zhurnal (RUS ISSN 0031-031X) 6729
Paleontologiia, Stratigrafiia i Litologiia (BGR ISSN 0204-7217) 6729
Paleontos (BEL ISSN 1377-4654) 6729
Paleopathology Newsletter (USA ISSN 0148-4737) 6729
• Paleorient (FRA ISSN 0153-9345) 6729
• Palestina Nu (SWE ISSN 1100-4746) 4177
• Palestine Exploration Quarterly (GBR ISSN 0031-0328) 410
• ➤ Palestine - Israel Journal of Politics, Economics and Culture (ISR ISSN 0793-1395) 7163
Palestine Refugees Today (AUT ISSN 0031-0336) 8061
Palestine Yearbook of International Law (NLD ISSN 1386-1972) 4937
Palestinian Documents *see* Al- Watha'iq al-Filastiniyyah 4326
Palestra/Bar (POL ISSN 0031-0344) 4755
Die Palette (AUT) 145
Paletten (SWE ISSN 0031-0352) 510
Palgrave Modern Novelists Series (GBR) 5348
▼ ➤ Paliativna Medicina a Liecba Bolesti (SVK ISSN 1337-6896) 5692
Palilia (DEU) 410
Palimpsestes. Textes de Reference (FRA ISSN 1274-9036) 5159
Palimpsestus (COL ISSN 1657-5083) 7991
• PALINET News (USA ISSN 0278-9469) 5063
Palingenesia (DEU ISSN 0552-9638) 2238
▼ Palisade Magazine (USA) 5079
Palitra Pedagoga (UKR ISSN 1680-449X) 2895
Palladio (ITA ISSN 0031-0379) 452
➤ Pallas (FRA ISSN 0031-0387) 2238
Pallas Athene (DEU ISSN 1439-9857) 7991
Pallet Digest (USA) 1051
Pallet Enterprise (USA ISSN 1065-3651) 3700
Pallet Enterprise. Buyer's Guide *see* Pallet Enterprise 3700
Pallet Profile Weekly (USA) 3714
Pallett and Case Industry *see* P A C 6712
• Palliative & Supportive Care (GBR ISSN 1478-9515) 5692
▼ • ➤ Palliative Care: Research and Treatment (NZL ISSN 1178-2242) 5977
• ➤ Palliative Medicine (GBR ISSN 0269-2163) 5693
Palliative Medicine and Rehabilitation *see* Palliativnaya Meditsina i Reabilitatsiya 6113
Palliativnaya Meditsina i Reabilitatsiya/Palliative Medicine and Rehabilitation (RUS) 6113
• Pallium (NLD ISSN 1389-2630) 5693
Pallottinische Studien zu Kirche und Welt (DEU) 7812
Pallottis Werk (DEU ISSN 0031-0395) 7668
Palm (LBR) 3789
Palm Beach Cottages & Gardens (USA) 3747
Palm Beach Design & Architectural Review (USA) 4548
Palm Beach Gazette (USA) 3557
Palm Beach Illustrated (USA ISSN 1047-5575) 3985
Palm Beach Society (USA ISSN 1045-7259) 3985
Palm Beach Young Society (USA) 7943
The Palm Beacher (USA) 5079
Palm Oil Developments (MYS ISSN 0127-3329) 145
Palm Oil Research Institute of Malaysia Occasional Paper *see* P O R I M Occasional Paper 145
• Palm Oil Technical Bulletin (MYS ISSN 1394-4983) 3144
Palm Springs Life (USA ISSN 0031-0425) 8746
Palm Springs Life Desert Guide (USA) 8746
Palmbaum (DEU ISSN 0943-545X) 5348
Palmebladet (NOR ISSN 1503-4593) 807
Palmer College of Chiropractic Alumni News *see* P C C Alumni News 2295
† Palmer's Company Cases (GBR ISSN 0267-5951) 8980
Palmer's Company Law (GBR ISSN 0142-341X) 4755
Palmer's Corporate Insolvency (GBR) 4755
Palmetto (USA ISSN 0276-4164) 3747
Palmetto Pharmacist (USA) 6866
PalmPower Magazine *see* Computing Unplugged 2570
Palms (USA ISSN 1523-4495) 807
▼ • Palo Alto Institute. Journal (USA ISSN 1948-7843) 7897
• ➤ Palo Alto Review (USA ISSN 1092-5619) 2895
Palomar (ITA ISSN 1590-1831) 4468
Palomar Italia *see* Palomar 4468
Palomino Horses (USA ISSN 0031-045X) 8295
Palomino Parade (USA) 8295
Palontorjuntatekniikka *see* Pelastustieto 3580
• Palstek (DEU ISSN 0936-5877) 8280
Paludicola (USA ISSN 1091-0263) 6729
Palyno-Bulletin *see* Palyno Bulletin 807
Palyno Bulletin (AUT ISSN 1816-4374) 807
• ➤ Palynology (USA ISSN 0191-6122) 6729
• Palynos (Online) (USA ISSN 1936-1718) 6729
➤ Pamatky Archeologicke/Archaeological Monuments (CZE ISSN 0031-0506) 410
• Pamatky Archeologicke. Bibliographical Register (Online) (CZE) 410
Pamatky Archeologicke. Bibliographical Register (Print) *see* Pamatky Archeologicke. Bibliographical Register (Online) 410
Pamatnik Narodniho Pisemnictvi. Sbornik (CZE ISSN 0231-5904) 5348
• Pambu (AUS) 4193
Pamiatky a Muzea (SVK ISSN 1335-4353) 4252
Pamiec i Sprawiedliwosc (POL ISSN 1427-7476) 4252
Pamietnik Literacki (POL ISSN 0031-0514) 5348
Pamietnik Slowianski (POL ISSN 0078-866X) 5348
➤ Pamietnik Teatralny (POL ISSN 0031-0522) 8475
Pamietnik Towarzystwa Lekarskiego Warszawskiego (POL ISSN 1233-2062) 5693
Pamietnikarstwo Polskie (POL ISSN 0137-3234) 4252
Pamietniki Muzyczne (POL) 6604
Pamphlet Architecture (USA) 452
Pampus (NLD ISSN 1871-3521) 5348
• Pamukkale Universitesi Egitim Fakultesi Dergisi (TUR ISSN 1301-0085) 2895
Pam'yat Stolit' (UKR ISSN 0869-3595) 410
➤ Pam'yatky Ukrainy: Istoriya ta Kul'tura/Ukrainian Heritage: History & Culture (UKR) 4252
Pamyatniki Kul'tury. Novye Otkrytiya/Monuments of Culture. New Discoveries (RUS) 510
Pamyatniki Otechestva (RUS ISSN 0207-2203) 4252
Pan *see* Pan und Vital 3855
Pan (FRA ISSN 1161-4137) 5159
Pan (GBR ISSN 1360-1563) 6604
Pan (ITA ISSN 0390-3141) 5159
Pan (MEX ISSN 0187-8492) 3675
• Pan-African Magazine (CAN) 3557
▼ • Pan African Medical Journal (UGA ISSN 1937-8688) 5693
The Pan - American (USA) 2296
Pan American Development Foundation. Annual Report (USA ISSN 0552-9913) 1603
Pan American Development Foundation News *see* P A D F News 1603
Pan American Health (USA ISSN 0377-5119) 7534
• Pan American Health Organization. Expanded Program on Immunization. Measles Surveillance in the Americas. Bulletin (USA ISSN 1564-0833) 5824
• Pan American Health Organization. Expanded Program on Immunization. Poliomyelitis Surveillance in the Americas. Bulletin (USA ISSN 1564-085X) 5824
Pan American Health Organization Newsletter *see* P A H O H I V Newsletter 5824
Pan American Health Organization. Proposed Program and Budget Estimates (USA ISSN 1012-9685) 7535
Pan American Health Organization. Scientific and Technical Publication (USA ISSN 1020-9492) 7535
Pan American Institute of Geography and History. Commission on History. Bibliografias (MEX ISSN 0078-8813) 4307
• ➤ Pan - American Journal of Aquatic Sciences (BRA ISSN 1809-9009) 2797
Pan American Journal of Public Health *see* Revista Panamericana de Salud Publica 7539
Pan American Sanitary Bureau. Annual Report of the Director (USA ISSN 0085-462X) 5693
Pan American Union. Bulletin *see* Americas (English Edition) 4442
▼ Pan Arab Journal of Oncology (JOR ISSN 2070-254X) 6032
▼ Pan Arab Journal of Voiding Dysfunction/Al-Magallat Al-'arabiyyat lil-Idhtrabat Al-Bawliyyat/Al- Majallat Al-'arabiyyat lil-Idhtrabat Al-Bawliyyat (EGY ISSN 1687-7896) 6273
Pan-Bladet *see* Panbladet 8980
Pan Directorio de Proveedores/Bread Caterers' Directory (MEX ISSN 0187-8506) 3675
Pan-European Associations (GBR ISSN 0265-458X) 7257
Pan-European Biological and Diversity Strategy Bulletin (FRA) 2624

Title

10726 PAPERS DE LA CATEDRA UNESCO ULRICH'S PERIODICALS

• Papers de la Catedra UNESCO (ESP ISSN 1577-8819) **7991**
Papers de Turisme (ESP ISSN 0214-8021) **8746**
Papers del Montgri (ESP ISSN 1137-6864) **6535**
• ➤ Papers: Explorations into Children's Literature (AUS ISSN 1034-9243) **5348**
Papers from the Annual Meeting of the Atlantic Provinces Linguistic Association *see* Atlantic Provinces Linguistic Association. Annual Meeting. Papers **5097**
Papers from the Institute of Archaeology *see* University College London. Institute of Archaeology. Papers **422**
▼ • Papers I E Med (Instituto Europeo del Mediterraneo) (ESP ISSN 1888-5357) **7257**
Papers in Austronesian Linguistics (AUS ISSN 1032-5077) **5159**
Papers in Japanese Studies *see* Michigan Papers in Japanese Studies **4186**
Papers in Laboratory Phonology (GBR) **5159**
† Papers in Leisure and Tourism Studies (GBR ISSN 0960-6629) **8980**
Papers in Linguistics from the University of Manchester (GBR ISSN 1363-4402) **5159**
Papers in Mediaeval Studies (CAN ISSN 0228-8605) **4253**
• Papers in Meteorology and Geophysics (JPN ISSN 0031-126X) **6393**
Papers in Museology (SWE ISSN 1103-0100) **6535**
† ➤ Papers in Organization (DNK ISSN 0906-0510) **8980**
Papers in Papuan Linguistics (AUS ISSN 1032-5107) **5159**
Papers in Pidgin and Creole Linguistics (AUS ISSN 0811-0026) **5159**
• ➤ Papers in Regional Science (USA ISSN 1056-8190) **7991**
Papers in Slavic Philology (USA ISSN 0161-8822) **5159**
Papers in Social Sciences (TWN) **7991**
Papers in Southeast Asian Linguistics (AUS ISSN 0078-9178) **5159**
Papers in Text Linguistics *see* Papiere zur Textlinguistik **5160**
Papers in the Administration of Development (GBR ISSN 0268-4020) **1603**
• Papers in the Politics of Global Competitiveness (GBR ISSN 1755-6740) **7163**
Papers in the Theory and Practice of Human Rights (GBR) **7213**
• ➤ Papers Lextra (ESP ISSN 1885-2785) **4755**
Papers of Remote Sensing Symposium *see* Rimoto Senshingu Shinpojumu Shiryo **4027**
Papers of Robert Morris, 1781-1784 (USA) **4308**
Papers of the Algonquian Conference/Actes du Congres des Algonquianistes *see* Algonquian Conference. Papers **323**
• Papers on Anthropology (EST ISSN 1406-0140) **351**
Papers on Fisheries Economics *see* Fiskerioekonomiske Smaaskrifter **3594**
Papers on French Seventeenth Century Literature (DEU ISSN 0343-0758) **5348**
Papers on Joyce (ESP ISSN 1135-0504) **5348**
• ➤ Papers on Language and Literature (USA ISSN 0031-1294) **5348**
• ➤ Papers on Social Representations. Thread of Discussion/Textes sur les Representations Sociales. Espace de Discussion (AUT ISSN 1021-5573) **7389**
• ➤ Papers on Surrealism (GBR ISSN 1750-1954) **511**
PapersIEMed *see* Papers I E Med **7257**
† • PaperTree Letter (USA ISSN 1180-9175) **8980**
PaperWeek International Reporter/Le Reporter de la Semaine Internationale du Papier (CAN) **6736**
Paperworker (USA ISSN 0363-6437) **4600**
PaperWorks *see* GiftMaker **8959**
Papeterie und Buero (CHE ISSN 1423-7016) **6736**
Papetier (CAN ISSN 0048-2889) **6736**
Le Papetier de France (FRA ISSN 0031-1324) **1854**
Les Papetieres du Quebec (CAN ISSN 0847-2645) **6736**
Papier aus Oesterreich (AUT ISSN 1011-0186) **6736**
Papier Buero Schreibwaren Spiel Magazin *see* P B S - Spiel Magazin **6735**
Papier Musique *see* A Contretemps **6541**
Papier-Toiture Asphalte *see* Canada. Statistics Canada. Asphalt Roofing **1045**
Papier und Folien *see* PackMittel **6735**
Papiere zur Textlinguistik/Papers in Text Linguistics (DEU ISSN 0341-3195) **5160**
Papiermacher B G (Berufsgenossenschaft) (DEU ISSN 1611-2393) **6737**
Papiermacher Magazin (DEU) **6737**
PapierRestaurierung *see* Journal of Paper Conservation **499**
Papierwaren, Buerobedarf, Schreibwaren Aktuell *see* P B S Aktuell **1853**
Papierwaren Buerobedarf Schreibwaren Report *see* P B S Report **1853**
Papieski Fakultet Teologiczny we Wroclawiu. Rozprawy Naukowe (POL) **7812**
Papilles (FRA ISSN 1165-2721) **3659**
• Papir (SVN ISSN 0350-6614) **6737**
Papir a Celuloza/Paper and Pulp (CZE ISSN 0031-1421) **6737**
Papirhandleren *see* Kontor/papir **1852**
Papirhandleren (NOR ISSN 0332-8929) **6737**
Papiripar (HUN ISSN 0031-1448) **6737**
Papiripari es Nyomdaipari Szakirodalmi Tajekoztato/Paper Industry & Printing Abstracts (HUN ISSN 0231-0740) **6740**
Papiro (DOM) **5039**
• Papotage (USA) **5233**
Papoum (FRA ISSN 1266-7528) **2206**
Papper & Kontor (SWE ISSN 1104-2400) **1854**
Papper och Massa *see* Nordisk Papper & Massa **6735**
Pappus (CAN ISSN 0710-0469) **3747**
paps (DEU ISSN 1432-8771) **6297**
Papua and New Guinea Education Gazette (PNG ISSN 0048-2919) **2895**
Papua and New Guinea Law Reports (PNG ISSN 0085-4689) **4958**
Papua New Guinea Banking Corporation. Annual Report (PNG) **1374**
Papua New Guinea Business *see* P N G Business **3926**
Papua New Guinea Coffee Journal *see* P N G Coffee Journal **3659**
Papua New Guinea. Department of Labour and Employment. Worker's Compensation Claims (PNG) **4530**
Papua New Guinea Institute of Medical Research. Monograph Series (PNG ISSN 0256-2901) **5693**
Papua New Guinea International Arrivals and Departures (PNG ISSN 1017-6551) **7313**
➤ Papua New Guinea Journal of Agriculture, Forestry and Fisheries (PNG ISSN 0256-954X) **145**
Papua New Guinea Journal of Education (PNG ISSN 0031-1472) **2896**
➤ Papua New Guinea Medical Journal (PNG ISSN 0031-1480) **5693**
Papua New Guinea National Bibliography (PNG ISSN 0252-8347) **633**
Papua New Guinea National Museum Record *see* P N G National Museum Record **4193**
Papua New Guinea. National Statistical Office. Abstract of Statistics (PNG ISSN 0310-5377) **8393**
Papua New Guinea. National Statistical Office. Annual Business Census (PNG ISSN 1023-6481) **1258**
Papua New Guinea. National Statistical Office. Building Statistics (PNG ISSN 0479-4826) **1048**
Papua New Guinea. National Statistical Office. Consumer Price Index (PNG ISSN 1017-6500) **8393**
Papua New Guinea. National Statistical Office. Domestic Factor Incomes, by Region and Province (PNG ISSN 1017-6403) **1258**
Papua New Guinea. National Statistical Office. Export Price Indexes (PNG ISSN 1017-6527) **1258**
Papua New Guinea. National Statistical Office. Government Finance Statistics (PNG ISSN 1017-6411) **1258**
Papua New Guinea. National Statistical Office. Gross Domestic Product and Expenditure (PNG ISSN 1017-639X) **1258**
Papua New Guinea. National Statistical Office. Household Expenditure Survey. Preliminary Bulletin (PNG) **4370**
Papua New Guinea. National Statistical Office. Import Price Indexes (PNG ISSN 1017-6543) **1258**
Papua New Guinea. National Statistical Office. International Trade - Exports (PNG ISSN 1017-6519) **1258**
Papua New Guinea. National Statistical Office. International Trade - Imports (PNG ISSN 1017-6535) **1258**
Papua New Guinea. National Statistical Office. Statistical Bulletin: Registered Motor Vehicles (PNG) **8528**
• Papua New Guinea Post-Courier (Online) (PNG ISSN 1563-5694) **3927**
Papua New Guinea Post-Courier Index *see* P N G Post-Courier Index **4587**
Papua New Guinea Times Index *see* P N G Times Index **4588**
Papua New Guinea University of Technology. Reporter (PNG ISSN 1019-5343) **2296**
Papyrologica Bruxellensia (BEL ISSN 0078-9402) **411**
† Papyrologica Castroctaviana (ITA) **8980**
Papyrologica Florentina (ITA ISSN 1824-6478) **5160**
➤ Papyrologica Lugduno-Batava (NLD ISSN 0169-9652) **5349**
Papyrologische Texte und Abhandlungen (DEU ISSN 0933-498X) **4155**
Papyrus (CAN ISSN 0820-2605) **2268**
• Papyrus (DNK ISSN 0903-4714) **4177**
Papyrus (JPN) **3901**
• Papyrus (USA) **5429**
Papyrus (West Hartford) (USA ISSN 1078-5841) **5349**
Par Avion (USA ISSN 1520-3611) **2354**
Par Golf (JPN) **8242**
Par Oneri (AUS ISSN 0810-0500) **6441**
par T U (DEU) **2296**
Para (DEU) **314**
Para Doxa *see* Paradoxa **5349**
Para phrase (CAN ISSN 1180-2537) **5349**
• Para Ti (ARG ISSN 0328-8501) **8879**
Parabas (IND ISSN 0031-1553) **5233**
Parabel (NOR ISSN 0808-1514) **6938**
† Parabiblos (ESP ISSN 1133-9756) **8980**
• Parabola (USA ISSN 0362-1596) **3621**
† Paraboles (FRA ISSN 0031-1561) **8980**
Parabolic Hyperbolic Or Elliptic Numerical Integration Code Series Journal of Computational Fluid Dynamics & its Applications *see* The P H O E N I C S Journal of Computational Fluid Dynamics & its Applications **3356**
• Parabrisas (ARG ISSN 0328-4387) **8597**
Parabrisas Guia Total de Rutas *see* Parabrisas **8597**
Parabrisas Libro de Los Tests *see* Parabrisas **8597**
Parabrisas Libro Guia Todos Los 4 x 4 *see* Parabrisas **8597**
El Paracaidista (USA) **7257**
• Parachute (CAN ISSN 0318-7020) **511**
Parachutist (USA ISSN 0031-1588) **8192**
Paracontact (CHE) **4078**
Parade (GBR ISSN 0031-160X) **3870**
Parade (IND) **3887**
• Parade (USA) **3985**
• Parade (ZAF ISSN 1819-8759) **8295**
Parade of Royalty (Year) (USA) **6812**
Parade Sauvage (FRA ISSN 0764-471X) **5349**
Paradeigmata (DEU) **6938**
Paradhikrit (IND ISSN 0972-3811) **1158**
• Paradigm Shift (Austin) (USA ISSN 1944-5458) **5349**
• Paradigm Shift (Kingston) (USA) **6647**
• Paradigma (VEN ISSN 1011-2251) **2896**
Paradis (FRA ISSN 1955-0960) **5079**
Paradise (PNG) **8785**
Paradise Family Guides: Big Island of Hawaii (USA ISSN 1552-9282) **8746**
Paradise Family Guides: Kauai (USA ISSN 1544-1407) **8746**
Paradise Family Guides: Maui (USA ISSN 1544-1377) **8746**
Paradise Golf (DEU ISSN 1618-5285) **8242**
Paradise Magazine (USA) **6297**
Paradise Traveller (DEU) **8746**
Paradiso (HND) **4468**
• Paradox (USA ISSN 1548-0593) **5349**
➤ Paradoxa (USA ISSN 1079-8072) **5349**
• ➤ Paradoxism (USA) **5349**
Parag (IND ISSN 0031-1642) **2206**
Paraglider (USA ISSN 1540-2185) **8192**
Paragoge Georgikon kai Ktenotrofikon Proionton Etous (Year) *see* Greece. National Statistical Service. Agricultural and Livestock Production (Year) **181**
• ➤ Paragrana (DEU ISSN 0938-0116) **351**
• ➤ Paragraph (GBR ISSN 0264-8334) **5349**
Paragraphes (CAN ISSN 0843-5235) **5349**
Paragraphic (CAN ISSN 0048-2935) **6173**
Paraguay (PRY ISSN 0257-7070) **633**
Paraguay. Centro de Promocion de las Exportaciones. Directorio de Exportadores - Export Directory (PRY) **1580**
Paraguay. Direccion General de Estadistica y Censos. Boletin Estadistico (PRY ISSN 0031-1677) **8393**
Paraguay. Ministerio de Industria y Comercio. Division de Registro y Estadistica Industrial. Encuesta Industrial (PRY ISSN 0085-4743) **1258**
Paraguay. Ministry of Industry and Trade. Investment Guide (PRY) **1643**
Paraguay Noticias (PRY) **7213**
Parakleet (NLD ISSN 0924-7688) **7770**
Paralegal (USA ISSN 0739-3601) **4755**
Paralegal Career Guide (USA) **4755**
Paralegal Educator (USA ISSN 1072-6527) **4755**
Paralegal School Directory (USA) **4755**
Paralegal's Guide to U.S. Government Jobs (USA ISSN 1040-3221) **4755**
Paraleli (BGR) **3805**
† Paralelo 37 (ESP ISSN 0210-3796) **8980**
• ➤ Parallax (GBR ISSN 1353-4645) **5349**
Parallax (USA ISSN 1549-0645) **3015**
Parallel and Distributed Computing and Systems (CAN ISSN 1027-2658) **2434**
Parallel and Distributed Computing Practices *see* International Journal of Computer Research **2425**
Parallel and Distributed Systems Report *see* P D S Report **5524**
Parallel and Large-Data Visualization and Graphics Symposium. Proceedings (USA ISSN 1543-4346) **2489**
• ➤ Parallel Computing (NLD ISSN 0167-8191) **2468**
Parallel Processing for Artificial Intelligence *see* Machine Intelligence and Pattern Recognition **2454**
• ➤ Parallel Processing Letters (SGP ISSN 0129-6264) **2468**
Paralleles (CHE ISSN 1015-7573) **5160**
† Paralleli (ITA ISSN 1121-5542) **8980**
Paralleli e Meridiani (ITA ISSN 1825-1528) **4253**
Paramagnitnyi Rezonans (RUS ISSN 0202-2257) **7029**
• Parameter Magazine (GBR ISSN 1754-3193) **5349**
• ➤ Parameters (Carlisle) (USA ISSN 0031-1723) **6441**
Parameters (Portland) (USA) **5233**
Parametric World (USA ISSN 1072-3803) **1298**
Parametro (ITA ISSN 0031-1731) **452**
Paramillo (VEN ISSN 0798-278X) **4468**
Parana, Brazil. Secretaria de Estado da Fazenda. Estatistica Economico-Financeira (BRA) **1258**
Parana em Paginas (BRA ISSN 0031-174X) **3804**
Parana Informacoes (BRA) **1510**
Paraninfo (HND) **7991**
Paranoia (USA) **7163**
Paranoid Bachelor Guy (USA) **7943**
The Paranormal Review (GBR ISSN 1369-0426) **6743**
Parapara Boletin Informativo (VEN) **7570**
Parapara Seleccion de Libros para Ninos y Jovenes (VEN ISSN 0798-1619) **7570**
Parapente Mag (FRA ISSN 1156-9743) **8327**
Parapharmex (FRA) **6866**
Paraplegie (CHE) **4078**
Paraplegiker (DEU ISSN 0723-5070) **4078**
• Parapluie (DEU ISSN 1439-1163) **4468**
Parapsychological Monographs (USA ISSN 0078-9437) **6743**
Parapsychology Foundation. Proceedings of International Conferences (USA) **6743**
Parapsychology-Psychic Science Reports (USA) **6743**
Parapsykologiske Notiser (NOR ISSN 0333-1172) **6743**
Parascope (USA ISSN 0738-1247) **4755**
Parashram Shakti (IND) **3887**
• ➤ Parasite (FRA ISSN 1252-607X) **894**
• ➤ Parasite Immunology (GBR ISSN 0141-9838) **5824**
▼ • ➤ Parasites & Vectors (GBR ISSN 1756-3305) **5948**
Parasitic Plants Magazine *see* Yakkoso Tsuchitorimochi no Tomo **823**
Parasitica (BEL ISSN 0031-1812) **696**
Parasitologia al Dia *see* Parasitologia Latinoamericana **894**
• Parasitologia Latinoamericana (CHL ISSN 0717-7704) **894**
▼ Parasitologists United Journal (EGY ISSN 1687-7942) **696**
Parasitology *see* Parazitologiya **5824**
• ➤ Parasitology (Cambridge) (GBR ISSN 0031-1820) **5824**
• ➤ Parasitology International (NLD ISSN 1383-5769) **5824**
• ➤ Parasitology Research (DEU ISSN 0932-0113) **894**
Parasitosis and Medical Entomology *see* Jishengchong yu Yixue Kunchong Xuebao **851**
Paraskino/Behind the Scenes (CYP) **3832**
• Parassitologia (ITA ISSN 0048-2951) **5824**
Parat (NOR ISSN 1504-4297) **4600**
• Paratesto (ITA ISSN 1824-6249) **7570**
➤ Parazitologiya/Parasitology (RUS ISSN 0031-1847) **5824**
De Parbode (SUR ISSN 1872-3292) **3954**
Parc National de La Vanoise. Travaux Scientifiques (FRA ISSN 0180-961X) **7897**
Parc National de Port Cros. Travaux Scientifiques/Port-Cros National Park. Scientific Reports (FRA ISSN 0241-8231) **2624**
Parc Natural del Delta de l'Ebre. Butlleti (ESP ISSN 1134-5578) **2624**
• Parcel (USA) **8508**
Parcel Shipping & Distribution *see* Parcel **8508**
Le Parchemin (BEL) **3778**
Le Parchemin. Recueil Genealogique et Heraldique (BEL) **3778**
Parchi Italia (ITA ISSN 1826-0462) **807**
Parchitalia *see* Parchi Italia **807**
➤ Parchment (CAN ISSN 1193-5146) **5349**
Parco Monte Barro. Quaderni (ITA ISSN 1825-7372) **697**
Parcours *see* In Stride **6022**
Parcs & Loisirs *see* Parks & Recreation Canada **4981**
Parcs et Reserves (BEL ISSN 1370-6322) **2624**
• PaRDeS (DEU ISSN 1614-6492) **7727**
Paregian Directory of Colleges (USA) **2961**
Paregian Directory of Independent - Private Schools (USA) **2961**
De Pareldiukerreeks (NLD ISSN 1872-2172) **5349**
Paremia (ESP ISSN 1132-8940) **3621**
• Parent & Child (USA ISSN 1070-0552) **2164**
Parent and Citizen Journal (AUS ISSN 1326-0669) **2896**
Parent and Preschooler Newsletter (USA ISSN 0887-0365) **2164**
Parent Cooperative Preschools International. Directory (USA) **2896**
Parent Guide (USA) **2164**
Parent Life *see* ParentLife **7770**
Parent News (USA ISSN 1077-274X) **4068**
Parent Pages (USA ISSN 1091-3173) **2164**
• Parent Paper (USA) **2164**
Parent Talk (GBR) **2164**
Parent Teacher Association Fundraising Essentials *see* P T A Fundraising Essentials **3029**
Parent-Teacher Association Perspectives *see* P T A Perspectives **2894**
Parent Teacher Organization Today *see* P T O Today **3029**
Parent.Teen (USA) **2164**
• The Parent Time (USA) **5079**
Parenteral & Enteral Nutrition *see* Changwai yu Changnei Yingyang **6656**
Parenteral Drug Association Journal of Pharmaceutical Science and Technology *see* P D A Journal of Pharmaceutical Science and Technology **6866**
Parenteral Drug Association Letter *see* P D A Letter **6866**
Parenteral Drug Association Technical Reports *see* P D A Technical Reports **6866**
† Parentesi (ITA) **8980**

Title

10728 PARTNERS' NEWS ULRICH'S PERIODICALS

Partners' News *see* SHARE (Birmingham) **7681**
• Partner's Report (New York, 1987) (USA ISSN 0892-4805) **4878**
• Partner's Report (New York, 1989) (USA ISSN 1043-7428) **1298**
Partner's Report for CPA Firm Owners *see* Partner's Report (New York, 1989) **1298**
Partner's Report for Law Firm Owners *see* Partner's Report (New York, 1987) **4878**
Partners Task Force for Gay & Lesbian Couples (USA) **4377**
• ➤ Partnership (CAN ISSN 1911-9593) **5039**
Partnership for Aboriginal Care. Annual Report (AUS ISSN 1832-2565) **8061**
• Partnership Online (GBR) **1158**
• Partnership Tax Planning & Practice (USA) **1938**
• Partnership Taxation (USA) **1938**
• Partnerships (NLD) **1938**
▼ • ➤ Partnerships (USA ISSN 1944-1061) **2997**
Partnery i Konkurenty *see* Partnery i Konkurenty. Laboratorium **6405**
Partnery i Konkurenty. Laboratorium (RUS ISSN 1813-9469) **6405**
• Partout (DEU) **3855**
Partridge, Quail and Francolin Specialist Group News *see* P Q F News **913**
Parts (ITA ISSN 1120-2179) **8598**
Parts & People (USA ISSN 1083-771X) **8598**
• Parts & People (Northwest Motor Edition) (USA) **8598**
Parts & Pieces (DEU ISSN 1862-2135) **8598**
Parts Connection Hot Line *see* Hot Line Parts Connection Monthly **5452**
The Parts Manager *see* DealersEdge Parts Manager **8577**
parTU *see* par T U **2296**
Party (NLD ISSN 1382-4449) **3915**
• Party & Paper Retailer (USA ISSN 0899-6008) **4981**
Party Construction *see* Dang Jian **7128**
Party History Research & Teaching *see* Dangshi Yanjiu yu Jiaoxue **7128**
Party Life (IND ISSN 0377-2667) **7164**
The Party Magazine (GBR ISSN 1479-9448) **3870**
Party Platter (USA) **2687**
• ➤ Party Politics (GBR ISSN 1354-0688) **7164**
▼ Party Sex (ARG ISSN 1851-331X) **6297**
Party Times *see* Progressive Party **1965**
PartyLine (USA) **32**
Partysan (DEU) **5079**
Pas a Pas (FRA ISSN 1631-963X) **3747**
Pas a Pas *see* Footsteps **8040**
Pas-de-Calais. Commission Departementale d'Histoire et d'Archeologie. Memoires (FRA ISSN 0996-4614) **4253**
Pasaa Journal (THA ISSN 0125-2488) **3075**
Pasadena Official Visitors Guide (USA) **8747**
Pasado y Memoria (ESP ISSN 1579-3311) **4253**
Pasajes (ESP ISSN 1575-2259) **7164**
Pasajes. Arquitectura y Critica (ESP ISSN 1575-1937) **452**
Pasajes Construccion *see* Pasajes. Arquitectura y Critica **452**
▼ Pasajes. Diseno (ESP ISSN 1889-1586) **452**
Pasarelas Internacionales (ESP ISSN 1136-0607) **2259**
Pasarkrant (NLD ISSN 0926-3810) **4187**
Paschim Banga (IND) **3887**
Paschim Bongal (IND) **3887**
† El Paseante (ESP ISSN 1130-0388) **8980**
Paseka (RUS) **145**
† Pashosh (ISR ISSN 0334-3022) **8980**
Pashto *see* Pushto **5163**
Pashto Academy. Monthly Journal (AFG) **5349**
Pasicrisie Belge (BEL ISSN 0031-2614) **4756**
Pasientstatistikk (Kongsvinger) *see* Norway. Statistisk Sentralbyraa. Pasientstatistikk **4114**
• Pasifika Interactions Project. Working Paper (NZL ISSN 1177-9063) **7164**
Pasinomie (BEL ISSN 0031-2630) **4756**
Paskin (EST) **2206**
Paso a Paso *see* Footsteps **8040**
Paso Fino Horse World (USA ISSN 1054-3201) **8295**
• Pasonariti Kenkyuu/Japanese Journal of Personality (JPN ISSN 1348-8406) **7389**
• PasOpp-Rapport (NOR ISSN 1504-3428) **5693**
Pasos (CRI ISSN 1016-9857) **7770**
• Pasos (ESP ISSN 1695-7121) **8747**
Pasport Ekspress (RUS) **8747**
Pasque Petals (USA ISSN 0031-2649) **5429**
Pasquino (USA ISSN 0031-2657) **2296**
† Pasquino Musicale (ITA) **8980**
Pass (GBR) **8598**
Pass Herald Ltd. (CAN ISSN 0710-3891) **3815**
Pass It On (USA ISSN 1942-0021) **4756**
Pass It On! (USA) **6604**
Pass Key to the G M A T *see* Barron's Pass Key to the G M A T **2968**
Passage (DNK ISSN 0901-8883) **5349**
Passage *see* Rehabilitatie **6180**
Passagem (DEU ISSN 1861-583X) **7991**
• PassageMaker (USA ISSN 1095-7286) **8280**
Passagen (Berlin) (DEU) **8785**
Passagen (Hildesheim) (DEU) **4468**
Passager (USA ISSN 1052-889X) **4053**
• Passages (USA ISSN 1933-5148) **3557**
▼ Passages a l'Act (FRA ISSN 1961-3458) **5349**
➤ Passages North (USA ISSN 0278-0828) **5350**
• Passaggi (ITA ISSN 1826-5219) **4468**
Passaic County Dental Society Newsletter (USA) **5860**
Passaic Review (USA ISSN 0731-4663) **5233**
Passaic River Review (USA) **2624**
Il Passatempo (ITA ISSN 1591-1349) **2896**
• Passato e Presente (ITA ISSN 1120-0650) **4253**
Passauer Bistumsblatt (DEU ISSN 0031-2681) **7668**
Passauer Neue Presse (DEU) **3855**
Passauer Reihe (DEU ISSN 0945-3849) **4518**
Passauer Universitaetsschriften zur Archaeologie (DEU ISSN 0945-327X) **411**
Passe-Murailles (FRA ISSN 1954-2356) **2945**
Passenger and Immigration Lists Index. Supplement (USA ISSN 0736-8267) **3779**
• Passenger Forecast (Online) (CAN) **8550**
Passenger Pigeon (USA ISSN 0031-2703) **913**
Passenger Services Conference Resolutions Manual (CAN ISSN 0256-3282) **8550**
Passenger Tariff Coordinating Conferences Resolutions Manual (CAN) **8550**
Passenger Terminal World (GBR ISSN 1362-0770) **8550**
Passenger Train Services Over Unusual Lines *see* Branch Line News **8615**
Passenger Transport (USA ISSN 0364-345X) **8508**
• Passenger Transport Monitor. Scotland (GBR ISSN 1752-413X) **8508**
• Passenger Transport Monitor. Wales (GBR ISSN 1752-4156) **8508**
Passenger Travel in U K *see* Key Note Market Review: Passenger Travel in the U K **1896**
Passenger Vehicle Guide (AUS) **8598**
Passengerboat *see* Ryokakusen **8659**
Passepartout (DNK ISSN 0908-5351) **511**
Passeport Canada. Rapport Annuel *see* Passport Canada. Annual Report **7257**
Passerelle Eco (FRA ISSN 1951-8749) **3459**
• Le Passeur (CAN ISSN 1708-1416) **5039**
Passi (ZAF ISSN 1990-2611) **3949**
Passie voor Luxe *see* Passion du Luxe **3801**
Passiflora (USA ISSN 1548-3061) **807**
Passigli Poesia (ITA ISSN 1824-5188) **5429**
The Passing Show (USA ISSN 1061-8112) **8475**
Passion *see* Passion du Luxe **3801**
Passion (GBR ISSN 1352-3473) **5233**
Passion (SWE ISSN 1653-8625) **3956**
▼ Passion 43eme (FRA ISSN 1961-4225) **4343**
▼ Passion Construction (FRA ISSN 1957-5696) **1029**
Passion du Luxe (BEL ISSN 1377-6347) **3801**
† Passion du Patchwork (FRA ISSN 1767-9567) **8980**
Passion Fruit *see* Passionfruit **8747**
Passion Intense (FRA ISSN 1773-4754) **5412**
Passion Lady (DEU) **590**
Passion Men (DEU) **590**
Passion Quarante-Troisieme *see* Passion 43eme **4343**
Passione Pesca in Acqua Dolce (ITA ISSN 1826-395X) **8327**
Passione Pesca in Mare (ITA ISSN 1826-3968) **8328**
Passionfruit (USA ISSN 1527-6945) **8747**
Passionist Youth *see* Gioventu Passionista **8959**
Passions Complices *see* Collection Passions Complices **5276**
Passive Activity Losses and At-Risk Rules (USA ISSN 1931-5759) **1298**
▼ Passive Incomes (ZAF ISSN 1996-1219) **1837**
Passivhaus Kompendium (DEU) **1029**
Passo a Passo *see* Footsteps **8040**
Passos *see* Tracce. Litterae Communionis **7690**
Passover Directory (USA) **7728**
Passport (CAN ISSN 1194-8302) **2296**
Passport (GBR ISSN 0960-3697) **5233**
• Passport (Columbus) (USA ISSN 1949-9760) **7257**
Passport (New York) (USA) **8747**
• Passport Canada. Annual Report (CAN ISSN 1719-914X) **7257**
• Passport Newsletter (USA ISSN 1095-6824) **8747**
Passport to World Band Radio (USA ISSN 0897-0157) **2361**
Password (DEU ISSN 0930-3693) **2532**
Password (USA ISSN 0031-2738) **4308**
Password *see* I S S A Journal **2514**
Past *see* Minalo **4153**
Past (GBR ISSN 0965-1381) **411**
• ➤ Past & Present (GBR ISSN 0031-2746) **4155**
Past & Present Supplements *see* Past & Present **4155**
Past Global Changes News *see* P A G E S News **3459**
➤ Past Imperfect (CAN ISSN 1192-1315) **4155**
Past, Present, and Future (USA ISSN 0895-0857) **4308**
Past, Present, Futures (USA) **1643**
Past Times: The Nostalgia Entertainment Newsletter (USA ISSN 1050-5504) **6509**
• The Past Uncovered (GBR ISSN 1364-324X) **411**
Pasta! (DEU) **3855**
Pasta *see* Tastes of Italia **3665**
Pasta (USA) **4365**
Pasta Journal (USA ISSN 8750-9393) **3659**
• Pasta Lovers Newsletter (USA) **4365**
Pastagens e Forragens (PRT ISSN 0870-6263) **145**
Paste (USA ISSN 1540-3106) **6604**
Paste-Up (USA) **6897**
Pastel (FRA ISSN 0996-4878) **6604**
• The Pastel Journal (USA ISSN 1524-9034) **511**
▼ • Pasteur Le Mag' (FRA ISSN 1957-2050) **5824**
Pasteur Le Magazine *see* Pasteur Le Mag' **5824**
Pastfinder (USA) **3779**
Pasticceria Internazionale (ITA ISSN 0392-4718) **3675**
▼ Pasticcio Quartz (USA ISSN 1941-949X) **511**
Pasticcio Zine *see* Pasticcio Quartz **511**
Pastila de Ras (ROM ISSN 1454-4113) **4343**
Pastizales (MEX ISSN 0304-2502) **295**
Pastoral Andina (PER) **7812**
• ➤ Pastoral Care in Education (GBR ISSN 0264-3944) **2896**
• Pastoral Lines (AUS ISSN 1834-2566) **3459**
Pastoral Liturgy (USA ISSN 1946-9586) **6604**
• Pastoral Music (USA ISSN 0363-6569) **6604**
Pastoral Music Notebook (USA ISSN 0145-6636) **6604**
Pastoral Patterns (USA ISSN 1079-4751) **7812**
• ➤ Pastoral Psychology (USA ISSN 0031-2789) **7389**
The Pastoral Review (GBR) **7812**
Pastoral Sciences *see* Counseling et Spiritualite **6644**
Pastoral Theology (USA ISSN 1098-3562) **7669**
Pastoralblaetter (DEU ISSN 0031-2800) **7669**
Pastoralblatt (DEU) **7812**
Pastorale Verkenningen. Extern Katern (NLD ISSN 1875-0850) **7669**
Pastoralia (GTM) **7669**
➤ Pastoraltheologie (DEU ISSN 0720-6259) **7669**
Pastoraltheologische Informationen (DEU ISSN 0555-9308) **7812**
Pastores (POL ISSN 1505-9634) **7812**
Pastos y Forrajes (CUB ISSN 0864-0394) **268**
Pastry Art & Design *see* Dessert Professional **3673**
Pasturas Tropicales (COL ISSN 1012-7410) **145**
Pasture Literature Monthly *see* Caoyuan **5270**
• Pasumai Vikatan (IND) **146**
Pata Travel News Asia - Pacific (SGP) **8747**
El Patagonico (ARG) **3791**
Il Patalogo (ITA) **8475**
Patchwork & Quilting (GBR ISSN 0268-5620) **6641**
Patchwork & Stitching (AUS) **6641**
Patchwork Magazin (DEU ISSN 1434-5080) **538**
Patchwork Patter (USA) **6641**
Patchwork Professional (DEU ISSN 1862-3115) **538**
Patchwork Spezial (DEU ISSN 1862-3123) **538**
Paten (DEU ISSN 0176-2982) **8061**
• Patent Abstracts in English (RUS) **6760**
Patent Abstracts of Bulgaria (BGR) **6760**
Patent and Trademark Institute of Canada. Annual Proceedings (CAN ISSN 0079-015X) **6755**
Patent and Trademark Office Notices (USA) **6755**
• Patent and Trademark Office Society. Journal (USA ISSN 0882-9098) **6755**
Patent Applications Handbook (USA) **6755**
Patent Attorneys and Agents Registered to Practice before the U.S. Patent and Trademark Office *see* Attorneys and Agents Registered to Practice before the U.S. Patent and Trademark Office **6745**
Patent Cooperation Treaty Gazette *see* P C T Gazette (Bilingual Edition) **6755**
Patent Cooperation Treaty Gazette (Bilingual Edition) *see* P C T Gazette (Bilingual Edition) **6755**
Patent Cooperation Treaty Handbook (GBR) **6755**
Patent Cooperation Treaty Newsletter *see* P C T Newsletter **6755**
• Patent Fast-Alert (GBR ISSN 1462-2394) **6866**
Patent Focus (GBR ISSN 1749-4176) **6756**
• Patent Focus (GBR) **6756**
Patent Journal Including Trademarks, Designs and Copyright (ZAF ISSN 0031-286X) **6756**
Patent Law Handbook (USA ISSN 0192-8198) **6756**
Patent Law: Legal and Economic Principles (USA) **6756**
• Patent Law Perspectives (USA) **6756**
The Patent Lawyer (USA ISSN 1549-9871) **6756**
Patent Legislation and Commentary (CAN ISSN 1910-4030) **4756**
• Patent Licensing Transactions (USA) **6756**
• Patent Litigation: Procedures & Tactics (USA) **6756**
Patent News *see* Tokkyo Nyusu **6758**
Patent- och Registreringsverkets Foerfattningssamling (SWE ISSN 0347-500X) **6756**
Patent Office. Annual Gazette *see* Tokkyocho Nenpo **6758**
Patent Office of the Republic of Bulgaria. Annual Report *see* Patentno Vedomstvo na Republika Bulgaria. Godishen Otchet **6756**
Patent Office Record *see* Canadian Patent Office Record **6747**
• Patent Office Rules and Practice (USA) **6756**
Patent Office Technical Society. Journal (IND) **6756**
• Patent Strategy and Management (USA ISSN 1532-0162) **4756**
• Patent, Trademark & Copyright Law Daily (USA ISSN 1535-1610) **6756**
Patent, Trademark and Copyright Laws (Year) (USA ISSN 0741-1219) **6756**
Patent, Trademark, and Copyright Regulations (USA) **6756**
Patent, Trademark, and Copyright Regulations. Supplement (USA) **6756**
Patent Update *see* Genetic Technology News **869**
• Patent World (GBR ISSN 0950-2513) **6756**
Patent Yearbook *see* Patent Focus **6756**
• Patentblatt (Online) (DEU) **6756**
• La Patente di Guida (ITA ISSN 1120-4176) **8598**
PatentEye (SWE ISSN 1403-2309) **6756**
Patentjoernaal Insluitende Handelsmerke, Modelle en Outeursreg *see* Patent Journal Including Trademarks, Designs and Copyright **6756**
Patentni Glasnik (SRB ISSN 0031-2908) **6756**
Patentno Vedomstvo na Republika Bulgaria. Godishen Otchet/Patent Office of the Republic of Bulgaria. Annual Report (BGR) **6756**
Patentno Vedomstvo na Republika Bulgaria. Ofitsialen Biuletin/The Official Gazette of the Patent Office of the Republic of Bulgaria (BGR) **6756**
Patents *see* Tokkyo **6758**
• Patents Abstracts (USA) **6801**
• Patents Abstracts of Japan (JPN) **6760**
• Patents and Design Journal (Online)/R'shumot. Yoman Happatentim w'haMidgamim (ISR) **6756**
Patents and Design Journal (Print) *see* Patents and Design Journal (Online) **6756**
Patents and Licensing (JPN ISSN 0388-7081) **6756**
Patents Office Journal (IRL ISSN 1393-1415) **6756**
• Patents, Trade Marks and Related Rights (AUS) **6756**
Patenttidning *see* Finland. Patentti- ja Rekisterihallitus. Patenttilehti **6750**
Patenty i Litsenzii (RUS) **6756**
The Pater Newsletter (USA ISSN 0264-8342) **5350**
• The Paterson Literary Review (USA ISSN 1938-4785) **5233**
Paterson's Licensing Acts (GBR ISSN 0269-3658) **4756**
• Path Consult (USA ISSN 1559-8675) **5693**
Path of Truth (ZAF ISSN 0031-2932) **7669**
• Pathfinder (Bethesda) (USA ISSN 1948-4569) **6441**
The Pathfinder (Lewiston) (USA) **2296**
• Pathfinder Business (GBR ISSN 1753-7355) **1158**
Pathfinders Travel (USA ISSN 1096-0708) **8747**
• ➤ Pathobiology (CHE ISSN 1015-2008) **5764**
Pathogenese und Klinik der Harnsteine (DEU ISSN 0174-4860) **6273**
▼ • ➤ PathoGenetics (GBR ISSN 1755-8417) **877**
Patholinguistica (DEU ISSN 0173-301X) **5160**
• ➤ Der Pathologe (DEU ISSN 0172-8113) **5693**
• ➤ Pathologica (ITA ISSN 0031-2983) **5693**
Pathological Physiology and Experimental Therapy *see* Patologicheskaya Fiziologiya i Eksperimental'naya Terapiya **5694**
Pathologie Biologie *see* Pathologie et Biologie **5693**
• ➤ Pathologie et Biologie (FRA ISSN 0369-8114) **5693**
Pathologie, Science, Formation *see* Collection Pathologie, Sciences, Formation **5598**
• Pathology (AUS) **5860**
• ➤ Pathology (GBR ISSN 0031-3025) **5693**
• ➤ Pathology and Laboratory Medicine (USA ISSN 1521-7418) **5910**
• Pathology and Oncology Research (NLD ISSN 1219-4956) **6032**
• Pathology Case Reviews (USA ISSN 1082-9784) **5694**
Pathology in Practice (GBR ISSN 1465-9131) **5694**
• ➤ Pathology International (AUS ISSN 1320-5463) **5694**
Pathology Lab Coding Alert *see* Pathology/Lab Coding Alert **4518**
• Pathology/Lab Coding Alert (USA ISSN 1947-6841) **4518**
• Pathology Patterns Reviews (USA ISSN 1542-2305) **5694**
• ➤ Pathology, Research and Practice (DEU ISSN 0344-0338) **5694**
• ➤ Pathophysiology (NLD ISSN 0928-4680) **926**
• ➤ Pathophysiology of Haemostasis and Thrombosis (CHE ISSN 1424-8832) **5940**
• Pathos Net (Online) (USA) **314**
PathWay (AUS ISSN 1449-793X) **5694**
• Pathway Interaction Database (GBR ISSN 1752-5519) **6032**
Pathway to God (IND ISSN 0971-927X) **7669**
† Pathways (AUS ISSN 1833-2307) **8980**
Pathways (CAN ISSN 0840-8114) **2624**
Pathways (Atlanta) (USA ISSN 1931-8219) **7770**
Pathways (Bethesda) (USA) **7389**
Pathways (Chestnut Hill) (USA ISSN 0899-9252) **7459**
Pathways (Maynardville) (USA ISSN 8755-4747) **4308**
Pathways (Middletown) (USA ISSN 1942-1044) **3779**
Pathways (Watsonville) (USA) **7702**
Pathways Across America (USA) **8328**
Pathways to Health (USA) **6938**
Pathways to Outdoor Communication (USA ISSN 1077-5110) **2625**
Pathways to Profitability (USA) **4548**
• The Patient (NZL ISSN 1178-1653) **5694**
▼ The Patient (USA) **4109**
• Patient Access Advisor (USA ISSN 1933-3307) **4109**
▼ • Patient Access Weekly Advisor (USA ISSN 1947-8992) **4109**
• Patient Care (CAN ISSN 0845-065X) **5694**
Patient Care (NLD ISSN 0770-4224) **5694**
• ➤ Patient Care for the Nurse Practitioner (Online) (USA) **5977**
• Patient Care Law Weekly (USA ISSN 1551-5257) **5694**
† • ➤ Patient Care: Primary Care Topics in Dermatology (USA) **8980**
Patient Centre Care (GBR ISSN 1477-481X) **4109**
• ➤ Patient Education and Counseling (IRL ISSN 0738-3991) **7535**
• Patient Education Management (USA ISSN 1087-0296) **5694**

Title

➤ Peabody Museum of Archaeology and Ethnology. Monographs (USA ISSN 1931-8812) **411**
➤ Peabody Museum of Archaeology and Ethnology. Papers (USA ISSN 0079-0303) **411**
➤ Peabody Museum of Natural History. Bulletin (USA ISSN 0079-032X) **7897**
Peabody Reflector (USA ISSN 0031-3459) **2296**
Peace (IND ISSN 0031-3467) **7708**
• ➤ Peace & Change (USA ISSN 0149-0508) **7258**
• ➤ Peace and Conflict (USA ISSN 1078-1919) **7389**
Peace and Conflict Issues Series (FRA) **7258**
• Peace and Conflict Studies (USA ISSN 1082-7307) **7258**
• ➤ Peace and Democracy in South Asia (MYS) **7258**
• Peace and Freedom (USA ISSN 0015-9093) **7258**
• Peace & Freedom (Spalding) (GBR ISSN 1351-1653) **5350**
Peace and Freedom News (GBR ISSN 0031-3491) **7258**
Peace & Order *see* Chang'an **7429**
Peace & Policy (JPN) **7258**
Peace and Security (AUT ISSN 1028-4885) **7258**
• Peace Arch News (CAN ISSN 0700-9003) **3815**
Peace Brigades International *see* Presence (Toronto) **8063**
Peace Brigades International. Newsletter *see* Presence (Toronto) **8063**
Peace Chronicle (USA) **7258**
• ➤ Peace, Conflict & Development (GBR ISSN 1742-0601) **7258**
Peace Conversion Times (USA) **7258**
• Peace Corps. Performance and Accountability Report (USA ISSN 1930-1251) **7258**
• Peace Corps Times (USA ISSN 0884-9196) **7258**
• Peace Economics, Peace Science and Public Policy (Online) (USA ISSN 1554-8597) **7164**
Peace Education Center Monthly of Peace and Justice Action (USA) **7258**
Peace Gazette (USA) **7258**
Peace Human Rights *see* Pace Diritti Umani **7213**
• Peace Magazine (CAN ISSN 0826-9521) **7258**
• Peace Matters (GBR ISSN 1350-3006) **7258**
• Peace News for Nonviolent Revolution (GBR ISSN 0031-3548) **7258**
• Peace Newsletter (USA ISSN 0735-4134) **7258**
Peace Office Newsletter (USA ISSN 0112-238X) **7740**
† Peace Plans (AUS) **8980**
Peace Press (USA) **5233**
• Peace, Prosperity & Democracy (USA ISSN 1533-1636) **7164**
Peace Psychology (USA ISSN 1935-4894) **7389**
• ➤ Peace Research (CAN ISSN 0008-4697) **7258**
• Peace Research Abstracts Journal (USA ISSN 0031-3599) **7200**
Peace Research Institute Frankfurt Reports *see* P R I F Reports **7257**
Peace Research Reviews (CAN ISSN 0553-4283) **7259**
• ➤ Peace Review (GBR ISSN 1040-2659) **7259**
Peace River Block Daily News (CAN) **3815**
Peace Studies *see* Heiwa Kenkyu **7240**
Peace Tax Fund Newsletter (USA ISSN 1065-254X) **7213**
• Peace Watch (USA ISSN 1080-9864) **7259**
Peacekeeper *see* Australian Peacekeeper and Peacemaker **8026**
Peacekeeping (GBR ISSN 1367-9880) **7259**
• ➤ Peacekeeping & International Relations (CAN ISSN 1187-3485) **7259**
Peacelinks (GBR) **7669**
† The Peacemaker (NZL) **8980**
• Peacework (USA ISSN 0748-0725) **7164**
Peach (DEU) **2206**
Peach - Times (USA ISSN 0031-3610) **245**
Peafowl Report (USA) **295**
Peak (CAN ISSN 0031-3629) **2296**
Peak (DEU ISSN 1613-8775) **8328**
• Peak (NOR ISSN 0806-7066) **3110**
The Peak (Hong Kong Edition) *see* The Peak (Singapore Edition) **5079**
The Peak (Indonesia Edition) *see* The Peak (Singapore Edition) **5079**
The Peak (Malaysia Edition) *see* The Peak (Singapore Edition) **5079**
The Peak (Singapore Edition) (SGP ISSN 0218-0480) **5079**
• Peak and Prairie (USA) **2625**
Peak District Journal of Natural History and Archaeology (GBR ISSN 1360-4422) **411**
Peak District Journal of Natural History and Archaeology. Special Publication (GBR ISSN 1369-3697) **411**
Peak District Magazine (GBR) **8747**
The Peak Selections of Timepieces (SGP) **4569**
Peake Studies (CHE ISSN 1013-1191) **5233**
Peaky Hide (USA ISSN 1091-8116) **5350**
➤ Pe'amim (ISR ISSN 0334-4088) **7728**
The Peanut Grower (USA ISSN 1042-9379) **245**
Peanut Industry Guide (USA ISSN 0740-2562) **205**
Peanut News (USA) **205**
Peanut Report (USA) **205**
➤ Peanut Science (Online) (USA ISSN 1943-7668) **245**
Pearce-Sellards Series (USA ISSN 0079-0354) **6535**
Pearl (USA) **5429**
Pearl Harbor Shipyard & I M F Log *see* Shipyard & I M F Log **6446**
Pearl Harbor Study Group Newsletter *see* P H S G Newsletter **6897**
Pearl Oyster (NCL ISSN 1021-1861) **3604**
Pearl River *see* Renmin Zhujiang **3364**
Pearl River Economy *see* Zhujiang Jingji **1198**
Pearls Magazine (USA) **6509**
▼ • Pearls of Travel Wisdom (USA ISSN 1948-1675) **8747**
Pearls of Wisdom (USA ISSN 1059-2350) **7669**
Pears Cyclopaedia (GBR ISSN 0079-0362) **3121**
Pearson Investment Letter (USA) **1644**
Peasants in History and Literature (AUS) **4469**
Peatland News (IRL ISSN 0791-2757) **2625**
Peatlands International (FIN ISSN 1455-8491) **6475**
Pebble (USA ISSN 0031-3696) **5429**
Pebble Beach (USA) **8747**
The Pecan Grower (USA ISSN 1044-9639) **245**
Pecan South (USA) **245**
Pechatnyi Dvor (RUS) **1159**
Peche. Annuaire *see* Fisheries. Yearbook **3613**
▼ La Peche aux Leurres Mer & Ocean (FRA ISSN 1957-3782) **8328**
La Peche en Mer (FRA ISSN 0295-5989) **3604**
▼ Peche & Innovations (FRA ISSN 1958-5144) **3604**
La Peche & les Poissons (FRA ISSN 0031-3718) **3604**
La Peche Europeenne *see* Fisheries and Aquaculture in Europe **3592**
Peche Maritime (FRA ISSN 0031-3726) **3604**
Peche Mouche (FRA ISSN 1282-5220) **8328**
Peches Canadiennes. Commerce International *see* Canadian Fisheries. International Trade **1554**
Peches Canadiennes. Debarquements *see* Canadian Fisheries. Landings **1882**
Les Peches Canadiennes. Produits et Stocks *see* Canadian Fisheries. Products and Inventories **1882**
Peches et Bateaux (FRA ISSN 1779-9651) **8328**
Peches et Oceans Canada. Plan de Gestion de Chasse au Phoque de l'Atlantic *see* Canada. Department of Fisheries and Oceans. Atlantic Seal Hunt Management Plan **3588**
Peches et Oceans. Serie de l'Education Generale (CAN ISSN 0837-4503) **3604**
Pecheur Belge (BEL ISSN 0770-2701) **3604**
Le Pecheur de France (FRA ISSN 0154-6953) **8328**
Le Pecheur de France. Peche pour Tous *see* Peches et Bateaux **8328**
Pecheur Romand (CHE) **8328**
Peckerwood (CAN ISSN 1182-6193) **5429**
Pecten (English Edition) (CAN ISSN 1185-5444) **6786**
Pecten (French Edition) (CAN ISSN 1185-5436) **6786**
Pecvnia (ESP ISSN 1699-9495) **1159**
Pedagogia (PRI ISSN 0031-3769) **2896**
Pedagogia e Vita (ITA ISSN 0031-3777) **2896**
Pedagogia Oggi (ITA ISSN 1827-0824) **2896**
Pedagogia para el Adiestramiento (MEX) **1702**
Pedagogia Social (ESP ISSN 1139-1723) **2896**
• Pedagogia Universitaria (CUB ISSN 1609-4808) **2896**
Pedagogia y Saberes (COL ISSN 0121-2494) **2896**
Pedagogicheskie Nauki (RUS ISSN 1728-8894) **2896**
Pedagogicheskii Kaleidoskop (RUS) **2896**
Pedagogicheskii Vestnik (RUS) **2896**
Pedagogicka a Psychologicka Diagnostika pro Ucitele na ZS (CZE ISSN 1801-8416) **3029**
Pedagogics Abstracts on Cards *see* Jiaoyuxue Wenzhai Ka **2934**
Pedagogie de la Traduction/Didactics of Translation (CAN) **5160**
• Pedagogie Medicale (FRA ISSN 1625-6484) **2997**
Pedagogie Specialisee (CHE ISSN 1420-1534) **3045**
Pedagogiek (NLD ISSN 1567-7109) **2896**
Pedagogiek in Praktijk (NLD ISSN 1382-3272) **2165**
• Pedagogies (USA ISSN 1554-480X) **3076**
Pedagogies Magazine (FRA ISSN 1953-5457) **2165**
Pedagogija (SRB ISSN 0031-3807) **2896**
Pedagogika (BGR) **3076**
➤ Pedagogika/Pedagogy (CZE ISSN 0031-3815) **2896**
• ➤ Pedagogika (LTU ISSN 1392-0340) **2897**
➤ Pedagogika (RUS ISSN 0869-561X) **2896**
Pedagogika Detstva (RUS) **2165**
Pedagogika Pracy (POL ISSN 0239-7757) **2945**
Pedagogische Studien (NLD ISSN 0165-0645) **2897**
➤ Pedagogisk Forskning i Sverige (SWE ISSN 1401-6788) **2897**
Pedagogisk-Psykologiska Problem (SWE ISSN 0346-5004) **7389**
• Pedagogiska Magasinet (SWE ISSN 1401-3320) **2897**
Pedagogues et Pedagogies (FRA ISSN 1255-2488) **2897**
Pedagogusok Lapja (HUN ISSN 0133-2260) **2897**
Pedagogy *see* Pedagogika **2896**
• ➤ Pedagogy (USA ISSN 1531-4200) **3076**
▼ • ➤ Pedagogy and the Human Sciences (USA ISSN 1941-7934) **7389**
• ➤ Pedagogy, Culture and Society (GBR ISSN 1468-1366) **3076**
Pedahohichna Hazeta (UKR) **2897**
Pedal (CAN ISSN 1191-2685) **8266**
Pedal Steel Newsletter (USA ISSN 1088-7954) **6604**
• Pedal Update (AUS ISSN 1321-1870) **8266**
Pedalpoint (USA ISSN 0272-9199) **6604**
Peddler (USA) **2640**
• Pedestrian Forum (USA ISSN 1944-8848) **8633**
Pedestrian Forum Newsletter *see* Pedestrian Forum **8633**
Pediater *see* Gyermekorvos Tovabbkepzes **6092**
• Il Pediatra (ITA ISSN 1970-4240) **6099**
Le Pediatre (FRA ISSN 0397-9180) **6099**
Pediatria (BGR ISSN 0479-7876) **6099**
Pediatria (COL ISSN 0031-3882) **6099**
Pediatria *see* Encyclopedie Medico-Chirurgicale. Pediatria **6091**
• Pediatria (PRY ISSN 1683-979X) **6099**
➤ Pediatria (SVK ISSN 1336-863X) **6099**
➤ Pediatria & Medycyna Rodzinna (POL ISSN 1734-1531) **6099**
Pediatria Atencion Primaria (ESP ISSN 1139-7632) **6099**
Pediatria Atual (BRA ISSN 0103-2712) **6099**
• Pediatria Catalana (ESP ISSN 1135-8831) **6099**
Pediatria Integral (ESP ISSN 1135-4542) **6099**
➤ Pediatria Moderna (BRA ISSN 0031-3920) **6099**
Pediatria Oggi Medica e Chirurgica (ITA ISSN 0391-898X) **6099**
➤ Pediatria Polska (POL ISSN 0031-3939) **6099**
➤ Pediatria pre Prax (SVK ISSN 1336-8168) **6099**
Pediatria Preventiva e Sociale (ITA ISSN 1970-8165) **7535**
• Pediatria Rural y Extrahospitalaria (ESP ISSN 1135-4410) **6099**
Pediatria Wspolczesna (POL ISSN 1507-5532) **6099**
• Pediatric Alert (USA ISSN 0160-0184) **6099**
• ➤ Pediatric Allergy and Immunology (GBR ISSN 0905-6157) **6099**
• ➤ Pediatric Allergy and Immunology. Supplementum (GBR ISSN 0906-5784) **6099**
Pediatric Allergy for Clinicians (JPN) **5765**
• ➤ Pediatric and Adolescent Medicine (CHE ISSN 1017-5989) **6099**
• ➤ Pediatric and Developmental Pathology (USA ISSN 1093-5266) **6100**
• ➤ Pediatric Annals (USA ISSN 0090-4481) **6100**
• ➤ Pediatric Asthma, Allergy & Immunology (USA ISSN 0883-1874) **6100**
† • The Pediatric Asthma Virtual Journal (GBR) **8980**
• ➤ Pediatric Blood & Cancer (USA ISSN 1545-5009) **6032**
• Pediatric Cardiac Surgery Annual of the Seminars in Thoracic and Cardiovascular Surgery (USA ISSN 1092-9126) **5797**
• ➤ Pediatric Cardiology (USA ISSN 0172-0643) **5797**
Pediatric Cardiology Today *see* Congenital Cardiology Today **5783**
† • Pediatric Case Reviews (USA ISSN 1532-9798) **8980**
• Pediatric Clinical Practice Guidelines & Policies (USA ISSN 1942-2024) **6100**
Pediatric Clinical Practice Guidelines and Policies *see* Pediatric Clinical Practice Guidelines & Policies **6100**
Pediatric Clinics Amsterdam (NLD ISSN 0928-7868) **6100**
• ➤ Pediatric Clinics of North America (USA ISSN 0031-3955) **6100**
• Pediatric Coder's Pink Sheet (USA ISSN 1941-8787) **6100**
• Pediatric Coding Alert (USA ISSN 1098-1799) **4518**
Pediatric Coding Companion *see* A A P Pediatric Coding Newsletter **6086**
• ➤ Pediatric Critical Care Medicine (USA ISSN 1529-7535) **6100**
Pediatric Dental Journal *see* Shoni Shikagaku Zasshi **5865**
• Pediatric Dental Journal (JPN ISSN 0917-2394) **5860**
• Pediatric Dentistry (USA ISSN 0164-1263) **5860**
Pediatric Dentistry Today (USA ISSN 1046-2791) **5860**
• ➤ Pediatric Dermatology (USA ISSN 0736-8046) **5880**
Pediatric Dermatology (Spanish Edition) (ESP ISSN 1136-534X) **5880**
• ➤ Pediatric Diabetes (DNK ISSN 1399-543X) **6100**
• ➤ Pediatric Diabetes Online (DNK ISSN 1399-5448) **6100**
Pediatric Dosage Handbook (USA ISSN 1533-578X) **6867**
Pediatric Drugs *see* Paediatric Drugs **6866**
• ➤ Pediatric Emergency Care (USA ISSN 0749-5161) **6100**
• Pediatric Emergency Medicine Practice (USA ISSN 1549-9650) **6100**
• Pediatric Emergency Medicine Reports (USA ISSN 1082-3344) **6070**
Pediatric Endocrinology, Diabetes and Metabolism *see* Endokrynologia, Diabetologia i Choroby Przemiany Materii Wieku Rozwojowego **5892**
➤ Pediatric Endocrinology Reviews (ISR ISSN 1565-4753) **5898**
• ➤ Pediatric Exercise Science (USA ISSN 0899-8493) **6100**
▼ • ➤ Pediatric Health (GBR ISSN 1745-5111) **6101**
Pediatric Health Monitor (USA ISSN 1067-9413) **6101**
• ➤ Pediatric Hematology & Oncology (GBR ISSN 0888-0018) **6101**
➤ Pediatric Hematology - Oncology Series (USA ISSN 1054-2086) **6032**
• ➤ The Pediatric Infectious Disease Journal (USA ISSN 0891-3668) **6101**
Pediatric Infectious Disease Journal International Newsletter *see* The Pediatric Infectious Disease Journal **6101**
• Pediatric Length of Stay by Diagnosis & Operation, United States (USA) **4114**
• ➤ Pediatric Nephrology (DEU ISSN 0931-041X) **6273**
• ➤ Pediatric Neurology (USA ISSN 0887-8994) **6101**
• ➤ Pediatric Neurosurgery (CHE ISSN 1016-2291) **6173**
• Pediatric News (USA ISSN 0031-398X) **6101**
Pediatric Nurse Practitioner (USA ISSN 0886-9006) **5977**
• ➤ Pediatric Nursing (USA ISSN 0097-9805) **5977**
Pediatric Nutrition Handbook (USA) **6101**
Pediatric Pathology & Molecular Medicine (Print Edition) *see* Fetal and Pediatric Pathology (Print Edition) **6092**
• Pediatric Pharmacotherapy (USA) **6101**
• ➤ Pediatric Physical Therapy (USA ISSN 0898-5669) **6101**
Pediatric Practice Advisor (USA) **4109**
• ➤ Pediatric Pulmonology (USA ISSN 8755-6863) **6101**
Pediatric Pulmonology. Supplement *see* Pediatric Pulmonology **6101**
• ➤ Pediatric Radiology (DEU ISSN 0301-0449) **6205**
Pediatric Rehabilitation *see* Developmental Neurorehabilitation **6108**
• ➤ Pediatric Research (USA ISSN 0031-3998) **6101**
Pediatric Review and Education Program Reference on CD-ROM *see* P R E P Reference on CD-ROM **6098**
• ➤ Pediatric Rheumatology Online Journal (USA ISSN 1546-0096) **6225**
Pediatric Surgery *see* Cocuk Cerrahisi Dergisi **6090**
• ➤ Pediatric Surgery International (DEU ISSN 0179-0358) **6255**
• Pediatric Surgery Update (PRI ISSN 1089-7739) **6255**
• ➤ Pediatric Transplantation (DNK ISSN 1397-3142) **6101**
Pediatric Transplantation. Supplement *see* Pediatric Transplantation **6101**
• Pediatriclinx (USA) **6102**
Pediatrics *see* Pediatriya **6102**
Pediatrics *see* Audio-Digest Pediatrics **6088**
Pediatrics (Chinese Edition) *see* Pediatrics (Spanish Edition) **6102**
Pediatrics (Chinese Edition) *see* Pediatrics (English Edition) **6102**
• ➤ Pediatrics (English Edition) (USA ISSN 0031-4005) **6102**
Pediatrics (Indian Edition) *see* Pediatrics (English Edition) **6102**
• Pediatrics (Italian Edition) (ITA ISSN 1120-7507) **6102**
• ➤ Pediatrics (Spanish Edition) (ESP ISSN 0210-5721) **6102**
▼ ➤ Pediatrics and Neonatology (TWN ISSN 1875-9572) **6102**
Pediatrics and Pediatric Surgery (Section 7 EMBASE) *see* Excerpta Medica. Section 7: Pediatrics and Pediatric Surgery **5746**
Pediatrics Edizione Italiana *see* Pediatrics (Italian Edition) **6102**
• Pediatrics for Parents (USA ISSN 0730-6725) **6102**
• ➤ Pediatrics in Review (USA ISSN 0191-9601) **6102**
• ➤ Pediatrics International (AUS ISSN 1328-8067) **6102**
Pediatrics of Japan *see* Shonika **6104**
Pediatrics On Call (USA ISSN 1556-6927) **6102**
Pediatrics Review and Education Program the Curriculum *see* P R E P, the Curriculum **6098**
▼ • Pediatrics Week (USA ISSN 1944-2637) **6102**
Pediatrie *see* Encyclopedie Medico-Chirurgicale. Pediatrie **6091**
Pediatrie Pratique (FRA ISSN 0993-9717) **6102**
• ➤ Pediatrie pro Praxi (CZE ISSN 1213-0494) **6102**
• ➤ Pediatriya/Pediatrics (RUS ISSN 0031-403X) **6102**
Pediatriya, Akusherstvo ta Ginekologiya (UKR ISSN 0031-4048) **6102**
• ➤ Pedobiologia (DEU ISSN 0031-4056) **246**
Pedologia Clinica (ESP ISSN 1578-0716) **6071**
➤ Pedologist/Pedorojisuto (JPN ISSN 0031-4064) **246**
Pedoman Masyarakat (MYS ISSN 0127-1717) **3907**
Pedoman Rakyat (MYS) **3907**
• Pedometron (NLD) **246**
Pedorojisuto *see* Pedologist **246**
• ➤ Pedosphere/Turang Quan (CHN ISSN 1002-0160) **2714**
Pedozoologica Hungarica (HUN ISSN 1785-1025) **960**
Pedralbes (ESP ISSN 0211-9587) **4253**
• Peel (USA) **6604**
Peep (USA) **5233**
Peeping Tom (GBR ISSN 0961-4400) **5446**
• The Peer Bulletin (CAN ISSN 1488-6774) **8061**
Peer Counsellor Journal *see* Compass (Victoria) **8035**
• Peer Health News (USA) **2165**
• Peer Review (USA ISSN 1541-1389) **2997**
The Peer Review Journal.com *see* The PRJ.com **5700**

Title

Pensamiento & Gestion (COL ISSN 1657-6276) **1785**
➤ Pensamiento Constitucional (PER ISSN 1027-6769) **7164**
▼ Pensamiento Cooperativo y Mutual (ARG ISSN 1851-4960) **1424**
Pensamiento Costarricense (CRI) **3830**
Pensamiento Economico (ARG ISSN 0325-5069) **1408**
Pensamiento Economico (HND) **1159**
Pensamiento Educativo (CHL ISSN 0717-1013) **2897**
Pensamiento Iberoamericano (ESP ISSN 0212-0208) **1510**
• Pensamiento Propio (NIC ISSN 1016-9628) **7991**
• ➤ Pensamiento Psicologico (COL ISSN 1657-8961) **7390**
Pensamiento Universitario (ARG ISSN 0327-9901) **2296**
Pensamiento y Accion (COL ISSN 0120-1190) **7897**
• Pensamiento y Cultura (COL ISSN 0123-0999) **5350**
Pensando o Brasil (BRA) **7991**
➤ Pensar (BRA ISSN 1519-8464) **4757**
• Pensar a Pratica (BRA ISSN 1415-4676) **8193**
Pensar Enfermagem (PRT ISSN 0873-8904) **5977**
▼ • Pensar la Publicidad (ESP ISSN 1887-8598) **32**
† Pensare Faenza/Thinking about Faenza (ITA) **8980**
➤ Pensares y Quehaceres (MEX ISSN 1870-4492) **6938**
La Pensee (Paris) (FRA ISSN 0031-4773) **7164**
Pensee Africaine (FRA ISSN 1779-7551) **351**
Pensee et Perspectives Africaines/African Thought and Perspectives (BEL ISSN 1379-213X) **7991**
Pensee Libre (USA ISSN 1716-3692) **5350**
• Pensee Plurielle (BEL ISSN 1376-0963) **8125**
Pensee Russe (FRA ISSN 0757-2239) **3557**
Il Pensiero (USA) **3557**
Il Pensiero (Naples) (ITA ISSN 1824-4971) **6938**
• Il Pensiero Economico Italiano (ITA ISSN 1122-8784) **1159**
➤ Il Pensiero Economico Moderno (ITA ISSN 1593-8522) **1547**
Pensiero Giuridico e Politico. Nuova Serie (ITA ISSN 1827-6741) **4757**
Il Pensiero Mazziniano (ITA ISSN 0031-482X) **7164**
• Il Pensiero Politico (Florence) (ITA ISSN 0031-4846) **7164**
Il Pensiero Politico (Rome) (ITA ISSN 1971-2375) **7164**
Il Pensiero Politico. Biblioteca (ITA ISSN 1122-0767) **7164**
Pensiero Politico Medievale (ITA ISSN 1825-2338) **4253**
Pensioen Actief (NLD ISSN 1567-3863) **1702**
Pensioen Advies (NLD ISSN 0925-496X) **1644**
• Pensioen Alert (NLD ISSN 1568-5799) **1702**
Pensioen Bulletin (NLD ISSN 0031-4854) **4518**
• Pensioen Jurisprudentie (NLD ISSN 1382-4015) **1702**
Pensioen Monografieen (NLD ISSN 1567-2654) **1702**
• Pensioenbrief (NLD ISSN 0929-8681) **1702**
PensioenBulletin *see* Pensioen Bulletin **4518**
Pensioenfonds Nederlandse Omroep Actueel. Pensioen *see* P N O Actueel. Pensioen **1701**
• Pensioengids (NLD ISSN 1383-617X) **1702**
The Pension Actuary *see* The A S P A Journal **4490**
• Pension & Benefits Daily (USA ISSN 1523-5718) **1702**
Pension and Benefits Daily *see* Pension & Benefits Daily **1702**
Pension and Benefits Reporter *see* Pension & Benefits Reporter **1702**
• Pension & Benefits Reporter (USA ISSN 1069-5117) **1702**
Pension and Benefits Update (USA) **1938**
• Pension & Benefits Week (USA ISSN 1088-8969) **1702**
Pension and Profit Sharing (USA) **1871**
• Pension Benefit Guaranty Corporation. Annual Report (USA ISSN 1936-5527) **1702**
• Pension Benefits (USA ISSN 1063-2476) **1702**
Pension Boards *see* United Church of Christ. Pension Boards (Annual Report) **7778**
Pension Coordinator (USA) **1871**
† • Pension Fund Litigation Reporter (USA ISSN 1052-9640) **8980**
• Pension Funds & Their Advisers (GBR ISSN 0140-6647) **4518**
Pension Funds CD-ROM *see* Pension Funds & Their Advisers **4518**
Pension Insurance Data Books *see* Pension Benefit Guaranty Corporation. Annual Report **1702**
• Pension Investment Report (USA) **1644**
Pension News *see* College Pension Plan. Pension News **1670**
Pension News *see* Municipal Pension Plan. Pension News **1698**
Pension News *see* Teachers' Pension Plan. Pension News **1710**
Pension News *see* Public Service Pension Plan. Pension News **1704**
• Pension Plan Guide (USA ISSN 0162-1637) **4518**
Pension Scheme Trustee (GBR ISSN 1353-1654) **1644**
Pensionaeren /PRO (SWE ISSN 0345-9225) **8061**
Pensioners Voice (GBR ISSN 0048-3281) **8061**
Las Pensiones de la Seguridad Social, en la C A V (ESP ISSN 1134-9883) **8061**
Pensionnoe Obespechenie (RUS) **8061**
Pensions *see* Key Note Market Report: Pensions **1895**
• ➤ Pensions (GBR ISSN 1478-5315) **1871**
Pensions Age (GBR ISSN 1366-8366) **4518**
• Pensions & Investments (USA ISSN 1050-4974) **1644**
Pensions Board. Annual Report and Accounts/Tuarascail Bhliantuil Agus Cuntais (IRL ISSN 1649-8690) **7460**
Pensions Compliance Briefing (GBR ISSN 1471-7999) **1871**
Pensions International (GBR ISSN 1464-7419) **1702**
Pensions Law and Practice with Precedents (GBR) **1702**
• Pensions Management (GBR ISSN 0269-7505) **1871**
Pensions Pocket Book (GBR ISSN 0965-5409) **1702**
Pensions Systems (GBR ISSN 0962-8487) **1871**
Pensions Today (GBR ISSN 0140-8526) **1644**
• Pensions Week (GBR ISSN 1366-8765) **1871**
Pensions World (GBR ISSN 0307-191X) **4518**
➤ The Pentagon (USA ISSN 0031-4870) **5524**
• Pentagon Brief (USA ISSN 1551-6679) **6441**
Pentagon Brief - Deutsche Ausgabe *see* Pentagon Brief **6441**
Pentagram (Bulgaarse Edition) (NLD ISSN 1871-1626) **7770**
Pentatette (USA) **5429**
Pentecostal Evangel *see* Today's Pentecostal Evangel **7742**
Pentecostal Messenger (USA ISSN 0031-4919) **7770**
Pentecostal Testimony (CAN ISSN 0031-4927) **7740**
Pentecote (FRA ISSN 1166-7095) **7812**
Penthouse (DEU) **6297**
† Penthouse (ESP) **8980**
Penthouse (FRA ISSN 0762-5006) **6297**
Penthouse (GBR ISSN 0950-0685) **6297**
Penthouse (GRC ISSN 1108-8087) **6297**
Penthouse (HKG) **6297**
Penthouse (HUN ISSN 1786-8890) **6297**
Penthouse (THA ISSN 1685-6465) **6297**
• Penthouse (USA ISSN 0090-2020) **6297**
Penthouse Forum (USA ISSN 1043-0210) **6297**
• Penthouse Letters (USA ISSN 0883-8798) **6297**
• Penthouse Variations (USA ISSN 0274-5143) **6297**
Penticton Herald (CAN ISSN 0844-2711) **3815**
• Penton's Military Electronics (USA) **3110**
• Penton's Welding Magazine (USA ISSN 1935-5572) **6343**
Pentru Patrie (ROM ISSN 1220-6792) **2663**
Pentukun (CHL ISSN 0717-1099) **351**
Penzenskaya Pravda (RUS) **3939**
Penzenskie Vesti (RUS) **3939**
Penzinger Museumsblaetter (AUT) **4253**
Penzugyi Szemle (HUN ISSN 0031-496X) **7460**
Peolpeu Jong'i Gi'sul/Technical Association of the Pulp and Paper Industry of Korea. Journal (KOR ISSN 0253-3200) **6737**
Peony *see* Mudan **5336**
People (AUS ISSN 1321-9847) **6297**
The People (GBR) **3968**
People (NGA ISSN 0048-329X) **3920**
The People (SYC ISSN 0031-4994) **7164**
• People (Kansas City) (USA ISSN 0031-501X) **3015**
• The People (Mountain View) (USA ISSN 0199-350X) **7164**
People (Nairobi, 1978) (KEN) **3902**
People (Nairobi, 1993) (KEN) **3902**
• People (New York) (USA ISSN 0093-7673) **3985**
People (Raleigh) (USA ISSN 0145-2932) **1702**
People and Countries *see* Lide a Zeme **4018**
People and Culture in Oceania (JPN ISSN 1349-5380) **4469**
People & Entertainment (NLD ISSN 1874-4869) **6604**
• ➤ People and Place (AUS ISSN 1039-4788) **8125**
People and Products (USA) **1900**
• People and Science (GBR ISSN 2040-3968) **7897**
• People & Strategy (USA ISSN 1946-4606) **1871**
People and the Word *see* Zmogus ir Zodis **5200**
People at the Peak (Malaysia Edition) (SGP) **645**
People at the Peak (Singapore Edition) (SGP ISSN 0219-7391) **645**
People Dynamics (ZAF ISSN 1019-6196) **1871**
• People en Espanol (USA ISSN 1096-5750) **3985**
People, Food & Land (USA) **246**
People for the Ethical Treatment of Animals, Inc.'s Animal Times (English Edition) *see* P E T A's Animal Times (English Edition) **321**
People for the Ethical Treatment of Animals Inc.'s Animal Times (German Edition) *see* P E T A's Animal Times (German Edition) **321**
People from the Past Series (GBR ISSN 0079-0729) **645**
People in Parking Directory *see* P I P Directory **8507**
• People in Power (GBR ISSN 0965-7517) **7164**
People Magazine *see* People (New York) **3985**
• People Management (GBR ISSN 1358-6297) **2897**
People 'n Pride (USA) **3392**
People News (MTQ ISSN 1950-3113) **3907**
People of Today *see* Debrett's People of Today **642**
▼ • ➤ People, Place and Policy Online (GBR ISSN 1753-8041) **8125**
People, Places & Plants (USA ISSN 1092-9223) **3747**
People Plant Connection (USA ISSN 1067-4276) **5695**
People Profiles (USA) **645**
People Style Watch (USA ISSN 1935-0457) **2260**
† The People Take the Lead (USA ISSN 0735-455X) **8980**
People to Know (Phoenix) (USA) **7603**
People United to Save Humanity. P.U.S.H.-Operation Push (USA ISSN 0048-332X) **5233**
People with Disabilities (USA) **4068**
People with Special Needs - Down Syndrome Report (USA ISSN 0731-566X) **3045**
People's Action (New Delhi) (IND) **8434**
People's Army *see* Ardyn Armi **5206**
People's Bible Studies (GBR ISSN 0967-6147) **7669**
People's China *see* Jinmin Chugoku **3825**
People's Court Daily *see* Renmin Fayuan Bao **4768**
People's Culture (USA ISSN 1071-7250) **5233**
People's Daily *see* Renmin Ribao **3827**
People's Daily. Index *see* Renmin Ribao Suoyin **4588**
People's Daily Online *see* Renminwang **3827**
People's Deputy *see* Nguoi Dai Bieu Nhan Dan **7159**
People's Education *see* Renmin Jiaoyu **2904**
The People's Friend (GBR ISSN 0262-2386) **8880**
People's Government of Beijing Municipality. Gazette *see* Beijing Shi Renmin Zhengfu Gongbao **7422**
The People's Guide to Mexico (USA ISSN 1099-5315) **8747**
Peoples in Atoms (JPN) **3173**
• The People's Korea (JPN ISSN 0031-5036) **7165**
Peoples Law (ZAF ISSN 1019-6722) **4757**
People's Liberation Army. General Hospital of Air Force. Journal *see* Kongjun Zongyiyuan Xuebao **5658**
People's Liberation Army. Naval General Hospital. Journal *see* Haijun Zongyiyuan Xuebao **5623**
People's Literature *see* Renmin Wenxue **5359**
People's Manifesto (IND ISSN 0971-1619) **7165**
• People's Medical Society Newsletter (USA ISSN 0736-4873) **2640**
People's Military Surgeon *see* Renmin Junyi **6256**
People's Music *see* Renmin Yinyue **6610**
† Peoples of the World (USA) **8980**
People's Photography *see* Renmin Sheying **6976**
People's Police *see* Renmin Jingcha **2667**
People's Post and Telecommunications News *see* Renmin Youdian Bao **2337**
People's Power (IND ISSN 0377-2713) **7165**
People's Procuratorial Work *see* Renmin Jiancha **4768**
People's Public Security Review *see* Renmin Gongan Bao **7538**
People's Railways *see* Renmin Tiedao **8624**
People's Republic of China. Ministry of Foreign Trade & Economic Cooperation. Bulletin *see* Zhonghua Renmin Gongheguo. Duiwai Maoyi Jingji Hezuobu. Xinwen Gongbao **1589**
People's Republic of China. Ministry of Foreign Trade & Economic Cooperation. Bulletin *see* Zhonghua Renmin Gongheguo. Duiwai Maoyi Jingji Hezuobu. Tongbao **1589**
People's Republic of China. National People's Congress. Standing Committee. Gazette *see* Zhonghua Renmin Gongheguo Quanguo Renmin Daibiao Dahui Changwu Weiyuanhui Gongbao **7478**
People's Republic of China Year Book (CHN ISSN 1000-9396) **3121**
People's Songletter (USA) **6604**
Peoples Spectator (AUS) **3795**
People's State *see* Ardyn Tor **7107**
People's Theatre *see* Giao Vien Nhan Dan **8471**
People's Tribune (USA ISSN 1081-4787) **7165**
People's Voice (CAN ISSN 1198-8657) **3815**
People's Voice (SDN) **7165**
People's Voice *see* Dwon Lwak **3963**
The People's Voice (USA ISSN 1939-6899) **3557**
• People's Weekly World (USA) **7165**
People's Will *see* Narodna Volya **3552**
People's Yellow River *see* Renmin Huang He **4026**
Pepino (PRI) **3931**
† Peppa Big Magazine (NLD ISSN 1873-9490) **8980**
• Pepperdine Dispute Resolution Law Journal (USA ISSN 1536-3090) **4757**
• ➤ Pepperdine Law Review (USA ISSN 0092-430X) **4757**
Pepper'n Salt (USA) **6812**
Peptide Chemistry (JPN ISSN 0388-3698) **741**
• Peptide Information (JPN ISSN 0385-8847) **718**
• ➤ Peptides (USA ISSN 0196-9781) **741**
Pepuchido Kagaku Toronkai Koen Yoshishu *see* Abstracts of Symposium on Peptide Chemistry **3612**
Pequena Diana (MEX) **538**
Pequenas Empresas Grandes Negocios (BRA ISSN 0104-2297) **1965**
Pequenas Piadas Grandes Negocios (BRA ISSN 1678-8001) **4982**
Pequenos Rumiantes (ESP ISSN 1888-4865) **295**
Pequod (SWE ISSN 1102-6499) **5350**
➤ Pequod (USA ISSN 0149-0516) **5350**
Pequot Times (USA) **6636**
Per *see* Per Salvare Palermo **511**
† Per il Sessantotto (ITA) **8980**
Per Jacobsson Foundation. Lectures (USA ISSN 0252-3108) **1374**
• ➤ Per la Filosofia (ITA ISSN 0394-4131) **6938**
• Per Leggere (ITA ISSN 1593-4861) **5350**
Per Linguam (ZAF ISSN 0259-2312) **5160**
Per Me (ITA ISSN 1129-2644) **7390**
• Per Musi (BRA ISSN 1517-7599) **6604**
Per Salvare Palermo (ITA ISSN 1970-5646) **511**
▼ Per Se (ESP ISSN 1888-5713) **5233**
Per Verba (ITA ISSN 1970-2159) **4253**
Pera News (GBR) **8434**
Peraba (IDN ISSN 0553-6448) **7812**
Perakende Fiyat Istatistikleri *see* Turkey. Turkiye Istatistik Kurumu. Perakende Fiyat Istatistikleri **8995**
Perangkaan Bulanan Getah Bagi Malaysia *see* Malaysia. Department of Statistics. Monthly Rubber Statistics, Malaysia **7828**
Perbadanan Perpustakaan Awam Selangor. Lapuran Tahunan *see* Selangor Public Library Corporation. Annual Report **5046**
Perbadanan Produktiviti Negara. Lapuran Tahunan *see* National Productivity Corporation, Malaysia. Annual Report **1780**
Perception (CAN ISSN 0704-5263) **8061**
• ➤ Perception (GBR ISSN 0301-0066) **7390**
Perception & Psychophysics *see* Attention, Perception & Psychophysics **7337**
Perceptions (CAN ISSN 1497-1011) **4377**
• Perceptions/Journal of International Affairs (TUR ISSN 1300-8641) **7165**
Perceptions (Duluth) (USA) **1374**
• ➤ Perceptual and Motor Skills (USA ISSN 0031-5125) **7390**
➤ O Percevejo (BRA ISSN 0104-7671) **8475**
Perchtoldsdorfer Pfarrbote (AUT ISSN 0031-5141) **7770**
Percorsi *see* Percorsi di Cultura Politica **7165**
Percorsi *see* Percorsi di Psicanalisi **7390**
Percorsi (ITA) **6938**
Percorsi di Cultura Politica (ITA ISSN 1594-4557) **7165**
Percorsi di Psicanalisi (ITA ISSN 1970-6049) **7390**
Percorsi in Ceramica (ITA) **452**
Percurso (BRA ISSN 0103-6815) **7390**
Percussion Creativ (DEU) **6604**
• Percussion News (USA ISSN 1534-9764) **6604**
• Percussive Notes (USA ISSN 0553-6502) **6604**
• Percutio (NZL ISSN 1177-5955) **5350**
Perdido (USA ISSN 1524-1610) **1159**
Pere ja Kodu (EST ISSN 1406-216X) **3836**
Pere Marquette Theology Lecture Series (USA) **7669**
• Peregrinations (USA ISSN 1554-8678) **511**
Peregrine (USA ISSN 0890-622X) **5429**
Peregrine Fund Newsletter (USA) **2625**
Peregrinus Cracoviensis (POL ISSN 1425-1922) **4023**
Perekhid IV (UKR ISSN 1609-946X) **5233**
Perekrestok (ARM) **2402**
Perennial Plants Quarterly Journal (USA) **3747**
Pererabotka i Marketing Medi: Oblasti dla Mezdunarodnogo Sotrudnicestva *see* Studies in the Processing, Marketing and Distribution of Commodities **8991**
Les Peres dans la Foi (BEL ISSN 0180-7439) **7669**
Perets' (UKR ISSN 0031-5176) **5233**
Perfect 10 (USA ISSN 1094-3927) **6297**
• ➤ Perfect Beat (GBR ISSN 1038-2909) **6605**
Perfect Flight (RUS) **8785**
† Perfect Girls (CZE ISSN 1801-500X) **8980**
Perfect Home (GBR ISSN 0966-6443) **4561**
Perfect Horse *see* John Lyons' Perfect Horse **8294**
Perfect Match Mariage/Guide de la Mariee (CAN ISSN 1705-0456) **8880**
• Perfect Sound Forever (USA) **6605**
• The Perfect Vision (USA ISSN 0895-4143) **2387**
▼ Perfect Wedding (GBR ISSN 1753-0458) **5561**
Perficit (ESP ISSN 0210-167X) **5160**
Perfidious Albion (GBR) **8193**
Perfil (CRI) **8880**
Perfil da Administracao Federal (BRA) **7460**
Perfil de Coyuntura Economica (COL) **1510**
Perfil Municipal (BRA ISSN 0100-8781) **7500**
Perfiles Contemporaneos (ARG) **645**
Perfiles de Salud de las Comunidades Hermanas de la Frontera Mexico - Estados Unidos/Sister Communities Health Profiles of the U S - Mexico Border (USA ISSN 1086-4539) **7549**
Perfiles Educativos (MEX ISSN 0185-2698) **2897**
• ➤ Perfiles Latinoamericanos (MEX ISSN 0188-7653) **7991**
Perfis (FIN ISSN 0359-2189) **5861**
Perfis Parlamentares (BRA) **645**
Performance (DEU) **1374**
Performance (GBR) **6786**
Performance (Canadian Opera Company Edition) (CAN) **6605**
Performance (Royal Thomson - Massey Hall Edition) (CAN) **511**
Performance Accessories (AUS ISSN 1832-6927) **32**
The Performance Advantage *see* A P I C S **1722**
Performance and Accountability Report *see* U.S. Securities and Exchange Commission. Performance and Accountability Report **1657**
Performance and Accountability Report *see* U.S. Department of Agriculture. Performance and Accountability Report **164**
Performance and Accountability Report *see* U.S. Department of Labor. Performance and Accountability Report **1712**
Performance and Accountability Report *see* U.S. Federal Trade Commission. Performance and Accountability Report **7473**

Title

Title

▼ new title   † ceased   ● electronic media   ➤ refereed

Title

Title

Title

Title

▼ *new title*   † *ceased*   ● *electronic media*   ➤ *refereed*

10744 PLANS ET LES RAPPORTS, GUIDE A L'INTENTION DES CONSEILS ULRICH'S PERIODICALS

Plans et les Rapports, Guide a l'Intention des Conseils Scolaires *see* Guide pour les Plans d'Education et la Communication des Resultats **2861**
• Plant (CAN ISSN 0845-4213) **1785**
The Plant (Westmount) (CAN) **2296**
Plant Action Pac *see* Plant **1785**
Plant Analysis Manual *see* Plant Analysis Procedures **247**
Plant Analysis Procedures (NLD) **247**
• ➤ Plant and Cell Physiology (GBR ISSN 0032-0781) **835**
Plant and Civil Engineer (GBR) **3280**
Plant and Construction Engineering (GBR) **3392**
Plant & Equipment (AUS ISSN 1449-6534) **5458**
† Plant & Equipment Guide (GBR) **8981**
Plant and Equipment Price Guide (GBR) **5458**
Plant and Laboratory Equipment Guide *see* Guia de la Industria: Equipo y Aparatos **5452**
▼ Plant & Machinery (IRL ISSN 2009-0226) **5458**
• ➤ Plant and Soil (NLD ISSN 0032-079X) **810**
• ➤ Plant and Vegetation (NLD ISSN 1875-1318) **2762**
Plant & Works Engineering (GBR ISSN 0262-0227) **3370**
Plant Automation *see* Plant **1785**
• ➤ Plant Biology (GBR ISSN 1435-8603) **810**
• ➤ Plant Biosystems (GBR ISSN 1126-3504) **810**
• Plant Biotechnology (JPN ISSN 1342-4580) **810**
• Plant Biotechnology Journal (GBR ISSN 1467-7644) **810**
▼ • ➤ Plant Biotechnology Reports (JPN ISSN 1863-5466) **769**
• ➤ Plant Breeding/Zeitschrift fuer Pflanzenzuechtung (DEU ISSN 0179-9541) **810**
• Plant Breeding Abstracts (GBR ISSN 0032-0803) **185**
Plant Breeding and Seed Science/Hodowla Roslin i Nasiennictwo (POL ISSN 1429-3862) **147**
• Plant Breeding Online (DEU ISSN 1439-0523) **810**
Plant Breeding Reviews (USA ISSN 0730-2207) **247**
Plant Brochure Guide *see* Plant **1785**
• ➤ The Plant Cell (USA ISSN 1040-4651) **810**
• ➤ Plant, Cell and Environment (GBR ISSN 0140-7791) **697**
• ➤ Plant Cell Reports (DEU ISSN 0721-7714) **811**
• ➤ Plant Cell, Tissue and Organ Culture (NLD ISSN 0167-6857) **835**
Plant Controls & Instrumentation *see* Plant **1785**
• ➤ Plant Disease (USA ISSN 0191-2917) **247**
➤ Plant Disease Research (IND ISSN 0970-4914) **811**
Plant Disease Research *see* Sigmulbyeong Yeon'gu **817**
• ➤ Plant Ecology (NLD ISSN 1385-0237) **811**
• ➤ Plant Ecology and Diversity (GBR ISSN 1755-0874) **811**
Plant Engineer (GBR ISSN 0032-0838) **3215**
Plant Engineer (JPN ISSN 0289-0178) **3392**
• The Plant Engineer E-Zine (USA) **3215**
• Plant Engineering (USA ISSN 0032-082X) **3215**
• Plant Engineering Product Supplier Guide (USA) **3215**
Plant Equipment Hire & Rates (ZAF) **1901**
Plant Fibers and Products *see* Zhongguo Maye **260**
• ➤ Plant Foods for Human Nutrition (USA ISSN 0921-9668) **6668**
Plant for Life (ZAF) **811**
Plant Gene Research (AUT ISSN 0175-2073) **877**
• ➤ Plant Genetic Resources (GBR ISSN 1479-2621) **247**
• Plant Genetic Resources Abstracts (GBR ISSN 0966-0100) **718**
• ➤ Plant Genetic Resources Newsletter (ITA ISSN 1020-3362) **811**
▼ • ➤ The Plant Genome (USA ISSN 1940-3372) **877**
• ➤ Plant Growth Regulation (NLD ISSN 0167-6903) **811**
Plant Growth Regulation Society of America Quarterly *see* P G R S A Quarterly **806**
• Plant Growth Regulator Abstracts (GBR ISSN 0305-9154) **185**
• ➤ The Plant Health Instructor (USA ISSN 1935-9411) **811**
• ➤ Plant Health Progress (USA ISSN 1535-1025) **811**
Plant Hire *see* Key Note Market Report: Plant Hire **1495**
Plant Journal *see* The Plant Journal **811**
• ➤ The Plant Journal (GBR ISSN 0960-7412) **811**
• Plant Managers Journal (GBR ISSN 1352-8637) **1785**
• Plant Methods (GBR ISSN 1746-4811) **811**
• ➤ Plant Molecular Biology (NLD ISSN 0167-4412) **697**
• ➤ Plant Molecular Biology Reporter (USA ISSN 0735-9640) **742**
Plant Mutation Reports (AUT) **248**
▼ • ➤ Plant Omics (AUS ISSN 1836-0661) **811**
• ➤ Plant Pathology (GBR ISSN 0032-0862) **811**
• The Plant Pathology Journal (KOR ISSN 1598-2254) **812**
• ➤ Plant Pathology Journal (PAK ISSN 1812-5387) **812**
• ➤ Plant Physiology (USA ISSN 0032-0889) **812**
• ➤ Plant Physiology and Biochemistry (FRA ISSN 0981-9428) **812**
Plant Physiology Communications *see* Zhiwu Shenglixue Tongxun **824**
Plant Press (USA) **3747**
Plant Production *see* Plant, Soil and Environment **147**
• ➤ Plant Production Science (JPN ISSN 1343-943X) **812**
• Plant Prospector (USA ISSN 1083-5636) **1901**
Plant Protection *see* Zhiwu Baohu **823**
Plant Protection *see* Novenyvedelem **244**
Plant Protection *see* Shokubutsu Boeki **252**
Plant Protection Bulletin (IND ISSN 0378-0449) **812**
Plant Protection Bulletin *see* Bitki Koruma Bulteni **222**
Plant Protection Bulletin *see* Zhiwu Baohuxuehui Huikan **260**
• ➤ Plant Protection Quarterly (AUS ISSN 0815-2195) **248**
Plant Protection Research Institute. Annual Report (ZWE) **248**
➤ Plant Protection Science (CZE ISSN 1212-2580) **248**
➤ Plant Resources of South-East Asia (NLD) **812**
Plant Resources of Tropical Africa Newsletter *see* P R O T A Newsletter **245**
▼ • Plant Root (JPN ISSN 1881-6754) **812**
Plant Safety & Maintenance (USA ISSN 1541-2407) **6684**
Plant Safety and Maintenance *see* Plant Safety & Maintenance **6684**
• ➤ Plant Science (IRL ISSN 0168-9452) **812**
• Plant Science Bulletin (USA ISSN 0032-0919) **812**
Plant Science Pamphlet (USA ISSN 1057-2422) **248**
• Plant Services (USA ISSN 0199-8013) **3392**
• ➤ Plant Signalling & Behavior (USA ISSN 1559-2316) **812**
➤ Plant, Soil and Environment (CZE ISSN 1214-1178) **147**
• ➤ Plant Species Biology (AUS ISSN 0913-557X) **812**
▼ Plant Stress (GBR ISSN 1749-0359) **813**
• ➤ Plant Systematics and Evolution (AUT ISSN 0378-2697) **813**
➤ Plant Systematics and Evolution. Supplement (AUT) **813**
Plant Tissue Culture *see* Plant Tissue Culture and Biotechnology **813**
• ➤ Plant Tissue Culture and Biotechnology (BGD ISSN 1817-3721) **813**
Plant Tissue Culture Manual (NLD) **769**
Plant User (GBR ISSN 0959-4361) **3747**
Plant Var/Feuille Suisse des Brevets, Dessins et Marques/Foglio Svizzero dei Brevetti, Disegni e Marchi (CHE ISSN 1660-2307) **6757**
Plant Varieties and Seeds Gazette (GBR ISSN 0048-4342) **248**
• Plant Varieties Journal (CAN ISSN 1188-1534) **3747**
• Plant Varieties Journal (CAN ISSN 1911-1479) **3747**
Plant Variety Protection (CHE ISSN 0257-9030) **248**
Plant Variety Protection *see* P V P **245**
▼ ➤ Plant Viruses (GBR ISSN 1749-6209) **813**
Plant World (GBR) **1029**
• ➤ Planta (DEU ISSN 0032-0935) **813**
Planta *see* Puranta **814**
• Planta Daninha (BRA ISSN 0100-8358) **813**
• ➤ Planta Medica (DEU ISSN 0032-0943) **6875**
➤ The Plantagenet Connection (USA ISSN 1081-1621) **4254**
Plantagenet Productions (GBR) **5351**
Plantarchy (USA ISSN 1558-8874) **5430**
Plantas, Flores e Jardins (BRA ISSN 1516-2419) **3747**
Plantation Society in the Americas (USA ISSN 0192-5059) **7992**
Plante si Flori *see* O Viata Frumoasa cu Plante si Flori **3753**
Plantebeskyttelsemidler (DNK ISSN 0108-4887) **248**
➤ Planter (MYS ISSN 0126-575X) **147**
Planters' Chronicle (IND ISSN 0032-0978) **3660**
Plantes & Sante (FRA ISSN 1157-7797) **314**
• Plantevaern Landbrug (DNK ISSN 1901-7812) **248**
• Plantfinder West (USA ISSN 1548-5080) **3747**
Planting and Breeding *see* Zhongzhi yu Yangzhi **260**
Plantman Magazine (IRL) **1029**
Plants *see* Dirk van der Werff's Plants **3728**
Plants & Gardens News (USA) **3747**
Plants & People (USA) **813**
Plantsman (USA) **3748**
• Plantula (VEN ISSN 1316-1547) **813**
Planung, Materialen, Praxis Konkrete Mathematik *see* P M P Konkrete Mathematik **3075**
Planung, Materialien, Praxis - Arbeit, Wirtschaft, Technik *see* P M P - A W T **3075**
Planung, Materialien, Praxis Grundschule *see* P M P Grundschule **3075**
Planung, Materialien, Praxis Klasse 5 - 10 *see* P M P Klasse 5 - 10 **3075**
Planung & Analyse (DEU ISSN 0724-9632) **1837**
Planung und Produktion (CHE) **3392**
Planungs-, Verkehrs- und Technikrecht (DEU ISSN 1615-813X) **4758**
Planungsrecht (DEU) **4423**
Planungsstudien (DEU ISSN 0079-2284) **1901**
Plaque N Care (DEU) **5861**
Plascon Colour (ZAF ISSN 1994-148X) **6720**
• ➤ Plasma and Fusion Research (JPN ISSN 1880-6821) **7035**
• ➤ Plasma Chemistry & Plasma Processing (USA ISSN 0272-4324) **3252**
• ➤ Plasma Devices and Operations (GBR ISSN 1051-9998) **7035**
▼ • ➤ Plasma Medicine (USA ISSN 1947-5764) **5940**
• ➤ Plasma Physics and Controlled Fusion (GBR ISSN 0741-3335) **7035**
• ➤ Plasma Physics Reports (RUS ISSN 1063-780X) **7035**
• ➤ Plasma Processes and Polymers (DEU ISSN 1612-8850) **7035**
Plasma Processing *see* Purazuma Puroseshingu Kenkyukai Puroshidingusu **7036**
• Plasma Science and Technology (GBR ISSN 1009-0630) **3252**
• ➤ Plasma Sources Science and Technology (GBR ISSN 0963-0252) **7035**
➤ Plasma Technology (NLD ISSN 1572-6061) **7035**
Plasmas and Polymers *see* Plasma Chemistry & Plasma Processing **3252**
• ➤ Plasmid (USA ISSN 0147-619X) **698**
• ➤ Plasmonics (USA ISSN 1557-1955) **7035**
Plast (ITA ISSN 0391-7401) **7096**
• Plast 21 (ESP ISSN 1131-7515) **7096**
Plast Panorama Scandinavia (DNK ISSN 0106-1720) **7096**
PlastDesign (ITA) **3370**
Plaster (SWE) **7096**
Plasterer and Cement Mason (USA ISSN 0032-1036) **4600**
• Plastforum (NOR ISSN 0809-5469) **7096**
• Plastforum (SWE ISSN 1653-557X) **7096**
Plastforum Nordica *see* Plastforum **7096**
Plastic Additives *see* Suliao Zhuji **7100**
• ➤ Plastic and Reconstructive Surgery (USA ISSN 0032-1052) **6255**
▼ Plastic Antinomy (USA ISSN 1937-7789) **512**
Plastic Art *see* Zaoxing Yishu **528**
Plastic Canvas Home & Holiday *see* Annie's Plastic Canvas **8930**
Plastic Canvas Today *see* Annie's Plastic Canvas **8930**
Plastic Cards in Europe (GBR ISSN 1474-709X) **1375**
Plastic Laminates Symposium. Proceedings (USA) **7096**
Plastic Molding Technology *see* Purasuchikku Seikei Gijutsu **7099**
Plastic Optical Fiber (USA ISSN 1064-1068) **2336**
• Plastic Optical Fiber Newsletter (USA) **2371**
• Plastic Packaging Innovation News (GBR ISSN 1745-6819) **6714**
Plastic Surgery News (USA ISSN 1043-4119) **6255**
• Plastic Surgery Practice Advisor (USA ISSN 1558-7312) **4109**
Plastic Surgery Products (USA ISSN 1084-1660) **6255**
• Plastic Surgical Nursing (USA ISSN 0741-5206) **5978**
Plastic Tower (USA ISSN 1066-6044) **5430**
Plastichem (SGP ISSN 0129-5195) **3252**
Plasticheskie Massy/Journal of the Plastic Compounds (RUS ISSN 0554-2901) **7096**
• Plasticidad y Restauracion Neurologica (MEX ISSN 1665-3254) **6174**
Plastico Industrial (BRA ISSN 1808-3528) **2128**
• Plastico Moderno (BRA ISSN 0102-1931) **7096**
• Plasticos em Revista (BRA ISSN 0032-1133) **7096**
Plasticos en Colombia (COL ISSN 0120-8624) **7096**
Plasticos Universales (ESP ISSN 0303-4011) **7096**
Plastics *see* Suliao **7100**
Plastics *see* Suoliao **7100**
Plastics *see* Gosei Jushi **7092**
Plastics (USA ISSN 0192-1789) **7096**
• Plastics, Additives and Compounding (GBR ISSN 1464-391X) **7096**
• Plastics Advisor (USA ISSN 1530-2393) **7096**
Plastics Advisor. Sourceguide *see* Plastics Advisor **7096**
Plastics Age/Purasuchikkusu Eji (JPN ISSN 0551-0503) **7096**
Plastics Age Encyclopedia (JPN) **7096**
Plastics and Rubber *see* Muanyag es Gumi **7095**
• Plastics and Rubber Asia (GBR ISSN 1360-1245) **7096**
• Plastics & Rubber Weekly (GBR ISSN 1356-7152) **7096**
† Plastics Board Industries Federation Magazine (GBR ISSN 1477-7398) **8981**
Plastics Brief: Thermoplastics Marketing Newsletter (USA ISSN 1041-083X) **7096**
Plastics Bulletin (HKG ISSN 1024-462X) **7096**
• Plastics Business News (USA ISSN 0734-1784) **7096**
Plastics Compounding Redbook (USA) **7097**
Plastics Conference Proceedings (Year) (USA) **7097**
• The Plastics Distributor & Fabricator Magazine (USA) **7097**
• Plastics Engineering (USA ISSN 0091-9578) **7097**
➤ Plastics Engineering Series (USA ISSN 1040-2527) **7097**
Plastics Fabricating & Forming (USA) **7097**
Plastics Focus (USA ISSN 0554-2952) **7097**
Plastics High Performance Packaging (BEL) **7097**
Plastics Hot Line (USA) **7097**
• Plastics Hotline (USA) **7097**
• Plastics in Canada (CAN ISSN 1198-225X) **7097**
Plastics in Canada Buyers' Guide (CAN) **7097**
Plastics Industry Directory (NZL ISSN 1176-9629) **2023**
Plastics Information Europe (DEU ISSN 0944-1395) **7097**
† • Plastics Insights (USA ISSN 1544-9475) **8981**
Plastics Machining and Fabricating *see* Plastics Machining & Fabricating **7097**
• Plastics Machining & Fabricating (USA ISSN 1527-277X) **7097**
Plastics Machining & Fabricating Illustrated Buying Guide *see* P M & F Illustrated Buying Guide **7096**
Plastics Molding and Fabricating *see* Plastics Molding & Fabricating (Online) **7097**
• Plastics Molding & Fabricating (Online) (USA) **7097**
Plastics Molding & Fabricating (Print) *see* Plastics Molding & Fabricating (Online) **7097**
• Plastics News (IND ISSN 0971-3689) **7097**
• Plastics News (USA ISSN 1042-802X) **7097**
• Plastics News China E-Weekly (USA) **7097**
• Plastics News International (AUS ISSN 1328-7451) **7097**
Plastics Newsletter (HKG) **7097**
Plastics Packaging Manufacturers *see* Business Ratio. Plastics Packaging Manufacturers **6708**
Plastics Processing *see* Key Note Market Report: Plastics Processing **7094**
Plastics Processors *see* Business Ratio Report. Plastics Processors (Year) **7091**
Plastics Recycling Update (USA ISSN 1052-4908) **3510**
Plastics, Rubber & Chemical Products (GBR) **2023**
Plastics, Rubber & Composites *see* Plastics, Rubber and Composites **7097**
• ➤ Plastics, Rubber and Composites (GBR ISSN 1465-8011) **7097**
Plastics Science and Technology *see* Suliao Keji **7100**
Plastics South East Asia Pacific *see* Plastics News International **7097**
Plastics Southern Africa (ZAF ISSN 0048-4385) **7098**
Plastics Southern Africa Buyers Guide (ZAF) **7098**
• Plastics Technology (USA ISSN 0032-1257) **7098**
Plastics Week (USA ISSN 1044-9663) **7098**
▼ • Plastics World Insight (USA ISSN 1949-4394) **7098**
PlasticsBrief: Design & Materials Newsletter (USA ISSN 1041-0821) **7098**
PlasticsBrief: Extrusion & Blow Molding Newsletter (USA ISSN 1041-0813) **7098**
PlasticsBrief: Injection Molding Newsletter (USA ISSN 1041-0791) **7098**
PlasticsBrief: Reinforced Plastic Edition (USA ISSN 0744-5296) **7098**
PlasticsNews.com *see* Plastics News **7097**
• ➤ Plasticulture (FRA ISSN 0257-9022) **7098**
Plastika i Guma (SRB ISSN 0351-8787) **7098**
Plastiquarian (GBR ISSN 1355-4859) **7098**
Plastiques & Caoutchoucs Magazine (FRA ISSN 1776-1395) **7098**
Plastische Chirurgie (DEU ISSN 1618-6214) **6255**
• Plastix (ITA ISSN 1824-8411) **7098**
Plastribution News (GBR) **7098**
Plastron Papers (USA) **321**
Plastverarbeiter (DEU ISSN 0032-1338) **7098**
Plate (USA ISSN 1541-7387) **3660**
Das Plateau (DEU ISSN 0938-6602) **512**
▼ Plateau (Richmond Hill) (USA ISSN 1942-6976) **6606**
➤ Plateau Journal (USA ISSN 1092-2814) **352**
• ➤ Platelets (London) (GBR ISSN 0953-7104) **5940**
Plates (Automobile License Plate Collectors Association) (USA ISSN 1554-6896) **4343**
Plates Magazine *see* Plates **4343**
▼ Plates to Pixels (USA ISSN 1943-8311) **6975**
• Platform (GBR ISSN 1751-0171) **8476**
Platform (Amsterdam) (NLD ISSN 1574-0226) **3558**
Platform (Yorkshire) (GBR ISSN 0143-8875) **8621**
Platform A (NLD) **4600**
Platform Biologica. Nieuwsbrief *see* Bio Update **96**
Platform Oil & Gas Technology Review (GBR) **6789**
Platform Papers (AUS ISSN 1449-583X) **8476**
• Platform Tennis News (Online) (USA) **8242**
Platform Tennis News (Print) *see* Platform Tennis News (Online) **8242**
Platforma Spartakusowcow (DEU) **7165**
Plating and Finishing *see* Diandu yu Jingshi **2113**
Plating and Surface Finishing (USA ISSN 0360-3164) **6328**
Platinum (Year) (GBR ISSN 0268-7305) **6329**
Platinum Business (ZAF ISSN 1994-8654) **1159**
Platinum Business News *see* Platinum Business **1159**
Platinum Magazin (DEU) **5080**
• Platinum Metals Review (Online) (GBR ISSN 1471-0676) **6329**
Platinum Privilege (AUS) **8748**
➤ Platon (GRC ISSN 1105-073X) **2239**
➤ Platonselskabets Skriftserie (DNK ISSN 0901-2583) **6944**
• Platou Report (NOR ISSN 0802-0213) **8656**
• Platow Boerse (DEU ISSN 1439-7684) **1644**
• Der Platow Brief (DEU ISSN 1431-3863) **1511**
• Platow Emerging Markets (DEU ISSN 1439-1473) **1644**
Platow Prognose (DEU) **1511**
Platte County Historical and Genealogical Society Bulletin (USA ISSN 1083-7736) **3779**
Platte Valley Review (USA ISSN 0092-4318) **2297**
Platteland (NLD ISSN 1574-2989) **147**
Plattelands Post Magazine (NLD ISSN 0922-2197) **147**
Plattform (CHE) **7770**

Link to your serials resources and content with ulrichsweb.com

Title

Title

Title

Title

▼ *new title*　　† *ceased*　　● *electronic media*　　➤ *refereed*

Title

10756 PRACTICAL MEXICAN TAX STRATEGIES ULRICH'S PERIODICALS

• Practical Mexican Tax Strategies (USA ISSN 1557-3680) **1939**
Practical Motorhome (GBR ISSN 1474-1830) **8329**
Practical Motorist (GBR ISSN 0960-2828) **8599**
• Practical Neurology (GBR ISSN 1474-7758) **6174**
The Practical Nomad (USA ISSN 1088-6419) **8748**
Practical Oncology Journal *see* Shiyong Zhongliuxue Zazhi **6034**
Practical Optometry *see* Clinical & Refractive Optometry **6040**
Practical Pain Management (USA ISSN 1541-5988) **5698**
Practical Papers for the Bible Translator *see* Bible Translator. Practical Papers **5099**
Practical Parenting (AUS) **2165**
Practical Parenting *see* Practical Parenting and Pregnancy **2166**
Practical Parenting and Pregnancy (GBR ISSN 1758-9045) **2166**
▼ Practical Pedal (USA) **8266**
Practical Pharmacy/Yakkyoku (JPN ISSN 0044-0035) **6876**
Practical Photography (GBR ISSN 0032-6445) **6975**
Practical Planning Law (GBR ISSN 1361-584X) **4904**
Practical Poultry (GBR ISSN 1743-0712) **297**
Practical Pre-School (GBR ISSN 1366-610X) **2898**
Practical Pregnancy *see* Practical Parenting **2165**
Practical Preventive Medicine *see* Shiyong Yufang Yixue **5714**
• ➤ Practical Procedures and Aesthetic Dentistry (USA ISSN 1534-6846) **5861**
Practical Project Execution Know How Reports (IND) **1645**
▼ Practical Promulgation (USA ISSN 1940-5707) **7536**
Practical Queensland Landscape Design, Construction and Maintenance (AUS ISSN 1037-0285) **3748**
Practical Radiology *see* Shiyong Fangshexue Zazhi **6208**
• The Practical Real Estate Lawyer (USA ISSN 8756-0372) **4759**
• Practical Research for Education (GBR ISSN 1751-2131) **2898**
Practical Rural Engineering Technology *see* Nongcun Shiyong Gongcheng Jishu **141**
• Practical Russia / Eurasia Tax Strategies (USA ISSN 1933-2718) **1939**
Practical Sailor (USA ISSN 0161-8059) **8280**
➤ Practical Spectroscopy Series (USA ISSN 0148-9054) **2104**
Practical Sportsman (USA ISSN 1067-5914) **8329**
Practical Stock Picker (USA) **1645**
Practical Strategies for Maintaining Safe Schools *see* Maintaining Safe Schools **3027**
• Practical Summaries in Acute Care (USA ISSN 1930-1103) **6071**
• The Practical Tax Lawyer (USA ISSN 0890-4898) **1939**
• Practical Tax Strategies (USA ISSN 1523-6250) **1939**
Practical Technology Education *see* Jissen Kyoiku **2873**
• Practical Theology (GBR ISSN 1756-073X) **7670**
• Practical Theology in South Africa (ZAF ISSN 1010-8017) **7670**
† Practical Tips for New York Law Enforcement (USA) **8982**
Practical Training (GBR) **1872**
• Practical Trust Precedents (GBR) **4905**
• Practical U.S. / Domestic Tax Strategies (USA) **1939**
• Practical U.S. / International Tax Strategies (USA ISSN 1523-2638) **1939**
Practical Video Photography (GBR ISSN 0267-8462) **6975**
Practical Web Design (GBR) **2566**
Practical Web Projects (GBR ISSN 1475-1380) **2566**
• Practical Welding Today (USA ISSN 1092-3942) **6329**
• Practical Will Precedents (GBR) **4905**
Practical Winery & Vineyard (USA ISSN 0739-8077) **609**
Practical Wireless (GBR ISSN 0141-0857) **2387**
Practical Woodworking (GBR ISSN 1758-5430) **1051**
Practical Woodworking & Routing *see* Practical Woodworking **1051**
Practical Writing *see* Yingyong Xiezuo **5403**
• Practically Primary (AUS ISSN 1324-5961) **3077**
PracticaOto-Rhino-Laryngologica *see* Jibi Inkoka Rinsho **6081**
Practice/Purakutisu (JPN ISSN 0289-4947) **5899**
• ➤ Practice (Abingdon) (GBR ISSN 0950-3153) **8062**
Practice (Carlton South) *see* Australian Optometry **6039**
• ➤ Practice and Evidence of Scholarship of Teaching and Learning in Higher Education (GBR ISSN 1750-8428) **2998**
• Practice and Procedure - High Court and Federal Court of Australia (AUS) **4959**
• Practice Before Federal Magistrates (USA) **4759**
• Practice Brief (AUS ISSN 1834-5484) **8062**
• Practice Development in Health Care (GBR ISSN 1475-9861) **5698**
▼ • Practice Exercises for the T O E F L (Test of English as a Foreign Language) (USA ISSN 1935-8512) **2998**
Practice in Foreign Economic Relations and Trade *see* Duiwai Jingmao Shiwu **1562**
Practice in Prosthodontics *see* Hotetsu Rinsho **5846**
Practice Management *see* Money Management **1368**
Practice Management (GBR ISSN 1479-2818) **5698**
Practice Management Notes *see* A A O M S Today **5832**
Practice Manager *see* Practice Management **5698**
• Practice Matters (USA ISSN 1545-6781) **8062**
Practice Monograph Series *see* Social Work Practice Monograph Series **8071**
• Practice Nurse (GBR ISSN 0953-6612) **5978**
• ➤ Practice Nursing (GBR ISSN 0964-9271) **5978**
Practice of Anti-Corrosion Protection *see* Praktika Protivokorrozionnoi Zashchity **6329**
Practice of Psychotherapy Series (GBR) **7391**
• ➤ Practice Periodical of Hazardous, Toxic and Radioactive Waste Management (USA ISSN 1090-025X) **3510**
• ➤ Practice Periodical on Structural Design and Construction (USA ISSN 1084-0680) **3281**
• ➤ Practice Reflexions (AUS ISSN 1834-3635) **8062**
• Practice under the California Corporation Securities Laws (USA) **4879**
Practice While You Play (USA) **8243**
Practices (USA ISSN 1059-7239) **453**
Practiciens et 3eme Age *see* Practiciens et Troisieme Age **4053**
Practiciens et Troisieme Age (FRA ISSN 0242-9772) **4053**
Practicing Anthropology (USA ISSN 0888-4552) **352**
• The Practicing C P A (USA ISSN 0885-6931) **1299**
Practicing Oil Analysis (USA ISSN 1536-3937) **6789**
• Practicing Planner (Chicago) (USA ISSN 1544-1261) **4424**
• ➤ The Practising Midwife (GBR ISSN 1461-3123) **6002**
• The Practitioner (GBR ISSN 0032-6518) **5698**
The Practitioner Inquiry Series (USA ISSN 1556-4509) **3077**
Practitioners 1040 Deskbook (USA ISSN 1056-9952) **1939**
Practitioner's British Columbia Taxes Annotated (Year) (CAN ISSN 1912-3124) **1940**
Practitioner's Guide Series (GBR) **8062**
The Practitioner's Guide to Consumer Bankruptcy (USA) **1376**
Practitioner's Guide to Trusts, Estates and Trust Returns (CAN ISSN 1910-6742) **4905**
Practitioner's Income Tax Act (CAN ISSN 1193-1701) **1940**
Practitioner's Manual of Patent Examining Procedure (USA ISSN 1942-0307) **4759**
Practitioners Publishing Company's Guide to P C A O B Audits *see* P P C's Guide to P C A O B Audits **1298**
Practitioners Publishing Company's Guide to Public Company Accounting Oversight Board Audits *see* P P C's Guide to P C A O B Audits **1298**
Practitioners Publishing Company's Guide to Quality Control. Compilation and Review *see* P C C's Guide to Quality Control. Compilation and Review **1298**
Practitioners Publishing Company's Guide to Related Parties (Including Variable Interest Entities) *see* P P C's Guide to Related Parties (Including Variable Interest Entities) **1298**
Practitioners Publishing Company's Guide to Risk-Based Audits of Construction Contractors *see* P P C's Guide to Risk-Based Audits of Construction Contractors **1298**
Practitioners Publishing Company's Guide to Risk-Based Audits of H U D Projects *see* P P C's Guide to Risk-Based Audits of H U D Projects **1298**
Practitioners Publishing Company's Guide to Sales and Use Tax Savings for Manufacturers *see* P P C's Guide to Sales and Use Tax Savings for Manufacturers **1298**
• Practitioner's Trademark Manual of Examining Procedure (USA ISSN 1523-3979) **6757**
Practyczny Poradnik Ksiegowego (POL ISSN 1640-9930) **1299**
Prader-Willi Fonds. Nieuws (NLD ISSN 1574-714X) **5698**
Praedica Verbum (DEU ISSN 0936-403X) **7670**
Praeger Illustrated Military History (USA ISSN 1547-206X) **6441**
Praeger Series in Political Communications (USA ISSN 1062-5623) **7172**
Praeger Series in Political Economy (USA ISSN 1072-2882) **7172**
Praeger Series in Presidential Studies (USA ISSN 1062-0931) **7173**
Praeger Series in Transformational Politics and Political Science (USA ISSN 1061-5261) **7173**
▼ Praeger Series on Contemporary Health and Living (USA ISSN 1932-8079) **5698**
▼ Praeger Series on Healing and Managing Injury and Disease (USA ISSN 1940-5804) **5698**
Praeger Series on Jewish and Israeli Studies (USA ISSN 1550-1159) **7728**
Praeger Series on the Ancient World (USA ISSN 1932-1406) **4156**
▼ Praeger Series on the Middle Ages (USA ISSN 1939-2508) **4254**
The Praeger Singer-Songwriter Collection (USA ISSN 1553-3484) **6607**
The Praeger Television Collection (USA ISSN 1549-2257) **8126**
Praehistoria (ARG ISSN 0327-9480) **4156**
Praehistoria (HUN ISSN 1586-7811) **4156**
Praehistorische Archaeologie in Suedosteuropa (DEU ISSN 0723-1725) **411**
• Praehistorische Zeitschrift (DEU ISSN 0079-4848) **412**
▼ • Praemis (DNK ISSN 1903-4725) **148**
Der Praeparator (DEU ISSN 0032-6542) **2625**
Praesent Service Institut Journal *see* P S I Journal **32**
Praesteforeningens Blad (DNK ISSN 0106-6218) **7771**
Praevention (DEU ISSN 0170-2602) **7536**
• Praevention und Gesundheitsfoerderung (DEU ISSN 1861-6755) **7536**
Praevention und Rehabilitation (DEU ISSN 0937-552X) **5698**
Praew (THA) **8880**
Pragati (IND ISSN 0032-6550) **5353**
Pragativadi (IND) **3887**
• The Prager Perspective (USA ISSN 1091-1960) **7728**
Prager Volkszeitung (CZE ISSN 0139-8792) **3559**
Prager Zeitung (CZE ISSN 1211-6998) **3832**
Pragmalinguistica (ESP ISSN 1133-682X) **5162**
Pragma's Product Profiles (USA) **2595**
• ➤ Pragmatic Case Studies in Psychotherapy (USA ISSN 1553-0124) **7391**
▼ • The Pragmatic Marketer (USA ISSN 1938-9752) **1837**
• The Pragmatic Marketing Update (USA) **1837**
➤ Pragmatics (BEL ISSN 1018-2101) **5162**
➤ Pragmatics and Beyond New Series (NLD ISSN 0922-842X) **5162**
• ➤ Pragmatics & Cognition (NLD ISSN 0929-0907) **5204**
Pragmatics and Discourse Analysis *see* Studies of Argumentation in Pragmatics and Discourse Analysis **5183**
Pragmatist (USA ISSN 0885-6699) **1547**
• ➤ Prague Bulletin of Mathematical Linguistics (CZE ISSN 0032-6585) **5204**
† • Prague Business Journal (CZE ISSN 1211-3514) **8982**
➤ Prague Economic Papers (CZE ISSN 1210-0455) **1160**
† Prague In Your Pocket (CZE ISSN 1213-2128) **8982**
Prague Leaders Magazine (CZE) **1160**
† Prague Linguistic Circle Papers/Travaux du Cercle Linguistique de Prague (NLD ISSN 1383-7583) **8982**
➤ Prague Medical Report (CZE ISSN 1214-6994) **5698**
• The Prague Post (CZE ISSN 1210-3934) **3832**
The Prague Tribune (CZE ISSN 1211-314X) **1161**
Pragya Features (IND) **1786**
• ➤ Pragyaan: Information Technology (IND ISSN 0974-5513) **2549**
➤ Pragyaan: Journal of Management (IND ISSN 0974-5505) **1786**
➤ Pragyaan: Mass Communication (IND ISSN 0974-5521) **2336**
The Prairie (USA) **2297**
• Prairie Business (USA) **1161**
Prairie Club Bulletin (USA ISSN 0032-6607) **2625**
The Prairie Dog (CAN ISSN 1199-9225) **3559**
• Prairie Farmer (USA) **297**
Prairie Farmers Catalogue (CAN ISSN 0831-2338) **213**
Prairie Fire (CAN ISSN 0821-1124) **5353**
▼ Prairie Fire (USA ISSN 1936-7082) **7173**
➤ Prairie Forum (CAN ISSN 0317-6282) **3461**
• The (Year) Prairie Garden (CAN ISSN 0315-6850) **3748**
Prairie Gleaner (USA ISSN 0032-6623) **3779**
Prairie Gold Rush (USA ISSN 0896-5617) **213**
Prairie Harvester (CAN ISSN 0383-7653) **2297**
➤ Prairie Journal (CAN ISSN 0827-2921) **5353**
Prairie Landscape Magazine (CAN ISSN 0820-6848) **454**
Prairie Messenger (CAN ISSN 0032-664X) **7813**
➤ The Prairie Naturalist (USA ISSN 0091-0376) **698**
Prairie News (USA) **3660**
Prairie Pedaler (CAN) **8266**
Prairie Pioneer (USA ISSN 1523-9233) **3779**
Prairie Profile (USA) **8748**
Prairie Provinces Water Board Annual Report (CAN ISSN 0704-8726) **8831**
Prairie Rose (USA ISSN 0032-6666) **5978**
• Prairie Schooner (USA ISSN 0032-6682) **5353**
• Prairie Sounds (CAN ISSN 0822-7500) **6607**
The Prairie Star (USA) **148**
Prairie Tales (CAN ISSN 1914-7198) **6510**
Praise & Prayer Calendar (AUS) **7670**
Prajamata Illustrated Weekly (IND) **3887**
Prajatantra (IND) **3887**
Prajavani (IND) **3887**
Prajna (IND ISSN 0554-9884) **2998**
➤ Prajnan (Pune) (IND ISSN 0970-8448) **1376**
Prakalpana Literature *see* Prakalpana Sahitya **5354**
Prakalpana Sahitya/Prakalpana Literature (IND) **5354**
Prakit Jain Institute Research Publication Series (IND ISSN 0554-9906) **7740**
Prakrit Text Society. Publications (IND) **5354**
Prakseologia (POL ISSN 0079-4872) **6944**
Praksis Oekonomi *see* Praxis Oekonomi **5699**
Prakticheskaya Bukhgalteriya (RUS) **1299**
Prakticheskii Marketing (RUS) **1837**
Prakticheskii Zhurnal dlya Uchitelya i Administratsii Shkoly/Practical Journal for a Teacher and Administration of the School (RUS) **3030**
Prakticka Gynekologia (SVK ISSN 1335-4221) **6002**
• Prakticka Prirucka pre Bezpecnostnych Technikov (SVK ISSN 1336-7668) **6684**
Prakticka Zena (CZE ISSN 0231-6471) **8880**
• ➤ Prakticke Lekarenstvi (CZE ISSN 1801-2434) **6876**
➤ Prakticky Lekar/General Practitioner (CZE ISSN 0032-6739) **5699**
• Prakticky Poradce v Danovych Otazkach (CZE ISSN 1212-8600) **1940**
Praktiese Teologie in S.A. *see* Practical Theology in South Africa **7670**
Praktijk (NLD ISSN 1871-8744) **2898**
▼ Praktijkblad Preventie (NLD ISSN 1876-4223) **6684**
Praktijkblad Salarisadministratie *see* Praktijkblad voor de Salarisadministratie **1872**
• Praktijkblad voor de Salarisadministratie (NLD ISSN 1384-5365) **1872**
Praktijkblad voor Medezeggenschap *see* OndernemingsRaad **1156**
Praktijkboek Arbeidsomstandigheden (NLD ISSN 1874-9801) **4759**
Praktijkboek Binnenvaart (NLD ISSN 1876-4274) **8657**
Praktijkboek Personeel, Organisatie en Ontwikkeling (NLD ISSN 1574-4884) **1872**
Praktijkboek voor Vennootschappen (BEL ISSN 0778-5895) **4879**
Praktijkcahiers Strafrecht (NLD ISSN 1574-3098) **4759**
• De Praktijkgids (NLD ISSN 0165-0025) **4759**
Praktijkgids Afvalstoffenkaarten (NLD ISSN 1872-1087) **3510**
• Praktijkgids Zorg en Inkomen (NLD ISSN 1871-0107) **4760**
Praktijkkompas Rundvee *see* V-Focus **303**
Praktijkkompas Varkens *see* V-Focus **303**
Praktijkserie Basisschoolmanagement (NLD ISSN 1573-4307) **3030**
Praktijkserie Schoolmanagement *see* Praktijkserie Basisschoolmanagement **3030**
† Praktijkserie Sociaal Recht (NLD) **8982**
Praktijkwijzer Toezicht en Opsporing (NLD ISSN 1874-5776) **7460**
• Praktik & Teori (SWE ISSN 1104-6570) **2898**
Praktika (DEU ISSN 0179-7298) **5163**
Praktika (HUN ISSN 1588-5518) **8880**
Praktika Protivokorrozionnoi Zashchity/Practice of Anti-Corrosion Protection (RUS) **6329**
Praktika Reklamy (RUS) **32**
Praktikan (SWE ISSN 1103-1727) **5699**
Der Praktiker (DEU ISSN 0554-9965) **6343**
Praktiki (GRC ISSN 1105-1477) **8880**
Praktiline Arvutikasutaja (EST) **3836**
• Der Praktische Gartenratgeber (DEU) **3748**
• Der Praktische Gartenratgeber Online (DEU) **3748**
• ➤ Praktische Metallographie (DEU ISSN 0032-678X) **6329**
Praktische Philosophie (DEU) **6944**
➤ Praktische Psychiatrie (DEU ISSN 0933-3851) **6174**
Der Praktische Schaedlingsbekaempfer (DEU ISSN 0032-6801) **249**
Praktische Theologie (DEU ISSN 0946-3518) **7671**
Praktische Theologie (NLD ISSN 0165-6511) **7671**
Praktische Theologie im Dialog (CHE ISSN 1422-4410) **7671**
➤ Der Praktische Tierarzt (DEU ISSN 0032-681X) **8805**
Praktischer Journalismus (DEU ISSN 1617-3570) **4582**
Praktisk Baatliv *see* Baatliv **8272**
• Praktisk Oekonomi & Finans (NOR ISSN 1501-0074) **1161**
Praktiskais Latvietis (LVA ISSN 1407-3358) **3905**
• ➤ Praktiske Grunde (DNK ISSN 1902-2271) **4470**
Praktiskt Butiksarbete (SWE ISSN 0345-9071) **3681**
Praline *see* Die Junge Praline **3851**
• ➤ Pramana (IND ISSN 0304-4289) **7035**
➤ Prameny a Studie (CZE ISSN 0862-8483) **148**
Prampra (IND) **3621**
Prana (NLD ISSN 0165-4373) **4470**
Prana Yoga Life (USA ISSN 0149-953X) **6944**
Pranab Jyoti (IND) **5234**
• Pranjana (IND ISSN 0971-9997) **1786**
Pranjana. The Journal of Management Awareness *see* Pranjana **1786**
Prantik (IND ISSN 0971-5932) **3887**
Prasar (IND) **2945**
Prashasnika (IND) **7460**
Prasine Europe *see* Green Europe **116**
Prataculture & Animal Husbandry *see* Caoye yu Xumu **283**
Pratah Kamal (IND) **3887**
Pratahkal (IND) **3887**
Pratap (Jalandhar) (IND) **3887**
Pratap (New Delhi) (IND) **3887**
Prather Bulletin (USA) **3779**
Pratibha India (IND ISSN 0970-2849) **5354**
† Pratica (ITA ISSN 1120-4575) **8982**
La Pratica Analitica (ITA ISSN 1120-9380) **7391**
Pratica Contabile (ITA ISSN 1594-0292) **1299**
Pratica e Criativa (PRT) **8880**
Pratica Lavoro (ITA ISSN 1592-5994) **1703**
Pratiche Linguistiche e Analisi di Testi Quaderni *see* P L A T Quaderni **5159**

Title

10758 PRELIMINARY DETERMINATION OF EPICENTERS, MONTHLY LISTING ULRICH'S PERIODICALS

Preliminary Determination of Epicenters, Monthly Listing *see* U.S. Geological Survey. National Earthquake Information Service. Preliminary Determination of Epicenters, Monthly Listing **2791**
Preliminary Overview of the Economies of Latin America and the Caribbean (CHL ISSN 1014-7802) **1512**
Preliminary Provincial and Territorial Government Health Expenditure Estimates *see* Estimations Preliminaires des Depenses de Sante des Gouvernements Provinciaux et Territoriaux **7516**
Preliminary Report of the Hakuho Maru Cruise (JPN) **2816**
Prelucrari la Cald (ROM ISSN 1224-452X) **6329**
Prelude (Calgary) (CAN ISSN 0381-890X) **6607**
Prelude (Toronto) (CAN) **6607**
• Premiata Salumeria Italiana (ITA ISSN 1121-9068) **3660**
Premices (FRA ISSN 1770-2488) **2208**
Premie Press (AUS ISSN 1832-1615) **2166**
Premiefoto Vereniging Oud Volendam *see* Stichting Volendams Museum. Museumjaarboek **4267**
Premier Essentials (USA) **3985**
▼ • Premier Guitar (USA ISSN 1945-077X) **6607**
Premier Hair *see* Ultimate Black Hair Guide **592**
Premier Hotels and Resorts *see* Premier Hotels + Resorts **4395**
• Premier Hotels + Resorts (USA) **4395**
Premier Rapport sur les Plans d'Action Annuels Produits par les Ministeres, les Organismes Publics et les Municipalites a l'Egard des Personnes Handicapees (CAN ISSN 1912-6271) **4069**
Premier Romance (USA) **4396**
Premier Spas (USA) **8748**
• Premier Stats (GBR ISSN 1754-0526) **8243**
Premier Telecard Magazine (USA ISSN 1081-4329) **4343**
Premiere *see* Keji Shangpin **3107**
Premiere (CZE ISSN 1212-8899) **6510**
Premiere (FRA ISSN 0399-3698) **6510**
Premiere (JPN) **6510**
Premiere (RUS) **6510**
Premiere (ZAF) **6510**
• Premiere (Korean Edition)/Peulimieo Han'gugpan (KOR ISSN 1228-081X) **6510**
• Premiere (Online) (USA) **6510**
▼ Premiere Dame (FRA ISSN 1962-3151) **3842**
Premiere Magazin (DEU) **2388**
Premiere Video Magazine (CAN) **2402**
Premieres Informations. Dossiers Statistiques *see* France. Direction de l'Animation de la Recherche, des Etudes et des Statistiques. Dossiers **1233**
• Premieres Informations et Premieres Syntheses (FRA ISSN 1253-1545) **4470**
▼ Premiers Secours Magazine (FRA ISSN 1961-0785) **4109**
Premio Internacional a la Investigacion en Alfabetizacion *see* International Award for Literacy Research **3025**
• Premise Wiring (USA ISSN 1521-3110) **2352**
Premise Wiring Newsletter *see* Premise Wiring **2352**
Premises and Facilities Management (GBR ISSN 0965-4739) **1854**
Premises Liability Alert (USA ISSN 1532-0197) **4760**
• Premises Liability Law and Practice (USA) **7604**
• Premises Liability Report (USA ISSN 1055-730X) **4760**
Premises Management *see* Croner's Premises Management **7588**
Premium (DEU) **8599**
Premium Games (BRA ISSN 1807-2151) **2481**
▼ Premium Incentive Products (USA) **32**
Premium Lagers, Beers & Ciders Plus *see* Key Note Market Report Plus. Premium Lagers, Beers & Ciders **606**
• Premium Links (USA) **2566**
Premium Marketing Club of New York, Inc. of N Y Newsletter *see* P M C of N Y Newsletter **1837**
• Premium Tax Collection (NZL ISSN 1177-4363) **4760**
Premonitions (GBR ISSN 0968-6185) **5446**
Premsela Nieuwsbrief *see* Premsela.org **512**
Premsela.org (NLD ISSN 1874-4605) **512**
Premsela Stichting *see* Premsela.org **512**
• ➤ Prenatal Diagnosis (GBR ISSN 0197-3851) **6002**
Prendre Soin Domicile (FRA ISSN 1772-8789) **8063**
Prenez l'Air Averti *see* Fly Smart **8541**
La Prensa *see* La Prensa on the Web **3821**
Prensa *see* Diario la Prensa **3875**
• La Prensa (MEX ISSN 1563-7662) **3910**
• La Prensa (NIC ISSN 1027-4588) **3920**
• La Prensa (PAN) **3927**
Prensa Confidencial (ARG ISSN 0032-7433) **1512**
† Prensa de la Industria Grafica (ESP) **8982**
• La Prensa de Minnesota (USA) **3559**
La Prensa de San Antonio (USA) **3559**
La Prensa del Rioja (ESP) **609**
• La Prensa Grafica (SLV ISSN 1605-1912) **3836**
• Prensa Hispana (Phoenix) (USA) **3559**
Prensa Latina (USA ISSN 1524-2803) **1512**
• La Prensa Libre (CRI) **3830**
• Prensa Libre (GTM) **3874**
Prensa Medica Argentina (ARG ISSN 0032-745X) **5699**
• Prensa Obrera (ARG) **7173**
• La Prensa on the Web (HND ISSN 1563-8898) **3821**
• La Prensa San Diego (USA ISSN 0738-9183) **3559**
Prensa Web *see* La Prensa **3927**
Prenses (TUR) **2208**
La Prensita (USA) **3559**
La Prensita de San Antonio (USA) **3559**
† • Prent (DNK ISSN 1603-9106) **8982**
Prentice-Hall Information and System Sciences Series (USA ISSN 0891-4559) **2549**
Prentice-Hall International Series in Optoelectronics (USA ISSN 0959-9118) **7084**
Prentice-Hall International Series in Systems and Control Engineering (USA ISSN 0892-4252) **2524**
Prentice-Hall Signal Processing Series (USA ISSN 1050-2769) **3393**
Prentice-Hall Software Series (USA ISSN 0891-4516) **2596**
Preodolenie (RUS ISSN 0869-477X) **4069**
• Prep Audio (USA ISSN 1559-0356) **6103**
Prep School (GBR ISSN 0963-8601) **2899**
• Prep Stars Recruiter's Handbook (USA) **8194**
Prep Talk *see* Pr E P Talk **1901**
Prep Traveler (USA ISSN 1554-2564) **8748**
▼ Prepa Magazine (FRA ISSN 1959-4860) **2998**
The Prepaid Press (USA ISSN 1934-5313) **2371**
Preparacion Para la Escuela *see* Ayudando a los Ninos a Aprender (Preparacion para la Escuela) **2829**
Preparacion Para La Lectura *see* Desarrollando la Lectura (Preparacidon Para la Lectura) **2841**
Preparation of Annual Disclosure Documents & S E C Update *see* Annual Disclosure Documents & S E C Update **4855**
Preparation X (USA) **3985**
• ➤ Preparative Biochemistry and Biotechnology (USA ISSN 1082-6068) **742**
• Prepared Foods (USA ISSN 0747-2536) **3660**
Prepared Foods. Wellness and Organic Ingredients Directory (USA) **3660**
Preparing for the California Notary Public Exam (USA ISSN 1097-2226) **4760**
† Preparing for the Future: E S A Technology Quarterly (NLD ISSN 1018-8657) **8982**
• Preparing Your Corporate Tax Returns (CAN ISSN 0713-8946) **1940**
Prepodavanie Istorii i Obshchestvoznaniya v Shkole (RUS) **4157**
Prepodavanie Istorii v Shkole (RUS ISSN 0132-0696) **4157**
Prepravni a Tarifni Vestnik/Transportation and Tariff News (CZE ISSN 0032-7514) **8508**
PrePress (DEU) **7580**
† Prepress (NLD ISSN 1386-2596) **8982**
Prepress Bulletin *see* I P A Bulletin **7323**
Preprints of Joint Conference on Nuclear Fusion *see* Kaku Yugo Rengo Koenkai Yokoshu **7068**
Preprints of Symposium on Liquid Crystals *see* Ekisho Toronkai Koen Yokoshu **2110**
• Presbyterian Banner (AUS ISSN 0729-3542) **7771**
Presbyterian Church (U.S.A.). Minutes of the General Assembly (USA) **7771**
Presbyterian Church in Canada. General Assembly. Acts and Proceedings (CAN ISSN 0079-4996) **7771**
Presbyterian College Magazine (USA ISSN 1071-4928) **2297**
The Presbyterian Herald (GBR ISSN 0032-7530) **7771**
Presbyterian Messenger (CMR) **7771**
The Presbyterian Outlook (USA ISSN 0032-7565) **7771**
• Presbyterian Record (CAN ISSN 0032-7573) **7771**
The Presbyterian Sun (USA) **7771**
Presbyterians Today (USA ISSN 1083-2181) **7771**
Presbyterion (USA ISSN 0193-6212) **7771**
Preschool Education *see* Xueqian Jiaoyu **2927**
Preschool Playhouse. Student Folder (USA ISSN 1550-9362) **7671**
Preschool Playhouse. Teacher Guide (USA ISSN 1550-9370) **7671**
Prescon South African Newsletter (ZAF) **1512**
• Prescott Area Newcomer's Guide (USA ISSN 1939-3504) **5080**
▼ • The Prescott Report (USA ISSN 1949-3320) **1838**
• Prescriber (GBR ISSN 0959-6682) **6876**
• Prescriber Update (NZL ISSN 1172-5648) **7536**
Prescriber's Letter (USA ISSN 1073-7219) **6876**
• Prescribing & Medicines Management (GBR ISSN 1479-3849) **6876**
Prescribing Reference for Obstetricians and Gynecologists *see* M P R (Obstetrician & Gynecologist Edition) **6859**
Prescription Drug User Fee Act. Financial Report to Congress *see* U.S. Department of Health and Human Services. Food and Drug Administration. Prescription Drug User Fee Act. Financial Report to Congress **7472**
Prescription For Healthy Living (USA) **8881**
Prescrire International (FRA ISSN 1167-7422) **6876**
• ➤ Presek (SVN ISSN 0351-6652) **7899**
Presenca Filosofica (BRA ISSN 0103-2283) **6945**
• ➤ Presence (USA ISSN 1054-7460) **2489**
Presence (Toronto) (CAN ISSN 1719-7155) **8063**
➤ Presence Africaine (FRA ISSN 0032-7638) **5234**
Presence Autochtone a Montreal (Year) (CAN ISSN 1910-0531) **3559**
Presence de Gabriel Marcel (FRA ISSN 1166-9993) **6945**
Presence de l'Enseignement Agricole Prive (FRA ISSN 0339-0055) **148**
• Presence Magazine (CAN ISSN 1188-5580) **7671**
Presence Sense Magazine (USA) **3985**
Presence Ukrainienne (FRA ISSN 1951-5588) **4254**
Presences (FRA ISSN 0981-1869) **1408**
Presences in Business (BEL ISSN 0779-8881) **1512**
Presencia (COL) **7671**
Presencia Ecumenica (VEN ISSN 0798-0256) **7671**
Presencia Negra (COL) **3559**
Presencia Universitaria (HND) **2998**
Presens (SWE ISSN 1403-7963) **8476**
Present (NLD ISSN 1874-9755) **7536**
Present State of Land Construction *see* Kokudo Kensetsu no Genkyo **1019**
Present Status of H T T R R & D *see* Koon Kogaku Shiken Kenkyu no Genjo **3170**
Present Truth and Herald of Christ's Epiphany (USA ISSN 0032-7700) **7740**
• Presentations (USA ISSN 1072-7531) **32**
Presente (DEU) **3821**
• Presente! (USA ISSN 1949-3223) **7260**
Presente e la Storia (ITA ISSN 1121-7499) **4254**
Presentia (VEN ISSN 1316-1857) **4470**
† Presenza (ITA ISSN 0478-1376) **8982**
Presenza Economica (VEN) **1409**
Presenza Tecnica (ITA ISSN 0390-329X) **3216**
Preser-vision *see* PreserVision **5040**
Preservation (USA ISSN 1090-9931) **454**
Preservation (Washington) *see* Preservation **454**
• Preservation Advocate (USA ISSN 1051-5755) **4157**
▼ ➤ Preservation Education & Research (USA) **4309**
Preservation Education Directory (USA ISSN 1049-619X) **5040**
Preservation Law Reporter (USA ISSN 0882-715X) **454**
Preservation New Mexico (USA) **4309**
Preservation New York (USA) **454**
Preservation Notes (USA ISSN 0885-7326) **454**
Preservation Perspective (USA) **454**
Preservation Progress (Charleston) (USA ISSN 0478-1392) **454**
Preservation Tech Notes (USA ISSN 0741-9023) **1029**
Preservation Tips (USA ISSN 1523-4967) **6536**
Preserve (CAN ISSN 1910-9342) **4309**
Preserved Bus *see* Bus & Coach Preservation **8491**
Preserved Milk (GBR ISSN 0141-223X) **268**
Preserving Christian Homes (USA ISSN 1098-3775) **7671**
PreserVision *see* PreserVision **5040**
• PreserVision (CAN ISSN 1719-7813) **5040**
PreShipment Testing (USA ISSN 1043-2841) **6714**
• The Presidency (USA ISSN 1099-3681) **2998**
President (JPN ISSN 0032-7751) **1786**
President and Planner (USA) **4840**
President Transport World (USA) **8508**
Presidential Design Awards (USA ISSN 1049-541X) **512**
Presidential Elections *see* Forsetakjoer **7136**
• ➤ Presidential Studies Quarterly (USA ISSN 0360-4918) **7173**
President's Cancer Panel. Report of the Chairman (USA ISSN 0739-9987) **6032**
• The President's Emergency Plan for AIDS Relief (USA ISSN 1939-3687) **7536**
President's Fiscal Year (Year) Budget (USA) **1940**
The Presidents' Journal (USA ISSN 8755-8939) **4309**
President's Letter *see* Arkansas Hospitals **4088**
President's National Urban Policy Report (USA ISSN 0163-8602) **4424**
President's Newsletter (CAN ISSN 1194-3319) **3077**
Presidio (USA) **5354**
➤ Preslia (CZE ISSN 0032-7786) **814**
➤ Presovska Univerzita. Fakulta Humanitnych a Prirodnych Vied. Geograficke Prace (SVK) **4025**
• Press (GBR ISSN 1475-0910) **7329**
• Press (Christchurch) (NZL ISSN 0113-9762) **3918**
• Press (Harrisburg) (USA ISSN 1523-6390) **4582**
Press and Information *see* As- Sihafa wal-I'lam **7265**
• The Press and Journal (GBR) **3870**
Press Circles *see* Xinwenjie **4586**
Press Council of India Review (IND) **4582**
Press Digest *see* Wenzhaibao **3829**
Press - Enterprise Wheels - Offroad - Waves *see* P E - W O W **8327**
The Press Gallery Guide (AUS ISSN 1449-9142) **7460**
Press Gazette (GBR ISSN 0041-5170) **4582**
Press - Graph (ESP ISSN 1695-2448) **7325**
Press in India (IND ISSN 0445-6653) **633**
Press News (USA) **4582**
Press News-Sugar Industry (IND) **185**
Press Now. Nieuwsbrief (NLD ISSN 1574-6275) **4582**
Press On (ZAF ISSN 1992-1659) **2208**
Press Pass (USA) **4582**
Press Release *see* Baolin **3822**
Press Release - Building Societies Association (GBR ISSN 0261-6416) **1048**
Press Review (CAN ISSN 0706-9286) **4582**
Press Watch (ROM ISSN 1454-2765) **4582**
Press Working/Puresu Gijutsu (JPN ISSN 0387-3544) **5458**
Die Presse (AUT) **3798**
La Presse (TUN) **3962**
Presse et Information *see* As- Sihafa wal-I'lam **7265**
Presse-Inter (BEL ISSN 0777-9909) **6647**
Presse Juridique (CAN ISSN 1192-862X) **4760**
La Presse Litteraire (FRA ISSN 1778-7882) **5354**
• ➤ La Presse Medicale (FRA ISSN 0755-4982) **5699**
La Presse Medicale (Italian Edition) (ITA ISSN 0393-0653) **5699**
• Presse - Papiers (ITA ISSN 1126-9197) **5163**
Presse-Portraets (DEU ISSN 0176-5248) **633**
La Presse Quebecoise (CAN ISSN 1719-8747) **4582**
Presse Report (DEU ISSN 0341-8073) **7570**
Presse Suisse. Journaux, Feuilles Officielles, Feuilles d'annonces. Periodiques s'adressant au Grand Public *see* Schweizer Presse. Zeitungen, Amtsblaetter, Anzeiger, Publikumszeitschriften **7579**
Presse und Sprache (DEU ISSN 0935-8064) **4582**
Presseblomster (DNK ISSN 0108-9943) **5234**
Pressedienst P D S (Partei des Demokratischen Sozialismus) (DEU) **7173**
Pressehandbuch (Year) (AUT) **7570**
Pressens Tidning *see* Medievaerlden **4580**
Pressesprecher (DEU ISSN 1612-7668) **32**
Presshistorisk Aarsbok (SWE ISSN 0282-020X) **4582**
Pressing, Laverie, Libre-Service (FRA ISSN 1253-8736) **2244**
Pressje (POL) **2998**
• Pressocolata e Tecnologia/P & T - Pressacolata e Tecnologia (ITA ISSN 1126-1498) **6329**
Presspective (CAN) **7325**
• Presstime (USA ISSN 0194-3243) **4582**
Pressure (DEU ISSN 1615-794X) **5797**
Pressure (Bethesda) (USA ISSN 0889-0242) **5699**
Prestations Familiales. Statistiques *see* Soutien aux Enfants. Statistiques **8084**
Prestige (CAN) **3816**
† Prestige (ITA ISSN 1122-4320) **8982**
▼ Prestige (ZAF ISSN 1996-708X) **8280**
Prestige (Piedmond) (CAN) **8194**
Prestige Audio Video *see* Audio Video Prestige **8152**
Prestige Corporate Interiors (GBR ISSN 1354-0181) **4549**
Prestige High Street Interiors (GBR) **4549**
Prestige Hong Kong (HKG) **5080**
Prestige Hotel and Restaurant Interiors (GBR ISSN 1354-4233) **4549**
Prestige Indonesia (IDN) **5080**
Prestige Magazine (USA ISSN 1547-1306) **8599**
Prestige Malaysia (MYS) **5080**
Prestige New York *see* Prestige Singapore **5080**
Prestige Singapore (SGP) **5080**
Prestige Thailand (THA) **5080**
• Preston Pipe & Tube Report (USA ISSN 1085-4274) **6789**
Preston Scoop (USA) **3779**
Prestuplenia i Osudeni Litsa (BGR) **8395**
Prestuplenie i Nakazanie (RUS ISSN 0869-6462) **7173**
• Presupuesto y Gasto Publico (ESP ISSN 0210-5977) **1940**
Pretentaine (FRA ISSN 1259-2242) **8126**
Pretextos (PER ISSN 1021-6480) **7173**
Pretium Journal of Economics, Business and Finance *see* Pretium Revista de Economia, Negocios y Finanzas **1161**
▼ • Pretium Revista de Economia, Negocios y Finanzas/Pretium Journal of Economics, Business and Finance (USA ISSN 1948-478X) **1161**
Pretoria News (ZAF ISSN 1016-3654) **3949**
Pretoria News Weekend *see* Pretoria News **3949**
▼ Pretoria Student Law Review (ZAF ISSN 1998-0280) **4760**
Pretoria Witwatersrand Vaal Provinsiale Koerant *see* P W V. Provinsiale Koerant **7459**
Pretoriana (ZAF) **4177**
▼ Pretorien (FRA ISSN 1955-8198) **4254**
Pretosia Cassellana (DEU ISSN 0936-8205) **4254**
Pretre et Pasteur (CAN ISSN 0383-8307) **7813**
Pretres Diocesains (FRA ISSN 0032-7956) **7813**
Pretrial Motions in Criminal Prosecutions (USA) **4896**
The Pretrial Reporter (USA ISSN 0193-4015) **2666**
Prets et Bourses *see* Loans and Bursaries **1366**
Prettig Weekend (NLD) **3915**
▼ • Pretty Boy Magazine (USA ISSN 1945-970X) **5080**
Pretty Pony Club (GBR ISSN 1460-0854) **2208**
Pretty Style (JPN) **2260**
Preussenland (DEU ISSN 0032-7972) **4254**
Preussische Allgemeine Zeitung (DEU) **3855**
Preussischer Kulturbesitz. Staatsbibliothek zu Berlin. Beitraege (DEU ISSN 0948-3853) **5040**
• Prevailing Winds (USA ISSN 1086-2692) **3985**
Prevalence (FRA ISSN 1627-3346) **5699**
• Prevalence (USA ISSN 1933-3811) **1786**
Prevencion (ESP ISSN 0034-8732) **7536**
Prevencion del Tabaquismo (ESP ISSN 1576-1959) **6217**
Prevenir *see* Guia Prevenir Salud **6987**
Prevenir es Salud (ESP ISSN 1133-3782) **6995**
Prevenir les Risques du Metier (FRA ISSN 0982-443X) **6684**
Prevent Blindness America. Annual Report (USA) **7536**
Prevent Blindness News (USA) **7536**

Title

10762 PROBLEMAS DEL DESARROLLO ULRICH'S PERIODICALS

• ➤ Problemas del Desarrollo (MEX ISSN 0301-7036) **1603**
Problemas y Soluciones (ARG) **4600**
Problemata (DEU) **6945**
Problemata Iberoamericana (DEU) **4470**
Problemata Literaria (DEU) **5354**
➤ Probleme de Informare si Documentare (ROM ISSN 0032-924X) **5040**
Probleme de Lingvistica Generala (ROM ISSN 0552-1645) **5163**
Probleme de Logica (ROM ISSN 1454-2366) **6945**
➤ Probleme de Pedagogie Contemporana (ROM ISSN 1220-8825) **2900**
➤ Probleme der Aegyptologie (NLD ISSN 0169-9601) **559**
Probleme der Dichtung (DEU ISSN 0555-2257) **5354**
Probleme der Ernaehrungs- und Lebensmittelwissenschaft (AUT ISSN 0301-7656) **6668**
Probleme der Kuestenforschung im Suedlichen Nordseegebiet (DEU ISSN 0343-7965) **7899**
➤ Probleme der Semiotik (DEU ISSN 0933-4483) **6945**
Probleme Ekonomike (ALB) **1161**
† Problemes Actuels de Biochimie Appliquee (FRA ISSN 0555-2354) **8982**
Problemes d'Amerique Latine (FRA ISSN 0765-1333) **4309**
Problemes des Genres Litteraires *see* Zagadnienia Rodzajow Literackich **5404**
➤ Problemes d'Histoire des Religions (BEL ISSN 0778-6735) **7813**
Problemes Economiques (FRA ISSN 0032-9304) **1161**
Problemes Philosophiques d'Aujourd'hui *see* Philosophical Problems Today **6941**
• Problemes Politiques et Sociaux (FRA ISSN 0015-9743) **7260**
Problemes Sociaux Zairois (COD ISSN 0379-3729) **8126**
† Problemi (ITA ISSN 0032-9339) **8982**
† I Problemi della Pedagogia (ITA ISSN 0032-9347) **8982**
• Problemi dell'Informazione (ITA ISSN 0390-5195) **8126**
† Problemi di Civilta (ITA) **8982**
Problemi di Critica Goldoniana (ITA ISSN 1127-2570) **5354**
Problemi di Gestione (ITA ISSN 0032-9363) **1786**
Problemi e Ricerche di Storia Antica (ITA ISSN 0079-5682) **2239**
Problemi na Bulgarskiya Folklor (BGR) **3621**
Problemi na Geografijata/Problems of Geography (BGR ISSN 0204-7209) **4025**
Problemi na Izkustvoto/Problems of Art (BGR ISSN 0032-9371) **513**
Problemi na Khigienata (BGR ISSN 0323-9179) **5700**
Problemi na Tekhnicheskata Kibernetika i Robotika/Problems of Engineering Cybernetics and Robotics (BGR ISSN 0204-9848) **2528**
The Problemist (GBR ISSN 0032-9398) **8194**
• Problemos (LTU ISSN 1392-1126) **6945**
Problemove Dite a Hra (CZE ISSN 1801-8351) **3045**
• ➤ Problems & Perspectives in Management (UKR ISSN 1727-7051) **1786**
➤ Problems in Contemporary Philosophy (USA ISSN 0898-0136) **6945**
† • ➤ Problems in General Surgery (USA ISSN 0739-8328) **8982**
Problems in the Teaching of History *see* Lishi Jiaoxue Wenti **4151**
Problems of Aging and Longevity *see* Problemy Stareniya i Dolgoletiya **4053**
Problems of Art *see* Problemi na Izkustvoto **513**
➤ Problems of Atomic Science and Technology. Series: Plasma Physics (UKR ISSN 1682-9344) **7071**
Problems of Biological, Medical and Pharmacological *see* Voprosy Biologicheskoi, Meditsinskoi, i Farmatsevticheskoi Khimii **711**
Problems of Building Growth *see* Problemy Rozwoju Budownictwa **1030**
Problems of Capitalism and Socialism (GBR ISSN 1365-7887) **7173**
Problems of Cryobiology *see* Problemy Kriobiologii **754**
Problems of Diffraction and Spreading of Waves *see* Problemy Difraktsii i Rasprostraneniya Voln **7089**
• ➤ Problems of Economic Transition (USA ISSN 1061-1991) **1161**
▼ • ➤ Problems of Education in the 21st Century (LTU ISSN 1822-7864) **2900**
Problems of Education in the Twenty-First Century *see* Problems of Education in the 21st Century **2900**
Problems of Endocrinology *see* Problemy Endokrinologii **5899**
Problems of Engineering Cybernetics and Robotics *see* Problemi na Tekhnicheskata Kibernetika i Robotika **2528**
Problems of Forestry Economics *see* Linye Jingji Wenti **3696**
Problems of Geography *see* Problemi na Geografijata **4025**
Problems of Health Resorts, Physiotherapy and Exercise Therapy *see* Voprosy Kurortologii, Fizioterapii i Lechebnoi Fizicheskoi Kul'tury **6117**
Problems of Infectious and Parasitic Diseases (BGR ISSN 0204-9155) **5825**
• ➤ Problems of Information Transmission (RUS ISSN 0032-9460) **2534**
Problems of Large Metropolitan Areas *see* Problemy Bol'shikh Gorodov **3461**
Problems of Medical Chemistry *see* Biomeditsinskaya Khimiya **727**
Problems of National Liberation (IND) **7173**
Problems of Nonlinear Analysis in Engineering Systems *see* Problemy Nelineinogo Analiza v Inzhenernykh Sistemakh **7900**
Problems of Nuclear Science and Engineering. Series: Physics of Radiation Damage and Radiation Materials Science *see* Voprosy Atomnoi Nauki i Tekhniki. Seriya: Fizika Radiatsionnykh Povrezhdenii i Radiatsionnoye Materialovedeniye **7073**
Problems of Nutrition *see* Voprosy Pitaniya **6671**
• ➤ Problems of Post-Communism (USA ISSN 1075-8216) **7173**
Problems of Programming *see* Problemy Programmirovaniya **2509**
Problems of Social Hygiene, Health Service and History of Medicine *see* Problemy Sotsialnoi Gigieny, Zdravookhraneniya, i Istorii Meditsiny **7536**
Problems of Tourism (POL ISSN 1230-1035) **8748**
Problems of Tuberculosis *see* Problemy Tuberkuleza i Boleznei Legkikh **6217**
Problems of Virology *see* Voprosy Virusologii **898**
Problems, Resources, and Issues in Mathematics Undergraduate Studies *see* P R I M U S **5524**
Problemy (POL ISSN 0032-9487) **7899**
➤ Problemy Alkoholizmu (POL ISSN 0032-9495) **2698**
Problemy Arktiki i Antarktiki (RUS ISSN 0555-2648) **6393**
Problemy Avyatsionnoi i Kosmicheskoi Tekhniki (RUS) **68**
Problemy Bol'shikh Gorodov/Problems of Large Metropolitan Areas (RUS ISSN 0233-5816) **3461**
• Problemy Dal'nego Vostoka (RUS ISSN 0131-2812) **4255**
Problemy Difraktsii i Rasprostraneniya Voln/Problems of Diffraction and Spreading of Waves (RUS ISSN 0202-2354) **7089**
Problemy Ekologii (POL ISSN 1427-3381) **698**
Problemy Eksploatacji (POL ISSN 1232-9312) **3393**
Problemy Endokrinologii/Problems of Endocrinology (RUS ISSN 0375-9660) **5899**
• Problemy H I V i A I D S (POL ISSN 1234-9496) **5825**
Problemy i Perspektyvy Upravlinnya v Ekonomitsi (UKR) **1786**
Problemy Informatiki i Energetiki (UZB) **8435**
Problemy Jakosci (POL ISSN 0137-8651) **6405**
• ➤ Problemy Kharchuvannya (UKR) **6668**
Problemy Kosmicheskoi Biologii (RUS ISSN 0555-2788) **698**
Problemy Kriobiologii/Problems of Cryobiology (UKR ISSN 1026-1230) **754**
Problemy Mashinostroeniya i Avtomatizatsii (RUS ISSN 0234-6206) **2463**
Problemy Mashinostroeniya i Nadezhnosti Mashin (RUS ISSN 0235-7119) **5458**
Problemy Medycyny Nuklearnej (POL ISSN 0860-3405) **6205**
Problemy Mekhaniki (UZB) **8435**
Problemy Nelineinogo Analiza v Inzhenernykh Sistemakh (RUS ISSN 1727-687X) **7900**
Problemy Opiekunczo-Wychowawcze (POL ISSN 0552-2188) **2900**
Problemy Osvoeniya Pustyn' (TKM ISSN 0032-9428) **148**
• ➤ Problemy Oswiaty i Wychowania (POL ISSN 1428-5991) **2900**
Problemy Peredachi Informatsii (RUS ISSN 0555-2923) **2534**
• ➤ Problemy Prochnosti (UKR ISSN 0556-171X) **3356**
Problemy Prognozirovaniya (RUS) **1512**
Problemy Programmirovaniya/Problems of Programming (UKR ISSN 1727-4907) **2509**
• Problemy Reproduktsii (RUS ISSN 1025-7217) **698**
Problemy Rodziny (POL ISSN 0552-2234) **8126**
Problemy Rozwoju Budownictwa/Problems of Building Growth (POL ISSN 0555-2966) **1030**
Problemy Severa (RUS ISSN 0555-2982) **633**
Problemy Sotsialnoi Gigieny, Zdravookhraneniya, i Istorii Meditsiny/Problems of Social Hygiene, Health Service and History of Medicine (RUS ISSN 0869-866X) **7536**
Problemy Spetsial'noi Elektrometallurgii (UKR ISSN 0131-1611) **6329**
Problemy Stareniya i Dolgoletiya/Problems of Aging and Longevity (UKR ISSN 0869-1703) **4053**
• Problemy Stomatoogii (KAZ) **5861**
Problemy Teorii i Praktiki Upravleniya (RUS ISSN 0257-9928) **1786**
➤ Problemy Terapii Monitorowanej (POL ISSN 0867-6348) **6115**
Problemy Transportu *see* Transport Problems **8515**
Problemy Tuberkuleza *see* Problemy Tuberkuleza i Boleznei Legkikh **6217**
Problemy Tuberkuleza i Boleznei Legkikh/Problems of Tuberculosis (RUS ISSN 1728-2993) **6217**
Problemy Turystyki (POL ISSN 0138-0478) **8748**
Problemy Upravleniya (RUS) **1786**
Problemy Upravleniya i Informatiki (UKR ISSN 1028-0979) **2463**
• ➤ Probus (DEU ISSN 0921-4771) **5163**
• ➤ ProCare (AUT ISSN 0949-7323) **5978**
ProCare Pulse (NZL ISSN 1176-9041) **7536**
Procedes de Recolte des Bois Utilises au Quebec dans les Forets du Domaine de l'Etat. Rapport Annuel (CAN ISSN 1499-1195) **3715**
Procedes de Recolte Utilises au Quebec dans les Forets du Domaine de l'Etat. Rapport Annuel *see* Procedes de Recolte des Bois Utilises au Quebec dans les Forets du Domaine de l'Etat. Rapport Annuel **3715**
▼ • ➤ Procedia Chemistry (NLD ISSN 1876-6196) **2077**
▼ • ➤ Procedia - Social and Behavioral Sciences (NLD ISSN 1877-0428) **7993**
Procedura Penale. Commenti (ITA ISSN 1970-2302) **4896**
Procedura Penale. Studi (ITA ISSN 1970-2299) **4896**
Procedural Aspects of International Law Monograph Series (USA ISSN 1873-6580) **4938**
Proceeding of Clinical Medicine *see* Linchuang Yiyao Shijian **5662**
Proceeding of I A I Congress (IDN) **1299**
Proceeding of I A I Convention (IDN) **1299**
Proceedings. Annual Symposium. Incremental Motion Control Systems and Devices *see* Symposium on Incremental Motion Control Systems and Devices. Proceedings **5460**
Proceedings - Beltwide Cotton Conferences *see* Beltwide Cotton Conferences. Proceedings **221**
Proceedings - Computer Security, Dependability and Assurance *see* Computer Security, Dependability and Assurance **2512**
Proceedings - Conference on Ground Water *see* Conference on Ground Water. Proceedings **2793**
Proceedings - Electrochemical Society *see* Electrochemical Society. Proceedings **2113**
Proceedings for the I F C Symposium *see* Kiso Kagaku Kenkyujo Koenkai Koenshu **2070**
Proceedings - IEEE Workshop on Computer Vision Beyond the Visible Spectrum *see* I E E E Workshop on Computer Vision Beyond the Visible Spectrum **2449**
• Proceedings in Applied Mathematics and Mechanics (DEU ISSN 1617-7061) **5526**
• Proceedings in Marine Science (NLD ISSN 1568-2692) **2816**
Proceedings - International Database Engineering and Applications Symposium *see* International Database Engineering and Applications Symposium **2521**
Proceedings Magazine *see* U S Naval Institute. Proceedings **6450**
Proceedings of Applied Radiation Chemistry Symposium *see* Oyo Hoshasen Kagaku Shinpojumu Koen Yoshishu **2139**
Proceedings of CASCON *see* C A S C O N Proceedings **2408**
Proceedings of Coastal Engineering, JSCE *see* Kaigan Kogaku Ronbunshu **3277**
Proceedings of Hydraulics Engineering *see* Suikogaku Ronbunshu **3364**
Proceedings of Infrastructure Planning *see* Doboku Keikakugaku Kenkyu Koenshu **3265**
▼ • Proceedings of Lex Informatica: Cyberlaw and I C T Conference (Information and Communications Technologies) (USA ISSN 1949-1344) **4896**
Proceedings of Meetings on Acoustics *see* Meetings on Acoustics. Proceedings **7088**
Proceedings of N E L S *see* North East Linguistic Society. Proceedings **5156**
Proceedings of Noise-Con *see* Noise-Con Proceedings **3489**
Proceedings of Panel Discussions for the Analysis of the Korean Economy *see* Korea Institute of Finance. Panel Discussions for the Analysis of the Korean Economy. Proceedings **1496**
➤ Proceedings of Parasitology (PAK ISSN 1018-2500) **895**
Proceedings of S S O R *see* S S O R Yokoshu **2444**
Proceedings of Science *see* P o S - Proceedings of Science **7896**
Proceedings of Symposium on Heteroatom Chemistry/Hetero Genshi Kagaku Toronkai Koen Yoshishu (JPN) **2117**
Proceedings of Symposium on Radiation Chemistry *see* Hoshasen Kagaku Toronkai Koen Yoshishu **2135**
Proceedings of Symposium on Solvent Extraction *see* Symposium on Solvent Extraction. Proceedings **2131**
Proceedings of Symposium on Water Resources and Environment *see* Mizu Shigen Kankyo Gakkai Kenkyu Taikai Koen Gaiyoshu **8829**
Proceedings of the A A J R *see* American Academy for Jewish Research. Proceedings of the A A J R **7717**
Proceedings of the A C S A Annual Meeting *see* Association of Collegiate Schools of Architecture. Proceedings of the Annual Meeting **434**
Proceedings of the American Catholic Philosophical Association *see* American Catholic Philosophical Association. Proceedings **6903**
Proceedings of the Annual Aquatic Toxicity Workshop *see* Aquatic Toxicity Workshop. Proceedings of the Annual **3483**
Proceedings of the Annual Conference on Magnetism and Magnetic Materials *see* Conference on Magnetism and Magnetic Materials. Proceedings **7009**
Proceedings of the Annual Institute on Labor Law Developments *see* Institute on Labor Law Developments. Annual Proceedings **8965**
Proceedings of the Annual International Logistics Symposium *see* S O L E - International Society of Logistics. Proceedings **8437**
Proceedings of the Annual Meeting - National Association of Schools of Music *see* National Association of Schools of Music. Proceedings of the Annual Meeting **6598**
Proceedings of the Annual Meeting of A A C E International *see* A A C E International Transactions **3179**
Proceedings of the Annual Meeting of the Western Society for French History *see* Western Society for French History. Proceedings of the Annual Meeting **8998**
Proceedings of the Annual Southeastern Symposium on System Theory *see* Southeastern Symposium on System Theory. Proceedings **2525**
Proceedings of the Annual Tulane Tax Institute *see* Tulane Tax Institute **1953**
Proceedings of the Antitrust Law Section Annual Meeting *see* New York State Bar Association. Antitrust Law Section Symposium **4745**
Proceedings of the British Academy *see* British Academy. Proceedings **384**
Proceedings of the... C C O P Annual Session (Part I) *see* Coordinating Committee for Geoscience Programmes in East and Southeast Asia. Annual Session. Proceedings. Part I **2704**
Proceedings of the Conference on Hazardous Waste Research *see* Conference on Hazardous Waste Research. Proceedings **3495**
Proceedings of the Court of Justice and the Court of First Instance of the European Communities *see* European Communities. Court of Justice and Court of First Instance. Proceedings **4950**
Proceedings of the Danish Institute at Athens *see* The Danish Institute at Athens. Proceedings **389**
Proceedings of the Eucarpia Congress *see* European Association for Research on Plant Breeding. Report of the Congress **3729**
• Proceedings of the Friesian School (USA) **6945**
Proceedings of the I E E E *see* Institute of Electrical and Electronics Engineers. Proceedings **3319**
Proceedings of the Illinois Medieval Association *see* Essays in Medieval Studies **4218**
Proceedings of the Institute of Marine Engineering, Science and Technology *see* Journal of Marine Design and Operations **8648**
Proceedings of the Institute of Marine Engineering, Science and Technology *see* Journal of Operational Oceanography **2809**
Proceedings of the International Conference on Business & Public Policy *see* Academy of Business & Public Policy. Proceedings of the International Conference **1056**
Proceedings of the International Conference on Lasers (Year) *see* International Conference on Lasers. Proceedings (Year) **7077**
Proceedings of the International Conference on Multichip Modules *see* International Conference on Multichip Modules. Proceedings **3104**
Proceedings of the International Cryogenic Engineering Conference *see* Cryogenics **7053**
• Proceedings of the Legislative Assembly for the Australian Capital Territory. Digest (AUS ISSN 1321-6163) **7460**
Proceedings of the National Academy of Sciences *see* National Academy of Sciences. Proceedings **7886**
Proceedings of the National Academy of Sciences of the United States of America *see* National Academy of Sciences. Proceedings **7886**
Proceedings of the Natural Philosophy Alliance *see* Natural Philosophy Alliance. Proceedings **6935**
Proceedings of the Nutrition Society *see* Nutrition Society. Proceedings **6667**
Proceedings of the Osaka Symposium on Flow Measuring Techniques *see* Nagare no Keisoku Oosaka Shinpojumu Koen Yoshishu **6404**
Proceedings of the Rabbinical Assembly *see* Rabbinical Assembly. Proceedings **8984**
Proceedings of the Royal Microscopical Society *see* Infocus Magazine **899**
Proceedings of the Sheep Veterinary Society *see* Sheep Veterinary Society. Proceedings **8807**
Proceedings of the South Carolina Historical Association *see* South Carolina Historical Association. Proceedings **4313**
Proceedings of the Symposium on Amylase *see* Amiraze Shinpojumu **751**
Proceedings of the Symposium on Photoelasticity *see* Nihon Kodansei Gakkai Kenkyu Happyo Koenkai Koen Ronbunshu **7081**
Proceedings of the Takeda Science Foundation Symposium on Bioscience *see* Takeda Science Foundation Symposium on Bioscience. Proceedings **707**
Proceedings of the Valencia International Meeting *see* Bayesian Statistics **8357**

Link to your serials resources and content with ulrichsweb.com

Title

10764 PROFESSIONAL & TRADE ASSOCIATIONS. DIRECTORY ULRICH'S PERIODICALS

Professional & Trade Associations. Directory (CAN ISSN 1914-105X) 2024
Professional & Trade Associations in the Toronto Region see Professional & Trade Associations. Directory 2024
Professional and Trade Organisations in India (IND ISSN 0079-5925) 2024
• Professional Animal Scientist (USA ISSN 1080-7446) 8805
Professional Apartment Management see Apartment Building Management Insider 7582
Professional Appraisers Information Exchange (USA) 368
• Professional Association for Cactus Development. Journal (USA ISSN 1938-663X) 814
• Professional Association of Canadian Theatres. Annual Report (CAN ISSN 1719-6973) 8476
Professional Association of Diving Instructors Member News see P A D I Member News 8192
Professional Aviation Maintenance Association News see P A M A News 67
• Professional Boatbuilder (USA ISSN 1043-2035) 8280
Professional Bowlers Association of America Tour Official Program (Year) see P B A Tour Official Program (Year) 8192
Professional Broking (GBR ISSN 1355-0519) 4519
Professional Builder (GBR) 1051
• Professional Builder (USA ISSN 1072-0561) 1030
† • Professional Builder's Home Plan Database CD-ROM (USA) 8982
Professional Builders Merchant (GBR ISSN 0967-2605) 1030
Professional Bull Rider see Pro Bull Rider 8194
Professional Business & Technical Management (GBR ISSN 1470-7799) 1787
• Professional Candy Buyer (USA ISSN 1090-1914) 3661
• Professional Car Care e-News (USA) 8599
• Professional Car Washing & Detailing (USA ISSN 1087-3260) 8599
Professional Careers Sourcebook (USA ISSN 1045-9863) 6702
• Professional Case Management (USA ISSN 1932-8087) 5978
Professional Caterer and Hotelkeeper (ZAF) 4396
• Professional Collector (USA) 1161
The Professional Databases Directory see Repertoire des Banques de Donnees Professionnelles 8985
Professional Deck Builder (USA ISSN 1545-181X) 1051
Professional Degree Programs in the Visual and Performing Arts see Peterson's Professional Degree Programs in the Visual and Performing Arts 511
• ➤ Professional Development (USA ISSN 1097-4911) 8063
• ➤ Professional Development in Education (GBR ISSN 1941-5257) 3077
Professional Development Series (AUS ISSN 1325-7706) 5979
• Professional Development Today (GBR ISSN 1460-8340) 3030
• Professional Distributor (USA ISSN 1553-6211) 3393
• Professional Door Dealer (USA) 1030
Professional Edge (CAN ISSN 0841-6427) 3216
Professional Editors' Group see PEGboard 7570
Professional Educator (AUS ISSN 1447-3607) 2900
• ➤ The Professional Educator (USA ISSN 0196-786X) 2900
Professional Electrician and Installer (GBR ISSN 1757-5729) 3328
Professional Engineer (IND ISSN 0033-0078) 3216
Professional Engineer see P E 3214
The Professional Engineer (Raleigh) (USA) 3216
Professional Engineer, Geologist, Geophysicist see The P E G G 3214
• Professional Engineering (GBR ISSN 0953-6639) 3393
† Professional Engineering Publishing. Engineering Research Series (GBR ISSN 1468-3938) 8982
Professional Ethics see Business & Professional Ethics Journal 6909
• Professional Ethics Report (USA ISSN 1045-8808) 6945
† Professional Farm Management Guidebook (AUS ISSN 0312-889X) 8982
Professional Fisherman see Ausmarine 3586
Professional Forester (CAN) 3700
Professional Fraternity Association Today see P F A Today 2268
• Professional Freelance Writers Directory (USA) 4582
Professional Fundraising (GBR ISSN 0961-5679) 8063
• Professional Gas Cooking (USA) 3661
• ➤ The Professional Geographer (USA ISSN 0033-0124) 4025
Professional Geologist (USA ISSN 0279-0521) 2762
Professional Golf Association Tour Partners see P G A Tour Partners 8242
Professional Golfers Association of America Magazine see P G A Magazine 8241
Professional Golfers' Association Profile see P G A Profile 8241
Professional Hairdresser (GBR ISSN 1757-5761) 590
Professional Heating and Plumbing Installer (GBR ISSN 1356-0840) 4125
Professional Institute of the Public Service of Canada. Communications (CAN ISSN 0318-0646) 7460
Professional Insurance Agent Connection see P I A Connection 4518
Professional Insurance Agents of Connecticut (USA ISSN 0883-1092) 4519
Professional Insurance Agents of New Jersey (USA ISSN 0883-1084) 4519
Professional Insurance Agents of New York (USA ISSN 0883-8240) 4519
• Professional Investor (GBR ISSN 0958-2541) 1645
Professional Investor Careers see Professional Investor 1645
• ➤ Professional Issues in Criminal Justice (USA ISSN 1932-1368) 4896
Professional Jeweler Magazine (USA ISSN 1097-5314) 4569
• The Professional Journal (USA) 2493
Professional Landscaper (GBR) 3748
• Professional Lawyer (USA ISSN 1042-5675) 4762
Professional Lectures (GBR ISSN 1476-6833) 2900
• Professional Liability Insurance (USA) 4519
Professional Liability Litigation Alert see Professional Liability Litigation @lert 4762
• Professional Liability Litigation @lert (USA ISSN 1938-9035) 4762
Professional Liability Reporter (USA ISSN 0145-3505) 4762
Professional Licensing Report (USA ISSN 1043-2051) 4762
Professional Lighting (CAN ISSN 1480-1930) 2336
Professional Lighting Design (DEU) 4562
• Professional Management Review (ZAF) 1838
• The Professional Manager (GBR ISSN 0969-6695) 1787
• Professional Mariner (USA ISSN 1066-2774) 8657
Professional Marketing (AUS ISSN 1327-1903) 1838
Professional Marketing (GBR ISSN 0969-1847) 1838
Professional Medical Assistant see C M A Today 5954
• The Professional Medical Journal (PAK ISSN 1024-8919) 5700
Professional Motor Factor (GBR ISSN 1757-5745) 8599
Professional Motor Mechanic (GBR ISSN 1757-5753) 8599
Professional Motorsport World (GBR) 8194
Professional Nanny & Childcare see Nursery World 2163
Professional Negligence and Liability Reports (GBR ISSN 1363-4577) 4762
• Professional Negligence Law Reporter (USA ISSN 1051-3744) 4762
• Professional Network (AUS) 3216
• Professional Newsbytes (USA) 1161
Professional Nurse see Nursing Times 5975
Professional Office Building Management (USA ISSN 1531-5975) 7604
Professional Officer (GBR) 1787
The Professional Painter & Decorator (GBR ISSN 0956-9235) 4549
Professional Papermaking (DEU ISSN 1612-0485) 6737
• Professional Pensions (GBR ISSN 1743-3320) 1645
• Professional Pest Controller (GBR) 7536
Professional Pest Manager (AUS) 249
Professional Photographer (GBR ISSN 1472-5339) 6976
• Professional Photographer (USA ISSN 1528-5286) 6975
Professional Photographer and Digital Pro see Professional Photographer 6976
Professional Photography see ProPhoto 6976
Professional Photography see Tsillum Miktso'i 8994
Professional Photography in Australasia see ProPhoto 6976
Professional Pilot Magazine (USA ISSN 0191-6238) 8550
Professional Practice Series (USA) 7391
† Professional Printer (GBR ISSN 0308-4205) 8982
Professional Production (DEU ISSN 0932-0393) 6510
• ➤ Professional Psychology: Research and Practice (USA ISSN 0735-7028) 7392
• Professional Publishing Report (USA ISSN 1095-2187) 7570
Professional Purchasing (USA ISSN 1070-0455) 1838
Professional Quilter (USA ISSN 0891-5237) 1965
Professional Reactor Operator Society. Communicator see The Communicator (Mishicot) 3166
Professional Relocation & Real Estate Directory (USA) 7604
• Professional Remodeler (USA ISSN 1521-9135) 1030
Professional Responsibility see B A R - B R I Bar Review. Professional Responsibility 4624
Professional Responsibility Standards, Rules and Statutes (USA ISSN 1085-7575) 4762
• Professional Retail Store Maintenance (USA ISSN 1099-9345) 1965
Professional Rodeo Cowboy Association Media Guide see P R C A Media Guide 8295
Professional Rodeo U S A see P R C A Media Guide 8295
Professional Roofing (USA ISSN 0896-5552) 1030
• ➤ Professional Safety (USA ISSN 0099-0027) 6684
† Professional, Sales & Technical Remuneration, Canada (USA ISSN 1042-4482) 8982
Professional Scholarly Publishing Bulletin see P S P Bulletin 7569
• ➤ Professional School Counseling (USA ISSN 1096-2409) 2900
Professional Scientist Remuneration Survey Report see A P E S M A / F A S T S Professional Scientist Remuneration Survey Report 6691
• Professional Security Magazine (GBR ISSN 1745-0950) 2666
• Professional Services Bulletin (USA) 1030
• Professional Services Management Journal (USA) 1787
Professional Services Review. Annual Report (AUS ISSN 1324-9371) 7536
• Professional Social Work (GBR ISSN 1352-3112) 8063
• Professional Sound (CAN ISSN 1186-1797) 6607
• Professional Sound (USA ISSN 1044-4793) 8154
Professional Speaker see Speaker (Tempe) 5176
Professional Sports Authenticator Population Report and Price Guide see P S A Population Report and Price Guide 4343
Professional Sports Authenticator Vintage Population Report see P S A Vintage Population Report 4343
Professional Sports Wives (USA) 8881
Professional Spraying (USA) 6720
Professional Staff Congress Clarion see P S C Clarion 2997
➤ Professional Studies Review (USA ISSN 1548-0704) 6702
Professional, Supervisory & Sales Compensation Survey (Year) (CAN) 6707
• Professional Surveyor (USA ISSN 0278-1425) 4025
Professional System (DEU ISSN 1437-2592) 1420
Professional Timing Service (USA) 1645
• Professional Tool and Equipment News (USA ISSN 1081-4485) 8599
Professional Tool & Equipment News see Professional Tool and Equipment News 8599
Professional Training Series (CHE ISSN 1020-1688) 7214
Professional Woman's Magazine (USA) 8881
• Professional Women and Minorities (USA ISSN 0190-1796) 6702
Professional Women Photographers Newsletter see P W P Newsletter 6972
Professional Wrestling Shu-kan (JPN) 8194
• Professionalism in Practice: The P A T Journal (Professional Association of Teachers) (GBR ISSN 1468-6759) 2900
Professionalita (ITA ISSN 0392-2790) 2998
• ➤ Professionalization of Exercise Physiology (USA ISSN 1099-5862) 927
Professionally Speaking (CAN ISSN 1206-8799) 2900
Professional's Handbook of Complementary & Alternative Medicines (USA ISSN 1522-0877) 314
Professione Allevatore (ITA ISSN 1825-3199) 297
Professione Avicunicoltore (ITA ISSN 1825-3245) 297
Professione Camionista (ITA ISSN 1126-2648) 8674
Professione Odontoiatria see Doctor Os 5842
• La Professione Sociale (ITA ISSN 1122-6307) 8063
Professione Suinicoltore (ITA ISSN 1593-571X) 297
• Professione Veterinaria (ITA ISSN 1121-1547) 8805
Professioneel Cateren (NLD ISSN 1871-1243) 4396
Professioneel Schoonmaken (NLD ISSN 1569-4968) 6684
Professionele Fotografie see P - F 6972
Professionelle Verpflegung Report see P V - Report 4395
Professioni Infermieristiche (ITA ISSN 0033-0205) 5979
Professions and Projects Register (ZAF) 1030
Professions Education Researcher Quarterly (USA ISSN 1052-7060) 2998
Professiya (RUS) 6702
Professor (PRT ISSN 0870-841X) 2900
The Professor in the Classroom (USA ISSN 1947-3664) 2998
• Professor Trim's Waistline (AUS) 6995
Professor Zamorra (DEU) 5446
Proffs (SWE ISSN 1103-3614) 8508
Proffsfoto see Cap & Design Proffsfoto 2483
Profi (DEU ISSN 0937-1583) 148
Profi (RUS) 6441
Profi Kosmetik (DEU ISSN 0944-4025) 596
Profi Raetsel see Freizeit Revue Profi Raetsel 8173
Profiel (NLD ISSN 1387-6112) 2945
Profiel (The Hague) (NLD ISSN 1875-404X) 1873
Profifoto (DEU ISSN 0721-9725) 6976
Profiinfo (DEU ISSN 1436-2066) 3145
Profil (AUT ISSN 1022-2111) 3798
Profil (CHE ISSN 1661-2248) 2260
• ➤ Profil (CZE ISSN 1212-9097) 6945
Profil' (RUS) 1162
Profil (Bad Harzburg) (DEU) 2297
Profil (Duesseldorf) (DEU ISSN 0945-7666) 2900
Profil (Stuttgart) (DEU ISSN 0941-0414) 2715
Profil de Localisation de l'Effectif, des Dirigeants, des Bureaux Centraux des Ministeres et des Sieges Sociaux des Organismes Gouvernementaux (CAN ISSN 1912-3515) 7460
Profil Extra (AUT) 3798
Profil Femme see Profil 2260
• Profilaktika Zabolevanii i Ukreplenie Zdorov'a/Diseases Prevention and Health Promotion (RUS) 6995
Profile (AUT) 5354
Profile (BHR) 3799
• ➤ Profile (COL ISSN 1657-0790) 3078
Profile see Audi Magazine 8556
• Profile (NZL ISSN 1176-3892) 2998
Profile see L A J C C Scene 1406
Profile (ZAF) 7461
ProFile (Atlanta) (USA ISSN 0190-8766) 454
The Profile (Conway) (USA) 2297
Profile (Leeds) (GBR) 5081
Profile (London) (GBR) 32
Profile (Los Angeles) (USA ISSN 1048-2989) 1409
• ➤ Profile (Norfolk) (USA ISSN 0145-112X) 6442
Profile (Omaha) (USA ISSN 0162-5241) 1409
Profile (Skokie) (USA) 1902
• Profile (Washington, D C) (USA ISSN 1933-0901) 1787
Profile (Wheaton) (USA) 7671
Profile of Canadian Youth in the Labour Market (CAN ISSN 1497-7222) 1703
• Profile of Electoral Districts (Online Edition) (CAN) 7482
Profile of State Chartered Banking (USA ISSN 0734-6638) 1376
Profile of the Nation (Farmington Hills) see Information Plus Reference Series. Profile of the Nation 8964
Profile Ontario see Perspective Ontario 1837
➤ Profiles (NLD ISSN 0924-1930) 6945
Profiles (USA ISSN 1530-3497) 7327
Profile's (Years) African Stock Exchange Handbook (ZAF) 1645
Profile's (Year) Financial Markets Handbook (ZAF) 1646
• Profiles in Diversity Journal (USA ISSN 1537-2103) 7214
• Profiles in Seizure Management (USA) 6174
Profile's J S E Results & Earnings see Profile's Results & Earnings 1646
Profiles Magazine (USA) 4562
Profiles of American Colleges see Barron's Profiles of American Colleges 2954
Profiles of Business Success. Burlington - Oakville Edition (CAN ISSN 1911-3951) 7604
Profiles of Business Success. Hamilton - Niagara Edition (CAN ISSN 1718-7591) 7604
Profiles of Business Success. Ontario North Edition (CAN ISSN 1718-7605) 7604
Profiles of Business Success. Ottawa Edition (CAN ISSN 1718-7613) 7604
Profiles of Business Success. Southwestern Ontario Edition (CAN ISSN 1911-396X) 7604
Profiles of Business Success. Toronto East Edition (CAN ISSN 1718-7621) 7604
Profiles of Business Success. Toronto West, Toronto North Edition (CAN ISSN 1911-3978) 7604
Profiles of Business Success. Vancouver Edition (CAN ISSN 1718-763X) 7604
Profiles of Business Success. Vancouver West Edition (CAN ISSN 1911-4192) 7604
▼ Profiles of California (USA ISSN 1940-3844) 3121
▼ Profiles of Connecticut and Rhode Island (USA ISSN 1938-5684) 3121
• ➤ Profiles of Drug Substances, Excipients and Related Methodology (USA ISSN 1871-5125) 6876
Profiles of Earnings in Cyprus: by Education, Occupation, Experience, Age, Sex and Sector (CYP) 1259
• Profiles of Ethnic Communities in Canada (CAN ISSN 1719-7376) 3559
Profiles of Florida (USA ISSN 1941-1952) 3121
Profiles of Governmental Excellence (USA ISSN 1553-8311) 7461
Profiles of Illinois (USA ISSN 1935-5866) 3121
▼ Profiles of Indiana (USA ISSN 1939-6007) 3121
Profiles of Massachusetts (USA ISSN 1935-4916) 3121
Profiles of Michigan (USA ISSN 1933-8279) 3122
Profiles of New Jersey (USA ISSN 1934-516X) 3122
Profiles of New York State (USA ISSN 1941-2436) 3122
▼ Profiles of North Carolina and South Carolina (USA ISSN 1934-6689) 3122
Profiles of Ohio (USA ISSN 1933-8058) 3122
• Profiles of Pennsylvania (USA ISSN 1934-5151) 3122
Profiles of People of Interest to Young Readers see Biography Today Performing Artists Series 641
Profiles of Regulatory Agencies in the U S and Canada (USA) 7461
Profiles of Success. Maritimes Edition (CAN ISSN 1718-3863) 7604
Profiles of Texas (USA ISSN 1932-7226) 3122
• Profiles of U S Hospitals (USA ISSN 1082-4200) 4109
▼ Profiles of Virginia (USA ISSN 1941-241X) 3122
▼ Profiles of Wisconsin (USA ISSN 1936-752X) 3122
Profiles of Worldwide Government Leaders see Worldwide Government Directory 7477
• Profiles of Worldwide Government Leaders (USA ISSN 1080-7063) 7173
Profile's Offshore Investing (ZAF ISSN 1729-0333) 1646

▼ new title   † ceased   • electronic media   ➤ refereed

Title

10766 PROGRESS IN NUCLEIC ACID RESEARCH AND MOLECULAR BIOLOGY ULRICH'S PERIODICALS

Progress in Nucleic Acid Research and Molecular Biology see Progress in Molecular Biology and Translational Science **698**
➤ Progress in Numerical Simulation for Microelectronics (CHE) **8435**
Progress in Nutrition (ITA ISSN 1129-8723) **6668**
➤ Progress in Obesity Research (Year) (GBR ISSN 0962-7936) **5700**
Progress in Obstetrics and Gynaecology (GBR ISSN 0261-0140) **6002**
Progress in Obstetrics and Gynecology see Xiandai Fuchanke Jinzhan **5732**
● ➤ Progress in Oceanography (GBR ISSN 0079-6611) **2816**
Progress in Oncology (USA ISSN 1535-9980) **6032**
➤ Progress in Optics (NLD ISSN 0079-6638) **7084**
● ➤ Progress in Organic Coatings (NLD ISSN 0300-9440) **6720**
● ➤ Progress in Orthodontics (DNK ISSN 1399-7513) **5862**
Progress in Orthodontics (ITA ISSN 1723-7785) **5861**
● Progress in Orthodontics Online (DNK ISSN 1600-9975) **5862**
➤ Progress in Osteoporosis (GBR ISSN 1615-4959) **5700**
● ➤ Progress in Palliative Care (GBR ISSN 0969-9260) **6032**
● ➤ Progress in Paper Recycling (USA ISSN 1061-1452) **6737**
● ➤ Progress in Particle and Nuclear Physics (GBR ISSN 0146-6410) **7071**
Progress in Pathology (GBR ISSN 0968-896X) **5700**
● ➤ Progress in Pediatric Cardiology (IRL ISSN 1058-9813) **5798**
† Progress in Pesticide Biochemistry and Toxicology (GBR ISSN 0887-6142) **8983**
Progress in Pharmaceutical and Biomedical Analysis (GBR ISSN 1464-3456) **6876**
Progress in Pharmaceutical Sciences see Yaoxue Jinzhan **6886**
● ➤ Progress in Photovoltaics (GBR ISSN 1062-7995) **3145**
➤ Progress in Phycological Research (GBR ISSN 0167-8574) **814**
● ➤ Progress in Physical Geography (GBR ISSN 0309-1333) **4025**
● ➤ Progress in Physical Organic Chemistry (USA ISSN 0079-6662) **2139**
● ➤ Progress in Physics (USA ISSN 1555-5534) **7036**
Progress in Physiological Sciences see Shengli Kexue Jinzhan **928**
● ➤ Progress in Planning (GBR ISSN 0305-9006) **4424**
Progress in Plant Protection see Postepy w Ochronie Roslin **147**
● ➤ Progress in Polymer Science (GBR ISSN 0079-6700) **2130**
Progress in Poultry "Through Research" (USA ISSN 1057-3232) **297**
➤ Progress in Probability (CHE ISSN 1050-6977) **5526**
† Progress in Protein - Lipid Interactions (NLD ISSN 0168-9614) **8983**
Progress in Protozoology (USA) **895**
● ➤ Progress in Psychobiology and Physiological Psychology (USA ISSN 0363-0951) **7392**
Progress in Pure and Applied Discrete Mathematics (NLD ISSN 0929-9017) **5526**
● ➤ Progress in Quantum Electronics (GBR ISSN 0079-6727) **3111**
● Progress in Reaction Kinetics and Mechanism (GBR ISSN 1468-6783) **2139**
● ➤ Progress in Respiratory Research (CHE ISSN 1422-2140) **6217**
● ➤ Progress in Retinal and Eye Research (GBR ISSN 1350-9462) **6050**
Progress in Robotics and Intelligent Systems (USA) **2456**
● ➤ Progress in Rubber, Plastics and Recycling Technology (GBR ISSN 1477-7606) **3254**
Progress in Self Psychology see International Journal of Psychoanalytic Self Psychology **7365**
Progress in Soil Science see Turangxue Jinzhan **2717**
● ➤ Progress in Solid State Chemistry (GBR ISSN 0079-6786) **2140**
Progress in Structural Engineering and Materials see Structural Control and Health Monitoring **7041**
● ➤ Progress in Surface Science (GBR ISSN 0079-6816) **7036**
➤ Progress in Surgery (CHE ISSN 0079-6824) **6256**
➤ Progress in Textiles: Science & Technology (IND) **8456**
Progress in the Chemistry of Organic Natural Products see Fortschritte der Chemie Organischer Naturstoffe **2123**
Progress in the Psychology of Language (GBR ISSN 0268-7364) **7392**
Progress in Tourism, Recreation and Hospitality Management (GBR ISSN 0952-5424) **8749**
● ➤ Progress in Transplantation (USA ISSN 1526-9248) **6256**
Progress in Veterinary Medicine see Dongwu Yixue Jinzhan **8796**
➤ Progress in Water Resources (GBR ISSN 1461-6513) **3216**
Progress: International Exchange in Trade, Science and Technology see Jinzhan: Guoji Maoyi yu Keji Jiaoliu **1573**
Progress Notes (USA) **7392**
Progress of Anatomical Sciences see Jiepou Kexue Jinzhan **923**
The Progress of Canada's Children and Youth (CAN ISSN 1910-6211) **2166**
Progress of Digestive Endoscopy (JPN ISSN 1348-9844) **5930**
Progress of Education in Saudi Arabia (SAU) **2935**
Progress of Nuclear Safety Research see Genshiryoku Anzensei Kenkyu no Genjo **7066**
Progress of Physics see Fortschritte der Physik **7013**
● ➤ Progress of Theoretical Physics/Riron Butsurigaku no Shinpo (JPN ISSN 0033-068X) **7036**
➤ Progress of Theoretical Physics. Supplement (JPN ISSN 0375-9687) **7036**
Progress Report - Asian Vegetable Research and Development Center see A V R D C Report **78**
● Progress Report on Alzheimer's Disease (USA ISSN 1935-1860) **4053**
Progress Reports see Rehabilitation R & D Progress Reports **6443**
Progress Research & Development (CAN) **7900**
† ● Progressi in Reumatologia (ITA ISSN 1129-8758) **8983**
Progressio (ZAF ISSN 0256-8853) **3078**
Progressio (English Edition) (ITA ISSN 0394-5936) **7672**
Progressio (French Edition) (ITA ISSN 0394-591X) **7672**
Progressio (Spanish Edition) (ITA ISSN 0394-5928) **7672**
Progression (CAN) **2269**
Progression (USA ISSN 1087-2744) **6608**
Progressiste, Avant-Gardiste see Looking Forward, Staying Ahead **6431**
● The Progressive (Madison) (USA ISSN 0033-0736) **7173**
Progressive Building (NZL ISSN 1173-9916) **1030**
● The Progressive Christian (USA ISSN 1934-7316) **7771**
Progressive Clinical Insights Journal see P C I Journal **5880**
Progressive Computer Software Advisor see P C S Advisor **2580**
The Progressive Dairyman (USA) **268**
● Progressive Distributor (USA ISSN 1531-7811) **1162**
● Progressive Engineer (USA) **3216**
Progressive Farmer (Midsouth) (USA) **148**
Progressive Farmer (Midwest) (USA ISSN 1073-0656) **148**
Progressive Farmer (Southeast) (USA) **148**
● Progressive Farmer (Southwest) (USA ISSN 0033-0760) **148**
Progressive Farming (PAK) **149**
Progressive Gifts see Progressive Gifts & Home Worldwide **4061**
Progressive Gifts & Home Worldwide (GBR) **4061**
Progressive Greetings (GBR) **4061**
● Progressive Grocer (New York, 2002) (USA) **3681**
Progressive Grocer's Marketing Guidebook (USA) **3661**
The Progressive Hay Grower (USA) **249**
Progressive Health News see Journal of Immunity **311**
● Progressive Librarian (USA ISSN 1052-5726) **5040**
Progressive Party (GBR) **1965**
Progressive Planning (USA ISSN 1559-9736) **4424**
● Progressive Populist (USA ISSN 1096-5971) **7174**
Progressive Purchasing (CAN) **1838**
● Progressive Railroading (USA ISSN 0033-0817) **8622**
Progressive Railroading's Car & Locomotive Yearbook & Buyers' Guide (USA ISSN 1534-3901) **8622**
Progressive Rentals (USA ISSN 8750-6106) **1787**
Progressive Retailing (ZAF ISSN 1607-9892) **1838**
The Progressive Review (Princeton) (USA) **3986**
Progressive Review (Washington D.C.) (USA ISSN 0889-2202) **5235**
Progressive Utilization Theory Press see P R O U T Press **3984**
Progresso Fotografico see P C Photo **6972**
Progresso Socio-Economico na America Latina. Relatorio see Economic and Social Progress in Latin America. Report **1479**
● Il Progresso Veterinario (ITA ISSN 1594-0810) **8805**
Prohibition History Notes (USA ISSN 1093-5975) **4309**
● ➤ Prohistoria (ARG ISSN 1514-0032) **4309**
ProHort (USA) **3748**
I Proini (USA ISSN 0749-3126) **3559**
Proizvodstvo i Ispol'zovaniye Elastomerov/Production and Utilization of Elastomers (RUS ISSN 0236-1639) **3254**
● Proizvodstvo i Oborot Etilivogo Spirta i Alkogol'noi Produktsii v Rossiiskoi Federatsii/Production and Turnover of Alcoholic Products in Russian Federation (RUS) **614**
Proizvodstvo i Realizatsiya Morozhenogo i Bystrozamorozhennykh Produktov/Production and Sales of Ice-Cream and Quick-Frozen Foods (RUS ISSN 1606-4305) **4125**
➤ Proizvodstvo Prokata (RUS ISSN 1684-257X) **6330**
Proizvodstvo Spirta i Likero-Vodochnykh Izdelii/Manufacture of Alcohol Liqueur and Vodka Products (RUS) **609**
Project (USA) **7174**
Project Action Products and Publications Resource Guide (USA) **8528**
Project Construct Connections (USA) **2900**
Project Control Professional (GBR ISSN 1750-371X) **3371**
Project Destiny Magazine (USA ISSN 1533-0656) **3559**
Project Feasibility cum Market Survey Report (IND) **1646**
Project Finance see Project Finance and Infrastructure Finance **1376**
● Project Finance and Infrastructure Finance (GBR ISSN 1756-7866) **1376**
Project Finance Book of Lists (Years) (GBR) **1259**
● Project Finance International (GBR ISSN 0967-5914) **1376**
Project Finance International Directory (GBR ISSN 1352-4062) **1376**
Project Finance Monthly (USA ISSN 1071-4324) **1787**
Project Finance Regional Report. Africa (GBR ISSN 1460-910X) **1512**
Project Finance Regional Report. Asia Pacific (GBR ISSN 1460-9045) **1512**
Project Finance Regional Report. Eastern Europe and Former Soviet Union (GBR ISSN 1460-9061) **1512**
Project Finance Regional Report. Latin America and Caribbean (GBR ISSN 1460-9096) **1512**
Project Finance Regional Report. Middle East (GBR ISSN 1460-9118) **1512**
Project Finance Regional Report. North America (GBR ISSN 1460-9088) **1512**
Project Finance Regional Report. South Asia (GBR ISSN 1460-9053) **1512**
Project Finance Regional Report. Western Europe (GBR ISSN 1460-907X) **1512**
Project Finance Report. B O O & B L T Projects (Build Operate Own & Build Lease Transfer) (GBR ISSN 1463-4406) **1376**
Project Finance Report. B O O & B O O T Projects (Build Operate Transfer & Build Operate Own Transfer) (GBR ISSN 1463-4414) **1377**
Project Finance Report. D B F O, D B O, D B O T and Turnkey Projects (Design Build Finance Operate, Design Build Operate, Design Build Operate Transfer) (GBR ISSN 1463-4430) **1377**
Project Finance Report. Privatisation (GBR ISSN 1463-4422) **1377**
Project Finance Sector Report. Commercial (GBR ISSN 1462-8333) **1512**
Project Finance Sector Report. Energy - Power (GBR ISSN 1462-8368) **1512**
Project Finance Sector Report. Industry (GBR ISSN 1462-8341) **1512**
Project Finance Sector Report. Infrastructure (GBR ISSN 1462-8376) **1512**
Project Finance Sector Report. Natural Resources (GBR ISSN 1462-835X) **1513**
Project Finance Yearbook (Years) (GBR ISSN 0968-2279) **1377**
● Project Gutenberg Newsletter (USA) **5354**
Project HOPE (USA) **7537**
Project Inform Fact Sheet (USA ISSN 1051-8924) **5825**
Project Inform Perspective see P I Perspective **5824**
Project Management (IRL) **1030**
● ➤ Project Management Journal (USA ISSN 8756-9728) **1787**
Project Management Network see P M Network **1785**
Project Manager (AUS) **1787**
● Project Manager Today (GBR ISSN 1366-6851) **1787**
▼ ● Project on Gobal Migration and Transnational Politics (USA ISSN 1941-7586) **7291**
Project Planning and Control for Construction (USA) **4424**
Project Plant (GBR) **5458**
Project Russia/Proekt Rossiya (RUS ISSN 1385-2043) **454**
Project Scotland (GBR) **1030**
Project Zinger (USA) **4582**
† Projecten ABCDelfland (NLD ISSN 1874-0014) **8983**
Projection (Montreal) (CAN) **3559**
Projection Monthly see Large Display Report **2384**
Projections (Cambridge) (USA ISSN 1535-6191) **7537**
▼ ● ➤ Projections (New York) (USA ISSN 1934-9688) **6510**
Projections of Education Statistics see U.S. Department of Education. National Center for Education Statistics. Projections of Education Statistics **2937**
Projectmanagementkalender (NLD ISSN 1874-8147) **1787**
Projecto I2 do P I D D A C. Boletim (Programa de Investimentos e Despesas de Desenvolvimento da Administracao Publica) (PRT ISSN 0870-4724) **6393**
Projector (CAN ISSN 0380-6863) **2297**
Projects and Profits (IND ISSN 0972-5334) **1787**
Projekt (CZE ISSN 1211-9490) **454**
Projekt (SVK ISSN 1335-2180) **454**
Projekt & Interieur see P I **452**
ProjektArbeit (DEU ISSN 1612-8753) **2900**
Projekte - Geschaeftschancen im Rahmen der Entwicklungszusammenarbeit (DEU) **1580**
Projektisisustus see Spaces **4550**
Projektmanagement (DEU ISSN 0942-1017) **1787**
Projektowanie i Systemy (POL ISSN 0239-3174) **8435**
Projet (FRA ISSN 0033-0884) **7993**
▼ Projet Construction Maison (FRA ISSN 1954-1864) **1030**
Projet Professionnel see Collection Projet Professionnel **1734**
Projeto Historia (BRA ISSN 0102-4442) **4157**
➤ Prokla (DEU ISSN 0342-8176) **8126**
† Prokto (DEU ISSN 1615-8733) **8983**
➤ Proktologia (POL ISSN 1640-5382) **5700**
● Prolegomena (CAN) **6945**
● ➤ Prolegomena (HRV ISSN 1333-4395) **6945**
PROles (RUS) **3700**
Proletaeren (SWE ISSN 0345-9578) **7174**
Proletarian Path (IND ISSN 0377-3086) **7174**
Proletarian Revolution (USA ISSN 0894-0754) **7174**
ProLibris (DEU ISSN 1430-7235) **5040**
ProLiteracy Worldwide. Annual Report (USA) **2945**
● Prologue (AUS ISSN 1834-6316) **8476**
● Prologue (College Park) (USA ISSN 0033-1031) **4309**
Prologue (Medford) (USA ISSN 0033-1007) **8476**
Prologue (Milwaukee) (USA) **8477**
Prologue (New York) (USA ISSN 1543-3595) **7771**
Prom Guide (USA) **2260**
Promacasa (MEX) **1030**
● Promax International (USA) **2388**
ProMed see ProMed Komplementaer **5700**
● ➤ ProMed Komplementaer (AUT ISSN 1866-5756) **5700**
Promenade (USA) **3986**
Promet (HRV ISSN 0353-5320) **3281**
Prometeo (COL ISSN 0121-2966) **5432**
Prometeo (ITA ISSN 0394-1639) **4470**
Promethean (Loudonville) (USA) **2297**
Promethean (Superior) (USA) **2297**
Promethee (BEL ISSN 0033-1082) **7900**
● ➤ Prometheus (Abingdon) (AUS ISSN 0810-9028) **2336**
Prometheus (London) (GBR ISSN 1464-3901) **4470**
Prometheus (New York) (USA) **2269**
▼ Prominent (USA ISSN 1940-9664) **3559**
Promise (USA) **5432**
Promising Practices in Research Use/Pratiques Prometteuses dans l'Utilisation de la Recherche (CAN ISSN 1719-3788) **5700**
● Promo (USA ISSN 1047-1707) **33**
● Promo Marketing (USA ISSN 1940-1256) **1838**
Promobil (DEU ISSN 0935-834X) **8599**
Promobil Extra (DEU ISSN 1860-2878) **8599**
Promobil Katalog (DEU) **8599**
● PromoDispatch (USA) **1838**
Promote Yourself with Better Grammar (USA) **6702**
Promoteur Zairois (COD) **1580**
● Promoting Health (GBR ISSN 1368-6445) **7537**
Promoting Machine Industry in Japan see Kikai Shinko **5454**
Promotion & Education see Global Health Promotion **7519**
Promotion Business (DEU ISSN 1864-1555) **33**
Promotion et Education see Global Health Promotion **7519**
Promotion Immobiliere (FRA ISSN 1760-1436) **7604**
Promotional Consultant (USA ISSN 1930-7357) **1838**
Promotional Marketing see Promo Marketing **1838**
Promotional Products Business (USA ISSN 1072-3293) **33**
Promotional Test Questions (USA) **2666**
● Promotions and Incentives (GBR ISSN 0266-7991) **1838**
ProMotor (NLD ISSN 1381-0154) **8266**
Promotor (POL ISSN 1426-6660) **6684**
● Promowear (USA ISSN 1538-5620) **2249**
Prompt (DEU) **4084**
Prompt (JPN ISSN 0910-7223) **2596**
● Prompt (Altadena) (USA) **2435**
● Prompt (Raleigh) (USA) **2435**
Promusica (PRT) **8154**
Promyshlennaya Energetika (RUS ISSN 0033-1155) **3145**
Promyshlennaya Okraska (RUS) **6720**
● ➤ Promyshlennaya Teplotekhnika/Industrial Heat Engineering (UKR ISSN 0204-3602) **3394**
Promyshlennoe i Grazhdanskoe Stroitel'stvo (RUS ISSN 0869-7019) **1162**
Promyshlennoe Stroitel'stvo (RUS ISSN 0033-118X) **1030**
Promyshlennost' Armenii (RUS ISSN 0033-1163) **1902**
Promyshlennost' Belorussii (RUS ISSN 0033-1171) **1902**
Promyshlennye A S U i Kontrolery (RUS ISSN 1561-1531) **5458**
Pronab (IND ISSN 0033-1201) **5235**
Pronto (ESP ISSN 1139-8566) **8881**
Prontuario Agroquimico (MEX) **249**
Prontuario de Especialidades Veterinarias (MEX) **8805**
Prontuario Internacional (MEX) **1377**
Prontuario Tecnico de la Construccion (VEN) **1030**
Proof (USA) **1838**
Proof Collectors Corner (USA) **6653**
Proof Monthly see P M **2295**
Proof Rock (USA ISSN 0889-9568) **5235**
Prooficinas (VEN) **1854**
● Proofs (USA ISSN 0033-1236) **5862**
● ➤ Prooftexts (USA ISSN 0272-9601) **5354**
Prop (AUT) **4343**
● Prop-Liners of America. Newsletter (USA) **68**
Propaganda (USA ISSN 0737-0776) **5081**

Link to your serials resources and content with ulrichsweb.com

Title

10768 PROVINCE OF NOVA SCOTIA. PUBLICATIONS ULRICH'S PERIODICALS

Province of Nova Scotia. Publications (CAN ISSN 0550-1792) **633**
Province of Ontario Annual Report and Financial Statements (CAN ISSN 1707-6633) **7461**
Province of the Cape of Good Hope Official Gazette *see* Wes-Kaap. Offisiele Koerant **7476**
Province of the Indian Ocean Support Association *see* P I O S A **7770**
• Provincetown Arts (USA ISSN 1053-5012) **513**
Provincia (ARG) **5432**
Provincia (ESP) **5432**
• ➤ Provincia (VEN ISSN 1317-9535) **7174**
Diario Provincia 23 (ARG) **3791**
• Provincia de Pontevedra. Boletin Oficial (ESP) **7501**
† Provincia di Forli in Cifre (ITA ISSN 0033-1902) **8983**
Provincia Nuova (ITA ISSN 1722-5523) **7461**
Provincial Auditor Saskatchewan. Report of the Provincial Auditor to the Legislative Assembly of Saskatchewan (CAN ISSN 1704-6610) **1940**
Provincial Capital Commission. Annual Report (CAN ISSN 0827-1089) **7461**
• Provincial China (GBR ISSN 1326-7612) **7261**
Provincial Crown Oil and Gas Royalties - Provincial Freehold Oil and Gas Production Taxes - Drilling Inactive Program (CAN) **6801**
Provincial Directory Cross-Canada *see* Canada's Legal Support Directory **4638**
Provincial Directory, Process Servers, Bailiffs, Investigators *see* Canada's Legal Support Directory **4638**
Provincial Drug Benefit Programs (CAN) **6876**
Provincial Farmer (IRL) **149**
▼ Provincial Gazette. Kwazulu-Natal Province (ZAF ISSN 1994-4551) **7461**
Provincial Geologists Journal (CAN) **2762**
Provincial Judges Journal/Journal des Juges Provinciaux (CAN ISSN 0709-5139) **4762**
Provincial Laboratory Newsletter (CAN ISSN 1910-9903) **3490**
• Provincial Legislation (ZAF ISSN 1560-165X) **4762**
Provincial Legislative Record (CAN ISSN 0835-0329) **7174**
Provincial Museum of Alberta. Archaeology Occasional Papers (CAN) **412**
Provincial Newsletter (CAN) **6608**
• Provincial Outlook (CAN ISSN 0827-5785) **1513**
Provincial Outlook, Executive Summary (CAN ISSN 0832-3542) **1513**
• Las Provincias (Alicante Edition) (ESP) **3953**
• Las Provincias (Valencia Edition) (ESP) **3953**
Las Provincias Digital *see* Las Provincias (Valencia Edition) **3953**
Las Provincias Digital *see* Las Provincias (Alicante Edition) **3953**
• Proving Medical Diagnosis and Prognosis (USA) **4763**
Provins (SWE ISSN 0280-9974) **5235**
Provinsiale Koerant - die Provinsie Transvaal *see* P W V. Provinsiale Koerant **7459**
Provintsial'nyi Reporter (RUS) **3940**
Provinzialinstitut fuer Westfaelische Landes- und Volksforschung des Landschaftsverbandes Westfalen-Lippe. Veroeffentlichungen (DEU) **4255**
Provisional National Accounts of Greece *see* Greece. National Statistical Service. Provisional National Accounts of Greece **1235**
Provisionaries (CAN ISSN 1910-958X) **7772**
Provisions in U S International Air Transport Agreements (USA) **8550**
ProVita (DEU ISSN 1433-6413) **6995**
ProVita Healthcare (DEU ISSN 1610-8507) **7537**
• Provizor (UKR) **6876**
Provning och Forskning *see* Teknik & Forskning **3222**
† • Provoke Newsletter (NZL ISSN 1176-9408) **8983**
ProWald (DEU ISSN 1868-1247) **3700**
ProWholesaler *see* Pro Wholesaler **1432**
Proximites (FRA ISSN 1955-8082) **7501**
▼ Proximity (USA ISSN 1944-9496) **513**
Proxy Rules Handbook *see* Securities Handbook Series. Proxy Rules Handbook **1650**
Proxy Solicitor Comparison Report (USA ISSN 1932-7293) **1646**
Proyeccion (ESP ISSN 0478-6378) **7672**
Proyeccion Humana (MEX) **5700**
• ➤ Proyecciones (CHL ISSN 0716-0917) **5526**
• Proyecciones (MEX ISSN 1606-7908) **2998**
Proyecto Hombre (ESP ISSN 1136-3177) **2698**
• Proyectos Quimicos (ESP ISSN 1887-1992) **2077**
Proyectos Quimicos Digital *see* Proyectos Quimicos **2077**
† Proza (ISR ISSN 0334-4975) **8983**
• Der Prozess-Rechts-Berater (DEU ISSN 1610-0859) **4840**
Prozessrecht Aktiv (DEU ISSN 1619-0262) **4763**
Prozessrechtliche Abhandlungen (DEU) **4763**
Prozesstechnik und Automation (DEU ISSN 1614-7200) **2463**
Prudence (IRL ISSN 1649-587X) **3894**
Prudent Investors Magazine (CAN) **1646**
The Prudent Speculator (USA ISSN 0743-0809) **1646**
➤ Prudentia (NZL ISSN 0110-487X) **4157**
Prudentia Iuris (ARG ISSN 0326-2774) **4763**
Prudential Insurance Company of America. Economic Forecast (USA) **1513**
Pruef mit (CHE) **2640**
Der Pruefingenieur (DEU ISSN 1430-9084) **3281**
Pruefungstraining fuer Steuerfachangestellte (DEU) **1940**
• Prumysl Ceske Republiky (CZE) **1259**
† Prumysl Potravin/Food Industry (CZE ISSN 0033-1988) **8983**
Pruttelpot (NLD ISSN 1876-178X) **8266**
• Prva Statisticna Objava/First Release (SVN ISSN 1580-4216) **8395**
Pryamurskie Vedomosti (RUS) **3940**
Pryazovskii Krai (RUS) **3940**
Prykordonnyk Ukrainy (UKR) **6442**
Przedszkolak (POL ISSN 1734-7416) **2166**
Przeglad Antropologiczny - Anthropological Review *see* Anthropological Review **325**
Przeglad Archeologiczny (POL ISSN 0079-7138) **412**
Przeglad Biblioteczny (POL ISSN 0033-202X) **5040**
Przeglad Dermatologiczny (POL ISSN 0033-2526) **5881**
Przeglad Dokumentacyjny Elektrotechniki (POL ISSN 0033-2062) **3233**
Przeglad Dokumentacyjny Instytutu Obrobki Skrawaniem *see* Instytut Obrobki Skrawaniem. Przeglad Dokumentacyjny **3232**
Przeglad Dokumentacyjny Materialow Ogniotrwalych i Ceramiki Specjalnej (POL ISSN 1232-9703) **2044**
Przeglad Elektrotechniczny (POL ISSN 0033-2097) **3328**
➤ Przeglad Epidemiologiczny (POL ISSN 0033-2100) **7537**
• Przeglad Eureka (POL) **7900**
Przeglad Filozoficzny Nowa Seria (POL ISSN 1230-1493) **6945**
• Przeglad Flebologiczny (POL ISSN 1232-7174) **5940**
Przeglad Funeralny (POL ISSN 1234-6306) **3720**
Przeglad Gastronomiczny (POL ISSN 0033-2119) **3661**
Przeglad Geodezyjny (POL ISSN 0033-2127) **2788**
Przeglad Geofizyczny/Review of Geophysics (POL ISSN 0033-2135) **2788**
➤ Przeglad Geograficzny/Geographical Review (POL ISSN 0033-2143) **4025**
Przeglad Geologiczny/Geological Review (POL ISSN 0033-2151) **2763**
• Przeglad Ginekologiczno-Poloniczy (POL ISSN 1731-8602) **6002**
Przeglad Glottodydaktyczny (POL ISSN 0137-544X) **5163**
Przeglad Gorniczy (POL ISSN 0033-216X) **6476**
Przeglad Historyczno-Wojskowy (POL ISSN 1640-6281) **6442**
Przeglad Historyczny (POL ISSN 0033-2186) **4157**
Przeglad Humanistyczny (POL ISSN 0033-2194) **4470**
Przeglad Komunikacyjny (POL ISSN 0033-2232) **8509**
Przeglad Lekarski (POL ISSN 0033-2240) **5700**
Przeglad Lesniczy (POL ISSN 0867-7468) **3700**
Przeglad Mechaniczny (POL ISSN 0033-2259) **3394**
Przeglad Menopauzalny/Menopause Review (POL ISSN 1643-8876) **6002**
Przeglad Mleczarski/Polish Dairy Journal (POL ISSN 0478-6599) **268**
Przeglad Muzykologiczny (POL ISSN 1643-3319) **6608**
Przeglad N A T O (Online) *see* N A T O Review (Online) **7156**
Przeglad Naukowej Literatury Rolniczej i Lesnej (POL ISSN 0079-7154) **249**
Przeglad Obrony Cywilnej (POL ISSN 0137-7213) **2228**
Przeglad Odlewnictwa (POL ISSN 0033-2275) **6330**
➤ Przeglad Organizacji (POL ISSN 0137-7221) **1787**
Przeglad Orientalistyczny (POL ISSN 0033-2283) **559**
Przeglad Papierniczy/Polish Paper Review (POL ISSN 0033-2291) **6737**
• Przeglad Pediatryczny (POL ISSN 0137-723X) **6103**
Przeglad Piekarski i Cukierniczy (POL ISSN 0033-2313) **3675**
Przeglad Pismiennictwa Teologicznego *see* Uniwersytet Opolski. Wydzial Teologiczny. Przeglad Pismiennictwa Teologicznego **7692**
Przeglad Podatkowy (POL ISSN 0867-7514) **1940**
Przeglad Policyjny (POL ISSN 0867-5708) **2666**
Przeglad Polityczny (POL ISSN 1232-6488) **5235**
Przeglad Polonijny (POL ISSN 0137-303X) **4255**
Przeglad Powszechny (POL ISSN 0209-1127) **5235**
Przeglad Prawa Handlowego (POL ISSN 1230-2996) **4879**
Przeglad Prawa Karnego (POL ISSN 0860-8903) **4897**
Przeglad Przyrodniczy (POL ISSN 1230-509X) **699**
➤ Przeglad Psychologiczny/Psychological Review (POL ISSN 0048-5675) **7392**
➤ Przeglad Religioznawczy (POL ISSN 1230-4379) **7672**
➤ Przeglad Rusycystyczny (POL ISSN 0137-298X) **5163**
Przeglad Sadowy (POL ISSN 0867-7255) **4763**
Przeglad Socjologiczny (POL ISSN 0033-2356) **8127**
Przeglad Spawalnictwa (POL ISSN 0033-2364) **6343**
• Przeglad Sportowy (POL ISSN 0137-9267) **8194**
Przeglad Statystyczny/Statistical Review (POL ISSN 0033-2372) **8395**
Przeglad Techniczny (POL ISSN 0137-8783) **8435**
Przeglad Techniki Rolniczej i Lesnej *see* Technika Rolnicza, Ogrodnicza, Lesna **214**
Przeglad Telekomunikacyjny i Wiadomosci Telekomunikacyjne/Telecommunication Review & Telecommunication News (POL ISSN 1230-3496) **2371**
➤ Przeglad Uniwersytecki (POL ISSN 0866-9961) **4470**
Przeglad Ustawodawstwa Gospodarczego/Economic Legislation Review (POL ISSN 0137-5490) **1513**
Przeglad Wielkopolski (POL ISSN 0860-7540) **3930**
Przeglad Wlokienniczy i Technik Wlokienniczy *see* Przeglad Wlokienniczy - Wlokno, Odziez, Skora **8456**
Przeglad Wlokienniczy - Wlokno, Odziez, Skora (POL ISSN 1731-8645) **8456**
• Przeglad Wojsk Lotniczych i Obrony Powietrznej (POL ISSN 0867-2075) **6442**
Przeglad Zachodni (POL ISSN 0033-2437) **7261**
Przeglad Zachodniopomorski (POL ISSN 0552-4245) **4470**
Przeglad Zbozowo - Mlynarski (POL ISSN 0033-2461) **275**
Przeglad Zoologiczny (POL ISSN 0033-247X) **960**
Przekroj (POL ISSN 0033-2488) **3930**
Przemysl Chemiczny (POL ISSN 0033-2496) **2077**
Przemysl Drzewny (POL ISSN 0373-9856) **3715**
Przemysl Fermentacyjny i Owocowo Warzywny (POL ISSN 0137-2645) **3661**
Przemysl Spozywczy (POL ISSN 0033-250X) **3661**
➤ Przemyslowy Instytut Elektroniki. Prace/Industrial Institute of Electronics. Proceedings (POL ISSN 0509-7053) **3111**
Przemyslowy Instytut Telekomunikacji. Prace (POL ISSN 0032-6283) **3111**
Przeszlosc Demograficzna Polski (POL ISSN 0079-7189) **7291**
• Przewodnik Bibliograficzny (POL ISSN 0033-2518) **634**
Przewodnik Katolicki (POL ISSN 0137-8384) **7813**
Przewodnik Twojego Biznesu (POL ISSN 1428-7617) **1162**
Przez Czern (POL ISSN 1509-1066) **5235**
Przy Stoliku (POL ISSN 1643-7365) **3681**
Przyjaciolka (POL ISSN 0033-2534) **8881**
Przyjaciolka Poleca (POL ISSN 1429-2009) **8881**
PS2 Magazine *see* P S 2 Magazine **2480**
▼ • Psaltiki (USA ISSN 1946-7540) **6608**
.psd (POL ISSN 1732-2200) **6980**
➤ Pseudepigrapha Veteris Testamenti Graece (NLD ISSN 0079-7197) **7672**
➤ Psi Chi Journal of Undergraduate Research (USA ISSN 1089-4136) **7392**
Psi Kusy (CZE) **6814**
▼ Psi Sporty (CZE ISSN 1802-1867) **6814**
• ➤ Psic (BRA ISSN 1676-7314) **7392**
➤ Psicanalise e Universidade/Psychoanalysis and University (BRA ISSN 1413-0556) **7392**
Psiche Donna (ITA ISSN 1591-1209) **6175**
• Psichiatri Oggi (ITA ISSN 1129-0846) **6175**
Psichiatria dell'Infanzia e dell'Adolescenza (ITA ISSN 0393-361X) **6175**
• ➤ Psichiatria di Comunita (ITA ISSN 1724-0751) **7392**
• Psichiatria di Consultazione (ITA ISSN 1127-395X) **6175**
➤ Psichiatria e Psicoterapia (Rome)/Analytic Psychotherapy and Psychopathology (ITA ISSN 1724-4919) **6175**
Psichiatria e Psicoterapia Analitica *see* Psichiatria e Psicoterapia (Rome) **6175**
Psichiatria e Territorio (ITA) **6175**
Psichiatria Generale e dell'Eta Evolutiva (ITA ISSN 0555-5299) **6175**
• Psichologija (LTU ISSN 1392-0359) **7392**
• Psico (BRA ISSN 0103-5371) **7392**
• Psico-USF (Psicologia Universidade Sao Francisco) (BRA ISSN 1413-8271) **7392**
• Psicoanalisi (Milan) (ITA ISSN 1971-0364) **7392**
Psicoanalisi Corporea (ITA ISSN 1828-0803) **6175**
• Psicoanalisi e Metodo (ITA) **7392**
• Psicoanalisi Forense (ITA ISSN 1591-2795) **6175**
• Psicoanalisis (ARG ISSN 0325-819X) **7392**
• Psicoanalisis: Ayer y Hoy (ARG ISSN 1668-3870) **6175**
• Psicobiettivo (ITA ISSN 0392-2952) **7392**
Psicodiagnostico de Rorschach (ARG ISSN 0327-2273) **7392**
• Psicodoc (ESP ISSN 1988-0073) **7417**
• Psicolgia Escolar e Educacional (BRA ISSN 1413-8557) **7392**
Psicologemas (ESP ISSN 1130-1481) **7392**
Psicologia (BRA ISSN 1518-5923) **7392**
Psicologia *see* Psicologia Practica **7393**
Psicologia (Braga) (PRT ISSN 0873-4976) **7392**
➤ Psicologia (Lisbon) (PRT ISSN 0874-2049) **7392**
Psicologia Argumento (BRA ISSN 0103-7013) **7392**
• Psicologia Clinica (BRA ISSN 0103-5665) **7392**
• Psicologia Clinica dello Sviluppo (ITA ISSN 1824-078X) **7392**
Psicologia.com *see* Revista Electronica de Psicologia **7404**
• ➤ Psicologia Conductual/Behavioral Psychology (ESP ISSN 1132-9483) **7392**
Psicologia Contemporanea (ITA ISSN 0390-346X) **7392**
• Psicologia della Salute (ITA ISSN 1721-0321) **7393**
▼ Psicologia dell'Educazione (ITA ISSN 1971-3711) **2900**
Psicologia dell'Educazione e della Formazione *see* Psicologia dell'Educazione **2900**
• ➤ Psicologia desde el Caribe (COL ISSN 0123-417X) **7393**
• Psicologia di Comunita (ITA ISSN 1827-5249) **8127**
Psicologia e Lavoro (ITA ISSN 0048-5691) **7393**
Psicologia e Scuola (ITA ISSN 0392-680X) **2901**
• Psicologia & Sociedade (BRA ISSN 0102-7182) **7993**
Psicologia e Societa (ITA ISSN 0394-2856) **7393**
Psicologia, Educacao e Cultura (PRT ISSN 0874-2391) **7393**
• Psicologia Educativa (ESP ISSN 1135-755X) **7393**
• Psicologia em Estudo (BRA ISSN 1413-7372) **7393**
• ➤ Psicologia em Revista (BRA ISSN 1677-1168) **7393**
Psicologia Iberoamericana (MEX ISSN 1405-0943) **7393**
Psicologia Italiana (ITA ISSN 0393-1064) **7393**
• Psicologia Politica (ESP ISSN 1138-0853) **7393**
Psicologia Practica (ESP ISSN 1576-5148) **7393**
• ➤ Psicologia: Reflexao e Critica (BRA ISSN 0102-7972) **7393**
➤ Psicologia Revista (BRA ISSN 1413-4063) **7393**
• Psicologia, Saude e Docencas (PRT ISSN 1645-0086) **7393**
• Psicologia sin Fronteras (ARG ISSN 1851-3441) **7393**
• Psicologia Sociale (ITA ISSN 1827-2517) **7993**
• ➤ Psicologia: Teoria e Pesquisa/Psychology: Theory and Research (BRA ISSN 0102-3772) **7393**
• ➤ Psicologia: Teoria e Pratica (BRA ISSN 1516-3687) **7393**
Psicologia. Text i Context (ESP ISSN 1130-8877) **7393**
• Psicologia U S P (Universidade de Sao Paulo) (BRA ISSN 0103-6564) **7393**
• Psicologia y Ciencia Social (MEX ISSN 1405-5082) **7393**
• Psicologia y Psicopedagogia (ARG ISSN 1515-1182) **2901**
• Psicologia y Salud (MEX ISSN 1405-1109) **7393**
Psicologia(s) *see* Psicologias **7393**
▼ • ➤ Psicologias/Psychologies (PRI ISSN 1948-559X) **7393**
Psicologias Revista *see* Psicologias **7393**
• ➤ Psicologica (ESP ISSN 0211-2159) **7393**
† Psicomotricidad (ESP ISSN 0213-0092) **8983**
Psicomotricita (ITA ISSN 1723-3844) **7393**
Psicooncologia (ESP ISSN 1696-7240) **6033**
• ➤ Psicopatologia (ESP ISSN 0211-5549) **6175**
• Psicopedagogia (BRA ISSN 0103-8486) **2901**
• Psicoperspectivas (Online) (CHL ISSN 0718-6924) **7393**
Psicoperspectivas (Print) *see* Psicoperspectivas (Online) **7393**
Psicosi *see* Rivista di Psichiatria **6183**
Psicosomatica *see* Riza Psicosomatica **5707**
• Psicotech (ITA ISSN 1828-5171) **7393**
Psicoterapia Cognitiva e Comportamentale (ITA ISSN 1126-1072) **7394**
• Psicoterapia e Scienze Umane (ITA ISSN 0394-2864) **6175**
Psicoterapia Psicoanalitica (ITA ISSN 1721-0135) **6175**
Psicoterapia, Psicoterapie (ITA ISSN 1828-5198) **6175**
• ➤ Psicothema: Revista de Psicologia (ESP ISSN 0214-9915) **7394**
Psiha (HRV ISSN 1330-8777) **7394**
➤ Psihijatrija Danas/Psychiatry Today (SRB ISSN 0350-2538) **6175**
➤ Psihofarmakologia i Biologiceskaa Narkologia/Psychopharmacology and Biological Narcology (RUS ISSN 1606-8181) **6876**
• Psihologija (SRB ISSN 0048-5705) **7394**
• Psihologijske Teme/Psychological Topics (HRV ISSN 1332-0742) **7394**
Psiholoska Obzorja/Horizons of Psychology (SVN ISSN 1318-1874) **7394**
Psihoterapija (HRV ISSN 0350-3186) **7394**
• Psikeba (ARG ISSN 1850-339X) **7394**
• Psikhe (CHL ISSN 0717-0297) **7394**
• ➤ Psikhologicheskii Zhurnal (RUS ISSN 0205-9592) **7394**
➤ Psikhologiya Zrelosti i Stareniya (RUS ISSN 0236-4999) **4053**
▼ • ➤ Psikiyatride Guncel Yaklasimlar/Current Approaches in Psychiatry (TUR ISSN 1309-0658) **6175**
Psiqiatria (MEX ISSN 0187-4543) **6175**
Psique (BRA ISSN 1677-3179) **6175**
Psique (COL ISSN 0121-8913) **6175**
➤ Psiquiatria Biologica (BRA ISSN 0104-7787) **6175**
• Psiquiatria Biologica (ESP ISSN 1134-5934) **6175**
Psiquiatria.com *see* Revista Electronica de Psiquiatria **6182**
Psiquis (MEX ISSN 0188-736X) **6175**
• Psittascene (GBR ISSN 1363-3368) **913**
Pskovskaya Pravda (RUS) **3940**
PSM3 *see* P S M 3 **2480**
Pso Magazin (DEU ISSN 0938-8532) **5881**
Psoriasis (ITA ISSN 1971-3843) **5862**
Psoriasis Advance (USA ISSN 1543-429X) **5881**
• Psoriasis Forum (USA ISSN 1089-3504) **5881**
Psoriasis in Practice (GBR ISSN 1477-3783) **5881**
Psoriasis Nyt (DNK ISSN 0909-2757) **5881**

▼ • Psoriasis Skinsights (USA ISSN 1939-6597) **5881**
Psoriasistidningen (SWE ISSN 1404-4056) **5881**
PSP *see* P S P **2480**
PSP Magazine Ufficiale *see* P S P Magazine Ufficiale **2480**
Psuhiatrike/Psychiatriki (GRC ISSN 1105-2333) **6175**
Psuhologia/Psychology (GRC ISSN 1106-5737) **7394**
PSWorld *see* P S World **2480**
Psy (NLD ISSN 1385-7630) **7394**
• ➤ PsyArt (USA ISSN 1088-5870) **7394**
• PsycCRITIQUES (Online) (USA ISSN 1554-0138) **7394**
Psych Discourse (USA ISSN 1091-4781) **7394**
• ➤ Psych. Pflege Heute (DEU ISSN 0949-1619) **6175**
• Psych Thoughts (USA ISSN 1540-1863) **7394**
Psychanalise et Traditions *see* G R A P P A F. Cahiers **6142**
• Psychanalyse (FRA ISSN 1770-0078) **7394**
La Psychanalyse a l'Ouvrage (FRA ISSN 1951-7599) **7394**
Psychanalyse et Ecriture (FRA ISSN 1951-7564) **5355**
Psychanalyse et Faits Sociaux (FRA ISSN 1778-5413) **7394**
Psychanalyse Magazine *see* Signes & Sens **8988**
Psychanalyse, Medecine et Societe (FRA ISSN 1767-3143) **6175**
• Psyche (BRA ISSN 1415-1138) **7394**
➤ Psyche (DEU ISSN 0033-2623) **7394**
• ➤ Psyche (Cambridge, 1874) (USA ISSN 0033-2615) **857**
• ➤ Psyche (Online) (USA) **7394**
Psyche (Staten Island) (USA ISSN 1539-8595) **5355**
Psyche & Brein (BEL) **7394**
Psyche en Geloof (NLD ISSN 1385-4585) **6175**
† Psyche et Natura (CZE ISSN 1213-3159) **8983**
Psyche und Soma (CHE ISSN 1661-7142) **5700**
PsychEd Up *see* Psychopharmacology Educational Update **6877**
▼ De Psychiater (Belgium Edition) (NLD) **6175**
De Psychiater (Dutch Edition) (NLD) **6176**
• ➤ Psychiatria/Psychiatry (POL ISSN 1732-9841) **6176**
Psychiatria (SVK ISSN 0113-423X) **6176**
Psychiatria Danubina (HRV ISSN 0353-5053) **6176**
Psychiatria et Neurologia Japonica *see* Seishin Shinkeigaku Zasshi **6184**
Psychiatria Fennica/Finnish Psychiatry (FIN ISSN 0079-7227) **6176**
Psychiatria Fennica. Monographs/Psychiatria Fennican Monografiasarja (FIN ISSN 0359-1034) **6176**
Psychiatria Fennica. Reports (FIN ISSN 0359-3207) **6176**
Psychiatria Fennican Monografiasarja *see* Psychiatria Fennica. Monographs **6176**
Psychiatria Hungarica (HUN ISSN 0237-7896) **6176**
• ➤ Psychiatria Polska (POL ISSN 0033-2674) **6176**
➤ Psychiatria pre Prax (SVK ISSN 1335-9584) **6176**
Psychiatric and Psychological Evidence (USA) **4763**
• ➤ Psychiatric Annals (USA ISSN 0048-5713) **6176**
Psychiatric Bulletin *see* The Psychiatrist **6177**
Psychiatric Care *see* The British Journal of Forensic Practice **5912**
• ➤ Psychiatric Clinics of North America (USA ISSN 0193-953X) **6176**
• ➤ Psychiatric Genetics (USA ISSN 0955-8829) **877**
Psychiatric Mental Health Nursing *see* Seishin Kango **6184**
• Psychiatric News (USA ISSN 0033-2704) **6176**
• ➤ Psychiatric Quarterly (USA ISSN 0033-2720) **6176**
• ➤ Psychiatric Rehabilitation Journal (USA ISSN 1095-158X) **6176**
Psychiatric Rehabilitation Skills *see* American Journal of Psychiatric Rehabilitation **6121**
• ➤ Psychiatric Services (USA ISSN 1075-2730) **6176**
• ➤ Psychiatric Times (USA ISSN 0893-2905) **6176**
• ➤ Psychiatrie (CZE ISSN 1211-7579) **6176**
Die Psychiatrie (DEU ISSN 1614-4864) **6176**
Psychiatrie *see* Tijdschrift voor Psychiatrie **6188**
• ➤ La Psychiatrie de l'Enfant (FRA ISSN 0079-726X) **6103**
Psychiatrie Francaise (FRA ISSN 0755-9755) **6177**
• ➤ Psychiatrie pro Praxi (CZE ISSN 1213-0508) **6177**
• Psychiatrie, Sciences Humaines, Neurosciences (FRA ISSN 1639-8319) **6177**
• ➤ Psychiatrie und Psychotherapie (AUT ISSN 1614-7189) **6177**
▼ • Psychiatrie und Psychotherapie up2date (DEU ISSN 1611-7867) **6177**
Psychiatriki *see* Psuhiatrike **6175**
Psychiatrische Pflege Heute *see* Psych. Pflege Heute **6175**
• ➤ Psychiatrische Praxis (DEU ISSN 0303-4259) **6177**
• ➤ Psychiatrische Praxis. Supplement (DEU ISSN 0934-3008) **6177**
• ➤ The Psychiatrist (GBR ISSN 1758-3209) **6177**
Psychiatry *see* Seishinka **6184**
Psychiatry *see* Psychiatria **6176**
• Psychiatry (Abingdon) (GBR ISSN 1476-1793) **6177**
• ➤ Psychiatry (Edgemont) (USA ISSN 1550-5952) **6177**
• ➤ Psychiatry (New York) (USA ISSN 0033-2747) **6177**
Psychiatry (Section 32 EMBASE) *see* Excerpta Medica. Section 32: Psychiatry **5746**
Psychiatry 2005 *see* Psychiatry (Edgemont) **6177**
▼ • Psychiatry Alerts N O S (Not Otherwise Specified) (USA ISSN 1559-5625) **6177**
• ➤ Psychiatry and Clinical Neurosciences (AUS ISSN 1323-1316) **6177**
Psychiatry Drug Alerts (USA ISSN 0894-4873) **6876**
† Psychiatry in Progress (USA) **8983**
• ➤ Psychiatry Investigation (KOR ISSN 1738-3684) **6177**
• ➤ Psychiatry On-Line (GBR ISSN 1359-7620) **6177**
• ➤ Psychiatry Psychology and Law (GBR ISSN 1321-8719) **6177**
• ➤ Psychiatry Research (IRL ISSN 0165-1781) **6178**
▼ Psychiatry Research Journal (USA ISSN 1939-5949) **6178**
• ➤ Psychiatry Research: Neuroimaging (IRL ISSN 0925-4927) **6178**
▼ • Psychiatry Research Review (NZL ISSN 1178-6183) **6178**
Psychiatry Series *see* Monographien aus dem Gesamtgebiete der Psychiatrie **6161**
Psychiatry Today *see* Psihijatrija Danas **6175**
† Psychiatry Update (EGY ISSN 1110-760X) **8983**
† Psychic (FRA ISSN 1779-2525) **8983**
Psychic News (GBR ISSN 0033-2801) **6743**
Psychic Reader (USA) **6743**
• ➤ PsychNology (ITA ISSN 1720-7525) **7394**
➤ Psycho-analytic Psychotherapy in South Africa (ZAF ISSN 1023-0548) **7394**
➤ Psycho-Lingua (IND ISSN 0377-3132) **5163**
Psycho-Logik (DEU ISSN 1861-4183) **6178**
• ➤ Psycho-Oncologie (FRA ISSN 1778-3798) **6033**
• ➤ Psycho-Oncology (GBR ISSN 1057-9249) **6033**
Psycho-Pedagogie (FRA ISSN 1255-1546) **7394**
Psycho - Social - Medicine *see* G M S Psycho - Social - Medicine **6142**
Psycho-social Update (AUS ISSN 1833-5659) **7394**
Psychoanalyse (BEL ISSN 0772-9219) **7394**
➤ Psychoanalyse en Cultuur/Psychoanalysis and Culture (NLD ISSN 0924-6290) **7395**
Psychoanalyse und Koerper (DEU) **7395**
➤ Psychoanalysis and Contemporary Thought (USA ISSN 0161-5289) **6178**
Psychoanalysis and Culture *see* Psychoanalyse en Cultuur **7395**
• ➤ Psychoanalysis and History (GBR ISSN 1460-8235) **4157**
Psychoanalysis and Psychotherapy (USA ISSN 1057-5723) **7395**
Psychoanalysis and University *see* Psicanalise e Universidade **7392**
• ➤ Psychoanalysis, Culture & Society (GBR ISSN 1088-0763) **7395**
Psychoanalytic Abstracts (Print) *see* PsycSCAN: Psychoanalysis (Online) **7417**
Psychoanalytic Crosscurrents (USA) **7395**
• ➤ Psychoanalytic Dialogues (USA ISSN 1048-1885) **7395**
• ➤ Psychoanalytic Inquiry (USA ISSN 0735-1690) **7395**
Psychoanalytic Perspectives (USA ISSN 1551-806X) **7395**
• ➤ Psychoanalytic Psychology (USA ISSN 0736-9735) **7395**
• ➤ Psychoanalytic Psychotherapy (GBR ISSN 0266-8734) **7395**
➤ Psychoanalytic Quarterly (USA ISSN 0033-2828) **7395**
• ➤ The Psychoanalytic Review (USA ISSN 0033-2836) **7395**
• ➤ Psychoanalytic Social Work (USA ISSN 1522-8878) **8063**
Psychoanalytic Study of the Child (USA ISSN 0079-7308) **7395**
• ➤ Psychoanalytische Blaetter (DEU ISSN 0945-7542) **6178**
Psychoanalytische Familientherapie (DEU ISSN 1616-8836) **7395**
Psychodrama Network News (USA) **7395**
Psychodrame (FRA ISSN 0245-9744) **6178**
• Psychodynamic Practice (Online) (GBR ISSN 1475-3626) **6178**
• ➤ Psychodynamic Practice (Print) (GBR ISSN 1475-3634) **6178**
➤ Psychodynamische Psychotherapie (DEU ISSN 1618-7830) **7395**
• Psychofenia (ITA ISSN 1722-8093) **7395**
➤ Psychogeriatria Polska/Polish Journal of Geriatric Psychiatry (POL ISSN 1732-2642) **4053**
• ➤ Psychogeriatrics (AUS ISSN 1346-3500) **7396**
• ➤ Psychologia/Pushikorogia (JPN ISSN 0033-2852) **7396**
➤ Psychologia a Patopsychologia Dietata (SVK ISSN 0555-5574) **7396**
Psychologia et Sociologia Religionum (SWE ISSN 0283-149X) **7672**
Psychologia, Etologia, Genetyka (POL) **7396**
Psychologica (PRT ISSN 0871-4657) **7396**
• ➤ Psychologica Belgica (BEL ISSN 0033-2879) **7396**
Psychological Aspects of Education - Current Trends *see* British Journal of Educational Psychology. Monograph Series II. Psychological Aspects of Education - Current Trends **7342**
• ➤ Psychological Assessment (USA ISSN 1040-3590) **7396**
• ➤ Psychological Bulletin (USA ISSN 0033-2909) **7396**
Psychological Cinema Register *see* P C R **7417**
Psychological Development and Education *see* Xinli fazhan yu Jiaoyu **7415**
Psychological Exploration *see* Xinlixue Tanxin **7415**
▼ • Psychological Injury and Law (USA ISSN 1938-971X) **7396**
• ➤ Psychological Inquiry (USA ISSN 1047-840X) **7396**
• ➤ Psychological Medicine (GBR ISSN 0033-2917) **6178**
† Psychological Medicine. Monograph Supplement (GBR ISSN 0264-1801) **8983**
• ➤ Psychological Methods (USA ISSN 1082-989X) **7396**
• Psychological Perspectives (USA ISSN 0033-2925) **7396**
• ➤ The Psychological Record (USA ISSN 0033-2933) **7396**
• ➤ Psychological Reports (USA ISSN 0033-2941) **7396**
• ➤ Psychological Research (DEU ISSN 0340-0727) **7396**
Psychological Research Journal (IND ISSN 0970-6097) **7397**
Psychological Research Reports *see* University of Turku. Psychological Research Reports **7414**
Psychological Review *see* Przeglad Psychologiczny **7392**
• ➤ Psychological Review (USA ISSN 0033-295X) **7397**
Psychological Science *see* Xinli Kexue **7415**
• ➤ Psychological Science (GBR ISSN 0956-7976) **7397**
• Psychological Science Agenda (USA ISSN 1057-0721) **7397**
• Psychological Science in the Public Interest (GBR ISSN 1529-1006) **7397**
• Psychological Services (USA ISSN 1541-1559) **7397**
Psychological Studies *see* Pszichologiai Tanulmanyok **7402**
• ➤ Psychological Studies (IND ISSN 0033-2968) **7397**
Psychological Topics *see* Psihologijske Teme **7394**
▼ • Psychological Trauma (USA ISSN 1942-9681) **7397**
Psychologie (Houten) *see* Netherlands Journal of Psychology **7386**
Psychologie Canadienne *see* Canadian Psychology **7344**
Psychologie Clinique (FRA ISSN 1145-1882) **7397**
Psychologie Clinique et Projective (FRA ISSN 1265-5449) **7397**
Psychologie de l'Interaction (FRA ISSN 1291-0600) **6178**
▼ Psychologie des Alltagshandelns/Psychology of Everyday Activity (AUT ISSN 1998-9970) **7397**
Psychologie Dnes (CZE ISSN 1212-9607) **7397**
• Psychologie du Travail et des Organisations (FRA ISSN 1420-2530) **7397**
• Psychologie & Gezondheid (NLD ISSN 1873-1791) **7397**
Psychologie & Education (FRA ISSN 1148-9502) **2901**
• Psychologie et Neuropsychiatrie du Vieillissement (FRA ISSN 1760-1703) **6178**
• Psychologie Francaise (FRA ISSN 0033-2984) **7397**
➤ Psychologie Heute (DEU ISSN 0340-1677) **7397**
➤ Psychologie in Erziehung und Unterricht (DEU ISSN 0342-183X) **2901**
Psychologie Magazine (NLD ISSN 1389-8051) **7398**
Psychologie Preventive (CAN ISSN 0714-3494) **7398**
Psychologie pro Praxi/Applied Industrial Psychology (CZE) **7398**
Psychologie Transpersonnelle *see* Collection Psychologie Transpersonnelle **7348**
Psychologie und Person (DEU ISSN 0079-7405) **7398**
Psychologie und Sport *see* Zeitschrift fuer Sportpsychologie **7416**
Psychologie v Ekonomicke Praxi *see* Psychologie pro Praxi **7398**
Psychologie Verstehen (DEU ISSN 0941-3049) **7398**
Psychologies *see* Xinli Yuekan **7415**
• Psychologies (ESP) **7398**
Psychologies (FRA ISSN 0032-1583) **8881**
Psychologies (GBR) **8881**
Psychologies *see* Psicologias **7393**
▼ Psychologies (ZAF ISSN 1993-2839) **7398**
Psychologies Magazine (ITA ISSN 1824-7822) **8881**
Psychologische Forschungsergebnisse (DEU ISSN 1435-666X) **7398**
• ➤ Psychologische Rundschau (DEU ISSN 0033-3042) **7398**
• ➤ The Psychologist (GBR ISSN 0952-8229) **7398**
• Psychologist Appointment (GBR) **7398**
The Psychologist in Wales (GBR ISSN 1468-4756) **7398**
• The Psychologist-Manager Journal (USA ISSN 1088-7156) **7398**
• Psychologists for Social Responsibility. Newsletter (USA) **7398**
Psychology *see* Xinlixue **7415**
Psychology *see* Psuhologia **7394**
Psychology *see* Pszichologia **7402**
Psychology: An IUPsyS Global Resource *see* International Journal of Psychology **7365**
• ➤ Psychology and Aging (USA ISSN 0882-7974) **4053**
• ➤ Psychology and Developing Societies (IND ISSN 0971-3336) **7398**
➤ Psychology & Education (USA ISSN 1553-6939) **7398**
Psychology and Health *see* Xinli yu Jiankang **6190**
• ➤ Psychology & Health (GBR ISSN 0887-0446) **7398**
• ➤ Psychology & Marketing (USA ISSN 0742-6046) **7398**
▼ • Psychology & Psychiatry Journal (USA ISSN 1944-2718) **7399**
• ➤ Psychology & Psychotherapy (GBR ISSN 1476-0835) **7399**
Psychology and Sociology of Sport: Current Selected Research (USA ISSN 0885-7423) **7399**
➤ Psychology Bulletin (ZAF) **7399**
Psychology Crime and Law *see* Psychology, Crime and Law **7399**
• ➤ Psychology, Crime and Law (GBR ISSN 1068-316X) **7399**
• ➤ Psychology, Health & Medicine (GBR ISSN 1354-8506) **7399**
• Psychology in Spain (ESP ISSN 1137-9685) **7399**
• ➤ Psychology in the Schools (USA ISSN 0033-3085) **7399**
▼ ➤ Psychology Journal (USA ISSN 1931-5694) **7399**
• ➤ Psychology of Addictive Behaviors (USA ISSN 0893-164X) **2698**
• Psychology of Aesthetics, Creativity, and the Arts (USA ISSN 1931-3896) **7399**
➤ The Psychology of Education Review (GBR ISSN 1463-9807) **2901**
Psychology of Everyday Activity *see* Psychologie des Alltagshandelns **7397**
• Psychology of Language and Communication (POL ISSN 1234-2238) **7399**
• Psychology of Learning and Motivation: Advances in Research and Theory (USA ISSN 0079-7421) **7399**
Psychology of Mathematics Education Conference. Proceedings *see* P M E Conference. Proceedings **3075**
• Psychology of Men & Masculinity (USA ISSN 1524-9220) **7399**
• ➤ Psychology of Music (GBR ISSN 0305-7356) **6608**
➤ Psychology of Programming Interest Group. Proceedings (GBR) **2509**
▼ • Psychology of Religion and Spirituality (USA ISSN 1941-1022) **7399**
▼ • Psychology of Sexualities (GBR ISSN 1941-9899) **7399**
• ➤ Psychology of Sport and Exercise (NLD ISSN 1469-0292) **7399**
• ➤ Psychology of Women Quarterly (USA ISSN 0361-6843) **7400**
Psychology of Women Section Review (GBR ISSN 1466-3724) **7400**
• ➤ Psychology, Public Policy, and Law (USA ISSN 1076-8971) **7400**
▼ • ➤ Psychology Research and Behavior Management (GBR ISSN 1179-1578) **6178**
Psychology Research Journal (IND) **7400**
• Psychology Review (GBR ISSN 1750-3469) **7400**
Psychology Science *see* Psychology Science Quarterly **7400**
• ➤ Psychology Science Quarterly (DEU ISSN 1866-6140) **7400**
Psychology Teaching Review (GBR ISSN 0965-948X) **7400**
Psychology: Theory and Research *see* Psicologia: Teoria e Pesquisa **7393**
• Psychology Today (USA ISSN 0033-3107) **7400**
Psychology Today's Blues Buster *see* Blues Buster **8937**
De Psycholoog (NLD ISSN 0033-3115) **7400**
† Psychomed (DEU ISSN 0935-2937) **8983**
• ➤ Psychometrika (USA ISSN 0033-3123) **7400**
• ➤ Psychomusicology (CAN ISSN 0275-3987) **6608**
• ➤ Psychoneuro (DEU ISSN 1611-9991) **6178**
• ➤ Psychoneuroendocrinology (GBR ISSN 0306-4530) **6178**
• Psychonomic Bulletin & Review (USA ISSN 1069-9384) **7400**
• ➤ Psychoonkologia (POL ISSN 1429-8538) **6178**
• ➤ Psychopathologie Africaine (SEN ISSN 0033-314X) **6179**
• ➤ Psychopathology (CHE ISSN 0254-4962) **6179**
• Psychopharm Review (USA ISSN 1936-9255) **6179**
• ➤ Psychopharmacology (DEU ISSN 0033-3158) **6876**
Psychopharmacology and Biological Narcology *see* Psihofarmakologia i Biologiceskaa Narkologia **6876**
• Psychopharmacology Bulletin (USA ISSN 0048-5764) **6877**
• Psychopharmacology Educational Update (USA ISSN 1553-8907) **6877**

Title

DIRECTORY 2010 PUBLICATIONS OF THE MODERN LANGUAGE ASSOCIATION OF 10771

Public Management and Policy Association Reports (GBR) **1941**
Public Management and Policy Association Review (GBR) **7174**
Public Management Bulletin (USA) **7462**
• Public Management Review (Online) (GBR ISSN 1471-9045) **1787**
• ➤ Public Management Review (Print) (GBR ISSN 1471-9037) **1787**
• The Public Manager (USA ISSN 1061-7639) **7462**
▼ • Public Marketing Idea (ESP ISSN 1988-7841) **1838**
Public Money (GBR) **1941**
• ➤ Public Money and Management (GBR ISSN 0954-0962) **7462**
† • Public Network Europe (GBR ISSN 0963-5084) **8983**
• ➤ Public Opinion Quarterly (GBR ISSN 0033-362X) **7174**
Public Opinion Report (USA) **7174**
• Public Opinion Research in the Government of Canada. Annual Report (CAN ISSN 1715-9067) **7462**
• Public Organization Review (USA ISSN 1566-7170) **1787**
• Public Papers of the Presidents of the United States (USA ISSN 0079-7626) **7462**
• ➤ Public Performance and Management Review (USA ISSN 1530-9576) **7462**
Public Personnel Law Bulletin *see* Public Employment Law Bulletin **7462**
• ➤ Public Personnel Management (USA ISSN 0091-0260) **1873**
Public Policy (AUS ISSN 1833-2110) **7174**
• Public Policy and Administration (GBR ISSN 0952-0767) **7462**
The Public Policy & Aging Report (USA ISSN 1055-3037) **4054**
Public Policy and Politics (GBR ISSN 1754-9590) **7462**
• Public Policy & Practice (USA ISSN 1540-1499) **7174**
Public Policy and Social Welfare (AUT) **7174**
• Public Policy Forum. Research Reports (USA) **7462**
• Public Policy Institute of California. Research Brief (USA ISSN 1933-6640) **7174**
Public Policy Institute of California Statewide Survey *see* P P I C Statewide Survey **7459**
➤ Public Policy Issues in Resource Management (USA ISSN 0079-7634) **1902**
• Public Policy Research (Online) (GBR ISSN 1744-540X) **1547**
• Public Policy Research (Print) (GBR ISSN 1744-5396) **1547**
Public Power (USA ISSN 0033-3654) **3161**
Public Power Weekly (USA ISSN 0747-3613) **3161**
Public Printer's Annual Report *see* U.S. Government Printing Office. Annual Report **7328**
• Public-Private Finance (GBR ISSN 1742-0334) **1377**
Public Private Partnership Bulletin *see* P P P Bulletin **1938**
Public Private Partnerships *see* Public Private Partnerships and P F I **4763**
Public Private Partnerships and P F I (Private Finance Initiative) (GBR) **4763**
Public Procurement Law Review (GBR ISSN 0963-8245) **7463**
• Public Pulse (USA ISSN 1053-9751) **1838**
Public Purpose (USA ISSN 1557-4946) **2999**
Public Radio Legal Handbook (USA) **2361**
▼ • ➤ Public Reason (ROM ISSN 2065-7285) **6945**
Public Relations Agency Insider *see* P R Agency Insider **31**
Public Relations Almanach *see* P R Almanach **31**
Public Relations Consultancies *see* Business Ratio. Public Relations Consultancies **22**
Public Relations Consultants Association Yearbook *see* P R C A Yearbook **31**
• Public Relations Forum (DEU ISSN 0949-8052) **33**
Public Relations Investor Relations *see* P R I R **31**
▼ • ➤ Public Relations Journal (Online) (USA ISSN 1942-4604) **33**
Public Relations Journal of India (IND ISSN 0033-3689) **33**
Public Relations Journal Register Issue *see* Public Relations Society of America Directory **2024**
Public Relations Magazin *see* P R - Magazin **31**
Public Relations News *see* P R News **31**
Public Relations Office of the Sugar Industry *see* P R O S I **3659**
Public Relations Office of the Sugar Industry. Annuaire (MUS) **3661**
Public Relations Praxis *see* P R - Praxis **31**
• Public Relations Quarterly (USA ISSN 0033-3700) **33**
Public Relations Report *see* P R Report **31**
• Public Relations Review (GBR ISSN 0363-8111) **33**
Public Relations Society of America Directory (USA) **2024**
• Public Relations Strategist (USA ISSN 1082-9113) **33**
• Public Relations Tactics (USA ISSN 1080-6792) **33**
Public Relations Week (UK Edition) *see* P R Week (UK Edition) **32**
Public Relations Week (US Edition) *see* P R Week (US Edition) **32**
Public Relations World *see* Gongguan Shijie **25**
Public Report - Ombudsman of British Columbia *see* British Columbia. Office of the Ombudsman. Public Report Series **7424**
Public Risk (USA ISSN 0891-7183) **1787**
• Public Roads (USA ISSN 0033-3735) **3281**
Public Safety Communications (USA ISSN 1526-1646) **7537**
Public Safety Funding Solution (USA) **7537**
• Public Safety I T (USA) **2679**
Public School Enrollment and Staff, New York State (USA ISSN 0197-2901) **3030**
Public School Programs (Year)/Programmes des Ecoles Publiques (CAN ISSN 0709-6607) **2901**
Public Sculpture of Britain (GBR) **513**
Public Sector (GBR) **3559**
• Public Sector (NZL ISSN 0110-5191) **7463**
Public Sector (USA) **7463**
Public Sector (Year) Information Systems & E-Business Spending (USA) **2435**
Public Sector Accounting *see* C I C A Public Sector Accounting Handbook **1283**
Public Sector Director *see* Moderngov **1780**
Public Sector Executive (GBR ISSN 1477-9331) **7463**
Public Sector IT Insight (GBR ISSN 1367-2290) **2435**
Public Sector Management/Management et Secteur Public (CAN ISSN 1183-1081) **7463**
▼ Public Sector Procurement (GBR ISSN 1754-7849) **7463**
• Public Sector Property (GBR ISSN 1460-7190) **1838**
• Public Sector Review (AUS) **7463**
Public Sector Review (Macclesfield) (GBR ISSN 1749-5784) **7463**
Public Sector Standard Conditions of Contract (Year) (SGP) **1030**
Public Sector Standard Conditions of Contract for Design and Build (Year) (SGP) **1030**
Public Sector Times (IRL ISSN 0790-1232) **7463**
Public Sector Voice (AUS) **4601**
Public Security (GBR) **2679**
Public Servant (GBR ISSN 1744-1781) **7463**
Public Servant (GUY) **7463**
Public Service Advertising *see* P S A **32**
Public Service Advertising Bulletin (USA) **33**
Public Service Alliance of Canada Union Update *see* P S A C Union Update **4600**
Public Service & Local Government *see* P S L G **7459**
Public Service Association Journal (NZL ISSN 0110-6945) **7463**
Public Service Board Bulletin *see* P S B Bulletin **8979**
• Public Service Commission of Canada. Annual Report (Online) (CAN ISSN 1912-0842) **7463**
• Public Service Commission of Canada. Annual Report (Print) (CAN ISSN 0701-7820) **7463**
• Public Service Commission of Canada. Annual Report. Highlights (CAN ISSN 1912-0613) **7463**
Public Service Commission of Canada. Appeal Board Decisions (CAN ISSN 0226-0360) **4851**
• Public Service Commission of Canada. Performance Report (CAN ISSN 1483-8850) **7463**
Public Service Human Resources Management Agency of Canada. Annual Report on Official Languages (Online) *see* Canada Public Service Agency. Annual Report on Official Languages (Online) **1857**
Public Service Human Resources Management Agency of Canada. Annual Report on Official Languages (Print) *see* Canada Public Service Agency. Annual Report on Official Languages (Print) **1857**
• Public Service Integrity Office. Annual Report to Parliament/Bureau de l'Integrite de la Fonction Publique. Rapport Annuel au Parlement (CAN ISSN 1709-7274) **7463**
Public Service Magazine (GBR ISSN 1460-8936) **4601**
Public Service Pension Plan Annual Report (CAN ISSN 1201-4192) **1646**
Public Service Pension Plan. Pension News (CAN ISSN 1912-4023) **1704**
Public Service Review. Central Government (GBR ISSN 1470-5257) **7463**
Public Service Review. Construction (GBR ISSN 1743-016X) **7463**
Public Service Review. D F I D *see* Public Service Review. Intenational Development **1604**
Public Service Review. Department of Trade and Industry (GBR ISSN 1474-8029) **7463**
Public Service Review. Department of Transport, Local Government and the Regions *see* Public Service Review. Transport, Local Government and the Regions **7501**
Public Service Review. Devolved Government (GBR ISSN 1473-9275) **7463**
Public Service Review. European Union (GBR ISSN 1472-3395) **7463**
Public Service Review. Finance (GBR ISSN 1478-6699) **7463**
Public Service Review. Health (GBR ISSN 1742-2078) **7537**
Public Service Review. Home Office (GBR ISSN 1469-6819) **2228**
Public Service Review. Intenational Development (GBR ISSN 1744-179X) **1604**
Public Service Review. P F I - P P P (Private Finance Initiative - Public Private Partnerships) (GBR ISSN 1471-6046) **1941**
Public Service Review. Transport, Local Government and the Regions (GBR ISSN 1478-2200) **7501**
Public Service Staff Relations Board Decisions *see* Public Service Staff Relations Board. Summaries of Decisions **7463**
Public Service Staff Relations Board. Summaries of Decisions (CAN ISSN 1499-6499) **7463**
• Public Service Staffing Tribunal Annual Report (Online) (CAN ISSN 1912-0699) **1873**
• Public Service Staffing Tribunal Annual Report (Print) (CAN ISSN 1912-0672) **1873**
Public Service Workplace (GBR ISSN 1466-2167) **1854**
Public Services Information Bulletin (GBR) **8064**
• ➤ Public Services Quarterly (USA ISSN 1522-8959) **5041**
▼ • ➤ Public Space (AUS ISSN 1835-0550) **4763**
A Public Space (USA ISSN 1558-965X) **5355**
Public Television Transcripts Index (USA ISSN 0897-9642) **2348**
▼ • Public Transport (DEU ISSN 1866-749X) **8509**
Public Transport International (Deutsche Ausgabe) *see* Public Transport International (French Edition) **8509**
Public Transport International (English Edition) *see* Public Transport International (French Edition) **8509**
Public Transport International (French Edition) (BEL ISSN 1029-1261) **8509**
Public Transport Market Assessment *see* Key Note Market Assessment. Public Transport **8502**
Public Transportation Fact Book (USA) **8528**
• Public Trustee. Annual Report (AUS ISSN 1441-2799) **4905**
• ➤ Public Understanding of Science (GBR ISSN 0963-6625) **7900**
Public Use of the National Park System (Washington) *see* U.S. National Park Service. Public Use of the National Park System: Fiscal Year Report **2630**
Public Utilities *see* Chengshi Gongyong Shiye **7429**
• Public Utilities Fortnightly (USA ISSN 1078-5892) **3510**
• Public Utilities Reports (USA ISSN 0196-7843) **3145**
Public Utilities Reports Utility Weekly *see* P U R Utility Weekly **3144**
Public Utility and Transportation Manual *see* Mergent Public Utility & Transportation Manual **7453**
• A Public Voice (Online) (USA) **2999**
• Public Works (USA ISSN 0033-3840) **7501**
Public Works and Constructions in Oita Prefecture. Outline *see* Doboku Kenchiku Gyosei no Gaiyo **3265**
• Public Works and Government Services Canada. Sustainable Development Strategy/Strategie de Developpement Durable (CAN ISSN 1912-5062) **1162**
• ➤ Public Works Management & Policy (USA ISSN 1087-724X) **7463**
Public Works Research Institute. Annual Report *see* Doboku Kenkyujo Nenpo **3265**
Public Works Research Institute. Journal of Research (JPN ISSN 0416-1351) **3281**
Public Works Research Institute. Proceedings *see* Doboku Kenkyujo Koenkai Koenshu **3265**
Public Works Research Institute. Proceedings of Meeting *see* Doboku Kenkyujo Kenkyu Happyokai Ronbunshu **3265**
Public Works Research Institute. Report *see* Doboku Kenkyujo Hokoku **3265**
Public Works Research Institute. Report of Research Results (JPN) **3281**
Public Works Research Institute. Technical Memorandum *see* Doboku Kenkyujo Shiryo **3265**
Public Works Research Institute. Technical Note *see* Doboku Kenkyujo Iho **3265**
Public Worlds Series (USA) **352**
Publicacion del C I F F y H *see* Centro de Investigaciones, Facultad de Filosofia y Humanidades. Publicacion **4447**
Publicacion del Distribuidor de Informatica *see* P V D **2493**
Publicacion I A A *see* Instituto Antartico Argentino. Publicacion **2710**
Publicaciones (ARG) **352**
• Publicaciones de Biologia. Serie Botanica (ESP ISSN 1130-9113) **814**
Publicaciones Matematicas del Uruguay (URY ISSN 0797-1443) **5526**
Publicaciones Recientes sobre la Union Europea Recibidas por la Biblioteca *see* Recent Publications on the European Union Received by the Library **7200**
• Publicaciones Seriadas Cubanas (CUB ISSN 0864-3598) **7570**
Publicaciones UNAM *see* Catalogo de Ventas **622**
➤ Publicacions Matematiques (ESP ISSN 0214-1493) **5526**
Publicacoes Culturais da Companhia (AGO) **7900**
The Publican Newspaper (GBR ISSN 1365-5817) **609**
➤ Publicar en Antropologia y Ciencias Sociales (ARG ISSN 0327-6627) **352**
Publicatieblad van de Europese Gemeenschappen. Serie L & C: Wetgeving, Mededelingen en Bekendmakingen *see* Official Journal of the European Union. L & C Series: Legislation and Information Notices (Quarterly Edition) **4937**
▼ Publicatiereeks Amsterdamse Monumenten (NLD ISSN 1875-7839) **412**
Publicatii din Romania (ROM) **634**
Publicatio U E P G. Ciencias Biologicas e da Saude (Universidade Estadual de Ponta Grossa) (BRA ISSN 1676-8485) **699**
Publicatio U E P G. Ciencias Exatas e da Terra, Ciencias Agrarias e Engenharias (Universidade Estadual de Ponta Grossa) (BRA ISSN 1676-8477) **7900**
Publicatio U E P G. Ciencias Humanas, Ciencias Sociais Aplicadas, Linguistica, Letras e Artes (Universidade Estadual de Ponta Grossa) (BRA ISSN 1676-8493) **4470**
Publication - Brome County Historical Society *see* Brome County Historical Society. Publication **4286**
Publication de la Revue Generale de Droit International Public (FRA ISSN 0035-3094) **4938**
A Publication Of The Corporate Counsel Section Of The New York State Bar Association *see* Inside (Albany) **4870**
Publication Profiles (CAN ISSN 0836-5024) **33**
Publication Speciale Canadienne des Sciences Halieutiques et Aquatiques *see* Canadian Special Publication of Fisheries and Aquatic Sciences **3588**
Publicationes Bibliothecae Academiae Scientiarum Hungaricae *see* Magyar Tudomanyos Akademia Konyvtaranak Kozlemenyei **7938**
➤ Publicationes Mathematicae (HUN ISSN 0033-3883) **5526**
Publicationes Universitatis Miskolciensis. Sectio Philosophica (HUN ISSN 1219-5448) **4471**
Publicationes Universitatis Miskolciensis. Series Juridica et Politica (HUN ISSN 0866-6032) **4763**
Publications de la Societe Archeologique du Jutland *see* Jysk Arkaeologisk Selskab. Skrifter **4236**
Publications de l'Institut Mathematique *see* Institut Mathematique. Publications **5494**
Publications de l'Institut Orientaliste de Louvain *see* Universite Catholique de Louvain. Institut Orientaliste. Publications **4189**
Publications et Bases de Donnees (LUX ISSN 1606-4879) **1259**
Publications from the Sado Museum *see* Sado Hakubutsukan Kenkyu Hokoku **7906**
Publications in Archaeology (USA ISSN 0270-1308) **2625**
Publications in Climatology (USA ISSN 0160-9599) **6393**
Publications in Medieval Studies (USA ISSN 0079-7677) **4255**
Publications in Modern Chinese Language and Literature (DEU ISSN 1574-4825) **5355**
Publications in the American West (USA ISSN 0085-5227) **4309**
• ➤ Publications of Astronomical Society of Japan/Nihon Tenmon Gakkai Obun Kenkyu Hokoku (JPN ISSN 0004-6264) **580**
Publications of Oulu University Library *see* Oulun Yliopiston Kirjaston Julkaisuja **5038**
➤ Publications of the American Dialect Society (USA ISSN 0002-8207) **5163**
Publications of the Astronomical Society of the Pacific *see* Astronomical Society of the Pacific. Publications **570**
Publications of the De Wulf-Mansion Centre *see* Ancient and Medieval Philosophy. Series 1, Publications of De Wulf-Mansion Centre **6904**
• Publications of the I R S (Online) (USA) **1941**
Publications of the Institute of Geophysics. A: Physics of the Earth's Interior *see* Polish Academy of Sciences. Institute of Geophysics. Publications. Series A: Physics of the Earth's Interior **2788**
Publications of the Institute of Geophysics. B: Seismology *see* Polish Academy of Sciences. Institute of Geophysics. Publications. Series B: Seismology **2788**
Publications of the Institute of Geophysics. C: Geomagnetism *see* Polish Academy of Sciences. Institute of Geophysics. Publications. Series C: Geomagnetism **2788**
Publications of the Institute of Geophysics. D: Physics of the Atmosphere *see* Polish Academy of Sciences. Institute of Geophysics. Publications. Series D: Physics of the Atmosphere **2788**
Publications of the Institute of Geophysics. E: Water Resources *see* Polish Academy of Sciences. Institute of Geophysics. Publications. Series E: Water Resources **2788**
Publications of the Institute of Geophysics. F: Planetary Geodesy *see* Polish Academy of Sciences. Institute of Geophysics. Publications. Series F: Planetary Geodesy **2788**
Publications of the Institute of Geophysics. M: Miscellanea *see* Polish Academy of Sciences. Institute of Geophysics. Publications. Series M: Miscellanea **2788**
Publications of the Mississippi Philological Association *see* Mississippi Philological Association. Publications **5334**
Publications of the Modern Language Association of America *see* P M L A **5347**

Title

10772 PUBLICATIONS OF THE NEWTON INSTITUTE ULRICH'S PERIODICALS

† Publications of the Newton Institute (GBR ISSN 1366-2651) **8983**
Publications of the Sir Thomas Browne Institute *see* Sir Thomas Browne Institute. Publications. New Series **8988**
Publications of the Society for Psychological Anthropology *see* Society for Psychological Anthropology. Publications **8989**
Publications of the Thoresby Society *see* Thoresby Society. Publications **4164**
Publications of the University of Aarhus *see* Acta Jutlandica **3833**
Publications of the University of Miskolc. Series F. Economic Sciences *see* Business Studies **1076**
Publications on English Themes *see* P O E T **5159**
Publications on English Themes *see* P O E T **5159**
➤ Publications on Ocean Development (NLD ISSN 0924-1922) **2816**
Publications on Russia and Eastern Europe of the School of International Studies, University of Washington *see* School of International Studies. Publications on Russia and Eastern Europe **7181**
Publications Recentes sur l'Union Europeenne Recues par la Bibliotheque *see* Recent Publications on the European Union Received by the Library **7200**
Publications Romanes et Francaises (CHE ISSN 0079-7812) **5355**
Publications Universitaires Europeennes. Serie 23: Theologie *see* European University Studies. Series 23: Theology **7963**
Publications Universitaires Europeennes. Serie 9: Lingua e Letteratura Italiana *see* Europaeische Hochschulschriften. Reihe 9: Italienische Sprache und Literatur **5117**
Publications Yearbook, Republic of China *see* Zhonghua Minguo Chuban Nianjian **7576**
Publicidad y Mercadeo (VEN) **33**
• Publico (MEX ISSN 1563-7778) **3910**
• Publicus (CHE ISSN 0080-7249) **7464**
Publiek Domein (NLD ISSN 1380-5525) **7900**
Publiek Rechtelijke Bedrijfsorganisatie Blad *see* P B O Blad **7459**
† Publieke Dienstverlening: Van Vandaag naar Morgen (NLD ISSN 1871-9384) **8983**
▼ Publieke Werken (NLD ISSN 1877-5543) **4424**
Publieke Zaken *see* Fact (Rotterdam) **1288**
PubLife *see* PubChef **4396**
Publik-Forum (DEU ISSN 0343-1401) **7672**
Publikatieblad van de Europese Gemeenschappen. C: Mededelingen en Bekendmakingen *see* Official Journal of the European Union **7256**
Publikatieblad van de Europese Gemeenschappen. C: Mededelingen en Bekendmakingen *see* Diario Oficial de las Comunidades Europeas. C: Comunicaciones e Informaciones **4923**
Publikatieblad van de Europese Gemeenschappen. L Serie: Wetgeving *see* Official Journal of the European Union. L Series: Legislation **7256**
Publikaties van de Faculteit der Historische en Kunstwetenschappen *see* Erasmus Universiteit. Faculteit der Historsiche en Kunstwetenschappen. Publikaties **4139**
Publikation foer Svenska Narkotikapolisfoereningen *see* Svenska Narkotikapolisfoereningen. Publikation **2669**
Publikationen der G K S S (DEU ISSN 1439-474X) **7900**
Publikationen der Universitaetsbibliothek Basel *see* Universitaetsbibliothek Basel. Publikationen **638**
Publikationen zur Zeitschrift fuer Germanistik (CHE ISSN 1660-0088) **5355**
Publio (USA ISSN 1934-8827) **5355**
Publiquip (CAN ISSN 0829-6359) **1030**
• Publish (BRA ISSN 0103-8869) **7580**
Publish (NLD ISSN 1566-1474) **2582**
• Publish (RUS ISSN 1560-5183) **7580**
Publish & Print (BEL ISSN 1377-5685) **7580**
Publish.de (DEU) **7570**
Publish Portugal (PRT) **7580**
Publisher (CAN ISSN 0380-8025) **7570**
The Publisher (NGA ISSN 0331-7714) **7570**
• Publisher (Online) (NZL ISSN 1177-6870) **7570**
• Publisher Plug-In (USA) **2566**
Publishers Association Brief *see* P A Brief **7569**
Publishers Association News Update *see* P A News Update **7569**
Publishers Association of the South Newsletter *see* P A S Newsletter **7569**
Publishers Association. Quarterly Statistics (GBR) **7570**
• Publishers' Auxiliary (USA ISSN 0048-5942) **4582**
• Publisher's Directory (USA ISSN 0742-0501) **7570**
• Publishers, Distributors & Wholesalers of the United States (USA ISSN 0000-0671) **2024**
Publishers Information Bureau Report (USA) **33**
• Publishers' International I S B N Directory (Year) (International Standard Book Number) (DEU ISSN 0939-1975) **7570**
• Publishers' International I S B N Directory Plus (International Standard Book Number) (DEU ISSN 0000-1716) **7571**
Publishers' Monthly (IND) **7571**
• Publisher's Report (USA ISSN 0884-3090) **7571**
• Publishers Weekly (USA ISSN 0000-0019) **7571**
Publishers Weekly Booklife *see* P W Booklife **7569**
Publishers Weekly Daily for Booksellers *see* P W Daily for Booksellers **7569**
Publishers Weekly Newsline *see* P W Newsline **7569**
Publishers Weekly Religion BookLine *see* P W Religion BookLine **7569**
• Publishers Weekly Rights Alert (USA) **7571**
Publishing & Printing *see* Chuban yu Yinshua **7558**
• Publishing Executive (USA ISSN 1558-9641) **7571**
Publishing for Intranets: Money Making Strategies for Reaching the Corporate Desktop (USA) **2503**
• Publishing For Library Markets (Year) (USA ISSN 1539-1213) **7571**
• Publishing for Professional Markets (USA ISSN 1523-7524) **7571**
• ➤ Publishing History (GBR ISSN 0309-2445) **7571**
• The Publishing Industry (GBR ISSN 1478-3274) **1902**
Publishing Law Update *see* PubLaw Update **4763**
Publishing Magazine (GBR) **7571**
Publishing News (GBR ISSN 0261-5398) **7571**
Publishing Pathways (GBR) **7571**
• Publishing Perspectives (USA) **7571**
• Publishing Poynters (USA) **1838**
Publishing Praxis (DEU ISSN 0948-1931) **7580**
Publishing Reference: New Readings *see* Chuban Cankao **7558**
Publishing Research *see* Chuban Faxing Yanjiu **7558**
• ➤ Publishing Research Quarterly (USA ISSN 1053-8801) **7571**
Publishing Scotland Yearbook (Year) (GBR) **7571**
• Publishing Today (New Delhi, 2006) (IND) **7571**
Publishing Work *see* Chuban Gongzuo **7558**
† Publitransport (ITA ISSN 0033-3999) **8983**
• Publituris (PRT) **8749**
• ➤ Publius (GBR ISSN 0048-5950) **7174**
• ➤ Publizistik (DEU ISSN 0033-4006) **2336**
Puchatkowe Zabawy (POL ISSN 1895-5665) **2209**
The Puck Review (USA ISSN 1934-323X) **5355**
Puckerbrush Review (USA ISSN 0890-3433) **5235**
➤ The Pudding Magazine (USA ISSN 0196-5913) **5432**
Puddler (USA ISSN 1073-8320) **2209**
Der Pudel Spiegel (DEU) **6814**
Pudhari (IND) **3887**
El Pueblo (PER) **3928**
Pueblo Continente (PER ISSN 1991-5837) **2901**
Pueblo Unido (USA) **7174**
Puente (PER ISSN 1810-6145) **2336**
Puentelibre (MEX ISSN 1405-1680) **513**
Puericultura Market (ESP ISSN 1134-038X) **4562**
La Puerta (PRY ISSN 1017-2815) **8881**
Puerta del Sol (USA ISSN 1041-2026) **3559**
Puertanueva (ESP ISSN 1132-7707) **2901**
Puertanueva. Anexo (ESP ISSN 1132-7715) **2901**
Puertas Abiertas (ARG ISSN 1669-8886) **5163**
Puerto del Sol (USA ISSN 0738-517X) **5355**
Puerto Rico. Bureau of Labor Statistics. Census of Manufacturing Industries of Puerto Rico *see* Census of Manufacturing Industries of Puerto Rico **1882**
Puerto Rico Business Review (PRI ISSN 0270-126X) **1377**
Puerto Rico, Culebra & Vieques *see* Rum & Reggae's Puerto Rico, Culebra & Vieques **8753**
Puerto Rico. Departamento de la Vivienda. Secretaria Auxiliar de Planification y Programacion. Informe Anual (PRI) **4424**
Puerto Rico. Department of Health. Boletin Estadistico (PRI) **8064**
Puerto Rico. Department of Health. Informe Estadistico de Facilidades de Salud (PRI) **4109**
Puerto Rico. Department of Health. Office of Health Statistics. Division of Statistics and Reports. Annual Vital Statistics Report/Informe Anual de Estadisticas Vitales (PRI) **7314**
Puerto Rico. Department of Labor. Directorio de Organizaciones del Trabajo (PRI) **4601**
Puerto Rico. Department of Labor. Empleo, Asalariado no Agricola en Puerto Rico (PRI) **1259**
Puerto Rico Economic Indicators (PRI) **1259**
Puerto Rico. Fisheries Research Laboratory. Technical Report (PRI) **3605**
• Puerto Rico Health Sciences Journal (PRI ISSN 0738-0658) **5700**
Puerto Rico Living (PRI ISSN 0033-4049) **3932**
Puerto Rico Official Industrial Directory (PRI ISSN 0090-3612) **2024**
Puerto Rico. Oficina de Estadisticas Agricolas. Boletin Semestral de Estadisticas Agricolas (PRI) **185**
Puerto Rico. Ports Authority. Statistical Summary (PRI) **8550**
Puerto Rico Report (USA ISSN 1541-5473) **7214**
Puerto Rico Tax Reporter (USA) **1941**
• Puerto Rico Taxes (USA ISSN 0735-7893) **1941**
Puerto Rico Travel & Tourism (PRI ISSN 1548-4769) **8749**
Puertos y Navieras *see* Puertos y Navieras y Transporte Maritimo **8657**
Puertos y Navieras y Transporte Maritimo (ESP ISSN 1695-8985) **8657**
➤ Puesta al Dia en Urgencias, Emergencias y Catastrofes (ESP ISSN 1576-0316) **6071**
Puff (DNK ISSN 0106-2018) **1030**
Pug Dog Club of America. Bulletin (USA) **6814**
Puget Consumers Co-op Sound Consumer *see* P C C Sound Consumer **6668**
• Puget Sound Business Journal (USA ISSN 8750-7757) **1162**
Puget Sound Co-Op Federation Newsletter (USA) **8064**
Puget Sound Computer User *see* Puget Sound ComputerUser **2582**
Puget Sound ComputerUser (USA ISSN 0886-8174) **2582**
• Puget Sound Consumers' Checkbook (USA ISSN 1542-3514) **2641**
Puget Sound Journey (USA ISSN 1540-5141) **8749**
Puget Sound Parent (USA) **2166**
Puget Sound Regional Council. Regional View (USA) **8633**
Puglia Imperiale Magazine (ITA ISSN 1828-9290) **8749**
Pugwash Occasional Papers (USA ISSN 1932-6297) **7261**
Pugyong Taehakkyo Haeyang Kwahak Kongdong Yon'guso Yon'gu Nonmunjip/Pukyong National University. Korea Inter-University Institute of Ocean Science. Contributions (KOR) **699**
Puhe ja Kieli/Speech and Language/Tal och Spraak (FIN ISSN 1458-3410) **5163**
Puhelin/Telephone (FIN ISSN 0048-5977) **2371**
Puig Castellar (ESP ISSN 0214-1000) **6536**
Puissance Maximale de l'Energie Electrique et Charge des Reseaux *see* Electric Power Capability and Load **3157**
Pukyong National University. Korea Inter-University Institute of Ocean Science. Contributions *see* Pugyong Taehakkyo Haeyang Kwahak Kongdong Yon'guso Yon'gu Nonmunjip **699**
➤ Pula (BWA ISSN 0256-2316) **7261**
Pulborough, Storrington and Steyning Guardian *see* Worthing Guardian **3873**
• La Pulce (ITA ISSN 1128-4684) **33**
Pulheimer Beitraege zur Geschichte und Heimatkunde (DEU ISSN 0171-3426) **4255**
Puli News (USA) **6814**
Pulicatieblad van de Europese Gemeenschappen. Bijlage. Handelingen *see* Diario Oficial de las Comunidades Europeas. Anexo Debates **4923**
Pulizia Industriale e Sanificazione (ITA ISSN 0393-1072) **7538**
Pull (USA) **8194**
The Puller (USA ISSN 8750-4219) **8194**
Pulmon (IND ISSN 0973-3809) **6217**
▼ Pulmonary Circulation (IND) **6218**
• ➤ Pulmonary Perspectives (USA) **6218**
• ➤ Pulmonary Pharmacology and Therapeutics (GBR ISSN 1094-5539) **6218**
• Pulmonary Physiology (USA ISSN 1540-7764) **5798**
• Pulmonary Reviews (USA ISSN 1086-4423) **6218**
Pulmonary Vascular Research Institute Review *see* P V R I Review **5797**
• ➤ Pulmonology (RUS ISSN 0869-0189) **6218**
• Pulmonology Coding Alert (USA ISSN 1529-6121) **4520**
Pulp (NZL ISSN 1174-460X) **2209**
Pulp & Paper *see* Pulp & Paper International **6737**
Pulp & Paper Buyers Guide (USA) **6737**
Pulp and Paper Buyers Guide *see* Pulp & Paper Buyers Guide **6737**
• Pulp & Paper Canada (CAN ISSN 0316-4004) **6737**
• Pulp & Paper Canada Annual Directory (CAN ISSN 0709-2563) **6737**
Pulp and Paper Company Profiles (Year) *see* Pulp & Paper Company Profiles (Year) **6737**
Pulp & Paper Company Profiles (Year) (USA) **6737**
† • Pulp & Paper Edge (AUS ISSN 1449-9703) **8983**
† • Pulp & Paper Europe (USA ISSN 1370-754X) **8983**
Pulp and Paper Industry Asia *see* P P I Asia **6735**
Pulp & Paper Industry Global Fact & Price Book *see* P P I Global Fact & Price Book **6735**
• Pulp and Paper Industry Technical Conference. Conference Record (USA ISSN 1041-7249) **6737**
Pulp and Paper Internaitonal European Company Profiles *see* P P I's European Company Profiles **6735**
• Pulp & Paper International (USA ISSN 0033-409X) **6737**
Pulp & Paper International's European Company Profiles *see* P P I's European Company Profiles **6735**
Pulp & Paper North American Factbook (USA) **6737**
• Pulp & Paper Project Update (USA) **6738**
Pulp and Paper Research Institute of Canada. Annual Report (CAN ISSN 0079-7960) **6738**
• Pulp and Paper Technical Association of Canada. Annual Meeting. Preprints A/Association Technique des Pates et Papiers du Canada. Congres Annuel. Pretires A (CAN ISSN 1494-7722) **6738**
Pulp and Paper Technical Association of Canada. Annual Meeting. Preprints B/Association Technique des Pates et Papiers du Canada. Congres Annuel. Pretires B (CAN) **6738**
Pulp and Paper Technical Association of Canada. Annual Meeting Preprints CD *see* Pulp and Paper Technical Association of Canada. Annual Meeting. Preprints A **6738**
Pulp & Paper Technical Association of Canada. Indices/Association Technique des Pates et Papiers du Canada. Listes (CAN) **6740**
Pulp and Paper Technical Association of Canada. Meeting. Preprint Book C (CAN ISSN 1494-4138) **6738**
Pulp and Paper Technical Association of Canada. News Bulletin (CAN ISSN 1493-017X) **6738**
• Pulp & Paper Week (USA ISSN 0738-0917) **6738**
Pulp & Paper Yearbook (ZAF) **6738**
Pulp Fictions (ZAF ISSN 1992-5174) **4851**
Pulp Tales (USA) **5414**
Pulping Conference. Proceedings *see* T A P P I Pulping Conference. Proceedings **6739**
Pulpit Helps (USA) **7672**
The Pulpit of Islam *see* Minbar al-Islam **7714**
Pulpit Resource (USA ISSN 0195-1548) **7672**
Puls (CZE ISSN 1211-7404) **8847**
Puls-Dossier (CHE ISSN 1424-6082) **6995**
Pul's Povolzh'ya (RUS) **3940**
Puls-Tip (CHE ISSN 1424-6090) **6995**
• Pulsar (AUT ISSN 1605-4652) **314**
Pulse *see* ProCare Pulse **7536**
Pulse (Bedford) (GBR ISSN 1476-6019) **2687**
The Pulse (Brighton) (GBR) **2297**
The Pulse (Cedar Falls) (USA ISSN 0033-4189) **5979**
Pulse (Cypress) (USA ISSN 0555-6953) **8805**
Pulse (Johannesburg) (ZAF ISSN 0256-6028) **3216**
Pulse (Lexington) (USA ISSN 1525-9226) **590**
• Pulse (London, 1959) (GBR ISSN 0048-6000) **5700**
Pulse (London) *see* Viewpoint (London, 1995) **6189**
• Pulse! (Washington) (USA) **1787**
• Pulse Berlin (DEU ISSN 1860-5451) **5355**
• Pulse Buyers Guide (ZAF ISSN 0256-6036) **3111**
Pulse International (PAK) **5700**
▼ Pulse Magazine (USA ISSN 1940-1604) **5081**
▼ • The Pulse Magazine (USA ISSN 1946-7257) **5979**
Pulse of the Planet (USA ISSN 1041-6773) **3461**
Pulse of Youth (IND ISSN 0033-4227) **2209**
Pulse Weekly (USA) **3986**
Pulsed Power Conference. Proceedings (USA) **3328**
Pulsepoint (CAN ISSN 1701-9125) **249**
Pulsional Revista de Psicanalise (BRA ISSN 1517-5316) **7402**
Pulso (ESP ISSN 1577-0338) **2901**
• Pulso (MEX ISSN 1605-0428) **3910**
• Pulso (Online) (USA) **4582**
• Pulso Analitico (BOL ISSN 1609-7076) **1513**
† Pulso Bursatil (ESP) **8983**
Pulso Digital *see* Pulso Semanario **3803**
• Pulso Semanario (BOL) **3803**
Der Pulsschlag (DEU) **4084**
Pulteney St. Survey (USA ISSN 0883-6590) **2297**
• The Pulver Report (USA) **2566**
Pumapunku (BOL) **352**
• Pump Industry Analyst (GBR ISSN 1359-6128) **5459**
Pump Price Report (USA) **6790**
Pump Talk (GBR) **3364**
• ➤ Pump Users Symposium. Proceedings (USA) **5459**
▼ Pumpe (NLD) **3364**
Pumpen *see* Informationsdienst F I Z Technik. Pumpen **3231**
Pumpen und Kompressoren (DEU ISSN 1611-4221) **3356**
Pumper (USA) **4125**
Pumps and Compressors *see* Pumpen und Kompressoren **3356**
Pumps & Hydraulics (USA ISSN 1559-5854) **3364**
• Pumps and Processes (USA) **3394**
Pumps and Systems (USA ISSN 1065-108X) **3394**
Pumuckl (DEU) **2209**
Pun American Newsletter (USA ISSN 1077-1948) **5355**
Pun Intended (USA) **5235**
Puna/Travail (ALB) **4601**
Puna Korero *see* Journal of Maori and Pacific Development **1600**
• Punch (GBR ISSN 0033-4278) **5235**
• Punch in International Travel and Entertainment Magazine (USA ISSN 1053-3842) **8749**
The Punch List (USA) **1704**
† Puncto! (DEU ISSN 1439-0019) **8983**
Punctuality Statistics Heathrow, Gatwick, Manchester, Birmingham, Luton and Stanstead - Full Analysis *see* Great Britain. Civil Aviation Authority. Punctuality Statistics Heathrow, Gatwick, Manchester, Birmingham, Luton and Stanstead - Full Analysis **8525**
Punctuality Statistics Heathrow, Gatwick, Manchester, Birmingham, Luton and Stanstead - Summary Analysis *see* Great Britain. Civil Aviation Authority. Punctuality Statistics Heathrow, Gatwick, Manchester, Birmingham, Luton and Stanstead - Summary Analysis **8525**
Punctuality Statistics - Summary Analysis *see* Great Britain. Civil Aviation Authority. Punctuality Statistics Heathrow, Gatwick, Manchester, Birmingham, Luton and Stanstead - Summary Analysis **8525**
† Puncture (USA ISSN 1047-4528) **8983**
• The Pundit (AUS ISSN 1833-7848) **6510**
Pundit (CAN ISSN 0712-1318) **5355**
† • Pungolo (ITA) **8983**
Pungolo del Sud (ITA ISSN 0033-4286) **3898**
† Pungolo Verde (ITA ISSN 0033-4294) **8983**
▼ • Punica Fides (ESP ISSN 1988-768X) **5163**
• ➤ Punishment & Society (GBR ISSN 1462-4745) **2666**
Punitive Damages (Charlottesville) (USA) **4879**
• Punitive Damages (Eagan) (USA ISSN 1547-9382) **4840**
Punitive Damages Overview *see* Mealey's Litigation Report: Insurance Bad Faith **4836**

Punjab Agricultural University. Journal of Research (IND ISSN 0048-6019) **149**
Punjab College of Technical Education Journal of Business Management *see* P C T E Journal of Business Management **1784**
Punjab College of Technical Education Journal of Computer Sciences *see* P C T E Journal of Computer Sciences **2434**
Punjab Cooperative Union. Review (PAK) **1424**
Punjab Fruit Journal (PAK ISSN 0033-4316) **3748**
Punjab Horticultural Journal (IND ISSN 0033-4324) **3748**
Punjab Journal of English Studies *see* P J E S. Punjab Journal of English Studies **5159**
Punjab Journal of Politics (IND ISSN 0253-3960) **7261**
• Punjab Kesari (IND) **3887**
Punjab Law Reporter (IND ISSN 0033-4332) **4764**
Punjab National Bank. Annual Report (IND ISSN 0304-8101) **1377**
Punjab University Indological Series (IND) **559**
Punjab University Journal of Mathematics (PAK ISSN 1016-2526) **5526**
➤ Punjab University Journal of Zoology (PAK ISSN 1016-1597) **961**
Punjabi Digest (IND) **3887**
Punjabi Sahitya (GBR) **5235**
Punjabi Tribune (IND) **3887**
Punjabrao Krishi Vidyapeeth Research Journal *see* P K V Research Journal **145**
Punsok Hwahak (PRK ISSN 0555-781X) **7900**
Punters' Way (SGP ISSN 0218-8813) **8296**
Puntex Dental (ESP ISSN 0212-1913) **5862**
Puntex Herbolisteria y Dietetica (ESP) **6668**
Puntex Medico (ESP) **5701**
Puntex Ortopedia (ESP) **6071**
† Punto (ITA ISSN 0391-3082) **8983**
Il Punto (Pavia) (ITA ISSN 1828-583X) **3898**
Punto 21 (URY ISSN 0797-4248) **2901**
Punto 7 Review (USA ISSN 1047-3726) **7993**
Punto Croce Facile e Veloce (ITA ISSN 1724-3998) **6641**
Punto Croce. La Grande Biblioteca delle Idee (ITA ISSN 1970-8289) **6641**
Punto de Contacto *see* Point of Contact **5352**
Punto de Cruz (ESP ISSN 1576-5873) **6641**
• Punto de Encuentro (BOL ISSN 1608-1579) **7672**
El Punto de las Artes (ESP ISSN 1130-0361) **513**
Punto de Partida (MEX ISSN 0033-4367) **5355**
• ➤ Punto de Vista (ARG ISSN 0326-3061) **4471**
Punto de Vista (BOL) **7174**
El Punto de Vista de Le Monde Diplomatique (ESP ISSN 1699-0080) **7174**
† Punto d'Incontro (ITA) **8983**
Punto Final Internacional (MEX ISSN 0188-1094) **7174**
Punto Inicial (PER) **1513**
• PuntoMarket (ESP ISSN 1575-3662) **6714**
Puntos de Estres Traumatico *see* Traumatic Stress Points Newsletter **6188**
Pupil Transportation News (USA ISSN 0730-5443) **8509**
Pupila: Libros de Nuestro Tiempo (URY ISSN 0079-8061) **4157**
Puppen und Spielzeug (DEU ISSN 0722-2408) **4061**
Puppenmachen (DEU ISSN 0949-0469) **4061**
The Puppet Master (GBR ISSN 0033-4413) **8477**
Puppeteer *see* Loutkar **8473**
• Puppetry Journal (USA ISSN 0033-443X) **8477**
Puppetry Yearbook (USA ISSN 1070-3624) **8477**
Puppies U S A (USA ISSN 1093-9377) **6814**
Puppy and Dog Basics *see* Puppy & Dog Basics **6814**
Puppy & Dog Basics (CAN ISSN 1719-5713) **6814**
Puppy Basics *see* Puppy & Dog Basics **6814**
Puppy in My Pocket and Friends (GBR ISSN 1463-9688) **2209**
Puppy Love (GBR ISSN 1465-2285) **6814**
Pupukahi/Harmoniously United (USA) **6442**
Pur (DEU) **7772**
Pur-Magazin (DEU) **5235**
➤ Purabhilekh - Puratatva/Archives - Archaeology (IND ISSN 0970-1923) **4187**
Puraimari - Kea/Primary Care (JPN ISSN 0914-8426) **5701**
Purakutisu *see* Practice **5899**
Purana Research Publications, Tuebingen (DEU ISSN 0931-9158) **559**
Puranta/Planta (JPN ISSN 0915-2059) **814**
Purasuchikku Seikei Gijutsu/Plastic Molding Technology (JPN ISSN 0289-4556) **7099**
Purasuchikkusu Eji *see* Plastics Age **7096**
Puratattva (IND ISSN 0970-2105) **412**
Purazuma Kagaku Godo Shinpojumu *see* Japanese Symposium on Plasma Chemistry. News **2066**
Purazuma Kagaku Godo Shinpojumu Abusutorak Utoshu *see* Japanese Symposium on Plasma Chemistry. Abstract Papers **2094**
Purazuma Kaku Yugo Gakkai Nenkai Yokai Yokoshu/Japan Society of Plasma Sciences and Nuclear Fusion Research. Preprints of Annual Meeting (JPN) **7071**
• ➤ Purazuma Kaku Yugo Gakkaishi/Journal of Plasma and Fusion Research (JPN ISSN 0918-7928) **7071**
Purazuma Puroseshingu Kenkyukai Puroshidingusu/Plasma Processing (JPN) **7036**
Purbachal (IND) **3887**
Purbottar (IND) **5235**
PurCanada *see* PureCanada **8749**
Purchase Guide of Japan (JPN) **1580**
Purchaser Stripout *see* Texas. Railroad Commission. Oil and Gas Division. Purchaser Stripout **6795**
Purchaser's Guide to the Music Industries (USA) **6608**
• Purchasing (IND ISSN 0014-6544) **1838**
• Purchasing (Newton) (USA ISSN 0033-4448) **1839**
Purchasing and Supply Rewards (GBR ISSN 0954-6774) **1704**
• Purchasing b2b (CAN ISSN 1497-1569) **1839**
Purchasing Group Users' Handbook (USA) **4520**
The Purchasing Law Handbook (CAN) **4879**
Purchasing Magazine's Buying Strategy Forecast *see* Buying Strategy Forecast **1809**
Purchasing Management Association of Philadelphia News *see* P M News **1837**
• Purchasing Management Bulletin (USA ISSN 1080-3203) **1839**
• Purchasing Power Parities and Real Expenditures/Parites de Pouvoir d'Achat et Depenses Reelles (FRA ISSN 1015-4639) **1513**
Purchasing Today *see* Inside Supply Management **1821**
Purdue Agricultural Economics Report (USA ISSN 1057-2201) **205**
• Purdue Alumnus (USA ISSN 0033-4502) **2297**
Purdue Exponent (USA) **2297**
Purdue Studies in Romance Literatures (USA) **5355**
Purdue University. Agricultural Experiment Station. Research Bulletin (USA ISSN 0363-6011) **149**
Purdue University. Cooperative Extension Service. B P (USA ISSN 1040-2357) **814**
• Purdue University. Cooperative Extension Service. F N R (USA ISSN 1057-2112) **149**
Purdue University. Cooperative Extension Service. H E (USA ISSN 1050-9755) **149**
• Purdue University. Indiana Water Resources Research Center. Annual Report (USA) **8831**
Purdue University Musical Organizations Notes *see* P M O Notes **6604**
Purdue University. Office of Manpower Studies. Manpower & Technical Education Requirements Reports (USA) **1704**
Purdue University. Road School. Proceedings of Annual Road School (USA ISSN 0079-8142) **8633**
Purdue University. School of Electrical and Computer Engineering. Annual Research Summary (USA) **3233**
Purdue University. Water Resources Research Center. Technical Report (USA ISSN 0555-8026) **8831**
• ➤ Pure and Applied Chemistry (USA ISSN 0033-4545) **2077**
• ➤ Pure and Applied Geophysics (CHE ISSN 0033-4553) **2788**
Pure and Applied Mathematics *see* Chuncui Shuxue yu Yingyong Shuxue **5478**
Pure and Applied Mathematics *see* Sunsu Mit Eung-yong Suhag **5540**
• ➤ Pure and Applied Mathematics (USA ISSN 0079-8169) **5526**
➤ Pure and Applied Mathematics: A Wiley Interscience Series of Texts, Monographs and Tracts (USA) **5526**
• Pure and Applied Mathematics Quarterly (USA ISSN 1558-8599) **5526**
➤ Pure and Applied Mathematics Series (USA ISSN 0079-8177) **5526**
Pure and Applied Mathematika Sciences (IND ISSN 0379-3168) **5526**
▼ Pure and Applied Undergraduate Texts (USA ISSN 1943-9334) **5526**
Pure Beauty (GBR ISSN 1478-162X) **590**
Pure Brightness *see* Qing Ming **5355**
Pure Canada *see* PureCanada **8749**
Pure Facts (USA) **6668**
Pure Fantasy (NLD ISSN 1574-177X) **5446**
The Pure Fundamentalist (USA ISSN 1536-2329) **1377**
Pure Inspiration (USA ISSN 1936-8682) **6647**
Pure Mathematics and Applications (HUN ISSN 1218-4586) **5527**
Pure Power (USA ISSN 1539-1264) **6995**
Pure Power *see* Consulting - Specifying Engineer **3185**
PureCanada (CAN ISSN 1912-3493) **8749**
▼ Purely Pontoons (USA ISSN 1936-1890) **8281**
Purer Genuss (DEU) **4549**
Puresu Gijutsu *see* Press Working **5458**
Puresutoresuto Konkurito/Journal of Prestressed Concrete (JPN ISSN 0387-1983) **1030**
Purge (GBR) **5432**
Purinergic Signaling (USA) **750**
• Purinergic Signalling (NLD ISSN 1573-9538) **699**
Purinto Kairo Gakkai Semina/Japan Institute of Printed Circuit. Seminar (JPN) **3328**
Purjehtija/Seglaren (FIN ISSN 0355-6980) **8281**
Purnasa (BGD) **5355**
• Puro Periodismo (PER) **4582**
Purongo Oranga Tangata *see* Social Report **8134**
Il Purosangue in Italia (ITA) **8296**
Purple *see* Purple Journal **4471**
Purple *see* Purple Fashion **3842**
Purple and Gold (USA ISSN 0734-3612) **2901**
Purple Dot Magazine (USA) **7606**
Purple Fashion (FRA ISSN 1766-8832) **3842**
Purple Heart Magazine (USA ISSN 0279-0653) **6442**
Purple Journal (FRA ISSN 1766-8840) **4471**
Purple Light Pavilion *see* Ziguangge **1535**
Purple Mountain Observatory. Publications *see* Zijinshan Tianwentai Taikan **584**
Purple Patch (GBR ISSN 0966-5609) **5432**
Purple Report (CAN) **1162**
Purple Sky (USA ISSN 1940-2112) **6608**
Purpose (USA ISSN 0163-7274) **7740**
Purpose Magazine (USA) **5081**
▼ • Purposeful Entrepreneur Times (USA ISSN 1948-2051) **1788**
• Purposeful Pondering Ezine (USA) **5081**
Pursuing Our Italian Names Together ers *see* P O I N T ers **3778**
Pursuit *see* Zhuiqiu **3830**
Pursuit (ZAF ISSN 1811-2986) **2260**
Pursuit - S I T U (USA) **6743**
Pursuit: The Fashion Index (ZAF) **2260**
Purushartha (FRA ISSN 0339-1744) **4187**
Purvanchal Prahari (IND) **3887**
Pusat Penelitian Atma Jaya. Laporan Penelitian Keagamaan *see* Atma Jaya Research Centre. Socio-Religious Research Report **7623**
Pusat Penelitian Atma Jaya. Penelitian Tentang Kebutuhan Kesehatan Masyarakat dan Sistem Peleyanan Kesehatan di Kecamatan Penjaringan *see* Atma Jaya Research Centre. Socio-Medical Research Report **5580**
Pusat Penelitian Atma Jaya. Studi Tentang Pengembangan Pendidikan *see* Atma Jaya Research Centre. Education Development Research Report **2828**
Pusat Penelitian Perkebunan Gula Indonesia. Annual Report/Indonesian Sugar Research Center. Annual Report (IDN ISSN 0216-9967) **249**
Pusat Penelitian Perkebunan Gula Indonesia. Bulletin/Indonesian Sugar Research Center. Bulletin (IDN ISSN 0125-9997) **249**
Push and Pull (GBR) **8622**
Pushcart Prize: Best of the Small Presses (USA ISSN 0149-7863) **5355**
Pushikorogia *see* Psychologia **7396**
Pushish/ha-yi Sathi *see* Iran Surface Coatings **1016**
Pushkin (RUS) **5355**
The Pushkin Journal (USA ISSN 1071-8214) **5355**
➤ Pushkin Review/Pushkinskii Vestnik (USA ISSN 1526-1476) **5355**
Pushkinskii Vestnik *see* Pushkin Review **5355**
Pushpi (IND) **3887**
Pushto (PAK ISSN 0555-8158) **5163**
• Pustaka: Bulletin Perpustakaan Negara (MYS ISSN 0128-8679) **5041**
Pustakala Pravrtti (LKA ISSN 1391-0000) **5041**
Pustakalaya (IND ISSN 0033-4693) **5041**
Puszcza Kampinoska (POL ISSN 1232-4043) **2625**
Put' i Putevoe Khozyaistvo (RUS ISSN 0033-4715) **8622**
• Put' i Voditel' (RUS) **8599**
Put' k Sebe (RUS ISSN 0136-0078) **4471**
Put Shaktjora (KGZ) **3904**
• Te Putara (NZL ISSN 1177-4665) **7464**
Puteshestvennik (RUS) **4982**
Puthiya Ulaham (LKA) **7672**
Puti k Bezopasnosti (RUS) **7993**
• Putian Gaodeng Zhuanke Xuexiao Xuebao (CHN ISSN 1008-7885) **7993**
Putishta/Roads (BGR ISSN 1310-6848) **8633**
Putnam County Genealogical Society Journal (USA ISSN 1940-3631) **3780**
Putnam County Heritage (USA) **4309**
Putnotransportni Proizshestvia v Republika Bulgaria (BGR) **8395**
Putt-Putt World (USA ISSN 1041-5785) **8243**
• Puu/Bois/Holz/Wood (FIN ISSN 0357-9484) **1051**
Puuha-Pete (FIN ISSN 1458-2023) **2209**
Puumies (FIN ISSN 0355-953X) **1051**
Puur Bouwen *see* BouwIQ **983**
Puzha Magazine (IND ISSN 0973-273X) **3887**
Puzle Japones (ESP ISSN 1699-1680) **4343**
Puzzel Varia (NLD) **4344**
• Puzzle (Online) (ESP ISSN 1696-8573) **5041**
• Puzzle (Print) (ESP) **5041**
Puzzle Selection (GBR ISSN 1351-2714) **4344**
Puzzler Christmas Annual (GBR ISSN 1745-1108) **4344**
Puzzler's Pocket Word Search (USA ISSN 1944-4303) **4344**
• Puzzling Evidence? (USA) **3986**
• Pyat' s Plyusom (RUS) **2166**
Pyatoe Koleso *see* 5 Koleso **8614**
Pyinnya Lawka Journal (MMR) **1788**
Pyke Practical Civil Court Precedents *see* Practical Civil Court Precedents **4959**
Pymatuning Symposia in Ecology (USA) **3461**
➤ Pynchon Notes (USA ISSN 0278-1891) **5355**
The Pyongyang Times (PRK) **7174**
Pyramid (USA ISSN 1070-0579) **8194**
Pyramid Media Catalog (USA) **6510**
Pyramida (SVK ISSN 0231-9047) **5355**
The Pyrates Way (USA ISSN 1932-023X) **4344**
Pyrenae: Cronica Arqueologica (ESP ISSN 0079-8215) **412**
Pyrenees (FRA ISSN 0033-474X) **4255**
Pyrenees Advocate (AUS ISSN 1834-4100) **3796**
Pyrenees Magazine (FRA ISSN 0998-3767) **8749**
• ➤ Pyrethrum Post (KEN ISSN 0048-6043) **814**
Pyro (FRA ISSN 1770-4456) **5432**
➤ The Pyrotechnic Literature Series (USA ISSN 1087-4402) **3254**
➤ The Pyrotechnic Reference Series (USA ISSN 1080-8027) **3254**
➤ Pyrotechnica (USA ISSN 0272-6521) **3254**
Pythagoras Foundation. Newsletter (NLD ISSN 1872-3233) **5527**
Pythian International (USA ISSN 0199-0144) **2269**
Pythian Record (CAN) **2269**
• The Python Papers (AUS ISSN 1834-3147) **2509**
• Pyttersen's Nederlandse Almanak (NLD ISSN 0079-8223) **3122**
• Q (DNK ISSN 1604-0511) **3834**
• Q (GBR ISSN 0955-4955) **6608**
Q *see* Q Magazine (Milford) **2698**
• Q A (Questione Agraria) (ITA ISSN 1971-4017) **205**
• Q A (Torino) (Quality Assurance) (ITA ISSN 1971-7415) **7538**
Q A E *see* Quality Assurance in Education **2901**
Q A E *see* Quarterly Architecture Essay **454**
Q A R *see* Queensland Archaeological Research **413**
• Q A Register (Quality Assessed) (GBR) **2025**
Q A S. Quaderni di Azione Sociale (ITA ISSN 1592-5277) **7175**
Q & S *see* Organizacoes & Sociedade **4468**
Q B R *see* Queensland Business Review **1163**
Q C Circle (Quality Control) (JPN ISSN 0914-5001) **1788**
Q C N *see* Queensland Chinese News **3796**
Q C R (Quaderni del Circolo Rosselli) (ITA ISSN 1123-9700) **2269**
Q C Review (Quality Control) (USA) **8064**
Q C W A Journal (Quarter Century Wireless Association) (USA) **2388**
Q D C *see* Recording for the Blind & Dyslexic. Quarterly Disk Catalog **4071**
Q D L F *see* Universita degli Studi di Firenze. Dipartimento di Linguistica. Quaderni **5190**
Q d S *see* Quaderni di Didattica della Scrittura **5164**
Q D T (Quintessence of Dental Technology) (USA ISSN 1060-1341) **5862**
Q E D (Quarterly Enterprise Digest) (GBR ISSN 0969-1162) **1965**
Q E J *see* Arquitectura del Paisaje **3723**
Q E R Cuba, Dominican Republic, Haiti, Puerto Rico *see* Country Report. Puerto Rico **1460**
• Q E X (USA ISSN 0886-8093) **2361**
Q F *see* Quincena Fiscal **1941**
Q F F I *see* Quick Frozen Foods International **3661**
• Q F F Weekly Bulletin (Queensland Farmers' Federation) (AUS ISSN 1834-4798) **149**
Q F H *see* Queensland Family Historian **3780**
Q F I R *see* Quarterly Financial Institution Ratings **1377**
Q G (Quaderni Giornale) (ITA ISSN 1971-1042) **7571**
Q G M J *see* Queensland Government Mining Journal **6477**
Q H *see* Mark Lipinski's Quilter's Home **6640**
Q H A Review (Queensland Hotels Association) (AUS ISSN 1320-954X) **4396**
Q I R *see* Quality Improvement Report **4109**
Q J A Journal (Queensland Justices Association) (AUS) **2667**
Q J B E *see* Quarterly Journal of Finance and Accounting **1163**
Q J E *see* The Quarterly Journal of Economics **1547**
• ➤ Q J I (Quarterly Journal of Ideology) (USA ISSN 0738-9752) **7175**
• ➤ Q J M (Quarterly Journal Medicine) (GBR ISSN 1460-2725) **5701**
Q J M A M *see* Quarterly Journal of Mechanics and Applied Mathematics **5527**
• Q: Journal of Sexual Orientation & Public Policy at Harvard (USA ISSN 1532-5385) **7464**
• Q Katolsk Ungdom (NOR ISSN 1503-8998) **7813**
Q L A Bulletin/Bulletin A B Q (Quebec Library Association) (CAN ISSN 0380-7150) **5041**
Q L D Administrative Law *see* Queensland Administrative Law **7464**
Q L I *see* Queensland Legal Indices **4824**
Q L R *see* Quinnipiac Law Review **4764**
The Q L S Journal *see* Queensland Law Society Journal (Online) **4764**
Q M *see* Quaker Monthly **7740**
Q M *see* Quiltmaker **6641**
Q M A *see* Quaderni del Museo Antoniano **6608**
Q M A *see* Quality Manager's Alert **1788**
Q M H C *see* Quality Management in Health Care **4110**
Q M J *see* Quality Management Journal **1788**
Q M - Quantitative Methoden in Forschung und Praxis (DEU) **1788**
Q M R *see* Qualitative Market Research **1839**
• Q Magazine (AUS ISSN 1449-499X) **4378**
• Q Magazine (GBR) **6608**
• Q Magazine (Flushing) (USA) **2297**
Q Magazine (Milford) (USA ISSN 1556-5319) **2698**
Q N M *see* Quilter's Newsletter Magazine **6641**
Q N U Journal *see* Queensland Nurse **5979**
Q-NewZ (NZL ISSN 0111-4158) **1788**
Q-Notes (USA) **4378**
• Q O G Working Paper Series (Quality of Government) (SWE) **7175**
Q O L Newsletter *see* Patient Reported Outcomes Newsletter **5694**
Q P *see* Quality Progress **1788**
Q P A Statistical Yearbook (Quarry Products Association) (GBR) **1048**
Q P L: Quaderni Patavini di Linguistica (ITA ISSN 1122-441X) **5163**
Q P - P Q: Quantum Probability and White Noise Analysis (SGP ISSN 1793-5121) **5527**
Q R *see* Qualitative Research **7994**
Q R *see* Qualified Remodeler **1031**

Title

▼ *new title* † *ceased* • *electronic media* ➤ *refereed*

Title

DIRECTORY 2010 QUEENSLAND COUNTRY LIFE 10777

• ➤ Quaternary Geochronology (NLD ISSN 1871-1014) **2763**
• ➤ Quaternary International (GBR ISSN 1040-6182) **2763**
➤ Quaternary Newsletter (GBR ISSN 0143-2826) **2763**
➤ Quaternary of South America and Antarctic Peninsula (GBR ISSN 0168-6305) **2763**
• Quaternary Perspective (IRL ISSN 0965-1357) **2763**
Quaternary Research *see* Daiyonki Kenkyu **2730**
• ➤ Quaternary Research (USA ISSN 0033-5894) **2763**
Quaternary Research Association. Field Guide Series (GBR ISSN 0261-3611) **2763**
Quaternary Research Association Technical Guide *see* Q R A Technical Guide **2763**
• ➤ Quaternary Science Reviews (GBR ISSN 0277-3791) **2763**
Quaternary Sciences *see* Disiji Yanjiu **2731**
➤ Quaternary Sciences Center Technical Report (USA ISSN 1043-335X) **7901**
Quaternary Studies in Poland *see* Studia Quaternaria **2770**
Quatre par Quatre Plus *see* 4 x 4 Plus (French Edition) **8614**
Quatre par Quatre Tout Terrain Magazine *see* 4 x 4 Magazine **8217**
• Les Quatre Saisons du Jardin Bio (FRA ISSN 1962-5790) **3748**
Les Quatre Saisons du Jardinage *see* Les Quatre Saisons du Jardin Bio **3748**
• Quatro Rodas (BRA ISSN 0033-5908) **8749**
Quattro Zampe (ITA ISSN 0394-5898) **6814**
Quattroruote (ITA ISSN 0033-5916) **8600**
Quattroruotine (ITA ISSN 1121-5550) **4344**
▼ • Quay (USA ISSN 1935-259X) **5356**
Al-Quds (ISR ISSN 1606-3678) **3559**
Que Choisir? (FRA ISSN 0033-5932) **2641**
Que Faire? (FRA ISSN 1762-1704) **8749**
Que Faire Apres le Bac (FRA ISSN 1969-9034) **2999**
• Que Leer (ESP ISSN 1136-3916) **5235**
Que Linda! (USA) **3559**
• Que Me Dices (ESP) **3953**
• Que Onda! (Dallas - Ft.Worth) (USA) **5081**
• Que Onda! (Houston) (USA) **5081**
• Que Onda! (San Antonio) (USA) **5081**
• Que Pasa (CHL ISSN 0716-3576) **3822**
Que Pasa (PRI ISSN 0192-9364) **8749**
Que Pasa? (VEN) **3994**
Que Pasa Florida Gulf Coast (USA) **3560**
• Que se Passe-t-il a la Mine Giant? (CAN ISSN 1910-2585) **6476**
Que Tal (GBR ISSN 0033-5940) **5164**
Que Tal? (ITA ISSN 1826-1566) **5164**
• Que Tal? in the Current Skies (USA) **580**
Quebec (Province). Commission des Services Juridiques. Rapport Annuel *see* Quebec. Commission des Services Juridiques. Rapport Annuel de Gestion **4764**
Quebec (Province). Commission des Valeurs Mobilieres du Quebec. Bulletin Hebdomadaire (CAN) **1646**
Quebec (Province). Department of Energy and Resources. Geological Reports (CAN) **2763**
Quebec (Province). Direction de l' Innovation et des Technologies. Cahier d'Information (CAN) **699**
Quebec (Province). Direction de l'Innovation et des Technologies. Activites (Year) *see* Quebec (Province). Direction de l'Innovation et des Technologies. Rapport d'Activites (Year) **699**
Quebec (Province). Direction de l'Innovation et des Technologies. Rapport d'Activites (Year) (CAN ISSN 1912-6980) **699**
Quebec (Province). Ministere de l'Agriculture, des Pecheries et de l'Alimentation. Compte Rendu (CAN) **3605**
Quebec (Province). Ministere de l'Agriculture. Rapport Annuel: Merite Agricole (CAN ISSN 0701-6557) **149**
Quebec (Province). Ministere de l'Education. Direction Generale du Financement et des Equipements. Regles Budgetaires des Commission Scolaires (CAN) **3030**
Quebec (Province). Ministere de l'Environnement et Faune. Rapport Annuel (CAN) **8329**
Quebec (Province). Ministere des Affaires Municipales, du Sport et du Loisir. Rapport Annuel de Gestion *see* Quebec (Province). Ministere des Affaires Municipales et des Regions. Rapport Annuel de Gestion **7464**
Quebec (Province). Ministere des Affaires Municipales et de la Metropole. Rapport Annuel *see* Quebec (Province). Ministere des Affaires Municipales et des Regions. Rapport Annuel de Gestion **7464**
Quebec (Province). Ministere des Affaires Municipales et de la Metropole. Rapport Annuel de Gestion *see* Quebec (Province). Ministere des Affaires Municipales et des Regions. Rapport Annuel de Gestion **7464**
• Quebec (Province). Ministere des Affaires Municipales et des Regions. Rapport Annuel de Gestion (CAN ISSN 1719-8631) **7464**
Quebec (Province). Ministere des Ressources Naturelles, de la Faune et des Parcs. Rapport Annuel de Gestion *see* Quebec (Province). Ministere des Ressources Naturelles et de la Faune. Rapport Annuel de Gestion **3145**
Quebec (Province). Ministere des Ressources Naturelles et de la Faune. Rapport Annuel de Gestion (CAN ISSN 1910-7005) **3145**
Quebec (Province). Ministere des Ressources Naturelles. Foret Quebec Direction de la Recherche Forestiere. Note de Recherche Forestiere (CAN ISSN 0834-4833) **3700**
Quebec (Province). Ministere des Ressources Naturelles. Rapport Annuel *see* Quebec (Province). Ministere des Ressources Naturelles et de la Faune. Rapport Annuel de Gestion **3145**
Quebec (Province). Ministere des Ressources Naturelles. Rapport Annuel de Gestion *see* Quebec (Province). Ministere des Ressources Naturelles et de la Faune. Rapport Annuel de Gestion **3145**
Quebec (Province). Ministere des Ressources Naturelles. Rapport des Geologues Residents sur l'Activite Miniere Regionale (CAN) **2763**
Quebec (Province). Office de la Langue Francaise. Rapport d'Activites (CAN ISSN 0707-1795) **5164**
Quebec (Province). Office de la Protection du Consommateur. Rapport Annuel (CAN) **2641**
Quebec (Province). Regie de l'Assurance-Maladie. Statistiques Annuelles (CAN ISSN 0226-5346) **4530**
• Quebec (Province). Services Documentaires Multimedia. Choix: Documentation Imprimee (CAN) **634**
• Quebec (Province). Services Documentaires Multimedia. D A V I D: Documentation Audiovisuelle (CAN) **634**
Quebec (Province). Services Documentation Multimedia. Choix Jeunesse: Documentation Imprimee *see* Quebec. Services Documentation Multimedia. Choix Jeunesse. Livres de Langue Francaise **634**
Le Quebec a Votre Portee (CAN ISSN 0836-0014) **3122**
Quebec Appeal Cases (CAN) **4764**
Quebec. Bulletin Regional sur le Marche du Travail *see* Capitale-Nationale. Bulletin Regional **1669**
• Quebec Business Directory (USA) **2025**
Quebec. Centre de Recouvrement. Rapport de Gestion *see* Quebec Province. Ministere de l'Emploi et de la Solidarite Sociale. Rapport Annuel de Gestion **6703**
Quebec Chronicle - Telegraph (CAN ISSN 0226-9252) **3816**
Quebec. Commission des Services Juridiques. Rapport Annuel de Gestion (CAN ISSN 1912-3833) **4764**
Quebec. Commission des Valeurs Mobilieres. Rapport Annuel *see* Quebec Province. Autorite des Marches Financiers. Rapport Annuel **1646**
Quebec. Commission des Valeurs Mobilieres. Rapport d'Activites *see* Quebec Province. Autorite des Marches Financiers. Rapport Annuel **1646**
Quebec. Conseil des Aines *see* Le Doyen **4043**
Quebec. Conseil Permanent de la Jeunesse. Plan Strategique (CAN ISSN 1912-4600) **2166**
Quebec. Conseil Superieur de la Langue Francaise. Bulletin (CAN ISSN 1709-9684) **5164**
Quebec. Conseil Superieur de la Langue Francaise. Rapport Annuel de Gestion (CAN ISSN 1708-2781) **7464**
Quebec Corporations Manual *see* Manuel des Corporations du Quebec **4875**
Quebec. Direction Generale des Peches et de l'Aquiculture Commerciales. Direction de l'Innovation et des Technologies. Activites (Year) *see* Quebec (Province). Direction de l'Innovation et des Technologies. Rapport d'Activites (Year) **699**
Quebec et Chaudiere-Appalaches. Bulletin Regional sur le Marche du Travail *see* Capitale-Nationale. Bulletin Regional **1669**
Quebec Farmers' Advocate (CAN ISSN 0714-9158) **149**
Quebec Folklore (CAN ISSN 1708-9662) **3621**
Quebec Francais (CAN ISSN 0316-2052) **3816**
▼ Quebec Franchise Magazine (CAN ISSN 1911-8384) **1965**
Quebec Habitation (CAN) **1031**
Quebec Home & School News (CAN ISSN 0033-5967) **2902**
Quebec Homeschooling Advisory Newsletter/Conseil pour l'Education a Domicile au Quebec (CAN) **2902**
Quebec Info (CAN ISSN 1198-7928) **3816**
Quebec. Inspecteur General des Institutions Financieres. Rapport Annuel *see* Quebec Province. Autorite des Marches Financiers. Rapport Annuel **1646**
Quebec. Inspecteur General des Institutions Financieres. Rapport Annuel de Gestion *see* Quebec Province. Autorite des Marches Financiers. Rapport Annuel **1646**
Quebec International (Sainte-Foy) (CAN ISSN 0847-494X) **3122**
Quebec Legislation on the Law of Financial Institutions *see* Legislation Quebecoise en Droit des Institutions Financieres **4874**
Quebec Library Association Bulletin *see* Q L A Bulletin **5041**
Quebec. Ministere de la Culture et des Communications. Rapport Annuel *see* Gestion du Ministere de la Culture et des Communications du Quebec. Rapport Annuel (Year) **7439**
Quebec. Ministere de la Famille et de l'Enfance. Rapport Annuel *see* Quebec Province. Ministere de l'Emploi et de la Solidarite Sociale. Rapport Annuel de Gestion **6703**
Quebec. Ministere de l'Agriculture, des Pecheries et de l'Alimentation. Direction Regionale de Quebec-Capitale-Nationale. Bilan des Regions (CAN ISSN 1910-0019) **205**
Quebec. Ministere de l'Education, du Loisir et du Sport. Rapport Annuel de Gestion (CAN ISSN 1715-8818) **2902**
Quebec. Ministere de l'Education. Rapport Annuel *see* Quebec. Ministere de l'Education, du Loisir et du Sport. Rapport Annuel de Gestion **2902**
Quebec. Ministere de l'Education. Rapport Annuel de Gestion *see* Quebec. Ministere de l'Education, du Loisir et du Sport. Rapport Annuel de Gestion **2902**
Quebec. Ministere de l'Emploi. Rapport Annuel *see* Quebec. Ministere du Travail. Rapport Annuel de Gestion (Year) **1704**
Quebec. Ministere de l'Environnement. Rapport Annuel *see* Quebec. Ministere du Developpement Durable, Environnement et Parcs. Rapport Annuel de Gestion **7464**
Quebec. Ministere de l'Environnement. Rapport Annuel de Gestion *see* Quebec. Ministere du Developpement Durable, Environnement et Parcs. Rapport Annuel de Gestion **7464**
Quebec. Ministere du Developpement Durable, Environnement et Parcs. Rapport Annuel de Gestion (CAN ISSN 1719-8607) **7464**
Quebec. Ministere du Developpement Economique, de l'Innovation et de l'Exportation. Rapport Annuel de Gestion (CAN ISSN 1719-9050) **1513**
Quebec. Ministere du Developpement Economique et Regional et de la Recherche. Rapport Annuel de Gestion *see* Quebec. Ministere du Developpement Economique, de l'Innovation et de l'Exportation. Rapport Annuel de Gestion **1513**
Quebec. Ministere du Revenu. Plan d'Action (CAN ISSN 1911-0642) **7464**
Quebec. Ministere du Travail. Rapport Annuel *see* Quebec. Ministere du Travail. Rapport Annuel de Gestion (Year) **1704**
Quebec. Ministere du Travail. Rapport Annuel de Gestion (Year) (CAN ISSN 1709-3678) **1704**
Quebec, Off the Beaten Path *see* Off the Beaten Path: Quebec **8744**
Quebec Pharmacie (CAN ISSN 0826-9874) **6877**
Quebec Province. Autorite des Marches Financiers. Rapport Annuel (CAN ISSN 1710-7725) **1646**
Quebec Province. Bureau du Verificateur General. Rapport Annuel de Gestion (CAN ISSN 1715-2798) **1941**
Quebec Province. Centre de Recouvrement. Rapport Annuel de Gestion *see* Quebec Province. Ministere de l'Emploi et de la Solidarite Sociale. Rapport Annuel de Gestion **6703**
Quebec Province. Commission des Normes du Travail. Rapport Annuel *see* Quebec Province. Commission des Normes du Travail. Rapport Annuel de Gestion **1704**
Quebec Province. Commission des Normes du Travail. Rapport Annuel de Gestion (CAN ISSN 1708-1157) **1704**
Quebec Province. Ministere de la Famille, des Aines et de la Condition Feminine. Rapport Annuel de Gestion (CAN ISSN 1718-0392) **8064**
Quebec Province. Ministere de la Famille et de l'Enfance. Rapport Annuel de Gestion *see* Quebec Province. Ministere de la Famille, des Aines et de la Condition Feminine. Rapport Annuel de Gestion **8064**
Quebec Province. Ministere de la Famille et de l'Enfance. Rapport Annuel de Gestion *see* Quebec Province. Ministere de l'Emploi et de la Solidarite Sociale. Rapport Annuel de Gestion **6703**
Quebec Province. Ministere de l'Emploi, de la Solidarite Sociale et de la Famille. Rapport Annuel de Gestion *see* Quebec Province. Ministere de l'Emploi et de la Solidarite Sociale. Rapport Annuel de Gestion **6703**
Quebec Province. Ministere de l'Emploi, de la Solidarite Sociale et de la Famille. Rapport Annuel de Gestion *see* Quebec Province. Ministere de la Famille, des Aines et de la Condition Feminine. Rapport Annuel de Gestion **8064**
Quebec Province. Ministere de l'Emploi et de la Solidarite Sociale. Rapport Annuel de Gestion *see* Quebec Province. Ministere de la Famille, des Aines et de la Condition Feminine. Rapport Annuel de Gestion **8064**
Quebec Province. Ministere de l'Emploi et de la Solidarite Sociale. Rapport Annuel de Gestion (CAN ISSN 1912-0931) **6703**
Quebec Province. Ministere de l'Immigration et des Communautes Culturelles. Rapport Annuel de Gestion (CAN ISSN 1719-3869) **7464**
Quebec Province. Ministere des Finances. Budget en Bref (CAN ISSN 1719-5969) **1941**
Quebec Province. Ministere des Finances. Budget in Brief *see* Quebec Province. Ministere des Finances. Budget en Bref **1941**
Quebec Province. Ministere des Relations avec les Citoyens et de l'Immigration. Rapport Annuel de Gestion *see* Quebec Province. Ministere de l'Immigration et des Communautes Culturelles. Rapport Annuel de Gestion **7464**
Quebec Province. Ministere des Relations Internationales. Rapport Annuel de Gestion. (CAN ISSN 1714-5457) **7464**
Quebec Province. Ministere des Ressources Naturelles et de la Faune. Plan Strategique (CAN ISSN 1910-7099) **2715**
Quebec Province. Ministere des Ressources Naturelles. Plan Strategique *see* Quebec Province. Ministere des Ressources Naturelles et de la Faune. Plan Strategique **2715**
Quebec Province. Securite du Revenu. Rapport Annuel de Gestion *see* Quebec Province. Ministere de l'Emploi et de la Solidarite Sociale. Rapport Annuel de Gestion **6703**
Quebec. Registraire des Entreprises. Rapport Annuel de Gestion *see* Quebec Province. Autorite des Marches Financiers. Rapport Annuel **1646**
Le Quebec Rural & Agricole (CAN ISSN 1911-9402) **149**
• Quebec Science (CAN ISSN 0021-6127) **7901**
• Quebec. Services Documentation Multimedia. Choix Jeunesse. Livres de Langue Francaise (CAN ISSN 1719-5284) **634**
Quebec Soccer (CAN ISSN 0228-6351) **8243**
Quebec Statistique (CAN ISSN 0834-5252) **8395**
• ➤ Quebec Studies (USA ISSN 0737-3759) **5356**
• Quebec Tax Reporter (CAN ISSN 0048-6299) **1941**
Quebec Vert (CAN ISSN 0705-6923) **3748**
The Quebecer (CAN ISSN 0824-2348) **7175**
Quebecer (French Edition) *see* The Quebecer **7175**
• Quebracho (ARG ISSN 0328-0543) **3700**
• Queen (USA ISSN 1538-5248) **4471**
Queen Mary and Westfield College. Department of Geography. Research Papers in Geography (GBR) **4025**
Queen Mary and Westfield College. Department of Geography. Working Papers (GBR) **4025**
Queen Mary College Students Union Handbook (GBR) **2999**
Queen of All Hearts (USA ISSN 0033-6017) **7672**
Queen Street Quarterly (CAN ISSN 1206-5498) **5235**
Queen Victoria Museum and Art Gallery. Annual Report (AUS ISSN 1039-8090) **6536**
The Queen Victoria Museum and Art Gallery, Launceston. Records (AUS ISSN 1441-6506) **6536**
Queen Victoria Museum and Art Gallery. Occasional Papers (AUS ISSN 1038-2224) **6536**
• Queen's Alumni Review (CAN ISSN 0843-8048) **2298**
• Queens. Ausgabe Mittelrhein (DEU) **3855**
Queen's Awards Magazine (GBR ISSN 1462-9704) **1580**
Queens Bar Bulletin (USA ISSN 0048-6302) **4764**
Queen's College the Wyvern Society Newsletter *see* In Aeternum **2287**
• Queens County Dental Society. Bulletin (USA ISSN 1527-3989) **5862**
Queen's File (GBR) **8195**
Queen's Gazette (CAN ISSN 0319-2725) **2999**
Queen's Journal (CAN) **2298**
• ➤ Queen's Law Journal (CAN ISSN 0316-778X) **4764**
Queen's Medical Review (CAN ISSN 0079-8789) **5702**
➤ Queen's Papers in Pure and Applied Mathematics (CAN ISSN 0079-8797) **5527**
Queens Parent (USA) **2166**
• ➤ Queen's Quarterly (CAN ISSN 0033-6041) **3816**
Queen's Regulations for the Army Amendments (GBR) **6442**
Queen's Regulations for the R.A.F. Amendments (GBR) **6442**
Queen's University at Kingston. Douglas Library. Occasional Papers (CAN ISSN 0075-6113) **5059**
Queen's University. Industrial Relations Centre. Queen's Papers in Industrial Relations Series (CAN ISSN 0838-6609) **1704**
Queen's University. Institute for Economic Research. Discussion Paper (CAN ISSN 0316-5078) **1163**
Queen's University of Belfast. Department of Environmental Planning. Occasional Paper (GBR) **4424**
Queensborough (USA ISSN 0033-6068) **1409**
Queensland Administrative Law (AUS) **7464**
• ➤ Queensland Archaeological Research (AUS ISSN 0814-3021) **413**
Queensland Asian News *see* Queensland Chinese News **3796**
Queensland Bookbinders' Guild. Newsletter (AUS ISSN 1035-1817) **7572**
Queensland Business Acumen *see* Acumen **1723**
Queensland Business Review (AUS ISSN 1448-7683) **1163**
• Queensland Caravan Parks & Touring Accomadation Directory (AUS) **8749**
• Queensland Chinese News/Sheng Huo Qing Bao (AUS ISSN 1449-843X) **3796**
Queensland Country Life (AUS ISSN 0033-6084) **3796**

Title

10778 QUEENSLAND COUNTRY WOMAN ULRICH'S PERIODICALS

Queensland Country Woman (AUS ISSN 0033-6092) **8881**
Queensland Court of Appeal Headnotes (AUS ISSN 1329-3346) **4824**
Queensland Dairyfarmer (AUS ISSN 0033-6106) **268**
Queensland. Department of Education. Research and Evaluation Unit. Educational Research Report (AUS) **2902**
• Queensland. Department of Education, Training and the Arts. Annual Report (AUS ISSN 1835-0402) **7464**
• Queensland. Department of Industrial Relations. Annual Report (AUS ISSN 1448-6873) **1704**
• Queensland. Department of Mines and Energy. Annual Report (AUS ISSN 1832-9462) **3145**
Queensland. Department of Primary Industries. Bulletin (AUS ISSN 0155-221X) **205**
Queensland. Department of Primary Industries. Conference and Workshop Series (AUS ISSN 0728-067X) **1902**
Queensland. Department of Primary Industries. Project Report (AUS ISSN 0727-6281) **149**
Queensland. Department of Primary Industries. Research Note (AUS ISSN 1035-9788) **3700**
Queensland Department of Primary Industries. Study Tour Report (AUS ISSN 0728-0696) **149**
Queensland Dog World (AUS) **6814**
• Queensland Energy Brief (AUS ISSN 1833-5187) **3145**
Queensland Environmental Practice Reporter (AUS ISSN 1323-7349) **4764**
Queensland Family Historian (AUS ISSN 0811-3394) **3780**
Queensland Farmer *see* North Queensland Register **3795**
Queensland Farmers' Federation Weekly Bulletin *see* Q F F Weekly Bulletin **149**
Queensland Fisherman (AUS ISSN 0812-9452) **3605**
Queensland Forest Service. Research Paper (AUS ISSN 1035-9796) **3700**
Queensland Forest Service. Research Report (AUS) **3700**
Queensland Forest Service. Technical Note (AUS ISSN 1035-9818) **3700**
Queensland Forest Service. Technical Paper (AUS ISSN 1035-9826) **3700**
Queensland Geology (AUS ISSN 1035-4840) **2763**
• Queensland Government Mining Journal (AUS) **6477**
† Queensland Graingrower (AUS ISSN 1321-1986) **8983**
Queensland Grains Outlook (AUS ISSN 1448-6040) **275**
• Queensland History Journal (AUS) **4194**
Queensland Hotels Association Review *see* Q H A Review **4396**
• Queensland Institute of Medical Research. Annual Report (AUS) **5702**
The Queensland Journal of Labour History (AUS ISSN 1832-9926) **4194**
Queensland Justices Association Journal *see* Q J A Journal **2667**
The Queensland Law Handbook (AUS) **4764**
Queensland Law Reporter (AUS ISSN 0726-0784) **4764**
• ➤ Queensland Law Society Journal (Online) (AUS ISSN 1833-8321) **4764**
Queensland Lawyer (AUS ISSN 0312-1658) **4764**
• Queensland Legal Indices (AUS) **4824**
• Queensland Master Plumber (AUS ISSN 0048-637X) **4125**
• Queensland Mines and Quarries Safety Performance and Health Report (AUS ISSN 1834-3708) **6477**
Queensland Museum, Brisbane. Memoirs. Cultural Heritage Series *see* Queensland Museum. Memoirs. Cultural Heritage Series **4471**
• ➤ Queensland Museum. Memoirs (AUS ISSN 0079-8835) **7901**
• ➤ Queensland Museum. Memoirs. Cultural Heritage Series (AUS ISSN 1440-4788) **4471**
➤ Queensland Naturalist (AUS ISSN 0079-8843) **699**
Queensland Newsagent (AUS) **4582**
Queensland - Northern Territory Nursery Register (AUS) **3748**
Queensland Nurse (AUS ISSN 0815-936X) **5979**
Queensland Nurses' Union. Union Update (AUS) **4601**
Queensland Planner (AUS ISSN 1326-3374) **4424**
Queensland Potters Association. Annual Report of the Directors (AUS ISSN 0728-0858) **2044**
Queensland Practice Papers *see* The College of Law Queensland Practice Papers. Volume 1 **4644**
Queensland Racing Magazine (AUS) **8297**
Queensland Reports (AUS ISSN 0726-3759) **4959**
• Queensland Resources Council. Annual Report (AUS ISSN 1449-2016) **6477**
• ➤ Queensland Review (AUS ISSN 1321-8166) **4194**
Queensland Rugby League News (AUS) **8243**
The Queensland Science Teacher (AUS) **3078**
Queensland Sentencing Manual (AUS) **4897**
The Queensland Shelter Quarterly (AUS ISSN 1832-6625) **4424**
Queensland Smart Farmer (AUS) **149**
Queensland Sower (AUS ISSN 1449-6372) **7672**
Queensland Street Car (AUS ISSN 1448-384X) **4344**
Queensland Studies Authority Quarterly *see* Q S A Quarterly **2901**
Queensland Taxi Magazine (AUS) **8509**
Queensland Teachers' Journal (AUS ISSN 0033-6238) **2902**
Queensland Teachers Professional Magazine *see* Queensland Teachers' Journal **2902**
Queensland Teachers Union Professional Magazine *see* Queensland Teachers' Journal **2902**
• Queensland. Tourism Queensland. Annual Report (AUS) **8749**
Queensland University Libraries Office of Cooperation News *see* Q U L O C News **5041**
• ➤ Queensland University of Technology Law and Justice Journal (AUS ISSN 1445-6230) **4764**
Queenstown Mirror *see* The Mirror (Queenstown-Lakes Edition) **3918**
Queer (DEU) **4378**
Queer Ramblings (USA ISSN 1552-4701) **4378**
Queerzine Explosion (USA) **4378**
➤ Queeste (NLD ISSN 0929-8592) **5356**
• QueHacer (PER ISSN 0250-9806) **7175**
Queirosiana (PRT ISSN 0872-1769) **5356**
• ➤ Quekett Journal of Microscopy (GBR ISSN 0969-3823) **900**
Quekett Microscopical Club. Bulletin (GBR ISSN 1350-9128) **900**
Quell (DEU) **5081**
Quelle Sante (FRA ISSN 1779-8469) **314**
Quelle Sterne-Info (DEU) **3855**
Quellen der Wissenschaftsgeschichte (DEU) **7901**
Quellen und Abhandlungen zur Mittelrheinischen Kirchengeschichte (DEU ISSN 0480-7480) **7672**
Quellen und Beitraege des Stadtarchivs Olpe (DEU ISSN 0947-4196) **4255**
Quellen und Beitraege zur Geschichte der Universitaet Jena (DEU) **2999**
Quellen und Beitraege zur Geschichte der Universitaet Wuerzburg (DEU ISSN 0481-3510) **2999**
Quellen und Beitraege zur Geschichte der Universitaet Wuerzburg. Beiheft (DEU ISSN 0084-3075) **2999**
Quellen und Darstellungen zur Geschichte von Stadt und Kreis Uelzen (DEU ISSN 0944-2995) **4255**
Quellen und Darstellungen zur Hansischen Geschichte (DEU ISSN 0931-4660) **4255**
Quellen und Darstellungen zur Schlesischen Geschichte (DEU ISSN 0481-3537) **4255**
➤ Quellen und Darstellungen zur Zeitgeschichte (DEU) **4157**
Quellen und Dokumente zur Geschichte der Berufsbildung in Deutschland (AUT) **2999**
• Quellen und Forschungen aus Italienischen Archiven und Bibliotheken (DEU ISSN 0079-9068) **4157**
Quellen und Forschungen zur Basler Geschichte (CHE ISSN 0079-9076) **4255**
Quellen und Forschungen zur Brandenburgischen und Preussischen Geschichte (DEU ISSN 0943-8629) **4255**
Quellen und Forschungen zur Geschichte des Dominikanerordens (DEU ISSN 0942-4059) **7813**
Quellen und Forschungen zur Geschichte Sachsen-Anhalts (AUT ISSN 1861-8561) **4255**
Quellen und Forschungen zur Hoechsten Gerichtsbarkeit im Alten Reich (AUT) **4764**
Quellen und Forschungen zur Lingener Geschichte (DEU ISSN 1439-8605) **4255**
➤ Quellen und Forschungen zur Literatur- und Kulturgeschichte (DEU ISSN 0946-9419) **5356**
Quellen und Forschungen zur Saechsischen Geschichte (DEU) **4255**
Quellen und Forschungen zur Suedsee. Reihe A: Quellen (DEU ISSN 1614-3388) **4187**
Quellen und Forschungen zur Suedsee. Reihe B: Forschungen (DEU ISSN 1610-5354) **4187**
Quellen und Materialien zur Saechsischen Geschichte und Volkskunde (DEU) **4255**
Quellen und Schrifttum zur Kulturgeschichte des Wiehengebirgsraumes. Reihe A (DEU ISSN 0947-4668) **413**
Quellen und Schrifttum zur Kulturgeschichte des Wiehengebirgsraumes. Reihe B (DEU ISSN 0947-4676) **413**
Quellen und Studien zur Geschichte der Pharmazie (DEU ISSN 0085-5367) **6877**
Quellen und Studien zur Geschichte des Oestlichen Europa (DEU ISSN 0170-3595) **4255**
➤ Quellen und Studien zur Philosophie (DEU ISSN 0344-8142) **6946**
Quellen und Untersuchungen zur Lateinischen Philologie des Mittelalters (DEU ISSN 0721-6203) **2239**
Quellen zur Geschichte des 19. und 20. Jahrhunderts (AUT) **4256**
Quellen zur Geschichte des Parlamentarismus und der Politischen Parteien. Dritte Reihe: Die Weimarer Republik (DEU ISSN 0931-0495) **7175**
Quellen zur Geschichte des Parlamentarismus und der Politischen Parteien. Erste Reihe: Von der Konstitutionellen Monarchie zur Parlamentarischen Republik (DEU ISSN 0481-3650) **7175**
Quellen zur Geschichte des Parlamentarismus und der Politischen Parteien. Vierte Reihe: Deutschland seit 1945 (DEU ISSN 0931-0614) **7175**
Quellen zur Geschichte des Parlamentarismus und der Politischen Parteien. Zweite Reihe: Militaer und Politik (DEU ISSN 0931-0274) **7175**
Quellen zur Geschichte Oberoesterreichs (AUT) **4256**
Quellen zur Geschichte und Landeskunde Ostmitteleuropas (DEU) **4256**
Quellen zur Khoisan Forschung *see* Research in Khoisan Studies **5166**
Quellen zur Rechtsvergleichung (DEU) **4959**
Quellen zur Regionalgeschichte (DEU ISSN 1439-8591) **4256**
Quellenkataloge zur Musikgeschichte (DEU ISSN 0079-905X) **6608**
Quellenschriften zur Westdeutschen Vor- und Fruehgeschichte (DEU ISSN 0079-9149) **413**
Quellenstudien zur Hadit- und Rechtsliteratur in Nordafrika (DEU ISSN 0942-6574) **7715**
Quellenwerke zur Alten Geschichte Amerikas (DEU ISSN 0079-9157) **4309**
† Quelli di Fuori (ITA ISSN 1825-2583) **8983**
Quem e Quem na Economia Brasileira (BRA ISSN 0102-7115) **2025**
➤ Quepo (PER ISSN 1022-5897) **814**
Quer Durch Antwerpen. Port and Shipping (DEU) **8657**
Quer Durch Bremen. Niedersaechsische Haefen (DEU ISSN 1617-9536) **8657**
Quer Durch Hamburg. Schiffahrt und Hafen (DEU ISSN 0936-0603) **8657**
Quer Durch Hamburg/Schleswig-Holstein. Spedition und Transport (DEU ISSN 1614-4554) **8509**
Quer Durch Hamburg. Spedition und Transport *see* Quer Durch Hamburg/Schleswig-Holstein. Spedition und Transport **8509**
Quer Durch Rotterdam. Port and Shipping (DEU) **8658**
• Quercus (ESP ISSN 0212-0054) **3461**
Quercus Review (USA ISSN 1543-4532) **5356**
Quercy Recherche (FRA ISSN 0335-3958) **4256**
• Querelles - net (DEU ISSN 1862-054X) **8127**
Querida (BRA ISSN 0104-334X) **2209**
Querida Especial (BRA ISSN 1413-3075) **2209**
Querida Super Stars (BRA ISSN 0104-6616) **2209**
➤ Querschnitte (DEU ISSN 0938-6130) **7772**
Querstand (AUT) **6608**
➤ Query (CAN ISSN 0380-240X) **2902**
• Quesnel Cariboo Observer (CAN ISSN 1195-5023) **3816**
Quest (GBR) **6299**
➤ Quest (HKG ISSN 1684-6206) **7672**
Quest (Barton) (AUS) **3371**
Quest (Boston) (USA ISSN 1070-244X) **7672**
Quest (Canberra City) (AUS ISSN 1448-4390) **2945**
• ➤ Quest (Champaign) (USA ISSN 0033-6297) **3078**
Quest (Diemen) (NLD ISSN 1573-4617) **7901**
➤ Quest (Grand Forks) (USA ISSN 1065-7738) **68**
➤ Quest (Leiden) (NLD ISSN 1011-226X) **6946**
Quest (Milton Keynes) (GBR ISSN 0963-4886) **7772**
• Quest (Tucson) (USA ISSN 1087-1578) **6180**
The Quest (Wheaton) (USA ISSN 1040-533X) **7740**
Quest. Special (NLD ISSN 1871-8094) **7901**
• Queste Istituzioni (ITA ISSN 1121-3353) **7175**
Questiio *see* S O R T **8398**
Question' Air (FRA ISSN 1963-2150) **6442**
Question Book, Income Tax Law for Accountants, Income Tax Law for Tax Agents (AUS ISSN 1440-0278) **1941**
Question de (FRA ISSN 0246-5434) **6743**
• Question d'Education (FRA ISSN 1953-7743) **2902**
Question d'Emploi *see* Question Emploi **6703**
▼ Question Emploi (FRA ISSN 1957-4614) **6703**
Question Mark (USA) **2667**
Question of Balance *see* E E O Trust Work & Life Awards (Series) **1676**
Question Pratique (FRA ISSN 1779-1626) **5081**
Question Psycho (FRA ISSN 1777-6988) **7402**
Question: Research@U N S W Magazine *see* Research @ U N S W **2904**
Question Sante (FRA ISSN 1771-1924) **7538**
La Questione Agraria *see* Q A **205**
Q A. La Questione Agraria *see* Q A **205**
Questione Agraria *see* Q A **205**
• Questione Giustizia (ITA ISSN 1720-4518) **4764**
La Questione Meridionale (ITA) **4471**
➤ La Questione Romantica (ITA ISSN 1125-0364) **5356**
Questiones Publicitarias (ESP ISSN 1133-6870) **1839**
• Questioni di Economia e Finanza (ITA ISSN 1972-6627) **1163**
Questioning Cities Series (GBR ISSN 1754-260X) **7994**
Questioning Techniques and Tactics (USA) **4959**
• ➤ Questions (USA ISSN 1541-4760) **6946**
† Questions Actuelles (FRA ISSN 1276-5910) **8983**
➤ Questions and Answers in General Topology (JPN ISSN 0918-4732) **5527**
Questions and Answers on Tax *see* Premium Tax Collection **4760**
Questions & Reponses Canadiennes *see* Canadian Notes & Queries **5270**
Questions Autochtones (FRA ISSN 1778-333X) **7175**
Questions Contemporaines (FRA ISSN 1286-8698) **8127**
Questions Contemporaines. Serie Globalisation et Sciences Sociales (FRA ISSN 1778-3429) **7994**
Questions d'Ados (FRA ISSN 1768-2428) **2166**
Questions de Femmes (FRA ISSN 1270-8887) **8881**
Questions de Parents (FRA ISSN 1275-4390) **2166**
Questions de Patrimoine *see* Heritage Matters **4295**
Questions de Vida Cristiana (ESP ISSN 0214-7769) **7672**
Questions d'Edition, Politique et Programmes de l'Edition du Livre, Rapport Annuel *see* Printed Matters, Book Publishing Policy and Programs Annual Report **5040**
• Questions d'Education (CAN ISSN 1710-5862) **2902**
Questions Internationales (FRA ISSN 1761-7146) **7261**
• ➤ Questions Liturgiques (BEL ISSN 0774-5524) **7673**
Questions Social (FRA ISSN 1951-0829) **7175**
Questions Sociales/Migrations/Sante *see* Source O C D E. Questions Sociales/Migrations/Sante **8006**
Quest'Italia (ITA ISSN 1970-3856) **4025**
Quetico Information Guide (CAN ISSN 1710-6370) **2625**
Quetico Provincial Park *see* Quetico Information Guide **2625**
Quetico. Visitor Information Guide *see* Quetico Information Guide **2625**
Quetta Times (PAK ISSN 0033-6386) **3926**
El Quetzal (USA ISSN 0162-7902) **6899**
• ➤ Queueing Systems (USA ISSN 0257-0130) **3328**
Qufu Normal University. Journal (Natural Science Edition) *see* Qufu Shifan Daxue Xuebao (Ziran Kexue Ban) **7994**
• Qufu Shifan Daxue Xuebao (Ziran Kexue Ban)/Qufu Normal University. Journal (Natural Science Edition) (CHN ISSN 1001-5337) **7994**
Qui Construit des Machines en Allemagne *see* Wer Baut Maschinen in Deutschland **3399**
Qui Economia (ITA) **1409**
Qui Est Qui au Cinema et a la Television au Canada *see* Who's Who in Canadian Film and Television (Year) **647**
Qui Est Qui en France *see* Who's Who in France **647**
Qui Fait Quoi? *see* Sonovision Qui Fait Quoi? **2028**
Qui Fait Quoi en Developpement International *see* Who's Who in International Development **1607**
• Qui Magazine (ITA ISSN 1828-2199) **3898**
• ➤ Qui Parle (USA ISSN 1041-8385) **4471**
Qui Quoi Quand (FRA ISSN 1296-591X) **4157**
† Qui Rai (ITA) **8983**
Qui Touring (ITA ISSN 0042-546X) **3898**
• Qui Transporte (FRA ISSN 1625-9777) **8509**
Quick (CAN) **4845**
Quick 123 *see* Quick123 **3968**
Quick & Crafty! (GBR ISSN 1746-6520) **538**
Quick & Easy Cooking *see* Family Circle Quick & Easy Cooking **4357**
Quick & Easy Crafts *see* Quick & Crafty! **538**
Quick and Easy Crochet (USA ISSN 0885-0631) **6641**
Quick and Easy Cross Stitch *see* Quick and Easy Stitch & Craft **6641**
Quick & Easy Decorating *see* Better Homes and Gardens Quick & Easy Decorating **4554**
Quick and Easy Painting (USA ISSN 1097-3761) **4344**
▼ Quick & Easy Recipes (USA ISSN 1941-5095) **4366**
Quick and Easy Stitch & Craft (GBR ISSN 1753-2213) **6641**
Quick & Light *see* Healthy Cooking **3646**
† Quick & Simple (USA ISSN 1556-7397) **8983**
• Quick Answers for Digital Photography (USA ISSN 1543-8201) **6976**
• Quick Answers for Microsoft Access (USA ISSN 1543-821X) **2596**
• Quick Answers for Microsoft Excel (USA ISSN 1543-8228) **2596**
• Quick Answers for Microsoft Visual Basic (USA ISSN 1543-7655) **2596**
• Quick Answers for Microsoft Windows X P (USA ISSN 1550-4360) **2596**
• Quick Answers for Microsoft Word (USA ISSN 1543-8236) **2596**
Quick Caller: Atlanta Air Cargo Directory (USA) **8550**
Quick Caller: Boston Area Air Cargo Directory (USA) **8550**
Quick Caller: Boston - New England Area Air Cargo Directory *see* Quick Caller: Boston Area Air Cargo Directory **8550**
Quick Caller: Chicago Area Air Cargo Directory (USA) **8550**
Quick Caller: Detroit Area Air Cargo Directory (USA) **8550**
Quick Caller: Los Angeles Area Air Cargo Directory (USA) **8550**
Quick Caller: Miami - Orlando - Florida Air Cargo Directory (USA) **8550**
Quick Caller: New York- New Jersey Metro Area Air Cargo Directory (USA) **8550**
Quick Caller: Pacific Northwest Area Air Cargo Directory (USA) **8550**
Quick Caller: San Francisco - Oakland Bay Area Air Cargo Directory (USA) **8550**
Quick Escapes: Boston (USA ISSN 1540-1545) **8749**
Quick Escapes: Chicago (USA ISSN 1540-9813) **8749**
Quick Escapes: Dallas/Fort Worth (USA ISSN 1540-4374) **8749**

Link to your serials resources and content with ulrichsweb.com

10780 R & S REPORT (HONOLULU) ULRICH'S PERIODICALS

R & S Report (Honolulu) see Hawaii. Department of Health. Research and Statistics Office. R & S Report 7307
R & T see Religion and Theology 7674
R and T see Road & Track 8601
R & W see Rotor & Wing 69
R & W - Reiniger und Waescher see R & W - Textilservice 2244
R & W - Textilservice (Reiniger und Waescher) (DEU ISSN 1611-468X) 2244
R + B see R + B Home 8983
R B see Reponses Bain 1032
R B A C see Revista Brasileira de Analises Clinicas 5910
R B A Insight (Retailer's Bakery Association) (USA) 3675
R B B see Revista Brasileira de Bioetica 700
R B C see Revista Brasileira de Contabilidade 1300
R B C see Revista de Bombas y Compresores 3364
R B C E H see Revista Brasileira de Ciencias do Envelhecimento Humano 4054
R B C F see B J P S Brazilian Journal of Pharmaceutical Sciences 6824
• R B C Letter (Royal Bank of Canada) (CAN) 1377
R B C S see Red Book Credit Services 3661
R B Congress Marketing (DEU) 1839
R B E see Revista Brasileira de Economia 1166
R B E P see Revista Brasileira de Estudos Pedagogicos 2905
R B F see Review of Behavioral Finance 1379
R B G O see Revista Brasileira de Ginecologia e Obstetricia 6003
† R + B Home (Renovate + Build) (AUS ISSN 1832-116X) 8983
R B Hotel-Marketing (DEU) 8750
R B I - Agro see Sociedade Brasileira de Agroinformatica 157
R B I Annual Report see Reserve Bank of India. Annual Report 1378
R + B Inside see R + B Home 8983
R B L see Review of Biblical Literature (Cumulative Edition) 7677
R B Luftfahrt Marketing (DEU) 8750
R B M see Revista Brasileira de Medicina 5704
R B M A Bulletin (Radiology Business Management Association) (USA) 6205
• ➤ R B M: A Journal of Rare Books, Manuscripts and Cultural Heritage (USA ISSN 1529-6407) 5041
• R B M News (Revue Europeenne de Biotechnologie Medicale) (FRA ISSN 1959-7568) 770
R B M Online see Reproductive BioMedicine Online 6002
• R B M S Newsletter (Association of College and Research Libraries, Rare Books and Manuscripts Section) (USA ISSN 0743-1481) 5041
R B Marketing (DEU ISSN 1863-8864) 8750
• R B O C Update (Regional Bell Operating Company) (USA) 2371
R + B Outside see R + B Home 8983
R B P G see Revista Brasileira de Pos - Graduacao 6703
R B P O see Revista Brasileira de Patologia Oral 5863
R B R H (Revista Brasileira de Recursos Hidricos) (BRA ISSN 1414-381X) 3364
R B R R Kale Memorial Lectures (IND) 7175
• R B. Revue Banque (FRA ISSN 1772-6638) 1377
• R B S E. Revista Brasileira de Sociologia da Emocao (BRA ISSN 1676-8965) 7402
The R B S Gazette (Rubber Band Society) (USA) 5357
R B U S see Revista Brasileira de Ultra - Sonografia 6207
R B W see Reviewer's Bookwatch (Online) 634
R B Weekender (Robinson-Blackmore Ltd.) (CAN) 2388
R B Z Weekly Economic Highlights (ZWE) 1377
R C see Ristorazione Collettiva 4397
R C see R C. Respiratory Care 6218
R C see Roofing Contractor 1034
R C A F Memorial Museum. Newsletter (Royal Canadian Air Force) (CAN ISSN 1910-7889) 6442
R C A Record (Rabbinical Council of America) (USA) 7728
R C A. Revista Cientifica Agropecuaria (ARG ISSN 0329-3602) 149
R C A Sermon Anthology see Rabbinical Council of America. Sermon Anthology 8984
R C A Technical Notes (USA ISSN 0483-7495) 2337
The R C Aircraft & Construction Guide (Radio Control) (GBR ISSN 1741-7791) 4344
R C Boat Modeler see Radio Control Boat Modeler 4344
▼ R C Buggy & Truggy (Remote Control) (USA ISSN 1943-9830) 4344
R/C Buyer's Guide see Radio Control Car Action Buyer's Guide 4345
R C C C Yearbook see Royal Caledonian Curling Club. Annual 8197
R C C Counselor (Religion Communicators Council) (USA) 33
R C C Koude & Luchtbehandeling (Refrigeration & Climate Control) (NLD ISSN 0925-630X) 4125
R C C M Bulletin see Research and Information in Complementary Medicine 5703
R C C Service Manuals (Radio College of Canada) (CAN) 3111
R C Car Action see Radio Control Car Action 4345
▼ R C Crawler (Radio Control) (USA ISSN 1944-0898) 4344
† R C D (Rock Compact Disc Magazine) (GBR ISSN 0965-190X) 8983
R C D A see R C D A Newsletter 7673
R C D A Newsletter (Religion in Communist Dominated Areas) (USA ISSN 2150-0274) 7673
R C Driver (Radio Control) (USA ISSN 1544-418X) 4344
R C E. Revista de Contratacion Electronica (ESP ISSN 1576-2033) 4764
R C E: Revue des Comites d'Entreprise et Equivalents see N V O Espace Elus 1698
R C E T J see Research Center for Educational Technology. Journal 3078
R C Excellence Magazine see R / C Excellence Magazine 4344
R / C Excellence Magazine (Radio Control) (USA) 4344
R/C Excellence Magazine see R / C Excellence Magazine 4344
R C - Freizeit (Radio Control) (DEU) 4344
R C G A Roster and Membership Services Directory see St. Louis Regional Chamber & Growth Association. Roster and Membership Services Directory 2029
R C G A's Directory of Saint Louis Large Employers see St. Louis Regional Chamber & Growth Association. Directory of St. Louis Large Employers 2029
• R C Heli (Radio Control) (USA ISSN 1559-7903) 8195
R C Heli Magazine see R C Heli 8195
R C I (Roofing, Cladding and Insulation) (GBR ISSN 0951-6263) 1031
R C I Directory see R C I 1031
R C I P see Reseau Canadien d'Information sur le Patrimoine 5043
R C I Premier (Resort Condominiums International) (USA ISSN 1099-6753) 4396
• R C I. Riscaldamento Climatizzazione Idronica (ITA ISSN 1120-8457) 3217
R C J Journal/R C J Kaiho (Reliability Center for Electronic Components of Japan) (JPN ISSN 0910-2787) 3111
R C J Kaiho see R C J Journal 3111
R C L see Resources for College Libraries 3000
R C M see Radio Commande Magazine 4344
R C M & E (Radio Control Models & Electronics) (GBR ISSN 0269-8307) 4344
R C M Annual Review (Royal College of Music) (GBR) 6608
• ➤ R C M Midwives (Royal College of Midwives) (GBR ISSN 1479-2915) 6002
R C M Top 3000 Charities (Year) see Top 3000 Charities (Year) 8075
R C Microflight see Radio Control Microflight 4345
R C Model see R C Model Auto 4344
R C Model see R C Model Aero 4344
R C Model see Modelbouw Aktueel 4341
R C Model Aero (Radio Controlled) (ESP ISSN 1578-4649) 4344
R C Model Auto (Radio Controlled) (ESP ISSN 1578-4630) 4344
R C Model World see Radio Control Model World 4345
R/C Modeler (Radio Control) (USA ISSN 0033-6866) 4344
R C - Monster - Action (Radio Controlled) (DEU) 4344
R / C Monster Trucks see Radio Control Car Action Monster Trucks 4345
R C N Institute. Report (Royal College of Nursing) (GBR) 5979
R C N P Annual Report (Research Center for Nuclear Physics) (JPN) 7071
R C O E see Ilustre Consejo General de Colegios de Ondotologos y Estomatologos de Espana. Revista 5847
R C O Update (Recycling Council of Ontario) (CAN) 3510
• R C R A Regulations and Keyword Index (Resource Conservation and Recovery Act) (USA ISSN 1074-1364) 3461
† • R C R Wireless News (USA ISSN 1533-0796) 8983
• R C. Respiratory Care (USA ISSN 0098-9142) 6218
R C: Revista de Responsabilidad Civil, Circulacion y Seguro (ESP ISSN 1133-6900) 4765
R C S Bulletin see Royal College of Surgeons of England. Bulletin 6257
R C Scale International (Radio Control) (GBR ISSN 1368-3179) 4344
▼ R C Sport Flyer (Radio Control) (USA ISSN 1941-3467) 4344
R C T L J see Rutgers Computer & Technology Law Journal 4845
R C T. Revista Colombiana de Telecomunicaciones see C I N T E L. Revista 2314
R d A see Recht der Arbeit 4766
† R D A Journal of Agricultural Science (Rural Development Administration) (KOR) 8983
R D A News (Riding for the Disabled Association of Australia) (AUS) 6115
R D B see Residential Design and Build 1033
R d C see Rivista del Cinematografo 6511
The R D C (PHL) 1513
R d E - Recht der Energiewirtschaft (DEU ISSN 0944-128X) 3145
R D Electronic see Research Disclosure 6757
• R D H (Registered Dental Hygienist) (USA ISSN 0279-7720) 5862
R D I P see Respiratory Disease in Practice 6218
R d M see Revista de Musicologia 6611
R d M see Rivista della Montagna 8330
R D M. Revista de Minas (ESP ISSN 1130-9644) 6477
R D M Z Info. Architecture en Stedebouw see Rijksdienst voor Archeologie, Cultuurlandschap en Monumenten. Brochure Cultuurhistorie 4426
R D M Z Info. Restauratie en Beheer see Rijksdienst voor Archeologie, Cultuurlandschap en Monumenten. Brochure Techniek 456
R D M Z Nieuwsbrief see Rijksdienst voor Archeologie, Cultuurlandschap en Monumenten. Nieuwsbrief 456
R D P see Reserve Bank of Australia. Research Discussion Paper 1378
R D P D D see McGill International Journal of Sustainable Development Law and Policy 4730
R D P Monitor (Reconstruction and Development Programme) (ZAF ISSN 1023-9286) 1646
R D P Vision (Reconstruction and Development Programme) (ZAF) 7464
R D S Occasional Papers see Research Development and Statistics Directorate. Occasional Papers 8128
R D T Info see Research E U 8436
R D U see Rotary Down Under 2269
R D U see Revista Digital Universitaria 2566
R D V see Recht der Datenverarbeitung 2515
R E (Real Estate) (NZL ISSN 1176-9718) 7606
• R E A (Red Espanola de Aerobiologia) (ESP ISSN 1135-4704) 699
R E A D Perspectives (Institute for Research in English Acquisition and Development) (USA ISSN 1091-6822) 2902
R E A L I D A D see Revista de Ciencias Sociales y Humanidades 1515
R E A L Journal see Washington and Lee Journal of Civil Rights and Social Justice 4844
R E A L. Yearbook (Research in English and American Literature) (DEU ISSN 0723-0338) 5357
R E A's Math Tutor for the S A T see Math Review for the S A T 2885
R E C E N F. Revista Tecnico Cientifica de Enfermagem (BRA ISSN 1677-7271) 5979
R E C E R C see Centre de Recherche et d'Etudes Catalanes. Revue 8093
R E C Focus (Reformed Ecumenical Council) (USA ISSN 1534-259X) 7772
• R E C I D T (Revista Electronica del Centro de Investigacion y Desarrollo Tecnico) (CUB ISSN 1684-6826) 8436
R E C I E L see Review of European Community and International Environmental Law 3463
R E C News Exchange (Reformed Ecumenical Council) (USA) 7772
R E C S A M Annual Report (Regional Centre for Education in Science and Mathematics) (MYS ISSN 0377-3450) 2902
R E C S A M News (Regional Centre for Education in Science and Mathematics) (MYS ISSN 0126-7612) 3078
† R E D (Revista de Educacion a Distancia) (ESP ISSN 1131-8783) 8983
R E D see Revista de la Educacion a Distancia 2906
R E D (Retail Equipment & Design) (GBR ISSN 1353-6087) 1839
R E D E N (Revista Espanola de Estudios Norteamericanos) (ESP ISSN 1131-9674) 4309
R E D E T I (Revista del Derecho de las Telecomunicacions e Infraestructuras) (ESP ISSN 1139-482X) 2503
• R E D I (Revista Electronica de Derecho Informatico) (PER ISSN 1576-7124) 4765
R E D. Revista de Entrenamiento Deportivo (ESP ISSN 1133-0619) 6995
R E D U. Revista (Red Estatal de Docencia Universitaria) (ESP ISSN 1696-1412) 2999
R E D V E T see Revista Electronica de Veterinaria 8806
R E E see Revue de l'Electricite et de l'Electronique 3329
R E E see Rural and Environmental Engineering 153
R E E Action (Real Estate Educators Association) (USA) 7606
R E E C see Revista Electronica de Ensenanza de las Ciencias 2906
R E E G see Russia - Eurasia Executive Guide 1581
R E E H see Revue Europeenne des Etudes Hebraiques 7729
R E E P see Review of Environmental Economics and Policy 7996
R E F A see Revue Economique et Financiere Ivoirienne 1515
R E F A Nachrichten (Reichsausschuss fuer Arbeitsstudien) (DEU ISSN 0033-6874) 1704
R E I C I S see Revista Espanola de Inovacion, Calidad e Ingenieria del Software 2436
R E I D Quarterly (Real Estate Investment Digest) (USA) 4520
R E I Q Journal (Real Estate Institute of Queensland) (AUS ISSN 1442-9683) 7606
† R E I R P R. Cahiers (Reseau Europeen Interdisciplinaire de Recherche sur Psychologie et Reanimation) (FRA ISSN 1025-3807) 8983
R E I S Report: Industrial Market Service (Real Estate Information Service) (USA) 7606
R E I S Report: Residential Market Service (Real Estate Information Service) (USA) 7606
R E I S Reports: Office Market Service (Real Estate Information Service) (USA) 7606
R E I S Reports: Retail Market Service (Real Estate Information Service) (USA) 7606
• The R E I T Investor (Real Estate Investment Trust) (USA) 1646
R E I T Review (Real Estate Investment Trust) (USA) 7606
R E I T Street (Real Estate Investment Trust) (USA) 7606
R E I T Watch (Real Estate Investment Trusts) (USA) 7606
• R E I T Week (Real Estate Investment Trust) (USA) 7606
• R E L C Journal (Regional English Language Centre) (GBR ISSN 0033-6882) 5164
R E L C Newsletter (Regional English Language Centre) (SGP ISSN 0217-3077) 5164
R E L I E F see Revue Electronique de Litterature Francaise 5362
• ➤ R E L I E V E: Revista Electronica de Investigacion y Evaluacion Educativa/Electronic Journal of Educational Research, Assessment and Evaluation (ESP ISSN 1134-4032) 2902
R E L I M see Revista Electronica de Literatura Mexicana 5361
R E M (Retail Entertainment Monthly) (AUS) 2403
R E M see Rangeland Ecology & Management 699
• R E M A (Revista Electronica de Medotologia Aplicadad) (ESP ISSN 1135-6855) 5527
➤ R E M E Journal (Royal Electrical & Mechanical Engineers) (GBR ISSN 0432-2924) 3394
R E M R A see Russia and Eurasia Military Review Annual 6444
R E M: The Real Estate Magazine (CAN ISSN 1201-1223) 7606
R E Magazine (Rural Electrification) (USA) 3161
R E N O Praxis (Rechtsanwalts- und Notariatsangestellten) (DEU) 4765
R.E. Olds Transportation Museum Newsletter (USA) 8509
R E P S Directory see Western Australian Resource Development Services. Directory 2034
R E R see Rental Equipment Register 1839
• R E R F Update (Online English Edition) (JPN) 6205
• R E R F Update (Online Japanese Edition) (JPN) 6205
➤ R E R I C International Energy Journal (Regional Energy Resources Information Center) (THA ISSN 0857-6173) 3145
• R E R Reports (Rental Equipment Register) (USA) 1839
R E. Review of Ethnology see International Union of Anthropological and Ethnological Sciences. Newsletter 343
R E S see The Review of English Studies 5360
R E S (New York) (Resource) (USA ISSN 1539-4654) 6976
R E S N A Conference. Proceedings (Rehabilitation Engineering & Assistive Technology Society of North America) (USA ISSN 1067-9111) 6115
R E S N A News (Rehabilitation Engineering and Assistive Technology Society of North America) (USA) 3045
• R E S P A News Monthly (Real Estate Settlement Procedures Act) (USA ISSN 1940-350X) 4765
R E S S see Revue Europeenne des Sciences Sociales 7998
• R E S S I (Revue Electronique Suisse de Science de l'Information) (CHE ISSN 1661-1802) 5041
R E T see Real Estate Technology 7610
• R E T E L (Revista de Toxicologia en Linea) (ARG ISSN 1668-091X) 7538
R E T N see Real Estate Technology News 7619
• R E T Revista de Toxicomanias (ESP ISSN 1136-0968) 2698
R E Today (Religious Education) (GBR ISSN 0266-7738) 2902
R E U (Revista de Ensenanza Universitaria) (ESP) 2902
R E U Technical Series (Regional Office for Europe) (ITA ISSN 1020-3737) 149
• R E V E R. Revista de Estudos da Religiao (BRA ISSN 1677-1222) 7673
R E V I S A see Revista Brasileira de Vigilancia Sanitaria 7539
† • ➤ R E: view (Rehabilitation and Education) (USA ISSN 0899-1510) 8983
• R E X E (Revista de Estudios y Experiencias en Educacion) (CHL ISSN 0717-6945) 2902
R F see Realidad Ferroviaria 8624
R F B & D Impact (Recording for the Blind & Dyslexic) (USA) 4084
R F B Survey see Remittances of Foreign Balances Survey 8551
R F Conseil (Revue Fiduciaire) (FRA ISSN 1167-7848) 1789
R F D (Rural Free Delivery) (USA ISSN 0149-709X) 4378
R F D A see Revue Francaise de Droit Administratif 4774
R F D News (USA ISSN 0481-5084) 149
R F D-TV (Rural Free Delivery) (USA ISSN 1948-027X) 2388

▼ new title † ceased • electronic media ➤ refereed

Title

▼ new title   † ceased   ● electronic media   ➤ refereed

Rakuno Gakuen Daigaku Kiyo. Shizen Kagaku Hen/Rakuno Gakuen University. Journal: Natural Science (JPN ISSN 0388-001X) 269
Rakuno Gakuen University. Cultural and Social Sciences see Rakuno Gakuen Daigaku Kiyo. Jinbun Shakai Kagaku Hen 149
Rakuno Gakuen University. Journal: Natural Science see Rakuno Gakuen Daigaku Kiyo. Shizen Kagaku Hen 269
▼ Ralahine Utopian Studies (GBR ISSN 1661-5875) 5357
Rally (IND ISSN 0048-668X) 7813
† Rally & Motori (ITA ISSN 1124-5409) 8984
Rally Jaaroverzicht (NLD ISSN 1874-0030) 8196
The Rally Leader (NZL) 2210
Rally Sport (GBR ISSN 0140-542X) 8600
Rally Sprint (ITA ISSN 1122-7141) 8196
Rallycourse (GBR ISSN 0265-2617) 8196
Rallye Monte-Carlo (ITA ISSN 1827-0778) 8600
Rallyes Magazine (FRA ISSN 1254-0331) 8196
Rallyes Magazine. Hors Serie see Rallyes Magazine 8196
• Ralph (AUS ISSN 1449-650X) 6299
Ralph (CAN ISSN 1203-0287) 5433
Ralph (USA) 5357
Ralph H. Blanchard Memorial Endowment Series (USA) 4520
Ralph's Review (USA) 5446
Ram (GRC ISSN 1107-8618) 2435
The Ram (USA) 2298
The Ram Page (USA) 2298
Ram - The Letter Box (USA) 5433
• Ramada Worldwide Directory (USA) 4396
Ramadan see Ad- Dustour 3901
Ramakrishna Mission Institute of Culture. Bulletin (IND ISSN 0971-2755) 4471
• ➤ The Ramanujan Journal (USA ISSN 1382-4090) 5527
• Ramanujan Mathematical Society. Journal (IND ISSN 0970-1249) 5528
• Ramanujan Mathematical Society. Lecture Notes Series (IND) 5528
Ramanujan Series on Little Mathematical Treasures see Little Mathematical Treasures 5509
Ramavtal (SWE) 1421
Ramazzini/Norwegian Journal of Occupational Medicine (NOR ISSN 0805-5238) 6685
Rambam (DNK ISSN 0907-2160) 3560
The Rambler (USA ISSN 1557-5322) 5357
• Rambles (USA) 514
Ramblings see Queer Ramblings 4378
Rambunctious Review (USA ISSN 0889-1664) 5357
Ramdam (FRA ISSN 1276-6267) 514
Ramp (USA ISSN 1541-4671) 6299
Rampant (NZL ISSN 1177-2581) 8064
The Rampant Colt (USA ISSN 1934-7421) 4345
Rampant Lion (USA ISSN 1076-4658) 4256
Die Rampe (AUT ISSN 1562-8272) 5357
Rampelyset (DNK ISSN 0107-1882) 8477
Rampike Magazine (CAN ISSN 0834-3551) 514
The Ram's Horn (CAN ISSN 0827-4053) 150
➤ Ram's Horn (USA ISSN 0272-2747) 5165
Ramuri (ROM ISSN 1220-6342) 3933
• ➤ Ramus (AUS ISSN 0048-671X) 2239
Ran (DEU ISSN 0004-7899) 7176
Ran/Kansai Society of Naval Architects, Japan. Bulletin see Kanrin 8649
Rana Blad (NOR) 3924
Ranch & Coast (Rancho Santa Fe) (USA ISSN 1543-589X) 3986
• Ranch & Rural Living Magazine (USA ISSN 1084-5402) 297
Ranch Express (IND) 3888
Rancher see Ganadero 287
Ranchero Courier (USA) 4345
• Ranchi Express (IND) 3888
Ranchi University Mathematical Journal (IND ISSN 0079-9602) 5528
Ranching Review see Revista Pecuaria 298
Rancho Santa Ana Botanic Garden Occasional Publications (USA ISSN 1094-1398) 814
Rand Afrikaans University Rapport see R A U - Rapport 2999
Rand Corporation. Annual Report (USA) 8436
• ➤ RAND Journal of Economics (USA ISSN 0741-6261) 1164
Rand McNally Business Traveler's Road Atlas (USA) 8750
Rand McNally Commercial Atlas and Marketing Guide (USA) 1839
Rand McNally Goode's World Atlas (USA) 4026
Rand McNally Motor Carriers' Road Atlas (USA) 8675
Rand McNally Road Atlas & Travel Guide (USA) 8750
Rand McNally Ultimate Road Atlas & Vacation Guide (USA) 8750
† Rand McNally World Facts & Maps (USA ISSN 1057-9834) 8984
Rand Publications Series (USA) 7901
• Rand Review (USA ISSN 1557-2897) 7176
Randa (ESP ISSN 0210-5993) 4471
Rande Extra (SVK ISSN 1336-2925) 7943
Rando Alpes see Alpes Magazine Balades et Randonnees 8302
Rando Pyrenees (FRA ISSN 1769-1400) 8330
Randolph-Macon College. Bulletin (USA) 2298
Random Flight Plan A F T N Address Book (Aeronautical Fixed Telecommunications Network) (GBR) 8550
• Random Lengths (USA ISSN 0483-9420) 3715
Random Lengths Big Book (USA ISSN 0891-7833) 3715
• Random Lengths International Report (USA ISSN 1532-1436) 3715
• Random Lengths Midweek Market Report (USA) 3715
• Random Lengths Yardstick (USA ISSN 1055-0895) 3709
Random Lengths Yearbook (USA ISSN 0485-9960) 3709
➤ Random Materials and Processes (NLD ISSN 0925-5850) 7036
Random Notes see Suibi 5383
• ➤ Random Operators and Stochastic Equations (DEU ISSN 0926-6364) 5528
• ➤ Random Structures & Algorithms (USA ISSN 1042-9832) 5528
Random Thoughts (CAN ISSN 0380-8114) 4345
Randonner a Cheval (FRA) 8330
• Randosukepu Kenkyu/Japanese Institute of Landscape Architecture. Journal (JPN ISSN 1340-8984) 3748
Randse Afrikaanse Universiteit. Jaarboek (ZAF) 2999
The Randy Reviewer (USA) 5236
Rang Tarang (IND) 3888
Rangahau Tane Ai Tane see G A P S S 8103
Ranganathan Institute of Library and Information Science for Applied Research Bulletin see R I L I S A R Bulletin 5041
Rangbhumi (IND) 6511
RANGE (Carson City) (USA ISSN 1093-3670) 5081
Range Management Newsletter (AUS ISSN 0812-4930) 150
Range Reminiscing (USA) 4309
Rangefinder (USA ISSN 0033-9202) 6976
• ➤ Rangeland Ecology & Management (USA ISSN 1550-7424) 699
• ➤ The Rangeland Journal (AUS ISSN 1036-9872) 2625
• Rangelands (USA ISSN 0190-0528) 297
Rangel's Reports (USA ISSN 0882-312X) 7261
The Ranger (GBR ISSN 1755-3709) 8266
Ranger (Amarillo) (USA) 2298
Ranger (Morristown) (USA) 4982
• Ranger Rick (USA ISSN 0738-6656) 2210
Ranger Rick Educator's Guide see Ranger Rick 2210
Rangerbred News (USA) 8297
Rangers (GBR ISSN 1463-9718) 8243
▼ The Ranger's Guide to Yellowstone (USA ISSN 1941-8485) 8750
Rangers Monthly see Rangers 8243
Rangers News (GBR ISSN 0965-111X) 8243
Rangers Now (USA) 7740
• ➤ Rangifer (NOR ISSN 0333-256X) 298
Rangifer. Report (NOR ISSN 0808-2359) 298
➤ Rangifer. Special Issue (NOR ISSN 0801-6399) 298
• Rangikainga (NZL ISSN 1177-5068) 8127
Rangitikei Mail (NZL) 3918
Rani Muthu (IND ISSN 0971-8826) 3888
Rank (GBR) 2260
Ranking Arizona (USA ISSN 1946-9179) 1965
Ranking of Investment Analysts (GBR) 1646
† Rankings & Estimates: Rankings of the States and Estimates of School Statistics (USA ISSN 1931-4809) 8984
Ranliao Gongye/Dyestuff Industry see Ranliao yu Ranse 2244
• ➤ Ranliao Huaxue Xuebao/Journal of Fuel Chemistry and Technology (CHN ISSN 0253-2409) 3254
• Ranliao yu Huagong (CHN ISSN 1001-3709) 3254
• Ranliao yu Ranse/Dyestuffs and Coloration (CHN ISSN 1672-1179) 2244
• Ranqi Wolun Shiyan yu Yanjiu/Gas Turbine Experiment and Research (CHN ISSN 1672-2620) 3217
• ➤ Ranshao Kexue yu Jishu/Journal of Combustion Science and Technology (CHN ISSN 1006-8740) 7056
Ransomer (GBR ISSN 0033-9245) 7813
• Rant Magazine (USA) 5236
➤ The Raoul Wallenberg Institute Human Rights Guides (NLD ISSN 1384-6442) 7214
The Raoul Wallenberg Institute Human Rights Library (NLD ISSN 1388-3208) 4851
The Raoul Wallenberg Institute New Authors Series (NLD ISSN 1574-8022) 4851
The Raoul Wallenberg Institute Series of Intergovernmental Human Rights Documentation (NLD ISSN 1566-7766) 4851
Rap Brasil (BRA ISSN 1517-1833) 6609
Rap Brasil Especial (BRA ISSN 1519-1567) 514
Rap & Groove (FRA ISSN 1966-6748) 6609
Rap Ireland (IRL) 6609
Rap Mag (FRA ISSN 1773-5858) 6609
• Rap Pages (USA ISSN 1063-1283) 6609
• Rap Sheet (USA) 6609
Rap U S see Rap & Groove 6609
Rap-Up (USA ISSN 1943-4006) 6609
➤ Rapa Nui Journal (USA ISSN 1040-1385) 352
• Rapaport Diamond Report (USA ISSN 0746-9829) 4569
• Rapid (CAN ISSN 1494-9172) 8330
• ➤ Rapid Communications in Mass Spectrometry (GBR ISSN 0951-4198) 2104
• Rapid Excavation and Tunneling Conference Proceedings (USA ISSN 1045-9065) 6330
Rapid Notice News Service (USA) 6899
† • Rapid Prototyping (USA ISSN 1544-9491) 8984
• ➤ Rapid Prototyping Journal (GBR ISSN 1355-2546) 3394
Rapid Readers Series (USA ISSN 0160-3949) 1164
Rapid Reports see Statisticne Informacije 8405
Rapid Technology eJournal see R T eJournal 1902
• Rapid Transit Monitor (GBR ISSN 1367-6040) 8509
• Rapidly Changing Face of Computing (USA ISSN 1520-8117) 2435
Raport Asupra Guvernarii/Policy Warning Report (ROM) 7176
Raport o Inflacji (POL ISSN 1640-0747) 1721
RapPages see Rap Pages 6609
Rappel (Charleroi Regional Edition) see Vers l'Avenir 3802
Rapport (FRA ISSN 0768-9756) 8509
• Rapport (GBR ISSN 1462-8007) 8064
Rapport (USA ISSN 1061-6861) 7572
• Rapport (ZAF ISSN 1017-1657) 3949
Rapport Annuel (Year) sur la Sante de la Population see Annual Report on the Health of the Population 7507
Rapport Annuel de C A N A F E see F I N T R A C Annual Report 1108
Rapport Annuel de Gestion see Quebec Province. Bureau du Verificateur General. Rapport Annuel de Gestion 1941
Rapport Annuel de Gestion (Year) (CAN ISSN 1709-6227) 7464
Rapport Annuel de Production des Peches Maritimes et des Cultures Marines see Office National Interprofessionnel des Produits de la Mer et de l'Aquaculture. Rapport Annuel 3604
Rapport Annuel du B S I F see O S F I Annual Report 7458
Rapport Annuel du Juge-Avocat General au Ministre de la Defense Nationale sur l'Administration de la Justice Militaire dans les Forces Canadiennes see Canada. Office of the Judge Advocate General. Annual Report of the Judge Advocate General to the Minister of National Defence on the Administration of Military Justice in the Canadian Forces 4971
Rapport Annuel du Secretaire General Interimaire aux Membres de la Commission Canadienne pour l'UNESCO see Canadian Commission for Unesco. Annual Report of the Secretary-General 4920
Rapport Annuel et Compte - Rendu Financier see Cameroon Development Corporation. Annual Report and Accounts 1882
Rapport Annuel sur la Cooperation au Developpement - Burundi (USA) 1604
Rapport Annuel sur l'Assistance au Developpement: Rwanda (RWA) 1604
Rapport Annuel sur le Commerce Exterieur des Produits de la Mer see Commerce Exterieur des Produits de la Mer et de l'Aquaculture 3589
Rapport Annuel sur l'Economie Syrienne (SYR ISSN 0079-9696) 1513
Rapport Annuel Sur les Ententes Federales-Provinciales Concernant le Progamme de Lutte Contre les Pluies Acides Dans l'Est du Canada see Federal - Provincial Agreements for the Eastern Canada Acid Rain Program. Annual Report 3431
Rapport Annuel sur l'Etat du Phenomene de la Drogue dans l'Union Europeenne see State of the Drugs Problem in the European Union. Annual Report 2699
Rapport Annuel sur l'Evolution de la Flotte de Peche see Belgium. Administration des Affaires Maritimes et de la Navigation. Rapport Annuel sur l'Evolution de la Flotte de Peche 8639
Rapport aux Gouvernements see Canadian Intergovernmental Conference Secretariat. Report to Governments 7428
Rapport Canadien a l'Industrie sur les Sciences Halieutiques et Aquatiques see Canadian Industry Report of Fisheries and Aquatic Sciences 3588
Rapport d'Activite du L I M S I see Laboratoire d'Informatique pour la Mecanique et les Sciences de l'Ingenieur. Rapport d'Activite 3208
Rapport d'Activite et Bilan des Activites de Prelevement et de Greffe en France see Agence de la Biomedecine. Rapport Annuel Bilan des Activites 5570
• Rapport d'Activite et de Developpement Durable (FRA ISSN 1769-4566) 8550
Rapport d'Activites des Entreprises du Secteur Moderne (COG) 1259
Rapport Depose au Parlement par le Ministre des Peches et des Oceans Concernant l'Administration de la Loi sur la Restructuration du Secteur des Peches de l'Atlantique pour l'Annee Financiere see Report to Parliament by the Minister of Fisheries and Oceans Respecting the Administration of the Atlantic Fisheries Restructuring Act 1942
Rapport des Plaintes see L' Application de la Procedure d'Examen des Plaintes et l'Amelioration de la Qualite des Services. Rapport Annuel 7508
Rapport d'Etape d'I R S C/Rx & D see Welcome to the C I H R - Rx & D Progress Report (Year) 6885
Rapport d'Exercice - D G-Bank see Deutsche Zentral-Genossenschaftsbank. Geschaeftsbericht 1335
• Le Rapport d'Inventaire National (CAN ISSN 1910-7056) 3462
Rapport du C S A R S see S I R C Report 7264
Rapport du Conseiller en Ethique sur les Activites du Bureau du Conseiller en Ethique see Report of the Ethics Counsellor on the Activities of the Office of the Ethics Counsellor 7465
Rapport du Directeur sur l'Activite et la Gestion du Bureau International des Poids et Mesures/Director's Report on the Activity and Management of the International Bureau of Weights and Measures (FRA ISSN 1606-3740) 6405
Rapport du Verificateur General a l'Assemblee Legislative see New Brunswick. Office of the Auditor General. Report of the Auditor General to the Legislative Assembly 7455
Rapport Federal sur les Indicateurs Comparables de la Sante see Les Canadiens et les Canadiennes en Sante 7511
Rapport fra S T I K K see Samarbejdsgruppen for Trafiksikkerhed i Kommunerne i Koebenhavns-Omraadet. Rapport 8634
Rapport fra Skogforskningen see Forskning fra Skog og Landskap 3691
Rapport General sur la Securite Sociale au Grand-Duche du Luxembourg see Luxembourg. Inspection Generale de la Securite Sociale. Rapport General sur la Securite Sociale au Grand-Duche de Luxembourg 4513
Rapport General sur l'Activite de l'Union Europeenne see General Report on the Activities of the European Union 3837
Rapport Integration (SWE ISSN 1651-1662) 7291
Rapport Mensuel sur l'Europe see Monthly Report on Europe 7253
Rapport Miljoe, Teknik och Lantbruk (SWE ISSN 1652-3237) 150
Rapport Mondial sur la Communication see Rapport Mondial sur la Communication et l'Information 2337
Rapport Mondial sur la Communication et l'Information (FRA) 2337
Rapport Mondial sur la Science see World Science Report 7930
Rapport Mondial sur l'Education see World Education Report 2926
Rapport Mondial sur l'Information see World Information Report 5055
Rapport om Arbeidsmarkedet see Arbeid og Velferd 1663
Rapport pour l'Exercice see Institut National pour l'Etude et la Recherche Agronomique. Rapport Annuel 122
• Rapport Statistique a l'Intention des Agents Immobiliers. Region Metropolitaine de Saguenay (CAN ISSN 1912-2365) 7618
• Rapport Statistique a l'Intention des Agents Immobiliers. Region Metropolitaine de Trois-Rivieres, Agglomeration de Shawinigan (CAN ISSN 1912-2381) 7618
• Rapport sur la Facturation Reciproque, Canada (CAN ISSN 1709-5298) 4110
Rapport sur la Politique Monetaire see Monetary Policy Report 1499
Rapport sur la Situation Demographique de la France (FRA) 7291
Rapport sur la Situation Sociale dans le Monde see Report on the World Social Situation (Year) 8128
Rapport sur l'Alimentation Mondiale see World Food Report 3668
Rapport sur l'Application de la Loi sur les Prestations d'Adaptation pour les Travailleurs see Report on the Administration of the Labour Adjustment Benefits Act 1705
Rapport sur le Commerce et le Developpement see Trade and Development Report 1584
• Rapport sur le Commerce Mondial (CHE ISSN 1813-811X) 1581
• Rapport sur le Developpement dans le Monde (USA ISSN 0271-1710) 1604
Rapport sur le Developpement en Afrique see African Development Report (Year) 1590
• Rapport sur le Marche Locatif. Faits Saillants. Alberta (CAN ISSN 1912-4805) 7606
• Rapport sur le Marche Locatif. Faits Saillants. Colombie-Britannique (CAN ISSN 1912-4821) 7606
• Rapport sur le Marche Locatif. Faits Saillants. Ile-du-Prince-Edouard (CAN ISSN 1912-3469) 7606
Rapport sur le Marche Locatif. Faits Saillants. Manitoba (CAN ISSN 1912-340X) 7606
• Rapport sur le Marche Locatif. Faits Saillants. Nouveau-Brunswick (CAN ISSN 1912-4899) 7606
• Rapport sur le Marche Locatif. Faits Saillants. Nouvelle-Ecosse (CAN ISSN 1912-3442) 7606
• Rapport sur le Marche Locatif. Faits Saillants. Ontario (CAN ISSN 1912-4848) 7606
• Rapport sur le Marche Locatif. Faits Saillants. Quebec (CAN ISSN 1912-4872) 7606
• Rapport sur le Marche Locatif. Faits Saillants. Saskatchewan (CAN ISSN 1912-4961) 7606
• Rapport sur le Marche Locatif. Faits Saillants. Terre-Neuve-et-Labrador (CAN ISSN 1912-3426) 7607
• Rapport sur le Marche Locatif. Faits Saillants. Yellowknife. Territories du Nord-Ouest (CAN ISSN 1912-4988) 7607

Title

10788 REAL ESTATE LAW LETTER ULRICH'S PERIODICALS

Real Estate Law Letter *see* Tennessee Real Estate Law Letter 4794
Real Estate Law Report (USA ISSN 0162-752X) 4765
Real Estate Law Reporter *see* New York Real Estate Law Reporter 4745
Real Estate Litigation (USA ISSN 2150-0916) 7609
Real Estate Magazine (NLD ISSN 1388-3887) 7609
Real Estate Market Facts (AUS) 7618
Real Estate Market in New Zealand. Provisional Report *see* New Zealand Real Estate Market. Summary Report 7602
Real Estate Mid-America *see* Real Estate Forum 7608
Real Estate Millionaire (CAN ISSN 1712-7246) 7609
• Real Estate New Jersey (USA ISSN 1942-4744) 7609
• Real Estate New York (USA ISSN 1079-1272) 1031
Real Estate News (CAN ISSN 0225-2783) 7609
Real Estate News (Brooklyn) (USA ISSN 1072-9364) 7609
Real Estate News (Chicago) (USA) 7609
Real Estate News and Buyers Guide (CAN) 7609
Real Estate Newsline (USA ISSN 0749-8640) 7609
Real Estate Outlook: Market Trends & Insights (USA) 7609
Real Estate Portfolio (USA) 7609
• Real Estate/Portfolio Strategist (USA) 7609
The Real Estate Professional (USA ISSN 0744-4516) 7609
Real Estate Professional's Tax Guide (USA) 7609
Real Estate Record (USA) 7609
• Real Estate Recording Guide (Online Edition) (USA) 7609
Real Estate, Renting and Business Activities Statistics *see* Norway. Statistisk Sentralbyraa. Statistikk over Eiendomsdrift, Forretningsmessig Tjenesteyting og Utleierivirksomhet 7618
Real Estate Research/Fudosan Kenkyu (JPN ISSN 0532-7776) 7609
• Real Estate Review (USA ISSN 0034-0790) 7609
Real Estate Salesperson's and Sub-Mortgage Broker's Pre-Licensing Course Manual *see* Real Estate Trading Services Licensing Course Manual 7610
Real Estate Securities Daily *see* Real Estate Daily: North America Edition 1647
Real Estate Settlement Procedures Act News Monthly *see* R E S P A News Monthly 4765
• Real Estate Software Guide (USA ISSN 1521-5512) 7619
Real Estate Solutions Guide *see* Florida Realtor 7591
• Real Estate Southern California (USA ISSN 1547-4186) 7609
Real Estate Tax Guide *see* Real Estate Professional's Tax Guide 7609
• Real Estate Taxation (USA ISSN 1538-3792) 7610
• Real Estate Technology (USA) 7610
• Real Estate Technology News (USA ISSN 1559-6249) 7619
Real Estate Times/Fangdichan Dao Bao (HKG ISSN 1012-3253) 7610
Real Estate Trading Services Licensing Course Manual (CAN ISSN 1715-9652) 7610
• Real Estate Transactions (USA ISSN 1070-6704) 1941
Real Estate Transactions: Condemnation Procedure and Techniques Forms (USA) 7610
Real Estate Transactions: Condominium Law and Practice Forms (USA) 7610
Real Estate Transactions: Purchase and Sale of Real Property (USA) 7610
Real Estate Transactions Series (USA) 7610
Real Estate Transactions: Tax Planning and Consequences (USA) 7610
Real Estate Victoria (CAN) 7610
• Real Estate Weekly (USA ISSN 1096-7214) 7610
▼ • Real Estate Weekly News (USA ISSN 1945-8339) 7610
Real Estatement (USA) 7610
Real Florida *see* Florida Parks & Wildlife 8704
Real Goods Solar Living Sourcebook *see* Gaiam Real Goods Solar Living Sourcebook 3176
The Real Groove (NZL ISSN 1172-2096) 6609
Real Health (USA) 6995
Real Health & Beauty (GBR ISSN 1465-2803) 8847
Real Hip-Hop Magazine *see* R H N Magazine 6608
Real Hip-Hop Network Magazine *see* R H N Magazine 6608
Real Homes (GBR ISSN 1464-4061) 4562
• Real Innovation Newsletter (USA ISSN 1933-9224) 1789
• Real Instituto El Cano de Estudios Internacionales y Estrategicos. Newsletter (ESP ISSN 1698-1944) 7261
• Real Instituto de Estudios Asturianos. Boletin (ESP ISSN 1133-5262) 4256
▼ • Real Law Central (USA ISSN 1940-1655) 7610
• Real Leaders (CAN ISSN 1912-225X) 8881
• Real Life (GBR) 7814
Real Life Decorating (USA) 4549
• Real Lives (GBR ISSN 1367-5486) 973
Real Living (PHL) 4549
Real Living (Sydney) (AUS ISSN 1833-0398) 4562
• Real Living with Diabetes (USA ISSN 1074-7648) 5899
• Real Living with Multiple Sclerosis (USA ISSN 1079-4220) 6180
Real Lottery Winning Guide (USA) 8196
Real Money (GBR ISSN 1468-5612) 1647
Real Parenting (THA) 2166
• Real Patronato sobre Discapacidad. Boletin (ESP ISSN 1696-0998) 4069
Real People (GBR ISSN 1748-8982) 3870
Real People (USA ISSN 1040-9335) 645
Real Pottery (GBR ISSN 0953-0436) 539
Real Property (USA ISSN 0445-4278) 7610
Real Property *see* B A R - B R I Bar Review. Real Property 4625
Real Property Institute (USA) 4765
Real Property Law Journal *see* N.Y. Real Property Law Journal 7601
Real Property Law Journal *see* N Y Real Property Law Section Journal 4738
Real Property Law Reporter (USA ISSN 0898-1698) 4765
Real Property, Probate and Trust Journal *see* Real Property, Trust and Estate Law Journal 4905
Real Property, Probate and Trust Law Newsletter (USA) 7610
Real Property, Probate and Trust News *see* R P P T News 4905
Real Property Reports (3rd Series) (CAN ISSN 0703-4687) 7610
• Real Property, Trust and Estate Law Journal (USA) 4905
• Real Simple (USA ISSN 1528-1701) 8881
Real Simple South Africa (ZAF ISSN 1816-5109) 4366
Real Sociedad Arqueologica. Boletin Arqueologico *see* Real Sociedad Arqueologica. Butlleti Arqueologic 413
Real Sociedad Arqueologica. Butlleti Arqueologic (ESP ISSN 1695-5862) 413
Real Sociedad Bascongada de los Amigos del Pais. Boletin (ESP ISSN 0211-111X) 7995
Real Sociedad Espanola de Historia Natural. Boletin. Actas (ESP ISSN 0583-7499) 699
Real Sociedad Espanola de Historia Natural. Boletin. Seccion Biologica (ESP ISSN 0366-3272) 699
Real Sociedad Espanola de Historia Natural. Boletin. Seccion Geologica (ESP ISSN 0583-7510) 2763
Real Sociedad Espanola de Historia Natural. Memorias (ESP ISSN 1132-0869) 7902
➤ Real Sociedad Espanola de Quimica. Anales (ESP ISSN 1575-3417) 2078
Real Sociedad Geografica. Boletin (ESP ISSN 0210-8577) 4026
Real Sociedad Matematica Espanola. Gaceta (ESP ISSN 1138-8927) 5528
Real Sports *see* Amy Love's Real Sports 8158
Real Time *see* RealTime 8477
Real-Time Engineering (USA ISSN 1076-4429) 2468
Real Time Engineering *see* Real-Time Engineering 2468
† • ➤ Real-Time Imaging (GBR ISSN 1077-2014) 8984
➤ Real-Time Safety Critical Systems (NLD ISSN 1572-5960) 2468
• ➤ Real-Time Systems (USA ISSN 0922-6443) 2524
• Real-Time Systems Symposium (USA ISSN 1052-8725) 2524
Real-Time Technology and Applications Symposium. Proceedings *see* I E E E Real-Time Technology and Applications Symposium. Proceedings 3291
• Real Times (USA ISSN 0275-4770) 3986
• Real Wealth Report (USA ISSN 1548-3347) 1378
Real Wives (GBR ISSN 1356-3394) 6299
Real Women (USA) 8881
• RealAdviser (GBR ISSN 1749-5717) 1647
• REALbasic Developer (USA ISSN 1540-3114) 2509
Reales Sitios (ESP ISSN 0486-0993) 455
• Realidad Economica (ARG ISSN 0325-1926) 1513
Realidad Economico-Social *see* Revista de Ciencias Sociales y Humanidades 1515
• Realidad Ferroviaria (ARG) 8624
Realidad Peruana (PER) 1513
REALIDAD: Revista de Ciencias Sociales y Humanidades *see* Revista de Ciencias Sociales y Humanidades 1515
Realidades (MEX) 8509
Realisa Son (USA) 2389
▼ Realisatie Milieudoelen (NLD ISSN 1874-7086) 3462
Realisations *see* Achievements 7418
Realisations du C R T C *see* C R T C Accomplishments 2314
Realit (CZE ISSN 1210-8308) 7610
Realites Cardiologiques (FRA ISSN 1145-1955) 5798
Realites Cliniques (FRA ISSN 0999-5021) 5863
Realites en Gynecologie-Obstetrique (FRA ISSN 1264-8809) 6002
▼ Realites en Nutrition (FRA ISSN 1958-1084) 6668
▼ Realites en Rhumatologie (FRA ISSN 1960-1980) 6225
Realites & Vaccinations (FRA ISSN 1777-3261) 5702
Realites Familiales (FRA ISSN 0220-9926) 8064
Realites Gabonaises (GAB ISSN 0486-106X) 7176
• Realites Industrielles (FRA ISSN 1148-7941) 6477
Realites Ophtalmologiques (FRA ISSN 1242-0018) 6050
Realites Pediatriques (FRA ISSN 1266-3697) 6103
Realites Therapeutiques en Dermato-Venerologie (FRA ISSN 1155-2492) 5881
• Realities (USA) 5433
Reality (IRL ISSN 0034-0960) 7814
Reality (NZL ISSN 1172-9236) 7673
Reality (Houston) (USA ISSN 1041-8199) 5863
Reality Now (CAN) 3462
Reality Now (USA ISSN 1041-8253) 5863
The Reality of Aid (Year) (GBR) 1604
Realizace Staveb (CZE ISSN 1802-0631) 1032
Realizations (Estrie) (CAN ISSN 1910-0159) 150
Realize (CAN) 4069
Realizm - Nowy Ustroj Spoleczno-Polityczny (POL ISSN 1426-2924) 7176
Reallexikon fuer Antike und Christentum (DEU) 7673
Reallexikon zur Byzantinischen Kunst (DEU) 514
Really Big Ten *see* Athlon's Big Ten Football 8221
• Realm (CAN) 6703
Realm (North American Edition) *see* Heritage 3866
Realms of Fantasy (USA ISSN 1078-1951) 5446
• RealPoetik (USA) 5433
Realschule in Deutschland (DEU ISSN 0945-4306) 2903
• RealScreen (CAN ISSN 1480-1434) 1164
• Realta Forense (ITA) 4766
Realta Nuova (ITA ISSN 0391-867X) 3898
• RealTime (AUS ISSN 1321-4799) 8477
RealTime and Onlinescreen *see* RealTime 8477
Realtime Magazine (ZAF) 3949
RealTime + Online Screen *see* RealTime 8477
The Realtor (Portland) (USA) 7610
• Realtor Magazine (USA ISSN 1522-0842) 7610
Realty and Building (USA ISSN 0034-1045) 7610
Realty Report (USA) 7610
Realty Stock Digest (USA) 1647
Realty Stock Review (USA ISSN 1075-7554) 1647
▼ • Realtyscorecard.com (USA ISSN 1949-0798) 7610
• ➤ Reanimation (FRA ISSN 1624-0693) 5773
Reappraisals, Canadian Writers (CAN ISSN 1189-6787) 5358
The Rear View Mirror (USA ISSN 1547-1594) 2269
• Reason (USA ISSN 0048-6906) 5236
Reason & Revelation (USA ISSN 1542-0922) 7772
A Reason for Hope (USA) 6180
➤ Reason in Practice (GBR ISSN 1473-589X) 6946
➤ Reason Papers (USA ISSN 0363-1893) 6946
Rebe und Wein (DEU ISSN 0034-1118) 609
Rebecca (SVK ISSN 1336-586X) 8881
▼ • Rebel Rodz (USA ISSN 1936-1777) 8600
Rebelde (ESP ISSN 1887-1186) 2210
• Rebell (Oslo. Trykt Utg.) (NOR ISSN 0802-3786) 7214
Rebis Chapbook Series (USA ISSN 0147-0396) 5433
Rebiun *see* Red de Bibliotecas Universitarias 8984
• Rebondir (FRA ISSN 1243-6267) 6703
• Rebuilding Wall Street (USA) 1164
➤ De Rebus (ZAF ISSN 0250-0329) 4766
Rebusache (ROM ISSN 1222-7013) 4345
Rebyu ng Agham Panlipunan ng Pilipinas *see* Philippine Social Sciences Review 4469
Rec Naroda (SRB ISSN 0034-1142) 5236
Recados do Coracao (BRA ISSN 1677-7433) 2210
• ➤ ReCall (GBR ISSN 0958-3440) 2469
Recambio Libre (ESP ISSN 1132-1490) 8600
• Recambios & Accesorios (ESP ISSN 1579-2404) 8600
Recanati Institute for Maritime Studies News *see* R I M S News 413
• Recap (GBR) 1378
Recap of Milk Receipts and Utilization in Montana (USA) 269
Receivables Management Services *see* Credit Management Magazine 8947
• The Receivables Report (USA ISSN 1060-0418) 1299
• Recensioni Filosofiche (ITA ISSN 1826-4654) 6946
Recent Advances in Anaesthesia and Intensive Care (GBR ISSN 1743-4017) 5773
Recent Advances in Animal Nutrition (GBR ISSN 0269-5642) 298
Recent Advances in Computational Chemistry (SGP) 2078
Recent Advances in Conductive Education (GBR ISSN 1476-2374) 2903
Recent Advances in Histopathology (GBR ISSN 0143-6953) 5702
Recent Advances in Human Biology (SGP) 699
Recent Advances in Ophthalmology *see* Yanke Xin Jinzhan 6053
Recent Advances in Paediatrics (GBR ISSN 0309-0140) 6103
• Recent Advances in Phytochemistry (USA ISSN 0079-9920) 814
Recent Advances in Surgery (GBR ISSN 0143-8395) 6256
† Recent Advances in Urology (GBR ISSN 1464-2883) 8984
Recent American History *see* Modern American History: the United States Since 1865 4304
Recent Demographic Developments in Europe and North America (FRA) 7291
➤ Recent Developments in Alcoholism (USA ISSN 0738-422X) 2698
Recent Developments in Colloids & Interface Research (IND) 2140
Recent Developments in International Banking and Finance (USA) 1378
Recent Developments of World Seismology *see* Guoji Dizhen Dongtai 2783
➤ Recent Economic Thought (NLD ISSN 0924-199X) 1548
Recent Ethics Opinions (USA ISSN 0276-055X) 4766
Recent Laws of Nepal (NPL ISSN 1017-1452) 4766
• ➤ Recent Patents on Anti-Cancer Drug Discovery (NLD ISSN 1574-8928) 6033
• ➤ Recent Patents on Anti-Infective Drug Discovery (NLD ISSN 1574-891X) 5765
▼ • ➤ Recent Patents on Biomedical Engineering (NLD ISSN 1874-7647) 6757
• ➤ Recent Patents on Biotechnology (NLD ISSN 1872-2083) 770
• ➤ Recent Patents on C N S Drug Discovery (Central Nervous System) (NLD ISSN 1574-8898) 6180
• ➤ Recent Patents on Cardiovascular Drug Discovery (NLD ISSN 1574-8901) 5798
▼ • ➤ Recent Patents on Chemical Engineering (NLD ISSN 1874-4788) 6757
▼ • ➤ Recent Patents on Computer Science (NLD ISSN 1874-4796) 6757
• ➤ Recent Patents on D N A & Gene Sequences (NLD ISSN 1872-2156) 3780
Recent Patents on DNA & Gene Sequences *see* Recent Patents on D N A & Gene Sequences 3780
• ➤ Recent Patents on Drug Delivery & Formulation (NLD ISSN 1872-2113) 6877
▼ • ➤ Recent Patents on Electrical Engineering (NLD ISSN 1874-4761) 6757
• ➤ Recent Patents on Endocrine, Metabolic & Immune Drug Discovery (NLD ISSN 1872-2148) 5765
• ➤ Recent Patents on Engineering (NLD ISSN 1872-2121) 3217
▼ • ➤ Recent Patents on Food, Nutrition & Agriculture (NLD ISSN 1876-1429) 6757
• ➤ Recent Patents on Inflammation & Allergy Drug Discovery (NLD ISSN 1872-213X) 5765
▼ • Recent Patents on Materials Science (NLD ISSN 1874-4648) 6757
▼ • ➤ Recent Patents on Mechanical Engineering (NLD ISSN 1874-477X) 6757
• ➤ Recent Patents on Nanatechnology (NLD ISSN 1872-2105) 7036
Recent Progress of Kanpo Medicine in Obstetrics and Gynecology *see* Sanfujinka Kanpo Kenkyu no Ayumi 6004
Recent Publications of the Southern Research Station *see* Compass (Asheville) 3412
Recent Publications on the European Union Received by the Library/Neuerscheinungen ueber die Europaeische Union Eingegangen in der Bibliothek/Nye Publikationer om den Europaeiske Union Modtaget af Biblioteket/Pubblicazioni Recenti sull'Unione Europea Recevute dalla Biblioteca/Publicaciones Recientes sobre la Union Europea Recibidas por la Biblioteca/Publications Recentes sur l'Union Europeenne Recues par la Bibliotheque (LUX ISSN 1024-011X) 7200
Recent Research Development in Chemical Engineering (IND) 3254
Recent Research Developments in Allergy, Asthma & Immunology (IND) 5765
Recent Research Developments in Analytical Biochemistry (IND) 744
Recent Research Developments in Analytical Chemistry (IND) 2104
Recent Research Developments in Antiviral Research (IND) 895
Recent Research Developments in Applied Physics (IND) 7036
Recent Research Developments in Applied Polymer Science (IND) 3254
Recent Research Developments in Bioenergetics (IND) 744
Recent Research Developments in Biophysical Chemistry (IND) 754
Recent Research Developments in Biophysics (IND) 755
Recent Research Developments in Biophysics & Biochemistry (IND) 755
Recent Research Developments in Cancer (IND) 6033
Recent Research Developments in Carbohydrate Research (IND) 744
Recent Research Developments in Chemical Engineering (IND) 3254
Recent Research Developments in Chemical Physics (IND) 2140
Recent Research Developments in Chemistry (IND) 2078
Recent Research Developments in Comparative Biochemistry and Physiology (IND) 744
Recent Research Developments in Crystal Growth (IND) 2112
Recent Research Developments in Ecology (IND) 3462
Recent Research Developments in Electro Analytical Chemistry (IND) 2104
Recent Research Developments in Electrochemistry (IND) 2114
Recent Research Developments in Endocrinology (IND) 5899
Recent Research Developments in Fluid Dynamics (IND) 7062
Recent Research Developments in Genetics (IND) 878
Recent Research Developments in Infection & Immunity (IND) 5825

Link to your serials resources and content with ulrichsweb.com

10792 REFERATIVNYI ZHURNAL. FARMAKOLOGIYA OBSHCHAYA. FARMAKOLOGIYA ULRICH'S PERIODICALS

Referativnyi Zhurnal. Farmakologiya Obshchaya. Farmakologiya Nervnoi Sistemy *see* Referativnyi Zhurnal. Farmakologiia Obshchaia. Khimioterapevtitcheskie Sredstva **6890**

• Referativnyi Zhurnal. Farmakologiya. Toksikologiya (RUS ISSN 0869-4109) **6890**

• Referativnyi Zhurnal. Financy. Banki. Strakhovanie (RUS) **1260**

• Referativnyi Zhurnal. Fitopatologiya (RUS ISSN 0202-9235) **718**

• Referativnyi Zhurnal. Fizicheskaya Khimiya: Khimicheskaya Termodinamika, Fizikokhimicheskii Analiz, Rastvory, Elektrokhimiya (RUS ISSN 0208-1636) **2095**

• Referativnyi Zhurnal. Fizicheskaya Khimiya: Kinetika, Kataliz, Fotokhimiya, Radyatsionnaya Khimiya, Plazmokhimiya (RUS ISSN 0208-1725) **2095**

• Referativnyi Zhurnal. Fizicheskaya Khimiya: Kristallokhimiya, Khimiya Tverdogo Tela, Gazy, Zhidkosti, Amorfnye Tela, Poverkhnostnye Yavleniya, Khimiya Kolloidov (RUS ISSN 0208-1717) **2095**

• Referativnyi Zhurnal. Fizika (RUS ISSN 0034-2343) **7049**

• Referativnyi Zhurnal. Fizika Elementarnykh Chastits i Teoriya Polei (RUS ISSN 0207-1401) **7049**

• Referativnyi Zhurnal. Fizika Gazov i Zhidkostei: Termodinamika i Statisticheskaya Fizika (RUS ISSN 0203-6002) **7049**

▼ • Referativnyi Zhurnal. Fizika Nanoob'ektov i Nanotekhnologiya (RUS) **7049**

• Referativnyi Zhurnal. Fizika Plazmy (RUS ISSN 0203-6010) **7049**

• Referativnyi Zhurnal. Fizika Tverdykh Tel: Elektricheskie Svoistva (RUS ISSN 0235-8867) **7049**

• Referativnyi Zhurnal. Fizika Tverdykh Tel: Magnitnye Svoistva (RUS ISSN 0235-8859) **7049**

• Referativnyi Zhurnal. Fizika Tverdykh Tel: Struktura i Dinamika Reshetki (RUS ISSN 0208-1679) **7049**

• Referativnyi Zhurnal. Fizika Zemli (RUS ISSN 0202-9456) **2720**

• Referativnyi Zhurnal. Fiziologiya Cheloveka i Zhivotnykh. Endokrinnaya Sistema, Razmnozhenie, Laktatsiya (RUS ISSN 0207-1460) **719**

• Referativnyi Zhurnal. Fiziologiya Cheloveka i Zhivotnykh. Krov', Limfa, Krovoobrashchenie, Dykhanie, Pochki (RUS ISSN 0207-1436) **719**

• Referativnyi Zhurnal. Fiziologiya Cheloveka i Zhivotnykh. Neirofiziologiya, Sensornye Sistemy, V N D, Nervno-Myshechnaya Sistema (RUS ISSN 0207-1444) **719**

• Referativnyi Zhurnal. Fiziologiya Cheloveka i Zhivotnykh. Obmen Veshchestv, Pitanie, Pishchevarenie (RUS ISSN 0208-2853) **719**

• Referativnyi Zhurnal. Fiziologiya Cheloveka i Zhivotnykh. Obshchie Problemy. Vozrastnaya Fiziologiya. Prikladnaya Fiziologiya. Termoregulyatsiya (RUS) **719**

• Referativnyi Zhurnal. Fiziologiya i Biokhimiya Rastenii (RUS ISSN 0202-4241) **719**

• Referativnyi Zhurnal. Generatory Pryamogo Preobrazovaniya Teplovoi i Khimicheskoi Energii v Elektricheskuyu (RUS ISSN 0203-5324) **3154**

• Referativnyi Zhurnal. Genetika Cheloveka (RUS ISSN 0202-9146) **719**

• Referativnyi Zhurnal. Genetika i Selektsiya Mikroorganizmov (RUS ISSN 0235-8913) **719**

• Referativnyi Zhurnal. Genetika i Selektsiya Sel'skokhozyaistvennykh Zhivotnykh (RUS ISSN 0235-8921) **719**

• Referativnyi Zhurnal. Genetika i Selektsiya Vozdelyvaemykh Rastenii (RUS ISSN 0202-9138) **719**

• Referativnyi Zhurnal. Geodeziya i Aeros'emka (RUS ISSN 0375-9717) **2720**

• Referativnyi Zhurnal. Geofizika (RUS ISSN 0034-236X) **2720**

• Referativnyi Zhurnal. Geografiya (RUS ISSN 0034-2378) **4036**

• Referativnyi Zhurnal. Geografiya Ameriki, Avstralii, Okeanii i Antarktiki (RUS ISSN 0202-9251) **4036**

• Referativnyi Zhurnal. Geografiya Rossiiskoi Federatsii (RUS) **4036**

Referativnyi Zhurnal. Geografiya Stran na Territorii Byvshego S S S R *see* Referativnyi Zhurnal. Geografiya Rossiiskoi Federatsii **4036**

• Referativnyi Zhurnal. Geografiya Zarubezhnoi Azii i Afriki (RUS ISSN 0202-926X) **4036**

• Referativnyi Zhurnal. Geografiya Zarubezhnoi Evropy (RUS ISSN 0202-9278) **4036**

• Referativnyi Zhurnal. Geokhimiya, Mineralogiya, Petrografiya (RUS ISSN 0202-9367) **2721**

• Referativnyi Zhurnal. Geologicheskie i Geokhimicheskie Metody Poiskov Poleznykh Iskopaemykh. Metody Razvedki i Otsenki Mestorozhdenii. Razvedotchnaya i Promyslovaya Geofizika (RUS ISSN 0202-9359) **2721**

• Referativnyi Zhurnal. Geologiya (RUS ISSN 0486-2309) **2721**

• Referativnyi Zhurnal. Geomagnetizm i Vysokie Sloi Atmosfery (RUS ISSN 0202-9448) **2721**

• Referativnyi Zhurnal. Gidroenergetika (RUS ISSN 0203-5332) **3154**

• Referativnyi Zhurnal. Gidrogeologiya, Inzhenernaya Geologiya, Merzlotovedenie (RUS ISSN 0202-9375) **2721**

• Referativnyi Zhurnal. Gornoe Delo (RUS ISSN 0034-2386) **6486**

• Referativnyi Zhurnal. Gornoe i Neftepromyslovoe Mashinostroenie (RUS ISSN 0373-6415) **6486**

• Referativnyi Zhurnal. Gorodskoi Transport (RUS ISSN 0202-9766) **8529**

• Referativnyi Zhurnal. Ikhtiologiya (RUS) **719**

• Referativnyi Zhurnal. Immunologiya. Allergologiya (RUS ISSN 0202-9154) **5750**

• Referativnyi Zhurnal. Informatika (RUS ISSN 0486-235X) **5059**

Referativnyi Zhurnal. Iskusstvennye Sooruzheniya na Avtomobil'nykh Dorogakh. Vypusk Svodnogo Toma *see* Referativnyi Zhurnal. Avtomobil'nye Dorogi. Otdel'nyi Vypusk **8528**

• Referativnyi Zhurnal. Issledovanie Kosmicheskogo Prostranstva (RUS ISSN 0034-2408) **76**

• Referativnyi Zhurnal. Issledovanie Zemli iz Kosmosa (RUS ISSN 0233-6480) **584**

• Referativnyi Zhurnal. Izdatel'skoe Delo i Poligrafiya (RUS ISSN 0235-2222) **7329**

• Referativnyi Zhurnal. Kadry, Ekonomika Obrazovaniya (RUS ISSN 0235-8832) **1260**

• Referativnyi Zhurnal. Kartografiya (RUS ISSN 0202-9294) **4036**

• Referativnyi Zhurnal. Khimicheskoe, Neftepererabatyvayuschchee i Polimernoe Mashinostroenie (RUS ISSN 0370-8098) **3233**

• Referativnyi Zhurnal. Khimiya (RUS ISSN 0486-2325) **2095**

• Referativnyi Zhurnal. Khimiya i Pererabotka Goryuchikh Iskopaemykh i Prirodnykh Gazov (RUS ISSN 0203-6169) **2095**

• Referativnyi Zhurnal. Khimiya i Tekhnologiya Pishchevykh Produktov (RUS ISSN 0235-3156) **2095**

• Referativnyi Zhurnal. Khimiya Vysokomolekuliarnykh Soedinenii (RUS ISSN 0203-6150) **2095**

• Referativnyi Zhurnal. Klinicheskaya Farmakologiya (RUS ISSN 0202-9162) **6890**

• Referativnyi Zhurnal. Kommunal'noe, Bytovoe i Torgovoe Oborudovanie (RUS ISSN 0484-2286) **5462**

• Referativnyi Zhurnal. Kompleksnye i Spetsyal'nye Razdely Mekhaniki (RUS ISSN 0203-5146) **7049**

• Referativnyi Zhurnal. Korroziya i Zashchita ot Korrozii (RUS ISSN 0131-3533) **6341**

• Referativnyi Zhurnal. Kotelnye Ustanovki i Vodopodgotovka (RUS ISSN 0203-5340) **3154**

• Referativnyi Zhurnal. Kvantovaya Elektronika. Krioelektronika. Golografiya (RUS ISSN 0235-215X) **7049**

Referativnyi Zhurnal. Legkaya Promyshlennost'. Tekhnologiya i Oborudovanie. Svodnyi Tom *see* Referativnyi Zhurnal. Legkaya Promyshlennost'. Tekhnologiya i Oborudovaniye. Otdel'nyi Vypusk **1260**

• Referativnyi Zhurnal. Legkaya Promyshlennost'. Tekhnologiya i Oborudovaniye. Otdel'nyi Vypusk (RUS ISSN 0034-2432) **1260**

† • Referativnyi Zhurnal. Lekarstvennye Rasteniya (RUS) **8984**

• Referativnyi Zhurnal. Lesovedenie i Lesovodstvo (RUS ISSN 0034-2440) **3709**

• Referativnyi Zhurnal. Lokomotivostroenie i Vagonostroenie (RUS ISSN 0202-9855) **8529**

• Referativnyi Zhurnal. Mashinostroitel'nye Materialy, Konstruktsii i Raschet Detalei Mashin. Gidroprivod (RUS ISSN 0034-2459) **3233**

Referativnyi Zhurnal. Mashiny i Oborudovanie dlya Tekstil'noi Promyshlennosti. Vypusk Svodnogo Toma *see* Referativnyi Zhurnal. Legkaya Promyshlennost'. Tekhnologiya i Oborudovaniye. Otdel'nyi Vypusk **1260**

Referativnyi Zhurnal. Matematicheskii Analiz (RUS ISSN 0202-9545) **5548**

Referativnyi Zhurnal. Matematika (RUS ISSN 0034-2467) **5548**

• Referativnyi Zhurnal. Materialy dlya Elektroniki (RUS ISSN 0235-2168) **3117**

• Referativnyi Zhurnal. Meditsina (RUS ISSN 0207-8643) **5750**

• Referativnyi Zhurnal. Meditsinskaya Geografiya (RUS ISSN 0034-2475) **5750**

• Referativnyi Zhurnal. Mekhanika (RUS ISSN 0034-2483) **3233**

• Referativnyi Zhurnal. Mekhanika Deformiruemogo Tverdogo Tela (RUS ISSN 0202-9693) **7049**

• Referativnyi Zhurnal. Mekhanika Zhidkosti i Gaza (RUS ISSN 0202-9707) **7049**

• Referativnyi Zhurnal. Mestorozhdeniya Goryuchikh Poleznykh Iskopaemykh (RUS ISSN 0202-9383) **6486**

• Referativnyi Zhurnal. Metallovedenie i Termicheskaya Obrabotka (RUS ISSN 0202-9626) **6341**

• Referativnyi Zhurnal. Metallurgicheskaya Teplotekhnika. Oborudovanie, Izmereniya, Kontrol i Avtomatizatsiya v Metallurgicheskom Proizvodstve (RUS ISSN 0202-9634) **6341**

• Referativnyi Zhurnal. Metallurgiya (RUS ISSN 0034-2491) **6341**

• Referativnyi Zhurnal. Metallurgiya Tsvetnykh Metallov (RUS ISSN 0203-5170) **6341**

• Referativnyi Zhurnal. Meteorologiya i Klimatologiya (RUS ISSN 0202-9308) **6400**

• Referativnyi Zhurnal. Metody Upravleniya Ekonomikoi (RUS ISSN 0235-8891) **1260**

• Referativnyi Zhurnal. Metrologiya i Izmeritel'naya Tekhnika (RUS ISSN 0034-2505) **6408**

• Referativnyi Zhurnal. Mikrobiologiya Obshchaya (RUS ISSN 0208-1466) **719**

• Referativnyi Zhurnal. Mikrobiologiya Prikladnaya (RUS) **719**

• Referativnyi Zhurnal. Mikrobiologiya Sanitarnaya i Meditsinskaya (RUS ISSN 0206-5517) **719**

• Referativnyi Zhurnal. Mirovaya Ekonomika. Sotsyal'no-Ekonomicheskoe Razvitie Stran Mira (RUS ISSN 0204-3807) **1260**

• Referativnyi Zhurnal. Molekulyarnaya Biologiya (RUS ISSN 0207-8619) **719**

• Referativnyi Zhurnal. Molekulyarnaya i Kletochnaya Immunologiya (RUS ISSN 0207-8627) **5750**

• Referativnyi Zhurnal. Morfologiya Cheloveka i Zhivotnykh. Antropologiya (RUS ISSN 0207-1428) **362**

• Referativnyi Zhurnal. Narkologicheskaya Toksikologiya (RUS) **2701**

• Referativnyi Zhurnal. Nasosostroenie i Kompressorostroenie. Kholodil'noe Mashinostroenie (RUS ISSN 0034-2513) **4128**

• Referativnyi Zhurnal. Nauchno-Tekhnicheskii Progress. Integratsiya Nauki s Proizvodstvom. Organizatsiya i Finansirovanie (RUS ISSN 0235-8824) **8447**

• Referativnyi Zhurnal. Nemetallicheskie Poleznye Iskopaemye (RUS ISSN 0202-9391) **2721**

• Referativnyi Zhurnal. Neorganicheskaya Khimiya. Kompleksnye Soedineniya. Radiokhimiya (RUS ISSN 0234-9639) **2095**

• Referativnyi Zhurnal. Netraditsionnye i Vozobnovlyaemye Istochniki Energii (RUS ISSN 0207-8635) **3154**

• Referativnyi Zhurnal. Obogashchenie Poleznykh Iskopaemykh (RUS ISSN 0202-9464) **6486**

• Referativnyi Zhurnal. Oborudovanie Pishchevoi Promyshlennosti (RUS ISSN 0034-2521) **5462**

• Referativnyi Zhurnal. Obshchaya Ekologiya. Biotsenologiya. Gidrobiologiya (RUS) **719**

• Referativnyi Zhurnal. Obshchaya Genetika (RUS) **719**

• Referativnyi Zhurnal. Obshchaya Geologiya (RUS ISSN 0202-9405) **2721**

• Referativnyi Zhurnal. Obshcheotraslevye Voprosy Sovershenstvovaniya Khozyaistvennogo Mekhanizma (RUS ISSN 0135-9789) **1260**

• Referativnyi Zhurnal. Obshchie Voprosy Energetiki. Energeticheskii Balans. Toplivo (RUS) **3154**

• Referativnyi Zhurnal. Obshchie Voprosy Fiziki i Fizicheskogo Eksperimenta (RUS ISSN 0207-138X) **7049**

• Referativnyi Zhurnal. Obshchie Voprosy i Teoreticheskie Osnovy Elektrotekhniki. Elektrobezopasnost' (RUS ISSN 0203-5197) **3329**

• Referativnyi Zhurnal. Obshchie Voprosy Khimicheskoi Tekhnologii (RUS ISSN 0203-607X) **2095**

• Referativnyi Zhurnal. Obshchie Voprosy Khimii. Fizicheskaya Khimiya. Stroenie Molekul (RUS ISSN 0208-1695) **2095**

Referativnyi Zhurnal. Obshchie Voprosy Matematiki. Matematicheskaya Logika. Teoriya Chisel. Algebra. Topologiya. Geometriya (RUS ISSN 0202-9553) **5549**

• Referativnyi Zhurnal. Obshchie Voprosy Mekhaniki. Obshchaya Mekhanika (RUS ISSN 0202-9715) **7049**

• Referativnyi Zhurnal. Obshchie Voprosy Patologicheskoi Anatomii (RUS) **719**

• Referativnyi Zhurnal. Okeanologiya. Gidrologiya Sushi. Glyatsiologiya (RUS ISSN 0202-9316) **2721**

• Referativnyi Zhurnal. Okhrana i Uluchshenie Gorodskoi Sredy (RUS ISSN 0868-460X) **3480**

• Referativnyi Zhurnal. Okhrana Prirody i Vosproizvodstvo Prirodnykh Resursov (RUS ISSN 0202-9332) **3480**

• Referativnyi Zhurnal. Onkologiya (RUS ISSN 0202-9197) **5750**

• Referativnyi Zhurnal. Onkologiya Eksperimental'naya (RUS) **5750**

• Referativnyi Zhurnal. Onkologiya Klinicheskaya (RUS ISSN 0869-4117) **5750**

• Referativnyi Zhurnal. Onkologiya: Terapiya Opukholei (RUS) **5750**

• Referativnyi Zhurnal. Optika i Yadernaya Fizika (RUS ISSN 0235-8875) **7049**

• Referativnyi Zhurnal. Organicheskaya Khimiya (RUS ISSN 0203-6088) **2095**

• Referativnyi Zhurnal. Organizatsiya i Bezopasnost' Dorozhnogo Dvizheniya (RUS ISSN 0202-9952) **8529**

• Referativnyi Zhurnal. Organizatsiya Upravleniya (RUS ISSN 0132-5639) **1260**

• Referativnyi Zhurnal. Pochvovedenie i Agrokhimiya (RUS ISSN 0034-2548) **185**

• Referativnyi Zhurnal. Pod'emno-Transportnoe Mashinostroenie (RUS ISSN 0202-9936) **3233**

• Referativnyi Zhurnal. Poroshkovaya Metallurgiya. Nanomaterialy, Pokrytiya i Plenki, Poluchaemye Fiziko-Metallurgicheskimi Metodami (RUS) **6341**

Referativnyi Zhurnal. Poroshkovaya Metallurgiya. Pokrytiya i Plenki, Poluchaemye Fiziko-Metallurgicheskimi Metodami *see* Referativnyi Zhurnal. Poroshkovaya Metallurgiya. Nanomaterialy, Pokrytiya i Plenki, Poluchaemye Fiziko-Metallurgicheskimi Metodami **6341**

Referativnyi Zhurnal. Pozharnaia Bezopasnost. Vypusk Svodnogo Toma *see* Referativnyi Zhurnal. Pozharnaya Okhrana. Otdel'nyi Vypusk **3582**

Referativnyi Zhurnal. Pozharnaia Okhrana. Vypusk Svodnogo Toma *see* Referativnyi Zhurnal. Pozharnaya Okhrana. Otdel'nyi Vypusk **3582**

• Referativnyi Zhurnal. Pozharnaya Okhrana. Otdel'nyi Vypusk (RUS ISSN 0202-9898) **3582**

Referativnyi Zhurnal. Pozharnaya Okhrana. Svodnyi Tom *see* Referativnyi Zhurnal. Pozharnaya Okhrana. Otdel'nyi Vypusk **3582**

• Referativnyi Zhurnal. Primenenie Matematicheskikh Metodov v Ekonomicheskikh Issledovaniyakh i Planirovanii (RUS ISSN 0868-4685) **1260**

• Referativnyi Zhurnal. Prirodnye Organicheskie Soedineniya i ikh Sinteticheskie Analogi (RUS ISSN 0235-3148) **2095**

Referativnyi Zhurnal. Problemy Funktsionirovaniya Rynochnogo Khoziaistva *see* Referativnyi Zhurnal. Financy. Banki. Strakhovanie **1260**

• Referativnyi Zhurnal. Prochnost' Konstruktsii i Materyalov (RUS ISSN 0203-5154) **1048**

• Referativnyi Zhurnal. Proektirovanie, Konstruirovanie, Tekhnologiya i Oborudovanie dlya Radiotekhnicheskogo Proizvodstva (RUS ISSN 0235-2109) **3117**

• Referativnyi Zhurnal. Programnoe Obespechenie (RUS ISSN 0234-9655) **2444**

• Referativnyi Zhurnal. Proizvodstvo Chuguna i Stali (RUS ISSN 0202-9650) **6341**

• Referativnyi Zhurnal. Prokatnoye i Volochil'noye Proizvodstvo (RUS ISSN 0202-9669) **6341**

• Referativnyi Zhurnal. Promyshlennyi Transport (RUS ISSN 0034-2556) **8529**

• Referativnyi Zhurnal. Psikhologiya (RUS ISSN 0869-4133) **7417**

• Referativnyi Zhurnal. Radiatsionnaya Biologiya (RUS ISSN 0131-355X) **719**

• Referativnyi Zhurnal. Radiofizika i Fizicheskie Osnovy Elektroniki (RUS ISSN 0202-9979) **7049**

• Referativnyi Zhurnal. Radiolokatsiya, Radionavigatsiya, Radioupravlenie, Televizionnaya Tekhnika (RUS ISSN 0235-2117) **3117**

• Referativnyi Zhurnal. Radiosvyaz'. Radioveshchanie. Televidenie (RUS ISSN 0235-2087) **2348**

• Referativnyi Zhurnal. Radiotekhnika (RUS ISSN 0034-267X) **3117**

• Referativnyi Zhurnal. Raketostroenie i Kosmicheskaya Tekhnika (RUS ISSN 0207-1371) **77**

• Referativnyi Zhurnal. Rastenievodstvo (Biologicheskie Osnovy) (RUS ISSN 0202-9200) **719**

• Referativnyi Zhurnal. Razrabotka Mestorozhdenii Tverdykh Poleznykh Iskopaemykh. Obshchie Problemy, Promyshlennost, Ekonomika, Stroitelstvo (RUS ISSN 0202-9480) **6486**

• Referativnyi Zhurnal. Razrabotka Mestorozhdenii Tverdykh Poleznykh Iskopaemykh. Osnovnye Protsessy (RUS ISSN 0202-9499) **6486**

• Referativnyi Zhurnal. Razrabotka Mestorozhdenii Tverdykh Poleznykh Iskopaemykh. Vspomogatelnye Protsessy (RUS ISSN 0202-9472) **6486**

• Referativnyi Zhurnal. Razrabotka Neftyanykh i Gazovykh Mestorozhdenii (RUS ISSN 0202-9502) **6801**

• Referativnyi Zhurnal. Rezanie Materyalov. Stanki i Instrumenty (RUS ISSN 0202-957X) **5462**

• Referativnyi Zhurnal. Risk i Bezopasnost' (RUS) **7549**

• Referativnyi Zhurnal. Robototekhnika (RUS ISSN 0208-001X) **5462**

• Referativnyi Zhurnal. Rudnye Mestorozhdeniya (RUS ISSN 0202-9413) **6477**

• Referativnyi Zhurnal. Seti i Sistemy Svyazi (RUS ISSN 0235-2095) **2348**

• Referativnyi Zhurnal. Silovaya Preobrazovatel'naya Tekhnika (RUS ISSN 0203-5219) **3117**

• Referativnyi Zhurnal. Sistemy, Pribory i Metody Kontrolya Kachestva Okruzhayushchei Sredy (RUS ISSN 0206-6149) **3480**

▼ • Referativnyi Zhurnal. Spintronika (RUS) **7049**

• Referativnyi Zhurnal. Stratigrafiya. Paleontologiya (RUS ISSN 0202-9421) **6731**

• Referativnyi Zhurnal. Stroitel'nye i Dorozhnye Mashiny (RUS ISSN 0484-2480) **3233**

Referativnyi Zhurnal. Stroitel'stvo i Ekspluatatsiya Avtomobilnykh Dorog. Vypusk Svodnogo Toma *see* Referativnyi Zhurnal. Avtomobil'nye Dorogi. Otdel'nyi Vypusk **8528**

• Referativnyi Zhurnal. Stroitelstvo Zheleznykh Dorog. Put' i Putevoe Khozyaistvo (RUS ISSN 0202-9863) **8529**

• Referativnyi Zhurnal. Sudostroenie (RUS ISSN 0132-2931) **8529**

• Referativnyi Zhurnal. Svarka (RUS ISSN 0131-3525) **6341**

• Referativnyi Zhurnal. Sverkhprovodimost' (RUS ISSN 0235-6856) **7049**

DIRECTORY 2010 REFRIGERATION EQUIPMENT INDUSTRY 10793

● Referativnyi Zhurnal. Svetotekhnika i Infrakrasnaya Tekhnika (RUS ISSN 0203-5200) **3233**
● Referativnyi Zhurnal. Svyaz' (RUS ISSN 0235-2079) **2348**
● Referativnyi Zhurnal. Tekhnicheskaya Ekspluatatsiya Podvizhnogo Sostava i Tyaga Poezdov (RUS ISSN 0202-9871) **8529**
● Referativnyi Zhurnal. Tekhnicheskaya Kibernetika (RUS) **2444**
† ● Referativnyi Zhurnal. Tekhnicheskii Analiz v Metalurgii (RUS ISSN 0202-9685) **8984**
● Referativnyi Zhurnal. Tekhnika Geologo-Razvedochnykh Rabot (RUS ISSN 0202-943X) **2721**
● Referativnyi Zhurnal. Tekhnologicheskie Aspekty Okhrany Okruzhayushchei Sredy (RUS ISSN 0206-6130) **3480**
● Referativnyi Zhurnal. Tekhnologiya i Oborudovanie Kuznechno-Shtampovochnogo Proizvodstva (RUS ISSN 0202-9596) **6341**
● Referativnyi Zhurnal. Tekhnologiya i Oborudovanie Lesozagotovitel'nogo, Derevoobrabatyvayushchego i Tsellyulozno-Bumazhnogo Proizvodstva (RUS ISSN 0208-1415) **6740**
● Referativnyi Zhurnal. Tekhnologiya i Oborudovanie Liteinogo Proizvodstva (RUS ISSN 0202-960X) **6341**
● Referativnyi Zhurnal. Tekhnologiya i Oborudovanie Mekhanosborochnogo Proizvodstva (RUS ISSN 0202-9618) **5462**
Referativnyi Zhurnal. Tekhnologiya i Organizatsiya Proizvodstva Tekstil'noi Promyshlennosti. Vypusk Svodnogo Toma *see* Referativnyi Zhurnal. Legkaya Promyshlennost'. Tekhnologiya i Oborudovaniye. Otdel'nyi Vypusk **1260**
● Referativnyi Zhurnal. Tekhnologiya Mashinostroeniya (RUS ISSN 0034-2599) **3234**
● Referativnyi Zhurnal. Tekhnologiya Neorganicheskikh Veshchestv i Materialov (RUS) **2095**
● Referativnyi Zhurnal. Tekhnologiya Organicheskikh Lekarstvennykh Veshchestv, Veterinarnykh Preparatov i Pestitsidov (RUS ISSN 0203-6134) **2095**
● Referativnyi Zhurnal. Tekhnologiya Organicheskikh Veshchestv (RUS ISSN 0203-6126) **2096**
● Referativnyi Zhurnal. Tekhnologiya Polimernykh Materyalov: Plastmassy, Ionoobmennye Materyaly (RUS ISSN 0208-1733) **2096**
● Referativnyi Zhurnal. Tekhnologiya Polimernykh Materyalov: Prirodnye Vysokomolekulyarnye Soedineniya. Khimiya i Pererabotka Drevesiny. Khimicheskie Volokna. Tekstil'nye Materialy. Bumaga. Kozha. Mekh (RUS ISSN 0208-1768) **2096**
● Referativnyi Zhurnal. Tekhnologiya Polimernykh Materyalov: Rezina, Lakokrasochnye Materialy i Organicheskie Pokrytiya. Vspomogatel'nye Materialy dlia Proizvodstva Polimerov i Izdelii iz Nikh (RUS ISSN 0208-1741) **2096**
● Referativnyi Zhurnal. Tekhnologiya Proizvodstva Produktov Bytovoi Khimii. Parfumeriya i Kosmetika (RUS ISSN 0235-3164) **2096**
● Referativnyi Zhurnal. Tekhnologiya Silikatnykh i Tugoplavkikh Nemetallicheskikh Materialov (RUS ISSN 0235-2206) **3234**
● Referativnyi Zhurnal. Teoreticheskaya Radiotekhnika. Antenny. Volnovody. Ob'emnye Rezonatory. Rasprostranenie Radiovoln (RUS ISSN 0235-2133) **3117**
● Referativnyi Zhurnal. Teoreticheskie i Obshchie Voprosy Geografii (RUS ISSN 0202-9324) **4036**
● Referativnyi Zhurnal. Teoreticheskie Osnovy Teplotekhniki. Promyshlennaya Teplotekhnika (RUS ISSN 0208-1431) **3154**
● Referativnyi Zhurnal. Teoriya Metallurgicheskikh Protsessov (RUS ISSN 0202-9677) **6341**
Referativnyi Zhurnal. Teoriya Veroyatnostei i Matematicheskaya Statistika (RUS ISSN 0202-9561) **5549**
● Referativnyi Zhurnal. Teplomassobmen (RUS ISSN 0203-6436) **3154**
● Referativnyi Zhurnal. Teplovye Elektrostantsii. Teplosnabzhenie (RUS ISSN 0203-5375) **3154**
● Referativnyi Zhurnal. Toksikologiya (RUS ISSN 0202-9219) **6890**
● Referativnyi Zhurnal. Traktory i Sel'skokhozyaistvennye Mashiny i Orudiya (RUS ISSN 0034-2602) **185**
● Referativnyi Zhurnal. Transport Promyshlennykh Predpriyatii. Logistika. Sklady. Avtomatizatsiya Pogruzochno-Razgruzochnykh Rabot (RUS) **8529**
Referativnyi Zhurnal. Trikotazhnaya, Shveinaya i Kozhevenno-Obuvnaya Promyshlennosti. Vypusk Svodnogo Toma *see* Referativnyi Zhurnal. Legkaya Promyshlennost'. Tekhnologiya i Oborudovaniye. Otdel'nyi Vypusk **1260**
● Referativnyi Zhurnal. Truboprovodnyi Transport (RUS ISSN 0034-2610) **3234**
● Referativnyi Zhurnal. Tsitologiya (RUS ISSN 0202-9103) **719**
● Referativnyi Zhurnal. Turbostroenie. Kotlostroenie (RUS ISSN 0034-2629) **3234**
● Referativnyi Zhurnal. Upravlenie Perevozochnym Protsessom na Zheleznykh Dorogakh (RUS ISSN 0202-988X) **8529**
Referativnyi Zhurnal. Upravlenie Vozdushnym Dvizheniem. Organizatsiya Perevozok *see* Referativnyi Zhurnal. Vozdushnyi Transport. Aeroporty **8529**
● Referativnyi Zhurnal. Virusologiya (RUS) **719**
● Referativnyi Zhurnal. Virusologiya. Mikrobiologiya (RUS ISSN 0201-5226) **719**
● Referativnyi Zhurnal. Vodnye Perevozki. Tekhnicheskaya Ekspluatatsiya i Remont Flota (RUS ISSN 0869-4001) **8529**
● Referativnyi Zhurnal. Vodnyi Transport (RUS ISSN 0484-2545) **8529**
● Referativnyi Zhurnal. Volokonno-Opticheskaya Svyaz' (RUS) **7049**
Referativnyi Zhurnal. Volokonno-Opticheskie Systemy *see* Referativnyi Zhurnal. Volokonno-Opticheskaya Svyaz' **7049**
● Referativnyi Zhurnal. Voprosy Tekhnicheskogo Progressa i Organizatsii Proizvodstva v Mashinostroenii (RUS ISSN 0034-2637) **3234**
● Referativnyi Zhurnal. Vozdushnyi Transport (RUS ISSN 0484-2561) **8529**
▼ ● Referativnyi Zhurnal. Vozdushnyi Transport. Aeroporty (RUS) **8529**
Referativnyi Zhurnal. Vychislitel'naya Matematika. Matematicheskaya Kibernetika (RUS ISSN 0235-2184) **5549**
● Referativnyi Zhurnal. Vychislitel'nye Mashiny i Sistemy (RUS ISSN 0234-9663) **2444**
Referativnyi Zhurnal. Vychislitel'nye Nauki (RUS ISSN 0235-1501) **2444**
● Referativnyi Zhurnal. Vzaimodeistvie Raznykh Vidov Transporta i Konteinernye Perevozki (RUS ISSN 0034-2645) **8529**
● Referativnyi Zhurnal. Yadernaya Fizika i Fizika Yadernykh Reaktorov (RUS ISSN 0203-6037) **7049**
† ● Referativnyi Zhurnal. Yadernye Reaktory (RUS ISSN 0034-2653) **8984**
● Referativnyi Zhurnal. Zheleznodorozhnyi Transport (RUS ISSN 0484-2596) **8529**
● Referativnyi Zhurnal. Zoologiya (RUS ISSN 0869-4052) **720**
● Referativnyi Zhurnal. Zoologiya Nazemnykh Pozvonochnykh. Obshchie Voprosy. Gerpetologiya (RUS) **961**
● Referativnyi Zhurnal. Zoologiya Nazemnykh Pozvonochnykh. Ornitologiya (RUS) **720**
● Referativnyi Zhurnal. Zoologiya Nazemnykh Pozvonochnykh. Teriologiya, Okhotovedenie, Zooparki (RUS) **720**
● Referativnyi Zhurnal. Zoologiya Obshchaya. Zoologiya Bespozvonochnykh (RUS) **720**
● Referativnyi Zhurnal. Zooparazitologiya (RUS) **720**
† Referatovy Vyber a Aktuality z Urologie/Abstracts of Urology (CZE ISSN 1212-320X) **8984**
Referatovy Vyber z Anesteziologie, Resuscitace a Intenzivni Mediciny/Abstracts of Anesthesiology and Resuscitation (CZE ISSN 1212-3048) **5750**
● Referatovy Vyber z Radiodiagnostiky (Online)/Abstracts of Radiology (CZE ISSN 1214-5068) **5750**
● Referatovy Vyber z Revmatologie (Online)/Abstracts of Rheumatology (CZE ISSN 1214-5076) **5750**
Referatovy Vyber z Revmatologie (Print) *see* Referatovy Vyber z Revmatologie (Online) **5750**
▼ Referee (SWE ISSN 1654-2169) **8330**
Referee (Franksville) (USA ISSN 0733-1436) **8196**
The Reference *see* Refarensu **4767**
● Reference and Research Book News (USA ISSN 0887-3763) **634**
Reference & User Services Association Update *see* R U S A Update **5042**
● ➤ Reference and User Services Quarterly (USA ISSN 1094-9054) **5042**
Reference Artisan (FRA ISSN 1628-5263) **539**
Reference Book - Argentina (USA ISSN 0080-0449) **1513**
Reference Book for World Traders (USA) **2025**
Reference Book of Corporate Managements *see* D & B Reference Book of Corporate Managements **1737**
Reference Book - Republic of South Africa (USA ISSN 0080-0457) **1513**
Reference Book Review (USA ISSN 0272-1988) **634**
Reference Books Bulletin (USA ISSN 8755-0962) **5042**
Reference Circulars *see* National Library Service. Reference Circulars **4083**
Reference Encyclopedia of the American Indian (USA ISSN 1071-3204) **6636**
Reference Environnement *see* Campagne et Environnement **2605**
Reference Files - Index to Hispanic Legislation *see* U.S. Library of Congress. Reference Files - Index to Hispanic Legislation **637**
Reference Files - National Union Catalog of Manuscript Collections *see* U.S. Library of Congress. Reference Files - National Union Catalog of Manuscript Collections **637**
Reference for Middle School Education *see* Zhongguo Jiaoxue Cankao **2928**
Reference for Primary School Teaching *see* Xiaoxue Jiaoxue Cankao **2927**
† Reference Guides to Archival and Manuscript Sources in World History (USA ISSN 1054-9110) **8984**
† Reference Guides to Archives and Manuscript Collections on Immigrant Culture (USA ISSN 0885-7555) **8984**
● Reference Guides to National Architecture (USA ISSN 1550-8315) **455**
† Reference Guides to State History and Research (USA) **8984**
● Reference Guides to the State Constitutions of the United States (USA) **4851**
● Reference Guides to the World's Cinema (USA ISSN 1090-8234) **6511**
● ➤ The Reference Librarian (USA ISSN 0276-3877) **5042**
Reference Manual on Scientific Evidence (USA) **4767**
Reference Materials and Documentation for Tax Credit Property Managers *see* L I H T C Property Management **7597**
Reference Materials for Study and Research *see* Xuexi yu Yanjiu **7197**
Reference Methods for Marine Pollution Studies (USA) **3490**
Reference Point (Annapolis) (USA) **8281**
Reference Point (Parsippany) (USA) **5042**
Reference Point: Food Industry Abstracts (USA ISSN 0889-2113) **3670**
Reference Probiotique (FRA ISSN 1957-326X) **269**
● Reference Reviews (GBR ISSN 0950-4125) **5042**
● Reference Reviews Europe (ITA ISSN 1124-6332) **5042**
Reference Service and Bibliography *see* Sanko Shoshi Kenkyu **5045**
● ➤ Reference Services Review (GBR ISSN 0090-7324) **5042**
The Reference Shelf (USA) **5042**
Reference Sources for Small and Medium-Sized Libraries (USA) **5059**
† Reference Sources for the Social Sciences and Humanities (USA ISSN 0730-3335) **8984**
● Referencen (DNK ISSN 0108-5913) **5042**
References to Contemporary Papers in Acoustics (USA ISSN 0163-0970) **7089**
Referencia (PRT ISSN 0874-0283) **5979**
● Referencias (ARG ISSN 0328-1507) **5043**
Referencias (VEN) **7214**
Referencias Criticas sobre Autores Chilenos (CHL ISSN 0716-1778) **634**
Referendum (GBR) **1965**
Referente (ARG) **5358**
Referrals of Children to Reporters and Children's Hearings (Year) (GBR) **8064**
Refiguring English Studies (USA ISSN 1073-9637) **3078**
● Refiner (USA ISSN 1556-9357) **6790**
Refinery and Petrochemical Plant Maintenance Conference. Technical Transcripts *see* N P R A Refinery and Petrochemical Plant Maintenance Conference. Technical Transcripts **6779**
Refining and Chemicals *see* Lianyou yu Huagong **6777**
Refining & Gas Processing Industry (USA ISSN 1062-5658) **6790**
Refining and Gas Processing Industry *see* Refining & Gas Processing Industry **6790**
Refinisher (AUS) **8601**
Reflectie (NLD ISSN 1574-2776) **7814**
● The Reflecting Community (USA) **7814**
● ➤ Reflecting Education (GBR ISSN 1746-9082) **2903**
Reflection (USA ISSN 0484-2650) **5358**
Reflection and Theory in the Study of Religion (USA) **7673**
Reflections (CAN ISSN 0384-0697) **5043**
Reflections (DEU) **5358**
● Reflections (FRA ISSN 1606-1276) **4471**
Reflections (GBR ISSN 0260-8499) **3870**
Reflections (Baltimore) (USA ISSN 1541-2075) **5358**
● ➤ Reflections (Cambridge) (USA ISSN 1524-1734) **1789**
Reflections (Corpus Christi) (USA ISSN 0732-488X) **3780**
● Reflections (Lakemba) (AUS ISSN 1449-2555) **7715**
● ➤ Reflections (Long Beach) (USA ISSN 1080-0220) **3045**
Reflections (Mishawaka) (USA ISSN 1075-7368) **7673**
Reflections (New Haven) (USA ISSN 0362-0611) **7673**
● Reflections (North Ryde) (AUS ISSN 0156-7799) **3078**
Reflections (University Center) (USA ISSN 1939-0548) **2298**
Reflections (Washington)/Reflejos (USA) **4309**
Reflections on Nursing Leadership (USA ISSN 1527-6538) **5979**
▼ Reflections on the Civil War Era (USA ISSN 1939-649X) **4310**
● ➤ Reflective Practice (GBR ISSN 1462-3943) **6947**
Reflector (BEL ISSN 1374-9218) **2210**
The Reflector (CAN) **2298**
Reflector (Amersfoort) (NLD ISSN 0034-2947) **4520**
Reflector (Doetinchem) (NLD ISSN 0926-8537) **8601**
● The Reflector Newsletter (USA ISSN 0034-2963) **580**
Reflejos *see* Reflections (Washington) **4309**
† Refleks (DNK ISSN 1604-5076) **8984**
Refleksion *see* Refleksion (Muslimernes Faellesraad) **7715**
Refleksion (Muslimernes Faellesraad) (DNK ISSN 1903-1106) **7715**
Le Reflet du Lac (CAN) **3816**
Le Reflet Week-End (CAN) **3816**
Reflets de la Physique (FRA ISSN 1953-793X) **7037**
Reflets et Nuances (FRA ISSN 1764-0709) **1032**
● ➤ Reflets et Perspectives de la Vie Economique (BEL ISSN 0034-2971) **1164**
● Reflex (CZE ISSN 0862-6634) **3832**
Reflex (DNK ISSN 0906-4664) **6947**
Reflex (SWE ISSN 1651-5471) **6180**
➤ Reflexao (BRA ISSN 0102-0269) **6947**
Reflexao e Acao (BRA ISSN 0103-8842) **2903**
Reflexen (SWE ISSN 0284-0707) **8634**
Reflexion (ESP ISSN 1130-5533) **7995**
Reflexion (NIC) **7214**
Reflexion Politica (COL ISSN 0124-0781) **7176**
● Reflexiones (CRI ISSN 1021-1209) **7995**
Reflexiones (Year) (USA ISSN 1098-0873) **3560**
Reflexiones del Batallismo (URY ISSN 0797-0005) **7995**
Reflexions (BEL ISSN 1371-676X) **7176**
Reflexions Historiques *see* Historical Reflections **4143**
Reflexzone (NLD ISSN 1380-3174) **6878**
Refmonde *see* Refworld **4939**
Refocus *see* Renewable Energy Focus **3146**
† Refolade (ITA) **8984**
● Reform (AUS ISSN 0313-153X) **4767**
Reform *see* Gaige **7965**
Reform (GBR ISSN 0306-7262) **7772**
Reform (HUN ISSN 0238-9037) **3877**
Reform *see* Al- Islah **7711**
† ● Reform (Kingston) (AUS ISSN 1329-184X) **8984**
Reform: An Overall View *see* Gaige Zongheng **1541**
Reform & Opening *see* Gaige yu Kaifang **7966**
Reform & Strategy *see* Gaige yu Zhanlue **7966**
Reform Judaism (USA ISSN 0482-0819) **7728**
● Reforma (MEX ISSN 1563-7697) **3910**
Reforma (RUS) **1164**
Reforma Agraria, Colonizacion y Cooperativas *see* Land Reform, Land Settlement and Cooperatives **202**
Reforma - Byulleten' Rossiiskogo Fonda Federal'nogo Imushchestva (RUS) **1164**
reforma.com *see* Reforma **3910**
Reforma - Mezhdunarodnyi Fond Ekonomicheskikh i Sotsyal'nykh Reform (RUS) **1164**
Reforma Newsletter (USA ISSN 0891-8880) **5043**
● ➤ Reforma y Democracia (VEN ISSN 1315-2378) **7465**
Reformatio (CHE) **7772**
● ➤ Reformation (GBR ISSN 1357-4175) **4256**
● Reformation and Renaissance Review (GBR ISSN 1462-2459) **7673**
Reformation & Revival (USA ISSN 1071-7277) **7673**
Reformation of Economic System *see* Jingji Tizhi Gaige **1719**
Reformation Texts with Translation (1350-1650). Theology and Piety (USA ISSN 1937-3708) **7772**
Reformation Today (GBR ISSN 0034-3048) **7772**
Reformationsgeschichtliche Studien und Texte (DEU ISSN 0171-3469) **7772**
Reformatorisch Dagblad (NLD ISSN 1566-6808) **3915**
Reformatus Egyhaz (HUN) **7772**
Reformatusok Lapja (HUN ISSN 0482-086X) **7772**
● Reforme (FRA ISSN 0223-5749) **7772**
Reforme Agraire, Colonisation et Cooperatives *see* Land Reform, Land Settlement and Cooperatives **202**
Reformed Ecumenical Council Focus *see* R E C Focus **7772**
Reformed Ecumenical Council News Exchange *see* R E C News Exchange **7772**
● Reformed Review (Online) (USA) **7772**
Reformed Theological Review (AUS ISSN 0034-3072) **7673**
Reformed World (CHE ISSN 0034-3056) **7772**
Reformed Worship (USA ISSN 0890-8583) **7772**
† Reformer (GBR ISSN 0034-3080) **8984**
The Reformer (GBR ISSN 1353-0461) **7176**
● Reformes Economiques (FRA ISSN 1813-2731) **1513**
reformiert (DEU) **7772**
Refractive Eye News (GBR ISSN 1478-3800) **6050**
● Refractive Eyecare (USA ISSN 1931-7905) **6050**
Refractive Eyecare for Ophthalmologists *see* Refractive Eyecare **6050**
Refractories *see* Taikabutsu **6334**
● ➤ Refractories and Industrial Ceramics (USA ISSN 1083-4877) **2045**
Refractories Applications and News (USA ISSN 1537-6443) **2045**
Refractories Engineer (GBR ISSN 1362-4547) **2045**
Refractory News (USA) **3254**
reFRESH (GBR) **4378**
Refresh Magazine *see* reFRESH **4378**
† Refrigeracion - Frial (ESP ISSN 1133-7761) **8984**
● Refrigerated and Frozen Foods (USA ISSN 1061-6152) **3662**
Refrigerated and Frozen Foods. Annual Buyers Guide *see* Refrigerated and Frozen Foods **3662**
● Refrigerated and Frozen Foods Retailer (USA ISSN 1552-3330) **3662**
● Refrigerated Stores and Container Terminals Classed with Lloyd's Register (GBR) **8658**
● Refrigerated Transporter (USA ISSN 0034-3129) **8675**
Refrigeration *see* Reito **4126**
Refrigeration & Air Conditioning *see* R A C **4125**
Refrigeration and Air Conditioning Yearbook (GBR ISSN 1465-7406) **4125**
Refrigeration & Climate Control Koude & Luchtbehandeling *see* R C C Koude & Luchtbehandeling **4125**
Refrigeration Equipment Industry *see* Business Ratio. The Refrigeration Equipment Industry **4117**

Title

• Regione del Veneto. Bollettino Ufficiale (ITA ISSN 1971-7989) 7465
• Regione Umbria. Bollettino Ufficiale (ITA) 7465
• Regionen: Statistisches Jahrbuch (Year) (LUX ISSN 1681-9292) 8396
• Le Regioni (ITA ISSN 0391-7576) 4767
Regionologiya (RUS ISSN 0131-5706) 7995
Regionology (RUS) 7995
Regions and Regionalism in History (GBR ISSN 1742-8254) 4257
• Regions: Annuaire Statistique (Year) (LUX ISSN 1681-9314) 8396
Les Regions Exportatrices du Quebec (CAN ISSN 1912-6867) 1432
• Regions: Statistical Yearbook (Year) (LUX ISSN 1681-9306) 8396
Regionsnytt (Ski) (NOR ISSN 1504-2707) 8064
Regionsrundschau R-19 (AUT) 3798
Regiony (POL ISSN 0137-8325) 5236
Regiony Rossii. Sotsial'no-Ekonomicheskie Pokazateli (Year) (RUS) 1260
RegiOpinie (East Edition) see De Status (East Edition) 1968
† RegiOpinie (Ed. Brabant/Zeeland) (NLD ISSN 1873-9504) 8984
RegiOpinie (Mid-Netherlands Edition) see De Status (Mid-Netherlands Edition) 1968
RegiOpinie (North Edition) see De Status (North Edition) 1968
† RegiOpinie (Northwest Netherlands Edition) (NLD ISSN 1872-4825) 8985
RegiOpinie (Randstad-North Edition) see De Status (Randstad-North Edition) 1968
RegiOpinie (Randstad-West Edition) see De Status (Randstad-West Edition) 1968
† RegiOpinie (Rhine Edition) (NLD ISSN 1872-4817) 8985
Regis College (USA) 2298
The Register (USA) 7610
The Register (Middletown) (USA ISSN 1556-4045) 1378
Register Development Research Projects Africa (SEN ISSN 0850-4008) 1604
• Register of African Mining (AUS) 6477
Register of Architects (GBR ISSN 0306-6967) 455
• Register of Australasian Petroleum (AUS ISSN 1441-5070) 6790
• Register of Australian Mining (AUS ISSN 0725-9158) 6477
Register of Commissioned and Warrant Officers of the United States Navy and Reserve Officers on Active Duty (USA ISSN 0193-8665) 6443
Register of Development Activities of the United Nations System (CHE ISSN 1012-7666) 7262
Register of Finnish Industry and Commerce see Kompass Finland 1574
• Register of Indo-Pacific Mining (AUS ISSN 1446-9898) 6477
• Register of International Shipowning Groups (GBR ISSN 1460-0625) 8658
• Register of Laws of the Arabian Gulf (NLD) 4939
Register of Manufacturers see South Africa. Statistics South Africa. Census of Manufacturing - Principal Statistics on a Regional Basis Part-I 1264
Register of Manufacturing Firms see Kenya. Central Bureau of Statistics. Register of Manufacturing Firms 1247
Register of Medical Practitioners, Interns and Dentists for the Republic of South Africa (ZAF) 5702
Register of Musicians in Education (GBR ISSN 0953-5330) 6610
Register of Offshore Units, Submersibles and Underwater Systems (GBR) 8658
Register of Patent Agents (GBR ISSN 1358-5355) 6757
Register of Performers & Composers (GBR) 6610
Register of Professional Private Music Teachers (GBR ISSN 0951-6239) 6610
Register of Ships (in Japanese Coastal Shipping Service) see Naiko Senpaku Meisaisho 8654
Register of Stunt - Action Co-ordinators and Performers (GBR ISSN 1742-3651) 8477
Register over Danske Patenter Udstedt i (Year) (DNK ISSN 0107-590X) 6757
Register over Gaellande S F S-Foerfattningar (SWE ISSN 0280-1647) 7465
Register til Aarsskriftet Witherloese (DNK ISSN 1903-4997) 4257
Registered Dental Hygienist see R D H 5862
Registered Homes and Services (GBR) 8065
Registered Master Builders House of the Year see House of the Year. South Island 1012
Registered Master Builders Placemakers House of the Year and Commercial Awards see House of the Year. South Island 1012
Registered Number & Wool Products Label and W P L Encyclopedia see R N and W P L Encyclopedia 1902
Registered Nurse (CAN ISSN 1484-0863) 5979
Registered Nurse see R N 5979
• Registered Nurse (USA ISSN 1932-8966) 5979
Registered Nurse CareerSearch see R N CareerSearch 5979
• Registered Nurses Association of Ontario. Annual Report (Online) (CAN ISSN 1719-6892) 5979
Registered Psychiatric Nurses' Association of Saskatchewan. R P News (CAN) 5979
• Registered Rep (USA ISSN 1539-7149) 1647
Registered Representative see Registered Rep 1647
Registrar General's Newsletter see Bionotes 661
Registratie (Weert) (NLD) 4520
Registratie van Voedselinfecties en -Vergiftigingen bij de Inspectie voor de Gezondheidszorg en Voedsel en Waren Autoriteit see Registratie van Voedselinfecties en -Vergiftigingen Onderzocht door G G D's en Regionale Inspecties Gezondheidsbescherming Keuringsdiensten van Waren 7538
Registratie van Voedselinfecties en -Vergiftigingen Onderzocht door G G D's en Regionale Inspecties Gezondheidsbescherming Keuringsdiensten van Waren (NLD ISSN 1574-4922) 7538
Registration and Election Laws of Maryland (USA) 7176
Registre Aeronautique International (FRA ISSN 0080-066X) 8551
Registre de l'I S S N (Edition sur Bande Magnetique) see I S S N Register (Tape) 8963
Registre des Residences Privees pour Personnes Agees avec Services (CAN ISSN 1718-4789) 8065
Registre Maritime (FRA ISSN 0152-9994) 8658
Registres (FRA ISSN 1274-2414) 8477
Registro Informatico dei Protesti (ITA) 1409
Registro Nacional de Leyes, Decretos y Otros Documentos (URY ISSN 0797-5457) 4767
Registro Oficial de Auditores de Cuentas. Anuario (ESP ISSN 1133-4819) 1299
Registry News (USA) 8297
Registry of Interpreters for the Deaf. National Convention Proceedings (USA) 4076
• Registry of the Federal Court of Canada. Performance Report (CAN ISSN 1483-7579) 4959
Registry of Toxic Effects of Chemical Substances see R T E C S 3500
Registry Review (USA ISSN 1067-0521) 7610
• Regiyanal'naya Gazeta (BLR) 3800
RegJo Niedersachsen (DEU ISSN 1614-2624) 1839
RegJo Suedniedersachsen (DEU ISSN 1615-5696) 1839
• Reglas Firmes, Justas y Constantes (USA ISSN 1542-7706) 2904
Reglement Provisoire de la Chambre des Communes see Standing Orders of the House of Commons Including the Conflict of Interest Code for Members 4852
Reglementation du Transport des Animaux Vivants see Live Animals Regulations 8547
Regles des Cours Federales see Loi sur les Cours Federales, L R C, 1985, Ch. F-7 4725
Regmi Research Series (NPL ISSN 0034-348X) 4187
Regnbuen see Neriusaaq 508
Le Regne Mineral (FRA ISSN 1259-4415) 2764
Il Regno (ITA ISSN 0034-3498) 7814
• Regnskabsstatistik for Akvakultur/Aquaculture Account Statistics (DNK ISSN 1901-3345) 3605
• Regnskabsstatistik for Oekologisk Jordbrug/Account Statistics of Organic Farming (DNK ISSN 1398-1951) 205
Regnum (DEU ISSN 0341-3322) 7814
Regnum Vegetabile (DEU ISSN 0080-0694) 815
Regroupement des Chercheurs-res en Histoire des Travailleurs et Travailleuses du Quebec. Bulletin (CAN ISSN 1187-6484) 4310
Regroupement des Gens d'Affaires de la Capitale Nationale. Repertoire des Membres (CAN ISSN 1910-300X) 1164
Regroupement Quebecois des Amis et Benevoles de Musees Info see R Q A B M Info 6536
• Regulacion y Gestion (ARG ISSN 1515-7210) 3217
† Regulae Benedicti Studia. Annuarium Internationale (DEU ISSN 0174-0091) 8985
Regulae Benedicti Studia. Supplementa see Regulae Benedicti Studia. Traditio et Receptio 7673
Regulae Benedicti Studia. Traditio et Receptio (DEU) 7673
• ➤ Regular and Chaotic Dynamics (RUS ISSN 1560-3547) 5528
Regularly Scheduled Deprogramming (USA) 6610
• Regulateri (IND) 1164
Regulating the City Newsletter (GBR) 7501
• Regulation (Washington, 1977) (USA ISSN 0147-0590) 7176
▼ • ➤ Regulation & Governance (AUS ISSN 1748-5983) 4767
Regulation & Listed Corporates see Regulation et Societes Cotees 1393
▼ • Regulation et Societes Cotees (FRA ISSN 1961-9065) 1393
Regulation C C Directory (Check Clearinghouse) (USA ISSN 1932-4375) 1378
▼ • Regulation & Asset Management (FRA ISSN 1955-2645) 1647
▼ • Regulation & Gestion d'Actifs (FRA ISSN 1955-2637) 1647
• Regulation of Foreign Banks (USA) 4939
Regulation of Insurance in the U K, Ireland and E U (GBR) 4520
Regulation of Insurance Law see Regulation of Insurance in the U K, Ireland and E U 4520
• Regulation of Investment Companies (USA) 1647
Regulation of Plant Growth & Development see Shokubutsu no Seichou Chousetsu 817
Regulation of the Gas Industry (USA) 6790
Regulation, Policy and Market Access Report see R P M Report 6877
Regulations see Norway. Direktoratet for Arbeidstilsynet. Forskrifter 6681
Regulations of South Africa see Juta's South African Regulations 4708
RegulationsMedizin (DEU ISSN 1430-7561) 5702
The Regulator and Professional Conduct Quarterly (GBR ISSN 1360-7286) 4767
Regulatory Affairs Bulletin (USA ISSN 0950-3374) 3500
Regulatory Affairs Focus see Regulatory Focus 5703
Regulatory Affairs Journal see The Regulatory Affairs Journal. Pharma 6878
• Regulatory Affairs Journal. Devices (GBR ISSN 0969-4129) 6878
• The Regulatory Affairs Journal. Pharma (GBR ISSN 1740-1240) 6878
Regulatory Briefing Service (USA) 3329
• Regulatory Focus (USA) 5703
Regulatory Guide to Canadian Television Programming Services (CAN ISSN 1910-3727) 2389
• ➤ Regulatory Peptides (NLD ISSN 0167-0115) 744
Regulatory Plan and Unified Agenda see Unified Agenda of Federal Regulatory and Deregulatory Actions 7473
• Regulatory Rapporteur (GBR ISSN 1742-8955) 1164
The Regulatory Reporting Handbook (USA ISSN 1090-2562) 1378
• Regulatory Research Perspectives (USA ISSN 1933-8791) 6878
• The Regulatory Review (NZL ISSN 1177-0953) 7465
Regulatory Review (Year) (GBR) 1260
The Regulatory Risk Management Handbook (USA ISSN 1090-2554) 1378
• Regulatory Risk Monitor (USA) 1378
• ➤ Regulatory Toxicology and Pharmacology (USA ISSN 0273-2300) 3500
• Regulatory Update (USA ISSN 1065-1896) 7099
Regulierungsbehoerde fuer Telekommunikation und Post. Amtsblatt (DEU ISSN 1434-8128) 2355
• Reguxing Shuzhi/Thermosetting Resin (CHN ISSN 1002-7432) 6720
Reha-Einkaufsfuehrer (DEU) 2025
Rehab & Community Care Management (CAN ISSN 1192-2508) 6115
Rehab and Therapy Products Review (USA ISSN 1078-8204) 5703
• Rehab Management (USA ISSN 0899-6237) 6115
➤ Rehabilitace a Fyzikalni Lekarstvi/Rehabilitation and Physical Medicine (CZE ISSN 1211-2658) 6226
Rehabilitacia/Rehabilitation (SVK ISSN 0375-0922) 6115
• ➤ Rehabilitacion (ESP ISSN 0048-7120) 6115
➤ Rehabilitacja Medyczna (POL ISSN 1427-9622) 6115
Rehabilitatie (NLD ISSN 1570-6303) 6180
Rehabilitation see Kang Fu 6112
• ➤ Die Rehabilitation (DEU ISSN 0034-3536) 6115
Rehabilitation see Rehabilitacia 6115
Rehabilitation (Tokyo, 1951) see Ryoiku 3046
Rehabilitation (Tokyo, 1953) see Rihabiriteshon 8066
Rehabilitation and Education view see R E: view 8983
Rehabilitation and Physical Medicine see Rehabilitace a Fyzikalni Lekarstvi 6226
Rehabilitation and Physical Medicine (Section 19 EMBASE) see Excerpta Medica. Section 19: Rehabilitation and Physical Medicine 5745
▼ • Rehabilitation Compensation Report (USA ISSN 1943-2445) 4110
• ➤ Rehabilitation Counseling Bulletin (USA ISSN 0034-3552) 4069
➤ Rehabilitation Education (USA ISSN 0889-7018) 3046
Rehabilitation Engineering & Assistive Technology Society of North America Conference. Proceedings see R E S N A Conference. Proceedings 6115
Rehabilitation Engineering and Assistive Technology Society of North America News see R E S N A News 3045
Rehabilitation Engineering Society of Japan. Proceedings of the Conference see Riha Kogaku Kanfarensu Koen Ronbunshu 3218
• ➤ Rehabilitation Nursing (USA ISSN 0278-4807) 5979
Rehabilitation of Cancer Victims see Aizheng Kangfu 6106
Rehabilitation Professional (USA) 6115
• ➤ Rehabilitation Psychology (USA ISSN 0090-5550) 7402
• Rehabilitation R & D Progress Reports (Research & Development) (USA ISSN 0882-7753) 6443
Rehabilitation Research. Report (CAN ISSN 1910-6831) 6115
▼ • Rehabilitation Research Review (NZL ISSN 1170-3415) 6115
Rehabilitation und Praevention (USA ISSN 0172-6412) 6115
Rehabilitering (NOR ISSN 0809-8298) 4110
Rehilete see Crisol Virtual 3908
Rehotnik (SVK ISSN 1335-6836) 3947
Reial Academia de Bones Lletres. Series Minor/Real Academia de Buenas Letras. Serie Minor (ESP ISSN 1695-5110) 5359
Reichenberger Heimatblatt (DEU ISSN 1438-8596) 3561
• Reichorui Kenkyu/Primate Research (JPN ISSN 0912-4047) 961
Reichsausschuss fuer Arbeitsstudien Nachrichten see R E F A Nachrichten 1704
Reichsbund Aktuell mit Sport (AUT) 3798
† Reid's Magazine (AUS ISSN 1832-4681) 8985
Reign of the Sacred Heart (USA ISSN 0048-7155) 7814
Reihe der Villa Vigoni (DEU ISSN 0936-8965) 7262
Reihe Germanistische Linguistik (DEU ISSN 0344-6778) 5166
Reihe Geschichtswissenschaften (DEU) 4158
Reihe Informationsmanagement im Engineering Karlsruhe (DEU ISSN 1860-5990) 3293
Reihe Juedische Moderne (DEU) 3561
Reihe Kommunikationswissenschaften (DEU) 2337
Reihe: Kulleraugen Studium (DEU ISSN 0933-1395) 6511
Reihe Kulturwissenschaften (DEU) 3561
Reihe Kunstgeschichte (DEU) 514
Reihe Maritim (DEU) 4257
Reihe Medizin und Gesellschaft (DEU) 5703
Reihe Politikwissenschaften (DEU) 7176
Reihe Politische Bildung (AUT) 7176
Reihe Religionswissenschaften (DEU) 7673
Reihe Siegen (DEU) 5359
Reihe Sozialwissenschaften (DEU) 7995
Reihe Sprach- und Literaturwissenschaften (DEU) 5166
Reihe Spurensuche (DEU ISSN 1862-0256) 5359
Reiki (NOR ISSN 1504-5595) 314
Reiki Magazin (DEU ISSN 1432-5063) 314
• Reiki News Magazine (USA ISSN 1539-6533) 314
Reikinytt see Reiki 314
Reil (COL) 8624
• Reimbursement Advisor (USA ISSN 0884-2795) 4110
Rein-Echos (FRA ISSN 1958-3184) 5703
• Reinardus (NLD ISSN 0925-4757) 5359
• Reindriftsnytt/Boazodoallu-oddasat (NOR ISSN 0333-4031) 298
• Reinforced Plastics (GBR ISSN 0034-3617) 7099
Reiniger und Waescher Textilservice see R & W - Textilservice 2244
Reinigungs Markt (DEU ISSN 1439-7544) 1854
ReinRaumTechnik (DEU ISSN 1439-4251) 3371
• Reinsurance (GBR ISSN 0048-7171) 4520
Reinsurance Basics (USA ISSN 1939-6740) 4520
Reinsurance Directory of Asia (SGP) 2025
Reinsurance Educator (USA ISSN 1053-5934) 4520
Reinsurance Law (GBR) 4520
▼ Reinsurance Law (USA ISSN 1946-0104) 4879
Reinsurance Report see Re Report 4520
• Reinsurance Reporter (USA ISSN 0034-3641) 4520
▼ • Reinsurance Roundtable Continuum (USA) 4520
Reintegratiewijzer (NLD ISSN 1871-2134) 1705
Reintegration Today (USA ISSN 1528-509X) 6180
Reinventing Democracy (GBR) 7176
Reinwardtia (IDN ISSN 0034-365X) 815
Reinwater (NLD ISSN 1573-9643) 3490
Reinwater Kwartaaltijdschrift see Reinwater 3490
Reis (NOR ISSN 1500-3701) 8751
Reis & Geniet (NLD ISSN 1574-3063) 8751
Reisbrief (NLD) 8751
Reisburo see Reisburo Actueel 8751
Reisburo Actueel (NLD ISSN 1871-9104) 8751
• Reise Aktuell (AUT) 8751
† Reise Bild (DEU ISSN 1611-6569) 8985
Reise-Dienst (DEU ISSN 0942-0517) 8751
• Reise Motorrad (DEU ISSN 0947-1375) 8267
Reise und Camping (AUT) 8751
• Reise und Preise (DEU ISSN 0932-4186) 8751
Reisebuero Bulletin see Travel One 8767
Reisefieber (DEU ISSN 0177-4050) 8751
Reiselust (DEU) 8751
Reisemagazin (AUT) 8751
Reisemobil International (DEU) 8601
Reisen & Geniessen (DEU) 8751
Reisen Exclusiv (DEU) 8751
Reisen in Deutschland: Reisefuehrer (DEU ISSN 0177-2953) 8751
Reisen in Deutschland: Zimmerkatalog (DEU ISSN 0177-2961) 8751
ReiseRecht aktuell (DEU ISSN 0944-7490) 8751
Reisetips (AUT) 8751
Der Reiseverkehr der Schweizer im Ausland/Touristes Suisses a l'Etranger (CHE) 8780
Reiseziele (DEU) 8751
De Reisgids (NLD ISSN 1569-0407) 8751
Reisinfo Express see Zakenreis Magazine 8777
• De Reiskrant (NLD ISSN 0777-0030) 8751
Reisrevue (NLD ISSN 1574-2105) 8751
Reisrevue Xtra see Reisrevue 8751
Reiten und Fahren St. Georg (DEU ISSN 0944-5854) 8297
Reiten und Zucht in Berlin-Brandenburg (DEU) 8297
Reiter Prisma (DEU ISSN 0722-0731) 8297
Reiter Revue International (DEU ISSN 0034-3692) 8297
Reiter und Pferde in Westfalen (DEU ISSN 0343-6861) 8297
Reiterjournal (DEU ISSN 0173-2404) 8297
Reito/Refrigeration (JPN ISSN 0034-3714) 4126
Reito to Kucho/Japan Refrigeration and Airconditioning Industry Association. Journal (JPN ISSN 0386-1538) 4126

10796 REITSPORT MAGAZIN FUER DAS PFERDELAND NIEDERSACHSEN ULRICH'S PERIODICALS

Reitsport Magazin fuer das Pferdeland Niedersachsen (DEU ISSN 1862-782X) **8297**
Reitsport Magazin fuer Hannover-Bremen *see* Reitsport Magazin fuer das Pferdeland Niedersachsen **8297**
Reitsport Weser-Ems (DEU) **8297**
REITStreet *see* R E I T Street **7606**
Der Reitwagen (AUT) **8267**
• Reizen (NLD ISSN 0921-0032) **8751**
▼ • Rejecta Mathematica (USA ISSN 1948-8351) **5528**
The Rejected Quarterly (USA ISSN 1525-2671) **5359**
Rejoice! (CAN) **7740**
• Rejs (POL ISSN 1507-1308) **8281**
Rejsebogen (Year) (DNK ISSN 0108-6812) **8751**
▼ Rejuvenate (IRL ISSN 1649-9425) **6256**
Rejuvenate (USA) **1789**
• ➤ Rejuvenation Research (USA ISSN 1549-1684) **4054**
Rekeningkunde S A *see* Accountancy S A **1276**
Rekexue Xuebao *see* Journal of Thermal Science **7055**
• Rekexue yu Jishu/Journal of Thermal Science and Technology (CHN ISSN 1671-8097) **7056**
• Rekhev (ISR) **8601**
Rekhev W'tahbura *see* Vehicles & Transportation **8519**
Rekishi Hyoron/History Review (JPN ISSN 0386-8907) **4187**
Rekishi to Jinbutsu/History and Personalities (JPN) **4158**
Rekishi to Tabi/History and Travel (JPN) **8751**
Rekishigaku Kenkyu *see* Journal of Historical Studies **4170**
Rekisho Nenpyo (JPN) **6400**
Reklaam is Succes (BEL) **34**
Reklama *see* Sostines Skelbimai **3906**
Reklama Nedeli (RUS) **1164**
Reklambyraaer i Sverige *see* Byraaboken **22**
Reklameforbrugsundersoegelsen *see* Det Danske Reklamemarked **24**
Reklameforbrugsundersoegelsen i Danmark *see* Det Danske Reklamemarked **24**
Reklamnyi Mir (KGZ) **3904**
Reklamodatel' (RUS) **1839**
Reknuus (ZAF ISSN 1683-1713) **1299**
Rekonstrukce (CZE ISSN 1801-1756) **1032**
Rekonstrukcie *see* Rekonstrukce **1032**
Rekord/Record (ZAF) **3949**
RekreaVakkrant (NLD ISSN 1389-3491) **4982**
RekreaVakkrant Extra *see* RekreaVakkrant **4982**
Relacao dos Advogados e das Sociedades de Advogados (PRT) **4768**
Relacao dos Advogados e das Sociedades de Advogados. Adenda *see* Relacao dos Advogados e das Sociedades de Advogados **4768**
• Relacion de Colegiados (ESP) **3281**
Relacion de Ingenieros de Caminos, Canales y Puertos *see* Relacion de Colegiados **3281**
Relaciones (ARG ISSN 0325-2221) **352**
➤ Relaciones (URY ISSN 0797-9754) **7402**
• Relaciones (Mexico City) (MEX ISSN 0188-2643) **8127**
• Relaciones (Zamora) (MEX ISSN 0185-3929) **4310**
Relaciones de Trabajo (VEN) **1705**
Relaciones Economicas Internacionales (ESP ISSN 1575-8133) **7262**
Relaciones Financieras (ESP ISSN 0486-3518) **1647**
Relaciones Industriales (DEU) **1705**
• Relaciones Internacionales (ESP ISSN 1699-3950) **7262**
• Relaciones Internacionales (MEX ISSN 0185-0814) **7262**
Relaciones Laborales (ESP ISSN 0213-0556) **1705**
Relaciones Laborales. Normativa Laboral y de Seguridad Social (ESP ISSN 1137-8611) **1705**
Relaciones Publicas *see* Revista Internacional de Comunicacion y Relaciones Publicas **34**
Relacoes Internacionais (BRA ISSN 1413-0149) **7262**
Relacoes Internacionais (PRT ISSN 1645-9199) **7262**
Relais *see* I N S E E Picardie Relais **1241**
Relais & Chateaux Magazin (DEU) **4396**
La Relance a l'Universite, Baccalaureat et Maitrise (CAN ISSN 1719-3877) **2999**
Relance a l'Universite, Baccalaureat, Maitrise et Doctorat, le Placement des Personnes Diplomees *see* La Relance a l'Universite, Baccalaureat et Maitrise **2999**
Relance Survey Vocational Training at the Secondary Level. Employment Situation of Graduates: (Year) Surveys (CAN ISSN 1718-3979) **2904**
ReLaSur *see* Revista de Relaciones Laborales en American Latina, Cono Sur **1705**
Relate News (GBR ISSN 0954-3406) **8065**
Relatewell (AUS ISSN 1327-7553) **8127**
• Relation (AUT ISSN 1025-2339) **8127**
Relation Client Magazine (FRA) **1839**
Relational Child & Youth Care Practice (CAN ISSN 1705-625X) **2166**
Relationen (DEU ISSN 1431-3669) **7262**
▼ Relationes (DEU ISSN 1867-3198) **7902**
• Relations (CAN ISSN 0034-3781) **8065**
Relations (HRV ISSN 1334-6768) **5359**
Relations Across Taiwan Straits *see* Liang'an Guanxi **7251**
Relations Elec (FRA) **3161**
Relations Financieres Internationales (BEL ISSN 1377-5669) **1581**
• ➤ Relations Industrielles/Industrial Relations (CAN ISSN 0034-379X) **1705**
Relations Industrielles au Canada *see* Industrial Relations Legislation in Canada **1688**
Relations Internationales (FRA ISSN 0335-2013) **7262**
Relations Presse (FRA ISSN 0246-7143) **34**
Relations Publiques Informations (FRA ISSN 0034-3811) **34**
• Relationship Marketing & Sales Strategies (USA ISSN 1535-5918) **1839**
Relative Values for Physicians (USA ISSN 1065-7681) **5703**
Relatively Seeking (USA ISSN 0747-5624) **3780**
Relatively Speaking (CAN ISSN 0701-8878) **3780**
Relatorio Anual Sobre a Evolucao do Fenomeno da Droga na Uniao Europeia *see* State of the Drugs Problem in the European Union. Annual Report **2699**
Relatorio D N O C S *see* Brazil. Departamento Nacional de Obras Contra as Secas. Relatorio **7423**
Relatorio Geral sobre a Actividade da Uniao Europeia *see* General Report on the Activities of the European Union **3837**
Relatorio Mensal de Economia (PRT ISSN 0871-9365) **1514**
• Relax! (HUN ISSN 1585-8642) **3877**
Relay (GBR ISSN 1357-0110) **5043**
Relay Magazine (USA) **3161**
Relazione Annuale Sull'evoluzione del Fenomeno della Droga nell'Unione Europea *see* State of the Drugs Problem in the European Union. Annual Report **2699**
Relazione Generale sull'Attivita dell'Unione Europea *see* General Report on the Activities of the European Union **3837**
Relea (Revista Latinoamerica de Estudios Avanzados) (VEN ISSN 1316-0486) **1514**
• Release (AUS ISSN 0157-3470) **2667**
Release (NLD ISSN 1871-9074) **6610**
Release 1.0 *see* Release 2.0 **2436**
• Release 2.0 (USA ISSN 1935-9446) **2436**
Release Magazine (USA) **6610**
Release Print (USA ISSN 0890-5231) **6511**
Release to the Membership (USA) **1647**
Relevamientos de Biodiversidad (URY ISSN 1510-0804) **3462**
Relevant (NLD ISSN 1381-2866) **6947**
Relevant (USA ISSN 1543-317X) **7674**
La Releve *see* La Nouvelle Releve **7160**
• Releve des Maladies Transmissibles au Canada (CAN) **5825**
Releve des Societes dont les Actions, Parts et Certificats sont Cotes en Bourse de Luxembourg/List of Companies of Which Shares, Parts and Foreign Share Certificates are Listed on the Luxembourg Stock Exchange (LUX) **1647**
• Reli Touping/Thermal Turbine (CHN ISSN 1672-5549) **3394**
• Reliability and Maintainability Symposium. Proceedings (USA ISSN 0149-144X) **3329**
Reliability Assessment (USA ISSN 0898-3933) **3161**
Reliability Center for Electronic Components of Japan Journal *see* R C J Journal **3111**
• ➤ Reliability Engineering & System Safety (GBR ISSN 0951-8320) **3217**
• Reliability: Theory & Applications/Nadyezhnost': Voprosy Teorii i Praktiki (USA ISSN 1932-2321) **3217**
• ➤ Reliable Computing (NLD ISSN 1385-3139) **2436**
• Reliable Plant (USA) **3371**
• Reliance (FRA ISSN 1774-9743) **6115**
Reliant Logistic News (CZE ISSN 1802-3746) **1902**
Reliant News *see* Reliant Logistic News **1902**
Relics (USA ISSN 0034-3897) **4310**
Relics and Museology *see* Wen Bo **6540**
• Relics from South (CHN ISSN 1004-6275) **413**
Relics of Sichuan *see* Sichuan Wenwu **416**
Relief (FRA ISSN 1166-5742) **7291**
• Relief and Rehabilitation Network Papers and Newsletter (GBR) **1604**
Relief, Boden, Palaeoklima (DEU ISSN 0720-4876) **2764**
ReliefWeb (CHE) **8065**
• Religiao & Sociedade (BRA ISSN 0100-8587) **7674**
Religie & Samenleving (NLD ISSN 1872-3497) **7674**
➤ Religio (CZE ISSN 1210-3640) **7674**
➤ Religiologiques (CAN ISSN 1180-0135) **7674**
Religion *see* Zongjiao **7697**
• ➤ Religion (GBR ISSN 0048-721X) **7674**
• ➤ Religion and American Culture (USA ISSN 1052-1151) **7674**
➤ Religion & Education (USA ISSN 1550-7394) **2904**
• ➤ Religion and Human Rights (NLD ISSN 1871-031X) **7674**
Religion and Human Rights Series (USA) **7814**
Religion and Law Review (IND ISSN 0971-3212) **4768**
➤ Religion and Literature (USA ISSN 0888-3769) **5359**
➤ Religion and Reason (DEU ISSN 0080-0848) **7674**
▼ Religion and Security Monograph Sieries (USA ISSN 1945-3256) **7674**
Religion & Society *see* Centre for Studies in Religion & Society **7630**
➤ Religion and Society (DEU ISSN 1437-5370) **7674**
• Religion and Society in Central and Eastern Europe (USA ISSN 1553-9962) **7674**
Religion and Society in Transition (DEU ISSN 1437-4641) **7674**
The Religion & Society Report (USA ISSN 0742-6984) **7674**
• ➤ Religion and the Arts (NLD ISSN 1079-9265) **7674**
Religion and the Social Order (NLD ISSN 1061-5210) **7674**
• ➤ Religion and Theology (NLD ISSN 1023-0807) **7674**
Religion Betrifft Uns (DEU ISSN 0936-5141) **7674**
Religion Communicators Council Counselor *see* R C C Counselor **33**
▼ • ➤ Religion Compass (GBR ISSN 1749-8171) **7674**
• Religion East & West (USA ISSN 1539-2430) **7674**
Religion for Peace (USA ISSN 1027-9369) **7674**
Religion, Health, and Healing (USA ISSN 1556-262X) **7674**
Religion Heute (DEU ISSN 0722-9151) **2904**
Religion in America (Cary) (USA ISSN 1556-4843) **7674**
Religion in American Life Update *see* R I A L Update **7673**
Religion in Communist Dominated Areas Newsletter *see* R C D A Newsletter **7673**
Religion in der Geschichte (DEU ISSN 1439-8753) **7674**
Religion in der Gesellschaft (DEU ISSN 1432-0304) **7675**
• Religion in Eastern Europe (USA ISSN 1069-4781) **7675**
Religion in Malawi (MWI) **7675**
Religion in the Americas Series (NLD ISSN 1542-1279) **7675**
• Religion in the News (USA ISSN 1525-7207) **4583**
• Religion Index One: Periodicals (USA ISSN 0149-8428) **7699**
Religion Indexes: Thesaurus (USA ISSN 0730-6350) **7675**
Religion Newswriters Association Newsletter *see* R N A Newsletter **4582**
Religion & Livsfraagor (RoL) (SWE ISSN 0347-2159) **2904**
▼ Religion, Politics, and Public Life (USA ISSN 1934-290X) **7176**
Religion - Politik - Gesellschaft in der Schweiz (CHE ISSN 1422-4429) **7675**
Religion, Science and the Environment (SGP) **3946**
• Religion - Staat - Gesellschaft (DEU ISSN 1438-955X) **7675**
• ➤ Religion, State and Society (GBR ISSN 0963-7494) **7675**
Religion Teacher's Journal (USA ISSN 0034-401X) **7675**
Religion Watch (USA ISSN 0886-2141) **7675**
† Religione e Scuola (ITA ISSN 1125-7156) **8985**
Religione e Societa (Rome) (ITA ISSN 0391-853X) **7814**
Religiones y Textos *see* Biblioteca de las Religiones **7627**
• Religioni e Societa (ITA ISSN 0394-9397) **7675**
Religions and Beliefs/Religions et Croyances (CAN) **7675**
Religions and Discourse (GBR ISSN 1422-8998) **7675**
Religions Contemporaines (FRA ISSN 1778-3453) **7675**
Religions et Croyances *see* Religions and Beliefs **7675**
Religions & Histoire (FRA ISSN 1772-7200) **7675**
➤ Religions in the Graeco-Roman World (NLD ISSN 0927-7633) **7675**
▼ • ➤ Religions of South Asia (GBR ISSN 1751-2689) **7740**
➤ Religionsgeschichtliche Versuche und Vorarbeiten (DEU ISSN 0939-2580) **7675**
Religionslaereren (DNK ISSN 0108-559X) **7675**
Religionspaedagogik an Berufsbildenden Schulen *see* R A B S **7772**
Religionspaedagogik in Einer Multikulturellen Gesellschaft (DEU) **7675**
Religionspaedagogik in Pluraler Gesellschaft (DEU) **7675**
➤ Religionspaedagogische Beitraege (DEU ISSN 0173-0339) **7814**
Religionsunterricht *see* R U **7813**
Religionsunterricht an Hoeheren Schulen (DEU ISSN 0341-8960) **7814**
Religionsvetenskapliga Studier fraan Gaevle (SWE ISSN 1652-7895) **7675**
➤ Religionsvidenskabeligt Tidsskrift (DNK ISSN 0108-1993) **7675**
Religionswissenschaftliche Reihe (DEU ISSN 0934-2192) **7675**
Religionswissenschaftliche Texte und Studien (DEU ISSN 0179-9215) **7675**
• ➤ Religious & Theological Abstracts (USA) **7699**
Religious Book Review Index (IND ISSN 0034-4060) **7699**
• Religious Conference Manager (USA ISSN 1050-2742) **7675**
Religious Consultancy (IND) **7675**
Religious Cultures in the World *see* Shijie Zongjiao Wenhua **7681**
• Religious Education (USA ISSN 0034-4087) **7676**
Religious Education Association. Annual Convention. Proceedings *see* Religious Education **7676**
Religious Education Today *see* R E Today **2902**
• Religious Freedom Reporter (USA ISSN 0275-3529) **4851**
Religious Funding Resource Guide (USA) **8065**
Religious Herald (USA ISSN 0738-7318) **7773**
▼ ➤ Religious History and Culture Series (NLD) **7676**
Religious Humanism (USA ISSN 0034-4095) **7676**
• The Religious Language Newsletter (E-mail Edition) (USA) **7676**
• The Religious Language Newsletter (Online Edition) (USA) **7676**
† • Religious Leaders of America (USA ISSN 1057-2961) **8985**
Religious Life (USA ISSN 0279-0459) **7814**
➤ Religious Life Review (IRL ISSN 0332-4346) **7814**
Religious Product News (USA) **1854**
Religious Representatives' Guide to Marriage in British Columbia (CAN ISSN 1912-3876) **5561**
➤ Religious Socialism (USA ISSN 0278-7784) **7177**
• ➤ Religious Studies (GBR ISSN 0034-4125) **7676**
• ➤ Religious Studies and Theology (GBR ISSN 0829-2922) **7676**
Religious Studies Journal (PHL ISSN 0115-6349) **7676**
Religious Studies News (USA ISSN 0885-0372) **7676**
• ➤ Religious Studies Review (USA ISSN 0319-485X) **7699**
Religious Trends (GBR) **7699**
† Religious Zionism in Action - Essays/Mesilot (ISR) **8985**
Religiya (GEO) **7676**
Relish (USA) **4366**
Relish of Culture *see* Wenhua Yule **4984**
Relix (USA ISSN 0146-3489) **6610**
▼ The Relo Report (USA) **7610**
† Reload (CZE ISSN 1214-617X) **8985**
Reload (NLD) **3915**
Relocation Journal *see* U.S. Sites and Development Relocation Journal **7614**
• Relocation Journal & Real Estate News (USA ISSN 1085-5289) **7610**
Relocation Link - York County, PA (USA) **3986**
The Relocation Report (USA ISSN 0275-7613) **1873**
Relojes (ESP) **4569**
Relojes y Estilograficas (ESP) **4569**
† Remainders' Book Italiano (ITA ISSN 0034-4176) **8985**
† Remanso (ESP ISSN 0034-4184) **8985**
➤ Remate de Males (BRA ISSN 0103-183X) **7995**
• ➤ Remedial and Special Education (USA ISSN 0741-9325) **3046**
• Remediation (USA ISSN 1051-5658) **3511**
Remediation Review (USA) **3511**
• Remediation Solutions (Print) (GBR ISSN 1747-5554) **3511**
Remedies *see* B A R - B R I Bar Review. Remedies **4625**
Remedies *see* Gilbert Law Summaries. Remedies **4952**
Remedium (RUS ISSN 1561-5936) **5703**
• Remedy (USA ISSN 1554-8767) **4054**
Remember Markham (CAN ISSN 1486-7842) **4310**
Remember That Song (USA ISSN 0889-8790) **6610**
Remembering Yesterday (USA ISSN 1524-2897) **4054**
Reminder List of Eligible Releases (USA) **6511**
Reminder Plus (USA) **34**
The Remington Report (USA ISSN 1070-3411) **5703**
Reminisce (USA ISSN 1057-2368) **3986**
Reminisce Extra (USA ISSN 1069-8957) **3986**
† • Remisis (FRA ISSN 0766-6500) **8985**
• Remittances of Foreign Balances Survey (CAN) **8551**
• Remix (USA ISSN 1532-1347) **6610**
Remnant of Israel (USA) **7814**
▼ Remnants of the Rails (USA ISSN 1949-033X) **8624**
Remodel (USA ISSN 1935-0678) **455**
Remodel Spokane Magazine (USA ISSN 1930-2142) **4549**
• Remodeling (USA ISSN 0885-8039) **1032**
Remodeling and Makeovers *see* Remodeling & Makeovers **455**
Remodeling & Makeovers (USA ISSN 1938-6907) **455**
Remodeling Ideas *see* Better Homes and Gardens Building & Remodeling **435**
Remodeling Ideas for Your Home *see* Remodel **455**
Remodeling Magazine (USA ISSN 1552-8677) **1032**
Remodeling News (Baltimore - Washington, DC Edition) *see* Remodeling News (Northern - Central New Jersey Edition) **1032**
Remodeling News (Greater Boston - New England Edition) *see* Remodeling News (Northern - Central New Jersey Edition) **1032**
Remodeling News (Greater Philadelphia - Delaware Edition) *see* Remodeling News (Northern - Central New Jersey Edition) **1032**
Remodeling News (Long Island - Metro New York Edition) *see* Remodeling News (Northern - Central New Jersey Edition) **1032**
Remodeling News (Northern - Central New Jersey Edition) (USA) **1032**

Link to your serials resources and content with ulrichsweb.com

DIRECTORY 2010 RENTAL MARKET REPORT. SASKATCHEWAN HIGHLIGHTS 10797

Remodeling News (Westchester, Rockaland, Putnam, Orange, Fairfield & New Haven Edition) *see* Remodeling News (Northern - Central New Jersey Edition) **1032**
Remodeling Online *see* Remodeling **1032**
Remodeling - Repair Construction Costs (USA) **1032**
➤ Remont, Vosstanovlenie, Modernizatsiya (RUS ISSN 1684-2561) **5459**
Remote Control Buggy & Truggy *see* R C Buggy & Truggy **4344**
Remote Gas Strategies *see* Gas Leads for Suppliers of Products and Services to the World Gas Community **6770**
Remote Imaging Group Journal (GBR) **2715**
▼ • Remote Sensing (CHE ISSN 2072-4292) **7037**
Remote Sensing and Digital Image Processing (NLD ISSN 1567-3200) **2489**
† Remote Sensing and Photogrammetry News (AUS ISSN 1441-7723) **8985**
Remote Sensing for Land & Resources *see* Guotu Ziyuan Yaogan **2709**
• Remote Sensing in Canada (CAN ISSN 0226-479X) **2715**
Remote Sensing Information *see* Yaogan Xinxi **4034**
➤ Remote Sensing of Earth Resources and Environment (NLD ISSN 0924-6010) **2715**
• ➤ Remote Sensing of Environment (USA ISSN 0034-4257) **4026**
Remote Sensing Society of Japan. Journal *see* Nihon Rimoto Senshingu Gakkaishi **4022**
Remote Sensing Technology and Application *see* Yaogan Jishu yu Yingyong **2718**
Remote Site and Equipment Management *see* Remote Site & Equipment Management **1032**
• Remote Site & Equipment Management (USA ISSN 1535-0347) **1032**
• Remote Site & Equipment Management e-Report (USA ISSN 1942-6232) **2337**
Remote Systems Technology Proceedings *see* Conference on Robotics and Remote Systems. Proceedings **2584**
Removals and Storage (GBR ISSN 0034-4265) **8509**
• La Remuneration des Expatries (FRA ISSN 1955-7523) **1873**
Remuneration in Europe (GBR) **1873**
Remuneration Report - Austria (USA) **1873**
Remuneration Report - Belgium (USA) **1873**
Remuneration Report - Denmark (USA) **1873**
Remuneration Report - Finland (USA) **1873**
Remuneration Report - France (USA) **1873**
Remuneration Report - Germany (USA) **1873**
Remuneration Report - Greece (USA) **1873**
Remuneration Report - Ireland (USA) **1873**
Remuneration Report - Italy (USA) **1873**
Remuneration Report - Luxembourg (USA) **1873**
Remuneration Report - Netherlands (USA) **1873**
Remuneration Report - Norway (USA) **1873**
Remuneration Report - Portugal (USA) **1873**
Remuneration Report - Spain (USA) **1873**
Remuneration Report - Sweden (USA) **1873**
Remuneration Report - Switzerland (USA) **1873**
Remuneration Report - Turkey (USA) **1873**
Remuneration Report - United Kingdom (USA) **1873**
• Remuneration Tribunal. Annual Report (AUS ISSN 0728-7216) **7465**
REN *see* Revista Economica do Nordeste **1515**
Ren che Zhi *see* Car and Driver **8571**
• Ren Energi (DNK ISSN 0108-9439) **3146**
Ren Idrett (NOR ISSN 1504-5188) **8196**
Ren Sheng (CHN) **973**
• Ren Viden (DNK ISSN 0908-3987) **3511**
• Ren yu Shengwuquan/Man and the Biosphere (CHN ISSN 1009-1661) **700**
Ren yu Ziran/Human and Nature (CHN ISSN 1671-3745) **7902**
➤ Renaessancestudier (DNK ISSN 0902-9907) **4257**
• Renaissance (PAK ISSN 1605-0045) **7715**
Renaissance (Greensboro) (USA) **5081**
Renaissance and Baroque: Studies and Texts (USA ISSN 0897-7836) **4257**
• ➤ Renaissance and Reformation/Renaissance et Reforme (CAN ISSN 0034-429X) **5359**
Renaissance and Reformation Texts in Translation (CAN) **5359**
Renaissance Bulletin (JPN ISSN 0388-0796) **5359**
• Renaissance Drama (USA ISSN 0486-3739) **8477**
Renaissance et Reforme *see* Renaissance and Reformation **5359**
† • ➤ Renaissance Forum (GBR ISSN 1362-1149) **8985**
La Renaissance Francaise (FRA ISSN 1251-7135) **4257**
Renaissance, Humanisme, Reforme *see* R H R **7994**
• Renaissance Learning (USA) **3078**
Renaissance Magazine (USA ISSN 1088-906X) **4257**
Renaissance Manuscript Studies (USA ISSN 0196-7037) **6610**
Renaissance Monographs (JPN) **5359**
Renaissance Noire *see* Black Renaissance **3523**
• Renaissance Papers (Year) (USA ISSN 0584-4207) **5359**
• ➤ Renaissance Quarterly (USA ISSN 0034-4338) **5359**
• ➤ Renaissance Studies (GBR ISSN 0269-1213) **4158**
Renaissance Studies Utrecht (NLD ISSN 0923-0084) **4158**
Renaissance Vocal and Instrumental Music *see* Music Archive Publications. Series C, Renaissance Vocal and Instrumental Music **6590**
Renal & Urology News (USA ISSN 1550-9478) **6273**
Renal Business Today (USA ISSN 1940-4646) **6273**
• ➤ Renal Failure (USA ISSN 0886-022X) **6273**
• ➤ Renal Society of Australasia Journal (AUS ISSN 1832-3804) **6274**
Renal Transplantation, Vascular Surgery *see* Jin Ishoku Kekkan Geka **6247**
Renalink (USA ISSN 1532-6195) **6274**
Renarres (CHL ISSN 0716-4637) **3715**
• ➤ Renascence (USA ISSN 0034-4346) **5359**
Renault Magazine (GBR ISSN 1469-4158) **8601**
• Rencai Kaifa/Talent Exploitation (CHN ISSN 1000-7628) **1874**
• Rencai Ziben/Human Capital (TWN) **1874**
Rencheng Huixun *see* Rencheng Jikan **7702**
Rencheng Jikan (TWN) **7702**
Renchengfo Jizazhi *see* Rencheng Jikan **7702**
Rencontre (CAN ISSN 0709-9487) **3561**
Rencontre (English Edition) *see* Rencontre **3561**
Rencontre avec l'Inde (IND ISSN 0970-4876) **4471**
• Rencontres (FRA ISSN 1955-2890) **5166**
Rencontres (MUS) **5359**
Rencontres Autour des Recherches sur les Ruminants (FRA ISSN 1279-6530) **150**
Les Rencontres de Normale Sup' (FRA ISSN 1770-2208) **4471**
Rencontres de Philosophie Medievale (BEL) **6947**
Rencontres Internationales de Geneve (CHE) **7995**
Rencontres Recherche Ruminants *see* Rencontres Autour des Recherches sur les Ruminants **150**
Rencontres sur l'Education *see* Encounters on Education **2853**
Rendemens *see* Arbo Rendement **1856**
Rendement (NLD ISSN 0926-3314) **1789**
Render (USA ISSN 0090-8932) **150**
Rendevenement (Dutch Edition) *see* Rendevenement (French Edition) **34**
Rendevenement (French Edition) (BEL ISSN 1372-3294) **34**
Rendez-Vous (LUX) **4982**
Les Rendez-Vous de l'Innovation (FRA ISSN 1779-2622) **6790**
Rendez-vous Jeunesse *see* Youth Rendez-Vous **2927**
➤ Rendezvous (USA ISSN 0034-4400) **4471**
Rendiconti Accademia Nazionale delle Scienze detta dei XL. Memorie di Scienze Fisiche e Naturali (ITA ISSN 0392-4130) **7037**
Rendiconti dell'Accademia Nazionale delle Scienze detta del XL. Parte I. Memorie di Matematica e Applicazioni (ITA ISSN 1128-8582) **5528**
Rendiconti dell'Istituto di Matematica dell'Universita di Trieste *see* Universita degli Studi di Trieste. Istituto di Matematica. Rendiconti **5543**
Rendiconti di Matematica e delle Sue Applicazioni (ITA ISSN 1120-7183) **5528**
Rendite Plus (DEU ISSN 1614-7545) **4054**
• ➤ Renditions (HKG ISSN 0377-3515) **559**
• ➤ Reneng Dongli Gongcheng/Journal of Engineering for Thermal Energy and Power (CHN ISSN 1001-2060) **3394**
• Renew (AUS ISSN 1327-1938) **3146**
• Renew (USA) **590**
• Renew Newsletter (GBR) **3146**
• Renewable Agriculture and Food Systems (Online) (GBR ISSN 1742-1713) **150**
• ➤ Renewable Agriculture and Food Systems (Print) (GBR ISSN 1742-1705) **150**
• Renewable & Sustainable Energy Reviews (GBR ISSN 1364-0321) **3146**
• ➤ Renewable Energy (GBR ISSN 0960-1481) **3146**
• Renewable Energy (Year) (GBR) **3146**
Renewable Energy Annual (Online) *see* U.S. Department of Energy. Energy Information Administration. Renewable Energy Annual (Online) **3149**
† Renewable Energy Bulletin (GBR ISSN 0306-364X) **8985**
Renewable Energy Canada (CAN ISSN 1912-0427) **3146**
• Renewable Energy Focus (GBR ISSN 1755-0084) **3146**
• Renewable Energy for Development (SWE ISSN 1101-8267) **3146**
Renewable Energy Journal (FRA ISSN 1276-7573) **3146**
• Renewable Energy Report (GBR ISSN 1355-6258) **3146**
• Renewable Energy Today (USA) **3146**
Renewable Energy Weekly *see* S N L Renewable Energy Week **3147**
• Renewable Energy World (USA ISSN 1462-6381) **3146**
Renewable Fuel News *see* Ethanol & Biodiesel News **3134**
▼ • Renewable Fuels Supply Americas (USA ISSN 1943-1449) **3254**
Renewable Resources and Recycling Economy *see* Zaisheng Ziyuan yu Xunhuan Jingji **3476**
Renewable Resources Journal (USA ISSN 0738-6532) **3462**
• Renewables Information (FRA ISSN 1816-0247) **3462**
Renewal (London) (GBR ISSN 0968-252X) **7177**
• Renewal Journal (AUS ISSN 1326-5857) **7741**
Renewal Magazine (USA) **7728**
• The Renewal Times (CAN ISSN 1705-3773) **6647**
reNews *see* re News **3145**
ReNews (Louisville) (USA) **7773**
Renfro Valley Bugle (USA ISSN 0034-4451) **6610**
Rengjoering og Vedlikehold *see* Renhold **1854**
Renglon (MEX ISSN 0188-5650) **7177**
Renglones (MEX ISSN 0186-4963) **7995**
• Rengong Jingti Xuebao/Journal of Synthetic Crystals (CHN ISSN 1000-985X) **2045**
Renhold (NOR ISSN 1501-987X) **1854**
Renholdsnytt *see* Renhold **1854**
Renkei Iryou/Healthcare Network Management (JPN ISSN 1880-2869) **4110**
Renkou Tongji Jikan/Demography Quarterly, Republic of China (TWN) **7314**
• Renkou Xuekan/Population Journal (CHN) **7291**
• Renkou Yanjiu/Population Research (CHN ISSN 1000-6087) **7291**
Renkou Yanjiu Tongxun/Population Newsletter (TWN ISSN 1018-3930) **7291**
• Renkou yu Fazhan (Beijing) (CHN ISSN 1674-1668) **7291**
† Renkou yu Fazhan (Chengdu)/Population and Development (CHN ISSN 1003-8426) **8985**
• Renkou yu Jihua Shengyu/Population and Family Planning (CHN ISSN 1004-8197) **7291**
• Renkou yu Jingji/Population & Economics (CHN ISSN 1000-4149) **7291**
Renkou yu Yousheng/Population and Better Birth *see* Jiankang Rensheng **7286**
➤ Renkou Zuekan/Journal of Population Studies (TWN ISSN 1018-3841) **7292**
Renkouxue yu Jihua Shengyu/Population Science and Family Planning (CHN ISSN 1005-4235) **7292**
• Renlei Gongxiaoxue/Chinese Journal of Ergonomics (CHN ISSN 1006-8309) **927**
• ➤ Renleixue Xuebao/Acta Anthropologica Sinica (CHN ISSN 1000-3193) **352**
• Renli Ziyuan Bao (CHN) **1874**
Renli Ziyuan Kaifa Guanli/Human Resources Development and Management (CHN ISSN 1009-7678) **1874**
Renmark Paringa District Hospital Board. Annual Report (AUS ISSN 1833-0428) **4110**
• Renmin Changjiang/Yangtze River (CHN ISSN 1001-4179) **4026**
Renmin Fayuan Bao/People's Court Daily (CHN) **4768**
Renmin Gongan Bao/People's Public Security Review (CHN) **7538**
• Renmin Gongan Bao. Jiaotong Anquan Zhoukan (CHN) **8634**
• Renmin Gongan Bao. Xiaofang Zhoukan (CHN) **3580**
• Renmin Gongan Bao. Zhian Baowei Zhoukan (CHN) **7538**
• Renmin Huabao (CHN ISSN 0448-9373) **3827**
• Renmin Huang He/People's Yellow River (CHN ISSN 1000-1379) **4026**
• Renmin Jiancha/People's Procuratorial Work (CHN ISSN 1004-4043) **4768**
• Renmin Jiaoyu/People's Education (CHN ISSN 0448-9365) **2904**
Renmin Jingcha/People's Police (CHN ISSN 1004-7506) **2667**
• Renmin Junyi/People's Military Surgeon (CHN ISSN 1000-9736) **6256**
• Renmin Luntan (CHN ISSN 1004-3381) **3827**
• Renmin Ribao/People's Daily (CHN ISSN 1672-8386) **3827**
Renmin Ribao (Suoyin Heding Ben) *see* Renmin Ribao **3827**
Renmin Ribao Suoyin/People's Daily. Index (CHN ISSN 1006-0065) **4588**
Renmin Sheying/People's Photography (CHN) **6976**
• Renmin Tiaojie (CHN ISSN 1002-7238) **4768**
Renmin Tiedao/People's Railways (CHN) **8624**
Renmin Wenxue/People's Literature (CHN ISSN 0258-8218) **5359**
• ➤ Renmin Yinyue/People's Music (CHN ISSN 0447-6573) **6610**
Renmin Youdian Bao/People's Post and Telecommunications News (CHN) **2337**
Renmin Zhengxie Bao/Journal of the C P P C C (CHN) **7465**
Renmin Zhongguo *see* Jinmin Chugoku **3825**
• Renmin Zhujiang/Pearl River (CHN ISSN 1001-9235) **3364**
• Renminwang (CHN) **3827**
Rennbahn Express *see* Xpress **5087**
Renninger's Antique Guide (USA) **368**
Rennrad (DEU ISSN 1861-2733) **8267**
Renota Rosaldo Lecture Series Monograph (USA ISSN 0883-3389) **4310**
Le Renouveau (BDI) **3805**
Renovalnvest *see* Renova!nvest **455**
Renova!nvest (CHE ISSN 1660-8577) **455**
Renovate & Extend (AUS ISSN 1832-8113) **4549**
Renovate Your House and Home (IRL ISSN 1649-4687) **1032**
Renovateur (SEN) **7177**
Renovatie (NLD ISSN 1873-9733) **4425**
Renovatie en Onderhoud *see* Cobouw **992**
Renovating Trade. N S W - A C T Edition (New South Wales - Australian Capital Territory) (AUS ISSN 1834-0466) **1032**
Renovating Trade. Queensland Edition *see* Renovating Trade. N S W - A C T Edition **1032**
Renovating Trade. Victoria Edition *see* Renovating Trade. N S W - A C T Edition **1032**
Renovatio (DEU ISSN 0340-8280) **7814**
Renovatio Imperii (DEU) **514**
Renovation *see* Renovation und Domizil **1032**
Renovation Actuelle *see* Chantiers et Renovation **991**
Renovation and Decor Magazine (CAN) **1032**
Renovation Bricolage (CAN ISSN 0381-0992) **4439**
Renovation Style (USA ISSN 1534-2093) **1032**
Renovation und Domizil (AUT) **1032**
Renovering & Drift - Brutto (DNK ISSN 1396-6820) **1032**
Renovering og Drift - Netto (DNK ISSN 1396-6812) **1032**
• Renquan (CHN ISSN 1009-6442) **7214**
• Rens og Vask (DNK ISSN 1397-2782) **2244**
Renseignements aux Collectionneurs *see* Information for Collectors **6465**
† Renseignements et Operations Speciales (FRA ISSN 1295-4896) **8985**
Renseignements sur le Tourisme. Bulletin (CAN ISSN 1910-1538) **8751**
Renseignements sur le Tourisme. Sommaire. Bulletin (CAN ISSN 1910-1554) **8751**
Renshen Yanjiu/Ginseng Studies (CHN ISSN 1671-1521) **150**
Rensheng 16-7 *see* Rensheng Shiliuqi **2210**
Rensheng Shiliuqi/At 16 or 17 in One's Life (CHN ISSN 1006-3099) **2210**
Rensheng yu Banlu/Life and Companions (CHN ISSN 1003-5001) **7995**
Rensselaer Engineer (USA ISSN 0034-4508) **8436**
Rensselaer Polytechnic (USA) **2298**
• Rent/Clean (SWE ISSN 0282-1168) **2244**
Rent Cases (IND) **4768**
Rent i Danmark (DNK ISSN 0906-270X) **1789**
• Rent Review and Lease Renewal (GBR ISSN 0263-7499) **7611**
Rent Review Hearings Board. Annual Report (CAN ISSN 0843-5073) **4425**
Renta Nacional de Espana (ESP ISSN 0408-3407) **7465**
Rental & Staging *see* Rental and Staging Systems **2025**
Rental & Staging Systems *see* Rental and Staging Systems **2025**
• Rental and Staging Systems (USA ISSN 1540-0638) **2025**
• Rental Equipment Register (USA ISSN 0034-4524) **1839**
Rental Equipment Register Reports *see* R E R Reports **1839**
• Rental Management (USA ISSN 1042-9085) **1839**
Rental Market Report. Alberta Highlights *see* Rapport sur le Marche Locatif. Faits Saillants. Alberta **7606**
Rental Market Report. British Columbia Highlights *see* Rapport sur le Marche Locatif. Faits Saillants. Colombie-Britannique **7606**
• Rental Market Report. Calgary (Online) (CAN ISSN 1912-5038) **7611**
Rental Market Report. Edmonton *see* Rapport sur le Marche Locatif. R M R d'Edmonton **7607**
Rental Market Report. Gatineau *see* Rapport sur le Marche Locatif. Gatineau **7607**
Rental Market Report. Hamilton C M A *see* Rapport sur le Marche Locatif. R M R de Hamilton **7607**
Rental Market Report. Kelowna *see* Rapport sur le Marche Locatif. Kelowna **7607**
Rental Market Report. Kitchener C M A *see* Rapport sur le Marche Locatif. Kitchener **7607**
Rental Market Report. London *see* Rapport sur le Marche Locatif. London **7607**
• Rental Market Report. Manitoba Highlights (CAN ISSN 1912-323X) **7611**
• Rental Market Report. Metro Victoria (CAN ISSN 1912-5488) **7611**
Rental Market Report. Montreal *see* Rapport sur le Marche Locatif. Montreal **7607**
Rental Market Report. New Brunswick Highlights *see* Rapport sur le Marche Locatif. Faits Saillants. Nouveau-Brunswick **7606**
Rental Market Report. Newfoundland and Labrador Highlights *see* Rapport sur le Marche Locatif. Faits Saillants. Terre-Neuve-et-Labrador **7607**
Rental Market Report. Northern Ontario *see* Rapport sur le Marche Locatif. Nord de l'Ontario **7607**
Rental Market Report. Northern Ontario *see* Rapport sur le Marche Locatif. Nord de l'Ontario **7607**
Rental Market Report. Nova Scotia Highlights *see* Rapport sur le Marche Locatif. Faits Saillants. Nouvelle-Ecosse **7606**
Rental Market Report. Ontario Highlights *see* Rapport sur le Marche Locatif. Faits Saillants. Ontario **7606**
Rental Market Report. Oshawa *see* Rapport sur le Marche Locatif. Oshawa **7607**
Rental Market Report. Ottawa (Online) *see* Rapport sur le Marche Locatif. Ottawa (Online) **7607**
Rental Market Report. Prince Edward Island Highlights *see* Rapport sur le Marche Locatif. Faits Saillants. Ile-du-Prince-Edouard **7606**
Rental Market Report. Quebec *see* Rapport sur le Marche Locatif. Quebec **7607**
Rental Market Report. Quebec Highlights *see* Rapport sur le Marche Locatif. Faits Saillants. Quebec **7606**
Rental Market Report. Regina *see* Rapport sur le Marche Locatif. R M R de Regina **7607**
Rental Market Report. Saguenay *see* Rapport sur le Marche Locatif. Saguenay **7607**
Rental Market Report. Saskatchewan Highlights *see* Rapport sur le Marche Locatif. Faits Saillants. Saskatchewan **7606**

Title

10798 RENTAL MARKET REPORT. SASKATOON ULRICH'S PERIODICALS

Rental Market Report. Saskatoon *see* Rapport sur le Marche Locatif. R M R de Saskatoon **7607**
• Rental Market Report. Sherbrooke (Online) (CAN ISSN 1912-6212) **7611**
• Rental Market Report. St. Catharines-Niagara (CAN ISSN 1912-6263) **7611**
• Rental Market Report. Toronto C M A (Census Metropolitan Area) (CAN ISSN 1912-6360) **7611**
Rental Market Report. Trois-Rivieres *see* Rapport sur le Marche Locatif. Trois-Rivieres **7607**
• Rental Market Report. Vancouver (Online) (CAN ISSN 1912-6646) **7611**
Rental Market Report. Vancouver (Print) *see* Rental Market Report. Vancouver (Online) **7611**
Rental Market Report. Windsor *see* Rapport sur le Marche Locatif. Windsor **7607**
Rental Market Report. Winnipeg *see* Rapport sur le Marche Locatif. R M R de Winnipeg **7607**
Rental Market Report. Yellowknife, Northern Territories. Highlights *see* Rapport sur le Marche Locatif. Faits Saillants. Yellowknife. Territories du Nord-Ouest **7607**
Rental Market Reports *see* Rapport sur le Marche Locatif. Halifax **7607**
• Rental Product News (USA ISSN 1067-0904) **1902**
Rental Report *see* Victoria, Australia. Department of Human Services. Office of Housing. Rental Report **4431**
Rental Staging & Services Guide & Product Directory *see* Rental and Staging Systems **2025**
Die Rentenversicherung (DEU ISSN 0340-5753) **4520**
Renters News (CAN) **7611**
Rentgenologia i Radiologia (BGR ISSN 0486-400X) **6207**
Renton & Brown's Criminal Procedure (GBR) **4897**
Renton & Brown's Criminal Procedure Legislation (GBR) **4897**
Renton & Brown's Statutory Offences (GBR) **4897**
Renton Historical Quarterly (USA) **4310**
La Rentree (CAN ISSN 1912-1334) **2904**
➤ Renwen ji Shehui Kexue Jikan/Journal of Social Sciences and Philosophy (TWN ISSN 1018-189X) **6947**
Renwen Qianzhan (TWN) **5359**
Renwen Yanjiu Xuebao (TWN ISSN 1990-441X) **4472**
• Renwen Zazhi/Journal of Humanities (CHN ISSN 0447-662X) **4472**
Renwu/Biographies, Reminiscences (CHN ISSN 1001-6635) **645**
Renxiang Sheying/Portrait Photography (CHN ISSN 1002-7211) **6976**
• Il Reo e il Folle (ITA ISSN 1828-6216) **2667**
Reoroji Toronkai Koen Yoshishu/Abstracts of Symposium on Rheology (JPN) **7049**
The Rep Report (USA) **8477**
• Repair Shop Product News (USA ISSN 1524-0428) **8601**
Reparation: Liability for Delict (GBR) **4768**
Reparatur-Daten Motorisierte Zweiraeder (DEU ISSN 1436-2848) **8601**
Reparatur-Daten P K W (DEU ISSN 1436-2856) **8601**
Reparatur- und A U - Daten Nutzfahrzeuge (DEU ISSN 1436-283X) **8601**
• Repatriation General Hospital. Annual Report (AUS ISSN 1832-9810) **7538**
• ➤ Repbase Reports (USA ISSN 1534-830X) **878**
† Repeat (NLD ISSN 0168-6542) **8985**
Repenser le Cinema (BEL ISSN 1379-8391) **6511**
Repercussions (USA ISSN 1067-2699) **6610**
Repere *see* Presence Magazine **7671**
• Repere (Online) (CAN ISSN 1206-1913) **16**
Repere (Print) *see* Repere (Online) **16**
Repere Social (CHE ISSN 1422-7924) **7995**
Reperes (Paris, 1947) (FRA ISSN 0761-4241) **514**
Reperes (Paris, 1970) (FRA ISSN 1157-1330) **5166**
Reperes en Geriatrie (FRA ISSN 1767-803X) **4054**
Reperes Ocean (FRA ISSN 1240-1153) **2817**
Reperes Statistiques (MAR ISSN 1113-738X) **1514**
Repertoire *see* Repertoire Magazine **1165**
• ➤ Repertoire Bibliographique de la Philosophie/Bibliografisch Repertorium van de Wijsbegeerte/International Philosophical Bibliography (BEL ISSN 0034-4567) **6963**
➤ Repertoire Bibliographique des Livres Imprimes en France (DEU ISSN 0085-5499) **634**
Repertoire Canadien des Conferences de Soins de Sante *see* Canadian Directory of Health Care Conferences **6278**
Repertoire Canadien des Psychologues Offrant des Services de Sante *see* Canadian Register of Health Service Providers in Psychology. Directory **6129**
Repertoire Canadien des Services d'Information et de Soutien sur l'Ensemble des Troubles Causes par l'Alcoolisme Foetale (E T C A F) *see* Directory of Fetal Alcohol Spectrum Disorder (F A S D) Information and Support Services in Canada **8037**
† Repertoire Chronologique d'Epigraphie Arabe (EGY) **8985**
• Repertoire de la Vie Francaise en Amerique (Online Edition) (CAN) **3561**
Repertoire de l'Administration Francaise (FRA ISSN 0765-0078) **7465**
Repertoire des Annuaires (FRA) **634**
Repertoire des Annuaires Europeens *see* Current European Directories **1981**
† • Repertoire des Banques de Donnees Professionnelles/The Professional Databases Directory (FRA ISSN 1147-7814) **8985**
Repertoire des Bibliotheques Specialisees dans l'Est du Canada *see* Directory of Special Libraries in Eastern Canada **5007**
Repertoire des Camps de Vacances/Directory of Accredited Camps (CAN ISSN 0316-1226) **8330**
Repertoire des Cartotheques de France (FRA) **4026**
Repertoire des Centres de Dialyse Participants au Canada *see* Directory of Participating Dialysis Centres, Transplant Centres and Organ Procurement Organizations in Canada **6267**
Repertoire des Colleges Prives du Quebec (CAN ISSN 1719-5519) **2904**
Repertoire des Designations d'Importance Historique Nationale *see* Directory of Designations of National Historic Significance **4137**
Repertoire des Fournisseurs de Services de Sante en Francais de Terre-Neuve-et-Labrador/ Directory of French Speaking Health Care Providers in Newfoundland and Labrador (CAN ISSN 1911-2327) **4110**
• Repertoire des Medecins de Famille Accoucheurs du Quebec (CAN ISSN 1910-2062) **6002**
Le Repertoire des Meilleurs sites Internet pour l'Amelioration de la Langue (CAN ISSN 1912-0605) **2904**
Repertoire des Organisations de Travailleurs et Travailleuses au Canada *see* Directory of Labour Organizations in Canada **4593**
Repertoire des Organismes Jeunesse du Quebec (CAN ISSN 1712-3089) **2166**
• Repertoire des Produits Disponibles au Quebec (CAN ISSN 1184-9916) **2025**
Repertoire des Publications Seriees Canadiennes *see* Canadian Serials Directory **5057**
Repertoire des Radiosignaux (FRA ISSN 0989-5981) **2363**
Repertoire des Services aux Victimes d'Actes Criminels *see* Directory of Services for Victims of Crime **8037**
Repertoire des Services Communautaires du Grand Montreal *see* Directory of Community Services of Greater Montreal **8037**
Repertoire des Textes Legislatifs et Reglementaires et des Reponses aux Questions Ecrites Concernant la Reunion (REU) **7177**
Repertoire des Universites Canadiennes (Year) *see* The Directory of Canadian Universities (Year) **2955**
Repertoire du Mouvement Quebecois des Camps Familiaux *see* Les Centres de Vacances Familiales **8309**
Repertoire du Notariat Defrenois (FRA ISSN 0224-2249) **4768**
Repertoire du Notariat Defrenois. Supplement Rapide (FRA ISSN 0224-2222) **4768**
Repertoire EnerGuide des Appareils Menagers *see* EnerGuide Appliance Directory **3129**
Repertoire General de l'Economie Finlandaise *see* Kompass Finland **1574**
Repertoire Industriel du Quebec *see* Scott's Quebec Industrial **2027**
Repertoire International *see* International Directory **2226**
Repertoire International de la Librairie Ancienne *see* International Directory of Antiquarian Booksellers **7563**
Repertoire International de la Philosophie et des Philosophes *see* International Directory of Philosophy and Philosophers **6925**
Repertoire International de la Presse Musicale (USA ISSN 0896-6079) **6632**
Repertoire International de la Presse Musicale du XIXe Siecle. Newsletter *see* Periodica Musica **6605**
Repertoire International de Litterature Musicale Abstracts of Music Literature *see* R I L M Abstracts of Music Literature **6632**
† Repertoire International des Banques de Donnees pour le Marketing et les Etudes (FRA ISSN 0982-3085) **8985**
Repertoire International des Dix-Huitiemistes *see* International Directory of Eighteenth-Century Studies **4457**
Repertoire International des Medievistes (BEL ISSN 0080-1151) **4257**
Repertoire International des Seiziemistes (FRA ISSN 1147-8209) **4257**
Repertoire International des Sources. Infoterra *see* International Directory of Sources. Infoterra **3441**
Repertoire Internationale d'Iconographie Musicale - Research Center for Music Iconography Inventory of Music Iconography *see* R I D I M - R C M I Inventory of Music Iconography **6608**
Le Repertoire Internet des Meilleurs Sites pour l'Amelioration de la Langue *see* Le Repertoire des Meilleurs sites Internet pour l'Amelioration de la Langue **2904**
• Repertoire Magazine (USA ISSN 1520-7587) **1165**
Repertoire Mondial des Ecoles de Medecine *see* World Directory of Medical Schools **5731**
Repertoire National des Services et Programmes Destines aux Hommes Qui Sont ou Ont Ete Victimes de Violence *see* National Directory of Services and Programs for Men Who Are or Have Been Victims of Violence **4107**
Repertoire Officiel *see* International Federation of Journalists and Travel Writers. Official List **8723**
Repertoire Officiel des Musees Canadiens et Institutions Connexes *see* Official Directory of Canadian Museums and Related Institutions **6535**
Repertoire Toponymique du Canada *see* Gazetteer of Canada **4007**
Repertorien zur Erforschung der Freuhen Neuzeit (DEU ISSN 0724-9578) **4257**
➤ Repertorio Americano (CRI ISSN 0252-8479) **5359**
Repertorio Aranzadi del Tribunal Constitucional (ESP ISSN 0212-2855) **4768**
Repertorio Aranzadi del Tribunal Constitucional (Quarterly Edition)/Decisions of the Constitutional Court (ESP ISSN 1139-0824) **4768**
Repertorio Cientifico (CRI ISSN 1021-6294) **7902**
• Repertorio Cronologico de Legislacion (ESP ISSN 0210-5780) **4768**
Repertorio Cronologico de Legislacion (Semi-weekly Edition) (ESP ISSN 1139-0387) **4768**
Repertorio Cronologico de Legislacion. Indices Auxiliares (ESP ISSN 1139-0379) **4825**
Repertorio de Consultas Tributarias (ESP ISSN 1137-5345) **4768**
Repertorio de Exportadores (ESP) **1409**
Repertorio de Importadores (ESP) **1409**
• Repertorio de Jurisprudencia (ESP ISSN 0210-5772) **4768**
Repertorio de Jurisprudencia. Indices Auxiliares (ESP ISSN 1139-059X) **4825**
Repertorio de Jurisprudencia Tributaria (ESP ISSN 1137-2982) **4768**
Repertorio de la Industria Quimica Espanola/Directory of the Spanish Chemical Industry (ESP) **2078**
Repertorio de Legislacion Tributaria (ESP ISSN 1138-8803) **4768**
• Repertorio de Medicina y Cirugia (COL ISSN 0121-7372) **6256**
Repertorio de Servicios IberoAmericanos de Documentacion e Informacion Educativas/Repertorio de Servicos Ibero-Americanos de Documentacao e Informacao Educativas (ESP ISSN 1010-2973) **5043**
Repertorio de Servicos Ibero-Americanos de Documentacao e Informacao Educativas *see* Repertorio de Servicios IberoAmericanos de Documentacion e Informacion Educativas **5043**
• Repertorio del Foro Italiano (CD-ROM) (ITA) **4768**
† Il Repertorio del Giornalismo Italiano (ITA) **8985**
Repertorio delle Macchine Agricole *see* Macchine e Motori Agricoli **212**
Repertorio General: La Ley (ARG) **4768**
Repertorio Mensual de Jurisprudencia (ESP ISSN 1134-7376) **4768**
Repertorio Siderurgico Latinoamericano (CHL) **2025**
Repertoriul Colectiv al Periodicelor Straine Intrate in Bibliotecile din Romania (ROM ISSN 1221-6860) **634**
Repertorium Columbianum (BEL) **4158**
Repertorium Plantarum Succulentarum (CHE ISSN 0486-4271) **815**
Repertory of Articles in the South African Archives Journal (ZAF) **5059**
Repertory Report (GBR ISSN 0142-6303) **8477**
• Repetitive Stress Injury Law Bulletin (USA ISSN 1094-3765) **4768**
† • Repetitive Stress Injury Litigation Reporter (USA ISSN 1067-0483) **8985**
• Repindex (PER ISSN 0252-7987) **3480**
Replacement Contractor (USA ISSN 1549-1986) **1032**
Replay (USA ISSN 0360-7348) **1902**
RePlay Magazine *see* Replay **1902**
Replica (USA ISSN 0146-2008) **3561**
• Replikk (NOR ISSN 0806-8593) **7995**
Reponse a Tout (FRA ISSN 1143-7693) **3842**
Reponse a Tout! Jeux (FRA ISSN 1297-5516) **3842**
Reponses a vos Questions (FRA ISSN 1761-1679) **7538**
Reponses Bain (FRA ISSN 1246-354X) **1032**
Reponses Cuisine (FRA ISSN 1636-1180) **1032**
Reponses Photo (FRA ISSN 1167-864X) **6976**
Report *see* Gozaresh **3891**
Report *see* Whangarei Report **3920**
Report *see* Cincinnati Bar Association. Report **4642**
Report (Latham) *see* New York State Nurses Association. Report **5971**
Report by H M Chief Inspector of Factories (GBR ISSN 0950-8430) **7538**
Report by the Auditor General on the Accounts of Lesotho (LSO ISSN 0085-2740) **1942**
Report Card on Cancer Care in Canada *see* Cancer Advocacy Coalition of Canada. Report Card on Cancer in Canada **6011**
The Report. Emerging Algeria *see* Emerging Algeria **1884**
The Report. Emerging Indonesia *see* Emerging Indonesia **1482**
The Report. Emerging Ukraine *see* Emerging Ukraine **1104**
Report EPS 9 *see* Arctic and Marine Oilspill Program Report **3404**
Report for the Year Ending - South African Astronomical Observatory *see* South African Astronomical Observatory. Annual Report **582**
Report from State Circle (USA) **7177**
Report from the Capital (USA ISSN 0364-6661) **7773**
Report from the National Council on Family Relations *see* National Council on Family Relations. Report **8122**
Report - Hastings Center *see* Hastings Center Report **5623**
Report Naturheilkunde (DEU ISSN 1435-1218) **314**
Report - Nevada Bureau of Mines and Geology *see* Nevada. Bureau of Mines and Geology. Report **2758**
• Report of a Vantage Conference (USA ISSN 0748-0571) **7262**
Report of Cases Determined in the Supreme Court and Court of Appeals of the State of New Mexico (Print) *see* New Mexico Reports and West's New Mexico Statutes (Premise CD-ROM) **4744**
Report of E-Commerce by Quarter *see* Jeonja Sang'geo'lae Tong'gye Josa Bo'goseo **1246**
Report of Educational Statistics *see* Delaware. State Board of Education. Report of Educational Statistics **3019**
Report of Environmental Radiology of Nuclear Fuel Cycle Facilities *see* Genshi Nenryo Saikuru Shisetsu Kankyo Hoshasento Jizen Chosa Hokokusho **3506**
Report of Marine Remote Sensing Technique *see* Kaiyo Enkaku Tansa. Kaiyo Rimoto Senshingu Gijutsu no Kenkyu. Kenkyu Seikashu **2810**
Report of Meeting on Firefly *see* Hotaru Kenkyu Taikai **848**
Report of Observation at the Meteorological Observation Tower *see* Kisho Kansokukyo Tetto Kansoku Shiryo **6359**
Report of Physiological Technology *see* Seirigaku Gijutsu Kenkyukai Hokoku **928**
Report of Research and Development of Medical Information System *see* Iryo Joho Shisutemu Kenkyu Kaihatsu Hokokusho **5641**
Report of Research Results, P W R I *see* Public Works Research Institute. Report of Research Results **3281**
• Report of Reviewable Deaths (AUS) **8065**
(Year) Report of Salaries and Employee Benefits Statistics Managerial and Professional Employees (Excluding Top Management) see Hong Kong Special Administrative Region of China. Census and Statistics Department. Report of Salaries and Employee Benefits Statistics Managerial and Professional Employees (Excluding Top Management) **1239**
Report of Studies Supported by Sankyo Foundation of Life Science *see* Sankyo Seimei Kagaku Kenkyu Shinko Zaidan Kenkyu Hokokushu **703**
Report of Study Group on International Issues, FAPRC *see* Food and Agricultural Policy Research Center. Study Group on International Issues. Report **113**
Report of Survey on Machine Tools Installation *see* Kosaku Kikai Setsubito Tokei Chosa Hokokusho **5454**
Report of the (Year) Business Trade and Services Survey (THA) **1260**
Report of the (Year) Industrial Census (THA) **1260**
Report of the (Year) Survey of Fertility in Thailand (THA) **1260**
Report of the Administrator of Tokelau (NZL ISSN 0111-6053) **7465**
Report of the Air Travel Complaints Commissioner *see* Air Travel Complaints Report (Print) **8535**
• Report of the Attorney General of the State of Montana (USA) **4768**
Report of the Auditor General on the Public Accounts of the Republic of Trinidad and Tobago (TTO) **1942**
Report of the Ethics Counsellor on the Activities of the Office of the Ethics Counsellor/Rapport du Conseiller en Ethique sur les Activites du Bureau du Conseiller en Ethique (CAN ISSN 1706-1806) **7465**
Report of the Federal Home Loan Mortgage Corporation *see* Federal Home Loan Mortgage Corporation. Report **1341**
Report of the Health and Welfare Survey (Year) *see* Thailand. National Statistical Office. Report of the Health and Welfare Survey (Year) **7549**
Report of the International Commission on the Work of Its (Year) Session, United Nations (CHE ISSN 0082-822X) **4768**
Report of the Judicial Branch, State of Connecticut *see* Connecticut. Judicial Branch. Biennial Report **4648**
Report of the Labor Force Survey, Whole Kingdom, Round Four (Year) (THA) **1260**
Report of the New Mexico Veteran's Service Commission *see* New Mexico. Veterans' Service Commission. Report **6439**
Report of the O P C W: On the Implementation of the Convention on the Prohibition of the Development, Production, Stockpiling and Use of Chemical Weapons and on Their Destruction *see* O P C W Annual Report **7160**
Report of the Ombudsman *see* New Brunswick. Office of the Ombudsman. Annual Report **7455**
• Report of the Quadrennial Defense Review (USA) **6443**
Report of the Research Center of Ion Beam Technology, Hosei University. Supplement (JPN ISSN 0914-2908) **3329**
Report of the Ross Conference on Pediatric Research *see* Ross Conference on Pediatric Research. Report **6669**

Report of the Ross Roundtable on Critical Approaches to Common Pediatric Problems in Collaboration with the Ambulatory Pediatric Association (USA ISSN 0737-7282) **6103**
• Report of the Secretary of the Commonwealth to the Governor and General Assembly of Virginia (USA ISSN 0145-1928) **7465**
Report of the Tarlton Law Library (USA ISSN 1935-1453) **5043**
Report of the U. S. Forest Service *see* U.S. Forest Service. Report **3706**
Report of Volcano Observation in Kyushu District *see* Kyushu Chiiki Kazan Kido Kansoku Jisshi Hokoku **2786**
Report on (Year) Establishment Survey on Manpower Training and Job Skills Requirements *see* Hong Kong Special Administrative Region of China. Census and Statistics Department. Report on (Year) Establishment Survey on Manpower Training and Job Skills Requirements **1239**
Report on Alcohol, Drugs, and Disability (USA) **2698**
Report on Annual Survey of Building, Construction and Real Estate Sectors *see* Hong Kong Special Administrative Region of China. Census and Statistics Department. Report on Annual Survey of Building, Construction and Real Estate Sectors **1046**
Report on Annual Survey of Industrial Production *see* Hong Kong Special Administrative Region of China. Census and Statistics Department. Report on Annual Survey of Industrial Production **1239**
Report on Annual Survey of Regional Offices Representing Overseas Companies in Hong Kong *see* Hong Kong Special Administrative Region of China. Census and Statistics Department. Report on Annual Survey of Regional Offices Representing Overseas Companies in Hong Kong **1239**
Report on Annual Survey of Storage, Communication, Financing, Insurance and Business Services *see* Hong Kong Special Administrative Region of China. Census and Statistics Department. Report on Annual Survey of Storage, Communication, Financing, Insurance and Business Services **1240**
Report on Annual Survey of Transport and Related Services *see* Hong Kong Special Administrative Region of China. Census and Statistics Department. Report on Annual Survey of Transport and Related Services **8526**
Report on Annual Survey on Information Technology Usage *see* Hong Kong Special Administrative Region of China. Census and Statistics Department. Report on Annual Survey on Information Technology Usage and Penetration in the Business Sector **1240**
Report on Applications for Orders Authorizing or Approving the Interception of Wire or Oral Communications *see* U.S. Administrative Office of the United States Courts. Report on Applications for Orders Authorizing or Approving the Interception of Wire or Oral Communications **4799**
• Report on Average Producers' Price - Agricultural Products (ETH) **185**
The Report on Business (USA) **1165**
Report on Business 1000 *see* Report on Business Magazine **1165**
• Report on Business Magazine (CAN ISSN 0827-7680) **1165**
Report on Customer Relationship Management *see* I O M A's Report on Customer Relationship Management **8963**
Report on Development Assistance to Ethiopia (ETH) **1604**
Report on Development Cooperation to the Democratic Republic of the Sudan (SDN) **1604**
• Report on Electronic Commerce (USA) **2566**
Report on Emotional and Behavioral Disorders in Youth *see* Report on Emotional & Behavioral Disorders in Youth **7402**
Report on Emotional & Behavioral Disorders in Youth (USA ISSN 1531-5479) **7402**
Report on Executive Remuneration (USA ISSN 1060-0205) **1874**
Report on General Household Survey *see* Nigeria. National Integrated Survey of Households. Report on General Household Survey **4436**
Report on Guatemala (USA ISSN 1043-3856) **7262**
Report on Half-Yearly Business Prospects Survey *see* Hong Kong Special Administrative Region of China. Census and Statistics Department. Report on Half-Yearly Business Prospects Survey **1240**
• Report on Healthcare Information Management (USA ISSN 1071-006X) **5703**
• The Report on I B M (USA ISSN 0742-5341) **2541**
Report on Industrial Census *see* Korea (Republic). National Statistical Office. Report on Industrial Census **1247**
The Report on Library Cooperation (USA ISSN 1047-3688) **5043**
Report on Managing Training & Development *see* I O M A's Report on Managing Training & Development **1865**
Report on Medical Guidelines & Outcomes Research *see* Disease Management Advisor **4092**
• Report on Medicare Compliance (USA ISSN 1094-3307) **4768**
• Report on Microsoft (USA ISSN 1072-9453) **2493**
Report on Mining and Manufacturing Survey. Enterprise *see* Gwang'eob. Jejoeob Tong'gye Josa Bo'goseo. Gi'eobche Pyeon **1236**
Report on Monthly Survey of Retail Sales *see* Hong Kong Special Administrative Region of China. Census and Statistics Department. Report on Monthly Survey of Retail Sales **8376**
Report on National Consumer Survey *see* Nigeria. National Integrated Survey of Households. Report on National Consumer Survey **1255**
Report on Ohio Mineral Industries (USA ISSN 0747-7333) **6477**
• Report on Operations under the Bretton Woods and Related Agreements Act (CAN ISSN 0849-3235) **1378**
Report on Passenger Road Transport in Zambia (ZMB) **8529**
• Report on Patient Privacy (USA ISSN 1539-6487) **4110**
Report on Pig Breeding in Poland *see* Stan Hodowli i Wyniki Oceny Swin **301**
• Report on Preschool Programs (USA ISSN 1544-9157) **3078**
• Report on Proposals (USA ISSN 1079-5332) **3581**
Report on Quarterly Survey of Restaurant Receipts and Purchases *see* Hong Kong Special Administrative Region of China. Census and Statistics Department. Report on Quarterly Survey of Restaurant Receipts and Purchases **4402**
• Report on Research Compliance (USA ISSN 1937-6634) **4769**
Report on Salary Surveys *see* I O M A's Report on Salary Surveys **1866**
• Report on Salary Surveys Yearbook (USA) **1874**
Report on Science and Human Rights *see* Science and Human Rights Newsletter **7215**
• Report on Science & Technology Indicators for Norway (NOR ISSN 1503-0857) **8396**
• Report on Small Scale Manufacturing Industries Survey (ETH) **1260**
Report on Technology of Iwate University *see* Iwate Daigaku Kogakubu Kenkyu Hokoku **3204**
Report on the Activities of O S P A R (GBR) **3462**
Report on the Activities of the Committee on Armed Services, United States Senate *see* United States Senate. House Armed Services Committee. Report on the Activities **6451**
Report on the Activities of the Committee on the Judiciary of the House of Representatives *see* United States House of Representatives. Committee on the Judiciary. Report on the Activities **4966**
Report on the Activities of the Committee on the Judiciary of the United States Senate during the Congress *see* United States Senate. Committee on the Judiciary. Report on the Activities during the Congress **4966**
Report on the Activities of the Oslo and Paris Commissions *see* Report on the Activities of O S P A R **3462**
Report on the Administration of the Firearms Act to the Solicitor General by the Registrar *see* Solicitor General on the Administration of the Firearms Act. Registrar's Report **2668**
Report on the Administration of the Labour Adjustment Benefits Act/Rapport sur l'Application de la Loi sur les Prestations d'Adaptation pour les Travailleurs (CAN ISSN 0828-4547) **1705**
Report on the Application of the Alternative Fuels Act (CAN ISSN 1493-2741) **4769**
Report on the Census of Wholesale, Retail Trade and Service Industry *see* To Somaeop Mit Sobisu Ch'ong Chosa Pogoso **1270**
Report on the Census on Basic Characteristics of Establishments *see* Sa'eobche Gicho Tong'gye Jo'sa Bo'go'seo. Jeon'gug Pyeon **1261**
Report on the Construction Work Survey *see* Geonseol'eob Tong'gye Jo'sa Bo'go'seo **1046**
Report on the Discharges from Municipal S T Ps in Ontario (Sewage Treatment Plants) (CAN ISSN 1183-8787) **3511**
Report on the Federal Columbia River Power System *see* Bonneville Power Administration. Annual Report **3125**
Report on the Human Rights Situation in Peru (USA) **7214**
Report on the Implementation of the Charter for the Protection of Children and Young People (USA ISSN 1559-4211) **2167**
Report on the Industrial Direct Discharges in Ontario (CAN ISSN 0838-519X) **3462**
Report on the Largest Companies in Finland *see* Talouselaman Raportti Suuryrityksista **1181**
Report on the Marketing of Tobacco in Andhra Pradesh (IND) **205**
Report on the Progress of Education in Pakistan *see* Development of Education in Pakistan **2842**
Report on the Quarterly Survey of Construction Output *see* Hong Kong Special Administrative Region of China. Census and Statistics Department. Report on the Quarterly Survey of Construction Output **1047**
Report on the Situation of Human Rights in Paraguay (USA) **7214**
• Report on the Situation on Human Rights in the Republic of Guatemala (USA) **7214**
Report on the Social Statistics Survey *see* Sahoe Tong'gye Jo'sa Bo'go'seo **7314**
Report on the Survey of Family Income & Expenditure in Taiwan Area *see* Taiwan, Republic of China. Executive Yuan. Directorate-General of Budget, Accounting & Statistics. Report on the Survey of Family Income & Expenditure in Taiwan Area **1721**
Report on the Survey of Wholesale and Retail Trade *see* Do So'maeob Tong'gye Jo'sa Bo'go'seo **1224**
Report on the Time Use Survey. Volume 1, Time Spent on Activities *see* Saenghwal Si'gan Jo'sa Bo'go'seo. Je 1 Gwon, Saenghwal Si'ganlyang Pyeon **7314**
Report on the Time Use Survey. Volume 2, Participation Rates in Activities by Time Intervals *see* Saenghwal Si'gan Jo'sa Bo'go'seo. Je 2 Gwon, Si'gan Dae'byeol Haengwija Biyul Pyeon **7292**
Report on the Total Salary Increase Budget Survey *see* Total Salary Increase Budget Survey **1876**
Report on the Transport Survey *see* Unsu'eob Tong'gye Jo'sa Bo'go'seo **8532**
Report on the Treatment of Offenders in Mauritius: Part 1: Prisons (MUS) **2667**
Report on the Treatment of Offenders in Mauritius: Part 2: Probation Service (MUS) **2667**
Report on the World Social Situation (Year) (USA ISSN 0082-8068) **8128**
Report on Tourism Statistics (Year) *see* Taiwan, Republic of China. Tourism Bureau. Report on Tourism Statistics (Year) **8781**
Report on Tourism Statistics in Tanzania (TZA ISSN 0564-836X) **8780**
Report on Trends in the State Courts *see* Future Trends in State Courts **4831**
Report on Urban Research *see* Toshi Kenkyu Hokoku **4428**
• Report on Wireless (CAN ISSN 1206-7628) **2337**
Report on World Affairs (GBR ISSN 0034-4737) **7177**
Report - Printing Department (Suva) *see* Fiji. Printing Department Report **4575**
➤ Report Psychologie (DEU ISSN 0344-9602) **7402**
Report Series in Physical Sciences (FIN ISSN 1239-4327) **7037**
Report to Business (USA) **2641**
Report to Congress on Abnormal Occurrences *see* U.S. Nuclear Regulatory Commission. Report to Congress on Abnormal Occurrences **3175**
Report to Congress on Acquisitions Made From Manufacturer Inside and Outside the United States, Fiscal Year (Year) *see* Defense Nuclear Facilities Safety Board. Report to Congress on Acquisitions Made From Manufacturer Inside and Outside the United States, Fiscal Year (Year) **6419**
Report to Congress on Export Credit Competition and the Export-Import Bank of the United States *see* Export-Import Bank of the United States. Report to Congress on Export Credit Competition and the Export-Import Bank of the United States **1340**
Report to Congress on the Youth Programs of the Family and Youth Services Bureau for Fiscal Years (Year) *see* Administration on Children, Youth and Families. Family and Youth Services Bureau. Report to Congress on the Youth Programs of the Family and Youth Services Bureau for Fiscal Years (Year) **7418**
Report to Governments *see* Canadian Intergovernmental Conference Secretariat. Report to Governments **7428**
• Report to Legal Management (USA ISSN 0191-863X) **1789**
Report to Parliament by the Minister of Fisheries and Oceans Respecting the Administration of the Atlantic Fisheries Restructuring Act (CAN ISSN 0839-9131) **1942**
Report to the Aerospace Profession *see* Society of Experimental Test Pilots. Symposium Proceedings **70**
Report to the Congress on Ocean Pollution, Overfishing, and Offshore Development *see* U.S. National Oceanic and Atmospheric Administration. Report to the Congress on Ocean Pollution, Overfishing, and Offshore Development **3491**
Report to the Governor - Arizona Commission on the Arts *see* Arizona Commission on the Arts. Report to the Governor (Year) **467**
Report to the Governor in Council. Status of Competition in Canadian Telecommunications Markets, Deployment/Accessibility of Advanced Telecommunications Infrastructure and Services *see* C R T C Telecommunications Monitoring Report **2314**
Report. United Western Communications *see* Citizens Centre Report **3807**
Report - University of Bergen. Geophysical Institute. Division A Physical Oceanography *see* University of Bergen. Institute of Geophysics. Department of Physical Oceanography. Report **2820**
Reportable A T C Occurrences *see* Great Britain. Civil Aviation Authority. Reportable A T C Occurrences **8543**
Reportable Accidents to U K Registered Aircraft and to Foreign Registered Aircraft in U K Airspace (Year) (GBR) **8551**
Reportable Diseases in Nova Scotia. Surveillance Report *see* Canada. Nova Scotia Department of Health. Notifiable Diseases in Nova Scotia. Surveillance Report **7511**
Reportable Occurrences *see* Great Britain. Civil Aviation Authority. Reportable Occurrences **8543**
Reportage (GBR ISSN 1350-4010) **4583**
Reportage (ITA ISSN 0034-4745) **5236**
• Reportage (USA) **4583**
Reportage Literature *see* Baogao Wenxue **4572**
• Reportage Media Magazine (AUS ISSN 1444-9803) **4583**
Reportages *see* Collection Reportages **4135**
† Reportback (GBR ISSN 1351-086X) **8985**
• El Reporte Delta (COL ISSN 0123-5338) **2566**
• Reporte Electoral (PER) **7177**
• Reporte Politico Policiaco (MEX ISSN 1606-7819) **1514**
• Reporte Tecnico de Vigilancia (CUB ISSN 1028-4362) **5703**
Reporter (BGD) **3800**
Reporter (BLZ) **3802**
• Reporter (SRB ISSN 1450-975X) **3945**
• Reporter (UKR) **3965**
The Reporter (Akron) (USA) **3561**
† The Reporter (Fuengirola) (ESP ISSN 1139-3823) **8985**
• The Reporter (Little Rock) (USA ISSN 1041-6757) **3030**
Reporter (Mankato) *see* Minnesota State University, Mankato Reporter **2292**
The Reporter (New York, 1966) (USA ISSN 1053-2676) **7728**
The Reporter (New York, 1971) (USA) **7728**
Reporter (River Forest) (USA) **2298**
Reporter (St. Louis) (USA ISSN 0360-7119) **7773**
The Reporter (Vestal) (USA) **7728**
The Reporter (Washington, 1977) *see* U.S. Air Force. Office of the Judge General. The Reporter **4972**
• The Reporter (Washington, D.C.) (USA) **7292**
Le Reporter de la Semaine Internationale du Papier *see* PaperWeek International Reporter **6736**
Reporter Doc (ESP ISSN 1133-9713) **2210**
Reportero Doc (ESP ISSN 1133-9721) **2210**
• Reportero Industrial (USA ISSN 0034-4818) **5459**
• Reportero Industrial Mexicano (USA) **2025**
• Reportes Tecnicos en Ingenieria del Software (ARG ISSN 1667-5002) **2596**
Reportorio da Industria, Comercio e Servicos de Portugal *see* Kompass Portugal **2011**
Reports and Papers in the Social Sciences (FRA ISSN 0080-1348) **7995**
Reports and Papers on Mass Communications Series (FRA ISSN 0080-1356) **8128**
Reports and Testimony *see* United States Government Accountability Office. Reports and Testimony **7474**
Reports from Uppsala University Linguistics *see* Uppsala University. Department of Linguistics. Reports **5192**
Reports in Mackinac History and Archaeology (USA) **4310**
▼ • ➤ Reports in Medical Imaging (GBR ISSN 1179-1586) **6207**
Reports in Public Health *see* Cadernos de Saude Publica **7511**
Reports Magazine *see* World Education Reports **8147**
Reports Magazine (USA) **2904**
Reports of Cases Decided in the Appellate Division of the Supreme Court, State of New York (USA ISSN 0276-9581) **4959**
Reports of Cases Decided in the Court of Appeals of the State of Georgia *see* Court of Appeals of Georgia. Reports of Cases **4948**
Reports of Cases Heard and Determined in the Appellate Division of the Supreme Court of the State of New York *see* Reports of Cases Decided in the Appellate Division of the Supreme Court, State of New York **4959**
Reports of Development of Shipbuilding Technique *see* Zosen Gijutsu Kenkyu Kaihatsu Kadai Chosho **8666**
Reports of Family Law (5th Series) (CAN ISSN 0317-4859) **4914**
Reports of Investigations - Illinois State Museum *see* Illinois. State Museum. Reports of Investigations **7864**
Reports of Morphology *see* Visnyk Morfolohii **5728**
• Reports of Patent, Design and Trade Mark Cases (GBR ISSN 0080-1364) **6757**
Reports of Psychiatria Fennica *see* Psychiatria Fennica. Reports **6176**
Reports of the Faculty of Science and Engineering, Mathematics *see* Saga University. Faculty of Science and Engineering. Department of Mathematics. Reports. Mathematics **5532**
Reports of the Fauna and Flora *see* University of Wisconsin Stevens Point. Museum of Natural History. Reports of the Fauna and Flora **7927**
Reports of the Research Laboratory, Asahi Glass Company, Ltd. *see* Asahi Garasu Kenkyu Hokoku **2037**
Reports of the U.S. Tax Courts (USA ISSN 8755-6294) **1942**
Reports on America *see* P R B Reports on America **7289**
Reports on Asian and African Studies (SWE ISSN 1404-0743) **5166**

Title

10800 REPORTS ON BUSINESS AND INFORMATICS ULRICH'S PERIODICALS

Reports on Business and Informatics (SWE ISSN 1403-7203) **1165**
Reports on Collection of Microbial Genetic Resources *see* Biseibutsu Iden Shigen Tansaku Shushu Chosa Hokokusho **882**
Reports on Geodesy (POL ISSN 0867-3179) **4026**
Reports on Historiographical Studies of Taiwan *see* Taiwan Wen Hsien **4189**
Reports on Mathematical Logic (POL ISSN 0137-2904) **5528**
• ➤ Reports on Mathematical Physics (GBR ISSN 0034-4877) **7037**
Reports on Measurement and Sensor Systems (DEU ISSN 1617-6553) **3356**
• Reports on Monastic Research (USA) **7814**
Reports on Philosophy (POL ISSN 0324-8712) **6947**
Reports on Polar and Marine Research *see* Berichte zur Polar- und Meeresforschung **2800**
Reports on Practical Oncology and Radiotherapy (POL ISSN 1507-1367) **6033**
• ➤ Reports on Progress in Physics (GBR ISSN 0034-4885) **7037**
Reports on Statistical Co-ordination *see* Sweden. Statistiska Centralbyraan. Meddelanden i Samordningsfraagor **8408**
Reports on the Rheumatic Diseases *see* Rheumatic Disease Topical Reviews **6226**
Reports on the Supplemental Security Income Program *see* U.S. Social Security Administration. Supplemental Security Income Program. Reports **4526**
Reports on the Survey of Level Reference Points *see* Suijun Kihyo Sokuryo Seikahyo **2721**
Reports Required by Congress: C I S Guide to Executive Communications (USA) **7465**
• Reports to the Nation on Our Changing Planet (USA) **3462**
Reprax (CHE) **6757**
Representants Diplomatiques, Consulaires et Autres au Canada *see* Diplomatic, Consular and other Representatives in Canada **7231**
• ➤ Representation (GBR ISSN 0034-4893) **7177**
Representation Case Law Guide Manual *see* U.S. Federal Labor Relations Authority. Representation Case Law Guide Manual **4800**
Representation Proceedings Case Handling Manual. Part 1 *see* U.S. Federal Labor Relations Authority. Representation Proceedings Case Handling Manual. Part 1 **4800**
Representation Proceedings Case Handling Manual. Part 2 *see* U.S. Federal Labor Relations Authority. Representation Proceedings Case Handling Manual. Part 2 **4800**
• Representation Theory (USA ISSN 1088-4165) **5528**
• ➤ Representations (USA ISSN 0734-6018) **4472**
Representations Books Series (USA) **7402**
Representative American Speeches (Year) (USA ISSN 0197-6923) **4472**
Representing Asylum Seekers (USA ISSN 1931-1508) **4769**
➤ Representing Children (GBR ISSN 1359-463X) **8065**
Representing the Child Client (USA) **4914**
RePrint *see* RePrint Consumables **7327**
▼ RePrint Consumables (USA ISSN 1948-786X) **7327**
Reprints in International Finance (USA ISSN 0080-1380) **1378**
Repro Bulletin (CHE) **7327**
• ➤ Reproduction (GBR ISSN 1470-1626) **700**
Reproduction. Abstract Series (GBR ISSN 1476-3990) **720**
• ➤ Reproduction and Contraception (SGP ISSN 1001-7844) **973**
Reproduction Bulletin (USA ISSN 0736-1238) **7327**
• ➤ Reproduction, Fertility and Development (AUS ISSN 1031-3613) **700**
Reproduction Furniture Market (GBR) **4562**
Reproduction Humaine et Hormones (FRA ISSN 0994-3919) **6002**
• ➤ Reproduction in Domestic Animals (DEU ISSN 0936-6768) **8805**
• Reproduction in Domestic Animals Online (DEU ISSN 1439-0531) **8805**
Reproduction in Domestic Animals. Supplement *see* Reproduction in Domestic Animals **8805**
Reproduction, Nutrition, Development *see* Animal **932**
➤ Reproduction. Supplement (GBR ISSN 1477-0415) **927**
Reproductions (PHL) **700**
Reproductive Biology (POL ISSN 1642-431X) **700**
• ➤ Reproductive Biology and Endocrinology (GBR ISSN 1477-7827) **5899**
Reproductive Biology and Phylogeny (USA) **700**
• ➤ Reproductive BioMedicine Online (GBR ISSN 1472-6483) **6002**
• Reproductive Health (GBR ISSN 1742-4755) **5703**
• ➤ Reproductive Health Matters (NLD ISSN 0968-8080) **8848**
Reproductive Health, Pregnancy Outcomes, Alberta *see* Alberta Reproductive Health, Pregnancies and Births **5985**
• ➤ Reproductive Medicine and Biology (JPN ISSN 1445-5781) **5703**
• ➤ Reproductive Sciences (USA ISSN 1933-7191) **6003**
• ➤ Reproductive Toxicology (USA ISSN 0890-6238) **927**
Reproduire (FRA ISSN 0245-3355) **6976**
➤ Reproduktivnoe Zdorov'ye Zhenshchiny (UKR) **6003**
Reprowatch (PHL ISSN 0117-7796) **973**
ReproWatch. Youth Edition (PHL ISSN 0119-044X) **973**
Reps, Groups, Distributors, Networks, Ad Agencies, Telco - D B S Guide *see* N A P T E Guide to North American Media **2385**
• Reptil Mag (FRA ISSN 1620-9540) **6814**
Reptil Zine (ESP) **6610**
Reptile & Amphibian Hobbyist (USA ISSN 1525-4712) **6814**
Reptile & Exotic Animal Care (GBR) **6814**
Reptile Care *see* Reptile & Exotic Animal Care **6814**
Reptile Life (CAN) **961**
Reptilen *see* Farmis-Reptilen **6842**
Reptiles (USA ISSN 1068-1965) **961**
Reptiles U S A (USA ISSN 1093-944X) **6814**
Reptilia (DEU ISSN 1431-8997) **961**
Reptilia (English Edition) (ESP ISSN 1138-4913) **961**
Reptilia (Italian Edition) (ESP ISSN 1699-3756) **961**
Reptilia (Spanish Edition) (ESP ISSN 1135-5832) **961**
Reptilian (GBR ISSN 0966-7911) **961**
• La Repubblica (ITA ISSN 0390-1076) **3898**
La Repubblica Napoletana del 1799 (ITA ISSN 1971-0542) **4257**
Republic Forge Company. Annual Report (IND ISSN 0304-811X) **1903**
Republic Medical Journal *see* Cumhuriyet Universitesi Tip Fakultesi Dergisi **5602**
Republic of Argentina. Ministry of Economy and Production, Secretariat of Economy Policy. Economic Report (ARG ISSN 1515-5471) **1514**
Republic of China (Taiwan). Government Information Office. Publication Annual *see* Zhonghua Minguo Chuban Nianjian **7576**
Republic of China Yearbook (Year) *see* Taiwan Yearbook (Year) **3122**
Republic of Kazakhstan. Ministry of Sciences and Higher Education. National Academy of Sciences. Reports *see* Kazakstan Respublikasynyn Gylym Akademiasynyn Baandamalary **7875**
† • The Republic of Korea Policy Series (KOR) **8985**
The Republic of Letters *see* News from the Republic of Letters **5341**
Republic of Mauritius. National Library. Annual Report (MUS ISSN 1694-0393) **5043**
Republic of Seychelles. Trades Tax Regulations (Year) (SYC) **1942**
• Republic of Singapore Government Gazette (SGP) **7465**
Republic of the Philippines. Bureau of Mines and Geo-Sciences. Annual Report (PHL ISSN 0116-2896) **6477**
Republic of the Philippines. Department of Public Information. Bureau of National and Foreign Information. Policy Statements *see* Republic of the Philippines. Office of the Press Secretary. Bureau of Communications Services. Policy Statements **7465**
• Republic of the Philippines. Office of the Press Secretary. Bureau of Communications Services. Policy Statements (PHL) **7465**
• La Republica (COL) **1378**
• La Republica (MEX ISSN 1607-1239) **3911**
• La Republica (Online) (PER ISSN 1605-3273) **3928**
• La Republica (Print) (PER ISSN 1605-3281) **3928**
• Republica Argentina. Ministerio de Economia y Produccion. Secretaria de Politica Economica. Informe Economico Trimestral (ARG) **1514**
Republica Croata *see* Republika Hrvatska **3561**
Republica de Cabo Verde. Boletim Oficial (CPV) **3789**
Republica de las Letras (ESP ISSN 1133-2158) **5359**
Republica de las Letras. Informes - Estudios (ESP ISSN 1135-6871) **5359**
• La Republica en Chiapas (MEX ISSN 1605-0479) **3911**
Le Republicain (MLI) **3907**
Republican Almanac (USA ISSN 0363-9290) **7177**
Republican Archives *see* Minguo Dang'an **4186**
Republican Englishman (GBR ISSN 0144-7548) **7177**
• Republican Liberty (USA) **7465**
Republican News *see* An Phoblacht **3894**
The Republican Woman (USA) **7177**
Republicki Zavod za Unapredjivanje Vaspitanja i Obrazovanja. Bibliografija (SRB ISSN 0351-6660) **2935**
Republika (HRV ISSN 0350-1337) **5236**
Republika Hrvatska/Republica Croata (ARG) **3561**
Republika Srbija. Mesecni Statisticki Pregled/Monthly Statistical Review (SRB ISSN 0354-205X) **8396**
Der Republikaner (DEU) **7177**
Die Republikein (NAM) **3913**
De Republikein (NLD ISSN 1574-1834) **7177**
Republique Centrafricaine. Journal Officiel (CAF) **1165**
Republique de Congo en Quelques Chiffres (COG) **7314**
Repulesi Szakirodalmi Tajekoztato/Aviation and Air Transport Abstracts (HUN ISSN 0231-3928) **8529**
Required Reading for Junior Middle Schools Students *see* Chuzhongsheng Bidu **2836**
• ➤ Requirements Engineering (GBR ISSN 0947-3602) **3293**
Requirements for Certification of Teachers, Counselors, Librarians, Administrators for Elementary and Secondary Schools (Year) (USA ISSN 1047-7071) **3030**
➤ Res (USA ISSN 0277-1322) **413**
Res *see* R E S (New York) **6976**
• Res (Stockholm, 1981) (SWE ISSN 1400-8971) **8751**
➤ Res Antiquae (BEL ISSN 1781-1317) **4158**
• ➤ Res Cogitans (DNK ISSN 1603-8509) **6947**
• Res Communes (USA) **3462**
Res et Jura Immobilia (BEL ISSN 0772-9588) **4769**
Res Forum (SWE ISSN 1403-297X) **8751**
Res Gesta (ARG ISSN 0325-772X) **4158**
• Res Gestae (USA ISSN 0557-9295) **4769**
• Res Ipsa Loquitur/Georgetown Law (USA ISSN 0838-8121) **4769**
Res och Trafik Forum *see* Trafik Forum **8513**
Res Orientales (BEL ISSN 1142-2831) **559**
• ➤ Res Publica (BEL ISSN 0486-4700) **7177**
Res Publica (ESP ISSN 1576-4184) **6947**
• ➤ Res Publica (NLD ISSN 1356-4765) **6947**
• Res Publica (SWE ISSN 0282-6062) **5236**
Res Publica (Bishkek) (KGZ) **3904**
• Res Publica Litterarum (ITA ISSN 1123-3990) **5359**
Res Publica Litterarum (USA ISSN 0275-4304) **5360**
• Res Publica Nowa (POL ISSN 1230-2155) **5236**
Res Socialis (CHE ISSN 1422-4437) **6947**
Resale Weekly (GBR ISSN 0034-5105) **1032**
Resam Forestier (CAN) **3715**
Reschtspflege. Reihe 1: Ausgewaehlte Zahlen fuer die Rechtspflege (DEU ISSN 0722-4834) **4825**
• Rescogitans (ITA ISSN 1828-7778) **6947**
• Rescol (CAN ISSN 1497-5572) **2950**
Rescol Hors Ligne *see* Rescol **2950**
Rescue (Kansas City) (USA ISSN 1049-586X) **8065**
• Rescue (Portland) (USA) **5081**
Rescue News (GBR ISSN 0950-5830) **413**
Rescue Publication (GBR ISSN 0309-4251) **413**
Rescues (NZL ISSN 1175-9968) **8281**
• Research (AUS ISSN 1834-4593) **7611**
Research (GBR ISSN 0969-6709) **1839**
Research (English Edition) *see* Research (German Edition) **6878**
Research (English Edition) *see* Research (Spanish Edition) **6878**
Research (German Edition) (DEU ISSN 0179-8618) **6878**
• Research (San Francisco) (USA ISSN 0192-172X) **1647**
Research (Spanish Edition) (DEU ISSN 1438-6747) **6878**
Research (University Park) *see* Research - Penn State **3000**
Research Accomplishments and Plans *see* National Center for Toxicological Research. Research Accomplishments and Plans **3500**
Research Advisor (USA ISSN 1096-1046) **5043**
• Research Africa (GBR ISSN 1751-617X) **4177**
• Research Alert (New York) (USA ISSN 0739-358X) **1839**
• Research Alert Yearbook (USA ISSN 1542-9172) **1840**
Research & Action Report (USA ISSN 1546-6434) **8902**
† Research and Bibliographical Guides in Criminal Justice (USA ISSN 1042-4636) **8985**
Research and Breeding Institute of Pomology, Holovousy. Scientific Papers of Pomology *see* Vyzkumny a Slechtitelsky Ustav Ovocnarsky Holovousy. Vedecke Prace Ovocnarske **258**
➤ Research and Clinical Center for Child Development. Annual Report (JPN ISSN 0386-8435) **2167**
Research & Development (DEU ISSN 0935-7238) **2715**
Research and Development *see* R & D Kobe Seiko Giho **6330**
Research & Development Associates for Military Food and Packaging Systems. Activities Report (USA ISSN 0198-0181) **6443**
Research and Development Brazilian Journal *see* Revista Brasileira de Pesquisa e Desenvolvimento **3174**
Research & Development Contracts Monthly *see* R & D Contracts Monthly **8983**
Research & Development Digest *see* R & D Digest **3145**
Research and Development Directions *see* R & D Directions **6877**
Research and Development Focus *see* R & D Focus **6877**
Research and Development Focus *see* R & D Focus **6343**
Research and Development Focus Drug News *see* R & D Focus Drug News **6877**
• ➤ Research and Development in Higher Education Series (AUS ISSN 0156-8884) **2999**
Research & Development in Industry (IND) **8436**
Research and Development in Ireland (IRL ISSN 0085-5545) **7902**
Research and Development in Japan Awarded the Okochi Memorial Prize (JPN ISSN 0289-9329) **8436**
Research and Development in New Zealand (NZL ISSN 1177-0295) **7938**
Research & Development Magazine *see* R & D Magazine **8436**
Research and Development News *see* Gijutsu Kaihatsu Nyusu **3309**
Research and Development Product Source Guide *see* R & D Product Source Telephone Directory **8436**
Research & Development Product Source Telephone Directory *see* R & D Product Source Telephone Directory **8436**
Research and Development Reporter (IND ISSN 0257-3245) **249**
Research and Development Rewards (GBR ISSN 1477-6235) **1705**
Research & Development Scoreboard *see* The (Year) R & D Scoreboard **1163**
Research and Exploration in Laboratory *see* Shiyanshi Yanjiu yu Tansuo **8438**
Research and Exposition in Mathematics (DEU) **5528**
Research and Industry (IND ISSN 0034-513X) **8436**
• Research and Information in Complementary Medicine (GBR ISSN 1358-6092) **5703**
Research and Issues in Music Education *see* R I M E **6608**
Research and Planning Unit Programme (Year) *see* Great Britain. Home Office. Research and Planning Unit. Programme (Year) **7442**
• ➤ Research and Practice for Persons with Severe Disabilities (USA ISSN 1540-7969) **4069**
Research and Practice in Adult Literacy Bulletin *see* R A P A L Bulletin **2945**
Research and Practice in Adult Literacy Journal *see* R A P A L Journal **2945**
Research and Practice in Alzheimer's Disease. Series (FRA ISSN 1284-8360) **4054**
Research and Practice in Forensic Medicine *see* Hoigaku no Jissai to Kenkyu **5914**
• ➤ Research and Practice in Human Resource Management (SGP ISSN 0218-5180) **1874**
• Research and Practice in Social Sciences (CAN ISSN 1715-4731) **7995**
• Research and Practice in Technology Enhanced Learning (SGP ISSN 1793-2068) **2436**
Research & Progress of Solid State Electronics *see* Guti Dianzixue Yanjiu yu Jinzhan **3100**
• Research and Public Policy Series (AUS ISSN 1326-6004) **2667**
Research and Scholarship in Composition (USA ISSN 1079-2554) **5360**
Research and Studies (CAN) **2935**
• ➤ Research and Teaching in Developmental Education (USA ISSN 1046-3364) **2904**
Research & Technology Transporter (USA) **8509**
• ➤ Research and Theory for Nursing Practice (USA ISSN 1541-6577) **5979**
Research and Theory in Educational Administration (USA ISSN 1537-3738) **3030**
Research Association for Nuclear Facility Decommissioning. Journal *see* Dekomisshoningu Giho **3166**
Research Association of Superconducting Magnetic Energy Storage. Research Report *see* Chodendo Enerugi Chozo Kenkyukai Kenkyu Hokokusho **7065**
Research at the Australian Institute of Sport (AUS ISSN 1449-7603) **8196**
• Research @ U N S W (University of New South Wales) (AUS) **2904**
Research Bibliographies and Checklists (GBR ISSN 1476-9700) **5408**
• Research Bulletin (AUS ISSN 1832-8385) **6180**
Research Bulletin *see* Boltan-e-Pizhuhishi **4445**
Research Bulletin for Home Economics *see* Nashrat Buhuth al-Iqtisad al-Manzili **4364**
Research Bulletin - Home Office Research and Statistics Department *see* Great Britain. Home Office. Research and Statistics Department. Research Bulletin **7442**
Research Bulletin of the Panjab University - Science *see* Panjab University Research Bulletin (Sciences) **7897**
Research Business Report (USA ISSN 1087-9641) **1840**
• The Research Buyer's Guide (Year) (GBR ISSN 1462-026X) **1840**
▼ • ➤ Research Center for Educational Technology. Journal (USA ISSN 1948-075X) **3078**
Research Center for Gas Industry in Cold District. Technical Report *see* Kanreichi Gijutsu Kenkyu Kaihatsu Senta Hokoku **6776**
Research Center for Nuclear Physics Annual Report *see* R C N P Annual Report **7071**
Research Centers Directory (USA ISSN 0080-1518) **7902**
Research Centers of the Black Sea Economic Cooperation. Ecological Bulletin *see* Nauchnye Tsentry Chernomorskogo Ekonomicheskogo Sotrudnichestva. Ekologicheskii Vestnik **3456**
• Research Centre for German and Austrian Exile Studies. Yearbook (NLD ISSN 1388-3720) **4257**
Research Committee for Graphic Simulation and Visualization of Multiphase Flow. Proceedings (JPN) **7084**
Research Committee of Essential Amino Acids. Reports *see* Hissu Aminosan Kenkyu **733**
➤ Research Communications in Alcohol & Substances of Abuse (USA ISSN 1080-8388) **6878**
➤ Research Communications in Biochemistry and Cell & Molecular Biology (USA ISSN 1087-111X) **744**

Title

▼ • Research Journal of Medical Sciences (PAK ISSN 1815-9346) **5703**
• Research Journal of Medicinal Plant (USA ISSN 1819-3455) **815**
• Research Journal of Medicine and Medical Sciences (PAK ISSN 1816-272X) **5703**
• Research Journal of Microbiology (USA ISSN 1816-4935) **895**
▼ • ➤ Research Journal of Mutagenesis (PAK ISSN 1994-7917) **878**
▼ • ➤ Research Journal of Obstetrics and Gynecology (PAK ISSN 1994-7925) **6003**
• Research Journal of Parasitology (USA ISSN 1816-4943) **6181**
▼ • Research Journal of Pharmacology (PAK ISSN 1815-9362) **6878**
Research Journal of Philosophy and Social Sciences (IND ISSN 0048-7325) **6947**
• Research Journal of Physics (USA ISSN 1819-3463) **7037**
• Research Journal of Phytochemistry (USA ISSN 1819-3471) **744**
▼ • Research Journal of Poultry Sciences (PAK ISSN 1993-5285) **298**
• Research Journal of Radiology (USA ISSN 1819-348X) **6207**
• Research Journal of Seed Science (USA ISSN 1819-3552) **250**
• Research Journal of Social Sciences (PAK ISSN 1815-9125) **7996**
• Research Journal of Soil Biology (USA ISSN 1819-3498) **700**
Research Journal of Textile and Apparel (HKG ISSN 1560-6074) **8456**
• Research Journal of Toxins (USA ISSN 1819-3560) **3501**
• Research Journal of Veterinary Sciences (USA ISSN 1819-1908) **8806**
Research Journal: Science (IND ISSN 0253-9306) **7902**
• Research Journal Telecommunication and Information Technology (PAK ISSN 1816-2738) **2337**
Research Laboratory for Nuclear Reactors. Bulletin (JPN ISSN 0387-6144) **3174**
Research Laboratory of Electronics Currents *see* R L E Currents **3112**
Research Laboratory of Engineering Materials. Report (JPN ISSN 0385-3799) **3356**
▼ • Research Letters in Biochemistry (USA ISSN 1687-6709) **744**
▼ • Research Letters in Chemical Engineering (USA ISSN 1687-6725) **3254**
▼ • ➤ Research Letters in Communications (USA ISSN 1687-6741) **2337**
▼ • ➤ Research Letters in Ecology (USA ISSN 1687-6768) **3462**
▼ • ➤ Research Letters in Electronics (USA ISSN 1687-6784) **3112**
▼ • ➤ Research Letters in Inorganic Chemistry (USA ISSN 1687-6806) **2118**
▼ • ➤ Research Letters in Materials Science (USA ISSN 1687-6822) **3356**
▼ • ➤ Research Letters in Nanotechnology (USA ISSN 1687-6849) **3217**
▼ • ➤ Research Letters in Optics (USA ISSN 1687-8175) **7084**
▼ • ➤ Research Letters in Organic Chemistry (USA ISSN 1687-6865) **2130**
▼ • ➤ Research Letters in Physical Chemistry (USA ISSN 1687-6873) **2140**
▼ • ➤ Research Letters in Physics (USA ISSN 1687-689X) **7037**
▼ • ➤ Research Letters in Signal Processing (USA ISSN 1687-6911) **3329**
• Research Letters in the Information and Mathematical Sciences (Online) (NZL ISSN 1177-6994) **5529**
Research Letters in the Information and Mathematical Sciences (Print) *see* Research Letters in the Information and Mathematical Sciences (Online) **5529**
Research Libraries Group DigiNews *see* R L G DigiNews **5042**
Research Libraries Group Focus (Online) *see* R L G Focus (Online) **5042**
Research Libraries Group News *see* R L G News **5042**
Research Links *see* Research Matters (Burnaby) **3000**
• Research Management Review (USA ISSN 1068-4867) **1790**
Research Materials on Ocean Economics *see* Kaiyo Sangyo Kenkyu Shiryo **1139**
• Research Matters (AUS ISSN 1448-6881) **7292**
• Research Matters (CAN ISSN 1203-3308) **2904**
Research Matters (GBR ISSN 1363-0105) **8065**
Research Matters (Burnaby) (CAN ISSN 1719-4520) **3000**
• Research Methodology in Strategy and Management (GBR ISSN 1479-8387) **1790**
• Research Money (CAN ISSN 0833-1677) **1378**
Research Monographs in French Studies (GBR ISSN 1466-8157) **5166**
Research Monographs on Human Population Biology (GBR ISSN 0957-2856) **7292**
• Research News (AUS ISSN 1447-3100) **1840**
Research News & Opportunities in Science and Theology (USA ISSN 1530-6410) **7902**
Research Note R M R S *see* U S D A Forest Service. Rocky Mountain Research Station. Research Note **3705**
Research Notes *see* V T T Tiedotteita **8444**
➤ Research Notes in Artificial Intelligence (USA ISSN 0268-7526) **2456**
▼ • ➤ Research Notes on Educational Effectiveness (USA ISSN 1940-3380) **2904**
Research Nurse *see* Research Practitioner **5910**
Research of Administration of N P Os *see* Shetuan Guanli Yanjiu **8068**
Research of Administration of Non-Profit Organizations *see* Shetuan Guanli Yanjiu **8068**
Research of Chinese Literature *see* Zhongguo Wenxue Yanjiu **5404**
Research of Environmental Sciences *see* Huanjing Kexue Yanjiu **3437**
Research of Modern Young People *see* Dangdai Qingnian Yanjiu **2150**
Research of Soil and Water Conservation *see* Shuitu Baochi Yanjiu **252**
Research on Accounting Ethics *see* Research on Professional Responsibility and Ethics in Accounting **1299**
• ➤ Research on Aging (USA ISSN 0164-0275) **4054**
• ➤ Research on Chemical Intermediates (NLD ISSN 0922-6168) **2078**
▼ Research on Chrysomelidae (NLD ISSN 1876-3111) **857**
Research on Contemporary Society *see* Aichi Shukutoku Daigaku Gendai Shakai Kenkyuuka Kenkyu Houkoku **8086**
➤ Research on Crops (IND ISSN 0972-3226) **250**
Research on Drug Actions and Interactions *see* Iyakuhin Sogo Sayo Kenkyu **6851**
Research on Economics and Management *see* Jingji yu Guanli Yanjiu **1763**
• Research on Emotion in Organizations (NLD ISSN 1746-9791) **7403**
Research on Financial and Economic Problems *see* Caijing Wenti Yanjiu **1323**
Research on France *see* Faguo Yanjiu **7964**
Research on Home Medicines *see* Kateiyaku Kenkyu **6857**
• Research on Language and Computation (NLD ISSN 1570-7075) **5166**
• ➤ Research on Language and Social Interaction (USA ISSN 0835-1813) **5166**
Research on Negotiation in Organizations (USA ISSN 1040-9556) **1790**
Research on Professional Responsibility and Ethics in Accounting (USA ISSN 1574-0765) **1299**
Research on Shanghai Macro-Micro Economy *see* Shanghai Zonghe Jingji **1721**
• ➤ Research on Social Work Practice (USA ISSN 1049-7315) **8128**
Research on Sociocultural Influences on Motivation and Learning (USA ISSN 1531-2828) **2904**
Research on Soft Science of Surveying and Mapping *see* Cehui Ruankexue Yanjiu **8940**
Research on Steroids (ITA ISSN 0370-7466) **6232**
• ➤ Research on Technological Innovation, Management and Policy (USA ISSN 0737-1071) **8436**
Research on Transport Economics *see* Recherche en Matiere d'Economie des Transports **8509**
Research on Women in Modern Chinese History *see* Jindai Zhongguo Funu Shi Yanjiu **4184**
Research Opportunities in Renaissance Drama (USA ISSN 0098-647X) **5360**
Research Oregon *see* Oregon Business Magazine **1157**
Research Organization for Information Science & Technology News *see* R I S T News **7901**
Research Paper (AUS ISSN 1832-0287) **5703**
Research Paper R M R S *see* U S D A Forest Service. Rocky Mountain Research Station. Research Paper **3705**
Research Paper S E *see* U S D A Forest Service. Southern Research Station. Research Paper **3705**
Research Paper S O *see* U S D A Forest Service. Southern Research Station. Research Paper **3705**
▼ Research Paper Series (SWE ISSN 1654-7322) **7676**
Research Papers in Banking and Finance *see* Institute of European Finance. School of Accounting, Banking and Economics. Research Papers in Banking and Finance **1355**
• ➤ Research Papers in Education (GBR ISSN 0267-1522) **2905**
Research Papers in Finance (GBR ISSN 1473-6462) **1378**
➤ Research Papers in Geography and Environmental Science (AUS) **4026**
• ➤ Research Papers in Management Studies (GBR) **1790**
Research Papers in Media and Cultural Studies (GBR ISSN 1367-8620) **2337**
Research Papers in Russian and East European Studies (GBR) **4257**
• Research Papers of the Parliamentary Library Service (AUS ISSN 1833-8771) **4769**
Research Partners *see* Research Matters (Burnaby) **3000**
Research - Penn State (USA) **3000**
• Research Perspectives/Perspectives sur la Recherche (CAN ISSN 1915-0091) **7903**
• ➤ Research Perspectives in Music Education (USA ISSN 1947-7457) **6610**
• ➤ Research Policy (NLD ISSN 0048-7333) **7903**
• Research, Policy and Planning (GBR ISSN 0264-519X) **8065**
▼ Research, Policy and Practice in Higher Education (NLD ISSN 1875-0842) **3000**
• Research Practitioner (USA ISSN 1528-0330) **5910**
Research Profiles in Aging (NLD ISSN 1567-7184) **4054**
Research Programme on Human Resources Development. Research Monograph (ZAF ISSN 1816-4226) **1874**
• ➤ Research Quarterly for Exercise and Sport (USA ISSN 0270-1367) **6995**
Research Reactor Institute. News *see* Genshiro Jikkenjo Dayori **7066**
Research Recommendations (USA ISSN 0893-4347) **1965**
Research Report *see* Research & Action Report **8902**
Research Report *see* Travel and Tourism Works for America **8766**
Research Report from the National Institute for Environmental Studies, Japan *see* Kokuritsu Kankyo Kenkyujo Kenkyu Hokoku **3449**
Research Report N I F S - Data Series *see* National Institute for Fusion Science. Research Report. Data Series **7069**
Research Report N I F S - Memo Series *see* National Institute for Fusion Science. Research Report. Memo Series **7069**
Research Report N I F S. TECH Series *see* National Institute for Fusion Science. Research Report. Tech Series **7027**
Research Report of Geological Survey and Landsubsidence in Chiba Prefecture *see* Chibaken Kogai Kenkyujo Chika Shigen Jiban Saigai Kenkyu Shiryo **2728**
Research Report of Meteorology and Climatology *see* Kikogaku Kishogaku Kenkyu Hokoku **6359**
Research Report of Revegetation in Tokyo Prefecture *see* Ryokka ni Kansuru Chosa Hokoku **2716**
Research Report of Utilization of Radiation by Irradiation Therapy Group *see* Hoshasen Riyo Kenkyukai Hokokusho, Shosha Riyo Gurupu **7066**
Research Report of Utilization of Radiation by Isotope User's Group *see* Hoshasen Riyo Kenkyukai Hokokusho, Aisotopu Riyo Gurupu **7066**
Research Report of Utilization of Radiation by Medical User's Group *see* Hoshasen Riyo Kenkyukai Hokokusho, Igaku Riyo Gurupu **6198**
Research Report of Waves *see* Haro Chosa Hokokusho **2805**
Research Report on Ptarmigan *see* Raicho Chosa Hokokusho **913**
Research Report P (USA ISSN 0361-5804) **150**
Research Report Series *see* S C R E Research Report **2908**
Research Reporter (HKG ISSN 1683-0733) **5806**
Research Reports from the Rockefeller Archive Center *see* Rockefeller University. Rockefeller Archive Center. Research Reports **4159**
Research Reports on Information Science and Electrical Engineering/Kyushu Daigaku Daigakuin Shisutemu Joho Kagaku Kiyo (JPN ISSN 1342-3819) **3329**
Research Reports on Information Science and Electrical Engineering of Kyshu University *see* Research Reports on Information Science and Electrical Engineering **3329**
Research Reports on Information Sciences. Series A, Mathematical Science (JPN ISSN 0912-2370) **2550**
Research Reports on Mathematical and Computing Sciences. Series B, Operations Research (JPN ISSN 1342-2804) **2550**
Research Reports on Mathematical and Computing Sciences. Series C, Computer Sciences (JPN ISSN 1342-2812) **2550**
Research Reports on Sport and Health *see* Liikunnan ja Kansanterveyden Edistamissaatio. Julkaisuja **6231**
▼ • Research Repository of Stringed Musical Instrument Technology (USA ISSN 1935-5742) **6610**
Research Results Digests *see* C T B S S P Research Results Digests **8669**
Research Review *see* Federal Reserve Bank of Boston. Research Review **1486**
Research Review *see* Gartner Group. Research Review **2543**
Research Review - Institute of African Studies *see* University of Ghana. Institute of African Studies. Research Review **5243**
Research Roundup (USA ISSN 8755-2590) **3030**
Research Society for American Periodicals Newsletter *see* R S A P Newsletter **634**
Research Society for Ayurveda in Japan. News *see* Ayuruveda Tsushin **307**
Research Society of Pakistan. Journal (PAK ISSN 0034-5431) **4187**
† • ➤ Research Strategies (GBR ISSN 0734-3310) **8985**
• Research Studies in Botany and Related Applied Fields (GBR ISSN 0951-6654) **815**
• ➤ Research Studies in Music Education (GBR ISSN 1321-103X) **6611**
Research Studies in Particle and Nuclear Technology (GBR) **7072**
Research Studies in Plant Science (GBR) **815**
Research Subject for Development Shipbuilding Techniques *see* Zosen Gijutsu Kenkyu Kaihatsu Kadaishu **8666**
Research Symposium Proceedings *see* Review of Futures Markets (Kent) **1166**
† Research Techniques in Nondestructive Testing (GBR ISSN 0277-7045) **8985**
• ➤ Research Technology Management (USA ISSN 0895-6308) **1790**
• Research Today (USA) **8806**
Research Triangle Institute Viewpoints *see* R T P Viewpoints **7901**
• Research U S A (USA ISSN 1544-466X) **7177**
Research Updates in Kidney and Urologic Health *see* Urologic Diseases Research Updates **6276**
Research Updates in Kidney and Urologic Health *see* Kidney Disease Research Updates **6270**
Research Work for the Period ... - Building Research Institute, Ibaraki *see* Kenchiku Kenkyujo Nenpo **1019**
• Research Works (USA ISSN 1937-173X) **4425**
Research World (NLD ISSN 1567-3073) **1840**
Researches Assisted by the Asahi Glass Foundation. Reports (CD-ROM) *see* Asahi Garasu Zaidan Josei Kenkyu Seika Hokoku (CD-ROM) **2050**
Researches in Chinese Economic History *see* Zhongguo Jingjishi Yanjiu **1551**
Researches in Classical and Modern Chinese Literature *see* Zhongguo Gudai, Jindai Wenxue Yanjiu **5404**
Researches in Foreign Literature *see* Waiguo Wenxue Yanjiu (Beijing) **5396**
Researches in Geography *see* Pizhuhish'ha-yi Jughrafiyayi **4024**
Researches in Management in Asia Series (IND) **1790**
Researches in Medical Education *see* Yixue Jiaoyu Tansuo **5733**
Researches in Modern and Contemporary Chinese Literature *see* Zhongguo Xiandai, Dangdai Wenxue Yanjiu **5404**
Researches of Wallonia *see* Les Chercheurs de la Wallonie **387**
Researches on Anatolian Art *see* Anadolu Sanati Arastirmalari **466**
Researches on Landsubsidence and Earthquake in Chiba Prefecture *see* Chibaken no Jiban Chinka to Jishin **3262**
Researches on the Hui *see* Huizu Yanjiu **3618**
Researchin' Ouachita - Calhoun Counties, Ar. (USA ISSN 8756-9817) **3780**
• Researching Law (USA ISSN 1059-4906) **4769**
Researching Markets, Industries, and Business Opportunities (USA ISSN 1067-0394) **1165**
Le Reseau *see* Network (Winnipeg) **8847**
• Reseau Canadien d'Information sur le Patrimoine (CAN ISSN 1910-2534) **5043**
Reseau Canadien d'Information sur le Patrimoine un Regard sur l'Annee *see* Canadian Heritage Information Network, the Year in Perspective **4134**
Le Reseau des Aires Protegees d'Environnement Canada. Rapport Annuel *see* Environment Canada's Protected Areas Network Annual Report **3421**
Reseau des Femmes de la F I I Q. Le Reseau *see* F I IQ Women's Network. Le Reseau **5958**
Reseau des S A D C du Quebec. Directory *see* Reseau des S A D C du Quebec. Directory of Members **1165**
Reseau des S A D C du Quebec. Directory of Members (CAN ISSN 1910-4340) **1165**
Reseau des S A D C du Quebec. Repertoire des Membres *see* Reseau des S A D C du Quebec. Directory of Members **1165**
Reseau Europeen de Sciences et Techniques Appliquees au Patrimoine Culturel. Revue *see* Pact **410**
Reseau Europeen Interdisciplinaire de Recherche sur Psychologie et Reanimation Cahiers *see* R E I R P R. Cahiers **8983**
Reseau Feministe Ruptures (FRA ISSN 1769-924X) **8882**
Reseau Femmes Ruptures. Bullletin *see* Reseau Feministe Ruptures **8882**
• Reseau Juridique Canadien VIH - SIDA. Plan Strategique (CAN ISSN 1910-8966) **5825**
Reseau Juridique Canadien VIH - SIDA. Rapport Annuel *see* Canadian HIV - AIDS Legal Network. Annual Report **4639**
• Reseau Juridique Canadien VIH-Sida. Rapport Annuel (CAN ISSN 1719-6132) **4769**
Reseau Mondial des Femmes pour les Droits sur la Reproduction *see* Women's Global Network for Reproductive Rights. Newsletter **8849**
• Reseau National des Sports de Nature. La Lettre (FRA ISSN 1958-5101) **8330**
• Reseaux (FRA ISSN 0751-7971) **8128**
Reseaux (Saint Cloud) *see* Reseaux V R D **1032**
Reseaux - Ciephum (BEL ISSN 0378-9926) **6947**
Reseaux et Systemes Repartis, Calculateurs Paralleles (FRA ISSN 1638-3672) **2503**
• Reseaux & Telecoms (FRA ISSN 1251-8964) **2337**
Reseaux: French Journal of Communication (GBR ISSN 0969-9864) **2337**
Reseaux V R D/Network (Voirie Reseaux Divers) (FRA ISSN 1772-4007) **1032**
Reseaux Voirie Reseaux Divers *see* Reseaux V R D **1032**
Reseller Business (ITA ISSN 1594-4018) **2511**

DIRECTORY 2010 RESTAURANG & STORHUSHAALL - NYTT 10803

Reseller News *see* New Zealand Reseller News **2493**
Reseller Quarterly (USA) **2511**
Reseller Weekly *see* Reseller Business **2511**
Reseller World Middle East (UAE) **2494**
† Resena (ESP ISSN 1578-9926) **8985**
Resena Biblica (ESP ISSN 1134-5233) **7676**
Resena de Literatura, Arte y Espectaculos *see* Resena **8985**
Resena Laboral (MEX ISSN 0302-5004) **1705**
Resenas Malacologicas (ESP ISSN 1576-933X) **815**
Reservations Services Manual (CAN) **8551**
Reserve & National Guard Magazine (USA) **6443**
• Reserve Bank of Australia. Annual Report (AUS ISSN 0484-5412) **1378**
• Reserve Bank of Australia. Bulletin (AUS ISSN 0725-0320) **1260**
Reserve Bank of Australia. Company Finance. Bulletin Supplement *see* Reserve Bank of Australia. Bulletin **1260**
Reserve Bank of Australia. Financial Flows. Bulletin Supplement *see* Reserve Bank of Australia. Bulletin **1260**
• Reserve Bank of Australia. Occasional Papers (AUS ISSN 0080-178X) **1378**
• Reserve Bank of Australia. Payments System Board. Annual Report (AUS ISSN 1442-939X) **1378**
• Reserve Bank of Australia. Research Discussion Paper (AUS ISSN 1320-7229) **1378**
Reserve Bank of Fiji. Annual Report (FJI) **1514**
Reserve Bank of Fiji. Monthly Economic Bulletin (FJI) **1514**
Reserve Bank of Fiji. News Review (FJI) **1514**
Reserve Bank of Fiji. Quarterly Review (FJI) **1514**
Reserve Bank of India. Annual Report (IND ISSN 0080-1801) **1378**
Reserve Bank of India. Bulletin (IND ISSN 0034-5512) **1378**
Reserve Bank of India. Bulletin. Weekly Statistical Supplement (IND) **1378**
Reserve Bank of India. Occasional Papers (IND ISSN 0972-7493) **1379**
Reserve Bank of India. Report on Currency and Finance (IND) **1379**
Reserve Bank of Malawi. Financial and Economic Review (MWI ISSN 0376-5725) **1514**
Reserve Bank of Malawi. Report and Accounts (MWI ISSN 0486-5383) **1379**
• Reserve Bank of New Zealand. Annual Report (NZL ISSN 0110-7070) **1379**
• Reserve Bank of New Zealand Bulletin (NZL ISSN 1174-7943) **1379**
• Reserve Bank of New Zealand. Discussion Paper Series (Online) (NZL ISSN 1177-7567) **1379**
Reserve Bank of New Zealand. Discussion Paper Series (Print) *see* Reserve Bank of New Zealand. Discussion Paper Series (Online) **1379**
• Reserve Bank of New Zealand. Monetary Policy Statement (NZL ISSN 1170-4829) **1514**
Reserve Bank of New Zealand. Research Papers (NZL ISSN 0110-523X) **1514**
• Reserve Bank of New Zealand. Statement of Intent (NZL ISSN 1176-6786) **1379**
Reserve Bank of Zimbabwe. Annual Report (ZWE ISSN 1024-2732) **1379**
Reserve Bank of Zimbabwe. Annual Report and Statements of Accounts for the Year *see* Reserve Bank of Zimbabwe. Annual Report **1379**
Reserve Bank of Zimbabwe. Monthly Bulletin (ZWE ISSN 1024-2740) **1379**
Reserve Bank of Zimbabwe. Quarterly Economic and Statistical Review (ZWE ISSN 0251-1819) **1379**
▼ The Reserve Force Volunteer (ZAF ISSN 1995-1973) **6443**
Reserve Forces Almanac (USA ISSN 0363-860X) **6443**
Reserves Naturelles *see* Natagora **910**
Reserves of Coal, Province of Alberta (CAN ISSN 0380-4275) **3146**
Reservofficeren (SWE ISSN 0284-625X) **6443**
Reservoir (CAN ISSN 1484-2238) **6790**
Reservoir Evaluation and Engineering *see* S P E Reservoir Evaluation and Engineering **6791**
Reset (ITA ISSN 1594-9893) **3898**
Resforum *see* Res Forum **8751**
The Reshaping of Psychoanalysis (USA ISSN 1059-3551) **7403**
Reshimat Havre Histadrut ha-Rabanim da-Amerika/Rabbinic Registry (USA ISSN 0098-468X) **7728**
Reshimat Ma'amarim be-Mada'e ha-Yahadut *see* Index of Articles on Jewish Studies (Online) **7698**
Reshimot (USA ISSN 1086-4490) **7728**
Residence *see* Jushe **4544**
Residence (NLD ISSN 0926-9592) **4549**
Residence (SWE ISSN 1404-8892) **4549**
Residence (USA) **7611**
Residence International (USA ISSN 1945-628X) **7611**
• Residency Program Connection (USA ISSN 1948-0555) **4110**
• Residency Program Director's Alert (USA ISSN 1545-0791) **4110**
Resident (USA) **3986**
The Resident Assistant (USA ISSN 1542-2186) **5980**
Resident of Registration Population *see* Jeon'gug Ju'min Deunglog In'gu Tong'gye **7311**
Residential (ESP) **5703**
• Residential Aged Care Coronial Communique (AUS ISSN 1834-318X) **8065**
Residential and Business Listing Phone Book (MUS ISSN 1694-0148) **2026**
• Residential Architect (USA ISSN 1093-359X) **455**
Residential Assessment Manual (CAN ISSN 1719-5276) **4425**
Residential Building Cost Guide (Year) *see* Residential Cost Handbook **1033**
Residential Care Homes Scotland. Statistical Information Note (GBR) **8083**
Residential Concrete (USA ISSN 1934-8177) **1032**
Residential Construction Costs (USA) **1032**
Residential Cost Data (USA) **1033**
Residential Cost Handbook (USA) **1033**
• Residential Design and Build (USA ISSN 1934-7553) **1033**
Residential Developer *see* Developer **1002**
Residential Developer Magazine (AUS ISSN 1833-2889) **7611**
• Residential Land Bulletin (AUS) **4425**
• Residential Lighting Magazine (USA ISSN 1072-1614) **4562**
Residential Property Journal *see* Royal Institution of Chartered Surveyors. Residential Property Journal **7611**
Residential Square Foot Building Costs (Year) (USA) **1033**
• Residential Systems (USA ISSN 1528-7858) **3112**
▼ • Residential Systems International (USA) **3112**
Residential Tenancies in Newfoundland and Labrador (CAN) **4425**
Residential Tenancy Act (CAN ISSN 1911-5822) **4425**
• ➤ Residential Treatment for Children & Youth (USA ISSN 0886-571X) **2167**
Residents of Farms and Rural Areas *see* Current Population Reports. Population Characteristics. Residents of Farms and Rural Areas **8947**
Residual Values (ZAF) **8601**
• Residuos (ESP) **3480**
Resilience (CAN ISSN 1718-407X) **7538**
• Resilog (CAN ISSN 0225-5804) **3511**
Resist Newsletter (USA ISSN 0897-2613) **7214**
Resistance (USA) **6611**
▼ • Resistance Studies Magazine (SWE ISSN 1654-7063) **7214**
Resistance Welder Manufacturers Association News *see* R W M A News **6343**
Resistant Pest Management (USA ISSN 1061-7795) **150**
Resistor (ESP ISSN 0211-0830) **3112**
Resoconti di Letteratura Italiana (ITA ISSN 1824-6273) **5360**
• reSolution (DEU) **7084**
Resolution Trust Corporation Report *see* R T C Report **7606**
Resolutions, Beliefs & Policies, Constitution and Bylaws (USA) **3030**
Resolutions Information and Guidelines (CAN ISSN 1912-4139) **8882**
Resolutions Information Book *see* Resolutions Information and Guidelines **8882**
Resolve National Newsletter (USA ISSN 1042-0290) **6003**
▼ Resolving Technology and Media Disputes Before Trial (USA ISSN 1944-8422) **6757**
Resonance (GEO) **3843**
Resonance *see* Tehuda **3086**
Resonance (USA) **6611**
Resonance (ZAF ISSN 1816-2428) **5703**
▼ Resonance Generale (FRA ISSN 1959-2108) **5433**
• ➤ Resonance - Journal of Science Education (IND ISSN 0971-8044) **7903**
Resonancias (PRI ISSN 1537-8292) **6611**
• ➤ Resonate (AUS) **6611**
Resonator Guitarist (USA) **6611**
Resort Condominiums International Premier *see* R C I Premier **4396**
Resort Development Law Reporter (USA) **4769**
Resort Life - Zimbali *see* Zimbali **5087**
Resort Living (USA ISSN 1541-7492) **7611**
Resort Management & Operations (USA) **4396**
Resort Newspaper *see* Kurortnaya Gazeta **4979**
The Resort Trades (USA) **8752**
Resort Weekly (CAN) **8752**
Resort Weekly *see* Kurortnaya Nedelya **3937**
• Resorts & Great Hotels (USA ISSN 1085-2573) **8752**
Resorts & Parks Purchasing Guide (USA ISSN 1065-0849) **4396**
Resorts and Spas *see* One+ **6282**
Resound (USA ISSN 0749-2472) **6611**
• ReSoundings (USA) **514**
Resource (AUS ISSN 1031-3796) **2905**
Resource (GBR ISSN 0143-2710) **7676**
• The Resource (GBR ISSN 0969-0409) **3462**
• ReSource (GBR ISSN 1473-7841) **7903**
Resource *see* Wageningen Update **2308**
The Resource (USA) **8675**
Resource (New York) *see* R E S (New York) **6976**
• Resource (Niles) (USA ISSN 1076-3333) **250**
Resource (San Francisco) (USA ISSN 1936-6485) **7728**
Resource (Wageningen) (NLD ISSN 1874-3625) **2298**
Resource Access Control Facility Update *see* R A C F Update **8983**
• ➤ Resource and Energy Economics (NLD ISSN 0928-7655) **3146**
† Resource and Environmental Biotechnology (GBR ISSN 1358-2283) **8985**
Resource Bulletin R M R S *see* U S D A Forest Service. Rocky Mountain Research Station. Resource Bulletin **3705**
Resource Center Bulletin *see* I R C News **7241**
Resource Center for Nonviolence. Center Report (USA) **7262**
Resource Conservation and Recovery Act Regulations and Keyword Index *see* R C R A Regulations and Keyword Index **3461**
Resource Development and Market *see* Ziyuan Kaifa yu Shichang **2634**
Resource Directory (USA ISSN 1931-8820) **8477**
Resource Directory for Ventilator-Assisted Living (Year) *see* Ventilator-Assisted Living **5728**
Resource Directory of Scientists and Engineers with Disabilities (USA) **645**
• ➤ Resource Geology (GBR ISSN 1344-1698) **2764**
Resource Guide & Fact Book *see* Sports Business Resource Guide & Fact Book **8207**
• Resource Guide for Starting and Growing a Small Business (USA) **1965**
• Resource Library (USA ISSN 1550-8420) **514**
Resource Library Magazine *see* Resource Library **514**
• Resource Links (CAN ISSN 1201-7647) **2210**
Resource Management (USA ISSN 0893-1828) **6443**
Resource Management and Recovery (GBR ISSN 1475-0791) **3511**
• Resource Management Journal (NZL ISSN 1175-1444) **4879**
Resource Management Theory & Practice (NZL ISSN 1177-1003) **4879**
Resource Material Series - U N A F E I *see* United Nations. Asia and Far East Institute for the Prevention of Crime and the Treatment of Offenders. Resource Material Series **2670**
• Resource Quantities and Pricing Guide (ZAF) **1033**
Resource Recovery Report (USA ISSN 0735-3081) **3511**
Resource Recycling *see* E-Scrap News **3505**
† Resource Sciences Interface (AUS ISSN 1039-5423) **8985**
• ➤ Resource Sharing & Information Networks (USA ISSN 0737-7797) **5043**
Resource Stocks *see* ResourceStocks **1647**
Resource: The Newsletter of the Section on Administration. American Physical Therapy Association *see* H P A Resource **4095**
▼ • Resource Week (USA ISSN 1945-8355) **1903**
Resources (CAN ISSN 0714-5918) **4769**
• Resources (USA) **2626**
Resources (Dayton) *see* The Influential Executive **26**
Resources (Fort Worth) (USA) **6790**
Resources (Nashville) (USA) **2641**
Resources (New York) (USA ISSN 1047-1286) **634**
• Resources (Washington) (USA ISSN 0048-7376) **2626**
Resources and Environment in the Yangtze Basin *see* Changjiang Liuyu Ziyuan yu Huanjing **3410**
• ➤ Resources, Conservation and Recycling (NLD ISSN 0921-3449) **3511**
• Resources, Energy and Development (IND ISSN 0973-0516) **3146**
Resources Environment & Engineering *see* Ziyuan Huanjing yu Gongcheng **3477**
• ➤ Resources for American Literary Study (USA ISSN 0048-7384) **5360**
• Resources for American Studies (GBR ISSN 1746-9414) **5043**
Resources for Change (USA ISSN 0147-7501) **2905**
• Resources for College Libraries (USA) **3000**
• ➤ Resources for Feminist Research/ Documentation sur la Recherche Feministe (CAN ISSN 0707-8412) **8902**
Resources for Nursing Research (GBR) **5980**
Resources for Radicals (CAN ISSN 1492-4234) **8128**
Resources for the Future. Annual Report (USA ISSN 0486-5561) **2626**
Resources for the Future Discussion Papers *see* R F F Discussion Papers **2625**
Resources for the Future News *see* R F F News **2625**
Resources Guide *see* Le Guide Ressources **6645**
Resources in Education (GBR ISSN 1754-2618) **2905**
• Resources in Education (USA ISSN 0098-0897) **2935**
The Resources of International Permaculture (USA ISSN 1070-4868) **700**
† Resources of Music Series (GBR) **8985**
Resources on Contemporary Issues (USA) **7996**
• ➤ Resources Policy (GBR ISSN 0301-4207) **3146**
Resources Processing *see* Kankyou Shigen Kougaku **6467**
Resources Science *see* Ziyuan Kexue **3477**
ResourceStocks (AUS ISSN 1441-9750) **1647**
Respiracion (ARG ISSN 0326-9116) **6218**
• ➤ Respiration (CHE ISSN 0025-7931) **6218**
Respiration *see* Tanaffos **6220**
Respiration and Circulation *see* Kokyu to Junkan **6215**
Respiration Research *see* Kokyu **6215**
Respiratory Care *see* Kokyuuki Kea **6216**
• Respiratory Care Clinics of North America (USA ISSN 1078-5337) **6218**
Respiratory Care Education Annual (USA) **6218**
Respiratory Disease *see* Today in Medicine. Respiratory Disease **6220**
Respiratory Disease in Practice (GBR ISSN 0262-7043) **6218**
Respiratory Diseases Research Centre. Annual Report (KEN) **6218**
Respiratory Management (USA ISSN 1932-7927) **6218**
• ➤ Respiratory Medicine (GBR ISSN 0954-6111) **6218**
Respiratory Medicine *see* Kokyuukika **6216**
• ➤ Respiratory Medicine C M E (GBR ISSN 1755-0017) **6218**
• Respiratory Medicine: C O P D Update (Chronic Obstructive Pulmonary Disease) (GBR ISSN 1745-0454) **6218**
Respiratory Medicine Extra *see* Respiratory Medicine C M E **6218**
Respiratory Molecular Medicine *see* Bunshi Kokyukibyo **6212**
➤ Respiratory Pharmacology and Pharmacotherapy (CHE) **6878**
• ➤ Respiratory Physiology & Neurobiology (NLD ISSN 1569-9048) **927**
• ➤ Respiratory Research (GBR ISSN 1465-9921) **6219**
• Respiratory Research Review (NZL ISSN 1178-6205) **6219**
• Respiratory Therapeutics Week (USA ISSN 1543-6659) **6219**
Respiratory Therapy (USA) **6219**
• ➤ Respirology (AUS ISSN 1323-7799) **6219**
The Responder (USA) **3462**
Responder Safety *see* Responder Safety **7538**
Responder Safety (USA) **7538**
Responding to Change *see* Opportunities **1431**
Responsa Meridiana (ZAF ISSN 0486-5588) **4769**
• La Responsabilita Civile (ITA ISSN 1824-7474) **4879**
• Responsabilita Civile e Previdenza (ITA ISSN 0391-187X) **4520**
Responsabilita e Risarcimento (ITA ISSN 1827-448X) **4879**
Responsabilite et Environnement (FRA ISSN 1268-4783) **3462**
Responsable Sante (FRA ISSN 1770-0914) **7538**
Response (AUS) **4110**
• Response (Los Angeles) (USA ISSN 1055-3703) **7728**
Response (New York, 1969) (USA ISSN 0034-5725) **7773**
Response (Seattle) (USA ISSN 1084-6093) **2298**
• Response Magazine (USA ISSN 1523-7656) **34**
Response to Terrorism (USA) **7177**
• Responsibilities of Insurance Agents and Brokers (USA) **4521**
• Responsibility (USA) **1165**
Responsible National Oceanographic Data Center Activity Report *see* R N O D C Activity Report **2816**
Responsible Organization Review *see* Revue de l'Organisation Responsable **1791**
Responsive Philanthropy (USA ISSN 1065-0008) **8065**
Respublika (BLR) **3800**
Respublika (LTU ISSN 1392-5873) **3906**
Respublika Armeniya (ARM ISSN 1029-8983) **3792**
Respublika Tatarstan (RUS) **3940**
Respuestas Educativas (ARG ISSN 1851-2291) **2905**
Ressouces Humaines Publiques *see* R H Publiques **8984**
Ressource en Sante et en Securite (CAN ISSN 1198-1237) **6685**
Ressources d'Habitation Privees de la Region de Montreal-Centre *see* Registre des Residences Privees pour Personnes Agees avec Services **8065**
Ressources Genetiques Forestieres *see* Forest Genetic Resources **3688**
Ressources Humaines *see* Collection Ressources Humaines **1858**
Ressources Marines et Formation *see* Fisheries Education and Training **3592**
Ressources Marines et Traditions *see* Traditional Marine Resource Management and Knowledge **3610**
• Ressources Naturelles Canada. Division de la Reglementation des Explosifs. Rapport aux Intervenants (CAN ISSN 1910-4405) **7538**
Ressources Naturelles Canada. Rapport au Parlement en Vertu de la Loi sur l'Efficacite Energetique (CAN ISSN 1491-0640) **3147**
Ressources Naturelles Canada. Secteur des Sciences de la Terre. Revue Annuelle (CAN ISSN 1709-5735) **2715**
Rest & Relaxation Cable & Satellite T V *see* R & R - A F N Cable & Satellite T V **2388**
Rest & Relaxation Entertainment Digest *see* R & R Entertainment Digest **6442**
Restatement of the Law Citations *see* Shepard's Restatement of the Law Citations **4964**
Restauracion Hoy (COL ISSN 0121-5264) **514**
• Restauracion News (ESP ISSN 1697-4603) **4396**
Restauracion y Rehabilitacion (ESP ISSN 1134-4571) **514**
Restaurang & Storhushaall - Nytt *see* Restaurangvaerlden **4396**

Title

Title

10806 REVIEW OF THE RIVER PLATE ULRICH'S PERIODICALS

Review of the River Plate (ARG ISSN 0034-6810) **1514**
Review of Tropical Plant Pathology (IND ISSN 0254-1300) **815**
Review of Tuberculosis for Public Health Nurse *see* Hokenfu no Kekkaku Tenbo **5960**
• ➤ Review of Urban & Regional Development Studies (AUS ISSN 0917-0553) **1604**
• ➤ Review of World Economics (DEU ISSN 1610-2878) **1166**
Review of World Inventions *see* Shijie Faming **7915**
Review on Liberal Arts/Kyoyo Ronshu (JPN ISSN 0288-1500) **4472**
• Reviewer's Bookwatch (Online) (USA) **634**
• Reviewing Sociology (GBR ISSN 0261-0272) **8128**
Reviews Chronicle *see* Litopys Retsenzii **5407**
Reviews for Primary Care (USA ISSN 1555-4635) **5703**
• Reviews in American History (USA ISSN 0048-7511) **4310**
• ➤ Reviews in Analgesia (USA ISSN 1542-961X) **5773**
➤ Reviews in Analytical Chemistry (ISR ISSN 0048-752X) **2105**
• ➤ Reviews in Anthropology (USA ISSN 0093-8157) **353**
▼ • ➤ Reviews in Aquaculture (USA ISSN 1753-5123) **2817**
• ➤ Reviews in Cardiovascular Medicine (USA ISSN 1530-6550) **5798**
➤ Reviews in Chemical Engineering (ISR ISSN 0167-8299) **3254**
• Reviews in Clinical Gerontology (GBR ISSN 0959-2598) **4054**
• ➤ Reviews in Computational Chemistry (USA ISSN 1069-3599) **2078**
➤ Reviews in Conservation (GBR ISSN 1817-2245) **2626**
➤ Reviews in Contemporary Pharmacotherapy (GBR ISSN 0954-8602) **6878**
• Reviews in Economic Geology (USA ISSN 0741-0123) **2764**
• Reviews in Endocrine & Metabolic Disorders (USA ISSN 1389-9155) **5899**
• ➤ Reviews in Engineering Geology (USA ISSN 0080-2018) **3281**
• Reviews in Environmental Science and Biotechnology (NLD ISSN 1569-1705) **770**
• ➤ Reviews in Fish Biology and Fisheries (NLD ISSN 0960-3166) **961**
• ➤ Reviews in Fisheries Science (USA ISSN 1064-1262) **3605**
Reviews in Fluorescence (USA ISSN 1573-8086) **2105**
Reviews in Food and Nutrition Toxicity (USA ISSN 1933-4486) **6668**
• Reviews in Gastroenterological Disorders (USA ISSN 1533-001X) **5930**
• ➤ Reviews in History (GBR ISSN 1749-8155) **4158**
Reviews in Infectious Diseases (USA ISSN 1548-3363) **5825**
➤ Reviews in Inorganic Chemistry (ISR ISSN 0193-4929) **2118**
• ➤ Reviews in Mathematical Physics (SGP ISSN 0129-055X) **7037**
• ➤ Reviews in Medical Microbiology (USA ISSN 0954-139X) **5703**
• ➤ Reviews in Medical Virology (GBR ISSN 1052-9276) **895**
• ➤ Reviews in Mineralogy and Geochemistry (USA ISSN 1529-6466) **6477**
• Reviews in Neurological Diseases (USA ISSN 1545-2913) **6181**
▼ Reviews in Obstetrics and Gynecology (USA ISSN 1941-2797) **6003**
• Reviews in Religion and Theology (GBR ISSN 1350-7303) **7677**
➤ Reviews in the Neurosciences (ISR ISSN 0334-1763) **6181**
• ➤ Reviews in Toxicology (NLD ISSN 1382-6980) **3501**
Reviews in Urology (USA ISSN 1523-6161) **6274**
▼ • Reviews of Accelerator Science and Technology (SGP ISSN 1793-6268) **7903**
Reviews of Environmental Contamination and Toxicology (USA ISSN 0179-5953) **3501**
• ➤ Reviews of Geophysics (USA ISSN 8755-1209) **2788**
• ➤ Reviews of Health Promotion and Education Online (FRA) **7538**
• ➤ Reviews of Modern Physics (USA ISSN 0034-6861) **7037**
Reviews of National Policies for Education (FRA ISSN 1563-4914) **3030**
➤ Reviews of Oculomotor Research (NLD ISSN 0168-8375) **6051**
• ➤ Reviews of Physiology, Biochemistry and Pharmacology (USA ISSN 0303-4240) **927**
Reviews of Plasma Chemistry (USA) **2078**
➤ Reviews of Plasma Physics (USA ISSN 0080-2050) **7037**
• Reviews on Advanced Materials Science (RUS ISSN 1605-8127) **3356**
Reviews on Environmental Health (ISR ISSN 0048-7554) **3463**
➤ Reviews on Heteroatom Chemistry (JPN ISSN 0915-6151) **2078**
Reviews on Immunoassay Technology (GBR ISSN 0952-7168) **5765**
• ➤ Reviews on Recent Clinical Trials (NLD ISSN 1574-8871) **5704**
▼ • Reviisori (FIN ISSN 1796-9212) **7466**
Reviista da A B R A P L I P *see* A B R A P L I P. Revista **5247**
Revija 92 (SRB ISSN 0353-507X) **3945**
Revija N A T O *see* N A T O Review (Online) **7156**
Revija o Konjih (SVN ISSN 1318-3109) **298**
Revija Obrazovanja (SRB ISSN 0351-0697) **2905**
Revija Rada (SRB) **7178**
Revija za Elementarno Izobrazevanje/Journal of Elementary Education (SVN ISSN 1855-4431) **2905**
Revija za Kriminalistiko in Kriminologijo (SVN ISSN 0034-690X) **2667**
Revija za Kriminologiju i Krivicno Pravo (SRB ISSN 1820-2969) **2667**
• ➤ Revija za Socijalnu Politiku (HRV ISSN 1330-2965) **8065**
Revija za Sociologiju/Sociological Review (HRV ISSN 0350-154X) **8128**
• Revised Consolidated Index (CAN ISSN 1910-2844) **4939**
• The Revised Uniform Partnership Act (USA ISSN 1524-2757) **4879**
• Revision & Regnskabsvaesen (DNK ISSN 0034-6918) **1300**
➤ Revisiones en Cancer (ESP ISSN 0213-8573) **6033**
• Le Revisioni dei Veicoli (ITA ISSN 1824-5617) **8510**
Revisioning Philosophy (USA ISSN 0899-9937) **6948**
The Revisionist (USA ISSN 1542-376X) **4158**
Revisionist History (SWE ISSN 0348-9078) **4257**
Revisions (USA) **6948**
Revisjon og Regnskap (NOR ISSN 0332-7795) **1300**
Revisor (NLD ISSN 0302-8852) **5236**
Revisor Posten (DNK ISSN 0108-9196) **1942**
• Revisorbladet (DNK ISSN 0106-5203) **1300**
Revisorhaandbogen *see* Revisorhaandbogen, Revision **1300**
Revisorhaandbogen *see* Revisorhaandbogen, Regnskab **1300**
• Revisorhaandbogen, Regnskab (DNK ISSN 1399-5995) **1300**
• Revisorhaandbogen, Revision (DNK ISSN 1399-5987) **1300**
• Revisorn Informerar (SWE ISSN 1402-6597) **1300**
Revista *see* Asociacion de Ferreterias, Pinturerias y Bazares de la Republica Argentina. Revista **1053**
La Revista (ARG) **3792**
• ReVista (Cambridge) (USA ISSN 1541-1443) **4310**
La Revista (Long Island City) (USA) **3561**
Revista 13 Grafico (GTM) **3874**
Revista 22 *see* 22 **3934**
Revista A B E N G E *see* Revista de Ensino de Engenharia **3217**
Revista A B I G R A F *see* Associacao Brasileira da Industria Grafica. Revista **7318**
Revista A B N T (Associacao Brasileira de Normas Tecnicas) (BRA ISSN 0102-9789) **6405**
Revista A B O Nacional (Associacao Brasileira de Odontologia) (BRA ISSN 0104-3072) **5863**
Revista A B R A V A (Associacao Brasileira de Refrigeracao, Ar Condicionado, Ventilacao e Aquecimento) (BRA ISSN 0100-9087) **4126**
• ➤ Revista A C B (Associacao Catarinense de Bibliotecarios) (BRA ISSN 1414-0594) **5043**
Revista A C I E M (Asociacion Colombiana de Ingenieros Electricistas, Mecanicos, Electronicos y Afines) (COL ISSN 0121-9715) **3217**
Revista A C O M A C (Asociacion de Comerciantes en Materiales para Construccion y Afines) (ARG) **1033**
Revista A C O R *see* Azucarera Cooperativa "Onesimo Redondo". Revista **220**
Revista A C P (PRT ISSN 0870-273X) **8601**
• ➤ Revista A D M (Asociacion Dental Mexicana) (MEX ISSN 0001-0944) **5863**
Revista A I B D A *see* Asociacion Interamericana de Bibliotecarios y Documentalistas Agricolas. Revista **4992**
• ➤ Revista A M R I G S (Associacao Medica do Rio Grande do Sul) (BRA ISSN 0102-2105) **5704**
Revista A S O C O L D R O (Asociacion Colombiana de Droguistas Detallistas) (COL ISSN 0121-9073) **6878**
Revista A T E M C O P *see* A T E M C O P **3258**
Revista Academica (BRA ISSN 0103-989X) **4472**
Revista Acento (ARG) **5433**
Revista Acodal (COL ISSN 0120-0798) **3512**
Revista Acta Medica de Puno *see* Acta Medica Puno **5566**
Revista Aerea (USA ISSN 0279-4519) **68**
Revista Aeronautica (COL ISSN 0034-6942) **68**
Revista Africa y Medio Oriente (CUB) **3789**
Revista Agronomia *see* Agronomia **87**
Revista Agronomica del Noroeste Argentino (ARG ISSN 0080-2069) **150**
Revista Agropecuaria (CRI ISSN 0048-7597) **150**
Revista Agropecuario de Manfredi y Marcos Juarez (ARG ISSN 0327-151X) **250**
Revista Agustiniana (ESP ISSN 0211-612X) **7814**
• ➤ Revista Alcance (Online) (BRA ISSN 1983-716X) **150**
Revista Alcance (Print) *see* Revista Alcance (Online) **150**
Revista Alentejana *see* Revista Alentejo **5236**
Revista Alentejo (PRT) **5236**
• ➤ Revista Alergia Mexico (MEX) **5765**
• Revista Alicantina de Estudios Ingleses (ESP ISSN 0214-4808) **5166**
Revista Amae Educando (BRA) **3030**
• Revista Ambiente & Agua (BRA ISSN 1980-993X) **3463**
Revista Analecta *see* Analecta **2826**
Revista ANAPORC *see* Asociacion Nacional de Porcinocultura Cientifica (A N A P O R C). Revista **279**
Revista Andaluza de Administracion Publica *see* Administracion de Andalucia **7487**
Revista Andaluza de Medicina del Deporte (ESP ISSN 1888-7546) **6232**
• Revista Andaluza de Patologia Digestiva (ESP ISSN 1988-317X) **5930**
• Revista Andina (PER ISSN 0259-9600) **7996**
Revista Anthropos (ESP ISSN 1137-3636) **4472**
Revista Anthropos. Extra (ESP ISSN 1138-0357) **4472**
Revista Apotepac *see* Asociacion Colombiana de Tecnicos de la Industria de la Pulpa, Papel y Carton. Revista **6732**
• Revista Aragonesa de Administracion Publica (ESP ISSN 1133-4797) **7466**
Revista Aranzadi de Derecho Ambiental (ESP ISSN 1695-2588) **4769**
Revista Aranzadi de Derecho y Proceso Penal *see* Revista de Derecho y Proceso Penal **4897**
Revista Archivo Arzobispal de Arequipa (PER) **5043**
Revista Argentina de Agrometeorologia (ARG ISSN 1666-017X) **6394**
Revista Argentina de Andrologia (ARG ISSN 1669-7618) **6274**
Revista Argentina de Anestesiologia (ARG ISSN 0370-7792) **5773**
Revista Argentina de Antropologia Biologica (ARG ISSN 1514-7991) **353**
Revista Argentina de Artroscopia (ARG ISSN 0328-1256) **6232**
Revista Argentina de Bibliotecologia (ARG ISSN 0329-5265) **5043**
Revista Argentina de Bioingenieria (ARG ISSN 0329-5257) **3217**
• Revista Argentina de Cardiologia (ARG ISSN 0034-7000) **5798**
Revista Argentina de Cardiologia (Suplemento) *see* Revista Argentina de Cardiologia **5798**
Revista Argentina de Ciencia Politica (ARG ISSN 0329-3092) **7178**
Revista Argentina de Ciencias Penales (ARG ISSN 0325-9501) **2667**
Revista Argentina de Cirugia (ARG ISSN 0048-7600) **6256**
• ➤ Revista Argentina de Cirugia Cardiovascular (ARG ISSN 1667-5738) **5798**
Revista Argentina de Cirugia Cardiovascular (Separata) *see* Revista Argentina de Cirugia Cardiovascular **5798**
Revista Argentina de Clinica Psicologica (ARG ISSN 0327-6716) **7403**
Revista Argentina de Coloproctologia (ARG ISSN 0326-9620) **5930**
Revista Argentina de Derecho Empresario (ARG ISSN 1669-4058) **4879**
➤ Revista Argentina de Dermatologia (ARG ISSN 0325-2787) **5881**
Revista Argentina de Documentacion Biomedica (ARG ISSN 1668-1967) **5043**
Revista Argentina de Economia Agraria (ARG ISSN 0327-3318) **205**
Revista Argentina de Economia y Ciencias Sociales (ARG ISSN 0328-2058) **1166**
Revista Argentina de Endocrinologia y Metabolismo (ARG ISSN 0326-4610) **5899**
Revista Argentina de Ensenanza de la Ingenieria (ARG ISSN 1515-5838) **2905**
Revista Argentina de Estudios Estrategicos (ARG ISSN 0326-6427) **6443**
Revista Argentina de Estudios Politicos (ARG) **7178**
▼ • ➤ Revista Argentina de Historiografia Linguistica (ARG ISSN 1852-1495) **5166**
• Revista Argentina de Humanidades y Ciencias Sociales (Online) (ARG ISSN 1669-1555) **7996**
Revista Argentina de Lactologia (ARG ISSN 0327-5418) **269**
• Revista Argentina de Linguistica (ARG ISSN 0326-6400) **5166**
Revista Argentina de Mastologia (ARG ISSN 0326-2219) **6256**
Revista Argentina de Micologia (ARG ISSN 0325-4755) **815**
• ➤ Revista Argentina de Microbiologia (ARG ISSN 0325-7541) **895**
• Revista Argentina de Neurocirugia (ARG ISSN 1668-9151) **6181**
• Revista Argentina de Neuropsicologia (ARG ISSN 1668-5415) **6181**
Revista Argentina de Osteologia (ARG ISSN 1666-5139) **6071**
Revista Argentina de Produccion Animal (ARG ISSN 0326-0550) **298**
Revista Argentina de Psicologia (ARG ISSN 0557-6466) **7403**
Revista Argentina de Psicopedagogia (ARG ISSN 1514-5603) **2905**
Revista Argentina de Psiquiatria y Psicologia de la Infancia y de la Adolescencia (ARG ISSN 0325-2434) **6181**
• Revista Argentina de Quemaduras (ARG ISSN 0326-4823) **6071**
Revista Argentina de Radiologia (ARG ISSN 0048-7619) **6207**
Revista Argentina de Residentes de Cirugia (ARG ISSN 0328-9206) **6256**
• Revista Argentina de Sociologia (ARG ISSN 1667-9261) **8128**
Revista Argentina de Transfusion (ARG ISSN 0325-6030) **5941**
Revista Argentina de Urologia (ARG ISSN 0327-3326) **6274**
Revista Argentina de Zoonosis y Enfermedades Infecciosas Emergentes (ARG ISSN 1851-3638) **7538**
Revista Argentina del Torax (ARG ISSN 0327-1595) **6219**
Revista Arhivelor (ROM ISSN 0034-7043) **4257**
▼ Revista Arquitectura & Diseno (CHL ISSN 0718-512X) **456**
• Revista Arvore (BRA ISSN 0100-6762) **3715**
Revista Asea Brown Boveri *see* A B B Review **3293**
Revista Astronomica (ARG ISSN 0374-4272) **580**
† Revista Asturiana de Economia (ESP ISSN 1134-8291) **8985**
Revista Atlantica *see* Revistatlantica de Poesia **5433**
Revista Atlantica-Mediterranea de Prehistoria y Arqueologia Social (ESP ISSN 1138-9435) **413**
Revista Atletismo (PRT) **8330**
Revista Austral de Ciencias Sociales (CHL ISSN 0717-3202) **7996**
Revista Ave Maria *see* Ave Maria **7785**
Revista Baiana de Saude Publica (BRA ISSN 0100-0233) **7538**
Revista Balear d'Arquitectura (ESP) **456**
Revista Banca Central (GTM) **1380**
Revista Bancaria Brasileira (BRA ISSN 0034-706X) **1380**
Revista Bancos y Bancarios de Colombia *see* Bancos y Bancarios de Colombia **1312**
Revista Barbie *see* Barbie **2178**
• Revista Bibliotecii Nationale a Romaniei (ROM ISSN 1224-0184) **5043**
Revista Bigott (VEN ISSN 1315-0588) **4472**
Revista Bilingue *see* Bilingual Review **2831**
Revista Bioanalisis (COL ISSN 1657-4680) **896**
• ➤ Revista Biologia (CUB ISSN 0864-3490) **700**
• Revista Biomedica (MEX ISSN 0188-493X) **5704**
La Revista Blanca F M R *see* La Rivista Bianca F M R **515**
Revista Boliviana de Derecho (BOL ISSN 2070-8157) **4770**
Revista Boliviana de Fisica (BOL ISSN 1562-3823) **7037**
Revista Boliviana de Investigacion (BOL) **7996**
Revista Bosque *see* Bosque **3685**
Revista Brasil Nuclear *see* Brasil Nuclear **3165**
Revista Brasileira de Administracao (BRA ISSN 1517-2007) **7466**
Revista Brasileira de Administracao Publica e de Empresas (BRA ISSN 1516-7429) **7466**
Revista Brasileira de Agrociencia (BRA ISSN 0104-8996) **150**
Revista Brasileira de Agrocomputacao (BRA ISSN 1676-0425) **151**
Revista Brasileira de Agrometeorologia (BRA ISSN 0104-1347) **6394**
Revista Brasileira de Alergia e Imunopatologia (BRA ISSN 0103-2259) **5765**
Revista Brasileira de Analise do Comportamento (BRA ISSN 1807-8338) **7403**
Revista Brasileira de Analise Transacional (BRA ISSN 1517-8668) **7403**
Revista Brasileira de Analises Clinicas (BRA ISSN 0370-369X) **5910**
• Revista Brasileira de Anestesiologia (BRA ISSN 0034-7094) **5773**
Revista Brasileira de Angiologia e Cirugia Vascular (BRA ISSN 0102-8537) **5798**
Revista Brasileira de Aplicacoes de Vacuo/Brazilian Journal of Vacuum Applications (BRA ISSN 0101-7659) **3394**
• Revista Brasileira de Aprendizagem Aberta a Distancia/Brazilian Review of Open and Distance Learning/Revista Brasilena de Aprendizaje Abierto y a Distancia (BRA ISSN 1806-1362) **2905**
Revista Brasileira de Armazenamento (BRA ISSN 0100-3518) **151**
Revista Brasileira de Atividade Fisica & Saude (BRA ISSN 1413-3482) **6996**
Revista Brasileira de Biblioteconomia e Documentacao (BRA ISSN 0100-0691) **5043**
• Revista Brasileira de Biociencias/Brazilian Journal of Biosciences (BRA ISSN 1679-2343) **700**
Revista Brasileira de Bioetica (BRA ISSN 1808-6020) **700**
• ➤ Revista Brasileira de Botanica/Brazilian Journal of Botany (BRA ISSN 0100-8404) **815**
Revista Brasileira de Cancerologia (BRA ISSN 0034-7116) **6033**
Revista Brasileira de Cardiologia Invasiva (BRA ISSN 0104-1843) **5798**
• ➤ Revista Brasileira de Cartografia (BRA ISSN 0560-4613) **4026**
• Revista Brasileira de Ciencia Avicola/Brazilian Journal of Poultry Science (BRA ISSN 1516-635X) **298**
• Revista Brasileira de Ciencia do Solo (BRA ISSN 0100-0683) **250**
Revista Brasileira de Ciencia e Movimento (BRA) **6232**

DIRECTORY 2010 REVISTA CHILENA DE MEDICINA LEGAL 10807

Revista Brasileira de Ciencia e Tecnologia Aquatica *see* Brazilian Journal of Aquatic Science and Technology **2793**
Revista Brasileira de Ciencia Politica (BRA ISSN 0103-3352) **7178**
Revista Brasileira de Ciencia Veterinaria (BRA ISSN 1413-0130) **8806**
Revista Brasileira de Ciencias Criminais (BRA ISSN 1415-5400) **4897**
Revista Brasileira de Ciencias da Saude (BRA ISSN 1678-054X) **5704**
● Revista Brasileira de Ciencias do Envelhecimento Humano (BRA ISSN 1679-7930) **4054**
Revista Brasileira de Ciencias do Esporte (BRA ISSN 0101-3289) **8196**
Revista Brasileira de Ciencias Farmaceuticas *see* B J P S Brazilian Journal of Pharmaceutical Sciences **6824**
● Revista Brasileira de Ciencias Morfologicas/Brazilian Journal of Morphological Sciences (BRA ISSN 0102-9010) **927**
● ➤ Revista Brasileira de Ciencias Sociais (BRA ISSN 0102-6909) **7996**
● Revista Brasileira de Cineantropometria & Desempenho Humano (BRA ISSN 1415-8426) **6996**
Revista Brasileira de Cirugia, Protese e Traumatologia Buco - Maxilo - Facial (BRA ISSN 0102-0900) **5863**
● Revista Brasileira de Cirurgia Cardiovascular/ Brazilian Journal of Cardiovascular Surgery (BRA ISSN 0102-7638) **5798**
Revista Brasileira de Cirurgia da Cabeca e Pescoco (BRA ISSN 0100-2171) **6256**
● Revista Brasileira de Coloproctologia (BRA ISSN 0101-9880) **6256**
Revista Brasileira de Comercio Exterior (BRA ISSN 0102-5074) **1581**
Revista Brasileira de Contabilidade (BRA ISSN 0104-8341) **1300**
➤ Revista Brasileira de Crescimento e Desenvolvimento Humano (BRA ISSN 0104-1282) **6103**
Revista Brasileira de Desenvolvimento Regional (BRA ISSN 1807-0167) **1515**
Revista Brasileira de Direito Ambiental (BRA ISSN 1807-9962) **4770**
Revista Brasileira de Direito Comparado (BRA ISSN 1517-2163) **4770**
➤ Revista Brasileira de Direito Constitucional (BRA ISSN 1678-9547) **4852**
Revista Brasileira de Direito Desportivo (BRA ISSN 1677-3756) **4770**
➤ Revista Brasileira de Direito Municipal (BRA ISSN 1808-5628) **4770**
➤ Revista Brasileira de Direito Processual (BRA ISSN 0100-2589) **4770**
Revista Brasileira de Direito Publico (BRA ISSN 1678-7072) **4770**
● Revista Brasileira de Economia (BRA ISSN 0034-7140) **1166**
Revista Brasileira de Economia de Empresas (BRA ISSN 1676-8000) **1166**
● Revista Brasileira de Educacao (BRA ISSN 1413-2478) **2905**
Revista Brasileira de Educacao a Distancia (BRA ISSN 0104-4141) **2905**
● Revista Brasileira de Educacao Especial (BRA ISSN 1413-6538) **3046**
● ➤ Revista Brasileira de Educacao Medica (BRA ISSN 0100-5502) **5704**
Revista Brasileira de Energia (BRA ISSN 0104-303X) **3147**
● ➤ Revista Brasileira de Enfermagem (BRA ISSN 0034-7167) **5980**
● ➤ Revista Brasileira de Engenharia Agricola e Ambiental (BRA ISSN 1415-4366) **151**
Revista Brasileira de Engenharia Biomedica (BRA ISSN 1517-3151) **5704**
Revista Brasileira de Engenharia. Caderno de Engenharia Eletrica (BRA ISSN 0102-2660) **3329**
Revista Brasileira de Engenharia. Caderno de Engenharia Naval (BRA ISSN 0102-2679) **3217**
Revista Brasileira de Engenharia. Caderno de Engenharia Nuclear (BRA ISSN 0102-7670) **3174**
Revista Brasileira de Engenharia Quimica (BRA ISSN 0102-9843) **3254**
● Revista Brasileira de Ensino de Bioquimica e Biologia Molecular (BRA ISSN 1677-2318) **744**
● Revista Brasileira de Ensino de Fisica (BRA ISSN 1806-1117) **7037**
● ➤ Revista Brasileira de Entomologia (BRA ISSN 0085-5626) **857**
● ➤ Revista Brasileira de Epidemiologia (BRA ISSN 1415-790X) **7538**
Revista Brasileira de Estatistica/Brazilian Statistical Journal (BRA ISSN 0034-7175) **8396**
▼ ➤ Revista Brasileira de Estudos Constitucionais (BRA ISSN 1981-6162) **4852**
● Revista Brasileira de Estudos de Populacao (BRA ISSN 0102-3098) **7292**
● ➤ Revista Brasileira de Estudos Pedagogicos (BRA ISSN 0034-7183) **2905**
Revista Brasileira de Estudos Politicos (BRA ISSN 0034-7191) **7178**
Revista Brasileira de Estudos Urbanos e Regionais (BRA ISSN 1517-4115) **456**
Revista Brasileira de Farmacia (BRA ISSN 0370-372X) **6878**
Revista Brasileira de Farmacognosia (BRA ISSN 0102-695X) **6878**
➤ Revista Brasileira de Financas (BRA ISSN 1679-0731) **1380**
Revista Brasileira de Fisiologia do Exercicio (BRA ISSN 1677-8510) **6996**
● ➤ Revista Brasileira de Fisioterapia (BRA ISSN 1413-3555) **6115**
● Revista Brasileira de Fruticultura (BRA ISSN 0100-2945) **250**
● Revista Brasileira de Geociencias (BRA ISSN 0375-7536) **2715**
● Revista Brasileira de Geofisica/Brazilian Journal of Geophysics (BRA ISSN 0102-261X) **2788**
Revista Brasileira de Geografia/Brazilian Geographic Journal (BRA ISSN 0034-723X) **4026**
Revista Brasileira de Geomorfologia (BRA ISSN 1519-1540) **2715**
Revista Brasileira de Gerenciamento de Projetos (BRA ISSN 1679-902X) **1790**
● Revista Brasileira de Gestao de Negocios (BRA ISSN 1806-4892) **1166**
● ➤ Revista Brasileira de Gestao e Desenvolvimento Regional (BRA ISSN 1809-239X) **1604**
● Revista Brasileira de Ginecologia e Obstetricia (BRA ISSN 0100-7203) **6003**
● Revista Brasileira de Hematologia e Hemoterapia (BRA ISSN 1516-8484) **5941**
● Revista Brasileira de Herbicidas (Online) (BRA ISSN 1517-9443) **250**
Revista Brasileira de Hipertensao (BRA ISSN 1519-7522) **5798**
Revista Brasileira de Hipnose (BRA ISSN 1516-232X) **5943**
● ➤ Revista Brasileira de Historia (BRA ISSN 0102-0188) **4310**
Revista Brasileira de Historia da Matematica (BRA ISSN 1519-955X) **5529**
Revista Brasileira de Historia de Educacao (BRA ISSN 1519-5902) **2905**
● Revista Brasileira de Horticultura Ornamental (BRA ISSN 1414-039X) **3749**
Revista Brasileira de Implantodontia (BRA ISSN 1413-5388) **5863**
Revista Brasileira de Informacao Bibliografica em Ciencias Sociais *see* B I B. Revista Brasileira de Informacao Bibliografica em Ciencias Sociais **616**
Revista Brasileira de Inovacao (BRA ISSN 1677-2504) **8436**
Revista Brasileira de Letras (BRA ISSN 1806-7352) **5360**
Revista Brasileira de Linguistica (BRA ISSN 0102-6798) **5166**
Revista Brasileira de Linguistica Aplicada (BRA ISSN 1676-0786) **5166**
➤ Revista Brasileira de Medicina (BRA ISSN 0034-7264) **5704**
● Revista Brasileira de Medicina do Esporte/Brazilian Journal of Sports Medicine (BRA ISSN 1517-8692) **6232**
Revista Brasileira de Medicina do Trabalho (BRA ISSN 1679-4435) **5704**
Revista Brasileira de Mercado de Capitais (BRA ISSN 0102-9797) **1167**
● Revista Brasileira de Meteorologia (BRA ISSN 0102-7786) **6394**
Revista Brasileira de Milho e Sorgo/Brazilian Journal of Maize and Sorghum (BRA ISSN 1676-689X) **275**
Revista Brasileira de Musica (BRA ISSN 0103-7595) **6611**
Revista Brasileira de Neurologia (BRA ISSN 0101-8469) **6181**
➤ Revista Brasileira de Neurologia e Psiquiatria (BRA ISSN 1414-0365) **6181**
Revista Brasileira de Nutricao Clinica (BRA ISSN 0103-7196) **6668**
Revista Brasileira de Oceanografia (BRA ISSN 1413-7739) **2817**
Revista Brasileira de Odontologia (BRA ISSN 0034-7272) **5863**
● Revista Brasileira de Oftalmologia (BRA ISSN 0034-7280) **6051**
Revista Brasileira de Oncologia Clinica (BRA ISSN 1806-6054) **6033**
Revista Brasileira de Orientacao Profissional (BRA ISSN 1679-3390) **6703**
● Revista Brasileira de Ortopedia/Brazilian Journal of Orthopaedics (BRA ISSN 0102-3616) **6072**
Revista Brasileira de Ortopedia Pediatrica (BRA ISSN 1518-8698) **6072**
● ➤ Revista Brasileira de Otorrinolaringologia (BRA ISSN 0034-7299) **6084**
● Revista Brasileira de Paleontologia (BRA ISSN 1519-7530) **6730**
➤ Revista Brasileira de Parasitologia Veterinaria/Brazilian Journal of Veterinary Parasitology (BRA ISSN 0103-846X) **8806**
● Revista Brasileira de Patologia Oral (BRA ISSN 1677-9630) **5863**
Revista Brasileira de Pesquisa e Desenvolvimento/Research and Development Brazilian Journal (BRA ISSN 0104-7698) **3174**
Revista Brasileira de Pesquisa em Educacao em Ciencias (BRA ISSN 1806-5104) **7903**
Revista Brasileira de Plantas Medicinais/Brazilian Journal of Medicinal Plants (BRA ISSN 1516-0572) **815**
Revista Brasileira de Politica e Administracao da Educacao (BRA ISSN 1678-166X) **2905**
● ➤ Revista Brasileira de Politica Internacional (BRA ISSN 0034-7329) **7262**
Revista Brasileira de Pos - Graduacao (BRA ISSN 1806-8405) **6703**
Revista Brasileira de Produtos Agroindustriais (BRA ISSN 1517-8595) **151**
Revista Brasileira de Protese - Periodontia - Oclusao (BRA ISSN 0104-9410) **5863**
● Revista Brasileira de Psicanalise (BRA ISSN 0486-641X) **7403**
Revista Brasileira de Psicodrama (BRA ISSN 0104-5393) **6181**
Revista Brasileira de Psicoterapia (BRA ISSN 1516-8530) **6181**
● ➤ Revista Brasileira de Psiquiatria (BRA ISSN 1516-4446) **6181**
Revista Brasileira de Recursos Hidricos *see* R B R H **3364**
Revista Brasileira de Reproducao Animal (Online) (BRA ISSN 0102-0803) **961**
Revista Brasileira de Reproducao Animal (Print) *see* Revista Brasileira de Reproducao Animal (Online) **961**
● ➤ Revista Brasileira de Reumatologia/Brazilian Journal of Rheumatology (BRA ISSN 0482-5004) **6226**
● Revista Brasileira de Risco e Seguro (BRA ISSN 1808-0723) **4521**
Revista Brasileira de Saude da Familia (BRA ISSN 1518-2355) **7538**
● Revista Brasileira de Saude e Producao Animal (BRA ISSN 1519-9940) **961**
Revista Brasileira de Saude Escolar/Brazilian Journal of School Health (BRA ISSN 1413-3415) **7538**
● Revista Brasileira de Saude Materno Infantil/Brazilian Journal of Mother and Child Health (BRA ISSN 1519-3829) **2167**
● Revista Brasileira de Saude Ocupacional (BRA ISSN 0303-7657) **6685**
● Revista Brasileira de Sementes/Brazilian Seed Journal (BRA ISSN 0101-3122) **250**
Revista Brasileira de Sexualidade Humana (BRA ISSN 0103-6122) **927**
Revista Brasileira de Terapia Comportamental e Cognitiva (BRA ISSN 1517-5545) **5704**
Revista Brasileira de Terapia Floral (BRA ISSN 1414-6231) **314**
● Revista Brasileira de Terapia Intensiva (BRA ISSN 0103-507X) **5704**
Revista Brasileira de Terapias Cognitivas/Brazilian Journal of Cognitive Therapies (BRA ISSN 1808-5687) **6181**
Revista Brasileira de Toxicologia (BRA ISSN 1415-2983) **3501**
Revista Brasileira de Ultra - Sonografia (BRA ISSN 1679-8953) **6207**
● Revista Brasileira de Videocirurgia (BRA ISSN 1678-7137) **6256**
Revista Brasileira de Vigilancia Sanitaria/Brazilian Journal of Health Surveillance (BRA ISSN 1807-8923) **7539**
Revista Brasileira de Xadrez Postal (BRA) **8196**
● Revista Brasileira de Zoociencias (BRA ISSN 1517-6770) **961**
Revista Brasileira de Zoologia *see* Zoologia (Curitiba) **969**
● Revista Brasileira de Zootecnia/Brazilian Journal of Animal Science (BRA ISSN 1516-3598) **8806**
Revista Brasileira e Latino - Americana de Marcapasso e Arritmia (BRA ISSN 0104-8317) **5798**
● Revista Brasileira em Promocao da Saude (BRA ISSN 1806-1222) **7539**
Revista Brasilena de Aprendizaje Abierto y a Distancia *see* Revista Brasileira de Aprendizagem Aberta a Distancia **2905**
Revista Brasindoor (BRA ISSN 1519-4108) **3463**
● Revista C & T (Ciencia y Tecnologia) (CHL ISSN 0717-2664) **7903**
● Revista C E N I C. Ciencias Biologicas (CUB ISSN 0253-5688) **700**
● Revista C E N I C. Ciencias Quimicas (CUB ISSN 1015-8553) **2078**
● ➤ Revista C E N I P E C (VEN ISSN 0798-9202) **2667**
Revista C N I (BRA ISSN 0104-1029) **1167**
Revista C V (ESP) **3147**
Revista Cadernos de Seguro *see* Cadernos de Seguro **4497**
Revista Cafetera de Colombia (COL ISSN 0120-2278) **3662**
Revista Camacol *see* Camara Colombiana de la Construccion. Revista **989**
Revista Camacol Valle *see* C A M A C O L Valle. Revista **3261**
Revista Caminhoneiro (BRA) **8675**
Revista Camoes *see* Camoes **4446**
➤ Revista Canadiense de Estudios Hispanicos (CAN ISSN 0384-8167) **5360**
● Revista Canaria de Estudios Ingleses (ESP ISSN 0211-5913) **5167**
Revista Canaria de Filosofia y Ciencia Social (ESP ISSN 0212-8780) **6948**
Revista C&T *see* Revista C & T **7903**
Revista Canopus *see* Canopus **573**
Revista Capital Cientifico (BRA ISSN 1679-1991) **7996**
● Revista Cartografica (MEX ISSN 0080-2085) **4026**
Revista Casa de la Mujer (CRI) **8902**
● Revista Casa Silva (COL ISSN 0121-4667) **5433**
Revista Castilla (ESP ISSN 0378-200X) **5361**
● Revista Catalana de Dret Privat (ESP ISSN 1695-5633) **4770**
● Revista Catalana de Dret Public (ESP ISSN 1885-5709) **4770**
Revista Catalana de Micologia (ESP ISSN 1135-1225) **700**
Revista Catalana de Musicologia (ESP ISSN 1578-5297) **6611**
Revista Catalana de Pedagogia (ESP ISSN 1695-5641) **2905**
Revista Catalana de Psicoanalisi (ESP ISSN 0212-9205) **7403**
Revista Catalana de Sociologia (ESP ISSN 1136-8527) **8128**
● ➤ Revista Catalana d'Ornitologia (ESP ISSN 1697-4697) **913**
Revista Catarinense de Odontologia (BRA ISSN 0100-7955) **5863**
La Revista Catolica (CHL ISSN 0716-033X) **7814**
Revista Cauce *see* Cauce **5105**
Revista Cearense de Odontologia (BRA ISSN 1677-7719) **5863**
Revista Ceciliana (BRA ISSN 1517-6363) **4472**
Revista CEJ *see* C E J. Revista **4635**
Revista Central de Sociologia (CHL ISSN 0718-4379) **7996**
Revista Centroamericana de Administracion Publica (CRI) **7466**
Revista Centroamericana de Economia (HND ISSN 0254-4210) **1515**
➤ Revista Ceres (BRA ISSN 0034-737X) **151**
● Revista Chacarera (PER) **8882**
● Revista Chapingo. Serie Ciencias Forestales y del Ambiente (MEX) **3700**
Revista Chapingo. Serie Horticultura (MEX ISSN 1027-152X) **3749**
Revista Chilena Cooperacion (CHL ISSN 0717-313X) **7466**
Revista Chilena de Administracion Publica (CHL ISSN 0717-070X) **7466**
Revista Chilena de Anatomia *see* International Journal of Morphology **5639**
Revista Chilena de Anestesia (CHL ISSN 0716-4076) **5774**
Revista Chilena de Antropologia (CHL ISSN 0716-3312) **353**
● Revista Chilena de Antropologia Visual (CHL ISSN 0717-876X) **353**
Revista Chilena de Cancerologia y Hematologia (CHL ISSN 0717-3210) **6033**
Revista Chilena de Cardiologia (CHL ISSN 0716-7105) **5798**
Revista Chilena de Ciencias Medico - Biologicas (CHL ISSN 0716-9337) **5704**
● Revista Chilena de Cirugia (CHL ISSN 0379-3893) **6256**
● Revista Chilena de Derecho (CHL ISSN 0716-0747) **4770**
Revista Chilena de Derecho Informatico (CHL ISSN 0717-9162) **4770**
Revista Chilena de Derecho Privado (CHL ISSN 0718-0233) **4841**
Revista Chilena de Dermatologia (CHL ISSN 0717-2273) **5881**
Revista Chilena de Diseno (CHL ISSN 0718-2430) **456**
Revista Chilena de Docencia e Investigacion en Salud (CHL ISSN 0717-1137) **2905**
Revista Chilena de Educacion Cientifica (CHL ISSN 0717-9618) **7903**
Revista Chilena de Educacion Matematica (CHL ISSN 0718-1213) **5529**
▼ Revista Chilena de Endocrinologia y Diabetes (CHL ISSN 0718-493X) **5899**
Revista Chilena de Enfermedades de Transmision Sexual (CHL ISSN 0716-4041) **5881**
● Revista Chilena de Enfermedades Respiratorias (CHL ISSN 0717-5698) **6219**
➤ Revista Chilena de Entomologia (CHL ISSN 0034-740X) **858**
● Revista Chilena de Epilepsia (CHL ISSN 0717-5337) **6181**
● ➤ Revista Chilena de Estudiantes de Medicina (CHL ISSN 0718-6711) **5704**
Revista Chilena de Fonoaudiologia (CHL ISSN 0717-4659) **6084**
Revista Chilena de Historia del Derecho (CHL ISSN 0716-5447) **4770**
● ➤ Revista Chilena de Historia Natural (CHL ISSN 0716-078X) **700**
➤ Revista Chilena de Historia y Geografia (CHL ISSN 0716-2812) **4310**
● Revista Chilena de Humanidades (CHL ISSN 0716-4181) **7996**
● Revista Chilena de Infectologia (CHL ISSN 0716-1018) **5825**
Revista Chilena de Ingenieria (CHL ISSN 0370-4009) **3217**
Revista Chilena de Investigacion Educacional (CHL ISSN 0717-0211) **2905**
● ➤ Revista Chilena de Literatura (CHL ISSN 0048-7651) **5361**
Revista Chilena de Medicina del Sueno (CHL ISSN 0718-4190) **6181**
Revista Chilena de Medicina Familiar (CHL ISSN 0717-5965) **5704**
Revista Chilena de Medicina Intensiva (CHL ISSN 0717-5833) **6072**
Revista Chilena de Medicina Legal (CHL ISSN 0716-1751) **5704**

Title

10808 REVISTA CHILENA DE NEUROCIRUGIA ULRICH'S PERIODICALS

• Revista Chilena de Neurocirugia (CHL ISSN 0716-4491) **6256**
• Revista Chilena de Neuropsicologia (CHL ISSN 0718-0551) **6181**
• Revista Chilena de Neuropsiquiatria (CHL ISSN 0034-7388) **6181**
• Revista Chilena de Nutricion (CHL ISSN 0716-1549) **6668**
Revista Chilena de Obesidad (CHL ISSN 0716-6931) **6668**
• Revista Chilena de Obstetricia y Ginecologia (CHL ISSN 0048-766X) **6003**
Revista Chilena de Obstetricia y Ginecologia Infantil y de la Adolescencia (CHL ISSN 0717-0815) **6003**
Revista Chilena de Ortodoncia (CHL ISSN 0716-3614) **5863**
Revista Chilena de Ortopedia y Traumatologia (CHL ISSN 0716-4548) **6072**
• Revista Chilena de Pediatria (CHL ISSN 0370-4106) **6103**
Revista Chilena de Periodoncia y Oseointegracion (CHL ISSN 0718-1140) **5863**
➤ Revista Chilena de Psicoanalisis (CHL ISSN 0716-3649) **7403**
Revista Chilena de Psicologia (CHL ISSN 0716-3630) **7403**
• Revista Chilena de Psicologia Clinica/Chilean Journal of Clinical Psychology (CHL ISSN 0718-3666) **7403**
• Revista Chilena de Psiquiatria y Neurologia de la Infancia y la Adolescencia (CHL) **6181**
• Revista Chilena de Radiologia (CHL ISSN 0717-201X) **6207**
Revista Chilena de Salud Publica (CHL ISSN 0717-3652) **7539**
• Revista Chilena de Semiotica (CHL ISSN 0717-3075) **5167**
• Revista Chilena de Tecnologia Medica (CHL ISSN 0716-0135) **5704**
Revista Chilena de Temas Sociologicos (CHL ISSN 0717-2087) **8128**
Revista Chilena de Terapia Ocupacional (CHL ISSN 0717-6767) **6115**
• Revista Chilena de Ultrasonografia (CHL ISSN 0717-3695) **6207**
Revista Chilena de Urologia (CHL ISSN 0716-0429) **6274**
Revista Chilena en Venta (CHL) **634**
• ➤ Revista Ciencia e Ingenieria Neogranadina (COL ISSN 0124-8170) **7903**
Revista Ciencia Policial (ESP) **2667**
Revista Ciencia y Tecnologia para la Salud Visual y Ocular (COL ISSN 1692-8415) **6051**
• ➤ Revista Ciencias de la Educacion (VEN ISSN 1316-5917) **2905**
• Revista Ciencias de la Salud (COL ISSN 1692-7273) **5704**
Revista Ciencias Exactas e Naturais (BRA ISSN 1518-0352) **7903**
Revista Ciencias Humanas *see* Ciencias Humanas **5210**
Revista Ciencias Sociais (BRA ISSN 1413-8999) **7996**
Revista Ciencias Sociales (ECU ISSN 0252-8681) **7996**
• Revista Ciencias Tecnicas Agropecuarias (CUB ISSN 1010-2760) **151**
Revista Cientifica (COL ISSN 0124-2253) **7903**
Revista Cientifica Alimentaria (PER ISSN 1990-9225) **3662**
Revista Cientifica de Informacion y Comunicacion (ESP ISSN 1696-2508) **2337**
• Revista Cientifica de U C E S (Universidad de Ciencias Empresariales y Sociales) (ARG ISSN 1514-9358) **1790**
Revista Cine Cubano *see* Cine Cubano **6492**
Revista Clinica de Ortodontia Dental Press (BRA ISSN 1676-6849) **5863**
• Revista Clinica Espanola (ESP ISSN 0014-2565) **5704**
• Revista Co-herencia (COL ISSN 1794-5887) **4472**
Revista Colombiana de Anestesiologia (COL ISSN 0120-3347) **5774**
➤ Revista Colombiana de Antropologia (COL ISSN 0486-6525) **353**
• Revista Colombiana de Biotecnologia (COL ISSN 0123-3475) **770**
• Revista Colombiana de Cancerologia (COL ISSN 0123-9015) **6033**
• Revista Colombiana de Cardiologia (COL ISSN 0120-5633) **5799**
• ➤ Revista Colombiana de Ciencias Pecuarias (COL ISSN 0120-0690) **8806**
• Revista Colombiana de Ciencias Quimico Farmaceuticas (COL ISSN 0034-7418) **6878**
• Revista Colombiana de Cirugia (COL ISSN 0120-856X) **6256**
Revista Colombiana de Cirugia Plastica y Reconstructiva (COL ISSN 0121-2729) **6256**
➤ Revista Colombiana de Educacion (COL ISSN 0120-3916) **2905**
Revista Colombiana de Entomologia (COL ISSN 0120-0488) **858**
Revista Colombiana de Estadistica (COL ISSN 0120-1751) **8396**
Revista Colombiana de Fisica (COL ISSN 0120-2650) **7037**
• ➤ Revista Colombiana de Gastroenterologia (COL ISSN 0120-9957) **5930**
Revista Colombiana de Investigacion Musical (COL) **6611**
• ➤ Revista Colombiana de Matematicas (COL ISSN 0034-7426) **5529**
Revista Colombiana de Neumologia (COL ISSN 0121-5426) **6219**
• ➤ Revista Colombiana de Obstetricia y Ginecologia (COL ISSN 0034-7434) **6003**
Revista Colombiana de Ortopedia y Traumatologia (COL ISSN 0120-8845) **6072**
Revista Colombiana de Psicologia (COL ISSN 0121-5469) **7403**
• Revista Colombiana de Psiquiatria (COL ISSN 0034-7450) **6181**
Revista Colombiana de Quimica (COL ISSN 0120-2804) **2078**
• ➤ Revista Colombiana de Reumatologia (COL ISSN 0121-8123) **6226**
Revista Colombiana de Sociologia (COL ISSN 0120-159X) **8128**
Revista Colombiana de Tecnologias de Avanzada (COL ISSN 1692-7257) **8436**
Revista Colombiana de Trabajo Social (COL ISSN 0121-2818) **8065**
Revista COMALFI *see* Sociedad Colombiana de Control de Malezas y Fisiologia Vegetal. Revista **253**
Revista Comechingonia *see* Comechingonia **388**
Revista Comercio (ECU) **1409**
Revista Comercio Portuense (PRT) **1432**
Revista Companero (URY) **7178**
• Revista Complutense de Educacion (ESP ISSN 1130-2496) **3000**
• Revista Complutense de Historia de America (ESP ISSN 1132-8312) **4310**
Revista Comunicacoes e Artes (BRA ISSN 0102-0897) **8128**
▼ • Revista Conatus (BRA ISSN 1981-7517) **6948**
Revista Conicyt *see* Revista C & T **7903**
• Revista Contabilidade & Financas (BRA ISSN 1519-7077) **1167**
Revista Contactor (CHL) **3329**
Revista Contribuciones Cientificas y Tecnologicas (CHL ISSN 0716-0127) **7903**
• Revista Corpoica (COL ISSN 0122-8706) **298**
• Revista Costarricense de Cardiologia (CRI ISSN 1409-4142) **5799**
• ➤ Revista Costarricense de Ciencias Medicas (CRI ISSN 0253-2948) **5704**
• Revista Costarricense de Salud Publica (CRI ISSN 1409-1429) **7539**
Revista Cotelco (COL ISSN 0121-7313) **4397**
Revista Crisol (CRI ISSN 1409-150X) **7903**
➤ Revista Critica de Ciencias Sociais (PRT ISSN 0254-1106) **7996**
Revista Critica de Derecho Inmobiliario (ESP ISSN 0210-0444) **4770**
• Revista Cubana de Angiologia y Cirugia Vascular (CUB ISSN 1682-0037) **5799**
• ➤ Revista Cubana de Ciencia Agricola (CUB ISSN 0034-7485) **151**
Revista Cubana de Ciencia Avicola (CUB ISSN 0138-6352) **298**
• Revista Cubana de Ciencias Matematicas (CUB ISSN 0256-5374) **5529**
Revista Cubana de Ciencias Sociales (CUB ISSN 0138-6425) **7996**
Revista Cubana de Ciencias Veterinarias (CUB ISSN 0048-7678) **8806**
• Revista Cubana de Cirugia (CUB ISSN 0034-7493) **6256**
Revista Cubana de Derecho (CUB ISSN 0864-165X) **4770**
• Revista Cubana de Educacion Medica Superior (CUB ISSN 0864-2141) **5704**
• Revista Cubana de Educacion Superior (CUB ISSN 0257-4314) **3000**
• Revista Cubana de Endocrinologia (CUB ISSN 0864-4462) **5900**
• Revista Cubana de Enfermeria (CUB ISSN 0864-0319) **5980**
• Revista Cubana de Estomatologia (CUB ISSN 0034-7507) **5863**
• Revista Cubana de Farmacia (CUB ISSN 0034-7515) **6878**
• Revista Cubana de Fisica (CUB ISSN 0253-9268) **7037**
• Revista Cubana de Genetica Medica (CUB ISSN 1682-6760) **878**
• Revista Cubana de Hematologia, Inmunologia y Hematerapia (CUB ISSN 0864-0289) **5941**
• Revista Cubana de Higiene y Epidemiologia (CUB ISSN 0253-1151) **7539**
• Revista Cubana de Informatica Medica (CUB ISSN 1684-1859) **5832**
• Revista Cubana de Investigaciones Biomedicas (CUB ISSN 0864-0300) **700**
Revista Cubana de Investigaciones Pesqueras. Boletines Bibliograficos (CUB) **3605**
• Revista Cubana de Medicina (CUB ISSN 0034-7523) **5704**
• Revista Cubana de Medicina General Integral (CUB ISSN 0864-2125) **5704**
• Revista Cubana de Medicina Intensiva y Emergencias (CUB ISSN 1810-2352) **6072**
• Revista Cubana de Medicina Militar (CUB ISSN 0138-6557) **5704**
• Revista Cubana de Medicina Tropical (CUB ISSN 0375-0760) **5825**
Revista Cubana de Meteorologia (CUB ISSN 0864-151X) **2715**
Revista Cubana de Nutricion y Alimentacion *see* Revista Cubana de Salud Publica **7539**
• Revista Cubana de Obstetricia y Ginecologia (CUB ISSN 0138-600X) **6003**
• Revista Cubana de Oftalmologia (CUB ISSN 0864-2176) **6051**
• Revista Cubana de Ortodoncia (CUB ISSN 0864-3784) **5863**
• Revista Cubana de Ortopedia y Traumatologia (CUB ISSN 0864-215X) **6072**
• Revista Cubana de Pediatria (CUB ISSN 0034-7531) **6103**
• Revista Cubana de Plantas Medicinales (CUB ISSN 1028-4796) **6878**
• Revista Cubana de Psicologia (CUB ISSN 0257-4322) **7403**
• Revista Cubana de Quimica (CUB ISSN 0258-5995) **2078**
Revista Cubana de Reproduccion Animal (CUB ISSN 0138-6700) **961**
• Revista Cubana de Reumatologia (CUB ISSN 1606-5581) **6226**
• Revista Cubana de Salud Publica (CUB ISSN 0864-3466) **7539**
• Revista Cubana del Arroz (CUB ISSN 1607-6273) **250**
Revista Cuestiones Economicas *see* Cuestiones Economicas **1334**
Revista Cultului Mozaic/Review of the Mosaic Creed (ROM ISSN 0034-754X) **7729**
Revista da A B E M *see* A B E M. Revista **6541**
Revista da A B E N O *see* A B E N O. Revista **5832**
Revista da A B O P *see* A B O P. Revista **6691**
Revista da A B R A L I N *see* A B R A L I N. Revista **5088**
Revista da A B R O *see* Associacao Brasileira de Radiologia Odontologica. Revista **5835**
Revista da A M R I G S *see* Revista A M R I G S **5704**
• ➤ Revista da Ajuris (BRA ISSN 1679-1363) **4770**
Revista da Armada (PRT ISSN 0870-9343) **6443**
Revista da Engenharia Termica (BRA ISSN 1676-1790) **3394**
• Revista da Escola de Minas (BRA ISSN 0370-4467) **3281**
Revista da Faculdade de Direito da Universidade Federal de Minas Gerais *see* Universidade Federal de Minas Gerais. Faculdade de Direito. Revista **4802**
Revista da Faculdade de Direito da Universidade Federal do Parana *see* Universidade Federal do Parana. Faculdade de Direito. Revista **4802**
Revista da Faculdade de Direito Milton Campos *see* Milton Campos. Faculdade de Direito. Revista **4734**
Revista da Faculdade Mineira de Direito (BRA ISSN 1808-9429) **4770**
Revista da Historia da Sociedade e da Cultura (PRT ISSN 1645-2259) **4472**
Revista da Imagem (Online) (BRA) **6207**
Revista da Imagem (Print) *see* Revista da Imagem (Online) **6207**
Revista da Industria (BRA) **1903**
Revista da Madeira (BRA ISSN 0034-7582) **3715**
Revista da S B O (Sociedade Brasileira de Ortodontia) (BRA ISSN 0103-5738) **5863**
Revista da TV *see* Diario Catarinese **3803**
Revista da TV *see* Zero Hora **3804**
Revista da Universidade dos Acores *see* Arquipelago. Serie Ciencias da Natureza **7837**
Revista d'Arqueologia de Ponent (ESP ISSN 1131-883X) **413**
Revista das Edicoes Africanas *see* African Publishing Review **7551**
Revista das Empresas (PRT) **1167**
Revista de Acustica (ESP ISSN 0210-3680) **7089**
• ➤ Revista de Administracao (BRA ISSN 0080-2107) **1790**
Revista de Administracao, Contabilidade e Economia *see* R A C E: Revista de Administracao, Contabilidade e Economia **1163**
• ➤ Revista de Administracao Contemporanea (BRA ISSN 1415-6555) **1790**
Revista de Administracao de Empresas *see* R A E **1788**
Revista de Administracao de Empresas Eletronica *see* R A E Eletronica **1163**
• ➤ Revista de Administracao Mackenzie (Online) (BRA ISSN 1678-6971) **1790**
† • ➤ Revista de Administracao Mackenzie (Print) (BRA ISSN 1518-6776) **8985**
Revista de Administracao Municipal (BRA ISSN 0034-7604) **7501**
• Revista de Administracao Publica (BRA ISSN 0034-7612) **7466**
• Revista de Administracion Publica (ESP ISSN 0034-7639) **7466**
Revista de Administracion Publica/Journal of Public Administration (MEX ISSN 0482-5209) **7466**
Revista de Administracion Publica (PRI ISSN 0034-7620) **7466**
Revista de Administracion Sanitaria Siglo XXI (ESP ISSN 1696-1641) **7539**
Revista de Administracion Tributaria *see* Tax Administration Review **1946**
Revista de Administration Publica Uruguaya (URY ISSN 0797-0056) **7466**
Revista de Aeronautica y Astronautica (ESP ISSN 0034-7647) **68**
• ➤ Revista de Agricultura (BRA ISSN 0034-7655) **151**
Revista de Agricultura Tropical (CRI ISSN 1409-438X) **151**
• Revista de Analisis Economico (CHL ISSN 0716-5927) **1515**
Revista de Analisis Transaccional y Psicologia Humanista (ESP ISSN 0212-9876) **7403**
Revista de Anillamiento (ESP ISSN 1139-5672) **913**
• ➤ Revista de Antiguos Alumnos (ESP ISSN 1138-2333) **1167**
• ➤ Revista de Antropologia (BRA ISSN 0034-7701) **353**
Revista de Antropologia (ECU ISSN 0557-8507) **353**
Revista de Antropologia (PER) **353**
• Revista de Antropologia Experimental (ESP ISSN 1578-4282) **353**
Revista de Antropologia Rural (CHL ISSN 0718-428X) **353**
• ➤ Revista de Antropologia Social (ESP ISSN 1131-558X) **353**
Revista de Antropologia y Arqueologia *see* Antipoda **328**
• Revista de APS (Atencao Primaria a Saude) (BRA ISSN 1516-7704) **7539**
• Revista de Aracnologia (ESP ISSN 1576-9518) **961**
Revista de Arbitragem e Mediacao (BRA ISSN 1679-6462) **4770**
Revista de Arqueologia (BRA ISSN 0102-0420) **413**
Revista de Arqueologia (ESP ISSN 0212-0062) **413**
• Revista de Arqueologia Americana (MEX) **413**
Revista de Arquitectura (ARG ISSN 0327-330X) **456**
• Revista de Arquitectura e Ingenieria (CUB ISSN 1990-8830) **456**
Revista de Artes Marciales Asiaticas (ESP ISSN 1885-8643) **8196**
Revista de Artes Visuales *see* Heterogenesis **493**
Revista de Asesoria para Cooperativas (PER) **1424**
† Revista de Atencion Temprana (ESP ISSN 1139-1170) **8985**
Revista de Bibliotecologia y Ciencias de la Informacion (CRI ISSN 1016-0396) **5043**
• Revista de Bioetica y Derecho (ESP ISSN 1886-5887) **4770**
Revista de Biologia (PRT ISSN 0034-7736) **700**
• Revista de Biologia e Ciencias de la Terra (BRA ISSN 1519-5228) **700**
• ➤ Revista de Biologia Marina y Oceanografia (CHL ISSN 0717-3326) **701**
• ➤ Revista de Biologia Tropical (CRI ISSN 0034-7744) **701**
Revista de Biomecanica (ESP ISSN 1575-5622) **750**
Revista de Bombas y Compresores (ESP ISSN 0210-2188) **3364**
• Revista de Calidad Asistencial (ESP ISSN 1134-282X) **5705**
Revista de Catalunya (ESP ISSN 0213-5876) **3953**
➤ Revista de Chimie (ROM ISSN 0034-7752) **2078**
Revista de Ciencia & Tecnologia (BRA ISSN 0103-8575) **7903**
• ➤ Revista de Ciencia Politica (CHL ISSN 0716-1417) **7262**
• Revista de Ciencia y Tecnologia (ARG ISSN 0329-8922) **7903**
Revista de Ciencias Administrativas y Financieras de la Seguridad Social *see* Gestion **8042**
• ➤ Revista de Ciencias Agrarias (PRT ISSN 0871-018X) **151**
• Revista de Ciencias Agrarias y Tecnologia de los Alimentos (Online) (ARG ISSN 1668-1940) **151**
Revista de Ciencias Agricolas *see* Agronomia Costarricense **88**
• Revista de Ciencias Clinicas (MEX) **5705**
Revista de Ciencias de la Actividad Fisica y Deportes *see* Revista de las Ciencias de la Actividad Fisica **8196**
• Revista de Ciencias de la Educacion (ESP ISSN 0210-9581) **2905**
Revista de Ciencias de la Salud (CHL ISSN 0717-2621) **701**
Revista de Ciencias del Ejercito y la Salud (CRI ISSN 1409-0724) **8196**
Revista de Ciencias Economicas (ARG) **1300**
Revista de Ciencias Economicas. Temas de Administracion *see* Administracion **1723**
Revista de Ciencias Farmaceuticas *see* Revista de Ciencias Farmaceuticas Basica e Aplicada **6879**
➤ Revista de Ciencias Farmaceuticas Basica e Aplicada (BRA ISSN 1808-4532) **6879**
Revista de Ciencias Humanas (Curitiba) (BRA ISSN 0104-0111) **7996**
• Revista de Ciencias Humanas (Federico Westphalen) (BRA ISSN 1518-4684) **2905**
Revista de Ciencias Humanas (Florianopolis) (BRA ISSN 0101-9589) **7996**
Revista de Ciencias Humanas (Vicosa) (BRA ISSN 1519-1974) **7996**
Revista de Ciencias Juridicas (ESP ISSN 1137-0912) **4770**
Revista de Ciencias Juridicas Sociales (ARG ISSN 0325-0601) **4770**
• ➤ Revista de Ciencias Medicas (Campinas) (BRA ISSN 1415-5796) **5705**
Revista de Ciencias Medicas (Caxias do Sul) (BRA ISSN 1678-3379) **5705**
Revista de Ciencias Medicas e Biologicas (BRA ISSN 1677-5090) **5705**
Revista de Ciencias Sociais (Fortaleza) (BRA ISSN 0303-9862) **7996**
Revista de Ciencias Sociais (Porto Alegre) (BRA ISSN 0102-8200) **7996**
Revista de Ciencias Sociales (ARG ISSN 0328-2643) **7997**
• Revista de Ciencias Sociales (CHL ISSN 0717-2257) **7996**

Title

Revista de Saude do Distrito Federal (BRA ISSN 0103-4480) **7539**
● ➤ Revista de Saude Publica (BRA ISSN 0034-8910) **7539**
● ➤ Revista de Senologia y Patologia Mamaria (ESP ISSN 0214-1582) **6003**
Revista de Serveis Personals Locals (ESP ISSN 1136-5560) **8065**
Revista de Servicios Sociales y Politica Social (ESP ISSN 1130-7633) **8129**
Revista de Sociologia (COL ISSN 0120-1212) **8129**
● ➤ Revista de Sociologia e Politica (BRA ISSN 0104-4478) **8129**
● Revista de Soria (ESP ISSN 0213-9731) **8065**
● Revista de Stinte Politice (ROM ISSN 1584-224X) **7178**
Revista de Teatro (BRA ISSN 0102-7336) **8477**
Revista de Tecnica Forense (URY ISSN 1510-4427) **5916**
Revista de Tecnologia Educativa (CHL ISSN 0259-5400) **2906**
Revista de Tecnologia Educativa (PER ISSN 0034-866X) **2950**
● Revista de Teledeteccion (ESP ISSN 1133-0953) **4037**
● ➤ Revista de Teoria y Didactica de las Ciencias Sociales (VEN ISSN 1316-9505) **7997**
● ➤ Revista de Toxicologia (ESP ISSN 0212-7113) **3501**
Revista de Toxicologia en Linea *see* R E T E L **7538**
Revista de Trabajo (VEN ISSN 0034-8988) **1705**
Revista de Trabajo Social *see* R T S **8064**
Revista de Transporte y Seguros (URY ISSN 0797-2954) **4521**
● ➤ Revista de Turism/Journal of Tourism (ROM ISSN 1844-2994) **8752**
Revista de Unelte si Echipamente *see* Unelte si Echipamente **5461**
● ➤ Revista de Universidad y Sociedad del Conocimiento (ESP ISSN 1698-580X) **2906**
● Revista de Urbanismo (CHL ISSN 0717-5051) **4425**
Revista de Urbanismo y Edificacion (ESP ISSN 1576-9380) **4425**
Revista de Urbanismo y Edificacion. Monografia *see* Revista de Urbanismo y Edificacion **4425**
Revista de Urologia (ESP ISSN 1696-1773) **6274**
Revista de Vinhos (PRT ISSN 0874-372X) **609**
Revista de Zoologia (MEX ISSN 0188-1884) **962**
▼ ● Revista Debates (BRA ISSN 1982-5269) **7178**
Revista del Archivo Nacional (CRI ISSN 1409-0279) **5043**
Revista del Area de Sanidad, Consumo y Calidad de la Vida (ESP ISSN 1132-273X) **3501**
Revista del Ateneo Puertorriqueno (PRI) **5361**
▼ ● ➤ La Revista del C C C (Centro Cultural de la Cooperacion) (ARG ISSN 1851-3263) **7997**
Revista del C I Z A S *see* Centro de Investigacion en Zonas Aridas y Semiaridas. Revista **100**
● Revista del Caucho (ESP ISSN 0212-2138) **7826**
Revista del Centro de Estudios Merindad de Tudela (ESP ISSN 1131-9577) **4472**
Revista del Centro de Investigacion *see* Universidad de la Salle. Centro de Investigacion. Revista **4479**
● Revista del Climaterio (MEX ISSN 1665-5060) **5705**
Revista del Colegio de Filosofia *see* Theoria **6957**
Revista del Comercio (CUB) **1432**
Revista del Derecho de las Telecomunicacions e Infraestructuras *see* R E D E T I **2503**
Revista del Derecho Industrial (ARG ISSN 0327-4039) **4772**
La Revista del Diario *see* Diario Las Americas **3530**
Revista del Ejercito (MEX ISSN 0034-9046) **6443**
Revista del Foro Canario (ESP ISSN 0211-0903) **4772**
Revista del Instituto de Estudios Cooperativos (ARG) **1380**
Revista del Instituto de Estudios Economicos *see* Instituto de Estudios Economicos. Revista **1491**
Revista del Instituto de Lengua y Cultura Espanolas *see* R I L C E **5165**
Revista del Instituto de Lengua y Cultura Espanolas Anejos *see* R I L C E. Anejos **5165**
▼ ● Revista del Laboratorio Clinico (ESP ISSN 1888-4008) **5705**
Revista del Magister en Antropologia y Desarrollo *see* Revista M A D **354**
Revista del Mercosur *see* Revista do Mercosul **7178**
Revista del Mexico Agrario (MEX ISSN 0034-9097) **151**
Revista del Museo Americanista (ARG) **6536**
Revista del Museo de La Plata. Seccion Antropologia *see* Museo de La Plata. Revista. Seccion Antropologia **348**
Revista del Museo de La Plata. Seccion Botanica *see* Museo de La Plata. Revista. Seccion Botanica **802**
Revista del Museo de La Plata. Seccion Geologia *see* Museo de La Plata. Revista. Seccion Geologia **2756**
Revista del Museo de La Plata. Seccion Paleontologia *see* Museo de La Plata. Revista. Seccion Paleontologia **6727**
Revista del Museo de La Plata. Seccion Zoologia *see* Museo de La Plata. Revista. Seccion Zoologia **956**
Revista del Museo y Centro de Estudios Historicos de la Facultad de Odontologia de Buenos Aires *see* Universidad de Buenos Aires. Facultad de Odontologia. Museo y Centro de Estudios Historicos. Revista **5868**
Revista del Patrimonio Mundial *see* World Heritage Review **4167**
● Revista del Poder Judicial (ESP ISSN 1139-2819) **4959**
Revista del Poder Judicial. Numero Especial *see* Revista del Poder Judicial **4959**
Revista del Profesor de Matematicas (CHL ISSN 0717-0882) **5529**
Revista del Suboficial (ARG ISSN 0327-6953) **6443**
Revista del Sur (URY ISSN 0797-4892) **7997**
Revista del V Centenario del Descubrimiento y de la Evangelizacion de America (ARG ISSN 0327-6511) **4311**
La Revista del Vidrio, Fachadas y Ventanas (USA) **2045**
Revista del Vidrio Hueco (ESP) **2045**
Revista del Vidrio Plano (ESP) **2045**
Revista Democracia (BRA) **7178**
Revista Dental de Chile (CHL ISSN 0716-1107) **5863**
Revista Dental Press de Estetica (BRA ISSN 1807-2488) **5863**
● ➤ Revista Dental Press de Ortodontia e Ortopedia Facial (BRA ISSN 1415-5419) **5863**
▼ Revista Dental Press de Periodontologia e Implantologia (BRA ISSN 1980-2269) **5863**
Revista Derecho del Estado *see* Revista de Derecho del Estado **4770**
● Revista Desafios (COL ISSN 0124-4035) **7262**
Revista Desarrollo y Sociedad *see* Desarrollo y Sociedad **1476**
Revista Design em Foco (BRA ISSN 1807-3778) **514**
Revista d'Estudis Catalans *see* Zeitschrift fuer Katalanistik **5199**
Revista d'Etnologia de Catalunya (ESP ISSN 1132-6581) **353**
Revista d'Historia Medieval (ESP ISSN 1131-7612) **4158**
Revista Dialogo Educacional (BRA ISSN 1518-3483) **2906**
Revista Dicas & Truques para Games (BRA ISSN 1808-9364) **2481**
● Revista Digital Art& (BRA ISSN 1806-2962) **4472**
● Revista Digital de Biblioteconomia e Ciencia da Informacao (BRA ISSN 1678-765X) **5043**
● Revista Digital Universitaria (MEX ISSN 1607-6079) **2566**
Revista Diners (COL ISSN 0121-0211) **3830**
Revista Diners (ECU) **8752**
Revista Diners - Mundo (CHL) **4397**
Revista d'Internet, Dret i Politica *see* Revista de Internet, Derecho y Politica **4771**
Revista Direito, Estado e Sociedade *see* Direito, Estado e Sociedade **4659**
➤ Revista Direito G V (Getulio Vargas) (BRA ISSN 1808-2432) **4772**
Revista Direito Mackenzie (BRA ISSN 1517-6851) **4772**
● Revista Discurso Juridico (BRA ISSN 1982-5412) **4772**
Revista Discursos *see* Discursos **4450**
Revista do Ar (PRT ISSN 0034-9208) **69**
Revista do CD-ROM (BRA ISSN 0104-8732) **2596**
Revista do Comercio de Cafe (BRA ISSN 0034-9224) **3662**
Revista do Couro (BRA ISSN 0103-5827) **4975**
Revista do Direito (BRA ISSN 0104-9496) **4772**
Revista do DVD (BRA ISSN 1519-8499) **2403**
Revista do Exercito Brasileiro (BRA ISSN 0101-7284) **6443**
Revista do I R B *see* I R B Revista **4505**
Revista do Instituto Superior de Teologia de Evora *see* Eborensia **7639**
Revista do Mercosul/Revista del Mercosur (BRA ISSN 0104-9178) **7178**
Revista do Patrimonio (BRA) **4311**
Revista do Rio de Janeiro - U E R J (BRA) **3804**
● Revista do Setor de Ciencias Agrarias (BRA ISSN 0100-607X) **151**
▼ ● Revista Doces (ESP ISSN 1988-804X) **2906**
Revista DocPop (BRA ISSN 0101-7217) **7292**
● Revista dos Tribunais (BRA ISSN 0034-9275) **4772**
Revista dos Vegetarianos (BRA ISSN 1980-0630) **6669**
Revista E A N *see* Escuela de Administracion de Negocios. Revista **1742**
Revista E C A *see* Estudios Centroamericanos **7962**
Revista E C M (Escuela Colombiana de Medicina) (COL ISSN 0121-0076) **5705**
● ➤ Revista e-Curriculum (BRA ISSN 1809-3876) **2906**
Revista E I A *see* Escuela de Ingenieria de Antioquia. Revista **3191**
Revista E M A (COL ISSN 0122-5057) **456**
Revista Eclesiastica Brasileira (BRA ISSN 0101-8434) **7677**
Revista Economia *see* Economia **1098**
● Revista Economia (VEN ISSN 1315-2467) **1167**
Revista Economica *see* I I E Revista **1121**
Revista Economica (Buenos Aires) (ARG) **1167**
Revista Economica (La Plata) (ARG ISSN 0013-0419) **1167**
● La Revista Economica de Catalunya (ESP ISSN 1135-819X) **1515**
Revista Economica do Nordeste (BRA ISSN 0100-4956) **1515**
Revista Ecuatoriana de Higiene y Medicina Tropical (ECU ISSN 0048-7775) **5825**
Revista Ecuatoriana de Historia Economica (ECU ISSN 1016-7994) **1167**
Revista Ecuatoriana de Medicina y Ciencias Biologicas (ECU ISSN 0034-9313) **5705**
➤ Revista Ecuatoriana de Neurologia (ECU ISSN 1019-8113) **6182**
Revista Educacao & Tecnologia (BRA ISSN 1516-280X) **8436**
➤ Revista Educacion y Pedagogia (COL ISSN 0121-7593) **2906**
Revista Educarte (CHL ISSN 0716-8535) **514**
Revista Eidisis (CHL ISSN 0717-0785) **5043**
● Revista Ekosol (CHL ISSN 0718-4433) **2906**
Revista El Agora U S B *see* El Agora U S B **6902**
Revista el Protesista Dental *see* El Protesista Dental **5862**
● Revista Electronica Actualidades Investigativas en Educacion (CRI ISSN 1409-4703) **2906**
● ➤ Revista Electronica Complutense de Investigacion en Educacion Musical (ESP ISSN 1698-7454) **6611**
Revista Electronica de Biomedicina *see* Electronic Journal of Biomedicine **5609**
● Revista Electronica de Ciencia Penal y Criminologia (ESP ISSN 1695-0194) **4897**
Revista Electronica de Derecho Informatico *see* R E D I **4765**
● Revista Electronica de Derecho Societario (ARG ISSN 1515-4599) **4772**
● Revista Electronica de Ensenanza de las Ciencias (ESP ISSN 1579-1513) **2906**
● Revista Electronica de Estudos Hegelianos (BRA ISSN 1980-8372) **6948**
Revista Electronica de Farmacia (BRA ISSN 1808-0804) **6879**
● Revista Electronica de Informatica en Terapia Ocupacional (ESP ISSN 1576-5385) **6115**
● ➤ Revista Electronica de Investigacion Educativa/Electronic Journal of Educational Research (MEX ISSN 1607-4041) **3000**
● ➤ Revista Electronica de Investigacion Educativa y Psicopedagogica/Electronic Journal of Research in Educational Psychology (ESP ISSN 1696-2095) **2906**
● Revista Electronica de Investigacion en Educacion en Ciencias (ARG ISSN 1850-6666) **2906**
Revista Electronica de Investigacion y Evaluacion Educativa *see* R E L I E V E: Revista Electronica de Investigacion y Evaluacion Educativa **2902**
● Revista Electronica de la Autopsia (ESP ISSN 1699-2334) **5916**
Revista Electronica de Linguistica Aplicada *see* Revista Espanola de Linguistica Aplicada **5167**
● Revista Electronica de Literatura Mexicana (MEX ISSN 1606-8521) **5361**
Revista Electronica de Medotologia Aplicadad *see* R E M A **5527**
Revista Electronica de Motivacion y Emocion *see* Revista Espanola de Motivacion y Emocion **7404**
● Revista Electronica de PortalesMedicos.com (ESP ISSN 1886-8924) **5705**
● Revista Electronica de Psicologia (ESP ISSN 1137-8492) **7404**
● Revista Electronica de Psiquiatria (ESP ISSN 1137-3148) **6182**
● ➤ Revista Electronica de Veterinaria (ESP ISSN 1695-7504) **8806**
Revista Electronica del Centro de Investigacion y Desarrollo Tecnico *see* R E C I D T **8436**
Revista Electronica del D I I C C *see* Ingenieria Informatica **2423**
Revista Electronica Discurso.org *see* Discurso.org **5112**
● ➤ Revista Electronica Iberoamericana sobre Calidad, Eficacia y Cambio en Educacion (ESP ISSN 1696-4713) **2906**
Revista Electronica Patrimonio: Lazer & Turismo *see* Patrimonio: Lazer & Turismo **8747**
Revista Electronica Universitaria de Formacion del Profesorado *see* Revista Interuniversitaria de Formacion del Profesorado **3000**
● Revista Electronica Video (CUB ISSN 1027-2135) **4472**
Revista Electrotecnica (ARG ISSN 0370-7857) **3329**
● Revista Eletronica de Enfermagem (BRA ISSN 1518-1944) **5980**
● ➤ Revista Eletronica do C E J U R (Centro de Estudos Juridicos) (BRA ISSN 1981-8386) **4772**
Revista Eletronica do CEJUR *see* Revista Eletronica do C E J U R **4772**
● Revista Empresa y Humanismo (ESP ISSN 1139-7608) **4472**
Revista Encuentro *see* Encuentro **7961**
Revista Encuentros (URY ISSN 0797-9517) **7997**
Revista Energetica/Energy Magazine (ECU ISSN 0254-8445) **3147**
Revista Energia Nucleara (ROM ISSN 1220-5508) **3174**
● Revista Enfermagem (BRA ISSN 0104-3552) **5980**
● Revista Enfoques (CHL ISSN 0718-0241) **7466**
▼ Revista Ensenarte (ARG ISSN 1851-488X) **2906**
Revista "Es" (ESP ISSN 0210-9689) **5167**
● ➤ Revista Escrita (BRA ISSN 1679-6888) **5361**
● Revista Escuela de Historia (ARG ISSN 1667-4162) **4311**
● Revista Espanola de Anestesiologia y Reanimacion (ESP ISSN 0034-9356) **5774**
Revista Espanola de Anestesiologia y Reanimation. Suplemento *see* Revista Espanola de Anestesiologia y Reanimacion **5774**
● Revista Espanola de Antropologia Americana (ESP ISSN 0556-6533) **353**
➤ Revista Espanola de Antropologia Biologica (ESP ISSN 1134-7368) **353**
Revista Espanola de Capital Riesgo/Journal of Private Equity and Venture Capital (ESP ISSN 1887-2697) **1648**
● Revista Espanola de Cardiologia (Online) (ESP ISSN 1579-2242) **5799**
● ➤ Revista Espanola de Cardiologia (Print) (ESP ISSN 0300-8932) **5799**
Revista Espanola de Cardiologia. Suplemento (ESP ISSN 1131-3587) **5799**
● Revista Espanola de Ciencia Politica (ESP ISSN 1575-6548) **7178**
● Revista Espanola de Cirugia Oral y Maxilofacial (ESP ISSN 1130-0558) **6256**
● ➤ Revista Espanola de Cirugia Ortopedica y Traumatologia (ESP ISSN 1888-4415) **6072**
Revista Espanola de Control Externo (ESP ISSN 1575-1333) **4772**
● Revista Espanola de Defensa (ESP ISSN 1131-5172) **6443**
● Revista Espanola de Derecho Administrativo (ESP ISSN 0210-8461) **4772**
Revista Espanola de Derecho Canonico (ESP ISSN 0034-9372) **7814**
● Revista Espanola de Derecho Constitucional (ESP ISSN 0211-5743) **4852**
Revista Espanola de Derecho Europeo (ESP ISSN 1579-6302) **4939**
Revista Espanola de Derecho Internacional (ESP ISSN 0034-9380) **4939**
Revista Espanola de Derecho Militar (ESP ISSN 0034-9399) **4972**
● Revista Espanola de Desarrollo y Cooperacion (ESP ISSN 1137-8875) **4772**
● ➤ Revista Espanola de Documentacion Cientifica (ESP ISSN 0210-0614) **5043**
● Revista Espanola de Drogodependencias (ESP ISSN 0213-7615) **2698**
➤ Revista Espanola de Ecografia Digestiva (ESP ISSN 1576-0545) **5930**
Revista Espanola de Economia *see* Spanish Economic Review **1519**
● Revista Espanola de Economia (ESP ISSN 0210-1025) **1167**
Revista Espanola de Economia de la Salud (ESP ISSN 1579-5772) **4110**
Revista Espanola de Educacion Comparada (ESP ISSN 1137-8654) **2906**
● ➤ Revista Espanola de Enfermedades Digestivas (ESP ISSN 1130-0108) **5930**
Revista Espanola de Enfermedades Digestivas. Suplemento *see* Revista Espanola de Enfermedades Digestivas **5930**
● Revista Espanola de Enfermedades Metabolicas Oseas (ESP ISSN 1132-8460) **5807**
Revista Espanola de Estudios Agrosociales y Pesqueros (ESP ISSN 1575-1198) **205**
➤ Revista Espanola de Estudios Canadienses (ESP ISSN 1132-7839) **7997**
Revista Espanola de Estudios Norteamericanos *see* R E D E N **4309**
● Revista Espanola de Filosofia Medieval (ESP ISSN 1133-0902) **6948**
● Revista Espanola de Financiacion y Contabilidad (ESP ISSN 0210-2412) **1380**
➤ Revista Espanola de Fisica (ESP ISSN 0213-862X) **7038**
● ➤ Revista Espanola de Geriatria y Gerontologia (ESP ISSN 0211-139X) **4054**
● ➤ Revista Espanola de Herpetologia (ESP ISSN 0213-6686) **962**
Revista Espanola de Historia Militar (ESP ISSN 1575-9059) **6443**
Revista Espanola de Homeopatia (ESP ISSN 1134-4024) **5807**
● Revista Espanola de Inovacion, Calidad e Ingenieria del Software (ESP ISSN 1885-4486) **2436**
● Revista Espanola de Investigacion Criminologica (ESP ISSN 1696-9219) **7539**
Revista Espanola de Investigacion de Marketing (ESP ISSN 1138-1442) **1841**
● ➤ Revista Espanola de Investigaciones Sociologicas (Spanish Edition) (ESP ISSN 0210-5233) **8129**
Revista Espanola de la Funcion Consultiva (ESP ISSN 1698-6849) **4772**
Revista Espanola de Linguistica (ESP ISSN 0210-1874) **5167**
● Revista Espanola de Linguistica Aplicada (ESP ISSN 0213-2028) **5167**
● Revista Espanola de Medicina Legal (ESP ISSN 0377-4732) **5916**
● ➤ Revista Espanola de Medicina Nuclear (ESP ISSN 0212-6982) **6207**
Revista Espanola de Micropaleontologia (ESP ISSN 0556-655X) **6730**
● Revista Espanola de Motivacion y Emocion (ESP ISSN 1576-4214) **7404**
Revista Espanola de Neuropsicologia (ESP ISSN 1139-9872) **7404**
Revista Espanola de Nutricion Comunitaria (ESP ISSN 1135-3074) **6669**

Title

▼ *new title*   † *ceased*   • *electronic media*   ➤ *refereed*

Title

10814 REVISTA PESCADOR ULRICH'S PERIODICALS

Revista Pescador (BRA ISSN 1413-6554) 8330
Revista Philosophica (CHL ISSN 0716-1913) 6949
• Revista Philosophos (BRA ISSN 1982-2928) 6949
• Revista Pilquen. Seccion Agronomia (Online) (ARG ISSN 1851-2852) 152
• Revista Pilquen. Seccion Ciencias Sociales (Online) (ARG ISSN 1851-3123) 7997
Revista Plantas Medicinales (CUB ISSN 0138-6492) 152
Revista Politica Comparada (ESP ISSN 0211-5581) 7179
• Revista Portuguesa de Cardiologia (PRT ISSN 0870-2551) 5799
Revista Portuguesa de Ciencia Criminal (PRT ISSN 0871-8563) 4897
Revista Portuguesa de Ciencia e Tecnologia *see* Electricidade 3304
Revista Portuguesa de Ciencias do Desporto/Portuguese Journal of Sports Sciences (PRT ISSN 1645-0523) 8196
Revista Portuguesa de Ciencias Veterinarias (PRT ISSN 0035-0389) 8806
• Revista Portuguesa de Educacao (PRT ISSN 0871-9187) 2907
Revista Portuguesa de Engenharia de Estructuras (PRT ISSN 0870-984X) 2789
• ➤ Revista Portuguesa de Estomatologia e Cirurgia Maxilo-Facial (PRT ISSN 0035-0397) 5864
• Revista Portuguesa de Farmacia (PRT ISSN 0484-811X) 6879
Revista Portuguesa de Filologia (PRT ISSN 0870-4139) 5168
➤ Revista Portuguesa de Filosofia (PRT ISSN 0870-5283) 6949
Revista Portuguesa de Filosofia. Suplemento Bibliografico *see* Revista Portuguesa de Filosofia 6949
Revista Portuguesa de Historia (PRT ISSN 0870-4147) 4158
Revista Portuguesa de Humanidades (PRT ISSN 0874-0321) 4472
• ➤ Revista Portuguesa de Marketing (PRT ISSN 0873-2949) 1841
Revista Portuguesa de Ortodoncia (PRT ISSN 0873-4569) 5864
Revista Portuguesa de Panificacao (PRT) 3675
Revista Portuguesa de Pedagogia (PRT ISSN 0870-418X) 2907
• Revista Portuguesa de Pneumologia (PRT ISSN 0873-2159) 6219
Revista Portuguesa de Psicanalise (PRT ISSN 0873-9129) 7405
Revista Portuguesa de Psicossomatica (PRT ISSN 0874-4696) 7405
Revista Portuguesa de Saude Publica (PRT ISSN 0870-9025) 7466
• Revista Portuguesa e Brasileira de Gestao (PRT ISSN 1677-2067) 1791
Revista Presencia *see* Presencia 7671
• Revista Probidad (SLV ISSN 1605-1939) 7179
Revista Proceso *see* Proceso 7173
• ➤ Producao (BRA ISSN 0103-6513) 1903
Revista Producao Online *see* Producao 1903
▼ • Revista Productos Naturales (CAN ISSN 1916-2413) 314
Revista Profissional dos Sectores da Saude Higiene e Beleza *see* Farmacia Distribuicao 6841
• Revista Propiedad Intelectual (VEN ISSN 1316-1164) 4880
Revista Publicidad y Mercadeo (COL ISSN 0120-5293) 34
• Revista Question (ARG ISSN 1669-6581) 4583
Revista Realidad e Rural/Rural Realty (BRA) 152
• Revista Red (MEX) 2503
Revista Referativa de Educacion (CUB) 2907
• ➤ Revista Regional de Aracatuba (BRA ISSN 0101-8140) 5864
Revista Relasur *see* Revista de Relaciones Laborales en American Latina, Cono Sur 1705
Revista - Review Interamericana (PRI ISSN 0360-7917) 5361
Revista Rodoviaria (BRA) 8634
Revista Rol de Enfermeria (ESP ISSN 0210-5020) 5980
Revista Rol de Enfermeria. Formacion Permanente *see* Revista Rol de Enfermeria 5980
Revista Roma e America. Diritto Romano Comune (COL) 4841
Revista Romana de Gerontologie si Geriatrie *see* Romanian Journal of Gerontology and Geriatrics 4055
Revista Romana de Materiale/Romanian Journal of Materials (ROM ISSN 1583-3186) 1033
Revista Romana de Medicina Muncii (ROM ISSN 1220-6067) 5706
Revista Romana de O R L (Oto-Rino-Laringologia) (ROM ISSN 1583-9443) 6085
Revista Romana de Pediatrie (ROM ISSN 1454-0398) 6103
• Revista Romana de Proprietate Industriala/Romanian Review for Industrial Property (ROM ISSN 1220-3009) 6758
Revista Romana de Psihoterapii Cognitive si Comportamentale (ROM ISSN 1582-6694) 7405
Revista Romana de Sah (ROM ISSN 1220-5516) 8196
• Revista Romana de Sociologie (ROM ISSN 1224-9262) 8129
Revista Romana de Statistica (ROM ISSN 1018-046X) 8396
• Revista Romana de Stiinte Politice/Romanian Journal of Political Science (ROM ISSN 1582-456X) 7179
Revista Romana de Studii Internationale/Romanian Journal of International Studies (ROM ISSN 1220-2908) 1581
† Revista Romana de Turism (ROM ISSN 1222-5428) 8985
Revista Romana de Ultrasonografie *see* Medical Ultrasonography 6203
Revista S A A P (Sociedad Argentina de Analisis Politico) (ARG ISSN 1666-7883) 7179
Revista S A D E, Cordoba *see* Sociedad Argentina de Escritores. Revista 5374
Revista S A I (Sociedad Antioquena de Ingenieros y Arquitectos) (COL ISSN 0120-5862) 3218
Revista S y D *see* Salud y Drogas 2698
• Revista Salud Publica y Nutricion (MEX ISSN 1870-0160) 7539
Revista Salus *see* Universidad de Carabobo. Facultad de Ciencias. Revista 5726
Revista Salvadorena de Ciencias Sociales (SLV ISSN 1019-9594) 7998
• Revista Saude.Com (BRA ISSN 1809-0761) 4110
➤ Revista Secao Judiciaria do Rio de Janeiro (BRA ISSN 1678-3085) 4773
Revista Semanal de Legislacion (ESP ISSN 0214-4549) 4773
Revista Servico de Administracao Militar (PRT ISSN 0377-4686) 6443
Revista Shinca (ARG ISSN 1851-3255) 413
Revista Signo (BRA ISSN 0101-1812) 4472
• ➤ Revista Signos (CHL ISSN 0035-0451) 5361
Revista Signos Vitales *see* Signos Vitales 5715
Revista Sindrome de Down (ESP ISSN 1132-1911) 6103
Revista Sistemas de la A C I S (COL ISSN 0120-5919) 2524
Revista Sobre Relaciones Industriales y Laborales (VEN ISSN 0798-197X) 1705
• ➤ Revista Soldagem & Inspecao (BRA ISSN 0104-9224) 6343
Revista Suiza (COL) 1409
Revista Sul-Americana de Engenharia Estructural (BRA ISSN 1806-3985) 3282
Revista Symposium *see* Symposium 4477
Revista T E D (Tecne Episteme y Didaxis) (COL) 8437
• Revista T O P E (Todo para Produccion y Equipamiento) (ESP) 5459
Revista Tachirense de Derecho (VEN ISSN 1316-6883) 4773
Revista Tamaulipas (MEX ISSN 0035-0486) 3911
Revista Teatro *see* Teatro 8481
Revista Technologia (BRA ISSN 1518-5540) 8437
Revista Tecnica de Cooperativismo en el Peru *see* Revista de Asesoria para Cooperativas 1424
Revista Tecnica de Distribucion, Mantenimiento y Limpiezas (ESP ISSN 1136-3010) 2244
Revista Tecnica de Enfermagem *see* Nursing 5972
Revista Tecnica de Peluqueria y Belleza *see* Peluquerias de Gran Seleccion 590
Revista Tecnica Portuguesa *see* Electricidade 3304
• Revista Tecnica Tributaria (ESP ISSN 0214-6010) 4773
Revista Tecnico-Cientifica Clima Interior, Confort y Control de Ambiente (ESP ISSN 0214-5804) 4126
Revista Tecnologia (BRA ISSN 0101-8191) 8437
Revista Tecnologia: Electroenergetica (CUB) 3329
Revista Tecnologia: Geologia (CUB) 2764
Revista Tecnologia: Mineria y Metalurgia (CUB) 6330
Revista Tecnologia: Quimica (CUB) 2079
Revista Tecnologica (BRA ISSN 1517-8048) 8437
• ➤ Revista Tecnologica (CUB ISSN 0864-1897) 8437
• Revista Teknokultura (PRI ISSN 1549-2230) 8129
Revista Telematica de Filosofia del Derecho (ESP ISSN 1575-7382) 4773
Revista Temas de Bioetica (COL) 878
Revista Temas Economicos y Sociales (BOL) 7998
➤ Revista Teologica Limense (PER ISSN 1026-0021) 7815
• Revista Terapia Manual (BRA ISSN 1677-5937) 6116
Revista Textil (BRA ISSN 0035-0524) 8456
Revista Texto & Contexto-Enfermagem *see* Texto & Contexto-Enfermagem 5983
• Revista Theomai (ARG ISSN 1666-2830) 3463
➤ Revista Tiempo y Espacio (CHL ISSN 0716-9671) 4158
Revista Tienda (ARG) 1841
Revista Trabajo Social (CHL ISSN 0716-2642) 8065
• Revista Tradumatica (ESP ISSN 1578-7559) 5168
Revista Trafico *see* Spain. Ministerio de Justicia e Interior. Direccion General de Trafico. Revista Trafico 8635
➤ Revista Transportes (BRA ISSN 1415-7713) 8510
Revista Tributaria e de Financas Publicas (BRA ISSN 1518-2711) 4773
Revista Tricontinental (CUB ISSN 0049-4682) 7262
• Revista Trimestral de Jurisprudencia (BRA ISSN 0035-0540) 4773
• Revista Turismo & Desenvolvimento (BRA ISSN 1645-9261) 8752
Revista U D (Universidad de Deusto) (ESP) 2298
Revista U I S Ingenierias (Universidad Industrial de Santander) (COL ISSN 1657-4583) 3282
Revista U N I B E de Ciencia y Cultura (Universidad Iberoamericana) (DOM ISSN 1015-440X) 7179
Revista Une *see* U N E 6407
Revista UNELLEZ de Ciencias y Tecnologia. Serie Produccion (Universidad Nacional Experimental de los Llanos Occidentales "Ezequiel Zamora") (VEN ISSN 1012-7054) 250
Revista Unibanco (PRT) 4366
Revista Union *see* Union 4604
Revista Universidad Cooperativa de Colombia (COL) 1380
• Revista Universidad E A F I T (Escuela de Administracion y Finanzas y Tecnologias) (COL ISSN 0120-341X) 1791
Revista Universidade Rural. Serie Ciencias da Vida (BRA ISSN 0104-7264) 701
Revista Universidade Rural. Serie Ciencias Humanas (BRA ISSN 0104-9259) 8129
Revista Universitaria (CHL ISSN 0250-3670) 3000
Revista Universitaria de Derecho Procesal (ESP ISSN 1130-1767) 4773
Revista Universitaria de Geografia (ARG ISSN 0326-8373) 4027
Revista Universitaria de Letras (ARG ISSN 0326-1166) 5168
Revista Universitaria de Psicoanalisis (ARG ISSN 1515-3894) 7405
Revista Universitaria de Publicidad y Relaciones Publicas (ESP ISSN 1130-5681) 34
• Revista Universo Contabil (BRA ISSN 1809-3337) 1300
• Revista Uruguaya de Cardiologia (URY ISSN 0797-0048) 5799
• Revista Uruguaya de Ciencia Politica (URY ISSN 0797-9789) 7179
Revista Uruguaya de Derecho de Familia (URY ISSN 0797-048X) 4914
Revista Uruguaya de Derecho Internacional Privado (URY ISSN 1510-0960) 4939
Revista Uruguaya de Derecho Procesal (URY ISSN 0797-0471) 4773
Revista Uruguaya de Enfermeria (URY ISSN 0797-6194) 5980
Revista Uruguaya de Epilepsia (URY ISSN 1510-7701) 6182
Revista Uruguaya de Estudios Internacionales (URY) 7263
Revista Uruguaya de Instrumentadores Quirurgicos (URY ISSN 0797-8855) 4489
Revista Uruguaya de Patologia Clinica (URY ISSN 0797-0307) 5706
Revista Uruguaya de Psicoanalisis (URY ISSN 0484-8268) 7405
Revista Uruguaya de Psicologia (URY ISSN 0797-4876) 7405
Revista Valenciana de Economia y Hacienda (ESP ISSN 1577-4163) 1380
Revista Valenciana d'Estudis Autonomics (ESP ISSN 0213-2206) 7502
Revista Varona (CUB) 2907
Revista Vasca de Administracion Publica (ESP ISSN 0211-9560) 7466
Revista Vasca de Derecho Procesal y Arbitraje (ESP ISSN 0214-7246) 4773
Revista Vasca de Economia Social/Gizarte Ekonomiaren Euskal Aldizkaria (ESP ISSN 1698-7446) 7998
• ➤ Revista Venezolana de Analisis de Coyuntura (VEN ISSN 1315-3617) 1515
Revista Venezolana de Ciencia Politica (VEN ISSN 0798-9881) 7179
• Revista Venezolana de Ciencias Sociales (VEN ISSN 1316-4090) 7998
Revista Venezolana de Cirugia (VEN ISSN 0378-6420) 6257
• Revista Venezolana de Economia y Ciencias Sociales (VEN ISSN 1315-6411) 1167
• Revista Venezolana de Endocrinologia y Metabolismo (VEN) 5900
Revista Venezolana de Estudios de la Mujer (VEN ISSN 1316-3701) 8902
➤ Revista Venezolana de Filosofia (VEN ISSN 1013-2368) 6949
• ➤ Revista Venezolana de Gerencia (VEN ISSN 1315-9984) 1791
• ➤ Revista Venezolana de Oncologia (VEN ISSN 0798-0582) 6033
Revista Venezolana de Urologia (VEN ISSN 0035-0591) 6274
• Revista Veterinaria (ARG ISSN 1668-4834) 8806
Revista Veterinaria Venezolana (VEN ISSN 0484-8284) 8806
➤ Revista Veterinaria y Zootecnica de Caldas (COL ISSN 0120-4114) 8806
Revista Viceversa (PAN) 4472
Revista Viet-Nam (CUB) 5237
Revista View *see* View Magazine 6052
▼ Revista Virtual de Derecho Procesal (COL ISSN 2011-2750) 4773
• Revista Virtual de Estudos da Linguagem - ReVEL (BRA ISSN 1678-8931) 5168
▼ • Revista Virtual de Quimica (BRA ISSN 1984-6835) 2079
• Revista Virtual Matematica, Educacion e Internet (CRI) 5529
Revista W I Z O *see* W I Z O Review 7731
Revista Werken *see* Werken 423
Revista www.com.br (BRA ISSN 1518-1561) 2566
▼ Revista Yoga Facil (ARG ISSN 1851-0175) 6996
Revistart (ESP ISSN 1134-7988) 515
• ➤ Revistas Otras Miradas (VEN ISSN 1317-5904) 7998
Revistas Temas y Propuestas *see* Temas y Propuestas 1182
Revistatlantica de Poesia (ESP ISSN 1133-0368) 5433
Revitalization (Chicago) (USA) 1167
Revitalization (Wilmore) (USA) 7773
• Revitec (ESP ISSN 0214-7394) 2244
Revival (GBR ISSN 1355-9966) 7263
• ➤ Revizni a Posudkove Lekarstvi/Health Insurance and Medical Review (CZE ISSN 1214-3170) 4110
• Revmatikeren (NOR ISSN 0800-5575) 6226
➤ Revmatologiia (BGR ISSN 1310-0505) 6226
• Revocable Trusts (USA) 4773
Revocatio Historiae (DEU ISSN 0936-7748) 4159
Revoluciones per Minuto (ESP) 6611
▼ Revolutic (FRA ISSN 1957-9241) 6611
Revolution (Bournemouth) (GBR) 2481
• Revolution (Chicago) (USA ISSN 1557-413X) 7179
• Revolution (London) (GBR ISSN 1460-5953) 1421
Revolution et Travail (DZA ISSN 0484-8365) 7179
▼ Revolution Motorcycle Mag (English Edition) (CAN ISSN 1913-0082) 8267
Revolution Motorcycle Mag (French Edition) *see* Revolution Motorcycle Mag (English Edition) 8267
Revolution Socialiste Antilles (MTQ ISSN 0755-2742) 1705
• ➤ Revolutionary Russia (GBR ISSN 0954-6545) 4257
Revolutionary Worker *see* Revolution (Chicago) 7179
Revolver (BEL ISSN 0085-5650) 5433
Revolver (USA ISSN 1527-408X) 6611
Revolver Magazine (AUS) 6611
Revolver Magazine (NLD ISSN 1871-8604) 6511
• ➤ Revstat Statistical Journal (PRT ISSN 1645-6726) 8396
La Revue (CAN ISSN 1719-864X) 3816
Revue *see* Schweizer Maschinenmarkt 5459
Revue *see* M S M 5455
† Revue (DEU ISSN 1862-295X) 8985
Revue (LUX ISSN 0035-0729) 8752
Revue A B B *see* A B B Review 3293
Revue A C E S M *see* C A E D H H Journal 4072
La Revue Administrative (FRA ISSN 0035-0672) 7466
† Revue AFRAM/AFRAM Review (FRA ISSN 1277-6408) 8985
Revue Africaine (FRA ISSN 1956-7820) 4473
Revue Africaine de Developpement *see* African Development Review 1590
Revue Africaine de Gestion et d'Evaluation Environnementales *see* African Journal of Environmental Assessment and Management 3493
Revue Africaine de la Protection des Vegetaux *see* African Journal of Plant Protection 216
La Revue Africaine de la Sante Reproductive *see* African Journal of Reproductive Health 8843
Revue Africaine de Sociologie *see* African Sociological Review 8086
Revue Africaine de Theologie (COD ISSN 1016-2461) 7815
Revue Africaine des Livres *see* Africa Review of Books 7551
Revue Africaine des Medias *see* Africa Media Review 8085
Revue Africaine des Sciences de l'Education/African Review of Educational Sciences (COD) 2907
Revue Agricole de l'Aube (FRA ISSN 0999-212X) 152
➤ Revue Agricole et Sucriere de Maurice/Agricultural and Sugar Review of Mauritius (MUS ISSN 0370-3576) 250
Revue Agricole pour l'Europe *see* Agricultural Review for Europe 8928
➤ Revue Andre Malraux Review (USA ISSN 0839-458X) 5362
Revue Annuelle des Industries Mecaniques et Electriques et de l'Automatisation *see* World Engineering Industries and Automation 3359
Revue Annuelle d'Histoire du Quatorzieme Arrondissement de Paris (FRA ISSN 0556-7335) 4258
Revue Archeologique (FRA ISSN 0035-0737) 414
Revue Archeologique de l'Ouest (FRA ISSN 0767-709X) 414
Revue Archeologique de l'Ouest. Supplement (FRA ISSN 1166-8261) 414
➤ Revue Archeologique de Picardie (FRA ISSN 0752-5656) 414
• Revue Archeologique du Centre de la France (Online) (FRA ISSN 1951-6207) 414
Revue Attaalim *see* Attaalim 2828
Revue Automobile (CHE ISSN 0035-0761) 8510
• Revue Automobile Medicale (FRA) 5706
Revue Avicole (FRA ISSN 0048-7902) 298
Revue B S T.com *see* Le Bois et sa Sous - Traitance 3710
Revue Belge d'Archeologie et d'Histoire de l'Art/Belgisch Tijdschrift voor Oudheidkunde en Kunstgeshiedenis (BEL ISSN 0035-077X) 515
➤ Revue Belge de Droit Constitutionnel (BEL ISSN 1374-2558) 4852
➤ Revue Belge de Droit International/Belgian Review of International Law/Belgisch Tijdschrift voor Internationaal Recht (BEL ISSN 0035-0788) 4939
➤ Revue Belge de Geographie/Belgian Journal of Geography/Belgisch Tijdschrift voor Geografie/Belgishe Zeitschrift fuer Geographie (BEL ISSN 1377-2368) 4027

Title

▼ *new title*   † *ceased*   ● *electronic media*   ➤ *refereed*

10818 REVUE ROUMAINE DE BIOLOGIE. SERIE BIOLOGIE VEGETALE ULRICH'S PERIODICALS

• Revue Roumaine de Biologie. Serie Biologie Vegetale (ROM ISSN 0250-5517) 815
➤ Revue Roumaine de Chimie/Romanian Journal of Chemistry (ROM ISSN 0035-3930) 2079
Revue Roumaine de Geographie (ROM ISSN 1220-5311) 4027
Revue Roumaine de Geologie (ROM ISSN 1220-529X) 2764
Revue Roumaine de Geophysique (ROM ISSN 1220-5303) 2789
• Revue Roumaine de Linguistique (ROM ISSN 0035-3957) 5168
• Revue Roumaine de Mathematiques Pures et Appliquees/Romanian Journal of Pure and Applied Mathematics (ROM ISSN 0035-3965) 5530
Revue Roumaine de Medecine Interne see Romanian Journal of Internal Medicine 5948
Revue Roumaine de Morphologie et Embryologie see Journal of Molecular and Cellular Pathology 683
• Revue Roumaine de Philosophie (ROM ISSN 1220-5400) 6949
Revue Roumaine de Physiologie see Romanian Journal of Physiology 927
• Revue Roumaine de Sciences Economiques (ROM ISSN 1220-5397) 1168
Revue Roumaine d'Endocrinologie see Acta Endocrinologica 5883
• Revue Roumaine des Sciences Techniques. Serie de Mecanique Appliquee (ROM ISSN 0035-4074) 3394
• Revue Roumaine des Sciences Techniques. Serie Electrotechnique et Energetique (ROM ISSN 0035-4066) 3329
Revue Roumaine d'Etudes Internationales (ROM ISSN 0048-8178) 7263
• Revue Roumaine d'Histoire (ROM ISSN 0556-8072) 4258
• Revue Roumaine d'Histoire de l'Art. Serie Beaux-Arts (ROM ISSN 0556-8080) 515
Revue Russe (FRA ISSN 1161-0557) 5362
Revue S T I C E F see Sciences et Technologies de l'Information et la Communication pour l'Education et la Formation 2437
• La Revue Sage - Femme (FRA ISSN 1637-4088) 6003
La Revue Salon Equip'Hotel see La Revue H R C 8985
Revue Schweiz Suisse Svizzera (CHE ISSN 1421-8909) 3959
Revue Scientifique du Bourbonnais et du Centre de la France (FRA ISSN 0370-7164) 7904
† Revue Scientifique et Technique de la Defense (FRA ISSN 0994-155X) 8985
Revue Scriptura, Nouvelle Serie (CAN ISSN 1495-9313) 7678
Revue Sentiers see Wander Revue 8340
Revue SEPTET see S E P T E T Revue 5171
Revue Slavistique see Rocznik Slawistyczny 5169
La Revue Socialiste (FRA ISSN 1294-2529) 7179
Revue Suisse (CHE) 3959
Revue Suisse d'Agriculture (CHE ISSN 0375-1325) 152
Revue Suisse d'Art et d'Archeologie see Zeitschrift fuer Schweizerische Archaeologie und Kunstgeschichte 425
Revue Suisse d'Assurances see Schweizerische Versicherungszeitschrift 4522
Revue Suisse de Droit International et de Droit Europeen see Schweizerische Zeitschrift fuer Internationales und Europaeisches Recht 4940
Revue Suisse de Jurisprudence see Schweizerische Juristen-Zeitung 4780
Revue Suisse de la Securite et de l'Environnement (CHE ISSN 0254-1262) 3463
Revue Suisse de l'Imprimerie see Typografische Monatsblaetter 7328
Revue Suisse de Medecine see Praxis 5699
Revue Suisse de Numismatique/Schweizerische Numismatische Rundschau (CHE ISSN 0035-4163) 6653
Revue Suisse de Science Politique see Schweizerische Zeitschrift fuer Politikwissenschaft 7181
Revue Suisse de Sociologie see Schweizerische Zeitschrift fuer Soziologie 8131
Revue Suisse de Viticulture, Arboriculture et Horticulture (CHE ISSN 0375-1430) 251
➤ Revue Suisse de Zoologie/Swiss Journal of Zoology (CHE ISSN 0035-418X) 962
Revue Suisse d'Economie Politique et de Statistique see Schweizerische Zeitschrift fuer Volkswirtschaft und Statistik 1171
Revue Suisse des Assurances Sociales et de la Prevoyance Professionnelle see Schweizerische Zeitschrift fuer Sozialversicherung und Berufliche Vorsorge 8067
Revue Suisse des Chorales see Schweizerische Chorzeitung 6615
Revue Suisse des Sciences de l'Education see Schweizerische Zeitschrift fuer Bildungswissenschaften 2910
Revue Suisse d'Histoire see Schweizerische Zeitschrift fuer Geschichte 4160
Revue Suisse pour Medecine et Traumatologie de Sports see Schweizerische Zeitschrift fuer Sportmedizin und Sporttraumatologie 6232
Revue Svetovej Literatury (SVK ISSN 0231-6269) 5237
Revue T E S L du Canada see T E S L Canada Journal 3083
† Revue Technique A P A V E (Associations de Proprietaires d'Appareils a Vapeur et Electriques) (FRA ISSN 1254-2075) 8985
Revue Technique Automobile (FRA ISSN 0017-307X) 8601
Revue Technique Carrosserie (FRA ISSN 0150-7206) 8601
Revue Technique Diesel (FRA ISSN 0037-2579) 8601
Revue Technique du Batiment see Revue Technique du Batiment et des Constructions Industrielles 1033
Revue Technique du Batiment et des Constructions Industrielles (FRA ISSN 0397-9296) 1033
Revue Technique du CETMEF see Centre d'Etudes Techniques Maritime et Fluviales. Revue Technique 8940
Revue Technique Luxembourgeoise (LUX ISSN 0035-4260) 8437
Revue Technique Machinisme Agricole (FRA ISSN 0223-0135) 214
• Revue Theologique de Louvain (BEL ISSN 0080-2654) 7815
➤ Revue Theologique de Louvain. Cahiers (BEL ISSN 0771-601X) 7815
Revue Theologique de Lugano see Rivista Teologica di Lugano 7815
Revue Thomiste (FRA ISSN 0035-4295) 7678
• Revue Tiers Monde (FRA ISSN 1293-8882) 7263
Revue Tocqueville see Tocqueville Review 8144
Revue Tricontinental see Revista Tricontinental 7262
Revue Trimestrielle de Droit Civil see R T D Civ 4841
Revue Trimestrielle de Droit Commercial et de Droit Economique (FRA ISSN 0244-9358) 4775
Revue Trimestrielle de Droit Europeen (FRA ISSN 0035-4317) 4775
Revue Trimestrielle de Droit Familial (BEL ISSN 0779-4711) 4914
➤ Revue Trimestrielle des Droits de l'Homme (BEL ISSN 0777-3579) 7214
Revue Trimestrielle sur le Marche du Travail et le Revenu see Quarterly Labour Market and Income Review 1873
Revue Tunisienne d'Administration Publique see R T A P 7464
Revue Tunisienne de Communication (TUN ISSN 0330-8480) 2337
Revue Tunisienne de Geographie (TUN ISSN 0330-9924) 4027
Revue Tunisienne de l'Energie (TUN ISSN 0330-7530) 3147
Revue Tunisienne de l'Equipement (TUN) 3282
Revue Tunisienne des Langues Vivantes see Al-Majallah at-Tunisiyyah lil-Lughat al-Hayyah 5149
Revue Tunisienne des Sciences Sociales (TUN ISSN 0035-4333) 7998
Revue Turque d'Hygiene et de Biologie Experimentale see Turk Hijiyen ve Deneysel Biyoloji Dergisi 6998
Revue U F A see U F A - Revue 164
• Revue UniRcoop (CAN ISSN 1705-2165) 7998
La Revue Universelle des Droits de l'Homme (DEU ISSN 0937-714X) 4852
Revue Valaisanne de Jurisprudence (CHE) 4775
Revue Valdotaine d'Histoire Naturelle (ITA ISSN 1120-1371) 7904
Revue Vervietoise d'Histoire Naturelle (BEL ISSN 0375-1465) 701
Revue Veterinaire Canadienne see Canadian Veterinary Journal 8795
• Revue VIH/SIDA, Droit et Politiques (Online) (CAN ISSN 1712-6258) 4775
• Revue VIH/SIDA, Droit et Politiques (Print) (CAN ISSN 1712-624X) 4775
Revue Zairoise de la Comptabilite see Conseiller Comptable 1917
La Revuo Orienta (JPN ISSN 0035-4406) 5168
Revuser (USA ISSN 1051-8118) 2574
Reward Management Rewards (GBR) 1706
• ReWater (AUS ISSN 1449-9800) 3512
Rewriting Indian and World History (IND) 4159
• ➤ Rexter (CZE ISSN 1214-7737) 7263
• El Rey (ARG ISSN 0326-0011) 8196
• Reykjavik Energi. Annual Report (ISL ISSN 1670-4991) 3394
Reykjavik Energy. Environmental Report (ISL ISSN 1670-5017) 3394
Reykjavik Port Handbook see Faxaflohafnir. Handbook 8643
Reynolds Records (USA ISSN 1057-6010) 3780
Reynolds Review (USA ISSN 0192-9569) 6331
Rez Biz (USA) 6636
Reza Gakkai Gakujutsu Koenkai Nenji Taikai Koen Yokoshu/Laser Society of Japan. Annual Meeting. Digest of Technical Papers (JPN ISSN 0913-6355) 7049
Reza Gakkai Kenkyukai Hokoku (JPN) 7084
Reza Gijutsu Sogo Kenkyujo Jigyo Hokokusho/Institute for Laser Technology. Report (JPN) 7084
Reza Gijutsu Sogo Kenkyujo Nenpo/Institute for Laser Technology. Annual Progress Report (JPN) 7084
Reza Kagaku/Abstracts of Riken Symposium on Laser Science (JPN) 7049
Reza Kako Gak-kai Kaishi (JPN) 3218
Reza Kako Gak-kai Ronbunshu/Japan Laser Processing Society. Proceedings (JPN) 3218
• ➤ Reza Kenkyu/Review of Laser Engineering (JPN ISSN 0387-0200) 7084
Reza Kurosu/Laser Cross (JPN ISSN 0914-9805) 7084
Reza Kyokai Uinta Semina/Japan Society of Laser Technology. Winter Seminar (JPN ISSN 0913-1361) 7084
Reza Kyokaishi/Laser (JPN ISSN 0916-7277) 7084
Reza no Kiso to Sono Oyo (JPN) 7084
Rezanie i Instrument (UKR ISSN 0370-808X) 7062
Rezepte mit Pfiff (DEU ISSN 0930-6579) 8882
Rezepte Pur (DEU ISSN 1861-9606) 4366
Rezidence (CZE ISSN 1214-5459) 4549
rfv.se see Dagens Socialfoersaekring 8036
Rhapsoidia (USA ISSN 1542-6823) 5362
➤ Rheedea (IND ISSN 0971-2313) 815
Rhein-Main Geht Aus! (Year) (DEU) 4397
Rhein-Neckar-Kind (DEU) 2167
• Rhein-Neckar-Zeitung (DEU) 3855
Rhein-Sieg-Kreis. Jahrbuch (DEU ISSN 0932-0377) 3856
Rhein-Zeitung (DEU) 3856
Rheinbahn Extra (DEU) 8624
Rheingau-Forum (DEU ISSN 0942-4474) 609
Der Rheingauer see Vivat 5086
Rheingolf Magazin (DEU) 8243
Rheingolf News see Rheingolf Magazin 8243
Rheingutebericht N R W (Nordrhein-Westfalen) (DEU ISSN 0939-0804) 8831
Rheinisch-Bergischer Kalender (DEU ISSN 0722-7671) 3622
Rheinisch-Pfaelzische Hotels and Gaststaetten (DEU ISSN 1430-0672) 4397
Rheinisch-Westfaelische Boerse zu Duesseldorf. Amtliches Kursblatt (DEU ISSN 0035-4457) 1648
Rheinisch-Westfaelische Technische Hochschule Aachen. Lehrstuhl und Institut fuer Wasserbau und Wasserwirtschaft. Mitteilungen (DEU ISSN 1437-8477) 2797
➤ Rheinisch-Westfaelische Zeitschrift fuer Volkskunde (DEU ISSN 0556-8218) 4258
Rheinisch-Westfaelischen Technischen Hochschule Aachen. Aerodynamisches Institut. Abhandlungen (DEU ISSN 0172-3898) 69
Rheinisch-Westfaelischen Technischen Hochschule Aachen Themen see R W T H - Themen 7901
Rheinisch-Westfaelischer Jaeger (DEU ISSN 0171-0796) 8330
Rheinisch-Westfaelisches Institut Materialien see R W I: Materialien 7994
Rheinisch-Westfaelisches Institut Schriftenreihe see R W I: Schriftenreihe 1164
Rheinische Ausgrabungen (DEU ISSN 0557-7853) 414
Rheinische Bauernzeitung (DEU ISSN 0344-5070) 152
Rheinische Freilichtmuseum - Landesmuseum fuer Volkskunde Kommern. Fuehrer und Schriften (DEU) 4258
Rheinische Friedrich-Wilhelms-Universitaet. Institut fuer Geodaesie und Geoinformation. Mitteilungen (DEU ISSN 0723-4325) 2764
Rheinische Friedrich-Wilhelms-Universitaet. Institut fuer Tierzuchtwissenschaft. Arbeiten (DEU ISSN 0724-1208) 298
Rheinische Heimatpflege (DEU ISSN 0342-1805) 4258
Rheinische Lebensbilder (DEU ISSN 0080-2670) 645
Rheinische Mundarten (DEU) 5168
Rheinische Post (DEU) 3856
Rheinische Vierteljahrsblaetter (DEU ISSN 0035-4473) 4258
Rheinischer Merkur (DEU ISSN 0942-6973) 3856
Rheinisches Aerzteblatt (DEU ISSN 0035-4481) 5706
Rheinisches Archiv (AUT ISSN 0933-5102) 4258
Rheinisches Genossenschaftsblatt (DEU) 152
➤ Rheinisches Jahrbuch fuer Volkskunde (DEU ISSN 0080-2697) 3622
Rheinisches Landesmuseum Bonn. Kataloge (DEU) 414
Rheinisches Museum fuer Philologie (DEU ISSN 0035-449X) 5168
Rheinisches Zahnaerzteblatt (DEU ISSN 0035-4503) 5864
Rheinland Aktuell (DEU ISSN 0344-5267) 186
Rheinland-Pfalz Heute (DEU ISSN 0174-2876) 7483
Rheinland-Pfalz. Ministerium fuer Bildung, Frauen und Jugend. Amtsblatt (DEU) 3030
Rheinland-Pfalz. Statistisches Landesamt Rheinland-Pfalz. Statistische Monatshefte (DEU ISSN 0174-2914) 7483
Rheinlands Reiter-Pferde (DEU) 8297
Die Rheinpfalz (DEU) 3856
• ➤ Rheologica Acta (DEU ISSN 0035-4511) 7062
Rheology Abstracts (GBR ISSN 0035-452X) 7050
Rheology Bulletin (GBR ISSN 1469-4999) 7062
Rheology Bulletin (USA ISSN 0035-4538) 7062
• Rheology Series (NLD ISSN 0169-3107) 7038
• RhetOn (AUT ISSN 1810-6250) 5362
Rhetoric (GBR) 5237
• Rhetoric & Public Affairs (USA ISSN 1094-8392) 5362
Rhetoric, Culture, and Social Critique (USA) 5362
• ➤ Rhetoric Review (USA ISSN 0735-0198) 5362
• ➤ Rhetoric Society Quarterly (USA ISSN 0277-3945) 5362
Rhetoric Study see Xiuci Xuexi 5196
• ➤ Rhetorica (USA ISSN 0734-8584) 5168
➤ Rhetorica Scandinavica (SWE ISSN 1397-0534) 5362
• Rhetorik (DEU ISSN 0720-5775) 3079
Rhetorik-Forschungen (DEU ISSN 0939-6462) 5362
Rheuma (ESP ISSN 0211-7274) 6226
Rheuma Aktuell see Osteoporose und Rheuma Aktuell 6225
Rheumatic Disease: In Practice (Series 4) (GBR ISSN 1469-3089) 6226
Rheumatic Disease Topical Reviews (GBR ISSN 1469-3097) 6226
• ➤ Rheumatic Diseases Clinics of North America (USA ISSN 0889-857X) 6226
Rheumatism (IND ISSN 0035-4546) 6226
Rheumatism see Turkish Journal of Rheumatology 6227
Rheumatologia (SVK ISSN 1210-1931) 6226
• The Rheumatologist (USA ISSN 1931-3268) 6226
• ➤ Rheumatology (CHE ISSN 0080-2727) 6226
Rheumatology see Ryumachika 6227
• Rheumatology (Online) (GBR ISSN 1462-0332) 6227
• ➤ Rheumatology (Print) (GBR ISSN 1462-0324) 6227
• ➤ Rheumatology International (DEU ISSN 0172-8172) 6227
• Rheumatology News (USA ISSN 1541-9800) 6227
Rhinegold Guide to Music Education (Years) see British Music Education Yearbook (Year) 6552
Rhino (USA ISSN 1521-8414) 5433
• ➤ Rhinology (NLD ISSN 0300-0729) 6085
Rhinology. Supplement see Rhinology 6085
Le Rhinolophe (CHE ISSN 1011-8098) 962
• ➤ Rhizome (AUS ISSN 1832-2328) 3000
• ➤ Rhizomes (USA ISSN 1555-9998) 4473
Rhoades and Langer, U S International Taxation and Tax Treaties see Rhoades & Langer, U S International Taxation and Tax Treaties 1942
• Rhoades & Langer, U S International Taxation and Tax Treaties (USA) 1942
Rhode Island: All-Industries see Harris Directory. Rhode Island All-Industries 2002
Rhode Island American Ballroom Dance Association Newsletter see R I A B D A Newsletter 2687
• Rhode Island Appellate Practice (USA) 4960
Rhode Island Bar Journal (USA ISSN 1079-9230) 4775
Rhode Island Beverage Journal (USA ISSN 0035-4562) 609
The Rhode Island Builder Report (USA) 1033
• Rhode Island Business Directory (USA ISSN 1048-7166) 2026
Rhode Island Catholic (USA ISSN 1938-8675) 7815
• Rhode Island Civil Practice and Procedure (USA) 4841
Rhode Island College Alumni Magazine (USA) 2299
• Rhode Island Criminal and Traffic Law Manual (USA ISSN 1536-2671) 4897
▼ Rhode Island Curiosities (USA ISSN 1935-6455) 8752
Rhode Island Dental Association. Newsletter (USA) 5864
Rhode Island. Department of Health. Vital Statistics (USA ISSN 0091-3073) 7314
• Rhode Island. Department of Labor & Training. Characteristics of the Insured Unemployed in Rhode Island (USA) 1706
• Rhode Island. Department of Labor & Training. Covered Employment & Wages in Rhode Island (USA) 1706
• Rhode Island. Department of Labor & Training. Directory of Labor Information (USA) 1706
Rhode Island. Department of Labor and Training. Employment Bulletin (USA) 1706
• Rhode Island. Department of Labor & Training. Establishment Employment in Rhode Island (USA) 1706
• Rhode Island. Department of Labor & Training. Local Area Unemployment Statistics (USA) 1706
• Rhode Island. Department of Labor & Training. Nonfarm Employment, Hour, and Earnings (USA) 1706
• Rhode Island. Department of Labor & Training. Occupational Employment Statistics (USA) 1706
• Rhode Island. Department of Labor & Training. Rhode Island 2006 - A Positive Outlook on Tomorrow's Workforce (USA) 1706
• Rhode Island. Department of Labor & Training. Rhode Island Employment Bulletin (USA) 1706
• Rhode Island. Department of Labor & Training. Rhode Island Statistical & Fiscal Digest (USA) 1706
Rhode Island Directory of Manufacturers (USA ISSN 0361-5103) 2026
• Rhode Island Education Laws and Rules Annotated (USA) 4775
• Rhode Island Employment Law Letter (USA ISSN 1086-0517) 4775
• Rhode Island Evidence Manual (USA) 4775
• Rhode Island Fire Law and Rules Annotated (USA) 3581
Rhode Island Genealogical Register (USA ISSN 0190-3055) 3780
Rhode Island Geological Survey. Bulletin (USA) 2764
The Rhode Island Government Owner's Manual (USA ISSN 1932-4669) 7467
Rhode Island Government Register (USA ISSN 1071-3395) 7467
Rhode Island History (USA ISSN 0035-4619) 4311
Rhode Island Jewish Herald (USA) 3561
Rhode Island Jewish Historical Association. Newsletter (USA ISSN 0897-0602) 4311

Title

Rikkyo University. Institute for Atomic Energy. Annual Report of Reactor Facilities *see* Genshiryoku Riyo Jisseki Hokoku **7066**
Rikkyo University. Institute for Atomic Energy. Annual Report of Reactor Utilization *see* Rikkyo Daigaku Genshiryoku Kenkyujo Genshiro Riyo Jisseki Hokoku **3174**
Rikkyo University. Institute for Atomic Energy. Report (JPN) **3174**
Rikkyo University. Institute for Atomic Energy. Seminar Proceedings *see* Rikkyo Daigaku Genshiryoku Kenkyujo Koenkai Ronbunshu **3174**
Rikogaku ni Okeru Doi Genso Kenkyu Happyokai Yoshishu/Annual Meeting on Radioisotopes in the Physical Sciences and Industries (JPN) **7072**
• Rikosseuraamusalan Strategiat (FIN ISSN 1458-7890) **4775**
• Riksaaklagarens Foerfattningssamling (Online) (SWE) **4775**
Riksantikvaren. Rapporter (NOR ISSN 0333-2551) **4426**
Riksantikvarieaembetet. Arkeologiska Undersoekningar. Skrifter (SWE ISSN 1102-187X) **414**
Riksdagens Aarsbok *see* Sveriges Riksdag. Aarsbok **7471**
Riksdagens Ledamoeter (SWE ISSN 1402-8239) **7179**
Riksfoereningen foer Laerarna i Moderna Spraak Lingua *see* L M S - Lingua **5138**
Riksfoersaekringsverkets Foerfattningssamling *see* Foersaekringskassans Foerfattningssamling **4503**
Riksskatteverkets Foerfattningssamling *see* Skatteverkets Foerfattningssamling **1943**
Rikstaecket (SWE) **6642**
Rikujo Kyogi (JPN) **8197**
Rikujo-Kyogi Magazine/Athletic Sports Magazine (JPN) **8197**
Rikusui Gaku Zasshi/Japanese Journal of Limnology (JPN ISSN 0021-5104) **2798**
➤ Rikusui Seibutsugakuho/Biology of Inland Waters (JPN ISSN 0286-8172) **701**
Rikuyo Nainen Kikan/Land Engine Manufacturers (JPN ISSN 0911-4858) **3394**
Rilke-Gesellschaft. Blaetter (DEU ISSN 1010-3597) **5363**
RiLUnE *see* Revue des Litteratures de l'Union Europeenne **5362**
• Rim (JPN ISSN 0916-0191) **1168**
Rimbaud Vivant (FRA ISSN 0999-1557) **5237**
Rime Magazine (USA ISSN 1546-086X) **5081**
➤ Rimjhim (MUS) **2210**
Rimmonim (ISR ISSN 0333-9637) **515**
Rimoto Senshingu Shinpojumu Shiryo/Papers of Remote Sensing Symposium (JPN) **4027**
Rimscope (USA) **4521**
• Rinascimento (ITA ISSN 0080-3073) **4473**
Rinascimento. Quaderni (ITA ISSN 0394-4387) **4473**
† Rinascita (ITA ISSN 0035-5380) **8985**
Rinboku no Ikushu/Forest Tree Breeding (JPN ISSN 0387-9119) **3701**
▼ • Rince (ARG ISSN 1851-3239) **1515**
Rincontro (CAN ISSN 0380-8416) **3561**
Rind im Bild (DEU) **298**
Rinder-Union-West Report *see* R U W Report **297**
Rinderproduktion *see* Masterrind **293**
• Rinderzucht Braunvieh (DEU ISSN 0948-9118) **299**
• Rinderzucht Fleckvieh (DEU ISSN 0948-7247) **299**
Rinderzucht und Milchproduktion (DEU) **299**
Ring *see* Sedm **5082**
➤ The Ring (POL ISSN 0035-5429) **913**
• The Ring (USA ISSN 0035-5410) **8197**
Ring and Rejoice *see* Ring and Rejoice! **6612**
Ring and Rejoice! (USA ISSN 1931-4779) **6612**
Ring Junger Buende. Mitteilungen (DEU) **2167**
Ring Rhetoric (USA) **8197**
• Ring Systems Handbook (USA ISSN 0742-5996) **2130**
Ringerikes Blad (NOR) **3924**
Ringette Canada. Official Rules (Years) (CAN) **8197**
Ringette Review (CAN) **8197**
Ringing and Migration (GBR ISSN 0307-8698) **913**
Ringing World (GBR ISSN 0035-5453) **6612**
Ringkasan Bulanan Pemerhatian Kajicuaca/Monthly Abstract of Meteorological Observations of Malaysia (MYS ISSN 0126-8872) **6400**
Ringkasan Tahunan Pemerhatian Kajicuaca/Malaysian Meteorological Service. Annual Summary of Meteorological Observations (MYS) **6394**
Ringkjoebing Amts Dagblad (DNK) **3834**
Ringmerkaren (NOR ISSN 0803-3927) **913**
Ringsaker Blad - Brumunddoelen (NOR) **3924**
Ringside (USA) **8197**
† Ringside Wrestling (USA ISSN 1089-618X) **8985**
Ringsider (GBR) **1168**
Ringsport (GBR ISSN 0037-6310) **8197**
Ringyo Shikenjo Kyushu Shijo Nenpo *see* Japan. Government Forest Experiment Station. Kyushu Branch. Annual Report **3694**
Rink (Ambler) (USA ISSN 1531-3042) **8197**
Rinksider (USA) **1791**
Rinpagaku/Japanese Journal of Lymphology (JPN ISSN 0910-4186) **5900**
Rinsho Biseibutsu Jinsoku Shindan Kenkyukaishi/Association for Rapid Method and Automation in Microbiology. Journal (JPN ISSN 0915-1753) **896**
Rinsho Byori *see* Japanese Journal of Clinical Pathology **5643**
Rinsho Eiyo/Japanese Journal of Clinical Nutrition (JPN ISSN 0485-1412) **6669**
Rinsho Fujinka Sanka/Clinical Gynecology and Obstetrics (JPN ISSN 0386-9865) **6003**
Rinsho Ganka/Japanese Journal of Clinical Ophthalmology (JPN ISSN 0370-5579) **6051**
Rinsho Gazo/Clinical Imagiology (JPN ISSN 0911-1069) **6207**
Rinsho Geka/Journal of Clinical Surgery (JPN ISSN 0386-9857) **6257**
Rinsho Hifuka/Japanese Journal of Clinical Dermatology (JPN ISSN 0021-4973) **5881**
Rinsho Hinyokika/Japanese Journal of Clinical Urology (JPN ISSN 0385-2393) **6274**
Rinsho Hoshasen/Japanese Journal of Clinical Radiology (JPN ISSN 0009-9252) **6207**
Rinsho Jui/Journal of Clinical Veterinary Medicine (JPN ISSN 0912-1501) **8807**
Rinsho Kagaku/Japanese Journal of Clinical Chemistry (JPN ISSN 0370-5633) **5707**
Rinsho Kango/Japanese Journal of Clinical Nursing, Monthly (JPN ISSN 0386-7722) **5980**
Rinsho Kensa/Journal of Medical Technology (JPN ISSN 0485-1420) **5910**
Rinsho Kensagaku Zasshi *see* Medical Technology **5672**
• Rinsho Ketsueki/Japanese Journal of Clinical Hematology (JPN ISSN 0485-1439) **5941**
Rinsho Koketsuatsu/Clinical Hypertension (JPN ISSN 1342-2154) **5799**
Rinsho Masui/Journal of Clinical Anesthesia (JPN ISSN 0387-3668) **5774**
Rinsho Men'eki/Clinical Immunology *see* Rinshou Men'eki Arerugika **5765**
Rinsho Noha/Clinical Electroencephalography (JPN ISSN 0485-1447) **6183**
Rinsho Seijimbyo *see* Seijimbyou to Seikatsu Shuukambyou **5711**
Rinsho Seikei Geka/Clinical Orthopaedic Surgery (JPN ISSN 0557-0433) **6072**
Rinsho Seishin Byori/Japanese Journal of Psychopathology (JPN ISSN 0389-3723) **7405**
Rinsho Seishin Igaku/Japanese Journal of Clinical Psychiatry (JPN ISSN 0300-032X) **6183**
• ➤ Rinsho Shinkeigaku/Clinical Neurology (JPN ISSN 0009-918X) **6183**
Rinsho Shinrigaku/Japanese Journal of Clinical Psychology (JPN ISSN 1345-9171) **6183**
Rinsho Shokaki Naika/Clinical Gastroenterology (JPN ISSN 0911-601X) **5930**
Rinsho Shoni Igaku *see* Journal of Clinical Pediatrics **6094**
Rinsho to Kenkyu/Japanese Journal of Clinical and Experimental Medicine (JPN ISSN 0021-4965) **5910**
Rinsho to Yakubutsu Chiryo/Clinics & Drug Therapy *see* Kurinikaru Purakutisu **5659**
Rinsho Toseki/Japanese Journal of Clinical Dialysis (JPN ISSN 0910-5808) **6274**
Rinsho Yakuri (JPN ISSN 0388-1601) **6879**
Rinshou Men'eki Arerugika/Clinical Immunology & Allergology (JPN ISSN 1881-1930) **5765**
Rinshou Ryuumachi/Clinical Rheumatology and Related Research (JPN ISSN 0914-8760) **6227**
Rinshou Shinrigaku Kenkyuu/Japanese Journal of Clinical Psychology (JPN ISSN 0035-5496) **7405**
• Rio (USA) **5363**
Rio Artes (BRA) **515**
Rio de Janeiro *see* Rum & Reggae's Rio de Janeiro **8753**
Rio de Janeiro, Brazil (State). Instituto Estadual do Livro. Divisao de Bibliotecas. Boletim Bibliografico (BRA) **634**
Rio de Janeiro Suplemento *see* Veja **3804**
Rio de la Plata (FRA ISSN 0982-0582) **5169**
➤ Rio Grande do Sul, Brazil. Fundacao de Economia e Estatistica. Indicadores Economicos F E E (BRA ISSN 0103-3905) **1515**
Rio Grande do Sul, Brazil. Procuradoria Geral do Estado. Revista (BRA ISSN 0101-1480) **4775**
• Rio Negro (ARG) **3792**
• Rio Observer (BRA) **8752**
• La Rioja. Boletin Oficial (ESP ISSN 1576-1126) **4775**
Riolering (NLD ISSN 1380-8613) **3512**
Rioleringswetenschap (NLD ISSN 1568-3788) **3512**
Rioleringswetenschap en Techniek *see* Rioleringswetenschap **3512**
† Riot (AUS ISSN 1832-9594) **8986**
Riot Magazine (USA) **2210**
• Riovale Jornal (BRA) **3804**
Rip It Up (NZL ISSN 0114-0876) **6612**
Ripe (CAN ISSN 1718-1305) **6976**
Ripley P. Bullen Monographs in Anthropology and History (USA ISSN 0271-6925) **414**
Ripon Magazine (USA ISSN 1058-1855) **2299**
Ripon Quarterly (USA ISSN 0094-7865) **7179**
The Ripple (CAN ISSN 1910-7196) **8281**
Ripples (AUS ISSN 1832-7516) **5363**
Ripsaw News (USA) **3986**
Ripsik (EST) **2210**
Riptide (AUS ISSN 1034-2346) **8330**
Riptide. Photo Annual *see* Riptide **8330**
Riron Butsurigaku no Shinpo *see* Progress of Theoretical Physics **7036**
➤ Riron to Hoho/Sociological Theory and Methods (JPN ISSN 0913-1442) **8130**
▼ Risafa Medical Digest (IRQ ISSN 2070-2027) **5707**
Al-Risalah (UAE) **7715**
Risalat al-Maktaba *see* Message of the Library **5032**
Risalat al-Masjid (OMN) **7715**
Risalat al-Mu'allim *see* Message of the Teacher **2993**
Risalat al Sina'a/Amman Chamber of Industry. Bimonthly Industrial Bulletin (JOR) **1409**
Risalat Al-Taqrib (IRN) **7715**
Risalatuh Thaqalayn (IRN) **7715**
RisControl (AUT) **4521**
Rise (USA) **8197**
▼ • Rise Up (USA) **3561**
Risen (USA) **6612**
RiseUp *see* Rise Up **3561**
Rishiri Kenkyu/Rishiri Studies (JPN ISSN 0919-9160) **4187**
Rishiri Studies *see* Rishiri Kenkyu **4187**
Risicoltore (ITA ISSN 0391-8688) **152**
Risiko Manager (DEU ISSN 1861-9363) **1168**
Rising Generation *see* Eigo Seinen **5114**
• The Rising Nepal (NPL ISSN 0259-1642) **3914**
Rising Sun (IND) **7179**
Rising Tide (USA ISSN 1072-5687) **7179**
The Rising Times (USA ISSN 1930-0832) **8066**
• Risk (GBR ISSN 0952-8776) **1380**
Risk *see* The British Journal of Diabetes and Vascular Disease **5884**
• Risk Abstracts (Online) (USA ISSN 1555-8436) **3481**
• ➤ Risk Analysis (USA ISSN 0272-4332) **5530**
Risk & Benefits Journal (Marina del Rey) (USA ISSN 1053-556X) **1791**
▼ • Risk and Decision Analysis (NLD ISSN 1569-7371) **1791**
Risk & Insurance *see* Risk & Insurance **4521**
• Risk & Insurance (USA ISSN 1050-9232) **4521**
• Risk and Regulation (GBR ISSN 1473-6004) **1168**
• Risk and Uncertainty Program Working Paper (AUS ISSN 1832-4258) **1168**
Risk: Australasian Risk Management *see* Risk Management **4521**
Risk-Based Decision Making in Water Resources (USA ISSN 1063-5076) **3282**
Risk Book Series (CHE ISSN 0254-3966) **7678**
• Risk Factor Method of Investing (USA) **1648**
• Risk Financing (USA) **4521**
• Risk, Fraud and Compliance (DEU) **2667**
Risk, Fraud and Governance *see* Risk, Fraud and Compliance **2667**
Risk Insight (ZAF) **4521**
Risk - It (AUS) **1301**
• Risk Management (AUS) **4521**
• ➤ Risk Management (GBR ISSN 1460-3799) **4521**
• Risk Management (USA ISSN 0035-5593) **4521**
Risk Management (ZAF ISSN 1817-6585) **6685**
Risk Management Alert (USA ISSN 1540-3998) **4880**
▼ • ➤ Risk Management and Healthcare Policy (GBR ISSN 1179-1594) **7540**
• Risk Management and Insurance Audit Techniques (USA) **4521**
• Risk Management and Insurance Review (USA ISSN 1098-1616) **4521**
Risk Management Association Annual Statement Studies *see* R M A Annual Statement Studies **1377**
Risk Management Association Journal *see* The R M A Journal **1377**
Risk Management Bulletin *see* Risk Transfer **1791**
Risk Management for Campus Recreation (CAN ISSN 1718-4606) **7540**
• Risk Management in Canadian Health Care (CAN ISSN 1488-0555) **4775**
Risk Management Magazine *see* Risk Management **4521**
• Risk Management Module (GBR ISSN 1749-7426) **5864**
• Risk Management Reports (Online) (USA) **4522**
Risk Management Reports (Print) *see* Risk Management Reports (Online) **4522**
Risk Manager (IRL) **2679**
• Risk Measurement Service (AUS ISSN 0812-8901) **1380**
Risk Measurement Service (GBR ISSN 0261-3344) **1380**
Risk Mitigation Executive (USA ISSN 1556-1569) **1791**
• Risk Policy Report (USA) **3463**
Risk Ratings Review *see* Country Risk Service. Risk Ratings Review **1619**
• The Risk Report (AUS ISSN 1327-6174) **1648**
• The Risk Report (USA) **4522**
Risk Retention Group Directory and Guide (USA) **4522**
• Risk Retention Reporter (USA ISSN 1063-357X) **4522**
• Risk Transfer (GBR) **1791**
• Risk Update (London, 1997) (GBR ISSN 1467-3886) **1581**
• The Risks Digest (USA) **2515**
▼ • Risks, Hazards & Crisis in Public Policy (USA ISSN 1944-4079) **7467**
RiskWatch (USA ISSN 0896-2308) **1791**
Risley Record (USA ISSN 1050-7922) **3780**
Risoe International Symposium on Materials Science. Proceedings (DNK ISSN 0907-0079) **6331**
Risoe News *see* Risoenyt **3174**
Risoe Nyt *see* Risoenyt **3174**
• Risoenyt (DNK ISSN 0108-0350) **3174**
Il Risorgimento (ITA ISSN 0035-5607) **4258**
Risorgimento. Idee e Realta (ITA ISSN 1828-5872) **4259**
• Risorsa Uomo (ITA ISSN 1128-0689) **7405**
• Il Risparmio (ITA ISSN 0035-5615) **1380**
Risque et Prevention (FRA ISSN 0982-8303) **7072**
† Risques & Management International (FRA ISSN 1760-2009) **8986**
Risques et Responsabilites Territoriales *see* La Lettre du Contentieux **7496**
• Risques Internationaux (FRA ISSN 1770-474X) **1581**
Riss (AUT ISSN 1019-1976) **7405**
Riss (Bergen) (NOR ISSN 1503-7436) **414**
• Riss (Trondheim) (NOR ISSN 0806-5063) **5363**
▼ Rissala (FRA ISSN 1954-1562) **7715**
Rissener Jahrbuch (DEU) **7179**
Rister Zollgesetze (DEU) **1581**
Ristik (EST) **8197**
Ristorante! (USA ISSN 1542-9601) **4397**
Ristorante *see* Primo Ristorante **3660**
I Ristoranti dell'Accademia (ITA ISSN 1972-2729) **4397**
Ristorazione Collettiva (ITA ISSN 1120-6039) **4397**
• Il Risveglio (ITA ISSN 1723-7599) **3898**
† Risveglio del Molise e del Mezzogiorno (ITA ISSN 0035-5623) **8986**
➤ Rit Fiskideildar/Marine Research Institute. Journal (ISL ISSN 0484-9019) **3606**
Rit L B H I (Landbunadarhaskoli Islands) (ISL ISSN 1670-5785) **152**
Rit Landbunadarhaskoli Islands *see* Rit L B H I **152**
RITA *see* R I T A **4084**
Ritchie County Historical Society Newsletter (USA) **3780**
Ritchie's Supreme Court Procedure, New South Wales *see* Ritchie's Uniform Civil Procedure N S W **4960**
• Ritchie's Uniform Civil Procedure N S W (New South Wales) (AUS) **4960**
Rite *see* Pastoral Liturgy **6604**
Ritenour News (USA) **2907**
Rites Egyptiens (BEL) **414**
Ritid (ISL ISSN 1670-0139) **4473**
Ritmennt (ISL ISSN 1027-4448) **5044**
Ritmo (ESP ISSN 0035-5658) **6612**
El Ritmo de la Noche (USA) **5081**
• Ritorno al Diritto (ITA ISSN 1827-0263) **4776**
▼ Ritratti di Donne Indimenticabili (ITA ISSN 1972-4063) **8902**
➤ Ritsumeikan Daigaku Rikogaku Kenkyujo Kiyo/Ritsumeikan University. Research Institute of Science and Engineering. Memoirs (JPN ISSN 0370-4254) **3218**
Ritsumeikan Economic Review *see* Ritsumeikan Keizaigaku **1168**
• Ritsumeikan Hogaku (JPN ISSN 0483-1330) **4940**
Ritsumeikan Keizaigaku/Ritsumeikan Economic Review (JPN ISSN 0288-0180) **1168**
• Ritsumeikan Law Review (International Edition) (JPN ISSN 0912-4322) **4940**
Ritsumeikan University. Research Institute of Science and Engineering. Memoirs *see* Ritsumeikan Daigaku Rikogaku Kenkyujo Kiyo **3218**
Rittenhouse (USA) **4489**
▼ Rittenhouse Magazine (USA) **3986**
▼ Ritter Rost (DEU) **2210**
The Ritual (GBR) **5414**
Ritual Magazine (GBR) **6299**
The Ritz-Carlton (USA) **8785**
Ritz Carlton Magazine (USA) **8752**
Rivaaj (USA ISSN 1947-8976) 5081
Rivages (FRA) **8659**
Rivarol (FRA ISSN 0035-5666) **7998**
† Rive Gauche Magazine (FRA ISSN 1141-4073) **8986**
• La Rivendita (ITA) **1033**
La Rivendita Show Building *see* Show Building **1035**
River (USA ISSN 1098-5956) **8330**
River Behaviour and Control (IND ISSN 0970-9258) **8831**
River Bend Library System. Report of the Director (USA ISSN 0080-3227) **5044**
River City Library Times (USA ISSN 0270-9104) **5044**
▼ • River City Tails (USA ISSN 1945-6751) **6814**
• The River News (AUS ISSN 1447-8501) **3796**
River Oak Review (USA ISSN 1074-3693) **5433**
River Plate Shipping Guide; Ship Owners', Masters' and Agents' Handbook, River Plate Ports *see* Centro de Navegacion. Handbook. River Plate Handbook for Shipowners and Agents **8641**
† • River Post (AUS) **8986**
• ➤ River Research and Applications (GBR ISSN 1535-1459) **8831**
• River Styx (USA ISSN 0149-8851) **5237**
River Talk (USA ISSN 1942-4752) **8281**
• River Teeth (USA ISSN 1544-1849) **5363**
River Watch (AUS ISSN 1031-4881) **3463**
Riverbed Haiku *see* Riverbed Haiku Anthology **5433**
▼ • Riverbed Haiku Anthology (USA ISSN 1941-434X) **5433**
La Riverego (CAN ISSN 0830-9574) **5169**
Riverfront (USA) **5237**
• Riverina Highlands Catchment Tumut/Gundagai/Adelong Region. Newsletter (AUS ISSN 1833-6604) **3463**
Riverlander Notes (AUS) **2626**

Title

Title

10824 ROMANIA PETROCHEMICALS REPORT ULRICH'S PERIODICALS

Romania Petrochemicals Report (GBR ISSN 1749-2416) 6790
Romania Pitoreasca (ROM ISSN 1221-0692) 8752
Romania the Source Book (Years) (ROM) 3933
Romanian Academic Society. Crisis Papers Collection (ROM) 7180
Romanian Academic Society. Working Papers Collection (ROM) 7180
Romanian Academy. Proceedings. Series A: Mathematics, Physics, Technical Sciences, Information Science (ROM ISSN 1454-9069) 5530
Romanian Academy. Proceedings. Series B: Chemistry, Life Sciences and Geosciences (ROM ISSN 1454-8267) 2079
Romanian Archives of Microbiology and Immunology (ROM ISSN 1222-3891) 896
• Romanian Astronomical Journal (ROM ISSN 1220-5168) 580
Romanian Business Journal (ROM ISSN 1223-6837) 1168
Romanian Business News (ROM) 1168
➤ Romanian Civilization (ROM ISSN 1220-7365) 4260
Romanian Civilization Studies (ROM ISSN 1223-1908) 4260
Romanian Cultural Studies (ROM ISSN 1454-3443) 4473
▼ The Romanian Echo (USA ISSN 1939-2974) 5082
• ➤ The Romanian Economic Journal (ROM ISSN 1454-4296) 1168
Romanian Film (ROM) 6511
Romanian Financial and Banking News *see* Romanian Business News 1168
Romanian Gymnastics (ROM ISSN 1453-1240) 8197
• Romanian Journal of Biochemistry (ROM ISSN 1582-3318) 744
• Romanian Journal of Biophysics (ROM ISSN 1220-515X) 755
Romanian Journal of Chemistry *see* Revue Roumaine de Chimie 2079
Romanian Journal of Endocrinology *see* Acta Endocrinologica 5883
• ➤ Romanian Journal of European Affairs (ROM ISSN 1582-8271) 7263
• Romanian Journal of Gastroenterology (ROM ISSN 1221-4167) 5930
Romanian Journal of Geophysics (ROM ISSN 1220-5680) 2789
Romanian Journal of Gerontology and Geriatrics/Revista Romana de Gerontologie si Geriatrie (ROM ISSN 0254-2307) 4055
Romanian Journal of Information Science and Technology (ROM ISSN 1453-8245) 2550
• Romanian Journal of Internal Medicine/Revue Roumaine de Medecine Interne (ROM ISSN 1582-3296) 5948
Romanian Journal of International Studies *see* Revista Romana de Studii Internationale 1581
Romanian Journal of Legal Medicine *see* Revista de Medicina Legala 5916
Romanian Journal of Materials *see* Revista Romana de Materiale 1033
➤ Romanian Journal of Meteorology (ROM ISSN 1223-1118) 6394
Romanian Journal of Mineral Deposits (ROM ISSN 1220-5648) 2715
Romanian Journal of Mineralogy (ROM ISSN 1220-5621) 2765
Romanian Journal of Morphology and Embryology *see* Journal of Molecular and Cellular Pathology 683
Romanian Journal of Neurology: Serie de Neurologie et Psychiatrie (ROM ISSN 1453-4134) 6183
Romanian Journal of Paleontology (ROM ISSN 1220-5656) 6730
➤ Romanian Journal of Petrology (ROM ISSN 1220-563X) 2765
• ➤ Romanian Journal of Physics (ROM ISSN 1221-146X) 7038
• Romanian Journal of Physiology (ROM ISSN 1223-4974) 927
Romanian Journal of Political Science *see* Revista Romana de Stiinte Politice 7179
Romanian Journal of Pure and Applied Mathematics *see* Revue Roumaine de Mathematiques Pures et Appliquees 5530
▼ • Romanian Journal of Regional Science (ROM ISSN 1843-8520) 7998
Romanian Journal of Society and Politics (ROM) 7180
Romanian Journal of Stratigraphy (ROM ISSN 1220-5664) 2765
Romanian Journal of Tectonics and Regional Geology (ROM ISSN 1221-4663) 2765
Romanian Language *see* Limba Romana 5144
Romanian Lepidopterological Society. Information Bulletin *see* Societatea Lepidopterologica Romana. Buletin de informare 859
• Romanian Panorama (ROM ISSN 1220-5028) 3933
• Romanian Patriarchate News Bulletin (ROM ISSN 1841-7663) 7706
➤ Romanian Physical Society. National Conference for Physics. Abstracts (ROM) 7072
• Romanian Report in Physics (ROM ISSN 1221-1451) 7038
• Romanian Review (ROM ISSN 0035-8088) 5237
Romanian Review for Industrial Property *see* Revista Romana de Proprietate Industriala 6758
• Romanian Travel Guide (ROM ISSN 1454-4423) 8753
• ➤ Romanic Review (USA ISSN 0035-8118) 5364
Romanica (ARG ISSN 0327-1102) 5169
Romanica (PRT ISSN 0872-5675) 5364
➤ Romanica et Comparatistica (DEU ISSN 0940-3736) 5364
➤ Romanica Gandensia (BEL ISSN 0080-3855) 5169
Romanica Gothoburgensia (SWE ISSN 0080-3863) 5169
Romanica Helvetica (DEU ISSN 0080-3871) 5169
Romanica Monacensia (DEU ISSN 0178-1294) 5364
Romanica Neapolitana (ITA ISSN 0391-1950) 5169
• Romanica Stockholmiensia (SWE ISSN 0557-2657) 5169
Romanice (DEU) 5364
• Romanische Bibliographie (DEU ISSN 0080-388X) 5201
• Romanische Bibliographie CD-ROM (DEU) 5201
• ➤ Romanische Forschungen (DEU ISSN 0035-8126) 5169
Romanistik (DEU ISSN 1860-1995) 5169
Romanistik in Geschichte und Gegenwart (DEU ISSN 0947-0565) 5169
Romanistik in Geschichte und Gegenwart. Beihefte (DEU ISSN 0947-0573) 5169
Romanistische Arbeitshefte (DEU ISSN 0344-676X) 5170
Romanistische Kongressberichte (DEU) 5170
Romanistische Texte und Studien (DEU ISSN 0176-8166) 5170
Romanistische Zeitschrift fuer Literaturgeschichte/Cahiers d'Histoire des Litteratures Romanes (DEU ISSN 0343-379X) 5364
• Romanistisches Jahrbuch (DEU ISSN 0080-3898) 5170
• ➤ Romanitas (PRI ISSN 1937-5697) 5364
Romano (BRA ISSN 1807-7331) 6299
Romanobarbarica (ITA ISSN 0391-285X) 2240
Romanoslavica (ROM ISSN 0557-272X) 5170
Les Romans Bleus (FRA ISSN 1951-5766) 2211
Romans d'Inspiration *see* Collection Romans d'Inspiration 5276
Romanserier og Selvbiografiske Serier (DNK ISSN 0106-8253) 5364
Romansk Filmklub (DNK ISSN 0902-1523) 6511
• Romansk Forum (Online) (NOR) 5170
Romansk Instituts Duplikerede Smaaskrifter *see* R I D S 5164
Romansk Instituts Duplikerede Smaaskrifter *see* R I D S 5164
• Romanske Skrifter (DNK ISSN 1395-4873) 5170
Romanske Stenarbejder (DNK ISSN 0107-2366) 515
The RoMANtic (USA ISSN 1093-894X) 6299
• Romantic Circles Praxis Series (USA ISSN 1528-8129) 5364
Romantic Country (USA ISSN 1946-0651) 4549
Romantic Days and Nights in New Orleans (USA ISSN 1540-1529) 8753
Romantic Escapes in the Caribbean (USA ISSN 1546-6833) 8753
Romantic Homes (USA ISSN 1086-4083) 4549
The Romantic Movement *see* English Language Notes 5290
Romantic Praxis: Theory and Criticism *see* Romantic Circles Praxis Series 5364
➤ Romantic Russia (USA ISSN 1521-1975) 5364
Romantic Shelters (USA) 3282
• ➤ Romantic Textualities (GBR ISSN 1748-0116) 5364
Romantic Times Book Club *see* Romantic Times Book Reviews 5412
• Romantic Times Book Reviews (USA ISSN 1933-0634) 5412
Romantic Traveling (USA ISSN 1053-0177) 8753
• Romanticism (GBR ISSN 1354-991X) 5364
• ➤ Romanticism and Victorianism on the Net (GBR) 5364
Romanticism in Perspective (GBR) 5412
Romanticism on the Net *see* Romanticism and Victorianism on the Net 5364
• Romantisme (FRA ISSN 0048-8593) 5364
Le Romantisme et Apres en France (GBR ISSN 1422-8696) 5364
Romantisme et Modernites (FRA ISSN 1169-2944) 5364
† The Romantist (ITA ISSN 0161-682X) 8986
Romantizm v Russkoi i Sovetskoi Literature (RUS) 5364
Romanwoche (DEU) 5412
† Romanwoche - Schicksale Hautnah (DEU) 8986
† I Romanzi d'Amore di Confessioni Donna (ITA ISSN 1722-7984) 8986
† I Romanzi Proibiti di Confessioni Donna (ITA ISSN 1721-5714) 8986
Romatizma *see* Turkish Journal of Rheumatology 6227
➤ Romatoloji ve Tibbi Rehabilitasyon Dergisi/Journal of Rheumatology and Medical Rehabilitation (TUR ISSN 1300-0691) 6227
Romboid (SVK ISSN 0231-6714) 5237
▼ Rome (USA ISSN 1937-044X) 8753
Rome (Year) (USA ISSN 1056-442X) 8753
Rome Directions (USA ISSN 1933-0723) 8753
Rome for Dummies (USA ISSN 1935-4363) 8753
RoMeO Nieuws (Rotterdams Openbaar Vervoer Museum en Exploitatie van Oldtimers) (NLD ISSN 1874-5407) 8510
Romford Observer (GBR ISSN 1350-5939) 3870
Romford Record (GBR ISSN 0306-1140) 4260
Romford Recorder (GBR ISSN 0961-3382) 3870
Romhorisont (SWE ISSN 0349-5590) 4260
Romney Sheep Breeders' Society. Handbook (GBR) 299
• Rompan Filas (MEX) 2908
Romsdals Budstikke (NOR) 3924
Romu (DNK ISSN 0107-928X) 6536
• Roncarelli Report on the Computer Animation Industry (CAN ISSN 1202-1156) 2489
Rond de Tafel *see* Vieren 7692
Rond Reuma (NLD ISSN 1566-6018) 6227
Ronda Iberia (ESP) 8785
De Ronde Vener (NLD ISSN 0012-558X) 3915
Rondell Programm (DEU) 6511
• Rondo (DEU) 6613
Rondo (FIN ISSN 0355-5054) 6613
Rondom de Leeuw (NLD ISSN 1873-3603) 4260
Rondom M S (NLD ISSN 1574-9215) 6183
Rondom Multiple Sclerose *see* Rondom M S 6183
Ronduit Insite (NLD ISSN 1570-470X) 7773
Ronduit Magazine *see* Ronduit Insite 7773
Ronen Seishin Igaku Zasshi/Japanese Journal of Geriatric Psychiatry (JPN ISSN 0915-6305) 4055
• Rongbaozhai/Rongbaozhai Studio (CHN ISSN 1009-0649) 515
Rongbaozhai Studio *see* Rongbaozhai 515
RonMay@themayreport.com *see* The May Report 3981
Rood (NLD ISSN 1574-2733) 7180
Roodkoper (NLD ISSN 1385-0334) 3915
Roof (GBR ISSN 0307-6911) 4426
Roofing (GBR) 1034
Roofing, Cladding and Insulation *see* R C I 1031
• Roofing Contractor (USA ISSN 1098-1519) 1034
Roofing Materials and Systems Directory (USA ISSN 1538-0130) 1034
Roofing Siding Insulation *see* R S I 1031
Roofs (NLD ISSN 1566-1458) 1034
Rooi Rose (ZAF ISSN 0035-8207) 8882
Rooilijn (NLD ISSN 1380-2860) 4027
Room (CAN ISSN 1914-4083) 5364
Room *see* IKEA Family Live 4543
Room (GBR ISSN 1460-0218) 4562
Room (THA ISSN 1685-7240) 4549
Room 5 (GBR ISSN 1472-1066) 4473
Room Five *see* Room 5 4473
Room of One's Own *see* Room 5364
ROOM, the National Council for Housing and Planning (GBR) 4426
• Roomers (AUS) 5364
▼ Rooms Outlast Us (USA ISSN 1947-5586) 5433
▼ Roomservice Pro (SWE ISSN 1654-059X) 1034
Roomuud (EST) 8197
Roopa - Lekha (IND ISSN 0035-8215) 539
Roope-Seta (FIN ISSN 0357-8755) 2211
Roopvati (IND) 5365
Roosevelt Island (USA ISSN 1946-3391) 8753
† Roost (AUS) 8986
• The Root (USA) 3561
Root & Branch (GBR) 6613
Root Cellar Preserves (USA ISSN 0748-6251) 3781
Root Directory (USA) 2583
Root Fodder Crop, Pulse and Oilseed Varieties Recommended List *see* Ireland. Department of Agriculture and Food. Root Fodder Crop, Pulse and Oilseed Varieties Recommended List (Year) 238
Rooting Around (USA) 3781
Rooting Around Huron (CAN ISSN 0847-401X) 3781
Roots and Branches (USA ISSN 0737-9242) 3781
Roots & Branches (USA ISSN 0893-4150) 3781
Roots & Leaves (USA ISSN 0748-2485) 3781
Roots & Rhythm Newsletter (USA) 6613
Roots & Shoots Quarterly (USA ISSN 0738-2391) 3781
Roots, Branches and Twigs (CAN ISSN 0831-5930) 3781
Roots-Key (USA ISSN 0895-6472) 3781
Roots Music (GBR) 6613
Roots of Empathy Link (CAN ISSN 1910-6351) 2908
▼ • Roots Zone (Online) (DNK ISSN 1902-8547) 6613
† • Roots Zone (Print) (DNK ISSN 1902-8539) 8986
• RootsWorld (USA) 6613
Ropa a Ropne Produkty *see* Ropa, Ropne Produkty a Zemni Plyn 6801
• Ropa, Ropne Produkty a Zemni Plyn (CZE) 6801
Ropanasuri (IDN ISSN 0216-0951) 6257
• Ropet fra Oest (NOR ISSN 0803-4729) 7773
• Rorschachiana (USA ISSN 1192-5604) 7405
Ros *see* Ros Paardenmagazine 8298
▼ Ros Paardenmagazine (NLD ISSN 1570-6257) 8298
La Rosa (ITA ISSN 1970-3546) 4473
Rosa Mundi (USA ISSN 1558-5972) 3749
• La Rosa Profunda (ESP ISSN 1699-4671) 5433
El Rosacruz (MEX ISSN 0035-8266) 6950
Rosai Rehabilitation Engineering Center. Annual Report *see* E I R E C Kenkyu Hokokushu 6108
Rosalie-Cadron-Jette Centre Newsletter *see* Centre Rosalie-Cadron-Jette. Bulletin 7791
Rosalie, Lumiere et Tendresse sur nos Pas *see* Centre Rosalie-Cadron-Jette. Bulletin 7791
Rosarian (CAN ISSN 1487-6876) 3749
Rosario de Maria (PRT ISSN 0035-8274) 7815
Il Rosario di Padre Pio (ITA ISSN 1824-1204) 7815
Il Rosario e la Nuova Pompei (ITA ISSN 0035-8282) 7815
Rosazea Journal (DEU) 5881
The Roscoe Pound Institute Civil Justice Digest *see* Civil Justice Digest 4828
Roscommon Champion (IRL) 3894
Roscommon Herald (IRL ISSN 1393-7642) 3894
Rosdorfer Mitteilungen (DEU) 7502
The Rose *see* The Rose Annual 3749
Rose al-Yusuf *see* Ruz al-Yusuf 5237
• The Rose & Thorn (USA) 5365
The Rose Annual (GBR ISSN 1751-1666) 3749
Rose Arranger's Bulletin (USA) 3749
• ➤ Rose Croix Journal (USA ISSN 1553-9156) 4473
Rose Exhibitors Forum (USA) 3749
Rose Hybridizers Association Newsletter (USA) 3749
• The Rose Sheet (USA ISSN 1530-1222) 596
The Rose Sheet on the Web *see* The Rose Sheet 596
Rosebud (USA ISSN 1072-1681) 5365
Rosemary Conley Diet & Fitness (GBR ISSN 1360-497X) 6996
The Rosengarten Report (USA) 3662
RosenKrieg (DEU) 8130
Rosenzweig-Jahrbuch/Rosenzweig Yearbook (DEU) 6950
Rosenzweig Yearbook *see* Rosenzweig-Jahrbuch 6950
Rosenzweigiana (DEU) 6950
• Rosetta (GBR ISSN 1752-1580) 415
Rosetum (ITA ISSN 1825-0718) 7815
Roseville Granite Bay Style *see* RosevilleGraniteBayStyle 5082
RosevilleGraniteBayStyle (USA) 5082
ROSEWELLness (USA) 6033
Roshan Pakistan (PAK) 3218
Roshia Kenkyu/Russian Studies (JPN ISSN 0918-7030) 7263
Roshni (IND) 8882
• Rosicrucian Digest (USA ISSN 0035-8339) 6950
Roskilde Kommune. Statistikken (DNK ISSN 0105-8339) 8397
Roskilde Universitetsbibliotek. Skriftserie (DNK ISSN 0105-564X) 5044
• Roskilde Universitetscenter. Center for Oestrigsk-Nordiske Kulturstudier. Smaaskrifter/Kleine Schriften vn Z OE N K (DNK ISSN 1600-9509) 4260
Roskilde Universitetscenter. Datalogisk Afdeling. Datalogiske Noter (DNK ISSN 0908-5491) 2436
Roskilde Universitetscenter. Datalogisk Afdeling. Datalogiske Skrifter (DNK ISSN 0109-9779) 2436
Roskilde Universitetscenter. Institut for Geography and International Development Studies. Kompendium (DNK ISSN 1395-3222) 4027
Roskilde Universitetscenter. Institut for Geography and International Development Studies. Research Reports (DNK ISSN 1395-1904) 4027
Roskilde Universitetscenter. Institut for Geography and International Development Studies. Working Papers (DNK) 4027
Roskilde Universitetscenter. Institut for Samfundsoekonomi og Planlaegning. Arbejdspapir (DNK ISSN 0108-2205) 8130
Roskilde Universitetscenter. Institut for Samfundsoekonomi og Planlaegning. Research Report (DNK ISSN 0105-8827) 1168
Roskilde Universitetscenter. Institute for Geography and International Development Studies. Meddelelser (DNK ISSN 1395-1963) 4027
Roskilde Universitetscenter. Lingvistgruppen. Rolig-Papir (DNK ISSN 0106-0821) 5170
Roskilde Universitscenter. International Development Studies. Occasional Paper (DNK ISSN 0907-2829) 1604
Roskill's Lithium Digest (GBR ISSN 0965-7711) 6331
Rosliny Ozdobne (POL ISSN 1730-2803) 3749
Il Rosone (ITA) 5237
Ross - Commercial Leases (GBR) 4880
Ross Conference on Pediatric Research. Report (USA ISSN 0557-3467) 6669
Ross County Genealogical Society Newsletter (USA) 3781
Ross Reports Television and Film *see* Call Sheet 2378
Ross Reports Television & Film *see* Call Sheet 2378
Rossica Nitriensia (SVK ISSN 1336-9091) 5365
➤ Rossica Olomucensia (CZE ISSN 0139-9268) 5170
➤ Rossica Society of Russian Philately Journal (USA ISSN 0035-8363) 6899
• ➤ Rossiiskaya Akademiya Meditsinskikh Nauk. Rossiiskii Onkologicheskii Nauchnyi Tsentr imeni N. N. Blokhina. Vestnik/Russian Academy of Medical Sciences. N. N. Blokhin Cancer Research Center. Herald (RUS ISSN 1726-9865) 6034
Rossiiskaya Akademiya Meditsinskikh Nauk. Vestnik (RUS ISSN 0869-6047) 5707
Rossiiskaya Akademiya Nauk. Bibliografiya Izdanii (RUS) 634
Rossiiskaya Akademiya Nauk. Dal'nevostochnoe Otdelenie. Vestnik/Russian Academy of Sciences. Far Eastern Branch. Bulletin (RUS ISSN 0869-7698) 8066
• ➤ Rossiiskaya Akademiya Nauk. Doklady (RUS ISSN 0869-5652) 7904
Rossiiskaya Akademiya Nauk. Institut Arkheologii. Kratkie Soobshcheniya (RUS) 415

DIRECTORY 2010 ROYAL ACADEMY OF ENGINEERING. ENGINEERING MANUFACTURING 10825

Rossiiskaya Akademiya Nauk. Institut Obshchei Fiziki. Trudy (RUS ISSN 0233-9390) **7038**
Rossiiskaya Akademiya Nauk. Institut Russkoi Literatury. Otdel Drevnerusskoi Literatury. Trudy (RUS ISSN 0130-464X) **5365**
Rossiiskaya Akademiya Nauk. Izvestiya. Energetika (RUS) **3394**
• Rossiiskaya Akademiya Nauk. Izvestiya. Fizika Zemli (RUS ISSN 1026-3527) **2789**
Rossiiskaya Akademiya Nauk. Izvestiya. Mekhanika Tverdogo Tela (RUS ISSN 1026-3519) **3395**
➤ Rossiiskaya Akademiya Nauk. Izvestiya. Mekhanika Zhidkosti i Gaza (RUS ISSN 0568-5281) **7062**
Rossiiskaya Akademiya Nauk. Izvestiya. Seriya Biologicheskaya (RUS ISSN 1026-3470) **701**
➤ Rossiiskaya Akademiya Nauk. Izvestiya. Seriya Fizicheskaya (RUS ISSN 1026-3489) **7038**
• Rossiiskaya Akademiya Nauk. Izvestiya. Seriya Fizika Atmosfery i Okeana (RUS ISSN 1023-6317) **6394**
Rossiiskaya Akademiya Nauk. Izvestiya. Seriya Geograficheskaya (RUS ISSN 0373-2444) **4027**
Rossiiskaya Akademiya Nauk. Izvestiya. Seriya Geologicheskaya (RUS) **2765**
Rossiiskaya Akademiya Nauk. Izvestiya. Seriya Khimicheskaya (RUS ISSN 1026-3500) **2079**
• Rossiiskaya Akademiya Nauk. Izvestiya. Seriya Literatury i Yazyka (RUS) **5365**
➤ Rossiiskaya Akademiya Nauk. Izvestiya. Seriya Matematicheskaya (RUS ISSN 1607-0046) **5530**
• Rossiiskaya Akademiya Nauk. Izvestiya. Teoriya i Systemy Upravleniya (RUS ISSN 1029-3620) **2528**
• Rossiiskaya Akademiya Nauk. Kolloidnyi Zhurnal (RUS ISSN 0023-2912) **2140**
• ➤ Rossiiskaya Akademiya Nauk. Okeanologiya (RUS ISSN 0030-1574) **2817**
Rossiiskaya Akademiya Nauk. Sibirskoe Otdelenie. Ob'edinennyi Institut Geologii, Geofiziki, i Mineralogii. Trudy (RUS ISSN 1027-3603) **2765**
• Rossiiskaya Akademiya Nauk. Vestnik (RUS ISSN 0869-5873) **7904**
Rossiiskaya Akademiya Nauk. Zoologicheskii Institut. Opredeliteli Zhyvotnykh (RUS) **962**
Rossiiskaya Akademiya Nauk. Zoologicheskii Institut. Trudy/Russian Academy of Sciences. Zoological Institute. Proceedings (RUS ISSN 0206-0477) **962**
Rossiiskaya Akademiya Sel'skokhozyaistvennykh Nauk. Doklady (RUS ISSN 0869-6128) **152**
Rossiiskaya Akademiya Sel'skokhozyaistvennykh Nauk. Vestnik (RUS ISSN 0869-3730) **152**
• Rossiiskaya Arkheologiya (RUS ISSN 0869-6063) **415**
Rossiiskaya Aziya (RUS) **4260**
Rossiiskaya Ekonomika: Prognozy i Tendentsii (RUS) **1516**
Rossiiskaya Federatsiya. Gazeta (RUS) **7180**
Rossiiskaya Federatsiya Segodnya (RUS) **7180**
• Rossiiskaya Gazeta (RUS ISSN 1560-0823) **3940**
• Rossiiskaya Gazeta Online (RUS ISSN 1606-5484) **3940**
Rossiiskaya Gosudarstvennaya Biblioteka. Nauchno-Issledovatel'skii Otdel Rukopisei. Zapiski (RUS ISSN 0132-3415) **5044**
Rossiiskaya Gosudarstvennaya Biblioteka. Otchety (RUS) **5044**
Rossiiskaya Gosudarstvennaya Biblioteka. Uchenye Trudy (RUS) **5044**
Rossiiskaya Muzykal'naya Gazeta (RUS) **6613**
• Rossiiskaya Okhotnich'ya Gazeta (RUS ISSN 1682-6981) **8331**
Rossiiskaya Pochta i Rasprostranenie Pechati (RUS) **4583**
Rossiiskaya Pravda (RUS) **3940**
Rossiiskaya Provintsiya (RUS ISSN 0869-8376) **3940**
➤ Rossiiskaya Rinologiya (RUS ISSN 0869-5474) **6085**
• Rossiiskaya Yustitsiya (RUS ISSN 0131-6761) **4776**
• Rossiiskie Vesti (RUS ISSN 1560-053X) **3940**
Rossiiskii Advokat (RUS) **4776**
Rossiiskii Chernobyl (RUS) **3940**
Rossiiskii Ekonomicheskii Zhurnal (RUS ISSN 0869-5202) **1168**
➤ Rossiiskii Fiziologicheskii Zhurnal im. Sechenova/Sechenov Physiological Journal (RUS ISSN 0869-8139) **928**
• Rossiiskii Fond Fundamental'nykh Issledovanii. Informatsionnyi Bulletin (RUS) **7904**
Rossiiskii Fond Fundamental'nykh Issledovanii. Vestnik (RUS ISSN 1605-8070) **1169**
Rossiiskii Fondovyi Rynok (RUS) **1169**
➤ Rossiiskii Khimicheskii Zhurnal (RUS) **2079**
Rossiiskii Kosmicheskii Byulleten' (RUS) **580**
Rossiiskii Kto Est' Kto (RUS) **645**
Rossiiskii Meditsinskii Zhurnal (RUS ISSN 0869-2106) **5707**
Rossiiskii Neftyanoi Byulleten' (RUS) **6790**
Rossiiskii Nematologicheskii Zhurnal *see* Russian Journal of Nematology **896**
Rossiiskii Obozrevatel' (RUS) **5044**
Rossiiskii Onkologicheskii Zhurnal/Russian Oncological Journal (RUS ISSN 1028-9984) **6034**
Rossiiskii Pediatricheskii Zhurnal/Russian Journal of Pediatrics (RUS ISSN 1560-9561) **6104**
Rossiiskii Psikhyatricheskii Zhurnal/Russian Journal of Psychiatry (RUS ISSN 1560-957X) **6183**
Rossiiskii Regional'nyi Press Byulleten' (RUS) **3940**
Rossiiskii Sotsyal'no-Politicheskii Vestnik (RUS) **7180**
• Rossiiskii Statisticheskii Yezhegodnik/Russian Statistical Yearbook (RUS) **1261**
Rossiiskii Stomatologicheskii Zhurnal/Russian Journal of Dentistry (RUS) **5864**
Rossiiskii Vestnik Akushera-Ginekologa (RUS ISSN 1726-6122) **6003**
• Rossiiskii Vestnik Perinatologii i Pediatrii (RUS ISSN 1027-4065) **6003**
Rossiiskii Zhurnal Kozhnykh i Venericheskikh Boleznei/Russian Journal of Skin and Sexually Transmitted Diseases (RUS ISSN 1560-9588) **5825**
• Rossiiskii Zhurnal Nauk o Zemle (Online) (RUS ISSN 1681-1194) **2715**
• Rossiiskii Zhurnal Nauk o Zemle (Print) (RUS ISSN 1681-1178) **2715**
• Rossiiskiye Politicheskiye Portrety (RUS ISSN 1606-1543) **7180**
Rossiisko-Amerikanskii Forum Obrazovaniia *see* Russian-American Education Forum **2908**
Rossiiskoe Obrazovanie (RUS) **2908**
Rossiiskoe Voennoe Obozrenie (RUS) **6444**
Rossing Magazine (NAM ISSN 0257-2001) **2626**
Rossiya (KGZ) **2211**
Rossiya (Year) (RUS) **1261**
Rossiya Dvadtsat' Odin *see* Rossiya XXI **1169**
Rossiya. Gazeta (RUS) **3940**
Rossiya i Mir: Nauka i Technologiya *see* Russia and World: Science and Technology **7906**
Rossiya i Musul'manskii Mir (RUS) **7180**
Rossiya i Sovremennyi Mir (RUS) **7263**
Rossiya i Strany Mira/Russia and Countries of the World (RUS) **1261**
Rossiya i Strany S N G/Russia and C I S Countries (Sodruzhestvo Nezavisimykh Gosudarstv) (RUS) **1261**
Rossiya Molodaya (RUS ISSN 0868-5789) **1169**
• Rossiya v Global'noi Politike (RUS ISSN 1810-6439) **7263**
• Rossiya v Tsifrakh (Year) (RUS) **1261**
• Rossiya Vybirayet (RUS ISSN 1606-1500) **7180**
Rossiya XXI (RUS ISSN 0869-8503) **1169**
Rossmoor News (USA) **5082**
Rostaniha/Botanical Journal of Iran (IRN ISSN 1608-4306) **815**
Roster & Government Guide (USA ISSN 1053-9530) **7180**
Roster and Statistics of Oklahoma Public and Institutional Libraries (USA) **5044**
Roster of Africa Social Scientists (SEN) **1604**
Roster of North American Rapid Transit Cars (Year) (USA) **8624**
Rostlinna Vyroba *see* Plant, Soil and Environment **147**
Rostlinolekar (CZE ISSN 1211-3565) **251**
Rostocker Beitraege zu Controlling und Rechnungswesen (DEU ISSN 1437-7802) **1791**
Rostocker Beitraege zur Demographie (DEU ISSN 1615-7273) **7292**
• Rostocker Mathematisches Kolloquium (DEU ISSN 0138-3248) **5530**
Rostocker Medizinrechtliche Reihe (DEU ISSN 1612-0523) **4777**
Rostocker Meeresbiologische Beitraege (DEU ISSN 0943-822X) **701**
Rostocker Rechtsgeschichtliche Reihe (DEU) **4777**
Rostocker Rechtswissenschaftliche Abhandlungen (DEU) **4777**
Rostocker Schriften zum Wirtschaftsrecht (DEU ISSN 1614-998X) **4880**
Rostria/Hemipterological Society of Japan. Transactions (JPN ISSN 0910-6839) **858**
† Rostrum (AUS) **8986**
Rostrum (ZAF ISSN 1026-4914) **858**
The Rostrum of Asclepius *see* To Vima tou Asklipiou **5728**
Rota (POL ISSN 0867-5872) **3079**
Rota Gene (USA ISSN 0730-5168) **3781**
Rotacion (ESP ISSN 0211-2892) **8659**
De Rotarian (NLD ISSN 0923-1552) **2269**
The Rotarian (USA ISSN 0035-838X) **2269**
Rotarian Monthly (TWN) **2269**
Le Rotarien (FRA) **2269**
El Rotario de Chile (CHL) **2269**
El Rotario Peruano (PER) **2269**
Rotarismo en Mexico (MEX) **2269**
Rotary (ITA) **2269**
Rotary Contact (BEL) **2269**
Rotary Dergisi (TUR) **2269**
• Rotary Down Under (AUS ISSN 0048-8631) **2269**
Rotary in Africa (ZAF) **2269**
Rotary Korea (KOR) **2269**
Rotary Magazin (DEU ISSN 1612-5983) **2269**
Rotary Magazine (GBR) **2269**
Rotary Magazine (Cairo) (EGY) **2269**
Rotary News *see* Rotary Smachar **2269**
Rotary-No-Tomo (JPN) **2269**
Rotary Smachar (IND) **2269**
Rotary Suisse-Liechtenstein (CHE) **2269**
Rotas do Mundo (PRT) **8753**
• Rotas & Destinos (PRT) **8753**
Rotblau (CHE ISSN 1660-0878) **8244**
Rote Fahne (DEU ISSN 0936-1421) **7180**
Das Rote Kreuz (AUT) **8066**
• Rote Liste (DEU) **6879**
Die Rote Mappe (DEU) **2626**
Rote Revue (CHE ISSN 1421-8763) **7180**
➤ Roteiro (BRA ISSN 0104-4311) **2908**
† Rotem (ISR ISSN 0333-9904) **8986**
Rotenburger Schriften (DEU) **4260**
Roter Morgen (DEU ISSN 0939-2947) **7180**
Rotes Kreuz (DEU ISSN 0938-9687) **8066**
ROTH Teien Journal of Japanese Gardening *see* Sukiya Living **3751**
Rothenberg Political Report *see* Political Report **7169**
Rothmans Football Yearbook (GBR ISSN 0080-4088) **8244**
Rothmans Rugby League Yearbook (GBR ISSN 0262-4745) **8244**
• The Rothschild Archive (GBR ISSN 1748-9148) **3781**
Rotifer News (AUS ISSN 1327-4007) **962**
Rotkreuz Magazin (DEU) **8066**
Die Rotkreuz-Schwester (DEU) **8066**
Rotkreuzmagazin (DEU) **8066**
▼ • ➤ Rotman International Journal of Pension Management (CAN ISSN 1916-9833) **1874**
La Rotonde (CAN ISSN 1481-0581) **2299**
Rotonews Fantasy Baseball Guide (Year) *see* The Fantasy Baseball Guide (Professional Edition) **8227**
Rotor (DEU ISSN 0935-8277) **4345**
Rotor and Wing *see* Rotor & Wing **69**
• Rotor & Wing (USA ISSN 1066-8098) **69**
Rotor & Wing Annual Buyer's Guide *see* Rotor & Wing **69**
Rotor Breeze (USA) **69**
• Rotor Roster (USA ISSN 1073-8274) **8551**
Rotorcraft (USA ISSN 1041-2735) **69**
Rotorua Review (NZL ISSN 1170-1560) **3919**
Rottenburger Jahrbuch fuer Kirchengeschichte (DEU ISSN 0722-7531) **4260**
Rotterdam Institute of Private Law (NLD ISSN 1873-9512) **4777**
Rotterdam Qualitime (NLD ISSN 1874-7604) **3916**
† Rotterdam Real Estate City Book (NLD ISSN 1871-5605) **8986**
Rotterdams Onderwijs Magazine (NLD ISSN 1386-2863) **3079**
The Rottweiler Quarterly (USA ISSN 1040-8037) **6814**
• Rotunda (CAN ISSN 0035-8495) **515**
Rotunda (USA ISSN 1071-9369) **2299**
Rotunda Delivery (IRL ISSN 1649-9174) **6004**
Rotunden (DNK ISSN 0908-6781) **3834**
Rotweinguide (Year) (AUT) **609**
Rotweiss (CHE ISSN 1661-304X) **8244**
Rotweissrot (AUT) **3798**
Roudou Anzen Eisei Sougou Kenkyujo Gijutsu Shishin/National Institute of Occupational Safety and Health. Technical Recommendation (JPN) **6685**
Rouge (FRA) **7180**
Rouge (GBR ISSN 0958-188X) **4378**
• Rouge et Noir (AUT) **8197**
• Rouge Magazine (AUS ISSN 1833-119X) **5365**
▼ Rough Beast (USA ISSN 1949-1093) **5365**
• The Rough Guide to Barcelona (USA ISSN 1931-0579) **8753**
▼ • The Rough Guide to Colorado (USA ISSN 1938-4866) **8753**
Rough Guide to Cyprus (GBR ISSN 1948-1403) **4324**
▼ • The Rough Guide to First-Time Africa (USA ISSN 1940-2430) **8753**
The Rough Guide to First-Time Asia (USA ISSN 1935-0619) **8753**
• The Rough Guide to MySpace and Online Communities (USA ISSN 1937-6154) **8130**
The Rough Guide to Norway (USA ISSN 1935-2387) **8753**
The Rough Guide to the Italian Lakes (USA ISSN 1933-4079) **8753**
The Rough Guide to Travel Survival (GBR ISSN 1931-2628) **8753**
▼ • The Rough Guide to Yellowstone and Grand Teton (USA ISSN 1940-2708) **8753**
• Rough Justice (USA ISSN 1934-7138) **5365**
Rough News (GBR) **8753**
• Rough Notes (USA ISSN 0035-8525) **4522**
Rough Rider (USA ISSN 0273-9453) **8602**
• Rough Stuff (USA ISSN 1931-9231) **515**
Rough Writer (USA) **2299**
Rougsoe Lokalhistoriske Forening. Aarsskrift (DNK ISSN 0106-5327) **4260**
• Roulei Yanjiu/Meat Research (CHN ISSN 1001-8123) **3662**
Rouleur (GBR ISSN 1752-962X) **8267**
Roulez sans Vous Faire Rouler *see* Lemon Aid Magazine **8589**
Round Robbins Newsletter. Friends of the Robbins Museum (USA) **415**
• ➤ The Round Table (GBR ISSN 0035-8533) **7263**
Round Table (Anderson) (USA) **7572**
The Round Table (Beloit) (USA ISSN 1053-5020) **2299**
Round the Table (USA ISSN 0161-7125) **4522**
• The Round Top Register (USA) **3987**
• The Round Up (USA ISSN 0744-5555) **2299**
Roundabout (NLD ISSN 1567-9799) **3919**
Roundalab Journal (USA) **2687**
Roundel (USA ISSN 0889-3225) **8602**
Rounder Mail Order (USA) **6613**
† Roundtable (AUS ISSN 1328-5335) **8986**
• The Roundtable (Southfield, Online) (USA) **8066**
Roundtable Report (USA) **7678**
▼ Roundtable Viewpoints (USA ISSN 1934-4236) **1791**
▼ Roundtable Viewpoints. Business Law (USA ISSN 1942-9592) **4880**
▼ Roundtable Viewpoints. Educational Leadership (USA ISSN 1937-1187) **3079**
▼ Roundtable Viewpoints. Physical Anthropology (USA ISSN 1940-9125) **354**
Roundtables in Plastic Surgery (USA ISSN 1546-6760) **6257**
Roundtables in Spine Surgery (USA ISSN 1552-4124) **6257**
• The Roundup Magazine (USA ISSN 1081-2229) **5365**
Roundy House (GBR) **5433**
• Roupin Weisheng/Meat Hygiene (CHN ISSN 1000-9876) **7540**
Roustabout Energy International (GBR ISSN 1750-967X) **6790**
Roustabout Magazine *see* Roustabout Energy International **6790**
Route (FRA ISSN 0035-8568) **8602**
Route 49 (DEU ISSN 1613-8600) **5082**
Route 66 *see* Road Trip U S A: Route 66 **8752**
Route 66 Magazine (USA ISSN 1069-1405) **3987**
Route Actualite/Road News (FRA ISSN 1156-4865) **8634**
Route Driver and Service Technician (USA ISSN 1522-7448) **8510**
The Router (GBR ISSN 1368-4752) **1051**
Routes du Monde *see* World Highways **8637**
Routes et Transports (CAN ISSN 0319-3780) **8634**
Routes - Roads (FRA ISSN 1011-1891) **8634**
• Routes to Action (GBR ISSN 1755-3393) **8267**
Les Routiers (FRA ISSN 0243-6795) **8675**
Routing *see* Practical Woodworking **1051**
Routledge Advances in International Political Economy (GBR) **1516**
Routledge Advances in Management and Business Studies (GBR) **1791**
Routledge Advances in Tourism (GBR) **8753**
Routledge Critical Thinkers (GBR) **5365**
Routledge E C P R Studies in European Political Science (European Consortium for Political Research) (GBR) **7263**
Routledge Explorations in Economic History (GBR ISSN 1359-7892) **1549**
Routledge I N E M Advances in Economic Methodology (International Network Economic Methodology) (GBR ISSN 1754-8721) **1169**
Routledge International Studies in Business History (GBR ISSN 1361-2174) **1549**
Routledge Medieval Casebooks (GBR) **4260**
Routledge Progress in Psychology (GBR ISSN 1361-2204) **7406**
Routledge Research E A D I Studies in Development (European Association of Development Research and Training Institutes) (GBR) **1605**
Routledge Research in Information Systems (GBR) **5063**
Routledge Studies in Business Organization and Networks (GBR ISSN 1359-8058) **1706**
Routledge Studies in Development and Society (GBR) **7998**
Routledge Studies in Development Economics (GBR ISSN 1359-7884) **1605**
Routledge Studies in Governance and Public Policy (GBR) **7180**
Routledge Studies in Information and Library Management Systems *see* Routledge Research in Information Systems **5063**
Routledge Studies in International Business and the World Economy (GBR ISSN 1359-7930) **1581**
Routledge Studies in International Information and Library Management Systems *see* Routledge Research in Information Systems **5063**
Routledge Studies in Middle Eastern Politics (GBR ISSN 1754-873X) **7264**
Routledge Studies in Slave and Post-Slave Societies and Cultures (GBR) **8130**
Routledge Studies in Small Business (GBR) **1966**
Routledge Studies in Social and Political Thought (GBR) **7180**
Routledge Studies in the European Economy (GBR ISSN 1359-7957) **1549**
Routledge Studies in the History of Economics (GBR ISSN 1359-7906) **1549**
Routledge Studies on China in Transition (GBR) **7998**
Rovartani Kozlemenyek *see* Folia Entomologica Hungarica **848**
Rover Blatt (DEU ISSN 0945-7259) **8197**
Rovesnik (RUS ISSN 0131-5994) **2211**
Roving Commissions (GBR ISSN 0485-5175) **8281**
Rowe Historical Society. Bulletin (USA ISSN 0882-7672) **4311**
Rowell Practical Food Manual *see* Practical Food Law Manual **4759**
• Rowena's Page (USA) **5365**
➤ Rowett Research Institute Annual Report (GBR ISSN 0952-7222) **6669**
Rowing & Regatta (GBR) **8281**
Rowley & Baker: International Mergers - The Antitrust Process *see* International Mergers - The Antitrust Process **4871**
Roy Adaptation Association Review *see* R A A Review **5979**
Royal Academy Magazine *see* R A Magazine **513**
Royal Academy of Dancing. Annual Report (GBR) **2687**
Royal Academy of Engineering. Engineering Manufacturing Lecture (GBR ISSN 1366-6487) **3218**

Title

10826 ROYAL ACADEMY OF ENGINEERING. MISCELLANEOUS REPORTS ULRICH'S PERIODICALS

Royal Academy of Engineering. Miscellaneous Reports (GBR) **3218**
Royal Academy of Engineering. Occasional Lectures (GBR) **3218**
Royal Academy of Engineering. Reports (GBR) **3218**
Royal Academy of Letters, History and Antiquities. Proceedings. Antiquarian Series *see* Kungliga Vitterhets Historie och Antikvitets Akademien. Handlingar. Antikvariska Serien **501**
Royal Academy of Letters, History and Antiquities. Proceedings. Historical Series *see* Kungliga Vitterhets Historie och Antikvitets Akademien. Handlingar. Historiska Serien **4239**
Royal Academy of Letters, History and Antiquities. Proceedings. Philological - Philosophical Series *see* Kungliga Vitterhets Historie och Antikvitets Akademien. Handlingar. Filologisk-Filosofiska Serien **5138**
Royal Academy of Medicine in Ireland. Bulletin (IRL) **5707**
Royal Aeronautical Directory of European Aviation (GBR) **8551**
Royal Agricultural Society of Natal. Royal Show Programme (ZAF) **152**
Royal Air Force News *see* R A F News **6442**
Royal Air Force Yearbook (GBR ISSN 1465-5829) **6444**
Royal Ambassador Leadership (USA ISSN 0893-5246) **7773**
• ➤ Royal Anthropological Institute. Journal (GBR ISSN 1359-0987) **354**
Royal Anthropological Institute. Occasional Paper (GBR ISSN 0080-4150) **354**
Royal Arch Mason (USA ISSN 0035-8649) **2269**
Royal Architectural Institute of Canada. Membership Directory (CAN ISSN 1489-6044) **456**
The Royal Army Medical Corps Magazine (GBR) **6444**
Royal Asiatic Society. Hong Kong Branch. Journal (HKG ISSN 0085-5774) **560**
• ➤ Royal Asiatic Society. Journal (GBR ISSN 1356-1863) **560**
Royal Asiatic Society. Malaysian Branch. Journal (MYS ISSN 0126-7353) **4188**
• ➤ Royal Astronomical Society. Monthly Notices (GBR ISSN 0035-8711) **580**
• Royal Astronomical Society. Monthly Notices. Letters (Online) (GBR ISSN 1745-3933) **580**
Royal Astronomical Society of Canada. Journal (CAN ISSN 0035-872X) **580**
Royal Astronomical Society of Canada. Observer's Handbook (CAN ISSN 0080-4193) **581**
Royal Australasian College of Dental Surgeons. Annals (AUS ISSN 0158-1570) **5864**
Royal Australian College of General Practitioners Training Program Victoria. Newsletter *see* R A C G P Training Program Victoria. Newsletter **5702**
Royal Australian Historical Society. Annual Report and Statement of Accounts *see* Royal Australian Historical Society. History Magazine **4194**
Royal Australian Historical Society. Annual Report and Statement of Accounts *see* Royal Australian Historical Society. Journal **4194**
• Royal Australian Historical Society. History Magazine (AUS ISSN 1031-9476) **4194**
• ➤ Royal Australian Historical Society. Journal (AUS ISSN 0035-8762) **4194**
Royal Auto *see* K A C B Auto Revue **8587**
Royal Automobile Club Europe for the Independent Traveller *see* R A C Europe for the Independent Traveller **8750**
Royal Automobile Club Inspected Hotel Guide Great Britain & Ireland *see* R A C Inspected Hotel Guide Great Britain & Ireland **8750**
Royal B C Museum. Annual Report (British Columbia) (CAN ISSN 1911-1231) **6536**
Royal Bank of Canada Letter *see* R B C Letter **1377**
Royal Bank of Trinidad and Tobago. Annual Report (TTO) **1381**
Royal Bath & West Show Catalogue (GBR) **152**
Royal Berkshire Life *see* Berkshire & Chilterns Life **3861**
Royal Book News (USA) **645**
Royal British Columbia Museum. Annual Report *see* Royal B C Museum. Annual Report **6536**
Royal British Legion Annual Report and Accounts (GBR) **6444**
Royal British Legion. Burckhurst Hill Branch. Newsletter *see* The Chronicle (Buckhurst Hill) **2265**
Royal Brunei Airlines Muhibah (BRN) **8785**
Royal Caledonian Curling Club. Annual (GBR ISSN 0080-4282) **8197**
Royal Canadian Air Force Memorial Museum. Newsletter *see* R C A F Memorial Museum. Newsletter **6442**
Royal Canadian College of Organists. Yearbook & Directory of Members (CAN ISSN 1701-7440) **6613**
Royal Canadian Military Institute. Members' News (CAN ISSN 1719-8844) **6444**
Royal Canadian Mint. Annual Report (CAN ISSN 0714-1211) **7467**
Royal Canadian Mounted Police. External Review Committee. Annual Report (CAN ISSN 0837-4589) **7467**
• Royal Canadian Mounted Police. External Review Committee. Performance Report (CAN ISSN 1483-9679) **7467**
• Royal Canadian Mounted Police. Gazette (Online) (CAN ISSN 1910-3441) **2667**
• Royal Canadian Mounted Police. Gazette (Print) (CAN ISSN 1196-6513) **2667**
• Royal Canadian Mounted Police. Performance Report (CAN ISSN 1483-6661) **7467**
Royal Canadian Mounted Police. Public Complaints Commission. Annual Report *see* Canada. Commission for Public Complaints Against the R C M P. Annual Report **7426**
Royal Canadian Mounted Police. Quarterly/G R C Revue Trimestrielle (CAN ISSN 0824-9415) **2667**
Royal College of Anaesthetists. Bulletin (GBR) **5774**
Royal College of Anaesthetists. Newsletter *see* Royal College of Anaesthetists. Bulletin **5774**
Royal College of General Practicioners. North & West London Faculty. Magazine *see* North & West London Journal of General Practice **5688**
Royal College of General Practitioners. North & West London Faculty. News (GBR ISSN 1476-4164) **5707**
Royal College of General Practitioners. Occasional Paper (GBR ISSN 1352-2450) **5707**
Royal College of General Practitioners. Policy Statement (GBR ISSN 0957-0357) **5707**
Royal College of General Practitioners. Practice Organisation Series (GBR) **5707**
Royal College of Midwives Midwives *see* R C M Midwives **6002**
Royal College of Music Annual Review *see* R C M Annual Review **6608**
Royal College of Nursing Institute. Report *see* R C N Institute. Report **5979**
Royal College of Obstetricians and Gynaecologists. Audit (GBR) **6004**
• Royal College of Physicians and Surgeons of U S A. Journal (USA) **5825**
• ➤ Royal College of Physicians of Edinburgh. Journal (GBR ISSN 1478-2715) **5707**
• Royal College of Psychiatrists. College Reports (GBR) **6183**
Royal College of Psychiatrists. Council Report *see* Royal College of Psychiatrists. College Reports **6183**
• Royal College of Speech and Language Therapists. Bulletin (GBR) **3046**
Royal College of Surgeons of Edinburgh. Journal *see* The Surgeon **6259**
• ➤ Royal College of Surgeons of England. Annals (GBR ISSN 0035-8843) **6257**
• Royal College of Surgeons of England. Bulletin (GBR ISSN 1473-6357) **6257**
Royal College of Surgeons of England. College and Faculty Bulletin *see* Royal College of Surgeons of England. Bulletin **6257**
Royal College of Veterinary Surgeons. Directory of Veterinary Practices (Year) (GBR ISSN 0966-6303) **8807**
Royal College of Veterinary Surgeons. Register of Members (Year) (GBR ISSN 1474-2063) **8807**
The Royal Dispatch (USA ISSN 1938-629X) **6814**
Royal Doulton Collectables (CAN ISSN 1714-9517) **2045**
Royal Economic Society. Conference Papers *see* The Economic Journal **1100**
Royal Electrical & Mechanical Engineers Journal *see* R E M E Journal **3394**
Royal Engineers Journal (GBR ISSN 0035-8878) **6444**
Royal Entomological Society of London. Symposia (GBR ISSN 0080-4363) **858**
▼ Royal Flush (DEU) **8197**
Royal Free and University College Medical School. Department of Obstetrics & Gynaecology. Newsletter (GBR) **6004**
Royal Gazette (Charlottetown) (CAN ISSN 0035-8908) **3817**
• The Royal Gazette (New Brunswick) (CAN ISSN 0703-8623) **7467**
• Royal Gazette Limited (BMU) **3802**
Royal Gazette Magazine *see* R G Magazine **3802**
Royal Gazette. Part 1 (CAN ISSN 1200-5649) **3817**
Royal Geographical Society of Queensland. Bulletin (AUS ISSN 1832-8830) **4027**
Royal Highland News (GBR) **152**
• Royal Historical Society. Annual Bibliography of British and Irish History (Online) (BEL) **4171**
† Royal Historical Society. Guides and Handbooks (GBR ISSN 0080-4398) **8986**
Royal Historical Society of Queensland. Bulletin (AUS ISSN 0035-8916) **4194**
Royal Historical Society of Queensland. Journal *see* Queensland History Journal **4194**
Royal Historical Society Studies in History (USA ISSN 0269-2244) **4260**
• Royal Historical Society. Transactions (GBR ISSN 0080-4401) **4260**
• Royal Holloway University of London. Department of Politics and International Relations. Politics and International Working Papers (GBR ISSN 1750-7308) **7264**
Royal Holloway University of London. Department of Social & Political Science. Occasional Papers (GBR) **7998**
Royal Horticultural Society Gardener's Diary *see* R H S Gardener's Diary **3748**
Royal Horticultural Society Plant Finder *see* R H S Plant Finder **3757**
Royal Humane Society. Annual Report (GBR) **8066**
Royal Institute for Inter-Faith Studies. Bulletin (JOR ISSN 1466-2361) **7715**
Royal Institute of British Architects Directory of Practices *see* R I B A Directory of Practices **455**
Royal Institute of British Architects Drawings Monographs *see* R I B A Drawings Monographs **455**
Royal Institute of British Architects Journal *see* R I B A Journal **455**
Royal Institute of British Architects. Members (GBR ISSN 0269-0829) **456**
Royal Institute of British Architects Product Selector (Year) *see* R I B A Product Selector (Year) **455**
Royal Institute of British Architects Sector Review. Conservation *see* R I B A Sector Review. Conservation **455**
Royal Institute of British Architects Sector Review. Education *see* R I B A Sector Review. Education **455**
Royal Institute of British Architects Sector Review. Government and Public *see* R I B A Sector Review. Government and Public **455**
Royal Institute of British Architects Sector Review. Houses and Housing *see* R I B A Sector Review. Houses and Housing **455**
Royal Institute of British Architects Sector Review. Industrial and Commercial *see* R I B A Sector Review. Industrial and Commercial **455**
Royal Institute of British Architects Sector Review. Interiors *see* R I B A Sector Review. Interiors **455**
Royal Institute of British Architects Sector Review. Sports and Leisure *see* R I B A Sector Review. Sports and Leisure **455**
• Royal Institute of International Affairs. Briefing Papers (GBR) **7264**
The Royal Institute of International Affairs. Conference Proceedings (GBR) **7264**
Royal Institute of Oil Painters. Exhibition Catalogue (GBR) **515**
➤ Royal Institute of Philosophy Conference (NLD ISSN 0923-0114) **6950**
• Royal Institute of Philosophy Supplement (GBR ISSN 1358-2461) **6950**
Royal Institute of Technology. Department of Aeronautical and Vehicle Engineering. Transactions/Kungliga Tekniska Hoegskolan. Institutionen foer Farkost och Flyg. Trita-A V E (SWE ISSN 1651-7660) **69**
The Royal Institute of Technology. Department of Aeronautical Structures and Materials. Report *see* Royal Institute of Technology. Department of Aeronautical and Vehicle Engineering. Transactions **69**
The Royal Institute of Technology. Department of Aeronautics. Report *see* Royal Institute of Technology. Department of Aeronautical and Vehicle Engineering. Transactions **69**
➤ Royal Institute of Technology. Department of Infrastructure. Transactions/Kungliga Tekniska Hoegskolan. Institutionen foer Infrastruktur. Trita-I N F R A. EX (SWE ISSN 1651-0194) **4027**
Royal Institute of Technology. Department of Structural Engineering. Trita - B K N. Bulletin (SWE ISSN 1103-4270) **3282**
Royal Institute of Technology. Department of Structural Engineering. Trita-B K N. Diploma Work *see* Kungliga Tekniska Hoegskolan. Institutionen foer Byggkonstruktion. Trita-B K N. Examensarbete **3277**
Royal Institute of Technology. Department of Structural Engineering. Trita-B K N. Report *see* Kungliga Tekniska Hoegskolan. Institutionen foer Byggkonstruktion. Trita-B K N. Rapport **3277**
Royal Institute of the Architects of Ireland Yearbook & Diary *see* R I A I Yearbook & Diary **454**
• Royal Institution of Chartered Surveyors. Commercial Property Journal (GBR ISSN 1754-9132) **7611**
Royal Institution of Chartered Surveyors Construction Journal *see* R I C S Construction Journal **1031**
Royal Institution of Chartered Surveyors. Contracts in Use (GBR ISSN 1369-5630) **1034**
Royal Institution of Chartered Surveyors Foundation. Research Papers *see* R I C S Foundation. Research Papers **3281**
Royal Institution of Chartered Surveyors. Geographical Directory (GBR ISSN 0956-7763) **2026**
Royal Institution of Chartered Surveyors Housing Market Survey. United Kingdom *see* R I C S Housing Market Survey. United Kingdom **4424**
• Royal Institution of Chartered Surveyors. Land Journal (GBR ISSN 1754-9094) **3464**
Royal Institution of Chartered Surveyors. List of Members (GBR ISSN 0951-4082) **2026**
Royal Institution of Chartered Surveyors Minerals Practice Skills Panel. Information Paper *see* R I C S Minerals Practice Skills Panel. Information Paper **3281**
Royal Institution of Chartered Surveyors Policy Unit Report *see* R I C S Policy Unit Report **3281**
Royal Institution of Chartered Surveyors Research Findings *see* R I C S Research Findings **3281**
• Royal Institution of Chartered Surveyors. Residential Property Journal (GBR ISSN 1754-9116) **7611**
➤ Royal Institution of Cornwall. Journal (GBR ISSN 0968-5936) **4260**
† Royal Institution of Great Britain. Proceedings (GBR ISSN 0035-8959) **8986**
Royal Institution of Great Britain. Record (GBR) **7904**
Royal Institution of Great Britain. Royal Institution Lectures (GBR) **7904**
• Royal Institution of Naval Architects. Transactions. Part A. International Journal of Maritime Engineering (GBR ISSN 1479-8751) **8659**
• Royal Institution of Naval Architects. Transactions. Part B. International Journal of Small Craft Technology (GBR ISSN 1740-0694) **8659**
Royal Irish Academy. Discovery Programme. Reports (IRL) **415**
Royal Irish Academy of Music. Prospectus (IRL) **6613**
• Royal Irish Academy. Proceedings. Section C: Archaeology, Celtic Studies, History, Linguistics and Literature (IRL ISSN 0035-8991) **415**
The Royal Life Saving Society U.K. Lifeguard (GBR ISSN 0968-7726) **7540**
Royal Melbourne Institute of Technology Business Students Association B S A Report *see* R M I T B S A Report **1163**
• Royal Melbourne Institute of Technology. Faculty of Business. Working Paper Series (AUS ISSN 1327-7448) **1169**
• ➤ Royal Meteorological Society. Quarterly Journal (GBR ISSN 0035-9009) **6394**
Royal Microscopical Society. Transactions (GBR ISSN 0962-7375) **900**
Royal Military Police Journal (GBR ISSN 0035-9025) **6444**
• ➤ Royal Musical Association. Journal (GBR ISSN 0269-0403) **6613**
Royal Musical Association. Newsletter (GBR ISSN 1461-9717) **6613**
➤ Royal Musical Association Research Chronicle (GBR ISSN 1472-3808) **6613**
Royal National Institute for the Blind. Busy Solicitors Digest (GBR) **4084**
• Royal National Institute for the Blind. Campaign News (GBR) **8066**
Royal National Institute for the Blind Gleanings *see* R N I B. Gleanings **7772**
Royal National Institute for the Blind. Information Leaflets (GBR ISSN 0080-4479) **4084**
Royal National Institute for the Blind Product Catalog *see* R N I B. Product Catalog **4084**
Royal National Institute for the Blind Scientific Enquiry *see* R N I B. Scientific Enquiry **4084**
• Royal National Institute for the Blind. Update (GBR ISSN 0969-0468) **8066**
➤ Royal Naval Medical Service. Journal (GBR ISSN 0035-9033) **5707**
Royal Naval Sailing Association Journal (GBR ISSN 0035-9041) **8281**
Royal Neighbor (USA ISSN 0035-905X) **2269**
Royal New Zealand College of General Practitioners. Workforce Series (NZL ISSN 1177-5971) **5707**
Royal New Zealand Foundation for the Blind. Outlook *see* Outlook (Auckland) **4084**
Royal Norwegian Society of Sciences and Letters. Publications *see* Kongelige Norske Videnskabers Selskab. Skrifter **7877**
➤ Royal Nova Scotia Historical Society. Journal (CAN ISSN 1486-5920) **4311**
Royal Numismatic Society. Special Publications (GBR ISSN 0080-4487) **6653**
Royal Ontario Museum. Annual Report (CAN ISSN 0082-5115) **6536**
Royal Philatelic Society of New Zealand. Annual Report (NZL) **6899**
Royal Philatelic Society of New Zealand. Bibliographic Series (NZL ISSN 1174-3921) **6901**
Royal Philatelic Society of New Zealand. Monograph Handbook (NZL ISSN 1176-693X) **6899**
Royal Photographic Society of Great Britain Journal *see* R P S Journal **6976**
Royal Purple (USA) **2299**
Royal School of Mines, London. Journal (GBR ISSN 0080-4495) **6478**
Royal Scottish Automobile Club Official Handbook (GBR) **8197**
Royal Scottish Country Dance Society Bulletin (GBR) **2687**
Royal Shakespeare Company. Publication (GBR) **5365**
Royal Society for Music History of The Netherlands. Review *see* Koninklijke Vereniging voor Nederlandse Muziekgeschiedenis. Tijdschrift **6583**
Royal Society for the Prevention of Accidents Occupational Safety & Health Journal *see* R O S P A Occupational Safety & Health Journal **6684**
Royal Society for the Prevention of Cruelty to Animals. Annual Review (GBR) **321**
Royal Society for the Prevention of Cruelty to Animals Science Group Review *see* R S P C A Science Group Review **321**
Royal Society for the Prevention of Cruelty to Animals. Trustees' Report and Accounts (GBR) **1301**
Royal Society for the Promotion of Health. Journal *see* Perspectives in Public Health **8061**
Royal Society of Antiquaries of Ireland. Journal (IRL ISSN 0035-9106) **415**
Royal Society of Arts Journal *see* R S A Journal **514**
Royal Society of British Artists. Publication (GBR) **515**

Title

Title

▼ new title   † ceased   ● electronic media   ➤ refereed

Ryoksagwahak/Historical Science (PRK) **4159**
Ryokunaisho/Japan Glaucoma Society. Journal (JPN ISSN 0917-4338) **6051**
Ryosei Hachurui Kenkyukaishi/Nippon Herpetological Journal (JPN ISSN 0285-287X) **962**
Rypins' Clinical Sciences Review (USA) **5708**
Ryska Huset (SWE ISSN 1651-8330) **5237**
Rytme (DNK ISSN 0107-6280) **6614**
• Rytmi (FIN ISSN 1239-1204) **6614**
Rytmus Zivota (CZE ISSN 1211-5649) **3832**
Ryugin Keizai Report (JPN ISSN 0916-3158) **1516**
Ryukoku Daigaku Ronshu/Ryukoku University. Journal (JPN ISSN 0287-6000) **3000**
Ryukoku University. Journal *see* Ryukoku Daigaku Ronshu **3000**
Ryukyu Daigaku Kogakubu Kiyo/University of the Ryukyus. Faculty of Engineering. Bulletin (JPN ISSN 0389-102X) **3218**
Ryukyu Daigaku Nogakubu Gakujutsu Hokoku *see* University of the Ryukyus. College of Agriculture. Science Bulletin **167**
Ryukyu Daigaku Rigakubu Kiyo *see* University of the Ryukyus. College of Science. Bulletin **5545**
Ryukyu Mathematical Journal (JPN ISSN 1344-008X) **5531**
Ryukyu Medical Journal (JPN) **5708**
Ryukyu no Konchu/Insects of Loochoos (JPN ISSN 0910-9889) **858**
Ryukyu Seifu Kachiku Eisei Shikenjo Kenkyu Hokoku *see* Okinawa-ken Kachiku Eisei Shikenjo Nenpo **8804**
Ryukyu Seifu Kachiku Eisei Shikenjo Nenpo *see* Okinawa-ken Kachiku Eisei Shikenjo Nenpo **8804**
Ryumachika/Rheumatology (JPN ISSN 0915-227X) **6227**
➤ Ryusan To Kogyo/Sulphuric Acid and Industry (JPN ISSN 0370-8047) **2079**
Ryuseijin Kaiho/Circular of Meteoric Dust (JPN ISSN 0385-0994) **581**
Ryutai Kogaku Bumon Koenkai Koen Ronbunshu/Fluids Engineering Conference (JPN) **3395**
Ryutai Rikigaku Koenkai Koenshu/Symposium on Fluid Mechanics. Proceedings (JPN) **3364**
Ryutai Seigyo Shinpojumu Koen Ronbunshu/Symposium on Fluid Control. Papers (JPN) **3395**
Ryutsu Netto Wakingu (JPN ISSN 1343-5566) **1841**
Rzecznik Praw Obywatelskich. Biuletyn (POL ISSN 0860-7958) **4841**
Rzeczpospolita (POL ISSN 0208-9130) **3930**
Rzeczy Teatralne (POL ISSN 1509-412X) **8477**
RZone *see* R - Zone **2210**
S (LVA ISSN 1407-3617) **3031**
▼ • ➤ S (NLD ISSN 1874-9062) **7406**
• The S A A Archaeological Record (Society for American Archaeology) (USA ISSN 1532-7299) **415**
S A A C E Directory of Firms/S A V R I Firmagids (South African Association of Consulting Engineers) (ZAF) **2026**
• S A A D Digest (Society for the Advancement of Anaesthesia in Dentistry) (GBR ISSN 0049-1160) **5864**
• S A A D Newsletter (Society for the Advancement of Anaesthesia in Dentistry) (GBR) **5864**
• S A A O Newsletter (South African Astronomical Observatory) (ZAF ISSN 1017-7787) **581**
S A A R C Journal of Educational Research (South Asian Association for Regional Cooperation) (LKA ISSN 1391-1880) **2908**
S A A R F A M P S *see* S A A R F All Media & Product Survey **38**
• S A A R F All Media & Product Survey (South Africa Advertising Research Foundation) (ZAF) **38**
• S A A R F Radio Audience Measurement Survey (South Africa Advertising Research Foundation) (ZAF) **2349**
• S A A R F Television Audience Measurement Survey (South Africa Advertising Research Foundation) (ZAF) **38**
S A A S Bulletin. Biochemistry and Biotechnology (Southern Association of Agricultural Scientists) (USA ISSN 1052-6781) **744**
S A & B Mag (Sustainable Architecture & Building) (CAN ISSN 1911-4230) **1034**
S A and N T Sower (South Australia and Northern Territory) (AUS ISSN 1832-5092) **7678**
The S A B Choir (Soprano, Alto, Bass) (USA ISSN 0744-0200) **6614**
S A B Info (Schweizerische Arbeitsgemeinschaft der Allgemeinen Oeffentlichen Bibliotheken) (CHE ISSN 1423-5595) **5044**
S A B R A O Journal of Breeding and Genetics (Society for the Advancement of Breeding Researches in Asia and Oceania) (THA ISSN 1029-7073) **153**
S A B R Bulletin (Society for American Baseball Research, Inc.) (USA) **8244**
S A B S Catalogue (South African Bureau of Standards) (ZAF ISSN 1018-4295) **6406**
S A B W O News *see* Blind S A News **4079**
S.A. Bakery and Confectionery Review *see* South African Bakery and Confectionery Review **3675**
➤ S A Banker (South African) (ZAF ISSN 0038-2000) **1381**
S A Baseball Digest (South African) (ZAF ISSN 1021-3570) **8244**
S A Besproeiing *see* S A Irrigation **251**
S A Builder (South African) (ZAF ISSN 0038-2027) **1034**
S A C *see* Symposium on Applied Computing **2438**
S A C (Supplemento ad Annuario Cracoviense) *see* Uniwersytet Jagiellonski. Oberwatorium Krakowskie. Rocznik Astronomiczny **583**
S A C Award Reporter (Securities Arbitration Commentator, Inc.) (USA ISSN 1526-2588) **1648**
S A C C *see* Australia. Bureau of Statistics. Standard Australian Classification of Countries (Online) **7301**
• S A C C Notes - Teaching Anthropology (Society for Anthropology in Community Colleges) (USA ISSN 1077-5714) **354**
S A C D. Journal des Auteurs (Societe des Auteurs et Compositeurs Dramatiques) (FRA ISSN 1769-4450) **8477**
S A C E Bulletin (Saskatchewan Association for Computers in Education) (CAN ISSN 0831-7925) **2951**
S A C I Slants (Sales Association of the Chemical Industry, Inc.) (USA) **2080**
• S A C N A S News (Society for Advancement of Chicanos and Native Americans in Science) (USA) **7906**
• S A C Newsmonthly (Southern Art and Crafts) (USA) **539**
S A C Review (Scottish Agricultural College) (GBR ISSN 1369-2143) **153**
† S A C S O S Newsletter (South Australian Coloured Sheep Owners' Society Inc.) (AUS) **8986**
S.A. Chef *see* Professional Caterer and Hotelkeeper **4396**
S A Co-op (South Africa) (ZAF) **153**
S A Complex News (South Africa) (ZAF) **7612**
• S A Computer Magazine (South Africa) (ZAF ISSN 1018-9564) **2436**
† S.A. Crafts (South Australia) (AUS ISSN 0819-2936) **8986**
S A Cricketer (South African) (ZAF ISSN 1022-6478) **8244**
S A Crime Quarterly (South Africa) (ZAF ISSN 1991-3877) **2668**
S A D C C Energy Bulletin (Southern African Development Coordination Conference, Energy Sector Technical & Administrative Unit) (AGO ISSN 1022-1913) **3147**
The S A D C Regional Business Climate Survey (Southern African Development Community) (ZAF ISSN 1993-3460) **1409**
• S A D E V Policy Brief (Swedish Agency for Development Evaluation) (SWE ISSN 1653-9257) **1605**
S A D E V. Report (Swedish Agency for Development Evaluation) (SWE ISSN 1653-9249) **1605**
S A D E V. Working Papers (Swedish Agency for Development Evaluation) (SWE ISSN 1654-045X) **1605**
S A Directory of Black Managers (South African) (ZAF) **2026**
S A Draughtsman *see* South African Draughtsman **8439**
S A Drums & Percussion *see* Drums & Percussion S A **6563**
S A E (Sammlung Arbeitsrechtlicher Entscheidungen) (DEU ISSN 0048-9069) **1706**
S A E A M S Index (Society of Automotive Engineers Aerospace Material Specifications) (USA ISSN 1055-3762) **3218**
S A E Ground Vehicle Lighting Standards Manual (Society of Automotive Engineers) (USA) **8602**
• S A E Handbook (CD-ROM) (Society of Automotive Engineers) (USA) **8602**
• S A E International Journal of Aerospace (Society of Automotive Engineers) (USA ISSN 1946-3855) **69**
• ➤ S A E International Journal of Commercial Vehicles (Society of Automotive Engineers) (USA ISSN 1946-391X) **8510**
• ➤ S A E International Journal of Engines (Society of Automotive Engineers) (USA ISSN 1946-3936) **8602**
• ➤ S A E International Journal of Fuels and Lubricants (Society of Automotive Engineers) (USA ISSN 1946-3952) **6790**
• S A E International Journal of Materials & Manufacturing (Society of Automotive Engineers) (USA ISSN 1946-3979) **3357**
• ➤ S A E International Journal of Passenger Cars - Electronic and Electrical Systems (Society of Automotive Engineers) (USA ISSN 1946-4614) **3329**
• ➤ S A E International Journal of Passenger Cars - Mechanical Systems (Society of Automotive Engineers) (USA ISSN 1946-3995) **3395**
S A E Journal *see* Society for the Anthropology of Europe. Journal **356**
• S A E Off-Highway Engineering (Society of Automotive Engineers) (USA ISSN 1528-9702) **8602**
S A E. Revista (Sociedad Argentina de Estadistica) (ARG ISSN 0329-5583) **8397**
S A E Special Publications (Society of Automotive Engineers) (USA ISSN 0099-5908) **3218**
• S A E Technical Papers (Society of Automotive Engineers) (USA ISSN 0148-7191) **8602**
S A E Transactions *see* S A E International Journal of Aerospace **69**
S A E Transactions *see* S A E International Journal of Commercial Vehicles **8510**
S A E Transactions *see* S A E International Journal of Passenger Cars - Mechanical Systems **3395**
S A E Transactions *see* S A E International Journal of Materials & Manufacturing **3357**
S A E Transactions *see* S A E International Journal of Fuels and Lubricants **6790**
S A E Transactions *see* S A E International Journal of Engines **8602**
S A E Transactions *see* S A E International Journal of Passenger Cars - Electronic and Electrical Systems **3329**
• S A E Update (Society of Automotive Engineers) (USA ISSN 0742-972X) **3395**
S A E UPdate (International Edition) *see* S A E Update **3395**
▼ • S A E Vehicle Engineering (Society of Automotive Engineers) (USA ISSN 1946-3227) **3218**
S A EconoInsight *see* South African EconoInsight **1177**
S A Electronics Buyer's Guide (South Africa) (ZAF ISSN 1025-1782) **3112**
S A F C E C Bulletin (South African Federation of Civil Engineering Contractors) (ZAF) **3282**
S A F E - D I Weekly (JPN ISSN 1348-2688) **6879**
S A F E Journal (Space and Flight Equipment) (USA ISSN 0191-6319) **69**
S A F E Magazine (Save Animals from Exploitation) (NZL ISSN 1174-9369) **321**
S A F E - Nachrichten (Salzburger Aktiengesellschaft fuer Energiewirtschaft) (AUT ISSN 0036-0708) **3329**
S A F E R E *see* Southern African Feminist Review **8903**
S A F E Series *see* S A F E Magazine **321**
➤ S A F E Symposium Proceedings (Space and Flight Equipment) (USA ISSN 0743-846X) **69**
S A F I S Extension Manual Series (Southeast Asian Fisheries Information Service) (PHL ISSN 1018-9734) **3606**
S A F M *see* South Australia's Future Mathematicians **5537**
S A F T O Annual Report/Suid-Afrikaanse Buitelandse Handelsorganisasie Jaarverslag (South African Foreign Trade Organisation) (ZAF ISSN 0081-2552) **1582**
S A Fitness Professionals *see* South African Fitness Professionals **6997**
S A Forestry (South African) (ZAF ISSN 1996-7349) **3701**
S A Fruit Journal (South African) (ZAF ISSN 1683-4577) **3749**
S A G A News (Smocking Arts Guild of America) (USA) **539**
S A G E Link (Seniors Association of Greater Edmonton) (CAN ISSN 1912-0087) **8066**
S A G E S Working Papers in Development (Print) *see* S S E E Working Papers in Development (Online) **354**
S.A. Game & Hunt *see* S.A. Wild & Jag **8331**
S A Gardening *see* South African Garden Guide **3750**
S A Geographical Journal *see* South Australian Geographical Journal **4029**
S A Geographical Papers *see* South Australian Geographical Papers **4029**
S A Graan/S A Grain (South Africa) (ZAF ISSN 1814-1676) **275**
S A Grain *see* S A Graan **275**
S A Guide to Working from Home (South Africa) (ZAF ISSN 1813-3088) **8882**
• S A H News (Society of Architectural Historians) (USA ISSN 1062-6301) **456**
S A H O News (Saskatchewan Association of Health Organizations) (CAN) **4111**
S A H P C *see* International Journal of High Performance Computing Applications **2592**
S A Holstein Joernaal *see* S A Holstein Journal **299**
S A Holstein Journal/S A Holstein Joernaal (South African) (ZAF) **299**
S A Holsteiner (South African) (ZAF ISSN 1561-3305) **299**
S A Horseman (South Africa) (ZAF ISSN 1818-9091) **299**
▼ S A Hot Rods (South Africa) (ZAF ISSN 1998-0272) **8198**
S A I L *see* Studies in American Indian Literatures **5380**
The S A I M A S (South African Institute of Management Services) (ZAF ISSN 1026-6550) **1792**
S A I Reeks (Suid - Afrikaanse Instituut) (NLD ISSN 0926-5783) **4177**
• ➤ S A I S Review (School of Advanced International Studies) (USA ISSN 0036-0775) **7264**
S A I S Studies on Africa (School of Advanced International Studies) (USA) **4177**
S A I T Journal (South Australian Institute of Teachers) (AUS) **3031**
S A I W Fusion (South African Institute of Welding) (ZAF) **6343**
S A Instrument & Control Buyer's Guide (South Africa) (ZAF ISSN 1025-272X) **8437**
S A Interior Design *see* Built **436**
S A Irrigation/S A Besproeiing (South African) (ZAF ISSN 0258-5081) **251**
S A J *see* Scottish Archaeological Journal **415**
S A J B L *see* South African Journal of Bioethics and Law **4785**
S A J C H *see* South African Journal of Child Health **6104**
➤ S A J C N (South African Journal of Clinical Nutrition) (ZAF ISSN 1607-0658) **6669**
S A J I A *see* The South African Journal of International Affairs **7266**
S A J I M *see* South African Journal of Information Management **1794**
S A J O G *see* South African Journal of Obstetrics and Gynaecology **6005**
S A Jewellery News (South Africa) (ZAF ISSN 1817-5333) **4569**
• S A Journal of Human Resource Management (South Africa) (ZAF ISSN 1683-7584) **1874**
• S A Journal of Industrial Psychology (South Africa) (ZAF ISSN 0258-5200) **7406**
S A Kitchens, Bedrooms & Bathrooms (South Africa) (ZAF) **4550**
S A Koops *see* S A Co-op **153**
S A L A L M Bibliography and Reference Series (Seminar on the Acquisition of Latin American Library Materials) (USA) **5059**
S A L A L M Newsletter (Seminar on the Acquisition of Latin American Library Materials) (USA ISSN 0098-6275) **634**
† S A L G Newsletter (South Asia Library Group) (GBR ISSN 0307-1456) **8986**
S A L I S Directory (Substance Abuse Librarians and Information Specialists) (USA) **5044**
S A L I S News (Substance Abuse Librarians and Information Specialists) (USA ISSN 1072-4567) **5044**
S A L L T *see* Studies in Toegepaste Linguistiek en Literatuurwetenskap **5183**
S A L S *see* Studien zur Anglistischen Literatur- und Sprachwissenschaft **5181**
S A L S in Brief (Southern Adirondack Library System) (USA) **5044**
S A L T Newsletter (Saskatchewan Association of Library Technicians) (CAN) **5044**
S A L T Newsletter *see* Society for Applied Learning Technology. Newsletter **2951**
The S A L T Programme for 11 to 13 (Sharing and Learning Together) *see* The GRID **7646**
The S A L T Programme for 3 to 4 (Sharing and Learning Together) (GBR ISSN 0968-5367) **7773**
The S A L T Programme for 5 to 7 (Sharing and Learning Together) (GBR ISSN 0968-5375) **7678**
The S A L T Programme for 8 to 10 (Sharing and Learning Together) (GBR ISSN 0968-5383) **7678**
The S A L T Programme for All Ages (Sharing and Learning Together) (GBR ISSN 0968-5405) **7773**
S A L Z (Saarlaendische Arbeitslosenzeitung) (DEU) **4601**
S A M A B *see* South African Museums Association. Bulletin **6537**
• S A M Advanced Management Journal (Society for Advancement of Management) (USA ISSN 0749-7075) **1792**
▼ • S A M e-Rapport (Seksjon for Anvendt Miljoeforskning-Marin) (NOR ISSN 1890-5153) **3490**
S A M - Forschungsberichte (Stroemungs- und Arbeitsverdraenger Maschinen) (DEU ISSN 1615-6587) **3357**
S A M H S A News (Substance Abuse and Mental Health Services Administration) (USA) **2698**
S A M International Management Conference. Proceedings (Society for Advancement of Management) (USA) **1792**
• ➤ S A M J South African Medical Journal (ZAF ISSN 0256-9574) **5708**
• S A M Magazine (Sales Advertising Marketing) (USA ISSN 1532-9550) **1841**
• ➤ S A M P E Journal (Society for the Advancement of Material and Process Engineering) (USA ISSN 0091-1062) **3357**
S A M P E Symposium Proceedings (Society for the Advancement of Material and Process Engineering) (USA) **3357**
▼ • ➤ S A M S A Journal of Pure and Applicable Mathematics (Southern Africa Mathematical Sciences Association) (LSO ISSN 1993-8594) **5531**
▼ S A M-U N I F O B Rapport (Seksjon for Anvendt Miljoeforskning-Universitetsforskning Bergen) (NOR ISSN 1504-9310) **3491**
S A Mango Growers' Association. Research Journal *see* Mango (Year) **242**
S A Meat - Vleis (South Africa) (ZAF) **3662**
S A Mining (South African) (ZAF) **6478**
• S A Motor (South Australia) (AUS ISSN 1030-8253) **8602**
S A Mountain Magazine (South Africa) (ZAF ISSN 1683-7444) **8331**
S A N C B News (South African National Council for the Blind) (ZAF) **4084**
• S A N D E C News (Department of Water and Sanitation in Developing Countries) (CHE ISSN 1420-5572) **3512**
S A N E *see* Sources from the Ancient Near East **4325**
S A N Journal of Electroacoustic Music *see* Journal of Electroacoustic Music **8968**
• S A N / L A N (Storage Area Network / Local Area Network) (USA) **2503**
S A N/L A N Newsletter *see* S A N / L A N **2503**

Title

S C Trend (South Carolina) (USA ISSN 1930-5591) **1169**
• S C U P E-mail News (Society for College and University Planning) (USA) **3000**
S C W *see* Syndicated Columnists Weekly **4085**
S C W E A Newsletter (Saskatchewan Career - Work Education Association) (CAN ISSN 0845-244X) **6703**
S Corporation Service (USA) **1942**
S Corporations *see* S Corporations: Tax Practice and Analysis **1942**
S Corporations (New York, 1983) (USA ISSN 0738-2448) **1942**
• S Corporations: Tax Practice and Analysis (USA) **1942**
S D *see* Strategic Direction **1179**
S D *see* Stochastics and Dynamics **8407**
S D *see* Stage Directions **8479**
S d A *see* Soluzioni di Assemblaggio **1904**
S D A D News (South Dakota Association for the Deaf) (USA ISSN 1089-4314) **4076**
S D A Journal (Saskatchewan Drama Association) (CAN) **8477**
S D A Nyt (Farum, 2005) *see* Fund & Fortid **394**
S D Abstracts *see* U S A I D in Africa **1606**
S D & I *see* Security Dealer & Integrator **1854**
S D B *see* Secure Destruction Business **3512**
S D Developments *see* U S A I D in Africa **1606**
S D E A Directory of Shopfittings and Display Equipment (Shop and Display Equipment Association) (GBR) **34**
S D H M *see* Structural Durability & Health Monitoring **3220**
S D I *see* Social Development Issues **8068**
S D I L J *see* San Diego International Law Journal **4940**
S D I News Service (IND) **1792**
S D. International Medical Review on Down Syndrome *see* S D. Revista Medica Internacional sobre la Sindrome de Down (Catalan Edition) **6183**
S D J *see* Symbian Developer's Journal **2599**
S D L P *see* Sustainable Development Law & Policy **3468**
S D M *see* Security Distributing & Marketing **1843**
S D M *see* San Diego **3987**
S D M S Sound News (Society of Diagnostic Medical Sonography) (USA ISSN 1543-0448) **6208**
S D P M A Petroleum Journal (South Dakota Petroleum Marketer) (USA) **6791**
S D P S Transactions *see* Journal of Integrated Design & Process Science **3205**
S D R *see* Spatio - Economic Development Record **4427**
S D. Revista Medica Internacional sobre el Sindrome de Down (Spanish Edition) *see* S D. Revista Medica Internacional sobre la Sindrome de Down (Catalan Edition) **6183**
S D. Revista Medica Internacional sobre la Sindrome de Down (Catalan Edition)/S D. International Medical Review on Down Syndrome (ESP ISSN 1138-011X) **6183**
S D S *see* Scuola dello Sport **8200**
• S D S C Education News (San Diego Supercomputer Center) (USA ISSN 1545-1372) **2436**
S D S U Alumnus (South Dakota State University) (USA) **2299**
S D S U Census Data Center. Newsletter (South Dakota State University) (USA) **7292**
S D S U Magazine (San Diego State University) (USA) **2299**
• S D Times (Software Development) (USA ISSN 1528-1965) **2596**
S D V Communicatief *see* Donorvoorlichting Communicatief **6242**
S E *see* dal Seme **227**
S E A *see* Sociedad Entomologica Argentina. Boletin Informativo **859**
S E A Abstracts (PHL) **7938**
S E A F D E C Newsletter (Southeast Asian Fisheries Development Center) (THA ISSN 0857-233X) **3606**
S E A I S I Newsletter (South East Asia Iron & Steel Institute) (MYS ISSN 0116-9645) **6331**
➤ S E A I S I Quarterly Journal (South East Asia Iron and Steel Institute) (MYS ISSN 0129-5721) **6331**
• S E A M E O Horizon (Southeast Asian Ministers of Education Organization) (THA ISSN 1513-1165) **2908**
S E A M E O Regional Language Centre. Anthology Series (Southeast Asian Ministers of Education Organization) (SGP ISSN 0129-8895) **5170**
S E A M E O Regional Language Centre Guidelines (Southeast Asian Ministers of Education Organization) (SGP ISSN 0129-7767) **5170**
S E A P O L Newsletter (Southeast Asian Programme on Ocean Law, Policy and Management) (THA) **4971**
S E A R *see* South East Asian Review **4188**
S E A S *see* Special Entry Access Schemes **3002**
S E A S Anniversary Meeting. Proceedings (S H A R E European Association) (CHE ISSN 0254-6213) **2550**
S E C *see* Secondant **2668**
S E C A C Review *see* Southeastern College Art Conference Review **518**
• S E C Accounting and Auditing Update Service (Securities and Exchange Commission) (USA) **1301**
• S E C Accounting Report (Securities and Exchange Commission) (USA ISSN 0146-485X) **1301**
• S E C Accounting Rules (Securities and Exchange Commission) (USA ISSN 0277-3953) **1648**
• S E C Compliance: Financial Reporting and Forms (Securities and Exchange Commission) (USA) **1648**
• S E C Disclosures Checklists (Securities and Exchange Commission) (USA) **1301**
• S E C Docket (Securities and Exchange Commission) (USA ISSN 0091-4061) **1648**
S E C E D Newsletter (Society for Earthquake and Civil Engineering Dynamics) (GBR ISSN 0967-859X) **3282**
• S E C News Digest (Securities and Exchange Commission) (USA ISSN 0364-6718) **1648**
➤ S E C O L A S Annals (Southeastern Council on Latin American Studies) (USA ISSN 0081-2951) **4311**
S E C Serramenti e Componenti *see* Serramenti+Design **1055**
S E C Today (Securities and Exchange Commission) (USA ISSN 0745-2667) **1301**
• S E D E R I (Sociedad Espanola de Estudios Renacentistas Ingleses) (ESP ISSN 1135-7789) **5170**
S E D M E (Small Enterprises Development, Management and Extension) (IND ISSN 0970-8464) **1966**
S E D O C (Servicio de Documentacao) (BRA ISSN 0036-1267) **7679**
S E E *see* Journal for Studies in Economics and Econometrics **1544**
S E E C Occasional Paper (Surrey Energy Economics Centre) (GBR) **1169**
S E E D S (Surrey Energy Economics Discussion Paper Series) (GBR ISSN 0952-8490) **1169**
S E E D S Technical Papers (Surrey Energy Economics Discussion Paper Series) (GBR) **1169**
S E E I R *see* Slavic & East European Information Resources **5048**
S E E J *see* Slavic and East European Journal **5174**
S E E J E (South - Eastern Europe Journal of Economics) (GRC ISSN 1109-8597) **1516**
S E E L *see* Survey of East European Law **4941**
S E E M *see* Emerging Europe Monitor. South East Europe **1482**
S E E P *see* Slavic and East European Performance **8478**
S E E R *see* South East Europe Review **8006**
S E F *see* Studies in Economics and Finance **1385**
S E F News (Stiftung Entwicklung und Frieden) (DEU ISSN 1437-2827) **1605**
S E F Policy Paper (Stiftung Entwicklung und Frieden) (DEU) **1605**
S E G Abstracts (Society of Exploration Geophysicists) (USA ISSN 0737-0164) **2789**
▼ • S E G Compilations (Society of Economic Geologists, Inc.) (USA ISSN 1939-1439) **2765**
S E G D Design (Society for Environmental Graphic Design) (USA ISSN 1551-4595) **530**
• S E G Newsletter (Society of Economic Geologists, Inc.) (USA ISSN 1550-297X) **2765**
S E G R A S *see* The C R A C Students' Guide to Graduate Studies in the U K **2970**
S E G Technical Program Expanded Abstracts *see* Society of Exploration Geophysicists. S E G Technical Program Expanded Abstracts **2790**
S E I *see* Science Education International **7909**
S E I *see* Structural Engineering International **3284**
S E I News (Sumitomo Electric Industries Ltd.) (JPN) **3329**
S E I S I D A *see* Sociedad Espanola Interdisciplinaria de S I D A. Publicacion Oficial **5826**
S E I Technical Review (Sumitomo Electric Industries) (JPN ISSN 1343-4349) **3329**
S E I Technical Review (Japanese Edition) *see* S E I Tekunikaru Rebyu **3330**
S E I Tekunikaru Rebyu/S E I Technical Review (Japanese Edition) (Sumitomo Electric Industries) (JPN ISSN 1343-4330) **3330**
S E I U Action (Service Employees International Union) (USA ISSN 1097-1009) **4601**
S E I U Update (Service Employees International Union) (USA) **4601**
S E I Working Papers (University of Sussex, Sussex European Institute) (GBR ISSN 1350-4649) **7998**
S E J *see* Scottish Educational Journal **2910**
S E J *see* Social Enterprise Journal **8133**
S E K E *see* International Journal of Software Engineering and Knowledge Engineering **2592**
S E K O Magasinet (Service och Kommunikation) (SWE ISSN 1400-7886) **7502**
S E L *see* Studies in English Literature 1500-1900 **5381**
S E L I M (Sociedad Espanola de Lengua y Literatura Inglesa Medieval) (ESP ISSN 1132-631X) **5171**
S E L J *see* Southeastern Environmental Law Journal **4785**
S E M A News (Specialty Equipment Market Association) (USA ISSN 0279-5051) **8603**
S E M A P. Revista (Sociedad de Enfermeria Madrilena de Atencion Primaria) (ESP ISSN 1577-242X) **5980**
S E M E R *see* Sociedad Espanola de Medicos de Residencias **5865**
• S E M E R G E N (Sociedad Espanola de Medicina Rural y Generalista) (ESP ISSN 1138-3593) **5708**
S E M Newsletter (Society for Ethnomusicology) (USA) **6614**
S E Magazine *see* N Z Today **8739**
S E N *see* Studies in Ethnicity and Nationalism **7187**
S E N C O Update (Special Educational Needs Coordinator) (GBR ISSN 1465-265X) **3046**
S E N Conference Proceedings (Subsea Engineering News) (GBR) **6791**
S E N R *see* Sustainability, Economics, and Natural Resources **1180**
S E N Report Series: Software Engineering *see* Software Engineering **2597**
• S E O / S E M Journal (Search Engine Optimization and Marketing) (USA) **2436**
S E P M Midyear Meeting. Abstracts (Society of Economic Paleontologists and Mineralogists) (USA ISSN 1052-8423) **6730**
S E P M Reprint Series (Society of Economic Paleontologists and Mineralogists) (USA ISSN 0731-759X) **6730**
▼ S E P T E T Revue (Societe d'Etudes des Pratiques et Theories en Traduction) (FRA ISSN 1962-4220) **5171**
S E R *see* Singapore Economic Review **1174**
S E R America (Service, Employment, Redevelopment) (USA ISSN 1063-1917) **1874**
S E R B Official Reporter (State Employment Relations Board) (USA ISSN 0894-3486) **4777**
S E R Bulletin (Sociaal-Economische Raad) (NLD ISSN 0920-4849) **1516**
• ➤ S E R en el 2000 (Seguridad Estrategia Regional) (ARG ISSN 0328-6126) **6444**
S E R Network Directory (Service, Employment, Redevelopment) (USA) **1874**
S E S C A *see* Australia. Bureau of Statistics. Standard Economic Sector Classifications of Australia (Online) **1210**
S E S D Newsletter (Science Education for Students with Disabilities) (USA) **2908**
• ➤ S E S H A e-Journal (Semiconductor Environmental Safety Health Association) (USA) **6685**
• ➤ S E S I Journal (Solar Energy Society of India) (IND ISSN 0970-2466) **3177**
S E S Journal *see* Pauses **1643**
S E S Newsletter (Saskatchewan Environmental Society) (CAN) **3464**
S E T Free (Society for the Eradication of Television) (USA) **2389**
• S E T Journal (Stock Exchange of Thailand) (THA ISSN 0859-709X) **1648**
S E T Newsletter (Stock Exchange of Thailand) (THA) **1649**
S E T P Technical Review *see* Society of Experimental Test Pilots. Symposium Proceedings **70**
S E T S - Julkaisu (Suomen Elokuvatutkimuksen Seura) (FIN ISSN 1237-2366) **6511**
• S E W (Sociaal-Economische Wetgeving) (NLD ISSN 0165-098X) **4777**
S E W *see* Sports Executive Weekly **8207**
S E W R P C Newsletter (Southeastern Wisconsin Regional Planning Commission) (USA ISSN 0584-4266) **4426**
S en B *see* Advies & Educatie **2824**
S en D *see* Socialisme en Democratie **7183**
S en V *see* Stedebouw & Ruimtelijke Ordening **4427**
S F *see* Superfunds **4524**
S F *see* Successful Farming **159**
S F & W B *see* Snack Food & Wholesale Bakery **3675**
S F B Post (Stichting Sociaal Fonds Bouwnijverheid) *see* Cordares Post **1673**
▼ • S F C Newsletter for Writers (Stories for Children) (USA ISSN 1945-8657) **2211**
• S F Commentary (Science Fiction) (AUS) **5446**
S F D S *see* Australia. Bureau of Statistics. Sales of Australian Wine and Brandy by Winemakers (Online) **614**
S F E N. Bulletin (Societe Francaise d'Energie Nucleaire) (FRA ISSN 1620-9583) **3174**
S F E N. Bulletin de Liaison *see* S F E N. Bulletin **3174**
S F E P Directory (Society of Freelance Editors and Proofreaders) (GBR ISSN 0960-5533) **7572**
S F E T H. Journal (Syndicat Francais des Entreprises de Travaux en Hauteur) (FRA ISSN 1761-6425) **1034**
S F I Report *see* Denmark. Socialforskningsinstituttet. Rapporter **8098**
S F Newsletter (Southern Forest Products Association) (USA) **3715**
• S F O - Stocks, Futures & Options Magazine (Stocks, Futures & Options) (USA) **1649**
S F R *see* Solid Fuel Review **6793**
S F R A Review (Science Fiction Research Association) (USA ISSN 1068-395X) **5446**
S F S L *see* Studies in Functional and Structural Linguistics **5182**
▼ S F S News (School of Foreign Service) (USA ISSN 1946-827X) **7264**
S F S - Tiedotus (Suomen Standardisoimisliitto ry) (FIN ISSN 0356-1089) **6406**
† • S F Status (Socialistisk Folkeparti) (DNK ISSN 0902-1612) **8986**
• S F T E Newsletter (Society of Flight Test Engineers) (USA) **69**
• S F T - Spiele Filme Technik (DEU) **6511**
S F Terra (Science Fiction) (NLD ISSN 0169-5770) **5446**
▼ ➤ S F U Educational Review (Simon Fraser University) (CAN ISSN 1916-050X) **2908**
S F X (Science Fiction Excitement) (GBR ISSN 0262-2971) **5446**
• S G B (Sports Goods Buyer) (USA ISSN 1548-7407) **8198**
S G B E Bulletin *see* Bioethica Forum **6907**
S G B Golf (Sports Goods Buyer) (GBR ISSN 1475-8636) **8244**
S G B Outdoor (Sports Goods Buyer) (GBR) **8331**
S G B UK (Sports Goods Buyer) (GBR ISSN 1465-6930) **8331**
S G B UK - Guide to the Trade (Sports Goods Buyer) (GBR ISSN 1466-0709) **8331**
S G B UK - Guide to the Trade *see* S G B UK - Guide to the Trade **8331**
S G C A Journal (Saskatchewan Gun Collectors Association) (CAN) **4345**
S G G E E Journal (Society for German Genealogy in Eastern Europe) (CAN ISSN 1712-7572) **3781**
S G G Revue (Schweizerische Gemeinnuetzige Gesellschaft) (CHE) **8130**
S G I A Journal (Screenprinting & Graphic Imaging Association International) (USA ISSN 1546-4431) **7327**
S G I A News (Screenprinting & Graphic Imaging Association International) (USA ISSN 1544-0060) **7327**
S G I Asia *see* Sporting Goods Intelligence Asia **1178**
S G I - Auto Fund. Annual Report (Saskatchewan Government Insurance) (CAN) **8634**
S G I Europe *see* Sporting Goods Intelligence Europe **1178**
• S G I M Forum (Society of General Internal Medicine) (USA ISSN 1940-2899) **5948**
S G I Market Facts Athletic Footwear & Apparel (Sporting Goods Intelligence) (USA ISSN 1931-7255) **1169**
• S G I - Nu (Statens Geotekniska Institut) (SWE ISSN 0283-0175) **2789**
• S G I Quarterly (Soka Gakkai International) (JPN ISSN 1341-6510) **7264**
S G M A Comprehensive Quarterly Sales Trends Report (Sporting Goods Manufacturers Association) (USA) **1842**
S G M A Today (Sporting Goods Manufacturers Association) (USA) **8198**
S G N *see* Shotgun News **8200**
S G P B Alert (Southern Growth Policies Board) (USA ISSN 8755-7282) **1516**
S G S L Network News *see* Sustainable Grazing on Saline Lands Network News **8991**
S G Suesswarenhandel *see* S G Sweets Global Network **3675**
S G Sweets Global Network (DEU ISSN 1863-1940) **3675**
▼ S G U Nschrift (Spolek Germanistu a Ucitelu Nemciny) (CZE ISSN 1802-3282) **5366**
S Gaugian (USA ISSN 0273-6241) **4345**
S H *see* Safety and Health **6685**
S H A R E European Association Anniversary Meeting. Proceedings *see* S E A S Anniversary Meeting. Proceedings **2550**
S H A R P News (Society for the History of Authorship Reading and Publishing) (GBR ISSN 1073-1725) **7572**
S H & C *see* Scottish Home and Country **8883**
S H E (Subject Headings for Engineering) (USA) **5045**
• S H E Alert (Safety Health Environment) (GBR ISSN 1741-475X) **6720**
S H E Alert Online *see* S H E Alert **6720**
S H E T A Newsletter (Saskatchewan Home Economics Teachers' Association) (CAN ISSN 0820-4535) **4366**
• ➤ S H I L A P (Sociedad Hispano-Luso-Americana de Lepidopterologia) (ESP ISSN 0300-5267) **858**
S H I T A Journal *see* Shokubutsu Kankyou Kougaku **156**
S H K Profi (Sanitaer Heizung Klima) (DEU) **4126**
S H M *see* Structural Health Monitoring **8439**
S H M *see* Studies in the History of Music **6621**
La S H M C. Bulletin *see* Revue d'Histoire Moderne et Contemporaine **4159**
S H M R Bulletin *see* Societe Historique de Meaux et sa Region. Bulletin **4265**
S H O T Business (Shooting, Hunting & Outdoor Trade) (USA ISSN 1081-8618) **8331**
S H O T Newsletter (Society for the History of Technology) (USA) **8437**
S H Q *see* Southwestern Historical Quarterly **4313**
S H R *see* Strategic H R Review **1875**
S H R *see* Southern Humanities Review **4475**
S H T *see* Supply House Times **4127**
S H V Gas Newsletter (Steenkolen Handelsvereniging) (NLD ISSN 1874-9704) **6791**
A S I *see* American Statistics Index **8344**
S I *see* Semiconductor International **3113**
S I *see* Symbolic Interaction **8008**
S I *see* Shooting Illustrated **8332**
S I A *see* Surface and Interface Analysis **2106**
S I A (Skogsindustriarbetaren) (SWE ISSN 0346-1033) **3715**
• S I A Andronews (Societa Italiana di Andrologia) (ITA ISSN 1970-8238) **6274**

Title

10834 S I W I PROCEEDINGS ULRICH'S PERIODICALS

S I W I Proceedings (Stockholm International Water Institute) (SWE ISSN 1404-2134) **8831**

S I Young (Schweizer Illustrierte) (CHE) **8882**

S J *see* Security Journal **2680**

S J *see* Sound Journal **8155**

S J C S *see* Scandinavian Journal of Caring Sciences **5710**

S J E A A *see* Stanford Journal of East Asian Affairs **561**

S J First (South Jersey) (USA) **8754**

S.J. Hall Lectureship in Industrial Forestry (USA ISSN 0080-5092) **3701**

S J I *see* Scandinavian Journal of Immunology **5765**

S J I L *see* Stanford Journal of International Law **4941**

S J L B F *see* Stanford Journal of Law, Business & Finance **4787**

S J M *see* Scandinavian Journal of Management **1792**

S J - Nytt (Statens Jaernvaegar) (SWE ISSN 0037-5985) **8624**

S J P E *see* Scottish Journal of Political Economy **1172**

S J P H *see* Scandinavian Journal of Public Health **5710**

S J R *see* The St. Louis Journalism Review **4584**

S J S *see* Scandinavian Journal of Statistics **8398**

S J T G *see* Singapore Journal of Tropical Geography **4028**

S J T R E M *see* Scandinavian Journal of Trauma, Resuscitation and Emergency Medicine **6072**

S Jo P *see* Scandinavian Journal of Psychology **7406**

S Journal (AUT) **1381**

S K A S (Suomen Keskiajan Arkeologian Seura) (FIN ISSN 1455-0334) **4261**

• ➤ S K A S E Journal of Theoretical Linguistics (Slovak Association for the Study of English) (SVK ISSN 1336-782X) **5171**

• S K I P Newsletter (Strategies with Kids - Information for Parents) (NZL ISSN 1177-4495) **2167**

S K R *see* Die Schweizerische Kommunal Revue **7468**

• S K S WebSelect (SIRS Knowledge Source) (USA) **2444**

S K T F!Tidningen (Sveriges Kommunaltjaenstemannafoerbund) (SWE ISSN 0280-6975) **7502**

S K V Info *see* Skatteverket Informerar **1943**

S K V -Nytt *see* Skatteaktuellt **1943**

S L *see* Strategy & Leadership **1795**

S L *see* Southern Lumberman **3716**

S L *see* Significant Living **7681**

• S L (Student Life) (ZAF ISSN 1682-5071) **2908**

S L A *see* Svensklararforeningens Arsskrift **5184**

S L A B (Sound and Literary Art Book) (USA ISSN 1559-288X) **5366**

S L A E I *see* Studies in Late Antiquity and Early Islam **7716**

S L A M. La Lettre (Syndicat de la Librairie Ancienne et Moderne) (FRA ISSN 1957-5262) **7572**

• S L A Salary Survey & Workplace Study (Year) (Special Libraries Association) (USA) **5045**

• S L A T E Newsletter (Online) (Support for the Learning and Teaching of English) (USA) **3079**

S L A T E Newsletter (Print) *see* S L A T E Newsletter (Online) **3079**

S L C *see* Seminaire Lotharingien de Combinatoire **5533**

S L C S *see* Studies in Language Companion Series **5182**

➤ S L D Experience (Severe Learning Difficulties) (GBR ISSN 1367-2460) **3046**

S L E N *see* Sri Lanka Engineering News **3220**

S L I G Buyers' Guide (Starting, Lighting, Ignition and Generating Systems) (USA) **3330**

S L I Newsletter *see* Fleur de Lis **3729**

S L I S Network *see* Indiana University. School of Library & Information Sciences. S L I S Network **5015**

S L J *see* Southern Literary Journal **5375**

S L J *see* School Library Journal **5046**

S L M (Sopra il Livello del Mare) (ITA ISSN 1592-792X) **2716**

S L Magazine *see* S L **2908**

• S L O County Farmer & Rancher Magazine (San Luis Obispo) (USA) **154**

S L Ohtuleht (EST ISSN 1406-6173) **3836**

S L R *see* Second Language Research **5172**

S L R *see* Scottish Languages Review **5172**

S L R *see* Sex Offender Law Report **4898**

The S L S Report *see* Laparoscopy Today **6251**

S L T *see* Southern Loggin' Times **3716**

S L T I *see* The Sign Language Translator and Interpreter **5174**

S L U *see* Supervisors Legal Update **1795**

S L U B Kurier (Saechsische Landesbibliothek) (DEU) **5045**

S L U - E I S S I F Newsletter (Saint Louis University - Extension Institute for Small-Scale Industries Foundation) (PHL ISSN 0115-8341) **1169**

S L U. Institutionen foer Husdjurens Miljoe och Haelsa. Rapport *see* Sveriges Lantbruksuniversitet. Institutionen foer Husdjurens Miljoe och Haelsa. Rapport **301**

The S L V G S News (Saint Lawrence Valley Genealogical Society) (USA ISSN 0890-1287) **3781**

S. London Auto Trader *see* South London Auto Trader **8604**

S M *see* Successful Meetings **1844**

• ➤ S M A D Electronical Journal Mental Health, Alcohol and Drugs (English Edition) (Saude Mental Alcool e Drogas) (BRA ISSN 1806-6992) **2698**

• ➤ S M A D Revista Electronica en Salud Mental, Alcohol y Drogas (Spanish Edition) (Saude Mental Alcool e Drogas) (BRA ISSN 1806-6984) **2698**

• ➤ S M A D Revista Electronica Saude Mental Alcool e Drogas (Saude Mental Alcool e Drogas) (BRA ISSN 1806-6976) **2698**

S M A R T *see* Studies in Medieval and Renaissance Teaching **5381**

➤ S M A R T Journal of Business Management Studies (Scientific Management and Advanced Research Trust) (IND ISSN 0973-1598) **1792**

S M A - The African Missonary *see* African Missionary **7782**

† S M A U News (ITA) **8986**

S M A Weighlog (Scale Manufacturers Association) (USA) **6406**

† S M B - Data (NOR ISSN 1504-0631) **8986**

• S M B Finance (Small & Midsized Business) (USA) **1966**

S M B Partner Community (Small and Medium Business) (USA ISSN 1933-8899) **1966**

S M C *see* Studies in Medieval Culture **4163**

S M D - Oberflaechenmontage-Technologie *see* Informationsdienst F I Z Technik. S M D - Oberflaechenmontage-Technologie **3117**

• S M E - I T Guide (Small and Medium-Sized Enterprise - Information Technology) (SGP) **1421**

S M E News (Society of Manufacturing Engineers) (USA) **3464**

S M E Research Database (Small Enterprise) (GBR) **1966**

• S M E Resource Guide (Society for Mining, Metallurgy, and Exploration Resource Guide) (USA ISSN 1087-0113) **6478**

• S M Es in New Zealand (Small to Medium Enterprises) (NZL ISSN 1178-3281) **1966**

S M H I Hydrologi (Sveriges Meteorologiska och Hydrologiska Institut) (SWE ISSN 0283-7722) **2798**

S M H I Meteorologi (Sveriges Meteorologiska och Hydrologiska Institut) (SWE ISSN 0283-7730) **6394**

S M H I Oceanografi (Sveriges Meteorologiska och Hydrologiska Institut) (SWE ISSN 0283-7714) **2817**

S M H I Rapporter. Meteorologi och Klimatologi/S M H I Reports. Meteorology and Climatology (Sveriges Meteorologiska och Hydrologiska Institut) (SWE ISSN 0347-2116) **6394**

S M H I Reports. Hydrology (Sveriges Meteorologiska och Hydrologiska Institut) (SWE ISSN 0283-1104) **2798**

S M H I Reports. Meteorology and Climatology *see* S M H I Rapporter. Meteorologi och Klimatologi **6394**

S M H I Reports. Oceanography (Sveriges Meteorologiska och Hydrologiska Institut) (SWE ISSN 0283-1112) **2817**

S M I - Tryck (Smittskyddsinstitutet) (SWE ISSN 1400-3473) **7540**

S M J R *see* Sales and Marketing Jobs Report **6703**

S M K Art Journal (Statens Museum for Kunst) (DNK ISSN 1604-9853) **516**

S M K Nieuwsbrief (Stichting Milieukeur) (NLD ISSN 1872-0536) **3464**

S M L Info (Suomen Markkinointiliitto) (FIN ISSN 1239-0143) **1842**

S M M Newsletter *see* Society for Marine Mammalogy Newsletter (Online) **964**

• S M N Newsletter (Sales Marketing Network) (USA) **1842**

S M - Nomer Odin (RUS) **3941**

S M P T E Journal *see* S M P T E Motion Imaging Journal **6511**

• S M P T E Motion Imaging Journal (Society of Motion Picture and Television Engineers) (USA ISSN 1545-0279) **6511**

S M Q *see* Services Marketing Quarterly **1843**

S M R *see* Sociological Methods & Research **8137**

S M R C Newsletter (Southwestern Mission Research Center, Inc.) (USA ISSN 0584-5025) **4311**

• S M R Commodity Charts (Security Market Research) (USA) **1649**

S M R H *see* Studies in Medieval and Renaissance History **4271**

S M R Rapport (Senter for Miljoe- og Ressursstudier) (NOR ISSN 0803-7132) **2626**

• S M R Stock Charts (Security Market Research) (USA) **1649**

S M S *see* Schiffe - Menschen - Schicksale **8660**

S M S *see* Le Specialiste de Medecine du Sport **6233**

S M S *see* Storage Management Solutions **2438**

† S M. Strumenti Musicali (ITA ISSN 1591-7045) **8986**

S M T (Security Management Today) (GBR ISSN 1368-5325) **2679**

S M T *see* Svensk Missionstidskrift **7776**

• S M T (Surface Mount Technology) (USA ISSN 1529-8930) **3112**

S M T - Surface Mount Technology (DEU ISSN 0947-0808) **3330**

• S M T Trends (Surface Mount Technology) (USA ISSN 0890-7900) **3112**

S M U K *see* Skate Magazine U K **8201**

• S M U Law Review (Southern Methodist University) (USA ISSN 1066-1271) **4777**

• S M U Science and Technology Law Review (Southern Methodist University) (USA ISSN 1949-2642) **4845**

S M U V Zeitung (Schweizerischer Metall- und Uhrenarbeitnehmer Verband) (CHE) **6331**

• S M Y A L News (Sexual Minority Youth Assistance League, Inc.) (USA ISSN 0895-3120) **4378**

• S magazine (Simplicity) (USA) **5082**

S N *see* Rivista di Suinicoltura **299**

S N *see* Skattenytt **1943**

S N *see* The Sporting News **8206**

S N A Boletin de Mercado (Sociedad Nacional de Agricultura) (CHL) **154**

S N A Boletin Economico (Sociedad Nacional de Agricultura) (CHL) **154**

S N A G Newsletter (Society of North American Goldsmiths) (USA) **539**

▼ S N A P (Sweets News and Products) (USA ISSN 1947-2374) **1034**

S N A Vocero Agricola (Sociedad Nacional de Agricultura) (CHL) **154**

• S N D Membership Directory (Society for News Design) (USA ISSN 1520-4278) **4583**

• S N D S Magazine (Society for News Design Scandinavia) (DNK ISSN 1901-8088) **4583**

S N D Update (Society for News Design) (USA ISSN 1520-426X) **4583**

S N E *see* EUROSIM - Simulation News Europe **2517**

S N E C M A Informations (Societe Nationale d'Etude et de Construction de Moteurs d'Aviation) (FRA ISSN 0750-7569) **69**

S N E S U P Bulletin (Syndicat National de l'Enseignement Superieur) (FRA) **3000**

S N E T A C. Journal *see* S F E T H. Journal **1034**

• S N F Bulletin (Samfunns- og Naeringslivsforskning A/S) (NOR ISSN 0803-3900) **8130**

• S N F - Rapport (Samfunns- og Naeringslivforskning) (NOR ISSN 0803-4036) **1169**

S N G A N S *see* Sylloge Nummorum Graecorum **6653**

S.N.G.: Obshchii Rynok (Sodruzhestvo Nezavisimykh Gosudarstv) (RUS) **1649**

S N G v (Year) (Sodruzhestvo Nezavisimykh Gosudarst) (RUS) **1261**

S N H Review (Scottish Natural Heritage) (GBR ISSN 1350-3111) **2626**

S N I C Bulletin *see* Singapore National Institute of Chemistry. Bulletin **2080**

• S N L Bank & Thrift Daily (Savings and Loans) (USA) **1381**

S N L Bank and Thrift Daily *see* S N L Bank & Thrift Daily **1381**

• S N L Bank & Thrift Weekly (Midwestern Edition) (Savings and Loans) (USA ISSN 1522-130X) **1381**

• S N L Bank & Thrift Weekly (Northeastern Edition) (Savings and Loans) (USA ISSN 1522-1296) **1381**

• S N L Bank & Thrift Weekly (Southern Edition) (Savings and Loans) (USA ISSN 1522-1288) **1381**

• S N L Bank & Thrift Weekly (Western Edition) (Savings and Loans) (USA ISSN 1522-127X) **1381**

The S N L Conversion Watch *see* S N L ConversionWatch (E-mail) **1381**

• S N L ConversionWatch (E-mail) (Savings and Loans) (USA) **1381**

• S N L Daily EnergyWatch (Savings and Loans) (USA ISSN 1535-850X) **1649**

▼ • S N L de Novo Watch (Savings and Loans) (USA ISSN 1935-4924) **1649**

• S N L Energy Coal Report (Savings and Loans) (USA ISSN 1554-5776) **3147**

▼ • S N L Energy Daily Gas Report (Savings and Loans) (USA ISSN 1937-1160) **1649**

S N L Energy F E R C Report *see* S N L - F E R C Report **3147**

• S N L Energy Gas Utility Week (Savings and Loans) (USA ISSN 1559-7148) **6791**

S N L Energy Power Daily *see* Power Daily **3144**

S N L Energy Renewable Energy Week *see* S N L Renewable Energy Week **3147**

• S N L - F E R C Report (Savings and Loans, Federal Energy Regulatory Commission) (USA ISSN 1931-6801) **3147**

• The S N L Financial Services Daily (E-mail) (Savings and Loans) (USA) **1649**

The S N L Financial Services Daily (Print) *see* The S N L Financial Services Daily (E-mail) **1649**

• S N L Insurance Daily (E-mail) (Savings and Loans) (USA) **1649**

S N L Insurance Mergers & Acquisitions Yearbook (Savings and Loans) (USA ISSN 1099-3215) **1649**

• S N L Insurance Quarterly (E-mail) (Savings and Loans) (USA) **1649**

• S N L Insurance Weekly (Life & Health Edition) (Savings and Loans) (USA ISSN 1098-8149) **1649**

S N L Insurance Weekly (Life and Health Edition) *see* S N L Insurance Weekly (Life & Health Edition) **1649**

• S N L Insurance Weekly (Property & Casualty Edition) (USA ISSN 1098-8130) **1649**

S N L Insurance Weekly (Property and Casualty Edition) *see* S N L Insurance Weekly (Property & Casualty Edition) **1649**

S N L Kagan Broadcast Investor: Deals & Finance *see* Broadcast Investor: Deals & Finance **1614**

S N L Kagan's Broadband Cable Financial Databook *see* Broadband Cable Financial Databook **2375**

S N L Real Estate Securities Daily (E-mail) *see* Real Estate Daily: North America Edition **1647**

• S N L Real Estate Securities Quarterly (Savings and Loans) (USA ISSN 1528-1582) **1649**

• S N L Real Estate Securities Weekly (Savings and Loans) (USA ISSN 1528-1604) **1649**

• S N L Renewable Energy Week (Savings and Loans) (USA ISSN 1555-8703) **3147**

S N L Securities Monthly Market Report *see* ThriftInvestor (E-mail) **1655**

S N M *see* Saturday Night Magazine **2300**

S N O P *see* Catholiques en France **7791**

• S N P Tech Reporter (Single Nucleotide Polymorphisms) (USA ISSN 1542-8737) **6879**

S N S Analys & Opinion (Studiefoerbundet Naeringsliv och Samhaelle) (SWE ISSN 1653-381X) **1169**

S N Supermarket News *see* Supermarket News **3681**

S N V Bulletin (Schweizerische Normen-Vereinigung) (CHE ISSN 0252-0389) **6406**

S Nami Bog (RUS) **7679**

S O *see* Strategic Outsourcing **1180**

S O *see* Super Onda **2215**

S O A Acquired Immunodeficiency Disease Syndrome Magazine *see* S O A Aids Magazine **5765**

S O A Aids Magazine (Sexueel Overdraagbare Aandoeningen) (NLD ISSN 1573-6369) **5765**

S O A Bulletin *see* S O A Aids Magazine **5765**

S O A I D S Magazine *see* S O A Aids Magazine **5765**

S O A P (Selly Oak Alternative Paper) (GBR ISSN 0261-1953) **5237**

• S O A R S Newsletter (Significant Opportunities in Atmospheric Research and Science) (USA ISSN 1948-2507) **6394**

S O A S Law Department Occasional Papers *see* University of London. School of Oriental and African Studies. School of Law. Occasional Paper **563**

S O A S Working Papers in Linguistics and Phonetics (School of Oriental and African Studies) (GBR) **5171**

S O A Web Services Journal *see* S O A World Magazine **2596**

• S O A World Magazine (Service-Oriented Architecture) (USA) **2596**

S O B E C C. Revista (Sociedade Brasileira de Enfermeiros de Centro Cirurgico) (BRA ISSN 1414-4425) **5980**

S O B S *see* The Site of Big Shoulders **5435**

S o C Bulletin (Society of Cartographers) (GBR ISSN 1469-5170) **4028**

• S O C E D Boletim (BRA ISSN 1808-0405) **8130**

• S O C M A Chemical Bond (Synthetic Organic Chemical Manufacturers Association) (USA) **2080**

S O C M Sentinel (Save Our Cumberland Mountains) (USA ISSN 0889-2415) **3464**

S O D I Livros. Analise (Sociedade Distribuidora de Livros e Publicacoes) (PRT ISSN 0870-3124) **7572**

S O E *see* Sociology of Education **2913**

S O E D *see* Samfunnsoekonomisk Debatt **1170**

S O E L K. Soenderjysk Laegekredsforening *see* Syddanske Laeger **8992**

La S O F C O T. Cahiers d'Enseignement (Societe Francaise de Chirurgie Orthopedique et Traumatologique) (FRA ISSN 0338-3849) **6257**

S O F I A *see* The State of World Fisheries and Aquacultures **3609**

S o F i d - Sozialwissenschaftlicher Fachinformationsdienst. Bevoelkerungsforschung (DEU ISSN 0942-2455) **7292**

S O F O *see* The State of the World's Forests **3703**

• S O H O Business Report (Small Office/Home Office) (CAN ISSN 1712-8145) **1170**

S O H O Life and Technology Today *see* SoHo Life and Technology Today **1968**

S O H O Market Analysis & Forecast: Targeting the Small Office - Home Office Online User (USA) **1421**

S O H O Market Analysis and Forecast: Targeting the Small Office - Home Office Online User *see* S O H O Market Analysis & Forecast: Targeting the Small Office - Home Office Online User **1421**

S O I Bulletin *see* U.S. Internal Revenue Service. Statistics of Income Bulletin **1272**

S O J *see* The Sydney Organ Journal **6622**

S O K Magasin *see* O S Magasinet **8191**

S O L *see* Nylink Connection **5037**

• S O L A (Scientific Online Letters on the Atmosphere) (JPN ISSN 1349-6476) **6394**

S O L E - International Society of Logistics. Proceedings (USA ISSN 0893-3499) **8437**

S O L G A Newsletter (Society of Lesbian and Gay Anthropologists) (USA ISSN 1547-5298) **354**

• S O N E T / S D H / M A N (Synchronous Optical Networking - Synchronous Digital Hierarchy - Metropolitan Area Network) (USA ISSN 1094-2785) **2338**

Title

Title

Salar Weekly (IND) **3888**
Salaries and Fringe Benefits: Benchmark Employee Compensation Report (USA) **7502**
Salaries and Fringe Benefits in Colorado Cities and Towns under 3,000 Population (USA) **7502**
Salaries and Fringe Benefits: Management Compensation Report (USA) **7502**
Salaries and Staff Issues in I T. Business Report *see* Benchmark of Salaries and Employment Trends in I T. Business Report (Year) **6693**
Salaries and Wages for Michigan Municipalities over 1,000 Population (USA) **1706**
• Salaries of Scientists, Engineers and Technicians (USA ISSN 0146-5015) **6703**
Salaris en Benefits *see* Gribb Salarisadviseur **1684**
▼ Salaris Pro (NLD ISSN 1873-9369) **1874**
De Salarisadviseur *see* Gribb Salarisadviseur **1684**
Salarisonderzoek Facility Management (NLD ISSN 1872-101X) **1707**
Salary Increase Survey Report (USA) **6703**
Salary Survey *see* Hospital Home Health **4100**
Salary Survey (Washington) (USA) **1516**
Salary Survey (Years) (Saint Louis) (USA) **1707**
• Sale and Altrincham Messenger (GBR) **3870**
▼ Sale & Pepe (SRB ISSN 1452-8363) **4366**
Sale e Pepe (ITA ISSN 0394-7580) **4366**
Sale of a Business (CAN ISSN 1912-0508) **4778**
Salecina - Beitraege zur Gesellschafts- und Kulturkritik *see* Beitraege zur Rechts-, Gesellschafts- und Kulturkritik **7950**
Salem County Historical Society. Quarterly Newsletter (USA ISSN 1535-0983) **4311**
• Salem Metro Labor Trends (USA) **1707**
Salem State Log (USA) **2300**
Sales (JPN) **1842**
Sales, Advertising and Marketing *see* SAM **1842**
Sales Advertising Marketing Magazine *see* S A M Magazine **1841**
The Sales Advisor (USA ISSN 1930-0085) **1842**
Sales and Bargains Report *see* The S & B Report **2249**
Sales and Bulk Transfers Under the U C C (Uniform Commercial Code) (USA) **4778**
Sales and Idea Book (USA) **34**
Sales & Marketing Digest (Belvidere) (USA) **1842**
Sales & Marketing Digest (New York) (USA) **1842**
Sales and Marketing Jobs Report (USA ISSN 1088-9523) **6703**
• Sales & Marketing Management (USA ISSN 0163-7517) **1842**
† Sales & Marketing Management Survey of Buying Power (USA ISSN 0361-1329) **8986**
Sales & Marketing Report (USA) **1842**
Sales and Marketing Strategies & News Ezine *see* The Competitive Advantage **1811**
• Sales & Service Excellence (USA) **1842**
• Sales and Service for an Unfair Advantage (USA) **1842**
• Sales and Use Tax Alert (USA) **1942**
Sales and Use Tax Answer Book (USA ISSN 1942-2105) **1942**
Sales & Use Tax Desk Book (USA ISSN 1064-1947) **1942**
• Sales & Use Tax Monitor (USA ISSN 1543-9895) **1942**
Sales and Use Tax Review (USA) **1942**
Sales Arena (GBR ISSN 1361-9691) **1842**
Sales Association of the Chemical Industry, Inc. Slants *see* S A C I Slants **2080**
• Sales Automation Success (USA ISSN 8756-8780) **1842**
• Sales Business (DEU ISSN 1616-7902) **1842**
Sales Counter (USA) **6976**
Sales Guide Cologne (DEU ISSN 0936-6709) **2026**
Sales Guide Ruhr (DEU ISSN 0947-4773) **2026**
Sales Insider (USA ISSN 1935-147X) **1903**
• Sales Lead Report (USA) **1842**
Sales Management (NLD ISSN 1381-0553) **1792**
Sales Manager (JPN) **1842**
Sales Marketing Network Newsletter *see* S M N Newsletter **1842**
Sales Memory Jogger (USA ISSN 1077-9329) **1842**
Sales of Natural Gas Liquids and Liquified Refinery Gases (Year) (USA ISSN 1937-9730) **6801**
Sales Promotion (CAN ISSN 1206-6435) **1842**
Sales Promotion (GBR ISSN 0957-6193) **1842**
† Sales Rep's Advisor (USA ISSN 0278-5048) **8986**
Sales Rewards (GBR ISSN 1472-9806) **1707**
Sales Tax Advices (IND ISSN 0036-3472) **1942**
Sales Ways (USA) **1842**
• SalesDoctors Magazine (USA) **1842**
• Salesian (USA ISSN 0036-3480) **7816**
Salesian Bulletin (IRL ISSN 0790-1216) **7816**
Salesian Bulletin *see* Salezijanski Vestnik **7816**
Salesianum (ITA ISSN 0036-3502) **7816**
Salesmanship *see* Dartnell's Salesmanship **1813**
Salezijanski Vestnik/Salesian Bulletin (SVN ISSN 0353-0477) **7816**
Salg og Markedsfoering *see* Sesam **1843**
Salg og Suksess *see* Sesam **1843**
➤ Salin - Agham (PHL ISSN 0116-9963) **3715**
Salina (ESP ISSN 1137-6651) **5366**
The Saline (USA ISSN 0893-3057) **3781**
• ➤ Saline Systems (GBR ISSN 1746-1448) **896**
Salir del Armario (ESP ISSN 1699-4418) **4378**
• SalirenBarcelona.com (ESP ISSN 1698-4641) **8754**
Salisbury Review (GBR ISSN 0265-4881) **5238**
Sally'Scout (DEU) **6614**
• ➤ Salmagundi (USA ISSN 0036-3529) **4474**
Salmanticensis (ESP ISSN 0036-3537) **7816**
Salmo Salar (CAN ISSN 0703-5810) **8331**
Salmon and Trout Association. Members' Handbook (GBR) **3607**
Salmon and Trout Association. Newsletter (GBR) **3607**
Salmon Arm Observer (CAN) **3817**
Salmon Farming (GBR ISSN 0951-9882) **3614**
Salmon Research Agency of Ireland Incorporated. Annual Report (IRL) **962**
Salmon, Trout & Sea Trout (GBR ISSN 0955-081X) **8331**
Salmon Trout Steelheader (USA ISSN 0029-3431) **8331**
• Salmonciencia (CHL ISSN 0718-5537) **3607**
▼ • Salmonella Dublin (DNK ISSN 1902-9306) **299**
Salmonella Surveillance Annual Summary *see* U.S. Centers for Disease Control. Salmonella Annual Summary **7544**
Salnamah-i Amari-i Kishvar *see* Iran Statistical Yearbook **8380**
Saloje (IRL ISSN 1649-7813) **3562**
Salome (NLD ISSN 1872-2857) **8882**
Salome (USA ISSN 0749-6435) **516**
• Salon (USA) **5238**
Salon Aeudun Sanomat (FIN ISSN 0782-5404) **3839**
▼ • Salon America Journal (USA ISSN 1934-4252) **516**
Salon City (USA) **590**
Salon.com *see* Salon **5238**
Salon i Elegancja (POL ISSN 1230-9656) **590**
Salon Magazine (CAN ISSN 1197-1495) **591**
Le Salon Orange (FRA ISSN 1962-5626) **516**
• Salon Today (USA ISSN 0743-6394) **591**
Salpafuerra (PRI) **4378**
Salpisma (GRC ISSN 0036-357X) **7773**
• Salsa Cubana (CUB ISSN 1024-946X) **6614**
• SalsaZine (USA) **3562**
• Salt (AUS ISSN 0816-0031) **7679**
† • Salt (DNK ISSN 0907-0974) **8986**
Salt (GBR) **5434**
Salt (NLD ISSN 1874-334X) **5082**
Salt (USA ISSN 0160-7537) **6976**
Salt and Highway Deicing Newsletter (USA) **8634**
Salt and Trace Minerals Newsletter (USA) **299**
Salt for Slugs (USA) **6614**
Salt Hill (USA ISSN 1078-8689) **5366**
• Salt Lake (USA ISSN 1524-7538) **3987**
Salt Lake City Messenger (USA ISSN 0586-7282) **7741**
Salt Lake City Service Directory *see* Salt Lake Living **4550**
Salt Lake Living (USA) **4550**
▼ Salt Life Magazine (USA ISSN 1938-906X) **8199**
• Salt Water Sportsman (USA ISSN 0036-3618) **8331**
Saltscapes (CAN ISSN 1492-3351) **5082**
Saltwater Fishing (AUS) **8331**
Saltwater Girl (ZAF ISSN 1605-7759) **8331**
Saltwater Girl Surf Magazine (ZAF ISSN 1818-9253) **8332**
Saltwater Sport Fishing *see* Sport Fishing Marine and Trailer Boats **3609**
Salud 2000 (ESP ISSN 0214-3615) **5708**
• Salud Bucal (ARG ISSN 0325-0741) **5864**
• ➤ Salud Colectiva (ARG ISSN 1669-2381) **7540**
• Salud de los Trabadores (VEN ISSN 1315-0138) **7540**
• La Salud en Durango (MEX) **5708**
• Salud en Tabasco (MEX ISSN 1405-2091) **7540**
• ➤ Salud Mental (MEX ISSN 0185-3325) **6183**
Salud para Todos (CRI) **2211**
Salud para Todos. Serie *see* Health for All Series **4096**
Salud Plus (USA ISSN 1535-7988) **3987**
Salud Problema (MEX ISSN 0187-3148) **5708**
• ➤ Salud Publica de Mexico/Public Health of Mexico (MEX ISSN 0036-3634) **7540**
† • Salud Publica y Educacion para la Salud (ESP ISSN 1578-858X) **8986**
Salud Rural (ESP ISSN 0212-646X) **5708**
† • Salud Total de la Mujer (ESP ISSN 1575-5371) **8986**
Salud U I S *see* Universidad Industrial de Santander. Revista. Salud **5726**
• Salud Uninorte (COL ISSN 0120-5552) **7541**
• Salud Vital (ARG ISSN 0329-1421) **6996**
Salud! y Buen Provecho/Cheers! and Bon Appetit (USA ISSN 1548-677X) **4398**
➤ Salud & Desarrollo Social (VEN ISSN 1690-4419) **7541**
• Salud y Drogas (ESP ISSN 1578-5319) **2698**
• Salud(i)Ciencia (ARG ISSN 1667-8982) **5709**
Saludos Hispanos (USA ISSN 0898-4875) **3562**
Saluki Club of America. Newsletter (USA) **6814**
† Salumaio e il Gastronomo (ITA) **8986**
Salus *see* Universidad de Carabobo. Facultad de Ciencias. Revista **5726**
Salus Online *see* Universidad de Carabobo. Facultad de Ciencias. Revista **5726**
• ➤ Salusvita (BRA ISSN 0101-9910) **5709**
† Salut (FRA ISSN 0397-7854) **8986**
• Salut (ZAF ISSN 1609-5014) **6444**
• Salute! (USA ISSN 1933-5318) **6444**
Salute *see* In Buona Salute Magazine **3539**
Salute (USA) **3987**
† Salute & Benessere (ITA ISSN 1594-6193) **8986**
† Salute e Benessere. Il Tuo Bambino (ITA ISSN 1722-0416) **8987**
Salute e Prevenzione (ITA ISSN 1592-0216) **7406**
• Salute e Societa (ITA ISSN 1723-9427) **7181**
Salute e Territorio (ITA ISSN 0392-4505) **8067**
Salute Naturale (ITA ISSN 1128-4366) **314**
▼ Salute to Freedom (USA ISSN 1942-6836) **6444**
Salvacion (CUB) **8067**
El Salvador *see* The P R S Group. Country Reports: El Salvador **1506**
Salvage Bids (USA ISSN 0036-3669) **4522**
Salvagemagazine *see* Uit de Brand **3581**
Il Salvagente (ITA ISSN 1123-7236) **2641**
Salvation Army Year Book (GBR ISSN 0080-567X) **7773**
Salvationist (GBR) **7773**
Salvationist.Ca (CAN ISSN 1718-5769) **7741**
Salve (ITA ISSN 1120-446X) **8848**
Salvo (USA) **4312**
Salvo (Chicago) (USA ISSN 1935-0171) **7741**
Salwator (POL ISSN 1426-0662) **7816**
Salz (AUT) **5434**
Salz & Pfeffer (CHE) **4398**
Salz & Technik (CHE) **4398**
Salzburg Studies in English: Jacobean Drama Studies *see* Mellen Studies in Literature: Jacobean Drama **5332**
Salzburg Studies in English Literature: Elizabethan & Renaissance Studies *see* Mellen Studies in Literature: Elizabethan and Renaissance Studies **5332**
Salzburg Studies in English Literature: Poetic Drama & Poetic Theory *see* Mellen Studies in Literature: Poetic Drama and Poetic Theory **5332**
Salzburg Studies in English Literature: Romantic Reassessment *see* Mellen Studies in Literature: Romantic Reassessment **5332**
Salzburger Aktiengesellschaft fuer Energiewirtschaft Nachrichten *see* S A F E - Nachrichten **3329**
Salzburger Beitraege zur Paracelsusforschung (AUT ISSN 0259-0794) **6950**
Salzburger Beitraege zur Sprach- und Kulturwissenschaft (AUT ISSN 1681-6439) **5171**
Salzburger Geographische Arbeiten (AUT) **4028**
Salzburger Geographische Materialien (AUT) **4028**
Salzburger Jahrbuch fuer Philosophie (AUT ISSN 0080-5696) **6950**
• Salzburger Nachrichten (AUT ISSN 1015-1303) **3798**
• Salzburger Nachrichten Online (AUT ISSN 1563-5473) **3798**
Salzburger Romanistische Schriften (DEU ISSN 0256-8578) **5366**
Salzburger Wirtschaft (AUT ISSN 0036-3677) **1409**
Sam (ESP) **299**
• SAM (Sales, Advertising and Marketing) (USA) **1842**
SAM-Forschungsberichte *see* S A M - Forschungsberichte **3357**
Sam Noble Oklahoma Museum of Natural History. Occasional Paper (USA ISSN 1526-3614) **7907**
Sam Nyied Sam *see* San Yue San **5366**
Sam Nyied Sam (Zhuang Edition) *see* San Yue San **5366**
Sam: Zhurnal dlya Umel'tsev (RUS ISSN 0869-7604) **6299**
Samachar Jagat (IND) **3888**
Samachar Sodh (IND) **3888**
Samachar Times (IND) **3888**
Samaj (IND) **3888**
Samaj Daily (NPL) **3914**
Samaj Nirikkhon (BGD) **7999**
Samaja Shodhana/Mangalore Sociology Association. Journal (IND) **8131**
Samajwad Daily (IND) **3888**
Samakaleen (IND) **3888**
Samakaleen Bharatiya Sahitya (IND) **5171**
Samakalina Bharatiya Sahitya/Contemporary Indian Literature (IND ISSN 0970-8367) **5366**
Sa'mang Won'in Tong'gye Yeonbo/Korea (Republic). National Statistical Office. Annual Report on the Cause of Death Statistics (KOR ISSN 1599-0486) **7292**
Samanyolu (TUR ISSN 1300-2511) **7716**
Samara State University. Vestnik. Natural Science Series. Biology *see* Samarskii Gosudarstvennyi Universitet. Vestnik. Estestvennonauchnaya Seriya. Biologiya **702**
Samara State University. Vestnik. Natural Science Series. Chemistry *see* Samarskii Gosudarstvennyi Universitet. Vestnik. Estestvennonauchnaya Seriya. Khimiya **2080**
Samara State University. Vestnik. Natural Science Series. Mathematical Modelling *see* Samarskii Gosudarstvennyi Universitet. Vestnik. Estestvennonauchnaya Seriya. Matematicheskoe Modelirovanie **5532**
Samara State University. Vestnik. Natural Science Series. Mathematics *see* Samarskii Gosudarstvennyi Universitet. Vestnik. Estestvennonauchnaya Seriya. Matematika **5532**
Samara State University. Vestnik. Natural Science Series. Mechanics *see* Samarskii Gosudarstvennyi Universitet. Vestnik. Estestvennonauchnaya Seriya. Mekhanika **7062**
Samara State University. Vestnik. Natural Science Series. Physics *see* Samarskii Gosudarstvennyi Universitet. Vestnik. Estestvennonauchnaya Seriya. Fizika **7039**
Samarbejdsgruppen for Trafiksikkerhed i Kommuneerne i Koebenhavns-Omraadet. Rapport (DNK ISSN 0105-6956) **8634**
Samarbete (FIN ISSN 0036-3715) **1424**
• Samaritan (POL ISSN 1425-5081) **7679**
Samariter (CHE) **5709**
• Samarskie Izvestiya (RUS) **3941**
Samarskii Gosudarstvennyi Universitet. Vestnik. Estestvennonauchnaya Seriya. Biologiya/Samara State University. Vestnik. Natural Science Series. Biology (RUS) **702**
Samarskii Gosudarstvennyi Universitet. Vestnik. Estestvennonauchnaya Seriya. Fizika/Samara State University. Vestnik. Natural Science Series. Physics (RUS) **7039**
• Samarskii Gosudarstvennyi Universitet. Vestnik. Estestvennonauchnaya Seriya. Khimiya/Samara State University. Vestnik. Natural Science Series. Chemistry (RUS) **2080**
Samarskii Gosudarstvennyi Universitet. Vestnik. Estestvennonauchnaya Seriya. Matematicheskoe Modelirovanie/Samara State University. Vestnik. Natural Science Series. Mathematical Modelling (RUS) **5532**
Samarskii Gosudarstvennyi Universitet. Vestnik. Estestvennonauchnaya Seriya. Matematika/Samara State University. Vestnik. Natural Science Series. Mathematics (RUS) **5532**
Samarskii Gosudarstvennyi Universitet. Vestnik. Estestvennonauchnaya Seriya. Mekhanika/Samara State University. Vestnik. Natural Science Series. Mechanics (RUS) **7062**
Samarskii Gosudarstvennyi Universitet. Vestnik. Gumanitarnaya Seriya. Ekonomika i Menedzhment (RUS) **1792**
Samarskii Gosudarstvennyi Universitet. Vestnik. Gumanitarnaya Seriya. Filosofiya (RUS) **6951**
Samarskii Gosudarstvennyi Universitet. Vestnik. Gumanitarnaya Seriya. Istoriya (RUS) **4261**
Samarskii Gosudarstvennyi Universitet. Vestnik. Gumanitarnaya Seriya. Literaturovedenie (RUS) **5366**
Samarskii Gosudarstvennyi Universitet. Vestnik. Gumanitarnaya Seriya. Sotsiologiya i Sotsial'naya Rabota (RUS) **8131**
Samarskii Gosudarstvennyi Universitet. Vestnik. Gumanitarnaya Seriya. Yazykoznanie (RUS) **5171**
Samarskii Kur'er (RUS) **3941**
• Samarskii Universitet (RUS) **3001**
Samarskoe Obozrenie (RUS) **3941**
Samaru Journal of Agricultural Research (NGA ISSN 0331-7285) **154**
Samaru Miscellaneous Papers (NGA ISSN 0080-5769) **154**
Samay Prabaha (IND) **3888**
Samaya (IND) **3888**
Sambad (IND) **3888**
Sambad Pratidin (IND) **3888**
Sambalpur University. Post-Graduate Department of Oriya. Journal (IND) **5366**
Sambo *see* El Universo **3835**
Sambodhi (IND) **560**
Sambre et Heure (BEL ISSN 0774-3548) **4160**
• Same-Day Surgery (USA ISSN 0190-5066) **6257**
• Same Sex Partnership Law Report (USA) **4914**
▼ Samedi Magazine (CAN ISSN 1914-623X) **5082**
Samefolket (SWE ISSN 0346-0320) **4261**
Samenes Venn (NOR ISSN 0809-5779) **7773**
SamenGevat (NLD ISSN 1875-0109) **7181**
Samenleving, Criminaliteit en Strafrechtspleging (BEL) **4778**
Samenwerkende Fondsen Midden- in Oost-Europa. Kwartaalblad *see* C N F Quarterly Journal **8938**
Samenwerkende Organisaties Vogelonderzoek Nederland Onderzoeksrapport *see* S O V O N Onderzoeksrapport **914**
Samenwerking Universitaire Reken Faciliteitennieuws *see* SURF Licentienieuws **2438**
Samenwerking Universitaire Rekenfaciliteiten (Utrecht) *see* SURF (Utrecht) **2567**
▼ Sametinget. Foerfattningssamling (SWE ISSN 1654-0549) **4852**
Samferdsel (NOR ISSN 0332-8988) **8634**
Samford Crimson (USA) **2300**
Samfundet Dansk Kirkesang. Aarskrift (DNK ISSN 0107-6736) **7773**
Samfundet til Udgivelse af Dansk Musik. Catalog (DNK) **6614**
• ➤ Samfundsoekonomen (DNK ISSN 0108-3937) **1170**
Samfundsvidenskabelig Serie *see* Acta Jutlandica. Samfundsvidenskabelig Serie **7945**
Samfunns- og Naeringslivforskning Rapport *see* S N F - Rapport **1169**
Samfunns- og Naeringslivsforskning A/S Bulletin *see* S N F Bulletin **8130**
Samfunnsoekonomen (NOR ISSN 1890-5250) **1170**
• Samfunnsoekonomisk Debatt (NOR ISSN 1502-5683) **1170**
• Samfunnssikkerhet (NOR ISSN 1503-7843) **2228**
• Samfunnsspeilet (NOR ISSN 0801-7603) **8150**
Samhaellsforskning (SWE ISSN 1654-8043) **3174**
Sami Instituhtta. Utredning (NOR ISSN 0809-6090) **8131**
Samiksa (IND ISSN 0971-3492) **7406**
Saminuorat (SWE ISSN 1652-201X) **3562**
• Samir Husni's Guide to New Consumer Magazines (USA ISSN 0000-1767) **7572**
Samiske Samlinger (NOR ISSN 0581-4480) **354**
• Samizdat (RUS) **5238**
Samkaleen Kala Aur Kavita (IND ISSN 0970-0986) **5434**
Samlarboken (SWE ISSN 1102-5212) **368**
Samlaren (SWE ISSN 0348-6133) **5408**
Samlarguiden (SWE ISSN 1653-9656) **4345**
Samlarnytt (SWE ISSN 0036-3790) **2269**

Title

10840 SAMLER OG ANTIKKBOERSEN ULRICH'S PERIODICALS

Samler og Antikkboersen (NOR ISSN 0805-0759) 368
Samlernyt *see* Oelkassen 608
Samleringen (DNK ISSN 0105-3442) 609
Samling af Afgoerelser fra Domstolen og Retten i Foerste Instans *see* Court of Justice and the Court of First Instance. Reports of Cases before the Court 4922
Samling af Afgoerelser fra Domstolen og Retten i Foerste Instans *see* Recueil de la Jurisprudence de la Cour de Justice et du Tribunal de Premiere Instance. Partie 1. Cour de Justice 4938
Samling af Afgoerelser fra Domstolen og Retten i Foerste Instans *see* Recueil de la Jurisprudence de la Cour de Justice et du Tribunal de Premiere Instance. Partie 2, Tribunal de Premiere Instance 4938
Samling af Afgoerelser fra Domstolen og Retten i Foerste Instans *see* Raccolta della Giurisprudenza della Corte e del Tribunale di Primo Grado. Parte 1. Corte di Giustizia 4938
Samling af Afgoerelser fra Domstolen og Retten i Foerste Instans *see* Raccolta della Giurisprudenza della Corte e del Tribunale di Primo Grado. Parte 2. Tribunale di Primo Grado 4938
Samling af Afgorelser. Personalesager *see* European Court Reports. Reports of European Community Staff Cases 4669
Sammelblatt fuer Rechtsvorschriften des Bundes und der Laender (DEU ISSN 0558-3624) 4778
Sammelbuch Griechischer Urkunden aus Aegypten (DEU) 2240
Sammenslutningen af Danske Fodplejere - Fagtidsskrift (DNK ISSN 0109-596X) 591
Sammler Markt International (DEU) 368
Sammlung Arbeitsrechtlicher Entscheidungen (AUT) 4778
Sammlung Arbeitsrechtlicher Entscheidungen *see* S A E 1706
Sammlung Bauaufsichtlich Eingefuehrte Technische Baubestimmungen (DEU) 1048
• Sammlung Bauaufsichtlich Eingefuehrte Technische Baubestimmungen CD-ROM (DEU) 1048
Sammlung Dalp (DEU ISSN 0080-5807) 4474
Sammlung der Entscheidungen des Bundesfinanzhofs (DEU ISSN 0342-197X) 1942
Sammlung der Rechtsprechung des Gerichtshofes und des Gerichts Erster Instanz *see* Raccolta della Giurisprudenza della Corte e del Tribunale di Primo Grado. Parte 1. Corte di Giustizia 4938
Sammlung der Rechtsprechung des Gerichtshofes und des Gerichts Erster Instanz *see* Court of Justice and the Court of First Instance. Reports of Cases before the Court 4922
Sammlung der Rechtsprechung des Gerichtshofes und des Gerichts Erster Instanz *see* Recueil de la Jurisprudence de la Cour de Justice et du Tribunal de Premiere Instance. Partie 1. Cour de Justice 4938
Sammlung der Rechtsprechung des Gerichtshofes und des Gerichts Erster Instanz *see* Recueil de la Jurisprudence de la Cour de Justice et du Tribunal de Premiere Instance. Partie 2, Tribunal de Premiere Instance 4938
Sammlung der Rechtsprechung des Gerichtshofes und des Gerichts Erster Instanz *see* Raccolta della Giurisprudenza della Corte e del Tribunale di Primo Grado. Parte 2. Tribunale di Primo Grado 4938
Sammlung der Rechtsprechung. Offentlicher Dienst *see* European Court Reports. Reports of European Community Staff Cases 4669
Sammlung des Gesamten Hessischen Abfallrechts und Sonstiger Regelungen zur Abfallwirtschaft in Hessen (DEU ISSN 0942-8933) 4841
Sammlung Groos (DEU ISSN 0344-0591) 3001
Sammlung Kurzer Grammatiken Germanischer Dialekte. Series A (DEU ISSN 0344-6646) 5171
Sammlung Metzler (DEU ISSN 0558-3667) 5366
➤ Sammlung Musikwissenschaftlicher Abhandlungen/Collection d'Etudes Musicologiques (DEU ISSN 0085-588X) 6614
Sammlung von Entscheidungen aus dem Sozialrecht (DEU ISSN 0342-2003) 8067
Sammlungen des Herder-Instituts zur Ostmitteleuropa-Forschung (DEU) 4261
Sammlungen zur Landkreisgeschichte (DEU) 4261
Samo Zdrowie (POL ISSN 1429-1568) 6996
• Samoa News (ASM) 3790
Le Samoa Post (NZL ISSN 1177-1712) 3919
Samojeden (DNK ISSN 0108-2736) 6814
Samolechenie (RUS) 314
Samolet (RUS ISSN 0869-5946) 70
Samolety Mira (RUS) 70
Samolyot/Aircraft (USA) 70
Samos (DEU ISSN 0080-5866) 415
Samoyed Quarterly (USA ISSN 0161-0651) 6815
Sampada (IND ISSN 0036-3871) 1516
Sampan (USA ISSN 0738-4467) 3562
Sampel (BEL ISSN 1374-6758) 5238
Sample Case (USA ISSN 0036-3898) 2269
Sample of Dutch F A D N (Farm Accountancy Data Network) (NLD ISSN 1876-2328) 206
Sample Registration Bulletin (IND ISSN 0258-0853) 8067
The Sampler (USA) 8831
Sampler and Antique Needlework Quarterly *see* Sampler & Antique Needlework Quarterly 6642
• Sampler & Antique Needlework Quarterly (USA ISSN 1061-6756) 6642
• Samples (DEU ISSN 1612-8001) 6614
Sampling Guide for Air Contaminants in the Workplace (CAN ISSN 1912-0818) 6686
• Sampling Theory in Signal and Image Processing (USA ISSN 1530-6429) 2538
Samplings (USA ISSN 1553-0876) 6642
Sampovisio (FIN ISSN 0786-2113) 1792
Samrat Ashok Technological Institute Journal of Science and Technology *see* S A T I Journal of Science and Technology 7906
Samruddhi (IND) 1409
Samskrita Pratibha (IND) 5366
Samskriti (IND ISSN 0971-0612) 7708
Samsom Accountancy Actualiteit *see* Samsom Actualite Comptable 1301
Samsom Actualite Comptable (BEL ISSN 0776-0590) 1301
Samsom Audit & Revisoraat (BEL ISSN 0773-8625) 1301
Samsom Besloten Vennootschappen met Beperkte Aansprakelijkheid (BEL ISSN 0778-127X) 1170
Samsom Concertation Sociale *see* Samsom Sociaal Overleg 1874
Samsom Cooperatieve Vennootschappen (BEL ISSN 0776-1511) 1170
Samsom Environnement et Gestion *see* Samsom Milieu & Bedrijf 3464
Samsom Fiscale Wenken (BEL ISSN 0776-1465) 1942
Samsom Geld en Onderneming (BEL ISSN 0778-1288) 1381
Samsom Milieu & Bedrijf (BEL ISSN 0775-3691) 3464
Samsom Naamloze Vennootschappen (BEL ISSN 0778-1261) 1170
Samsom Personal Computer (Dutch Edition) *see* Info Media Net (Flemish Edition) 2576
Samsom Professions Liberales *see* Samsom Vrije Beroepen 1170
Samsom Signaux Fiscaux *see* Samsom Fiscale Wenken 1942
Samsom Sociaal Overleg (BEL ISSN 0774-7217) 1874
Samsom Societe Anonyme *see* Samsom Naamloze Vennootschappen 1170
Samsom Societe Cooperative *see* Samsom Cooperatieve Vennootschappen 1170
Samsom Societe Privee a Responsabilite Limitee *see* Samsom Besloten Vennootschappen met Beperkte Aansprakelijkheid 1170
Samsom Sportsecretaris (BEL ISSN 0775-7883) 8199
Samsom Subsidie-Info (BEL ISSN 0778-6158) 1903
Samsom Vrije Beroepen (BEL ISSN 0776-4383) 1170
Samsoms Aandrijfkrant *see* Aandrijven & Besturen 3258
Samspill *see* Nytt om E U-Forskningen 4467
Samspraak (SWE) 5171
Samsung Journal of Innovative Technology (KOR ISSN 1738-7752) 8437
• Samtid (DNK ISSN 1600-8510) 7999
• Samtiden (NOR ISSN 0036-3928) 5238
Samudra. Dossier (BEL) 3607
Samudra Report (English Edition) (BEL ISSN 1016-5568) 3607
Samudra Report (French Edition) (BEL ISSN 1016-555X) 3607
Samudra Revista (BEL ISSN 1016-5576) 3607
• Samuel Beckett Today - Aujourd'hui (NLD ISSN 0927-3131) 5366
Samuel French Basic Catalogue of Plays and Musicals (USA ISSN 0361-6495) 8478
Samuel H. Kress Foundation. Annual Report (USA ISSN 0581-4766) 516
† Samuel Neaman Institute for Advanced Studies in Science and Technology. Annual Report (ISR ISSN 0792-1896) 8987
Samui Magazine (THA) 3962
Samupakara Vigrahaya (LKA) 1424
Samvadadhvam (IND ISSN 0581-4790) 8398
Samvardhana (LKA) 1516
Samvet Shikhar (IND) 3888
• Samvirke (DNK ISSN 0036-3944) 3834
Samyukta Karnataka (IND) 3888
• San Antonio Business Journal (USA ISSN 0895-1551) 1170
San Antonio District Dental Society Newsletter (USA) 5864
San Antonio Focus (USA) 3987
San Antonio Magazine (USA) 3987
The San Antonio Register (USA) 3562
San Bernardino County Library. Newsletter (USA) 5045
San Carlos Publications. Series A: Humanities (PHL) 4474
San Diegan (USA) 8754
• San Diego (USA ISSN 0734-6727) 3987
• San Diego Business Journal (USA ISSN 8750-6890) 1170
(Year) San Diego Chargers Official Yearbook (USA) 8245
• The San Diego Coast Real Estate Report (USA) 7612
San Diego Commerce (USA) 7612
San Diego County Commerce and Industry Directory *see* Harris Directory. San Diego County Commerce and Industry Directory 2002
San Diego Creative Directory (USA ISSN 1063-9144) 2026
• San Diego Daily Transcript (USA) 4778
San Diego Downtown (USA) 5082
• San Diego Earth Times (USA) 3464
San Diego Family Magazine (USA) 2167
San Diego Home - Garden Lifestyles (USA ISSN 1073-6891) 4550
San Diego International Law Journal (USA ISSN 1539-7904) 4940
San Diego Jewish Times (USA ISSN 0891-5814) 7729
• San Diego Law Review (USA ISSN 0036-4037) 4778
San Diego Lawyer (USA ISSN 1096-1887) 4778
San Diego Leaves & Saplings (USA ISSN 0740-4417) 3781
San Diego Living Metro (USA) 4550
San Diego Magazine *see* San Diego 3987
San Diego Masterplanner (USA ISSN 1542-4782) 8067
San Diego Meeting and Convention Planner's Guide *see* San Diego Meeting & Convention Planner's Guide 6282
San Diego Meeting & Convention Planner's Guide (USA) 6282
• San Diego Metropolitan Magazine (USA) 1170
San Diego Museum of Man. Ethnic Technology Notes (USA ISSN 0080-5890) 354
San Diego Museum of Man. Papers (USA ISSN 0080-5904) 354
San Diego Navy Dispatch (USA) 6445
San Diego Numismatic Society. Bulletin (USA ISSN 0036-4053) 6653
San Diego Padres Official Yearbook (USA) 8245
San Diego Pets Magazine (USA) 6815
San Diego Physician (USA ISSN 0036-4061) 5709
San Diego Region. Info Bulletin. Population & Housing Estimates (USA) 4436
The San Diego Review (USA) 5238
San Diego Service Directory *see* South Bay Living 4550
San Diego Service Directory *see* North San Diego Living 4548
➤ San Diego Society of Natural History. Proceedings (USA ISSN 1059-8707) 7907
San Diego Sound Post (USA ISSN 0036-407X) 4602
San Diego State University Magazine *see* S D S U Magazine 2299
San Diego Supercomputer Center Education News *see* S D S C Education News 2436
San Diego Visitors Planning Guide (USA) 8754
San Diego Visitors Pocket Guide (USA) 8754
• San Diego Voice & Viewpoint (USA) 3562
San Diego Westways (USA ISSN 1540-5230) 8754
San-eob Yeon-gu-won. Jiyeog Gyeongje *see* Jiyeog Gyeongje 1132
San Fernando (ESP) 7502
San Fernando News Observer *see* The Valleys News Observer 3570
• San Fernando Valley Business Journal (USA ISSN 1526-0712) 1170
San Fernando Valley Service Directory *see* Valley Living (San Fernando, Conejo, Simi Valley) 4552
San Fernando Valley Service Directory *see* Valley Living 4552
San Franc *see* San Francisco 3987
• San Francisco (USA ISSN 1097-6345) 3987
San Francisco (Year) (USA ISSN 1056-4403) 8754
San Francisco 49ers GameDay Insider Magazine (USA) 8245
San Francisco 49ers (Year) Official Yearbook (USA) 8245
The San Francisco Almanac (USA ISSN 1053-1696) 1966
• San Francisco Arts Monthly (USA) 6536
• San Francisco Attorney (USA ISSN 0744-9348) 4778
† The San Francisco Bay Area JobBank (USA ISSN 1098-9889) 8987
San Francisco Bay Area Rapid Transit District. Annual Report (USA ISSN 0362-2800) 8510
San Francisco Bay Area Sanyo Group Newsletter (USA) 2583
San Francisco Bay Conservation and Development Commission. Annual Report (USA ISSN 0085-5898) 2626
San Francisco Bay Times (USA) 4378
San Francisco Bay View (USA ISSN 1520-7285) 3562
San Francisco Berlitz Travel Guide *see* Berlitz San Francisco Pocket Guide 8687
The San Francisco Book (USA) 8754
San Francisco Bride (USA) 5561
• San Francisco Business Times (USA ISSN 0890-0337) 1432
San Francisco Chronicle Index (USA ISSN 0893-2425) 4588
San Francisco Craft and Folk Art Museum. Report (USA) 516
San Francisco Daily Journal (USA ISSN 1059-2636) 4778
• San Francisco Downtown (USA ISSN 1087-5638) 3987
• ➤ San Francisco Estuary and Watershed Science (USA ISSN 1546-2366) 8831
San Francisco Forty Niners GameDay Insider Magazine *see* San Francisco 49ers GameDay Insider Magazine 8245
San Francisco Fresh Fruit and Vegetable Wholesale Market Prices (USA) 206
San Francisco Giftcenter and JewelryMart Buyer's Guide (USA) 4061
San Francisco Guide (USA) 8754
The San Francisco Jung Institute Library Journal *see* Jung Journal 7382
San Francisco Law Review (USA ISSN 1083-2319) 4778
San Francisco Medicine (USA ISSN 0361-705X) 5709
San Francisco Meeting & Event Planner's Guide *see* San Francisco Meeting and Event Planner's Guide 6282
San Francisco Meeting and Event Planner's Guide (USA) 6282
San Francisco - North Bay Service Directory *see* North Bay Living 4548
San Francisco Post (USA) 3562
▼ San Francisco Professional Travel Planner's Guide (USA) 8754
San Francisco Service Directory *see* Bay Living 4532
San Francisco State University Series in Philosophy (USA ISSN 1067-0017) 6951
San Francisco Visitors Planning Guide (USA) 8754
San Francisco Wholesale Fruit and Vegetable Report (USA) 206
San Francisco Wholesale Ornamental Crops Report (USA ISSN 0273-6004) 154
San Francisco with Kids *see* Fodor's Family San Francisco with Kids 8705
• ➤ San Joaquin Agricultural Law Review (USA ISSN 1055-422X) 4778
San Joaquin Metro Reporter *see* Metro Reporter 3550
San Joaquin Parents Paper (USA) 2167
San Jose (USA) 3987
• San Jose Film & Video Production Handbook - Directory (USA) 6511
San Jose Post-Record (USA ISSN 0036-4185) 4778
San Jose Sharks Magazine (USA) 8199
San Juan Islands *see* A FalconGuide to the San Juan Islands 8680
The San Juans Beckon (USA) 8754
San Juans Pocket Magazine (USA) 3987
San Khau/Theatre (VNM) 8478
San Luis Obispo County Farmer & Rancher Magazine *see* S L O County Farmer & Rancher Magazine 154
San Luis Valley Historian (USA ISSN 0036-4215) 4312
San Marcos (PER ISSN 0254-8151) 516
San Marino (Repubblica) Bollettino Ufficiale (SMR ISSN 0036-4223) 7467
San Marino (Repubblica). Dipartimento Affari Esteri. Notizia (SMR) 7467
San Miguel Writer (MEX) 5238
▼ San Pedro River Review (USA ISSN 1944-5954) 5366
San Sebastiano (ITA) 8067
San Sun (JPN) 2260
La San Vincenzo in Italia (ITA) 7816
San Yue San/Sam Nyied Sam (CHN ISSN 1003-6458) 5366
Sana (ROM ISSN 1584-2746) 8848
Sanagan's Encyclopedia of Words and Phrases, Legal Maxims (CAN ISSN 1719-8690) 4778
Sananda (IND) 3888
Sananjalka (Helsinki) *see* Sykelaeinen 3469
➤ Sananjalka (Turku) (FIN ISSN 0558-4639) 5171
Sanchar (IND) 3888
Sancho el Sabio (ESP ISSN 1131-5350) 354
Una Sancta (DEU ISSN 0342-1465) 7679
Sancta Crux (AUT) 4261
Sanctiecapaciteit (NLD ISSN 1871-4420) 4898
Sancties (NLD ISSN 0925-0530) 2668
Sanctorum (ITA ISSN 1824-2367) 7816
Sanctuary Circles (USA) 7741
Sand Addiction (USA ISSN 1940-3860) 8268
Sand Dune Research *see* Nihon Sakyu Gakkaishi 2759
The Sand Paper (USA) 4346
Sand Sports Magazine (USA ISSN 1096-1941) 8603
Sandakania (MYS ISSN 0128-5939) 3701
† Sandalion (ITA ISSN 0392-5099) 8987
Sandara/League (USA ISSN 8750-2348) 3562
Sandbach Chronicle (GBR ISSN 0964-7309) 3870
• The Sandbar (USA ISSN 1947-3966) 3465
Sandbar Lake, Information Guide (CAN ISSN 1710-3207) 8754
Sandbox Magazine (USA) 516
• Sandbox Web-Zine (USA) 516
Sandebudet (SWE ISSN 1403-2457) 7773
Sandefjords Blad (NOR) 3924
Sandesh (IND) 3888
• Sandeviften (DNK ISSN 0108-9315) 914
➤ Sandgrouse (GBR ISSN 0260-4736) 914
Sandhills Review (USA ISSN 1061-3579) 5367
The Sandhurst Conference Series (GBR ISSN 1468-1153) 7264
Sandhya Aajkaal (IND) 3888
Sandhya Jyoti Darpan (IND) 3888
Sandhya Ranchi Express (IND) 3888
Sandhya Times (IND) 3888
• Sandhya Times (NPL) 3914
Sandia National Laboratories. Report (USA) 7907
Sandia Review of Books (USA) 7572
SanDiego360 (USA) 3987
Sandip (BGD) 3800
Sandlapper (USA ISSN 1046-3267) 3987
The S&M Utopian Guardian *see* The SandMUtopian Guardian 4982
▼ Sandmaennchen (DEU) 2211

The SandMUtopian Guardian (USA ISSN 1087-6316) **4982**
Sandnats (GBR ISSN 1367-7039) **2626**
† Sandorama (German-French Edition) (CHE ISSN 1422-6472) **8987**
The SandPaper (USA ISSN 0194-5904) **4982**
Sandpiper (USA) **914**
Sandpiper (Bendigo) (AUS ISSN 1449-9606) **7816**
▼ Sandra Lee Semi-Homemade (USA ISSN 1943-8060) **4366**
● Sandstone Review (GBR ISSN 1743-7059) **516**
Sandton Central Essential Directory (ZAF ISSN 1818-815X) **8754**
Sanduq Abu Dhabi lil-Inma' al-Iqtisadi al-Arabi. Al-Taqrir al-Sanawi/Abu Dhabi Fund for Arab Economic Development. Annual Report (UAE) **1605**
Sandwich & Snack News (GBR) **3662**
Sandwich Historical Society. Annual Excursion (USA ISSN 0361-1426) **4312**
Sandy Parker Reports (USA ISSN 1064-0029) **4975**
† Sane e Belle (ITA ISSN 1722-5825) **8987**
Sane Research Report *see* Research Bulletin **6180**
● Saneamento Ambiental (BRA ISSN 0103-7056) **3465**
San'eob Misaengmul Haghoeji/Korean Journal of Applied Microbiology and Biotechnology *see* Han'gug Mi'saengmul Saengmyeong Gong Haghoeji **886**
● San'eob Saengsan Tong'gye/Korea (Republic). National Statistical Office. Monthly Industrial Product Statistics (KOR ISSN 1228-8047) **1261**
San'eob Saengsan Yeonbo/Korea (Republic). National Statistical Office. Annual Report on Monthly Industrial Production Statistics (KOR ISSN 1228-9078) **1262**
San'eob Yeon'gu - San'eob Yeon'guweon/Journal of Industrial Competitiveness (KOR ISSN 1225-7265) **1170**
Sanford Evans Gold Book of Motorcycle Data & Used Prices (CAN ISSN 0705-1840) **8268**
Sanford Evans Gold Book of Older Car Prices (CAN ISSN 1197-6950) **8603**
Sanford Evans Gold Book of Snowmobile Data and Used Prices (CAN ISSN 0318-9422) **8219**
Sanford Evans Gold Book of Used Car Prices (CAN ISSN 0381-8179) **8603**
Sanford Evans Gold Book. Supplement to Both the Car and Truck Data Guides (CAN ISSN 1717-1865) **8603**
▼ Sanfrancisco & Northern Carolina (USA ISSN 1937-0458) **8754**
Sanfujinka Chiryo/Obstetrical and Gynecological Therapy (JPN ISSN 0558-471X) **6004**
Sanfujinka Kanpo Kenkyu no Ayumi/Recent Progress of Kanpo Medicine in Obstetrics and Gynecology (JPN ISSN 0913-865X) **6004**
Sanfujinka Maikuro Sajari Gakkai Zasshi/Japanese Journal of Gynecological Microsurgery *see* Nihon Seishoku Geka Gakkai Zasshi **6000**
Sanfujinka no Jissai/Obstetrical and Gynecological Practice (JPN ISSN 0558-4728) **6004**
Sanfujinka no Sekai/World of Obstetrics and Gynecology (JPN ISSN 0386-9873) **6004**
Sanfujinka Shujutsu/Gynecologic and Obstetric Surgery (JPN ISSN 0915-8375) **6004**
Sang Tao/Creativity (VNM) **1170**
● Sang Thrombose Vaisseaux (FRA ISSN 0999-7385) **5941**
● Sangaku Renkeigaku/Japan Society for Intellectual Production. Journal (JPN ISSN 1349-6913) **7907**
Sangaku Shashin Nenkan (JPN) **6976**
Sangbad Bichitra (USA ISSN 1542-5657) **3562**
Sangeet Natak (IND ISSN 0036-4339) **6614**
Sangeet Research Academy. Journal *see* Ninad **6599**
● Sanger-Hilsen/Singers' Greetings (USA) **6614**
Sangkakala Peradilan (IDN ISSN 0303-321X) **4778**
† Sangre (ESP ISSN 0036-4355) **8987**
Sangre de Cristo Newsnotes (USA) **7816**
Sangyo Anzen Kenkyujo Kenkyu Hokoku/National Institute of Industrial Safety. Research Report (JPN ISSN 0911-6923) **6686**
● Sangyo Chishitsu Kagaku Kenkyujo Kenkyu Nenpo/Institute of Industrial Geological Sciences. Annual Report (JPN) **2765**
● Sangyo Eiseigaku Zasshi (JPN ISSN 1341-0725) **6686**
Sangyo Gijutsu Joho Yokkaichi/Industrial and Technological Information of Yokkaichi City (JPN ISSN 0036-4371) **8437**
Sangyo Ika Daigaku Zasshi (JPN ISSN 0387-821X) **6686**
Sangyo Keiei Kenkyujoho/Journal of Industry and Management of Industrial Management Institute (JPN ISSN 0288-0059) **1792**
Sangyo Kikai/Industrial Machinery (JPN ISSN 0558-4809) **5459**
Sangyo Kikai Shinpo/Industrial Machinery News (JPN) **5459**
Sangyo Kunren *see* Industrial Training **1752**
Sangyo Sharyo/Industrial Vehicles (JPN ISSN 0036-4398) **8603**
Sangyo to Denki/Industry and Electricity (JPN ISSN 0387-2319) **3330**
Sangyo Tokushin (Yosetupan) (JPN) **6343**
Sani Naturalmente *see* Essere & Benessere **8954**
Sanidad Animal Mundial en (Year) *see* World Animal Health in (Year) **8815**
Sanilec (Dutch Edition) (BEL) **1034**
Sanilec (French Edition) (BEL) **1034**
Sanissimi (ITA ISSN 1828-0226) **5709**
Sanita Pubblica *see* Sanita Pubblica e Privata **7541**
Sanita Pubblica e Privata (ITA ISSN 1722-7194) **7541**
Sanitaer Heizung Klima Profi *see* S H K Profi **4126**
Sanitaer und Heizung News (DEU) **4126**
Sanitaer und Heizungs Report (DEU ISSN 0344-9122) **4126**
Sanitaer- und Heizungstechnik (DEU ISSN 0036-4401) **4126**
● Sanitaetshandbuch CD (AUT) **5709**
Sanitair - Dakwerk *see* Sanitaire - Couverture **4126**
Sanitair & Tegel Specialist (NLD ISSN 1387-019X) **4562**
Sanitair Studio *see* Badkamer Studio **4554**
Sanitaire - Couverture/Sanitair - Dakwerk (BEL) **4126**
Sanitar Blech Zentralheizung Monteur *see* S B Z - Monteur **4126**
Sanitaristas (ESP) **4562**
● Sanitary Maintenance (USA ISSN 0036-4436) **1842**
Sanitary Tableware, Artistic Ceramics Suppliers Book (ITA) **4126**
Sanitation Canada (CAN ISSN 0225-6134) **3512**
Saniya (AZE) **3799**
Sanj Samachar (IND) **3889**
Sanjevani (IND) **3889**
Sanjiao Wenxian (NLD ISSN 1566-1997) **7741**
Sanjiao Zhou (CHN ISSN 1003-9643) **5367**
● Sanjin Dushi Bao (CHN) **3827**
Sanken Giho/Sanken Technical Report (JPN ISSN 0285-9815) **3330**
Sanken Technical Report *see* Sanken Giho **3330**
Sankhya *see* Sankhya: The Indian Journal of Statistics **8398**
● ➤ Sankhya: The Indian Journal of Statistics (IND ISSN 0972-7671) **8398**
Sanko Shoshi Kenkyu/Reference Service and Bibliography (JPN ISSN 0385-3306) **5045**
Sankofa (USA ISSN 1544-0885) **2167**
Sankt Gallen Studien zum Wettbewerbs- und Immaterialgueterrecht (CHE) **4779**
St. Galler Bauer (CHE ISSN 1424-6341) **154**
St. Galler Hauseigentuemer (CHE) **7612**
St. Galler Studien zum Privat-, Handels- und Wirtschaftsrecht (CHE) **4779**
St. Galler Studien zur Politikwissenschaft (CHE) **7181**
St. Gallisch - Appenzellische Gewerbe Zeitung (CHE) **1842**
Sankt Gallische Naturwissenschaftliche Gesellschaft. Berichte (CHE) **7907**
St. Hallvard (NOR ISSN 0036-2859) **4261**
St. Hubertus (AUT ISSN 0036-2875) **8332**
St. Pauli Nachrichten (DEU) **6299**
Sankt-Peterburgskaya Panorama (RUS) **1034**
● Sankt-Peterburgskie Vedomosti (RUS) **3941**
● Sankt-Peterburgskii Universitet (RUS ISSN 1681-1941) **3031**
Sankt-Peterburgskii Universitet. Uchenye Zapiski. Seriya Geologicheskikh Nauk (RUS) **2765**
➤ Sankt-Peterburgskii Universitet. Vestnik. Seriya 1. Matematika, Mekhanika, Astronomiya (RUS ISSN 1025-3106) **5532**
➤ Sankt-Peterburgskii Universitet. Vestnik. Seriya 10. Prikladnaya Matematika, Informatika, Protsessy Upravleniya (RUS ISSN 1811-9905) **5532**
➤ Sankt-Peterburgskii Universitet. Vestnik. Seriya 11. Meditsina (RUS ISSN 1818-2909) **5709**
➤ Sankt-Peterburgskii Universitet. Vestnik. Seriya 2. Istoriya (RUS ISSN 1812-9323) **4160**
Sankt-Peterburgskii Universitet. Vestnik. Seriya 2. Istoriya, Yazykoznanie, Literaturovedenie *see* Sankt-Peterburgskii Universitet. Vestnik. Seriya 2. Istoriya **4160**
➤ Sankt-Peterburgskii Universitet. Vestnik. Seriya 3. Biologiya (RUS ISSN 1025-8604) **703**
➤ Sankt-Peterburgskii Universitet. Vestnik. Seriya 4. Fizika, Khimiya (RUS ISSN 1024-8579) **7039**
➤ Sankt-Peterburgskii Universitet. Vestnik. Seriya 5. Ekonomika (RUS ISSN 1026-356X) **1170**
➤ Sankt-Peterburgskii Universitet. Vestnik. Seriya 6. Filosofiya, Politologiya, Sotsiologiya, Psikhologiya, Pravo (RUS ISSN 1560-1390) **4474**
➤ Sankt-Peterburgskii Universitet. Vestnik. Seriya 7. Geologiya, Geografiya (RUS ISSN 1029-7456) **2765**
➤ Sankt-Peterburgskii Universitet. Vestnik. Seriya 8. Menedzhment (RUS ISSN 1605-7953) **1792**
➤ Sankt-Peterburgskii Universitet. Vestnik. Seriya 9. Filologiya, Vostokovedenie, Zhurnalistika (RUS ISSN 1813-1921) **5171**
Sankt-Peterburgskoe Ekho (RUS) **3941**
Sankt-Peterburgskoe Obshchestvo Estestvoispytatelei. Trudy (RUS ISSN 1028-5970) **703**
St. Poeltner Dioezesanblatt (AUT ISSN 0036-3162) **7679**
St. Stefaner Gemeindenachrichten (AUT) **7502**
Sankyo Research Laboratories. Annual Report (JPN ISSN 1341-741X) **6879**
Sankyo Seimei Kagaku Kenkyu Shinko Zaidan Kenkyu Hokokushu/Report of Studies Supported by Sankyo Foundation of Life Science (JPN) **703**
Sanlam se Ekonomiese Oorsig *see* Sanlam's Economic Survey **1516**
Sanlam's Economic Survey (ZAF) **1516**
Sanmarg (Calcutta) (IND) **3889**
Sannivedana (LKA) **8131**
Sanquin. Scientific Report (NLD ISSN 1574-1664) **5941**
Sanrim Gwahag Nonjib/F R I Journal of Forest Science (KOR ISSN 1225-9667) **3701**
▼ ● Sans Frontieres (FRA ISSN 1961-7070) **5709**
Sans Serif *see* Serif **7328**
Sans Tache (USA) **3781**
Sanshi-Konchu Biotec *see* Sanshi Konchuu Baiotekku **858**
Sanshi. Konchu Nogyo Gijutsu Kenkyusho Shiryo/National Institute of Sericultural and Entomological Science. Miscellaneous Publication (JPN ISSN 0915-2679) **858**
● Sanshi Konchuu Baiotekku (JPN ISSN 1881-0551) **858**
Sanskriti (IND ISSN 0581-4758) **4474**
Sansouken Keiryou Hyoujun Houkoku (JPN ISSN 1347-1473) **6406**
Sansouken Today (JPN ISSN 1880-0041) **7907**
● Sant Pau (ESP ISSN 0211-0873) **4111**
Sant Sipahi (IND) **7741**
Santa (LVA ISSN 1407-1584) **3905**
Santa Barbara Magazine (USA ISSN 0744-5199) **3987**
Santa Barbara Museum of Natural History. Contributions in Anthropology (USA) **355**
Santa Barbara Museum of Natural History. Contributions in Science (USA ISSN 0099-5894) **962**
Santa Barbara Museum of Natural History. Museum Bulletin (USA) **6537**
Santa Barbara Portuguese Studies (USA ISSN 1077-5943) **4261**
● Santa Clara Computer and High Technology Law Journal (USA ISSN 0882-3383) **4779**
Santa Clara County Connections (USA ISSN 0895-6103) **3781**
● Santa Clara Journal of International Law (USA) **4940**
● Santa Clara Law Review (USA ISSN 0146-0315) **4779**
Santa Clara Valley Lifestyles (USA) **5082**
Santa Claus *see* Better Homes and Gardens Santa Claus (Year) **532**
Santa Cruz Action Network. Newsletter (USA) **4426**
The Santa Cruz Comic News (USA ISSN 1932-9628) **7181**
Santa Cruz County History Journal (USA ISSN 1081-681X) **4312**
Santa Cruz Operation Magazine *see* S C O Magazine **8986**
● Santa Fe Institute. Bulletin (USA ISSN 1058-7608) **3001**
● Santa Fe Institute. Working Papers (USA) **7907**
The Santa Fean Magazine (USA ISSN 1046-2708) **3987**
Santa Justa Klan (ESP ISSN 1885-8635) **2211**
Santa Monica Review (USA ISSN 0899-9848) **5367**
Santa Rosa News (USA ISSN 0894-783X) **3562**
Santag (DEU ISSN 0940-0265) **560**
Santakuti Vedic Research Series (IND ISSN 0080-6137) **4188**
● Santalka/Coactivity (LTU ISSN 1822-430X) **5171**
Santana (USA) **8281**
Sant'Anna News (ITA ISSN 1593-5442) **2300**
Sante (FRA ISSN 1950-0440) **5709**
Sante (NLD ISSN 1380-7889) **8882**
Sante (Montrouge) *see* Cahiers d'Etudes et de Recherches Francophones. Sante **5591**
Sante Animale Mondiale en (Year) *see* World Animal Health in (Year) **8815**
La Sante C'est Alimentaire (CAN ISSN 1719-9263) **6669**
Sante Conjuguee (BEL ISSN 1372-6064) **5709**
● La Sante de la Population Canadienne (CAN ISSN 1708-7694) **7541**
La Sante de l'Abeille (FRA ISSN 0036-4568) **154**
Sante de l'Homme (FRA ISSN 0151-1998) **5709**
● ➤ Sante Decision Management (FRA ISSN 1960-8748) **5709**
Sante du Pied (FRA ISSN 1961-571X) **6072**
Sante Environnement (FRA ISSN 1958-9719) **7541**
Sante et Cafe (FRA ISSN 1959-1578) **5709**
Sante et Environnement *see* Sante Environnement **7541**
Sante & Ressources (FRA ISSN 1778-6673) **5709**
Sante et Services Sociaux au Quebec (CAN ISSN 1203-3669) **7541**
Sante et Systemique *see* Sante Decision Management **5709**
Sante et Travail *see* Sante Travail **7541**
Sante Famille Magazine (FRA ISSN 1954-2062) **4084**
Sante Femme *see* Healthy Woman **8846**
Sante Integrative (FRA ISSN 1961-3768) **5709**
● Sante Magazine (FRA ISSN 0397-0329) **6996**
Sante Mentale (FRA ISSN 1273-7208) **6183**
➤ Sante Mentale au Quebec (CAN ISSN 0383-6320) **7406**
† Sante Pays de la Loire (FRA ISSN 1270-850X) **8987**
Sante pour Tous. Serie *see* Health for All Series **4096**
Sante Pratique (FRA ISSN 1952-5745) **5709**
Sante Publique (FRA ISSN 0995-3914) **7541**
Sante Publique. Bulletin (CAN ISSN 1911-5784) **7541**
Sante Quebec (CAN ISSN 1180-3983) **5980**
Sante Travail (FRA ISSN 1956-5488) **7541**
▼ Sante Zen (FRA ISSN 1960-7377) **6996**
Santekhnika (RUS ISSN 1609-9559) **4126**
Santemagazine.fr *see* Sante Magazine **6996**
Santeria Ciencia y Religion (MEX) **7741**
Santi (IND) **7708**
† I Santi (ITA ISSN 1970-6006) **8987**
Santi e Beati. Eroi della Fede (ITA ISSN 1970-4755) **7816**
● Santiago (CUB ISSN 0048-9115) **5238**
Santiago Canyon College Faculty Writers *see* S C C Faculty Writers **5365**
● Santiago Times (CHL) **7215**
Il Santo (ITA ISSN 0391-7819) **7816**
† Il Santo dei Voli (ITA ISSN 0036-4606) **8987**
● ➤ Santo Tomas Journal of Medicine (SGP ISSN 0371-3520) **5709**
Santorini Guide (GRC) **8754**
Santuario de Aparecida (BRA ISSN 0036-4614) **7679**
Il Santuario della Madonna delle Rocche (ITA ISSN 0036-4622) **7816**
Sanwa Bank. Corporate Communications Department. Annual Report (JPN) **1381**
Sanwa Shinbun/Sanwa Times (JPN) **3395**
Sanwa Times *see* Sanwa Shinbun **3395**
Sanwarudo *see* SunWorld **2574**
● Sanwen/Prose Monthly (CHN ISSN 0257-5809) **5367**
Sanwen Baijia (CHN ISSN 1003-6652) **5367**
● Sanwen Haiwaiban/Prose Overseas Edition (CHN ISSN 1005-7323) **5367**
Sanwen Xuankan (CHN ISSN 1003-272X) **5367**
● Sanxia Daxue Xuebao (Renwen Shehui Kexue Ban)/China Three Gorges University. Journal (Humanities & Social Sciences) (CHN ISSN 1672-6219) **4474**
● Sanxia Daxue Xuebao (Ziran Kexue Ban)/China Three Gorges University. Journal (Natural Sciences) (CHN ISSN 1672-948X) **7907**
● Sanxia Huanjing yu Shengtai/Environment and Ecology in the Three Gorges (CHN ISSN 1674-2842) **3465**
San'yo Denki Giho/Sanyo Technical Review (JPN ISSN 0285-516X) **3330**
Sanyo Kasei News (JPN ISSN 0036-4649) **2080**
Sanyo Source (USA) **2583**
Sanyo Technical Review *see* San'yo Denki Giho **3330**
● Sanyuefeng/Spring Breezes (CHN ISSN 1003-109X) **2338**
Sao Paulo (BRA ISSN 0036-4657) **3804**
Sao Paulo (City) Arquivo Municipal. Revista (BRA ISSN 0034-9216) **4312**
Sao Paulo. Biblioteca Mario de Andrade. Revista *see* Biblioteca Mario de Andrade. Revista **619**
● Sao Paulo em Perspectiva (BRA ISSN 0102-8839) **7999**
● Sao Paulo Journal of Mathematical Sciences (BRA) **5532**
● ➤ Sao Paulo Medical Journal (BRA ISSN 1516-3180) **5709**
Sao Paulo Suplemento *see* Veja **3804**
Sao Paulo Yearbook (BRA) **1409**
Sao Tome e Principe. Reparticao Provincial dos Servicos de Estatistica. Boletin Trimestral de Estatistica (STP) **8398**
➤ Saobracaj (SRB ISSN 0558-6208) **8634**
Saopcenja - Pliva *see* Medicus **5675**
Saothar (IRL ISSN 0332-1169) **4261**
@sap *see* Analyses of Social Issues and Public Policy **8087**
Sapere (ITA ISSN 0036-4681) **7907**
Sapeur-Pompier (FRA ISSN 0036-469X) **3581**
Sapheneia (CHE ISSN 1421-7899) **2240**
SAPIENS *see* Surveys and Perspectives Integrating Environment and Society **7921**
Sapiens (VEN ISSN 1317-5815) **355**
Sapientia (ARG ISSN 0036-4703) **6951**
● Sapientia (Aberdeen) (GBR) **7181**
Sapienza (ITA ISSN 0036-4711) **6951**
● La Sapienza della Croce (ITA ISSN 1120-7825) **7816**
SAPinfo.net *see* S A P Spectrum **2524**
Sapio (JPN) **1171**
➤ Sapostavitelno Ezikoznanie/Contrastive Linguistics (BGR ISSN 0204-8701) **5171**
● The Sapper (GBR) **6445**
Sapperloot (NLD ISSN 1574-3055) **5367**
Sapporo District Meteorological Observatory. Journal *see* Sapporo Kanku Kisho Kenkyukaishi **6394**
Sapporo District Meteorological Observatory. Technical Report *see* Sapporo Kanku Kishodai Gijutsu Jiho **6394**
Sapporo Igaku Zasshi/Sapporo Medical Journal (JPN ISSN 0036-472X) **5709**
Sapporo Ika Daigaku Igakubu Jinbun Shizen Kagaku Kiyo/Sapporo Medical University. School of Medicine. Journal of Liberal Arts and Sciences (JPN ISSN 1343-0920) **4474**
Sapporo Ika Daigaku Kiyo *see* Sapporo Igaku Zasshi **5709**
Sapporo Kanku Kisho Kenkyukaishi/Sapporo District Meteorological Observatory. Journal (JPN) **6394**
Sapporo Kanku Kishodai Gijutsu Jiho/Sapporo District Meteorological Observatory. Technical Report (JPN) **6394**
Sapporo Medical Journal *see* Sapporo Igaku Zasshi **5709**
Sapporo Medical University. School of Medicine. Journal of Liberal Arts and Sciences *see* Sapporo Ika Daigaku Igakubu Jinbun Shizen Kagaku Kiyo **4474**
Sapporo-shi Seishonen Kagakukan Kiyo (JPN ISSN 0914-2401) **7907**

Title

▼ *new title*   † *ceased*   ● *electronic media*   ➤ *refereed*

Title

▼ *new title*   † *ceased*   ● *electronic media*   ➤ *refereed*

Title

Title

Title

10852 SDU WETTENVERZAMELING. STRAF(PROCES)RECHT ULRICH'S PERIODICALS

Sdu Wettenverzameling. Straf(proces)recht see Sdu Wettenverzameling. Strafprocesrecht **4898**
Sdu Wettenverzameling. Strafprocesrecht (NLD ISSN 1871-5370) **4898**
† Sdu Wettenverzameling Verzekeringsrecht (NLD ISSN 1874-7299) **8987**
SE A M E O Regional English Language Centre. Annual Report (Southeast Asian Ministers of Education Organization) (SGP ISSN 0129-7716) **5172**
• Se A M K (FIN ISSN 1457-2397) **3001**
Se & Hoer (SWE ISSN 1104-909X) **2364**
• Se og Hoer (DNK ISSN 0901-9545) **3834**
• Se og Hoer (NOR ISSN 0809-4519) **3924**
Se Vuoi (ITA ISSN 0036-9950) **7680**
The Sea (GBR ISSN 0308-2253) **8660**
Sea see Aegir **3583**
Sea see Umi **5391**
Sea (USA ISSN 0746-8601) **8282**
The Sea (USA) **2817**
The Sea & Safety see Umi to Anzen **2819**
• Sea & Shore (USA ISSN 1550-1434) **7541**
Sea and Sky see Umi to Sora **6397**
• Sea & Yachting (GRC ISSN 1106-8892) **8282**
Sea Angler (GBR ISSN 0306-6568) **8332**
Sea Breezes (GBR ISSN 0036-9977) **8660**
Sea Canoeist (NZL ISSN 1177-4177) **8282**
➤ Sea Chest (USA ISSN 0582-3471) **8660**
• Sea Classics (USA ISSN 0048-9867) **8660**
Sea Coast see Kaigan **3276**
Sea Fisheries Institute. Reports/Morski Instytut Rybacki w Gdyni. Prace (POL ISSN 0209-097X) **3607**
Sea Fishing Today (GBR ISSN 0265-024X) **8332**
Sea Grant College Technical Report see University of Wisconsin. Sea Grant College Program. Technical Report **2820**
Sea Grant Extension Program Newsletter (USA) **3607**
▼ • Sea Grant Law & Policy Journal (USA ISSN 1947-3982) **4971**
Sea History (USA ISSN 0146-9312) **4160**
Sea History Gazette (USA ISSN 0896-1646) **8660**
▼ Sea Island Weddings Magazine (USA ISSN 1935-8024) **5561**
Sea Kayaker (USA ISSN 0829-3279) **8282**
SeA M K see Se A M K **3001**
▼ • SeA M K International Journal (Seinajoen Ammattikorkeakoulu) (FIN ISSN 1796-9719) **3001**
Sea Magazine see Sea **8282**
Sea Mass Traveler (USA) **8755**
Sea of Knowledge see Xue Hai **8016**
▼ Sea of Red (USA ISSN 1941-7071) **8245**
• Sea Power (USA ISSN 0199-1337) **6445**
Sea Shelters (USA) **7612**
Sea Spray (NZL ISSN 1173-9479) **8282**
• Sea Technology (USA ISSN 0093-3651) **3219**
Sea Technology Buyers Guide - Directory (USA ISSN 1094-2424) **3219**
Sea Tow Lifelines (USA ISSN 1546-010X) **8282**
• ➤ Seabird (GBR ISSN 1757-5842) **914**
Seacoast Living (USA) **5082**
Seacole Research Papers see Mary Seacole Research Center. Research Papers **5969**
➤ The Seafarer (GBR ISSN 0037-007X) **8660**
Seafarers Log (USA ISSN 1086-4636) **4602**
• Seafood Business (USA ISSN 0889-3217) **3607**
Seafood Export Journal (IND ISSN 0037-010X) **3607**
• Seafood International (GBR ISSN 0268-1293) **3607**
Seafood New Zealand (NZL ISSN 1172-4633) **3607**
† • Seafood Price-Current (USA ISSN 0270-417X) **8987**
• Seafood Price-Current (E-mail) (USA) **3607**
Seafood Processing & Packaging International see Seafood International **3607**
Seafood Trend Newsletter (USA ISSN 1057-2708) **3607**
Seaford House Papers (GBR) **6445**
• Seafriends (NZL ISSN 1177-4983) **2627**
Seagull Theatre Quarterly (IND) **8478**
Seaham Star see Washington Star **3872**
Seaham Star see Houghton Star **2287**
Seahorse International Sailing (GBR) **8282**
Seal Facts/Faits sur les Phoques (CAN ISSN 1914-1009) **3607**
Seal News (USA) **6899**
Sealandair (CAN ISSN 0048-9883) **6445**
Sealants (USA) **6720**
Seales Cayman Letter (CYM) **1650**
• SeaLetter Cruise Magazine (USA) **8755**
• Sealift (Online) (USA) **6445**
• Sealing Technology (GBR ISSN 1350-4789) **6720**
Seamless Steel Tube and Pipe Monthly (GBR ISSN 1749-3757) **6331**
Sean Alexander's The Vital Edge see The Vital Edge **1800**
Seaplane Base Directory see S P A Water Landing Directory **69**
Seaplane Pilots Association Water Landing Directory see S P A Water Landing Directory **69**
Seaport: New York's History Magazine (USA ISSN 0743-6246) **4312**
Seaposter (USA ISSN 0048-9891) **6899**
Search (IND) **1517**
Search (IRL ISSN 0332-0618) **7774**
• Search (Washington DC) (USA ISSN 1943-1848) **7680**
Search (York) (GBR ISSN 0958-3467) **8067**
Search: Agriculture (USA ISSN 0362-2754) **155**
• Search Aids (GBR ISSN 1479-599X) **5046**
• Search & Discovery (USA) **6791**
• Search and Rescue (USA ISSN 1544-7308) **7541**
Search and Rescue Scene see S A R S C E N E **7540**
Search and Rescue Society of British Columbia News see S.A.R. News **7540**
Search and Rescue Statistics see S A R Statistics **8529**
• Search and Seizure Bulletin (USA ISSN 0037-0193) **2668**
Search and Seizure Checklists (USA ISSN 1045-8719) **4898**
• Search and Seizure Law Report (USA ISSN 0095-1005) **4898**
▼ Search Dog News (USA ISSN 1947-7449) **6815**
Search Engine Optimization and Marketing / S E M Journal see S E O / S E M Journal **2436**
• Search Engine Report (USA) **2566**
• Search Engine Watch (USA) **2566**
Search Guide see Federal Research in Progress Database **3192**
Search Light (USA ISSN 1059-9843) **3782**
• Search Marketing Standard (USA) **1843**
• Search Soft Base (USA) **2597**
Search the Scriptures (NGA ISSN 0795-8994) **7680**
Searchable Big Book of Library Grant Money see The Big Book of Library Grant Money **4997**
SearchEngineWatch see Search Engine Watch **2566**
• Searcher (CAN ISSN 0037-041X) **4602**
• The Searcher (GBR ISSN 0955-9221) **4346**
Searcher (Burbank) (USA ISSN 0037-0401) **3782**
The Searcher (Hualapai) (USA) **6647**
• Searcher (Medford) (USA ISSN 1070-4795) **2532**
The Searcher (Olyphant) (USA ISSN 1086-3591) **3782**
Searching for Scruggs (USA ISSN 1053-3907) **3782**
• Searching for the Truth (KHM) **4160**
Searching Together (USA ISSN 0739-2281) **7774**
Searchlight see Search Light **3782**
Searchlight (Hallaton) (GBR) **4085**
Searchlight (Ilford) (GBR ISSN 0262-4591) **7182**
Searchlight (W. Hollywood) (USA ISSN 1932-2526) **7541**
Searchlight on the City Council (USA) **7502**
Searchlight on the State Constitution (USA) **7468**
Searchlines see Association News! (Fort Collins) **7508**
SearchLites (USA ISSN 1096-5599) **581**
Searchnotes (USA ISSN 1061-2467) **3782**
Searchword Special (GBR ISSN 1354-6023) **4346**
• SeaRead (AUS ISSN 1834-6774) **3465**
Seas to Mulberry Fields see Cangsang **4180**
Seashore Trolley Museum Dispatch (USA) **6537**
Seaside Post News Sentinel (USA) **3563**
Season see Sezon **5370**
Season Magazine (USA) **3988**
Season of Champions Fact Book see Canadian Curling Association. Fact Book **8164**
Season of Wonder see Liguorian **7804**
Seasonal Missalette (USA) **7817**
▼ The Seasonal Review (USA ISSN 1948-0016) **5238**
Seasonal Trader (USA) **1650**
Seasons see ON Nature **2623**
Seasons (NLD ISSN 0929-1636) **3750**
Seasons (RUS) **5082**
Seasons - Center Focus see N J Audubon **2619**
Seasons - Center Focus see New Jersey Birds **911**
† Seasons Engeland (NLD ISSN 1871-8124) **8987**
Season's Greetings (USA ISSN 1079-8307) **1843**
Seasons Keuken see Seasons Engeland **8987**
Seasons Keuken see Seasons Koken & Eten **8987**
Seasons Keuken see Seasons **3750**
† Seasons Koken & Eten (NLD ISSN 1871-8116) **8987**
Seasons Tuinen see Seasons **3750**
Seasons Tuinen see Seasons Koken & Eten **8987**
Seasons Tuinen see Seasons Engeland **8987**
Seaswells (USA) **5369**
Seatalk (AUS ISSN 1322-6479) **6445**
• Seatrade (GBR ISSN 1476-3680) **8660**
Seatrade Week Newsfront (GBR) **8660**
• Seattle (USA ISSN 1081-4469) **5082**
Seattle Arts (USA) **517**
Seattle Bride (USA) **5561**
Seattle Chinese Post (USA ISSN 0745-2322) **3563**
Seattle Compass (USA) **8755**
• Seattle Daily Journal Of Commerce (USA) **1172**
Seattle Folklore Society Newsletter (USA ISSN 0037-0460) **3622**
Seattle Gay News (USA) **4379**
Seattle Genealogical Society. Bulletin (USA ISSN 0559-2526) **3782**
Seattle Genealogical Society Bulletin (USA) **3782**
Seattle Homes and Lifestyles (USA ISSN 1525-7711) **5082**
† The Seattle JobBank (USA ISSN 1098-9897) **8987**
• ➤ Seattle Journal for Social Justice (USA ISSN 1544-1245) **7215**
Seattle - King County Dental Society. Journal see Seattle - King County Dental Society Quarterly **5865**
Seattle - King County Dental Society Quarterly (USA) **5865**
The Seattle Medium (USA ISSN 0746-5394) **3563**
Seattle Metropolitan (USA ISSN 1931-2792) **3988**
Seattle Opera Magazine (USA) **6615**
Seattle Professional Engineering Employees Association Spotlite see S P E E A Spotlite **4601**
Seattle / Puget Sound Service Directory see Northwest Living **4548**
➤ Seattle Review (USA ISSN 0147-6629) **5369**
Seattle Theology and Ministry Review (USA ISSN 1536-7533) **7680**
Seattle Treatment Education Project Newsletter see S T E P Newsletter **5826**
Seattle Treatment Education Project Zine see S T E P Zine **5826**
• ➤ Seattle University. Law Review (USA ISSN 1078-1927) **4781**
• Seattle Weekly (USA ISSN 0898-0845) **3988**
Seattle's Child (USA) **2168**
• SeaWaves Today in History (CAN ISSN 1710-6966) **6445**
Seaways (GBR ISSN 0144-1019) **8660**
Seaways' Ships in Scale (USA ISSN 1065-8904) **4346**
Seaweed Research and Utilisation (IND ISSN 0971-7560) **2817**
SeaWIFS Postlaunch Technical Report Series (Sea-Viewing Wide Field-of-View Sensor) (USA ISSN 1522-8789) **2817**
SeaWIFS Technical Report Series see SeaWIFS Postlaunch Technical Report Series **2817**
Sechenov Physiological Journal see Rossiiskii Fiziologicheskii Zhurnal im. Sechenova **928**
Secheresse see Science et Changements Planetaires - Secheresse **3465**
Sechzig - Na und? (DEU) **3856**
Secolul 20 (ROM ISSN 0037-0517) **5369**
Secolul Douazecilea see Secolul 20 **5369**
Secom Annual Report (Year) (JPN) **2680**
Second Circuit Review (USA) **4960**
The Second Class of Guangdong see Guangdong Di-er Ketang **2191**
Second District Dental Society. Bulletin (USA ISSN 0037-055X) **5865**
Second Grade Studies Weekly (USA ISSN 1550-3070) **2911**
Second Guess (USA) **3988**
Second Hand see Deuteros Kheri **8257**
Second Home (USA) **7612**
Second Home Journal see 2nd Home Journal **7616**
Second Home Specialist see 2nd Home Specialist **7616**
Second Impressions (CAN ISSN 0834-9304) **7328**
Second Language Acquisition (GBR ISSN 1754-2642) **5172**
Second Language Learning (USA) **5172**
• ➤ Second Language Research (GBR ISSN 0267-6583) **5172**
Second Line (USA ISSN 0037-0576) **6615**
Second Opinion (Atlanta) (USA ISSN 1068-2953) **5807**
Second Order (NGA ISSN 0048-9964) **6951**
Second Penny (CAN ISSN 0702-0783) **8883**
† Second Shift (GBR ISSN 1351-3591) **8987**
Second Sight (USA ISSN 1937-6944) **4111**
Second Skin (NLD ISSN 1872-9363) **2249**
A Second Wind Newsletter (USA) **6219**
Seconda Navigazione (ITA ISSN 1972-2745) **6951**
• Secondamano (Bologna - Modena - Reggio) (ITA ISSN 1124-9900) **34**
• Secondamano (Genova) (ITA ISSN 1124-9897) **34**
• Secondamano (Milan) (ITA ISSN 1124-9927) **35**
• Secondamano (Monza - Brianza) (ITA ISSN 1124-9870) **35**
• Secondamano (Parma) (ITA ISSN 1120-5237) **35**
• Secondamano (Piacenza) (ITA ISSN 1120-5245) **35**
Secondamano (Savona) (ITA ISSN 1825-1226) **35**
• Secondamano (Turin) (ITA ISSN 1124-9919) **35**
Secondant (NLD ISSN 1574-5732) **2668**
The Secondary Assembly File (GBR ISSN 1361-6145) **3081**
Secondary English Magazine (GBR ISSN 1460-5015) **3081**
Secondary Headship (GBR ISSN 1749-1908) **3033**
Secondary Market of Government Securities (BGR) **1517**
• Secondary Marketing Executive (USA ISSN 0891-2947) **1382**
Secondary School Education see Zhongxue Jiaoyu **2929**
Secondary Teachers Guide to FREE Curriculum Materials (USA) **2935**
Il Secondo Rinascimento (ITA) **7999**
Seconds Magazine (USA ISSN 1052-5025) **5369**
SecondWind (USA ISSN 1548-7806) **5434**
Seconsight see Second Sight **4111**
Secours Catholique et Developpement. Rapport d'Activites et Compte-Rendu Financier (Year) (TCD) **1605**
• Secrecy News (USA ISSN 1939-1986) **7468**
• The Secret Pens (USA) **5447**
The Secret Place (USA ISSN 0037-0606) **7774**
▼ La Secretaire de Direction (FRA ISSN 1962-4352) **1854**
• Secretaria de Deporte de la Nacion. Boletin de Investigacion (ARG ISSN 1851-345X) **8200**
Secretaria Permanente del Tratado General de Integracion Economica Centroamericana. Boletin Estadistico (GTM) **7201**
Secretaria Permanente del Tratado General de Integracion Economica Centroamericana. Boletin Informativo (GTM) **1605**
Secretaria Permanente del Tratado General de Integracion Economica Centroamericana. Cuadernos (GTM) **1582**
Secretariat (AUS ISSN 1329-0940) **6184**
Secretariat des Conferences Intergouvernementales Canadiennes. Rapport aux Gouvernements see Canadian Intergovernmental Conference Secretariat. Report to Governments **7428**
Secretariat du Conseil du Tresor. Budget des Depenses. Partie III: Rapport sur les Plans et les Priorites see Canada. Treasury Board Secretariat. Estimates. Part III: Report on Plans and Priorities **7428**
Secretariat of the Pacific Community Agricultural News see S P C Agricultural News **154**
Secretariat of the Pacific Community. Oceanic Fisheries Programme. Standing Committee on Tuna and Billfish. Report (NCL) **3607**
Secretariat of the Pacific Community Tuna Fishery Yearbook see S P C Tuna Fishery Yearbook **3606**
Secretariat Permanent des Organisations Non Gouvernementales. Echo see Echo du S P O N G **3119**
Secretariat Permanent des Organisations Non Gouvernementales. Rapport d'Activites (BFA) **3122**
Secretaries Year Book (THA ISSN 0857-1163) **1707**
Secretary of Energy Annual Report to Congress (USA) **8603**
Secretary Work see Mishu Gongzuo **1852**
Secretary's Companion see Mishu Zhi You **1852**
Secretele Bucatariei (ROM ISSN 1454-7503) **4367**
Secrets d'Artisans (FRA ISSN 1627-8283) **539**
Secrets d'Artiste (FRA ISSN 1953-2296) **517**
Secrets d'Ateliers (FRA ISSN 1763-9867) **539**
Secrets de Cuisine (FRA ISSN 1952-000X) **4367**
Les Secrets de l'Artiste (FRA ISSN 0993-5347) **517**
Secrets d'Etats (FRA ISSN 1778-5359) **7182**
▼ Les Secrets du Temple (FRA ISSN 1961-6287) **6951**
Secrets of a Successful Chrysler Warranty Audit (USA) **8603**
Secrets of a Successful G M Warranty Audit (General Motors) (USA) **8603**
Secrets of Getting Organized (USA ISSN 1933-2696) **4367**
• Secretum Online (ITA ISSN 1970-7754) **3898**
• Section 16 Service (USA) **4880**
• Section 504 Compliance Advisor (USA ISSN 1094-3730) **3046**
Section 504 Compliance Handbook (USA ISSN 1068-6533) **4069**
Section Distribution de Produits et Services Financiers see L' Autorite des Marches Financiers. Bulletin **1309**
Section Five Hundred and Four Compliance Handbook. Supplement see Section 504 Compliance Handbook **4069**
Section Indemnisation see L' Autorite des Marches Financiers. Bulletin **1309**
Section Information Generale see L' Autorite des Marches Financiers. Bulletin **1309**
Section Institutions Financieres see L' Autorite des Marches Financiers. Bulletin **1309**
Section of Cataloguing News see S C A T News **5045**
Section of Children's Libraries News see S C L News **5045**
Section on Cataloguing News see S C A T News **5045**
Section Valeurs Mobilieres see L' Autorite des Marches Financiers. Bulletin **1309**
Sector Alimentario en Mexico (Year) (MEX) **3663**
Sector Customs Tariff Guidebooks (USA) **1582**
Sector Electrico en Mexico (MEX ISSN 0186-050X) **3161**
Sector Publico Empresarial de la Comunidad Autonoma de Euskadi (ESP) **1172**
Sectorbestuur Onderwijsarbeidsmarkt. Nieuwsbrief (NLD ISSN 1871-2657) **3033**
Secuencia (MEX ISSN 0186-0348) **4312**
Secuencias see Secuencias de Arquitectura y Construccion **456**
Secuencias (ESP ISSN 1134-6795) **6512**
Secuencias de Arquitectura y Construccion (ESP ISSN 0213-6724) **456**
▼ Secular Homeschooling (USA) **2911**
Secular Humanist Bulletin (USA ISSN 1063-2611) **7680**
† • Seculive Magazine (FRA ISSN 1957-231X) **8987**
Secure Computing Infosecurity News Magazine see S C Magazine (US Edition) **2516**
Secure Computing Magazine (Asia Pacific Edition) see S C Magazine (Asia Pacific Edition) **2516**
Secure Computing Magazine (UK/Europe Edition) see S C Magazine (UK/Europe Edition) **2516**
Secure Computing Magazine (US Edition) see S C Magazine (US Edition) **2516**
• Secure Destruction Business (USA) **3512**
Secure Magazine (USA) **1650**
Secure Signals (USA) **2390**
• Secured Lender (USA ISSN 0888-255X) **1382**
Secured Lending see Finance Handbook. Volume 1: Secured Lending **1343**
• Secured Transactions Guide (USA) **1650**
Secured Transactions Monthly see Clark's Secured Transactions Monthly **1327**
• Secured Transactions Under the U C C (USA) **4781**

10854 SEGNOCINEMA ULRICH'S PERIODICALS

SegnoCinema (ITA ISSN 0393-3865) **6512**
Segodnya (LVA) **3905**
• Segodnya (UKR ISSN 1606-5395) **3965**
Segodnya i Zavtra (RUS) **3941**
Segodnyashnaya Gazeta (RUS) **3941**
Segredos de Cozinha (PRT) **4367**
† I Segreti dei Pescatori (ITA ISSN 1828-3608) **8987**
I Segreti del Mare (ITA ISSN 1828-6062) **2818**
† I Segreti della Pesca Dolce (ITA ISSN 1825-7178) **8987**
† I Segreti della Pesca Mare (ITA ISSN 1825-716X) **8987**
▼ I Segreti delle Piante Aromatiche (ITA ISSN 1971-6745) **816**
Segretissimo (ITA ISSN 1120-5253) **5412**
▼ Segretissimo S A S (ITA ISSN 1973-6630) **5415**
• Segue (USA) **6615**
• Segue (Middletown) (USA ISSN 1939-263X) **5369**
Segunda Juventud (USA ISSN 1539-0179) **4055**
Seguridad Estrategia Regional en el 2000 *see* S E R en el 2000 **6444**
Seguridad Nuclear *see* Alfa **3180**
Seguridad Radiologica (ARG ISSN 0327-3849) **7072**
Seguridad Social (BOL) **4522**
Seguridad Social (COL) **4522**
Seguridad Social (MEX ISSN 0379-0304) **8067**
Seguridad y Defensa (VEN) **6445**
Seguridad y Medio Ambiente (ESP ISSN 1888-5438) **6687**
Segurinotas (MEX) **1793**
Seguritecnia (ESP ISSN 0210-8747) **2680**
Seguros (URY ISSN 0797-3527) **4522**
Segusium (ITA) **4474**
• Sehepunkte (DEU ISSN 1618-6168) **4160**
Seher.no *see* Se og Hoer **3924**
Sehhatuk Alyoum (SAU ISSN 1319-4607) **5711**
▼ Sehnsucht (USA ISSN 1940-5537) **5369**
➤ Sei Marianna Ika Daigaku Kiyo/St. Marianna University School of Medicine. Bulletin (JPN ISSN 1341-674X) **5711**
Sei Roka Kango Gakkaishi/St. Luke's Society for Nursing Research. Journal (JPN ISSN 1344-1922) **5981**
Seibt Catalogo de la Industria Alemana *see* Seibt Industriekatalog **2027**
Seibt Directory of German Industries *see* Seibt Industriekatalog **2027**
• Seibt Industriekatalog (DEU ISSN 0723-3159) **2027**
• Seibt Medizinische Technik (DEU ISSN 0940-9270) **5711**
• Seibt Oberflaechentechnik (DEU ISSN 0933-8047) **7062**
Seibt Repertoire de l'industrie Allemande *see* Seibt Industriekatalog **2027**
• Seibt Umwelt Technik (DEU) **3465**
• Seibt Verpackungstechnik (DEU ISSN 1431-5556) **6715**
Seibu Zosenkai Kaiho/West-Japan Society of Naval Architects. Transactions *see* Nihon Sempaku Kaiyou Kougakkai Rombunshuu **8655**
Seibu Zosenkai Ronbun Kogai/West Japan Society of Naval Architects. Abstracts from Research Report (JPN) **8530**
• ➤ Seibutsu Butsuri (JPN ISSN 0582-4052) **755**
• Seibutsu Butsuri Kagaku/Physico-Chemical Biology (JPN ISSN 0031-9082) **745**
Seibutsu Fukuoka/Biologia Fukuoka (JPN ISSN 0286-7761) **703**
Seibutsu Kagaku/Biological Science (JPN ISSN 0045-2033) **703**
Seibutsu Kagaku Nyusu/Biological Science News (JPN ISSN 0385-5996) **703**
Seibutsu Kenkyu/Japan Association of Biology Education. Research Report (JPN) **703**
Seibutsu Kino Kankei Shiryoshu/Findings of Biofunctional Chemistry (JPN) **745**
Seibutsu Kogaku Kaishi (JPN ISSN 0919-3758) **896**
➤ Seibutsu Kyoiku/Japanese Journal of Biological Education (JPN ISSN 0287-119X) **703**
Seibutsu Seisangaku Kenkyu/Applied Biological Science *see* Seibutsuken Kagaku **703**
Seibutsu Shiiku Kenkyukai Kaishi/Aquarium and Terrarium Animals (JPN ISSN 0917-1606) **703**
Seibutsu Shiryo Bunseki/Journal of Analytical Bio-Science (JPN ISSN 0913-3763) **703**
• Seibutsu to Kisho (JPN ISSN 1346-5368) **6395**
Seibutsugakushi Kenkyu/Japanese Journal of the History of Biology (JPN ISSN 0386-9539) **703**
Seibutsuken Kagaku/Biosphere Science (JPN ISSN 1348-1371) **703**
• Seicento & Settecento (ITA ISSN 1828-2148) **5369**
Seiche (USA ISSN 8755-4682) **8831**
• Seicho/Journal of Growth (JPN ISSN 0287-7775) **703**
Seicho Kagaku Kyokai Kenkyu Nenpo/Foundation for Growth Science. Annual Research Reports (JPN ISSN 0386-7617) **703**
Seidenki Gakkai Koen Ronbunshu/Institute of Electrostatics. Proceedings of Annual Meeting (JPN ISSN 1342-1492) **7039**
Seidenki Gakkaishi (JPN ISSN 0386-2550) **7039**
Seiji Keizai Shigaku/Journal of Historical Studies (JPN ISSN 0286-4266) **4160**
Seijimbyou to Seikatsu Shuukambyou/Journal of Adult Diseases (JPN ISSN 1347-0418) **5711**
Seijo Daigaku Keizai Kenkyu *see* Seijo University Economic Papers **1172**
Seijo University Economic Papers/Seijo Daigaku Keizai Kenkyu (JPN ISSN 0387-4753) **1172**
Seika Seipan (JPN) **3675**
Seikagaku/Japanese Biochemical Society. Journal (JPN ISSN 0037-1017) **745**
Seikaku Shinrigaku Kenkyu *see* Pasonariti Kenkyuu **7389**
• Seikatsu Eisei/Urban Living and Health Association. Journal (JPN ISSN 0582-4176) **6996**
Seikatsu Kagaku Ronso/Review of Living Science (JPN ISSN 0288-6146) **704**
Seikatsu Kankyou Kagaku Kenkyuujo Kenkyuu Houkoku/Institute of Living and Environmental Sciences. Annual Report (JPN ISSN 1346-6534) **704**
Seikatsu to Fukushi (JPN ISSN 1341-6677) **8067**
Seikatsu to Kankyo/Life and Environment (JPN ISSN 0037-1025) **3465**
Seikei Geka/Orthopedic Surgery (JPN ISSN 0030-5901) **6072**
Seikei-geka Kango/Japanese Journal of Orthopedic Nursing (JPN ISSN 1342-4718) **5981**
• Seikei Geka to Saigai Geka/Orthopedics and Traumatology (JPN ISSN 0037-1033) **6072**
Seikei Kakou/Japan Society of Polymer Processing. Journal (JPN ISSN 0915-4027) **7099**
Seikei Kisho Kansokujo Hokoku/Seikei Meteorological Observatory. Yearly Data Report (JPN ISSN 0388-3515) **6400**
Seikei Meteorological Observatory. Yearly Data Report *see* Seikei Kisho Kansokujo Hokoku **6400**
Seiken N S T Shinpojumu Koen Ronbunshu (Numerical Simulation Turbulence) (JPN) **2518**
Seiki Technical News (JPN ISSN 0288-8785) **3395**
Seilas (NOR ISSN 0803-0553) **8282**
• Seilmagasinet (NOR ISSN 1501-8105) **8282**
Seimei Kagaku Kenkyujo Kiyo/Sophia Life Science Bulletin (JPN ISSN 0288-1578) **704**
Seimitsu Chosa Hokokusho/Metal Mining Agency of Japan. Close Examination Report (JPN ISSN 0286-7184) **6479**
Seimitsu Kogakkai Taikai Gakujutsu Koenkai Koen Ronbunshu/The Japan Society for Precision Engineering. Proceedings of the Meeting (JPN) **3219**
• Seimitsu Kogakkaishi/The Japan Society for Precision Engineering. Journal (JPN ISSN 0912-0289) **3219**
Le Sein *see* Imagerie de la Femme **5633**
Seinajoen Ammattikorkeakoulu. Julkaisusarja. A, Tutkimuksia (FIN ISSN 1456-1735) **3001**
Seinajoen Ammattikorkeakoulu. Julkaisusarja. B, Raportteja ja Selvityksia/Seinajoki Polytechnic. Publications. B. Research Reports (FIN ISSN 1456-1743) **3001**
• Seinajoen Ammattikorkeakoulu. Julkaisusarja. C, Oppimateriaaleja/Seinajoki Polytechnic. Publications. C. Teaching Materials (FIN ISSN 1456-1751) **3001**
Seinajoen Ammattikorkeakoulu. Julkaisusarja. D, Opinnaytteita (FIN ISSN 1456-176X) **3002**
Seinajoki Polytechnic. Publications. B. Research Reports *see* Seinajoen Ammattikorkeakoulu. Julkaisusarja. B, Raportteja ja Selvityksia **3001**
Seinajoki Polytechnic. Publications. C. Teaching Materials *see* Seinajoen Ammattikorkeakoulu. Julkaisusarja. C, Oppimateriaaleja **3001**
Seinan Gakuin Daigaku Kokusai Bunka Ronshu/Seinan Journal of Cultures (JPN ISSN 0913-0756) **4474**
Seinan Journal of Cultures *see* Seinan Gakuin Daigaku Kokusai Bunka Ronshu **4474**
Seine (USA) **963**
Seiri Shinrigaku to Seishin Seirigaku/Japanese Journal of Physiological Psychology and Psychophysiology (JPN ISSN 0289-2405) **7407**
Seirigaku Gijutsu Kenkyukai Hokoku/Report of Physiological Technology (JPN ISSN 0285-3299) **928**
• Seirigaku Kenkyujo Nenpo/National Institute for Physiological Sciences. Annual Report (JPN) **928**
Seisaku Kagaku/Policy Science (JPN ISSN 0919-4851) **7182**
• Seisan Kenkyu/Production Research (JPN ISSN 0037-105X) **8438**
Seisan to Denki/Production and Electricity (JPN ISSN 0285-6204) **3330**
Seisanzai/Industrial Marketing (JPN) **1843**
Seishin Hoken Kenkyu/Journal of Mental Health (JPN ISSN 0915-065X) **6184**
• Seishin Igaku/Clinical Psychiatry (JPN ISSN 0488-1281) **6184**
Seishin Igaku Institute of Psychiatry. Bulletin *see* Seishin Igaku Kenkyujo Gyosekishu **6184**
Seishin Igaku Kenkyujo Gyosekishu/Seishin Igaku Institute of Psychiatry. Bulletin (JPN ISSN 0080-8547) **6184**
• Seishin Kango/Psychiatric Mental Health Nursing (JPN ISSN 1343-2761) **6184**
Seishin Ryoho/Japanese Journal of Psychotherapy (JPN ISSN 0916-8710) **6184**
Seishin Shinkeigaku Zasshi/Psychiatria et Neurologia Japonica (JPN ISSN 0033-2658) **6184**
➤ Seishin Studies (JPN ISSN 0037-1084) **4474**
Seishinka/Psychiatry (JPN ISSN 1347-4790) **6184**
Seishinka Chiryogaku/Japanese Journal of Psychiatric Treatment (JPN ISSN 0912-1862) **6184**
Seismic Engineering (USA ISSN 1069-0891) **3395**
• ➤ Seismic Instruments (USA ISSN 0747-9239) **2789**
Seismic Interpretation Series (USA ISSN 1043-2175) **2789**
Seismicheskie Pribory *see* Seismic Instruments **2789**
Seismicity and Seismic Hazard *see* Jishin Saigai Yosoku no Kenkyu **2784**
Seismological and Geomagnetic Observation and Research *see* Dizhen Dici Guance yu Yanjiu **2779**
Seismological and Volcanological Annual Report in Hokkaido *see* Hokkaido Jishin Kazan Nenpo **2783**
Seismological and Volcanological Bulletin of Japan *see* Jishin, Kazan Geppo. Katarogu-hen (CD-ROM) **2784**
Seismological and Volcanological Monthly Report in Hokkaido *see* Hokkaido Jishin Kazan Geppo **2783**
• Seismological Bulletin (PRT) **2789**
• ➤ Seismological Research Letters (USA ISSN 0895-0695) **2789**
• ➤ Seismological Society of America. Bulletin (USA ISSN 0037-1106) **2789**
Seismological Society of Japan. Journal *see* Jishin **2784**
Seismological Society of Japan. Newsletter *see* Nihon Jishin Gakkai Nyusu Reta **2787**
Seismological Society of Japan. Programme and Abstracts (JPN) **2721**
Seismology and Geology *see* Dizhen Dizhi **2779**
Seismostoikoe Stroitel'stvo. Bezopasnost' Sooruzhenii/Earthquake Engineering (RUS) **2789**
➤ Seitai no Kagaku/Medical Science (JPN ISSN 0370-9531) **704**
Seitai Zairyo *see* Baiomateriaru **655**
➤ Seitaibunsi Kaiseki Kenkyu Senta Dayori (JPN ISSN 1344-6924) **745**
Seitaigaku Kenkyu *see* Ecological Review **670**
Seitaigakuteki Eiyogaku Kenkyu/Japanese Association for Ecological Nutrition Research. Annals (JPN ISSN 0286-0198) **704**
➤ Seitenwechsel (DEU ISSN 0930-3308) **8200**
Seitetsu Kenkyu *see* Nippon Steel Technical Report **6327**
Seitseman Paivaa *see* 7 Paivaa **3839**
Seiva (BRA ISSN 0037-1122) **155**
Seiyo Kotengaku Kenkyu/Journal of Classical Studies (JPN ISSN 0582-4524) **2240**
➤ Seiyoshigaku/Studies in Western History (JPN ISSN 0386-9253) **4263**
Seizieme Siecle (FRA ISSN 1774-4466) **5369**
Seizonken Kenkyuu *see* Sustainable Humanosphere **3469**
• ➤ Seizure - European Journal of Epilepsy (GBR ISSN 1059-1311) **6184**
• Sejler (DNK ISSN 1902-1925) **8282**
Sejleravisen *see* Albatroz **8271**
Sejleravisen Albatros *see* Albatroz **8271**
Sejlerbladet *see* Sejler **8282**
Sekai/World (JPN ISSN 0582-4532) **7182**
Sekai CD-ROM Soran (JPN ISSN 0915-9088) **635**
Sekai Kaihatsu Hokoku *see* World Development Report **1608**
Sekai Kaihatsu Hokoku *see* Rapport sur le Developpement dans le Monde **1604**
Sekai Kowan Jijo Sokuho/World Port Journal (JPN ISSN 1340-4229) **8660**
Sekai no Genshiryoku Hatsuden Kaihatsu no Doko/Nuclear Power Plants in the World (JPN ISSN 0915-0692) **3174**
Sekai no Kansen/Ships of the World (JPN) **6445**
Sekai no Kessakuki/Famous Airplanes of the World (JPN) **70**
Sekai no Norinsuisan/World Agriculture, Forestry and Fisheries (JPN ISSN 0387-4338) **155**
Sekei Saigai Geka/Orthopaedic Surgery and Traumatology (JPN ISSN 0387-4095) **6072**
Sekichu Henkei/Spinal Deformity (JPN ISSN 0911-6826) **6072**
Sekigai Raman Bunkenshu/Infrared and Raman Spectroscopy (JPN) **2141**
Sekitar Perpustakaan (MYS ISSN 0127-1172) **5046**
Sekitsui Sekizui Janaru/Spine and Spinal Cord (JPN ISSN 0914-4412) **6072**
Sekiyu Gakkai Seisei Koenkai/J P I Petroleum Refining Conference (JPN) **6791**
Sekiyu Gijutsu Kyokaishi/Japanese Association for Petroleum Technology. Journal (JPN ISSN 0370-9868) **6791**
Sekizui Geka/Spinal Surgery (JPN ISSN 0914-6024) **6072**
Sekkei Shinpojumu Koen Ronbunshu/Design Symposium. Proceedings (JPN) **3395**
Sekko, Sekkai, Semento, Chikyu Kankyo no Kagaku *see* Society of Inorganic Materials, Japan. Journal **2118**
Seko/Architectural Product Engineering (JPN ISSN 0389-1879) **1035**
Sekretariat (POL ISSN 1425-5782) **1854**
Sekretariat pod Lupou (SVK ISSN 1336-6092) **1793**
Sekretarskoe Delo (RUS) **1172**
Sekrety Serca (POL ISSN 1426-2819) **5412**
Seksjon for Anvendt Miljoeforskning-Marin Rapport *see* S A M e-Rapport **3490**
Seksjon for Anvendt Miljoeforskning-Universitetsforskning Bergen Rapport *see* S A M-U N I F O B Rapport **3491**
Seksten:Ni *see* 16:9 **6517**
➤ Seksuologia Polska (POL ISSN 1731-6677) **5711**
Sektor Erziehung (CHE) **3033**
Sekundaer-Rohstoffe (DEU ISSN 0176-2656) **5459**
Selamta/Greetings (GBR) **8785**
Selangor Public Library Corporation. Annual Report/Perbadanan Perpustakaan Awam Selangor. Lapuran Tahunan (MYS) **5046**
Selber Machen Garten (DEU) **3750**
† Selber Planen (DEU) **8987**
SelberMachen (DEU ISSN 0171-614X) **4346**
• Selbst ist der Mann (DEU ISSN 0037-1157) **4439**
Der Selbstaendige (DEU ISSN 0939-0081) **1966**
Selbsthilfe (DEU ISSN 0724-5572) **8067**
• Selbstmanagement-Letter (DEU ISSN 1863-530X) **7407**
† Selbstorganisation. Jahrbuch fuer Komplexitaet in den Natur-, Sozial- und Geisteswissenschaften (DEU ISSN 0939-0952) **8987**
Selbstpsychologie/Self Psychology (DEU ISSN 1615-343X) **7407**
Selbstverwaltungsrecht der Sozialversicherung (DEU ISSN 0943-9196) **8067**
Selbstzeugnisse der Neuzeit (AUT) **4263**
➤ Selbyana (USA ISSN 0361-185X) **816**
• Selcuk Journal of Applied Mathematics (TUR ISSN 1302-7980) **5533**
Selcuk Universitesi Fen-Edebiyat Fakultesi Edebiyat Dergisi (TUR ISSN 1300-4921) **5369**
• Selcuk Universitesi. Fen-Edebiyat Fakultesi. Fen Dergisi/Selcuk University. Science and Art Faculty. Journal of Science (TUR ISSN 1300-4905) **7913**
• Selcuk Universitesi Ilahiyat Fakultesi Dergisi (TUR ISSN 1300-5057) **7716**
• ➤ Selcuk Universitesi Sosyal Bilimler Enstitusu Dergisi/Selcuk University. Institute of Social Sciences. Journal (TUR ISSN 1302-1796) **7999**
Selcuk University. Institute of Social Sciences. Journal *see* Selcuk Universitesi Sosyal Bilimler Enstitusu Dergisi **7999**
Selcuk University. Science and Art Faculty. Journal of Science *see* Selcuk Universitesi. Fen-Edebiyat Fakultesi. Fen Dergisi **7913**
Selden Society, London. Handbook: Publications, List of Members and Rules (GBR) **4781**
Selden Society, London. Lectures (GBR ISSN 1363-4216) **4781**
Selden Society, London. Main (Annual) Series (GBR ISSN 0265-0657) **4781**
Selden Society, London. Supplementary Series (GBR ISSN 1363-4224) **4782**
➤ Seleccion (ESP ISSN 0214-8927) **6233**
Selecciones Avicolas (ESP ISSN 0210-0541) **300**
Selecciones de Bioetica (COL ISSN 1657-8856) **6951**
Selecciones de Fornituras (ESP) **2249**
Selecciones de Prensa *see* Colegio Oficial de Psicologos de Madrid. Selecciones de Prensa **7417**
Selecciones de Teologia (ESP ISSN 0037-119X) **7680**
• Selecciones del Reader's Digest (Chilean Edition) (CHL ISSN 0037-1203) **3822**
• Selecoes do Reader's Digest (Portuguese Edition) (PRT ISSN 0871-8679) **3931**
Selecoes Economicas/Jitsugyo no Burajiru (BRA) **1605**
Select (GBR ISSN 0959-8367) **6616**
Select (New York) (USA) **7573**
† Select Bibliography of Danish Works on the History of Towns Published (DNK ISSN 0105-9475) **8987**
Select Furniture and Interiors of Ireland (IRL ISSN 0791-9301) **4562**
Select Home Designs (CAN ISSN 0833-1103) **1035**
Select in Furness (GBR ISSN 1750-659X) **8755**
Select Index to South African Literature in English *see* N E L M Index Series **5408**
• SELECT Journal (USA ISSN 1556-7915) **2532**
Selecta (USA ISSN 1096-5882) **5082**
• ➤ Selecta Mathematica (CHE ISSN 1022-1824) **5533**
Selected and Annotated Bibliography of Reference Materials in Consumer Credit (USA ISSN 0077-4014) **1262**
Selected Bibliographies on Ageing (GBR ISSN 0267-0348) **4058**
Selected Book Reviews (USA) **2437**
Selected Books of the Year *see* Aarets Bedste Bogarbejde **7550**
† Selected Borrowings in Immediately Available Funds of Large Commercial Banks (USA) **8987**
Selected Case Law Abstracts (ZAF) **4782**
Selected Current Aerospace Notices *see* S C A N **69**
Selected Excellent Compositions from Nationwide Middle Schools (High School Edition) *see* Quanguo Zhongxue Youxiu Zuowen Xuan (Gaozong Ban) **5164**
Selected Excellent Compositions from Nationwide Middle Schools (Junior High School Edition) *see* Quanguo Zhongxue Youxiu Zuowen Xuan (Chuzong Ban) **2901**
Selected Federal Taxation Statutes and Regulations (USA ISSN 1075-9832) **1942**
• Selected Interest Rates (USA ISSN 1934-1393) **1382**
• Selected Laws and Regulations of Tennessee Financial Institutions (USA) **4881**
Selected Legendary Literature *see* Chuanqi Wenxue Xuankan **5273**
Selected Manpower Statistics (USA ISSN 0501-9427) **1262**
Selected Novellas *see* Zhongpian Xiaoshuo Xuankan **5405**

Selected Novels see Changpian Xiaoshuo Xuankan 5272
Selected Papers From the Annual Meeting see Society of Christian Ethics. Journal 7682
Selected Papers in School Finance (USA ISSN 0162-9697) 3033
Selected Papers of Engineering Chemistry and Metallurgy (CHN ISSN 1007-2365) 6331
Selected Periodicals for the Medical Library (USA) 5750
Selected Popular Literature see Beiyue Feng 5261
Selected Rand Abstracts (USA ISSN 0037-1343) 7939
Selected Readings in Computer Graphics (DEU ISSN 0948-3950) 2489
• Selected Readings in General Surgery (USA) 6258
Selected Readings in Oral and Maxillofacial Surgery (USA ISSN 1044-7032) 6258
Selected Readings in Plastic Surgery (USA ISSN 0739-5523) 6258
➤ Selected Reports in Ethnomusicology (USA ISSN 0361-6622) 6616
Selected Research in Microfiche (USA) 7913
Selected Stories see Xiaoshuo Xuankan 5402
➤ Selected Tables in Mathematical Statistics (USA ISSN 0094-8837) 5533
Selected Topics in Electronics and Systems (SGP ISSN 1793-1274) 3219
➤ Selected Topics in Mass Spectrometry (USA) 2105
Selected Topics in Quantum Electronics see I E E E Journal on Selected Topics in Quantum Electronics 3102
➤ Selected Topics in Superconductivity (USA) 7039
Selected Topics of Electronics and Micromechatronics/Ausgewaehlte Probleme der Elektronik und Mikromechatronik (DEU ISSN 1618-7539) 3330
Selected Translations in Mathematical Statistics and Probability (USA ISSN 0065-9274) 5533
Selected Vital Statistics and Health Status Indicators. Annual Report (CAN ISSN 1188-3642) 7314
➤ Selected Works of Juan Luis Vives (NLD ISSN 0921-0717) 4263
Selected Works of Taiwan and Hong Kong Literature see Taigang Wenxue Xuankan 5384
Selected Works of Young Writers see Xiao Zuojia Xuankan 5402
Selection (DEU) 4367
Selection (GBR) 1874
Selection and Development Review see Assessment & Development Matters 1726
Selection du Reader's Digest (Belgian-French Edition) (BEL ISSN 0037-1408) 3801
Selection du Reader's Digest (French Edition) (FRA ISSN 0037-1386) 3842
Selection du Reader's Digest (Swiss-French Edition) (CHE ISSN 0037-1394) 3959
Selections Avicoles (FRA) 300
Selections from B M J (South Asia Edition) (British Medical Journal) (IND) 5711
Selections from Educational Records of the Government of India (IND) 2911
Selections from University News (IND) 3002
Selections of Pupil Composition see Xiaoxuesheng Zuowen Xuankan 5196
† Selective and Preliminary List of Danish Jazz Clubs (DNK ISSN 1396-0911) 8987
Selective Inventory of Social Science Information and Documentation Services (FRA) 7999
A Selective Listing of Learning Resources (CAN ISSN 1719-7589) 2911
Selectivo (ESP ISSN 1695-7237) 596
The Selector.com Architects Handbook (AUS ISSN 1832-5696) 456
Selektsiya i Nasinnytstvo (UKR) 816
Selektsiya i Semenovodstvo (RUS ISSN 0037-1459) 252
Selenium - Tellurium Development Association. Bulletin (BEL ISSN 1024-4204) 6331
Selenium - Tellurium Development Association. Symposium Proceedings (BEL) 6331
Selenology (USA) 581
† Selezionando S I P (Societa Italiana per l'Esercizio delle Telecomunicazioni P.A.) (ITA) 8987
† Selezione dal Reader's Digest (Italian Edition) (ITA ISSN 0037-1483) 8987
Selezione di Elettronica (ITA ISSN 1129-6941) 3113
• Selezione Tessile (Milan) (ITA ISSN 1125-5579) 8456
• Self (USA ISSN 0149-0699) 8883
Self (China Edition) see Yueji 8892
Self-Adhesive Materials and Markets Bulletin (GBR ISSN 1361-1631) 7099
Self, Agency and Society (GBR) 8131
• ➤ Self and Identity (GBR ISSN 1529-8868) 7407
Self & Society (GBR ISSN 0306-0497) 7407
The Self-Assessment Checklist. Hospitals (USA ISSN 1543-6942) 7541
➤ Self-Care, Dependent-Care & Nursing (USA) 5981
Self-Catering Getaways see A A Self-Catering Getaways 8679
Self Catering Holiday Guide (GBR) 8755
Self-Catering Holidays in Britain (GBR) 8755
• Self-Employed America (USA ISSN 1041-8741) 1966
Self-Employed Country (USA) 1966
Self-Employment Update (USA ISSN 0736-1912) 1966
Self-Help 2000 (USA) 7407
Self-Help and Psychology Magazine see Self-Help Magazine 8067
• Self-Help Magazine (USA) 8067
Self Help Reporter Newsletter see Self-Help 2000 7407
The Self-Help Sourcebook (USA ISSN 8756-1425) 8067
Self-Help Two Thousand see Self-Help 2000 7407
▼ Self Improvement Magazine (USA ISSN 1941-6083) 6647
Self-Knowledge (GBR ISSN 0037-1556) 6951
Self / Nonself see Self Nonself 5766
▼ • ➤ Self Nonself (USA ISSN 1938-2030) 5766
Self Psychology see Selbstpsychologie 7407
• The Self Publishing Magazine (GBR ISSN 1752-9433) 7573
The Self-Publishing Manual (USA) 7573
Self Publishing Update (USA ISSN 0736-1882) 2338
Self-Realization (USA ISSN 0037-1564) 7741
Self-Reliance (IND) 252
Self-Reliant (USA ISSN 0745-7170) 7182
Self Serbis/Self Service Review (GRC ISSN 1105-4972) 1843
//Self Serve (USA) 1172
Self Service Review see Self Serbis 1843
Self-Storage Almanac (USA) 1432
(Year) Self-Storage Development Handbook see Development Handbook 1427
Self Storage Journal (USA ISSN 1044-9590) 1966
Self-Storage Legal Review (USA ISSN 1073-4465) 7612
Self-Storage Now (USA) 1432
Self Study of Teaching and Teacher Education Practices (NLD ISSN 1875-3620) 3081
SelfBuild & Design (GBR ISSN 1471-1079) 1051
Selgeren see Sesam 1843
Selides (CYP) 3832
Selim see S E L I M 5171
Sell Out (ITA) 2390
• Selling (USA ISSN 1069-1952) 1793
The Selling Advantage (USA ISSN 1046-9036) 1172
• Selling Christmas Decorations (USA ISSN 0037-1602) 4061
Selling Crusing (GBR) 8755
Selling Elegance (USA) 3750
• Selling Essentials (USA ISSN 1946-1062) 1793
† • Selling Financial Services (GBR ISSN 1462-3552) 8987
• Selling Halloween (USA) 4061
Selling Long-Haul (GBR ISSN 0959-6496) 8755
• Selling Power (USA ISSN 1093-2216) 1843
Selling Short Breaks & Holidays see Short Breaks & Holidays 8756
• Selling to Seniors (USA ISSN 1050-382X) 1843
Sell!ng see Selling 1793
➤ Sellowia (BRA ISSN 0375-1651) 816
Sell's Marina Guide (GBR ISSN 0969-8191) 8282
† Sell's Marine Industry Buyers' Guide (GBR ISSN 1362-7783) 8987
† • Sell's Products & Services Directory (GBR ISSN 0957-8889) 8987
Selly Oak Alternative Paper see S O A P 5237
Selskab for Nordisk Filologi. Aarsberetning see Studier in Nordisk 5182
➤ Selskabet til Historiske Kildeskrifters Oversaettelse (DNK ISSN 1399-5820) 4161
Sel'skaya Molodezh (RUS ISSN 0203-3569) 2212
Sel'skaya Nov' (RUS ISSN 0582-5164) 252
Sel'skaya Shkola/Rural School (RUS) 2911
Sel'skaya Zhizn' (RUS) 539
Sel'skii Mekhanizator (RUS ISSN 0131-7393) 214
Sel'skoe Khozyaistvo Uzbekistana (UZB) 1517
Sel'skoe Stroitel'stvo (RUS ISSN 0201-4211) 1035
Sel'skohozjstvennyj obzor Evropy see Agricultural Review for Europe 8928
Sel'skokhozyaistvennaya Literatura (RUS) 186
Selskostopanska Tekhnika (BGR ISSN 0037-1718) 214
Seltskond (EST ISSN 1406-3085) 3837
Selvatica (USA) 5238
• Selvedge (GBR ISSN 1742-254X) 6642
† De Selvstaendige (DNK ISSN 1399-8935) 8987
Sem' Dnei (RUS) 3941
• Sem' Dnei (Minsk) (BLR) 3800
Sem Fronteiras (NLD ISSN 1872-356X) 3563
Semaian (NLD ISSN 0924-4840) 4188
Semaien (Leiden) see Semaian 4188
Semaine a Berne see Bern Events 8687
Semaine a Rome see Settimana a Roma 8755
Semaine Africaine (COG ISSN 0488-2024) 7817
Semaine Judiciaire (CHE) 4782
Semaine Juridique (Edition Generale) see La Semaine Juridique. Edition Generale 4782
• La Semaine Juridique. Edition Generale (FRA ISSN 0242-5777) 4782
• La Semaine Juridique. Entreprise et Affaires (FRA ISSN 1290-5119) 4881
• La Semaine Juridique. Notariale et Immobiliere (FRA ISSN 0242-5785) 4782
• La Semaine Juridique. Social (FRA ISSN 1774-7503) 4782
Semaine Quebecoise des Personnes Handicapees. Bilan see Semaine Quebecoise des Personnes Handicapees. Rapport d'Evaluation 4069
Semaine Quebecoise des Personnes Handicapees. Rapport d'Evaluation (CAN ISSN 1719-6299) 4069
Semaine Sociale Lamy (FRA ISSN 0223-4637) 4782
Semaine Veterinaire (FRA ISSN 0396-5015) 8807
Semaines (FRA ISSN 1953-5201) 517
† Semajna Bulteno (DNK ISSN 0108-3759) 8987
Semana (COL) 3830
• Semana (ESP ISSN 0037-1793) 3953
La Semana (Boston) (USA) 3563
Semana Economica (PER ISSN 0254-816X) 1172
• Semana Informatica (PRT ISSN 0871-6218) 2538
La Semana Medica (ARG ISSN 0370-9590) 5712
Semana Medica (PRT) 5711
Semana Politica (MEX) 5238
Semana Politica (Morelia) see La Voz de Michoacan 3912
Semana Vitivinicola (ESP ISSN 0037-184X) 252
• Semanal Oleo (ESP ISSN 0472-8807) 3663
Semanal TV see Mashal 3926
• Semanario (ARG ISSN 0326-0429) 3792
Semanario Economico (PRT ISSN 0872-1688) 1172
Semanario El Sol see El Sol 3792
Semanario Infantil Pionero (CUB) 7182
Semanario Para el Inversionista (MEX) 1382
• Semanario Universidad (CRI) 2300
Semantics and Linguistic Theory Conferences. Proceedings (USA) 5173
▼ • ➤ Semantics & Pragmatics (USA ISSN 1937-8912) 5173
Semaphore Signal (USA) 2525
Semaphores and Signs (GBR) 5173
➤ Semata (ESP ISSN 1137-9669) 4474
▼ • Sembrando Ideas (CHL ISSN 0718-4956) 3002
Semeador Baptista (PRT ISSN 0037-1874) 7774
Semeia see Semeia Studies 7680
• ➤ Semeia Studies (NLD ISSN 1567-200X) 7680
Semeinyi Doktor/Family Doctor (RUS ISSN 1562-0093) 5712
• Semen (FRA ISSN 0761-2990) 5173
Semences et Progres (FRA ISSN 0395-8930) 275
Sementi Elette see dal Seme 227
Semento, Konkurito Ronbunshu (JPN ISSN 0916-3182) 1035
Semergen see S E M E R G E N 5708
Semestrale di Studi e Ricerche di Geografia (ITA ISSN 1125-5218) 4028
Semi-Weekly Called Bond Record see Standard & Poor's Semi-Weekly Called Bond Record 1653
• Semiannual Report to the Congress (USA ISSN 1930-4439) 7468
Semicerchio (ITA ISSN 1123-4075) 5434
Semicolon Login Colon see ;login: 2523
† • Semiconductor Business News (USA ISSN 1523-7184) 8987
Semiconductor Electronics Journal (THA ISSN 0125-1015) 3113
Semiconductor Environmental Safety Health Association Journal see S E S H A e-Journal 6685
Semiconductor F P D World (JPN) 3113
Semiconductor Fabtech (GBR ISSN 1355-8633) 3113
Semiconductor Industry Association. (Year) Annual Report & Directory (USA) 3113
Semiconductor Industry News see Handotai Sangyo Shinbun 3100
• Semiconductor Innovation Letter (USA) 7052
• Semiconductor International (USA ISSN 0163-3767) 3113
• Semiconductor International SemiSource (USA ISSN 1931-9657) 3113
Semiconductor Magazine see Banna 5260
Semiconductor News (PAK ISSN 1561-1418) 3330
Semiconductor Optoelectronics see Bandaoti Guangdian 7051
• Semiconductor Photonics and Technology (CHN ISSN 1007-0206) 7084
Semiconductor Physics, Quantum Electronics & Optoelectronics see Fizika Napivprovidnikiv Kvantova ta Optoelektronika 7051
Semiconductor Reliability News (USA) 3113
Semiconductor Research see Handotai Kenkyu 3100
Semiconductor Research Institute. Report see Handotai Kenkyujo Hokoku 3100
• ➤ Semiconductor Science and Technology (GBR ISSN 0268-1242) 3113
Semiconductor Technology see Bandaoti Jishu 3296
• Semiconductor Today (GBR ISSN 1752-6639) 3330
• ➤ Semiconductors (RUS ISSN 1063-7826) 7039
➤ Semiconductors and Semimetals (GBR ISSN 0080-8784) 3330
• ➤ Semigroup Forum (USA ISSN 0037-1912) 5533
Semikhondaktoe Ilekthronik see Semiconductor Electronics Journal 3113
Semikolon (DNK ISSN 1398-7763) 7680
• Semikolon (Aarhus C) (DNK ISSN 1600-8529) 5369
Semina see Farmasia 6841
Semina (Londrina) (BRA ISSN 0101-3742) 2300
Seminaire de Probabilites (DEU ISSN 0720-8766) 5533
• ➤ Seminaire Lotharingien de Combinatoire (FRA ISSN 1286-4889) 5533
▼ Seminaire Magazine (FRA ISSN 1957-4207) 1843
• ➤ Seminaires et Congres (FRA ISSN 1285-2783) 5534
• ➤ Seminar (CAN ISSN 0037-1939) 5369
• Seminar (New Delhi) (IND ISSN 0971-6742) 7182
Seminar Arghiriade (ROM ISSN 0255-8718) 5534
Seminar for Arabian Studies. Proceedings (GBR ISSN 0308-8421) 416
Seminar Hausarztpraxis (DEU ISSN 1430-4023) 5712
Seminar Klostermann see KlostermannRoteReihe 7981
• ➤ Seminar.net (NOR ISSN 1504-4831) 2911
Seminar of Differential Equations see Seminarul of Ecuatii Functionale 5534
Seminar of Ilia Vekua Institute of Applied Mathematics see Ilia Vekuas Saxelobis Gamoqenebit'i Mat'ematikis Institutis Seminaris Moxsenebebi 5492
Seminar on Dravidian Linguistics. Proceedings (IND) 5173
Seminar on Electrochemistry in Boundary Region. Proceedings see Kyokai Ryoiki ni Okeru Denki Kagaku Semina 2114
Seminar on Fixed Point Theory Computation and Applications (ROM ISSN 1583-5022) 5534
Seminar on Mathematical Sciences (JPN) 5534
Seminar on Miscellaneous Problems and Breakthroughs of Soil Mechanics and Foundation Engineering. Proceedings see Doshitsu Kiso ni Kansuru Shomondai to Kaiketsusaku Koshukai Koen Shiryo 3265
Seminar on Oxidation see Yukagaku Sanka Semina 3257
Seminar on Petroliferous Basins of India. Proceedings (IND) 6792
Seminar on the Acquisition of Latin American Library Materials Bibliography and Reference Series see S A L A L M Bibliography and Reference Series 5059
Seminar on the Acquisition of Latin American Library Materials. Microfilming Projects Newsletter (USA ISSN 0080-8857) 5047
Seminar on the Acquisition of Latin American Library Materials Newsletter see S A L A L M Newsletter 634
Seminar on the Acquisition of Latin American Library Materials. Papers (USA) 5047
Seminar Reporteur (IND ISSN 0970-6755) 7913
† Seminari in Dermatologia (ITA ISSN 1121-1881) 8988
Seminari Romani di Cultura Greca (ITA ISSN 1129-5953) 2240
Seminaria Pa'lante (CUB) 5238
Seminario de Analisis Numerico (ESP ISSN 1130-1376) 5534
Seminario de Arqueologia y Etnologia Turolense. Revista (ESP ISSN 1136-8187) 416
➤ Seminario de Arte Aragones (ESP ISSN 0487-3491) 517
Seminario de Estudios de Arte y Arqueologia. Boletin (ESP ISSN 0210-9573) 517
• Seminario de Filologia Vasca Julio de Urquijo. Anuario/Julio de Urquijo Euskal Filologiarako Mintegiaren Urtekaria/The Julio de Urquijo Seminar on Basque Philology. Journal (ESP ISSN 0582-6152) 5173
Seminario Folclore e Cultura Popular. Serie Encontros e Estudos (BRA) 3622
Seminario Iberoamericano de Matematicas. Publicaciones (ESP ISSN 1136-3894) 5534
Seminario Matematico di Messina. Rendiconti (ITA ISSN 0390-6167) 5534
▼ Seminario Politicas Urbanas, Gestion Territorial y Ambiental para el Desarrollo Local (ARG ISSN 1851-3506) 4426
Seminarios Complutenses de Derecho Romano (ESP ISSN 1135-7673) 4842
Seminarios de Estratigrafia. Serie Monografias (ESP ISSN 0211-2256) 2766
Seminarium (VAT ISSN 0582-6314) 7817
• Seminars in Anesthesia, Perioperative Medicine and Pain (USA ISSN 1547-9951) 5774
• ➤ Seminars in Arthritis and Rheumatism (USA ISSN 0049-0172) 6227
• Seminars in Arthroplasty (USA ISSN 1045-4527) 6072
Seminars in Avian and Exotic Pet Medicine see Journal of Exotic Pet Medicine 8800
• Seminars in Breast Disease (USA ISSN 1092-4450) 6004
• ➤ Seminars in Cancer Biology (GBR ISSN 1044-579X) 928
• Seminars in Cardiothoracic and Vascular Anesthesia (USA ISSN 1089-2532) 5799
• ➤ Seminars in Cell and Developmental Biology (GBR ISSN 1084-9521) 836
• Seminars in Colon and Rectal Surgery (USA ISSN 1043-1489) 6258
• ➤ Seminars in Cutaneous Medicine and Surgery (USA ISSN 1085-5629) 5881
• ➤ Seminars in Diagnostic Pathology (USA ISSN 0740-2570) 5712
• ➤ Seminars in Dialysis (USA ISSN 0894-0959) 6274
• ➤ Seminars in Fetal & Neonatal Medicine (GBR ISSN 1744-165X) 6004
• ➤ Seminars in Hearing (USA ISSN 0734-0451) 6085
• ➤ Seminars in Hematology (USA ISSN 0037-1963) 5941
• ➤ Seminars in Immunology (GBR ISSN 1044-5323) 5766
• ➤ Seminars in Immunopathology (DEU ISSN 1863-2297) 5766
• Seminars in Inflammatory Bowel Disease (CAN ISSN 1496-8290) 5931
• Seminars in Integrative Medicine (USA ISSN 1543-1150) 5712
• ➤ Seminars in Interventional Radiology (USA ISSN 0739-9529) 6208

Title

Seminars in Laparoscopic Surgery *see* Surgical Innovation **6260**
• ➤ Seminars in Liver Disease (USA ISSN 0272-8087) **5931**
• Seminars in Medical Practice (USA) **5712**
• Seminars in Musculoskeletal Radiology (USA ISSN 1089-7860) **6208**
• ➤ Seminars in Nephrology (USA ISSN 0270-9295) **6274**
• ➤ Seminars in Neurology (USA ISSN 0271-8235) **6184**
• ➤ Seminars in Nuclear Medicine (USA ISSN 0001-2998) **6208**
Seminars in Nutrition (USA ISSN 0898-5995) **6669**
• ➤ Seminars in Oncology (USA ISSN 0093-7754) **6034**
• Seminars in Oncology Nursing (USA ISSN 0749-2081) **5981**
• Seminars in Ophthalmology (GBR ISSN 0882-0538) **6051**
• Seminars in Orthodontics (USA ISSN 1073-8746) **5865**
• ➤ Seminars in Pain Medicine (USA ISSN 1537-5897) **6185**
• Seminars in Pediatric Infectious Diseases (USA ISSN 1045-1870) **6104**
• Seminars in Pediatric Neurology (USA ISSN 1071-9091) **6185**
• Seminars in Pediatric Surgery (USA ISSN 1055-8586) **6258**
• ➤ Seminars in Perinatology (USA ISSN 0146-0005) **6104**
• ➤ Seminars in Plastic Surgery (USA ISSN 1535-2188) **6258**
➤ Seminars in Preventive and Alternative Medicine (USA ISSN 1556-4061) **5712**
• ➤ Seminars in Radiation Oncology (USA ISSN 1053-4296) **6034**
Seminars in Radiologic Technology *see* Continuing Education in Radiologic Technology **6194**
• ➤ Seminars in Reproductive Medicine (USA ISSN 1526-8004) **5900**
• ➤ Seminars in Respiratory and Critical Care Medicine (USA ISSN 1069-3424) **6219**
• ➤ Seminars in Roentgenology (USA ISSN 0037-198X) **6208**
• ➤ Seminars in Speech and Language (USA ISSN 0734-0478) **6085**
• Seminars in Spine Surgery (USA ISSN 1040-7383) **6073**
Seminars in Surgical Oncology *see* Journal of Surgical Oncology **6250**
• Seminars in Thoracic and Cardiovascular Surgery (USA ISSN 1043-0679) **6258**
• ➤ Seminars in Thrombosis and Hemostasis (USA ISSN 0094-6176) **5941**
• ➤ Seminars in Ultrasound, C T and M R I (Computerized Tomography and Magnetic Resonance) (USA ISSN 0887-2171) **6208**
Seminars in Urologic Oncology *see* Urologic Oncology **6036**
Seminars in Vascular Medicine *see* Seminars in Thrombosis and Hemostasis **5941**
• Seminars in Vascular Surgery (USA ISSN 0895-7967) **6258**
Seminars, Workshops & Classes (USA ISSN 0740-2791) **2945**
Seminarul de Operatori Liniari si Analiza Armonica *see* Universitatea din Timisoara. Facultatea de Matematica. Seminarul de Operatori Liniari si Analiza Armonica **5544**
Seminarul of Ecuatii Functionale/Seminar of Differential Equations (ROM ISSN 0255-8874) **5534**
• Seminary Ridge Review (USA ISSN 1526-0674) **7774**
• Seminole Tribune (USA ISSN 0891-8252) **3563**
† Semiosfera (ESP ISSN 1134-3974) **8988**
Semiosis (MEX ISSN 0187-9316) **5173**
Semiotic and Cognitive Studies (BEL) **6951**
➤ Semiotic Review of Books (CAN ISSN 0847-1622) **4474**
• ➤ Semiotica (DEU ISSN 0037-1998) **5173**
Semiotics and the Human Sciences (USA ISSN 1054-8386) **5173**
Semiotique Appliquee *see* Applied Semiotics **5095**
➤ Semiotique et Bible (FRA ISSN 0154-6902) **7680**
Semiquasi Review (USA) **5434**
SemiSource *see* Semiconductor International SemiSource **3113**
➤ Semitic Study Series (NLD ISSN 0169-9911) **5173**
Semitica (FRA ISSN 0373-630X) **4474**
▼ • Semitica et Classica (BEL ISSN 2031-5937) **2240**
Semitica et Semitohamitica Berolinensia (DEU ISSN 1616-525X) **5173**
Semitica Viva (DEU ISSN 0931-2811) **5173**
Semitica Viva - Series Didactica (DEU ISSN 0935-7556) **5173**
Semittimes (DEU ISSN 0941-8180) **3563**
Semper (AUS) **2300**
Semper (BEL) **5712**
Semper Fi (USA ISSN 1933-2327) **6445**
Sempervivum Society. Newsletter (GBR ISSN 0950-9771) **3750**
Sempex (FRA) **6880**
† Semplice (ITA) **8988**
Sempre Pronto (PRT ISSN 0037-203X) **2911**
Sem'ya (RUS) **8131**
Sem'ya i Shkola (RUS ISSN 0131-7377) **2911**
Sem'ya. Zemlya. Urozhai (RUS) **155**
• ➤ Sen/Sleep (POL ISSN 1641-6007) **7407**
Sen-i Kougyo Yoran/Japan Textile Industry. Directory (JPN) **8464**
• Sen Shakthi (LKA) **7182**
Senat du Canada. Deliberations du Comite Senatorial Permanent des Droits de la Personne *see* Senate of Canada. Standing Senate Committee on Human Rights. Proceedings **7215**
Senate Debate Indexes *see* Debates of the Senate of Canada. Hansard **7433**
Senate Election Law Guidebook (USA ISSN 0740-9834) **4782**
Senate of Canada. Standing Committee on Energy, the Environment and Natural Resources. Proceedings (CAN ISSN 1187-8800) **3465**
• Senate of Canada. Standing Committee on Legal and Constitutional Affairs. Proceedings (CAN ISSN 0576-3835) **4852**
Senate of Canada. Standing Senate Committee on Aboriginal Peoples. Proceedings (CAN ISSN 0846-9261) **7215**
• Senate of Canada. Standing Senate Committee on Human Rights. Proceedings/Senat du Canada. Deliberations du Comite Senatorial Permanent des Droits de la Personne (CAN ISSN 1700-1315) **7215**
• Senate of Canada. Standing Senate Committee on Social Affairs, Science and Technology. Proceedings (CAN ISSN 0826-7839) **7468**
Senate of Canada. Subcommittee on Communications. Proceedings (CAN ISSN 1209-5648) **2338**
Senate of Canada. Subcommittee on Transportation Safety. Proceedings (CAN ISSN 1209-563X) **8510**
Senate of Canada. Subcommittee on Veterans Affairs. Proceedings/Deliberations du Sous-Comite des Affaires des Anciens Combattants (CAN ISSN 0848-5038) **8067**
The Senator (USA) **2300**
Senator Raetsel *see* Freizeit Revue Senator Raetsel **8174**
Senckenberg Buecher (DEU ISSN 0341-4108) **7913**
Senckenberg Gesellschaft fuer Naturforschung. Abhandlungen (DEU ISSN 1868-0356) **704**
† ➤ Senckenbergiana Biologica (DEU ISSN 0037-2102) **8988**
Senckenbergiana Lethaea *see* Palaeobiodiversity and Palaeoenvironments **6727**
Senckenbergiana Maritima *see* Marine Biodiversity **2811**
Senckenbergischen Naturforschenden Gesellschaft. Abhandlungen *see* Senckenberg Gesellschaft fuer Naturforschung. Abhandlungen **704**
Senda Senior (ESP ISSN 1576-4982) **5082**
Sendai Astronomiaj Reportoj (JPN ISSN 0386-0817) **581**
Sendai Denpa Kogyo Koto Senmon Gakko Kenkyu Kiyo/Sendai National College of Technology. Research Report (JPN ISSN 0386-4243) **7999**
Sendai District Meteorological Observatory. Proceedings of the Meeting *see* Sendai Kanku Chosa Kenkyukai Shiryo **6395**
Sendai District Meteorological Observatory. Technical Data *see* Sendai Kanku Gijutsu Shiryo **6395**
Sendai District Meteorological Observatory. Unusual Meteorological Report *see* Sendai Kanku Ijo Kisho Hokoku **6395**
Sendai Kanku Chosa Kenkyukai Shiryo/Sendai District Meteorological Observatory. Proceedings of the Meeting (JPN) **6395**
Sendai Kanku Gijutsu Shiryo/Sendai District Meteorological Observatory. Technical Data (JPN) **6395**
Sendai Kanku Ijo Kisho Hokoku/Sendai District Meteorological Observatory. Unusual Meteorological Report (JPN) **6395**
Sendai Municipal Institute of Public Health. Report *see* Sendai-shi Eisei Kenkyujoho **7541**
Sendai National College of Technology. Research Report *see* Sendai Denpa Kogyo Koto Senmon Gakko Kenkyu Kiyo **7999**
Sendai Nuclear Power News *see* Genshiryoku Koho Sendai **3167**
Sendai-shi Eisei Kenkyujoho/Sendai Municipal Institute of Public Health. Report (JPN ISSN 0916-7226) **7541**
Sendbote des Hl. Antonius *see* Messaggero di Sant' Antonio **7806**
Sendebar (ESP ISSN 1130-5509) **5173**
Senden Kaigi (JPN) **35**
Sendero (PRY) **7817**
Sendero (USA ISSN 1538-3695) **5369**
• Sendrom (TUR ISSN 1016-5134) **5712**
† Sendtnera (DEU ISSN 0944-0178) **8988**
Seneca, het Journaal (NLD ISSN 1874-9763) **7541**
• Seneca Review (USA ISSN 0037-2145) **5434**
Seneca Searchers (USA ISSN 1046-5545) **3782**
Senegal. Archives du Senegal. Rapport Annuel (SEN ISSN 0850-010X) **5047**
Senegal. Centre de Recherche Oceanographique. Document Scientifique (SEN ISSN 0850-1602) **2818**
Senegal en Chiffres (SEN) **4178**
Senegal. Liste du Corps Diplomatique (SEN) **7265**
Senegal. Ministere de l'Economie, des Finances et du Plan. Banque de Donnees Economiques et Financieres (SEN) **1262**
Senegal. Ministere de l'Economie, des Finances et du Plan. Bulletin Economique et Statistique (SEN) **1262**
Senegal. Ministere de l'Economie, des Finances et du Plan. Comptes Economiques (SEN ISSN 0850-1009) **1517**
Senegal. Ministere de l'Economie, des Finances et du Plan. Dossiers Documentaires (SEN) **1262**
Senegal. Ministere de l'Economie, des Finances et du Plan. Enquete Demographique et Sante II (Year) (SEN) **8083**
Senegal. Ministere de l'Economie, des Finances et du Plan. Enquete Emploi, Sous Emploi et Chomage (SEN) **8084**
Senegal. Ministere de l'Economie, des Finances et du Plan. Enquete sur la Planification Familiale en Milieu Urbain (SEN) **973**
Senegal. Ministere de l'Economie, des Finances et du Plan. Enquete sur les Priorites: Dimensions Sociales de l'Ajustement (Year) (SEN) **8084**
Senegal. Ministere de l'Economie, des Finances et du Plan. Indice de la Production Industrielle (SEN ISSN 0850-1203) **1262**
Senegal. Ministere de l'Economie, des Finances et du Plan. Indice des Prix a la Consommation (SEN) **1262**
Senegal. Ministere de l'Economie, des Finances et du Plan. Note d'Analyse du Commerce Exterieur (SEN) **1262**
Senegal. Ministere de l'Economie, des Finances et du Plan. Note de Conjoncture (SEN) **1262**
Senegal. Ministere de l'Economie, des Finances et du Plan. Population du Senegal (SEN) **8084**
Senegal. Ministere de l'Economie, des Finances et du Plan. Population du Senegal: Structure par Age et Sexe et Projection (SEN) **7314**
Senegal. Ministere de l'Economie, des Finances et du Plan. Rapport d'Analyse par Region (SEN) **7314**
Senegal. Ministere de l'Economie, des Finances et du Plan. Rapport National (SEN) **7314**
Senegal. Ministere de l'Economie, des Finances et du Plan. Rapport sur les Perspectives Economiques (SEN) **1262**
Senegal. Ministere de l'Economie, des Finances et du Plan. Recensement General de la Population et de l'Habitat (SEN) **7315**
Senegal. Ministere de l'Economie, des Finances et du Plan. Repertoire des Villages par Region (SEN) **7315**
Senegal. Ministere de l'Economie, des Finances et du Plan. Resultats Provisoires (SEN) **7315**
Senegal. Ministere de l'Economie, des Finances et du Plan. Situation Economique Regionale (SEN) **1262**
Senegal. Ministere de l'Economie, des Finances et du Plan. Tableau de Bord de la Situation Sociale (SEN) **8084**
Senegal. Ministere de l'Economie, des Finances et du Plan. Tableau de Bord de l'Economie Senegalaise (SEN) **1262**
➤ Sengyakhak-Hoeji/Korean Journal of Pharmacognosy (KOR ISSN 0253-3073) **6880**
• ➤ Sen'i Gakkaishi/Society of Fiber Science and Technology, Japan. Journal (JPN ISSN 0037-9875) **8457**
• Sen'i Kikai Gakkaishi/Textile Machinery Society of Japan. Journal (JPN ISSN 0371-0580) **8457**
Sen'i Seihin Shohi Kagaku/Japan Research Association for Textile End-Uses. Journal (JPN ISSN 0037-2072) **8457**
• Senior (NOR ISSN 1504-324X) **8131**
Senior Advocate *see* Fifty Plus Advocate **3766**
Senior Advocate (USA) **4055**
The Senior Beacon (USA) **4055**
Senior Bulletin (ZAF) **4055**
• The Senior Care Acquisition Report (USA ISSN 1089-1412) **1172**
Senior Care Investor *see* The SeniorCare Investor **1172**
• Senior Care Management (USA ISSN 1098-822X) **7541**
Senior Circuit (USA) **4055**
Senior Citizens Secretariat *see* Seniors' News **8068**
Senior Counseling Letter (USA) **4522**
The Senior Courier (USA) **5082**
▼ Senior Directions Magazine (USA ISSN 1938-5048) **4055**
• The Senior Executive Report (USA ISSN 1536-1020) **1382**
• Senior High Core Collection (USA) **5047**
Senior High School Library Catalog *see* Senior High Core Collection **5047**
Senior Lawyer *see* The Voice of Experience **4809**
Senior Life (GBR ISSN 1367-8213) **8067**
Senior Life (USA) **3988**
Senior Life Health Monitor (USA ISSN 1542-8192) **4055**
Senior Lifestyles (CAN ISSN 1911-6411) **4055**
Senior Living (CAN ISSN 1911-6373) **4055**
Senior Living (Vancouver and Lower Mainland) (CAN ISSN 1911-639X) **4055**
▼ • Senior Living Business (USA ISSN 1938-6613) **1793**
Senior Living Magazine (Glendale) (USA) **4055**
Senior Magazine (USA) **4055**
Senior Market Advisor (USA ISSN 1530-874X) **1843**
Senior Media Directory (USA ISSN 1047-4692) **2338**
Senior Membership Horizons (USA) **4055**
The Senior Messenger (USA) **4055**
Senior Musician (USA ISSN 1046-4158) **6616**
• Senior Net (ESP ISSN 1887-0732) **2566**
The Senior News (USA) **4055**
Senior News (USA) **4055**
Senior News Long Island *see* 50 Plus Senior News **4058**
Senior Observer (USA ISSN 1064-3605) **5082**
Senior Plus Newspaper (CAN) **4055**
Senior Positive! (USA) **4055**
Senior Reflections (USA) **4055**
Senior Scene (USA) **4055**
• Senior Secondary Assessment Board of South Australia Art Show (AUS ISSN 1832-4401) **517**
• Senior Secondary Assessment Board of South Australia Technology Show (AUS ISSN 1832-4827) **8438**
Senior Services Guide *see* What's Up? Annapolis **5086**
• Senior.sk (SVK ISSN 1336-9059) **4055**
Senior Softball News (USA ISSN 1934-922X) **8245**
Senior Softball - USA News *see* Senior Softball News **8245**
Senior Solutions Advisor *see* Boomer Advisor **4042**
Senior Style (NZL ISSN 1177-4711) **8131**
Senior Sun (USA) **3147**
Senior Times (Columbus) (USA) **4055**
Senior Times (Montreal) (CAN ISSN 0846-6238) **4055**
Senior Times (Spokane) (USA) **4055**
Senior Tribune (USA ISSN 0149-7413) **4055**
Senior Views (USA) **4055**
Senior Voice (USA ISSN 0741-2894) **4055**
• Senior World Online (USA) **4055**
• The SeniorCare Investor (USA) **1172**
Senioren Aktiv (DEU) **4055**
Senioren-Blickpunkt (DEU) **4055**
Senioren Contact (NLD ISSN 1871-9090) **6703**
Senioren Echo (DEU) **4055**
Senioren Leichtathletik (DEU) **8332**
Senioren Magazin Hamburg (DEU) **4056**
Senioren Magazine *see* Came Magazine **8939**
Senioren Ratgeber (DEU ISSN 0934-9936) **4056**
Senioren Tanzen (DEU) **2687**
Senioren Zeitschrift (DEU ISSN 0722-5725) **7468**
SENIORity (USA) **4056**
Seniormagasinet *see* Senior **8131**
Seniornet Newsline (USA) **2566**
• Seniorpolitikk.no (NOR ISSN 1503-9404) **8068**
SeniorProof (NLD ISSN 1574-6232) **7541**
Seniors Advisory Council for Alberta. Update *see* Seniors Advisory Council for Alberta. Update Newsletter **8068**
Seniors Advisory Council for Alberta. Update Newsletter (CAN ISSN 1912-6999) **8068**
Seniors' Advocate (CAN ISSN 0831-4365) **4056**
Seniors Association of Greater Edmonton Link *see* S A G E Link **8066**
The Seniors Coaliton Advocate *see* Advocate (Virginia) **4038**
• Seniors' Guide to Federal Programs and Services (CAN ISSN 1191-6737) **7468**
Seniors Housing & Care Journal (USA ISSN 1941-7187) **4056**
Seniors' Housing Update (CAN ISSN 1188-1828) **4426**
Seniors in Canada *see* Les Aines au Canada **8024**
Seniors' News (CAN ISSN 1719-4075) **8068**
Seniors' Organizations in Alberta. Directory (CAN ISSN 1912-3299) **8068**
The Seniors Review (CAN) **4056**
Seniors' Statistical Profile (CAN ISSN 1719-4121) **8398**
Seniors Voice (USA) **4056**
Seniors Voice of Ocala *see* Seniors Voice **4056**
▼ • Seniors Vox (FRA ISSN 1956-2845) **4056**
Senjo ni Kansuru Shinpojumu/Symposium of Cleaning (JPN ISSN 0919-4231) **3255**
Senjski Zbornik (HRV ISSN 0582-673X) **4263**
• Senkyo Gakkai Kiyou/Review of Electoral Studies (JPN ISSN 1348-8783) **7182**
• Senkyo Kenkyu/Japanese Journal of Electoral Studies (JPN ISSN 0912-3512) **7182**
Senlin Caiyun Kexue *see* Senlin Gongcheng **3715**
• Senlin Fanghuo/Forest Fire Prevention (CHN ISSN 1002-2511) **3581**
• Senlin Gongan (CHN ISSN 1009-8038) **3702**
• Senlin Gongcheng/Forest Engineering (CHN) **3715**
• Senlin yu Renlei/Forest and Human Kind (CHN ISSN 1002-9990) **3702**
Senmon Toshokan/Japan Special Libraries Association. Bulletin (JPN ISSN 0385-0188) **5047**
Senmonryouri/Specialty Foods (JPN) **3663**
Sennacieca Revuo (FRA ISSN 1248-2293) **7265**
Sennaciulo (FRA ISSN 1163-0442) **5173**
Sennke/Tohuku Plant Association. News (JPN ISSN 0385-3985) **816**
• Senologie (DEU ISSN 1611-6453) **8848**
Senpaku Gijutsu Kenkyujo Happyo Ronbun Hyodaishu/Ship Research Institute. List of Papers (JPN) **8660**
Senpaku Gijutsu Kenkyujo Kenkyu Happyokai Koenshu/Ship Research Institute. Reports of Meeting (JPN ISSN 0285-7332) **8660**
Senpaku Gijutsu Kenkyujo Kikan Doryokubu Kiyo/Ship Research Institute. Power and Energy Engineering Division. Memoirs (JPN) **8660**
Senpaku Gijutsu Kenkyujo Nenpo/Ship Research Institute. Annual Report (JPN) **8660**
Senpaku Kaihatsu Giho/Ship Research Report (JPN ISSN 0916-8672) **8660**
Senri Ethnological Studies (JPN ISSN 0387-6004) **355**
▼ S'Enrichir Magazine (FRA ISSN 1959-0504) **1382**

Sensa (HRV) 591
▼ Sensa (SRB) 591
• SensAbility (USA ISSN 1549-0106) 3219
• Sensations Magazine (USA ISSN 1053-9115) 5434
Senses (DEU ISSN 1612-2038) 591
† Senses (DEU ISSN 1616-6582) 8988
Senses (USA ISSN 1935-6811) 8883
• ➤ The Senses and Society (GBR ISSN 1745-8927) 7999
• ➤ Senses of Cinema (AUS ISSN 1443-4059) 6512
Senshoku Kogyo/Dyeing Industry (JPN ISSN 0370-9574) 8457
Senshu Keizaigaku Ronshu/Economic Bulletin of the Senshu University (JPN ISSN 0386-4383) 1172
Senshu Shizen Kagaku Kiyo/Senshu University. Association of Natural Science. Bulletin (JPN ISSN 0386-5827) 7913
Senshu Syogaku Ronshu/Commercial Review of Senshu University (JPN ISSN 0386-5819) 1172
Senshu University. Association of Natural Science. Bulletin see Senshu Shizen Kagaku Kiyo 7913
➤ Sensibilities (AUS ISSN 1323-8418) 5369
† • The Sensible Sound (USA ISSN 0199-4654) 8988
• ➤ Sensing and Imaging (USA ISSN 1557-2064) 4489
▼ • ➤ Sensing and Instrumentation for Food Quality and Safety (USA ISSN 1932-7587) 3663
Sensitivity Matters (AUS ISSN 1445-2774) 5766
Sensor Array and Multichannel Signal Processing. I E E E Workshop (USA ISSN 1551-2282) 2466
Sensor Business Digest see Sensor Technology 2528
• ➤ Sensor Letters (USA ISSN 1546-198X) 3330
Sensor Magazin (DEU ISSN 0945-6899) 3113
Sensor Report (CHE ISSN 0179-9592) 4490
• ➤ Sensor Review (GBR ISSN 0260-2288) 5459
• Sensor Technology (USA ISSN 8756-4017) 2528
Sensor World see Chuan'ganqi Shijie 3090
➤ Sensornye Sistemy (RUS ISSN 0235-0092) 6185
• ➤ Sensors (CHE ISSN 1424-8220) 2105
• Sensors (Online) (USA) 4490
† • Sensors (Print) (USA ISSN 0746-9462) 8988
Sensors (Year). Proceedings see I E E E Sensors. Proceedings 2421
Sensors and Actuators (USA ISSN 1054-6693) 3395
• ➤ Sensors and Actuators A: Physical (CHE ISSN 0924-4247) 7052
• ➤ Sensors and Actuators B: Chemical (CHE ISSN 0925-4005) 2114
➤ Sensors and Materials (JPN ISSN 0914-4935) 7039
• ➤ Sensors & Transducers (CAN ISSN 1726-5479) 3357
Sensor's Buyers Guide (USA ISSN 1042-2757) 4490
Sensors Series (GBR ISSN 0964-0339) 7084
Sensors Update see Advanced Micro- and Nanosystems 2445
† ➤ Sensory Formations (GBR ISSN 1741-4725) 8988
Sensory Integration Special Interest Section Quarterly (USA ISSN 1093-7250) 6116
• ➤ Sensuous Knowledge (NOR ISSN 1890-2154) 517
Sensus van Welsynsorganisasies see South Africa. Statistics South Africa. Census of Social, Recreational and Personal Services - Welfare Organisations 8084
Sensus Water Journal (USA ISSN 0892-9548) 8831
➤ Sentairui Kenkyu/Bryological Research (JPN ISSN 1343-0254) 816
Sentan Gijutsu Koenkai/Lecture on Advanced Laser Technology (JPN ISSN 0915-1079) 7084
Sentan Kako Gijutsu/Advanced Machining Technology (JPN ISSN 0914-8698) 3395
Sentan Seimei Ikagaku Kenkyuujo Houkoku/Tokyo Women's Medical College. Institute of Advanced Biomedical Engineering & Science. Reports (JPN ISSN 1347-7110) 751
Sentei Tosho Somokuroku see Catalogue of Books Recommended for Libraries 622
Sentence (USA ISSN 1545-5378) 5434
Sentences Arbitrales de la Fonction Publique (CAN ISSN 0823-3322) 4782
Sentencias de Tribunales Superiores de Justicia y Audiencias Provinciales y Otros Tribunales (Bi-weekly Edition) (ESP ISSN 1136-3967) 4782
Sentencias de Tribunales Superiores de Justicia y Audiencias Provinciales y Otros Tribunales (Quarterly Edition) see Sentencias de Tribunales Superiores de Justicia y Audiencias Provinciales y Otros Tribunales (Bi-weekly Edition) 4782
Sentencias en Apelacion de las Audiencias Provinciales (ESP ISSN 0210-3427) 4782
Sentencing Practice see Morrison: Sentencing Practice 4736
• Sentencing Snapshots (AUS ISSN 1832-6153) 4960
Sentencing Trends and Issues see Sentencing Trends & Issues 4825
• Sentencing Trends & Issues (AUS ISSN 1449-6607) 4825
Senter for Internasjonalisering av Hoejere Utdanning Publikasjoner see S I U. Publikasjoner 3000
Senter for Miljoe- og Ressursstudier Rapport see S M R Rapport 2626
Senter for Studier av Holocaust og Livssynsminoriteter Senteret. Temahefte see H L-Senteret. Temahefte 4225
Sentier Chasse - Peche (CAN ISSN 0711-7957) 8332
• Sentieri Selvaggi Online (ITA) 6512
The Sentimentalist (USA ISSN 1542-2259) 5082
The Sentinel (CAN ISSN 1711-3989) 2270
Sentinel (IND) 3889
The Sentinel (Castlegar) (CAN) 2300
The Sentinel (Halifax) (CAN) 2300
Sentinel Investment Letter (USA) 1651
Sentinel Security Assessments see Jane's Sentinel Security Assessments 2678
Sentinella Agricola (ITA ISSN 0037-234X) 155
• Sentura (DNK ISSN 1398-6562) 6512
Seo'bi'seu Eob Hwaldong Ji'su see Seobiseu-eob Saengsan Jisu (Online) 1262
• Seobiseu-eob Saengsan Jisu (Online)/Korea (Republic). National Statistical Office. Monthly Report on the Service Industry Activity Index (KOR ISSN 2005-1603) 1262
Seobiseu Eob Saengsan Jisu (Print) see Seobiseu-eob Saengsan Jisu (Online) 1262
Seo'eo Seo'mun Yeon'gu see Seu'pein Eo'munhag 5173
Seolbi Gonghag Nonmunjib see International Journal of Air-Conditioning and Refrigeration 4122
Seolgye Gyeong'gi/Architecture & Design Competition (KOR ISSN 1228-7970) 456
• Seoul Business Letter (KOR) 1172
† Seoul Daehag'gyo Nonghag Yeon'gu/Seoul National University Journal of Agricultural Sciences (KOR ISSN 1013-4077) 8988
Seoul Economic Daily see Seoul Gyeongje Sinmun 1172
• Seoul Gyeongje Sinmun/Seoul Economic Daily (KOR) 1172
• ➤ Seoul Journal of Business (KOR ISSN 1226-9816) 1172
• Seoul Journal of Economics (KOR ISSN 1225-0279) 1172
Seoul Journal of Korean Studies (KOR ISSN 1225-0201) 560
† Seoul National University. Faculty Papers. C & D, Science and Technology Series, Medicine and Pharmacy Series (KOR) 8988
† Seoul National University. Faculty Papers. E, Biology and Agriculture Series (KOR) 8988
Seoul National University Forests. Research Bulletin/Nyensubrim Nyengu Bogo: Seoul Daihaggyo Nongkwa Daihag (KOR ISSN 1010-8289) 3702
Seoul National University Journal of Agricultural Sciences see Seoul Daehag'gyo Nonghag Yeon'gu 8988
Separation see G I T Spezial Separation 2100
• ➤ Separation and Purification Reviews (USA ISSN 1542-2119) 2105
Separation and Purification Reviews (Online) see Separation and Purification Reviews 2105
• ➤ Separation and Purification Technology (GBR ISSN 1383-5866) 3255
Separation Processes Service Bulletin see S P S Bulletin 8986
• ➤ Separation Science and Technology (USA ISSN 0149-6395) 2105
Separation Science and Technology (San Diego) (USA ISSN 1877-1718) 2105
Sephardic Heritage see Erensia Sefardi 7721
Sephardic Scholar (USA ISSN 0278-2251) 7729
▼ SepinNet. Responsabilidad Civil y Seguro (ESP ISSN 1888-0444) 4522
SepinNET Revista. Propiedad Horizontal (ESP ISSN 1886-9033) 7612
• ➤ Seppyo/Japanese Society of Snow and Ice. Journal (JPN ISSN 0373-1006) 2716
Seppyo Hokushin'etsu/Japanese Society of Snow and Ice. Hokushin'etsu Branch. Journal (JPN ISSN 0918-1474) 6395
▼ • Seppyou Kenkyuu Taikai Kouen Youshishuu/Summaries of J S S I & J S S E Joint Conference on Snow and Ice Research (JPN ISSN 1883-0870) 3219
Sept Jours see 7 Club News 3820
September Days Club News (USA) 8755
Septentrion (BEL ISSN 0771-8934) 3801
Septentrion (HTI) 3875
Septimo Dia see Momento 3909
The Septs (USA ISSN 1049-1783) 3782
Septuagint and Cognate Studies see Septuagint and Cognate Studies Series 7680
Septuagint and Cognate Studies Series (NLD ISSN 1044-6761) 7680
Septuagint Commentary Series (NLD ISSN 1572-3755) 7680
• ➤ Sepu/Chinese Journal of Chromatography (CHN ISSN 1000-8713) 7084
Seqer Herg'le N'si'a. Heleq A see Israel. Central Bureau of Statistics. Survey of Travelling Habits 8779
Seqer Masa'iyot see Israel. Central Bureau of Statistics. Survey of Trucks 8527
Sequels (USA) 5059
Sequences (CAN ISSN 0037-2412) 6512
Sequences (FRA ISSN 0983-3919) 5434
• Sequential Analysis (USA ISSN 0747-4946) 8399
Sequoia Genealogical Society. Newsletter (USA) 3782
SER-bulletin see S E R Bulletin 1516
Ser Padres/Being Parents (USA ISSN 1558-5867) 8883
Ser Padres Bebe (ESP) 2168
Ser Padres Hoy (ESP) 2168
† Ser Similia Santini (ITA) 8988
▼ • Serafi (ESP ISSN 1888-3362) 5047
† Il Serafico (ITA) 8988
Seramiasht (AFG) 8068
Seramikkusu see Ceramics Japan 2039
Se'ra'miseuteu (KOR ISSN 1226-976X) 2045
Serangga (MYS ISSN 1394-5130) 858
Serb World U S A (USA ISSN 8756-5579) 3563
Serbia see Srbija 3566
Serbia and Montenegro see Country Profile. Montenegro 8945
Serbia and Montenegro see Country Profile. Serbia 8946
• Serbia & Montenegro Autos Report (GBR ISSN 1749-0138) 8603
• Serbia & Montenegro Defence & Security Report (GBR ISSN 1749-1614) 6445
• Serbia & Montenegro Food & Drink Report (GBR ISSN 1749-2939) 1172
▼ Serbia Freight Transport Report (GBR ISSN 1752-7929) 8510
Serbia Information Technology Report see Business Monitor International. Information Technology Country Reports 2491
▼ The Serbia Insurance Report (GBR ISSN 1754-2197) 4522
Serbian Academy of Sciences and Arts. Department of Technical Sciences. Scientific Meetings (SRB) 7913
Serbian Archives of Medicine see Srpski Arhiv za Celokupno Lekarstvo 5717
• Serbian Astronomical Journal (SRB ISSN 1450-698X) 581
• Serbian Chemical Society. Journal (SRB ISSN 0352-5139) 2080
Serbian Dental Journal see Stomatoloski Glasnik Srbije 5866
➤ Serbian Journal of Electrical Engineering (SRB ISSN 1451-4869) 3330
▼ • Serbian Journal of Sports Sciences (SRB ISSN 1820-6301) 8200
• ➤ Serbian Studies (USA ISSN 0742-3330) 4475
Serbian Supreme Court Law Practice. Bulletin see Vrhovni Sud Srbije. Bilten Sudske Prakse 4810
Serbische Rechtsquellen see Izvori Srpskog Prava 4698
Serbska Sula (DEU ISSN 0138-2497) 2911
• Serbske Nowiny (DEU ISSN 0138-2640) 3563
Serdalo (RUS) 3941
Serdica (BGR ISSN 1310-6600) 5534
Serdica Mathematicae Publicationes see Serdika Matematichesko Spisanie 5534
Serdika Matematichesko Spisanie/Serdica Mathematicae Publicationes (BGR ISSN 0204-4110) 5534
Y Seren (GBR) 5238
Serendipity (USA) 1966
Serengeti Wildlife Research Centre. Report (TZA) 704
▼ • Serenity Matters (USA ISSN 1947-0606) 6647
Sergeant see Serzhant 6446
† Sergei (CZE ISSN 1213-9548) 8988
Sergej (DEU ISSN 1437-3718) 4379
Sergej Baden-Wuerttemberg (DEU ISSN 1861-3764) 4379
Sergej Franken (DEU ISSN 1610-7721) 4379
• Sergej Magazin (DEU) 4379
Sergent-Major see Feldwebel 6421
Sergente Maggiore see Feldwebel 6421
† Seri Magazine (FRA ISSN 0999-7903) 8988
Seriados de T V (BRA) 2390
Serial Books see Black Dog Publishing. Serial Books. Design 435
Serial Books. Architecture and Urbanism see Architecture and Urbanism 430
Serial Fan see Club Rythm' and Blues 6557
Serial Report (USA) 6512
• Serials (Online) (GBR ISSN 1475-3308) 5047
• Serials (Print) (GBR ISSN 0953-0460) 5047
• The Serials Directory (USA) 635
• Serials-eNews (GBR ISSN 1476-0576) 5047
• Serials-eNews (N A S I G Edition) (GBR ISSN 1746-9775) 5047
Serials Holdings in Newfoundland Libraries (CAN ISSN 0709-0536) 635
Serials in the British Library (GBR ISSN 0260-0005) 5059
• ➤ The Serials Librarian (USA ISSN 0361-526X) 5047
Serials Monograph (GBR ISSN 0141-1810) 5047
• ➤ Serials Review (GBR ISSN 0098-7913) 5047
Serica (GBR ISSN 0266-0822) 8457
Sericologia (FRA ISSN 0250-3980) 858
• Sericulture & Silk Industry Statistics (Year) (IND) 8464
Sericulture Bulletin see Cansang Tongbao 100
† Seridim (ISR ISSN 0333-6174) 8988
Serie Antropologia see Instituto de Estudios Peruanos. Documentos de Trabajo. Serie Antropologia 343
Serie Arquetipo (ARG ISSN 1851-5916) 5369
Serie Capistrano de Abreu (BRA) 7265
Serie Conservacion de la Naturaleza (ARG ISSN 0325-9625) 2627
Serie Cuadernos de Reencuentro see Reencuentro 2999
Serie de Cocina por Luis Ripoli (ESP) 3663
Serie de Estudios en Ciencias de la Educacion (CHL ISSN 0718-2880) 2911
Serie de informes del M A B see M A B Report Series 3451
▼ • Serie de Informes Tecnicos (ESP ISSN 1988-8074) 5173
Serie de Teoria Juridica y Filosofia del Derecho (COL) 4782
Serie d'Ecriture (USA ISSN 0269-0179) 5369
Serie des Rapports du M A B see M A B Report Series 3451
Serie di Matematica e Fisica (ITA ISSN 0391-3252) 5534
Serie Documentos de Politica see Instituto de Estudios Peruanos. Documentos de Trabajo. Serie Documentos de Politica 7143
Serie Economia see Instituto de Estudios Peruanos. Documentos de Trabajo. Serie Economia 1125
Serie: Educacion y Mercosur (URY ISSN 0797-650X) 2911
Serie Ensaios e Monografias - IEPG see Escola Superior de Teologia. Instituto Ecumenico de Pos-Graduacao. Serie Ensaios e Monografias 7641
Serie Estudios B C R A see Banco Central de la Republica de Argentina. Serie Estudios 1311
Serie Estudios Literarios (CRI) 5369
Serie Estudos Penitenciarios (BRA) 2668
Serie Etnohistoria see Instituto de Estudios Peruanos. Documentos de Trabajo. Serie Etnohistoria 343
Serie EU Jurisprudentie (NLD ISSN 1574-8472) 1793
Serie EU Wetgeving, Rechtspraak en Documentatie (NLD ISSN 1573-2002) 4782
Serie F A O, Apprentissage Agricole see F A O Better Farming Series 109
Serie Fraude en Integriteit (NLD ISSN 1871-6105) 4782
Serie Guias de los Estudios Universitarios (ESP) 2962
Serie Historia see Instituto de Estudios Peruanos. Documentos de Trabajo. Serie Historia 4298
Serie Internationale d' Analyse Numerique see International Series of Numerical Mathematics 5498
Serie Investigaciones Sociales (BOL) 8131
Serie Kureren (DNK ISSN 0109-3797) 517
Serie Legislacion Laboral (CUB) 1707
Serie Linguistica see Instituto de Estudios Peruanos. Documentos de Trabajo. Serie Linguistica 5128
Serie Linguistica Peruana (PER ISSN 1022-1506) 5173
Serie Literatura (ESP ISSN 1699-440X) 8478
Serie los Departamentos see Uruguay. Direccion de Educacion. Serie los Departamentos 2924
Serie Mejores Cultivos see F A O Better Farming Series 109
Serie Mujer (PER) 8883
Serie Novaterra (ESP) 2716
Serie Nuestra America (MEX) 4475
Serie Onderneming en Recht (NLD ISSN 1574-1060) 4782
Serie Pedagogique de l'Institut Linguistique de Louvain see Institut de Linguistique de Louvain. Serie Pedagogique 5127
Serie Praktijkhandleidingen (NLD ISSN 1573-3920) 4782
Serie Protagonistas (ARG ISSN 1851-2321) 5369
Serie Recht en Praktijk see Recht en Praktijk 4766
Serie Saint-Exupery (FRA ISSN 1621-0581) 5369
Serie Seminarios FONASA (Fondo Nacional de Salud) (CHL ISSN 0718-4204) 5712
Serie Sociologia, Politica see Instituto de Estudios Peruanos. Documentos de Trabajo. Serie Sociologia, Politica 8107
Serie Talleres I E P see Instituto de Estudios Peruanos. Documentos de Trabajo. Serie Talleres 1889
Serie Teoria y Practica del Teatro see Teoria y Practica del Teatro 8481
Serie Vie Locale (FRA ISSN 0586-9889) 7182
† • Seriekatalog, Skoenlitteratur (DNK ISSN 1601-135X) 8988
Serieparaden (SWE) 2212
Series A: Human and Social Sciences see Mu'tah lil-Buhuth wal-Dirasat. Al-Silsilah A: Al-'Ulum al-Insaniyyah wal-Ijtima'iyyah 4465
Series Arcaeologica see Masarykova Univerzita. Filozoficka Fakulta. Sbornik Praci. M: Rada Archeologicka 405
Series B: Natural and Applied Sciences see Mu'tah lil-Buhuth wal-Dirasat. B: Al-Silsilah B: Al-'Ulum al-Tabi'iyyah wal-Tatbiqiyyah 7884
➤ Series de Quimica Oceanografia. Serie I. Monografias (ESP ISSN 1130-4766) 2818
➤ Series de Quimica Oceanografica. Serie II. Cuadernos (ESP ISSN 1130-4774) 2818
Series Desenvolvimento Brasileiro see Brazil Development Series 1880
➤ Series Entomologica (NLD ISSN 0924-4611) 858
Series Estadisticas Seleccionadas de Centroamerica y Panama (GTM) 1262
Series in Algebra (SGP) 5534
Series in American Constitutionalism see S U N Y Series in American Constitutionalism 7181
Series in Analysis (SGP ISSN 1793-1126) 5534
Series in Anxiety and Related Disorders (NLD ISSN 1574-9037) 6185
Series in Approximations and Decompositions (SGP) 5534
Series in Automation (SGP ISSN 0218-0197) 2464
Series in Biostatistics (SGP) 5534
Series in Broadband Communications (DEU ISSN 1431-9306) 2338
Series in Clinical and Community Psychology (USA ISSN 0146-0846) 7407

Title

▼ new title † ceased • electronic media ➤ refereed

DIRECTORY 2010 SHALLOW WATER ANGLER 10859

• Seton Hall Circuit Review (USA ISSN 1942-5171) **4782**
† Seton Hall Constitutional Law Journal (USA) **8988**
Seton Hall Journal of Diplomacy and International Relations *see* The Whitehead Journal of Diplomacy and International Relations **7273**
• Seton Hall Journal of Sports and Entertainment Law (USA ISSN 1931-4825) **4782**
• Seton Hall Law Review (USA ISSN 0586-5964) **4782**
• Seton Hall Legislative Journal (USA ISSN 0361-8951) **4782**
Setsudai Jinbun Kagaku *see* Setsunan University. Review of Humanities and Social Sciences **4475**
Setsunan Hogaku *see* Setsunan University. Law Review **4782**
Setsunan University. Journal of Business Administration and Information/Keiei Joho Kenkyu (JPN ISSN 1340-2617) **1173**
Setsunan University. Law Review/Setsunan Hogaku (JPN ISSN 0915-1265) **4782**
Setsunan University. Review of Humanities and Social Sciences/Setsudai Jinbun Kagaku (JPN ISSN 1341-9315) **4475**
Sette *see* 7 **9000**
Sette e Religioni (ITA ISSN 1590-4601) **7681**
Sette Giorni (ROM ISSN 1582-4292) **3934**
Setters, Incorporated (USA ISSN 0886-3997) **6815**
Settimana (ITA) **7817**
Settimana a Roma/Semaine a Rome/Week in Rome (ITA ISSN 0040-6295) **8755**
La Settimana Fiscale (ITA ISSN 1826-2643) **1942**
† Settimana Giuridica (ITA ISSN 0392-7253) **8988**
La Settimana Veterinaria (ITA ISSN 1825-3253) **8807**
Settimana Vip *see* Vip **6516**
Settimanale di Piu (ITA ISSN 1824-0348) **3898**
• Setting (ITA ISSN 1124-3899) **7407**
Setting Course (USA ISSN 1941-1510) **7182**
Setting Future Directions (NZL ISSN 1177-3456) **7913**
Setting Up Enterprises in Japan (JPN) **1651**
Settlement, Payment, E-money & E-trading Development *see* S P E E D **1381**
Settlement Publications *see* Setlementtijulkaisuja **7681**
Settlement Services Today (USA) **4522**
Settlements Information Network Africa Newsletter (KEN ISSN 1012-7771) **4426**
➤ The Settler (USA ISSN 0488-4965) **4312**
Settler (ZAF ISSN 1015-2393) **3949**
Settlin' In (USA) **7612**
Seu Sucesso (BRA ISSN 1678-4332) **5083**
Seu'pein Eo'munhag/Estudios Hispanicos (KOR ISSN 1738-2130) **5173**
• Seupoceu Gwahag (KOR ISSN 1225-7656) **8200**
Seura (FIN ISSN 0358-8017) **3839**
➤ Sevartham (IND ISSN 0970-8324) **3889**
Sevashram News (GBR ISSN 1463-4309) **5238**
• Seve (FRA ISSN 1765-8888) **5712**
▼ • Se7en (USA ISSN 1937-2558) **8200**
Seven Ball Magazine *see* 7 Ball Magazine **6631**
Seven by Seven Magazine *see* 7 x 7 Magazine **3993**
Seven County Farm and Home News (USA ISSN 0192-4184) **155**
• Seven Days (USA) **3988**
Seven - Eleven Japan. (Year) Annual Report (JPN) **1903**
Seven Fifty Bulletin *see* 750 Bulletin **8614**
Seven Hundred Six/Seven Hundred Nine Preparation and Planning Guide *see* 706/709 Preparation and Planning Guide **1956**
Seven Stars of I L E *see* Seven Stars of Institute of Laser Engineering **3174**
Seven Stars of Institute of Laser Engineering (JPN ISSN 0288-7703) **3174**
Seven Zero Four *see* 704 **5087**
• Seventeen (USA ISSN 0037-301X) **8883**
Seventeen (Colombia Edition) (COL) **8883**
Seventeen (Malaysia Edition) (MYS) **2212**
Seventeen (Mexico Edition) (COL) **8883**
Seventeen (Russia Edition) (RUS ISSN 1682-2404) **2212**
Seventeen (South Africa Edition) (ZAF ISSN 1729-0104) **2212**
Seventeen (Venezuela Edition) (COL) **8883**
Seventeen Philippines (PHL ISSN 0118-7023) **8883**
Seventeen Sixty Six *see* 1766 **2310**
• ➤ The Seventeenth Century (GBR ISSN 0268-117X) **5369**
• ➤ Seventeenth Century French Studies (GBR ISSN 0265-1068) **5369**
Seventeenth Century Music (USA ISSN 1054-6022) **6616**
• ➤ Seventeenth - Century News (USA ISSN 0037-3028) **5369**
Seventeenth Century Review (USA) **2270**
Seventeenth - Century Texts and Studies (USA ISSN 0893-6900) **5370**
Seventh Circuit Review (USA) **4960**
Seventh Sky and Seventh Sky People (CHE) **8200**
Seventy Eight Quarterly *see* 78 Quarterly **6631**
Seventy six pyro *see* '76 Pyro **3258**
Severe Learning Difficulties Experience *see* S L D Experience **3046**
• Severe Magazine (USA) **3988**
• Severn Trent Plc. Annual Report and Accounts (Year) (GBR) **8831**
Severn Trent Water. Drinking Water Quality (Year) (GBR) **8831**
Severnaya Pravda (RUS) **3941**
Severni Morava (CZE ISSN 0231-6323) **4263**
Severniak (BGR ISSN 1310-8085) **5370**
Severnside - South Wales Salary Survey (GBR) **1707**
Severnye Prostory (RUS ISSN 0233-7762) **3941**
Severnyi Kavkaz (RUS) **4263**
Severnyi Krai (RUS) **3941**
Severo-Kavkazskii Nauchnyi Tsentr Vysshei Shkoly. Obshchestvennye Nauki. Izvestiya/North-Caucasus Scientific Center of High School. Social Science. News (RUS ISSN 0321-3056) **4263**
Severo-Kavkazskii Nauchnyi Tsentr Vysshei Shkoly. Tekhnicheskie Nauki. Izvestiya/North-Caucasus Scientific Center of High School. Technical Science. News (RUS ISSN 0321-2653) **8438**
Severoceskou Prirodou (CZE ISSN 0231-9705) **816**
Severomorskie Vesti (RUS) **4986**
Sevres (FRA ISSN 1169-2537) **539**
• Sew Beautiful (USA ISSN 1063-9160) **6642**
Sew News (USA ISSN 0273-8120) **2260**
Sew News Holidays (USA) **2249**
Sew Simple (USA ISSN 1944-3943) **4367**
▼ Sew Stylish (USA ISSN 1935-8482) **6642**
Sew Today (GBR ISSN 1351-6477) **6642**
Sew Up the Holidays *see* Sew News Holidays **2249**
Sewanee (USA) **2300**
➤ Sewanee Mediaeval Studies (USA ISSN 0896-1638) **4263**
The Sewanee Purple (USA) **2300**
• The Sewanee Review (USA ISSN 0037-3052) **5370**
• Sewanee Theological Review (USA ISSN 1059-9576) **7774**
Sewells Pay Guide (Year) (GBR) **8603**
Sewer Sense (USA) **4126**
Sewing Quilting & Embroidery Professional *see* S Q E Professional **6642**
Sewing Savvy *see* Clotilde's Sewing Savvy **6637**
Sewing Today (USA) **2260**
Sewing With Butterick (GBR ISSN 0950-3625) **2260**
Sewing with Butterick - Vogue Patterns - Weddings (GBR ISSN 1467-3339) **2260**
Sewing World (GBR ISSN 1352-013X) **6642**
SEx (GBR) **6299**
• ➤ Sex Education (GBR ISSN 1468-1811) **2911**
Sex Education Matters (GBR ISSN 1353-1689) **2212**
• Sex, Etc. (USA) **6299**
Sex Herald *see* SexHerald **6299**
Sex Information and Education Council of Canada Newsletter *see* S I E C C A N Newsletter **3031**
Sex Kontakt Magazin (CZE ISSN 1211-4502) **6299**
▼ Sex, Love and Psychology (USA ISSN 1554-222X) **7407**
Sex Offender Law Report (USA ISSN 1529-0697) **4898**
• ➤ Sex Roles (USA ISSN 0360-0025) **7407**
Sex Talk (GBR ISSN 1749-8325) **973**
Sex Woche (DEU) **6299**
• SexHerald (USA ISSN 1933-7426) **6299**
• Sexing the Political (USA) **8902**
Sexodrama (POL ISSN 1230-9761) **5412**
Sexologi (NOR ISSN 1503-7088) **355**
• Sexologia y Sociedad (CUB ISSN 1025-6512) **8131**
• ➤ Sexologies (FRA ISSN 1158-1360) **6004**
• Sexpol (ESP ISSN 0214-042X) **8131**
• Sexpressions (CAN ISSN 1718-4231) **973**
† Sexrande (CZE ISSN 1213-7634) **8988**
➤ Sexta Feira (BRA ISSN 1415-689X) **355**
Sextant (CHE) **8282**
• ➤ Sexual Abuse (USA ISSN 1079-0632) **7407**
Sexual Abuse by Professionals (USA) **4782**
▼ ➤ Sexual Abuse in Australia and New Zealand (AUS ISSN 1833-8488) **7407**
• ➤ Sexual Addiction & Compulsivity (USA ISSN 1072-0162) **7407**
• ➤ Sexual and Relationship Therapy (GBR ISSN 1468-1994) **7407**
Sexual Assault Report (USA ISSN 1096-0155) **2668**
• Sexual Assault Trials (USA) **4898**
Sexual Confessions (USA) **6299**
Sexual Cultures (USA) **8132**
▼ • ➤ Sexual Development (CHE ISSN 1661-5425) **878**
Sexual Forum *see* Stag Sexual Forum **6300**
Sexual Harassment Litigation Reporter *see* Andrews Litigation Reporter: Sexual Harassment **4827**
Sexual Harrassment (USA) **4782**
• ➤ Sexual Health (AUS ISSN 1448-5028) **5826**
Sexual Health Agenda *see* Sex Talk **973**
Sexual Health Exchange *see* Exchange on HIV/AIDS, Sexuality and Gender **5813**
▼ • Sexual Health Research Review (NZL) **5712**
• Sexual Intelligence (USA) **6299**
Sexual Medizin (Ausgabe Oesterreich) *see* Psyche und Soma **5700**
Sexual Minority Youth Assistance League, Inc. News *see* S M Y A L News **4378**
• ➤ Sexual Offender Treatment (DEU ISSN 1862-2941) **7408**
• ➤ Sexual Plant Reproduction (DEU ISSN 0934-0882) **817**
• Sexual Science (Online) (USA) **8132**
Sexualidade e Planeamento Familiar (PRT ISSN 0872-7023) **8132**
▼ • Sexualidades (USA ISSN 1938-6419) **4379**
• ➤ Sexualis Lex (AUS ISSN 1447-4522) **4782**
• ➤ Sexualities (GBR ISSN 1363-4607) **7408**
• Sexuality & Culture (USA ISSN 1095-5143) **8132**
• ➤ Sexuality and Disability (USA ISSN 0146-1044) **5712**
Sexuality and Literature (USA ISSN 0893-6889) **5370**
• ➤ Sexuality, Reproduction & Menopause (USA ISSN 1546-2501) **6004**
• ➤ Sexuality Research and Social Policy (USA ISSN 1553-6610) **5712**
• ➤ Sexually Transmitted Diseases (USA ISSN 0148-5717) **5881**
• ➤ Sexually Transmitted Infections (GBR ISSN 1368-4973) **5881**
• Sexually Transmitted Infections in New Zealand (NZL ISSN 1176-0796) **5826**
Sexually Transmitted Infections Lab Surveillance *see* S T I Lab Surveillance **5826**
Sexualmedizin (Ausg. Schweiz) *see* Psyche und Soma **5700**
† Sexualmedizin fuer den Arzt (DEU) **8988**
Sexueel Overdraagbare Aandoeningen Acquired Immunodeficiency Disease Syndrome Magazine *see* S O A Aids Magazine **5765**
Sexueel Overdraagbare Aandoeningen Aids Magazine *see* S O A Aids Magazine **5765**
Sexuologie (DEU ISSN 0944-7105) **5712**
Sexwoche *see* Sex Woche **6299**
Sexy (DEU) **6299**
Sexy N Y C (USA) **6299**
• Seybold Publications. Bulletin (USA ISSN 1091-1898) **7580**
• The Seybold Report (USA ISSN 1533-9211) **7580**
Seychelles. Department of Finance. Economic Indicators (SYC) **1262**
Seychelles. Department of Finance. National Accounts (SYC) **1262**
Seychelles. Department of Finance. Statistical Bulletin. (SYC) **8399**
Seychelles. Department of Finance. Statistics Division. Statistical Abstract (SYC) **8399**
Seychelles Fishing Authority. Annual Report (SYC) **3608**
Seychelles Fishing Authority. Technical Report (SYC) **3608**
Seychelles. Management and Information Systems Division. Tourism and Migration Statistics (SYC) **8780**
Seychelles. Ministry of Finance. Budget Address (SYC) **7468**
• The Seychelles Nation (SYC) **3945**
Seychelles. President's Office. Statistics Division. Agriculture Survey (SYC) **186**
Seychelles. President's Office. Statistics Division. Census (SYC) **7315**
Seychelles. President's Office. Statistics Division. Employment & Earnings (SYC) **1262**
Seychelles. President's Office. Statistics Division. External Trade (SYC) **1262**
Seychelles. President's Office. Statistics Division. Household Expenditure Survey (SYC) **1262**
Seychelles. President's Office. Statistics Division. Population and Vital Statistics (SYC) **7315**
Seychelles. President's Office. Statistics Division. Production Indicators (SYC) **1262**
Seychelles. President's Office. Statistics Division. Retail Prices (SYC) **1262**
Seychelles. President's Office. Statistics Division. Statistical Abstract (SYC) **1262**
Seychelles. Statistics Division. Statistical Bulletin. Tourism (SYC) **8780**
Seychelles. Statistics Division. Statistical Bulletin. Visitor Survey (SYC) **8780**
Seychelles Today (SYC) **3945**
Seychelles Trade Report (SYC) **1582**
Seychelles Tuna Bulletin (SYC) **3608**
Seychelles Weekend Nation (SYC) **3945**
Seychellois (SYC) **155**
• Seymour Lecture in Biography (AUS ISSN 1833-329X) **645**
Sezon/Season (BGR) **5370**
Sfinx (DNK ISSN 0105-7618) **4325**
Sfoglialibro (ITA ISSN 1120-253X) **7573**
• Sfuoi Fornes (Online) (ITA) **5238**
Sfuoi Fornes (Print) *see* Sfuoi Fornes (Online) **5238**
SGUNschrift *see* S G U Nschrift **5366**
Shaanxi Archives *see* Shaanxi Dang'an **5047**
Shaanxi Daily *see* Shaanxi Ribao **3827**
Shaanxi Dang'an/Shaanxi Archives (CHN ISSN 1003-7268) **5047**
• Shaanxi Guangbo Dianshi Daxue Xuebao/Shaanxi Radio and T V University Journal (CHN ISSN 1008-4649) **2364**
Shaanxi Huabao/Shaanxi Pictorial (CHN ISSN 1001-0440) **3827**
Shaanxi Institute of Technology. Journal *see* Shaanxi Ligong Xueyuan Xuebao (Ziran Kexue Ban) **7914**
Shaanxi Institute of Traditional Chinese Medicine. Journal *see* Shaanxi Zhongyi Xueyuan Xuebao **5712**
Shaanxi Journal of Traditional Chinese Medicine *see* Shaanxi Zhongyi **314**
• Shaanxi Keji Daxue Xuebao (Ziran Kexue Ban)/Shaanxi University of Science & Technology. Journal (Natural Science Edition) (CHN) **7914**
• Shaanxi Ligong Xueyuan Xuebao (Shehui Kexue Ban) (CHN) **8000**
• Shaanxi Ligong Xueyuan Xuebao (Ziran Kexue Ban)/Shaanxi Institute of Technology. Journal (CHN ISSN 1673-2944) **7914**
Shaanxi Pictorial *see* Shaanxi Huabao **3827**
Shaanxi Radio and T V University Journal *see* Shaanxi Guangbo Dianshi Daxue Xuebao **2364**
• Shaanxi Ribao/Shaanxi Daily (CHN) **3827**
Shaanxi Shifan Daxue Jixu Jiaoyu Xuebao/Shaanxi Normal University. Journal of Further Education *see* Dangdai Jiaoshi Jiaoyu **2940**
• Shaanxi Shifan Daxue Xuebao (Zhexue Shehui Kexue Ban)/Shanxi Normal University. Journal (Philosophy and Social Sciences Edition) (CHN ISSN 1672-4283) **6951**
• Shaanxi Shifan Daxue Xuebao (Ziran Kexue Ban)/Shanxi Normal University. Journal (Natural Science Edition) (CHN ISSN 1672-4291) **7914**
Shaanxi University of Science & Technology. Journal (Natural Science Edition) *see* Shaanxi Keji Daxue Xuebao (Ziran Kexue Ban) **7914**
• Shaanxi Yixue Zazhi (CHN ISSN 1000-7377) **5712**
• Shaanxi Zhongyi/Shaanxi Journal of Traditional Chinese Medicine (CHN ISSN 1000-7369) **314**
• Shaanxi Zhongyi Xueyuan Xuebao/Shaanxi Institute of Traditional Chinese Medicine. Journal (CHN ISSN 1002-168X) **5712**
Al-Shabakah (LBN) **4983**
• Shabbat Shalom (USA) **3563**
Shadan Hojin Nihon Kokusai Kogyo Shoyuken Hogo Kyokai Geppo/International Association for the Protection of Industrial Property. Japanese Group. Journal (Japanese Edition) *see* International Association for the Protection of Intellectual Property. Japanese Group. Journal (Japanese Edition) **6753**
Shade Tree (USA ISSN 0037-3133) **3750**
• Shades (USA ISSN 1540-5370) **3563**
• Shades Beyond Gray (USA) **5370**
• Shades of Grey (USA) **4263**
Shadis (USA) **8200**
The Shadow (USA) **8068**
† • Shadowed Realms (AUS ISSN 1832-0651) **8988**
Shadows (NZL ISSN 1170-9758) **6208**
Shaheed Beheshti University. Faculty of Dentistry. Journal (IRN) **5865**
➤ Al-Shahid/The Martyr (LBY) **4325**
Shahid Chamran University Educational Journal (IRN) **3002**
Shahmatnyi Informator *see* Sahovski Informator **8198**
† Shai Maritime Magazine (ISR) **8988**
Shakai Fukushi no Doko (JPN) **8068**
➤ Shakai Gengo Kagaku/Japanese Journal of Language in Society (JPN ISSN 1344-3909) **5173**
Shakai Jinruigaku Nenpo (JPN ISSN 0387-2483) **355**
Shakai Kagaku/The Social Sciences (JPN ISSN 0419-6759) **8000**
Shakai Kagaku Kenkyu/Social Sciences Journal (JPN ISSN 0387-3307) **8000**
Shakai Keizai Shigaku *see* Socio-Economic History **1549**
Shakai Shimpo (JPN) **7182**
Shakai Shinrigaku Kenkyu/Japanese Journal of Social Psychology (JPN ISSN 0916-1503) **7408**
Shakai to Rinri (JPN ISSN 1344-0616) **6951**
Shakaigaku Hyoron *see* Japanese Sociological Review **8111**
Shakaigaku Nenshi (JPN ISSN 0288-7126) **8132**
Shakaigaku Ronso/Journal of Sociology (JPN ISSN 0582-933X) **8132**
Shaken Baby Alliance (USA) **2168**
Shaker Quarterly (USA ISSN 0582-9348) **7741**
Shakers World Magazine (USA ISSN 1087-0466) **3563**
• ➤ Shakespeare (GBR ISSN 1745-0926) **5370**
• ➤ Shakespeare Bulletin (USA ISSN 0748-2558) **8478**
Shakespeare in Performance (GBR) **5370**
• ➤ Shakespeare in Southern Africa (ZAF ISSN 1011-582X) **5370**
➤ Shakespeare International Yearbook (GBR ISSN 1465-5098) **5370**
Shakespeare Jahrbuch (DEU ISSN 1430-2527) **5370**
• Shakespeare Newsletter (USA ISSN 0037-3214) **5370**
• Shakespeare Oxford Newsletter (USA ISSN 1525-6863) **5370**
▼ The Shakespeare Papers (USA ISSN 1942-7417) **5434**
Shakespeare, Petrarch, Sidney, Milton & Hopkins *see* S P S M & H **5434**
• ➤ Shakespeare Quarterly (USA ISSN 0037-3222) **5370**
• Shakespeare Studies (JPN ISSN 0582-9402) **5370**
• ➤ Shakespeare Studies (USA ISSN 0582-9399) **5370**
• Shakespeare Survey (GBR ISSN 0080-9152) **5370**
Shakespeare: The Critical Tradition (GBR) **5370**
† Shakespeare Worldwide (USA ISSN 0914-1677) **8988**
Shakespeare Yearbook (USA ISSN 1045-9456) **5370**
Shakespearean Criticism (USA ISSN 0883-9123) **5371**
Shakhmatna Misl (BGR) **8200**
Shakhmaty v Rossii (RUS) **8200**
Shale Shaker (USA ISSN 0037-3257) **2767**
• Shallow Water Angler (USA ISSN 1932-5304) **8332**

Title

Shanghai Journal of Translators *see* Shanghai Keji Fanyi **5173**
• ➤ Shanghai Keji Fanyi/Shanghai Journal of Translators (CHN ISSN 1000-6141) **5173**
• Shanghai Kouqiang Yixue/Shanghai Journal of Stomatology (CHN ISSN 1006-7248) **5931**
• Shanghai Kuaiji/Shanghai Accounting (CHN ISSN 1007-5135) **1301**
Shanghai Legal World *see* Shanghai Fayuan **4783**
• Shanghai Ligong Daxue Xuebao (CHN ISSN 1007-6735) **8438**
• Shanghai Ligong Daxue Xuebao (Shehui Kexue Ban)/University of Shanghai For Science and Technology. Journal (Social Science) (CHN ISSN 1009-895X) **8000**
Shanghai Literature *see* Shanghai Wenxue **5371**
Shanghai Lixue/Shanghai Mechanics (CHN ISSN 0254-0053) **7062**
Shanghai Machine Tool *see* Shanghai Jichuang **5459**
Shanghai Maritime University. Journal *see* Shanghai Haishi Daxue Xuebao **8660**
Shanghai Mechanics *see* Shanghai Lixue **7062**
Shanghai Medical & Pharmaceutical Journal *see* Shanghai Yiyao **5713**
Shanghai Medical Imaging *see* Shanghai Yixue Yingxiang **5713**
Shanghai Medical Journal *see* Shanghai Yixue **5713**
Shanghai Metals (Nonferrous Fascicule) *see* Shanghai Jinshu (Youse Fence) **6331**
• Shanghai Nongye Xuebao/Acta Agriculturae Shanghai (CHN ISSN 1000-3924) **155**
Shanghai Normal University. Journal (Philosophy & Social Sciences) *see* Shanghai Shifan Daxue Xuebao (Zhexue Shehui Kexue Ban) **8000**
Shanghai Packaging *see* Shanghai Baozhuang **6715**
Shanghai Philately *see* Shanghai Jiyou **6899**
Shanghai Physical Education Institute. Journal *see* Shanghai Tiyu Xueyuan Xuebao **2911**
Shanghai Polytechnic College of Urban Management. Journal *see* Shanghai Chengshi Guanli Zhiye Jishu Xueyuan Xuebao (Dangdai Jianshe) **1035**
• Shanghai Qiye/Shanghai Enterprise (CHN ISSN 1004-7808) **1432**
Shanghai Quality *see* Shanghai Zhiliang **1903**
Shanghai Ribao *see* Shanghai Daily **3827**
Shanghai Second Medical University. Journal *see* Shanghai Jiaotong University. Journal **8438**
Shanghai Second Polytechnic University. Journal *see* Shanghai Di-er Gongye Daxue Xuebao **7914**
Shanghai Securities News *see* Shanghai Zhengquan Bao **1651**
Shanghai Shangxueyuan Xuebao/Shanghai Business School. Journal (CHN ISSN 1673-324X) **1173**
Shanghai Shangye Zhiye Jishu Xueyuan Xuebao/Shanghai Commercial Polytechnic. Journal *see* Shanghai Shangxueyuan Xuebao **1173**
Shanghai Shehui Kexueyuan Xueshu Jikan/Shanghai Academy of Social Sciences. Quarterly Journal *see* Shehui Kexue (Shanghai) **8001**
Shanghai Shengwu Yixue Gongcheng/Shanghai Journal of Biomedical Engineering *see* Shengwu Yixue Gongchengxue Jinzhan **751**
• Shanghai Shibo/EXPO 2010 Shanghai (CHN ISSN 1673-307X) **1173**
• Shanghai Shifan Daxue Xuebao (Zhexue Shehui Kexue Ban)/Shanghai Normal University. Journal (Philosophy & Social Sciences) (CHN ISSN 1004-8634) **8000**
• Shanghai Shifan Daxue Xuebao (Ziran Kexue Ban)/Shanghai Teachers University. Journal (Natural Sciences) (CHN ISSN 1000-5137) **7914**
Shanghai Shizhuang Bao/Shanghai Fashion Times (CHN) **2261**
• Shanghai Shuichan Daxue Xuebao/Shanghai Fisheries University. Journal (CHN ISSN 1004-7271) **3608**
• Shanghai Star (CHN) **3827**
Shanghai Statistical Yearbook (Year) (HKG) **8399**
Shanghai Statistics *see* Shanghai Tongji **8399**
Shanghai Stories *see* Shanghai Gushi **5371**
Shanghai Studies on C C P History and Construction *see* Shanghai Dangshi yu Dangjian **7182**
Shanghai T V Weekly *see* Shanghai Dianshi **2390**
Shanghai Tatler (HKG) **3827**
Shanghai Teachers University. Journal (Natural Sciences) *see* Shanghai Shifan Daxue Xuebao (Ziran Kexue Ban) **7914**
Shanghai Textile Science and Technology *see* Shanghai Fangzhi Keji **8457**
• Shanghai Tiyu Xueyuan Xuebao/Shanghai Physical Education Institute. Journal (CHN ISSN 1000-5498) **2911**
• Shanghai Tongji/Shanghai Statistics (CHN ISSN 1006-2726) **8399**
Shanghai Touzi/Shanghai Investment (CHN ISSN 1005-7552) **1651**
• Shanghai Tuke/Shanghai Coatings (CHN ISSN 1009-1696) **6720**
• Shanghai University. Journal/Shanghai Daxue Xuebao (Yingwen Ban) (CHN ISSN 1007-6417) **7914**
Shanghai University. Journal (Natural Science Edition) *see* Shanghai Daxue Xuebao (Ziran Kexue Ban) **7914**
Shanghai University of Engineering Science. Journal *see* Shanghai Gongcheng Jishu Daxue Xuebao **3219**
Shanghai University of Finance and Economics. Journal *see* Shanghai Caijing Daxue Xuebao **1173**
Shanghai Wednesday *see* Shanghai Xingqisan **3827**
Shanghai Weekly *see* Shanghai Yizhou **3827**
• Shanghai Wenxue/Shanghai Literature (CHN ISSN 1001-8026) **5371**
Shanghai Xiju/Shanghai Drama (CHN ISSN 0559-7277) **8478**
• Shanghai Xingqisan/Shanghai Wednesday (CHN) **3827**
• Shanghai Xingzheng Xueyuan Xuebao/Shanghai Administration Institute. Journal (CHN ISSN 1009-3176) **8000**
• Shanghai Xumu Shouyi Tongxun/Shanghai Journal of Animal Husbandry and Veterinary Medicine (CHN ISSN 1000-7725) **8807**
• Shanghai Yingyong Jishu Xueyuan Xuebao (Ziran Kexue Ban) (CHN ISSN 1671-7333) **7914**
• Shanghai Yishujia/Shanghai Artists (CHN) **8478**
• Shanghai Yixue/Shanghai Medical Journal (CHN ISSN 0253-9934) **5713**
• Shanghai Yixue Jianyan Zazhi/Shanghai Journal of Medical Laboratory Sciences (CHN ISSN 1001-2087) **5911**
• Shanghai Yixue Yingxiang/Shanghai Medical Imaging (CHN ISSN 1008-617X) **5713**
• Shanghai Yiyao/Shanghai Medical & Pharmaceutical Journal (CHN ISSN 1006-1533) **5713**
Shanghai Yizhou/Shanghai Weekly (CHN) **3827**
• Shanghai Yufang Yixue/Shanghai Journal of Preventive Medicine (CHN ISSN 1004-9231) **5713**
• Shanghai Zhengquan Bao/Shanghai Securities News (CHN) **1651**
• Shanghai Zhenjiu Zazhi/Shanghai Journal of Acupuncture and Moxibustion (CHN ISSN 1005-0957) **315**
• Shanghai Zhiliang/Shanghai Quality (CHN ISSN 1004-7816) **1903**
• Shanghai Zhongxue Shuxue/School Mathematics in Shanghai (CHN ISSN 1672-7495) **5535**
• Shanghai Zhongyiyao Zazhi/Revista de Medicina Tradicional China de Shanghai/Revue de Medecine Traditionnelle Chinoise/Shanghai Journal of Traditional Chinese Medicine (CHN ISSN 0559-7269) **315**
• Shanghai Zonghe Jingji/Economic Forum (CHN ISSN 1005-2240) **1721**
Shangjie Daokan/Commercial World Guide (CHN ISSN 1671-3443) **1173**
• Shanglu Daobao (CHN) **8755**
Shangpin Pingjie/Review on Commodity *see* Target **5084**
• Shangqiu Shifan Xueyuan Xuebao/Shangqiu Teachers College (CHN ISSN 1008-2662) **3002**
Shangqiu Teachers College *see* Shangqiu Shifan Xueyuan Xuebao **3002**
Shangqiu Vocational and Technical College. Journal *see* Shangqiu Zhiye Jishu Xueyuan Xuebao **8000**
• Shangqiu Zhiye Jishu Xueyuan Xuebao/Shangqiu Vocational and Technical College. Journal (CHN ISSN 1671-8127) **8000**
• Shangri-la (NPL ISSN 1605-9263) **8785**
Shangrila *see* Shangri-la **8785**
▼ Shangwu Luxing/Business Travel (CHN ISSN 1673-8551) **8755**
• Shangwu Zhoukan/Business Watch Magazine (CHN ISSN 1009-4865) **1173**
Shangye Gushi/World of Economy and Trade (CHN ISSN 1673-8160) **1173**
Shangye Jingji/Commercial Economy *see* Maoyi Jingji **1431**
• Shangye Jingji yu Guanli/Economics and Business Administration (CHN ISSN 1000-2154) **1793**
Shangye Qiye Guanli/Management of Commercial Enterprise (CHN ISSN 1005-4367) **1793**
• Shangye Yanjiu/Commercial Research Editorial Department (CHN ISSN 1001-148X) **1173**
Shangying Huabao/Shanghai Film Pictorial (CHN ISSN 0559-7331) **6513**
Shanhua/Mountain Blossoms (Guizhou) (CHN ISSN 0559-7218) **5371**
Shannon Zimmerman's Motley Fool Champion Funds *see* Motley Fool Champion Funds **1641**
Shans (RUS) **5238**
Shanti *see* Santi **7708**
• Shantou Daxue Xuebao (Renwen Kexue Ban)/Shantou University. Journal (Humanities & Social Sciences Edition) (CHN ISSN 1001-4225) **4475**
• Shantou Daxue Xuebao (Ziran Kexue Ban)/Shantou University. Journal (Natural Science Edition) (CHN ISSN 1001-4217) **7914**
• Shantou Daxue Yixueyuan Xuebao/Shantou University Medical College. Journal (CHN ISSN 1007-4716) **5713**
Shantou Special Economic Zone Yearbook (Year) (HKG) **1262**
Shantou University. Journal (Humanities & Social Sciences Edition) *see* Shantou Daxue Xuebao (Renwen Kexue Ban) **4475**
Shantou University. Journal (Natural Science Edition) *see* Shantou Daxue Xuebao (Ziran Kexue Ban) **7914**
Shantou University Medical College. Journal *see* Shantou Daxue Yixueyuan Xuebao **5713**
Shanxi Adult Education *see* Shanxi Chengren Jiaoyu **2946**
Shanxi Agricultural University. Journal (Social Science Edition) *see* Shanxi Nongye Daxue Xuebao (Shehui Kexue Ban) **8000**
• Shanxi Agriculture/Shanxi Nongye (CHN ISSN 1006-9739) **155**
• Shanxi Cai-Jing Daxue Xuebao (Gaodeng Jiaoyu Ban)/Shanxi Finance and Economics University. Journal (Higher Education Edition) (CHN ISSN 1008-7362) **3002**
• Shanxi Caijing Daxue Xuebao/Shanxi Finance and Economics University. Journal (CHN ISSN 1007-9556) **1173**
• Shanxi Caizheng Shuiwu Zhuanke Xuexiao Xuebao/Shanxi Finance and Tax College. Journal (CHN ISSN 1008-9306) **1943**
• Shanxi Chengren Jiaoyu/Shanxi Adult Education (CHN ISSN 1004-6747) **2946**
Shanxi College of Traditional Chinese Medicine. Journal *see* Shanxi Zhongyi Xueyuan Xuebao **5713**
Shanxi Cooking Coal Science & Technology *see* Shanxi Jiaomei Keji **6479**
Shanxi Daily *see* Shanxi Ribao **3827**
• Shanxi Daxue Xuebao (Shehui Kexue Ban)/Shanxi University. Journal (Social Science Edition) (CHN ISSN 1000-5935) **8000**
• Shanxi Daxue Xuebao (Ziran Kexue Ban)/Shanxi University. Journal (Natural Science Edition) (CHN ISSN 0253-2395) **7914**
• Shanxi Dianli/Shanxi Electric Power (CHN ISSN 1671-0320) **3161**
Shanxi Difang Zhi *see* Cangsang **4180**
• Shanxi Dizhen/Earthquake Research in Shanxi (CHN ISSN 1000-6265) **2789**
Shanxi Education *see* Shanxi Jiaoyu **2911**
Shanxi Education Newspaper *see* Shanxi Jiaoyu Bao **2911**
Shanxi Electric Power *see* Shanxi Dianli **3161**
Shanxi Finance and Economics University. Journal *see* Shanxi Caijing Daxue Xuebao **1173**
Shanxi Finance and Economics University. Journal (Higher Education Edition) *see* Shanxi Cai-Jing Daxue Xuebao (Gaodeng Jiaoyu Ban) **3002**
Shanxi Finance and Tax College. Journal *see* Shanxi Caizheng Shuiwu Zhuanke Xuexiao Xuebao **1943**
Shanxi Folk Literature *see* Shanxi Minjian Wenxue **5371**
Shanxi Fruits *see* Shanxi Guoshu **155**
• Shanxi Gaodeng Xuexiao Shehui Kexue Xuebao/Social Sciences Journal of Colleges of Shanxi (CHN ISSN 1008-6285) **8000**
• Shanxi Guoshu/Shanxi Fruits (CHN ISSN 1005-345X) **155**
Shanxi Huabao/Shanxi Pictorial (CHN ISSN 0559-717X) **3827**
• Shanxi Jiaomei Keji/Shanxi Cooking Coal Science & Technology (CHN ISSN 1672-0652) **6479**
• Shanxi Jiaoyu/Shanxi Education (CHN ISSN 1004-6739) **2911**
Shanxi Jiaoyu Bao/Shanxi Education Newspaper (CHN) **2911**
Shanxi Journal of Traditional Chinese Medicine *see* Shanxi Zhongyi **315**
Shanxi Keji Bao/Shanxi Science and Technology Gazette (CHN) **7914**
Shanxi Library Journal *see* Jintu Xuekan **5020**
Shanxi Literature *see* Shanxi Wenxue **5371**
Shanxi Medical Journal *see* Shanxi Yiyao Zazhi **6880**
Shanxi Medical University. Journal *see* Shanxi Yike Daxue Xuebao **5713**
Shanxi Medical University. Journal (Preclinical Medical Education Edition) *see* Shanxi Yike Daxue Xuebao (Jichu Yixue Jiaoyu Ban) **2911**
Shanxi Meteorological Quarterly *see* Shanxi Qixiang **6395**
Shanxi Minjian Wenxue/Shanxi Folk Literature (CHN) **5371**
• Shanxi Nongmin Bao (CHN) **3827**
Shanxi Nongye *see* Shanxi Agriculture **155**
• Shanxi Nongye Daxue Xuebao (Shehui Kexue Ban)/Shanxi Agricultural University. Journal (Social Science Edition) (CHN ISSN 1671-816X) **8000**
• Shanxi Nongye Daxue Xuebao (Ziran Kexue Ban)/Shanxi University of Agriculture. Journal (Natural Science Edition) (CHN ISSN 1671-8151) **7914**
Shanxi Normal University. Journal (Natural Science Edition) *see* Shaanxi Shifan Daxue Xuebao (Ziran Kexue Ban) **7914**
Shanxi Normal University. Journal (Philosophy and Social Sciences Edition) *see* Shaanxi Shifan Daxue Xuebao (Zhexue Shehui Kexue Ban) **6951**
Shanxi Pictorial *see* Shanxi Huabao **3827**
• Shanxi Qixiang/Shanxi Meteorological Quarterly (CHN ISSN 1004-5732) **6395**
• Shanxi Ribao/Shanxi Daily (CHN) **3827**
Shanxi Science and Technology Gazette *see* Shanxi Keji Bao **7914**
• Shanxi Shi-Da Tiyu Xueyuan Xuebao/Shanxi Teachers University. Physical Education Institute. Journal (CHN ISSN 1008-8571) **6996**
• Shanxi Shi-da Xuebao (Shehui Kexue Ban)/Shanxi Teachers University. Journal (Social Science Edition) (CHN ISSN 1001-5957) **8000**
• Shanxi Shifan Daxue Xuebao (Ziran Kexue Ban)/Shanxi Teacher's University. Journal (Natural Science Edition) (CHN ISSN 1009-4490) **7914**
• Shanxi Shuitu Baochi Keji/Soil and Water Conservation Science and Technology in Shanxi (CHN ISSN 1008-0120) **2627**
Shanxi Teacher's University. Journal (Natural Science Edition) *see* Shanxi Shifan Daxue Xuebao (Ziran Kexue Ban) **7914**
Shanxi Teachers University. Journal (Social Science Edition) *see* Shanxi Shi-da Xuebao (Shehui Kexue Ban) **8000**
Shanxi Teachers University. Physical Education Institute. Journal *see* Shanxi Shi-Da Tiyu Xueyuan Xuebao **6996**
Shanxi University. Journal (Natural Science Edition) *see* Shanxi Daxue Xuebao (Ziran Kexue Ban) **7914**
Shanxi University. Journal (Social Science Edition) *see* Shanxi Daxue Xuebao (Shehui Kexue Ban) **8000**
Shanxi University of Agriculture. Journal (Natural Science Edition) *see* Shanxi Nongye Daxue Xuebao (Ziran Kexue Ban) **7914**
• Shanxi Wanbao (CHN) **3827**
Shanxi Wenxue/Shanxi Literature (CHN ISSN 0257-5906) **5371**
• Shanxi Yike Daxue Xuebao/Shanxi Medical University. Journal (CHN ISSN 1007-6611) **5713**
• Shanxi Yike Daxue Xuebao (Jichu Yixue Jiaoyu Ban)/Shanxi Medical University. Journal (Preclinical Medical Education Edition) (CHN ISSN 1008-7249) **2911**
Shanxi Yixueyuan Xuebao/Shanxi Medical College. Journal *see* Shanxi Yike Daxue Xuebao **5713**
• ➤ Shanxi Yiyao Zazhi/Shanxi Medical Journal (CHN ISSN 0253-9926) **6880**
Shanxi Zhigong Yixueyuan Xuebao (CHN ISSN 1671-0126) **2911**
• Shanxi Zhongyi/Shanxi Journal of Traditional Chinese Medicine (CHN ISSN 1000-7156) **315**
• Shanxi Zhongyi Xueyuan Xuebao/Shanxi College of Traditional Chinese Medicine. Journal (CHN ISSN 1671-0258) **5713**
Shao Nu/Young Girl (CHN ISSN 1001-5590) **2212**
Shaoguan University. Journal *see* Shaoguan Xueyuan Xuebao **8000**
• Shaoguan Xueyuan Xuebao/Shaoguan University. Journal (CHN) **8000**
Shaolin yu Taiji (CHN ISSN 1003-5176) **8200**
Shaonan Shaonu/Boys and Girls (CHN ISSN 1004-7875) **5371**
Shaonian Bao/Juvenile Press (CHN) **2212**
• Shaonian Ertong Yanjiu/Adolescent Studies (CHN ISSN 1002-9915) **2168**
• Shaonian Kexue/The Science for Juvenile (CHN ISSN 1004-0080) **2212**
Shaonian Kexue Huabao/Juvenile Scientific Pictorial (CHN ISSN 1000-7776) **2212**
Shaonian Wenyi (Nanjing) (CHN ISSN 1002-0365) **2212**
• Shaonian Wenyi (Shanghai)/Juvenile Literature (CHN ISSN 1004-0889) **2212**
Shaonian Zuowen Fudao (CHN ISSN 1005-5231) **5371**
Shaoxing University. Journal *see* Shaoxing Weli Xueyuan Xuebao **8000**
• Shaoxing Weli Xueyuan Xuebao/Shaoxing University. Journal (CHN ISSN 1008-293X) **8000**
Shaoyang Gaodeng Zhuanke Xuexiao Xuebao/Shaoyang College. Journal *see* Shaoyang Xueyuan Xuebao (Shehui Kexue Ban) **8000**
Shaoyang Gaodeng Zhuanke Xuexiao Xuebao/Shaoyang College. Journal *see* Shaoyang Xueyuan Xuebao (Ziran Kexue Ban) **7914**
Shaoyang Shifan Gaodeng Zhuanke Xuexiao Xuebao/Shaoyang Teachers College. Journal *see* Shaoyang Xueyuan Xuebao (Shehui Kexue Ban) **8000**
Shaoyang Shifan Gaodeng Zhuanke Xuexiao Xuebao/Shaoyang Teachers College. Journal *see* Shaoyang Xueyuan Xuebao (Ziran Kexue Ban) **7914**
Shaoyang University. Journal (Natural Science) *see* Shaoyang Xueyuan Xuebao (Ziran Kexue Ban) **7914**
• Shaoyang Xueyuan Xuebao (Shehui Kexue Ban) (CHN) **8000**
• Shaoyang Xueyuan Xuebao (Ziran Kexue Ban)/Shaoyang University. Journal (Natural Science) (CHN ISSN 1672-7010) **7914**
Shaoyang Xueyuan Xuebao/Shaoyang University. Journal *see* Shaoyang Xueyuan Xuebao (Ziran Kexue Ban) **7914**
Shaoyang Xueyuan Xuebao/Shaoyang University. Journal *see* Shaoyang Xueyuan Xuebao (Shehui Kexue Ban) **8000**
Shape (DEU ISSN 1422-9188) **8848**
• Shape (HUN ISSN 1585-7379) **8848**
Shape (POL ISSN 1509-8834) **8848**
• Shape (USA ISSN 0744-5121) **8848**
Shape (Singapore Edition) (SGP) **6996**
The Shape of Enrichment (USA ISSN 1088-8152) **321**
Shape Presents Fit Pregnancy *see* Fit Pregnancy **5990**
Shape South Africa (ZAF) **8848**

Title

10862 SHAPE. THE COMPLETE WORKOUT GUIDE ULRICH'S PERIODICALS

Shape. The Complete Workout Guide (ZAF ISSN 1991-6132) **6996**
Shape Up (DEU ISSN 0949-2380) **6996**
Shape-Up (NOR ISSN 0803-222X) **6996**
Shape Up Trainer's Only (DEU) **6996**
ShapeUp *see* Shape-Up **6996**
Shaping Up (GBR) **6996**
Shapu Giho/Sharp Technical Journal (JPN ISSN 0285-0362) **3113**
Shara Bara (KAZ) **3902**
Share (CAN ISSN 0709-4647) **3563**
Share (NLD ISSN 1872-2598) **2437**
Share (USA ISSN 0192-7418) **7817**
• SHARE (Birmingham) (GBR ISSN 1367-6741) **7681**
Share (French Edition) *see* Share **2437**
Share (German Edition) *see* Share **2437**
Share (Italian Edition) *see* Share **2437**
Share (Spanish Edition) *see* Share **2437**
▼ • Share Buybacks (GBR ISSN 1753-9323) **1651**
Share Europe Spring Conference. Proceedings (CHE ISSN 1028-284X) **2550**
Share European Association. Anniversary Meeting. Proceedings *see* S E A S Anniversary Meeting. Proceedings **2550**
• The Share Guide (USA) **315**
Share International (USA ISSN 0169-1341) **6647**
Share Market Review *see* Sanchar **3888**
• Share Purchases (GBR ISSN 1754-8306) **1651**
Share the Earth Newsletter (USA) **3466**
Shared Journey (CAN ISSN 1912-7464) **3564**
• ShareDebate International (USA ISSN 1054-0695) **8000**
Shareholder *see* Aktiespararen **1609**
Shareholder Remedies in Canada (CAN) **1651**
Shareholders, Form 10-K. Banking Supplement (USA) **1383**
• Shareowner (CAN ISSN 1704-1082) **1651**
SharePoint Advisor *see* Databased Advisor Magazine **2554**
Shares *see* Smart Investor **1651**
Shares (GBR ISSN 1468-1102) **1651**
Shares Investment (SGP ISSN 0218-8716) **1651**
Shari'ah (JOR) **7716**
Sharing *see* Fenyou **8863**
Sharing (St. Charles) (USA) **7408**
Sharing and Learning Together Programme for 3 to 4 *see* The S A L T Programme for 3 to 4 **7773**
Sharing and Learning Together Programme for 5 to 7 *see* The S A L T Programme for 5 to 7 **7678**
Sharing and Learning Together Programme for 8 to 10 *see* The S A L T Programme for 8 to 10 **7678**
Sharing and Learning Together Programme for All Ages *see* The S A L T Programme for All Ages **7773**
Sharing God's Word (GBR ISSN 1471-5015) **7774**
Sharing Ideas News Magazine (USA ISSN 0886-1501) **5371**
Sharing News (NLD ISSN 1874-9712) **1843**
• Sharing Solutions (USA) **4085**
Sharing the Practice (USA ISSN 0193-8274) **7681**
Sharing the Victory (USA ISSN 0745-1245) **7681**
Sharing Times (USA) **8132**
Sharjah Commercial Directory/Dalil al-Sharqah al-Tijari (UAE) **2027**
Sharjah Exporter - Importer Directory/Daleel Al Sariqah Lil Mosaddireen wa Al-Mostawrideen (UAE) **2027**
Shark Fear, Shark Awareness (USA) **963**
• Shark News (GBR ISSN 1361-7397) **963**
Sharp Technical Journal *see* Shapu Giho **3113**
• SharpMan.com (USA) **6299**
• Al-Sharq (QAT) **3932**
Al-Sharq (SAU) **3944**
Sharq Al-Andalus (ESP ISSN 0213-3482) **560**
• Al-Sharq al-Awsat (SAU ISSN 1319-0814) **3912**
Al-Sharqiyyah Elle (SAU) **8883**
Sharqiyyat *see* ZemZem **4280**
Shashin Sokuryo to Rimoto Senshingu/Photogrammetry and Remote Sensing (JPN ISSN 0285-5844) **4028**
Shatranj Samarat (IND) **8200**
• Shattered (USA ISSN 1559-7571) **8883**
Shattered Magazine *see* Shattered **8883**
Shattered Wig Review (USA) **5434**
▼ Shaun das Schaf (DEU) **2213**
Shaver Focus (CAN ISSN 0315-6915) **300**
Shavian (GBR ISSN 0037-3346) **5371**
Shavings (USA ISSN 0734-0680) **8282**
• Shavings (South Dartmouth) (USA ISSN 1949-9655) **1903**
† Ha-Shavu'a (ISR) **8988**
• ➤ Shaw (USA ISSN 0741-5842) **5371**
SHAW Annual *see* Shaw **5371**
Shaw Historical Library. Journal (USA ISSN 0889-0277) **4312**
• Shaw Magazine (USA) **5238**
Shaw Society Newsletter (GBR) **5371**
Shawcross & Beaumont Air Law (GBR) **8551**
Shaw's Directory of Courts in the United Kingdom (GBR ISSN 0264-312X) **4960**
Shaw's Directory of Tribunals and Regulatory Bodies (GBR ISSN 1356-6415) **4960**
Shaw's Local Government Directory (GBR ISSN 1462-821X) **7502**
Shbut *see* Shvut **3564**
• Shchit i Mech (RUS ISSN 0236-3496) **8200**
She (GBR ISSN 0037-3370) **8883**
† She (NLD ISSN 1873-9261) **8988**
She (POL ISSN 1505-4578) **8848**
SHE (USA) **6513**
• SHE Caribbean (LCA) **8883**
She-ke yu Jingji Xinxi/Social Sciences and Economic Information *see* Jingji yu Shehui Fazhan (Nanning) **1494**
• Sheaf (CAN) **2300**
• Shearsman (GBR) **5371**
The Shed (NZL ISSN 1177-0457) **4367**
Sheep! *see* Sheep Magazine **300**
Sheep and Beef Industry Mid-season Review *see* Meat and Wool Boards' Economic Service. Sheep and Beef Industry Mid-season Review **203**
• Sheep & Beef New Season Outlook (NZL) **300**
Sheep & Beef News (GBR ISSN 1749-4087) **300**
• Sheep & Goat Health Report (USA) **300**
Sheep and Goats *see* U.S. Department of Agriculture. National Agricultural Statistics Service. Sheep and Goats (Print) **8995**
Sheep and Goats in Humid West Africa (ETH) **300**
Sheep / Beef Notes *see* Sheep & Beef News **300**
Sheep Breeder and Sheepman (USA ISSN 0037-3400) **300**
Sheep Canada (CAN ISSN 0702-8881) **300**
The Sheep Farmer (GBR ISSN 0141-2434) **300**
Sheep Magazine (USA ISSN 0279-9200) **300**
Sheep Veterinary Society. Proceedings (GBR ISSN 1367-1138) **8807**
• Sheep's Back to Mill (AUS ISSN 1449-1532) **8457**
Sheep's Back to Mill Statistics *see* Sheep's Back to Mill Statistics Yearbook **8464**
• Sheep's Back to Mill Statistics Yearbook (AUS) **8464**
Sheerness Times Guardian (GBR ISSN 0964-1394) **3870**
Sheet Metal and Fabricator/Shito Metaru (JPN) **6332**
Sheet Metal Industries Buyers' Guide (GBR) **6344**
Sheet Metal Journal (CAN) **6344**
Sheet Metal School *see* Shito Metaru Sukuru **6332**
Sheet Music Magazine (USA ISSN 1548-9108) **6616**
Sheet Music Magazine. Standard Piano - Guitar Edition (USA ISSN 0273-6462) **6616**
Sheetfed Operations Quarterly (USA) **7328**
Sheffield Archaeological Monographs (GBR ISSN 1362-6752) **416**
• Sheffield Birds Study Group. Bulletin (GBR) **914**
Sheffield Chamber of Commerce. Business directory (GBR) **1409**
Sheffield City Press (GBR) **3870**
Sheffield Currency (NZL ISSN 1176-8770) **1874**
• Sheffield Electronic Press (GBR) **6616**
Sheffield Hallam University, Centre for Regional Economic and Social Research Lecture Series *see* C R E S R Lecture Series **1445**
Sheffield Hallam University, Centre for Regional Economic and Social Research Planning and Property Series *see* C R E S R Planning and Property Series **1445**
Sheffield Hallam University, Centre for Regional Economic and Social Research Research Paper *see* C R E S R Research Paper **1445**
Sheffield Hallam University, Centre for Regional Economic and Social Research Social Policy Paper *see* C R E S R Social Policy Paper **8029**
Sheffield Hallam University, Centre for Regional Economic and Social Research Supertram Impact Series *see* C R E S R Supertram Impact Series **1445**
Sheffield Hallam University. Engineering Education Research Group. Proceedings (GBR) **3219**
The Sheffield Mercury Newspaper (GBR) **3870**
Sheffield Newsletter *see* Sheffield Currency **1874**
Sheffield University Annual Report (GBR) **3002**
Sheffield University Calendar (GBR ISSN 0307-6202) **3002**
Sheffield University Postgraduate Prospectus (GBR) **3002**
Sheffield University Undergraduate Prospectus (GBR) **3002**
• Shehui/Society (CHN ISSN 1004-8804) **8000**
Shehui Baozhang Zhidu/Social Security System (CHN ISSN 1007-0613) **8068**
Shehui - Jiating/Society - Family (CHN) **3827**
• Shehui Kexue (Shanghai)/Social Sciences (CHN ISSN 0257-5833) **8001**
• Shehui Kexue Jikan/Social Science Journal (CHN ISSN 1001-6198) **8001**
• Shehui Kexue Yanjiu/Social Science Research (CHN ISSN 1000-4769) **8001**
Shehui Kexue Yanjiu (Zhongwen Ban) (USA ISSN 1551-6342) **8001**
• Shehui Kexue Zhanxian/Social Science Front (CHN ISSN 0257-0246) **8001**
Shehui Kexue Zonglun/Studies in Social Sciences (CHN ISSN 1001-3431) **8001**
➤ Shehui Lilun Xuebao/Journal of Social Theory (SGP ISSN 1099-4882) **8132**
Shehui Xinli Kexue/Science of Social Psychology (CHN) **4783**
Shehui Zhuyi Jingji Lilun yu Shijian/Socialist Economic Theory and Practice (CHN ISSN 1005-4294) **1173**
Shehui Zhuyi Luncong/Collected Essays on Socialism (CHN ISSN 1009-7554) **7182**
Shehuixue/Sociology (CHN ISSN 1001-344X) **8132**
Shehuixue Wenzhai Ka/Sociology Abstracts on Cards (CHN ISSN 1009-7414) **8150**
• Shehuixue Yanjiu/Sociological Studies (CHN ISSN 1002-5936) **8132**
• Shehuizhuyi Yanjiu (Wuhan)/Studies on Socialism (CHN ISSN 1001-4527) **7182**
➤ Sheila-Na-Gig (USA ISSN 1083-1274) **5434**
Shekel (USA) **6653**
▼ Shekinah (DEU) **6743**
Shelburne Securities Forecast (USA) **1651**
Shelby County Ancestors (USA ISSN 8756-131X) **3782**
Shelby County Historical Society. The Quarterly (USA ISSN 1055-2006) **4312**
Shelby County Urban Development Report (USA) **4427**
Shelby Exchange (USA ISSN 1086-8720) **3782**
▼ The Shelby Report of the Midwest (USA ISSN 1947-2749) **3681**
Shelby Report of the Southeast (USA ISSN 0194-1968) **3681**
Shelby Report of the Southwest (USA ISSN 0192-916X) **3681**
▼ The Shelby Report of the West (USA ISSN 1945-2217) **3663**
Sheldon Family Association Quarterly (USA ISSN 1063-956X) **3782**
Sheldon's Major Stores & Chains (USA) **1843**
Shelf Action (USA) **3663**
† • Shelf Life (AUS ISSN 1325-7919) **8988**
Shelf Life (GBR) **5047**
Shelf Life (USA) **5238**
• ShelfImpact! (USA) **6715**
ShelfLife (IRL ISSN 1393-0753) **3663**
• Shelflife (Jupiter) (USA ISSN 1935-5246) **5047**
Shelflife (Princeton) (USA ISSN 1528-7971) **5173**
Shelfmark (ZWE ISSN 0037-3494) **635**
The Shell *see* La Conchiglia **8943**
• Shell Chemicals Magazine (GBR ISSN 1747-0706) **3255**
Shell Tourist Guide to South Africa (ZAF) **8755**
Shell-Venster (NLD ISSN 1389-0859) **6792**
Shellac Export Promotion Council. Annual Report (IND ISSN 0304-8179) **6721**
Sheller's Directory of Clubs, Books, Periodicals and Dealers (USA ISSN 0085-607X) **963**
† Shellfish Information Leaflet (GBR ISSN 0144-2104) **8988**
• Shellfish News (GBR) **3608**
Shells of Kyushu *see* Kyushu no Kai **953**
• Shelter (USA ISSN 0164-6559) **1035**
Shelter Quarterly *see* The Queensland Shelter Quarterly **4424**
• Shelterforce (USA ISSN 0885-9612) **4427**
Shelter's Housing Law Update (GBR ISSN 1740-4231) **4783**
Sheltie International (USA ISSN 0745-2012) **6815**
• Sheltie Pacesetter (USA ISSN 0744-6608) **6815**
Shem Tov (CAN ISSN 0843-6924) **3782**
Shemot (GBR ISSN 0969-2258) **3782**
Shemp! (USA) **6616**
Shems (USA ISSN 1550-3089) **3564**
Shenandoah (USA ISSN 0037-3583) **5238**
Shenandoah Newsletter (USA) **3564**
Shenandoah Valley *see* The Shenandoah Valley & Mountains of the Virginias **8755**
The Shenandoah Valley and Mountains of the Virginias *see* The Shenandoah Valley & Mountains of the Virginias **8755**
The Shenandoah Valley & Mountains of the Virginias (USA ISSN 1559-940X) **8755**
Shenandoah Valley Folk Art and Heritage Center Newsletter (USA ISSN 1096-3014) **3782**
Shenaton Hidrologi Le-Yisrael *see* Hydrological Yearbook of Israel **2795**
Shenaton Statisti Le-Nimele Yisra'el *see* Yearbook of Israel Ports Statistics **8999**
Shenaton Statisti le-Yisrael *see* Israel. Central Bureau of Statistics. Statistical Abstract of Israel **8381**
▼ Shenbian Kexue/Science Around Us (CHN ISSN 1673-0941) **2912**
Sheng Huo Qing Bao *see* Queensland Chinese News **3796**
Shenghua Yaowu Zazhi *see* Zhongguo Shenghua Yaowu Zazhi **6887**
Shenghuo Chuangzao/Life - Creation (CHN) **3828**
• Shenghuo Ribao/Life Daily (CHN) **3828**
• Shenghuo yu Jiankang/Life & Health (CHN ISSN 1009-3613) **6996**
Shenghuobao/Life News (CHN) **3828**
Shenghuobao Hedingben *see* Shenghuobao **3828**
• Shengjingjibing yu Jingshen Weisheng/Nervous Diseases and Mental Hygiene (CHN ISSN 1009-6574) **6185**
• ➤ Shengli Kexue Jinzhan/Progress in Physiological Sciences (CHN ISSN 0559-7765) **928**
• ➤ Shengli Xuebao/Acta Physiologica Sinica (CHN ISSN 0371-0874) **928**
Shengli zhi Guang *see* Victorious **7192**
• Shengming de Huaxue/Chemistry of Life (CHN ISSN 1000-1336) **745**
• Shengming Kexue/Chinese Bulletin of Life Sciences (CHN ISSN 1004-0374) **704**
• Shengming Kexue Yanjiu/Life Science Research (CHN ISSN 1007-7847) **704**
• Shengming Kexue Yiqi/Life Science Instruments (CHN ISSN 1671-7929) **704**
• Shengming Shijie/Life World (CHN ISSN 1673-0437) **817**
• Shengsixue Yanjiu/Journal of Life-and-Death Studies (TWN ISSN 1812-7274) **4475**
• Shengtai Duli Xuebao/Asian Journal of Ecotoxicolog (CHN ISSN 1673-5897) **3466**
Shengtai Huanjing yu Baohu/Ecological Environment and Protection (CHN ISSN 1007-0508) **3466**
Shengtai Jingji/Ecological Economy (CHN ISSN 1671-4407) **1173**
• ➤ Shengtai Xuebao/Acta Ecologica Sinica (CHN ISSN 1000-0933) **3466**
• Shengtai yu Nongcun Huanjing Xuebao/Journal of Ecology and Rural Environment (CHN ISSN 1673-4831) **3466**
• ➤ Shengtaixue Zazhi/Chinese Journal of Ecology (CHN ISSN 1000-4890) **3466**
• ➤ Shengwu Duoyangxing/Chinese Biodiversity (CHN ISSN 1005-0094) **704**
• ➤ Shengwu Gongcheng Xuebao/Chinese Journal of Biotechnology (CHN ISSN 1000-3061) **770**
• Shengwu Guke Cailiao yu Linchuang Yanjiu/Orthopaedic Biomechanics Materials and Clinical Study (CHN ISSN 1672-5972) **6073**
• ➤ Shengwu Huaxue yu Shengwu Wuli Jinzhan/Progress in Biochemistry and Biophysics (CHN ISSN 1000-3282) **745**
• Shengwu Jishu/Biotechnology (CHN ISSN 1004-311X) **770**
• Shengwu Jishu Tongbao/Bulletin of Biological Technology (CHN ISSN 1002-5464) **770**
• Shengwu Jishu Tongxun/Letters in Biotechnology (CHN ISSN 1009-0002) **770**
• Shengwu Shuxue Xuebao/Journal of Biomathematics (CHN ISSN 1001-9626) **704**
• Shengwu Yixue Gongcheng yu Linchuang/Biomedical Engineering & Clinical Medicine (CHN ISSN 1009-7090) **5713**
• Shengwu Yixue Gongchengxue Jinzhan/Progress in Biomedical Engineering (CHN ISSN 1674-1242) **751**
• Shengwu Yixue Gongchengxue Zazhi/Journal of Biomedical Engineering (CHN ISSN 1001-5515) **5713**
Shengwuxue Jiaoxue *see* Biology Teaching **660**
• ➤ Shengwuxue Tongbao/Bulletin of Biology (CHN ISSN 0006-3193) **704**
• Shengwuxue Zazhi/Journal of Biology (CHN ISSN 1008-9632) **704**
• Shengwuzhi Huaxue Gongcheng/Biomass Chemical Engineering (CHN ISSN 1673-5854) **3255**
• Shengxue Jishu/Technical Acoustics (CHN ISSN 1000-3630) **7089**
• ➤ Shengxue Xuebao/Chinese Journal of Acoustics (CHN ISSN 0371-0025) **7089**
• Shengzhi Yixue Zazhi/Journal of Reproductive Medicine (CHN ISSN 1004-3845) **6004**
• Shengzhi yu Biyun (CHN ISSN 0253-357X) **973**
Shenji Wenzhai/Auditor's Digest (CHN ISSN 1008-3243) **1301**
• Shenji Yanjiu/Auditing Studies (CHN ISSN 1002-4239) **1301**
• ➤ Shenji Yuekan (CHN ISSN 1672-8939) **1301**
Shenjian/God Sword (CHN ISSN 1004-4752) **5371**
• Shenjing Jiepouxue Zazhi/Chinese Journal of Neuroanatomy (CHN ISSN 1000-7547) **6185**
Shenjing Kexue Tongbao (Yinwen Ban) *see* Neuroscience Bulletin **6169**
Shenyang Agricultural University. Journal *see* Shenyang Nongye Daxue Xuebao **155**
• Shenyang Daxue Xuebao/Shenyang University. Journal (CHN ISSN 1008-9225) **8001**
• Shenyang Gongye Daxue Xuebao/Shenyang University of Technology. Journal (CHN ISSN 1000-1646) **7915**
▼ • ➤ Shenyang Gongye Daxue Xuebao (Shehui Kexue Ban)/Shenyang Institute of Technology. Journal (Social Science Edition) (CHN ISSN 1674-0823) **8001**
Shenyang Gongye Xueyuan Xuebao/Shenyang Institute of Technology. Journal *see* Shenyang Gongye Daxue Xuebao (Shehui Kexue Ban) **8001**
Shenyang Gongye Xueyuan Xuebao/Shenyang Institute of Technology. Journal *see* Shenyang Gongye Daxue Xuebao **7915**
• Shenyang Hangkong Gongye Xueyuan Xuebao/Shenyang Institute of Aeronautical Engineering. Journal (CHN ISSN 1007-1385) **70**
• Shenyang Huagong Xueyuan Xuebao/Shenyang Institute of Chemical Technology. Journal (CHN ISSN 1004-4639) **7915**
Shenyang Institute of Aeronautical Engineering. Journal *see* Shenyang Hangkong Gongye Xueyuan Xuebao **70**
Shenyang Institute of Chemical Technology. Journal *see* Shenyang Huagong Xueyuan Xuebao **7915**
Shenyang Institute of Technology. Journal (Social Science Edition) *see* Shenyang Gongye Daxue Xuebao (Shehui Kexue Ban) **8001**
• Shenyang Jianzhu Daxue Xuebao (Shehui Kexue Ban)/Shenyang Jianzhu University. Journal (Social Science Edition) (CHN ISSN 1673-1387) **457**
• Shenyang Jianzhu Daxue Xuebao (Ziran Kexue Ban)/Shenyang Jianzhu University. Journal (Natural Science Edition) (CHN) **7915**
Shenyang Jianzhu Gongcheng Xueyuan Xuebao (Shehui Kexue Ban)/Shenyang Architectural and Civil Engineering University. Journal (Social Science) *see* Shenyang Jianzhu Daxue Xuebao (Shehui Kexue Ban) **457**
Shenyang Jianzhu Gongcheng Xueyuan Xuebao (Ziran Kexue Ban)/Shenyang Architecture and Civil Engineering University. Journal (Natural Science Edition) *see* Shenyang Jianzhu Daxue Xuebao (Ziran Kexue Ban) **7915**
Shenyang Jianzhu University. Journal (Natural Science Edition) *see* Shenyang Jianzhu Daxue Xuebao (Ziran Kexue Ban) **7915**

Shenyang Jianzhu University. Journal (Social Science Edition) *see* Shenyang Jianzhu Daxue Xuebao (Shehui Kexue Ban) **457**
• Shenyang Ligong Daxue Xuebao/Shenyang Ligong University. Transactions (CHN) **7915**
Shenyang Ligong University. Transactions *see* Shenyang Ligong Daxue Xuebao **7915**
Shenyang Medical College. Journal *see* Shenyang Yixueyuan Xuebao **5713**
• Shenyang Nongye Daxue Xuebao/Shenyang Agricultural University. Journal (CHN ISSN 1000-1700) **155**
• Shenyang Nongye Daxue Xuebao (Shehui Kexue Ban) (CHN ISSN 1008-9713) **8001**
Shenyang Normal University. Journal (Natural Science Edition) *see* Shenyang Shifan Daxue Xuebao (Ziran Kexue Ban) **7915**
Shenyang Normal University. Journal. (Social Science Edition) *see* Shenyang Shifan Daxue Xuebao (Shehui Kexue Ban) **8001**
Shenyang Pharmaceutical University. Journal *see* Shenyang Yaoke Daxue Xuebao **6880**
Shenyang Physical Education Institute. Journal *see* Shenyang Tiyu Xueyuan Xuebao **2912**
• ➤ Shenyang Shifan Daxue Xuebao (Shehui Kexue Ban)/Shenyang Normal University. Journal. (Social Science Edition) (CHN) **8001**
• ➤ Shenyang Shifan Daxue Xuebao (Ziran Kexue Ban)/Shenyang Normal University. Journal (Natural Science Edition) (CHN ISSN 1673-5862) **7915**
Shenyang Shifan Xueyuan Xuebao (Shehui Kexue Ban) *see* Shenyang Shifan Daxue Xuebao (Shehui Kexue Ban) **8001**
Shenyang Shifan Xueyuan Xuebao (Ziran Kexue Ban) *see* Shenyang Shifan Daxue Xuebao (Ziran Kexue Ban) **7915**
• Shenyang Tiyu Xueyuan Xuebao/Shenyang Physical Education Institute. Journal (CHN ISSN 1004-0560) **2912**
Shenyang University. Journal *see* Shenyang Daxue Xuebao **8001**
Shenyang University of Technology. Journal *see* Shenyang Gongye Daxue Xuebao **7915**
• ➤ Shenyang Yaoke Daxue Xuebao/Shenyang Pharmaceutical University. Journal (CHN ISSN 1006-2858) **6880**
Shenyang Yinyue Xueyuan Xuebao *see* Yuefu Xin Sheng **6630**
• Shenyang Yixueyuan Xuebao/Shenyang Medical College. Journal (CHN ISSN 1008-2344) **5713**
• Shenzangbing yu Touxi Shenyizhi Zazhi/Nephrosis - Dialysis and Renal Transplantation (CHN ISSN 1006-298X) **6274**
Shenzhen Commercial News *see* Shenzhen Shangbao **1582**
• Shenzhen Daxue Xuebao (Ligong Ban)/Shenzhen University. Journal (Science & Engineering Edition) (CHN ISSN 1000-2618) **7915**
• Shenzhen Daxue Xuebao (Renwen Sheke Ban)/Shenzhen University. Journal (Humanities, Social Sciences Edition) (CHN ISSN 1000-260X) **2912**
Shenzhen Fengcai/Shenzhen Panorama Weekly (CHN) **3828**
Shenzhen Journal of Integrated Traditional and Western Medicine *see* Shenzhen Zhongxiyi Jiehe Zazhi **5713**
Shenzhen Panorama Weekly *see* Shenzhen Fengcai **3828**
Shenzhen Polytechnic. Journal *see* Shenzhen Zhiye Jiezhu Xueyuan Xuebao **7915**
Shenzhen Shangbao/Shenzhen Commercial News (CHN) **1582**
Shenzhen Special Economic Zone Daily *see* Shenzhen Tequbao **3828**
Shenzhen Statistical Yearbook *see* Shenzhen Tongji Nianjian (Year) **1262**
• Shenzhen Tequbao/Shenzhen Special Economic Zone Daily (CHN) **3828**
Shenzhen Today (HKG) **1517**
Shenzhen Tongji Nianjian (Year)/Shenzhen Statistical Yearbook (HKG) **1262**
Shenzhen University. Journal (Humanities, Social Sciences Edition) *see* Shenzhen Daxue Xuebao (Renwen Sheke Ban) **2912**
Shenzhen University. Journal (Science & Engineering Edition) *see* Shenzhen Daxue Xuebao (Ligong Ban) **7915**
Shenzhen Wanbao (CHN) **3828**
• Shenzhen Zhiye Jiezhu Xueyuan Xuebao/Shenzhen Polytechnic. Journal (CHN ISSN 1672-0318) **7915**
• Shenzhen Zhongxiyi Jiehe Zazhi/Shenzhen Journal of Integrated Traditional and Western Medicine (CHN ISSN 1007-0893) **5713**
Shenzhou Chuanqi (CHN) **5371**
• Shenzhou Xueren/China's Scholars Abroad (CHN ISSN 1002-6738) **3002**
Shepard's Acts and Cases by Popular Names (USA) **4783**
• Shepard's Alabama Case Name Citator (USA ISSN 1052-570X) **4960**
Shepard's Alabama Case Names Citations *see* Shepard's Alabama Case Name Citator **4960**
• Shepard's Alabama Citations (USA ISSN 0730-3572) **4960**
Shepard's Alaska Case Names Citations *see* Shepard's Alaska Case Names Citator **4960**
Shepard's Alaska Case Names Citator (USA ISSN 1052-5696) **4960**
• Shepard's Alaska Citations (USA ISSN 0488-6097) **4960**
Shepard's Arizona Case Names Citations *see* Shepard's Arizona Case Names Citator **4960**
Shepard's Arizona Case Names Citator (USA ISSN 1052-567X) **4960**
• Shepard's Arizona Citations (USA ISSN 0730-3629) **4960**
Shepard's Arkansas Case Names Citations *see* Shepard's Arkansas Case Names Citator **4783**
• Shepard's Arkansas Case Names Citator (USA ISSN 1052-5688) **4783**
• Shepard's Arkansas Citations (USA ISSN 0730-3637) **4960**
Shepard's Atlantic Reporter Citations (USA ISSN 0730-2053) **4960**
Shepard's Bankruptcy Case Name Citations *see* Shepard's Bankruptcy Case Name Citator **1383**
Shepard's Bankruptcy Case Name Citator (USA ISSN 1048-0587) **1383**
• Shepard's Bankruptcy Citations (USA ISSN 0730-1936) **1383**
Shepard's California Annotations *see* Shepard's California Citations **4960**
Shepard's California Case Names Citations *see* Shepard's California Case Names Citator **4960**
• Shepard's California Case Names Citator (USA ISSN 1048-0757) **4960**
• Shepard's California Citations (USA ISSN 0730-3661) **4960**
Shepard's California Citations Statutes *see* Shepard's California Citations **4960**
• Shepard's California Reporter Citations (USA ISSN 0559-7781) **4960**
Shepard's Citations. C F R *see* Shepard's Code of Federal Regulations Citations **4783**
Shepard's Citations. Federal Law *see* Shepard's Federal Tax Citator **4961**
Shepard's Citations. Federal Reporter *see* Shepard's Federal Citations **4783**
Shepard's Citations. Federal Rules *see* Shepard's Federal Rules Citations **4961**
Shepard's citations. Federal Supplement *see* Shepard's Federal Citations **4783**
• Shepard's Citations for Annotations (USA ISSN 1047-9163) **4960**
Shepard's Citations. Illinois Decisions, Northeast Reporter, Illinois Statutes *see* Shepard's Illinois Citations **4961**
Shepard's Citations. Illinois Official, Illinois Statutes *see* Shepard's Illinois Citations **4961**
Shepard's Citations. Louisiana Cases *see* Shepard's Louisiana Citations **4962**
Shepard's Citations. Massachusetts *see* Shepard's Massachusetts Citations **4962**
Shepard's Citations. Michigan *see* Shepard's Michigan Citations **4962**
Shepard's Citations. New Jersey Cases, New Jersey Statutes *see* Shepard's New Jersey Citations **4962**
Shepard's Citations. Ohio Case Citations *see* Shepard's Ohio Citations **4963**
Shepard's Citations. Ohio Case Citations Archive. Ohio Statutes *see* Shepard's Ohio Citations **4963**
Shepard's Citations. Pennsylvania Official Cases, Pennsylvania Statutes *see* Shepard's Pennsylvania Citations **4963**
Shepard's Citations. Pennsylvania Unofficial Cases, Pennsylvania Statutes *see* Shepard's Pennsylvania Citations **4963**
Shepard's Citations. S C Statutes, W V Statutes *see* Shepard's South Carolina Citations **4964**
Shepard's Citations. S C Statutes, W V Statutes *see* Shepard's West Virginia Citations **4964**
Shepard's Citations. Tennessee *see* Shepard's Tennessee Citations **4964**
Shepard's Citations. Texas Cases *see* Shepard's Texas Citations **4964**
Shepard's Citations. Texas Statutes *see* Shepard's Texas Citations **4964**
Shepard's Citations. Virginia *see* Shepard's Virginia Citations **4964**
• Shepard's Code of Federal Regulations Citations (USA ISSN 0730-465X) **4783**
Shepard's Colorado Case Names Citations *see* Shepard's Colorado Case Names Citator **4960**
Shepard's Colorado Case Names Citator (USA ISSN 1052-5653) **4960**
• Shepard's Colorado Citations (USA ISSN 0730-2096) **4960**
Shepard's Connecticut Case Names Citations *see* Shepard's Connecticut Case Names Citator **4960**
Shepard's Connecticut Case Names Citator (USA ISSN 1052-5661) **4960**
• Shepard's Connecticut Citations (USA ISSN 0730-3688) **4961**
Shepard's Criminal Justice Citations (USA ISSN 0363-0978) **4898**
Shepard's Delaware Case Names Citations *see* Shepard's Delaware Case Names Citator **4961**
Shepard's Delaware Case Names Citator (USA ISSN 1082-0329) **4961**
• Shepard's Delaware Citations (USA ISSN 0730-5869) **4961**
Shepard's District of Columbia Case Names Citations *see* Shepard's District of Columbia Case Names Citator **4961**
Shepard's District of Columbia Case Names Citator (USA ISSN 1052-5645) **4961**
• Shepard's District of Columbia Citations (USA ISSN 0730-5877) **4961**
• Shepard's Employment Law Citations (USA ISSN 1087-349X) **1707**
• Shepard's Environmental Law Citations (Federal) (USA ISSN 1088-9280) **4961**
Shepard's Federal Circuit Table Citations (USA) **4783**
Shepard's Federal Citations (USA ISSN 0730-4633) **4783**
• Shepard's Federal Energy Law Citations (USA ISSN 0746-312X) **4783**
• Shepard's Federal Law Citations in Selected Law Reviews (USA ISSN 0094-9531) **4783**
• Shepard's Federal O S H A Citations (Occupational Safety and Health) (USA) **4961**
• Shepard's Federal Rules Citations (USA ISSN 1048-0838) **4961**
Shepard's Federal Statute Citations (USA ISSN 1089-411X) **4783**
• Shepard's Federal Tax Citator (USA ISSN 1092-275X) **4961**
Shepard's Florida Case Names Citations *see* Shepard's Florida Case Names Citator **4961**
• Shepard's Florida Case Names Citator (USA ISSN 1048-096X) **4961**
• Shepard's Florida Citations (USA ISSN 0730-3718) **4961**
• Shepard's Georgia Citations (USA ISSN 0730-3742) **4961**
Shepard's Hawaii Case Name Citator (USA ISSN 1052-5920) **4961**
Shepard's Hawaii Case Names Citations *see* Shepard's Hawaii Case Name Citator **4961**
• Shepard's Hawaii Citations (USA ISSN 0730-5885) **4961**
• Shepard's Idaho Citations (USA ISSN 0730-5893) **4961**
Shepard's Illinois Case Names Citations *see* Shepard's Illinois Case Names Citator **4961**
• Shepard's Illinois Case Names Citator (USA ISSN 1048-0765) **4961**
• Shepard's Illinois Citations (USA ISSN 0730-3904) **4961**
• Shepard's Immigration and Naturalization Citations (USA ISSN 0746-3138) **4783**
• Shepard's Indiana Citations (USA ISSN 0730-3831) **4961**
• Shepard's Intellectual Property Law Citations (USA ISSN 1087-1268) **4783**
Shepard's Iowa Case Names Citations *see* Shepard's Iowa Case Names Citator **4961**
Shepard's Iowa Case Names Citator (USA ISSN 1052-5947) **4961**
• Shepard's Iowa Citations (USA ISSN 0730-3866) **4961**
• Shepard's Kansas Citations (USA ISSN 0730-3947) **4961**
Shepard's Kentucky Case Names Citations *see* Shepard's Kentucky Case Names Citator **4961**
• Shepard's Kentucky Case Names Citator (USA ISSN 1052-5963) **4961**
• Shepard's Kentucky Citations (USA ISSN 0730-3971) **4961**
• Shepard's Labor Arbitration Citations (USA ISSN 1049-5096) **4961**
• Shepard's Labor Law Citations (USA ISSN 1086-976X) **1707**
• Shepard's Law Review Citations (USA ISSN 0582-9887) **4783**
Shepard's Louisiana Case Names Citations *see* Shepard's Louisiana Case Names Citator **4962**
• Shepard's Louisiana Case Names Citator (USA ISSN 1048-0773) **4962**
• Shepard's Louisiana Citations (USA ISSN 0730-4005) **4962**
• Shepard's Maine Citations (USA ISSN 0730-5923) **4962**
Shepard's Maryland Case Names Citator (USA ISSN 1052-598X) **4962**
• Shepard's Maryland Citations (USA ISSN 0730-403X) **4962**
Shepard's Massachusetts Case Name Citator (USA ISSN 1048-0692) **4962**
Shepard's Massachusetts Case Names Citations *see* Shepard's Massachusetts Case Name Citator **4962**
• Shepard's Massachusetts Citations (USA ISSN 0730-4064) **4962**
Shepard's Michigan Case Names Citations *see* Shepard's Michigan Case Names Citator **4962**
Shepard's Michigan Case Names Citator (USA ISSN 1048-0684) **4962**
• Shepard's Michigan Citations (USA ISSN 0730-4102) **4962**
• Shepard's Military Justice Citations (USA ISSN 0163-1101) **4972**
• Shepard's Minnesota Citations (USA ISSN 0730-4145) **4962**
Shepard's Mississippi Case Names Citations *see* Shepard's Mississippi Case Names Citator **4962**
• Shepard's Mississippi Case Names Citator (USA ISSN 1052-6323) **4962**
• Shepard's Mississippi Citations (USA ISSN 0488-6119) **4962**
Shepard's Missouri Case Names Citations *see* Shepard's Missouri Case Names Citator **4962**
• Shepard's Missouri Case Names Citator (USA ISSN 1048-0676) **4962**
• Shepard's Missouri Citations (USA ISSN 0730-417X) **4962**
Shepard's Montana Case Names Citations *see* Shepard's Montana Case Names Citator **4962**
Shepard's Montana Case Names Citator (USA ISSN 1082-927X) **4962**
• Shepard's Montana Citations (USA ISSN 0730-5931) **4962**
Shepard's Nebraska Case Names Citations *see* Shepard's Nebraska Case Names Citator **4962**
Shepard's Nebraska Case Names Citator (USA ISSN 1052-6315) **4962**
• Shepard's Nebraska Citations (USA ISSN 0730-594X) **4962**
Shepard's Nevada Case Names Citations *see* Shepard's Nevada Case Names Citator **4962**
Shepard's Nevada Case Names Citator (USA ISSN 1052-6307) **4962**
• Shepard's Nevada Citations (USA ISSN 0730-5974) **4962**
Shepard's New Hampshire Case Names Citations *see* Shepard's New Hampshire Case Names Citator **4962**
Shepard's New Hampshire Case Names Citator (USA ISSN 1048-0668) **4962**
• Shepard's New Hampshire Citations (USA ISSN 0730-5982) **4962**
Shepard's New Jersey Case Names Citations *see* Shepard's New Jersey Citations **4962**
Shepard's New Jersey Case Names Citations *see* Shepard's New Jersey Case Names Citator **4962**
Shepard's New Jersey Case Names Citator (USA ISSN 1048-065X) **4962**
• Shepard's New Jersey Citations (USA ISSN 0730-420X) **4962**
• Shepard's New Mexico Citations (USA ISSN 0730-6008) **4962**
• Shepard's New York Court of Appeals Case Names Citator (USA ISSN 1048-0781) **4963**
• Shepard's New York Court of Appeals Citations (USA ISSN 0730-4277) **4963**
• Shepard's New York Miscellaneous Case Names Citator (USA ISSN 1046-7092) **4963**
• Shepard's New York Miscellaneous Citations (USA ISSN 0730-4269) **4963**
• Shepard's New York Statute Citations (USA ISSN 0730-4242) **4963**
• Shepard's New York Supplement Citations (USA ISSN 0730-4234) **4963**
• Shepard's New York Supreme Court Appellate Division Case Names Citator (USA ISSN 1048-079X) **4963**
Shepard's New York Supreme Court Appellate Division Citations *see* Shepard's New York Supreme Court Citations **4963**
• Shepard's New York Supreme Court Citations (USA ISSN 0730-4285) **4963**
• Shepard's North Carolina Citations (USA ISSN 0730-2126) **4963**
• Shepard's North Dakota Citations (USA ISSN 0730-6016) **4963**
• Shepard's Northeastern Reporter Citations (USA ISSN 0730-1979) **4963**
Shepard's Northwestern Reporter Case Names Citations *see* Shepard's Northwestern Reporter Case Names Citator **4963**
Shepard's Northwestern Reporter Case Names Citator (USA ISSN 1088-4572) **4963**
• Shepard's Northwestern Reporter Citations (USA ISSN 0730-4706) **4963**
• Shepard's Ohio Citations (USA ISSN 0730-4293) **4963**
• Shepard's Ohio Unreported Appellate Citations (USA ISSN 1084-7987) **4963**
Shepard's Oklahoma Case Names Citations *see* Shepard's Oklahoma Case Names Citator **4963**
Shepard's Oklahoma Case Names Citator (USA ISSN 1052-6277) **4963**
• Shepard's Oklahoma Citations (USA ISSN 0730-4323) **4963**
• Shepard's Oregon Citations (USA ISSN 0730-4358) **4963**
• Shepard's Pacific Reporter Citations (USA ISSN 0730-1987) **4783**
Shepard's Pennsylvania Case Name Citations *see* Shepard's Pennsylvania Case Names Citator **4963**
Shepard's Pennsylvania Case Names Citator (USA ISSN 1048-0544) **4963**
• Shepard's Pennsylvania Citations (USA) **4963**
Shepard's Professional and Judicial Conduct Citations (USA ISSN 0730-6229) **4963**
Shepard's Puerto Rico Case Names Citations *see* Shepard's Puerto Rico Citations **4964**
Shepard's Puerto Rico Case Names Citations *see* Shepard's Puerto Rico Case Names Citator **4964**
Shepard's Puerto Rico Case Names Citator (USA ISSN 1052-6641) **4964**
Shepard's Puerto Rico Citations (USA ISSN 0730-6261) **4964**
Shepard's Restatement of the Law Citations (USA ISSN 0730-4641) **4964**
Shepard's Rhode Island Case Names Citations *see* Shepard's Rhode Island Case Names Citator **4964**
Shepard's Rhode Island Case Names Citator (USA ISSN 1084-7979) **4964**
• Shepard's Rhode Island Citations (USA ISSN 0730-6024) **4964**
Shepard's South Carolina Case Names Citations *see* Shepard's South Carolina Case Names Citator **4964**

Title

10864 SHEPARD'S SOUTH CAROLINA CASE NAMES CITATOR ULRICH'S PERIODICALS

• Shepard's South Carolina Case Names Citator (USA ISSN 1052-665X) **4964**
• Shepard's South Carolina Citations (USA ISSN 0730-6059) **4964**
• Shepard's South Dakota Citations (USA ISSN 0730-6032) **4964**
• Shepard's Southeastern Reporter Citations (USA ISSN 0730-4692) **4964**
• Shepard's Southern Reporter Citations (USA ISSN 0730-1944) **4964**
• Shepard's Southwestern Reporter Citations (USA ISSN 0730-1952) **4964**
• Shepard's Tennessee Citations (USA ISSN 0730-4439) **4964**
• Shepard's Texas Case Names Citator (USA ISSN 8750-1120) **4964**
• Shepard's Texas Citations (USA ISSN 0730-4463) **4964**
• Shepard's Uniform Commercial Code Case Citations (USA ISSN 1048-1273) **4783**
Shepard's Uniform Commercial Code Citations (USA ISSN 0745-5925) **4783**
• Shepard's United States Administrative Citations (USA ISSN 0582-9909) **4783**
Shepard's United States Administrative Law Citations *see* Shepard's United States Administrative Citations **4783**
• Shepard's United States Patents and Trademarks Case Name Citator (USA ISSN 1075-7317) **4783**
Shepard's Utah Case Names Citations *see* Shepard's Utah Case Names Citator **4964**
Shepard's Utah Case Names Citator (USA ISSN 1084-7847) **4964**
• Shepard's Utah Citations (USA ISSN 0730-6083) **4964**
Shepard's Vermont Case Names Citations *see* Shepard's Vermont Case Names Citator **4964**
Shepard's Vermont Case Names Citator (USA ISSN 1084-760X) **4964**
• Shepard's Vermont Citations (USA ISSN 0730-6091) **4964**
Shepard's Virginia Case Names Citations *see* Shepard's Virginia Case Names Citator **4964**
• Shepard's Virginia Case Names Citator (USA ISSN 1052-6676) **4964**
• Shepard's Virginia Citations (USA ISSN 0730-4498) **4964**
Shepard's Washington Case Name Citations *see* Shepard's Washington Case Names Citator **4964**
Shepard's Washington Case Names Citator (USA ISSN 1048-0536) **4964**
• Shepard's Washington Citations (USA ISSN 0730-4528) **4964**
Shepard's West Virginia Case Names Citations *see* Shepard's West Virginia Case Names Citator **4964**
• Shepard's West Virginia Case Names Citator (USA ISSN 1052-6684) **4964**
• Shepard's West Virginia Citations (USA ISSN 0730-4579) **4964**
• Shepard's Wisconsin Citations (USA ISSN 0730-4552) **4964**
Shepard's Wisconsin Express Citations *see* Shepard's Wisconsin Citations **4964**
• Shepard's Wyoming Citations (USA ISSN 0730-6105) **4965**
Shepards's West Virginia Citations and Annotations *see* Shepard's West Virginia Citations **4964**
Shephard's Air Ambulance Handbook *see* Shephard's Public Service Aviation Handbook **8551**
Shephard's Civil Helicopter Handbook (GBR ISSN 1365-649X) **8551**
Shephard's Defence & Public Service Helicopter *see* Defence Helicopter **52**
Shephard's Electronic Warfare Handbook (GBR ISSN 1461-6203) **3331**
Shephard's Inflight Handbook (GBR ISSN 1461-619X) **8785**
Shephard's Military Helicopter Handbook (GBR ISSN 1365-6600) **8551**
Shephard's Police Aviation Handbook *see* Shephard's Public Service Aviation Handbook **8551**
Shephard's Public Service Aviation Handbook (GBR) **8551**
Shephard's Regional Aviation Handbook *see* Low-Fare and Regional Aviation **8548**
Shephard's Unmanned Vehicles Handbook (GBR ISSN 1351-3478) **70**
The Shepherd (GBR ISSN 0260-0382) **7706**
The Shepherd (USA ISSN 8750-7897) **300**
The Shepherd College Picket (USA) **2300**
The Shepherd's Voice (USA ISSN 1945-4783) **2213**
Sheppard's Book Dealers in British Isles (GBR ISSN 0950-0715) **7573**
Sheppard's Book Dealers in India and the Orient (GBR) **7573**
Sheppard's Book Dealers in Japan (GBR) **7573**
Sheppard's Bookdealers in Australia and New Zealand (GBR ISSN 0962-2764) **7573**
Sheppard's Bookdealers in Europe (GBR ISSN 0963-0171) **7573**
Sheppard's Bookdealers in North America (GBR ISSN 0269-1469) **7573**
Sheppard's International Directory of Ephemera Dealers (GBR) **7573**
Sheppard's International Directory Print & Map Sellers (GBR ISSN 0963-9721) **7573**
▼ • Shepreneur (USA ISSN 1948-0121) **1173**
Sher-i-Punjab (IND) **3889**
Sherbet (GBR) **5083**
Sherbondy Beacon (USA ISSN 8755-0547) **3782**
Shereese Hair & Beauty Magazine (USA ISSN 1558-898X) **591**
• Sheriff Magazine (USA ISSN 1070-8170) **2668**
Sheriff Services Selected Operating Procedures (CAN) **4783**
Sherkin Comment (IRL ISSN 0791-2447) **3608**
Sherlock Holmes Journal (GBR ISSN 0037-3621) **5415**
Sherlockian Tidbits (USA ISSN 1040-4937) **5415**
Sherman County, for the Record (USA ISSN 1086-2269) **4312**
Sherman's Travel (USA ISSN 1932-9113) **8755**
Sheshunoff Bank Ownership News *see* Bank Operations and Technology Alert **1315**
Sheshunoff Credit Union Asset/Liability Management Report *see* Credit Union Asset/Liability Management Report **1333**
The Sheshunoff N A F C U's Regulatory Compliance Report *see* N A F C U's Credit Union Regulatory Compliance Report **4876**
Shest'desat Chetyre - Shakhmatnoe Obozrenie *see* 64 - Shakhmatnoe Obozrenie **8217**
Shestnadtsat': Vse, Chto Vy Khotite Znat' o Sekse, no Boites' Sprosit' (RUS) **8883**
Shetland Bird Report (GBR ISSN 1364-4149) **914**
Shetland Fishing News (GBR ISSN 1366-4425) **3608**
Shetland Life (GBR ISSN 0260-5732) **3870**
De Shetland Pony (NLD ISSN 1384-0568) **8298**
Shetland Pony Stud-Book Society Magazine (GBR) **8298**
Shetland Times (GBR ISSN 0969-5656) **3870**
Shetlandsponnyn (SWE ISSN 1104-7860) **8298**
Shetu-Bondha (GBR) **5371**
▼ • Shetuan Guanli Yanjiu/Research of Administration of N P Os (CHN ISSN 1674-1323) **8068**
Shevchenko Scientific Society. Memoirs *see* Naukove Tovarystvo Imeni Shevchenka. Zapysky **3553**
Shevut *see* Shvut **3564**
• Shewai Shuiwu/International Taxation in China (CHN ISSN 1006-3056) **1943**
Sheying Shijie/Photography World (CHN ISSN 1002-6770) **6976**
Sheying yu Shexiang/Photo & Video (CHN ISSN 1006-4788) **6976**
Sheying Zhiuou/The Photographers' Company (CHN ISSN 1004-0153) **6976**
Sheyingjia Zazhi/Photographers International (TWN ISSN 1019-9608) **6976**
• Shezhi/Journal of Snake (CHN ISSN 1001-5639) **5713**
• Shi (CHN ISSN 1005-1848) **2261**
• Shi-hua Jishu/Petrochemical Industry Technology (CHN ISSN 1006-0235) **6792**
Shi Jie Guan Dao Gong Cheng Hui Gu *see* W P R **1042**
Shi Shen/Poems Deity (CHN) **5434**
Shi Yue/October (CHN ISSN 0257-5841) **5371**
Shia World (GBR) **7716**
Shiah (PAK) **7716**
Shiatsu Society News (GBR) **6116**
Shiawassee County Genealogical Society. Journal (USA ISSN 0735-8016) **3782**
Shibaura Institute of Technology. Research Laboratory of Engineering. Report/Shibaura Kogyo Daigaku. Kogaku Kenkyujo (JPN ISSN 0915-4566) **3219**
Shibaura Kogyo Daigaku. Kogaku Kenkyujo *see* Shibaura Institute of Technology. Research Laboratory of Engineering. Report **3219**
Shibukitsubo/Niigata Shell Club. Report (JPN ISSN 0917-7159) **963**
Shichang Bao/Market News (CHN) **1843**
Shichang Guancha. Guanggaozhu *see* Guanggaozhu Shichang Guancha **26**
Shichang Yingxiao/Marketing (CHN ISSN 1009-1351) **1843**
Shichang Yingxiao Wenzhai Ka/Marketing Abstracts on Cards (CHN) **1843**
Shichang yu Xiaofei Bao/Market and Consumers (CHN) **1173**
• Shichang Zhoukan/Market Weekly (CHN ISSN 1008-4428) **1173**
Shichokaku Kyoiku/Audio-Visual Education (JPN ISSN 0037-3664) **2912**
Shida Shokubutsu Bunken Mokuroku/Bibliography of Pteridophytes by Japanese Fernists (JPN) **720**
Shidai (CHN ISSN 1003-6679) **3828**
Shidai Fengcai/Modern Elegance (CHN ISSN 1004-8294) **3828**
• Shidai Jianzhu/Time + Architecture (CHN ISSN 1005-684X) **3282**
Shidai Jiaoyu/Modern Education (CHN ISSN 1672-8181) **2912**
Shidai Jiemei/Modern Sisters (CHN ISSN 1002-7459) **8883**
• Shidai Jinrong/Finance Times (CHN ISSN 1672-8661) **1383**
Shidai Wenxue (CHN) **5371**
• Shidao/Teacher Doctrines (CHN ISSN 1672-2655) **3082**
• Shidi Kexue/Wetland Science (CHN ISSN 1672-5948) **3466**
➤ The Shield (PAK ISSN 1991-8410) **6996**
Shield & Diamond (USA ISSN 8750-7536) **2300**
The Shield of Freedom (USA ISSN 1559-4807) **6446**
Shifra Stein's Day Trips from Austin (USA ISSN 1535-8232) **8756**
Shifra Stein's Day Trips from Kansas City (USA ISSN 1538-4993) **8756**
Shifra Stein's Day Trips from Phoenix, Tucson, and Flagstaff (USA ISSN 1543-0499) **8756**
Shifra Stein's Day Trips from San Antonio (USA ISSN 1545-0333) **8756**
Shifra Stein's Day Trips from San Antonio and Austin *see* Shifra Stein's Day Trips from Austin **8756**
Shifra Stein's Day Trips from San Antonio and Austin *see* Shifra Stein's Day Trips from San Antonio **8756**
Shifra Stein's Daytrips from Cincinnati *see* Day Trips from Cincinnati **8697**
Shift (NZL ISSN 1177-0775) **8603**
• Shift (Institute of Noetic Sciences) (USA) **7915**
Shifter Kart Illustrated (CAN) **4347**
Shiga Daigaku Kyoiku Gakubu Kiyo. Kyoiku Kagaku/Shiga University. Faculty of Education. Memoirs. Pedagogic Science (JPN ISSN 1342-9280) **2912**
Shiga Daigaku Kyoiku Gakubu Kiyo. Shizen Kagaku/Shiga University. Faculty of Education. Memoirs. Natural Science (JPN ISSN 1342-9272) **7915**
Shiga Daigaku Kyoikugakubu Kosho Jisshu Shisetsu Ronbunshu/Shiga University. Faculty of Education. Institute of Lake Sciences. Annual Report (JPN ISSN 0914-3068) **2798**
Shiga Ika Daigaku Zasshi/Shiga University of Medical Science. Journal (JPN ISSN 0912-3016) **5713**
Shiga Kenritsu Biwako Bunkakan Kenkyu Kiyo/Biwako Bunkakan. Annual Report (JPN ISSN 0289-7636) **2798**
Shiga-kenritsu Tanki Daigaku Gakujutsu Zasshi/Shiga Prefectural Junior College. Scientific Reports (JPN ISSN 0371-3385) **214**
Shiga Prefectural Junior College. Scientific Reports *see* Shiga-kenritsu Tanki Daigaku Gakujutsu Zasshi **214**
Shiga Prefecture. Monthly Report of Meteorology *see* Shigaken Kisho Geppo **6395**
Shiga Shizen Kyoiku Kenkyu Shisetsu Kenkyu Gyoseki/Institute of Nature Education in Shiga Heights. Bulletin (JPN ISSN 0389-9128) **2716**
Shiga University. Faculty of Education. Institute of Lake Sciences. Annual Report *see* Shiga Daigaku Kyoikugakubu Kosho Jisshu Shisetsu Ronbunshu **2798**
Shiga University. Faculty of Education. Memoirs. Natural Science *see* Shiga Daigaku Kyoiku Gakubu Kiyo. Shizen Kagaku **7915**
Shiga University. Faculty of Education. Memoirs. Pedagogic Science *see* Shiga Daigaku Kyoiku Gakubu Kiyo. Kyoiku Kagaku **2912**
Shiga University of Medical Science. Journal *see* Shiga Ika Daigaku Zasshi **5713**
Shigaken Biwako Kenkyujo Nyusu *see* Oumia **2797**
Shigaken Kisho Geppo/Shiga Prefecture. Monthly Report of Meteorology (JPN) **6395**
Shigaku *see* Odontology **5858**
Shigaku Zasshi *see* Historical Journal of Japan **4183**
➤ Shigen Chishitsu (JPN ISSN 0918-2454) **2767**
Shigen Energi Kenkyukai Koenshu/Proceedings on Study of Resources and Energy (JPN) **3147**
Shigen Kagaku Kenkyujo *see* Tokyo Institute of Technology. Research Laboratory of Resources Utilization. Report **8443**
Shigen Shori Gijutsu *see* Kankyou Shigen Kougaku **6467**
• Shigen Sozai/Mining and Materials Processing Institute of Japan. Journal (JPN ISSN 0916-1740) **6479**
Shigen to Kankyo/National Institute for Resources and Environment. Journal (JPN ISSN 0916-9997) **3466**
• ➤ Shigong Jishu/Construction Technology (CHN ISSN 1002-8498) **457**
• Shigong Qiye Guanli/Construction Enterprise Management (CHN ISSN 1001-9251) **1793**
Shigyo Taimusu/Paper Industry (JPN ISSN 0912-5019) **6738**
Shih Tzu Bulletin (USA) **6815**
Shih Tzu Reporter (USA ISSN 1040-5801) **6815**
Shih Yueh P'ing Lun *see* October Review **7160**
• Shihezi Daxue Xuebao (Zhexue Shehui Kexue Ban)/Shihezi University. Journal (Philosophy and Social Science) (CHN ISSN 1671-0304) **6952**
• Shihezi Daxue Xuebao (Ziran Kexue Ban)/Shihezi University. Journal (Natural Science) (CHN ISSN 1007-7383) **7915**
Shihezi University. Journal (Natural Science) *see* Shihezi Daxue Xuebao (Ziran Kexue Ban) **7915**
Shihezi University. Journal (Philosophy and Social Science) *see* Shihezi Daxue Xuebao (Zhexue Shehui Kexue Ban) **6952**
Shihezi Yixueyuan Xuebao/Shihezi Medical College. Journal *see* Nongken Yixue **5687**
• Shihua Jishu Yu Yingyong/Petrochemical Technology and Application (CHN ISSN 1009-0045) **6792**
Shiji/Century (CHN ISSN 1005-4715) **3828**
Shijian Pinlu Xuebao/Journal of Time and Frequency (CHN) **6406**
Shijiazhuang Railway Institute. Journal *see* Shijiazhuang Tiedao Xueyuan Xuebao **8511**
• Shijiazhuang Tiedao Xueyuan Xuebao/Shijiazhuang Railway Institute. Journal (CHN ISSN 1006-3226) **8511**
Shijiazhuang Vocational Technology Institute. Journal *see* Shijiazhuang Zhiye Jishu Xueyuan Xuebao **8001**
• Shijiazhuang Zhiye Jishu Xueyuan Xuebao/Shijiazhuang Vocational Technology Institute. Journal (CHN ISSN 1009-4873) **8001**
Shijie Bolan/World Expo (CHN ISSN 1003-0271) **3828**
• ➤ Shijie Dianxin/World Telecommunications (CHN ISSN 1001-4802) **2338**
• Shijie Dianying/World Cinema (CHN ISSN 1002-9966) **6513**
• Shijie Dianzi Yuanqijian/Global Electronics China (CHN ISSN 1006-7604) **3113**
• Shijie Dizhen Gongcheng/World Earthquake Engineering (CHN ISSN 1007-6069) **3282**
Shijie Dizhen Yicong/Translated World Seismology (CHN ISSN 1003-3238) **2789**
Shijie Ertong/World Children (CHN) **2168**
Shijie Faming/Review of World Inventions (CHN ISSN 1003-1049) **7915**
Shijie Gangtie/World Iron & Steel (CHN ISSN 1672-9587) **6332**
• Shijie Haiyun/World Shipping (CHN ISSN 1006-7728) **8660**
Shijie Hangkong Hangtian Bolan/Aerospace World *see* Shuzi Jungong **70**
• Shijie Hanxue/World Sinology (CHN ISSN 1007-0028) **3564**
• Shijie Hanyu Jiaoxue/Chinese Teaching in the World (CHN ISSN 1002-5804) **5173**
• Shijie Hedizhi Kexue/World Nuclear Geoscience (CHN ISSN 1672-0636) **2767**
• Shijie Hexin Yixue Qikan Wenzhai (Erkexue Fence)/Digest of the World Core Medical Journals (Pediatrics) (CHN) **5713**
• Shijie Hexin Yixue Qikan Wenzhai (Fuchang Kexue Fence)/Digest of the World Core Medical Journals (Obstetrics/Gynecology) (CHN) **6004**
• Shijie Hexin Yixue Qikan Wenzhai (Pifubingxue Fence)/Digest of the World Core Medical Journals (Dermatology) (CHN) **5882**
• Shijie Hexin Yixue Qikan Wenzhai (Shengjingbingxue Fence)/Digest of the World Core Medical Journals (Clinical Neurology) (CHN) **6185**
• Shijie Hexin Yixue Qikan Wenzhai (Weichangbingxue Fence)/Digest of the World Core Medical Journals (Gastroenterology) (CHN) **5931**
• Shijie Hexin Yixue Qikan Wenzhai (Xinzangbeingxue Fence)/Digest of the World Core Medical Journals (Cardiolog) (CHN) **5799**
• Shijie Hexin Yixue Qikan Wenzhai (Yankexue Fence)/Digest of the World Core Medical Journals (Ophthalmology) (CHN) **6051**
• Shijie Huanjing/World Environment (CHN ISSN 1003-2150) **3466**
• Shijie Huaren Xiaohua Zazhi/World Chinese Journal of Digestology (CHN ISSN 1009-3079) **5931**
• Shijie Jianzhu Daobao/World Architecture Herald (CHN ISSN 1000-8373) **457**
• Shijie Jingji (CHN ISSN 1002-9621) **1173**
Shijie Jingji *see* Shijie Jingjixue **1721**
Shijie Jingji Daokan/Guide to World Economy (CHN ISSN 1671-3419) **1173**
• Shijie Jingji Wenhui/World Economic Papers (CHN ISSN 0488-6364) **1173**
• Shijie Jingji Yanjiu/World Economy Study (CHN ISSN 1007-6964) **1517**
Shijie Jingjixue/World Economics (CHN ISSN 1009-7511) **1721**
Shijie Junshi/World Military Affairs (CHN ISSN 1002-4891) **6446**
• Shijie Keji Yanjiu yu Fazhan/World Research and Development on Science and Technology (CHN ISSN 1006-6055) **7915**
• Shijie Kexue (CHN ISSN 1000-0968) **7915**
• Shijie Kexue Jishu/World Science and Technology (CHN ISSN 1003-1898) **7915**
Shijie Liangshi Baogao *see* World Food Report **3668**
• Shijie Linchuang Yaowu/World Clinical Drugs (CHN ISSN 1672-9188) **6880**
• Shijie Lishi/World History (CHN ISSN 1002-011X) **4161**
• Shijie Meishu/World Art (CHN ISSN 1000-8683) **517**
• Shijie Minzu/World Ethno-National Studies (CHN ISSN 1006-8287) **355**
Shijie Nongyao/World Pesticides (CHN ISSN 1009-6485) **252**
• Shijie Nongye/World Agriculture (CHN ISSN 1002-4433) **156**
• Shijie Redai Nongye Xinxi/World Tropical Agriculture Information (CHN ISSN 1009-1726) **156**
Shijie Ribao (Monterey Park)/World Journal (Los Angeles) (USA ISSN 0740-1108) **3564**
Shijie Ribao (New York) (USA) **3564**
Shijie Ribao (San Francisco)/World Journal (San Francisco Edition) (USA ISSN 0747-5071) **3564**
• Shijie Shizhuang Zhiyuan/Elle China (CHN ISSN 1006-1169) **8883**
Shijie Suidao *see* Xiandai Suidao Jishu **1043**
• Shijie Tiyu Zhoubao/World Sports News (CHN) **8200**
† Shijie Tushu/World Books (CHN ISSN 1000-0097) **8988**
Shijie Weichangbingxue Zazhi (Yingwen) *see* World Journal of Gastroenterology **5932**

Title

Title

Sicilia Parra (USA ISSN 8755-6987) **8001**
Sicilia Tempo (ITA) **3898**
Sickle & Sheaf (USA ISSN 8750-6866) **2270**
Siculorum Gymnasium (ITA ISSN 0037-458X) **4475**
Sicurezza (ITA) **2681**
† Sicurezza Digitale (ITA ISSN 1723-5065) **8988**
Sicurezza Urbana (ITA ISSN 1972-8360) **2668**
Sid Cato's Newsletter on Annual Reports (USA ISSN 1083-6721) **1651**
SiD Fiskeren *see* 3F Fiskeren **4606**
➤ Sida: Botanical Miscellany (USA ISSN 0883-1475) **817**
Sida: Contributions to Botany *see* Botanical Research Institute of Texas. Journal **781**
SIDAahora (USA) **5826**
Sidcup & Blackfen Times (GBR ISSN 0964-3524) **3871**
• ➤ Side Effects of Drugs Annual (NLD ISSN 0378-6080) **6881**
• Side-Line Magazine (BEL) **6616**
Side-Line Music Magazine *see* Side-Line Magazine **6616**
Side-Saddle News *see* Aside World **8287**
Side X Side Action Magazine (USA) **8268**
Sidekicks (USA) **8245**
Sidelines (USA) **2301**
Sidemount Reporter (CAN ISSN 0037-4601) **4347**
Siden Saxo (DNK ISSN 0109-6028) **4263**
Siderealist (USA) **567**
Siderurgia Brasileira. Relatorio de Diretoria (BRA) **6332**
Sidmouth Herald (GBR ISSN 0968-1779) **3871**
Sidney Haughton Memorial Lectures (ZAF) **6730**
➤ Sidney Journal (USA ISSN 1480-0926) **5372**
Sidra (ISR ISSN 0334-6986) **7729**
Sidwaya (BFA ISSN 1013-655X) **3805**
Der Siebdruck (DEU ISSN 0178-2835) **7328**
Sieben Sky Magazin *see* 7sky Magazin **3959**
Sieben Tage *see* 7 Tage **3861**
Siebenbuergische Familienforschung (DEU ISSN 0175-761X) **3782**
Siebenbuergische Zeitung (DEU) **4263**
Siebenstern (DEU) **2627**
Siedlung und Eigenheim (AUT) **4427**
Siedlung und Eigenheim (DEU ISSN 0174-3600) **4427**
Sieg Tech (DEU ISSN 0934-9391) **8439**
Siegburger Studien (DEU) **4263**
Siegel's New York Law Digest *see* New York State Law Digest **4745**
Siegener Beitraege (DEU ISSN 1431-6684) **4263**
➤ Siegener Forschungen zur Romanischen Literatur- und Medienwissenschaft (DEU ISSN 1433-7983) **5372**
Siegener Periodikum zur Internationalen Empirischen Literaturwissenschaft *see* S P I E L **5366**
Siegener Schriften zur Kanonforschung (DEU ISSN 1614-578X) **5372**
Siegener Zeitung (DEU) **3856**
• Siegessaeule (DEU ISSN 0943-7657) **4379**
Siegrunen (USA ISSN 0733-0367) **6446**
• Siempre! (MEX ISSN 0185-0784) **5239**
Siempre Mujer (USA ISSN 1556-2638) **8883**
Siempre Peru (BOL) **7265**
• Sierra (USA ISSN 0161-7362) **2627**
• Sierra Atlantic (USA ISSN 0164-825X) **2627**
Sierra Carriers Newsletter (USA) **8332**
Sierra Heritage (USA ISSN 0886-6503) **3988**
Sierra Leone. Central Statistics Office. Annual Statistical Digest (SLE) **8399**
Sierra Leone Journal of Education (SLE ISSN 0022-0582) **2912**
Sierra Leone. Library Board. Report (SLE ISSN 0583-2268) **5047**
Sierra Leone. Ministry of Education. Monthly Newsletter (SLE) **2912**
Sierra Leone. Ministry of Education. Report (SLE ISSN 0080-9551) **2912**
Sierra Leone Newsletter (SLE) **3790**
Sierra Leone Publications (SLE) **5059**
Sierra Leone Trade Journal (SLE ISSN 0037-4768) **1433**
Sierra Nevada College Review *see* The Sierra Nevada Review **5372**
The Sierra Nevada Review (USA ISSN 1945-8460) **5372**
Sierra Report (CAN ISSN 1194-6148) **2627**
▼ SierraStyle Weddings (USA) **5561**
Siesta Nacional (BOL) **5372**
• Siete Dias (MEX ISSN 1563-7980) **3911**
Siete Dias *see* 7 Dias **3821**
Siete Dias Ilustrados (ARG ISSN 0037-4784) **3792**
Siete Dias Medicos (ESP ISSN 0214-3011) **5715**
Siete Dies *see* 7 Dies **3954**
Sieviete (LVA ISSN 0868-4715) **8884**
SiF News (GBR ISSN 1362-9905) **6721**
Sifre Ya'ats Hadashim/New Reference Books (ISR ISSN 0334-5262) **635**
Sifriya Laam (ISR ISSN 0037-4792) **5372**
Sifrut Yeladim Vanoar (ISR ISSN 0334-276X) **2213**
• Sift (AUS ISSN 1833-8194) **6479**
• Sight and Sound (GBR ISSN 0037-4806) **6513**
Sight and Sound News (AUS) **4111**
Sight Lecture (USA) **8551**
Sighthound Review (USA ISSN 8750-1953) **6815**
Sightline (GBR ISSN 0265-9808) **8478**
Sightlines (New York) (United States Institute for Theatre Technology, Inc. Sightlines) (USA ISSN 1048-955X) **8478**
Sights and Sounds (USA) **4076**
• Sigletter (USA) **5715**
• El Siglo (CHL) **3822**
• El Siglo (DOM ISSN 1605-3710) **3835**
• El Siglo (PAN) **3927**
Siglo 19 (MEX ISSN 0187-8530) **4312**
• Siglo XXI Ciencia and Tecnologia (CHL ISSN 0716-8136) **7916**
Siglo Cero (ESP ISSN 0210-1696) **7408**
• El Siglo de Durango (MEX ISSN 1563-7336) **3911**
• El Siglo de Torreon (MEX ISSN 1563-7344) **3911**
• Siglo Diecinueve (ESP ISSN 1136-2308) **5173**
El Siglo Digital *see* El Siglo **3927**
† El Siglo Que Viene (ESP ISSN 0214-3216) **8988**
Sigma (CHE ISSN 0037-4857) **4523**
Sigma (LUX ISSN 1018-5739) **8399**
• Sigma (NLD ISSN 0166-6967) **1793**
Sigma Phi Epsilon Journal (USA ISSN 0097-6563) **2301**
Sigma Research. Briefing Paper *see* Sigma Research. Original Research Report **4379**
• Sigma Research. Original Research Report (GBR ISSN 1754-5447) **4379**
Sigma-Serien (DNK ISSN 1399-1337) **5372**
Sigma Series in Pure Mathematics (DEU ISSN 0936-8272) **5536**
Sigma XI Newsletter (USA) **7916**
Sigma Zetan (USA ISSN 0080-9578) **7916**
† • Sigmapascal (USA) **8988**
Sigmul Bunryu Hag-hoeji/Korean Journal of Plant Taxonomy (KOR ISSN 1225-8318) **817**
• ➤ Sigmul Saengmyeong Gong Haghoeji/Korean Journal of Plant Biotechnology (KOR ISSN 1598-6365) **770**
• Sigmulbyeong Yeon'gu/Research in Plant Disease (KOR ISSN 1598-2262) **817**
Sign (CZE ISSN 1211-8605) **1843**
Sign+ *see* Sign + Silkscreen Magazine **7328**
Sign & Graphics (ZAF) **35**
Sign & Street Furniture Industry *see* Financial Survey. Sign & Street Furniture Manufacturers & Distributors **1994**
Sign and Street Furniture Manufacturers *see* Business Ratio Report: Sign and Street Furniture Manufacturers **22**
• Sign Builder Illustrated (USA ISSN 0895-0555) **35**
• Sign Business (USA ISSN 0893-9888) **35**
• ➤ Sign Language and Linguistics (Online) (NLD ISSN 1569-996X) **5173**
• ➤ Sign Language Studies (USA ISSN 0302-1475) **5174**
▼ ➤ The Sign Language Translator and Interpreter (GBR ISSN 1750-3981) **5174**
Sign Language Typology Series (NLD ISSN 1874-7833) **4076**
Sign Line *see* Sign **1843**
• Sign Media Canada (CAN ISSN 1718-3006) **530**
• Sign of the Times (USA ISSN 0891-6926) **5239**
Sign + Silkscreen Magazine (NLD ISSN 1871-6741) **7328**
• ➤ Sign Systems Studies/Trudy po Znakovym Sistemam (EST ISSN 1406-4243) **5174**
▼ Sign Tech (USA ISSN 1946-4746) **35**
• Sign Update (GBR) **35**
Sign World (GBR ISSN 0049-0466) **35**
Signa (ESP ISSN 1133-3634) **5174**
• ➤ Signa Vitae (HRV ISSN 1334-5605) **6104**
Signaal *see* Staal (The Hague) **1384**
• Signal (CAN ISSN 0228-9091) **6687**
• Signal (DEU ISSN 0721-6831) **6034**
Signal (UKR) **8511**
Signal (Boulder) (USA ISSN 1948-2493) **6395**
Signal 8-2 (USA ISSN 0037-5012) **2668**
Signal and Data Processing of Small Targets (USA ISSN 1082-1244) **3331**
▼ • Signal, Image and Video Processing (GBR ISSN 1863-1703) **2403**
• Signal International (FIN ISSN 0037-4970) **4347**
Signal Journal (USA ISSN 1535-1696) **5372**
• Signal Magazine (Fairfax) (USA ISSN 0037-4938) **2338**
• Signal Mountain (USA) **4312**
▼ • Signal Processing (MYS ISSN 1985-2339) **2437**
• ➤ Signal Processing (NLD ISSN 0165-1684) **2464**
Signal Processing Advances in Wireless Communications *see* I E E E Workshop on Signal Processing Advances in Wireless Communications. Proceedings **2324**
Signal Processing and its Applications (USA) **2466**
• ➤ Signal Processing: Image Communication (NLD ISSN 0923-5965) **2535**
Signal Processing Report (SWE ISSN 1100-8105) **3331**
Signal Smoke (USA ISSN 1931-9282) **914**
Signal Stenographique (CHE) **1854**
Signal to Noise (USA) **6616**
• ➤ Signal Transduction (DEU ISSN 1615-4053) **836**
Signal Transduction Knowledge Environment *see* Science Signaling **7911**
Signal und Draht (DEU ISSN 0037-4997) **8625**
➤ Signale (DEU ISSN 1615-1364) **1174**
Signalen uit de Binnenstad (NLD ISSN 1874-3390) **4427**
Signaler (NOR ISSN 0801-6674) **5239**
Signalering Ethiek en Gezondheid (NLD ISSN 1871-5184) **6952**
Signaleringsrapport Hulpmiddelen (NLD ISSN 1871-0794) **6116**
Signalman's Journal (USA ISSN 0037-5020) **4602**
Signal'naya Informatsiya. Khimiya Vody (RUS ISSN 0202-8948) **2096**
Signal'naya Informatsiya. Toksikologiya Lekarstvennaya (RUS ISSN 0233-6588) **6890**
signalpenpals.net *see* Signal International **4347**
Signals (AUS ISSN 1033-4688) **6537**
Signals (USA) **1966**
• Signals from the Future (USA ISSN 1084-4600) **8132**
Signaltheorie (DEU ISSN 1619-6864) **2464**
Signature (BEL) **1174**
Signature (CAN ISSN 0843-0640) **2912**
Signature (JPN) **8756**
Signature (KEN) **8756**
Signature (SGP) **8756**
Signature *see* S I Gnature (Greensboro) **2437**
Signature (Mahwah) (USA ISSN 1091-5222) **5865**
Signature Exclusive (GRC) **8756**
Signatures (USA) **2301**
Signcraft (USA ISSN 0270-4757) **35**
Signes d'Aujourd'hui (FRA ISSN 0338-2052) **6616**
Signes des Ameriques (CAN) **3564**
Signes du Present (MAR ISSN 0851-4909) **1174**
† Signes & Sens (FRA ISSN 1778-7793) **8988**
Signes Musiques (FRA ISSN 1151-4051) **6616**
Signes V itaux d'Ottawa *see* Ottawa's Vital Signs **8124**
Signewrist (USA) **3581**
• Significance (GBR ISSN 1740-9705) **8399**
Significant Data for Directors (USA ISSN 1528-1671) **1793**
Significant Incidents of Political Violence Against Americans *see* Political Violence Against Americans **2664**
▼ Significant Living (USA ISSN 1944-6330) **7681**
Significant Opportunities in Atmospheric Research and Science Newsletter *see* S O A R S Newsletter **6394**
Signifikation (DEU ISSN 1435-795X) **8132**
• Signis Media (BEL ISSN 1726-0426) **6513**
† Signmaking (CZE ISSN 1212-0588) **8988**
SIGNmatters *see* British Deaf News **4072**
Signo (BOL ISSN 0258-2112) **4475**
Signo (ESP ISSN 1134-1165) **6952**
Signo y Pensamiento (COL ISSN 0120-4823) **4475**
➤ Signo y Sena (ARG ISSN 0327-8956) **5174**
Il Signore degli Anelli. Scacchi da Collezione (ITA ISSN 1970-0407) **8200**
▼ Le Signore del Thriller (ITA ISSN 1971-8160) **5415**
Signos (CUB ISSN 0252-8606) **3622**
Signos (PER ISSN 1022-789X) **7681**
▼ • Signos Ele (ARG ISSN 1851-4863) **5174**
Signos Filosoficos (MEX ISSN 1665-1324) **6952**
Signos Historicos (MEX ISSN 1665-4420) **4161**
Signos Linguisticos (MEX ISSN 1665-1316) **5174**
Signos Literarios (MEX ISSN 1870-4050) **5372**
Signos Universitarios (ARG ISSN 0326-3932) **3002**
Signos Vitales (SLV ISSN 1729-2042) **5715**
Signotica (BRA ISSN 0103-7250) **5372**
The Signpost (USA) **2301**
Signpost for Northwest Trails (USA ISSN 8750-1600) **8332**
▼ • ➤ Signs (DNK ISSN 1902-8822) **6952**
Signs (NLD ISSN 1871-2770) **6616**
• ➤ Signs (USA ISSN 0097-9740) **8903**
Signs Canada *see* Sign Media Canada **530**
Signs Magazine (GBR ISSN 0264-8814) **1433**
Signs of the Times (GBR) **7681**
Signs of the Times (JPN ISSN 0037-5055) **7681**
Signs of the Times (USA ISSN 0037-5063) **35**
• Signs of the Times & Screen Printing en Espanol (USA ISSN 1091-0832) **7328**
Signtech *see* Sign Tech **35**
Signum (FIN ISSN 0355-0036) **5048**
• Signum (SWE ISSN 0347-0423) **7817**
• Sigpum San'eob gwa Yeong'yang/Food Industry and Nutrition (KOR ISSN 1226-3338) **6669**
SIGS: Managing Object Technology Series *see* S I G S: Managing Object Technology Series **8437**
SIGSPATIAL Special *see* S I G S P A T I A L Special **2436**
Sigtuna Museers Skriftserie (SWE ISSN 0280-8439) **6537**
Sigtuna Museum. Meddelanden och Rapporter (SWE ISSN 1401-4645) **4161**
• Sigurnost/Safety (HRV ISSN 0350-6886) **7542**
As-Sihafa wal-I'lam/Press and Information/Presse et Information (LBN) **7265**
Sihai (CHN ISSN 1001-0165) **5372**
Sihatak *see* Sehhatuk Alyoum **5711**
▼ Al-Sihhat al-Mihaniyyat wa-al-Salamat fi al-Munsha'at al-Ta'limiyyat/Occupational Health and Safety in Educational Establishments. Newsletter (EGY ISSN 1687-868X) **6116**
Siirtolaisuus/Migration (FIN ISSN 0355-3779) **7292**
Siirtolaisuustutkimuksia. A (FIN ISSN 0356-9659) **7293**
Al-Sijil al-Shahri li-Ahdath al-Alam/Monthly Record of World Events (UAE) **7265**
As-Sijil ash-Shahri li-Ahdath Dawlat al-Imarat al-Arabiyyah al-Muttahidah/Monthly Record for the Events of the United Arab Emirates (UAE) **7468**
Sika/Pig (FIN ISSN 0037-5101) **300**
Sikania (ITA ISSN 1123-7058) **8756**
Sikelika. Serie Archeologica (ITA ISSN 0392-0909) **416**
Sikelika. Serie Storica (ITA ISSN 0392-0917) **4161**
The Sikh Courier International (GBR) **7741**
• ➤ Sikh Formations (GBR ISSN 1744-8727) **7741**
Sikh Messenger (GBR ISSN 0266-9153) **7741**
➤ Sikh Review (IND ISSN 0037-5128) **7681**
• SIKids.com (USA) **2213**
Sikiliza (TZA) **7774**
• Sikkerhedsrapport (DNK ISSN 1901-6247) **8625**
• Det Sikkerhetspolitiske Bibliotek/Security Policy Library/Die Sicherheitpolitische Bibliothek (NOR ISSN 0802-6602) **7265**
• Sikkert! (NOR ISSN 1890-064X) **7542**
Sikp'um Kwahak/Food Science and Industry (KOR) **3664**
Siksha - O - Sahitya (IND ISSN 0037-5160) **2912**
Sikuleo o Tuvalu *see* Tuvalu Echoes **3963**
Sila i Krasota (RUS) **5372**
Silabario (ARG ISSN 1514-4100) **5372**
Silac (CUB ISSN 1028-4389) **6258**
Silage U K (GBR ISSN 0957-2805) **275**
Silarus (ITA ISSN 0037-5179) **5239**
▼ • ➤ Silence (GBR) **745**
▼ Silence, ca Pousse (FRA ISSN 1957-2190) **3750**
• Silencer (GBR) **6616**
Silencio (PRI ISSN 1938-0585) **5372**
Sileno (ESP ISSN 1137-2001) **517**
Silenos (ESP ISSN 1888-279X) **7408**
• The Silent Advocate (USA ISSN 0037-5187) **4076**
The Silent Reminder (USA) **7774**
Silent Sports (USA ISSN 0882-9640) **8201**
Silent Voices (USA) **5372**
Silesia (DEU) **4263**
Silesia Antiqua (POL ISSN 0080-9594) **416**
Silesian Studies *see* Studia Slaskie **4476**
• Silgo 21 (MEX) **3911**
Silhouet *see* Silhouet **6185**
• Silhouet (NLD ISSN 1872-4396) **6185**
Silhouet/Vizier *see* Silhouet **6185**
• Silhouette (CAN ISSN 0841-2596) **5239**
Silhouette (GBR) **8785**
Silhouette Donna (ITA ISSN 1124-1721) **8884**
• Siliao Bolan/Feed Panorama (CHN ISSN 1001-0084) **275**
Siliao Guangjiao/Feed China (CHN) **275**
• Siliao Yanjiu/Feed Research (CHN ISSN 1002-2813) **275**
• Siliao yu Xumu (CHN ISSN 1006-6314) **275**
Silica *see* HarrisMartin Columns. Silica **4684**
Silicates Industriels (BEL ISSN 0037-5225) **2045**
▼ • Silicon (NLD ISSN 1876-990X) **2118**
• Silicon Alley Daily (USA) **2566**
• ➤ Silicon Chemistry (NLD ISSN 1569-0660) **2118**
• Silicon Chip (AUS ISSN 1030-2662) **2541**
Silicon Iran (USA) **2566**
Silicon Magazine *see* Polygon **2481**
• Silicon Valley Daily (USA) **1174**
Silicon Valley North *see* National Capital Scan **1152**
Silicon Valley North Alberta *see* National Capital Scan **1152**
Silicon Valley North British Columbia *see* National Capital Scan **1152**
Silicon Valley North Ottawa *see* National Capital Scan **1152**
Silicon Valley North Toronto *see* National Capital Scan **1152**
• The Silicon Valley Real Estate Report (USA) **7612**
• Silicon Valley - San Jose Business Journal (USA ISSN 1532-7469) **1174**
▼ • Silicon Valley Tails (USA ISSN 1945-6794) **6815**
Siliconeer (USA ISSN 1528-9273) **3564**
• Siliconindia (USA ISSN 1091-9503) **2494**
Silja Magazine (FIN ISSN 1235-2640) **8756**
Silk *see* Sichou **8457**
Silk Export Bulletin (IND) **8457**
Silk Road *see* Sichou zhi Lu **8756**
• Silk Road (USA ISSN 1931-6933) **5372**
Silk Screen *see* Sign + Silkscreen Magazine **7328**
Silkroad (Hong Kong) (HKG) **8785**
➤ Silliman Journal (PHL ISSN 0037-5284) **7916**
Sillon (USA) **156**
Sillon Belge (BEL) **156**
Sillon des Landes et des Pyrenees. Edition 64 (FRA ISSN 0152-6456) **156**
Silmu *see* Hyva Hengitys **6214**
Silnicni Obzor (CZE ISSN 0322-7154) **8634**
Silos a grain du Canada *see* Grain Elevators in Canada **272**
▼ • Silpakorn University. Science and Technology Journal (THA ISSN 1905-9159) **7916**
Silsilat Tatwir al-Ihsa'At *see* F A O Statistical Development Series **8369**
Sil's'ka Shkola (UKR) **2912**
Sil's'ke Budivnytstvo (RUS ISSN 0037-5322) **156**
Sil's'ki Obrii (UKR ISSN 0235-635X) **156**
• Sil's'ki Visti (UKR) **3965**
Silueta de Mujer (ESP ISSN 1576-5490) **8848**
Silurian News (USA) **4583**
➤ Silva (ESP ISSN 1579-7392) **5372**
Silva Balcanica (BGR ISSN 1311-8706) **3702**
• Silva Belgica (BEL ISSN 0776-7153) **3702**
• ➤ Silva Fennica (FIN ISSN 0037-5330) **3702**
Silva Fennica. Monographs (FIN ISSN 1457-7356) **3702**
➤ Silva Gabreta (CZE ISSN 1211-7420) **858**
• ➤ Silva Lusitana (PRT ISSN 0870-6352) **3702**
➤ Silvae Genetica (DEU ISSN 0037-5349) **817**
Silver (USA ISSN 0899-6105) **369**
➤ The Silver Age (USA ISSN 1070-972X) **5372**
Silver & Blue (USA ISSN 1054-3031) **2301**
Silver Baron's Money Fever (USA) **1651**
Silver Flower/Ginka (JPN) **4347**
Silver Institute Letter (USA ISSN 0730-8132) **6479**
Silver Kris (SGP ISSN 0129-606X) **8786**
Silver Screen (CAN ISSN 0846-3131) **2490**
• The Silver Sheet (USA ISSN 1093-281X) **5715**
Silver Styles (HKG) **4569**
Silver Web (USA ISSN 1082-8370) **5372**

Title

Title

10872 SKELETAL RADIOLOGY ULRICH'S PERIODICALS

• ➤ Skeletal Radiology (DEU ISSN 0364-2348) **6208**
Skenbladet (SWE ISSN 0281-109X) **8625**
• Skene (MEX ISSN 1605-4105) **8478**
Skepsis (DEU ISSN 1105-1582) **6952**
Skepsis (NOR ISSN 0803-2718) **6743**
• The Skeptic (AUS ISSN 0726-9897) **6743**
• ➤ Skeptic (USA ISSN 1063-9330) **6743**
Skeptical Briefs (USA ISSN 1060-216X) **6743**
• Skeptical Inquirer (USA ISSN 0194-6730) **6743**
Skeptics India (IND) **6952**
➤ Skeptiker (DEU ISSN 0936-9244) **6647**
Skeptikko (FIN ISSN 0786-2571) **6952**
Sketch (CAN ISSN 1910-9776) **3002**
Sketch (USA) **5373**
Sketch Book (USA) **517**
• Sketches (USA) **517**
The SketchPad (USA) **518**
Ski (CHE ISSN 1420-0333) **8332**
Ski (FRA ISSN 1763-5535) **8332**
• Ski (USA ISSN 0037-6159) **8333**
• Ski Area Management (USA ISSN 0037-6175) **8333**
Ski Austria (AUT) **8333**
Ski Canada (CAN ISSN 0702-701X) **8333**
Ski Canada Buyer's Guide (CAN) **8333**
Ski Francais *see* Ski **8332**
Ski Industry Letter (USA ISSN 0197-3479) **8333**
Ski Journal (DEU) **8333**
Ski Journal *see* Skui Janaru **8334**
▼ The Ski Journal (USA ISSN 1935-3219) **8333**
Ski Magazine (NLD ISSN 0169-2364) **8333**
Ski Nautique Magazine (FRA ISSN 0183-3367) **8333**
Ski Patrol Magazine (USA ISSN 0890-6076) **8201**
• Ski Press (CAN ISSN 1490-7755) **8333**
Ski Press (Europe Edition) *see* Ski Press **8333**
Ski Press (German Edition) *see* Ski Press **8333**
Ski Press U S A (United States of America) (USA) **8333**
Ski Presse (French Edition) *see* Ski Press **8333**
Ski Racing (USA ISSN 0037-6213) **8201**
Ski Special (GBR ISSN 0954-9765) **8333**
Ski-Sport *see* SkiSport **8333**
Ski Survey (GBR ISSN 0955-8225) **8333**
Ski the West (CAN) **8333**
Ski Tour Operators Association Annual Business Survey (Year) (USA) **1517**
Ski Trax (CAN) **8333**
Ski Watch Atlas (USA) **8333**
Ski Writers Bulletin (USA) **4583**
Skidmore News (USA) **2301**
The Skier and Snowboarder (GBR ISSN 1475-7451) **8333**
• Skier News (USA ISSN 1094-0960) **8333**
Skieur Magazine (FRA ISSN 1266-9210) **8333**
Skif (KAZ) **3902**
Skiing (DEU) **8333**
• Skiing Magazine (USA ISSN 0037-6264) **8333**
† Skilaeufer (DEU ISSN 0930-1194) **8988**
† Skill (USA ISSN 0279-2028) **8988**
➤ The Skill Journal (GBR) **3046**
Skill New Zealand. Insight *see* Manu Mataurangа **8972**
• Skillings' Mining Review (USA ISSN 0037-6329) **6479**
Skills at Work (ZAF ISSN 1815-3666) **1707**
Skills For Lawyers (GBR ISSN 1353-6648) **4784**
SkillsU S A Champions (Vocational Industrial Clubs of America) (USA ISSN 1539-834X) **2913**
Skim (CAN ISSN 1910-2372) **518**
SkiMagazin (DEU ISSN 0353-4724) **8333**
Skimbaaja (FIN ISSN 0359-0569) **8333**
▼ • Skin (JOR ISSN 1998-7684) **2261**
Skin & Aging (USA ISSN 1096-0120) **4056**
• Skin & Allergy News (USA ISSN 0037-6337) **5882**
Skin & Ink (USA ISSN 1071-7684) **591**
Skin Art (USA ISSN 1061-3013) **518**
Skin Cancer (JPN ISSN 0915-3535) **6034**
• Skin Cancer (PRT ISSN 0871-2549) **6034**
Skin Cancer Foundation Journal (USA ISSN 0898-6665) **6034**
Skin Care Campaign News *see* Campaign News (Online) **8029**
Skin Deep (GBR ISSN 0966-4351) **518**
Skin Deep (USA) **591**
Skin Deep (Evergreen) (USA ISSN 1941-2495) **591**
Skin Diseases & Therapy *see* Hifu Shikkan Saishin no Chiryo **5877**
• Skin Inc. (USA ISSN 0898-6525) **5882**
Skin Pharmacology and Applied Skin Physiology *see* Skin Pharmacology and Physiology **6881**
• ➤ Skin Pharmacology and Physiology (CHE ISSN 1660-5527) **6881**
• ➤ Skin Research and Technology (DNK ISSN 0909-752X) **5882**
• Skin Therapy Letter (CAN ISSN 1201-5989) **5882**
Skin Two (GBR ISSN 0962-9297) **5083**
† • ➤ Skinmed (USA ISSN 1540-9740) **8988**
Skinned Knuckles (USA ISSN 0164-3509) **4347**
Skip (AUT) **6513**
Skip Shot (USA ISSN 1946-8490) **8201**
Skipper (DEU ISSN 0721-4472) **8282**
Skipperen (DNK ISSN 0900-9132) **8662**
• Skipping Stones (USA ISSN 0899-529X) **2213**
Skipsfartens Innkjoepsbok (NOR) **8662**
• Skipsrevyen (NOR ISSN 0800-2282) **8662**
Skirnir (ISL ISSN 0256-8446) **5373**
• Skirt! Magazine (USA ISSN 1946-5165) **8884**
SkiSport (NOR ISSN 0333-3973) **8333**
Skitrax (CAN ISSN 1191-2677) **8333**
Skive-egnens Jul (DNK ISSN 0106-2697) **4263**
Skive Folkeblad (DNK) **3834**
Skivebogen (DNK ISSN 0107-721X) **4263**
Sklar a Keramik/Glass and Ceramics Maker (CZE ISSN 0037-637X) **2045**
Sklaverei, Knechtschaft, Zwangsarbeit (DEU ISSN 1860-9317) **2240**
Sko (Norway) (NOR ISSN 0802-653X) **7942**
Sko & Mode (SWE ISSN 1653-7793) **7942**
Sko - Shoes & More (DNK ISSN 0909-3826) **7942**
Skocken (SWE ISSN 1652-4780) **6815**
Skoda Revue (CZE ISSN 1801-934X) **8603**
Skoena Hem (SWE ISSN 1401-5013) **4562**
† Skoenne Hjem (DNK ISSN 0106-8679) **8988**
Skog och Forskning *see* Skogsliv **3702**
• Skog & Industri (SWE ISSN 1654-8523) **3715**
Skog & Saag (SWE ISSN 1101-8003) **3715**
Skog & Trae (SWE ISSN 1403-6398) **3702**
Skogeieren (NOR ISSN 0037-6396) **3702**
Skogeiernytt *see* Allskog **3683**
Skogen (SWE ISSN 0037-640X) **3702**
Skogindustri (NOR ISSN 0800-8582) **6738**
Skogsbruket (FIN ISSN 0037-6434) **3702**
Skogsforskningsinstitutet. Skogsstatistisk Aarsbok *see* Metsatilastollinen Vuosikirja **3709**
• Skogshistoriska Saellskapet. Aarsskrift (SWE ISSN 1650-0962) **3702**
• Skogshistoriska Tidender (SWE ISSN 1401-9485) **3702**
Skogsindustriarbetaren *see* S I A **3715**
Skogsindustriarbetaren *see* S I A **3715**
Skogsindustrierna *see* Skog & Industri **3715**
Skogsindustrierna. Annual Publication *see* Skogsindustriernas Aarsskrift **3715**
Skogsindustrierna. Jahresschrift *see* Skogsindustriernas Aarsskrift **3715**
Skogsindustrierna. Rapport Annuel *see* Skogsindustriernas Aarsskrift **3715**
Skogsindustriernas Aarsskrift (SWE ISSN 1104-6678) **3715**
Skogsindustrins Tekniska Forskningsinstitut Annual Review *see* S T F I Annual Review **6738**
Skogsindustrins Tekniska Forskningsinstitut Kontakt (English Edition) *see* S T F I - Kontakt (English Edition) **6738**
Skogsindustrins Tekniska Forskningsinstitut Report. PUB *see* S T F I Report. PUB **6738**
Skogsliv (SWE ISSN 1653-6568) **3702**
Skogssport (SWE ISSN 0346-1297) **8333**
Skogurinn (ISL) **3702**
Skohandlaren *see* Sko & Mode **7942**
Skol Vaerlden *see* Skolvaerlden **2913**
Skol Vreizh- l'Ecole Bretonne. Nouvelle Serie (FRA ISSN 0755-8848) **4263**
Skola a Pravo (CZE ISSN 1801-836X) **3033**
Skolan i Norden (Print Edition) *see* Skolen i Norden (Online) **2913**
Skolans Artikelservice (SWE ISSN 0037-6469) **635**
• Skolavardan (ISL ISSN 1670-0163) **2913**
Skolbarn *see* Grundskoletidningen **2861**
• Skolebiblioteket (DNK ISSN 0105-9556) **5048**
Skolebiblioteksaarbog (DNK ISSN 0900-9582) **5048**
Skolefokus *see* Utdanning **2924**
Skoleledelse (DNK ISSN 1902-438X) **3033**
▼ • Skoleledernyt (DNK ISSN 1902-5912) **2913**
• Skolen i Norden (Online) (DNK ISSN 1602-8155) **2913**
Skolepsykologi (NOR ISSN 0333-0389) **2913**
Skolhaelsan (SWE ISSN 0284-284X) **5981**
Skolhistoriskt Arkiv (FIN ISSN 0489-0760) **4263**
Skolledaren (SWE ISSN 0037-6515) **2913**
Skolledningsnytt *see* Chef & Ledarskap **3019**
Skolnytt (SWE ISSN 1653-3119) **3033**
➤ Skolska Fyzika (CZE ISSN 1211-1511) **7040**
Skolske Novine (HRV ISSN 0037-6531) **2913**
Skolvaerlden (SWE ISSN 0037-6566) **2913**
† Skoop (NLD) **8988**
Skopet *see* Kulturmagasinet Skopet **8970**
Skorstensfejaremaestaren (SWE ISSN 0346-1351) **3581**
Skorstensfejermesteren (DNK ISSN 1396-0091) **4126**
Skotaville African Classics Series (ZAF) **5373**
Skotaville Black Theology Series (ZAF) **7681**
Skotaville Children's Book Series (ZAF) **5373**
Skotaville Graphic Series (ZAF) **518**
Skotaville History Series (ZAF) **5373**
Skoter Racing *see* Snoeskoter med Racing **8334**
Skov & Land (DNK ISSN 1399-4751) **3703**
• Skov og Natur (DNK ISSN 1602-1908) **7917**
Skoven (DNK ISSN 0106-8539) **3703**
Skoven Nyt (DNK ISSN 0902-6061) **3703**
Skraedderi (SWE ISSN 0346-1386) **2249**
Skribuak (ESP ISSN 1578-486X) **2913**
➤ Skrien (NLD ISSN 0166-1787) **6513**
Skrift for Historisk Forening for Sundeved (DNK ISSN 0908-3537) **4263**
Skrifter fra Aarhus Universitet *see* Acta Jutlandica **3833**
Skrifter fra Landslaget for Lokalhistorie (NOR ISSN 0802-0434) **4263**
➤ Skrifter med Historiska Perspektiv (SWE ISSN 1652-2761) **4161**
Skrifter Roerande Uppsala Universitet. B, Inbjudningar (SWE ISSN 0566-3091) **2301**
Skrifter Roerande Uppsala Universitet. C, Organisation och Historia (SWE ISSN 0502-7454) **3002**
Skrifter Utgivna af Historiska Samfundet i Aabo (FIN ISSN 0356-1496) **4263**
Skrifter Utgivna av Riksarkivet (SWE ISSN 1402-4705) **4264**
Skrifter Utgivna av Stiftelsen Hallands Laensmuseer, Halmstad och Varberg (SWE ISSN 0282-4922) **4264**
▼ • Skriftserie foer Funktionshinder (SWE ISSN 1654-8221) **4069**
Skriftserie i Vaardvetenskap (SWE ISSN 1653-6533) **5981**
Skript (NLD ISSN 0165-7518) **4161**
Skrivlustan (SWE ISSN 1400-5050) **5373**
Skrjancek (SVN ISSN 1408-5763) **2371**
Skui Janaru/Ski Journal (JPN) **8334**
Skul Thai (THA) **3962**
• Skulabladid (FRO ISSN 1395-0061) **2913**
Skull (USA) **2270**
• ➤ Skull Base (USA ISSN 1531-5010) **6258**
Skulptur Veksoelund (DNK ISSN 0107-4911) **518**
Skunk (DEU) **2213**
Skvaerriggerne (NOR ISSN 0809-6287) **8662**
Sky (GBR) **2390**
• Sky (USA ISSN 0734-8967) **8786**
Sky and Marine *see* Sora to Umi **70**
Sky and Space (AUS ISSN 1035-932X) **581**
• Sky & Telescope (USA ISSN 0037-6604) **581**
Sky & Telescope's Weekly News Bulletin *see* Sky & Telescope **581**
Sky Blue Programme (GBR) **8245**
Sky Calendar *see* Abrams Planetarium Sky Calendar **568**
Sky Customer (IRL) **2390**
Sky Guide Africa South (ZAF) **581**
• ➤ SKY Journal of Linguistics/Linguistic Association of Finland. Journal/ Sprakvetenskapliga Foreningen i Finland. Tidskrift (Suomen Kielitieteellinen Yhdistys) (FIN ISSN 1456-8438) **5174**
Sky Magazine *see* Sky **8786**
Sky Model (ITA ISSN 1593-2087) **4347**
▼ Sky Sport (NZL ISSN 1177-4924) **8201**
Sky Watch *see* SkyWatch **581**
Sky Watcher (JPN ISSN 0911-7652) **581**
Sky Waves *see* SkyWaves **7681**
Skydd & Saekerhet/Safety and Security (SWE ISSN 0283-5452) **2681**
• Skydive (GBR ISSN 1470-5249) **8334**
Skydiving (USA ISSN 0192-7361) **8201**
Skye Terrier Club of America. Bulletin (USA ISSN 1072-8899) **6815**
Skylark (USA) **5239**
Skylark (Saskatoon) (CAN ISSN 0226-353X) **5174**
Skylark Food Science Institute. Study for Food under the Supporting Program. Annual Report *see* Shoku ni Kansuru Josei Kenkyu Chosa Hokokusho **6669**
• Skylife (TUR) **8786**
Skylights (AUT) **8786**
Skylights (USA) **8551**
Skyline (USA) **4028**
Skyline Magazine *see* Skyline Review **5239**
• Skyline Review (USA ISSN 1940-6533) **5239**
Skyliner (CAN) **8334**
• The Skyliner (USA) **8603**
Skylines (AUT) **8786**
Skylines (GBR) **8786**
Skyllis (DEU ISSN 1436-3372) **416**
SkyMag (GBR) **2390**
Skynet Web Magazine (BEL ISSN 1376-4411) **2566**
SkyNews (CAN ISSN 0840-8939) **581**
Skyport (GBR) **70**
Skyrevue (AUT) **70**
Skyrslur og Reikningar Felagatal *see* Skirnir **5373**
Skyscraper (USA) **5083**
Skytteanska Samfundets Aarsbok *see* Thule **3957**
• Skyttebladet (DNK ISSN 0037-6663) **8201**
Skyview (Analogue) (GBR ISSN 1473-2246) **2390**
• SkyWatch (USA ISSN 1089-4888) **581**
Skywatchers Almanac (Year) (USA ISSN 0889-9614) **581**
SkyWaves (AUS) **7681**
Skyways (IND ISSN 0970-8502) **70**
Skyways (USA ISSN 1051-6956) **70**
Skyways (ZAF) **8786**
† Skyweek (DEU ISSN 1430-4201) **8988**
• Skywings (GBR) **8334**
Skywriters (USA) **5435**
Skywritings (JAM) **8786**
Slack (DEU) **8201**
Slaegt og Stavn (DNK ISSN 0107-539X) **3783**
Slaekt och Bygd (FIN ISSN 0780-8763) **3783**
Slaekt och Haevd (SWE ISSN 0489-1090) **3783**
Slaekt och Haevd (Terjaerv) (FIN ISSN 0783-1803) **4264**
Slaektforskaren (FIN ISSN 1235-2365) **3783**
Slaektforskarnas Aarsbok (SWE) **3783**
Slaekthistoriskt Forum (SWE ISSN 0280-3984) **3783**
SlagersWereld (NLD ISSN 1382-3345) **3664**
➤ Slagmark (DNK ISSN 0108-8084) **3834**
• Slagteriernes Forskningsinstitut/Danish Meat Research Institute (DNK ISSN 1604-7842) **3664**
Slagteriernes Forskningsinstitut. Aarsberetning *see* Slagteriernes Forskningsinstitut **3664**
Slainte (IRL ISSN 1393-483X) **7542**
Slam (AUS ISSN 1036-3483) **8334**
• Slam (New York) (USA ISSN 1072-625X) **8245**
Slamm (USA) **6617**
Slammer (FIN ISSN 1239-9035) **8334**
The Slanker Report (USA) **1651**
Slant (Conway) *see* Slant: A Journal of Poetry **5435**
Slant (Madison) (USA) **2301**
Slant 6 News (USA) **8603**
➤ Slant: A Journal of Poetry (USA ISSN 0893-7095) **5435**
Slap (USA) **8201**
Slap Skateboard Magazine *see* Slap **8201**
Slash Magazine (USA) **518**
Slash Slash Self Service *see* //Self Serve **1172**
Slask Opolski (POL ISSN 0867-6070) **3930**
Slaski Kwartalnik Historyczny "Sobotka" (POL ISSN 0037-7511) **4161**
Slaskie Sprawozdania Archeologiczne (POL ISSN 0520-9250) **416**
Slaskie Studia Historyczno-Teologiczne (POL ISSN 0137-3447) **7817**
Slate (CAN ISSN 0821-2287) **518**
The Slate (IRL) **3894**
• Slate (USA ISSN 1091-2339) **5239**
• Slate & Style (USA ISSN 1536-4321) **4085**
Slate on Paper *see* Slate **5239**
Slava (SVN ISSN 0353-3158) **5174**
Slava i Chest' (UKR) **6446**
Slava. Posebna Izdaja (SVN ISSN 1318-5748) **5174**
Slava Sevastopolya (UKR) **3965**
• The Slave River Journal (CAN ISSN 0707-4964) **3817**
Slave River Journal Interactive *see* The Slave River Journal **3817**
• ➤ Slavery and Abolition (GBR ISSN 0144-039X) **4161**
Slavia (CZE ISSN 0037-6736) **5174**
Slavia (ITA) **4475**
Slavia Antiqua (POL ISSN 0080-9993) **416**
▼ ➤ Slavia Centralis (SVN ISSN 1855-6302) **5174**
Slavia Meridionalis (POL ISSN 1233-6173) **5174**
➤ Slavia Occidentalis (POL ISSN 0081-0002) **5174**
Slavia Orientalis (POL ISSN 0037-6744) **5174**
Slavic Almanac (ZAF) **5373**
• ➤ Slavic & East European Information Resources (USA ISSN 1522-8886) **5048**
• ➤ Slavic and East European Journal (USA ISSN 0037-6752) **5174**
Slavic and East European Performance (USA ISSN 1069-2800) **8478**
Slavic and Eastern European Section Newsletter *see* Association of College and Research Libraries. Slavic and Eastern European Section Newsletter **4992**
Slavic Gospel News (AUS) **7741**
• ➤ Slavic Review (USA ISSN 0037-6779) **8002**
• Slavic Studies (JPN ISSN 0562-6579) **3564**
Slavic Survey *see* Slovansky Prehled **7183**
Slavica *see* Universitatis Debreceniensis de Ludovico Kossuth Nominatae. Instituti Philologiae Slavicae. Annales. Slavica **5191**
Slavica *see* Polska Akademia Nauk. Instytut Slawistyki. Prace Slawistyczne **5162**
Slavica Gandensia (BEL ISSN 0771-1395) **3564**
Slavica Gothoburgensia (SWE ISSN 0081-0010) **5174**
Slavica Helvetica (CHE ISSN 0171-7316) **5174**
Slavica Litteraria (CZE ISSN 1212-1509) **5373**
➤ Slavica Lundensia (SWE ISSN 0346-8712) **5174**
• ➤ Slavica Slovaca (SVK ISSN 0037-6787) **5175**
Slavische Cahiers (NLD ISSN 1871-3262) **5373**
Slavische Propylaeen (DEU ISSN 0583-5402) **5373**
Slavisticeskij Zbornik *see* Zbornik Matice Srpske za Slavistiku **5198**
➤ Slavisticna Revija (SVN ISSN 0350-6894) **5175**
Slavistische Beitraege (DEU ISSN 0583-5429) **5175**
Slavistische Studienbuecher. Neue Folge (DEU ISSN 0583-5445) **5175**
Slavna Nadeje/Glorious Hope (USA ISSN 0700-5202) **7775**
Slavolinguistica (DEU) **5175**
• ➤ Slavonic and East European Review (GBR ISSN 0037-6795) **5373**
• ➤ Slavonica (GBR ISSN 1361-7427) **5373**
• Slavyanovedenie (RUS ISSN 0869-544X) **4264**
Slavyanskaya Filologiya (RUS ISSN 0134-9023) **5175**
• Slayage (USA ISSN 1546-9212) **5447**
Sleaze Nation (GBR ISSN 1460-4736) **5239**
Sleazenation *see* Sleaze Nation **5239**
▼ Slechticke Romance (CZE ISSN 1802-8616) **5412**
Sledheads (USA) **8334**
Sledovatel' (RUS) **4965**
Sleek (DEU) **518**
Sleep *see* Sen **7407**
• Sleep (USA ISSN 0161-8105) **6185**
• ➤ Sleep and Biological Rhythm (AUS ISSN 1446-9235) **5715**
• ➤ Sleep and Breathing (DEU ISSN 1520-9512) **6185**
• ➤ Sleep and Hypnosis (TUR ISSN 1302-1192) **6186**
Sleep & Duwvaart (NLD ISSN 1386-3797) **8662**
• ➤ Sleep Medicine (NLD ISSN 1389-9457) **6186**
• Sleep Medicine Clinics (USA ISSN 1556-407X) **6186**
Sleep Medicine Clinics: Continuing Medical Education Supplements *see* Sleep Medicine Clinics **6186**
• ➤ Sleep Medicine Reviews (FRA ISSN 1087-0792) **6186**
• Sleep Research (Los Angeles, 1998) (USA ISSN 1096-214X) **928**
• Sleep Review (USA ISSN 1531-3034) **7408**
Sleep Savvy (USA ISSN 1538-702X) **1844**
• Sleeper (GBR ISSN 1476-4075) **4398**
Sleeper News (USA ISSN 1523-4142) **3783**
Sleeper Queries (USA) **3783**
Sleeping Fish (USA) **5373**
Sleepy Time (USA) **4398**
• Slektsveven (NOR ISSN 0809-6082) **3783**
• Slesvigland (Online) (DNK) **4264**

Slesvigland (Print) *see* Slesvigland (Online) **4264**
Sletten *see* D T U Avisen **8419**
Sleutelgat (BEL ISSN 0771-6001) **5175**
Slezske Zemske Muzeum. Casopis. Serie A. Vedy Prirodni (CZE ISSN 1211-3026) **2716**
Slezske Zemske Muzeum. Casopis. Serie B. Vedy Historicke (CZE ISSN 0323-0678) **4264**
† Slezske Zemske Muzeum. Casopis. Serie C. Dendrologie (CZE ISSN 0323-0724) **8988**
➤ Slezsky Sbornik/Acta Silesiaca (CZE ISSN 0037-6833) **8132**
▼ Slice Magazine (USA ISSN 1938-6923) **5373**
• A Slice of Stale Pizza (AUS) **6617**
Slightly West (USA) **5373**
The Sligo Champion (IRL) **3894**
• Sligo Weekender (IRL ISSN 1393-8800) **3894**
Slim at Home (GBR ISSN 1753-0245) **6669**
Slimmer *see* Slim at Home **6669**
Slimming *see* Slimming & Health **6669**
Slimming (GBR ISSN 0144-8129) **6669**
Slimming & Health (AUS) **6669**
Slingervel (ZAF ISSN 0037-685X) **7775**
Slipstream (Niagara Falls) (USA ISSN 0749-0771) **5435**
Slitz (SWE ISSN 0283-1503) **3956**
Slo-Pitch Game (USA) **8245**
Slo-Pitch News (USA) **8245**
• Sloan-C View (USA ISSN 1541-2806) **3082**
Sloan's Green Guide to Antiquing in New England (USA ISSN 1051-6719) **369**
• Slobids'kyi Krai (UKR) **3965**
• Slobodna Dalmacija (HRV ISSN 0350-4662) **3831**
Slobodno Poduzetnistvo (HRV ISSN 1330-2833) **1174**
Sloejd (DNK ISSN 0106-9608) **539**
• Sloejdforum (SWE ISSN 0346-0509) **539**
Slot Manager *see* SlotManager **8201**
SlotManager (USA ISSN 1949-9728) **8201**
Slouch (USA) **5373**
➤ Slovak Academy of Sciences. Geophysical Institute. Contributions to Geophysics and Geodesy (SVK ISSN 1335-2806) **2789**
Slovak American *see* Slovak v Amerike **3564**
The Slovak American Newsletter (USA) **3564**
Slovak Archeology *see* Slovenska Archeologia **416**
Slovak Association for the Study of English Journal of Theoretical Linguistics *see* S K A S E Journal of Theoretical Linguistics **5171**
Slovak Catholic Falcon (USA ISSN 0897-8107) **7817**
Slovak Ethnology *see* Slovensky Narodopis **355**
Slovak Foreign Policy Affairs *see* International Issues & Slovak Foreign Policy Affairs **7243**
• ➤ Slovak Geological Magazine (SVK ISSN 1335-096X) **2716**
Slovak Heritage Live (CAN ISSN 1198-6077) **3564**
Slovak Hydrometeorological Institut. Meteorological Journal *see* Slovensky Hydrometeorologicky Ustav. Meteorologicky Casopsis **6395**
➤ Slovak Journal of Animal Science (SVK ISSN 1335-3683) **300**
Slovak Language *see* Slovenska Rec **5175**
Slovak Language and Literature in the School *see* Slovensky Jazyk a Literatura v Skole **3082**
Slovak Life *see* Slovensky Zivot **3565**
Slovak Literature *see* Slovenska Literatura **5373**
Slovak Music (SVK) **6617**
Slovak Press Digest (USA ISSN 0037-6914) **3564**
Slovak Republic *see* The P R S Group. Country Reports: Slovak Republic **1509**
Slovak Review (SVK ISSN 1335-0544) **5373**
Slovak Seismographic Stations: Bratislava, Srobarova, Hurbanovo and Skalnate Pleso. Bulletin (SVK ISSN 0139-9349) **2789**
Slovak Sociological Review *see* Sociologia **8135**
• The Slovak Spectator (SVK ISSN 1335-9843) **5239**
Slovak Studies Association. Newsletter (USA) **4264**
Slovak Theater *see* Slovenske Divadlo **8478**
Slovak v Amerike/Slovak American (USA ISSN 0199-6819) **3564**
Slovakia (Economist Intelligence Unit) *see* Country Forecast. Slovakia **7122**
Slovakia: A General Briefing *see* Eastern Europe Newsletter - Briefing. Slovakia **7131**
• Slovakia Autos Report (GBR ISSN 1749-0154) **8603**
• Slovakia Defence & Security Report (GBR ISSN 1749-1630) **6446**
• Slovakia Food & Drink Report (GBR ISSN 1749-2955) **1174**
Slovakia Freight Transport Report (GBR ISSN 1750-5240) **8511**
Slovakia Petrochemicals Report (GBR ISSN 1749-2459) **6793**
Slovanske Historicke Studie (CZE ISSN 0081-007X) **4264**
Slovanske Studie (SVK ISSN 0583-564X) **4264**
Slovansky Prehled/Slavic Survey (CZE ISSN 0037-6922) **7183**
Slovene Ethnological Society. Bulletin *see* Slovensko Etnolosko Drustvo. Glasnik **355**
Slovene Linguistic Studies *see* Slovenski Jezik **5175**
➤ Slovene Studies (USA ISSN 0193-1075) **4264**
Slovenia: A General Briefing *see* Eastern Europe Newsletter - Briefing. Slovenia **7131**
• Slovenia Autos Report (GBR ISSN 1749-0162) **8604**
• Slovenia Defence & Security Report (GBR ISSN 1749-1649) **6446**
• Slovenia Food & Drink Report (GBR ISSN 1749-2963) **1175**
Slovenia Freight Transport Report (GBR ISSN 1750-5259) **8511**
Slovenia in Figures *see* Slovenia v Stevilkah **8399**
Slovenia Information Technology Report *see* Business Monitor International. Information Technology Country Reports **2491**
• Slovenia v Stevilkah/Slovenia in Figures (SVN ISSN 1318-3745) **8399**
Slovenian Academy of Sciences and Arts. Yearbook *see* Slovenska Akademija Znanosti in Umetnosti. Letopis **518**
• Slovenian Economic Mirror (SVN ISSN 1318-3826) **1517**
Slovenian Journal of Forestry *see* Gozdarski Vestnik **3692**
➤ Slovenian Society for Nondestructive Testing. International Conference Proceedings (SVN) **3395**
• ➤ Slovenian Veterinary Research/Slovenski Veterinarski Zbornik (SVN ISSN 1580-4003) **8807**
Slovenija (SVN ISSN 0353-118X) **3565**
• Slovenka (SVK ISSN 0231-6676) **8884**
Slovenska Akademia Vied. Archeologicky Ustav. Studijne Zvesti (SVK ISSN 0560-2793) **416**
Slovenska Akademija Znanosti in Umetnosti. Letopis/Slovenian Academy of Sciences and Arts. Yearbook (SVN ISSN 0374-0315) **518**
Slovenska Akademija Znanosti in Umetnosti. Razred za Filoloske in Literarne Vede. Razprave/Academia Scientiarum et Artium Slovenica. Classis 2, Philologia et Litterae. Dissertationes (SVN ISSN 0560-2920) **5175**
Slovenska Akademija Znanosti in Umetnosti. Razred za Naravoslovne Vede. Razprave/Academia Scientiarum et Artium Slovenica. Classis 4: Historia Naturalis. Dissertationes (SVN ISSN 0352-5090) **7917**
Slovenska Archeologia/Slovak Archeology (SVK ISSN 1335-0102) **416**
Slovenska Archivistika (SVK ISSN 0231-6722) **4264**
• Slovenska Bibliografija. A. Serijske Publikacije (SVN ISSN 0353-1724) **635**
• Slovenska Bibliografija. Knjige (SVN ISSN 0353-1716) **635**
Slovenska Drzava (CAN ISSN 0037-6957) **7183**
Slovenska Hudba (SVK ISSN 1335-2458) **6617**
Slovenska Literatura/Slovak Literature (SVK ISSN 0037-6973) **5373**
† • Slovenska Narodna Bibliografia (SVK ISSN 1335-2202) **8988**
Slovenska Numizmatika (SVK ISSN 0081-0088) **6653**
Slovenska Rec/Slovak Language (SVK ISSN 0037-6981) **5175**
➤ Slovenske Divadlo/Slovak Theater (SVK ISSN 0037-699X) **8478**
Slovenske Lesokruhy *see* Les Slovenske Lesokruhy **3703**
Les Slovenske Lesokruhy (SVK ISSN 1337-088X) **3703**
Slovenske Lesokruhy & Les *see* Les Slovenske Lesokruhy **3703**
Slovenske Narodne Muzeum. Zbornik. Archeologia (SVK) **416**
Slovenske Narodne Muzeum. Zbornik. Etnografia (SVK ISSN 0139-5475) **4264**
Slovenske Narodne Muzeum. Zbornik. Historia (SVK ISSN 0139-5378) **4264**
Slovenske Narodne Muzeum. Zbornik. Prirodne Vedy/Acta Rerum Naturalium Musei Nationalis Slovenici Bratislava (SVK ISSN 0139-5424) **705**
Slovenske Narodne Noviny (SVK ISSN 0862-8823) **3947**
Slovenske Pohlady (SVK) **5373**
Slovenske Pohlady na Literaturu a Umenie (SVK ISSN 0037-7007) **5373**
Slovenski Cebelar (SVN ISSN 0350-4697) **156**
• ➤ Slovenski Jezik/Slovene Linguistic Studies (SVN ISSN 1408-2616) **5175**
Slovenski Veterinarski Zbornik *see* Slovenian Veterinary Research **8807**
Slovensko (SVK ISSN 0231-7303) **3947**
➤ Slovensko Etnolosko Drustvo. Glasnik/Slovene Ethnological Society. Bulletin (SVN ISSN 0351-2908) **355**
Slovensky Chirurg *see* Miniinvazivna Chirurgia a Endoskopia, Chirurgia Sucasnosti **6252**
Slovensky Hydrometeorologicky Ustav. Meteorologicky Casopsis/Slovak Hydrometeorological Institut. Meteorological Journal (SVK ISSN 1335-339X) **6395**
Slovensky Jazyk a Literatura v Skole/Slovak Language and Literature in the School (SVK ISSN 1335-2040) **3082**
➤ Slovensky Narodopis/Slovak Ethnology (SVK ISSN 1335-1303) **355**
Slovensky Stenograf (SVK ISSN 0231-6978) **1854**
Slovensky Zivot/Slovak Life (ARG ISSN 0326-3193) **3565**
Slovgas (SVK ISSN 1335-3853) **6793**
Slovit (ITA ISSN 1826-6371) **3565**
Slovo (BLR) **7681**
Slovo (FRA ISSN 0183-6080) **560**
Slovo (HRV ISSN 0583-6255) **5373**
• Slovo (UKR) **3965**
• ➤ Slovo (London) (GBR ISSN 0954-6839) **8002**
• Slovo (Moscow) (RUS ISSN 0868-4855) **5374**
• ➤ Slovo a Slovesnost/Word and Speech (CZE ISSN 0037-7031) **5175**
Slovo a Smysl/Word & Sense (CZE ISSN 1214-7915) **5374**
Slovo i Chas (UKR ISSN 1027-5673) **5374**
Slovo Kyrgyzstana (KGZ) **3904**
Slovo Neftyannika (RUS) **6793**
Slovo Prosvity (UKR) **7706**
Slov'yans'ke Viche - XX! Stolittya (UKR) **5239**
Slow (ITA) **3664**
Slow Baking (DEU ISSN 1860-7802) **3675**
Slow Cooker Favorites *see* All-Time Favorites: Slow Cooker **4351**
▼ Slow Cooker Favorites (USA ISSN 1935-0724) **4367**
Slow Cooking (USA ISSN 1938-6885) **4367**
Slowem i Ksztaltem (POL ISSN 1426-6628) **518**
Slownik Biograficzny Polskich Nauk Medycznych XX Wieku (POL) **5715**
Slowo (POL ISSN 1230-8668) **7817**
Slowo i Liturgia (USA ISSN 0892-5100) **7817**
Slowo Wsrod Nas (POL ISSN 0867-7573) **7817**
Slug & Lettuce (USA) **6617**
Slugs and Snails (GBR) **4085**
Slunicko (CZE ISSN 0231-7222) **2213**
Sluzba Bozja (HRV ISSN 0037-7074) **7681**
Sluzben Vesnik na Republika Makedonija (MKD ISSN 0354-1622) **7468**
Sluzbeni Glasnik Opcine Rovinj (HRV ISSN 0037-7120) **7502**
Sluzhba (RUS) **6446**
Sluzhba Bezopasnosti (RUS) **6446**
Sluzhba Bezopasnosti (UKR) **6446**
Sly (USA ISSN 1555-4694) **6300**
Smaabedrifter i Fokus (NOR ISSN 1502-8232) **1966**
Smaak *see* Smaakwereld **4367**
Smaak, het Magazine *see* Smaakwereld **4367**
Smaakwereld (NLD ISSN 1871-8701) **4367**
Smaalands - Tidningen (SWE) **3956**
Smaaskogsnytt (SWE ISSN 0348-2685) **3703**
SmackDown! Magazine *see* W W Magazine **8215**
Smaerta (SWE ISSN 1402-1048) **5981**
Smag (DEU) **3856**
Smak (NLD ISSN 1872-2326) **2168**
• ➤ Small (DEU ISSN 1613-6810) **3357**
Small and Medium Business Partner Community *see* S M B Partner Community **1966**
Small and Medium-Sized Enterprise - Information Technology Guide *see* S M E - I T Guide **1421**
Small & Midsized Business Finance *see* S M B Finance **1966**
Small & Midsized Businesses Finance *see* S M B Finance **1966**
Small Animal Practice (Baltimore) (USA ISSN 0894-3710) **8807**
Small Arms *see* Qingbingqi **6442**
• ➤ Small Axe (USA ISSN 0799-0537) **5239**
Small Boats (USA ISSN 1933-6152) **8282**
Small Business (GBR ISSN 0262-3102) **1966**
Small Business *see* Piccola Impresa **8981**
Small Business Advisor (USA ISSN 1069-9619) **1966**
The Small Business Advisor: Software News (USA) **1421**
• The Small Business Advocate (Austin) (USA) **1966**
Small Business Advocate (Brooklyn) (USA) **1966**
Small Business Advocate (Washington) (USA ISSN 1045-7658) **1966**
Small Business Banking News (USA) **1966**
Small Business Bibliography (USA ISSN 0502-5133) **1263**
Small Business Bulletin (Worcester) (USA ISSN 0893-8326) **1967**
• Small Business Canada Magazine (CAN ISSN 1481-7357) **1967**
Small Business Computing & Communications (USA ISSN 1523-3057) **2583**
• Small Business Economic Trends (USA ISSN 1080-0816) **1517**
• ➤ Small Business Economics (USA ISSN 0921-898X) **1967**
• The Small Business Economy (USA ISSN 1932-3573) **1967**
Small Business Environmental Advocate (USA) **3466**
Small Business Executive Report (USA) **1967**
Small Business Insights (USA) **1967**
Small Business Investment Companies Directory and Handbook of Small Business Finance *see* S B I C Directory and Handbook of Small Business Finance **1966**
• Small Business Issues (GBR) **1967**
• The Small Business Journal (Cincinnati) (USA) **1967**
• Small Business Journal (Lansing) (USA ISSN 1084-3639) **1967**
• Small Business Leader (USA) **1967**
Small Business Magazine (USA) **1967**
Small Business Monthly *see* Atlanta Small Business Monthly **1956**
Small Business News (USA ISSN 0279-8395) **1967**
• Small Business News - Dayton (USA) **1967**
Small Business News Report (USA) **1967**
Small Business News - Washington D.C. (USA) **1967**
• Small Business Opportunities (USA ISSN 1071-8087) **1967**
Small Business or Entrepreneurial Related Newsletters, Publications & Periodicals, Etc. (USA) **1967**
Small Business Preferential Subcontracts Opportunities Monthly (USA ISSN 0887-4050) **2028**
Small Business Profiles (Washington, D.C.) (USA ISSN 1066-646X) **1967**
• Small Business Quarterly (CAN ISSN 1205-9099) **1263**
• Small Business Sourcebook (USA ISSN 0883-3397) **1967**
• Small Business Stats (AUS ISSN 1833-3869) **1967**
Small Business Tax and Finance (GBR ISSN 0953-9506) **1943**
• Small Business Tax News (USA) **1967**
• Small Business Tax Review (USA ISSN 0276-5322) **1943**
• Small Business Tax Strategies (USA ISSN 1935-1992) **1967**
Small Business Times *see* BizTimes (Milwaukee) **1068**
Small Business U S A (USA ISSN 0898-4972) **1967**
Small Business World (ZAF) **1967**
Small Business World Magazine (CAN ISSN 0835-4251) **1967**
Small Businesses & Banks Market Assessment *see* Key Note Market Assessment. Small Businesses & Banks **1963**
Small Businesses and Their Banks (GBR) **1383**
Small Caps Profits (FRA ISSN 1955-0251) **1651**
Small Carnivore Conservation (CHE ISSN 1019-5041) **2627**
Small Change (IND ISSN 0973-4511) **1383**
The Small City and Regional Community (USA ISSN 0194-2735) **7183**
Small Claim Manual (CAN) **4784**
Small Claims Guide for Town & Village Courts *see* New York Small Claims Guide **4745**
Small Claims Rules *see* Civil Rules **4829**
Small Community Quarterly (USA) **7502**
Small Corporate Offering Registration Report *see* S C O R Report **1648**
Small Craft Advisory (USA ISSN 1066-2383) **8282**
Small Domestic Electrical Appliances *see* Key Note Market Report: Small Domestic Electrical Appliances **4559**
Small Enterprise Development *see* Enterprise Development & Microfinance **1959**
Small Enterprise Research Database *see* S M E Research Database **1966**
Small Enterprise Research Report (GBR ISSN 1742-9773) **1967**
Small Enterprises Development, Management and Extension *see* S E D M E **1966**
• Small Farm Digest (USA) **156**
Small Farm News (USA) **156**
Small Farm Today (USA ISSN 1079-9729) **156**
Small Farmer's Journal (USA ISSN 0743-9989) **156**
Small Farms (AUS ISSN 1441-3701) **157**
Small Firm Business (USA ISSN 1552-3470) **1967**
Small Flows Quarterly (USA ISSN 1528-6827) **7542**
Small Fruits Review *see* International Journal of Fruit Science **237**
• ➤ Small Group Research (USA ISSN 1046-4964) **7408**
Small Homes *see* New Small Homes **8976**
Small Hydro Power *see* Xiao Shuidian **3164**
Small Industries Development Organization. Annual Report (TZA) **1967**
Small Luxury Hotels (USA) **4398**
Small Nitrogenous Fertilizer Plant *see* Xiao Danfei **259**
• Small Office (USA) **2583**
Small Office/Home Office Business Report *see* S O H O Business Report **1170**
Small Office Home Office Life and Technology Today *see* SoHo Life and Technology Today **1968**
• Small or Rural Hospitals Update (Online Edition) (USA) **4111**
Small or Rural Hospitals Update (Print Edition) *see* Small or Rural Hospitals Update (Online Edition) **4111**
▼ • Small Plant News (USA ISSN 1942-7085) **3664**
Small Pond *see* Small Pond Magazine of Literature **5374**
• Small Pond Magazine of Literature (USA ISSN 0037-721X) **5374**
• Small Press Book Review (Online) (USA) **7574**
Small Press Creative Explosion (USA) **5374**
† Small Press Listings (GBR) **8988**
• Small Press Record of Books in Print (USA ISSN 0148-9720) **7579**
• Small Press Review (Online) (USA ISSN 1949-2731) **7574**
Small Press Review (Print) *see* Small Press Review (Online) **7574**
Small Publisher (USA ISSN 1081-1133) **7574**
Small Publishers Association of North America Connection *see* S P A N Connection **7572**
Small-Publishers Exchange *see* S P E X **7572**
• ➤ Small Ruminant Research (NLD ISSN 0921-4488) **300**
Small Ruminant Research Network Newsletter (KEN) **301**
▼ • Small Scale Digital Device Forensics Journal (USA ISSN 1941-6164) **2675**
Small-Scale Forest Economics, Management and Policy *see* Small-Scale Forestry **3703**
• ➤ Small-Scale Forestry (NLD ISSN 1873-7617) **3703**
Small Scale Industries *see* S S I **1966**
Small Scale Industries Envoy (IND) **1967**
Small-Scale Industries: South Eastern and Benue Plateau States of Nigeria (NGA) **1967**
Small Ships (GBR ISSN 0262-480X) **8662**
Small Side Team Games and Potted Sports (GBR) **8201**

Title

▼ *new title*   † *ceased*   ● *electronic media*   ➤ *refereed*

Title

Social Sciences Index (WilsonWeb) *see* Social Sciences Index **8021**
Social Sciences Journal *see* Shakai Kagaku Kenkyu **8000**
Social Sciences Journal of Colleges of Shanxi *see* Shanxi Gaodeng Xuexiao Shehui Kexue Xuebao **8000**
Social Sciences Perspectives in Higher Education *see* Gaoxiao Sheke Dongtai **7966**
Social Sciences Research Journal (IND ISSN 0251-348X) **8004**
Social Scientist (IND ISSN 0970-0293) **8004**
Social Scientist (NGA ISSN 0081-0487) **8004**
Social Security/Bitahon Sotziyali (ISR ISSN 0334-231X) **4523**
Social Security (USA ISSN 0148-1967) **4523**
Social Security Administration Publications on CD-ROM *see* S S A Publications on CD-ROM **4522**
Social Security and Health Reports *see* Sosiaali- ja Terveysturvan Katsauksia **8005**
• Social Security Bulletin (USA ISSN 0037-7910) **4523**
Social Security Bulletin. Annual Statistical Supplement Tables *see* Annual Statistical Supplement to the Social Security Bulletin **8080**
Social Security Bulletin. Annual Statistical Supplement Tables *see* Social Security Bulletin **4523**
Social Security Documentation: African Series (CHE ISSN 0379-704X) **4523**
Social Security Documentation: Asia and Pacific Series (CHE ISSN 1013-4484) **4523**
Social Security Documentation. Caribbean Series (CHE ISSN 0254-0576) **4523**
Social Security Documentation: European Series (CHE ISSN 1564-507X) **4523**
• Social Security Excellence (LawDesk) (USA) **4523**
Social Security Explained (USA ISSN 0277-0539) **8069**
• Social Security Handbook (Washington, DC) (USA ISSN 0361-5200) **4523**
Social Security Insurance Recipients by State and County (Year) *see* S S I Recipients by State and County (Year) **4522**
• Social Security Law & Practice (USA) **4523**
Social Security Legislation (Year) (GBR) **8069**
Social Security Panorama *see* Panorama de Seguridad Social **8061**
Social Security Plus *see* Social Security Excellence (LawDesk) **4523**
Social Security Practice Advisory (USA) **4523**
• Social Security Practice Guide (USA) **4523**
Social Security Programs in the United States (USA ISSN 1073-1415) **8069**
Social Security Programs Throughout the World *see* Social Security Programs Throughout the World. Americas **8069**
Social Security Programs Throughout the World. Africa (USA ISSN 1936-6477) **8069**
• Social Security Programs Throughout the World. Americas (USA ISSN 1936-8712) **8069**
• Social Security Programs Throughout the World. Asia and the Pacific (USA) **8069**
Social Security Programs Throughout the World. Europe (USA) **8069**
† Social Security Reporter (AUS ISSN 0817-3524) **8988**
• Social Security Statistics, Canada and Provinces (CAN ISSN 1189-5594) **8069**
Social Security System *see* Shehui Baozhang Zhidu **8068**
• ➤ Social Semiotics (GBR ISSN 1035-0330) **6952**
Social Service *see* Social Fokus **8069**
Social Service Administration Magazine *see* S S A Magazine **8067**
Social Service and Related Laws of North Carolina (USA) **8069**
Social Service Jobs (USA) **6703**
• ➤ Social Service Review (USA ISSN 0037-7961) **8069**
• Social Services Abstracts (USA) **8084**
Social Services Bulletin (GBR ISSN 0964-9891) **8084**
• Social Services Bulletin (USA) **8070**
Social Services Law Bulletin *see* Social Services Bulletin **8070**
• Social Services Parliamentary Monitor (GBR ISSN 1462-9933) **8070**
Social Services Research (GBR ISSN 1351-5586) **8070**
Social Services Research & Information Unit. Report (No.) (GBR ISSN 0952-9772) **8070**
Social Services Research & Information Unit. Reports and Occasional Papers (GBR) **8070**
Social Services Statistics for Wales (GBR) **8084**
Social Services Yearbook (GBR ISSN 0307-093X) **8070**
Social Situation and Economy of Romania (ROM ISSN 1224-8177) **8399**
The Social Situation in the European Union (LUX ISSN 1681-1658) **8134**
Social Statistics in Nigeria (NGA ISSN 0189-6067) **8021**
➤ Social Strategies (CHE ISSN 1423-9531) **8134**
• ➤ The Social Studies (USA ISSN 0037-7996) **8005**
Social Studies and the Young Learner (USA ISSN 1056-0300) **3082**
➤ Social Studies Journal (USA ISSN 0886-9286) **3082**
• ➤ Social Studies of Science (GBR ISSN 0306-3127) **7917**
The Social Studies Professional (USA ISSN 0586-6235) **3082**
• ➤ Social Studies Review (USA ISSN 1056-6325) **8005**
➤ The Social Studies Texan (USA ISSN 1056-4675) **3082**
• Social Sudies Research and Practice (USA ISSN 1933-5415) **8134**
Social Survey Division Omnibus Survey *see* O N S Omnibus Survey **7288**
• Social Text (USA ISSN 0164-2472) **8134**
Social Theory: A Bibliographic Series (USA ISSN 0887-3577) **8150**
• ➤ Social Theory & Health (GBR ISSN 1477-8211) **8134**
• ➤ Social Theory and Practice (USA ISSN 0037-802X) **6952**
Social Thought *see* Journal of Religion and Spirituality in Social Work **8051**
➤ Social Thought and Research (USA ISSN 1094-5830) **8134**
Social Transformations in Chinese Societies (NLD ISSN 1871-2673) **8134**
Social Trends (ROM ISSN 1454-4466) **8399**
Social Trygghet i de Nordiska Laenderna *see* Social Tryghed i de Nordiske Lande **8070**
• Social Tryghed i de Nordiske Lande/Social Trygghet i de Nordiska Laenderna/Sosiaali Trygghet i de Nordiska Land (DNK ISSN 1395-7546) **8070**
Social Welfare (IND ISSN 0037-8038) **8070**
Social Welfare and Health Care Expenditure *see* Sosiaali- ja Terveysmenot **8084**
▼ Social Welfare: Fighting Poverty and Homelessness (USA ISSN 1937-3295) **8070**
Social Welfare, Fighting Poverty and Homelessness *see* Social Welfare: Fighting Poverty and Homelessness **8070**
Social Welfare History Group. Newsletter (USA ISSN 0560-3870) **8070**
Social Work *see* Socialno Delo **8071**
• ➤ Social Work (USA ISSN 0037-8046) **8070**
• ➤ Social Work/Maatskaplike Werk (ZAF ISSN 0037-8054) **8070**
• ➤ Social Work Abstracts (USA ISSN 1070-5317) **8084**
• ➤ Social Work and Christianity (USA ISSN 0737-5778) **7681**
Social Work and Social Issues (USA ISSN 0081-055X) **8070**
• ➤ Social Work and Social Sciences Review (GBR ISSN 0953-5225) **8070**
† Social Work and Social Welfare Yearbook (GBR ISSN 0957-3623) **8988**
• ➤ Social Work and Society (DEU ISSN 1613-8953) **8070**
• ➤ Social Work Education (GBR ISSN 0261-5479) **8070**
† Social Work Education Reporter (USA ISSN 0037-8062) **8988**
Social Work Forum (IND ISSN 0583-7065) **8070**
• ➤ Social Work Forum (USA ISSN 1536-691X) **8070**
Social Work in a Changing World (GBR) **8070**
• ➤ Social Work in Health Care (USA ISSN 0098-1389) **8070**
• ➤ Social Work in Mental Health (USA ISSN 1533-2985) **8071**
• ➤ Social Work in Public Health (USA ISSN 1937-1918) **8071**
Social Work Monographs (GBR ISSN 1363-0059) **8071**
• Social Work Now (NZL ISSN 1173-4906) **8071**
➤ Social Work Perspectives (USA) **8071**
Social Work Practice (ZAF) **8071**
Social Work Practice Monograph Series (USA ISSN 8756-5013) **8071**
Social Work Practice with Children and Families (USA) **7409**
• ➤ Social Work Research (USA ISSN 1070-5309) **8071**
Social Work Research Centre. Research Reports (GBR) **8071**
Social Work Research Centre. Working Papers (GBR) **8071**
Social Work Review *see* Aotearoa New Zealand Social Work Review **8025**
Social Work Services Group. Community Service (GBR) **8071**
Social Work Services Group. Statistical Bulletin (GBR ISSN 0144-5081) **8071**
• Social Work Today (USA ISSN 1540-420X) **8071**
• ➤ Social Work with Groups (USA ISSN 0160-9513) **8071**
• Socialarbeit in Europa/European Interests (IRL) **8134**
Sociale Cohesie in Nederland (NLD ISSN 1872-5252) **8134**
Sociale Dienst Nieuws (NLD) **8071**
Sociale Dienst Post (NLD) **8071**
• Sociale Interventie (NLD ISSN 0926-3977) **8134**
Sociale Kaart Geestelijke Gezondheidszorg (NLD ISSN 1873-9970) **7542**
• Sociale Psychiatrie (NLD ISSN 1386-3541) **6186**
• De Sociale Staat van Nederland (NLD ISSN 1570-3606) **8071**
Sociale Statistieken - Nationaal Instituut voor de Statistiek *see* Belgium. Nationaal Instituut voor de Statistiek. Sociale Statistieken **8081**
Sociale Verzekering *see* Documentatie Orgaan Sociale Verzekering **4501**
Sociale Verzekeringsbank. Jaarbericht (NLD ISSN 1871-5176) **8071**
Sociale Werkvoorziening Journaal *see* S W Journaal **1706**
† ➤ Sociale Wetenschappen (NLD ISSN 0037-8097) **8989**
• Sociale Ydelser, Hvem, Hvad, og Hvornaar (DNK ISSN 0107-5047) **4523**
Sociale Zekerheid *see* Zakboekje Sociale Zekerheid **4529**
Sociale Zekerheid Bulletin *see* S Z Bulletin **8067**
Sociale Zekerheid en Besluit Bovenwettelijke Werkloosheidsregeling voor Onderwijspersoneel (NLD ISSN 1574-4094) **1707**
Sociales *see* Heraldo de Saltillo **3909**
Socialfoerfattningar (SWE ISSN 0037-8100) **8071**
Socialfoersaekring *see* Dagens Socialfoersaekring **8036**
Socialfoersaekring/Social Insurance (SWE ISSN 1104-0688) **4523**
Socialfoersaekringen Aarsredovisning foer Budgetaaret (Year) *see* Sweden. Foersaeksringskassan. Aarsredovisning **4524**
Socialia (DEU ISSN 1435-6651) **8134**
• ➤ Socialiniai Mokslai (LTU ISSN 1392-0758) **8005**
➤ Socialinis Darbas (LTU ISSN 1648-4789) **8005**
• Socialism and Democracy (GBR ISSN 0885-4300) **7183**
Socialism and Health (GBR ISSN 0037-8119) **7542**
Socialism and Liberation (USA ISSN 1930-3017) **7183**
Socialisme *see* Reflexions **7176**
Socialisme en Democratie (NLD ISSN 0037-8135) **7183**
Socialismo & Politica (PRT) **7183**
➤ Socialismo y Participacion (PER ISSN 0252-8827) **7183**
Socialist (USA ISSN 0884-6154) **7183**
Socialist Affairs (GBR ISSN 0049-0946) **7183**
Socialist Economic Theory and Practice *see* Shehui Zhuyi Jingji Lilun yu Shijian **1173**
Socialist Federal Republic of Yugoslavia. Statistical Yearbook *see* Statisticki Godisnjak Srbije i Crne Gore **8405**
Socialist Forum (USA ISSN 0037-8194) **7183**
➤ Socialist History (GBR ISSN 0969-4331) **4161**
Socialist History Working Papers (GBR ISSN 1363-7827) **4161**
Socialist India (IND ISSN 0037-8208) **7183**
Socialist Lawyer (GBR ISSN 0954-3635) **4784**
Socialist Nation (LKA) **7183**
➤ Socialist Perspective (IND ISSN 0970-8863) **7183**
Socialist Register (GBR ISSN 0081-0606) **7183**
Socialist Republic of Vietnam. Office Gazette *see* Cong Bao **7431**
• Socialist Review (GBR) **7183**
• Socialist Standard (GBR ISSN 0037-8259) **7183**
Socialist Studies (GBR) **7183**
➤ Socialist Studies Bulletin/Bulletin d'Etudes Socialistes (CAN ISSN 0830-9086) **8005**
Socialist Viewpoint (USA ISSN 1535-5438) **7184**
Socialist Worker (CAN ISSN 0836-7094) **7184**
• Socialist Worker (GBR ISSN 1475-9705) **7184**
Socialist Worker (IRL ISSN 1649-6655) **7184**
The Socialist Worker (USA ISSN 0885-1468) **7184**
Socialist Worker Monthly Review *see* Unity **7191**
El Socialista (NIC) **7184**
Socialisten Weekend (DNK ISSN 1396-6367) **7184**
Socialistisk Debatt (SWE ISSN 0346-1491) **7184**
Socialistisk Folkeparti Status *see* S F Status **8986**
• Socialistisk Information (DNK ISSN 0108-1861) **7184**
Sociallovgivning (DNK ISSN 1901-0400) **4969**
Socialmanagement *see* Sozialwirtschaft **8072**
Socialmedicinsk Tidskrift (SWE ISSN 0037-833X) **5715**
Socialmedicinsk Tidskrift Skriftserie *see* Socialmedicinsk Tidskrift **5715**
Socialna a Charitativna Sluzba (SVK ISSN 1336-8915) **8071**
Socialna Pedagogika (SVN ISSN 1408-2942) **8134**
Socialna Prevencia (SVK ISSN 1336-9679) **8071**
Socialni Politika *see* Prace & Socialni Politika **8062**
➤ Socialni Studia (CZE ISSN 1214-813X) **8135**
➤ Socialno Delo/Social Work (SVN ISSN 0352-7956) **8071**
• Socialpaedagogen (DNK ISSN 0105-5399) **8071**
Socialpolitik (SWE ISSN 1104-6376) **8071**
Socialraadgiveren (DNK ISSN 0108-6103) **8071**
Socialreformen (DNK ISSN 1398-4403) **8135**
Socialreformen 1-2 og Aktivlovene. Supplementsbind *see* Socialreformen **8135**
Socialsektor. Nyhedsbrev *see* Voksne **8997**
Socialvetenskaplig Tidskrift (SWE ISSN 1104-1420) **8071**
• ➤ Sociation Today (USA ISSN 1542-6300) **8135**
• Sociedad (ARG ISSN 0327-7712) **8005**
Sociedad Americana de Oftalmologia y Optometria. Archivos/American Society for Ophthalmology and Optometry. Archives (COL ISSN 0037-8364) **6051**
Sociedad Andaluza de Entomologia. Boletin (ESP ISSN 1578-1666) **859**
• ➤ Sociedad Andaluza de Traumatologia y Ortopedia. Revista (ESP ISSN 0212-0771) **6073**
• Sociedad Antioquena de Ornitologia. Boletin (COL ISSN 0123-9082) **914**
• Sociedad Argentina de Botanica. Boletin (ARG ISSN 0373-580X) **817**
Sociedad Argentina de Diabetes. Revista (ARG ISSN 0325-5247) **5900**
Sociedad Argentina de Educacion Matematica. Boletin (ARG ISSN 1666-3934) **5536**
Sociedad Argentina de Escritores. Revista (ARG ISSN 0328-6363) **5374**
Sociedad Argentina de Estadistica Revista *see* S A E. Revista **8397**
Sociedad Argentina de Estudios Geograficos. Anales (ARG ISSN 0374-0323) **4028**
Sociedad Argentina de Estudios Geograficos. Boletin (ARG ISSN 0325-2698) **4028**
Sociedad Argentina de Estudios Geograficos. Contribuciones Cientificas (ARG) **4028**
▼ • Sociedad Argentina de Estudios Medievales. Boletin (ARG ISSN 1851-3689) **4161**
Sociedad Argentina de Ginecologia Infanto Juvenil. Revista (ARG ISSN 0328-7947) **6005**
Sociedad Argentina de Linguistica. Revista (ARG ISSN 0327-8794) **5175**
Sociedad Argentina de Psicoanalisis. Revista (ARG ISSN 1514-089X) **6186**
Sociedad Argentina de Sexualidad Humana Revista Argentina de Sexualidad Humana *see* S A S H. Revista Argentina de Sexualidad Humana **6285**
➤ Sociedad Argentina para la Investigacion de Productos Aromaticos. Anales (ARG) **818**
Sociedad Bolivariana de Venezuela. Revista (VEN ISSN 0037-8402) **4312**
Sociedad Boliviana de Historia Natural. Revista (BOL) **705**
• ➤ Sociedad Botanica de Mexico. Boletin (MEX ISSN 0366-2128) **818**
• Sociedad Brasileira de Meteorologia. Boletim (BRA ISSN 1676-014X) **6395**
Sociedad Canaria de Oftalmologia. Archivos (ESP ISSN 0211-2698) **6051**
Sociedad Castellonense de Cultura. Boletin (ESP ISSN 0210-1475) **4264**
Sociedad Chilena de Arqueologia. Bulletin (CHL ISSN 0716-5730) **416**
Sociedad Chilena de Ciencia de Computacion. Boletin (CHL ISSN 0716-7784) **2438**
Sociedad Chilena de Ciencia de Computacion. Conferencia Internacional/Chilean Computer Science Society. International Conference (CHL) **2474**
• Sociedad Chilena de Ciencia de Computacion. Revista (CHL ISSN 0717-4276) **2438**
Sociedad Chilena de Ingenieria Hidraulica. Revista (CHL ISSN 0716-3746) **3364**
Sociedad Chilena de Odontopediatria. Revista (CHL ISSN 0718-395X) **5865**
Sociedad Chilena de Quimica. Boletin *see* The Chilean Chemical Society. Journal **2058**
➤ Sociedad Cientifica Argentina. Anales (ARG ISSN 0037-8437) **7917**
Sociedad Colombiana de Control de Malezas y Fisiologia Vegetal. Revista (COL ISSN 0120-0682) **253**
Sociedad Colombiana de Endocrinologia. Revista (COL ISSN 0120-1182) **5900**
Sociedad Colombiana de Oftalmologia. Revista (COL ISSN 0120-0453) **6052**
Sociedad Colombiana de Psicoanalisis. Revista (COL ISSN 0120-0445) **6186**
Sociedad de Biologia de Concepcion. Boletin (CHL ISSN 0037-850X) **705**
Sociedad de Ciencias Naturales la Salle. Memoria (VEN ISSN 0037-8518) **7917**
Sociedad de Enfermeria Madrilena de Atencion Primaria Revista *see* S E M A P. Revista **5980**
Sociedad de Estudios Vascos. Boletin (ESP ISSN 0213-8670) **355**
Sociedad de Estudios Vascos. Cuadernos de Seccion. Ciencias Medicas *see* Osasunaz **5691**
Sociedad de Estudios Vascos. Memoria (ESP) **355**
Sociedad de Ingenieros. Informaciones y Memorias (PER) **3220**
Sociedad de la Informacion para America Latina y el Caribe Boletin *see* I N F O L A C. Boletin **5014**
Sociedad de Matematica de Chile. Boletin *see* Sociedad de Matematica de Chile. Notas **5536**
Sociedad de Matematica de Chile. Notas (CHL ISSN 0716-1298) **5536**
Sociedad de Obstetricia y Ginecologia de Buenos Aires. Revista (ARG ISSN 0037-8542) **6005**
Sociedad de Psiquiatria y Neurologia de la Infancia y Adolescencia. Revista *see* Revista Chilena de Psiquiatria y Neurologia de la Infiancia y la Adolescencia **6181**
Sociedad Ecuatoriana de Investigaciones Historicas y Geograficas. Memoria (ECU) **4312**
• Sociedad Entomologica Aragonesa. Boletin (ESP ISSN 1134-6094) **859**
Sociedad Entomologica Aragonesa. Manuales and Tesis (ESP ISSN 1576-9526) **859**
• Sociedad Entomologica Argentina. Boletin Informativo (ARG ISSN 1515-1557) **859**
• ➤ Sociedad Entomologica Argentina. Revista (ARG ISSN 0373-5680) **859**
Sociedad Espanola de Automoviles de Turismo. Memoria y Balance (ESP) **8756**
Sociedad Espanola de Briologia. Boletin (ESP ISSN 1132-8029) **818**
Sociedad Espanola de Ceramica y Vidrio. Boletin (ESP ISSN 0366-3175) **2045**
• Sociedad Espanola de Enfermeria Nefrologica. Revista (ESP ISSN 1139-1375) **6275**

Sociedad Espanola de Estudios Renacentistas Ingleses *see* S E D E R I **5170**
• Sociedad Espanola de Farmacia Hospitalaria. Boletin Informativo (ESP ISSN 1130-8230) **6881**
Sociedad Espanola de Hidrologia Medica. Boletin (ESP ISSN 0214-2813) **5716**
† Sociedad Espanola de Horticultura. Revista (ESP) **8989**
Sociedad Espanola de Italianistas. Revista (ESP ISSN 1576-7787) **4475**
Sociedad Espanola de Lengua y Literatura Inglesa Medieval *see* S E L I M **5171**
Sociedad Espanola de Malacologia. Noticiario (ESP ISSN 1131-527X) **818**
Sociedad Espanola de Medicina Rural y Generalista *see* S E M E R G E N **5708**
Sociedad Espanola de Medicos de Residencias (ESP ISSN 1579-4938) **5865**
▼ Sociedad Espanola de Medicos de Residencias. Boletin (ESP ISSN 1887-5866) **5865**
† Sociedad Espanola de Musicologia. Boletin (ESP ISSN 0210-1440) **8989**
• Sociedad Espanola de Oftalmologia. Archivos (ESP ISSN 0365-6691) **6052**
Sociedad Espanola de Virologia. Publicacion Oficial *see* Virologia **5828**
• ➤ Sociedad Espanola del Dolor. Revista (ESP ISSN 1134-8046) **5774**
Sociedad Espanola del Rorschach y Metodos Proyectivos. Revista (ESP ISSN 1130-4561) **7409**
• Sociedad Espanola Interdisciplinaria de S I D A. Publicacion Oficial (Sindrome de Inmunodeficiencia Adquirida) (ESP ISSN 1130-1597) **5826**
Sociedad Espanola para el Procesamiento del Lenguaje Natural. Boletin *see* Procesamiento del Lenguaje Natural **5163**
Sociedad Geografica de Colombia. Boletin (COL ISSN 0037-8577) **4029**
Sociedad Geografica de Lima, Peru. Boletin (PER ISSN 0037-8585) **4029**
Sociedad Geologica de Espana. Revista (ESP ISSN 0214-2708) **2767**
➤ Sociedad Geologica del Peru. Boletin (PER ISSN 0079-1091) **2767**
• Sociedad Geologica Mexicana. Boletin (MEX ISSN 1405-3322) **2767**
Sociedad Herpetologica Mexicana. Publicaciones (MEX ISSN 0188-6835) **963**
Sociedad Hispano-Luso-Americana de Lepidopterologia *see* S H I L A P **858**
Sociedad Iberoamericana de Informacion Cientifica Csalud *see* S I I Csalud **5708**
Sociedad Interamericana de Planificacion. Ediciones S I A P (ARG) **4427**
Sociedad Latinoamericana de Historia de la Ciencia y la Tecnologia. Boletin Informativo (COL ISSN 0185-5107) **7917**
• Sociedad Malacologica del Uruguay. Comunicaciones (URY ISSN 0037-8607) **963**
• ➤ Sociedad Matematica Mexicana. Boletin (MEX ISSN 0037-8615) **5536**
Sociedad Mexicana de Fisica. Boletin (MEX ISSN 0187-4713) **7040**
Sociedad Mexicana de Geografia y Estadistica. Boletin (MEX ISSN 0049-1004) **4036**
Sociedad Mexicana de Historia Natural. Revista (MEX ISSN 0370-7415) **2716**
Sociedad Mexicana de Lepidopterologia. Revista (MEX ISSN 0187-022X) **859**
Sociedad Mexicana de Mecanica de Suelos. Boletin (MEX ISSN 0185-4003) **3283**
Sociedad Micologica de Madrid. Boletin (ESP ISSN 0214-140X) **818**
Sociedad Nacional de Agricultura Boletin de Mercado *see* S N A Boletin de Mercado **154**
Sociedad Nacional de Agricultura Boletin Economico *see* S N A Boletin Economico **154**
Sociedad Nacional de Agricultura Vocero Agricola *see* S N A Vocero Agricola **154**
Sociedad Nacional de Mineria. Boletin Minero (CHL ISSN 0378-0961) **6479**
Sociedad Nuclear Espanola. Revista *see* Nuclear Espana **3171**
Sociedad Odontologica de la Plata. Revista (ARG ISSN 1514-9943) **5865**
Sociedad Oftalmologica de Madrid. Boletin (ESP ISSN 1132-3701) **6052**
• Sociedad Paraguaya de Cardiologia. Revista (PRY ISSN 1817-762X) **5799**
Sociedad Peruana de Historia. Serie: Actos Academicos (PER) **4312**
• Sociedad Peruana de Medicina Interna. Revista (PER ISSN 1681-9721) **5948**
Sociedad "Puig Adam" de Profesores de Matematicas. Boletin (ESP ISSN 1135-0261) **5536**
• ➤ Sociedad Quimica de Mexico. Revista (MEX ISSN 0583-7693) **2080**
Sociedad Quimica del Peru. Boletin *see* Sociedad Quimica del Peru. Revista **2080**
• Sociedad Quimica del Peru. Revista (PER ISSN 1810-634X) **2080**
Sociedad Rural Argentina. Anales (ARG ISSN 0037-8631) **301**
Sociedad Rural Argentina. Boletin (ARG ISSN 0037-864X) **157**
Sociedad Rural Argentina. Memoria (ARG ISSN 0081-0630) **301**
Sociedad Sueca de Americanistas. Revista *see* Acta Americana **322**
Sociedad Uruguaya (URY ISSN 0081-0649) **8135**
Sociedad Uruguaya de Egiptologia. Revista (URY ISSN 1510-3218) **416**
Sociedad Uruguaya de Geologia. Revista (URY ISSN 0797-2997) **2767**
• ➤ Sociedad Valenciana de Patologia Digestiva. Revista (ESP ISSN 1136-1956) **5931**
Sociedad Valenciana de Pediatria. Boletin (ESP ISSN 0489-3824) **6104**
Sociedad Vasco-Navarra de Pediatria. Boletin (ESP ISSN 0037-8658) **6104**
• Sociedad Venezolana de Espeleologia. Boletin (VEN ISSN 0583-7731) **2767**
Sociedad Venezolana de Fitopatologia. Revista Oficial *see* Fitopatologia Venezolana **788**
Sociedad Venezolana de Gastroenterologia. Revista *see* G E N **5923**
Sociedad Venezolana de Geologos. Boletin (VEN ISSN 0583-774X) **2767**
Sociedad Venezolana de Historia de la Medicina. Revista (VEN ISSN 0560-4567) **5716**
Sociedad Venezolana de Microbiologia. Boletin *see* Sociedad Venezolana de Microbiologia. Revista **896**
• Sociedad Venezolana de Microbiologia. Revista (VEN) **896**
Sociedad & Conocimiento (CHL ISSN 0717-991X) **8135**
Sociedad y Religion (ARG ISSN 0326-9795) **7682**
Sociedad y Utopia (ESP ISSN 1133-6706) **8135**
Sociedad Zoologica del Uruguay. Boletin (URY ISSN 0255-4402) **963**
Sociedade Brasileira de Agroinformatica (BRA ISSN 1517-3267) **157**
Sociedade Brasileira de Automatica *see* S B A **2463**
Sociedade Brasileira de Biomecanica (BRA ISSN 1518-8191) **3395**
➤ Sociedade Brasileira de Cancerologia. Revista (BRA ISSN 1415-6725) **6034**
Sociedade Brasileira de Cirurgia Plastica. Revista (BRA ISSN 1516-2001) **6258**
Sociedade Brasileira de Clinica Medica. Revista (BRA ISSN 1679-1010) **5716**
Sociedade Brasileira de Direito Internacional. Boletim (BRA ISSN 0103-8451) **4941**
Sociedade Brasileira de Economia Politica. Revista (BRA ISSN 1415-1979) **7184**
Sociedade Brasileira de Enfermeiros de Centro Cirurgico Revista *see* S O B E C C. Revista **5980**
Sociedade Brasileira de Estudos sobre Discos Voadores. Boletim (BRA ISSN 0037-8666) **70**
Sociedade Brasileira de Farmacia Hospitalar. Revista (BRA ISSN 1808-4540) **6881**
• Sociedade Brasileira de Fonoaudiologia (BRA ISSN 1516-8034) **6085**
Sociedade Brasileira de Geografia. Boletim (BRA ISSN 0037-8674) **4029**
• Sociedade Brasileira de Hematologia e Hemoterapia. Boletim (BRA ISSN 1516-2451) **5941**
Sociedade Brasileira de Historia da Ciencia. Boletim (BRA ISSN 0103-1899) **7917**
Sociedade Brasileira de Historia da Ciencia. Revista (BRA ISSN 0103-7188) **7917**
Sociedade Brasileira de Infermeiros Pediatras. Revista (BRA ISSN 1676-3793) **5981**
• ➤ Sociedade Brasileira de Matematica. Boletim, Nova Serie/Brazilian Mathematical Society. Bulletin, New Series (DEU ISSN 1678-7544) **5536**
• Sociedade Brasileira de Medicina Tropical. Revista (BRA ISSN 0037-8682) **5826**
Sociedade Brasileira de Musicologia. Boletim (BRA) **6617**
Sociedade Brasileira de Pesquisa Historica Revista *see* S B P H. Revista **4311**
Sociedade Brasileira de Telecomunicacoes. Revista (BRA ISSN 0102-986X) **2339**
Sociedade Broteriana. Anuario (PRT ISSN 0373-4641) **818**
Sociedade Broteriana. Boletim (PRT ISSN 0081-0657) **818**
Sociedade de Geografia de Lisboa. Boletim (PRT ISSN 0037-8690) **4029**
Sociedade de Lingua Portuguesa. Boletim (PRT ISSN 0049-1039) **5175**
Sociedade Distribuidora de Livros e Publicacoes Livros. Analise *see* S O D I Livros. Analise **7572**
• Sociedade e Cultura (BRA ISSN 1415-8566) **8005**
• Sociedade e Estado (BRA ISSN 0102-6992) **8135**
• Sociedade e Natureza (BRA ISSN 0103-1570) **4029**
Sociedade e Territorio (PRT ISSN 0873-6308) **8135**
Sociedade Entomologica do Brasil. Anais *see* Neotropical Entomology **855**
• Sociedade Paranaense de Matematica. Boletim (BRA ISSN 0037-8712) **5537**
Sociedade Portuguesa de Contabilidade. Boletim (PRT) **1302**
Sociedade Portuguesa de Entomologia. Boletim (PRT ISSN 0870-7227) **859**
Sociedade Portuguesa de Entomologia. Boletim. Suplemento (PRT ISSN 0871-0554) **859**
Sociedade Portuguesa de Malacologia. Publicacoes Ocasionais (PRT ISSN 0870-7308) **963**
Sociedade Portuguesa de Matematica. Boletim (PRT ISSN 0872-3672) **5537**
Sociedade Psicanalitica de Porto Alegre. Revista de Psicanalise (BRA ISSN 1413-4438) **7409**
Sociedades Brasileiras *see* Societes Bresiliennes **8989**
Sociedades Cotizadas en Bolsa (ESP) **1651**
• Le Societa (ITA ISSN 1591-2094) **8135**
• Societa 24. Banca Dati (ITA ISSN 1828-1273) **4881**
• Societa Astronomica Italiana. Memorie/Italian Astronomical Society. Journal (ITA ISSN 0037-8720) **581**
† Societa Chimica Italiana. Bollettino (ITA ISSN 0393-4594) **8989**
Societa Dalmata di Storia Patria. Atti e Memorie (ITA) **4264**
• La Societa degli Individui (ITA ISSN 1590-7031) **4475**
Societa degli Ingegneri e degli Architetti in Torino. Atti e Rassegna Tecnica (ITA ISSN 0004-7287) **3283**
Societa dei Naturalisti e Matematici di Modena. Atti (ITA ISSN 0365-7027) **5537**
Societa di Ortopedia e Traumatologia dell'Italia Meridionale ed Insulare Atti e Memorie *see* S O T I M I. Atti e Memorie **6072**
Societa di Studi Romagnoli. Guide (ITA ISSN 0081-0681) **4264**
Societa di Studi Valdesi. Bollettino (ITA ISSN 0037-8739) **4264**
Societa di Sudi Fiorentini. Bollettino (ITA ISSN 1129-8200) **4475**
Societa e Conflitto (ITA) **7184**
Societa e Diritto *see* Nova24 Review **4877**
• Societa e Storia (ITA ISSN 0391-6987) **4161**
Societa Economica di Chiavari. Atti (ITA) **8072**
Societa Entomologica Italiana. Bollettino (ITA ISSN 0373-3491) **859**
Societa Entomologica Italiana. Memorie (ITA ISSN 0037-8747) **859**
Societa Filosofica Italiana. Bollettino (ITA ISSN 1129-5643) **6952**
Societa Friulana di Archeologia. Bollettino (ITA ISSN 1828-2121) **416**
• Societa Geografica Italiana. Bollettino (ITA ISSN 0037-8755) **4029**
Societa Geografica Italiana. Memorie (ITA ISSN 0391-5190) **4029**
Societa Geologica Italiana. Bollettino (ITA ISSN 0037-8763) **2767**
Societa Geologica Italiana. Memorie (ITA ISSN 0375-9857) **2767**
Societa Istriana di Archeologia e Storia Patria. Atti e Memorie (ITA ISSN 0392-0321) **416**
Societa Italiana Attivita Regolatorie News *see* S I A R News **5708**
Societa Italiana di Andrologia Andronews *see* S I A Andronews **6274**
Societa Italiana di Buiatria. Atti *see* Buiatria **8794**
Societa Italiana di Ecografia Ostetrico-Ginecologica News *see* S I E O G News **6004**
• Societa Italiana di Farmacia Ospedaliera. Bollettino (ITA ISSN 0037-8798) **6881**
Societa Italiana di Fisica. Atti di Conferenze/Italian Physical Society. Conference Proceedings (ITA ISSN 1122-1437) **7040**
• Societa Italiana di Fisica. Nuovo Cimento B. Basic Topics in Physics (ITA ISSN 1594-9982) **7040**
• Societa Italiana di Fisica. Nuovo Cimento C. Colloquia on Physics (ITA ISSN 1124-1896) **7040**
• ➤ Societa Italiana di Fisica. Rivista del Nuovo Cimento (ITA ISSN 0393-697X) **7040**
Societa Italiana di Fotogrammetria e Topografia. Bollettino (ITA) **4029**
Societa Italiana di Ginecologia e Ostetrica Notizie *see* S I G O Notizie **6004**
➤ Societa Italiana di Malacologia. Bollettino Malacologico (ITA ISSN 0394-7149) **963**
Societa Italiana di Malacologia. Lavori (ITA ISSN 1121-3604) **963**
Societa Italiana di Malacologia. Notiziario (ITA ISSN 1121-161X) **963**
Societa Italiana di Matematica Applicata e Industriale lecture Notes *see* S I M A I e-lecture Notes **5532**
• Societa Italiana di Medicina Generale (ITA ISSN 1724-1375) **5716**
Societa Italiana di Patologia Ittica. Bollettino *see* Ittiopatologia **680**
Societa Italiana di Scienze Farmaceutiche (S I S F) Documenti *see* S I S F Documenti **8986**
Societa Italiana di Scienze Naturali e del Museo Civico di Storia Naturale. Atti (ITA ISSN 0037-8844) **7917**
Societa Italiana di Scienze Naturali e del Museo Civico di Storia Naturale. Memorie (ITA ISSN 0376-2726) **7917**
Societa Italiana per il Progresso delle Scienze. Atti della Riunione (ITA ISSN 0371-0424) **7917**
† Societa Letteraria di Verona. Bollettino (ITA) **8989**
† Societa Medico-Chirurgica della Provincia di Cremona. Bollettino (ITA ISSN 1121-1342) **8989**
Societa Medico-Chirurgica di Modena. Bollettino (ITA ISSN 0366-3434) **6259**
Societa Paleontologica Italiana. Bollettino (ITA ISSN 0375-7633) **6730**
Societa per gli Studi Storici, Archeologici ed Artistici della Provincia di Cuneo. Bollettino (ITA ISSN 0392-0402) **416**
† Societa Piemontese di Archeologia e Belle Arti. Bollettino (ITA) **8989**
Societa Reggiana di Studi Storici. Biblioteca. Fonti e Studi (ITA ISSN 1827-2576) **4264**
Societa Romana di Storia Patria. Archivio (ITA ISSN 0391-6952) **6617**
Societa Sarda di Scienze Naturali. Bollettino (ITA ISSN 0392-6710) **7917**
Societa Savonese di Storia Patria. Atti e Memorie (ITA ISSN 0392-033X) **4264**
† Societa Storica Maremmana. Bollettino (ITA ISSN 0583-8002) **8989**
Societa Storica Valtellinese. Bollettino (ITA ISSN 1591-0342) **4161**
Societa, Territorio, Ambiente (ITA) **8135**
Societa Tiburtina di Storia e d'Arte. Atti e Memorie (ITA ISSN 0394-1663) **416**
Societa Ticinese di Scienze Naturali. Bollettino (CHE ISSN 0379-1254) **7917**
Societa Ticinese di Scienze Naturali. Memorie (CHE ISSN 1421-5586) **7917**
• Societa Toscana di Scienza Naturali. Atti. Serie A (Abiologica) (ITA ISSN 0365-7655) **7917**
• Societa Toscana di Scienza Naturali. Atti. Serie B (Biologica) (ITA ISSN 0365-7450) **705**
Societa Veneziana di Scienze Naturali. Lavori (ITA ISSN 0392-9450) **7917**
• Societal (FRA ISSN 1274-3356) **1517**
Societas (CHL) **8005**
† Societas & Lex (ESP ISSN 1578-3804) **8989**
Societas Internationalis Odonatologica. Rapid Communications (NLD ISSN 0926-3551) **705**
• ➤ Societas pro Fauna et Flora Fennica. Memoranda (FIN ISSN 0373-6873) **705**
Societas Qualitatis (JPN ISSN 0918-5542) **3220**
Societas Uralo-Altaica. Veroeffentlichungen (DEU ISSN 0340-6423) **5175**
➤ Societat Catalana de Biologia. Treballs (ESP ISSN 0212-3037) **705**
Societat Catalana de Filosofia. Anuari (ESP ISSN 1130-4383) **6952**
Societat Catalana de Geografia. Treballs (ESP ISSN 1133-2190) **4264**
Societat Catalana de Lepidopterologia. Butlleti (ESP ISSN 1132-7669) **859**
Societat Catalana de Lepidopterologia. Treballs (ESP ISSN 0210-6159) **859**
• Societat Catalana de Matematiques. Butlleti (ESP ISSN 0214-316X) **5537**
Societat Catalana de Matematiques Noticies *see* S C M - Noticies **5531**
Societat Catalana de Pedagogia. Butlleti *see* Revista Catalana de Pedagogia **2905**
Societat d'Historia Natural de les Balears. Bolleti (ESP ISSN 0212-260X) **7917**
Societat d'Historia Natural de les Balears. Monografie (ESP) **705**
Societat d'Onomastica. Butlleti Interior (ESP ISSN 0213-4098) **5175**
Societat Paleontologica d'Elx. Seccion Paleontologica. Revista (ESP ISSN 1135-7665) **6730**
Societat Paleontologica d'Elx. Seccion Vertebrados Actuales. Revista (ESP ISSN 1576-9550) **6730**
Societat Valenciana de Psicologia. Anuari de Psicologia (ESP ISSN 1135-1268) **7409**
Societatea Lepidopterologica Romana. Buletin de informare/Romanian Lepidopterological Society. Information Bulletin (ROM ISSN 1221-5244) **859**
• Societatea Numismatica Romana. Buletinul (ROM ISSN 1012-0890) **6653**
Societati Listate (ROM) **1176**
• ➤ Societatis Geologorum Poloniae. Annales/Journal of the Geological Society of Poland/Polskie Towarzystwo Geologiczne. Rocznik (POL ISSN 0208-9068) **2767**
Societatis Historiae Medicinae Fenniae. Annales *see* Hippokrates **5628**
Societatis Litterarum Estonicae in Svecia. Annales *see* Eesti Teadusliku Seltsi Rootsis. Aastaraamat **3955**
Societatis Litterarum Humaniorum Regiae Upsaliensis. Annales *see* Kungliga Humanistiska Vetenskapssamfundet i Uppsala. Aarsbok **4185**
† Societats Catalanes de Fisica, Quimica, Matematiques i Tecnologia. Butlleti (ESP ISSN 1130-4758) **8989**
Societe *see* Society **8135**
Societe (USA ISSN 1050-1940) **7741**
Societe Academiques du Boulonnais. Memoires. Serie Histoire Naturel (FRA) **6730**
➤ Societe Algerienne de Chimie. Journal/Algerian Chemical Society. Journal (DZA ISSN 1111-4797) **2080**
Societe Americaine de Philosophie de Langue Francaise. Bulletin *see* Journal of French Philosophy **6928**
Societe Archeologique de Touraine. Bulletin (FRA ISSN 1153-2521) **417**
Societe Archeologique de Touraine. Memoires (FRA ISSN 1149-4670) **417**
Societe Archeologique et Historique de la Charente. Bulletins et Memoires (FRA ISSN 0244-9412) **4264**
Societe Archeologique et Historique de l'Orleanais. Bulletin (FRA ISSN 0337-579X) **417**
Societe Archeologique et Historique de Tarn et Garonne. Bulletin (FRA ISSN 1295-232X) **417**
Societe Archeologique, Historique, Litteraire et Scientifique du Gers. Bulletin Trimestriel (FRA ISSN 0037-8895) **417**
Societe Belge de Photogrammetrie - Teledetection et Cartographie. Bulletin Trimestriel (BEL) **4029**
Societe Belge d'Ophtalmologie. Bulletin (BEL ISSN 0081-0746) **6052**

Title

10878 SOCIETE BIBLIOGRAPHIQUE DU CANADA. CAHIERS ULRICH'S PERIODICALS

Societe Bibliographique du Canada. Cahiers *see* Bibliographical Society of Canada. Papers **618**
Societe Calviniste de France. Revue Reformee (FRA ISSN 0035-3884) **7775**
Societe Canadienne de la Croix-Rouge. Services Transfusionnels. Rapport Annuel *see* Canadian Red Cross Society. Blood Services. Annual Report **5935**
Societe Canadienne de Medecine Transfusionnelle. Bulletin *see* Canadian Society for Transfusion Medicine. Bulletin **5935**
Societe Canadienne de Pediatrie. Rapport Annuel *see* Canadian Paediatric Society. Annual Report **6089**
Societe Canadienne de Physiologie Vegetale. Bulletin *see* Canadian Society of Plant Physiologists. Bulletin **783**
Societe Canadienne de Rhumatologie. Journal *see* Canadian Rheumatology Association. Journal **6222**
Societe Canadienne des Etudes Bibliques. Bulletin *see* Canadian Society of Biblical Studies. Bulletin **7630**
Societe Canadienne des Postes. Rapport Annuel *see* Canada Post Corporation. Annual Report **7427**
Societe Canadienne des Sciences Judiciaires Journal *see* Canadian Society of Forensic Science Journal **4640**
Societe Canadienne d'Etudes Ethniques. Bulletin *see* C E S A. Bulletin **8938**
• Societe Canadienne d'Histoire de l'Eglise Catholique. Bulletin (CAN ISSN 1484-7450) **7817**
Societe Canadienne d'Hypotheques et de Logement. Statistiques Mensuelles sur l'Habitation *see* Canada Mortgage and Housing Corporation. Monthly Housing Statistics **4434**
Societe Clinique des Hopitaux de Bruxelles. Bulletins et Comptes Rendus *see* Acta Clinica Belgica **5565**
Societe d'Agriculture, Commerce, Sciences et Arts du Departement de la Marne. Memoires *see* Etudes Marnaises **4451**
Societe d'Amenagement Regional. Rapport Annuel *see* Regional Development Corporation. Annual Report **1514**
Societe d'Anthropologie de Paris. Bulletins & Memoires (FRA ISSN 0037-8984) **355**
Societe d'Archeologie et d'Histoire du Pays de Lorient. Bulletin (FRA ISSN 1763-1203) **4264**
Societe d'Art et d'Histoire du Diocese de Liege. Bulletin (BEL ISSN 0776-1295) **518**
Societe d'Assurance-Depots du Canada. Rapport Annuel *see* Canada Deposit Insurance Corporation. Annual Report **4497**
Societe de Biologie. Journal *see* Biologie Aujourd'hui **659**
Societe de Botanique du Nord de la France. Bulletin (FRA ISSN 0037-9034) **818**
Societe de Developpement de la Zone de Commerce International de Montreal a Mirabel. Rapport Annuel *see* Societe de Developpement de la Zone de Commerce International de Montreal a Mirabel. Rapport Annuel d'Activites **1582**
Societe de Developpement de la Zone de Commerce International de Montreal a Mirabel. Rapport Annuel d'Activites (CAN ISSN 1719-4040) **1582**
Societe de Geographie de Marseille. Bulletin (FRA ISSN 1622-3691) **4029**
Societe de la Bourse de Luxembourg. Cote Officielle de la Bourse de Luxembourg (Bi-monthly)/Luxembourg Stock Exchange. Official Price List (LUX) **1651**
Societe de la Bourse de Luxembourg. Cote Officielle de la Bourse de Luxembourg (Daily)/Luxembourg Stock Exchange. Official Price List (LUX) **1651**
Societe de la Bourse de Luxembourg. Cote Officielle de la Bourse de Luxembourg (Monthly)/Luxembourg Stock Exchange. Official Price List (LUX) **1651**
Societe de la Bourse de Luxembourg. Cote Officielle de la Bourse de Luxembourg (Weekly)/Luxembourg Stock Exchange. Official Price List (LUX) **1651**
Societe de la Bourse de Luxembourg. Fact Book (LUX) **1651**
Societe de la Bourse de Luxembourg. Faits et Chiffres/Luxembourg Stock Exchange. Facts and Figures (LUX) **1263**
Societe de la Bourse de Luxembourg. Rapport Annuel/Luxembourg Stock Exchange. Annual Report (LUX) **1651**
Societe de la Bourse des Valeurs de Casablanca. Statistiques Mensuelles (MAR) **1263**
Societe de l'Ecole des Chartes. Memoires et Documents (CHE ISSN 1158-6060) **4162**
Societe de l'Histoire de l'Art Francais. Bulletin (FRA ISSN 0301-4126) **518**
Societe de l'Histoire de Paris et de l'Ile-de-France. Bulletin (FRA ISSN 1148-7968) **4264**
Societe de l'Histoire du Protestantisme Francais. Bulletin (FRA ISSN 0037-9050) **7775**
Societe de l'Industrie Minerale. Guide des Mines et Carrieres (FRA ISSN 1163-5959) **6479**
• ➤ Societe de Linguistique de Paris. Bulletin (BEL ISSN 0037-9069) **5175**
➤ Societe de Linguistique de Paris. Memoires (Nouvelle Serie) (BEL ISSN 1256-9976) **5175**
• ➤ Societe de Pathologie Exotique. Bulletin (FRA ISSN 0037-9085) **5716**
Societe de Pathologie Exotique et de ses Filiales. Bulletin *see* Societe de Pathologie Exotique. Bulletin **5716**
Societe de Pharmacie de Bordeaux. Bulletin (FRA ISSN 0037-9093) **6881**
Societe de Physique et d'Histoire Naturelle de Geneve. Memoires (CHE ISSN 0252-7960) **7918**
Societe d'Egyptologie. Bulletin (CHE ISSN 0255-6286) **4178**
Societe d'Emulation de Montbeliard. Bulletin et Memoires (FRA ISSN 1162-8774) **4264**
Societe d'Emulation des Cotes-d'Armor (FRA ISSN 1251-9103) **4264**
Societe d'Emulation des Cotes-d'Armor. Memoires de l'Annee (Year) *see* Societe d'Emulation des Cotes-d'Armor **4264**
Societe d'Emulation du Bourbonnais. Bulletin (FRA ISSN 0037-9158) **417**
Societe des Alcools du Quebec. Rapport Annuel (CAN ISSN 0845-924X) **2699**
• ➤ Societe des Americanistes. Journal (FRA ISSN 0037-9174) **356**
Societe des Amis de Marcel Proust et des Amis de Combray. Bulletin *see* Bulletin Marcel-Proust **5267**
Societe des Amis du Chateau et des Musees de Blois. Bulletin *see* Chateau et des Musees de Blois. Cahiers **6522**
Societe des Amis du Vieux Strasbourg. Annuaire (FRA ISSN 0986-2684) **4427**
Societe des Amis du Vieux Toulon et de sa Region. Bulletin (FRA ISSN 1148-8549) **4264**
Societe des Antiquaires de l'Ouest. Bulletin *see* Revue Historique du Centre Ouest **4258**
Societe des Antiquaires de l'Ouest et des Musees de Poitiers. Memoires (FRA ISSN 1257-032X) **4265**
Societe des Antiquaires de Picardie. Bulletin Trimestriel (FRA ISSN 0037-9204) **4265**
Societe des Antiquaires de Picardie. Memoires. Series in 8 (FRA ISSN 0399-1717) **4265**
Societe des Auteurs, Compositeurs, Editeurs pour la Gerance des Droits de Reproduction Mecanique. Bulletin (FRA ISSN 0081-0843) **4784**
Societe des Auteurs et Compositeurs Dramatiques Journal des Auteurs *see* S A C D. Journal des Auteurs **8477**
Societe des Etudes Litteraires, Scientifiques et Artistiques du Lot. Bulletin (FRA ISSN 0755-2483) **4265**
Societe des Etudes Oceaniennes. Bulletin (AUS ISSN 0373-8957) **356**
Societe des Explorateurs et des Voyageurs Francais. Annuaire General (FRA ISSN 0081-086X) **4029**
Societe des Explorateurs Francais (FRA ISSN 1765-6370) **4029**
Societe des Francs-Bibliophiles. Annuaire (FRA ISSN 0081-0878) **7574**
Societe des Gens de Lettres. Feuilleton (FRA ISSN 1287-2687) **5374**
Societe des Naturalistes Luxembourgeois. Bulletin (LUX ISSN 0304-9620) **705**
• Societe des Oceanistes. Journal (FRA ISSN 0300-953X) **8005**
Societe des Oceanistes. Publications (FRA ISSN 0081-0894) **8005**
Societe des Poetes Francais. Annuaire (FRA ISSN 0081-0908) **5435**
Societe des Poetes Francais. Bulletin Trimestriel (FRA ISSN 0296-6867) **5435**
Societe des Sciences et des Lettres de Lodz. Bulletin (POL ISSN 0459-6854) **7918**
Societe des Sciences Historiques & Naturelles de la Corse. Bulletin (FRA ISSN 1154-7472) **7918**
Societe des Sciences Historiques et Naturelles de Semur en Auxois et des Fouilles d'Alesia. Bulletin (FRA ISSN 0989-9200) **4265**
Societe des Sciences, Lettres et Arts de Bayonne. Bulletin (FRA) **5374**
Societe des Sciences Mathematiques de Roumanie. Bulletin Mathematique (ROM ISSN 1220-3874) **5537**
➤ Societe des Sciences Medicales du Grand-Duche de Luxembourg. Bulletin (LUX ISSN 0037-9247) **5716**
➤ Societe des Sciences Naturelles de la Charente-Maritime. Annales (FRA ISSN 0373-9929) **914**
Societe des Sciences Naturelles de l'Ouest de la France. Bulletin (FRA ISSN 0758-3818) **963**
Societe des Sciences Naturelles et d'Archeologie de Toulon et du Var. Annales (FRA ISSN 0153-9299) **7918**
Societe d'Ethnozootechnie. Lettre (FRA ISSN 1151-1737) **963**
Societe d'Etude des Sciences Naturelles de Nimes et du Gard. Bulletin (FRA ISSN 0755-1924) **7918**
Societe d'Etude des Sciences Naturelles de Vaucluse. Bulletin (FRA ISSN 1148-8565) **7918**
La Societe d'Etudes Anglo-Americaines des Dix-Septieme et Dix-Huitieme Siecles. Bulletin (FRA ISSN 0291-3798) **5374**
Societe d'Etudes des Pratiques et Theories en Traduction Revue *see* S E P T E T Revue **5171**
Societe d'Etudes Historiques de la Nouvelle-Caledonie. Bulletin (NCL ISSN 0766-0278) **4194**
Societe d'Etudes Linguistiques et Anthropologiques de France *see* Bibliotheque de la S E L A F **5100**
Societe d'Etudes Linguistiques et Anthropologiques de France. Applications et Transferts (BEL ISSN 0755-9291) **5175**
➤ Societe d'Etudes Linguistiques et Anthropologiques de France. Numero Special (BEL ISSN 0249-7069) **5175**
Societe d'Etudes Scientifiques de l'Anjou. Bulletin (FRA ISSN 0153-9361) **7918**
Societe d'Etudes Scientifiques de l'Anjou. Bulletin Trimestriel (FRA) **7918**
Societe d'Etudes Scientifiques de l'Anjou. Memoires (FRA ISSN 0750-6473) **7918**
Societe d'Habitation du Quebec. Rapport Annuel (CAN ISSN 0714-6159) **4427**
Societe d'Histoire de France. Annuaire (FRA ISSN 0081-0940) **4265**
Societe d'Histoire de la Guadeloupe. Bulletin (GLP ISSN 0583-8266) **4312**
Societe d'Histoire et d'Archaeologie de Geneve. Bulletin (CHE ISSN 1017-849X) **417**
Societe d'Histoire et d'Archeologie de la Goele. Bulletin d'Information (FRA ISSN 0081-0967) **417**
Societe d'Histoire et d'Archeologie de Vichy et des Environs. Bulletin (FRA ISSN 1153-3277) **417**
Societe d'Histoire et d'Archeologie. Memoires et Documents. Serie in 4 (CHE) **417**
Societe d'Histoire et d'Archeologie. Memoires et Documents. Serie in 8 (CHE ISSN 1017-8511) **417**
Societe d'Histoire et de Genealogie du Plateau-Mont-Royal. Bulletin (CAN ISSN 1912-5070) **3783**
Societe d'Histoire et d'Epistemologie des Sciences de la Vie. Bulletin (FRA ISSN 1279-7243) **705**
Societe d'Histoire Naturelle de Colmar. Bulletin (FRA ISSN 0374-0706) **818**
Societe d'Histoire Naturelle de Toulouse. Bulletin (FRA ISSN 0758-4113) **705**
Societe d'Histoire Naturelle des Ardennes. Bulletin (FRA ISSN 0373-8442) **705**
Societe d'Histoire Naturelle du Doubs. Bulletin (FRA ISSN 0753-4655) **7918**
Societe d'Histoire Naturelle du Pays de Montbeliard. Bulletin (FRA ISSN 0755-2491) **818**
Societe d'Histoire Naturelle et des Amis du Museum d'Autun. Bulletin Trimestriel (FRA ISSN 0291-8390) **7918**
Societe d'Horticulture et d'Histoire Naturelle de l'Herault. Annales (FRA ISSN 0373-8701) **7918**
➤ Societe Entomologique de France. Annales (FRA ISSN 0037-9271) **859**
➤ Societe Entomologique de France. Bulletin (FRA ISSN 0037-928X) **859**
Societe Entomologique de France. Memoires (FRA ISSN 1285-5545) **859**
Societe Entomologique de Mulhouse. Bulletin (FRA ISSN 0373-4544) **859**
Societe Entomologique du Nord de la France. Bulletin (FRA ISSN 0395-7306) **859**
Societe Entomologique du Quebec. Memoires (CAN ISSN 0071-0784) **859**
Societe Entomologique Suisse. Bulletin. *see* Schweizerische Entomologische Gesellschaft. Mitteilungen **858**
Societe Financiere Internationale. Rapport Annuel *see* International Finance Corporation. Annual Report **1356**
Societe Finno-Ougrienne. Journal *see* Suomalais-Ugrilaisen Seuran Aikakauskirja **357**
Societe Finno-Ougrienne. Memoires *see* Suomalais-Ugrilaisen Seuran Toimituksia **357**
➤ Societe Francaise de Chimie. Annuaire (FRA ISSN 0996-8083) **2080**
Societe Francaise de Chirurgie Orthopedique et Traumatologique Cahiers d'Enseignement *see* La S O F C O T. Cahiers d'Enseignement **6257**
Societe Francaise de Chirurgie Orthopedique et Traumatologique. Conferences d'Enseignement (FRA ISSN 0081-1033) **6073**
Societe Francaise de Microbiologie. Bulletin (FRA ISSN 0998-9188) **896**
Societe Francaise de Numismatique. Bulletin (FRA ISSN 0037-9344) **6653**
• Societe Francaise de Parasitologie. Bulletin (FRA ISSN 1626-0384) **896**
Societe Francaise de Philosophie. Bulletin (FRA ISSN 0037-9352) **6953**
Societe Francaise de Photogrammetrie et de Teledetection. Bulletin *see* Revue Francaise de Photogrammetrie et de Teledetection **4027**
Societe Francaise de Photographie. Bulletin (FRA ISSN 1254-6380) **6977**
Societe Francaise de Physique. Annuaire (FRA ISSN 0081-1076) **7040**
Societe Francaise de Physique. Bulletin *see* Reflets de la Physique **7037**
Societe Francaise de Psychanalyse Adlerienne. Bulletin (FRA ISSN 1953-6623) **7409**
Societe Francaise d'Egyptologie. Bulletin (FRA ISSN 0037-9379) **417**
Societe Francaise d'Energie Nucleaire Bulletin *see* S F E N. Bulletin **3174**
Societe Francaise des Architectes. Bulletin (FRA) **457**
Societe Francaise d'Histoire des Hopiteaux. Revue (FRA ISSN 1255-250X) **5716**
➤ Societe Francaise du Vide. Proceedings (FRA) **7040**
Societe Francaise Shakespeare. Actes du Congres (FRA ISSN 0750-5299) **5374**
Societe Franco-Japonaise de Biologie. Bulletin/Nichifutsu Seibutsu Gakkaishi (JPN ISSN 0081-1106) **705**
Societe Fribourgeoise des Sciences Naturelles. Bulletin (CHE ISSN 0366-3256) **7918**
Societe Genealogique Canadienne-Francaise. Memoires (CAN ISSN 0037-9387) **3783**
Societe Generale de Belgique. Rapport - Report (BEL ISSN 0081-1114) **1383**
Societe Generale de Presse et d'Editions. Index (FRA) **4583**
Societe Generale Suisse d'Histoire. Bulletin *see* Schweizerische Gesellschaft fuer Geschichte. Bulletin **4160**
• Societe Geographique de Liege. Bulletin (BEL ISSN 0770-7576) **4029**
• Societe Geologique de France. Bulletin (FRA ISSN 0037-9409) **2767**
➤ Societe Geologique de France. Memoires (FRA ISSN 0249-7549) **2767**
Societe Geologique de Normandie et des Amis du Museum du Havre. Bulletin (FRA ISSN 1768-3572) **2767**
Societe Geologique du Nord. Annales (FRA ISSN 0767-7367) **2768**
La Societe Guernesiaise. Report and Transactions (GBR ISSN 0144-1973) **4265**
Societe Herpetologique de France. Bulletin (FRA ISSN 0754-9962) **963**
Societe Herpetologique de France. Bulletin de Liaison *see* Societe Herpetologique de France. Bulletin **963**
Societe Historique Acadienne. Cahiers (CAN ISSN 0049-1098) **4312**
Societe Historique de Meaux et sa Region. Bulletin (FRA ISSN 1775-8882) **4265**
Societe Historique de Saint-Boniface. Bulletin (CAN ISSN 0384-0158) **4312**
La Societe Historique du Canada. Brochures Ethniques (CAN ISSN 1483-9512) **4162**
Societe Historique du Madawaska. Revue (CAN ISSN 0820-0793) **4313**
• Societe Historique du Marigot, Longueuil. Cahier (CAN ISSN 0711-0529) **4313**
Societe Historique et Archeologique dans le Limbourg. Publications/Limburgs Geschied- en Oudheidkundig Genootschap. Jaarboek (NLD ISSN 0167-6652) **4265**
Societe Historique et Archeologique de Pontoise, du Val d'Oise et du Vexin. Memoires (FRA ISSN 1148-8085) **4265**
Societe Historique et Archeologique du Perigord. Bulletin (FRA ISSN 1141-135X) **4265**
Societe Historique Nicolas Denys. Revue d'Histoire (CAN ISSN 0381-9388) **4313**
Societe Imperiale des Naturalistes de Moscou. Section Geologique. Bulletin *see* Moskovskoe Obshchestvo Ispytatelei Prirody. Geologicheskii Otdel. Byulleten **2756**
Societe Industrielle de Mulhouse. Bulletin (FRA ISSN 0037-9441) **8439**
Societe Internationale Arthurienne. Bulletin Bibliographique *see* International Arthurian Society. Bibliographical Bulletin **5407**
Societe Internationale de Conchyliologie. Bulletin (CHE ISSN 0259-9678) **963**
Societe Internationale des Amis de Montaigne. Nouveau Bulletin (FRA ISSN 0037-9182) **5374**
Societe Internationale d'Etudes Yourcenariennes. Bulletin (FRA ISSN 0987-7940) **5374**
Societe J.K. Huysmans. Bulletin (FRA ISSN 1148-862X) **5239**
Societe Jean Bodin pour l'Histoire Comparative des Institutions. Recueils (BEL ISSN 0998-0601) **1176**
Societe Jersiaise. Annual Bulletin (GBR ISSN 0141-1942) **4475**
La Societe Jules Verne. Bulletin (FRA ISSN 0986-2226) **4265**
Societe Liegeoise de Musicologie. Bulletin (BEL) **6617**
➤ Societe Linguistique de Paris. Collection Linguistique (BEL) **5201**
Societe Linneenne de Bordeaux. Bulletin (FRA ISSN 0750-6848) **963**
Societe Linneenne de Lyon. Bulletin Mensuel (FRA ISSN 0366-1326) **705**
Societe Litteraire de la Poste et de France Telecom. Missives (FRA ISSN 1169-212X) **5239**
• ➤ Societe Mathematique de France. Bulletin (FRA ISSN 0037-9484) **5537**
Societe Mathematique de France. Journee Annuelle (FRA) **5537**
➤ Societe Mathematique de France. Memoires (FRA ISSN 0249-633X) **5537**
Societe Militaire du Canton de Geneve. Bulletin (CHE) **6446**
Societe Mycologique de France. Bulletin Trimestriel (FRA ISSN 0395-7527) **818**
Societe Nationale des Chemins de Fer Belges. Bulletin des Acquisitions *see* Nationale Maatschappij van Belgische Spoorwegen. Informatie en Aanwinsten **8528**
Societe Nationale des Chemins de Fer Belges. Rapport Annuel (BEL ISSN 0081-119X) **8625**

DIRECTORY 2010 SOCIETY FOR TECHNICAL COMMUNICATION. ANNUAL CONFERENCE 10879

Societe Nationale des Sciences Naturelles et Mathematiques de Cherbourg. Memoires (FRA ISSN 0374-9231) **7918**

Societe Nationale d'Etude et de Construction de Moteurs d'Aviation Informations *see* S N E C M A Informations **69**

Societe Nationale d'Etude et de Promotion Industrielle. Bulletin d'Information Industrielle (SEN) **1904**

Societe Neophilologique de Helsinki. Bulletin *see* Neuphilologischer Verein in Helsinki. Mitteilungen **5155**

Societe Neophilologique de Helsinki. Memoires (FIN ISSN 0355-0192) **5175**

Societe Neuchateloise de Geographie. Bulletin (CHE ISSN 0373-3076) **356**

Societe Neuchateloise des Sciences Naturelles. Bulletin (CHE ISSN 0366-3469) **705**

Societe Nucleaire Canadienne. Sommaires du Congres *see* Canadian Nuclear Society. Annual Conference Summaries **3166**

Societe Odontologique de Paris. Journal. (FRA ISSN 1285-3933) **5865**

Societe Philomatique Vosgienne. Bulletin *see* Memoire des Vosges **4244**

Societe pour le Developpement Minier de la Cote d'Ivoire. Rapport Annuel (CIV ISSN 0250-3697) **6479**

Societe pour l'Etude de l'Architecture au Canada. Journal *see* Society for the Study of Architecture in Canada. Journal **457**

Societe Prehistorique Ariege - Pyrenees. Bulletin (FRA ISSN 1764-1020) **417**

➤ Societe Prehistorique Francaise. Bulletin (FRA ISSN 0249-7638) **417**

Societe Prehistorique Francaise. Memoires (FRA ISSN 1950-2133) **417**

▼ Societe Protectrice des Animaux. Lettre (FRA ISSN 1961-0548) **321**

Societe Quebecoise de Recherche en Musique Cahiers *see* S Q R M. Cahiers **6614**

Societe Quebecoise de Science Politique. Bulletin/Canadian Political Science Association. Bulletin (CAN ISSN 0832-008X) **7184**

Societe Radio-Canada. Rapport Annuel *see* C B C / Radio Canada Annual Report **2314**

Societe Rencesvals. Bulletin Bibliographique (BEL ISSN 0583-8797) **5408**

Societe Royale Belge d'Entomologie. Bulletin (BEL ISSN 1374-8297) **859**

Societe Royale Belge d'Entomologie. Memoires (BEL ISSN 0376-2025) **859**

Societe Royale d'Archeologie, d'Histoire et de Folklore de Nivelles et du Brabant Wallon. Annales (BEL) **417**

Societe Royale de Lettres de Lund. Bulletin *see* Kungliga Humanistiska Vetenskapssamfundet i Lund. Aarsberattelse **5319**

Societe Royale d'Economie Politique de Belgique. Seances (BEL) **1176**

Societe Royale des Sciences de Liege. Bulletin (BEL ISSN 0037-9565) **7918**

Societe Royale du Canada. Annuaire *see* Royal Society of Canada. Calendar **7904**

Societe Royale Le Vieux-Liege. Bulletin (BEL ISSN 0776-1309) **4265**

Societe Royale Le Vieux-Liege. Chronicle. Sites et Monuments (BEL ISSN 1371-0753) **4265**

Societe Saint-Jean-Baptiste de Montreal. Information Nationale (CAN ISSN 0537-6211) **8135**

Societe Scientifique de Bretagne. Bulletin (FRA ISSN 0037-9581) **7918**

La Societe Scientifique et Litteraire de Cannes et de l'Arrondissement de Grasse. Annales (FRA ISSN 0995-9181) **7918**

Societe Speleologique de Grece. Bulletin Trimestriel *see* Greek Speleological Society. Deltion **2745**

Societe Suisse de Chronometrie. Actes de la Journee d'Etude (CHE ISSN 1023-2680) **4569**

Societe Suisse de Chronometrie. Actes du Congres de Chronometrie (CHE ISSN 1023-2699) **4569**

Societe Suisse de Chronometrie. Bulletin (CHE ISSN 1016-2011) **4569**

Societe Suisse des Americanistes. Bulletin/Schweizerische Amerikanisten-Gesellschaft. Bulletin (CHE ISSN 0582-1592) **356**

Societe Theophile Gautier. Bulletin (FRA ISSN 0221-7945) **5374**

➤ Societe Vaudoise des Sciences Naturelles. Bulletin (CHE ISSN 0037-9603) **7918**

Societe Vaudoise des Sciences Naturelles. Memoires (CHE ISSN 0037-9611) **7918**

Societe Veterinaire Pratique de France. Bulletin (FRA ISSN 1635-3501) **8807**

➤ Societe Zoologique de France. Bulletin (FRA ISSN 0037-962X) **963**

➤ Societe Zoologique de France. Memoires (FRA ISSN 0750-747X) **964**

• ➤ Societes (BEL ISSN 0765-3697) **8135**

Societes Africaines et Diaspora (FRA ISSN 1275-4099) **8135**

Societes Americaines: Repertoire des Sources de Documentation *see* American Companies: Guide to Sources of Information **1200**

Societes Arabes et Musulmanes (FRA ISSN 1151-843X) **4325**

† Societes Bresiliennes/Sociedades Brasileiras (FRA ISSN 1629-825X) **8989**

• Societes Contemporaines (FRA ISSN 1150-1944) **8135**

Societes d'Histoire et d'Archeologie de la Meuse. Bulletin (FRA ISSN 0525-1249) **4265**

Societes d'Ophtalmologie de France. Bulletin (FRA ISSN 0081-1270) **6052**

Societes en Changement (FRA ISSN 1773-5440) **8135**

Societes en Mouvement (FRA ISSN 1148-5833) **8135**

➤ Societes & Representations (FRA ISSN 1262-2966) **8005**

† • Societies Without Borders (NLD ISSN 1871-8868) **8989**

• Society/Societe (CAN ISSN 0381-1794) **8135**

Society *see* Shehui **8000**

Society (IND) **3889**

• ➤ Society (USA ISSN 0147-2011) **8005**

Society (Hong Kong) (HKG) **3875**

• ➤ Society and Animals (NLD ISSN 1063-1119) **321**

• ➤ Society and Business Review (GBR ISSN 1746-5680) **8135**

Society and Change (IND ISSN 0970-5279) **8005**

Society and Commerce (IND ISSN 0300-4546) **1433**

➤ Society and Culture in East-Central Europe (USA ISSN 1549-1706) **4265**

Society and Economy *see* Tarsadalom es Gazdasag **8992**

• ➤ Society and Economy (HUN ISSN 1588-9726) **1176**

Society and Economy in Central and Eastern Europe *see* Society and Economy **1176**

Society and Leisure *see* Loisir et Societe **4980**

• ➤ Society and Natural Resources (USA ISSN 0894-1920) **3466**

Society and Politics in Africa (USA ISSN 1083-3323) **8135**

• Society and Welfare/Hevra u-Revaha (ISR ISSN 0334-4029) **8072**

Society - Family *see* Shehui - Jianting **3827**

Society Farsarotul Newsletter (USA ISSN 1042-3230) **3565**

Society for Advancement of Chicanos and Native Americans in Science News *see* S A C N A S News **7906**

Society for Advancement of Management Advanced Management Journal *see* S A M Advanced Management Journal **1792**

Society for Advancement of Management International Management Conference. Proceedings *see* S A M International Management Conference. Proceedings **1792**

Society for American Archaeology Archaeological Record *see* The S A A Archaeological Record **415**

Society for American Archaeology. Special Publications Series (USA) **417**

Society for American Baseball Research, Inc. Bulletin *see* S A B R Bulletin **8244**

• Society for American Music. Bulletin (USA) **6617**

▼ • ➤ Society for American Music. Journal (GBR ISSN 1752-1963) **6617**

Society for American Music. Membership Directory and Handbook (USA) **6617**

Society for Anthropology in Community Colleges Notes - Teaching Anthropology *see* S A C C Notes - Teaching Anthropology **354**

Society for Antibacterial and Antifungal Agents, Japan. Abstracts of the Meeting *see* Nihon Bokin Bobai Gakkai. Nenji Taikai Yoshishu **717**

Society for Applied Anthropology. Newsletter (USA) **356**

• Society for Applied Learning Technology. Newsletter (USA) **2951**

† ➤ Society for Applied Microbiology. Symposium Series (GBR ISSN 1467-4734) **8989**

Society for Applied Spectroscopy. Membership Directory *see* Applied Spectroscopy **2098**

Society for Archaeological Sciences Bulletin *see* S A S Bulletin **415**

Society for Armenian Studies. Journal (USA ISSN 0747-9301) **3565**

➤ Society for Army Historical Research. Journal (GBR ISSN 0037-9700) **6446**

Society for Atomic Collision Research. Circular *see* Genshi Shototsu Sakyura **7066**

Society for Biomaterials. Annual Meeting Proceedings (USA) **745**

Society for Buddhist-Christian Studies. Newsletter (USA ISSN 1934-080X) **7682**

Society for Business Ethics. Membership Directory (USA ISSN 1930-6652) **1176**

Society for Business Ethics. Newsletter (USA ISSN 1932-4677) **6953**

Society for Chemical Regulation of Plants. Proceedings of Annual Meeting *see* Shokubutsu Kagaku Chosetsu Gakkai Taikai Kenkyu Happyo Kirokushu **817**

Society for Clinical and Experimental Hypnosis Focus *see* S C E H Focus **5943**

Society for College and University Planning mail News *see* S C U P E-mail News **3000**

Society for Commercial Archeology. Journal (USA) **457**

Society for Commercial Archeology. News (USA ISSN 1069-0492) **457**

Society for Common Insights. Journal (USA) **7682**

Society for Companion Animal Studies. Journal (GBR ISSN 1363-464X) **322**

Society for Cryobiology. News Notes (USA ISSN 1069-3610) **705**

Society for Earthquake and Civil Engineering Dynamics Newsletter *see* S E C E D Newsletter **3282**

Society for Environmental Exploration. Frontier Vietnam Forest Research Programme. Technical Report (GBR ISSN 1369-8796) **3703**

Society for Environmental Graphic Design Design *see* S E G D Design **530**

Society for Ethnomusicology Newsletter *see* S E M Newsletter **6614**

Society for Ethnomusicology. Special Series (USA) **6617**

Society for Experimental Biology. Symposia (GBR ISSN 0081-1386) **705**

➤ Society for Experimental Mechanics. Annual Proceedings (USA ISSN 1046-6789) **3357**

† Society for General Microbiology. Symposium (GBR ISSN 0081-1394) **8989**

Society for German - American Studies. Newsletter (USA ISSN 0741-5753) **5374**

Society for German Genealogy in Eastern Europe Journal *see* S G G E E Journal **3781**

Society for Gynecologic Investigation. Journal (Print) *see* Reproductive Sciences **6003**

Society for Health Systems. Journal (USA ISSN 1043-1721) **6687**

Society for Historical Archaeology Newsletter (USA ISSN 0037-9735) **417**

➤ Society for Historical Archaeology. Special Publication Series (USA ISSN 0898-0004) **417**

➤ Society for History in the Federal Government. Occasional Papers (USA) **4313**

Society for Imaging Science and Technology Annual Conference. Proceedings *see* I S & T Annual Conference. Proceedings **6969**

Society for Imaging Science and Technology Non-impact Printing Proceedings *see* I S & T Non-impact Printing Proceedings **6969**

Society for Imaging Science and Technology Symposium on Electronic Imaging: Science and Technology. Abstracts *see* I S & T - S P I E Symposium on Electronic Imaging: Science and Technology. Abstracts **6969**

Society for Imaging Science and Technology. Technical Symposium on Pre-press, Proofing, & Printing (USA) **6977**

➤ Society for In Vitro Biology. Proceedings (USA) **928**

Society for Industrial and Applied Mathematics Journal on Applied Dynamical Systems *see* S I A M Journal on Applied Dynamical Systems **5531**

Society for Industrial and Applied Mathematics Journal on Applied Mathematics *see* S I A M Journal on Applied Mathematics **5531**

Society for Industrial and Applied Mathematics Journal on Computing *see* S I A M Journal on Computing **5555**

Society for Industrial and Applied Mathematics Journal on Control and Optimization *see* S I A M Journal on Control and Optimization **5531**

Society for Industrial and Applied Mathematics Journal on Discrete Mathematics *see* S I A M Journal on Discrete Mathematics **5531**

Society for Industrial and Applied Mathematics Journal on Financial Mathematics *see* S I A M Journal on Financial Mathematics **5531**

Society for Industrial and Applied Mathematics Journal on Imaging Sciences *see* S I A M Journal on Imaging Sciences **7084**

Society for Industrial and Applied Mathematics Journal on Mathematical Analysis *see* S I A M Journal on Mathematical Analysis **5531**

Society for Industrial and Applied Mathematics Journal on Matrix Analysis and Applications *see* S I A M Journal on Matrix Analysis and Applications **5531**

Society for Industrial and Applied Mathematics Journal on Numerical Analysis *see* S I A M Journal on Numerical Analysis **5531**

Society for Industrial and Applied Mathematics Journal on Optimization *see* S I A M Journal on Optimization **5531**

Society for Industrial and Applied Mathematics Journal on Scientific Computing *see* S I A M Journal on Scientific Computing **5532**

Society for Industrial and Applied Mathematics Miscellaneous Titles in Applied Mathematics *see* S I A M Miscellaneous Titles in Applied Mathematics **5532**

Society for Industrial and Applied Mathematics Monographs on Mathematical Modeling and Computation *see* S I A M Monographs on Mathematical Modeling and Computation **5532**

Society for Industrial and Applied Mathematics News *see* S I A M News **5532**

Society for Industrial and Applied Mathematics Proceedings *see* S I A M - A M S Proceedings **5531**

Society for Industrial and Applied Mathematics Proceedings in Applied Mathematics *see* S I A M Proceedings in Applied Mathematics **5532**

Society for Industrial and Applied Mathematics Review *see* S I A M Review **5532**

Society for Industrial and Applied Mathematics Studies in Applied and Numerical Mathematics *see* S I A M Studies in Applied and Numerical Mathematics **5532**

Society for Industrial Archeology Newsletter (USA ISSN 0160-1067) **8439**

Society for Industrial Microbiology Industrial Microbiology News *see* S I M Industrial Microbiology News **770**

Society for Information Display International Symposium. Applications Seminar Notes *see* S I D International Symposium. Applications Seminar Notes **2489**

Society for Information Display International Symposium. Digest of Technical Papers *see* S I D International Symposium. Digest of Technical Papers **2444**

Society for Information Display International Symposium. Seminar Lecture Notes *see* S I D International Symposium. Seminar Lecture Notes **2489**

• Society for Information Display. Journal (USA ISSN 1071-0922) **2490**

Society for Information Management Network *see* S I M Network **2550**

• ➤ Society for Integrative Oncology. Journal (CAN ISSN 1715-894X) **6034**

Society for Interdisciplinary Studies Internet Digest *see* S I S Internet Digest **8986**

Society for International Hockey Research. Newsletter (CAN ISSN 1910-1414) **8202**

Society for International Ministries Now *see* S I M Now **7679**

Society for Italian Historical Studies. Newsletter (USA ISSN 0081-1424) **4265**

Society for Japanese Blood Programme. Journal *see* Ketsueki Jigyo **5939**

• Society for Marine Mammalogy Newsletter (Online) (USA) **964**

• Society for Medieval Archaeology Newsletter (GBR ISSN 1740-7036) **417**

➤ Society for Mining, Metallurgy, and Exploration, Inc. Transactions (USA ISSN 1075-8623) **6479**

Society for Mining, Metallurgy, and Exploration Resource Guide Resource Guide *see* S M E Resource Guide **6478**

➤ Society for Modeling and Simulation International. Transactions (USA ISSN 0740-6797) **2518**

• ➤ Society for Musicology in Ireland. Journal (IRL ISSN 1649-7341) **6617**

Society for Nautical Research. Newsletter *see* Mariner's Mirror **4152**

Society for Near Eastern Studies in Japan. Bulletin *see* Oriento **558**

• Society for Neuroscience. Abstract Viewer & Itinerary Planner (USA) **6186**

Society for New Testament Studies. Monograph Series (GBR ISSN 0081-1432) **7682**

Society for News Design Membership Directory *see* S N D Membership Directory **4583**

Society for News Design Scandinavia Magazine *see* S N D S Magazine **4583**

Society for News Design Update *see* S N D Update **4583**

Society for Old Testament Study. Book List (GBR ISSN 0081-1440) **7699**

Society for Pacific Coast Native Iris Almanac *see* S P C N I Almanac **3749**

Society for Pentecostal Studies. Newsletter (USA) **7775**

Society for Photographic Education. Quarterly Newsletter (USA ISSN 0748-6413) **6977**

Society for Post-Medieval Archaeology. Monograph (GBR ISSN 1740-4924) **417**

• Society for Post-Medieval Archaeology. Newsletter (GBR ISSN 1357-8340) **417**

Society for Promoting Christian Knowledge International Study Guide *see* S P C K International Study Guide **7679**

Society for Promoting Training of Women. Annual Report (GBR) **8884**

Society for Psychical Research. Journal (GBR ISSN 0037-9751) **6743**

Society for Psychical Research. Proceedings (GBR ISSN 0081-1475) **6744**

† Society for Psychological Anthropology. Publications (GBR ISSN 1367-4102) **8989**

• Society for Range Management. International Rangeland Congress. Abstracts of Papers (USA ISSN 0163-173X) **186**

Society for Renaissance Studies. Bulletin (GBR ISSN 0264-8571) **5374**

Society for Research in Asiatic Music. Journal *see* Toyo Ongaku Kenkyu **6624**

Society for Research in Asiatic Music. Newsletter *see* Toyo Ongaku Gakkai Kaiho **6623**

• ➤ Society for Research in Child Development. Monographs (USA ISSN 0037-976X) **7409**

Society for Research in Child Development Newsletter *see* S R C D Newsletter **2167**

Society for Research into Higher Education News *see* S R H E News **3001**

• Society for Romanian Studies Newsletter (USA) **4265**

Society for Scholarly Publishing Bulletin *see* S S P Bulletin **7572**

Society for Science on Form. Bulletin *see* Katachi no Kagakkaiho **7874**

Society for Sedimentary Geology. Special Publication (USA ISSN 1060-071X) **2768**

Society for Slovene Studies. Documentation Series (USA) **4265**

Society for Slovene Studies. Letter (USA) **4475**

➤ Society for Spanish and Portuguese Historical Studies. Bulletin (USA ISSN 0739-182X) **4265**

Society for Technical Communication. Annual Conference Proceedings (USA) **2339**

Title

10880 SOCIETY FOR THE ADVANCEMENT OF ANAESTHESIA IN DENTISTRY ULRICH'S PERIODICALS

Society for the Advancement of Anaesthesia in Dentistry Digest *see* S A A D Digest **5864**
Society for the Advancement of Anaesthesia in Dentistry Newsletter *see* S A A D Newsletter **5864**
Society for the Advancement of Breeding Researches in Asia and Oceania Journal of Breeding and Genetics *see* S A B R A O Journal of Breeding and Genetics **153**
Society for the Advancement of Material and Process Engineering Journal *see* S A M P E Journal **3357**
Society for the Advancement of Material and Process Engineering Symposium Proceedings *see* S A M P E Symposium Proceedings **3357**
Society for the Advancement of Scandinavian Study. News and Notes (USA ISSN 0891-7477) **8005**
Society for the Advancement of Travel for the Handicapped News *see* S A T H News **8754**
• Society for the Anthropology of Europe. Journal (USA ISSN 1535-5632) **356**
Society for the Eradication of Television Free *see* S E T Free **2389**
Society for the History of Authorship Reading and Publishing News *see* S H A R P News **7572**
Society for the History of Social and Economic Thought. Annual Bulletin *see* Keizaigakushi Gakkai Nenpo **1546**
Society for the History of Technology Newsletter *see* S H O T Newsletter **8437**
Society for the Medical Application of Carbon Thirteen. Bulletin *see* 13 C Igaku **5739**
Society for the Performing Arts (USA) **8478**
Society for the Philosophic Study of the Contemporary Visual Arts Newsletter *see* S P S C V A Newsletter **6511**
Society for the Preservation of New England Antiquities's Historic Houses in New England *see* S P N E A's Historic Houses in New England **456**
Society for the Promotion of Byzantine Studies. Publication (GBR) **4265**
Society for the Promotion of Construction Engineering. Annual Report *see* Kensetsu Kogaku Kenkyu Shinkokai Nenpo **3277**
➤ Society for the Study of Architecture in Canada. Journal/Societe pour l'Etude de l'Architecture au Canada. Journal (CAN ISSN 1486-0872) **457**
Society for the Study of Egyptian Antiquities. Journal (CAN ISSN 0383-9753) **417**
➤ Society for the Study of Human Biology. Symposium Series (GBR ISSN 0954-7800) **928**
➤ Society for the Study of Metaphysical Religion. Journal (USA ISSN 1545-7338) **6953**
Society for the Study of Southern Literature. Newsletter (USA ISSN 0197-8071) **5374**
Society for the Study of Symbolic Interaction Notes *see* S S S I Notes **8130**
Society for Underwater Technology. News (GBR ISSN 1352-8289) **2818**
Society for Values in Higher Education. Monograph Series (USA) **3002**
Society for Values in Higher Education. Newsletter (USA) **3002**
Society for Veterinary Epidemiology and Preventive Medicine. Proceedings of a Meeting (GBR ISSN 0956-7496) **8807**
Society in Transition *see* South African Review of Sociology **8140**
Society Matters (AUS) **7682**
Society Matters (GBR ISSN 1756-5928) **7612**
Society News *see* S A G E Link **8066**
Society News (Icelandic-American Society of New York) *see* Icelandic - American Society of New York. Society News **3538**
▼ • Society Now (GBR ISSN 1758-2121) **8005**
Society of Actuaries. Transactions: Reports of Mortality and Morbidity Experience (USA) **4523**
• Society of Actuaries. Yearbook (USA) **4523**
Society of Allied Weight Engineers, Inc. Newsletter *see* S A W E Newsletter **69**
• Society of American Foresters. National Convention. Proceedings (CD-ROM) (USA) **3703**
Society of American Registered Architects Scope *see* S A R A Scope **456**
Society of American Value Engineers Inc. Proceedings *see* S A V E Proceedings **1792**
Society of Animal Artists Newsletter (USA) **518**
Society of Antiquaries of London. Occasional Papers (GBR ISSN 0953-7155) **417**
Society of Antiquaries of London. Research Committee. Reports (GBR ISSN 0953-7163) **417**
Society of Antiquaries of Newcastle upon Tyne. Monograph Series (GBR ISSN 0265-1785) **4265**
Society of Antiquaries of Newcastle upon Tyne. Record Series (GBR) **4265**
➤ Society of Antiquaries of Scotland. Monograph Series (GBR ISSN 0263-3191) **4265**
➤ Society of Antiquaries of Scotland. Proceedings (GBR ISSN 0081-1564) **4265**
Society of Archer-Antiquaries. Journal (GBR ISSN 0560-6152) **8202**
• ➤ Society of Architectural Historians. Journal (USA ISSN 0037-9808) **457**
Society of Architectural Historians News *see* S A H News **456**
• Society of Architectural Historians of Great Britain. Newsletter (GBR) **457**
Society of Architectural Historians of Great Britain. Occasional Paper (GBR) **457**
• ➤ Society of Archivists. Journal (GBR ISSN 0037-9816) **5048**
Society of Archivists. Newsletter (GBR ISSN 0142-2278) **5048**
Society of Atmospheric Electricity of Japan. Journal *see* Taiki Denki Gakkaishi **6396**
Society of Atmospheric Electricity of Japan. Proceedings *see* Taiki Denki Kenkyu **6396**
Society of Automotive Engineers Aerospace Material Specifications Index *see* S A E A M S Index **3218**
Society of Automotive Engineers Ground Vehicle Lighting Standards Manual *see* S A E Ground Vehicle Lighting Standards Manual **8602**
Society of Automotive Engineers Handbook (CD-ROM) *see* S A E Handbook (CD-ROM) **8602**
Society of Automotive Engineers International Journal of Aerospace *see* S A E International Journal of Aerospace **69**
Society of Automotive Engineers International Journal of Commercial Vehicles *see* S A E International Journal of Commercial Vehicles **8510**
Society of Automotive Engineers International Journal of Engines *see* S A E International Journal of Engines **8602**
Society of Automotive Engineers International Journal of Fuels and Lubricants *see* S A E International Journal of Fuels and Lubricants **6790**
Society of Automotive Engineers International Journal of Materials & Manufacturing *see* S A E International Journal of Materials & Manufacturing **3357**
Society of Automotive Engineers International Journal of Passenger Cars - Electronic and Electrical Systems *see* S A E International Journal of Passenger Cars - Electronic and Electrical Systems **3329**
Society of Automotive Engineers International Journal of Passenger Cars - Mechanical Systems *see* S A E International Journal of Passenger Cars - Mechanical Systems **3395**
Society of Automotive Engineers of Japan. Journal *see* Jidosha Gijutsu **8587**
Society of Automotive Engineers of Japan. Transactions *see* Jidosha Gijutsukai Ronbunshu **8587**
Society of Automotive Engineers Off-Highway Engineering *see* S A E Off-Highway Engineering **8602**
Society of Automotive Engineers Special Publications *see* S A E Special Publications **3218**
Society of Automotive Engineers Technical Papers *see* S A E Technical Papers **8602**
Society of Automotive Engineers Update *see* S A E Update **3395**
Society of Automotive Engineers Vehicle Engineering *see* S A E Vehicle Engineering **3218**
Society of Basque Studies in America. Journal (USA ISSN 1042-3834) **4265**
Society of Biblical Literature and Exegesis. Journal *see* Journal of Biblical Literature **7654**
Society of Biblical Literature. Disseration Series *see* Academia Biblica **7619**
Society of Biblical Literature Forum *see* The S B L Forum **7678**
Society of Biblical Literature. Symposium Series (NLD ISSN 1569-3627) **7682**
Society of Biological Chemists Newsletter *see* S B C Newsletter **745**
Society of Biological Chemists. Proceedings (IND ISSN 0300-0486) **745**
Society of Biomechanisms. Journal *see* Baiomekanizumu Gakkaishi **752**
Society of Biomechanisms. Proceedings of the Annual Meeting *see* Baiomekanizumu Gakujutsu Koenkai Yokoshu **752**
Society of California Archivists Newsletter (San Francisco) *see* S C A Newsletter (San Francisco) **5045**
Society of Cardiovascular Anesthesiologists. Annual Meeting Proceedings (USA) **5774**
• Society of Cardiovascular Anesthesiologists. Newsletter (USA) **5774**
Society of Cartographers Bulletin *see* S o C Bulletin **4028**
Society of Children's Book Writers & Illustrators Bulletin *see* S C B W I Bulletin **7572**
Society of Christian Ethics. Annual *see* Society of Christian Ethics. Journal **7682**
• ➤ Society of Christian Ethics. Journal (USA ISSN 1540-7942) **7682**
Society of College, National & University Libraries Annual Library Statistics *see* S C O N U L Annual Library Statistics **5059**
Society of College, National & University Libraries Focus *see* S C O N U L Focus **5059**
Society of Colonial Wars. Bulletin (USA) **4313**
Society of Composers Inc. Journal of Music Scores *see* S C I Journal of Music Scores **6614**
Society of Composers Newsletter (USA ISSN 1088-033X) **6617**
Society of Cosmetic Chemists of Japan. Journal (JPN ISSN 0387-5253) **596**
Society of Cypriot Studies. Bulletin/Kypriakai Spoudai (CYP ISSN 0081-1580) **4265**
Society of Decorative Painters. Business & Teacher Directory (Year) *see* Business & Teacher Directory (Year) **532**
➤ Society of Depreciation Professionals. Journal (USA ISSN 1067-8689) **1302**
Society of Design Administration. National Publication (USA) **457**
Society of Diagnostic Medical Sonography Sound News *see* S D M S Sound News **6208**
• Society of Economic Geologists. Guidebook Series (CD-ROM) (USA ISSN 1547-3104) **2768**
† • Society of Economic Geologists. Guidebook Series (Print) (USA ISSN 1547-3090) **8989**
Society of Economic Geologists, Inc. Compilations *see* S E G Compilations **2765**
Society of Economic Geologists, Inc. Newsletter *see* S E G Newsletter **2765**
• Society of Economic Geologists. Special Publications Series (USA ISSN 1547-3112) **2768**
Society of Economic Paleontologists and Mineralogists Midyear Meeting. Abstracts *see* S E P M Midyear Meeting. Abstracts **6730**
Society of Economic Paleontologists and Mineralogists Reprint Series *see* S E P M Reprint Series **6730**
Society of Economic Paleontologists and Mineralogists. Special Publication *see* Society for Sedimentary Geology. Special Publication **2768**
• Society of Editors Briefing (GBR) **4583**
Society of Engineers for Mineral Springs. Journal *see* Onsen Kogakkaishi **2760**
Society of Experimental Test Pilots. Symposium Proceedings (USA ISSN 0742-3705) **70**
Society of Exploration Geophysicists Abstracts *see* S E G Abstracts **2789**
Society of Exploration Geophysicists. Expanded Abstracts with Biographies *see* Society of Exploration Geophysicists. S E G Technical Program Expanded Abstracts **2790**
Society of Exploration Geophysicists. Geophysical Development Series (USA ISSN 1046-0586) **2790**
Society of Exploration Geophysicists. Geophysics Reprint Series (USA ISSN 0734-5631) **2790**
Society of Exploration Geophysicists. International Meeting. Abstracts *see* S E G Abstracts **2789**
Society of Exploration Geophysicists. International Meeting. Proceedings (USA) **2790**
Society of Exploration Geophysicists of Japan. Conference. Proceedings *see* Butsuri Tansa Gakkai Gakujutsu Koenkai Koen Ronbunshu **2778**
• Society of Exploration Geophysicists. S E G Technical Program Expanded Abstracts (USA) **2790**
➤ Society of Exploration Geophysicists. Special Publications (Symposia) Series (USA) **2790**
Society of Federal Linguists. Newsletter (USA) **5175**
Society of Fiber Science and Technology, Japan. Journal *see* Sen'i Gakkaishi **8457**
Society of Flight Test Engineers. Annual Symposium Proceedings (USA ISSN 1050-9690) **70**
Society of Flight Test Engineers Newsletter *see* S F T E Newsletter **69**
Society of Folk Dance Historians. Report to Members (USA) **2687**
Society of Freelance Editors and Proofreaders Directory *see* S F E P Directory **7572**
Society of General Internal Medicine Forum *see* S G I M Forum **5948**
Society of Geomagnetism and Earth, Planetary and Space Sciences. News *see* Chikyu Denjiki Chikyu Wakuseiken Gakkai Kaiho **2779**
Society of Geomagnetism and Earth, Planetary and Space Sciences. Preprints of the Meeting *see* Chikyu Denjiki Chikyu Wakuseiken Gakkai Koenkai Koen Yokoshu **2779**
Society of Glass and Ceramic Decorators. Membership Directory (USA) **2045**
Society of Glass and Ceramic Decorators. TechNotebook (USA) **2045**
Society of Government Economists. Bulletin (USA) **1176**
Society of Government Meeting Planners. Newsletter (USA) **6282**
Society of Graphic Artists. Publication (GBR) **7328**
Society of Heating, Air-Conditioning and Sanitary Engineering of Japan. Journal *see* Kuki Chowa Eisei Kogaku **7530**
Society of Heating, Air-conditioning and Sanitary Engineers of Japan. Transactions *see* Kuuki Chouwa, Eisei Kogakkai Ronbunshuu **4123**
Society of High Technology in Agriculture. Journal *see* Shokubutsu Kankyou Kougaku **156**
Society of Independent Professional Earth Scientists. Newsletter (USA ISSN 0037-9913) **2717**
Society of Industrial and Office Realtors. Professional Report (USA) **7612**
➤ Society of Inorganic Materials, Japan. Journal/Sekko, Sekkai, Semento, Chikyu Kankyo no Kagaku (JPN ISSN 1345-3769) **2118**
Society of Instrument and Control Engineers. Journal *see* Keisoku to Seigyo **6403**
Society of Instrument and Control Engineers Journal of Control, Measurement, and System Integration *see* S I C E Journal of Control, Measurement, and System Integration **2436**
Society of Instrument and Control Engineers. Transactions *see* Keisoku Jido Seigyo Gakkai Ronbunshu **3207**
Society of Insurance Research News *see* S I R News **4522**
• Society of Insurance Research. Research Review (USA ISSN 0899-5346) **4523**
Society of Irish Foresters. Journal *see* Irish Forestry **3694**
Society of Japanese Virologists. Proceedings of the Annual Meeting *see* Nihon Uirusu Gakkai Sokai Enzetsu Shoroku **894**
Society of Japanese Women Scientists. News *see* Nihon Josei Kagakusha no Kai Nyusu **8877**
• ➤ Society of Laparoendoscopic Surgeons. Journal (USA ISSN 1086-8089) **6259**
• ➤ Society of Leather Technologists and Chemists. Journal (GBR ISSN 0144-0322) **4975**
Society of Lesbian and Gay Anthropologists Newsletter *see* S O L G A Newsletter **354**
Society of Magnetic Resonance in Medicine. Proceedings of Annual Conference *see* Jiki Kyomei Igakkai Puroguramu **6200**
Society of Maine Archivists. Newsletter (USA) **5048**
Society of Malawi Journal (MWI ISSN 0037-993X) **7918**
Society of Management Accountants of Canada. Annual Report (CAN) **1302**
Society of Manufacturing Engineers News *see* S M E News **3464**
Society of Manufacturing Engineers. Technical Paper AD (USA ISSN 0361-8765) **3357**
Society of Manufacturing Engineers. Technical Paper EE (USA ISSN 0191-0841) **3358**
Society of Manufacturing Engineers. Technical Paper EM (USA ISSN 0161-1852) **3358**
Society of Manufacturing Engineers. Technical Paper FC (USA ISSN 0161-1844) **3358**
Society of Manufacturing Engineers. Technical Paper IQ (USA ISSN 0161-1860) **3358**
Society of Manufacturing Engineers. Technical Paper MF (USA ISSN 0191-085X) **3358**
Society of Manufacturing Engineers. Technical Paper MR (USA ISSN 0161-1879) **3358**
Society of Manufacturing Engineers. Technical Paper MS (USA ISSN 0161-6382) **3358**
Society of Manufacturing Engineers. Technical Paper TE (USA ISSN 0161-1887) **3358**
Society of Maritime Arbitrators. Award Service (USA) **8662**
Society of Materials Engineering for Resources. International Journal (JPN ISSN 1347-9725) **3220**
Society of Materials Engineering for Resources of Japan. Journal *see* Sozai Busseigaku Zasshi **3358**
Society of Materials Science, Japan. Journal *see* Zairyo **3360**
Society of Mexican American Engineers & Scientists *see* M A E S **3208**
Society of Motion Picture and Television Engineers Motion Imaging Journal *see* S M P T E Motion Imaging Journal **6511**
Society of Motor Manufacturers and Traders. Monthly Statistical Review (GBR) **8530**
Society of Naval Architects and Marine Engineers. Transactions (USA ISSN 0081-1661) **8662**
Society of Non-Traditional Technology. Journal *see* Mito Kagaku Gijutsu **8432**
Society of North American Goldsmiths Newsletter *see* S N A G Newsletter **539**
Society of Otorhinolaryngology and Head-Neck Nurses. Update (USA) **6085**
Society of Petroleum Engineers *see* S P E **3395**
Society of Petroleum Engineers, Inc. Drilling & Completion *see* S P E Drilling & Completion **6791**
Society of Petroleum Engineers, Inc. Journal *see* S P E Journal **6791**
Society of Petroleum Engineers, Inc. Production & Operations *see* S P E Production & Operations **6791**
Society of Petroleum Engineers, Inc. Projects, Facilities & Construction *see* S P E Projects, Facilities & Construction **6791**
Society of Petroleum Engineers, Inc. Reservoir Evaluation and Engineering *see* S P E Reservoir Evaluation and Engineering **6791**
Society of Petroleum Engineers. Paper (USA ISSN 0362-0980) **3255**
• Society of Petroleum Engineers. Reprint Series (USA ISSN 0891-0901) **6793**
Society of Petroleum Engineers Review *see* S P E Review **6791**
Society of Photo Finishing Engineers Newsletter *see* S P F E Newsletter **6976**
Society of Photo-optical Instrumentation Engineers Milestone Series *see* S P I E Milestone Series **7084**
Society of Photo-Optical Instrumentation Engineers Reviews *see* S P I E Reviews **7084**
Society of Photographer and Artist Representatives. Member Directory (USA) **6977**
Society of Photographer and Artist Representatives. Newsletter (USA) **6977**
Society of Photographic Science and Technology of Japan. Journal *see* Nihon Shashin Gakkaishi **6972**
Society of Plant Protection of North Japan. Annual Report *see* Kita Nihon Byogaichu Kenkyukaiho **240**
• Society of Plastics Engineers. Annual Technical Conference (Antec). Proceedings (USA) **7100**

Link to your serials resources and content with ulrichsweb.com

Title

DIRECTORY 2010 SOTSIAL'NYE I GUMANITARNYE NAUKI. OTECHESTVENNAYA I 10883

● Solski Razgledi (SVN ISSN 1318-1483) **2913**
● ➤ Solsko Polje/The School Field (SVN ISSN 1581-6036) **2913**
Solstice (CAN ISSN 1718-1577) **5374**
● ➤ Solstice (USA ISSN 1059-5325) **5537**
● Solstice (Palm Desert) (USA ISSN 1948-1624) **5374**
➤ Solubility Data Series (USA ISSN 0191-5622) **2081**
● Soluciones (PER ISSN 1606-1047) **3928**
● Soluciones Avanzadas (MEX ISSN 0188-8048) **1421**
Solunar Bite Times (NZL ISSN 1177-5807) **8335**
▼ ● Solution Manager Expert (USA ISSN 1945-032X) **2438**
Solution Zone *see* SolutionZone **2481**
Solutions (AUS ISSN 1449-9428) **1176**
Solutions (CAN ISSN 1719-9743) **1176**
Solutions! *see* Paper360 **6736**
Solutions (Denver) (USA ISSN 1543-5733) **1383**
● Solutions Integrator (BRA ISSN 1415-8884) **2494**
▼ Solutions Logiciels (FRA ISSN 1959-7630) **1794**
Solutions Reseaux (FRA ISSN 1627-7244) **2503**
Solutions Unix-Linux (FRA ISSN 1764-4372) **2598**
SolutionZone (GBR) **2481**
Soluzioni di Assemblaggio (ITA) **1904**
Solvay Pharmaceuticals Conferences (NLD ISSN 1566-7685) **6881**
● Solve (AUS ISSN 1832-651X) **8439**
Solve It Logically Special (GBR ISSN 0964-9913) **4347**
● ➤ Solvent Extraction and Ion Exchange (USA ISSN 0736-6299) **2105**
➤ Solvent Extraction Research and Development, Japan (JPN ISSN 1341-7215) **2130**
Solving Problems in the Teaching of Literacy (USA) **7409**
● Solvista (GBR ISSN 1465-038X) **5447**
Soma (USA ISSN 0896-5005) **5239**
† Somae Panmae-aeg Tonggye/Korea (Republic). National Statistical Office. Annual Report on the Consumer Price Index (KOR ISSN 1976-8370) **8989**
Somatic Inkblot Society Journal of Projective Psychology & Mental Health *see* S I S Journal of Projective Psychology & Mental Health **7406**
Somatics (USA ISSN 0147-5231) **6997**
● ➤ Somatosensory and Motor Research (GBR ISSN 0899-0220) **928**
Somborske Novine (SRB ISSN 0038-1276) **3945**
▼ ● La Sombrereria (ESP ISSN 1988-7698) **5239**
▼ Some Assembly Required (USA ISSN 1935-2956) **5374**
Some Friends (USA) **5374**
Some Important Statistics on Slovenia *see* Pomembnejsi Statisticni Podatki o Sloveniji **8394**
Some Other Magazine (USA) **5375**
Somersault Gymnastics Magazine (AUS ISSN 1833-427X) **8202**
Somerset and Dorset Notes and Queries (GBR ISSN 0049-1306) **4266**
Somerset Archaeology and Natural History (GBR ISSN 0081-2056) **418**
Somerset Birds (GBR ISSN 0081-2048) **914**
Somerset Business (GBR) **1517**
Somerset Country Gardener (GBR) **3750**
Somerset Farmer (GBR ISSN 0038-1314) **157**
Somerset Life (GBR ISSN 1476-1238) **3871**
▼ Somerset Life (USA ISSN 1941-238X) **539**
Somerset Magazine *see* Somerset Life **3871**
Somerset Memories (USA ISSN 1939-5000) **540**
Somerset Past (USA) **3783**
Somerset Record Society (GBR ISSN 1355-4689) **3871**
Somerset Studio (USA ISSN 1096-5823) **540**
Somerset Workshop (USA ISSN 1937-9722) **540**
● Something About the Author (USA ISSN 0276-816X) **5375**
Something for the Weekend *see* s four w **8198**
Sommaire Annuel des Donnees sur la Recolte de Poissons et de Mammiferes Marins dans les Territoires du Nord-Ouest (CAN ISSN 1183-9554) **3608**
Sommaire Chronologique des Niveaux d'Eau. Quebec *see* Canada. Inland Waters Directorate. Historical Water Levels Summary. Quebec **2793**
Sommaire des Realisations *see* Realizations (Estrie) **150**
Sommaire Statistique du B S T des Evenements Aeronautiques *see* T S B Statistical Summary of Aviation Occurrences **7549**
Sommaire Statistique du B S T, Evenements Maritimes *see* T S B Statistical Summary, Marine Occurrences **8531**
Sommaires de la Jurisprudence *see* Canadian Current Law Case Digests **4639**
Sommelier (CZE ISSN 1212-4001) **4398**
Sommelier (ESP) **610**
▼ Sommelier Journal (USA ISSN 1944-074X) **610**
Sommelier Magazin (DEU ISSN 1615-5114) **610**
➤ Sommerfeltia (NOR ISSN 0800-6865) **818**
Sommerfeltia. Supplement (NOR ISSN 0802-8478) **818**
Sommets *see* U de S **2304**
● Somnial Times (USA) **6647**
Somno - Journal (DEU ISSN 1611-0706) **5716**
● Somnologie/Somnology (DEU ISSN 1432-9123) **5716**
Somnology *see* Somnologie **5716**
● Somogyi Hirlap (HUN ISSN 0865-9125) **3877**
Somogyi Hirlap Gratisz (HUN ISSN 1585-8693) **3877**
Somogyi Hirlap. Vasarnap Reggel (HUN ISSN 1419-0176) **3877**
Somontano (ESP ISSN 1132-8924) **4162**
Somos (NIC) **8884**
● Somos Jovenes (CUB ISSN 0864-0564) **2168**
Sonar Transducers Conference. Proceedings (GBR) **7089**
▼ ● Sonar4 Science Fiction and Horror Ezine (USA ISSN 1948-0830) **5447**
Sondages (FRA ISSN 0489-7293) **8139**
Sondenhaeuser Verband Zeitung *see* S V Zeitung **2299**
Sonderbaende zur Theologischen Zeitschrift (CHE ISSN 0067-4907) **7682**
Sonderpaedagogik (DEU ISSN 0342-7366) **3046**
Sonderpaedagogik in Bayern (DEU ISSN 1860-0220) **3046**
Sonderpaedagogik in Forschung und Praxis (DEU ISSN 1618-6028) **3046**
➤ Sonderpaedagogische Foerderung (DEU ISSN 1611-1540) **2913**
Sondersprachenforschung (DEU ISSN 1430-0214) **5176**
Sondheim Magazine *see* Sondheim News **6617**
Sondheim News (GBR ISSN 1470-2401) **6617**
● The Sondheim Review (USA ISSN 1076-450X) **8479**
Sondreposten *see* Armer & Bein **4077**
Sonerasound (FIN) **2339**
Sonet Newsletter *see* S O N E T / S D H / M A N **2338**
Song and Popular Culture *see* Lied und Populaere Kultur **6584**
Song Liao Jin Yuanshi/History of Song, Liao, Jin and Yuan Dynasties (CHN ISSN 1001-263X) **4188**
Song of Zion (USA ISSN 0273-2920) **6617**
Song Post *see* Songu Posuto **914**
● Songklanakarin Journal of Science and Technology (THA) **7918**
● Songliao Xuekan (Ziran Kexue Ban) (CHN ISSN 1000-1840) **7918**
Songlines (GBR ISSN 1464-8113) **6617**
Songs Monthly *see* Gequ **6569**
Songu Posuto/Song Post (JPN) **914**
Songwriter's Market (USA ISSN 0161-5971) **6617**
Songwriter's Monthly (USA ISSN 1525-6138) **8154**
The Sonia Sanchez Literary Review *see* B Ma **5259**
Sonic (DEU ISSN 1613-4451) **6617**
Sonic (ITA ISSN 1828-6186) **6617**
Sonic Arts Network Journal *see* Journal of Electroacoustic Music **8968**
● Sonic Seducer (DEU) **6617**
Sonic the Comic (GBR ISSN 0969-3041) **5447**
● Sonika (MEX) **6617**
● Sonitron (ESP ISSN 1133-0260) **3114**
● Sonne (DEU ISSN 0721-0094) **582**
Sonne, Wind und Waerme (DEU ISSN 1861-938X) **3177**
Sonnenenergie (CHE ISSN 0379-6256) **3177**
Sonnenenergie (DEU ISSN 0172-3278) **3177**
Der Sonntag (Leipzig) (DEU ISSN 0232-5527) **7775**
Der Sonntag (Limburg) (DEU ISSN 1617-6421) **7817**
Sonntag Aktuell (DEU) **3857**
● Sonntags Blick (CHE ISSN 1421-4350) **3959**
Sonntagsanzeiger (DEU) **3857**
Sonntagsblatt (Leer) (DEU) **7775**
Sonntagsblatt (Muenchen) (DEU ISSN 0722-3145) **7775**
Sonntagsblatt - Gemeindeblatt fuer Muenchen und Oberbayern (DEU ISSN 0722-2831) **7775**
SonntagsBlick *see* Sonntags Blick **3959**
Der Sonntagsbrief *see* Christlicher Digest **7633**
† Sonntagsdienste (DEU ISSN 0176-862X) **8989**
Sonntagsgruss und Besinnung (DEU) **7775**
● SonntagsZeitung (CHE ISSN 1420-7222) **3959**
Sono Magazine (FRA ISSN 0243-4938) **8154**
SonoAce-International (RUS) **6208**
● Sonoma (USA ISSN 1937-0377) **8756**
Sonoma Business *see* NorthBay Biz **1155**
Sonoma County Herald-Recorder (USA) **1176**
➤ Sonoma County Physician (USA ISSN 1087-8807) **5716**
Sonoma County Women's Voices (USA) **8903**
Sonoma Mandala (USA) **5375**
The Sonoma Searcher (USA ISSN 1065-1217) **3783**
Sonora Review (USA ISSN 0275-5203) **5375**
Sonoran Quarterly (USA ISSN 1075-1386) **818**
● Sonoran Tails (USA ISSN 1945-6816) **6815**
Sonorensis (USA ISSN 0277-4887) **7919**
Sonovision (FRA ISSN 0768-956X) **2339**
Sonovision Qui Fait Quoi? (FRA ISSN 1166-6609) **2028**
Sons and Daughters Reflector *see* S & D Reflector **3781**
Sons of Italy News (USA ISSN 0038-1446) **2270**
Sons of Italy Times (USA ISSN 0038-1454) **3565**
Sons of Norway Viking *see* Viking Magazine for the Members of Sons of Norway **3571**
Sons of the American Revolution Magazine (USA ISSN 0161-0511) **4313**
➤ Sonus (USA ISSN 0739-229X) **6617**
▼ Sony Magazine (GBR ISSN 1755-9391) **3871**
Sony Technical Reports (JPN ISSN 0916-7153) **3114**
Sonyeon Hangug Ilbo (KOR) **2213**
Sonyon Dong-A (KOR) **2213**
Soochow Journal of Chinese Studies (TWN ISSN 1027-1163) **560**
Soochow Journal of Economics and Business (TWN ISSN 0259-3769) **1176**
Soochow Journal of Foreign Languages and Literatures (TWN ISSN 0259-3777) **5176**
Soochow Journal of History (TWN ISSN 1025-0689) **4188**
Soochow Journal of Japanese Language Teaching/Dongwu Riyu Jiaoyu Xuebao (TWN) **5176**
Soochow Journal of Mathematics (TWN ISSN 0250-3255) **5537**
Soochow Journal of Philosophical Studies/Dongwu Zhexue Xuebao (TWN) **6953**
Soochow Journal of Political Science/Dongwu Zhengzhi Xuebao (TWN ISSN 1019-8636) **7184**
Soochow Journal of Social Work (TWN ISSN 1026-4493) **8072**
Soochow Journal of Sociology/Dongwu Shehui Xuebao (TWN ISSN 1019-0449) **8005**
Soochow Law Review (TWN ISSN 0259-3750) **4784**
Soohak Kwa Moolli *see* Suhak Kwa Mulli **7042**
Sooke News Mirror (CAN) **3817**
Sooner Catholic (USA) **7817**
Sooner L P G Times (USA ISSN 0038-1500) **6793**
Sooners Illustrated (USA ISSN 0279-3288) **8202**
Soosiana (HUN ISSN 0133-7971) **964**
Sooty (GBR ISSN 1362-2862) **2213**
Sopa de Letras Fantasticas (ARG ISSN 1514-4437) **4347**
Sopas Pocket (ARG ISSN 1514-6030) **4347**
Sopas Pocket. Extra (ARG ISSN 1515-033X) **4347**
● Sophia (FIN ISSN 1238-5484) **4171**
● ➤ Sophia (NLD ISSN 0038-1527) **7682**
Sophia (California) (USA ISSN 0194-7958) **7817**
Sophia (Tokyo, 1984) (JPN) **8884**
Sophia (Virginia) (USA ISSN 1521-1231) **7682**
Sophia Circle (USA) **8884**
Sophia English Studies *see* Jochi Eigo Bungaku Kenkyu **5132**
Sophia Kokyuroku in Mathematics *see* Jochi Daigaku Sugaku Kokyuroku **5499**
Sophia Life Science Bulletin *see* Seimei Kagaku Kenkyujo Kiyo **704**
Sophia Linguistica (JPN ISSN 0287-5357) **5176**
Sophia Magazine (NLD ISSN 1871-9279) **7716**
● The Sophist (USA ISSN 1559-8764) **3002**
● Sophisticated Groom (USA) **5561**
The Sophisticated Investor (USA) **1652**
Sophisticate's Black Hair (USA ISSN 1042-5276) **591**
Sophisticate's Hairstyle Guide (USA ISSN 1041-7125) **591**
Sophistication in Westchester (USA) **5083**
The Sophist's Bane (USA ISSN 1948-6901) **3002**
Sophoshare (NLD ISSN 0929-0753) **3331**
● Sopi Online (SEN) **7184**
Sopp- og Nyttevekster (NOR ISSN 1504-4165) **818**
Sopra il Livello del Mare *see* S L M **2716**
Soprano, Alto, Bass Choir *see* The S A B Choir **6614**
Soprintendenza Archeologica di Pompei. Cataloghi (ITA) **418**
Soprintendenza Archeologica di Pompei. Monografie (ITA) **418**
Soprintendenza Archeologica di Pompei. Studi (ITA ISSN 1828-1907) **418**
Soprintendenza per i Beni Culturali della Valle d'Aosta. Quaderni (ITA) **518**
SoQ *see* Southern Quarterly **4476**
Sora to Umi/Sky and Marine (JPN ISSN 0289-3347) **70**
Sorbifolia (FIN ISSN 0359-3568) **818**
Sorby Natural History Society. Newsletter (GBR ISSN 0038-1551) **7919**
The Sorby Record (GBR ISSN 0260-2245) **7919**
● ➤ Sorites (ESP ISSN 1135-1349) **6953**
● Sorkins Directory of Business & Government (Chicago Edition) (USA ISSN 1055-906X) **1904**
Sorkins Directory of Business & Government (Kansas City Edition) *see* Sorkins Directory of Business & Government (Chicago Edition) **1904**
Sorkins Directory of Business & Government (St. Louis Edition) *see* Sorkins Directory of Business & Government (Chicago Edition) **1904**
Soroptimist of the Americas *see* Best for Women **8027**
Soroush (Monthly) (IRN) **3892**
Soroush (Weekly) (IRN) **3892**
Sorpresa! (ESP ISSN 1139-1588) **3953**
Sorrisi e Canzoni T V *see* T V Sorrisi e Canzoni **2394**
Sorte Pletter (DNK ISSN 1395-3354) **8634**
Sortenversuchsergebnisse (AUT ISSN 1018-1954) **157**
▼ ● Sortuz (ESP ISSN 1988-0847) **4784**
Soryushiron Kenkyu/Study of Elementary Particles (JPN ISSN 0371-1838) **7072**
SOS du Jardinier (FRA ISSN 1778-6886) **3750**
Sosei (JPN ISSN 0288-4348) **5716**
Sosei to Kako/Japan Society for Technology of Plasticity. Journal (JPN ISSN 0038-1586) **8439**
➤ Soshiki Baiyo Kenkyu/Tissue Culture Research Communications (JPN ISSN 0912-3636) **836**
Soshiki Kagaku/Organizational Science (JPN ISSN 0286-9713) **1794**
Soshiki Saibo Kagaku Koshukai/Course Text of Histochemistry and Cytochemistry (JPN) **836**
Soshiki Saibogaku Kiroku *see* Archives of Histology and Cytology **827**
Soshioroji (JPN ISSN 0584-1380) **8139**
Sosiaali- ja Terveydenhuollon Tilastollinen Vuosikirja/Statistical Yearbook on Social Welfare and Health Care/Statistisk Aarsbok foer Social- och Haelsovaerden (FIN ISSN 1458-1671) **8084**
● Sosiaali- ja Terveysmenot (FIN ISSN 1458-5286) **8084**
● Sosiaali- ja Terveysturvan Katsauksia/Social Security and Health Reports (FIN ISSN 1238-5069) **8005**
● Sosiaali- ja Terveysturvan Tutkimuksia/Studies in Social Security and Health (FIN ISSN 1238-5050) **8005**
➤ Sosiaalilaaketieteellinen Aikakauslehti (FIN ISSN 0355-5097) **5716**
Sosiaaliturva (FIN ISSN 0785-4625) **8084**
Sosiaalyurva Suomessa *see* Sosiaali- ja Terveysmenot **8084**
Sosial- og Helsedirektoratet. Rapport *see* Utviklingstrekk i Helse- og Socialsektoren **8076**
Sosial Trygghet i de Nordiske Land *see* Social Tryghed i de Nordiske Lande **8070**
Sosiale og Oeknomiske Studier (NOR ISSN 0801-3845) **8139**
Sosialisma Mpiasa (MDG) **4602**
● Sosiolog-Nytt (NOR ISSN 0333-3205) **8139**
➤ Sosiologi i Dag (NOR ISSN 0332-6330) **8139**
Sosiologia (FIN ISSN 0038-1640) **8139**
➤ Sosiologisk Aarbok. Ny Serie (NOR ISSN 0808-288X) **8139**
● Sosiologisk Tidsskrift/Journal of Sociology (NOR ISSN 0804-0486) **8139**
† Il Sospiro del Tifoso (ITA) **8989**
● Sostenible? (ESP ISSN 1139-966X) **8005**
Sostines Skelbimai (LTU ISSN 1822-1904) **3906**
Sostoanie mnogostoronnih soglasenij o regulirovanii vooruzenij i razoruzenii - Organizacia Obedinennyh Nacij *see* United Nations Disarmament Yearbook **7270**
Sostoyaniye Prirodnoi Sredy Belarusi/The State of Natural Environment of Belarus (BLR) **3467**
Sosyal Bilimler Dergisi/Journal of Social Sciences (TUR) **8006**
➤ Sosyoekonomi (TUR ISSN 1305-5577) **1176**
Sot (ALB) **7184**
Sot la Nape (ITA ISSN 0038-1659) **5239**
Sotahistoriallinen Aikakauskirja/Journal of Military History (FIN ISSN 0357-816X) **6447**
Sotainvalidi (FIN ISSN 0049-1349) **8072**
SOTECH *see* Special Operations Technology **6447**
● Soter (LTU ISSN 1392-7450) **7682**
Sotheby's International Preview (USA ISSN 0267-6915) **1433**
† Sotheby's International Realty Domain (USA ISSN 1521-2459) **8989**
Sotheby's Newsletter *see* Newsletter - Sotheby's **508**
Sotilasaikakauslehti/Finnish Military Review (FIN ISSN 0038-1675) **6447**
➤ Sotilaslaaketieteellinen Aikakauslehti/Annales Medicinae Militaris Fenniae (FIN ISSN 0300-8797) **5716**
Sotsialni Tendentsii (BGR ISSN 1311-2422) **8399**
Sotsial'no-Ekonomicheskoe Polozhenie Dal'nevostochnogo Federal'nogo Okruga/Socio-Economic Situation of the Far Eastern Federal Region (RUS) **1263**
Sotsial'no-Ekonomicheskoe Polozhenie Privolzhskogo Federal'nogo Okruga/Socio-Economic Situation of the Volga Federal Region (RUS) **1263**
● Sotsial'no-Ekonomicheskoe Polozhenie Rossii/Social and Economic Situation in Russia (RUS) **1263**
Sotsial'no-Ekonomicheskoe Polozhenie Severo-Zapadnogo Federal'nogo Okruga/Socio-Economic Situation of the North-Western Federal Region (RUS) **1263**
Sotsial'no-Ekonomicheskoe Polozhenie Sibirskogo Federal'nogo Okruga/Socio-Economic Situation of the Siberian Federal Region (RUS) **1263**
Sotsial'no-Ekonomicheskoe Polozhenie Tsentral'nogo Federal'nogo Okruga/Socio-Economic Situation of the Central Federal Region (RUS) **1263**
Sotsial'no-Ekonomicheskoe Polozhenie Ural'skogo Federal'nogo Okruga/Socio-Economic Situation of the Ural Federal Region (RUS) **1263**
Sotsial'no-Ekonomicheskoe Polozhenie Yuzhnogo Federal'nogo Okruga/Socio-Economic Situation of the Southern Federal Region (RUS) **1263**
Sotsial'no-Gumanitarnye Znaniya (RUS) **8006**
● Sotsialno Osiguriavane (BGR) **4523**
Sotsial'noe Partnerstvo (RUS) **1707**
Sotsial'nye i Gumanitarnye Nauki. Otechestvennaya i Zarubezhnaya Literatura. Ekonomika (RUS) **1263**
Sotsial'nye i Gumanitarnye Nauki. Otechestvennaya i Zarubezhnaya Literatura. Filosofiya (RUS) **6963**
Sotsial'nye i Gumanitarnye Nauki. Otechestvennaya i Zarubezhnaya Literatura. Gosudarstvo i Pravo (RUS) **4825**
Sotsial'nye i Gumanitarnye Nauki. Otechestvennaya i Zarubezhnaya Literatura. Istoriya (RUS) **4171**
Sotsial'nye i Gumanitarnye Nauki. Otechestvennaya i Zarubezhnaya Literatura. Literaturovedenie (RUS) **5408**
Sotsial'nye i Gumanitarnye Nauki. Otechestvennaya i Zarubezhnaya Literatura. Naukovedenie (RUS) **7939**
Sotsial'nye i Gumanitarnye Nauki. Otechestvennaya i Zarubezhnaya Literatura. Sotsiologiya (RUS) **8150**

Title

10884 SOTSIAL'NYE I GUMANITARNYE NAUKI. OTECHESTVENNAYA I ULRICH'S PERIODICALS

Sotsial'nye i Gumanitarnye Nauki. Otechestvennaya i Zarubezhnaya Literatura. Yazykoznanie (RUS ISSN 1560-5078) **5202**
Sotsial'nye i Gumanitarnye Nauki. Zarubezhnaya Literatura. Vostokovedenie i Afrikanistika (RUS) **564**
Sotsiologicheski Problemi (BGR ISSN 0324-1572) **8139**
• ➤ Sotsiologicheskie Issledovaniya (RUS ISSN 0132-1625) **8139**
• Sotsiologicheskii Forum/Russian Sociological Forum (RUS) **8140**
• Sotsiologicheskii Zhurnal (RUS ISSN 1562-2495) **8140**
➤ Sotsiologiya (BLR) **8140**
Sotsiologiya Meditsiny (RUS ISSN 1728-2810) **5716**
Sotsiolohiya: Teoriya, Metody, Marketinh (UKR) **8140**
• Sotsionika, Mentologiya i Psikhologiya Lichnosti (UKR ISSN 1680-4325) **8140**
➤ Sotsyal'naya i Klinicheskaya Psikhyatriya (RUS ISSN 0869-4893) **6186**
Sotsyal'naya Zashchita (RUS ISSN 0868-4960) **8140**
Sotsyal'naya Zashchita Naseleniya. Seriya. Organizatsiya Sotsyal'nogo Obespecheniya Pensionerov (RUS) **8140**
Sotsyal'naya Zashchita Naseleniya. Seriya. Protezirovanie i Protezostroenie (RUS) **8140**
Sotsyal'naya Zashchita Naseleniya. Seriya. Sotsyal'naya Pomoshch' Sem'e i Detyam (RUS) **8140**
Sotsyal'naya Zashchita Naseleniya. Seriya. Sotsyal'no Bytovoe Obsluzhivanie Pensionerov i Invalidov (RUS) **8140**
Sotsyal'naya Zashchita Naseleniya. Seriya. Vrachebno-Trudovaya Ekspertiza. Sotsyal'no-Trudovaya Reabelitatsiya Invalidov (RUS) **8140**
• La Souche (CAN ISSN 0827-1046) **3783**
Soudage dans le Monde *see* Welding in the World **6345**
Le Soudanais (MLI) **3907**
Soudni Rozhledy (CZE ISSN 1211-4405) **4784**
Soudobe Dejiny/Contemporary History (CZE ISSN 1210-7050) **4266**
Soudure *see* Schweisstechnik **6344**
Souffle de Perse (FRA ISSN 1157-7460) **5435**
The Soul (DEU) **6617**
Soul (San Jose) (USA) **5083**
Soul (Washington, New Jersey) (USA ISSN 0038-1756) **7817**
Soul Access Kiteboarding Magazine *see* Access Kiteboarding Magazine **8156**
Soul & Spirit (GBR ISSN 1754-0186) **6647**
Soul Bag (FRA ISSN 0398-9089) **6618**
Soul of Martial Arts *see* Wuhun **8216**
• Soul Purpose Magazine (AUS ISSN 1833-7465) **7682**
Soul Rydah Magazine (USA ISSN 1930-8353) **8268**
• Souls (USA ISSN 1099-9949) **8140**
Sound & Communication Systems International (GBR ISSN 1358-9164) **8154**
Sound & Communications (USA ISSN 0038-1845) **8155**
Sound & Hi Fi *see* Echos kai Hi Fi **6564**
Sound & Image (AUS ISSN 1032-3899) **2391**
Sound and Literary Art Book *see* S L A B **5366**
Sound & Recording (DEU) **8155**
• Sound and Vibration (USA ISSN 1541-0161) **3395**
• Sound & Video Contractor (USA ISSN 0741-1715) **8155**
• Sound & Vision (USA ISSN 1537-5838) **8155**
Sound and Vision *see* Sound & Vision **8155**
Sound & Vision Buyers' Guide *see* Sound & Vision Buyers' Guide **8155**
Sound & Vision Buyers' Guide (USA ISSN 1537-0798) **8155**
Sound & Vision H D T V Guide (High Definition Television) (USA ISSN 1931-0951) **2391**
Sound Arts (NZL ISSN 1177-4371) **6618**
• Sound Business (USA ISSN 1048-2970) **1176**
Sound Choice (USA ISSN 8756-6176) **6618**
Sound Collector (USA ISSN 1523-4851) **6618**
• Sound Computing (USA) **4078**
Sound Consumer *see* P C C Sound Consumer **6668**
Sound Effects (USA) **4076**
Sound Historian (USA ISSN 1077-2979) **4313**
• ➤ Sound Ideas (Online) (NZL) **6618**
Sound Ideas (Print) *see* Sound Ideas (Online) **6618**
Sound Investing Basics (USA) **1652**
• ➤ Sound Journal (GBR ISSN 1474-354X) **8155**
• The Sound Magazine (CAN) **5375**
Sound of Malaysian's Musician/Ta Ma Ko Yu Chih Sheng (MYS) **6618**
• Sound on Sound (GBR ISSN 0951-6816) **6618**
Sound Post (USA ISSN 0749-0755) **6618**
Sound Recording (CAN ISSN 0847-1223) **7089**
Sound Stage *see* SoundStage **6618**
Sound Technology Promotion Foundation. Research Report *see* Kenkyu Josei Jigyo Josei Kenkyu Seika Hokoku Gaiyo **7088**
Sound Telegraph (AUS) **3796**
Sound Views (USA) **6618**
Sound Vision Install (GBR ISSN 1755-8387) **8155**
Soundboard (USA ISSN 0145-6237) **6618**
Soundcheck (DEU ISSN 0936-0689) **6618**
Soundi (FIN ISSN 0785-0891) **6618**
Sounding Board (CAN ISSN 0381-5471) **1176**
Sounding Board (GBR ISSN 1464-6730) **8155**
• ➤ Soundings (GBR ISSN 1362-6620) **5239**
Soundings *see* B T Soundings **4041**
▼ Soundings (USA ISSN 1940-3399) **6618**
• Soundings (Essex) (USA ISSN 1526-8268) **8283**
Soundings (Milwaukee) (USA ISSN 0888-4072) **4313**
Soundings (Minneapolis) (USA ISSN 0194-8040) **7775**
Soundings (Norfolk) (USA) **6447**
Soundings (Notre Dame) (USA) **6953**
➤ Soundings (Portland) (USA ISSN 0038-1861) **4475**
Soundings East (USA ISSN 1082-5851) **5375**
• Soundings Trade Only (USA ISSN 0194-8369) **8283**
Soundless Sound *see* Anahata Nada **7621**
Soundoff! (USA) **6447**
Sounds Australian *see* Resonate **6611**
• Sounds Great! (GBR ISSN 1360-2861) **6618**
Sounds of Death Magazine (USA) **6618**
Sounds of Lexington (USA) **4076**
Sounds of Truth and Tradition (USA ISSN 0038-187X) **7817**
• Soundscape (AUS ISSN 1607-3304) **3491**
† • Soundscapes Relaxing Music (ITA) **8989**
• SoundStage (CAN) **6618**
▼ • The Soundtrack (GBR ISSN 1751-4193) **6513**
Soundtrack (USA ISSN 1042-0649) **6618**
Soundview Executive Book Summaries (USA ISSN 0747-2196) **1794**
The Soup Market *see* Key Note Market Report. Soup Market **3652**
† Soupis Zahranicnich Casopisu Dochazejicich do C R a S R v Roce.../List of Foreign Periodicals Acquired in Czech and Slovak Libraries in (Year) (CZE ISSN 1212-3870) **8989**
† Soupis Zahranicnich Casopisu Objednanych do C R a S R v Roce (...)/List of Foreign Periodicals Ordered in Czech and Slovak Libraries in (Year) (CZE ISSN 1212-3889) **8989**
Soup's Cheap or Almost Free Recipe Newsletter (USA) **4367**
• The Source (AUS ISSN 1833-2501) **3467**
➤ Source (DEU ISSN 0947-0174) **4785**
The Source *see* Jazz Research Journal **6579**
Source (IRL) **6977**
The Source (NLD ISSN 1572-4018) **7574**
▼ • The Source (NZL ISSN 1178-3265) **8400**
The Source (USA) **8832**
The Source (Abington) (USA) **3681**
The Source (New York, 1988) (USA ISSN 1063-2085) **6618**
The Source (Princeton) (USA) **2028**
The Source (Schaumburg) (USA ISSN 1932-7862) **4111**
Source (Seattle) (USA ISSN 0744-8333) **7682**
Source Book *see* Source Book: Social and Health Services in the Greater New York Area **8072**
Source Book of American State Legislation (USA ISSN 0730-1154) **7184**
Source Book of Health Insurance Data (USA ISSN 0073-148X) **4523**
Source Book: Social and Health Services in the Greater New York Area (USA ISSN 0740-4549) **8072**
• ➤ Source Code for Biology and Medicine (GBR ISSN 1751-0473) **705**
The Source Guide (USA) **2364**
Source Journals in Metals and Materials (USA ISSN 0968-1043) **6332**
The Source Latino *see* The Source (New York, 1988) **6618**
Source Magazine (GBR ISSN 1369-2224) **6977**
Source Material of Finnish History *see* Suomen Historian Laehteitae **4272**
Source Materials on the History of Science in India (IND) **7919**
➤ Source: Notes in the History of Art (USA ISSN 0737-4453) **518**
Source O C D E Base de Donnees des Telecommunications de l'O C D E *see* O E C D Telecommunications and Internet Statistics **2348**
• Source O C D E. Developpement Urbain, Rural et Regional (Organisation de Cooperation et de Developpement Economiques) (FRA ISSN 1729-0635) **1176**
Source O C D E. Economie Territoriale *see* Source O C D E. Developpement Urbain, Rural et Regional **1176**
• Source O C D E. Finance et Investissement / Assurance et Retraites (Organisation de Cooperation et de Developpement Economiques) (FRA ISSN 1683-237X) **1383**
• Source O C D E. Fiscalite (Organisation de Cooperation et de Developpement Economiques) (FRA ISSN 1683-2434) **1943**
• Source O C D E. Gouvernance (Organisation de Cooperation et de Developpement Economiques) (FRA ISSN 1683-2388) **1176**
Source O C D E Indicateurs du Commerce International et de la Competitivite *see* Source O E C D. International Trade and Competitiveness Statistics **8989**
• Source O C D E. Questions Sociales/Migrations/ Sante (Organisation de Cooperation et de Developpement Economiques) (FRA ISSN 1683-2426) **8006**
Source O C D E Rentabilite des Banques *see* O E C D Banking Statistics **1256**
• Source O C D E. Science et Technologies de l'Information (Organisation de Cooperation et de Developpement Economiques) (FRA ISSN 1683-2418) **2550**
Source O C D E Statistiques de l'Education *see* O E C D Education Statistics **2935**
Source O C D E Statistiques des Investisseurs Institutionnels *see* Source O E C D. Institutional Investors Statistics **8989**
Source O C D E Statistiques des Migrations Internationales *see* O E C D International Migration Statistics **1256**
Source O C D E Statistiques des Perspectives Economiques de l'O C D E *see* O E C D Economic Outlook: Statistics and Projections **1256**
Source O C D E Statistiques des Services *see* O E C D Statistics on International Trade in Services **1257**
Source O C D E Statistiques Mensuelles du Commerce International *see* Source O E C D. Monthly International Trade Aggregates **1263**
• Source O C D E. Statistiques: Sources et Methodes (Organisation de Cooperation et de Developpement Economiques) (FRA ISSN 1684-3142) **8400**
• Source O C D E. Transports (Organisation de Cooperation et de Developpement Economiques) (FRA ISSN 1683-2469) **8511**
• Source O E C D. Agriculture & Food (Organisation for Economic Cooperation and Development (O E C D)) (FRA ISSN 1608-0149) **206**
Source O E C D. Agriculture and Food Statistics *see* O E C D Agriculture Statistics **184**
Source O E C D. Bank Profitability Statistics *see* O E C D Banking Statistics **1256**
Source O E C D. Economic Outlook *see* O E C D Economic Outlook: Statistics and Projections **1256**
• Source O E C D. Education & Skills (Organisation for Economic Cooperation and Development (O E C D)) (FRA ISSN 1608-0165) **2914**
Source O E C D. Education at a Glance. O E C D Database *see* O E C D Education Statistics **2935**
Source O E C D. Education Statistics *see* O E C D Education Statistics **2935**
• Source O E C D. Emerging Economies (Organisation for Economic Cooperation and Development (O E C D)) (FRA ISSN 1608-0173) **1176**
• Source O E C D. Employment (Organisation for Economic Cooperation and Development (O E C D)) (FRA ISSN 1608-0181) **1708**
Source O E C D. Employment Statistics *see* O E C D Employment and Labour Market Statistics **1256**
• Source O E C D. Energy (Organisation for Economic Cooperation and Development (O E C D)) (FRA ISSN 1608-019X) **3147**
• Source O E C D. Environment & Sustainable Development (Organisation for Economic Cooperation and Development (O E C D)) (FRA ISSN 1608-0211) **3467**
• Source O E C D. Finance & Investment/Insurance & Pensions (Organisation for Economic Cooperation and Development (O E C D)) (FRA ISSN 1608-022X) **1383**
• Source O E C D. General Economics & Future Studies (Organisation for Economic Cooperation and Development (O E C D)) (FRA ISSN 1608-0238) **1177**
Source O E C D. General Economies & Future Studies *see* Source O E C D. General Economics & Future Studies **1177**
• Source O E C D. Governance (Organisation for Economic Cooperation and Development (O E C D)) (FRA ISSN 1608-0246) **1177**
Source O E C D. I T C S *see* International Trade by Commodities Statistics **1244**
• Source O E C D. Industry, Services & Trade (Organisation for Economic Cooperation and Development (O E C D)) (FRA ISSN 1608-0203) **1582**
† • Source O E C D. Institutional Investors Statistics (Organisation for Economic Cooperation and Development) (FRA ISSN 1608-1072) **8989**
• Source O E C D. Insurance Statistics (Organisation for Economic Cooperation and Development) (FRA ISSN 1681-2026) **4530**
Source O E C D. International Direct Investment Statistics *see* O E C D International Direct Investment Statistics (Online) **1256**
Source O E C D. International Migration Statistics *see* O E C D International Migration Statistics **1256**
† • Source O E C D. International Trade and Competitiveness Statistics/Source O C D E Indicateurs du Commerce International et de la Competitivite (Organisation for Economic Cooperation and Development) (FRA ISSN 1608-1145) **8989**
Source O E C D. Main Economic Indicators *see* Main Economic Indicators **1250**
• Source O E C D. Measuring Globalisation Statistics (Organisation for Economic Cooperation and Development) (FRA ISSN 1608-1293) **1263**
• Source O E C D. Monthly International Trade Aggregates/Source O C D E Statistiques Mensuelles du Commerce International (Organisation for Economic Cooperation and Development (O E C D)) (FRA ISSN 1608-1226) **1263**
• Source O E C D. National Accounts & Historical Statistics (Organisation for Economic Cooperation and Development (O E C D)) (FRA ISSN 1681-2018) **1263**
• Source O E C D. National Accounts Statistics (Organisation for Economic Cooperation and Development) (FRA ISSN 1608-1188) **1264**
• Source O E C D. Nuclear Energy (Organisation for Economic Cooperation and Development (O E C D)) (FRA ISSN 1608-0262) **3174**
• Source O E C D. Revenue Statistics of O E C D Member Countries (Organisation for Economic Cooperation and Development) (FRA ISSN 1608-1099) **1264**
Source O E C D. S T A N Industry Analysis Database *see* S T A N: O E C D Structural Analysis Statistics **1261**
Source O E C D. Science and Technology Database *see* O E C D Science, Technology and R & D Statistics **3233**
Source O E C D. Services Statistics *see* O E C D Statistics on International Trade in Services **1257**
Source O E C D. Social Expenditure Database *see* O E C D Social Expenditure Statistics **1257**
Source O E C D. Social Issues & Migration *see* Source O E C D. Social Issues/Migration/ Health **8006**
• Source O E C D. Social Issues/Migration/Health (Organisation for Economic Cooperation and Development) (FRA) **8006**
Source O E C D. Structural Statistics for Industry and Services (Online) *see* Structural and Demographic Business Statistics (Online) **1268**
Source O E C D. Telecommunications Database *see* O E C D Telecommunications and Internet Statistics **2348**
Source O E C D. Territorial Economy *see* Source O E C D. Urban, Rural and Regional Development **1177**
• Source O E C D. Urban, Rural and Regional Development (Organisation for Economic Cooperation and Development) (FRA ISSN 1729-0619) **1177**
Sourcebook of County Asset/Lien Records *see* The Sourcebook to Public Record Information **7469**
Sourcebook of County Court Records *see* The Sourcebook to Public Record Information **7469**
• Sourcebook of Criminal Justice Statistics (USA ISSN 0360-3431) **2675**
Sourcebook of Federal Courts, U.S. District and Bankruptcy *see* The Sourcebook to Public Record Information **7469**
Sourcebook of State Public Records *see* The Sourcebook to Public Record Information **7469**
The Sourcebook to Public Record Information (USA ISSN 1932-1309) **7469**
• SourceMex (USA ISSN 1054-8890) **1518**
SourceOECD Employment *see* Source O E C D. Employment **1708**
SourceOECD Energy *see* Source O E C D. Energy **3147**
SourceOECD Nuclear Energy *see* Source O E C D. Nuclear Energy **3174**
• Sources (CAN ISSN 0700-480X) **2028**
Sources (Richmond Heights) (USA) **6332**
Sources (Tampa) (USA) **8202**
Sources+Design (USA) **457**
Sources and Methods. Labour Statistics (CHE ISSN 1014-9856) **1264**
➤ Sources and Studies in the History of Mathematics and Physical Sciences (USA) **5537**
Sources Chretiennes (FRA ISSN 0750-1978) **7682**
Sources Classiques (FRA ISSN 1169-2936) **5375**
Sources de Droit Serbe *see* Izvori Srpskog Prava **4698**
Sources d'Emission des Principaux Contaminants Atmospheriques. Guide de Declaration a l'Inventaire National des Rejets de Polluants (CAN ISSN 1708-0118) **3491**
Sources d'Histoire Medievale (FRA ISSN 0398-3811) **4266**
• Sources Ejournal (USA) **3988**
Sources et Travaux d'Histoire Haut-Pyreneenne (FRA ISSN 0248-5516) **4266**
Sources for African History (NLD ISSN 1570-8721) **4178**
➤ Sources for Biblical and Theological Study (USA ISSN 1931-0943) **7682**
Sources from the Ancient Near East (USA ISSN 0732-6424) **4325**
The Sources HotLink (CAN ISSN 1480-2821) **35**
Sources in the History of Mathematics and Physical Sciences (USA ISSN 0172-6315) **5537**
† Sources of Contemporary Jewish Thought/Mekevot (ISR ISSN 0082-4585) **8989**
Sources of Cornish History (GBR) **4266**
• Sources of Custom-Produced Books (USA ISSN 1535-1505) **5048**
Sources, Queries & Reviews *see* Missouri Sources, Queries and Reviews **8974**
• Sourcingmag.com (USA) **1794**
• Sourcingmag Insights (USA ISSN 1930-269X) **1794**
Sourd Journal (BEL) **4076**
Sournal *see* Sourd Journal **4076**
Sourozh (GBR ISSN 0950-2742) **7706**
Sous Fashion in Lingerie (DEU) **2261**
Sous le Vent (FRA ISSN 1951-3941) **5375**
Sous le Vent. Classiques (FRA ISSN 1951-395X) **5375**

Link to your serials resources and content with ulrichsweb.com

▼ *new title*   † *ceased*   • *electronic media*   ➤ *refereed*

Title

South African Journal for Research in Sport, Physical Education and Recreation *see* Suid-Afrikaanse Tydskrif vir Navorsing in Sport, Liggaamlike Opvoedkunde en Ontspanning **6997**
- ➤ South African Journal of African Languages (ZAF ISSN 0257-2117) **5176**
- South African Journal of Agricultural Extension/Suid-Afrikaanse Tijdskrif vir Landbouvoorligting (ZAF ISSN 0301-603X) **157**
- ➤ South African Journal of Anaesthesiology and Analgesia (ZAF ISSN 1027-9148) **5774**
- ➤ South African Journal of Animal Science (ZAF ISSN 0375-1589) **301**
- ▼ ● South African Journal of Bioethics and Law (ZAF ISSN 1999-7639) **4785**
- ➤ South African Journal of Botany (NLD ISSN 0254-6299) **818**
- South African Journal of Business Management/Suid-Afrikaanse Tydskrif vir Bedryfsleiding (ZAF ISSN 0378-9098) **1794**
- South African Journal of Chemical Engineering (ZAF ISSN 1026-9185) **3255**
- ● South African Journal of Chemistry/Suid-Afrikaanse Tydskrif vir Chemie (ZAF ISSN 0379-4350) **2081**
- ▼ ● ➤ South African Journal of Child Health (ZAF ISSN 1994-3032) **6104**

South African Journal of Clinical Nutrition *see* S A J C N **6669**
- ● ➤ South African Journal of Criminal Justice/Suid-Afrikaanse Tydskrif vir Strafregspleging (ZAF ISSN 1011-8527) **4898**
- ➤ South African Journal of Critical Care (ZAF) **6073**
- ➤ The South African Journal of Diabetes and Vascular Disease (ZAF ISSN 1811-6515) **5800**
- ➤ South African Journal of Economic and Management Sciences (ZAF ISSN 1015-8812) **1794**
- ● ➤ South African Journal of Economic History (ZAF ISSN 1011-3436) **1549**
- ● ➤ South African Journal of Economics/Suid-Afrikaanse Tydskrif vir Ekonomie (AUS ISSN 0038-2280) **1177**
- ● South African Journal of Education/Suid-Afrikaanse Tydskrif vir Opvoedkunde (ZAF ISSN 0256-0100) **2914**
- ➤ South African Journal of Environmental Law and Policy (ZAF ISSN 1023-1765) **3467**

South African Journal of Ethnology *see* Anthropology Southern Africa **327**
- ● ➤ South African Journal of Geology (ZAF ISSN 1012-0750) **2768**
- ● ➤ South African Journal of Higher Education (ZAF ISSN 1011-3487) **3002**
- South African Journal of Industrial Engineering (ZAF ISSN 1012-277X) **3371**
- ● South African Journal of Information Management (GBR ISSN 1560-683X) **1794**
- ● ➤ The South African Journal of International Affairs (GBR ISSN 1022-0461) **7266**
- ➤ South African Journal of Labour Relations (ZAF ISSN 0379-8410) **1708**
- ● ➤ South African Journal of Library and Information Science (ZAF ISSN 0256-8861) **5048**

South African Journal of Marine Science *see* African Journal of Marine Science **3583**
- ● ➤ South African Journal of Musicology/Suid-Afrikaanse Tydskrif vir Musiekwetenskap (ZAF ISSN 0258-509X) **6618**
- ➤ South African Journal of Obstetrics and Gynaecology (ZAF ISSN 0038-2329) **6005**
- ● ➤ South African Journal of Philosophy (ZAF ISSN 0258-0136) **6953**

South African Journal of Physiotherapy (ZAF ISSN 0379-6175) **6116**
- ➤ South African Journal of Plant and Soil (ZAF ISSN 0257-1862) **254**
- ➤ South African Journal of Psychiatry (ZAF ISSN 1608-9685) **6186**
- ● ➤ South African Journal of Psychology/Suid-Afrikaanse Tydskrif vir Sielkunde (ZAF ISSN 0081-2463) **7409**

South African Journal of Radiology (ZAF ISSN 1027-202X) **6208**
- ● ➤ South African Journal of Science/Suid-Afrikaanse Tydskrif vir Wetenskap (ZAF ISSN 0038-2353) **7919**
- ➤ South African Journal of Surgery/Suid-Afrikaanse Joernaal vir Chirurgie (ZAF ISSN 0038-2361) **6259**
- ● ➤ South African Journal of Wildlife Research/Suid-Afrikaanse Tydskrif vir Natuurnavorsing (ZAF ISSN 0379-4369) **2627**
- ● South African Journal on Human Rights (ZAF ISSN 0258-7203) **7215**

South African Labour Bulletin (ZAF ISSN 0377-5429) **1708**
- ● South African Labour Law Reports (ZAF ISSN 1017-0618) **1708**
- ● South African Labour Library (ZAF ISSN 1022-8349) **1708**

South African Labour Statistics (ZAF) **1266**
South African Lapidary Magazine (ZAF ISSN 0038-237X) **2717**
- ● South African Law Journal (ZAF ISSN 0038-2388) **4785**
- ● The South African Law Reports/Suid-Afrikaanse Hofverslae (ZAF ISSN 0038-2396) **4785**

South African Library. Quarterly Bulletin *see* National Library of South Africa. Quarterly Bulletin **5034**
South African Licensee's Guardian (ZAF ISSN 0489-8567) **4398**
South African Machine Tool Review (ZAF ISSN 0036-0848) **5459**
The South African Magazine (ZAF ISSN 1813-5781) **3950**
South African Mango Growers' Association Yearbook *see* Mango (Year) **242**
South African Market News (USA) **1582**
South African Mathematical Society. Notices (ZAF) **5537**
South African Mechanical Engineer (ZAF ISSN 0038-2442) **3395**
● South African Medical Research Council. Annual Report and Health Impact Report (ZAF) **5716**
● South African Mercantile Law Journal/Suid-Afrikaanse Tydskrif vir Handelsreg (ZAF ISSN 1015-0099) **4785**
South African Mining *see* S A Mining **6478**
South African Mining World *see* Mining World **6473**
South African Museum. Annals *see* African Natural History **651**
South African Museums Association. Bulletin (ZAF ISSN 0370-8314) **6537**
South African Music (ZAF ISSN 1815-3623) **6618**
South African Music Teacher/Suid-Afrikaanse Musiekonderwyser (ZAF ISSN 0038-2493) **6618**
● South African National Bibliography (Online) (ZAF) **635**
South African National Council for the Blind. Biennial Report (ZAF) **4085**
South African National Council for the Blind News *see* S A N C B News **4084**
South African National Tuberculosis Association Annual Report *see* S.A.N.T.A. Annual Report **6219**
South African National Tuberculosis Association T B and Health News *see* S.A.N.T.A. T B and Health News **6219**
South African Observer (ZAF ISSN 0038-2515) **7184**
● ➤ South African Optometrist/Suid-Afrikaanse Oogkundige (ZAF ISSN 0378-9411) **6052**
South African Paddler (ZAF ISSN 1817-1931) **8283**
● South African Pharmaceutical Journal/Suid-Afrikaanse Tydskrif vir Apteekwese (ZAF ISSN 0257-8719) **6881**
South African Pharmaceutical Journal *see* S A Pharmaceutical Journal **6879**
South African Pharmacist's Assistant *see* S A Pharmacist's Assistant **6879**
South African Philatelist (ZAF ISSN 0038-2566) **6899**
South African Poultry Bulletin (ZAF ISSN 0257-201X) **301**
South African Psychiatry Review *see* African Journal of Psychiatry **6120**
South African Publiekreg *see* S A Publiekreg **4777**
The South African Radiographer (ZAF ISSN 0258-0241) **6208**
South African Rates and Data *see* S A R A D **34**
▼ ● South African Real Estate Investor Magazine (ZAF ISSN 1995-655X) **7612**
South African Refrigeration and Airconditioning *see* S A Refrigeration and Airconditioning **4126**
South African Reserve Bank. Annual Economic Report/Suid-Afrikaanse Reserwebank. Jaarlikse Ekonomiese Verslag (ZAF ISSN 0081-2528) **1518**
▼ South African Reserve Bank. Conference Series (ZAF ISSN 1993-0895) **1383**
● South African Reserve Bank. Financial Stability Review (ZAF ISSN 1811-2226) **1383**
South African Reserve Bank. Monthly Release of Selected Data/Suid-Afrikaanse Reserwebank. Maandelikse Vrystelling van Uitgesoekte Gegewens (ZAF) **1266**
South African Reserve Bank. Quarterly Bulletin/Suid-Afrikaanse Reserwebank. Kwartaalblad (ZAF ISSN 0038-2620) **1383**
South African Reserve Bank. Report of the Ordinary General Meeting of Shareholders/Suid-Afrikaanse Reserwebank. Verslag van die Gewone Algemene Vergadering van Aandeelhouers (ZAF) **1383**
● ➤ South African Review of Sociology (ZAF) **8140**
South African Road Federation Official Newsletter (ZAF) **8635**
South African Rugby (ZAF) **8246**
South African Rugby News *see* S A Rugby News **8244**
South African Shipping News and Fishing Industry Review *see* Southern African Shipping News **8662**
South African Society for Agricultural Extension. Conference Proceedings/Suid-Afrikaanse Vereniging vir Landbouvoorligting. Konferensiehandelinge (ZAF) **157**
South African Society of Bank Officials News *see* S A S B O News **1381**
➤ South African Society of Pathologists. Congress Brochure (ZAF) **6282**
➤ South African Statistical Journal/Suid-Afrikaanse Statistiese Tydskrif (ZAF ISSN 0038-271X) **8402**
South African Statistics (ZAF ISSN 0081-2544) **8402**
● South African Studies (ZAF ISSN 1025-4315) **4171**
South African Sugar Association Experiment Station. Annual Report (ZAF ISSN 0375-2682) **254**

South African Sugar Association Experiment Station. Bulletin (ZAF) **254**
South African Sugar Association Experiment Station. Herbicide Guide (ZAF) **254**
South African Sugar Journal (ZAF ISSN 0038-2728) **3664**
South African Sugar Technologists' Association. Annual Congress *see* South African Sugar Technologists' Association. Proceedings **254**
● ➤ South African Sugar Technologists' Association. Proceedings (ZAF ISSN 0373-045X) **254**
● South African Theatre Journal (ZAF ISSN 1013-7548) **8479**
South African Timber Homes and Projects (ZAF ISSN 1813-4270) **457**
South African Translators' Institute. Journal *see* Muratho **5153**
South African Transport (ZAF ISSN 0038-2760) **8511**
South African Tunnelling (ZAF ISSN 0255-058X) **3283**
South African Typographical Journal/Suid-Afrikaanse Tipografiese Joernaal (ZAF ISSN 0038-2787) **4602**
➤ South African Veterinary Association. Scientific Journal (ZAF) **8807**
● South African Weather Service. Climate Summary of South Africa/Suid-Afrika. Weerburo. Klimaatopsomming van Suidelike Afrika (ZAF ISSN 1992-2566) **6395**
South African Woman Golfer *see* S A Woman Golfer **8244**
South African Worker *see* S A Worker **4601**
➤ South African Yearbook of International Affairs (ZAF ISSN 1026-5651) **7266**
South African Yearbook of International Law/Suid-Afrikaanse Jaarboek vir Volkereg (ZAF ISSN 0379-8895) **4941**
South Africa's Film & DVD Magazine *see* Movie & D V D **6507**
South America, Central America and the Caribbean (Year) (GBR ISSN 0268-0661) **7184**
● South America Report (USA ISSN 1082-183X) **1582**
South American Explorer (USA ISSN 0889-7891) **8757**
South American Explorer's Club Catalog (USA) **8757**
South American Handbook (Year) (GBR ISSN 0309-4529) **8757**
South American Ports Handbook (ARG) **8662**
South & North of the Yangtse River *see* Dajiang Nanbei **4181**
● ➤ South Asia (AUS ISSN 0085-6401) **4188**
● ➤ South Asia Economic Journal (IND ISSN 1391-5614) **1518**
● South Asia Graduate Research Journal (USA) **3565**
South Asia Library Group Newsletter *see* S A L G Newsletter **8986**
▼ ● ➤ South Asia Multidisciplinary Academic Journal (FRA ISSN 1960-6060) **8006**
South Asia News (USA) **4188**
● ➤ South Asia Research (IND ISSN 0262-7280) **560**
South Asian *see* Dongnanya **548**
➤ South Asian Anthropologist (IND ISSN 0257-7348) **356**
† South Asian Archaeology (NLD) **8989**
South Asian Association for Regional Cooperation Journal of Educational Research *see* S A A R C Journal of Educational Research **2908**
▼ ● South Asian Diaspora (GBR ISSN 1943-8192) **560**
● South Asian Economic Abstracts (IND) **1266**
South Asian Journal (PAK) **3565**
● ➤ South Asian Journal of Management (IND ISSN 0971-5428) **1794**
South Asian Journal of Psychology (BGD ISSN 1025-773X) **7409**
South Asian Language Review (IND ISSN 0971-0485) **5176**
● South Asian Magazine for Action and Reflection (Online Edition) (USA ISSN 1940-8382) **3565**
South Asian Magazine for Action and Reflection (Print Edition) *see* South Asian Magazine for Action and Reflection (Online Edition) **3565**
● South Asian Management Abstracts (IND) **1266**
South Asian Minority Affairs (PAK) **7215**
● ➤ South Asian Popular Culture (GBR ISSN 1474-6689) **356**
➤ South Asian Review (USA ISSN 0275-9527) **5375**
South Asian Reviews and Abstracts (LKA) **8006**
➤ South Asian Social Scientist (IND ISSN 0970-3764) **560**
● South Asian Studies (DEU ISSN 0584-3170) **561**
➤ South Asian Studies (GBR ISSN 0266-6030) **4188**
South Asian Studies (IND ISSN 0038-285X) **561**
South Asian Studies (PAK ISSN 1026-678X) **4188**
South Asian Studies (SWE ISSN 1653-8129) **561**
South Asian Studies Quarterly *see* Nanya Yanjiu Jikan **557**
● ➤ South Asian Survey (IND ISSN 0971-5231) **4188**
▼ ● The South Asian Times (USA ISSN 1941-9333) **3565**
The South Asian Voice (CAN) **3565**
South Atlantic Modern Language Association Awards (USA) **5375**

South Atlantic Quarterly *see* S A Q: The South Atlantic Quarterly **5237**
● ➤ South Atlantic Review (USA ISSN 0277-335X) **5375**
South Australia and Northern Territory and N T Sower *see* S A and N T Sower **7678**
South Australia and Northern Territory Sower *see* S A and N T Sower **7678**
South Australia Crafts *see* S.A. Crafts **8986**
● South Australia. Department for Families and Communities. Annual Report (AUS ISSN 1832-8938) **8072**
South Australia. Department for Transport, Urban Planning, and the Arts. Metropolitan Adelaide Development Program (AUS) **3467**
● South Australia. Department of Further Education, Employment, Science and Technology. Annual Report (AUS ISSN 1449-6437) **1708**
● South Australia. Department of Health. Annual Report (AUS ISSN 1833-0002) **7542**
● South Australia. Department of Housing and Urban Development. Adelaide Statistical Division. Land Monitoring Report. Land Sales, Prices, Land Division and Land Stocks Statistics (AUS) **3467**
South Australia. Department of Housing and Urban Development. Population Projections by Statistical Division - Data Sheets (AUS) **7293**
South Australia. Department of Human Services. Annual Report (Online Edition) *see* South Australia. Department for Families and Communities. Annual Report **8072**
● South Australia. Department of Trade and Economic Development. Annual Report (AUS ISSN 1832-0791) **1582**
● South Australia. Department of Transport Energy and Infrastructure. Annual Report (AUS ISSN 1832-9055) **7469**
● South Australia. Independent Gambling Authority. Annual Report (AUS ISSN 1832-3839) **8202**
South Australia Motor *see* S A Motor **8602**
● South Australia Nursery Register *see* Victoria, South Australia, Tasmania Nursery Register **3753**
● South Australia. Office of the Guardian for Children and Young People. Annual Report (AUS ISSN 1833-9484) **8072**
South Australian Baker and Pastrycook (AUS) **3675**
South Australian Builder (AUS ISSN 0157-938X) **1036**
South Australian Coloured Sheep Owners' Society Inc. Newsletter *see* S A C S O S Newsletter **8986**
South Australian Community Housing Authority. Annual Report *see* South Australian Housing Trust. Annual Report **4427**
† South Australian Electrical Contractor (AUS ISSN 0038-2892) **8989**
South Australian Flute News (AUS) **6618**
South Australian Football Budget (AUS ISSN 1834-5506) **8246**
The South Australian Genealogist (AUS ISSN 0311-2756) **3783**
South Australian Geographer (AUS ISSN 1440-2998) **4029**
● ➤ South Australian Geographical Journal (AUS ISSN 1030-0481) **4029**
South Australian Geographical Papers (AUS ISSN 0811-6504) **4029**
● The South Australian Government Gazette (AUS ISSN 0038-2906) **7469**
The South Australian Grower *see* The South Australian Grower **254**
The South Australian Grower (AUS) **254**
● South Australian Housing Trust. Annual Report (AUS ISSN 0728-7933) **4427**
South Australian Humanist Post (AUS) **6953**
South Australian Institute of Teachers Journal *see* S A I T Journal **3031**
South Australian Museum. Records. Monograph Series (AUS ISSN 1035-7939) **7919**
South Australian Naturalist (AUS ISSN 0038-2965) **7919**
➤ South Australian Ornithologist (AUS ISSN 0038-2973) **914**
South Australian Pamphlets of Verse (AUS ISSN 0726-3872) **5435**
South Australian Research and Development Institute Impacts *see* S A R D I Impacts **153**
South Australian Research and Development Institute Research Report Series *see* S A R D I Research Report Series **153**
● South Australian State Reports (AUS ISSN 0049-1470) **4785**
South Australian Volunteering (AUS ISSN 1033-3177) **8072**
South Australian Water. Annual Report *see* S A Water. Annual Report **7467**
South Australian Water. Drinking Water Quality Report *see* S A Water. Drinking Water Quality Report **8831**
South Australian Water. Sustainability Report *see* S A Water. Sustainability Report **8831**
South Australia's Future Mathematicians (AUS) **5537**
South Bank University. Faculty of Humanities and Social Science. Social Science Research Papers (GBR) **8140**
South Bay Living (USA) **4550**
▼ South Bay Living (Santa Clara County) (USA) **4550**
South Bay - Los Angeles Service Directory *see* South Bay Living (Santa Clara County) **4550**
● The South Beach Diet Newsletter (USA ISSN 1553-5509) **6669**

Title

DIRECTORY 2010 SOUTHERN CALIFORNIA GUIDE 10889

• The South Shore Journal (USA ISSN 1933-8163) **5375**
South Shore Living (USA) **5083**
➤ The South Slav Journal (GBR ISSN 0141-6146) **4266**
South Sound Magazine (USA) **5083**
South Suburban Citizen (USA) **3565**
South Suburban Genealogical and Historical Society Newsletter *see* S S G H S Newsletter **3781**
South Suburban Genealogical and Historical Society Research Series *see* S S G H S Research Series **3781**
South Suburban Standard (USA) **3565**
• South Sudan Food Security Update (USA ISSN 1947-0819) **1605**
South Swedish Placename Society. Journal *see* Sydsvenska Ortnamnssaellskapet. Aarsskrift **5184**
South Taranaki Star (NZL) **3916**
• South Texas Automotive Report (USA) **8604**
South Texas Catholic (USA ISSN 0745-9343) **7817**
• South Texas Law Review (USA ISSN 1052-343X) **4785**
South Tyne Star *see* Washington Star **3872**
South Tyne Star *see* Houghton Star **2287**
South Valley Medical Journal *see* Sohag Medical Journal **5716**
South Valley University. Faculty of Arts. Bulletin/Magallat Kulliyyat al-Adab bi-Qina (EGY ISSN 1110-614X) **5375**
South Waikato News (NZL ISSN 1170-1242) **3919**
South Wales Business Directory (GBR) **1410**
South Wales Caterer (GBR) **4398**
South Wales Ports Tides Tables (GBR) **2818**
South West Auto Trader (GBR ISSN 0958-238X) **8604**
South West Building and Construction (GBR) **1036**
South West Coast Path (GBR) **8757**
South West Economy Trends and Prospects (GBR) **1519**
South West Farmer (GBR) **158**
The South-West Irish Sea Survey (GBR) **705**
South West Salary Survey (GBR) **1708**
South West Tourist News *see* The Standard (Warrnambool) **8990**
South Western Catholic History (GBR ISSN 0269-8390) **7817**
South Western Electricity News *see* S W E B News **3330**
South Wind *see* Nanfeng **5338**
South Wind Through Window *see* Nan Feng Chuang **7254**
South Yorkshire Chambers of Commerce Directory *see* Sheffield Chamber of Commerce. Business directory **1409**
Southall Gazette *see* Ealing & Acton Gazette **3864**
Southampton and Fareham Chamber of Commerce and Industry Directory (GBR) **1410**
Southampton City News (GBR) **3871**
Southampton Oceanography Centre. Annual Report (GBR) **2818**
Southampton Oceanography Centre. Cruise Report (GBR ISSN 1461-7684) **2818**
Southampton Oceanography Centre. Report (GBR ISSN 1461-7668) **2818**
Southampton Port Tide Tables (GBR) **2818**
Southampton Record Series (GBR ISSN 0584-4029) **4266**
Southanpton Tide Tables *see* Tide Tables **8663**
• Southbank Cityscope (AUS) **7618**
Southbay Times (USA ISSN 1556-1038) **3988**
SouthCoast Wine (USA) **610**
• Southcon Conference Record (USA ISSN 1087-8785) **3395**
• Southeast Asia Building (SGP ISSN 0218-0782) **1036**
• Southeast Asia Construction (SGP ISSN 0217-4685) **1036**
Southeast Asia Development Corporation Berhad. Reports and Accounts (MYS) **1605**
Southeast Asia Journal (PHL ISSN 0038-3600) **2914**
Southeast Asia Microfilms Newsletter (MYS ISSN 0129-511X) **4188**
➤ Southeast Asia Papers (USA) **561**
Southeast Asia Program Series (USA) **561**
Southeast Asia Series (USA) **561**
• Southeast Asian Affairs (SGP ISSN 0377-5437) **7184**
Southeast Asian Architecture. Journal (SGP ISSN 0218-9593) **457**
Southeast Asian Archives (MYS ISSN 0085-6509) **4189**
• ➤ Southeast Asian Bulletin of Mathematics (HKG ISSN 0129-2021) **5537**
Southeast Asian Bulletin of Mathematics Online *see* Southeast Asian Bulletin of Mathematics **5537**
Southeast Asian Fisheries Development Center. Aquaculture Department. Report (PHL ISSN 0116-712X) **3608**
Southeast Asian Fisheries Development Center Newsletter *see* S E A F D E C Newsletter **3606**
Southeast Asian Fisheries Development Center. Special Publication (THA) **3608**
Southeast Asian Fisheries Development Center. Training Department. Research Paper Series (THA) **3608**
Southeast Asian Fisheries Information Service Extension Manual Series *see* S A F I S Extension Manual Series **3606**
Southeast Asian Institutions of Higher Learning *see* Association of Southeast Asian Institutions of Higher Learning. Handbook: Southeast Asian Institutions of Higher Learning **2968**
• Southeast Asian Journal of Tropical Medicine and Public Health (THA ISSN 0125-1562) **5826**
Southeast Asian Language Text Series (USA) **5176**
Southeast Asian Ministers of Education Organisation. Regional Centre for Education in Science and Mathematics. Governing Board Meeting. Final Report (MYS ISSN 0126-8155) **3082**
Southeast Asian Ministers of Education Organisation. Regional Centre for Education in Science and Mathematics. Library Accession List (MYS ISSN 0126-7590) **2936**
Southeast Asian Ministers of Education Organization Horizon *see* S E A M E O Horizon **2908**
Southeast Asian Ministers of Education Organization Regional English Language Centre. Annual Report *see* S E A M E O Regional English Language Centre. Annual Report **5172**
Southeast Asian Ministers of Education Organization Regional Language Centre. Anthology Series *see* S E A M E O Regional Language Centre. Anthology Series **5170**
Southeast Asian Ministers of Education Organization Regional Language Centre Guidelines *see* S E A M E O Regional Language Centre Guidelines **5170**
Southeast Asian Programme on Ocean Law, Policy and Management Newsletter *see* S E A P O L Newsletter **4971**
Southeast Asian Studies *see* Nanyang Wenti Yanjiu **557**
Southeast Asian Studies *see* Dongnanya Yanjiu **548**
Southeast Asian Translation Data *see* Nanyang Ziliao Yicong **557**
† Southeast C-Store Journal (USA) **8989**
Southeast Case Research Journal (USA ISSN 1938-2154) **1177**
Southeast China National Defence Medical Science. Journal *see* Dongnan Guofang Yiyao **5606**
Southeast Communication *see* Dongnan Chuanbo **2319**
• Southeast Construction (Florida Edition) (USA ISSN 1546-9808) **1036**
Southeast - East Asian English Publications in Print (JPN) **7579**
• Southeast Environmental Directory (USA ISSN 1082-7196) **2628**
Southeast Equine Monthly (USA) **8298**
Southeast European and Black Sea Studies *see* Journal of Southeast European and Black Sea Studies **7249**
• Southeast Farm Press (USA ISSN 0194-0937) **158**
• Southeast Farm Press Daily (USA) **254**
• Southeast Food Service News (USA ISSN 0199-2805) **3664**
Southeast Louisiana Review (USA) **4313**
• Southeast Machinery & Industrial News (USA) **5460**
Southeast Real Estate Business (USA ISSN 1530-6097) **7612**
The Southeast Review *see* Sundog (Tallahassee) **5436**
➤ Southeast Review of Asian Studies (USA ISSN 1083-074X) **561**
Southeast Singles Association Quarterly Publication (USA) **7944**
Southeast States Petroleum Industry (USA) **6793**
Southeast Texas Business Monthly (USA) **1410**
Southeast Transaction Guide: Florida, Georgia and Alabama *see* Southeast Transaction Guide: Florida, Georgia & Alabama **4785**
• Southeast Transaction Guide: Florida, Georgia & Alabama (USA) **4785**
• Southeast University. Journal (CHN ISSN 1003-7985) **7919**
Southeast University. Journal (Medical Science Edition) *see* Dongnan Daxue Xuebao (Yixue Ban) **5606**
Southeast University. Journal (Natural Science Edition) *see* Dongnan Daxue Xuebao (Ziran Kexue Ban) **7851**
Southeast University. Journal (Philosophy and Social Science) *see* Dongnan Daxue Xuebao (Zhexue Shehui Kexue Ban) **7960**
▼ Southeast Wealth Management Business (USA ISSN 1939-6112) **1652**
Southeastern Adventures (USA) **8757**
• ➤ Southeastern Archaeology (USA ISSN 0734-578X) **418**
➤ Southeastern Association of Fish and Wildlife Agencies. Proceedings (USA ISSN 0276-7929) **3609**
Southeastern Biology (USA ISSN 1533-8436) **706**
Southeastern College Art Conference Review (USA ISSN 1043-5158) **518**
• Southeastern Cooperative Wildlife Disease Study Briefs (USA) **2628**
Southeastern Council on Latin American Studies Annals *see* S E C O L A S Annals **4311**
• Southeastern Environmental Law Journal (USA) **4785**
• ➤ Southeastern Europe/Europe du Sud-Est (NLD ISSN 0094-4467) **4266**
Southeastern Football *see* Athlon's Southeastern Football **8221**
Southeastern Football *see* Lindy's Southeastern Football **8237**
Southeastern Front (USA ISSN 0886-067X) **518**
• ➤ Southeastern Geographer (USA ISSN 0038-366X) **4029**
➤ Southeastern Geology (USA ISSN 0038-3678) **2769**
Southeastern Historical Keyboard Society. Newsletter (USA ISSN 1522-5879) **6618**
➤ Southeastern Journal of Music Education (USA ISSN 1047-9635) **6618**
Southeastern Law Librarian (USA ISSN 0272-7560) **5048**
• ➤ Southeastern Librarian (USA ISSN 0038-3686) **5048**
• ➤ Southeastern Naturalist (USA ISSN 1528-7092) **818**
Southeastern Newsline (USA) **5048**
Southeastern Oil Review (USA) **6793**
Southeastern Peanut Farmer (USA ISSN 0038-3694) **254**
Southeastern Regional Association of Teacher Educators Journal *see* S R A T E Journal **2909**
Southeastern Society of Pediatric Dentistry. Journal *see* The Journal of Pediatric Dental Care **5853**
• Southeastern Symposium on System Theory. Proceedings (USA ISSN 0094-2898) **2525**
▼ ➤ Southeastern Teacher Education Journal (USA ISSN 1945-3744) **2914**
Southeastern V H F Society Conference Proceedings (Very High Frequency) (USA) **2364**
Southeastern Virginia Jewish News (USA) **7729**
Southeastern Wisconsin Regional Planning Commission Newsletter *see* S E W R P C Newsletter **4426**
Southeasterner (USA ISSN 0038-3716) **4584**
• ➤ Southerly (AUS ISSN 0038-3732) **5375**
Southern *see* Southern Chinese News **3565**
† • Southern Accents (USA ISSN 0149-516X) **8989**
Southern Adirondack Library System in Brief *see* S A L S in Brief **5044**
Southern Africa Mathematical Sciences Association Journal of Pure and Applicable Mathematics *see* S A M S A Journal of Pure and Applicable Mathematics **5531**
Southern Africa Monitor *see* Africa Monitor. Southern Africa **1435**
• Southern Africa Monthly Regional Bulletin (USA ISSN 0966-8802) **7184**
Southern Africa. Political and Economic Monthly (ZWE ISSN 1017-9208) **7266**
Southern Africa Political Economy Series Seminar and Occasional Paper Series *see* S A P E S Seminar and Occasional Paper Series **7264**
Southern Africa Report (ZAF ISSN 1016-4731) **3950**
Southern Africa Vexillological Association Newsletter *see* S A V A Newsletter **3781**
Southern African Association for Research in Mathematics, Science and Technology. Journal *see* African Journal of Mathematics, Science and Technology Education **5467**
Southern African Association of Geomorphologists. Newsletter (ZAF) **2769**
• Southern African Books in Print (ZAF) **635**
Southern African Books in Print on CD-ROM *see* Southern African Books in Print **635**
• ➤ Southern African Business Review (Online) (ZAF ISSN 1998-8125) **1177**
Southern African Business Review (Print) *see* Southern African Business Review (Online) **1177**
Southern African Development Community Regional Business Climate Survey *see* The S A D C Regional Business Climate Survey **1409**
Southern African Development Coordination Conference, Energy Sector Technical & Administrative Unit Energy Bulletin *see* S A D C C Energy Bulletin **3147**
• Southern African Feminist Review (ZWE ISSN 1024-9451) **8903**
➤ Southern African Field Archaeology (ZAF ISSN 1019-5785) **418**
The Southern African Forestry Journal *see* Southern Forests **3703**
➤ Southern African Humanities (ZAF ISSN 1681-5564) **418**
Southern African Journal of Child and Adolescent Mental Health *see* Journal of Child and Adolescent Mental Health **6150**
Southern African Journal of Critical Care *see* South African Journal of Obstetrics and Gynaecology **6005**
Southern African Journal of Critical Care *see* S A J C N **6669**
Southern African Journal of Critical Care *see* The Journal of Endocrinology, Metabolism and Diabetes of South Africa **5896**
Southern African Journal of Critical Care *see* South African Journal of Psychiatry **6186**
Southern African Journal of Critical Care *see* Cardiovascular Journal of Africa **5781**
Southern African Journal of Critical Care *see* S A M J South African Medical Journal **5708**
➤ Southern African Journal of Demography (ZAF ISSN 1682-4482) **7293**
➤ Southern African Journal of Epidemiology and Infection (ZAF ISSN 1015-8782) **5882**
Southern African Journal of Gerontology (ZAF ISSN 1019-8016) **4056**
• Southern African Journal of H I V Medicine (ZAF ISSN 1608-9693) **5826**
Southern African Journal of Human Immunodeficiency Virus Medicine *see* Southern African Journal of H I V Medicine **5826**
➤ Southern African Journal of Mathematics and Science Education (BWA ISSN 1022-4572) **5537**
• ➤ Southern African Linguistics and Applied Language Studies (ZAF ISSN 1607-3614) **5176**
Southern African P R J *see* Southern African Public Relations Journal **35**
Southern African Plant Pathology (ZAF) **818**
Southern African Public Relations Journal (ZAF) **35**
Southern African Shipping News (ZAF) **8662**
Southern African Tourism Update (ZAF) **8757**
Southern African Tourism Update's Buyers' Guide & Who's Who for Southern African Tourism Products (ZAF) **2028**
Southern African Travel Guide (ZAF) **8757**
Southern Africa's Travel News Weekly (ZAF) **8757**
Southern Alumni (USA) **2301**
Southern Anthropological Society. Proceedings (USA ISSN 0081-2994) **356**
Southern Argus (AUS ISSN 1834-3902) **3796**
Southern Art and Crafts Newsmonthly *see* S A C Newsmonthly **539**
Southern Association for Women Historians. Newsletter (USA) **4162**
Southern Association of Agricultural Scientists Bulletin. Biochemistry and Biotechnology *see* S A A S Bulletin. Biochemistry and Biotechnology **744**
Southern Association of Colleges and Schools. Proceedings (USA ISSN 0038-3813) **3002**
Southern Auto Trader (GBR ISSN 0958-2398) **8604**
Southern Baby (USA) **4367**
Southern Bankers Directory (USA ISSN 0734-7812) **1384**
Southern Baptist Convention. Annual (USA ISSN 0081-3001) **7775**
Southern Baptist Convention Life *see* S B C Life **7773**
• Southern Baptist Educator (USA ISSN 0038-3848) **7775**
The Southern Baptist Journal of Theology (USA ISSN 1520-7307) **7775**
• Southern Baptist Periodical Index (USA ISSN 0081-3028) **7699**
Southern Baptist Periodical Index on CD-ROM *see* Southern Baptist Periodical Index **7699**
Southern Bays (NZL ISSN 1177-0279) **4194**
▼ Southern Beauty (USA ISSN 1934-6204) **591**
Southern Bell Views (USA ISSN 0038-3856) **2371**
Southern Beverage Journal (USA ISSN 0193-0613) **610**
Southern Beverage Journal. Florida Edition (USA) **610**
Southern Beverage Journal. Georgia Edition (USA) **610**
• Southern Beverage Journal. South Carolina Edition (USA) **610**
• Southern Beverage Journal. Tennessee Edition (USA) **610**
• Southern Biomedical Engineering Conference. Proceedings (USA ISSN 1086-4105) **706**
Southern Bird (NZL ISSN 1175-1916) **914**
Southern Birds (ZAF ISSN 1018-7634) **914**
Southern Boating (USA ISSN 0192-3579) **8283**
Southern Brazilian Journal of Chemistry (BRA ISSN 0104-5431) **2081**
Southern Breeze (USA) **3988**
Southern Building Code Congress. Standard Building Code (USA) **1036**
Southern Building Code Congress. Standard Gas Code (USA) **1036**
Southern Building Code Congress. Standard Mechanical Code (USA) **1036**
Southern Building Code Congress. Standard Plumbing Code (USA) **1036**
Southern Business & Development Magazine (USA ISSN 1067-8751) **1178**
➤ Southern Business & Economic Journal (USA) **1178**
Southern Business Times Magazine *see* S B T Magazine **1169**
Southern CA Business *see* Harris Directory. Southern C A Business **2002**
• Southern California Academy of Sciences. Bulletin (USA ISSN 0038-3872) **7919**
Southern California & Las Vegas *see* TourBook: Southern California and Las Vegas **8762**
Southern California Anthology *see* Southern California Review **5375**
Southern California Association of Law Libraries Newsletter *see* S C A L L Newsletter **5044**
Southern California Association of Marine Invertebrate Taxonomists Newsletter *see* S C A M I T Newsletter **962**
Southern California Bride *see* Modern Bride Southern California **5560**
• Southern California Business Directory (USA ISSN 1061-2181) **2028**
• Southern California Business Directory and Buyers Guide (USA ISSN 0093-3090) **2028**
Southern California Business Trends *see* The Chamber Voice **1399**
▼ • ➤ Southern California Chinese American Environmental Protection Association. Online Journal (USA ISSN 1944-8945) **3467**
Southern California Coastal Water Research Project. Annual Report (USA) **3512**
Southern California Curiosities (USA ISSN 1547-8920) **8757**
Southern California Golf (USA) **8246**
• Southern California Guide (USA ISSN 0038-3902) **8757**

Title

10890 SOUTHERN CALIFORNIA HEALTH CARE WORKERS ULRICH'S PERIODICALS

Southern California Health Care Workers (USA) **4602**
• Southern California Home and Outdoor (USA) **4550**
Southern California Horticultural Society. Newsletter (USA) **3750**
• Southern California Interdisciplinary Law Journal (USA ISSN 1077-0704) **4786**
• ➤ Southern California Law Review (USA ISSN 0038-3910) **4786**
Southern California Magazine (USA) **3988**
Southern California Media Directory (USA) **35**
▼ Southern California Meetings + Events (USA) **6282**
Southern California Paleontological Society. Bulletin (USA ISSN 0160-4937) **6730**
Southern California Physician (USA ISSN 1533-9254) **5717**
Southern California Psychiatrist (USA ISSN 1047-6334) **6186**
➤ Southern California Quarterly (USA ISSN 0038-3929) **4313**
▼ Southern California Real Estate Magazine (USA ISSN 1940-5766) **7613**
Southern California Regional Industrial Buying Guide *see* Regional Industrial Buying Guide. Southern California **2025**
Southern California Renewal Communities Spirit *see* S C R C Spirit **7816**
Southern California Review (USA ISSN 1946-8784) **5375**
• Southern California Review of Law and Social Justice (USA ISSN 1935-2778) **8903**
Southern California Safety Institute Safety Monitor *see* S C S I Safety Monitor **6685**
Southern California Section of American Chemical Society *see* S C A L A C S **2080**
Southern California Senior Life (USA) **4056**
Southern California Teamster (USA ISSN 0038-3953) **4602**
Southern California Update (USA) **4379**
Southern California's Divorce Magazine (CAN ISSN 1481-9155) **8140**
Southern Caterer Update (GBR) **4398**
Southern Caver (AUS ISSN 0157-8464) **2769**
Southern Changes (USA ISSN 0193-2446) **7215**
Southern China Journal of Dermato-Venereology *see* Lingnan Pifu-xingbingke Zazhi **5880**
Southern Chinese News (USA) **3565**
Southern Christian Family (USA ISSN 1529-6024) **7682**
Southern City (USA ISSN 0361-7130) **7502**
Southern Climate and Pasture Outlook *see* Otago Climate and Pasture Update **6393**
• ➤ Southern Communication Journal (USA ISSN 1041-794X) **2339**
Southern Communicator (AUS ISSN 1832-0120) **2339**
• Southern Communities (USA) **4427**
Southern Comparative Literature Association Newsletter *see* S C L A Newsletter **5365**
Southern Country (AUS) **158**
Southern Courier (AUS) **3796**
Southern Cross (AUS ISSN 1445-0089) **7775**
Southern Cross (ZAF ISSN 0038-4011) **7818**
Southern Cross (San Diego) (USA ISSN 0745-0257) **7818**
Southern Cross (Savannah) (USA) **7818**
➤ Southern Cross University Law Review (AUS ISSN 1329-3737) **4786**
Southern Cultural Forum *see* Nanfang Wentan **5338**
• Southern Cultures (USA ISSN 1068-8218) **4475**
• Southern Cyclist (USA) **8268**
Southern Daily *see* Nanfang Ribao **3826**
Southern Demographic News (USA) **7293**
The Southern Digest (USA ISSN 1540-7276) **2301**
• Southern District Crime Statistics (NZL ISSN 1178-1645) **2675**
Southern District Statistics *see* Southern District Crime Statistics **2675**
Southern Echoes (USA ISSN 0735-6870) **3783**
• ➤ Southern Economic Journal (USA ISSN 0038-4038) **1178**
Southern Economic Review (IND) **1178**
Southern Economist (IND ISSN 0038-4046) **1178**
Southern Engineer (USA ISSN 0038-4054) **3220**
Southern Exposure (Carbondale) (USA) **5048**
Southern Exposure (Durham) (USA ISSN 0146-809X) **5239**
Southern Exposure (Talladega) (USA ISSN 0038-4070) **6977**
Southern Farm & Ranch (USA) **7613**
Southern Farmer (USA ISSN 1541-2008) **158**
Southern Fisheries (AUS ISSN 1321-2249) **3609**
Southern Forest Products Association Newsletter *see* S F Newsletter **3715**
Southern Forest Tree Improvement Conference. Proceedings (USA ISSN 0361-784X) **3703**
• ➤ Southern Forests (ZAF ISSN 2070-2620) **3703**
Southern Friend (USA ISSN 0743-7439) **4313**
Southern Gameplan (USA) **8202**
Southern Gaming (USA) **8202**
Southern Genealogist's Exchange Quarterly *see* Southern Genealogist's Exchange Society Quarterly **3783**
• Southern Genealogist's Exchange Society Quarterly (USA ISSN 1933-1010) **3783**
Southern Golf - Landscape & Resort Management (USA) **3750**
Southern Growth (Charleston) (USA) **3988**
Southern Growth (Research Triangle Park) (USA) **1519**
Southern Growth Policies Board Alert *see* S G P B Alert **1516**
Southern Hemisphere Forestry Journal *see* Southern Forests **3703**
• Southern Hemisphere Winter Summary (USA ISSN 1932-0418) **6395**
Southern Historian (USA ISSN 0738-5102) **4313**
➤ Southern History (GBR ISSN 0142-4688) **4266**
Southern Home Designs Memphis (USA) **4550**
▼ • Southern Home Organizers. Online Magazine (USA ISSN 1947-2188) **4367**
† Southern Home Plans (USA) **8989**
Southern Horse and Rider (USA ISSN 1931-7131) **8298**
Southern Horseman (USA ISSN 0093-3929) **8298**
Southern Hospitality Magazine (USA ISSN 1556-1313) **4398**
• Southern Hum (USA ISSN 1932-4804) **5375**
• ➤ Southern Humanities Review (USA ISSN 0038-4186) **4475**
Southern Illinois University at Carbondale. Center for Archaeological Investigations. Occasional Paper (USA) **418**
Southern Illinois University at Carbondale. Center for Archaeological Investigations. Research Paper (USA) **418**
Southern Illinois University at Carbondale. Center for Archaeological Investigations. Visiting Scholar Conference (USA) **418**
Southern Illinois University at Carbondale. Library. Bibliographic Contributions (USA) **635**
Southern Illinois University at Carbondale. Materials Technology Center. Conference Proceedings (USA) **3358**
Southern Illinois University at Edwardsville. Regional Research and Development Services. Report: Private Sector Investments (USA) **4427**
• ➤ Southern Illinois University Law Journal (USA ISSN 0145-3432) **4786**
Southern Indiana Genealogical Society Quarterly (USA ISSN 0747-8453) **3783**
➤ Southern Indiana Review (USA ISSN 1932-6866) **5375**
The Southern Instructor (GBR) **8604**
➤ Southern Jewish History (USA ISSN 1521-4206) **7729**
Southern Journal (USA) **4313**
• ➤ Southern Journal of Applied Forestry (USA ISSN 0148-4419) **3703**
▼ Southern Journal of Entrepreneurship (USA ISSN 1935-8695) **1178**
Southern Journal of Linguistics (USA) **5176**
• ➤ The Southern Journal of Philosophy (USA ISSN 0038-4283) **6953**
• Southern Lady (USA ISSN 1525-8580) **5083**
Southern Lady Presents Tea Time *see* Tea Time (Birmingham) **611**
Southern Landscape & Turf (USA ISSN 8755-2256) **3751**
➤ Southern Law Journal (USA ISSN 1056-2184) **4786**
Southern Lifestyles (USA) **4056**
• ➤ Southern Literary Journal (USA ISSN 0038-4291) **5375**
Southern Literary Studies (USA) **5375**
Southern Livestock Review (USA) **301**
• Southern Living (USA ISSN 0038-4305) **3988**
Southern Living Decorating Step by Step (USA ISSN 1077-887X) **4550**
Southern Living Garden Annual (USA ISSN 1048-2318) **3751**
Southern Living Home for the Holidays (USA) **4367**
Southern Living House Plans (USA ISSN 1057-3429) **457**
Southern Living Summertime (USA) **4367**
Southern Living Vacations (USA ISSN 1074-0945) **8757**
Southern Living Weddings (USA) **5561**
• Southern Loggin' Times (USA ISSN 0744-2106) **3716**
• Southern Lumberman (USA ISSN 0038-4313) **3716**
▼ • Southern Med Review (NZL ISSN 1174-2704) **6881**
• ➤ Southern Medical Journal (USA ISSN 0038-4348) **5717**
Southern Metals *see* Nanfang Jinshu **6327**
Southern Methodist University Law Review *see* S M U Law Review **4777**
• Southern Methodist University School of Law. Brief (USA ISSN 0006-9965) **4786**
Southern Methodist University Science and Technology Law Review *see* S M U Science and Technology Law Review **4845**
Southern MotoRacing (USA ISSN 0049-1616) **8202**
Southern Nature. Hampshire and Isle of Wight Edition (GBR ISSN 1358-1848) **2628**
Southern Nature. Surrey, Sussex and Brighton and Hove Edition (GBR ISSN 1478-7733) **2628**
Southern Nature. Thames and Chilterns Edition (GBR ISSN 1358-1856) **2628**
• Southern New England Roundtable Symposium Law Journal (USA) **4786**
• Southern New Mexico Online Magazine (USA) **8757**
Southern News and Views (USA ISSN 0038-4380) **2301**
† • Southern Ocean Review (NZL ISSN 1178-8607) **8989**
• Southern Online Journal of Nursing Research (USA ISSN 1538-0696) **5982**
Southern Oregon Heritage (USA ISSN 1082-2003) **4313**
Southern Orthopaedic Association. Journal *see* Journal of Surgical Orthopaedic Advances **6066**
Southern P H C Magazine (USA) **4127**
Southern Partisan (USA ISSN 0739-1714) **3989**
Southern Perspectives (Print Edition) *see* Around the South (Online Edition) **8089**
Southern Plumbing, Heating, Cooling *see* Southern P H C Magazine **4127**
Southern Poetry Review (USA ISSN 0038-447X) **5435**
• Southern Political Report (USA ISSN 0739-3938) **7184**
Southern Poverty Law Center Report *see* S P L C Report **7215**
Southern Power System Technology *see* Nanfang Dianwang Jishu **3160**
Southern Purchaser (USA ISSN 0049-1624) **1844**
• ➤ Southern Quarterly (USA ISSN 0038-4496) **4476**
Southern Queensland Forestry News (AUS ISSN 1448-4005) **3703**
• Southern Queries (USA ISSN 1048-8057) **3783**
Southern Railways (IND ISSN 0038-450X) **8625**
• Southern Regional Education Board. Annual Report (USA ISSN 0081-3060) **3033**
Southern Regional Education Board Fact Book on Higher Education *see* S R E B Fact Book on Higher Education **3001**
Southern Regional Industrial Directory (USA) **3371**
• The Southern Register (USA ISSN 0895-5573) **4313**
Southern Reporter (GBR ISSN 1355-9346) **3871**
Southern Research Institute. Annual Report (USA) **7919**
• Southern Review (AUS ISSN 0038-4526) **8140**
• The Southern Review (USA ISSN 0038-4534) **5375**
• Southern Review of Books (USA ISSN 1559-971X) **7574**
Southern Rockies & Wyoming Report *see* Southern Rockies Report **3147**
Southern Rockies Report (USA) **3147**
Southern Rodder (USA) **8604**
Southern Roots & Shoots (USA ISSN 0895-2876) **3783**
Southern Runner (USA ISSN 0744-3439) **8202**
Southern Rural Development Center Series *see* S R D C Series **4426**
• ➤ Southern Rural Sociology (USA ISSN 0885-3436) **8140**
The Southern Seminary Magazine (USA ISSN 0040-7232) **7775**
Southern Shipper (USA ISSN 1054-7150) **8663**
▼ • Southern Shopper (USA ISSN 1944-6799) **5083**
Southern Sierran (USA ISSN 1073-6875) **2628**
• ➤ Southern Social Studies Journal (USA ISSN 1047-7942) **8006**
Southern Sociologist (USA ISSN 0038-4577) **8140**
Southern South America (ARG ISSN 0327-6597) **8757**
• Southern Spaces (USA ISSN 1551-2754) **4476**
Southern Speed Magazine (USA) **8202**
• Southern Sporting Journal (USA ISSN 1097-2978) **8335**
Southern Star (IND) **3889**
The Southern Star (IRL) **3894**
➤ Southern Stars (NZL ISSN 0049-1640) **582**
➤ Southern Studies (USA ISSN 0735-8342) **8006**
Southern Sudan Food Security Update *see* South Sudan Food Security Update **1605**
Southern Sun (AUS) **8757**
Southern Surgical Association. Transactions (USA ISSN 0891-3633) **6259**
Southern Technology Site *see* Area Development Site & Facility Planning **4403**
Southern Textile News (USA ISSN 0038-4607) **8457**
• Southern Theatre (USA ISSN 0584-4738) **8479**
Southern Tour Magazine (USA ISSN 1556-2476) **5083**
Southern Transylvania In Your Pocket (ROM) **8757**
• Southern University Law Review (USA ISSN 0099-1465) **4786**
Southern Voice (USA ISSN 1088-1840) **4379**
Southern Weed Science Society. Proceedings (USA ISSN 0362-4463) **254**
Southern Weekly (AUS) **3796**
Southern Women: The Intersection of Race, Class and Gender (USA) **8903**
▼ • Southern Women's Review (USA ISSN 1947-976X) **5376**
Southern Yangtze University. Journal (Humanities & Social Sciences Edition) *see* Jiangnan Daxue Xuebao (Renwen Shehui Kexue Ban) **4458**
SouthFloridaC E O Magazine (USA) **1178**
Southland Express (NZL) **3919**
Southland Golf Magazine (USA) **8246**
• Southland Times (NZL ISSN 0112-9910) **3919**
Southpaw Activities (USA) **8246**
The South's Best Bed and Breakfasts *see* The South's Best Bed & Breakfasts **8757**
The South's Best Bed & Breakfasts (USA ISSN 1093-9059) **8757**
• Southscan (GBR ISSN 0952-7524) **7184**
The Southside Virginian (USA ISSN 0736-5683) **3783**
Southsider Magazine (USA) **5083**
Southwest Academy of Management. Annual Meeting Proceedings (USA) **1794**
Southwest Academy of Management Newsletter (USA) **1794**
Southwest Agricultural University. Journal (Natural Science) *see* Xinan Nongye Daxue Xuebao (Ziran Kexue Ban) **7931**
Southwest Agricultural University. Journal (Social Science Edition) *see* Xi'nan Nongye Daxue Xuebao (Shehui Kexue Ban) **8016**
SouthWest Airlines Spirit Magazine (USA ISSN 1066-1581) **8786**
• Southwest Art (USA ISSN 0192-4214) **518**
Southwest Baptist University Omnibus (USA) **2301**
Southwest Blues Magazine (USA) **6618**
Southwest Booster (CAN ISSN 0832-185X) **3817**
Southwest China *see* Zhongguo Xinan **1198**
Southwest China Journal of Agricultural Sciences *see* Xinan Nongye Xuebao **171**
• Southwest Contractor (USA ISSN 1064-6914) **1036**
Southwest Digest (USA) **3565**
Southwest Economy *see* Federal Reserve Bank of Dallas Southwest Economy **1342**
Southwest Environment Research News (USA ISSN 1547-027X) **3467**
• Southwest Farm Press (USA ISSN 0194-0945) **158**
• Southwest Farm Press Daily (USA) **254**
Southwest Finance *see* Xi'nan Jinrong **1391**
Southwest Florida Business (USA) **1178**
Southwest Fly Fishing (USA ISSN 1536-8505) **8335**
Southwest Hydrology (USA ISSN 1552-8383) **2798**
Southwest Institute for Research on Women Newsletter *see* S I R O W Newsletter **8902**
• ➤ Southwest Jiaotong University. Journal (CHN ISSN 1005-2429) **7919**
Southwest Jiaotong University. Journal (Social Sciences) *see* Xi'nan Jiaotong Daxue Xuebao (Shehui Kexue Ban) **8016**
• Southwest Journal of Business and Economics (USA ISSN 8750-4294) **1178**
• ➤ The Southwest Journal of Criminal Justice (USA ISSN 1939-442X) **2669**
• ➤ Southwest Journal of Linguistics (USA ISSN 0737-4143) **5176**
➤ Southwest Journal on Aging (USA ISSN 1070-6127) **4056**
Southwest Kansas Register (USA ISSN 0038-4690) **7818**
• Southwest Machinery & Industrial News (USA) **5460**
▼ Southwest Meetings + Events (USA) **6282**
Southwest Normal University. Journal (Natural Sciences Edition) *see* Xi'nan Shifan Daxue Xuebao (Ziran Kexue Ban) **7931**
➤ Southwest Philosophy Review. Journal (USA ISSN 0897-2346) **6953**
Southwest Region Rotary Report (USA) **3147**
Southwest Research Institute. Annual Report (USA) **3220**
• The Southwest Review (USA ISSN 0038-4712) **5240**
Southwest Sage (USA) **5376**
Southwest Stockman (USA ISSN 1050-9526) **301**
Southwest Style (USA) **4550**
Southwest Symposium on Mixed-Signal Design (USA) **2466**
Southwest University for Nationalities. Journal (Natural Science Edition) *see* Xinan Minzu Daxue Xuebao (Ziran Kexue Ban) **7931**
Southwest University for Nationalities. Journal (Philosophy, Social Science Edition) *see* Xinan Minzu Daxue Xuebao (Zhexue Shehui Kexue Ban) **8016**
Southwest University. Journal (Humanities and Social Sciences Edition) *see* Xi'nan Daxue Xuebao (Shehui Kexue Ban) **8016**
Southwest University of Political Science and Law. Journal *see* Xi'nan Zheng-Fa Daxue Xuebao **4816**
Southwest University of Science and Technology. Journal *see* Xi'nan Keji Daxue Xuebao **3227**
Southwest Wealth Management Business *see* Texas Wealth Management Business (Print) **8993**
Southwestern (Georgetown) (USA ISSN 0038-4852) **2301**
• Southwestern American Literature (USA ISSN 0049-1675) **5376**
Southwestern Anthropological Association Newsletter (USA) **356**
Southwestern Archivist (USA ISSN 1056-1021) **5048**
➤ Southwestern Business Administration Journal (USA ISSN 1554-7892) **1178**
Southwestern Directory of Expert Witnesses & Consultants *see* A L M Experts. Southwestern Directory **4608**
• Southwestern Economic Review (USA ISSN 1941-7683) **1519**
➤ Southwestern Entomologist (USA ISSN 0147-1724) **859**
➤ Southwestern Entomologist. Supplement (USA ISSN 1055-8799) **859**
Southwestern Federation of Archaeological Societies. Transactions (USA) **418**
Southwestern Financial Directory (USA ISSN 1082-8923) **1384**
• Southwestern Historical Quarterly (USA ISSN 0038-478X) **4313**
▼ Southwestern Illinois Living (USA) **4550**
Southwestern Illinois Living Service Directory *see* Southwestern Illinois Living **4550**
Southwestern Journal of International Law (USA) **4941**

➤ Southwestern Journal of Theology (USA ISSN 0038-4828) **7682**
• ➤ Southwestern Law Review (USA ISSN 1944-3706) **4786**
Southwestern Lore (USA ISSN 0038-4844) **418**
➤ Southwestern Mass Communication Journal (USA ISSN 0891-9186) **4584**
Southwestern Mission Research Center, Inc. Newsletter *see* S M R C Newsletter **4311**
Southwestern Musician (USA ISSN 0162-380X) **6618**
• ➤ Southwestern Naturalist (USA ISSN 0038-4909) **7919**
Southwestern News (USA ISSN 0038-4917) **7775**
Southwestern Review (USA ISSN 0276-7155) **5376**
➤ Southwestern Studies. Monographs (USA ISSN 0081-315X) **4313**
Southwestern Union Record (USA) **7775**
The Southwest's Best Bed & Breakfasts (USA ISSN 1521-7299) **8757**
Soutien aux Enfants. Statistiques (CAN ISSN 1912-743X) **8084**
Souvenir Building Collector (USA ISSN 1092-4353) **4347**
Souvenir Card Journal (USA) **4347**
Souvenir Francais (FRA) **4162**
• Souvenirs, Gifts, and Novelties (USA ISSN 1521-4249) **4061**
Souveraen (DEU) **5083**
Sou'wester (CAN ISSN 0049-1705) **3609**
Sou'wester (Edwardsville) (USA ISSN 0098-499X) **5376**
• Sou'wester (South Bend) (USA ISSN 0038-4984) **4314**
Sovac Series on Social Security *see* Kluwer Sovac Series on Social Security **1932**
Soveltavan Psykologian Monografioita (FIN ISSN 0783-408X) **7409**
Sovereign (GBR) **8604**
Sovereign Assessment Monthly (USA) **1652**
Sovereignty Lectures (GBR) **7185**
Sovershenno Sekretno (RUS) **3941**
Sovetskaya Pravda (RUS) **7185**
• Sovetskaya Rossiya (RUS) **3941**
Sovetskaya Sibir' (RUS) **4266**
• Sovetskii Sakhalin (RUS) **4266**
Sovetskii Sport (RUS ISSN 0233-4283) **8202**
Sovety Potrebitelyam, Reitingi, Obzory, Situatsii *see* S P R O S **2641**
Soviet (Russian) Military Experience (GBR ISSN 1462-0944) **6447**
Soviet (Russian) Military Theory and Practice (GBR) **6447**
Soviet Analyst (GBR ISSN 0049-1713) **7185**
• ➤ The Soviet and Post Soviet Review (NLD ISSN 1075-1262) **4266**
Soviet Biographical Service (USA) **645**
Soviet Maritime Newsletter (GBR ISSN 1464-1046) **8663**
Soviet Metal Technology (USA ISSN 0561-2454) **6332**
Sovmestnye Predpriyatiya *see* Joint Ventures **1132**
Sovremennaya Dramaturgiya (RUS ISSN 0207-7698) **8479**
Sovremennaya Elektrometallurgiya (UKR ISSN 0233-7681) **6332**
Sovremennaya Elektronika (RUS) **3114**
Sovremennaya Meditsina. Teoriya i Praktika (RUS) **5717**
Sovremennaya Pediatriya (UKR) **6104**
Sovremennaya Stomatologiya (BLR) **5866**
➤ Sovremennaya Stomatologiya (UKR) **5866**
Sovremennoe Domovodstvo (RUS) **4914**
Sovremennye Problemy Toksikologii *see* Suchasni Problemy Toksykolohii **6881**
Sower (USA) **3046**
The Sower (ZAF ISSN 0038-5980) **7682**
• The Sowetan (ZAF ISSN 1016-3697) **3950**
Sowetan Soccer Guide (ZAF ISSN 1028-2920) **8246**
Soweto Mix (ZAF) **3950**
Soweto Today (ZAF) **3950**
† SoWi (DEU) **8989**
• sowieso (DEU) **2213**
Sowiniec (POL ISSN 1425-1965) **4266**
Sow's Ear Poetry Review (USA ISSN 1535-5462) **5435**
The Soy Connection (USA) **254**
• (Year) Soya & Oilseed Bluebook (USA ISSN 1099-7970) **254**
• Soybean (AUS ISSN 1834-3546) **254**
• Soybean Abstracts (Online) (GBR) **720**
Soybean Digest *see* Corn and Soybean Digest **225**
• Soybean Genetics Newsletter (Online Edition) (USA ISSN 1930-8981) **878**
Soybean Genetics Newsletter (Print Edition) *see* Soybean Genetics Newsletter (Online Edition) **878**
Soybean: Inland Northern N S W Planting Guide *see* Soybean **254**
Soybean: North Coast N S W Planting Guide *see* Soybean **254**
Soybean Science *see* Dadou Kexue **227**
Soybean South (USA) **254**
Soybean: Southern N S W Planting Guide *see* Soybean **254**
Soyuz (BLR) **3800**
Sozai Busseigaku Zasshi/Society of Materials Engineering for Resources of Japan. Journal (JPN ISSN 0919-9853) **3358**
Sozial (DEU ISSN 1861-1281) **8072**
Sozial Agenda *see* Social Agenda **1707**
• Sozial.Geschichte (CHE ISSN 1660-2870) **5240**
Sozial- und Kulturwissenschaftliche Materialien (AUT) **8006**
Sozial- und Praeventivmedizin *see* International Journal of Public Health **5639**
Sozial- und Wirtschaftshistorische Studien (AUT) **1549**
Sozial- und Wirtschaftspolitik (NLD ISSN 1871-8841) **7185**
Sozial- und Wirtschaftspolitik. Zusammenfassung *see* Sozial- und Wirtschaftspolitik **7185**
Sozial- und Zeitgeschichte des Sports *see* SportZeit **8209**
Sozialarbeit in Oesterreich (AUT ISSN 1019-7729) **8072**
Sozialarbeiterbrief (DEU ISSN 1435-8220) **8072**
Sozialcourage (DEU ISSN 1613-8538) **8072**
Soziale Arbeit (DEU ISSN 0490-1606) **8072**
Soziale Fortschritt (LUX) **4602**
Soziale Innovation (CHE ISSN 1661-6871) **8006**
Soziale Medizin (CHE) **7542**
Soziale Orientierung (DEU ISSN 0720-6917) **8006**
▼ • Soziale Passagen (DEU ISSN 1867-0180) **8006**
Soziale Psychiatrie (Deutsche Gesellschaft fuer Soziale Psychiatrie e.V.) (DEU ISSN 0937-2628) **6186**
Soziale Selbstverwaltung (DEU ISSN 0038-6057) **4524**
Soziale Sicherheit (AUT ISSN 0038-6065) **4524**
Soziale Sicherheit (DEU ISSN 0490-1630) **8072**
➤ Soziale Systeme (DEU ISSN 0948-423X) **8140**
➤ Soziale Welt (DEU ISSN 0038-6073) **8140**
Sozialer Arbeitsschutz (DEU) **1708**
• ➤ Sozialer Fortschritt (DEU ISSN 0038-609X) **8006**
Sozialer Sinn (DEU ISSN 1439-9326) **8140**
Soziales Seminar Informationen (DEU ISSN 0584-5882) **7818**
• Sozialextra (DEU ISSN 0931-279X) **8006**
▼ Sozialgeographie Kompakt (DEU) **8006**
Sozialgeographische Bibliothek (DEU ISSN 1860-3955) **8006**
• Die Sozialgerichtsbarkeit (DEU ISSN 0943-1462) **8006**
Sozialgesetzbuch: Allgemeiner Teil (DEU ISSN 0934-4136) **4842**
Sozialgesetzbuch: Arbeitsfoerderung (DEU ISSN 1434-5374) **4842**
Sozialgesetzbuch: Gemeinsame Vorschriften (DEU ISSN 0934-4144) **4842**
Sozialgesetzbuch: Gesetzliche Krankenversicherung (DEU ISSN 0936-4773) **4842**
Sozialgesetzbuch: Gesetzliche Rentenversicherung (DEU ISSN 0937-3853) **4842**
Sozialgesetzbuch: Gesetzliche Unfallversicherung (DEU ISSN 1432-4768) **4842**
Sozialgesetzbuch: Grundsicherung fuer Arbeitsuchende (DEU) **4842**
Sozialgesetzbuch: Kinder- und Jugendhilfe (DEU ISSN 0940-2810) **4842**
Sozialgesetzbuch: Pflegeversicherung (DEU ISSN 0947-6873) **4842**
Sozialgesetzbuch: Rehabilitation und Teilhabe Behinderter Menschen (DEU) **4842**
Sozialgesetzbuch: Sozialhilfe (DEU) **4842**
Sozialgesetzbuch: Verwaltungsverfahren und Schutz der Sozialdaten (DEU ISSN 0934-4152) **4842**
Sozialgesetzbuch: Zusammenarbeit der Leistungstraeger und ihre Beziehungen zu Dritten (DEU ISSN 0934-4160) **4842**
Sozialhilfe- und AsylbewerberleistungsRecht (DEU ISSN 1618-6265) **4941**
Sozialistische Erziehung (AUT ISSN 0038-6146) **2914**
Der Sozialistische Kaempfer (AUT ISSN 0038-6162) **7185**
Sozialistische Politik und Wirtschaft *see* S P W **7181**
Sozialistische Zeitung (DEU ISSN 0932-8750) **7185**
Sozialmagazin (DEU ISSN 0340-8469) **8072**
Sozialmarkt Aktuell (DEU ISSN 1439-4057) **1794**
Sozialoekonomische Schriften zur Ruralen Entwicklung (DEU ISSN 0175-2464) **207**
Sozialpaedagogik in Forschung und Praxis (DEU ISSN 1615-1151) **8006**
➤ Sozialpaedagogische Impulse (AUT ISSN 1023-6929) **8006**
• Sozialphysik (AUT ISSN 1990-3553) **8140**
Sozialpolitische Informationen (DEU ISSN 0341-1117) **7185**
Sozialpolitische Monografien (AUT ISSN 1990-732X) **8072**
Sozialpolitische Schriften (DEU ISSN 0584-5998) **8006**
Sozialpsychiatrische Informationen (DEU ISSN 0171-4538) **7409**
Sozialrecht Aktuell (DEU ISSN 1434-7261) **8072**
Sozialrecht & Praxis (DEU ISSN 0939-401X) **8072**
Sozialversicherung Aktuell (AUT) **8072**
• Sozialversicherungs-Berater (DEU ISSN 0936-9198) **1794**
Sozialversicherungsrecht - Rechtsprechung/Droit des Assurances Sociales - Jurisprudence (CHE ISSN 1022-8047) **4786**
Sozialversicherungsrechtliche Entscheidungen (AUT) **4786**
Sozialwirtschaft (DEU ISSN 1613-0707) **8072**
Sozialwirtschaft Aktuell (DEU ISSN 1619-2427) **8072**
Sozialwissenschaften und Berufspraxis (DEU ISSN 0724-3464) **8007**
Sozialwissenschaftliche Literaturrundschau (DEU ISSN 0175-6559) **8007**
Sozialwissenschaftliche Materialien *see* Sozial- und Kulturwissenschaftliche Materialien **8006**
Sozialwissenschaftliche Schriften (DEU ISSN 0935-4808) **8007**
Sozialwissenschaftliche Studien zu Internationalen Problemen/Social Science Studies on International Problems (DEU ISSN 0584-603X) **8007**
Sozialwissenschaftliche Studiengesellschaft Rundschau *see* S W S - Rundschau **7999**
Sozialwissenschaftlicher Studienkreis fuer Internationale Probleme Bulletin *see* S S I P - Bulletin **8130**
Sozialwissenschaftliches Institut der Bundeswehr Arbeitspapiere *see* S O W I Arbeitspapiere **7998**
Sozialwissenschaftliches Institut der Bundeswehr. Vortraege (DEU ISSN 0177-9141) **8007**
Sozialwissenschaftliches Journal (DEU ISSN 1862-9695) **8007**
SoziO (NLD ISSN 1872-0072) **8073**
➤ Soziolinguistik und Sprachkontakt (DEU ISSN 0938-670X) **5176**
Soziologiazko Euskal Koadernoak/Cuadernos Sociologicos Vascos (ESP ISSN 1575-7005) **8141**
• ➤ Soziologie (DEU ISSN 0340-918X) **8141**
Soziologische Abhandlungen (DEU ISSN 0584-6048) **8141**
➤ Soziologische Revue (DEU ISSN 0343-4109) **8141**
Soziologische Schriften (DEU ISSN 0584-6064) **8141**
Soziologisches Jahrbuch *see* Annali di Sociologia (Trent) **8087**
Soziooekonomische Forschungen (CHE) **8007**
• Soz:mag (CHE ISSN 1660-3346) **8141**
Soznanie i Fizicheskaya Real'nost' (RUS ISSN 1027-4359) **8007**
Sozo no Sekai/World of the Creation (JPN) **3467**
• Sp.gov (BRA ISSN 1807-3131) **7469**
Sp V - Spektrum fuer Versicherungsrecht (DEU ISSN 1438-3381) **4524**
Spa Concept (DEU ISSN 1862-2011) **591**
Spa Destinations (CAN ISSN 1186-8848) **8757**
Spa Finder *see* Luxury SpaFinder Magazine **6992**
Spa Guide - Wellness & Beauty (DEU) **591**
Spa Life (AUS ISSN 1833-2528) **5083**
Spa Life, the Ultimate Lifestyle, Vitality Wellness Bliss *see* Spa Life **5083**
Spa Magazine (USA) **6997**
Spa Management (CAN ISSN 1199-0600) **4398**
Spa Manager *see* Spa Concept **591**
Spa Specs (USA) **6997**
Spa Worldwide Guide *see* Spa Magazine **6997**
• Space (HKG) **458**
Space *see* Gong'gan **443**
Space (NZL ISSN 1177-1224) **2914**
Space *see* Kongjian **448**
Space (USA) **4562**
Space Age Times (USA ISSN 0738-0968) **70**
• ➤ Space & Culture (USA ISSN 1206-3312) **4029**
Space and Flight Equipment Journal *see* S A F E Journal **69**
Space and Flight Equipment Symposium Proceedings *see* S A F E Symposium Proceedings **69**
• Space & Missile Defense Report (Email) (USA) **6447**
Space and Naval Warfare Systems Center San Diego. Technical Document (USA) **6447**
Space and Naval Warfare Systems Center San Diego. Technical Report (USA) **6447**
• ➤ Space and Polity (GBR ISSN 1356-2576) **7185**
Space and Security News (USA ISSN 1071-2569) **70**
The Space Architecture *see* Prostranstvoto Arkhitektura **454**
▼ Space Autodefinidos (ARG ISSN 1851-3840) **8202**
Space Autograph News (USA ISSN 1069-6016) **4347**
➤ The Space Between (USA ISSN 1551-9309) **5376**
Space Business International (GBR ISSN 1462-8112) **70**
• Space Calendar (USA ISSN 0741-1731) **70**
• Space Careers (GBR) **6703**
Space Coast C I L News (Center for Independent Living) (USA) **4111**
• SPACE.com (USA) **71**
• ➤ Space Communications (NLD ISSN 0924-8625) **71**
• Space Congress. Proceedings (USA ISSN 0584-6099) **71**
• Space Daily (AUS) **71**
• Space Daily. Newsletter (AUS) **71**
Space Exploration *see* Taikong Tansuo **72**
Space Exploration (Farmington Hills) *see* Information Plus Reference Series. Space Exploration **59**
• Space Fax Daily (USA ISSN 1048-2652) **71**
Space in Japan (JPN) **71**
† • Space Industry News (AUS ISSN 1329-4857) **8989**
• Space Mart (AUS) **71**
Space Medicine & Medical Engineering *see* Hangtian Yixue yu Yixue Gongcheng **58**
Space News (New York) (USA) **71**
• Space News International (USA ISSN 1937-1462) **71**
Space Observer (USA) **6447**
• ➤ Space Policy (GBR ISSN 0265-9646) **71**
Space Research Co-Operative Association Jimukyokuho *see* S P A R C Jimukyokuho **581**
Space Research in Japan (JPN) **582**
Space Research in Norway (Year) (NOR ISSN 0801-9517) **7919**
• Space Research Journal (USA ISSN 1819-3382) **71**
Space Research Organization Netherlands. Annual Report (NLD ISSN 1873-9032) **71**
• Space Research Today (GBR ISSN 1752-9298) **71**
Space Review (GBR ISSN 1366-6827) **71**
Space Safety and Rescue (Year) (USA) **71**
• Space Science News (USA) **71**
• ➤ Space Science Reviews (NLD ISSN 0038-6308) **582**
Space Science Series (USA ISSN 1053-8534) **582**
Space Security (CAN ISSN 1910-8680) **71**
Space Technology (London) (GBR) **71**
Space Technology and Applications International Forum (Year) (USA) **71**
• Space Technology Japan (JPN ISSN 1347-3832) **71**
➤ Space Technology Library (NLD ISSN 0924-4263) **71**
Space Times (USA ISSN 1933-2793) **71**
Space Today (USA ISSN 0889-6054) **71**
• Space: UK (GBR) **71**
Space View (DEU ISSN 0949-8273) **5447**
• ➤ Space Weather (USA ISSN 1542-7390) **582**
Spacecraft Environment Engineering *see* Hangtianqi Huanjing Gongcheng **58**
Spacecraft Recovery & Remote Sensing *see* Hangtian Fanhui yu Yaogan **58**
• Spaceflight (GBR ISSN 0038-6340) **72**
Spaceflight Dynamics (Year) *see* A A S / G S F C International Symposium on Spaceflight Dynamics **40**
Spaceflight Mechanics (USA ISSN 1081-6003) **72**
Spaces (FIN ISSN 1797-1020) **4550**
Spaces (GBR ISSN 1740-679X) **4550**
Spaces of Kansas City (USA) **1036**
• Spaces of Utopia (PRT ISSN 1646-4729) **5376**
• Spacewarn Bulletin (USA) **72**
SpaceWatch (USA ISSN 1076-609X) **72**
Spadchyna (BLR) **4476**
Spadcyna/Heritage (BLR ISSN 0236-1019) **4266**
Spaetantike - Fruehes Christentum - Byzanz. Reihe A: Grundlagen und Monumente (DEU) **4325**
Spaetantike - Fruehes Christentum - Byzanz. Reihe B: Studien und Perspektiven (DEU) **4325**
Spagehetti Junction (GBR) **2301**
Spagna Contemporanea (ITA ISSN 1121-7480) **4266**
Spain (Year) (USA ISSN 1055-565X) **8757**
Spain 21 (USA) **8757**
Spain. Agencia Tributaria. Informacion Estadistica sobre el Comercio Exterior (ESP) **1582**
Spain and Portugal *see* Fodor's Portugal **8708**
• Spain Autos Report (GBR ISSN 1749-0197) **8604**
Spain Berlitz Travel Guide *see* Berlitz Spain Pocket Guide **8687**
• Spain. Boletin Oficial del Estado (ESP ISSN 0212-033X) **7469**
Spain. Direccion General de Comercio Exterior. Coleccion Cuadernos de Information del SOIVRE (ESP) **1433**
Spain. Direccion General de Comercio Interior. Coleccion Estudios (ESP) **1433**
† Spain. Direccion General de Correos y Telecomunicacion. Boletin Oficial de Correos y Telecomunicacion (ESP) **8989**
Spain. Direccion General de la Produccion Agraria. Campana Algodonera (ESP) **254**
† Spain. Direccion General de Pesca Maritima. Publicaciones Tecnicas (ESP) **8989**
Spain. Direccion General del Servicio Juridico del Estado. Anales *see* Abogacia General del Estado. Anales **4608**
• Spain Food & Drink Report (GBR ISSN 1749-2998) **1178**
Spain Freight Transport Report (GBR ISSN 1750-5283) **8511**
Spain Gourmetour (ESP ISSN 0214-2937) **4398**
Spain in Figures *see* Espana en Cifras **7306**
Spain. Instituto Nacional de Industria. Informe Anual (ESP) **1178**
Spain. Instituto Tecnologico Geominero de Espana. Coleccion Memorias (ESP) **2769**
Spain. Instituto Tecnologico Geominero de Espana. Coleccion Temas Geologicos - Mineros (ESP) **2717**
Spain. Instituto Tecnologico Geominero de Espana. Informes (ESP) **2769**
Spain. Ministerio Asuntos Exteriores. Direccion General de Cooperacion Tecnica Internacional. Sintesis de Informacion Sobre Organismos Internacionales (ESP) **6282**
Spain. Ministerio de Agricultura, Pesca y Alimentacion. Boletin (ESP) **158**
Spain. Ministerio de Agricultura, Pesca y Alimentacion. Boletin de Precios de Productos Pesqueros (ESP) **3614**
Spain. Ministerio de Agricultura, Pesca y Alimentacion. Boletin de Sanidad Vegetal: Plagas (ESP ISSN 0213-6910) **254**
Spain. Ministerio de Agricultura, Pesca y Alimentacion. Boletin Mensual de Estadistica Agraria (ESP ISSN 0211-9897) **186**

Title

10892 SPAIN. MINISTERIO DE AGRICULTURA, PESCA Y ALIMENTACION ULRICH'S PERIODICALS

Spain. Ministerio de Agricultura, Pesca y Alimentacion. Instituto de Reforma y Desarrollo Agrario. Hojas Divulgadoras (ESP) **158**
Spain. Ministerio de Agricultura Pesca y Alimentacion. Secretaria General Tecnica. Anuario de Estadistica Agroalimentaria (ESP ISSN 1576-4869) **186**
Spain. Ministerio de Defensa. Boletin Oficial (ESP ISSN 0213-2753) **6447**
Spain. Ministerio de Economia y Hacienda. Boletin de Informacion Trimestral (ESP ISSN 1132-0052) **1519**
Spain. Ministerio de Economia y Hacienda. Boletin Oficial (ESP ISSN 0212-5897) **7469**
Spain. Ministerio de Economia y Hacienda. Delegacion del Gobierno en Campsa. El Petroleo en la C E E (Comunidad Economica Europea) (ESP) **6793**
Spain. Ministerio de Economia y Hacienda. Delegacion del Gobierno en Campsa. Memoria (ESP) **6793**
Spain. Ministerio de Economia y Hacienda. Direccion General de Seguros. Balances y Cuentas (ESP) **1944**
Spain. Ministerio de Economia y Hacienda. Estadisticas Presupuestarias y Fiscales (ESP) **1266**
Spain. Ministerio de Economia y Hacienda. Memoria Estadistica. Seguros Privados (ESP) **8402**
Spain. Ministerio de Educacion y Cultura. Boletin (ESP) **2914**
Spain. Ministerio de Educacion y Cultura. Guia (ESP) **2914**
Spain. Ministerio de Fomento. Anuario Estadistico (ESP ISSN 1887-0872) **7316**
• Spain. Ministerio de Fomento. Revista (Madrid, 2001) (ESP ISSN 1577-4589) **3467**
Spain. Ministerio de Fomento y Ministerio de Medio Ambiente. Revista *see* Spain. Ministerio de Fomento. Revista (Madrid, 2001) **3467**
Spain. Ministerio de Industria. Resultados de la Encuesta de Coyuntura Industrial: Sector Industrial (ESP) **1904**
Spain. Ministerio de Industria, Turismo y Comercio. Informe (ESP ISSN 1885-7000) **1519**
Spain. Ministerio de Justicia. Boletin de Informacion (ESP ISSN 0211-4267) **4786**
• Spain. Ministerio de Justicia e Interior. Direccion General de Trafico. Revista Trafico (ESP) **8635**
Spain. Ministerio de Justicia e Interior. Documentacion Juridica (ESP ISSN 0210-3419) **4786**
Spain. Ministerio de la Vivienda. Boletin Oficial (ESP ISSN 0490-3323) **4427**
Spain. Ministerio de la Vivienda. Estadistica de la Industria de la Construccion (ESP ISSN 0561-4902) **1048**
Spain. Ministerio de la Vivienda. Serie 3: Vivienda (ESP) **7469**
• Spain. Ministerio de Trabajo y Asuntos Sociales. Revista (ESP ISSN 1137-5868) **1708**
Spain. Ministerio del Interior. Direccion General de Trafico. Anuario Estadistico de Accidentes (ESP ISSN 1575-3298) **8530**
Spain. Ministerio del Interior. Direccion General de Trafico. Anuario Estadistico General (ESP ISSN 1575-3395) **8530**
Spain. Ministerio del Interior. Revista de Documentacion (ESP ISSN 1132-7863) **4786**
Spain. Ministerio Fiscal. Revista (ESP ISSN 1135-0628) **4786**
• Spain. Registro Mercantil. Boletin Oficial (ESP ISSN 0214-9958) **1178**
† Spain. Senado. Temas (ESP) **8989**
† Spain. Senado. Textos Normativos (ESP) **8989**
Spain: The Business Link (USA) **1582**
Spajanie Metali i Tworzyw w Praktyce (POL ISSN 1732-1425) **6344**
Spal (ESP ISSN 1133-4525) **418**
➤ Span (FJI ISSN 0313-1459) **5376**
Span (London) (GBR) **7682**
Spandauer Volksblatt (DEU) **3857**
Spanende Fertigungsverfahren und Werkzeugmaschinen, Drehen, Fraesen, Hobeln, Bohren, Abtragen *see* Informationsdienst F I Z Technik. Spanende Fertigungsverfahren und Werkzeugmaschinen, Drehen, Fraesen, Hobeln, Bohren, Abtragen **3231**
Spanglish Times (USA ISSN 1933-0227) **3565**
• Spaniels in the Field (USA ISSN 1043-5034) **6815**
Spanische Forschungen der Goerresgesellschaft. Reihe 1: Gesammelte Aufsaetze zur Kulturgeschichte Spaniens (DEU ISSN 0342-1058) **4266**
Spanische Forschungen der Goerresgesellschaft. Reihe 2: Monographien (DEU ISSN 0081-3494) **4266**
Spanish Accounting Review *see* Revista de Contabilidad **1300**
Spanish Balance of Payments *see* The Spanish Balance of Payments and International Investment Position **1944**
• The Spanish Balance of Payments and International Investment Position (ESP ISSN 1698-8566) **1944**
Spanish Bibliography of Scientific Journals in Social Sciences and Humanities *see* Bibliografia Espanola de Revistas Cientificas de Ciencias Sociales y Humanidades **8020**
Spanish Books in Print *see* Libros en Venta en Hispanoamerica y Espana **629**
Spanish Classical Texts (USA) **5376**
Spanish Daily News *see* Popular **3558**
• ➤ Spanish Economic Review/Revista Espanola de Economia (DEU ISSN 1435-5469) **1519**
Spanish Herald (AUS ISSN 0725-1831) **3565**
Spanish Homes Magazine (GBR ISSN 1471-6607) **7613**
• Spanish in Context (NLD ISSN 1571-0718) **5376**
Spanish International Transport Newspaper *see* Portnewspaper **8508**
• ➤ Spanish Journal of Agricultural Research (ESP ISSN 1695-971X) **158**
Spanish Journal of Chemotherapy *see* Revista Espanola de Quimioterapia **5910**
• The Spanish Journal of Psychology (ESP ISSN 1138-7416) **7409**
Spanish Language Books for Children & Young Adults (USA) **7579**
Spanish Language Literature Review *see* Oil, Gas & Petrochem Equipment **6784**
Spanish Magazine (GBR ISSN 1741-1564) **8757**
Spanish Official Chamber of Commerce in Australia. Spanish - Australian Trade (AUS) **1410**
▼ Spanish Perspectives on English and American Literature, Communication and Culture (CHE ISSN 1662-2383) **5376**
Spanish Property News *see* Spanish Homes Magazine **7613**
Spanish Studies (GBR ISSN 0144-3771) **5376**
➤ Spanish Yearbook of International Law (NLD ISSN 0928-0634) **4941**
Spanish Yellow Pages (USA) **2028**
• Spank! Youth Culture Online (CAN) **6618**
Spanner (London, 1974) (GBR ISSN 0584-8067) **5240**
Spanner N Y C (USA) **518**
Spanning (NLD ISSN 1574-986X) **7185**
Spanning Presbyterians in Aotearoa New Zealand. *see* S P A N Z **7773**
Spanning the Centuries of Hawkesbury's History (AUS ISSN 1833-9905) **4194**
Spansklaererforeningen. Informationer (DNK ISSN 0109-307X) **5176**
† Spar Network (GBR) **8989**
† SparCo (ESP) **8989**
• Spare Time (USA ISSN 0038-6499) **1652**
Sparebankbladet/Norwegian Savings Bank News (NOR ISSN 0038-6502) **1384**
Sparetime *see* Baxiaoshi Yiwai **3822**
Spargel und Erdbeer Profi (DEU ISSN 1616-2439) **254**
Spark *see* Xing Huo **5402**
Spark (IND) **5435**
Spark *see* Tsog **5390**
• The Spark (NZL ISSN 1177-0724) **7185**
• Spark (London) (GBR ISSN 1749-5008) **4427**
Spark (Market Harborough) (GBR) **4085**
Spark (New York) (USA ISSN 0024-0591) **7741**
• Spark (Washington) (USA ISSN 1945-9890) **582**
Sparkasse (DEU ISSN 0038-6561) **1384**
† Sparkassen-Magazin (DEU ISSN 1435-8379) **8989**
Sparkassen-Markt (DEU ISSN 0943-3953) **1384**
Die Sparkassen-Zeitung (DEU ISSN 1612-3743) **1384**
Sparkassenfachbuch (Year) (DEU ISSN 0561-5402) **1384**
Sparkle Magazine (KEN) **2213**
Sparkle World (GBR ISSN 1742-0873) **2213**
Sparkle World (USA ISSN 1556-0775) **2213**
Sparks (USA) **518**
Sparks (Grand Rapids) (USA) **8479**
• Sparks (West Chester) (USA ISSN 1077-4149) **5376**
Sparoeversikt (SWE ISSN 1101-4709) **1519**
Sparraaja (FIN ISSN 1457-0637) **1904**
➤ Sparta (GBR ISSN 1751-0007) **2240**
Spartacist (USA ISSN 0038-6596) **7185**
Spartacist (Japanese Edition) (JPN) **7185**
Spartacist Canada (CAN ISSN 0229-5415) **7185**
Spartacist Ireland (IRL) **7185**
Spartacist South Africa (ZAF) **7185**
Spartaco (ITA) **7185**
Spartacus International Gay Guide (DEU ISSN 0167-479X) **4379**
Spartacus Traveler *see* SpartacusTraveler **8757**
SpartacusTraveler (DEU ISSN 1862-7943) **8757**
Spartakist (DEU ISSN 0173-7430) **7185**
Spartan (USA) **8246**
Spartan Daily (USA) **2301**
Spartanburg Magazine (USA) **3989**
Sparta's Journey *see* Sparta **2240**
Spasmagazine *see* Sante Integrative **5709**
Spass mit Musik *see* Playmusic **6606**
• Spatial Business Newsletter (AUS ISSN 1324-2008) **4037**
• Spatial Cognition and Computation (USA ISSN 1387-5868) **7409**
• ➤ Spatial Economic Analysis (GBR ISSN 1742-1772) **1178**
Spatial Practices (NLD ISSN 1871-689X) **4162**
Spatial Structures *see* Kongjian Jiegou **3277**
Spatial Vision *see* Seeing and Perceiving **5555**
Spatial Vision Perspectives (NLD) **518**
• Spa_tien (CHE ISSN 1661-383X) **5376**
Spatio - Economic Development Record (IND ISSN 0971-4944) **4427**
Spatz (DEU) **2213**
Spawn (BRA ISSN 1413-3350) **2214**
Spazio Casa (ITA ISSN 1120-4516) **4562**
† Spaziolegno (ITA ISSN 1120-4788) **8989**
SpazioSport (ITA ISSN 1125-1905) **8202**
SPC-A Annual *see* Australian Maritime Issues **6413**
Speak Out (RUS ISSN 1810-2336) **5240**
Speak Out/Khulumani/Taurai (ZWE) **8903**
Speak Out! (Canterbury) (GBR ISSN 1026-4345) **5176**
Speak Out! (London) (GBR) **8479**
Speak Up (BRA ISSN 0104-2238) **5176**
Speak Up! (CAN ISSN 0383-9370) **7185**
Speak Up (ESP ISSN 0214-1418) **5176**
• Speak Up (ITA ISSN 1120-4583) **5176**
Speak Up Interactive *see* Speak Up **5176**
Speakeasy (FRA ISSN 0221-833X) **5240**
The Speaker (Bridgewater) (USA) **3565**
Speaker (Tempe) (USA ISSN 1934-9076) **5176**
• Speaker and Gavel (Online Edition) (USA) **2914**
Speaker and Gavel (Print Edition) *see* Speaker and Gavel (Online Edition) **2914**
Speakers Academy *see* Academy Magazine **5089**
Speakers' Papers: Speeches from the Gold and Silver Institutes' (Year) Annual Meeting (USA) **6479**
Speakin' Out News (USA) **3565**
• ➤ Speaking English (GBR ISSN 1465-153X) **5177**
Speaking of "Columbias" (USA ISSN 0038-6626) **301**
Speaking of Fire (USA ISSN 1076-5441) **3581**
Speaking of Safety (USA) **7542**
Speaking Out (JPN ISSN 0915-6690) **3467**
Speaking Relatively (USA ISSN 0884-8610) **3783**
Spear (NGA ISSN 0038-6634) **3921**
† • SPEaR Bulletin (NZL ISSN 1176-161X) **8989**
• The Spear Report (USA ISSN 1535-7309) **1652**
• Spear Shaker Review (USA ISSN 0894-8852) **5376**
Spearhead (KEN) **7682**
Spearhead (Mayfield) (USA) **8283**
Spearhead (Moneta) (USA) **6447**
Spear's W M S *see* Spear's Wealth Management Survey **1384**
Spear's Wealth Management Survey (GBR) **1384**
SpecCheck (GBR ISSN 1357-4752) **2045**
Specchio (CAN) **3565**
Lo Specchio *see* Almanacco dello Specchio **5416**
Specchio (ITA ISSN 1972-8123) **3898**
Specchio Economico (ITA) **1519**
Speciaal (NLD ISSN 1574-7239) **1708**
Special (CHE) **4398**
Special (GBR ISSN 0966-4831) **3046**
SPeCiaL *see* S P C L **3916**
Special Antieke Bouwmaterialen (BEL ISSN 1784-7915) **1036**
Special Art Floral (FRA ISSN 1636-3345) **3751**
Special Astrophysical Observatory. Bulletin *see* Astrophysical Bulletin **571**
Special Badkamers & Keukens (BEL ISSN 1782-6454) **1036**
• ➤ Special Care in Dentistry (USA ISSN 0275-1879) **5866**
Special Casting & Non-ferrous Alloys *see* Tezhong Zhuzao Ji Youse Hejin **6335**
▼ Special Cheval (FRA ISSN 1958-8518) **8298**
▼ Special Chiens (FRA ISSN 1959-0970) **6815**
• Special Children (GBR ISSN 0951-6875) **3047**
▼ Special Cloture Portes & Barrieres (BEL ISSN 1784-794X) **1036**
Special Collections in Children's Literature (USA) **2174**
Special Cuisines & Salles de Bain (BEL ISSN 1784-0112) **1036**
• Special Data Issue (USA ISSN 1082-3417) **7469**
Special Delivery *see* Odtey Bichig **8507**
• Special Delivery (USA ISSN 1083-5008) **6005**
Special Derniere - Le Meilleur (FRA ISSN 1632-0700) **8298**
• The Special Ed Advocate Newsletter (USA ISSN 1538-3202) **4069**
Special Edition (USA) **6300**
Special Edition Press (USA) **3565**
Special Education Coding Criteria (CAN ISSN 1911-4311) **3047**
Special Education Handbook (GBR ISSN 1367-6334) **3033**
• Special Education Law and Litigation Treatise (USA) **3047**
• Special Education Law Bulletin (USA ISSN 1542-4995) **3047**
• Special Education Law Monthly (USA ISSN 1094-3773) **3047**
Special Education Law Report (USA) **3047**
Special Education Law Update (USA) **3047**
• Special Education News (USA) **3047**
➤ Special Education Perspectives (AUS) **3047**
• Special Education Report (USA ISSN 1553-4294) **3047**
Special Education Technology Practice (USA ISSN 1524-2765) **3047**
† Special Education Today (USA ISSN 1080-1375) **8989**
• Special Educational Needs Abstracts (GBR ISSN 0954-0822) **2936**
Special Educational Needs Coordinator Update *see* S E N C O Update **3046**
• The Special Educator (USA ISSN 1047-1618) **3047**
Special Effects & Stunts Guide (USA ISSN 1045-0750) **6513**
• Special Entry Access Schemes (AUS ISSN 1832-6552) **3002**
• Special Events Magazine (USA ISSN 1079-1264) **4398**
Special Features in Vegetation Science *see* Journal of Vegetation Science **799**
▼ Special Finance Insider (USA) **8604**
▼ Special Immobilier (FRA ISSN 1961-6228) **7613**
Special Interest Autos (USA ISSN 0049-1845) **8604**
Special Interest Divisions. Division 7, Aural Rehabilitation and its Instrumentation *see* Perspectives on Aural Rehabilitation and its Instrumentation **4076**
Special Interest Group Artifical Intelligence Conference Proceedings *see* S I G A R T Conference Proceedings **2456**
Special Interest Group Electronic Commerce Gecom Newsletter *see* S I Gecom Newsletter **1421**
Special Interest Group Embedded Systems Newsletter *see* S I G B E D Newsletter **2436**
Special Interest Group for Documentation Newsletter *see* S I G D O C Newsletter **2524**
Special Interest Group for Documentation Proceedings *see* S I G D O C Proceedings **2338**
Special Interest Group Gnature (Greensboro) *see* S I Gnature (Greensboro) **2437**
Special Interest Group Graphics Computer Graphics and Interactive Techniques *see* S I G G R A P H Computer Graphics and Interactive Techniques **2489**
Special Interest Group Group Bulletin *see* S I G Group Bulletin **2524**
Special Interest Group Information Technology Education Newsletter *see* S I G I T E Newsletter **3079**
Special Interest Group Mobility of Systems, Users, Data and Computing MC2R *see* S I G M O B I L E MC2R **2436**
Special Interest Group Multimedia Conference Proceedings *see* S I G M M Conference Proceedings **2489**
Special Interest Group on Ada Ada Annual International Conference. Proceedings *see* S I G Ada Annual International Conference. Proceedings **2596**
Special Interest Group on Algorithms and Computation Theory News *see* S I G A C T News **2464**
Special Interest Group on Computer and Human Interaction Bulletin *see* S I G C H I Bulletin **8151**
Special Interest Group on Computer Architecture Computer Architecture News *see* S I G A R C H Computer Architecture News **2468**
Special Interest Group on Computer Graphics and Interactive Techniques Conference Abstracts and Applications *see* S I G G R A P H Conference Abstracts and Applications **2489**
Special Interest Group on Computer Graphics and Interactive Techniques Electronic Art and Animation Catalog *see* S I G G R A P H Electronic Art and Animation Catalog **530**
Special Interest Group on Computer Science Education Bulletin Inroads *see* S I G C S E Bulletin Inroads **2951**
Special Interest Group on Design Automation Newsletter (Online) *see* S I G D A Newsletter (Online) **2464**
Special Interest Group on Electromagnetic Analysis and Design for Printed Circuits. Technical Report *see* Denji Tokusei o Koryoshita Purinto Kiban Sekkei Kenkyu Bukai Yokoshu **3298**
Special Interest Group on Embedded Systems Review *see* S I G B E D Review **2509**
Special Interest Group on Information Retrieval Forum *see* S I G I R Forum **2550**
Special Interest Group on Knowledge Discovery & Data Mining Explorations *see* S I G K D D Explorations **2436**
Special Interest Group on Knowledge Discovery and Data Mining Explorations *see* S I G K D D Explorations **2436**
Special Interest Group on Management of Data Record *see* S I G M O D Record **2532**
Special Interest Group on Measurement and Evaluation Performance Evaluation Review *see* S I G M E T R I C S Performance Evaluation Review **2474**
Special Interest Group on Microarchitecture Newsletter (Online) *see* S I G M I C R O Newsletter (Online) **2436**
Special Interest Group on Spatial Information Special *see* S I G S P A T I A L Special **2436**
Special Interest Group on University Computing Centers User Services Conference. Proceedings *see* S I G U C C S User Services Conference. Proceedings **2436**
Special Interest Group Synergy *see* S I G Synergy **2908**
Special Interest Groups Managing Object Technology Series *see* S I G S: Managing Object Technology Series **8437**
Special Investment Situations (USA) **1652**
Special Issues for Chinese Export Commodities Fair/Zhongguo Chukou Shangpin Jiaoyihui Tekan (HKG) **1844**
▼ Special Kernthema Bedrijfsvoering (NLD ISSN 1875-3949) **3033**
Special Kernthema Good Governance (NLD ISSN 1872-1591) **3033**
Special Kernthema Huisvesting (NLD ISSN 1875-4295) **3033**
Special Libraries Association Salary Survey & Workplace Study (Year) *see* S L A Salary Survey & Workplace Study (Year) **5045**
Special Libraries Association. Social Science Division. Bulletin (USA ISSN 1041-7737) **5048**

Title

10894 SPIEL UND THEATER ULRICH'S PERIODICALS

Spiel und Theater (DEU ISSN 0038-7509) **8479**
Spielbox (DEU ISSN 0721-6777) **8202**
Spielcasino (DEU ISSN 1432-3788) **8202**
Spielen und Lernen (DEU ISSN 0344-8754) **2914**
Spielfilmliste (DEU ISSN 0071-4933) **6514**
• Spielmagazin (DEU) **8202**
Spielmittel (DEU ISSN 0174-1772) **4061**
Der Spielplan (DEU ISSN 0038-7517) **8479**
▼ SpielRaeume der Antike (DEU ISSN 1866-7805) **4162**
Das Spielzeug (DEU ISSN 0038-7525) **4061**
Spielzeug International (DEU ISSN 1861-7689) **4061**
Spiesser (DEU ISSN 1617-8963) **5083**
Spijs en Drank *see* Nest (Dutch Edition) **3801**
Spike! (GBR) **8246**
Spike *see* Student Impact **2302**
Spike (HKG) **5240**
• The Spike (USA) **3565**
Spike Art Quarterly (AUT ISSN 1813-6281) **518**
Spil (NLD ISSN 0165-6252) **254**
Spildevandsteknisk Tidsskrift (DNK ISSN 0108-0466) **3512**
Spill Reporting Procedures Guide (USA ISSN 1056-5264) **3512**
† • ➤ Spill Science & Technology Bulletin (GBR ISSN 1353-2561) **8989**
Spill Technology Newsletter/Bulletin de la Lutte contre les Deversements (CAN ISSN 0381-4459) **7919**
SpIN *see* Space Industry News **8989**
De Spin *see* Stuifmeel **8073**
• Spin (USA ISSN 0886-3032) **6619**
Spin-Off (USA ISSN 0198-8239) **540**
Spin Report (DEU ISSN 1612-4898) **751**
Spin to Win Rodeo (USA ISSN 1096-9772) **8298**
Spin to Win Rodeo Magazine (USA) **8298**
Spinal Column (Atlanta) (USA) **6073**
Spinal Connection (USA) **6073**
• ➤ Spinal Cord (GBR ISSN 1362-4393) **6186**
Spinal Cord Injury Life (USA) **4078**
Spinal Cord Injury Nursing *see* S C I Nursing **5708**
Spinal Cord Injury Psychosocial Process *see* S C I Psychosocial Process **7406**
Spinal Deformity *see* Sekichu Henkei **6072**
Spinal Network (USA) **4069**
Spinal Surgery *see* Sekizui Geka **6072**
Spinalkanalen *see* Columna **5804**
Spincraft Pattern Newsletter (USA) **6642**
Spindel *see* The Southern Journal of Philosophy **6953**
• Spindet (DNK ISSN 1603-7979) **5177**
• ➤ Spine (Philadelphia, 1976) (USA ISSN 0362-2436) **6073**
• Spine-Affiliated Society Meeting Abstracts (USA ISSN 1548-2545) **5807**
Spine and Spinal Cord *see* Sekitsui Sekizui Janaru **6072**
Spine Art *see* SpineArt **8989**
Spine Arthroplasty Society Journal *see* S A S Journal **6257**
• The Spine Journal (NLD ISSN 1529-9430) **6073**
† SpineArt (DEU ISSN 1613-7140) **8989**
• Spinifex (AUS) **2628**
• Spinner (NZL) **3919**
Spinner (USA ISSN 0730-2657) **4314**
Spinning Jenny (USA ISSN 1082-1406) **5435**
Spinning Magazine (ITA ISSN 1828-9460) **8335**
Spinoff (USA ISSN 0148-2203) **8439**
Spinoza *see* N W O-Spinozapremies **7885**
Spiral of Time *see* Spirale der Zeit **8903**
Spirale (CAN ISSN 0225-9044) **4476**
➤ Spirale (FRA ISSN 0994-3722) **2914**
• Spirale (Ramonville Saint-Agne) (FRA ISSN 1278-4699) **2168**
▼ Spirale der Zeit/Spiral of Time (DEU ISSN 1864-5275) **8903**
Spire (CAN) **5435**
Spiridon Laufmagazin (DEU ISSN 0171-6298) **6997**
Spirit (CAN) **3565**
Spirit (DEU ISSN 1432-9468) **8202**
Spirit (Joplin) (USA ISSN 1098-1039) **7775**
Spirit (Metairie) (USA) **8073**
Spirit (St. Paul) (USA ISSN 1040-3868) **7682**
Spirit & Destiny (GBR ISSN 1478-4343) **8884**
Spirit & Life (USA ISSN 0038-7592) **7818**
Spirit and Life (USA ISSN 1088-9191) **7818**
The Spirit Guide to Spellcraft (AUS ISSN 1833-2552) **6744**
Spirit Journal *see* F. Paul Pacult's Spirit Journal **603**
Spirit Magazine (CAN ISSN 1703-8448) **3566**
Spirit of Aborginal Youth Magazine *see* S A Y Magazine **3562**
• Spirit of Aloha (USA ISSN 0199-7092) **8786**
Spirit of Books (USA ISSN 1077-6648) **7699**
• The Spirit of Bosnia (USA ISSN 1931-4957) **3566**
• Spirit of Service (USA) **4085**
Spirit of Success Magazine (USA) **3664**
Spirit of the Plains Magazine (USA ISSN 1948-0857) **7682**
• Spirit of the Season (GBR ISSN 1748-5088) **7818**
▼ Spirit of the West (USA ISSN 1940-5898) **8758**
Spirit Plus Magazine (USA) **4056**
The Spirit Tales of Silver Wolf and His People (USA ISSN 1546-7090) **6636**
The Spirit That Moves Us (USA ISSN 0364-4014) **5376**
• Spirita (Online) (DEU) **7683**
• Spiritan Horizons (USA ISSN 1933-1762) **7818**
• SpiritLed Woman (Online) (USA) **7683**
SpiritLed Woman (Print) *see* SpiritLed Woman (Online) **7683**
Spiritual Book News (USA ISSN 0038-7606) **7574**
Spiritual Counterfeits Project, Inc Journal *see* S C P Journal **7679**
Spiritual Counterfeits Project, Inc Newsletter *see* S C P Newsletter **7679**
Spiritual Frontiers Fellowship International Journal (USA) **6744**
Spiritual Frontiers Fellowship International Newsletter (USA) **6744**
The Spiritual Healer (GBR ISSN 0038-7622) **7683**
Spiritual Information Bulletin (CAN) **6744**
• Spiritual Life (USA ISSN 0038-7630) **7683**
▼ • Spiritual Living Digest (USA ISSN 1938-1875) **7683**
Spiritualita (ITA ISSN 1825-3563) **7683**
La Spiritualita Cristiana (ITA) **7683**
Spirituality (IRL ISSN 1393-273X) **7818**
Spirituality & Health (USA ISSN 1520-5444) **315**
† • Spirituality and Health International (GBR ISSN 1743-1867) **8989**
• Spirituality for Today (USA) **7683**
De Spirituele Krant *see* Imagine **6924**
Spirituele Scheurkalender (NLD ISSN 1871-5494) **7409**
Der Spirituosen- und Weinhandel (DEU ISSN 0038-7657) **610**
• Spiritus (FRA ISSN 0038-7665) **7683**
• Spiritus (USA ISSN 1533-1709) **7683**
Spirou (BEL ISSN 0771-8071) **2214**
Spirula (NLD ISSN 1566-063X) **964**
Spisanie Statistika (BGR ISSN 1310-7410) **8402**
Spisy Archeologickeho Ustavu A V C R Brno *see* Ceska Akademie Ved. Archeologicky Ustav. Spisy **387**
Spisy Masarykovy Univerzity v Brne. Filozoficka Fakulta *see* Masarykova Univerzita. Filozoficka Fakulta. Spisy **6933**
Spitaeler Alters Pflegeheime (CHE) **8073**
Spitball (USA ISSN 8755-741X) **5376**
• The Spitting Image (USA) **5376**
➤ Spixiana (DEU ISSN 0341-8391) **964**
Spixiana Supplemente (DEU ISSN 0177-7424) **964**
Splash (AUS) **8335**
Splash (DEU ISSN 1861-4434) **8202**
Splash! (Boston) (USA) **3467**
Splash! (Colorado Springs) (USA ISSN 1099-8306) **8202**
Splash (Costa Mesa) (USA ISSN 0898-8951) **8283**
Splash Magazine (MEX) **6815**
• Splendid (USA) **6619**
Splendour (IND ISSN 0972-5296) **6744**
Spletka.net (SVN ISSN 1580-3457) **2567**
• Splinter Magazine (GBR ISSN 1747-0781) **6619**
• Splints & Co/Tidsskrift med Nordisk Poesi paa Nettet (DNK ISSN 1396-867X) **5435**
Splitsko-Makarska Nadbiskupija. Vjesnik (HRV ISSN 0042-7659) **7683**
Splitting Heirs (CAN ISSN 1206-4688) **3783**
Spoehn Schleswig-Holstein (DEU) **1052**
Spokane Area Chamber of Commerce. Directory of Organizations (USA) **1410**
Spokane Business Interaction (USA ISSN 1074-3065) **1410**
Spokane Journal of Business *see* Journal of Business (Spokane) **1360**
▼ Spokane Metro Magazine (USA ISSN 1943-1015) **5083**
Spokane, Washington. Official Gazette (USA ISSN 0038-7711) **7502**
• Spoke (CAN ISSN 0844-4862) **2301**
Spoke (NZL ISSN 1177-018X) **8268**
▼ • Spoken Magazine (USA ISSN 1559-3533) **3566**
Spokeout (IRL ISSN 1393-8517) **4078**
The Spokesman (GBR ISSN 1367-7748) **7266**
• Spokesman (San Antonio) (USA) **6447**
Spokesman Online *see* Spokesman (San Antonio) **6447**
▼ SpokeWrite (USA ISSN 1946-0562) **5376**
Spola (ITA ISSN 1970-4186) **5240**
▼ Spolecnost Pratel Starozitnosti. Casopis (CZE ISSN 1803-1382) **4267**
Spoleczenstwo Otwarte (POL ISSN 0867-0412) **8007**
Spolek Germanistu a Ucitelu Nemciny Nschrift *see* S G U Nschrift **5366**
Spolem (POL ISSN 0038-7746) **1944**
• Spolia (ITA ISSN 1824-727X) **5376**
Spolia Berolinensia (DEU ISSN 0931-4040) **4267**
Spolia Zeylanica/National Museums of Sri Lanka. Bulletin (LKA ISSN 0081-3745) **7920**
Sponge Bob *see* Sungerbob Karepantolon **2215**
SpongeBob Schwammkopf (DEU) **2214**
▼ SpongyaBob Kockanadrag (HUN ISSN 1788-5566) **2214**
Spon's Architects' & Builders' Price Book (Year) (GBR ISSN 0306-3046) **1037**
Spon's Civil Engineering and Highway Works Price Book (GBR ISSN 0957-171X) **3283**
Spon's External Works and Landscape Price Book (GBR) **1037**
Spon's Landscape & External Works Pricebook *see* Spon's External Works and Landscape Price Book **1037**
Spon's Mechanical & Electrical Services Price Book (GBR ISSN 0305-4543) **1037**
Sponsors (DEU ISSN 1432-8925) **35**
Sponsors' Update *see* Community Works **2647**
Sponsorship and Funding Directory *see* Sponsorship and Funding Guide **35**
Sponsorship and Funding Guide (GBR) **35**
Sponsorship News (GBR ISSN 0263-3809) **8202**
The Sponsorship Report (CAN ISSN 1201-5326) **8073**
Sponsorship Strategy: Evidentiary Tactics for Winning Jury Trials *see* Winning Jury Trials: Trial Tactics and Sponsorship Strategy **4967**
▼ • Spontaneous Generations (CAN ISSN 1913-0465) **4162**
Spoon (USA) **2261**
➤ Spoon River Poetry Review (USA) **5435**
Het Spoor (BEL ISSN 0773-5901) **8625**
Spoor & Tram *see* Spoor en Tram **8625**
Spoor en Tram (NLD ISSN 1871-7004) **8625**
Spoor en Trein *see* Spoor en Tram **8625**
Spor (NOR ISSN 0801-5376) **4267**
• ➤ Spor Hekimligi Dergisi/Turkish Journal of Sports Medicine (TUR ISSN 1300-0551) **6233**
† Spor ve Tip (TUR ISSN 1300-5278) **8989**
Sporditaht (EST ISSN 1406-1244) **3837**
Spore (NLD ISSN 1011-0054) **207**
Sport (BEL ISSN 0038-7770) **8202**
Sport *see* Schweizerische Zeitschrift fuer Sportmedizin und Sporttraumatologie **6232**
Sport (CHE) **8202**
Sport (CZE ISSN 1210-8383) **8203**
Sport (FIN ISSN 1458-7122) **6997**
Le Sport (FRA ISSN 1264-6806) **8203**
† Sport (FRA ISSN 1764-1756) **8989**
• Sport (GBR) **8203**
Sport (NOR ISSN 0333-3639) **8203**
Sport (POL ISSN 0137-9305) **8203**
Sport (Warsaw) (POL ISSN 1506-6398) **8203**
Sport Adapte Magazine (FRA ISSN 1157-6421) **8203**
Sport Adressbuch (DEU) **2028**
Sport Africain (COD) **8203**
Sport Aktiv (CHE) **8203**
The Sport Americana Price Guide to Baseball Collectibles (USA) **4347**
The Sport Americana Team Baseball Card Checklist (USA ISSN 0743-9563) **4347**
The Sport Americana Team Football and Basketball Card Checklist (USA) **4347**
Sport & E U Newsletter *see* Sport & E U Review **8203**
• ➤ Sport & E U Review (European Union) (GBR ISSN 2040-5847) **8203**
Sport and Exercise Psychology Review (GBR ISSN 1745-4980) **7409**
• The Sport and Exercise Scientist (GBR ISSN 1754-3444) **6997**
Sport & Fitnes (SVK ISSN 1337-1827) **8203**
Sport and Recreation Information Group Bulletin (GBR ISSN 0267-3304) **4983**
Sport and Science *see* Sport i Nauka **8204**
Sport & Science *see* Tiyu yu Kexue **8212**
Sport & Strategie *see* Sport en Strategie **8203**
Sport & Street Collezioni *see* Collezioni Sport & Street **2252**
Sport and the Law Journal (GBR ISSN 1353-0127) **4786**
† Sport and Tuning Markt (DEU) **8989**
Sport & Wellness Management (CZE ISSN 1802-6931) **1844**
Sport Artikel Zeitung Bike *see* S A Z Bike **1841**
Sport Artikel Zeitung Sport *see* S A Z Sport **1841**
Sport Artikel Zeitung Sportsfashion Magazin *see* S A Z Sportsfashion Magazin **2260**
Sport Auto (DEU ISSN 0940-4287) **8604**
Sport Auto (FRA ISSN 0151-6353) **8203**
Sport Auto (GRC ISSN 1109-7035) **8604**
Sport Auto Magazine (LBN) **8604**
Sport Auto, Virage Auto, Champion *see* Sport Auto **8203**
Sport Auto, Virage Auto, Champion *see* Sport Auto **8203**
• Sport Aviation (USA ISSN 0038-7835) **72**
Sport- Baeder- Freizeitbauten (DEU ISSN 0344-6492) **8203**
Sport Bestuur & Management (NLD ISSN 1389-3130) **8203**
• Sport Bild (DEU ISSN 0934-3369) **8203**
Sport Cardiology (ITA ISSN 1591-1195) **6233**
➤ Sport Commerce and Culture (GBR ISSN 1741-0916) **8203**
Sport Compact Car (USA ISSN 1062-9629) **8604**
• Sport Diver (USA ISSN 1077-985X) **8203**
Sport dlya Vsekh (RUS) **8203**
Sport & Medicina (ITA ISSN 0392-9647) **6233**
• ➤ Sport, Education and Society (GBR ISSN 1357-3322) **8203**
Sport-Ekspress (RUS) **8203**
Sport-Ekspress. Zhurnal (RUS) **8203**
➤ Sport & Geneeskunde (NLD ISSN 1874-6659) **6233**
Sport & Recreatie Management (NLD ISSN 1386-0445) **8246**
▼ Sport en Strategie (NLD ISSN 1875-2357) **8203**
Sport et Plein Air (FRA ISSN 0397-4707) **8335**
Sport et Responsabilite (FRA ISSN 1957-6498) **8203**
Sport et Vie (FRA ISSN 1152-9563) **8203**
▼ • ➤ Sport, Ethics and Philosophy (GBR ISSN 1751-1321) **8203**
Sport Extra *see* Do It! **8170**
Sport First (GBR) **8203**
Sport Fish Currents Newsletter *see* Alaska Department of Fish and Game. Sport Fish Division's Newsletter **8302**
• Sport Fishing (USA ISSN 0896-7369) **8335**
• Sport Fishing BC News (British Columbia) (CAN) **8204**
Sport Fishing Marine and Trailer Boats (AUS) **3609**
Sport Fishing Marine & Trailer Boats *see* Sport Fishing Marine and Trailer Boats **3609**
Sport Flying (NZL ISSN 1176-2136) **72**
Sport Health (AUS ISSN 1032-5662) **6233**
• ➤ Sport History Review/Revue de l'Histoire des Sports (USA ISSN 1087-1659) **8204**
Sport i Nauka/Sport and Science (BGR ISSN 1310-3393) **8204**
† Sport im Spiegel (DEU) **8989**
Sport in Berlin (DEU ISSN 0931-8240) **8204**
Sport in der Heutigen Zeit (DEU) **8204**
Sport in Hessen (DEU) **8204**
• ➤ Sport in History (GBR ISSN 1746-0263) **8204**
• ➤ Sport in Society (GBR ISSN 1743-0437) **8204**
Sport in the Global Society (GBR ISSN 1368-9789) **8204**
Sport-Inform (DEU ISSN 1438-3152) **8204**
Sport International (BEL ISSN 1013-4700) **8204**
Sport International (NLD ISSN 0169-6084) **8204**
† Sport Journal (DEU) **8989**
• ➤ The Sport Journal (USA ISSN 1543-9518) **8204**
Sport Karate International (USA ISSN 1064-6507) **8204**
• Sport Klub (RUS ISSN 1027-9644) **8204**
Sport, Kultur und Gesellschaft (DEU ISSN 1864-0168) **4162**
Sport Life (ESP) **8204**
Sport Literate (USA ISSN 1082-3247) **5240**
Sport Lokaal (NLD ISSN 1872-2210) **8204**
Sport Magazin (CZE ISSN 1214-3677) **8204**
Sport Magazin (ROM ISSN 1221-3349) **8204**
Sport Magazin *see* Sport & Fitnes **8203**
Sport Magazine *see* Sport Magazine - Foot Magazine **8204**
Sport Magazine - Foot Magazine (BEL ISSN 1376-9081) **8204**
Sport Magazine - Voetbal Magazine *see* Sport Magazine - Foot Magazine **8204**
▼ Sport Management Education Journal (USA ISSN 1938-6974) **8204**
• ➤ Sport Management Review (GBR ISSN 1441-3523) **1794**
Sport Market Forecasts (GBR ISSN 1472-0663) **8204**
Sport Marketing Europe (NLD ISSN 1873-720X) **1844**
• ➤ Sport Marketing Quarterly (USA ISSN 1061-6934) **8204**
Sport Med' (FRA ISSN 0993-1252) **6233**
Sport Na MnoGo.ru (RUS) **8204**
• Sport-Orthopadie - Sport-Traumatologie (DEU ISSN 0949-328X) **6233**
Sport Partner (NLD ISSN 1381-9283) **8204**
Sport Pilot *see* E A A Sport Pilot & Light Sport Aircraft **53**
Sport Pilot & Light Sport Aircraft *see* E A A Sport Pilot & Light Sport Aircraft **53**
Sport Pilot F A A Knowledge Test (Federal Aviation Administration) (USA ISSN 1933-4109) **72**
Sport Pilot Syllabus (USA ISSN 1933-4095) **72**
Sport Place International (USA ISSN 0888-9589) **8205**
Sport Plus (CAN ISSN 0828-9581) **8205**
Sport Premiere Magazine (FRA ISSN 0992-7697) **8205**
• ➤ The Sport Psychologist (USA ISSN 0888-4781) **7409**
Sport-Report (DEU ISSN 0722-0405) **8205**
Sport Rider (USA ISSN 1065-7649) **8268**
Sport Rocketry (USA ISSN 1076-2701) **4347**
• Sport Scene (Online) (USA) **8205**
• Sport Science & Physical Education Bulletin (DEU ISSN 1728-5666) **6997**
• ➤ Sport Sciences for Health (ITA ISSN 1824-7490) **6997**
Sport Sciences International (DEU ISSN 0939-3706) **8205**
Sport Scolaire *see* Equilibre **8171**
Sport Shop News (USA) **8205**
Sport Show (DEU ISSN 0931-8178) **8205**
Sport Specijal (SRB ISSN 1820-2802) **8205**
• Sport Strategies Hebdo (FRA ISSN 1772-7693) **8205**
• Sport Summit Sports Business Directory (USA) **2029**
• Sport Supplement (USA) **8205**
• Sport Thesaurus (CAN ISSN 0831-6317) **8219**
• Sport Truck (USA ISSN 1044-7903) **8675**
Sport Tuning Magazine (USA) **8604**
† Sport & Co. (DEU) **8989**
Sport und Design Drachen (DEU ISSN 0945-5507) **4347**
• Sport und Fitness (DEU ISSN 0176-4136) **8205**
Sport und Gesellschaft/Sports and Society (DEU ISSN 1610-3181) **8141**
Sport und Mehr (DEU ISSN 1616-7783) **8205**
Sport und Mobilitaet mit Rollstuhl (DEU) **8205**
Sport und Mode (DEU ISSN 0049-1926) **8205**
• ➤ Sport- und Praeventivmedizin (AUT ISSN 1867-1977) **6233**
Sport Universitario (ITA ISSN 0490-5113) **8205**
Sport Utility, Truck & Van Buyer's Guide *see* Motor Trend Sport Utility, Truck & Van Buyer's Guide **8593**
Sport Utility Vehicle Magazine *see* S U V Magazine **8603**
Sport-Welt (DEU ISSN 1430-1008) **8205**
† Sport & Medicina (ESP ISSN 1130-0183) **8989**
Sport Z *see* Nissan Sport **8595**
Sportaccom (NLD ISSN 0922-4270) **8205**
Sportamo (MUS) **8205**

Title

Title

10898 STAEDTE- UND KREISSTATISTIK RUHRGEBIET ULRICH'S PERIODICALS

• Staedte- und Kreisstatistik Ruhrgebiet (DEU) 1267
Staedteforschung (AUT) 8007
Der Staedtetag (DEU ISSN 0038-9048) 7503
Der Staedtische (CHE) 7503
Staerke see Starch 2130
Stafette (DEU ISSN 0174-5832) 2214
➤ Staff and Educational Development International (IND ISSN 0971-9008) 2914
Staff Development in Indian Universities (Year) (IND) 3002
• The Staff Educator (USA ISSN 1937-755X) 4111
• Staff Leader (USA ISSN 0897-8484) 1875
Staff of Scottish Social Work Departments (GBR ISSN 0260-5457) 8073
Staff Organizations Round Table Bulletin see S O R T Bulletin 5045
Staff Status (USA) 6815
Staff Studies for the World Economic Outlook see International Monetary Fund. World Economic and Financial Surveys 1358
Staff Studies for the World Economic Outlook see International Monetary Fund. World Economic Outlook 1493
Staff Studies for the World Economic Outlook see International Monetary Fund. Global Financial Stability Report 1358
Staff Working Papers Series see United Nations Children's Fund. Programme Division. Staff Working Papers Series 8075
Staffel Aktuell (DEU) 7185
• Staffetta News (ITA) 6793
Staffetta Prezzi (ITA) 6793
• Staffetta Quotidiana (ITA) 6793
Staffing Industry Analysts, Inc. Review see S I Review 1874
Staffing Industry Report (USA ISSN 1051-3051) 1875
Staffing Industry Supplier Directory (USA ISSN 1553-8168) 1875
Staffing Industry Supplier Directory & Buyers Guide see Staffing Industry Supplier Directory 1875
• Staffing Law Digest (USA) 1875
• Staffing Management (USA ISSN 1555-2586) 1875
• Staffing Success (USA ISSN 1530-6011) 1875
➤ Staffordshire Archaeological and Historical Society. Transactions (GBR ISSN 1479-6368) 418
Staffordshire Archaeological Studies (GBR ISSN 0266-4992) 418
Staffordshire Farmer (GBR ISSN 0955-0267) 158
• Staffordshire Life (GBR ISSN 0963-3545) 5083
➤ Staffordshire Studies (GBR ISSN 0950-1630) 4267
Staffordshire University. Division of Economics. Working Papers (GBR) 1179
Staffrider (ZAF ISSN 0258-7211) 5435
Staffroom Guide to School Journeys (GBR ISSN 0953-9115) 2914
Stafo-Nytt (NOR ISSN 0800-658X) 1708
Stag Sexual Forum (ZAF ISSN 1022-3096) 6300
• The Stage (GBR) 2391
Stage (ZMB) 8479
Stage and Screen Studies (GBR ISSN 1660-2560) 8479
Stage & Studio (USA ISSN 1042-9409) 6619
• Stage Directions (USA ISSN 1047-1901) 8479
† • ➤ Stage of the Art (USA ISSN 1080-7268) 8990
Stage Screen & Radio (GBR ISSN 0969-6652) 4602
Stage Steps (GBR ISSN 1460-4620) 8479
• Stage Whispers (AUS ISSN 1321-5965) 8479
Stagebill (USA) 8479
Stagebill Family (USA) 2214
Stagecast - Irish Stage and Screen Directory (IRL) 8479
Stagecraft see Wutai Yishu 6629
StageReport (DEU) 1844
Stages (USA ISSN 1041-6048) 8479
StageWorks (CAN) 8479
Stagnito's New Products Magazine see New Products Magazine 3657
Stahl (DEU ISSN 0941-0821) 6332
• Stahl und Eisen (DEU ISSN 0340-4803) 6332
• Stahlbau (DEU ISSN 0038-9145) 3283
Stahlbau - Nachrichten (DEU ISSN 0176-3083) 1037
Der Stahlformenbauer (DEU) 3371
Stahlmarkt (DEU ISSN 0178-6571) 6332
Stahlreport (DEU ISSN 0942-9336) 6332
The Stained Finger (USA) 4347
• Stained Glass (USA ISSN 1067-8867) 540
Stainless India (IND ISSN 0971-9482) 6332
Stainless Steel (ZAF ISSN 0038-917X) 6332
Stainless Steel Buyer's Guide (Year) (ZAF) 6332
Stainless Steel Databook (GBR ISSN 0953-7228) 6332
Stainless Steel Focus (GBR ISSN 1478-1824) 6332
Stainless Steel Industry (GBR ISSN 0306-2988) 6333
Stainless Steel Market Information (GBR) 1794
Stainless Steel Review (GBR ISSN 1460-2628) 6333
• Stainless Steel World (NLD ISSN 1383-7184) 6333
Stair Society (GBR) 4787
Stajerski Tednik (SVN ISSN 1581-6257) 3947
The Stakeholder (GBR ISSN 1367-9759) 7185
Stakeholder Pensions: A Practical Guide (GBR) 4881
• Stakeholder Satisfaction (GBR ISSN 1749-088X) 1794
Stal' (RUS ISSN 0038-920X) 6333
Stal & Akker (NLD ISSN 1386-1379) 254
Stalactite (CHE ISSN 0038-9226) 2769
Stalker (USA ISSN 0882-7311) 3784
• Stalkin' Kin (USA) 3784
Stall (USA ISSN 0888-7411) 2301
Stallcup's Electrical Calculations Simplified (USA ISSN 1934-4627) 3331
Stallcup's Electrical Grounding and Bonding Simplified (USA ISSN 1933-480X) 3331
Stallcup's Master Electrician's Study Guide (USA ISSN 1931-6003) 3581
• Stallion Directory (USA ISSN 1055-2979) 8298
Stallions see Stodhestar 8299
Stam Cel Transplantaties Contact (NLD ISSN 1871-4005) 5948
† Stambog over Shetland Ponyer (DNK ISSN 0900-5846) 8990
Stamford Plus see Stamfordplus 3989
Stamfordplus (USA ISSN 1948-0865) 3989
Stamm (DEU ISSN 0942-3869) 635
Stamp and Coin Digest (USA) 6899
Stamp & Coin Mart (GBR ISSN 0956-6627) 4348
Stamp Auction News see Mekeel's and Stamps Magazine 6897
Stamp Duties South Australia (AUS) 1944
Stamp Duties Western Australia (AUS) 1944
Stamp Exchangers Annual Directory (USA) 6899
Stamp It! (USA) 540
Stamp Lover (GBR ISSN 0038-9277) 6900
Stamp Magazine (GBR ISSN 0307-6679) 6900
Stamp Mail (GBR ISSN 0953-5241) 6900
Stamp News Australasia (AUS ISSN 1448-1014) 6900
• La Stampa (ITA ISSN 1122-1763) 3898
La Stampa. CD-ROM see La Stampa 3898
La Stampa. D V D see La Stampa 3898
▼ Stampe Botaniche dell' 800 (ITA ISSN 1971-2103) 519
Stampe Botaniche dell' Ottocento see Stampe Botaniche dell' 800 519
The Stampers' Sampler (USA ISSN 1096-5688) 540
• Stampi (ITA ISSN 1121-063X) 8439
† Stampi e Design (ITA ISSN 1592-3541) 8990
Stamping and Papercraft (AUS) 540
Stamping Arts & Crafts see Scrap & Stamp Arts 539
• Stamping Journal (USA ISSN 1091-2460) 6333
Stampington Inspirations (USA ISSN 1532-1894) 541
• Stamps (USA ISSN 0038-9358) 6900
• Stamps.Net (USA) 6900
• Stamps of India (IND ISSN 0972-3587) 6900
Stamps on Stamps Centenary Unit Signal see S O S Signal 6899
Stamps World (IND ISSN 0255-8254) 6900
Stan Hodowli i Wyniki Oceny Swin/Report on Pig Breeding in Poland (POL ISSN 0239-5096) 301
▼ • ➤ Stance (USA ISSN 1943-1880) 6953
Stand (NLD ISSN 1872-3225) 3283
Stand (Leeds) (GBR ISSN 2041-4056) 5377
Stand By (USA) 4602
Stand By (Louisville) (USA) 4602
Stand Firm (USA ISSN 1085-7966) 7775
▼ • The Stand Out Newsletter (USA ISSN 1949-3355) 1844
Stand Point see StandPoint 8903
Stand To! (GBR ISSN 0261-6548) 4267
De Stand van de Rechtenstudie in Nederland (NLD ISSN 1872-1907) 3002
De Stand van het Notariaat in Nederland (NLD ISSN 1873-9563) 4787
Stand van Zaken see Dialoog 5890
De Standaard (NLD ISSN 1874-0553) 3033
De Standaard Plus see De Standaard 3033
• Der Standard (AUT ISSN 1560-6155) 3798
Standard (GHA ISSN 0038-9374) 7818
The Standard (HKG) 1179
The Standard (MWI) 3906
The Standard see Zimbabwe Standard 3996
• The Standard (Boston) (USA ISSN 0038-9390) 4524
The Standard (Elliot Lake) (CAN ISSN 0827-6609) 3817
• Standard (Hope) (CAN ISSN 0841-3614) 3817
• The Standard (St. Catharines) (CAN ISSN 0837-3434) 3817
† The Standard (Warrnambool) (AUS ISSN 0812-9762) 8990
Standard (Washington) see The Weekly Standard 7193
• Standard Acquisition Clauses and Conditions (CAN ISSN 1910-8710) 1179
Standard and Poor's 500 Indexes of the Securities Markets - Flash Report see Standard & Poor's 500 Indexes of the Securities Markets - Flash Report 1652
Standard & Poor's 500 Indexes of the Securities Markets - Flash Report (USA ISSN 1088-8373) 1652
Standard and Poor's Analyst's Handbook see Standard & Poor's Analyst's Handbook 1652
Standard & Poor's Analyst's Handbook (USA) 1652
† Standard & Poor's Bankratings Service (USA) 8990
Standard and Poor's Bond Guide see Standard & Poor's Bond Guide 1652
• Standard & Poor's Bond Guide (USA ISSN 0277-3988) 1652
Standard and Poor's Canadian Focus see Standard & Poor's Canadian Focus 1652
Standard & Poor's Canadian Focus (USA ISSN 1076-0318) 1652
Standard & Poor's Corporate Registered Bond Interest Record see Standard & Poor's Corporate Registered Bond Interest Record 1652
• Standard & Poor's Corporate Registered Bond Interest Record (USA) 1652
† • Standard & Poor's Corporation Records. Current News Edition (USA ISSN 0196-4674) 8990
Standard and Poor's Current Statistics see Standard & Poor's Current Statistics 1652
Standard & Poor's Current Statistics (USA ISSN 1940-1949) 1652
Standard & Poor's Current Statistics Statistical Service see Standard & Poor's Current Statistics 1652
Standard & Poor's Daily Stock Price Record. American Stock Exchange (USA ISSN 0737-4127) 1652
Standard & Poor's. Daily Stock Price Record. N A S D A Q (National Association of Securities Dealers Automated Quotations) (USA ISSN 1072-3846) 1652
Standard and Poor's. Daily Stock Price Record. NASDAQ see Standard & Poor's. Daily Stock Price Record. N A S D A Q 1652
† Standard & Poor's Directory of Dividend Reinvestment Plans (USA ISSN 1062-5607) 8990
Standard & Poor's Dividend Record (Annual) (USA) 1384
• Standard & Poor's Dividend Record (Daily) (USA ISSN 0196-4658) 1652
Standard & Poor's Dividend Record (Quarterly) (USA) 1652
Standard & Poor's Dividend Record (Weekly) (USA) 1652
Standard & Poor's Emerging Stock Markets Factbook (USA ISSN 1530-678X) 1384
Standard & Poor's Financial Institutions Ratings. Europe, Asia, Oceania (USA ISSN 1055-0070) 1652
Standard and Poor's Financial Institutions Ratings. Europe, Asia, Oceania see Standard & Poor's Financial Institutions Ratings. Europe, Asia, Oceania 1652
Standard & Poor's Financial Institutions Ratings. North America (USA ISSN 1060-3468) 1653
Standard and Poor's Financial Institutions Ratings. North America see Standard & Poor's Financial Institutions Ratings. North America 1653
• Standard & Poor's Global Project Finance Yearbook (USA ISSN 1932-4138) 1384
Standard & Poor's Index Directory see S & P Index Directory 1648
† Standard & Poor's Industry Reports (USA ISSN 1088-2847) 8990
• Standard & Poor's Industry Surveys (USA ISSN 0196-4666) 1653
Standard & Poor's Institutional Equity Research (USA ISSN 1090-3933) 1653
Standard and Poor's Institutional Equity Research see Standard & Poor's Institutional Equity Research 1653
Standard & Poor's - Lipper Mutual Fund Profiles see Mutual Fund Profiles 8975
Standard and Poor's New Issues Research see Standard & Poor's New Issues Research 1653
Standard & Poor's New Issues Research (USA) 1653
• Standard & Poor's Register of Corporations, Directors and Executives (USA ISSN 0361-3623) 1794
Standard & Poor's Security Dealers of North America (USA ISSN 1087-3325) 1653
Standard & Poor's Semi-Weekly Called Bond Record (USA ISSN 0737-299X) 1653
† Standard & Poor's Smallcap 600 Guide (USA ISSN 1085-6927) 8990
Standard and Poor's Smallcap 600 Guide see Standard & Poor's Smallcap 600 Guide 8990
• Standard & Poor's Stock Guide (USA ISSN 0737-4135) 1653
• Standard & Poor's Stock Reports (USA ISSN 1097-4490) 1653
Standard & Poor's Stock Reports Bound Quarterly see Standard & Poor's Stock Reports Bound Quarterly 1653
• Standard & Poor's Stock Reports Bound Quarterly (USA) 1653
Standard and Poor's Stock Reports. N A S D A Q and Regional Exchanges see Standard & Poor's Stock Reports. N A S D A Q and Regional Exchanges 1653
• Standard & Poor's Stock Reports. N A S D A Q and Regional Exchanges (National Association of Securities Dealers Automated Quotations) (USA) 1653
Standard & Poor's Stock Reports. Over the Counter see Standard & Poor's Stock Reports 1653
Standard & Poor's Trendline Current Market Perspectives (USA ISSN 1088-890X) 1653
Standard and Poor's Trendline Current Market Perspectives see Standard & Poor's Trendline Current Market Perspectives 1653
Standard Bearer (Sacramento) (USA ISSN 0038-9447) 7775
• Standard Catalog of Baseball Cards (USA ISSN 1935-0546) 8209
Standard Catalog of Baseball Cards (Modern Edition) see Standard Catalog of Baseball Cards 8209
Standard Catalog of Baseball Cards (Vintage Edition) see Standard Catalog of Baseball Cards 8209
Standard Catalog of World Coins. 1901-2000 (USA ISSN 1939-814X) 6653
Standard Catalog of World Coins. 1901-Present see Standard Catalog of World Coins. 1901-2000 6653
▼ Standard Catalog of World Coins. 2001-Date (USA ISSN 1935-4339) 6653
Standard Catalogue of British Coins (GBR) 6653
Standard Chartered. Fact Book (GBR) 1384
• Standard Corporation Descriptions (Year) (USA) 1653
• Standard Directory of Advertisers (Advertising Agencies) (USA) 2029
† • Standard Directory of Advertisers (Business Classifications Edition) (USA ISSN 1048-2415) 8990
Standard Directory of Advertisers (Geographic Edition) see Standard Directory of Advertisers (Advertising Agencies) 2029
Standard Encyclopedia of Carnival Glass Price Guide (USA ISSN 1933-3242) 540
• Standard Federal Tax Reporter (USA) 1944
Standard First Aid, C P R and A E D (Cardiopulmonary Resuscitation - Automated External Defibrillator) (USA ISSN 1931-9509) 5717
• Standard for Health Care Facilities (USA ISSN 1931-4078) 3581
• Standard Freeholder (CAN ISSN 0842-0351) 3817
Standard Guide to Cars & Prices see Collector Car Price Guide 8575
Standard Highway Signs see Standard Highway Signs as Specified in the Manual on Uniform Traffic Control Devices 8511
Standard Highway Signs as Specified in the Manual on Uniform Traffic Control Devices (USA) 8511
Standard Industrial Classification of Economic Activities (Year) see Great Britain. Central Statistical Office. Standard Industrial Classification of Economic Activities (Year) 1235
Standard Lesson Commentary King James Version (USA) 7683
Standard Methods for the Examination of Dairy Products (USA ISSN 8755-3554) 269
• Standard Methods for the Examination of Water and Wastewater (USA ISSN 8755-3546) 8832
• Standard.no (NOR) 6406
• Standard Periodical Directory (USA ISSN 0085-6630) 635
Standard Rate & Data Service Business Publication Advertising Source see S R D S Business Publication Advertising Source 38
Standard Rate and Data Service Cable Source see S R D S T V & Cable Source 39
Standard Rate & Data Service Circulation (Year) see S R D S Circulation (Year) 34
Standard Rate & Data Service Consumer Magazine Advertising Source see S R D S Consumer Magazine Advertising Source 39
Standard Rate & Data Service Direct Marketing List Source see S R D S Direct Marketing List Source 39
Standard Rate and Data Service Hispanic Media & Market Source see S R D S Hispanic Media & Market Source 39
Standard Rate & Data Service Interactive Advertising Source see S R D S Interactive Advertising Source 34
Standard Rate & Data Service International Guide. Business Publications. Europe see S R D S International Guide. Business Publications. Europe 39
Standard Rate & Data Service International Media Guide. Business Publications. Asia-Pacific/Middle East/Africa see S R D S International Media Guide. Business Publications. Asia-Pacific/Middle East/Africa 39
Standard Rate & Data Service International Media Guide. Newspapers Worldwide see S R D S International Media Guide. Newspapers Worldwide 39
Standard Rate & Data Service Lifestyle Market Analyst (Online) see S R D S Lifestyle Market Analyst (Online) 1261
Standard Rate & Data Service Mexican Audiovisual Media Rates & Data see S R D S Mexican Audiovisual Media Rates & Data 39
Standard Rate & Data Service Mexican Print Media Rates & Data see S R D S Mexican Print Media Rates & Data 39
Standard Rate & Data Service Newspaper Advertising Source see S R D S Newspaper Advertising Source 39
Standard Rate & Data Service Out-of-Home Advertising Source see S R D S Out-of-Home Advertising Source 39
Standard Rate & Data Service Print Media Production Source (Online) see S R D S Print Media Production Source (Online) 39
Standard Rate & Data Service Radio Advertising Source see S R D S Radio Advertising Source 39
Standard Rate & Data Service Technology Media Source see S R D S Technology Media Source 39
Standard Rate and Data Service The Bullet see S R D S The Bullet 8986

Title

10900 STATE AND FEDERAL WAGE HOUR COMPLIANCE GUIDE ULRICH'S PERIODICALS

State and Federal Wage Hour Compliance Guide *see* State & Federal Wage Hour Compliance Guide **1708**
• State and Federal Water Programs (USA) **8832**
• State & Local Communications Report (USA ISSN 1538-7534) **2339**
State and Local Government *see* State & Local Government (Washington) **7470**
• State & Local Government (Washington) (USA) **7470**
State and Local Government Collective Bargaining Settlements *see* Major Collective Bargaining Settlements in State and Local Government **8972**
• State & Local Government Computer News (USA) **7486**
• State and Local Government Finances (USA) **1944**
State and Local Government Information Security *see* State & Local Government Information Security **7470**
• State & Local Government Information Security (USA) **7470**
• ➤ State and Local Government Review (USA ISSN 0160-323X) **7503**
State and Local Government Special Studies *see* Current Governments Reports: State and Local Government Special Studies **8947**
State and Local Health Law Weekly *see* State & Local Health Law Weekly **4788**
• State & Local Health Law Weekly (USA ISSN 1551-5605) **4788**
State and Local Law News *see* State & Local Law News **7503**
State & Local Law News (USA ISSN 1078-7356) **7503**
➤ The State and Local Tax Lawyer (USA ISSN 1093-6785) **4788**
• State & Local Taxes (USA ISSN 1084-7588) **1944**
• State and Local Taxes (Online) (USA) **1944**
State and Local Taxes (Print) *see* State and Local Taxes (Online) **1944**
State & Local Taxes Weekly *see* State and Local Taxes (Online) **1944**
• State and Metropolitan Area Data Book (USA ISSN 0276-6566) **7316**
State and Metropolitan Area Employment and Unemployment (USA) **1519**
The State and Needs of Education. Annual Report *see* L' Etat et les Besoins de l'Education. Rapport Annuel **2854**
State and Regional Associations of the United States (USA ISSN 1044-324X) **2029**
State and Society *see* M'dina VaHevra **7154**
State Archives of Assyria Bulletin (ITA ISSN 1120-4699) **418**
State Archives of Assyria Cuneiform Texts (FIN ISSN 1455-2345) **4325**
State Archives of Assyria Literary Texts (FIN ISSN 1457-9189) **4325**
State Archives of Assyria Studies (FIN ISSN 1235-1032) **4325**
State Arts Agency Directory (USA) **519**
▼ • State Attorneys General News (USA ISSN 1942-3357) **4788**
• State B E A R F A C T S (Year) Alabama (State Bureau of Economic Analysis Regional Fact Sheet) (USA ISSN 1938-484X) **1267**
• State B E A R F A C T S (Year) Alaska (State Bureau of Economic Analysis Regional Fact Sheet) (USA ISSN 1938-5811) **1267**
• State B E A R F A C T S (Year) Arizona (State Bureau of Economic Analysis Regional Fact Sheet) (USA ISSN 1938-8853) **1267**
• State B E A R F A C T S (Year) Arkansas (State Bureau of Economic Analysis Regional Fact Sheet) (USA ISSN 1938-8861) **1267**
• State B E A R F A C T S (Year) California (State Bureau of Economic Analysis Regional Fact Sheet) (USA ISSN 1939-1684) **1267**
State Backgrounder (USA ISSN 1042-5446) **7185**
State Bank of India. Annual Report (IND) **1384**
State Bank of India. Economic Newsletter (IND) **1519**
State Bank of India. Indian Economic Newsletter (IND) **1519**
State Bank of India. Monthly Review (IND ISSN 0039-0003) **1519**
State Bank of Pakistan. Annual Report (PAK ISSN 0081-444X) **1384**
State Bank of Pakistan. Bulletin (PAK ISSN 0039-0011) **1384**
State Bank of Pakistan. Equity Yields on Ordinary Shares (PAK) **1267**
State Bank of Pakistan. Export Receipts (PAK ISSN 0585-1009) **1583**
State Bank of Pakistan. Index Numbers of Stock Exchange Securities (PAK ISSN 0081-4466) **1267**
State Bank of Pakistan. State Bank News (PAK ISSN 0561-8738) **1384**
State Bank of Pakistan. Statistics on Co-Operative Banks (PAK ISSN 0039-0569) **1267**
State Bank of Pakistan. Statistics on Scheduled Banks (PAK ISSN 0039-0577) **1267**
State Bar Association of North Dakota. Note Pad (USA) **4788**
State Bar News *see* State Bar News (Albany) **4788**
State Bar News (Albany) (USA ISSN 0363-0331) **4788**
State Bar of New Mexico. Bar Bulletin (USA ISSN 1062-6611) **4788**
State Bar of New Mexico. Bar Journal (USA ISSN 1084-9793) **4788**
State Bar of South Dakota. Newsletter (USA) **4788**
State Bar of Wisconsin. Construction and Public Contract Law Section. Newsletter (USA) **4788**
State Bar of Wisconsin. Government and Administrative Law Section. News *see* Administrative and Local Government Law News **4846**
State Bar of Wisconsin. Government Lawyers Division News (USA) **4788**
State Bar of Wisconsin. Individual Rights & Responsibilities Section. Newsletter (USA) **4788**
State-by-State Health Care Collection Laws and Regulations (USA ISSN 1530-745X) **4788**
State-By-State Mortgage Lending Alert. Eastern Region (USA ISSN 1556-2867) **1653**
State Capitals Newsletters *see* Motor Vehicle Regulation - State Capitals **8593**
State Capitals Newsletters. Alcoholic Beverage Control *see* Alcoholic Beverage Control - State Capitals **4613**
State Capitals Newsletters. Economic Development *see* Economic Development - State Capitals **1480**
State Capitals Newsletters. Family Relations *see* Family Relations - State Capitals **4910**
State Capitals Newsletters. Federal Action Affecting the States *see* Federal Action Affecting the States - State Capitals **4671**
State Capitals Newsletters. Highway Financing & Construction *see* Highway Financing & Construction - State Capitals **4687**
State Capitals Newsletters. Insurance Regulation *see* Insurance Regulation - State Capitals **4508**
State Capitals Newsletters. Lottery, Parimutuel & Casino Regulation *see* Lottery, Parimutuel & Casino Regulation - State Capitals **4725**
State Capitals Newsletters. Public Assistance & Welfare Trends *see* Public Assistance & Welfare Trends - State Capitals **4763**
State Capitals Newsletters. Taxation and Revenue Policies *see* Taxation and Revenue Policies - State Capitals **1950**
State Capitals Newsletters. Taxes - Property *see* Property Taxes & School Funding - State Capitals **1940**
• State Capitols Report (USA) **7470**
State Chamber News (USA) **1179**
State College (USA ISSN 0886-361X) **3989**
State Commercial - Residential Codes (USA) **4427**
State Committee of the Russian Federation. Current Statistical Survey (RUS) **1179**
• State Constitutional Law (USA) **4852**
State Constitutional Law Bulletin (USA) **4852**
State Construction Quarterly Briefing *see* U.S. State Construction Quarterly Briefing **1041**
State Court Clerks and County Courthouses *see* Directory of State Court Clerks & County Courthouses (Year) **4950**
• State Court Sentencing of Convicted Felons (USA) **4898**
State Directory of Kentucky (USA ISSN 0585-1173) **7470**
State Domestic Product of Himachal Pradesh (IND) **1267**
State - E P A Agreements. Annual Report (USA ISSN 0275-2271) **3467**
The State Education Standard (USA ISSN 1540-8000) **3033**
State Employment Relations Board Official Reporter *see* S E R B Official Reporter **4777**
State Engineers (LKA) **3220**
• State Environment Daily (USA ISSN 1535-1637) **3467**
• State Expediture on Science & Technology (IRL) **7920**
State Fact Finder (USA ISSN 1079-7149) **7470**
State Farming *see* Allami Gazdasag **90**
State Fiscal Brief (New York) (USA) **7470**
State Fiscal Capacity and Effort (USA ISSN 1042-6027) **1944**
State Gazette *see* Durzhaven Vestnik **3804**
• State Gazette Business News (BGR) **1179**
State Geological and Natural History Survey of Connecticut. Bulletin (USA ISSN 0095-8638) **2769**
State Geologists Journal (USA ISSN 0039-0089) **2769**
• State Government Finances (Online) (USA) **1267**
State Government News *see* State News (Lexington) **7470**
• State Government Tax Collections (Online) (USA ISSN 1933-8805) **1944**
• State Health Care Regulatory Developments (USA ISSN 1073-8886) **4111**
† • State Health Monitor (USA ISSN 1522-5348) **8990**
State Health Notes (Online Edition) (USA) **7542**
State Health Notes (Print Edition) *see* State Health Notes (Online Edition) **7542**
• (Year) State Health Profiles (USA) **7549**
• State Health Watch (USA ISSN 1074-4754) **7542**
State Highway Forecast *see* Transit New Zealand's 10-Year State Highway Plan **8636**
State Highway Plan *see* Transit New Zealand's 10-Year State Highway Plan **8636**
The State Hornet (USA) **2302**
State House Watch (USA ISSN 1070-7719) **7470**
State Housing Development Authority Review *see* M S H D A Review **4419**
• State Income Tax Alert (USA) **1944**
State Income Tax Alert (Atlanta) (USA ISSN 1088-2898) **1944**
• State Income Tax Monitor (USA ISSN 1551-1162) **1944**
State Information *see* Toriyn Medeelel **7472**
† State Information Directory (Year) (USA ISSN 1530-0188) **8990**
State Institute of Education, Rajasthan. Annual Report (IND) **2914**
• State Investment in Science & Technology (Year) (IRL) **7920**
State Investment Portfolio. (Juneau) *see* Alaska. Department of Revenue. State Investment Portfolio **1610**
• The State Journal (USA ISSN 1521-8767) **1179**
State Judicial Clerkship Directory (USA) **4965**
➤ State, Law and Society (GBR ISSN 1354-5957) **7185**
State Laws and Published Ordinances, Firearms (USA ISSN 0276-7651) **4788**
State Legislative Report (Denver) (USA ISSN 0735-8733) **7185**
State Legislative Report (Washington, DC) (USA) **8884**
State Legislative Sourcebook (USA ISSN 0898-7297) **7470**
• State Legislatures (USA ISSN 0147-6041) **7186**
• State Magazine (USA ISSN 1099-4165) **7266**
State Medical Licensure Requirements and Statistics (Year) (USA ISSN 1549-4055) **5717**
State Municipal League Directory (USA ISSN 0898-8374) **7503**
• State Net Capitol Journal (USA ISSN 1521-8457) **7470**
The State News (USA) **2302**
• State News (Lexington) (USA ISSN 1549-3628) **7470**
State of America's Children Yearbook (Year) (USA ISSN 1084-3191) **8073**
State of Black America (USA ISSN 0148-6985) **7215**
• State of California Commission on the Status of Women (USA) **8903**
• The State of California Labor (USA ISSN 1541-9037) **1708**
• The State of Canada's Forests (CAN ISSN 1196-1589) **3703**
State of Connecticut. Law Revision Commission. Annual Report (USA) **4788**
• State of Education in New Zealand (NZL ISSN 1177-6374) **2914**
State of Food and Agriculture (USA ISSN 0081-4539) **158**
State of Greek Industry in (Year) (GRC ISSN 0072-7458) **1904**
• The State of Hawaii Data Book (USA ISSN 1932-4693) **1267**
State of Hawaii Data Book, a Statistical Abstract (Print) *see* The State of Hawaii Data Book **1267**
The State of High Definition Television (USA ISSN 1549-5582) **2391**
The State of Higher Education (UGA ISSN 1819-6551) **3002**
• The State of Home Video (USA) **2403**
State of Louisiana Public Documents (USA ISSN 0099-2410) **7470**
State of Montana Investment Program. Report on Audit *see* Montana. Office of the Legislative Auditor. State of Montana Board of Investments. Report on Examination of Financial Statements **7453**
The State of Natural Environment of Belarus *see* Sostoyaniye Prirodnoi Sredy Belarusi **3467**
State of Nebraska Annual Budgetary Report *see* State of Nebraska. Annual Budgeting Report **1944**
State of Nebraska. Annual Budgeting Report (USA) **1944**
State of Nebraska. Comprehensive Annual Financial Report (USA) **1944**
State of Nebraska Uniform Crime Report (USA ISSN 0090-3221) **2669**
State of New York City's Municipal Hospital System (USA ISSN 0895-688X) **4111**
State of Ohio. Department of Natural Resources. Division of Geological Survey. Report of Investigations (USA ISSN 0097-5680) **2769**
• The State of Our Environment Hawke's Bay (NZL ISSN 1177-1186) **3467**
The State of Our Fisheries (NZL ISSN 1177-3812) **7470**
The State of Reading (USA ISSN 1077-3584) **2914**
State of Safety Report (CAN ISSN 1719-5179) **7542**
The State of Small Business: A Report of the President Transmitted to the Congress *see* The Small Business Economy **1967**
• State of Small Business and Entrepreneurship in Atlantic Canada (CAN ISSN 1193-3550) **1968**
• State of South Dakota. Office of the Attorney General. Official Opinions (USA ISSN 0361-0292) **7503**
State of Tennessee. Department of Conservation. Division of Geology. Bulletin (USA ISSN 0096-7866) **2769**
State of the Art (USA) **596**
• State of the Arts (AUS ISSN 1443-721X) **6537**
State of the Beaches (AUS ISSN 1833-5896) **3467**
• The State of the Drugs Problem in the Acceding and Candidate Countries to the European Union (LUX) **2699**
State of the Drugs Problem in the European Union and Norway. Annual Report *see* State of the Drugs Problem in the European Union. Annual Report **2699**
State of the Drugs Problem in the European Union. Annual Report (LUX ISSN 1609-6150) **2699**
State of the Environment in Denmark, Illustrated Summary *see* Natur og Miljoe, Illustreret Sammenfatning **3455**
State of the Environment Report for Manitoba (CAN ISSN 1185-5762) **2628**
State of the Environment Reporting Series *see* State of the Environment Reporting Series Discussion Paper **3467**
• State of the Environment Reporting Series Discussion Paper (AUS ISSN 1834-3074) **3467**
State of the Environment Reporting Series Technical Paper (AUS ISSN 1834-3082) **3467**
State of the Environment: Selected Topics; Report of the Executive Director *see* United Nations Environment Programme. The State of the World Environment **3472**
• State of the Family (AUS ISSN 1832-5564) **8141**
State of the Future (USA) **7186**
The State of the Market (GBR) **1519**
The State of the Nation's Housing (USA ISSN 1932-4715) **4427**
• State of the Net (IRL ISSN 1649-850X) **2567**
State of the Planet *see* Science Magazine's State of the Planet **3465**
State of the Regions: A Baseline for the Century of the Region - A Progress Report (USA) **7470**
State of the State Banking System (USA ISSN 1053-3435) **1384**
• State of the Uganda Economy (UGA ISSN 1993-9752) **1519**
State of the Union (USA) **2270**
State of the Wild (USA ISSN 1556-0619) **3467**
• State of the World (USA ISSN 0887-364X) **3467**
• State of the World's Children (USA ISSN 0251-9100) **8073**
The State of the World's Forests (ITA ISSN 1020-5705) **3703**
• The State of Waste and Recycling in Queensland (AUS ISSN 1834-3651) **3512**
The State of Working America (USA ISSN 1054-2159) **1519**
The State of World Fisheries and Aquacultures (ITA ISSN 1020-5489) **3609**
State of World Population (USA) **7294**
State Plan for Developmental Disabilities (USA ISSN 0743-5916) **8073**
State Planning Newsletter (USA) **8403**
• ➤ State Politics & Policy Quarterly (USA ISSN 1532-4400) **7186**
State Press (USA) **2302**
• State Profile (USA ISSN 1044-4947) **1519**
State Profiles (USA ISSN 1524-3958) **8403**
State Rankings (USA ISSN 1057-3623) **4436**
State Reports. Western Australia (AUS ISSN 0158-1996) **4788**
State Revenue News (USA ISSN 1542-0523) **6900**
▼ State Securities. Blue Sky Statutes Annotated (USA ISSN 1942-0293) **4881**
• State Services Commission. Annual Report (NZL ISSN 1176-8304) **7503**
State Statistical Trends (USA ISSN 1099-6486) **8403**
State Tax Alert *see* Payroll Practitioner's State Tax Alert **1938**
State Tax Cases Reports - All States (USA) **1944**
State Tax Collections and Rates (USA) **1944**
▼ State Tax Essentials (USA ISSN 2150-3990) **1944**
• State Tax Guide (USA ISSN 0162-1777) **1944**
State Tax Guide Report Bulletin: All States *see* All States Tax Guide **1910**
• State Tax Notes (USA ISSN 1057-8404) **1944**
State Tax One Disc *see* State Tax Onedisc **1944**
• State Tax Onedisc (USA ISSN 1089-8891) **1944**
• State Tax Review (USA ISSN 0162-1750) **1945**
State Tech (USA ISSN 1559-5277) **7486**
• State Telephone Regulation Report (USA ISSN 0741-8388) **2371**
State to State (USA) **4788**
• State Transportation Statistics (USA) **8530**
• The State Trials (ZAF ISSN 1683-2728) **4965**
State Trooper Exam *see* Master the State Trooper Exams **6701**
State University of New York at Albany. Institute for Mesoamerican Studies. Monograph Series (USA) **356**
• State University of New York at Albany. Update (USA) **2302**
State University of New York at Binghamton. Center for Medieval and Early Renaissance Studies. Acta (USA ISSN 0361-7491) **4162**
State University of New York Librarians Association Newsletter *see* S U N Y L A Newsletter **5045**
State University of New York Series in American Constitutionalism *see* S U N Y Series in American Constitutionalism **7181**
State University of New York Series in Feminist Criticism and Theory *see* S U N Y Series in Feminist Criticism and Theory **5366**
State University of New York Series in Medieval Studies *see* S U N Y Series in Medieval Studies **5366**
State University of New York Series in Native American Religions *see* S U N Y Series in Native American Religions **7741**

DIRECTORY 2010 STATISTICAL YEARBOOK OF SICHUAN 10901

State University of New York Series in Postmodern Culture *see* S U N Y Series in Postmodern Culture **5366**
State University of West Georgia. Studies in the Social Sciences (USA ISSN 0081-8682) **8007**
State Veterinary Journal *see* Government Veterinary Journal **8798**
• State Water. Annual Report (AUS) **8832**
• State Water Report (AUS ISSN 1833-640X) **8832**
State World *see* State of the World **3467**
• State Yellow Book (USA ISSN 0899-2207) **7470**
Stateco (FRA ISSN 0224-098X) **1267**
Statehouse Observer (USA ISSN 0091-1402) **7470**
Stateline (USA) **1384**
Stateline Midwest (USA) **7186**
Statement (NLD ISSN 1874-9593) **7613**
Statement *see* Colorado Language Arts Society. Statement **3055**
Statement *see* Statement (Calabasas) **3989**
The Statement *see* The Michigan Daily **2292**
Statement (Calabasas) (USA ISSN 1934-1784) **3989**
Statement (Fredonia) (USA) **2302**
Statement of Financial Accounting Concepts (USA ISSN 0276-1378) **1302**
Statement of Financial Accounting Standards (USA ISSN 0746-7486) **1302**
Statement of Treaties and International Agreements *see* United Nations. Statement of Treaties and International Agreements **7271**
Statement of Votes - General Election and By-Election (CAN ISSN 0227-9207) **7186**
• Statements (AUS) **3468**
Staten Island Historian (USA ISSN 0039-0232) **4314**
Staten Island Institute of Arts and Sciences News *see* S I I A S News **4473**
Statenet Capitol Journal News & Views from California *see* State Net Capitol Journal **7470**
Statens Arbeidsmiljoeinstitutt Rapport (Online Edition) *see* S T A M I-Rapport (Online Edition) **6685**
• Statens Beredning foer Medicinsk Utvaerdering. S B U Alert-Rapport (SWE ISSN 1652-7151) **5717**
• Statens Beredning foer Medicinsk Utvaerdering. S B U - Rapport (SWE ISSN 1400-1403) **5717**
Statens Energimyndighet. Energimarknadsinspetion. Aarsrapport (SWE ISSN 1653-8684) **3148**
Statens Folkhaelsoinstitut. Rapport (SWE ISSN 1651-8624) **7542**
Statens Geotekniska Institut Nu *see* S G I - Nu **2789**
Statens Geotekniska Institut. Rapport/Swedish Geotechnical Institute. Report (SWE ISSN 0348-0755) **2790**
Statens Historiska Museums Utstaellningskatalog (SWE ISSN 1404-4870) **6537**
Statens Institut foer Kommunikationsanalys Kommunikationer *see* S I K A Kommunikationer **8529**
Statens Institut foer Kommunikationsanalys Rapport *see* S I K A Rapport **8510**
Statens Institut foer Kommunikationsanalys Statistik *see* S I K A Statistik **8397**
Statens Institut foer Kommunikationsanalys Statistiska Meddelanden *see* S I K A Statistiska Meddelanden **8398**
Statens Institut for Folkesundhed. Beretning (DNK ISSN 1601-3956) **5717**
Statens Institut for Folkesundhed Fs Groenlandsskrifter *see* S I Fs Groenlandsskrifter **5708**
• Statens Institutionsstyrelse. Allmaen SiS-Rapport (SWE ISSN 1404-2584) **8073**
• Statens Institutionsstyrelse. Forskningsrapport (SWE ISSN 1404-2576) **8073**
Statens Invandrarverks Foerfattningssamling *see* Migrationsverkets Foerfattningssamling **7287**
Statens Jaernvaegar Nytt *see* S J - Nytt **8624**
Statens Jordbruksverk. Rapport (SWE ISSN 1102-3007) **158**
Statens Jordbruksverks Foerfattningssamling *see* Djurskyddsmyndigheten. Foerfattningssamling **319**
Statens Museum for Kunst Art Journal *see* S M K Art Journal **516**
Statens Museum for Kunst. Journal *see* S M K Art Journal **516**
Statens Musiksamlingar. Musikmuseet. Rapporter (SWE ISSN 0282-6534) **6619**
Statens Musiksamlingar. Musikmuseet. Skrifter (SWE ISSN 0282-8952) **6619**
Statens Musiksamlingar. Svenskt Visarkiv. Handlingar (SWE ISSN 0081-9824) **6619**
Statens Musiksamlingar. Svenskt Visarkiv. Meddelanden (SWE ISSN 0081-9832) **6619**
Statens Musiksamlingar. Svenskt Visarkiv. Skrifter (SWE ISSN 0081-9840) **6619**
Statens Offentliga Utredningar (SWE ISSN 0375-250X) **7470**
Statens Pensjonsfond - Utland *see* Norges Bank Investment Management. Aarsrapport **1502**
Statens Raad foer Kaernavfallsfraagor. Rapport (SWE ISSN 1653-820X) **3512**
Statens Serum Institut, Centrale Afdeling for Sygehushygiejne Nyt *see* C A S - Nyt **4089**
• Statens Straalskyddsinstitut. S S I-Rapport (SWE ISSN 0282-4434) **7470**
Statens Vaeg- och Transportforskningsinstitut EC Research *see* V T I EC Research **8636**
Statens Vaeg- och Transportforskningsinstitut Facts and Figures. Annual Report *see* V T I Facts and Figures. Annual Report **8636**
Statens Vaeg- och Transportforskningsinstitut Konferens *see* V T I Konferens **8636**
Statens Vaeg- och Transportforskningsinstitut Meddelande *see* V T I Meddelande **8636**
Statens Vaeg- och Transportforskningsinstitut Rapport *see* V T I Rapport **8636**
Statens Vaeg- och Transportforskningsinstitut Saertryck *see* V T I Saertryck **8636**
Statens Vaeg- och Transportforskningsinstitut Siffror *see* V T I i Siffror **8636**
Statens Veterinaermedicinska Anstalt. Aarsberaettelse *see* Statens Veterinaermedicinska Anstalt. Aarsredovisning **8807**
• Statens Veterinaermedicinska Anstalt. Aarsredovisning (SWE) **8807**
Statens Veterinaermedicinska Anstalt Vet *see* S V A Vet **8807**
The States and Small Business: A Directory of Programs and Activities (USA ISSN 0742-843X) **1968**
• States News Service (USA) **7186**
States of Health (USA ISSN 1524-4830) **4056**
The Statesman (IND) **3889**
Statesman (NGA) **7186**
Statesman (PAK ISSN 0039-0313) **3926**
• The Statesman (Spiegel Grove) (USA) **6537**
Statesman (Wantagh) (USA) **2302**
Statesman Weekly (IND ISSN 0039-0321) **3889**
The Statesman's Year-Book (Year) (USA ISSN 0081-4601) **7201**
• Statewatch (GBR ISSN 0961-7280) **7215**
• Statewatch European Monitor (Online) (GBR ISSN 1745-0276) **7215**
• Stateways (USA ISSN 0279-2133) **610**
Gli Stati Uniti d'Europa (Bari)/Les Etats Unis d'Europe/The Unitred States of Europe/Die Vereinigten Staaten von Europa (ITA ISSN 1825-4985) **7266**
• Static (GBR ISSN 1754-5374) **519**
▼ Static (USA ISSN 1947-4393) **3989**
Static Line (USA ISSN 1059-7468) **6447**
Station Listing Guide (USA) **2391**
Station Log (USA) **6537**
• Station Reporter (CAN) **8605**
Station Solution Zone *see* Station SolutionZone **2481**
Station SolutionZone (GBR) **2481**
Station to Station (DEU ISSN 0177-4913) **3857**
Stationary Engine (GBR ISSN 0264-4061) **3220**
Stationery (Personal & Office) *see* Key Note Market Report: Stationery (Personal & Office) **1852**
Stationery & Office Buyers' Guide (TWN) **1854**
Stationery and Office Products Buyer's Guide *see* Stationery & Office Buyers' Guide **1854**
Stationery & Office Products S A (ZAF) **1854**
Stationery and Office Supplies (TWN) **1854**
Stationery & Office Update (GBR ISSN 1475-8644) **1854**
Stationery Distributors *see* Business Ratio. Stationery Distributors **1850**
Stationery Manufacturers *see* Business Ratio. Stationery Manufacturers **1850**
Stationery News (AUS ISSN 1033-758X) **1855**
• Stationery Office Monthly Catalogue (GBR ISSN 1367-5184) **636**
• Statistica & Applicazioni (ITA ISSN 1824-6672) **8403**
Statistica e Metrica Italiana (ITA ISSN 1591-6693) **8403**
• ➤ Statistica Neerlandica (GBR ISSN 0039-0402) **8403**
• ➤ Statistica Sinica (TWN ISSN 1017-0405) **8403**
• Statistical Abstract (Year) of Ethiopia (ETH ISSN 0425-4279) **8403**
Statistical Abstract of Israel *see* Israel. Central Bureau of Statistics. Statistical Abstract of Israel **8381**
Statistical Abstract of Latin America (USA ISSN 0081-4687) **7201**
Statistical Abstract of Maharashtra State (IND ISSN 0081-4709) **8403**
Statistical Abstract of Oklahoma (USA ISSN 0191-0310) **1267**
Statistical Abstract of Rajasthan (IND ISSN 0081-4717) **8403**
Statistical Abstract of the Democratic Socialist Republic of Sri Lanka (LKA ISSN 0259-8086) **8403**
Statistical Abstract of the United States (Large Print Edition) (USA ISSN 1063-1690) **8403**
Statistical Abstract of the United States (Library Edition) *see* Statistical Abstract of the United States (Large Print Edition) **8403**
• Statistical Abstract of the United States (Year) (USA ISSN 0081-4741) **7176**
▼ • Statistical Analysis and Data Mining (USA ISSN 1932-1864) **8403**
Statistical Analysis System Com *see* S A S Com **2596**
➤ Statistical and Social Inquiry Society of Ireland. Journal (IRL ISSN 0081-4776) **8403**
Statistical Annuals: List of I E G Library Holdings (IND) **636**
• Statistical Applications in Genetics and Molecular Biology (USA ISSN 1544-6115) **878**
Statistical Bulletin *see* Arab Institute for Training & Research in Statistics. Statistical Bulletin **8347**
Statistical Bulletin (Year) *see* Notiziario Statistico (Year) **8528**
Statistical Code of Practice for the Bank of England *see* Bank of England. Statistical Code of Practice **1314**
▼ • ➤ Statistical Communications in Infectious Diseases (USA ISSN 1948-4690) **5827**
Statistical Computation and Simulation *see* Journal of Statistical Computation and Simulation **2443**
• Statistical Computing and Graphics (USA) **2444**
Statistical Data on Commercial Banks in Thailand (THA) **1267**
Statistical Days *see* Statisticni Dnevi **8405**
Statistical Digest of the Services Sector *see* Hong Kong Special Administrative Region of China. Census and Statistics Department. Statistical Digest of the Services Sector **1240**
Statistical Focus on Wales (GBR ISSN 1362-3575) **8404**
A Statistical Focus on Wales: The Valleys (GBR) **8404**
A Statistical Focus on Wales: Women (GBR) **8404**
† Statistical Handbook (USA ISSN 1020-0991) **8990**
Statistical Handbook of Tamil Nadu (IND) **8404**
Statistical Handbook of the Philippines (PHL) **8404**
Statistical Handbook on Aging Americans (USA) **4059**
• Statistical Highlights of U.S. Agriculture (USA) **186**
Statistical Indicators for Asia and the Pacific (THA ISSN 0252-4457) **1267**
† Statistical Indicators of Short Term Economic Changes in E.C.E. Countries (USA ISSN 0251-0073) **8990**
• Statistical Inference for Stochastic Processes (NLD ISSN 1387-0874) **5538**
Statistical Institute of Jamaica. Consumer Price Indices Bulletin (JAM) **1267**
Statistical Institute of Jamaica. Demographic Statistics (JAM) **7316**
Statistical Institute of Jamaica. External Trade (JAM) **1267**
Statistical Institute of Jamaica. External Trade Annual Review (JAM) **1267**
Statistical Institute of Jamaica. External Trade Monthly Bulletin (JAM) **1267**
Statistical Institute of Jamaica. National Income and Product (JAM) **1267**
Statistical Institute of Jamaica. Pocketbook of Statistics (JAM) **8404**
Statistical Institute of Jamaica. Statistical Abstract (JAM) **8404**
Statistical Institute of Jamaica. Statistical Review (JAM) **8404**
Statistical Journal of the International Association for Official Statistics *see* International Association for Official Statistics. Statistical Journal **8379**
Statistical Masterfile *see* Statistical Reference Index **8404**
Statistical Messages *see* Statisticna Sporocila **8405**
• ➤ Statistical Methodology (NLD ISSN 1572-3127) **5538**
• ➤ Statistical Methods and Applications (DEU ISSN 1618-2510) **8404**
• ➤ Statistical Methods in Medical Research (GBR ISSN 0962-2802) **8404**
Statistical Modeling and Decision Science (USA) **5538**
• ➤ Statistical Modelling (IND ISSN 1471-082X) **5538**
Statistical News *see* Great Britain. Central Statistical Office. Statistical News **8374**
Statistical Newsletter (THA) **8404**
Statistical Office of the European Communities. Agricultural Prices (LUX ISSN 0254-3834) **186**
Statistical Office of the European Communities. Bulletin of Energy Prices (LUX ISSN 0256-6362) **3154**
Statistical Office of the European Communities. Gas Prices *see* Gas and Electricity Market Statistics **3152**
Statistical Office of the European Communities. National Accounts Yearbook (LUX ISSN 0081-4911) **1267**
Statistical Office of the European Communities. Quarterly National Accounts (LUX ISSN 1010-1764) **1267**
Statistical Office of the European Communities. Statistical Studies and Surveys (LUX) **1267**
Statistical Office of the European Communities. Statistical Yearbook. Agriculture (LUX) **186**
Statistical Office of the European Communities. Transport, Communications, Tourisme - Annuaire Statistique (LUX ISSN 0257-2419) **8530**
• ➤ Statistical Papers/Statistische Hefte (DEU ISSN 0932-5026) **8404**
Statistical Pocket-Book of Afghanistan (AFG ISSN 0302-2099) **8404**
Statistical Pocket-Book of Serbia and Montenegro (SRB) **8404**
Statistical Pocket Book of the Democratic Socialist Republic of Sri Lanka (LKA ISSN 0585-1777) **8404**
Statistical Pocket Book of the Islamic Republic of Iran (IRN) **8404**
Statistical Pocket-Book of Yugoslavia *see* Statistical Pocket-Book of Serbia and Montenegro **8404**
Statistical Pocketbook of Bangladesh (BGD) **8404**
Statistical Pocketbook of Hungary *see* Magyar Statisztikai Zsebkonyv **8386**
• Statistical Pocketbook of Indonesia/Buku Saku Statistik Indonesia (IDN ISSN 0126-3595) **8404**
Statistical Portrait of Slovenia in the E U *see* Statisticni Portret Slovenije v E U **8405**
Statistical Profile of Iowa (USA) **8404**
A Statistical Profile of Nova Scotia Seniors *see* Seniors' Statistical Profile **8398**
Statistical Record (GBR ISSN 0307-0093) **8219**
† Statistical Record of Black America (USA ISSN 1051-8002) **8990**
Statistical Record of the Environment (USA) **3481**
Statistical Reference Book of Republic of Bulgaria *see* Statisticheski Spravochnik na Republika Bulgaria **8405**
• Statistical Reference Index (USA ISSN 0885-6834) **8404**
• Statistical Report. Distilled Spirits (USA ISSN 1946-4509) **614**
• Statistical Report for Real Estate Agents. Saguenay Metropolitan Area (CAN ISSN 1912-2357) **7618**
• Statistical Report for Real Estate Agents. Trois-Rivieres Census Metropolitan Area. Shawinigan Census Agglomeration (CAN ISSN 1912-2373) **7619**
Statistical Report of Region (THA) **1267**
Statistical Report on Visitor Arrivals to Indonesia (IDN ISSN 0854-6886) **8780**
Statistical Report. Rural Telecommunications Borrowers *see* U.S. Department of Agriculture. Rural Utilities Service. Statistical Report. Rural Telecommunications Borrowers **2373**
▼ • Statistical Reports (ESP ISSN 1988-7825) **8404**
Statistical Review *see* Przeglad Statystyczny **8395**
Statistical Review of Coal in Canada (CAN ISSN 0707-2767) **6479**
Statistical Review of Government in Utah (USA) **7483**
Statistical Review of the Canadian Automotive Industry *see* Automotive Trade **1211**
Statistical Review of Tourism in Hong Kong (HKG ISSN 0377-5704) **8780**
• ➤ Statistical Science (USA ISSN 0883-4237) **8404**
▼ Statistical Science and Interdisciplinary Research (SGP ISSN 1793-6195) **8405**
Statistical Series *see* Hagtidindi **8375**
Statistical Service *see* Standard & Poor's Current Statistics **1652**
Statistical Service. Security Price Index Record (USA) **1653**
Statistical Society of Australia. Newsletter (AUS ISSN 0314-6820) **8405**
Statistical Sources and Methods (CHE ISSN 0255-3465) **1267**
Statistical Studies *see* Voprosy Statistiki **1274**
Statistical Supplement to the Federal Reserve Bulletin *see* Federal Reserve Bulletin. Statistical Supplement **8956**
Statistical Survey of the East African Community Institutions (KEN ISSN 0377-5712) **1267**
Statistical Synthesis of Chile (CHL ISSN 0716-2464) **1267**
Statistical Tables for the Federal Judiciary *see* Administrative Office of the United States Courts. Statistics Division. Statistical Tables for the Federal Judiciary (Online) **4820**
Statistical Tables of Public Nuisance, Tokyo (JPN) **3481**
Statistical Year Book of Indonesia (IDN ISSN 0126-2912) **7316**
Statistical Yearbook Compendium of the Republic of Cuba (CUB) **8405**
Statistical Yearbook for Asia and the Pacific/Annuaire Statistique pour l'Asie et le Pacifique (THA ISSN 0252-3655) **1267**
Statistical Yearbook for Latin America and the Caribbean *see* Anuario Estadistico de America Latina y el Caribe **8345**
Statistical Yearbook for the Copenhagen Region *see* Statistisk Aarbog for Hovedstadsregionen **8990**
Statistical Yearbook for the Faroe Islands *see* Arbok fyri Foeroyar **8347**
Statistical Yearbook of Administrative Districts of Sweden *see* Aarsbok foer Sveriges Kommuner **7478**
Statistical Yearbook of Algeria *see* Annuaire Statistique de l'Algerie **8345**
Statistical Yearbook of Bangladesh (BGD ISSN 0302-2374) **8405**
Statistical Yearbook of Brazil *see* Anuario Estatistico do Brasil **8347**
Statistical Yearbook of China's Industrial Economy *see* Zhongguo Gongye Jingji Tongji Nianjian **1275**
Statistical Yearbook of Copenhagen *see* Kobenhavns Statistiske Aarbog **8969**
Statistical Yearbook of Estonia *see* Eesti Statistika Aastaraamat **8367**
Statistical Yearbook of Foresty *see* Metsatilastollinen Vuosikirja **3709**
Statistical Yearbook of Greece (GRC ISSN 0081-5071) **8405**
Statistical Yearbook of Guangdong (Year) (HKG) **1267**
Statistical Yearbook of Hungary *see* Magyar Statisztikai Evkonyv **8386**
Statistical Yearbook of Iceland *see* Landshagir **8385**
• Statistical Yearbook of Ireland (IRL ISSN 1649-1408) **8405**
Statistical Yearbook of Jamaica (JAM ISSN 0304-0992) **8405**
Statistical Yearbook of Romania *see* Anuarul Statistic al Romaniei **8347**
Statistical Yearbook of Sichuan *see* Sichuan Tongji Nianjian **8399**

Title

DIRECTORY 2010 STEILACOOM HISTORICAL MUSEUM QUARTERLY 10903

Statistisch Tijdschrift - Nationaal Instituut voor de Statistiek *see* Belgium. Nationaal Instituut voor de Statistiek. Statistisch Tijdschrift **1214**
Statistisch Zakjaarboek - Nationaal Instituut voor de Statistiek *see* Belgium. Nationaal Instituut voor de Statistiek. Statistisch Zakjaarboek **1214**
Statistische Hefte *see* Statistical Papers **8404**
Statistische Information/Informations Statistiques (CHE) **7483**
Statistische Mitteilungen der Stadt Wien. Neue Folge (AUT) **8406**
Statistische Monatshefte Schleswig-Holstein (DEU ISSN 0947-7373) **7503**
Statistische Nachrichten der Stadt Nuernberg (DEU ISSN 0944-1492) **7483**
Statistischer Jahresbericht der Stadt Muenster (DEU) **7316**
Statistischer Monatsbericht der Stadt Augsburg (DEU) **8406**
Statistischer Vierteljahresbericht Hannover (DEU ISSN 0930-3782) **7483**
Statistischer Wochendienst (DEU ISSN 0177-2554) **8406**
Statistisches Amt des Saarlandes. Kurzbericht *see* Statistisches Amt Saarland. Statistische Berichte A **7483**
Statistisches Amt Saarland. Statistische Berichte A (DEU ISSN 1864-2594) **7483**
Statistisches Amt Saarland. Statistische Berichte B (DEU ISSN 1864-2268) **7483**
Statistisches Amt Saarland. Statistische Berichte C (DEU) **7484**
Statistisches Amt Saarland. Statistische Berichte D (DEU) **7484**
Statistisches Amt Saarland. Statistische Berichte E (DEU) **7484**
Statistisches Amt Saarland. Statistische Berichte F (DEU ISSN 1864-2276) **7484**
Statistisches Amt Saarland. Statistische Berichte G (DEU) **7484**
Statistisches Amt Saarland. Statistische Berichte H (DEU) **7484**
Statistisches Amt Saarland. Statistische Berichte J (DEU) **7484**
Statistisches Amt Saarland. Statistische Berichte K (DEU) **7484**
Statistisches Amt Saarland. Statistische Berichte L (DEU ISSN 1864-2608) **7484**
Statistisches Amt Saarland. Statistische Berichte M (DEU) **7484**
Statistisches Amt Saarland. Statistische Berichte N (DEU) **7484**
Statistisches Amt Saarland. Statistische Berichte P (DEU ISSN 1864-2616) **7484**
Statistisches Amt Saarland. Statistische Berichte Q (DEU) **7484**
Statistisches Amt Saarland. Veroeffentlichungsverzeichnis (DEU ISSN 1438-3411) **7484**
Statistisches Jahrbuch Berlin (DEU ISSN 0081-5322) **8407**
Statistisches Jahrbuch der Eisen- und Stahlindustrie (DEU ISSN 0081-5365) **6341**
Statistisches Jahrbuch der Schweiz/Annuaire Statistique de la Suisse (CHE ISSN 0081-5330) **8407**
Statistisches Jahrbuch der Stadt Augsburg (DEU ISSN 0931-9239) **8407**
Statistisches Jahrbuch der Stadt Koeln (DEU ISSN 0178-160X) **7484**
Statistisches Jahrbuch der Stadt Nuernberg (DEU ISSN 0944-1514) **7484**
• Statistisches Jahrbuch der Stadt Wien (AUT ISSN 0259-6083) **8407**
Statistisches Jahrbuch Deutscher Gemeinden (DEU ISSN 0081-5349) **7484**
• Statistisches Jahrbuch fuer die Bundesrepublik Deutschland (DEU ISSN 0943-5743) **8407**
Statistisches Jahrbuch fuer die Republik Oesterreich (AUT ISSN 1811-6760) **8407**
Statistisches Jahrbuch Fuerstentum Liechtenstein (LIE ISSN 0259-4676) **8407**
Statistisches Jahrbuch Muenchen (DEU ISSN 0720-3314) **7484**
• Statistisches Jahrbuch Schleswig-Holstein (DEU ISSN 0487-6423) **8407**
Statistisches Jahrbuch ueber Ernaehrung, Landwirtschaft und Forsten der Bundesrepublik Deutschland (DEU ISSN 0072-1581) **186**
Statistisches Landesamt Hamburg. Ein Stadtportraet in Zahlen (DEU) **7484**
Statistisches Landesamt Hamburg. Statistisches Jahrbuch (DEU ISSN 1438-8480) **7484**
Statistisches Landesamt Rheinland-Pfalz. Statistisches Taschenbuch (DEU ISSN 0948-5074) **7484**
Statistisches Landesamt Saarland. Statistische Berichte B *see* Statistisches Amt Saarland. Statistische Berichte B **7483**
Statistisches Landesamt Saarland. Statistische Berichte C *see* Statistisches Amt Saarland. Statistische Berichte C **7484**
Statistisches Landesamt Saarland. Statistische Berichte D *see* Statistisches Amt Saarland. Statistische Berichte D **7484**
Statistisches Landesamt Saarland. Statistische Berichte E *see* Statistisches Amt Saarland. Statistische Berichte E **7484**
Statistisches Landesamt Saarland. Statistische Berichte F *see* Statistisches Amt Saarland. Statistische Berichte F **7484**
Statistisches Landesamt Saarland. Statistische Berichte G *see* Statistisches Amt Saarland. Statistische Berichte G **7484**
Statistisches Landesamt Saarland. Statistische Berichte H *see* Statistisches Amt Saarland. Statistische Berichte H **7484**
Statistisches Landesamt Saarland. Statistische Berichte J *see* Statistisches Amt Saarland. Statistische Berichte J **7484**
Statistisches Landesamt Saarland. Statistische Berichte K *see* Statistisches Amt Saarland. Statistische Berichte K **7484**
Statistisches Landesamt Saarland. Statistische Berichte L *see* Statistisches Amt Saarland. Statistische Berichte L **7484**
Statistisches Landesamt Saarland. Statistische Berichte M *see* Statistisches Amt Saarland. Statistische Berichte M **7484**
Statistisches Landesamt Saarland. Statistische Berichte N *see* Statistisches Amt Saarland. Statistische Berichte N **7484**
Statistisches Landesamt Saarland. Statistische Berichte P *see* Statistisches Amt Saarland. Statistische Berichte P **7484**
Statistisches Landesamt Saarland. Statistische Berichte Q *see* Statistisches Amt Saarland. Statistische Berichte Q **7484**
Statistisches Taschenbuch Baden-Wuerttemberg (DEU) **7484**
Statistisches Taschenbuch der Stadt Wien (AUT ISSN 0259-7985) **8407**
Statistisches Taschenbuch Muenchen (DEU ISSN 0173-0029) **7484**
Statistisk Aarbog, Danmark *see* Denmark. Danmarks Statistik. Statistisk Aarbog **8366**
† Statistisk Aarbog for Hovedstadsregionen/Statistical Yearbook for the Copenhagen Region (DNK ISSN 0906-2211) **8990**
Statistisk Aarsbok foer Social- och Haelsovaerden *see* Sosiaali- ja Terveydenhuollon Tilastollinen Vuosikirja **8084**
Statistisk Aarsbok foer Sverige/Statistical Yearbook of Sweden (SWE ISSN 0081-5381) **8407**
† • Statistisk Tiaars-Oversigt for Koebenhavns Kommune (DNK ISSN 0107-6744) **8990**
• ➤ Statny Geologicky Ustav Dionyza Stura. Geologicke Prace. Spravy (SVK ISSN 0433-4795) **2769**
• Stato e Mercato (ITA ISSN 0392-9701) **7186**
Statoil Magasin (NOR ISSN 0804-8266) **6793**
Stats *see* American Statistical Association. Stats **8344**
Stats Baseball Scorecard *see* S T A T S (Year) Baseball Scorecard **8245**
Stats Basketball Scorecard *see* S T A T S (Year) Basketball Scorecard **8245**
Stats - Monthly Statistical and Marketing Digest (ZAF ISSN 0379-8836) **8407**
➤ Stats- og Livsformer (DNK ISSN 1395-3672) **8007**
Statsautoriserede Revisorer Skat *see* S R - Skat **1942**
Statsautoriseret Revisor-Skat *see* S R - Skat **1942**
• Statsbiblioteket. Arbejdspapirer (DNK ISSN 1399-5332) **5049**
Statsbiblioteket Lige Nu! *see* Lige Nu! **5030**
Statsnoekkelen (Year) (NOR ISSN 1503-9358) **7470**
Statspack *see* Program for Adolescent Life Management **2698**
Statstjaenstemannen *see* S T Press **1706**
➤ Statsvetenskaplig Tidskrift (SWE ISSN 0039-0747) **7186**
➤ Statsvetenskapliga Foreningen i Uppsala. Skrifter/Uppsala Political Science Association. Publications (SWE ISSN 0346-7538) **7186**
Statsvetenskapliga Foreningen i Uppsala. Skrifter *see* Statsvetenskapliga Foreningen i Uppsala. Skrifter **7186**
Status (DNK ISSN 0109-0798) **1179**
Status (GRC ISSN 1107-8588) **6300**
• Status (HRV ISSN 1331-2251) **6619**
• Status (ISR ISSN 0792-6839) **1794**
Status (SWE ISSN 0346-1823) **7542**
De Status (East Edition) (NLD) **1968**
De Status (Mid-Netherlands Edition) (NLD) **1968**
De Status (North Edition) (NLD) **1968**
De Status (Randstad-North Edition) (NLD) **1968**
De Status (Randstad-West Edition) (NLD) **1968**
Status-Kvo (UKR) **3965**
The Status of Black Atlanta (USA ISSN 1081-9142) **8007**
• Status of Coral Reefs of the World (Year) (AUS ISSN 1447-6185) **3468**
Status of Nuclear Fusion Research and Development *see* Kaku Yugo Kenkyu Kaihatsu no Genjo **7068**
Status of the American Public School Teacher (USA ISSN 0734-5062) **3033**
Status of Women and Employment Equity in Ontario School Boards (CAN ISSN 1183-0735) **2915**
Status of Women Canada. Perspectives/Condition Feminine Canada. Perspectives (CAN ISSN 0836-0111) **8884**
The Status of Women in the States (USA ISSN 1932-2437) **8903**
Status og Visioner (DNK ISSN 0905-0035) **7542**
Status Report (Washington) *see* Insurance Institute for Highway Safety. Status Report **7526**
• Statusline (USA ISSN 1072-3404) **5049**
• Statut et Gestion des Personnels Medicaux et Hospitaliers (FRA ISSN 1957-603X) **4111**
Statut Social des Travailleurs Independants (BEL) **4524**
• ➤ Statute Law Review (GBR ISSN 0144-3593) **4788**
• ➤ Statutes and Decisions: The Laws of the U S S R & Its Successor States (USA ISSN 1061-0014) **4788**
Statutes and Notifications (IND ISSN 0039-0763) **4788**
Statutes and Regulations Alberta *see* Canada. Federal Court of Canada. Statutes and Regulations Canada. Statutes and Regulations Alberta **4638**
Statutes of Alberta (CAN ISSN 0823-3489) **4788**
Statutes of Alberta Judicially Considered *see* Statutes of Alberta **4788**
Statutes of Manitoba (CAN ISSN 1196-2356) **4788**
Statutes of New Zealand (NZL ISSN 0111-5626) **4788**
Statutes of Nova Scotia (CAN ISSN 0708-3386) **4788**
• Statutes of Ontario/Lois de l'Ontario (CAN ISSN 0843-8994) **4789**
Statutes of Quebec (CAN ISSN 0712-4422) **4789**
Statutes of Saskatchewan (CAN ISSN 0840-2043) **4789**
• Statutes of South Africa (Print) (ZAF) **4789**
Statutes of the Province of British Columbia (CAN ISSN 0225-9494) **4789**
Statutes of the Province of Newfoundland (CAN ISSN 0709-1346) **4789**
Statutes of the Yukon Territory (CAN ISSN 0823-4949) **4789**
• Statutes of Zimbabwe (ZAF ISSN 1682-1033) **4789**
Statutes, Regulations and Case Law Protecting Individuals with Disabilities (USA) **1708**
Statutory Instruments List *see* Great Britain. H.M.S.O. Statutory Instruments List **625**
• Statuts des Medecins Hospitaliers (FRA ISSN 1958-2730) **4111**
Statuutenzakboekje Overheidspersoneel (BEL ISSN 1377-4204) **7470**
• StatZing Primary (NZL) **2915**
• StatZing Secondary (NZL) **3082**
Staub- und Silikosebericht Nordrhein-Westfalen (DEU) **3491**
Der Staudengarten (DEU ISSN 0178-837X) **3751**
Staufenbiel Das M B A - Studium (DEU) **1794**
Staufenbiel I T (Information Technology) (DEU) **1421**
Staufenbiel Ingenieure (DEU) **3220**
Staufenbiel Karrieremagazin (DEU) **6704**
Staufenbiel Management Nachwuchs (DEU) **1794**
Staufenbiel-Newsletter fuer Berufseinstieg & Karriere *see* Staufenbiel Karrieremagazin **6704**
➤ Stauffenburg Aktuell (DEU ISSN 1439-2224) **5240**
➤ Stauffenburg Bibliothek (DEU) **5377**
➤ Stauffenburg Colloquium (DEU ISSN 0940-3795) **5377**
➤ Stauffenburg Discussion (DEU ISSN 0948-3357) **3015**
➤ Stauffenburg Einfuehrungen (DEU ISSN 0948-3365) **5178**
➤ Stauffenburg Festschriften (DEU ISSN 1433-2752) **5377**
➤ Stauffenburg Handbuecher (DEU) **5377**
➤ Stauffenburg Interpretation (DEU ISSN 1439-0183) **5377**
➤ Stauffenburg Linguistik (DEU ISSN 1430-4139) **5178**
➤ Stauffenburg Medien (DEU ISSN 1435-1048) **2339**
Stauros Notebook *see* Suffering **7686**
Stavanger Aftenblad (NOR ISSN 0804-8991) **3925**
Stavanger Museum. Aarbok (NOR ISSN 0333-0656) **519**
Stavanger Museum. Skrifter (NOR ISSN 0333-0664) **6537**
Stavba (CZE ISSN 1210-9568) **458**
Stavba Automobilu *see* Automobil Revue **8563**
Stavebne Hmoty (SVK ISSN 1336-6041) **1037**
Stavebne Materialy (SVK ISSN 1336-7617) **1037**
Stavebni Materialy (DEU ISSN 0949-2275) **1037**
Stavebnictvo a Byvanie (SVK ISSN 1336-0191) **1037**
Stavitel (CZE ISSN 1210-4825) **458**
Stavn (DNK ISSN 0904-3683) **4267**
• Stavropol'skaya Pravda (RUS) **3941**
Stavropol'skie Gubernskie Vedomosti (RUS) **7503**
Stavropol'skii Meridian (RUS) **3941**
• Stay Free! (USA ISSN 1547-2663) **8007**
Stayer (NOR ISSN 1890-1190) **6233**
Staying Alive (GBR ISSN 1354-2249) **7542**
Staying at a Lighthouse (USA ISSN 1541-8987) **8758**
Staying on Track (USA ISSN 1049-9024) **8625**
Staying Safe on the Job (USA ISSN 1080-0395) **6687**
Stazione Sperimentale del Vetro. Rivista (ITA ISSN 0391-4259) **2045**
StB, StBv Handbuch *see* Steuerberater Handbuch **1945**
• Stealth (AUS ISSN 1443-0401) **6619**
Steam and Stone (CAN) **4314**
Steam Automobile (USA ISSN 0561-9726) **8605**
Steam Days (GBR ISSN 0269-0020) **8625**
• Steam Engine Time (AUS) **5448**
Steam Heritage Guide (Year) (GBR) **8511**
Steam Heritage Museums & Rally Guide (Year) *see* Steam Heritage Guide (Year) **8511**
Steam Passenger Service Directory (USA ISSN 0081-542X) **8625**
Steam Railway (GBR ISSN 0143-7232) **8625**
Steam Railway News (GBR ISSN 0953-5292) **8625**
† Steam Traction (USA) **8990**
Steam Traction Engine (GBR ISSN 1746-0026) **5460**
† Steam World (GBR ISSN 0959-0897) **8990**
➤ Steamboat Bill (USA ISSN 0039-0844) **8663**
Steamboat Magazine (USA ISSN 0743-2267) **3989**
Steamboating (USA ISSN 1056-6422) **8283**
Steamshovel Press (USA ISSN 1062-3795) **4162**
Stearns Newsletter (USA ISSN 1046-4387) **6619**
Steaua (ROM ISSN 0039-0852) **5377**
Stedebouw en Architectuur (NLD ISSN 1380-9393) **1037**
Stedebouw & Ruimtelijke Ordening (NLD ISSN 1384-6531) **4427**
Stedelijk Museum Zutphen en Museum Henriette Polak. Informatieblad *see* Regionaal Historisch Centrum Zutphen en Het Museum Henriette Polak. Kwartaalblad **6536**
Stedelijke en Regionale Verkenningen (NLD ISSN 0928-7353) **4427**
Stedenbouw (NLD) **4427**
• Stedfast (GBR) **7776**
Steed *see* Jun Ma **5316**
• ➤ Steel & Composite Structures (KOR ISSN 1229-9367) **6333**
Steel Art (ITA ISSN 1721-1395) **4348**
Steel Australia (AUS ISSN 1447-5359) **1037**
Steel Authority of India Ltd., Bhilai Steel Plant Magazine *see* B S P Magazine **6306**
Steel Bridge Yearbook *see* Kyoryo Nenkan **3278**
Steel Bulletin - Bhilai Darshan *see* Steel Bulletin - Panorama **6333**
Steel Bulletin - Panorama/Steel Bulletin - Bhilai Darshan (IND) **6333**
Steel Construction (AUS ISSN 0049-2205) **1037**
Steel Construction (ZAF) **1037**
▼ Steel Construction - Design and Research (DEU) **1037**
Steel Construction New Zealand (NZL ISSN 1177-3855) **1037**
Steel Design/Construction Metallique (CAN ISSN 0712-9092) **458**
Steel Digest (USA) **6333**
Steel Frame *see* Tekkotsu **1040**
• Steel Grips (DEU ISSN 1866-8453) **6333**
• ➤ Steel in Translation (USA ISSN 0967-0912) **6333**
Steel Industry of Japan (year) (JPN) **6333**
Steel Industry Update (USA ISSN 1063-4339) **6333**
† The Steel Market and Prospects (USA ISSN 1020-8887) **8990**
▼ • Steel Market Update (USA ISSN 1942-9002) **6333**
▼ • Steel Markets Daily (USA ISSN 1935-7354) **1179**
Steel Markets Monthly (GBR ISSN 0964-7694) **6333**
Steel Metals & Mineral International (IND) **6333**
Steel News *see* Inline (Finnish Edition) **1054**
Steel News (USA) **6333**
Steel News (London) (GBR) **6333**
Steel News (Newport) (GBR) **6333**
Steel News (Scunthorpe Edition) (GBR) **6333**
Steel News (Sheffield) (GBR) **6333**
Steel News (Teesside Edition) (GBR) **6333**
Steel News Investor *see* Inline (Finnish Edition) **1054**
Steel Pipe *see* Gangguan **6313**
Steel Press *see* Forge Press **2284**
† Steel Profile (AUS ISSN 0726-0865) **8990**
Steel R T D Newsletter (BEL ISSN 1029-8916) **6333**
➤ Steel Research International (DEU ISSN 1611-3683) **6333**
Steel Scenario (IND) **6333**
• Steel Statistical Yearbook (Year) (BEL ISSN 0771-2871) **6341**
• Steel Times International (GBR ISSN 0143-7798) **6334**
Steel Tower *see* Tetto **3285**
Steel Traders of the World (GBR ISSN 0308-8006) **6334**
Steel Tube and Pipe Monthly (GBR ISSN 1743-1883) **6334**
• Steel, Tubular Products and Steel Wire (CAN ISSN 1719-9506) **1904**
• Steel Week (GBR ISSN 1359-1681) **6479**
Steelabor *see* U S W@Work **4604**
Steelmasters (FRA ISSN 1251-3431) **4348**
Steen en Marmer *see* Pierre et Marbre **2762**
Steenkolen Handelsvereniging Gas Newsletter *see* S H V Gas Newsletter **6791**
• Steenstrupia (DNK ISSN 0375-2909) **964**
† The Steering Wheel (USA ISSN 0039-1298) **8990**
Stefan University. Bulletin (USA ISSN 1098-1632) **7920**
➤ The Stefan University Journal of Genomic Medicine (USA ISSN 1528-4883) **878**
➤ Stefan University Press Series on Achievements in Physics (USA ISSN 1097-9298) **7041**
▼ • Stefan University Press Series on the Greats of the World (USA ISSN 1944-8090) **645**
Stefanus (DEU) **7683**
Steget *see* Unik **6189**
Steiermaerkische Landesbibliothek. Arbeiten (AUT) **636**
Steiermaerkisches Landesarchiv. Mitteilungen (AUT ISSN 0434-3883) **4267**
Steigenberger Journal (DEU) **4398**
Steilacoom Historical Museum Quarterly (USA) **4314**

Title

▼ new title † ceased • electronic media ➤ refereed

DIRECTORY 2010 STORMTRACK 10905

† Stimme der Befreiten Kirche (DEU ISSN 0938-541X) 8990
Stimme der Maertyrer (DEU ISSN 1618-4114) 7683
Stimme der Maertyrer - H M K Kurier see Stimme der Maertyrer 7683
Stimme der Wahrheit see In Spirit 7761
Stimme und Weg (DEU ISSN 0944-2766) 6447
Stimmen der Zeit (DEU ISSN 0039-1492) 7818
Stimuleringsfonds Nederlandse Culturele Omroepproducties. Actueel (NLD ISSN 1873-9083) 2391
Stimuleringsfonds Nederlandse Culturele Omroepproducties. Het Fonds In. . . see Stimuleringsfonds Nederlandse Culturele Omroepproducties. Actueel 2391
Stimuleringsprogramma Doorstroom van Dagbesteding naar Werk. Nieuwsbrief see Werk en Handicap 1714
Stimulus (AUT ISSN 1028-1509) 5178
Stimulus (NLD ISSN 0929-0591) 6116
• Stimulus (NZL ISSN 1171-7920) 7683
Stin see S T I N 2586
Sting (CAN) 158
Sting (USA ISSN 0890-9229) 8209
Stint (DEU ISSN 0933-646X) 5377
Stires Family Newsletter (USA ISSN 1522-7758) 3784
Stirpes (USA ISSN 0039-1522) 3784
Stirrings (GBR) 6620
Stirrings Still (USA ISSN 1551-0433) 5377
▼ • Stitch Innovation Series (NZL ISSN 1178-3486) 1904
Stitch With The Embroiderers Guild (GBR ISSN 1467-6648) 6642
Stitcher's World see Cross-Stitch & Needlework 6638
• Stitches (USA ISSN 0899-5893) 2250
Stjaernurmakaren (SWE ISSN 1104-8999) 4569
Stjoerdalens Blad (NOR) 3925
StLouis at Home see St. Louis at Home 4562
Sto Plus Jedna see 100+1 3833
Stobaeana (SWE ISSN 1104-5957) 964
• ➤ Stochastic Analysis and Applications (USA ISSN 0736-2994) 5538
• ➤ Stochastic Environmental Research and Risk Assessment (DEU ISSN 1436-3240) 3364
Stochastic Modelling and Applied Probability (USA) 5538
• ➤ Stochastic Models (USA ISSN 1532-6349) 8407
• ➤ Stochastic Processes and Their Applications (NLD ISSN 0304-4149) 5538
• ➤ Stochastics (GBR ISSN 1744-2508) 5538
• ➤ Stochastics and Dynamics (SGP ISSN 0219-4937) 8407
Stock and Custom (USA) 8605
Stock and Land (AUS ISSN 1321-0157) 158
Stock Car Racing (USA ISSN 0734-7340) 8209
† Stock Car REV (USA ISSN 1540-2193) 8990
Stock Exchange Daily Official List (GBR) 1653
Stock Exchange of Thailand. Fact Book (THA) 1653
Stock Exchange of Thailand Journal see S E T Journal 1648
Stock Exchange of Thailand. Monthly Review (THA ISSN 0125-1139) 1653
Stock Exchange of Thailand Newsletter see S E T Newsletter 1649
Stock Exchange Official Directory (IND ISSN 0971-3808) 2029
Stock Exchange Weekly Official Intelligence (GBR) 1653
• Stock Footage Index (Year) (GBR) 6977
Stock Guide see Standard & Poor's Stock Guide 1653
• Stock Index U K / Europe (Year) (GBR) 6977
• Stock Index U S A (Year) (GBR) 6977
Stock Journal (AUS ISSN 1321-1919) 301
Stock Market see Fondov Pazar 1624
Stock Market Annual (IRL ISSN 1649-7414) 1653
Stock Market in Thailand (THA) 2790
The Stock Market Magazine (IRL ISSN 1649-8801) 1653
Stock Market Yearbook (IND) 1384
Stock Number Survey as at Thirty June see Meat and Wool Boards' Economic Service. Stock Number Survey as at 30 June 203
Stock Photo Deskbook (USA ISSN 0897-6287) 6977
† Stock Photo Fees and Terms of Business in Europe (DEU) 8991
Stock Photo Fees in Europe see Stock Photo Fees and Terms of Business in Europe 8991
Stock Selector (USA) 1653
Stock Summary (Monthly Edition) (USA ISSN 1080-3157) 1653
Stock Summary (Semi-annual Edition) see Stock Summary (Monthly Edition) 1653
Stock Trader's Almanac (USA ISSN 1553-4812) 1654
• The Stockade (NZL ISSN 0110-4926) 4194
Stockeman's Hall of fame see Stockman's News 4194
Stockgrower Digest (CAN ISSN 0820-4683) 301
Stockholm Center for Organizational Research Rapportserie see S C O R E Rapportserie 7181
Stockholm Cinema Studies (SWE ISSN 1653-4859) 6514
Stockholm Economic Studies. Pamphlet Series (SWE ISSN 0585-3540) 1179
• Stockholm Environmental Institute. Report Series (SWE ISSN 1651-7229) 3148
Stockholm Fest och Moeten see Sthlm Fest & Moeten 4367
Stockholm In Your Pocket (SWE) 8758
• Stockholm International Arbitration Review (USA ISSN 1558-271X) 4941
Stockholm International Peace Research Institute Chemical & Biological Warfare Studies see S I P R I Chemical & Biological Warfare Studies 7264
Stockholm International Peace Research Institute Policy Paper see S I P R I Policy Paper 7264
Stockholm International Peace Research Institute Research Report see S I P R I Research Report 7264
Stockholm International Peace Research Institute Update see S I P R I Update 7264
Stockholm International Peace Research Institute Yearbook see S I P R I Yearbook 7264
Stockholm International Water Institute Proceedings see S I W I Proceedings 8831
The Stockholm Journal of East Asian Studies (SWE ISSN 0284-883X) 561
Stockholm Lectures in Educology (SWE ISSN 1651-1670) 2915
Stockholm New (SWE ISSN 1402-7496) 3957
Stockholm Oriental Studies (SWE ISSN 0585-3559) 561
Stockholm School of Economics/ Ekonomiska Forskningsinstitutet Working Paper Series in Business Administration see S S E/E F I Working Paper Series in Business Administration 1170
Stockholm School of Economics. Ekonomiska Forskningsinstitutet Working Paper Series in Economics and Finance see S S E/E F I Working Paper Series in Economics and Finance 1170
Stockholm Slavic Studies (SWE ISSN 0585-3575) 5178
Stockholm Stock Exchange. Annual Report (SWE) 1654
Stockholm Studies in Baltic Languages (SWE ISSN 0281-5478) 5178
Stockholm Studies in Classical Archaeology (SWE ISSN 0562-1062) 2240
Stockholm Studies in Comparative Religion (SWE ISSN 0562-1070) 7683
Stockholm Studies in Economic History (SWE ISSN 0346-8305) 1179
Stockholm Studies in Educational Psychology (SWE ISSN 0562-1089) 7410
Stockholm Studies in English (SWE ISSN 0346-6272) 5178
Stockholm Studies in Ethnology (SWE ISSN 1653-851X) 8141
Stockholm Studies in Finnish Language and Literature (SWE ISSN 0346-7392) 5178
Stockholm Studies in History of Art (SWE ISSN 0491-0850) 519
Stockholm Studies in History of Literature (SWE ISSN 0491-0869) 5377
Stockholm Studies in Human Geography (SWE ISSN 0349-7003) 4162
Stockholm Studies in Linguistics see Stockholms Universitet. Institutionen foer Linguistics. Monographs 5178
Stockholm Studies in Modern Philology see Studier i Modern Spraakvetenskap 5182
Stockholm Studies in Philosophy (SWE ISSN 0491-0877) 6953
➤ Stockholm Studies in Politics (SWE ISSN 0346-6620) 7186
Stockholm Studies in Psychology (SWE ISSN 0585-3591) 7410
Stockholm Studies in Russian Literature (SWE ISSN 0346-8496) 5377
Stockholm Studies in Social Work (SWE ISSN 0281-2851) 8073
Stockholm Studies in Sociology (SWE ISSN 0491-0885) 8141
Stockholm Studies in Statistics (SWE ISSN 0280-4018) 8407
Stockholm Studies in the History of Ideas (SWE ISSN 1100-9667) 6953
➤ Stockholm Studies of Curriculum Studies (SWE ISSN 1403-4972) 2915
Stockholm Theatre Studies (SWE ISSN 1400-2132) 8479
Stockholm Universitet. Pedagogiska Institutionen. Utvecklingspsykologiska Seminariet. Skriftserien (SWE ISSN 1652-5639) 7410
• Stockholm University. Department of Economics. Working Papers (SWE ISSN 1404-7667) 1179
Stockholm Water Front (SWE ISSN 1102-7053) 8832
Stockholmer Germanistische Forschungen (SWE ISSN 0491-0893) 5178
Stockholms-Foeretagaren (SWE) 519
Stockholms Stadsmuseum. Kulturmiljoeavdelingen. Arkeologisk Rapport (SWE ISSN 1650-9579) 418
Stockholms Universitet. Institutionen foer Linguistics. Monographs (SWE ISSN 0348-2812) 5178
Stockholms Universitet. Institutionen foer Lingvistik. Papers (SWE ISSN 0348-3223) 6620
Stockholms Universitet. Konstvetenskapliga Institutionen. Skriftserie (SWE ISSN 1401-3398) 519
Stockholms Universitet. Pedagogiska Institutionen. Forskningsrapport (SWE ISSN 0280-0314) 2915
Stockholms Universitet. Pedagogiska Institutionen. Seminariet om Miljoepedagofik och Kunskapsbilding. Rapport (SWE ISSN 0281-6296) 2915
• Stockholms Universitet. Statsvetenskapliga Institutionen. Quotas - a Key to Equality. Working Paper Series (SWE ISSN 1652-7755) 8903
Stockholmstidningen (SWE ISSN 1402-8069) 7186
• Stockhom Environment Institute. EcoSanRes Programme. Publications Series (SWE ISSN 1653-4328) 3468
• StockHouse Online (CAN) 1654
Stockley's Drug Interactions (GBR ISSN 1752-3605) 6881
The Stocklists (GBR ISSN 0950-5024) 8457
The Stocklists and News Service for Carpet and Floorcovering Buyers see The Stocklists 8457
Stockman - Grass Farmer (USA ISSN 0899-1057) 301
Stockman's News (AUS) 4194
Stockport Heritage Magazine (GBR ISSN 0957-3771) 4268
Stockpot (GBR) 4399
Stocks (CHE ISSN 1424-7739) 1654
Stocks (USA ISSN 1945-0133) 1654
• Stocks, Bonds, Bills and Inflation (Year) Yearbook (USA ISSN 1047-2436) 1654
Stocks, Bonds, Bills and Inflation Yearbook (Valuation Edition) (USA ISSN 1523-343X) 1654
Stocks, Futures & Options Stocks, Futures & Options Magazine see S F O - Stocks, Futures & Options Magazine 1649
The Stockton Family Newsletter (USA ISSN 0883-9050) 3784
• Stockton News (GBR) 7503
Stodhestar/Hengste/Stallions (ISL ISSN 1670-4789) 8299
Stoeberiet (DNK ISSN 0039-1549) 6334
Stoeperitidende (NOR ISSN 0039-1824) 6334
Stoff R (DEU ISSN 1613-3919) 4789
StoffR see Stoff R 4789
➤ Stoffwechselmanagement (DEU) 6669
Stofnun Sigurdar Nordals - Frettabref (ISL ISSN 1021-8440) 5178
Stoke City Southern Supporters Club (GBR ISSN 1752-8534) 8247
Stokvel Times (ZAF ISSN 1991-041X) 1384
Stolichnye Novosti (UKR) 3965
Stoma (PRT ISSN 0870-4287) 5866
Stomach and Intestine see I to Cho 5926
• Stomatolog (UKR) 5866
Stomatologicheskii Forum (RUS) 5866
• Stomatologicheskii Vestnik (RUS) 5866
• ➤ Stomatologie (AUT ISSN 0946-3151) 5866
➤ Stomatologija (LTU ISSN 1392-8589) 5866
• Stomatologiya/Dentistry (RUS ISSN 0039-1735) 5866
Stomatologiya Rossii (RUS) 5866
Stomatology see Kouqiang Yixue 5854
➤ Stomatoloski Glasnik Srbije/Serbian Dental Journal (SRB ISSN 0039-1743) 5866
• Stomatos (BRA ISSN 1519-4442) 5866
Stomp and Stammer (USA) 6620
Stone see Fireplace Specialist 1008
▼ • Stone (GBR ISSN 1754-1026) 2769
Stone (USA) 3989
Stone Age Institute Publication Series (USA) 418
Stone and Cox General Insurance Register (CAN ISSN 0380-223X) 4524
Stone and Cox Life Insurance Tables (CAN ISSN 0835-2933) 4524
Stone & Stein (ITA) 1038
Stone Business (USA) 1038
Stone-Campbell Journal (USA ISSN 1097-6566) 7776
▼ Stone Canoe (USA ISSN 1934-9963) 5378
Stone Center for Developmental Services and Studies. Work in Progress (USA ISSN 1046-3674) 8903
The Stone Circle (USA ISSN 1931-3381) 5378
Stone Federation Handbook and Directory see Stone Specifiers Guide 1038
† Stone Magazine (USA ISSN 1525-4909) 8991
Stone Plus (DEU ISSN 1434-4378) 1038
Stone Review see Stone, Sand & Gravel Review 6480
Stone, Sand & Gravel Review (USA) 6480
• Stone Soup (USA ISSN 0094-579X) 2215
Stone Specifiers Guide (GBR) 1038
• Stone World (USA ISSN 1052-6994) 6480
Stoneham Catalogue of British Stamps (GBR ISSN 0142-615X) 6900
Stones and Bones Newsletter (USA) 418
Stone'S Journal see Philadelphia Sunday Sun 3557
Stone's Justices' Manual (GBR ISSN 0269-3682) 4789
• Stoney Creek News (CAN ISSN 0834-7433) 3818
Stoney Creek News (Stoney Creek, 1948) see Stoney Creek News 3818
Stonnington History News see Local History News 4193
▼ Stoomschip Vereeniging (NLD ISSN 1875-0265) 8663
Stoomtractie (NLD ISSN 1382-8649) 8625
De Stoomtram (NLD ISSN 1382-8770) 8625
Stop (ITA ISSN 1121-1288) 3899
Stop (SVK ISSN 0139-6501) 8605
Stop (SVN ISSN 0351-8094) 3947
Stop Arnaques (FRA ISSN 1770-359X) 2641
Stop Breathing (USA) 5084
Stop Press (GBR) 2915
Stop Press Magazine (GBR) 7328
Stop Press News Digest see Stop Press 2915
Stop Watch (USA ISSN 1942-2113) 8675
Stopanski Pregled/Economic Review (MKD ISSN 0039-1816) 1179
Stoppa Rasismen (SWE ISSN 0281-5893) 3566
Stopress (IRL) 540
Stopwatcher (USA) 8209
Storage see TechTarget Magazin 2516
• Storage (USA ISSN 1549-6783) 2438
Storage (Des Moines) (USA ISSN 1939-1579) 4550
Storage & Entertainment (USA ISSN 1547-2809) 2339
Storage & Government (USA ISSN 1547-4682) 2532
Storage and Process see Baoxian yu Jiagong 94
Storage and Processing of Farm Products see Khranenie i Pererabotka Sel'khozsyr'ya 130
Storage Area Network / Local Area Network / L A N see S A N / L A N 2503
Storage Battery see Chikudenchi 3297
† Storage Inc (USA ISSN 1524-6558) 8991
Storage Magazine (NLD ISSN 1570-9930) 2541
Storage Management (USA ISSN 1090-0799) 2538
Storage Management Solutions (USA ISSN 1097-5152) 2438
Storage News (RUS) 2532
Den Store 4x4-guiden see 4x4guiden 8614
Store Check Distributiegids Food see Store Check Foodgids 3681
Store Check Foodgids (BEL ISSN 1781-877X) 3681
Store Check Guide de la Distribution Alimentaire see Store Check Guide Food 3681
Store Check Guide Food (BEL ISSN 1781-8907) 3681
Store et Showroom see Retail Update Magazine 1841
Store Planning & Design Review (USA ISSN 0896-8772) 4551
• Store Satsinger (NOR ISSN 0809-6139) 4476
Store Windows (USA ISSN 1086-704X) 35
• Stores (USA ISSN 0039-1867) 1844
Stores & Shops (DEU ISSN 1430-4082) 1179
Stores et Fermetures (FRA ISSN 0183-455X) 1038
Stores of the Year (USA ISSN 0192-8732) 4551
Storia Amministrazione Costituzione (ITA ISSN 1126-5825) 7470
Storia. Contributi (ITA ISSN 1724-1367) 4162
Storia del Pensiero Economico see Storia del Pensiero Economico. Nuova Serie 1549
• Storia del Pensiero Economico. Nuova Serie (ITA ISSN 1828-1990) 1549
† Storia del Turismo. Annale (Year) (ITA ISSN 1825-6848) 8991
Storia della Miniatura. Studi e Documenti (ITA ISSN 0081-5845) 519
Storia della Storiografia/Geschichte der Geschichtsschreibung/Histoire de l'Historiographie/History of Historiography (ITA ISSN 0392-8926) 4268
• Storia dell'Arte (ITA ISSN 0392-4513) 519
Storia dell'Arte e della Critica d'Arte (ITA) 519
• Storia delle Donne (ITA ISSN 1826-7513) 8903
Storia delle Dottrine Politiche. Saggi e Ricerche (ITA ISSN 1971-1255) 7186
Storia delle Religioni (ITA) 7683
Storia dell'Ebraismo in Italia (ITA ISSN 1122-0716) 7730
• Storia di Venezia (ITA ISSN 1825-5132) 4268
Storia di Venezia Rivista see Storia di Venezia 4268
Storia e Civilta (ITA ISSN 1824-5897) 4268
Storia e Critica (ITA ISSN 1120-0669) 4268
Storia e Diritto. Studi (ITA ISSN 1724-1103) 4162
• Storia e Furturo (ITA ISSN 1720-190X) 4162
Storia e Letteratura (ITA) 5378
Storia e Memoria (ITA ISSN 1121-9742) 4268
• Storia e Problemi Contemporanei (ITA ISSN 1120-4206) 4268
Storia e Regione see Geschichte und Region 4223
† Storia e Societa (ITA) 8991
Storia e Storie al Femminile (ITA ISSN 1826-9192) 4162
Storia e Teoria Politica (ITA ISSN 1825-3482) 4162
Storia Illustrata (Bologna) (ITA ISSN 1826-0977) 4162
• Storia in Lombardia (ITA ISSN 1828-2008) 4268
Storia in Rete (ITA ISSN 1826-817X) 4162
Storia, Letteratura e Arte nel Mezzogiorno (ITA) 4268
Storia Militare (ITA ISSN 1122-5289) 6447
Storia Universale dell'Arte (ITA ISSN 1724-1359) 519
• Storia Urbana (ITA ISSN 0391-2248) 4428
Storiadentro (ITA) 4268
• Storica (ITA ISSN 1125-0194) 4268
• Storicamente (ITA ISSN 1825-411X) 4162
Storie al Femminile see Storia e Storie al Femminile 4162
Storie d'Italia (ITA ISSN 1824-6761) 5378
Storie Regionali (ITA ISSN 1970-7851) 5378
Stories & Anecdotes see Jingu Chuanqi 3619
Stories & Anecdotes (Magic Fantasy) see Jinggu Chuanqi (Qihuan) 5444
▼ • Stories for Children Magazine (USA ISSN 1945-8649) 2215
Stories for Children Newsletter for Writers see S F C Newsletter for Writers 2211
Stories from C P C History see Dangshi Tiandi 7128
Stories from the Hills (USA ISSN 0081-5861) 5378
Stories of Relics see Wenwu Chunqiu 423
• Storiografia (ITA ISSN 1128-2339) 4162
• Stork (DNK ISSN 1604-2050) 2915
• Storm Data (USA ISSN 0039-1972) 6395
Stormarnspiegel (DEU) 7683
• Stormtrack (USA) 6395

Title

10906 STORMWATER ULRICH'S PERIODICALS

Stormwater (USA) 3283
Storrs Agricultural Experiment Station. Bulletin (USA ISSN 0097-1251) 158
Storrs Agricultural Experiment Station. Research Report (USA ISSN 0069-8997) 158
Story (CZE ISSN 1211-1848) 8885
Story (HRV ISSN 1333-5863) 2391
Story (HUN ISSN 1419-0354) 8885
Story (NLD ISSN 0165-5078) 3916
Story (ROM ISSN 1583-6525) 8884
Story (SRB) 3945
The Story (Delaware) (USA) 7776
• The Story Bag (USA) 3082
Story Box (FRA ISSN 1366-901X) 2215
Story of China see Zhongguo Gushi 5404
Story Quarterly see StoryQuarterly 5378
Story Rhyme Greeting Letters (USA) 5378
Story Rhyme Newsletter for Schools (USA ISSN 1087-755X) 2215
Story Samphlet of Five Stories (USA) 2215
Story Selection see Gushihui 5303
Story Teller see Gushi Jia 5303
Story Time Stories That Rhyme Newsletter (USA ISSN 1045-5515) 2215
Story Writer see Xiaoshuojia 8999
Storyboard (GUM ISSN 1059-7492) 5435
Storyhead Magazine (USA ISSN 1071-3336) 5240
• StoryQuarterly (USA ISSN 1041-0708) 5378
Storyteller (CAN ISSN 1198-614X) 5378
• Storytelling (USA ISSN 1536-0555) 5378
Storytelling Magazine (USA ISSN 1048-1354) 5378
• ➤ Storytelling, Self, Society (USA ISSN 1550-5340) 5378
• Storyworks (USA ISSN 1068-0292) 3082
▼ • ➤ Storyworlds (USA ISSN 1946-2204) 5378
Stosunki Miedzynarodowe (Warsaw, 1982) (POL ISSN 0209-0961) 7266
• Stosunki Miedzynarodowe (Warsaw, 1999) (POL ISSN 1509-3077) 7266
Stosunki.pl see Stosunki Miedzynarodowe (Warsaw, 1999) 7266
Stout Research Centre for New Zealand Studies. Treaty of Waitangi Research Unit. Occasional Papers Series (NZL ISSN 1177-2077) 7216
Stout Research Centre. Treaty of Waitangi Research Unit. Occasional Papers Series see Stout Research Centre for New Zealand Studies. Treaty of Waitangi Research Unit. Occasional Papers Series 7216
Stoutonia (USA) 2302
Stovall Journal (USA ISSN 0199-3070) 3784
Stowage and Segregation Guide to I M D G Code (DEU ISSN 0934-6260) 8663
• Stp - Digest (DEU ISSN 1439-5967) 8439
Straaleverninfo (NOR ISSN 0806-895X) 7542
• Straalevernrapport/N R P A Report (NOR ISSN 0804-4910) 7543
Straalskyddsnytt see Bq 7423
• ➤ Strabismus (London) (GBR ISSN 0927-3972) 6052
• The Strad (GBR ISSN 0039-2049) 6620
Strada (London) (GBR) 5084
Strada Maestra (ITA) 4162
▼ • The Straddler (USA ISSN 1945-8096) 5240
Le Strade (ITA ISSN 0373-2916) 3283
• Strade Aperte (ITA ISSN 0039-2057) 2946
• Strade & Autostrade (ITA ISSN 1723-2155) 3283
† Lo Stradone (ITA) 8991
Strafblad (NLD ISSN 1567-2581) 4898
StraFo - Strafverteidiger Forum (DEU ISSN 0947-9252) 4898
Strafrecht der Wirtschaft (DEU) 4881
Strafrecht en Strafvordering (NLD ISSN 1574-4051) 4898
Strafrecht in Forschung und Praxis (DEU ISSN 1615-8148) 4789
Strafrecht und Kriminologie (DEU ISSN 0720-6860) 2669
Strafrechtliche Abhandlungen (DEU ISSN 0720-7271) 2669
➤ Der Strafverteidiger (DEU ISSN 0720-1605) 4898
Strafvordering op Straat (NLD ISSN 1872-0951) 4789
Strafwetboek en Wetboek van Strafverordering/Code de Procedure Penale (BEL ISSN 1379-0145) 4898
Strahlenschutz (AUT ISSN 1024-7092) 5718
Strahlenschutz (DEU ISSN 0935-4905) 6687
Strahlenschutz in Forschung und Praxis (DEU ISSN 0081-5888) 6687
Strahlenschutzkommission. Veroeffentlichungen (DEU ISSN 0179-2075) 3174
StrahlenschutzPraxis (DEU ISSN 0947-434X) 6687
Strahlentelex mit Elektrosmog-Report (DEU) 3501
• ➤ Strahlentherapie und Onkologie (DEU ISSN 0179-7158) 6209
Straight 25 (ZAF) 8336
• Straight Furrow (NZL ISSN 0112-6202) 214
Straight Line: The World of Direct Marketing (USA) 1844
Straight No Chaser (GBR ISSN 0958-8124) 6620
Straight Talk (GBR ISSN 0267-3282) 2699
Straight Talk (Jupiter) (USA) 3989
Straight Talk (Pleasantville) (USA ISSN 1062-0095) 2215
Straight Through Processing Magazine see S T P Magazine 1381
Straight Tip see U F R A Straight Tip 3581
▼ • Straight Up (USA ISSN 1942-4523) 610
Straightalk (USA ISSN 1061-2858) 7730
• StraightTalk (USA ISSN 1051-9521) 1519
• Strain (GBR ISSN 0039-2103) 3358
The Strain (USA) 5378
Strait see Haixia 5303
Strait City Daily see Haixia Dushi Bao 3824
Strait Herald Fujian see Haixia Daobao 3824
Strait Journal of Preventive Medicine see Haixia Yufang Yixue Zazhi 5623
Strait Pharmaceutical Journal see Haixia Yaoxue 6845
Strait Talk (CAN ISSN 1482-602X) 3468
• Straits Times (SGP) 3946
Straits Times (Weekly Overseas Edition) (SGP) 3946
Strakhovoe Delo (RUS) 4524
Strakhovoe Revyu (RUS) 4524
Stralsunder Beitraege zur Archaeologie, Geschichte, Kunst und Volkskunde in Vorpommern (DEU ISSN 1611-0447) 4268
Strana Lyubvi. Roman v Fotografiyakh (RUS) 6977
The Strand (CAN ISSN 0710-4537) 2302
† Strand & Berge (DEU) 8991
Strand Magazine (GBR) 5436
The Strand Magazine (Birmingham) (USA ISSN 1523-8709) 5415
Strand Magazine (Myrtle Beach) (USA) 8758
• Strand Three (USA) 8141
• Strandgut (DEU) 6514
• Strandpost (DEU) 3857
Strandsitteren (NOR ISSN 1504-5641) 4268
De Strandvlo (BEL ISSN 0773-3542) 964
Strange Attractor (GBR ISSN 0966-3347) 5448
• Strange Horizons (USA) 5448
• Strange Magazine (USA ISSN 0894-8968) 964
Strange Tales (USA) 5448
Stranger see Lo Straniero 5240
Strangpressen von Metallen see Informationsdienst F I Z Technik. Strangpressen von Metallen 6339
Strani Jezici (HRV ISSN 0351-0840) 5178
Strani Pravni Zivot/Foreign Law Review (SRB ISSN 0039-2138) 4789
Lo Straniero/Etranger/Extranjero/Fremde/Stranger (ITA ISSN 1123-8542) 5240
Stranitsa/A Page (BGR ISSN 1310-9081) 5378
Stranitsy. Bogoslovie, Kul'tura, Obrazovanie/Pages: Theology, Culture, Education (RUS ISSN 1562-1421) 7818
Strapazin (CHE ISSN 1424-2575) 519
Strasbourg In Your Pocket (FRA ISSN 1630-4578) 8758
Strasse und Autobahn (DEU ISSN 0039-2162) 3283
Strasse und Verkehr (CHE ISSN 0039-2189) 3283
Strassen- und Gebietsverzeichnis Hamburg (DEU) 7484
Strassen- und Tiefbau (DEU ISSN 0039-2197) 3283
Strassenatlas Deutschland und Europa (DEU) 8758
Strassenbahn Magazin (DEU ISSN 0340-7071) 8625
Strassenbau A-Z (DEU ISSN 0943-4577) 8635
Strassengueterverkehr (AUT ISSN 0029-9073) 8511
Strassentransport (CHE) 8625
• StrassenverkehrDirekt C D (DEU ISSN 1862-0981) 4789
Strassenverkehrsrecht (DEU ISSN 1613-1096) 4789
• Strassenverkehrsrecht Texte CD (DEU) 4789
Strassenverkehrstechnik (DEU ISSN 0039-2219) 8635
Strassenverkehrsunfaelle in der Schweiz/Accidents de la Circulation Routiere en Suisse (CHE ISSN 0259-5192) 8605
Strassenwaerter (DEU) 8635
De Strata Francigena (ITA) 4162
Strata Management Licensing Course Manual (CAN ISSN 1715-8389) 7613
Strata. Serie 1. Communication (FRA ISSN 0761-2443) 2769
• Strata Titles N S W (AUS) 4789
Strata Titles New South Wales see Strata Titles N S W 4789
Strategi og Ledelse see Computerworld 2414
† Strategia (ITA) 8991
Strategic 100 (NZL ISSN 1177-0104) 1795
Strategic Adult Ministries Journal (USA) 7944
Strategic Ageing (AUS ISSN 1325-4359) 4056
Strategic and Combat Studies Institute Occasional Papers see S C S I Occasional Papers 6444
† • Strategic and Defence Studies Centre. Newsletter (AUS) 8991
• ➤ Strategic and Defence Studies Centre. Working Papers (AUS ISSN 0158-3751) 6447
Strategic Approaches: Renewing the Response see Canada's Report on HIV/AIDS 7511
Strategic Asia (USA ISSN 1933-6462) 1179
• Strategic Audit of Victorian Government Agencies' Environmental Management Systems (AUS ISSN 1832-3294) 3468
• Strategic Balance in the Middle East (CYP) 7266
Strategic Change see Briefings in Entrepreneurial Finance 1729
Strategic Commentary see Start-Up 5717
Strategic Commentary Online see Start-Up 5717
• Strategic Comments (GBR ISSN 1356-7888) 7186
• Strategic Communication Management (GBR ISSN 1363-9064) 1795
Strategic Datalinks (CAN) 7266
• Strategic Direction (GBR ISSN 0258-0543) 1179
• Strategic Display Outlook (USA) 3114
Strategic Employee Publications; Editor'S Workshopnewsletter see Corporate Writer & Editor 2318
▼ • ➤ Strategic Entrepreneurship Journal (GBR ISSN 1932-4391) 1795
Strategic Europe (FRA) 1583
• Strategic Finance (USA ISSN 1524-833X) 1302
• Strategic Financial Planning (USA ISSN 1934-7103) 4112
• Strategic H R Review (Human Resource) (GBR ISSN 1475-4398) 1875
Strategic Health Care Marketing (USA ISSN 0749-5153) 1844
Strategic: Housing, Financial, Community Partners (USA) 1384
Strategic Human Resources (CAN ISSN 1910-4375) 1875
Strategic Human Resources Compensation News see Strategic Human Resources 1875
• Strategic Insights (USA ISSN 1938-1670) 6448
• Strategic Intelligence Review (GBR ISSN 1753-9668) 1519
Strategic Investment (USA ISSN 1543-8848) 1654
• ➤ Strategic Management Journal (GBR ISSN 0143-2095) 1795
• Strategic News Service (USA) 2339
Strategic One Hundred see Strategic 100 1795
• Strategic Organization (GBR ISSN 1476-1270) 1795
▼ • ➤ Strategic Outsourcing (GBR ISSN 1753-8297) 1180
Strategic Partners Report see Genetic Technology News 869
Strategic Perspectives (PAK) 6448
Strategic Plan see United States Mint. Strategic Plan 1187
Strategic Plan see U.S. Federal Trade Commission. Strategic Plan 7473
Strategic Plan see U.S. Department of Justice. Office of the Attorney General. Strategic Plan 2670
• Strategic Planning for Energy and the Environment (USA ISSN 1048-5236) 3148
Strategic Planning for Magazine Executives (USA) 7574
• Strategic R M (Risk Management) (USA ISSN 1551-6881) 4524
• ➤ Strategic Review for Southern Africa/Strategiese Oorsig vir Suider Afrika (ZAF ISSN 1013-1108) 7267
Strategic Sales Management (USA) 1844
• ➤ Strategic Studies (PAK ISSN 1029-0990) 7267
Strategic Study of Shandong Economics see Shandong Jingji Zhanlue Yanjiu 1721
• ➤ Strategic Survey (GBR ISSN 0459-7230) 7267
Strategic Technotes (USA) 1180
Strategic Weapon Systems see Jane's Strategic Weapon Systems 6428
Strategie (CZE ISSN 1210-3756) 1180
Strategie (SVK ISSN 1335-2016) 1180
Strategie (Ottawa) see Strategy (Ottawa) 5718
Strategie de Developpement Durable see Public Works and Government Services Canada. Sustainable Development Strategy 1162
Strategie de Developpement Durable see Public Health Agency of Canada. Sustainable Development Strategy 1902
• Strategie de Developpement Durable d'Environnement Canada (CAN ISSN 1912-080X) 3468
Strategie d'Emploi pour les Jeunes Inuits et des Premieres Nations. Rapport Annuel see First Nations and Inuit Youth Employment Strategy. Annual Report 1682
Strategie Small Caps see Small Caps Profits 1651
Strategie- und Informationsmanagement (DEU ISSN 0934-4179) 1795
Strategie und Technik (DEU ISSN 1860-5311) 6448
Strategies (FRA ISSN 0180-6424) 35
Strategies see M A R Hedge 1638
• ➤ Strategies (Reston) (USA ISSN 0892-4562) 3083
• Strategies (Secaucus) (USA) 3033
Strategies and Tactics in Organic Synthesis (USA ISSN 1874-6004) 2131
• Strategies for Health Care Compliance (USA ISSN 1542-2844) 7543
Strategies for inner and outer beauty see Highlights on Inner/Outer Beauty 589
Strategies for inner/outer beauty see Highlights on Inner/Outer Beauty 589
• Strategies For Nurse Managers (USA ISSN 1535-847X) 5982
Strategies for Policy in Science and Education see Strategii na Obrazovatelnata i Nauchnata Politika 2946
Strategies for Success (USA ISSN 1933-4885) 4789
• Strategies for Success in Dental Practice Management (USA) 5866
• ➤ Strategies in Trauma and Limb Reconstruction (ITA ISSN 1828-8936) 6073
• Strategies Newsletter (FRA) 1844
Strategies with Kids - Information for Parents Newsletter see S K I P Newsletter 2167
Strategiese Oorsig vir Suider Afrika see Strategic Review for Southern Africa 7267
➤ Strategii na Obrazovatelnata i Nauchnata Politika/Strategies for Policy in Science and Education (BGR ISSN 1310-0270) 2946
Strategique (FRA ISSN 0224-0424) 6448
Strategique Logistique (FRA ISSN 1249-2965) 1904
Strategisches Management (DEU ISSN 1617-7762) 1795
Strategist (USA) 8209
• Strategy (CAN ISSN 1187-4309) 1844
Strategy (IND ISSN 0973-2977) 1180
Strategy see Commerce (Winston-Salem) 1400
Strategy (Khartoum) (SDN ISSN 1818-1619) 1605
• Strategy (Ottawa) (CAN ISSN 0847-2181) 5718
• Strategy and Innovation (USA ISSN 1543-7760) 1180
• ➤ Strategy & Leadership (GBR ISSN 1087-8572) 1795
Strategy and Management see Zhanlue yu Guanli 1802
Strategy and Risk Management S + R M (GBR) 1795
Strategy and Tactics (USA ISSN 1040-886X) 6448
Strategy & Tactics Magazine (Special Edition) (USA ISSN 0736-654X) 6448
• Strategy + Business (USA ISSN 1083-706X) 1180
• Strategy for Peace U.S. Foreign Policy Conference. Report (USA ISSN 0748-9641) 7267
Strategy Player (GBR ISSN 1471-6119) 2481
Strategy Plus see Computer Games 2475
Stratford City Gazette (CAN ISSN 1717-0095) 3818
Stratford Festival (CAN ISSN 0085-6770) 8479
Strathclyde Papers on Government and Politics (GBR ISSN 0264-1496) 7470
Strathclyde Papers on Sociology and Social Policy (GBR ISSN 1356-0522) 8141
Strathclyde Regional Council. Annual Report & Financial Statement (GBR ISSN 0266-0172) 7470
Strathclyde Telegraph (GBR ISSN 0039-2243) 2302
• Stratigrafiya, Geologicheskaya Korrelyatsiya (RUS ISSN 0869-592X) 2769
• Stratigraphy (CAN) 2769
• ➤ Stratigraphy (USA ISSN 1547-139X) 2769
• ➤ Stratigraphy and Geological Correlation (RUS ISSN 0869-5938) 2769
Stratiotiki Epitheorisis/Military Revue (GRC) 6448
Stratos (USA ISSN 1539-7777) 8786
Stratton Magazine (USA ISSN 1064-1629) 3989
Stratus (CHE) 6395
Straub Foundation. Proceedings (USA ISSN 1080-5222) 5718
Straubinger Tagblatt (DEU) 3857
Strawberry Handbook see Berry Yearbook and Buyer's Guide 221
Strax (NLD ISSN 1574-261X) 6953
Strays (GBR ISSN 0143-8859) 3784
Straz/Guard (USA ISSN 1075-931X) 3566
Strazak (POL ISSN 0562-1666) 3581
▼ Strazak Sam (POL ISSN 1898-861X) 2215
Strazh Baltiki (RUS) 3941
Stream (GBR ISSN 0307-9074) 8832
Stream of History (USA ISSN 0562-1690) 4314
Streaming Business Magazin (DEU ISSN 1618-2723) 2599
Streaming Media (USA ISSN 1531-7315) 2567
• Streaming Media Advertising Forecast (Year) (USA) 35
Streaming Media Industry Sourcebook (USA) 2352
• Streaming Media Xtra (USA) 2567
• Streamline (CAN ISSN 1705-5989) 3468
Streamline (USA) 458
Streamlined Sales and Use Tax (USA ISSN 1933-5547) 1946
➤ Streams of William James (USA ISSN 1541-4647) 6953
Streatham Mercury (GBR) 3871
Strecha nad Hlavou see Living 4545
Strecker Museum News (USA) 6537
• ➤ Stredoevropske Politicke Studie/Central European Political Studies Review (CZE ISSN 1212-7817) 7186
Stree (IND) 3889
Streek Nuus see Noordwes Noordkaap StreekNuus 3949
De Streekkrant (BEL ISSN 1375-6982) 3801
Street (CZE ISSN 1214-8989) 5084
Street and Smith's Baseball see Street & Smith's Baseball 8247
Street & Smith's Baseball (USA) 8247
Street & Smith's College Basketball (USA ISSN 1522-5836) 8247
Street and Smith's College Basketball see Street & Smith's College Basketball 8247
Street & Smith's College Football (USA) 8247
Street and Smith's College Football see Street & Smith's College Football 8247
Street & Smith's National College Basketball see Street & Smith's College Basketball 8247
Street and Smith's Pro Basketball see Street & Smith's Pro Basketball 8247
Street & Smith's Pro Basketball (USA) 8247
Street and Smith's Pro Football see Street & Smith's Pro Football 8247
Street & Smith's Pro Football (USA ISSN 1053-2641) 8247
• Street & Smith's SportsBusiness Journal (USA ISSN 1098-5972) 8209
Street Artists' Newsletter (USA) 519
Street Beat (USA) 2481
Street Beat Quarterly (USA ISSN 1069-5478) 8073
Street Chopper (USA ISSN 1548-6540) 8268
Street Commodores (AUS ISSN 1329-1475) 8605
Street Commodores Car of the Year (Year) see Street Commodores 8605
Street Customs (USA) 8209
▼ Street Desirez Magazine (USA ISSN 1949-3541) 8209
Street Fords (AUS) 8605
• Street Machine (AUS ISSN 0810-0187) 8511
Street Machine & American Car World see American Car World 8490
▼ Street Monsters (FRA ISSN 1956-3841) 8268
Street Motors (BRA ISSN 1807-5746) 8605

Street n' Strip Performance (USA ISSN 1931-7670) **8605**
Street News (USA) **3989**
Street of Dreams *see* American Dream Homes **975**
• Street Rights N S W (New South Wales) (AUS ISSN 1834-4496) **8073**
Street Rod & Sport Truck (GBR ISSN 0965-7061) **8605**
Street Rod Builder (USA ISSN 1528-4166) **8605**
Street Rodder (USA ISSN 0112-1669) **8209**
Street Rodder Presents: A Guide to Building Street Rods (USA) **8605**
Street Scenes (USA) **3003**
Street Sheet (USA ISSN 1064-4504) **8073**
Street Style *see* Street **5084**
Street Talk (USA) **8073**
Street Thunder (USA ISSN 1557-5640) **8605**
Street Trenz Magazine *see* Streettrenz Magazine **8605**
Street Trucks (USA ISSN 1525-1918) **8605**
Streetfighters (GBR ISSN 0961-9453) **8268**
Streets, Towns and Places Directory (AUS ISSN 1832-0686) **5049**
• Streettrenz Magazine (USA ISSN 1550-462X) **8605**
Streetwear Today (DEU ISSN 1860-9996) **2261**
Streetwise Confidential (GBR ISSN 1748-5177) **1844**
Streetwise Profits *see* Streetwise Confidential **1844**
† Streetwize Communications (AUS) **8991**
Strehlow Research Centre. Occassional Papers (AUS ISSN 1327-9858) **3566**
Streife (DEU ISSN 0585-4202) **2669**
Streiflicht (DEU) **4112**
Streiflichter (Karben) (DEU ISSN 1612-9687) **4268**
Streiflichter (Kraichtal) (DEU) **7683**
Streit (DEU ISSN 0175-4467) **7216**
Strelitzia (ZAF ISSN 1025-322X) **818**
Stremez (MKD ISSN 0039-2294) **5240**
• ➤ Strength and Conditioning Journal (USA ISSN 1524-1602) **6997**
Strength for the Day (USA) **7776**
• Strength, Fracture and Complexity (NLD ISSN 1567-2069) **7063**
• ➤ Strength of Materials (USA ISSN 0039-2316) **3358**
Strengthening Farming (CAN ISSN 1209-8965) **159**
• ➤ Stress (GBR ISSN 1025-3890) **5718**
➤ Stress and Emotion (USA ISSN 1053-2161) **7410**
• Stress and Health (Online) (GBR ISSN 1532-2998) **6187**
• ➤ Stress and Health (Print) (GBR ISSN 1532-3005) **6187**
• Stress Club (USA ISSN 1933-9186) **7410**
Stress in Modern Society (USA ISSN 0884-870X) **8141**
Stress Management for Law Enforcement (USA) **2669**
Stress Research Reports *see* Stressforskningsrapporter **7410**
Stress, Trauma and Crisis *see* Journal of Loss & Trauma **7376**
• Stressed Out Nurses Weekly (USA ISSN 1947-8968) **5982**
• ➤ Stressforskningsrapporter/Stress Research Reports (SWE ISSN 0280-2783) **7410**
Streven (BEL ISSN 0039-2324) **3801**
➤ Striae (SWE ISSN 0345-0074) **2769**
Strick und Haekelmode (DEU) **8885**
Strictly Nothing But (USA) **6620**
Strictly Slots (USA ISSN 1527-5027) **8209**
Stride (IND ISSN 0039-2340) **3889**
Stridsropet (SWE ISSN 0346-1890) **7683**
Strigunok (RUS) **4983**
Strijdkreet (NLD ISSN 0167-1006) **7776**
Striker Magazine (USA) **8247**
Striker West (USA) **8247**
Striking Home (USA ISSN 1093-8923) **2583**
Strilen (NOR) **3925**
Strindbergiana (SWE ISSN 0282-8006) **5378**
String (GBR) **5448**
String Figure Magazine (USA ISSN 1087-1527) **8210**
➤ Stringendo (AUS ISSN 1327-6808) **6620**
Stringer (RUS) **3941**
Stringing (USA ISSN 1932-6386) **540**
• Strings (USA ISSN 0888-3106) **6620**
• Strings and Squares (DNK ISSN 0906-1061) **2688**
† Strip (CZE ISSN 1211-8842) **8991**
STRIP! (DNK ISSN 1398-0742) **519**
The Stripe (USA) **6448**
Stripes Jobs (USA) **1709**
Stritch Medicine (USA) **2302**
• Strive (USA) **8848**
Strive: Action, Sports & Supplements Issue *see* Strive **8848**
➤ Strix/Nihon Yacho no Kai Kenkyu Hokoku (JPN ISSN 0910-6901) **915**
Strix *see* Nya Soendagsnisse Strix **5232**
• Stroemninger (DNK ISSN 1902-777X) **6793**
Stroemungs- und Arbeitsverdraenger Maschinen Forschungsberichte *see* S A M - Forschungsberichte **3357**
Stroemungs- und Kolbenmaschinen *see* Informationsdienst F I Z Technik. Stroemungs- und Kolbenmaschinen **3231**
Stroitel'naya Gazeta (RUS) **1038**
Stroitel'naya Mekhanika i Raschet Sooruzhenii (RUS ISSN 0039-2383) **3358**
Stroitelni Materiali i Silikatna Promishlenost (BGR) **1038**
Stroitel'noe Vedomosti (RUS) **458**
Stroitel'nye i Dorozhnye Mashiny (RUS ISSN 0039-2391) **5460**
Stroitel'nye Materyaly (RUS ISSN 0585-430X) **1038**
Stroitel'stvo (BGR ISSN 0562-1852) **1038**
Stroitel'stvo Gradat/Construction & City (BGR) **4428**
• Stroitel'stvo i Nedvizhimost' (BLR) **1038**
Stroitel'stvo Neftyanykh i Gazovykh Skvazhin na Sushe i na More/Construction of Oil and Gas Wells on Dry Land and Offshore (RUS ISSN 0130-3872) **6793**
➤ Strojarstvo (HRV ISSN 0562-1887) **3396**
Strojarstvo (SVK ISSN 1335-2938) **3220**
➤ Strojnicky Casopis/Mechanical Engineering Magazine (SVK ISSN 0039-2472) **3396**
▼ Strojnik Mechanik (SVK ISSN 1337-6888) **3396**
➤ Strojniski Vestnik/Journal of Mechanical Engineering (SVN ISSN 0039-2480) **3396**
• ➤ Stroke (USA ISSN 0039-2499) **5800**
Stroke (Selected Articles Edition) *see* Stroke **5800**
Stroke and Nervous Diseases *see* Zuzhong yu Shenjing Jibing **6191**
Stroke, Clinical Update (USA ISSN 1049-7463) **5800**
Stroke Club International Bulletin (USA) **5800**
• Stroke Connection Magazine (USA) **5800**
• Stroke News (GBR ISSN 1360-8371) **6116**
Stroke Smart (USA) **5800**
Strokes (USA) **8210**
Strolic Furlan (ITA ISSN 1120-916X) **3622**
Strolling Astronomer *see* Association of Lunar and Planetary Observers. Journal **569**
Strom (CHE ISSN 1421-6698) **3331**
• Strom Magazin (DEU) **3161**
➤ Stromata (ARG ISSN 0049-2353) **6953**
• Strombus (BRA ISSN 0104-7531) **964**
Strommarkt Deutschland (DEU ISSN 1436-3410) **3331**
Strompraxis (DEU ISSN 0340-7519) **3331**
Strong-Motion Earthquake Records in Japan/Kyoshin Kiroku (JPN ISSN 0563-7902) **2790**
Stronger Together (NZL ISSN 1177-2018) **8073**
Stronica Snieznicka (POL ISSN 1509-3360) **5240**
Strooidak (ZAF) **7776**
Strophes (USA) **5436**
• Structural and Demographic Business Statistics (Online) (FRA ISSN 1991-7899) **1268**
• Structural and Demographic Business Statistics (Print)/Statistiques Structurelles et Demographiques des Entreprises (FRA ISSN 1996-2517) **1268**
• ➤ Structural and Multidisciplinary Optimization (DEU ISSN 1615-147X) **3293**
• ➤ Structural Change and Economic Dynamics (NLD ISSN 0954-349X) **1549**
• ➤ Structural Chemistry (USA ISSN 1040-0400) **2081**
• ➤ Structural Concrete (GBR ISSN 1464-4177) **3283**
• Structural Control and Health Monitoring (GBR ISSN 1545-2255) **7041**
• ➤ The Structural Design of Tall and Special Buildings (GBR ISSN 1541-7794) **3284**
• Structural Durability & Health Monitoring (USA ISSN 1930-2983) **3220**
Structural Engineer (GBR ISSN 1466-5123) **3284**
Structural Engineer (USA ISSN 1525-6251) **3284**
• ➤ Structural Engineering and Mechanics (KOR ISSN 1225-4568) **3396**
Structural Engineering Documents (CHE ISSN 0254-6302) **3284**
• Structural Engineering / Earthquake Engineering (JPN ISSN 0289-8063) **3284**
• Structural Engineering International (CHE ISSN 1016-8664) **3284**
Structural Engineering Report (CAN ISSN 0319-0110) **3284**
Structural Engineering Series *see* Kozo Kogaku Shirizu **3277**
Structural Engineers *see* Jiegou Gongchengshi **3274**
Structural Engineers Association of California. Proceedings (USA) **3220**
• Structural Equation Modeling (USA ISSN 1070-5511) **7410**
• ➤ Structural Health Monitoring (GBR ISSN 1475-9217) **8439**
• Structural Integrity & Durability (USA ISSN 1551-3750) **3220**
▼ • Structural Longevity (USA ISSN 1944-611X) **3284**
Structural Mover (USA ISSN 1054-1195) **3284**
• ➤ Structural Safety (NLD ISSN 0167-4730) **3284**
Structural Statistics for Industry and Services *see* Structural and Demographic Business Statistics (Print) **1268**
Structural Statistics for Industry and Services (Online) *see* Structural and Demographic Business Statistics (Online) **1268**
• ➤ Structural Survey (GBR ISSN 0263-080X) **1038**
Structural Technology 1 *see* General Structures **443**
Structural Technology 2 *see* General Structures **443**
• ➤ Structure (USA ISSN 0969-2126) **706**
• ➤ Structure and Bonding (DEU ISSN 0081-5993) **2081**
Structure and Dynamics of Molecular Systems (NLD) **7041**
Structure and Finances of U.S. Farms *see* U.S. Department of Agriculture. Economic Research Service. Structure and Finances of U.S. Farms **207**
• ➤ Structure & Infrastructure Engineering (GBR ISSN 1573-2479) **3220**
Structure des Industries Canadiennes. Tranches de Revenu *see* Canadian Business Patterns. Revenue Ranges **1079**
Structure of the Japanese Auto Parts Industry (JPN) **1519**
Structure of the Japanese Electronics Industry (JPN) **3114**
Structure Painting (JPN ISSN 1346-6364) **3284**
Structure with Folding & Design *see* Structure **706**
Structured Cabling *see* Network Cabling **2386**
Structured Finance International *see* Total Securitization **1386**
▼ The Structured Finance Service Provider Guide (USA ISSN 1939-4276) **2029**
• Structured Products (GBR ISSN 1745-4611) **1654**
Structured Query Language Server Executive *see* S Q L Server Executive **2532**
Structured Query Language Server Magazin *see* S Q L Server Magazin **2509**
Structured Query Language Server Magazine *see* S Q L Server Magazine **2509**
Structured Query Language Server Solutions *see* S Q L Server Solutions **2509**
Structured Query Language Server Update *see* S Q L Server Update **2509**
➤ Structures and Materials (GBR ISSN 1462-6055) **3358**
• Structuring Buy - Sell Agreements (USA) **4881**
• Structuring Foreign Investment in U.S. Real Estate (NLD) **4789**
• The Structurist (CAN ISSN 0081-6027) **519**
Struggle *see* Fendou **7135**
Struggle *see* Fen Tou **5216**
Struggle (USA ISSN 1094-9399) **5240**
Struktur und Wachstum. Reihe Absatzwirtschaft (DEU ISSN 0579-5923) **1844**
Struktur und Wachstum. Reihe Industrie (DEU ISSN 0536-1621) **1519**
• Strukturstatistik (DNK ISSN 1601-717X) **1709**
Struma (BGR) **5378**
Strumenti (Milan) (ITA ISSN 1825-1625) **8141**
Strumenti (Rome) (ITA ISSN 0390-4296) **458**
Strumenti & Musica (ITA ISSN 0039-260X) **6620**
Strumenti Bibliografici (ITA ISSN 1973-0799) **5049**
• Strumenti Critici (ITA ISSN 0039-2618) **5378**
Strumenti di Diritto Comparato (ITA ISSN 1827-6350) **4789**
Strumenti di Lessicografia Letteraria Italiana (ITA ISSN 1122-0708) **5436**
Strumenti di Riferimento *see* Istituto Superiore di Sanita. Notiziario **7527**
Strumenti per il Lavoro Psico - Sociale ed Educativo (ITA ISSN 1827-6369) **2915**
Strumenti per la Formazione (ITA ISSN 1970-5867) **2915**
† Strumenti per le Scienze della Formazione. Teorie dell'Educazione (ITA ISSN 1970-5859) **8991**
• Strut (USA) **8885**
Strutter Magazine (CAN) **6620**
Strzal (POL ISSN 1644-4906) **8210**
Stuart Magazine (USA) **3989**
Stubbs Gazette (Scottish Edition) *see* Stubbs Gazette. Scotland **1795**
• Stubbs Gazette. Northern Ireland (Online) (IRL ISSN 1756-9214) **1795**
Stubbs Gazette. Northern Ireland (Print) *see* Stubbs Gazette. Northern Ireland (Online) **1795**
• Stubbs Gazette. Scotland (IRL ISSN 1756-9222) **1795**
Stubs (Metro NY) (USA ISSN 0081-6051) **8479**
• Stuck In Traffic (USA) **3989**
Stud and Stable (AUS ISSN 0311-8215) **8299**
Stud. Jur (DEU ISSN 0932-5360) **4789**
† • Stud Med (DNK ISSN 0039-2634) **8991**
The Studebaker Family (USA) **3784**
Studencheskii Meridian/Student Meridian (RUS ISSN 0321-3803) **2215**
The Student/L-Istudent (MLT) **2302**
• Student (SRB ISSN 1451-656X) **2302**
Student (ZAF ISSN 0258-9044) **3003**
The Student (Lincoln) (USA ISSN 0039-2677) **7683**
Student Acceleration in Florida Public Education (USA) **3033**
Student Accountant (GBR ISSN 1473-0979) **1302**
Student Action (IND) **2302**
Student Action in Engineering (USA ISSN 0899-5427) **3396**
• The Student Advocate (USA) **3047**
• Student Affairs Journal Online (USA) **2302**
• Student Affairs Today (USA ISSN 1098-5166) **3003**
• The Student Aid Audio Guide (USA) **2915**
• Student Aid News (USA ISSN 0194-2212) **3003**
• Student & Graduate Magazine (GBR ISSN 1745-0934) **3331**
Student & Youth Travel Association's Student & Youth Traveler *see* S Y T A's Student & Youth Traveler **8754**
Student & Youth Traveler *see* S Y T A's Student & Youth Traveler **8754**
Student Assistance Journal (USA ISSN 1042-6388) **2699**
• Student B M J (British Medical Journal) (GBR ISSN 0966-6494) **5718**
➤ Student Bar Review (IND ISSN 0972-6543) **4789**
Student British Medical Journal *see* Student B M J **5718**
Student Career Skills Development Program. Job Catalogue (CAN ISSN 1719-4180) **6704**
Student Choice (ZAF) **3033**
Student Choir Director's Library (RUS) **6620**
Student Collegiate Outlook of U S A Talent *see* S C O U T **8244**
• Student Companion to Classic Writers (USA ISSN 1522-7979) **5378**
Student Direct (GBR) **2302**
• Student Direct (NZL ISSN 1177-9020) **3221**
• Student Discipline Law Bulletin (USA ISSN 1542-4952) **3033**
Student Echo (USA) **2302**
• Student Economic Review (IRL) **1180**
Student Filmmakers (USA) **6514**
Student Financial Aid Handbook. Student Eligibility *see* Federal Student Aid Handbook. Student Eligibility **3022**
Student Financing of Graduate and First-Professional Education *see* U.S. Department of Education. National Center for Education Statistics. Student Financing of Graduate and First-Professional Education **3006**
Student Group Tour Magazine (USA) **8758**
Student Guide (GBR) **3968**
• The Student Guide (USA) **2915**
Student Hack (GBR) **2302**
Student Helpbooks Series (GBR) **2915**
• Student Impact (GBR) **2302**
• ➤ Student Law Review (GBR ISSN 0961-0391) **4790**
• Student Lawyer (Chicago) (USA ISSN 0039-274X) **4790**
• Student Leader (USA ISSN 1070-9657) **2302**
Student Leadership Journal (USA ISSN 1073-8487) **7683**
Student Life *see* S L **2908**
Student Life (St. Louis) (USA ISSN 0039-2758) **2302**
The Student Magazine (GBR ISSN 1471-6291) **2915**
Student Mathematical Library (USA ISSN 1520-9121) **5538**
Student Meridian *see* Studencheskii Meridian **2215**
Student Movement (USA) **2302**
• Student Net (USA) **2302**
Student Pages Ireland (GBR) **3003**
Student Paths (USA) **3083**
• Student Pharmacist (USA ISSN 1559-7210) **6881**
• Student Press Law Center Report (USA ISSN 0160-3825) **4790**
• Student Press Review (USA ISSN 1523-729X) **4584**
• Student Printz (USA) **2302**
Student Pulsen (SWE) **2302**
Student Sports *see* S P A R Q Magazine **8198**
Student Studying Abroad *see* Liuxuesheng **2884**
Student Summer Job Action *see* Summer Work Experience **6704**
The Student Times (GBR) **2302**
Student Times International (PAK ISSN 0039-2790) **2302**
Student Traveller (CAN ISSN 1201-9569) **8758**
Student und Praktikant (DEU ISSN 0721-8672) **6881**
Student Voice (USA ISSN 0039-2804) **2302**
Student Writing Journal (CAN) **5240**
Student Xpress (IRL ISSN 1393-9947) **2915**
Studenten Kurier (DEU ISSN 0931-0444) **2915**
Studenterhaandbogen (DNK ISSN 0108-1020) **3003**
• Studenthandboken (SWE ISSN 1402-6104) **3003**
Studentidrott (SWE ISSN 0283-3883) **8210**
Studentliv (SWE) **2915**
Students' Law Society Students Law Journal *see* U M A Students Law Journal **4799**
Student's Representative Council Bulletin *see* S R C Bulletin **2299**
Students with Disabilities and Special Education (USA ISSN 1076-0911) **3047**
Students World (GHA) **2302**
Studi (e Testi) Italiani (ITA ISSN 1724-3653) **4476**
Studi Africanistici - Serie Ciado - Sudanese (ITA ISSN 1828-5910) **4476**
Studi Arceviesi (ITA) **4268**
Studi Bitontini (ITA ISSN 0392-1727) **4268**
† Studi Bompiani (ITA ISSN 1970-5840) **8991**
Studi Bompiani. Spettacolo e Comunicazione *see* Studi Bompiani **8991**
Studi Bresciani (ITA ISSN 1121-6557) **4268**
Studi Cattolici (ITA ISSN 0039-2901) **7818**
Studi Celtici (ITA ISSN 1828-1540) **4476**
† • Studi Classici e Orientali (ITA ISSN 0081-6124) **8991**
Studi Critici sulle Scienze (ITA) **7920**
• Studi Culturali (ITA ISSN 1824-369X) **4476**
Studi Danteschi (ITA ISSN 0391-7835) **5378**
Studi Danteschi (Ravenna) (ITA) **5378**
Studi di Diritto del Lavoro (ITA ISSN 1970-2507) **1709**
• Studi di Egittologia e di Papirologia (ITA ISSN 1724-6156) **4325**
• Studi di Estetica (ITA ISSN 0585-4733) **6953**
Studi di Filologia Italiana (ITA ISSN 0392-5110) **5178**
• Studi di Filologia Moderna (ITA ISSN 1828-8987) **5178**
• Studi di Glottodidattica (ITA ISSN 1970-1861) **5178**
Studi di Grammatica Italiana (ITA ISSN 0391-4151) **5178**

Title

10908 STUDI DI LESSICOGRAFIA ITALIANA ULRICH'S PERIODICALS

Studi di Lessicografia Italiana (ITA ISSN 0392-5218) **5179**
Studi di Letteratura Francese (ITA ISSN 0585-4768) **5378**
Studi di Letteratura Ispano-Americana (ITA ISSN 1128-2355) **5378**
Studi di Metrica Classica (ITA ISSN 0081-6159) **2240**
Studi di Musica Veneta (ITA ISSN 0394-4417) **6620**
Studi di Musica Veneta. Archivio Alfredo Casella. Studi (ITA) **6620**
Studi di Musica Veneta. Archivio Camillo Togni. Studi (ITA ISSN 1973-8579) **6620**
Studi di Musica Veneta. Archivio Luigi Nono. Studi (ITA ISSN 1973-8560) **6620**
Studi di Musica Veneta. Archivio Nino Rota. Studi (ITA ISSN 1973-8552) **6620**
Studi di Musica Veneta. Quaderni Vivaldiani (ITA) **6620**
Studi di Paletnologia *see* Bullettino di Paletnologia Italiana **331**
Studi di Psicologia dell'Educazione (ITA ISSN 0393-6163) **2915**
Studi di Scienze della Comunicazione *see* Studies in Communication Sciences **8141**
• Studi di Sociologia (ITA ISSN 0039-291X) **8141**
Studi di Storia dell'Arte (ITA ISSN 1123-5683) **519**
† Studi di Storia e Storiografia (ITA ISSN 1824-677X) **8991**
➤ Studi di Teologia (ITA ISSN 1125-7326) **7776**
† • Studi Duemilleschi (ITA ISSN 1593-0750) **8991**
† Studi e Documenti di Architettura (ITA ISSN 0301-6455) **8991**
Studi e Materiali di Archeologia Greca (ITA) **419**
Studi e Materiali di Storia delle Religioni (ITA ISSN 0393-8417) **7683**
• Studi e Problemi di Critica Testuale (ITA ISSN 0049-2361) **5179**
Studi e Ricerche di Geografia (ITA ISSN 1971-4823) **4030**
Studi e Ricerche sui Giacimenti Terziari di Bolca (ITA ISSN 0587-1239) **6731**
Studi e Ricerche sulla Storia, la Cultura e la Letteratura degli Ebrei d'Italia *see* Italia **3541**
Studi e Saggi (ITA ISSN 1972-0084) **5378**
Studi e Saggi Linguistici (ITA ISSN 0085-6827) **5179**
Studi e Testi (ITA ISSN 1828-5856) **4476**
† Studi e Testi dell'Antichita (ITA) **8991**
† Studi e Testi di Letteratura Italiana (ITA) **8991**
† Studi e Testi di Storia e Critica dell'Arte (ITA) **8991**
Studi e Testi per il Corpus dei Papiri Filosofici Greci e Latini *see* Corpus dei Papiri Filosofici Greci e Latini **2233**
Studi e Testi per la Storia della Musica (ITA ISSN 1122-0686) **6620**
Studi e Testi per la Storia della Tolleranza in Europa (ITA) **4268**
Studi e Testi per la Storia Religiosa del Cinquecento (ITA ISSN 1122-0694) **7684**
† Studi Eblaiti (ITA ISSN 0393-0246) **8991**
Studi Economici (ITA ISSN 0039-2928) **1180**
† Studi Economico - Giuridici (ITA ISSN 1971-5692) **8991**
Studi Ecumenici (ITA ISSN 0393-3687) **7684**
Studi Ellenistici (ITA ISSN 1828-5864) **2240**
Studi Emigrazione/Emigration Studies (ITA ISSN 0039-2936) **7294**
Studi Etruschi (ITA ISSN 0075-1472) **4268**
Studi Etruschi (ITA ISSN 0391-7762) **4268**
Studi Europei (ITA ISSN 1123-8623) **6953**
Studi Filosofici (ITA ISSN 1124-1047) **6953**
Studi Francesi (ITA ISSN 0039-2944) **5179**
Studi Germanici (ITA ISSN 0039-2952) **5378**
Studi Giorgioneschi (ITA ISSN 1826-2597) **519**
Studi Goriziani (ITA ISSN 0392-1735) **8007**
Studi Interdisciplinari sulla Famiglia (ITA ISSN 1827-5397) **8141**
• Studi Ispanici (ITA ISSN 0585-492X) **5378**
• Studi Italiani (ITA ISSN 1121-0621) **5378**
Studi Italiani di Filologia Classica (ITA ISSN 0039-2987) **5179**
Studi Italiani di Linguistica Teorica ed Applicata (ITA ISSN 0390-6809) **5179**
Studi Italo - Tedeschi. Villa Vigoni (ITA ISSN 1122-4304) **4268**
• Studi Junghiani (ITA ISSN 1828-5147) **7410**
• Studi Kantiani (ITA ISSN 1123-4938) **6953**
• Studi Latinoamericani/Estudios Latinoamericanos (ITA ISSN 1827-1499) **5179**
• Studi Linguistici Italiani (ITA ISSN 0394-3569) **5179**
• ➤ Studi Lingustici e Filologici Online (ITA ISSN 1724-5230) **5179**
Studi Magrebini. Nuova Serie (ITA) **4178**
• Studi Mariniani (ITA ISSN 1125-0321) **5436**
† Studi Marittimi (ITA ISSN 0392-5021) **8991**
Studi Medievali (ITA ISSN 0391-8467) **4268**
Studi Medievali. Estratti (ITA) **4171**
Studi Mediolatini e Volgari (ITA ISSN 0585-4962) **5179**
Studi Micenei ed Egeo Anatolici (ITA ISSN 1126-6651) **356**
• Studi Musicali (ITA ISSN 0391-7789) **6620**
• Studi Nordici (ITA ISSN 1128-0107) **5379**
• Studi Novecenteschi (ITA ISSN 0303-4615) **5379**
• Studi Organizzativi (ITA ISSN 0391-8769) **1795**
Studi Orientali e Linguistici (ITA ISSN 1720-2353) **5179**
Studi Parlamentari e di Politica Costituzionale (ITA ISSN 0303-9714) **4790**
Studi Parmensi (ITA ISSN 0562-2646) **4790**
Studi per l'Ecologia del Quaternario (ITA ISSN 0392-6788) **356**
Studi Pergolesiani (ITA ISSN 1826-8021) **6620**
Studi Pergolesiani *see* Pergolesi Studies **6605**
• Studi Petrarcheschi (ITA ISSN 1128-2045) **5379**
Studi Piacentini (ITA ISSN 1125-1972) **4268**
Studi Pichiani (ITA) **4268**
➤ Studi Piemontesi (ITA ISSN 0392-7261) **4476**
Studi Pucciniani (ITA ISSN 1724-2401) **6620**
† Studi Ricerche Documentazione (ITA) **8991**
• Studi Rinascimentali (ITA ISSN 1724-6164) **5379**
Studi Romagnoli (ITA ISSN 0081-6205) **4268**
Studi Romagnoli. Estratti di Sezione (ITA ISSN 0081-6213) **4268**
Studi Romagnoli. Quaderni (ITA ISSN 0081-6221) **4268**
• Studi Romani (ITA ISSN 0039-2995) **4162**
Studi Salentini (ITA ISSN 0039-3002) **4268**
• Studi Secenteschi (ITA ISSN 0081-6248) **5379**
Studi Senesi (ITA ISSN 0039-3010) **4790**
Studi Settecenteschi (ITA ISSN 0392-7326) **4162**
• Studi Slavistici (ITA ISSN 1824-761X) **5179**
Studi Storici/Historical Studies (ITA ISSN 0039-3037) **4163**
Studi Storici della Valdinievole (ITA ISSN 1825-2575) **4268**
Studi Storici dell'Ordine dei Servi di Maria *see* Ordine dei Servi di Maria. Studi Storici **7810**
† Studi Storici e Religiosi (ITA ISSN 1122-5564) **8991**
Studi sul Boccaccio (ITA ISSN 0585-4997) **5379**
† Studi sul Fascismo Repubblicano (ITA) **8991**
Studi sul Petrarca (ITA ISSN 1824-6796) **5379**
• Studi sul Settecento e l'Ottocento (ITA ISSN 1828-2156) **4476**
Studi sul Settecento Romano (ITA ISSN 1124-3910) **519**
Studi sulla Cultura dell'Antico (ITA ISSN 1827-7675) **419**
Studi sulla Cultura dell'Italia Meridionale e Italo-Americana *see* Studies in Southern Italian and Italian-American Culture **8142**
Studi sulla Questione Criminale (ITA ISSN 1590-5837) **2669**
Studi sull'Educazione (ITA ISSN 0392-2146) **2915**
Studi sull'Integrazione Europea (ITA ISSN 1970-0903) **7267**
Studi Tanatologici/Etudes Thanatologiques/Thanatological Studies (ITA ISSN 1971-5684) **6954**
Studi Tassiani (ITA ISSN 0081-6256) **5379**
Studi Trentini di Scienze Naturali. Acta Biologica (ITA ISSN 0392-0542) **706**
Studi Trentini di Scienze Naturali. Acta Geologica (ITA ISSN 0392-0534) **2770**
Studi Umanistici Piceni (ITA ISSN 1126-4764) **4476**
Studi Urbinati. Serie A: Diritto (ITA ISSN 0039-307X) **4790**
Studi Urbinati. Serie B: Scienze Umane e Sociali (ITA ISSN 1125-2057) **8007**
• Studi Veneziani (ITA ISSN 0392-0437) **4268**
Studi Verdiani (ITA ISSN 0393-2532) **6620**
Studi Versiliesi (ITA ISSN 1825-2567) **4268**
Studi Vetrallesi (ITA ISSN 1826-4379) **4476**
Studi Vivaldiani (ITA ISSN 1594-0012) **646**
• Studi Zancan (ITA ISSN 1591-2965) **8007**
† ➤ Studia Ad Corpus Hellenisticum Novi Testamenti (NLD ISSN 0169-801X) **8991**
Studia Africana (GHA ISSN 0163-2965) **3566**
Studia Albanica (ALB ISSN 0585-5047) **5179**
Studia Amstelodamensia ad Epigraphicam, Ius Antiquum et Papyrologicam Pertinentia/Studies in Ancient Law and Society (NLD ISSN 1875-5038) **419**
• ➤ Studia Anglica Posnaniensia (POL ISSN 0081-6272) **5179**
Studia Anglistica Upsaliensis (SWE ISSN 0562-2719) **5179**
Studia Anthropologica (BEL) **356**
Studia Anthroponymica Scandinavica (SWE ISSN 0280-8633) **5179**
Studia Archaeologica (ESP ISSN 0210-976X) **419**
Studia Archaeologica (ITA ISSN 0081-6299) **419**
Studia Archaeologica Septentrionalia (FIN ISSN 0786-5066) **419**
Studia Aristotelica (ITA ISSN 0081-6310) **6954**
Studia Arqueologica (ESP) **419**
Studia Augustana (DEU ISSN 0938-9652) **4268**
Studia Austriaca (ITA ISSN 1593-2508) **5179**
Studia Austro-Polonica (POL ISSN 0860-2883) **4163**
Studia Balcanica (BGR) **4269**
Studia Baltica Stockholmiensia (SWE ISSN 0282-5066) **5179**
† ➤ Studia Biblica (NLD ISSN 0169-9954) **8991**
Studia Biblica (Rome) (ITA ISSN 1970-545X) **7684**
➤ Studia Biblica Upsaliensia (SWE ISSN 1101-878X) **7684**
Studia Bibliothecae Wittockianae (NLD ISSN 1570-2189) **7574**
Studia Bobolanum (POL ISSN 1642-5650) **7818**
Studia Botanica (ESP ISSN 0211-9714) **818**
Studia Botanica Hungarica (HUN ISSN 0301-7001) **818**
Studia Byzantina Upsaliensia (SWE ISSN 0283-1244) **4269**
• ➤ Studia Canonica/Canon Law (CAN ISSN 0039-310X) **7818**
Studia Carande (ESP ISSN 1138-6355) **8141**
Studia Cartesiana (NLD ISSN 0921-9919) **6954**
• Studia Celtica (GBR ISSN 0081-6353) **5179**
Studia Celtica Upsaliensia (SWE ISSN 1104-5515) **4269**
† Studia Chemica (ESP ISSN 0370-923X) **8991**
Studia Choreologica (POL ISSN 1508-1354) **2688**
Studia Classica et Neolatina (POL ISSN 1733-4012) **2240**
➤ Studia Comeniana et Historica (CZE ISSN 0323-2220) **4269**
Studia Comitatensia (HUN ISSN 0133-3046) **6537**
Studia Copernicana (POL ISSN 0081-6701) **7920**
➤ Studia Copernicana - Brill Series (NLD ISSN 0925-6806) **582**
➤ Studia Croatica (ARG ISSN 0326-7997) **3566**
Studia Cultorologica *see* Divinatio **4450**
Studia Demograficzne (POL ISSN 0039-3134) **7294**
Studia Demotica (BEL) **2240**
➤ Studia Diplomatica (BEL ISSN 0770-2965) **7267**
➤ Studia Dipterologica (DEU ISSN 0945-3954) **859**
➤ Studia Dipterologica. Supplement (DEU ISSN 1433-4968) **860**
Studia do Dziejow Dawnego Uzbrojenia i Ubioru Wojskowego (POL ISSN 0137-5733) **6448**
Studia Ekonomiczne (POL) **1519**
Studia Ekonomiczne (Bialystok) *see* Optimum **1157**
Studia Ephemeridis Augustinianum (ITA) **7818**
▼ Studia et Documenta (ITA ISSN 1970-4879) **7818**
➤ Studia et Documenta ad Iura Orientis Antiqui Pertinentia (NLD ISSN 0169-8168) **561**
Studia et Documenta Historiae et Iuris (VAT ISSN 1026-9169) **4163**
Studia et Testimonia Antiqua (DEU ISSN 0585-5136) **4476**
Studia Ethnographica Friburgensia (CHE ISSN 1422-4453) **357**
Studia Ethnographica Upsaliensia (SWE ISSN 0491-2705) **357**
Studia Ethnologica Croatica (HRV ISSN 1330-3627) **357**
Studia Ethnologica Upsaliensia (SWE ISSN 0346-900X) **357**
Studia Etymologica Cracoviensia (POL ISSN 1427-8219) **5179**
Studia Fennica. Ethnologica (FIN ISSN 1235-1954) **357**
Studia Fennica. Folkloristica (FIN ISSN 1235-1946) **3622**
Studia Fennica. Historica (FIN ISSN 1458-526X) **4269**
Studia Fennica. Linguistica (FIN ISSN 1235-1938) **5179**
Studia Fennica Stockholmiensia (SWE ISSN 0284-4273) **5179**
• ➤ Studia Forestalia Suecica (SWE ISSN 0039-3150) **3703**
Studia Formosiana (DEU) **561**
Studia Francisci Scholten Memoriae Dicata (NLD ISSN 0081-6396) **419**
Studia Franciszkanskie (POL ISSN 0860-0775) **7818**
Studia Friburgensia (CHE ISSN 1015-3497) **7684**
➤ Studia Geologica Polonica (POL ISSN 0081-6426) **2770**
Studia Geologica Salmanticensia (ESP ISSN 0211-8327) **2770**
Studia Geomorphologica Carpatho-Balcanica (POL ISSN 0081-6434) **2790**
• ➤ Studia Geophysica et Geodaetica (USA ISSN 0039-3169) **2790**
Studia Geotechnica et Mechanica (POL ISSN 0137-6365) **3221**
Studia Germanica Gandensia (BEL ISSN 0081-6442) **5179**
➤ Studia Germanica Gedanensia (POL ISSN 1230-6045) **5379**
Studia Germanica Posnaniensia (POL ISSN 0137-2467) **5379**
Studia Germanica Universitatis Vesprimiensis (AUT ISSN 1417-4340) **5179**
Studia Germanistica Upsaliensia (SWE ISSN 0585-5160) **5379**
Studia Ghisleriana. Serie I. Studi Giuridici (ITA ISSN 1129-714X) **4790**
Studia Graeca et Latina Gothoburgensia (SWE ISSN 0081-6450) **2240**
Studia Graeca et Latina Lundensia (SWE ISSN 1100-7931) **2240**
Studia Graeca Stockholmiensia (SWE ISSN 0585-5187) **5180**
Studia Graeca Upsaliensia (SWE ISSN 0562-2743) **2240**
Studia Grammatica (DEU ISSN 0081-6469) **5180**
Studia Halleriana (CHE) **4269**
➤ Studia Hellenistica (BEL ISSN 0779-3448) **2240**
➤ Studia Hibernica (IRL ISSN 0081-6477) **5180**
Studia Historiae Academiae Scientarium *see* Prace z Archivu Akademie Ved. Rada A, B, C, D **7899**
Studia Historiae Ecclesiasticae (ZAF ISSN 1017-0499) **7684**
Studia Historiae Oeconomicae (POL ISSN 0081-6485) **1549**
Studia Historica *see* Masarykova Univerzita. Filozoficka Fakulta. Sbornik Praci. C: Rada Historicka **4242**
Studia Historica (FIN ISSN 0081-6493) **4269**
Studia Historica (ITA ISSN 0081-6507) **4269**
† Studia Historica et Philologica: Sectio Romanica (ITA ISSN 0391-4143) **8991**
† Studia Historica et Philologica: Sectio Slavica (ITA ISSN 0390-4393) **8991**
† Studia Historica et Philologica: Sectio Slavo-Romanica (ITA ISSN 0391-416X) **8991**
Studia Historica. Historia Antigua (ESP ISSN 0213-2052) **4269**
Studia Historica. Historia Contemporanea (ESP ISSN 0213-2087) **4269**
Studia Historica. Historia Medieval (ESP ISSN 0213-2060) **4269**
Studia Historica. Historia Moderna (ESP ISSN 0213-2079) **4269**
Studia Historica Jyvaskylaensia (FIN ISSN 0081-6523) **4269**
Studia Historica Lundensia (SWE ISSN 1650-755X) **4163**
➤ Studia Historica Septentrionalia (FIN ISSN 0356-8199) **4269**
Studia Historica Slavo-Germanica (POL ISSN 0301-6420) **4269**
Studia Historica Slovaca (SVK ISSN 0585-5225) **4269**
➤ Studia Historica Slovenica (SVN ISSN 1580-8122) **4269**
Studia Historica Upsaliensia (SWE ISSN 0081-6531) **4269**
Studia Historico-Ecclesiastica Upsaliensia (SWE ISSN 0562-2751) **7684**
Studia Historyczne (POL ISSN 0025-1429) **4269**
Studia Humaniora (DEU) **5379**
• ➤ Studia Humaniora Tartuensia (EST ISSN 1406-6203) **4476**
Studia Humanistyczne/Contributions to Humanities (POL ISSN 1732-2189) **4476**
Studia Hungarica Stockholmiensia (SWE ISSN 0585-525X) **5379**
Studia i Materialy do Dziejow Teatru Polskiego (POL ISSN 0208-404X) **8479**
Studia i Materialy do Dziejow Wielkopolski i Pomorza (POL ISSN 0081-654X) **4269**
Studia i Materialy do Dziejow Zup Solnych w Polsce (POL ISSN 0137-530X) **419**
Studia i Materialy do Historii Wojskowosci (POL ISSN 0562-2786) **6448**
Studia i Materialy do Teorii i Historii Architektury i Urbanistyki (POL ISSN 0081-6566) **458**
➤ Studia Imagologica (NLD ISSN 0927-4065) **5379**
➤ Studia in Veteris Testamenti Pseudepigrapha (NLD ISSN 0169-8125) **7684**
Studia Indoeuropaea Upsaliensia (SWE ISSN 0346-6469) **5180**
Studia Informatica (POL ISSN 1642-0489) **2464**
Studia Instituti Anthropos (CHE ISSN 0570-3085) **357**
Studia Interdisciplinaria Aenipontana (AUT ISSN 2070-6405) **5180**
• ➤ Studia Iranica (BEL ISSN 0221-5004) **561**
➤ Studia Iranica. Cahiers (BEL ISSN 0993-8699) **561**
Studia Iranica Upsaliensia (SWE ISSN 1100-326X) **5180**
† Studia Irenica (DEU ISSN 0081-6663) **8991**
• Studia Islamica (FRA ISSN 0585-5292) **7716**
Studia Islandica (ISL ISSN 0258-3828) **5180**
Studia Iuridica Auctoriatate Universitatis Pecs Publicata (HUN ISSN 0324-5934) **4790**
Studia Jezykoznawcze (POL ISSN 0208-8665) **5202**
▼ Studia Judaeoslavica (NLD ISSN 1876-6153) **7730**
➤ Studia Judaica (DEU ISSN 0585-5306) **7730**
• ➤ Studia Judaica (POL ISSN 1506-9729) **4269**
Studia Judaica (ROM ISSN 1221-5163) **7730**
Studia Judaica Cracoviensia (POL) **4269**
Studia Juridica (ITA ISSN 0081-6698) **4790**
Studia Juridica Stockholmiensia (SWE ISSN 0562-2840) **4790**
Studia Kieleckie (POL ISSN 0137-4354) **4269**
Studia Kognitywne/Etudes Cognitives (POL ISSN 1641-9758) **5180**
Studia Latina Stockholmiensia (SWE ISSN 0491-2764) **5180**
Studia Latina Upsaliensia (SWE ISSN 0562-2859) **5180**
➤ Studia Leibnitiana (DEU ISSN 0039-3185) **6954**
Studia Leibnitiana. Sonderhefte (DEU ISSN 0341-0765) **6954**
Studia Leibnitiana. Supplementa (DEU ISSN 0303-5980) **6954**
• ➤ Studia Linguistica (GBR ISSN 0039-3193) **5180**
Studia Linguistica Germanica (DEU ISSN 1861-5651) **5180**
➤ Studia Litteraria (HUN ISSN 0562-2867) **5379**
Studia Litteraria Polono-Slavica (POL ISSN 1231-8922) **5379**
➤ Studia Liturgica (USA ISSN 0039-3207) **7684**
• ➤ Studia Logica (NLD ISSN 0039-3215) **6954**
Studia Lomzynskie (POL ISSN 0860-7249) **4269**
Studia Lulliana (ESP ISSN 1132-130X) **4269**
Studia Marina Sinica *see* Haiyang Kexue Jikan **2805**
Studia Maritima (POL ISSN 0137-3587) **4163**
• ➤ Studia Mathematica (POL ISSN 0039-3223) **5538**
Studia Mediewistyczne (POL ISSN 0039-3231) **6954**
Studia Mediterranea (ITA ISSN 1970-5395) **8007**
Studia Mediterranea. Series Hethaea (ITA ISSN 1970-5441) **8007**
Studia Melitensia (DEU ISSN 0943-7908) **561**
Studia Metodologiczne. Dissertationes Methodologicae (POL ISSN 0039-324X) **6954**
Studia Missionalia (ITA ISSN 0080-3987) **7741**
Studia Monastica (ESP ISSN 0039-3258) **7818**
➤ Studia Moralia (ITA ISSN 0081-6736) **7684**
Studia Multiethnica Upsaliensia (SWE ISSN 0282-6623) **3566**
Studia Musica (FIN ISSN 0788-3757) **6620**

Studia Musicologica *see* Musicologica Brunensia **6594**
● Studia Musicologica (HUN ISSN 1788-6244) **6620**
Studia Musicologica Academiae Scientiarum Hungaricae *see* Studia Musicologica **6620**
● ➤ Studia Musicologica Norvegica (NOR ISSN 0332-5024) **6620**
Studia Musicologica Upsaliensia. Nova Series (SWE ISSN 0081-6744) **6620**
Studia Mystica (USA ISSN 0161-7222) **6954**
● ➤ Studia Mythologica Slavica (SVN ISSN 1408-6271) **3566**
➤ Studia nad Dawnym Wojskiem, Bronia i Barwa (POL ISSN 1231-1707) **4269**
Studia nad Rodzina (POL ISSN 1429-2416) **7818**
Studia nad Sztuka Renesansu i Baroku/Studies in Art of Renaissance and Baroque (POL) **519**
Studia nad Zagadnieniami Gospodarczymi i Spolecznymi Ziem Zachodnich (POL ISSN 0081-6752) **4269**
➤ Studia Naturae. Wydawnictwa Naukowe (POL) **2628**
Studia Naturalia (HUN ISSN 1215-5365) **7920**
● ➤ Studia Neophilologica (NOR ISSN 0039-3274) **5180**
† Studia Oecologica (ESP ISSN 0211-4623) **8991**
Studia Oeconomiae Negotiorum (SWE ISSN 0586-884X) **1549**
Studia Oecumenica (POL ISSN 1643-2762) **7684**
Studia Oecumenica Friburgensia (CHE ISSN 1662-6540) **7818**
➤ Studia Orientalia (FIN ISSN 0039-3282) **561**
● Studia Orientalia Christiana. Collectanea (ISR) **7684**
Studia Orientalia Christiana. Monographiae (ISR) **7684**
➤ Studia Orientalia Lundensia (SWE ISSN 0281-4528) **561**
Studia Orientalia. Supplementa *see* Studia Orientalia **561**
Studia Paedagogica (BEL) **2915**
Studia Paedagogica *see* Masarykova Univerzita. Filozoficka Fakulta. Sbornik Praci. U: Rada Pedagogicka **2885**
Studia Patavina (ITA ISSN 0039-3304) **7684**
➤ Studia Patristica (BEL) **7684**
Studia Pedagogiczne (POL ISSN 0081-6795) **2915**
Studia Philologiae Scandinavicae Upsaliensia (SWE ISSN 0081-6809) **5180**
Studia Philologica Jyvaskylaensia (FIN ISSN 0585-5462) **5180**
Studia Philologica Salmanticensia (ESP ISSN 0210-5438) **5180**
The Studia Philonica Annual (USA ISSN 1052-4533) **7730**
Studia Philosophiae Christianae (POL ISSN 0585-5470) **7818**
Studia Philosophiae Religionis (SWE ISSN 0346-5446) **6954**
Studia Philosophica (CHE ISSN 0081-6825) **6954**
Studia Philosophica *see* Masarykova Univerzita. Filozoficka Fakulta. Sbornik Praci. B: Rada Filozoficka **6933**
● ➤ Studia Philosophica (EST ISSN 1406-0000) **6954**
Studia Philosophica Estonica *see* Studia Philosophica **6954**
Studia Philosophica. Supplementum *see* Studia Philosophica **6954**
Studia Philosophica Upsaliensia (SWE ISSN 0585-5497) **6954**
➤ Studia Phoenicia (BEL) **4325**
Studia Phonetica Posnaniensia (POL ISSN 0860-2085) **5180**
Studia Phonologica/Onsei Kagaku Kenkyu (JPN ISSN 0300-1067) **5180**
Studia Picena (ITA ISSN 0392-1719) **4269**
Studia Plockie (POL) **7819**
Studia Pneumologica et Phthiseologica (CZE ISSN 1213-810X) **6220**
Studia Podlaskie (POL ISSN 0867-1370) **4270**
Studia Poetica (HUN ISSN 0209-9403) **5379**
Studia Pohl (ITA) **561**
Studia Poliana (ESP ISSN 1139-6660) **6954**
Studia Politicae (ARG ISSN 1669-7405) **7267**
Studia Polityczne (POL ISSN 1230-3135) **7186**
Studia Polonijne (POL ISSN 0137-5210) **7294**
Studia Polono-Judaica. Series Bibliographica (POL ISSN 1230-0306) **4171**
Studia Polono-Judaica. Series Fontium (POL ISSN 1233-6777) **4270**
Studia Polono-Judaica. Series Librorum Congressus (POL ISSN 1230-5014) **4171**
Studia Praehistorica (BGR ISSN 0204-9880) **419**
➤ Studia Prawnicze (POL ISSN 0039-3312) **4790**
Studia Prawno-Ekonomiczne (POL ISSN 0081-6841) **4790**
Studia Psychologica (BEL) **7410**
Studia Psychologica (POL ISSN 1642-2473) **7410**
➤ Studia Psychologica (SVK ISSN 0039-3320) **7410**
Studia Psychologica Clinica Upsaliensia (SWE ISSN 1100-3278) **6187**
● Studia Psychologica et Paedagogica. Series Altera (SWE ISSN 0346-5926) **2915**
Studia Psychologica Upsaliensia (SWE ISSN 0586-8858) **7410**
➤ Studia Psychologiczne (POL ISSN 0081-685X) **7410**
Studia Quaternaria (POL ISSN 1641-5558) **2770**

Studia Regionalia *see* Polska Akademia Nauk. Komitet Przestrzennego Zagospodarowania Kraju. Studia **4424**
Studia Regionalia *see* Polska Akademia Nauk. Komitet Przestrzennego Zagospodarowania Kraju. Studia Regionalia **4424**
Studia Regionalne i Lokalne (POL) **1180**
Studia Religiologica *see* Uniwersytet Jagiellonski. Zeszyty Naukowe. Studia Religiologica **7692**
➤ Studia Romanica de Debrecen. Series Linguistica (HUN) **5180**
➤ Studia Romanica de Debrecen. Series Litteraria (HUN) **5379**
Studia Romanica et Anglica Zagrabiensia (HRV ISSN 0039-3339) **5180**
Studia Romanica Posnaniensia (POL ISSN 0137-2475) **5379**
Studia Romanica Upsaliensia (SWE ISSN 0562-3022) **5180**
● ➤ Studia Rosenthaliana (BEL ISSN 1781-7838) **7730**
Studia Rossica (POL ISSN 0239-3506) **5379**
Studia Rossica Posnaniensia (POL ISSN 0081-6884) **5379**
Studia Russica (HUN ISSN 0139-0287) **5379**
● ➤ Studia Scientiarum Mathematicarum Hungarica (HUN ISSN 0081-6906) **5538**
➤ Studia Semiotyczne (POL ISSN 0137-6608) **5180**
Studia Semitica Neerlandica (NLD ISSN 0081-6914) **7776**
Studia Semitica Upsaliensia (SWE ISSN 0585-5535) **5180**
➤ Studia Silensia (ESP ISSN 0210-8739) **7684**
Studia Slaskie/Silesian Studies (POL ISSN 0039-3355) **4476**
● Studia Slavica Academiae Scientiarum Hungaricae (HUN ISSN 0039-3363) **5181**
Studia Slavica Finlandensia (FIN ISSN 0781-3333) **5379**
Studia Slavica Savariensia (HUN ISSN 1216-0016) **5181**
Studia Slavica Upsaliensia (SWE ISSN 0562-3030) **5181**
Studia Slovenica (SVN ISSN 0585-5543) **4270**
➤ Studia Slovenica. Special Series (SVN ISSN 0081-6922) **4270**
Studia Socialia (ITA) **8008**
Studia Societatis Scientiarum Torunensis. Sectio C. Geografia et Geologia (POL ISSN 0082-5549) **4030**
Studia Societatis Scientiarum Torunensis. Sectio G. Physiologia (POL ISSN 0082-5581) **928**
Studia Societatis Scientiarum Torunensis. Sectio H. Medicina (POL ISSN 0860-9594) **5718**
Studia Sociologica (CZE) **8141**
Studia Sociologica Upsaliensia (SWE ISSN 0585-5551) **8141**
Studia Socjologiczne (POL ISSN 0039-3371) **8141**
Studia Spinozana (DEU ISSN 0179-3896) **6954**
Studia Staropolskie (POL ISSN 0081-6949) **5379**
Studia Statistica Upsaliensia (SWE ISSN 1104-1560) **8407**
Studia Sumiro-Hungarica (USA ISSN 0585-5578) **357**
Studia Teologiczne (POL ISSN 0239-801X) **7819**
Studia Teologiczno-Historyczne Slaska Opolskiego (POL ISSN 0137-3420) **7684**
Studia Theodisca (ITA ISSN 1593-2478) **4476**
● ➤ Studia Theologica (GBR ISSN 0039-338X) **7684**
Studia Theologica Holmiensia (SWE ISSN 1401-1557) **7684**
Studia Theologica Lundensia (SWE ISSN 0491-2853) **7684**
Studia Theologica Varsaviensia (POL ISSN 0585-5594) **7819**
Studia Transylvanica (AUT) **4270**
Studia Troica (DEU ISSN 0942-7635) **419**
➤ Studia Turcica Upsaliensia (SWE ISSN 0346-6477) **5181**
Studia Turcologica Cracoviensia/Cracow Turkological Studies (POL ISSN 1425-1973) **561**
Studia Ubezpieczeniowe (POL ISSN 0137-9704) **4524**
▼ ➤ Studia Universitatis "Babes-Bolyai". Bioethica (ROM ISSN 1843-598X) **6954**
➤ Studia Universitatis "Babes-Bolyai". Biologia (ROM ISSN 1221-8103) **706**
➤ Studia Universitatis "Babes-Bolyai". Chemia (ROM ISSN 1224-7154) **2081**
➤ Studia Universitatis "Babes-Bolyai". Dramatica (ROM ISSN 1842-2799) **8479**
➤ Studia Universitatis "Babes-Bolyai". Educatio Artis Gymnasticae (ROM ISSN 1453-4223) **6997**
➤ Studia Universitatis "Babes-Bolyai". Ephemerides (ROM ISSN 1224-872X) **7186**
➤ Studia Universitatis "Babes-Bolyai". Geographia (ROM ISSN 1221-079X) **4030**
● ➤ Studia Universitatis "Babes-Bolyai". Geologia (ROM ISSN 1221-0803) **2770**
➤ Studia Universitatis "Babes-Bolyai". Historia (ROM ISSN 1220-0492) **4163**
● ➤ Studia Universitatis "Babes-Bolyai". Informatica (ROM ISSN 1224-869X) **5049**
➤ Studia Universitatis "Babes-Bolyai". Jurisprudentia (ROM ISSN 1220-045X) **4790**
➤ Studia Universitatis "Babes-Bolyai". Mathematica (ROM ISSN 0252-1938) **5538**
▼ ➤ Studia Universitatis "Babes-Bolyai". Musica (ROM ISSN 1844-4369) **6621**

➤ Studia Universitatis "Babes-Bolyai". Negotia (ROM ISSN 1224-8738) **1180**
➤ Studia Universitatis "Babes-Bolyai". Oeconomica (ROM ISSN 1220-0506) **1180**
Studia Universitatis "Babes-Bolyai". Philologia (ROM ISSN 1220-0484) **5181**
➤ Studia Universitatis "Babes-Bolyai". Philosophia (ROM ISSN 1221-8138) **6954**
➤ Studia Universitatis "Babes-Bolyai". Physica (ROM ISSN 0258-8730) **7041**
➤ Studia Universitatis "Babes-Bolyai". Politica (ROM ISSN 1224-8711) **7186**
➤ Studia Universitatis "Babes-Bolyai". Psychologia - Paedagogia (ROM ISSN 1221-8111) **2915**
➤ Studia Universitatis "Babes-Bolyai". Sociologia (ROM ISSN 1224-8703) **8141**
➤ Studia Universitatis "Babes-Bolyai". Studia Europaea (ROM ISSN 1224-8746) **8008**
➤ Studia Universitatis "Babes-Bolyai". Theologia Catholica (ROM ISSN 1224-8754) **7819**
➤ Studia Universitatis "Babes-Bolyai". Theologia Catholica Latina (ROM ISSN 1582-2524) **7741**
➤ Studia Universitatis "Babes-Bolyai". Theologia Graeco-Catholica Varadiensis (ROM ISSN 1454-8933) **7741**
➤ Studia Universitatis "Babes-Bolyai". Theologia Orthodoxa (ROM ISSN 1224-0869) **7706**
➤ Studia Universitatis "Babes-Bolyai". Theologia Reformata Transylvanica (ROM ISSN 1582-5418) **7684**
Studia Uralica (DEU ISSN 0259-0808) **5181**
Studia Uralica Upsaliensia (SWE ISSN 1101-7430) **5181**
Studia Uralo-Altaica (NLD ISSN 0133-4239) **5181**
Studia Wschodnioslowianskie (POL ISSN 1642-557X) **5181**
➤ Studia z Automatyki i Informatyki (POL) **2464**
Studia z Dziejow Rosji i Europy Srodkowo-Wschodniej (POL ISSN 1230-5057) **4270**
➤ Studia z Filologii Polskiej i Slowianskiej (POL ISSN 0081-7090) **5181**
Studia z Historii Sztuki (POL ISSN 0081-7104) **519**
Studia z Okresu Oswiecenia (POL ISSN 0081-7112) **5379**
Studia z Zakresu Inzynierii (POL ISSN 0137-5393) **3284**
Studia Zamorensia (ESP ISSN 0214-736X) **4163**
➤ Studia Zrodloznawcze (POL ISSN 0081-7147) **4171**
Studie Archeologickeho Ustavu A V C R *see* Ceska Akademie Ved. Archeologicky Ustav. Studie **387**
Studie-Cirkeln *see* Cirkeln **2837**
Studie en Stage in het Buitenland (NLD ISSN 1871-1332) **3003**
Studie en Werk (NLD ISSN 1872-387X) **1709**
Studie o Rukopisech (CZE ISSN 0585-5691) **4270**
▼ Studiebijbel Magazine (NLD ISSN 1876-4096) **7684**
● Studiefinancieringsschijf (NLD ISSN 1570-9205) **3003**
Studiefoerbundet Naeringsliv och Samhaelle Analys & Opinion *see* S N S Analys & Opinion **1169**
● Studiehefte i Landbrukspolitikk (NOR ISSN 1504-3401) **159**
Het Studiehuis *see* Dossier Kennis en Media **8951**
Studiekring Offerhaus *see* Studiekring Prof. Mr. J. Offerhaus **4941**
Studiekring Prof. Mr. J. Offerhaus (NLD ISSN 1572-3968) **4941**
Studien des Bonner Zentrums fuer Religion und Gesellschaft *see* Bonner Zentrum fuer Religion und Gesellschaft. Studien **7628**
Studien und Berichte (DEU ISSN 0076-5627) **2915**
● Studien- und Berufswahl (DEU ISSN 0302-6299) **3003**
Studien und Gutachten aus dem Institut fuer Staatslehre, Staats- und Verwaltungsrecht der Freien Universitaet Berlin *see* Freie Universitaet Berlin. Institut fuer Staatslehre, Staats- und Verwaltungsrecht. Studien und Gutachten **7438**
Studien und Materialen zur Geschichte der Philosophie (DEU ISSN 0585-5802) **6954**
Studien und Materialen zur Musikwissenschaft (DEU ISSN 0941-9403) **6621**
Studien und Mitteilungen zur Geschichte des Benediktinerordens und Seiner Zweige (DEU ISSN 0303-4224) **7819**
Studien und Mitteilungen zur Geschichte des Benediktinerordens und Seiner Zweige. Ergaenzungsband (DEU ISSN 0722-253X) **7819**
Studien und Quellen zur Postgeschichte. Reihe A: Forschungen (DEU ISSN 0720-4183) **2355**
Studien und Quellen zur Postgeschichte. Reihe B: Faksimiledrucke (DEU ISSN 0720-4191) **2355**
Studien und Quellen zur Versgeschichte (DEU ISSN 0585-5810) **5436**
Studien und Texte (DEU ISSN 0938-6432) **4270**
Studien und Texte zum Mittelalter und der Fruehen Neuzeit (DEU ISSN 1617-3953) **4270**
Studien und Texte zur Erforschung der Konservatismus (DEU ISSN 1439-3743) **7186**
➤ Studien und Texte zur Geistesgeschichte des Mittelalters (NLD ISSN 0169-8028) **6954**
Studien und Texte zur Keltologie (DEU ISSN 1431-3049) **5181**
Studien und Texte zur Kirchengeschichte und Geschichte (AUT) **7776**
Studien und Texte zur Sozialgeschichte der Literatur (DEU ISSN 0174-4410) **5380**
● Studien von Zeitfragen (Online Edition) (DEU ISSN 1619-8417) **4163**

Studien zu den Bogazkoey-Texten (DEU ISSN 0585-5853) **5181**
Studien zu den Bogazkoey-Texten. Beihefte (DEU ISSN 0936-0468) **5181**
Studien zu Finanzen, Geld und Kapital (DEU ISSN 0939-5113) **1384**
Studien zu Fundmuenzen der Antike (DEU) **1384**
● Studien zu Gesundheit, Medizin und Gesellschaft (DEU ISSN 1862-7412) **5718**
Studien zu Grund- und Menschenrechten (DEU ISSN 1435-9154) **7216**
Studien zu Policey und Policeywissenschaft (DEU ISSN 1612-7730) **4790**
Studien zu Politik und Verwaltung (AUT) **4790**
Studien zu Religionspaedagogik und Pastoralgeschichte (DEU ISSN 1611-6771) **7819**
Studien zu Sprache und Technik (DEU ISSN 0935-5472) **5181**
Studien zum 18. Jahrhundert (DEU) **6954**
Studien zum Achtzehnten Jahrhundert *see* Studien zum 18. Jahrhundert **6954**
Studien zum Altaegyptischen Totenbuch (DEU) **561**
Studien zum Amerikanischen Dokumentarfilm (DEU) **6514**
Studien zum Bildungswesen Mittel- und Osteuropaeischer Staaten (DEU ISSN 1435-9847) **3033**
Studien zum Familienrecht (DEU ISSN 1613-0995) **4914**
Studien zum Gewerblichen Rechtsschutz und zum Urheberrecht (DEU ISSN 1613-3994) **6758**
Studien zum Internationalen Privat- und Zivilprozessrecht sowie zum U N Kaufrecht (DEU ISSN 1613-0987) **4941**
Studien zum Kleinen Deutschen Sprachatlas (DEU) **5181**
Studien zum Konsumentenverhalten (DEU ISSN 1613-9100) **1904**
Studien zum Neuen Testament und Seiner Umwelt. Serie A (AUT ISSN 1027-3360) **7684**
Studien zum Physiklernen (DEU ISSN 1435-5280) **7041**
Studien zum Planungs- und Verkehrsrecht (DEU ISSN 1860-8876) **8511**
Studien zum Regionalismus in Europa (DEU ISSN 1436-5227) **8008**
Studien zum Sozialrecht (DEU ISSN 1614-6700) **4842**
Studien zum Suedosteuropasprachatlas (DEU) **5181**
Studien zum Verwaltungsrecht (DEU ISSN 1613-1002) **4790**
Studien zum Voelker- und Europarecht (DEU ISSN 1613-0979) **4941**
Studien zum Zivilrecht (DEU ISSN 1613-0952) **4790**
Studien zur Agrar- und Umweltpolitik (DEU ISSN 0945-4675) **159**
Studien zur Allgemeinen und Romanischen Sprachwissenschaft (DEU ISSN 0934-3725) **5181**
➤ Studien zur Altaegyptischen Kultur (DEU ISSN 0340-2215) **2240**
Studien zur Altaegyptischen Kultur. Beihefte (DEU ISSN 0934-7879) **2240**
Studien zur Anglistik und Amerikanistik (DEU ISSN 1610-4978) **5380**
Studien zur Anglistischen Literatur- und Sprachwissenschaft (DEU) **5181**
† Studien zur Antiken Philosophie (NLD ISSN 0921-9129) **8991**
Studien zur Archaeologie in Ostmitteleuropa (DEU ISSN 1617-5549) **419**
Studien zur Aussereuropaeischen Christentumsgeschichte/Studies in the History of Christianity in the Non-Western World (DEU) **7684**
Studien zur Berufspaedagogik (DEU ISSN 1610-6962) **2946**
Studien zur Bibliotheksgeschichte (AUT ISSN 1012-5841) **5049**
Studien zur Christlichen Religions- und Kulturgeschichte (CHE) **7684**
Studien zur Datenbankforschung (DEU ISSN 1435-6279) **2532**
Studien zur Demographie und Bevoelkerungsentwicklung (DEU ISSN 1610-9775) **7294**
➤ Studien zur Deutschen Grammatik (DEU ISSN 0342-359X) **5181**
➤ Studien zur Deutschen Kunstgeschichte (DEU ISSN 0081-7228) **519**
Studien zur Deutschen Literatur (DEU ISSN 0081-7236) **5380**
Studien zur Deutschen Literatur des 19 und 20 Jahrhunderts *see* Studien zur Deutschen und Europaeischen Literatur des 19 und 20 Jahrhunderts **5380**
Studien zur Deutschen Sprache (DEU) **5181**
Studien zur Deutschen und Europaeischen Literatur des 19 und 20 Jahrhunderts (DEU ISSN 0946-9168) **5380**
Studien zur Deutschlandfrage (DEU ISSN 0720-6887) **4270**
➤ Studien zur Deutschsprachigen Gegenwartsliteratur/Studies in Contemporary German Literature (DEU ISSN 0946-7459) **5380**
Studien zur Englischen Literatur- und Kulturwissenschaft/Studies in English Literary and Cultural History (DEU) **5380**
Studien zur Englischen Philologie, Neue Folge (DEU ISSN 0081-7244) **5181**

Title

Studien zur Erwachsenenbildung (DEU ISSN 1435-652X) **2946**
Studien zur Europaeischen Integration (DEU ISSN 1618-2847) **7267**
Studien zur Familienforschung (DEU ISSN 1435-6775) **8141**
Studien zur Filmgeschichte (DEU ISSN 0175-9590) **6514**
Studien zur Fuggergeschichte (DEU ISSN 0340-7195) **4270**
Studien zur Geistesgeschichte (DEU) **8008**
Studien zur Geographischen Entwicklungsforschung (DEU ISSN 1618-3657) **8141**
Studien zur Germanistik (DEU ISSN 1610-8604) **5380**
Studien zur Germanistik, Anglistik und Komparatistik (DEU ISSN 0340-594X) **5380**
Studien zur Germanistik und Anglistik (DEU ISSN 0721-4065) **5380**
Studien zur Gerontologie (DEU ISSN 1435-6813) **4056**
▼ Studien zur Geschichte der Deutschen Forschungsgemeinschaft (DEU) **4270**
Studien zur Geschichte der Katholischen Moraltheologie (DEU ISSN 0081-7295) **7819**
Studien zur Geschichte der Musiktheorie (DEU) **6621**
Studien zur Geschichte der Wissenschaften in Basel. Neue Folge (CHE) **4270**
Studien zur Geschichte des Alltags (DEU ISSN 0944-954X) **4270**
Studien zur Geschichte des Bayerischen Rundfunks (DEU ISSN 1619-120X) **2364**
Studien zur Geschichte des Neunzehnten Jahrhunderts (DEU ISSN 0081-7309) **4163**
Studien zur Geschichte Nordwest-Griechenlands (DEU ISSN 1432-7228) **2240**
Studien zur Geschichte und Kultur Nordwesteuropas (DEU ISSN 1617-3112) **4270**
Studien zur Geschichtsforschung der Neuzeit (DEU ISSN 1435-6627) **4163**
Studien zur Geschichtsforschung des Altertums (DEU ISSN 1435-6600) **4163**
Studien zur Geschichtsforschung des Mittelalters (DEU ISSN 1435-6619) **4163**
Studien zur Gewerbe- und Handelsgeschichte der Vorindustriellen Zeit (DEU ISSN 1615-4282) **4270**
Studien zur Historischen Migrationsforschung (DEU) **7294**
Studien zur Indologie und Iranistik (DEU ISSN 0341-4191) **4189**
Studien zur Interkulturellen Kommunikation *see* Studies in Intercultural Communication **8142**
Studien zur Interkulturellen Mediation (DEU ISSN 1611-5902) **5181**
Studien zur Interkulturellen Philosophie/Etudes de Philosophie Interculturelle/Studies in Intercultural Philosophy (NLD ISSN 0928-141X) **6954**
Studien zur International und Interkulturell Vergleichenden Erziehungswissenschaft (DEU ISSN 1612-2003) **8008**
Studien zur Internationalen Politik (DEU ISSN 1433-8858) **7267**
➤ Studien zur Kinderpsychoanalyse (DEU ISSN 0255-6715) **7410**
Studien zur Kindheits- und Jugendforschung (DEU ISSN 1435-6791) **2168**
Studien zur Kirchengeschichte (DEU ISSN 1611-0277) **7819**
➤ Studien zur Kirchengeschichte Niedersachsens (DEU ISSN 0938-5924) **7684**
Studien zur Koelner Kirchengeschichte (DEU ISSN 0562-3359) **4270**
Studien zur Konflikt- und Friedensforschung (DEU ISSN 1619-5175) **7267**
Studien zur Kredit- und Finanzwirtschaft (DEU ISSN 1861-0951) **1384**
➤ Studien zur Kulturkunde (DEU ISSN 0170-3544) **357**
Studien zur Kulturpolitik (DEU ISSN 1611-700X) **8008**
Studien zur Kunst am Oberrhein (DEU ISSN 1617-3961) **519**
Studien zur Kunstgeschichte (DEU ISSN 0175-9558) **519**
† Studien zur Literatur der Moderne (DEU ISSN 0340-9023) **8991**
Studien zur Literaturwissenschaft (DEU ISSN 1615-7664) **5380**
Studien zur Migrationsforschung (DEU ISSN 1618-6095) **7294**
Studien zur Modernen Geschichte (DEU ISSN 0178-8310) **4163**
Studien zur Musik (DEU ISSN 0172-7904) **6621**
Studien zur Musikgeschichte des Neunzehnten Jahrhunderts (DEU ISSN 0081-7341) **6621**
Studien zur Musikwissenschaft (DEU ISSN 0930-9578) **6621**
Studien zur Musikwissenschaft (Hamburg) (DEU ISSN 1613-1185) **6621**
Studien zur Mustererkennung (DEU) **5181**
Studien zur Oesterreichischen Philosophie (NLD ISSN 0167-4102) **6954**
Studien zur Ostasiatischen Schriftkunst (DEU ISSN 0170-3684) **519**
Studien zur Pastoralliturgie (DEU ISSN 0341-6909) **7819**
Studien zur Phaenomenologie und Praktischen Philosophie (DEU ISSN 1866-4814) **6955**
Studien zur Philosophie des 18. Jahrhunderts (DEU ISSN 0171-7278) **6955**
Studien zur Politischen Wirklichkeit (AUT ISSN 1814-5604) **7186**
Studien zur Praevention in Allergologie, Berufs- und Umweltdermatologie (DEU) **5882**
† ➤ Studien zur Problemgeschichte der Antiken und Mittelalterlichen Philosophie (NLD ISSN 0169-9857) **8991**
Studien zur Psychiatrieforschung (DEU ISSN 1435-6503) **6187**
Studien zur Rechtswissenschaft (DEU ISSN 1435-6821) **4790**
Studien zur Regionalgeschichte (DEU ISSN 1615-0422) **4270**
Studien zur Reiseliteratur- und Imagologieforschung (DEU ISSN 1430-4899) **5380**
Studien zur Romanischen Sprachwissenschaft und Interkulturellen Kommunikation (DEU ISSN 1436-1914) **5181**
Studien zur Romanistik (DEU ISSN 1610-756X) **5181**
Studien zur Schizophrenieforschung (DEU ISSN 1435-6317) **6187**
Studien zur Schulpaedagogik (DEU ISSN 1435-6538) **2915**
Studien zur Slavistik (DEU ISSN 1610-4986) **5181**
Studien zur Stadt- und Verkehrsplanung (DEU ISSN 1437-7845) **4428**
Studien zur Stressforschung (DEU ISSN 1435-6805) **7410**
Studien zur Theologie und Geschichte (DEU) **7819**
Studien zur Theologie und Praxis der Seelsorge (DEU ISSN 0935-5898) **7776**
Studien zur Theologischen Ethik (CHE ISSN 0379-2366) **7684**
Studien zur Theoretischen Linguistik (DEU ISSN 0178-126X) **5181**
Studien zur Traditionellen Musik Japans (DEU) **6621**
➤ Studien zur Translation (DEU ISSN 0948-1494) **5182**
➤ Studien zur Umwelt des Neuen Testaments (DEU) **7684**
Studien zur Umweltpolitik (DEU ISSN 1611-1826) **7186**
Studien zur Umweltpsychologie (DEU ISSN 1861-1494) **7410**
Studien zur Volksliedforschung (DEU ISSN 0930-8636) **3622**
Studien zur Wiener Geschichte. Jahrbuch des Vereins fuer Geschichte der Stadt Wien (AUT) **4270**
Studien zur Wirtschaftsinformatik (DEU ISSN 1435-6295) **1421**
Studien zur Zeitgeschichte (Hamburg) (DEU ISSN 1435-6635) **4163**
➤ Studien zur Zeitgeschichte (Munich) (DEU) **4163**
Studien zur Zeitgeschichte und Sicherheitspolitik/Studies in Contemporary History and Security Policy (CHE ISSN 1422-8327) **7267**
Studienangebote Deutscher Hochschulen (DEU ISSN 1434-727X) **2962**
Studienbibliographien Sprachwissenschaft (DEU ISSN 0938-8648) **5182**
Studienbuecher der Geographie (DEU ISSN 1618-9175) **4030**
Studienbuecher Deutsch als Fremdsprache (DEU ISSN 0171-7596) **5182**
Studienbuecher zur Publizistik- und Kommunikationswissenschaft (AUT ISSN 1814-5655) **8141**
Studienfuehrer *see* Fachhochschule Muenchen. Studienfuehrer **2981**
Studienfuehrer (DEU) **7470**
Studienfuehrer Mathematik (DEU) **5539**
Studienhaus fuer Keltische Sprachen und Kulturen. Schriften (DEU ISSN 1613-9976) **5182**
Studienkreis zur Erforschung und Vermittlung der Geschichte des Deutschen Widerstands 1933-1945. Informationen (DEU ISSN 0938-8672) **4270**
Studienreihe Arbeitsrecht (AUT) **2029**
Studienreihe Arbeitsrechtliche Forschungsergebnisse *see* Arbeitsrechtliche Forschungsergebnisse **1664**
Studienreihe Konfliktforschung (AUT ISSN 1814-568X) **7267**
Studienreihe Wirtschaftsrechtliche Forschungsergebnisse *see* Wirtschaftsrechtliche Forschungsergebnisse **1195**
Studienstiftung. Jahresbericht (DEU) **3047**
Studiepockets Privaatrecht *see* Monografieen Privaatrecht **4736**
Studier av Inter-Religioesa Relationer/Studies on Inter-Religious Relations (SWE ISSN 1650-8718) **7685**
➤ Studier fra Sprog- og Oldtidsforskning (DNK ISSN 0107-9212) **2241**
Studier i Ide- och Laerdomshistoria (SWE ISSN 0348-212X) **2915**
Studier i Kommunikation och Medier (SWE ISSN 1401-9701) **4584**
Studier i Modern Spraakvetenskap/Stockholm Studies in Modern Philology (SWE ISSN 0585-3583) **5182**
Studier i Nordisk Filologi (FIN ISSN 0356-0376) **5182**
Studier in Nordisk (DNK ISSN 1601-4715) **5182**
Studiereeks Burgerlijk Procesrecht (NLD ISSN 1873-0574) **4790**
Studiereeks Burgerlijk Recht (NLD ISSN 1875-0605) **4842**
Studiereeks Nederlands-Antilliaans en Arubaans Recht (NLD ISSN 1568-1076) **4941**
Studieren fuer Europa (DEU) **2962**
Studieren in Goettingen (DEU) **2302**
Studieren in Hessen (DEU ISSN 0179-9355) **2962**
Studieren nach dem Studium (DEU) **3003**
Studierende an den Universitaeren Hochschulen/Etudiants des Hautes Ecoles Suisses (CHE ISSN 1661-3341) **3003**
➤ Studies (IRL ISSN 0039-3495) **7920**
Studies about Languages *see* Kalbu Studijos **5136**
Studies and Documents *see* New Testament Tools, Studies and Documents **7666**
Studies and Facsimiles of Netherlandish Illuminated Manuscripts (NLD) **519**
Studies and Materials on the Settlement of International Disputes (NLD ISSN 1387-2990) **4941**
Studies and Reports in Hydrology Series (FRA ISSN 0081-7449) **2798**
Studies and Research in Geology *see* Studii si Cercetari de Geologie **2770**
Studies and Surveys in Comparative Education (FRA ISSN 0251-5865) **2915**
Studies di Gestalt Therapy (ITA ISSN 1972-4241) **6187**
▼ • ➤ Studies for the Learning Society (LTU ISSN 1736-7085) **2946**
Studies in 19th Century British Literature *see* Studies in Nineteenth-Century British Literature **5436**
Studies in 20th and 21st Century European History (DNK ISSN 1398-1862) **4270**
Studies in 20th and 21st Century Literature *see* Studies in Twentieth and Twenty-First Century Literature **5382**
Studies in 20th Century British Literature *see* Studies in Twentieth-Century British Literature **5382**
Studies in Accounting Research (USA ISSN 0586-5050) **1302**
Studies in Adolescent Development (GBR ISSN 1466-4801) **7410**
Studies in Adult Education (TZA ISSN 0856-0560) **2946**
Studies in Aesthetics (SWE ISSN 1100-035X) **6955**
Studies in African and African-American Culture (USA ISSN 0890-4847) **4178**
Studies in African and Afro-American Culture *see* Studies in African and African-American Culture **4178**
➤ Studies in African Linguistics (USA ISSN 0039-3533) **5182**
Studies in African Literature Series (USA) **5380**
Studies in Afrotropical Zoology (BEL ISSN 1780-1311) **964**
Studies in Agricultural Economics (HUN ISSN 1418-2106) **207**
Studies in Air Power (GBR ISSN 1368-5597) **6448**
Studies in American Culture *see* Studies in Popular Culture **8142**
• ➤ Studies in American Fiction (USA ISSN 0091-8083) **5380**
Studies in American History (USA ISSN 1930-3912) **4163**
• ➤ Studies in American Humor (USA ISSN 0095-280X) **5241**
• ➤ Studies in American Indian Literatures (USA ISSN 0730-3238) **5380**
• ➤ Studies in American Jewish Literature (USA ISSN 0271-9274) **3566**
Studies in American Literary Realism and Naturalism (USA) **5380**
Studies in American Literature and Culture: Literary Criticism in Perspective (USA ISSN 1556-9101) **5380**
• ➤ Studies in American Naturalism (USA ISSN 1931-2555) **5380**
• ➤ Studies in American Political Development (GBR ISSN 0898-588X) **7186**
➤ Studies in American Religion (USA) **7685**
Studies in Anabaptist and Mennonite History (USA ISSN 0081-7538) **7741**
Studies in Ancient Chronology (GBR ISSN 0952-4975) **419**
Studies in Ancient Greek Narrative (NLD ISSN 1574-2687) **5380**
Studies in Ancient Law and Society *see* Studia Amstelodamensia ad Epigraphicam, Ius Antiquum et Papyrologicam Pertinentia **419**
➤ Studies in Ancient Medicine (NLD ISSN 0925-1421) **5718**
Studies in Ancient Oriental Civilization (USA ISSN 0081-7554) **4325**
Studies in Anglesey History (GBR ISSN 0585-6515) **4270**
Studies in Anglo-Saxon History (USA ISSN 0950-3412) **4270**
Studies in Antiquity *see* Antik Tanulmanyok **2230**
Studies in Applied Economics and Rural Institutions (DEU ISSN 0177-0160) **1605**
➤ Studies in Applied Electromagnetics and Mechanics (NLD ISSN 1383-7281) **3331**
Studies in Applied Ethics (NLD) **6955**
Studies in Applied International Economics (SGP) **1384**
Studies in Applied Linguistics and Literary Theory *see* Studies in Toegepaste Linguistiek en Literatuurwetenskap **5183**
• ➤ Studies in Applied Mathematics (Malden) (USA ISSN 0022-2526) **5539**
• ➤ Studies in Applied Mechanics (NLD ISSN 0922-5382) **7063**
Studies in Arabic Language and Literature (DEU ISSN 0939-818X) **5182**
Studies in Arabic Literature *see* Brill Studies in Middle Eastern Literatures **5266**
Studies in Archaeological Science (USA) **419**
➤ Studies in Art and Religious Interpretation (USA) **520**
• ➤ Studies in Art Education (USA ISSN 0039-3541) **520**
Studies in Art History *see* Taidehistoriallisia Tutkimuksia **521**
Studies in Art of Renaissance and Baroque *see* Studia nad Sztuka Renesansu i Baroku **519**
➤ Studies in Asian Art and Archaeology (NLD ISSN 1380-782X) **561**
➤ Studies in Asian Thought and Religion (USA) **7742**
➤ Studies in Astronautics (NLD ISSN 0926-7093) **72**
▼ • Studies in Australasian Cinema (GBR ISSN 1750-3175) **6514**
Studies in Australian Banking & Finance Series. Banking and Financial Institutions Law (AUS) **1384**
Studies in Austrian Literature, Culture and Thought (USA) **5380**
➤ Studies in Avian Biology (USA ISSN 0197-9922) **915**
Studies in Belgian Economic History (BEL) **1549**
➤ Studies in Bible and Early Christianity (USA) **7685**
Studies in Biblical Greek (USA ISSN 0897-7828) **5182**
Studies in Biblical Literature (Atlanta) (USA ISSN 1570-1999) **7685**
Studies in Biblical Literature (New York) (USA ISSN 1089-0645) **7685**
• ➤ Studies in Bibliography (USA ISSN 0081-7600) **636**
Studies in Bibliography and Booklore (USA ISSN 0039-3568) **7699**
➤ Studies in Bilingualism (NLD ISSN 0928-1533) **5182**
Studies in Bioethics and Research Ethics (SWE ISSN 1402-3148) **6955**
Studies in Book and Print Culture (CAN ISSN 1716-0626) **7574**
Studies in British & American Literature/Ei-Beibungaku (JPN ISSN 0286-9853) **5380**
Studies in British Art (USA) **520**
➤ Studies in British History (USA) **4270**
Studies in Browning and His Circle (USA ISSN 0095-4489) **5380**
Studies in Business Administration *see* Kauppatieteiden Osaston Tutkimuksia **1139**
• ➤ Studies in Business and Economics (QAT ISSN 1818-1228) **1180**
➤ Studies in Business and Society (USA ISSN 0081-7635) **1180**
Studies in Business Cycles (USA ISSN 0081-7643) **1549**
Studies in Calligraphy *see* Shufa Yanjiu **8988**
• ➤ Studies in Canadian Literature/Etudes en Litterature Canadienne (CAN ISSN 0380-6995) **5380**
Studies in Central European Histories (NLD ISSN 1547-1217) **4270**
• ➤ Studies in Christian Ethics (GBR ISSN 0953-9468) **7685**
• ➤ Studies in Christian-Jewish Relations (USA ISSN 1930-3777) **7685**
➤ Studies in Christian Mission (NLD ISSN 0924-9389) **7685**
➤ Studies in Church and State (USA) **7685**
Studies in Church History (GBR ISSN 0424-2084) **7685**
Studies in Church History (USA ISSN 1074-6749) **7685**
Studies in Cistercian Art and Architecture (USA ISSN 1555-4058) **520**
Studies in Classical Archaeology *see* Stockholm Studies in Classical Archaeology **2240**
Studies in Classics (USA) **2241**
Studies in Cognitive Systems (NLD ISSN 0924-0780) **7410**
Studies in Communication (SWE ISSN 0280-5634) **2339**
• ➤ Studies in Communication Sciences/Studi di Scienze della Comunicazione (CHE ISSN 1424-4896) **8141**
Studies in Communications (USA ISSN 0275-7982) **2339**
† Studies in Comparative Corporate and Financial Law (NLD ISSN 1566-0435) **8991**
➤ Studies in Comparative Economic Policies (NLD ISSN 0927-5460) **1549**
Studies in Comparative Education (FRA ISSN 1020-7333) **2915**
• ➤ Studies in Comparative International Development (USA ISSN 0039-3606) **8008**
Studies in Comparative Literature (GBR ISSN 1466-8173) **5380**
† ➤ Studies in Comparative Literature (USA ISSN 0081-7775) **8991**
➤ Studies in Comparative Religion (USA) **7685**
Studies in Composition and Rhetoric (USA ISSN 1080-5397) **5381**
• Studies in Computational Intelligence (DEU ISSN 1860-949X) **2456**
• ➤ Studies in Computational Mathematics (NLD ISSN 1570-579X) **5539**

Title

Title

10914 SUBSTANCE ABUSE LIBRARIANS AND INFORMATION SPECIALISTS ULRICH'S PERIODICALS

Substance Abuse Librarians and Information Specialists Directory *see* S A L I S Directory **5044**
Substance Abuse Librarians and Information Specialists News *see* S A L I S News **5044**
▼ • ➤ Substance Abuse: Research and Treatment (NZL ISSN 1178-2218) **2699**
• ➤ Substance Abuse Treatment, Prevention, and Policy (GBR ISSN 1747-597X) **2699**
• ➤ Substance Use and Misuse (USA ISSN 1082-6084) **2699**
Subsurface Sensing Technologies and Applications *see* Sensing and Imaging **4489**
SubTel Forum *see* Submarine Telecoms Forum **2339**
Subterrain (CAN) **5241**
Subterranean Biology (FRA) **706**
Subterranean Sociology Newsletter (USA ISSN 0039-4394) **8142**
• Subtitled (AUT ISSN 1991-9913) **6977**
➤ Subtle Energies and Energy Medicine (USA ISSN 1099-6591) **7042**
Subtropical Plant Science *see* Yaredai Zhiwu Kexue **823**
Subtropical Plant Science (USA) **3751**
Subtropics (USA ISSN 1559-0704) **5383**
• Suburb Magazine (IRL ISSN 1649-0541) **3894**
Suburban (CAN ISSN 0226-9686) **3818**
Suburban Essex Magazine (USA) **4983**
Suburban Family (USA) **3989**
Suburban Focus *see* Chicago Suburban Focus **5068**
Suburban Golf (USA) **8247**
Suburban Lifestyle (USA) **7613**
Suburban Real Estate News (East of Boston) (USA) **7613**
Suburban Real Estate News (Maine) (USA) **7613**
Suburban Real Estate News (North of Boston) (USA) **7613**
Suburban Real Estate News (South of Boston) (USA) **7613**
Suburban Real Estate News (West of Boston) (USA) **7613**
• Suburban Scene (USA ISSN 1941-3904) **5084**
Suburban Voice (USA) **6621**
• Subway (DEU ISSN 1618-6370) **6621**
Succeed Magazine (USA) **2946**
• Succes d'Estime (USA ISSN 1536-5492) **8885**
Succes- en Faalfactoren in het V M B O (NLD ISSN 1874-7310) **2916**
Success *see* Success from Home **1968**
• Success (New York) (USA ISSN 0745-2489) **6704**
Success from Failure (USA) **1654**
Success from Home (USA ISSN 1936-0177) **1968**
Success in Soccer (DEU ISSN 1438-0153) **8247**
Success Magazine Ltd (USA ISSN 1942-0536) **1795**
Success Magazine's Working at Home (USA) **1968**
• Success Online Weekly (USA) **2567**
Success Orientation (USA) **1795**
Successful Attitudes (USA ISSN 0746-9861) **3989**
The Successful California Accountant (USA ISSN 1078-0106) **1302**
Successful Cost Control Strategies for C E Os, Managers, & Administrators (USA ISSN 1533-7170) **1795**
Successful Dealer (USA ISSN 0161-6080) **8675**
The Successful Dilettante (USA ISSN 1935-4886) **6647**
• Successful Farming (USA ISSN 0039-4432) **159**
Successful Fund Raising (USA ISSN 1070-9061) **8073**
▼ • Successful Fund Raising (Schools Edition) (USA ISSN 1944-5938) **8073**
Successful Hunter (USA ISSN 1541-6259) **8336**
• Successful Job Accommodation Strategies (USA ISSN 1082-9210) **1709**
Successful Litigation Techniques (USA) **4791**
Successful Living with Diabetes (USA) **5900**
• Successful Meetings (USA ISSN 0148-4052) **1844**
Successful Officer Call Strategies (USA ISSN 1523-6196) **1385**
Successful Promotions (USA ISSN 1941-7098) **1845**
• The Successful Registrar (USA ISSN 1534-7710) **3003**
Successful Sales & Marketing Strategies *see* Relationship Marketing & Sales Strategies **1839**
• Successful Schmoozing (USA) **1845**
• Successful Searching on DIALOG (USA) **5049**
Successful Student (USA) **2168**
Successful Supervisor *see* Dartnell's Successful Supervisor **1737**
Successful Trade Show Strategies (USA ISSN 1535-4113) **1433**
SuccessGuide Worldwide (Year) (USA) **3566**
• Succession Law and Practice N S W (AUS) **4905**
Successor of China (Overseas Edition) *see* Zhonghua Ernu (Haiwaiban) **648**
Succulenta (NLD ISSN 0039-4467) **3751**
Sucesos (PAN) **2669**
Such & Find Kraftfahrzeug (DEU ISSN 0937-8030) **8605**
• ➤ Suchasni Problemy Toksykolohii/Sovremennye Problemy Toksikologii (UKR ISSN 1609-0446) **6881**
Suchasnist' (UKR ISSN 0585-8364) **5241**
➤ Sucht (DEU ISSN 0939-5911) **2699**
• ➤ Suchtmedizin in Forschung und Praxis (DEU ISSN 1437-5567) **2699**
Suchtreport (DEU ISSN 0930-8350) **2699**
• ➤ Suchttherapie (DEU ISSN 1439-9903) **2699**
La Sucrerie Belge (BEL ISSN 0770-9404) **254**
Sud *see* Autre Sud **5417**
Sud Hebdo (SEN) **3790**
Sud. Il Sole 24 Ore (ITA ISSN 1724-0794) **3899**
Sud in Europa (ITA ISSN 1825-6112) **4941**
• Sud Nord (FRA ISSN 1265-2067) **8008**
• Sud Ouest (FRA) **3842**
Sud-Ouest Europeen (FRA ISSN 1276-4930) **4030**
▼ Sud Provence Cote d'Azur (FRA ISSN 1962-4204) **8758**
Sudan *see* The P R S Group. Country Reports: Sudan **1509**
Sudan Church Review (GBR) **7742**
Sudan Commercial Bank. Report of the Board of Directors (SDN) **1385**
Sudan Cotton Bulletin (SDN ISSN 0562-5033) **8457**
Sudan Cotton Review (SDN ISSN 0562-5068) **255**
Sudan Democratic Gazette (GBR ISSN 1359-9291) **7187**
Sudan. Department of Statistics. Foreign Trade Statistics (SDN ISSN 0585-8488) **1268**
Sudan. Department of Statistics. Internal Trade and Other Statistics (SDN ISSN 0377-0125) **1268**
Sudan. Department of Statistics. National Income Accounts and Supporting Tables (SDN ISSN 0377-1652) **1721**
Sudan. Department of Statistics. Statistical Yearbook (SDN) **8407**
Sudan Development Studies Review (SDN) **1605**
Sudan. Economic and Social Research Council. Occasional Paper (SDN) **8008**
➤ Sudan Engineering Society. Journal (SDN ISSN 0585-8615) **3221**
Sudan Environment (SDN ISSN 1010-1675) **3468**
Sudan Journal of Administration and Development (SDN) **7471**
Sudan Journal of Economic and Social Studies (SDN ISSN 0377-5828) **8008**
Sudan Journal of Food Science and Technology (SDN ISSN 0254-0789) **3664**
Sudan Law Journal and Reports (SDN ISSN 0585-8631) **4791**
Sudan. Ministry of Finance and National Economy. Annual Budget Speech, Proposals for the General Budget and the Development Budget (SDN) **7471**
Sudan. Ministry of Finance and National Economy. Economic and Financial Research Section. Economic Survey (SDN) **1520**
Sudan. Ministry of Finance and National Economy. General Budget: Review, Presentation and Analysis (SDN) **7471**
Sudan. National Centre for Research. Documentation and Information Centre. Library Information Bulletin (SDN) **5049**
Sudan. National Council for Research. Economic and Social Research Council. Bibliographies (SDN) **1269**
Sudan. National Council for Research. Economic and Social Research Council. Bulletin (SDN) **8008**
Sudan. National Council for Research. Economic and Social Research Council. Research Methods (SDN) **8008**
Sudan. National Council for Research. Economic and Social Research Council. Research Report (SDN) **8008**
Sudan. National Council for Research. Science Policy and Annual Report (SDN) **7920**
Sudan News Agency *see* S U N A **3954**
Sudan News Agency. Weekly Review/Wakatlat al-Sudan Lil-Anba. Weekly Review (SDN) **3790**
Sudan Notes and Records (SDN ISSN 0375-2984) **4325**
Sudan Research Information Bulletin (SDN ISSN 0453-8129) **4477**
Sudan Science Abstracts (SDN ISSN 0255-4054) **7939**
Sudan Silva (SDN ISSN 0562-5122) **3703**
Sudan Society/Mujtama (SDN ISSN 0562-5130) **357**
Sudan Studies Association Bulletin (USA ISSN 1941-3629) **4178**
Sudan Studies Series (GBR) **8008**
Sudan Trade Directory (GBR) **1520**
▼ Sudan Working Papers (NOR ISSN 1890-5056) **8142**
Sudan Yearbook of Agricultural Statistics (SDN) **186**
Sudanese Business (SDN) **1433**
Sudanese Journal of Dermatology (SDN ISSN 1815-3941) **5882**
• ➤ Sudanese Journal of Ophthalmology (SDN ISSN 1858-540X) **6052**
Sudanese Journal of Public Health/Al-Majallat al-Sudaniyyat li-l-Sihhat al'ammat (SDN ISSN 1990-7567) **7543**
• ➤ Sudanic Africa (NOR ISSN 0803-0685) **4178**
Sudanic Africa. Texts and Sources (NOR ISSN 0809-2397) **4178**
Sudanow (SDN ISSN 0378-8059) **4325**
Sudarushka (RUS) **8885**
• Sudbury Star (CAN ISSN 0839-2544) **3818**
Sudden Weekly *see* Huran Yizhou **3875**
Sudebna Praktika *see* Vurkhoven Kasatsionen Sud na Republika Bulgaria. Bulletin **4967**
† ➤ Sudebnik (GBR ISSN 1362-3710) **8991**
Sudebno-Meditsinskaya Ekspertiza/Medico-Legal Expert Testimony (RUS ISSN 0039-4521) **5917**
Sudetendeutsche Akademie der Wissenschaften und Kuenste. Schriften (DEU ISSN 1610-4196) **7920**
Sudha (IND) **3889**
Sudhi Sahitya (IND) **7708**
➤ Sudhoffs Archiv (DEU ISSN 0039-4564) **7921**
Sudhoffs Archiv. Beihefte (DEU ISSN 0341-0773) **7921**
▼ Sudinfos Courses (FRA ISSN 1771-2734) **8299**
▼ Sudoeste (CHL ISSN 0718-5154) **1605**
Sudokhodstvo (UKR) **8663**
Sudostroenie/Shipbuilding (RUS ISSN 0039-4580) **8663**
Sudsupda (THA) **2215**
Sudura (ROM ISSN 1453-0384) **6344**
Suecoromana (ITA ISSN 1102-7940) **4271**
• Sued-Afrika (DEU ISSN 1430-4791) **8758**
Sued Magazin (CHE) **3959**
Suedafrikanische Exporteure *see* South African Exporters **1582**
Sueddeutsche Apotheker-Zeitung *see* Deutsche Apotheker Zeitung **6832**
Sueddeutsche Gemeinschaftsverband. Nachrichten (DEU) **2270**
Sueddeutsche Wohnwirtschaft *see* Huas und Grund. Ausgabe Baden **4414**
• Sueddeutsche Zeitung (DEU ISSN 0174-4917) **3857**
Sueddeutsche Zeitung Wissen *see* S Z Wissen **7906**
Sueddeutscher Molkerei- und Kaeserei-Adresskalender (DEU ISSN 0724-3235) **269**
Sueddeutscher Verkehrskurier (DEU) **8625**
Sueddeutsches Baumagazin *see* Baumagazin **980**
Suedkurier (DEU) **3858**
➤ Suedost-Europa (DEU ISSN 0722-480X) **7187**
➤ Suedost-Forschungen (DEU ISSN 0081-9077) **4271**
Suedostasien Aktuell *see* Journal of Current Southeast Asian Affairs **7146**
Der Suedostdeutsche (DEU) **3858**
➤ Suedostdeutsche Historische Kommission. Buchreihe (DEU) **4271**
Suedostdeutsche Vierteljahresblaetter (DEU ISSN 0562-5297) **4271**
Suedostdeutsches Archiv *see* Danubiana Carpathica **4213**
Suedostdeutsches Kulturwerk. Veroeffentlichungen. Reihe A: Kultur und Dichtung (DEU) **4271**
Suedostdeutsches Kulturwerk. Veroeffentlichungen. Reihe B: Wissenschaftliche Arbeiten (DEU) **4271**
Suedostdeutsches Kulturwerk. Veroeffentlichungen. Reihe C: Erinnerungen und Quellen (DEU) **4271**
Suedostdeutsches Kulturwerk. Veroeffentlichungen. Reihe D: Kleine Suedostreihe (DEU) **4271**
Suedostdeutsches Kulturwerk. Veroeffentlichungen. Reihe E: Miscellanea (DEU) **4271**
Suedosteuropa Aktuell (DEU) **4272**
Suedosteuropa Aktuell *see* Dow Jones Suedosteuropa Aktuell **1477**
Suedosteuropa - Bibliographie (DEU ISSN 0081-9131) **636**
Suedosteuropa Brief (DEU) **1520**
Suedosteuropa - Jahrbuch (DEU ISSN 0081-914X) **4272**
Suedosteuropa - Mitteilungen (DEU ISSN 0340-174X) **4272**
Suedosteuropa - Schriften (DEU ISSN 0081-9158) **4272**
Suedosteuropa - Studien (DEU ISSN 0081-9166) **4272**
➤ Suedosteuropaeische Arbeiten (DEU ISSN 0933-6850) **4272**
Suedthueringer Zeitung (DEU) **3858**
Suedthueringische Wirtschaft (DEU) **1410**
Suedtiroler Landwirt (ITA ISSN 1120-5857) **159**
Suedwest Presse (DEU) **3858**
Suedwestdeutsche Schuetzenzeitung (DEU) **8210**
Suedwestdeutscher Einzelhandel (Freiburg) (DEU) **2364**
Suedwestdeutscher Einzelhandel (Stuttgart) (DEU) **7942**
Suedwestfaelische Wirtschaft (DEU ISSN 0039-4637) **1410**
Suedwestfunk Journal (DEU) **2364**
SuedZeit (DEU ISSN 1438-2814) **1605**
Der Suelchgau (DEU ISSN 0940-4325) **4272**
Suelo Pelvico (ESP ISSN 1885-0642) **6005**
Suelos Ecuatoriales (COL ISSN 0562-5351) **2717**
Suessetania (ESP ISSN 1130-7722) **5184**
Suesswaren (DEU ISSN 0721-0825) **3675**
Suesswarenproduktion (DEU) **3676**
Suesswarentaschenbuch (DEU ISSN 0721-9504) **3676**
• Sueste (MEX) **3911**
Suevica (DEU ISSN 0941-0988) **5383**
Suez Canal University Medical Journal (EGY ISSN 1110-6999) **5718**
Suez Canal Veterinary Medicine Journal/Magallat Tibb Bitari Qanat al-Suwis (EGY ISSN 1110-6298) **8807**
• Suffering (USA ISSN 1557-9751) **7686**
• The Suffering Child (ITA ISSN 1721-5471) **6104**
Suffolk Academy of Law. Journal (USA ISSN 0888-2142) **4791**
Suffolk Alumni Magazine (USA ISSN 1556-8970) **2916**
Suffolk & Norfolk Life (GBR ISSN 1359-2408) **3871**
Suffolk Birds (GBR ISSN 0264-5793) **915**
• Suffolk Business Directory (GBR) **2029**
Suffolk County Agricultural News (USA ISSN 0039-467X) **159**
Suffolk County Archaeological Association. Newsletter (USA ISSN 1079-2198) **419**
Suffolk Dental Bulletin *see* Suffolk Dentistry **5866**
Suffolk Dentistry (USA) **5866**
Suffolk Farmer (GBR ISSN 0955-0275) **159**
Suffolk Institute of Archaeology and History. Newsletter (GBR ISSN 0143-4896) **419**
➤ Suffolk Institute of Archaeology and History. Proceedings (GBR ISSN 0262-6004) **419**
The Suffolk Journal *see* Suffolk Journal **4983**
• Suffolk Journal (GBR ISSN 1751-3294) **4983**
Suffolk Journal & East Anglian Life *see* Suffolk Journal **4983**
Suffolk Journal of Trial & Appellate Advocacy (USA ISSN 1535-3419) **4791**
Suffolk Jumbo Free Ads (GBR ISSN 1744-3415) **3968**
Suffolk Natural History (GBR ISSN 0144-2244) **964**
Suffolk Norfolk Life *see* Suffolk & Norfolk Life **3871**
Suffolk Scene (GBR) **159**
Suffolk Sheep Society Flock Book (GBR) **301**
Suffolk Stud Book (GBR) **8299**
• ➤ Suffolk Transnational Law Review (USA ISSN 1072-8546) **4941**
• ➤ Suffolk University Law Review (USA ISSN 0039-4696) **4791**
Sufi (GBR ISSN 0955-7385) **7716**
➤ Sufism (USA ISSN 1534-2379) **7410**
Sufu (TWN) **5049**
Sugaku/Mathematics (JPN ISSN 0039-470X) **5539**
Sugaku Expositions (USA ISSN 0898-9583) **5539**
Sugaku Kyoiku Gakujutsu Zasshi *see* Hiroshima Journal of Mathematics Education **5491**
Sugaku Semina/Sugaku Seminar (JPN ISSN 0386-4960) **5539**
Sugaku Seminar *see* Sugaku Semina **5539**
Sugakushi Kenkyu/Journal of the History of Mathematics, Japan (JPN ISSN 0386-9555) **5539**
Suganitam (IND ISSN 0971-6475) **5539**
† Sugar (DEU ISSN 1860-0042) **8991**
Sugar (GBR ISSN 1355-9672) **2215**
Sugar and Spice (GBR) **4085**
▼ • Sugar & Spice Magazine (USA ISSN 1946-536X) **8885**
Sugar & Sweetener *see* Situation & Outlook Report. Sugar & Sweetener **206**
Sugar Bulletin (USA ISSN 0039-4726) **3664**
Sugar Cane International (GBR ISSN 1468-6031) **159**
Sugar Crops of China *see* Zhongguo Tangliao **173**
Sugar Economy *see* Zuckerwirtschaft Europa **3668**
Sugar, Food Product, Vegetable Oils, Wheat Product, Fats, Soaps (IND) **3664**
Sugar in Parliament (IND) **255**
• Sugar Industry Abstracts (GBR ISSN 0957-5022) **3670**
Sugar Industry Journal Buyer's Guide (GBR) **3665**
Sugar Journal (USA ISSN 0039-4734) **3665**
Sugar Kids (NLD ISSN 1574-7115) **5900**
Sugar Milling Research Institute. Annual Report (ZAF) **3665**
Sugar Needle (USA) **3676**
Sugar Processing Research Conference. Proceedings (USA ISSN 0730-6490) **159**
Sugar Producer (USA ISSN 0199-8498) **159**
• ➤ Sugar Series (NLD ISSN 0167-7675) **3665**
• ➤ Sugar Tech (IND ISSN 0972-1525) **3665**
Sugarbeet Grower (USA ISSN 0039-4750) **255**
Sugarcane Farmers' Bulletin (PHL ISSN 0039-4769) **159**
Suge no Kai Kaiho/Japanese Cyperaceae Newsletter (JPN ISSN 0917-1347) **819**
Sugei Pazuru (JPN) **5539**
Suggested References for Dam Safety Programs (USA) **3284**
Suggested State Legislation (USA ISSN 0070-1157) **4852**
Suggestion (USA) **7411**
† Suggestions Shoe Models for Man (ITA) **8991**
† Suggestions Shoe Models for Woman (ITA) **8991**
Suggestopaedisk Forening. Nyhedsbrev (DNK ISSN 1903-475X) **2916**
Sughrona Bemata (GRC ISSN 1105-3208) **7819**
Sugino News *see* Sugino Nyusu **5460**
Sugino Nyusu/Sugino News (JPN) **5460**
Suhaag (CAN) **5561**
Suhag Gyoyug/Mathematical Education (KOR ISSN 1225-1380) **5539**
Suhag Gyoyug Nonchong - Han'gug Suhag Gyoyug Haghoe/Studies in Mathematical Education (KOR ISSN 1229-1021) **2916**
Suhag Gyo'yug Nonmunjib/Communication of Mathematical Education (KOR ISSN 1226-6663) **2916**
• Suhag Gyo'yug Yeon'gu/Research in Mathematical Education (KOR ISSN 1226-6191) **2916**
Suhaj Medical Journal *see* Sohag Medical Journal **5716**
Suhak Kwa Mulli (PRK ISSN 0371-0688) **7042**
Suhayl (ESP ISSN 1576-9372) **7921**
Sui Yuan Wen Hsien (TWN ISSN 1017-2297) **3566**
Suibi/Random Notes (CHN ISSN 1000-7903) **5383**
Suicidal Behavior: A Survey of Oregon High School Students, (Year) (USA ISSN 1520-5681) **8142**
• ➤ Suicide and Life-Threatening Behavior (USA ISSN 0363-0234) **7411**
Suicide Prevention Information New Zealand News *see* S P I N Z News **7540**
• ➤ Suicidologi (NOR ISSN 1501-6994) **6187**
Suid-Afrika. Statistieke. Jaarverslag *see* South Africa. Statistics South Africa. Annual Report (Online Edition) **8400**
Suid-Afrika. Weerburo. Daaglikse Weerbulletin *see* South Africa. Weather Bureau. Daily Weather Bulletin **6395**
Suid-Afrika. Weerburo. Jaarlikse Weerverslag *see* South Africa. Weather Bureau. Yearly Weather Report **6395**

DIRECTORY 2010 SUMMERTIME FLOODLIGHT 10915

Suid-Afrika. Weerburo. Klimaatopsomming van Suidelike Afrika see South African Weather Service. Climate Summary of South Africa **6395**
Suid-Afrika. Weerburo. Tegniese Verhandeling see South Africa. Weather Bureau. Technical Paper **6395**
Suid-Afrikaanse Akademie vir Wetenskap en Kuns. Nuusbrief (ZAF ISSN 0039-4807) **7921**
• ➤ Suid-Afrikaanse Argiefblad/South African Archives Journal (ZAF ISSN 1012-2796) **5049**
Suid-Afrikaanse Buitelandse Handelsorganisasie Jaarverslag see S A F T O Annual Report **1582**
Suid-Afrikaanse Historiese Joernaal see South African Historical Journal **4178**
Suid-Afrikaanse Hofverslae see The South African Law Reports **4785**
Suid - Afrikaanse Instituut Reeks see S A I Reeks **4177**
Suid-Afrikaanse Instituut van Siviele Ingenieurs. Joernaal see South African Institution of Civil Engineering. Journal **3283**
Suid-Afrikaanse Instituut vir Sweiwese. Nasionale Register see South African Institute of Welding. National Register **2028**
Suid-Afrikaanse Jaarboek vir Volkereg see South African Yearbook of International Law **4941**
Suid-Afrikaanse Joernaal van Wetenskap see South African Journal of Science **7919**
Suid-Afrikaanse Joernaal vir Chirurgie see South African Journal of Surgery **6259**
Suid-Afrikaanse Kerkorrelistevereniging. Jaarblad see Vir die Musiekleier **6627**
Suid-Afrikaanse Kultuurhistoriese Museum. Annale/South African Cultural History Museum. Annals (ZAF ISSN 1010-9226) **4178**
Suid-Afrikaanse Museum. Annale see African Natural History **651**
Suid-Afrikaanse Musiekonderwyser see South African Music Teacher **6618**
Suid-Afrikaanse Oogkundige see South African Optometrist **6052**
Suid Afrikaanse Rekenaartydskrif see South African Computer Journal **2438**
Suid-Afrikaanse Reserwebank. Jaarlikse Ekonomiese Verslag see South African Reserve Bank. Annual Economic Report **1518**
Suid-Afrikaanse Reserwebank. Kwartaalblad see South African Reserve Bank. Quarterly Bulletin **1383**
Suid-Afrikaanse Reserwebank. Maandelikse Vrystelling van Uitgesoekte Gegewens see South African Reserve Bank. Monthly Release of Selected Data **1266**
Suid-Afrikaanse Reserwebank. Verslag van die Gewone Algemene Vergadering van Aandeelhouers see South African Reserve Bank. Report of the Ordinary General Meeting of Shareholders **1383**
Suid-Afrikaanse Statistiese Tydskrif see South African Statistical Journal **8402**
Suid-Afrikaanse Strafregverslae see The South African Criminal Law Reports **4898**
Suid-Afrikaanse Tijdskrif vir Landbouvoorligting see South African Journal of Agricultural Extension **157**
Suid-Afrikaanse Tipografiese Joernaal see South African Typographical Journal **4602**
Suid-Afrikaanse Tydskrif vir Apteekwese see South African Pharmaceutical Journal **6881**
Suid-Afrikaanse Tydskrif vir Bedryfsleiding see South African Journal of Business Management **1794**
Suid-Afrikaanse Tydskrif vir Chemie see South African Journal of Chemistry **2081**
Suid-Afrikaanse Tydskrif vir Ekonomie see South African Journal of Economics **1177**
Suid-Afrikaanse Tydskrif vir Etnologie see Anthropology Southern Africa **327**
Suid-Afrikaanse Tydskrif vir Handelsreg see South African Mercantile Law Journal **4785**
Suid-Afrikaanse Tydskrif vir Musiekwetenskap see South African Journal of Musicology **6618**
Suid-Afrikaanse Tydskrif vir Natuurnavorsing see South African Journal of Wildlife Research **2627**
Suid Afrikaanse Tydskrif vir Natuurwetenskap en Tegnologie (ZAF ISSN 0254-3486) **7921**
• ➤ Suid-Afrikaanse Tydskrif vir Navorsing in Sport, Liggaamlike Opvoedkunde en Ontspanning/South African Journal for Research in Sport, Physical Education and Recreation (ZAF ISSN 0379-9069) **6997**
Suid-Afrikaanse Tydskrif vir Opvoedkunde see South African Journal of Education **2914**
Suid-Afrikaanse Tydskrif vir Seewetenskap see African Journal of Marine Science **3583**
Suid-Afrikaanse Tydskrif vir Sielkunde see South African Journal of Psychology **7409**
Suid-Afrikaanse Tydskrif vir Strafregspleging see South African Journal of Criminal Justice **4898**
Suid-Afrikaanse Tydskrif vir Veekunde see South African Journal of Animal Science **301**
Suid-Afrikaanse Tydskrif vir Wetenskap see South African Journal of Science **7919**
Suid-Afrikaanse Vereniging vir Landbouvoorligting. Konferensiehandelinge see South African Society for Agricultural Extension. Conference Proceedings **157**
Suid-Afrikaanse Wette see Jutastat's South African Statutes **4708**
Suido Jigyo Nenpo/Annual Statistics of Water Works (JPN) **8843**
Suido Kyokai Zasshi/Journal of Water Works Association (JPN ISSN 0371-0785) **8832**
Suido no Chi/Japanese Society of Irrigation, Drainage and Rural Engineering. Journal (JPN ISSN 1882-2770) **159**
Suijun Kihyo Sokuryo Seikahyo/Reports on the Survey of Level Reference Points (JPN) **2721**
Suikogaku ni Kansuru Kaki Kenshukai Kogishu/Summer Seminar on Hydraulic Engineering. Lecture Notes (JPN) **3364**
Suikogaku Ronbunshu/Proceedings of Hydraulics Engineering (JPN ISSN 0916-7374) **3364**
Suimon Mizu Shigen Gakkai Nyusu/Japan Society of Hydrology and Water Resources News (JPN) **2798**
• Suimon Mizu Shigen Gakkaishi/Japan Society of Hydrology and Water Resources. Journal (JPN ISSN 0915-1389) **2798**
Suimon Tekkan/Hydraulic Gate and Penstock (JPN ISSN 0562-5548) **3364**
Suinocultura Industrial (BRA ISSN 0100-9125) **301**
Suiri Jikken Senta Hokoku/Environmental Research Center. Bulletin (JPN ISSN 0385-907X) **3468**
Suiri Kagaku/Water Science (JPN ISSN 0039-4858) **8832**
Suiri Kenkyushitsu Ronbunshu/Hydraulic Reports (JPN) **3364**
Suiriho (JPN ISSN 0914-4218) **159**
Suiro Tsuho see Japan. Maritime Safety Agency. Hydrographic Department. Notices to Mariners **8648**
Suirobu Giho/Technical Bulletin on Hydrography (JPN ISSN 0288-5301) **2798**
Suis (ESP ISSN 1699-7867) **8807**
Suisan Daigakko Kenkyu Hokoku/National Fisheries University. Journal (JPN ISSN 0370-9361) **3609**
Suisan Kai/Fisheries World (JPN ISSN 0039-4866) **3609**
Suisan Kaiyo Kenkyu/Japanese Society of Fisheries Oceanography. Bulletin (JPN ISSN 0916-1562) **3609**
Suisan Kogaku/Fisheries Engineering (JPN ISSN 0916-7617) **3609**
Suisan Kogaku Kenkyujo Giho/National Research Institute of Fisheries Engineering. Technical Report (JPN ISSN 1341-8750) **3609**
Suisan Kogaku Kenkyujo Kenkyu Hokoku/National Research Institute of Fisheries Engineering. Bulletin (JPN ISSN 0388-9718) **3609**
Suisan Sougou Kenkyuu Senta Kenkyuu Houkoku/Fisheries Research Agency. Bulletin (JPN ISSN 1346-9894) **3609**
Suisanzoshoku/Aquaculture (JPN ISSN 0371-4217) **3609**
Suiso Energi Sisutemu/Hydrogen Energy Systems Society of Japan. Journal (JPN ISSN 1341-6995) **3148**
Suisse Magazine (FRA ISSN 1768-1367) **5084**
• Suitcase (USA ISSN 1085-2484) **5241**
• Suite (ITA) **4399**
Suite see Prince George's Suite **5080**
• Suite Benessere (ITA ISSN 1722-6147) **5084**
Suites (CAN) **2302**
Suizhi Jiaoyu (Xiaoxue Ban)/Quality Education (Primary School Edition) (CHN ISSN 1009-7597) **2916**
Suizhi Jiaoyu (Zhongxue Ban)/Quality Education (Middle School Edition) (CHN) **2916**
➤ Suizidprophylaxe (DEU ISSN 0173-458X) **6187**
Suizo/Japan Pancreas Society. Journal (JPN ISSN 0913-0071) **5949**
Suizo Carne y Leche (MEX ISSN 1025-2568) **301**
Sujaneshu (BGD) **5383**
Al Sukaria (SDN) **3665**
Sukeltajan Maailma (FIN ISSN 1238-2574) **8210**
Sukh Datta (IND ISSN 0039-4882) **6998**
Sukiya Living (USA ISSN 1942-4094) **3751**
Sukizofurenia Furontia see Schizophrenia Frontier **6184**
➤ Al-Sukkaryoun/The Diabetics (SAU ISSN 1319-7266) **5900**
Sukoyaka Kenpo (JPN) **4524**
Suksa May (LAO) **3033**
Suktara (IND) **2215**
Sukutieto (FIN ISSN 0788-1673) **3784**
Sukuviesti (FIN ISSN 0357-9492) **4272**
• Sul Ponticello (ESP ISSN 1697-6886) **6621**
Sulco (USA) **159**
• ➤ Suleyman Demirel Universitesi Ilahiyat Fakultesi Dergisi/University of Suleyman Demirel. Faculty of Divinity. Review (TUR ISSN 1300-9672) **7686**
➤ Sulfur (USA ISSN 0730-305X) **5383**
• Suliao/Plastics (CHN ISSN 1001-9456) **7100**
• Suliao Keji/Plastics Science and Technology (CHN ISSN 1005-3360) **7100**
• Suliao Zhuji/Plastic Additives (CHN ISSN 1672-6294) **7100**
Sulinet Magazine (HUN ISSN 1418-5288) **3877**
▼ Sulla Via del Catai (ITA ISSN 1970-3449) **4189**
Sullivan County Historical Society, Inc (USA ISSN 1935-3715) **3784**
Sullivan County Travel Guide (USA) **8758**
Sulloge Nomologias. Upallelikes Upothedeis see European Court Reports. Reports of European Community Staff Cases **4669**
Sulloge tes Nomologias tou Dikasteriou Kai Tou Protodikeiou see Raccolta della Giurisprudenza della Corte e del Tribunale di Primo Grado. Parte 2. Tribunale di Primo Grado **4938**
Sulloge tes Nomologias tou Dikasteriou Kai Tou Protodikeiou see Recueil de la Jurisprudence de la Cour de Justice et du Tribunal de Premiere Instance. Partie 2, Tribunal de Premiere Instance **4938**
Sulloge tes Nomologias tou Dikasteriou Kai Tou Protodikeiou see Recueil de la Jurisprudence de la Cour de Justice et du Tribunal de Premiere Instance. Partie 1. Cour de Justice **4938**
Sulloge tes Nomologias tou Dikasteriou Kai Tou Protodikeiou see Court of Justice and the Court of First Instance. Reports of Cases before the Court **4922**
Sulloge tes Nomologias tou Dikasteriou Kai Tou Protodikeiou see Raccolta della Giurisprudenza della Corte e del Tribunale di Primo Grado. Parte 1. Corte di Giustizia **4938**
Sully's Living Without see Living Without **5076**
• Sulphur (GBR ISSN 0039-4890) **3256**
➤ Sulphur in Agriculture (USA ISSN 0160-0680) **159**
Sulphur Industry Directory (GBR) **2081**
Sulphur Recovery Databook (GBR) **3256**
Sulphur River Literary Review (USA ISSN 1073-5933) **5436**
Sulphuric Acid and Industry see Ryusan To Kogyo **2079**
Sulphuric Acid Databook (GBR) **3256**
Sultan (IND) **4189**
Sultanate of Oman Business Directory (Year) (OMN) **2029**
Sulur (ISL) **3622**
Sum News (USA) **1302**
Suma (ESP ISSN 1130-488X) **5539**
Suma (URY ISSN 0797-0064) **1520**
Suma Administrativa (COL ISSN 0123-5532) **1795**
Suma Psicologia UST (Universidad de Santo Tomas) (CHL ISSN 0718-0446) **7411**
• Suma Psicologica (COL ISSN 0121-4381) **7411**
Sumai to Denka/Amenity & Electrification (JPN ISSN 1346-8472) **3331**
Suman Saurabh (IND ISSN 0971-149X) **2215**
Sumario Mineral (BRA ISSN 0101-2053) **6480**
➤ Sumarski List (HRV ISSN 0373-1332) **3703**
• Sumava (CZE ISSN 0862-5166) **3468**
† Suministros Industriales (ESP) **8991**
Sumitomo Bank. Annual Report (JPN ISSN 0910-1403) **1385**
Sumitomo Chemical Review see Sumitomo Kagaku Tokushugo **2081**
Sumitomo Corporation. Annual Report (JPN) **1583**
Sumitomo Corporation News (JPN ISSN 0914-322X) **3901**
Sumitomo Electric Industries Ltd. News see S E I News **3329**
Sumitomo Electric Industries Technical Review see S E I Technical Review **3329**
Sumitomo Electric Industries Tekunikaru Rebyu see S E I Tekunikaru Rebyu **3330**
Sumitomo Kagaku Tokushugo/Sumitomo Chemical Review (JPN ISSN 0387-1312) **2081**
Sumitomo Keikinzoku Giho/Sumitomo Light Metal Technical Reports (JPN ISSN 0039-4963) **6334**
Sumitomo Kinzoku/Sumitomo Metals (JPN ISSN 0371-411X) **6334**
Sumitomo Light Metal Technical Reports see Sumitomo Keikinzoku Giho **6334**
Sumitomo Metal Industries. Annual Report (JPN) **6334**
Sumitomo Metals see Sumitomo Kinzoku **6334**
Sumitomo Mitsui Construction Co., Ltd. Technical Research Institute. Reports see Mitsui Sumitomo Kensetsu Gijutsu Kenkyuujo Houkoku **1024**
Sumitomo Quarterly (JPN ISSN 0912-7712) **3901**
Sumitomo Search (JPN ISSN 0585-9131) **6334**
Summa + (ARG ISSN 0327-9022) **458**
Summa see Summa Animali da Compagnia **8807**
Summa see Summa Animali da Reddito **8807**
Summa Animali da Compagnia (ITA ISSN 1828-5538) **8807**
Summa Animali da Reddito (ITA ISSN 1828-5546) **8807**
Summa Mas see Summa + **458**
• ➤ Summa Phytopathologica (BRA ISSN 0100-5405) **819**
Summa Summarum (DEU ISSN 1434-2901) **8073**
• Summaries of Arkansas Cotton Research (USA ISSN 1941-160X) **255**
Summaries of Arkansas Cotton Research in Progress in (Year) see Summaries of Arkansas Cotton Research **255**
Summaries of J S S I & J S S E Joint Conference on Snow and Ice Research see Seppyou Kenkyuu Taikai Kouen Youshishuu **3219**
• Summary Health Statistics for the U.S. Population (USA ISSN 1938-9892) **8407**
• Summary Health Statistics for U.S. Adults (USA ISSN 1933-0138) **7549**
• Summary Health Statistics for U.S. Children (USA ISSN 1931-2970) **7549**
† Summary Information on Master of Social Work Programs (USA ISSN 0145-7314) **8991**
• Summary Judgments in Texas (USA) **4965**
Summary Justice S A see Summary Justice South Australia **2669**
Summary Justice South Australia (AUS) **2669**
Summary of Activities. A Report of the Committee on Standards of Official Conduct, United States House of Representatives see U.S. House of Representatives. Committee on Standards of Official Conduct. Summary of Activities. Report **7473**
Summary of Agreements Filed in F Y (Year) see U.S. Federal Trade Commission. Bureau of Competition. Summary of Agreements Filed in F Y (Year) **6883**
Summary of Alaska Legislation (USA) **4791**
Summary of Canadian Transit Statistics (CAN ISSN 1199-1755) **8511**
Summary of Congress (USA ISSN 0146-2156) **7187**
Summary of International Travel to the United States (USA) **8780**
Summary of Labor Arbitration Awards (USA ISSN 0039-5005) **4602**
Summary of Meteorological Observations in Hong Kong (Year) (HKG) **6396**
• Summary of State Laws and Regulations Relating to Distilled Spirits (CD-ROM) (USA) **610**
Summary of State Laws and Regulations Relating to Distilled Spirits (Print Edition) see Summary of State Laws and Regulations Relating to Distilled Spirits (CD-ROM) **610**
• Summary of World Broadcasts. Part 1: Former Soviet Union (Daily) (GBR ISSN 1350-8148) **1520**
• Summary of World Broadcasts. Part 1: Former Soviet Union (Weekly Economic Report) (GBR) **1520**
• Summary of World Broadcasts. Part 2: Central Europe, the Balkans (Daily) (GBR ISSN 1352-1365) **1520**
• Summary of World Broadcasts. Part 2: Central Europe, the Balkans (Weekly Economic Report) (GBR ISSN 1352-1373) **1520**
• Summary of World Broadcasts. Part 3: Asia - Pacific (Daily) (GBR ISSN 1352-139X) **1520**
• Summary of World Broadcasts. Part 3: Asia - Pacific (Weekly Economic Report) (GBR ISSN 1352-1403) **1520**
• Summary of World Broadcasts. Part 4: Middle East (Daily) (GBR ISSN 1350-8199) **1520**
• Summary of World Broadcasts. Part 4: Middle East (Weekly Economic Report) (GBR ISSN 1350-8202) **1520**
• Summary of World Broadcasts. Part 5: Africa, Latin America and the Caribbean (Daily) (GBR ISSN 1350-8245) **1521**
• Summary of World Broadcasts. Part 5: Africa, Latin America and the Caribbean (Weekly Economic Report) (GBR ISSN 1350-8253) **1521**
• Summary Offences Queensland (AUS) **4898**
Summary Report of Fluid Power Technology see Kenkyu Jisshi Gaikyo Hokokusho **3387**
Summary: State Transportation Profile see State Transportation Statistics **8530**
▼ Summation (Ripon) (USA ISSN 1943-6734) **5539**
• ➤ Summer Academe (USA ISSN 1091-8515) **3003**
• Summer Assessment - Winter Assessment (Year) (USA) **3161**
Summer Athenaeum see The Daily Athenaeum **2280**
Summer Computer Simulation Conference. Proceedings (USA ISSN 0094-7474) **2518**
Summer Fun Book see The City Pages **3972**
Summer Institute of Linguistics and The University of Texas at Arlington Publications in Linguistics (USA) **5184**
Summer Institute of Linguistics, Australian Aborigines and Islanders Branch Bibliography see S I L - A A I B Bibliography **8986**
Summer Institute of Linguistics, Australian Aborigines and Islanders Branch Occasional Papers see S I L - A A I B Occasional Papers **5171**
Summer Institute of Linguistics Electronic Survey Reports see S I L Electronic Survey Reports **5171**
Summer Institute of Linguistics. Serie Linguistica (BRA ISSN 0102-6526) **5184**
• Summer Institute of Linguistics. University of North Dakota Session. Work Papers (USA ISSN 0361-4700) **5184**
Summer Jobs for (Year) (USA) **6704**
Summer Jobs in Canada see The Canadian Summer Job Directory **6694**
Summer Programs for Kids and Teenagers see Summer Programs for Kids & Teenagers **8758**
Summer Programs for Kids & Teenagers (USA ISSN 1934-6794) **8758**
Summer Seminar on Hydraulic Engineering. Lecture Notes see Suikogaku ni Kansuru Kaki Kenshukai Kogishu **3364**
Summer Seminar on New Topics in Naval Architecture see Kaki Koza Atarashii Zozengaku **8649**
Summer Symposium of Operation Research Yokoshu see S S O R Yokoshu **2444**
Summer Theatre Directory (Year) (USA ISSN 0884-5840) **8480**
Summer Times (USA) **4983**
Summer Vanguard see Vanguard (Portland) **2308**
• Summer Work Experience (CAN ISSN 1912-1636) **6704**
➤ Summerhill (IND) **8008**
Summers Dining Guide see What's Up? Annapolis **5086**
• Summertime Floodlight (GBR ISSN 1352-870X) **2946**

Title

▼ *new title* † *ceased* • *electronic media* ➤ *refereed*

10916 SUMMERVILLE POST ULRICH'S PERIODICALS

Summerville Post (USA ISSN 0743-2585) **7503**
The Summit (AUS ISSN 0312-7044) **7819**
• Summit (CAN ISSN 1481-4935) **7471**
Summit (USA) **2302**
The Summit Collection (USA) **36**
Summons (USA ISSN 0039-5072) **4791**
Sumo World (JPN) **8210**
Sumo Wrestling (Tokyo, 1949) (JPN) **8210**
Sumo Wrestling (Tokyo, 1954) (JPN) **8210**
Sumptuous (AUS ISSN 1832-1224) **3665**
Sumter Black Post (USA) **3566**
Sumu (JPN ISSN 1347-2577) **458**
• The Sun (AUS) **7742**
The Sun *see* Taiyang Bao **3875**
• The Sun (IND) **3889**
The Sun (NGA ISSN 0795-7475) **3921**
Sun (Boca Raton) (USA) **3989**
The Sun (Chapel Hill) (USA ISSN 0744-9666) **5241**
• Sun (London) (GBR ISSN 0307-2681) **3871**
Sun (Montreal) (CAN) **3818**
Sun and Moon Tables for Ghana *see* Ghana. Meteorological Department. Sun and Moon Tables for Ghana **6353**
Sun & Skin News (USA) **5882**
Sun & Wind Energy (DEU ISSN 1861-2741) **3177**
Sun Belt Building Journal (USA ISSN 0745-354X) **1038**
Sun Belt Journal (USA) **1180**
Sun Dog *see* Sundog (Tallahassee) **5436**
Sun Golf (USA) **8247**
Sun Guide to the Flat (GBR ISSN 0955-0488) **8299**
Sun Guide to the Jumps (GBR ISSN 0955-0496) **8299**
Sun Lakes Life (USA) **4056**
Sun Life (USA) **4056**
Sun Living (CYM) **8758**
• Sun Reporter (USA ISSN 0890-0930) **3567**
▼ Sun Residences (FRA ISSN 1957-2778) **7613**
Sun Sign Book (USA ISSN 0737-6154) **567**
Sun Tennis Magazine (USA) **8247**
• Sun Times (CAN ISSN 0839-5152) **3818**
Sun Valley Home Design *see* Sun Valley Magazine **3989**
Sun Valley Magazine (USA ISSN 1076-8599) **3989**
Sun World *see* SunWorld **2574**
Sun World *see* SunWorld **2504**
Sun Yat-sen Cultural Foundation Bulletin/Chung Shan Hsueh Shu Wen Hua Ch'i K'an (TWN ISSN 0300-3302) **8008**
Sun Yat-sen Journal of Humanities *see* Zhongshan Renwen Xuebao **4483**
Sun Yat-sen University. Journal (Medical Sciences Edition) *see* Zhongshan Daxue Xuebao (Yixue Kexue Ban) **5739**
Sun Yat-sen University. Journal (Social Science Edition) *see* Zhongshan Daxue Xuebao (Shehui Kexue Ban) **8019**
Sun Yatsen University Forum *see* Zhongshan Daxue Xuebao Luncong **8019**
Sunaparant (IND) **3889**
Sunbelt Foodservice (USA ISSN 1069-3475) **3665**
Sunbelt Vending and O C S (USA) **3665**
Sunbelt W2K Newsflash *see* W2K News **2504**
➤ The Sunbird (AUS ISSN 1037-258X) **915**
➤ Sunceva Energija/Solar Energy (HRV ISSN 0351-2797) **3177**
† Sund og Slank (DNK ISSN 1901-1288) **8991**
Sunday (IND) **3889**
Sunday (USA ISSN 0039-5161) **7686**
Sunday Age *see* The Age **3793**
• Sunday Business (GBR ISSN 1362-1947) **1180**
• The Sunday Business Post (IRL ISSN 0791-2617) **1180**
Sunday Citizen (GBR) **3871**
Sunday Digest (USA ISSN 0039-5188) **7686**
Sunday Examiner *see* The Examiner **3794**
Sunday Examiner (HKG) **7819**
The Sunday Express (GBR) **3871**
Sunday Express (LBR) **3790**
Sunday Gleaner (JAM ISSN 0039-520X) **3995**
Sunday Guardian (TTO) **3995**
• Sunday Herald (GBR ISSN 1465-8771) **3871**
Sunday Herald-Sun (AUS ISSN 1038-3425) **3796**
Sunday Hours *see* Kyriatikis Ores **3832**
Sunday Independent (IRL ISSN 0039-5218) **3894**
The Sunday Independent (ZAF ISSN 1024-9575) **3950**
• Sunday Life (GBR ISSN 1360-2772) **3871**
Sunday Luxury (USA) **3989**
Sunday Magazine (AUS) **4983**
• Sunday Mail (AUS ISSN 1322-5243) **3796**
• Sunday Mail (GBR ISSN 0307-5877) **3871**
Sunday Mail (ZMB) **3995**
Sunday Mail (ZWE ISSN 1996-384X) **3996**
• Sunday Mail (Adelaide) (AUS ISSN 1039-4184) **3793**
Sunday Mail (Entertainment Supplement) *see* Sunday Mail **3871**
Sunday Mainichi (JPN ISSN 0039-5234) **3901**
• Sunday Mercury (GBR ISSN 0039-5242) **3871**
• Sunday Mirror (GBR ISSN 0956-8077) **3871**
Sunday Missal for Young Catholics (CAN ISSN 1715-6149) **7819**
Sunday Morning Post Magazine (HKG) **3875**
Sunday Nation (KEN ISSN 1025-1251) **3902**
• Sunday News (NZL ISSN 1170-0882) **3919**
The Sunday News (ZWE ISSN 1814-4233) **3996**
The Sunday Observer (IND) **3889**
The Sunday Observer (Bombay Edition) *see* The Sunday Observer **3889**
The Sunday Observer (New Delhi Edition) *see* The Sunday Observer **3889**
Sunday People (LBR) **3790**
The Sunday Post (GBR ISSN 0307-5753) **3871**
Sunday Post (PAK ISSN 0039-5277) **3926**
Sunday Post (Online Edition) *see* Kantipur Online **3913**
Sunday Stabroek *see* Stabroek News **1179**
The Sunday Standard (KEN) **3902**
Sunday Standard (Harare) (ZWE) **3996**
Sunday Star (BGD) **3800**
Sunday Star *see* Toronto Star **3818**
Sunday Star (MYS) **3907**
• Sunday Star Times (NZL ISSN 1172-9740) **3919**
Sunday Student Post (TWN) **3960**
Sunday Sun *see* Toronto Sun **3818**
Sunday Sun (GBR ISSN 0039-5315) **3871**
Sunday Sun Television Magazine (Calgary) (CAN) **2391**
• Sunday Telegraph (GBR ISSN 0307-269X) **3871**
• Sunday Territorian (AUS ISSN 0815-9572) **3796**
• Sunday Times (AUS ISSN 1442-9527) **3796**
• The Sunday Times (GBR ISSN 0956-1382) **3871**
Sunday Times (KEN) **3902**
Sunday Times (LKA) **3954**
Sunday Times (MLT) **3907**
Sunday Times (NGA ISSN 0331-2658) **3921**
The Sunday Times (SGP) **3946**
• Sunday Times (ZAF ISSN 0039-5331) **3950**
Sunday Times Magazine (AUS) **5084**
Sunday Times of Zambia (ZMB) **3995**
Sunday Tribune (IRL ISSN 0332-1940) **3895**
Sunday Tribune (NGA ISSN 0331-2569) **3921**
• Sunday Tribune (ZAF ISSN 1016-6939) **3950**
Sunday Vanguard *see* Tien Phong Chu Nhat **2217**
The Sunday Vision (UGA) **3963**
Sunday World. Northern Ireland Edition (IRL) **3871**
Sunday World. Republic of Ireland Edition (IRL) **3895**
Sundazed Tymes (USA) **6621**
Sunderland Star *see* Washington Star **3872**
Sunderland Star *see* Houghton Star **2287**
• Sundhed, Teknologi, Informatik (DNK ISSN 1901-5283) **5718**
Sundhedsstatistikken (Koebenhavn) *see* Sundhedsstatistikken (Year) **4114**
Sundhedsstatistikken (Year) (DNK ISSN 0909-4156) **4114**
The Sundial (USA) **2302**
Sundog (Tallahassee) (USA ISSN 0735-7133) **5436**
Sundsvalls Tidning (SWE ISSN 1104-005X) **3925**
Sunduq al-Naqd al-Duwalil. Al-Qadaya al-Iqtisadiyyat *see* International Monetary Fund. Economic Issues **1571**
The Sunflower (Bismarck) (USA ISSN 0192-8988) **255**
The Sunflower (Wichita) (USA) **2303**
Sunflower and Oilseeds Grower (AUS) **3751**
Sungerbob Karepantolon/Sponge Bob (TUR) **2215**
Sunglass Association of America. Newsletter (USA) **2250**
Sunhwan'gi *see* Korean Circulation Journal **5795**
Sunjata (MLI) **3790**
Sunjet (CYP ISSN 1011-1727) **8786**
Sunkist Report *see* Newslink (Sherman Oaks) **243**
Sun'n Fun (DEU) **8758**
Sunnhetsbladet (NOR ISSN 0332-7434) **6998**
Sunnhordland (NOR) **3925**
• Sunnmoersposten (NOR ISSN 1503-9056) **3925**
Sunnseit'n (AUT) **8758**
Sunny South News (CAN ISSN 0714-5306) **3818**
Sunny Speaks English (CZE ISSN 1802-1395) **2215**
Sunny Times (DEU) **8786**
Sunraysia Daily (AUS) **3796**
• Sunrise (USA ISSN 0562-6048) **6956**
Sunrise Magazine (USA) **5982**
• Sunset (USA ISSN 0039-5404) **3989**
Sunset (Birminham) (USA) **5084**
Sunset 250 Best Selling Home Plans (USA) **1038**
Sunset Best Selling Home Plans (USA) **458**
Sunset Best-Selling One-Story Home Plans *see* Sunset Best Selling Home Plans **458**
Sunset Holiday Entertaining (USA) **4368**
Sunset Living 101 (USA) **5084**
Sunset Recipe Annual (Year) (USA ISSN 0896-2170) **4368**
Sunset Small Backyard Secrets (USA) **3751**
• Sunshine Artist (USA ISSN 1081-6542) **520**
Sunshine Bulletin (USA ISSN 0728-909X) **2270**
Sunshine Coast Living (ZAF ISSN 1815-2953) **5084**
Sunshine Express (AUS ISSN 0726-5093) **8625**
Sunshine Girl *see* Jiankang Nuhai **6990**
➤ Sunshine State T E S O L Journal (Teachers of English to Speakers of Other Languages) (USA ISSN 1934-7030) **2916**
• Sunstone (USA ISSN 0363-1370) **7742**
Sunsu Mit Eung-yong Suhag/Pure and Applied Mathematics (KOR ISSN 1226-0657) **5540**
Sunt Foernuft (SWE ISSN 0039-5455) **1946**
Sunwear (USA ISSN 1087-299X) **6052**
• SunWorld/Sanwarudo (JPN ISSN 0918-5453) **2574**
• SunWorld (USA ISSN 1091-8914) **2504**
• SunZine - About Queensland Australia (AUS) **1180**
➤ Suo (FIN ISSN 0039-5471) **3704**
Suoliao/Plastics (CHN) **7100**
Suomalainen Teologinen Kirjallisuusseura. Julkaiau (FIN ISSN 0356-9349) **7686**
Suomalainen Tiedeakatemia. Vuosikirja/Academia Scientiarum Fennica. Yearbook (FIN ISSN 0356-6927) **7921**
Suomalais-Ugrilaisen Seuran Aikakauskirja/Gebiete der Finnischen Voelkerschaften. Ethnographische Forschungen/Societe Finno-Ougrienne. Journal (FIN ISSN 0355-0214) **357**
Suomalais-Ugrilaisen Seuran Kansatieteellisia Julkaisuja/Travaux Ethnographiques de la Societe Finno-Ougrienne (FIN ISSN 0359-7679) **357**
Suomalais-Ugrilaisen Seuran Toimituksia/Societe Finno-Ougrienne. Memoires (FIN ISSN 0355-0230) **357**
Suomalaisen Kirjallisuuden Seura. Toimituksia (FIN ISSN 0355-1768) **5383**
• Suomen Akatemia. Julkaisuja/The Academy of Finland. Publications (FIN ISSN 0358-9153) **7921**
➤ Suomen Antropologi/Antropologi i Finland/Finnish Anthropological Society. Journal (FIN ISSN 0355-3930) **357**
Suomen Antropologisen Seura. Toimituksia/Finnish Anthropological Society. Transactions (FIN ISSN 0356-0481) **357**
Suomen Arkkitehtiliitto. Vuosikirja (FIN ISSN 0787-3840) **458**
Suomen Atomiteknillinen Seura Ydintekniikka *see* A T S Ydintekniikka **3164**
Suomen Autolehti (FIN ISSN 0355-2691) **8605**
Suomen Elainlaakarilehti/Finsk Veterinaertidskrift (FIN ISSN 0039-5501) **8807**
Suomen Elokuvatutkimuksen Seura Julkaisu *see* S E T S - Julkaisu **6511**
• Suomen Evankelis-Luterilainen Kirkko. Kirkkohallituksen Yleiskirje (Online) (FIN ISSN 1797-0326) **7776**
Suomen Evankelis-Luterilainen Kirkko. Kirkkohallituksen Yleiskirje (Print) *see* Suomen Evankelis-Luterilainen Kirkko. Kirkkohallituksen Yleiskirje (Online) **7776**
Suomen Geodeettisen Laitos. Julkaisuja/Finnisches Geodaetisches Institut. Veroeffentlichungen/ Finnish Geodetic Institute. Publications (FIN ISSN 0085-6932) **2790**
Suomen Geodeettisen Laitos. Tiedonantoja/Finnish Geodetic Institute. Reports (FIN ISSN 0355-1962) **2790**
• Suomen Golflehti (FIN ISSN 0784-5502) **8247**
Suomen Hammaslaakarilehti/Finlands Tandlaekartidning/Finnish Dental Journal (FIN ISSN 0355-4090) **5866**
Suomen Historiallinen Seura. Kasikirjoja (FIN ISSN 0081-9417) **4171**
Suomen Historian Laehteitae/Source Material of Finnish History (FIN ISSN 0081-9425) **4272**
• Suomen Joukkovelkakirjalainat/Finlaendska Masskuldebrevslaan/Finnish Bond Issues (FIN ISSN 0781-4437) **1654**
Suomen Kalapaikkaopas (FIN ISSN 0789-6638) **8336**
Suomen Kalastuslehti (FIN ISSN 0039-5528) **3609**
Suomen Kalatalous (FIN ISSN 0085-6940) **3609**
Suomen Kasvatustieteellinen Seura. Kasvatusalan Tutkimuksia/Finnish Educational Research Association. Research in Educational Sciences (FIN ISSN 1458-1094) **2916**
Suomen Kaukolampo ry L. Raportti *see* Energiateollisuus ry L. Raportti **3128**
Suomen Keskiajan Arkeologian Seura *see* S K A S **4261**
Suomen Kielitieteellinen Yhdistys Journal of Linguistics *see* SKY Journal of Linguistics **5174**
Suomen Kielitieteellisen Yhdistyksen Aikakauskirja *see* SKY Journal of Linguistics **5174**
➤ Suomen Kioriallisen Seura. Toimituksia (FIN ISSN 0356-0759) **7686**
Suomen Kirkkohistoriallinen Seura. Vuosikirja/Finska Kyrkohistoriska Samfundet. Aarskrift (FIN ISSN 0356-0767) **7686**
• Suomen Kuvalehti (FIN ISSN 0039-5552) **3839**
Suomen Kuvalehti Gourmet (FIN ISSN 1459-8728) **4368**
Suomen Kuvalehti Mies (FIN ISSN 1459-871X) **3839**
• ➤ Suomen Laakarilehti/Finlands Laekartidning/Finnish Medical Journal (FIN ISSN 0039-5560) **5718**
Suomen Laakarilehti. Eripainos *see* Suomen Laakarilehti **5718**
Suomen Laaketieteen Historian Seura. Vuosokirja *see* Hippokrates **5628**
Suomen Lehdisto/Finlands Press (FIN ISSN 0039-5587) **4584**
Suomen Logopedis-Foniatrinen Aikakauslehti *see* Puhe ja Kieli **5163**
• Suomen Maksutase (Online) (FIN ISSN 1456-5838) **1904**
Suomen Maksutase (Print) *see* Suomen Maksutase (Online) **1904**
• Suomen Maksutase. Vuositilasto/Finland's Balance of Payments. Annual Statistics/Finlands Betalningsbalans (FIN ISSN 1238-8424) **1904**
Suomen Markkinointiliitto Info *see* S M L Info **1842**
Suomen Merimuseo. Nautica Fennica (FIN ISSN 1235-9122) **6537**
• Suomen Metsateollisuuden Keskusliitto. Metsateollisuuden Vuosikirja (FIN ISSN 0780-4717) **3704**
Suomen Muinaismuistoyhdistyksen Aikakauskirja/Finska Fornminnesfoereningens Tidskrift (FIN ISSN 0355-1822) **419**
Suomen Musiikkikirjastoyhdistys. Julkaisusarja (FIN ISSN 0784-0322) **6621**
Suomen Pankin Keskustelualoitteita *see* Bank of Finland Research Discussions Papers **1314**
• Suomen Pankki. Rahoitusmarkkinat. Tilastokatsaus/Bank of Finland. Statistical Review. Financial Markets/Finlands Bank. Statistisk Oeversikt. Finansmarknaden (FIN ISSN 1795-7575) **1269**
Suomen Pankki. Tilastokatsaus. Rahoitusmarkkinat. Euroina *see* Suomen Pankki. Rahoitusmarkkinat. Tilastokatsaus **1269**
• Suomen Pankki. Tutkimuksia. Sarja A/Bank of Finland. Expository Studies. A (FIN ISSN 1238-1683) **1385**
• Suomen Pankki. Tutkimuksia. Sarja E/Bank of Finland. Scientific Monographs (FIN ISSN 1238-1691) **1385**
• Suomen Pankki. Tutkimustiedote (FIN ISSN 1457-5809) **1385**
• Suomen Pankki. Vuosikertomus (FIN ISSN 1239-9329) **1385**
Suomen Queer-Tutkimuksen Seura *see* S Q S **8130**
Suomen Riista (FIN ISSN 0355-0656) **3609**
Suomen Sanomalehtien Mikrofilmit/Microfilmed Newspapers of Finland (FIN ISSN 0355-4074) **4588**
Suomen Shakki (FIN ISSN 0355-8096) **8210**
Suomen Siipikarja (FIN ISSN 1238-9889) **301**
Suomen Silta/Finland Bridge (FIN ISSN 0039-5625) **3839**
Suomen Soveltavan Kielitieteen Yhdistyks (AFinLA). Julkaisuja (FIN ISSN 0781-0318) **5184**
Suomen Soveltavan Kielitieteen Yhdistyks (AFinLA). Vuosikirja (FIN ISSN 0781-030X) **5184**
Suomen Standardisoimisliitto ry Tiedotus *see* S F S - Tiedotus **6406**
Suomen Standardisoimisliitto. S F S - Kasikirja (FIN ISSN 0780-7961) **6407**
• Suomen Standardisoimisliitto. S F S - Luettelo/Finnish Standards Association. S F S Catalogue (FIN ISSN 1239-1735) **6407**
Suomen Standardisoimisliitto. S F S - Luettelo. Taydennysluettelo/Finnish Standards Association. S F S Catalogue. Cumulative Supplement (FIN ISSN 0780-766X) **6407**
Suomen Sukututkimusseura. Julkaisuja/Genealogiska Samfundet i Finland. Skrifter (FIN ISSN 0355-3175) **4272**
Suomen Sukututkimusseura. Vuosikirja (FIN ISSN 0355-3183) **3784**
Suomen Tekniikan Historian Seura. Julkaisuja/Teknikhistoriska Samfundet. S T H Publikationer (FIN ISSN 1456-7415) **3221**
Suomen Tukkukauppa (FIN ISSN 0355-7820) **1583**
Suomen Ulko-ja Turvallisuuspolitiikka (FIN ISSN 1455-1497) **7267**
Suomen Vakuutusvuosikirja/Finnish Insurance Yearbook (FIN ISSN 0356-7826) **4524**
• Suomen Ymparisto/Finnish Environment/Miljoen i Finland (FIN ISSN 1238-7312) **3468**
• Suomen Ymparistokeskus. Raportteja/Finnish Environment Institute. Reports (FIN ISSN 1796-1718) **3491**
Suomenmaa (Helsinki) (FIN ISSN 0356-3588) **3839**
Suomenmaa (Oulu) *see* Suomenmaa (Helsinki) **3839**
Suomi (AUS) **3567**
Suomi - U S A (FIN ISSN 0782-8454) **7267**
Suosikki (FIN ISSN 0355-4260) **2215**
Suowei Jishu/Journal of Micrographics *see* Shuzi Yu Suowei Yingxiang **6980**
Super! (ROM ISSN 1454-9808) **3934**
Super (USA) **3114**
Super 7 (USA ISSN 1542-2461) **4348**
• Super 8 Motel International Directory (USA) **4399**
Super 8 Sammler (DEU) **6515**
Super A M (USA) **520**
▼ The Super Advisor (USA ISSN 1945-4503) **6687**
Super Auto (ESP) **8605**
• Super Campo (ARG ISSN 0328-4247) **159**
• Super Chevy (USA ISSN 0146-2628) **8605**
Super Consciousness Magazine *see* SuperConsciousness Magazine **6647**
† Super Console (ITA ISSN 1594-2511) **8991**
Super Console PlayStation *see* Super Console **8991**
Super Eight Motel International Directory *see* Super 8 Motel International Directory **4399**
• Super Express (POL ISSN 0867-8723) **3930**
Super Feniks (HRV ISSN 1330-8602) **8210**
Super Floral Retailing (USA) **3757**
Super Food Ideas (AUS ISSN 1448-9546) **3665**
Super Foto Naturaleza (ESP) **6977**
Super Foto Practica (ESP ISSN 1136-5544) **6977**
Super Funds *see* Superfunds **4524**
• Super Illu (DEU ISSN 1433-9900) **3858**
Super Interessante (PRT) **3931**
• Super L C C S (Library of Congress Classification Schedules) (USA ISSN 1088-1611) **5049**
Super Looper (USA ISSN 1069-5508) **8336**
Super Map (BHS) **8758**
Super Marketing *see* SuperMarketing **3682**
Super Moto Tecnica *see* MotoTecnica **8264**
Super Motores Magazine (PRT) **8605**
Super Nanny (GBR) **2169**
Super Onda (USA ISSN 1548-9302) **2215**
Super Play (SWE ISSN 1401-8519) **2391**
Super Play Special *see* Super Play **2391**
Super Pop (ESP) **2215**
Super-Raetsel (DEU) **8210**
• Super Review (AUS ISSN 1324-5295) **1385**
Super Rod (USA ISSN 1528-4158) **8605**
Super Science *see* SuperScience **3083**
Super Seven *see* Super 7 **4348**

Super Six (GBR ISSN 1749-8244) **2215**
Super Street (USA) **8605**
Super Streetbike (USA ISSN 1934-4996) **8268**
Super T V (DEU ISSN 0863-3614) **2391**
Super T V (POL ISSN 1230-9788) **2391**
† Super T V Raetsel Magazin (DEU) **8991**
Super Tennis Magazine (ITA) **8248**
Super TV *see* Super T V **2391**
Super V W (FRA) **8606**
• Superannuation Determination (AUS ISSN 1449-8685) **1946**
Superb Storyteller for Infants *see* You'er Gushing Dawan **2223**
Superba (ITA ISSN 0039-5706) **8210**
SuperBasket (ITA ISSN 0393-7852) **8248**
SuperBike (GBR ISSN 0262-8457) **8268**
† Supercar (NLD ISSN 1875-4317) **8991**
Supercar Year (GBR ISSN 1469-3283) **8606**
Supercars (NOR) **8606**
Supercharger (USA) **8606**
• Supercomputing Proceedings (USA ISSN 1063-9535) **2525**
Superconducting Magnetic Energy Storage *see* Chodendo Energi Chozo Kenkyukai **7065**
• ➤ Superconductor Science & Technology (GBR ISSN 0953-2048) **7042**
• Superconductor Week (USA ISSN 0894-7635) **7042**
▼ • SuperConsciousness Magazine (USA ISSN 1948-917X) **6647**
Superficies (ESP ISSN 1575-8400) **6334**
Superficies y Vacios (MEX ISSN 1665-3521) **3358**
Superfoot Mag (FRA ISSN 1767-9966) **8248**
Superfund Innovative Technology Evaluation Program Annual Report to Congress *see* U.S. Environmental Protection Agency. Office of Research and Development. Superfund Innovative Technology Evaluation Program. Annual Report to Congress **7473**
• Superfund Report (USA ISSN 1049-6149) **3512**
Superfund Update (USA) **3468**
Superfunds (AUS ISSN 0729-3828) **4524**
• Superintendencia de Bancos e Instituciones Financieras. Informe Anual (CHL) **1385**
• Superintendencia de Bancos e Instituciones Financieras. Informe de Gestion (CHL) **1385**
• Superintendencia de Bancos e Instituciones Financieras. Memoria (CHL) **1385**
Superintendent of Financial Institutions. Report (CAN ISSN 0839-9115) **1385**
Superintendent of Insurance Annual Report (CAN) **4524**
Superintendent's Profile & Product Service Directory (USA) **3284**
Superintending for Contractors: How to Bring Jobs in on Time, on Budget (USA) **1038**
• Superinteressante (BRA ISSN 0104-1789) **3804**
Superior Catholic Herald (USA) **7819**
Superior Equipment of Pollution Prevention *see* Yushu Kogai Boshi Sochi **3493**
• Superior Sentinel (CAN ISSN 1911-4346) **3818**
SuperKuma (EST) **8210**
SuperKuma (LVA) **8210**
• ➤ Superlattices and Microstructures (GBR ISSN 0749-6036) **2081**
Supermarkedshaandbogen (Year)/Supermarkets and Other Large Grocery Stores (DNK ISSN 0903-868X) **1968**
Supermarket *see* Market **1830**
Supermarket and Retailer (ZAF ISSN 0049-2590) **3681**
• Supermarket News (USA ISSN 0039-5803) **3681**
Supermarket Own Labels *see* Key Note Market Assessment. Supermarket Own Labels **1827**
• Supermarket Strategic Alert (USA ISSN 1053-3648) **3682**
• SuperMarketing (GBR ISSN 0261-4251) **3682**
Supermarkets and Other Large Grocery Stores *see* Supermarkedshaandbogen (Year) **1968**
Supermarkets & Superstores *see* Key Note Market Report: Supermarkets & Superstores **3680**
Supermarktwijngids *see* Superwijngids **610**
Supermercado Moderno (BRA) **1845**
Supermoto (CZE ISSN 1212-2408) **8606**
Supermoto One (FRA ISSN 1779-5486) **8268**
SuperMoto Racer Magazine (USA ISSN 1932-6068) **8268**
Supernet Magazine (ESP ISSN 1135-6340) **2599**
SuperPorts (GBR ISSN 1468-439X) **8283**
SuperReds *see* Manchester United SuperReds **8238**
▼ Supersafemark Guia de Referencia Rapida las Mejores Practicas de Seguridad e Higiene en la Venta Directa de Alimentos al Consumidor (USA ISSN 2150-6639) **6687**
• SuperScience (USA) **3083**
† Superspy T V (CZE ISSN 1802-3169) **8991**
Superstar (DEU ISSN 1433-8122) **6621**
† Superstar Wrestlers (USA ISSN 0887-1035) **8991**
▼ • Superstition Review (USA ISSN 1938-324X) **5383**
• Supertele (ESP) **2391**
Supertrax International (CAN ISSN 1195-4965) **8336**
• Supervisie en Coaching (NLD ISSN 1572-0306) **1795**
Supervisie in Opleiding en Beroep *see* Supervisie en Coaching **1795**
• Supervising Scientist Report (AUS ISSN 1325-1554) **2628**
• Supervision (DEU ISSN 1431-7168) **1709**
• Supervision (USA ISSN 0039-5854) **1709**
Supervision Test and Cost of Construction *see* Jianzhu Jiandu Jiance yu Zaojia **1017**
• Supervisor Safety Alert (USA ISSN 1548-002X) **6687**
• Supervisor's Guide to Employee Performance Reviews (USA) **1875**
Supervisor's Guide to Employment Practices (USA ISSN 1069-4978) **1875**
† Supervisor's Guide to Ergonomics (USA ISSN 1549-7348) **8991**
The Supervisor's Guide to O S H A Regulations (Occupational Health and Safety Administration) (USA ISSN 1522-8711) **6687**
Supervisors Legal Update (USA ISSN 1521-8066) **1795**
Supervisor's Memory Jogger (USA ISSN 1077-9337) **1795**
Supervisory and Management Survey (USA) **1709**
Supervisory Insights (USA ISSN 1932-3034) **1385**
Superwijngids (NLD ISSN 1877-7538) **610**
Supesu Purazuma Kenkyukai (JPN) **7042**
Supima Association of America Newsletter (USA) **159**
Suplemento de Estudios Clasicos. Serie de Traducciones (ESP ISSN 0425-3477) **2241**
Suplemento de Estudios Clasicos. Serie Textos (ESP ISSN 0423-4820) **2241**
Suplemento de Urania *see* Urania **583**
Suplemento Literario de Minas Gerais (BRA ISSN 0102-065X) **5383**
Suplementos de Revista de Neurologia *see* Revista de Neurologia **6182**
Supochu Dong-A/Sports Dong-A (KOR) **8210**
Supplement *see* Nederlandsche Commissie voor Internationale Natuurbescherming. Mededelingen **3456**
Supplement *see* National Faculty Directory **3028**
Supplement au Dictionnaire de la Bible (FRA) **7686**
Supplement au Registre Maritime (FRA ISSN 0153-6001) **8663**
Supplement de Vol, Canada *see* Canada Flight Supplement **50**
Supplement du Bulletin des Statistiques du Travail (CHE ISSN 0378-5505) **1269**
Supplement Industry Executive *see* Nutrition Industry Executive **6666**
Supplement til FSRs Afgiftslove med Noter *see* F S Rs Skatte- og Afgiftslove. Supplement **1923**
Supplement till Norsk Skattelovsamling *see* Rett til Kildene **1942**
Supplement to Both the Motor Vehicle and Truck Data Books *see* Sanford Evans Gold Book. Supplement to Both the Car and Truck Data Guides **8603**
Supplement to Employment, Hours, and Earnings: States and Areas *see* Employment, Hours, and Earnings: States and Areas **8953**
A Supplement to Oncology *see* Oncology **6030**
A Supplement to Oncology News International *see* Oncology News International **6030**
Supplement Trimestriel au Registre Maritime (FRA ISSN 0153-6052) **8663**
➤ Supplementa Byzantina (DEU ISSN 0933-5080) **2241**
Supplemental Climatological Data, Late Reports and Corrections. Alabama *see* Climatological Data. Alabama **6349**
Supplemental Climatological Data, Late Reports and Corrections. California *see* Climatological Data. California **6350**
Supplemental Climatological Data, Late Reports and Corrections. Colorado *see* Climatological Data. Colorado **6350**
Supplemental Climatological Data, Late Reports and Corrections. Florida *see* Climatological Data. Florida **6350**
Supplemental Climatological Data, Late Reports and Corrections. Georgia *see* Climatological Data. Georgia **6350**
Supplemental Climatological Data, Late Reports and Corrections. Kentucky *see* Climatological Data. Kentucky **6350**
Supplemental Climatological Data, Late Reports and Corrections. Louisiana *see* Climatological Data. Louisiana **6350**
Supplemental Climatological Data, Late Reports and Corrections. Maryland & Delaware *see* Climatological Data. Maryland and Delaware **6350**
Supplemental Climatological Data, Late Reports and Corrections. New Jersey *see* Climatological Data. New Jersey **6351**
Supplemental Climatological Data, Late Reports and Corrections. New York *see* Climatological Data. New York **6351**
Supplemental Climatological Data, Late Reports and Corrections. Puerto Rico & Virgin Islands *see* Climatological Data. Puerto Rico and Virgin Islands **6400**
Supplemental Climatological Data, Late Reports and Corrections. Virginia *see* Climatological Data. Virginia **6351**
Supplemental Security Income Monthly Statistics (USA) **4530**
Supplemental Security Income Program. Reports *see* U.S. Social Security Administration. Supplemental Security Income Program. Reports **4526**
Supplemental Tidal Predictions, Anchorage, Nikishka, Seldovia, and Valdez, Alaska (USA ISSN 0270-8876) **2818**
Supplementary Prescribing in Practice (GBR ISSN 1742-5395) **6882**
† Supplementary Service to European Taxation (NLD ISSN 0039-5927) **8991**
Supplementi all'Italian Heart Journal *see* Giornale Italiano di Cardiologia **5787**
Supplements a Iranica Antiqua *see* Iranica Antiqua Supplementa **399**
Supplements to Clinical Neurophysiology *see* Clinical Neurophysiology. Supplement **6132**
Supplementum Epigraphicum Graecum (NLD ISSN 0920-8399) **2241**
(Year) Supplier Diversity Information Resource Guide (USA ISSN 1541-8618) **2029**
• Supplier Global Resource (USA ISSN 1933-1789) **36**
Supplier Member Directory (USA) **6793**
Supplier Selection and Management Report *see* Supplier Selection & Management Report **1845**
• Supplier Selection & Management Report (USA ISSN 1046-3771) **1845**
• Supply & Demand Chain Executive (USA ISSN 1548-3142) **1796**
Supply and Demand Chain Executive *see* Supply & Demand Chain Executive **1796**
Supply and Demand for Scientists and Engineers *see* Supply & Demand Indicators for New Science and Engineering Doctorates **6704**
Supply & Demand Indicators for New Science and Engineering Doctorates (USA) **6704**
Supply and Demand of Electric Power in Japan *see* Denryoku Jukyu no Gaiyo **3299**
Supply and Disposition of Crude Oil and Natural Gas (CAN ISSN 1488-4771) **6801**
Supply and Distribution of Registered Nurses in Canada *see* Workforce Trends of Registered Nurses in Canada **5984**
Supply Chain Brain *see* SupplyChainBrain **1583**
Supply Chain Business (GBR ISSN 1744-9960) **1796**
Supply Chain E-business (USA ISSN 1529-8167) **1796**
• Supply Chain Europe (GBR ISSN 1742-447X) **1845**
• ➤ Supply Chain Forum (FRA ISSN 1625-8312) **8511**
▼ • Supply Chain Magasinet (DNK ISSN 1902-8075) **1796**
• ➤ Supply Chain Management (GBR ISSN 1359-8546) **1796**
Supply Chain Management Expert *see* S C M Expert **1792**
• Supply Chain Management Review (USA ISSN 1521-9747) **1796**
Supply Chain Management Supply Chain Magazine *see* S C M Supply Chain Magazine **1842**
Supply Chain Pharmafile (GBR) **6882**
• Supply Chain Review (AUS ISSN 1832-553X) **1904**
• Supply Chain Risk Report (USA ISSN 1930-4935) **1796**
• Supply Chain Solutions (USA ISSN 1557-5128) **1845**
• Supply Chain Strategy (USA ISSN 1557-9522) **1796**
Supply Chain Today (ZAF) **5460**
Supply, Distribution, Manufacturing and Service *see* Supply, Distribution, Manufacturing & Service **6794**
Supply, Distribution, Manufacturing & Service (USA) **6794**
• Supply House Times (USA ISSN 0039-5935) **4127**
The Supply Line *see* Chemistry & Industry **2057**
Supply Line (USA ISSN 8750-0124) **4348**
Supply Lines (USA) **8832**
• Supply Management (GBR ISSN 1362-2021) **1845**
Supply Manual *see* Guide des Approvisionnements **7443**
Supply Post (CAN) **3704**
Supply Side Inside Cosmeceuticals *see* Supply-Side Inside Cosmeceuticals **596**
▼ Supply-Side Inside Cosmeceuticals (USA) **596**
SupplyChainBrain (USA ISSN 1949-2693) **1583**
Support and Assistance Update (USA) **2916**
• Support for Learning (GBR ISSN 0268-2141) **3047**
Support for the Learning and Teaching of English Newsletter (Online) *see* S L A T E Newsletter (Online) **3079**
• Support Insight (GBR) **1421**
Support Line (USA ISSN 1067-3768) **6669**
• Support Net (USA ISSN 1940-4107) **5766**
Support to Sector Associations Program, a 'Sound' Program *see* Programme d'Aide aux Associations Sectorielles, un Programme a l'Ecoute **6607**
Support World *see* H D I Support World **2419**
Supported Employment InfoLines (USA ISSN 1047-952X) **8073**
Supporters MagAZine (NLD ISSN 1876-455X) **8248**
• ➤ Supportive Cancer Therapy (USA ISSN 1543-2912) **6034**
• ➤ Supportive Care in Cancer (DEU ISSN 0941-4355) **6034**
Supportive Lifestyles News (USA) **6648**
• Suppression Matters Under Massachusetts Law (USA ISSN 1934-5607) **4791**
• ➤ Supramolecular Chemistry (GBR ISSN 1061-0278) **2081**
Supreme and District Courts Practice N S W *see* N S W Civil Practice & Procedure **4838**
Supreme Court Act 59 of 1959 and the Magistrates' Court Act 32 of 1944 (ZAF) **4965**
Supreme Court Bulletin (USA ISSN 0199-5030) **4965**
• Supreme Court Cases (IND ISSN 0039-5951) **4965**
Supreme Court Cases (Criminal) (IND ISSN 0253-6544) **4898**
Supreme Court Cases (Labour and Services) (IND ISSN 0253-6552) **4965**
Supreme Court Cases Full Text on CD-ROM *see* Supreme Court Cases **4965**
• Supreme Court Debates (USA ISSN 1099-5390) **4852**
• ➤ Supreme Court Economic Review (USA ISSN 0736-9921) **4965**
Supreme Court History Program Yearbook (Year) (AUS ISSN 1833-5667) **4852**
• Supreme Court Law Review (CAN ISSN 0228-0108) **4791**
Supreme Court Monthly Review (PAK ISSN 0585-9794) **4965**
Supreme Court of Appeal of the Republic of Bulgaria. Bulletin *see* Vurkhoven Kasatsionen Sud na Republika Bulgaria. Bulletin **4967**
• Supreme Court of Canada Decisions (CAN ISSN 0709-5600) **4965**
Supreme Court of Canada Practice Guide (CAN ISSN 1206-3193) **4965**
Supreme Court of Canada Reports Service (CAN) **4965**
Supreme Court of Nigeria. Monthly Judgments (NGA ISSN 1595-7632) **4965**
Supreme Court of the United States. Individual Slip Opinions (USA) **4791**
• Supreme Court of the United States. Journal (USA ISSN 0270-9805) **4791**
Supreme Court of the United States. Preliminary Prints. Advance Sheets (USA) **4791**
Supreme Court Record (USA ISSN 0892-810X) **4791**
• ➤ The Supreme Court Review (USA ISSN 0081-9557) **4965**
Supreme Court Year Book *see* Supreme Court Yearbook **8991**
† Supreme Court Yearbook (USA ISSN 1054-2701) **8991**
Supreme Islamic Authorities. Herald *see* Rijaset Islamske Zajednice u Bosni i Hercegovini. Glasnik **7715**
Supreme People's Court of the People's Republic of China. Bulletin *see* Zhonghua Renmin Gongheguo Zuigao Renmin Fayuan Gongbao **4820**
• El Sur (MEX ISSN 1605-0401) **3911**
• El Sur de Campeche (MEX ISSN 1563-8642) **3911**
• El Sur del Sur (ARG) **3792**
• Sur in English (ESP) **3954**
Sur - International Journal on Human Rights *see* Sur - Revista Internacional de Direitos Humanos **7216**
Sur la Mise en Oeuvre de l'Aide Exterieure de la Commission Europeenne. Situation au (Annee). Rapport Annuel *see* On the Implementation of the European Commission's External Assistance (Year). Annual Report **1602**
Sur la Route (FRA ISSN 1771-9941) **4030**
Sur l'Administration et l'Application des Dispositions de la Loi sur les Peches Relatives a la Protection de l'Habitat du Poisson et a la Prevention de la Pollution. Rapport Annuel au Parlement *see* On the Administration and Enforcement of the Fish Habitat Protection and Pollution Prevention Provisions of the Fisheries Act. Annual Report to Parliament **3604**
• ➤ Sur - Revista Internacional de Direitos Humanos/Sur - International Journal on Human Rights (BRA ISSN 1806-6445) **7216**
Sura (RUS) **5383**
Surah (IRN) **5383**
Suraj Mukhi (PAK) **5241**
Surb-Khach (UKR) **4477**
Surchhanda (IND) **6621**
Surco Argentina (USA) **159**
Surco Latinoamericana (USA) **159**
Surco Mexicana (USA) **159**
Surcos de Aragon (ESP ISSN 1699-4744) **159**
Surdites (FRA ISSN 1962-5189) **4076**
• Sure! (ITA ISSN 1126-9227) **5184**
Diario El Sureno *see* El Sureno **3792**
El Sureno (ARG) **3792**
Surety Bonding Supplement *see* A B C Today **974**
Surf (DEU ISSN 1436-5618) **8336**
SURF (Utrecht) (Samenwerking Universitaire Rekenfaciliteiten) (NLD ISSN 1570-632X) **2567**
Surf a Vela (ESP ISSN 1135-3775) **8336**
Surf & Ski (GRC) **8210**
SURF Cahier *see* SURF (Utrecht) **2567**
▼ SURF Licentienieuws (NLD ISSN 1875-340X) **2438**
Surf 'n Beach (NLD ISSN 1872-5546) **8336**
Surf Report (USA ISSN 0270-2630) **8336**
Surf Session (FRA ISSN 0767-7987) **8210**
SURF Special *see* SURF (Utrecht) **2567**
Surface *see* Hyomen **2135**
• Surface (USA ISSN 1091-806X) **3990**
• ➤ Surface and Coatings Technology (CHE ISSN 0257-8972) **2106**
➤ Surface and Colloid Science (USA ISSN 0081-9573) **2141**
• ➤ Surface and Interface Analysis (GBR ISSN 0142-2421) **2106**
Surface & Panel (USA) **4562**

Title

DIRECTORY 2010 SVENSK SKIDSPORTSKI & BOARD MAGAZINE 10919

Survey Report on Sales & Marketing Personnel Compensation *see* Survey Report on Marketing Personnel Compensation **1709**
Survey Report on Sales & Marketing Personnel Compensation *see* Survey Report on Sales Personnel Compensation **1709**
• Survey Report on Sales Personnel Compensation (USA) **1709**
• Survey Report on Supervisory Management Compensation (USA ISSN 1930-4277) **1796**
Survey Report on Technician and Skilled Trades Personnel Compensation *see* Survey Report on Technician & Skilled Trades Personnel Compensation **1876**
• Survey Report on Technician & Skilled Trades Personnel Compensation (USA ISSN 1558-0733) **1876**
Survey Report on Variable Pay Programs (USA) **1876**
Survey Research (USA) **8142**
▼ • ➤ Survey Research Methods (DEU ISSN 1864-3361) **8008**
• ➤ Survey Review (GBR ISSN 0039-6265) **3284**
• Survey Serbia & Montenegro (SRB ISSN 1451-477X) **3945**
Survey - Smaller Companies Sector (GBR) **1654**
Surveying *see* Maanmittaus **3278**
• ➤ Surveying and Land Information Science (USA ISSN 1538-1242) **4030**
• Surveying the Digital Future (USA ISSN 1557-1823) **2567**
Surveyor (GBR) **3284**
Surveys, Analysis, Modelling and Mapping Research Programme. Occasional Paper (ZAF ISSN 1726-507X) **4030**
† Surveys and Development Plans of Industry in Israel/Hata'asiyah Be-Yisrael (ISR ISSN 0081-9743) **8991**
▼ • ➤ Surveys and Perspectives Integrating Environment and Society (DEU ISSN 1993-3800) **7921**
Surveys and You *see* Hong Kong Special Administrative Region of China. Census and Statistics Department. Surveys and You **7284**
Surveys in Applied and Industrial Mathematics *see* Obozrenie Prikladnoi i Promyshlennoi Matematiki **5522**
Surveys in Applied Mathematics (USA ISSN 1082-622X) **5540**
• Surveys in Approximation Theory (USA ISSN 1555-578X) **5540**
Surveys in Differential Geometry (USA ISSN 1052-9233) **5540**
• ➤ Surveys in Geophysics (NLD ISSN 0169-3298) **2790**
• ➤ Surveys in Mathematics and its Applications (ROM ISSN 1843-7265) **5540**
• ➤ Surveys in Operations Research and Management Science (NLD ISSN 1876-7354) **2438**
Surveys of Applied Economics (USA) **1180**
Surveys of Consumers (USA ISSN 0085-3410) **1521**
Surveys of International Air Transport Fares and Rates (CAN) **8552**
Surveys of Science Resources Series. Federal Scientists and Engineers *see* Federal Scientists and Engineers **1861**
Surveys on Mathematics for Industry *see* European Journal of Applied Mathematics **5486**
Survivability - Vulnerability Information Analysis Center Bulletin *see* S U R V I A C Bulletin **69**
Survival (POL ISSN 1730-5241) **8336**
• ➤ Survival (Abingdon) (GBR ISSN 0039-6338) **7268**
Survival (London, 1993) (GBR ISSN 1353-0488) **357**
Survival (Year) (GBR) **3567**
• Survival News (USA ISSN 1551-8876) **5827**
Survival Skills for Scholars (IND) **2916**
Survivor *see* Mopheme **3905**
Survivors Outreach Series (USA) **8142**
Susacka Revija (HRV ISSN 1330-1306) **5241**
† Su'san Gwahag Yeon'gu/Fisheries Science Research (KOR ISSN 1226-1858) **8991**
Susanna Solo Bimbi (ITA ISSN 1129-1281) **2169**
Susel *see* Tanssiviihde **2688**
Sushama (IND ISSN 0039-6370) **5383**
Sushiki Shori/Communications for Symbolic and Algebraic Manipulation (JPN ISSN 0919-1410) **5540**
Sushmita (IND) **5383**
Susong Faxue, Sifa Zhidu/Studies of Procedural Law, Studies of Judicial Systems (CHN ISSN 1007-0516) **4965**
▼ • Suspense Magazine (USA ISSN 1947-492X) **5383**
▼ Susquehanna Business Life (USA) **1180**
Susquehanna Heritage (USA ISSN 1541-5112) **4314**
Susquehanna Life (USA ISSN 1520-8788) **3990**
Susquehanna River Basin Commission. Annual Report (USA ISSN 0094-6427) **8832**
Susquehanna Style (USA ISSN 1540-0875) **3990**
Susquehanna Today (USA) **2303**
Sussex, East Surrey and South East Auto Trader (GBR ISSN 1364-5994) **8606**
Sussex European Institute Working papers *see* S E I Working Papers **7998**
• Sussex Inletter (AUS ISSN 1832-1828) **3796**
Sussex Life (GBR ISSN 0039-6397) **3872**
• Sussex Past and Present (GBR ISSN 1357-7417) **420**
➤ Sussex Record Society (GBR) **4272**
Sussidi Patristici (ITA) **7819**
▼ • Sustainability (CHE ISSN 2071-1050) **3468**
▼ Sustainability (IRL ISSN 2009-0854) **3491**
Sustainability (SWE ISSN 1654-8329) **3491**
▼ • Sustainability (USA ISSN 1937-0695) **3468**
▼ • Sustainability Accounting, Management and Policy Journal (GBR ISSN 2040-8021) **1302**
Sustainability, Economics, and Natural Resources (NLD ISSN 1871-6121) **1180**
• Sustainability Matters (AUS ISSN 1834-917X) **3512**
Sustainability Report (CAN ISSN 1912-0923) **3163**
Sustainability Research Institute Papers *see* S R I Papers **3464**
• Sustainability Science (JPN ISSN 1862-4065) **7921**
Sustainability Science Abstracts *see* C S A Sustainability Science Abstracts **3477**
Sustainability Science and Engineering (NLD ISSN 1871-2711) **7921**
• ➤ Sustainability: Science, Practice, & Policy (USA ISSN 1548-7733) **7921**
Sustainable Agriculture Programme. Gatekeeper Series *see* International Institute for Environment and Development. Sustainable Agriculture Programme. Gatekeeper Series **123**
Sustainable Agriculture Programme. Research Series *see* International Institute for Environment and Development. Sustainable Agriculture Programme. Hidden Harvest Research Series. **201**
Sustainable Architecture & Building Mag *see* S A & B Mag **1034**
• Sustainable Brands Weekly (USA) **3468**
• Sustainable Building (GBR ISSN 1753-2825) **3148**
Sustainable Business (GBR ISSN 1756-8633) **3468**
• Sustainable Business Investor - America (GBR ISSN 1472-0019) **1654**
Sustainable Business Investor - Worldwide (GBR ISSN 1742-2981) **1654**
• Sustainable Business News (USA) **3468**
• ➤ Sustainable Development (GBR ISSN 0968-0802) **3468**
▼ • Sustainable Development Digest (USA ISSN 1939-7097) **3468**
• Sustainable Development Law & Policy (USA ISSN 1552-3721) **3468**
• Sustainable Development Strategy (CAN ISSN 1912-4783) **3567**
• Sustainable Development U K (GBR ISSN 1479-5043) **3469**
• Sustainable Facility (USA ISSN 1934-6980) **3148**
• Sustainable Fisheries Livelihoods Programme Newsletter (ITA) **3609**
Sustainable Forest Management Network. Projects and Publications Guide (CAN ISSN 1718-0163) **3704**
Sustainable Forest Management Network. Research Program *see* Sustainable Forest Management Network. Projects and Publications Guide **3704**
† Sustainable Grazing on Saline Lands Network News (AUS ISSN 1832-0937) **8991**
Sustainable Humanosphere (JPN ISSN 1880-6503) **3469**
• Sustainable Industries Journal (USA ISSN 1549-8670) **1180**
• Sustainable Ireland (GBR) **3512**
• Sustainable Land Development Today (USA ISSN 1938-1050) **1038**
• Sustainable Land Use Change in the Northwest Provinces of China. Research Reports (AUS ISSN 1449-7433) **1521**
Sustainable Management of Sediment Resources (NLD ISSN 1872-1990) **2798**
• Sustainable Sourcing Weekly (USA) **3469**
The Sustainable Times (CAN ISSN 1201-8384) **1709**
Sustainable Urban Areas (NLD ISSN 1574-6410) **1038**
The Sustainable World (GBR ISSN 1476-9581) **3469**
Sustainable World Series (USA) **3469**
• Sustaining Regions (AUS ISSN 1446-2974) **8142**
• Sustaining Repositories (AUS ISSN 1834-1098) **5049**
Sustrai (ESP ISSN 0213-330X) **3609**
• Sustrans (Organization). Annual Review (GBR ISSN 1755-3636) **1302**
Sustrans Active Travel News *see* Active Travel News **8253**
Sustrans Volunteer Rangers Newsletter *see* The Ranger **8266**
The Sutler (USA ISSN 1059-6976) **3784**
Sutton Bridge Annual Review (GBR ISSN 0309-2968) **207**
Sutureline (USA) **6260**
Suured Ruudud (EST) **8210**
Suuri Kasityolehti (FIN ISSN 1236-3855) **6642**
Suuri Ristikko (FIN ISSN 0357-2366) **8210**
Suvorovskii Natisk (RUS) **6448**
• Suvremena Lingvistika (HRV ISSN 0586-0296) **5184**
➤ Suvremena Psihologija (HRV ISSN 1331-9264) **7411**
Suvremena Trgovina (HRV ISSN 1330-0180) **1845**
Suvremeni Promet (HRV ISSN 0351-1898) **8552**
Suvremenna Meditsina/Modern Medicine (BGR ISSN 0562-7192) **5719**
Suvremennik/Contemporary (BGR ISSN 0204-6962) **5383**
Suvremenno Pravo (BGR) **4791**
• Suxing Gongcheng Xuebao/Journal of Plasticity Engineering (CHN ISSN 1007-2012) **3256**
Suzhi Jiaoyu Dacankao/Political Education (CHN ISSN 1672-0237) **7187**
• Suzhi Jiaoyu Luntan (CHN) **2916**
Suzhou Art & Design Technology Institute. Journal *see* Suzhou Gongyi Meishu Zhiye Jishu Xueyuan Xuebao **520**
Suzhou College of Education. Journal *see* Suzhou Jiaoyu Xueyuan Xuebao **2916**
• Suzhou Daxue Xuebao (Gongke Ban)/Suzhou University. Journal (Engineering Science Edition) (CHN ISSN 1673-047X) **8457**
• Suzhou Daxue Xuebao (Yixue Ban)/Suzhou University Journal of Medical Science (CHN ISSN 1673-0399) **5719**
• ➤ Suzhou Daxue Xuebao (Zhexue Shehui Kexue Ban)/Suzhou University. Journal (Philosophy and Social Sciences) (CHN ISSN 1001-4403) **8008**
• Suzhou Daxue Xuebao (Ziran Kexue Ban)/Suzhou University. Journal (Natural Science Edition) (CHN ISSN 1000-2073) **7921**
• Suzhou Gongyi Meishu Zhiye Jishu Xueyuan Xuebao/Suzhou Art & Design Technology Institute. Journal (CHN ISSN 1672-3848) **520**
• Suzhou Jiaoyu Xueyuan Xuebao/Suzhou College of Education. Journal (CHN ISSN 1008-7931) **2916**
• Suzhou Keji Xueyuan Xuebao (Gongcheng Jishu Ban)/University of Science and Technology of Suzhou. Journal (Engineering and Technology) (CHN ISSN 1672-0679) **3221**
Suzhou Keji Xueyuan Xuebao (Shehui Kexue Ban)/University of Science and Technology of Suzhou. Journal (Social Science) (CHN) **8008**
• Suzhou Keji Xueyuan Xuebao (Ziran Kexue Ban)/University of Science and Technology of Suzhou. Journal (Natural Science) (CHN ISSN 1672-0687) **7921**
Suzhou University. Journal (Engineering Science Edition) *see* Suzhou Daxue Xuebao (Gongke Ban) **8457**
Suzhou University. Journal (Medical Edition) *see* Suzhou Daxue Xuebao (Yixue Ban) **5719**
Suzhou University. Journal (Natural Science Edition) *see* Suzhou Daxue Xuebao (Ziran Kexue Ban) **7921**
Suzhou University. Journal (Philosophy and Social Sciences) *see* Suzhou Daxue Xuebao (Zhexue Shehui Kexue Ban) **8008**
Suzhou University Journal of Medical Science *see* Suzhou Daxue Xuebao (Yixue Ban) **5719**
• Suzhou Xueyuan Xuebao (CHN ISSN 1673-2006) **7921**
Suzhou Yixueyuan Xuebao/Suzhou Institute of Medical Sciences. Journal *see* Suzhou Daxue Xuebao (Yixue Ban) **5719**
Suzi Deveraux International Fan Club (USA) **6621**
➤ Suzugamine Joshi Tandai Kenkyu Shuho. Shizen Kagaku/Suzugamine Women's College. Bulletin. Natural Science (JPN ISSN 0389-5025) **7921**
Suzugamine Women's College. Bulletin. Natural Science *see* Suzugamine Joshi Tandai Kenkyu Shuho. Shizen Kagaku **7921**
Suzuken Memorial Foundation. Research Papers *see* Ikagaku Oyo Kenkyu Zaidan Kenkyu Hokoku **7524**
Suzukuri/Asa Zoological Park News (JPN ISSN 0389-6838) **964**
Suzy Gershman's Born to Shop: Hong Kong, Shanghai & Beijing (USA) **8759**
Suzy Gershman's Born to Shop: Paris (USA) **8759**
Svadba (SVK ISSN 1335-7697) **5561**
• Svadba.sk (SVK ISSN 1336-3360) **5561**
Svampe (DNK ISSN 0106-7451) **819**
† Svantevit (DNK ISSN 0106-5378) **8991**
† S'vara (USA ISSN 1044-0011) **8991**
Svarochnoe Proizvodstvo (RUS ISSN 0491-6441) **6344**
SvB *see* Svensk Bokhandel **7574**
SvB *see* Svenskans Beskrivning **5184**
Sve o Tebi! (HRV ISSN 1330-9455) **2215**
Sve Tebi *see* Sve o Tebi! **2215**
Sveamaal (SWE ISSN 1101-7597) **7187**
Svedi Nas, Sud'ba (RUS ISSN 1560-6988) **4477**
Sveiseaktuelt (NOR ISSN 0804-2489) **6344**
Sveitarsjodareikningar/Local Government Finance (ISL ISSN 1017-6357) **1269**
Sveitarstjornarkosningar/Local Government Elections (ISL ISSN 1021-5646) **7187**
Sveitarstjornarmal (ISL ISSN 0255-8459) **7503**
Svensk Aakeritidning (SWE ISSN 1404-1022) **8675**
• Svensk Annonstaxa (SWE ISSN 0491-6522) **636**
• Svensk Annonstaxa Online (SWE) **7579**
Svensk Arkivtidskrift *see* Tema Arkiv **1797**
Svensk Bergs- & Brukstidning (SWE ISSN 0039-6435) **6480**
• ➤ Svensk Biblioteksforskning (Online) (SWE ISSN 1653-5235) **5049**
Svensk Biblioteksforskning (Print) *see* Svensk Biblioteksforskning (Online) **5049**
Svensk Bokfoerteckning (Print edition) *see* Nationalbibliografin - Boecker **631**
• Svensk Bokhandel (SWE ISSN 0039-6451) **7574**
Svensk Botanisk Tidskrift (SWE ISSN 0039-646X) **819**
Svensk Bridge (SWE ISSN 0282-4809) **8210**
Svensk Curling (SWE ISSN 0346-2048) **8336**
Svensk Damtidning (SWE ISSN 0039-6486) **8885**
➤ Svensk Exegetisk Aarsbok (SWE ISSN 1100-2298) **7686**
Svensk Fallskaermssport (SWE ISSN 0280-011X) **8210**
Svensk Familjeterapi (SWE ISSN 1100-3421) **6187**
• Svensk Fastighetsindikator (SWE ISSN 1102-9218) **7613**
Svensk Fastighetstidning *see* Fastighetstidningen **7590**
Svensk Fiskhandel (SWE ISSN 0346-2072) **3609**
➤ Svensk Flyghistorisk Tidskrift (SWE ISSN 1100-9837) **72**
Svensk Foerfattningssamling (SWE ISSN 0346-5845) **4791**
Svensk Foersaekring/Swedish Insurance (SWE ISSN 1102-1330) **4524**
Svensk Foersaekringsaarsbok *see* Svensk Foersaekring **4524**
Svensk Froetidning (SWE ISSN 0346-2099) **255**
Svensk Geografisk Aarsbok/Swedish Geographical Yearbook (SWE ISSN 0081-9808) **4030**
Svensk Golf (SWE ISSN 0346-2102) **8248**
Svensk Golfguide (SWE ISSN 1100-3758) **8248**
Svensk Gris med Knorr (SWE ISSN 1650-5077) **301**
• Svensk Handelstidning Justitia (SWE ISSN 0039-6575) **1946**
Svensk Handelstidning Justitia. Aarsfakta (SWE ISSN 1403-011X) **1946**
Svensk Handikapptidskrift (SWE ISSN 0346-2129) **8074**
• Svensk Historia (SWE ISSN 1652-4632) **4272**
• Svensk Historisk Bibliografi (Online Edition) (SWE) **4171**
Svensk Hjortavel (SWE ISSN 1101-198X) **301**
Svensk Hotellrevy (SWE ISSN 0346-2137) **4399**
Svensk Idrott (SWE ISSN 0049-2663) **8210**
Svensk Idrottsmedicin (SWE ISSN 1103-7652) **6234**
Svensk Innebandy (SWE ISSN 0283-2208) **8210**
Svensk Jakt (SWE ISSN 0039-6583) **8336**
Svensk Jakt Nyheter *see* Svensk Jakt **8336**
Svensk Juristtidning (SWE ISSN 0039-6591) **4965**
Svensk Kaernbraenslehantering. Plantsundersoekningar *see* Svensk Kaernbraenslehantering. S K B P **3512**
Svensk Kaernbraenslehantering. S K B F U D-Program (Forskning, Utveckling och Demonstration) (SWE ISSN 1104-8395) **3512**
• Svensk Kaernbraenslehantering. S K B P (SWE ISSN 1651-4416) **3512**
Svensk Kaernbraenslehantering. S K B R D & D-Programme *see* Svensk Kaernbraenslehantering. S K B F U D-Program **3512**
• Svensk Kaernbraenslehantering. S K B Rapport (SWE ISSN 1402-3091) **3175**
• Svensk Kaernbraenslehantering. Technical Report (SWE ISSN 1404-0344) **3175**
Svensk Kirurgi (SWE ISSN 0346-847X) **6260**
Svensk Konstvetenskaplig Bibliografi *see* Konsthistorisk Tidskrift **500**
Svensk Leksaksrevy (SWE ISSN 0039-6621) **4061**
• Svensk Leverantoerstidning (SWE ISSN 0283-7803) **1845**
Svensk Linje (SWE ISSN 0346-2161) **7187**
Svensk Medicin (SWE ISSN 0284-5342) **5719**
Svensk Medicinhistorisk Tidskrift/Swedish Journal of History of Medicine (SWE ISSN 1402-9871) **5719**
Svensk Medicinhistorisk Tidskrift. Supplement *see* Svensk Medicinhistorisk Tidskrift **5719**
Svensk Missionstidskrift/Swedish Missiological Themes (SWE ISSN 0346-217X) **7776**
• Svensk Musik (Online) (SWE) **6621**
Svensk Musik (Print) *see* Svensk Musik (Online) **6621**
Svensk Mykologisk Tidskrift (SWE ISSN 1653-0357) **819**
• Svensk Numismatisk Tidskrift (SWE ISSN 0283-071X) **6653**
Svensk Oe N H Tidskrift (SWE ISSN 1400-0121) **6085**
Svensk-Oesterbottniska Samfundet. Skrifter (FIN ISSN 0473-8063) **4272**
Svensk Papperstidning *see* S P C I Svensk Papperstidning **6738**
Svensk Papperstidning *see* Nordisk Papperstidning **6735**
Svensk Pastoraltidskrift *see* S P T: Svensk Pastoraltidskrift **7679**
Svensk Patenttidning/Swedish Patent Gazette (SWE ISSN 0346-2196) **6758**
Svensk Patenttidnings Kumulerade Namnregister/Swedish Patent Gazette's Accumulated Name Register (SWE ISSN 0347-898X) **6758**
• Svensk Periodicafoerteckning. (Online)/Current Swedish Periodicals (SWE) **636**
Svensk Periodicafoerteckning (Print edition) *see* Svensk Periodicafoerteckning. (Online) **636**
Svensk Polis (SWE ISSN 0562-7370) **2669**
• Svensk Reklamtaxa (SWE ISSN 0282-0919) **636**
• Svensk Reklamtaxa Online (SWE) **7579**
Svensk Religionshistorisk Aarsskrift (SWE ISSN 0283-0302) **7686**
Svensk Sjoefartstidning/Scandinavian Shipping Gazette (SWE ISSN 0039-6702) **8663**
• Svensk Sjukhustandlaekartidning (SWE ISSN 0348-0011) **5867**
Svensk Skattetidning (SWE ISSN 0346-2218) **1946**
Svensk Skidsport *see* Svensk SkidsportSki & Board Magazine **8336**
Svensk SkidsportSki & Board Magazine (SWE) **8336**

Title

▼ *new title* † *ceased* • *electronic media* ➤ *refereed*

Title

T D C Annual Review *see* Transportation Development Centre. Annual Review **8516**
T D C. Textes et Documents pour la Classe *see* Centre National de Documentation Pedagogique. Textes et Documents pour la Classe. **2835**
T D F Sightlines (Theatre Development Fund) (USA) **8480**
T D I and U I Laws of Rhode Island *see* Temporary Disability Insurance and Unemployment Insurance Laws of Rhode Island **4525**
T D - I H K Magazin (Tuerkisch-Deutsche Industrie- und Handelskammer) (DEU) **1410**
T D I National Directory of T T Y Numbers (Year) *see* The Blue Book (Year) T D I National Directory & Resource Guide **4072**
T D M Kenkyu/Japanese Journal of Therapeutic Drug Monitoring (Therapeutic Drug Monitoring) (JPN ISSN 0911-1026) **6882**
T D O *see* The Doctor's Office **4092**
T D O D *see* Training & Development Organisations Directory **2920**
T D R *see* Trade and Development Report **1584**
• T D R (The Drama Review) (USA ISSN 1054-2043) **8480**
T D R I Quarterly Review (Thailand Development Research Institute) (THA ISSN 0857-2968) **1181**
T D Repoto *see* Technology Development Report **3115**
▼ • T D Securities Melbourne Institute Monthly Inflation Gauge (AUS ISSN 1836-4268) **1521**
T Design (ITA ISSN 1825-3091) **2262**
T E *see* Trusts and Estates (Springfield) **4906**
T E A *see* Transport Engineering in Australia **3285**
T E A L Manitoba Journal (Teaching English as an Additional Language) (CAN ISSN 1914-1726) **5185**
T E A M *see* Tertiary Education and Management **3005**
T E A M Club Newsletter (Tellington-Jones Equine Awareness Method) (USA) **8299**
T E A M Horizons (Evangelical Alliance Mission) (USA ISSN 0163-3422) **7687**
T E A News *see* Teach **2917**
T E A Newsletter (Tucson Education Association) (USA ISSN 0039-8306) **2917**
T E A R Times (The Evangelical Alliance Relief) (GBR ISSN 0955-2324) **8074**
T E A R Topics (The Evangelical Alliance Relief) (GBR ISSN 0955-3738) **8074**
T E A S *see* Twayne's English Authors Series **5391**
T E B A *see* T E B A News **1521**
T E B A News (Turkish Ekonomik Basin Ajansi) (TUR) **1521**
T E C (Teens Erleben Christus) (DEU) **2215**
T E C (Transport Environnement Circulation) (FRA ISSN 0397-6513) **8635**
T E C *see* New Caledonia. Institut de la Statistique et des Etudes Economiques. Tableaux de l'Economie Caledonienne **1254**
T E C *see* Teaching Exceptional Children **3048**
T E C Advanced Engineering Information (Toyo Engineering Corporation) (JPN) **3221**
T E C O R *see* The Environmental Contract Opportunity Report **7435**
T E D (The Electrical Distributor) (USA ISSN 1067-3806) **3332**
T E D D Y *see* T E R I Energy Data Directory and Yearbook **2029**
T E Financial Strategies *see* T E Wealth Strategies **1654**
T E I *see* Taiwan Electronics Industry **3114**
T E J O - Tutmonde (Tutmonda Esperantista Junulara Organizo) (NLD) **2215**
• T E L E M A S P Bulletin (Texas Law Enforcement Management and Administrative Statistics Program) (USA ISSN 1075-3702) **2675**
T E L J *see* Tulane Environmental Law Journal **3471**
T E M A *see* Tendencias em Matematica Aplicada e Computacional **5541**
t.e.m.p.l.e. Magazine (USA) **3990**
T E N *see* Trophy & Engraving News **1855**
T E N *see* Transportation Equipment News **8676**
➤ T E N (Trends in Evidence-Based Neuropsychiatry) (USA) **6187**
T E N Annual Directory *see* Transportation Equipment News Annual Directory **8676**
T E N C O N (I E E E Region 10 Conference). Proceedings (Trends in Electronics Conference) (USA ISSN 0886-1420) **2439**
T E N / M E T Newsletter (Tanzania Education Network / Mtandao wa Elimu Tanzania) (TZA ISSN 1821-5025) **2917**
T E Notes (USA ISSN 1054-514X) **646**
• T E O N A N A C A T L (USA ISSN 1543-1681) **819**
➤ T E P S A Journal (Texas Elementary Principals and Supervisors Association) (USA ISSN 0300-6433) **3034**
• T E Q (USA) **8440**
T E R *see* The Tertiary Education Report **3005**
T E R I Energy Data Directory and Yearbook (Tata Energy Research Institute) (IND) **2029**
T E R I Information Digest on Energy and Environment *see* T I D E E **3148**
• T E R I Newswire (Tata Energy Research Institute) (IND ISSN 0971-6661) **3154**
T E S *see* Australia. Department of the Treasury. Tax Expenditures Statement **1911**
T E S *see* Times Educational Supplement **2920**
T E S E *see* Teacher Education and Special Education **3048**
T E S G *see* Tijdschrift voor Economische en Sociale Geografie **4031**
T E S L Canada Journal/Revue T E S L du Canada (CAN ISSN 0826-435X) **3083**
• ➤ T E S L - E J (Teaching English as a Second Language - Electronic Journal) (USA ISSN 1072-4303) **5185**
T E S L Manitoba *see* T E A L Manitoba Journal **5185**
T E S L Reporter (Teaching English as a Second Language) (USA ISSN 0886-0661) **3083**
T E S L Talk (Teachers of English as a Second Language) (CAN ISSN 0700-1584) **3083**
T E S O L A N Z Journal (NZL ISSN 1172-9694) **5185**
➤ T E S O L in Context (Teachers of English to Speakers of Other Languages) (AUS ISSN 1030-8385) **3015**
T E S O L Placement Bulletin (Print Edition) *see* T E S O L Placement E-Bulletin **5185**
• T E S O L Placement E-Bulletin (Teachers of English to Speakers of Other Languages) (USA) **5185**
• ➤ T E S O L Quarterly (Teachers of English to Speakers of Other Languages) (USA ISSN 0039-8322) **5185**
• T E S S (The Educational Software Selector) (USA) **2951**
T E T Y C *see* Teaching English in the Two-Year College **3004**
T.E. Trabajadores de la Ensenanza *see* Trabajadores de la Ensenanza **2920**
T E U B R G Working Paper Series (GBR ISSN 1462-6292) **1521**
T E Wealth Strategies (CAN ISSN 1910-1899) **1654**
T F I *see* Journal of Taxation and Regulation of Financial Institutions **1363**
• T F I Advocate (The Fertilizer Institute) (USA) **255**
T F J *see* Armed Forces Journal **6411**
T F K *see* Time for Kids Big Picture (Grades K-1) **2217**
T F K *see* Time for Kids News Scoop **2217**
T F M Monitor (Training for Ministries) (ZAF) **7687**
T F N *see* Techno - File News **2567**
T F R *see* III - Vs Review **3116**
T F R I Conference Proceedings (Taiwan Fisheries Research Institute) (TWN ISSN 1018-4538) **3609**
T F S Pack + Plast *see* Pack + Plast **6712**
T F W *see* Tattoos For Women **521**
• T F W M Newsletter (CAN) **8440**
T G *see* Tropical Grasslands **255**
† T G (Tapicerias Gancedo) (ESP ISSN 0210-3761) **8992**
T G *see* Transforming Government **7472**
T G A-Fachplaner (DEU ISSN 1610-5656) **4127**
• T G A News (Australian Government Department of Health and Ageing, Therapeutic Goods Administration) (AUS ISSN 1325-8559) **6882**
• T G A News (Print Edition) (Therapeutic Goods Administration) (AUS ISSN 1327-6662) **6882**
T G A - Report (Technische Gebaeudeausruestung) (AUT ISSN 1019-4118) **3396**
T G C *see* Today's Garden Center **3757**
T G G *see* The Greatest Game **8234**
T.G.I.F. Casting News (USA) **6704**
T G L. Tijdschrift voor Geestelijk Leven (BEL ISSN 1370-6691) **7687**
T G M Echo (Turngemeinde 1861 e.V.) (DEU) **8211**
T G O *see* The Great Outdoors **8316**
T H B *see* Toy & Hauler Business **8269**
T H B Deutsche Schiffahrtszeitung (Taeglicher Hafen Bericht) (DEU ISSN 1618-5234) **8663**
T H E *see* Times Higher Education **3005**
• T H E Focus (Technological Horizons in Education) (USA) **2951**
• T H E Journal (Technological Horizons in Education) (USA ISSN 0192-592X) **2951**
T H E M A A. Lettre d'Information *see* Manip **8473**
T H E S A Newsletter (Teachers of Home Economics Specialist Association) (CAN ISSN 0702-7133) **3083**
T H & M A (Tijdschrift voor Hoger Onderwijs en Management) (NLD ISSN 1380-7110) **3034**
• T H E's Newsletter (Technological Horizons in Education) (USA) **2951**
T H - Extra (SVK ISSN 1335-4442) **3947**
T H J L P *see* Texas Hispanic Journal of Law and Policy **4794**
T H L I (Textwissenschaft Theologie Hermeneutik Literaturanalyse Informatik) (DEU ISSN 0941-0570) **7687**
T H M C F Technical Report (Thorne & Hatfield Moors Conservation Forum) (GBR ISSN 1468-2087) **2628**
T H R *see* Tilburg Hisstorische Reeks **4273**
T H R *see* The Hollywood Reporter **6502**
T H R A P & P *see* Tasmanian Historical Research Association. Papers and Proceedings **4194**
T H R C Newsletter (Texas Humanities Resource Center) (USA) **4477**
† T H S Health Summary (Times Health Supplement) (GBR ISSN 0266-9056) **8992**
T H S la Revue des Addictions (Toxicomanies, Hepatites, Sida) (FRA ISSN 1624-0898) **5827**
T H S News (Theatre Historical Society) (USA ISSN 1948-0253) **8480**
T I A - M M T A Directory and Desk Reference (Telecommunications Industry Association - MultiMedia Telecommunications Association) (USA) **2029**
T I A Update (Transportation Intermediaries Association) (USA) **8512**
T I A Z *see* Pedagogiek in Praktijk **2165**
• T I B (Trae-Industri-Byg) (DNK ISSN 1903-7104) **1052**
T i B S *see* Trends in Biochemical Sciences **746**
T I B ung *see* Handymag **8961**
T I C L Journal *see* Torts, Insurance & Compensation Law Section Journal **4797**
T I D E *see* T I D E E **3148**
• T I D E E (Teri Information Digest on Energy and Environment) (IND ISSN 0972-6721) **3148**
T I D Touristik Kontakt (DEU) **8759**
T I E *see* The International Educator **3013**
T I E Online *see* The International Educator **3013**
T I E S *see* Theoretical Issues in Ergonomics Science **3223**
• T I E S (Online) (Technology, Innovation and Entrepreneurship for Students) (USA) **8440**
T I E S (Print) *see* T I E S (Online) **8440**
T I F *see* Tidskrift i Fortifikation **3285**
T I F F A Freight Forwarding Handbook (Thai International Freight Forwarders Association) (THA) **8663**
T I G G *see* Trends in Glycoscience and Glycotechnology **2132**
T I H *see* Toxicology and Industrial Health **3502**
T I J S A T *see* Thammasat International Journal of Science and Technology **7923**
T I L *see* The International Lawyer **4931**
T I L J *see* Texas International Law Journal **4942**
T I M *see* Technisch Info Magazine **8441**
T I M (SVN ISSN 0040-7712) **2215**
• T I M News (Technologie Information Medien) (AUT ISSN 1992-6146) **2352**
T I M S. Bulletin *see* Tabbin Institute for Metallurgical Studies. Bulletin **6480**
• T I M S S Australia Monograph (Third International Mathematics and Science Study) (AUS ISSN 1834-4224) **2917**
T I M Trade Interactive Multimedia (ITA) **2339**
T I N F O N (NLD ISSN 0927-8982) **2917**
T I N S Neurotoxins Supplement *see* Neurotoxins **6170**
T I P *see* Textverarbeitung, Informationsverarbeitung, Praesentation **1855**
T I P *see* The Industrial-Organizational Psychologist **7362**
T I P A *see* Travaux Interdisciplinaires du Laboratoire Parole et Langage d'Aix-en-Provence **5189**
T I P der Woche (Trends Infos Praktisches) (DEU) **3858**
T I P L J *see* Texas Intellectual Property Law Journal **4794**
T I P R O Target Newsletter (Texas Independent Producers & Royalty Owners Association) (USA) **7471**
T I P S *see* Topical Issues in Procurement Series **7472**
T I P S Journal *see* The International Permaculture Solutions Journal **2615**
T I R E L *see* The Institutional Real Estate Letter **7596**
T I R Southern Africa (ZAF) **8759**
T.I.S. *see* Technologies de l'Information et Societe **8441**
T I S *see* Trends im Stellenmarkt **6704**
T I S *see* The International Soroptimist **2267**
T I S *see* Il Corriere Termo Idro Sanitario **4118**
T I S S E C *see* A C M Transactions on Information and System Security **2511**
T I S T R Research News (Thailand Institute of Scientific and Technological Research) (THA) **7922**
T I S - Tiefbau, Ingenieurbau, Strassenbau (DEU ISSN 0941-1038) **3284**
T J *see* Journal of Creation **7654**
T J *see* Training Journal **1876**
T J C I L *see* Tulsa Journal of Comparative & International Law **4942**
T J C L C R *see* Texas Journal on Civil Liberties and Civil Rights **4843**
T J L P *see* Tennessee Journal of Law & Policy **4793**
T J O G E L *see* Texas Journal of Oil, Gas & Energy Law **4881**
T J S T E L *see* Temple Journal of Science, Technology & Environmental Law **4793**
T J T *see* Toronto Journal of Theology **7690**
T J W L *see* Texas Journal of Women and the Law **4794**
T K (ESP ISSN 1136-7679) **5049**
T K Aktuell (Techniker Krankenkasse) (DEU ISSN 0176-1536) **4524**
T K R *see* The Key Reporter **2289**
T L *see* Trailer Life **8338**
T + L *see* Travel + Leisure **8765**
T L *see* Teacher Librarian **2918**
T L C P *see* Transnational Law & Contemporary Problems **4798**
T L C: The Waiting Room Magazine (ZAF) **4112**
T L Catho (Tous en Ligne) (FRA ISSN 1763-8321) **2215**
T L E (Theorie Litterature Enseignement) (FRA ISSN 0295-1843) **5384**
T L E *see* The Leading Edge (Tulsa) **2786**
• T L Infobits (Teaching and Learning) (USA ISSN 1931-3144) **3004**
T L J *see* Tribal Law Journal **4798**
T L L *see* The Licensing Letter **6754**
T L N *see* Toutes les Nouvelles de l'Hotellerie et du Tourisme **8993**
T L N *see* Truman Lake News **3991**
T L Notre Hebdo *see* T L Catho **2215**
T L O *see* The Learning Organization **1869**
T L R *see* The Leisure Review **4980**
T L R *see* Tax Law Review **4792**
T L R *see* Texas Law Review **4794**
T L R *see* Tulsa Law Review **4798**
T L R M O U S *see* Texas Law Review Manual on Usage and Style **4794**
• T L S (Times Literary Supplement) (GBR ISSN 0307-661X) **5384**
T L Technical Journal *see* Dianxin Yanjiu **3300**
T L - Teknikeren (Teknisk Landsforbund) (DNK ISSN 0901-7917) **8440**
T M *see* Technische Mitteilungen fuer Genietruppen **6448**
T M (Trans Media) (DEU) **5241**
T M (DNK) **6300**
T M (Travel Management) (JPN) **8759**
T M *see* Team Management Briefings **1797**
T M (Amsterdam) (Theatermaker) (NLD ISSN 1567-8628) **8480**
T M A *see* Tijdschrift voor Milieuschade en Aansprakelijkheidsrecht **3470**
T M A (Tijdschrift voor Mediterrane Archeologie) (NLD ISSN 0922-3312) **420**
• T M A Directory of Cigarette Brands (Tobacco Merchants Association of the United States, Inc.) (USA) **8487**
• T M A Executive Summary (Tobacco Merchants Association) (USA) **8487**
• T M A International Tobacco Guide (Tobacco Merchants Association) (USA) **8487**
• T M A Issues Monitor (Tobacco Merchants Association) (USA) **8487**
• T M A Leaf Bulletin (Tobacco Merchants Association) (USA) **8487**
• T M A Legislative Bulletin (Tobacco Merchants Association) (USA) **8487**
• T M A Newsline (Telecommunications Managers Association) (GBR) **2340**
• T M A Tobacco Barometer (Tobacco Merchants Association) (USA) **8487**
• T M A Tobacco Barometer: Smoking, Chewing, Snuff (Tobacco Merchants Association) (USA) **8487**
• T M A Tobacco Tax Guide (Tobacco Merchants Association) (USA) **8487**
• T M A Tobacco Trade Barometer (Tobacco Merchants Association) (USA ISSN 0495-6753) **8487**
• T M A Tobacco Weekly (Tobacco Merchants Association) (USA) **8487**
• T M A Trademark Report (Tobacco Merchants Association) (USA) **8487**
• T M A World Alert (Tobacco Merchants Association) (USA) **8487**
• T M A World Consumption & Production (Tobacco Merchants Association) (USA) **8487**
T M A World Consumption and Production *see* T M A World Consumption & Production **8487**
T M & E *see* Transportation Management & Engineering **8516**
A T M and Financial Self-Service Executive Summary *see* A T M & Financial Self-Service Executive Summary **1305**
T M & I H *see* Tropical Medicine & International Health **5827**
T M. Automaailma *see* T M. Tekniikan Maailma. Automaailma **8606**
• ➤ T M C Academic Journal (Technology, Management and Communications) (SGP ISSN 1793-6020) **8440**
T M Catalogo (Transporte Mundial) (ESP) **8675**
T M D *see* Today's Medical Developments **5722**
T M D M *see* Training & Management Development Methods **1798**
T M E *see* The Mathematics Educator **3072**
T M E Educator *see* The Mathematics Educator **3072**
T M H *see* Target Machinery & Hardware **5460**
T M I *see* Treasury Management International **1799**
T M I Focus (The Monroe Institute) (USA) **3004**
• T M J Nihon Gaku Kansetsu Gakkai Zasshi (JPN ISSN 0915-3004) **6073**
T M J Update: A Current Review of Temporomandibular Joint Developments (USA ISSN 0885-9191) **5719**
T M M. Timarit um Menningn og Manntif *see* Timarit Mals og Menningar **5242**
T M O *see* Tijdschrift voor Medisch Onderwijs **3005**
T M R *see* The Metaphysical Review **5227**
T M R *see* The Melbourne Review **1148**
T M R *see* The Marketing Report **1833**
T M R *see* The Medieval Review **4243**
T M R *see* The Monday Review **2994**
The T M R Weekly Post/L' Hebdo de Ville Mont-Royal (CAN) **3818**
T M Rakennusmaailma (FIN ISSN 1459-1839) **1039**
• ➤ T M S Letters (USA ISSN 1550-2570) **6334**
• T M T Advisor (Telecommunications, Media, and Technology) (USA ISSN 1551-6911) **2340**
T M T China Weekly *see* Interfax. T M T China Weekly **2326**
• T M. Tekniikan Maailma (FIN ISSN 0355-4287) **2641**

Title

10926 T M. TEKNIIKAN MAAILMA. AUTOMAAILMA ULRICH'S PERIODICALS

T M. Tekniikan Maailma. Automaailma (FIN ISSN 0786-2016) **8606**
T M. Transporte Mundial (ESP ISSN 1139-9384) **8675**
T Magazine (USA) **8248**
T N & A *see* Tydskrif vir Nederlands en Afrikaans **5189**
T N B *see* The New Bookbinder **7568**
T N Cs *see* Transnational Corporations **1585**
T N I Briefing Series *see* Transnational Institute. Briefing Series **7189**
T N J *see* Transplant Nurses Journal **5983**
T N L Research Guide Series *see* Philippines. National Library. T N L Research Guide Series **633**
T N Menuiserie - Miroiterie - Metallerie *see* Techniques Nouvelles **1055**
† T N N Outdoors (USA ISSN 1531-6335) **8992**
T N O Building and Construction Research. Annual Report (NLD) **1039**
T N O Jaarverslag *see* Nederlandse Organisatie voor Toegepast Natuurwetenschappelijk Onderzoek. Jaarverslag **7891**
T N O Magazine (Toegepast Natuurwetenschappelijk Onderzoek) (NLD ISSN 1386-5447) **7922**
T N O Magazine (Dutch Edition) *see* T N O Magazine. T N O Informatie- en Communicatietechnologie **2439**
T N O Magazine (Dutch Edition) *see* T N O Magazine. T N O Ruimte en Infrastructuur **3285**
T N O Magazine (Dutch Edition) *see* T N O Magazine. T N O Kwaliteit van Leven **7543**
T N O Magazine (Dutch Edition) *see* T N O Magazine. T N O Industrie en Techniek **1905**
T N O Magazine (Dutch Edition) *see* T N O Magazine. T N O Defensie en Veiligheid **7471**
T N O Magazine. T N O Defensie en Veiligheid (Toegepast Natuurwetenschappelijk Onderzoek) (NLD ISSN 1871-0840) **7471**
T N O Magazine. T N O Industrie en Techniek (Toegepast Natuurwetenschappelijk Onderzoek) (NLD ISSN 1871-0824) **1905**
T N O Magazine. T N O Informatie- en Communicatietechnologie (Toegepast Natuurwetenschappelijk Onderzoek) (NLD ISSN 1871-0859) **2439**
T N O Magazine. T N O Kwaliteit van Leven (Toegepast Natuurwetenschappelijk Onderzoek) (NLD ISSN 1871-0832) **7543**
T N O Magazine. T N O Ruimte en Infrastructuur (Toegepast Natuurwetenschappelijk Onderzoek) (NLD ISSN 1871-0816) **3285**
T N R *see* The New Republic **5230**
T N S *see* Tisk News Service **3990**
T N T *see* Tandlaegernes Nye Tidsskrift **2169**
▼ T N T (FRA ISSN 1957-4193) **6448**
T N T Magazine (DEU) **6515**
T N T Magazine (GBR) **3872**
T N T Magazine *see* Truck 'N Trailer Magazine **8677**
• T N T Magazine Australia (AUS) **8759**
T N W *see* Southern Africa's Travel News Weekly **8757**
T O A R *see* The Original Art Report **510**
T O C H I *see* A C M Transactions on Computer - Human Interaction **2470**
T O C L *see* A C M Transactions on Computational Logic **2405**
T O C S *see* A C M Transactions on Computer Systems **2519**
• T O C S - I N (Tables of Contents of Interest to Classicists) (CAN) **2242**
T O D S *see* A C M Transactions on Database Systems **2529**
• T O G (Terapia Ocupacional Galicia) (ESP ISSN 1885-527X) **6116**
T O G *see* The Obstetrician & Gynaecologist **6001**
T O I S *see* A C M Transactions on Information Systems **1413**
T O J D E *see* Turkish Online Journal of Distance Education **3086**
• ➤ T O J E T (The Turkish Online Journal of Educational Technology) (TUR ISSN 1303-6521) **3083**
T O K K *see* Tijdschrift voor Orthopedagogiek, Kinderpsychiatrie en Klinische Kinderpsychologie **6188**
T O N Y Kids *see* Time Out New York Kids **8761**
The T O N Y Reading Supplement (USA) **5384**
• ➤ T O P (DEU ISSN 1134-5764) **5540**
• T O P. Tijdschrift voor de Ondernemingsrechtpraktijk (NLD ISSN 1570-6613) **4792**
T O S E M *see* A C M Transactions on Software Engineering and Methodology **2587**
T O T *see* The Off-Trader **1643**
T og V *see* Teknologi & Verkstedindustri **3371**
T P (Telovychovny Pracovnik) (CZE ISSN 1212-1061) **6998**
A T P *see* Annals of Tropical Paediatrics **6087**
T P *see* Timber Processing **3716**
T P *see* Top Producer **163**
T P A Messenger *see* Texas Press Messenger **4584**
T P A S Notes (Tenant Participation Advisory Service) (GBR ISSN 0261-197X) **4428**
T P A Speedletter (Texas Pharmacy Association) (USA ISSN 1096-9268) **6882**
T P & D Forum (Year) (Technical Processing and Documentation) (JPN ISSN 0918-404X) **5049**
T P Annales *see* T P de France. Annales **7471**
T P D Annual Report (Technisch Physische Dienst) (NLD) **7042**
T P D Annual Report *see* T P D Jaarverslag **7042**
T P D Jaarverslag/T P D Annual Report (Technisch Physische Dienst) (NLD) **7042**
T P de France. Annales (Travaux Publics) (FRA ISSN 1254-5678) **7471**
• ➤ T P E Digitaal (Tijdschrift Politieke Ekonomie) (NLD ISSN 1875-8797) **7187**
T P H *see* The Public Historian **4157**
T P J *see* The Tube & Pipe Journal **6336**
T P L *see* The Philadelphia Lawyer **4758**
T.P.L. News (Toronto Public Library) (CAN ISSN 0039-8470) **5049**
T P M *see* Team Performance Management **1797**
T P M. Testing Psicometria Metodologia (ITA ISSN 1720-0121) **1876**
T P N *see* Telecom Plus International **2340**
▼ • T P O (Treatment Plant Operator) (USA) **3513**
T P P *see* Australian Tenancy Practice and Precedents **4624**
T P Plus (TransitPulse) (USA) **8512**
T P Q *see* Text and Performance Quarterly **5386**
T P Q OnLine *see* The Pittsburgh Quarterly (Pittsburgh, 1991) **5351**
T P R *see* Tijdschrift voor Privaatrecht **4796**
T P S Bulletin *see* Thomas Paine Society Bulletin **7188**
T P S Extra *see* Theorie und Praxis der Sozialpaedagogik. Extra **2169**
T P S S Cooperative Effort News (Takoma Park-Silver Spring) (USA ISSN 1933-1398) **3469**
T P Tecnica del Punto *see* Tecnica del Punto **2250**
T plus D *see* T+ D **1876**
▼ • T Q (Transportation Quarterly) (USA ISSN 1946-1976) **4792**
T Q H A Newsletter (USA) **8299**
• ➤ The T Q M Journal (Total Quality Management) (GBR ISSN 1754-2731) **1797**
The T Q M Magazine *see* The T Q M Journal **1797**
T Q S News (Tonatiuh-Quinto Sol) (USA ISSN 1045-8875) **5384**
A T R *see* Australian Target Rifle **8305**
T R *see* Tourism Review **8764**
T R A C Annual Report (Transvaal Rural Action Committee) (ZAF) **7216**
T R A C E (Travaux et Recherches dans les Ameriques du Centre) (MEX ISSN 0185-6286) **357**
T R A C E News (Teachers of Religion and Christian Ethics) (CAN ISSN 1196-6777) **7687**
T R A F F I C Bulletin (Trade Records Analysis of Flora and Fauna in Commerce) (GBR ISSN 0267-4297) **2628**
T R C Spectral Data - 1 H Nuclear Magnetic Resonance (Thermodynamics Research Center) (USA ISSN 1088-1468) **2106**
➤ T R C Spectral Data - 13 C Nuclear Magnetic Resonance (Thermodynamics Research Center) (USA ISSN 1088-1506) **2106**
➤ T R C Spectral Data - Infrared (Thermodynamics Research Center) (USA ISSN 1088-7989) **2106**
T R C Spectral Data - Mass (Thermodynamics Research Center) (USA ISSN 1088-1476) **2106**
T R C Spectral Data - Raman (Thermodynamics Research Center) (USA ISSN 1088-1484) **2106**
➤ T R C Spectral Data - Ultraviolet (Thermodynamics Research Center) (USA ISSN 1088-1492) **2106**
➤ T R C Thermodynamic Tables - Hydrocarbons (Thermodynamics Research Center) (USA) **2141**
➤ T R C Thermodynamic Tables - Non-Hydrocarbons (Thermodynamics Research Center) (USA) **2106**
• T R Daily (USA ISSN 1082-9350) **2340**
T R E *see* Theory and Research in Education (Print) **2919**
T R E - Annual Lapidei (Territorio Restauro Edilizia) (ITA) **1039**
T R E - European Building Magazine (Territorio - Restauro - Edilizia) (ITA) **1039**
T R E S L *see* Texas Review of Entertainment and Sports Law **4795**
T R I M *see* Trends in Information Management **5051**
T R I M Bulletin (Tax Reform Immediately) (USA) **1946**
T R I News (Tropical Resources Institute) (USA) **3704**
T R I P *see* The Resources of International Permaculture **700**
T R I P Rapport (Transfusie Reacties in Patienten) (NLD ISSN 1873-8869) **5941**
• T R I P South (Travel Reference Information Planner) (USA ISSN 1067-926X) **8759**
T R I Public Data Release *see* Toxics Release Inventory. Public Data Release **3470**
• T R I S Electronic Bibliographic Data Base (Transportation Research Information Services) (USA) **8530**
T R I U M F Annual Report Scientific Activities (Tri-University Meson Facility) (CAN) **7072**
T R I U M F Financial and Administrative Annual Report (Tri-University Meson Facility) (CAN) **7072**
• The T R I Z Journal/Theory of Inventive Problem Solving Journal (Teoriya Reshniya Izobretatelskikg Zadatch) (USA ISSN 1543-8813) **1181**
T R J *see* Textile Research Journal **8460**
• T R L News (Transport Research Laboratory) (GBR) **8635**
• T R L Reports (Transport Research Laboratory) (GBR ISSN 0968-4107) **8635**
T R L State of the Art Review (Transport Research Laboratory) (GBR) **8635**
T R N *see* Tasmanian Rail News **8625**
T R N *see* Technology Research News **8442**
T R News (Transportation Research) (USA ISSN 0738-6826) **8512**
T R O L *see* The Review of Litigation **4769**
T R O L P *see* Texas Review of Law & Politics **4795**
T R O S (Tijdschrift voor Ruimtelijke Ordening en Stedebouw) (BEL ISSN 1371-8274) **1039**
T R P *see* Australia. Department of the Treasury. Treasury Research Papers **1438**
T R Q (GBR) **3872**
T R Transfer (CHE ISSN 1023-0823) **8440**
T R - Wissen (CHE ISSN 1023-3377) **8440**
T R Y M - TSP Version *see* Australia. Bureau of Statistics. Treasury Model of the Australian Economy - TSP Version **1210**
• T R's Last-Mile Telecom Report (USA ISSN 1530-2113) **2340**
• T R's Online Census (Telecommunications Reports) (USA ISSN 1538-845X) **7580**
• T R's State Newswire...with T R Insight (Telecommunications Reports) (USA ISSN 1542-3328) **2340**
T S *see* Tijdschrift voor Tijdschriftstudies **7574**
T S *see* Theological Studies **7689**
T S A Hebdo *see* T S A Mensuel **8074**
• T S A Mensuel (Travail Social Actualites) (FRA) **8074**
T S B *see* The Sophist's Bane **3002**
T S B A BoardTalk (USA) **3034**
T S B Annual Report to Parliament/B S T Rapport Annuel au Parlement (Transportation Safety Board) (CAN ISSN 1709-2841) **7471**
• T S B Statistical Summary, Marine Occurrences (Transportation Safety Board of Canada) (CAN ISSN 1191-7245) **8531**
• T S B Statistical Summary of Aviation Occurrences (Transportation Safety Board of Canada) (CAN ISSN 1482-6992) **7549**
T S B Statistical Summary, Railway Occurrences (Transportation Safety Board) (CAN ISSN 1196-8702) **7549**
T S C A - T S C A T S *see* Toxic Substances Control Act: Report to Congress for Fiscal Year **3501**
• T. S. Elrieos Yeon'gu (KOR ISSN 1225-5912) **5384**
➤ T S I Journal of Particle Instrumentation (USA) **3396**
T S I. Technique et Sciences Informatiques (FRA ISSN 0752-4072) **2528**
T S J *see* Tolstoy Studies Journal **5389**
T S J *see* Training and Simulation Journal **6449**
T S L *see* Tijdschrift voor Sociaal Wetenschappelijk Onderzoek van de Landbouw **207**
T S L *see* The Sporting Life **8206**
T S M *see* The Security Magazine **2680**
T S M. Techniques Sciences Methodes *see* Techniques Sciences Methodes, Genie Urbain Genie Rural **3469**
T S M Techniques Sciences Methodes, Genie Urbain Genie Rural *see* Techniques Sciences Methodes, Genie Urbain Genie Rural **3469**
▼ T S Mag (FRA ISSN 1960-2251) **1855**
T S N Fantasy Football *see* The Sporting News Fantasy Football **8246**
† T S O / I S P F Update (Time Sharing Option / Interactive System Productivity Facility) (USA) **8992**
T S P *see* The Sport Psychologist **7409**
T S Q *see* Toronto Slavic Quarterly **5389**
T S Q *see* Technical Services Quarterly **5050**
T S R *see* Third Sector Review **8010**
T S T *see* Terahertz Science & Technology **7923**
T S T A Advocate (Texas State Teachers Association) (USA ISSN 0279-022X) **2917**
T S T. Transportes, Servicios y Telecomunicaciones (ESP ISSN 1578-5777) **8512**
T S Today (Trading Standards) (GBR ISSN 1475-1364) **1845**
T S Vgg 1848 Stadecken - Elsheim. Vereinsnachrichten (DEU) **8211**
➤ T S W Development & Embryology (The Scientific World) (USA ISSN 1749-4958) **707**
• ➤ T S W Holistic Health & Medicine (The Scientific World) (USA ISSN 1749-494X) **315**
• ➤ T S W Urology (The Scientific World) (USA ISSN 1747-8049) **6275**
• T-Shirt Business Info Mapping Newsletter (USA ISSN 1053-6493) **1968**
T T Circuit Assen (Tourist Trophy) (NLD ISSN 1873-9636) **8211**
T T G *see* T M A Tobacco Tax Guide **8487**
• T T G Asia (SGP) **8759**
T T G - B T M I C E China (SGP) **6282**
T T G China *see* Luyebao **8731**
† T T G Directory (Travel Trade Gazette) (GBR) **8992**
T T G Europa *see* Travel Trade Gazette Europa **8994**
• T T G India (Travel Trade Gazette) (SGP) **8759**
• T T G M I C E (Travel Trade Gazette Meetings, Incentives, Conferences and Exhibitions) (SGP) **6282**
T T G M I C E Planner (Travel Trade Gazette Meetings, Incentives, Conferences and Exhibitions) (SGP) **6283**
T T G Meetings, Incentives, Conferences and Exhibitions *see* T T G M I C E **6282**
T T G Travel Trade Gazette Europa *see* Travel Trade Gazette Europa **8994**
T T G - U K & Ireland *see* Travel Trade Gazette U K & Ireland **8768**
T T I *see* Textile Technology Index **8464**
T T I City Reports (Travel and Tourism Intelligence) (GBR ISSN 1465-7694) **8759**
T T I Country Reports *see* Country Reports **8695**
T T I Q *see* Tsetse and Trypanosomiasis Information Quarterly **5828**
• T T J (Timber Trades Journal) (GBR ISSN 1740-701X) **3716**
T T J - Timber and Wood Products *see* T T J **3716**
T T K K ja Co *see* Tekhne **3004**
T T K Radio Science and Engineering Publications/Teknillinen Korkeakoulu. Radiolaboratorio. Julkaisu S (Teknillinen Korkeakoulu) (FIN ISSN 1797-4364) **2364**
T T K. Technical Report *see* Tokyo Tekkotsu Kyoryo. Gijutsuho **3285**
T T L *see* Tuttolibri Tempo Libero **7575**
T T M (Truck en Transport Management) (NLD ISSN 1380-2852) **8675**
T T N *see* Table Tennis News **8248**
T T O S Bulletin (Toy Train Operating Society) (USA ISSN 0095-3059) **4348**
T T O S Order Board (Toy Train Operating Society) (USA) **4348**
T T P I Trade Gazette (Tasmanian Trade Protective Institute) (AUS ISSN 0011-1716) **1433**
T T - Profile *see* Bosch-Zuender **1880**
T T R *see* Tocqueville Review **8144**
T T R A News (Travel and Tourism Research Association) (USA ISSN 1080-837X) **8759**
T T R. Traduction Terminologie Redaction (CAN ISSN 0835-8443) **5185**
T T Y ja Co *see* Tekhne **3004**
T. Tennis (JPN) **8337**
T Three *see* T3 **2439**
T U *see* Teknisk Ukeblad **8443**
• T U B A - A R/Turkish Academy of Sciences Journal of Archaeology (Tukiye Bilimler Akademisi Arkeoloji Dergisi) (TUR ISSN 1301-8566) **420**
T U C General Council Report *see* Trades Union Congress. General Council Report **4603**
T U C News (Trades Union Congress of Ghana) (GHA) **4603**
T U F S *see* Tokyo University of Foreign Studies **5188**
T U I A F P W Information (Trade Union International of Agricultural Forestry and Plantation Workers) (RUS) **4603**
T U Intern (Technische Universitaet) (DEU) **2303**
T U M J *see* Tehran University Medical Journal **5720**
T U News (Tingley's United) (USA) **3784**
T U S E D *see* Journal of Turkish Science Education **7873**
T U S Info (Turn- und Sportverein) (DEU ISSN 0179-0153) **8211**
T U S T *see* Tunnelling and Underground Space Technology **3224**
T U S Vereinsnachrichten (Turn- und Sportvereinigung Gaarden von 1875 e.V.) (DEU) **8211**
• T U Spektrum (DEU ISSN 0946-1817) **3221**
T U T (Textiles a Usages Techniques) (FRA ISSN 1161-9317) **8457**
T U X (Torvolds Unix) (USA) **2525**
T U - Zeitschrift fuer Technik im Unterricht (DEU ISSN 0342-6254) **8440**
T Ue V Autoreport (DEU) **8606**
T Ue V Journal *see* T Ue V Sued Journal **8440**
T Ue V Sued Journal (T Ue V Sued AG) (DEU ISSN 1863-8198) **8440**
T V 14 (DEU) **2391**
T V 2 (CHE) **2391**
T V 4Wochen (DEU) **2391**
T V 4x7 (DEU) **2391**
T V 7 (RUS ISSN 1726-0876) **2391**
T V 7 Dias (PRT) **2392**
T V 7 Jours (CAN ISSN 1192-7615) **2392**
T V 8 (CHE ISSN 1424-991X) **2392**
T V A Report *see* Tennessee Valley Authority. Report **2798**
T V A Z. Tijdschrift van de Vereniging van Artsen in de Swakzinnigenzorg *see* Tijdschrift voor Artsen voor Verstandelijk Gehandicapten **6188**
T V & Cable Factbook *see* Television and Cable Factbook **2396**
T V & Film Extras (USA) **2392**
T V and Film Literature *see* Dian Jiang Ying Shi **8950**
T V & Satellite Week (GBR) **2392**
T V & Satellite Week. Midlands - Wales and West *see* T V & Satellite Week **2392**
T V & Satellite Week. North West - Anglia *see* T V & Satellite Week **2392**
T V & Satellite Week. North West - Border *see* T V & Satellite Week **2392**
T V & Satellite Week. Northwest - Ulster *see* T V & Satellite Week **2392**
T V & Satellite Week. South - Southwest *see* T V & Satellite Week **2392**
T V & Satellite Week. Yorkshire - Tyne - Tees *see* T V & Satellite Week **2392**
T V & Video World (IND) **2392**
T V Anzeiger (DEU) **2392**
T V Apotheke (DEU) **6882**

T V Apotheken Spiegel (DEU) 2392
T V - Arena (DEU ISSN 1862-930X) 2392
T V B (Tijdschrift voor Verzorging en Beheer) (NLD ISSN 0167-0018) 4056
T V B E see Television Broadcast Europe 2397
T V B Europe see Television Broadcast Europe 2397
T V - Bladet see Kristianstadsbladet 3956
T v C see Tijdschrift voor Consumentenrecht en Handelspraktijken 2641
T V Cablu see T V Satelit 2394
T V Choice (Central Edition) see T V Choice (London, Anglia & Central Edition) 2392
T V Choice (London & Anglia Edition) see T V Choice (London, Anglia & Central Edition) 2392
▼ T V Choice (London, Anglia & Central Edition) (GBR ISSN 1758-4124) 2392
T V Choice (North Edition) see T V Choice (London, Anglia & Central Edition) 2392
T V Choice (Scotland Edition) see T V Choice (London, Anglia & Central Edition) 2392
T V Choice (South & South West Edition) (GBR ISSN 1745-9346) 2392
T V Choice (Ulster Edition) see T V Choice (London, Anglia & Central Edition) 2392
T V Digital (DEU ISSN 1613-7221) 2392
T V Dimensions (USA ISSN 0884-1098) 2392
T V direkt (DEU ISSN 1616-8992) 2392
T V Diskurs (DEU ISSN 1433-9439) 2169
T V Duel & Film (CZE ISSN 1214-4770) 2392
T V E T see Technical and Vocational Education and Training 3004
T V Easy (GBR ISSN 1747-1133) 2392
T V Executive (USA ISSN 0736-2986) 2392
T V Familie (BEL ISSN 1371-8185) 3802
T V Film (NLD ISSN 1574-1176) 2392
T V Film Memorabilia (Television) (GBR ISSN 1753-6693) 4348
T V Gaido/T V Guide (JPN) 2392
T V Grandes Chaines (FRA ISSN 1767-0519) 2392
T V Guia (PRT ISSN 0871-7362) 2392
▼ T V Guide (DEU) 2392
T V Guide see T V Gaido 2392
The T V Guide (NZL ISSN 1170-3776) 2392
T V Guide (SAU) 2392
• T V Guide (USA ISSN 0039-8543) 2392
• T V Guide (Canadian Edition) (Online) (CAN) 2392
T V Guide (Canadian Edition) (Print) see T V Guide (Canadian Edition) (Online) 2392
T V - Guiden Programbladet (NOR ISSN 1890-0488) 2392
T V Hebdo (CAN ISSN 0039-8551) 2392
T V Highlights (DEU) 2393
T V Hits (AUS ISSN 1032-2973) 2215
• T V Hits (GBR ISSN 0958-2363) 2393
T V Hits Hot! see Hot! 2382
T V Hoeren und Sehen (DEU ISSN 0940-0656) 2393
• T V info (DEU) 2393
• T V International (Television) (GBR) 2393
• T V International Daily (Online) (GBR) 2393
• T V International Daily (Print) (GBR ISSN 1086-5675) 2393
• T V International Sourcebook (Year) (GBR ISSN 1082-3913) 2393
T V J see The Veterinary Journal 8812
T V K 1877 Echo (Turnverein 1877 e.V. Essen-Kupferdreh) (DEU) 8211
T V Karstadt (DEU) 2393
† T V Key (ITA) 8992
T V Klar (DEU ISSN 0945-5981) 2393
T V Krant (NLD ISSN 0927-3204) 2393
† T V Life (DEU) 8992
T V Life (JPN) 2393
T V M see Trib Magazine 8994
T V Magazin (CZE ISSN 1210-5120) 2393
T V Magazine (CAN ISSN 0316-2397) 2393
T V Magazine (JPN) 2393
T V Mais (PRT ISSN 0872-3559) 2393
T V Mania (ROM ISSN 1584-0336) 2393
▼ T V Max (CZE ISSN 1801-8912) 2393
T V Max (SVK ISSN 1336-9512) 2393
• T V Media (AUT) 2393
T V Mini (CZE) 2393
T V Movie (DEU ISSN 0945-6007) 2393
▼ T V Movie Digital (DEU) 2393
† T V Movie Multimedia (DEU) 8992
T V Neu (DEU ISSN 0949-4502) 2393
T V News (New York) (USA) 2393
T V News Weekly see Dazhong Dianshi 2379
T V Notas (USA) 2393
T V Now (IRL ISSN 1393-9475) 2393
T V Observer (GBR) 2393
T V Oko (SVK ISSN 1335-910X) 2393
T V P - Fachzeitschrift fuer Textilveredlung und Promotion (DEU ISSN 1613-2505) 8458
T V P P A News (Tennessee Valley Public Power Association) (USA ISSN 1547-5158) 3332
T V Piccolino (DEU) 2393
T V Plus (CZE ISSN 1212-6500) 2393
T V Plus (USA) 2394
T V Plus! (ZAF) 2393
† • T V Program Investor (USA ISSN 0885-2340) 8992
T V pur (DEU) 2394
T V Quick (Central Edition) see T V Quick (London, Anglia and Central Edition) 2394
T V Quick (HTV Edition) see T V Quick (London, Anglia and Central Edition) 2394
T V Quick (London and Anglia Edition) see T V Quick (London, Anglia and Central Edition) 2394
▼ T V Quick (London, Anglia and Central Edition) (GBR ISSN 1758-4132) 2394
T V Quick (North Edition) see T V Quick (London, Anglia and Central Edition) 2394
T V Quick (Scottish & Grampian Edition) see T V Quick (London, Anglia and Central Edition) 2394
T V Quick (South and South West Ed.) (GBR ISSN 1745-932X) 2394
T V Quick (Ulster Edition) see T V Quick (London, Anglia and Central Edition) 2394
T V Research see Dianshi Yanjiu 2380
T V Revue (CZE ISSN 1212-2998) 2394
T V Satelit (ROM ISSN 1221-6453) 2394
▼ T V Schlau (DEU) 2394
T V Sept Jours see T V 7 Jours 2392
T V Sete Dias see T V 7 Dias 2392
T V Sorrisi e Canzoni (ITA ISSN 0038-156X) 2394
T V Special (SVN ISSN 1408-0877) 2394
• T V Spielfilm (DEU ISSN 0938-8729) 2394
T V Spielfilm XXL (DEU) 2394
• T V Sportsfile (USA) 8211
T V Star (CZE ISSN 1801-4860) 2394
• T V Station Deals & Finance Databook (USA ISSN 1542-9164) 2394
T V Station Deals and Finance Databook see T V Station Deals & Finance Databook 2394
T V Story see Stars 2391
T V Story (ROM ISSN 1583-6533) 2394
T V Svet (SVK ISSN 1336-9369) 2394
T V T see T V Technology 2394
T V taeglich (CHE) 2394
• T V Technology (USA ISSN 0887-1701) 2394
T V Technology (Asia-Pacific Edition) see T V Technology 2394
T V Technology (European Edition) see T V Technology 2394
T V Technology (Japanese Edition) see T V Technology 2394
T V Technology (Latin American Edition) see T V Technology 2394
T V Technology America Latina (USA) 2394
T V Technology and Production. European Edition (USA) 2394
T V Technology. Asia-Pacific Edition (USA) 2394
T V Technology Nihongo Ban (USA) 2394
T V Telescope (CAN) 2394
T V Times (GBR ISSN 0962-1660) 2394
T V Today (DEU ISSN 0948-2717) 2394
T V Today (USA) 2394
▼ T V Today Digital (DEU) 2394
▼ T V! Top (DEU) 2394
T V Translators Engineering Data Base in Order by State, Channel, Call (USA) 2349
T V Translators Engineering Data Base in Order by State, City, Channel (USA) 2349
T V Trends (USA) 2395
• T V und Serien (DEU ISSN 1438-0250) 2395
T V V L Magazine (Tijdschrift Vereniging voor Verwarming en Luchtbehandeling) (NLD ISSN 1380-5428) 4127
T V V S see Ondernemingsrecht 4752
T V Vier (CHE) 2395
T V Week (AUS ISSN 0810-249X) 2395
T V Week (HKG) 2395
T V Week Magazine (CAN) 2395
T V World (CAN) 2395
† T V World (DEU) 8992
† T V Wrestlers (USA ISSN 1053-041X) 8992
T V y Novelas (USA ISSN 0188-0683) 2395
T V y Video (USA) 2340
▼ T V Year (USA ISSN 1935-7486) 2395
T v Z: Tijdschrift voor Verpleegkundigen (NLD ISSN 1380-3425) 5982
T V Zone (GBR ISSN 0957-3844) 2395
T V Zone Special (GBR ISSN 0960-8230) 2395
T W/Convention Industry (Tagungs-Wirtschaft) (DEU ISSN 0342-7951) 6283
T W see Tissue World 6739
• T W 3 (The Whole Wired World) (USA ISSN 1094-8104) 5384
T W A R O News (Asian Regional Organisation of the International Textile Garment and Leather Workers' Federation) (JPN) 8458
T W A S see Twayne's World Authors Series 5391
T W I Bulletin (GBR) 6344
• T W I C E (This Week in Consumer Electronics) (USA ISSN 0892-7278) 3114
T W I T see This Week in Texas 4379
T W I W see This Week in Washington (Online) 7188
T W M Newsletter see Technologies for Worship 8442
T W O (Two Wheels Only) (GBR ISSN 1473-9674) 8269
T W Q see Third World Quarterly 1606
T W Q see The Washington Quarterly 7273
T W S (Tanken Wassen Shoppen) (NLD ISSN 1871-9414) 6794
T W S Actualiteit (Tweetalige Wetboeken Story-Scientia Actualiteit) (BEL ISSN 0778-9572) 4792
T W S Annual Report see The Wilderness Year (Year) 2632
T W TagungsRegionen (DEU) 6283
T W U Express (Transport Workers Union of America) (USA ISSN 0039-8659) 4603
T Y A Today (Theatre for Young Audiences) (USA) 8480
T Y R (USA ISSN 1538-9413) 3623
T Z see Trail Zone 8338
T Z (DEU) 3858
T Z B (Technicke Zariadenia Budov) (SVK ISSN 1210-356X) 4127
T Z T A (CAN ISSN 1912-2004) 3567
T Z T A International Newspaper see T Z T A 3567
• T-Zero Xpandizine (USA) 5384
T3 (Tomorrow's Technology Today) (DNK ISSN 1603-595X) 8440
T3 (Tomorrow's Technology Today) (GBR ISSN 1364-2642) 3114
T3 (Tomorrow's Technology Today) (ITA ISSN 1825-2427) 3114
T3 (Tomorrow's Technology Today) (PHL) 3114
T3 (ZAF ISSN 1684-7008) 2439
T3 - Technical Textile Technology (USA ISSN 1553-944X) 8458
• T3 - Transport Technology Today (USA) 8512
Ta Kung Pao (HKG ISSN 0039-8675) 3875
Ta Ma Ko Yu Chih Sheng see Sound of Malaysian's Musician 6618
Taag/Trains (SWE ISSN 0039-8683) 8625
Taal & Arbeidsmarkt see Taal en Arbeidsmarkt 8992
† Taal en Arbeidsmarkt (NLD ISSN 1871-7322) 8992
➤ Taal en Tongval (NLD ISSN 0039-8691) 5185
Taal van het Jaar (Ed. Van Dale Lexicografie) see Van Dale Jaarboek Taal (Year) 5193
Taalbeheersing in de Praktijk see Over Taal 5158
Die Taalgenoot (ZAF ISSN 0039-8705) 5241
Taalkalender (NLD ISSN 1871-6504) 5185
Taalkundige see Linguiste 5145
Taamuli (TZA ISSN 0049-2817) 7187
Taasiot see Ta'asiyot 5460
Ta'asiyot (ISR ISSN 0792-1322) 5460
Taasiyot see Ta'asiyot 5460
At-Ta'awin/Cooperation (SAU) 3912
Tabac see Tabak 8487
† Il Tabacco (ITA ISSN 1124-3791) 8992
• Tabaccologia (ITA ISSN 1970-1187) 8487
Tabak/Tabac (CHE ISSN 0039-8721) 8487
Tabak Plus Gemak (NLD ISSN 1566-8142) 8487
Die Tabak Zeitung (DEU ISSN 0049-2825) 8488
Der Tabakwaren-Grosshandel (DEU) 8488
Tabanque (ESP ISSN 0214-7742) 2917
Tabaret (CAN ISSN 1187-8622) 2303
Tabasco Hoy (MEX ISSN 1563-700X) 3911
Tabbin Institute for Metallurgical Studies. Bulletin/Al-Nasrat al-'Imiyyat li-Ma'had al-Tibin lil-Dirasat al-Ma'danit (EGY ISSN 1110-2519) 6480
Tabco Bulletin (USA) 3034
• Tabelbilag til Landsforsoegene (DNK ISSN 0908-0813) 255
Tabellae Ansatae see Bound & Lettered 479
The Taber Times (CAN) 3818
Taber's Cyclopedia Medical Dictionary (USA ISSN 1065-1357) 5719
Tabeto. Anexo (ESP ISSN 1138-4069) 4272
Tabi-Meijin/Excellent Vacationers (JPN) 8759
Tabi - Meijin see Tabi-Meijin 8759
Tabi ni Deyo (JPN) 8759
Tabi to Tetsudo (JPN) 8759
Tabibok/Your Doctor (LBN) 5720
Tabla Redonda (ARG) 5436
Tablas (CUB) 5384
Table et Cadeau (FRA ISSN 0039-8780) 4563
Table of International Telex Relations and Traffic (CHE ISSN 0074-9052) 2371
Table of Sunrise, Sunset, Twilight, Moonrise and Moonset (PHL ISSN 0115-3307) 582
Table Quebecoise sur l'Herbe a Poux see Le Flash Herbe a Poux 7517
Table Rock Lake Vacation - Service and Relocation Guide (USA) 8759
Table Ronde Francaise. Annuaire see Table Ronde Francaise. Guide 4272
Table Ronde Francaise. Guide (FRA ISSN 1953-132X) 4272
Table Ronde Nationale sur l'Environnement et l'Economie. Revue see National Round Table on the Environment and the Economy. Review (Print) 3454
Table Ronde Nationale sur l'Environnement et l'Economie. Revue see National Round Table on the Environment and the Economy. Review (Online) 3454
Table Tennis News (GBR ISSN 0039-8799) 8248
Table Tennis World see Pingpang Shijie 8242
Tableau (BEL) 4965
Tableau (NLD ISSN 0166-4492) 521
Tableau (Fredericton) (CAN ISSN 0845-8081) 6537
Tableau (Winnipeg) (CAN) 6537
Tableau Economique de la Reunion (REU ISSN 0994-415X) 1521
• Tableau Synthese sur les Professions et Metiers en Demande (CAN ISSN 1719-5543) 6704
Tableaux de l'Economie Caledonienne see New Caledonia. Institut de la Statistique et des Etudes Economiques. Tableaux de l'Economie Caledonienne 1254
Tableaux de l'Economie Polynesienne (PYF ISSN 0765-1104) 1269
Tableaux Economiques de l'Ile-de-France. Edition (Year) see Tableaux Economiques Regionaux 1521
Tableaux Economiques de Midi-Pyrenees (FRA ISSN 0291-8692) 1269
Tableaux Economiques Regionaux (FRA ISSN 1635-0529) 1521
Tableaux Economiques Regionaux: Guadeloupe (Year) (GLP ISSN 0999-1271) 1269
Tableaux Economiques Regionaux: Guyane (Year) (GUF ISSN 0999-128X) 1269
Tableaux Economiques Regionaux: Martinique (Year) (FRA ISSN 0999-1409) 1269
The Tablelander Newspaper (AUS) 3796
Tablelands Advertiser (AUS) 3796
Tables de Mortalite, Canada, Provinces et Territoires see Life Tables, Canada, Provinces and Territories 8385
Tables for Tertiary Planning Units: Quarters, Households and Population by Type of Quarters see Hong Kong Special Administrative Region of China. Census and Statistics Department. Hong Kong (Year) Population By-Census. Tables for Tertiary Planning Units: Quarters, Households and Population by Type of Quarters 7309
Tables Legislatives Mensuelles (BEL ISSN 0778-905X) 4792
Tables of Contents of Interest to Classicists see T O C S - I N 2242
Tables of Redemption Values for United States Series E E Savings Bond and Series I Savings Bonds see U.S. Department of the Treasury. Bureau of Public Debt. Tables of Redemption Values for United States Series E E Savings Bond and Series I Savings Bonds 1657
Tables of Redemption Values for United States Series E Savings Bond and Savings Notes see U.S. Department of the Treasury. Bureau of Public Debt. Tables of Redemption Values for United States Series E Savings Bond and Savings Notes 1953
The Tablet (GBR ISSN 0039-8837) 7687
† Tablet (NZL ISSN 0110-4853) 8992
▼ • Tablet (New York, 2009) (USA) 3567
The Tablet (New York) (USA ISSN 0039-8845) 7819
Tabletalk (USA ISSN 1064-881X) 7776
• Tablets and Capsules (USA ISSN 1549-9928) 6882
Tableware International (GBR ISSN 0143-7755) 2046
Tabloid (ITA) 4584
Tabloid di Ortopedia (ITA ISSN 1970-741X) 6073
Tabloid Radiologia (ITA ISSN 1971-0690) 6209
• Tabo Kikai/Turbomachinery (JPN ISSN 0385-8839) 3396
Tabo Kikai Koenkai/Turbomachinery Society of Japan. Proceedings (JPN) 3396
Tabona (ESP ISSN 0213-2818) 420
• ➤ Taboo (USA ISSN 1080-5400) 2917
Tabor (SVN ISSN 0492-1127) 2169
Tabor Drums News (USA) 3784
Tabortuz (SVK) 2215
Tabu (NLD ISSN 0165-9200) 5185
Tabu Tattoo (USA) 521
➤ Tabula (ESP ISSN 1132-6506) 5050
Tabula (HUN ISSN 1419-3310) 357
• Tabula Rasa (COL ISSN 1794-2489) 4477
• Tabularia (FRA ISSN 1630-7364) 4272
• Taburet (RUS) 4563
Tac News (USA) 8211
• Il Tacco d'Italia (ITA ISSN 1971-6605) 3899
Il Taccuino dell'Azionista (ITA ISSN 0082-1446) 1654
• tachles (CHE ISSN 1660-3540) 3567
Tachograf (CZE ISSN 1211-5827) 8512
Tachometer (DEU) 8606
Tacis Programme. Contract Information Update see European Commission. Tacis Programme. Contract Information Update 1595
Tack 'n Togs Buyers Guide (USA) 8299
Tack 'n Togs Merchandising (USA ISSN 0149-3442) 8299
Tackett Family Journal (USA ISSN 1052-7753) 3784
Tackle & Guns (GBR ISSN 0955-7695) 8337
Tackle Talk International (GBR) 3609
• Tacoma Daily Index (USA) 1181
Tacoma - Pierce County Chamber of Commerce Update (USA) 1410
• Tacoma Reporter (USA) 6622
Tacoma Trainsheet (USA) 8625
Tacoma True Citizen (USA) 3567
• Tactical Knives (USA ISSN 1079-865X) 4348
• Tactical Response (USA ISSN 1543-8856) 2669
The Tactile Mind (USA ISSN 1540-6938) 5384
Tactique & Strategie (BEL ISSN 1373-3672) 1797
Tadias (USA ISSN 1936-9638) 3567
Tae Kwon Do & Korean Martial Arts (GBR) 8211
Tae Kwon Do Spiegel (DEU) 8211
Tae Kwon Do Times (USA) 8211
† Taeckkolmia (DEU ISSN 0171-3558) 8992
• Taeglich Kress (DEU) 2340
Taegliche Praxis (DEU ISSN 0494-464X) 5720
Taegliche Rundschau (DEU) 4272
Taeglicher Hafen Bericht Deutsche Schiffahrtszeitung see T H B Deutsche Schiffahrtszeitung 8663
Taegu University. Research Institute for Special Education. Journal see Teugsu Gyoyug Yeon-gu 3048
• Taehan Chonghyong Oekwa Hakhoechi/Korean Orthopedic Association. Journal (KOR) 6073
• Taehan Kanho/Korean Nurse (KOR ISSN 0047-3618) 5982
Taehan Pangsason Uihakhoe Chapchi (KOR ISSN 0301-4029) 6209
Taehan P'ibu Kwahakhoe Chi/Korean Journal of Dermatology (KOR ISSN 0494-4739) 5882
Taehan Pogon Yongu/Korean Public Health Research (KOR ISSN 1738-3897) 7543

Title

10928 TAEHAN SIN'GYONG CHONGSIN UIHAK HOEJI ULRICH'S PERIODICALS

Taehan Sin'gyong Chongsin Uihak Hoeji/Korean Neuropsychiatric Association. Journal (KOR ISSN 1015-4817) **6187**
Taehan Songhyong Oekwa Hakhoe Chi/Korean Society of Plastic and Reconstructive Surgery. Journal (KOR ISSN 1015-6402) **6260**
Taehan Uisa Hyophoe Chi/Korean Medical Association. Journal (KOR) **5720**
Taekwondo Aktuell (DEU) **8211**
Taekwondo Spiegel *see* Tae Kwon Do Spiegel **8211**
Taenk/Think (DNK ISSN 1604-6307) **2641**
Taenk og test *see* Taenk **2641**
▼ Taenk, Penge (DNK ISSN 1903-7457) **2641**
Taenk plus Test *see* Taenk **2641**
Taenk + Test *see* Taenk **2641**
Taetigkeitsbericht des Verkehrs Arbeitsinspektorates fuer das Jahr (Year) (AUT) **8531**
Taetowier Magazin *see* TaetowierMagazin **521**
TaetowierMagazin (DEU ISSN 1614-9394) **521**
TAFELINK *see* T A F E Link (Online) **2946**
Taft and the University of Cincinnati Series in Latin American and Hispanic American Theatre (USA) **8480**
Taft Memorial Fund and University of Cincinnati Series in Latin American and Hispanic Theatre *see* Taft and the University of Cincinnati Series in Latin American and Hispanic American Theatre **8480**
Taft Monthly Portfolio (USA) **8074**
Tag (DEU) **3858**
Tag der Juristischen Fakultaet (DEU ISSN 1438-0439) **4792**
• Tag des Herrn (DEU ISSN 0492-1283) **7819**
Tag fuer Tag (DEU) **7328**
Tagblatt (CHE ISSN 1424-2869) **3959**
• Tageblatt (LUX) **3906**
• Tages-Anzeiger (CHE ISSN 1422-9994) **3959**
Tageslicht (DEU) **3332**
Die Tagespost (DEU ISSN 1615-8415) **3858**
• TagesSatz (DEU) **3858**
Der Tagesspiegel (DEU) **3858**
• Die Tageszeitung (DEU ISSN 0941-1526) **3858**
Die Tageszeitung (Ausg. West) *see* Die Tageszeitung **3858**
Tagore International (IND) **5384**
Tagungen der Gesellschaft fuer Umweltrecht *see* Gesellschaft fuer Umweltrecht. Tagungen **3433**
Tagungen zur Ostmitteleuropa-Forschung (DEU) **4272**
Tagungs-Wirtschaft *see* T W **6283**
Tahdet (Year) (FIN ISSN 0355-9459) **582**
Tahdet ja Avaruus (FIN ISSN 0355-9467) **582**
Taheke (EST ISSN 0134-2266) **2215**
Al-Tahirah (IRN ISSN 1019-0791) **7716**
Tahiti Beach Press (PYF ISSN 1157-349X) **8759**
Tahiti Today (PYF) **3842**
Tahoe Quarterly (USA ISSN 1930-0719) **5084**
Tahqiqat e Eqtesadi (English Edition) (IRN ISSN 1010-657X) **1181**
Tahqiqat-i Iqtisadi (Chap-i Farsi) *see* Tahqiqat e Eqtesadi (English Edition) **1181**
Tahqiqat Kishavarzai-i Iran *see* Iran Agricultural Research **123**
Tahtitieteellinen Yhdistys Ursa. Maailmankaikkeus (FIN ISSN 1456-8381) **582**
Tahtitieteellinen Yhdistys Ursa. Ursan Julkaisuja (FIN ISSN 0357-7937) **582**
Tahtitieteen Vuosikirja *see* Tahtitieteellinen Yhdistys Ursa. Maailmankaikkeus **582**
• Tahtivaeltaja/No Mercy (FIN ISSN 0781-271X) **5448**
Tahudromos (GRC ISSN 1108-6181) **3874**
• Tai-Bun Tong-Sin/Taiwanese Writing Forum (USA) **5185**
T'ai Chi (USA ISSN 0730-1049) **562**
Tai Chi & Alternative Health (GBR ISSN 1355-8307) **562**
• Tai Sheng/Voice of Taiwan (CHN ISSN 1002-9788) **3567**
T'ai-wan Chiao Yu/Taiwan Education Review (TWN) **2917**
T'ai Wan Jen Lei Hsueh K'an *see* Taiwan Journal of Anthropology **3567**
Tai-wan Sheng Chiao T'ung T'ung Chi Nien Pao *see* Taiwan Annual Statistical Report of Transportation **8531**
Tai-wan Sheng Ho-tso Chin-k'u. Annual Report. *see* Cooperative Bank of Taiwan. Annual Report **1329**
T'ai Wan Shou I Hsueh Tsa Chih *see* Taiwan Shouyixue Zazhi **8808**
Tai-wan Tang Yeh Yen Chiu So Nien Pao *see* Taiwan Sugar Research Institute. Annual Report **255**
Taian Shi-Zhuan Xuebao *see* Taishan Xueyuan Xuebao **8009**
Taichung District Agricultural Improvement Station. Bulletin *see* Taizhong-qu Nongye Gailiang Chang Yanjiu Huibao **160**
➤ Taida Lishi Xuebao/Historical Inquiry (TWN ISSN 1991-2498) **4189**
Taide (FIN ISSN 0039-8977) **521**
Taidehistoriallisia Tutkimuksia/Studies in Art History (FIN ISSN 0355-1938) **521**
• Taideteollinen Korkeakoulu. Julkaisusarja. F, Tyopaperit/University of Art and Design Helsinki. Publication Series. F, Working Papers (FIN ISSN 1455-8955) **521**
Taidian Gongcheng Yuekan (TWN ISSN 0494-5468) **3161**
Taiei Toshi News (GBR) **1654**
Taieri Herald (NZL ISSN 1170-1331) **3919**
† Taifa (ESP ISSN 0214-0527) **8992**
Taifa Uganda Empya (UGA) **3963**
Taifu Jumapili (KEN) **3902**
Taigai Junkan Gijutsu/Journal of Extra-Corporeal Technology (JPN ISSN 0912-2664) **5720**
Taigang Wenxue Xuankan/Selected Works of Taiwan and Hong Kong Literature (CHN ISSN 1002-753X) **5384**
Taiheiyo Cement Kenkyu Hokoku (JPN ISSN 1344-8773) **3285**
Taiheiyo Gakkai Shi *see* Pacific Society. Journal **351**
Taiiku no Kagaku/Journal of Health, Physical Education and Recreation (JPN ISSN 0039-8985) **3083**
• Taiikugaku Kenkyu/Japan Journal of Physical Education, Health and Sport Sciences (JPN ISSN 0484-6710) **2917**
Taijiquan Journal (USA ISSN 1528-6290) **8211**
Taikabutsu/Refractories (JPN ISSN 0039-8993) **6334**
Taiki Denki Gakkaishi/Society of Atmospheric Electricity of Japan. Journal (JPN ISSN 1882-0549) **6396**
Taiki Denki Kenkyu/Society of Atmospheric Electricity of Japan. Proceedings (JPN ISSN 0286-3405) **6396**
Taiki Hoshano Kansoku Seiseki/Bulletin of Atmospheric Radioactivity (JPN ISSN 0447-3884) **6396**
➤ Taiki Kankyo Gakkaishi/Japan Society for Atmospheric Environment (JPN ISSN 1341-4178) **3491**
Taikiken Shinpojumu *see* Symposium on Atmosphere **6396**
• Taikong Tansuo/Space Exploration (CHN ISSN 1009-6205) **72**
Tail Ends (USA ISSN 1083-2572) **6300**
Tail Spins (USA) **6622**
† Tailgate (USA ISSN 1529-4021) **8992**
➤ Tailoring Biotechnologies (NLD ISSN 1574-1990) **771**
Tails *see* Capital Tails **6805**
TAIMEX *see* (Year) Directory of Taiwan's Leading Manufacturers and Exporters **1988**
Tainan District Agricultural Reserach and Extension Station. Research Bulletin *see* Tainan-qu Nongye Gailiangchang Yanjiu Huibao **160**
Tainan Mook *see* Aiyue **3960**
Tainan-qu Nongye Gailiangchang Yanjiu Huibao/Tainan District Agricultural Reserach and Extension Station. Research Bulletin (TWN) **160**
Tainaya Vlast' (RUS ISSN 1563-3845) **6744**
• Taipan (DEU ISSN 0949-7420) **1654**
Taipan (USA ISSN 1062-1016) **1654**
Taipei Hilton (TWN) **4399**
Taipei Hua K'an/Taipei Pictorial (TWN ISSN 0039-9051) **3960**
Taipei Journal *see* Taiwan Journal **3960**
Taipei Pictorial *see* Taipei Hua K'an **3960**
Taipei Review *see* Taiwan Review **3960**
Taipei Traders Information System (TWN) **2029**
Taira (FRA ISSN 1145-3559) **5384**
Al-Tairan al-Madani/Civil Aviation (UAE) **72**
Tairyoku Igaku Kenkyujo Hokoku *see* Tairyoku Kenkyu **6998**
• ➤ Tairyoku Kagaku/Japanese Journal of Physical Fitness and Sports Medicine (JPN ISSN 0039-906X) **6998**
Tairyoku Kenkyu/Physical Fitness Research Institute. Bulletin (JPN ISSN 0389-9071) **6998**
Taisei Kensetsu Gijutsu Kenkyujoho/Taisei Technical Research Report (JPN ISSN 0387-2254) **1039**
Taisei Quarterly (JPN ISSN 0285-5445) **1039**
Taisei Technical Research Report *see* Taisei Kensetsu Gijutsu Kenkyujoho **1039**
➤ Taisekigaku Kenkyu/Sedimentological Society of Japan. Journal (JPN ISSN 1342-310X) **2770**
Taishan University. Journal *see* Taishan Xueyuan Xuebao **8009**
• Taishan Xueyuan Xuebao/Taishan University. Journal (CHN ISSN 1672-2590) **8009**
• Taishan Yixueyuan Xuebao/Acta Academiae Medicinae Taishan (CHN ISSN 1004-7115) **5720**
Taisho Daigaku Sogo Bukkyo Kenkyujo Nenpo/Institute for Comprehensive Studies of Buddhism. Annual (JPN ISSN 0388-645X) **7702**
Taitei Ziliao/Taiwan Railway (TWN ISSN 1011-6850) **8625**
Taito (FIN ISSN 1235-6875) **540**
Taitoalvari (FIN ISSN 1458-7424) **2917**
Taiwan *see* The P R S Group. Country Reports: Taiwan **1509**
Taiwan Agricultural Information *see* Taiwan Nongye Qingkuang **160**
Taiwan Agricultural Research Institute. Annual Report (TWN ISSN 0494-5263) **160**
Taiwan Agricultural Research Institute. Research Summary (TWN) **160**
Taiwan Agricultural Research Institute. Special Publication (TWN ISSN 1026-3802) **160**
Taiwan Annual Statistical Report of Transportation/Tai-wan Sheng Chiao T'ung T'ung Chi Nien Pao (TWN) **8531**
Taiwan Association of Orthodontists. Journal *see* Zhonghua Minguo Chi'e Jiaozheng Xuehui Zazhi **5870**
• Taiwan Autos Report (GBR ISSN 1749-0200) **8606**
Taiwan Beer Life Magazine *see* Kuanle Shangqing Xiuxian Jikan **606**
• Taiwan Bicycles & Parts Guide (Year) (TWN ISSN 1024-8943) **2029**
• Taiwan Buyers' Guide (CD-ROM) (TWN) **2029**
Taiwan Chemical Importers' Directory (Year) (TWN) **3256**
Taiwan Chemical Producers' Directory (Year) (TWN) **3256**
Taiwan Communique (USA ISSN 1027-3999) **7216**
Taiwan Computer (TWN) **2541**
Taiwan Diqu Daomi Shengchanliang Diaocha Baogao *see* Quanguo Daomi Shengchanliang Diaocha Baogao **249**
Taiwan Dizhi Xilie/Taiwan Geology Series (TWN) **2770**
Taiwan Economic Forum *see* Taiwan Jingji Lunheng **1181**
• The Taiwan Economic News (TWN ISSN 1563-9533) **1181**
Taiwan Economy (TWN ISSN 0255-5697) **1521**
Taiwan Education Review *see* T'ai-wan Chiao Yu **2917**
Taiwan Electronics Industry (TWN ISSN 0257-8166) **3114**
Taiwan Environmental Industry *see* Huanbao Chanye **3437**
Taiwan Export Express (TWN) **1583**
Taiwan Exporters (TWN) **1583**
Taiwan Exports (TWN ISSN 0494-5336) **1583**
Taiwan Fisheries Research Institute Conference Proceedings *see* T F R I Conference Proceedings **3609**
• Taiwan Food & Drink Report (GBR ISSN 1749-3005) **1181**
Taiwan Freight Transport Report (GBR ISSN 1750-5291) **8512**
Taiwan Furniture (TWN) **4563**
Taiwan Fuwuye Fazhan Jianxun/Taiwan Service Industry Development Newsletter (TWN) **1181**
Taiwan Geology Series *see* Taiwan Dizhi Xilie **2770**
Taiwan Gongcheng Jie *see* Gongcheng **3194**
Taiwan Gonggong Weisheng Zazhi/Taiwan Journal of Public Health (TWN) **7543**
• Taiwan Haixia/Journal of Oceanography in Taiwan Strait (CHN ISSN 1000-8160) **2818**
• Taiwan Hand Tools Buyers' Guide (TWN ISSN 1024-8978) **2029**
Taiwan Hardware (TWN) **1055**
Taiwan Industrial Panorama (TWN ISSN 0039-9108) **1905**
Taiwan Industrial Suppliers (TWN) **2029**
• ➤ Taiwan Institute of Chemical Engineers. Journal (NLD ISSN 1876-1070) **3256**
Taiwan International Trade (TWN ISSN 0257-8158) **1583**
• Taiwan Jiating Yixue Zazhi (TWN ISSN 1682-3281) **5720**
Taiwan Jingji *see* Taiwan Economy **1521**
Taiwan Jingji Lunheng/Taiwan Economic Forum (TWN ISSN 1727-8627) **1181**
Taiwan Jingqi Zhibiao (TWN ISSN 1023-2109) **1181**
• Taiwan Journal (TWN) **3960**
• ➤ Taiwan Journal of Anthropology/T'ai Wan Jen Lei Hsueh K'an (TWN ISSN 1727-1878) **3567**
Taiwan Journal of East Asian Studies (TWN) **562**
• Taiwan Journal of English Literature (TWN) **5384**
Taiwan Journal of Forest Science *see* Taiwan Linye Kexue **3704**
• ➤ Taiwan Journal of Linguistics (TWN ISSN 1729-4649) **5185**
Taiwan Journal of Public Health *see* Taiwan Gonggong Weisheng Zazhi **7543**
Taiwan Journal of Sociology *see* Taiwan Shehui Xuekan **8142**
Taiwan Journal of Theology *see* Taiwan Shenxue Lukan **7687**
Taiwan Kunchong/Formosan Entomologist (TWN ISSN 1680-7650) **860**
Taiwan Lighting (TWN) **4563**
➤ Taiwan Linye Kexue/Taiwan Journal of Forest Science (TWN ISSN 1026-4469) **3704**
Taiwan Literature English Translation Series (USA ISSN 1097-5845) **5384**
Taiwan Machinery (TWN) **5460**
Taiwan Merchandise (TWN) **1583**
Taiwan Merchandise Japanese Special *see* Taiwan Merchandise **1583**
Taiwan Mission Quarterly (TWN) **7776**
Taiwan Museum of Art Newsletter/Guanxun Zazhi (TWN) **6537**
• Taiwan New Economy Newsletter/Taiwan Xinjingji Jianxun (TWN) **1181**
Taiwan Next Magazine *see* Taiwan Yizhoukan **3960**
Taiwan Nongye Huaxue yu Shipin Kexue/Taiwanese Journal of Agricultural Chemistry and Food Science (TWN ISSN 1605-2471) **3665**
Taiwan Nongye Qingkuang/Taiwan Agricultural Information (CHN) **160**
Taiwan Nongye Yanjiu (TWN ISSN 0022-4847) **160**
Taiwan Petrochemicals Report (GBR ISSN 1749-2483) **6794**
Taiwan Product Guide (Year) (USA ISSN 1055-9116) **2029**
Taiwan Railway *see* Taitei Ziliao **8625**
Taiwan Renkou Tongji Jikan/Taiwan Demography Quarterly Republic of Taiwan *see* Renkou Tongji Jikan **7314**
Taiwan-Report (DEU) **562**
Taiwan. Republic of China. Balance of Payments Quarterly *see* Zhonghua Minguo Guoji Shouzhi Pinghengbiao Jibao **1392**
Taiwan, Republic of China. Executive Yuan. Directorate-General of Budget, Accounting & Statistics. Monthly Bulletin of Statistics (TWN ISSN 0577-8670) **8408**
Taiwan, Republic of China. Executive Yuan. Directorate-General of Budget, Accounting & Statistics. National Income in Taiwan Area, R.O.C. (TWN ISSN 0257-5671) **1269**
Taiwan, Republic of China. Executive Yuan. Directorate-General of Budget, Accounting & Statistics. Quarterly National Economic Trends, Taiwan Area (TWN ISSN 0257-5663) **1521**
Taiwan, Republic of China. Executive Yuan. Directorate-General of Budget, Accounting & Statistics. Report on the Survey of Family Income & Expenditure in Taiwan Area (TWN ISSN 1011-694X) **1721**
Taiwan, Republic of China. Executive Yuan. Directorate-General of Budget, Accounting & Statistics. Social Indicators in Taiwan Area (Year) (TWN ISSN 0257-5736) **8408**
Taiwan. Republic of China. Financial Statistics Monthly *see* Zhonghua Minguo Jinrong Tongji Yuebao **1275**
• Taiwan, Republic of China. Financial Supervisory Commission. Annual Report (TWN ISSN 1816-5176) **1385**
Taiwan, Republic of China. Machinery and Electrical Apparatus Industry Yearbook/Chung Hua Min Kuo Chi Ch'i yu Tien Kung Ch'i Ts'ai Nien Chien (TWN) **3114**
Taiwan, Republic of China. Ministry of Communication. Tourism Bureau. Annual Report (TWN) **8781**
Taiwan, Republic of China. Ministry of Economic Affairs, Central Geological Survey. Annual Report *see* Jingjibu. Zhongyang Dizhi Diaochasuo. Nianbao **2749**
Taiwan, Republic of China. Ministry of Economic Affairs. Central Geological Survey. Bulletin *see* Jingjibu Zhongyang Diszhi Diaochasuo Huikan **2749**
Taiwan, Republic of China. Ministry of Economic Affairs. Central Geological Survey. Special Publication *see* Jingjibu. Zhongyang Dizhi Diaochasuo. Tekan **2749**
Taiwan, Republic of China. Ministry of Finance. Banking Bureau. Annual Report *see* Taiwan, Republic of China. Financial Supervisory Commission. Annual Report **1385**
Taiwan, Republic of China. Ministry of Finance. Bureau of Monetary Affairs. Annual Report (TWN) **1385**
Taiwan, Republic of China. Ministry of Finance. Department of Statistics. Monthly Statistics of Exports and Imports/Chin Ch'u K'ou Mao I T'ung Chi Yueh Pao (TWN) **1270**
Taiwan, Republic of China. Ministry of Finance. Department of Statistics. Yearbook of Tax Statistics (TWN) **1270**
Taiwan, Republic of China. Ministry of Finance. Insurance Bureau. Annual Report *see* Taiwan, Republic of China. Financial Supervisory Commission. Annual Report **1385**
Taiwan, Republic of China. Ministry of Finance. Securities and Futures Bureau. Annual Report *see* Taiwan, Republic of China. Financial Supervisory Commission. Annual Report **1385**
• Taiwan, Republic of China. National Science Council. Annual Report (TWN ISSN 1023-442X) **7922**
Taiwan, Republic of China. Tourism Bureau. Report on Tourism Statistics (Year) (TWN) **8781**
• Taiwan Review (TWN ISSN 1727-5148) **3960**
Taiwan Service Industry Development Newsletter *see* Taiwan Fuwuye Fazhan Jianxun **1181**
Taiwan Shehui Xuekan/Taiwan Journal of Sociology (TWN) **8142**
Taiwan-sheng Tainan-qu Nongye Gailiang Chang. Yanjiu Huibao/Tainan District Agricultural Improvement Station. Research Bulletin *see* Tainan-qu Nongye Gailiangchang Yanjiu Huibao **160**
Taiwan Shenxue Lukan/Taiwan Journal of Theology (TWN ISSN 0251-4788) **7687**
• Taiwan Shenxueyuan Yuanxun (TWN) **7687**
T'aiwan Shih-yu Ti-chih *see* Petroleum Geology of Taiwan **6787**
Taiwan Shouyixue Zazhi/Taiwan Veterinary Journal (TWN ISSN 1682-6485) **8808**
Taiwan Shuichan Xuehui Kan/Fisheries Society of Taiwan. Journal (TWN ISSN 0379-4180) **3609**
• Taiwan Statistical Data Book (TWN ISSN 1016-2224) **7294**
Taiwan Studies Newsletter (USA ISSN 1048-2342) **562**
Taiwan Study *see* Taiwan Yanjiu **8009**
Taiwan Sugar (TWN ISSN 0492-1712) **3665**
➤ Taiwan Sugar Research Institute. Annual Report/Tai-wan Tang Yeh Yen Chiu So Nien Pao (TWN ISSN 0255-5581) **255**
• Taiwan Telecom (TWN) **2340**
Taiwan Telecom Directory (TWN) **2030**
Taiwan Textile Industry Guide (TWN) **8458**
Taiwan Toy Buyer's Guide *see* Taiwan Toys & Children's Articles Buyers' Guide **4061**
• Taiwan Toys & Children's Articles Buyers' Guide (TWN) **4061**
Taiwan Trade Opportunities (TWN ISSN 1028-1126) **1583**
Taiwan Transportation Equipment Guide (TWN) **8512**
Taiwan Veterinary Journal *see* Taiwan Shouyixue Zazhi **8808**
Taiwan Wen Hsien/Reports on Historiographical Studies of Taiwan (TWN ISSN 1016-457X) **4189**

Taiwan Wenxian see Taiwan Wen Hsien 4189
Taiwan Xiaohua Xiyi Xuehui Zazhi/Gastroenterological Society of Taiwan. Journal (TWN) 5931
Taiwan Xinjingji Jianxun see Taiwan New Economy Newsletter 1181
Taiwan Yanjiu/Taiwan Study (CHN ISSN 1006-6683) 8009
Taiwan Yearbook (Year) (TWN) 3122
• Taiwan Yellow Pages (TWN ISSN 0379-7910) 2030
Taiwan Yinhang Jikan see Bank of Taiwan Quarterly 1441
Taiwan Yixue Renwen Xuekan see Formosan Journal of Medical Humanities 4453
• Taiwan Yizhoukan/Taiwan Next Magazine (TWN) 3960
Taiwan Zhinan see Directory of Taiwan 624
TaiwanContact (DEU) 1583
Taiwanese Journal of Agricultural Chemistry and Food Science see Taiwan Nongye Huaxue yu Shipin Kexue 3665
Taiwanese Journal of Australian Studies see Aozhou Yanjiu 7221
• Taiwanese Journal of Mathematics (TWN ISSN 1027-5487) 5540
• ➤ Taiwanese Journal of Obstetrics and Gynecology (HKG ISSN 1028-4559) 6005
Taiwanese Journal of Studies for Science, Technology, and Medicine see Keji, Yiliao yu Shehui 7875
Taiwanese Writing Forum see Tai-Bun Tong-Sin 5185
• ➤ Taiwania (TWN ISSN 0372-333X) 707
• Taiyang Bao/The Sun (HKG ISSN 1560-3342) 3875
• Taiyang Neng Xuebao/Acta Energiae Solaris Sinica (CHN ISSN 0254-0096) 3178
Taiyang Wang see Taiyang Bao 3875
• Taiyangneng/Solar Energy (CHN ISSN 1003-0417) 3178
Taiyo Enerugi/Solar Energy (JPN) 3178
Taiyo Yuden Giho/Needs & Seeds (JPN ISSN 0911-5439) 3332
Taiyokei Kagaku Shinpojumu (JPN) 584
• Taiyuan Daxue Xuebao/Taiyuan University. Journal (CHN ISSN 1671-5977) 2917
• Taiyuan Keji Daxue Xuebao/Taiyuan University of Science and Technology. Journal (CHN ISSN 1673-2057) 7922
• Taiyuan Ligong Daxue Xuebao/Taiyuan University of Technology. Journal (CHN ISSN 1007-9432) 8440
• Taiyuan Ligong Daxue Xuebao (Shehui Kexue Ban)/Taiyuan University of Technology. Journal (Social Sciences Edition) (CHN ISSN 1009-5837) 8009
• Taiyuan Shifan Xueyuan Xuebao (Ziran Kexue Ban) (CHN ISSN 1672-2027) 7922
• Taiyuan Shifan Zhuanke Xuexiao Xuebao/Taiyuan Teachers College. Journal (CHN ISSN 1008-6994) 2917
Taiyuan Teachers College. Journal see Taiyuan Shifan Zhuanke Xuexiao Xuebao 2917
Taiyuan University. Journal see Taiyuan Daxue Xuebao 2917
Taiyuan University of Science and Technology. Journal see Taiyuan Keji Daxue Xuebao 7922
Taiyuan University of Technology. Journal see Taiyuan Ligong Daxue Xuebao 8440
Taiyuan University of Technology. Journal (Social Sciences Edition) see Taiyuan Ligong Daxue Xuebao (Shehui Kexue Ban) 8009
Taiyuan Zhongxing Jixie Xueyuan Xuebao/Taiyuan Heavy-Machinery Institute. Journal see Taiyuan Keji Daxue Xuebao 7922
• Taizhong-qu Nongqing Yuekan (TWN) 160
Taizhong-qu Nongye Gailiang Chang Yanjiu Huibao/Taichung District Agricultural Improvement Station. Bulletin (TWN ISSN 0255-5905) 160
Taizhong-qu Nongye Zhuanxun (TWN) 160
Taizhou Polytechnical Institute. Journal see Taizhou Zhiye Jishu Xueyuan Xuebao 7922
• Taizhou Zhiye Jishu Xueyuan Xuebao/Taizhou Polytechnical Institute. Journal (CHN ISSN 1671-0142) 7922
The Taj Magazine (IND) 8759
Tajikistan Economic Review (TJK) 1521
Takahama Atomic Power Plant. Environment Monitoring Report see Takahama Genshiryoku Hatsudenjo Kankyo Hoshano Kanshi Kekka Hokokusho 3175
Takahama Genshiryoku Hatsudenjo Kankyo Hoshano Kanshi Kekka Hokokusho/Takahama Atomic Power Plant. Environment Monitoring Report (JPN) 3175
Takahe (NZL ISSN 0114-4138) 5385
Takao Museum of Natural History. Science Report see Tokyo-to Takao Shizen Kagaku Hakubutsukan Kenkyu Hokoku 7924
Takaoka Rebyu/Takaoka Review (JPN ISSN 0385-9630) 3332
Takaoka Review see Takaoka Rebyu 3332
Takayama Junior College. Memoirs see Takayama Tanki Daigaku Kenkyu Kiyo 7922
Takayama Tanki Daigaku Kenkyu Kiyo/Takayama Junior College. Memoirs (JPN ISSN 0386-6890) 7922
• Takbeer (PAK ISSN 1605-3788) 3926
Takbir see Takbeer 3926
• Take! (DEU ISSN 0947-5656) 2216
Take 10 see Take Ten 540
Take 5 (AUS ISSN 1449-6216) 8885
Take a Break (GBR ISSN 0958-983X) 8885
Take a Break's Big Value Codebreakers (GBR ISSN 1476-6477) 4348
Take a Break's Code Breakers (GBR ISSN 1366-1302) 4348
Take a Break's Crisscrosses (GBR ISSN 1461-4901) 4348
Take a Break's Fate & Fortune (GBR ISSN 1476-1041) 567
Take a Break's Fiction Feast (GBR ISSN 1463-5364) 5415
† Take a Break's Kids' Stuff (GBR ISSN 1466-7703) 8992
Take a Break's Picture Arrowwords (GBR ISSN 1463-0656) 4348
Take a Break's Quick-X-Words (GBR ISSN 1362-2528) 4348
Take a Break's Special Series (GBR ISSN 1742-6014) 3872
Take a Break's Take a Crossword (GBR ISSN 0968-8277) 4348
Take a Break's Take a Puzzle (GBR ISSN 0963-1208) 4348
Take a Break's Wordsearches (GBR ISSN 1361-5068) 4348
Take a Break's Wordsearches Collection (GBR ISSN 1474-1857) 4348
Take a Crossword see Take a Break's Take a Crossword 4348
Take A Hike Los Angeles see Moon Outdoors: Take A Hike Los Angeles 8738
Take a Hike New York City see Moon Outdoors: Take a Hike New York City 8739
Take A Hike Seattle see Moon Outdoors: Take A Hike Seattle 8739
Take a Puzzle see Take a Break's Take a Puzzle 4348
• Take Charge (Email) (USA) 5931
Take Charge (Print) see Take Charge (Email) 5931
• The Take - Charge Assistant (USA ISSN 1080-0387) 1797
Take Five see Take 5 8885
The Take Home Trade see Key Note Market Report: The Take Home Trade 1895
Take It Easy (FRA ISSN 0754-1678) 5241
Take Off (DNK ISSN 0107-1270) 8759
Take One (USA) 2403
Take Pride! Community see Take Pride! Community Magazine 3567
• Take Pride! Community Magazine (USA ISSN 1096-6625) 3567
Take Ten (USA ISSN 1939-5019) 540
Takeda Science Foundation Symposium on Bioscience. Proceedings (JPN) 707
Takenaka Gijutsu Kenkyu Hokoku/Takenaka Technical Research Report (JPN ISSN 0374-4663) 1039
Takenaka Technical Research Report see Takenaka Gijutsu Kenkyu Hokoku 1039
The Takeover Stock Report (USA) 1654
The Takeover Stock Report Europe (USA) 1654
• Takeovers (GBR ISSN 1753-7185) 4881
• Takeovers and Reconstructions in Australia (AUS) 4881
Takeovers, Offers and New Issues (GBR) 1181
Takie jest Zycie! (POL ISSN 1641-1706) 8885
Taking Sides: Clashing Views and Controversial Issues in 20th Century American History (USA ISSN 1554-3218) 4314
Taking Sides: Clashing Views and Controversial Issues in Classroom Management (USA ISSN 1554-3226) 3083
Taking Sides: Clashing Views in Criminal Justice (USA ISSN 1557-6361) 2669
▼ Taking Sides: Clashing Views in Energy and Society (USA ISSN 1944-7469) 3148
Taking Sides: Clashing views in Human Sexuality (USA ISSN 1940-2422) 7411
Taking Sides: Clashing Views in Lifespan Development (USA ISSN 1559-2642) 7411
Taking Sides: Clashing Views in Public Policy, Justice, and the Law (USA ISSN 1557-7074) 4792
Taking Sides: Clashing Views on Controversial Bioethical Issues (USA ISSN 1091-8809) 5720
Taking Sides: Clashing Views on Controversial Economic Issues (USA ISSN 1094-7612) 1521
Taking Sides: Clashing Views on Controversial Educational Issues (USA ISSN 1091-8817) 2917
Taking Sides: Clashing Views on Controversial Environmental Issues (USA ISSN 1091-8825) 3469
Taking Sides: Clashing Views on Controversial Issues African Issues (USA ISSN 1545-5327) 3790
Taking Sides: Clashing Views on Controversial Issues in American History (USA ISSN 1091-8833) 4314
Taking Sides: Clashing Views on Controversial Issues in American History since 1945 see Taking Sides: Clashing Views and Controversial Issues in 20th Century American History 4314
Taking Sides: Clashing Views on Controversial Issues in Business Ethics and Society (USA ISSN 1091-1006) 1181
Taking Sides: Clashing Views on Controversial Issues in Cognitive Science (USA ISSN 1548-7555) 7411
Taking Sides: Clashing Views on Controversial Issues in Crime and Criminology (USA ISSN 1098-5379) 2669
Taking Sides: Clashing Views on Controversial Issues in Cultural Anthropology (USA ISSN 1541-9207) 357
Taking Sides: Clashing Views on Controversial Issues in Drugs and Society (USA ISSN 1094-7566) 2700
Taking Sides: Clashing Views on Controversial Issues in Family and Personal Relationships (USA) 8142
Taking Sides: Clashing Views on Controversial Issues in Food and Nutrition (USA ISSN 1547-1802) 6669
Taking Sides: Clashing Views on Controversial Issues in Health and Society (USA ISSN 1094-7531) 7543
Taking Sides: Clashing Views on Controversial Issues in Human Sexuality see Taking Sides: Clashing views in Human Sexuality 7411
Taking Sides: Clashing Views on Controversial Issues in Management (USA ISSN 1552-4477) 1797
Taking Sides: Clashing Views on Controversial Issues in Mass Media and Society (USA ISSN 1084-4651) 8142
Taking Sides: Clashing Views on Controversial Issues in Race and Ethnicity (USA) 3567
Taking Sides: Clashing Views on Controversial Issues in Religion (USA ISSN 1541-8448) 7687
Taking Sides: Clashing Views on Controversial Issues in Social Psychology (USA ISSN 1550-6169) 7411
Taking Sides: Clashing Views on Controversial Issues in World Politics (USA ISSN 1094-754X) 7268
Taking Sides: Clashing Views on Controversial Legal Issues (USA ISSN 1098-5395) 4792
Taking Sides: Clashing Views on Controversial Moral Issues (USA ISSN 1094-7604) 7411
Taking Sides: Clashing Views on Controversial Political Issues (USA ISSN 1080-580X) 7187
Taking Sides: Clashing Views on Controversial Psychological Issues (USA ISSN 1098-5409) 7411
Taking Sides: Clashing Views on Controversial Social Issues (USA) 8142
Taking Sides: Clashing Views on Latin American Issues (USA ISSN 1932-9296) 4314
Taking Stock (Leeds) (GBR ISSN 0966-6745) 5050
Taking Up a Franchise (GBR) 1968
De Takkeling (NLD ISSN 1380-3735) 915
Takko Town Hospital. Annual Report see Akahige 4087
Takoma Park-Silver Spring Cooperative Effort News see T P S S Cooperative Effort News 3469
Takuma Denpa Kogyo Koto Senmon Gakko. Kenkyu Kiyo/Takuma National College of Technology. Bulletin (JPN ISSN 0388-2926) 3332
Takuma National College of Technology. Bulletin see Takuma Denpa Kogyo Koto Senmon Gakko. Kenkyu Kiyo 3332
Takusa see Taxa 965
• Tal Cual (VEN) 3994
† Tal fra Koebenhavns Kommune, Statistisk Kontor (DNK ISSN 1397-6567) 8992
Tal och Spraak see Puhe ja Kieli 5163
• Tal og Data, Medicin og Sundhedsvaesen/Facts, Medicine and Health Care, Denmark (DNK ISSN 0107-1181) 6882
• Tal om Forskning (DNK ISSN 1601-7196) 8408
• Tal om Landbruget (DNK ISSN 0109-6923) 186
Tala Industrial Relations Bulletin (PHL) 1710
• Tala Lelei (NZL ISSN 1177-3820) 7543
• ➤ Talanta (NLD ISSN 0039-9140) 2106
Talbot Times (CAN ISSN 0827-2816) 3784
Talbotania (GBR ISSN 0141-3589) 3784
Talbot's Student Planning Book (USA) 3004
• Talebones (USA ISSN 1084-7197) 5448
De Talen (NLD ISSN 0922-1166) 5185
Talent Exploitation see Rencai Kaifa 1874
Talent in Action see Billboard's Year-End Awards Issue 6549
Talent in Motion (USA) 5084
Talent Magazine (USA) 2270
Talent Management (USA) 1876
➤ TalentEd (AUS ISSN 0815-8150) 3048
Talento (ITA ISSN 1120-6683) 4477
Talents (CHN ISSN 1007-7391) 3828
• Tales From the Terminal Room (GBR ISSN 1467-338X) 2567
Tales of the Paradise Ridge (USA ISSN 0496-7607) 4314
Tales of the Twelve (CAN ISSN 0713-3901) 6537
• Talia Dixit (ESP ISSN 1886-9440) 5185
Talijanska Privreda Danas (HRV) 1181
Talim-O-Tarbiat (PAK ISSN 0039-9175) 2216
• Talimu Nongken Daxue Xuebao/Journal of Tarim University. Journal (CHN ISSN 1009-0568) 7922
▼ Talisman (ARG ISSN 1851-3328) 567
• Talisman (GBR ISSN 1474-4945) 2946
Talisman (USA ISSN 0898-8684) 5436
Talk (GBR ISSN 0049-2906) 4076
Talk Greenville (USA) 3990
• Talk of the Tyne (GBR ISSN 1357-891X) 8248
Talk Radio - Talk TV (USA) 2364
Talk Show Host Directory and Resource Guide (USA) 2030
Talk Show Yearbook (USA) 2395
• Talk Story (USA) 3623
Talkabout (BEL ISSN 0774-0557) 5185
Talkabout (USA) 6815
Talkers Magazine (USA) 2364
Talking Book Review (USA) 7574
• Talking Book Topics (USA ISSN 0039-9183) 4085
Talking Books in the Public Library Systems of Metropolitan Toronto (CAN ISSN 0380-2973) 5050
Talking Business (GBR) 2340
Talking Economics Monthly see Associative Economics Monthly 1536
Talking Electronics (AUS ISSN 0811-3742) 3114
➤ Talking Images (GBR ISSN 1744-9901) 6515
Talking Leaves (Eugene) (USA ISSN 1076-3635) 707
Talking Machine Review International (GBR) 8155
• Talking Native Title (AUS ISSN 1446-2508) 7471
Talking Pictures (GBR ISSN 0964-8364) 6515
Talking Point (GBR) 3083
• Talking Points (Urbana) (USA ISSN 1522-6115) 3083
• Talking Points (Washington, DC) (USA) 7268
† ➤ Talking Politics (GBR ISSN 0955-8780) 8992
Talking River Review (USA ISSN 1093-5460) 5385
Talking Sense (GBR) 8074
† Talking Stick Magickal Journal (GBR ISSN 1464-2042) 8992
Talking Straight With Your Teenager see Straight Talk (Pleasantville) 2215
Talking Things see Beszelo Targyak 5262
Talking to the Boss (USA ISSN 1067-067X) 1181
Talkline Business (DEU) 2340
Talkliner (DEU) 2340
Tall Magazine (USA ISSN 1545-6463) 3990
• Tall og Fakta/Figures and Facts. Drugs and Health Care (NOR ISSN 1503-352X) 6882
Tall og Fakta. Kortversjon see Legemiddel og Helsetjeneste 6858
Tall Timbers Fire Ecology Conference. Proceedings (USA) 3704
Tall Timbers Research Station. Miscellaneous Publication (USA ISSN 0496-764X) 3704
Talladega Student Star (USA) 2303
Talladegan (USA) 2303
▼ Tallaght Echo (IRL ISSN 1649-9611) 3895
Tallahassee Magazine (USA) 3990
Tallahassee's Boomers & Seniors (USA) 4056
Tallahassee's Family Forum (USA) 2169
Taller (NIC ISSN 0039-9221) 5385
• ➤ Taller de Letras (CHL ISSN 0716-0798) 5385
† Taller d'Historia (ESP ISSN 1133-4959) 8992
Taller Literario (PRI) 5385
Talleres en Comunicacion (ESP) 8512
Tallinn (EST ISSN 1406-0078) 3567
Tallinn In Your Pocket (EST ISSN 1406-2690) 8759
Tallinn Technical University. Preprints (EST) 5540
Tallinn Technical University. Reports (EST) 3285
Tallinn Technical University. Theses (EST ISSN 1406-4774) 3256
Tallinn This Week (EST ISSN 1406-1171) 3837
➤ Tallow Light (USA ISSN 0049-2914) 4314
Tally-Ho (USA) 6815
Tallyho see The Thunderbolt (Luke) 6449
• Taloha (MDG ISSN 0496-7801) 6538
Talomestari (FIN ISSN 0785-6318) 1039
The Talon (University of Southern Mississippi) (USA) 2303
Talotekniikka (FIN ISSN 1236-5173) 4127
▼ • Talouden Nakymat (FIN ISSN 1797-3759) 1386
Talouselama (FIN ISSN 0356-5106) 1181
Talouselaman Raportti Suuryrityksista (FIN ISSN 0780-5969) 1181
• Taloussanomat (Online) (FIN ISSN 1797-3813) 1386
Taloussanomat (Print) see Taloussanomat (Online) 1386
Taloustaito (FIN ISSN 0788-9135) 1946
Taloustaito Yritys (FIN ISSN 1457-4195) 1946
Talyllyn News (GBR ISSN 0300-3272) 8625
Tam Kernewek (USA ISSN 1085-1267) 3567
Tam Magazine (USA) 5448
Tama Zoological Park. Annual Report see Tokyoto Tama Dobutsu Koen Jigyo Gaiyo 965
Tamagawa University. Faculty of Agriculture. Bulletin (JPN ISSN 0082-156X) 160
Tamaqua (USA) 5241
• ➤ Tamara (USA ISSN 1532-5555) 8009
• Tamarack Magazine (CAN ISSN 1183-7950) 8337
• Tamara's Kitchen (AUS) 3676
Tamashagaran (IRN ISSN 1024-2244) 8248
Tambara (PHL ISSN 0117-6323) 8009
Tambour Battant (FRA ISSN 1771-2890) 4056
Tameike no Shizen/Nature of Irrigation Pond (JPN ISSN 0915-6550) 255
Tameiou Sunohes. Etesia Ekthese see Cohesion Fund. Annual Report (Year) 1083
Tamid (ESP ISSN 1138-5561) 5185
Tamil Arasu (IND ISSN 0039-9280) 3890
Tamil Ceithi Malar (IND) 2303
Tamil Chamber of Commerce. Journal (IND) 1410
Tamil Civilization (IND) 4189
Tamil Kalai (IND) 4189
Tamil Nadu. Department of Statistics. Annual Statistical Abstract (IND ISSN 0082-1578) 8408
Tamil Nadu. Department of Statistics. Season and Crop Report (IND ISSN 0082-1586) 187
Tamil Nadu Industrial Development Corporation. Annual Report (IND) 1905
Tamil Nadu Information (IND ISSN 0039-9310) 7471
Tamil Nadu Journal of Co-operation (IND ISSN 0377-8002) 1424

Title

DIRECTORY 2010 TAUBENMARKT, DIE SPORTAUBE 10931

Tanzania. National Agricultural Research Programme. Project Report (TZA) **255**
Tanzania National Bibliography (TZA ISSN 0856-003X) **636**
Tanzania. National Bureau of Statistics. Migration Statistics (TZA) **7316**
Tanzania. National Bureau of Statistics. Quarterly Statistical Bulletin (TZA ISSN 0039-9469) **8408**
Tanzania. National Bureau of Statistics. Survey of Employment (TZA) **1270**
Tanzania. National Bureau of Statistics. Survey of Industrial Production (TZA) **1270**
Tanzania News Review (TZA ISSN 0856-017X) **3961**
Tanzania Notes & Records (TZA ISSN 0039-9485) **3961**
Tanzania Official Gazette (TZA ISSN 0856-0323) **7471**
Tanzania. Planning Commission. Macro Planning Department. Hali Ya Uchumi Wa Taifa - Annual Economic Survey (TZA) **1905**
Tanzania Political Economy Series (TZA ISSN 1821-5653) **1710**
➤ Tanzania Publishing House. Inaugural Lecture Series (TZA) **7187**
Tanzania Railways Corporation. Habari za Reli (TZA) **8625**
Tanzania Trade Currents (TZA ISSN 0856-2105) **1583**
Tanzania Zamani (TZA ISSN 0039-9507) **4163**
Tanzanian Bankers Journal (TZA) **1386**
Tanzanian Mathematical Bulletin (TZA ISSN 0856-065X) **5540**
Tanzanian Studies (TZA) **4178**
Tanzen (DEU ISSN 0724-1062) **2688**
Tanzer Talk (CAN) **8283**
Tanzforschung (DEU ISSN 0940-1008) **2688**
Tanzspiegel (DEU ISSN 0931-5640) **2688**
Tanzwissenschaft (DEU ISSN 1431-9918) **2688**
• Taoci Yanjiu/Ceramics Studies Journal (CHN ISSN 1000-9892) **2046**
Taoci Yanjiu yu Zhiye Jiaoyu/Ceramic Research and Vocational Education (CHN ISSN 1672-2965) **2046**
Taos Magazine (USA ISSN 0895-6065) **8781**
Tap Chi Ca Dao/Ca Dao Magazine (USA) **3567**
Tap Chi Cong San/Communist Review (VNM) **7187**
Tap Chi Tac Pham Van Hoc (VNM) **5385**
Tap Chi Van Hoc/Literature Magazine (VNM ISSN 0494-6928) **5385**
Tap Roots (USA ISSN 0494-6944) **3784**
• Tap San Tu Tuong (AUS ISSN 1443-766X) **3567**
Tape Medical Bulletin (GBR) **5720**
Tape Op (USA) **8155**
Tapestry (USA) **7687**
Tapezierer und Raumausstatter (AUT) **4563**
Tapia (ESP ISSN 1131-656X) **4792**
Tapia (TTO ISSN 1010-4720) **5241**
Tapicerias Gancedo *see* T G **8992**
Tapikitanga O Apa (NZL ISSN 1176-9130) **3567**
Tapir Conservation (CHE) **2628**
Tapol (GBR ISSN 1356-1154) **7216**
Tapori (USA ISSN 0882-5424) **2216**
Tapout Magazine (USA ISSN 1937-108X) **8211**
Tapovan Prasad (IND ISSN 0971-3964) **7708**
Tapping Technology (USA) **4078**
TapRoot *see* Taproot Reviews **5385**
➤ Taproot Literary Review (USA ISSN 1520-8729) **5385**
• Taproot Reviews (USA) **5385**
Taptoe (NLD ISSN 0039-9604) **2216**
Taptoe Zomerboek *see* Taptoe Zomerspeurboek **2216**
Taptoe Zomerspeurboek (NLD ISSN 1875-0877) **2216**
Taqrir al-Iqtisadi - Bank al-Kuwayt al-Markazi *see* Central Bank of Kuwait. Economic Report **1446**
Al Taqrir al-Niha'i-Barnamag al-Insan Wa-al-Muhit al-Hayawi (al-Mab) *see* M A B Report Series **3451**
Al Taqrir al-Tanafusiyyat al-'arabiyyat *see* At Taqrir at-Tanafusiyyat al-'arabiyyat **1521**
At Taqrir at-Tanafusiyyat al-'arabiyyat/Arab Competitiveness Report (KWT ISSN 1814-2141) **1521**
▼ Tar (USA ISSN 1943-3794) **521**
Tar Heel Junior Historian (USA ISSN 0496-8913) **4314**
Tar Heel Nurse (USA ISSN 0039-9620) **5982**
▼ Tar Heel Tip-Off (USA ISSN 1942-0714) **8248**
Tar River Poetry (USA ISSN 0740-9141) **5436**
Tara (CHE) **6715**
Tara i Upakovka (RUS ISSN 0131-6907) **6715**
Tarab (USA ISSN 1547-5530) **6622**
• Taranaki Daily News (NZL ISSN 1176-7596) **3919**
Taranga (IND) **3890**
Tarantulas of the World (DEU ISSN 1431-7990) **964**
Tarbell's Teacher's Guide (USA ISSN 0082-1713) **7687**
Tarbiya (ESP ISSN 1132-6239) **2917**
At-Tarbiyat Li-l-Gami 2000 *see* E F A - 2000 **2843**
➤ At-Tarbiyyah/Education (QAT) **2917**
At-Tarbiyyah/Education (UAE) **2917**
Tarbiz (ISR ISSN 0334-3650) **7730**
Tarbut (USA) **3567**
Tarchna (ITA ISSN 1970-3147) **420**
Tarchna. Supplementi *see* Tarchna **420**
Tarcin (TUR) **8885**
• Tarcutta Valley Network Landcare Newsletter (AUS ISSN 1833-8895) **3469**
The Tardieu Series (NLD ISSN 0924-610X) **5720**
Tarea (PER ISSN 0252-8819) **2917**
➤ Tareas (PAN ISSN 0494-7061) **8009**
Tarex (FRA) **6882**
Targa Newfoundland (CAN ISSN 1911-2335) **8211**
Target (CHN) **5084**
Target (IND) **2216**
Target (KEN) **7687**
• ➤ Target (NLD ISSN 0924-1884) **5185**
Target (Wheeling) (USA ISSN 1051-1636) **1905**
Target Advertising News (KWT) **36**
Target Arson: Update (USA) **4524**
Target Atlanta (USA ISSN 1081-6623) **5084**
Target City & Finance (GBR ISSN 1477-2337) **7503**
Target Data Compilation Report (HKG) **1181**
Target Gun (GBR ISSN 0143-8751) **8211**
Target Intelligence Report (HKG) **1386**
• Target M D (Muscular Dystrophy) (GBR) **4078**
Target Machinery & Hardware (TWN) **5460**
• Target Marketing (USA ISSN 0889-5333) **1845**
➤ Target Organ Toxicology Series (USA ISSN 1073-0842) **3501**
Target World Drug Delivery News (GBR ISSN 1475-6870) **6882**
• ➤ Targeted Oncology (FRA ISSN 1776-2596) **6035**
Targets in Heterocyclic Systems. Chemistry and Properties (ITA ISSN 1724-9449) **2131**
Targum Online: The Daily Targum on the Web *see* Daily Targum **2281**
Targumic and Cognate Studies. Newsletter (USA ISSN 0704-5905) **7730**
Tariefadvies voor de Levering van Warmte aan Kleinverbruikers (NLD ISSN 1874-7515) **3148**
Tarievenboek *see* Kluwer Tarievenboek **1932**
➤ Tarif Aktuell (DEU ISSN 0944-1824) **7471**
Tarif Media (FRA ISSN 0038-9579) **36**
Tarif Pieces Detachees (FRA ISSN 0153-9205) **8512**
Tariffs *see* Tariffs **3148**
Tariffs (CAN ISSN 1910-1201) **3148**
Tariffs Effective as of October 1 *see* Tariffs **3148**
• The Tarifica Alert (Email) (GBR) **1583**
The Tarifica Alert (Print) *see* The Tarifica Alert (Email) **1583**
La Tarification en Assurance Automobile. Rapport *see* La Tarification en Assurance Automobile. Rapport Annuel **4524**
La Tarification en Assurance Automobile. Rapport Annuel (CAN ISSN 1712-9389) **4524**
Tarifs *see* Tariffs **3148**
• Les Tarifs d'Honoraires des Medecins. Canada. Rapport (CAN ISSN 1706-1571) **1710**
Tarih Dergisi (TUR ISSN 1015-1818) **4272**
Tarih Incelemeleri Dergisi (TUR ISSN 0257-4152) **4325**
Tarikh (NGA ISSN 0331-5134) **4178**
• Tarim Bilimleri Dergisi/Journal of Agricultural Sciences (TUR ISSN 1300-7580) **160**
Tarjeta (MEX) **7471**
Tarjman (IND) **3890**
Tarjuman al-Hadith (PAK) **7716**
Tarlac College of Technology. Annual Report of the President (PHL) **3004**
• Tarmac Topics (AUS ISSN 1833-6116) **72**
Tarnowskie Studia Teologiczne (POL ISSN 0239-4472) **7819**
Tarokalok (BGD) **3800**
▼ • Tarot World Magazine (USA ISSN 1938-5056) **6648**
Tarraco (ESP ISSN 0211-7916) **4030**
Tarralla (AUS ISSN 1832-0708) **5385**
† • ➤ Tarsadalom es Gazdasag/Society and Economy (HUN ISSN 1588-9734) **8992**
Tarsadalom es Gazdasag Kozep-es Kelet-Europaban *see* Tarsadalom es Gazdasag **8992**
• Tarsadalomkutatas/Social Science Research (HUN ISSN 0231-2522) **8143**
Tarsie (ITA ISSN 1970-5360) **420**
The Tartan (USA ISSN 0890-3107) **3004**
Tartan Book Sales Catalog (USA) **7574**
Tarun Bharat (Belgaum) (IND) **3890**
Tarun Bharat (Nagpur) (IND) **3890**
Tarun Mitra (IND) **3890**
Tarzan (JPN) **6300**
Tasa-Arvo (FIN ISSN 0784-6789) **8885**
Tascabili Hesperides (ITA) **5385**
Taschenbuch der Auktionspreise Alter Buecher (DEU) **636**
Taschenbuch der Frauenpresse (DEU) **8903**
Taschenbuch der Giesserei-Praxis (DEU ISSN 0082-1772) **6334**
Taschenbuch der Pflanzenarztes (DEU ISSN 0082-1799) **255**
Taschenbuch der Telekom Praxis *see* Jahrbuch der Telekom Praxis **2328**
Taschenbuch des Metallhandels (DEU) **6334**
Taschenbuch des Oeffentlichen Lebens (DEU ISSN 0082-1829) **7484**
• Taschenbuch des Oeffentlichen Lebens. Europa und Internationale Zusammenschluese (DEU ISSN 1433-9293) **7484**
Taschenbuch des Textil- und Lederwareneinzelhandels *see* Taschenbuch des Textileinzelhandels **8458**
Taschenbuch des Textileinzelhandels (DEU ISSN 1864-7189) **8458**
Taschenbuch fuer Agrarjournalisten (DEU ISSN 0082-1845) **160**
Taschenbuch fuer Bergingenieure (DEU) **6480**
Taschenbuch fuer den Tunnelbau (DEU) **3285**
Taschenbuch fuer die Bundeswehrverwaltung (DEU) **4972**
Taschenbuch fuer die Textil-Industrie (DEU ISSN 0082-1896) **8458**
Taschenbuch fuer Hauseigentuemer (DEU ISSN 0933-3894) **4428**
Taschenbuch Karosserie & Fahrzeugtechnik (DEU) **8606**
Taschenbuch Magazin (DEU) **7574**
Taschenbuecher zur Musikwissenschaft (DEU ISSN 0082-1969) **6622**
Taschenlexikon Arbeitsrechtlicher Entscheidungen (DEU ISSN 0937-0951) **1710**
Taschenlexikon Bau- und Architektenrechtlicher Entscheidungen (DEU ISSN 0935-7211) **1039**
Taschenlexikon Haftpflichtrechtlicher Entscheidungen (DEU ISSN 0934-3032) **4898**
Taschenlexikon Handwerksrechtlicher Entscheidungen (DEU ISSN 0935-9001) **4792**
Taschenlexikon Miet- und Wohnungsrechtlicher Entscheidungen (DEU ISSN 0936-5249) **4792**
Taschenlexikon Personalrechtlicher Entscheidungen des Oeffentlichen Dienstes (DEU ISSN 0935-9990) **4842**
Taschenlexikon Schul- und Hochschulrechtlicher Entscheidungen (DEU ISSN 1430-225X) **2917**
Taschenlexikon Sozialversicherungsrechtlicher Entscheidungen (DEU ISSN 0934-3059) **8074**
Taschenlexikon Staats- und Verwaltungsrechtlicher Entscheidungen (DEU) **7471**
Taschenlexikon Steuerrechtlicher Entscheidungen (DEU ISSN 0934-3229) **1946**
Taschenlexikon Versicherungsrechtlicher Entscheidungen (DEU ISSN 0936-5257) **4525**
Taschenstatistik der Schweiz (Year)/Memento Statistique de la Suisse (Year) (CHE) **8408**
Tashkent Lecture Notes (DEU) **1550**
At-Tashkil (UAE) **521**
▼ Task-Based Language Teaching (NLD ISSN 1877-346X) **5185**
Task Force Quarterly (USA) **5720**
• ➤ Tasks for Vegetation Science (NLD ISSN 0167-9406) **819**
Taskuristikko (FIN ISSN 0356-1577) **8211**
• Tasman District Crime Statistics (NZL ISSN 1178-1629) **2675**
Tasman District Statistics *see* Tasman District Crime Statistics **2675**
Tasmania. Anti-Discrimination Commission. Annual Report *see* Tasmania. Office of the Anti-Discrimination Commissioner. Annual Report **1710**
• Tasmania. Department of Economic Development and Tourism. Annual Report (AUS) **1181**
Tasmania. Department of Economic Development. Annual Report *see* Tasmania. Department of Economic Development and Tourism. Annual Report **1181**
• Tasmania. Department of Premier and Cabinet. Annual Report (AUS ISSN 1448-9023) **7471**
• Tasmania. Department of Primary Industries and Water. Annual Report (AUS ISSN 1834-0997) **3469**
• Tasmania. Department of Primary Industries, Water and Environment. Annual Report (AUS ISSN 1327-7081) **7471**
Tasmania. Department of Primary Industries, Water and Environment. Water Assessment and Planning Branch. Report Series (AUS ISSN 1449-5996) **8832**
• Tasmania. Department of Treasury and Finance. Budget Papers (AUS ISSN 1833-7406) **1946**
• Tasmania. Hobart Water. Annual Report (AUS) **3491**
• Tasmania. Mineral Resources. Geological Survey Bulletins (AUS) **2770**
Tasmania. Mineral Resources. Report (AUS) **2770**
Tasmania Nursery Register *see* Victoria, South Australia, Tasmania Nursery Register **3753**
• Tasmania. Office of the Anti-Discrimination Commissioner. Annual Report (AUS) **1710**
• Tasmania. Office of the State Service Commissioner. Annual Report (AUS ISSN 1448-9066) **7471**
Tasmanian Ancestry (AUS ISSN 0159-0677) **3784**
• ➤ Tasmanian Aquaculture and Fisheries Institute. Technical Report (AUS ISSN 1441-8487) **3610**
Tasmanian Baptist Advance (AUS ISSN 0815-6964) **7776**
Tasmanian Budget Documents *see* Tasmania. Department of Treasury and Finance. Budget Papers **1946**
Tasmanian Business Reporter (AUS) **1410**
The Tasmanian Catholic (AUS) **7819**
➤ Tasmanian Certificate of Education Manual (AUS) **3034**
• Tasmanian Conservationist (AUS ISSN 0725-0355) **2628**
• Tasmanian Government Gazette (AUS ISSN 0039-9795) **7471**
Tasmanian Historical Research Association. Papers and Proceedings (AUS ISSN 0039-9809) **4194**
➤ Tasmanian Historical Studies (AUS ISSN 1324-048X) **4194**
Tasmanian Manufacturers Directory (AUS ISSN 0314-8696) **2030**
Tasmanian Master Builder (AUS) **1039**
➤ Tasmanian Naturalist (AUS ISSN 0819-6826) **707**
• Tasmanian Numismatist (AUS ISSN 0817-4075) **6653**
Tasmanian Pen Craft (AUS ISSN 1832-200X) **521**
Tasmanian Rail News (AUS ISSN 1321-0238) **8625**
Tasmanian Reports (AUS ISSN 0085-7106) **4965**
• Tasmanian State Service Evaluation Report (AUS ISSN 1834-3023) **7471**
Tasmanian Trade Protective Institute Trade Gazette *see* T T P I Trade Gazette **1433**
The Tasmanian Tramp (AUS ISSN 0157-2938) **8337**
• Tasmanian Travelways (AUS) **8759**
Tasmanian University Law Review *see* University of Tasmania Law Review **4805**
• Tasmania's Financial Management Reform Strategy (AUS ISSN 1832-262X) **1386**
Tassels and Tails (USA) **6815**
Taste *see* Gefsi **3644**
Taste! (NLD ISSN 1574-3020) **610**
Taste *see* Taste Snowboard Magazine **8337**
Taste (NZL) **4368**
Taste *see* Williams-Sonoma Taste **3667**
Taste (ZAF ISSN 1728-8789) **4368**
Taste Cornwall Magazine *see* Inside Cornwall **8721**
• Taste for Life (USA ISSN 1521-2904) **5084**
Taste of Home (USA ISSN 1071-5878) **4368**
▼ Taste of Home Christmas (USA ISSN 1948-8386) **4368**
Taste of Home Healthy Cooking (USA ISSN 1942-5988) **3665**
Taste of Home's America's Family Recipes (USA ISSN 1930-1685) **4368**
Taste of Home's Cooking for 2 (USA ISSN 1557-3664) **4368**
Taste of Home's Cooking for Two *see* Taste of Home's Cooking for 2 **4368**
Taste of Home's Diabetic Cookbook (USA ISSN 1554-0103) **4368**
Taste of Home's Favorite Brand Name Recipes (USA ISSN 1554-0111) **4368**
Taste of Home's Light & Tasty *see* Taste of Home Healthy Cooking **3665**
Taste of Home's Quick Cooking *see* Taste of Home's Simple and Delicious **4368**
Taste of Home's Simple and Delicious (USA ISSN 1931-6232) **4368**
A Taste of Scotland Guide (Year) (GBR) **8759**
Taste of the South (USA) **4368**
• Taste Shropshire (GBR ISSN 1752-3648) **4399**
Taste Shropshire & the Marches *see* Taste Shropshire **4399**
Taste Snowboard Magazine (NLD ISSN 1574-7549) **8337**
• Tastenwelt (DEU ISSN 0946-3658) **6622**
The Taster of Wine and Food (ITA) **610**
Tastes of Italia (USA ISSN 1547-2000) **3665**
The Tasting Panel Magazine *see* Patterson's The Tasting Panel Magazine **609**
• Tastings (USA) **3665**
Tastings E-Zine *see* Tastings **3665**
† • Tasty Bits from the Technology Front (USA) **8992**
Taswiq Al-Ziraiy *see* Agricultural Marketing **192**
† Tat-Tarbut (ISR ISSN 0793-5439) **8992**
Tata Chombo (NIC) **3623**
Tata Energy Research Institute Energy Data Directory and Yearbook *see* T E R I Energy Data Directory and Yearbook **2029**
Tata Energy Research Institute Newswire *see* T E R I Newswire **3154**
Tata Search (IND ISSN 0971-5975) **6480**
Tatarstan (RUS ISSN 0869-5083) **3942**
Tate (London) *see* Tate Etc **521**
• Tate Etc (GBR ISSN 1743-8853) **521**
Tate Gallery Liverpool. Critical Forum Series (GBR) **6538**
Tate Liverpool Critical Forum *see* Tate Gallery Liverpool. Critical Forum Series **6538**
• Tate Papers (GBR ISSN 1753-9854) **521**
Tate Trails (USA ISSN 0893-309X) **3784**
Tatehamodoki/Miyazaki Entomological Society. Journal (JPN ISSN 0917-3102) **860**
▼ Tathaastu (USA ISSN 1937-4917) **315**
Tatler (GBR ISSN 0263-7162) **3872**
Tatouage (FRA ISSN 1289-5369) **521**
Tatra Eagle *see* Tatrzanski Orzel **3568**
Tatra Mountains Mathematical Publications (SVK ISSN 1210-3195) **5540**
Tatry (SVK ISSN 1335-6828) **3469**
Tatrzanski Orzel/Tatra Eagle (USA ISSN 0039-9914) **3568**
Tatsachen und Zahlen (DEU ISSN 1619-2877) **8606**
Tattersall's Club Magazine *see* Tattler Magazine **2270**
• I Tatti Studies (ITA ISSN 0393-5949) **4272**
The Tattler (CAN ISSN 1914-0827) **3469**
Tattler Magazine (AUS) **2270**
Tattoo (USA ISSN 1041-3146) **521**
Tattoo 1 Tribal *see* Tattoo One **521**
▼ Tattoo Annual (USA ISSN 1945-8991) **591**
Tattoo Flash (USA ISSN 1079-9443) **521**
Tattoo One (ITA ISSN 1591-1772) **521**
Tattoo Planet (USA) **521**
Tattoo Revue (USA ISSN 1525-7819) **521**
Tattoo Savage (USA ISSN 1072-8384) **521**
Tattoo Scene Live (DEU ISSN 1438-2083) **521**
Tattoos *see* Tattoos For Men **521**
• Tattoos.Com Ezine (CAN) **521**
Tattoos For Men (USA ISSN 1070-7247) **521**
Tattoos For Women (USA ISSN 1088-2456) **521**
TattooStyle (DEU ISSN 1614-9408) **521**
Tattootime (USA) **521**
➤ Tattvadipah/Academy of Sanskrit Research. Journal (IND) **8009**
Tau Beta Pi. Bulletin (USA ISSN 8755-5670) **3221**
Tauaki Whakamaunga Atu *see* National Library of New Zealand. Statement of Intent **5034**
Taubenmarkt, Die Sportaube (DEU ISSN 1862-9504) **6815**

Title

10932 TAUBER INSTITUTE FOR THE STUDY OF EUROPEAN JEWRY SERIES ULRICH'S PERIODICALS

Tauber Institute for the Study of European Jewry Series (USA ISSN 1942-8456) **4272**
Tauber-Zeitung (DEU) **3858**
• Taubman Center for State and Local Government. Report (USA) **7471**
The Taubman Center Report *see* Taubman Center for State and Local Government. Report **7471**
➤ Taubman Lectures in Jewish Studies (USA) **7730**
Tauch-Brille (DEU) **8211**
Tauchen (DEU ISSN 0170-4001) **8211**
Taula (ESP ISSN 0214-6657) **6956**
Taunton Tool Guide (USA ISSN 1930-9589) **1052**
Taunton's Fine Cook *see* Taunton's Fine Cooking **4368**
Taunton's Fine Cooking (USA ISSN 1072-5121) **4368**
Taunton's Fine Gardening (USA) **3751**
• Taunton's Fine Homebuilding (USA ISSN 1096-360X) **1039**
• Taunton's Fine Woodworking (USA ISSN 0361-3453) **1052**
Taunton's Threads *see* Threads **6642**
Taupo Times (NZL ISSN 1170-1072) **3919**
Taupo Weekender (NZL ISSN 1170-1366) **3919**
Taurai *see* Speak Out **8903**
Taurus (ARG ISSN 1515-3037) **8808**
Taurus Top 16 (USA) **1654**
Tausch (CHE ISSN 0937-9150) **5385**
➤ Tautosakos Darbai/Folklore Studies (LTU ISSN 1392-2831) **3623**
Tauwetter (DEU ISSN 1618-0550) **7819**
Tavira (ESP ISSN 0214-137X) **2917**
Tavlatok (HUN ISSN 1215-282X) **7819**
Tavricheskie Vedomosti (UKR) **3965**
Tavricheskii Zhurnal Psikhiatrii/Acta Psychiatrica, Psychoterapeutica et Etologica Tavrica (UKR) **6187**
Tavrida Pravoslavnaya (UKR) **7706**
Tawagoto (USA ISSN 1047-4250) **7687**
Tawantinsuyu (AUS ISSN 1324-5686) **357**
• ➤ Al-Tawhid (IRN ISSN 0267-968X) **7716**
At-Tawzi'/Distribution (UAE) **6794**
• Tax (GBR ISSN 1752-959X) **1946**
Tax Accounting (USA) **1302**
Tax Administration Review/Revista de Administracion Tributaria (PAN ISSN 1684-9434) **1946**
• Tax Administrators News (Online) (USA) **1946**
Tax Administrators News (Print) *see* Tax Administrators News (Online) **1946**
Tax-Advantaged Securities Law Report (USA) **4881**
➤ Tax Adviser (GBR ISSN 1472-4502) **1947**
• The Tax Adviser (USA ISSN 0039-9957) **1947**
† • Tax Analyst Microfiche Database (USA) **8992**
Tax Analysts Chief Counsel Advice Service *see* Chief Counsel Advice Service **1917**
Tax Analysts Onedisc *see* Basic Onedisc **1912**
▼ • Tax and Accounting Center (USA ISSN 1947-3923) **1947**
Tax & Business Adviser (USA) **1302**
Tax and Company Law Forms *see* Chartac Tax and Company Law Forms **1284**
Tax and Wealth Strategies for Family Businesses (USA ISSN 1931-7468) **1181**
Tax Aspects of Bankruptcy Law and Practice (USA) **4792**
Tax Aspects of Litigation (CAN ISSN 1910-4022) **4792**
Tax Aspects of Owning a Home (USA ISSN 1931-5163) **1947**
Tax Audit & Accountancy (BEL ISSN 1782-8007) **1947**
Tax - Benefit Position of Employees *see* Taxing Wages **1951**
Tax - Benefit Position of Production Workers *see* Taxing Wages **1951**
Tax Breaks (CAN ISSN 1196-5142) **1947**
Tax Breaks (ZAF) **1947**
Tax Careers (GBR ISSN 1743-713X) **6704**
Tax Case Report (GBR) **1947**
Tax Controversies: Audits, Investigations, Trials (USA) **1947**
• Tax Court Decisions (USA) **1947**
• Tax Court Reports (USA ISSN 0162-1815) **1947**
Tax Credit Advisor (USA ISSN 1065-3678) **1947**
• Tax Credit Housing Management Insider (USA ISSN 1527-2311) **1947**
Tax Deductions For Businesses and Self-Employed Individuals *see* 422 Tax Deductions For Businesses and Self-Employed Individuals **1970**
The Tax Directory *see* The Tax Directory. Corporate Tax Managers Worldwide **1947**
The Tax Directory *see* The Tax Directory. Government Officials Worldwide **1947**
• The Tax Directory. Corporate Tax Managers Worldwide (USA) **1947**
• The Tax Directory. Government Officials Worldwide (USA) **1947**
• Tax, Estate & Financial Planning for the Elderly (USA) **4056**
Tax, Estate and Financial Planning for the Elderly *see* Tax, Estate & Financial Planning for the Elderly **4056**
Tax, Estate & Financial Planning for the Elderly: Forms and Practice (USA) **4057**
Tax, Estate and Financial Planning for the Elderly: Forms and Practice *see* Tax, Estate & Financial Planning for the Elderly: Forms and Practice **4057**
Tax Examples and Scenarios (NZL ISSN 1176-175X) **1947**
• The Tax Executive (USA ISSN 0040-0025) **1947**
• Tax-Exempt Organization Alert! (USA ISSN 1536-4704) **1947**
Tax Expenditures Statement *see* Australia. Department of the Treasury. Tax Expenditures Statement **1911**
Tax Facts 1 *see* Tax Facts on Insurance & Employee Benefits **4525**
Tax Facts 2 *see* Tax Facts on Investments **1654**
• Tax Facts on Insurance & Employee Benefits (USA) **4525**
• Tax Facts on Investments (USA) **1654**
• Tax Features (USA ISSN 1069-711X) **1947**
Tax File (GBR) **1302**
• Tax for the Owner-Manager (CAN ISSN 1496-0419) **1947**
Tax Foundation. Background Papers (USA ISSN 1527-0408) **1947**
Tax Foundation. Federal Tax Burdens and Expenditures by State (USA) **1947**
Tax Foundation. Federal Tax Burdens by State *see* Tax Foundation. Federal Tax Burdens and Expenditures by State **1947**
• Tax Foundation. Special Reports (USA ISSN 1068-0306) **1947**
• Tax Fraud and Evasion (USA) **1947**
Tax Fraud: Audits, Investigations, Prosecutions *see* Tax Controversies: Audits, Investigations, Trials **1947**
• Tax-Free Trader & Travel Retail World (GBR ISSN 1361-9519) **1583**
Tax Guide for College Teachers and Other College Personnel (USA ISSN 0190-7522) **1947**
Tax Handbook (ZAF) **1947**
Tax Haven Reporter Newsletter (BHS) **1947**
• Tax Havens of the World (BHS) **1947**
Tax Havens of the World (USA) **1948**
† Tax Hotline (USA ISSN 0279-4446) **8992**
Tax Ideas (USA ISSN 0279-2109) **1948**
• Tax Incentives Alert (USA ISSN 1540-8302) **1948**
Tax Insight (GBR ISSN 0263-9076) **1948**
The Tax Journal (GBR ISSN 0954-7274) **1948**
Tax Journal Digest *see* W G & L Tax Journal Digest **1954**
• Tax Justice Focus (GBR ISSN 1746-7691) **1948**
Tax Law Dictionary (USA) **4792**
• Tax Law Review (USA ISSN 0040-0041) **4792**
Tax Laws and Regulations of People's Republic of China *see* Zhonghua Renmin Gongheguo Shuishou Fagui Gonggao **1956**
• ➤ The Tax Lawyer (USA ISSN 0040-005X) **4792**
Tax Letter *see* C P A Client Tax Letter **1914**
Tax Library *see* Premium Tax Collection **4760**
• Tax Library/Belastingbiblioteek (ZAF ISSN 1017-1193) **1948**
Tax Magazine (AUT ISSN 1819-5741) **1948**
• Tax Management Compensation Planning Journal (USA ISSN 0747-8607) **1797**
• Tax Management Country Portfolios (GBR) **1948**
• Tax Management Estates, Gifts and Trusts Journal (USA ISSN 0886-3547) **1655**
Tax Management Estates, Gifts & Trusts Journal *see* Tax Management Estates, Gifts and Trusts Journal **1655**
• Tax Management Financial Planning Journal (USA ISSN 8756-1360) **1386**
† • Tax Management Financial Products Report (USA ISSN 1087-2922) **8992**
• Tax Management Foreign Income Portfolios (USA) **1948**
• Tax Management I R S Forms (USA) **1948**
† • Tax Management I R S Practice and Policy (USA) **8992**
• Tax Management I R S Practice & Policy Adviser Reporter (Online) (USA) **1948**
• Tax Management Interactive Forms for Windows (USA ISSN 1930-899X) **1948**
• Tax Management International Forum (GBR ISSN 0143-7941) **1948**
• Tax Management International Journal (USA ISSN 0090-4600) **1948**
• Tax Management International Programme (GBR) **1948**
• Tax Management Memorandum (USA ISSN 0148-8295) **1948**
Tax Management Portfolios *see* U.S. Internal Revenue Service. Tax Management Portfolios **1953**
• Tax Management Primary Sources (USA ISSN 0738-5285) **1948**
• Tax Management Real Estate Journal (USA ISSN 8755-0628) **7613**
Tax Management Tax Practice Plus for Windows (CD-ROM) *see* Tax Practice Plus (DVD) **1949**
• Tax Management Tax Practice Series Bulletin (USA ISSN 1083-7345) **1948**
• Tax Management Transfer Pricing Portfolio Series (USA ISSN 0494-8270) **1948**
• Tax Management Transfer Pricing Report (USA ISSN 1063-2069) **1948**
• Tax Management U S Income (USA) **1948**
• Tax Management Weekly Report (USA ISSN 0884-6057) **1948**
• Tax Management Weekly State Tax Report (USA ISSN 1534-1550) **1949**
• Tax Management's Multistate Tax Portfolio Series (USA ISSN 1083-2289) **1949**
Tax News (USA ISSN 0279-0211) **1949**
• Tax News Service (Online) (NLD) **1949**
† • Tax News Service (Print) (NLD ISSN 0040-0076) **8992**
• Tax Notes (USA ISSN 0270-5494) **1949**
• Tax Notes International (USA ISSN 1048-3306) **1949**
† • Tax Notes International Weekly News (USA ISSN 1058-3971) **8992**
Tax Notes Today *see* Tax Notes **1949**
Tax Outlook (USA) **1302**
Tax Penalties and Interest (USA) **4792**
Tax Planning (IND) **1949**
• Tax Planning for Closely Held Corporations (Online) (USA) **1949**
• Tax Planning for Corporations and Shareholders (USA) **1949**
• Tax Planning for Corporations and Shareholders: Forms (USA) **4881**
• Tax Planning for S Corporations (USA) **4792**
• Tax Planning for the Alternative Minimum Tax (USA) **1949**
• Tax Planning International (GBR ISSN 0309-7900) **1949**
• Tax Planning International Asia-Pacific Focus (GBR) **1949**
• Tax Planning International E-Commerce (GBR) **1949**
• Tax Planning International European Tax Service (GBR ISSN 1754-1646) **1949**
Tax Planning International European Union Focus *see* Tax Planning International European Tax Service **1949**
Tax Planning International Taxgram *see* Tax Management International Forum **1948**
Tax Planning International Taxgram *see* Tax Planning International **1949**
• Tax Planning International Transfer Pricing (GBR ISSN 1472-0841) **1949**
Tax Planning Strategies (USA ISSN 1541-8871) **1949**
Tax.point (IRL ISSN 1649-7848) **1949**
• Tax Policy and the Economy (USA ISSN 0892-8649) **1949**
• Tax Practice (USA ISSN 1086-0088) **1949**
Tax Practice Deskbook (USA) **1949**
• Tax Practice Plus (DVD) (USA ISSN 1944-4923) **1949**
Tax Practitioner's Diary (GBR ISSN 0269-3720) **1949**
• Tax Profile (CAN ISSN 0827-3677) **1950**
Tax Rates & Tables *see* Tax Rates and Tables (Pyrmont) **1950**
• Tax Rates and Tables (Pyrmont) (AUS ISSN 1441-7596) **1950**
Tax Reform Immediately Bulletin *see* T R I M Bulletin **1946**
• Tax Resources Tax Tips Email Update (USA) **1950**
Tax Rules of Practice *see* U.S. Internal Revenue Service. Tax Rules of Practice **1953**
Tax Savings Report (USA) **1950**
• Tax Savvy for Small Business (USA ISSN 1939-3040) **4792**
• ➤ Tax Specialist (AUS ISSN 1329-1203) **1950**
Tax Statutes and Statutory Instruments (GBR ISSN 0960-6785) **1950**
Tax Strategies *see* Practical Tax Strategies **1939**
Tax Strategies *see* Practical European Tax Strategies **1939**
The Tax Strategist (USA ISSN 1559-5307) **1386**
Tax Talk (USA) **1950**
Tax Times (IND ISSN 0040-0122) **1950**
Tax Tips for Seamen *see* Seafarers Log **4602**
• Tax Tool Box (NZL ISSN 1177-4134) **4793**
• Tax Treaties (New York) (USA) **1950**
• Tax Treaties (Riverwoods) (USA ISSN 0414-0176) **1950**
• Tax Treaties Data Base on CD-ROM (NLD) **1950**
† Tax Treatment of Cross-Border Donations (NLD) **8992**
† The Tax Treatment of Transfer Pricing (NLD) **8992**
Tax Treaty Briefing (GBR ISSN 1468-3113) **1950**
• Tax Update (ZAF) **1950**
Tax-Vyapar (IND) **1950**
Tax Watch (USA) **1950**
➤ Taxa (JPN ISSN 1342-2367) **965**
• Taxable Sales in California. Sales and Use Tax Annual Report (USA ISSN 0095-2753) **1950**
• Taxation (GBR ISSN 0040-0149) **1950**
Taxation (IND) **1950**
Taxation (PAK ISSN 0040-0157) **1950**
Taxation *see* Journal of Taxation **1932**
Taxation 2 (GBR ISSN 1746-1359) **6704**
Taxation and Economy *see* Shuiwu yu Jingji **1383**
Taxation & Investment in Canada *see* Canada - Taxation & Investment **1915**
† Taxation & Investment in Mexico (NLD) **8992**
† Taxation & Investment in South Africa (NLD) **8992**
Taxation & Investment in the Caribbean *see* Caribbean - Taxation & Investment **1916**
Taxation & Investment in the People's Republic of China *see* China - Taxation & Investment **1917**
Taxation and Regulation of Financial Institutions *see* Journal of Taxation and Regulation of Financial Institutions **1363**
• Taxation and Revenue Policies - State Capitals (USA) **1950**
Taxation for Employment Specialists (GBR) **1950**
• ➤ Taxation in Australia (AUS ISSN 0494-8343) **1950**
Taxation in Latin America *see* Latin America - Taxation & Investment **1933**
Taxation Law Reports (IND) **1950**
Taxation of Companies and Company Reconstructions (GBR) **1950**
Taxation of Employees (ZAF) **1950**
Taxation of Executive Compensation: Planning and Practice (USA) **1302**
• Taxation of Exempt Organizations (USA) **1950**
• Taxation of Exempts (USA ISSN 1537-4238) **1950**
• Taxation of Financial Institutions (USA) **1951**
Taxation of Intellectual Property: Tax Planning Guide (USA) **6758**
Taxation of Mining Operations (USA) **1951**
Taxation of Mutual Fund Trusts and Corporations in Canada (CAN ISSN 1719-086X) **4881**
The Taxation of Permanent Establishments *see* Permanent Establishments **1939**
Taxation of Public Utilities (USA) **1951**
Taxation of Securities Transactions (USA) **1951**
Taxation Research *see* Shuiwu Yanjiu **1943**
Taxation Research Journal *see* Touzi Yanjiu **1952**
Taxation Structure of Pakistan (PAK) **1951**
Taxation Today (NZL ISSN 1178-2277) **1302**
• TaxBase (USA) **1951**
• TaxCore (USA ISSN 1532-5229) **1951**
Taxes (GBR ISSN 0960-7323) **1951**
Taxes (Madison) (USA) **1951**
Taxes and Investment in Asia and the Pacific *see* Asia-Pacific - Taxation & Investment Database **1911**
Taxes and Investment in the Middle East *see* Middle East - Taxation & Investment **1935**
• Taxes and Trade International (USA) **1583**
• Taxes on Parade (USA ISSN 0162-3486) **1951**
Taxes - Property - State Capitals *see* Property Taxes & School Funding - State Capitals **1940**
• Taxes - The Tax Magazine (USA) **1951**
• TaxFacts Online (USA) **1655**
Taxi (DEU ISSN 1437-0336) **8606**
Taxi (DNK ISSN 1903-1300) **8512**
▼ • El Taxi (ESP ISSN 1888-4520) **8512**
Taxi (GBR ISSN 0049-304X) **8512**
Taxi (NOR ISSN 0332-5881) **8512**
Taxi & Livery Management (USA) **8512**
Taxi & Livery Management *see* Transportation Leader **8765**
• Taxi Globe (GBR ISSN 1468-6643) **8512**
Taxi Heute (DEU ISSN 0174-3775) **8606**
Taxi Idag (SWE ISSN 0283-5576) **8512**
Taxi Kurier (DEU) **8606**
Taxi Libre (ESP) **8512**
Taxi News (CAN ISSN 0834-3489) **8512**
Taxi Talk (USA) **8512**
Taxila Institute of Asian Civilizations. Quaid-i-Azam University. Publications (PAK) **4189**
Taxinews (GBR ISSN 0040-0254) **8512**
• Taxing Wages/Situation des Ouvriers au Regard de l'Impot et des Transferts Sociaux (FRA ISSN 1995-3844) **1951**
The TaxLetter (CAN ISSN 0821-3704) **1951**
Taxlex (AUT ISSN 1813-4432) **1951**
Taxline (GBR ISSN 0965-8726) **1951**
• ➤ Taxon (AUT ISSN 0040-0262) **819**
Taxpayer (ZAF ISSN 0040-0270) **1951**
TaxPro Journal (USA ISSN 1536-5875) **1951**
TaxPro Monthly (USA ISSN 1535-5896) **1951**
Tay Valley Family Historian (GBR ISSN 0267-9884) **3784**
➤ Taylor (USA ISSN 1073-4376) **3004**
Taylor Talk (Online) (USA) **7574**
Taylor Talk (Print) *see* Taylor Talk (Online) **7574**
▼ The Taylor Trust (USA ISSN 1948-2078) **5385**
• Taylorology (USA) **6515**
Taylor's Encyclopedia of Government Officials, Federal and State (USA ISSN 0082-2183) **7188**
➤ Tayside and Fife Archaeological Journal (GBR ISSN 1360-5550) **420**
Tayside Farmer (GBR) **161**
Tayyarut *see* Israel. Central Bureau of Statistics. Tourism **8779**
Tazta *see* T Z T A **3567**
Tbilisi (GEO) **3843**
• ➤ Tbilisi International Center of Mathematics and Informatics. Bulletin (GEO ISSN 1512-0082) **5540**
➤ Tbilisi International Centre of Mathematics and Informatics. Lecture Notes (GEO ISSN 1512-0511) **5540**
Tbilisi Ivane Javakhishvili State University. Seminar of Ilia Vekua Institute of Applied Mathematics. Reports *see* Ilia Vekuas Saxelobis Gamoqenebit'i Mat'ematikis Institutis Seminaris Moxsenebebi **5492**
Tbilisskii Universitet. Institut Prikladnoi Matematiki. Doklady *see* Ilia Vekuas Saxelobis Gamoqenebit'i Mat'ematikis Institutis Seminaris Moxsenebebi **5492**
Tchad et Culture (TCD ISSN 0049-3066) **3790**
Tchad Mise a Jour de la Securite Alimentaire *see* Chad Food Security Update **1592**
Tchahert/Torch (LBN ISSN 0040-0297) **7706**
Tchebec (CAN ISSN 0834-7050) **915**
Tchelet *see* Azure **5208**
† Tchibo Club-Magazin (DEU) **8992**
Tchin Tchin (CAN ISSN 1910-9253) **610**
• Te Awamutu Courier (NZL ISSN 1170-1099) **3919**
• Te Awatea Review (NZL ISSN 1176-5259) **2669**
Te Deum (USA) **7776**
Te Deum Today (USA) **7776**
Te M A (FRA ISSN 1956-7405) **207**
Te M a *see* Tempo Materia Architettura **8993**
• Te Mangai Paho. Annual Report (NZL) **2340**
Te Puke Times (NZL ISSN 1170-1102) **3919**
Te Rarangi Pukapuka Matua O Aotearoa *see* New Zealand National Bibliography **632**
• ➤ Te Reo (NZL ISSN 0494-8440) **5185**
• Te Rito News (NZL ISSN 1177-7826) **8074**

DIRECTORY 2010 TECHLINKS 10933

Te Tari Puna Ora O Aotearoa. Iti Rearea/New Zealand Childcare Association. Newsletter (NZL) **2917**
Te Tari Puna Ora O Aotearoa. Itirearea *see* Te Tari Puna Ora O Aotearoa. Iti Rearea **2917**
Te Tari Puna Ora o Aotearoa/New Zealand Childcare Association. Report to Annual Conference *see* New Zealand Childcare Association. Report to Annual Conference **2891**
Tea *see* Chaye **3630**
Tea (KEN ISSN 1015-7174) **3665**
Tea. A Magazine (USA ISSN 1079-4611) **3665**
Tea Abstracts/Chaye Wenzhai (CHN ISSN 1001-3652) **3670**
● Tea and Coffee Trade Journal (USA ISSN 0040-0343) **3665**
Tea & Harrisburg Champion *see* The Champion **3972**
Tea Directory (IND) **611**
Tea in Fujian *see* Fujian Chaye **232**
Tea in Texas (USA ISSN 1937-1640) **611**
Tea Journal (IND) **3665**
Tea Research Association. Advisory Bulletin (IND ISSN 0375-3077) **611**
Tea Research Association. Memorandum (IND) **611**
Tea Research Association. Occasional Scientific Papers (IND) **611**
Tea Research Association. Tocklai Experimental Station. Scientific Annual Report (IND ISSN 0564-6723) **611**
Tea Research Foundation. Annual Report (MWI) **3665**
Tea Research Foundation of Kenya. Annual Technical Report (Year) (KEN) **3665**
Tea Research Foundation. Quarterly Newsletter (MWI) **161**
▼ The Tea Room (USA ISSN 1945-4066) **3666**
Tea Room Guide & Digest (USA ISSN 1539-7025) **3666**
Tea Science and Technology *see* Chaye Kexue Jishu **224**
Tea Talk (USA ISSN 1076-3457) **3666**
Tea Time (Birmingham) (USA ISSN 1559-212X) **611**
Tea Times *see* Cha Bolan **3630**
Teach (USA ISSN 1538-2907) **2917**
● Teach Kids! (USA ISSN 1554-7779) **7776**
▼ Teach Kids! Essentials (USA ISSN 1941-6172) **7777**
▼ Teach Primary! (GBR ISSN 1756-6509) **3084**
Teach Yourself Chinese *see* Zhongwen Zixue Zhidao **5199**
Teach Yourself English *see* Yinyu Zixue **5197**
● Teacher (AUS ISSN 1449-9274) **2917**
Teacher *see* Jiaoshi **2872**
Teacher *see* Opettaja **2894**
Teacher *see* Laeraren **2881**
The Teacher (GBR ISSN 0040-0408) **2917**
The Teacher (GHA) **3084**
The Teacher (MLT ISSN 1028-5717) **2917**
Teacher (Halifax) (CAN ISSN 0382-408X) **3034**
● Teacher (Vancouver) (CAN ISSN 0841-9574) **2917**
Teacher Certification Requirements in all Fifty States (USA ISSN 1063-7508) **2917**
● ➤ Teacher Development (GBR ISSN 1366-4530) **3084**
Teacher Doctrines *see* Shidao **3082**
Teacher Education (IND ISSN 0379-3400) **2917**
➤ Teacher Education and Practice (USA ISSN 0890-6459) **3084**
● ➤ Teacher Education and Special Education (USA ISSN 0888-4064) **3048**
Teacher Education in Uganda *see* Makerere University. Faculty of Education. Handbook **2993**
● ➤ Teacher Education Quarterly (USA ISSN 0737-5328) **3084**
Teacher Education Reports (USA) **2917**
Teacher Education Research *see* Jiaoshi Jiaoyu Yanjiu **2873**
● ➤ The Teacher Educator (USA ISSN 0887-8730) **3004**
Teacher in Charge of Class *see* Banzhuren **3052**
● Teacher Leadership (GBR ISSN 1750-7367) **2917**
● ➤ Teacher Librarian (USA ISSN 1481-1782) **2918**
Teacher Magazine (IRL) **3084**
● Teacher Magazine (USA ISSN 1046-6193) **3084**
Teacher of Mathematics in Primary School *see* Xiaoxue Shuxue Jiaoshi **5547**
▼ Teacher Professional Development Sourcebook (USA ISSN 1934-6212) **3084**
The Teacher Retirement Laws of the State of Arkansas (USA) **1710**
▼ ● ➤ Teacher-Scholar (USA ISSN 1938-0453) **2918**
Teacher Supply and Demand in Florida (USA) **2918**
Teacher Supply and Demand in the United States *see* Educator Supply and Demand in the United States **3022**
● The Teacher Trainer (GBR ISSN 0951-7626) **3084**
Teacher Update (GBR) **3084**
Teachers *see* For Teachers **3023**
● ➤ Teachers and Teaching (GBR ISSN 1354-0602) **3084**
Teachers & Writers (USA ISSN 0739-0084) **3084**
The Teacher's Calendar (USA ISSN 1533-0362) **3084**
● Teachers' Choices (USA) **2174**
Teachers' College and University. Journal of Science *see* Gao-shi Li-ke Xuekan **7857**
Teachers College Qingdao University. Journal *see* Qingdao Daxue Shifan Xueyuan Xuebao **7993**
● ➤ Teachers College Record (USA ISSN 0161-4681) **2918**
Teachers' Guide to Overseas Teaching (USA) **5185**
Teacher's Guide to Study Resources (GBR ISSN 0306-3836) **3084**
Teacher's Helper (Grade 1 Edition) *see* Teacher's Helper (Kindergarten Edition) **3084**
Teacher's Helper (Grades 2-3 Edition) *see* Teacher's Helper (Kindergarten Edition) **3084**
Teacher's Helper (Grades 4-5 Edition) *see* Teacher's Helper (Kindergarten Edition) **3084**
Teacher's Helper (Kindergarten Edition) (USA ISSN 1078-6570) **3084**
Teacher's Interaction (USA ISSN 0894-7821) **7777**
Teacher's Internet Pages *see* International Education Webzine **2868**
Teacher's Introduction Series *see* National Council of Teachers of English. Teacher's Introduction Series **3074**
Teachers Journal (NGA) **2918**
Teachers' Money Matters (CAN ISSN 0829-917X) **3034**
Teachers of English as a Second Language Talk *see* T E S L Talk **3083**
Teachers of English to Speakers of Other Languages in Context *see* T E S O L in Context **3015**
Teachers of English to Speakers of Other Languages Placement E-Bulletin *see* T E S O L Placement E-Bulletin **5185**
Teachers of English to Speakers of Other Languages Quarterly *see* T E S O L Quarterly **5185**
● Teachers of History in the Universities of the United Kingdom (GBR) **4163**
Teachers of Home Economics Specialist Association Newsletter *see* T H E S A Newsletter **3083**
Teachers of Religion and Christian Ethics News *see* T R A C E News **7687**
Teachers of the World (IND ISSN 0863-0070) **2918**
Teachers of Vision (USA) **7687**
Teachers' Pension Plan Annual Report (CAN ISSN 1198-7057) **1655**
Teachers' Pension Plan. Pension News (CAN ISSN 1912-4015) **1710**
Teachers' Pension Plan. Report to Members (CAN ISSN 1912-3868) **1710**
Teacher's Pet Term Paper (USA ISSN 1078-4179) **7294**
Teachers' Retirement Allowances Fund. Annual Report (CAN ISSN 1910-6467) **1710**
Teacher's World (BGD ISSN 0040-0521) **2918**
▼ ● ➤ Teaching American Literature (USA ISSN 2150-3974) **5385**
● Teaching & Learning (CAN ISSN 1703-2598) **2918**
● Teaching and Learning (GBR ISSN 1479-7976) **3084**
● ➤ Teaching and Learning (USA ISSN 0887-9486) **3084**
● ➤ Teaching and Learning in Medicine (USA ISSN 1040-1334) **5720**
● Teaching and Learning in Nursing (USA ISSN 1557-2013) **5982**
Teaching and Learning Infobits *see* T L Infobits **3004**
Teaching and Learning of All Subjects in Primary School *see* Xiaoxue Geke Jiaoyuxue **3088**
Teaching and Learning of Chemistry in Middle School *see* Zhongxue Huaxue Jiaoyuxue **2084**
Teaching and Learning of Chinese in Middle School *see* Zhongxue Yuwen Jiaoyuxue **5200**
Teaching and Learning of Foreign Language in Middle School *see* Zhongxue Waiyu Jiaoyuxue **5199**
Teaching and Learning of Mathematics in Middle School *see* Zhongxue Shuxue Jiaoyuxue **5547**
Teaching & Learning of Physical Education *see* Tiyu Jiaoxue **2920**
Teaching and Learning of Physics in Middle School *see* Zhongxue Wuli Jiaoyuxue **7047**
Teaching and Learning of Politics and Other Subjects in Middle School *see* Zhongxue Zhengzhi Ji Qita Geke Jiaoyue **2929**
Teaching and Research *see* Jiaoxue yu Yanjiu **3066**
● ➤ Teaching and Teacher Education (GBR ISSN 0742-051X) **3084**
● The Teaching Artist Journal (USA ISSN 1541-1796) **521**
● Teaching Business & Economics (GBR ISSN 1367-3289) **1181**
Teaching Business Ethics *see* Journal of Business Ethics **1134**
● ➤ Teaching Children Mathematics (USA ISSN 1073-5836) **3085**
● Teaching Citizenship (GBR ISSN 1474-9335) **7188**
➤ Teaching Earth Sciences (GBR ISSN 0957-8005) **2770**
● ➤ Teaching Education (GBR ISSN 1047-6210) **2918**
Teaching Educational Psychology (USA) **2918**
Teaching English as a Second Language - Electronic Journal *see* T E S L - E J **5185**
Teaching English as a Second Language Reporter *see* T E S L Reporter **3083**
Teaching English as a Second or Foreign Language *see* T E S L - E J **5185**
Teaching English as an Additional Language Manitoba Journal *see* T E A L Manitoba Journal **5185**
Teaching English for Specific Purposes Journal (PHL ISSN 0116-8037) **5186**
Teaching English in China *see* C E L E A Journal **5102**
● Teaching English in the Two-Year College (USA ISSN 0098-6291) **3004**
● Teaching English with Technology (POL ISSN 1642-1027) **2951**
● ➤ Teaching Exceptional Children (USA ISSN 0040-0599) **3048**
● Teaching Exceptional Children Plus (USA ISSN 1553-9318) **3048**
Teaching for Social Justice Series (USA) **2918**
● Teaching for Success (USA ISSN 1084-0427) **3085**
● ➤ Teaching Geography (GBR ISSN 0305-8018) **4030**
Teaching Geography. Occasional Paper (GBR ISSN 0305-9464) **4030**
Teaching German *see* Die Unterrichtspraxis **5192**
Teaching Guide *see* Listen **2696**
● Teaching History (AUS ISSN 0040-0602) **3085**
● ➤ Teaching History (GBR ISSN 0040-0610) **3085**
● ➤ Teaching History: A Journal of Methods (USA ISSN 0730-1383) **3085**
● ➤ Teaching in Higher Education (GBR ISSN 1356-2517) **3004**
Teaching Languages, Literatures, and Cultures (USA ISSN 1092-3225) **2918**
The Teaching Librarian (CAN ISSN 1188-679X) **3085**
Teaching Mathematics (AUS ISSN 0313-7767) **5541**
● ➤ Teaching Mathematics and Its Applications (GBR ISSN 0268-3679) **5541**
● Teaching Music (USA ISSN 1069-7446) **6622**
Teaching of English (USA) **3085**
Teaching of History and Geography in Middle School *see* Zhongxue Lishi, Dili Jiaoxue **2929**
● The Teaching of Mathematics (SRB ISSN 1451-4966) **5541**
● ➤ Teaching of Psychology (USA ISSN 0098-6283) **7411**
● ➤ Teaching Philosophy (USA ISSN 0145-5788) **6956**
● The Teaching Professor (USA ISSN 0892-2209) **3004**
➤ Teaching Public Administration (GBR ISSN 0144-7394) **7471**
● ➤ Teaching Science (AUS ISSN 1449-6313) **2918**
Teaching Science (GBR ISSN 0263-6107) **7922**
● ➤ Teaching Sociology (USA ISSN 0092-055X) **8143**
● ➤ Teaching Statistics (GBR ISSN 0141-982X) **2936**
Teaching Texts in Law and Politics (USA ISSN 1083-3447) **4793**
Teaching the New English (GBR ISSN 1754-9728) **5186**
Teaching Theatre (USA ISSN 1077-2561) **8480**
● ➤ Teaching Theology and Religion (GBR ISSN 1368-4868) **7687**
● Teaching Thinking Magazine (GBR ISSN 1470-6105) **3085**
Teaching Times for Educators (ZAF ISSN 1819-6667) **2918**
Teaching Today (GBR ISSN 0968-3062) **2918**
Teaching Tolerance (USA ISSN 1066-2847) **3085**
▼ Teaching with Compassion, Competence, Commitment (USA ISSN 1936-7872) **2918**
Teaching Young Children (USA ISSN 1554-6004) **2918**
Teagasc Annual Report (IRL ISSN 0791-4695) **161**
Teagasc Research Report (IRL ISSN 0791-7376) **161**
Team (London, 1959) (GBR ISSN 0969-5141) **5186**
Team and Trail (USA) **6816**
Team Baseball Card Checklist *see* The Sport Americana Team Baseball Card Checklist **4347**
Team Canada Inc. Achievements Report *see* Team Canada Inc. Annual Report **1583**
● Team Canada Inc. Annual Report (CAN ISSN 1704-1368) **1583**
Team Canada Inc. Business Plan *see* Team Canada Inc. Annual Report **1583**
Team Football and Basketball Card Checklist *see* The Sport Americana Team Football and Basketball Card Checklist **4347**
● ➤ Team in Practice (GBR ISSN 1741-9379) **5867**
Team Intelligence (USA) **8211**
Team Kids *see* TeamKids **2169**
Team Line-Up (USA) **8211**
Team Management Briefings (USA ISSN 1069-6539) **1797**
Team Marketing Report (USA ISSN 1097-119X) **1845**
Team N Y I Magazine (USA) **2918**
Team of Advocates for Special Kids Newsletter (USA) **4070**
● ➤ Team Performance Management (GBR ISSN 1352-7592) **1797**
● Team Spiegel (DEU ISSN 1868-1948) **8808**
Team Talk (GBR ISSN 0963-049X) **8248**
Team Tracker *see* National Football League Team Tracker **2204**
● TeamKids (USA ISSN 1555-953X) **2169**
● Teamster (USA ISSN 1083-2394) **4603**
Teamster Convoy Dispatch (USA ISSN 0738-8330) **4603**
Teamwork (Chicago) *see* Dartnell's Teamwork **1859**
Teamwork (German Edition) (DEU ISSN 1435-330X) **5867**
● Teamwork (Italian Edition) (ITA ISSN 1825-2214) **5867**
Teamwork Special (DEU) **5868**
Teanga (IRL ISSN 0332-205X) **5186**
Teangeolas (IRL ISSN 0332-0294) **5186**
Tear (USA) **521**
Tear Sheet (USA) **2262**
Tear Topics *see* T E A R Topics **8074**
Tearaway Magazine (NZL ISSN 0113-3403) **2216**
Tearmann (IRL ISSN 1649-1009) **161**
Tears (GBR) **3004**
Teatar/Theatre (BGR) **8480**
Teater 1 (DNK ISSN 0905-3026) **8480**
Teater. Muusika. Kino (EST ISSN 0207-6535) **8480**
Teaterforum (SWE ISSN 0347-8890) **8480**
Teaterhoegskolan. Aarsberaettelse *see* Teatterikorkeakoulu. Vuosikertomus **3004**
† Teatermagasinet ARTE Nyt (Arbejdernes Teaterorganisation) (DNK ISSN 1397-9426) **8992**
● Teatertidningen (SWE ISSN 1101-9107) **8480**
Teatr (POL ISSN 0040-0769) **8481**
Teatr (RUS ISSN 0131-6885) **8481**
➤ Teatr (USA ISSN 1535-6159) **8481**
Teatr Lalek (POL ISSN 0239-667X) **8481**
Teatral'naya Zhizn' (RUS ISSN 0131-6915) **8481**
● Teatro (ESP ISSN 1132-2233) **8481**
Teatro (NIC) **8481**
Teatro al Sur (ARG ISSN 1514-7916) **8481**
† Teatro Archivio (ITA) **8992**
Teatro C E L C I T (ARG) **8481**
Teatro del Mundo (ARG ISSN 1851-6378) **8481**
Teatro del Siglo de Oro: Bibliografias y Catalogos (DEU) **5385**
Teatro del Siglo de Oro: Ediciones Criticas (DEU) **5385**
Teatro del Siglo de Oro: Estudios de Literatura (DEU) **5385**
Il Teatro di Shakespeare (ITA ISSN 1825-4918) **5385**
Teatro en Latinoamerica (DEU) **8481**
Teatro. Studi e Testi (ITA ISSN 1122-0678) **8481**
Teatro XXI (ARG ISSN 0328-9230) **8481**
● TeatroMese (ITA ISSN 1128-7500) **8481**
Los Teatros (ARG) **8481**
Teatrulazi (ROM ISSN 1220-4676) **8481**
Teatterikorkeakoulu. Acta Scenica (FIN ISSN 1238-5913) **8481**
Teatterikorkeakoulu. Julkaisusarja (FIN ISSN 0783-3385) **8481**
● Teatterikorkeakoulu. Vuosikertomus/Teaterhoegskolan. Aarsberaettelse/Theatre Academy of Finland. Annual Report (FIN ISSN 1456-0828) **3004**
Teatur/Theater (BGR ISSN 0204-6253) **8481**
Teazer (GBR ISSN 1355-1485) **6300**
Teazer Just 18 (GBR ISSN 1365-8557) **6300**
Tebeto (ESP ISSN 1134-430X) **4272**
Tebiwa (USA) **357**
Tec-man (IND) **8440**
Tec21/Ingegneri e Architetti Svizzeri/Ingenieurs et Architectes Suisses (CHE ISSN 1424-800X) **458**
TecAgri News (USA) **215**
● TecBahia (BRA ISSN 0104-3285) **8440**
TecChannel (DEU) **2439**
● The Tech (USA ISSN 0148-9607) **2303**
Tech Almanac (USA ISSN 1548-5668) **7486**
● Tech Beat (USA) **2675**
● Tech Capital (USA ISSN 1094-673X) **1394**
Tech Coast (USA) **1181**
Tech Collegian (USA) **2303**
● Tech Confidential (USA ISSN 1556-8326) **1386**
● Tech Connection (USA) **2675**
● Tech Decisions for Insurance (USA ISSN 1542-8923) **4531**
● Tech Directions (USA ISSN 1062-9351) **3085**
Tech Employers *see* Vault Guide to the Top Tech Employers **1713**
● Tech Europe (BEL ISSN 1021-4232) **2352**
Tech Home Builder *see* TecHome Builder **1039**
Tech I Q (USA ISSN 1930-9546) **2525**
Tech International (ITA) **6052**
● The Tech Log (GBR) **72**
Tech - N J (USA) **8440**
Tech Sample (USA) **5720**
Tech Smart *see* TechSmart **2439**
● Tech Talk (USA) **8808**
Tech Talk (USA) **6407**
Tech Tips (PHL ISSN 0116-4333) **8440**
● Tech Tips Monthly (USA) **2567**
Tech Topics (USA ISSN 1062-077X) **2303**
Tech Transfer (USA ISSN 1062-5240) **8512**
Tech Troglodyte (USA ISSN 0733-575X) **2771**
● TechCapital (USA) **2567**
TechComp Review (USA) **1797**
TechConnect (USA) **1521**
TechFacts (USA) **2403**
TechIQ *see* Tech I Q **2525**
Techjobs Magazine (USA) **6704**
● TechJournal South (USA) **1182**
● TechKnow Times (USA ISSN 1089-2176) **2567**
Techletter (USA ISSN 0883-8828) **7543**
Techline (USA ISSN 0896-3215) **2395**
TechLink: Air Pollution (USA ISSN 1069-3939) **3491**
TechLink: Automotive and Road Transportation (USA ISSN 1069-3904) **8606**
TechLink: Solid and Hazardous Waste (USA ISSN 1069-3947) **3513**
TechLink: Transportation Safety (USA ISSN 1069-3912) **8512**
Techlinks (USA ISSN 1537-288X) **8440**

Title

10934 TECHMANTRA ULRICH'S PERIODICALS

TechMantra (USA) **1655**
TechMax (DEU) **8440**
Techne (BRA ISSN 0104-1053) **1039**
Techne (FRA ISSN 1254-7867) **6538**
Techne (ITA ISSN 1121-757X) **5436**
• Techne: Research in Philosophy and Technology (USA) **6956**
Technet *see* TechNet Magazine **2599**
TechNet Magazine (NLD) **2439**
TechNet Magazine (USA ISSN 1551-2770) **2599**
Techni-Porc (FRA ISSN 0181-6764) **302**
Technic *see* Journal of Operating Department Practice **6249**
Technica (CHE ISSN 0040-0866) **8440**
Technica (FRA ISSN 0184-4067) **1182**
Technica Didactica (DEU ISSN 0949-8109) **8440**
Technical Acoustics *see* Shengxue Jishu **7089**
Technical Adviser *see* Money Management **1368**
Technical Aid to the Disabled Journal (AUS ISSN 0725-2919) **4070**
• Technical Analysis of Stocks & Commodities (USA ISSN 0738-3355) **1655**
Technical Analysis of Stocks & Commodities (Year) (USA ISSN 1060-328X) **1655**
Technical and Commercial Message (NGA) **3221**
Technical and Further Education Link (Online) *see* T A F E Link (Online) **2946**
Technical & Skilled Trade Personnel Report (USA) **1710**
Technical and Vocational Education and Training (NLD ISSN 1871-3041) **3004**
Technical Association of Refractories, Japan. Journal (JPN) **6334**
Technical Association of the Graphic Arts Newsletter *see* T A G A Newsletter **7328**
Technical Association of the Graphic Arts Proceedings *see* T A G A Proceedings **7328**
Technical Association of the Pulp and Paper Industry Coating & Graphic Arts Conference Proceedings *see* T A P P I Coating & Graphic Arts Conference Proceedings **6738**
Technical Association of the Pulp and Paper Industry Coating Conference Proceedings *see* T A P P I Coating Conference Proceedings **6738**
Technical Association of the Pulp and Paper Industry Directory *see* T A P P I Directory **6738**
Technical Association of the Pulp and Paper Industry Engineering & Papermakers Conference *see* T A P P I Engineering & Papermakers Conference **6738**
Technical Association of the Pulp and Paper Industry Finishing and Converting Conference. Proceedings (Year) *see* T A P P I Finishing and Converting Conference. Proceedings (Year) **6738**
Technical Association of the Pulp and Paper Industry Hot Melt Conference (Year) *see* T A P P I Hot Melt Conference (Year) **6738**
Technical Association of the Pulp and Paper Industry International Corrugated Containers Conference and Trade Fair. Proceedings *see* T A P P I International Corrugated Containers Conference and Trade Fair. Proceedings **6738**
Technical Association of the Pulp and Paper Industry International Environmental Conference & Exhibit. Proceedings *see* T A P P I International Environmental Conference & Exhibit. Proceedings **3469**
Technical Association of the Pulp and Paper Industry International Pan Pacific Conference. Proceedings *see* T A P P I International Pan Pacific Conference. Proceedings **6739**
Technical Association of the Pulp and Paper Industry International Process & Product Quality Conference Proceedings (Year) *see* T A P P I International Process & Product Quality Conference Proceedings (Year) **6739**
Technical Association of the Pulp and Paper Industry Journal *see* T A P P I Journal **6739**
Technical Association of the Pulp and Paper Industry Nonwood Plant Fiber Pulping Progress Report *see* T A P P I Nonwood Plant Fiber Pulping Progress Report **6739**
Technical Association of the Pulp and Paper Industry Nonwovens Conference. Proceedings (Year) *see* T A P P I Nonwovens Conference. Proceedings (Year) **6739**
Technical Association of the Pulp and Paper Industry of Korea. Journal *see* Peolpeu Jong'i Gi'sul **6737**
Technical Association of the Pulp and Paper Industry of Southern Africa Journal *see* T A P P S A Journal **6739**
Technical Association of the Pulp and Paper Industry Polymers, Laminations & Coatings Conference. Proceedings (Year) *see* T A P P I Polymers, Laminations & Coatings Conference. Proceedings (Year) **6739**
Technical Association of the Pulp and Paper Industry Process Control Conference. Proceedings (Year) *see* T A P P I Process Control Conference. Proceedings (Year) **6739**
Technical Association of the Pulp and Paper Industry Pulping Conference. Proceedings *see* T A P P I Pulping Conference. Proceedings **6739**
Technical Association of the Pulp and Paper Industry Recycling Symposium *see* (Year) T A P P I Recycling Symposium **6739**
Technical Association of the Pulp and Paper Industry Technical Information Papers *see* T A P P I Technical Information Papers **6739**
Technical Association of the Pulp and Paper Industry Test Methods *see* T A P P I Test Methods **6739**
Technical Brief (USA ISSN 1053-8860) **8481**
Technical Bulletin, Committee for Coordination of Joint Prospecting for Mineral Resources in Asian Offshore Areas (CCOP) *see* Committee for Coordination of Joint Prospecting for Mineral Resources in Asian Offshore Areas. Technical Bulletin **2729**
Technical Bulletin - Department of Natural Resources (Madison) *see* Wisconsin. Department of Natural Resources. Technical Bulletin Series **2633**
Technical Bulletin on Hydrography *see* Suirobu Giho **2798**
Technical Bulletin Vevey (CHE ISSN 1012-294X) **8440**
Technical Choice *see* Techniki Eklogi **3332**
• ➤ Technical Communication (USA ISSN 0049-3155) **2340**
• ➤ Technical Communication Quarterly (USA ISSN 1057-2252) **3085**
† Technical Computing (AUS ISSN 1038-5231) **8992**
• Technical Computing Magazine (GBR ISSN 1355-9907) **2439**
Technical Conference on Artificial Insemination and Reproduction. Proceedings (USA ISSN 0190-4531) **269**
Technical Conference Proceedings - Irrigation Association *see* Irrigation Association. Technical Conference Proceedings **238**
Technical Data Bulletin *see* A S H R A E Technical Data Bulletin **3372**
Technical Diagnostics and Nondestructive Testing (GBR) **6344**
Technical Diagnostics and Nondestructive Testing *see* Tekhnicheskaya Diagnostika i Nerazrushayushchii Kontrol' **7043**
Technical Economic Digest *see* Muszaki-Gazdasagi Magazin **1252**
Technical Education & Training Abstracts *see* Vocational Education & Training Abstracts **2937**
• Technical Guidebook (USA) **7328**
Technical Ideas *see* Tekhnicheska Misal **3222**
Technical Information Digest (IND) **6480**
Technical Information in Mie Prefecture: Machine and Metal Series *see* Gijutsu Joho Mie. Kikai Kinzoku Hen **5452**
Technical Insights. Client Studies (USA) **8440**
Technical Instructions for the Safe Transport of Dangerous Goods by Air (CAN) **8552**
Technical Journal *see* Teknik Dergi **3285**
Technical Journal of Bacteriology *see* Saikingaku Gijutsu Sosho **896**
• Technical Literature Abstracts (Warrendale) (USA) **8531**
• Technical Literature Abstracts: Automotive (USA ISSN 1094-1568) **6801**
• Technical Literature Abstracts: Catalysts - Zeolites (Online) (USA) **2096**
• Technical Literature Abstracts: Fuel Reformulation (USA ISSN 1087-1454) **2096**
• Technical Literature Abstracts: Health & Environment (Online) (USA) **3481**
• Technical Literature Abstracts: Oilfield Chemicals (Online) (USA) **6801**
• Technical Literature Abstracts: Petroleum Refining & Petrochemicals (Online) (USA) **6801**
• Technical Literature Abstracts: Petroleum Substitutes (Online) (USA) **6801**
• Technical Literature Abstracts: Tribology (USA ISSN 1087-1462) **2096**
Technical Papers for the Bible Translator *see* Bible Translator. Technical Papers **5099**
Technical Papers in Hydrology Series (FRA ISSN 0082-2310) **2798**
• ➤ Technical Physics (RUS ISSN 1063-7842) **7042**
• ➤ Technical Physics Letters (RUS ISSN 1063-7850) **7042**
Technical Processing and Documentation Forum (Year) *see* T P & D Forum (Year) **5049**
† Technical Product Update (DNK ISSN 0900-3762) **8992**
Technical Publications by J A E R I Staff (JPN) **3175**
Technical Quarterly *see* Technical Quarterly & the M B A A Communicator **611**
• Technical Quarterly & the M B A A Communicator (Master Brewers Association of the Americas) (USA ISSN 1558-0628) **611**
Technical Report of I S E I, Series A *see* I S E I Technical Report. Series A **2709**
Technical Report of I S E I, Series B *see* I S E I Technical Report. Series B **2709**
Technical Report of I S E I, Series C *see* I S E I Technical Report. Series C **2709**
Technical Report of Kirin (JPN ISSN 0916-6491) **611**
Technical Report of Medical Ultrasound Engineering *see* Kiso Gijutsu Kenkyu Bukai Shiryo **6202**
Technical Report of Remotely Operated Vehicle *see* R O V Chosa Hokokusho **2816**
Technical Research Centre of Finland. Annual Report *see* V T T Annual Report **3226**
Technical Research Institute News *see* Gijutsu Kenkyujo Dayori **3309**
Technical Research Institute. Technical Reports *see* Gijutsu Kenkyujoho **3268**
Technical Research Report of Hazama Corporation *see* Hazama Kenkyu Nenpo (CD-ROM) **3268**
• Technical Review Middle East/Al-Nashrah al-Tiqniyyah al-sharq al-awsat (GBR ISSN 0267-5307) **8441**
Technical Review Sulzer (CHE ISSN 1420-7559) **3222**
Technical Reviews *see* Notre Dame Technical Review **3213**
Technical Sciences (POL ISSN 1505-4675) **8441**
• Technical Services Law Librarian (USA ISSN 0195-4857) **5050**
• ➤ Technical Services Quarterly (USA ISSN 0731-7131) **5050**
Technical Soaring (USA ISSN 0744-8996) **72**
Technical Supplement *see* Mobile Electronics **2334**
Technical Supplement *see* Administrative Notes **4987**
Technical Support *see* National Systems Programmers Association Technical Support **2508**
Technical Tax Proposals (GBR) **1386**
• Technical Textile Markets (GBR ISSN 0959-9185) **8458**
Technical Textiles *see* Technische Textilien **8458**
• Technical Textiles International (GBR ISSN 0964-5993) **8458**
• Technical Tips Online (GBR ISSN 1366-2120) **707**
Technical Trends (USA ISSN 0889-9525) **1655**
Technical University in Zvolen. Faculty of Forestry. Collection of Scientific Works *see* Acta Facultatis Forestalis, Zvolen **3682**
Technical University of Chalmer. Doctoral Thesis. New Series *see* Chalmers Tekniska Hoegskola. Doktorsavhandlingar. Ny Serie **3184**
Technical University of Kosice. Transactions (GBR ISSN 0960-6076) **8441**
➤ Technical University of Lodz. Scientific Bulletin. Physics (POL ISSN 1505-1013) **7042**
Technical University of Sofia. Proceedings *see* Tehniceskia Universitet Sofiya. Godisnik **3397**
• Technicalities (USA ISSN 0272-0884) **5050**
Technic'Baie (FRA ISSN 1956-3132) **1039**
• ➤ Technicheskaya Akustika (Online) (RUS ISSN 1819-2408) **7089**
➤ Technichna Elektrodynamika (UKR ISSN 1607-7970) **3332**
• Technician (USA ISSN 1072-1916) **2303**
Technician and Skilled Trades Personnel Report - Geographic Edition (USA) **1876**
Technician News & Satellite Journal (USA ISSN 1092-9592) **3115**
Le Technicien d'Agriculture Tropicale (FRA ISSN 0298-3540) **161**
Le Technicien du Film (FRA ISSN 1963-2304) **6515**
Technicka Univerzita vo Zvolene. Lesnicka Fakulta. Zbornik Vedeckych Prac *see* Acta Facultatis Forestalis, Zvolen **3682**
Technicke Zariadenia Budov *see* T Z B **4127**
• Technicky Tydenik (CZE ISSN 0040-1064) **5460**
Techniek en Bouw in de Kijker *see* Kijkkez Techniek & Bouw **3277**
Technik (CZE ISSN 1210-616X) **8441**
Technik am Bau *see* T A B **4127**
• Technik in Bayern (DEU ISSN 1432-6035) **3222**
Technik in Hessen *see* Technik und Mensch **3222**
Technik Report (AUT ISSN 0377-1725) **3397**
Technik und Einkauf (DEU ISSN 1860-1901) **1845**
Technik und Mensch (DEU ISSN 1611-5546) **3222**
Technika (HUN ISSN 0040-1110) **636**
➤ Technika (SRB ISSN 0040-2176) **5460**
Technika Chlodnicza i Klimatyzacyjna (POL ISSN 1231-188X) **4127**
Technika Chronika/Annales Techniques (GRC ISSN 0040-4764) **7922**
Technika Morska *see* Marine Technology Transactions **3363**
➤ Technika Poszukiwan Geologicznych, Geosynoptyka i Geotermia/Exploration Technology, Geosynoptics and Geothermal Energy (POL) **2771**
Technika Rolnicza *see* Technika Rolnicza, Ogrodnicza, Lesna **214**
Technika Rolnicza, Ogrodnicza, Lesna (POL ISSN 1732-1719) **214**
Technikart Magazine (FRA) **5241**
TechnikDialog (DEU) **8441**
Techniker Krankenkasse Aktuell *see* T K Aktuell **4524**
• Technikfolgenabschaetzung (DEU ISSN 1619-7623) **8441**
Technikgeschichte (DEU ISSN 0040-117X) **8441**
Techniki Eklogi/Technical Choice (GRC) **3332**
Techniki Komputerowe (POL ISSN 0239-8044) **2528**
Technikon Forum (ZAF) **3004**
Technikphilosophie (DEU) **6956**
Die Technikstunde (DEU) **2946**
† Technion - Israel Institute of Technology. Abstracts of Research Theses (ISR ISSN 0792-7355) **8992**
Technion - Israel Institute of Technology, Department of Aeronautical Engineering Report *see* T.A.E. Report **8992**
† Technion Magazine (ISR ISSN 0040-1188) **8992**
Technique *see* Teknika **6480**
Technique (Atlanta) (USA) **2303**
Technique (Indianapolis) (USA ISSN 0748-5999) **8211**
Technique (San Diego) (USA ISSN 1043-4658) **707**
Technique Agricole *see* Schweizer Landtechnik **154**
Technique Chaussure Maroquinerie *see* T C M **4975**
Technique et Management *see* Industrie Technique et Management **1752**
Technique of Self-Defense *see* Boji **8162**
• Techniques (USA ISSN 1527-1803) **2918**
Techniques and Equipment for Environmental Pollution Control *see* Huanjing Wuran Zhili Jishu yu Shebei **3487**
• ➤ Techniques and Instrumentation in Analytical Chemistry (NLD ISSN 0167-9244) **2106**
Techniques Chirgicales. Tete et Cou *see* Encyclopedie Medico-Chirurgicale. Techniques Chirurgicales. Tete et Cou **6242**
Techniques Chirurgicales - Appareil Digestif *see* Encyclopedie Medico-Chirurgicale. Techniques Chirurgicales. Appareil Digestif **6242**
Techniques Chirurgicales - Chirurgie Vasculaire *see* Encyclopedie Medico-Chirurgicale. Techniques Chirurgicales. Chirurgie Vasculaire **6242**
Techniques Chirurgicales. Thorax *see* Encyclopedie Medico-Chirurgicale. Techniques Chirurgicales. Thorax **6242**
Techniques de Developpement Personnel (FRA ISSN 1295-1552) **7411**
• Techniques de l'Ingenieur. Analyse et Caracterisation (FRA ISSN 1762-8717) **3256**
• Techniques de l'Ingenieur. Constantes Physico-Chimiques (FRA ISSN 0245-9604) **3256**
• Techniques de l'Ingenieur. Construction (FRA ISSN 0245-9590) **3285**
• Techniques de l'Ingenieur. Documents Numeriques - Gestion de Contenu (FRA ISSN 1953-4957) **2510**
Techniques de l'Ingenieur. Energies. La Lettre (FRA ISSN 1954-1031) **3148**
Techniques de l''Ingenieur. Environnement. La Lettre *see* Techniques de l'Ingenieur. Risques Industriels et Environnement. La Lettre **3371**
• Techniques de l'Ingenieur. Genie Electrique (FRA ISSN 0992-5449) **3332**
• Techniques de l'Ingenieur. Le Traitement du Signal et ses Applications (FRA ISSN 1953-4671) **2340**
• Techniques de l'Ingenieur. Maintenance (FRA ISSN 1776-0186) **3222**
• Techniques de l'Ingenieur. Materiaux Fonctionnels (FRA ISSN 1776-0178) **3222**
Techniques de l'Ingenieur. Materiaux Metalliques (FRA ISSN 1762-8733) **3358**
• Techniques de l'Ingenieur. Physique-Chimie (FRA ISSN 1776-016X) **3256**
• Techniques de l'Ingenieur. Qualite et Securite au Laboratoire (FRA ISSN 1954-5800) **3222**
• Techniques de l'Ingenieur. Reseaux et Telecommunications (FRA ISSN 1953-4647) **2340**
Techniques de l'Ingenieur. Reseaux sans fil *see* Techniques de l'Ingenieur. Reseaux sans Fil **3332**
Techniques de l'Ingenieur. Reseaux sans Fil (FRA) **3332**
▼ Techniques de l'Ingenieur. Risques Industriels et Environnement. La Lettre (FRA ISSN 1957-2891) **3371**
Techniques de l''Ingenieur. Risques Industriels. La Lettre *see* Techniques de l'Ingenieur. Risques Industriels et Environnement. La Lettre **3371**
• Techniques de l'Ingenieur. Securite des Systemes d'Information (FRA ISSN 1953-4663) **2516**
Techniques de l'Ingenieur. Securite des Systemes d'Information. La Lettre (FRA ISSN 1771-1061) **2516**
• Techniques de l'Ingenieur. Technologies Logicielles Architectures des Systemes (FRA ISSN 1953-4655) **2468**
Techniques de Presse *see* W A N - I F R A Magazine **7329**
Techniques Documentaires (FRA ISSN 1779-9813) **2551**
Techniques & Culture (FRA ISSN 0248-6016) **358**
Techniques et marches Avicoles *see* Te M A **207**
Techniques et Methodes des Laboratoires des Ponts et Chaussees. Methode (FRA ISSN 1167-489X) **3285**
Techniques & Pratique du Sport (FRA ISSN 1952-580X) **8248**
Techniques Hospitalieres (FRA ISSN 1166-8385) **4112**
• ➤ Techniques in Coloproctology (ITA ISSN 1123-6337) **5931**
• ➤ Techniques in Coloproctology (Online) (ITA ISSN 1128-045X) **5931**
Techniques in Diagnostic Pathology (USA ISSN 1056-7208) **5911**
• ➤ Techniques in Foot & Ankle Surgery (USA ISSN 1536-0644) **6260**
• ➤ Techniques in Gastrointestinal Endoscopy (USA ISSN 1096-2883) **5931**
• Techniques in Hand & Upper Extremity Surgery (USA ISSN 1089-3393) **6261**
• Techniques in Knee Surgery (USA ISSN 1536-0636) **6261**
Techniques in Marine Environmental Sciences *see* I C E S Techniques in Marine Environmental Sciences **677**
• Techniques in Ophthalmology (USA ISSN 1542-1929) **6052**
• ➤ Techniques in Orthopaedics (USA ISSN 0885-9698) **6073**
• Techniques in Protein Chemistry (USA ISSN 1080-8914) **2131**
• ➤ Techniques in Regional Anesthesia and Pain Management (USA ISSN 1084-208X) **5774**
• Techniques in Shoulder and Elbow Surgery (USA ISSN 1523-9896) **6261**

Title

• Telos (ESP ISSN 1132-0877) **6956**
• ➤ Telos (USA ISSN 0090-6514) **6956**
➤ Telos (VEN ISSN 1317-0570) **4477**
• Telos (Madrid) (ESP ISSN 0213-084X) **2439**
Telovychovny Pracovnik *see* T P **6998**
Telstra Corporation Limited. Annual Report (AUS) **2342**
Telugu Akademi Language Monograph Series (IND) **5186**
Telugu Naadi (USA ISSN 1559-7008) **3568**
Telugu Nadi *see* Telugu Naadi **3568**
• Telugu Vaani/Voice of Telugus (IND) **5385**
• Telva (ESP ISSN 0212-2375) **2262**
Telview Express *see* Market View **2369**
Tema (BRA ISSN 0103-8338) **3804**
Tema (CAN ISSN 0381-9582) **5186**
Tema (HUN ISSN 1587-4168) **3666**
▼ • Tema (Territorio Mobilita Ambiente) (ITA ISSN 1970-9889) **459**
Tema Arkiv (SWE ISSN 1102-3597) **1797**
• Tema Farmacia (ITA ISSN 1827-3718) **6882**
Tema International (USA) **4379**
• TEMA - Technology and Management (DEU) **8447**
Tema Verde (ARG) **2628**
Tema y Variaciones de Literatura (MEX) **5385**
Temamagasinet for Foraeldre om... *see* Magasinet Voksne for Barn **7383**
TemaNord (DNK ISSN 0908-6692) **7188**
Temas (CUB ISSN 0864-134X) **3831**
Temas (ESP) **8009**
• Temas (USA ISSN 0040-2869) **3565**
• Temas Agrarios (COL ISSN 0122-7610) **161**
Temas Americanistas (ESP ISSN 0212-4408) **4314**
Temas de Actualidad (PER) **8009**
Temas de Antropologia Aragonesa/Aragonese Anthropology (ESP ISSN 0212-5552) **358**
Temas de Arquitectura (ESP ISSN 1698-8671) **459**
• Temas de Coyuntura (VEN ISSN 1316-5003) **8009**
Temas de Derecho Publico (COL) **4852**
Temas de Educacion (COL) **2919**
Temas de Estetica y Arte (ESP ISSN 0214-6258) **522**
† Temas de Historia y Politica Contemporaneas (ESP) **8992**
Temas de Orientacion Agropecuaria (COL ISSN 0049-3333) **161**
Temas de Psicoanalisis (ESP ISSN 1137-7682) **7411**
Temas del Senado *see* Spain. Senado. Temas **8989**
Temas Economicos (VEN ISSN 0495-0615) **1182**
Temas Economicos, Trabajos y Negocios *see* Ercilla **3821**
Temas Juridicos (COL) **4793**
Temas Laborales (ESP ISSN 0213-0750) **1710**
• Temas Medievales (ARG ISSN 0327-5094) **4164**
Temas para el Debate (ESP ISSN 1134-6574) **7188**
Temas Sobre la Profesionalizacion Militar en la Republica Dominicana (DOM) **6448**
Temas Sociales (BOL ISSN 0040-2915) **8143**
Temas Sociales (CRI ISSN 0492-6471) **8074**
Temas Subjectividad y Procesos Sociales (MEX ISSN 0188-9273) **8009**
Temas Teatro (ARG ISSN 1851-619X) **8481**
• Temas Tributarios de Actualidad Fiscal (ESP ISSN 1576-5032) **1951**
Temas y Problemas de Comunicacion (ARG ISSN 1514-2159) **2342**
Temas y Propuestas (ARG) **1182**
• Teme (SRB ISSN 0353-7919) **8143**
Temel ve Uygulamali Bilmler Dergisi *see* Journal of Pure and Applied Sciences **8968**
➤ Temenos (FIN ISSN 0497-1817) **7688**
Temenos Academy Review (GBR ISSN 1461-779X) **5385**
Temi di Predicazione - Omelie (ITA ISSN 1124-0431) **7688**
† Temi e Profili del Novecento (ITA) **8992**
† Temi - Tendenze Moda Italia (ITA) **8993**
Temiskaming Speaker (CAN ISSN 0832-3054) **3818**
Temoignage Chretien (FRA ISSN 0244-1462) **5241**
Temoignage Chretien de la Reunion (REU) **7819**
Temoignages & Dossiers (FRA ISSN 1770-4774) **1606**
Temoins de Notre Histoire (BEL ISSN 1147-436X) **4273**
Temp Medieval *see* Mittelalter (Basel) **7600**
Temp Slave (USA) **6704**
† Tempe Informations (FRA ISSN 0338-1811) **8993**
Temperature Controlled Storage and Distribution Industry Buyers Guide *see* T C S & D - U K Industry Buyers Guide **3665**
† Templari (ITA ISSN 1592-7997) **8993**
Templarium *see* Le Medieviste Magazine **4243**
The Temple (USA) **5436**
Temple David Bulletin (ZAF ISSN 0040-2966) **7730**
• Temple International and Comparative Law Journal (USA ISSN 0889-1915) **4942**
• Temple Journal of Science, Technology & Environmental Law (USA) **4793**
• Temple Law Review (USA ISSN 0899-8086) **4793**
Temple News (USA) **2303**
• Temple Political & Civil Rights Law Review (USA ISSN 1062-5887) **4852**
• Temple Review (USA) **2303**
• Templer Record (AUS ISSN 1328-9187) **7688**
• Tempo (BRA ISSN 1413-7704) **4314**
† Tempo! (CZE ISSN 1212-6454) **8993**
• Tempo (IDN ISSN 0126-4273) **3891**
• Il Tempo (ITA) **3899**
Tempo (MOZ ISSN 0258-0837) **3913**
Tempo (NAM) **3913**
Tempo (POL ISSN 0137-933X) **8211**
• Tempo (TUR ISSN 1300-588X) **3963**
Tempo (USA ISSN 0040-3016) **6622**
• Tempo (London, 1939) (GBR ISSN 0040-2982) **6622**
Tempo (London, 1947) (GBR) **3872**
Tempo (Stockholm) (SWE ISSN 1650-4224) **1797**
Tempo Brasileiro (BRA ISSN 0102-8782) **2919**
Tempo Economico (PRT) **1182**
• Tempo Exterior (ESP ISSN 1579-6582) **7188**
† • Tempo Materia Architettura (ITA) **8993**
Tempo Medicina (PRT) **5721**
• Tempo Medico (ITA ISSN 0492-6749) **5721**
Tempo Medico Bis *see* Tempo Medico **5721**
† Tempo Nuovo (ITA ISSN 1128-2967) **8993**
† Tempo Pollino (ITA) **8993**
Tempo Psicanalitico (BRA ISSN 0101-4838) **7411**
• ➤ Tempo Social (BRA ISSN 0103-2070) **8143**
Tempora (DEU ISSN 1433-2078) **7716**
Tempora (ESP ISSN 0211-8939) **2919**
Temporadas de la Musica Clasica (ESP ISSN 0213-6031) **6622**
Temporale (CHE ISSN 1016-0809) **522**
Temporary Disability Insurance and Unemployment Insurance Laws of Rhode Island (USA ISSN 1931-2695) **4525**
Temporis Signa (ITA ISSN 1970-514X) **420**
Temporis Novos (ESP ISSN 1137-6945) **3954**
Tempra 365 (DEU ISSN 1614-7634) **1876**
• Le Temps (CHE ISSN 1423-3967) **3959**
Le Temps (TUN ISSN 0330-9983) **3962**
Temps Course Mag (FRA ISSN 1766-9057) **8337**
Le Temps de l'Histoire *see* Revue d'Histoire de l'Enfance Irreguliere **2167**
Temps d'Educacio (ESP ISSN 0214-7351) **2919**
• Le Temps des Medias (FRA ISSN 1764-2507) **2342**
Temps et Espace des Arts (FRA ISSN 1778-591X) **459**
Temps Libre Magazine (FRA ISSN 1778-8412) **3842**
Les Temps Modernes (FRA ISSN 0040-3075) **5241**
➤ Le Temps Mondial/World Time (GBR ISSN 1350-4134) **7268**
Le Temps Philosophique (FRA ISSN 1245-2998) **6956**
▼ • Temps Zero (CAN ISSN 1913-5963) **5186**
➤ Tempus (AUS ISSN 1323-6040) **358**
Tempus (ESP ISSN 1132-0958) **4273**
Tempus (MEX) **4314**
Tempus *see* Lake Effect (Erie) **5223**
Tempus (USA ISSN 1946-2271) **4164**
Ten (USA ISSN 1554-7469) **1386**
Ten Best Censored Stories *see* 10 Best Censored Stories **4586**
• Ten Dance (DEU) **6622**
Ten-Day Marine Report *see* Kishocho Kaiyo Junpo **6359**
Ten-Day Marine Report of the East China Sea *see* Nishinhon Kaikyo Junpo **6392**
Ten Forty Preparation *see* 1040 Preparation and Planning Guide **1956**
Ten Forty Report *see* TaxPro Monthly **1951**
Ten - Four *see* 10 - 4 **2672**
Ten Ten Magazine *see* 1010 Magazine **5088**
Ten Thousand Steps Working Paper Series *see* 10,000 Steps Working Paper Series **8019**
Ten Thousand Things (USA) **3990**
Ten Thousand Words! (USA ISSN 1063-9063) **6515**
Tena (HRV ISSN 1331-7806) **8885**
• The Tenagra Apogee (USA) **2439**
Tenant/Inquilino (USA ISSN 0040-3083) **7613**
Tenant Participation Advisory Service Notes *see* T P A S Notes **4428**
Tenant Times (USA) **4428**
Tendance Deco (CHE) **4551**
Tendance Recettes Magazine (FRA ISSN 1950-3075) **4368**
Tendances (FRA ISSN 1951-4468) **1522**
• Tendances de la Main-d'Oeuvre des Infirmieres et Infirmiers Autorises au Canada (Online) (CAN ISSN 1912-0265) **5982**
• Tendances de la Main-d'Oeuvre des Infirmieres et Infirmiers Autorises au Canada (Print) (CAN ISSN 1709-7525) **5982**
• Tendances de la Main-d'Oeuvre des Infirmieres et Infirmiers Psychiatriques Autorises au Canada (CAN ISSN 1711-0459) **5982**
Tendances des Marches. Hebdo *see* Te M A **207**
Tendances R H (Ressources Humaines) (CAN ISSN 1715-0132) **6704**
• Tendances Regionales (FRA) **1522**
Tendances Regionales Lorraine (Print) *see* Tendances Regionales **1522**
Tendances Ressources Humaines *see* Tendances R H **6704**
• Tendances Sociales Canadiennes (CAN ISSN 0831-5701) **7316**
Tendances Vin (BEL ISSN 1783-984X) **611**
Tendences des Migrations Internationales *see* Perspectives des Migrations Internationales **7289**
Tendencia (BRA ISSN 0495-0879) **1905**
▼ Tendencias (ARG ISSN 1851-6793) **4584**
Tendencias (MEX) **1182**
Tendencias Economicas y Financieras (ARG) **1182**
• Tendencias em Matematica Aplicada e Computacional (BRA ISSN 1677-1966) **5541**
• Tendenze Nuove (ITA) **4112**
Tendenzfarben D I H *see* D M I Colour + Man **2253**
Tenders Estimating Data Service (SGP) **1040**
Tenders Gazette (NZL ISSN 0111-2767) **5460**
Tendo (DNK ISSN 1902-9179) **7777**
Tendril (USA ISSN 0197-890X) **5436**
† Tenedores y Estrellas (ESP ISSN 0213-2982) **8993**
Tenews *see* Truck Equipment News **8677**
Tenir-too (KGZ) **3904**
Tenis (CZE ISSN 0862-6766) **8248**
➤ Tenisu Janaru/Tennis Journal (JPN) **8248**
Tenji Mainichi *see* Mainichi Shinbun **3900**
• Tenkan Kenkyu (JPN ISSN 0912-0890) **6187**
Tenki/Meteorological Society of Japan. Weather (JPN ISSN 0546-0921) **6396**
Tenkizu/Daily Weather Maps (JPN) **6396**
Tenmon Gaido/Guide to Astronomy (JPN ISSN 0288-1977) **582**
Tenmon Geppo/Astronomical Herald (JPN ISSN 0374-2466) **582**
Tenmon Kaiho/Astronomical Circular (JPN ISSN 0388-5852) **582**
Tennen Gasu Kankei Shiryo/Natural Gas Resources (JPN) **6794**
Tennen Yuki Kagobutsu Toronkai Koen Yoshishu/Symposium on the Chemistry of Natural Products. Symposium Papers (JPN) **2131**
▼ The Tennenbaum Institute Series on Enterprise Systems (NLD ISSN 1874-737X) **1797**
The Tennent's Lager Scottish Football Review (GBR) **8248**
Tennesseana Editions (USA ISSN 1930-1367) **4314**
Tennessee *see* Official Tennessee Vacation Guide **8745**
• ➤ Tennessee Academy of Science. Journal (USA ISSN 0040-313X) **7922**
Tennessee Agent (USA ISSN 1081-566X) **4525**
Tennessee Agri Science (USA) **161**
Tennessee: All-Industries *see* Harris Directory. Tennessee All-Industries **2002**
Tennessee Alumnus (USA ISSN 0040-3156) **2303**
Tennessee Ancestors (USA ISSN 0882-0635) **3784**
Tennessee Anthropological Association. Miscellaneous Paper (USA) **358**
Tennessee Anthropological Association. Newsletter (USA ISSN 0196-0377) **358**
Tennessee Archivist (USA ISSN 1528-6436) **5050**
Tennessee Association of Health, Physical Education, Recreation and Dance. Newsletter (USA) **6998**
Tennessee Attorneys Directory & Buyers Guide *see* Tennessee Attorneys Directory and Buyers Guide **4793**
• Tennessee Attorneys Directory and Buyers Guide (USA ISSN 0742-4329) **4793**
• Tennessee Attorneys Memo (USA ISSN 0194-1259) **4793**
Tennessee Automobile Liability Insurance (USA ISSN 1942-2938) **4525**
• The Tennessee Banker (USA ISSN 0040-3199) **1386**
• Tennessee Bar Journal (USA ISSN 0497-2325) **4793**
• Tennessee Business Directory (USA ISSN 1042-8801) **2030**
Tennessee Cities and Counties Graphic Performance Analysis *see* Tennessee Cities & Counties Graphic Performance Analysis **7484**
Tennessee Cities & Counties Graphic Performance Analysis (USA ISSN 1935-5491) **7484**
Tennessee Code Annotated Advance Annotation Service (USA ISSN 0747-7074) **4793**
Tennessee Compilation of Selected Laws on Children, Youth and Families (USA ISSN 1548-9671) **4914**
• Tennessee Concrete Magazine (USA) **1040**
The Tennessee Conservationist (USA ISSN 0040-3202) **2629**
• Tennessee Construction News Weekly. Knoxville & Vicinity (USA ISSN 1084-9580) **1040**
Tennessee Construction News Weekly. Knoxville and Vicinity *see* Tennessee Construction News Weekly. Knoxville & Vicinity **1040**
Tennessee Construction News Weekly. Memphis and Vicinity *see* Tennessee Construction News Weekly. Memphis & Vicinity **1040**
• Tennessee Construction News Weekly. Memphis & Vicinity (USA ISSN 1084-9572) **1040**
Tennessee Construction News Weekly. Nashville and Vicinity *see* Tennessee Construction News Weekly. Nashville & Vicinity **1040**
• Tennessee Construction News Weekly. Nashville & Vicinity (USA ISSN 1084-9556) **1040**
Tennessee Consumer Protection Act (USA ISSN 1550-3658) **2641**
Tennessee Consumer Protection Act and Related Laws *see* Tennessee Consumer Protection Act **2641**
• Tennessee Corporations, Partnerships and Associations Law Annotated (USA) **4881**
Tennessee County News (USA) **7471**
• Tennessee Criminal Laws Annotated (USA) **4898**
• Tennessee Criminal Offenses, Vehicles and Related Statutes (USA) **4898**
Tennessee Dental Association. Journal (USA ISSN 0040-3385) **5868**
Tennessee. Department of Safety. Annual Report (USA ISSN 0095-1994) **8635**
Tennessee. Division of Geology. Report of Investigations (USA ISSN 0497-2074) **2771**
Tennessee Education (USA ISSN 0739-0408) **3034**
• Tennessee Employment Law Letter (USA ISSN 1531-6580) **4793**
Tennessee Family Adventure Guide *see* Fun with the Family in Tennessee **8712**
Tennessee Family Law Letter (USA ISSN 0890-5355) **4914**
Tennessee Farm Bureau News (USA ISSN 1062-8983) **161**
➤ Tennessee Folklore Society. Bulletin (USA ISSN 0040-3253) **3623**
▼ Tennessee Football (USA) **8248**
Tennessee Genealogical Magazine (USA) **3784**
Tennessee Genealogy & History (USA) **3784**
• Tennessee Government Officials Directory (USA) **7503**
Tennessee. Higher Education Commission. Biennial Report (USA) **3004**
➤ Tennessee Historical Quarterly (USA ISSN 0040-3261) **4314**
Tennessee Holiday Guide & Travel Planner (GBR ISSN 1360-7189) **8760**
• Tennessee Home & Farm (USA) **161**
Tennessee Hospitals & Health Systems (USA) **4112**
The Tennessee Journal (USA ISSN 0194-1240) **7471**
Tennessee Journal of Law & Policy (USA ISSN 1940-4131) **4793**
Tennessee Journal of Practice and Procedure (USA) **4793**
• Tennessee Jurisprudence (USA) **4794**
Tennessee. Labor Market Information Directory (USA ISSN 0749-9930) **1710**
Tennessee Law of Damages (USA) **4842**
• Tennessee Law of Evidence (USA) **4965**
• Tennessee Law Review (USA ISSN 0040-3288) **4794**
Tennessee Librarian (Print) *see* Tennessee Libraries (Online) **5050**
• Tennessee Libraries (Online) (USA ISSN 1935-7052) **5050**
Tennessee Living *see* Southern Living **3988**
The Tennessee Magazine (USA ISSN 0492-746X) **3990**
• Tennessee Manufacturers Register (USA ISSN 1082-0248) **2030**
Tennessee: Manufacturing *see* Harris Directory. Tennessee Manufacturing **2002**
Tennessee Medicine (USA ISSN 1088-6222) **5721**
• Tennessee Motor Vehicle Laws Annotated (USA) **8513**
Tennessee Musician (USA ISSN 0040-3334) **6622**
Tennessee Native Plant Society. Newsletter (USA) **820**
➤ Tennessee Nurse (USA ISSN 1055-3134) **5982**
• Tennessee Parent - Teacher Bulletin (USA) **2919**
Tennessee Pattern Jury Instructions (USA ISSN 1935-5254) **4898**
Tennessee Pharmacist (USA ISSN 1047-0166) **6882**
Tennessee Philological Bulletin (USA ISSN 0735-0783) **5186**
• Tennessee Public Acts (Year) (USA) **7503**
Tennessee Public Library Directory and Statistics (Year) (USA) **5060**
Tennessee Public Works (USA ISSN 0892-5380) **7503**
Tennessee Real Estate Law Letter (USA ISSN 1059-5090) **4794**
• Tennessee Register (USA ISSN 1041-1569) **7819**
Tennessee Restauranteur (USA) **4399**
Tennessee School Boards Association Bulletin *see* T S B A BoardTalk **3034**
Tennessee School Boards Journal (USA ISSN 0747-6159) **3034**
Tennessee School Directory *see* M D R's Tennessee School Directory **2960**
Tennessee Sportsman (USA) **8337**
Tennessee State Agent Handbook (USA) **4525**
Tennessee Statistical Abstract (USA ISSN 0082-2760) **8408**
Tennessee Tax Guide (USA ISSN 0742-0757) **1951**
Tennessee Tax Guide and Tax Calendar *see* Tennessee Tax Guide **1951**
Tennessee Tax Service (USA) **1951**
Tennessee. The Labor Market Report (USA) **1710**
Tennessee Tort Law Letter (USA ISSN 1079-6215) **4842**
Tennessee Torts Case Finder (USA) **4842**
• Tennessee Town and City (USA ISSN 0040-3415) **7503**
▼ Tennessee Trial Law Report (USA ISSN 1946-987X) **4794**
• Tennessee Tribune (USA ISSN 1067-5280) **3568**
Tennessee Trucking News (USA) **8675**
Tennessee Valley Authority. Annual Report (USA ISSN 0363-101X) **2629**
Tennessee Valley Authority. Report (USA) **2798**
• Tennessee Valley Outdoors (USA ISSN 1077-4572) **8337**
Tennessee Valley Public Power Association News *see* T V P P A News **3332**
Tennessee Warbler (USA) **915**
Tennessee Wildlife (USA ISSN 0886-1269) **965**
• The Tennessee Williams Annual Review (USA ISSN 1097-6035) **5385**
Tennessee Williams Literary Journal (USA) **5386**
Tennessee Workers' Comp Reporter (USA ISSN 1526-3665) **4525**
• Tennessee Workers' Compensation Laws (USA) **1710**
Tennessee's Business (USA ISSN 0735-1135) **1968**
• Tennis (USA ISSN 0040-3423) **8248**
Tennis a Fondo (ESP ISSN 1575-1074) **8211**
Tennis de Table Magazine (FRA ISSN 0984-421X) **8248**

Link to your serials resources and content with ulrichsweb.com

DIRECTORY 2010 TEST JAHRBUCH (YEAR) 10939

Tennis Echo (BEL) **8248**
Tennis & Coach (NLD ISSN 0928-9372) **8248**
Tennis Illustrated (New York) (USA ISSN 1057-6851) **8248**
Tennis Info (FRA ISSN 0221-8127) **8248**
• Tennis Italiano (ITA ISSN 0393-0890) **8248**
† Tennis-Jahrbuch (DEU) **8993**
Tennis Journal *see* Tenisu Janaru **8248**
Tennis Life (USA ISSN 1545-6609) **8248**
Tennis Life en Espanol (USA ISSN 1548-8462) **8248**
Tennis Life Magazine *see* Tennis Life **8248**
Tennis Magazin (DEU ISSN 0176-8794) **8248**
Tennis Magazine (FRA ISSN 0396-6267) **8248**
Tennis Magazine (JPN) **8248**
Tennis Magazine (NLD ISSN 1571-4284) **8248**
Tennis Midwest (USA) **8248**
Tennis Nordwest (DEU) **8248**
Tennis Oggi (ITA ISSN 1721-419X) **8249**
Tennis Plus (RUS ISSN 0130-9439) **8249**
Tennis Revue (FRA ISSN 1774-6787) **8249**
• Tennis Server Interactive (USA) **8249**
Tennis Today (GBR ISSN 0140-5497) **8249**
Tennis U S T A (USA) **8249**
▼ Tennis View (USA ISSN 1937-7894) **8249**
• Tennis Week (USA ISSN 0194-9098) **8249**
Tennis World *see* Wangqiu Tiandi **8251**
Tennis World (GBR ISSN 0040-3474) **8249**
Tennisavisen (DNK ISSN 1902-4134) **8249**
† • Tennismagasinet (DNK ISSN 1602-8740) **8993**
TennisPro Magazine (USA) **8249**
Tennissport (DEU ISSN 0937-9681) **8249**
Tennyson Research Bulletin (GBR ISSN 0082-2841) **5386**
Tennyson Society (England). Monographs (GBR ISSN 0082-285X) **5386**
Tennyson Society (England). Occasional Papers (GBR ISSN 0307-3572) **5386**
Tennyson Society (England). Report (GBR ISSN 0082-2868) **5386**
Tenor (IND) **5386**
TenPercent (USA) **4379**
Tenqqara (MYS) **5386**
Tenrag (AUS) **5541**
Tenri Igaku Kiyo/Tenri Medical Bulletin (JPN ISSN 1344-1817) **5721**
Tenri Medical Bulletin *see* Tenri Igaku Kiyo **5721**
Tenrikyo (JPN ISSN 0040-3482) **7742**
➤ Tenside Surfactants Detergents (DEU ISSN 0932-3414) **2141**
• ➤ Tenso (USA ISSN 0890-3352) **5386**
Tensor (JPN ISSN 0040-3504) **5541**
Tentacle (CHE ISSN 0958-5079) **2629**
Tenth Muse *see* 10th Muse **5439**
Tentoonstellingsboekje (NLD ISSN 0920-7430) **6538**
Tenzone (ESP ISSN 1576-9216) **5386**
• Teocomunicacao (BRA ISSN 0103-314X) **7819**
Teollisuuden Keskusliitto. Jasenluettelo/ Confederation of Finnish Industries. List of Members/Finlands Industrifoerbund. Medlemsfoerteckning (FIN ISSN 0781-6987) **2030**
Teologia (ARG ISSN 0328-1396) **7688**
Teologia (HUN ISSN 0133-1779) **7819**
Teologia (ITA ISSN 1120-267X) **7688**
Teologia Espiritual (ESP ISSN 0495-1549) **7688**
Teologia I U S I (VEN) **7688**
Teologia y Catequesis (ESP ISSN 0212-1964) **7688**
• Teologia y Vida (CHL ISSN 0049-3449) **7820**
➤ Teologicka Reflexe (CZE ISSN 1211-1872) **7777**
➤ Teologinen Aikakauskirja/Teologisk Tidskrift (FIN ISSN 0040-3555) **7688**
Teologisk Serie *see* Acta Jutlandica. Teologisk Serie **7620**
Teologisk Tidskrift *see* Teologinen Aikakauskirja **7688**
• Aarhus Universitet. Det Teologiske Facultet. Aarsskrift (DNK ISSN 1603-337X) **7688**
• ➤ Teorema (ESP ISSN 0210-1602) **6956**
• ➤ Teoreticheskaya i Eksperimental'naya Khimiya (UKR ISSN 0497-2627) **2082**
Teoreticheskaya i Matematicheskaya Fizika (RUS ISSN 0564-6162) **7043**
Teoreticheskie Osnovy Khimicheskoi Tekhnologii (RUS ISSN 0040-3571) **3256**
• Teori og Aestetik (DNK ISSN 0908-8865) **5386**
Teoria (ITA ISSN 1122-1259) **6956**
Teoria Critica (ESP ISSN 1134-9018) **5386**
• Teoria de la Educacion (ESP ISSN 1130-3743) **2919**
Teoria di Diritto e dello Stato (ITA ISSN 1721-8098) **4794**
• Teoria e Critica della Regolazione Sociale (ITA ISSN 1970-5476) **8143**
• Teoria e Pratica na Engenharia Civil (BRA ISSN 1518-6393) **3285**
Teoria Literaria: Texto y Teoria (NLD ISSN 0921-2523) **5241**
• Teoria Politica (ITA ISSN 0394-1248) **7188**
Teoria y Practica del Teatro (DEU) **8481**
Teoria y Practica del Teatro (ESP ISSN 1698-6369) **8481**
Teoria y Realidad Constitucional (ESP ISSN 1139-5583) **4853**
➤ Teorie & Modelli (ITA ISSN 0393-2834) **5541**
Teorie e Oggetti della Filosofia (ITA ISSN 1973-1507) **6957**
Teorie e Oggetti delle Scienze Sociali (ITA ISSN 1972-0637) **8143**
➤ Teorie Vedy/Theory of Science (CZE ISSN 1210-0250) **7923**
➤ Teorija in Praksa (SVN ISSN 0040-3598) **8009**
Teorijska i Primenjena Mehanika *see* Theoretical and Applied Mechanics **7063**
Teoriya Funktsii Kompleksnogo Peremennogo i Kraevye Zadachi (RUS) **5541**
Teoriya i Praktika Fizicheskoi Kul'tury (RUS ISSN 0040-3601) **3086**
Teoriya Mekhanizmov i Mashin (UKR ISSN 0321-4419) **7063**
Teoriya Reshniya Izobretatelskikg Zadatch Journal *see* The T R I Z Journal **1181**
Te'oriya Uvikoret *see* Te'oriya Uviqoret **8143**
➤ Te'oriya Uviqoret/Theory and Criticism (ISR ISSN 0792-7223) **8143**
Teoriya Veroyatnostei i ee Primeneniya (RUS ISSN 0040-361X) **5541**
Teoriya Veroyatnostei i Matematicheskaya Statistika *see* Theory of Probability and Mathematical Statistics **5541**
Teoros (CAN ISSN 0712-8657) **8760**
Teosofi (FIN ISSN 0355-8045) **6957**
Teploenergetika (RUS ISSN 0040-3636) **3397**
Teplofizika i Aeromekhanika (RUS ISSN 0869-8635) **7056**
• Teplofizika Vysokikh Temperatur (RUS ISSN 0040-3644) **7043**
Tequ Jiaoyu *see* Tequ Xiaoxuesheng **2216**
• Tequ Jingji/Special Zone Economy (CHN ISSN 1004-0714) **1182**
† Tequ Jingji yu Konggaotai Jingji/Economy in S E Z and Hong Kong, Macao and Taiwan (CHN ISSN 1008-3286) **8993**
Tequ Wenxue/Special Zone Literature (CHN ISSN 1003-6881) **5386**
Tequ Xiaoxuesheng (CHN) **2216**
Tequ yu Gang-Ao Jingji/S E Zs & Hongkong-Macao Economy *see* Qianji Qianyan **1162**
Tequesta (USA ISSN 0363-3705) **4314**
† Tera Forum (CZE ISSN 1802-2294) **8993**
▼ • Terahertz Science & Technology (USA ISSN 1941-7411) **7923**
Teranga (FRA ISSN 1767-9370) **8786**
• ➤ Terapevticheskii Arkhiv/Therapeutic Archives (RUS ISSN 0040-3660) **5721**
Terapia (POL ISSN 1230-3917) **5721**
• Terapia Familiare (ITA ISSN 0391-2868) **4914**
Terapia Ocupacional Galicia *see* T O G **6116**
• Terapia Psicologica (CHL ISSN 0716-6184) **7412**
Teratogenesis, Carcinogenesis, and Mutagenesis *see* Birth Defects Research. Part B: Developmental and Reproductive Toxicology **5587**
Teratology *see* Birth Defects Research. Part A: Clinical and Molecular Teratology **662**
➤ Terazniejszosc, Czlowiek, Edukacja (POL ISSN 1505-8808) **2919**
Terceira Margem (BRA ISSN 1413-0378) **4477**
• Tercer Millenio (CHL ISSN 0717-229X) **4584**
La Tercera (CHL) **3822**
Tere (VEN ISSN 1856-0970) **2919**
Terebi Gijutsu/Television Techniques & Electronics (JPN ISSN 0497-2791) **3115**
Terefere (HUN ISSN 1587-3145) **8885**
Terematikusu Shinpojumu/Telematics Symposium (JPN) **2342**
• TERENA Compendium of National Research and Education Networks in Europe (Trans-European Research and Education Networking Association) (NLD ISSN 1569-447X) **3004**
Teresa de Jesus (ESP) **7820**
Teresianum (VAT ISSN 0392-4556) **7820**
➤ Terezinske Listy (CZE ISSN 0232-0452) **4273**
Teri Information Digest on Energy and Environment *see* T I D E E **3148**
Teri Information Monitor on Environmental Science (IND ISSN 0971-8192) **3469**
Teri Newswire *see* T E R I Newswire **3154**
• Teriscope (IND) **3148**
Terme (ESP ISSN 0213-6678) **4164**
• Termeszet Vilaga (HUN ISSN 0040-3717) **7923**
Termeszetbuvar (HUN ISSN 0866-1510) **707**
Terminal (FRA ISSN 0997-5551) **2439**
• Terminal (Kiev) (UKR) **6794**
Terminal Fright (CAN ISSN 1080-6873) **5448**
Terminal Member Directory (USA) **6794**
Terminfo (FIN ISSN 0358-7517) **5186**
Termino (USA ISSN 0742-4531) **5386**
Terminogramme (CAN ISSN 0225-3194) **5186**
Terminologie (CAN ISSN 0225-1981) **5186**
➤ Terminologie et Traduction (LUX ISSN 0256-7873) **5186**
Terminologies Nouvelles (BEL ISSN 1015-5716) **5186**
➤ Terminologija (LTU ISSN 1392-267X) **5186**
• ➤ Terminology (NLD ISSN 0929-9971) **5186**
Terminology and Knowledge Engineering (DEU) **2551**
Terminology and Lexicography Research and Practice (NLD ISSN 1388-8455) **5186**
Terminology Standardization and Information Technology *see* Shuyu Biaozhunhua yu Xinxi Jishu **2550**
• Terminometro (CD-ROM) (FRA ISSN 1683-7681) **5186**
• Terminometro (French Edition) (FRA ISSN 1609-9931) **5186**
• Terminometro (Italian Edition) (FRA ISSN 1609-994X) **5186**
• Terminometro (Portuguese Edition) (FRA ISSN 1609-9958) **5186**
• Terminometro (Romanian Edition) (FRA ISSN 1609-9966) **5186**
• Terminometro (Spanish Edition) (FRA ISSN 1609-9923) **5186**
Terminometro. Hors-Serie/Terminometro. Numero Especial (FRA ISSN 1683-7673) **5186**
Terminometro. Numero Especial *see* Terminometro. Hors-Serie **5186**
• Terminus (USA ISSN 1540-1871) **5386**
Termite *see* Shiroari **858**
• Termium (CAN ISSN 1191-7288) **5186**
TermNet News (AUT ISSN 0251-5253) **5186**
Termodinamica Applicata (ITA) **7056**
Termoelektrichestvo *see* Journal of Thermoelectricity **3159**
Termoelektrichestvo *see* Termoelektryka **3161**
Termoelektryka (UKR ISSN 1726-7714) **3161**
• ➤ Termotehnika (SRB ISSN 0350-218X) **3148**
Terneuzen-Vlissingen Port Handbook *see* Zeeland Seaports Port Handbook **8666**
Ternopil's'ka Hazeta (UKR) **3965**
Terpsichore (DEU ISSN 1434-0771) **2688**
• Terpsichore (DNK ISSN 1395-4601) **2688**
Terpsichore ONline *see* Terpsichore **2688**
Terra *see* Os Caminhos da Terra **2605**
Terra (DEU) **965**
Terra (FIN ISSN 0040-3741) **4030**
• Terra (MEX ISSN 0187-5779) **161**
Terra (ROM ISSN 0373-9570) **7923**
Terra (USA) **2717**
• ➤ Terra (VEN ISSN 1012-7089) **4031**
Terra (Barcelona, 1993) (ESP ISSN 1134-461X) **4031**
La Terra (Barcelona) (ESP ISSN 0212-5684) **161**
Terra (Finistere Edition) (FRA ISSN 1950-8476) **161**
Terra (Utrecht) (NLD ISSN 1574-9711) **2629**
† Terra Abstracts (GBR ISSN 0954-4887) **8993**
➤ Terra Antartica (ITA ISSN 1122-8628) **2717**
• Terra Daily (AUS) **2717**
Terra d'Este (ITA ISSN 1127-2910) **4273**
† Terra e Sole (ITA ISSN 0040-3768) **8993**
• Terra e Vita (ITA ISSN 0040-3776) **161**
Terra Economica (FRA ISSN 1953-8049) **1182**
• ➤ Terra et Aqua (NLD ISSN 0376-6411) **8663**
• Terra Firma (GBR) **8760**
Terra Grischuna - Graubuenden (CHE ISSN 1011-5196) **3470**
• Terra Incognita (BEL ISSN 1783-1180) **420**
• Terra Incognita (ESP ISSN 1576-754X) **5241**
Terra Indigena (BRA ISSN 0103-2437) **3568**
Terra Livre (BRA ISSN 0102-8030) **4031**
Terra Medica Nova (RUS ISSN 0868-7161) **5721**
Terra Nostra (DEU ISSN 0946-8978) **2771**
• ➤ Terra Nova (GBR ISSN 0954-4879) **2717**
Terra Nova *see* The New Earth Reader **6936**
• ➤ Terra Nova Online (GBR ISSN 1365-3121) **2717**
Terra Nueva Etapa *see* Terra **4031**
Terra Plana (CHE ISSN 0257-6686) **8760**
Terra Poetica (USA) **5436**
Terra Ticinese (CHE) **8760**
Terra Trentina (ITA ISSN 0492-7885) **161**
• Terrace Standard (CAN ISSN 0841-9264) **3818**
• ➤ Terrae Incognitae (GBR ISSN 0082-2884) **4164**
• TerraGreen (IND ISSN 0974-5688) **3470**
• ➤ Terrain (FRA ISSN 0760-5668) **358**
Terrain (Berkeley) (USA ISSN 1526-8322) **3470**
• Terrain.Org (Tucson) (USA ISSN 1932-9474) **2629**
Terralia (ESP ISSN 1138-6223) **161**
TerraTech *see* Wasser, Luft und Boden **3474**
† Terrazzi e Balconi (ITA ISSN 1825-7666) **8993**
Terre (FRA ISSN 0040-3814) **7188**
Terre & Nature (CHE ISSN 1422-3619) **161**
Terre Dauphinoise (FRA ISSN 1279-2853) **161**
La Terre de Chez Nous (CAN ISSN 0040-3830) **161**
Terre de Chez Nous (FRA) **161**
Terre de Provence (FRA ISSN 1627-1041) **8760**
Terre des Momes (FRA ISSN 1778-3240) **2216**
Terre Humaine (FRA ISSN 0492-7915) **358**
Terre Indienne (FRA ISSN 1159-7100) **5386**
Terre Information Magazine (FRA ISSN 0995-6999) **6448**
Terre Magazine *see* Terre Information Magazine **6448**
Terre Malgache/Tany Malagasy (MDG ISSN 0563-1637) **255**
Terre Sauvage (FRA ISSN 0981-4140) **2629**
Terre Valaisanne (CHE) **161**
Terrebonne Life Lines (USA ISSN 0735-2794) **3784**
Terrell Trails (USA ISSN 0884-2108) **3785**
Terres Cathares *see* Cathares Espace & Patrimoine **4002**
Terres d'Amerique (FRA ISSN 1272-1085) **5386**
Terres d'Ariege (FRA ISSN 0750-8093) **161**
• Terres de Bourgogne (FRA) **255**
Terres de Bourgogne (Edition Cote d'Or) *see* Terres de Bourgogne **255**
Terres de Bourgogne (Edition Nievre) *see* Terres de Bourgogne **255**
Terres de Bourgogne (Edition Yonne) *see* Terres de Bourgogne **255**
Terres des Savoie (FRA ISSN 1634-2046) **161**
Terres en Vues/Assi Nukuan (CAN ISSN 1192-4373) **541**
Terres et Gens d'Islam (FRA ISSN 1761-211X) **7716**
▼ Terrestrial and Aquatic Environmental Toxicology (GBR ISSN 1749-0324) **3501**
▼ • Terrestrial Arthropod Review (NLD ISSN 1874-9828) **965**
▼ • Terrestrial Ecology (USA ISSN 1936-7961) **707**
▼ Terriciae Litterature (FRA ISSN 1957-3650) **5386**
Der Terrier (DEU) **6816**
The Terrier Times (NLD ISSN 1871-1847) **6816**
Terrier Type (USA ISSN 0199-6495) **6816**
Territoire en Movement (FRA ISSN 1954-4863) **4031**
▼ Territoire Originel (FRA ISSN 1956-340X) **8760**
Territoires (FRA ISSN 0991-2428) **7503**
Territoires en Mutation (FRA ISSN 1278-4249) **1182**
Territorial Economy *see* Source O E C D. Urban, Rural and Regional Development **1177**
The Territories of the Russian Federation (GBR ISSN 1465-461X) **7188**
Il Territorio (ITA ISSN 1121-0532) **3899**
Territorio (Milano) (ITA ISSN 1825-8689) **459**
Territorio e Ambiente Lariano, Edilizia e Architettura *see* T A L E & A **458**
Territorio Restauro Edilizia Annual Lapidei *see* T R E - Annual Lapidei **1039**
Territorio - Restauro - Edilizia European Building Magazine *see* T R E - European Building Magazine **1039**
Territoris (ESP ISSN 1139-2169) **4031**
• Terror Response Technology Report (Email) (USA) **2228**
Terror Response Technology Report (Print) *see* Terror Response Technology Report (Email) **2228**
• ➤ Terrorism and Political Violence (GBR ISSN 0954-6553) **7268**
Terrorism & Security Monitor *see* Jane's Terrorism & Security Monitor **7247**
Terrorism and Weapons of Mass Destruction and Disruption *see* Weapons of Mass Destruction and Terrorism **7273**
Terrorism: Documents of International and Local Control (USA ISSN 1062-4007) **2228**
➤ Terrorism: Documents of International and Local Control. Second Series (USA ISSN 1064-9352) **2228**
• Terrorism in the United States (USA) **2669**
• Terrorism Update (USA) **2228**
Terrorism Watch Report *see* Jane's Terrorism Watch Report **7247**
Terrorizer (GBR ISSN 1350-6978) **6622**
• Terry Family Historian (Online) (USA) **3785**
† Terry Tracings (USA ISSN 1076-9854) **8993**
Terry Tracings Surname Booklet *see* Terry Tracings **8993**
➤ Tertiaersprachen (DEU ISSN 1439-1031) **5187**
Tertiaire *see* Economie et Management **1540**
• ➤ Tertiary Education and Management (GBR ISSN 1358-3883) **3005**
Tertiary Education and Training Victoria (AUS) **2946**
• The Tertiary Education Report (AUS) **3005**
Tertiary Education Strategy. Monitoring Report (NZL ISSN 1176-9238) **3034**
• ➤ Tertium Comparationis (DEU ISSN 0947-9732) **3015**
➤ Tertium Datur (BEL) **6957**
Tertulia (PRI) **4477**
Teruel (ESP ISSN 0210-3524) **8009**
Terugblik 40-45 (NLD ISSN 0924-8803) **4273**
Terugvordering en Verhaal Memo *see* Memo Terugvordering en Verhaal **4515**
• Terve Elama (FIN ISSN 0789-8789) **7543**
Tervis Pluss (EST ISSN 1406-300X) **6998**
Terviseleht (EST) **5721**
† Terza Pagina (ITA) **8993**
† Terzo Millennio verso l'Antropocrazia (ITA ISSN 1126-8069) **8993**
Terzo Occhio (ITA ISSN 0390-0355) **522**
Terzo Settore (ITA ISSN 1724-210X) **1182**
• Teshu Gang/Special Steel (CHN ISSN 1003-8620) **6335**
Tesi Gregoriana (ITA) **7820**
Tesinsko (CZE ISSN 0139-7605) **4273**
• Tesisat Muhendisligi (TUR ISSN 1300-3399) **1040**
† Teson (ESP ISSN 1130-8338) **8993**
Tesori d'Abruzzo (ITA ISSN 1970-7029) **8760**
I Tesori dell'Antico Egitto (ITA ISSN 1970-1381) **4178**
Tesori di Citta (ITA ISSN 1971-0321) **522**
• Tesouro Informatizadoo da Lingua Galela (ESP ISSN 1988-7345) **5187**
• Tesouro Medieval Informatizado da Lingua Galega (ESP ISSN 1888-4261) **5187**
➤ Tessera (CAN ISSN 0840-4631) **8903**
Tesseris Trochoi *see* 4 Trochoi **8613**
TesserisTrochoi Test *see* 4 Trochoi Test **8613**
Tessinger Zeitung (CHE) **3959**
Test (DEU ISSN 0040-3946) **2641**
• ➤ Test (DEU ISSN 1133-0686) **8408**
Test *see* Global S M T & Packaging **1886**
Test Aankoop Magazine (BEL ISSN 0772-9413) **2641**
Test Achats Magazine *see* Test Aankoop Magazine **2641**
Test & Kauf *see* Chip Test & Kauf **2635**
Test & Measurement Korea *see* Test & Measurement World **3332**
• Test & Measurement News (USA) **2541**
• Test & Measurement World (USA ISSN 0744-1657) **3332**
Test and Measurement World *see* Test & Measurement World **3332**
Test & Measurement World Automotive Test Report *see* Automotive & Aerospace Test Report **3296**
Test & Measurement World Buyer's Guide (USA) **3332**
Test Engineering & Management (USA ISSN 0193-4120) **72**
Test Focus (ZAF ISSN 1990-6072) **2599**
Test Gezondheid *see* Test Sante **7543**
Test Jahrbuch (Year) (DEU) **2641**

Title

▼ new title *† ceased* *• electronic media* *➤ refereed*

10940 TEST MEASURE RECORD ULRICH'S PERIODICALS

Test Measure Record see Radio Comms Asia-Pacific 2362
Test Measure Record see Voice and Data 2344
Test Measure Record see What's New in Electronics 3116
Test Measure Record see Electrical Solutions 3094
• Test Methods for Evaluating Solid Waste. Physical/Chemical Methods (USA) 3470
Test Methods for Pressure Sensitive Adhesive Tapes (USA) 3256
Test Sante (BEL ISSN 1370-0650) 7543
Testcard (DEU) 6623
Testdriven (ZAF ISSN 1812-6685) 8606
The Tester (USA) 6448
• The Testers' Network (USA) 2599
Testi e Commenti (ITA ISSN 1828-5848) 2241
Testi e Discorsi (ITA ISSN 1971-0313) 5187
Testi e Documenti di Letteratura e di Lingua (ITA ISSN 1970-3902) 5386
† Testi e Studi Umanistici (ITA) 8993
Testify Sister Magazine (USA ISSN 1932-7382) 8885
† Testifying Expert (USA ISSN 1071-7595) 8993
Testimoni (ITA) 7688
Testimonia Siciliae Antiqua (ITA ISSN 0392-1328) 420
Testimonial Privileges (USA) 4794
• Testimonianze (ITA ISSN 0040-3989) 5241
Testimonios Revolucionarios see Coleccion Testimonios Revolucionarios 7117
Testimony Magazine (GBR) 7688
Testing and Balancing Journal see T A B Journal 1039
Testing and Evaluation of Life-Saving Appliances see International Maritime Organization. Testing and Evaluation of Life-Saving Appliances 8647
Testing Technology (USA) 6335
Testing Technology International see Automotive Testing Technology International 3374
• Testnyt (DNK ISSN 1604-6803) 1797
• Testo (ITA ISSN 1123-4660) 4477
Testosterone (USA) 6998
Tests in Microfiche (USA ISSN 0161-2573) 2919
Tests in Print (USA ISSN 0361-025X) 7412
† Tests of Agrochemicals and Cultivars (GBR ISSN 0951-4309) 8993
• Testzentrale Testkatalog (DEU) 7417
Tete Beche (FRA ISSN 1159-1293) 2216
Tetra Tech Incorporated. Technical Report (USA) 8443
• ➤ Tetrahedron (GBR ISSN 0040-4020) 2131
• ➤ Tetrahedron: Asymmetry (GBR ISSN 0957-4166) 2131
• ➤ Tetrahedron Letters (GBR ISSN 0040-4039) 2131
Tetrahedron Organic Chemistry Series (NLD ISSN 1460-1567) 2131
Tetsu Taisha Kenkyukai Puroguramu Shorokushu/Conference on Current Topics for Iron Metabolism. Program and Abstracts (JPN) 746
➤ Tetsu to Hagane/Iron and Steel Institute of Japan. Journal (JPN ISSN 0021-1575) 6335
Tetsudo Pikutoriaru/Railway Pictorial (JPN ISSN 0040-4047) 8626
• Tetsudo Saibane. Shinpojumu Ronbunshu (CD-ROM)/Railway Cybernetics. Symposium. Papers (JPN) 2528
Tetsudo Sharyoto Seisan Dotai Tokei Geppo/Monthly Survey on Current Rolling Stock Production (JPN) 8531
Tetsudo Sharyoto Seisan Dotai Tokei Nenpo/Annual Survey on Current Rolling Stock Production (JPN) 8531
Tettigonia/Nihon Chokushirui Gakkai Kaishi (JPN ISSN 1341-6707) 860
Tetto/Steel Tower (JPN) 3285
• Tetu (FRA ISSN 1265-3578) 4379
Teubner-Archiv zur Mathematik (DEU ISSN 0233-0962) 5541
Teubner Skripten zur Mathematischen Stochastik (DEU ISSN 1615-4193) 5541
Teubner Skripten zur Numerik (DEU ISSN 1615-4207) 5541
Teubner Studienbuecher Bauwesen (DEU ISSN 1615-2352) 1040
Teubner Studienbuecher Chemie (DEU ISSN 0941-3677) 2082
Teubner Studienbuecher Elektrotechnik (DEU ISSN 1615-2794) 3332
Teubner Studienbuecher Maschinenbau (DEU ISSN 1615-1747) 3397
Teubner Studienbuecher Mathematik (DEU ISSN 1615-3405) 5541
Teubner Studienbuecher Philologie (DEU ISSN 1615-2247) 5386
Teubner Studienbuecher Physik (DEU ISSN 1615-3766) 7043
Teubner Studienbuecher Wirtschaftswissenschaften (DEU ISSN 1615-3898) 1182
Teubner Texte zur Informatik (DEU ISSN 1615-4584) 2551
Teubner-Texte zur Mathematik (DEU ISSN 0138-502X) 5541
Teubner-Texte zur Physik (DEU ISSN 0233-0911) 7043
• Teugsu Gyoyug Yeon-gu/Taegu University. Research Institute for Special Education. Journal (KOR ISSN 1225-9802) 3048
† Teuraebeul Teureideu Jeoneol/Travel Trade Journal (KOR ISSN 1225-8075) 8993
Tev Fema (TGO) 8885
TeVe Blad (BEL ISSN 0770-2396) 2397
• TeVeo (PRY ISSN 1026-6062) 8885
Tevere (ITA ISSN 1592-8594) 2771
Teviskes Ziburiai/Lights of the Homeland (CAN ISSN 0040-4063) 3568
Tevyne (USA ISSN 0040-4071) 3568
Tex (DEU ISSN 0720-1303) 2303
Tex Home (ITA) 4551
The Texan see The Social Studies Texan 3082
Texan Veteran News (USA) 6448
Texarkana U S A Journal (USA ISSN 1549-6317) 3785
Texarkana U S A Quarterly see Texarkana U S A Journal 3785
Texas A & M Battalion see The Battalion 2274
➤ Texas A & M University. College of Geosciences. Contributions in Oceanography (USA ISSN 0069-9640) 2818
Texas A & M University. Department of Oceanography. Technical Report (USA ISSN 0272-6076) 2818
Texas A & M University Library Notes (USA ISSN 0040-4136) 5050
Texas A & M University. Sea Grant College Program. Report (USA) 2818
Texas A F L - C I O News (USA) 4603
Texas Advocate see A Second Wind Newsletter 6219
Texas Aggie (USA ISSN 0747-1661) 2303
Texas Agricultural Statistics (USA) 187
Texas Agriculture. North Texas Regional Edition see Texas Agriculture. West Texas Regional Edition 8993
† Texas Agriculture. West Texas Regional Edition (USA ISSN 0162-3001) 8993
Texas AgriNews (USA) 162
Texas: All-Industries see Harris Directory. Texas All-Industries 2002
Texas Almanac see (Years) Texas Almanac and State Industrial Guide 8409
(Years) Texas Almanac and State Industrial Guide (USA ISSN 0363-4248) 8409
Texas Annotated Civil Practice and Remedies Code (USA ISSN 1933-2726) 4842
Texas Annotated Property Code (USA ISSN 1931-6062) 7613
Texas Apartment Association News & Views see T A A News & Views 4428
• Texas Apartments (USA ISSN 1939-0076) 7613
Texas Archeological Society. Bulletin (USA ISSN 0082-2930) 420
Texas Archeological Society. Special Publication (USA ISSN 0495-2944) 420
Texas Archeology (USA ISSN 0082-2949) 420
Texas Architect (USA ISSN 0040-4179) 459
Texas Association for Health, Physical Education, Recreation and Dance Journal see T A H P E R D Journal 6998
Texas Association of Family and Consumer Sciences Research Journal see T A F C S Research Journal 4368
Texas Automotive Report see South Texas Automotive Report 8604
Texas Automotive Report see North Texas Automotive Report 8596
• Texas Banking (USA ISSN 0885-6907) 1386
Texas Banking Red Book (USA) 1386
• Texas Banking Redbook (USA) 1386
• Texas Bar Journal (USA ISSN 0040-4187) 4794
• Texas Books in Review (USA ISSN 0739-3202) 636
Texas Brangus (USA) 302
• Texas Builder (USA ISSN 0164-8012) 1040
• Texas Business Directory (USA ISSN 1053-6698) 2030
• Texas Business Review (USA ISSN 0040-4209) 1182
Texas Case Names Citator see Shepard's Texas Case Names Citator 4964
Texas Catholic (USA ISSN 0899-6296) 7820
Texas Catholic Herald (USA) 7820
Texas Child Care (USA ISSN 1049-9466) 2169
• Texas Chiropractic College Magazine (USA) 5807
Texas Christian University Magazine see T C U Magazine 2303
Texas Cities and Counties Graphic Performance Analysis see Texas Cities & Counties Graphic Performance Analysis 7484
Texas Cities & Counties Graphic Performance Analysis (USA ISSN 1935-5440) 7484
Texas Civil Engineer (USA ISSN 0040-4292) 3285
• Texas Civil Trial Guide (USA) 4842
Texas Classical Association's Journal see T C A's Journal 2241
• Texas Co-op Power (USA) 1425
Texas Coach (USA ISSN 0040-4241) 8211
Texas Coastal Enthusiast (USA) 3990
Texas Conchologist (USA ISSN 0885-1263) 965
• Texas Construction (USA ISSN 1077-1867) 1040
Texas Construction Law Manual (USA) 4794
• Texas Construction News Weekly Covering Fort Worth and Vicinity (USA ISSN 1521-7000) 1040
Texas Contemporary Criminal Procedure see Texas Law Enforcement Handbook 4899
• Texas Contractor (USA ISSN 0192-9216) 1040
• Texas Cooking Online (USA) 3666
Texas County Directory see County Progress 7432
• Texas Courthouse Guide (USA ISSN 1546-8143) 4794
• Texas Court's Charge Reporter (USA) 4965
Texas Crimes & Consequences see O'Connor's Texas Crimes & Consequences 4896
Texas Criminal and Motor Vehicle Code (USA ISSN 1930-8051) 4898
• Texas Criminal Law & Motor Vehicle Handbook (USA ISSN 1055-1913) 4794
Texas Criminal Law and Motor Vehicle Handbook see Texas Criminal Law & Motor Vehicle Handbook 4794
• Texas Criminal Practice Guide (USA) 4898
• Texas D O (USA ISSN 0275-1453) 5807
Texas Dental Assistants Association. Bulletin (USA) 5868
➤ Texas Dental Journal (USA ISSN 0040-4284) 5868
Texas. Department of Criminal Justice. Institutional Division. Research Report (USA ISSN 0095-1900) 2669
Texas. Department of Health. Annual Report (USA) 7543
Texas. Department on Aging. Annual Report (USA) 8074
Texas Director (USA) 3720
Texas Discovery Forms (USA) 4965
• Texas Drunk Driving Law (USA) 4794
Texas Education Review (USA ISSN 1531-7722) 3005
Texas Elementary Principals and Supervisors Association Journal see T E P S A Journal 3034
• Texas Employment Law (USA ISSN 1938-016X) 1710
• Texas Employment Law Letter (USA ISSN 1046-9214) 4794
Texas Energy Reporter (USA ISSN 0739-8050) 3148
† • Texas Environmental Compliance Update (USA ISSN 1075-2595) 8993
Texas Environmental Law Journal (USA) 4794
• Texas Estate Planning (USA) 4905
Texas Estate Planning Statutes (USA ISSN 1545-6447) 4905
• Texas Evidentiary Foundations (USA) 4966
Texas F F A Magazine see Texas F F A News 162
Texas F F A News (USA) 162
Texas Facts (USA ISSN 0899-7349) 3122
• Texas Family Law Reporter (USA ISSN 0743-9342) 4914
• Texas Family Physician (USA ISSN 0098-1052) 5721
Texas Farm & Ranch (USA) 7613
Texas Film and Media Studies Series (USA ISSN 1557-5896) 6515
Texas Finance Code (USA ISSN 1559-9213) 4794
Texas Finance Report (USA ISSN 1063-0376) 1386
• Texas Fire Chief (USA) 3581
• Texas Fish & Game (USA ISSN 0887-4174) 8337
Texas Folklore Society. Publications (USA ISSN 0082-3023) 3623
Texas Food Merchant (USA ISSN 0040-4322) 3682
Texas Football Magazine (USA) 8249
Texas Foreclosure: Law and Practice (USA) 7613
Texas Future Farmers of America News see Texas F F A News 162
• Texas Gardener (USA ISSN 0744-0987) 3751
Texas Golfer Magazine (USA) 8249
The Texas Gulf Historical & Biographical Record (USA ISSN 0563-2897) 4314
• ➤ Texas Heart Institute Journal (USA ISSN 0730-2347) 5800
Texas Hereford (USA ISSN 0744-4761) 302
Texas High Technology Directory (USA ISSN 0896-9779) 2030
• Texas Highways (USA ISSN 0040-4349) 8760
• Texas Hispanic Journal of Law and Policy (USA ISSN 1547-4887) 4794
Texas Hispanic Magazine (USA ISSN 1055-2944) 3568
Texas Hispanic News (USA) 3568
Texas Historian (USA ISSN 0022-6602) 4314
• Texas HIV - STD Update (USA) 5827
Texas Home Economist see T A F C S Research Journal 4368
• Texas Hospital Law (USA) 4794
Texas Humanities Resource Center Newsletter see T H R C Newsletter 4477
Texas Hunting Directory (USA) 8337
Texas Independent Producers & Royalty Owners Association Target Newsletter see T I P R O Target Newsletter 7471
Texas Instruments Technical Journal (USA ISSN 0893-7877) 3223
• Texas Insurance Law & Litigation Alert (USA ISSN 1552-5147) 4525
Texas Insurance Law and Litigation Alert see Texas Insurance Law & Litigation Alert 4525
• Texas Intellectual Property Law Journal (USA ISSN 1068-1000) 4794
• Texas International Law Journal (USA ISSN 0163-7479) 4942
Texas Jewish Post (USA ISSN 0040-439X) 7730
Texas Journal of Agriculture and Natural Resources (USA ISSN 0891-5466) 162
Texas Journal of Business Law (USA ISSN 1547-3619) 4881
Texas Journal of Chiropractic (USA) 5807
• Texas Journal of Corrections (USA) 2669
• The Texas Journal of Distance Learning (USA ISSN 1546-8992) 3086
• Texas Journal of Oil, Gas & Energy Law (USA ISSN 1559-2189) 4881
Texas Journal of Plumbing-Heating-Cooling (USA) 4127
➤ Texas Journal of Political Studies (USA ISSN 0191-0930) 7188
• ➤ Texas Journal of Science (USA ISSN 0040-4403) 7923
• Texas Journal of Women and the Law (USA ISSN 1058-5427) 4794
• Texas Journal on Civil Liberties and Civil Rights (USA ISSN 1930-2045) 4843
• Texas Journey (USA) 8606
• Texas Labor Market Review (USA) 1710
• Texas Law Enforcement Handbook (USA) 4899
Texas Law Enforcement Management and Administrative Statistics Program Bulletin see T E L E M A S P Bulletin 2675
Texas Law of Oil and Gas (USA) 4794
• ➤ Texas Law Review (USA ISSN 0040-4411) 4794
Texas Law Review Manual on Usage and Style (USA) 4794
Texas Law Review Texas Rules of Form (USA) 4795
Texas Lawman (USA ISSN 0040-442X) 2669
• Texas Lawyer (USA ISSN 0267-8306) 4795
Texas Legion Times (USA) 2270
Texas Legislative Guide (USA ISSN 1931-0897) 4795
Texas Legislative Handbook (USA ISSN 0193-2322) 4795
• Texas Library Journal (USA ISSN 0040-4446) 5050
Texas Linguistic Forum (USA ISSN 0741-2576) 5187
• Texas Litigation Guide (USA) 4795
Texas Litigation Reader (USA) 4795
Texas Living see Southern Living 3988
Texas Lone Star (USA ISSN 0749-9310) 3034
• Texas Manufacturers Register (USA ISSN 0743-1163) 2030
Texas: Manufacturing see Harris Directory. Texas Manufacturing 2002
Texas-Marshal (CZE ISSN 1214-0333) 5412
Texas Mason (USA) 2270
• Texas Medicine (USA ISSN 0040-4470) 5721
▼ Texas Meetings + Events (USA) 6283
Texas Memorial Museum. Bulletin (USA ISSN 0082-3074) 6538
Texas Memorial Museum. Miscellaneous Papers (USA ISSN 0082-3082) 6538
Texas Memorial Museum. Museum Notes (USA) 6538
Texas Memorial Museum. Speleological Monographs (USA) 2771
• Texas Monthly (USA ISSN 0148-7736) 3990
▼ Texas Motions in Limine (USA ISSN 1941-9740) 4966
• Texas Municipal Zoning Law (USA) 4795
• Texas Music (USA) 6623
The Texas Music Industry Directory (USA ISSN 1062-6646) 2030
• Texas Music Online (USA) 6623
Texas Native Plant Society News (USA) 3751
Texas. Natural Resources Information System. Newsletter (USA) 3470
Texas Natural Resources Reporter (USA ISSN 0197-2340) 8832
Texas Neighbors (USA) 162
▼ • Texas Neuroscience Review (USA ISSN 1941-6652) 6187
Texas Notary Law Primer (USA ISSN 1097-5462) 4795
Texas Nursing (USA ISSN 0095-036X) 5982
Texas Nursing Voice (USA) 5983
Texas Oil and Gas Law Journal (USA ISSN 0950-3285) 4795
• Texas On-Site Insights (USA) 8832
Texas Optometry (USA ISSN 0738-7644) 6052
Texas Ornithological Society. Bulletin (USA ISSN 0040-4543) 915
Texas Outdoors Journal (USA ISSN 1082-5940) 8337
Texas Paleontology Series (USA ISSN 0738-2464) 6731
Texas Pan American Series (USA) 3568
Texas Parks and Wildlife Department. Management Data Series (USA) 2629
Texas Parks & Wildlife Magazine (USA ISSN 0040-4586) 2629
Texas Parks & Wildlife Outdoor Annual (USA) 3990
Texas Penal Code and Related Statutes Flip Code (USA) 4899
Texas Personal Injury Reporter see Texas Torts Update 4843
Texas Petro Facts (USA) 6801
Texas Petroleum and C-Store Journal (USA ISSN 1087-9048) 6794
Texas Petroleum Industry (USA) 6794
➤ Texas Pharmacy (USA ISSN 0362-7926) 6882
Texas Pharmacy Association Speedletter see T P A Speedletter 6882
• Texas Pharmacy Laws and Regulations (USA ISSN 1930-983X) 4795
The Texas Philatelist (USA ISSN 0893-2670) 6900
• Texas Poetry Journal (USA ISSN 1554-4931) 5436
Texas Pollution Report (USA ISSN 1063-0406) 3491
Texas Population Perspective (USA) 7294
• Texas Practice Series (USA) 4795
Texas Practice Series. Consumer Rights and Remedies (USA) 2641
Texas Press Messenger (USA ISSN 1521-7523) 4584

DIRECTORY 2010 TEXTOS Y ESTUDIOS DE MUJERES 10941

● Texas Probate, Estate, and Trust Administration (USA) **4905**
➤ Texas Professional Engineer (USA ISSN 0040-4632) **3223**
● Texas Propane (USA ISSN 1081-4051) **6794**
Texas Property Code and Related Texas Codes *see* Texas Annotated Property Code **7613**
Texas Public Employee (USA ISSN 0040-4640) **7471**
Texas Public Library Directory (USA) **5050**
Texas Public Library Statistics (USA ISSN 0082-3120) **5060**
Texas Public Library Summary (USA) **5060**
Texas Public School Law Bulletin *see* Texas School Law Bulletin **4795**
Texas Public Sector *see* Texas Staff Directory **7471**
Texas. Railroad Commission. Oil and Gas Division. Annual Report (USA) **6794**
Texas. Railroad Commission. Oil and Gas Division. Crude Oil and Gas Nominations (USA) **6794**
Texas. Railroad Commission. Oil and Gas Division. Crude Oil Nominations and Purchases (USA) **6794**
Texas. Railroad Commission. Oil and Gas Division. Drilling Permit Index (USA) **6794**
Texas. Railroad Commission. Oil and Gas Division. Gas Lease Index (USA) **6794**
Texas. Railroad Commission. Oil and Gas Division. Gas Production Ledger (USA) **6794**
Texas. Railroad Commission. Oil and Gas Division. Gas Proration Schedule (USA) **6794**
Texas. Railroad Commission. Oil and Gas Division. Gas Purchaser (USA) **6794**
Texas. Railroad Commission. Oil and Gas Division. Gatherer Stripout (USA) **6794**
Texas. Railroad Commission. Oil and Gas Division. Notices of Hearings and Orders (USA) **6794**
Texas. Railroad Commission. Oil and Gas Division. Oil and Gas Field Names (USA) **6794**
Texas. Railroad Commission. Oil and Gas Division. Oil and Gas Notices and Forms (USA) **6794**
Texas. Railroad Commission. Oil and Gas Division. Oil Lease Index (USA) **6794**
Texas. Railroad Commission. Oil and Gas Division. Oil Leases and Gas Wells by District and Operator (USA) **6794**
Texas. Railroad Commission. Oil and Gas Division. Oil Production Ledger (USA) **6794**
Texas. Railroad Commission. Oil and Gas Division. Oil Proration Schedule (USA) **6794**
Texas. Railroad Commission. Oil and Gas Division. Operator Stripout (USA) **6794**
Texas. Railroad Commission. Oil and Gas Division. P-5 Organization Directory (USA) **6795**
Texas. Railroad Commission. Oil and Gas Division. Prorated Gas Fields - Monthly Schedule (USA) **6795**
Texas. Railroad Commission. Oil and Gas Division. Purchaser Stripout (USA) **6795**
Texas Real Estate Business (USA ISSN 1555-9173) **7613**
Texas Realtor (USA ISSN 1068-1248) **7613**
Texas Recreational Fresh and Saltwater Fishing Guide (Year) (USA) **8337**
● Texas Recycler Market News (USA) **1968**
● Texas Register (USA ISSN 0362-4781) **4795**
Texas Reports *see* West's Jury Verdicts. Texas Reports **4967**
● Texas Restaurant Industry Operations Report (USA ISSN 1935-5084) **4399**
● Texas Review (USA ISSN 0885-2685) **5386**
● Texas Review of Entertainment and Sports Law (USA ISSN 1533-1903) **4795**
● Texas Review of Law & Politics (USA ISSN 1098-4577) **4795**
Texas Rules of Civil Procedure (USA) **4843**
▼ ● Texas Saltwater Fishing Magazine (USA ISSN 1935-9586) **8337**
Texas Scenic Drives *see* Scenic Driving Texas **8755**
● Texas School Directory (USA ISSN 0363-4566) **2962**
Texas School Directory *see* M D R's Texas School Directory **2960**
● Texas School Law Bulletin (USA) **4795**
Texas Shores (USA ISSN 0747-0959) **3470**
● Texas Speech Communication Journal (USA ISSN 0363-8782) **5187**
Texas Sporting Journal (USA) **8337**
Texas Sportsman (USA ISSN 0279-8875) **8337**
Texas Staff Directory (USA ISSN 1942-5589) **7471**
● Texas State Agent Handbook (USA) **4525**
● Texas State Directory (USA ISSN 0363-7530) **7471**
Texas State Genealogical Society. Newsletter (USA ISSN 1081-616X) **3785**
Texas State Teachers Association Advocate *see* T S T A Advocate **2917**
● ➤ Texas Studies in Literature and Language (USA ISSN 0040-4691) **5386**
Texas Study of Secondary Education Research Bulletin (USA ISSN 0040-4705) **2919**
Texas Surplus Line Reporter (USA) **4525**
● Texas Talk (USA) **3048**
● Texas Tech Administrative Law Journal (USA ISSN 1942-9789) **4795**
Texas Tech Journal of Texas Administrative Law *see* Texas Tech Administrative Law Journal **4795**
● ➤ Texas Tech Law Review (USA ISSN 0564-6197) **4795**
● Texas Technology (USA) **8443**
Texas Techsan Magazine (USA) **2303**
Texas Theatre Journal (USA ISSN 1555-6832) **8481**
The Texas Thoroughbred (USA ISSN 0164-6168) **8299**
● Texas Torts and Remedies (USA) **4843**
● Texas Torts Update (USA) **4843**
Texas Tour Guide (USA) **2629**
Texas TourBook *see* TourBook: Texas **8762**
Texas Town & City (USA ISSN 1084-5356) **7472**
Texas Transaction Guide *see* Texas Transaction Guide: Legal Forms **4795**
● Texas Transaction Guide: Legal Forms (USA) **4795**
● Texas Transportation Researcher (USA ISSN 0040-4748) **8513**
Texas Traveler (USA) **8760**
● The Texas Triangle (USA) **4379**
† Texas Vehicle Laws Flip Code (USA) **8993**
Texas Veterinarian (USA ISSN 1071-0566) **8808**
Texas Vital Statistics (USA ISSN 0495-257X) **7316**
● Texas Water Resources (USA ISSN 0744-1320) **8832**
● Texas Water Resources Institute. Technical Report (USA ISSN 0275-5483) **8833**
● Texas Water Savers (USA) **8833**
Texas Water Utilities Journal (USA ISSN 1051-709X) **8833**
▼ ● Texas Wealth Management Business (Online) (USA) **1655**
† ● Texas Wealth Management Business (Print) (USA) **8993**
● Texas Weekly (USA ISSN 0890-5924) **7472**
● Texas Wesleyan Law Review (USA ISSN 1081-5449) **4795**
Texas Woman's News (USA) **8885**
Texas Woman's University. School of Library and Information Studies. Alumnae Newsletter (USA) **2303**
Texas Workers' Comp Advisor (USA ISSN 1527-1439) **1710**
Texas Workers' Comp Reporter (USA ISSN 1544-4341) **4881**
† Texas Workers' Compensation Law: A Guide to Practice Before Commission and Courts (USA) **8993**
Texas Zoning and Land Use Forms (USA) **7613**
Texbel International (BEL ISSN 1375-7814) **8458**
TexDecor *see* Textile Network **8460**
Texelse Courant (NLD ISSN 1385-5719) **3916**
Texeltoerist Magazine (NLD ISSN 1385-5735) **8760**
● TeXhax Digest (USA) **7328**
Texincon (IND ISSN 0970-5686) **8458**
▼ ● Texoma Living (USA ISSN 1937-2906) **5084**
Texpress (NLD ISSN 0040-4772) **8458**
TexReport (ZAF) **8459**
Texscope *see* Texscope: U S A Textile Industry Overview **8459**
Texscope: U S A Textile Industry Overview (USA ISSN 0092-3540) **8459**
● ➤ Text (AUS ISSN 1327-9556) **5386**
Text *see* Text & Talk **4477**
Text (DEU ISSN 1420-1496) **5386**
Text (SWE ISSN 0345-0112) **636**
Text (USA ISSN 0736-3974) **5386**
● ➤ Text and Performance Quarterly (GBR ISSN 1046-2937) **5386**
➤ Text and Presentation (USA ISSN 1054-724X) **8481**
● ➤ Text & Talk (DEU ISSN 1860-7330) **4477**
Text-Critical Studies (NLD ISSN 1569-3619) **7688**
Text Intern (DEU ISSN 0173-9018) **2342**
Text. Kritische Beitraege *see* Text **5386**
Text, Speech and Language Technology (NLD ISSN 1386-291X) **5187**
➤ Text Technology (CAN ISSN 1053-900X) **7580**
➤ Text, Translation, Computational Processing (DEU ISSN 1861-4272) **5204**
Text und Kontext (DEU ISSN 0933-4769) **5386**
➤ Text & Kontext (DNK ISSN 0105-7014) **5386**
➤ Text & Kontext. Sonderreihe (DNK ISSN 0105-7065) **5386**
Text und Kritik (DEU ISSN 0040-5329) **5386**
Text und Kritik. Sonderband *see* Text und Kritik **5386**
Textbook for Grinding Academy *see* Guraindingu Akademi Tekisuto **3378**
Textbook Letter (USA) **3086**
Textbook of Lectures on Surface Science *see* Hyomen Kagaku Kiso Koza **7015**
Textbook of Seminar on Surface Science *see* Hyomen Kagaku Semina **7015**
Textbook on Criminal Law (GBR) **4899**
Textbooks for Knowledge Organization (DEU ISSN 0944-8152) **5050**
Texte (AUT ISSN 0254-7902) **6187**
Texte (CAN ISSN 0715-8920) **5387**
Texte der Hethiter (DEU ISSN 0173-4865) **4164**
Texte des Fachbereich Allgemeinwissenschaften (DEU) **8009**
Texte des Spaeten Mittelalters und der Fruehen Neuzeit (DEU ISSN 0563-3079) **5387**
Texte et l'Idee (FRA ISSN 0981-1907) **5387**
Texte und Arbeiten zum Neutestamentlichen Zeitalter *see* T A N Z **7687**
Texte & Kontexte (DEU ISSN 0170-1096) **7688**
Texte und Materialen aus der Mindener Museum (DEU ISSN 1615-049X) **4273**
➤ Texte und Materialen zur Zeitgeschichte (DEU) **4164**
Texte und Studien zum Antiken Judentum (DEU ISSN 0721-8753) **7730**
Texte und Studien zur Mittelhochdeutschen Heldenepik (DEU ISSN 1611-7581) **5387**
Texte und Studien zur Wissenschaftsgeschichte (DEU) **6957**
Texte und Textgeschichte (DEU ISSN 0174-4429) **5387**
Texte und Untersuchungen zur Archivpflege (DEU) **4273**
Texte und Untersuchungen zur Englischen Philologie (DEU ISSN 0178-1383) **4477**
Texte und Untersuchungen zur Germanistik und Skandinavistik (DEU ISSN 0721-4286) **5387**
Texte und Untersuchungen zur Geschichte der Altchristlichen Literatur (DEU ISSN 0082-3589) **7688**
Texte zum Umwelttechnik und Oekologie im Bauwesen (DEU) **3470**
Texte zur Forschung (DEU ISSN 0174-0474) **6957**
Texte zur Kunst (DEU ISSN 0940-9459) **522**
Texte zur Populaeren Musik (DEU) **6623**
➤ Texte zur Rechtspolitik (AUT ISSN 1434-9078) **4795**
Texte zur Sozialpsychologie (DEU) **7412**
Texte zur Wissenschaftlichen Weltauffassung (AUT ISSN 1433-7185) **6957**
Texter fraan Migrations- och Etnicitetsseminariet (SWE ISSN 1651-453X) **8143**
Texter om Forskningsmetod (SWE ISSN 1401-2588) **3086**
Texter om Konstruktion av Normalitet, Genus och Etnicitet (SWE ISSN 1653-3062) **8143**
Textes Arabes et Etudes Islamiques (EGY ISSN 0257-4136) **7716**
Textes de la Renaissance (FRA ISSN 1262-2842) **4273**
Textes de Litterature Moderne et Contemporaine (FRA ISSN 1259-4490) **5387**
† Textes d'Interet General (FRA ISSN 0429-4769) **8993**
Textes et Contre-Textes (FRA ISSN 1627-7112) **5187**
Textes et Etudes du Moyen Age (BEL) **4273**
➤ Textes et Etudes Liturgiques/Studies in Liturgy (BEL) **7688**
Textes et Etudes sur l'Orient Chretien/Musus wa-Dirasat fi al-Sharq al-Masihi (LBN ISSN 1682-8615) **7688**
Textes et Manuscrits (FRA ISSN 0242-7206) **5387**
† Textes et Traductions d'Auteurs Orientaux (EGY ISSN 1110-001X) **8993**
Textes, Etudes, Congres (BEL) **4273**
Les Textes Legaux et les Commentaires (BEL) **4525**
Textes Litteraires *see* Exeter Textes Litteraires **5294**
Textes Litteraires Francais (CHE ISSN 0257-4063) **5387**
Textes sur les Representations Sociales. Espace de Discussion *see* Papers on Social Representations. Thread of Discussion **7389**
➤ Textiel Beheer (NLD ISSN 0929-2012) **2244**
Textielhistorische Bijdragen (NLD ISSN 1384-0398) **8459**
Textielreiniging *see* Textielverzorging **2244**
Textielverzorging (BEL ISSN 1780-1052) **2244**
TextielVisie (NLD ISSN 0168-9940) **8459**
Textil (DEU ISSN 1615-7052) **2262**
Textil (DNK ISSN 0040-4837) **8459**
Textil (VEN) **8459**
Textil-Bekleidung (DEU ISSN 0492-9934) **8459**
Textil Expres Noticias (ESP) **8459**
Textil Expres Suplementos (ESP) **8459**
● Die Textil-Industrie und Ihre Helfer (DEU ISSN 0082-3627) **8459**
Textil Mitteilungen (DEU ISSN 0342-2224) **8459**
Textil-Revue (CHE ISSN 0040-4861) **8459**
Textil- und Bekleidungstechnik, Textilveredlung, Textilmaschinenbau *see* Informationsdienst F I Z Technik. Textil- und Bekleidungstechnik, Textilveredlung, Textilmaschinenbau **8463**
Textil und Unterricht (DEU ISSN 1619-8840) **8459**
Textil Vestido (MEX) **2250**
● Textil-Wirtschaft (DEU ISSN 0040-487X) **8459**
Textil Zurnal (CZE ISSN 1210-4078) **2250**
Textilarbeit und Werken (CHE ISSN 1422-1187) **2919**
Textile/La Revue Canadienne du Textile (CAN ISSN 1490-8530) **8459**
● ➤ Textile (GBR ISSN 1475-9756) **8459**
Textile Abstract *see* Fangzhi Wenzhai **8463**
Textile Accessories *see* Fangzhi Qicai **8450**
Textile Analysis Bulletin Service (USA ISSN 0894-8267) **8459**
Textile and Apparel of Australasia (AUS ISSN 1323-661X) **8464**
Textile Asia (HKG ISSN 0049-3554) **8459**
Textile Asia Index (HKG) **8464**
Textile Association (India). Journal (IND ISSN 0368-4636) **8459**
Textile Auxiliaries *see* Yinran Zhuji **8463**
Textile Blue Book *see* Davison's Textile Blue Book **8449**
Textile Clothing Weekly *see* Fangzhi Fuzhuang Zhoukan **8450**
Textile Exports - Turkey *see* Exports Home Textile **1565**
Textile Fibre Forum (AUS ISSN 0818-6308) **8459**
Textile Forum (Deutsche Ausgabe) (DEU ISSN 1431-3510) **8459**
Textile forum (English edition) *see* Textile Forum (Deutsche Ausgabe) **8459**
● ➤ Textile History (GBR ISSN 0040-4969) **8459**
Textile Horizons (GBR ISSN 1353-6184) **8459**
Textile India Progress (IND ISSN 0970-6887) **8460**
Textile Industries Buyers Guide for Southern Africa (ZAF) **8460**
Textile Industries Dyegest Southern Africa (ZAF ISSN 0254-0533) **8460**
Textile Industry *see* Tekstilna Industrija **8458**
Textile Industry & Trade Journal (IND ISSN 0040-4993) **8460**
Textile Information Condensed *see* Texincon **8458**
Textile Insight (USA) **8460**
● ➤ Textile Institute. Journal (GBR ISSN 0040-5000) **8460**
Textile Institute. Journal. Part 2. Textile Economics, Management, and Marketing (GBR) **8460**
Textile Institute. Journal. Part 3. Annual Special Issue (GBR) **8460**
Textile Institute. World Conference (GBR) **8460**
Textile Labour Cost Comparison - International (USA) **8460**
Textile Leader (CHE ISSN 1016-7536) **8460**
Textile Machinery (IND ISSN 0040-5035) **8460**
Textile Machinery Society of Japan. Journal *see* Sen'i Kikai Gakkaishi **8457**
Textile Magazine (IND ISSN 0040-5078) **8460**
Textile Month *see* Textile Month International **8460**
● Textile Month International (GBR ISSN 2040-5162) **8460**
Textile Museum Bulletin (USA) **6538**
➤ The Textile Museum Journal (USA ISSN 0083-7407) **8460**
Textile Network (DEU ISSN 1612-5096) **8460**
Textile News (IND ISSN 0040-5124) **8460**
Textile News - Handlooms and Handicrafts Report (IND) **8460**
● Textile Outlook International (GBR ISSN 0268-4764) **8460**
Textile Perspectives *see* The Quilter **6641**
● Textile Progress (GBR ISSN 0040-5167) **8460**
Textile Red Book *see* A T I Official North American Textile Red Book **8447**
● Textile Rental (USA ISSN 0195-0118) **2250**
Textile Rental, Launderers and Dry Cleaners *see* Business Ratio Report. Textile Rental, Launderers & Dry Cleaners (Year) **2242**
● ➤ Textile Research Journal (GBR ISSN 0040-5175) **8460**
● ➤ Textile Science and Technology (NLD ISSN 0920-4083) **8461**
Textile Science Research *see* Fangzhi Kexue Yanjiu **8450**
Textile Technology Digest *see* Textile Technology Index **8464**
● Textile Technology Index (USA) **8464**
Textile Times International (GBR ISSN 0957-1639) **8461**
● Textile Topics (Online) (USA) **8461**
Textile Topics (Print) *see* Textile Topics (Online) **8461**
➤ Textile Trends (IND ISSN 0040-5205) **8461**
Textile View (NLD ISSN 1384-5306) **8461**
Textile View2 Magazine *see* View2 **8462**
● Textile World (USA ISSN 0040-5213) **8461**
Textile World Asia/Yazhou Fangzhi Shijie (USA ISSN 1546-4598) **8461**
Textile World - Carpet & Rug *see* Textile World **8461**
Textile World Latina *see* Textile World **8461**
Textile World - Textile Maintenance & Engineering *see* Textile World **8461**
Textiles a Usages Techniques *see* T U T **8457**
Textiles Africains *see* African and Middle East Textiles **8447**
Textiles Eastern Europe (GBR ISSN 1354-5981) **8461**
Textiles Magazine (GBR ISSN 1367-1308) **8461**
● Textiles Panamericanos (USA ISSN 0049-3570) **8461**
Textiles para el Hogar (ESP ISSN 0211-7975) **8461**
Textiles South East Asia (GBR ISSN 1743-3231) **8461**
➤ Textiles That Changed the World (GBR ISSN 1477-6294) **8461**
Textilia (NLD ISSN 0040-5264) **8461**
Textilkunst International (DEU ISSN 0934-3342) **8461**
Textillaren *see* Tekstiiliopettaja **8458**
Textilpflege Schweiz (CHE ISSN 1422-3430) **2244**
Textilstunde (DEU) **6642**
Textilstunde II (DEU) **6642**
Textilveredlung (CHE ISSN 0040-5310) **8461**
Textilveredlung *see* Informationsdienst F I Z Technik. Textilveredlung **8463**
Textilwirtschaft *see* Textil-Wirtschaft **8459**
TextilWirtschaft Season (DEU) **2250**
Textintern *see* Text Intern **2342**
† Texto (FRA ISSN 1278-4362) **8993**
● Texto! (FRA ISSN 1773-0120) **5187**
● Texto & Contexto-Enfermagem (BRA ISSN 0104-0707) **5983**
➤ Texto Critico (MEX ISSN 0185-0830) **5387**
● Texto e Contexto (COL ISSN 0120-5455) **5187**
Texto y Teoria: Estudios Culturales (NLD) **5387**
Textos (USA ISSN 1086-8704) **5387**
Textos de Cultura e Comunicacao (BRA ISSN 0104-0324) **2342**
Textos de Didactica de la Lengua y de la Literatura *see* Articles de Didactica de la Llengua i de la Literatura **5096**
● Textos de la CiberSociedad (ESP ISSN 1577-3760) **2439**
● Textos & Contextos (BRA ISSN 1679-2041) **8074**
● Textos sobre Envelhecimento (BRA ISSN 1517-5928) **4057**
Textos y Estudios Coloniales y de la Independencia (DEU) **5387**
Textos y Estudios de Mujeres (ESP) **5387**

Title

Themenbrief Export und Zoll *see* Export und Zoll **1564**
Themenbrief Logistik und Lager *see* Logistik und Lager **8971**
† Themenbrief Mitarbeiterfuehrung (DEU ISSN 1615-9535) **8993**
Themenhefte Gemeinde (DEU ISSN 1862-8028) **7688**
Themenhefte Gemeindearbeit *see* Themenhefte Gemeinde **7688**
• Der Themenplan (DEU ISSN 0946-4077) **7574**
Themenzentrierte Interaktion (DEU ISSN 0934-5272) **7412**
Themepark (GBR) **8760**
Themes Canadiens *see* Canadian Issues **4446**
Themes in Biblical Narrative (NLD ISSN 1388-3909) **7688**
Themes in Islamic Studies (NLD ISSN 1389-823X) **7716**
Themes in Theatre (NLD ISSN 1871-8736) **8483**
Themis *see* Revue Juridique Themis **4775**
Themis (USA) **2303**
Themis Rechtsgeleerdheid Magazijn *see* Rechtsgeleerd Magazijn Themis **4766**
ThemNews (ZAF ISSN 1991-8968) **4349**
Theo (DEU) **7777**
▼ Theo Knippenberg's Bulkboekvandemaand (NLD ISSN 1876-4169) **5387**
• Theo-Web. Zeitschrift fuer Religionpaedagogik (DEU ISSN 1863-0502) **7688**
Theodor-Fontane-Gesellschaft. Schriften (DEU ISSN 1861-4396) **5387**
Theodor-Litt-Jahrbuch (DEU ISSN 1439-1805) **8009**
Theodor-Storm-Gesellschaft. Schriften (DEU ISSN 0082-3880) **5388**
Theodore M. Hesburgh Lectures on Ethics and Public Policy (USA) **7188**
Theodore Roosevelt Association Journal (USA ISSN 0161-8423) **646**
Theoforum (CAN ISSN 1495-7922) **7688**
† Theokratia: Jahrbuch der Franz Delitzsch - Arbeitsgemeinschaft (NLD ISSN 0169-8370) **8993**
Theologia (GRC ISSN 0049-3635) **7706**
Theologia (SWE ISSN 1652-9480) **7688**
Theologia Reformata (NLD ISSN 0040-5612) **7777**
Theologiai Szemle (HUN ISSN 0133-7599) **7688**
Theologica Xaveriana (COL ISSN 0120-3649) **7820**
Theological Book Review (GBR ISSN 0954-2191) **7688**
Theological College of Northern Nigeria Research Bulletin *see* T C N N Research Bulletin **7687**
• ➤ Theological Education (USA ISSN 0040-5620) **7689**
Theological Journal Library CD *see* Westminster Theological Journal **7694**
Theological Journal Library CD *see* Bibliotheca Sacra **7748**
Theological Journal Library CD *see* Trinity Journal **7691**
Theological Journal Library CD *see* Evangelical Theological Society. Journal **7756**
Theological Journal Library CD *see* Master's Seminary Journal **7766**
Theological Journal Library CD *see* Emmaus Journal **7755**
Theological Journal Library CD *see* Journal of Christian Apologetics **7762**
▼ • Theological Librarianship (USA ISSN 1937-8904) **5050**
Theological Renewal (GBR ISSN 0308-6089) **7777**
• Theological Review (LBN ISSN 0379-9557) **7689**
• ➤ Theological Studies (USA ISSN 0040-5639) **7689**
Theological Times (GBR ISSN 0049-3651) **7777**
Theologie der Dritten Welt (DEU ISSN 0930-0341) **7689**
Theologie der Gegenwart (DEU ISSN 0342-1457) **7689**
➤ Theologie fuer die Praxis (DEU ISSN 0939-5121) **7777**
• Theologie.Geschichte (DEU ISSN 1862-1678) **7689**
Theologie Interkulturell und Studium der Religionen *see* Intercultural Theology and Study of Religions **7650**
Theologie - Religionswissenschaft (DEU ISSN 1862-6157) **7689**
Theologie und Dienst (DEU) **7689**
Theologie & Empirie (NLD ISSN 1381-2033) **7689**
Theologie und Glaube (DEU ISSN 0049-366X) **7820**
Theologie und Hochschule (DEU ISSN 1863-1215) **7820**
Theologie und Philosophie (DEU ISSN 0040-5655) **7820**
Theologika (PER ISSN 1022-5390) **7689**
• Theologiques (CAN ISSN 1188-7109) **7689**
Theologisch Debat (NLD ISSN 1572-5057) **7689**
Theologisch-Praktische Quartalschrift (DEU ISSN 0040-5663) **7689**
Theologische Beitraege (DEU ISSN 0342-2372) **7689**
➤ Theologische Bibliothek Toepelmann (DEU ISSN 0563-4288) **7689**
Theologische Dissertationen (CHE ISSN 0082-3902) **7689**
Theologische Hochschule Chur. Schriftenreihe (CHE) **7689**
Theologische Literaturzeitung (DEU ISSN 0040-5671) **7689**
Theologische Quartalschrift (DEU ISSN 0342-1430) **7820**
Theologische Revue (DEU ISSN 0040-568X) **7820**
• Theologische Rundschau (DEU ISSN 0040-5698) **7689**
Theologische Studien (DEU ISSN 1433-4534) **7689**
Theologische Texte und Studien (DEU ISSN 0941-8717) **7689**
Theologische Zeitschrift (CHE ISSN 0040-5701) **7689**
Theologisches Gespraech (DEU ISSN 1431-200X) **7689**
• Theology (GBR ISSN 0040-571X) **7689**
Theology and Culture Newsletter (USA) **7689**
➤ Theology and Medicine (NLD ISSN 0928-8783) **7689**
• ➤ Theology and Science (GBR ISSN 1474-6700) **7689**
• ➤ Theology and Sexuality (GBR ISSN 1355-8358) **7690**
Theology Digest (USA ISSN 0040-5728) **7690**
Theology for Ministry (USA ISSN 1934-8711) **7777**
Theology News and Notes (USA ISSN 1529-899X) **7777**
• ➤ Theology Today (USA ISSN 0040-5736) **7690**
TheOne Magazine (USA) **5084**
• Theophilos (BRA ISSN 1676-1332) **7690**
Theoreme (FRA ISSN 1159-7941) **6515**
• ➤ Theoretical and Applied Climatology (AUT ISSN 0177-798X) **6396**
Theoretical and Applied Economics *see* Economie Teoretica si Aplicata **1101**
• ➤ Theoretical and Applied Fracture Mechanics (NLD ISSN 0167-8442) **7063**
• ➤ Theoretical and Applied Genetics (DEU ISSN 0040-5752) **878**
Theoretical and Applied Lingusitics at Kobe Shoin (JPN ISSN 1343-4535) **5187**
➤ Theoretical and Applied Mechanics/Teorijska i Primenjena Mehanika (SRB ISSN 1450-5584) **7063**
Theoretical and Applied Mechanics Japan (Online) *see* Theoretical and Applied Mechanics Japan (Print) **7063**
• Theoretical and Applied Mechanics Japan (Print) (JPN ISSN 1348-0693) **7063**
➤ Theoretical and Computational Acoustics (SGP) **7050**
• Theoretical and Computational Chemistry (NLD ISSN 1380-7323) **2082**
• ➤ Theoretical and Computational Fluid Dynamics (DEU ISSN 0935-4964) **7063**
• ➤ Theoretical and Empirical Researches in Urban Management (ROM ISSN 2065-3913) **4428**
• ➤ Theoretical and Experimental Chemistry (USA ISSN 0040-5760) **2082**
• ➤ Theoretical and Mathematical Physics (USA ISSN 0040-5779) **7043**
• Theoretical Anthropology (AUT ISSN 1024-5804) **358**
Theoretical Aspects of Rationality and Knowledge (USA ISSN 1525-3430) **2456**
• ➤ Theoretical Biology and Medical Modelling (GBR ISSN 1742-4682) **707**
• Theoretical Chemical Engineering (DEU ISSN 0960-5053) **3234**
➤ Theoretical Chemistry (USA ISSN 0082-3961) **2082**
• ➤ Theoretical Chemistry Accounts (DEU ISSN 1432-881X) **2082**
• ➤ Theoretical Computer Science (NLD ISSN 0304-3975) **2601**
• ➤ Theoretical Criminology (GBR ISSN 1362-4806) **2670**
▼ • Theoretical Ecology (NLD ISSN 1874-1738) **3470**
Theoretical Ecology Series (NLD ISSN 1875-306X) **707**
Theoretical Economics *see* Lilun Jingjixue **1546**
• ➤ Theoretical Economics (USA ISSN 1933-6837) **1550**
• ➤ Theoretical Foundations of Chemical Engineering (RUS ISSN 0040-5795) **3256**
Theoretical Front of Higher Education Institutes *see* Gaoxiao Lilun Zhanxian **2982**
• Theoretical Inquiries in Law (ISR ISSN 1565-1509) **4795**
Theoretical Investigation *see* Lilun Tantao **7983**
• ➤ Theoretical Issues in Ergonomics Science (GBR ISSN 1463-922X) **3223**
• ➤ Theoretical Linguistics (DEU ISSN 0301-4428) **5187**
• ➤ Theoretical Medicine and Bioethics (NLD ISSN 1386-7415) **5721**
Theoretical Physics Seminar in Trondheim (NOR ISSN 0803-4222) **7043**
Theoretical Platform of Tibetan Developement *see* Xizang Fazhan Luntan **7197**
• ➤ Theoretical Population Biology (USA ISSN 0040-5809) **707**
Theoretical Studies In Literature and Art *see* Wenyi Lilun Yanjiu **5398**
Theoretical Studies in Second Language Acquisition (USA ISSN 1051-6670) **5187**
Theoretische Untersuchungen zur Architektur (DEU ISSN 1434-5919) **459**
• Theoria (CHL ISSN 0717-196X) **3005**
• ➤ Theoria (ESP ISSN 0495-4548) **6957**
• ➤ Theoria (GBR ISSN 0040-5825) **6957**
Theoria (MEX) **6957**
• ➤ Theoria (USA ISSN 0040-5817) **4477**
➤ Theoria (Denton) (USA ISSN 1554-1312) **6623**
Theoria et Historia Scientiarum (POL ISSN 0867-4159) **7923**
Theorie in den Biowissenschaften *see* Theory in Biosciences **707**
Theorie Litterature Enseignement *see* T L E **5384**
Theorie und Geschichte der Buergerlichen Gesellschaft (DEU) **8143**
Theorie und Geschichte der Literatur und der Schoenen Kuenste (DEU ISSN 0563-4415) **5388**
➤ Theorie und Praxis der Sozialen Arbeit (DEU ISSN 0342-2275) **8074**
Theorie und Praxis der Sozialpaedagogik (DEU ISSN 0342-7145) **2169**
Theorie und Praxis der Sozialpaedagogik. Extra (DEU ISSN 1439-1872) **2169**
Theorie und Vermittlung der Sprache (DEU ISSN 0724-9144) **5187**
Theories of Representation and Difference (USA) **6515**
Theorists of Myth (USA) **5388**
• ➤ Theory and Applications of Categories (CAN ISSN 1201-561X) **5541**
➤ Theory and Applications of Transport in Porous Media (NLD ISSN 0924-6118) **7043**
Theory and Criticism *see* Te'oriya Uviqoret **8143**
Theory and Criticism of Literature and Art *see* Wenyi Pinglun yu Piping **5245**
• ➤ Theory and Decision (USA ISSN 0040-5833) **8009**
➤ Theory and Decision Library. Series A: Philosophy and Methodology of the Social Sciences (NLD ISSN 0921-3384) **8009**
➤ Theory and Decision Library. Series B: Mathematical and Statistical Methods (NLD ISSN 0921-3392) **5541**
➤ Theory and Decision Library. Series C: Game Theory, Mathematical Programming and Operations Research (NLD ISSN 0924-6126) **5556**
➤ Theory and Decision Library. Series D: System Theory, Knowledge Engineering and Problem Solving (NLD ISSN 0921-3406) **2528**
• Theory & Event (USA ISSN 1092-311X) **7188**
Theory and History of Literature Series (USA) **5388**
Theory and Modernization *see* Lilun yu Xiandaihua **7983**
➤ Theory and Practice (USA ISSN 0741-6156) **6623**
• Theory and Practice of Logic Programming (GBR ISSN 1471-0684) **2510**
• ➤ Theory & Psychology (GBR ISSN 0959-3543) **7412**
Theory and Research *see* Theory and Research in Social Education **3086**
Theory and Research in Education (Online) *see* Theory and Research in Education (Print) **2919**
• ➤ Theory and Research in Education (Print) (GBR ISSN 1477-8785) **2919**
• ➤ Theory and Research in Social Education (USA ISSN 0093-3104) **3086**
• ➤ Theory & Science (USA ISSN 1527-5558) **8143**
• ➤ Theory and Society (NLD ISSN 0304-2421) **8143**
• ➤ Theory, Culture & Society (GBR ISSN 0263-2764) **8143**
Theory, Culture & Society. Supplement *see* Theory, Culture & Society **8143**
Theory Front *see* Lilun Qianyan **7152**
▼ • ➤ Theory in Action (USA ISSN 1937-0229) **8010**
• ➤ Theory in Biosciences/Theorie in den Biowissenschaften (DEU ISSN 1431-7613) **707**
• ➤ Theory into Practice (USA ISSN 0040-5841) **2919**
Theory Into Practice - Digital *see* Theory into Practice **2919**
• Theory of Computing (USA ISSN 1557-2862) **2439**
• ➤ Theory of Computing Systems (USA ISSN 1432-4350) **2601**
Theory of Inventive Problem Solving Journal *see* The T R I Z Journal **1181**
• ➤ Theory of Probability and Its Applications/Zeoriya Veroyatnostei i ee Primeneniya (USA ISSN 0040-585X) **5541**
• Theory of Probability and Mathematical Statistics (USA ISSN 0094-9000) **5541**
Theory of Science *see* Teorie Vedy **7923**
➤ Theory out of Bounds Series (USA) **4478**
Theos (DEU ISSN 1435-6864) **7690**
Theosofia (NLD ISSN 0040-5868) **6957**
TheoSophia (NZL ISSN 1177-8032) **6957**
➤ Theosophical History (USA ISSN 0951-497X) **7742**
Theosophical Movement (IND ISSN 0040-5884) **6957**
Theosophie Heute (DEU ISSN 0177-8005) **7742**
Theosophist (IND ISSN 0972-1851) **7742**
Theosophy (USA ISSN 0040-5906) **6957**
Theosophy in Australia (AUS ISSN 1038-1139) **7742**
Theosophy in New Zealand *see* TheoSophia **6957**
• ThePosition (USA) **6301**
Thera (FRA) **6882**
▼ • ➤ Therapeutic Advances in Cardiovascular Disease (GBR ISSN 1753-9447) **5800**
▼ • Therapeutic Advances in Chronic Disease (GBR ISSN 2040-6223) **5721**
▼ • ➤ Therapeutic Advances in Gastroenterology (GBR ISSN 1756-283X) **5932**
▼ • Therapeutic Advances in Hematology (GBR ISSN 2040-6207) **5941**
▼ • Therapeutic Advances in Medical Oncology (GBR ISSN 1758-8340) **6035**
▼ • Therapeutic Advances in Musculoskeletal Disease (GBR ISSN 1759-720X) **6073**
▼ • ➤ Therapeutic Advances in Neurological Disorders (GBR ISSN 1756-2856) **6187**
▼ • ➤ Therapeutic Advances in Respiratory Disease (GBR ISSN 1753-4658) **6220**
▼ • ➤ Therapeutic Advances in Urology (GBR ISSN 1756-2872) **6275**
Therapeutic Apheresis *see* Therapeutic Apheresis and Dialysis **6275**
• ➤ Therapeutic Apheresis and Dialysis (AUS ISSN 1744-9979) **6275**
Therapeutic Archives *see* Terapevticheskii Arkhiv **5721**
Therapeutic Communities *see* Community, Culture and Change **6911**
• ➤ Therapeutic Drug Monitoring (USA ISSN 0163-4356) **6882**
Therapeutic Drug Monitoring Kenkyu *see* T D M Kenkyu **6882**
Therapeutic Goods Administration News (Print Edition) *see* T G A News (Print Edition) **6882**
• ➤ Therapeutic Guidelines. Analgesic (AUS) **5774**
• ➤ Therapeutic Guidelines. Antibiotic (AUS ISSN 1329-5039) **5721**
• ➤ Therapeutic Guidelines. Cardiovascular (AUS ISSN 1327-9513) **5800**
• ➤ Therapeutic Guidelines. Dermatology (AUS ISSN 1440-6357) **5882**
• ➤ Therapeutic Guidelines. Endocrinology (AUS ISSN 1327-9505) **5900**
• ➤ Therapeutic Guidelines. Gastrointestinal (AUS) **5932**
• ➤ Therapeutic Guidelines. Neurology (AUS ISSN 1327-9491) **6187**
• ➤ Therapeutic Guidelines. Palliative Care (AUS) **5721**
• ➤ Therapeutic Guidelines. Psychotropic (AUS ISSN 1441-5178) **6188**
• ➤ Therapeutic Guidelines. Respiratory (AUS ISSN 1441-516X) **6220**
Therapeutic Patient Education *see* Education Therapeutique du Patient **6108**
Therapeutic Plasmapheresis *see* Nihon Afereshisu Gakkai Zasshi **5940**
• ➤ Therapeutic Recreation Journal (USA ISSN 0040-5914) **6998**
Therapeutic Research (JPN ISSN 0289-8020) **5721**
• ➤ Therapeutics and Clinical Risk Management (Online) (GBR ISSN 1178-203X) **6882**
† • ➤ Therapeutics and Clinical Risk Management (Print) (NZL ISSN 1176-6336) **8993**
• Therapeutics Letter (CAN) **5721**
• ➤ Therapeutische Umschau (CHE ISSN 0040-5930) **5721**
Therapeutisches Reiten (DEU ISSN 0942-7546) **8299**
• ➤ Therapie (FRA ISSN 0040-5957) **5721**
• Therapie Familiale (CHE ISSN 0250-4952) **6188**
Therapie Kreativ (DEU ISSN 1434-8977) **7412**
Therapie und Praxis (DEU ISSN 1432-7872) **6116**
Therapies Naturelles (FRA ISSN 1953-9770) **315**
Therapiewoche (CHE ISSN 1424-1900) **5721**
The Therapist (USA ISSN 1540-2770) **7412**
Therapists Report (USA ISSN 1061-4362) **7412**
• ➤ Therapy (GBR ISSN 1475-0708) **5911**
• ➤ Therapy Today (GBR ISSN 1748-7846) **7412**
Therese de Lisieux (FRA ISSN 1168-5638) **7820**
Theriaca (DNK ISSN 0082-4003) **6882**
• ➤ Theriogenology (USA ISSN 0093-691X) **8808**
Thermal Air *see* Thermalair Householder **8760**
Thermal and Nuclear Power *see* Karyoku Genshiryoku Hatsuden **3176**
• Thermal Engineering (RUS ISSN 0040-6015) **3397**
• Thermal Medicine/Japanese Journal of Hyperthermic Oncology (JPN ISSN 1882-2576) **6035**
▼ • Thermal News (USA ISSN 1937-1152) **4127**
▼ • Thermal News e-Report (USA ISSN 1938-0860) **3332**
Thermal Phenomena in Electronic Systems *see* Intersociety Conference on Thermal Phenomena in Electronic Systems. Proceedings **2466**
• ➤ Thermal Science (SRB ISSN 0354-9836) **3148**
Thermal Science and Engineering (JPN ISSN 0918-9963) **7056**
Thermal Turbine *see* Reli Touping **3394**
Thermalair (NZL ISSN 1170-1374) **8760**
Thermalair *see* Thermalair Householder **8760**
Thermalair Householder (NZL) **8760**
† • ThermalNet (GBR ISSN 1750-8363) **8993**
Thermiek (NLD ISSN 0040-6023) **72**
• ➤ Thermochimica Acta (NLD ISSN 0040-6031) **2141**
➤ Thermodynamics at Texas A & M (USA) **2141**
Thermodynamics Research Center Spectral Data - 1 H Nuclear Magnetic Resonance *see* T R C Spectral Data - 1 H Nuclear Magnetic Resonance **2106**
Thermodynamics Research Center Spectral Data - 13 C Nuclear Magnetic Resonance *see* T R C Spectral Data - 13 C Nuclear Magnetic Resonance **2106**
Thermodynamics Research Center Spectral Data - Infrared *see* T R C Spectral Data - Infrared **2106**
Thermodynamics Research Center Spectral Data - Mass *see* T R C Spectral Data - Mass **2106**

Title

Thermodynamics Research Center Spectral Data - Raman see T R C Spectral Data - Raman 2106
Thermodynamics Research Center Spectral Data - Ultraviolet see T R C Spectral Data - Ultraviolet 2106
Thermodynamics Research Center Thermodynamic Tables - Hydrocarbons see T R C Thermodynamic Tables - Hydrocarbons 2141
Thermodynamics Research Center Thermodynamic Tables - Non-Hydrocarbons see T R C Thermodynamic Tables - Non-Hydrocarbons 2106
➤ Thermology International (AUT ISSN 1560-604X) 7056
Thermometer Binnenstad Groningen (NLD ISSN 1874-5253) 7503
➤ Thermophysical Properties/Nihon Netsu Bussei Shinpojumu Koen Ronbunshu (JPN ISSN 0911-1743) 7057
• Thermophysics and Aeromechanics (RUS ISSN 0869-8643) 7057
Thermosetting Resin see Reguxing Shuzhi 6720
Thesaurismata (ITA ISSN 0082-4097) 4164
Thesaurus (COL ISSN 0040-604X) 5187
Thesaurus - American Petroleum Institute see American Petroleum Institute. Thesaurus 6799
Thesaurus Linguae Etruscae (ITA ISSN 1824-0631) 5187
Thesaurus of Metallurgical Terms (USA ISSN 1052-7877) 6335
TheScientificWorldJournal see The Scientific World Journal 7913
These Days (USA) 7777
Theses and Dissertations Accepted for Higher Degrees in Nigerian Universities (NGA ISSN 0082-4100) 3005
• Theses and Other Publications of the University of Copenhagen (DNK ISSN 1603-0338) 636
Thesis (GRC ISSN 1107-7999) 7268
Thesis (RUS) 8010
Thesis Abstracts (IND ISSN 0379-3990) 187
• ➤ Thesis Eleven (GBR ISSN 0725-5136) 7188
• TheStandard.com (USA) 2567
TheStreet.com Ratings' Consumer Guide to Automobile Insurance (USA ISSN 1934-4333) 4525
TheStreet.com Ratings' Consumer Guide to Elder Care Choices (USA ISSN 1934-435X) 8074
TheStreet.com Ratings' Consumer Guide to Homeowners Insurance (USA ISSN 1934-4368) 4525
TheStreet.com Ratings' Consumer Guide to Long-term Care Insurance (USA ISSN 1934-4155) 4525
TheStreet.com Ratings' Consumer Guide to Medicare Prescription Drug Coverage (USA ISSN 1934-4147) 4525
TheStreet.com Ratings' Consumer Guide to Medicare Supplement Insurance (USA ISSN 1934-4120) 4525
TheStreet.com Ratings' Consumer Guide to Term Life Insurance (USA ISSN 1934-4139) 4525
TheStreet.com Ratings' Consumer Guide to Variable Annuities (USA ISSN 1934-4341) 1655
TheStreet.com Ratings' Guide to Banks and Thrifts (USA ISSN 1935-0058) 1386
TheStreet.com Ratings' Guide to Bond and Money Market Mutual Funds (USA ISSN 1935-004X) 1655
TheStreet.com Ratings' Guide to Closed-End Mutual Funds see TheStreet.com Ratings' Guide to Exchange-Traded Funds 1655
TheStreet.com Ratings' Guide to Common Stocks (USA ISSN 1935-0031) 1655
TheStreet.com Ratings' Guide to Exchange-Traded Funds (USA ISSN 1936-9840) 1655
• TheStreet.com Ratings' Guide to Health Insurers (USA ISSN 1940-4123) 4525
TheStreet.com Ratings' Guide to HMOs and Health Insurers see TheStreet.com Ratings' Guide to Health Insurers 4525
TheStreet.com Ratings' Guide to Life and Annuity Insurers (USA ISSN 1937-6626) 4525
TheStreet.com Ratings' Guide to Life, Health, and Annuity Insurers see TheStreet.com Ratings' Guide to Life and Annuity Insurers 4525
TheStreet.com Ratings' Guide to Property and Casualty Insurers (USA ISSN 1935-5327) 4525
TheStreet.com Ratings' Guide to Stock Mutual Funds (USA ISSN 1935-2050) 1655
TheStreet.com Ratings' Ultimate Guided Tour of Stock Investing (USA ISSN 1935-5300) 1655
➤ Theta (GBR ISSN 0953-0738) 5541
Theta (NLD) 7742
➤ Theta Alpha Kappa. Journal (USA ISSN 8756-4785) 7690
Theta Market Research Reports (USA) 5721
Thexis see Marketing Review St. Gallen 1833
They Won't Stay Dead (USA) 6515
Thieme Almanac (USA) 315
▼ Thieme Refresher Innere Medizin (DEU ISSN 1616-9654) 5949
Thieme Refresher Neurologie (DEU ISSN 1616-9646) 6188
Thieme Refresher Pneumologie (DEU ISSN 1616-9662) 6220
Thieu Nien Tien Phong/Young Pioneers (VNM) 2216
Thikana see Saptahika Thikana 7181
Thin Air (USA) 5388
Thin Film Device see Hakumaku Denshi Debaisu Nenkan 3309
• ➤ Thin Films and Nanostructures (USA) 7043
• ➤ Thin Solid Films (CHE ISSN 0040-6090) 7043
• ➤ Thin-Walled Structures (GBR ISSN 0263-8231) 3397
Things (GBR ISSN 1356-921X) 5242
Think (CAN ISSN 1718-2662) 3005
Think see Taenk 2641
• Think (London) (GBR ISSN 1477-1756) 6957
Think Again (CZE) 8760
Think & Discover (USA ISSN 1542-9784) 2216
Think Business (USA ISSN 1947-0096) 1182
Think in English (ESP ISSN 1139-5370) 5187
Think India (IND ISSN 0971-1260) 3223
▼ Think Journal (USA ISSN 1943-1473) 5388
Think On (USA ISSN 1066-601X) 3785
Think Tank Directory (USA ISSN 1063-3340) 7188
• ➤ Thinking (USA ISSN 0190-3330) 6957
Thinking about Faenza see Pensare Faenza 8980
• ➤ Thinking & Reasoning (GBR ISSN 1354-6783) 7412
Thinking and Wisdom see Siwei yu Zhihui 8002
† • Thinking Business (AUS ISSN 1833-363X) 8993
Thinking in Colour see I Q 5307
Thinking Mission (GBR ISSN 0143-8514) 7690
• Thinking Skills and Creativity (GBR ISSN 1871-1871) 2919
▼ • Thique (USA ISSN 1935-3480) 6301
Third Age New Zealand see Savvy 8987
The Third Alternative see Black Static 5440
Third Bed see 3rd Bed 5439
Third Branch (USA ISSN 0040-6120) 4966
Third Century Methodism (USA ISSN 1092-7085) 7777
Third Circuit Digest (USA ISSN 1043-1470) 4966
➤ Third Coast (USA ISSN 1520-8206) 5388
Third Degree (CAN ISSN 0843-7092) 2303
The Third Degree (USA ISSN 0040-6139) 5415
• ➤ Third Education Group Review (USA ISSN 1557-2870) 2919
Third Eye (USA ISSN 0198-800X) 5436
Third Floor see 3rd Floor 529
• Third Indicator (USA) 5050
Third International Mathematics and Science Study Australia Monograph see T I M S S Australia Monograph 2917
Third Muse Poetry Journal see 3rd Muse Poetry Journal 5439
Third Party Rx (USA) 6883
Third Rail (USA ISSN 0741-5958) 5242
Third Reich Study Group Bulletin (USA) 6900
• Third Sector (GBR ISSN 1355-6371) 8074
Third Sector (GBR) 8074
➤ Third Sector Review (AUS ISSN 1323-9163) 8010
Third Space see Thirdspace (Online) 8903
• ➤ Third Text (GBR ISSN 0952-8822) 522
Third Wave Magazine see Di San Bo 2589
Third Way (Harrow) (GBR ISSN 0309-3492) 7690
Third Way (London) (GBR ISSN 0959-5031) 7188
➤ Third World Economics (MYS ISSN 0128-4134) 1182
Third World Forum (USA ISSN 0317-0659) 7188
Third World Impact (GBR) 3568
Third World in Perspective (USA ISSN 0885-2200) 7188
Third World Law Journal see Boston College Third World Law Journal 4918
• ➤ Third World Legal Studies (Year) (USA ISSN 0895-5018) 4942
• ➤ Third World Quarterly (GBR ISSN 0143-6597) 1606
Third World Resource Directory (USA ISSN 1074-3154) 7188
Third World Resurgence see Revista del Sur 7997
• ➤ Thirdspace (Online) (CAN ISSN 1499-8513) 8903
Thirdspace (Print) see Thirdspace (Online) 8903
Thirdworld (PAK ISSN 1018-8991) 1606
The Thirsk Weekly News (GBR ISSN 1749-5954) 3968
Thirst see Zhazhda 5404
Thirst (USA) 5388
Thirteen (USA) 2397
Thirteen Minutes (USA) 8886
Thirteenth Moon (Albany) see 13th Moon 5405
Thirteenth Moon (San Francisco) (USA) 5448
Thirteenth Warrior Review see The 13th Warrior Review 5247
Thirty Day Notice - Tenant Tattler see 30 Day Notice - Tenant Tattler 7616
Thirty Days in the Church and in the World see 30 Days in the Church and in the World 7824
Thirty-three Metal Producing see Metal Producing & Processing 6323
Thirty-two B - J see 32 B - 32 J 4606
Thirty-two E Events see 32 E Events 4606
Thirty Up see 30up 6302
This Active Life (USA ISSN 1526-7148) 4057
This Caring Business (GBR ISSN 0268-4047) 8074
• This England (GBR ISSN 0040-6171) 8760
This Is Austin (USA ISSN 1934-4686) 5084
This Is Bahrain and What's On (BHR) 3799
This Is Botswana (BWA) 8760
This Is Bristol and Bath (GBR) 3872
This is Greenland (DVD) (GRL) 1433
This is Greenland (Print) see This is Greenland (DVD) 1433
This Is Indianapolis (USA) 8760
• This Is London (GBR ISSN 0040-6198) 8760
This Is Malawi (MWI ISSN 0563-4784) 1522
This is Manitoba, Fishing and Hunting Adventures see Manitoba. Fishing & Hunting Adventures 8732
This is Manitoba, Vacation Guide see Manitoba Vacation Guide 8732
This Is Mexico (MEX) 8760
This Is N E C (Year) (JPN ISSN 0910-3732) 2342
This Is Qatar (QAT) 8760
This Is the Spinal Tap Zine (USA ISSN 1083-0057) 6623
• This Is True (USA ISSN 1521-1932) 4584
This Is Vietnam (HKG) 8760
• This Just In (USA) 3990
• This Magazine (CAN ISSN 1491-2678) 7188
This Month in Mississippi (USA) 4379
• This Old House (USA ISSN 1086-2633) 1040
This Old House Guide to Interiors (USA) 4551
This Quarter (GBR ISSN 1354-327X) 1182
This Rock (USA ISSN 1049-4561) 7820
• This Week (USA) 6396
This Week Big Island (USA ISSN 0191-8354) 8760
This Week in Berne see Bern Events 8687
This Week in Brisbane (AUS ISSN 0817-6159) 8760
This Week in Business (CAN ISSN 0838-7087) 1182
This Week in Canberra (AUS ISSN 0817-6140) 8760
This Week in Cleveland (USA ISSN 1093-5924) 8760
This Week in Consumer Electronics see T W I C E 3114
This Week in Darwin (AUS ISSN 1442-7168) 8760
This Week in Melbourne (AUS ISSN 0817-6124) 8760
This Week in Sydney (AUS ISSN 0817-6175) 8760
This Week in Tasmania (AUS ISSN 0817-6132) 8761
This Week in Texas (USA) 4379
This Week in the Poconos (USA) 8761
• This Week in Washington (Online) (USA) 7188
This Week in Washington (Print) see This Week in Washington (Online) 7188
This Week in Western North Carolina (USA) 8761
This Week Kauai (USA ISSN 0191-8362) 8761
This Week Magazine (AUS) 8761
This Week Magazine (USA) 4983
This Week Maui (USA ISSN 0191-8370) 8761
This Week Oahu (USA) 8761
• This Week's Finds in Mathematical Physics (USA) 7043
Thisted Dagblad (DNK) 3835
• The Thistle (USA) 3990
The Thistle & Shamrock (USA ISSN 1055-436X) 6623
• Thjodarbuskapurinn (ISL ISSN 1670-1968) 1182
• Thoi Bao Kinh Te Vietnam (VNM) 1182
• Thoi Bao Kinh Te Vietnam Online (VNM ISSN 1563-8812) 1182
Thoi Bao Kinh Te Vietnam Tu Van Tieu Dung see Tu Van Tieu Dung 3994
Thoi Bao USA (USA ISSN 1946-1461) 3568
Thoi Bao vi Tinh Sai Gon see ComputerWorld 2414
Thoi Trang Tre/New Fashion (VNM) 8886
▼ Thomas a Gozmozdony (HUN ISSN 1789-5553) 2216
Thomas & Friends (GBR ISSN 1467-7288) 2216
Thomas Bulletin (NLD ISSN 1381-5377) 3086
Thomas Burke Memorial Washington State Museum. Research Report (USA ISSN 1046-4891) 6538
Thomas California Civil Courtroom Handbook and Desktop Reference see California Civil Courtroom Handbook and Desktop Reference 4828
Thomas Cook (DEU) 8761
Thomas Cook Overseas Timetable (GBR ISSN 0144-7475) 8513
Thomas Corbishley Lectures see Corbishley Memorial Lecture 7228
Thomas Edward Lawrence Notes see T E Notes 646
Thomas Food and Beverage Market Place see Food & Beverage Market Place 1995
Thomas Goode Jones Law Review see Jones Law Review 4699
➤ Thomas Hardy Journal (GBR ISSN 0268-5418) 5388
➤ Thomas Hardy Year Book (GBR ISSN 0082-416X) 5388
➤ Thomas Instituut Utrecht Series (BEL) 7690
The Thomas J. Herzfeld Encyclopedia of Closed-End Funds (USA ISSN 1055-9035) 1655
• Thomas Jefferson Law Review (USA ISSN 1090-5278) 4899
• Thomas M Cooley Journal of Practical and Clinical Law (USA ISSN 1097-0800) 4795
• Thomas M. Cooley Law Review (USA ISSN 1060-1007) 4796
Thomas Mann Gesellschaft. Blaetter (CHE ISSN 0082-4186) 5388
Thomas Mann Jahrbuch (DEU ISSN 0935-6983) 5388
Thomas Mann Studien (DEU ISSN 0563-4822) 5388
Thomas Paine Society Bulletin (GBR ISSN 0965-1411) 7188
† • Thomas Register (USA) 8993
Thomas the Tank Engine and Friends Collected (GBR ISSN 0964-3850) 2216
Thomas und Seine Freunde (DEU) 2217
• ➤ Thomas Wolfe Review (USA ISSN 0276-5683) 5388
Thomas Wolfe Society. Proceedings (USA) 5388
• ThomasNet.com (USA) 2030
• ➤ Thomist (USA ISSN 0040-6325) 7820
Thomistic Papers (USA ISSN 0898-4417) 7820
Thompson on Real Property, Thomas Edition (USA) 4905
Thompson's N C L B Advisor (No Child Left Behind) (USA ISSN 1930-3483) 3034
Thompson's Special Ed Advisor (USA ISSN 1930-3475) 3048
Thom's Commercial Directory (IRL ISSN 0082-4224) 2030
• Thom's Dublin & County Street Directory (IRL) 4031
Thomson Biomedical Business & Technology see Biomedical Business & Technology 5585
Thomson Financial Directory of Independent Investment Research see Directory of Independent Investment Research 1621
Thomson H R (DNK ISSN 1902-3146) 1797
Thomson H R Update see Thomson H R 1797
• Thomson Merger News (USA) 1394
Thomson Regulation Check Clearinghouse Directory see Regulation C C Directory 1378
Thomson Tax Q & A (AUS ISSN 1449-6976) 1951
Thomson World Bank Directory. 1-Vol Edition see World Bank Directory 2035
• Thomson's Blue Book (USA ISSN 1078-8522) 1386
† • Thomson's Corporations Law Academic Alert (AUS ISSN 1834-6103) 8993
• Thomson's Liquor Guide (AUS ISSN 0313-0568) 2641
• ➤ The Thoracic and Cardiovascular Surgeon (DEU ISSN 0171-6425) 6261
The Thoracic and Cardiovascular Surgeon. Supplement see The Thoracic and Cardiovascular Surgeon 6261
• Thoracic Surgery Clinics (USA ISSN 1547-4127) 6261
Thoracic Surgery News (USA ISSN 1558-0156) 6261
Thoracic Surgical Science see G M S Thoracic Surgical Science 6244
• ➤ Thorax (GBR ISSN 0040-6376) 6220
• Thoreau Society Bulletin (USA ISSN 0040-6406) 5388
➤ Thoresby Society. Publications (GBR ISSN 0082-4232) 4164
Thorikos (BEL ISSN 0775-3411) 420
Thorikos Guides see Thorikos 420
Thorndike Encyclopedia of Banking and Financial Tables (USA ISSN 0196-7762) 1386
Thorndyke File (USA ISSN 0145-5575) 5412
Thorne & Hatfield Moors Conservation Forum Technical Report see T H M C F Technical Report 2628
Thorny Locust (USA ISSN 1094-0154) 5388
The Thorny Trail (USA ISSN 0094-0844) 3785
➤ Thoroton Society of Nottinghamshire. Transactions (GBR ISSN 0309-9210) 420
Thoroughbred (USA) 8283
Thoroughbred Racing Associations. Directory and Record Book (USA ISSN 0082-4240) 8299
Thoroughbred Times (USA ISSN 0887-2244) 8299
† • Thorpe - R O M (AUS ISSN 1038-3395) 8993
Thorslunde Ishoej Lokalhistoriske Forening (DNK ISSN 0902-6592) 4273
Thorvaldsens Museum. Meddelelser (DNK ISSN 0085-7262) 6538
Thot (BRA ISSN 1413-893X) 6957
Thought see Shiso (Tokyo) 4475
• Thought & Action (USA ISSN 0748-8475) 3005
Thought and Words see Ssu yu Yen 4476
Thought Magazine (USA) 5388
• Thoughtline (USA) 6957
Thoughts see Misli 7807
Thoughts (ZAF ISSN 1818-9059) 7543
• Thoughts about Things Magazine (USA) 3990
Thoughts for All Seasons (USA ISSN 0886-6481) 5242
▼ • Thoughtsmith (USA ISSN 1947-5489) 5388
Thoughtsmith Magazine see Thoughtsmith 5388
Thousand Biggest Companies in Colombia see Las Mil Empresas Mas Grandes de Colombia 2017
Thozhil Vanniga Mudaleedu (IND) 162
Thraco-Dacica (ROM ISSN 0259-1081) 4273
• Thrasher (USA ISSN 0889-0692) 8212
• Threads (USA ISSN 0882-7370) 6642
Threatened Birds of Africa and Related Islands (GBR) 915
Threatened Birds of the Americas (GBR) 915
Threatened Species Occasional Publication (NZL ISSN 1170-3709) 3470
Threatened Species Recovery Plan Series (NZL ISSN 1170-3806) 3470
Three-by-Three Magazine see 3 x 3 Magazine 529
Three C Media see 3CMedia 2346
Three C Online see 3 C On-line 2570
Three Counties Farming Review (GBR) 162
Three D see 3 D 2490
Three D Artist see 3 D Artist 2490
Three Dog Night News (USA) 2270
▼ Three Dollar Squirrel (USA ISSN 1948-7118) 5388
Three F M see 3 F M 4086
Three - Fives Review see III - Vs Review 3116
Three Forks of Muddy Creek (USA ISSN 0094-9698) 4315
Three G Bulletin see 3 G Bulletin 2374
Three G Mobile see 3 G Wireless Broadband 2346
Three-Hundred and Sixty Degrees see 360 Degrees 1199
Three Hundred Six Thousand Ninety see 306090 462
Three Hundred Sixty Degrees see 360 2225

Title

Tidskrift foer Queerforskning i Finland *see* S Q S **8130**
Tidskrift foer Schack (SWE ISSN 0040-6848) **8212**
Tidskrift foer Svensk Antikvarisk Forskning *see* Fornvaennen **394**
Tidskrift foer Sveriges Domarefoerbund (SWE ISSN 1102-2752) **4796**
Tidskrift foer Visuell Konst *see* Heterogenesis **493**
➤ Tidskrift for Sygeplejeforskning (DNK ISSN 0900-3002) **5983**
Tidskrift i Fortifikation (SWE ISSN 0040-6937) **3285**
Tidskrift i Gymnastik och Idrott *see* Idrott & Haelse **8178**
Tidskrift i Sjoevaesendet (SWE ISSN 0040-6945) **6449**
Tidskriften 00tal om Litteratur och Konst *see* 00tal **5405**
Tidskriften Biblis *see* Biblis **7553**
• Tidskriften Bioenergi (SWE ISSN 1403-6746) **3223**
➤ Tidskriften Doktorn (SWE ISSN 1651-5161) **5722**
Tidskriften Filmkonst *see* Filmkonst **6500**
Tidskriften Filmkrets *see* Filmkrets **6500**
Tidskriften Folkuniversitetet (SWE ISSN 1400-190X) **3005**
Tidskriften Golf till Tak *see* Golv till Tak **4557**
Tidskriften Heimdal (SWE ISSN 0040-6988) **7189**
Tidskriften Hjaernstorm *see* Hjaernstorm **493**
Tidskriften Jabbok *see* Jabbok **7652**
Tidskriften Kraftsport *see* Tynglyftaren **8213**
• Tidskriften Kuba (SWE ISSN 1402-8638) **4315**
Tidskriften Laboratoriet *see* Laboratoriet **5908**
Tidskriften Munskaenken *see* Munskaenken med Vinjournalen **607**
Tidskriften Nyliberalen *see* Nyliberalen **7160**
Tidskriften Oeverlaekaren *see* Sjukhuslaekaren **5715**
Tidskriften Opera (SWE ISSN 1651-3770) **6623**
• Tidskriften Svenskt Konsthantverk (SWE ISSN 1652-3687) **540**
Tidskriften Vaegmaestaren *see* Vaegmaestaren **8519**
Tidskriften Vest *see* Vest **7928**
Tidsperspektiv (SWE ISSN 1404-8280) **420**
• ➤ Tidsskrift for Arbejdsliv (DNK ISSN 1399-1442) **1710**
• Tidsskrift for Biavl (DNK ISSN 0900-0801) **162**
Tidsskrift for Boerne- og Ungdomskultur (DNK ISSN 0907-6581) **2169**
Tidsskrift for Dansk Faareavl *see* Faar **286**
Tidsskrift for Dansk Politi *see* Dansk Politi **2650**
Tidsskrift for Dansk Sundhedsvaesen (DNK ISSN 0909-6388) **4112**
• ➤ Tidsskrift for Eiendomsrett (NOR ISSN 1504-3495) **4905**
• ➤ Tidsskrift for Erstatningsrett (NOR ISSN 1503-6782) **4881**
• Tidsskrift for Familierett, Arverett og Barnevernrettslige Spoergsmaal (NOR ISSN 1503-2965) **4914**
• ➤ Tidsskrift for Forretningsjus (NOR ISSN 0805-4355) **4882**
Tidsskrift for Groenlands Retsvaesen/The Greenland Law Reports (GRL ISSN 0040-6880) **4796**
• ➤ Tidsskrift for Islamforskning (DNK ISSN 1901-9580) **7716**
• Tidsskrift for Jordemoedre (DNK ISSN 0106-1836) **6005**
Tidsskrift for Jordmoedre (NOR ISSN 1503-3244) **6005**
Tidsskrift for Kaninavl (DNK ISSN 0900-3401) **302**
Tidsskrift for Kirke, Religion, Samfunn *see* Nordic Journal of Religion and Society **7666**
➤ Tidsskrift for Kjoennsforskning (NOR ISSN 0809-6341) **8903**
Tidsskrift for Kognitiv Terapi (NOR ISSN 1504-3142) **7412**
➤ Tidsskrift for Kulturforskning (NOR ISSN 1502-7473) **358**
Tidsskrift for Landoekonomi (DNK ISSN 0040-7119) **162**
Tidsskrift for Miljoe (DNK ISSN 1603-8398) **4796**
Tidsskrift for Museumsformidling *see* Dansk Tidsskrift for Museumsformidling **6523**
• Tidsskrift for Psykisk Helsearbeid (NOR ISSN 1503-6707) **6188**
• Tidsskrift for Rettsvitenskap (NOR ISSN 0040-7143) **4796**
• ➤ Tidsskrift for Samfunnsforskning (NOR ISSN 0040-716X) **8010**
• Tidsskrift for Skatter og Afgifter (DNK ISSN 0908-8431) **1951**
Tidsskrift for Soevaesen (DNK ISSN 0040-7186) **6449**
• Tidsskrift for Sprogforskning (DNK ISSN 1603-5925) **5187**
• ➤ Tidsskrift for Strafferett (NOR ISSN 1502-685X) **4899**
• Tidsskrift for Teologi og Kirke (NOR ISSN 0040-7194) **7777**
• ➤ Tidsskrift for Ungdomsforskning (NOR ISSN 1502-7759) **2169**
Tidsskrift for Velferdsforskning (NOR ISSN 0809-2052) **8074**
Tidsskrift med Nordisk Poesi paa Nettet *see* Splints & Co **5435**
Tidsskrift om Islam & Kristendom (DNK ISSN 1902-5823) **7690**
Tidsskriftet Antropologi *see* Antropologi **328**
Tidsskriftet den Frie Laererskole (DNK ISSN 1903-5632) **2919**
Tidsskriftet Groenland *see* Groenland (Charlottenlund) **4013**
Tidsskriftet Sykepleien *see* Sykepleien **5982**
Tidsspegel *see* Medvind **2886**
Tie ja Liikenne (FIN ISSN 0355-7855) **3285**
Tie Lines (USA) **2250**
Tiebreak/Swedish Tennis (SWE ISSN 1653-2546) **8249**
• ➤ Tiedao Gongcheng Xuebao/Railway Engineering Society. Journal (CHN ISSN 1006-2106) **8626**
• Tiedao Jianzhu/Railway Engineering (CHN ISSN 1003-1995) **8626**
• Tiedao Jianzhu Jishu/Railway Construction Technology (CHN ISSN 1009-4539) **8626**
• Tiedao Jiche Cheliang/Railway Locomotive & Car (CHN ISSN 1008-7842) **8626**
• Tiedao Jingguan Gaodeng Zhuanke Xuexiao Xuebao/Railway Police College. Journal (CHN) **8626**
• Tiedao Jishu Jiandu/Railway Quality Control (CHN ISSN 1006-9178) **8626**
Tiedao Keyanbao (CHN) **8626**
• Tiedao Laodong Anquan Weisheng yu Huan-bao/Railway Occupational Safety Health & Environmental Protection (CHN ISSN 1003-1197) **8626**
Tiedao Laodong Weisheng Tongxun *see* Tiedao Laodong Anquan Weisheng yu Huan-bao **8626**
Tiedao Shi-Yuan Xuebao (Ziran Kexueban)/Suzhou Railway Teachers College. Journal *see* Suzhou Keji Xueyuan Xuebao (Ziran Kexue Ban) **7921**
• Tiedao Tongxin Xinhao/Railway Signalling & Communication (CHN ISSN 1000-7458) **8626**
• ➤ Tiedao Xuebao/China Railway Society. Journal (CHN ISSN 1001-8360) **8626**
Tiedao Yixue/Railway Medical Journal *see* Xiandai Yixue **5732**
• Tiedao Yunshu yu Jingji/Railway Transportation and Economics (CHN ISSN 1003-1421) **8626**
Tiedao Zhishi/Railway Knowledge (CHN ISSN 1000-0372) **8626**
• Tiedao Zhuangxie yu Jizhuangxiang Yunshu/Railway Freight Transport (CHN ISSN 1004-2024) **8626**
Tiede (FIN ISSN 1457-9030) **7923**
➤ Tiede ja Ase (FIN ISSN 0358-8882) **6449**
Tiede & Edistys (FIN ISSN 0356-3677) **3839**
• Tiedepolitiikka (FIN ISSN 0782-0674) **7189**
Tiedonantaja (FIN ISSN 0356-1631) **3839**
Tiefbau (DEU ISSN 0944-8780) **1040**
Tiefkuehl Compact (DEU ISSN 1619-327X) **3666**
Tiefkuehl-Report (DEU ISSN 0941-9128) **4127**
• Tielu Jisuanji Yingyong/Railway Computer Application (CHN ISSN 1005-8451) **8626**
Tiem (NLD ISSN 1572-5472) **1798**
• El Tiempo (COL) **3830**
Tiempo *see* Tiempo de Hoy **3954**
Tiempo (GBR ISSN 0962-7030) **3470**
Tiempo (GTM) **3874**
• Tiempo (HND) **3875**
El Tiempo (USA) **3568**
Tiempo (USA) **3568**
• Tiempo (Chihuahua) (MEX ISSN 1563-8960) **3911**
Tiempo Actual (CRI) **3920**
Tiempo de Educar (MEX ISSN 1665-0824) **2919**
• Tiempo de Hoy (ESP ISSN 0213-1951) **3954**
• Tiempo de Paz (ESP ISSN 0212-8926) **7268**
• Tiempo Fueguino (ARG) **3792**
Tiempo Latino News *see* The Urban Latino News (San Francisco) **3570**
• Tiempo Libre (MEX ISSN 1405-5406) **3911**
El Tiempo Libre (USA) **3568**
• Tiempo y Escritura (MEX) **4164**
Tiempo y Espacio (VEN) **4315**
• Los Tiempos (BOL ISSN 1563-8200) **3803**
Tiempos de America (ESP ISSN 1138-1310) **4315**
Tiempos de Ciencia (MEX ISSN 0186-5730) **7923**
Tiempos del Mundo (New York) *see* Tiempos del Mundo. Edicion Hemisferica **3792**
Tiempos del Mundo (Washington, DC) *see* Tiempos del Mundo. Edicion Hemisferica **3792**
Tiempos del Mundo. Argentina (ARG) **3792**
• Tiempos del Mundo. Bolivia (BOL ISSN 1605-0789) **3803**
• Tiempos del Mundo. Chile (CHL) **3822**
• Tiempos del Mundo. Edicion Hemisferica (USA ISSN 1932-5290) **3792**
• Tiempos del Mundo. Guatemala (GTM ISSN 1605-0797) **3874**
• Tiempos del Mundo. Mexico (MEX ISSN 1605-0843) **3911**
• Tiempos del Mundo. Nicaragua (NIC ISSN 1605-0649) **3821**
• Tiempos del Mundo. Paraguay (PRY ISSN 1605-086X) **3927**
Tiempos Medicos (ESP ISSN 0210-9999) **5722**
• Tiempos Modernos (ESP ISSN 1699-7778) **4164**
Tiempos Nuevos (HND) **3875**
Tien Phong/Vanguard (VNM) **7189**
Tien Phong Chu Nhat/Sunday Vanguard (VNM) **2217**
Tien Phong Cuoi Thang/Monthly Vanguard (VNM) **2217**
Tiengemeten Nieuws *see* Tij Schrift Tiengemeten **8993**
Das Tier (CHE ISSN 1017-1576) **965**
Tier - A B C (DEU ISSN 1864-3531) **6816**
† Tier Bild (DEU ISSN 1610-7160) **8993**
Tier International (DEU) **965**
Tieraerztliche Praxis. Ausgabe G: Grosstiere - Nutztiere (DEU ISSN 1434-1220) **8808**
➤ Tieraerztliche Praxis. Ausgabe K: Kleintiere - Heimtiere (DEU ISSN 1434-1239) **8808**
➤ Tieraerztliche Umschau (DEU ISSN 0049-3864) **8808**
Tieraerztlicher Central-Anzeiger *see* Berliner und Muenchener Tieraerztliche Wochenschrift **8794**
• Tierarzthelferin Konkret (DEU ISSN 1614-8754) **8808**
• Tierarztliche-Hochschule-Anzeiger (DEU ISSN 0720-2237) **8808**
Tierarztliche Hochschule-Forschung fuers Leben (DEU ISSN 0947-0956) **8808**
Tiere - Freunde fuers Leben (DEU) **965**
Tiere in Unserer Welt (DEU) **965**
† Tiere Unsere Besten Freunde (DEU) **8993**
Tierfreund (DEU ISSN 0342-3018) **2629**
Tiergarten Schoenbrunn - Geschichte (AUT ISSN 1994-5116) **965**
Tierische Nebenprodukte Nachrichten (DEU) **3513**
• La Tierra (ESP) **162**
La Tierra (USA ISSN 0163-0695) **420**
Tierra Adentro (CHL ISSN 0717-1609) **162**
Tierra Amiga (URY ISSN 0797-8871) **3470**
Tierra Firme (VEN ISSN 0798-2968) **8010**
Tierra Grande (USA ISSN 1070-0234) **7614**
Tierra Nuestra, Visiones Latinoamericanos (NIC) **3821**
• Tierra Tropical (CRI ISSN 1659-2751) **3470**
Tierra y Tecnologia (ESP ISSN 1131-5016) **2771**
Tierras de Leon (ESP ISSN 0495-5773) **3954**
➤ Das Tierreich (DEU ISSN 0040-7305) **965**
Tierschuetzer *see* Tier - A B C **6816**
Tierwelt (CHE) **915**
➤ Tierwelt Deutschlands (DEU ISSN 0082-4305) **965**
▼ Tierwelt Heute (DEU ISSN 1863-9569) **6816**
Tieteen Kuvalehti *see* Illustreret Videnskab **7865**
Tieteen Kuvalehti *see* Illustrerad Vetenskap **7864**
Tieteen Kuvalehti *see* Illustrert Vitenskap **7865**
• Tieteessa Tapahtuu (FIN ISSN 0781-7916) **7923**
• Tietitekniikkaa Yliopistlle (FIN ISSN 1796-8607) **2439**
Tietoa Euroopasta *see* Documentation Europeene **8366**
Tietoaika *see* Tieto&Trendit **8409**
• Tieto&Trendit (FIN ISSN 1795-9799) **8409**
• Tietokone (FIN ISSN 0359-4947) **2583**
• Tietolinja (FIN ISSN 1239-9132) **5050**
Tietosuoja/Dataskydd (FIN ISSN 0786-5767) **4853**
Tietoviikko (FIN ISSN 0359-8543) **2439**
Tiferet (USA) **5389**
† Tiffany (DEU ISSN 0949-5525) **8993**
Tiffany (HUN ISSN 0865-4158) **5412**
† Tiffany Duo (DEU ISSN 0949-5533) **8993**
Tiffany Lieben und Lachen (DEU ISSN 1616-7287) **5412**
Tiffany Sexy (DEU ISSN 1439-9490) **5412**
Tiflologia per l'Integrazione (ITA ISSN 1825-1374) **4085**
The Tiger (USA) **2303**
Tiger Beat (USA ISSN 1932-796X) **2217**
Tiger Paper (THA ISSN 1014-2789) **2629**
Tiger Tales (USA) **8607**
Tigermaedchen (DEU) **2217**
▼ Tigers (Year) Corner (USA ISSN 1942-1400) **8249**
Tigertail (USA ISSN 1545-5025) **5436**
Tiggers Spielekiste (DEU) **2217**
Tight Lines *see* Stywe Lyne **8336**
Le Tigre (FRA ISSN 1778-9796) **3842**
TiHo-Anzeiger *see* Tierarztliche-Hochschule-Anzeiger **8808**
TiHo-Forschung fuers Leben *see* Tierarztliche Hochschule-Forschung fuers Leben **8808**
Tij Schrift (NLD ISSN 1872-0242) **2629**
† Tij Schrift Tiengemeten (NLD ISSN 1871-9252) **8993**
Al-Tijarah (UAE) **1410**
Al-Tijarah (Jeddah) (SAU) **1410**
• De Tijd (BEL ISSN 0772-0890) **1183**
Tijding (NLD ISSN 0167-1057) **7742**
Tijdingen *see* Boek.Bedrijf - V B V B **7553**
Tijdingen (NLD ISSN 1872-3446) **2629**
• Tijdschrift Aanbestedingsrecht (NLD ISSN 1573-9910) **7614**
Tijdschrift Administratie (NLD ISSN 1388-2635) **1798**
Tijdschrift Antropologie en Ontwikkelingsstudies (NLD ISSN 1873-6092) **358**
Tijdschrift Conflicthantering (NLD ISSN 1872-0765) **4796**
Tijdschrift Controlling (NLD ISSN 1389-7713) **1302**
Tijdschrift der Openbare Werken van Belgie *see* Annales des Travaux Publics de Belgique **3259**
Tijdschrift Erfrecht (NLD ISSN 1874-1681) **4905**
Tijdschrift Financieel Management *see* Finance & Control **1342**
Tijdschrift Financieel Management (Amsterdam) (NLD) **1798**
Tijdschrift Financiering, Zekerheden en Involventiepraktijk (NLD) **4882**
Tijdschrift Fiscaal Ondernemingsrecht *see* Fiscaal Ondernemingsrecht **1925**
Tijdschrift Geestelijke Verzorging (NLD ISSN 1567-3499) **6188**
Tijdschrift GezondheidsVoorlichting *see* G **7518**
Tijdschrift Jeugdbeleid (NLD ISSN 1873-9482) **2169**
Tijdschrift Kanker (NLD ISSN 0923-8018) **6035**
Tijdschrift Klinische Psychologie (BEL ISSN 1378-8647) **7412**
Tijdschrift Lucht (NLD ISSN 1871-4773) **3491**
Tijdschrift Luchtrecht *see* Journaal Luchtrecht **63**
Tijdschrift Management en Informatie *see* Management Executive **1775**
Tijdschrift Ontwikkelings Studies, Kop of Munt *see* Tijdschrift Antropologie en Ontwikkelingsstudies **358**
Tijdschrift over Angst en Depressie *see* Silhouet **6185**
Tijdschrift Overheid en Personeel (NLD ISSN 1874-5962) **4796**
Tijdschrift Politieke Ekonomie Digitaal *see* T P E Digitaal **7187**
Tijdschrift Rechtsdocumentatie (BEL ISSN 0771-0704) **4825**
Tijdschrift Schrijven *see* Schrijven Magazine **5368**
Tijdschrift van de Periodieke Pers *see* Revue de la Presse Periodique **4583**
Tijdschrift van de Politierechters *see* Journal des Juges de Police **4699**
Tijdschrift van de Post *see* Revue de la Poste **2355**
Tijdschrift van de Vrederechters *see* Journal des Juges de Paix **4699**
Tijdschrift Vereniging voor Verwarming en Luchtbehandeling Magazine *see* T V V L Magazine **4127**
Tijdschrift Vervoerswetenschap (NLD ISSN 1571-9227) **8513**
Tijdschrift voor Agrarisch Recht (NLD ISSN 1874-9674) **162**
• Tijdschrift voor Ambtenarenrecht (NLD ISSN 0168-5848) **4796**
Tijdschrift voor Antilliaans Recht - Justicia (ANT ISSN 1382-0222) **4796**
Tijdschrift voor Arbeidsvraagstukken (NLD ISSN 0169-2216) **1710**
Tijdschrift voor Artsen voor Verstandelijk Gehandicapten (NLD ISSN 1871-6172) **6188**
• Tijdschrift voor Bedrijfs- en Verzekeringsgeneeskunde (NLD ISSN 0929-600X) **5722**
Tijdschrift voor Bedrijfsadministratie *see* Accounting **8928**
Tijdschrift voor Belgisch Burgerlijk Recht/Revue Generale de Droit Civil Belge (BEL ISSN 0775-2814) **4843**
Tijdschrift voor Belgisch Handelsrecht *see* Revue de Droit Commercial Belge **4774**
Tijdschrift voor Bestuurswetenschappen en Publiekrecht (BEL ISSN 0040-7437) **4796**
▼ ➤ Tijdschrift voor Bloedtransfusie/Journal of Blood Transfusion (NLD ISSN 1875-9424) **5941**
Tijdschrift voor Boek- en Bibliotheekwezen *see* Quaerendo **7571**
Tijdschrift voor Bouwrecht en Onroerend Goed (BEL ISSN 1781-989X) **1040**
Tijdschrift voor Civiele Rechtspleging (NLD ISSN 0929-8649) **4843**
Tijdschrift voor Clientgerichte Psychotherapie (NLD ISSN 1380-7161) **7412**
Tijdschrift voor Coaching (NLD ISSN 1877-0959) **1798**
• Tijdschrift voor Communicatiewetenschap (NLD ISSN 1384-6930) **2342**
Tijdschrift voor Consumentenrecht *see* Tijdschrift voor Consumentenrecht en Handelspraktijken **2641**
• Tijdschrift voor Consumentenrecht en Handelspraktijken (NLD ISSN 1871-3947) **2641**
Tijdschrift voor Criminologie (NLD ISSN 0165-182X) **2670**
Tijdschrift voor de Leefomgeving *see* Werkplaats voor de Leefomgeving **169**
Tijdschrift voor de Onderwijspraktijk *see* School en Wet **3031**
Het Tijdschrift voor de Politie (NLD ISSN 0165-0122) **2670**
Tijdschrift voor de Preventie, Verzuim en Reintegratie *see* B G Magazine **1666**
Tijdschrift voor de Rechterlijke Macht *see* Trema **4798**
† Tijdschrift voor de Sociale Sector (NLD ISSN 0921-2116) **8993**
➤ Tijdschrift voor Diergeneeskunde/Netherlands Journal of Veterinary Science (NLD ISSN 0040-7453) **8808**
Tijdschrift voor Economie en Management *see* Review of Business and Economics **1165**
• ➤ Tijdschrift voor Economische en Sociale Geografie/Journal of Economic and Social Geography (GBR ISSN 0040-747X) **4031**
Tijdschrift voor Effectenrecht *see* Tijdschrift voor Financieel Recht **1951**
• ➤ Tijdschrift voor Entomologie (NLD ISSN 0040-7496) **860**
Tijdschrift voor Ergonomie (NLD ISSN 0921-4348) **6688**
• Tijdschrift voor Familie- en Jeugdrecht (NLD ISSN 0165-0084) **4915**
➤ Tijdschrift voor Fertiliteitsonderzoek (NLD ISSN 0921-7304) **6005**
Tijdschrift voor Filosofie (BEL ISSN 1370-575X) **6957**
Tijdschrift voor Financieel Recht (NLD ISSN 1574-7913) **1951**
• Tijdschrift voor Fiscaal Recht (BEL) **1951**
Tijdschrift voor Formeel Belastingrecht (NLD ISSN 1389-9112) **4882**
Tijdschrift voor Gemeenterecht (BEL ISSN 0775-3217) **7504**
Tijdschrift voor Genderstudies (NLD ISSN 1388-3186) **8903**
• ➤ Tijdschrift voor Geneeskunde (BEL ISSN 0371-683X) **5722**

Title

• Tochka Zoru (UKR) **3965**
Tochu Kaso/Cordyceps (JPN ISSN 0911-1271) **820**
• Tocqueville Connection (USA) **3842**
Tocqueville Reeks (NLD ISSN 1871-160X) **7189**
• ➤ Tocqueville Review/Revue Tocqueville (CAN ISSN 0730-479X) **8144**
TOCS-IN *see* T O C S - I N **2242**
Toda Kensetsu Gijutsu Kenkyu Hokoku/Toda Technical Research Report (JPN ISSN 0910-917X) **1040**
Toda Technical Research Report *see* Toda Kensetsu Gijutsu Kenkyu Hokoku **1040**
Todai Suisan Jikkenjo Gyoseki/University of Tokyo. Faculty of Agriculture. Fisheries Laboratory. Contributions (JPN ISSN 0495-7903) **3610**
➤ Todas as Letras (BRA ISSN 1517-1000) **5389**
Today *see* Jintian **3826**
Today *see* Danas **5213**
† Today (NZL) **8993**
Today *see* Jintian **5313**
Today (Boston, 1977) (USA) **2439**
Today (Buffalo) (USA) **7412**
Today (Lawson) (AUS ISSN 1030-0295) **7777**
Today & Tomorrow (USA) **3990**
• Today at N A S A (U.S. National Aeronautics and Space Administration, Public Affairs Office) (USA) **72**
† Today Fax (ITA) **8993**
Today I Love English (ESP ISSN 1578-3081) **5187**
Today in Africa (KEN) **7742**
Today in Cardiology *see* Cardiology Today **5780**
Today in English (FRA ISSN 1154-5992) **2217**
Today in Medicine. Diabetology and Endocrinology (USA ISSN 1042-2838) **5900**
Today in Medicine. Family Practice (USA ISSN 1054-8521) **5722**
Today in Medicine. Gastroenterology (USA ISSN 1048-6771) **5932**
Today in Medicine. Internal Medicine Report (USA ISSN 1048-6755) **5949**
Today in Medicine. Musculoskeletal Disorders *see* Today in Medicine. Musculoskeletal Medicine **6227**
Today in Medicine. Musculoskeletal Medicine (USA ISSN 1048-6763) **6227**
Today in Medicine. Obstetrics & Gynecology (USA ISSN 1053-7651) **6005**
Today in Medicine. Respiratory Disease (USA ISSN 1042-2846) **6220**
Today in Mississippi (USA ISSN 1052-2433) **3161**
Today leader *see* Young Adult Today. Leader Guide **7695**
Today Literary Magazine *see* Jintian **5313**
Today Morning Express *see* Jinri Zaobao **3826**
Today Nurse *see* Dangdai Hushi **5957**
• Today on AgWeb (USA) **162**
Today Science and Technology *see* Jinri Keji **7871**
Today World Trade Opportunities Digest (SGP) **1584**
• Today@nasa.gov (USA) **72**
Today's Anaesthetist (GBR ISSN 0969-0166) **5774**
Today's Arizona Woman (Scottsdale) (USA) **8886**
Today's Arizona Woman Business Directory (USA) **2031**
Today's Astrologer (USA ISSN 1067-1439) **567**
▼ Today's Auto Guide (USA ISSN 1947-5128) **8607**
Today's Black Woman (USA ISSN 1099-582X) **8886**
Today's Bluesuit Mom (USA ISSN 1547-2280) **8886**
Today's Bride (CAN ISSN 0226-1758) **5561**
• Today's C P A (USA ISSN 0889-4337) **1302**
Today's Caregiver (USA) **4057**
Today's Catholic (Fort Wayne) (USA ISSN 0891-1533) **7820**
Today's Catholic (San Antonio) (USA ISSN 0745-3612) **7820**
• Today's Catholic Teacher (USA ISSN 0040-8441) **2920**
Today's Challenge (NGA ISSN 0189-0557) **7742**
• Today's Chicago Woman (USA ISSN 1071-3786) **8886**
Today's Child (USA ISSN 1524-5896) **2169**
Today's Chiropractic *see* Today's Chiropractic Lifestyle **5807**
• Today's Chiropractic Lifestyle (USA ISSN 1931-7085) **5807**
• Today's Christian (USA ISSN 1547-5085) **3991**
Today's Christian Doctor (USA) **5722**
Today's Christian Man (USA ISSN 1538-6775) **7777**
Today's Christian Teen (USA ISSN 1537-0135) **7690**
† • Today's Christian Woman (USA ISSN 0163-1799) **8993**
Today's Creative Home Arts (USA ISSN 1539-1183) **522**
Today's Dads (USA ISSN 1062-1768) **4915**
Today's Diet & Nutrition (USA ISSN 1559-5110) **6669**
Today's Dietitian (USA ISSN 1540-4269) **6669**
Today's Emergency (GBR ISSN 1360-1938) **6074**
• Today's Engineer (USA) **3333**
• Today's F D A (Florida Dental Association) (USA ISSN 1048-5317) **5868**
Today's F F A (Future Farmer) (USA) **162**
Today's Facility Manager (USA ISSN 1059-0307) **1855**
Today's Family (USA) **2169**
Today's Family Home Plans (USA ISSN 1059-5252) **459**
Today's Farm (IRL ISSN 0791-4660) **162**
Today's Farmer (USA ISSN 0739-0092) **162**
Today's Feed Lotting (AUS ISSN 1034-6147) **275**
▼ Today's Financial Women (USA ISSN 1935-7842) **1386**
† Today's Fishkeeper (GBR ISSN 1475-8709) **8993**
Today's Garden Center (USA ISSN 1553-0868) **3757**
Today's Golfer (GBR ISSN 0955-4939) **8249**
Today's Grocer (USA ISSN 1529-4420) **3682**
Today's Groom (USA) **5561**
Today's Health and Wellness (USA ISSN 1531-8044) **6998**
Today's Health & Wellness *see* Today's Health and Wellness **6998**
Today's Health Care (USA) **5722**
▼ Today's Home Educator Magazine (USA ISSN 1944-0197) **3086**
Today's Hospital Gift Shop Business (USA ISSN 1082-0434) **1846**
• Today's Hospitalist (USA) **4112**
Today's Insurance Professionals (USA ISSN 1538-0963) **4525**
Today's Investor (USA ISSN 1042-8127) **1655**
▼ • Today's Israel (USA ISSN 1935-5025) **8761**
Today's Lawyer (USA) **4797**
† Today's Lifestyles Home Plans (USA) **8993**
Today's Light (USA ISSN 1084-4775) **7777**
Today's Lighting Distributor (USA) **4563**
Today's Living (HKG ISSN 1018-578X) **4551**
Today's Manager (SGP) **1798**
• Today's Medical Developments (USA ISSN 1941-8817) **5722**
Today's Missal (USA ISSN 0199-8803) **7820**
Today's O E A (Oregon Education Association) (USA ISSN 1525-3589) **2920**
• Today's Officer (Alexandria) (USA ISSN 1541-5252) **6449**
Today's Outlook (LBN) **1522**
Today's Parent *see* Canadian Today's Parent **2146**
Today's Parent (IRL) **2169**
• Today's Parent, Baby & Toddler (CAN ISSN 1498-2625) **2169**
• Today's Parent, Pregnancy & Birth (CAN ISSN 1702-8590) **6005**
Today's Parent Toronto! *see* Canadian Today's Parent **2146**
Today's Parish *see* Today's Parish Minister **7820**
Today's Parish Minister (USA ISSN 1936-7465) **7820**
Today's Pawnbroker (USA ISSN 1068-090X) **1655**
Today's Pentecostal Evangel (USA ISSN 1540-9643) **7742**
• Today's Photographer International (USA) **6977**
Today's Pilot (GBR) **72**
Today's Playground (USA) **2169**
Today's Railways (GBR ISSN 1354-2753) **8626**
Today's Readings (USA ISSN 1098-7975) **7777**
• Today's Refinery (USA ISSN 1048-0935) **6795**
Today's Reports *see* United States Government Accountability Office. Today's Reports **7474**
• Today's School Psychologist (USA ISSN 1098-9277) **7412**
• ➤ Today's Science on File (USA ISSN 1059-9274) **7923**
Today's Single (USA ISSN 0748-7355) **7944**
Today's Supervisor (USA ISSN 0734-3302) **6688**
Today's SurgiCenter *see* SurgiStrategies **4112**
Today's Therapeutic Trends (USA ISSN 0741-2320) **5722**
Today's Truck & Sport Utility Performance (USA) **8607**
• Today's Trucking (CAN ISSN 0837-1512) **8676**
Today's Trustee (ZAF ISSN 1818-1783) **1656**
Today's Value Investor (USA) **1656**
Today's Vintage Magazine (USA) **369**
▼ Today's Wound Clinic (USA ISSN 1938-6311) **6074**
• Today's Zaman (TUR) **3963**
▼ Toddler (USA ISSN 1935-2751) **2169**
Toddlers' Pictorial *see* You'er Huabao **2223**
Toden/Tokyo Electric Power Company. Journal (JPN ISSN 0285-6247) **3333**
Toden Repoto/Tokyo Electric Power Company. Report (JPN) **3161**
Todo es Historia (ARG ISSN 0040-8611) **4164**
Todo Hospital (ESP ISSN 0212-1972) **4112**
Todo para Bebes (ARG ISSN 1669-5461) **2169**
Todo Perros (ESP ISSN 1134-7252) **6816**
Todo Plantas (ESP) **3752**
Todos Amigos (ITA ISSN 0997-0282) **5187**
• Todotransporte (ESP ISSN 0212-8357) **8513**
Todotransporte Digital *see* Todotransporte **8513**
• Todovida (URY ISSN 1510-1061) **315**
Toeff (CHE ISSN 1424-0149) **8269**
Toegang tot de Psychotherapie Internationaal (NLD ISSN 1566-0273) **7412**
Toegangscontrole *see* Weekblad Facilitair & Gebouwbeheer **1801**
Toegepast Natuurwetenschappelijk Onderzoek Magazine *see* T N O Magazine **7922**
Toegepast Natuurwetenschappelijk Onderzoek Magazine. T N O Defensie en Veiligheid *see* T N O Magazine. T N O Defensie en Veiligheid **7471**
Toegepast Natuurwetenschappelijk Onderzoek Magazine. T N O Industrie en Techniek *see* T N O Magazine. T N O Industrie en Techniek **1905**
Toegepast Natuurwetenschappelijk Onderzoek Magazine. T N O Informatie- en Communicatietechnologie *see* T N O Magazine. T N O Informatie- en Communicatietechnologie **2439**
Toegepast Natuurwetenschappelijk Onderzoek Magazine. T N O Kwaliteit van Leven *see* T N O Magazine. T N O Kwaliteit van Leven **7543**
Toegepast Natuurwetenschappelijk Onderzoek Magazine. T N O Ruimte en Infrastructuur *see* T N O Magazine. T N O Ruimte en Infrastructuur **3285**
Toegepaste Plantwetenskap *see* Applied Plant Science **776**
Toej (DNK ISSN 0107-0290) **2262**
Toelvumal (ISL ISSN 1021-724X) **2440**
Toen (NLD ISSN 1872-0099) **5050**
• Toensbergs Blad (NOR) **3925**
† Toer (NLD ISSN 1568-8763) **8993**
Toeractief (NLD ISSN 1573-0298) **8761**
Toerismee (NLD ISSN 0169-5738) **8761**
Toerusting *see* Toer **8993**
Toets (NLD ISSN 1872-5589) **7543**
Toetssteen (NLD ISSN 1871-3742) **3034**
Tof! (NLD ISSN 1871-1898) **4070**
Toga Calabrese (ITA ISSN 0040-8654) **4797**
Together *see* Gezondheid Samen Delen **1596**
Together (USA) **7690**
Together (Glendora) (USA ISSN 1937-4992) **7690**
Together (London, 1992) (GBR ISSN 0967-3857) **4603**
Together with Children (GBR ISSN 1361-1429) **7777**
• Toggolino (DEU) **2217**
Togo Dialogue (TGO) **3790**
Togo. Direction de la Meteorologie Nationale. Resume Annuel du Temps (TGO) **6396**
Togo. Direction de la Meteorologie Nationale. Resume Mensuel du Temps (TGO) **6396**
Togo. Direction de la Statistique. Bulletin Mensuel de Statistique (TGO) **8409**
Togo. Ministry of Economy and Finance. Bulletin de Statistiques (TGO) **1270**
Tohkai Orthopaedic Society of Traumatology. Journal *see* Tohkai Seikei Geka Gaisho Kenkyu Kaishi **6074**
• ➤ Tohkai Seikei Geka Gaisho Kenkyu Kaishi/Tohkai Orthopaedic Society of Traumatology. Journal (JPN ISSN 0915-2253) **6074**
• ➤ Tohkai Sekitsui Geka/Journal of Tohkai Spinal Surgery (JPN ISSN 0913-476X) **6074**
Toho Daigaku Rigakubu Seibutsu Gakka Gyoseki Hokoku/Toho University. Faculty of Science. Department of Biology. Research Report (JPN) **708**
Toho Gakuen Daigaku Kenkyu Kiyo/Toho Gakuen School of Music Faculty Bulletin (JPN ISSN 0385-5627) **6623**
Toho Gakuen School of Music Faculty Bulletin *see* Toho Gakuen Daigaku Kenkyu Kiyo **6623**
Toho Gakuho/Dongfang Xuebao (JPN ISSN 0304-2448) **562**
Toho Igakkai Zasshi *see* Toho University Medical Society. Journal **5723**
Toho Shukyo/Journal of Eastern Religions (JPN ISSN 0495-7180) **7690**
Toho University. Faculty of Science. Department of Biology. Research Report *see* Toho Daigaku Rigakubu Seibutsu Gakka Gyoseki Hokoku **708**
• ➤ Toho University Medical Society. Journal/Toho Igakkai Zasshi (JPN ISSN 0040-8670) **5723**
Tohogaku/Eastern Studies (JPN ISSN 0495-7199) **562**
Tohoku Association of Construction. News *see* Kokudo Kotsu Geppo Tohoku **1019**
Tohoku Chiho Choki Yoho Sokuho/Bulletin of Long Range Weather Forecasting of Tohoku District (JPN) **6396**
Tohoku Chiho Kisho Kenkyukaishi/Journal of Meteorological Research of Tohoku District (JPN ISSN 0563-6493) **6396**
Tohoku Daigaku Denki Tsushin Kenkyujo Chobisai Denshi Kairo Jikken Shisetsu Kenkyu Hokoku/Tohoku University. Research Institute of Electrical Communication. Laboratory for Microelectronics. Annual Report (JPN ISSN 0917-8600) **3115**
➤ Tohoku Daigaku Dentsu Danwakai Kiroku (JPN ISSN 0385-7719) **3333**
Tohoku Daigaku Kagaku Keisoku Kenkyujo Hokoku/Tohoku University. Research Institute for Scientific Measurements. Bulletin (JPN ISSN 0040-8689) **6407**
Tohoku Daigaku Kagaku Keisoku Kenkyujo Kenkyu Hokoku/Tohoku University. Research Institute for Scientific Measurements. Annual Report (JPN) **6407**
Tohoku Daigaku Kenkyujo Hokoku. A-shu: Butsurigaku, Kagaku, Yakingaku *see* Tohoku University. Science Reports of the Research Institutes. Series A: Physics, Chemistry, and Metallurgy **7043**
Tohoku Daigaku Kogakubu Zairyo Kyodo Kenkyu Shisetsu Hokoku *see* Tohoku University. Research Institute for Strength and Fracture of Materials. Reports **3359**
Tohoku Daigaku Rigakubu Chishitsugaku Koseibutsugaku Kyoshitsu Kenkyu Hobun Hokoku/Tohoku University. Faculty of Science. Institute of Geology and Paleontology. Contributions (JPN ISSN 0082-4658) **2771**
Tohoku Daigaku Rika Hokoku. Dai 3-shu, Gansekigaku Kobutsugaku Koshogaku *see* Tohoku University. Science Reports. Series 3: Mineralogy, Petrology and Economic Geology **6480**
Tohoku Daigaku Rika Hokoku, Dai-7-shu, Chirigaku *see* Tohoku University. Science Reports. Series 7: Geography **4031**
Tohoku Daigaku Ryutai Kagaku Kenkyujo Hokoku/Tohoku University. Institute of Fluid Science. Memoirs (JPN ISSN 0916-2860) **7043**
Tohoku Daigaku Sozai Kogaku Kenkyujo Iho/Tohoku University. Institute for Advanced Materials Processing. Bulletin (JPN ISSN 0919-4827) **6335**
Tohoku Denryoku K.K. Kenkyu Kiho/Tohoku Electric Power Co. Research Laboratory. Report (JPN ISSN 0285-5496) **3161**
Tohoku District Meteorological Observatory. Technical News *see* Tohoku Gijutsu Dayori **6396**
Tohoku Electric Power Co., Inc. Annual Report (Year) (JPN) **3333**
Tohoku Electric Power Co. Research Laboratory. Report *see* Tohoku Denryoku K.K. Kenkyu Kiho **3161**
Tohoku Engineering *see* Tohoku Gijutsu **3285**
Tohoku Engineering Office. Technical Materials *see* Tohoku Gijutsu Jimusho Gijutsu Shiryo **3285**
Tohoku Gakuin Daigaku Kogakubu Kenkyu Hokoku/Tohoku Gakuin University. Science and Engineering Reports (JPN ISSN 0286-5904) **3223**
Tohoku Gakuin Daigaku Ronshu. Eigo, Eibungaku *see* Tohoku Gakuin University Review **5389**
Tohoku Gakuin University Economic Review *see* Touhoku Gakuin Daigaku Keizaigaku Ronshuu **1183**
Tohoku Gakuin University Review/Tohoku Gakuin Daigaku Ronshu. Eigo, Eibungaku (JPN ISSN 0385-406X) **5389**
Tohoku Gakuin University. Science and Engineering Reports *see* Tohoku Gakuin Daigaku Kogakubu Kenkyu Hokoku **3223**
➤ Tohoku Geophysical Journal (JPN ISSN 0040-8794) **2791**
Tohoku Gijutsu/Tohoku Engineering (JPN) **3285**
Tohoku Gijutsu Dayori/Tohoku District Meteorological Observatory. Technical News (JPN ISSN 0289-3126) **6396**
Tohoku Gijutsu Jimusho Gijutsu Shiryo/Tohoku Engineering Office. Technical Materials (JPN) **3285**
Tohoku - Hokuriku Sugaku Kyoiku Kisoteki Kenkyu Hokoku (JPN ISSN 0913-221X) **5541**
Tohoku Igaku Zasshi *see* Tohoku Medical Journal **5723**
Tohoku Institute of Technology. Memoirs. Series 1. Science and Engineering *see* Tohoku Kogyo Daigaku Kiyo, 1. Rikogaku Hen **3223**
Tohoku Institute of Technology. Memoirs. Series 2: Humanities and Social Science (JPN ISSN 0285-3825) **4478**
Tohoku Journal of Agricultural Research (JPN ISSN 0040-8719) **255**
• ➤ The Tohoku Journal of Experimental Medicine (JPN ISSN 0040-8727) **5911**
Tohoku Journal of Obstetrics and Gynecology *see* Nihon Sanka Fujinka Gakkai Tohoku Rengo Chiho Bukai Kaishi **6000**
Tohoku Kogyo Daigaku Kiyo, 1. Rikogaku Hen/Tohoku Institute of Technology. Memoirs. Series 1. Science and Engineering (JPN ISSN 0285-3817) **3223**
Tohoku Kogyo Gijutsu Kenkyujo Hokoku *see* Tohoku National Industrial Research Institute. Reports **8443**
Tohoku Konchu/Journal of Entomology in Tohoku District (JPN ISSN 0913-5847) **860**
• ➤ Tohoku Mathematical Journal/Tohoku Sugaku Zasshi (JPN ISSN 0040-8735) **5541**
Tohoku Medical Journal/Tohoku Igaku Zasshi (JPN ISSN 0040-8700) **5723**
Tohoku National Industrial Research Institute. Reports/Tohoku Kogyo Gijutsu Kenkyujo Hokoku (JPN ISSN 0919-8881) **8443**
Tohoku no Dengen/Electric Power Resources in Tohoku District (JPN) **3161**
Tohoku no Koroni/Tohoku Society for Microbiology. Journal (JPN ISSN 0288-9463) **896**
Tohoku no Nogyo Kisho/Bulletin of the Agricultural Meteorology of Tohoku District (JPN ISSN 0287-1173) **6396**
Tohoku no Shizen/Nature of Tohoku (JPN ISSN 0910-7177) **7923**
Tohoku no Yuki to Seikatsu/Snow and Life in Tohoku (JPN ISSN 0917-6217) **2791**
➤ Tohoku Psychologica Folia (JPN ISSN 0040-8743) **7412**
Tohoku Seikei Saigai Geka Kiyo *see* Touhoku Seikei Saigai Geka Gakkai Zasshi **6074**
Tohoku Seikei Saigai Geka Kiyo/Tohoku Archives of Orthopaedic Surgery and Traumatology *see* Touhoku Seikei Saigai Geka Gakkai Zasshi **6074**
Tohoku Society for Microbiology. Journal *see* Tohoku no Koroni **896**
Tohoku Sugaku Zasshi *see* Tohoku Mathematical Journal **5541**
Tohoku University. Faculty of Science. Institute of Geology and Paleontology. Contributions *see* Tohoku Daigaku Rigakubu Chishitsugaku Koseibutsugaku Kyoshitsu Kenkyu Hobun Hokoku **2771**
Tohoku University. Institute for Advanced Materials Processing. Bulletin *see* Tohoku Daigaku Sozai Kogaku Kenkyujo Iho **6335**
Tohoku University. Institute of Fluid Science. Memoirs *see* Tohoku Daigaku Ryutai Kagaku Kenkyujo Hokoku **7043**

Title

10950 TOHOKU UNIVERSITY. INSTITUTE OF FLUID SCIENCE. REPORTS ULRICH'S PERIODICALS

Tohoku University. Institute of Fluid Science. Reports (JPN ISSN 0916-2879) **7043**
Tohoku University Museum. Bulletin (JPN ISSN 1346-2040) **6538**
Tohoku University. Record of Electrical and Communication Engineering Conversazione *see* Tohoku Daigaku Dentsu Danwakai Kiroku **3333**
Tohoku University. Research Institute for Scientific Measurements. Annual Report *see* Tohoku Daigaku Kagaku Keisoku Kenkyujo Kenkyu Hokoku **6407**
Tohoku University. Research Institute for Scientific Measurements. Bulletin *see* Tohoku Daigaku Kagaku Keisoku Kenkyujo Hokoku **6407**
Tohoku University. Research Institute for Strength and Fracture of Materials. Reports/Tohoku Daigaku Kogakubu Zairyo Kyodo Kenkyu Shisetsu Hokoku (JPN ISSN 0563-6590) **3359**
Tohoku University. Research Institute of Electrical Communication. Laboratory for Microelectronics. Annual Report *see* Tohoku Daigaku Denki Tsushin Kenkyujo Chobisai Denshi Kairo Jikken Shisetsu Kenkyu Hokoku **3115**
Tohoku University. Research Institute of Electrical Communication. Technical Report (JPN) **2342**
➤ Tohoku University. Science Reports of the Research Institutes. Series A: Physics, Chemistry, and Metallurgy/Tohoku Daigaku Kenkyujo Hokoku. A-shu: Butsurigaku, Kagaku, Yakingaku (JPN ISSN 0040-8808) **7043**
Tohoku University. Science Reports. Series 3: Mineralogy, Petrology and Economic Geology/Tohoku Daigaku Rika Hokoku. Dai 3-shu, Gansekigaku Kobutsugaku Koshogaku (JPN ISSN 0371-3903) **6480**
Tohoku University. Science Reports. Series 7: Geography/Tohoku Daigaku Rika Hokoku, Dai-7-shu, Chirigaku (JPN ISSN 0375-7854) **4031**
Tohoku University. Science Reports. Series 8: Physics and Astronomy (JPN ISSN 0388-5607) **7043**
Tohu Ahurea mo Aotearoa *see* Cultural Indicators for New Zealand **8148**
Tohuku Plant Association. News *see* Sennke **816**
Toike Oike (CAN ISSN 0049-4038) **3223**
The Toiler (GMB) **3843**
Toiletries & Cosmetics Industry *see* Business Ratio. The Toiletries & Cosmetics Industry **593**
Toiletries Plus Market Report *see* Key Note Plus Market Report. Toiletries **1896**
Toimielinhakemisto. Kuka Kukin on Euroopan Unionissa? *see* Interinstitutional Directory. Who's Who in the European Union? **643**
Toimisto *see* Portaali **1854**
• Toison d'Or (BEL ISSN 0040-8832) **4273**
Toit ja Toitumine *see* Food And Nutrition **3637**
La Toja (ESP) **4399**
Tojikiston (TJK) **3961**
• Tok Blong Pasifik (CAN ISSN 1196-8206) **8010**
Tokai Daigaku Kaiyo Kagaku Hakubutsukan Nenpo/Tokai University. Marine Science Museum. Annual Report (JPN ISSN 0287-2099) **2818**
Tokai Daigaku Kaiyo Kenkyujo Kenkyu Hokoku/Tokai University. Institute of Oceanic Research and Development. Bulletin (JPN ISSN 0289-680X) **2819**
Tokai Daigaku Kaiyo Kenkyujo Nenpo/Tokai University. Institute of Oceanic Research and Development. Annual Report (JPN ISSN 0287-1467) **2819**
Tokai Daigaku Kiyo. Bungakubu/Tokai University. Faculty of Letters. Bulletin (JPN ISSN 0563-6760) **4478**
Tokai Daigaku Kiyo. Gaikokugo Kyoiku Senta/Tokai University. Foreign Language Center. Bulletin (JPN ISSN 0389-3081) **5188**
Tokai Fossil Society. Journal *see* Kaseki no Tomo **6726**
• Tokai Journal of Experimental and Clinical Medicine (Online) (JPN) **5723**
Tokai Journal of Experimental and Clinical Medicine (Print) *see* Tokai Journal of Experimental and Clinical Medicine (Online) **5723**
Tokai Journal of Obstetrics and Gynecology *see* Tokai Sanka Fujinka Gakkai Zasshi **6005**
Tokai Sanka Fujinka Gakkai Zasshi/Tokai Journal of Obstetrics and Gynecology (JPN ISSN 0915-7204) **6005**
Tokai University. Faculty of Engineering. Proceedings (JPN ISSN 0388-0788) **3223**
Tokai University. Faculty of Letters. Bulletin *see* Tokai Daigaku Kiyo. Bungakubu **4478**
Tokai University. Foreign Language Center. Bulletin *see* Tokai Daigaku Kiyo. Gaikokugo Kyoiku Senta **5188**
Tokai University. Institute of Oceanic Research and Development. Annual Report *see* Tokai Daigaku Kaiyo Kenkyujo Nenpo **2819**
Tokai University. Institute of Oceanic Research and Development. Bulletin *see* Tokai Daigaku Kaiyo Kenkyujo Kenkyu Hokoku **2819**
Tokai University. Marine Science Museum. Annual Report *see* Tokai Daigaku Kaiyo Kagaku Hakubutsukan Nenpo **2818**
Tokai University. Marine Science Museum. Journal *see* Umi no Hakubutsukan **2819**
Tokai University. School of Information Technology and Electronics. Proceedings *see* Toukai Daigaku kiyou. Denshi Jouhou Gakubu **2551**
Tokai University. School of Marine Science and Technology. Journal *see* Umi, Shizen to Bunka **2819**
Tokai University. School of Science. Proceedings (JPN ISSN 0919-5025) **7923**
Tokan Gijutsu Nyusu/Tokyo District Meteorological Observatory. Technical Information News (JPN ISSN 0385-0625) **6396**
Tokei Joho *see* National Federation of Statistical Associations of Japan. Monthly Statistics of Japan **8389**
➤ Tokei Suri/Institute of Statistical Mathematics. Proceedings (JPN ISSN 0912-6112) **5549**
Tokei Suri Kenkyujo Kenkyuu Kyouiku Katsudou Houkoku (JPN) **8409**
Tokei Suri Kenkyujo Kenkyuu Ripooto/Institute of Statistical Mathematics. Research Report. General Series (JPN) **8409**
• Tokei Suri Kenkyujo Nyuusu/I S M News (JPN) **8409**
Tokei Suri Kenkyuzyo Kenkyu Ripoto/Institute of Statistical Mathematics. Research Report. General Series (JPN) **5542**
Tokeibu Shuyo/Head and Neck Cancer (JPN ISSN 1349-5747) **6035**
• Tokelau National Bibliography (NZL ISSN 1170-800X) **636**
Token and Medal Society Journal *see* T A M S Journal **6653**
Token Geppo/Token Monthly (JPN) **1040**
Token Monthly *see* Token Geppo **1040**
Tokin Electronics *see* Tokin Erekutoronikusu **3115**
Tokin Erekutoronikusu/Tokin Electronics (JPN) **3115**
• Tokion (JPN) **3901**
Tokion (USA ISSN 1939-3822) **5085**
Tokkyo/Patents (JPN ISSN 0285-3353) **6758**
Tokkyo Nyusu/Patent News (JPN ISSN 0385-9142) **6758**
Tokkyocho Nenpo/Patent Office. Annual Gazette (JPN) **6758**
• ➤ Toko-Ginecologia Practica (ESP ISSN 0040-8867) **6005**
Toksikologicheskii Vestnik/Toxicological Review (RUS ISSN 0869-7922) **3501**
Tokugikon/Japanese Patent Office Society. Journal (JPN) **6758**
Tokushima Daigaku Gakugei Kiyo/Tokushima University. Journal of Gakugei (JPN ISSN 0495-7601) **4478**
Tokushima Daigaku Sogo Kagakubu Ningen Shakai Bunka Kenkyu/Tokushima University. Faculty of Integrated Arts and and Sciences. Journal (JPN ISSN 0919-9411) **4478**
Tokushima Kagakushi Zasshi/Tokushima Society for the History of Science. Journal (JPN ISSN 0912-0599) **7923**
Tokushima-ken Kisho Geppo/Tokushima Prefecture. Monthly Report of Meteorology (JPN ISSN 0916-5231) **6396**
Tokushima-ken Shizen Hogo Kyokai Chosa Hokoku (JPN) **2629**
Tokushima Kenritsu Hakubutsukan Kenkyu Hokoku/Tokushima Prefectural Museum. Bulletin (JPN ISSN 0916-8001) **6538**
Tokushima Prefectural Museum. Bulletin *see* Tokushima Kenritsu Hakubutsukan Kenkyu Hokoku **6538**
Tokushima Prefecture. Monthly Report of Meteorology *see* Tokushima-ken Kisho Geppo **6396**
Tokushima Society for the History of Science. Journal *see* Tokushima Kagakushi Zasshi **7923**
Tokushima University. Faculty of Integrated Arts and Sciences. Journal *see* Tokushima Daigaku Sogo Kagakubu Ningen Shakai Bunka Kenkyu **4478**
Tokushima University. Journal of Gakugei *see* Tokushima Daigaku Gakugei Kiyo **4478**
Tokushima University. Journal of Mathematics *see* University of Tokushima. Journal of Mathematics **5545**
Tokushu Chorui Chosa (JPN) **915**
Tokushu Kyoiku Kenkyu Shisetsu Kenkyu Nempo/RIEEC Annual Report *see* Tokushu Kyouiku Kenkyuu Shisetsu Kenkyuu Houkoku **2920**
Tokushu Kyoiku Kenkyu Shisetsu Kenkyusei Kenkyu Hokoku *see* Tokushu Kyouiku Kenkyuu Shisetsu Kenkyuu Houkoku **2920**
Tokushu Kyokugaku Kenkyu/Japanese Journal of Special Education (JPN ISSN 0387-3374) **3048**
Tokushu Kyouiku Kenkyuu Shisetsu Kenkyuu Houkoku/Research Institute for the Education of Exceptional Children. Research Report (JPN ISSN 1346-910X) **2920**
Tokyo Art Directors Club Annual (JPN) **36**
Tokyo City Guide Tour Companion (JPN) **8761**
Tokyo Club Papers *see* Tokyo Kokusai Kenkyu Kurabu Ronbunshu **7268**
Tokyo Daigaku Aisotopu Sogo Senta Nyusu/University of Tokyo. Radioisotope Center. News (JPN ISSN 0916-3328) **3175**
Tokyo Daigaku Chokoatsu Denshi Kenbikyoshitsu Nenpo/University of Tokyo. Annual Report of High Voltage Electron Microscope (JPN ISSN 0387-4990) **7052**
Tokyo Daigaku Daigakuin Rigakukeikenkyuka Rigakubu Butsurigaku Kyoshitsu Nenji Kenkyu/University of Tokyo. School of Science. Department of Physics. Annual Report (JPN ISSN 0910-0709) **7043**
Tokyo Daigaku Genshiryoku Kenkyu Sogo Senta Nyusu/University of Tokyo. Research Center for Nuclear Science and Technology. News (JPN ISSN 0916-152X) **3175**
Tokyo Daigaku Jishin Kenkyujo Iho *see* University of Tokyo. Earthquake Research Institute. Bulletin **2791**
Tokyo Daigaku Kaiyo Kenkyujo *see* University of Tokyo. Ocean Research Institute. Bulletin **2820**
Tokyo Daigaku Kogakubu. Denki Kogaku Denshi Kogaku Iho/University of Tokyo. Electrical and Electronic Engineering Departments. Bulletin (JPN ISSN 0563-7929) **3333**
Tokyo Daigaku. Kogakubu. Doboku Kogakka. Ronbun Shuroku/University of Tokyo. Faculty of Engineering. Department of Civil Engineering. Transactions (JPN) **3285**
Tokyo Daigaku Kogakubu Kogakukei Kenkyuka Kiyo *see* University of Tokyo. School of Engineering. Journal **3225**
Tokyo Daigaku Rigakubu Chikaku Kagaku Jikken Shisetsu Iho/Laboratory for Earthquake Chemistry. Bulletin (JPN ISSN 0910-688X) **2717**
Tokyo Daigaku Rigakubu Fuzoku Rinkai Jikkenjo Nenpo/University of Tokyo. Misaki Marine Biological Station. Annual Report (JPN) **2819**
Tokyo Daigaku Shiryo Hensanjo kenkyu Kiyo/Historiographical Institute. Research Annual (JPN ISSN 0917-2416) **4164**
➤ Tokyo Daigaku Teoin Senta Dayori/University of Tokyo. Cryogenic Center. Report (JPN ISSN 1341-1810) **7057**
Tokyo Denki Daigaku Kogakubu Kenkyu Hokoku *see* Tokyo Denki University. Faculty of Engineering. Research Reports **3223**
Tokyo Denki Daigaku Rikogakubu Kiyo *see* Tokyo Denki University. Faculty of Science and Engineering. Research Activities **3223**
Tokyo Denki Daigaku Sogo Kenkyujo Nenpo/Tokyo Denki University. Research Institute for Technology. Annual Report (JPN) **3333**
Tokyo Denki University. Faculty of Engineering. General Education. Research Reports (JPN ISSN 0288-5530) **8010**
Tokyo Denki University. Faculty of Engineering. Research Reports/Tokyo Denki Daigaku Kogakubu Kenkyu Hokoku (JPN ISSN 0389-617X) **3223**
Tokyo Denki University. Faculty of Science and Engineering. Research Activities/Tokyo Denki Daigaku Rikogakubu Kiyo (JPN ISSN 0388-1989) **3223**
Tokyo Denki University. Research Institute for Technology. Annual Report *see* Tokyo Denki Daigaku Sogo Kenkyujo Nenpo **3333**
Tokyo Dental Association. Journal *see* Tokyo-to Shika Ishikai Zasshi **5868**
• Tokyo Dental College. Bulletin/Tokyo Shika Daigaku Obun Kiyo (JPN ISSN 0040-8891) **5868**
Tokyo Dental College Society Journal *see* Shika Gakuho **5865**
Tokyo District Meteorological Observatory. Geophysical Notes *see* Tokyo Kanku Chiho Kisho Kenkyukaishi **6396**
Tokyo District Meteorological Observatory. Technical Information News *see* Tokan Gijutsu Nyusu **6396**
Tokyo District Meteorological Observatory. Unusual Meteorological Report *see* Tokyo Kanku Ijo Kisho Hokoku **6396**
Tokyo Electric Power Company. Journal *see* Toden **3333**
Tokyo Electric Power Company. Report *see* Toden Repoto **3161**
Tokyo Gakugei Daigaku Kiyo. Dai 2-bumon, Jimbun Kagaku/Tokyo Gakugei University. Bulletin. Series 2, Humanities *see* Toukyou Gakugei Daigaku Kiyou. Jimbun Shakai Kagakukei. 1 **4478**
Tokyo Gakugei Daigaku Kiyo. Dai 3-bumon, Shakai Kagaku/Tokyo Gakugei University. Bulletin. Series 3, Social Sciences *see* Toukyou Gakugei Daigaku Kiyou. Jimbun Shakai Kagakukei. 2 **4478**
Tokyo Gakugei Daigaku Tokushu Kyoiku Kenkyu Shisetsu Hokoku/R I E E C Report (JPN ISSN 0386-3271) **3048**
Tokyo Gakugei University. Bulletin. Educational Sciences *see* Toukyou Gakugei Daigaku Kiyou. Sougou Kyouiku Kagakukei **2920**
Tokyo Gakugei University. Bulletin. Humanities and Social Sciences. 1 *see* Toukyou Gakugei Daigaku Kiyou. Jimbun Shakai Kagakukei. 1 **4478**
Tokyo Gakugei University. Bulletin. Humanities and Social Sciences. 2 *see* Toukyou Gakugei Daigaku Kiyou. Jimbun Shakai Kagakukei. 2 **4478**
Tokyo Geijutsu Daigaku Bijutsu Gakubu Kiyo/Tokyo National University of Fine Arts and Music. Faculty of Fine Arts. Bulletin (JPN ISSN 0563-8151) **522**
Tokyo Heart Journal *see* Shinposuru Shinzo Kenkyu **5799**
Tokyo Ika Daigaku Zasshi/Tokyo Medical University. Journal (JPN ISSN 0040-8905) **5723**
Tokyo Ika Shika Daigaku Seitai Zairyo Kogaku Kenkyujo Hokoku/Tokyo Medical and Dental University. Institute of Biomaterials and Bioengineering. Reports (JPN ISSN 1345-2886) **5723**
Tokyo Institute of Polytechnics. Faculty of Engineering. Academic Reports *see* Tokyo Kogei Daigaku Kogakubu Kiyo **3223**
Tokyo Institute of Technology. Department of Civil Engineering. Technical Report *see* Tokyo Kogyo Daigaku. Doboku Kogakka. Kenkyu Hokoku **3285**
Tokyo Institute of Technology. Precision and Intelligence Laboratory. Bulletin *see* Tokyo Kogyo Daigaku Seimitsu Kogaku Kenkyujo Yoran **5460**
Tokyo Institute of Technology. Research Laboratory of Resources Utilization. Report/Shigen Kagaku Kenkyujo (JPN ISSN 0495-8055) **8443**
Tokyo Isshukan (JPN) **3901**
Tokyo Jikeikai Ika Daigaku Zasshi *see* Jikeikai Medical Journal **5644**
Tokyo Joshi Daigaku Kiyo. Ronshu. Kagaku Bumon Hokoku/Tokyo Woman's Christian University. Science Reports (JPN ISSN 0386-4006) **7923**
➤ Tokyo Joshi Ika Daigaku Zasshi/Tokyo Women's Medical University. Journal (JPN ISSN 0040-9022) **5723**
Tokyo Journal (JPN ISSN 0289-811X) **3901**
➤ Tokyo Journal of Mathematics (JPN ISSN 0387-3870) **5542**
Tokyo Journal of Obstetrics and Gynecology *see* Nihon Sanka Fujinka Gakkai Tokyo Chiho Bukai Kaishi **6000**
Tokyo Kanku Chiho Kisho Kenkyukaishi/Tokyo District Meteorological Observatory. Geophysical Notes (JPN ISSN 0289-310X) **6396**
Tokyo Kanku Ijo Kisho Hokoku/Tokyo District Meteorological Observatory. Unusual Meteorological Report (JPN) **6396**
Tokyo Kasei Daigaku Kenkyu Kiyo. 1. Junbun Shakai Kagaku/Tokyo Kasei University. Bulletin. 1. Cultural and Social Science (JPN) **8010**
Tokyo Kasei Daigaku Kenkyu Kiyo. 2 Shizen Kagaku/Tokyo Kasei University. Bulletin. Natural Sciences (JPN) **7923**
Tokyo Kasei University. Bulletin. 1. Cultural and Social Science *see* Tokyo Kasei Daigaku Kenkyu Kiyo. 1. Junbun Shakai Kagaku **8010**
Tokyo Kasei University. Bulletin. Natural Sciences *see* Tokyo Kasei Daigaku Kenkyu Kiyo. 2 Shizen Kagaku **7923**
Tokyo Keizai University. Journal (JPN ISSN 0493-4091) **1183**
Tokyo Kogei Daigaku Kogakubu Kiyo/Tokyo Institute of Polytechnics. Faculty of Engineering. Academic Reports (JPN ISSN 0387-6055) **3223**
Tokyo Kogyo Daigaku. Doboku Kogakka. Kenkyu Hokoku/Tokyo Institute of Technology. Department of Civil Engineering. Technical Report (JPN ISSN 0289-1743) **3285**
Tokyo Kogyo Daigaku Seimitsu Kogaku Kenkyujo Yoran/Tokyo Institute of Technology. Precision and Intelligence Laboratory. Bulletin (JPN ISSN 1343-8719) **5460**
Tokyo Kokusai Kenkyu Kurabu Ronbunshu/Tokyo Club Papers (JPN ISSN 0916-3085) **7268**
Tokyo Kumo Danwakai Kaishi *see* Kishidaia **853**
Tokyo Les Nouvelles Municipales *see* Tokyo Metropolitan News **7504**
Tokyo Medical and Dental University. Institute of Biomaterials and Bioengineering. Reports *see* Tokyo Ika Shika Daigaku Seitai Zairyo Kogaku Kenkyujo Hokoku **5723**
Tokyo Medical Association. Journal *see* Tokyo-to Ishikai Zasshi **5723**
Tokyo Medical University. Journal *see* Tokyo Ika Daigaku Zasshi **5723**
Tokyo Metropolis. Monthly Report of Meteorology *see* Tokyoto Kisho Geppo **6396**
Tokyo Metropolitan Industrial Technology Research Institute. Bulletin *see* Tokyo Toritsu Sangyo Gijutsu Kenkyujo Kenkyu Hokoku **8443**
Tokyo Metropolitan Institute for Neurosciences. Annual Report *see* Tokyo-to Shinkei Kagaku Sogo Kenkyujo Nenpo **6188**
Tokyo Metropolitan Institute of Technology. Memoirs *see* Tokyo Toritsu Kagaku Gijutsu Daigaku Kenkyu Hokoku **8443**
Tokyo Metropolitan Isotope Research Center. Annual Report *see* Tokyo Toritsu Aisotopu Sogo Kenkyujo Nenpo **3175**
Tokyo Metropolitan News (JPN ISSN 0916-7951) **7504**
Tokyo Metropolitan Research Laboratory of Public Health. Annual Report *see* Tokyo Toritsu Eisei Kenkyujo Kenkyu Nenpo **5723**
Tokyo Metropolitan University. Annual Report of Research on the Ogasawara (Bonin) Islands *see* Ogasawara Kenkyu Nenpo **7895**
➤ Tokyo Metropolitan University Bulletin of Natural History (JPN ISSN 0918-3760) **7924**
Tokyo Metropolitan University. Department of Geography. Geographical Reports/Tokyo Toritsu Daigaku Chirigaku Kenkyu Obun Hokoku (JPN ISSN 0386-8710) **4031**
Tokyo Metropolitan University. Graduate School of Engineering. Annual Report (JPN) **3223**
Tokyo Metropolitan University. Graduate School of Engineering. Memoirs (JPN ISSN 1343-8743) **3223**
Tokyo - Mitsubishi Review (JPN ISSN 1342-2340) **1386**
Tokyo National Research Institute of Cultural Properties. Department of Performing Arts. Journal *see* Geino no Kagaku **8471**

Tokyo National University of Fine Arts and Music. Faculty of Fine Arts. Bulletin *see* Tokyo Geijutsu Daigaku Bijutsu Gakubu Kiyo **522**
Tokyo Nogyo Daigaku Aisotopu Senta Kenkyu Hokoku/Tokyo University of Agriculture. Isotope Center. Bulletin (JPN ISSN 0916-8621) **7072**
➤ Tokyo Nogyo Daigaku Nogaku Shuho/Tokyo University of Agriculture. Journal of Agricultural Science (JPN ISSN 0375-9202) **162**
Tokyo Noko Daigaku Nenpo *see* Tokyo University of Agriculture and Technology. Annual Report **255**
Tokyo Rika Daigaku Kenkyu Ronbunshu/Science University of Tokyo. Collected Papers (JPN ISSN 0918-0753) **7924**
Tokyo Shika Daigaku Obun Kiyo *see* Tokyo Dental College. Bulletin **5868**
Tokyo Shosen Daigaku Kenkyu Hokoku. Shizen Kagaku/Tokyo University of Mercantile Marine. Journal. Natural Sciences (JPN ISSN 0493-4474) **7924**
Tokyo Spider Study Group. Bulletin *see* Kishidaia **853**
Tokyo Suisan Daigaku Ronshu *see* Tokyo University of Fisheries. Report **3610**
Tokyo Surgical Society. Abstracts *see* Geka Shudankai Shorokushu **5747**
Tokyo Tekkotsu Kyoryo. Gijutsuho/T T K. Technical Report (JPN ISSN 0911-825X) **3285**
Tokyo Time Out (JPN) **3901**
Tokyo-to Ishikai Zasshi/Tokyo Medical Association. Journal (JPN ISSN 0040-8956) **5723**
Tokyo-to no Shizen (JPN ISSN 0288-2329) **7924**
Tokyo-to Shika Ishikai Zasshi/Tokyo Dental Association. Journal (JPN ISSN 0912-4462) **5868**
Tokyo-to Shinkei Kagaku Sogo Kenkyujo Nenpo/Tokyo Metropolitan Institute for Neurosciences. Annual Report (JPN) **6188**
Tokyo-to Takao Shizen Kagaku Hakubutsukan Kenkyu Hokoku/Takao Museum of Natural History. Science Report (JPN ISSN 0286-8768) **7924**
Tokyo Toritsu Aisotopu Sogo Kenkyujo Nenpo/Tokyo Metropolitan Isotope Research Center. Annual Report (JPN ISSN 0563-8488) **3175**
Tokyo Toritsu Daigaku Chirigaku Kenkyu Obun Hokoku *see* Tokyo Metropolitan University. Department of Geography. Geographical Reports **4031**
• Tokyo Toritsu Eisei Kenkyujo Kenkyu Nenpo/Tokyo Metropolitan Research Laboratory of Public Health. Annual Report (JPN ISSN 0082-4771) **5723**
Tokyo Toritsu Kagaku Gijutsu Daigaku Kenkyu Hokoku/Tokyo Metropolitan Institute of Technology. Memoirs (JPN ISSN 0913-8897) **8443**
Tokyo Toritsu Sangyo Gijutsu Kenkyujo Kenkyu Hokoku/Tokyo Metropolitan Industrial Technology Research Institute. Bulletin (JPN ISSN 1344-4867) **8443**
Tokyo University of Agriculture and Technology. Annual Report/Tokyo Noko Daigaku Nenpo (JPN ISSN 0563-8313) **255**
Tokyo University of Agriculture. Isotope Center. Bulletin *see* Tokyo Nogyo Daigaku Aisotopu Senta Kenkyu Hokoku **7072**
Tokyo University of Agriculture. Journal of Agricultural Science *see* Tokyo Nogyo Daigaku Nogaku Shuho **162**
Tokyo University of Fisheries. Journal/Tokyo Suisan Daigaku Kenkyu Hokoku *see* Toukyou Kaiyou Daigaku Kenkyuu Houkoku **3610**
Tokyo University of Fisheries. Report/Tokyo Suisan Daigaku Ronshu (JPN ISSN 0563-8372) **3610**
▼ Tokyo University of Foreign Studies (NLD ISSN 1877-6248) **5188**
Tokyo University of Marine Science and Technology. Journal *see* Toukyou Kaiyou Daigaku Kenkyuu Houkoku **3610**
Tokyo University of Mercantile Marine. Journal. Natural Sciences *see* Tokyo Shosen Daigaku Kenkyu Hokoku. Shizen Kagaku **7924**
Tokyo University of Science News (JPN) **3901**
Tokyo Woman's Christian University. Science Reports *see* Tokyo Joshi Daigaku Kiyo. Ronshu. Kagaku Bumon Hokoku **7923**
Tokyo Women's Medical College. Institute of Advanced Biomedical Engineering & Science. Reports *see* Sentan Seimei Ikagaku Kenkyuujo Houkoku **751**
Tokyo Women's Medical University. Journal *see* Tokyo Joshi Ika Daigaku Zasshi **5723**
Tokyoko Haro Kansoku Nenpo/Annual Report of Observation Waves in Tokyo Bay (JPN ISSN 0916-4820) **2819**
Tokyoto Kisho Geppo/Tokyo Metropolis. Monthly Report of Meteorology (JPN ISSN 0916-524X) **6396**
Tokyoto News *see* Tokyo Metropolitan News **7504**
Tokyoto Tama Dobutsu Koen Jigyo Gaiyo/Tama Zoological Park. Annual Report (JPN) **965**
Tokyu Construction Technical Reports *see* Tokyu Kensetsu Gijutsu Kenkyujoho **1040**
Tokyu Kensetsu Gijutsu Kenkyujoho/Tokyu Construction Technical Reports (JPN ISSN 0285-4546) **1040**
Toldot (ARG ISSN 1514-9072) **3785**
Toldot (DEU) **3568**
Toledo Area Parent News (USA) **2170**
Toledo Bar Association Newsletter (USA ISSN 0493-4571) **4797**
• Toledo Business Journal (USA) **1183**
Toledo City Journal (USA ISSN 0040-9065) **7504**
▼ Toledo History Museum Quarterly (USA ISSN 1937-3910) **0**
Toledo Jewish News (USA ISSN 0040-9081) **3568**
The Toledo Journal (USA) **3568**
➤ Toledo Journal of Great Lakes' Law, Science & Policy (USA ISSN 1097-9328) **4797**
Toledo Legal News (USA) **4797**
Toledo Medicine (USA) **5723**
Toledo Museum News *see* Toledo Museum of Art Members Newsletter **6538**
Toledo Museum of Art. Annual Report *see* Toledo Museum of Art Members Newsletter **6538**
Toledo Museum of Art Members Newsletter (USA) **6538**
Tolerie (FRA ISSN 0985-5637) **6335**
Toletum (ESP ISSN 0210-6310) **4273**
Toletvm *see* Toletum **4273**
• Tolkien Studies (USA ISSN 1547-3155) **5389**
Tolkoty (RUS) **8886**
Toll - Free Phone Book U S A (Year) (USA ISSN 1092-0285) **2031**
Toll Industry Statistics (Year) (USA) **8531**
Toll N Z. Annual Report (New Zealand) (NZL) **8626**
Tolley Swan National Survey of Company Car Schemes (GBR) **4882**
Tolley's Capital Gains Tax (GBR ISSN 0143-1633) **1952**
Tolley's Communications Law *see* Communications Law (Haywards Heath) **2316**
Tolley's Company Law & Insolvency (GBR ISSN 1475-1887) **4882**
Tolley's Company Law Bulletin (GBR ISSN 1369-5924) **4882**
Tolley's Construction Newsletter *see* Tottel's Construction Newsletter **1041**
Tolley's Corporation Tax (GBR ISSN 0305-8921) **1952**
Tolley's Employment Law-Line Newsletter *see* Tolley's Employment Law Newsletter **1876**
Tolley's Employment Law Newsletter (GBR ISSN 1747-6070) **1876**
Tolley's Health and Safety at Work Handbook (GBR ISSN 1366-2856) **6688**
Tolley's Income Tax (GBR ISSN 0305-893X) **1952**
Tolley's Inheritance Tax (GBR ISSN 0952-0791) **1952**
Tolley's Insolvency Law & Practice *see* Corporate Rescue and Insolvency **4651**
Tolley's Journal of Immigration, Asylum and Nationality Law *see* Tottel's Journal of Immigration, Asylum and Nationality Law **4942**
Tolley's Payroll Handbook (GBR ISSN 1365-5590) **1876**
Tolley's Pensions Administrator's and Trustee's Newsletter (GBR ISSN 1742-0393) **1710**
Tolley's Pensions Law Handbook (GBR) **4882**
Tolley's Practical Audit & Accounting (GBR ISSN 1367-1871) **1302**
Tolley's Practical National Insurance Contributions Newsletter (GBR ISSN 1477-8610) **4525**
Tolley's Practical Tax Newsletter (GBR ISSN 1475-2352) **1952**
Tolley's Practical V A T (Value Added Tax) (GBR ISSN 0951-176X) **1952**
Tolley's Social Security & State Benefits (GBR ISSN 0950-9259) **1952**
Tolley's Tax Cases (Year) (GBR) **1952**
Tolley's Tax Computations (GBR ISSN 0950-2343) **1952**
Tolley's Tax Data (Year) (GBR ISSN 0262-4583) **1952**
Tolley's Tax Guide (GBR ISSN 0950-9267) **1952**
Tolley's Tax Investigations (GBR ISSN 0959-681X) **1952**
Tolley's Tax Tables (Year) (GBR ISSN 0307-6687) **1952**
Tolley's Taxation in the Republic of Ireland *see* Tottel's Taxation in the Republic of Ireland **1952**
Tolley's Taxation of Employments *see* Tottel's Taxation of Employments **1952**
Tolley's Trust Law International (GBR ISSN 0962-2624) **4797**
Tolley's V A T Cases (Year) (Value Added Tax) (GBR ISSN 0962-0044) **1952**
Tolley's V A T Planning (Year) (Value Added Tax) (GBR ISSN 0957-2651) **1952**
Tolley's Value Added Tax (GBR ISSN 0957-2643) **1952**
Toll's Pennsylvania Crimes Code Annotated (USA ISSN 1931-2334) **4899**
Toll's Pennsylvania Crimes Code Annotated 2d *see* Toll's Pennsylvania Crimes Code Annotated **4899**
Tollways (USA) **8635**
Tolnai Konyvtaros (HUN ISSN 0133-8358) **5050**
• Tolnai Nepujsag (HUN ISSN 0865-9028) **3877**
Tolnai Nepujsag Gratisz *see* Tolnai Nepujsag **3877**
Tolnai Nepujsag. Vasarnap Reggel *see* Tolnai Nepujsag **3877**
Tolon (RUS) **4478**
Tolstoy Foundation News (USA) **8074**
➤ Tolstoy Studies Journal (CAN ISSN 1044-1573) **5389**
• Tolstyi Tsentralno-Aziatskii Zhurnal (KGZ) **3904**
Tolvuheimur (ISL ISSN 1025-5516) **2583**
Tom' (RUS) **3942**
Tom & Jerry (CZE ISSN 1211-6491) **2217**
Tom & Jerry (FIN ISSN 0357-6493) **2217**
Tom & Jerry *see* All New Tom & Jerry **2175**
Tom & Jerry (HRV ISSN 1330-9315) **2217**
† Tom & Jerry (LTU ISSN 1392-2645) **8993**
Tom & Jerry (LVA ISSN 1407-0863) **2217**
Tom es Jerry (HUN ISSN 1419-9289) **2217**
Tom i Jerry (POL ISSN 1897-3264) **2217**
Tom i Jerry Czyli Kot i Mysz *see* Tom i Jerry **2217**
Tom ja Jerry (EST ISSN 1406-3034) **2217**
Tom ja Jerry *see* Tom & Jerry **2217**
Tom Peters Fast Forward (USA ISSN 1089-5949) **1798**
Tom si Jerry (ROM ISSN 1224-8797) **2217**
• Tomahawk (Indianapolis) (USA ISSN 0741-5435) **2304**
The Tomahawk of Alpha Sigma Phi *see* Tomahawk (Indianapolis) **2304**
Tomart's Action Figure Digest (USA ISSN 1056-8697) **4061**
Tomart's Disneyana Update (USA ISSN 1074-1518) **4061**
Tomas Rivera Policy Institute. Policy Brief (USA ISSN 1523-0104) **3568**
Tomato Genetics Cooperative Report (USA) **820**
The Tomato Magazine (USA ISSN 1093-3980) **255**
• Tomatrax (AUS ISSN 1833-9034) **6623**
Tomb Raider *see* Lara Croft Tomb Raider **502**
Tomb Raider - Witchblade (GBR ISSN 1466-0997) **522**
Tombo/Acta Odonatologica (JPN ISSN 0495-8314) **860**
The Tombstone (USA ISSN 0893-7664) **3785**
The Tombstone Epitaph (USA) **4315**
▼ Tombstone Times (USA ISSN 1942-096X) **3991**
▼ Tomek i Przyjaciele (POL ISSN 1898-651X) **2217**
Tomis (ROM ISSN 1220-8167) **3934**
• Tommy Iseskogs Arbetsraettliga Nyhetsbrev (SWE ISSN 1101-7880) **4603**
Tomodachi (AUS ISSN 0157-3764) **1584**
Tomoegumi Iron Works Technical Report *see* Tomoegumi Tekkojo Giho **1041**
Tomoegumi Tekkojo Giho/Tomoegumi Iron Works Technical Report (JPN) **1041**
† • Tomorrow (DEU ISSN 1436-9192) **8993**
• Tomorrow (SWE ISSN 1102-0938) **3470**
Tomorrow (USA) **1710**
Tomorrow's Business Leader (USA ISSN 0279-9685) **6704**
Tomorrow's Christian Graduate (USA ISSN 1093-6238) **6704**
▼ Tomorrow's Manukau (NZL ISSN 1177-5688) **8074**
Tomorrow's News (CAN ISSN 1911-0987) **8075**
• Tomorrow's News Today (USA) **1386**
Tomorrow's Pharmacist (GBR ISSN 1470-5761) **6883**
• Tomorrow's Technician (USA ISSN 1539-9532) **8607**
Tomorrow's Technology Today *see* Australian T3 **8416**
▼ • Tomorrow's Technology Transfer (USA ISSN 1946-0619) **2951**
• TomPaine.common Sense (USA) **5242**
Toms un Dzerijs *see* Tom & Jerry **2217**
Tomsk State Pedagogical University. Bulletin *see* Tomskii Gosudarstvennyi Pedagogicheskii Universitet. Vestnik **2920**
Tomskaya Neft' (RUS) **6795**
Tomskie Pravoslavnye Vedomosti (RUS) **7706**
• ➤ Tomskii Gosudarstvennyi Pedagogicheskii Universitet. Vestnik/Tomsk State Pedagogical University. Bulletin (RUS ISSN 1609-624X) **2920**
TON (NLD ISSN 1871-1790) **8513**
Ton - Video Report (DEU ISSN 0948-9185) **8155**
Tonan Ajia Kenkyu *see* South East Asian Studies **8006**
Tonatiuh-Quinto Sol News *see* T Q S News **5384**
Tonbridge & Tunbridge Wells K M Extra (GBR) **3872**
Tone (Auckland) (NZL ISSN 1175-2459) **3115**
Tones & Notes (USA) **6623**
Tonfan Tiyu Ribao/Oriental Sports Daily (CHN) **8212**
Tong de Jiagong he Xiaoshou: ke Jinxing Guoji Hezuo de Lingyu *see* Studies in the Processing, Marketing and Distribution of Commodities **8991**
The Tonga Chronicle/Kalonikali Tonga (TON) **3962**
• Tonghua Shifan Xueyuan Xuebao/Tonghua Teachers College. Journal (CHN ISSN 1008-7974) **2920**
Tonghua Teachers College. Journal *see* Tonghua Shifan Xueyuan Xuebao **2920**
Tonghua yu Chuanshuo/Fairy Tales and Legends (CHN) **2218**
Tong'il Yeon'gu Noncong/Korean Journal of Unification Studies (KOR ISSN 1225-6064) **562**
• Tongji Daxue Xuebao (Shehui Kexue Ban)/Tongji University. Journal (Social Science Section) (CHN ISSN 1009-3060) **8010**
• Tongji Daxue Xuebao (Yixue Ban)/Tongji University. Journal (Medical Science) (CHN) **5723**
• Tongji Daxue Xuebao (Ziran Kexue Ban)/Tongji University. Journal (Natural Science) (CHN) **7924**
Tongji University. Journal (Medical Science) *see* Tongji Daxue Xuebao (Yixue Ban) **5723**
Tongji University. Journal (Natural Science) *see* Tongji Daxue Xuebao (Ziran Kexue Ban) **7924**
Tongji University. Journal (Social Science Section) *see* Tongji Daxue Xuebao (Shehui Kexue Ban) **8010**
Tongji Yanjiu/Statistics Research (CHN ISSN 0496-4225) **8409**
Tongji yu Jingsuan/Statistics and Accurate Calculation (CHN ISSN 1009-7651) **8409**
• Tongmei Keji/Datong Coal Mining Administration. Science and Technology (CHN ISSN 1000-4866) **6480**
Tongqu (CHN ISSN 1674-1560) **2218**
• Tongweisu/Journal of Isotopes (CHN ISSN 1000-7512) **7072**
Tongxin KeJi Shangqing *see* Global Sources Telecom Products **2322**
• Tongxin Shijie/Communications World (CHN ISSN 1009-1564) **2342**
• Tongxin Xuebao/China Institute of Communications. Journal (CHN ISSN 1000-436X) **2342**
• Tongxin yu Xinxi Jishu/Communication & Information Technology (CHN ISSN 1672-0164) **2342**
Tongxinyuan *see* Concentric **5277**
Tongxun he Jisuanji *see* Journal of Communication and Computer **2351**
• Tongye Gongcheng/Copper Engineering (CHN ISSN 1009-3842) **6335**
• Tongyi Luntan/United Tribune (CHN ISSN 1003-0484) **8010**
The Toni Morrison Newsletter (USA) **5242**
Tonic (GBR ISSN 0260-7425) **6623**
Tonight *see* Jinwanbao **3826**
Toniq (DEU ISSN 1613-4435) **6623**
Tonmeister Informationen (DEU) **8155**
Tonneru to Chika/Tunnels and Underground (JPN ISSN 0285-631X) **3285**
▼ • The Tonopah Review (USA ISSN 1947-5527) **5436**
• Tonos Digital (ESP ISSN 1577-6921) **5389**
Tonovi (HRV ISSN 0352-9711) **2920**
• El Tonto del Pueblo (BOL ISSN 1609-6819) **8483**
Tonyobyo/Japan Diabetes Society. Journal (JPN ISSN 0021-437X) **5900**
Tonyobyo to Kekkan *see* Complication **5944**
Tooele Valley Magazine (USA ISSN 1523-4770) **8761**
▼ Toogezer (FRA ISSN 1961-6309) **1606**
Took (USA) **5242**
Tool (DEU) **1041**
Tool and Alloy Steels (IND ISSN 0377-9408) **6335**
• Tool & Equipment Rental Guide (USA ISSN 1933-4931) **1183**
Tool Engineer *see* Kikai to Kogu **3387**
Tool Engineering *see* Gongju Jishu **3378**
Tool Guide *see* Taunton Tool Guide **1052**
• Toolbox Ondernemingsraad (NLD ISSN 1573-3769) **1710**
Tooling and Manufacturing Association. Purchasing Guide (USA) **1905**
Tooling and Production *see* Tooling & Production **5460**
• Tooling & Production (USA ISSN 0040-9243) **5460**
Toolkit Arbocommunicatie *see* Toolkit Personeelcommunicatie **4797**
Toolkit Medezeggenschap (NLD ISSN 1871-8574) **1876**
Toolkit Personeelcommunicatie (NLD ISSN 1871-2827) **4797**
Toolroom Directory (GBR) **5460**
Tools 4 Music (DEU ISSN 1613-4443) **8155**
Tools and Shops *see* Tools & Shops **1052**
• Tools & Shops (USA) **1052**
Tools & Techniques of Employee Benefit and Retirement Planning (USA ISSN 1930-3572) **1711**
• Tools of the Trade (USA ISSN 1534-2425) **1041**
TooN/SpeZiaal *see* SpeZiaal **2914**
Toorts (NLD ISSN 0165-9839) **2946**
Top (GBR) **6623**
Top (Benningen) (DEU) **2218**
Top 10 Restaurants (USA ISSN 1555-2381) **4399**
Top 100 Cable Systems *see* Multichannel News **2385**
Top 100 Cable Systems *see* Broadcasting & Cable **2376**
Top 100 Retailers Report and Annual Industry Directory *see* Casual Living **4555**
Top 1000 Charities in Scotland (Year) (GBR ISSN 1468-957X) **8075**
▼ Top 150 Schweizer Medien (CHE ISSN 1661-8483) **36**
▼ • Top 30 Global Media Owners (GBR ISSN 1753-9714) **2342**
• Top 3000 Charities (Year) (GBR ISSN 1470-7845) **8075**
• Top 400 Contractors Sourcebook (USA) **1041**
Top 5 (BRA) **1846**
Top 50 European Media Owners (GBR ISSN 0968-2155) **2343**
• The Top 500 Design Firms Sourcebook (USA) **3223**
Top 500 Foreign Trade Companies in China (CHN) **1584**
Top 500 Italian Wine Producers (Year) (ITA) **611**
The Top 5000 European Companies (Year) (GBR) **2031**
The Top 5000 Global Companies (Year) (GBR) **2031**
Top Accounting Issues for C P E Course (Continuing Professional Education) (USA ISSN 1933-3544) **1303**
Top Agrar: Ausgabe B (DEU ISSN 0936-8302) **162**
Top Agrar: Ausgabe R (DEU ISSN 0936-8310) **162**
Top Agrar: Ausgabe S (DEU ISSN 0936-8329) **162**
Top Agrar: Ausgabe S - R (DEU ISSN 0342-2399) **162**
Top Agrar Oesterreich (DEU) **162**
Top Alerte (FRA ISSN 1956-7383) **3842**

DIRECTORY 2010 TRADUZIONE, SOCIETA E CULTURA 10955

Toyooki Engineering Review see Toyooki Giho 3224
Toyooki Giho/Toyooki Engineering Review (JPN ISSN 0285-175X) 3224
Toyosato Museum of Entomology. Bulletin (JPN ISSN 1342-1263) 860
Toyoshi-Kenkyu/Journal of Oriental Researches (JPN ISSN 0386-9059) 4189
Toyota (JPN) 8608
Toyota and Automotive Electronics (JPN) 8608
Toyota and Automotive Safety (JPN) 8608
• Toyota Chuo Kenkyujo R & D Rebyu/R & D Review of Toyota C R D L (JPN ISSN 0385-1508) 3224
Toyota Engine Technology (JPN) 8608
Toyota Foundation Occasional Report (JPN ISSN 0285-9033) 5389
Toyota Gijutsu (JPN ISSN 0916-7501) 8608
Toyota Magazin (DEU) 8608
Toyota Motor Corporation. Annual Report (JPN) 8608
Toyota Technical Review (JPN ISSN 0917-3706) 8608
Toys (DEU) 4062
Toys & Games see Key Note Market Report: Toys & Games 1895
Toys and Games Imports America Directory (CAN) 4062
Toyuncak (TUR) 1183
TPEdigitaal see T P E Digitaal 7187
• TQ (ESP ISSN 1139-658X) 5542
Tr A C see Trends in Analytical Chemistry 2107
Tr A C Compendium Series see Trends in Analytical Chemistry (Library Edition) 2107
TR7 (CHE) 2398
Tra Arte e Teologia (ITA ISSN 1970-3465) 7690
Tra Noi (ITA) 2304
Tra Storia e Cronaca (ITA ISSN 1827-6393) 4478
• Trabajadores (CUB ISSN 0864-0432) 1711
Trabajadores de la Ensenanza (ESP ISSN 1131-9615) 2920
Trabajadores Digital see Trabajadores 1711
Trabajo (COL) 1711
Trabajo (DOM ISSN 0564-0334) 1711
Trabajo (ESP ISSN 1136-3819) 1711
Trabajo en el Mundo see World Labour Report 1716
Trabajo Social (MEX ISSN 0188-1396) 8075
Trabajo Social (Colombia) (COL ISSN 0123-4986) 8075
• Trabajo Social Hoy (ESP ISSN 1134-0991) 8075
• Trabajo Social y Salud (ESP ISSN 1130-2976) 8075
• Trabajo y Sociedad (ARG ISSN 1514-6871) 1711
Trabajos de Antropologia (ESP ISSN 0210-1483) 358
Trabajos de Arqueologia Navarra (ESP ISSN 0211-5174) 421
• Trabajos de Geologia (ESP ISSN 0474-9588) 2771
• Trabajos de Prehistoria. Nueva Serie (ESP ISSN 0082-5638) 421
Trabajos del Colegio Andino (PER ISSN 1022-0941) 8010
Trabajos del Museo Arqueologico de Ibiza (ESP ISSN 1130-8095) 6538
Trabajos Monograficos sobre la Independencia de Norteamerica (ESP) 4315
Trabalho (AGO ISSN 0564-0342) 1711
• Trabalho, Educacao e Saude (BRA ISSN 1678-1007) 1711
Trabalhos de Antropologia e Etnologia (PRT ISSN 0304-243X) 358
➤ Trabalhos em Linguistica Aplicada (BRA ISSN 0103-1813) 5188
A Trabe de Ouro (ESP ISSN 1130-2674) 5242
Traber-Rundschau (DEU ISSN 0175-162X) 8299
Tracce. Litterae Communionis (ITA ISSN 1128-9333) 7690
Trace (London) (GBR ISSN 1366-1752) 6624
Trace (New York, 1947) (USA) 7328
Trace (New York, 1998) (USA) 5085
Trace Elements and Electrolytes (DEU ISSN 0946-2104) 2115
• ➤ Trace Metals and Other Contaminants in the Environment (NLD ISSN 1875-1121) 3503
Trace Metals in the Environment see Trace Metals and Other Contaminants in the Environment 3503
Tracer (CAN ISSN 1911-4184) 3785
Tracer (JPN ISSN 0289-9906) 3175
The Tracer (Cincinnati) (USA ISSN 8756-8462) 3785
Tracer (Fairview Park) (USA ISSN 1057-6258) 3785
Tracers (USA ISSN 1073-0206) 6209
Traces (CHE) 3224
Traces (FRA ISSN 0041-0276) 5436
Traces see Tracce. Litterae Communionis 7690
Traces (Glasgow) (USA ISSN 0882-2158) 3785
Traces (Ithaca) (USA ISSN 1533-3426) 5188
Traces (Jackson) (USA) 2629
Traces (Paris) see Tracce. Litterae Communionis 7690
Traces in the Sand (USA) 3785
➤ Traces of Indiana and Midwestern History (USA ISSN 1040-788X) 4315
Tracht und Brauch/Costumes et Coutumes (CHE) 4274
Tracings (USA) 3785
Track (DNK ISSN 1602-0510) 2218
Track 7 (NLD ISSN 1574-7697) 7690
Track a Word (GBR ISSN 0954-9552) 4349
Track & Field see Tianjing 8337
Track and Field and Cross Country Rules Book (USA ISSN 1042-878X) 8337
Track and Field Case Book (USA) 8337
Track and Field Coaches Review see Coaches Review 8309
Track & Field News (USA ISSN 0041-0284) 8337
Track and Field Officials Manual (USA) 8337
• Track & Race Cars (GBR ISSN 1742-1934) 8212
Track & Signal (AUS ISSN 1327-418X) 8626
Track and Tire (USA) 1041
Track Coach (USA ISSN 1085-8792) 8338
Track Magazine (USA ISSN 1527-5035) 8299
Track Newsletter (USA ISSN 0041-0306) 8338
Track to Track (AUS ISSN 1832-360X) 8299
• Track Topics (USA) 8299
Track Yearbook & Buyers' Guide (USA) 8626
Track Yearbook and Buyers' Guide see Track Yearbook & Buyers' Guide 8626
• Tracker (GBR) 1846
• The Tracker (USA ISSN 0041-0330) 6624
Tracking Eastern Europe (USA ISSN 1051-7197) 1522
Tracking in Crawford County, Ohio (USA) 3785
Tracking Japan (USA ISSN 1075-7686) 7268
• Tracking Report (USA ISSN 1553-0787) 7543
The Tracking Way (USA ISSN 1554-852X) 5389
Tracks (AUS ISSN 1032-3317) 8338
• Tracks (USA ISSN 1547-6979) 6624
Tracks (Cardiff) (GBR) 6624
Tracks and Traces (USA) 3785
Track's Monday Report (USA) 8299
Trackside (AUS) 8212
Trackside Magazine (USA ISSN 1050-558X) 8212
Tract Messenger (USA ISSN 0041-0357) 4085
Tractatenblad van het Koninkrijk der Nederlanden (NLD ISSN 0920-2218) 7268
▼ Tracteur Retro (FRA ISSN 1962-4344) 214
▼ Tracteurs Passion et Collection (FRA ISSN 1960-7873) 214
Traction (GBR ISSN 1354-2680) 8626
Traction Annual see Traction 8626
Tractor (GBR ISSN 1751-343X) 214
Tractor & Farm Machinery Trader (GBR ISSN 0262-8090) 214
Tractor & Farming Heritage see Tractor 214
Tractor and Implement Swap Meet see Tractor Shop 214
Tractor & Machinery (GBR ISSN 1357-3101) 214
Tractor Power see Traktor Power 214
Tractor Shop (USA ISSN 1549-6988) 214
† Tractor Tom (NLD ISSN 1872-1583) 8993
Trad Magazine (FRA ISSN 0995-3280) 6624
Trade-a-Boat (AUS ISSN 1449-6305) 8283
Trade-a-Boat (NZL) 8664
• Trade-a-Plane (USA ISSN 0041-0365) 73
Trade Action Monitoring System (USA) 1433
Trade and Commerce (CAN ISSN 0049-4321) 1433
† Trade and Customs World Directory (USA ISSN 1093-8885) 8993
• Trade and Development Report (CHE ISSN 0255-4607) 1584
• Trade and Employment Effects of the Andean Trade Perference Act (USA) 1584
• Trade & Forfaiting Review (GBR ISSN 1465-136X) 1584
Trade and Industry see Majallat al-Tijara wal-Sina'a 1407
• Trade and Investment Monitor (CAN ISSN 1496-1938) 1433
Trade and Professional Associations in California (USA) 2031
• Trade & Traveler (HKG) 8765
Trade Associations and Professional Bodies of the Continental European Union (GBR) 2031
Trade Associations & Professional Bodies of the United Kingdom and Eire (GBR) 2031
Trade Bianco (ITA) 2031
• Trade Book Publishing (Year): Analysis by Category (USA) 7575
Trade Briefing Paper (USA ISSN 1932-3670) 1183
Trade Cases (USA ISSN 1045-5191) 1433
Trade Channel (Consumer Products Edition) (NLD) 1584
Trade Channel (Technical Products Edition) (NLD) 1584
Trade Chronicle (PAK ISSN 0041-0411) 1905
Trade Commerce & Industry Weekly Bulletin (IND) 1433
• Trade Connections (USA) 1584
Trade Consumer Electronics (ITA) 1846
Trade Dimensions' Directory of Convenience Stores (USA ISSN 1521-902X) 3666
Trade Dimensions' Directory of Mass Merchandisers (USA) 2031
Trade Dimensions' Retail Tenant Directory (USA) 7614
Trade Directories of the World (USA ISSN 0564-0482) 2031
† Trade Directory for Denmark/Annuaire de l'Exportation du Danemark/Anuario de la Exportacion de Dinamarca/Daenischer Handelskalender (DNK ISSN 0109-467X) 8994
Trade Directory of Mexico (USA) 1584
Trade Dress Protection (USA) 6758
Trade Fairs International (DEU ISSN 1437-4250) 6283
† Trade Fax (USA ISSN 1086-7341) 8994
• Trade Finance (GBR ISSN 1464-8873) 1387
Trade Finance. The Guide to the Emerging Markets see The Citi World Official Agency Guide 1327
Trade Finance. The Guide to the Emerging Markets see Trade Finance 1387
Trade Focus (ETH) 1410
Trade Forums (SGP) 1584
Trade Home Entertainment (ITA ISSN 1826-4840) 2403
Trade International Digest (GBR ISSN 1476-9905) 1584
• Trade-It (GBR ISSN 0960-8885) 8608
Trade Journal Recap (USA) 522
Trade-Mark Business Network News (USA) 1183
The Trade Marks Handbook (GBR) 6758
Trade Marks Journal/Journal des Marques de Commerce (CAN ISSN 0041-0438) 6758
• Trade Marks Journal (GBR ISSN 0041-0446) 6758
• Trade Marks, Trade Names and Unfair Competition (GBR) 6758
Trade Monitor (USA) 1433
• Trade Negotiations Insights (CHE ISSN 1682-6744) 1584
† Trade News (ITA) 8994
Trade News (NZL) 2031
Trade Opportunity (TWN) 1410
Trade Pages (TWN) 1584
Trade Policy Agenda and Annual Report of the President of the United States on the Trade Agreements Program (USA ISSN 1064-9263) 1433
Trade Policy Analysis (USA ISSN 1932-3689) 1584
• Trade Policy Research (CAN ISSN 1702-5524) 1584
Trade Policy Review (CHE ISSN 1014-7411) 1584
• Trade Practices Law (AUS) 4882
Trade Practices Law Journal (AUS ISSN 1039-3277) 4882
Trade Records Analysis of Flora and Fauna in Commerce Bulletin see T R A F F I C Bulletin 2628
Trade Regulation (USA) 4797
• Trade Regulation Reporter (USA) 1433
Trade Regulation Reports see Trade Regulation Reporter 1433
Trade Report on Diskette (BLZ) 2031
Trade Review (USA) 6624
• Trade Roundup.com (CAN) 1584
• Trade Secrets (USA) 1968
Trade Secrets Law (USA) 4882
Trade Secrets Throughout the World (USA) 2031
• Trade Services Directory & Guide (USA ISSN 1531-006X) 1584
Trade Services Directory and Guide see Trade Services Directory & Guide 1584
† Trade Shows & Exhibits Schedule (USA) 8994
• Trade Shows Worldwide (USA ISSN 1046-4395) 6283
• Trade Topics (AUS ISSN 1449-9851) 1584
Trade Union Advisor (USA ISSN 1058-0557) 4603
Trade Union Courier (USA ISSN 0041-0497) 4603
Trade Union Handbook (USA ISSN 1053-7007) 4603
Trade Union International of Agricultural Forestry and Plantation Workers Information see T U I A F P W Information 4603
Trade Union Record (IND ISSN 0041-0535) 4603
Trade Unions in India (IND ISSN 0445-6289) 4603
Trade Unions International of Agricultural, Forestry and Plantation Workers. Bulletin (RUS) 3704
Trade Unions International of Chemical, Oil and Allied Workers. Information Bulletin (HUN) 4603
Trade Unions International of Chemical, Oil and Allied Workers. International Trade Conference. Documents (HUN ISSN 0084-1544) 4603
Trade Unions International of Workers of the Building Wood and Building Materials Industries Bulletin see U I T B B Bulletin 4603
Trade Update see Canada's State of Trade (Year) 1554
Trade Weekly (TWN) 1584
Trade Winds (USA) 2250
Trade Winds Monthly (TWN ISSN 0259-9880) 1585
• Trade Winners (TWN) 2494
The Trade with Beverages/Der Handel mit Getraenken (DEU) 611
The Trade with Building Materials/Der Handel mit Baumaterial (DEU) 1041
• Trade with Greece (GRC ISSN 0041-0543) 1411
Trade with Italy (USA ISSN 0041-0551) 1411
Trade Yellow Pages (Year) (TWN) 2031
• Tradeline Exclusive Reports (USA ISSN 1541-8634) 1041
Tradelink (Chinese Edition) see Shang lian: Xinjiapo Changshang Gonghui Changnian Zhinan 2027
Tradelink - S C I Annual Directory (Year) (Singapore Confederation of Industries) (SGP) 2031
Trademark Digest see Allen's Trademark Digest 4613
Trademark Law Handbook (USA ISSN 0731-5813) 4797
Trademark Law Practice Forms (USA) 6758
Trademark Manual of Examining Procedure see U.S. Patent and Trademark Office. Trademark Manual of Examining Procedure 6759
Trademark Practice Throughout the World (USA) 6759
• Trademark Register of the United States (USA ISSN 0082-5786) 6759
Trademark Registration Practice (USA) 6759
Trademark Report see T M A Trademark Report 8487
• The Trademark Reporter (USA ISSN 0041-056X) 6759
Trademark Trial and Appeal Board Manual of Procedure (USA) 6759
• Trademark World (GBR ISSN 0950-2564) 6759
Trademarks Throughout the World (USA) 6759
Tradenames see The Business Who's Who Australian Products and Tradenames Guide 8938
• Tradequip International (USA) 6795
The Trader (GBR ISSN 0955-0828) 1846
Trader Monthly (GBR ISSN 1749-4842) 1656
Trader-Source (USA ISSN 1556-1992) 1656
• Traders Magazine (USA ISSN 0894-7295) 1387
Trader's Option (USA) 1656
Trader's World Magazine (USA ISSN 1045-7690) 1656
TradersJournal (DEU ISSN 1613-5555) 1656
• Trades Union Congress. General Council Report (GBR) 4603
Trades Union Congress of Ghana News see T U C News 4603
Trades Union Press Service (GBR ISSN 0144-5049) 1711
Tradeshow (USA ISSN 0145-5559) 36
Tradeshow Week see Tradeshow Week Data Book (Year) 1846
• Tradeshow Week (USA ISSN 0733-0170) 36
Tradeshow Week 200 see Tradeshow 36
• Tradeshow Week Data Book (Year) (USA ISSN 0000-1023) 1846
Tradeshow Week's Buyer's Guide (USA ISSN 1099-3061) 36
Tradeshow Week's Major Exhibit Hall Directory (USA) 36
Tradeweek (CAN) 1585
• TradeWinds (NOR ISSN 0803-9364) 8664
Tradewinds (USA) 8338
Tradewinds Archive see TradeWinds 8664
• Tradewinds - The Network for Portugal (GBR) 1585
TradeWinds Today see TradeWinds 8664
Tradicion Popular (GTM ISSN 0252-872X) 3623
➤ Tradicion Revista (USA ISSN 1093-0973) 522
Tradiciones de Guatemala/Traditions of Guatemala (GTM ISSN 0564-0571) 358
▼ • Tradicioun (FRA ISSN 1958-7813) 3623
Trading Cards (USA ISSN 1060-9970) 4349
Trading in Metals (GBR ISSN 0264-8199) 6335
Trading Law Newsletter (GBR) 1585
Trading Post (USA ISSN 1043-7665) 4349
Trading Standards Today see T S Today 1845
Trading Technology Week see Dealing with Technology 1392
Tradisjon see Tidsskrift for Kulturforskning 358
Traditie (NLD ISSN 1382-4104) 3623
Traditio (USA ISSN 0362-1529) 4274
➤ Traditio Exegetica Graeca (BEL) 7690
Tradition (USA ISSN 1071-1864) 6624
• Tradition (New York) (USA ISSN 0041-0608) 7731
• Tradition & Discovery (USA ISSN 1057-1027) 6958
Traditional Boats & Tall Ships (GBR ISSN 1466-2477) 8283
Traditional Building (USA ISSN 0898-0284) 1041
Traditional Chinese Architecture and Gardens see Gujian Yuanlin Jishu 444
Traditional Chinese Drug Research & Clinical Pharmacology see Zhongyao Xinyao yu Lingchuang Yaoli 6888
Traditional Chinese Medicinal Research see Zhongyi Yanjiu 5739
Traditional Chinese Medicine University of Hunan. Journal see Hunan Zhongyiyao Daxue Xuebao 5631
Traditional Chinese Novel see Zhanghui Xiaoshuo 5404
➤ Traditional Dwellings and Settlements Review (USA ISSN 1050-2092) 459
• Traditional Home (USA ISSN 0883-4660) 4551
Traditional Karate (GBR) 8212
Traditional Marine Resource Management and Knowledge (NCL ISSN 1025-7497) 3610
Traditional Medical Systems (IND ISSN 0970-5031) 5723
Traditional Music Maker see Music Maker 6591
Traditional Parent (USA) 2170
Traditional Quiltworks see Quiltworks Today 6642
Traditional Rod & Kulture Illustrated (USA ISSN 1932-1007) 4349
Traditional South Asian Medicine (DEU ISSN 1618-1522) 5723
Traditional Southern Home Plan see Southern Home Plans 8989
Traditional Style see Better Homes and Gardens Traditional Style 4533
Traditional Woodworking see British Woodworking 1049
➤ Traditiones (SVN ISSN 0352-0447) 358
Traditions (USA ISSN 1081-3098) 2304
Traditions (Uniondale) (USA ISSN 1089-506X) 3568
Traditions of Christian Spirituality Series (USA) 7820
Traditions of Guatemala see Tradiciones de Guatemala 358
Traditionsverband Ehemaliger Schutz- und Ueberseetruppen. Mitteilungsblatt (DEU ISSN 1430-0613) 4274
Tradizione Cattolica (ITA) 7820
† Tradizione nella Ristorazione Italiana (ITA ISSN 1122-3510) 8994
Tradizioni Italiane (ITA ISSN 1970-3716) 3623
• Traducao em Revista (BRA ISSN 1808-5989) 5188
Traduction Automatique Documents see T A Documents 5185
Traduire (FRA ISSN 0395-773X) 5188
Tradurin (FRO ISSN 1601-8990) 2343
† Traduzione, Societa e Cultura (ITA) 8994

Title

➤ Transport i Khranenie Nefteproduktov/ Transportation and Storage of Petroleum Products (RUS) **6795**
Transport i Suobshchenia (BGR) **8409**
• Transport iDag (SWE ISSN 1654-2118) **8514**
Transport iDag och i Trafik *see* Transport iDag **8514**
Transport iDag och i Trafik *see* Logistik iDag **1773**
• ➤ Transport in Porous Media (NLD ISSN 0169-3913) **2083**
Transport Info Hebdo (FRA ISSN 1774-8917) **8515**
Transport, Infrastructure and Logistics Conference Proceedings *see* TRAIL Conference Proceedings **8513**
Transport, Infrastructure and Logistics Studies in Transportation Science *see* TRAIL Studies in Transportation Science **8513**
Transport Inside (NOR ISSN 1503-5921) **8515**
Transport: International Transport Treaties (NLD) **8515**
Transport-Journalen (SWE ISSN 0348-3118) **8627**
Transport Law & Policy Journal (GBR) **4798**
Transport-Magasinet (DNK ISSN 0908-0570) **8515**
Transport Magazine *see* Transporte Magazine **8517**
Transport Management (GBR) **8515**
Transport Management (ZAF) **8515**
Transport Manager's and Operator's Handbook (GBR ISSN 0958-1561) **8515**
Transport Manager's Handbook and Trucker's Guide (ZAF ISSN 1015-5287) **8676**
Transport Miejski *see* Transport Miejski i Regionalny **8636**
Transport Miejski i Regionalny (POL ISSN 1732-5153) **8636**
Transport Museums (POL ISSN 0137-4435) **8515**
Transport. Navigation Interieure *see* Belgium. Institut National de Statistique. Transport. Navigation Interieure **8522**
Transport News (GBR ISSN 0969-1022) **8515**
Transport News Digest (GBR ISSN 0306-2252) **8676**
Transport-Nytt *see* Transportnytt **8664**
Transport of Goods by Road in Great Britain (GBR ISSN 0954-2647) **8676**
Transport og Logistik *see* D T L Magasinet **8670**
• ➤ Transport Policy (GBR ISSN 0967-070X) **8515**
▼ • Transport Problems/Problemy Transportu (POL ISSN 1896-0596) **8515**
➤ Transport Processes in Engineering (NLD ISSN 0923-5280) **3397**
Transport Przemyslowy (POL ISSN 1640-5455) **8515**
Transport Public (FRA ISSN 0397-474X) **8515**
Transport Research Foundation. Fellowship Lecture (GBR ISSN 1475-2298) **8636**
Transport Research Laboratory News *see* T R L News **8635**
Transport Research Laboratory Reports *see* T R L Reports **8635**
Transport Research Laboratory State of the Art Review *see* T R L State of the Art Review **8635**
Transport Retort (GBR ISSN 0965-6707) **8515**
Transport Review *see* Contractor (Leederville) **999**
• ➤ Transport Reviews (GBR ISSN 0144-1647) **8515**
Transport Routier (CAN ISSN 1494-6564) **8676**
Transport Rundschau (CHE ISSN 1423-2707) **8676**
• Transport Safety Pro Advisor (USA ISSN 1550-2074) **8515**
• Transport Salaried Staff Journal (GBR ISSN 0041-1531) **1711**
• Transport Security Advisor (USA ISSN 1539-3232) **8515**
Transport Statistics Great Britain (GBR ISSN 0144-8021) **8531**
• ➤ Transport Theory and Statistical Physics (USA ISSN 0041-1450) **7044**
Transport Ticket Society. Journal (GBR ISSN 0144-347X) **8515**
Transport-Tidende *see* Danmarks Transport-Tidende **8494**
• Transport Topics (USA ISSN 0041-1558) **8676**
Transport Trends (GBR) **8515**
Transport Ukrainy. Normativnoye Regulirovaniye *see* Transport Ukrayiny. Normatyvne Rehuliuvannia **8515**
Transport Ukrayiny. Normatyvne Rehuliuvannia (UKR) **8515**
Transport v Rossii (Year) (RUS) **8531**
Transport Workers Union of America Express *see* T W U Express **4603**
Transport Workers Union. Triennial Report (MYS) **8515**
Transport World *see* President Transport World **8508**
Transport Yearbook (Year) (GBR) **8515**
Transportarbetaren/Transportworker (SWE ISSN 0492-004X) **8515**
Transportas *see* Transport **8514**
• ➤ Transportation (USA ISSN 0049-4488) **8515**
Transportation *see* Transportation Equipment News **8676**
Transportation (Farmington Hills) *see* Information Plus Reference Series. Transportation **8964**
Transportation (Springfield) (USA) **7050**
Transportation Accident Briefs (USA) **8531**
Transportation Accident Briefs. Aviation (USA) **8531**
Transportation Accident Briefs. Highway (USA) **8531**
Transportation Accident Briefs. Marine (USA) **8531**
Transportation Accident Briefs. Pipeline (USA) **6801**
Transportation Accident Briefs. Railroads (USA) **8531**
Transportation Accident Reports (USA) **8531**
Transportation Accident Reports. Aircraft (USA) **8531**
Transportation Accident Reports. Highway (USA) **8531**
Transportation Accident Reports. Marine (USA) **8531**
Transportation Accident Reports. Pipeline (USA) **6801**
Transportation Accident Reports. Railroads (USA) **8531**
• Transportation Alternatives (USA ISSN 1524-1912) **8636**
Transportation and Economy *see* Un'yu to Keizai **8519**
Transportation and Storage of Petroleum Products *see* Transport i Khranenie Nefteproduktov **6795**
Transportation and Tariff News *see* Prepravni a Tarifni Vestnik **8508**
Transportation & Technologies (FRA ISSN 1295-7097) **8516**
Transportation Appeal Tribunal of Canada. Performance Report (CAN ISSN 1714-129X) **8516**
Transportation Association of Canada News *see* T A C News **8512**
Transportation Association of Canada Search *see* T A C Search **8512**
Transportation Builder (USA ISSN 1043-4054) **8636**
▼ • Transportation Business Journal (USA ISSN 1945-8436) **8516**
Transportation Committee Quarterly *see* T Q **4792**
• Transportation Development Centre. Annual Review (CAN ISSN 0840-9854) **8516**
Transportation Energy Research (USA ISSN 0885-8330) **3154**
Transportation Equipment News (USA ISSN 1532-0294) **8676**
Transportation Equipment News Annual Directory (USA) **8676**
Transportation Executive Update (USA ISSN 0897-8077) **8676**
Transportation Improvement Program (USA) **8636**
Transportation in America (USA ISSN 0889-0889) **8516**
Transportation in Canada. Annual Report (CAN ISSN 1484-2351) **8516**
Transportation in Canada. Report Highlights/Transports au Canada. Points Saillants du Rapport (CAN ISSN 1483-2496) **8516**
Transportation, Infrastructure and Logistics Reports in Transportation Planning *see* TRAIL Reports in Transportation Planning **8513**
Transportation, Infrastructure and Logistics Thesis Series *see* TRAIL Thesis Series **1846**
Transportation Intermediaries Association Update *see* T I A Update **8512**
• ➤ Transportation Journal (USA ISSN 0041-1612) **8516**
Transportation Law Institute Papers and Proceedings (USA ISSN 1071-5312) **4798**
• ➤ Transportation Law Journal (USA ISSN 0049-450X) **4798**
Transportation Leader (USA) **8765**
▼ • Transportation Letters (USA ISSN 1942-7867) **8516**
• Transportation Management & Engineering (USA ISSN 1537-0259) **8516**
Transportation Management Today (USA ISSN 1097-6280) **8676**
Transportation of Dangerous Goods Act. Annual Report (CAN ISSN 1719-7848) **8516**
• ➤ Transportation Planning and Technology (GBR ISSN 0308-1060) **8516**
• Transportation Professional (GBR ISSN 1478-4467) **3285**
• Transportation Quarterly (USA ISSN 0278-9434) **8516**
Transportation Quarterly *see* T Q **4792**
Transportation Recruiting and Retention Insights *see* Keller's Transportation Recruiting and Retention Insights **8672**
Transportation Research Board. Annual Meeting Proceedings (USA) **8516**
Transportation Research Board. Bibliography *see* National Research Council. Transportation Research Board. Bibliography **8528**
Transportation Research Board. State-of-the-Art Report (USA ISSN 0892-6891) **8516**
Transportation Research Circular (USA ISSN 0097-8515) **8516**
➤ Transportation Research, Economics and Policy (NLD ISSN 1572-4387) **8516**
➤ Transportation Research Forum. Journal (USA ISSN 1046-1469) **8516**
Transportation Research Information Services Electronic Bibliographic Data Base *see* T R I S Electronic Bibliographic Data Base **8530**
Transportation Research News *see* T R News **8512**
• ➤ Transportation Research. Part A: Policy & Practice (GBR ISSN 0965-8564) **8516**
• ➤ Transportation Research. Part B: Methodological (GBR ISSN 0191-2615) **8517**
• ➤ Transportation Research. Part C: Emerging Technologies (GBR ISSN 0968-090X) **8517**
• ➤ Transportation Research. Part D: Transport & Environment (GBR ISSN 1361-9209) **8517**
• ➤ Transportation Research. Part E: Logistics and Transportation Review (GBR ISSN 1366-5545) **8517**
• ➤ Transportation Research. Part F: Traffic Psychology and Behaviour (GBR ISSN 1369-8478) **8517**
➤ Transportation Research Record (USA ISSN 0361-1981) **8636**
Transportation Safety Board Annual Report to Parliament *see* T S B Annual Report to Parliament **7471**
Transportation Safety Board of Canada Annual Report *see* T S B Annual Report to Parliament **7471**
• Transportation Safety Board of Canada. Business Plan (CAN ISSN 1910-2682) **8517**
• Transportation Safety Board of Canada. Performance Report (CAN ISSN 1483-7773) **7472**
Transportation Safety Board of Canada Statistical Summary, Marine Occurrences *see* T S B Statistical Summary, Marine Occurrences **8531**
Transportation Safety Board of Canada Statistical Summary of Aviation Occurrences *see* T S B Statistical Summary of Aviation Occurrences **7549**
Transportation Safety Board Statistical Summary, Railway Occurrences *see* T S B Statistical Summary, Railway Occurrences **7549**
Transportation Safety Information Report (USA ISSN 0276-8852) **8517**
Transportation Safety Recommendations (USA ISSN 8756-4408) **7543**
Transportation Safety Reflexions. Air (CAN ISSN 1499-2442) **8517**
Transportation Safety Reflexions. Pipeline (CAN ISSN 1499-2450) **8636**
Transportation Safety Reflexions. Rail (CAN ISSN 1498-9980) **8517**
Transportation Safety Special Reports (USA) **7543**
Transportation Safety Training Newsletter *see* Keller's Transportation Safety Training Newsletter **8501**
• ➤ Transportation Science (USA ISSN 0041-1655) **8517**
Transportation Security Directory & Handbook *see* The Grey House Transportation Security Directory & Handbook **8497**
• Transportation Telephone Tickler (USA ISSN 1078-4241) **2031**
• Transportation Topics (USA) **8636**
• Transportation Watch (USA ISSN 1542-6122) **8517**
• Transporte 3 (ESP ISSN 0210-5047) **8517**
• Transporte Aereo & Turismo (ESP ISSN 0211-9633) **8765**
Transporte Automotor (URY) **8608**
• Transporte Magazine/Transport Magazine (USA) **8517**
El Transporte Maritimo en... *see* Review of Maritime Transport **8658**
Transporte Mundial Catalogo *see* T M Catalogo **8675**
Transporte Profesional (ESP) **8517**
Transporte Tres *see* Transporte 3 **8517**
Transporte y Logistica Terrestre (ESP ISSN 1576-0642) **8517**
Transporte y Vias de Comunicacion (CUB ISSN 0258-6029) **8517**
• Transporter och Kommunikationer/Transport and Communications (SWE ISSN 1403-7912) **8517**
Los Transportes y los Servicios Postales (ESP ISSN 1577-1377) **8517**
• Transportes y Turismo (MEX ISSN 0188-8013) **8517**
Transporteur (CAN ISSN 0229-4362) **7777**
Transportforskningskommissionen. Rapport (SWE ISSN 0347-0970) **8518**
Transportforum (NOR ISSN 0803-6640) **8518**
Transportista (USA ISSN 1934-3264) **8676**
TransportMarkt (DEU ISSN 0176-358X) **8518**
• Transportmetrica (HKG ISSN 1812-8602) **8518**
Transportnoe Stroitel'stvo (RUS ISSN 0131-4300) **8627**
† Transportnyt (DNK ISSN 0109-128X) **8994**
Transportnytt (SWE ISSN 0041-1523) **8664**
Transportoekonomisk Institutt. Aarsberetning (NOR) **8627**
Transport+Opslag *see* Transport & Opslag **8514**
Transportrecht (DEU ISSN 0174-559X) **8518**
Transports (FRA ISSN 0564-1373) **8518**
Transports *see* Source O C D E. Transports **8511**
Transports Actualites (FRA ISSN 0151-5861) **8518**
Transports au Canada. Points Saillants du Rapport *see* Transportation in Canada. Report Highlights **8516**
• Transports Canada. Strategie de Developpement Durable (CAN ISSN 1912-8142) **8518**
Transports Internationaux & Logistique (FRA ISSN 1766-8255) **8518**
➤ Transports Urbains (FRA ISSN 0397-6521) **8518**
TransportVisie (NLD ISSN 1381-690X) **8676**
Transportworker *see* Transportarbetaren **8515**
Transportzakboekje (BEL) **8518**
Transsexual Voice (USA) **4379**
Transtalk (ZAF) **8518**
Transterra Business Brief (GBR) **1183**
Transterra Human Resources Review (GBR ISSN 1353-5730) **1876**
Transvaal Computaform *see* Computaform **8289**
Transvaal Gardener (ZAF ISSN 0041-1744) **3752**
Transvaal Museum. Annale *see* Transvaal Museum. Annals **7924**
Transvaal Museum. Annals/Transvaal Museum. Annale (ZAF ISSN 0041-1752) **7924**
Transvaal Museum. Monographs (ZAF ISSN 0255-0172) **965**
The Transvaal Philatelist (GBR ISSN 0267-789X) **6900**
Transvaal Rugby (ZAF) **8249**
Transvaal Rural Action Committee Annual Report *see* T R A C Annual Report **7216**
➤ Transversal (AUT ISSN 1607-629X) **7731**
Transversales (CHE ISSN 1424-5868) **8011**
† Transversales (FRA ISSN 0988-8705) **8994**
Transversales (Paris) (FRA ISSN 1772-5216) **8011**
Transversales Immobilieres (FRA ISSN 1958-136X) **7614**
Transversales Science Culture (FRA ISSN 1145-5284) **8144**
Transversalites (FRA ISSN 1286-9449) **3842**
Transworld B M X *see* Ride B M X **8267**
Transworld Business (USA ISSN 1552-227X) **1183**
Transworld Identity Research Series (USA) **358**
Transworld Motocross (USA ISSN 1533-6212) **8269**
• Transworld Skateboarding (USA ISSN 0748-7401) **8338**
Transworld Skateboarding Business *see* Transworld Business **1183**
• Transworld Snowboarding (USA ISSN 1046-4611) **8338**
Transworld Snowboarding Business *see* Transworld Business **1183**
• Transworld Surf (USA ISSN 1532-9402) **8212**
Transworld Surf Business *see* Transworld Business **1183**
Transylvania University of Brasov. Buletin. Series A (ROM ISSN 1223-9631) **3397**
Transylvania University of Brasov. Bulletin. Series B (ROM ISSN 1223-964X) **5542**
Transylvanian Review (ROM ISSN 1221-1249) **4274**
• ➤ Transylvanian Review of Systematical and Ecological Research (ROM ISSN 1841-7051) **3471**
Transzport (HUN ISSN 1217-9582) **8608**
Tranvia Essay (DEU) **5390**
Tranvia Kino (DEU) **6515**
Tranvia Sur (DEU) **4478**
Tranz Rail.Holdings Limited. Annual Report *see* Toll N Z. Annual Report **8626**
• Trap & Field (USA ISSN 0041-1760) **8338**
▼ • Trap Shooting U S A (GBR ISSN 1946-7613) **8338**
Trap Shooting USA *see* Trap Shooting U S A **8338**
Trapana (ESP ISSN 0213-8069) **4274**
• Trapezikos/Bank Employee (CYP ISSN 1015-6585) **1183**
Trapper and Predator Caller *see* Trapper & Predator Caller **8338**
Trapper & Predator Caller (USA ISSN 8750-233X) **8338**
Traps (USA ISSN 1942-6054) **6624**
Trasgressioni (ITA ISSN 0394-1418) **7189**
• Trash Talk (USA ISSN 1556-7648) **3513**
Trash Talk Tip of the Week *see* Trash Talk **3513**
† Trasmissioni di Potenza (ITA ISSN 1122-5025) **8994**
Trasporti & Cultura (ITA ISSN 1971-6524) **8518**
Trasporti Europei *see* European Transport - Trasporti Europei **8495**
• Trasporti News (ITA) **8518**
▼ Trasporto Commerciale (ITA ISSN 1971-1603) **8518**
• Il Trasporto e la Gestione dei Rifiuti (ITA ISSN 1828-597X) **3513**
Il Trasporto e lo Smaltimento dei Rifiuti *see* Il Trasporto e la Gestione dei Rifiuti **3513**
Trastienda (ARG) **522**
• Trastornos Adictivos (ESP ISSN 1575-0973) **2700**
• Trastornos Adictivos. Monografico (ESP ISSN 1578-262X) **2700**
▼ • Trastornos de la Conducta Alimenticia (ESP ISSN 1887-2778) **6670**
Tratado de Ginecologia - Obstetricia *see* Encyclopedie Medico-Chirurgicale. Ginecologia - Obstetricia **5989**
Tratado de Kinesiterapia - Medicina Fisica *see* Encyclopedie Medico-Chirurgicale. Kinesiterapia - Medicina Fisica **6108**
Tratado de Pediatria *see* Encyclopedie Medico-Chirurgicale. Pediatria **6091**
Tratamientos Termicos (ESP ISSN 1132-0346) **6335**
• Trattamenti e Finiture (ITA ISSN 0041-1833) **6721**
† Trattati di Architettura (ITA ISSN 0082-6006) **8994**
Trattati e Manuali (ITA ISSN 1970-3430) **646**
Trattato di Anestesia - Rianimazione *see* Encyclopedie Medico-Chirurgicale. Anestesia - Rianimazione **5771**
Trattato di Diritto Privato (ITA ISSN 1724-1049) **4882**
Trattato di Ginecologia - Ostetricia *see* Encyclopedie Medico-Chirurgicale. Ginecologia - Ostetricia **5989**
Trattato di Medicina Riabilitativa *see* Encyclopedie Medico-Chirurgicale. Medicina Riabilitativa **6108**
Trattori (ITA ISSN 1720-3503) **214**
▼ Traum-Prinzessin (DEU) **2218**
• Trauma (ESP ISSN 1888-6116) **6188**
• ➤ Trauma (GBR ISSN 1460-4086) **6074**
Trauma (MEX ISSN 1405-1001) **6074**
Trauma *see* Travma **6074**
† Trauma (USA ISSN 0564-1470) **8994**
• Trauma and Loss: Research and Interventions (USA ISSN 1534-0333) **7413**
La Trauma de la Comunicacion (ARG ISSN 1668-5628) **2343**
Trauma Patient Management Problems *see* Patient Management Problems in Trauma and Critical Care **6070**

Title

10960 TREASURY MANAGEMENT INTERNATIONAL ULRICH'S PERIODICALS

Treasury Management International (GBR ISSN 0967-523X) **1799**
• TreasuryLog (AUT) **1387**
Treaties and Documents *see* Razprave in Gradivo **3560**
Treating Tobacco Use and Dependence (USA ISSN 1530-6402) **2700**
• Treatise on Environmental Law (USA) **4843**
Treatise on Health Care Law (USA) **4798**
➤ Treatise on Materials Science & Technology (USA ISSN 0161-9160) **3359**
Treatise on Zoology: Anatomy, Taxonomy, Biology - The Crustacea (NLD) **965**
• ➤ Treatment (USA) **7413**
Treatment Guidelines (Italian Edition) (ITA ISSN 1722-3407) **6883**
• Treatment Guidelines from The Medical Letter (USA ISSN 1541-2784) **5724**
Treatment Manuals for Practitioners (USA) **7413**
Treatment Manuals for Real World Clinicians (USA) **7413**
Treatment Plant Operator *see* T P O **3513**
Treatment Research News *see* Addiction Treatment Research News **2690**
• TreatmentUpdate (CAN ISSN 1181-7186) **5827**
Treaty Council News (USA) **3568**
• Treballs d'Arqueologia (ESP ISSN 1134-9263) **421**
Treballs d'Ictiologia i Herpetologia (ESP ISSN 1130-6130) **965**
† Trebo (ESP ISSN 1133-0287) **8994**
† Le Trebuchet (FRA ISSN 0246-8476) **8994**
Trece Oko (SRB ISSN 0354-9682) **7924**
Tred (NLD ISSN 0169-6173) **7942**
Tredyffrin Easttown History Quarterly (USA ISSN 1938-5676) **4315**
▼ Tree and Forestry Science and Biotechnology (GBR ISSN 1752-3753) **3704**
• Tree Care Industry (USA ISSN 1059-0528) **3704**
Tree City U S A Bulletin (USA) **3704**
The Tree Climber (Aberdeen) (USA ISSN 1069-3882) **3785**
Tree Climber (Alliance) (USA ISSN 1060-8680) **3785**
Tree Farmer (USA ISSN 1553-7749) **3705**
Tree-Fruit Production Guide for Interior Districts *see* British Columbia. Ministry of Agriculture Fisheries and Food. Tree Fruit Production Guide for Interior Districts **223**
• ➤ Tree Genetics & Genomes (DEU ISSN 1614-2942) **820**
Tree House Canadian Family (CAN ISSN 1485-0729) **2170**
• Tree Huggin John's Civil War Ezine (USA) **4315**
• Tree Line (AUS ISSN 1833-5845) **3705**
Tree News (GBR ISSN 0263-3469) **3705**
Tree Nut Authority. Report (MWI) **255**
• ➤ Tree Physiology (GBR ISSN 0829-318X) **820**
Tree-Ring Research (USA ISSN 1536-1098) **820**
• Tree Services (USA ISSN 1555-1008) **459**
Tree Shaker (USA ISSN 0893-2069) **3785**
• Tree Talk (USA ISSN 0736-7678) **3785**
Tree Talks (USA ISSN 0041-2201) **3785**
Tree Tracer (CAN ISSN 0841-2642) **3786**
Tree Tracers (USA ISSN 0162-1440) **3786**
Treeline *see* Tree Line **3705**
Treelines (CAN ISSN 0847-9224) **3705**
• ➤ Trees (DEU ISSN 0931-1890) **820**
Trees (GBR ISSN 0041-221X) **3705**
Trees & Forebears (CAN ISSN 1499-8548) **3786**
† Trees and Natural Resources (AUS ISSN 0814-4680) **8994**
Trees from the Grove (USA ISSN 1046-6339) **3786**
Trees of Wilson (USA ISSN 1550-0721) **3786**
The Treesearcher (USA) **3786**
• Treeworker (USA ISSN 1529-4854) **3705**
Treff (DEU ISSN 0177-4719) **2218**
Treffen (DEU ISSN 1438-6631) **421**
Treffpunkt (CHE) **6301**
Treffpunkt 55plus (DEU) **4057**
Treffpunkt Bad Windsheim (DEU) **3859**
Treffpunkt Bibel - Leiterheft *see* DasHauskreisMagazin - Leiterheft **2940**
Treffpunkt Bibliothek (CHE ISSN 0255-3570) **7575**
Treffpunkt Boulevard (CHE) **3959**
Treffpunkt Jugendpresse (DEU) **4584**
• Treffpunkt Kino (DEU ISSN 0942-430X) **6515**
Treffpunkt: Musik (DEU) **6624**
Treffpunkt Sparkasse (DEU) **1387**
Trefle/Kim (CHE) **2218**
The Trefoil (GBR ISSN 0041-2244) **8886**
▼ 30,000 Revoluciones (ARG ISSN 1851-5045) **7189**
Trek Magazine (CAN ISSN 1498-2250) **2304**
Trek Magazine (FRA ISSN 1295-8913) **8769**
Trekker (NLD ISSN 1877-3893) **214**
Trekker en Werktuig *see* Trekker **214**
Trekkers World *see* Allmountain **8682**
Trekkerskrant (BEL) **8769**
Trekkingbike (DEU ISSN 1860-1421) **8269**
Treklang *see* Treklangen **8994**
† Treklangen (DNK ISSN 0109-0003) **8994**
• Trelleborgs Allehanda (SWE ISSN 1104-0114) **3957**
Trellis (CAN ISSN 0380-1470) **3752**
Trellis Singles Magazine (USA) **5085**
Trema (NLD ISSN 0167-5478) **4798**
Tremplin (BEL ISSN 0041-2279) **2218**
• Tren de Sombras (ESP ISSN 1699-2717) **6515**
Trenchless Australasia (AUS ISSN 1832-0562) **3285**
• ➤ Trenchless Technology (USA ISSN 1064-4156) **3224**
Trenchless Technology International *see* Trenchless Technology **3224**
• Trenchless World (GBR ISSN 1756-4093) **3285**
Trencianske Noviny (SVK ISSN 0139-5068) **3947**
• Trend (AUT ISSN 0049-4623) **1184**
Trend (IND) **5390**
• Trend (SVK ISSN 1335-0684) **1184**
Trend (Berlin) (DEU ISSN 0177-0780) **1184**
Trend (Wuerburg) (DEU) **3859**
Trend Aktuell Survey Data (DEU) **1184**
Trend-Boutique (NLD ISSN 0165-4438) **1846**
Trend Creatief (NLD ISSN 1874-6918) **2250**
† Trend Discotec (ITA ISSN 1129-4264) **8994**
Trend Frisuren (DEU ISSN 1614-9629) **592**
The Trend in Engineering (USA ISSN 0041-2317) **3224**
Trend Invest (AUT) **1656**
• Trend Letter (USA ISSN 1093-5428) **1522**
• Trend Magazine (USA) **3991**
Trend Marketing (CZE ISSN 1214-9594) **1846**
Trend Monitor Reports. Communications (GBR ISSN 0963-0317) **2343**
Trend Setter (USA ISSN 1069-2274) **8608**
Trend & Tradition (DEU ISSN 1619-8069) **4399**
Trendi (FIN ISSN 0786-9282) **8886**
TrendInfo (DEU ISSN 0948-2652) **7485**
Trendletter (DEU ISSN 0941-5289) **1184**
Trendline Daily Action Stock Charts (Weekly) (USA ISSN 0277-4968) **1656**
• TrendLines (USA) **6704**
Trendrapport Bewegen en Gezondheid (NLD ISSN 1871-3467) **7543**
• Trends (BEL ISSN 0776-3387) **5085**
Trends (CAN ISSN 0847-5482) **2936**
Trends (ZWE ISSN 1814-4268) **4983**
Trends (Chicago) (USA ISSN 1533-9556) **4975**
Trends (Duesseldorf) (DEU) **4569**
† Trends (Frankfurt) (DEU ISSN 0942-1300) **8994**
Trends (Stellenbosch) *see* University of Stellenbosch. Bureau for Economic Research. Trends **1434**
Trends (Washington, 1969) (USA) **7543**
Trends & Fun (DEU) **3859**
Trends and Issues in Crime and Criminal Justice (AUS ISSN 0817-8542) **2670**
Trends and Issues in East Asia (JPN ISSN 1345-0026) **1184**
† Trends and Issues in Postsecondary English Studies (USA ISSN 1527-4241) **8994**
• Trends & Predictions Analyst (USA) **6744**
Trends and Statistics *see* British Hospitality **4382**
Trends bij Banken *see* Ondernemingsanalyses. Trends bij Banken **8979**
Trends bij Verzekeringsmaatschappijen *see* Ondernemingsanalyses. Trends bij Verzekeringsmaatschappijen **8979**
Trends Collezioni (ITA ISSN 1124-2957) **8461**
Trends Health *see* Shishang Jiankang - Nushi **8848**
Trends Home *see* Shishang Jiaju **4550**
Trends im Stellenmarkt (DEU ISSN 1433-6901) **6704**
Trends in Adjusting (USA ISSN 0041-2384) **4525**
▼ • ➤ Trends in Agricultural Economics (PAK ISSN 1994-7933) **207**
• ➤ Trends in Amplification (USA ISSN 1084-7138) **6085**
• ➤ Trends in Analytical Chemistry (NLD ISSN 0165-9936) **2107**
• ➤ Trends in Analytical Chemistry (Library Edition) (NLD ISSN 0167-2940) **2107**
• Trends in Applied Sciences Research (USA ISSN 1819-3579) **7924**
Trends in Applied Spectroscopy (IND ISSN 0972-4516) **7085**
Trends in Autonomic Pharmacology (GBR ISSN 0197-0569) **6883**
Trends in Bedrijfs- en Verzekeringsgeneeskunde (NLD ISSN 1871-9376) **4525**
• ➤ Trends in Biochemical Sciences (GBR ISSN 0968-0004) **746**
▼ • ➤ Trends in Bioinformatics (PAK ISSN 1994-7941) **826**
• Trends in Biomaterials & Artificial Organs (IND ISSN 0971-1198) **4078**
• ➤ Trends in Biotechnology (GBR ISSN 0167-7799) **771**
Trends in Cancer Research (IND ISSN 0973-1040) **6035**
➤ Trends in Carbohydrate Chemistry (IND) **2132**
Trends in Cardiology & Vascular Disease (GBR ISSN 1464-4460) **5801**
• ➤ Trends in Cardiovascular Medicine (USA ISSN 1050-1738) **5801**
• ➤ Trends in Cell Biology (GBR ISSN 0962-8924) **837**
Trends in Chemical Engineering (IND ISSN 0972-4478) **3256**
Trends in Chemical Physics (IND ISSN 0972-4346) **2142**
▼ • ➤ Trends in Classics (DEU ISSN 1866-7473) **2241**
• ➤ Trends in Cognitive Sciences (GBR ISSN 1364-6613) **7413**
Trends in de Chemie *see* Ondernemingsanalyses. Trends in de Chemie **8979**
Trends in de Metaal- en Elektro-industrie *see* Ondernemingsanalyses. Trends in de Metaal- en Elektro-industrie **8979**
Trends in de Voedings- en Genotmiddelen-industrie *see* Ondernemingsanalyses. Trends in de Voedings- en Genotmiddelenindustrie **8979**
• Trends in Domestic Box Office (USA ISSN 1930-1464) **6515**
• ➤ Trends in Ecology & Evolution (GBR ISSN 0169-5347) **708**
Trends in Electronics Conference (I E E E Region 10 Conference). Proceedings *see* T E N C O N (I E E E Region 10 Conference). Proceedings **2439**
Trends in Employment and Wages Covered by Unemployment Insurance (USA) **1711**
• ➤ Trends in Endocrinology and Metabolism (GBR ISSN 1043-2760) **5900**
Trends in Europe and North America (CHE ISSN 1020-5799) **1550**
Trends in Evidence-Based Neuropsychiatry *see* T E N **6187**
• ➤ Trends in Food Science & Technology (GBR ISSN 0924-2244) **3666**
Trends in Food Shopping Market Assessment *see* Key Note Market Assessment. Trends in Food Shopping **3679**
• Trends in G H G Sources and Sinks in Canada (Greenhouse Gas) (CAN ISSN 1910-8877) **3471**
• ➤ Trends in Genetics (GBR ISSN 0168-9525) **879**
➤ Trends in Glycoscience and Glycotechnology (JPN ISSN 0915-7352) **2132**
Trends in Heat and Mass Transfer (IND ISSN 0973-2446) **7057**
Trends in Heat, Mass & Momentum Transfer *see* Trends in Heat and Mass Transfer **7057**
Trends in Heterocyclic Chemistry (IND ISSN 0972-432X) **2132**
Trends in Higher Education *see* Trends **2936**
• ➤ Trends in Immunology (GBR ISSN 1471-4906) **5766**
Trends in Indian Health *see* U.S. Department of Health and Human Services. Indian Health Service. Trends in Indian Health **6636**
Trends in Information Management (IND ISSN 0973-4163) **5051**
Trends in Inorganic Chemistry (IND ISSN 0972-4338) **2118**
Trends in Journal Subscriptions (GBR ISSN 0958-5354) **7575**
Trends in Language Acquisition Research (NLD ISSN 1569-0644) **5189**
• Trends in Law Library Management and Technology (USA ISSN 0893-6773) **5051**
Trends in Leisure Activities Market Assessment *see* Key Note Market Assessment. Trends in Leisure Activities **1893**
➤ Trends in Linguistics. Documentation (DEU ISSN 0179-8251) **5189**
➤ Trends in Linguistics. Studies and Monographs (DEU ISSN 1861-4302) **5189**
Trends in Logic - Studia Logica Library (NLD ISSN 1572-6126) **6958**
• Trends in Managing Water and Waste Water Treatment (USA) **3513**
▼ • Trends in Medical Research (USA ISSN 1819-3587) **5724**
➤ Trends in Medicine (ITA ISSN 1594-2848) **6883**
Trends in Medieval Philology (DEU ISSN 1612-443X) **5390**
Trends in Metals & Materials Engineering *see* Jae'lyo Ma'dang **6318**
• ➤ Trends in Microbiology (GBR ISSN 0966-842X) **896**
• ➤ Trends in Molecular Medicine (GBR ISSN 1471-4914) **5724**
▼ • ➤ Trends in Molecular Sciences (PAK ISSN 1994-5469) **2132**
Trends in Neurophysiology *see* Actualites Neurophysiologiques **6119**
• ➤ Trends in Neurosciences (GBR ISSN 0166-2236) **6189**
Trends in Neurosciences. Supplement *see* Neurotoxins **6170**
• Trends in Optics and Photonics Series (USA ISSN 1094-5695) **7085**
• Trends in Organized Crime (USA ISSN 1084-4791) **2670**
• ➤ Trends in Parasitology (GBR ISSN 1471-4922) **897**
• ➤ Trends in Pharmacological Sciences (GBR ISSN 0165-6147) **6883**
Trends in Photochemistry & Photobiology (IND ISSN 0972-4532) **2142**
Trends in Physical Chemistry (IND ISSN 0972-4435) **2142**
• ➤ Trends in Plant Science (GBR ISSN 1360-1385) **820**
Trends in Private Investment in Developing Countries (USA ISSN 1018-208X) **1606**
▼ Trends in Regenerative Medicine (USA) **5724**
• Trends in Reportable Sexually Transmitted Diseases in the United States (USA ISSN 1933-1541) **5882**
Trends in Social Security (CHE ISSN 1019-4126) **4526**
Trends in Southeast Asia (SGP ISSN 0082-6316) **7269**
• Trends in Telephone Service (USA ISSN 1937-4453) **2373**
• Trends in the Hotel Industry. U S A Edition (USA ISSN 0276-5357) **4399**
Trends in the Sciences *see* Gakujutsu no Doko **7857**
• Trends in the Well-Being of America's Children and Youth (USA ISSN 1932-3735) **2170**
Trends in Transport *see* Ondernemingsanalyses. Trends in Transport **8979**
• Trends in Urology, Gynaecology & Sexual Health (GBR ISSN 1362-5306) **6275**
Trends in Vacuum Science & Technology (IND ISSN 0972-4486) **7044**
Trends Infos Praktisches der Woche *see* T I P der Woche **3858**
The Trends Journal (USA ISSN 1065-2094) **1184**
Trends Magazine (CAN) **1184**
Trends Magazine (USA ISSN 1062-8266) **8809**
Trends of Recent Researches on the History of China *see* Zhongguoshi Yanjiu Dongtai **4191**
• Trends Online (USA) **6397**
• Trends - Tendances (BEL ISSN 0776-3395) **5085**
Trends Time *see* Shishang Shijian **3828**
• Trendsetters.com (USA) **2567**
TrendSportWissenschaft (DEU ISSN 1435-9944) **8212**
Trendy Africa (USA ISSN 1938-8462) **3568**
Trendy Girl (ITA ISSN 1827-6571) **592**
Trendz (IND ISSN 0973-2195) **5724**
Trendz (USA) **4570**
† Trenet (ESP) **8994**
I Treni (ITA) **8627**
➤ Trenie i Iznos (BLR ISSN 0202-4977) **3397**
Trennial Directory of Members *see* Centennial Biographical Directory of Members **7114**
Trent Geographical Papers (GBR ISSN 1365-7798) **4031**
Trent University. Centre for Health Studies. Showcase (CAN ISSN 1912-4341) **3005**
Trent University. Institute for Health Studies. Showcase *see* Trent University. Centre for Health Studies. Showcase **3005**
Trenta Buone Idee *see* 30 Buone Idee **4553**
Trenta Giorni *see* 30 Giorni **7824**
Trente (CAN ISSN 0384-9325) **4584**
Trente Journees Qui Ont Fait la France *see* Les Journees Qui Ont Fait la France **4236**
Trente Jours (CHE) **3959**
Trente Millions d'Amis *see* 30 Millions d'Amis **6817**
Trente-neuf-quarante-cinq Magazine *see* 39 - 45 Magazine **6455**
Trente-six Mille Communes *see* 36000 Communes **7505**
Trentino (ITA ISSN 0391-8785) **3471**
Trenton Courier Advocate *see* Trenton Trentonian **3819**
• Trenton Trentonian (CAN) **3819**
Trentonian & Tri-County News (CAN) **3819**
Treoir (IRL ISSN 0790-004X) **6624**
Trepleie *see* Trevennen **3752**
† Tres 60 Bodyboard (ESP) **8994**
Tres Continentes (PRT) **4478**
Tres Sesenta *see* 3sesenta **8343**
Tresearch (IRL ISSN 1649-8917) **163**
Tresors du Bouddhisme (FRA ISSN 1623-8613) **7702**
Tresors Monetaires (FRA ISSN 0223-4300) **6653**
† Trespass to Try Title (USA) **8994**
Trestnepravni Revue (CZE ISSN 1213-5313) **4899**
Tretii Vzglyad (RUS) **3942**
Tretzevents (ESP ISSN 1134-3427) **2218**
Treubia (IDN ISSN 0082-6340) **965**
Treveccan (USA) **2304**
Trevennen (NOR ISSN 1504-6028) **3752**
• Trevithick Society. Journal (GBR ISSN 0308-2644) **8444**
Trevithick Society. Quarterly Newsletter (GBR) **8444**
• Trevor Reid, M B A - Law Student Blog (Master in Business Administration) (USA ISSN 1947-119X) **4798**
Trevor Reid M B A - Law Student Blog *see* Trevor Reid, M B A - Law Student Blog **4798**
Trezvost' i Kul'tura/Abstinence and Culture (RUS ISSN 0234-6192) **8144**
Tri-Alphametic Puzzles (NZL ISSN 1176-9483) **8212**
• Tri-City Computing Magazine (USA ISSN 1081-1109) **2440**
Tri-City Genealogical Society. Bulletin (USA ISSN 0496-1803) **3786**
• Tri-City News (CAN ISSN 0839-4741) **3819**
Tri-County Bulletin (USA) **3569**
Tri-County Genealogy (USA ISSN 0896-419X) **3786**
Tri-County Woman (USA) **8886**
• Tri - M News (USA) **6624**
Tri-Ology Technical Report (Online) (USA) **163**
Tri-Ology Technical Report (Print) *see* Tri-Ology Technical Report (Online) **163**
Tri-Son News (USA) **6624**
Tri-State Bluegrass Association Band and Festival Guide (USA ISSN 0735-4711) **6624**
Tri-State Business Times (USA ISSN 1065-6170) **1184**
Tri-State Dairy Nutrition Conference. Proceedings (USA) **269**
Tri State Defender (USA) **3569**
Tri-State Food News (USA ISSN 0041-249X) **3682**
Tri-State Livestock News (USA) **302**
Tri-State Neighbor (USA) **163**
Tri-State Packet (USA ISSN 0740-896X) **3786**
Tri-State SportsLook (USA ISSN 1934-3256) **8212**
Tri-University Meson Facility Annual Report Scientific Activities *see* T R I U M F Annual Report Scientific Activities **7072**
Tri-University Meson Facility Financial and Administrative Annual Report *see* T R I U M F Financial and Administrative Annual Report **7072**
The Tri-Valley Townsman *see* Ye Olde Tri-Valley Townsman **3993**

Title

10962 TRNAVSKE NOVINY ULRICH'S PERIODICALS

Trnavske Noviny see T H - Extra 3947
• La Trobe University. Annual Research Report (Online) (AUS ISSN 1833-1270) 2920
• La Trobe University Library News (AUS ISSN 0155-8471) 5051
Troca see Trochus 3610
Trocadero (ESP ISSN 0214-4212) 4164
Trochus (NCL ISSN 1025-7454) 3610
Trockenbau Akustik (DEU ISSN 0179-8006) 1041
Troedler- und Sammler- Journal (DEU ISSN 1618-5242) 369
Troellaskagatidindi see Baejarposturinn 3877
Troender - Avisa (NOR) 3925
• Troenderbladet (NOR) 3925
Trofeo a la Vaquera (ESP) 5085
Trofeo Armas de Caza (ESP ISSN 1886-2233) 8338
Trofeo Caza (ESP ISSN 1699-7492) 8338
Trofeo Caza Mayor (ESP) 8338
Trofeo Doma Clasica (ESP) 8299
Trofeo Golf (ESP) 8249
Trofeo Nautica (ESP ISSN 1699-2776) 8283
Trofeo Nieve (ESP ISSN 1886-2136) 8338
Trofeo Perros de Caza (ESP) 8338
Trofeo Pesca (ESP ISSN 1699-2768) 8338
▼ Trofeo Pesca Mar (ESP ISSN 1889-0695) 8338
Trofeo Todo Caballo (ESP ISSN 1579-234X) 8299
Trofima kai Pota/Food & Beverages (GRC ISSN 1106-3718) 611
• Troianalexandrina (BEL ISSN 1577-5003) 5390
Trois-cent-trois see 303 529
Trois Fois Passera see 3 Fois Passera 2224
Trois Pommes (FRA ISSN 0768-3979) 2218
Troisdorfer Jahreshefte (DEU) 4274
Trojmiejska Akademicka Siec Komputerowa Quaterly see T A S K Quaterly 2504
Trolley Fare (USA ISSN 1041-9632) 6538
Trolley Wire (AUS ISSN 0155-1264) 8518
Trolleybus Magazine (GBR ISSN 0266-7452) 8518
Trollhaettans Tidning (SWE ISSN 1104-0122) 3957
Le Trombinoscope. Union Europeenne see Eurosource 624
Troms Folkeblad (NOR) 3925
Tromsoe (NOR) 3925
• Tromsoe Geophysical Observatory. Reports (NOR ISSN 1504-1174) 6397
Tromsoe Museum. Rapportserie. Fellesserie see Tromura. Fellesserie 6538
Tromsoe Museum. Rapportserie. Kulturhistorie see Tromura. Kulturhistorie 4274
Tromsoe Museum. Rapportserie. Museologi see Tromura. Museologi 6538
Tromsoe Museum. Rapportserie, Naturvitenskap see Tromura. Naturvitenskap 7925
Tromsoe Museum. Skrifter (NOR ISSN 0085-7394) 6538
Tromsoe University Working Papers on Language & Linguistics see Nordlyd 5156
Tromura. Fellesserie (NOR ISSN 0332-7647) 6538
Tromura. Kulturhistorie (NOR ISSN 0333-2802) 4274
Tromura. Museologi (NOR ISSN 0332-6543) 6538
Tromura. Naturvitenskap (NOR ISSN 0332-6195) 7925
Tronderlagets Aarbok see Aarbok 3515
Trondhjems Turistforening. Aarbok see Tur-Glede 8769
• TropAg & Rural (GBR) 187
Tropelias (ESP ISSN 1132-2373) 5390
Tropenbos Series (NLD ISSN 1383-6811) 3705
† Tropeninstituut (NLD ISSN 0167-708X) 8994
Der Tropenlandwirt see Journal of Agriculture and Rural Development in the Tropics and Subtropics 126
➤ Trophoblast Research (USA ISSN 0891-9925) 6005
Trophy & Engraving News (GBR ISSN 0266-3295) 1855
Trophy Rooms Around the World (CAN) 8213
• Tropi-Ties E-Zine & Catalog (USA) 8769
Tropic Oceanology see Redai Haiyang Xuebao 2816
Tropical Agricultural Research (LKA ISSN 1016-1422) 163
➤ Tropical Agriculture (TTO ISSN 0041-3216) 163
• Tropical Agriculturist (LKA ISSN 0041-3224) 163
• ➤ Tropical and Subtropical Agroecosystems (MEX ISSN 1870-0462) 163
• ➤ Tropical Animal Health and Production (NLD ISSN 0049-4747) 8809
➤ Tropical Biodiversity (IDN ISSN 0854-1566) 708
Tropical Biomedicine (MYS ISSN 0127-5720) 5724
Tropical Bryology Research Reports (GBR ISSN 1468-8158) 820
• Tropical Coasts (PHL ISSN 0117-9756) 3491
▼ • ➤ Tropical Conservation Science (USA ISSN 1940-0829) 821
Tropical Cyclones (Year) see Hong Kong Observatory. Tropical Cyclones (Year) 6354
Tropical Dental Journal see Odonto-Stomatologie Tropicale 5858
Tropical Disease Research News (CHE ISSN 1028-5911) 5827
• Tropical Diseases Bulletin (GBR ISSN 0041-3240) 5751
• ➤ Tropical Doctor (GBR ISSN 0049-4755) 5827
Tropical Ecology (IND ISSN 0564-3295) 821
Tropical Fish (GBR ISSN 1471-9517) 4349
Tropical Fish Hobbyist (USA ISSN 0041-3259) 4349
Tropical Forages Program Annual Report see Programa de Forrajes Tropicales. Informe Bianual 148
• Tropical Forest Update (JPN ISSN 1022-5439) 3705
Tropical Forestry Papers (GBR ISSN 0141-9668) 3705
• Tropical Forestry Reports (FIN ISSN 0786-8170) 3705
• ➤ Tropical Freshwater Biology (NGA ISSN 0795-0101) 3610
Tropical Fruit News (USA ISSN 1075-6108) 3752
Tropical Fruits Newsletter (TTO ISSN 1024-1957) 163
The Tropical Garden (USA) 3752
Tropical Gastroenterology (IND ISSN 0250-636X) 5932
Tropical Geography see Redai Dili 4026
➤ Tropical Grasslands (AUS ISSN 0049-4763) 255
• Tropical Journal of Obstetrics and Gynaecology (NGA ISSN 0189-5117) 6005
• ➤ Tropical Journal of Pharmaceutical Research (NGA) 6883
Tropical Lepidoptera see Tropical Lepidoptera Research 860
➤ Tropical Lepidoptera Research (USA ISSN 1941-7659) 860
➤ Tropical Medicine/Nettai Igaku (JPN ISSN 0041-3267) 5827
• Tropical Medicine and Health (JPN ISSN 1348-8945) 5827
• Tropical Medicine and Hygiene News (USA ISSN 0041-3275) 5827
• ➤ Tropical Medicine & International Health (GBR ISSN 1360-2276) 5827
Tropical Medicine: Science and Practice (GBR) 5724
• ➤ Tropical Oceanography (BRA ISSN 1679-3005) 708
Tropical Pesticides Research Institute. Annual Report (TZA ISSN 0082-6642) 255
▼ • Tropical Plant Biology (USA ISSN 1935-9756) 821
• ➤ Tropical Plant Pathology (BRA ISSN 1982-5676) 821
Tropical Resources Institute News see T R I News 3704
† • ➤ Tropical Science (GBR ISSN 0041-3291) 8994
Tropical Timber Market Report (JPN) 3716
Tropical Timbers (GBR ISSN 0269-980X) 3716
▼ Tropical Treasures (USA ISSN 1936-1378) 3752
• ➤ Tropical Veterinarian (NGA ISSN 0794-4845) 8809
• ➤ Tropical Zoology (ITA ISSN 0394-6975) 965
Tropical Zoology. Special Issue (ITA ISSN 1121-919X) 965
Tropicos (VEN ISSN 1316-7219) 7413
Tropics/Nettai Kenkyu (JPN ISSN 0917-415X) 708
• ➤ Tropicultura (BEL ISSN 0771-3312) 256
• Tropinet (USA) 2629
Tropische und Subtropische Pflanzenwelt (DEU ISSN 0302-9417) 821
TropMed Seminars on Tropical Medicine. Proceedings (THA) 5828
Tropolitan (USA) 2304
Tropos (USA ISSN 1044-8209) 5390
TROS see T R O S 1039
Trostberger Tagblatt (DEU) 3859
Trot (CAN ISSN 0704-0733) 8299
Trots Allt (SWE ISSN 1101-914X) 5243
Trott-war (DEU) 3859
Il Trottatore (ITA) 8299
Der Trotter (DEU ISSN 1860-9031) 8769
Trotter Review (USA ISSN 1070-695X) 3569
Trotting and Pacing Guide (USA ISSN 0083-3509) 8299
Trotwaer see De Moanne 5335
Trotzdem (AUT ISSN 0041-3356) 7189
Troubadour (NLD) 6958
Trouble and Strife (GBR ISSN 1352-027X) 8903
• Troubled Company Prospector (USA) 1846
• Troubled Company Reporter (USA ISSN 1520-9474) 1184
• Troubled Company Reporter - Asia Pacific (USA ISSN 1520-9482) 1184
• Troubled Company Reporter - Europe (USA ISSN 1529-2754) 1184
• Troubled Company Reporter - Latin America (USA ISSN 1529-2746) 1184
Troubles (CHE) 7189
TroubleShooter (NLD) 2440
Trout (USA ISSN 0041-3364) 2629
• Trout (Auckland) (NZL) 5243
Trout and Salmon (GBR ISSN 0041-3372) 8338
Trout Fisherman (GBR ISSN 0142-9108) 8338
Trout News see Finfish News 3591
Trout Production see U.S. Department of Agriculture. National Agricultural Statistics Service. Trout Production 3614
Trout Unlimited see Trout 2629
Trouvailles (FRA) 522
Trouw (NLD) 3916
Trowel (CAN ISSN 0702-2204) 1041
• Trowel and Sword (AUS ISSN 0813-796X) 7691
• Trubadur (POL ISSN 1642-3399) 6624
Truboprovodnyi Transport Nefti/Oil Pipeline Transport (RUS ISSN 0869-8740) 6795
Truboprovody i Ekologiya (RUS) 2629
Trubus (IDN ISSN 0126-0057) 163
Truck (GBR ISSN 0308-0641) 8676
Truck & see Gruzovik & 8497
† Truck and Bus (AUS ISSN 0041-3380) 8994
Truck and Bus Engineering see Truck & Bus Engineering 3224
▼ • Truck & Bus Engineering (USA ISSN 1946-7117) 3224
Truck & Bus, South Africa (ZAF ISSN 0258-9281) 8676
Truck & Business (Dutch Edition) (BEL ISSN 0772-5000) 8676
Truck & Business (French Edition) see Truck & Business (Dutch Edition) 8676
• Truck & Driver Magazine (GBR ISSN 0966-3533) 8676
▼ Truck and Equipment Post (USA ISSN 1947-9751) 8677
Truck & Plant Trader (GBR ISSN 1745-624X) 8677
• Truck & S U V Performance (USA ISSN 1534-2107) 8677
Truck and S U V Performance see Truck & S U V Performance 8677
• Truck & Trailer (CAN ISSN 0319-7492) 8677
Truck & Trailer Australia (AUS ISSN 1445-7806) 8677
Truck and Trailer Magazine see Truck 'N Trailer Magazine 8677
Truck and Van Guide see Black Book. Truck and Van Guide 1975
• Truck Blue Book (USA ISSN 0273-9402) 8677
Truck Blue Book Residual Value Guide (USA) 8677
Truck Builder (USA ISSN 1532-3889) 3224
Truck Data Book (CAN ISSN 0564-3392) 8677
Truck Driver's Handbook (GBR) 8608
Truck en Transport Management see T T M 8675
Truck Equipment News (USA) 8677
Truck Equipment Outlook (USA) 8677
Truck-Frame & Axle Repair Association News & Topics see T A R A News & Topics 8675
Truck Identification Book (USA ISSN 0889-3888) 8677
Truck Logger (CAN ISSN 0834-0285) 3717
Truck Magazin (CZE ISSN 1214-4185) 8677
Truck-Magazin Motor und Sport (DEU) 8677
Truck Market (DEU) 8677
Truck-Mobiles (DEU ISSN 1434-4106) 8677
Truck Model World (GBR ISSN 0958-0530) 4349
Truck Modell (DEU ISSN 0944-5897) 4349
• Truck 'N Trailer Magazine (USA) 8677
• Truck News (CAN ISSN 0712-2683) 8677
• Truck Paper (USA) 8677
Truck Parts & Service (USA ISSN 0895-3856) 8677
† Truck Race Book (DEU) 8994
Truck, Race, Cycle and Rec Marketplace (USA) 8608
Truck Safety Manager Report (USA ISSN 1559-2480) 8677
Truck Sport Book (DEU) 8677
Truck Sport Guide (DEU) 8677
▼ Truck Sport Magazin (DEU ISSN 1865-0988) 8677
Truck Trader see Truck & Plant Trader 8677
Truck Trader (GBR) 8677
Truck Trader (NZL) 8677
Truck Trader (USA) 8677
Truck Trend see Motor Trend's Truck Trend 8593
† Truck Trial Guide (DEU) 8994
• Truck West (CAN ISSN 1185-3409) 8677
Truckbody & Trailer see New Zealand Truckbody & Trailer 8673
Trucker (DEU ISSN 0946-3216) 8677
• The Trucker (USA ISSN 1526-0127) 8677
Trucker (Prague) (CZE ISSN 1335-4531) 8677
Trucker's Connection (USA) 8677
• Truckers Guide (NOR ISSN 1504-3487) 8678
• Truckers News (USA ISSN 1040-2284) 8678
Truckers News en Espanol see Transportista 8676
• The Trucker's Page (USA) 8678
• Truckin' (USA ISSN 0277-5743) 8678
Truckin' Life (AUS ISSN 0155-9648) 8678
Trucking (GBR ISSN 1740-066X) 8678
• Trucking Activity Report (USA ISSN 1942-2784) 8531
• Trucking Economic Review (USA ISSN 1942-2806) 8531
• Trucking in Canada (CAN ISSN 0829-8947) 8678
Trucking Minnesota (USA) 8678
Trucking Permit Guide (USA) 8678
• Trucking Technology (USA ISSN 1524-1009) 8678
• Trucking Times (Year) (USA ISSN 1935-6331) 8678
Trucks (USA ISSN 1553-7811) 8678
Trucks & Details (DEU ISSN 1860-3424) 4350
Trucks and Tanks Magazine see T N T 6448
Trucksalon (CZE ISSN 1212-334X) 8608
Truckstar (NLD ISSN 1382-9017) 8678
Truckstop Travel Plaza (USA) 1968
TruckWerk (NLD ISSN 1874-9097) 8678
• Truckworld Online! (USA) 8678
Trud (BGR ISSN 0205-1338) 3805
• Trud (RUS ISSN 1025-1189) 3942
Trud i Pravo (BGR) 1711
Trud i Pravo (RUS) 1711
Trud i Zanyatost' v Rossii (Year) (RUS) 1270
Trud. Subbotnii Vypusk (RUS) 1711
Trudbenik (MKD ISSN 0041-3437) 4603
• Trudovi Otnoshenia (BGR) 4843
Trudovoe Pravo (RUS) 1711
Trudy A A N I I see A A N I I. Trudy 3996
Trudy O A O Ts N I I S see Nauchno-Issledovatel'skii Institut Transportnogo Stroitel'stva. Trudy 8506
Trudy po Znakovym Sistemam see Sign Systems Studies 5174
Trudy Tsagi (RUS) 7063
True Buddha News see Zhen Fo Bao 7703
True Confessions (USA ISSN 0041-3488) 5415
True Crime (ITA ISSN 1824-9973) 5415
True Crime Monthly (GBR ISSN 0261-264X) 5412
True Detective (GBR ISSN 0262-4133) 5412
True Experience (USA ISSN 0199-0012) 5415
True Girl (USA) 2218
True Love (USA ISSN 0041-3550) 5412
True Love see True Love. East Africa 5412
True Love (ZAF) 8886
True Love Babe (ZAF ISSN 1819-8031) 8886
True Love. East Africa (ZAF ISSN 1812-6650) 5412
True Love. West Africa (ZAF ISSN 1813-1379) 5085
True North Volleyball (CAN) 8213
True Romance (USA ISSN 0199-0020) 5412
True Story (USA ISSN 0195-3117) 5412
The True Vine (USA ISSN 1043-7878) 7706
▼ • True Wealth Magazine (USA) 1184
True West (USA ISSN 0041-3615) 4315
Truite Mag (FRA ISSN 1292-6078) 8338
Truly Fine (USA) 5390
Truly Portable (USA) 2573
TrumaH (DEU ISSN 0935-1035) 3569
▼ • Truman Lake News (USA ISSN 1947-7627) 3991
• ➤ Truman Review (USA) 2304
Trump World (USA ISSN 1543-2432) 5085
The Trumpet (CAN) 2170
The Trumpet (New York) (USA) 522
Trumpet and Brass Programs (Year) (USA ISSN 1061-8856) 6624
• The Trumpeter (CAN ISSN 0832-6193) 3471
Trumpeter (USA ISSN 0148-673X) 6900
The Trumpeter (Crestview) (USA ISSN 1934-2179) 3752
The Trumpeter (Westbrook) (USA ISSN 1524-6132) 8483
Truppendienst (AUT ISSN 0041-3658) 6449
• Truro Daily News (CAN ISSN 1711-9081) 3819
The Trust (CAN ISSN 0381-9612) 3048
Trust (DEU ISSN 1615-4347) 6625
Trust Administration and Taxation (USA) 4905
Trust and Estate Practitioner see Private Client Practitioner 4905
Trust and Investment Services Positions see Survey Report on Financial Institutions Compensation. Trust and Investment Services Positions 1654
Trust and Verify (GBR ISSN 0966-9221) 7269
Trust Department Administration and Operations (USA) 4905
Trust for African Rock Art Newsletter see T A R A Newsletter 357
Trust in Focus (AUS ISSN 1834-1527) 4436
Trust Institutions (Year) Directory see Wealth Management Resource Guide 1390
Trust pour la Preservation de l'A V.CA. Rapport Annuel see A V Preservation Trust of Canada. Annual Report 6488
The Trust Regulatory Handbook (USA ISSN 1090-2511) 1387
Trust Regulatory News (USA ISSN 1068-4301) 1387
The Trusted Professional (USA) 1303
• Trustee (USA ISSN 0041-3674) 4112
The Trustee (USA ISSN 1085-3170) 5051
Trustee Quarterly (USA ISSN 0271-9746) 2920
A Trustee's Handbook see Loring, a Trustee's Handbook 4903
Trustee's Reports and Accounts see Royal Society for the Prevention of Cruelty to Animals. Trustees' Report and Accounts 1301
Trusteeship (USA ISSN 1068-1027) 3005
• Trusts (NLD) 1953
Trusts see B A R - B R I Bar Review. Trusts 4901
• Trusts & Estates (GBR ISSN 1472-6475) 4906
• Trusts & Estates (USA ISSN 0041-3682) 1656
Trusts & Estates see Trusts and Estates (Springfield) 4906
• ➤ Trusts and Estates (Springfield) (USA) 4906
Trusts and Estates Law & Tax Journal see Trusts and Estates Law Journal 4906
Trusts and Estates Law Journal (GBR ISSN 1464-7478) 4906
Trusts & Estates Law Section Newsletter see Trusts and Estates Law Section Newsletter 4906
• ➤ Trusts and Estates Law Section Newsletter (USA ISSN 1530-3896) 4906
Trusts and Succession Service (GBR) 4798
• Trusts & Trustees (GBR ISSN 1363-1780) 4906
The Truth (NGA ISSN 0331-5975) 7716
Truth see Adevarul 3932
The Truth (USA) 2670
The Truth (Philadelphia) (USA ISSN 0041-3690) 4526
The Truth at Last (USA) 5243
Truth in Action (USA) 6958
Truth-in-Lending Manual (USA) 1387
Truth of Life (USA) 6958
▼ • Truth Points (USA ISSN 1943-6645) 7777
• Truth Seeker (USA ISSN 0041-3712) 6958
• Truth vs. Tradition (USA) 7777
Trux (USA) 8678
Try It Yourself Hair (USA ISSN 1076-8092) 592
Try Us see National Minority and Women-Owned Business Directory 2018
Try Us - National Minority and Women-Owned Business Directory see National Minority and Women-Owned Business Directory 2018
Try Us - National Women-Owned Business Directory see National Minority and Women-Owned Business Directory 2018
Trybuna (POL ISSN 0867-0536) 3930
Trybuna (UKR ISSN 0868-8117) 3965
Trybuna Gornicza (POL ISSN 1231-9996) 6480
• Trybuna Slaska (POL ISSN 0867-4507) 3930

Title

10964 LA TUNISIE MEDICALE ULRICH'S PERIODICALS

• ➤ La Tunisie Medicale (TUN ISSN 0041-4131) **5724**
Tunnel (DEU ISSN 0722-6241) **3286**
• The Tunnel (USA) **7216**
• Tunnel Business Magazine (USA ISSN 1553-2917) **3286**
Tunnel Construction and Piling (GBR) **3286**
† Tunnel Management International (GBR ISSN 1463-242X) **8994**
Tunnel Safety International *see* Tunnel Management International **8994**
Tunnelbau *see* Taschenbuch fuer den Tunnelbau **3285**
Tunnelling Activities in Japan (JPN) **3286**
Tunnelling & Trenchless Construction *see* Trenchless World **3285**
• ➤ Tunnelling and Underground Space Technology (GBR ISSN 0886-7798) **3224**
Tunnels & Tunnelling Buyer's Guide (GBR ISSN 1756-7882) **3286**
• Tunnels & Tunnelling International (GBR ISSN 1369-3999) **3286**
Tunnels & Tunnelling No-Dig Technology (GBR) **3286**
Tunnels and Underground *see* Tonneru to Chika **3285**
Tunnels et Ouvrages Souterrains (FRA ISSN 0399-0834) **3286**
T'unot D'rakhim 'im Nifga'im *see* Israel. Central Bureau of Statistics. Road Accidents with Casualties. Part 2 **8527**
Il Tuo Bambino *see* Salute e Benessere. Il Tuo Bambino **8987**
Tuoi Tre/The Youth (VNM ISSN 1012-0637) **3994**
Tuoi Tre Chu Nhat/The Youth on Sunday (VNM ISSN 1560-1412) **3994**
• Tuph (DEU ISSN 1862-5525) **5243**
Tur-Glede (NOR ISSN 1503-7460) **8769**
Turan-Energy. Contracts (AZE) **4798**
Turan-Enerzhi. Kontrakty *see* Turan-Energy. Contracts **4798**
Turan-Finance (AZE) **1387**
Turan Information Agency. Analytical Bulletin (AZE) **5243**
Turan Information Agency. Cultural Issue *see* Informatsionnoe Agentstvo Turan. Kulturnyi Vestnik **3798**
Turan Information Agency. Daily Economic Bulletin (AZE) **1522**
Turan Information Agency. Daily Political - Eventual (AZE) **3799**
Turan Information Agency. Energy Annual Report (AZE) **6795**
Turan Information Agency. Macroeconomic Indexes (AZE) **1522**
Turan Information Agency. Monthly Economic Review (AZE) **1522**
Turan Informatsionnoe Agentstvo. Analiticheskii Byulletin *see* Turan Information Agency. Analytical Bulletin **5243**
Turan Informatsionnoe Agentstvo. Ezhemesyachnoe Ekonomicheskoe Obozrenie *see* Turan Information Agency. Monthly Economic Review **1522**
Turan Informatsionnoe Agentstvo. Makroekonomicheskie Pokazateli *see* Turan Information Agency. Macroeconomic Indexes **1522**
Turan-Transport (AZE) **8518**
• Turang/Soil (CHN ISSN 0253-9829) **2717**
• Turang Feiliao/Soils and Fertilizers (CHN ISSN 1002-0616) **256**
Turang Qinshi yu Shuitu Baochi Xuebao/Journal of Soil Erosion and Soil and Water Conservation *see* Shuitu Baochi Xuebao **252**
Turang Quan *see* Pedosphere **2714**
• ➤ Turang Xuebao/Acta Pedologica Sinica (CHN ISSN 0564-3929) **2717**
Turangi Chronicle (NZL ISSN 1170-1250) **3919**
Turangxue Jinzhan/Progress in Soil Science (CHN ISSN 0254-010X) **2717**
Al-Turath al-Urthuduksi *see* At- Turath al-Urthuduksi **7706**
At-Turath al-Urthuduksi/Orthodox Legacy (LBN ISSN 1814-7038) **7706**
Turath wa-Funun/Heritage and Arts (UAE) **3623**
• Turbine (NZL ISSN 1177-5203) **5243**
• Turbine Airliner Fleet Survey (GBR ISSN 1366-6703) **8552**
Turbine Technology *see* Qilunji Jishu **3394**
Turbine Technology Directory (GBR ISSN 1747-6046) **3148**
Turbo (FIN ISSN 1795-0546) **8608**
Turbo (PRT ISSN 0874-0534) **8608**
Turbo & High Tech Performance (USA ISSN 0894-5039) **8608**
Turbo and High Tech Performance *see* Turbo & High Tech Performance **8608**
Turbomachinery *see* Tabo Kikai **3396**
• Turbomachinery International (USA ISSN 0149-4147) **3398**
Turbomachinery International Handbook (USA ISSN 0748-0903) **3398**
Turbomachinery Society of Japan. Proceedings *see* Tabo Kikai Koenkai **3396**
• ➤ Turbomachinery Symposium. Proceedings (USA) **5460**
• Turboprop Storage Update (GBR ISSN 1366-6797) **8552**
• Turbozine (USA) **8608**
➤ Turbulence (POL ISSN 0860-7222) **6407**
• ➤ Turcica (BEL ISSN 0082-6847) **562**
Turcologica (DEU ISSN 0177-4743) **562**
Turdiye'de ve Dunyada Otomasyon/Automation in Turkey and the World *see* Otomasyon **1157**
Turf & Recreation (CAN ISSN 1186-0170) **3752**
• Turf Central (USA ISSN 1059-6348) **3752**
Turf Craft (AUS ISSN 0819-8632) **3752**
Turf Digest (NZL) **8299**
Turf digest Weekender *see* Turf Digest **8299**
Turf Grass Trends *see* TurfGrass Trends **3752**
Turf News (USA ISSN 0899-417X) **256**
• Turf North (USA ISSN 1092-1192) **3752**
• Turf South (USA ISSN 1058-3254) **3752**
• Turf West (USA ISSN 1071-4995) **3752**
Turfanological Research *see* Tulufanxue Yanjiu **4165**
• TurfGrass Trends (USA ISSN 1076-7207) **3752**
Turfnet (USA ISSN 1940-5812) **8249**
Turfroute Informatieblad (NLD ISSN 1574-4159) **8283**
• Turia (ESP ISSN 0213-4373) **5390**
• Turiaso (ESP ISSN 0211-7207) **7821**
Turicum (CHE ISSN 0254-3710) **3959**
Turin (American Edition) (USA ISSN 1932-5738) **8769**
Turisguia (PAN) **8769**
• ➤ Turismo (Online) (BRA ISSN 1983-7151) **8769**
† • Turismo (Print) (BRA ISSN 1415-6393) **8994**
Turismo d'Affari (ITA ISSN 1723-4182) **8769**
• Turismo d'Italia (ITA) **8769**
• Turismo & Attualita (ITA) **8769**
Turismo em Analise (BRA ISSN 0103-5541) **8769**
Turismo en Navarra (ESP ISSN 1130-1627) **8769**
† Turismo Gradese (ITA) **8994**
Turismo in Calabria Magazine (ITA ISSN 1970-0245) **8769**
Turismo Rural (ESP ISSN 1699-275X) **8769**
† Turismo Rural y Agroturismo en la Comunidad Valenciana (ESP ISSN 1135-0067) **8994**
• Turismo y Ocio (ESP) **8769**
Turismo&benessere (ITA ISSN 1970-1225) **8769**
Turismohotel (PRT) **8769**
Turismul in Romania/Tourism in Romania (ROM ISSN 1223-7515) **8781**
Turist (RUS ISSN 0131-7040) **8769**
Turist (SWE ISSN 0041-4190) **8769**
Turista (CZE ISSN 0139-5467) **8770**
Turistampa (MEX) **8770**
Turistfoerer (DNK ISSN 0108-8734) **8770**
Turistfoererforeningen. Medlemsliste *see* Turistfoerer **8770**
Turisticke Novine (SRB ISSN 0041-4204) **8770**
Turisver (PRT) **8770**
Turizam (HRV ISSN 0494-2639) **8770**
Turizm Dunyasi (TUR ISSN 1303-4731) **4399**
Turizm Istatistikleri *see* Turkey. Turkiye Istatistik Kurumu. Turizm Istatistikleri (Year) **8781**
Turizmus (HUN ISSN 0237-5249) **8770**
Turizmus Trend/Tourism Trend (HUN ISSN 1786-4585) **8770**
Turizum/Tourism (BGR) **8410**
Turjuman (MAR ISSN 1113-1292) **5189**
Turk Anesteziyoloji ve Reanimasyon Dernegi Dergisi *see* Turkiye Klinikleri Anesteziyoloji Reanimasyon Dergisi **5774**
† Turk Arkeoloji Dergisi/Turkish Review of Archaeology (TUR ISSN 0564-5042) **8994**
• ➤ Turk Biyokimya Dergisi/Turkish Journal of Biochemistry (TUR ISSN 1303-829X) **746**
Turk Biyoloji Dergisi *see* Turkish Journal of Biology **708**
Turk Botanik Dergisi *see* Turkish Journal of Botany **821**
▼ • ➤ Turk Dermatoloji Dergisi/Turkish Journal of Dermatology (TUR ISSN 1307-7635) **5882**
Turk Dili Arastirmalari Yilligi Belleten (TUR ISSN 0564-5050) **5391**
Turk Dili Dil ve Edebiyat Dergisi (TUR ISSN 1300-2155) **5391**
† Turk Etnografya Dergisi/Turkish Review of Ethnography (TUR ISSN 0082-6898) **8994**
Turk Folkloru Arastirmalari (TUR ISSN 1015-4868) **3623**
Turk Gastroenteroloji Dergisi *see* The Turkish Journal of Gastroenterology **5932**
Turk Geriatri Dergisi *see* Turkish Journal of Geriatrics **4057**
Turk Hematoloji-Onkoloji Dergisi/Turkish Journal of Hematology and Oncology *see* U H O D **6036**
Turk Hijiyen ve Deneysel Biyoloji Dergisi/Revue Turque d'Hygiene et de Biologie Experimentale/Turkish Bulletin of Hygiene and Experimental Biology (TUR) **6998**
• Turk Idare Dergisi/Journal of Turkish Administration (TUR ISSN 0041-3925) **7472**
Turk Kulturu (TUR ISSN 1300-3372) **562**
Turk Kulturu Arastirmalari (TUR ISSN 0564-5093) **562**
Turk Kulturu Incelemeleri Dergisi/Journal of Turkish Cultural Studies (TUR) **358**
• ➤ Turk Mikrobiyoloji Cemiyeti Dergisi/Turkish Microbiological Society. Journal (TUR ISSN 0258-2171) **897**
Turk Muhendislik ve Cevre Bilimleri Dergisi *see* Turkish Journal of Engineering and Environmental Sciences **3224**
Turk Nukleer Tip Dergisi *see* Turkish Journal of Nuclear Medicine **6209**
• ➤ Turk Oftalmoloji Gazetesi/Turkish Journal of Ophthalmology (TUR ISSN 1300-0659) **6052**
Turk Ortodonti Dergisi/Turkish Journal of Orthodontics (TUR ISSN 1300-3550) **5868**
• ➤ Turk Otolarengoloji Arsivi/Turkish Archives of Otolaryngology (TUR ISSN 0304-4793) **6086**
• ➤ Turk Pediatri Arsivi/Turkish Archives of Pediatrics (TUR ISSN 1306-0015) **6105**
• Turk Psikiyatri Dergisi (TUR ISSN 1300-2163) **6189**
• ➤ Turk Silahli Kuvvetler Koruyucu Hekimlik Bilgisi/T A F. Preventive Medicine Bulletin (TUR ISSN 1303-734X) **5724**
• Turk Tarih Kurumu. Belgeler (TUR ISSN 0041-4247) **4325**
Turk Tarih Kurumu. Belleten (TUR ISSN 0041-4255) **4325**
Turk Tarim ve Ormancilik Dergisi *see* Turkish Journal of Agriculture and Forestry **163**
• Turk Uroloji Dergisi/Turkish Journal of Urology (TUR ISSN 1300-5804) **6275**
Turk Zooloji Dergisi *see* Turkish Journal of Zoology **965**
• Turkbilig/Turkbilig Journal Turcology Studies (TUR ISSN 1302-6011) **4478**
Turkbilig Journal Turcology Studies *see* Turkbilig **4478**
• ➤ Turkderm (TUR) **5882**
Turkey (TUR ISSN 1300-2260) **1185**
Turkey *see* The P R S Group. Country Reports: Turkey **1509**
Turkey (Princeton, N.J.) *see* Berlitz Turkey Pocket Guide **8687**
Turkey and Turkey Hunting *see* Turkey & Turkey Hunting **8339**
Turkey & Turkey Hunting (USA ISSN 1067-4942) **8339**
• Turkey Autos Report (GBR ISSN 1749-0227) **8609**
• Turkey Business Forecast Report (GBR ISSN 1745-0748) **1522**
Turkey Call (USA ISSN 1064-6094) **915**
† Turkey. Devlet Istatistik Enstitusu. Aylik Istatistik Bulteni/Turkey. Turkish Statistical Institute. Monthly Bulletin of Statistics (TUR ISSN 0041-4263) **8994**
• Turkey Food & Drink Report (GBR ISSN 1749-3021) **1185**
Turkey Freight Transport Report (GBR ISSN 1750-5313) **8518**
† Turkey: Hotels - Camping (TUR) **8994**
Turkey Hunting Strategies (USA) **8339**
Turkey in Statistics (Year) (TUR ISSN 1300-4328) **8410**
Turkey Industry Magazine (TUR ISSN 1303-636X) **5460**
Turkey Information Technology Report *see* Business Monitor International. Information Technology Country Reports **2491**
▼ Turkey Insurance Report (GBR ISSN 1752-8399) **4526**
Turkey Petrochemicals Report (GBR ISSN 1749-2505) **6795**
Turkey Quarterly Forecast Report *see* Turkey Business Forecast Report **1522**
▼ Turkey Real Estate Yearbook (NLD ISSN 1873-989X) **7614**
Turkey. State Institute of Statistics. Publications and Electronic Services Catalogue *see* Turkey. Turkiye Istatistik Kurumu. Yayinlay ve Elektronik Hizmetler Katalogu **1271**
Turkey Tracks (USA) **4315**
† Turkey. Turkish Statistical Insitute. Census of Industry and Business Establishments - 2nd Stage Results, Trade (TUR) **8994**
Turkey. Turkish Statistical Institute. Agricultural Structure; Production, Price, Value (Year) *see* Turkey. Turkiye Istatistik Kurumu. Tarimsal Yapi; Uretim, Fiyat, Deger (Year) **187**
Turkey. Turkish Statistical Institute. Annual Manufacturing Industry Statistics *see* Turkey. Turkiye Istatistik Kurumu. Yillik Imalat Sanayi Istatistikleri **8995**
Turkey. Turkish Statistical Institute. Budgets - Municipal and Special Provincial Administrations and Villages (Year) *see* Turkey. Turkiye Istatistik Kurumu. Butceler - Belediyeler, Il Ozel Idarler ve Koyler (Year) **7485**
Turkey. Turkish Statistical Institute. Building Construction Statistics *see* Turkey. Turkiye Istatistik Kurumu. Bina Insaat Istatistikleri **8994**
Turkey. Turkish Statistical Institute. Census of Agriculture. Agricultural Holdings (Households) *see* Turkey. Turkiye Istatistik Kurumu. Genel Tarim Sayimi. Tarimsal Isletmeler (Hanehalki) **187**
† Turkey. Turkish Statistical Institute. Census of Industry and Business Establishments - 1st Stage Results (TUR ISSN 1300-7173) **8994**
† Turkey. Turkish Statistical Institute. Census of Industry and Business Establishments - 2nd Stage Results, Large Scale Manufacturing Industries (TUR) **8994**
† Turkey. Turkish Statistical Institute. Census of Industry and Business Establishments - 2nd Stage Results, Service, Hotel, Restaurant, Guest House, Cafe (TUR) **8994**
† Turkey. Turkish Statistical Institute. Census of Industry and Business Establishments - 2nd Stage Results, Small-Scale Manufacturing Industries (TUR) **8994**
Turkey. Turkish Statistical Institute. Census of Population. Administrative Division *see* Turkey. Turkiye Istatistik Kurumu. Genel Nufus Sayimi. Idari Bolunus **7316**
Turkey. Turkish Statistical Institute. Census of Population. Internal Migration by Permanent Residence *see* Turkey. Turkiye Istatistik Kurumu. Genel Nufus Sayimi; Goc Istatistikleri (Year) **7316**
Turkey. Turkish Statistical Institute. Census of Population; Migration Statistics (Year) *see* Turkey. Turkiye Istatistik Kurumu. Genel Nufus Sayimi; Goc Istatistikleri (Year) **7316**
Turkey. Turkish Statistical Institute. Census of Population. Preliminary Results *see* Turkey. Turkiye Istatistik Kurumu. Genel Nufus Sayimi. Gecici Sonuclar **7316**
Turkey. Turkish Statistical Institute. Census of Population. Social and Economic Characteristics of Population *see* Turkey. Turkiye Istatistik Kurumu. Genel Nufus Sayimi. Nufusan Sosyal ve Ekonomik Nitelikleri **7317**
Turkey. Turkish Statistical Institute. Cultural Statistics (Year) *see* Turkey. Turkiye Istatistik Kurumu. Kultur Istatistikleri (Year) **8410**
Turkey. Turkish Statistical Institute. Death Statistics; Provincial and District Centers (Year) *see* Turkey. Turkiye Istatistik Kurumu. Olum Istatistikleri; Il ve Ilce Merkezlerinde (Year) **7317**
Turkey. Turkish Statistical Institute. Divorce Statistics *see* Turkey. Turkiye Istatistik Kurumu. Bosanma Istatistikleri **5563**
Turkey. Turkish Statistical Institute. Elections of Local Administrations *see* Turkey. Turkiye Istatistik Kurumu. Mahalli Idareler Secimi **7485**
Turkey. Turkish Statistical Institute. Environmental Statistics - Air Pollution *see* Turkey. Turkiye Istatistik Kurumu. Gevre Istatistikleri - Hava Kirliligi **8994**
Turkey. Turkish Statistical Institute. Final Accounts - Municipalities and Special Provincial Administrations (Year) *see* Turkey. Turkiye Istatistik Kurumu. Kesin Hesaplar - Belediyeler ve Il Ozel Idareleri (Year) **7485**
Turkey. Turkish Statistical Institute. Fishery Statistics (Year) *see* Turkey. Turkiye Istatistik Kurumu. Su Urunleri Istatistikleri (Year) **3614**
Turkey. Turkish Statistical Institute. Foreign Trade by Transport System *see* Turkey. Turkiye Istatistik Kurumu. Tasimacelik Acisindan Turkiye'nin Dis Ticaeti **8995**
Turkey. Turkish Statistical Institute. Foreign Trade Statistics Yearbook *see* Turkey. Turkiye Istatistik Kurumu. Dis Ticaret Istatistikleri Yilligi **1270**
Turkey. Turkish Statistical Institute. Gas and Water Statistics *see* Turkey. Turkiye Istatistik Kurumu. Gaz ve Su Istatistikleri **8994**
Turkey. Turkish Statistical Institute. General Election of Representatives; Province and District Results (Year) *see* Turkey. Turkiye Istatistik Kurumu. Milletvekili Genel Secimi Il ve Ilce Sonuclari (Year) **7201**
Turkey. Turkish Statistical Institute. Gross National Product Results, News Bulletin *see* Turkey. Turkiye Istatistik Kurumu. Gayri Safi Milli Hasila, Haber Bulteni **1270**
Turkey. Turkish Statistical Institute. Household Budget Survey Consumption Expenditures (Year) *see* Turkey. Turkiye Istatistik Kurumu. Hanehalki Butce Arastirmasi Turketim Harcamalari (Year) **1271**
Turkey. Turkish Statistical Institute. Household Income Distribution (Year) *see* Turkey. Turkiye Istatistik Kurumu. Hanehalki Butce Arastirmasi Gelir Dagilimi (Year) **1270**
Turkey. Turkish Statistical Institute. Household Labor Force Statistical (Year) *see* Turkey. Turkiye Istatistik Kurumu. Hanehalki Isgucu Istatistikleri (Year) **1271**
Turkey. Turkish Statistical Institute. Industrial Production Indexes (Quarterly) *see* Turkey. Turkiye Istatistik Kurumu. Sanayi Uretim Indeksi (Donemler Itibariyle) **8995**
Turkey. Turkish Statistical Institute. Judicial Statistics *see* Turkey. Turkiye Istatistik Kurumu. Adalet Istatistikleri **4825**
Turkey. Turkish Statistical Institute. Marriage Statistics (Year) *see* Turkey. Turkiye Istatistik Kurumu. Evlenme Istatistikleri (Year) **5563**
Turkey. Turkish Statistical Institute. Methodology Explanation of Trade Price and Quantity Indexes (TUR) **1270**
Turkey. Turkish Statistical Institute. Mining Statistics *see* Turkey. Turkiye Istatistik Kurumu. Maden Istatistikleri **8995**
Turkey. Turkish Statistical Institute. Monthly Bulletin of Statistics *see* Turkey. Devlet Istatistik Enstitusu. Aylik Istatistik Bulteni **8994**
Turkey. Turkish Statistical Institute. Monthly Economic Indicators *see* Turkey. Turkiye Istatistik Kurumu. Aylik Ekonomik Gostergeler **1270**
Turkey. Turkish Statistical Institute. Monthly Summary of Foreign Trade *see* Turkey. Turkiye Istatistik Kurumu. Aylik Dis Ticaret Ozeti **8994**
Turkey. Turkish Statistical Institute. National Education Statistics; Adult Education (Year) *see* Turkey. Turkiye Istatistik Kurumu. Milli Egitim Istatistikleri; Yaygin Egitim (Year) **2936**
Turkey. Turkish Statistical Institute. National Educational Statistics Formal Education *see* Turkey. Turkiye Istatistik Kurumu. Milli Egitim Istatistikleri Orgun Egitim **2936**
Turkey. Turkish Statistical Institute. Prices Received by Farmers *see* Turkey. Turkiye Istatistik Kurumu. Ciftcinin Eline Gecen Fiyatlar **8994**

Title

10966 TURKISH JOURNAL OF OPHTHALMOLOGY ULRICH'S PERIODICALS

Turkish Journal of Ophthalmology see Turk Oftalmoloji Gazetesi 6052
Turkish Journal of Orthodontics see Turk Ortodonti Dergisi 5868
• ➤ Turkish Journal of Pediatrics (TUR ISSN 0041-4301) 6105
Turkish Journal of Physical Medicine and Rehabilitation see Turkiye Fiziksel tip ve Rehabilitasyon Dergisi 6116
• ➤ Turkish Journal of Physics (TUR ISSN 1300-0101) 7044
Turkish Journal of Physiotherapy Rehabilitation see Fizyoterapi Rhabilitasyon 6109
Turkish Journal of Population Studies see Nufusbilim Dergisi 8978
Turkish Journal of Psychiatry see Turk Psikiyatri Dergisi 6189
• ➤ Turkish Journal of Rheumatology/Romatizma (TUR ISSN 1300-5286) 6227
Turkish Journal of Sports Medicine see Spor Hekimligi Dergisi 6233
Turkish Journal of Surgery see Ulusal Cerrahi Dergisi 6262
Turkish Journal of Trauma & Emergency Surgery see Ulusal Travma Dergisi 4112
Turkish Journal of Tuberculosis & Thorax see Tuberkoloz ve Toraks 5949
Turkish Journal of Urology see Turk Uroloji Dergisi 6275
Turkish Journal of Vascular Surgery see Damar Cerrahi Dergisi 6241
• ➤ Turkish Journal of Veterinary and Animal Sciences/Doga Turk Veterinerlik ve Hayvancilik Dergisi (TUR ISSN 1300-0128) 8809
• ➤ Turkish Journal of Zoology/Turk Zooloji Dergisi (TUR ISSN 1300-0179) 965
Turkish Microbiological Society. Journal see Turk Mikrobiyoloji Cemiyeti Dergisi 897
Turkish National Bibliography see Turkiye Bibliyografyasi 8995
• ➤ Turkish Online Journal of Distance Education (TUR ISSN 1302-6488) 3086
The Turkish Online Journal of Educational Technology see T O J E T 3083
• Turkish Policy Quarterly (TUR ISSN 1303-5754) 7269
• Turkish Probe (TUR ISSN 1300-073X) 3963
Turkish Public Administration Annual (TUR ISSN 0251-2955) 7472
Turkish Respiratory Journal (TUR ISSN 1302-7786) 6220
† Turkish Review (TUR ISSN 1010-8874) 8995
Turkish Review of Archaeology see Turk Arkeoloji Dergisi 8994
• Turkish Review of Balkan Studies (TUR) 4325
Turkish Review of Ethnography see Turk Etnografya Dergisi 8994
• Turkish Review of Eurasian Studies (TUR) 4274
• Turkish Review of Middle East Studies (TUR) 4326
Turkish Society of Algology. Journal see Agri 6120
• ➤ Turkish Studies (GBR ISSN 1468-3849) 7269
Turkish Studies Association Bulletin see Turkish Studies Association Journal 4326
Turkish Studies Association Journal (USA) 4326
Turkish Thoracic Journal see Turks Toraks Dergisi 5949
The Turkish Times (USA ISSN 1043-0164) 3569
➤ Turkish Yearbook of Human Rights (TUR ISSN 1300-1809) 7216
Turkish Yearbook of International Relations/Milletlerarasi Munasebetler Turk Yilligi (TUR ISSN 0544-1943) 7189
Turkistalous (FIN ISSN 0355-0575) 4975
† ➤ Turkiyat Mecmuasi (TUR ISSN 0085-7432) 8995
Turkiye (TUR) 3963
† • Turkiye Bibliyografyasi/Turkish National Bibliography (TUR ISSN 0041-4328) 8995
Turkiye Cocuk (TUR) 2218
Turkiye Cocuk Dergisi see Turkiye Cocuk 2218
• Turkiye Cumhuriyet Merkez Bankasi. Aylik Bulten/Central Bank of the Republic of Turkey. Quarterly Bulletin (TUR ISSN 1300-4565) 1387
• Turkiye Entomoloji Dergisi/Turkish Journal of Entomology (TUR ISSN 1010-6960) 860
• ➤ Turkiye Fiziksel tip ve Rehabilitasyon Dergisi/Turkish Journal of Physical Medicine and Rehabilitation (TUR ISSN 1302-0234) 6116
† Turkiye Is Bankasi. Review of Economic Conditions (TUR ISSN 0034-6500) 8995
Turkiye Istatistik Dernegi Istatistik Dergisi (TUR ISSN 1300-4077) 8410
Turkiye Jeoloji Bulteni see Geological Bulletin of Turkey 2738
• Turkiye Klinikleri Anesteziyoloji Reanimasyon Dergisi/Turkish Anesthesiology and Reanimation Society. Journal (TUR ISSN 1304-0499) 5774
➤ Turkiye Klinikleri Jinekoloji Obstetrik/Anatolian Journal of Gynecology and Obstetrics (TUR ISSN 1300-0306) 6005
• Turkiye Klinikleri Tip Bilimleri Dergisi/Turkish Journal of Medical Science (TUR ISSN 1300-0292) 5725
† Turkiye Makaleler Bibliyografyasi/Bibliography of Articles in Turkish Periodicals (TUR ISSN 0041-4344) 8995
Turkiye Muhendislik Haberleri (TUR ISSN 0049-4852) 3286
Turkiye Orman, Topraksu, Tarim ve Tarim Sanayii Isciler Sendikasi. Tarim-is see Turkish Forestry, Land Irrigation, Agriculture and Agricultural Industry Workers' Union. Tarim-is 4603
Turkiye Turing ve Otomobil Kurumu Belleteni (TUR) 8770
Turkluk Bilgisi Arastirmalari see Journal of Turkish Studies 4322
Turkmen Yupek Ely (TKM) 3963
Turkmenistan (TKM) 3963
Turkmenistan see The P R S Group. Country Reports: Turkmenistan 1509
Turkmenistan Health Care see Turkmenistanyn Lukmancylygy 7543
Turkmenistan News (TKM) 3963
Turkmenistan Ylymlar Akademiasynyn Habarlary. Biologik Ylymlaryn Seriasy/Academy of Sciences of the Turkmenistan. Series of Biological Sciences. Proceedings (TKM ISSN 1026-3292) 708
Turkmenistanyn Lukmancylygy/Turkmenistan Health Care (TKM) 7543
Turkmenistanyn oba Khozhalygy (TKM ISSN 0868-7560) 163
Turkologie und Tuerkeikunde (DEU ISSN 0934-4403) 562
Turkologischer Anzeiger/Turkology Annual (AUT ISSN 0255-5425) 564
Turkology Annual see Turkologischer Anzeiger 564
• Turks Toraks Dergisi/Turkish Thoracic Journal (TUR ISSN 1302-7808) 5949
Turmschreiber Kalender (DEU ISSN 0723-8177) 5391
Turn-Ons (USA) 6301
Turn Ons Presents: Lusty Sex (USA) 5391
Turn-Ons Presents: Sticky Sex (USA) 6301
Turn Out (USA) 3581
Turn- und-Sportverein Info see T U S Info 8211
Turn- und Sportvereinigung Gaarden von 1875 e.V. Vereinsnachrichten see T U S Vereinsnachrichten 8211
Turnaround Letter (USA ISSN 1056-0173) 1656
Turnarounds & Workouts (USA ISSN 0889-1699) 4799
Turnarounds and Workouts see Turnarounds & Workouts 4799
Turnarounds & Workouts. The Supplement see Turnarounds & Workouts 4799
➤ The Turnbull Library Record (NZL ISSN 0110-1625) 4194
Turnen in Hessen (DEU ISSN 1861-1338) 8213
Turnen in Rheinland-Pfalz (DEU) 8213
Turnen und Sport (DEU ISSN 0945-666X) 8213
Der Turnermusiker (DEU ISSN 1439-524X) 6625
Turner's Syndrome News (CAN) 8848
Turngemeinde 1861 e.V. Echo see T G M Echo 8211
Turning Over a New Leaf (USA) 5801
Turning Point (USA) 3161
Turning Point Christian Worldview Series (USA ISSN 1930-1324) 7691
Turning Points (USA ISSN 0274-8894) 1656
▼ • The Turning Revolution (USA ISSN 1936-4423) 5460
Turning the Tide (AUS) 2630
• Turning the Tide (USA ISSN 1082-6491) 7190
• Turning Wheel (USA ISSN 1065-058X) 7702
Turning Wheels (USA ISSN 1052-3251) 8609
Turnverein 1877 e.V. Essen-Kupferdreh 1877 Echo see T V K 1877 Echo 8211
Turok's Choice (USA ISSN 1052-3170) 6625
Turps Banana (GBR ISSN 1749-3994) 523
Turtle see Turtle Magazine for Preschool Kids 2218
• Turtle and Tortoise Newsletter (USA ISSN 1526-3096) 965
• Turtle Island News (CAN ISSN 1204-1645) 3569
• Turtle Magazine for Preschool Kids (USA ISSN 0191-3654) 2218
Turtle Mountain Country (USA) 8770
Turtle Soup (USA) 4399
Turub Yliopisto. Historian Laitos. Julkaisu (FIN ISSN 0357-2129) 4274
Turun Historiallinen. Arkisto (FIN ISSN 0085-7440) 4274
Turun Sanomat (FIN ISSN 0356-133X) 3839
Turun Yliopisto. Julkaisuja. Sarja A. I. Astronomica - Chemica - Physica - Mathematica/Annales Universitatis Turkuensis (FIN ISSN 0082-7002) 7925
Turun Yliopisto. Julkaisuja. Sarja A. II. Biologica - Geographica - Geologica/Annales Universitatis Turkuensis (FIN ISSN 0082-6979) 708
Turun Yliopisto. Julkaisuja. Sarja B. Humaniora/Annales Universitatis Turkuensis (FIN ISSN 0082-6987) 4478
Turun Yliopisto. Julkaisuja. Sarja C. Scripta Lingua Fennica Edita/Annales Universitatis Turkuensis (FIN ISSN 0082-6995) 4479
Turun Yliopisto. Julkaisuja. Sarja D. Medica - Odontologica/Annales Universitatis Turkuensis (FIN ISSN 0355-9483) 5725
Turun Yliopisto. Kirjasto. Julkaisuja (FIN ISSN 0082-7010) 5051
Turun Yliopisto. Kulttuurien Tutkimuksen Laitoksen. Arkistot. Julkaisuja (FIN ISSN 1795-3863) 4479
Turun Yliopisto. Psykologian Tutkimuksia (FIN ISSN 0356-8741) 7413
Turun Yliopisto. Taydennyskoulutuskeskus. Julkaisu. A (FIN ISSN 0788-7906) 3005
Turvallisuus (FIN ISSN 0782-7571) 2681
Turystyka (POL ISSN 1425-4832) 8770
Tus Rollos (MEX) 2218
Tusaayaksat (CAN ISSN 0836-3005) 3569
▼ Tuscan Style (USA ISSN 1938-9558) 4551
Tuscany & Umbria see Karen Brown's Tuscany & Umbria 8727
Tuscarawas Pioneer Footprints (USA ISSN 1047-6873) 3786
Tusculum Review (USA ISSN 1555-2020) 2304
Tush Magazine (DEU) 592
Tushu Qingbao Gongzuo see Tushuguan Qingbao Gongzuo 5051
• Tushu Qingbao Zhishi/Knowledge of Library and Information Science (CHN ISSN 1003-2797) 5051
➤ Tushu Zixum Xuekan/Journal of Library and Information Studies (TWN ISSN 1606-7509) 5051
• Tushuguan Gongzuo yu Yanjiu/Library Work and Study (CHN ISSN 1005-6610) 5051
• ➤ Tushuguan Jianshe/Library Development (CHN ISSN 1004-325X) 5051
• Tushuguan Jie/Library World (CHN ISSN 1005-6041) 5051
Tushuguan Luntan (CHN ISSN 1002-1167) 5051
• Tushuguan Qingbao Gongzuo/Library and Information Service (CHN ISSN 0252-3116) 5051
• Tushuguan Xuebao/Journal of Library Science in China (CHN ISSN 1002-1884) 5051
Tushuguan Xuekan/Library Journal (CHN ISSN 0256-9671) 5051
Tushuguan Yuan/Librarians (CHN) 5051
Tushuguanxue, Xinxi Kexue, Ziliao Gongzuo/Library Science, Information and Data Collection (CHN ISSN 1005-4189) 5051
Tushuguanxue yu Zixun Kexue see Journal of Library & Information Science 5022
Tusind og Seksogtres see 1066 4281
Tussen Duin en Dijk (NLD ISSN 1570-7261) 821
Tussenstand see Achilles 8156
Tutela (ITA ISSN 0393-7798) 8075
Tutkijaliito. Julkaisusarja (FIN ISSN 0357-4083) 3839
Tutmonda Esperantista Junulara Organizo Tutmonde see T E J O - Tutmonde 2215
• ➤ Tutor (ITA ISSN 1971-7296) 6105
Tutor (ZAF ISSN 1021-9617) 3005
Tutorial Texts in Optical Engineering (USA ISSN 1017-6993) 7085
Tutti Fotografi (ITA ISSN 0041-4395) 6978
Tutti Insieme (ITA ISSN 0984-1466) 5189
Tuttitalia (GBR ISSN 0957-1752) 5189
Tutto Aerei (ITA ISSN 1724-2665) 4350
Tutto Casali & Case (ITA ISSN 1824-9949) 4551
† Tutto Codici (ITA) 8995
Tutto Discoteca Dance (ITA) 6625
Tutto Mountain Bike (ITA ISSN 1120-5873) 8269
† Tutto Playstation (ITA) 8995
Tutto Scooter (ITA ISSN 1125-6141) 8269
Tutto Treno (ITA ISSN 1124-4232) 4350
Tutto Treno & Storia (ITA ISSN 1724-2657) 4350
Tutto Treno Modellismo (ITA ISSN 1724-2649) 4350
Tutto Treno Tema (ITA ISSN 1724-2630) 4350
Tutto Tuning (ITA ISSN 1971-0240) 8609
Tutto Wrestling Magazine (ITA ISSN 1826-0195) 8213
† Tuttociclismo (ITA ISSN 1121-3884) 8995
Tuttodove see Tuttolibri Tempo Libero 7575
Tuttodove see Specchio 3898
Tuttodove see La Stampa 3898
Tuttofuoristrada Osservatore Motoristico (ITA) 8609
• Tuttoindici (ITA ISSN 1122-5009) 4882
Tuttolibri Tempo Libero (ITA ISSN 1828-4590) 7575
Tuttomoto (ITA ISSN 0393-7879) 8269
Tuttopesce (ITA ISSN 1826-4239) 8339
† TuttoPista (ITA ISSN 1124-5395) 8995
Tuttorally (ITA ISSN 1124-5387) 8269
Tuttorario (ITA ISSN 1824-7229) 8770
Tuttoscienze see La Stampa 3898
Tuttoscienze see Tuttolibri Tempo Libero 7575
Tuttoscienze see Specchio 3898
Tuttoscuola (ITA ISSN 0391-7967) 2921
Tuttosport (ITA ISSN 0041-4441) 8213
Tuttotrasporti (ITA ISSN 1121-5585) 8678
Tuttoturismo (ITA ISSN 0392-8020) 8770
Tutzinger Blaetter (DEU ISSN 0930-732X) 7778
Tutzinger Studien (DEU ISSN 0564-9021) 7190
Tuvalu Echoes (TUV) 3963
Tuzok (HUN ISSN 1416-020X) 915
Tuzolto (SVK ISSN 1336-4375) 3581
▼ Tuzolto Sam (HUN ISSN 1789-6614) 2218
TV Choice. South & South West Edition see T V Choice (South & South West Edition) 2392
TV Digital see T V Digital 2392
TV Familie see T V Familie 3802
TV Film see T V Film 2392
TV Hits see T V Hits 2393
TV International Daily see T V International Daily (Print) 2393
Tv Kethetes (HUN ISSN 1585-3586) 2398
TV Klar see T V Klar 2393
TV Life see T V Life 8992
TV Movie see T V Movie 2393
TV Movie Digital see T V Movie Digital 2393
TV pur see T V pur 2394
TV Quick see T V Quick (London, Anglia and Central Edition) 2394
TV Schlau see T V Schlau 2394
TV Soap (AUS) 2398
TV Spielfilm see T V Spielfilm 2394
TV Spielfilm XXL see T V Spielfilm XXL 2394
TV Times. Thames - LWT, C4, BBC1 and BBC2 see T V Times 2394
TV Today see T V Today 2394
TV Today Digital see T V Today Digital 2394
TV Week (N.S.W. Edition) see T V Week 2395
TV Y Mas (USA) 2398
TV14 see T V 14 2391
TV2 see T V 2 2391
TV7 see T V 7 2391
TV8 see T V 8 2392
Tvaerdrag (SWE ISSN 0281-2657) 7190
• Tvaersnitt (SWE ISSN 0348-7997) 4479
† Tvai (ISR ISSN 0041-4549) 8995
Tvar (CZE ISSN 0862-657X) 5243
• Tvarminne Studies (FIN ISSN 0358-3406) 720
TVDiskurs see T V Diskurs 2169
Tvedestrandsposten (NOR) 3925
TVemserie see Seriados de T V 2390
Tverskaya 13 (RUS) 3942
Tverskaya Starina (RUS) 369
Tverskaya Zhizn' (RUS) 3942
TVguide (CHE) 2398
TVinfo see T V info 2393
TVM.info see Trib Magazine 8994
TVmania see T V Mania 2393
Tvoe Zdorov'ye (UKR ISSN 1817-8987) 8848
Tvoi Den (RUS) 3942
Tvoi Malysh (UKR ISSN 1729-5017) 2170
TVOntario. Annual Report see TVOntario. Annual Report Card 2398
TVOntario. Annual Report Card (CAN ISSN 1716-4400) 2398
Tvorchestvo (RUS ISSN 0131-6877) 523
Tvoriva Dramatika (CZE ISSN 1211-8001) 8483
Tvr-het (HUN ISSN 0864-9251) 2398
Tvr Usjag (HUN ISSN 1419-0931) 2398
TV!Top see T V! Top 2394
Tvuj Svet (CZE ISSN 1802-1824) 8886
TVVier see T V Vier 2395
Twaalf Maanden see 12 Maanden 2173
Twainian (USA ISSN 0041-4573) 5391
Twayne's English Authors Series (USA ISSN 0564-559X) 5391
Twayne's World Authors Series (USA ISSN 0564-5603) 5391
➤ De Tweede Ronde (NLD ISSN 0166-1868) 5391
Tweeduizendvijfentwintig see 2025 4058
Tweenagers Market Assessment see Key Note Market Assessment. Tweenagers 1828
Tweenies Magazine (GBR ISSN 1467-7423) 2218
• Tweetalige Losbladige Wetboeken (BEL) 4799
Tweetalige Wetboeken Story-Scientia Actualiteit Actualiteit see T W S Actualiteit 4792
Tweewieler (NLD ISSN 0165-1943) 8269
Twelve Sixty Two Banner see 1262 Banner 4606
Twelve Step Rag (USA) 2700
Twelve Twenty Fifth see 1220 Fifth 6540
Twentelife (NLD ISSN 1574-2555) 8770
Twentieth Century American Jewish Writers (USA ISSN 0897-7844) 5391
Twentieth Century Architecture (GBR ISSN 1353-1964) 459
• ➤ Twentieth Century British History (GBR ISSN 0955-2359) 4274
• ➤ Twentieth-Century China (USA ISSN 1521-5385) 4189
▼ ➤ Twentieth Century Communism (GBR ISSN 1758-6437) 7190
Twentieth Century History Review see 20th Century History Review 4168
➤ Twentieth Century Japan: The Emergence of a World Power (USA) 4189
• Twentieth-Century Literary Criticism (USA ISSN 0276-8178) 5391
• ➤ Twentieth Century Literature (USA ISSN 0041-462X) 5391
• ➤ Twentieth Century Music (GBR ISSN 1478-5722) 6625
Twenty 3 Magazine (USA ISSN 1930-4234) 5391
Twenty by Twenty Magazine see 20 x 20 Magazine 5406
Twenty C F R Nineteen Ten O S H A General Industry Regulations Book see 20 C F R 1910 O S H A General Industry Regulations Book 6689
Twenty-First Century see 21 Shiji 2930
Twenty-First Century Business Review see 21 Shiji Shangye Pinglun 1199
Twenty First Century Christian Magazine see 21st Century Christian Magazine 7697
• Twenty-First Century Papers (USA ISSN 1545-6161) 4479
Twenty-first Century Retirement (USA) 1656
Twenty-First Century Science and Technology see 21st Century Science & Technology (Online) 7935
• ➤ Twenty - First Century Society (GBR ISSN 1745-0144) 8011
Twenty-First, the V X M Network see 21st, the V X M Network 2441
Twenty-Five Beautiful Homes see 25 Beautiful Homes 4553
Twenty-Five Years of Teaching Philosophy on CD-ROM see Teaching Philosophy 6956
Twenty Four see 24 7001
24x7 (USA ISSN 1091-1626) 4112
Twenty Four Frames see 24 Frames 6517
Twenty-four Frames Per Second see 24 Frames Per Second 6517
Twenty-Four/Seven see 24/7 4281
Twenty-Four - Seven Magazine see 24/7 Magazine 3993

10968 U D C MAGAZINE ULRICH'S PERIODICALS

U D C Magazine (United Daughters of the Confederacy) (USA) **2270**
U D H R *see* The Universal Declaration of Human Rights **7218**
U D I *see* Urban Design International **4430**
U D I Directory of Electric Power Producers and Distributors *see* Platt's U D I Directory of Electric Power Producers and Distributors **3160**
U D I International Directory of Electric Power Producers and Distributors *see* Platt's International Directory of Electric Power Producers and Distributors **3160**
U D I Who's Who at Electric Power Plants (Utility Data Institute) (USA) **3162**
U D M Law Review *see* University of Detroit Mercy Law Review **4804**
U D N *see* Lianhe Bao **3960**
• ➤ U D O Agricola. Revista Cientifica (Universidad de Oriente) (VEN ISSN 1317-9152) **163**
U D T Forum (GBR ISSN 1479-5574) **6449**
U D T Newsletter (Universal Dataflow and Telecommunications) (CAN ISSN 1010-9501) **5051**
U D T Series on Data Communication Technologies and Standards for Libraries (Universal Dataflow and Telecommunications) (CAN ISSN 1018-0311) **5063**
• U de S (Universite de Sherbrooke) (CAN ISSN 1913-8164) **2304**
A u E *see* Arbeiten und Editionen zur Mittleren Deutschen Literatur **5256**
• U E A Action (Utah Education Association) (USA ISSN 0042-1413) **2921**
U E Business Review (College of Business Administration) (PHL ISSN 0042-0158) **1799**
U E F A Flash (Union of European Football Associations) (CHE) **8250**
U E G Publication (Underwater Engineering Group) (GBR ISSN 0268-2303) **3224**
U E Law Journal (University of the East) (PHL) **4799**
• U E News (University of the East) (PHL) **3005**
U E News (United Electrical Radio and Machine Workers of America) (USA ISSN 0041-5065) **4603**
U E R J. Boletim (Universidade do Estado do Rio de Janeiro) (BRA) **2921**
U E R - Revue Technique *see* E B U Technical Review **2319**
U E T Research Journal *see* Pakistan Journal of Engineering and Applied Sciences **3214**
• ➤ U E Today (University of the East) (PHL ISSN 0118-3931) **2921**
U F A - Revue (CHE ISSN 1420-5025) **164**
U F A W Animal Welfare Research Report (Universities Federation for Animal Welfare) (GBR ISSN 0956-1137) **322**
U F A W Annual Report and Accounts (Universities Federation for Animal Welfare) (GBR ISSN 0263-4600) **322**
U F A W Handbook on the Care and Management of Laboratory Animals (Universities Federation for Animal Welfare) (GBR) **322**
U F A W News-Sheet (Universities Federation for Animal Welfare) (GBR ISSN 0566-8700) **322**
• U F C Nyt (DNK ISSN 1901-4279) **8144**
U F C V (Union Francaise des Centres de Vacances Loisirs) (FRA) **1711**
U F C W Local 1500 (USA) **4603**
U F C W Local 174 (United Food & Commercial Workers) (USA) **4603**
U F C W Local 27 Reporter (United Food & Commercial Workers) (USA) **4603**
U F C W Local 876 News *see* Advocate (Madison Heights) **4589**
U F C W Reporter *see* U F C W Local 27 Reporter **4603**
U F E S Revista de Odontologia (Universidade Federal do Espirito Santo) (BRA ISSN 1516-6228) **5868**
• U F F. Departamento de Psicologia. Revista (Universidade Federal Fluminense) (BRA ISSN 0104-8023) **7413**
U F O (Unidentified Flying Object) (BRA ISSN 1414-1833) **73**
U F O (USA) **73**
• U F O - Aktuellt (Unidentified Flying Object) (SWE ISSN 0284-9291) **73**
• U F O Digest (Unidentified Flying Object) (USA) **73**
U F O Documento (BRA ISSN 1808-5636) **73**
U F O Encounter (Unidentified Flying Object) (AUS) **6648**
U F O Especial (BRA ISSN 0103-7153) **73**
U F O Journal Of Facts (USA) **73**
• U F O Logist Magazine (Unidentified Flying Object) (AUS ISSN 1833-4962) **6648**
U F O Magazine (Unidentified Flying Object) (GBR ISSN 0966-1107) **5448**
U F O Magazine (USA) **73**
U F O Magazine *see* U F O **73**
† U F O Network (ITA ISSN 1128-6709) **8995**
U F O Newsclipping Service (Unidentified Flying Object) (USA) **73**
U F O. Notiziario (Unidentified Flying Objects) (ITA) **73**
U F O - Nyt (DNK ISSN 0049-4976) **73**
U F O Vision (DNK ISSN 0902-2341) **73**
▼ • U F P E. Revista de Enfermagem on Line (Universidade Federal de Pernambuco) (BRA ISSN 1981-8963) **5983**
U F R *see* Ugeskrift for Retsvaesen **4800**
U F R *see* Ugeskrift for Retsvaesen **4800**
U F R A Straight Tip (Utah Fire and Rescue Academy) (USA ISSN 1932-2356) **3581**
U F S Aktuell (Unabhaengigen Finanzsenates) (AUT ISSN 1729-9101) **1953**
U G A Grazier (United Graziers Association of Queensland) (AUS) **302**
U G A News *see* Crossroads (Salt Lake City) **3763**
• U G A - R X (USA) **6883**
U G I Corporation. Annual Report (USA) **1185**
U G I Corporation News (USA) **1185**
U G R A Mitteilungen (CHE ISSN 1019-4754) **7328**
• U H O D/International Journal of Hematology and Oncology (TUR ISSN 1306-133X) **6036**
U H P *see* Uluslararasi Hukuk ve Politika **4943**
U - Haul News (USA) **8678**
U I A Newsletter (Union Internationale des Architectes) (FRA) **459**
U i C *see* Up in Cumming Magazine **5085**
U I C Alumni Magazine (University of Illinois at Chicago) (USA ISSN 1067-4969) **2305**
U I C C International Calendar of Meetings on Cancer (Union Internationale Contre le Cancer) (CHE) **6283**
U I C C International Directory of Cancer Institutes and Organizations (Union Internationale Contre le Cancer) (CHE) **6036**
U I C Newsletter *see* Australian Uranium Association. Newsletter **6457**
U i D (Union in Deutschland) (DEU) **7190**
U I Data Summary (Unemployment Insurance) (USA ISSN 1932-3794) **4530**
• U I E Annual Report (UNESCO Institute for Education) (DEU) **2921**
U I E Handbooks (UNESCO, Institute for Education) (DEU) **3034**
U I E Reports *see* U I P - Berichte **3034**
U I E S P. Bulletin *see* I U S S P. Newsletter **7284**
U I E Studies in Education (UNESCO, Institute for Education) (DEU) **2921**
U I E Studies Series (UNESCO, Institute for Education) (DEU) **2921**
U I M *see* Underground Infrastructure Management **3286**
U I P - Berichte/Dossiers I U E/U I E Reports (UNESCO Institut fuer Paedagogik) (DEU ISSN 1014-9880) **3034**
• U I S Bulletin (Online) (Union Internationale de Speleologie) (FRA) **2771**
U I S Bulletin (Print) *see* U I S Bulletin (Online) **2771**
U I T B B Bulletin (Trade Unions International of Workers of the Building Wood and Building Materials Industries) (FIN) **4603**
U I T C *see* The Universe in the Classroom **3086**
U I U C D C S. Report Series (University of Illinois at Urbana-Champaign, Department of Computer Science) (USA) **2440**
U J D S - Studier (Universitets-Jubilaeets Danske Samfund) (DNK ISSN 0109-2804) **4274**
U J M S *see* Upsala Journal of Medical Sciences **5727**
U J Q (Uncle Jam Quarterly) (USA) **5243**
U K (GBR) **4274**
U K *see* Universiteitskrant Groningen **2306**
U K A E A. Culham Laboratory Reports (United Kingdom Atomic Energy Agency) (GBR) **3175**
U K - A I P *see* United Kingdom Aeronautical Information Publication **8552**
U K A S Directory of Accredited Laboratories (United Kingdom Accreditation Service) (GBR) **6407**
• U K - Ability Magazine (GBR ISSN 1748-5800) **4070**
U K Ability Magazine *see* U K - Ability Magazine **4070**
U K Additional Requirements and Special Conditions (United Kingdom) (GBR) **8552**
U K AIDS Directory (GBR) **5828**
U K Air Almanac (United Kingdom) (GBR ISSN 1747-3624) **73**
U K Airprox (P) Involving Commercial Air Transport (GBR ISSN 1365-7453) **8552**
• U K Alcohol Alert (GBR ISSN 2040-5340) **2700**
• U K and Irish Dividend & Interest Record (GBR ISSN 1470-918X) **1387**
U K & U S A (USA ISSN 0893-2107) **1411**
U K Annual Financial News Summary (GBR) **1185**
U K Autos Report *see* United Kingdom Autos Reports **8609**
U K Biotechnology (GBR ISSN 1756-5448) **1387**
The U K Biotechnology Directory *see* BioCommerce Data's Business Profile Series. Volume 4: The U K Biotechnology Directory **757**
U K Biotechnology Finance Guide *see* U K Biotechnology **1387**
• U K Book Publishing Industry Statistics Yearbook (Year) (United Kingdom) (GBR) **7575**
U K Broadcast Media (GBR ISSN 1470-3157) **2398**
U K Building Costs Handbook *see* Hutchins' U K Building Costs Handbook (Year) **1013**
U K Business & Professional Magazines Directory (GBR ISSN 1470-3122) **1185**
U K Business Confidence Monitor (United Kingdom) (GBR ISSN 1749-0782) **1303**
U K C E E D Discussion Paper (U K Centre for Economic and Environmental Development) (GBR) **3471**
U K C H Religious Trends *see* Religious Trends **7699**
The U K Cable Report (Year) (GBR) **2032**
U K Centre for Economic and Environmental Development Bulletin (GBR ISSN 0268-7402) **3471**
U K Centre for Economic and Environmental Development Discussion Paper *see* U K C E E D Discussion Paper **3471**
• U K Christian Handbook (Year) (GBR ISSN 0952-4061) **7691**
U K Christian Handbook Religious Trends *see* Religious Trends **7699**
U K Clearings Directory (GBR) **1387**
• U K Competition Law Reports (United Kingdom) (GBR ISSN 1467-7784) **4799**
U K Consumer Directory (GBR) **7579**
U K Consumer Magazines Directory *see* U K Consumer Directory **7579**
† The U K Consumer Marketplace (Year) (GBR ISSN 1749-5733) **8995**
U K Counselling and Psychotherapy Directory (GBR) **2032**
• U K Directory of Property Developers, Investors & Financiers (United Kingdom) (GBR ISSN 1363-2655) **7614**
U K Dividend & Interest Record *see* U K and Irish Dividend & Interest Record **1387**
U K E A *see* United Kingdom Economic Accounts **1273**
U K E N *see* U K Environment News **3491**
U K E R N A News (United Kingdom Education and Research Network Association) *see* J A N E T News **2988**
• U K Economic Brief (Online) (United Kingdom) (GBR ISSN 1749-5474) **1522**
U K Economic Brief (Print) *see* U K Economic Brief (Online) **1522**
• U K Employment Alert (United Kingdom) (USA) **4799**
U K Energy Sector Indicators (Year) (United Kingdom) (GBR) **3148**
• U K Environment News (GBR ISSN 1368-924X) **3491**
U K Excellence (United Kingdom) (GBR ISSN 1460-1095) **1185**
U K Excellence Magazine *see* U K Excellence **1185**
U K Financial Services (GBR ISSN 1746-6121) **1387**
U K Financial Services Sector Guide *see* U K Financial Services **1387**
U K Freelance Directory (GBR ISSN 1470-3149) **4584**
U K Freight Transport Report *see* United Kingdom Freight Transport Report **8518**
• U K Gas Report (GBR ISSN 1352-7924) **3148**
U K Higher Education. Europe Unit. Annual Report (GBR) **3006**
➤ U K Higher Education Research Yearbook (Year) (GBR) **3006**
U K Highways Specification Index (GBR ISSN 1743-5307) **8636**
U K Holiday Guide (GBR) **8770**
• U K Housing Review (GBR ISSN 1740-8075) **4429**
• U K Human Rights Reports (United Kingdom) (GBR ISSN 1469-168X) **7216**
U K - I S E S Meeting (International Solar Energy Society) (GBR ISSN 0956-5299) **3178**
U K Income Tax Service (GBR ISSN 1743-0488) **1953**
U K Investment Bulletin (GBR ISSN 1461-6785) **1656**
U K Iron and Steel Industry. Annual Statistics (GBR ISSN 0952-5505) **6341**
U K Irrigation (GBR ISSN 1474-8754) **8833**
U.K. Irrigation Association Quarterly (GBR) **256**
U K Journal of Mines and Minerals (GBR ISSN 0952-2409) **6480**
U K Kompass Buyers Guides *see* Kompass Advertising Extracts **2011**
U K Kompass Regional Sales Guide (GBR) **2032**
U K Kompass Register Company Information *see* Kompass. Company Information **2011**
U K Kompass Register Industrial Trade Names *see* Kompass. Industrial Trade Names **2011**
U K Kompass Register Parents & Subsidiaries *see* Kompass. Parents and Subsidiaries **2011**
U K Kompass Register Parents and Subsidiaries *see* Kompass. Parents and Subsidiaries **2011**
U K Kompass Register Products & Services *see* Kompass. Products and Services **2011**
U K Kompass Register Products and Services *see* Kompass. Products and Services **2011**
† U K Laboratory (USA ISSN 1460-3055) **8995**
U K Media Directory (GBR ISSN 0968-2678) **2032**
U K Media Town by Town (GBR ISSN 0968-2686) **4584**
U K Media Yearbook (GBR ISSN 0968-2198) **2343**
U K Monthly Index *see* I P D U K Monthly Property Index **1629**
U K Motor Industry *see* Key Note Market Review: Motor Industry **1896**
➤ U K Nature Conservation (GBR ISSN 0963-8083) **2630**
U K Newspaper Directory (GBR ISSN 1470-3114) **4584**
• U K Nonlinear News (GBR) **5542**
U K O L N Newsletter (U.K. Office for Library and Information Networking) (GBR ISSN 0963-7354) **5051**
U K O L U G Newsletter (U K Online Users Group) (GBR) **2353**
U.K. Office for Library and Information Networking Newsletter *see* U K O L N Newsletter **5051**
• U.K. Official Publications Online (GBR) **636**
U K Oil & Gas Law (United Kingdom) (GBR) **6795**
• U K Online Investing News (GBR) **1656**
• U K Online Investing Report (GBR) **1656**
U K Online Users Group Newsletter *see* U K O L U G Newsletter **2353**
U K Petrochemicals Report *see* United Kingdom Petrochemicals Report **6796**
• U K Plastics Directory (GBR ISSN 1358-6599) **7100**
U K Plastics Recycling Directory (GBR) **7100**
U K Police Directory (Year) (United Kingdom) (GBR ISSN 1742-3015) **2670**
U K Press Gazette *see* Press Gazette **4582**
U K Preview (United Kingdom) (GBR ISSN 1473-5989) **6739**
U K Printing (United Kingdom) (GBR) **7328**
▼ U K Property (GBR ISSN 1756-0659) **7614**
The U K R & D Scoreboard (Year) *see* The (Year) R & D Scoreboard **1163**
• U K R I News (United Kingdom and Republic of Ireland) (GBR) **3162**
• U K Retail Briefing (GBR) **1185**
U K Retail Pocket Book *see* The Retail Pocket Book **1840**
• U K Retail Report (GBR ISSN 1465-9212) **1846**
U K S M A Council's Report and Financial Statements (U K Spring Manufacturers' Association) (GBR) **1905**
U K Scanning Directory (GBR) **2364**
U K Sea Fisheries Statistics (GBR ISSN 1357-9533) **3614**
U K Service Sector. SDM 28, Retail Sales *see* Retail Sales **1261**
U K Shipping Contacts (GBR ISSN 1463-9092) **2032**
U K Space Index (GBR ISSN 1462-8600) **73**
U K Special Education Directory (GBR) **3048**
U K Spring Manufacturers' Association Council's Report and Financial Statements *see* U K S M A Council's Report and Financial Statements **1905**
U K Steel Exports (GBR) **6336**
U K Steel Imports (GBR) **6336**
• U K Surface Coatings Handbook (GBR ISSN 1353-8942) **6721**
U K Survey of Salaries and Benefits (GBR) **1877**
U K Television Forecasts (GBR) **2398**
U K Textile Industry Directory (GBR ISSN 1476-2781) **2032**
The U K Tourist: Statistics (Year) (GBR ISSN 1351-5535) **8781**
U K Trends (Year) (GBR) **4399**
U K - U S Trade Directory (Year) (GBR) **1411**
U K Upstream Petroleum Database (GBR) **6795**
➤ U K Vet. Companion Animal (United Kingdom) (GBR ISSN 1464-4630) **8809**
U K Vet. Livestock (United Kingdom) (GBR ISSN 1464-262X) **8809**
U K W - Berichte (Ultrakurzwellen) (DEU ISSN 0177-7513) **2364**
The U K Water Industry: Water Statistics (Year) (United Kingdom) (GBR ISSN 1467-5714) **8843**
U K Weekly Financial News Summary (GBR) **1185**
▼ U K Wives (GBR ISSN 1756-6150) **6301**
U K Writer (United Kingdom) (GBR ISSN 1748-9385) **5391**
U K Youth (GBR) **2170**
U K's Regional Charity Finder *see* Will to Charity Group. The Regional Charity Finder **8078**
U L A - Nachrichten (Union der Leitenden Angestellten) (DEU ISSN 0932-9234) **1877**
U L C Exchange (Urban Libraries Council) (USA) **5051**
U L C News (Universal Life Church) (USA) **7742**
U L D Technical Manual (Unit Load Devices) (CAN ISSN 0849-6811) **8552**
U L I ... Real Estate Forecast (Urban Land Institute) (USA ISSN 1091-918X) **7614**
U L L I C O Bulletin (Union Labor Life Insurance Co.) (USA ISSN 0041-5189) **4526**
U L S - Israel *see* Union List of Serials in Israel Libraries **638**
U L S Today (United Lutheran Society) (USA) **7778**
• U L S Universe (University Libraries Section) (USA ISSN 1539-2619) **5052**
• U L V A C Technical Journal (ULtimate in VACuum) (JPN ISSN 0910-6189) **3398**
• U - Laff Seattle Comedy (USA) **8483**
• U M A N A News (Ukrainian Medical Association of North America) (USA) **5725**
• U M A P Journal (Undergraduate Mathematics Applications Project) (USA ISSN 0197-3622) **5542**
U M A Students Law Journal (Students' Law Society) (MWI) **4799**
• U M B C AgentNews (USA) **2599**
U M C Study Guide *see* Uniform Mechanical Code Study Guide **1041**
U M Connection (United Methodist) (USA) **7778**
U M E (AUS ISSN 1037-5872) **459**
U M I. Notiziario *see* Unione Matematica Italiana. Notiziario **5543**
U M I S T Control Systems Centre Series (University of Manchester Institute of Science and Technology) (GBR) **2464**
• ➤ U M K C Law Review (University of Missouri at Kansas City) (USA ISSN 0047-7575) **4799**
U M R C C Newsletter *see* Upper Mississippi River Conservation Committee. Newsletter **8834**

● U M T R I Research Review (University of Michigan, Transportation Research Institute) (USA ISSN 0739-7100) **8518**

U Magazine (IRL ISSN 0791-2692) **3895**

● U - Magazine (University) (USA ISSN 1084-3043) **3006**

U Magazine (London) (GBR) **4603**

U-Mail (DEU) **2305**

● U Maine Today (USA ISSN 1537-8721) **2921**

U Mass Magazine see University of Massachusetts Magazine **2307**

U Mut Maya (USA) **359**

● U N A M Gaceta (Universidad Nacional Autonoma de Mexico) (MEX ISSN 0186-2863) **3006**

U N A M Gaceta. Agenda see U N A M Gaceta **3006**

● U N A M Hoy (Universidad Nacional Autonoma de Mexico) (MEX ISSN 0188-6630) **3006**

● U N A M. Instituto de Ciencias del Mar y Limnologia. Anales (Universidad Nacional Autonoma de Mexico, Instituto de Investigaciones Juridicas) (MEX ISSN 0185-3287) **2819**

U N A M. Instituto de Ciencias del Mar y Limnologia. Publicaciones Especiales see U N A M. Instituto de Ciencias del Mar y Limnologia. Anales **2819**

† U N A New Z (United Nations Association of New Zealand) (NZL ISSN 1173-3543) **8995**

U N A U L A (Universidad Autonoma Latinoamericana) (COL) **5243**

● U N A - U S A E-News Update (United Nations Association of the United States of America) (USA) **7269**

U N A - U S A E-Newsletter see U N A - U S A E-News Update **7269**

● U N A - U S A Policy Brief. Occational Papers (USA) **7269**

● ➤ U N B Law Journal (CAN ISSN 0836-6632) **4799**

U N C Medical Bulletin (University of North Carolina) (USA ISSN 1941-6334) **5725**

U N C R D Annual Report (English Edition) (United Nations Centre for Regional Development) (JPN ISSN 1020-3478) **1606**

U N C R D Annual Report (Nihonban) see U N C R D Annual Report (English Edition) **1606**

U N C R D Newsletter (United Nations Centre for Regional Development) (JPN ISSN 0379-0347) **1606**

U N C Sea Grant Publication see University of North Carolina Sea Grant College Program. Sea Grant Publication **2820**

● U N C T A D Commodity Yearbook (United Nations Conference on Trade and Development) (USA ISSN 1012-0793) **1271**

● U N C T A D Discussion Papers Series (United Nations Conference on Trade and Development) (CHE ISSN 1014-546X) **1585**

● U N C T A D Handbook of Statistics/Manuel de Statistiques de la C N U C E D (United Nations Conference on Trade and Development) (CHE ISSN 1020-7988) **1271**

U N C T A D News (United Nations, Conference on Trade and Development) (USA) **1585**

U N C T A D Occasional Papers (United Nations Conference on Trade and Development) (CHE) **1606**

† U N C T A D Review (United Nations Conference on Trade and Development) (USA ISSN 1014-370X) **8995**

U N C T A D Series on Issues in International Investment Agreements (United Nations Conference on Trade and Development) (CHE) **1656**

● U N Chronicle (United Nations) (USA ISSN 0251-7329) **7269**

U N D A L R see University of Notre Dame Australia Law Review **4804**

● U N D P Quarterly Report (United Nations Development Programme) (MNG) **1606**

● U N E (ESP ISSN 0213-9510) **6407**

● U N E B I Boletin (Unidad de Educacion Bilingue Intercultural Boletin) (PER ISSN 1682-4873) **3015**

● The U N E Law Journal (AUS) **4799**

● U N E P Chemicals Newsletter (United Nations Environment Programme) (CHE ISSN 1564-9032) **3257**

● U N E P Chemicals Newsletter Online (CHE ISSN 1564-9024) **3257**

● U N E P Regional Seas Reports and Studies (United Nations Environment Programme) (KEN ISSN 1014-8647) **2819**

● U N E P Year Book (United Nations Environment Programme) (KEN) **3471**

U N F P A (Year) Report see United Nations Population Fund. Annual Report **7295**

U N H C R Global Appeal (Year) (United Nations High Commissioner for Refugees) (CHE) **7269**

U N H C R Global Report (Year) (United Nations High Commissioner for Refugees) (CHE) **7269**

U N I C E M Annuaire Officiel (Union Nationale des Industries de Carrieres et Materiaux de Construction) (FRA) **1041**

● U N I D O Annual Report (United Nations Industrial Development Organization) (AUT ISSN 0258-8137) **1606**

● U N I D O Links (United Nations Industrial Development Organization) (AUT ISSN 1020-2781) **1606**

U N I D O Links. Al-Tab'at al-'Arabiyyat see U N I D O Links **1606**

U N I D O Links. Ed. Espanola see U N I D O Links **1606**

U N I D O Links. Ed. Francaise see U N I D O Links **1606**

U N I D O Links. Russkoe Izd. see U N I D O Links **1606**

U N I D O Links. Zhongguohua see U N I D O Links **1606**

U N I M A R C Manual - Bibliographic Format (DEU) **5052**

U N I M A - U S A Guide to Membership see U N I M A - U S A Membership Directory **523**

U N I M A - U S A Membership Directory (Union Internationale de la Marionette) (USA ISSN 1931-8847) **523**

● ➤ U N I M E P. Revista de Administracao (Universidade Metodista de Piracicaba) (BRA ISSN 1679-5350) **1799**

➤ U N I S A Latin American Report (University of South Africa) (ZAF ISSN 0256-6060) **4315**

U N I S A Psychologia see New Voices in Psychology **7388**

● ➤ U N I S C I Discussion Papers (Unidad de Investigacion sobre Cooperacion y Seguridad Internacional) (ESP ISSN 1696-2206) **7269**

● ➤ U N I T A R e-Journal (Universiti Tun Abdul Razak) (MYS ISSN 1511-7219) **8011**

U N I T. Le Journal see Transversales Immobilieres **7614**

U N I X Review's Performance Computing (USA) **2599**

● U N L V Gaming Research & Review Journal (University of Nevada, Las Vegas) (USA ISSN 1535-7589) **8213**

U N L V Journal of Anthropology (University of Nevada Las Vegas) (USA ISSN 1520-4340) **359**

● U N L V Journal of Hospitality, Tourism & Leisure Science (University of Nevada Las Vegas) (USA ISSN 1546-3273) **4399**

● U N L V Magazine (University of Nevada Las Vegas) (USA) **2305**

● U N M C Discover (University of Nebraska Medical Center) (USA) **5725**

● U N News (United Nations) (USA) **7269**

U N O (NZL ISSN 1176-9211) **5085**

U N O (Waikato Edition) (NZL ISSN 1176-922X) **5085**

▼ U N O (Wellington Edition) (NZL ISSN 1177-8946) **5085**

U N O S Update (United Network for Organ Sharing) (USA ISSN 1077-8268) **6262**

U N R I S D informa see U N R I S D News **8011**

U N R I S D infos see U N R I S D News **8011**

● U N R I S D News (United Nations Research Institute for Social Development) (CHE ISSN 1020-6825) **8011**

➤ U N R I S D Programme Paper Series (United Nations Research Institute for Social Development) (CHE) **8011**

U N Reform Campaigner (United Nations) (USA) **7269**

● U N S W Compendium of Good Practice in Learning and Teaching (University of New South Wales) (AUS ISSN 1449-7166) **2921**

U N S W Law Journal see University of New South Wales Law Journal **4804**

U N Special (United Nations) (CHE) **7504**

U N U C I. Rivista (Unione Nazionale Ufficiali in Congedo d'Italia) (ITA ISSN 0041-5375) **6449**

U N U - M E R I T Working Paper Series (United Nations University, Maastricht Economic Research Institute on Innovation and Technology) (NLD ISSN 1871-9864) **1185**

● U N Volunteer News (DEU ISSN 1564-8184) **1606**

● ➤ U O C. Papers (Universitat Oberta de Catalunya) (ESP ISSN 1885-1541) **8011**

U O L T J see University of Ottawa Law & Technology Journal **4804**

● U & D (Underhaall & Driftsaekerhet) (SWE ISSN 0280-8072) **3224**

U of L (University of Louisville) (USA) **2305**

U of T. University of Toronto magazine see University of Toronto Magazine **2307**

U P (USA ISSN 1541-5996) **8552**

U P C see Uniform Plumbing Code **4127**

The U.P. Catholic (USA ISSN 1063-4525) **7821**

U P E C (Union de Periodistas de Cuba) (CUB) **7575**

U P E N (University of Port Elizabeth Newspaper) (ZAF ISSN 0041-5405) **2305**

▼ U P F Today (Universal Peace Federation) (USA ISSN 1943-2933) **7269**

U P Irrigation Research Institute. Annual Report (IND ISSN 0080-4045) **8833**

U P Irrigation Research Institute. Technical Memorandum (IND ISSN 0080-4053) **8833**

● U P Newsletter (PHL ISSN 0117-245X) **2305**

U P O J see University of Pennsylvania Orthopaedic Journal (Online Edition) **6074**

U.P. Punjab Samachar (IND) **3890**

U P R (Umwelt- und Planungsrecht) (DEU ISSN 0721-7390) **3471**

U P R A Normande Informations see Normande **295**

▼ ● ➤ U P R Working Papers in Linguistics/Cuadernos de Linguistica de la Universidad de Puerto Rico (Universidad de Puerto Rico) (USA ISSN 1942-0919) **5190**

U P S Teamster (United Parcel Service) (USA ISSN 1551-8973) **8678**

U P T C. Cuadernos de Linguistica Hispanica (Universidad Pedagogica y Tecnologica de Colombia) (COL ISSN 0121-053X) **5190**

● U P. Universita Progetto see V S la Rivista **2924**

U Q A M Journal (Universite du Quebec a Montreal) (CAN) **2305**

U R A C Directory of Accredited Organizations and Resource Guide (Utilization Review Accreditation Commission) (USA ISSN 1559-4920) **7544**

● U R B - Info (CAN ISSN 1719-8186) **4429**

U R B S Informazioni (ITA) **8250**

● ➤ U R I S A Journal (Urban and Regional Information Systems Association) (USA ISSN 1045-8077) **2551**

U R I S A Marketplace (USA) **6704**

● U R I S A News (Urban and Regional Information Systems Association) (USA ISSN 0749-9531) **2551**

● U R P E Newsletter (Union for Radical Political Economics) (USA ISSN 0743-1694) **1185**

U R S S Embajada. Boletin de Informacion see Embajada de la Federacion de Rusia. Boletin Informativo **7232**

U R - V O X (USA) **5437**

U R W A Quarterly Newsletter (Upper Raritan Watershed Association) (USA) **2630**

U S see Ufficiostile **4551**

U S 1 (USA) **4983**

U S 1 Directory (USA) **2032**

U S 1 Worksheets (USA ISSN 0362-7012) **5391**

U S A (USA ISSN 0890-8648) **4429**

U S A A Magazine (United Services Automobile Association) (USA) **1387**

The U S A and Canada (Year) (GBR ISSN 0956-0904) **7190**

U S A and Europe in Business (GBR ISSN 1351-1637) **1585**

U.S.A. Auto Scene Oakland (USA) **8609**

U S A B A Agenda (United States Association for Blind Athletes) (USA) **8213**

➤ The U S A Body Psychotherapy Journal (USA ISSN 1538-960X) **7413**

U S A Boxing see United States Amateur Boxing. Annual Guide **8214**

U S A Boxing News (USA) **8213**

U S A Boxing: Official Rules see United States Amateur Boxing. Official Rules **8214**

U S A C (Universidad de San Carlos de Guatemala) (GTM ISSN 1015-339X) **7925**

U S A C News (United States Auto Club) (USA ISSN 0744-4702) **8213**

U S A Cycling (USA ISSN 1524-525X) **8269**

U S A D S F Bulletin see U S A Deaf Sports Federation Bulletin **4076**

U S A Deaf Sports Federation Bulletin (USA ISSN 1528-6681) **4076**

U S A Equestrian see Equestrian **8290**

U S A F Medical Service Digest (United States Air Force) (USA) **5725**

U S A Financial News (USA) **1656**

U S A for Business Travelers (USA ISSN 0883-251X) **8770**

● U S A Gymnastics (USA ISSN 0748-6006) **8213**

● U S A Hockey Annual Guide (USA) **8213**

U S A Hockey Magazine (USA ISSN 1551-6741) **8213**

U S A Hockey. Playing Rules Handbook (USA) **8213**

U S A I D Developments (U.S. Agency for International Development, Multimedia Communications Division) (USA) **1606**

● U S A I D in Africa (United States Agency for International Development) (USA ISSN 1931-2849) **1606**

U.S. A I P see Aeronautical Information Publication **42**

U S A Journal (CAN ISSN 1198-9599) **8770**

U S A Junior Hockey Magazine (USA) **8214**

U S A N and the U S P Dictionary of Drug Names see U S P Dictionary of U S A N and International Drug Names **6884**

U S A Real Estate see Who's Who Legal. U S A Real Estate **7616**

U S A Record (Uniformed Sanitationmen's Association) (USA ISSN 0041-5464) **4604**

U S A Roller Sports (USA ISSN 1532-8929) **8214**

U S A Softball Magazine (USA) **8250**

U.S.A. Statistics in Brief (Online) see U.S.A. Statistics in Brief (Print) **8995**

† U.S.A. Statistics in Brief (Print) (USA ISSN 1559-789X) **8995**

U S A Studien (DEU ISSN 1434-1905) **8011**

U S A Studies Weekly - 1865 to Present (USA ISSN 1934-9246) **4315**

U S A Studies Weekly - Eighteen Sixty Five to Present see U S A Studies Weekly - 1865 to Present **4315**

U S A Studies Weekly. Explorers to the Present (USA ISSN 1556-357X) **4315**

U S A Table Tennis Magazine (USA ISSN 1089-1870) **8250**

U S A Textile Industry Overview see Texscope: U S A Textile Industry Overview **8459**

● U S A Today (Valley Stream) (USA ISSN 0161-7389) **2921**

U S A Today (Year) Golf Almanac (USA) **8250**

● U S A Today Index (USA ISSN 0893-2409) **4588**

U S A Today Now Personal Technology (USA ISSN 1558-1845) **3115**

U S A Today Source Guide (USA) **2032**

● U S A Today Sports Weekly (USA ISSN 1541-5228) **8250**

U S A Triathlon Life see Triathlon Life **8213**

U S A Triathlon Times see Triathlon Life **8213**

U S A Turkish Times (United States of America) (USA ISSN 1559-579X) **3569**

U S A Volleyball. Officiating Guidebook (USA) **8250**

U S A Volleyball. Sports Quotes (USA) **8250**

U S A Volleyball. Volleyball Case Book (USA) **8250**

● U S A Weekend (USA) **3991**

● U S Ad Review (USA ISSN 1070-9096) **36**

U.S. Administrative Office of the United States Courts. Report on Applications for Orders Authorizing or Approving the Interception of Wire or Oral Communications (USA ISSN 0097-7977) **4799**

The U.S. African American Market (USA ISSN 1930-515X) **1846**

U S African Voice (United States) (USA ISSN 1088-7385) **3569**

U.S. Agency for International Development. Annual Report (USA) **1606**

U.S. Agency for International Development. Congressional Presentation, Fiscal Year (USA ISSN 0276-6469) **1606**

U.S. Agency for International Development, Multimedia Communications Division Developments see U S A I D Developments **1606**

U.S. Agency for International Development. Office of Housing and Urban Programs. Abstracts (USA ISSN 1049-0507) **4436**

U.S. Agricultural Research Service. A R S - N C (Agricultural Research Service. North Central Region) (USA ISSN 0092-1785) **164**

U.S. Agricultural Trade Update see Situation & Outlook Report. U.S. Agricultural Trade Update **206**

U.S. Air Force Academy. Institute for National Security Studies. Book Series (USA) **6449**

U.S. Air Force Academy. Institute for National Security Studies. Occasional Paper (USA) **6449**

U.S. Air Force Institute of Technology. Report (USA) **6449**

U.S. Air Force Medical Service Digest see U S A F Medical Service Digest **5725**

● U.S. Air Force. Office of the Judge General. The Reporter (USA ISSN 0193-8134) **4972**

U S Airgun (USA) **8214**

● U S Airline Salary Survey (USA) **73**

U.S.Airport Activity Statistics see Airport Activity Statistics of Certified Air Carriers **8536**

U S and Asia Statistical Handbook (USA ISSN 1059-4418) **1271**

The U S Archer (USA ISSN 0738-9949) **8214**

U.S. Arms Control and Disarmament Agency. Annual Report (USA ISSN 8755-7819) **7269**

U.S. Army Corps of Engineers. Coastal Engineering Research Center. Miscellaneous Report see Coastal Engineering Research Center. Miscellaneous Report **2802**

U.S. Army Corps of Engineers. Hydrologic Engineering Center. Research Document (USA) **8833**

U.S. Army Corps of Engineers. Hydrologic Engineering Center. Technical Paper (USA) **8833**

U.S. Army Corps of Engineers. Hydrologic Engineering Center. Training Document (USA ISSN 0160-9386) **8833**

U.S. Army Corps of Engineers. Hydrological Engineering Center. Project Report (USA) **8833**

U.S. Army Corps of Engineers. Waterways Experiment Station. Environmental Laboratory. Completion Report (USA) **2798**

U.S. Army Corps of Engineers. Waterways Experiment Station. Geotechnical Laboratory. Technical Report see U.S. Army Engineer Research and Development Center. Technical Report **3286**

U.S. Army. Corps of Engineers. Waterways Experiment Station. Miscellaneous Paper C (USA ISSN 0193-1253) **8833**

U.S. Army. Corps of Engineers. Waterways Experiment Station. Miscellaneous Paper D (USA ISSN 0730-1170) **8833**

U.S. Army. Corps of Engineers. Waterways Experiment Station. Miscellaneous Paper E (USA ISSN 0193-1261) **8833**

U.S. Army. Corps of Engineers. Waterways Experiment Station. Miscellaneous Paper EL (USA) **8833**

U.S. Army. Corps of Engineers. Waterways Experiment Station. Miscellaneous Paper GL (USA ISSN 0275-424X) **3286**

U.S. Army. Corps of Engineers. Waterways Experiment Station. Miscellaneous Paper H (USA ISSN 0193-1288) **3364**

U.S. Army. Corps of Engineers. Waterways Experiment Station. Miscellaneous Paper M (USA ISSN 0193-130X) **3224**

U.S. Army. Corps of Engineers. Waterways Experiment Station. Miscellaneous Paper N (USA ISSN 0193-127X) **3364**

U.S. Army. Corps of Engineers. Waterways Experiment Station. Miscellaneous Paper S (USA ISSN 0193-1296) **3364**

U.S. Army. Corps of Engineers. Waterways Experiment Station. Miscellaneous Paper Y (USA ISSN 0271-4167) **3224**

U.S. Army Engineer Research and Development Center. Technical Report (USA) **3286**

Title

10970 U.S. ARMY ENGINEERING RESEARCH AND DEVELOPMENT CENTER ULRICH'S PERIODICALS

U.S. Army Engineering Research and Development Center. Construction Engineering Research Laboratory. Special Report (USA) **3286**
U.S. Army Materiel Command. Annual Historical Review (USA) **6449**
• U.S. Army Medical Department. Journal (USA ISSN 1524-0436) **5725**
U S Association Executive (USA ISSN 0740-2678) **1799**
U S B B Y Newsletter *see* United States Board on Books for Young People. Newsletter **7575**
• U S B E and Information Technology (USA) **3224**
U S B E Back Issues Shelf List (United States Book Exchange) (USA) **7575**
U S B E: For Members Only (United States Book Exchange) (USA) **5052**
U S B L Nytt (Ungdommens Selvbyggerlag) (NOR) **7614**
U S B W A Tip-Off (United States Basketball Writers Association) (USA ISSN 0041-5472) **8250**
• U S Banker (USA ISSN 0148-8848) **1657**
• The U S Beer Market: Impact Databank Review and Forecast (USA ISSN 1059-6887) **611**
U.S. Beltie News (USA) **302**
The U S Biotechnology Directory *see* BioCommerce Data's Business Profile Series. Volume 1: The U S Biotechnology Directory **757**
• U.S. Bond Strategy (CAN ISSN 1912-8908) **1657**
U S Bowler (USA) **8250**
U.S. Brookhaven National Laboratory, Upton, N.Y. Brookhaven Highlights *see* Brookhaven Highlights **3165**
U.S. Bureau of Alcohol, Tobacco and Firearms. Explosives Incidents (USA ISSN 0273-5032) **2670**
• U.S. Bureau of Alcohol, Tobacco and Firearms. Quarterly Bulletin (USA ISSN 1057-9958) **2670**
U.S. Bureau of Labor Statistics. Bulletin (USA ISSN 0082-9021) **1271**
• U.S. Bureau of Labor Statistics. C P I Detailed Report (Online) (Consumer Price Index) (USA ISSN 1948-4062) **1522**
† • U.S. Bureau of Labor Statistics. C P I Detailed Report (Print) (Consumer Price Index) (USA ISSN 0095-926X) **8995**
† • U.S. Bureau of Labor Statistics. Monthly Labor Review (USA ISSN 0098-1818) **8995**
U.S. Bureau of Labor Statistics. National Compensation Survey (USA) **1271**
• U.S. Bureau of Labor Statistics. National Office News Releases (USA) **1271**
† U.S. Bureau of Labor Statistics. P P I Detailed Report (USA ISSN 1543-3145) **8995**
U.S. Bureau of Labor Statistics. Reports (USA) **1271**
U.S. Bureau of Labor Statistics. Reprint Series (USA) **1271**
U.S. Bureau of Labor Statistics. Southwest Statistical Summary (USA) **1271**
• U.S. Bureau of Land Management. Public Land Statistics (USA ISSN 0082-9110) **4436**
• U.S. Bureau of Mines. Mineral Industry Surveys (Online Edition) (USA) **6480**
U.S. Bureau of Mines. Mineral Industry Surveys - Commodities: Nickel (Online) *see* U.S. Geological Survey. Mineral Resources Program. Mineral Industry Surveys. Nickel **6488**
U.S. Bureau of Mines. Mineral Industry Surveys - Commodities: Phosphate Rock (Online) *see* U.S. Geological Survey. Mineral Resources Program. Mineral Industry Surveys. Marketable Phosphate Rock, Crop Year **1907**
U.S. Bureau of Mines. Mineral Industry Surveys - Commodities: Vanadium (Online Edition) *see* U.S. Geological Survey. Mineral Resources Program. Mineral Commodity Summaries. Vanadium **1907**
U.S. Bureau of Mines Minerals and Materials Information on CD-ROM *see* U.S. Geological Survey. Mineral Resources Program. Minerals and Materials Information CD-ROM **6488**
U.S. Bureau of Reclamation. Annual Report (USA ISSN 0887-4980) **2630**
U.S. Bureau of Reclamation. Engineering and Research Center. Report *see* U.S. Bureau of Reclamation. Reclamation Service Center. Report **8833**
U.S. Bureau of Reclamation. Engineering Monograph (USA) **3364**
U.S. Bureau of Reclamation. Reclamation Service Center. Report (USA) **8833**
U.S. Bureau of Reclamation. Technical Report (USA) **8833**
† • U.S. Bureau of the Census. (Year) Economic Census. Census of Retail Trade (Print) (USA) **8995**
• U.S. Bureau of the Census. (Year) Economic Census. Construction (Online) (USA) **1049**
† • U.S. Bureau of the Census. (Year) Economic Census. Construction (Print) (USA) **8995**
• U.S. Bureau of the Census. (Year) Economic Census. Information (Online) (USA) **1271**
• U.S. Bureau of the Census. (Year) Economic Census. Manufacturing (Online) (USA) **1271**
† • U.S. Bureau of the Census. (Year) Economic Census. Manufacturing (Print) (USA) **8995**
• U.S. Bureau of the Census. (Year) Economic Census. Mining (Online) (USA) **6486**
† • U.S. Bureau of the Census. (Year) Economic Census. Mining (Print) (USA) **8995**
• U.S. Bureau of the Census. (Year) Economic Census. Retail Trade (Online) (USA) **1271**
• U.S. Bureau of the Census. (Year) Economic Census. Transportation and Warehousing (Online) (USA) **1271**
† • U.S. Bureau of the Census. (Year) Economic Census. Transportation and Warehousing (Print) (USA) **8995**
• U.S. Bureau of the Census. (Year) Economic Census. Utilities (Online) (USA) **1271**
• U.S. Bureau of the Census. (Year) Economic Census. Wholesale Trade (Online) (USA) **1271**
U.S. Bureau of the Census. Annual Capital Expenditures (Print) *see* U.S. Bureau of the Census. Annual Capital Expenditures Survey **1271**
• U.S. Bureau of the Census. Annual Capital Expenditures Survey (USA) **1271**
• U.S. Bureau of the Census. Census of Population and Housing (Online) (USA) **7317**
U.S. Bureau of the Census. City Employment *see* City Employment (Online) **8941**
U.S. Bureau of the Census. City Government Finances *see* City Government Finances **8941**
U.S. Bureau of the Census. County Government Finances *see* County Government Finances **8946**
• U.S. Bureau of the Census. Current Housing Reports. H-130, Market Absorption of Apartments (USA ISSN 0363-8286) **4429**
U.S. Bureau of the Census. Current Population Reports. Consumer Income *see* Current Population Reports: Series P-60, Consumer Income **7305**
U.S. Bureau of the Census. Current Population Reports. Population Characteristics *see* Current Population Reports: Series P-20, Population Characteristics (Print) **7305**
† • U.S. Bureau of the Census. Current Population Reports. Population Characteristics. Geographical Mobility (USA) **8995**
U.S. Bureau of the Census. Current Population Reports. Population Characteristics. School Enrollment: Social and Economic Characteristics of Students *see* Current Population Reports. Population Characteristics. School Enrollment in the United States **7305**
U.S. Bureau of the Census. Current Population Reports. Population Estimates and Projections *see* Current Population Reports: Series P-25, Population Estimates and Projections **7305**
U.S. Bureau of the Census. Current Population Reports. Special Studies *see* Current Population Reports. Series P-23, Special Studies **7305**
U.S. Bureau of the Census. Governmental Finances *see* State and Local Government Finances **1944**
• U.S. Bureau of the Census. Governments Division. Local Government Employment and Payroll Data (USA) **1271**
• U.S. Bureau of the Census. Governments Division. Public Education Finances (USA) **2936**
U.S. Bureau of the Census. Guide to Foreign Trade Statistics (Online) *see* Guide to Foreign Trade Statistics (Online) **1236**
U.S. Bureau of the Census. Public Employment *see* Current Governments Reports: Public Employment **8947**
• U.S. Bureau of the Census. Schedule B: Statistical Classification of Domestic and Foreign Commodities Exported From the United States (USA) **1585**
U.S. Bureau of the Census. State Government Finances *see* State Government Finances (Online) **1267**
U.S. Bureau of the Census. U.S. Merchandise Trade: Exports, General Imports, and Imports for Consumption - Standard International Trade Classification Revision 3 - Commodity by Country *see* U.S. Merchandise Trade. F T 925, Exports, General Imports, and Imports for Consumption - Standard International Trade Classification Revision 3 - Commodity by Country **8995**
U.S. Business Directory (NLD) **1411**
• The U S Business Directory (USA) **2032**
• U.S. Business Journal (USA) **1185**
• U S Business Review (USA ISSN 1552-6313) **1185**
U S C A *see* United States Code Annotated **4801**
U S C A Croquet Directory (United States Croquet Association) (USA) **8250**
U S C A Croquet News (United States Croquet Association) (USA) **8250**
U S C Engineer (University of Southern California) (USA) **3224**
U S C Health Affairs (University of Southern California) (USA) **7544**
U S C I D Newsletter (United States Committee on Irrigation and Drainage) (USA ISSN 1083-1320) **8833**
U S C I S Annual Report *see* U.S. Citizenship and Immigration Services. Annual Report **7294**
• U S C I S Monthly (United States Citizenship and Immigration Services) (USA ISSN 1944-5199) **7294**
U S C I S Today *see* U S C I S Monthly **7294**
U S C O L D Newsletter (U S Committee on Large Dams) (USA ISSN 0041-5480) **8833**
U S C S Log (Universal Ship Cancellation Society) (USA ISSN 0279-6139) **6900**
U S C T A News (United States Combined Training Association) (USA ISSN 0744-0103) **8299**
U S C T Civil War Digest (United States Colored Troops) (USA ISSN 1947-7384) **4315**
U S C Trojan Family (University of Southern California) (USA ISSN 8750-7927) **2305**
▼ ➤ U S C W C Journal on Wireless Communications (U.S. Center for Wireless Communications) (USA ISSN 1932-9881) **2343**
• U S Captive (GBR ISSN 1751-0678) **4526**
• U S Cardiovascular Disease (United States) (GBR ISSN 1752-7627) **5801**
U.S. Cardiovascular Disease *see* U S Cardiovascular Disease **5801**
• U S Catholic (USA ISSN 0041-7548) **7821**
• U S Catholic Historian (USA ISSN 0735-8318) **7821**
• U S Catholic Mission Handbook (USA) **7821**
• U.S. Census Bureau. Annual Benchmark Report for Wholesale Trade (USA) **1272**
† • U.S. Census Bureau. Census Catalog and Guide (USA) **8995**
U.S. Census Bureau. Current Business Reports. Annual Benchmark Report for Wholesale Trade (Online) *see* U.S. Census Bureau. Annual Benchmark Report for Wholesale Trade **1272**
• U.S. Census Bureau. Economic Census (USA) **1272**
U.S. Census Bureau. FT900, U.S. International Trade in Goods and Services *see* U.S. International Trade in Goods and Services **1586**
U.S. Census Bureau. Governments Division. Federal Programs Branch. Federal Aid to States for Fiscal Year *see* Federal Aid to States for Fiscal Year **7436**
U.S. Census Bureau. Governments Division. Finances of Employee Retirement Systems of State and Local Governments *see* Finances of Selected State and Local Government Employee Retirement Systems (Online) **7437**
• U.S. Census Bureau. Nonemployer Statistics (USA ISSN 1940-090X) **1272**
U.S. Census Bureau. U.S. Bureau of Economic Analysis. News *see* U.S. International Trade in Goods and Services **1586**
U.S. Center for Wireless Communications Journal on Wireless Communications *see* U S C W C Journal on Wireless Communications **2343**
U.S. Centers for Disease Control. Abortion Surveillance (USA ISSN 0094-0933) **974**
U.S. Centers for Disease Control. Abortion Surveillance. Annual Summary (USA) **973**
• U.S. Centers for Disease Control and Prevention. Morbidity and Mortality Weekly Report. Recommendations and Report (USA ISSN 1057-5987) **7544**
U.S. Centers for Disease Control. Congenital Malformations Surveillance (USA ISSN 0092-5594) **5828**
U.S. Centers for Disease Control. Malaria Surveillance Report (USA ISSN 0501-8390) **5828**
• U.S. Centers for Disease Control. Reported Tuberculosis in the United States (USA) **6220**
• U.S. Centers for Disease Control. Salmonella Annual Summary (USA ISSN 1930-8396) **7544**
U.S. Centers for Disease Control. Salmonella Surveillance. Annual Summary *see* U.S. Centers for Disease Control. Salmonella Annual Summary **7544**
U.S. Centers for Disease Control. Sexually Transmitted Disease Surveillance (USA) **5882**
U.S. Chamber of Commerce. (Year) Employee Benefits Study (USA) **1877**
U.S. Chamber of Commerce. Analysis of Workers' Compensation Laws (Year) (USA ISSN 0191-118X) **1711**
U.S. Chamber of Commerce. Association Agenda (USA) **1411**
U S Chemical Industry Statistical Handbook (USA ISSN 1061-9143) **2096**
• U S - China Education Review (USA ISSN 1548-6613) **2921**
• U S - China Foreign Language (USA ISSN 1539-8080) **5190**
U S - China Law Review *see* Mei Zhong Fa Lu Ping Lun **4732**
• U S - China Review (USA ISSN 0164-3886) **7269**
U.S. Chinese International Journal of Traumatology *see* Mei Zhong Guo ji Chuang Shang za Zhi **6067**
U.S. Chinese Journal of Medical Progress and Clinical Medicine *see* Meiguo Zhonghua Yixue Jinzhan yu Linchuang Zazhi **5678**
• U.S. Citizenship and Immigration Services. Annual Report (USA) **7294**
U.S. Coast Guard Engineering, Electronics & Logistics Quarterly (USA ISSN 1931-4051) **3224**
U.S. Coast Guard. Environmental Protection Newsletter (USA) **3471**
U.S. Coast Guard Marine Safety Council. Proceedings *see* Marine Safety and Security Council. Proceedings **6432**
U.S. Coast Guard. Marine Safety Manual. Volume 1: Administration And Management (USA) **6449**
U.S. Coast Guard. Marine Safety Manual. Volume 10: Interagency Agreements and Acronyms (USA) **6449**
U.S. Coast Guard. Marine Safety Manual. Volume 2: Materiel Inspection (USA) **6449**
U.S. Coast Guard. Marine Safety Manual. Volume 3: Marine Industry Personnel (USA) **6449**
U.S. Coast Guard. Marine Safety Manual. Volume 4: Technical (USA) **6449**
U.S. Coast Guard. Marine Safety Manual. Volume 5: Investigations (USA) **6449**
• U.S. Coast Guard. Marine Safety Manual. Volume 6: Ports and Waterways Activities (USA) **6450**
U.S. Coast Guard. Marine Safety Manual. Volume 7: Port Security (USA) **6450**
U.S. Coast Guard. Marine Safety Manual. Volume 9: Environmental Protection (USA) **6450**
U.S. Coast Guard. Navigation and Vessel Inspection Circulars (USA) **8664**
U.S. Coast Guard No. 515. Rules and Regulations for Foreign Vessels Operating in the Navigable Waters of the United States. Volume #1, Navigation and Navigable Waters (USA ISSN 1931-2504) **4971**
U.S. Coast Guard No. 515. Rules and Regulations for Foreign Vessels Operating in the Navigable Waters of the United States. Volume 2, Shipping (USA ISSN 1931-2512) **4971**
U.S. Coast Guard. Office of Research and Development. Report *see* U.S. Coast Guard. Research and Development Center. Report **8664**
U.S. Coast Guard. Register of Officers (USA ISSN 0364-8753) **6450**
U.S. Coast Guard. Report *see* U.S. Coast Guard. Research and Development Center. Report **8664**
U.S. Coast Guard. Research and Development Center. Report (USA) **8664**
U.S. Coast Guard Systems Times *see* U.S. Coast Guard Engineering, Electronics & Logistics Quarterly **3224**
U.S. Coastal Engineering Research Center Cular *see* The C E R Cular **2801**
U.S. Coastal Engineering Research Center. Instruction Reports (USA) **2819**
U.S. Coastal Engineering Research Center. Miscellaneous Papers *see* Coastal Engineering Research Center. Miscellaneous Report **2802**
U.S. Coastal Engineering Research Center. Special Report (USA ISSN 0276-492X) **3364**
U.S. Coastal Engineering Research Center. Technical Reports (USA) **2819**
U.S. Code Congressional and Administrative News (USA ISSN 1548-6885) **4800**
U S Coin Collector (USA) **6653**
U.S. Commission on Civil Rights. Clearinghouse Publications (USA ISSN 0082-9641) **7216**
U.S. Commission on Civil Rights. Consultations and Conferences (USA) **7216**
U.S. Commission on Civil Rights. Hearings (USA) **7216**
U.S. Commission on Civil Rights. Staff Reports (USA) **7216**
U.S. Commission on Civil Rights. State Advisory Committee Reports. Alabama (USA) **7216**
U.S. Commission on Civil Rights. State Advisory Committee Reports. Alaska (USA) **7216**
U.S. Commission on Civil Rights. State Advisory Committee Reports. Arizona (USA) **7216**
U.S. Commission on Civil Rights. State Advisory Committee Reports. Arkansas (USA) **7216**
U.S. Commission on Civil Rights. State Advisory Committee Reports. California (USA) **7216**
U.S. Commission on Civil Rights. State Advisory Committee Reports. Colorado (USA) **7216**
U.S. Commission on Civil Rights. State Advisory Committee Reports. Connecticut (USA) **7216**
U.S. Commission on Civil Rights. State Advisory Committee Reports. Delaware (USA) **7216**
U.S. Commission on Civil Rights. State Advisory Committee Reports. District of Columbia (USA) **7216**
U.S. Commission on Civil Rights. State Advisory Committee Reports. Florida (USA) **7216**
U.S. Commission on Civil Rights. State Advisory Committee Reports. Georgia (USA) **7216**
U.S. Commission on Civil Rights. State Advisory Committee Reports. Hawaii (USA) **7216**
U.S. Commission on Civil Rights. State Advisory Committee Reports. Idaho (USA) **7216**
U.S. Commission on Civil Rights. State Advisory Committee Reports. Illinois (USA) **7216**
U.S. Commission on Civil Rights. State Advisory Committee Reports. Indiana (USA) **7217**
U.S. Commission on Civil Rights. State Advisory Committee Reports. Iowa (USA) **7217**
U.S. Commission on Civil Rights. State Advisory Committee Reports. Joint Reports (USA) **7217**
U.S. Commission on Civil Rights. State Advisory Committee Reports. Kansas (USA) **7217**
U.S. Commission on Civil Rights. State Advisory Committee Reports. Kentucky (USA) **7217**
U.S. Commission on Civil Rights. State Advisory Committee Reports. Louisiana (USA) **7217**
U.S. Commission on Civil Rights. State Advisory Committee Reports. Maine (USA) **7217**
U.S. Commission on Civil Rights. State Advisory Committee Reports. Massachusetts (USA) **7217**
U.S. Commission on Civil Rights. State Advisory Committee Reports. Michigan (USA) **7217**
U.S. Commission on Civil Rights. State Advisory Committee Reports. Minnesota (USA) **7217**
U.S. Commission on Civil Rights. State Advisory Committee Reports. Missouri (USA) **7217**
U.S. Commission on Civil Rights. State Advisory Committee Reports. Montana (USA) **7217**
U.S. Commission on Civil Rights. State Advisory Committee Reports. Nebraska (USA) **7217**
U.S. Commission on Civil Rights. State Advisory Committee Reports. Nevada (USA) **7217**

DIRECTORY 2010 U.S. DEPARTMENT OF EDUCATION. NATIONAL CENTER FOR EDUCATION 10971

U.S. Commission on Civil Rights. State Advisory Committee Reports. New Hampshire (USA) **7217**

U.S. Commission on Civil Rights. State Advisory Committee Reports. New Jersey (USA) **7217**

U.S. Commission on Civil Rights. State Advisory Committee Reports. New Mexico (USA) **7217**

U.S. Commission on Civil Rights. State Advisory Committee Reports. New York (USA) **7217**

U.S. Commission on Civil Rights. State Advisory Committee Reports. North Carolina (USA) **7217**

U.S. Commission on Civil Rights. State Advisory Committee Reports. North Dakota (USA) **7217**

U.S. Commission on Civil Rights. State Advisory Committee Reports. Ohio (USA) **7217**

U.S. Commission on Civil Rights. State Advisory Committee Reports. Oklahoma (USA) **7217**

U.S. Commission on Civil Rights. State Advisory Committee Reports. Pennsylvania (USA) **7217**

U.S. Commission on Civil Rights. State Advisory Committee Reports. Rhode Island (USA) **7217**

U.S. Commission on Civil Rights. State Advisory Committee Reports. South Carolina (USA) **7217**

U.S. Commission on Civil Rights. State Advisory Committee Reports. South Dakota (USA) **7217**

U.S. Commission on Civil Rights. State Advisory Committee Reports. Tennessee (USA) **7217**

U.S. Commission on Civil Rights. State Advisory Committee Reports. Texas (USA) **7217**

U.S. Commission on Civil Rights. State Advisory Committee Reports. Utah (USA) **7217**

U.S. Commission on Civil Rights. State Advisory Committee Reports. Vermont (USA) **7217**

U.S. Commission on Civil Rights. State Advisory Committee Reports. Virginia (USA) **7217**

U.S. Commission on Civil Rights. State Advisory Committee Reports. Washington (USA) **7217**

U.S. Commission on Civil Rights. State Advisory Committee Reports. West Virginia (USA) **7217**

U.S. Commission on Civil Rights. State Advisory Committee Reports. Wisconsin (USA) **7217**

U.S. Commission on Civil Rights. State Advisory Committee Reports. Wyoming (USA) **7217**

U.S. Commission on Civil Rights. Statutory and Interim Reports (USA) **7217**

U S Committee on Large Dams Newsletter *see* U S C O L D Newsletter **8833**

U.S. Congress. C R I *see* Congressional Record Index **7431**

• U.S. Congress. Congressional Directory (USA ISSN 0160-9890) **7190**

U.S. Congress: Mental Health (USA) **6189**

U.S. Congress. Reports on Public Bills (USA) **7472**

U.S. Congressional Record (Permanent Edition) *see* Congressional Record **7118**

U.S. Congressional Serial Set (USA ISSN 1931-2822) **7472**

U.S. Construction Quarterly Briefing *see* U.S. State Construction Quarterly Briefing **1041**

• U S Consumer Electronics Sales and Forecasts (USA) **3115**

U.S. Copyright Office. Annual Report of the Register of Copyrights (USA ISSN 0090-2845) **6759**

U.S. Corporations Doing Business Abroad (USA ISSN 1066-1778) **1585**

U S Court and Track Builders Association Newsline (USA) **1041**

U.S. Court of International Trade. Reports (USA ISSN 0740-9540) **1585**

U S Credit (GBR ISSN 1741-8380) **1387**

• U S Crude Oil, Natural Gas and Natural Gas Liquids Reserves (Year) Annual Report (Online) (USA) **6795**

U.S. - Cuba Policy Report (USA ISSN 1093-099X) **7269**

• U.S. Custom House Guide: Ports of Entry and U.S. Import Regulations (USA ISSN 1531-0108) **1585**

• U.S. Custom House Guide: U.S. Harmonized Tariff Schedule (USA ISSN 1531-0086) **1585**

U.S. Customs and Border Protection Today *see* Frontline **1566**

U S Customs and International Trade Guide (USA) **4943**

U S D A Broiler Market News Report (USA ISSN 1522-0567) **302**

U S D A Egg & Poultry Weekly Review (USA ISSN 1520-6114) **302**

U S D A Egg Market News Report (USA ISSN 1520-6122) **302**

U S D A Forest Service. Northeastern Research Station. Research Paper (USA) **3705**

U S D A Forest Service. Pacific Northwest Research Station. Research Paper P N W (USA) **3705**

U S D A Forest Service. Pacific Southwest Research Station. Research Paper (USA) **3705**

U S D A Forest Service. Research Note I N T *see* U S D A Forest Service. Rocky Mountain Research Station. Research Note **3705**

U S D A Forest Service. Rocky Mountain Research Station. Annual Western International Forest Disease Work Conference. Proceedings (USA ISSN 0273-3978) **3705**

U S D A Forest Service. Rocky Mountain Research Station. General Technical Report (United States Department of Agriculture) (USA) **3705**

U S D A Forest Service. Rocky Mountain Research Station. New Publications (USA ISSN 0748-1438) **3705**

U S D A Forest Service. Rocky Mountain Research Station. Research Note (USA) **3705**

• U S D A Forest Service. Rocky Mountain Research Station. Research Paper (USA) **3705**

U S D A Forest Service. Rocky Mountain Research Station. Resource Bulletin (USA ISSN 0888-9708) **3705**

U S D A Forest Service. Southern Research Station. Research Paper (USA) **3705**

U S D A - N A S S (USA) **187**

• U.S.D.A. National Lamb Market Summary (USA) **302**

• U S D A News (U.S. Department of Agriculture) (USA) **164**

U S D A Poultry Market News. Annual Summary (USA) **302**

U S D A Poultry Market News. Monthly Summary (USA ISSN 0891-8309) **302**

U S D A Turkey Market News Report (USA ISSN 1522-0575) **302**

• U S D A Weekly Retail Lamb and Veal Feature Activity (USA) **207**

• U S D A Weekly Retail Pork Feature Activity (USA) **207**

• U S D A Weekly Veal Market Summary (USA) **207**

U S Defense Budget Forecast *see* Market Intelligence Reports: U S Defense Budget Forecast **6434**

U.S. Department of Agriculture. Agricultural Economic Reports (USA ISSN 0083-0445) **207**

U.S. Department of Agriculture. Agricultural Marketing Service. Cotton Program. Cotton Quality Crop (USA ISSN 0098-7026) **207**

• U.S. Department of Agriculture. Agricultural Marketing Service. Cotton Program. Cotton Quality Crop (Monthly) (USA) **207**

U.S. Department of Agriculture. Agriculture Handbook (USA ISSN 0065-4612) **164**

U.S. Department of Agriculture. Agriculture Information Bulletin (USA ISSN 0065-4639) **164**

• U S Department of Agriculture. Agriculture Research Service Quarterly Report (USA) **164**

U.S. Department of Agriculture. Animal and Plant Health Inspection Service. Veterinary Services. Foreign Animal Diseases Report (USA ISSN 0091-8199) **8809**

• U.S. Department of Agriculture. Board of Contract Appeals. Annual Report (USA) **164**

• U.S. Department of Agriculture. Budget Summary and Annual Performance Plan (USA) **164**

U.S. Department of Agriculture. Economic Research Service. Structure and Finances of U.S. Farms (USA) **207**

• U.S. Department of Agriculture. Forest Service. Engineering Field Notes (Online) (USA) **3705**

U.S. Department of Agriculture. Forest Service. Engineering Field Notes (Print) *see* U.S. Department of Agriculture. Forest Service. Engineering Field Notes (Online) **3705**

U.S. Department of Agriculture. Forest Service. Forest Products Laboratory. Research Note FPL (USA ISSN 0163-3643) **3705**

U.S. Department of Agriculture Forest Service. Pacific Southwest Research Station. General Technical Report P S W (USA ISSN 0196-2094) **3706**

U.S. Department of Agriculture. Forest Service. Volunteer Opportunities (Year) (USA) **3706**

U.S. Department of Agriculture. Home and Garden Bulletin (USA ISSN 0073-3075) **3753**

U.S. Department of Agriculture. Home Economics Research Report (USA ISSN 0073-3113) **4368**

U.S. Department of Agriculture. Marketing Research Report (USA ISSN 0082-9781) **207**

U.S. Department of Agriculture. Miscellaneous Publication (USA ISSN 0097-0212) **164**

U.S. Department of Agriculture. National Agricultural Statistics Service. Ag. Newsletter (USA) **4379**

• U.S. Department of Agriculture. National Agricultural Statistics Service. Agricultural Chemical Usage (USA) **187**

• U.S. Department of Agriculture. National Agricultural Statistics Service. Agricultural Prices (USA ISSN 0002-1601) **187**

• U.S. Department of Agriculture. National Agricultural Statistics Service. Agricultural Statistics (USA ISSN 0082-9714) **187**

• U.S. Department of Agriculture. National Agricultural Statistics Service. Broiler Hatchery (Online) (USA ISSN 1949-1840) **187**

• U.S. Department of Agriculture. National Agricultural Statistics Service. Catfish Processing (USA) **3614**

• U.S. Department of Agriculture. National Agricultural Statistics Service. Catfish Production (Online) (USA ISSN 1948-271X) **3614**

• U.S. Department of Agriculture. National Agricultural Statistics Service. Cattle (Online) (USA ISSN 1948-9099) **187**

U.S. Department of Agriculture. National Agricultural Statistics Service. Cattle (Print) *see* U.S. Department of Agriculture. National Agricultural Statistics Service. Cattle (Online) **187**

• U.S. Department of Agriculture. National Agricultural Statistics Service. Cattle on Feed (USA ISSN 0364-202X) **187**

• U.S. Department of Agriculture. National Agricultural Statistics Service. Cherry Production (USA) **187**

• U.S. Department of Agriculture. National Agricultural Statistics Service. Chickens and Eggs (USA ISSN 1076-3945) **187**

• U.S. Department of Agriculture. National Agricultural Statistics Service. Citrus Fruits (USA ISSN 0883-2870) **187**

• U.S. Department of Agriculture. National Agricultural Statistics Service. Cold Storage (USA ISSN 0091-1267) **187**

• U.S. Department of Agriculture. National Agricultural Statistics Service. Cotton Ginnings (USA ISSN 0093-4313) **188**

• U.S. Department of Agriculture. National Agricultural Statistics Service. Cranberries (USA ISSN 0196-884X) **188**

• U.S. Department of Agriculture. National Agricultural Statistics Service. Crop Production (USA ISSN 0363-8561) **188**

• U.S. Department of Agriculture. National Agricultural Statistics Service. Crop Progress (USA) **188**

• U.S. Department of Agriculture. National Agricultural Statistics Service. Crop Values (USA ISSN 0884-2329) **188**

• U.S. Department of Agriculture. National Agricultural Statistics Service. Dairy Products (Online) (USA ISSN 1949-0399) **188**

† • U.S. Department of Agriculture. National Agricultural Statistics Service. Dairy Products (Print) (USA ISSN 0093-1446) **8995**

• U.S. Department of Agriculture. National Agricultural Statistics Service. Dairy Products Prices (USA) **188**

U.S. Department of Agriculture. National Agricultural Statistics Service. Delaware Weekly Crop and Weather Report *see* U.S. Department of Agriculture. National Agricultural Statistics Service. Maryland & Delaware Weekly Crop and Weather Report **188**

• U.S. Department of Agriculture. National Agricultural Statistics Service. Egg Products (USA ISSN 0145-3904) **188**

• U.S. Department of Agriculture. National Agricultural Statistics Service. Farm Labor (Online) (USA ISSN 1949-0909) **188**

† • U.S. Department of Agriculture. National Agricultural Statistics Service. Farm Labor (Print) (USA ISSN 0363-8545) **8995**

• U.S. Department of Agriculture. National Agricultural Statistics Service. Farm Numbers and Land in Farms (USA) **188**

• U.S. Department of Agriculture. National Agricultural Statistics Service. Farm Production Expenditures (USA ISSN 0191-0531) **188**

• U.S. Department of Agriculture. National Agricultural Statistics Service. Floriculture Crops (USA ISSN 0272-6793) **188**

• U.S. Department of Agriculture. National Agricultural Statistics Service. Grain Stocks (Online) (USA ISSN 1949-0925) **256**

• U.S. Department of Agriculture. National Agricultural Statistics Service. Hogs and Pigs (USA ISSN 0565-2189) **188**

• U.S. Department of Agriculture. National Agricultural Statistics Service. Honey (USA) **188**

• U.S. Department of Agriculture. National Agricultural Statistics Service. Hop Stocks (Online) (USA ISSN 1949-1484) **188**

† • U.S. Department of Agriculture. National Agricultural Statistics Service. Hop Stocks (Print) (USA) **8995**

U.S. Department of Agriculture. National Agricultural Statistics Service. Livestock Slaughter (USA ISSN 0499-0544) **188**

• U.S. Department of Agriculture. National Agricultural Statistics Service. Maryland & Delaware Weekly Crop and Weather Report (USA ISSN 1948-6677) **188**

• U.S. Department of Agriculture. National Agricultural Statistics Service. Meat Animals: Production, Disposition and Income (USA ISSN 0748-0318) **188**

• U.S. Department of Agriculture. National Agricultural Statistics Service. Milk Production (USA ISSN 0026-4202) **188**

• U.S. Department of Agriculture. National Agricultural Statistics Service. Mink (USA ISSN 0749-8683) **188**

• U.S. Department of Agriculture. National Agricultural Statistics Service. Mushrooms (USA ISSN 0197-6281) **188**

U.S. Department of Agriculture. National Agricultural Statistics Service. Noncitrus Fruits and Nuts (USA ISSN 1057-7912) **188**

• U.S. Department of Agriculture. National Agricultural Statistics Service. Peanut Stocks and Processing (Online) (USA ISSN 1949-1875) **188**

• U.S. Department of Agriculture. National Agricultural Statistics Service. Potato Stocks (USA ISSN 1057-7882) **189**

• U.S. Department of Agriculture. National Agricultural Statistics Service. Potatoes and Potato Stocks (USA) **189**

• U.S. Department of Agriculture. National Agricultural Statistics Service. Poultry Slaughter (Online) (USA ISSN 1949-1581) **189**

U.S. Department of Agriculture. National Agricultural Statistics Service. Poultry Slaughter (Print) *see* U.S. Department of Agriculture. National Agricultural Statistics Service. Poultry Slaughter (Online) **189**

• U.S. Department of Agriculture. National Agricultural Statistics Service. Quarterly Hogs and Pigs (USA ISSN 1949-1921) **189**

• U.S. Department of Agriculture. National Agricultural Statistics Service. Restricted Use Pesticides (USA ISSN 1083-3714) **189**

• U.S. Department of Agriculture. National Agricultural Statistics Service. Rice Stocks (Online) (USA ISSN 1949-1603) **189**

• U.S. Department of Agriculture. National Agricultural Statistics Service. Sheep and Goats (Online) (USA ISSN 1949-1611) **189**

† • U.S. Department of Agriculture. National Agricultural Statistics Service. Sheep and Goats (Print) (USA ISSN 0094-3851) **8995**

• U.S. Department of Agriculture. National Agricultural Statistics Service. Trout Production (USA) **3614**

• U.S. Department of Agriculture. National Agricultural Statistics Service. Turkey Hatchery (Online) (USA ISSN 1949-1964) **189**

• U.S. Department of Agriculture. National Agricultural Statistics Service. Turkeys Raised (USA ISSN 1949-1972) **189**

• U.S. Department of Agriculture. National Agricultural Statistics Service. United States and Canadian Cattle (USA) **189**

• U.S. Department of Agriculture. National Agricultural Statistics Service. United States and Canadian Hogs and Pigs (USA ISSN 1949-1956) **189**

• U.S. Department of Agriculture. National Agricultural Statistics Service. Vegetables (USA ISSN 0193-6603) **189**

U.S. Department of Agriculture News *see* U S D A News **164**

U.S. Department of Agriculture. North Central Forest Experiment Station. Research Paper N C (USA ISSN 0888-9686) **3706**

• U.S. Department of Agriculture. Performance and Accountability Report (USA) **164**

U.S. Department of Agriculture. Production Research Reports (USA ISSN 0082-979X) **207**

U.S. Department of Agriculture. Program Aid (USA ISSN 0276-0185) **207**

U.S. Department of Agriculture. Rural Business - Cooperative Service. Cooperative Information Reports (USA ISSN 0742-9487) **164**

U.S. Department of Agriculture. Rural Business - Cooperative Service. Cooperative Statistics (USA) **189**

U.S. Department of Agriculture. Rural Business - Cooperative Service. Research Reports (USA ISSN 0742-9509) **207**

U.S. Department of Agriculture. Rural Business - Cooperative Service. Service Report (USA) **164**

U.S. Department of Agriculture. Rural Information Center. Publication Series (USA ISSN 1056-9685) **164**

U.S. Department of Agriculture. Rural Utilities Service. Statistical Report. Rural Telecommunications Borrowers (USA) **2373**

U.S. Department of Agriculture. Technical Bulletin (USA ISSN 0082-9811) **164**

U.S. Department of Commerce. Latin American - Caribbean Business Department Center. Bulletin (USA) **1606**

U.S. Department of Commerce, National Technical Information Service Title Index *see* N T I S Title Index **7200**

• U.S. Department of Defense. Defense Security Cooperation Agency. D S C A Facts Book. Foreign Military Sales, Foreign Military Construction Sales and Military Assistance Facts (Online Edition) (USA) **6450**

U.S. Department of Defense Dictionary of Military and Associated Terms (USA ISSN 1048-7557) **6450**

• U.S. Department of Defense. Index of Specifications and Standards (USA ISSN 0363-8464) **6408**

U.S. Department of Defense. Index of Specifications and Standards: Part 1, Alphabetical Listing (USA) **6407**

U.S. Department of Defense. Index of Specifications and Standards: Part 2, Numeric Listing (USA) **6408**

U.S. Department of Defense. Index of Specifications and Standards: Part 3, Federal Supply Class Listing (USA) **6408**

U.S. Department of Defense. Index of Specifications and Standards: Part 4, Numerical Listing of Cancelled Documents (USA) **6408**

U.S. Department of Defense, Manufacturing Technology Information Analysis Center Current Awareness Bulletin *see* M T I A C Current Awareness Bulletin **3388**

U.S. Department of Defense. Report of the Secretary of Defense to the President and the Congress (USA) **6450**

• U.S. Department of Education. National Center for Education Statistics. Academic Libraries (Online) (USA) **3006**

U.S. Department of Education. National Center for Education Statistics. Academic Libraries (Print) *see* U.S. Department of Education. National Center for Education Statistics. Academic Libraries (Online) **3006**

U.S. Department of Education. National Center for Education Statistics. Digest of Education Statistics (USA ISSN 0502-4102) **2936**

• U.S. Department of Education. National Center for Education Statistics. Dropout Rates in the United States (USA) **2936**

Title

10972 U.S. DEPARTMENT OF EDUCATION. NATIONAL CENTER FOR EDUCATION ULRICH'S PERIODICALS

• U.S. Department of Education. National Center for Education Statistics. Early Estimates of Public Elementary and Secondary Education Statistics (USA) **2921**

U.S. Department of Education. National Center for Education Statistics. Fall Enrollment in Higher Education (USA ISSN 0362-5036) **3006**

• U.S. Department of Education. National Center for Education Statistics. Postsecondary Institutions in the United States: Fall (Year) and Degrees and Other Awards Conferred (USA) **2936**

• U.S. Department of Education. National Center for Education Statistics. Projections of Education Statistics (USA ISSN 0502-4110) **2937**

• U.S. Department of Education. National Center for Education Statistics. Student Financing of Graduate and First-Professional Education (USA) **3006**

U.S. Department of Energy Acquisition Regulation *see* Accounting for Government Contracts: Federal Acquisition Regulation **7418**

U.S. Department of Energy. D O E Symposium Series (USA ISSN 0164-2022) **3148**

• U.S. Department of Energy. Energy Information Administration. Annual Coal Report (Year) (USA) **6480**

• U.S. Department of Energy. Energy Information Administration. Annual Energy Outlook (Year) (USA ISSN 0740-4190) **3154**

• U.S. Department of Energy. Energy Information Administration. Annual Energy Review (Year) (USA ISSN 0740-3909) **3148**

U.S. Department of Energy. Energy Information Administration. Coal Industry Annual (Year) *see* U.S. Department of Energy. Energy Information Administration. Annual Coal Report (Year) **6480**

• U.S. Department of Energy. Energy Information Administration. Electric Power Annual (Year) (Online Edition)/Electric Power Annual (Year) (Online Edition) (USA ISSN 1936-3893) **3162**

• U.S. Department of Energy. Energy Information Administration. Electric Power Monthly (Online Edition) (USA) **3162**

• U.S. Department of Energy. Energy Information Administration. Electric Sales, Revenue, and Average Price (USA ISSN 1930-3750) **3155**

• U.S. Department of Energy. Energy Information Administration. International Energy Outlook (USA ISSN 1051-6360) **3149**

• U.S. Department of Energy. Energy Information Administration. International Petroleum Monthly (Online) (USA ISSN 1934-8509) **6795**

• U.S. Department of Energy. Energy Information Administration. Monthly Energy Review (Online) (USA) **3162**

• U.S. Department of Energy. Energy Information Administration. Natural Gas Annual (Year) (Online Edition) (USA) **6795**

• U.S. Department of Energy. Energy Information Administration. Natural Gas Monthly (Online) (USA) **6796**

• U.S. Department of Energy. Energy Information Administration. Petroleum Marketing Annual (Year) (USA ISSN 1936-5454) **6796**

• U.S. Department of Energy. Energy Information Administration. Petroleum Marketing Monthly (Online) (USA ISSN 1936-5926) **6796**

• U.S. Department of Energy. Energy Information Administration. Petroleum Supply Annual (Year) (Online) (USA ISSN 1936-6922) **6796**

• U.S. Department of Energy. Energy Information Administration. Petroleum Supply Monthly (Online Edition) (USA ISSN 1936-6949) **6796**

• U.S. Department of Energy. Energy Information Administration. Quarterly Coal Report (Online) (USA ISSN 1936-6531) **6486**

• U.S. Department of Energy. Energy Information Administration. Renewable Energy Annual (Online) (USA) **3149**

• U.S. Department of Energy. Energy Information Administration. Short-Term Energy Outlook (Online) (USA ISSN 1943-684X) **3149**

• U.S. Department of Energy. Energy Information Administration. Weekly Coal Production (USA) **6480**

• U.S. Department of Energy. Energy Information Administration. Weekly Petroleum Status Report (Online) (USA) **6796**

• U.S. Department of Energy. Energy Information Administration. Weekly U.S. Coal Production Overview (USA) **3149**

• U.S. Department of Energy. National Petroleum Technology Office. Publication List (USA) **6802**

U.S. Department of Energy. Reports (USA) **3149**

• U.S. Department of Energy. Western Area Power Administration. Annual Performance Report (USA) **3149**

U.S. Department of Energy. Western Area Power Administration. Annual Report (USA) **3149**

• U.S. Department of Health and Human Services. Centers for Medicare & Medicaid Services. Data Compendium (Online) (USA) **7544**

• U.S. Department of Health and Human Services. Food and Drug Administration. Prescription Drug User Fee Act. Financial Report to Congress (USA) **7472**

U.S. Department of Health and Human Services. Food and Drug Administration. Prescription Drug User Fee Act. Performance Report to Congress (USA) **7472**

• U.S. Department of Health and Human Services. Grants Administration Manual (USA) **7472**

U.S. Department of Health and Human Services. Indian Health Service. Trends in Indian Health (USA ISSN 1095-2896) **6636**

U.S. Department of Health and Human Services. National Center for Health Statistics. Advance Data from Vital and Health Statistics (USA ISSN 0147-3956) **7549**

• U.S. Department of Health and Human Services. National Center for Health Statistics. International Health Data Reference Guide (USA) **5751**

• U.S. Department of Health and Human Services. National Center for Health Statistics. National Vital Statistics Reports (USA ISSN 1551-8922) **7317**

U.S. Department of Homeland Security Daily Open Source Infrastructure Report *see* D H S Daily Open Source Infrastructure Report **7432**

• U.S. Department of Homeland Security. Privacy Office. (Year) Annual Freedom of Information Act Report to the Attorney General of the United States (USA) **4800**

• U.S. Department of Homeland Security. Privacy Office. Report to Congress (USA) **7472**

U.S. Department of Housing and Urban Development. Annual Report (USA ISSN 0565-2820) **4429**

U.S. Department of Housing and Urban Development. Characteristics of F H A Single-Family Mortgages: Selected Sections on National Housing Act (USA ISSN 0193-1660) **4429**

U.S. Department of Housing and Urban Development. F H A Home Mortgage Insurance Operations: State, County and M S A - P M S A (USA ISSN 0743-4464) **4437**

U.S. Department of Housing and Urban Development. F H A Homes (USA) **4437**

U.S. Department of Housing and Urban Development. F H A Homes (Supplement) (USA) **4437**

U.S. Department of Housing and Urban Development. F H A Monthly Report of Operations. Project Insurance Programs (USA ISSN 0145-5656) **4437**

U.S. Department of Housing and Urban Development. F H A Report of Insurance Operations under Home Mortgage Programs for (Month) (USA) **4437**

U.S. Department of Housing and Urban Development. F H A Trends of Home Mortgage Characteristics (USA ISSN 0364-2666) **4437**

U.S. Department of Housing and Urban Development. Secretary's Essays (USA) **4429**

U.S. Department of Justice. Antitrust Division. Manual (USA) **4882**

• U.S. Department of Justice. Attorney General of the United States. Annual Report (USA ISSN 0148-5229) **4800**

• U.S. Department of Justice. Bureau of Justice Statistics. Crime and Justice Data (USA) **2675**

• U.S. Department of Justice. Bureau of Justice Statistics. Criminal Victimization (USA) **2675**

• U.S. Department of Justice. National Drug Intelligence Center. National Drug Threat Assessment (USA ISSN 1940-4778) **2700**

U.S. Department of Justice. Office of Information and Privacy. Freedom of Information Case List (USA ISSN 0163-9390) **4800**

U.S. Department of Justice. Office of Juvenile Justice and Delinquency Prevention. Annual Report (USA) **2670**

U.S. Department of Justice. Office of Legal Counsel. Opinions (USA ISSN 0270-2134) **4800**

• U.S. Department of Justice. Office of the Attorney General. Strategic Plan (USA) **2670**

U.S. Department of Justice. Opinions of Attorney General *see* U.S. Department of Justice. Office of Legal Counsel. Opinions **4800**

U.S. Department of Labor. Accountability Report *see* U.S. Department of Labor. Performance and Accountability Report **1712**

U.S. Department of Labor. Annual Report Fiscal Year (Year). Report on Performance and Accountability *see* U.S. Department of Labor. Performance and Accountability Report **1712**

U.S. Department of Labor. Bureau of International Labor Affairs. Findings on the Worst Forms of Child Labor *see* The Department of Labor's (Year) Findings on the Worst Forms of Child Labor **2150**

U.S. Department of Labor. Bureau of Labor Statistics. Major Programs (USA ISSN 0160-2985) **1523**

• U.S. Department of Labor. Bureau of Labor Statistics. News. Multifactor Productivity Trends (USA ISSN 1931-8626) **1272**

U.S. Department of Labor, Bureau of Labor Statistics Releases: Demographic Data Book for States and Large Metropolitan Areas *see* B L S Releases: Demographic Data Book for States and Large Metropolitan Areas **1439**

U.S. Department of Labor, Bureau of Labor Statistics Reports on Employee Benefits in the United States *see* B L S Reports on Employee Benefits in the United States **1666**

U.S. Department of Labor, Bureau of Labor Statistics Update *see* B L S Update **1212**

U.S. Department of Labor. Employee Retirement Income Security Act. Report to Congress (USA ISSN 0271-1567) **1711**

U.S. Department of Labor. Employment & Training Administration. Training and Employment Report of the Secretary of Labor (USA) **1712**

• U.S. Department of Labor. Performance and Accountability Report (USA) **1712**

• U.S. Department of Labor. Service Contract Act Directory of Occupations (USA) **1185**

U.S. Department of State. Diplomatic List (USA ISSN 0012-3099) **7269**

U.S. Department of State Indexes of Living Costs Abroad, Quarters Allowances, and Hardship Differentials (USA ISSN 1058-0018) **1272**

• U.S. Department of State. Key Officers of Foreign Service Posts (USA ISSN 0023-0790) **7269**

U.S. Department of State. Library. Commercial Library Program. Publications List (USA) **7201**

• U.S. Department of State. Quarterly Report (USA) **1523**

U.S. Department of State. Standardized Regulations (Government Civilians, Foreign Areas) (USA ISSN 1057-9990) **4800**

U.S. Department of State. Treaties and Other International Acts Series (USA ISSN 0083-0186) **4943**

U.S. Department of State. Treaties in Force (USA ISSN 0083-0194) **4943**

U.S. Department of the Interior. A L J Decisions (USA) **7472**

U.S. Department of the Interior. Decisions (USA ISSN 0011-7331) **7472**

U.S. Department of the Interior. Fish and Wildlife Service. Fish and Wildlife Technical Report (USA ISSN 0899-3505) **3610**

• U.S. Department of the Interior. Geological Survey. Mineral Resources Program. Mineral Industry Surveys. Cement (USA) **6486**

U.S. Department of the Interior. I B I A Citator - Descriptive Word Index (USA) **7472**

U.S. Department of the Interior. Interior Board of Contract Appeals (USA) **7472**

U.S. Department of the Interior. Interior Board of Indian Appeals (USA) **7472**

U.S. Department of the Interior. Interior Board of Land Appeals (USA) **7472**

U.S. Department of the Interior. Listing of Appeals Docketed by the Board of Land Appeals (USA) **7472**

U.S. Department of the Interior. Minerals Management Service. Alaska Outer Continental Shelf Region. Report (USA) **3471**

U.S. Department of the Interior. Minerals Management Service. O C S Report (USA) **6480**

U.S. Department of the Navy. Naval Research Laboratory. Memorandum Report (USA ISSN 0502-3378) **6450**

• U.S. Department of the Treasury. Bureau of Public Debt. Monthly Statement of the Public Debt of the United States (USA ISSN 0364-1015) **1388**

U.S. Department of the Treasury. Bureau of Public Debt. Tables of Redemption Values for United States Series E E Savings Bond and Series I Savings Bonds (USA) **1657**

U.S. Department of the Treasury. Bureau of Public Debt. Tables of Redemption Values for United States Series E Savings Bond and Savings Notes (USA) **1953**

• U.S. Department of the Treasury. Financial Management Service. Daily Treasury Statement (USA ISSN 0145-0239) **1953**

• U.S. Department of the Treasury. Financial Management Service. Financial Connection (USA) **1388**

• U.S. Department of the Treasury. Financial Management Service. Financial Report of the United States Government (USA) **7472**

• U.S. Department of the Treasury. Financial Management Service. Monthly Treasury Statement of Receipts and Outlays of the United States Government (USA ISSN 0364-1007) **1388**

U.S. Department of the Treasury. Financial Management Service. United States Government Annual Report and Appendix (USA ISSN 0884-1063) **1953**

• U.S. Department of Transportation. Federal Railroad Administration. Office of Safety Analysis. Railroad Safety Statistics. Annual Report (Year) (USA ISSN 1931-860X) **8532**

U.S. Department of Transportation. Intelligent Vehicle Highway Systems Projects (USA) **8636**

U.S. Department of Transportation. National Highway Traffic Safety Administration. Equal Employment Opportunity and Affirmative Employment for Minorities, Women, and People with Disabilities (USA) **7217**

U.S. Department of Transportation. National Transportation Statistics. Annual (USA ISSN 0161-8628) **8532**

U.S. Department of Transportation. Technology Sharing Program. Report *see* U.S. Federal Transit Administration. Technology Sharing Program. Report **8518**

• U.S. Department of Veterans Affairs. Fiscal Year (Year) Performance and Accountability Report (USA) **6450**

U.S. Direct Investment Abroad (USA ISSN 0730-9848) **1585**

• U.S. Directory of Entertainment Employers (USA ISSN 1079-6797) **2032**

• The U S Distilled Spirits Market: Impact Databank Review and Forecast (USA) **611**

U.S. District Court Federal Filings Alert (USA ISSN 0742-1087) **4966**

• U.S. Domestic Business and Convention Travel (USA) **8770**

U S E N I X Conference Proceedings (USA ISSN 1049-5606) **2504**

U S E T Foundation News (United States Equestrian Team) (USA) **8300**

U S E T Gaming (United South and Eastern Tribes) (USA) **4983**

• U.S. Economic Development Administration. Annual Report (USA ISSN 0565-4408) **1906**

U.S. Economy, the 25 Year Focus (USA ISSN 1534-8156) **1523**

U.S. Endocrine Disease *see* U S Endocrine Disease **5901**

• U S Endocrine Disease (United States) (GBR ISSN 1753-4062) **5901**

U.S. Environmental Protection Agency. Clean Water: Report to Congress (USA ISSN 0092-9433) **3471**

U.S. Environmental Protection Agency. Ecological Research Series (USA ISSN 1052-2468) **708**

U.S. Environmental Protection Agency. Office of Pesticide Programs. CBI Review (USA) **256**

• U.S. Environmental Protection Agency. Office of Research and Development. Superfund Innovative Technology Evaluation Program. Annual Report to Congress (USA) **7473**

U.S. Environmental Protection Agency. Pesticides Enforcement Division. Notices of Judgment under Federal Insecticide, Fungicide, and Rodenticide Act (USA ISSN 0083-0518) **256**

U.S. Environmental Protection Agency. Report (USA) **3471**

U.S. Equal Employment Opportunity Commission. Annual Report (USA ISSN 0565-4688) **1712**

U.S. Equal Employment Opportunity Commission. Equal Opportunity Report. Job Patterns for Minorities and Women in Private Industry (USA ISSN 0083-0526) **6707**

U S Equity Sector Strategist *see* U S Equity Strategy **1657**

U S Equity Sector Strategy *see* U S Equity Strategy **1657**

U S Equity Sector Strategy. Weekly Bulletin *see* U S Equity Strategy. Weekly Bulletin **1657**

• U S Equity Strategy (United States) (CAN ISSN 1912-4287) **1657**

• U S Equity Strategy. Weekly Bulletin (United States) (CAN ISSN 1912-4295) **1657**

U.S. Excise Tax Guide *see* U.S. Master Excise Tax Guide **1953**

• U.S. Export Administration Regulations (USA ISSN 0094-8411) **7473**

U.S. Export Directory (USA ISSN 1080-9414) **1585**

U.S. Export Regulations *see* Official Export Guide: U.S. Export Regulations **1579**

• U S Export Sales Reports (USA ISSN 0145-0352) **1585**

U S - Exportbestimmungen (United States) (DEU ISSN 1611-4000) **1585**

† • U.S. Exports of Merchandise (CD-ROM) (USA ISSN 1057-8773) **8995**

• U.S. Exports of Merchandise (DVD-ROM) (USA) **1272**

• U S F A National Newsletter (Email) (United States Fencing Association, Inc.) (USA) **8214**

U S F A National Newsletter (Print) *see* U S F A National Newsletter (Email) **8214**

U S F A Rule Book: U S & International Rules (United States Fencing Association, Inc.) (USA) **8214**

U S F B Informations (Union Suisse des Fabricants de Boites de Montres) (CHE) **4570**

U S F M L J *see* University of San Francisco Maritime Law Journal **4971**

U S F Oracle (University of South Florida) (USA) **2305**

• U.S. Farm Credit Administration. Performance and Accountability Report (USA ISSN 1934-113X) **208**

U.S. Federal Aviation Administration Aviation News *see* F A A Aviation News **8540**

U.S. Federal Aviation Administration. National Aviation System: Development and Capital Needs (USA) **8552**

U.S. Federal Aviation Administration. Systems Research and Development. Report F A A - R D (USA) **77**

U.S. Federal Bureau of Investigation. (Year) Bombing Incidents (USA) **2670**

U.S. Federal Communications Commission. I N F Bulletins (USA ISSN 0083-0607) **2343**

U.S. Federal Communications Commission Record *see* F C C Record **2320**

U.S. Federal Deposit Insurance Corp., Division of Insurance and Research Summary of Deposits. Bank & Thrift Branch Office Data Book. Central Region *see* F D I C. Summary of Deposits. Bank & Thrift Branch Office Data Book. Central Region **1340**

U.S. Federal Deposit Insurance Corp., Division of Insurance and Research Summary of Deposits. Bank & Thrift Branch Office Data Book. Midwest Region *see* F D I C. Summary of Deposits. Bank & Thrift Branch Office Data Book. Midwest Region **1340**

DIRECTORY 2010 U.S. GEOLOGICAL SURVEY. MINERAL RESOURCES PROGRAM 10973

U.S. Federal Deposit Insurance Corp., Division of Insurance and Research Summary of Deposits. Bank & Thrift Branch Office Data Book. National *see* F D I C. Summary of Deposits. Bank & Thrift Branch Office Data Book. National **1341**

U.S. Federal Deposit Insurance Corp., Division of Insurance and Research Summary of Deposits. Bank & Thrift Branch Office Data Book. Northeast Region *see* F D I C. Summary of Deposits. Bank & Thrift Branch Office Data Book. Northeast Region **1341**

U.S. Federal Deposit Insurance Corp., Division of Insurance and Research Summary of Deposits. Bank & Thrift Branch Office Data Book. Southeast Region *see* F D I C. Summary of Deposits. Bank & Thrift Branch Office Data Book. Southeast Region **1341**

U.S. Federal Deposit Insurance Corp., Division of Insurance and Research Summary of Deposits. Bank & Thrift Branch Office Data Book. Southwest Region *see* F D I C. Summary of Deposits. Bank & Thrift Branch Office Data Book. Southwest Region **1341**

U.S. Federal Deposit Insurance Corp. Enforcement Decisions and Orders (Online) *see* F D I C Enforcement Decisions and Orders (Online) **1340**

U.S. Federal Deposit Insurance Corp. Quarterly *see* F D I C Quarterly **1340**

U.S. Federal Deposit Insurance Corp. State Profile, Alabama *see* F D I C State Profile, Alabama **1228**

U.S. Federal Deposit Insurance Corp. State Profile, Alaska *see* F D I C State Profile, Alaska **1228**

U.S. Federal Deposit Insurance Corp. State Profile, Arizona *see* F D I C State Profile, Arizona **1228**

U.S. Federal Deposit Insurance Corp. State Profile, Arkansas *see* F D I C State Profile, Arkansas **1228**

U.S. Federal Deposit Insurance Corp. State Profile, California *see* F D I C State Profile, California **1228**

U.S. Federal Deposit Insurance Corp. State Profile, Colorado *see* F D I C State Profile, Colorado **1228**

U.S. Federal Deposit Insurance Corp. State Profile, Connecticut *see* F D I C State Profile, Connecticut **1228**

U.S. Federal Deposit Insurance Corp. State Profile, Hawaii *see* F D I C State Profile, Hawaii **1229**

U.S. Federal Deposit Insurance Corp. State Profile, Idaho *see* F D I C State Profile, Idaho **1229**

U.S. Federal Deposit Insurance Corp. State Profile, Illinois *see* F D I C State Profile, Illinois **1229**

U.S. Federal Deposit Insurance Corp. State Profile, Indiana *see* F D I C State Profile, Indiana **1229**

U.S. Federal Deposit Insurance Corp. State Profile, Iowa *see* F D I C State Profile, Iowa **1229**

U.S. Federal Deposit Insurance Corp. State Profile, Kansas *see* F D I C State Profile, Kansas **1229**

U.S. Federal Deposit Insurance Corp. State Profile, Kentucky *see* F D I C State Profile, Kentucky **1229**

U.S. Federal Deposit Insurance Corp. State Profile, Louisiana *see* F D I C State Profile, Louisiana **1229**

U.S. Federal Deposit Insurance Corp. State Profile, Maine *see* F D I C State Profile, Maine **1229**

U.S. Federal Deposit Insurance Corp. State Profile, Maryland and Washington, D.C. *see* F D I C State Profile, Maryland and Washington, D.C. **1229**

U.S. Federal Deposit Insurance Corp. State Profile, Massachusetts *see* F D I C State Profile, Massachusetts **1229**

U.S. Federal Deposit Insurance Corp. State Profile, Michigan *see* F D I C State Profile, Michigan **1229**

U.S. Federal Deposit Insurance Corp. State Profile, Minnesota *see* F D I C State Profile, Minnesota **1229**

U.S. Federal Deposit Insurance Corp. State Profile, Mississippi *see* F D I C State Profile, Mississippi **1229**

U.S. Federal Deposit Insurance Corp. State Profile, Missouri *see* F D I C State Profile, Missouri **1229**

U.S. Federal Deposit Insurance Corp. State Profile, Montana *see* F D I C State Profile, Montana **1229**

U.S. Federal Deposit Insurance Corp. State Profile, Nebraska *see* F D I C State Profile, Nebraska **1229**

U.S. Federal Deposit Insurance Corp. State Profile, Nevada *see* F D I C State Profile, Nevada **1229**

U.S. Federal Deposit Insurance Corp. State Profile, New Hampshire *see* F D I C State Profile, New Hampshire **1229**

U.S. Federal Deposit Insurance Corp. State Profile, New Jersey *see* F D I C State Profile, New Jersey **1229**

U.S. Federal Deposit Insurance Corp. State Profile, New Mexico *see* F D I C State Profile, New Mexico **1229**

U.S. Federal Deposit Insurance Corp. State Profile, New York *see* F D I C State Profile, New York **1229**

U.S. Federal Deposit Insurance Corp. State Profile, North Carolina *see* F D I C State Profile, North Carolina **1229**

U.S. Federal Deposit Insurance Corp. State Profile, North Dakota *see* F D I C State Profile, North Dakota **1229**

U.S. Federal Deposit Insurance Corp. State Profile, Ohio *see* F D I C State Profile, Ohio **1229**

U.S. Federal Deposit Insurance Corp. State Profile, Oklahoma *see* F D I C State Profile, Oklahoma **1229**

U.S. Federal Deposit Insurance Corp. State Profile, Oregon *see* F D I C State Profile, Oregon **1229**

U.S. Federal Deposit Insurance Corp. State Profile, Pennsylvania *see* F D I C State Profile, Pennsylvania **1229**

U.S. Federal Deposit Insurance Corp. State Profile, Puerto Rico and the U.S. Virgin Islands *see* F D I C State Profile, Puerto Rico and the U.S. Virgin Islands **1229**

U.S. Federal Deposit Insurance Corp. State Profile, Rhode Island *see* F D I C State Profile, Rhode Island **1229**

U.S. Federal Deposit Insurance Corp. State Profile, South Carolina *see* F D I C State Profile, South Carolina **1229**

U.S. Federal Deposit Insurance Corp. State Profile, South Dakota *see* F D I C State Profile, South Dakota **1229**

U.S. Federal Deposit Insurance Corp. State Profile, Tennessee *see* F D I C State Profile, Tennessee **1229**

U.S. Federal Deposit Insurance Corp. State Profile, Texas *see* F D I C State Profile, Texas **1229**

U.S. Federal Deposit Insurance Corp. State Profile, Utah *see* F D I C State Profile, Utah **1229**

U.S. Federal Deposit Insurance Corp. State Profile, Vermont *see* F D I C State Profile, Vermont **1108**

U.S. Federal Deposit Insurance Corp. State Profile, Virginia *see* F D I C State Profile, Virginia **1229**

U.S. Federal Deposit Insurance Corp. State Profile, Washington *see* F D I C State Profile, Washington **1229**

U.S. Federal Deposit Insurance Corp. State Profile, West Virginia *see* F D I C State Profile, West Virginia **1229**

U.S. Federal Deposit Insurance Corp. State Profile, Wisconsin *see* F D I C State Profile, Wisconsin **1229**

U.S. Federal Deposit Insurance Corp. State Profile, Wyoming *see* F D I C State Profile, Wyoming **1230**

U.S. Federal Deposit Insurance Corp. Statistics on Banking *see* F D I C Statistics on Banking **1230**

U.S. Federal Deposit Insurance Corp. Summary of Deposits (Online) *see* F D I C. Summary of Deposits. Bank & Thrift Branch Office Data Book. Midwest Region **1340**

U.S. Federal Deposit Insurance Corp. Summary of Deposits (Online) *see* F D I C. Summary of Deposits. Bank & Thrift Branch Office Data Book. Central Region **1340**

U.S. Federal Deposit Insurance Corp. Summary of Deposits (Online) *see* F D I C. Summary of Deposits. Bank & Thrift Branch Office Data Book. Southwest Region **1341**

U.S. Federal Deposit Insurance Corp. Summary of Deposits (Online) *see* F D I C. Summary of Deposits. Bank & Thrift Branch Office Data Book. Northeast Region **1341**

U.S. Federal Deposit Insurance Corp. Summary of Deposits (Online) *see* F D I C. Summary of Deposits. Bank & Thrift Branch Office Data Book. National **1341**

U.S. Federal Deposit Insurance Corp. Summary of Deposits (Online) *see* F D I C. Summary of Deposits. Bank & Thrift Branch Office Data Book. Southeast Region **1341**

U.S. Federal Deposit Insurance Corporation. Merger Decisions (USA ISSN 0884-1187) **1388**

U.S. Federal Deposit Insurance Corporation. News Releases (USA) **1388**

U.S. Federal Deposit Insurance Corporation. Trust Assets of Banks and Trust Companies (USA ISSN 0278-5692) **1388**

• U.S. Federal Election Commission. Annual Report (USA ISSN 0145-7284) **7190**

U.S. Federal Highway Administration. Highway Planning Technical Reports (USA ISSN 0073-2184) **3286**

• U.S. Federal Highway Administration. Highway Statistics (USA ISSN 0095-344X) **8532**

• U.S. Federal Highway Administration. Monthly Motor Fuel Reported by States (USA) **6802**

U.S. Federal Highway Administration. Monthly Motor Gasoline Reported by States *see* U.S. Federal Highway Administration. Monthly Motor Fuel Reported by States **6802**

• U.S. Federal Labor Relations Authority. Litigation Manual (USA) **4800**

U.S. Federal Labor Relations Authority Reports of Case Decisions. F S I P Releases and Administrative Law Judge Decisions *see* F L R A Reports of Case Decisions. F S I P Releases and Administrative Law Judge Decisions **4848**

U.S. Federal Labor Relations Authority. Representation Case Law Guide Manual (USA) **4800**

U.S. Federal Labor Relations Authority. Representation Proceedings Case Handling Manual. Part 1 (USA) **4800**

U.S. Federal Labor Relations Authority. Representation Proceedings Case Handling Manual. Part 2 (USA) **4800**

U.S. Federal Labor Relations Authority. Representation Proceedings Hearing Officer's Guide (USA) **4800**

U.S. Federal Maritime Commission. Annual Report (USA ISSN 0083-0755) **8664**

U.S. Federal Mediation and Conciliation Service. Annual Report (USA ISSN 0196-9927) **1712**

• U.S. Federal Reserve System. Annual Report (USA ISSN 0083-0887) **1388**

• U.S. Federal Reserve System. Consumer Credit (USA) **1388**

U.S. Federal Reserve System. Research Library - Recent Acquisitions (USA ISSN 0145-0301) **636**

† U.S. Federal Reserve System. Selected Interest and Exchange Rates. Weekly Series of Charts (USA ISSN 0364-8370) **8995**

U.S. Federal Reserve System. Staff Studies (USA) **1388**

• U.S. Federal Trade Commission. Bureau of Competition. Summary of Agreements Filed in F Y (Year) (USA) **6883**

U.S. Federal Trade Commission. Court Decisions Pertaining to the Federal Trade Commission (USA) **1433**

U.S. Federal Trade Commission. Federal Trade Commission Decisions *see* U.S. Federal Trade Commission. Federal Trade Commission Decisions, Findings, Orders and Stipulations **1434**

U.S. Federal Trade Commission. Federal Trade Commission Decisions, Findings, Orders and Stipulations (USA) **1434**

• U.S. Federal Trade Commission. Performance and Accountability Report (USA) **7473**

• U.S. Federal Trade Commission. Performance Plan, Fiscal Year (Year) through Fiscal Year (Year), and President's Management Agenda (USA) **7473**

U.S. Federal Trade Commission. Performance Report *see* The F T C in (Year) **1428**

• U.S. Federal Trade Commission. Strategic Plan (USA) **7473**

U.S. Federal Transit Administration. Annual Report on New Starts (USA) **8518**

U.S. Federal Transit Administration. Grant Assistance Program. Fiscal Year Statistical Summaries *see* Grant Assistance Program. Fiscal Year Statistical Summaries **8525**

U.S. Federal Transit Administration. National Planning and Research Program. Technical Assistance Briefs (USA) **8636**

U.S. Federal Transit Administration. National Transit Planning and Research Program. Project Directory (USA) **8636**

U.S. Federal Transit Administration. Technology Sharing Program. Report (USA) **8518**

U.S. Federal Transit Administration. Transit Cooperative Research Program. Research Results Digest *see* Transit Cooperative Research Program. Research Results Digest **8513**

U S Firms in Germany/Amerikanische Unternehmen in Deutschland (USA) **2032**

U.S. Fish and Wildlife Service. Division of Federal Aid. Sport Fish and Wildlife Restoration Program Update (USA) **965**

U.S. Fish and Wildlife Service. Division of Law Enforcement. Annual Report *see* U.S. Fish and Wildlife Service. Office of Law Enforcement. Annual Report **2670**

U.S. Fish and Wildlife Service. National Survey of Fishing, Hunting and Wildlife - Associated Recreation (USA ISSN 0736-6450) **8219**

• U.S. Fish and Wildlife Service. Office of Law Enforcement. Annual Report (USA ISSN 1559-9337) **2670**

• U.S. Fish and Wildlife Service. Recovery Report to Congress (USA) **2630**

• U.S. Fixed Income Analyst (CAN ISSN 1711-1455) **1657**

U.S. Fixed Income Monthly *see* U.S. Fixed Income Analyst **1657**

• The U.S. Food Marketing System (USA ISSN 1932-4650) **1846**

U.S. Foreign Affairs on CD-ROM (USA ISSN 1075-993X) **7269**

U.S. Foreign Trade Highlights (Online) (USA ISSN 1932-376X) **1585**

U.S. Foreign Trade Highlights (Print) *see* U.S. Foreign Trade Highlights (Online) **1585**

U.S. Forest Service. Annual Report N E (USA ISSN 0083-2480) **3706**

U.S. Forest Service. General Technical Report N C (USA ISSN 1075-7937) **3706**

U.S. Forest Service. General Technical Report N E (USA ISSN 0748-1314) **3706**

U.S. Forest Service. General Technical Report P N W (USA ISSN 0887-4840) **3706**

U.S. Forest Service. General Technical Report W O (USA ISSN 0197-6109) **3706**

U.S. Forest Service. North Central Forest Experiment Station. List of Publications (USA) **3709**

• U.S. Forest Service. Pacific Southwest Forest and Range Experiment Station. Research Note P S W (Pacific South West) (USA ISSN 0196-3376) **3706**

U.S. Forest Service. Report (USA ISSN 0272-1007) **3706**

U S Forest Service. Research Note N C (USA ISSN 0361-2449) **3706**

U.S. Forest Service. Resource Bulletin N C (USA ISSN 0565-873X) **3706**

U.S. Forest Service. Resource Bulletin N E (USA ISSN 0748-1357) **3706**

U.S. Forest Service. Resource Bulletin P N W (USA ISSN 0748-1284) **3706**

U.S. Forest Service. Rocky Mountain Research Station. New Publications (USA) **3706**

U.S. Forest Service. Southern Research Station. Technical Publication R8-TP (USA ISSN 0749-5536) **3706**

The U.S. Forumeer Today *see* A G I F Forumeer **3515**

U.S. Futures Update *see* Platt's Oilgram Price Report (Online) **6789**

U S G A Green Section Record (United States Golf Association) (USA ISSN 0041-5502) **3753**

• U S G A Turfgrass and Environmental Research Online (United States Golf Association) (USA ISSN 1541-0277) **821**

U.S.G.S. Water Resources Data for Texas *see* Water Resources Data for Texas **8839**

U S G S Water Resources Data. Virginia *see* Water Resources Data for Virginia **8839**

• U S Gastroenterology Review (United States) (GBR ISSN 1754-5056) **5932**

U.S. General Accounting Office. Abstracts of Reports and Testimony: Fiscal Year (Year) *see* United States Government Accountability Office. Abstracts of Reports and Testimony: Fiscal Year (Year) **7474**

U.S. General Accounting Office. Monthly List of G A O Reports *see* U.S. General Accounting Office. Office of Public Affairs. Month in Review (Online) **7485**

• U.S. General Accounting Office. Office of Public Affairs. Month in Review (Online) (USA ISSN 1936-6620) **7485**

U.S. General Accounting Office, Office of Public Affairs. Reports and Testimony *see* U.S. General Accounting Office. Office of Public Affairs. Month in Review (Online) **7485**

U.S. General Accounting Office. Reports and Testimony *see* United States Government Accountability Office. Reports and Testimony **7474**

• U.S. General Services Administration. Catalog of Federal Domestic Assistance (USA ISSN 0097-7799) **7473**

U.S. Geological Survey. Board on Geographic Names. Decisions on Geographic Names in the United States (USA ISSN 0363-6828) **4031**

U.S. Geological Survey. Bulletin (USA ISSN 0083-1093) **2771**

U.S. Geological Survey Bulletin (USA ISSN 8755-531X) **2771**

U. S. Geological Survey Circular (USA ISSN 1067-084X) **2771**

U.S. Geological Survey. Completion Report (USA) **2771**

U.S. Geological Survey. Factsheet (USA) **4031**

• U.S. Geological Survey. Mineral Resources Mineral Industry Surveys. Fluorspar (USA) **6486**

• U.S. Geological Survey. Mineral Resources Program. Mineral Commodity Summaries. Barite (USA) **1906**

• U.S. Geological Survey. Mineral Resources Program. Mineral Commodity Summaries. Boron (USA) **1906**

• U.S. Geological Survey. Mineral Resources Program. Mineral Commodity Summaries. Bromine (USA) **1906**

• U.S. Geological Survey. Mineral Resources Program. Mineral Commodity Summaries. Cadmium (USA) **6487**

• U.S. Geological Survey. Mineral Resources Program. Mineral Commodity Summaries. Chromium (USA) **1906**

• U.S. Geological Survey. Mineral Resources Program. Mineral Commodity Summaries. Clays (USA) **1906**

• U.S. Geological Survey. Mineral Resources Program. Mineral Commodity Summaries. Construction Sand and Gravel (USA) **1906**

• U.S. Geological Survey. Mineral Resources Program. Mineral Commodity Summaries. Dimension Stone (USA) **1906**

• U.S. Geological Survey. Mineral Resources Program. Mineral Commodity Summaries. Feldspar (USA) **1906**

• U.S. Geological Survey. Mineral Resources Program. Mineral Commodity Summaries. Gemstones (USA) **1906**

• U.S. Geological Survey. Mineral Resources Program. Mineral Commodity Summaries. Graphite (Natural) (USA) **1906**

• U.S. Geological Survey. Mineral Resources Program. Mineral Commodity Summaries. Helium (USA) **1906**

• U.S. Geological Survey. Mineral Resources Program. Mineral Commodity Summaries. Iodine (USA) **1906**

• U.S. Geological Survey. Mineral Resources Program. Mineral Commodity Summaries. Iron and Steel (USA) **1906**

• U.S. Geological Survey. Mineral Resources Program. Mineral Commodity Summaries. Iron and Steel Scrap (USA) **1906**

• U.S. Geological Survey. Mineral Resources Program. Mineral Commodity Summaries. Iron and Steel Slag (USA) **1906**

Title

▼ *new title* † *ceased* • *electronic media* ➤ *refereed*

Title

10976 U.S. NATIONAL SCIENCE FOUNDATION. SELECTED DATA ON ULRICH'S PERIODICALS

U.S. National Science Foundation. Selected Data on Students and Postdoctorals in Science & Engineering *see* U.S. National Science Foundation. Division of Science Resources Statistics. Graduate Students and Postdoctorates in Science and Engineering **2937**
U.S. National Science Foundation. State Award Summary, Fiscal Year (Year) (USA) **7942**
• U.S. National Toxicology Program. Report on Carcinogens (USA ISSN 1551-8272) **6036**
U.S. National Transportation Safety Board. Aircraft Accident Reports (USA) **8552**
U.S. Natural Resouces Conservation Service. Annual Report (USA) **8833**
U.S. Natural Resources Conservation Service. National Engineering Handbook Sections (USA ISSN 0083-3304) **256**
U.S. Natural Resources Conservation Service. Soil Survey Investigation Reports (USA ISSN 0083-3320) **256**
U.S. Natural Resources Conservation Service. Technical Publications (USA ISSN 0083-3339) **256**
U S Naval Academy Alumni Association. Register of Alumni (USA) **2305**
U.S. Naval Biodynamics Laboratory. Report *see* National Biodynamics Laboratory. Report **750**
U.S. Naval Facilities Engineering Command. Report (USA) **6450**
U.S. Naval Health Research Center Report *see* N H R C Report **6162**
• U S Naval Institute. Proceedings (USA ISSN 0041-798X) **6450**
U.S. Naval Postgraduate School. Technical Report (USA) **8444**
U.S. Naval Research Laboratory. Marine Meteorology Division. Memorandum Report (USA) **6397**
U.S. Naval Research Laboratory. Report (USA) **7925**
U.S. Naval Surface Warfare Center. Carderock Division. Report (USA) **6450**
• U S Neurological Disease (United States) (GBR ISSN 1752-816X) **6189**
U.S. Neurological Disease *see* U S Neurological Disease **6189**
• U S News & World Report (USA ISSN 0041-5537) **3991**
U.S. News & World Report Digital Edition *see* U S News & World Report **3991**
U.S. News Ultimate Guide to Law Schools (USA ISSN 1934-4759) **2962**
U.S. News Ultimate Guide to Medical Schools *see* Ultimate Guide to Medical Schools **2962**
U.S. Northeast: All-Industries *see* Harris Directory. U.S. Northeast All-Industries **2002**
U.S. Northeast: Manufacturing *see* Harris Directory. U.S. Northeast Manufacturing **2002**
U.S. Notary Reference Manual (USA ISSN 1527-3512) **4800**
U.S. Nuclear Energy Institute. Nuclear Energy Info (USA) **3175**
U.S. Nuclear Regulatory Commission. Annual Report to Congress (USA ISSN 0363-7956) **3175**
U.S. Nuclear Regulatory Commission. Occupational Radiation at Commercial Nuclear Power Reactors and Other Facilities. Annual Report (USA) **6688**
U.S. Nuclear Regulatory Commission. Office of Enforcement. Enforcement Actions (USA ISSN 1056-9030) **7544**
U.S. Nuclear Regulatory Commission. Publications (USA) **3175**
U S Nuclear Regulatory Commission Regulatory Guide Series: Division 10 - General (USA) **7050**
U.S. Nuclear Regulatory Commission. Report to Congress on Abnormal Occurrences (USA ISSN 0748-4151) **3175**
U.S. Nuclear Regulatory Commission. Rules and Regulations (USA) **3175**
U.S. Nuclear Regulatory Commission. Rules and Regulations for Medical Licensees (USA) **6209**
U.S. Nuclear Regulatory Commission. Water Reactor Safety Research Information Meeting. Proceedings (USA) **3175**
• U.S. Nuclear Regulatory Commission. Weekly Information Report (USA ISSN 1056-9065) **3175**
U S O Annual Report (United Service Organizations) (USA ISSN 0082-8556) **8075**
U S O of Metropolitan New York (United Service Organizations) (USA) **3991**
U.S. Oceanographic Data Center. Annual Report (USA ISSN 0730-3610) **2819**
U.S. Office of Personnel Management. Negotiability Determinations by the Federal Labor Relations Authority (USA) **1712**
U.S. Office of Personnel Management. Notice and Posting System (USA) **1877**
U.S. Office of Personnel Management Operating Manuals. Qualification Standards for General Schedule Positions (USA) **1877**
U.S. Office of Personnel Management Operating Manuals. The Federal Wage System (USA) **1877**
U.S. Office of Personnel Management Operating Manuals. The Federal Wage System Nonappropriated Fund (USA) **1877**
U.S. Office of Personnel Management Operating Manuals. The Guide to Processing Personnel Actions (USA) **1877**
• U.S. Office of Personnel Management. Performance and Accountability Report for Fiscal Year (USA) **1877**
U.S. Office of Personnel Management. Personnel Systems and Oversight Group. Federal Civilian Workforce Statistics. Occupations of Federal White-Collar and Blue-Collar Workers (USA ISSN 0739-1404) **1272**
▼ • U.S. Office of Private Sector Initiatives. Peace Corps. Partnership (USA ISSN 1946-3634) **8075**
U.S. Office of the Comptroller of the Currency. Annual Report (USA) **1953**
• U.S. Office of the Comptroller of the Currency. Interpretations and Actions (USA) **1953**
• U.S. Office of the Comptroller of the Currency. Quarterly Journal (Online) (USA ISSN 1934-1261) **1953**
U.S. Office of the Comptroller of the Currency. Report of Operations *see* U.S. Office of the Comptroller of the Currency. Annual Report **1953**
U.S. Office of the Comptroller of the Currency. Survey of Credit Underwriting Practices (USA) **1388**
U.S. Office of the Federal Register. Federal Register. *see* Federal Register **4673**
U.S. Office of the Federal Register. Federal Register: What It Is and How to Use It (USA) **4800**
The U S Offshore Funds Directory (USA) **1586**
• U S Offshore Oil Company Contact List (USA ISSN 1089-3253) **6796**
U.S. Oncological Disease *see* U S Oncological Disease **6036**
• U S Oncological Disease (United States) (GBR ISSN 1753-4011) **6036**
U S Outdoor Drama (USA) **8484**
† • U S P - D I. Vol. 1. Drug Information for the Health Care Professional (United States Pharmacopeia) (USA ISSN 0740-4174) **8995**
• U S P - D I. Vol. 2. Advice for the Patient (United States Pharmacopeia) (USA ISSN 0740-6916) **6883**
U S P - D I. Vol. 3. Approved Drug Products and Legal Requirements (United States Pharmacopeia) (USA ISSN 1045-8298) **6884**
U S P Dictionary of U S A N and International Drug Names (United States Pharmacopeial Convention and the United States Adopted Names) (USA ISSN 1076-4275) **6884**
• U S P. Geologia. Serie Cientifica (Universidade de Sao Paulo) (BRA ISSN 1519-874X) **2771**
U S P. Geologia. Serie Didactica (Universidade de Sao Paulo) (BRA ISSN 1677-7549) **2772**
U S P. Geologia. Serie Especial (Universidade de Sao Paulo) (BRA ISSN 1676-7829) **2772**
U S P - Menschen im Marketing (DEU) **1847**
U S P N F *see* United States Pharmacopeia. National Formulary **6884**
U S P - N F *see* United States Pharmacopeia. National Formulary **6884**
U S P - N F. Supplement (United States Pharmacopeia National Formulary) (USA) **6884**
• U S P Pharmacists' Pharmacopeia (United States Pharmacopeial) (USA ISSN 1930-2908) **6884**
• U S P Quality Review (United States Pharmacopeia) (USA) **6884**
• U S P S Journal (Unitarian Society for Psychical Studies) (GBR) **6744**
U.S. Pacific Northwest: All-Industries *see* Harris Directory. U.S. Pacific Northwest All-Industries **2002**
U.S. Pacific Northwest: Manufacturing *see* Harris Directory. U.S. Pacific Northwest Manufacturing **2002**
U.S. Patent and Trademark Office. Classification Bulletins (USA ISSN 0083-3010) **6759**
U.S. Patent and Trademark Office. Guide for the Preparation of Patent Drawings (USA) **6759**
U.S. Patent and Trademark Office. Index of Patents Issued (USA ISSN 0362-0719) **6759**
U.S. Patent and Trademark Office. Index of Trademarks Issued (USA ISSN 0099-0809) **6761**
U.S. Patent and Trademark Office. Manual of Classification (USA) **6759**
U.S. Patent and Trademark Office. Manual of Patent Examining Procedure (USA ISSN 0364-2453) **6759**
• U.S. Patent and Trademark Office. Official Gazette. Trademarks (USA ISSN 0360-5132) **6759**
U.S. Patent and Trademark Office. Patent and Trademark Office Review *see* U.S. Patent and Trademark Office. Performance and Accountability Report **6759**
U.S. Patent and Trademark Office. Performance and Accountability Report (USA) **6759**
U.S. Patent and Trademark Office. Products and Services (USA) **6759**
U.S. Patent and Trademark Office. Technology Assessment and Forecast: Publications (USA) **6759**
• U.S. Patent and Trademark Office. Trademark Manual of Examining Procedure (USA) **6759**
U.S. Patent Classification Definitions (USA) **6759**
U S Patents Quarterly *see* United States Patents Quarterly **6759**
U.S. Peace Corps. Annual Report (USA ISSN 0083-3088) **7270**
U S Petrochemicals Report *see* United States Petrochemicals Report **6796**
• ➤ U S Pharmacist (USA ISSN 0148-4818) **6884**
U.S. Pharmacy Staff Compensation Survey (USA ISSN 1933-6314) **1712**
U S Piper (USA ISSN 0041-8048) **6336**
U.S. Policy & Politics (USA ISSN 1931-6534) **7190**
U S Q R *see* Union Seminary Quarterly Review **7778**
• U S Rail News (USA ISSN 0275-3758) **8627**
U.S. Railroad Retirement Board. Annual Report (USA ISSN 0891-8066) **1712**
U.S. Railroad Retirement Board. Quarterly Benefit Statistics (USA) **1273**
U S Real Estate Register (USA ISSN 8755-1608) **7614**
U.S. Regulatory Reporter (USA ISSN 0749-5005) **7544**
• U S Residential Real Estate Market Report (USA ISSN 1945-6565) **7614**
U.S. Respiratory Disease *see* U S Respiratory Disease **6220**
• U S Respiratory Disease (United States) (GBR ISSN 1753-4089) **6220**
U.S. Rocker Magazine (USA) **6625**
U S Rowing (United States) (USA ISSN 1094-1231) **8283**
U S S E A Update (USA ISSN 0741-4587) **74**
U S S Henrico A P A - 45 Reunion Association. Newsletter (USA) **6450**
U S S Reports (United Seamen's Service) (USA) **8664**
U S Sailing (USA ISSN 1545-2794) **8284**
U S Sailing Directory (USA) **8284**
U.S. Saint Lawrence Seaway Development Corporation. Annual Report (USA ISSN 0558-194X) **8664**
U.S. Scientist and Engineers (USA ISSN 0163-2302) **7925**
U.S. Securities and Exchange Commission. Annual Report *see* U.S. Securities and Exchange Commission. Performance and Accountability Report **1657**
U.S. Securities and Exchange Commission. Decisions and Reports (USA ISSN 0083-3223) **1657**
U.S. Securities and Exchange Commission. Judicial Decisions (USA ISSN 0083-3231) **1657**
U.S. Securities and Exchange Commission. Official Summary of Security Transactions and Holdings (USA ISSN 0364-2267) **1657**
• U.S. Securities and Exchange Commission. Performance and Accountability Report (USA) **1657**
• U.S. Senate. Calendar of Business (USA ISSN 0364-5886) **7473**
U.S. Senate. Committee on Foreign Relations. Legislative Activities Report (USA ISSN 0146-9371) **7270**
• U.S. Senate. Committee on Foreign Relations. Membership and Jurisdiction of Subcommittees (USA) **7473**
• U.S. Senate. Committee on Governmental Affairs. Rules of Procedure of the Committee on Homeland Security and Governmental Affairs, United States Senate/Rules of Procedure of the Committee on Homeland Security and Governmental Affairs, United States Senate (USA) **7473**
U.S. Senate. Committee on Small Business and Entrepreneurship. Legislative Calendar (USA) **7473**
• U S Silver Summary (USA) **6488**
U.S. Sites and Development (USA) **7614**
U.S. Sites and Development Annual Directory (USA) **7614**
U.S. Sites and Development Relocation Journal (USA) **7614**
U.S. Sites Magazine (USA) **7614**
U.S. Small Business Administration. Annual Report (USA ISSN 0083-3274) **1968**
U.S. Small Business Administration. Office of the Inspector General. Semi-Annual Report (USA ISSN 0742-3802) **1968**
U S Social Policy Shareholder Resolutions in (Year) (USA ISSN 1095-6395) **1657**
• U.S. Social Security Administration. Compilation of the Social Security Laws (USA) **4526**
• U.S. Social Security Administration. Supplemental Security Income Program. Reports (USA) **4526**
U.S. Soil Conservation Service. Annual Report *see* U.S. Natural Resouces Conservation Service. Annual Report **8833**
U.S. Southeast: All-Industries *see* Harris Directory. U.S. Southeast All-Industries **2002**
U.S. Southeast: Manufacturing *see* Harris Directory. U.S. Southeast Manufacturing **2002**
• U. S. Stamp News (USA ISSN 1082-9423) **6901**
U.S. State Construction Quarterly Briefing (USA ISSN 1933-5644) **1041**
U.S. Supreme Court Education Cases (USA) **3034**
U.S. Supreme Court Employment Cases (USA) **1712**
U.S. Supreme Court. Journal *see* Supreme Court of the United States. Journal **4791**
U S Survey of Business Expectations (USA) **1908**
U S T A Sires and Dams (United States Trotting Association) (USA) **8300**
U S T A Year Book (United States Trotting Association) (USA ISSN 0083-3517) **8300**
U S T O A Desk Reference *see* Travel Weekly **8768**
U.S. Tax Cases (USA ISSN 0277-402X) **1953**
U S Tax-Stamp Review (USA) **6901**
U S Taxation of International Operations (USA) **1953**
U S Tech (USA) **3115**
U S Tobacco Tax Guide *see* T M A Tobacco Tax Guide **8487**
U S Tobacco Trade Barometer *see* T M A Tobacco Trade Barometer **8487**
U S Tobacco Weekly *see* T M A Tobacco Weekly **8487**
U S Toy Collector Magazine (USA ISSN 1044-1344) **369**
• U.S. Trade with Puerto Rico and U.S. Possessions (USA) **1586**
U S Transactions Monthly (USA) **1388**
U S Transactions Prime Customer Quarterly (USA) **1388**
U S Transactions Small Business Quarterly (USA) **1388**
• U S U Newsletter (Uniformed Services University of the Health Sciences) (USA ISSN 1943-040X) **6450**
U.S. Urban Initiatives Anti-Crime Program. Annual Report to Congress (USA ISSN 0272-8974) **2670**
U.S. Virgin Islands Government Register (USA) **7473**
U S W at Work *see* U S W@Work **4604**
U S W @ Work *see* U S W@Work **4604**
U S Water News (USA ISSN 0749-1980) **8833**
U.S. Waterborne Exports and General Imports *see* Foreign Trade Reports. U.S. Waterborne Exports and General Imports (Online Edition) **1566**
• The U S Wine Market: Impact Databank Review and Forecast (USA) **611**
U S W@Work (United Steel Workers) (USA ISSN 1931-6658) **4604**
• U S Youth Bowler (USA) **8250**
U S Youth Soccer (USA) **8250**
U T (Universitas Tarraconensis) (ESP ISSN 1135-1438) **2921**
U T (HRV ISSN 1330-6766) **8770**
† U T A International (Umwelt Technologie Aktuell) (DEU ISSN 1431-1062) **8995**
U T B (Uni-Taschenbuecher) (DEU ISSN 0340-7225) **7691**
U T C *see* Douanerechtspraak **1920**
U T D Action *see* U T D Edge **2921**
U T D Edge (United Teachers of Dade) (USA ISSN 1557-4814) **2921**
U T D Today *see* U T D Edge **2921**
U T Daily Beacon (University of Tennessee at Knoxville) (USA) **2305**
• U T E P Magazine (University of Texas at El Paso) (USA ISSN 1946-8466) **2305**
U T F Science (DEU) **6336**
U T - I C E P P *see* University of Tokyo. International Center for Elementary Particle Physics **7045**
U T L J *see* University of Toronto Law Journal **4805**
U T Q *see* University of Toronto Quarterly **4481**
▼ • U T S A Discover (University of Texas at San Antonio) (USA) **7925**
† • ➤ The U T S Law Review (University of Technology, Sydney) (AUS ISSN 1442-4959) **8995**
U T S P Annual Report *see* Urban Transportation Showcase Program. Annual Review **8519**
➤ U T S Shopfront Monograph Series (University of Technology, Sydney) (AUS ISSN 1834-2027) **8144**
U T U News (United Transportation Union) (USA ISSN 0098-5937) **4604**
U., the National College Magazine *see* U - Magazine **3006**
U - The Union Magazine (USA ISSN 1932-6971) **5085**
• ➤ U - Turn E - Zine (USA) **523**
U Tz'ib (GTM) **359**
U U & Me! *see* U U World **7742**
U U Fellowship Focus (Unitarian Universalist) (USA ISSN 1930-7306) **7742**
U U M N Notes (Unitarian Universalist Musician's Network) (USA ISSN 1047-6601) **6625**
• U U World (USA ISSN 1532-7450) **7742**
U V P Report (Umweltvertraeglichkeitspruefung Gesellschaft e.V.) (DEU ISSN 0933-0690) **3471**
U V S O R Activity Report (Ultraviolet Synchrotron Orbital Radiation Facility) (JPN ISSN 0911-5730) **7072**
• U V Vaest Rapport (SWE ISSN 1404-2029) **421**
U W F *see* UmweltWirtschaftsForum **1186**
U W I Students' Law Review (University of the West Indies) (BRB ISSN 1022-985X) **4800**
U W J *see* The Utah Water Journal **8835**
• U W M Post (University of Wisconsin Milwaukee) (USA ISSN 1524-0517) **2305**
U X U *see* Underground Experts United **5448**
U Z Magazine (Universitaire Ziekenhuis) (BEL ISSN 0777-9364) **4112**
U25 (USA) **1388**
Ubi Caritas et Amor *see* U C E A **4379**
Ubique (USA ISSN 0049-500X) **4031**
▼ ➤ Ubiquitous Learning (AUS ISSN 1835-9795) **3086**
• Ubiquity (USA ISSN 1530-2180) **8444**
Ubisi Mail (ZAF ISSN 1815-1582) **164**
Ubu (FRA ISSN 1255-7196) **8484**
• Ubuntu (Dutch Edition) (Online) (NLD) **8075**
Ubuntu (Dutch Edition) (Print) *see* Ubuntu (Dutch Edition) (Online) **8075**

Title

• ➤ Ukrains'kyi Medychnyi Chasopys/Ukrainian Medical Journal/Ukrainskii Meditsinskii Zhurnal (UKR ISSN 1562-1146) **5725**
➤ Ukrains'kyi Naukovo-Medychnyi Molodizhnyi Zhurnal/Ukrainian Scientific Medical Youth Journal (UKR ISSN 1996-353X) **5725**
➤ Ukrains'kyi Neirokhirurhichnyi Zhurnal (UKR ISSN 1810-3154) **6262**
• ➤ Ukrains'kyi Pul'monolohichnyi Zhurnal/Ukrainian Journal of Pulmonology/Ukrainskii Pul'monologicheskii Zhurnal (UKR) **6220**
• ➤ Ukrains'kyi Radiolohichnyi Zhurnal (UKR ISSN 1027-3204) **6209**
Ukrainskyi Referatyvnyi Zhurnal. Seriya 1. Pryrodnychi Nauky, Medytsyna/Ukrainian Journal of Abstracts. Ser. 1. Prirodnici Nauki, Medicine (UKR ISSN 1561-1086) **7939**
Ukrainskyi Referatyvnyi Zhurnal. Seriya 2. Tehnika, Promyslovist', Sil's'ke Hospodarstvo/Ukrainian Journal of Abstracts. Ser. 2. Engineering, Industry, Agriculture. (UKR ISSN 1561-1094) **3234**
Ukrainskyi Referatyvnyi Zhurnal. Seriya 3. Sotsial'ni ta Humanitarni Nauky, Mystetstvo/Ukrainian Journal of Abstracts. Ser. 3. Social Sciences and Humanities, Art (UKR ISSN 1561-1108) **8021**
• Ukrains'kyi Revmatolohichnyi Zhurnal (UKR) **6227**
Ukrains'kyi Teatr (UKR ISSN 0207-7159) **8484**
Ukrains'kyi Zhurnal Fizychnoi Optyky *see* Ukrainian Journal of Physical Optics **7085**
Ukrains'kyi Zhurnal z Problem Medytsyny Pratsi (UKR) **6688**
Ukrstenice *see* Lisa. Ukrstenice **8186**
Uktubar *see* October **3836**
Ukulima wa Kisasa/Modern Farming (TZA ISSN 0856-0838) **164**
UKW-Berichte *see* U K W - Berichte **2364**
Ul'anovskaya Pravda (RUS) **3942**
Ulastirma Istatistikleri Ozeti *see* Turkey. Turkiye Istatistik Kurumu. Ulastirma Istatistikleri Ozeti (Year) **8532**
Ulbandus Review (USA ISSN 0163-450X) **5190**
Ulica Sezamkowa *see* Sesame Street **2212**
L'Ulivo (ITA) **7821**
➤ Uljarstvo (SRB ISSN 0351-9503) **3666**
• Ulkopoliittinen Instituutti. U P I Report (FIN ISSN 1458-994X) **7270**
• Ulkopoliittinen Instituutti. U P I Working Papers (FIN ISSN 1456-1360) **7270**
Ulkopolitiikka/Finnish Journal of Foreign Affairs/Utrikespolitik (FIN ISSN 0501-0659) **7270**
L'Ull Critic (ESP ISSN 1138-4573) **5391**
Ullern Avis - Akersposten (NOR) **3925**
• Ullmann's Encyclopedia of Industrial Chemistry (DEU ISSN 1435-6007) **2083**
Ulm und Oberschwaben (DEU ISSN 0342-2364) **4275**
Ulmer Sprachstudien (DEU ISSN 1435-6953) **5190**
➤ Uloom-e-Islamiyah (PAK) **7716**
Uloom e Islamiyah *see* Uloom-e-Islamiyah **7716**
Ulpia Noviomagus (NLD ISSN 1872-4000) **421**
• Ulrich's Periodicals Directory (USA ISSN 0000-2100) **638**
• Ulrichsweb.com (USA) **7579**
Ulster Architect International *see* U.A. International **459**
Ulster Bride (GBR) **5561**
† Ulster Builder and Allied Trades Journal (GBR) **8995**
• Ulster Business (GBR ISSN 1363-2507) **1186**
Ulster Business Journal (GBR) **1186**
Ulster County Gazette (USA) **4315**
Ulster Editions and Monographs (GBR ISSN 0954-3392) **5391**
Ulster Farmer (GBR) **164**
Ulster Folklife (GBR ISSN 0082-7347) **3623**
Ulster Food Trader (GBR) **3666**
• Ulster Gazette and Armagh Standard (GBR) **3872**
Ulster Grocer (GBR) **3682**
Ulster Journal of Archaeology (GBR ISSN 0082-7355) **421**
• ➤ The Ulster Medical Journal (GBR ISSN 0041-6193) **5725**
Ulster Nation (GBR) **7190**
Ulster News Letter (GBR) **3872**
Ulster Tatler (GBR ISSN 0049-5107) **3872**
† • ➤ UltiBASE Journal (AUS ISSN 1443-7023) **8995**
L'Ultima Crociata (ITA) **4275**
• Ultima Decada (CHL ISSN 0717-4691) **8145**
Ultima Moda (MEX ISSN 0041-6223) **2262**
Ultimate Accessories Guide: Auto Performance Accessories *see* Performance Accessories **32**
Ultimate Athlete (USA ISSN 1541-8170) **8214**
Ultimate Audio (USA ISSN 1093-3182) **8155**
Ultimate Baseball Scouting Guide *see* Sporting News Ultimate Baseball Scouting Guide **8247**
Ultimate Beauty (ESP) **8886**
Ultimate Black Hair Guide (USA ISSN 1523-4231) **592**
The Ultimate Car Book (Year) *see* Ultimate Car Book (Year) **2642**
Ultimate Car Book (Year) (USA) **2642**
Ultimate Collection For Men *see* For Men Ultimate Collection **6290**
• Ultimate D V D (Digital Video Disc) (GBR) **6516**
Ultimate D V D Solo (GBR ISSN 1748-5436) **6516**
• Ultimate E-Mail (USA) **2567**
Ultimate Grappling *see* Ultimate M M A **8214**
The Ultimate Guide (GBR) **3006**
Ultimate Guide to Buying Wine *see* Wine Spectator Magazine's Ultimate Guide to Buying Wine **8998**
Ultimate Guide to Law Schools *see* U.S. News Ultimate Guide to Law Schools **2962**
Ultimate Guide to Medical Schools (USA ISSN 1935-2204) **2962**
Ultimate Guided Tour of Stock Investing *see* TheStreet.com Ratings' Ultimate Guided Tour of Stock Investing **1655**
• Ultimate H R Manual (Human Resources) (CAN ISSN 1716-2149) **1877**
Ultimate Health (IRL ISSN 1393-922X) **7544**
Ultimate Home Design (USA) **459**
• Ultimate Home Plan Collection (USA) **1041**
Ultimate Human Resources Manual *see* Ultimate H R Manual **1877**
ULtimate in VACuum Technical Journal *see* U L V A C Technical Journal **3398**
▼ Ultimate Italian (USA ISSN 1942-7999) **4368**
▼ Ultimate Jet (FRA ISSN 1960-8578) **74**
The Ultimate Kauai Guidebook (USA ISSN 1550-7114) **8770**
Ultimate M M A (Mixed Martial Arts) (USA ISSN 1944-5709) **8214**
Ultimate Marvel (USA ISSN 1540-0093) **2219**
Ultimate Mobility (USA) **2583**
• Ultimate Motorcycling (USA ISSN 1945-9580) **8269**
Ultimate New Car Guide *see* Automobile Magazine's Ultimate New Car Guide **8563**
Ultimate P C (GBR ISSN 1368-5317) **2482**
Ultimate P C Strategies (GBR) **2482**
Ultimate Pursuits *see* U P **8552**
➤ Ultimate Reality and Meaning (CAN ISSN 0709-549X) **6958**
▼ Ultimate Slow Cooker (USA ISSN 1945-3620) **4368**
Ultimate Sports Baseball (USA ISSN 1075-5659) **8250**
Ultimate Sports Basketball (USA) **8250**
Ultimate Sports Pro Football (USA ISSN 1076-2930) **8250**
Ultimo (AUT) **3798**
Ultimo (Kiel) (DEU) **3859**
Ultimo (Luebeck) (DEU) **3859**
Ultimo (Muenster) (DEU) **5243**
➤ Ultimo Andar (BRA ISSN 1415-899X) **7691**
Ultra-Fit (GBR ISSN 0957-0616) **6999**
Ultra Fit Australia *see* Ultra Fit Magazine **6999**
Ultra Fit Magazine (AUS) **6999**
Ultra-FIT Magazine *see* Ultra Fit Magazine **6999**
Ultra-FIT Magazine *see* Ultra-Fit **6999**
Ultra Jovem (BRA ISSN 1519-3527) **2219**
➤ Ultra Scientist of Physical Sciences (IND ISSN 0970-9150) **7925**
Ultra V W (GBR) **8609**
• Ultra W W W Magazine (BEL) **6625**
Ultra-Wideband, Short-Pulse Electromagnetics. Proceedings (USA) **3333**
UltraFlight Magazine (USA) **74**
Ultragarsas/Ultrasound (LTU ISSN 1392-2114) **6209**
Ultrakurzwellen Berichte *see* U K W - Berichte **2364**
Ultralight Flying! (USA ISSN 0883-7937) **74**
• ➤ Ultramicroscopy (NLD ISSN 0304-3991) **7044**
Ultrapure Water (USA ISSN 0747-8291) **8833**
UltraRunning (USA ISSN 0744-3609) **8339**
• ➤ Ultraschall in der Medizin (DEU ISSN 0172-4614) **5725**
Ultraschall in der Medizin. Supplement *see* Ultraschall in der Medizin **5725**
• ➤ Ultrasonic Imaging (USA ISSN 0161-7346) **6209**
• Ultrasonic Inspection in Engineering Series (GBR) **3372**
Ultrasonic Technology *see* Choonpa Techno **7087**
• ➤ Ultrasonics (NLD ISSN 0041-624X) **7089**
• ➤ Ultrasonics Sonochemistry (NLD ISSN 1350-4177) **7089**
Ultrasonido (ARG) **6209**
➤ Ultrasonografia (POL) **6209**
• Ultrasound (GBR ISSN 1742-271X) **6209**
Ultrasound *see* Ultragarsas **6209**
• Ultrasound Clinics (USA ISSN 1556-858X) **6209**
Ultrasound Clinics: Continuing Medical Education Supplement *see* Ultrasound Clinics **6209**
• ➤ Ultrasound in Medicine & Biology (USA ISSN 0301-5629) **709**
• ➤ Ultrasound in Obstetrics and Gynecology (GBR ISSN 0960-7692) **6005**
Ultrasound in Obstetrics & Gynecology. Supplement *see* Ultrasound in Obstetrics and Gynecology **6005**
Ultrasound International (IND ISSN 0971-6874) **6210**
• ➤ Ultrasound Quarterly (USA ISSN 0894-8771) **6210**
• ➤ Ultrastructural Pathology (GBR ISSN 0191-3123) **6036**
Ultraviolet Synchrotron Orbital Radiation Facility Activity Report *see* U V S O R Activity Report **7072**
Ultreya (USA ISSN 0041-6258) **7821**
Ulula (USA ISSN 0747-8011) **5190**
Al 'ulum al-Iqtisadiyyat/Economic Sciences (IRQ ISSN 1814-9669) **1186**
Ulum al-Miyah *see* Water Science **8840**
➤ Ulum-e-Islamia (PAK ISSN 2073-5146) **7716**
• ➤ Ulum va-Tiknuluzhi-i Pulimir/Iranian Journal of Polymer Science and Technology (IRN ISSN 1016-3255) **3257**
Ulum wa-Funun al-Musiqa/Music Science and Art (EGY ISSN 1110-7804) **6625**
• ➤ Ulusal Cerrahi Dergisi/Turkish Journal of Surgery (TUR ISSN 1300-0705) **6262**
Ulusal Travma Dergisi/Turkish Journal of Trauma & Emergency Surgery (TUR ISSN 1300-6738) **4112**
Ulusal Travma ve Acil Cerrahi Dergisi *see* Ulusal Travma Dergisi **4112**
• ➤ Uluslararasi Hukuk ve Politika/The Review of International Law and Politics (TUR ISSN 1305-5208) **4943**
• Uluslararasi Iliskiler/Journal of International Relations (TUR ISSN 1304-7310) **7270**
Uluslararasi Iliskiler Dergisi *see* Uluslararasi Iliskiler **7270**
• ➤ Uluslararasi Insan Bilimleri Dergisi/International Journal of Human Sciences (TUR ISSN 1303-5134) **8011**
Uluslararasi Sosyal Arastirmalar Dergisi *see* Journal of International Social Research **7979**
Uluslararasiiliskiler *see* Uluslararasi Iliskiler **7270**
Ulysse (FRA ISSN 0990-7068) **8770**
Ulysses (DEU ISSN 1860-2371) **3859**
Umafrika (ZAF ISSN 0041-6274) **7691**
U_mag (DEU) **5085**
U_magazine *see* U_mag **5085**
Umak Tonga *see* Eumak Dong-A **6565**
Uman (OMN) **3926**
The UMass Lowell Connector (University of Massachusetts) (USA) **2305**
➤ UmBau (AUT ISSN 0256-2529) **459**
Umbauen und Modernisieren (DEU) **4551**
Umbauen und Renovieren (CHE ISSN 1423-6508) **4551**
Umbr(a) (USA ISSN 1087-0830) **7413**
Umbral (PAN) **5391**
• Umbral Universitario (COL ISSN 1692-3375) **7925**
Umbrales (ARG) **5243**
† • Umbrella (USA ISSN 0160-0699) **8995**
• Umbsebenzi (ZAF) **7190**
Um:druck (AUT ISSN 1991-5365) **523**
▼ Umeaa Studies in Cognitive Science (SWE ISSN 1654-2568) **5190**
Umeaa Studies in Linguistics (SWE ISSN 1650-254X) **5190**
Umeaa Studies in Philosophy (SWE ISSN 1650-1748) **6958**
Umeaa Studies in Sociology (SWE ISSN 1100-3553) **8145**
Umeaa Universitet. Institutionen foer Arkeologi och Samiska Studier. Arkeologiska Studier (SWE ISSN 1104-3520) **421**
Umeaa Universitet. Institutionen foer Arkeologi och Samiska Studier. Studia Archaeologica Universitatis Umensis (SWE ISSN 1100-7028) **421**
Umeaa Universitet. Institutionen foer Kultur och Medier. Rapportserien (SWE ISSN 1650-4801) **36**
Umeaa Universitet. Medical Dissertations (SWE ISSN 0346-6612) **5725**
Umeaa Universitet. Pedagogiska Institutionen. Akademiska Avhandlingar (SWE ISSN 0281-6768) **2921**
Umeaa Universitet. Pedagogiska Institutionen. Pedagogiska Rapporter/Educational Reports (SWE ISSN 1403-6169) **2921**
▼ • Umeaa Working Papers in Peace and Conflict Studies (SWE ISSN 1654-2398) **7190**
▼ • Umeaa Working Papers in Political Science (SWE ISSN 1654-238X) **7190**
➤ Umeni/Art (CZE ISSN 0049-5123) **523**
Umfeld (AUT ISSN 1015-8529) **7190**
Umformtechnik (DEU ISSN 0300-3167) **6336**
Umformtechnik und Werkzeugmaschinen - Pressen, Schmieden, Waelzen, Ziehen, Biegen, Sintern *see* Informationsdienst F I Z Technik. Umformtechnik und Werkzeugmaschinen - Pressen, Schmieden, Waelzen, Ziehen, Biegen, Sintern **3231**
The Umhlanga Globe (ZAF) **3950**
Umi *see* La Mer **689**
Umi/Sea (JPN) **5391**
Umi no Hakubutsukan/Tokai University. Marine Science Museum. Journal (JPN ISSN 0386-4197) **2819**
Umi no Kenkyu (JPN ISSN 0916-8362) **2819**
Umi no Kisho/Marine Meteorology (JPN ISSN 0287-5276) **6397**
Umi, Shizen to Bunka/Tokai University. School of Marine Science and Technology. Journal (JPN ISSN 1348-7620) **2819**
Umi to Anzen (JPN ISSN 0912-7437) **2819**
Umi to Ningen/Toba Maritime Museum. Annual (JPN ISSN 0385-5597) **2819**
➤ Umi to Sora/Marine Meteorological Society. Journal (JPN ISSN 0503-1567) **6397**
Umjetnost Rijeci/Word Art (HRV ISSN 0503-1583) **5391**
Umlozi (ZAF) **3950**
Al-Umm (LBN ISSN 2072-9774) **8886**
Umma *see* Ha'Umma **3895**
Umma (TZA ISSN 0856-0854) **5391**
Umoja (USA ISSN 0363-3160) **3569**
Umpqua Trapper (USA ISSN 0041-6339) **4315**
Umrisse *see* Baukultur **980**
• Der Umsatz-Steuer-Berater (DEU ISSN 1439-6777) **1953**
Umsatzsteuer B M F - B F H (Bundesministerium der Finanzen - Bundesfinanzhof) (DEU) **1953**
Umsatzsteuer-Kartei *see* Umsatzsteuer B M F - B F H **1953**
Umsatzsteuer-Rundschau (DEU ISSN 0341-8669) **1954**
Umsatzsteuer- und Verkehrsteuer-Recht (DEU ISSN 0935-7998) **1954**
Umsatzsteuergesetz (DEU ISSN 0940-8738) **1954**
Umsebenzi (ZAF ISSN 0814-0693) **7190**
Umthombo Wamandla (ZAF ISSN 0378-4134) **7778**
Umthunywa (ZWE ISSN 1814-4276) **3996**
Umuhinzi - Mworozi (RWA) **164**
• Umwelt (DEU ISSN 0041-6355) **3491**
Umwelt (DEU ISSN 0343-1460) **3471**
Umwelt - Bildung - Forschung (DEU ISSN 1434-3762) **3471**
Umwelt fur Europaer *see* Environment for Europeans **3421**
Umwelt Journal (AUT) **3471**
Umwelt - Kommunale Oekologische Briefe *see* UmweltBriefe **3472**
† Umwelt-Service (DEU) **8995**
Umwelt Technologie Aktuell International *see* U T A International **8995**
Umwelt und Betrieb (DEU ISSN 0938-3298) **3471**
Umwelt und Bildung (AUT ISSN 1818-7188) **8011**
Umwelt und Gesundheit (DEU ISSN 0945-7526) **5766**
Umwelt- und Planungsrecht *see* U P R **3471**
Umwelt- und Technikrecht (DEU ISSN 0933-6494) **3471**
Umweltbericht. Teil 1: Qualitaet (DEU ISSN 1618-4165) **3472**
Umweltbericht. Teil 2: Politische Bewertung (DEU ISSN 1618-4173) **3472**
Umweltbrief (DEU ISSN 0948-5953) **2630**
† Umweltbrief (Berlin) (BRD ISSN 0343-1312) **8995**
• UmweltBriefe (DEU ISSN 1866-0037) **3472**
Umweltbundesamt. Berichte (DEU ISSN 0171-1911) **3472**
Umweltbundesamt. Jahresbericht (DEU ISSN 0720-2830) **3472**
Umweltbundesamt. Texte (DEU ISSN 0722-186X) **3149**
Umweltdelikte (DEU ISSN 0946-3143) **3472**
Umweltforschungsplan (DEU ISSN 0173-1947) **3472**
UmweltMagazin *see* Umwelt **3491**
Umweltmagazin (DEU ISSN 0173-363X) **3472**
• ➤ Umweltmedizin in Forschung und Praxis (DEU ISSN 1430-8681) **5726**
† Umweltpraxis (DEU ISSN 1616-5829) **8995**
Umweltprobenbank des Bundes (DEU ISSN 1431-4584) **3472**
Umweltpsychologie (DEU ISSN 1434-3304) **7413**
• Umweltradioaktivitaet in der Bundesrepublik Deutschland (DEU ISSN 1864-2810) **3513**
Umweltrecht (DEU ISSN 0938-0329) **3472**
Umweltrecht in Forschung und Praxis (DEU ISSN 1617-7436) **3472**
Umweltschutz (AUT ISSN 0049-5131) **7544**
Umweltschutz und Umwelttechnik, Luftreinhaltung, Gewaesserschutz, Abfallentsorgung, Messtechnik *see* Informationsdienst F I Z Technik. Umweltschutz und Umwelttechnik, Luftreinhaltung, Gewaesserschutz, Abfallentsorgung, Messtechnik **3479**
Umweltstunde *see* Sachunterricht Kreativ **3464**
Umweltvertraeglichkeitspruefung Gesellschaft e.V. Report *see* U V P Report **3471**
• ➤ UmweltWirtschaftsForum (DEU ISSN 0943-3481) **1186**
• ➤ Umweltwissenschaften und Schadstoff-Forschung (DEU ISSN 0934-3504) **3492**
† • Un Magazine (AUS ISSN 1449-6747) **8995**
The Unabashed Librarian (USA ISSN 0049-514X) **5052**
Unabhaengige Bauernstimme (DEU ISSN 0934-4632) **164**
Unabhaengige Brandschutzzeitschrift *see* Feuerwehr **3576**
Unabhaengigen Finanzsenates Aktuell *see* U F S Aktuell **1953**
▼ • The Unabridged Life Ezine (USA ISSN 1944-6411) **5391**
UNANewZ *see* U N A New Z **8995**
➤ Una's Lectures (USA ISSN 1549-1293) **4479**
• Unasylva (ITA ISSN 0041-6436) **3706**
Unausforschlicher Reichtum (DEU ISSN 0041-6444) **7691**
An Unauthorized Guide to Fire-King Glasswares (USA ISSN 1935-0627) **2046**
Unavicoltura (ITA ISSN 1593-1005) **302**
Unbound *see* Unbound: Harvard Journal of the Legal Left **4800**
• Unbound: Harvard Journal of the Legal Left (USA ISSN 1932-3808) **4800**
Uncensored (NZL ISSN 1177-0236) **3919**
Uncensored Amateur Swinger (USA) **6301**
Uncensored: U S Edition *see* Uncensored **3919**
Uncertainty Theory in Artificial Intelligence Series (GBR) **2456**
▼ Uncinetto Facile Facile (ITA ISSN 1971-9353) **6642**
Unclaimed Property Law and Reporting Forms (USA) **4800**
• Unclassified Report to Congress on the Acquisition of Technology Relating to Weapons of Mass Destruction and Advanced Conventional Munitions (USA) **6450**
Uncle Jam Quarterly *see* U J Q **5243**
Uncle Sally's Magazin (DEU) **6625**
• Uncommon Sense (USA) **4315**

10980 L' UNION AGRICOLE ULRICH'S PERIODICALS

L'Union Agricole (FRA ISSN 0244-8459) **164**
Union Agricole de la Haute-Vienne (FRA) **164**
Union & Actions *see* Union and Actions **1969**
Union and Actions (BEL) **1969**
Union. Ausgabe Baden-Wuerttemberg *see* Union **7190**
Union. Ausgabe Berlin *see* Union **7190**
Union. Ausgabe Brandenburg *see* Union **7190**
Union. Ausgabe Bremen *see* Union **7190**
Union. Ausgabe Hamburg *see* Union **7190**
Union. Ausgabe Hessen *see* Union **7190**
Union. Ausgabe Mecklenburg-Vorpommern *see* Union **7190**
Union. Ausgabe Niedersachsen *see* Union **7190**
Union. Ausgabe Nordrhein-Westfalen *see* Union **7190**
Union. Ausgabe Saar *see* Union **7190**
Union. Ausgabe Sachsen *see* Union **7190**
Union. Ausgabe Sachsen-Anhalt *see* Union **7190**
Union. Ausgabe Schleswig-Holstein *see* Union **7190**
Union. Ausgabe Thueringen *see* Union **7190**
Union Bank of Finland. Annual Report (FIN ISSN 0355-0133) **1388**
Union Bank of Switzerland International Finance *see* U B S International Finance **1387**
Union Catalog of Motion Picture Music (USA) **6625**
Union Catalog of Serials *see* Katalog Induk Majalart **10**
Union College (USA) **3006**
Union Connection (USA) **2922**
• Union Contract Law Bulletin (USA ISSN 1096-3995) **1712**
Union County Family *see* New Jersey Family (Mountainside) **2162**
• Union County Family (USA) **2170**
Union County Heritage (USA ISSN 1536-1993) **3786**
Union Craftsman (USA ISSN 1092-7417) **4604**
Union de Detallistas de Alimentacion Press *see* U D A Press **8995**
L'Union de Fait *see* Living Common Law **4912**
Union de l'Europe Occidentale. Institut d'Etudes de Securite. Publications Occasionelles *see* European Union Institute for Security Studies. Occasional Papers **7234**
Union de Periodistas de Cuba *see* U P E C **7575**
Union de Universidades de America Latina. Gaceta (MEX ISSN 0185-2779) **3006**
Union Democracy Review (USA ISSN 1077-5080) **4604**
Union Departementale des Syndicats d'Entrepreneurs et d'Artisans du Batiment et des Travaux Publics de la Haute-Garonne. Officiel du Batiment (FRA) **1041**
Union der Leitenden Angestellten Nachrichten *see* U L A - Nachrichten **1877**
Union des Cadres et Ingenieurs. Lettre *see* F O - Cadres **4594**
Union des Caisses Nationales de Securite Sociale Bulletin Juridique *see* U C A N S S. Bulletin Juridique **4799**
Union des Cantons de l'Est (CAN) **3819**
Union des Chambres de Commerce et Etablissements Gestionnaires d'Aeroport. Statistics on Airport Traffic (FRA) **8532**
Union des Industries et Entreprises de l'Eau et de l'Environnement. Annuaire (FRA ISSN 0069-2603) **3472**
Union des Oenologues de France. Annuaire (FRA ISSN 1771-7914) **256**
Union des Physiciens. Bulletin *see* Le B U P Physique Chimie **7838**
Union des Producteurs Suisses. Journal (CHE) **164**
Union des Professions Immobilieres de Belgique. Bulletin Mensuel - Maandblad (BEL) **7614**
Union des Superieures Majeurs de France. Annuaire (FRA ISSN 0396-2393) **7691**
Union des Syndicats des PME du Caoutchouc et de la Plasturgie (FRA ISSN 1635-0502) **7827**
L'Union Edition Web *see* L' Union **3790**
Union Europea Aranzadi (ESP ISSN 1579-0452) **4801**
Union Europea. Boletin *see* European Union. Bulletin **1485**
Union Europea. Indice Anual (ESP ISSN 1135-5425) **4801**
Union Europea. Indice Mensual (ESP ISSN 1134-0231) **4801**
Union Europea. Noticias (ESP ISSN 1133-8660) **4801**
Union Europea. Revista de Derecho (ESP ISSN 1695-1085) **4801**
Union Europea y de la Competencia. Gaceta Juridica (ESP ISSN 1575-2054) **4801**
Union Europeenee. Bulletin *see* European Union. Bulletin **1485**
Union Farmer (CAN ISSN 0041-6878) **164**
Union for Radical Political Economics Newsletter *see* U R P E Newsletter **1185**
Union Francaise des Centres de Vacances Loisirs *see* U F C V **1711**
Union Francaise des Oenologues. Annuaire *see* Union des Oenologues de France. Annuaire **256**
Union Girondine des Vins de Bordeaux (FRA ISSN 0242-6706) **256**
Union Herald (MYS ISSN 0049-528X) **4604**
Union Herald, Inc. (USA) **4604**
Union in Deutschland *see* U i D **7190**
Union Internacional de Telecomunicaciones. Biblioteca Central. Lista de Revistas *see* International Telecommunication Union. Central Library. List of Periodicals **2348**
Union Internacional de Telecomunicaciones. Biblioteca Central. Lista de Adquisiciones Recientes *see* International Telecommunication Union. Central Library. List of Recent Acquisitions **2348**
Union Internacional de Telecomunicaciones. Informe sobre las Actividades *see* International Telecommunication Union. Report on the Activities **2368**
Union Internacional de Telecomunicaciones. Lista de Publicaciones Anuales *see* International Telecommunication Union. List of Annuals **2348**
Union Internationale Contre le Cancer International Calendar of Meetings on Cancer *see* U I C C International Calendar of Meetings on Cancer **6283**
Union Internationale Contre le Cancer International Directory of Cancer Institutes and Organizations *see* U I C C International Directory of Cancer Institutes and Organizations **6036**
Union Internationale de la Marionette Membership Directory *see* U N I M A - U S A Membership Directory **523**
Union Internationale de Speleologie Bulletin (Online) *see* U I S Bulletin (Online) **2771**
Union Internationale des Architectes Newsletter *see* U I A Newsletter **459**
Union Internationale des Associations d'Alpinisme. Bulletin *see* International Union of Alpine Associations. Bulletin **8724**
Union Internationale des Chemins de Fer. Supplementary Statistics (Year) (FRA) **8532**
Union Internationale des Telecommunications. Bibliotheque Centrale. Liste des Acquisitions Recentes *see* International Telecommunication Union. Central Library. List of Recent Acquisitions **2348**
Union Internationale des Telecommunications. Bibliotheque Centrale. Liste des Periodiques *see* International Telecommunication Union. Central Library. List of Periodicals **2348**
Union Internationale des Telecommunications. Listes des Publications Annuelles *see* International Telecommunication Union. List of Annuals **2348**
Union Internationale des Telecommunications. Rapport des Activites *see* International Telecommunication Union. Report on the Activities **2368**
Union Jack (USA ISSN 1077-3479) **3570**
Union Labor Journal (USA ISSN 0894-7775) **4604**
Union Labor Life Insurance Co. Bulletin *see* U L L I C O Bulletin **4526**
Union Labor News (USA ISSN 0041-6924) **4604**
• Union Labor Report Newsletter (USA ISSN 1542-9628) **4604**
Union Libre (ESP ISSN 1137-1250) **3954**
Union List of Scientific and Technical Periodicals in Zambia (ZMB) **638**
• Union List of Serials in Israel Libraries (ISR ISSN 0333-5321) **638**
Union List of Technical Reports, Standards and Patents in Engineering (USA) **3224**
The Union Magazine *see* U - The Union Magazine **5085**
Union Mail *see* New York Metro Area Postal Union. Union Mail **2354**
• Union Matematica Argentina. Noticiero (ARG ISSN 1514-9560) **5543**
• ➤ Union Matematica Argentina. Revista (ARG ISSN 0041-6932) **5543**
Union Matters (CAN ISSN 0845-8839) **4604**
Union Membership and Earnings Data Book (USA ISSN 1087-8629) **4604**
• Union Nationale Culture et Bibliotheques pour Tous. Notes Bibliographiques (FRA ISSN 0468-8678) **5060**
Union Nationale des Entrepreneurs Platriers-Plaquistes, Staffeurs et Stucateurs. Bulletin (FRA) **1041**
Union Nationale des Industries de Carrieres et Materiaux de Construction Annuaire Officiel *see* U N I C E M Annuaire Officiel **1041**
Union Nationale du Commerce de Gros en Fruits et Legumes. Bulletin (FRA) **165**
• Union Newsletter (English Edition) (FRA ISSN 1727-7914) **6220**
• Union Newsletter (French Edition) (FRA ISSN 1727-7922) **6220**
• Union Newsletter (Spanish Edition) (FRA ISSN 1727-7930) **6221**
Union of American Hebrew Congregations. State of Our Union (USA ISSN 0363-3810) **7731**
Union of American Physicians and Dentists Report *see* U A P D Report **4603**
Union of British Columbia Municipalities. Minutes of Annual Convention (CAN ISSN 0082-7746) **7473**
Union of Councils for Jews in the Former Soviet Union Membership Report *see* U C S J Membership Report **7731**
Union of Councils for Jews in the Former Soviet Union Monitor *see* U C S J Monitor **7731**
Union of European Football Associations. Bulletin (CHE ISSN 0501-1590) **8250**
Union of European Football Associations Flash *see* U E F A Flash **8250**
Union of European Football Associations. Handbook of U E F A (CHE ISSN 0570-2070) **8250**
Union of Forestry and Timber Industry Workers. Bulletin (BGR) **3706**
Union of International Associations. Documents *see* Collection of Documents for the Study of International Non-Governmental Relations **4920**
Union of Japanese Scientists and Engineers. Reports of Statistical Application Research (JPN ISSN 0034-4842) **5543**
Union of the Electricity Industry. Congress Proceedings (BEL) **3333**
Union of Yugoslav Composers' Organizations. Letter. Bulletin *see* Savez Organizacija Kompozitora Jugoslavije. Pismo **6615**
Union Paysanne de la Correze (FRA ISSN 1141-0175) **165**
Union Plus (USA ISSN 1089-6937) **3991**
La Union Politica (MEX) **7190**
Union Postal Universal. Actas *see* Union Postale Universelle. Actes **2355**
Union Postale (CHE ISSN 0041-7009) **2355**
Union Postale Universelle. Actes (CHE ISSN 0252-3973) **2355**
Union Postale Universelle. Statistique des Services Postaux (CHE ISSN 0252-3752) **2355**
Union Presse (FRA ISSN 0398-5369) **7575**
• Union Recorder (AUS ISSN 0041-7017) **2305**
Union Register (USA ISSN 0274-970X) **4604**
Union Roots (USA ISSN 1068-9427) **3786**
➤ Union Seminary Quarterly Review (USA ISSN 0362-1545) **7778**
Union Signal (USA ISSN 0041-7033) **2700**
Union Sociale (FRA ISSN 0041-7041) **8075**
Union Sociale des Oeuvres Privees *see* Union Sociale **8075**
Union Suisse des Fabricants de Boites de Montres Informations *see* U S F B Informations **4570**
Union Topics (USA) **4604**
Union Update *see* Queensland Nurses' Union. Union Update **4601**
• Union Wire (USA) **4604**
L'Unione dei Segretari (ITA ISSN 0394-8390) **4604**
Unione Europea. Bollettino *see* European Union. Bulletin **1485**
Unione Matematica Italiana. Bollettino (ITA ISSN 1972-6724) **5543**
Unione Matematica Italiana. Bollettino. Sezione A: La Matematica nella Societa e nella Cultura *see* La Matematica nella Societa e nella Cultura **5510**
Unione Matematica Italiana. Bollettino. Sezione B: Articoli di Ricerca Matematica *see* Unione Matematica Italiana. Bollettino **5543**
Unione Matematica Italiana. Bollettino. Supplemento. Fisica Matematica *see* Unione Matematica Italiana. Bollettino **5543**
• Unione Matematica Italiana. Notiziario (ITA ISSN 0393-0998) **5543**
Unione Nazionale Ufficiali in Congedo d'Italia Rivista *see* U N U C I. Rivista **6449**
L'Unione Sarda (ITA ISSN 1128-6857) **3899**
The Unioneer (USA) **4604**
Uniongram (USA) **3034**
Unionist *see* Al Ittihadi **3789**
Unionist (New York) (USA ISSN 0041-7092) **4604**
UniPress (DEU ISSN 0937-6496) **3006**
Unique Cars (AUS ISSN 1449-6682) **8609**
Unique Concepts and Events *see* U C E **2262**
Unique Homes (USA ISSN 0747-7465) **7614**
• Unique Opportunities (USA ISSN 1059-6100) **5726**
Unique Woman (USA) **8887**
Unir (FRA ISSN 0985-1798) **3842**
Unir Cine Media (SEN ISSN 0253-5858) **8145**
Unir Cinema (SEN ISSN 0253-195X) **6516**
Unir: Echo de Saint Louis (SEN ISSN 0253-584X) **5392**
Unisa Latin American Report *see* U N I S A Latin American Report **4315**
Unisa Psychologia *see* New Voices in Psychology **7388**
Uniscene (DEU) **2305**
Uniscene Hannover (DEU) **2305**
• UniSci (USA) **7925**
Uniscope (CAN ISSN 1181-8409) **2306**
• UniServe Science. Annual Report (AUS) **7925**
† • UniServe Science News (AUS ISSN 1329-7724) **8996**
• UniServe Science News (Online) (AUS ISSN 1329-1645) **7925**
• UniServe Science. Symposium Proceedings (AUS) **7925**
UniServe Science. Workshop Proceedings *see* UniServe Science. Symposium Proceedings **7925**
Unisono - Schweizerische Blasmusikzeitung (CHE) **6625**
UniSpiegel (Hamburg) (DEU) **3006**
Unispiegel (Heidelberg) (DEU ISSN 0171-4880) **3006**
• UniSwa Journal of Agriculture (SWZ ISSN 1021-0873) **165**
UniSwa Research Journal (SWZ ISSN 1017-7442) **4479**
Unisys News (JPN ISSN 0915-051X) **2494**
• The Unit Circle (USA) **5243**
Unit Costs of Health & Social Care (GBR ISSN 1368-230X) **8075**
Unit Investment Trusts *see* Mergent Unit Investment Trusts **1639**
Unit Investment Trusts Service Manuals (USA) **1657**
Unit Investment Trusts Weekly Reports (USA) **1657**
Unit Load Devices Technical Manual *see* U L D Technical Manual **8552**
Unit Load Management (USA) **1799**
Unit Scheme and Conservation Order Outlines (CAN) **2630**
• L'Unita (ITA ISSN 0391-7002) **7190**
Unita e Carismi (ITA) **7821**
† Unita Proletaria (ITA ISSN 0390-038X) **8996**
The Unitarian (GBR ISSN 0049-531X) **7743**
Unitarian and Free Christian Churches. Handbook and Directory of the General Assembly (GBR) **7743**
• Unitarian Historical Society, London. Transactions (GBR ISSN 0082-7800) **7743**
Unitarian Society for Psychical Studies Journal *see* U S P S Journal **6744**
➤ Unitarian Universalist Christian (USA ISSN 0362-0492) **7743**
• Unitarian Universalist Directory (USA ISSN 0082-7827) **7743**
Unitarian Universalist Fellowship Focus *see* U U Fellowship Focus **7742**
Unitarian Universalist Musician's Network Notes *see* U U M N Notes **6625**
Unitarian Universalist Service. Service Committee News *see* Rights Now **7741**
Unitarian Universalist World *see* U U World **7742**
Unitarische Blaetter (DEU ISSN 0932-0180) **7691**
• ➤ Unitas (PHL ISSN 0041-7149) **523**
Unitas/Lien Ho Wen Hsueh (TWN) **5243**
Unitas Fratrum (DEU ISSN 0344-9254) **7778**
Unite (CAN ISSN 1718-1178) **7190**
Unite de Programmation du Ministere. Bulletin de Conjoncture (HTI) **1523**
Unite des Chretiens (FRA ISSN 1248-9646) **7691**
Unite - Dignite - Travail: Programme Triennal d'Investissement de l'Etat (CAF) **1273**
• UNITE HERE! (USA) **4604**
Unitec. Annual Report (NZL) **3006**
Unitec Institute of Technology. Annual Report *see* Unitec. Annual Report **3006**
Unitec Institute of Technology. Research and Development Report *see* Advance **2965**
United Against Cruelty to Animals *see* U A C T A **322**
United Arab Emirates *see* The P R S Group. Country Reports: United Arab Emirates **1509**
United Arab Emirates. Al-Masraf al-Markazi. Al-Mulhiq al-Ihsa'i/United Arab Emirates. Central Bank. Statistical Supplement (UAE) **1273**
United Arab Emirates. Al-Masraf al-Markazi. Al-Nashrah al-Iqtisadiyyah/United Arab Emirates. Central Bank. Economic Bulletin (UAE) **1388**
United Arab Emirates. Al-Masraf al-Markazi. Al-Taqrir al-Sanawi/United Arab Emirates. Central Bank. Annual Report (UAE) **1954**
United Arab Emirates. Al-Qiyadah al-Aamah lil-Quwwat al-Musallihah. Majallah al-Tibbiyyah/United Arab Emirates. General Command for the Armed Forces. Medical Journal (UAE) **5726**
• United Arab Emirates Autos Report (GBR ISSN 1749-0243) **8609**
United Arab Emirates. Business Directory (UAE) **2032**
United Arab Emirates Business Forecast Report *see* The U A E Business Forecast Report **1522**
United Arab Emirates. Central Bank. Annual Report *see* United Arab Emirates. Al-Masraf al-Markazi. Al-Taqrir al-Sanawi **1954**
United Arab Emirates. Central Bank. Economic Bulletin *see* United Arab Emirates. Al-Masraf al-Markazi. Al-Nashrah al-Iqtisadiyyah **1388**
United Arab Emirates. Central Bank. Statistical Supplement *see* United Arab Emirates. Al-Masraf al-Markazi. Al-Mulhiq al-Ihsa'i **1273**
• United Arab Emirates Defence & Security Report (GBR ISSN 1749-1738) **6450**
• United Arab Emirates Food & Drink Report (GBR ISSN 1749-3048) **1186**
United Arab Emirates Freight Transport Report (GBR ISSN 1750-533X) **8518**
United Arab Emirates. General Command for the Armed Forces. Medical Journal *see* United Arab Emirates. Al-Qiyadah al-Aamah lil-Quwwat al-Musallihah. Majallah al-Tibbiyyah **5726**
United Arab Emirates. Ministry of Education. Annual Report *see* United Arab Emirates. Wizarat al-Tarbiyyah wal-Ta'lim. Al-Taqrir al-Sanawi **3034**
United Arab Emirates. Official Gazette *see* Al-Jaridah ar-Rasmiyyah li-Dawlat al-Imarat al-Arabiyyah al-Muttahidah **7447**
United Arab Emirates Petrochemicals Report (GBR ISSN 1749-2521) **6796**
United Arab Emirates Quarterly Forecast Report *see* The U A E Business Forecast Report **1522**
United Arab Emirates University. Faculty of Science. Journal/Jami'at al-Imarat al-Arabiyyah al-Muttahidah. Kulliyyat al-Ulum. Majallah (UAE ISSN 1021-0806) **7925**
United Arab Emirates. Wizarat al-Tarbiyyah wal-Ta'lim. Al-Taqrir al-Sanawi/United Arab Emirates. Ministry of Education. Annual Report (UAE) **3034**
United Arab Republic Journal of Animal Production *see* Egyptian Journal of Animal Production **285**
United Arab Republic Journal of Microbiology *see* Egyptian Journal of Microbiology **884**
United Association Journal (USA ISSN 0041-7181) **4604**
United Association Journal *see* U A Journal **4603**
United Association Manufacturers' Representatives, Inc. Confidential Bulletin *see* U A M R Confidential Bulletin **1905**

United Association Manufacturers' Representatives Newsletter *see* U A M R Newsletter **1185**
United Automobile, Aerospace, and Agricultural Implement Workers of America (Washington) Washington Report *see* U A W Washington Report **4603**
United Bank Limited. Economic Journal (PAK) **1523**
United Baptist Convention of the Atlantic Provinces. Yearbook (CAN ISSN 0082-7843) **7778**
United Bible Societies. Bulletin (GBR ISSN 0041-719X) **7691**
United Caprine News (USA ISSN 0164-9353) **302**
United Church News (USA ISSN 0882-7214) **7778**
The United Church Observer (CAN ISSN 0041-7238) **7778**
United Church of Canada. Year Book and Directory (CAN ISSN 0848-4449) **7778**
United Church of Christ, Commission for Racial Justice Reporter *see* C R J Reporter **3524**
United Church of Christ. Pension Boards (Annual Report) (USA ISSN 0360-9782) **7778**
United Cities *see* Cites Unies **7227**
United Daily News *see* Lianhe Bao **3960**
United Daughters of the Confederacy Magazine *see* U D C Magazine **2270**
United Electrical Radio and Machine Workers of America News *see* U E News **4603**
United Engineering Foundation Annual Report (USA) **3224**
United Evening News *see* Lianhe Wanbao **3960**
United Food & Commercial Workers Local 174 *see* U F C W Local 174 **4603**
United Food & Commercial Workers Local 27 Reporter *see* U F C W Local 27 Reporter **4603**
United Free Church of Scotland. Handbook (GBR ISSN 0082-7908) **7778**
United Graziers Association of Queensland Grazier *see* U G A Grazier **302**
United in Christ *see* Unidos en Cristo **7821**
United Kingdom Accreditation Service Directory of Accredited Laboratories *see* U K A S Directory of Accredited Laboratories **6407**
United Kingdom Additional Requirements and Special Conditions *see* U K Additional Requirements and Special Conditions **8552**
United Kingdom Aeronautical Information Publication (GBR) **8552**
United Kingdom Air Almanac *see* U K Air Almanac **73**
United Kingdom and Republic of Ireland News *see* U K R I News **3162**
United Kingdom Atomic Energy Agency Culham Laboratory Reports *see* U K A E A. Culham Laboratory Reports **3175**
United Kingdom Atomic Energy Authority, Corporate Communication Service Times *see* A E A Times **3164**
United Kingdom. Audit Commission. Executive Briefing (GBR) **1303**
United Kingdom. Audit Commission. Report & Accounts (Year) (GBR) **1388**
United Kingdom. Audit Commission. Reports (GBR) **1388**
• United Kingdom Autos Reports (GBR ISSN 1749-0251) **8609**
United Kingdom Balance of Payments *see* Great Britain. Central Statistical Office. United Kingdom Balance of Payments **1235**
United Kingdom Book Publishing Industry Statistics Yearbook (Year) *see* U K Book Publishing Industry Statistics Yearbook (Year) **7575**
United Kingdom Business Confidence Monitor *see* U K Business Confidence Monitor **1303**
United Kingdom Competition Law Reports *see* U K Competition Law Reports **4799**
• United Kingdom Defence & Security Report (GBR ISSN 1749-1746) **6451**
• United Kingdom. Department for Education and Skills. Research Report (GBR) **2922**
United Kingdom. Department of Health and Social Security. Reports on Health and Social Subjects (GBR ISSN 0300-8045) **7544**
United Kingdom. Department of the Environment. Marine Research Programme. Report (GBR ISSN 1367-3548) **2819**
United Kingdom. Department of Transport, Local Government, and the Regions. Planning Policy Guidance Notes (GBR) **8518**
United Kingdom Directory of Property Developers, Investors & Financiers *see* U K Directory of Property Developers, Investors & Financiers **7614**
United Kingdom Economic Accounts *see* United Kingdom Economic Accounts **1273**
• ➤ United Kingdom Economic Accounts (GBR ISSN 1350-4401) **1273**
United Kingdom Economic Brief (Online) *see* U K Economic Brief (Online) **1522**
United Kingdom Employment Alert *see* U K Employment Alert **4799**
United Kingdom Energy Sector Indicators (Year) *see* U K Energy Sector Indicators (Year) **3148**
United Kingdom Environment News *see* U K Environment News **3491**
United Kingdom Excellence *see* U K Excellence **1185**
The United Kingdom Financial Analysis Service (GBR) **6796**
• United Kingdom Food & Drink Report (GBR ISSN 1749-3056) **1186**
• United Kingdom Franchise Directory (GBR ISSN 0265-279X) **1847**
United Kingdom Freight Transport Report (GBR ISSN 1750-5348) **8518**
United Kingdom Human Rights Reports *see* U K Human Rights Reports **7216**
United Kingdom Input - Output Analyses (GBR ISSN 1475-7354) **1273**
United Kingdom Insider Dealmakers Guides *see* Insider Dealmakers Guides. United Kingdom **1354**
United Kingdom Irrigation *see* U K Irrigation **8833**
† United Kingdom Law Review (NLD ISSN 1385-173X) **8996**
United Kingdom Minerals Yearbook (GBR ISSN 0957-4697) **6482**
• United Kingdom. Ministry of Defence. Contracts Bulletin (GBR ISSN 0269-0365) **6451**
• United Kingdom. Ministry of Defence. Defence Contracts Bulletin (GBR ISSN 1479-3865) **6451**
United Kingdom. Ministry of Defence. Defence Estate Organisation. Design and Maintenance Guide (GBR) **6451**
United Kingdom. Ministry of Defence. Defence Estate Organisation. Specification (GBR) **6451**
United Kingdom. Ministry of Defence. News (GBR ISSN 0951-8053) **1186**
United Kingdom National Accounts *see* Great Britain. Central Statistical Office. United Kingdom National Accounts **1235**
United Kingdom Oil & Gas Law *see* U K Oil & Gas Law **6795**
United Kingdom Petrochemicals Report (GBR ISSN 1749-253X) **6796**
United Kingdom plc. (GBR ISSN 1747-5155) **2032**
United Kingdom Police Directory (Year) *see* U K Police Directory (Year) **2670**
United Kingdom Preview *see* U K Preview **6739**
United Kingdom Printing *see* U K Printing **7328**
United Kingdom Trade Bulletin Imports and Exports of Fish & Fish Products (GBR ISSN 0963-9446) **3610**
United Kingdom Vet. Companion Animal *see* U K Vet. Companion Animal **8809**
United Kingdom Vet. Livestock *see* U K Vet. Livestock **8809**
United Kingdom Waste Management Industry Report (GBR ISSN 1366-8293) **3513**
United Kingdom Water Industry: Water Statistics (Year) *see* The U K Water Industry: Water Statistics (Year) **8843**
United Kingdom Writer *see* U K Writer **5391**
United Knitwear Manufacturers League. Bulletin (USA) **2250**
United Languages (CAN) **3570**
United Lumbee Nation Times (USA) **3570**
United Lutheran Society Today *see* U L S Today **7778**
United Malays National Organisation. Annual Report (MYS) **7190**
United Methodist Church. General Minutes of the Annual Conferences (USA ISSN 0503-3551) **7778**
United Methodist Connection *see* U M Connection **7778**
The United Methodist Directory and Index Resources *see* The (Year) United Methodist Directory & Index Resources **7700**
United Methodist Life (USA ISSN 1081-079X) **7778**
United Methodist Reporter (USA ISSN 0737-5581) **7778**
• United Mine Workers Journal (USA ISSN 0041-7327) **4604**
United Moms Charity Association Newsletter *see* Mama Lianyihui Jianxun **2160**
United Nations. Asia and Far East Institute for the Prevention of Crime and the Treatment of Offenders. Resource Material Series (JPN ISSN 0256-5471) **2670**
• United Nations Association in Canada. Liaison (CAN) **7270**
United Nations Association of New Zealand New Z *see* U N A New Z **8995**
United Nations Association of the Republic of China Newsletter (TWN ISSN 0457-8074) **7270**
United Nations Association of the United States of America News Update *see* U N A - U S A E-News Update **7269**
The United Nations Blue Books Series (USA ISSN 1813-260X) **7270**
• United Nations. Bulletin on Narcotics (USA ISSN 0007-523X) **2700**
United Nations Centre for Human Settlements. Bibliographic Notes (KEN ISSN 0257-7216) **4437**
United Nations Centre for Regional Development Annual Report (English Edition) *see* U N C R D Annual Report (English Edition) **1606**
United Nations Centre for Regional Development Newsletter *see* U N C R D Newsletter **1606**
• United Nations Children's Fund. Annual Report (USA ISSN 0254-2447) **8075**
United Nations Children's Fund. Programme Division. Staff Working Papers Series (USA ISSN 1013-3178) **8075**
United Nations Chronicle *see* Lianheguo Jishi **7251**
United Nations Chronicle *see* U N Chronicle **7269**
United Nations Commission on International Trade Law. Report on the Work of Its Session (AUT ISSN 0251-9127) **4943**
• United Nations Commission on International Trade Law. Yearbook (AUT ISSN 0251-4265) **4943**
United Nations Conference of European Statisticians. Statistical Standards and Studies (CHE ISSN 0069-8458) **8412**
United Nations Conference on the Standardization of Geographical Names. Report (USA) **4031**
United Nations Conference on Trade and Development Commodity Yearbook *see* U N C T A D Commodity Yearbook **1271**
United Nations Conference on Trade and Development Discussion Papers Series *see* U N C T A D Discussion Papers Series **1585**
United Nations Conference on Trade and Development Handbook of Statistics *see* U N C T A D Handbook of Statistics **1271**
United Nations, Conference on Trade and Development News *see* U N C T A D News **1585**
United Nations Conference on Trade and Development Occasional Papers *see* U N C T A D Occasional Papers **1606**
• United Nations Conference on Trade and Development: Proceedings (CHE) **1586**
United Nations Conference on Trade and Development Review *see* U N C T A D Review **8995**
United Nations Conference on Trade and Development Series on Issues in International Investment Agreements *see* U N C T A D Series on Issues in International Investment Agreements **1656**
United Nations. Conference on Trade and Development. Trade and Development Board. Official Records (USA ISSN 0503-4108) **1606**
United Nations. Conference on Trade and Development. Trade and Development Board. Official Records. Supplements (USA) **7270**
† United Nations Congress on the Prevention of Crime and the Treatment of Offenders. Report (USA ISSN 0082-8025) **8996**
• United Nations. Demographic Yearbook/Annuaire Demographique (USA ISSN 0082-8041) **7294**
United Nations. Demographic Yearbook. Supplement *see* United Nations. Demographic Yearbook **7294**
† United Nations. Department of International Economic and Social Affairs. Statistical Office. Construction Statistic Yearbook (USA ISSN 0257-9073) **8996**
United Nations. Department of Public Information. Programme Update (USA) **7270**
United Nations Development Programme. Office of Development Studies. Discussion Paper Series (USA) **3472**
• United Nations Development Programme. Oslo Governance Centre. Update (NOR ISSN 1504-2103) **4943**
United Nations Development Programme Quarterly Report *see* U N D P Quarterly Report **1606**
• United Nations Disarmament Yearbook (USA ISSN 0252-5607) **7270**
United Nations. Economic and Social Commission for Asia and the Pacific. Asian Population Studies Series (THA ISSN 0066-8451) **7294**
United Nations. Economic and Social Commission for Asia and the Pacific. Development Papers (THA ISSN 0255-9250) **2630**
United Nations Economic and Social Commission for Asia and the Pacific. Statistical Newsletter (THA ISSN 0252-3647) **1273**
United Nations. Economic and Social Commission for Asia and the Pacific. Water Resources Series (THA ISSN 0082-8130) **8834**
United Nations Economic and Social Commission for Western Asia. National Accounts Studies of the E S C W A Region *see* Dirasat al-Hisabat al-Qawmiyyat li-Mintaqat al-Lagnat al-Iqtisadiyyat wa-al-Igtima'iyyat li-Garbi Asiya **1092**
United Nations. Economic and Social Commission for Western Asia Population Bulletin *see* E S C W A Population Bulletin **7282**
United Nations. Economic and Social Commission for Western Asia. Review of Transport in E S C W A Member Countries (LBN ISSN 1020-5772) **8519**
United Nations. Economic and Social Council. Annexes (USA) **1186**
United Nations Economic and Social Council. Disarmament Study Series (USA ISSN 1014-2177) **7270**
United Nations. Economic and Social Council. Index to Proceedings (USA ISSN 0082-8084) **7201**
• United Nations. Economic and Social Council. Official Records (USA ISSN 0082-8092) **7270**
United Nations Economic and Social Council. Official Records. Supplements and Special Supplements (USA) **1186**
United Nations. Economic and Social Council. Resolutions and Decisions (USA ISSN 0251-9410) **1186**
United Nations Economic and Social Council. Summary Records of Plenary Meetings (USA) **1186**
United Nations Economic Commission for Africa. Annual Report (ETH) **1606**
United Nations Economic Commission for Africa. Biennial Report of the Executive Secretary (ETH ISSN 0252-2128) **1606**
United Nations Economic Commission for Africa. Statistical Newsletter (ETH) **1273**
United Nations. Economic Commission for Asia and the Pacific. Energy Resources Development Series (THA ISSN 0252-4368) **3149**
• United Nations. Economic Commission for Europe. Economic Studies (CHE ISSN 1014-4994) **1523**
United Nations. Economic Commission for Europe. Energy Series (CHE ISSN 1014-7225) **3149**
United Nations. Economic Commission for Europe. Information (CHE ISSN 0253-0090) **1186**
United Nations. Economic Commission for Europe. Statistical Journal *see* International Association for Official Statistics. Statistical Journal **8379**
United Nations Economic Commission for Latin America and the Caribbean Notes *see* E C L A C Notes **1594**
United Nations Educational, Scientific and Cultural Organization Asia Bunka News Bulletin *see* UNESCO Asia Bunka News Bulletin **3901**
United Nations Educational, Scientific and Cultural Organization Association - U S A Newsletter *see* UNESCO Association - U S A Newsletter **7270**
United Nations Educational, Scientific and Cultural Organization Centro de Documentacion Cultural, Havana. Informaciones Trimestrales *see* UNESCO Centro de Documentacion Cultural, Havana. Informaciones Trimestrales **4479**
United Nations Educational, Scientific and Cultural Organization Collection of Representative Works *see* UNESCO Collection of Representative Works **5392**
United Nations Educational, Scientific and Cultural Organization. Comision Nacional Cubana. Boletin *see* UNESCO Comision Nacional Cubana. Boletin **4479**
United Nations Educational, Scientific and Cultural Organization Databases *see* UNESCO Databases **638**
United Nations Educational, Scientific and Cultural Organization. International Hydrological Programme: Operational Hydrology Programme: Yearbook Federal Republic of Germany *see* UNESCO Internationales Hydrologisches Programm: Operationelles Hydrologisches Programm: Jahrbuch Bundesrepublik Deutschland **8995**
United Nations Educational, Scientific and Cultural Organization Nairobi Bulletin *see* UNESCO Nairobi Bulletin **7925**
United Nations Educational, Scientific and Cultural Organization Records of the General Conference. Proceedings *see* UNESCO Records of the General Conference. Proceedings **7270**
United Nations Educational, Scientific and Cultural Organization Records of the General Conference. Resolutions *see* UNESCO Records of the General Conference. Resolutions **7270**
United Nations Educational, Scientific and Cultural Organization Regional Office for Science and Technology for Latin America and the Caribbean. Boletin *see* UNESCO Regional Office for Science and Technology for Latin America and the Caribbean. Boletin **8444**
United Nations Educational, Scientific and Cultural Organization Report of the Director - General on the Activities of the Organization *see* UNESCO Report of the Director - General on the Activities of the Organization **7270**
United Nations Educational, Scientific and Cultural Organization: Resolutions and Decisions *see* UNESCO: Resolutions and Decisions **8011**
United Nations Educational, Scientific and Cultural Organization Scientific Maps and Atlases and Other Related Publications *see* UNESCO Scientific Maps and Atlases and Other Related Publications **638**
United Nations Educational, Scientific and Cultural Organization Statistical Reports and Studies Series *see* UNESCO Statistical Reports and Studies Series **8412**
United Nations Educational, Scientific and Cultural Organization Statistics on Science and Technology *see* UNESCO Statistics on Science and Technology **7939**
United Nations Educational, Scientific and Cultural Organization Studies on Books and Reading *see* UNESCO Studies on Books and Reading **7575**
United Nations Educational, Scientific and Cultural Organization World Heritage Desk Diary (Year) *see* UNESCO World Heritage Desk Diary (Year) **4165**
United Nations Environment Programme Chemicals Newsletter *see* U N E P Chemicals Newsletter **3257**
United Nations Environment Programme. Governing Council. Report on the Work of its Session (KEN) **3472**
United Nations Environment Programme, Mediterranean Action Plan Technical Reports Series *see* M A P Technical Reports Series **2811**
United Nations Environment Programme Regional Seas Reports and Studies *see* U N E P Regional Seas Reports and Studies **2819**
United Nations Environment Programme. The State of the Environment; Report of the Executive Director *see* United Nations Environment Programme. The State of the World Environment **3472**
United Nations Environment Programme. The State of the World Environment (KEN ISSN 1014-5990) **3472**
United Nations Environment Programme Year Book *see* U N E P Year Book **3471**

Title

10982 UNITED NATIONS. GENERAL ASSEMBLY. ANNEXES ULRICH'S PERIODICALS

United Nations. General Assembly. Annexes (USA) **7271**
United Nations. General Assembly. Index to Proceedings (USA ISSN 0082-8157) **7201**
United Nations. General Assembly. Official Records (USA) **7271**
United Nations. General Assembly. Provisional Records (USA) **7271**
† United Nations General Assembly: Report of the Australian Delegation (AUS ISSN 0814-1967) **8996**
United Nations Handbook (Year) (NZL ISSN 0110-1951) **7271**
United Nations High Commissioner for Refugees Global Appeal (Year) *see* U N H C R Global Appeal (Year) **7269**
United Nations High Commissioner for Refugees Global Report (Year) *see* U N H C R Global Report (Year) **7269**
United Nations High Commissioner for Refugees. Mid-Year Progress Report (CHE) **7271**
United Nations High Commissioner for Refugees. Special Reports (CHE) **7271**
United Nations. Human Rights Committee. Official Records (CHE ISSN 1020-3508) **7217**
United Nations Industrial Development Organization Annual Report *see* U N I D O Annual Report **1606**
United Nations Industrial Development Organization Links *see* U N I D O Links **1606**
• United Nations. International Trade Statistics Yearbook (USA ISSN 1010-447X) **1273**
United Nations Interregional Crime and Justice Research Institute. Issues and Reports Series/Institut Interregional de Recherche des Nations Unies sur la Criminalite et la Justice. Serie Themes et Rapports (ITA ISSN 1020-1548) **2670**
† United Nations Interregional Crime and Justice Research Institute. Publication (ITA) **8996**
• United Nations Issues Conference. Report (USA ISSN 0743-9180) **7271**
• United Nations Juridical Yearbook (USA ISSN 0082-8297) **4943**
United Nations Law Report (USA ISSN 1082-8222) **4943**
• United Nations. Multilateral Treaties Deposited with the Secretary - General (USA ISSN 0255-724X) **4943**
United Nations. National Accounts Statistics. Analysis of Main Aggregates (USA ISSN 0259-3017) **1273**
† United Nations. National Accounts Statistics. Government Accounts and Tables (USA ISSN 0259-3009) **8996**
• United Nations. National Accounts Statistics. Main Aggregates and Detailed Tables (USA ISSN 0259-3025) **1273**
United Nations News *see* U N News **7269**
• United Nations of the Next Decade Conference. Report (USA ISSN 0748-433X) **7271**
United Nations, Office for the Coordination of Humanitarian Affairs News *see* O C H A News **4937**
• United Nations. Office on Drugs and Crime. Global Illicit Drug Trends (AUT) **2700**
United Nations. Population and Vital Statistics Report (USA ISSN 0251-0030) **7317**
United Nations Population Fund. Annual Report (USA) **7295**
United Nations. Population Studies (USA ISSN 0082-805X) **7295**
United Nations Postal Administration Philatelic Bulletin (USA) **6901**
United Nations Publications (USA) **7190**
United Nations Reform Campaigner *see* U N Reform Campaigner **7269**
• United Nations Regional Cartographic Conference for Asia and the Pacific. Report (USA) **4031**
United Nations Regional Cartographic Conference for the Americas. Report (USA) **4031**
United Nations Relief and Works Agency for Palestine Refugees in the Near East. Report of the Commissioner-General (USA ISSN 0082-8386) **8075**
• United Nations. Report of the Secretary-General on the Work of the Organization (USA ISSN 0082-8173) **4943**
United Nations. Reports of International Arbitral Awards/Nations Unies. Recueil des Sentences Arbitrales (USA ISSN 0251-7833) **4801**
United Nations Research Institute for Social Development News *see* U N R I S D News **8011**
United Nations Research Institute for Social Development Programme Paper Series *see* U N R I S D Programme Paper Series **8011**
United Nations. Resolutions and Decisions Adopted by the General Assembly During Its Session (USA ISSN 0252-7014) **4943**
United Nations. Security Council. Index to Proceedings (USA ISSN 0082-8408) **7201**
United Nations. Security Council. Official Records (USA ISSN 0082-8416) **7271**
United Nations. Security Council. Official Records. Supplement (USA ISSN 0257-067X) **7271**
United Nations Special *see* U N Special **7504**
United Nations. Statement of Treaties and International Agreements/Nations Unies. Releve des Traites et Accords Internationaux (USA ISSN 0251-7582) **7271**
• United Nations Statistical Office. Monthly Bulletin of Statistics (USA ISSN 0041-7432) **8412**
United Nations. Statistical Papers. Series A, Population and Vital Statistics Report *see* United Nations. Population and Vital Statistics Report **7317**
• United Nations. Statistical Yearbook (USA ISSN 0082-8459) **8413**
• United Nations Statistics on CD-ROM (USA ISSN 1020-1114) **8413**
United Nations. Supplement to the Statistical Yearbook and the Monthly Bulletin of Statistics *see* United Nations Statistical Office. Monthly Bulletin of Statistics **8412**
United Nations. Supplement to the Statistical Yearbook and the Monthly Bulletin of Statistics *see* United Nations. Statistical Yearbook **8413**
• United Nations System Standing Committee on Nutrition. News (CHE ISSN 1564-3743) **6670**
United Nations. Treaty Series (USA ISSN 0379-8267) **4943**
United Nations. Treaty Series. Cumulative Index (USA ISSN 0252-5321) **4825**
United Nations. Trusteeship Council. Index to Proceedings (USA ISSN 0082-8491) **7201**
United Nations. Trusteeship Council. Official Records/Proces-Verbaux Officiels - Nations Unies, Conseil de Tutelle (USA ISSN 0082-8505) **7271**
United Nations. Trusteeship Council. Official Records. Annexes - Sessional Fascicle (USA) **7271**
United Nations. Trusteeship Council. Official Records. Resolutions (USA) **7271**
United Nations. Trusteeship Council. Official Records. Supplements (USA ISSN 0082-8513) **7271**
United Nations. Trusteeship Council. Official Records. Verbatim Records of Plenary Meetings (USA) **7271**
The United Nations University. Geothermal Training Programme. Reports *see* Geothermal Training in Iceland **2783**
United Nations University, Maastricht Economic Research Institute on Innovation and Technology Working Paper Series *see* U N U - M E R I T Working Paper Series **1185**
United Nations University. Work in Progress (JPN ISSN 0259-4285) **1606**
United Nations University, World Institute for Development Economics Research Angle *see* W I D E R Angle **1607**
United Nations Weekly Report (USA ISSN 0746-6455) **7271**
• United Nations. Yearbook (USA ISSN 0082-8521) **7271**
United Network for Organ Sharing Update *see* U N O S Update **6262**
United News (GBR) **269**
United Parcel Service Teamster *see* U P S Teamster **8678**
• United Planter's Association of Southern India. Annual Report (IND ISSN 0972-3129) **256**
United Planters' Association of Southern India. Tea Scientific Department. Bulletin (IND ISSN 0498-1308) **256**
United Planting Association of Malaysia. Annual Report (MYS ISSN 0304-8349) **208**
United Reformed Church History Society. Journal (GBR ISSN 0049-5433) **7778**
United Reformed Church in the United Kingdom. United Reformed Church Year Book (GBR) **7778**
United Reformed Church Pocket Diary (GBR) **7778**
United Reformed Church, Yorkshire Province, Provincial Handbook (GBR) **7778**
United Review (GBR ISSN 1355-6983) **8250**
United Schools International. Documents of the Biennial Conference (IND ISSN 0503-4663) **3015**
United Schools Organisation of India. Annual Report (IND) **2922**
United Seamen's Service Reports *see* U S S Reports **8664**
United Service Institution of India Journal *see* U S I Journal **6450**
United Service Organizations Annual Report *see* U S O Annual Report **8075**
United Service Organizations of Metropolitan New York *see* U S O of Metropolitan New York **3991**
United Services Automobile Association Magazine *see* U S A A Magazine **1387**
United Society for the Propagation of the Gospel. Yearbook (GBR) **7691**
United South and Eastern Tribes Gaming *see* U S E T Gaming **4983**
United States (Year) (USA ISSN 0883-2501) **8770**
United States African Voice *see* U S African Voice **3569**
United States Agency for International Development in Africa *see* U S A I D in Africa **1606**
United States. Agricultural Statistics Board. Wool and Mohair *see* U.S. Department of Agriculture. National Agricultural Statistics Service. Sheep and Goats (Online) **189**
United States Air Force Medical Service Digest *see* U S A F Medical Service Digest **5725**
United States Air Forces Europe Yearbook (GBR ISSN 1465-5837) **6451**
United States Amateur Boxing. Annual Guide (USA) **8214**
United States Amateur Boxing. Official Rules (USA) **8214**
United States Animal Health Association. Proceedings of the Annual Meeting (USA ISSN 0082-8750) **8809**
United States Anti-Apartheid Newsletter (USA ISSN 1054-3481) **7218**
• United States. Appalachian Regional Commission. Office of Inspector General. Semiannual Report (USA) **1187**
United States Association for Blind Athletes Agenda *see* U S A B A Agenda **8213**
• United States Attorneys Annual Statistical Report (USA ISSN 1940-4859) **4825**
• United States Attorney's Bulletin (USA ISSN 0566-0785) **4801**
• United States Attorneys' Manual (USA) **4801**
United States Auto Club News *see* U S A C News **8213**
United States Autos Reports (GBR ISSN 1749-026X) **8609**
United States Banker *see* U S Banker **1657**
United States Basketball Writers Association Tip-Off *see* U S B W A Tip-Off **8250**
United States Board on Books for Young People. Newsletter (USA) **7575**
United States Bond Strategy *see* U.S. Bond Strategy **1657**
United States Book Exchange Back Issues Shelf List *see* U S B E Back Issues Shelf List **7575**
United States Book Exchange For Members Only *see* U S B E: For Members Only **5052**
United States. Bureau of Agricultural Economics. Farm Product Prices *see* U.S. Department of Agriculture. National Agricultural Statistics Service. Agricultural Prices **187**
United States Cardiovascular Disease *see* U S Cardiovascular Disease **5801**
United States Citizenship and Immigration Services Monthly *see* U S C I S Monthly **7294**
United States Coast Pilot 2, Atlantic Coast, Cape Cod to Sandy Hook (USA ISSN 0363-695X) **2819**
United States Coast Pilot. 7, Pacific Coast. California, Oregon, Washington, and Hawaii (USA ISSN 0098-9002) **2819**
• United States Code Annotated (USA ISSN 1084-5267) **4801**
United States Code Annotated (LawDesk CD-ROM Edition) *see* United States Code Annotated **4801**
United States Code Annotated (Premise CD-ROM Edition) *see* United States Code Annotated **4801**
• United States Code Unannotated (USA) **4801**
United States Colored Troops Civil War Digest *see* U S C T Civil War Digest **4315**
United States Combined Training Association News *see* U S C T A News **8299**
United States Committee on Irrigation and Drainage Newsletter *see* U S C I D Newsletter **8833**
United States Conference of Mayors. Annual Meeting (USA) **7504**
United States Conference of Mayors. Projects and Services (USA) **7504**
United States Congress. House Committee on Agriculture. Report on Activities (USA ISSN 0739-9995) **208**
United States Congressional Serial Set Catalog *see* Monthly Catalog of United States Government Publications **7482**
United States: Cotton Quality Reports for Ginnings *see* U.S. Department of Agriculture. Agricultural Marketing Service. Cotton Program. Cotton Quality Crop (Monthly) **207**
United States Council for International Business. Newsletter (USA) **1411**
United States Croquet Association Croquet Directory *see* U S C A Croquet Directory **8250**
United States Croquet Association Croquet News *see* U S C A Croquet News **8250**
United States Cross-Country Coaches Association. Annual Business Meeting. Minutes (USA) **8214**
United States Department of Agriculture Forest Service. Rocky Mountain Research Station. General Technical Report *see* U S D A Forest Service. Rocky Mountain Research Station. General Technical Report **3705**
• United States. Department of Energy. Office of Energy Efficiency and Renewable Energy. Budget in Brief (USA ISSN 1930-7136) **3149**
United States Department of Transportation. Office of Inspector General. Semiannual Report to the Congress (USA ISSN 8755-4836) **8519**
• United States. Department of Veterans Affairs. Health Services Research and Development Service. Forum (USA ISSN 1931-9134) **6451**
United States Earthquakes (USA ISSN 0091-1429) **2791**
United States Endocrine Disease *see* U S Endocrine Disease **5901**
United States Equestrian Team Foundation News *see* U S E T Foundation News **8300**
United States Equity Strategy *see* U S Equity Strategy **1657**
United States Equity Strategy. Weekly Bulletin *see* U S Equity Strategy. Weekly Bulletin **1657**
United States Exportbestimmungen *see* U S - Exportbestimmungen **1585**
• United States. Federal Housing Finance Board. Office of Inspector General. Semiannual Report (USA ISSN 1944-138X) **7473**
• United States. Federal Library and Information Center Committee. Annual Report (USA ISSN 1933-124X) **5052**
United States Fencing Association, Inc. National Newsletter (Email) *see* U S F A National Newsletter (Email) **8214**
United States Fencing Association, Inc. Rule Book: U S & International Rules *see* U S F A Rule Book: U S & International Rules **8214**
United States Foreign Policy (USA ISSN 0270-370X) **7271**
United States Gastroenterology Review *see* U S Gastroenterology Review **5932**
United States. General Accounting Office. Office of Public Affairs. Month in Review (Print) *see* U.S. General Accounting Office. Office of Public Affairs. Month in Review (Online) **7485**
• United States. General Services Administration. Office of Intergovernmental Solutions. Newsletter (USA ISSN 1559-6699) **7473**
United States - German Economic Yearbook (Year) (USA) **1411**
United States Golf Association Green Section Record *see* U S G A Green Section Record **3753**
United States Golf Association Turfgrass and Environmental Research Online *see* U S G A Turfgrass and Environmental Research Online **821**
United States Government Accountability Office. Abstracts of Reports and Testimony: Fiscal Year (Year) (USA) **7474**
• United States Government Accountability Office. Decisions of the Comptroller General of the United States (USA ISSN 0011-7323) **7474**
• United States Government Accountability Office. Month in Review (USA) **7474**
• United States Government Accountability Office. Reports and Testimony (USA) **7474**
• United States Government Accountability Office. Today's Reports (USA) **7474**
• United States Government Manual (USA ISSN 0092-1904) **7190**
• United States Government Policy and Supporting Positions (USA ISSN 1559-467X) **7474**
United States History *see* Annual Editions: United States History **4283**
United States House of Representatives. Committee on Appropriations. Report of Committee Activities (USA ISSN 0147-3883) **7474**
United States House of Representatives. Committee on Banking and Financial Services. Legislative Calendar *see* United States House of Representatives. Committee on Finance. Legislative Calendar **7474**
United States House of Representatives. Committee on Finance. Legislative Calendar (USA) **7474**
United States House of Representatives. Committee on Rules. Legislative Calendar (USA ISSN 0190-5805) **7474**
United States House of Representatives. Committee on Small Business. Legislative Calendar (USA ISSN 0161-6633) **4853**
United States House of Representatives. Committee on the Budget. Activities and Summary Report (USA ISSN 0276-7139) **7474**
United States House of Representatives. Committee on the Judiciary. Legislative Calendar (USA ISSN 0364-4294) **7474**
United States House of Representatives. Committee on the Judiciary. Report on the Activities (USA ISSN 0362-109X) **4966**
United States House of Representatives. Committee on Veterans' Affairs. Activities Report (USA ISSN 0738-4793) **6451**
United States House of Representatives. Committee on Veterans' Affairs. Legislative Calendar (USA ISSN 0364-4200) **6451**
United States House of Representatives. Committee on Ways and Means. Legislative Calendar (USA ISSN 0364-9644) **7474**
† United States Import Trade Law (USA) **8996**
United States Importers Product Guide (USA ISSN 1062-8339) **2032**
➤ United States in the World: Foreign Perspectives (USA) **7271**
United States Infectious Diseases *see* U S Infectious Diseases **5828**
United States Institute of Peace. Special Report (USA ISSN 1932-412X) **7191**
• United States - Italy Trade Directory (USA ISSN 0502-5842) **2032**
• United States. J William Fulbright Foreign Scholarship Board. Annual Report (USA ISSN 1930-6164) **3015**
• United States Law Week (USA ISSN 0148-8139) **4801**
United States Law Week Summary and Analysis (USA ISSN 0190-5252) **4801**
United States Lighthouse Society. Bulletin (USA) **4165**
United States Medical Licensing Exam Road Map: Emergency Medicine *see* U S M L E Road Map: Emergency Medicine **5725**
United States Medical Licensing Exam Road Map: Immunology *see* U S M L E Road Map: Immunology **5725**
United States Merit Systems Protection Board. Decisions (USA ISSN 0731-4450) **4853**
United States - Mexico Border Health Association. News - Noticias (USA) **7544**

† • United States-Mexico Law Journal (USA ISSN 1089-8948) **8996**
United States Military Posture (USA ISSN 0148-060X) **6451**
• United States Mint Annual Report (Online) (USA) **1388**
• United States Mint. Strategic Plan (USA ISSN 1939-8689) **1187**
United States Mint. World Coinage Report (USA) **6653**
United States Musculoskeletal Review *see* U S Musculoskeletal Review **6074**
• United States N L R B Online (USA) **1712**
United States. National Aeronautics and Space Administration. Headquarters Directory (USA ISSN 1056-909X) **74**
United States Neurological Disease *see* U S Neurological Disease **6189**
United States Oceanborne Foreign Trade Routes (USA ISSN 0161-8830) **8664**
United States of America Turkish Times *see* U S A Turkish Times **3569**
United States Oncological Disease *see* U S Oncological Disease **6036**
United States Participation in the United Nations (USA ISSN 0083-0208) **7271**
United States Participation in the United Nations (USA ISSN 1931-2830) **7474**
United States Patent. Plant (USA ISSN 1068-5472) **6759**
• United States Patents Quarterly (USA ISSN 0041-803X) **6759**
United States Petrochemicals Report (GBR ISSN 1749-2548) **6796**
• United States Pharmacopeia. National Formulary (USA ISSN 0195-7996) **6884**
United States Pharmacopeia National Formulary Supplement *see* U S P - N F. Supplement **6884**
United States Pharmacopeia Quality Review *see* U S P Quality Review **6884**
United States Pharmacopeia Vol. 1. Drug Information for the Health Care Professional *see* U S P - D I. Vol. 1. Drug Information for the Health Care Professional **8995**
United States Pharmacopeia Vol. 2. Advice for the Patient *see* U S P - D I. Vol. 2. Advice for the Patient **6883**
United States Pharmacopeia Vol. 3. Approved Drug Products and Legal Requirements *see* U S P - D I. Vol. 3. Approved Drug Products and Legal Requirements **6884**
United States Pharmacopeial Convention and the United States Adopted Names Dictionary of U S A N and International Drug Names *see* U S P Dictionary of U S A N and International Drug Names **6884**
United States Pharmacopeial Pharmacists' Pharmacopeia *see* U S P Pharmacists' Pharmacopeia **6884**
United States Pilots Association News (USA) **74**
United States Polo Association. Yearbook (USA ISSN 0083-3118) **8250**
• United States Population Projections by Age, Sex, Race, and Hispanic Origin (USA) **7317**
United States Respiratory Disease *see* U S Respiratory Disease **6220**
United States Rowing *see* U S Rowing **8283**
United States School Laws and Rules (USA ISSN 1078-2443) **4801**
United States Senate. Committee on Agriculture, Nutrition and Forestry. Legislative Calendar (USA ISSN 0147-4103) **7474**
United States Senate. Committee on Banking, Housing, and Urban Affairs. Legislative Calendar (USA ISSN 0364-4197) **7474**
United States Senate. Committee on Energy and Natural Resources. Legislative Calendar (USA ISSN 0161-0058) **4853**
United States Senate. Committee on Finance. Legislative Calendar (USA ISSN 0364-4162) **1389**
United States Senate. Committee on Foreign Policy. Legislative Calendar (USA ISSN 0364-4243) **7474**
United States Senate. Committee on Governmental Affairs. Legislative Calendar (USA ISSN 0147-6572) **7474**
United States Senate. Committee on Rules and Administration. Legislative Calendar (USA ISSN 0364-4154) **7474**
United States Senate. Committee on the Judiciary. Legislative and Executive Calendar (USA ISSN 0364-6947) **4966**
United States Senate. Committee on the Judiciary. Report on the Activities during the Congress (USA ISSN 0742-4078) **4966**
United States Senate. Committee on Veterans' Affairs. Legislative Calendar (USA ISSN 0364-8176) **6451**
United States Senate. House Armed Services Committee. Legislative Calendar (USA ISSN 0364-4146) **4853**
• United States Senate. House Armed Services Committee. Report on the Activities (USA ISSN 0363-0706) **6451**
United States Space Foundation. National Space Symposium Proceedings Reports (USA) **74**
The United States Specialist (USA ISSN 0164-923X) **6901**
United States Squash Racquets Association. Official Year Book (USA ISSN 0083-3398) **8250**
United States Stamp Catalogue (GBR ISSN 0142-9949) **6901**
United States State Construction Quarterly Briefing *see* U.S. State Construction Quarterly Briefing **1041**
United States Statutes at Large (USA ISSN 0083-3401) **4801**
United States Student Association. Legislative Update (USA) **3006**
United States Supreme Court Cases and Comments: Criminal Law and Procedure (USA) **4801**
• United States Supreme Court Reports (Lawyer's Edition) (USA ISSN 0161-8261) **4966**
• United States Tax Court Reports (USA ISSN 0040-0017) **1954**
United States Telephone Association. Holding Company Report (USA) **2373**
United States Telephone Association. Statistics of the Local Exchange Carriers (USA ISSN 0896-0585) **2349**
United States Tennis Association. Yearbook (USA ISSN 0196-5425) **8250**
United States Treaties and Other International Agreements (USA ISSN 0083-3487) **4943**
United States Trotting Association Sires and Dams *see* U S T A Sires and Dams **8300**
United States Trotting Association Year Book *see* U S T A Year Book **8300**
United States Youth Bowler *see* U S Youth Bowler **8250**
United Steel Workers Work *see* U S W@Work **4604**
United Steelworkers of America. Information (CAN ISSN 0566-0963) **4604**
United Synagogue Review *see* C J: Voices of Conservative/Masorti Judaism **7719**
United Teachers of Dade Edge *see* U T D Edge **2921**
United Technologies. Annual Report (USA ISSN 0149-3965) **8552**
United Times *see* Lianhe Shibao **3826**
United Towns News. Newsletter (FRA) **7504**
United Transportation Union News *see* U T U News **4604**
United Tribune *see* Tongyi Luntan **8010**
United Utilities. Annual Report & Accounts (GBR) **8834**
United Voice/Voz Unida (USA) **4604**
United Way of America. Annual Report (USA ISSN 0190-9630) **8075**
United We Stand (GBR ISSN 1369-9202) **8339**
Unitedland (USA) **7614**
Uniter (CAN ISSN 0041-817X) **2306**
Unites & Guerriers (FRA ISSN 1778-6762) **4165**
Uniting Care Wesley News *see* UnitingCare Wesley News **8075**
Uniting Church Studies (AUS ISSN 1323-6377) **7778**
Uniting World (AUS) **7691**
• UnitingCare Wesley News (AUS ISSN 1832-1925) **8075**
The Unitred States of Europe *see* Gli Stati Uniti d'Europa (Bari) **7266**
• Units (USA ISSN 0744-1681) **4429**
Unity (CAN ISSN 0829-4216) **3570**
Unity *see* Tuanjie Bao **7189**
Unity (GBR) **4604**
Unity (NZL ISSN 1176-9327) **7191**
Unity (Albany) (USA) **4604**
Unity Magazine (USA ISSN 0162-3567) **7743**
Unity: United Newsletter (USA) **4379**
Univeristaetsbibliothek Basel. Schriften (CHE ISSN 1422-7517) **5052**
▼ Univers de la Danse (FRA ISSN 1956-5542) **2688**
Univers de la France et des Pays Francophones (FRA ISSN 0768-4258) **4275**
Univers Historique (FRA ISSN 0083-3673) **7925**
† Univers Mac (FRA ISSN 1767-4085) **8996**
Univers Macworld *see* Univers Mac **8996**
▼ L'Univers Psychologique (FRA ISSN 1956-0206) **7413**
• El Universal (COL) **3830**
El Universal *see* El Universal en Linea **3927**
• ➤ Universal Access in the Information Society (DEU ISSN 1615-5289) **2353**
Universal Availability of Publications Newsletter *see* U A P Newsletter **5051**
Universal Business Directories. Victoria. Goulburn Valley Business to Business Directory (AUS) **2032**
Universal Dataflow and Telecommunications. Bulletin *see* U D T Newsletter **5051**
Universal Dataflow and Telecommunications Newsletter *see* U D T Newsletter **5051**
Universal Dataflow and Telecommunications Series on Data Communication Technologies and Standards for Libraries *see* U D T Series on Data Communication Technologies and Standards for Libraries **5063**
The Universal Declaration of Human Rights (NLD ISSN 1569-5174) **7218**
Universal Door/P'u Men (TWN) **7702**
• El Universal en Linea (PAN ISSN 1605-0983) **3927**
Universal Esperanto Association. Kongresa Libro *see* Kongresa Libro **6281**
The Universal Healthcare Almanac (USA ISSN 1069-6725) **8413**
Universal Justice (NLD) **4801**
Universal Life Church News *see* U L C News **7742**
Universal Message (PAK) **7716**
Universal Military Abstracts (IND ISSN 0970-3403) **6455**
Universal net.Connect (GBR) **2599**
Universal Peace Federation Today *see* U P F Today **7269**
Universal Postal Union. Acts *see* Union Postale Universelle. Actes **2355**
Universal Proutist (USA) **6648**
Universal Ship Cancellation Society Log *see* U S C S Log **6900**
Universal Subject Locator (CAN ISSN 1206-3126) **4825**
Universalia (PER ISSN 1810-1100) **8011**
Universalist (GBR ISSN 0267-6648) **7743**
† Universal's Popular Plants and Flowers Series. Cottage Garden and Fragrant Plants (AUS ISSN 1039-8279) **8996**
† Universal's Popular Plants and Flowers Series. Fruits, Vegetables and Herbs (AUS ISSN 1039-9526) **8996**
† Universal's Popular Plants and Flowers Series. Plants for Containers and Courtyards (AUS ISSN 1039-9534) **8996**
† Universal's Popular Plants and Flowers Series. Plants for Shade and Watergardens (AUS ISSN 1039-9542) **8996**
† Universal's Popular Plants and Flowers Series. Trees, Shrubs and Ground Covers (AUS ISSN 1039-8260) **8996**
Universario (URY) **3994**
Universe (AUS ISSN 0049-5506) **583**
Universe *see* Vesmir **4033**
The Universe (GBR ISSN 0041-8226) **7821**
Universe *see* Wszechswiat **7930**
• The Universe in the Classroom (USA ISSN 0890-6866) **3086**
• ➤ Universia Business Review (ESP ISSN 1698-5117) **1799**
Universida de Cadiz. Anales (ESP ISSN 0213-1595) **3006**
Universidad (CRI) **2306**
Universidad (MEX ISSN 0188-3976) **7925**
Universidad (NIC) **3006**
• Universidad Academia Humanismo Cristiano. Revista (CHL ISSN 0717-1846) **4479**
Universidad Autonoma de Baja California. Instituto de Investigaciones Oceanologicas. Reporte Mensual (MEX ISSN 0187-7305) **2819**
Universidad Autonoma de Baja California. Instituto de Investigaciones Oceanologicas. Reporte Tecnico (MEX ISSN 0187-7046) **2819**
Universidad Autonoma de Baja California Sur. Area de Ciencias del Mar. Serie Cientifica (MEX) **2820**
Universidad Autonoma de Baja California Sur. Revista de Investigacion Cientifica. Serie Ciencias del Mar (MEX ISSN 0188-9591) **2820**
• Universidad Autonoma de Centro America. Actas Academicas (CRI ISSN 1017-7507) **2306**
Universidad Autonoma de Madrid. Coleccion de Estudios (ESP ISSN 1577-1806) **2922**
Universidad Autonoma de Madrid. Facultad de Derecho. Anuario (ESP ISSN 1575-8427) **4801**
Universidad Autonoma de Nuevo Leon. Centro de Investigaciones Economicas. Boletin Bimestral (MEX ISSN 0041-8498) **1187**
Universidad Autonoma de Nuevo Leon. Facultad de Ciencias Biologicas. Publicaciones Tecnicas (MEX) **965**
Universidad Autonoma de San Luis Potosi. Instituto de Geologia. Folleto Tecnico (MEX ISSN 0581-5207) **2772**
Universidad Autonoma de Santo Domingo. Direccion de Investigaciones. D I C Boletin (DOM) **7925**
Universidad Autonoma de Yucatan. Revista (MEX ISSN 0186-7180) **4479**
Universidad Autonoma del Pacifico. Seminario de Estudios de la Significacion. Topicos del Seminario (MEX) **5392**
Universidad Autonoma Latinoamericana *see* U N A U L A **5243**
Universidad Autonoma Metropolitana - Azcapotzalco, Departamento de Humanidades Azcapotzalco. Coordinacion de Servicios de Computo. Boletin *see* U A M - Azcapotzalco. Coordinacion de Servicios de Computo. Boletin **2440**
Universidad Boliviana Juan Misael Saracho. Informe de Labores. (BOL) **3006**
Universidad Boliviana Tecnica de Oruro, Instituto de Investigaciones Economicas Revista *see* I I E Revista **1121**
Universidad Catolica de Chile. Facultad de Teologia. Anales (CHL ISSN 0069-3596) **7821**
Universidad Catolica Nuestra Senora de la Asuncion. Centro de Estudios Antropologicos. Suplemento Antropologico (PRY ISSN 0378-9896) **359**
• Universidad Central de Venezuela. Centro de Estudios del Desarrollo. Cuadernos del C E N D E S (VEN ISSN 1012-2508) **8145**
➤ Universidad Central de Venezuela. Facultad de Agronomia. Revista (VEN ISSN 0041-8285) **165**
Universidad Central de Venezuela. Facultad de Agronomia. Revista Alcance (VEN ISSN 0376-0030) **165**
Universidad Central de Venezuela. Facultad de Ciencias Juridicas y Politicas. Revista (VEN) **4801**
Universidad Central de Venezuela. Facultad de Ciencias Veterinarias. Revista (VEN ISSN 0258-6576) **8809**
➤ Universidad Central de Venezuela. Facultad de Farmacia. Revista (VEN ISSN 0041-8307) **6884**
➤ Universidad Central de Venezuela. Facultad de Ingenieria. Revista (VEN ISSN 0798-4065) **3225**
• Universidad Central de Venezuela. Facultad de Medicina. Revista (VEN ISSN 0798-0469) **5726**
Universidad Central de Venezuela. Instituto de Ciencias Penales y Criminologicas. Anuario (VEN ISSN 0507-570X) **2670**
Universidad Central de Venezuela. Instituto de Estudios Hispanoamericanos. Anuario (VEN ISSN 1315-0049) **4315**
Universidad Central del Ecuador. Biblioteca General. Bibliografia Ecuatoriana (ECU) **638**
Universidad Central del Ecuador. Instituto de Derecho Comparado. Boletin (ECU) **4801**
Universidad Central del Ecuador. Instituto de Estudios Administrativos. Boletin (ECU) **1799**
Universidad Central del Ecuador. Instituto de Investigaciones Economicas. Boletin Economia (ECU) **1523**
➤ Universidad, Ciencia y Tecnologia (VEN ISSN 1316-4821) **3225**
• Universidad Complutense. Anales de Geografia (ESP ISSN 0211-9803) **4032**
Universidad Complutense. Clinicas Urologicas (ESP ISSN 1133-0414) **6275**
• Universidad Complutense. Estudios Ingleses (ESP ISSN 1133-0392) **5190**
Universidad Complutense. Facultad de Derecho. Revista *see* Foro **4676**
Universidad de Alcala de Henares. Departamento de Geografia. Serie Geografica (ESP ISSN 1136-5277) **4032**
Universidad de Alicante. Anales. Literatura Espanola *see* Anales de Literatura Espanola **5254**
• Universidad de Antioquia. Departamento de Antropologia. Boletin de Antropologia (COL ISSN 0120-2510) **359**
Universidad de Antioquia. Departamento de Historia. Coleccion Papeles de Trabajo (COL) **4479**
• ➤ Universidad de Antioquia. Facultad de Ingenieria. Revista (COL ISSN 0120-6230) **3225**
Universidad de Antioquia. Facultad de Odontologia. Revista (COL ISSN 0121-246X) **5868**
➤ Universidad de Antioquia. Revista (COL ISSN 0120-2367) **4479**
Universidad de Antofagasta.Facultad de Medicina y Odontologia. Revista (CHL ISSN 0718-3275) **5726**
Universidad de Barcelona. Instituto de Arqueologia y Prehistoria. Publicaciones Eventuales (ESP ISSN 0067-4184) **421**
Universidad de Bogota Jorge Tadeo Lozano. Museo del Mar. Informe (COL ISSN 0120-8063) **709**
• Universidad de Buenos Aires. Centro de Estudios de Sociologia del Trabajo. Documentos de Trabajo (ARG ISSN 1666-4884) **8145**
Universidad de Buenos Aires. Facultad de Agronomia. Revista (ARG ISSN 0325-9250) **165**
• Universidad de Buenos Aires. Facultad de Filosofia y Letras. Boletin Informativo (ARG) **6958**
Universidad de Buenos Aires. Facultad de Odontologia. Museo y Centro de Estudios Historicos. Revista (ARG ISSN 1515-372X) **5868**
• Universidad de Buenos Aires. Facultad de Psicologia. Anuario de Investigaciones (ARG ISSN 0329-5885) **7413**
Universidad de Buenos Aires. Instituto de Historia Antigua Oriental. Coleccion Estudios (ARG) **4326**
Universidad de Buenos Aires. Instituto de Historia Antigua Oriental. Revista (ARG ISSN 0325-1209) **4326**
Universidad de Caldas. Facultad de Filosofia. Revista (COL ISSN 0120-1492) **6958**
Universidad de Caldas. Museo de Historia Natural. Boletin Cientifico (COL ISSN 0123-3068) **7925**
Universidad de Cantabria. Departamento de Matematicas, Estadistica y Computacion. Publicacion (ESP) **5543**
Universidad de Cantabria. Departamento de Matematicas, Estadistica y Computacion. Publicacion. Serie Computacion (ESP) **5543**
• Universidad de Carabobo. Facultad de Ciencias. Revista (VEN ISSN 1316-7138) **5726**
• Universidad de Chile. Anales (CHL ISSN 0365-7779) **5243**
▼ • Universidad de Chile. Centro de Estudios de la Justicia. Revista Electronica (CHL ISSN 0718-4735) **4801**
Universidad de Chile. Departamento de Geologia. Serie Comunicaciones (CHL ISSN 0069-357X) **2718**
Universidad de Chile. Facultad de Ciencias Economicas y Administrativas. Biblioteca. Lista de Memorias y Libros Seleccionados (CHL) **1273**
Universidad de Chile. Facultad de Ciencias Economicas y Administrativas. Desarrollo (CHL) **1187**
• Universidad de Chile. Facultad de Ciencias Fisicas y Matematicas. Boletin Informativo (CHL ISSN 0717-8891) **5543**
• Universidad de Chile. Facultad de Medicina. Boletin Informativo (CHL ISSN 0717-8905) **5726**
• Universidad de Chile. Facultad de Odontologia. Revista (CHL ISSN 0716-8500) **5868**

Title

10984 UNIVERSIDAD DE CIENCIAS APLICADAS Y AMBIENTALES REVISTA ULRICH'S PERIODICALS

Universidad de Ciencias Aplicadas y Ambientales Revista *see* U D C A. Revista **8444**
Universidad de Cuenca. Anales (ECU ISSN 0041-8390) **5243**
Universidad de Extremadura. Facultad de Derecho. Anuario (ESP ISSN 0213-988X) **4801**
Universidad de Extremadura. Facultad de Filosofia y Letras. Anuario de Estudios Filologicos (ESP ISSN 0210-8178) **5190**
• Universidad de Gotumburgo. Instituto Ibero Americano. Anales (SWE ISSN 1101-4148) **4315**
Universidad de Granada. Boletin (ESP ISSN 0210-5454) **3006**
Universidad de Granada. Catedra Francisco Suarez. Anales (ESP ISSN 0008-7750) **6958**
• ➤ Universidad de Granada. Cuadernos de Arte (ESP ISSN 0210-962X) **523**
➤ Universidad de Granada. Facultad de Derecho. Revista (ESP ISSN 0212-8217) **4801**
Universidad de Granada. Revista de Educacion (ESP ISSN 0214-0489) **2922**
Universidad de Guadalajara. Instituto de Astronomia y Meteorologia. Boletin Informativo Mensual (MEX ISSN 0185-2752) **583**
Universidad de Guadalajara. Instituto de Botanica. Boletin (MEX ISSN 0187-7054) **821**
Universidad de Guayaquil. Escuela de Diplomacia. Revista (ECU) **7271**
Universidad de Jaen. Facultad de Ciencias Experimentales. Monografias (ESP) **821**
Universidad de Jaen. Facultad de Humanidades. Revista (ESP ISSN 1133-2999) **4479**
Universidad de la Habana. Direccion de Extension Universitaria. Revista (CUB) **3006**
Universidad de la Laguna. Anuarios (ESP ISSN 0212-8047) **5190**
Universidad de la Laguna. Coleccion Estudios de Historia (ESP) **4275**
Universidad de la Laguna. Facultad de Ciencias. Anales (ESP ISSN 0075-7721) **7926**
Universidad de la Laguna. Facultad de Derecho. Anales (ESP ISSN 0075-773X) **4801**
• Universidad de la Republica. Estadisticas Basicas (URY ISSN 1510-8031) **8413**
Universidad de la Republica. Facultad de Agronomia. Boletin (URY ISSN 0077-1260) **165**
Universidad de la Republica. Facultad de Ciencias Economicas y de Administracion. Instituto de Estadistica. Indice de Precios al Consumidor (URY ISSN 0041-8439) **8413**
Universidad de la Republica. Facultad de Ciencias Economicas y de Administracion. Revista (URY ISSN 0378-9918) **1187**
Universidad de la Republica. Facultad de Derecho. Revista (URY ISSN 0797-8316) **4801**
Universidad de la Republica. Facultad de Humanidades y Ciencias. Revista. Serie Ciencias Antropologicas (URY ISSN 0250-6564) **359**
Universidad de la Republica. Facultad de Humanidades y Ciencias. Revista. Serie Ciencias Biologicas (URY ISSN 0250-653X) **709**
Universidad de la Republica. Facultad de Humanidades y Ciencias. Revista. Serie Ciencias de la Tierra (URY ISSN 0250-6521) **2718**
Universidad de la Republica. Facultad de Humanidades y Ciencias. Revista. Serie Ciencias Exactas (URY ISSN 0255-9188) **5543**
Universidad de la Republica. Facultad de Humanidades y Ciencias. Revista. Serie Filosofia (URY ISSN 0258-1841) **6958**
Universidad de la Republica. Facultad de Humanidades y Ciencias. Revista. Serie Historia (URY ISSN 0255-9196) **4316**
Universidad de la Republica. Facultad de Humanidades y Ciencias. Revista. Serie Letras (URY ISSN 0250-6556) **5392**
Universidad de la Republica. Facultad de Humanidades y Ciencias. Revista. Serie Linguistica (URY ISSN 0250-6548) **5190**
Universidad de la Republica. Facultad de Humanidades y Ciencias. Revista. Serie Musicologia (URY) **6625**
Universidad de la Republica. Facultad de Medicina. Anales (URY ISSN 0365-2297) **5726**
Universidad de la Republica. Instituto de Administracion. Boletin (URY) **1799**
Universidad de la Republica. Instituto de Administracion. Cuaderno (URY ISSN 0077-1287) **1799**
Universidad de La Rioja. Boletin Europeo (ESP ISSN 1138-2457) **4943**
Universidad de la Salle. Centro de Investigacion. Revista (MEX ISSN 1405-6690) **4479**
• Universidad de las Palmas de Gran Canaria. Boletin Oficial (ESP) **3006**
Universidad de Leon. Facultad de Derecho. Anales (ESP ISSN 1137-2702) **4801**
Universidad de Les Illes Balears. Facultad de Derecho. Cuadernos (ESP ISSN 0214-6932) **4801**
Universidad de los Andes. Cuadernos de Filosofia y Letras (COL ISSN 0120-0992) **5437**
• ➤ Universidad de Los Andes. Facultad de Ciencias Juridicas y Politicas. Anuario de Derecho (VEN ISSN 0076-6550) **4802**
Universidad de Los Andes. Instituto de Geografia y Conservacion de Recursos Naturales. Cuadernos Geograficos (VEN ISSN 0076-6569) **4032**
Universidad de Malaga. Departamento de Arte. Boletin de Arte *see* Boletin de Arte **479**
Universidad de Medellin. Facultad de Ciencias Administrativas. Revista (COL ISSN 0465-4773) **7474**
Universidad de Medellin. Revista (COL ISSN 0120-5692) **3006**
• Universidad de Mexico (MEX ISSN 0185-1330) **2922**
Universidad de Murcia. Anales de Biologia (ESP ISSN 1138-3399) **709**
Universidad de Murcia. Anales de Biologia. Seccion Biologia Molecular y Microbiana (ESP) **709**
Universidad de Murcia. Anales de Derecho (ESP ISSN 0210-539X) **4802**
Universidad de Murcia. Anales de Filologia Francesa (ESP ISSN 0213-2958) **5190**
Universidad de Murcia. Anales de Historia Contemporanea (ESP ISSN 0212-6559) **4275**
Universidad de Murcia. Anales de Prehistoria y Arqueologia (ESP ISSN 0213-5663) **4275**
Universidad de Murcia. Catedra de Teatro. Cuadernos (ESP) **8484**
Universidad de Murcia. Estudios Romanicos (ESP ISSN 0210-4911) **5190**
Universidad de Murcia. Miscelanea Medieval Murciana (ESP ISSN 0210-4903) **4275**
• Universidad de Murcia. Papeles de Geografia (ESP ISSN 0213-1781) **4032**
Universidad de Navarra. Cuadernos de Arqueologia (ESP ISSN 1133-1542) **421**
Universidad de Navarra. Departamento de Literatura Espanola. Coleccion Publicaciones (ESP) **5392**
Universidad de Navarra. Documentos Medievales (ESP ISSN 0070-6930) **4275**
Universidad de Navarra. Escuela de Arquitectura. Coleccion de Arquitectura (ESP ISSN 0078-8732) **459**
Universidad de Navarra. Escuela de Bibliotecarias. Coleccion Bibliotecarias (ESP ISSN 0078-8740) **5052**
Universidad de Navarra. Facultad de Ciencias de la Educacion. Coleccion (ESP) **2922**
Universidad de Navarra. Facultad de Ciencias de la Informacion. Coleccion de Trabajo (ESP) **4584**
Universidad de Navarra. Facultad de Ciencias de la Informacion. Manuales: Periodismo (ESP ISSN 0078-8783) **4584**
Universidad de Navarra. Facultad de Derecho Canonico. Manuales: Derecho Canonico (ESP ISSN 0078-8759) **7691**
• ➤ Universidad de Navarra. Publicaciones de Biologia. Serie Zoologia (ESP ISSN 0213-313X) **966**
Universidad de Oriente Agricola. Revista Cientifica *see* U D O Agricola. Revista Cientifica **163**
Universidad de Oriente. Instituto Oceanografico Biblioteca. Boletin Bibliografico (VEN ISSN 0590-3343) **2721**
Universidad de Panama. Centro de Investigacion Juridica. Anuario (PAN) **4966**
Universidad de Panama. Centro de Investigacion Juridica. Boletin de Informacion Juridica (PAN) **4966**
Universidad de Panama. Centro de Investigacion Juridica. Jurisprudencia Constitutional (PAN) **4853**
Universidad de Panama. Centro de Investigacion Juridica. Legislacion Panamena. Indices Cronologicos y Analitico de Leyes (o Decretos Ejecutivos) (PAN) **4966**
Universidad de Panama. Departamento de Bibliotecologia. Boletin (PAN) **5052**
Universidad de Panama. Facultad de Administracion Publica y Comercio. Revista (PAN) **7474**
Universidad de Panama. Facultad de Derecho y Ciencias Politicas. Cuadernos (PAN) **7191**
Universidad de Puerto Rico. Centro de Investigaciones Sociales. Informe Anual (PRI) **8145**
Universidad de Puerto Rico. Revista Juridica (PRI ISSN 0886-2516) **4802**
Universidad de Puerto Rico Working Papers in Linguistics *see* U P R Working Papers in Linguistics **5190**
Universidad de San Carlos Anual (GTM) **4479**
Universidad de San Carlos de Guatemala *see* U S A C **7925**
Universidad de San Carlos de Guatemala. Facultad de Medicina Veterinaria y Zootecnia Revista (GTM ISSN 0375-0884) **8809**
Universidad de San Carlos. Revista (GTM) **523**
Universidad de Santiago de Chile. Facultad de Humanidades. Cuadernos de Humanidades (CHL) **4479**
Universidad de Santiago de Chile. Facultad de Humanidades. Revista (CHL ISSN 0717-1404) **4479**
Universidad de Sevilla. Filosofia y Letras (ESP) **6958**
Universidad de Sevilla. Instituto Garcia Oviedo. Cuadernos (ESP) **1187**
Universidad de Sevilla. Instituto Garcia Oviedo. Publicaciones (ESP ISSN 0582-8929) **4825**
Universidad de Sevilla. Serie: Arquitectura (ESP) **459**
Universidad de Sevilla. Serie: Arte (ESP) **523**
Universidad de Sevilla. Serie: Biblioteca Universitaria (ESP) **638**
Universidad de Sevilla. Serie: Ciencias (ESP ISSN 0559-6645) **7926**
Universidad de Sevilla. Serie: Ciencias de la Educacion (ESP) **2922**
Universidad de Sevilla. Serie: Ciencias Economicas y Empresariales (ESP) **1187**
Universidad de Sevilla. Serie: Derecho (ESP) **4802**
Universidad de Sevilla. Serie: Farmacia (ESP ISSN 0214-1442) **6884**
Universidad de Sevilla. Serie: Filosofia y Psicologia (ESP) **6958**
Universidad de Sevilla. Serie: Historia y Geografia (ESP) **4165**
Universidad de Sevilla. Serie: Ingenieria (ESP) **3225**
Universidad de Sevilla. Serie: Linguistica (ESP) **5190**
Universidad de Sevilla. Serie: Literatura (ESP) **5392**
Universidad de Sevilla. Serie: Medicina (ESP) **5726**
Universidad de Sevilla. Serie: Premios Literarios (ESP) **5392**
Universidad de Sevilla. Serie: Testimonio Universitario (ESP) **3007**
▼ Universidad de Talca. Escuela de Arquitectura. Revista (CHL ISSN 0718-5278) **459**
Universidad de Tarapaca. Facultad de Ingenieria. Revista *see* Ingeniare **3379**
▼ Universidad de Tolima. Boletin Estadistico (COL ISSN 2011-2866) **2937**
Universidad de Valparaiso. Facultad de Arquitectura. Revista *see* Margenes **449**
Universidad de Valparaiso. Instituto de Oceanologia. Publicaciones Ocasionales (CHL ISSN 0716-159X) **2820**
• ➤ Universidad de Zaragoza. Departamento de Filologia Inglesa y Alemana. Miscelanea (ESP ISSN 1137-6368) **4316**
Universidad de Zaragoza. Escuela Universitaria de Ciencias de la Salud. Anales (ESP ISSN 1139-7101) **6999**
Universidad de Zaragoza. Facultad de Medicina. Archivos (ESP ISSN 0558-6291) **5726**
Universidad de Zaragoza. Museo de Paleontologia. Memorias (ESP ISSN 0214-2023) **6731**
Universidad del Aconcagua. Facultad de Economia y Ciencias Comerciales. Revista (ARG ISSN 0326-7059) **1187**
Universidad del Cauca. Facultad de Ciencias de la Salud. Revista (COL ISSN 0124-308X) **5726**
Universidad del Norte. Centro de Estudios Regionales. Documentos (COL ISSN 0121-2346) **359**
Universidad del Norte. Centro de Estudios Regionales. Monografias (COL ISSN 0122-0179) **359**
Universidad del Norte. Division de Investigaciones y Proyectos. Anuario Cientifico (COL) **7926**
▼ Universidad del Valle. Escuela de Estudios Literarios. Cuadernos de Posgrado (COL ISSN 2011-2505) **5392**
• Universidad del Valle. Museo de Entomologia. Boletin (COL ISSN 0121-733X) **860**
• ➤ Universidad del Zulia. Centro de Investigaciones Biologicas. Boletin (VEN ISSN 0375-538X) **709**
• ➤ Universidad del Zulia. Facultad de Agronomia. Revista (VEN ISSN 0378-7818) **165**
• ➤ Universidad del Zulia. Facultad de Ciencias Veterinarias. Revista Cientifica (VEN ISSN 0798-2259) **8809**
Universidad del Zulia. Facultad de Derecho. Revista (VEN) **4802**
• ➤ Universidad del Zulia. Facultad de Ingenieria. Revista Tecnica (VEN ISSN 0254-0770) **3225**
➤ Universidad del Zulia. Facultad Experimental de Ciencias. Ciencias (VEN ISSN 1315-2076) **7926**
Universidad del Zulia. Revista (VEN ISSN 0041-8811) **4479**
• Universidad Europea de Madrid. Boletin Juridico (ESP ISSN 1576-1789) **4802**
Universidad Industrial de Santander. Boletin de Geologia (COL ISSN 0120-0283) **2772**
Universidad Industrial de Santander. Revista - Humanidades (COL ISSN 0120-095X) **4479**
• ➤ Universidad Industrial de Santander. Revista. Salud (COL ISSN 0121-0807) **5726**
Universidad Interamericana de Puerto Rico. Recinto de San German. Revista de Ciencias Sociales e Historia. Anales (PRI) **8012**
• ➤ Universidad Interamericana de Puerto Rico. Revista Juridica (PRI ISSN 0041-851X) **4802**
Universidad Internacional Menendez Pelayo. Publicaciones (ESP ISSN 0080-6145) **3007**
Universidad Javeriana. Facultad de Teologia. Coleccion Teologia Hoy (COL) **7691**
Universidad Metropolitana de Ciencias de la Educacion. Departamento de Filosofia. Archivos (CHL ISSN 0718-4255) **6958**
Universidad Metropolitana de Ciencias de la Educacion. Revista (CHL ISSN 0717-3105) **2922**
Universidad Nacional Autonoma de Honduras. Instituto de Investigaciones Economicas y Sociales. Boletin (HND ISSN 0252-8770) **8012**
Universidad Nacional Autonoma de Mexico. Anuario de Geografia (MEX ISSN 0185-1322) **4032**
Universidad Nacional Autonoma de Mexico. Centro de Estudios Clasicos. Cuadernos (MEX) **2241**
Universidad Nacional Autonoma de Mexico. Centro de Estudios Mayas. Cuadernos (MEX ISSN 0187-9049) **4316**
Universidad Nacional Autonoma de Mexico. Escuela Nacional de Artes Plasticas. Revista (MEX ISSN 0188-9583) **523**
Universidad Nacional Autonoma de Mexico. Facultad de Arquitectura. Revista (MEX) **459**
Universidad Nacional Autonoma de Mexico. Facultad de Derecho de Mexico. Revista (MEX ISSN 0185-1810) **4802**
• Universidad Nacional Autonoma de Mexico. Facultad de Medicina. Gaceta (MEX ISSN 0186-2987) **5726**
• Universidad Nacional Autonoma de Mexico. Facultad de Medicina. Revista (MEX ISSN 0026-1742) **5726**
• Universidad Nacional Autonoma de Mexico. Facultad de Quimica. Gaceta (MEX) **2083**
Universidad Nacional Autonoma de Mexico Gaceta *see* U N A M Gaceta **3006**
Universidad Nacional Autonoma de Mexico Hoy *see* U N A M Hoy **3006**
Universidad Nacional Autonoma de Mexico. Instituto de Geofisica. Boletin Sismologico (MEX) **2791**
Universidad Nacional Autonoma de Mexico. Instituto de Geofisica. Monografias (MEX ISSN 0076-7204) **2791**
• ➤ Universidad Nacional Autonoma de Mexico. Instituto de Geografia. Investigaciones Geograficas (MEX ISSN 0188-4611) **4032**
Universidad Nacional Autonoma de Mexico. Instituto de Geografia. Serie Varia (MEX ISSN 0185-7444) **4032**
Universidad Nacional Autonoma de Mexico. Instituto de Geologia. Boletin (MEX ISSN 0185-5530) **2772**
Universidad Nacional Autonoma de Mexico. Instituto de Investigaciones Bibliografica. Instrumenta Bibliographica (MEX ISSN 0185-0067) **5052**
Universidad Nacional Autonoma de Mexico. Instituto de Investigaciones Bibliograficas. Boletin (MEX ISSN 0006-1719) **638**
Universidad Nacional Autonoma de Mexico. Instituto de Investigaciones Esteticas. Monografias de Arte (MEX ISSN 0185-1799) **523**
Universidad Nacional Autonoma de Mexico. Instituto de Investigaciones Esteticas. Monografias. Serie Mayor (MEX ISSN 0188-0861) **4479**
Universidad Nacional Autonoma de Mexico. Instituto de Investigaciones Historicas. Serie Bibliografica (MEX ISSN 0076-7301) **4316**
Universidad Nacional Autonoma de Mexico. Instituto de Investigaciones Historicas. Serie Culturas Mesoamericanas (MEX ISSN 0076-7328) **4316**
Universidad Nacional Autonoma de Mexico. Instituto de Investigaciones Historicas. Serie Documental (MEX ISSN 0076-731X) **4316**
Universidad Nacional Autonoma de Mexico. Instituto de Investigaciones Historicas. Serie Historia de la Ciencia y la Tecnologia (MEX) **7926**
Universidad Nacional Autonoma de Mexico. Instituto de Investigaciones Historicas. Serie Historia General (MEX ISSN 0076-7352) **4316**
Universidad Nacional Autonoma de Mexico. Instituto de Investigaciones Historicas. Serie Historia Moderna y Contemporanea (MEX) **4316**
Universidad Nacional Autonoma de Mexico. Instituto de Investigaciones Historicas. Serie Historia Novohispana (MEX ISSN 0076-7379) **4316**
Universidad Nacional Autonoma de Mexico. Instituto de Investigaciones Historicas. Serie Historiadores y Cronistas (MEX ISSN 0076-7387) **4316**
Universidad Nacional Autonoma de Mexico. Instituto de Investigaciones Juridicas Instituto de Ciencias del Mar y Limnologia. Anales *see* U N A M. Instituto de Ciencias del Mar y Limnologia. Anales **2819**
Universidad Nacional Autonoma de Mexico. Instituto de Matematicas. Anales (MEX ISSN 0185-0644) **5543**
Universidad Nacional Autonoma de Mexico. Instituto de Matematicas. Monografias (MEX ISSN 0187-4780) **5543**
Universidad Nacional Autonoma de Mexico. Revista *see* Universidad de Mexico **2922**
Universidad Nacional. Centro de Estudios Generales. Cuaderno de Estudio (CRI) **4479**
Universidad Nacional de Agraria. Taller de Estudios Andinos. Serie Costa Central (PER) **256**
Universidad Nacional de Asuncion. Escuela de Bibliotecologia. Informaciones (PRY) **5052**
➤ Universidad Nacional de Asuncion. Facultad de Ciencias Exactas y Naturales. Memoria (PRY) **7926**
Universidad Nacional de Colombia. Centro de Estudios Folkloricos. Monografias (COL ISSN 0067-9534) **3623**
Universidad Nacional de Colombia. Facultad de Arquitectura. Revista (COL ISSN 0120-2669) **459**
• Universidad Nacional de Colombia. Facultad de Medicina. Revista (COL ISSN 0120-0011) **5726**
• Universidad Nacional de Cordoba. Facultad de Ciencias Medicas. Escuela de Salud Publica. Revista (ARG ISSN 0327-3741) **7544**
Universidad Nacional de Cordoba. Facultad de Derecho y Ciencias Sociales. Revista de la Facultad (ARG) **4802**
Universidad Nacional de Cordoba. Revista (ARG ISSN 0370-7687) **2922**
• Universidad Nacional de Cuyo. Facultad de Ciencias Agrarias. Revista (ARG ISSN 0370-4661) **165**
Universidad Nacional de Cuyo. Facultad de Ciencias Economicas. Revista (ARG ISSN 0041-8668) **1187**

Universidad Nacional de Educacion a Distancia. Centro Asociado de Barbastro. Anales (ESP ISSN 0213-117X) **3007**
Universidad Nacional de Educacion a Distancia. Ciencias (ESP ISSN 1137-9537) **7926**
Universidad Nacional de Educacion a Distancia. Facultad de Derecho. Boletin (ESP) **4802**
Universidad Nacional de Ingenieria. Facultad de Ciencias. Revista (PER ISSN 1813-3894) **3225**
• ➤ Universidad Nacional de Jujuy. Facultad de Humanidades y Ciencias Sociales. Cuadernos (ARG ISSN 0327-1471) **8012**
Universidad Nacional de la Pampa. Facultad de Agronomia. Revista (ARG ISSN 0326-6184) **165**
➤ Universidad Nacional de la Plata. Facultad de Agronomia. Revista (ARG ISSN 0041-8676) **165**
Universidad Nacional de la Plata. Revista (ARG ISSN 0041-8625) **4479**
Universidad Nacional de la Rioja Ciencia *see* UNLar Ciencia **7927**
• Universidad Nacional de Rosario. Centro de Investigaciones de Filosofia Juridica y Filosofia Social. Revista (ARG) **4802**
Universidad Nacional de Rosario. Facultad de Ciencias Medicas. Revista (ARG ISSN 0375-0752) **5726**
Universidad Nacional de Rosario. Instituto de Fisiografia y Geologia. Boletin (ARG ISSN 1666-115X) **4032**
Universidad Nacional de Salta. Facultad de Ciencias Naturales. Catedra Manejo de Fauna. Publicaciones Tecnicas (ARG ISSN 0327-4853) **966**
Universidad Nacional de Tucuman. Departamento de Historia. Revista (ARG) **4316**
Universidad Nacional de Tucuman. Instituto de Ingenieria Electrica. Revista (ARG ISSN 0082-6693) **3333**
Universidad Nacional del Centro del Peru. Anales Cientificos (PER) **3007**
Universidad Nacional del Centro del Peru. Cuadernos Universitarios. Serie: Estudios Andinos del Centro (PER) **359**
Universidad Nacional del Litoral. Boletin (ARG) **3007**
Universidad Nacional del Litoral. Facultad de Ciencias de la Administracion. Revista (ARG) **7474**
Universidad Nacional del Litoral. Facultad de Ciencias Economicas Comerciales y Politicas (ARG) **1187**
Universidad Nacional del Sur. Escuela de Perfeccionamiento en Investigacion Operativa. Revista (ARG ISSN 0329-7322) **1799**
Universidad Nacional Federico Villareal. Departamento de Ciencias Historico Sociales. Publicaciones (PER) **4316**
Universidad Nacional Mayor de San Marcos. Facultad de Ciencias Economicas. Revista (PER) **1187**
• ➤ Universidad Nacional Mayor de San Marcos. Facultad de Medicina. Anales (PER ISSN 1025-5583) **5726**
▼ • Universidad Pablo de Olavide. Centro de Sociologia y Politicas Locales. Documentos de Trabajo (ESP ISSN 1988-8090) **8145**
Universidad Pedagogica Nacional. Facultad de Ciencia y Tecnologia. Revista *see* Revista T E D **8437**
Universidad Pedagogica y Tecnologica de Colombia. Centro de Estudios Economicos. Apuntes del C E N E S (COL ISSN 0120-3053) **1187**
Universidad Pedagogica y Tecnologica de Colombia Cuadernos de Linguistica Hispanica *see* U P T C. Cuadernos de Linguistica Hispanica **5190**
Universidad Peruana Cayetano Heredia. Boletin (PER) **3007**
Universidad Pontificia Bolivariana. Facultad de Administracion de Empresas. Revista (COL ISSN 0121-0688) **1799**
Universidad Pontificia Bolivariana. Facultad de Derecho y Ciencias Politicas. Revista (COL ISSN 0120-3886) **4802**
Universidad Pontificia Bolivariana. Facultad de Trabajo Social. Revista (COL ISSN 0121-1722) **8075**
Universidad Pontificia Bolivariana. Revista (COL ISSN 0120-1115) **5392**
Universidad Pontificia Comillas de Madrid. Publicaciones. Serie 1: Estudios (ESP) **7821**
Universidad Tecnologica del Choco. Revista (COL ISSN 1657-3498) **8444**
• Universidad Veracruzana. Gaceta (MEX ISSN 1405-5163) **3007**
• Universidad Veracruzana. Revista Medica (MEX ISSN 1870-3267) **5726**
Universidad y Ciencia (MEX ISSN 0186-2979) **7926**
Universidad y Cooperativismo (COL ISSN 0120-3789) **1523**
➤ Universidad y Empresa (COL ISSN 0124-4639) **1799**
Universidad y Salud (COL ISSN 0124-7107) **5726**
Universidad y Sociedad *see* Sociedad & Conocimiento **8135**
Universidade da Coruna. Facultade de Dereito. Anuario (ESP ISSN 1138-039X) **4802**
Universidade de Alfenas. Revista (BRA ISSN 1413-3547) **8012**
Universidade de Coimbra. Boletim do Arquivo (PRT ISSN 0872-5632) **5052**
Universidade de Coimbra. Faculdade de Direito. Boletim (PRT ISSN 0303-9773) **4944**
Universidade de Coimbra. Faculdade de Direito. Boletim de Ciencias Economicas (PRT ISSN 0870-4252) **1187**
Universidade de Coimbra. Museu e Laboratorio Mineralogico e Geologico. Publicacoes. Memorias e Noticas (PRT ISSN 0373-6474) **2772**
Universidade de Fortaleza. Centro de Ciencias da Saude. Revista *see* Revista Brasileira em Promocao da Saude **7539**
➤ Universidade de Lisboa. Faculdade de Letras. Revista (PRT ISSN 0870-6336) **5392**
Universidade de Lisboa. Instituto Botanico. Artigo de Divulgacao (PRT ISSN 0066-8079) **821**
➤ Universidade de Santiago de Compostela. Monografias (ESP) **7926**
Universidade de Sao Paulo. Boletim de Botanica (BRA ISSN 0302-2439) **821**
Universidade de Sao Paulo. Departamento de Sociologia. Serie Bibliografia (BRA) **8151**
Universidade de Sao Paulo. Departamento de Sociologia. Serie Escritos (BRA ISSN 0104-6713) **8145**
• Universidade de Sao Paulo. Escola de Enfermagem. Revista (BRA ISSN 0080-6234) **5983**
➤ Universidade de Sao Paulo. Faculdade de Direito. Revista (BRA ISSN 0303-9838) **4802**
Universidade de Sao Paulo. Faculdade de Economia e Administracao. Biblioteca. Boletim (BRA) **638**
Universidade de Sao Paulo. Faculdade de Educacao. Revista *see* Educacao e Pesquisa **2845**
Universidade de Sao Paulo Geologia. Serie Cientifica *see* U S P. Geologia. Serie Cientifica **2771**
Universidade de Sao Paulo Geologia. Serie Didactica *see* U S P. Geologia. Serie Didactica **2772**
Universidade de Sao Paulo Geologia. Serie Especial *see* U S P. Geologia. Serie Especial **2772**
Universidade de Sao Paulo. Hospital das Clinicas. Revista *see* Clinics **5598**
Universidade de Sao Paulo. Instituto de Estudos Brasileiros. Revista (BRA ISSN 0020-3874) **8012**
Universidade de Sao Paulo. Instituto de Matematica e Estatistica. Resenhas *see* Sao Paulo Journal of Mathematical Sciences **5532**
Universidade de Sao Paulo. Instituto Oceanografico. Publicacao Especial (BRA ISSN 0100-5146) **2820**
Universidade de Sao Paulo. Instituto Oceanografico. Relatorio de Cruzeiros (BRA ISSN 0100-5197) **2820**
Universidade de Sao Paulo. Instituto Oceanografico. Relatorios Tecnicos (BRA ISSN 1413-7747) **2820**
• Universidade de Sao Paulo. Museu Paulista. Anais (BRA ISSN 0101-4714) **4316**
Universidade de Sao Paulo. Museu Paulista. Colecao. Serie de Arqueologia (BRA) **421**
Universidade de Sao Paulo. Museu Paulista. Colecao. Serie de Etnologia (BRA) **359**
Universidade de Sao Paulo. Museu Paulista. Colecao. Serie de Geografia (BRA) **4032**
Universidade de Sao Paulo. Museu Paulista. Colecao. Serie de Historia (BRA) **4316**
Universidade de Sao Paulo. Museu Paulista. Colecao. Serie de Mobiliario (BRA) **6539**
Universidade de Sao Paulo. Museu Paulista. Colecao. Serie de Numismatica (BRA) **6653**
Universidade de Sao Paulo. Psicologia *see* Psicologia U S P **7393**
Universidade de Sao Paulo. Revista de Administracao *see* Revista de Administracao **1790**
Universidade de Sao Paulo. Revista de Terapia Ocupacional (BRA ISSN 1415-9104) **6117**
Universidade do Amazonas. Revista. Serie: Ciencias Humanas (BRA ISSN 0103-9024) **8012**
Universidade do Estado do Rio de Janeiro Boletim *see* U E R J. Boletim **2921**
• Universidade do Grande Rio. Instituto de Humanidades. Revista Electronica (BRA ISSN 1678-3182) **4479**
• Universidade do Porto. Faculdade de Letras. Geografia (PRT ISSN 0871-1666) **4032**
• Universidade do Porto. Faculdade de Letras. Historia (PRT ISSN 0871-164X) **4165**
• Universidade do Porto. Faculdade de Letras. Linguas e Literaturas (PRT ISSN 0871-1682) **5190**
• Universidade do Porto. Faculdade de Letras. Sociologia (PRT ISSN 0872-3419) **8145**
Universidade Estadual de Campinas. Centro de Memoria. Boletim (BRA ISSN 0103-5452) **4479**
➤ Universidade Estadual Paulista. Revista de Odontologia (BRA ISSN 0101-1774) **5868**
Universidade Federal da Bahia. Faculdade de Odontologia. Revista (BRA ISSN 0101-8418) **5868**
Universidade Federal de Goias. Publicacao (BRA) **3007**
Universidade Federal de Minas Gerais. Corpo Discente. Revista Literaria. (BRA ISSN 0079-9327) **5392**
➤ Universidade Federal de Minas Gerais. Faculdade de Direito. Revista (BRA ISSN 0304-2340) **4802**
Universidade Federal de Minas Gerais. Faculdade de Odontologia. Arquivos em Odontologia (BRA ISSN 1516-0939) **5868**
Universidade Federal de Pelotas. Departamento de Pesquisa e Pos-Graduacao. Trabalhos Publicados: Resumos (BRA ISSN 0102-731X) **2306**
Universidade Federal de Pernambuco. Anuario Estatistico (BRA) **2937**
Universidade Federal de Pernambuco. Departamento de Geologia. Serie B. Estudos e Pesquisas (BRA) **2718**
Universidade Federal de Pernambuco Revista de Enfermagem on Line *see* U F P E. Revista de Enfermagem on Line **5983**
Universidade Federal de Santa Catarina. Museu de Antropologia. Anais (BRA ISSN 0101-451X) **359**
Universidade Federal do Ceara. Centro de Ciencias da Saude. Revista de Medicina/Federal University of Ceara. School of Medicine. Journal of Medicine (BRA ISSN 0100-1302) **5726**
Universidade Federal do Ceara. Centro de Tecnologia. Boletim Trimestral (BRA) **8444**
Universidade Federal do Ceara. Departamento de Ciencias Sociais e Filosofia. Documentos (BRA ISSN 0041-8870) **8012**
Universidade Federal do Espirito Santo Revista de Odontologia *see* U F E S Revista de Odontologia **5868**
Universidade Federal do Para. Relatorio Anual (BRA) **3007**
• Universidade Federal do Parana. Faculdade de Direito. Revista (BRA ISSN 0104-3315) **4802**
Universidade Federal do Rio de Janeiro. Departamento de Microbiologia Geral. Anais de Microbiologia (BRA ISSN 0485-1854) **746**
➤ Universidade Federal do Rio de Janeiro. Instituto de Matematica. Estudos e Comunicacoes (BRA ISSN 0103-1015) **5543**
➤ Universidade Federal do Rio de Janeiro. Instituto de Matematica. Memorias de Matematica (BRA ISSN 0102-6631) **5549**
Universidade Federal do Rio de Janeiro. Instituto de Matematica. Textos de Metodos Matematicos (BRA ISSN 0103-491X) **5543**
Universidade Federal do Rio Grande do Norte. Centro de Biociencias. Departamento de Oceanografia e Limnologia. Boletim (BRA ISSN 0100-7068) **709**
Universidade Federal do Rio Grande do Norte. Departamento de Geologia. Boletim (BRA ISSN 0101-5400) **2772**
➤ Universidade Federal do Rio Grande do Sul. Instituto de Biociencias. Boletim (BRA ISSN 0102-597X) **709**
Universidade Federal do Rio Grande do Sul. Instituto de Geociencias. Pesquisas em Geociencias (BRA) **2718**
Universidade Federal Fluminense Departamento de Psicologia. Revista *see* U F F. Departamento de Psicologia. Revista **7413**
Universidade Metodista de Piracicaba Revista de Administracao *see* U N I M E P. Revista de Administracao **1799**
Universidade Nova de Lisboa. Faculdade de Ciencias Sociais e Humanas. Revista (PRT ISSN 0871-2778) **8012**
Universidade Tecnica de Lisboa. Faculdade de Arquitectura. Cadernos (PRT ISSN 1645-2844) **459**
Universidade Tecnica de Lisboa. Faculdade de Medicina Veterinaria. Anais (PRT ISSN 0873-5522) **8809**
Universidade Tecnica de Lisboa. Instituto Superior de Economia e Gestao. Estudos de Economia (PRT ISSN 0870-1326) **1187**
Universidades (MEX ISSN 0041-8935) **3007**
L'Universita (ITA ISSN 1828-4647) **2306**
Universita Cattolica del Sacro Cuore. Annuario (ITA ISSN 0393-7186) **2922**
Universita Cattolica del Sacro Cuore. Facolta di Agraria. Annali (ITA ISSN 0540-049X) **165**
† Universita Cattolica del Sacro Cuore. Istituto di Storia Antica. Contributi (ITA) **8996**
Universita degli Studi di Bergamo. Dipartimento di Lingue e Letterature Neolatine. Collana (ITA ISSN 1972-2419) **5392**
Universita degli Studi di Bologna. Istituto di Entomologia Guido Grandi. Bollettino *see* Bulletin of Insectology **841**
Universita degli Studi di Cagliari. Facolta di Lettere e Filosofia. Annali (ITA) **4479**
† Universita degli Studi di Cagliari. Facolta di Magistero. Annali (ITA) **8996**
Universita degli Studi di Cagliari. Facolta di Scienze. Seminario. Rendiconti (ITA ISSN 0370-727X) **7926**
Universita degli Studi di Catania. Dipartimento di Architettura ed Urbanistica. Quaderno (ITA ISSN 1970-237X) **459**
† Universita degli Studi di Ferrara. Istituto di Geologia. Pubblicazioni (ITA) **8996**
† Universita degli Studi di Ferrara. Istituto di Mineralogia. Annali. Nuova Serie. Sezione: Scienze della Terra (ITA) **8996**
Universita degli Studi di Firenze. Dipartimento di Italianistica. Studi e Testi (ITA ISSN 1825-3415) **5190**
Universita degli Studi di Firenze. Dipartimento di Linguistica. Quaderni (ITA ISSN 1122-0619) **5190**
Universita degli Studi di Firenze. Dipartimento di Progettazione dell'Architettura. Quaderni (ITA) **459**
† Universita degli Studi di Firenze. Istituto di Statistica. Documentazione (ITA ISSN 0041-896X) **8996**
➤ Universita degli Studi di Genova. Dipartimento di Archeologia e Filologia Classica "F. Della Corte". Pubblicazioni (ITA) **5190**
Universita degli Studi di Genova. Istituto Botanico Hanbury. Pubblicazioni (ITA ISSN 1828-4558) **821**
† Universita degli Studi di Genova. Istituto di Medievistica. Collana Storica di Fonti e Studi (ITA) **8996**
Universita degli Studi di Genova. Musei e Istituti Biologici. Bollettino (ITA ISSN 0373-4110) **709**
† Universita degli Studi di Lecce. Bollettino di Storia della Filosofia (ITA ISSN 0390-0614) **8996**
Universita degli Studi di Lecce. Centro di Studi Papirologici. Gli Album (ITA ISSN 1970-6316) **4178**
Universita degli Studi di Lecce. Dipartimento di Filologia, Linguistica e Letteratura. Collana (ITA) **5190**
Universita degli Studi di Macerata. Facolta di Lettere e Filosofia. Annali (ITA ISSN 0076-1818) **422**
Universita degli Studi di Messina. Facolta di Economia. Annali (ITA) **1550**
† Universita degli Studi di Milano. Annuario (ITA) **8996**
Universita degli Studi di Milano. Istituto d'Igiene. Quaderni (ITA ISSN 1827-4161) **6999**
Universita degli Studi di Modena. Seminario Matematico e Fisico. Atti *see* Universita di Modena e Reggio Emilia. Seminario Matematico e Fisico. Atti **5543**
Universita degli Studi di Napoli. Dipartimento di Discipline Storiche. Pubblicazione (ITA) **4165**
Universita degli Studi di Napoli. Dipartimento di Discipline Storiche. Quaderni (ITA ISSN 1828-9517) **4165**
† Universita degli Studi di Napoli. Facolta di Lettere e Filosofia. Annali (ITA ISSN 0469-5461) **8996**
Universita degli Studi di Napoli "Federico II" Portici. Facolta di Agraria. Annali (ITA ISSN 1720-2647) **165**
Universita degli Studi di Napoli Parthenope. Facolta di Scienze e Tecnologie. Annali (ITA) **7926**
Universita degli Studi di Padova. Dipartimento di Storia. Confronta *see* Confronta **4136**
Universita degli Studi di Padova. Facolta di Lettere e Filosofia. Opuscoli Accademici (ITA ISSN 0078-7728) **5392**
Universita degli Studi di Padova. Facolta di Lettere e Filosofia. Pubblicazioni (ITA ISSN 1122-0449) **5392**
Universita degli Studi di Palermo. Istituto di Filologia Greca. Quaderni (ITA ISSN 0078-8627) **5190**
† Universita degli Studi di Parma. Centro Studi e Archivio della Comunicazione. Archivi del Progretto - Collana (ITA) **8996**
† Universita degli Studi di Parma. Centro Studi e Archivio della Comunicazione. Cataloghi (ITA) **8996**
† Universita degli Studi di Parma. Facolta di Economia e Commercio. Studi e Ricerche (ITA) **8996**
Universita degli Studi di Parma. Facolta di Medicina Veterinaria. Annali (ITA ISSN 0393-4802) **8809**
Universita degli Studi di Parma. Istituto di Storia dell'Arte. Cataloghi (ITA) **523**
➤ Universita degli Studi di Parma. Rivista di Matematica (ITA ISSN 0035-6298) **5543**
• Universita degli Studi di Pavia. Scientifica Acta. Quaderni del Dottorato (ITA ISSN 0394-2309) **7926**
Universita degli Studi di Perugia. Dipartimento di Economia, Finanza e Statistica. Quaderni (ITA ISSN 1825-0211) **1187**
Universita degli Studi di Perugia. Dipartimento di Economia. Quaderni *see* Universita degli Studi di Perugia. Dipartimento di Economia, Finanza e Statistica. Quaderni **1187**
† Universita degli Studi di Perugia. Facolta di Agraria. Annali (ITA ISSN 0374-4981) **8996**
† Universita degli Studi di Perugia. Facolta di Medicina e Chirurgia. Annali (ITA ISSN 0365-2270) **8996**
Universita degli Studi di Pisa. Facolta di Medicina Veterinaria di Pisa. Annali (ITA ISSN 0365-4729) **8809**
Universita degli Studi di Roma. Facolta di Architettura. Bolletino della Biblioteca (ITA ISSN 0392-2898) **459**
Universita degli Studi di Roma. Seminario di Archeologia e Storia dell'Arte Greca e Romana. Studi Miscellanei (ITA) **2241**
Universita degli Studi di Salerno. Dipartimento di Scienze Economiche e Statistiche. Quaderni (ITA ISSN 1971-3045) **1187**
Universita degli Studi di Salerno. Dipartimento di Scienze Economiche e Statistiche. Ricerche (ITA ISSN 1971-3037) **1187**
Universita degli Studi di Salerno. Dipartimento di Scienze Economiche e Statistiche. Working Papers (ITA ISSN 1971-3029) **1187**
Universita degli Studi di Salerno. Sezione Atti, Convegni, Miscellanee. Pubblicazioni (ITA ISSN 1824-212X) **4479**
Universita degli Studi di Sassari. Dipartimento di Storia. Collana (ITA ISSN 1828-3004) **4165**

Title

Title

10988 UNIVERSITE DE GRENOBLE. U F R DE LETTRES. RECHERCHES ULRICH'S PERIODICALS

Universite de Grenoble. U F R de Lettres. Recherches et Travaux (FRA ISSN 0151-1874) **5393**
Universite de Lausanne. Faculte des Lettres. Publications (CHE ISSN 0041-915X) **5393**
Universite de Lausanne. Institut de Linguistique et des Sciences du Langage. Bulletin (CHE ISSN 1023-134X) **5191**
Universite de l'Etat a Gand. Service de Linguistique Francaise. Travaux de Linguistique *see* Travaux de Linguistique **5189**
Universite de Liege. Faculte de Philosophie et Lettres. Bibliotheque (BEL ISSN 0768-5475) **4480**
Universite de Liege. Faculte de Philosophie et Lettres. Publications du Service de Prehistoire (BEL) **4480**
Universite de Liege. Faculte des Sciences Appliquees. Collection des Publications (BEL ISSN 0075-9333) **8444**
Universite de Lille III. Lexique (FRA ISSN 0756-7138) **5191**
Universite de Lome. Annales. Serie Science (TGO) **709**
• Universite de Lome. Journal de la Recherche Scientifique (TGO) **7926**
Universite de Lubumbashi. Centre de Linguistique Theorique et Appliquee. Africanistique (COD) **5191**
Universite de Lubumbashi. Centre de Linguistique Theorique et Appliquee. Bulletin de Liaison, Enseignment des Langues (COD) **5191**
Universite de Lubumbashi. Centre de Linguistique Theorique et Appliquee. Linguistique et Sciences Humaines. Bulletin d'Information (COD) **5191**
Universite de Madagascar. Etablissement d'Enseignement Superieur des Sciences. Annales: Serie Sciences de la Nature et Mathematiques (MDG ISSN 0374-549X) **7926**
Universite de Madagascar. Musee d'Art et d'Archeologie. Travaux et Documents (MDG) **523**
Universite de Marne-la-Vallee. Travaux et Recherches (FRA ISSN 1298-1786) **4480**
Universite de Moncton. Revue (CAN ISSN 0316-6368) **3819**
Universite de Montreal. Centre de Recherches en Developpement Economique. Cahier (CAN ISSN 0821-4441) **1607**
Universite de Montreal. Faculte de Medecine Veterinaire. Annuaire (CAN ISSN 0383-8455) **8810**
Universite de Montreal. Groupe de Recherche Interdisciplinaire en Sante. Rapport (CAN ISSN 0830-890X) **7544**
• Universite de Nancy II. Centre de Recherches et d'Applications Pedagogiques en Langues. Melanges (FRA ISSN 0077-2712) **3086**
Universite de Nantes. Centre de Recherches en Histoire Internationale et Atlantique. Enquetes et Documents (FRA ISSN 1775-2981) **4275**
Universite de Nantes. Laboratoire Subatech. Rapport Interne (FRA) **7072**
Universite de Neuchatel. Faculte des Lettres. Recueil de Travaux (CHE ISSN 0077-7633) **5393**
Universite de Paix (BEL) **7271**
Universite de Paris. Institut de Statistique. Annales *see* Annales de l'I S U P **5548**
Universite de Paris VI. Institut de Statistique. Publications *see* Annales de l'I S U P **5548**
Universite de Poitiers. Centre d'Etudes Superieures de Civilisation Medievale. Publications (FRA ISSN 0184-7899) **4165**
Universite de Provence. Arts. Histoire des Arts (FRA ISSN 1779-7284) **523**
➤ Universite de Provence. Centre d'Aix. Cahiers d'Etudes Germaniques (FRA ISSN 0751-4239) **4480**
➤ Universite de Reims. Institut de Geographie. Travaux (FRA ISSN 0048-7163) **4032**
Universite de Saint Etienne. Centre Jean Palerne. Memoires (FRA ISSN 0223-9469) **4480**
• Universite de Sherbrooke. Revue de Droit (CAN ISSN 0317-9656) **4802**
Universite de Sidi Bel Abbes. Annales de Mathematiques (DZA ISSN 1111-5556) **5544**
Universite de Skopje. Faculte des Sciences Economique. Annuaire *see* Univerzitet vo Skoplje. Ekonomskiot Fakultet. Godisnik **1190**
Universite de Sofia. Faculte de Philosophie. Annuaire *see* Sofiiski Universitet Sv. Kliment Ohridski. Fakultet po Pedagogika. Godishnik **3082**
Universite de Sofia. Faculte des Lettres Classiques et Modernes. Annuaire *see* Sofiiski Universitet Sv. Kliment Ohridski. Fakultet po Klasicheski i Novi Filologii. Godishnik **5176**
Universite de Sofia. Faculte des Mathematiques et de Mecanique. Annuaire *see* Sofiiski Universitet Sv. Kliment Ohridski. Fakultet po Matematika i Informatika. Godishnik. Kniga 2. Mekhanika **5537**
Universite de Strasbourg II. Centre de Philologie et Litteratures Romanes. Actes et Colloques (FRA ISSN 0081-5918) **5191**
Universite de Strasbourg II. Institut de Phonetique. Travaux (FRA ISSN 0039-2235) **5191**
Universite de Tunis. Ecole Normale Superieure. Section A: Lettres et Sciences Humaines. Serie 1: Langue et Litterature (TUN) **5393**
Universite de Yaounde. Faculte de Droit et des Sciences Economiques. Economie Generale (CMR) **1550**
Universite de Yaounde. Faculte des Lettres et Sciences Humaines. Annales. Serie Lettres (CMR ISSN 1012-1757) **4480**
Universite de Yaounde. Faculte des Lettres et Sciences Humaines. Annales. Serie Sciences Humaines (CMR ISSN 1012-1765) **4480**
Universite de Yaounde. Faculte des Sciences. Annales (CMR ISSN 0566-201X) **7926**
Universite des Sciences Sociales de Toulouse. Annales *see* Universite des Sciences Sociales de Toulouse. Droit Ecrit **8012**
Universite des Sciences Sociales de Toulouse. Droit Ecrit (FRA ISSN 1634-8664) **8012**
Universite d'Istanbul. Faculte Forestiere. Revue *see* Istanbul Universitesi Orman Fakultesi Dergisi, Seri A **3694**
• Universite d'Ottawa, Centre de Recherche en Civilisation Canadienne-Francaise. Rapport Annuel (CAN ISSN 1910-2089) **4316**
Universite d'Ottawa. Centre de Recherche et d'Enseignement sur les Droits de la Personne. Droits de la Personne/Human Rights Research and Education Bulletin (CAN ISSN 0826-7766) **7218**
Universite du Benin. Journal de la Recherche Scientifique *see* Universite de Lome. Journal de la Recherche Scientifique **7926**
Universite du Burundi. Revue (BDI ISSN 0250-5509) **3805**
Universite du Quebec a Montreal Journal *see* U Q A M Journal **2305**
Universite du Quebec a Rimouski. Departement des Sciences de l'Education. Monographie (CAN ISSN 1914-1610) **3007**
Universite Francois-Rabelais de Tours. Groupe de Recherches Anglo-Americaines. Publication (FRA ISSN 0997-4970) **5393**
Universite Laval. Archives de Folklore (CAN ISSN 0085-5243) **3623**
Universite Laval. Departement d'Exploitation et Utilisation des Bois. Note de Recherches (CAN ISSN 0079-8355) **3717**
Universite Laval. Departement d'Exploitation et Utilisation des Bois. Note Technique (CAN ISSN 0079-8363) **3717**
Universite Laval. Laboratoire de Recherches Sociologiques. Collection Rapports de Recherche (CAN ISSN 1914-1629) **8145**
Universite Laval. Laboratoire de Recherches Sociologiques. Rapports de Recherche *see* Universite Laval. Laboratoire de Recherches Sociologiques. Collection Rapports de Recherche **8145**
Universite Laval. Les Cahiers d'Histoire (CAN ISSN 0701-4031) **4165**
Universite Laval. Revue Juridique *see* Universite Laval. Revue Juridique des Etudiants et Etudiantes **4803**
Universite Laval. Revue Juridique des Etudiants et Etudiantes (CAN ISSN 0845-9401) **4803**
Universite Libre de Bruxelles. Centre d'Etudes de Recherche Operationnelle. Cahiers/Operations Research, Statistics and Applied Mathematics (BEL ISSN 0008-9737) **1799**
Universite Libre de Bruxelles. Faculte de Philosophie et Lettres. Annales d'Histoire de l'Art et d'Archeologie (BEL ISSN 0771-2723) **523**
➤ Universite Libre de Bruxelles. Faculte de Philosophie et Lettres. Travaux (BEL) **4480**
Universite Libre de Bruxelles. Groupe d'Etude du Dix-Huitieme Siecle. Etudes sur le Dix-Huitieme Siecle *see* Etudes sur le Dix-Huitieme Siecle **4218**
Universite Libre de Bruxelles. Institut de Philosophie. Annales (FRA ISSN 0771-4963) **6959**
Universite Libre de Bruxelles. Institut de Sociologie. Annee Sociale (BEL ISSN 0066-2380) **8145**
➤ Universite Libre de Bruxelles. Institut des Langues Vivantes et de Phonetique. Etudes et Travaux (BEL ISSN 1373-1149) **5191**
➤ Universite Libre de Bruxelles. Revue de Droit (BEL ISSN 0779-5572) **4803**
Universite Marien Ngouabi. Annales (COG) **3007**
Universite Nationale de Cote d'Ivoire, Centre Ivoirien de Recherches Economiques et Sociales Cahiers *see* C I R E S Cahiers **1078**
Universite Nationale du Rwanda. Revue Scientifique du Droit/Law Review (RWA) **4803**
Universite Nationale du Zaire, Kinshasa. Faculte de Droit. Annales (COD) **4803**
Universite Nationale du Zaire, Kinshasa. Institut de Recherches Economiques et Sociales. Document du Mois (COD) **1523**
Universite Nationale du Zaire, Kinshasa. Institut de Recherches Economiques et Sociales. Lettre Mensuelle (COD) **1187**
Universite Paul Sabatier. Faculte des Sciences. Annales (FRA ISSN 0240-2963) **5544**
Universite Saint-Joseph. Faculte des Lettres et des Sciences Humaines. Recherches. Serie A: Langue Arabe et Pensee Islamique (LBN) **7716**
Universite Saint-Joseph. Faculte des Lettres et des Sciences Humaines. Recherches. Serie B: Orient Chretien (LBN) **562**
Universite Saint Joseph. Melanges (LBN ISSN 0253-164X) **4480**
Universite Sportive d'Ete. Cahiers (FRA ISSN 0298-7201) **8214**
Universite Syndicaliste (FRA ISSN 0751-5839) **3007**
Universite Technique de Zvolen. Faculte des Forets. Collection des Travaux Scientifiques *see* Acta Facultatis Forestalis, Zvolen **3682**
Universiteit Gent. Centrum voor Onkruidonderzoek. Mededeling (BEL ISSN 0435-950X) **256**
Universiteit Gent. Faculteit van de Landbouwkundige en Toegepaste Biologische Wetenschappen. Mededelingen *see* Communications in Agricultural and Applied Biological Sciences **762**
Universiteit te Gent. Sterrenkundig Observatorium. Mededelingen (BEL) **583**
Universiteit te Gent. Sterrenkundig Observatorium. Mededelingen: Meteorologie en Geofysica (BEL) **6397**
Universiteit Utrecht. Universiteit Media Bulletin (NLD) **3007**
Universiteit van Amsterdam. Duitsland Instituut Amsterdam. Forschungsberichte (NLD ISSN 1574-065X) **4275**
Universiteit van Amsterdam. Instituut voor Fonetische Wetenschappen. Proceedings (NLD ISSN 0167-5613) **5191**
Universiteit van Pretoria. Instituut vir Strategiese Studies. Ad Hoc Publikasie *see* University of Pretoria. Institute for Strategic Studies. Ad Hoc Publication **7272**
Universiteit van Pretoria. Jaarverslag *see* University of Pretoria. Annual Report **2307**
➤ Universiteit van Stellenbosch. Annale (ZAF ISSN 1018-0761) **7926**
Universiteitskrant Groningen (NLD ISSN 0920-7368) **2306**
• Universites (CAN ISSN 0226-7454) **3007**
Universites (FRA ISSN 1258-195X) **3007**
Universites. Chimie (FRA ISSN 1288-8788) **2083**
Universites. Droit (FRA ISSN 1287-0099) **4803**
Universites. Economie (FRA ISSN 1292-1440) **1187**
Universites. Electronique (FRA ISSN 1296-1515) **3333**
Universites. Geographie (FRA ISSN 1286-9791) **4032**
Universites. Histoire (FRA ISSN 1288-927X) **4165**
Universites. Informatique (FRA ISSN 1298-227X) **2440**
Universites. Lettres (FRA ISSN 1296-1795) **5393**
Universites. Lettres Classiques (FRA ISSN 1624-1789) **5393**
Universites. Mathematiques (FRA ISSN 1288-877X) **5545**
Universites. Mathematiques Appliquees (FRA ISSN 1630-0211) **5545**
Universites. Mechanique (FRA ISSN 1292-1807) **3398**
Universites. Physique (FRA ISSN 1294-0348) **7044**
Universites. Sciences de la Vie et de la Terre (FRA ISSN 1292-1459) **7926**
Universites. Statistiques Sciences Humaines (FRA ISSN 1630-0165) **8084**
Universitet i Oslo. Pedagogisk Forskningsinstitutt. Rapport (NOR ISSN 0800-6113) **2922**
Universitet po Arhitektura, Stroitelstvo i Geodezia. Godisnik (BGR ISSN 1310-814X) **460**
Universitet po Khranitelni Tekhnologii. Nauchni Trudove (BGR ISSN 0477-0250) **3666**
Universitet Rossiiskoi Akademii Obrazovaniya. Vestnik (RUS) **3007**
• Universitetet for Miljoe- og Biovitenskap. Doctor Philosophia Thesis (NOR ISSN 1503-1667) **165**
• Universitetet for Miljoe- og Biovitenskap. Doctor Scientiarum Theses (NOR ISSN 0802-3220) **165**
Universitetet for Miljoe- og BioVitenskap. Institutt for Matematiske Realfag og Teknologi. I M T-Rapport (NOR) **7926**
Universitetet for Miljoe- og BioVitenskap. Institutt for Plante- og Miljoevitenskap. Rapport (NOR ISSN 1504-3584) **256**
Universitetet i Bergen. Arkeologiske Avhandlinger og Rapporter *see* U B A S, Nordisk **421**
Universitetet i Bergen. Arkeologiske Avhandlinger og Rapporter *see* U B A S, Hovedfag/Master **421**
Universitetet i Bergen. Arkeologiske Avhandlinger og Rapporter *see* U B A S, International **421**
Universitetet i Bergen Arkeologiske Skrifter Hovedfag/Master *see* U B A S, Hovedfag/Master **421**
Universitetet i Bergen Arkeologiske Skrifter Nordisk *see* U B A S, Nordisk **421**
Universitetet i Bergen. Department of Mediastudies. Rapport *see* Universitetet i Bergen. Institutt for Informasjons- og Medievitenskap. Rapport **8145**
Universitetet i Bergen. Filosofisk Institutt. Filosofiske Smuler (NOR ISSN 1504-3460) **6959**
Universitetet i Bergen. Filosofisk Institutt. Skriftserie *see* Universitetet i Bergen. Filosofisk Institutt. Filosofiske Smuler **6959**
Universitetet i Bergen. Institutt for Administrasjon og Organisasjonsvitenskap. Notat (NOR ISSN 0803-0200) **7474**
Universitetet i Bergen. Institutt for Administrasjon og Organisasjonsvitenskap. Rapport (NOR ISSN 0803-0219) **1187**
Universitetet i Bergen. Institutt for Informasjons- og Medievitenskap. Rapport (NOR ISSN 1504-1697) **8145**
Universitetet i Bergen. Institutt for Medievitenskap. I M V Utgivelse *see* Universitetet i Bergen. Institutt for Informasjons- og Medievitenskap. Rapport **8145**
Universitetet i Bergen. Institutt for Medievitenskap. Publikasjon *see* Universitetet i Bergen. Institutt for Informasjons- og Medievitenskap. Rapport **8145**
• Universitetet i Oslo. ARENA - Senter for Europaforskning. Report (Advanced Research on the Europeanisation of the Nation State) (NOR ISSN 0807-3139) **8012**
• Universitetet i Oslo. ARENA - Senter for Europaforskning. Working Papers (Advanced Research on the Europeanisation of the Nation State) (NOR ISSN 0805-5130) **8012**
• Universitetet i Oslo. Helseoekonomisk Forskningsprogram. Working Paper (NOR ISSN 1501-9071) **8075**
Universitetet i Oslo. Institutt for Helseledelse og Helseoekonomi. Rapport (NOR ISSN 1504-1751) **4112**
Universitetet i Oslo. Institutt for Kriminologi og Rettssosiologi. Bokserien (NOR ISSN 0809-7488) **2670**
Universitetet i Oslo. Institutt for Kriminologi og Rettssosiologi. Skriftserie *see* Universitetet i Oslo. Institutt for Kriminologi og Rettssosiologi. Bokserien **2670**
Universitetet i Oslo. Institutt for Menneskerettigheter. Research Notes *see* Universitetet i Oslo. Norsk Senter for Menneskerettigheter. Research Notes **7218**
Universitetet i Oslo. Institutt for Menneskerettigheter. Working Papers *see* Universitetet i Oslo. Norsk Senter for Menneskerettigheter. Research Notes **7218**
Universitetet i Oslo. Institutt for Menneskerettigheter. Working Papers *see* Nordem Report **7213**
Universitetet i Oslo. Institutt for Offentlig Rett. Skriftserie (NOR ISSN 0803-2106) **4853**
Universitetet i Oslo. Institutt for Sosialantropologi. Hovedfagsstudentenes Aarbok *see* Betwixt & Between **330**
• Universitetet i Oslo. InterMedia. Rapport (NOR ISSN 1502-7198) **8145**
Universitetet i Oslo. Kulturhistorisk Museum. Fornminneseksjonen. Varia (NOR ISSN 1504-3266) **4275**
➤ Universitetet i Oslo. Kulturhistorisk Museum. Skrifter/University of Oslo. Museum of Cultural Heritage. Occasional Papers (NOR ISSN 1504-3258) **422**
Universitetet i Oslo. Kulturhistoriske Museer. Fornminneseksjonen. Varia *see* Universitetet i Oslo. Kulturhistorisk Museum. Fornminneseksjonen. Varia **4275**
Universitetet i Oslo. Kulturhistoriske Museer. Skrifter *see* Universitetet i Oslo. Kulturhistorisk Museum. Skrifter **422**
• Universitetet i Oslo. Norsk Senter for Menneskerettigheter. Research Notes (NOR ISSN 1504-0062) **7218**
• Universitetet i Oslo. Oekonomisk Institut. Memorandum (NOR ISSN 0809-8786) **1187**
Universitetet i Oslo. Senter for Barne- og Ungdomspsykiatri. Monografiserien *see* Universitetet i Oslo. Sogn Senter for Barne- og Ungdomspsykiatri. Monografiserien **6189**
Universitetet i Oslo. Senter for Helseadministrasjon. Rapport *see* Universitetet i Oslo. Institutt for Helseledelse og Helseoekonomi. Rapport **4112**
Universitetet i Oslo. Senter for Studier i Vikingtid og Nordisk Middelalder. Skriftserie *see* Moeteplass Middelalder **4246**
Universitetet i Oslo. Senter for Teknologi, Innovasjon og Kultur. Reprints (NOR ISSN 1501-9888) **8145**
Universitetet i Oslo. Senter for Teknologi, Innovasjon og Kultur. Working Papers (NOR ISSN 1501-8040) **8444**
Universitetet i Oslo. Sogn Senter for Barne- og Ungdomspsykiatri. Monografiserien (NOR ISSN 1504-2537) **6189**
Universitetet i Stavanger. Doktor Ingenioer-Avhandling *see* University of Stavanger. PhD Thesis UiS **3225**
Universitetet i Stavanger. Notater (NOR ISSN 1504-4939) **3225**
Universitetet i Tromsoe. Senter for Samiske Studier. Skrifter (NOR ISSN 0804-6093) **5243**
Universitetet i Trondheim. Norges Tekniske Hoegskole. Institutt for Uorganisk Kjemi. Avhandling (NOR) **2118**
Universitetets Statistiske Institut. Research Report (DNK ISSN 0105-9645) **8413**
Universitets-Jubilaeets Danske Samfund. Skriftserie (DNK ISSN 0105-449X) **5191**
Universitets-Jubilaeets Danske Samfund Studier *see* U J D S - Studier **4274**
• Universitetsavisen (DNK ISSN 0106-7141) **3008**
Universitetshistorisk Serie *see* Acta Jutlandica. Universitetshistorisk Serie **3833**
Universitetslaeraren (SWE ISSN 0282-4973) **2922**
Universitexts (USA ISSN 0172-5939) **5545**
Universiti Kebangsaan Malaysia. Jurnal Perubatan (MYS ISSN 0127-1075) **5727**
Universiti Kebangsaan Malaysia. Lapuran Tahunan - Annual Report (MYS) **2922**
Universiti Tun Abdul Razak Journal *see* U N I T A R e-Journal **8011**
Universities Acacdemic Pension Plan (Year) Annual Report (CAN ISSN 0842-2788) **1713**
Universities and Colleges Admissions Service Annual Report *see* U C A S Annual Report **2962**

DIRECTORY 2010 UNIVERSITY OF CALCUTTA. BUSINESS STUDIES 10989

Universities' and Colleges' Staff Development Agency Green Papers (GBR) **3008**
Universities' and Colleges' Staff Development Agency Handbooks (GBR) **3008**
Universities' and Colleges' Staff Development Agency Occasional Longer Briefing Papers (GBR) **3008**
Universities' and Colleges' Staff Development Agency Resource Packs and Disks (GBR) **3008**
Universities Art Association of Canada. Journal/Association d'Art des Universites du Canada. Journal (CAN ISSN 0315-940X) **523**
Universities Federation for Animal Welfare Animal Welfare Research Report *see* U F A W Animal Welfare Research Report **322**
Universities Federation for Animal Welfare Annual Report and Accounts *see* U F A W Annual Report and Accounts **322**
Universities Federation for Animal Welfare Handbook on the Care and Management of Laboratory Animals *see* U F A W Handbook on the Care and Management of Laboratory Animals **322**
Universities Federation for Animal Welfare News-Sheet *see* U F A W News-Sheet **322**
Universities Handbook (Year) (IND ISSN 0377-6336) **2962**
• The Universities Safety & Health Association. Digest (GBR) **7544**
Universities Safety Association. Digest *see* The Universities Safety & Health Association. Digest **7544**
Universities Telephone Directory (Year)/Bottin des Universites (year) (CAN ISSN 0847-3536) **3008**
• University (PHL ISSN 0042-0360) **2306**
• University Affairs/Affaires Universitaires (CAN ISSN 0041-9257) **3008**
University and Polytechnic Libraries Book and Journal Spending (GBR ISSN 0965-6804) **7575**
• ➤ University Avenue Undergraduate Journal of Economics (USA) **1187**
University Aviation Association. Newsletter (USA) **8552**
• ➤ The University Bookman (USA ISSN 0041-9265) **7575**
University Bristol Calendar (GBR) **3008**
▼ University Business (GBR ISSN 1756-0225) **3008**
• University Business (USA ISSN 1097-6671) **3008**
• University Business Daily (USA) **3008**
• University Casebook Series (USA) **4803**
University Casebook Series. Tarlock, Corbridge and Getches' Water Resource Management, a Casebook in Law and Public Policy (USA) **8834**
University Casebook Series. Waltz & Park's Evidence (USA) **4803**
University Casebook Series. Waltz & Park's Evidence. Supplement *see* University Casebook Series. Waltz & Park's Evidence **4803**
University Casebook Series. Weinstein, Mansfield, Abrams & Berger's Evidence (USA) **4803**
University Chemistry *see* Daxue Huaxue **2059**
University Chemistry Education (Online) *see* Chemistry Education Research and Practice **2057**
The University Chronicle (USA) **2306**
University College Cork Calendar (IRL ISSN 0332-0863) **3008**
University College Dublin Connections *see* U C D Connections **2304**
• University College Dublin Law Review (IRL ISSN 1649-1327) **4803**
University College London Classics Newsletter (GBR) **4480**
University College London. Department of Economics. Discussion Papers in Economics (GBR ISSN 1350-6722) **1188**
• University College London. Eastman Academy. Newsletter (GBR) **5868**
University College London. Institute of Archaeology. Papers (GBR ISSN 0965-9315) **422**
University College London. Laws Newsletter (GBR) **4803**
• University College London. Library News Online (GBR) **5052**
University College London Working Papers in Linguistics *see* U C L Working Papers in Linguistics **5190**
University College of the North (Year) Annual Academic Report (CAN ISSN 1910-2755) **3008**
University College of the North. Annual Report (CAN ISSN 1912-0540) **3008**
University Computing and Information Services Newsletter (CAN ISSN 0829-5425) **2440**
University Computing Centre Newsletter *see* U C C Newsletter **2440**
University Continuing Education Association. Membership Directory (USA) **2947**
University Corporation for Atmospheric Research Annual Report *see* U C A R. Annual Report **6397**
University Corporation for Atmospheric Research Quarterly *see* U C A R Quarterly **6397**
University Council for Educational Administration Monograph Series *see* U C E A Monograph Series **3034**
University Daily *see* The Daily Toreador **2281**
• University Daily Kansan (USA ISSN 0746-4967) **2306**
University Dunarea de Jos of Galati. Annals *see* Universitatea "Dunarea de Jos" din Galati. Analele. Fascicula I. Economie **1550**
University Education Science *see* Daxue Jiaoyu Kexue **2977**
The University Examiner (IRL) **2306**
University Faculty For Life. Proceedings *see* Life and Learning **6932**
University Gazette (USA) **2306**
University Geographer (NGA ISSN 0083-3975) **4032**
• University - Government - Industry - Micro-Nano Symposium. Proceedings (USA) **3115**
University - Government - Industry - Microelectronics Symposium. Proceedings *see* University - Government - Industry - Micro-Nano Symposium. Proceedings **3115**
University Graduate Destinations *see* NZUniPostgradReport **1701**
University Graduate Destinations *see* NZUniGradReport **1701**
University Graduate Destinations *see* NZUniGradStats **1701**
University - Industry Grants and Awards Guide *see* Medical Research Council of Canada. Grants and Awards Guide **5671**
• University Law Review Project (USA) **4825**
University Libraries Section Universe *see* U L S Universe **5052**
University Magazine *see* U - Magazine **3006**
The University Magazine (USA) **2306**
University Manager (CAN ISSN 1484-2173) **3034**
University Marine Biological Station Millport. Annual Report (GBR) **709**
University Marine Biological Station. Occasional Publication (GBR) **709**
University Messenger (USA) **3991**
University News (IND ISSN 0566-2257) **3008**
University News *see* University of Auckland News **2306**
The University News (USA) **2306**
University of Aarhus. Department of Computer Science. PhD Dissertation *see* D A I M I PhD Dissertation **2416**
University of Aberdeen. Annual Report (GBR ISSN 0305-8824) **2306**
University of Aberdeen. Department of Economics. Discussion Paper (GBR ISSN 0960-443X) **1188**
University of Aberdeen. Department of Land Economy. Discussion Paper (GBR ISSN 0953-3575) **2630**
University of Aberdeen. Report of the Library Committee (GBR ISSN 0515-0809) **5052**
University of Aberdeen. Staff Lists (GBR ISSN 0263-5968) **2962**
University of Aberdeen. Undergraduate Prospectus (GBR ISSN 0140-4016) **3008**
University of Aberdeen. University Library. Occasional Publications (GBR ISSN 0144-638X) **5053**
University of Addis Ababa. Institute of Ethiopian Studies. Ethiopian Publications *see* Ethiopian Publications: Books, Pamphlets, Annuals and Periodical Articles **624**
University of Agder. Doctoral Dissertations (NOR ISSN 1504-9272) **8012**
• University of Agricultural Sciences and Veterinary Medicine Cluj-Napoca. Bulletin. Agriculture (ROM ISSN 1843-5246) **165**
• University of Agricultural Sciences and Veterinary Medicine Cluj-Napoca. Bulletin. Animal Science and Biotechnology (ROM ISSN 1843-5262) **8810**
• University of Agricultural Sciences and Veterinary Medicine Cluj-Napoca. Bulletin. Horticulture (ROM ISSN 1843-5254) **165**
• University of Agricultural Sciences and Veterinary Medicine Cluj-Napoca. Bulletin. Veterinary Medicine (ROM ISSN 1843-5270) **8810**
University of Agricultural Sciences, Bangalore. Annual Report (IND ISSN 0067-3455) **165**
University of Agricultural Sciences, Bangalore. Collaborative Series (IND) **166**
University of Agricultural Sciences, Bangalore. Current Research (IND) **166**
University of Agricultural Sciences, Bangalore. Educational Series (IND) **166**
University of Agricultural Sciences Bangalore Extension Series *see* U A S Extension Series **163**
University of Agricultural Sciences, Bangalore. Information Series (IND) **166**
University of Agricultural Sciences Bangalore Miscellaneous Series *see* U A S Miscellaneous Series **163**
University of Agricultural Sciences, Bangalore. Research Monograph Series (IND) **166**
University of Agricultural Sciences, Bangalore. Research Review Series (IND) **166**
University of Agricultural Sciences, Bangalore. Technical Information Series (IND) **166**
University of Agricultural Sciences, Bangalore. Technical Series (IND) **166**
University of Agricultural Sciences, Bangalore. U A S Textbook Series (IND) **166**
• University of Akureyri. Faculty of Business Administration. Working Paper Series (ISL ISSN 1670-5394) **1188**
University of Alabama at Birmingham Visual Arts Gallery. Papers *see* U A B Visual Arts Gallery. Papers **6539**
University of Alabama at Birmingham Visual Arts Gallery. Selections from the Permanent Selection *see* U A B Visual Arts Gallery. Selections from the Permanent Selection **6539**
University of Alabama Reporter *see* U A B Reporter **3086**
➤ University of Alaska. Anthropological Papers (USA ISSN 0041-9354) **359**
University of Alaska at Fairbanks Alumnus *see* U A F Alumnus **2304**
➤ University of Alaska. Biological Papers (USA ISSN 0568-8604) **709**
University of Alaska. Biological Papers. Special Reports (USA ISSN 0161-3243) **709**
University of Alaska. Institute of Social and Economic Research. Research Summary (USA) **8145**
University of Alaska. Mineral Industry Research Laboratory. Annual Report of Research Progress (USA ISSN 0568-8760) **6482**
University of Alaska Museum. Annual Report (USA ISSN 0093-7436) **6539**
University of Alaska Sea Grant College Program. Education Publication (USA) **7926**
University of Alaska Sea Grant College Program. Marine Advisory Bulletin (USA) **3610**
University of Alberta. Centre for Criminological Research. Discussion Papers (CAN ISSN 0824-5134) **2671**
University of Alberta. Centre for Subatomic Research. Progress Report (CAN ISSN 1193-9796) **3175**
University of Alberta. Department of Computing Science. Technical Reports (CAN ISSN 0316-4683) **2440**
University of Alberta. Studies in Geography. Monographs (CAN) **4032**
• University of Alexandria. Faculty of Medicine. Bulletin (EGY ISSN 1110-0834) **5727**
➤ University of Alexandria. Faculty of Science. Bulletin (EGY ISSN 0568-9619) **7927**
University of Allahabad. Education Department. Researches and Studies (IND ISSN 0084-621X) **2922**
University of Ankara. Faculty of Medicine. Journal *see* Ankara Universitesi. Tip Fakultesi. Mecmuasi **5574**
University of Ankara. Faculty of Science. Communications. Series A1: Mathematics and Statistics (TUR ISSN 1303-5991) **5545**
• University of Ankara. Faculty of Science. Communications. Series A2-A3: Physics, Engineering Physics, Electronic Engineering and Astronomy (TUR ISSN 1303-6009) **3225**
• University of Ankara. Faculty of Science. Communications. Series B: Chemistry and Chemical Engineering (TUR ISSN 1303-6017) **2083**
• University of Ankara. Faculty of Science. Communications. Series C: Biology, Geological Engineering and Geophysical Engineering (TUR ISSN 1303-6025) **2772**
University of Ankara. Faculty of Veterinary Medicine. Journal *see* Ankara Universitesi Veteriner Fakultesi Dergisi **8792**
University of Arizona. Agricultural Experiment Station. Research Report (USA ISSN 0092-4369) **166**
➤ University of Arizona. Anthropological Papers (USA ISSN 0066-7501) **359**
• University of Arkansas at Little Rock Law Review (USA ISSN 1527-5787) **4803**
University of Arkansas. Cooperative Extension Service. Fact Sheet (USA ISSN 1057-1779) **8284**
University of Arkansas. Cooperative Extension Service. M P (USA ISSN 1057-1876) **166**
University of Art and Design Helsinki. Publication Series. F, Working Papers *see* Taideteollinen Korkeakoulu. Julkaisusarja. F, Tyopaperit **521**
• ➤ University of Auckland Business Review (NZL ISSN 1174-9946) **1188**
• University of Auckland. Calendar (NZL ISSN 0112-8337) **3008**
† University of Auckland. Department of Economics. Policy Discussion Papers (NZL ISSN 0112-9759) **8996**
University of Auckland. Department of Economics. Working Paper Series (NZL ISSN 1174-0884) **1188**
University of Auckland. Department of Geography and Environmental Science. Occasional Publication (NZL ISSN 1175-8457) **4032**
University of Auckland. Department of Geography. Occasional Publication *see* University of Auckland. Department of Geography and Environmental Science. Occasional Publication **4032**
• University of Auckland. Department of International Business. Discussion Paper Series (NZL ISSN 1177-4991) **1188**
• University of Auckland. Department of Mathematics. Report Series (NZL ISSN 1173-0889) **5545**
† University of Auckland. Department of Sociology. Working Papers in Sociology (NZL ISSN 1173-2636) **8996**
University of Auckland Historical Society. Annual *see* University of Auckland. Historical Society Annual. Histeria! **4194**
University of Auckland. Historical Society Annual. Histeria! (NZL ISSN 1176-3094) **4194**
University of Auckland News (NZL) **2306**
University of Auckland. School of Business Papers (NZL ISSN 1177-9292) **1188**
• University of Auckland. School of Engineering. Report (NZL ISSN 0111-0136) **3225**
• The University of Baltimore Intellectual Property Law Journal (USA ISSN 1081-5058) **6759**
• University of Baltimore Journal of Environmental Law (USA ISSN 1062-6212) **4803**
• ➤ University of Baltimore Law Forum (USA) **4803**
• University of Baltimore Law Review (USA ISSN 0091-5440) **4803**
• University of Basrah. Marine Science Centre Newsletter (IRQ ISSN 1814-9308) **966**
University of Belgrade. Faculty of Electrical Engineering. Publications Series: Automatic Control/Univerziteta u Beogradu. Elektrotehnickog Fakulteta. Publikacije Serija: Automatika (SRB ISSN 0354-124X) **3333**
University of Belgrade. Faculty of Electrical Engineering. Publications. Series: Engineering Physics/Univerziteta u Beogradu. Elektrotehnicki Fakultet. Publikacije. Serija: Tehnicka Fizika (SRB ISSN 0354-0162) **7044**
University of Belgrade. Faculty of Electrical Engineering. Publications. Series: Mathematics *see* Applicable Analysis and Discrete Mathematics **5471**
University of Belgrade. Faculty of Law. Annals *see* Univerzitet u Beogradu. Pravni Fakultet. Anali **4805**
University of Benin. Library. Annual Report (NGA) **5053**
University of Bergen Archaeological Series International *see* U B A S, International **421**
• University of Bergen. Department of Applied Mathematics. Report (NOR ISSN 0084-778X) **5545**
University of Bergen. Department of Economics. Working Papers in Economics. (Online) (NOR ISSN 1890-0968) **1188**
University of Bergen. Department of Economics. Working Papers in Economics. (Print) *see* University of Bergen. Department of Economics. Working Papers in Economics. (Online) **1188**
• University of Bergen. Department of Mathematics. Statistical Report (NOR ISSN 0333-1865) **5545**
• University of Bergen. Department of Pure Mathematics. Report (NOR ISSN 0332-5407) **5545**
University of Bergen. Institute of Geophysics. Department of Physical Oceanography. Report (NOR ISSN 0525-4760) **2820**
University of Bergen. Reports in Meteorology and Oceanography (NOR ISSN 1502-5519) **6397**
University of Birmingham. Centre for Urban and Regional Studies. Occasional Papers (GBR ISSN 0067-8953) **4429**
University of Birmingham. Centre for Urban and Regional Studies. Research Memorandum (GBR ISSN 0306-4034) **4429**
University of Birmingham. Centre for Urban and Regional Studies. Urban and Regional Studies (GBR ISSN 0067-8961) **4429**
University of Birmingham. Centre for Urban and Regional Studies. Working Paper (GBR) **4429**
University of Birmingham. Department of Economics. Discussion Papers (GBR) **1550**
University of Birmingham. Department of Social Policy and Social Work. Working with Poverty Series (GBR) **8076**
University of Birmingham. Health Services Management Centre. Handbook Series (GBR ISSN 0963-5599) **4112**
➤ University of Birmingham. Institute for Advanced Research in Arts and Social Sciences. Occasional Paper (GBR) **4480**
University of Birmingham. School of Public Policy. Occasional Papers (GBR) **7191**
University of Bombay. Journal (IND ISSN 0304-2286) **8012**
• University of Bradford. Annual Report (GBR) **3008**
➤ University of Bradford. Development and Project Planning Centre. Bradford Development Papers (GBR) **1607**
University of Bradford. School of Management. Working Paper Series (GBR) **1799**
University of Brighton. Business School. Occasional Papers Series (GBR) **1188**
University of Bristol. Department of Economics. Discussion Papers (GBR ISSN 1362-3850) **1188**
University of Bristol. Newsletter (GBR ISSN 0143-1951) **2306**
University of British Columbia. Department of Economics. Discussion Paper (CAN ISSN 0317-0144) **1188**
University of British Columbia. Department of Geological Sciences. Report (CAN ISSN 0705-3207) **2772**
University of British Columbia. Faculty of Forestry. Annual Report (CAN ISSN 1188-9837) **3706**
University of British Columbia. Institute of Oceanography. Data Report (CAN ISSN 0068-1830) **2820**
• ➤ University of British Columbia Law Review (CAN ISSN 0068-1849) **4803**
University of British Columbia. Physics Society. Journal (CAN) **7044**
➤ University of Cairo. Faculty of Medicine. Medical Journal/Al-Majallah al-Tibbiyyah Li-Jami'at Al-Qahirah (EGY ISSN 0045-3803) **5727**
University of Calcutta. Business Studies (IND ISSN 0970-9657) **1188**

Title

▼ *new title* † *ceased* • *electronic media* ➤ *refereed*

10990 UNIVERSITY OF CALCUTTA. DEPARTMENT OF ENGLISH. JOURNAL ULRICH'S PERIODICALS

University of Calcutta. Department of English. Journal (IND) **5393**
University of Calcutta. Department of Sociology. Journal (IND ISSN 0971-0663) **8145**
University of Calgary. Archaeological Association. Archaeological Conference. Proceedings (CAN ISSN 0822-2967) **422**
University of Calgary. Department of Civil Engineering Research Report (CAN) **3286**
• University of Calgary. Department of Mathematics and Statistics. Research Papers (CAN) **5545**
University of Calgary Gazette *see* OnCampus **2295**
University of California at Berkeley. Archaeological Research Facility. Contributions (USA ISSN 0068-5933) **422**
➤ University of California at Berkeley. Center for Chinese Studies. Series (USA) **4189**
➤ University of California at Berkeley. Center for Japanese Studies. Series (USA) **3901**
University of California at Berkeley. Fisher Center for Real Estate and Urban Economics. Reprint Series (USA ISSN 0068-5968) **7614**
University of California at Berkeley. Fisher Center for Real Estate and Urban Economics. Working Paper (USA) **7614**
• University of California at Berkeley. Institute of Transportation Studies. Review (USA ISSN 0192-3994) **8519**
University of California at Berkeley. International and Area Studies. Exploratory Essays (USA) **7271**
University of California at Berkeley. International and Area Studies. Policy Papers in International Affairs (USA ISSN 0731-6321) **7271**
University of California at Berkeley. International and Area Studies. Research Series (USA ISSN 0068-6093) **7271**
University of California at Davis. Game Bird Workshop. Proceedings (USA) **915**
University of California at Los Angeles Bulletin of Law and Technology *see* U C L A Bulletin of Law and Technology **4799**
➤ University of California at Los Angeles. Center for Medieval and Renaissance Studies. Contributions (USA ISSN 0068-6239) **4165**
➤ University of California at Los Angeles. Center for Medieval and Renaissance Studies. Publications (USA ISSN 0068-6220) **4165**
➤ University of California at Los Angeles. Clark Library Professorship. Monographic Series (USA) **4480**
University of California at Los Angeles Entertainment Law Review *see* U C L A Entertainment Law Review **4799**
University of California at Los Angeles. Fowler Museum of Cultural History. Monograph Series (USA) **6539**
University of California at Los Angeles. Fowler Museum of Cultural History. Occasional Papers (USA) **6539**
University of California at Los Angeles. Institute of Archaeology. Monograph Series (USA) **422**
University of California at Los Angeles. Institute of Industrial Relations. Monograph and Research Series (USA ISSN 0739-439X) **1713**
University of California at Los Angeles. James S. Coleman African Studies Center. Newsletter (USA) **4178**
University of California at Los Angeles Journal of International Law and Foreign Affairs *see* U C L A Journal of International Law and Foreign Affairs **4943**
University of California at Los Angeles Journal of Islamic and Near Eastern Law *see* U C L A Journal of Islamic and Near Eastern Law **4799**
University of California at Los Angeles Journal of Law and Technology *see* U C L A Journal of Law and Technology **4799**
University of California at Los Angeles. Latin American Center. Reference Series (USA ISSN 0068-6263) **4316**
University of California at Los Angeles Latin American Studies Latin American Studies *see* U C L A Latin American Studies **4315**
University of California at Los Angeles Law Review *see* U C L A Law Review **4799**
University of California at Los Angeles Pacific Basin Law Journal *see* U C L A Pacific Basin Law Journal **4799**
University of California at Los Angeles Women's Law Journal *see* U C L A Women's Law Journal **4799**
University of California at Oakland. Division of Agriculture and Natural Resources. Leaflet (USA ISSN 1079-9753) **166**
University of California at San Francisco Magazine *see* U C S F Magazine **5725**
University of California at Santa Barbara Daily Nexus *see* U C S B Daily Nexus **2304**
University of California, Berkeley. Center for Latin American Studies. Policy Papers (USA ISSN 1552-9665) **7271**
University of California, Berkeley. Center for Slavic & East European Studies. Newsletter (USA ISSN 1536-4003) **4275**
University of California, Berkeley. Department of Economics. Working Paper (USA ISSN 1932-4286) **1188**
• University of California, Berkeley. Wellness Letter (USA ISSN 0748-9234) **6999**
University of California. Center for Southeast Asia Studies. Monograph (USA) **4189**
University of California Davis Journal of Juvenile Law and Policy *see* U C Davis Journal of Juvenile Law and Policy **2170**
University of California Davis Law Review *see* U C Davis Law Review **4799**
University of California Davis Magazine *see* U C Davis Magazine **3005**
• University of California Hastings College of Law. Public Law Research Institute. Reports (USA) **7474**
• University of California. Institute of Governmental Studies Library. Accessions List (USA ISSN 0041-9443) **7485**
University of California. Institute of Transportation Studies. Library References (USA ISSN 0068-6115) **8532**
University of California, Los Angeles Dissertations in Linguistics *see* U C L A Dissertations in Linguistics **5189**
University of California Los Angeles Journal of Environmental Law and Policy *see* U C L A Journal of Environmental Law and Policy **3471**
University of California, Los Angeles Occasional Papers in Linguistics *see* U C L A Occasional Papers in Linguistics **5189**
University of California, Los Angeles Working Papers in Linguistics *see* U C L A Working Papers in Linguistics **5189**
University of California Los Angeles Working Papers in Phonetics *see* U C L A Working Papers in Phonetics **5190**
University of California, Los Angeles Working Papers in Phonology *see* U C L A Working Papers in Phonology **5190**
University of California, Los Angeles Working Papers in Syntax and Semantics *see* U C L A Working Papers in Syntax and Semantics **5190**
University of California Publications in Botany *see* Constancea **784**
† University of California Publications in Engineering (USA ISSN 0096-9311) **8996**
• ➤ University of California Publications in Entomology (USA ISSN 0068-6417) **860**
➤ University of California Publications in Folklore and Mythology (USA ISSN 0068-6247) **3623**
• ➤ University of California Publications in Geological Sciences (USA ISSN 0068-645X) **2718**
• ➤ University of California Publications in Linguistics (USA ISSN 0068-6484) **5191**
University of California Publications in Philosophy (USA ISSN 0749-1883) **6959**
• ➤ University of California Publications in Zoology (USA ISSN 0068-6506) **966**
University of California Riverside *see* U C R **2304**
➤ University of California, Riverside. Center for Water Resources. Contributions (USA) **8834**
University of California, San Diego Guardian *see* U C S D Guardian **2304**
University of California, Santa Cruz. Institute for Marine Sciences. Special Publication (USA) **2820**
University of California. Seismographic Stations. Bulletin (USA ISSN 0041-946X) **2791**
University of Cambridge. Department of Applied Economics. Working Papers (GBR ISSN 0956-862X) **1188**
• University of Cambridge. Department of Engineering. Annual Report (GBR) **3225**
University of Cambridge. Department of Land Economy. Discussion Paper (GBR) **4429**
University of Cambridge. Faculty of Economics and Politics. Research Paper (GBR) **1188**
University of Cambridge. Institute of Criminology. Cropwood Occasional Papers (GBR) **2671**
• University of Canterbury. Annual Report (NZL ISSN 1171-5774) **3008**
• University of Canterbury. Computer Science and Software Engineering. Technical Report (NZL ISSN 1178-5624) **2599**
† University of Canterbury. Department of Economics. Discussion Paper (NZL ISSN 1171-0705) **8996**
• University of Canterbury. Department of Economics. Working Paper (NZL ISSN 1178-5616) **1188**
University of Cape Coast. Institute of Education. Journal (GHA ISSN 0855-0883) **2922**
University of Cape Town. Committee for Undergraduate Education in Science. Colloquium Series (ZAF) **7927**
University of Cape Town. Department of Geological Sciences. Precambrian Research Unit. Bulletin (ZAF) **2772**
University of Cape Town. Department of Obstetrics and Gynaecology. Annual Report (ZAF ISSN 0254-184X) **6006**
• ➤ University of Cape Town. Research Report (ZAF) **3008**
University of Central England in Birmingham. Faculty of Computing & Information Studies. Research Papers (GBR) **2551**
University of Central England in Birmingham. Faculty of the Built Environment. Research Paper Series (GBR) **4429**
University of Central England in Birmingham. School of Planning. Working Paper Series (GBR) **4429**
• ➤ University of Central Florida Undergraduate Research Journal (USA ISSN 1947-8836) **4480**
➤ University of Chemical Technology and Metallurgy. Journal (BGR ISSN 1311-7629) **3257**
University of Chemical Technology. Annual *see* University of Chemical Technology and Metallurgy. Journal **3257**
University of Chicago. Biological Sciences Division. Pritzker School of Medicine. Alumni Association. Magazine *see* Medicine on the Midway **2291**
• University of Chicago. Center for Research in Security Prices. Working Paper Series (USA ISSN 1931-2997) **1389**
➤ University of Chicago. Geography Research Papers (USA ISSN 1054-206X) **4032**
• ➤ University of Chicago Law Review (USA ISSN 0041-9494) **4803**
University of Chicago Law School. Record *see* Law School Record **8970**
• University of Chicago Legal Forum (USA ISSN 0892-5593) **4803**
University of Chicago Magazine (USA ISSN 0041-9508) **2306**
University of Chicago Oriental Institute. Publications (USA ISSN 0069-3367) **4326**
University of Chicago Oriental Institute Seminars (USA ISSN 1559-2944) **422**
The University of Chicago Publications in Anthropology. Social Anthropological Series (USA ISSN 1942-8421) **359**
University of Chicago Record (USA ISSN 0362-4706) **3008**
➤ University of Chicago Studies in Library Science (USA ISSN 0069-3375) **5053**
• ➤ University of Cincinnati Law Review (USA ISSN 0009-6881) **4803**
University of Cincinnati Office of Information Technologies Now! *see* U C it Now! **2951**
University of Colorado. Business Research Division. Annual Business - Economic Outlook Forum (USA) **1523**
➤ University of Colorado. Institute of Arctic and Alpine Research. Occasional Papers (USA ISSN 0069-6145) **7927**
• University of Colorado Law Review (USA ISSN 0041-9516) **4803**
University of Connecticut. Center for Real Estate and Urban Economic Studies. Annual Report (USA ISSN 0589-381X) **7614**
➤ University of Connecticut. Institute of Water Resources. Report Series (USA ISSN 0069-9063) **8834**
University of Connecticut. Institute of Water Resources. Wetlands Conference. Proceedings (USA) **8834**
➤ University of Copenhagen. Department of Asian Studies. Occasional Papers (DNK) **562**
University of Copenhagen. Department of Physical Oceanography. Report (DNK) **2820**
• University of Copenhagen. Department of Theoretical Statistics. Annual Report (Online Edition) (DNK) **5549**
University of Copenhagen. Institute of Economics. Discussion Papers (DNK ISSN 0902-6452) **1188**
University of Copenhagen. Niels Bohr Institute, Oersted Laboratory. Report (DNK ISSN 0908-617X) **7044**
University of Craiova. Annals. Mathematics and Computer Science Series *see* Universitatea din Craiova. Analele. Seria: Matematica, Informatica **5544**
University of Dallas, Graduate School of Management Chronicle *see* G S M Chronicle **2284**
University of Dar es Salaam. Botany Department. Departmental Herbarium Publications (TZA) **821**
University of Dar es Salaam. Bureau of Resource Assessment and Land Use Planning. Annual Report (TZA ISSN 0084-960X) **3472**
University of Dar es Salaam. Bureau of Resource Assessment and Land Use Planning. Research Paper (TZA ISSN 0084-9626) **3472**
University of Dar es Salaam. Bureau of Resource Assessment and Land Use Planning. Research Report (TZA ISSN 0084-9634) **3472**
University of Dar es Salaam. Faculty of Agriculture, Forestry and Veterinary Science. Annual Record of Research (TZA) **166**
• University of Dar es Salaam Library Journal (TZA ISSN 0856-1818) **5053**
University of Dar es Salaam. Theatre Arts Department. Annual Report (TZA) **8484**
• University of Dayton Law Review (USA ISSN 0162-9174) **4803**
University of Delaware. College of Agricultural Sciences. Longwood Graduate Program Seminars *see* Longwood Graduate Program Seminars **800**
University of Delaware. Disaster Research Center. Dissertations (USA) **2228**
University of Delaware. Disaster Research Center. Final Project Reports (USA) **2228**
University of Delaware. Disaster Research Center. Miscellaneous Reports (USA) **2228**
University of Delaware. Disaster Research Center. Preliminary Papers (USA) **2228**
➤ University of Delaware. Disaster Research Center. Report Series (USA) **2228**
University of Delaware Messenger (USA) **2306**
University of Delaware. Student Center. Review (USA) **2306**
University of Denver Clarion (USA) **2306**
University of Denver Journal (USA) **2306**
University of Denver Water Law Review *see* Water Law Review **8837**
• University of Detroit Mercy Law Review (USA ISSN 1058-4323) **4804**
University of Dhaka. Department of Law. Journal (BGD) **4804**
University of Dundee Students Association Handbook (GBR) **3008**
University of Dundee. Tayside Centre for General Practice. Asthma Research Unit. Progress Report (GBR) **5766**
University of Durban-Westville. Institute for Social and Economic Research. Annual Report (ZAF ISSN 0377-8533) **8012**
University of Durham. Centre for European Studies. Working Papers (GBR) **8012**
• University of Durham. Department of Economics and Finance. Working Paper (GBR) **1389**
University of East Anglia. Accounts (GBR ISSN 0308-6771) **3034**
University of East Anglia. Annual Report of the Vice-Chancellor (GBR ISSN 0546-6660) **3034**
University of East Anglia. Calendar (GBR ISSN 0305-3326) **2962**
University of East Anglia. Librarian's Annual Report *see* University of East Anglia. Librariany Annual Report **5053**
University of East Anglia. Librariany Annual Report (GBR ISSN 1465-5632) **5053**
University of East Anglia. Prospectus (GBR ISSN 0308-6763) **2962**
• University of East Anglia. School of Development Studies. Working Papers (Online) (GBR ISSN 1756-7904) **8012**
University of East Anglia. School of Development Studies. Working Papers (Print) *see* University of East Anglia. School of Development Studies. Working Papers (Online) **8012**
University of East Anglia. School of Economic and Social Studies. Economics Research Centre. Discussion Paper (GBR ISSN 0956-7895) **1188**
University of East London. Centre for New Ethnicities Research. Working Paper (GBR) **8012**
University of Eastern Philippines. Research Center. Report (PHL ISSN 0070-8259) **2922**
University of Edinburgh Bulletin (GBR) **2306**
University of Edinburgh. Department of Archaeology. Occasional Papers (GBR ISSN 0144-3313) **422**
University of Edinburgh. Department of Archaeology. Project Papers (GBR ISSN 0266-1799) **422**
University of Edinburgh. Department of Politics. Working Paper Series (GBR) **7271**
• University of Edinburgh. Economics. Discussion Papers (GBR ISSN 1749-4427) **1188**
University of Edinburgh Journal (GBR ISSN 0041-9567) **2306**
University of Electro-Communications. Bulletin *see* Denki Tsushin Daigaku Kiyo **2318**
University of Electronic Science and Technology of China. Journal *see* Dianzi Keji Daxue Xuebao **8420**
University of Electronic Science and Technology of China. Journal (Social Sciences Edition) *see* Dianzi Keji Daxue Xuebao (Shehui Kexue Xuebao) **7959**
University of Engineering and Technology. Research Bulletin (PAK) **3286**
University of Engineering and Technology Taxila. Technical Journal (PAK ISSN 1813-1786) **3225**
University of Essex. Department of Accounting and Financial Management. Working Paper Series (GBR ISSN 1368-8286) **1303**
University of Essex. Department of Economics. Discussion Paper Series (GBR ISSN 0950-0464) **1188**
University of Essex. Department of Language & Linguistics. Essex Research Reports in Linguistics *see* Essex Research Reports in Linguistics **5116**
University of Exeter. Discussion Papers in Economics (GBR) **1188**
University of Florida. Department of Accounting. Accounting Series (USA ISSN 0071-6065) **1303**
University of Florida. Food and Resource Economics Department. Economic Information Report (USA ISSN 0886-4845) **208**
University of Florida. Institute of Food and Agricultural Sciences. Florida Agricultural Experiment Station. Circular (USA ISSN 0734-8452) **166**
• ➤ The University of Florida Journal of Anthropology (USA) **359**
University of Florida Journal of Law & Public Policy *see* Journal of Law & Public Policy **4702**
University of Florida Monographs. Humanities (USA ISSN 0071-6189) **4480**
University of Florida Monographs. Social Sciences (USA ISSN 0071-6197) **8012**
University of Fribourg. Series in Computer Science (CHE ISSN 0940-9580) **2440**
University of Galati Dunarea de Jos. Annals. Fascicle III. Electrotechnics, Electronics, Automatic Control and Informatics *see* Universitatea "Dunarea de Jos" din Galati. Analele. Fascicula III. Electrotehnica, Electronica, Automatica, Informatica **3115**
University of Georgia. Agricultural Experiment Stations. Southern Cooperative Series Bulletin (USA ISSN 0096-8498) **257**
University of Georgia. College of Agriculture. Cooperative Extension Service. Leaflet (USA ISSN 0090-2764) **166**

DIRECTORY 2010 UNIVERSITY OF LOUISVILLE LAW REVIEW 10991

University of Georgia. Cooperative Extension Service. Bulletin (USA ISSN 0092-9077) **166**
University of Georgia. Georgia Agricultural Experiment Stations. Research Bulletin (USA) **166**
• University of Georgia. Georgia Agricultural Experiment Stations. Research Report (Online) (USA) **166**
• University of Georgia. Georgia Agricultural Experiment Stations. Research Reports (Print) (USA) **166**
University of Georgia. Institute of Ecology. Annual Report (USA ISSN 0094-9205) **3472**
University of Ghana. Institute of African Studies. Collected Language Notes (GHA) **5191**
University of Ghana. Institute of African Studies. Local Studies Series (GHA ISSN 0533-8646) **359**
University of Ghana. Institute of African Studies. Research Review (GHA ISSN 0020-2703) **5243**
University of Ghana. Institute of Statistical, Social and Economic Research. Discussion Papers (GHA) **8012**
University of Ghana. Institute of Statistical, Social and Economic Research. Technical Publication Series (GHA) **1273**
➤ University of Ghana Law Journal (GHA ISSN 0041-9605) **4804**
University of Ghana Population Studies *see* Ghana Population Studies **7283**
University of Glasgow. Department of Archaeology. Occasional Paper Series (GBR) **422**
• University of Glasgow. Newsletter (GBR ISSN 0267-6311) **3008**
• University of Goeteborg. Center for Public Sector Research. Working Papers (SWE ISSN 1653-3895) **7474**
University of Gothenburg. Department of Sociology. Monograph (SWE ISSN 1100-3618) **8145**
University of Groningen. Groningen Growth and Development Centre. Research Memorandum (NLD) **1188**
University of Guelph. Department of Land Resource Science. Progress Report (CAN ISSN 0085-1329) **257**
University of Guelph Library. Collection Update (CAN ISSN 0226-3300) **5053**
University of Hartford Observer (USA ISSN 0747-3028) **2306**
University of Hawaii. Industrial Relations Center. Occasional Publications (USA ISSN 0073-1226) **1713**
• University of Hawaii Law Review (USA ISSN 0271-9835) **4804**
University of Hawaii. Matsunga Institute for Peace. Annual Report (USA) **7272**
University of Hawaii. Sea Grant College Program. Technical Report (USA) **2820**
➤ University of Hawaii. Water Resources Research Center. Technical Report (USA ISSN 0073-1307) **8834**
University of Healing. Syllabus (USA ISSN 0733-0375) **2922**
University of Helsinki. Department of Animal Science. Publications *see* Helsingin Yliopisto. Kotielaintieteen Laitos. Julkaisuja **288**
University of Helsinki. Department of Applied Sciences of Education. Research Report *see* Helsingin Yliopisto. Soveltavan Kasvatustieteen Laitos. Tukimuksia **2863**
University of Helsinki. Department of Applied Zoology. Reports *see* Helsingin Yliopisto. Soveltavan Elaintieteen Laitos. Julkaisuja **945**
University of Helsinki. Department of Economics and Management. Publications *see* Helsingin Yliopisto. Taloustieteen Laitos. Julkaisuja **1118**
University of Helsinki. Department of Economics and Management. Working Papers *see* Helsingin Yliopisto. Taloustieteen Laitos. Selvityksia **1118**
University of Helsinki. Department of Education. Research Bulletin (FIN ISSN 0359-5749) **2922**
University of Helsinki. Department of Forest Ecology. Publications *see* Helsingin Yliopisto. Metsaekologian Laitos. Julkaisuja **3692**
University of Helsinki. Faculty of Veterinary Medicine. Publications *see* Helsingin Yliopisto. Elainlaaketieteellinen Tiedekunta. Julkaisuja **8798**
University of Helsinki. Institute for Co-operative Studies. Publications (FIN ISSN 0356-1364) **1425**
University of Helsinki. Institute of Seismology. Publications (FIN ISSN 0079-774X) **2791**
University of Hertfordshire. Business School. Working Paper Series (GBR) **1188**
University of Hertfordshire. Numerical Optimisation Centre. Technical Report (GBR ISSN 1366-5251) **5545**
University of Hong Kong. Centre of Asian Studies. Bibliographies and Research Guides (HKG ISSN 0441-1900) **564**
University of Hong Kong. Centre of Asian Studies. Occasional Papers and Monographs (HKG ISSN 0378-2689) **563**
University of Houston Series in Mexican American Studies (USA) **3570**
University of Hull. Department of Sociology and Social Anthropology. Occasional Papers (GBR) **8145**
University of Ibadan. Institute of Education. Annual Report (NGA ISSN 0331-0817) **2922**
University of Ibadan. Institute of Education. Occasional Publications (NGA ISSN 0073-4314) **2923**
University of Ibadan. Library. Annual Report (NGA ISSN 0073-4322) **5053**
University of Ibadan. Library. Library Record (NGA ISSN 0046-8436) **5053**
University of Ibadan. Student Affairs Office. Student Handbook of Information on University Policies and Practices (NGA ISSN 0331-0809) **3008**
University of Iceland Bibliography *see* Haskola Islands. Ritaskra **2862**
• ➤ University of Iceland. Centre for Small State Studies. Occasional Paper (ISL ISSN 1670-4290) **1188**
• ➤ University of Iceland. Centre for Small State Studies. Working Paper (ISL ISSN 1670-4304) **1188**
University of Iceland. Institute of Business Research. Working Paper Series *see* Haskoli Islands. Vidskiptafraedistofnun. Working Paper Series **1117**
University of Iceland. Institute of Economic Studies. Working Paper Series (ISL ISSN 1670-0090) **1550**
University of Idaho. Agricultural Experiment Station. Bulletin (USA) **166**
University of Idaho. Agricultural Experiment Station. Research Bulletin (USA ISSN 0097-0689) **166**
University of Idaho Argonaut *see* Argonaut (Moscow) **2272**
University of Idaho. Forest, Wildlife and Range Experiment Station, Moscow. Station Bulletin (USA ISSN 0073-4586) **2630**
University of Idaho. Water Resources Research Institute. Annual Report (USA ISSN 0073-4616) **8834**
University of Ife. Faculty of Arts. Lecture Series (NGA) **4480**
University of Illinois at Chicago Alumni Magazine *see* U I C Alumni Magazine **2305**
University of Illinois at Chicago. College of Dentistry. Alumni Report (USA ISSN 1088-9108) **2306**
University of Illinois at Urbana-Champaign. Center for International Education and Research in Accounting. Monographs (USA ISSN 0073-5191) **1303**
• University of Illinois at Urbana-Champaign. College of Commerce and Business Administration. Office of Research. Results (USA ISSN 1097-5438) **1188**
University of Illinois at Urbana-Champaign. Cooperative Extension Service. Circular (USA ISSN 0360-9812) **166**
University of Illinois at Urbana-Champaign. Department of Agricultural Economics. Agricultural Finance Program Report (USA ISSN 0073-5213) **208**
University of Illinois at Urbana-Champaign. Department of Agricultural Economics. Lease Shares and Farm Returns (USA) **208**
University of Illinois at Urbana-Champaign, Department of Computer Science Report Series *see* U I U C D C S. Report Series **2440**
University of Illinois at Urbana-Champaign, Department of Theoretical and Applied Mechanics Report *see* T & A M Report **3358**
• University of Illinois at Urbana-Champaign. Engineering Experiment Station. Summary of Engineering Research (USA ISSN 0073-5280) **3225**
University of Illinois at Urbana-Champaign. Graduate School of Library and Information Science. Newsletter (USA) **5053**
University of Illinois at Urbana-Champaign. Graduate School of Library and Information Science. Occasional Papers (USA ISSN 0276-1769) **5053**
University of Illinois at Urbana-Champaign. School of Art and Design. Newsletter (USA) **523**
University of Illinois at Urbana-Champaign. Water Resources Center. Annual Report (USA ISSN 0073-5434) **8834**
➤ University of Illinois at Urbana-Champaign. Water Resources Center. Research Report (USA ISSN 0073-5442) **8834**
University of Illinois at Urbana-Champaign. Water Resources Center. Special Reports (USA ISSN 0733-0502) **8834**
University of Illinois. Institute of Government and Public Affairs. Working Papers (USA) **7504**
• ➤ University of Illinois Journal of Law, Technology and Policy (USA ISSN 1532-3242) **4804**
• ➤ University of Illinois Law Review (USA ISSN 0276-9948) **4804**
University of Illinois. School of Architecture - Building Research Council. Council Notes (USA) **1042**
University of Illinois. School of Architecture - Building Research Council. Technical Notes (USA ISSN 0073-5426) **1042**
• University of Iowa. Libraries. News! (USA) **5053**
University of Iowa. School of Library and Information Science. News (USA) **5053**
University of Istanbul. Faculty of Forestry. Review *see* Istanbul Universitesi Orman Fakultesi Dergisi, Seri A **3694**
University of Istanbul. Faculty of Science. The Journal of Mathematics *see* Istanbul Universitesi. Fen Fakultesi. Matematik Dergisi **8967**
University of Istanbul. Faculty of Veterinary Medicine. Journal *see* Istanbul Universitesi. Veteriner Fakultesi Dergisi **8800**
• University of Joensuu. Department of Computer Science and Statistics. Dissertations (FIN ISSN 1796-8100) **2440**
University of Joensuu. Department of Computer Science. Dissertations *see* University of Joensuu. Department of Computer Science and Statistics. Dissertations **2440**
University of Joensuu. Department of Sociology. Studies in Sociology *see* Joensuun Yliopisto. Sosiologian Laitos. Sosiologian Turkimuksia **8111**
University of Jos. Centre for Development Studies. Development Studies Review (NGA) **1523**
University of Jyvaskyla. Department of Mathematics and Statistics. Dissertations *see* Jyvaskylan Yliopisto. Matematiikan ja Tilastotieteen Laitos. Vaitokset **5507**
➤ University of Jyvaskyla. Department of Mathematics and Statistics. Report (FIN ISSN 1457-8905) **5545**
University of Jyvaskyla. Department of Mathematics. Report *see* University of Jyvaskyla. Department of Mathematics and Statistics. Report **5545**
University of Jyvaskyla. Department of Music. Research Reports *see* Jyvaskylan Yliopisto. Musiikin Laitos. Julkaisusarja. A, Tutkielmia ja Raportteja **6581**
University of Jyvaskyla. Department of Physics. Preprints (FIN) **7044**
University of Jyvaskylan. Department of Biological and Environmental Sciences. Research Reports *see* Jyvaskylan Yliopisto. Bio- ja Ymparistotieteiden Laitos. Tiedonantoja **685**
University of Kansas. Center for East Asian Studies. International Studies: East Asian Series. Reference Series (USA ISSN 0070-8070) **4189**
University of Kansas. Center for East Asian Studies. International Studies: East Asian Series. Research Series (USA ISSN 0070-8062) **4190**
➤ University of Kansas. Department of Anthropology. Publications in Anthropology (USA ISSN 0085-2457) **359**
University of Kansas Humanistic Studies (USA ISSN 0085-2473) **4480**
• University of Kansas Law Review (USA ISSN 0083-4025) **4804**
University of Kansas Libraries. Library Series. (USA ISSN 0075-5001) **5053**
➤ University of Kansas. Natural History Museum. Scientific Papers (USA ISSN 1094-0782) **7927**
• ➤ University of Kansas. Paleontological Contributions. New Series (USA ISSN 1046-8390) **6731**
University of Kansas Publications in Anthropology *see* University of Kansas. Department of Anthropology. Publications in Anthropology **359**
University of Karachi. Department of Geography. Geographical Papers (PAK ISSN 1991-8739) **4032**
University of Kashmir. Annual Report (IND) **3008**
University of Keele. Department of Economics. Working Paper (GBR ISSN 1352-8955) **1188**
University of Kentucky. Agricultural Experiment Station. Bulletin (USA ISSN 0097-0891) **166**
University of Kentucky. Agricultural Experiment Station. Progress Report (USA ISSN 0361-154X) **166**
University of Kentucky. Agricultural Experiment Station. Regulatory Bulletin (USA ISSN 0096-7343) **166**
University of Kentucky Art Museum Newsletter (USA) **6539**
University of Kentucky. College of Agriculture. Cooperative Extension Service. H O (USA ISSN 1057-2988) **3753**
University of Kentucky. Cooperative Extension Service. A G R (USA ISSN 0095-2486) **166**
University of Kentucky. Cooperative Extension Service. A S C (USA ISSN 0095-2494) **166**
University of Kentucky Libraries. Occasional Papers (USA ISSN 0743-8915) **5053**
University of Kentucky. Water Resources Research Institute. Research Report (USA ISSN 0277-884X) **8834**
University of Kerala. Department of Tamil. Research Papers (IND) **5192**
University of Khartoum. Development Studies and Research Centre. Discussion Papers (SDN) **1607**
University of Khartoum. Development Studies and Research Centre. Monograph Series (SDN) **1607**
University of Khartoum. Development Studies and Research Centre. Occasional Papers (SDN) **1607**
University of Khartoum. Library Bulletin (SDN) **5053**
University of KwaZulu-Natal, Centre for Social and Development Studies Working Papers *see* C S D S Working Papers **7952**
University of KwaZulu-Natal. Institute for Social and Economic Research. Report *see* I S E R Report **7971**
University of KwaZulu-Natal. School of Development Studies. Policy Brief (ZAF ISSN 1607-2715) **1607**
• University of La Verne Law Review (USA ISSN 1944-382X) **4915**
University of Lagos. Human Resources Research Unit. Monograph (NGA) **7295**
University of Lagos. Inaugural Lecture Series (NGA ISSN 0075-7659) **4480**
University of Lagos. Library. Annual Report (NGA ISSN 0075-7705) **5053**
University of Lausanne. Institut de Linguistique et des Sciences du Langage. Cahiers (CHE ISSN 1019-9446) **5192**
University of Leeds. Computing Based Learning Unit. C B L U Technical Reports (GBR) **2440**
University of Leeds. Department of Civil Engineering. Research Monographs in Tropical Public Health Engineering (GBR) **3286**
University of Leeds. Department of Colour Chemistry and Dyeing. Report (GBR) **2244**
University of Leeds. Department of Linguistics and Phonetics. Leeds Working Papers in Linguistics *see* Leeds Working Papers in Linguistics **5143**
University of Leeds. Department of Linguistics and Phonetics. Leeds Working Papers in Linguistics and Phonetics *see* Leeds Working Papers in Linguistics and Phonetics **5143**
University of Leeds. Leeds University Business School. Discussion Paper Series (GBR ISSN 1461-0264) **1188**
University of Leeds. School of Geography. Working Paper (GBR) **4032**
University of Leeds. School of Sociology and Social Policy. Research Working Paper (GBR) **8145**
University of Leeds. Universities Association for Continuing Education. Conference Proceedings (GBR) **2947**
University of Leicester. Centre for European Economic Studies. Discussion Papers in European Economic Studies (GBR ISSN 1363-8211) **1188**
University of Leicester. Department of Geography. Faculty of Social Sciences. Discussion Papers in Geography (GBR ISSN 1363-7207) **4032**
➤ University of Leicester Discussion Papers in Mass Communications (GBR ISSN 1363-7185) **8145**
University of Leicester Discussion Papers in Politics (GBR ISSN 1363-7177) **7191**
University of Leicester. Quality Audit Report (GBR) **3008**
• University of Leicester. X-Ray Astronomy Group. Special Report (GBR) **583**
University of Leiden. Department of Pottery Technology. Newsletter *see* Leiden Journal of Pottery Studies **403**
University of Liverpool Calendar (GBR ISSN 0305-9227) **3008**
University of Liverpool Post Graduate Prospectus (GBR) **2963**
University of Liverpool Prospectus (GBR ISSN 0268-2362) **3008**
University of Ljubljana. Biotechnical Faculty. Research Reports *see* Acta Agriculturae Slovenica **216**
➤ University of Lodz. Department of Logic. Bulletin of the Section of Logic (POL ISSN 0138-0680) **5545**
University of London. Australian Studies Centre. Working Papers in Australian Studies *see* London Papers in Australian Studies **3548**
University of London. Contemporary China Institute. Research Notes and Studies (GBR ISSN 0308-6119) **563**
University of London Heath Clark Lectures (GBR ISSN 0073-1536) **5727**
• University of London. Institute of Classical Studies. Bulletin (GBR ISSN 0076-0730) **2241**
University of London. Institute of Classical Studies. Bulletin Supplement (GBR ISSN 0076-0749) **2241**
University of London. Institute of Commonwealth Studies. Annual Report (GBR ISSN 0076-0781) **8012**
University of London. Institute of Commonwealth Studies. Collected Seminar Papers (GBR ISSN 0076-0773) **8012**
▼ • University of London. Institute of Education. Occasional Papers in Work-Based Learning (GBR ISSN 1753-0385) **2923**
University of London. Institute of Education. Viewpoint (GBR ISSN 1476-6841) **2923**
University of London. Institute of Germanic Studies. Bithell Memorial Lectures (GBR ISSN 0144-9850) **5393**
➤ University of London. Institute of Germanic Studies. Bithell Series of Dissertations (GBR ISSN 0266-7932) **5393**
University of London. Institute of Germanic Studies. Library Publications (GBR ISSN 0076-0803) **5408**
➤ University of London. Institute of Germanic Studies. Publications (GBR ISSN 0076-0811) **5393**
University of London. Pensions Institute. Discussion Papers (GBR ISSN 1367-580X) **1188**
• ➤ University of London. School of Oriental and African Studies. Bulletin (GBR ISSN 0041-977X) **4480**
University of London. School of Oriental and African Studies. School of Law. Occasional Paper (GBR ISSN 1362-4911) **563**
University of London. School of Slavonic and East European Studies. Library. Bibliographical Guides (GBR ISSN 0140-7260) **638**
University of London. Sir Robert Menzies Centre for Australian Studies. Working Paper (GBR) **8012**
• University of Louisville Law Review (USA) **4915**

Title

10992 UNIVERSITY OF LUND. ARCHEOLOGICAL INSTITUTE. PAPERS ULRICH'S PERIODICALS

University of Lund. Archeological Institute. Papers. Yearbook/Meddelande fraan Lunds Universitet Historiska Museum (SWE) **422**
University of Lund. Department of Archaeology and Ancient History. Report Series (SWE ISSN 0281-3440) **4165**
• University of Lund. Faculty of Medicine. Doctoral Dissertation Series (SWE ISSN 1652-8220) **5727**
University of Lund. Institute of Archaeology. Annual Report (SWE ISSN 0284-5393) **422**
University of Maine. Cooperative Extension. Publications Catalog (USA) **638**
University of Maine Law Review *see* Maine Law Review **4727**
University of Maine. Sea Grant Publication (USA) **966**
University of Maine Today *see* U Maine Today **2921**
University of Malawi Libraries. Bulletin (MWI) **5053**
University of Malawi Libraries. Report to the Senate on the University Libraries (MWI ISSN 0085-3038) **5053**
University of Malta. Annual Report (MLT) **3008**
• ➤ University of Manchester. Department of Computer Science. Technical Report Series (GBR ISSN 1361-6153) **2440**
University of Manchester. Department of Planning and Landscape. Occasional Papers (GBR) **4429**
University of Manchester. Faculty of Law. Working Papers (GBR) **4804**
University of Manchester Institute of Science and Technology Control Systems Centre Series *see* U M I S T Control Systems Centre Series **2464**
University of Manchester, Manchester Centre for Political Thought Working Paper Series *see* M A N C E P T Working Paper Series **7152**
University of Manchester. S P A Working Paper (GBR ISSN 1363-0687) **4032**
University of Manchester. School of Arts, Histories and Cultures. Working Papers in Economic and Social History *see* Manchester Papers in Economic and Social History **7984**
University of Manchester. School of Economic Studies. Discussion Paper (GBR) **1523**
University of Manchester. School of Economic Studies. Farm Business Unit. Bulletin (GBR) **208**
University of Manchester. Spatial Policy Analysis Working Paper *see* University of Manchester. S P A Working Paper **4032**
• ➤ University of Manchester. The Centre for International Politics. Working Paper Series (GBR ISSN 1754-2839) **7272**
University of Manila Law Gazette (PHL ISSN 0041-9796) **4804**
University of Manitoba. Alumni Journal (CAN ISSN 0706-9847) **2306**
University of Manitoba Anthropology Papers (CAN ISSN 0227-0072) **359**
University of Manitoba. Faculty of Agricultural and Food Sciences. Annual Progress Review (CAN) **166**
University of Manitoba Libraries. Annual Report (CAN ISSN 1719-8534) **5053**
University of Manitoba. Transport Institute. Occasional Paper (CAN ISSN 0841-8659) **8519**
University of Manitoba. Transport Institute. Quadrennial Report (CAN) **8519**
University of Manitoba. Transport Institute. Research Bulletin (CAN ISSN 0845-762X) **8519**
University of Manitoba. Transport Institute. Study Report (CAN) **8519**
University of Maryland Center for Environmental and Estuarine Studies. Chesapeake Biological Laboratory. Report *see* University of Maryland Center for Environmental Science. Chesapeake Biological Laboratory. Report **709**
University of Maryland Center for Environmental Science. Chesapeake Biological Laboratory. Report (USA) **709**
University of Maryland. College of Library and Information Services. Technical Report Series (USA) **5053**
University of Maryland. Cooperative Extension Service. Fact Sheet (USA ISSN 0093-0091) **166**
• University of Maryland Law Journal of Race, Religion, Gender and Class (USA ISSN 1554-4796) **4804**
University of Maryland. Medical Alumni Association. Bulletin (USA ISSN 1048-9606) **2306**
University of Maryland. Sea Grant Program. Publications (USA) **2820**
University of Maryland. Sea Grant Program. Technical Report (USA) **2820**
University of Massachusetts Lowell Connector *see* The UMass Lowell Connector **2305**
University of Massachusetts Magazine (USA) **2307**
University of Mauritius. Annual Report (MUS) **3009**
University of Mauritius. Journal: Law, Management & Social Science (MUS ISSN 1694-0350) **4804**
University of Mauritius. Journal: Social Sciences, Humanities, Law and Management *see* University of Mauritius. Journal: Law, Management & Social Science **4804**
University of Mauritius Research Journal. Science & Technology (MUS ISSN 1694-0342) **7927**
• University of Melbourne. Department of Economics. Research Paper (AUS ISSN 1832-2417) **1188**
University of Melbourne. Department of Electrical Engineering. Research Report (AUS ISSN 0085-3259) **3333**
➤ University of Memphis. Anthropological Research Center. Occasional Papers (USA ISSN 0564-8602) **359**
University of Memphis. Center for Research on Women. Center News (USA) **8904**
University of Memphis. Center for Research on Women. Curriculum Integration Series (USA) **8904**
University of Memphis. Center for Research on Women. Research Papers (USA) **8904**
• University of Memphis Law Review (USA ISSN 1080-8582) **4804**
• University of Miami. Business Law Review (USA) **4804**
University of Miami, Coral Gables. Law Center. Philip E. Heckering Institute on Estate Planning. Annual *see* Heckerling Institute on Estate Planning. Annual **4903**
† • University of Miami Entertainment & Sports Law Review (USA ISSN 1051-2225) **8996**
University of Miami. International and Comparative Law Review *see* International & Comparative Law Review **4929**
• University of Miami Law Review (USA ISSN 0041-9818) **4804**
University of Miami. Rosenstiel School of Marine & Atmospheric Science. Technical Report (USA) **6397**
➤ University of Michigan. Division of Research Development and Administration. Research News (USA ISSN 0041-9842) **3009**
➤ University of Michigan. Herbarium. Contributions (USA ISSN 0091-1860) **821**
University of Michigan. International Institute. Journal *see* I I **7240**
• University of Michigan Journal of Law Reform (USA ISSN 0363-602X) **4804**
University of Michigan. Museum of Anthropology. Anthropological Papers (USA ISSN 0076-8367) **359**
University of Michigan. Museum of Anthropology. Memoirs (USA ISSN 0076-8375) **359**
University of Michigan. Museum of Anthropology. Technical Reports (USA ISSN 0196-8297) **359**
➤ University of Michigan. Museum of Paleontology. Contributions (USA ISSN 0097-3556) **6731**
➤ University of Michigan. Museum of Paleontology. Papers on Paleontology (USA ISSN 0148-3838) **6731**
➤ University of Michigan. Museum of Zoology. Miscellaneous Publications (USA ISSN 0076-8405) **966**
➤ University of Michigan. Museum of Zoology. Occasional Papers (USA ISSN 0076-8413) **966**
University of Michigan. Museum of Zoology. Special Publications (USA ISSN 1053-6477) **966**
➤ University of Michigan. Museums of Art and Archaeology. Bulletin (USA ISSN 0270-1642) **6539**
University of Michigan. Population Studies Center. Report (USA) **7295**
University of Michigan. Population Studies Center. Research Report Series (USA) **7295**
University of Michigan. School of Dentistry. Alumni Bulletin (USA ISSN 0887-4387) **5868**
University of Michigan, Transportation Research Institute Research Review *see* U M T R I Research Review **8518**
University of Minnesota, Center for Advanced Feminist Studies Quarterly *see* C A F S Quarterly **8894**
University of Minnesota. Center for Cognitive Sciences. Report (USA) **3034**
University of Minnesota. Center for Cognitive Sciences. Report and Fellowship Offerings *see* University of Minnesota. Center for Cognitive Sciences. Report **3034**
University of Minnesota. Center for Natural Resource Policy and Management. Working Papers (USA) **8834**
University of Minnesota. Economic Development Center. Bulletin (USA) **1188**
University of Miskolc Bulletin. Series F. Economic Sciences *see* Business Studies **1076**
University of Miskolc. Publications. Physics *see* Computational and Applied Physics **7009**
University of Miskolc. Publications. Series A, Mining *see* University of Miskolc. Publications. Series A, Mining. Process Engineering **6482**
University of Miskolc. Publications. Series A, Mining *see* University of Miskolc. Publications. Series A, Mining. Petroleum and Natural Gas **6796**
University of Miskolc. Publications. Series A, Mining *see* University of Miskolc. Publications. Series A, Mining. Mining and Geotechnology **6482**
University of Miskolc. Publications. Series A, Mining. Mining and Geotechnology (HUN ISSN 1417-5428) **6482**
University of Miskolc. Publications. Series A, Mining. Petroleum and Natural Gas (HUN ISSN 1417-5401) **6796**
University of Miskolc. Publications. Series A, Mining. Process Engineering (HUN ISSN 1417-541X) **6482**
University of Miskolc. Publications. Series B, Metallurgy (HUN ISSN 1219-4255) **6336**
University of Miskolc. Publications. Series C, Mechanical Engineering (HUN ISSN 1217-3010) **3398**
University of Miskolc. Publications. Series D. Natural Sciences *see* Computational and Applied Physics **7009**
University of Miskolc. Publications. Series D. Natural Sciences. Mathematics *see* Miscolc Mathematical Notes **5518**
➤ University of Missouri at Columbia. Museum of Anthropology. Miscellaneous Publications in Anthropology (USA) **359**
University of Missouri at Columbia. Museum of Anthropology. Museum Briefs (USA ISSN 0362-1235) **359**
University of Missouri at Kansas City Law Review *see* U M K C Law Review **4799**
➤ University of Missouri Monographs in Anthropology (USA) **359**
University of Missouri Observatory. Publications (USA ISSN 1942-7255) **583**
University of Montana. Forest and Conservation Experiment Station, Missoula. Miscellaneous Publications (USA ISSN 0888-6229) **3706**
University of Montana. Forest and Conservation Experiment Station, Missoula. Research Notes (USA ISSN 0077-1163) **3706**
University of Nairobi. Institute for Development Studies. Consultancy Reports (KEN) **1607**
University of Nairobi. Institute for Development Studies. Discussion Paper (KEN ISSN 0547-1788) **1607**
University of Nairobi. Institute for Development Studies. Occasional Paper (KEN) **1607**
University of Nairobi. Institute for Development Studies. Working Paper (KEN ISSN 1015-6704) **4179**
University of Namibia, Social Sciences Division Discussion Papers *see* S S D Discussion Papers **7998**
University of Namibia, Social Sciences Division Research Reports *see* S S D Research Reports **7998**
University of Natal. Centre for Social and Development Studies. Annual Report (ZAF) **8012**
University of Natal. Centre for Social and Development Studies. C S D S Research Reports (ZAF) **8013**
University of Natal. Centre for Social and Development Studies. Publication Catalogue (ZAF) **8013**
University of Nebraska. Agricultural Experiment Station. Miscellaneous Publication (USA) **167**
University of Nebraska. Agricultural Research Division. Research Bulletin (USA ISSN 1042-2889) **167**
University of Nebraska Medical Center Discover *see* U N M C Discover **5725**
• University of Nebraska State Museum. Bulletin (USA ISSN 0093-6812) **709**
University of Nebraska State Museum. Museum Notes (USA ISSN 0041-9885) **6539**
University of Nebraska. Water Center. Annual Report of Activities (USA) **8834**
University of Nevada. Basque Studies Program Newsletter (USA ISSN 1047-2932) **3570**
University of Nevada, Las Vegas Gaming Research & Review Journal *see* U N L V Gaming Research & Review Journal **8213**
University of Nevada Las Vegas Journal of Anthropology *see* U N L V Journal of Anthropology **359**
University of Nevada Las Vegas Journal of Hospitality, Tourism & Leisure Science *see* U N L V Journal of Hospitality, Tourism & Leisure Science **4399**
University of Nevada Las Vegas Magazine *see* U N L V Magazine **2305**
University of Nevada. Seismological Laboratory. Bulletin (USA ISSN 0092-4288) **2791**
University of New Brunswick Law Journal *see* U N B Law Journal **4799**
• University of New England. Annual Report (AUS ISSN 0375-4588) **3009**
University of New England. Centre for Ecological Economics & Water Policy Research. Occasional Papers (No.) (AUS) **8834**
† University of New England. Centre for Water Policy Research. Discussion Papers (No.) (AUS ISSN 1038-3859) **8996**
University of New England. Centre for Water Policy Research. Resources Policy (AUS) **8834**
The University of New England Law Journal *see* The U N E Law Journal **4799**
• University of New England. School of Economic Studies, Econometrics Discipline. Working Papers in Econometrics and Applied Statistics (Online) (AUS ISSN 1449-0633) **8413**
† • University of New England. Teaching & Learning Centre. Updates (AUS ISSN 1443-3435) **8996**
➤ University of New Hampshire Magazine (USA) **2307**
University of New Hampshire. Sea Grant College Program. Report (USA) **2820**
University of New Mexico Art Museum. Bulletin (USA ISSN 0077-8583) **6539**
University of New Mexico. C I R T Newsletter (Computer & Information Resources & Technology) (USA) **2440**
University of New Mexico. Division of Government Research. Monograph Series (USA ISSN 0194-2670) **7474**
➤ University of New Mexico. Institute of Meteoritics. Special Publication (USA ISSN 0085-3968) **583**
University of New Mexico. Latin American and Iberian Institute. Research Paper Series (USA) **8013**
University of New Mexico. Latin American Institute. Research Paper Series *see* University of New Mexico. Latin American and Iberian Institute. Research Paper Series **8013**
University of New Mexico. Museum of Southwestern Biology. Occasional Papers (USA ISSN 0749-2421) **709**
University of New Mexico. Office of Research Services. Research Notes (USA) **3009**
The University of New South Wales at the Australian Defence Force Academy . Alumni Newsletter *see* Australian Defence Force Academy . Alumni Newsletter **8933**
University of New South Wales. College of Fine Arts. Newsletter *see* Incubate **496**
University of New South Wales Compendium of Good Practice in Learning and Teaching *see* U N S W Compendium of Good Practice in Learning and Teaching **2921**
• University of New South Wales. Handbook (AUS) **2923**
• ➤ University of New South Wales Law Journal (AUS ISSN 0313-0096) **4804**
University of New South Wales Law Journal Forum *see* University of New South Wales Law Journal **4804**
University of New South Wales. Library. Annual Report (AUS ISSN 0313-427X) **5053**
University of New South Wales. Postgraduate Handbook (Print) *see* University of New South Wales. Handbook **2923**
University of New South Wales. School of Civil Engineering. U N I C I V Reports. Series R (AUS ISSN 0077-880X) **3286**
University of New South Wales. School of Economics. Discussion Paper (AUS ISSN 1323-8949) **1189**
University of New South Wales. Undergraduate Handbook (Print) *see* University of New South Wales. Handbook **2923**
University of New South Wales. Water Research Laboratory, Manly Vale. Laboratory Research Reports (AUS ISSN 0077-8818) **8834**
University of New South Wales. Water Research Library. Water Information Update (AUS) **8843**
University of Newcastle. Agricultural Society. Journal (GBR ISSN 0267-8640) **167**
University of Newcastle. Department of Electrical and Computer Engineering. Technical Report EE (AUS) **2474**
University of Newcastle. Transport Operations Research Group. Research Report (GBR ISSN 1467-5110) **8519**
University of Newcastle upon Tyne. Calendar (GBR ISSN 0545-8005) **2963**
University of Newcastle-upon-Tyne. Computing Science. Technical Report Series (GBR) **2440**
University of Newcastle upon Tyne. Department of Agricultural Economics and Food Marketing. Report (GBR ISSN 0963-6536) **167**
University of Newcastle-upon-Tyne. Department of Town and Country Planning. Working Paper Series (GBR ISSN 0951-385X) **7474**
University of Nigeria. Annual Report (NGA ISSN 0331-1686) **3009**
• University of Nigeria. College of Medicine. Journal (NGA) **5727**
University of Nigeria. Inaugural Lecture Series (NGA) **1189**
University of Nijmegen. Research Report (NLD ISSN 1873-9644) **3009**
University of North Carolina, Chapel Hill. Institute of Statistics. Mimeo Series (USA ISSN 0078-1495) **8413**
University of North Carolina Medical Bulletin *see* U N C Medical Bulletin **5725**
• University of North Carolina School of Law Banking Institute (USA ISSN 1096-7249) **4804**
University of North Carolina Sea Grant College Program. Sea Grant Publication (USA ISSN 0893-0058) **2820**
University of North Carolina. Water Resources Research Institute. Report (USA ISSN 0078-1525) **8834**
University of North Dakota. Alumni Review (USA ISSN 0895-5409) **2307**
➤ University of North Dakota. Institute for Ecological Studies. Research Report (USA) **3472**
University of North Dakota. School of Medicine. The Review *see* North Dakota Medicine **5688**
University of Northumbria at Newcastle. Built Environment Research Group. Research Report (GBR) **3472**
• ➤ University of Notre Dame Australia Law Review (AUS ISSN 1441-9769) **4804**
University of Notre Dame. Department of Mathematics. Mathematical Lectures (USA ISSN 0076-5341) **5545**
University of Notre Dame. Department of Theology. Liturgical Studies (USA ISSN 0076-003X) **7821**
University of Notre Dame. Studies in the Philosophy of Religion (USA) **7692**
• University of Nottingham Business School. Discussion Papers (GBR) **1189**
• ➤ University of Nottingham. International Centre for Corporate Social Responsibility. Research Paper Series (GBR ISSN 1479-5116) **1189**
University of Occupational and Environmental Health. Journal *see* Sangyo Ika Daigaku Zasshi **6686**

DIRECTORY 2010 UNIVERSITY OF STOCKHOLM. DEPARTMENT OF PSYCHOLOGY 10993

University of Oerebro. Center for Feminist Social Studies. Working Papers see Oerebro Universitet. Centrum foer Feministika Samhaellsstudier. Arbetsrapport **8902**
University of Oerebro. Department of Education. Reports see Oerebro Universitet. Pedagogiska Institutionen. Rapporter **3075**
University of Ondokuz Mayis Journal of Medicine see Ondokuz Mayis Universitesi Tip Dergisi **5690**
University of Oradea. Annals. Economic Science see Universitatea din Oradea. Analele. Stiinte Economice **1187**
➤ University of Oregon Anthropological Papers (USA ISSN 0078-6071) **359**
University of Osaka Prefecture. Bulletin. Series A: Engineering and Natural Sciences/Osaka-furitsu Daigaku Kiyo, A. Kogaku, Shizen Kagaku (JPN ISSN 1342-3258) **3225**
▼ • ➤ University of Oslo. ARENA - Centre for European Studies. RECON Online Working Paper (Advanced Research on the Europeanisation of the Nation State. Reconstituting Democracy in Europe) (NOR ISSN 1504-6907) **7191**
• University of Oslo. Institute of Mathematics. Statistical Research Report (Online) (NOR) **5545**
University of Oslo. Museum of Cultural Heritage. Occasional Papers see Universitetet i Oslo. Kulturhistorisk Museum. Skrifter **422**
• University of Otago. Department of Computer Science. Technical Report (NZL ISSN 1178-3192) **2440**
• University of Otago. Department of Information Science. Information Science Discussion Paper Series (Online) (NZL ISSN 1177-455X) **2551**
• University of Otago. Economics Discussion Papers (NZL ISSN 0111-1760) **1189**
• University of Otago Magazine (NZL ISSN 1175-8147) **2307**
University of Otago Press. Newsletter (NZL) **7575**
University of Ottawa Law & Technology Journal see University of Ottawa Law & Technology Journal **4804**
• ➤ University of Ottawa Law & Technology Journal/Droit & Technologie de l'Universite d'Ottawa. Revue (CAN ISSN 1710-6028) **4804**
University of Oulu. Department of Information Processing Science. Series A, Research Papers (FIN ISSN 0786-8413) **2538**
University of Oxford. Centre for Criminological Research. Occasional Paper (GBR) **2671**
University of Oxford. Centre for Criminological Research. Probation Studies Unit Report (GBR) **2671**
• University of Oxford. Department of Economics. Discussion Paper Series (GBR ISSN 1471-0498) **1189**
University of Oxford. Department of Engineering Science. Report (GBR ISSN 0308-3683) **3225**
University of Oxford. Environmental Change Unit. Research Reports (GBR) **3472**
University of Oxford. European Humanities Research Centre. Special Lecture Series (GBR ISSN 1466-8165) **5393**
University of Oxford. Examination Regulations (GBR ISSN 1750-7170) **3009**
➤ University of Oxford. School of Geography. Research Papers (GBR ISSN 0305-8190) **4032**
University of Papua New Guinea. Department of Geography. Occasional Papers in Geography (PNG) **4032**
University of Papua New Guinea. Department of Physics. Technical Paper (PNG ISSN 0085-4735) **7044**
University of Pennsylvania. Journal of Business and Employment Law see University of Pennsylvania. Journal of Business Law **4882**
† • University of Pennsylvania Journal of Business and Employment Law (USA ISSN 1940-8064) **8996**
University of Pennsylvania. Journal of Business Law (USA ISSN 1945-2934) **4882**
• University of Pennsylvania. Journal of Constitutional Law (USA ISSN 1521-2823) **4853**
University of Pennsylvania. Journal of International Economic Law see University of Pennsylvania. Journal of International Law **4944**
• ➤ University of Pennsylvania. Journal of International Law (USA ISSN 1938-0283) **4944**
University of Pennsylvania. Journal of Labor and Employment Law see University of Pennsylvania Journal of Business and Employment Law **8996**
University of Pennsylvania. Journal of Labor and Employment Law see University of Pennsylvania. Journal of Business Law **4882**
University of Pennsylvania. Journal of Law and Social Change (USA) **4804**
• ➤ University of Pennsylvania. Law Review (USA ISSN 0041-9907) **4805**
• ➤ University of Pennsylvania Orthopaedic Journal (Online Edition) (USA) **6074**
University of Pennsylvania. Working Papers in Linguistics (USA ISSN 1524-9549) **5192**
University of Peshawar. Geological Bulletin see Journal of Himalayan Earth Sciences **2750**
• ➤ University of Petrosani. Annals. Electrical Engineering (ROM ISSN 1454-8518) **3333**
• ➤ University of Petrosani. Annals. Mechanical Engineering/Universitatea din Petrosani. Annals. Mechanical Engineering (ROM ISSN 1454-9166) **3398**
• ➤ University of Petrosani. Annals. Mining Engineering/Universitatea din Petrosani. Annals. Mining Engineering (ROM ISSN 1454-9174) **6482**
• ➤ University of Petrosani. Annals. Physics (ROM ISSN 1454-5071) **7045**
• ➤ University of Petrosani. Economics. Annals (ROM ISSN 1582-5949) **1189**
➤ University of Petrosani. Social Sciences. Annals (ROM ISSN 1582-1501) **8013**
• The University of Pittsburg. Journal of Technology Law and Policy (USA) **4805**
University of Pittsburgh. Department of Anthropology. Memoirs in Latin American Archaeology (USA) **422**
• ➤ University of Pittsburgh Law Review (USA ISSN 0041-9915) **4805**
University of Poona. Centre of Advanced Study in Sanskrit. Doctoral Theses and Other Sanskrit & Prakrit Publications (IND) **5192**
University of Poona. Centre of Advanced Study in Sanskrit. Publications (IND ISSN 0079-3809) **5192**
University of Poona. Centre of Advanced Study in Sanskrit. Sanskrit and Prakrit Studies (IND) **5192**
University of Port Elizabeth Newspaper see U P E N **2305**
University of Port Elizabeth. Publications. Bibliographies (ZAF) **4485**
University of Port Elizabeth. Publications. General Series (ZAF ISSN 0079-3957) **4480**
University of Port Elizabeth. Publications. Inaugural and Emeritus Addresses (ZAF ISSN 0085-5022) **4480**
University of Port Elizabeth. Publications. Research Papers (ZAF ISSN 0079-3965) **4480**
University of Port Elizabeth. Publications. Symposia, Seminars, and Lectures (ZAF ISSN 0031-7349) **4480**
University of Port Elizabeth. Publications. U P E Prestige Lectures (ZAF) **4481**
University of Portsmouth, Centre for the Economics and Management of Aquatic Resources Miscellaneous Publications see C E M A R E Miscellaneous Publications **3587**
University of Portsmouth, Centre for the Economics and Management of Aquatic Resources Reports see C E M A R E Reports **3587**
University of Portsmouth. Centre for the Economics & Management of Aquatic Resources. Research Papers (GBR) **3611**
University of Portsmouth. School of Languages and Area Studies. Working Papers in Linguistics (GBR ISSN 1355-1817) **5192**
University of Pretoria. Annual Report/Universiteit van Pretoria. Jaarverslag (ZAF ISSN 0259-1871) **2307**
➤ University of Pretoria. Institute for Strategic Studies. Ad Hoc Publication/Universiteit van Pretoria. Instituut vir Strategiese Studies. Ad Hoc Publikasie (ZAF) **7272**
University of Puerto Rico. Agricultural Experiment Station. Bulletin (PRI ISSN 0163-8238) **167**
➤ University of Puerto Rico. Journal of Agriculture (PRI ISSN 0041-994X) **167**
University of Puerto Rico. Sea Grant College Program. Report (PRI) **2630**
University of Qatar. Annual Statistical Report for the School Year see Jami'at Qatar. Al-Taqrir al-Ihsa'i al-Sanawi lil-Aam al-Jami'i **2934**
University of Qatar. Documentation and Humanities Research Centre. Journal see Journal of the Documentation and Humanities Research Centre **4461**
University of Qatar. Faculty of Humanities and Social Sciences. Journal see Gami'at Qatar. Kulliyyat al-Insaniyyat Wa-al-'ulum al-Igtima'iyyat. Magallat **4453**
University of Queensland. Calendar Series. Vol.1: Yearbook see University of Queensland. Yearbook **3009**
• University of Queensland, Department of Economics. Discussion Papers (AUS ISSN 1833-1068) **1189**
† • University of Queensland. Doctor of Philosophy Handbook (Online) (AUS) **8996**
† • University of Queensland. East Asian Economic Research Group. Discussion Paper Series (AUS ISSN 1833-1076) **8996**
• University of Queensland. East Asian Economic Research Group. Discussion Paper Series (Online) (AUS) **1189**
University of Queensland, L E R G. Discussion Paper see University of Queensland, Labour Economics Research Group. Discussion Paper **1189**
• University of Queensland, Labour Economics Research Group. Discussion Paper (AUS ISSN 1832-8741) **1189**
• ➤ University of Queensland Law Journal (AUS ISSN 0083-4041) **4805**
• University of Queensland. School of Economics. Annual Report (AUS ISSN 1832-8652) **1189**
University of Queensland. Yearbook (AUS) **3009**
University of Rajasthan. South Asian Studies Centre. Annual Report (IND ISSN 0304-8233) **563**
University of Rajasthan. Studies in Sanskrit and Hindi (IND ISSN 0448-1712) **5393**
University of Reading. Department of Agricultural and Food Economics. Farm Business Data (GBR ISSN 0557-6911) **208**
University of Reading. Department of Agricultural and Food Economics. Occasional Papers (GBR) **208**
University of Reading. Department of Economics. Discussion Papers in Economics and Management (GBR ISSN 1366-8226) **1189**
• University of Reading. Department of Geography. Geographical Papers Series (GBR ISSN 0305-5914) **4033**
University of Reading. Graduate Centre for Medieval Studies. Annual Proceedings see Reading Medieval Studies **4256**
University of Regina. Annual Report (CAN ISSN 1912-2799) **3009**
University of Regina. President's Report to the Community see University of Regina. Annual Report **3009**
University of Rhode Island. Library. Library Letter (USA) **5053**
University of Rhode Island. Sea Grant College Program. Marine Memorandum Series (USA) **2820**
University of Rhode Island. Sea Grant College Program. Marine Technical Report Series (USA) **2820**
University of Rhode Island. Sea Grant College Program. Publications (USA) **3611**
University of Rhode Island. Sea Grant College Program. Report (USA) **3611**
University of Rhode Island. Water Resources Center. Annual Report (USA) **8834**
• University of Richmond Law Review (USA ISSN 0566-2389) **4805**
University of Rijeka. Law Faculty. Collected Papers see Sveuciliste u Rijeci. Pravni Fakultet. Zbornik **4791**
➤ University of Rijeka. Technical Faculty. Engineering Review (HRV ISSN 1330-9587) **3333**
University of Riyadh. Central Library. Accession List (SAU) **5060**
University of Rochester Library Bulletin (USA ISSN 0041-9974) **5053**
• University of St. Thomas Law Journal (USA ISSN 1549-2028) **4805**
University of St. Thomas Magazine (USA) **2307**
• University of San Francisco Law Review (USA ISSN 0042-0018) **4805**
University of San Francisco Magazine (USA) **2307**
• University of San Francisco Maritime Law Journal (USA ISSN 1061-3331) **4971**
University of Santo Tomas. Faculty of Civil Law. Law Review (PHL ISSN 0047-5734) **4843**
University of Santo Tomas. Graduate School. Journal of Graduate Research (PHL ISSN 0047-5742) **8013**
University of Santo Tomas Journal of Graduate Research see University of Santo Tomas. Graduate School. Journal of Graduate Research **8013**
University of Sarajevo. Department of Agricultural and Food Sciences. Works see Univerzitet u Sarajevu. Poljoprivredni Fakultet. Radovi **167**
• University of Science and Technology Beijing. Journal (CHN ISSN 1005-8850) **6483**
University of Science and Technology Beijing. Journal (Social Sciences Edition) see Beijing Keji Daxue Xuebao (Shehui Kexue Ban) **7950**
University of Science and Technology. Journal see Journal of Science and Technology **7873**
University of Science and Technology of China. Journal see Zhongguo Kexue Jishu Daxue Xuebao **7934**
University of Science and Technology of Suzhou. Journal (Engineering and Technology) see Suzhou Keji Xueyuan Xuebao (Gongcheng Jishu Ban) **3221**
University of Science and Technology of Suzhou. Journal (Natural Science) see Suzhou Keji Xueyuan Xuebao (Ziran Kexue Ban) **7921**
University of Science and Technology of Suzhou. Journal (Social Science) see Suzhou Keji Xueyuan Xuebao (Shehui Kexue Ban) **8008**
University of Shanghai For Science and Technology. Journal (Social Science) see Shanghai Ligong Daxue Xuebao (Shehui Kexue Ban) **8000**
University of Sheffield. Diary of Events (GBR) **2307**
University of Sheffield. Newsletter (GBR) **2307**
University of Sheffield. School of Mathematics and Statistics. Research Report (GBR) **5545**
University of Sheffield. School of Nursing and Midwifery. Research Report (GBR) **5983**
University of Sierra Leone. Fourah Bay College. Institute of Marine Biology and Oceanography. Bulletin (SLE) **2820**
University of Sind. Research Journal. Science Series (PAK ISSN 0080-9624) **7927**
University of Sindh Arts Research Journal see International Research Journal of Arts & Humanities **497**
University of Singapore. History Society. Journal (SGP ISSN 0217-913X) **4190**
University of South Africa Latin American Report see U N I S A Latin American Report **4315**
University of South Africa. Verloren van Themaat Centre for Public Law Studies. Environmental Law Series (ZAF) **3472**
† • University of South Australia. Centre of Business Analysis and Research. Working Paper (Online) (AUS ISSN 1443-2943) **8996**
University of South Australia. School of Computer and Information Science Stemic see C I Stemic **2408**
† University of South Bohemia in Ceske Budejovice. Faculty of Agriculture. Collection of Scientific Papers. Series for Animal Sciences (CZE ISSN 1212-558X) **8996**
University of South Bohemia in Ceske Budejovice. Faculty of Agriculture. Collection of Scientific Papers. Series for Crop Sciences see Journal of Agrobiology **238**
University of South Carolina. Belle W. Baruch Library in Marine Science and Coastal Research. Collected Papers (USA) **2820**
University of South Carolina. Institute of Archeology and Anthropology. Annual Report (USA ISSN 0162-5799) **422**
University of South Florida Oracle see U S F Oracle **2305**
University of Southampton. Department of Aeronautics and Astronautics. Technical Report (GBR) **74**
University of Southampton. Department of Economics. Discussion Papers in Economics and Econometrics (GBR ISSN 0966-4246) **1189**
University of Southampton. Department of Geography. Discussion Papers (GBR ISSN 0140-9875) **4033**
University of Southampton. Department of Management. Discussion Papers (GBR ISSN 1356-3548) **1799**
University of Southampton, Institute of Sound and Vibration Research Technical Memoranda see I S V R Technical Memoranda **7087**
University of Southampton, Institute of Sound and Vibration Research Technical Reports see I S V R Technical Reports **7087**
University of Southern California Engineer see U S C Engineer **3224**
University of Southern California Health Affairs see U S C Health Affairs **7544**
University of Southern California. Law Center. Bibliography Series (USA) **4825**
University of Southern California Sea Grant Program. Report (USA) **2820**
University of Southern California Sea Grant Program. Technical Report (USA) **710**
University of Southern California Trojan Family see U S C Trojan Family **2305**
University of Southern Denmark Studies in History and Social Sciences/Byhistoriske Skrifter/Fynske Studier (DNK ISSN 1602-5962) **4275**
University of Southern Denmark Studies in Linguistics (DNK ISSN 1602-5113) **5192**
University of Southern Denmark Studies in Literature (DNK ISSN 0078-3323) **5393**
University of Southern Mindanao Research and Development Journal see U S M R & D Journal **164**
† • University of Southern Queensland. Handbook (AUS ISSN 1037-1818) **8996**
University of Southwestern Louisiana History Series see U S L History Series **4165**
University of St. Andrews. Centre for Research into Industry, Enterprise, Finance and the Firm. Discussion Paper Series (GBR ISSN 1364-453X) **1189**
University of Stavanger. PhD Thesis UiS (NOR ISSN 1890-1387) **3225**
• University of Stellenbosch. Bureau for Economic Research. Building and Construction (ZAF ISSN 0258-9265) **1042**
• University of Stellenbosch. Bureau for Economic Research. Economic Prospects (ZAF ISSN 0259-4862) **1523**
University of Stellenbosch. Bureau for Economic Research. Manufacturing Survey (ZAF ISSN 0258-9338) **1189**
• University of Stellenbosch. Bureau for Economic Research. Retail Survey (ZAF) **1847**
• University of Stellenbosch. Bureau for Economic Research. Trends (ZAF ISSN 0379-6191) **1434**
University of Stellenbosch. Bureau for Economic Research. Update (ZAF) **1523**
University of Sterling. Department of Economics. Discussion Papers in Economics, Finance and Investment (GBR ISSN 0962-4090) **1189**
University of Stirling. Department of Computing Science and Mathematics. Technical Report (GBR) **5556**
University of Stockholm. Center for Pacific Asia Studies. Occasional Paper (SWE ISSN 0284-1541) **4190**
University of Stockholm. Center for Pacific Asia Studies. Working Papers (SWE ISSN 0284-155X) **4190**
University of Stockholm. Department of Meteorology. Report A P (Atmospheric Physics) (SWE ISSN 0280-4441) **6397**
University of Stockholm. Department of Meteorology. Report C M (Chemical Meteorology) (SWE ISSN 0280-445X) **6397**
University of Stockholm. Department of Meteorology. Report D M (Dynamic Meteorology) (SWE ISSN 0349-0467) **6397**
University of Stockholm. Department of Psychology. Report (Print) see University of Stockholm. Department of Psychology. Reports (Online) **7414**

Title

• University of Stockholm. Department of Psychology. Reports (Online) (SWE) **7414**
University of Stockholm. Institute for International Economic Studies. Annual Report (SWE ISSN 1104-4195) **1189**
• University of Stockholm. Institute for International Economic Studies. Monograph Series (SWE ISSN 0346-6892) **1189**
• University of Stockholm. Institute for International Economic Studies. Seminar Papers (SWE ISSN 1653-610X) **1586**
University of Strathclyde. Department of Marketing. Working Paper Series (GBR) **1847**
University of Strathclyde. Fraser of Allander Institute for Research on the Scottish Economy. Quarterly Economic Commentary (GBR ISSN 0306-7866) **1189**
University of Strathclyde. University Review (GBR) **3009**
University of Suleyman Demirel. Faculty of Divinity. Review *see* Suleyman Demirel Universitesi Ilahiyat Fakultesi Dergisi **7686**
• University of Surrey. Department of Economics. Discussion Papers in Economics (Online) (GBR ISSN 1749-5075) **1189**
➤ University of Sussex. Centre for Continuing Education. Occasional Paper (GBR ISSN 0306-1108) **2947**
University of Sussex. Institute of Development Studies. Policy Briefing Paper *see* I D S Policy Briefing **1597**
University of Sussex. Institute of Education. Research Report Series (GBR) **2923**
• ➤ University of Sussex Journal of Contemporary History (GBR) **4165**
University of Sussex. School of Social Sciences. Economics Discussion Paper (GBR) **1189**
University of Sussex, Sussex European Institute Working Papers *see* S E I Working Papers **7998**
University of Swaziland Journal of Agriculture *see* UniSwa Journal of Agriculture **165**
University of Swaziland Research Journal *see* UniSwa Research Journal **4479**
University of Swaziland, Swaziland Institute for Educational Research Bulletin *see* S I E R Bulletin **2908**
University of Sydney. Annual Report (AUS ISSN 0313-4474) **3009**
• University of Sydney. Archives Record (AUS ISSN 0310-4729) **4194**
† University of Sydney. Department of Agricultural Economics. Research Report. (AUS ISSN 0817-8771) **8996**
University of Sydney. Gazette *see* Sydney Alumni Magazine **2303**
• University of Sydney. Institute of Transport and Logistics Studies. Working Paper (AUS ISSN 1832-570X) **8519**
University of Sydney Library Newsletter *see* Discover **5007**
• ➤ University of Sydney Papers in T E S O L (Teachers of English to Speakers of Other Languages) (AUS ISSN 1834-3198) **2923**
• University of Sydney. School of Economics and Political Science. Working Papers. Discipline of Econometrics and Business Statistics (AUS ISSN 1449-7174) **1189**
• University of Sydney. School of Economics and Political Science. Working Papers. Discipline of Economics (AUS ISSN 1446-3806) **1189**
• University of Sydney. School of Economics and Political Science. Working Papers. Discipline of Political Economy (AUS ISSN 1446-3814) **7191**
University of Sydney, Speleological Society Bull *see* S U S S Bull **2765**
➤ University of Szeged. Acta Cybernetica (HUN ISSN 0324-721X) **2528**
University of Tabriz. Faculty of Human and Social Sciences. Publication/Daneshgah-e Tabriz. Daneshkade-ye Ulume Ensani va Ijtima'i. Nashriyeh (IRN) **4481**
University of Tampere. Department of Sociology and Social Psychology. B, Working Papers *see* Tampereen Yliopisto. Sosiologian ja Sosiaalipsykologian Laitos. B, Tyoraportteja **8142**
University of Tampere. Department of Sociology and Social Psychology. Series A, Research Papers *see* Tampereen Yliopisto. Sosiologian ja Sosiaalipsykologian Laitos. A, Tutkimuksia **8142**
• University of Tartu. Faculty of Economics and Business Administration. Working Paper Series (EST ISSN 1406-5967) **1189**
➤ University of Tasmania. Centre for Environmental Studies. Environmental Studies Project Report (AUS ISSN 0811-580X) **2630**
➤ University of Tasmania. Centre for Environmental Studies. Occasional Paper (AUS ISSN 1034-1412) **3472**
† University of Tasmania. Centre for Environmental Studies. Working Papers (AUS ISSN 0313-5780) **8996**
• ➤ University of Tasmania Law Review (AUS ISSN 0082-2108) **4805**
University of Tasmania. Law School. Occasional Papers (AUS) **4805**
• University of Technology, Sydney. Annual Report (AUS ISSN 1031-8690) **3009**
• University of Technology, Sydney. Calendar (AUS ISSN 1030-5947) **3009**
University of Technology, Sydney. Faculty of Business Handbook *see* University of Technology, Sydney. Handbook **2923**
University of Technology, Sydney. Faculty of Design Architecture and Building Handbook *see* University of Technology, Sydney. Handbook **2923**
University of Technology, Sydney. Faculty of Education. Faculty of Education Handbook *see* University of Technology, Sydney. Handbook **2923**
University of Technology, Sydney. Faculty of Law Handbook *see* University of Technology, Sydney. Handbook **2923**
University of Technology, Sydney. Faculty of Nursing, Midwifery and Health Handbook *see* University of Technology, Sydney. Handbook **2923**
University of technology, Sydney. Faculty of Science Handbook *see* University of Technology, Sydney. Handbook **2923**
• University of Technology, Sydney. Handbook (AUS) **2923**
University of Technology, Sydney Law Review *see* The U T S Law Review **8995**
University of Technology, Sydney Shopfront Monograph Series *see* U T S Shopfront Monograph Series **8144**
University of Technology, Sydney. U T S Faculty of Humanities and Social Sciences Handbook *see* University of Technology, Sydney. Handbook **2923**
University of Technology, Sydney. U T S Information Technology Handbook *see* University of Technology, Sydney. Handbook **2923**
University of Technology, Sydney. U T S Institute for International Studies Handbook *see* University of Technology, Sydney. Handbook **2923**
University of Teesside. School of Science and Technology. Technical Report (GBR) **8444**
➤ University of Teheran. Central Library. Library Bulletin/Daneshgah-e Tehran. Ketabkhane-Ye Markazi. Nashriye-Ye Ketabkhaneh (IRN ISSN 0497-1000) **5053**
University of Teheran. Faculty of Letters and Humanities. Bulletin of Iranian Studies/Daneshgah-e Tehran. Daneshkade-Ye Adabiyat va 'olum-e Ensani. Majalle-Ye Iranshenasi (IRN) **4326**
University of Tehran. Faculty of Engineering. Journal (IRN ISSN 1026-0803) **3225**
University of Tehran. Faculty of Veterinary Medicine. Journal *see* Majallah-i Danishkadah-i Dampizishki **8802**
University of Tehran. Journal of Science (International Edition) *see* Iranian International Journal of Science **7868**
University of Tennessee at Knoxville Daily Beacon *see* U T Daily Beacon **2305**
University of Tennessee at Knoxville, Municipal Technical Advisory Service Salary and Fringe Benefit Survey *see* The (Year) M T A S Salary and Fringe Benefit Survey **1696**
University of Texas at Austin. Applied Research Laboratories. Technical Report (USA) **7045**
University of Texas at Austin. Bureau of Business Research. Research Monograph Series (USA) **1189**
➤ University of Texas at Austin. Bureau of Economic Geology. Annual Report (USA ISSN 0082-3287) **2772**
➤ University of Texas at Austin. Bureau of Economic Geology. Geological Circular (USA ISSN 0082-3309) **2772**
➤ University of Texas at Austin. Bureau of Economic Geology. Guidebook (USA ISSN 0363-4132) **2772**
➤ University of Texas at Austin. Bureau of Economic Geology. Mineral Resource Circulars (USA ISSN 0082-3333) **2772**
➤ University of Texas at Austin. Bureau of Economic Geology. Other Publications (USA) **2772**
➤ University of Texas at Austin. Bureau of Economic Geology. Report of Investigations (USA ISSN 0888-6725) **2772**
• ➤ University of Texas at Austin. Center for Research in Water Resources. Technical Report Series (Online) (USA) **8834**
University of Texas at Austin. General Libraries. Library Bulletin (USA ISSN 0277-450X) **5053**
University of Texas at Austin. General Libraries. Newsletter (USA ISSN 0362-854X) **5053**
• University of Texas at Austin. Graduate School of Library and Information Science. Alumni News (USA) **5053**
University of Texas at Austin. Tarlton Law Library. Legal Bibliography Series (USA ISSN 0085-7092) **4826**
University of Texas at El Paso Magazine *see* U T E P Magazine **2305**
University of Texas at San Antonio Discover *see* U T S A Discover **7925**
University of Texas, Austin. Lyndon B. Johnson School of Public Affairs. Policy Research Project Report Series (USA ISSN 0196-0369) **7191**
University of Texas, Austin. Lyndon B. Johnson School of Public Affairs. Working Paper Series (USA) **7474**
• University of Texas. M.D. Anderson Cancer Center. Research Report (USA) **6036**
• University of the District of Columbia Law Review (USA ISSN 1539-5693) **4805**
University of the District of Columbia. Water Resources Research Center. Report (USA) **8834**
University of the East Law Journal *see* U E Law Journal **4799**
University of the East News *see* U E News **3005**
University of the East Research Bulletin (PHL) **3009**
University of the East Today *see* U E Today **2921**
University of the North. Department of Bantu Languages. Communications (ZAF ISSN 0302-7481) **5192**
University of the Orange Free State. Institute for Contemporary History. Annual Report (ZAF) **4179**
University of the Philippines. Asian Center. Monograph Series (PHL ISSN 0079-9238) **4190**
University of the Philippines at Los Banos. Agrarian Reform Institute. Occasional Papers (PHL) **167**
University of the Philippines. College of Public Administration. Local Government Studies (PHL) **7504**
University of the Philippines. College of Public Administration. Public Administration Occasional Papers and Special Studies Series (PHL) **7474**
University of the Philippines Gazette (PHL) **3009**
University of the Philippines. Institute of Library Science. Newsletter (PHL ISSN 0300-3612) **5053**
University of the Punjab. Institute of Geology. Geological Bulletin (PAK ISSN 0079-8037) **2773**
➤ University of the Punjab. Journal of Research: Humanities (PAK ISSN 1812-1128) **4481**
University of the Ryukyus. College of Agriculture. Science Bulletin/Ryukyu Daigaku Nogakubu Gakujutsu Hokoku (JPN ISSN 0370-4246) **167**
University of the Ryukyus. College of Science. Bulletin/Ryukyu Daigaku Rigakubu Kiyo (JPN ISSN 0286-9640) **5545**
University of the Ryukyus. Faculty of Engineering. Bulletin *see* Ryukyu Daigaku Kogakubu Kiyo **3218**
University of the Sciences in Philadelphia. Bulletin (USA ISSN 1524-8348) **6884**
University of the South Pacific. Marine Studies Programme. Technical Report (FJI ISSN 1018-2896) **966**
University of the South Pacific. Publications (FJI ISSN 1011-5129) **638**
University of the West Indies. Annual Report on Cocoa Research (TTO) **257**
University of the West Indies. Institute of Social and Economic Research. Occasional Bibliography Series (JAM) **8021**
University of the West Indies. Institute of Social and Economic Research. Working Papers (JAM) **8145**
University of the West Indies Students' Law Review *see* U W I Students' Law Review **4800**
University of the West Indies, Trinidad. Institute of Social & Economic Research. Occasional Papers: General Series (TTO) **8013**
University of the West Indies, Trinidad. Institute of Social & Economic Research. Occasional Papers: Human Resources Series (TTO) **1713**
University of the West Indies. Vice-Chancellor's Report (JAM ISSN 0799-0006) **3009**
University of the West of England (Bristol), Faculty of Art, Media and Design. Newsletter: Artists' Books Exhibitions at the Library *see* Book Arts Newsletter **479**
University of the West of England. Faculty of Economics and Social Science. School of Economics. Working Papers (GBR) **1190**
University of the West of England. Faculty of the Built Environment. Working Paper (GBR) **4429**
University of the Witwatersrand. African Studies Institute. Seminar Papers (ZAF) **4179**
➤ University of the Witwatersrand. Institute for Advanced Social Research. Seminar Papers (ZAF) **8013**
University of the Witwatersrand, Johannesburg. Library. Archival Series (ZAF) **5060**
University of the Witwatersrand, Johannesburg. Library. Occasional Publications (ZAF) **5053**
University of the Witwatersrand, Johannesburg. School of Mechanical Engineering. Research Reports (ZAF) **3398**
➤ University of Tokushima. Faculty of Engineering. Bulletin (JPN ISSN 0040-8883) **3225**
University of Tokushima. Faculty of Integrated Arts and Sciences. Natural Science Research *see* Shizen Kagaku Kenkyu (Tokushima) **7916**
University of Tokushima. Journal of Mathematics (JPN ISSN 1346-7387) **5545**
➤ University of Tokushima. Social Science Research (JPN) **8013**
University of Tokyo. Annual Report of High Voltage Electron Microscope *see* Tokyo Daigaku Chokoatsu Denshi Kenbikyoshitsu Nenpo **7052**
University of Tokyo. Cryogenic Center. Report *see* Tokyo Daigaku Teion Senta Dayori **7057**
University of Tokyo. Department of Astronomy. Contributions (JPN ISSN 0563-8038) **583**
University of Tokyo. Department of Geography. Bulletin (JPN ISSN 0082-478X) **4033**
University of Tokyo. Earthquake Research Institute. Bulletin/Tokyo Daigaku Jishin Kenkyujo Iho (JPN ISSN 0040-8972) **2791**
University of Tokyo. Earthquake Research Institute. Special Bulletin (JPN ISSN 0915-0862) **2791**
University of Tokyo. Electrical and Electronic Engineering Departments. Bulletin *see* Tokyo Daigaku Kogakubu. Denki Kogaku Denshi Kogaku Iho **3333**
University of Tokyo. Engineering Research Institute. Annual Report *see* Sogo Shikenjo Nenpo **3220**
University of Tokyo. Faculty of Agriculture. Fisheries Laboratory. Contributions *see* Todai Suisan Jikkenjo Gyoseki **3610**
University of Tokyo. Faculty of Engineering. Department of Civil Engineering. Collected Papers (JPN ISSN 0495-7806) **3286**
University of Tokyo. Faculty of Engineering. Department of Civil Engineering. Transactions *see* Tokyo Daigaku. Kogakubu. Doboku Kogakka. Ronbun Shuroku **3285**
University of Tokyo. Institute for Solid State Physics. Neutron Scattering Laboratory. Activity Report on Neutron Scattering Research (JPN ISSN 1343-0297) **7073**
University of Tokyo. Institute for Solid State Physics. Technical Report. Series A (JPN ISSN 0082-4798) **7045**
University of Tokyo. Institute for Solid State Physics. Technical Report. Series B (JPN ISSN 0082-4801) **7045**
University of Tokyo. Institute of Medical Science. Annual Report (JPN ISSN 0918-8495) **5911**
University of Tokyo. International Center for Elementary Particle Physics (JPN ISSN 0917-754X) **7045**
University of Tokyo. Misaki Marine Biological Station. Annual Report *see* Tokyo Daigaku Rigakubu Fuzoku Rinkai Jikkenjo Nenpo **2819**
➤ University of Tokyo. Ocean Research Institute. Bulletin/Tokyo Daigaku Kaiyo Kenkyujo (JPN ISSN 0564-6898) **2820**
University of Tokyo. Ocean Research Institute. Publication List (JPN) **2820**
University of Tokyo. Radioisotope Center. News *see* Tokyo Daigaku Aisotopu Sogo Senta Nyusu **3175**
University of Tokyo. Research Center for Nuclear Science and Technology. News *see* Tokyo Daigaku Genshiryoku Kenkyu Sogo Senta Nyusu **3175**
University of Tokyo. School of Engineering. Journal/Tokyo Daigaku Kogakubu Kogakukei Kenkyuka Kiyo (JPN ISSN 1344-2929) **3225**
University of Tokyo. School of Science. Department of Physics. Annual Report *see* Tokyo Daigaku Daigakuin Rigakukeikenkyuka Rigakubu Butsurigaku Kyoshitsu Nenji Kenkyu **7043**
University of Tokyo. University Museum. Bulletin (JPN ISSN 0910-481X) **7927**
University of Tokyo. University Museum. Material Reports (JPN ISSN 0910-2566) **6539**
University of Tokyo. University Museum. Monograph (JPN ISSN 1346-6356) **6539**
• University of Toledo Law Review (USA ISSN 0042-0190) **4805**
University of Toronto *see* University of Toronto Magazine **2307**
• University of Toronto Bulletin (CAN) **2307**
University of Toronto Conference on Editorial Problems *see* Conference on Editorial Problems: University of Toronto **8943**
• University of Toronto Faculty of Law Review (CAN ISSN 0381-1638) **4805**
University of Toronto. Institute for Aerospace Studies. Graduate Studies and Research Progress Report (CAN ISSN 1483-457X) **74**
University of Toronto. Institute for Policy Analysis. Annual Report (CAN ISSN 0703-6949) **1190**
• University of Toronto. Institute for Policy Analysis. Working Paper Series (CAN ISSN 0829-4909) **1190**
• ➤ University of Toronto Law Journal (CAN ISSN 0042-0220) **4805**
• University of Toronto Magazine (CAN ISSN 1499-0040) **2307**
• ➤ University of Toronto. Medical Journal (CAN ISSN 0833-2207) **5727**
• ➤ University of Toronto Quarterly (CAN ISSN 0042-0247) **4481**
University of Toronto Romance Series (CAN ISSN 0082-5336) **5393**
University of Transkei. Department of Information Science. Occasional Papers (ZAF ISSN 1021-1500) **2551**
University of Tsukuba. Institute of Geoscience. Annual Report (JPN ISSN 0285-3175) **2791**
University of Tsukuba. Institute of Geoscience. Science Reports. Section A: Geographical Sciences (JPN ISSN 0388-6174) **4033**
University of Tsukuba. Institute of Geoscience. Science Reports. Section B: Geological Sciences (JPN ISSN 0388-6182) **2773**
University of Tsukuba. Institute of Physics. Annual Report *see* Tsukuba Daigaku Butsurigakukei Nenji Kenkyu Hokoku **7044**
University of Tsukuba. Report of Coastal Observation *see* Tsukuba Daigaku Engan Kansoku Hokoku **2819**
University of Tsukuba. Shimoda Marine Research Center. Contributions (JPN) **2820**
University of Tsukuba. Sugadaira Montane Research Center. Bulletin *see* Tsukuba Daigaku Sugadaira Kogen Jikken Senta Kenkyu Hokoku **2717**
University of Turku *see* UTUonline **3009**

DIRECTORY 2010 UNIWERSYTET JAGIELLONSKI. ZESZYTY NAUKOWE. PRACE PEDAGOGICZNE 10995

University of Turku. Department of English. Anglicana Turkuensia (FIN ISSN 1236-4754) **5393**
University of Turku. Psychological Research Reports (FIN ISSN 0359-0216) **7414**
University of Turku. Publications of the Institute of History. General History (FIN ISSN 0784-9257) **4165**
University of Ulster. School of the Built Environment. Real Estate Studies Unit. Occasional Paper (GBR) **7614**
➤ University of Utah Anthropological Papers (USA ISSN 0083-4947) **359**
University of Utah. Microwave Device and Physical Electronics Laboratory Quarterly Report (USA ISSN 0026-2870) **3115**
University of Vaasa. Proceedings. Discussion Papers (FIN ISSN 0358-870X) **1550**
University of Vaasa. Proceedings. Reports *see* Vaasan Yliopiston Julkaisuja. Selvityksia ja Raportteja **1550**
University of Vaasa. Proceedings. Reprint Series (FIN ISSN 0782-9388) **1190**
University of Vaasa. Proceedings. Research Papers *see* Vaasan Yliopisto. Julkaisuja. Tutkimuksia **1550**
University of Vaasa. Proceedings. Research Papers. Administrative Science *see* Vaasan Yliopisto. Julkaisuja. Tutkimuksia. Hallintotiede **7475**
University of Vaasa. Proceedings. Research Papers. Linguistics *see* Vaasan Yliopisto. Julkaisuja. Tutkimuksia. Kielitiede **5193**
University of Vaasa. Proceedings. Research Papers. Mathematics *see* Vaasan Yliopisto. Julkaisuja. Tutkimuksia. Matematiikka **5546**
University of Vaasa. Proceedings. Teaching Aid Series *see* Vaasan Yliopisto. Julkaisuja. Opetusjulkaisuja **1550**
University of Venice. Department of Applied Mathematics. Working Papers (ITA ISSN 1828-6887) **5545**
† University of Virginia. Center for Oceans Law and Policy. Annual Seminar (NLD ISSN 1052-1216) **8996**
University of Virginia. Declaration (USA) **2307**
• University of Virginia Magazine (USA ISSN 1559-985X) **2307**
University of Virginia Medical Center. Claude Moore Health Sciences Library. Annual Report (USA ISSN 8755-2043) **5053**
University of Waikato. Antarctic Research Unit. Report (NZL ISSN 0110-2192) **2773**
• University of Waikato. Department of Accounting. Working Paper Series (NZL ISSN 1173-7182) **1303**
• University of Waikato. Department of Computer Science. Working Paper Series (Online) (NZL ISSN 1177-777X) **2440**
University of Waikato. Department of Computer Science. Working Paper Series (Print) *see* University of Waikato. Department of Computer Science. Working Paper Series (Online) **2440**
University of Waikato. Department of Earth and Ocean Sciences. Occasional Report (NZL ISSN 1177-3871) **2718**
University of Waikato. Department of Earth Sciences. Occasional Report *see* University of Waikato. Department of Earth and Ocean Sciences. Occasional Report **2718**
• University of Waikato. Department of Societies and Cultures. Occasional Paper Series (NZL ISSN 1177-4266) **8145**
University of Waikato. Department of Strategic Management and Leadership. Working Papers Series *see* University of Waikato. Department of Strategy and Human Resource Management. Working Paper Series **1877**
University of Waikato. Department of Strategy and Human Resource Management. Working Paper Series (NZL ISSN 1177-066X) **1877**
• University of Waikato. Population Studies Centre. Discussion Papers (NZL ISSN 1172-6210) **7295**
University of Waikato. Statement of Objectives *see* Profile **2998**
University of Waikato. Statement of Objectives & Profile *see* Profile **2998**
University of Wales, Aberystwyth. Undergraduate Prospectus (GBR) **2963**
University of Wales at Aberystwyth. Library Report/Prifysgol Cymru Aberystwyth. Adroddiad y Llyfrgell (GBR) **5053**
University of Wales. Cardiff Business School. Discussion Papers in Accounting and Finance (Print) *see* Cardiff Business School. Working Papers in Accounting and Finance **1284**
University of Wales. Department of Maritime Studies and International Transport. Occasional Papers (GBR ISSN 0967-5566) **8664**
University of Wales. School of Social and Administrative Studies. Social Research Unit. Guide (GBR) **8013**
➤ University of Wales. Welsh Institute of Rural Studies. Working Paper (GBR ISSN 1368-2326) **8145**
University of Warwick Library. Occasional Publications. (GBR) **5053**
University of Warwick Newsletter (GBR) **3009**
University of Washington. Applied Physics Laboratory. Report (USA) **7045**
University of Washington. Applied Physics Laboratory. Technical Report (USA) **7045**
University Of Washington Daily (USA) **2307**
University of Washington. Fisheries Research Institute. Report *see* University of Washington. School of Aquatic and Fishery Sciences. Technical Report **710**
University of Washington Publications on Asia *see* School of International Studies. Publications on Asia **4188**
University of Washington. School of Aquatic and Fishery Sciences. Technical Report (USA) **710**
University of Washington. Working Papers in Linguistics (USA ISSN 0892-8886) **5192**
University of Waterloo Bibliography Series (CAN ISSN 0829-948X) **5060**
University of Waterloo Biology Series (CAN ISSN 0317-3348) **710**
University of Waterloo Courier (CAN ISSN 0227-2199) **2307**
University of Waterloo. Department of Geography. Occasional Papers (CAN) **4033**
University of Waterloo. Department of Geography. Publication Series (CAN ISSN 0843-7378) **4033**
University of Waterloo. Gazette (CAN ISSN 0042-031X) **2923**
University of Waterloo. Solid Mechanics Division. Papers (CAN ISSN 0317-7130) **3359**
University of Waterloo. Solid Mechanics Division. Reports (CAN ISSN 0317-7114) **3359**
University of Waterloo. Solid Mechanics Division. Studies Series (CAN ISSN 0318-3122) **3359**
• University of Western Australia. Business School. Economics. Discussion Paper (AUS) **1190**
University of Western Australia. Department of Organisational and Labour Studies. Discussion Paper (AUS ISSN 1328-3219) **1713**
• ➤ University of Western Australia Law Review (AUS ISSN 0042-0328) **4805**
University of Western Australia. School of Music. Music Monograph (AUS ISSN 0726-3929) **6625**
University of Western Ontario. The Gazette (CAN ISSN 0841-2715) **2307**
➤ University of Western Sydney Law Review (AUS ISSN 1446-9294) **4805**
University of Westminster. Centre for the Study of Democracy Perspectives *see* C S D Perspectives **7224**
University of Westminster. Faculty of Business, Management and Social Studies. Research Working Paper Series (GBR) **1190**
University of Windsor. Department of Economics. Discussion Paper Series (CAN) **1190**
University of Wisconsin at Madison. Applied Population Laboratory. Economic Series (USA) **7295**
University of Wisconsin at Madison. Center for Demography and Ecology Working Paper *see* C D E Working Paper **7278**
• University of Wisconsin at Madison. Center for South Asia. Newsletter (USA) **3086**
University of Wisconsin at Madison. College of Engineering. Annual Report (USA ISSN 0193-9637) **3226**
University of Wisconsin at Madison. Institute for Research on Poverty. Reprint Series (USA ISSN 0084-0769) **8013**
• University of Wisconsin at Madison. Institute for Research on Poverty. Special Report Series (USA ISSN 0275-2980) **8013**
University of Wisconsin. Department of French & Italian. Newsletter (USA) **2307**
University of Wisconsin, Madison. Applied Population Laboratory. Population Notes (USA ISSN 0084-0734) **7295**
University of Wisconsin, Madison. Applied Population Laboratory. Population Series (USA ISSN 0084-0742) **7295**
• University of Wisconsin, Madison. Institute for Research on Poverty. Discussion Papers (USA) **8013**
University of Wisconsin, Madison. Land Tenure Center. Reprint (USA ISSN 0084-0807) **208**
• University of Wisconsin-Milwaukee. Center for Latin America. Discussion Paper Series (USA ISSN 0084-0831) **4316**
University of Wisconsin - Milwaukee. Center for Latin American and Caribbean Studies. Occasional Paper (USA) **7272**
University of Wisconsin-Milwaukee. Field Station Bulletin (USA) **710**
University of Wisconsin-Milwaukee. Language and Area Center for Latin America. Center Discussion Paper *see* University of Wisconsin-Milwaukee. Center for Latin America. Discussion Paper Series **4316**
University of Wisconsin Milwaukee Post *see* U W M Post **2305**
University of Wisconsin. Sea Grant College Program. Technical Report (USA ISSN 0191-3336) **2820**
➤ University of Wisconsin Stevens Point. Museum of Natural History. Reports of the Fauna and Flora (USA) **7927**
University of Wollongong. Annual Report (AUS ISSN 1036-7535) **3035**
University of Wollongong. Postgraduate Calendar (AUS ISSN 1036-7985) **2307**
University of Wollongong. Research Profile (AUS) **2307**
University of Wollongong. Undergraduate Calendar (AUS ISSN 1036-2371) **2307**
University of York. Centre for Defence Economics. Research Monograph Series (GBR) **6451**
• University of York. Department of Economics and Related Studies. Discussion Papers in Economics (GBR ISSN 1367-3653) **1190**
University of York. Department of Politics. Working Paper (GBR) **7191**
University of York. Index of Private Rents and Yields (GBR ISSN 1468-6147) **8076**
University of York. Institute of Advanced Architectural Studies. Research Papers (GBR ISSN 0306-0624) **460**
• University of York. Social Policy Research Unit. Research Works (GBR ISSN 1749-3854) **8076**
University of Zambia. Centre for Continuing Education. Report of the Annual Resident Tutors' Conference (ZMB) **2947**
University of Zambia. School of Humanities and Social Sciences. Annual Report (ZMB) **8013**
University of Zimbabwe Business Review *see* Business Review **1730**
University of Zimbabwe. Institute of Mining Research. Report (ZWE ISSN 0254-2951) **6483**
The University Pacer (USA) **2307**
University Press Books for Public and Secondary School Libraries *see* University Press Books Selected for Public and Secondary School Libraries **5060**
University Press Books Selected for Public and Secondary School Libraries (USA ISSN 1537-5218) **5060**
University Publishing *see* Daxue Chuban **7559**
The University Record (IRL) **2307**
University Research on European Integration *see* Recherches Universitaires sur l'Integration Europeenne **7261**
University Scope (USA) **2307**
University Student *see* Daxuesheng **2977**
University Times (Charlotte) (USA) **2307**
University Urban Programs (USA) **8145**
• El Universo (ECU) **3835**
Universo (ESP ISSN 1135-2876) **583**
L'Universo (ITA ISSN 0042-0409) **4033**
Universo (MEX ISSN 0374-0501) **583**
Universo del Buho (MEX) **7191**
• Universo Diagnostico (CUB ISSN 1682-6779) **5727**
▼ Universo Holistico (ESP ISSN 1888-3885) **315**
• Universo Online (USA) **583**
Universo Visual (BRA) **6052**
Universos (ESP ISSN 1698-6083) **8013**
Universul (ROM ISSN 1454-931X) **3934**
Universul Cartii (ROM ISSN 1221-8685) **3934**
• Universum (CHL ISSN 0716-498X) **8013**
• Univert Outaouais (CAN ISSN 1912-1792) **3472**
• ➤ Univerza v Ljubljani. Filozofska Fakulteta. Oddelek za Geografijo. Dela (SVN ISSN 0354-0596) **4033**
† ➤ Univerzita Karlova. Lekarska Fakulta Hradec Kralove. Lekarske Zpravy (CZE ISSN 0457-4206) **8996**
Univerzita Komenskeho. Filozoficka Fakulta. Zbornik: Graecolatina et Orientalia (SVK ISSN 0083-4114) **2241**
Univerzita Komenskeho. Filozoficka Fakulta. Zbornik: Historica (SVK ISSN 0083-4122) **4165**
Univerzita Komenskeho. Filozoficka Fakulta. Zbornik: Kniznicna a Informacna Veda (SVK) **5053**
Univerzita Komenskeho. Filozoficka Fakulta. Zbornik: Logica et Methodologica (SVK) **6959**
Univerzita Komenskeho. Filozoficka Fakulta. Zbornik: Musaica (SVK ISSN 0083-4130) **524**
Univerzita Komenskeho. Filozoficka Fakulta. Zbornik: Paedagogica (SVK ISSN 0083-4165) **2923**
Univerzita Komenskeho. Filozoficka Fakulta. Zbornik: Philologica (SVK ISSN 0083-4173) **5192**
Univerzita Komenskeho. Filozoficka Fakulta. Zbornik: Philosophica (SVK ISSN 0083-4181) **6959**
Univerzita Komenskeho. Filozoficka Fakulta. Zbornik: Psychologica (SVK ISSN 0083-419X) **7414**
Univerzita Komenskeho. Filozoficka Fakulta. Zbornik: Zurnalistika (SVK ISSN 0083-422X) **4584**
Univerzita Komenskeho. Pedagogicka Fakulta. Katedra Specialnej Pedagogiky. Zbornik. Paedagogica Specialis (SVK) **3049**
Univerzita Komenskeho. Pedagogicke Fakulta v Trnave. Zbornik. Spolocenske Vedy. Historia (SVK ISSN 0139-5548) **4275**
Univerzita Komenskeho. Ustav Marxizmu-Leninizmu. Zbornik: Politicka Ekonomia (SVK ISSN 0139-5521) **1550**
Univerzita Komenskeho. Ustav Marxizmu-Leninizmu. Zbornik: Vedecky Komunizmus (SVK) **8013**
Univerzitet Danas (BIH ISSN 0042-0425) **3009**
Univerzitet "Kiril i Metodi" Skopje. Prirodno-Matematicki Fakultet. Godisen Zbornik (MKD ISSN 0351-7241) **5545**
Univerzitet u Beogradu. Elektrotehnicki Fakultet. Publikacije. Serija: Elektronika, Telekomunikacije, Automatika (SRB ISSN 0351-2177) **3115**
Univerzitet u Beogradu. Filozofski Fakultet. Anali (SRB ISSN 0522-8468) **6959**
Univerzitet u Beogradu. Pravni Fakultet. Anali (SRB ISSN 0003-2565) **4805**
Univerzitet u Kragujevcu. Prirodno-Matematicki Fakultet. Zbornik Radova *see* Kragujevac Journal of Mathematics **5508**
Univerzitet u Novom Sadu. Filozofski Fakultet. Godisnjak (SRB ISSN 0374-0730) **6959**
Univerzitet u Sarajevu. Doktorske Disertacije. Rezimei (BIH) **2937**
➤ Univerzitet u Sarajevu. Poljoprivredni Fakultet. Radovi/University of Sarajevo. Department of Agricultural and Food Sciences. Works (BIH ISSN 0033-8583) **167**
Univerzitet u Sarjevu. Bilten *see* Univerzitet u Sarajevu. Doktorske Disertacije. Rezimei **2937**
➤ Univerzitet u Zagrebu. Pravni Fakultet. Zbornik (HRV ISSN 0350-2058) **4805**
Univerzitet vo Skopje. Ekonomskiot Fakultet. Godisnik/Universite de Skopje. Faculte des Sciences Economique. Annuaire (MKD) **1190**
Univerziteta u Beogradu. Elektrotehnicki Fakultet. Publikacije. Serija: Elektroenergetika (SRB ISSN 0351-4749) **3333**
Univerziteta u Beogradu. Elektrotehnicki Fakultet. Publikacije. Serija: Tehnicka Fizika *see* University of Belgrade. Faculty of Electrical Engineering. Publications. Series: Engineering Physics **7044**
Univerziteta u Beogradu. Elektrotehnickog Fakulteta. Publikacije Serija: Automatika *see* University of Belgrade. Faculty of Electrical Engineering. Publications Series: Automatic Control **3333**
➤ Uniwerstytet Slaski w Katowicach. Prace Naukowe. Landform Analysis (POL ISSN 1429-799X) **2799**
Uniwersytet Ekonomiczny we Wroclawiu. Prace Naukowe (POL ISSN 1899-3192) **1190**
Uniwersytet Ekonomiczny we Wroclawiu. Prace Naukowe. Seria: Monografie i Opracowania (POL) **1190**
Uniwersytet im. Adama Mickiewicza. Akustyka (POL ISSN 0554-8039) **7090**
Uniwersytet im. Adama Mickiewicza. Antropologia (POL ISSN 0137-1460) **360**
Uniwersytet im. Adama Mickiewicza. Archeologia (POL ISSN 0554-8195) **422**
Uniwersytet im. Adama Mickiewicza. Astronomia (POL ISSN 0554-8233) **583**
Uniwersytet im. Adama Mickiewicza. Biologia (POL ISSN 0554-811X) **710**
Uniwersytet im. Adama Mickiewicza. Chemia (POL ISSN 0554-8241) **2083**
Uniwersytet im. Adama Mickiewicza. Filologia Angielska (POL ISSN 0554-8144) **5192**
Uniwersytet im. Adama Mickiewicza. Filologia Klasyczna (POL ISSN 0554-8160) **5192**
Uniwersytet im. Adama Mickiewicza. Filozofia - Logika (POL) **6959**
Uniwersytet im. Adama Mickiewicza. Fizyka (POL ISSN 0554-825X) **7045**
Uniwersytet im. Adama Mickiewicza. Geografia (POL ISSN 0554-8128) **4033**
Uniwersytet im. Adama Mickiewicza. Geologia (POL ISSN 0239-7560) **2773**
Uniwersytet im. Adama Mickiewicza. Historia Sztuki (POL ISSN 0556-1019) **524**
Uniwersytet im. Adama Mickiewicza. Prawo (POL ISSN 0083-4262) **4806**
Uniwersytet im. Adama Mickiewicza. Psychologia-Pedagogika (POL ISSN 0083-4254) **2923**
Uniwersytet im. Adama Mickiewicza w Poznaniu. Filologia Rosyjska (POL ISSN 0137-1452) **5393**
Uniwersytet im. Adama Mickiewicza. Zoologia (POL ISSN 0554-8136) **966**
Uniwersytet Jagiellonski. Instytut Botaniki. Prace Botaniczne/Jagellonian University. Institute of Botany. Botanical Papers (POL ISSN 1509-9156) **821**
Uniwersytet Jagiellonski. Instytut Filologii Wschodnioslowianskiej. Katedra Literatury i Kultury Rosyjskiej. Prace (POL) **5393**
Uniwersytet Jagiellonski. Instytut Geografii i Gospodarki Przestrzennej. Prace Geograficzne (POL ISSN 1644-3586) **4033**
• Uniwersytet Jagiellonski. Oberwatorium Krakowskie. Rocznik Astronomiczny/S A C (Supplemento ad Annuario Cracoviense) (POL) **583**
Uniwersytet Jagiellonski. Oberwatorium Krakowskie. Rocznik Astronomiczny. Dodatek Miedzynarodowy *see* Uniwersytet Jagiellonski. Oberwatorium Krakowskie. Rocznik Astronomiczny **583**
➤ Uniwersytet Jagiellonski. Osrodek Badan Prasoznawczych. Zeszyty Prasoznawcze (POL ISSN 0555-0025) **4584**
Uniwersytet Jagiellonski. Wydzial Prawa i Administracji. Monografie (POL) **4806**
Uniwersytet Jagiellonski. Zeszyty Naukowe. Acta Chimica (POL ISSN 0867-1095) **2083**
• Uniwersytet Jagiellonski. Zeszyty Naukowe. Acta Mathematica (POL ISSN 0860-0120) **5545**
Uniwersytet Jagiellonski. Zeszyty Naukowe. Opuscula Musealia (POL ISSN 0239-9989) **6539**
Uniwersytet Jagiellonski. Zeszyty Naukowe. Prace Archeologiczne (POL ISSN 0083-4300) **422**
Uniwersytet Jagiellonski. Zeszyty Naukowe. Prace Etnograficzne (POL ISSN 0083-4327) **360**
Uniwersytet Jagiellonski. Zeszyty Naukowe. Prace Historyczne (POL ISSN 0083-4351) **4275**
Uniwersytet Jagiellonski. Zeszyty Naukowe. Prace Historyczno-Literackie (POL ISSN 0083-436X) **5394**
Uniwersytet Jagiellonski. Zeszyty Naukowe. Prace Jezykoznawcze (POL ISSN 0083-4378) **5192**
Uniwersytet Jagiellonski. Zeszyty Naukowe. Prace Pedagogiczne/Universitas Iagellonica Acta Scientiarum Litterarumque. Schedae Paedagogicae (POL ISSN 0239-5436) **2923**

Title

10996 UNIWERSYTET JAGIELLONSKI. ZESZYTY NAUKOWE. PRACE POLONIJNE ULRICH'S PERIODICALS

Uniwersytet Jagiellonski. Zeszyty Naukowe. Prace Polonijne/Universitas Iagellonica. Acta Scientiarum Litterarumque. Polonia Extranea (POL ISSN 0137-2416) 4275
Uniwersytet Jagiellonski. Zeszyty Naukowe. Prace Prawnicze/Universitas Iagellonica. Acta Scientiarum Litterarumque. Schedae Iuridicae (POL ISSN 0083-4394) 4806
Uniwersytet Jagiellonski. Zeszyty Naukowe. Prace Psychologiczne (POL ISSN 0239-5428) 7414
Uniwersytet Jagiellonski. Zeszyty Naukowe. Prace z Bibliotekoznawstwa i Informacji Naukowej/Jagiellonian University. Studies in Librarianship and Information Science (POL ISSN 1230-7025) 5053
Uniwersytet Jagiellonski. Zeszyty Naukowe. Prace z Nauk Politycznych (POL ISSN 0137-2378) 7191
Uniwersytet Jagiellonski. Zeszyty Naukowe. Prace z Wynalazczosci i Ochrony Wlanosci Intelektualnej/Universitas Iagellonica Acta Scientiarum Litterarumque. Opera quae ad Arten Inventionis et ad Defensionem Domini Intellectualis Spectant (POL ISSN 0137-236X) 4806
Uniwersytet Jagiellonski. Zeszyty Naukowe. Studia Religiologica/Universitas Iagellonica. Acta Scientiarum Litterarumque. Studia Religiologica (POL ISSN 0137-2432) 7692
Uniwersytet Opolski. Biblioteka Glowna. Rocznik (POL ISSN 1506-588X) 5054
Uniwersytet Opolski. Wydzial Teologiczny. Czlowiek - Rodzina - Spoleczenstwo (POL) 8145
Uniwersytet Opolski. Wydzial Teologiczny. Przeglad Pismiennictwa Teologicznego (POL ISSN 1425-7998) 7692
Uniwersytet Opolski. Wydzial Teologiczny. Studia Biblijne. Scriptura Sacra (POL ISSN 1428-7218) 7692
Uniwersytet Opolski. Zeszyty Naukowe. Chemia (POL ISSN 1640-131X) 2083
Uniwersytet Opolski. Zeszyty Naukowe. Ekonomia (POL ISSN 1234-5369) 1523
Uniwersytet Opolski. Zeszyty Naukowe. Filologia Angielska (POL ISSN 1427-6445) 5192
Uniwersytet Opolski. Zeszyty Naukowe. Filologia Polska (POL ISSN 1427-2644) 5394
Uniwersytet Opolski. Zeszyty Naukowe. Filologia Rosyjska (POL ISSN 1425-3410) 5394
Uniwersytet Opolski. Zeszyty Naukowe. Fizyka (POL) 7045
Uniwersytet Opolski. Zeszyty Naukowe. Historia (POL ISSN 1425-3399) 4275
Uniwersytet Opolski. Zeszyty Naukowe. Jezykoznawstwo (POL ISSN 1427-6461) 5192
Uniwersytet Opolski. Zeszyty Naukowe. Nauki Techniczne (POL ISSN 1427-6623) 3226
Uniwersytet Opolski. Zeszyty Naukowe. Pedagogika (POL ISSN 1426-689X) 3086
Uniwersytet Opolski. Zeszyty Naukowe. Prace Germanistyczne (POL ISSN 1509-2178) 5394
Uniwersytet Opolski. Zeszyty Naukowe. Seria A. Filologia Germanska see Uniwersytet Opolski. Zeszyty Naukowe. Prace Germanistyczne 5394
Uniwersytet Opolski. Zeszyty Naukowe. Seria A. Nauki Spoleczno-Polityczne (POL ISSN 1427-6437) 8013
Uniwersytet Opolski. Zeszyty Naukowe. Studia i Monografie (POL ISSN 1233-6408) 4481
Uniwersytet Opolski. Zeszyty Naukowe. Stylistyka (POL) 5192
Uniwersytet Przyrodniczy we Wroclawiu. Zeszyty Naukowe (POL ISSN 1897-208X) 167
Uniwersytet Przyrodniczy we Wroclawiu. Zeszyty Naukowe. Bibliografie (POL) 189
Uniwersytet Przyrodniczy we Wroclawiu. Zeszyty Naukowe. Konferencje (POL) 167
Uniwersytet Przyrodniczy we Wroclawiu. Zeszyty Naukowe. Monografie (POL) 167
● Uniwersytet Przyrodniczy we Wroclawiu. Zeszyty Naukowe. Rolnictwo (POL ISSN 1897-2098) 167
Uniwersytet Przyrodniczy we Wroclawiu. Zeszyty Naukowe. Rozprawy (POL) 167
Uniwersytet Slaski w Katowicach. Prace Naukowe. Acta Biologica Silesiana (POL ISSN 0860-2441) 710
➤ Uniwersytet Slaski w Katowicach. Prace Naukowe. Annales Mathematicae Silesianae (POL ISSN 0860-2107) 5545
➤ Uniwersytet Slaski w Katowicach. Prace Naukowe. Folia Philosophica (POL ISSN 1231-0913) 6959
➤ Uniwersytet Slaski w Katowicach. Prace Naukowe. Geographia: Studia et Dissertationes (POL ISSN 0208-5054) 4033
➤ Uniwersytet Slaski w Katowicach. Prace Naukowe. Geologia (POL ISSN 0208-5534) 2773
➤ Uniwersytet Slaski w Katowicach. Prace Naukowe. Kras i Speleologia (POL ISSN 0137-5482) 2773
➤ Uniwersytet Slaski w Katowicach. Prace Naukowe. Neophilologica (POL ISSN 0208-5550) 5192
➤ Uniwersytet Slaski w Katowicach. Prace Naukowe. Problemy Prawa Karnego (POL ISSN 0208-5577) 4899
➤ Uniwersytet Slaski w Katowicach. Prace Naukowe. Problemy Prawne Handlu Zagranicznego (POL ISSN 0208-5496) 4944
➤ Uniwersytet Slaski w Katowicach. Prace Naukowe. Psychologia. Badania i Aplikacje (POL ISSN 1428-8664) 7414
➤ Uniwersytet Slaski w Katowicach. Prace Naukowe. Rusycystyczne Studia Literaturoznawcze (POL ISSN 0208-5038) 5394
➤ Uniwersytet Slaski w Katowicach. Prace Naukowe. Z Problematyki Prawa Pracy i Polityki Socjalnej (POL ISSN 0208-5003) 4806
➤ Uniwersytet Warminsko-Mazurski. Prace Jezykoznawcze (POL ISSN 1509-5304) 5192
➤ Uniwersytet Warminsko-Mazurski w Olsztynie. Biuletyn Naukowy (POL ISSN 1640-1395) 7927
Uniwersytet Warminsko-Mazurski w Olsztynie. Rozprawy i Monografie (POL ISSN 1509-3018) 7927
Uniwersytet Wroclawski. Instytut Geograficzny. Prace. Seria A: Geografia Fizyczna (POL ISSN 0137-107X) 4033
Uniwersytet Wroclawski. Instytut Geograficzny. Prace. Seria B: Geografia Spoleczna i Ekonomiczna (POL ISSN 0137-1088) 4033
Uniwersytet Wroclawski. Instytut Geograficzny. Prace. Seria C: Meteorologia i Klimatologia (POL) 6397
Uniwesytet Opolski. Zeszyty Naukowe. Matematyka (POL ISSN 1426-6881) 5545
UniWorld/UniMonde (CAN ISSN 1183-725X) 3009
UNIX Computer World (PRT) 2599
UNIX Magazine (JPN ISSN 0913-0748) 2599
● UNIX Update (USA) 2599
UNIX Video Quarterly (USA) 2599
● UnixNT (GBR ISSN 1473-0693) 2599
● Unjust Dismissal (USA) 1713
Unknown see Doe 5069
● Unknown Magazine (USA ISSN 1096-3790) 6744
Unknown Public (GBR) 6625
● UNLar Ciencia (Universidad Nacional de la Rioja) (ARG ISSN 1515-5005) 7927
Unleashed (USA ISSN 1536-8904) 5085
● Unlikely Stories (USA) 5437
▼ Unlimited (CAN) 1190
Unlimited (GBR) 1855
● Unlimited (NZL ISSN 1174-7366) 1799
UnlimitedNet see Unlimited 1799
Unlinked Anonymous Prevalence Monitoring Programme in the United Kingdom (GBR) 5828
Unmanned Aerial Vehicles and Targets see Jane's Unmanned Aerial Vehicles and Targets 63
▼ ● Unmanned Maritime Vehicles and Systems (GBR ISSN 1759-717X) 6451
● ➤ Unmanned Systems (USA ISSN 0892-4023) 6451
● Unmarried America (USA) 7944
Unmuzzled Ox (USA ISSN 0049-5557) 5437
Unnat Krishi (IND) 167
Unnatkrishi/Progress in Agriculture (IND ISSN 0566-2540) 167
Unnayan Bitarka (BGD) 5192
Unnerluussisuunerup. -Imut Ukiumoortumik Nalunaarusiaaa. Kalaallit Nunaanni Politit Pillugit Naammagittaalliuutit Suliarineqarnerat see Rigsadvokaten. Beretning, Behandling af Klager over Politiet i Groenland 2667
Uno (ESP ISSN 1133-9853) 5545
● Uno Mas Uno (MEX ISSN 0188-3615) 3911
Uno Mismo (ARG ISSN 1669-3795) 7414
Uno Mismo (MEX ISSN 0188-395X) 6999
Uno por Uno (ESP ISSN 1133-8121) 7414
UNO. Waikato Lifestyle Magazine see U N O (Waikato Edition) 5085
The Unofficial Guide to Disneyland (USA ISSN 1053-248X) 8770
● Unquote (GBR ISSN 0967-4616) 1657
Unrestrained! (CAN) 6625
The Unrorean (USA) 5437
Unscheduled Events (USA ISSN 0042-0468) 8145
Unschoolers Network (USA ISSN 1057-1043) 3086
Unsearchable Riches (USA ISSN 0042-0476) 7692
Unser Arbeitsbrief (DEU) 2170
Unser Baby (DEU) 2170
† Unser Betrieb (DEU ISSN 0343-8198) 8996
Unser Bocholt (DEU ISSN 0566-2575) 3859
Unser Dorfblaettchen (DEU) 7191
Unser Erstes Baby Kommt see Geburtsvorbereitung 2153
Unser Garten (DEU) 3753
Unser Haus (DEU) 4551
Unser Hund (DEU) 6816
Unser Land (Passau) (DEU) 167
Unser Neustadt (AUT ISSN 0042-0484) 2630
Unser Niederland (DEU ISSN 1433-5859) 4275
Unser Oberschlesien (DEU ISSN 0343-5113) 4275
Unser Oe T B Turnen (AUT) 8214
Unser Pferd (DEU ISSN 0342-7331) 8300
Unser Rassehund (DEU) 6816
Unser Schaffen (AUT ISSN 0042-0492) 4086
Unser Tsait (USA ISSN 0042-0506) 7731
Unser Wald (DEU ISSN 0935-7017) 3706
Unser Wanderbote (DEU) 8214
Unsere Alte Liebe (DEU) 8284
Unsere Archive (DEU) 4166
Unsere Eintracht see Eintracht Frankfurt 8227
● Unsere Familie (DEU ISSN 0945-5027) 7743
Unsere Gemeinde (DEU ISSN 0042-0522) 4076
Unsere Generation (AUT) 8076
Unsere Heimat (AUT ISSN 1017-2696) 4276
Unsere Heimat (Wohlen) (CHE) 4276
Unsere Hunde (AUT) 6816
Unsere Jagd (DEU ISSN 0566-2621) 8339
Unsere Jugend (DEU ISSN 0342-5258) 2170
Unsere Kirche - Der Weg - Sonntagsgruss (DEU) 7778
Unsere Post (DEU ISSN 0941-8431) 3859
Unsere Stadt (DEU) 7191
Unsere Tiere Daheim (DEU) 6816
● Unsere Welt (CHE ISSN 1423-6826) 7272
Unsere Windhunde (DEU) 6816
Unsere Wirtschaft (DEU ISSN 1439-829X) 1411
Unsigned Showcase (GBR ISSN 1478-7563) 6625
▼ Unsigned the Magazine (USA) 6625
● Unstrung Insider (USA) 2373
● Unsu'eob Tong'gye Jo'sa Bo'go'seo/Korea (Republic). National Statistical Office. Report on the Transport Survey (KOR ISSN 1599-063X) 8532
Unter Einem Dach (DEU) 4526
Unter Uns (DEU) 4086
Unterhaltung fuer Friedrichstadt und die Angraenzende Gegend (DEU ISSN 0933-3428) 4276
Unternehmen der Zukunft (DEU ISSN 1439-2585) 1190
Unternehmen Stellen Sich Vor (DEU) 6704
Unternehmens-Steuern Aktuell (DEU ISSN 1611-6011) 1954
† Unternehmensberater (DEU ISSN 1435-5418) 8996
Unternehmensfinanzierung (DEU) 1190
Unternehmensfuehrung und Logistik (DEU ISSN 1437-711X) 1908
Unternehmenskybernetik in der Praxis (DEU ISSN 1615-8431) 1799
Unternehmensrechnung und Insolvenzwesen (DEU ISSN 1616-9247) 1389
Unternehmer (AUT ISSN 0042-0581) 7544
Der Unternehmer (CHE ISSN 1422-8866) 1425
Unternehmer Magazin (DEU ISSN 0173-3664) 1799
UnternehmerBrief Bauwirtschaft (DEU) 1042
Die Unternehmerin (DEU ISSN 0938-3875) 1190
Die Unternehmung (CHE ISSN 0042-059X) 1799
Die Unternehmung im Markt (DEU ISSN 0566-2710) 1550
Unterricht Arbeit und Technik (DEU ISSN 1438-8987) 3087
Unterricht Biologie (DEU ISSN 0341-5260) 710
Unterricht Chemie (DEU) 2083
Unterricht Physik (DEU) 7045
Unterricht Wirtschaft (DEU ISSN 1616-1076) 3087
Unterrichten mit Geographie Aktuell (DEU ISSN 0948-1966) 4033
Unterrichtsblaetter fuer die Bundeswehrverwaltung (DEU ISSN 0042-0611) 7474
● Die Unterrichtspraxis/Teaching German (USA ISSN 0042-062X) 5192
Unterrichtswissenschaft (DEU ISSN 0340-4099) 2923
Untersuchung zur Arbeit von Planern (AUT ISSN 1992-1888) 1042
Untersuchungen ueber das Spar-, Giro- und Kreditwesen. Abteilung A: Wirtschaftswissenschaft see Studien zur Kredit- und Finanzwirtschaft 1384
Untersuchungen ueber das Spar-, Giro- und Kreditwesen. Abteilung B: Rechtswissenschaft (DEU ISSN 0720-7352) 1389
Untersuchungen ueber Gruppen und Verbaende (DEU ISSN 0566-2753) 1425
Untersuchungen zur Deutschen Literaturgeschichte (DEU ISSN 0083-4564) 5394
➤ Untersuchungen zur Gegenwartskunde Suedosteuropas (DEU) 4276
Untersuchungen zur Oesterreichischen Literatur des 20. Jahrhunderts see Zur Neueren Literatur Oesterreichs 5405
Untersuchungen zur Ordnungstheorie und Ordnungspolitik (DEU) 1190
Untersuchungen zur Sprach- und Literaturgeschichte der Romanischen Voelker (DEU ISSN 0083-4580) 5192
Untersuchungen zur Textheorie see Research in Text Theory 5166
Untersuchungen zur Wirtschafts-, Sozial- und Technikgeschichte (DEU ISSN 0170-1657) 8013
Unterwasser (DEU ISSN 0947-9155) 8214
● UnterWasserWelt (DEU) 8214
Unterwegs (Munich) (DEU ISSN 0930-1313) 7692
Unterwegs (Stuttgart) (DEU ISSN 1436-607X) 7778
Untitled (GBR ISSN 0969-9716) 524
Untitled (USA) 5437
Untold (GBR ISSN 1462-6497) 5085
Unwired (ZAF ISSN 1991-217X) 2440
Un'yu to Keizai/Transportation and Economy (JPN ISSN 0287-8305) 8519
Unzip see C J P Magazine 4976
Unzip XS see C J P XS 4976
Unzipped Monthly (USA ISSN 1096-2182) 6301
Uo/Fishes (JPN ISSN 0388-5461) 966
UofL see U of L 2305
Uomini & Business (ITA ISSN 1124-2108) 1190
Uomini Comunicazione (ITA ISSN 1825-5825) 4584
Uomini Comunicazione P A (Pubblica Amministrazione) (ITA ISSN 1825-5833) 7475
Uomini & Storie (ITA ISSN 1127-4107) 8145
Uomini e Trasporti (ITA ISSN 1592-0534) 8519
† Uomo (ITA ISSN 1591-7177) 8996
Uomo Citta Territorio (ITA ISSN 0394-5669) 3899
Uomo Collezioni see Collezioni Uomo 2253
L'Uomo Nero (ITA ISSN 1828-4663) 8484
Uomo Vogue (ITA ISSN 1120-7760) 2262
Uongozi: Journal of Management Development (TZA ISSN 0856-1435) 1799
Uova di Porcellana da Collezionare (ITA ISSN 1828-7506) 540
Uozu Aquarium. Annual Report see Uozu Shuizokukan Nenpo 3611
Uozu Shuizokukan Nenpo/Uozu Aquarium. Annual Report (JPN ISSN 0917-9631) 3611
Up (SWE ISSN 1401-8659) 524
Up Beat (GBR) 7692
Up - Date (THA ISSN 0858-6934) 7927
Up-date (THA) 1411
Up Here (CAN ISSN 0828-4253) 4983
Up in Cumming Magazine (USA) 5085
● Up Magazine (GBR) 6625
Up Magazine (NLD) 6625
● UP Magazine (USA ISSN 1935-1615) 5243
Up Rope (USA) 8339
Up the Gatineau! (CAN ISSN 0700-933X) 3786
Up to Date (GBR ISSN 1358-8923) 2373
Up-to-Date Construction Guide see Constru-Guia al Dia 994
Up-to-Date Price Magazine (USA) 1847
Up2 Scrap (NZL ISSN 1176-8495) 4350
Upbeat (GBR) 6625
Upbeat (USA) 6626
Upchurch Bulletin (USA ISSN 0270-465X) 3786
Update (DEU) 3859
Update see Library and Information Update 5027
Update (GBR ISSN 1479-7380) 6626
† ● Update (NZL ISSN 1176-6964) 8996
Update (PRT ISSN 0871-620X) 5727
Update see Up - Date 7927
● Update (UAE) 8664
Update see Society of Otorhinolaryngology and Head-Neck Nurses. Update 6085
● The Update (USA) 2599
Update (Bielefeld) (DEU) 3859
Update (Birmingham) (USA) 6221
Update (Chicago) (USA) 8076
Update (London) (GBR) 6626
† Update (New York) (USA) 8996
● ➤ Update (Online) (USA ISSN 1945-0109) 6626
Update (Pretoria) see Satour National Grading and Classification Scheme Update 8754
UPDATE (Reston) (USA) 6999
Update (Sacramento) (California Dental Association) (USA ISSN 1942-4353) 5868
Update (San Diego) (USA) 4380
Update (Smithsonian Institution Traveling Exhibition Service) (USA ISSN 0272-0345) 6539
Update (South African Edition) (ZAF ISSN 0258-929X) 5727
Update (Stellenbosch) see University of Stellenbosch. Bureau for Economic Research. Update 1523
● Update (Virginia) (USA) 3682
● Update (Washington, 1977) (USA ISSN 0160-9203) 5054
Update (Washington, D.C.) (USA ISSN 1534-8865) 4806
Update C S L (USA) 5054
● Update for Primary Care (GBR ISSN 1742-8947) 5727
● Update in Anaesthesia (GBR ISSN 1353-4882) 5774
Update. Journal of Postgraduate General Practice see General Practice Update 5619
Update of Personal Trust Asset Trends Among U.S. Banks (USA ISSN 1931-5325) 1389
Update on Analytical Studies Research see Mise a Jour des Etudes Analytiques 8388
● ➤ Update on Cancer Therapeutics (NLD ISSN 1872-115X) 6036
Update on Reduced-risk Pesticides in Canada see Mise a Jour sur les Pesticides a Risque Reduit au Canada 7531
Update on the Courts (USA ISSN 1066-0194) 4966
Update, Southern Air see Breathe (Birmingham) 6212
Update Standards see British Standards Institution. Update Standards 6747
Update to A Selective History of the Crego Family (USA ISSN 1085-0953) 3786
Updatebulletin Flexibiliteit in Arbeidsrelaties (NLD ISSN 1567-2417) 1713
Updates see University of New England. Teaching & Learning Centre. Updates 8996
Updates (Columbus) (USA) 4399
Updates at N R S A see Updates@nrsa 2718
Updates in Dermatology see Physician Forum 5696
† Updates in Lymphomatous Meningitis (GBR ISSN 1744-196X) 8996
● Updates in Therapeutics (USA ISSN 1948-1136) 6884
Updates@nrsa (IND ISSN 0973-1725) 2718
Updating Master Tax Pack see Tax Tool Box 4793
Updating School Board Policies (USA ISSN 1081-8286) 3035
● Upfront (GBR ISSN 0956-0742) 1607
Upfront see Red Rag 298
Upgrade (GBR) 8786
Upgrade (USA ISSN 1937-2493) 2599
▼ Upgrade (Birmingham) (USA ISSN 1940-1043) 5085
● Upgrade (English Edition) (ESP ISSN 1684-5285) 8444
Upholstery Design & Management see Upholstery Manufacturing (Mt. Morris) 4563
● Upholstery Journal (USA ISSN 1072-5628) 8462
● Upholstery Manufacturing (Mt. Morris) (USA ISSN 1556-990X) 4563
The Upland Almanac (USA ISSN 1541-597X) 8339
Uplift (IND ISSN 0377-6352) 8076

➤ Uttar Pradesh Journal of Zoology (IND ISSN 0256-971X) **966**
Uttar Pradesh Rozgar Digest (IND) **1713**
Uttar Pradesh. State Planning Institute. Quarterly Bulletin of Statistics (IND ISSN 0042-1626) **8413**
Uttar Ujala (IND) **3890**
Uttarakhanda Bharati (IND) **4190**
▼ • UTUonline (University of Turku) (FIN ISSN 1797-4461) **3009**
Utusan Sarawak (MYS) **3907**
• Utveier (NOR ISSN 1503-8386) **7191**
• Utviklingen i Norsk Kosthold (NOR ISSN 1504-5072) **6670**
• Utviklingstrekk i Helse- og Socialsektoren (NOR ISSN 1890-1468) **8076**
Uudenmaan Alueen Insinoori see Uudenmaan Insinoori Ins. **4604**
Uudenmaan Insinoori Ins. (FIN ISSN 1796-1211) **4604**
Uudistuva Konttori see Portaali **1854**
▼ Uusi Insinoori (FIN ISSN 1796-8178) **4604**
Uusi Nainen (FIN ISSN 0500-8476) **8887**
Uusimaa (FIN ISSN 0357-1858) **3839**
• Uutispaeivae Demari (FIN ISSN 1457-9545) **3839**
Uw Eigen Drogist (NLD ISSN 1574-6089) **6884**
• Uxbridge Times-Journal (CAN ISSN 0834-7336) **3819**
• De Uytvaert (NLD ISSN 1381-9135) **8770**
Uzbek Journal of Biology see Uzbekskii Biologicheskii Zhurnal **710**
Uzbek Journal on Chemistry see O'zbekiston Kimyo Jurnali **2075**
Uzbek Tili Va Adabieti (UZB ISSN 0134-2258) **5394**
Uzbekiston Matematika Zhurnali see Uzbekskii Matematicheskii Zhurnal **7045**
Uzbekiston Neft va Gaz Zhurnal (UZB) **6796**
Uzbekiston Ovozi (UZB) **3994**
Uzbekiston Respublikasi Khikumatining Karorlary Tuplami (UZB) **7191**
Uzbekskii Biologicheskii Zhurnal/O'zbekiston Biologiya Jurnali/Uzbek Journal of Biology (UZB ISSN 0042-1685) **710**
Uzbekskii Fizicheskii Zhurnal (UZB ISSN 1025-8817) **7045**
Uzbekskii Khimicheskii Zhurnal see O'zbekiston Kimyo Jurnali **2075**
Uzbekskii Matematicheskii Zhurnal/Uzbekiston Matematika Zhurnali (UZB ISSN 1027-3433) **7045**
• Uzlet & Siker (HUN ISSN 1588-5909) **1190**
Az Uzlettars (HUN ISSN 1786-9048) **1190**
Uzuri (USA ISSN 1932-1430) **2262**
Uzytkowanie Gruntow, Powierzchnia Zasiewow i Poglowie Zwierzat Gospodarskich see Poland. Glowny Urzad Statystyczny. Uzytkowanie Gruntow, Powierzchnia Zasiewow i Poglowie Zwierzat Gospodarskich **185**
Die V (AUT) **4380**
V (CZE ISSN 1213-7375) **3833**
V 8 Bathurst Magazine (AUS ISSN 1444-4003) **8214**
V-8 Times (USA ISSN 0274-5003) **369**
V A A see Veterinary Anaesthesia and Analgesia **8811**
The V A C Magazine see Collective **482**
V A C R O Reporter (Victorian Association for the Care and Resettlement of Offenders) (AUS ISSN 1039-9216) **2671**
V A G see Voting Assistance Guide **7192**
➤ V A H P E R D Journal (Virginia Association for Health, Physical Education and Dance) (USA ISSN 0739-4586) **6999**
• V A M A S. Bulletin (Versailles on Advanced Materials and Standards) (GBR ISSN 1016-2178) **6407**
• V A M Bulletin (Validated Analytical Measurements) (GBR ISSN 0957-1914) **2107**
V A M P (NLD ISSN 1874-1797) **5727**
V A N see Virginia Appalachian Notes **3786**
V A N see Vernacular Architecture Newsletter **460**
V A-Nytt (NOR ISSN 1503-6073) **8835**
V A R see Visual Arts Research **525**
V A R Business see C R N **2510**
• V A R D S Report (Variable Annuity Research & Data Service) (USA ISSN 1049-6173) **4526**
• V A R World (Value Added Reselling) (GBR ISSN 1358-7927) **2033**
V A S E see Virginia Sports and Entertainment Law Journal **4809**
V A S S A Journal (Vernacular Architecture Society of South Africa) (ZAF ISSN 1562-5257) **460**
V A T Briefing (Value Added Tax) (GBR ISSN 0964-5632) **1954**
V A T Gram see Butterworths V A T Gram **1914**
V A T I S Update. Biotechnology (Value Added Technology Information Service) (IND ISSN 0971-5622) **751**
V A T I S Update. Food Processing (Value Added Technology Information Services) (IND ISSN 0971-5649) **3666**
V A T I S Update. Non-Conventional Energy (Value Added Technology Information Service) (IND ISSN 0971-5630) **3178**
V A T I S Update. Ozone Layer Protection (Value Added Technology Information Service) (IND ISSN 0971-5657) **3473**
V A T I S Update. Waste Technology (Value Added Technology Information Service) (IND ISSN 0971-5665) **3513**
V A T Service see Croner's Reference Book for V A T **1918**
• V A T T Nyt (Valtion Taloudellinen Tutkimuskeskus) (FIN ISSN 1236-0716) **1190**
V A V - Nytt see Svenskt Vatten **8832**
V & A Magazine (Victoria & Albert) (GBR ISSN 1465-8291) **6539**
V & S see Viaggiesapori **8772**
V & S Priser, Anlaeg Netto see Anlaeg Netto **976**
V & S Priser, Beskrivelsestekster see Beskrivelsestekster **981**
V & S Priser, Bygningsdele see Bygningsdele **988**
V & S Priser, Groenland see Groenland **1010**
V & S Priser, Husbygning Brutto see Husbygning Brutto **1013**
V & S Priser, Husbygning Netto see Husbygning Netto **1013**
V & S Priser, Miljoe see Miljoe **1024**
V & S Priser. Renovering og Drift - Brutto see Renovering & Drift - Brutto **1032**
V & S Priser, Renovering og Drift - Netto see Renovering og Drift - Netto **1032**
V B see Video Business **2403**
• V B A News Journal (Virginia Bar Association) (USA ISSN 1522-0974) **4806**
V B B A Magazin (Vereinigung der Beschaeftigten der Berufs- und Arbeitsmarktdienstleister) (DEU) **4605**
V B B Magazin (Verband der Beamten der Bundeswehr) (DEU ISSN 1437-8094) **6451**
V B Net Advisor see Databased Advisor Magazine **2554**
V B O B Magazin (Verband der Beschaeftigten der Obersten und Oberen Bundesbehoerden) (DEU ISSN 1437-997X) **7475**
V B O Bulletin see F E B Bulletin **1885**
V B O I Magazine see F M T Gezondheidszorg **1744**
V B. Verzekeringsblad see Het Verzekeringsblad **4527**
V B - Vorbeugender Brandschutz see Brandverhuetung und Feuersicherheit **3575**
V - Byggaren (SWE ISSN 0283-5363) **3287**
V-Byggaren see S V R Medlemsblad **4601**
V C A Journal see Victorian Canine Association Journal **6816**
V C A Nieuws (Veiligheids Checklist Aannemers) (NLD ISSN 1573-2169) **6688**
V C H Kurier (Verband Christlicher Hotels) (DEU) **4399**
V C Info (Vereinigung Cockpit) (DEU) **8552**
V.C.O.T. see Veterinary and Comparative Orthopaedics and Traumatology **8811**
V C Oe Magazin (Verkehrsclub Oesterreich) (AUT) **8519**
V C Q see Visual Communication Quarterly **2344**
† V C S Resource Update (Vision Community Services) (USA) **8996**
V D B Mitteilungen (Verein Deutscher Bibliothekare) (DEU ISSN 1617-1071) **5054**
V D B U M - Information (Verband der Baumaschinen-Ingenieure und -Meister e.V.) (DEU ISSN 0940-3035) **1042**
V D B Zeitung (Verband Deutscher Buechsenmacher und Waffenfachhaendler) (DEU) **8214**
V D C - Nachrichten (Verband Deutscher Chemo Techniker und Chemisch - Technischer Association) (DEU) **1411**
V D E - Dialog (Verband der Elektrotechnik, Elektronik, Informationstechnik e.V.) (DEU ISSN 1618-422X) **3333**
V D E Fachberichte (Verband der Elektrotechnik, Elektronik, Informationstechnik) (DEU ISSN 0340-4161) **3333**
V D F Fuehrungskraft see Perspektiven (Cologne) **6475**
V D G S A News (Viola da Gamba Society of America, Inc.) (USA ISSN 0506-306X) **6626**
V D I (Venda & Distribuicao Informatica) (PRT) **2440**
V D I - Berichte (Verein Deutscher Ingenieure e.V.) (DEU ISSN 0083-5560) **3226**
V D I Informationsdienst. Blechbearbeitung see Informationsdienst F I Z Technik. Blechbearbeitung **6315**
V D I Informationsdienst. Drahtherstellung und Drahterzeugnisse see Informationsdienst F I Z Technik. Drahtherstellung und Drahterzeugnisse **3230**
V D I - Nachrichten (Verein Deutscher Ingenieure) (DEU ISSN 0042-1758) **3226**
• V D I - Z (Verein Deutscher Ingenieure) (DEU ISSN 0042-1766) **3226**
V d K Zeitung (Verband der Kriegsbeschaedigten, Kriegshinterbliebenen und Sozialrentner Deutschlands) (DEU) **8076**
V d K Zeitung. Ausgabe Hamburg - Schleswig-Holstein see V d K Zeitung **8076**
V d K Zeitung. Ausgabe Hessen see V d K Zeitung **8076**
V d K Zeitung. Ausgabe Mittelfranken see V d K Zeitung **8076**
V d K Zeitung. Ausgabe Niederbayern see V d K Zeitung **8076**
V d K Zeitung. Ausgabe Niederrhein see V d K Zeitung **8076**
V d K Zeitung. Ausgabe Nordbaden see V d K Zeitung **8076**
V d K Zeitung. Ausgabe Nordwuerttemberg see V d K Zeitung **8076**
V d K Zeitung. Ausgabe Oberbayern see V d K Zeitung **8076**
V d K Zeitung. Ausgabe Oberfranken see V d K Zeitung **8076**
V d K Zeitung. Ausgabe Oberpfalz see V d K Zeitung **8076**
V d K Zeitung. Ausgabe Rheinland see V d K Zeitung **8076**
V d K Zeitung. Ausgabe Rheinland-Pfalz see V d K Zeitung **8076**
V d K Zeitung. Ausgabe Saarland see V d K Zeitung **8076**
V d K Zeitung. Ausgabe Schwaben see V d K Zeitung **8076**
V d K Zeitung. Ausgabe Suedbaden see V d K Zeitung **8076**
V d K Zeitung. Ausgabe Unterfranken see V d K Zeitung **8076**
V d K Zeitung. Ausgabe Westfalen see V d K Zeitung **8076**
V d K Zeitung. Ausgabe Westfalen-Lippe see V d K Zeitung **8076**
V d L see Verniciatura del Legno **1052**
V D L - Journal (Verband Deutscher Akademiker fur Landwirtschaft, Ernahrung und Landespflege) (DEU ISSN 0724-2344) **167**
V D M A Nachrichten (Verband Deutscher Maschinen- und Anlagenbau e.V.) (DEU ISSN 1616-4598) **5461**
V d R Bulletin (Verband der Restauratoren e.V.) (DEU ISSN 1432-6876) **422**
V d R - Schriftenreihe zur Restaurierung und Grabungstechnik (DEU) **422**
V D T A News (Vacuum Dealers Trade Association) (USA) **1847**
V D T A Phone Directory and Product Guide (Vacuum Dealers Trade Association) (USA) **1847**
V D V Magazin (DEU) **3287**
V D V World (Voice Data Video) (USA) **2343**
V D W F im Dialog (Verband Deutscher Werkzeug- und Formenbauer e.V.) (DEU ISSN 1860-4935) **3372**
V E 6 (CAN ISSN 0049-5778) **2364**
• V E A News (Virginia Education Association) (USA ISSN 0042-1790) **2924**
V E Bulletin (Voluntary Euthanasia) (AUS ISSN 1321-0599) **6959**
V E D D Forum (Verband Evangelischer Diakonen- und Diakoninnen-Gemeinschaften in Deutschland e.V.) (DEU ISSN 1431-2549) **7778**
V E I Actualites see Ville - Ecole - Integration Actualites **7295**
V E L A see Venture Equity Latin America **1658**
V E L K D - Informationen (Vereinigte Evangelisch - Lutherische Kirche Deutschlands, Lutherisches Kirchenamt) (DEU ISSN 1617-0741) **7778**
V E O Journal (Verband der Elektrizitaetswerke Oesterreich) (AUT ISSN 1026-9339) **3333**
V E R T I C Annual Report see V E R T I C Matters **7272**
V E R T I C Brief (Verification Research, Training and Information Centre) (GBR ISSN 1740-8083) **7272**
V E R T I C Matters (Verification Research, Training and Information Centre) (GBR) **7272**
V E + T see Vogue Entertaining + Travel **4984**
V E T N E T - E C E R. Proceedings (Vocational Education and Training NETwork - European Conference of Education Research) (GBR) **2924**
V-Eight Times see V-8 Times **369**
V F A Jahrbuch (Vereinigung Freischaffender Architekten) (DEU) **460**
V F D B (Vereinigung zur Foerderung des Deutschen Brandschutzes) (DEU ISSN 1868-6540) **3257**
V F D B - Zeitschrift see V F D B **3257**
V F E D Aktuell (Verband fuer Ernaehrung und Diaetetik e.V.) (DEU) **6670**
V F G - Forum (Vlaamse Federatie van Gemeentesecretarissen) (BEL ISSN 1378-9872) **7504**
V F I Update (Vintners Federation of Ireland) (IRL) **611**
V F M see Victoria Fishing Monthly **8339**
V F M see Video Film Music **2403**
V F T-aktuelt (NOR ISSN 0807-111X) **6336**
V F V see La Revista del Vidrio, Fachadas y Ventanas **2045**
V F W Auxiliary see Ladies Auxiliary V F W **2267**
• V F W Magazine (Veterans of Foreign Wars of the United States) (USA ISSN 0161-8598) **6451**
V F Z (Vieh und Fleisch Handelszeitung) (DEU ISSN 0722-3668) **303**
V-Focus (NLD ISSN 1574-1575) **303**
• V G (Verdens Gang) (NOR ISSN 0805-5203) **3925**
V G (Trykt utg.) see V G **3925**
V G A Nachrichten (Verband der Geschaftsstellenleiter der Assekuranz) (DEU ISSN 0170-9690) **4526**
V G B Kraftwerkstechnik (Technische Vereinigung der Grosskraftwerksbetreiber e.V.) (DEU ISSN 0372-5715) **3333**
V G B PowerTech see V G B Kraftwerkstechnik **3333**
V G D see Victorian Government Directory **7475**
V G Monographs in Mass Spectrometry (GBR ISSN 0965-6758) **2107**
V G S Newsletter (Virginia Genealogical Society) (USA ISSN 1084-5852) **3786**
V G S Nieuws see V G S Nieuwsbrief **7504**
V G S Nieuwsbrief (Vereniging van Gemeentesecretarissen) (NLD ISSN 1380-5398) **7504**
V-gram (USA ISSN 0896-8454) **74**
V H see Victorian Humanist **6960**
V H E T T A Journal see Victorian Journal of Home Economics **4369**
V H E T T A News (Victorian Home Economics & Textiles Teachers Association) (AUS) **4369**
V H F Communications (Very High Frequency) (GBR ISSN 0177-7505) **2364**
V H J O E see Visible Human Journal of Endoscopy **5949**
• V H L Family Forum (Von Hippel-Lindau Disease) (USA ISSN 1066-4130) **6189**
V H L Krant (Von Hippel Lindau) (NLD ISSN 1872-1516) **5727**
V H N see Vierteljahresschrift fuer Heilpaedagogik und Ihre Nachbargebiete **3049**
V H T L Zeitung (CHE) **1190**
V H W Mitteilungen (Verband Hochschule und Wissenschaft) (DEU) **7927**
➤ V I A (USA ISSN 1048-292X) **5244**
V I A (Mission Viejo) (Vision In Action) (USA ISSN 1543-3463) **6648**
V I A Magazin (Verband der Initiativgruppen in der Auslaenderarbeit e.V.) (DEU ISSN 0943-1985) **7218**
V I B S see Value Inquiry Book Series **6959**
V I C Medical Update (Vitamin Information Centre) (ZAF) **6670**
The V I F M Review (Victorian Institute of Forensic Medicine) (AUS ISSN 1448-5842) **5917**
V I J see Victorians Institute Journal **5244**
V I K - Mitteilungen (Verband der Industriellen Energie- und Kraftwirtschaft eV) (DEU ISSN 0341-2318) **3149**
V I M A G azine (Vereniging van Importeurs van Machines en Gereedschappen voor de Metaalindustrie Magazine) (NLD ISSN 1380-0639) **3398**
• V I M P Report (Victorian Initiative for Minerals and Petroleum) (AUS ISSN 1323-4536) **2773**
• ➤ V I N E (Very Informal Newsletter on Library Automation) (GBR ISSN 0305-5728) **5064**
V I N E (London, Online) see V I N E **5064**
• V I N N O V A Analys (SWE ISSN 1651-355X) **1799**
V I N N O V A Debatt see V I N N O V A Forum **1800**
• V I N N O V A Forum (SWE ISSN 1651-3541) **1800**
V I N N O V A Innovation i Fokus see V I N N O V A Analys **1799**
V I N N O V A Meddelande see V I N N O V A Rapport **1800**
• V I N N O V A Policy (SWE ISSN 1651-3568) **1800**
• V I N N O V A Rapport (SWE ISSN 1650-3104) **1800**
V I O see Vrijwillige Inzet Onderzocht **8077**
V I P (Very Irish People) (IRL) **3895**
V I P see Vip **6516**
V I P (NLD ISSN 0926-3241) **2538**
V.I.P. Address Book see (Year) V I P Address Book **36**
(Year) V I P Address Book (USA ISSN 1043-0261) **36**
V I P Address Book Update (USA) **36**
V I P International Golf Edition (Very Important Persons) (DEU) **8770**
V I P International Honeymooner (Very Important Persons) (DEU ISSN 1610-0824) **8771**
V I P International Traveller (Very Important Persons) (DEU ISSN 1617-3910) **8771**
V I P International Traveller Gold Edition (Very Important Persons) (DEU) **8771**
• V I P Newsletter (Virtual Intellectual Property) (USA) **6759**
V I P Premier (RUS) **8013**
V.I.Pets (CAN) **6816**
V I R see Vietnam Investment Review **1192**
V J B O see The Virtual Journal for Biomedical Optics **710**
V J I L see Virginia Journal of International Law **4944**
V J M's Jazz & Blues Mart (GBR ISSN 1360-8924) **6626**
V J S P L see Virginia Journal of Social Policy & the Law **4809**
V K S S Connect (Vedomstvennye Korporativnye Sistemy Seti) (RUS ISSN 1563-194X) **2343**
V L A K - Verslag (Vlaardings Archeologisch Kantoor) (NLD ISSN 1872-521X) **422**
V L A Newsletter (Online) (Virginia Library Association) (USA) **5054**
V L A Newsletter (Print) see V L A Newsletter (Online) **5054**
V L A Shipping List (Online) (Virginia Library Association) (USA) **5054**
V L A Shipping List (Print) see V L A Shipping List (Online) **5054**
V L B see Verzeichnis Lieferbarer Buecher **638**
V L B R see Virginia Law & Business Review **4809**
• V L C T News (Vermont League of Cities & Towns) (USA) **7504**
• ➤ The V L D B Journal (Very Large Data Bases) (DEU ISSN 1066-8888) **2532**
V L K see Verzeichnis Lieferbarer Kaufmedien **8997**
V L R see Vehicle Recovery Link **8678**
• ➤ V L S I Design (Very Large Scale Integration) (USA ISSN 1065-514X) **2474**
V L S I Society of India Vision see V S I Vision **2474**
• V M (FIN ISSN 0355-4295) **8609**

Title

V M (Vauxhall Motors) (GBR) **8609**
V M *see* Vision Monday **6053**
V M *see* Voices from the Middle **3087**
V M *see* Virtual Mentor **5728**
V M & R D *see* Visual Merchandising & Retail Design **36**
• V M & S D (Visual Merchandising & Store Design) (USA ISSN 1072-9666) **4551**
V M B G - Mitteilungen (Ausgabe B G M S) *see* V M B G - Mitteilungen (Ausgabe B G M) **1425**
▼ V M B G - Mitteilungen (Ausgabe B G M) (Vereinigung der Metall-Berufsgenossenschaften) (DEU ISSN 1866-7201) **1425**
V M B G - Mitteilungen (Ausgabe N M B G) *see* V M B G - Mitteilungen (Ausgabe B G M) **1425**
V M B O - Reeks (NLD ISSN 1567-5815) **2924**
V M C Voice (Volunteers for Morris County) (USA) **8076**
• V M E and Critical Systems (USA ISSN 1941-3807) **2525**
V M E Bus Systems *see* V M E and Critical Systems **2525**
V M F (Vieilles Maisons Francaises) (FRA) **460**
V M I X *see* Vibe **6626**
V M P *see* Video - Medicina Primaria **5728**
V M R G Kwaliteitseisen en Adviezen en V R M G Branchegids (Vereniging Metalen Ramen en Gevelbranche) (NLD ISSN 1874-7523) **1042**
V M R Standard Used Car Prices (USA ISSN 1069-8779) **8610**
V M T *see* Voedingsmiddelentechnologie **3667**
• V M T's Ingredientenwijzer (Year) (NLD) **3666**
• V Magazine (USA ISSN 1539-185X) **524**
V Man (Visionaire) (USA ISSN 1546-0835) **6301**
V-Marketing *see* Chenggong Yingxiao **1810**
V N A B Newsletter (Visiting Nurse Association of Brooklyn) (USA) **5983**
V N C *see* Vermont Nurse Connection **5983**
V N G-Magazine (Vereniging van Nederlandse Gemeenten) (NLD ISSN 1566-1636) **7504**
V N R C Bulletin (Vermont Natural Resources Council) (USA) **3473**
V N R C Vermont Environmental Report (Vermont Natural Resources Council) (USA) **3473**
V N Times (Veterinary Nursing) (GBR ISSN 1471-1044) **8810**
V N U Annual Report *see* Verenigde Nederlandse Uitgeversbedrijven. Annual Report **7575**
• V N U Newswire (GBR) **2440**
V N V A Krant *see* V A M P **5727**
V N Vrij Nederland (NLD ISSN 0165-666X) **3916**
V N W Nieuws (Verzameling van Nederlandse Wetgeving) (NLD ISSN 1380-8478) **4806**
V O (Voortgezet Onderwijs) (NLD ISSN 1873-1163) **3035**
V O A Magazine (Vereniging van Ondernemingen in Alphen aan den Rijn) (NLD ISSN 1872-4841) **1800**
V O B S Magazin (Vereinigung fuer Organisation und Betriebsfuehrung Selbstaendiger e.V.) (DEU) **8076**
V O D and I T V Investor *see* V O D & I T V Investor **1657**
• V O D & I T V Investor (Video on Demand and Interactive Television) (USA ISSN 1541-3306) **1657**
V O-Flits (Voortgezet Onderwijs) (NLD ISSN 1873-118X) **3035**
V O H D *see* Verzeichnis der Orientalischen Handschriften in Deutschland **563**
V O H D Supplementbaende *see* Verzeichnis der Orientalischen Handschriften in Deutschland. Supplementbaende **563**
V O I C E (Victory Over Incontinence/Continence Education) (AUS) **6999**
V O I P Business News (Voice Over Internet Protocol) (USA) **2343**
V O M Jaarboek *see* Vereniging voor Overheidsmanagement. Jaarboek **1877**
V O N Canada Annual Report (Year) (Victorian Order of Nurses) (CAN) **5983**
V O N Canada Report (CAN ISSN 0846-135X) **5983**
• V O N Magazine (Voice on the Net) (USA ISSN 1547-6251) **2567**
V O Y A *see* Voice of Youth Advocates **2171**
V & S Generalbeskrivelse (DNK) **1847**
V & S Generalbeskrivelse. Supplement (DNK) **1847**
V og S Priser, Anlaeg Brutto *see* Anlaeg Brutto **976**
V & S Regler for Opmaaling af Byggeri (DNK) **1847**
V P B Almanak *see* Elsevier V P B Almanak **1922**
V P B Gids (Vennootschapsbelasting) (NLD ISSN 1574-1397) **1954**
V P C Newsletter *see* Victorian Parents Council. Newsletter **2924**
V P Magazine (USA ISSN 1553-8273) **1191**
V P N *see* Bijzijn **5953**
V P N *see* Veterinary Practice News **8813**
V P O D Zeitung (Verband des Personals Oeffentlicher Dienste) (CHE) **7504**
V P R *see* Virginia Policy Review **7192**
• V Q (Vite Qualita) (ITA ISSN 1825-6082) **257**
V Q Presents Tattoo Annual *see* Tattoo Annual **591**
V Q Vite, Vino & Qualita *see* V Q **257**
V R *see* Victorian Reports **4808**
V R *see* Visual Resources **525**
† V R (Video Registrare) (ITA ISSN 0394-2384) **8996**
V R A Bulletin *see* Visual Resources Association Bulletin **525**
V R B - Informatie (Vereniging van Religieus - Wetenschappelijke Bibliothecarissen) (BEL ISSN 0777-6306) **5054**
V R Forecaster (USA) **1657**
V R - Future (DEU) **1191**
• V R in the Schools (Virtual Reality) (USA) **2518**
V R M E *see* Visions of Research in Music Education **6627**
V R News (Virtual Reality) (GBR ISSN 1360-3485) **2490**
V R O M-Inspectie. Jaarplan (Volkshuisvesting Ruimtelijke Ordening en Milieu) (NLD ISSN 1874-0103) **1042**
V R O M-Raad. Work Programme (Volkshuisvesting Ruimtelijke Ordening en Milieubeheer) (NLD) **3473**
• V R S (Verkehrsrechts-Sammlung) (DEU ISSN 0342-2496) **4826**
V R - Verpackungs-Rundschau (DEU ISSN 0341-7131) **6715**
• V S A Case Study Series (Volunteer Service Abroad) (NZL ISSN 1177-5025) **1607**
• V S A M Revue (Verband Schweizerischer Angestelltenvereine der Maschinen- und Elektroindustrie) (CHE) **3226**
† V S A M Update (Virtual Storage Access Method) (USA) **8996**
V S A Magazine *see* Vista **8077**
V S A O Journal (Verband Schweizerischer Assistenz- und Oberaerzte) (CHE ISSN 1422-2086) **5727**
V S A Papers *see* Violin Society of America. Papers **6627**
• V S D (Vendredi Samedi Dimanche) (FRA ISSN 1278-916X) **3842**
V S D *see* Vehicle System Dynamics **3399**
• V S D (Viernes Sabado Domingo) (PER ISSN 1605-3346) **3928**
V S D - Mitteilungen (Verband der Schweizer Druckindustrie) (CHE) **7328**
V S F - Bulletin (Vereinigung Schweizerischer Formularhersteller) (CHE) **7328**
V S I G - Mitteilungen/Informations V S I G (Vereinigung des Schweizerischen Import- und Grosshandels) (CHE) **1586**
V S I Vision (V L S I Society of India) (IND ISSN 0973-3515) **2474**
V S J *see* Visual Systems Journal **2510**
V S la Rivista (Valore Scuola) (ITA ISSN 1827-0247) **2924**
V S O Newsletter (Virginia Society of Ornithology) (USA ISSN 1081-0218) **915**
V S Q *see* Voodoo Souls Quarterly **5396**
V S R *see* Vertical Systems Reseller **1847**
• V S T (Vie Sociale et Traitements) (FRA ISSN 0396-8669) **2924**
† • ➤ V S T E Journal (Virginia Society for Technology in Education) (USA) **8996**
V S T X *see* Vacation St. Croix **8771**
• ➤ V S W G - Vierteljahrschrift fuer Sozial- und Wirtschaftsgeschichte (DEU ISSN 0340-8728) **8013**
V Serdtse Evropy *see* Im Herzen Europas **5220**
V Svobodnyi Vecher (BLR) **3800**
• V T A C Guide (Victorian Tertiary Admissions Centre) (AUS) **3009**
V T E *see* Verbindungstechnik in der Elektronik und Feinwerktechnik **8997**
V T F - Post (Verein fuer Tonbandstimmenforschung e.V.) (DEU ISSN 0174-3538) **6744**
V T I Aktuellt (Vaeg-och Transportforskningsinstitut) (SWE ISSN 0347-9382) **8636**
V T I EC Research (Statens Vaeg- och Transportforskningsinstitut) (SWE ISSN 1403-4905) **8636**
V T I Facts and Figures. Annual Report (Statens Vaeg- och Transportforskningsinstitut) (SWE) **8636**
V T I i Siffror (Statens Vaeg- och Transportforskningsinstitut) (SWE) **8636**
• V T I Konferens (Statens Vaeg- och Transportforskningsinstitut) (SWE ISSN 1104-7267) **8636**
V T I Meddelande (Statens Vaeg- och Transportforskningsinstitut) (SWE ISSN 0347-6049) **8636**
• V T I Rapport (Statens Vaeg- och Transportforskningsinstitut) (SWE ISSN 0347-6030) **8636**
➤ V T I Saertryck (Statens Vaeg- och Transportforskningsinstitut) (SWE ISSN 1102-626X) **8636**
V.T. Krishnamachari Memorial Lecture Series (IND) **1191**
V T M S *see* Vehicle Thermal Management Systems Conference Proceedings **3359**
V T M S Conference Proceedings on CD-ROM *see* Vehicle Thermal Management Systems Conference Proceedings **3359**
V T M Science/Science, Technology and We (Veda, Technika a My) (CZE ISSN 1214-4754) **2219**
V T T Annual Report (Valtion Teknillinen Tutkimuskeskus) (FIN) **3226**
V T T Magazine (Velo Tout Terrain) (FRA ISSN 0299-4208) **8270**
• V T T Tiedotteita/Meddelanden/Research Notes (Valtion Teknillinen Tutkimuskeskus) (FIN ISSN 1235-0605) **8444**
V T T Toimintakertomus (Valtion Teknillinen Tutkimuskeskus) (FIN ISSN 0358-1861) **3226**
V T Wonen (NLD ISSN 0165-5175) **4983**
V-Twin (USA ISSN 1088-1557) **8270**
V-Twin Annual (USA ISSN 1932-8052) **8270**
V-Twin Magazine Presents the New Bike Builder's Handbook for Harley-Davidson and V-Twin Owners *see* Bike Builder's Handbook for Harley-Davidson and V-Twin Owners **8255**
V U G *see* The Virtual University Gazette **2947**
V U L R *see* Valparaiso University Law Review **4806**
• V U - Owners (USA) **2567**
V u R *see* Verbraucher und Recht **7615**
V U U Informer (Virginia Union University) (USA) **2307**
V V *see* VigneVini **257**
V V *see* Verwarming en Ventilatie **4127**
V V A O Magazine (Vereniging van Vrouwen met Hogere Opleiding) (NLD ISSN 1871-9481) **2307**
The V V A Veteran (Vietnam Veterans of America) (USA ISSN 1069-0220) **6451**
V V E C Power Circuit (USA ISSN 1933-2513) **3162**
V V O Basisvorming *see* Nieuwsbrief Onderbouw **8977**
V V O Flits *see* V O-Flits **3035**
V V O Magazine *see* V O **3035**
V V P (Verenigde Verzekerings Per) (NLD ISSN 1388-2724) **4526**
V V S *see* H V A C Magasinet **4120**
• V V S - Aktuelt (NOR ISSN 0802-5258) **4127**
V V S - Forum (Varme Vatten Sanitet) (SWE ISSN 0346-4644) **4127**
V V S og El Horisont *see* Installatoer Horisont **4121**
V V W C A Newsletter (Vintage Volkswagen Club of America) (USA) **369**
V W A (CHE ISSN 0259-6512) **5394**
V W-Autogramm (Volkswagen AG) (DEU) **1713**
The V W Autoist (Volkswagen) (USA) **8610**
V W Camper & Commercial *see* Volkswagen Camper & Commercial **8611**
V W D - Chemie Aktuell (Print Edition) *see* Dow Jones Chemie Aktuell **1477**
V W D Maerkte der Welt *see* Maerkte der Welt **1577**
V W D - Vieh und Fleisch (Vereinigte Wirtschaftsdienste GmbH) (DEU ISSN 0723-8037) **1657**
† V W Golf & Co. Scene (DEU ISSN 1611-0374) **8996**
V W Golf + (Volkswagen) (GBR ISSN 1751-4770) **8610**
V W S Bulletin (NLD ISSN 1385-562X) **8076**
V W Scene International (DEU ISSN 0942-3257) **8610**
• V W Speed (Volkswagen) (DEU ISSN 1433-4542) **8610**
V W Z (Verkehrswirtschaftliche Zahlen) (DEU ISSN 0083-5021) **8636**
V X I Technology *see* L X I Connexion **3107**
V Z Z-Mededeling (Vereniging voor Zoogdierkunde en Zoogdierbescherming) (NLD ISSN 0924-5111) **966**
V02 Magazine (FRA) **8214**
V6 Magasinet *see* Vaeddeloebsbladet **8300**
V64-Guiden (SWE) **8300**
V75-Guiden (SWE) **8300**
V8 Bathurst *see* V 8 Bathurst Magazine **8214**
V8 - Magazine (FIN ISSN 0780-2102) **8610**
▼ VA Jewish Life (USA ISSN 1942-3292) **7731**
Vaabenhistorisk Tidsskrift (DNK ISSN 0506-337X) **369**
Vaabenhistoriske Aarboeger (DNK ISSN 0108-707X) **369**
Vaaler og Svinndal Historielag. Aarbok (NOR ISSN 1503-5220) **4276**
Vaapenbrevet (NOR ISSN 0809-8638) **3786**
Vaar Bostad *see* Hem & Hyra **4412**
Vaar Energi (NOR ISSN 1502-7848) **3162**
Vaar Faagelvaerld (SWE ISSN 0042-2649) **915**
Vaar Foeda (SWE ISSN 0042-2657) **6670**
Vaar Fuglefauna (NOR ISSN 0332-5601) **915**
Vaar Konst *see* Antik & Auktion **362**
Vaar Trygghet (SWE) **7218**
Vaara Hundar *see* Koiramme **6810**
Vaara Hundar (SWE ISSN 0042-269X) **6816**
Vaara Katter (SWE ISSN 1404-3181) **6816**
• Vaara Tonaaringar (SWE ISSN 1654-8507) **7414**
Vaaraantari Rani (IND ISSN 0971-8559) **3890**
• ➤ Vaard i Norden/Nursing Science and Research in the Nordic Countries (NOR ISSN 0107-4083) **5983**
Vaardfacket (SWE ISSN 0347-0911) **5983**
Vaardfoerbundet Kanalen *see* Kanalen **5968**
Vaare Nyttevekster *see* Sopp- og Nyttevekster **818**
Vaare Rovdjur (SWE ISSN 1102-6111) **966**
• Vaare Veger (NOR ISSN 0376-7272) **3287**
Vaaronnavisa *see* Vaaronnavisa for Nord-Norge **168**
• Vaaronnavisa for Nord-Norge (NOR ISSN 1504-5706) **168**
Vaaronnavisa Nordpaa *see* Vaaronnavisa for Nord-Norge **168**
• Vaart Foersvar (SWE ISSN 0042-2800) **6451**
Vaart Land (NOR ISSN 0805-5424) **3925**
Vaart Vern (NOR ISSN 0042-2037) **6451**
Vaasan Yliopisto. Julkaisuja. Opetusjulkaisuja/University of Vaasa. Proceedings. Teaching Aid Series (FIN ISSN 1455-4321) **1550**
Vaasan Yliopisto. Julkaisuja. Opetusjulkaisuja. Alutiede (FIN ISSN 1456-9795) **4033**
Vaasan Yliopisto. Julkaisuja. Opetusjulkaisuja. Liiketaloustiede (FIN ISSN 1456-2170) **1800**
Vaasan Yliopisto. Julkaisuja. Tutkimuksia/University of Vaasa. Proceedings. Research Papers (FIN ISSN 0788-6667) **1550**
Vaasan Yliopisto. Julkaisuja. Tutkimuksia. Aluetiede (FIN ISSN 1459-6318) **3473**
Vaasan Yliopisto. Julkaisuja. Tutkimuksia. Hallintotiede/University of Vaasa. Proceedings. Research Papers. Administrative Science (FIN ISSN 0788-6675) **7475**
Vaasan Yliopisto. Julkaisuja. Tutkimuksia. Julkisoikeus (FIN ISSN 1239-4335) **4853**
Vaasan Yliopisto. Julkaisuja. Tutkimuksia. Kansantaloustiede (FIN ISSN 0788-6683) **1191**
Vaasan Yliopisto. Julkaisuja. Tutkimuksia. Kielitiede/University of Vaasa. Proceedings. Research Papers. Linguistics (FIN ISSN 0788-6691) **5193**
Vaasan Yliopisto. Julkaisuja. Tutkimuksia. Liiketaloustiede (FIN ISSN 0788-6705) **1800**
Vaasan Yliopisto. Julkaisuja. Tutkimuksia. Maantiede *see* Vaasan Yliopisto. Julkaisuja. Tutkimuksia. Aluetiede **3473**
Vaasan Yliopisto. Julkaisuja. Tutkimuksia. Matematiikka/University of Vaasa. Proceedings. Research Papers. Mathematics (FIN ISSN 0788-6721) **5546**
Vaasan Yliopisto. Julkaisuja. Tutkimuksia. Oikeustiede (FIN ISSN 0788-673X) **4806**
Vaasan Yliopisto. Julkaisuja. Tutkimuksia. Sosiaali- ja Terveyshallinto (FIN ISSN 1238-8629) **2671**
Vaasan Yliopisto. Julkaisuja. Tutkimuksia. Sosiologia (FIN ISSN 0788-6748) **8146**
Vaasan Yliopiston Julkaisuja. Selvityksia ja Raportteja/University of Vaasa. Proceedings. Reports (FIN ISSN 1238-7118) **1550**
Vaatturi (FIN ISSN 0356-8083) **2250**
Vaba Eesti Sona/Free Estonian Word (USA ISSN 8755-5808) **3570**
Vaba Eestlane/Free Estonia (CAN ISSN 0837-0672) **3570**
Vacances Actives, Vacances Hiver (FRA) **4400**
Vacances de Luxe (FRA ISSN 1953-5937) **8771**
• Vacances Pratiques (FRA ISSN 1778-9699) **8771**
Vacant Urban Residential Land Survey *see* Enquete sur les Terrains Residentiels Vacants en Milieu Urbain, Mise a Jour **4410**
Vacanta ta Perfecta (ROM ISSN 1841-5288) **8771**
Vacare Deo (ITA ISSN 0394-7807) **7821**
Vacation Agent (USA) **8771**
Vacation & Travel (USA) **8771**
Vacation Homes *see* Robb Report Vacation Homes **7611**
Vacation Industry Review (USA ISSN 1052-0848) **8771**
Vacation Ownership World (USA ISSN 1088-8071) **7614**
Vacation St. Croix (USA) **8771**
Vacation St. Thomas & St. John (USA) **8771**
Vacation Work's Overseas Summer Jobs *see* Directory of Overseas Summer Jobs **1988**
Vacationer (JAM) **8771**
Vacations (USA ISSN 0894-9093) **8771**
Vacaturemarkt M K B *see* Arbeidsmarkt M K B **1663**
• Vaccari Magazine (ITA ISSN 1120-6934) **6901**
• Vaccimonitor (CUB ISSN 1025-028X) **5727**
• Vaccinate Adults (USA ISSN 1525-7061) **7544**
• Vaccinate Women (USA ISSN 1538-196X) **8848**
• ➤ Vaccine (GBR ISSN 0264-410X) **5766**
Vaccine and Immunization News (USA ISSN 1564-0728) **5828**
▼ The Vaccine Quarterly (USA ISSN 1935-5653) **5727**
Vaccine. Supplement *see* Vaccine **5766**
• Vaccine Weekly (USA ISSN 1074-2921) **6884**
▼ Vaccines in Practice (GBR ISSN 1757-9724) **5828**
Vachan (BGR) **3570**
Vacher's Parliamentary Companion *see* Vacher's Quarterly **7475**
• Vacher's Quarterly (GBR ISSN 1744-7178) **7475**
Vacunacion Hoy (MEX) **6105**
• Vacunas (ESP ISSN 1576-9887) **5766**
Vacuum *see* Zhenkong **3334**
• ➤ Vacuum (GBR ISSN 0042-207X) **7045**
Vacuum Dealers Trade Association News *see* V D T A News **1847**
Vacuum Dealers Trade Association Phone Directory and Product Guide *see* V D T A Phone Directory and Product Guide **1847**
Vacuum Science and Technology *see* Zhenkong Kexue yu Jishu **3400**
Vacuum Society of Japan. Journal *see* Shinku **7040**
Vade Mecum: Begroting van de Sociale Bescherming (Year)/Social Protection Budget (BEL ISSN 1378-2622) **7475**
Vade Mecum: Begroting van de Sociale Zekerheid *see* Vade Mecum: Begroting van de Sociale Bescherming (Year) **7475**
Vade Mecum: Begrotingscontrole (Year)/Budget Control (BEL ISSN 1375-4394) **7475**
Vade Mecum: Budget de la Protection Sociale (Year) *see* Vade Mecum: Begroting van de Sociale Bescherming (Year) **7475**
Vade Mecum: Controle Budetaire (Year) *see* Vade Mecum: Begrotingscontrole (Year) **7475**
Vadeboncoeur Collection of Images (USA ISSN 1543-9313) **524**
• Vademecum Bursatil (PER) **1657**
Vademecum del Grupo Bitacora (COL ISSN 0123-6180) **8146**
• Vademecum Deutscher Lehr- und Forschungsstaetten. Staetten der Forschung (DEU ISSN 0083-5080) **7927**
Vademecum Financiele Jaarverslaggeving (NLD ISSN 1872-177X) **1303**

Title

Title

11004 VERBAND DER ELEKTRIZITAETSWERKE OESTERREICH JOURNAL ULRICH'S PERIODICALS

Verband der Elektrizitaetswerke Oesterreich Journal see V E O Journal **3333**
Verband der Elektrotechnik, Elektronik, Informationstechnik e.V. Dialog see V D E - Dialog **3333**
Verband der Elektrotechnik, Elektronik, Informationstechnik Fachberichte see V D E Fachberichte **3333**
Verband der Geographen an Deutschen Hochschulen. Rundbrief Geographie (DEU) **4033**
Verband der Geschaftsstellenleiter der Assekuranz Nachrichten see V G A Nachrichten **4526**
Verband der Industriellen Energie- und Kraftwirtschaft eV Mitteilungen see V I K - Mitteilungen **3149**
Verband der Initiativgruppen in der Auslaenderarbeit e.V. Magazin see V I A Magazin **7218**
Verband der Kriegsbeschaedigten, Kriegshinterbliebenen und Sozialrentner Deutschlands Zeitung see V d K Zeitung **8076**
Verband der Privaten Bausparkassen. Jahrbuch (DEU ISSN 1612-9555) **1042**
Verband der Restauratoren e.V. Bulletin see V d R Bulletin **422**
Verband der Schweizer Druckindustrie Mitteilungen see V S D - Mitteilungen **7328**
Verband der Versicherungsunternehmen Oesterreichs. Jahresbericht (AUT) **8076**
Verband des Personals Oeffentlicher Dienste Zeitung see V P O D Zeitung **7504**
Verband des Wurttemburgischen Verkehrsgewerbes. Sueddeutscher Verkehrsurier (DEU) **8627**
Verband Deutscher Akademiker fur Landwirtschaft, Ernahrung und Landespflege Journal see V D L - Journal **167**
Verband Deutscher Archivarinnen und Archivare. Fachgruppe 6. Mitteilungen (DEU) **7191**
Verband Deutscher Buechsenmacher und Waffenfachhaendler Zeitung see V D B Zeitung **8214**
Verband Deutscher Chemo Techniker und Chemisch - Technischer Association Nachrichten see V D C - Nachrichten **1411**
Verband Deutscher Fischereiverwaltungsbeamter und Fischereiwissenschaftler. Schriftenreihe (DEU ISSN 0944-7881) **3611**
Verband Deutscher Maschinen- und Anlagenbau e.V. Nachrichten see V D M A Nachrichten **5461**
Verband Deutscher Werkzeug- und Formenbauer e.V. im Dialog see V D W F im Dialog **3372**
Verband Evangelischer Diakonen- und Diakoninnen-Gemeinschaften in Deutschland e.V. Forum see V E D D Forum **7778**
Verband fuer Ernaehrung und Diaetetik e.V. Aktuell see V F E D Aktuell **6670**
Verband fuer Schiffbau und Meerestechnik. Jahresbericht (DEU) **8664**
Verband Hochschule und Wissenschaft Mitteilungen see V H W Mitteilungen **7927**
Verband Schweizerischer Angestelltenvereine der Maschinen- und Elektroindustrie Revue see V S A M Revue **3226**
Verband Schweizerischer Assistenz- und Oberaerzte Journal see V S A O Journal **5727**
Verbands-Handbuch (DEU ISSN 0934-9022) **2270**
Verbands Management (CHE) **1800**
Verbandsgemeinde Edenkoben. Amtsblatt (DEU) **7504**
Verbandsnachrichten Steuerberater (DEU) **1954**
• Verbatim (Chicago) (USA ISSN 0162-0932) **5193**
• Verbatim (Mahwah) (USA ISSN 1524-2706) **5869**
Verbicide (USA) **6626**
† Verbindungstechnik in der Elektronik und Feinwerktechnik (DEU ISSN 0946-7777) **8997**
Verbon van Belgische Ondernemingen. Jaarlijks Verslag see Federation des Entreprises de Belgique. Rapport Annuel **1885**
Verbondsnieuws voor de Belgische Sierteelt (BEL ISSN 0771-3851) **3707**
Verbraucher Aktuell (DEU) **2642**
Verbraucher Konkret (DEU ISSN 1435-3547) **2642**
Verbraucher und Recht (DEU ISSN 0930-8369) **7615**
Verbraucherrecht Kompakt (DEU ISSN 1611-9541) **4807**
Verbraucherschutz, Produktsicherheit, Umweltschutz (DEU ISSN 0948-8464) **2642**
Verbrauchserhebung. Ausgaben und Einnahmen der Privaten Haushalte/Enquete sur la Consommation les Depenses et les Revenus des Menages Prives (CHE) **1273**
Verbruik van Beton- en Metselzand en Gebroken Grind (NLD ISSN 1574-5848) **1042**
Verbum (DEU ISSN 0042-3696) **7692**
† • ➤ Verbum (HUN ISSN 1585-079X) **8997**
Verbum see Narthex **2889**
➤ Verbum et Ecclesia (ZAF ISSN 1609-9982) **7692**
Verbum Nobile (POL ISSN 1230-4573) **3786**
Verbundwerkstoffe und Faserverstaerkte Werkstoffe see Informationsdienst F I Z Technik. Verbundwerkstoffe und Faserverstaerkte Werkstoffe **3231**
Verdad y Vida (ESP ISSN 0042-3718) **6960**
Verdad y Vida (GTM) **7218**
▼ Verdak (HUN ISSN 2060-1689) **2219**
Verdandisten (SWE ISSN 0346-3869) **2700**
Verdant (USA ISSN 1936-5616) **3473**
▼ Verdant Hills of Connecticut (USA ISSN 1938-6443) **5086**
• Verdant Reflections (USA ISSN 1545-049X) **822**
Verdauungskrankheiten (DEU ISSN 0174-738X) **5728**
Verde Ambiente (ITA ISSN 1122-6102) **3473**
Verde Oggi (ITA ISSN 1126-5418) **8771**
Verde Olivo (CUB ISSN 0506-6913) **5244**
Verdens Gang see V G **3925**
• Verdensmagasinet X (NOR ISSN 1503-4879) **7192**
Verdi (ITA ISSN 0042-3734) **6626**
Verdi Forum (USA ISSN 1943-7056) **6626**
Verdi Publik see Ver.di Publik **2642**
• The Verdict (AUS ISSN 1449-9207) **4807**
Verdict Search California see VerdictSearch California **4807**
Verdict Search Employment Law see VerdictSearch Employment Law **1713**
Verdict Search Illinois see VerdictSearch Illinois **8997**
Verdict Search National see VerdictSearch National **4807**
Verdict Search New York see VerdictSearch New York **4807**
Verdict Search Texas see VerdictSearch Texas **4807**
Verdicts, Settlements and Tactics see Verdicts, Settlements & Tactics **4966**
Verdicts, Settlements & Tactics (USA ISSN 1041-0740) **4966**
• VerdictSearch California (USA ISSN 1545-1984) **4807**
VerdictSearch Employment Law (USA ISSN 1931-4280) **1713**
VerdictSearch Florida (USA) **4807**
† VerdictSearch Illinois (USA ISSN 1931-4310) **8997**
VerdictSearch Medical Malpractice (USA) **4843**
VerdictSearch National (USA ISSN 1549-6058) **4807**
VerdictSearch National Reporter see VerdictSearch National **4807**
VerdictSearch New Jersey (USA) **4807**
• VerdictSearch New York (USA ISSN 1545-0635) **4807**
VerdictSearch Pennsylvania (USA) **4807**
VerdictSearch Products Liability (USA) **4807**
• VerdictSearch Texas (USA ISSN 1545-0643) **4807**
† VerdictSearch Texas Evaluator (USA) **8997**
Verdolay (ESP ISSN 1130-9776) **6539**
Verdraengte Musik (DEU ISSN 0942-1246) **6626**
Vereeniging Nederlandsch Historisch Scheepvaart Museum te Amsterdam. Jaarboek (NLD ISSN 1387-1536) **8664**
Vereeniging tot Beoefening van Geldersche Geschiedenis, Oudheidkunde en Recht. Werken (NLD ISSN 0929-9858) **4276**
• Der Verein (DEU ISSN 0937-4574) **2270**
Verein der am Rohkakaohandel Beteiligten Firmen. Geschaftsbericht (DEU) **3666**
Verein Deutscher Bibliothekare Mitteilungen see V D B Mitteilungen **5054**
Verein Deutscher Ingenieure see V D I - Z **3226**
Verein Deutscher Ingenieure e.V. Berichte see V D I - Berichte **3226**
Verein Deutscher Ingenieure. Informationsdienst. Instandhaltung see Informationsdienst F I Z Technik. Instandhaltung **3230**
Verein Deutscher Ingenieure Nachrichten see V D I - Nachrichten **3226**
Verein Deutscher Kohlenimporteure. Jahresbericht (DEU ISSN 0302-4938) **6483**
Verein Deutscher Zementwerke. Forschungsinstitut der Zementindustrie. Taetigkeitsbericht (DEU ISSN 0507-6714) **1042**
Verein fuer Augsburger Bistumsgeschichte. Jahrbuch (DEU ISSN 0341-9916) **4276**
Verein fuer die Geschichte Berlins. Mitteilungen (DEU) **4276**
➤ Verein fuer Geschichte an der Universitaet G H Paderborn. Mitteilungen (DEU ISSN 1437-6660) **4276**
Verein fuer Geschichte der Stadt Nuernberg. Mitteilungen (DEU ISSN 0083-5579) **4276**
Verein fuer Geschichte des Bodensees und Seiner Umgebung. Schriften (DEU ISSN 0342-2070) **4277**
Verein fuer Hamburgische Geschichte. Veroeffentlichungen (DEU ISSN 0931-0231) **4277**
Verein fuer Hamburgische Geschichte. Zeitschrift (DEU ISSN 0083-5587) **4277**
➤ Verein fuer Heimatkunde im Landkreis Birkenfeld und der Heimatfreunde Oberstein. Mitteilungen (DEU ISSN 0341-6992) **4277**
Verein fuer Luebeckische Geschichte und Altertumskunde. Zeitschrift (DEU ISSN 0083-5609) **4277**
Verein fuer Niederdeutsche Sprachforschung. Korrespondenzblatt (DEU ISSN 0342-0752) **5193**
Verein fuer Pointer und Setter. News (DEU ISSN 1610-8612) **6816**
Verein fuer Rheinische Kirchengeschichte. Schriftenreihe (DEU) **7692**
Verein fuer Socialpolitik - Gesellschaft fuer Wirtschafts- und Sozialwissenschaften. Schriften see Verein fuer Socialpolitik. Schriften **8013**
Verein fuer Socialpolitik. Schriften (DEU) **8013**
Verein fuer Thueringische Geschichte. Zeitschrift (DEU ISSN 0943-9846) **4277**
Verein fuer Tonbandstimmenforschung e.V. Post see V T F - Post **6744**
Verein fuer Volkskunde in Wien. Sonderschriften. (AUT) **3623**
Verein fuer Wasser-, Boden- und Lufthygiene. Schriftenreihe (DEU ISSN 0300-8665) **2630**
Verein Hamburger Exporteure. Rundschreibendienst fuer Mitgliedsunternehmen (DEU) **1586**
Verein Oberpfaelzisches Bauernmuseum. Mitteilungen (DEU) **168**
Verein Saechsischer Ornithologen. Mitteilungen (DEU ISSN 0942-7872) **915**
Verein Thueringer Ornithologen. Mitteilungen und Informationen (DEU ISSN 0940-6700) **915**
Verein und Management (DEU ISSN 0943-285X) **1800**
➤ Verein zum Schutz der Bergwelt. Jahrbuch (DEU ISSN 0171-4694) **2630**
Verein zur Foerderung eines Deutschen Forschungsnetzes Mitteilungen see D F N Mitteilungen **2533**
Vereinigte Evangelisch - Lutherische Kirche Deutschlands, Lutherisches Kirchenamt Informationen see V E L K D - Informationen **7778**
Vereinigte Westfaelische Adelsarchive. Veroeffentlichung (DEU ISSN 1618-7377) **4277**
Vereinigte Wirtschaftsdienste GmbH Vieh und Fleisch see V W D - Vieh und Fleisch **1657**
Die Vereinigten Staaten von Europa see Gli Stati Uniti d'Europa (Bari) **7266**
Vereinigung Cockpit Info see V C Info **8552**
Vereinigung der Beschaeftigten der Berufs- und Arbeitsmarktdienstleister Magazin see V B B A Magazin **4605**
Vereinigung der Metall-Berufsgenossenschaften Mitteilungen (Ausgabe B G M) see V M B G - Mitteilungen (Ausgabe B G M) **1425**
Vereinigung des Schweizerischen Import- und Grosshandels Mitteilungen see V S I G - Mitteilungen **1586**
Vereinigung Freischaffender Architekten Jahrbuch see V F A Jahrbuch **460**
Vereinigung fuer Organisation und Betriebsfuehrung Selbstaendiger e.V. Magazin see V O B S Magazin **8076**
Vereinigung Oesterreichischer Bibliothekarinnen und Bibliothekare. Mitteilungen (AUT ISSN 1022-2588) **5054**
Vereinigung Pro Sihltal. Jahrheft (CHE ISSN 1660-0673) **4277**
Vereinigung Schweizerischer Formularhersteller Bulletin see V S F - Bulletin **7328**
Vereinigung Schweizerischer Strassenfachleute. Forschungsberichte (CHE) **8637**
Vereinigung zur Foerderung des Deutschen Brandschutzes see V F D B **3257**
Vereinte Nationen (DEU ISSN 0042-384X) **7272**
Verejna Sprava (SVK ISSN 1337-0448) **7475**
Verena (DEU ISSN 0940-9297) **6642**
Verena (RUS ISSN 1560-5388) **6643**
Verena (UKR) **6643**
Verena Kreativ (DEU) **6643**
Verena Kreativ Ostern (DEU) **6643**
Verena Kreativ Weihnachten (DEU) **6643**
Verenigde Nederlandse Uitgeversbedrijven. Annual Report (NLD) **7575**
Verenigde Verzekerings Per see V V P **4526**
Vereniging Arabische Volbloedpaarden Stamboek in Nederland. Nieuwsbrief see A V S Magazine **8286**
Vereniging Kleine Dorpen Groningen. Nieuwsbrief see Nijsblad veur t Grunneger Pladdelaand **4421**
Vereniging Metalen Ramen en Gevelbranche Kwaliteitseisen nen Adviezen en V R M G Branchegids see V M R G Kwaliteitseisen nen Adviezen en V R M G Branchegids **1042**
Vereniging "Oud-Wageningen". Historische Reeks (NLD) **4277**
Vereniging van Gemeentesecretarissen Nieuwsbrief see V G S Nieuwsbrief **7504**
Vereniging van Nederlandse Gemeenten Magazine see V N G-Magazine **7504**
Vereniging van Ondernemingen in Alphen aan den Rijn Magazine see V O A Magazine **1800**
Vereniging van Religieus - Wetenschappelijke Bibliothecarissen Informatie see V R B - Informatie **5054**
Vereniging van Vrienden en Vriendinnen van Dekema State. Nieuwsbrief (NLD ISSN 1574-7336) **460**
Vereniging van Vrienden van Het Museum Het Rembrandthuis. Kroniek see Kroniek van Het Rembrandthuis **500**
Vereniging van Vrienden van Museum Het Valkhof. Nieuwsbrief (NLD ISSN 1872-6585) **6539**
Vereniging van Vrouwen met Hogere Opleiding Magazine see V V A O Magazine **2307**
Vereniging van Vrouwen met Hogere Opleiding. Nieuwsbrief (NLD ISSN 1567-6668) **2308**
Vereniging voor Arbeidsrecht. Geschriften (NLD ISSN 0167-6946) **1713**
Vereniging voor Arbeidsrecht. Reeks see Vereniging voor Arbeidsrecht. Geschriften **1713**
Vereniging voor Christelijk Wetenschappelijk Onderwijs. Contact see VU-Windesheim **3009**
Vereniging voor Kinderpostzegels en Maximafilie. Bulletin (NLD ISSN 1574-7271) **6901**
Vereniging voor Overheidsmanagement. Jaarboek (NLD ISSN 1872-0528) **1877**
Vereniging voor Zoogdierkunde en Zoogdierbescherming Mededeling see V Z Z-Mededeling **966**
Vereniging Vrienden van het Gymnasium. Mededelingen see Amphora **3050**
Verenigingsblad Waffel see Waffel **7218**
Verenigingsmonitor (NLD ISSN 1871-9929) **8214**
Vereninging van Importeurs van Machines en Gereedschappen voor de Metaalindustrie Magazine azine see V I M A G azine **3398**
Verfahrensberichte zur Abwasserbehandlung (DEU ISSN 0934-5949) **3492**
Verfahrenstechnik (DEU ISSN 0175-5315) **3257**
Verfahrenstechnik Marktuebersicht (DEU) **3257**
• Verfahrenstechnische Berichte/Chemical and Process Engineering Abstracts (DEU ISSN 0042-3890) **3234**
Verfassung und Recht in Uebersee (DEU ISSN 0506-7286) **4807**
Verfassung und Verfassungswirklichkeit (DEU ISSN 0083-5676) **7192**
Verfassungen der Laender Afrikas sowie des Nahen und Mittleren Ostens (DEU) **4853**
Verfassungsrecht in Forschung und Praxis (DEU ISSN 1616-9794) **4853**
VergabeNews (DEU ISSN 1430-421X) **4843**
VergabeRecht (DEU ISSN 1617-1063) **7504**
Vergaderwijzer (NLD ISSN 1573-2150) **1847**
➤ Vergilius (USA ISSN 0506-7294) **2242**
Vergleichende Gesellschaftsgeschichte und Politische Ideengeschichte (AUT ISSN 1814-5671) **7192**
Vergleichende Paedagogische Chinaforschung (DEU ISSN 0943-1748) **3015**
Vergleichende Untersuchungen zur Kontinentaleuropaeischen und Anglo-Amerikanischen Rechtsgeschichte see Comparative Studies in Continental and Anglo-American Legal History **4647**
De Vergulde Swaen Mededelingenkrant (NLD ISSN 1571-9766) **4166**
De Vergulde Swaen Vrijwilligerskrant see De Vergulde Swaen Mededelingenkrant **4166**
• ➤ Verhaltenstherapie (CHE ISSN 1016-6262) **6189**
Verhaltenstherapie und Psychosoziale Praxis (DEU ISSN 0721-7234) **7414**
Verhaltenstherapie und Verhaltensmedizin (DEU ISSN 1865-9985) **6189**
Verhandelingen. Klasse van de Kunsten (BEL ISSN 0770-0849) **524**
Verhandelingen. Klasse van de Menswetenschappen (BEL ISSN 0770-0997) **4481**
Verhandelingen. Klasse van de Natuurwetenschappen (BEL ISSN 0770-7665) **7927**
Verhandlungen der Deutschen Gesellschaft fuer Pathologie see Deutsche Gesellschaft fuer Pathologie. Verhandlungen **5604**
Verhandlungen des Deutschen Geographentages (DEU ISSN 0083-5684) **4033**
Verhandlungen des Naturwissenschaftlichen Vereins in Hamburg see Naturwissenschaftlicher Verein in Hamburg. Verhandlungen **957**
Verhuetet Unfaelle see Papiermacher B G **6737**
Verification Organisations Directory (Year) (GBR) **7272**
Verification Research, Training and Information Centre Brief see V E R T I C Brief **7272**
Verification Research, Training and Information Centre Briefing Paper see V E R T I C Brief **7272**
Verification Research, Training and Information Centre Matters see V E R T I C Matters **7272**
Verification Yearbook (GBR ISSN 1477-3759) **7272**
• Verifiche (ITA ISSN 0391-4186) **6960**
† Verifiche e Proposte (ITA) **8997**
Verifiche. Pubblicazioni (ITA) **6960**
Verifiche. Quaderni (ITA) **6960**
Une Veritable Amie see A Friend Indeed **8864**
• Veritas (BRA ISSN 0042-3955) **3804**
Veritas (HRV ISSN 0352-5708) **7821**
• Veritas (MEX) **3009**
Veritas (PER ISSN 1684-7822) **2924**
Veritas (USA) **8013**
Verite des Mythes (FRA ISSN 0993-3794) **4481**
Verkauf Schweiz (CHE) **1434**
Verkaufsleiter Service (DEU ISSN 0178-5893) **1800**
VerkaufsProfi (DEU ISSN 1860-8167) **8610**
Verkeerskunde (NLD ISSN 0377-8495) **8637**
Verkeersongevallen in Nederland see Netherlands. Ministerie van Verkeer en Waterstaat. Directoraat-Generaal Rijkswaterstaat. Adviesdienst Verkeer en Vervoer. Verkeersongevallen in Nederland **8528**
Verkeersongevallen op de Openbare Weg met Doden of Gewonden see Belgium. Nationaal Instituut voor de Statistiek. Gezondheid. Verkeersongevallen op de Openbare Weg met Doden en Gewonden in (Year) **7547**
De Verkeersonveiligheid in Nederland tot en met (NLD ISSN 1874-3226) **7475**
Verkeersrecht - Jurisprudentie/Droit de la Circulation - Jurisprudence (BEL ISSN 0773-171X) **8519**
Verkeersveiligheid (BEL ISSN 0776-9628) **8532**
Verkehr (AUT ISSN 0254-5314) **8637**
Verkehr in Zahlen (DEU) **8532**
Verkehr und Technik (DEU ISSN 0340-4536) **8637**
Verkehr und Umwelt (AUT ISSN 1019-7346) **8519**
Verkehrs Rundschau. Ausgabe A (DEU ISSN 0341-2148) **8519**
Verkehrs Rundschau. Ausgabe B (DEU ISSN 0940-0184) **8519**
Verkehrs und Staatspersonal (CHE) **8519**
Der Verkehrsanwalt (DEU ISSN 1866-993X) **4807**
Verkehrsblatt (DEU ISSN 0342-4013) **8637**
Verkehrsclub Oesterreich Oe Magazin see V C Oe Magazin **8519**
Verkehrsdienst (DEU ISSN 0341-4388) **8637**

DIRECTORY 2010 VERY BEST OF MEGA BOOBS 11005

Verkehrsgeschichtliche Blaetter (DEU ISSN 0232-9042) **8627**
Das Verkehrsgewerbe (DEU ISSN 0938-7803) **8519**
Das Verkehrsgewerbe Nordrhein-Westfalen (DEU ISSN 1866-2536) **8519**
Das Verkehrsgewerbe Westfalen-Lippe *see* Das Verkehrsgewerbe Nordrhein-Westfalen **8519**
Verkehrspolitik in Forschung und Praxis (DEU ISSN 1612-5134) **7475**
Verkehrspsychologischer Informationsdienst (AUT ISSN 0042-4048) **8637**
Verkehrsrecht Aktuell (DEU ISSN 1615-3995) **8519**
Verkehrsrechtliche Mitteilungen (DEU ISSN 0342-6734) **8519**
Verkehrsrechts-Sammlung *see* V R S **4826**
Verkehrssicherheitsreport (DEU) **8610**
Verkehrstechnik in der Schweiz (CHE) **8532**
Verkehrsunfall und Fahrzeugtechnik (DEU ISSN 0724-2050) **8610**
Verkehrsverband Oberaargau. Offizielles Bulletin (CHE) **8637**
Verkehrswirtschaftliche Zahlen *see* V W Z **8636**
Verket foer Innovationssystem Analys *see* V I N N O V A Analys **1799**
Verket foer Innovationssystem Forum *see* V I N N O V A Forum **1800**
Verket foer Innovationssystem Policy *see* V I N N O V A Policy **1800**
Verket foer Innovationssystem Rapport *see* V I N N O V A Rapport **1800**
Verkhovnaya Rada Avtonomnoi Respubliki Krym. Normativno-Pravovye Akty (UKR) **4853**
Verkhovnyi Sud Rossiiskoi Federatsii. Byulleten (RUS ISSN 0321-0170) **4807**
Verkhovnyi Sud Ukrainy. Visnyk (UKR) **4807**
Verko (SWE ISSN 0283-4669) **3399**
Verksamhet och Foervaltning *see* Oikeusministerion Toiminta ja Hallinto **4752**
• Verkstadskontakt (SWE ISSN 1101-0002) **3359**
Verkstadstidningen (SWE ISSN 0346-6434) **3399**
Verkstaederna (SWE ISSN 1651-0682) **5461**
Verkuendigung und Forschung (DEU ISSN 0342-2410) **7692**
Verlage (DEU ISSN 1439-0736) **7575**
• Verlage - Vertretungen - Auslieferungen (Year) (DEU ISSN 0948-7697) **638**
Verlagsauslieferungen (DEU ISSN 0945-473X) **638**
Verlagsvertretungen (DEU ISSN 0944-3754) **638**
Vermeidung und Verwertung von Reststoffen (DEU ISSN 0947-1499) **4807**
† Vermeil (FRA ISSN 1625-7464) **8997**
Der Vermessungsingenieur *see* V D V Magazin **3287**
Der Vermieter (DEU ISSN 1434-9442) **7615**
Der Vermieter-Brief (DEU ISSN 1431-9055) **7615**
Vermietertipps Konkret! (DEU) **7615**
Vermilion Standard (CAN) **3819**
Vermoegen & Steuern (DEU ISSN 1437-0441) **1389**
Der Vermoegensberater (DEU) **2642**
† Vermogensrapportage Ziekenfondsen (NLD ISSN 1874-6403) **8997**
Vermogensrechtelijke Analyses *see* Vermogensrechtelijke Annotaties **4882**
Vermogensrechtelijke Annotaties (NLD ISSN 1574-0269) **4882**
Vermont Academy of Arts and Sciences. Student Symposium and Annual Conference. Occasional Papers (USA) **524**
Vermont. Agricultural Experiment Station, Burlington. Research Report M P (USA ISSN 0083-5706) **168**
Vermont. Agricultural Experiment Station, Burlington. Station Bulletin Series (USA ISSN 0083-5714) **168**
Vermont. Agricultural Experiment Station, Burlington. Station Pamphlet Series (USA ISSN 0083-5722) **168**
Vermont. Agricultural Experiment Station, Burlington. Technical Notes (USA) **168**
Vermont Agricultural Experiment Station. Research Report (USA ISSN 1058-1162) **168**
Vermont: All-Industries *see* Harris Directory. Vermont All-Industries **2003**
Vermont Bar Journal (USA) **4807**
Vermont Bar Journal and Law Digest *see* Vermont Bar Journal **4807**
• Vermont Business Directory (USA ISSN 1048-7174) **2033**
• Vermont Business Magazine (USA ISSN 0897-7925) **1191**
Vermont Buyer's Guide (USA) **2033**
Vermont Catholic Tribune (USA ISSN 0042-4145) **7821**
Vermont Cities & Counties Graphic Performance Analysis (USA ISSN 1935-5483) **7485**
Vermont Cities and Counties Graphic Performance Analysis *see* Vermont Cities & Counties Graphic Performance Analysis **7485**
Vermont. Commissioner of Banking Insurance and Securities. Annual Report of the Bank Commissioner (USA) **1389**
Vermont Criminal Code Annotated (USA) **4899**
• Vermont Criminal, Motor Vehicles & Related Statutes (USA) **4807**
Vermont Criminal, Motor Vehicles and Related Statutes *see* Vermont Criminal, Motor Vehicles & Related Statutes **4807**
• Vermont Cynic (USA ISSN 0892-3132) **2308**
Vermont. Department of Employment & Training. Labor Market Bulletin (USA) **1273**
Vermont Department of Libraries News (USA) **5054**
Vermont Division of Geology and Mineral Resources. Bulletin (USA) **2773**
Vermont Division of Geology and Mineral Resources. Economic Geology Report (USA) **2773**
Vermont Division of Geology and Mineral Resources. Geology of State Parks (USA) **2773**
Vermont Division of Geology and Mineral Resources. Open-File Report (USA) **2773**
Vermont Division of Geology and Mineral Resources. Special Bulletin (USA) **2773**
Vermont Division of Geology and Mineral Resources. Special Publication (USA) **2773**
Vermont Division of Geology and Mineral Resources. Studies in Vermont Geology (USA) **2773**
Vermont Economic Development Authority. Annual Report (USA) **1908**
• Vermont Employment Law Letter (USA ISSN 1086-7597) **4808**
Vermont Environment Monitor (USA) **3473**
• Vermont Family Law (Year) (USA) **4915**
Vermont Genealogy (USA ISSN 1086-2439) **3786**
Vermont Golf (USA ISSN 1058-8442) **8250**
Vermont Government Register (USA ISSN 1071-3379) **7475**
Vermont Green Mountain Guide (USA) **8771**
Vermont Hiking *see* Foghorn Outdoors. Vermont Hiking **8710**
• Vermont History (USA ISSN 0042-4161) **4316**
• Vermont Journal of Environmental Law (USA ISSN 1936-4253) **4808**
Vermont Jury Instructions: Civil and Criminal (USA) **4966**
Vermont Labor Market (USA) **1713**
• Vermont Law Review (USA ISSN 0145-2908) **4808**
Vermont League of Cities & Townsm News *see* V L C T News **7504**
Vermont Life (USA ISSN 0042-417X) **3992**
• Vermont Magazine (USA ISSN 1044-940X) **3992**
Vermont Manufacturers Directory *see* Harris Directory. Vermont Manufacturing **8961**
• Vermont Manufacturers Register (USA ISSN 1522-2004) **2033**
Vermont: Manufacturing *see* Harris Directory. Vermont Manufacturing **8961**
Vermont Manufacturing & Wholesale - Distributor Directory (USA) **1908**
Vermont Maturity Magazine (USA) **4057**
• Vermont - N E A Today (USA) **2924**
Vermont Natural Resources Council Bulletin *see* V N R C Bulletin **3473**
Vermont Natural Resources Council. Bulletin (USA) **3473**
Vermont Natural Resources Council Vermont Environmental Report *see* V N R C Vermont Environmental Report **3473**
• Vermont Nurse Connection (USA ISSN 1529-4609) **5983**
Vermont Outdoors Magazine *see* Outdoors Magazine **8327**
Vermont Philatelist (USA ISSN 1053-9204) **6901**
Vermont Planning, Development and Land Use Laws Annotated (USA ISSN 1534-8377) **7615**
Vermont Rules of Court *see* Court Rules Pamphlet(s). Vermont Rules of Court, State and Federal **4652**
Vermont School Directory *see* M D R's School Directory. Vermont **2960**
Vermont Science Newsletter (USA) **168**
Vermont Sports Today (USA) **8215**
Vermont Year Book (USA ISSN 0083-5781) **2033**
▼ • Vermont's Local Banquet (USA ISSN 1946-0295) **3667**
• ➤ Vernacular Architecture (GBR ISSN 0305-5477) **460**
Vernacular Architecture Newsletter (USA ISSN 1071-4898) **460**
Vernacular Architecture Society of South Africa Journal *see* V A S S A Journal **460**
• La Verne Magazine (USA ISSN 1055-3894) **2308**
▼ • Verniana (ISR ISSN 1565-8872) **5394**
Vernice (ITA) **5244**
Verniciatura del Legno (ITA ISSN 0393-4373) **1052**
Verniciatura Industriale (ITA ISSN 0048-8348) **6721**
Vernieuwing *see* Zone (Assen) **2929**
Vernissage (CAN ISSN 1481-4943) **6539**
Vernissage (DEU ISSN 1434-5986) **524**
Vernissage *see* Il Giornale dell'Arte **491**
† • Vernon Coleman's Newsletter (GBR) **8997**
• Vernon's Annotated Missouri Statutes (Premise CD-ROM Edition) (USA) **4808**
Vernon's Annotated Texas Statutes and Codes (USA) **4808**
Vero (ITA ISSN 1826-0748) **4983**
Vero Home & Design (USA) **4552**
Vero Life (USA ISSN 1522-4287) **5086**
Veroeffentlichung des Vorgeschichtlichen Seminars Marburg *see* Philipps-Universitaet Marburg. Vorgeschichtliches Seminar. Veroeffentlichungen **411**
Veroeffentlichungen an den Berufsakademie Baden-Wuerttemberg - Fachrichtung Versicherung *see* Berufsakademie Baden-Wuerttemberg. Fachrichtung Versicherung. Veroeffentlichungen **4495**
Veroeffentlichungen aus dem Kreisarchiv Guetersloh *see* Kreisarchiv Guetersloh. Veroeffentlichungen **4238**
Veroeffentlichungen aus den Archiven Preussischer Kulturbesitz (AUT ISSN 0930-8849) **8013**
Veroeffentlichungen der Abteilung fuer Slavische Sprachen und Literaturen *see* Freie Universitaet Berlin. Osteuropa-Institut. Slavistische Veroeffentlichungen **5298**
† Veroeffentlichungen der Astronomischen Institut der Universitaet Bonn (BRD ISSN 0340-9821) **8997**
Veroeffentlichungen der Berufsakademie Mannheim, Fachrichtung Versicherung *see* Berufsakademie Mannheim. Fachrichtung Versicherung. Veroeffentlichungen **4495**
Veroeffentlichungen der Hamburger Gesellschaft zur Foerderung des Versicherungswesens *see* Hamburger Gesellschaft zur Foerderung des Versicherungswesens. Veroeffentlichungen **4504**
Veroeffentlichungen des Deutschen Vereins fuer Versicherungswissenschaft *see* Deutscher Verein fuer Versicherungswissenschaft. Veroeffentlichungen **4501**
Veroeffentlichungen des Forschungsinstituts fuer Wirtschaftspolitik an der Universitaet Mainz *see* Universitaet Mainz. Forschungsinstitut fuer Wirtschaftspolitik. Veroeffentlichungen **1187**
Veroeffentlichungen des Frankreich-Zentrums *see* Frankreich-Zentrum. Veroeffentlichungen **4221**
Veroeffentlichungen des Instituts fuer Historische Landesforschung der Universitaet Goettingen *see* Universitaet Goettingen. Institut fuer Historische Landesforschung. Veroeffentlichungen **4275**
Veroeffentlichungen des Leibniz-Archivs (DEU ISSN 0440-2766) **4277**
Veroeffentlichungen des Max-Reger-Institutes (DEU ISSN 0543-1735) **6626**
Veroeffentlichungen des Ostfaelischen Instituts der Deuregio Ostfalen *see* Ostfaelische Institut der Deuregio Ostfalen. Veroeffentlichungen **4252**
Veroeffentlichungen Naturkundemuseum Leipzig *see* Naturkundemuseum Leipzig. Veroeffentlichungen **6534**
Veroeffentlichungen zur Brandenburgischen Landesarchaeologie (DEU ISSN 1860-5869) **4166**
Veroeffentlichungen zur Musikforschung (DEU) **6626**
Veroeffentlichungen zur Verfassungsgeschichte von Baden-Wuerttemberg seit 1945 (DEU) **4808**
• Verona Fedele (ITA ISSN 0042-4242) **7821**
Verona Illustrata (ITA ISSN 1120-3226) **8771**
Veronica (CZE ISSN 1213-0699) **2631**
Veronica (NLD) **2398**
Veronika (RUS) **8887**
Verordnung ueber Allgemeine Bedingungen fuer die Gasversorgung von Tarifkunden *see* Niederdruckanschlussverordnung - Gasgrundversorgungsverordnung **6781**
Verordnung ueber Allgemeine Bedingungen fuer die Versorgung mit Wasser (DEU ISSN 0933-2499) **8835**
Die Verpackung (CHE ISSN 0042-4277) **6715**
Verpakken (NLD ISSN 0167-9686) **6715**
Verpakkingsmanagement (NLD ISSN 1382-0583) **6715**
VerpflegungsManagement (DEU) **3667**
Verpleegkunde (NLD ISSN 0920-3273) **5983**
Verpleegkundig Perspectief *see* Nederlands Tijdschrift voor Evidence Based Practice **5684**
Verre Actualites *see* Verre & Menuiserie Actualites **2046**
Verre & Menuiserie Actualites (FRA ISSN 1772-3108) **2046**
Verre Plat (FRA ISSN 1773-1933) **2046**
Vers Demain (CAN ISSN 0042-434X) **7821**
Vers la Vie *see* Ensemble pour Agir **4065**
Vers l'Avenir (BEL) **3802**
Vers l'Education Nouvelle (FRA ISSN 0151-1904) **2924**
Versailles on Advanced Materials and Standards Bulletin *see* V A M A S. Bulletin **6407**
Versailles Project on Advanced Materials and Standards. Bulletin *see* V A M A S. Bulletin **6407**
Der Versandhausberater (DEU ISSN 0049-5999) **1847**
Versants (FRA ISSN 0256-9604) **5394**
Versatile Modular E-bus Extensions for Instrumentation & Peripheral Component Interface Extensions for Instrumentation Newsletter *see* VXIbus & PXI Newsletter **3334**
Verscheurkalender (NLD ISSN 1572-3623) **5394**
▼ Het Verschil (NLD ISSN 1875-1245) **8215**
Verschleiss und Lebensdauer, Reibung *see* Informationsdienst F I Z Technik. Verschleiss und Lebensdauer, Reibung **3231**
Verse (USA ISSN 0268-3830) **5394**
Verses *see* Cikan **6556**
Verses (USA ISSN 1059-6240) **5395**
† Versicherung und Allfinanz (DEU ISSN 1610-8019) **8997**
Versicherungs Betriebswirt (DEU ISSN 0178-9813) **4527**
• Versicherungs-Jahrbuch (DEU ISSN 0172-3979) **4527**
VersicherungsForum (DEU ISSN 0933-3061) **4527**
Versicherungskatalog (DEU) **4527**
Versicherungsmagazin (DEU ISSN 1616-1963) **4527**
Versicherungsmedizin (DEU ISSN 0933-4548) **5728**
Die VersicherungsPraxis (DEU ISSN 0170-2440) **4527**
• Versicherungsrecht (DEU ISSN 0342-2429) **4527**
Versicherungsrecht Schriftenreihe (DEU ISSN 1431-6463) **4527**
Versicherungsreport (DEU ISSN 0170-1924) **4527**
Versicherungsvermittlung (DEU ISSN 0049-6014) **4527**
Versicherungsvertrieb (DEU ISSN 1860-6210) **4527**
• Versicherungswirtschaft (DEU ISSN 0042-4358) **4527**
Version (MEX ISSN 0188-8242) **7192**
Versions Francaises *see* Collection Versions Francaises **5276**
Versiya (RUS) **6452**
Verslas/Business: Theory & Practice (LTU ISSN 1648-0627) **1800**
Verslas teor. prakt. *see* Verslas **1800**
Verslaving *see* Tijdschrift voor Verslaving **2700**
Verslo Zinios (LTU ISSN 1392-2807) **3906**
Verslunarskyrslur/External Trade (ISL ISSN 1017-6365) **1273**
Verso Arts et Lettres (FRA ISSN 1270-0614) **524**
Verso e Reverso (BRA ISSN 0103-1414) **4481**
▼ Verso Sud (ITA ISSN 1972-2583) **7192**
Die Versorgungsverwaltung (DEU ISSN 0935-1558) **8076**
Versorgungswirtschaft (DEU ISSN 0042-4382) **3334**
VersR-Schriftenreihe *see* Versicherungsrecht Schriftenreihe **4527**
Verstaerker, Oszillatoren und Filter *see* Informationsdienst F I Z Technik. Verstaerker, Oszillatoren und Filter **2348**
Versterking Kwaliteitsborging Diervoedersector/ Enhancing Quality Assurance in the Animal Feed Sector (NLD ISSN 1871-3580) **168**
• Versty (RUS ISSN 1560-9782) **3943**
Vert (PRT ISSN 0873-8025) **8339**
Vertebrata Palasiatica *see* Gujizhui Dongwu Xuebao **945**
Vertebrate Paleobiology and Paleoanthropology (USA) **6731**
Vertebrate Pest Conference. Proceedings (USA ISSN 0507-6773) **257**
Vertebrate Zoology (DEU ISSN 1864-5755) **966**
Vertex (ARG ISSN 0327-6139) **6189**
Vertex (ESP ISSN 0042-4420) **8339**
• Vertex (SWE ISSN 0346-4164) **2308**
Vertical (FRA ISSN 1764-6243) **8339**
• Vertical File Index (USA ISSN 0042-4439) **17**
Vertical, Roc *see* Vertical **8339**
• Vertical Systems Reseller (USA ISSN 1547-9943) **1847**
Vertice (PRT ISSN 0042-4447) **5244**
• Vertice (SLV ISSN 1605-1866) **3836**
Vertientes (MEX ISSN 1405-7867) **5728**
• Vertiflite (USA ISSN 0042-4455) **74**
• VertigO (CAN ISSN 1492-8442) **3473**
Vertigo (FRA ISSN 0985-1402) **6516**
Vertigo (GBR ISSN 0968-7904) **6516**
Vertikal'nyi Mir (RUS) **3943**
Vertraeglich Reisen (DEU ISSN 1862-3859) **8771**
Vertrauliche Mitteilungen aus Politik, Wirtschaft und Geldanlage (DEU) **1191**
Der Vertrauliche UnternehmerBrief (DEU) **1800**
† Das Vertriebene Landvolk (DEU ISSN 0342-6769) **8997**
Vertriebswirtschaftliche Abhandlungen (DEU ISSN 0409-1728) **1800**
Verve (Toronto) (CAN ISSN 1700-1005) **2219**
Vervoer. Binnenscheepvaart Jaar ... *see* Belgium. Nationaal Instituut voor de Statistiek. Vervoer. Binnenscheepvaart (Jaar) **8522**
Vervoer Gevaarlijke Stoffen door de Lucht *see* Handboek I C A O **8544**
Vervoer Gevaarlijke Stoffen over de Binnenwateren *see* Handboek Accord Europeen Relatif au Transport International des Marchandises Dangereuses par voie de Navigation du Rhin **8497**
Vervoer Gevaarlijke Stoffen over de Spoorwegen *see* Handboek Regeling Vervoer over de Spoorweg Gevaarlijke Stoffen / Reglement Concernant le Transport International Ferroviaire des Marchandises Dangereuses **8618**
Vervoer Gevaarlijke Stoffen over de Weg *see* Handboek Regeling Vervoer over Land van Gevaarlijke Stoffen / Accord Europeen Relatif au Transport International des Marchandises Dangereuses par Route **8671**
Vervoer Gevaarlijke Stoffen over Zee *see* Handboek International Maritime Dangerous Goods **8645**
Vervoer, Verkeer Gebrachte Nieuwe Tweedehands Motorvoert - Nationaal Instituut voor de Statistiek *see* Belgium. Nationaal Instituut voor de Statistiek. Vervoer. In het Verkeer Gebrachte Nieuwe en Tweedehands Motorvoertuigen in (Year) **8522**
Vervoerstatistieken. Motorvoertuigenpark - Nationaal Instituut voor de Statistiek *see* Belgium. Nationaal Instituut voor de Statistiek. Vervoerstatistieken. Motorvoertuigenpark op (Year) **8522**
• Die Verwaltung (DEU ISSN 0042-4498) **7475**
Die Verwaltung der Stadt Wien *see* Die Leistungen der Stadt Wien **7451**
➤ Verwaltung und Management (DEU ISSN 0947-9856) **4808**
Verwaltungsarchiv (DEU ISSN 0042-4501) **4808**
Verwaltungsblaetter fuer Baden-Wuerttemberg (DEU ISSN 0720-2407) **7504**
Verwaltungsrundschau (DEU ISSN 0342-5592) **4808**
Verwaltungszeitung Baden-Wuerttemberg (DEU) **4808**
Verwarming en Ventilatie (NLD ISSN 0042-451X) **4127**
Very Best of Mega Boobs (GBR ISSN 1461-2895) **6301**

Title

11006 VERY HIGH FREQUENCY COMMUNICATIONS ULRICH'S PERIODICALS

Very High Frequency Communications *see* V H F Communications **2364**
Very Important Persons International Golf Edition *see* V I P International Golf Edition **8770**
Very Important Persons International Honeymooner *see* V I P International Honeymooner **8771**
Very Important Persons International Traveller *see* V I P International Traveller **8771**
Very Important Persons International Traveller Gold Edition *see* V I P International Traveller Gold Edition **8771**
Very Informal Newsletter on Library Automation *see* V I N E **5064**
Very Irish People *see* V I P **3895**
Very Large Data Bases Journal *see* The V L D B Journal **2532**
Very Large Scale Integration Design *see* V L S I Design **2474**
▼ Very Light Jets (USA) **74**
Very Short Introductions (GBR) **4481**
Verzameling der Uitvindingsoctrooien *see* Recueil des Brevets d'Invention **6757**
Verzameling Milieuwetgeving (NLD ISSN 1574-5805) **3473**
Verzameling Nederlandse Belastingwetgeving *see* Wetteksten **1955**
Verzameling van Nederlandse Wetgeving Nieuws *see* V N W Nieuws **4806**
Verzameling Wetgeving Notariaat *see* Wetgeving Notariaat **4814**
Verzeichnis der Konsularischen Vertretungen in Oesterreich (AUT) **7272**
Verzeichnis der Orientalischen Handschriften in Deutschland (DEU ISSN 0506-7936) **563**
Verzeichnis der Orientalischen Handschriften in Deutschland. Supplementbaende (DEU ISSN 0506-7944) **563**
• Verzeichnis der Versandhandels (DEU) **2033**
Verzeichnis Liechtensteiner Entscheidungen (LIE) **4808**
• Verzeichnis Lieferbarer Buecher/German Books in Print (DEU ISSN 0067-8899) **638**
• Verzeichnis Lieferbarer Buecher - CD-ROM/German Books in Print on CD-ROM (DEU ISSN 1610-4242) **638**
† Verzeichnis Lieferbarer Kaufmedien (DEU ISSN 1432-9700) **8997**
Verzeichnis Rheinland-Pfaelzischer Recht- und Verwaltungsvorschriften (DEU) **4808**
Verzekerd van Cijfers (NLD ISSN 1875-0788) **4527**
Verzekerings-Archief (NLD ISSN 0042-4528) **4527**
Het Verzekeringsblad (NLD ISSN 0165-7909) **4527**
Verzekeringsnieuws (BEL) **4527**
De Verzekeringswereld (BEL ISSN 0772-5825) **4527**
Verzuim en Reintegratie *see* Praktijkblad Preventie **6684**
Verzuim en Vervanging in het Onderwijs (NLD ISSN 1875-094X) **2924**
Verzuim en Vervanging in het Onderwijs (Amsterdam) (NLD ISSN 1875-144X) **2924**
Verzuim Onder Personeel in het Onderwijs *see* Verzuim en Vervanging in het Onderwijs (Amsterdam) **2924**
Verzuim Onder Personeel in het Onderwjs (Zoetermeer) *see* Verzuim en Vervanging in het Onderwijs **2924**
Ves' Transport (UKR) **8519**
• Ves' Transport Onlain (UKR) **8520**
• Ves' Transport za Nedeliu (UKR) **8520**
Vesak (AUS ISSN 1036-4471) **7703**
Veselye Kartinki (RUS ISSN 0320-8044) **2219**
Veselye Kartinki: Izdanie dlya Vzroslykh (RUS) **2170**
Veselye Kartinki o Prirode (RUS) **2219**
Veselye Medvezhata (RUS) **2219**
▼ Vesi-Instituutti. Julkaisuja (FIN ISSN 1796-7376) **8835**
Vesitalous (FIN ISSN 0505-3838) **8835**
➤ Vesmir/Universe (CZE ISSN 0042-4544) **4033**
Vespertine Press (USA ISSN 1555-1288) **5395**
The Vessel *see* Die Erdekruik **7640**
➤ Vest/Journal for Sciene and Technology Studies (SWE ISSN 0283-6025) **7928**
Vesta (JPN ISSN 0918-0214) **3667**
Vestal Review (USA ISSN 1552-6178) **5395**
VestBio (NOR ISSN 1504-3878) **3611**
• Vested Interest (USA) **4527**
Vesteraalens Avis (NOR) **3925**
Vesterheim News (USA) **3570**
Vesterheim Rosemaling Letter (USA) **524**
Vesterheim Woodworking Newsletter (USA) **1052**
Vesteuropa Frimaerkekatalog *see* A F A Vesteuropa Frimaerkekatalog **6891**
Vestfynsk Hjemstavn (DNK ISSN 0108-6391) **4277**
Vesti (DEU ISSN 1439-8613) **3570**
Vesti (SRB ISSN 0354-2866) **5054**
Vesti (Surgut) (RUS) **3943**
Vesti Akademii Agrarnykh Navuk (BLR) **168**
Vesti Issyk-Kulya (KGZ) **3904**
Vesti Nedelja Plus (EST ISSN 1406-2240) **3837**
• Vesti Otechestva (RUS ISSN 1606-1527) **3943**
Vesti v Elektroenergetike/Electric Power's News (RUS) **3162**
Vestigia (CHE ISSN 1021-156X) **6960**
Vestigia Bibliae (CHE) **7692**
Vestigia Rapporten (NLD ISSN 1573-9406) **423**
Vestir (PRT) **2250**
Vestkusten (USA ISSN 1073-6883) **3570**
Vestkyst Fiskeren *see* Fiskerbladet **3594**
Vestlandsk Landbruk (NOR ISSN 0332-9690) **168**
Vestlandsnytt (NOR) **3925**
Vestnik (RUS) **3943**
• ➤ Vestnik (USA ISSN 1930-286X) **8013**
Vestnik A C (SVN) **8610**
Vestnik ALROSA *see* Almazy Rossii Sakha. Vestnik **1610**
➤ Vestnik Arkhivista (RUS) **5054**
Vestnik Arkhivov Armenii *see* Banber Hayastani Arkhivneri **4203**
Vestnik AsEkO (Assotsiatsiya Ekologicheskoye Obrazovaniye) (RUS) **4481**
Vestnik Aviatsii i Kosmonavtiki (RUS) **74**
Vestnik Banka Rosii (RUS) **1389**
Vestnik Banka Rossii *see* Tsentral'nyi Bank Rossiiskoi Federatsii. Vestnik **1387**
Vestnik Chernobylya/Visnyk Chornobylya (UKR) **3966**
• ➤ Vestnik Dermatologii i Venerologii/Annals of Dermatology and Venereology (RUS ISSN 0042-4609) **5882**
• Vestnik Drevnei Istorii/Journal of Ancient History (RUS ISSN 0321-0391) **4166**
Vestnik Ekonomiki (RUS) **1524**
Vestnik Elektroenergetiki (RUS ISSN 0869-6497) **3162**
Vestnik Evrazii (RUS) **4277**
Vestnik Granitsy Rossii (RUS) **4277**
Vestnik Gumanitarnoi Nauki (RUS) **4481**
• ➤ Vestnik Khirurgii im. I.I. Grekova/I.I. Grekov Annals of Surgery (RUS ISSN 0042-4625) **6262**
Vestnik Mashinostroeniya (RUS ISSN 0042-4633) **3359**
• Vestnik Molodych Uchenych. Ekonomicheskiye Nauki (RUS ISSN 1609-5588) **1191**
• Vestnik Molodych Uchenych. Filologicheskiye Nauki (RUS ISSN 1609-5383) **5193**
• ➤ Vestnik Molodych Uchenych. Fizicheskiye Nauki (RUS ISSN 1609-5375) **7045**
Vestnik Molodych Uchenych. Fiziologiya *see* Vestnik Molodych Uchenych. Nauki o Zhizni **928**
• Vestnik Molodych Uchenych. Istoricheskiye Nauki (RUS ISSN 1609-5391) **4166**
• Vestnik Molodych Uchenych. Nauki o Zhizni (RUS) **928**
• Vestnik Molodych Uchenych. Neorganicheskaya Khimiya (RUS) **2118**
• Vestnik Molodych Uchenych. Prikladnaya Matematika i Mekhanika (RUS ISSN 1605-2099) **5546**
• Vestnik Molodych Uchenych. Tekhnicheskiye Nauki (RUS ISSN 1561-7408) **8445**
Vestnik Moskovskogo Universiteta. Seriya 1. Matematika. Mekhanika *see* Moskovskii Gosudarstvennyi Universitet. Vestnik. Seriya 1: Matematika i Mekhanika **5519**
Vestnik Moskovskogo Universiteta. Seriya 10. Zhurnalistika *see* Moskovskii Gosudarstvennyi Universitet. Vestnik. Seriya 10: Zhurnalistika **4580**
Vestnik Moskovskogo Universiteta. Seriya 11. Pravo *see* Moskovskii Gosudarstvennyi Universitet. Vestnik. Seriya 11: Pravo **4736**
Vestnik Moskovskogo Universiteta. Seriya 12. Politicheskie Nauki *see* Moskovskii Gosudarstvennyi Universitet. Vestnik. Seriya 12: Politicheskie Nauki **7155**
Vestnik Moskovskogo Universiteta. Seriya 13. Vostokovedenie *see* Moskovskii Gosudarstvennyi Universitet. Vestnik. Seriya 13: Vostokovedenie **556**
Vestnik Moskovskogo Universiteta. Seriya 14. Psikhologiya *see* Moskovskii Gosudarstvennyi Universitet. Vestnik. Seriya 14: Psikhologiya **7386**
Vestnik Moskovskogo Universiteta. Seriya 15. Vychislitel'naya Matematika i Kibernetika *see* Moskovskii Gosudarstvennyi Universitet. Vestnik. Seriya 15. Vychislitel'naya Matematika i Kibernetika **2527**
Vestnik Moskovskogo Universiteta. Seriya 16. Biologiya *see* Moskovskii Gosudarstvennyi Universitet. Vestnik. Seriya 16: Biologiya **690**
Vestnik Moskovskogo Universiteta. Seriya 17. Pochvovedenie *see* Moskovskii Gosudarstvennyi Universitet. Vestnik. Seriya 17: Pochvovedenie **242**
Vestnik Moskovskogo Universiteta. Seriya 18. Sotsiologiya i Politologiya *see* Moskovskii Gosudarstvennyi Universitet. Vestnik. Seriya 18: Sotsiologiya i Politologiya **8121**
Vestnik Moskovskogo Universiteta. Seriya 19. Lingvistika i Mezhkul'turnaya Kommunikatsiya *see* Moskovskii Gosudarstvennyi Universitet. Vestnik. Seriya 19: Lingvistika i Mezhkul'turnaya Kommunikatsiya **5152**
Vestnik Moskovskogo Universiteta. Seriya 2. Khimiya *see* Moskovskii Gosudarstvennyi Universitet. Vestnik. Seriya 2: Khimiya **2073**
Vestnik Moskovskogo Universiteta. Seriya 20. Pedagogicheskoe Obrazovanie *see* Moskovskii Gosudarstvennyi Universitet. Vestnik. Seriya 20: Pedagogicheskoe Obrazovanie **2887**
Vestnik Moskovskogo Universiteta. Seriya 3. Fizika. Astronomiya *see* Moskovskii Gosudarstvennyi Universitet. Vestnik. Seriya 3: Fizika i Astronomiya **7026**
Vestnik Moskovskogo Universiteta. Seriya 4. Geologiya *see* Moskovskii Gosudarstvennyi Universitet. Vestnik. Seriya 4: Geologiya **2756**
Vestnik Moskovskogo Universiteta. Seriya 5. Geografiya *see* Moskovskii Gosudarstvennyi Universitet. Vestnik. Seriya 5: Geografiya **4019**
Vestnik Moskovskogo Universiteta. Seriya 6. Ekonomika *see* Moskovskii Gosudarstvennyi Universitet. Vestnik. Seriya 6: Ekonomika **1150**
Vestnik Moskovskogo Universiteta. Seriya 7. Filosofiya *see* Moskovskii Gosudarstvennyi Universitet. Vestnik. Seriya 7: Filosofiya **6935**
Vestnik Moskovskogo Universiteta. Seriya 8. Istoriya *see* Moskovskii Gosudarstvennyi Universitet. Vestnik. Seriya 8: Istoriya **4154**
Vestnik Moskovskogo Universiteta. Seriya 9. Filologiya *see* Moskovskii Gosudarstvennyi Universitet. Vestnik. Seriya 9: Filologiya **5152**
Vestnik Mostostroeniya (RUS) **3287**
Vestnik N A C R K *see* Natsional'nyi Yadernyi Tsentr Respubliki Kazakhstan. Vestnik **7069**
Vestnik Nedeli (RUS) **3943**
Vestnik Obrazovaniya (RUS) **6705**
Vestnik Obshchestvennykh Nauk *see* Lraber Hasarakakan Gitut'yunneri **4464**
Vestnik Oftal'mologii/Annals of Ophthalmology (RUS ISSN 0042-465X) **6052**
• Vestnik Otorinolaringologii/Annals of Otorhinolaryngology (RUS ISSN 0042-4668) **6086**
Vestnik Profsoyuzov (RUS ISSN 0869-480X) **4605**
Vestnik Psikhosotsyal'noi i Korrektsionno-Reabilitatsionnoi Raboty (RUS) **8076**
➤ Vestnik Rentgenologii i Radiologii/Annals of Roentgenology and Radiology (RUS ISSN 0042-4676) **6210**
Vestnik Rossiiskogo Onkologicheskogo Nauchnogo Tsentra imeni N.N. Blohina R A M N *see* Rossiiskaya Akademiya Meditsinskikh Nauk. Rossiiskii Onkologicheskii Nauchnyi Tsentr imeni N. N. Blokhina. Vestnik **6034**
Vestnik S i b A D I *see* S i b A D I. Vestnik **8510**
➤ Vestnik Samarskogo Gosudarstvennogo Tekhnicheskogo Universiteta. Seriya: Fiziko-Matematicheskie Nauki (RUS ISSN 1991-8615) **5546**
Vestnik SibADI *see* S i b A D I. Vestnik **8510**
Vestnik StAR *see* Stomatologicheskii Vestnik **5866**
Vestnik Svyazi (RUS ISSN 0320-8141) **2343**
Vestnik Travmatologii i Ortopedii im. N.N. Priorova (RUS ISSN 0869-8678) **6075**
Vestnik Volgotankera (RUS) **3943**
Vestnik Vozdushnogo Flota (RUS ISSN 1025-6768) **74**
Vestnik Vysshei Shkoly (RUS ISSN 0321-0383) **1191**
• Vestnik Zoologii/Visnyk Zoologii/Zoological Record (POL ISSN 0084-5604) **967**
Vestnytt (NOR) **3925**
Vestochki *see* Kogalymskie Vesti **3936**
Vesuv *see* Il Vesuvio **8997**
† Il Vesuvio (ITA ISSN 0393-6147) **8997**
Vet Impulse *see* VetImpulse **8814**
Vet Journal (AUT ISSN 1029-5321) **8810**
Vet-Med Report (DEU) **8810**
• ➤ Vet On-Line (GBR ISSN 1360-1962) **8810**
• Vet Scan (IND ISSN 0973-6980) **8810**
• Vetaffairs (AUS ISSN 0819-8934) **6452**
Vete a Saber! (ESP ISSN 1130-7471) **2924**
• Vetenskapsraadet. Rapportserie (SWE ISSN 1651-7350) **4481**
Vetenskapssocieteten i Lund. Aarsbok/New Society of Letters at Lund. Yearbook (SWE ISSN 0349-053X) **4481**
Vetenskapssocieteten in Lund. Skrifter/The New Society of Letters at Lund. Publications (SWE ISSN 0347-1772) **4481**
Veter Stranstvii (RUS ISSN 0132-9022) **5395**
Vetera Christianorum (ITA ISSN 1121-9696) **423**
Veteraan Boer *see* The Veteran Farmer **215**
Veteran (DEU) **369**
Veteran (RUS) **6452**
Veteran (USA ISSN 0042-4765) **6452**
Veteran Auto es Motor (HUN ISSN 1417-1406) **8610**
Veteran Car (GBR ISSN 0042-4781) **8610**
The Veteran Farmer/Veteraan Boer (ZAF) **215**
Veteran Granitsy (RUS) **6452**
Veteran og Sportsbil *see* Veteranvognposten **369**
Veteranposten (SWE ISSN 1102-8610) **8076**
Veterans' Bulletin (USA) **2270**
Veteran's Business Journal (USA ISSN 1548-4149) **1969**
The Veterans Day *see* Tomorrow **1710**
Veteran's Enterprise (USA) **6705**
Veterans for Peace Journal (USA ISSN 1063-9381) **7272**
• Veterans for Peace Newsletter (USA) **7272**
Veteran's Observer (USA) **6452**
Veterans of Foreign Wars of the United States. Annual Convention Proceedings (USA) **6452**
Veterans of Foreign Wars of the United States Magazine *see* V F W Magazine **6451**
Veterans of the Vietnam War (USA) **6452**
Veteran's View (USA ISSN 1054-0962) **6452**
Veteran's Vision (USA) **6705**
The Veterans' Voice (USA) **6452**
Veterans' Voices (USA ISSN 0504-0779) **5395**
Veteranvognposten (NOR ISSN 1890-257X) **369**
• Veterinaer Spiegel (DEU ISSN 0940-8711) **8810**
• Veterinaerinstituttet. Rapportserie (NOR ISSN 0809-9197) **8810**
Veterinaerkongressen (SWE ISSN 1654-9848) **8810**
Veterinaermoetet *see* Veterinaerkongressen **8810**
Veterinaria (ITA ISSN 0394-3151) **8810**
Veterinaria Argentina (ARG ISSN 0326-4629) **8810**
➤ Veterinaria e Zootecnia (BRA ISSN 0102-5716) **8810**
• Veterinaria em Foco (BRA ISSN 1679-5237) **8810**
• ➤ Veterinaria Mexico (MEX) **8810**
Veterinaria Noticias (BRA ISSN 0104-3463) **8810**
Veterinaria Pratica Equina (ITA ISSN 1825-3229) **8810**
• ➤ Veterinaria Tropical (VEN ISSN 0379-8275) **8811**
The Veterinarian (AUS ISSN 1447-9168) **8811**
• Veterinarija ir Zootechnika (LTU ISSN 1392-2130) **967**
Veterinarius (CAN ISSN 0830-1743) **8811**
Veterinariya (RUS ISSN 0042-4846) **8811**
Veterinarna Meditsina/Veterinary Medicine (BGR ISSN 1310-5825) **8811**
Veterinarnaya Gazeta (RUS) **8811**
Veterinarni Klinika (CZE ISSN 1214-6080) **8811**
• ➤ Veterinarni Lekar (CZE ISSN 1214-3774) **8811**
• ➤ Veterinarni Medicina/Veterinary Medicine - Czech (CZE ISSN 0375-8427) **8811**
• ➤ Veterinarski Arhiv (HRV ISSN 0372-5480) **8811**
Veterinarski Glasnik (SRB ISSN 0350-2457) **8811**
Veterinarstvi (CZE ISSN 0506-8231) **8811**
▼ Veterinary Advantage (USA ISSN 1948-0288) **8811**
• ➤ Veterinary Anaesthesia and Analgesia (GBR ISSN 1467-2987) **8811**
• ➤ Veterinary and Comparative Oncology (GBR ISSN 1476-5810) **8811**
➤ Veterinary and Comparative Orthopaedics and Traumatology (DEU ISSN 0932-0814) **8811**
• ➤ Veterinary and Human Toxicology (USA ISSN 0145-6296) **3503**
• Veterinary Bulletin (GBR ISSN 0042-4854) **8816**
Veterinary Business Journal (GBR ISSN 1474-1652) **8811**
• ➤ Veterinary Clinical Pathology (USA ISSN 0275-6382) **8812**
• ➤ Veterinary Clinics of North America: Equine Practice (USA ISSN 0749-0739) **8812**
• ➤ Veterinary Clinics of North America: Exotic Animal Practice (USA ISSN 1094-9194) **8812**
• ➤ Veterinary Clinics of North America: Food Animal Practice (USA ISSN 0749-0720) **8812**
• ➤ Veterinary Clinics of North America: Small Animal Practice (USA ISSN 0195-5616) **8812**
Veterinary Council of New Zealand. Annual Report *see* Veterinary Council of New Zealand. Handbook. Code of Professional Conduct **8812**
Veterinary Council of New Zealand. Handbook & Code of Professional Conduct *see* Veterinary Council of New Zealand. Handbook. Code of Professional Conduct **8812**
• Veterinary Council of New Zealand. Handbook. Code of Professional Conduct (NZL ISSN 1176-0028) **8812**
• ➤ Veterinary Dermatology (GBR ISSN 0959-4493) **8812**
Veterinary Dermatology. Supplement *see* Veterinary Dermatology **8812**
• ➤ Veterinary Economics (USA ISSN 0042-4862) **1969**
Veterinary Economics Firstline *see* Firstline **8797**
➤ Veterinary Focus (FRA) **6816**
Veterinary Focus (Dutch Edition) *see* Veterinary Focus **6816**
Veterinary Focus (Dutch Edition) *see* Waltham Focus (Japanese Edition) **6816**
➤ Veterinary Forum (USA ISSN 1047-6326) **8812**
Veterinary Heritage (USA ISSN 1096-5904) **8812**
Veterinary History (GBR ISSN 0301-6943) **8812**
• ➤ Veterinary Immunology and Immunopathology (NLD ISSN 0165-2427) **8812**
• Veterinary Institute, Pulawy. Bulletin (POL ISSN 0042-4870) **8812**
• ➤ The Veterinary Journal (GBR ISSN 1090-0233) **8812**
Veterinary Medical Review (USA ISSN 1059-0994) **8813**
Veterinary Medical Society. Record (PAK ISSN 1728-9459) **8813**
Veterinary Medicine *see* Veterinarna Meditsina **8811**
The Veterinary Medicine (PAK ISSN 1728-9440) **8813**
• ➤ Veterinary Medicine (USA ISSN 8750-7943) **8813**
Veterinary Medicine - Czech *see* Veterinarni Medicina **8811**
Veterinary Medicine. Proceedings (PAK ISSN 1728-9432) **8813**
• ➤ Veterinary Microbiology (NLD ISSN 0378-1135) **897**
• ➤ Veterinary Neurology and Neurosurgery (USA ISSN 1526-2073) **8813**
Veterinary Nurse *see* New Zealand Veterinary Nurse **8803**
Veterinary Nursing Times *see* V N Times **8810**
• ➤ Veterinary Ophthalmology (GBR ISSN 1463-5216) **8813**
• ➤ Veterinary Parasitology (NLD ISSN 0304-4017) **8813**
• ➤ Veterinary Pathology (USA ISSN 0300-9858) **8813**
Veterinary Pathology. Supplement *see* Veterinary Pathology **8813**
Veterinary Practice (GBR ISSN 0042-4897) **8813**
The Veterinary Practice (PAK ISSN 1728-9416) **8813**
Veterinary Practice News (USA ISSN 1528-6398) **8813**
Veterinary Practice News Sourcebook *see* Veterinary Practice News **8813**
Veterinary Practitioner (IND ISSN 0972-4036) **8813**
• ➤ Veterinary Quarterly (NLD ISSN 0165-2176) **8813**

• ➤ Villanova Journal of Law and Investment Management (Online) (USA) **1658**
• ➤ Villanova Law Review (USA ISSN 0042-6229) **4808**
• Villanova Sports & Entertainment Law Journal (USA) **4809**
• Villanova Women's Law Forum (USA) **4809**
Ville, Castelli e Palazzi (ITA ISSN 1593-5043) **8772**
Ville de Montreal. Economic Report (CAN ISSN 1910-9369) **1192**
Ville & Casali (ITA ISSN 1121-8479) **7615**
Ville e Castelli Sposi (ITA ISSN 1593-5035) **5561**
Ville - Ecole - Integration (FRA) **7295**
• Ville - Ecole - Integration Actualites (FRA ISSN 1291-7222) **7295**
Ville & Transports (FRA ISSN 1774-3869) **8520**
Une Ville, Un Pays (FRA ISSN 1159-0769) **4277**
Ville Venete (ITA ISSN 1827-6377) **460**
VilleGiardini (ITA ISSN 0042-6237) **460**
VilleGiardini. Repertorio *see* VilleGiardini **460**
Villes en Mouvement *see* Collection Villes en Mouvement **8094**
➤ Villes en Parallele (FRA ISSN 0242-2794) **4033**
Villes et Ports/Cities and Ports (FRA ISSN 1018-6735) **1586**
Villivarsa (FIN ISSN 0781-5638) **8300**
Villmarksliv (NOR ISSN 0332-7442) **8339**
Vilniaus Gedimino Technikos Universitetas. Filologija *see* Santalka **5171**
Vilniaus Universitetas. Ekonomika *see* Ekonomika **1103**
Vilniaus Universitetas. Psichologija *see* Psichologija **7392**
Vilniaus Universiteto Biblioteka (LTU ISSN 1648-9799) **5054**
Vil'nius (LTU) **5395**
Vilnius Conference on Probability Theory and Mathematical Statistics. Proceedings *see* Probability Theory and Mathematical Statistics **5526**
Vilnius In Your Pocket (LTU ISSN 1392-0057) **8772**
Vil'nyi Holos (UKR) **3966**
Vilt- och Fiskeriforskningsinstitutet. Fiskundersoekningar *see* Kalatutkimuksia **3600**
Viltforum (SWE ISSN 1400-1667) **2631**
Vily (CZE ISSN 1801-6316) **2219**
Vily (RUS) **4984**
Vim & Vigor (USA ISSN 0886-6554) **6999**
• To Vima/Tribune (GRC) **3874**
• To Vima tou Asklipiou/The Rostrum of Asclepius (GRC ISSN 1109-4486) **5728**
Vin och Mat *see* Allt om Vin & Mat **4351**
Vin och Sprit (SWE ISSN 1400-6715) **611**
Vinatorul si Pescarul Roman (ROM ISSN 1220-4617) **8339**
• ➤ Vincentian Chair of Social Justice. Presentations (USA ISSN 1097-2560) **8077**
Vinculos (CRI ISSN 0304-3703) **360**
• Vinculum (AUS ISSN 0157-759X) **5546**
Vindformation *see* Megawatt **3178**
• Vindmoelleindustrien. Aarsberetning (Year) (DNK) **3178**
Vindue mod Oest (DNK ISSN 0902-4344) **8014**
• Vinduet (NOR ISSN 0042-6288) **5395**
• The Vine (AUS) **3667**
Vine Wine Country (USA) **5086**
Vinegar Connoisseurs International. Newsletter (USA ISSN 1524-4377) **4369**
† Vinetec (FRA ISSN 0221-301X) **8997**
Vineyard/Vreshta (USA) **7706**
Vineyard and Winery Management (USA ISSN 1047-4951) **257**
Vineyard & Winery Management. Desktop Products Guide *see* Desktop Products Guide **1984**
Vingt-quatre Heures *see* 24 Heures (Montreal) **3821**
Vingt-quatre Images *see* 24 Images **6517**
Vingtaine (JPN) **8887**
• Vingtieme Siecle (FRA ISSN 0294-1759) **4277**
• Vinguiden (Online) (DNK) **611**
Vinho Magazine (BRA ISSN 1516-2648) **611**
Viniflhor Infos (FRA ISSN 1951-0349) **3667**
Vinimaya/Bank Management Education (IND ISSN 0970-8456) **1389**
Vinnaya Karta (RUS) **611**
▼ Vinni ta jogo Druzi/Winnie the Pooh (UKR ISSN 1994-1323) **2219**
Vinnijs Puks (LVA ISSN 1407-3390) **2219**
Vinnumarkadur/Labor Market Statistics (ISL ISSN 1024-0020) **1274**
Vino y Gastronomia (ESP ISSN 1131-5997) **611**
Vinodelie i Vinogradarstvo/Winemaking and Viticulture (RUS) **611**
Vinograd Gospodnji (SRB ISSN 0353-1783) **7707**
• VinoTeQ (ESP ISSN 1887-2794) **611**
Vins d'Alsace (FRA ISSN 0042-6334) **612**
Vins & Gastronomie (FRA ISSN 0982-8656) **4369**
Vins et Sante (FRA ISSN 1955-8104) **6670**
Vins Magazine (FRA) **612**
Vinski (FIN ISSN 1459-4137) **5395**
† Vintage (AUS ISSN 1442-780X) **8997**
Vintage Airplane (USA ISSN 0091-6943) **74**
The Vintage & Classic Baseball Collector (USA ISSN 1082-7927) **4350**
Vintage Bicycle Quarterly *see* Bicycle Quarterly **8254**
Vintage Boating Life (USA ISSN 1542-0248) **8284**
Vintage Commercial Vehicles *see* Heritage Commercials **8498**
The Vintage Ford (USA ISSN 0042-6350) **369**
• Vintage Guitar (USA ISSN 1056-8581) **6626**
Vintage Guitar Magazine (USA ISSN 1067-2605) **6626**
Vintage Magazines Price Guide *see* Antique Trader Vintage Magazines Price Guide **363**
Vintage Motor Cycle (GBR) **8270**
Vintage Motorsport (USA ISSN 1052-8067) **8215**
Vintage Muskoka (CAN ISSN 1481-3807) **4350**
• Vintage News (GBR) **4350**
Vintage Point *see* Vantage Point **5911**
Vintage Racecar Journal and Market Report (USA ISSN 1535-556X) **8611**
Vintage Record Mart (GBR) **8155**
Vintage Roadscene (GBR ISSN 0266-8947) **8637**
Vintage Spirit (GBR ISSN 1477-1276) **4277**
Vintage Tractor (GBR ISSN 0263-7529) **215**
Vintage Triumph (USA ISSN 0147-9695) **8611**
Vintage Truck (USA ISSN 1543-5059) **8678**
• The Vintage Truck and Fire Engine Monthly (USA) **4350**
Vintage Volkswagen Club of America Newsletter *see* V V W C A Newsletter **369**
▼ Vintager (USA ISSN 1935-9926) **612**
Vintners Federation of Ireland Update *see* V F I Update **611**
Vinum (DEU ISSN 0177-2570) **612**
Vinum (ITA ISSN 1824-2715) **612**
➤ Vinyar Tengwar (USA ISSN 1054-7606) **5395**
Vinyls and Polymers *see* Enbi to Porima **2122**
Die Viola (DEU ISSN 0172-9098) **6626**
Viola (SWE ISSN 0042-6407) **3753**
Viola da Gamba Society of America, Inc. News *see* V D G S A News **6626**
➤ Viola da Gamba Society of America. Journal (USA ISSN 0507-0252) **6626**
Viola d'Amore Society of America. Newsletter (USA) **6626**
• ➤ Violence Against Women (USA ISSN 1077-8012) **8146**
• Violence & Abuse Abstracts (USA ISSN 1077-2197) **8151**
• ➤ Violence and Victims (USA ISSN 0886-6708) **8146**
Violence Conjugale. Statistiques *see* La Criminalite Commise dans un Contexte Conjugal au Quebec. Statistiques **2649**
Violence Familiale au Canada, Un Profil Statistique *see* Canada. Statistics Canada. Family Violence in Canada, a Statistical Profile **8081**
Violent Kin (USA ISSN 1064-5071) **2671**
Violet Miranda, Girl Pirate (CAN ISSN 1910-2380) **2219**
Violin Society of America. Journal (USA ISSN 0148-6845) **6627**
Violin Society of America. Papers (USA ISSN 1556-5092) **6627**
Viomichaniki Economiki Epitheorissis *see* Oikonomike Biomehanike Epitheorese **1900**
Vip (ITA ISSN 1828-7204) **6516**
Vip Exame (BRA ISSN 0104-737X) **6301**
Vipasca (PRT ISSN 0872-1653) **423**
Viper Magazine (USA) **8611**
Vir die Musiekleier (ZAF ISSN 1999-3412) **6627**
† Virages (FRA ISSN 1150-4919) **8997**
• ➤ Viral Immunology (USA ISSN 0882-8245) **5766**
• ➤ Virchows Archiv (DEU ISSN 0945-6317) **710**
Virgats (AUS ISSN 1030-7699) **3571**
Virgil Society. Proceedings (GBR ISSN 0968-2112) **2242**
Virgin Blue Voyeur (AUS ISSN 1444-1632) **8786**
Virgin Islands (U.S.). Department of Labor. Annual Report. Fiscal Year (VIR) **1713**
Virgin Islands (U.S.). Department of Labor. Bureau of Labor Statistics. Labor Market Review (VIR ISSN 8756-1638) **1274**
• Virgin Islands Blue Book (VIR ISSN 1931-2865) **8772**
Virgin Islands Business Journal (VIR) **1524**
Virgin Islands Labor Market Review *see* Virgin Islands (U.S.). Department of Labor. Bureau of Labor Statistics. Labor Market Review **1274**
Virgin Islands Playground (VIR) **8772**
Virgin Islands Port Authority. Annual Report (VIR) **8664**
Virgin Islands Port Authority Directory (VIR) **8664**
• Virgin Islands Zoning, Building and Housing Laws and Regulations (USA) **7615**
• Virgin Meat (USA) **5395**
Virginia (Charlottesville) *see* University of Virginia Magazine **2307**
Virginia (Gwynn) (USA ISSN 1071-9849) **8772**
Virginia Agriculture Commodity Newsletter (USA ISSN 1064-4067) **168**
Virginia: All-Industries *see* Harris Directory. Virginia All-Industries **2003**
Virginia Appalachian Notes (USA ISSN 0739-3482) **3786**
Virginia Association for Health, Physical Education and Dance Journal *see* V A H P E R D Journal **6999**
Virginia Banking (USA) **1389**
Virginia Baptist Register (USA ISSN 0083-6311) **7779**
Virginia Bar Association News Journal *see* V B A News Journal **4806**
Virginia Beverage Journal (USA ISSN 1054-6561) **612**
Virginia Builder (USA ISSN 1552-8715) **1042**
• Virginia Business (USA ISSN 0888-1340) **1192**
• Virginia Business Directory (USA ISSN 1047-2711) **2033**
Virginia Campground Directory (USA) **8339**
Virginia CapitolConnections (USA ISSN 1076-4577) **7476**
Virginia Carolina Peanut News (USA) **3667**
Virginia Cattleman (USA) **303**
Virginia Circuit Court Judges Benchbook - Civil *see* Virginia Civil Benchbook for Judges and Lawyers **4843**
Virginia Circuit Court Judges Benchbook - Criminal *see* Virginia Criminal Benchbook for Judges and Lawyers **4899**
Virginia Circuit Court Opinions (USA ISSN 0885-4289) **4809**
• Virginia Cities & Counties Graphic Performance Analysis (USA ISSN 1935-5645) **7485**
Virginia Civil Benchbook for Judges and Lawyers (USA ISSN 1098-0784) **4843**
• Virginia Civil Procedure (USA) **4844**
• Virginia Climate Advisory (Online) (USA) **6397**
Virginia Corporation Law (USA) **4882**
• Virginia Criminal and Traffic Law Manual (USA ISSN 1530-1400) **4899**
Virginia Criminal and Traffic Law Manual on CD-ROM *see* Virginia Criminal and Traffic Law Manual **4899**
Virginia Criminal Benchbook for Judges and Lawyers (USA) **4899**
Virginia Criminal Law and Motor Vehicle Handbook (USA) **4899**
Virginia Criminal Law and Procedure (USA) **4899**
• Virginia Criminal Law Case Finder (USA) **4899**
Virginia Criminal Procedure *see* Virginia Practice Series **4809**
• Virginia Crops and Livestock (USA ISSN 0744-513X) **257**
Virginia Curiosities (USA ISSN 1932-734X) **8772**
Virginia Dental Journal (USA ISSN 0049-6472) **5869**
Virginia. Department of Agriculture and Consumer Services. Office of the Consumer Affairs. Bulletin (USA ISSN 1058-4765) **168**
Virginia Department of Transportation Bulletin (USA) **8637**
Virginia. Division of Mineral Resources. Publications (USA ISSN 0160-4643) **6483**
Virginia Domestic Relations & Related Laws Annotated (USA) **4915**
• Virginia Domestic Relations Handbook (USA) **4915**
• Virginia Economic Development Review (USA ISSN 1550-3313) **1192**
Virginia Economic Indicators (USA ISSN 0042-6490) **1524**
Virginia Economic Journal (USA ISSN 1085-1046) **1192**
• Virginia Economic Trends (USA ISSN 1528-2406) **1524**
Virginia Education Association News *see* V E A News **2924**
Virginia Educational Directory (USA ISSN 0083-6354) **2924**
• Virginia Employment Law Letter (USA ISSN 1042-461X) **4809**
Virginia Engineer (USA ISSN 0504-4251) **3226**
➤ Virginia English Bulletin (USA ISSN 0504-426X) **5193**
Virginia Environmental Endowment. Annual Report (USA ISSN 0191-4049) **3473**
• ➤ Virginia Environmental Law Journal (USA ISSN 1045-5183) **3473**
Virginia Episcopalian (USA ISSN 1535-3621) **7779**
Virginia Extension (USA ISSN 0745-7200) **8445**
Virginia Facts (USA ISSN 1054-8351) **3122**
• Virginia Family Physician (USA ISSN 0194-1119) **5728**
Virginia Farm Bureau News (USA) **168**
▼ Virginia Fire & Rescue (USA) **3581**
Virginia Forests (USA ISSN 0740-011X) **3707**
Virginia Fruit and Vegetable Bulletin (USA ISSN 1064-4075) **208**
Virginia Fruit and Vegetable Market Information (USA ISSN 1064-4083) **257**
Virginia Game & Fish (USA ISSN 0897-8794) **8339**
Virginia Game, Inland Fish and Boat Laws (USA) **2631**
Virginia Game, Inland Fish, and Dog Laws *see* Virginia Game, Inland Fish and Boat Laws **2631**
Virginia Gardener (USA ISSN 1541-8383) **3753**
Virginia Gardener Newsletter (USA ISSN 1068-5510) **3753**
Virginia Genealogical Society Newsletter *see* V G S Newsletter **3786**
† Virginia Genealogist (USA ISSN 0300-645X) **8997**
Virginia Golfer (USA ISSN 1094-3021) **8250**
Virginia Hay Clearing House (USA ISSN 1065-5948) **275**
Virginia Historical Society. Documents (USA ISSN 0083-6389) **4317**
Virginia Historical Society. History Notes (USA) **4317**
Virginia Horse Council Newsletter (USA) **8300**
• Virginia Industrial Directory (USA ISSN 0882-3219) **2033**
Virginia Institute of Marine Science. Educational Series (USA ISSN 0083-6427) **710**
Virginia Institute of Marine Science, Gloucester Point. Special Report in Applied Marine Science and Ocean Engineering (USA ISSN 0882-7427) **2820**
Virginia Institute of Marine Science. Marine Resources Advisory Series (USA ISSN 0083-6435) **710**
Virginia Institute of Marine Science. Special Scientific Report (USA ISSN 0083-6443) **710**
• Virginia Insurance Case Finder (USA) **4527**
Virginia Is for Lovers Travel Guide (USA) **8772**
Virginia Jewish Life *see* VA Jewish Life **7731**
† The Virginia JobBank (USA ISSN 1098-9900) **8997**
Virginia Journal of Education (USA ISSN 0270-837X) **2924**
• ➤ Virginia Journal of International Law (USA ISSN 0042-6571) **4944**
• Virginia Journal of Law and Technology (USA ISSN 1522-1687) **4809**
➤ Virginia Journal of Science (USA ISSN 0042-658X) **7928**
• Virginia Journal of Social Policy & the Law (USA ISSN 1068-7955) **4809**
Virginia Landlord - Tenant Law *see* Virginia Landlord - Tenant Laws and Rules Annotated **7615**
• Virginia Landlord - Tenant Laws and Rules Annotated (USA) **7615**
• Virginia Law & Business Review (USA ISSN 1930-627X) **4809**
• ➤ Virginia Law Review (USA ISSN 0042-6601) **4809**
• Virginia Law Weekly (USA ISSN 0042-661X) **4809**
• Virginia Lawyer (USA ISSN 0899-9473) **4809**
The Virginia Lawyer (USA) **4809**
Virginia Lawyer Register *see* Virginia Lawyer **4809**
• Virginia Lawyer's Weekly (USA ISSN 0897-4772) **4809**
Virginia Legionnaire (USA) **2270**
Virginia Liberty (USA) **7192**
• Virginia Libraries (USA ISSN 1086-9751) **5054**
Virginia Library Association Newsletter (Online) *see* V L A Newsletter (Online) **5054**
Virginia Library Association Shipping List (Online) *see* V L A Shipping List (Online) **5054**
• Virginia Living (USA ISSN 1543-9984) **3992**
• Virginia Magazine of History and Biography (USA ISSN 0042-6636) **4317**
• Virginia Manufacturers Directory (USA ISSN 1065-2493) **2033**
Virginia: Manufacturing *see* Harris Directory. Virginia Manufacturing **2003**
Virginia Marine Resource Bulletin (USA) **3611**
Virginia Maritimer (USA) **8664**
Virginia Medical Law Report (USA) **5728**
• Virginia Mental Health, Mental Retardation, Substance Abuse and Related Law Annotated (USA ISSN 1546-8844) **6189**
Virginia Minerals (USA ISSN 0042-6652) **6483**
• Virginia Model Jury Instructions - Civil (USA) **4966**
• Virginia Model Jury Instructions - Criminal (USA) **4967**
Virginia Museum of Fine Arts Calendar (USA ISSN 1084-676X) **6539**
Virginia Native Plant Society. Bulletin (USA ISSN 1085-9632) **822**
Virginia News Letter (USA) **7476**
• Virginia Nurses Today (USA ISSN 1084-4740) **5983**
Virginia Objections at Trial (USA) **4967**
Virginia Outdoors Plan (Year) (USA) **2631**
Virginia P H C Image *see* Image (Suffolk) **4120**
• Virginia P T A Bulletin (Parents and Teachers Association) (USA ISSN 0042-6709) **2924**
• Virginia Personal Injury Forms (USA) **4844**
The Virginia Pharmacist (USA ISSN 0042-6717) **6885**
▼ • Virginia Policy Review (USA ISSN 2150-3206) **7192**
Virginia Polytechnic Institute and State University. Department of Geological Sciences. Geological Guidebooks (USA ISSN 0507-1259) **2773**
Virginia Polytechnic Institute and State University. Sardo Pallet and Container Research Laboratory. Laboratory Report (USA) **3717**
• Virginia Polytechnic Institute and State University. Virginia Agricultural Experiment Station. Bulletin (Online) (USA) **168**
• Virginia Polytechnic Institute and State University. Virginia Agricultural Experiment Station. Information Series (USA) **169**
• Virginia Practice Series (USA ISSN 1931-0781) **4809**
Virginia Practice Series. Probate Handbook (USA ISSN 1930-3041) **4906**
Virginia Probate and Related Laws Annotated *see* Virginia Probate & Related Laws Annotated **4906**
Virginia Probate & Related Laws Annotated (USA) **4906**
Virginia Probate Handbook *see* Virginia Practice Series. Probate Handbook **4906**
• Virginia Quarterly Review (USA ISSN 0042-675X) **5244**
Virginia Register Index (USA) **7476**
Virginia Register of Regulations (USA) **4809**
• Virginia Review (USA ISSN 0732-9156) **7505**
Virginia Rules Annotated (USA ISSN 0747-7090) **4967**
Virginia School Boards Association Newsletter (USA ISSN 0042-6776) **3035**
Virginia School Directory *see* M D R's Virginia School Directory **2960**
• Virginia School Law Deskbook (USA) **4809**
Virginia Sea Grant Consortium. Publications (USA) **2820**
➤ Virginia Social Science Journal (USA ISSN 0507-1305) **8014**
Virginia Society for Technology in Education Journal *see* V S T E Journal **8996**
Virginia Society of Ornithology Newsletter *see* V S O Newsletter **915**
• Virginia Sports and Entertainment Law Journal (USA ISSN 1556-9799) **4809**

Title

▼ *new title* † *ceased* • *electronic media* ➤ *refereed*

11010 VIRGINIA STATE AGENT HANDBOOK ULRICH'S PERIODICALS

Virginia State Agent Handbook (USA) **4527**
Virginia State Documents (USA) **638**
• ➤ Virginia Tax Review (USA ISSN 0735-9004) **1954**
Virginia Tech (USA ISSN 0274-9904) **3009**
Virginia Tech Collegiate Times (USA) **2308**
Virginia Tech Research (USA ISSN 0731-9649) **3009**
A Virginia Title Examiner's Manual (USA) **7615**
• Virginia Torts Case Finder (USA) **4844**
Virginia Town & City (USA ISSN 0042-6784) **7505**
• Virginia Trial Lawyers Association. Journal (USA ISSN 1047-2134) **4809**
Virginia Turfgrass Journal (USA) **257**
Virginia Union University Informer *see* V U U Informer **2307**
Virginia United Methodist Advocate (USA ISSN 0891-5598) **7779**
Virginia: Virginia Workmen's Compensation Act Annotated *see* Virginia Workers' Compensation **1713**
Virginia. Water Resources Research Center. Bulletin (USA ISSN 0097-2584) **8835**
Virginia Wildlife (USA ISSN 0042-6792) **2631**
Virginia Wildlife Federation. Federation Record (USA) **2631**
▼ Virginia Wine Lover (USA ISSN 1940-8161) **612**
Virginia Woolf Bulletin (GBR ISSN 1465-2579) **5395**
• Virginia Woolf Miscellany (USA ISSN 0736-251X) **5395**
Virginia Workers' Compensation (USA) **1713**
The Virginia Workers' Compensation Act Annotated (USA ISSN 1539-543X) **1713**
† Virginia Workers' Compensation Case Finder (USA) **8997**
Virginia Workmen's Compensation Act Annotated *see* The Virginia Workers' Compensation Act Annotated **1713**
Virginia's Blue Ridge, Including the Shenandoah Valley *see* Insiders' Guide to Virginia's Blue Ridge, Including the Shenandoah Valley **8723**
Virginia's Health (USA ISSN 0199-1345) **7544**
Virginia's Local Economies: Central Shenandoah, P D No. 6 (Shenandoah Valley Area) (Planning District) (USA) **1434**
Virginia's Local Economies: Mount Rogers, P D No. 3 (Bristol - Galax Area) (Planning District) (USA) **1434**
Virginia's Press (USA ISSN 0887-5227) **4585**
Virginie (MUS) **8887**
Virgule (FRA ISSN 1760-2300) **2219**
† Viridiana (ESP ISSN 1132-9041) **8997**
Viridis Report (GBR ISSN 1478-0143) **8637**
➤ Virittaaja (FIN ISSN 0042-6806) **5194**
Virksomheden ved Sygehuse *see* Sygehusstatistik (Year) **4114**
Virologia (ESP ISSN 1133-0384) **5828**
• ➤ Virologica Sinica (DEU ISSN 1674-0769) **897**
• Virologie (FRA ISSN 1267-8694) **897**
• ➤ Virology (USA ISSN 0042-6822) **897**
• Virology and AIDS Abstracts (USA ISSN 0896-5919) **720**
• ➤ Virology Journal (GBR ISSN 1743-422X) **5728**
▼ • ➤ Virology: Research and Treatment (NZL ISSN 1178-122X) **897**
• ➤ Virtual and Physical Prototyping (GBR ISSN 1745-2759) **3399**
• Virtual Attorney.com (USA) **4845**
• Virtual Baguette (FRA) **3842**
• The Virtual Birder (USA) **915**
Virtual Business *see* Ei Magazine **2556**
• Virtual Flyshop (USA) **8340**
• The Virtual Gardener (CAN) **3753**
Virtual Instruments (USA ISSN 1932-1384) **6627**
Virtual Intellectual Property Newsletter *see* V I P Newsletter **6759**
• Virtual Journal (FRA) **4482**
• The Virtual Journal for Biomedical Optics (USA ISSN 1931-1532) **710**
• Virtual Journal of Applications of Superconductivity (USA ISSN 1553-9636) **7046**
▼ • Virtual Journal of Atomic Quantum Fluids (USA ISSN 1935-4061) **7073**
• ➤ Virtual Journal of Biological Physics Research (USA ISSN 1553-9628) **7046**
• ➤ Virtual Journal of Nanoscale Science & Technology (USA ISSN 1553-9644) **7046**
▼ • Virtual Journal of Nanotechnology Environment, Health & Safety (USA) **3226**
• ➤ Virtual Journal of Orthodontics (Online) (ITA ISSN 1128-6547) **5869**
• Virtual Journal of Quantum Information (USA ISSN 1553-961X) **7051**
• Virtual Journal of Ultrafast Science (USA ISSN 1553-9601) **7046**
• Virtual Medical Worlds (NLD ISSN 1388-722X) **5832**
• Virtual Mentor (USA ISSN 1937-7010) **5728**
▼ • Virtual Poetry Project (USA ISSN 1947-9409) **5437**
• The Virtual Portfolio (Online) (USA) **530**
• ➤ Virtual Reality (GBR ISSN 1359-4338) **2490**
Virtual Reality in the Schools *see* V R in the Schools **2518**
Virtual Reality News *see* V R News **2490**
Virtual Reality Society of Japan. Journal *see* Nihon Bacharu Riariti Gakkaishi **2433**
Virtual Reality Society of Japan. Transactions *see* Nihon Bacharu Riariti Gakkai Ronbunshi **2432**
Virtual Storage Access Method Update *see* V S A M Update **8996**
• The Virtual University Gazette (USA ISSN 1099-4262) **2947**
• ➤ Virtual University Journal (GBR ISSN 1460-7441) **2470**
• Virtual Vermont Internet Magazine (USA) **8772**
Virtual World *see* Lumi Virtuale **5444**
• Virtualia (MEX ISSN 1605-5780) **2440**
▼ • ➤ Virtualities (USA ISSN 1941-7373) **3009**
• Virtualization Journal (USA) **2490**
▼ Virtualization Review (USA) **2441**
• Virtually Gardening (USA) **3753**
• Virtuelt Center for Sundhedsinformatik. Technical Report (DNK ISSN 1397-9507) **5728**
Virtuoso Life (USA) **8772**
▼ • Virulence (USA) **5828**
Virus (DEU) **6516**
Virus *see* Uirusu **897**
Virus (NLD ISSN 1574-2016) **2947**
• Virus Bulletin (GBR ISSN 0956-9979) **2516**
• ➤ Virus Genes (USA ISSN 0920-8569) **897**
➤ Virus Infections of Vertebrates (NLD ISSN 1388-3852) **8815**
Virus Report (JPN ISSN 1349-6956) **5828**
• ➤ Virus Research (NLD ISSN 0168-1702) **897**
Virus Research. Supplement *see* Virus Research **897**
Virus Watch (AUS) **2516**
• Virus Weekly (USA ISSN 1531-6424) **5828**
▼ • Viruses (CHE ISSN 1999-4915) **897**
Vis-a-Vis (DEU ISSN 0942-8615) **1192**
• Vis.A.Vis (Online) (USA) **8887**
Vis.A.Vis (Print) *see* Vis.A.Vis (Online) **8887**
Visa Competences (FRA ISSN 1952-3637) **1877**
Visability (GBR ISSN 0961-9879) **3049**
Visage (CAN) **592**
Visakhapatnam *see* Fishing Chimes **3593**
Visalaandhra (IND) **3890**
Visao (PRT ISSN 0872-3540) **3931**
• ➤ Visao Academica (BRA ISSN 1518-5192) **6885**
➤ Visao Global (BRA ISSN 1516-2982) **8014**
Visao Junior (PRT) **2220**
Visao Juridica (BRA ISSN 1679-6454) **4809**
Visao Sete (PRT) **3931**
VisCom Quarterly *see* Visual Communication Quarterly **2344**
Viseo (DEU) **3859**
Vishal Karnatak (IND) **3890**
Vishva Jyoti (IND ISSN 0505-7523) **6960**
Vishva Samskrtam (IND) **5395**
Vishva Vicharamala (IND) **563**
Vishveshvaranand Indological Journal (IND ISSN 0507-1410) **4482**
Vishveshvaranand Indological Paper Series (IND ISSN 0083-6613) **4190**
Vishveshvaranand Indological Series (IND ISSN 0083-6621) **5194**
Vishveshvaranand Vedic Research Institute. Research and General Publications (IND) **563**
Vishwa Manav (IND) **3890**
Vishwakarma (IND ISSN 0042-6881) **3226**
Vishwamitra (IND) **3890**
VISI (ZAF ISSN 1810-4703) **4552**
VISI Colour *see* Plascon Colour **6720**
Visibility (USA ISSN 1084-4228) **8340**
Visible (FRA ISSN 1778-042X) **6960**
➤ Visible Evidence Series (USA) **8146**
• ➤ The Visible Hand (USA ISSN 1559-8802) **1192**
• Visible Human Journal of Endoscopy (USA ISSN 1559-4017) **5949**
Visible Human Journal of Endosonography *see* Visible Human Journal of Endoscopy **5949**
• Visible Language (USA ISSN 0022-2224) **5194**
➤ Visible Religion (NLD ISSN 0169-5606) **7693**
Visicom (CHE ISSN 1422-9609) **7328**
Visie *see* A C W Visie **4589**
Visie (NLD ISSN 0921-7711) **7779**
Visier (DEU ISSN 0933-4491) **8340**
Visier Special (DEU ISSN 0948-0528) **8340**
Visindafelag Islendinga - Radstefnurit (ISL ISSN 1010-7193) **7928**
Visindafelag Islendinga. Rit/Icelandic Scientific Society. Occasional Papers (ISL ISSN 0376-2599) **7928**
Visio (FIN ISSN 0780-4199) **2398**
Visio (NLD ISSN 1872-0633) **6052**
• Vision (AUS) **7779**
Vision (CAN ISSN 1183-7780) **1713**
Vision (CHE ISSN 1420-2468) **7928**
➤ Vision (IND) **1800**
Vision (MEX) **5244**
† Vision (NZL ISSN 1174-9784) **8997**
Vision *see* Science Vision **7911**
• Vision (UAE) **3967**
Vision (USA ISSN 1492-7799) **7743**
Vision (Chicago) (USA ISSN 1083-0804) **7693**
Vision (Costa Mesa) (USA) **7693**
† • Vision (Dearborn) (USA ISSN 1544-3531) **8997**
Vision (Greensboro) (USA) **3035**
Vision (Milwaukee) (USA ISSN 1527-2370) **7822**
Vision (Rivonia) (ZAF ISSN 1814-781X) **2631**
Vision & Aging (USA) **6053**
• Vision Care Product News (USA ISSN 1549-6716) **6053**
Vision Community Services Resource Update *see* V C S Resource Update **8996**
• Vision de Futuro (ARG ISSN 1669-7634) **1800**
▼ Vision Durable (CAN) **1192**
Vision - Ere (CAN ISSN 1718-4274) **8077**
• Vision Gerencial (VEN ISSN 1317-8822) **1800**
Vision In Action (Mission Viejo) *see* V I A (Mission Viejo) **6648**
Vision Magazine (GBR) **7731**
Vision Magazine (PHL ISSN 0042-692X) **524**
The Vision Maker (USA ISSN 1088-1824) **2398**
• Vision Monday (USA ISSN 1054-7665) **6053**
Vision of Wildlife, Ecotourism and the Environment in Southern Africa *see* Vision (Rivonia) **2631**
Vision On (GBR) **5437**
• ➤ Vision Research (GBR ISSN 0042-6989) **6053**
• Vision Systems Design (USA ISSN 1089-3709) **3226**
➤ Vision Tecnologica (VEN ISSN 1315-0855) **6796**
• Vision Update (USA ISSN 1554-3048) **6053**
Visionair (NLD ISSN 1569-7533) **8340**
Visionaire (USA ISSN 1071-5266) **2262**
Visionary (USA) **6053**
Visionen (DEU ISSN 1434-1921) **7693**
Visionere *see* Vision - Ere **8077**
Visiones Cientificas (CHL ISSN 0716-677X) **7928**
Visiones de la Educacion (CHL ISSN 0718-0888) **2925**
• Visions (DEU) **6627**
Visions (Kansas City) (USA ISSN 1050-7221) **3571**
▼ • Visions (Kentwood) (USA ISSN 1948-1497) **6705**
Visions (Mount Laurel) (USA) **1908**
Visions (St. Louis) (USA) **6053**
Visions (San Francisco) (USA) **7414**
Visions (Stillwater) (USA) **208**
Visions (Tallahassee) (USA ISSN 1087-9382) **2925**
Visions in Leisure and Business (USA ISSN 0277-5204) **8772**
Visions International (USA) **5437**
• Visions of Australia (AUS) **8772**
• Visions of Glory Magazine (USA) **7779**
• ➤ Visions of Research in Music Education (USA ISSN 1938-2065) **6627**
Visions sur l'Art Quebec Inc. Annual Report (CAN ISSN 1719-6361) **4086**
Visions sur l'Art Quebec Inc. Rapport Annuel *see* Visions sur l'Art Quebec Inc. Annual Report **4086**
• Visions: The Journal of Rogerian Nursing Science (USA ISSN 1072-4532) **5983**
Visions West - National Center for American Western Art (USA) **6539**
VisIT (DEU ISSN 1616-8240) **2551**
Visit Africa (FRA ISSN 1774-7155) **8786**
• Visit Denmark (DNK ISSN 1604-5807) **8772**
Visit Detroit (USA ISSN 1541-5562) **8772**
Visit Florida (GBR) **8772**
• Visitador Medico (ESP ISSN 1695-4394) **6885**
El Visitante de Puerto Rico (PRI ISSN 1526-8616) **7822**
Visite Actuelle (FRA ISSN 1258-4711) **6885**
• Visite Deco (FRA ISSN 1774-6760) **4552**
▼ Visite Pharma (FRA ISSN 1954-1988) **6885**
Le Visiteur (FRA ISSN 1265-7034) **460**
Visiting Arts (GBR ISSN 1368-5236) **524**
Visiting Fireman (USA) **3581**
Visiting Nurse Association of Brooklyn Newsletter *see* V N A B Newsletter **5983**
Visiting Scholar Directory (USA) **3015**
• Visitor (DNK ISSN 1602-7183) **4400**
Visitor (IRL ISSN 0790-6056) **8772**
Visitor (UAE ISSN 1816-7861) **8772**
• Visitor (USA) **7693**
Visitor (Grantham) *see* In Part **7761**
Visitor (St. Cloud) (USA) **7822**
Visitor Days (IRL) **8772**
Visitor Magazine (CAN ISSN 0839-1335) **8772**
• ➤ Visitor Studies (USA ISSN 1064-5578) **7414**
Visitor Vacation Guide (JAM) **8772**
A Visitor's Guide to Colonial & Revolutionary New England (USA ISSN 1937-9609) **8772**
Visjon (NOR ISSN 0809-8565) **315**
• Vismandsrapport (DNK ISSN 1600-3888) **2631**
Vismandsrapporten *see* Dansk Oekonomi **1476**
Visnyk *see* Herald (Winnipeg) **7704**
Visnyk *see* Ukrainian Medical Association of North America. Journal **5725**
Visnyk/Herald (USA ISSN 0042-7004) **5244**
Visnyk Chornobylya *see* Vestnik Chernobylya **3966**
Visnyk Farmatsii (UKR ISSN 1562-7241) **6885**
Visnyk Knyzhkovoi Palaty *see* Knyzhkova Palata Ukrainy. Visnyk **7565**
• ➤ Visnyk Morfolohii/Reports of Morphology (UKR ISSN 1818-1295) **5728**
Visnyk Zoologii *see* Vestnik Zoologii **967**
Visnywerheid-Navorsingsinstituut. Jaarverslag van die Direkteur *see* Fishing Industry Research Institute. Annual Report of the Director **3636**
Visoka Uciteljska Skola u Zadru. Zbornik Radova *see* Sveuciliste u Zadru. Strueni Odjel za Izobrazbu Ueitelja i Odgojitelja Predskolske Djece. Zbornik Radova **2916**
Visserij in Cijfers (NLD ISSN 0921-4283) **3614**
Visserij in Europa *see* Fisheries and Aquaculture in Europe **3592**
Visserijnieuws (NLD ISSN 1380-5061) **3611**
Vissha Geodeziia (BGR ISSN 0324-1114) **2774**
Visslingar & Rop (SWE ISSN 1401-5307) **8484**
Vista (GBR ISSN 1362-7163) **2671**
Vista (NZL ISSN 1176-9904) **8077**
Vista (Dallas) (USA) **1524**
Vista (Indianapolis) (USA) **7693**
Vista (Regina) (CAN ISSN 0828-7023) **6539**
Vista (Saskatoon) (CAN ISSN 0382-0289) **4369**
Vista Magazine (USA ISSN 0733-5746) **3571**
Vistas *see* iN.SG **2325**
Vistascript (DEU ISSN 0947-4552) **8146**
Vistazo (ECU ISSN 0042-7128) **3835**
Visti Iz Sarseliu (FRA ISSN 0083-6672) **8014**
Visti Ukrayins'kykh Inzheneriv/Ukrainian Engineering News (USA ISSN 0042-7136) **3226**
Visto (ITA ISSN 1120-4486) **3899**
• Visual (ESP ISSN 1133-0422) **524**
Visual and Performing Arts *see* Peterson's Professional Degree Programs in the Visual and Performing Arts **511**
• ➤ Visual Anthropology (USA ISSN 0894-9468) **360**
• Visual Anthropology Review (USA ISSN 1058-7187) **360**
Visual Art in Japan *see* Nihon no Bijutsu **509**
Visual Artist's Collective Magazine *see* Collective **482**
Visual Arts News (CAN ISSN 0704-0512) **524**
• ➤ Visual Arts Research (USA ISSN 0736-0770) **525**
• Visual Arts Trends (USA) **525**
• Visual Arts Trends Es (USA) **525**
† Visual Basic Developer (USA ISSN 1552-5341) **8997**
• Visual Basic Journal (ITA ISSN 1123-8534) **2510**
† Visual C++ Developer (USA ISSN 1079-0608) **8997**
Visual C Plus Plus Developer *see* Visual C++ Developer **8997**
• ➤ Visual Cognition (GBR ISSN 1350-6285) **7414**
• ➤ Visual Communication (GBR ISSN 1470-3572) **2343**
• ➤ Visual Communication Quarterly (USA ISSN 1555-1393) **2344**
Visual Communications and Image Processing (USA ISSN 1018-8770) **7085**
➤ Visual Communications Journal (USA ISSN 0507-1658) **525**
• ➤ The Visual Computer (DEU ISSN 0178-2789) **2490**
Visual Convergence (CAN ISSN 1480-5545) **2404**
• ➤ Visual Culture & Gender (USA ISSN 1936-1912) **525**
• Visual Culture in Britain (GBR ISSN 1471-4787) **525**
Visual Dermatology (JPN) **5883**
• Visual Diagnosis of Child Abuse on CD-ROM (USA ISSN 1532-4443) **6105**
• ➤ Visual Impairment Research (GBR ISSN 1388-235X) **4086**
† Visual J Plus Plus Informant (USA) **8997**
➤ Visual Literacy Newsletter (USA) **3087**
Visual Literacy Review (USA) **3087**
• Visual Mathematics (SRB) **5546**
Visual Merchandising & Retail Design (IND) **36**
Visual Merchandising & Store Design *see* V M & S D **4551**
• ➤ Visual Neuroscience (GBR ISSN 0952-5238) **6189**
• ➤ Visual Resources (GBR ISSN 0197-3762) **525**
• Visual Resources Association Bulletin (USA ISSN 1046-9001) **525**
• ➤ Visual Studies (GBR ISSN 1472-586X) **8146**
• Visual Studio Developer (USA) **2510**
Visual Studio Magazine (USA ISSN 1537-002X) **2441**
Visual Studio .NET Developer *see* Visual Studio Developer **2510**
Visual Systems Journal (GBR ISSN 1369-2992) **2510**
† Visual-X (DEU) **8997**
Visualization Society of Japan. Transactions *see* Kashika Jouhou Gakkai Rombunshuu Gappon **7874**
▼ ➤ Visualizing the Middle Ages (NLD ISSN 1874-0448) **4277**
Visually Speaking (CAN ISSN 1205-0024) **3087**
Visuell (DEU ISSN 0720-4841) **6978**
• Visuell International (DEU ISSN 1438-3012) **6978**
Visuelle Geschichtskultur (DEU) **4166**
Visuellt (SWE ISSN 1404-3386) **525**
Visuelt (NOR ISSN 0803-8236) **7329**
Visva - Bharati Journal of Philosophy (IND ISSN 0042-7187) **6960**
Visva - Bharati Patrika (IND ISSN 0042-7179) **5395**
➤ Visva - Bharati Quarterly (IND ISSN 0042-7195) **5244**
Viswa Rachana/World Writing (IND ISSN 0042-7209) **5395**
Viswarachana *see* Viswa Rachana **5395**
• Viszeralchirurgie (DEU ISSN 1435-3067) **6262**
• ➤ Viszeralmedizin (CHE ISSN 1662-6664) **5932**
Vita (DEU ISSN 1612-5177) **6285**
Vita (GRC ISSN 1108-6033) **6999**
Vita (HRV ISSN 1330-8297) **8848**
Vita (POL ISSN 1505-9294) **6999**
La Vita Casalese (ITA ISSN 1826-1787) **3899**
Vita Cattolica (ITA ISSN 0042-7233) **7822**
Vita Consacrata (ITA ISSN 0042-7330) **7693**
Vita dell'Infanzia (ITA ISSN 0042-7241) **2925**
• Vita e Pensiero (ITA ISSN 0042-725X) **5244**
Vita e Salute (ITA ISSN 0042-7268) **6999**
† Vita e Salute Junior (ITA) **8997**
† Vita Fratrum (DEU) **8997**
Vita Giuseppina (ITA ISSN 0042-7276) **7822**
• Vita in Campagna (ITA ISSN 1120-3005) **5086**
La Vita in Cristo e nella Chiesa (ITA ISSN 0042-7284) **7822**
† Vita Italiana (Rome)/Italy' Life/Leben in Italien/Vie Italienne (ITA ISSN 0504-5010) **8997**
† Vita Italiana. Cultura e Scienza (ITA ISSN 0394-6940) **8997**
† Vita Italiana. Documenti e Informazioni (ITA ISSN 0507-1712) **8997**
† Vita Italiana. Quaderni (ITA ISSN 1125-3355) **8997**

DIRECTORY 2010 VOCE DELL'EMIGRANTE 11011

† Vita Italiana. Speciale (ITA ISSN 1120-5520) **8997**
† Vita Italiana. Speciale. Istituzioni e Comunicazione (ITA ISSN 1120-5512) **8997**
† Vita Italiana. Temi (ITA ISSN 1120-5504) **8997**
• Vita Latina (BEL ISSN 1781-5231) **5194**
Vita Notarile (ITA ISSN 1824-1484) **4882**
Vita Notarile Esperienze Giuridiche *see* Vita Notarile **4882**
Vita Nuova (ITA ISSN 1825-2923) **7822**
Vita Ospedaliera (ITA ISSN 0391-1470) **4112**
Vita Pastorale (ITA) **7693**
Vita Regularis (DEU) **7822**
La Vita Scolastica (ITA ISSN 0042-7349) **2925**
† Vita Sindacale Bergamasca (ITA ISSN 0042-7357) **8997**
Vita. Traditsii, Meditsina, Zdorov'e (RUS ISSN 1562-0433) **5728**
• Vita Trentina (ITA) **3899**
Vitae (COL ISSN 0121-4004) **6885**
Vitae (JPN) **711**
• Vitae (VEN ISSN 1317-987X) **5728**
• ➤ Vitae Scholasticae (USA ISSN 0735-1909) **646**
Vitaform' (FRA ISSN 2101-8308) **6670**
Vitajte Doma *see* Vitejte Doma **4369**
Vital (DEU ISSN 0507-1747) **6999**
Vital (FRA ISSN 1638-5012) **8887**
• Vital (GBR ISSN 1741-7503) **5869**
Vital (USA ISSN 0279-8905) **8887**
▼ • Vital (Crawley) (GBR ISSN 1755-6465) **1192**
▼ Vital (Sioux Falls) (USA ISSN 1942-5961) **6796**
Vital and Health Statistics. Series 1. Programs and Collection Procedures *see* U.S. National Center for Health Statistics. Vital and Health Statistics. Series 1. Programs and Collection Procedures **7549**
Vital and Health Statistics. Series 10. Data from the Health Interview Survey *see* U.S. National Center for Health Statistics. Vital and Health Statistics. Series 10. Data from the Health Interview Survey **7549**
Vital and Health Statistics. Series 11. Data from the Health and Nutrition Examination Survey see U.S. National Center for Health Statistics. Vital and Health Statistics. Series 11. Data from the National Health Examination Survey, the Health and Nutrition Examination Surveys, and the Hispanic Health and Nutrition Examination Survey **7549**
Vital and Health Statistics. Series 13. Data on Health Resources Utilization *see* U.S. National Center for Health Statistics. Vital and Health Statistics. Series 13. Data on Health Resources Utilization **7544**
Vital and Health Statistics. Series 14. Data on Health Resources *see* U.S. National Center for Health Statistics. Vital and Health Statistics. Series 14. Data on Health Resources **7549**
Vital and Health Statistics. Series 2. Data Evaluation and Methods Research *see* U.S. National Center for Health Statistics. Vital and Health Statistics. Series 2. Data Evaluation and Methods Research **7549**
Vital and Health Statistics. Series 20. Data on Mortality *see* U.S. National Center for Health Statistics. Vital and Health Statistics. Series 20. Data on Mortality **7549**
Vital and Health Statistics. Series 21. Data on Natality, Marriage, and Divorce *see* U.S. National Center for Health Statistics. Vital and Health Statistics. Series 21. Data on Natality, Marriage, and Divorce **7549**
Vital and Health Statistics. Series 23. Data from the National Survey of Family Growth *see* U.S. National Center for Health Statistics. Vital and Health Statistics. Series 23. Data from the National Survey of Family Growth **7550**
Vital and Health Statistics. Series 24. Compilations of Data on Natality, Mortality, Divorce, and Induced Terminations of Pregnancy *see* U.S. National Center for Health Statistics. Vital and Health Statistics. Series 24. Compilations of Data on Natality, Mortality, Divorce, and Induced Terminations of Pregnancy **7550**
Vital and Health Statistics. Series 3. Analytical Studies *see* U.S. National Center for Health Statistics. Vital and Health Statistics. Series 3. Analytical and Epidemiological Studies **7550**
Vital and Health Statistics. Series 4. Documents and Committee Report *see* U.S. National Center for Health Statistics. Vital and Health Statistics. Series 4. Documents and Committee Report **7550**
Vital and Health Statistics. Series 5. Comparative International Vital and Health Statistics Reports *see* U.S. National Center for Health Statistics. Vital and Health Statistics. Series 5. Comparative International Vital and Health Statistics Reports **7550**
Vital and Health Statistics. Series 6. Cognition and Survey Measurement *see* U.S. National Center for Health Statistics. Vital and Health Statistics. Series 6. Cognition and Survey Measurement **7417**
▼ • The Vital Edge (USA ISSN 1949-0356) **1800**
Vital Issues (USA ISSN 1056-6368) **7192**
Vital Link (CAN ISSN 1497-9659) **3087**
Vital Magazine *see* Vital **5869**
Vital News *see* Florida. Department of Health. Vital News **7307**
The Vital Record (USA ISSN 1543-1436) **3786**
Vital Signs *see* Ottawa's Vital Signs **8124**
• Vital Signs (Cambridge) (USA) **7544**
Vital Signs (Fresno) (USA) **5728**
Vital Signs (Pueblo) (USA) **5983**
• Vital Signs (Years) (USA ISSN 1075-0576) **3473**
Vital Signs Pharmacy Services Newsletter (USA ISSN 0739-9588) **6885**
• Vital Speeches of the Day (USA ISSN 0042-742X) **4585**
Vital Statistics *see* Nova Scotia. Department of Health. Vital Statistics. Annual Report **7288**
Vital Statistics, Idaho *see* Idaho. Department of Health and Welfare. Vital Statistics (Year) **7548**
Vital Statistics of Iowa (USA ISSN 0161-8695) **7317**
• Vital Statistics of the United States (USA ISSN 1931-2873) **7550**
Vital Statistics on Congress (USA ISSN 0896-9469) **7485**
Vital Textile Literature (Year) (USA) **8464**
Vital Woman Magazine (USA ISSN 1547-9285) **7779**
▼ VitalCare (USA) **6075**
▼ Vitale (ESP ISSN 1888-4687) **5728**
Vitalia (NLD ISSN 1874-0278) **5932**
Vitalida Ahora (USA) **6999**
Vitality (ITA ISSN 1120-4591) **6670**
Vitality (USA ISSN 1074-5831) **6999**
Vitality Digest (USA) **5728**
Vitality Magazine (CAN ISSN 1180-0291) **315**
Vitamin B (BGR ISSN 1310-8441) **5437**
Vitamin Information Centre Medical Update *see* V I C Medical Update **6670**
Vitamin Retailer (USA) **6885**
Vitamin Schast'ya (RUS) **8887**
Vitamins *see* Bitamin **6826**
• ➤ Vitamins and Hormones (USA ISSN 0083-6729) **6885**
Vitamins & Supplements Market Assessment *see* Key Note Market Assessment. Vitamins & Supplements **1893**
Vitarelle (DEU) **6999**
Vitchyzna (UKR ISSN 0042-7470) **5244**
Vite Qualita *see* V Q **257**
Vitebskii Kur'er (BLR) **3800**
Vitejte Doma (CZE ISSN 1214-4061) **4369**
• Viten fra Skog og Landskap (NOR ISSN 1890-159X) **3707**
▼ • Vitenskapskomiteen for Mattrygghet. Rapport (NOR ISSN 1504-694X) **8077**
Vitex (GBR ISSN 1470-0123) **822**
Viti (FRA ISSN 0757-4673) **257**
Viti Vinicole (FRA ISSN 0244-4860) **257**
Viticultura Enologia Profesional (ESP ISSN 1131-5679) **257**
Viticulture en Val de Loire (FRA ISSN 1151-1109) **258**
• Viticulture Notes (USA) **258**
Vitiligo Information (DEU) **5883**
➤ Vitis (DEU ISSN 0042-7500) **258**
Vitis - V E A *see* Vitis - Viticulture and Oenology Abstracts (Online) **258**
• Vitis - Viticulture and Oenology Abstracts (Online) (DEU) **258**
Vitreous Enameller (GBR ISSN 0042-7519) **2046**
Vitriini (FIN ISSN 0357-749X) **4400**
Vitrina *see* Vitrina. Mir Supremarketa **3667**
• La Vitrina (USA) **525**
Vitrina Chitayushchei Rossii (RUS) **5395**
Vitrina i Torgovyi Dizain (RUS) **525**
Vitrina. Mir Supremarketa (RUS) **3667**
Vitrina. Restorannyi Biznes (RUS) **4400**
Vitrine *see* Museumtijdschrift **6533**
Vitrine (Sint-Michielsgestel) *see* Viataal Magazine **4076**
La Vitrine. Bulletin (CAN ISSN 1910-1252) **1713**
▼ Vitrines & Meubles Miniatures (FRA ISSN 1957-6358) **4350**
• Vitruvian Perspectives (USA ISSN 1932-5681) **4482**
Viva (ARG ISSN 1514-9668) **3792**
† Viva! (DEU ISSN 1862-152X) **8997**
▼ Viva (DEU) **6627**
Viva (NLD ISSN 0165-4462) **2171**
Viva! (POL ISSN 1426-9554) **3930**
Viva! (ROM ISSN 1454-6922) **8887**
Viva (SRB ISSN 0354-0332) **8887**
Viva (UAE ISSN 1812-7703) **8887**
Viva! (UKR ISSN 1811-8984) **3966**
Viva (USA) **8773**
Viva Africa (TZA) **1524**
Viva Baby *see* Viva Mama **2171**
▼ Viva Cuisine (FRA ISSN 1958-1955) **4369**
Viva Leve (BRA ISSN 1806-3551) **6999**
Viva Mais (BRA ISSN 1517-0934) **8887**
Viva Mama (NLD ISSN 1875-2446) **2171**
Viva Origino (JPN ISSN 0910-4003) **711**
Viva Vida com Saude *see* Saude! **6996**
Viva Voce (DEU ISSN 1439-0612) **8904**
Viva! Wydanie Specjalne *see* Viva! **3930**
Vivace! (AUS) **6627**
† Vivacious (USA ISSN 1946-6471) **8997**
Vivacious Magazine *see* Vivacious **8997**
Vivaista (ITA) **3757**
Vivant (NLD ISSN 1574-2962) **1954**
Vivant Univers *see* Enjeux Internationaux **7232**
Vivant Univers. Edition Suisse *see* Enjeux Internationaux **7232**
Vivarium (ITA ISSN 1825-9952) **7693**
• ➤ Vivarium (NLD ISSN 0042-7543) **4277**
Vivat (DEU ISSN 1860-5001) **5086**
Vivat Hussar (FRA) **6452**
Vivaverdi (ITA ISSN 1972-6694) **7575**
Vive (AUS ISSN 1328-9225) **8887**
† Vive + (AUS ISSN 1832-2298) **8997**
Vive (USA ISSN 1534-6056) **8887**
Vive - Gesundheit Erleben! (DEU) **6999**
Vive la Difference (GBR ISSN 0260-3993) **3571**
▼ Vive la Vie! (FRA ISSN 1960-9701) **3842**
Vive Magazine *see* Came Magazine **8939**
Vive Plus *see* Vive + **8997**
➤ Vivek (IND ISSN 0970-8618) **2456**
Vivekananda Kendra Patrika (IND ISSN 0970-9053) **4482**
Vivekananda Vedanta Society of Chicago. Bulletins (USA) **6960**
Vivenda Exclusive (NLD) **7615**
Vivens Homo (ITA ISSN 1123-5470) **7822**
Viver Light (BRA ISSN 1516-9723) **6670**
Viver Sani e Belli (ITA) **6999**
† Vivere (ITA ISSN 1121-8673) **8997**
Vivere a - Living in Milano *see* Vivere a Milano **8773**
Vivere a Milano/Living in Milano (ITA) **8773**
Viverito (DEU) **5086**
Vives (NLD ISSN 1389-8566) **3087**
ViVi (Chinese Edition)/Weini Shishang (Guoji Zhongwen Ban) (TWN) **8888**
ViVi (Japanese Edition) (JPN) **8888**
Vivi il Cinema *see* Vivilcinema **6516**
Vivid Magazine (USA ISSN 1930-5540) **3571**
• Vivienda/Dwelling (ARG ISSN 0505-7981) **460**
Vivilcinema (ITA) **6516**
Vivimilano (ITA ISSN 1120-5296) **3899**
Vivir *see* Vivir con Salud **6999**
Vivir con Salud (ESP ISSN 1697-7122) **6999**
Vivir Mejor (ARG ISSN 1515-8519) **6670**
Vivir Nuevos Tiempos *see* Plus es Mas **4365**
Vivliographika (GRC ISSN 0302-1181) **5054**
• VIVmag (USA ISSN 1933-8856) **8888**
Vivo (POL ISSN 1232-9665) **6627**
Vivre (FRA ISSN 0249-0358) **6036**
† Vivre au Feminin (FRA ISSN 1634-8028) **8997**
Vivre avec les Oiseaux (FRA ISSN 1248-2056) **915**
Vivre en Eglise (CAN ISSN 1492-9295) **7822**
Vivre en Famille (FRA ISSN 1773-8164) **7414**
† Vivre en Harmonie (FRA ISSN 0042-7608) **8997**
Vivre Ensemble (CAN ISSN 0823-2687) **7822**
Vivre Ensemble (FRA ISSN 1152-6653) **3049**
Vivre et Agir *see* Tambour Battant **4056**
Vivre & Communiquer (FRA ISSN 1952-0778) **7414**
Vivre Ma Maison (Edition Alpes de Haute-Provence, Hautes-Alpes, Bouches du Rhone, Vaucluse) (FRA ISSN 1968-0090) **1042**
Vivre Ma Maison (Edition Aude, Pyrenees-Orientales) (FRA ISSN 1777-6848) **1042**
Vivre Ma Maison (Edition Bouches-du-Rhone, Vaucluse) *see* Vivre Ma Maison (Edition Alpes de Haute-Provence, Hautes-Alpes, Bouches du Rhone, Vaucluse) **1042**
▼ Vivre Ma Maison (Edition Dordogne, Gironde, Lot-et-Garonne) (FRA ISSN 1955-0979) **1042**
Vivre Ma Maison (Edition Gard Herault) (FRA ISSN 1769-0021) **1042**
Vivre Ma Maison Aquitaine *see* Vivre Ma Maison (Edition Dordogne, Gironde, Lot-et-Garonne) **1042**
• Vivre Nice (FRA ISSN 1959-6375) **4984**
Vivre Plus (FRA ISSN 1953-0447) **4057**
Vixen *see* Vibe Vixen **8997**
Viz *see* Viz Comic **5244**
Viz Comic (GBR ISSN 0952-7966) **5244**
Vizantijskij Vremennik (RUS ISSN 0132-3776) **7928**
Vizier (NLD ISSN 1574-7247) **7693**
Vizier *see* Silhouet **6185**
Vizsla News (USA ISSN 0747-4636) **6816**
Vizugyi Kozlemenyek (HUN ISSN 0042-7616) **3399**
• Vjesnik (HRV ISSN 0350-3305) **3831**
• ➤ Vjesnik Bibliotekara Hrvatske (HRV ISSN 0507-1925) **5054**
Vjesnik Drzavnog Arhiva u Rijeci *see* Drzavni Arhiv u Rijeci. Vjesnik **4215**
Vjesnik H M D *see* Hrvatsko Matematicko Drustvo. Vjesnik **5491**
Vjesnik I N A - Naftaplin (HRV) **6796**
Vjesnik Rada (HRV ISSN 0042-7632) **1714**
Vjesnik za Arheologiju i Historiju Dalmatinsku *see* Vjesnik za Arheologiju i Povijest Dalmatinsku **423**
• Vjesnik za Arheologiju i Povijest Dalmatinsku (HRV ISSN 1845-7789) **423**
Vkusno i Polezno (RUS) **4369**
VKVisie *see* Reflectie **7814**
➤ Vlaams Diergeneeskundig Tijdschrift/Flemish Veterinary Journal (BEL ISSN 0303-9021) **8815**
Vlaams Jurist Vandaag (BEL) **4809**
Vlaams Tijdschrift voor Overheidsmanagement (BEL ISSN 1373-0509) **7476**
Vlaams Tijdschrift voor Sportbeheer (BEL ISSN 0770-9420) **8215**
Vlaamse Bedrijfssport (BEL) **8215**
Vlaamse Federatie van Gemeentesecretarissen Forum *see* V F G - Forum **7504**
Vlaamse Filmpjes (BEL ISSN 0773-1027) **2220**
De Vlaamse Gids (BEL ISSN 0042-7675) **5244**
De Vlaamse Ondernemer (BEL) **1192**
Vlaamse Stam (BEL ISSN 0774-5486) **3787**
Vlaanderen (BEL ISSN 0042-7683) **525**
Vlaardings Archeologisch Kantoor Verslag *see* V L A K - Verslag **422**
• ➤ Vladikavkazskii Matematicheskii Zhurnal (RUS ISSN 1683-3414) **5546**
• Vladivostok (RUS) **3943**
Vladivostok Eshche *see* Vladivostok **3943**
Vlaggentijdschrift Vexilla Nostra (NLD) **3787**
Vlakna a Textil/Fibres and Textiles (SVK ISSN 1335-0617) **8462**
Vlast' (RUS) **7192**
Vlasta (CZE ISSN 0139-6617) **8888**
Vlasta Magazin (CZE ISSN 1212-1290) **8888**
Vlastivedne Muzeum v Olomouci. Zpravy (CZE ISSN 1212-1134) **4277**
Vlastivedny Sbornik Novojicinska (CZE ISSN 1214-8032) **4277**
Vlastivedny Sbornik Okresu Novy Jicin *see* Vlastivedny Sbornik Novojicinska **4277**
➤ Vlastivedny Vestnik Moravsky (CZE ISSN 0323-2581) **4278**
† Vlastivedny Zpravodaj Podbrdska (CZE) **8997**
Vlees Plus *see* Vakblad Vlees en Vers **303**
Vlees&Vers *see* Vakblad Vlees en Vers **303**
† Vleeswetgeving Compact (NLD ISSN 1874-7736) **8997**
Vliegende Hollander (NLD ISSN 0042-7705) **6452**
Vliesstoff Nonwoven International (DEU ISSN 0935-6347) **8462**
Vlinders (NLD ISSN 0923-1846) **861**
Vloer Technisch Magazine (NLD ISSN 1381-9763) **1052**
VM. Vauhdin Maailma *see* V M **8609**
V:Magazine *see* Amaze Magazine **585**
Vmax (Velocity Maximum) (DNK ISSN 1399-2864) **8611**
VME and Critical Systems *see* V M E and Critical Systems **2525**
VMEbus Extensions for Instrumentation & PCI Extensions for Instrumentation Newsletter *see* VXIbus & PXI Newsletter **3334**
VMobile (FRA ISSN 1777-7801) **8611**
Vneshnaya Torgovlya (RUS ISSN 0321-057X) **1586**
Vneshneekonomicheskaya Deyatel'nost': Sovremennaya Praktika, Problemy, Perspektivy (RUS) **1524**
Vneshneekonomicheskie Svyazi Rossii (RUS ISSN 0236-1426) **1524**
Vneshneekonomicheskii Byulleten' (RUS) **1524**
• Vneshneekonomicheskoye Obozreniye (RUS ISSN 1606-1616) **1586**
➤ Vnitrni Lekarstvi (CZE ISSN 0042-773X) **5728**
• Vo I P (Voice Over Internet Protocol) (USA ISSN 1559-7350) **2567**
Vo Slavu Rodiny (BLR) **3800**
VO2 Max (NZL ISSN 1176-8134) **8215**
Vocable (FRA ISSN 0763-9686) **5194**
Vocabula Bound Quarterly *see* The Vocabula Review **5194**
• The Vocabula Review (USA ISSN 1542-7080) **5194**
Vocabulaire des Grands Ecrivains Francais *see* Lettres Numeriques **5144**
• Vocal Journal (AUS ISSN 1445-5080) **6705**
VocalPoint (CAN) **8077**
Vocare (USA ISSN 1945-2381) **7779**
➤ Vocarstvo/Journal of Pomology (SRB ISSN 1820-5054) **258**
• Vocation Sage - Femme (FRA ISSN 1634-0760) **6006**
Vocational and Technical Schools. East (USA ISSN 1541-1478) **2963**
Vocational Careers Sourcebook (USA ISSN 1060-5630) **6705**
• Vocational Education & Training Abstracts (GBR ISSN 1943-0272) **2937**
Vocational Education and Training NETwork - European Conference of Education Research Proceedings *see* V E T N E T - E C E R. Proceedings **2924**
• Vocational Education and Training Research Database (Online) (AUS) **2937**
Vocational Education and Training Research Database (Print) *see* Vocational Education and Training Research Database (Online) **2937**
➤ Vocational Evaluation and Career Assessment Professionals Journal (USA) **6705**
Vocational Evaluation and Work Adjustment Journal (Colorado Springs, 2002) *see* Vocational Evaluation and Career Assessment Professionals Journal **6705**
Vocational Rehabilitation of Disabled Persons Act Annual Report (CAN ISSN 1187-2535) **4070**
Vocational Training Council. Annual Report (HKG) **2947**
Vocational Training Information Bulletin (LUX) **6705**
Vocational Training News *see* Career and Technical Education Advisor **6694**
▼ • Vocations and Learning (NLD ISSN 1874-785X) **6705**
Vocations and Prayers (USA ISSN 1075-6663) **7822**
La Voce (ITA ISSN 0042-7780) **3899**
Voce (JPN) **8888**
La Voce (ZAF) **3571**
† Voce Bruzia (ITA ISSN 0042-7802) **8997**
La Voce degli Italiani (GBR ISSN 0042-7810) **3571**
Voce degli Italo Canadesi (CAN ISSN 0842-9715) **3571**
Voce dei Berici (ITA) **7822**
La Voce del Lago (ITA ISSN 1826-0365) **3899**
La Voce del Tabaccaio (ITA ISSN 0042-7829) **8488**
La Voce della Campania *see* La Voce delle Voci **7192**
† Voce della Fiera (ITA ISSN 0042-7837) **8997**
† Voce della Regione (ITA) **8997**
La Voce della U I L (Unione Italiana del Lavoro) (ITA) **4605**
• La Voce delle Voci (ITA) **7192**
• Voce dell'Emigrante (ITA ISSN 0394-8153) **8077**

Title

Title

Vreme (SRB ISSN 0353-8028) **3945**
Vremya (Almaty) (KAZ) **3902**
Vremya (Kemerovo) (RUS) **4605**
Vremya i Den'gi (RUS) **1192**
Vremya i My (RUS) **5396**
• Vremya MN (Moskovskie Novosti) (RUS ISSN 1029-8487) **3943**
• Vremya Novostei (RUS ISSN 1605-8844) **3943**
• Vremya po Grinvichu (KAZ) **3902**
Vreshta *see* Vineyard **7706**
Vrhovni Sud Srbije. Bilten Sudske Prakse/Serbian Supreme Court Law Practice. Bulletin (SRB ISSN 0354-4109) **4810**
Vriend *see* Viataal Magazine **4076**
Vriendenkrant *see* Ecomare Bericht **2609**
Vriendin (NLD ISSN 1387-5663) **8888**
Vrij Nederland *see* V N Vrij Nederland **3916**
Vrij Zicht *see* Ad Interim **8928**
De Vrijdenker (NLD ISSN 1872-1478) **6960**
De Vrije Fries (NLD ISSN 0923-6279) **4278**
De Vrije Gedachte *see* De Vrijdenker **6960**
Vrije Tijd Wonen *see* V T Wonen **4983**
Vrije Universiteit. Faculteit der Economische Wetenschappen en Econometrie. Research Memorandum (NLD ISSN 0927-0132) **1550**
Vrije Universiteit. Juridische Reeks (NLD ISSN 0921-450X) **4810**
† Het Vrije Woord (NLD ISSN 1574-0854) **8998**
➤ Vrijetijdstudies (NLD ISSN 1384-2439) **4984**
Vrijheid en Democratie *see* Liber **7151**
Vrijwillige Inzet Onderzocht (NLD ISSN 1573-3785) **8077**
Vritta Vidya (IND) **4585**
Vroegop (NLD ISSN 1873-409X) **460**
Vrouekeur (ZAF ISSN 1726-0698) **3950**
▼ Vrouw (NLD ISSN 1875-6026) **8888**
Vrouw en Politiek *see* CDA.nl **7114**
Vrouw en Wereld (BEL) **8888**
Vrouw Vandaag (NLD ISSN 1387-2966) **8888**
Vrouwen Advies Commissies Nieuws *see* WoonKwaliteit **1043**
Vrouwen van Nu (NLD ISSN 1872-0579) **8888**
Vrouwenbelangen (NLD ISSN 0925-482X) **8888**
VrouwenMode (NLD ISSN 1570-825X) **2263**
Die Vrye Afrikaan (ZAF ISSN 1814-6635) **3950**
Vrystaatse Onderwysnuus *see* Free State Educational News **2858**
Vse dlya Bukhgaltera (RUS) **1303**
Vse Pro Dum - Byt - Zahradu - Hobby (CZE ISSN 1214-8210) **4552**
Vselennaya i My (RUS) **583**
Vsemirnaya Assambleya Zdravookhraneniya i Ispolnitel'nogo Komiteta. Sbornik Rezolyutsii i Reshenii *see* World Health Organization. Handbook of Resolutions and Decisions of the World Health Assembly and the Executive Board. **7545**
Vsemirnaya Meteologicheskaya Organizatsiya. Komissiya po Osnovnym Sistemam. Okonchatel'nyi Sokrashchennyi Otchet (No) Sessii *see* World Meteorological Organization. Commission for Basic Systems. Abridged Final Report of the (No.) Session **6398**
Vsemirnaya Meteorologicheskaya Organizatsiya. Godovoi Otchet (CHE ISSN 0250-8893) **6397**
Vsemirnaya Meteorologicheskaya Organizatsiya. Komissiya po Atmosfernym Naukam. Okonchatel'nyi Sokrashchennyi Otchet (No) Sessii *see* World Meteorological Organization. Commission for Atmospheric Sciences. Abridged Final Report of the (No.) Session **6398**
Vsemirnaya Meteorologicheskaya Organizatsiya. Komissiya po Aviatsionnoi Meteorologii. Okonchatel'nyi Sokrashchennyi Otchet (No) Sessii *see* World Meteorological Organization. Commission for Aeronautical Meteorology. Abridged Final Report of the (No.) Session **6398**
Vsemirnaya Meteorologicheskaya Organizatsiya. Komissiya po Gidrologii. Okonchatel'nyi Sokrashchennyi Otchet (No) Sessii *see* World Meteorological Organization. Commission for Hydrology. Abridged Final Report of the (No.) Session **6399**
Vsemirnaya Meteorologicheskaya Organizatsiya. Komissiya po Morskoi Meteorologii. Okonchatel'nyi Sokrashchennyi Otchet (No) Sessii *see* World Meteorological Organization. Commission for Marine Meteorology. Abridged Final Report of the (No.) Session **6399**
Vsemirnaya Meteorologicheskaya Organizatsiya. Komissiya po Priboram i Metodam Nablyudenii. Okonchatel'nyi Sokrashchennyi Otchet (No) Sessii *see* World Meteorological Organization. Commission for Instruments and Methods of Observation. Abridged Final Report of the (No.) Session **6399**
Vsemirnaya Meteorologicheskaya Organizatsiya Komissiya po Sel'skokhozyaistvennoi Meteorologii. Okonchatel'nyi Sokrashchennyi Otchet (No) Sessii *see* World Meteorological Organization. Commission for Agricultural Meteorology. Abridged Final Report of the (No.) Session **6398**
Vsemirnaya Meteorologicheskaya Organizatsiya. Kongress. Sokrashechennyi Otchet s Rezolyutsiyami *see* World Meteorological Organization. Congress. Abridged Report with Resolutions **6399**
Vsemirnaya Meteorologicheskaya Organizatsiya. Regional'naya Assotsiatsiya II (Aziya). Okonchatel'nyi Sokrashchennyi Otchet (No.) Sessii *see* World Meteorological Organization. Regional Association II (Asia). Abridged Final Report of the (No.) Session **6399**
Vsemirnaya Meteorologicheskaya Organizatsiya. Sessiya Ispolnitel'nogo Soveta. Sokrashchennyi Otchet s Rezolyutsiyami (CHE ISSN 1011-3673) **6397**
Vsemirnaya Organizatsiya Zdravookhraneniya. Byulleten' *see* World Health Organization. Bulletin **5731**
Vsemirnaya Organizatsiya Zdravookhraneniya. Seriya Tekhnicheskikh Dokladov (CHE ISSN 0250-8737) **5729**
Vserossiiskii Nauchno-Issledovatel'skii Institut Morskogo Rybnogo Khozyaistva i Okeanografii (V N I R O). Trudy (RUS) **2820**
Vserossiiskii Nauchno-issledovatel'skii Institut Zheleznodorozhnovo Transporta. Vestnik (RUS ISSN 0869-8163) **8627**
Vserossiiskii Soyuz Strakhovshikov. Vestnik (RUS) **4527**
Vserossiiskii Vystavochnyi Tsentr (RUS) **6539**
• ➤ Vserossiiskoe Mineralogicheskoe Obshchestvo. Zapiski/Russian Mineralogical Society. Proceedings (RUS ISSN 0869-6055) **2774**
➤ Vsesvitnya Literatura v Serednikh Navchal'nykh Zakladakh Ukrainy (UKR) **5396**
• Vsichko za Knigata (BGR ISSN 1310-4047) **7575**
Vspomogatel'nye Istoricheskie Distsipliny (RUS ISSN 0130-0865) **4278**
Vstrechi (USA ISSN 0888-5257) **5437**
Vsya Evropa (DEU) **5086**
VTM *see* Vloer Technisch Magazine **1052**
VU-Windesheim (NLD ISSN 1574-9924) **3009**
• Vue Weekly (CAN) **6627**
Vuelo (MEX) **8786**
Vulcan (GBR ISSN 0958-4293) **4380**
Vulcan Historical Review (USA ISSN 1097-6957) **4166**
† Vulkanen (DNK ISSN 0108-691X) **8998**
• ➤ Vulnerable Children and Youth Studies (GBR ISSN 1745-0128) **2171**
• Vulpia (USA ISSN 1540-3599) **822**
Vulture News (ZAF ISSN 1606-7479) **916**
Vunshna Turgovia na Republika Bulgaria/Foreign Trade in the Republic of Bulgaria (BGR ISSN 1311-2260) **8413**
Vuollerim 6000 Aar. Arkeologiska Rapporter (SWE ISSN 1651-3525) **423**
Vuoriteollisuus *see* Materia **6469**
Vuosiraportti Euroopan Unionin Huumeongelmasta *see* State of the Drugs Problem in the European Union. Annual Report **2699**
Vuoto *see* Vuoto, Scienza e Tecnologia **7192**
Vuoto, Scienza e Tecnologia (ITA ISSN 0391-3155) **7192**
Vurkhoven Kasatsionen Sud na Republika Bulgaria. Bulletin/Supreme Court of Appeal of the Republic of Bulgaria. Bulletin (BGR ISSN 1311-2880) **4967**
Vuzovskie Vesti (RUS) **2925**
VXIbus & PXI Newsletter (USA) **3334**
Vy i Vash Magazin (RUS) **1969**
Vyapar (IND) **1192**
Vyapar (Gujarati Edition) (IND ISSN 0042-9325) **1192**
Vyapar Bharati (IND) **3890**
Vyapar Drishti (IND) **3890**
Vyapar Kesari (IND) **3890**
Vyapar Sandesh (IND) **3891**
Vyapari-Mitra (IND) **1954**
Vyatskii Krai (RUS) **3943**
Vyavasaya Keralam (IND) **1434**
Vyber Kulturnich Vyroci (Online) (CZE ISSN 1803-6953) **638**
Vyber Kulturnich Vyroci (Print) *see* Vyber Kulturnich Vyroci (Online) **638**
Vyber z Rozhodnuti Sudneho Dvora Europskych Spolocenstiev (SVK ISSN 1336-5312) **4967**
• Vybrane Ekonomicke Vysledky Malych a Strednich Subjektu C R v Letech (Years) (CZE) **1274**
• Vychislitel'nye Metody i Programirovaniye/ Numerical Methods and Programming (RUS ISSN 0507-5386) **2510**
• Vychislitel'nye Tekhnologii (RUS ISSN 1560-7534) **2474**
Vychodoslovenske Muzeum v Kosiciach. Sbornik. Seria A. Prirodne Vedy *see* Natura Carpatica **2713**
• Vyroba Vybranych Vyrobku v Prumyslu C R za Rok (Year) (Ceska Republika) (CZE) **1274**
Vyrobne Inzinierstvo/Manufacturing Engineering (SVK ISSN 1335-7972) **3372**
Vyrocne Spravy o Cinnosti Muzei na Slovensku (SVK) **6539**
➤ Vyshcha Osvita Ukrainy (UKR) **2925**
Vyshchiy Arbitrazhniy Sud Ukrainy. Visnyk (UKR) **4810**
Vyshka (AZE) **1192**
Vysoka Skola Banska - Technicka Univerzita Ostrava. Sbornik Vedeckych Praci: Rada Elektrotechnicka (CZE ISSN 1210-048X) **3334**
† • Vysoka Skola Banska - Technicka Univerzita Ostrava. Sbornik Vedeckych Praci: Rada Hornicko-Geologicka (CZE ISSN 0474-8476) **8998**
Vysoka Skola Banska - Technicka Univerzita Ostrava. Sbornik Vedeckych Praci: Rada Hutnicka/Institute of Mining and Metallurgy. Transactions: Metallurgical Series (CZE ISSN 0474-8484) **6336**
Vysoka Skola Banska - Technicka Univerzita Ostrava. Sbornik Vedeckych Praci: Rada Strojni (CZE ISSN 1210-0471) **3399**
Vysoka Skola Lesnicka a Drevarska vo Zlovene. Drevarska Fakulta. Zbornik Vedeckych Prac (SVK ISSN 0232-0029) **3707**
Vysokomolekulyarnye Soedineniya. Kratkie Soobshcheniya (RUS) **2142**
• Vysokomolekulyarnye Soedineniya. Seriya A i Seriya B (RUS ISSN 1023-3091) **2142**
➤ Vysokomolekulyarnye Soedineniya. Seriya C (RUS) **2084**
• Vysokyi Zamok (UKR) **3966**
Vyssee obrazovanie v Evrope *see* Higher Education in Europe **2984**
Vysshaya i Sredniaya Professional'naya Shkola v Rossii i Za Rubezhom (RUS) **3009**
Vyssheye Obrazovanie v Rossii (RUS ISSN 0869-3617) **3010**
Vysshii Arbitrazhnyi Sud Rossiiskoi Federatsii. Vestnik (RUS ISSN 0869-7426) **4810**
Vytapeni, Vetrani, Instalace (CZE ISSN 1210-1389) **4127**
Vytis/Knight (USA ISSN 0042-9384) **2270**
➤ Vytvarna Vychova (CZE ISSN 1210-3691) **2925**
Vytvarnictvo, Fotografia, Film (SVK ISSN 0042-9392) **525**
Vytvarny Zivot (SVK ISSN 0139-7214) **525**
Vyziva a Potraviny (CZE ISSN 1211-846X) **6671**
† ➤ Vyziva a Spotreba Potravin v Cislech (CZE ISSN 1212-0022) **8998**
➤ Vyzkumny a Slechtitelsky Ustav Ovocnarsky Holovousy. Vedecke Prace Ovocnarske/ Research and Breeding Institute of Pomology, Holovousy. Scientific Papers of Pomology (CZE ISSN 0231-6900) **258**
† Vyzkumny Ustav Spoju. Sbornik Praci (CZE ISSN 0231-6951) **8998**
Vyzkumy v Cechach (CZE ISSN 0862-2930) **423**
Vyzov (RUS ISSN 0868-9520) **7218**
Vyzvol'nyi Shlyakh/Liberation Path (GBR ISSN 0042-9422) **5244**
• Vzglyad (KAZ) **3902**
• W (CAN ISSN 1912-8398) **5396**
• W (USA ISSN 0162-9115) **8888**
• W A A C Newsletter (Western Association for Art Conservation) (USA ISSN 1052-0066) **525**
W A A P Book of the Year (World Association for Animal Production) (NLD ISSN 1574-1125) **303**
W A Business News *see* West Australian Business News **1587**
• ➤ The W A C Journal (Writing Across the Curriculum) (USA ISSN 1544-4929) **3087**
W A D (We'ar Different) (FRA ISSN 1626-5394) **2220**
W A D *see* World Aerospace Database **75**
W A D E Journal (World Association of Document Examiners) (USA) **2671**
W A D E S Herald (Western Alcohol and Drugs Education Society (W A D E S)) (GBR) **2700**
W A D. Hors-Serie (We'ar Different) (FRA ISSN 1630-3903) **2220**
W A E N T *see* World Articles in Ear Nose and Throat **6086**
W A F *see* Weather and Forecasting **6398**
W.A. Grower (AUS ISSN 0042-9465) **169**
• W A H M (Work at Home Moms) (USA) **8888**
The W A H M magazine *see* The Work-at-Home Parent Magazine **1969**
W A M *see* Wireless America Magazine **2344**
• W A M News (Wyoming Association of Municipalities) (USA) **7505**
W A M R *see* The World Arbitration and Mediation Review **4816**
W A N A T C A Yearbook *see* West Australian Nut and Tree Crop Association. Yearbook **259**
W A N D Bulletin (Women's Action for New Directions) (USA) **8888**
W A N - I F R A Magazine (DEU) **7329**
W A O W *see* We Are One World **2221**
W A Organic Life (Western Australia) (AUS ISSN 1834-3570) **3753**
W A P D A News (Water and Power Development Authority) (PAK) **8835**
• W A P Magazin (Wireless Application Protocol) (DEU) **2344**
W A R *see* World Accounting Report **1304**
W A R *see* West Africa Review **4179**
W A S I (Writers and Artists Services International) (MWI) **525**
W A S Newsletter (World Archaeological Society) (USA ISSN 0738-8063) **423**
W A S O Frauen (DEU) **8888**
W A Z *see* Westdeutsche Allgemeine Zeitung **3860**
• W A Z Online (DEU) **3859**
W Akcji (POL ISSN 1643-7373) **3582**
W & J Magazine (Washington & Jefferson College) (USA ISSN 8750-8133) **2308**
W & L Magazine (Washington and Lee University) (USA ISSN 0042-952X) **2308**
W & S (DEU ISSN 1612-3360) **2671**
• W & V (Werben und Verkaufen) (DEU ISSN 0042-9538) **37**
W & W P *see* Wood & Wood Products **3717**
W A's Best Kitchens and Bathrooms (Western Australia) (AUS ISSN 1834-2906) **4552**
W B *see* Resource (Wageningen) **2298**
W B C News (Witwatersrand Bird Club) (ZAF ISSN 0250-1481) **916**
W B E R *see* The World Bank Economic Review **1525**
W B F In Action (Workmen's Benefit Fund of the United States of America) (USA ISSN 1061-1444) **4527**
W B F O (Wohnbauforschung in Oesterreich) (AUT ISSN 0042-9562) **4431**
W B K Forschungsberichte (Institut fuer Werkzeugmaschinen und Betriebstechnik) (USA ISSN 0724-4967) **3226**
W B M *see* Weed Biology and Management **258**
• W B M (Wine Business Magazine) (AUS ISSN 1832-5068) **612**
W B N *see* Weekly Book Newsletter (Online) **7576**
W C *see* Walls & Ceilings **1042**
W C A T in Focus *see* W S I A T in Focus **1714**
• W C & P International (Water Conditioning & Purification) (USA ISSN 1097-1726) **8835**
W C B Newsletter and Bulletin (Worshipful Company of Butchers) (GBR ISSN 1358-5118) **3667**
W C C *see* What's Working in Credit & Collection **4883**
W C C F L *see* West Coast Conference on Formal Linguistics. Proceedings **5195**
W C C Focus (World Council of Churches) (CHE) **7693**
W C C I Newsletter *see* World Council for Curriculum and Instruction. Newsletter **3088**
W C C News (World Council of Churches) (CHE) **7693**
W C C Publications (World Council of Churches) (CHE) **7693**
W C E R Highlights *see* W C E R Research Highlights **3087**
• W C E R Research Highlights (Wisconsin Center for Education Research) (USA) **3087**
W C E T Journal *see* World Council of Enterostomal Therapists Journal **5932**
W C G S Newsletter *see* Wetzel County Genealogical Society. Newsletter **3787**
W C G S Updates (Wake County Genealogical Society) (USA ISSN 1526-0771) **3787**
W C J *see* Women & Criminal Justice **4900**
W.C.J. Meredith Memorial Lectures (CAN ISSN 0509-5166) **4810**
W C J O *see* Workers' Compensation Journal of Ohio **7477**
W C M *see* Woodall's Campground Management **8342**
W C N *see* Workers Compensation N S W **1715**
W C N Commercial News (USA ISSN 0047-5068) **1586**
W C O *see* Workers' Compensation Outlook **4528**
• W C O News (World Customs Organization) (BEL ISSN 1782-1851) **7476**
W C P S Quarterly (Women's Caucus for Political Science) (USA) **7218**
W C R A News (West Coast Railway Association) (CAN ISSN 1204-072X) **8627**
W C S Canada Conservation Reports *see* Conservation Report **2607**
W C V A Annual Report/Adroddiad Blynyddol C G G C (Wales Council for Voluntary Action) (GBR) **8077**
W C Y *see* The World Competitiveness Yearbook **1525**
W D *see* Wind Directions **3178**
W D A Journal (Wisconsin Dental Association) (USA ISSN 1080-6989) **5869**
• W D C - M A R E Reports (World Data Center for Marine Environmental Sciences) (DEU ISSN 1611-6577) **3492**
W D I *see* World Development Indicators **1587**
W D L News (Workers Defense League, Inc.) (USA) **1714**
W D M in Action (World Development Movement) (GBR) **1607**
W E *see* World Englishes **5196**
W E A Legend (Wilderness Education Association) (USA ISSN 1062-0435) **2631**
W E A News (Wyoming Education Association) (USA) **2925**
• ➤ W E A Theological News (World Evangelical Alliance) (AUS ISSN 0260-3705) **7693**
W E & T *see* Water Environment & Technology **3492**
W E B Du Bois Institute Series (USA) **3571**
W E F A Industrial Monitor (Wharton Econometric Forecasting Associates) (USA ISSN 1093-6580) **1192**
• W E F Highlights (Water Environment Federation) (USA ISSN 1087-3384) **3474**
W E F Proceedings *see* Water Environment Federation. Proceedings **3492**
W E H O Magazine (Where Everything Hip Originates) (USA) **3992**
W E M *see* Water and Environment Magazine **8837**
W E O *see* International Monetary Fund. World Economic Outlook **1493**
W E P *see* West European Politics **7273**
W E P Z A Newsletter (World Economic Processing Zones Association) (USA ISSN 0887-9990) **1586**
W E R *see* Water Environment Research **3493**
W E S *see* Work, Employment & Society **8147**
W E S A Newsletter (Wisconsin Electronic Sales and Service Association) (USA) **1969**
W E S T P A C Information (Western Pacific) (FRA ISSN 1020-4598) **2820**

Link to your serials resources and content with ulrichsweb.com

DIRECTORY 2010 W S D A NEWS 11015

W E T A Magazine (Washington Educational Telecommunications Association) (USA ISSN 1041-2700) **2398**
W E T News *see* Water & Effluent Treatment News **8836**
W E T R *see* Wine Equalisation Tax Ruling **1955**
• W.E. Upjohn Institute for Employment Research. Staff Working Papers (USA) **1714**
• W.E. Upjohn Institute for Employment Research. Technical Reports (USA) **1714**
▼ • W E V A Journal (World Electric Vehicle Association) (BEL) **8611**
W. Europe (USA) **8888**
W F B Review (World Fellowship of Buddhists) (THA) **7703**
W F D Y News (World Federation of Democratic Youth) (HUN ISSN 0049-8076) **2220**
W F I *see* Window Fabricator and Installer **1043**
W F L A R *see* Wichita Falls Literature & Art Review **5398**
W f m (Woodmen of the World Fraternal Magazine) (USA ISSN 1933-057X) **4527**
W F S Quarterly (Women in the Fire Service) (USA ISSN 1071-1767) **3582**
W F T (Werkstoff Forschung und Technik) (USA ISSN 0940-7804) **3226**
W G A Geschaeftsbericht (Wirtschaftsvereinigung Gross- und Aussenhandel Hamburg e.V.) (DEU ISSN 0042-966X) **1586**
W G and L Tax Journal Digest *see* W G & L Tax Journal Digest **1954**
W G & L Tax Journal Digest (Warren, Gorham and Lamont) (USA ISSN 1075-0223) **1954**
W G & S *see* Western Grower and Shipper **259**
W G C *see* Women, Girls & Criminal Justice **2672**
W G I *see* World Gas Intelligence **6797**
† W G O - Monatshefte fuer Osteuropaeisches Recht (DEU ISSN 0042-9678) **8998**
• W G S Newsletter (Working Group on Software) (NLD ISSN 0921-0490) **2599**
W H *see* Women & Health **8849**
W H A T T E-Journal *see* World Hospitality and Tourism Trends **8776**
W H B A *see* Western Horse Breeders Annual **8300**
W H I N en Espanol *see* Workers' Health International Newsletter **6689**
W H M I S at Work (Workplace Hazardous Materials Information System) (CAN ISSN 1703-0935) **6688**
W H M I S Compliance Manual (Workplace Hazardous Materials Information Systems) (CAN) **6688**
• W H O Drug Information (World Health Organization) (CHE ISSN 1010-9609) **7545**
W H O Food Additives Series (World Health Organization) (CHE ISSN 0300-0923) **3667**
• W H O Pharmaceuticals Newsletter (World Health Organization) (CHE ISSN 1564-1120) **6885**
W H O Regional Publications. European Series *see* World Health Organization Regional Publications. European Series **7545**
• ➤ W H O Technical Report Series (World Health Organization) (CHE ISSN 0512-3054) **5729**
W H Q *see* Welsh Housing Quarterly **4431**
W H Q *see* The Western Historical Quarterly **4317**
W H R *see* What's Working in Human Resources **1877**
W I A P S *see* Women in Asia Publication Series **8904**
W I A S News (Women in Atmospheric Sciences) (USA ISSN 1949-4327) **2774**
W I B G Journal *see* Women In and Beyond the Global **8904**
W I D *see* Australian and New Zealand Wine Industry Directory **598**
W I D *see* Washington Information Directory (Year) **7193**
W I D Bulletin (Women and International Development) (USA ISSN 1077-145X) **7218**
• W I D E R Angle (United Nations University, World Institute for Development Economics Research) (FIN ISSN 1238-9544) **1607**
W I D E R Series *see* Studies in Development Economics and Policy **1180**
W I D Forum (Women and International Development) (USA ISSN 0888-7772) **7218**
The W I D H H Wave (Western Institute for the Deaf & Hard of Hearing) (CAN ISSN 1713-8906) **4077**
W I F I S Aktuell (Wissenschaftliches Forum fuer Internationale Sicherheit) (DEU ISSN 1867-3015) **7272**
W I F - Wirtschaft, Information, Fortbildung (AUT) **1389**
W I Genealogical Council Newsletter (Wisconsin) (USA) **3787**
W I I W Current Analyses and Country Profiles (Wiener Institut fuer Internationale Wirtschaftsvergleiche) (AUT) **1607**
➤ W I I W Forschungsberichte/W I I W Research Reports (Wiener Institut fuer Internationale Wirtschaftsvergleiche) (AUT ISSN 1025-8930) **1607**
W I I W Monographien *see* W I I W Monographs **1607**
W I I W Monographs/W I I W Monographien (Wiener Institut fuer Internationale Wirtschaftsvergleiche) (AUT) **1607**
W I I W Research Reports *see* W I I W Forschungsberichte **1607**
W I I W Working Papers (Wiener Institut fuer Internationale Wirtschaftsvergleiche) (AUT) **1607**
W I J *see* Australian and New Zealand Wine Industry Journal **598**
W I K - Zeitschrift fuer die Sicherheit der Wirtschaft (DEU ISSN 1615-455X) **2671**
W I L J *see* Wisconsin International Law Journal **4944**
W I L L A *see* Women in Literacy and Life Assembly **8904**
W I N *see* The World of Irish Nursing & Midwifery **5984**
W I N *see* Woman's International Net **8890**
W I N D O W. Western Indian Ocean Waters (FRA ISSN 1024-4158) **2821**
W I N H E C Journal *see* World Indigenous Nations Higher Education Consortium. Journal **3010**
The W I N Informer (Writers Information Network) (USA) **7575**
• W I N News (Women's International Network) (USA ISSN 0145-7985) **8904**
W I P O Magazine (World Intellectual Property Organization) (CHE ISSN 1020-7074) **6760**
W I R (DEU) **1389**
W I R *see* World Industrial Reporter **5461**
W I R - Wirtschaft in Rostock (DEU) **1192**
• W I S E/N I R S Nuclear Monitor (World Information Service on Energy/Nuclear Information and Resource Service) (NLD ISSN 1570-4629) **3175**
W I S E News Communique *see* W I S E/N I R S Nuclear Monitor **3175**
† W I S E R (Whitlam Institute for Social and Economic Research) (AUS ISSN 1321-3067) **8998**
W I S E Women's News (Women's International Studies Europe) (NLD ISSN 1380-0701) **8904**
W I S O (Wirtschafts- und Sozialpolitische) (AUT ISSN 1012-3059) **8014**
W I S O - Dokumente (Wirtschafts- und Sozialpolitische) (AUT) **8014**
W I S O SteuerBrief (DEU ISSN 0948-0625) **1954**
W I T (Women In Touch) (USA) **8888**
W.I.T.C.H. (Will, Irma, Taranee, Cornelia, Hay Lin) (BGR ISSN 1312-1537) **2220**
W.I.T.C.H. (Will, Irma, Taranee, Cornelia, Hay Lin) (CZE ISSN 1213-6190) **2220**
W.I.T.C.H. (Will, Irma, Taranee, Cornelia, Hay-Lin) (DEU) **2220**
W.I.T.C.H. (Will, Irma, Taranee, Cornelia, Hay Lin) (DNK) **2220**
W.I.T.C.H. (Will, Irma, Taranee, Cornelia, Hay Lin) (EST ISSN 1736-4124) **2220**
W.I.T.C.H. (Will, Irma, Taranee, Cornelia, Hay Lin) (FIN ISSN 1458-9036) **2220**
W.I.T.C.H. (Will, Irma, Taranee, Cornelia, Hay Lin) (HRV ISSN 1334-2169) **2220**
W.I.T.C.H. (Will, Irma, Taranee, Cornelia, Hay Lin) (HUN ISSN 1587-8600) **2220**
W.I.T.C.H. (Will, Irma, Taranee, Cornelia, Hay Lin) (ITA ISSN 1592-0143) **2220**
W.I.T.C.H. (Will, Irma, Taranee, Cornelia, Hay Lin) (LTU) **2220**
W.I.T.C.H. (Will, Irma, Taranee, Cornelia, Hay Lin) (LVA ISSN 1691-1660) **2220**
† W.I.T.C.H. (NLD ISSN 1571-1870) **8998**
W.I.T.C.H. (Will, Irma, Taranee, Cornelia, Hay-Lin) (NOR ISSN 1502-7554) **2220**
W.I.T.C.H. (Will, Irma, Taranee, Cornelia, Hay Lin) (PHL) **2220**
W.I.T.C.H. (Will, Irma, Taranee, Cornelia, Hay Lin) (PRT) **2220**
W.I.T.C.H. (Will, Irma, Taranee, Cornelia, Hay Lin) (ROM ISSN 1583-722X) **2220**
W.I.T.C.H. (Will, Irma, Taranee, Cornelia, Hay-Lin) (SWE ISSN 1650-7479) **2220**
W.I.T.C.H. (Will, Irma, Taranee, Cornelia, Hay Lin) (TUR) **2220**
W I T C H Mag (FRA ISSN 1638-7945) **2220**
▼ W.I.T.C.H. Styl (CZE ISSN 1802-3118) **2220**
W I T S: 1 (Wisconsin Introductions to Scandinavia) (USA ISSN 0742-7018) **3571**
W I T S: 2 (Wisconsin Introductions to Scandinavia) (USA ISSN 0742-7026) **3571**
• W I T Transactions on Biomedicine and Health (Wessex Institute of Technology) (GBR ISSN 1747-4485) **5729**
• W I T Transactions on Ecology and the Environment (Wessex Institute of Technology) (GBR ISSN 1746-448X) **3474**
• W I T Transactions on Engineering Sciences (Wessex Institute of Technology) (GBR ISSN 1746-4471) **3226**
• W I T Transactions on Information and Communication Technologies (Wessex Institute of Technology) (GBR ISSN 1746-4463) **2353**
• W I T Transactions on Modelling and Simulation (Wessex Institute of Technology) (GBR ISSN 1746-4064) **2518**
• W I T Transactions on the Built Environment (Wessex Institute of Technology) (GBR ISSN 1746-4498) **3287**
W I - Wohnungswirtschaftliche Informationen (DEU ISSN 0179-7948) **7615**
W I Z O Review (Women's International Zionist Organization) (ISR ISSN 0042-9732) **7731**
W In D *see* World Interior Design **4553**
W-Info Wirtschaftsmagazin (DEU) **1192**
W J A S *see* World Journal of Agricultural Sciences **170**
W J B Chiltern's Orange Tax Guide (GBR) **1954**
W J C *see* Western Journal of Communication **5195**
W J L G S *see* Wisconsin Journal of Law, Gender & Society **4815**
W J M L L *see* Web Journal of Modern Language Linguistics **5194**
W J R *see* Watch & Jewelry Review **4570**
• W K C News Bulletin (Working Kelpie Council) (AUS) **6816**
• W K Kellogg Foundation Annual Report (USA ISSN 0889-7956) **1192**
W K S B (Waermeschutz, Kaelteschutz, Schallschutz, Brandschutz) (DEU ISSN 0341-0293) **4127**
W K W Magazin *see* Wiener Klinisches Magazin **5730**
• ➤ W L A (War, Literature & the Arts) (USA ISSN 1949-9752) **5396**
W L A Newsletter (Wisconsin Library Association) (USA ISSN 0746-5785) **5054**
W L B *see* Wasser, Luft und Boden **3474**
W L B Report (Wasser, Luft und Boden) (DEU ISSN 0343-3153) **3474**
W L D J *see* WebLogic Developer's Journal **2510**
W L F *see* Villanova Women's Law Forum **4809**
W L J *see* Washburn Law Journal **4810**
W L J *see* Hastings Women's Law Journal **4685**
W L J *see* U C L A Women's Law Journal **4799**
W L R *see* Washington Law Review **4811**
W L R *see* Water Law Review **8837**
W L R *see* Widener Law Review **4814**
W L R *see* Washington Literary Review (Online) **5437**
W L T Magazine *see* World Literature Today **5400**
W M A S H (Year) *see* A C M International Workshop on Wireless Mobile Applications and Services on W L A N Hotspots **2310**
• W M Allgemeine Verlosungstabelle (Wertpapier-Mitteilungen) (DEU ISSN 0342-6874) **1389**
W M B (Women Mean Business) (IRL ISSN 1649-8062) **1714**
W M H & D *see* Women's Mental Health & Development **8849**
W M J *see* Wisconsin Medical Journal **5731**
W M O Bulletin (World Meteorological Organization) (CHE ISSN 0042-9767) **6397**
W M O Magazine (Wet Maatschappelijke Ondersteuning) (NLD ISSN 1873-6653) **4070**
W M O Magazine. Nieuwsbrief (Wet Maatschappelijke Ondersteuning) (NLD ISSN 1873-670X) **4070**
W M R *see* Waste Management and Research **3513**
W M S *see* Word and Music Studies **6628**
• W M Teil II: Nachrichten ueber Deutsche Festverzinsliche Werte (Wertpapier-Mitteilungen) (DEU ISSN 0342-6939) **1389**
W M Teil IIb: Sammelliste Gekuendigter und Verloster Wertpapiere (Wertpapier-Mitteilungen) (DEU ISSN 0944-6303) **1389**
W M Teil III: Nachrichten ueber Deutsche Aktien, Anteile, Genussscheine, Kuxe *see* W M Teil III: Nachrichten ueber Deutsche Aktien, Anteile, Genussscheine, Kuxe und Optionsscheine **1389**
• W M Teil III: Nachrichten ueber Deutsche Aktien, Anteile, Genussscheine, Kuxe und Optionsscheine (Wertpapier-Mitteilungen) (DEU ISSN 0944-3568) **1389**
W M Teil IV: Zeitschrift fuer Wirtschafts- und Bankrecht (Wertpapier-Mitteilungen) (DEU ISSN 0342-6971) **4810**
• W M Teil Va: Nachrichten ueber Auslaendische Aktien, Anteile, Optionsscheine und Aktienaehnliche Werte (Wertpapier-Mitteilungen) (DEU ISSN 0944-1026) **1389**
W M Teil Va: Nachrichten ueber Auslaendische Aktien und Aktienaehnliche Werte *see* W M Teil Va: Nachrichten ueber Auslaendische Aktien, Anteile, Optionsscheine und Aktienaehnliche Werte **1389**
• W M Teil Vb: Nachrichten ueber Auslaendische Festverzinsliche Wertpapiere (Wertpapier Mitteilungen) (DEU ISSN 0342-7005) **1389**
W M Teil VI: Nachrichten ueber Optionen und Futures (Wertpapier Mitteilungen) (DEU ISSN 0937-4108) **1390**
W M W *see* Wiener Medizinische Wochenschrift **5730**
W M W Skriptum (Wiener Medizinische Wochenschrift) (AUT) **5729**
W M - Wohnungswirtschaft und Mietrecht (DEU ISSN 0173-1564) **4810**
W N *see* Wetgeving Notariaat **4814**
W N B & C *see* What's New in Benefits & Compensation **1877**
W N C Business Journal (Western North Carolina) (USA) **1193**
W N I I *see* What's New in Industry **2034**
W N N R *see* World News & Nursing Report **5984**
W N O Kaiyo Kiko Gaiyo/Marine Climatological Summary (JPN) **6397**
W N Y F (With New York Firefighters) (USA ISSN 0042-9775) **3582**
• W N Y L R C Watch Newsletter (Western New York Library Resources Council) (USA) **5054**
W.News (DEU) **1411**
W O B L *see* Wohnrechtliche Blaetter **4815**
W O E *see* Writing on the Edge **5401**
W O M Journal (World of Music) (DEU) **6627**
W O R L D (Women Organized to Respond to Life-Threatening Diseases) (USA ISSN 1538-0726) **8848**
W O T N *see* Window on the News **7743**
W O T R O. Annual Report *see* Stichting voor Wetenschappelijk Onderzoek van de Tropen. Annual Report **4030**
W O W (GBR) **7779**
W O W Magazine (Women on Wheels) (GBR) **8270**
W O Z Zakboekje *see* W O Z Zakboekje. Jurisprudentie **1390**
W O Z Zakboekje *see* W O Z Zakboekje. Wetgeving **1390**
W O Z Zakboekje. Jurisprudentie (Wet Waardering Onroerende Zaken) (NLD ISSN 1573-9864) **1390**
W O Z Zakboekje. Wetgeving (Wet Waardering Onroerende Zaken) (NLD ISSN 1573-9856) **1390**
W P (Wij Poppenspelers) (NLD ISSN 1871-4161) **8484**
W P *see* Journal of Women, Politics & Policy **7148**
W P A *see* Writing Program Administration **3010**
W P A *see* Working People's Advocate **7194**
W P A Bulletin (Wyoming Press Association) (USA) **4585**
W P A News (World Pheasant Association) (GBR ISSN 0963-3278) **916**
W P A News - E-mail (Western Publications Association) (USA) **7576**
W P A S Museletter (Washington Performing Arts Society) (USA ISSN 0092-4113) **6627**
W P A Series. Evidence and Experience in Psychiatry (World Psychiatry Association) (GBR) **6189**
W P C & T *see* Working Papers in Composition & T E S O L **5195**
W P C C *see* Westminster Papers in Communication and Culture **2344**
W P C R *see* Working Papers in Communication Research **8147**
W P E S *see* A C M Workshop on Privacy in the Electronic Society. Proceedings **4846**
W P F Reports *see* Program on Intrastate Conflict Report **7993**
W P I Journal (Worcester Polytechnic Institute) (USA ISSN 0148-6128) **3226**
W P K Magazin (Wirtschaftsprueferkammer) (DEU) **1303**
• W P N R (Weekblad voor Privaatrecht, Notariaat en Registratie) (NLD ISSN 0165-8476) **4810**
W P P I Monthly (Wedding & Portrait Photographers International) (USA) **6978**
• W P R (World Plumbing Review) (AUS ISSN 1833-3303) **1042**
W P T Poker (World Poker Tour) (GBR ISSN 1749-8473) **8215**
W Q *see* The Wilson Quarterly **5245**
W Q P *see* Water Quality Products **8838**
• W R (Woon Recht) (NLD ISSN 1381-6942) **7615**
▼ • W R (Writing) (USA ISSN 1948-4763) **5396**
W R C News and Announcements (Water Resources Center) (USA) **8835**
W R C Progress Reports (Welding Research Council) (USA) **6344**
The W R E N Magazine (Wyoming Rural Electric News) (USA ISSN 1098-2876) **3162**
W R F Comment (Work Research Foundation) (CAN ISSN 0821-1248) **7693**
➤ W R I Journal (Welding Research Institute) (IND ISSN 0970-4477) **6344**
W R L A Buyers' Guide & Product Source Directory *see* Directory and Product Source Guide **3711**
W R L A Directory *see* Directory and Product Source Guide **3711**
• W R News. Grade 3 Edition (Weekly Reader) (USA) **2220**
W R News. Grade 3 Edition (Large Print) (Weekly Reader) (USA) **2220**
W R News. Senior Edition (Weekly Reader) (USA) **2220**
W R News. Senior Edition (Large Print) (Weekly Reader) (USA) **2221**
W R P *see* Wettbewerb in Recht und Praxis **4814**
W R P - Waescherei- und Reinigungspraxis (DEU ISSN 0938-9067) **2244**
W R R *see* Water Resources Research **8840**
• W R R I News (Water Resources Research Institute) (USA ISSN 0549-799X) **8835**
W R R I Report *see* University of North Carolina. Water Resources Research Institute. Report **8834**
W R R I Report (New Mexico Water Resources Research Institute) (USA ISSN 0731-7557) **8835**
W R R Rapporten (Wetenschappelijke Raad voor het Regeringsbeleid) (NLD) **7192**
W R R Verkenningen (Wetenschappelijke Raad voor het Regeringsbeleid) (NLD ISSN 1572-1159) **7192**
W R R Webpublicaties (Wetenschappelijke Raad voor het Regeringsbeleid) (NLD) **8146**
▼ W R Science (Weekly Reader) (USA ISSN 1942-2121) **7928**
• W S A (World Sports Activewear) (GBR ISSN 1356-644X) **2250**
W S A Today (World Shoe Association) (USA ISSN 1940-8269) **7942**
W S D A Membership Directory & Resource Guide (Washington State Dental Association) (USA) **5869**
W S D A News (Washington State Dental Association) (USA ISSN 1064-0835) **5869**

Title

W S E A S Transactions on Acoustics and Music (World Scientific and Engineering Academy and Society) (GRC ISSN 1109-9577) **6627**
W S E A S Transactions on Advances in Engineering Education (World Scientific and Engineering Academy and Society) (GRC ISSN 1790-1979) **3226**
▼ W S E A S Transactions on Applied and Theoretical Mechanics (World Scientific and Engineering Academy and Society) (GRC ISSN 1991-8747) **7064**
➤ W S E A S Transactions on Biology and Biomedicine (World Scientific and Engineering Academy and Society) (GRC ISSN 1109-9518) **711**
W S E A S Transactions on Business and Economics (World Scientific and Engineering Academy and Society) (GRC ISSN 1109-9526) **1193**
W S E A S Transactions on Circuits and Systems (World Scientific and Engineering Academy and Society) (GRC ISSN 1109-2734) **3115**
W S E A S Transactions on Communications (World Scientific and Engineering Academy and Society) (GRC ISSN 1109-2742) **2344**
➤ W S E A S Transactions on Computers (World Scientific and Engineering Academy and Society) (GRC ISSN 1109-2750) **2441**
➤ W S E A S Transactions on Computers Research (World Scientific and Engineering Academy and Society) (GRC ISSN 1991-8755) **2441**
W S E A S Transactions on Electronics (World Scientific and Engineering Academy and Society) (GRC ISSN 1109-9445) **3115**
W S E A S Transactions on Environment and Development (World Scientific and Engineering Academy and Society) (GRC ISSN 1790-5079) **3474**
W S E A S Transactions on Fluid Mechanics (World Scientific and Engineering Academy and Society) (GRC ISSN 1790-5087) **7064**
W S E A S Transactions on Heat and Mass Transfer (World Scientific Engineering Academy and Society) (GRC ISSN 1790-5044) **7057**
W S E A S Transactions on Information Science and Applications (World Scientific and Engineering Academy and Society) (GRC ISSN 1790-0832) **2551**
W S E A S Transactions on Mathematics (World Scientific and Engineering Academy and Society) (GRC ISSN 1109-2769) **5546**
W S E A S Transactions on Mathematics and Computers in Biology and Biomedicine *see* W S E A S Transactions on Biology and Biomedicine **711**
➤ W S E A S Transactions on Power Systems (World Scientific and Engineering Academy and Society) (GRC ISSN 1790-5060) **3162**
➤ W S E A S Transactions on Signal Processing (World Scientific and Engineering Academy and Society) (GRC) **7090**
➤ W S E A S Transactions on Systems (World Scientific and Engineering Academy and Society) (GRC ISSN 1109-2777) **5546**
W S E A S Transactions on Systems and Controls (World Scientific and Engineering Academy and Society) (GRC ISSN 1991-8763) **5546**
W S E Monthly Bulletin *see* Gielda Papierow Wartosciowych. Biuletyn Miesieczny **1626**
W S G Discussion Papers (Institut fuer Wirtschafts- und Sozialgeography) (AUT) **4034**
W S I A T in Focus (Workplace Safety and Insurance Appeals Tribunal) (CAN ISSN 1480-5731) **1714**
W S I Mitteilungen (Wirtschafts- und Sozialwissenschaftliches Institut) (DEU ISSN 0342-300X) **8014**
▼ W S J (Wall Street Journal) (USA) **5086**
W S N *see* Wisconsin Snowmobile News **8342**
W S S A Grapevine (Wine and Spirits Shippers Association) (USA) **612**
• W S S A Meeting Abstracts (Online) (Weed Science Society of America) (USA) **189**
• W S S A Newsletter (Weed Science Society of America) (USA) **258**
W S S C C Catalogue of Documents and Publications (Water Supply and Sanitation Collaborative Council) (CHE) **8835**
W S S Reports *see* Water Software Systems Research Reports **3334**
W S S Research Series (Water Software Systems) (GBR) **3334**
W T *see* Women & Therapy **7415**
W T *see* World Trade: WT100 **1588**
W T - Blue Sky Region (Wynterblue Thunder) (CAN ISSN 1719-573X) **5437**
W T E & T E *see* World Transactions on Engineering and Technology Education **2926**
W t F *see* Welcome to Finland **8774**
W T G S Bulletin *see* West Texas Geological Society. Bulletin **2774**
W T G Tourism News (Where to Go) (ZMB) **8773**
W T N *see* Washington Telecom Newswire **3992**
W T O Annual Report (World Trade Organisation) (CHE ISSN 1020-4997) **1586**
W T O Focus (Online) (CHE ISSN 1563-9088) **1586**
W T O Focus (Print) *see* W T O Focus (Online) **1586**
W T O News (World Tourism Organization) (ESP ISSN 1014-7276) **8773**
• W T O Reporter (World Trade Organization) (USA ISSN 1529-4153) **1587**
W T O Update (World Trade Organization) (IND) **1411**
• W T O World Tourism Barometer (World Tourism Organization) (ESP ISSN 1728-9246) **8781**
W T Online *see* Washington Technology **7486**
W T T E R C Travel & Tourism (World Travel & Tourism Environment Research Centre) (GBR) **8773**
W T U S M Bulletin of Science and Technology *see* Cehui Xinxi yu Gongcheng **4002**
• W T Werkstattstechnik (DEU ISSN 1436-5006) **8445**
W U F A (Writers Union of Free Afghanistan) (PAK ISSN 1016-7846) **4190**
W U G (Wyzszy Urzad Gorniczy) (POL ISSN 1505-0440) **6483**
W V A Views & Visions (Wisconsin Vocational Association) (USA) **2947**
W V D A News (West Virginia Dental Association) (USA) **5869**
W V School Journal *see* West Virginia School Journal **2926**
W V T Handbuch zum Literaturwissenschaftlichen Studium (Wissenschaftlicher Verlag Trier) (DEU) **5396**
W V, the Magazine of Emerging Writers (Writer's Voice) (USA) **5396**
• W W 2 Today (World War II) (USA) **4166**
W W B *see* Wet Werk en Bijstand (Doetinchem) **7477**
W W B Inkomen Memo *see* Memo W W B Inkomen **1697**
W W B Monitor (Wet Werk en Bijstand) (NLD ISSN 1874-4885) **7476**
W W B Reintegratie Memo *see* Memo W W B Reintegratie **8055**
• W W D (Women's Wear Daily) (USA ISSN 0149-5380) **2250**
W W E Divas (Year) (World Wrestling Entertainment, Inc.) (USA) **6301**
▼ W W E Kids Magazine (World Wrestling Entertainment, Inc.) (USA ISSN 1941-7047) **2221**
W W E Raw *see* W W Magazine **8215**
W W F (World Wide Fund) (JPN ISSN 0916-7846) **2631**
W W F India Quarterly (World Wide Fund) (IND ISSN 0971-2666) **3474**
W W F Journal (World Wildlife Fund) (DEU) **2631**
W W F News (World Wildlife Fund) (USA ISSN 0254-3893) **2631**
W W F Transparent (DEU) **2364**
W W I *see* Water and Wastewater International **8837**
W W I Aero (World War I Aeroplanes, Inc.) (USA ISSN 0736-198X) **74**
W W II History (USA ISSN 1539-5456) **4317**
W W M *see* Waste Disposal and Water Management in Australia **3513**
W W Magazine (World Wrestling Entertainment, Inc.) (USA ISSN 1933-4524) **8215**
W W S M *see* What's Working in Sales Management **1801**
W W T - Wasserwirtschaft Wassertechnik (DEU) **8835**
W W W *see* Wacker Werk & Wirken **2084**
• W W W (World Wide Web) (MEX) **2567**
• W W W (World Wide Web) (POL ISSN 1428-2879) **2567**
• W W W Backstage (USA) **6516**
W - Weekly (USA) **6627**
W Z B Forschung (Wissenschaftszentrum Berlin fuer Sozialforschung) (DEU ISSN 0932-3481) **8021**
• W Z B - Mitteilungen (Wissenschaftszentrum Berlin fuer Sozialforschung) (DEU ISSN 0174-3120) **8014**
• ➤ W Z B Papers (Wissenschaftszentrum Berlin fuer Sozialforschung) (DEU) **8014**
• W2K News (USA) **2504**
▼ Waag Society Magazine (NLD ISSN 1876-1550) **4585**
Die Waage (DEU ISSN 0017-4874) **3859**
Waarderingsinstructie (NLD ISSN 1871-1960) **4810**
Waarnemingenverslag Dagvlinders, Libellen en Sprinkhanen *see* Waarnemingenverslag Ongewervelden **967**
Waarnemingenverslag Ongewervelden (NLD ISSN 1871-8191) **967**
Waarvan Akte (BEL ISSN 0929-4082) **4810**
• Wabanaki Legal News (USA) **4969**
Wabash County Historical Society Newsletter (USA ISSN 0889-5503) **4317**
Wabash Valley Generations (USA) **3787**
WaBoLu Hefte (DEU ISSN 0175-4211) **3474**
• ➤ Wacana (AUS) **3010**
▼ Waccamaw (USA ISSN 1944-5431) **5396**
Wachtlijsten in het (Voortgezet) Speciaal Onderwijs *see* Wachtlijsten in het Speciaal en Voortgezet Speciaal Onderwijs **2925**
Wachtlijsten in het Speciaal en Voortgezet Speciaal Onderwijs (NLD ISSN 1875-2063) **2925**
Wachtlijsten Speciaal en Voortgezet Speciaal Onderwijs *see* Wachtlijsten in het Speciaal en Voortgezet Speciaal Onderwijs **2925**
Wackenberger Echo (DEU) **4431**
Wacker Werk & Wirken (DEU) **2084**
Wacker World-Wide *see* Wacker Werk & Wirken **2084**
Waco Heritage and History (USA ISSN 1072-3447) **4317**
Waconda Roots and Branches (USA ISSN 8755-2167) **3787**
• Wad-al-Hayara (ESP ISSN 0214-7092) **423**
➤ Wadabagei (USA ISSN 1091-5753) **3571**
Wadden Sea Ecosystem (DEU ISSN 0946-896X) **2631**
Wadden Sea Newsletter (Online) (DEU) **2631**
Wadden Sea Newsletter (Print) *see* Wadden Sea Newsletter (Online) **2631**
Waddenbulletin *see* Waddenmagazine **2631**
Waddenmagazine (NLD ISSN 1572-3453) **2631**
• Wade Research Foundation Reports (USA ISSN 1940-0659) **7928**
Wade World (USA ISSN 0898-5421) **3787**
Wader Study Group. Bulletin (GBR ISSN 0260-3799) **916**
Wadi ar-Rafidayn li-'ulum al-Bihar. Magalla/Marina Mesopotamica (IRQ ISSN 1815-2058) **967**
Waegen, Dosieren und Mischen (DEU ISSN 1435-2176) **6407**
Waeller Heimat (DEU ISSN 0931-2889) **3859**
Waelzlager *see* Informationsdienst F I Z Technik. Waelzlager **3231**
Waerland (DEU ISSN 0944-3509) **6999**
Waerme (CHE) **4127**
Waermebehandlung von Werkstoffen *see* Informationsdienst F I Z Technik. Waermebehandlung von Werkstoffen **3231**
Der Waermebehandlungsmarkt (DEU ISSN 0943-8025) **3359**
Waermeschutz, Kaelteschutz, Schallschutz, Brandschutz *see* W K S B **4127**
• WaferNews (USA) **7052**
Waffel (NLD ISSN 1874-0944) **7218**
Das Waffen-Arsenal (DEU) **6453**
Waffenmarkt Intern (DEU ISSN 0177-1221) **8215**
Waffenwelt (DEU ISSN 0177-1299) **8215**
The WAG (USA ISSN 1931-6364) **3992**
Wag Magazine (USA) **6816**
• ➤ Wagadu (USA ISSN 1545-6196) **8904**
• Wage Formation (SWE ISSN 1651-4750) **1714**
Wage, Hour & Leave Report (USA ISSN 1537-6389) **1714**
Wage, Hour and Leave Report *see* Wage, Hour & Leave Report **1714**
Wage-Price Law & Economics Review (USA ISSN 0361-6665) **1721**
Wage-Setting Decision and Reasons for Decision (AUS ISSN 1834-1381) **1714**
Wage Settlements Bulletin (CAN ISSN 1186-6640) **1714**
Wageningen Update (NLD ISSN 1874-2475) **2308**
• Wages and Hours: Law & Practice (USA) **1714**
Wages and Hours: Law and Practice *see* Wages and Hours: Law & Practice **1714**
† Wagga Wagga and District Historical Society. Journal (AUS ISSN 0085-7858) **8998**
Wagner (GBR ISSN 0963-3332) **6627**
▼ • The Wagner Journal (GBR ISSN 1755-0173) **5396**
Wagner Latin American Newsletter (USA ISSN 0198-7496) **4317**
Wagner News (GBR ISSN 0261-3468) **6627**
Wagner-Spectrum *see* WagnerSpectrum **6627**
WagnerSpectrum (DEU ISSN 1614-9459) **6627**
Wagnis (AUT ISSN 1727-0561) **7576**
Wagon Tracks (USA ISSN 1547-7703) **4317**
Wagoner Journal (USA) **3787**
Wah Wah (NLD ISSN 1872-5368) **6627**
• Wahine (USA) **8340**
The Wahkaw (USA ISSN 0743-6483) **3787**
• The Wahlstrom Report (USA) **37**
Wahre Geschichten (DEU ISSN 0944-6273) **5413**
Wahre Geschichten Raetsel (DEU) **8215**
Die Wahrheit (AUT ISSN 0042-9996) **7192**
Wahrnehmungen und Spuren Altaegyptens (DEU ISSN 1864-0052) **4179**
Al-Wa'i (UAE) **2221**
Waigani Seminar. Papers (PNG ISSN 0085-7866) **4194**
• Waiguo Jiaoyu Yanjiu/Studies in Foreign Education (CHN ISSN 1006-7469) **2925**
• Waiguo Jingji yu Guanli/Foreign Economies and Management (CHN ISSN 1001-4950) **1800**
• Waiguo Wenxue/Foreign Literature (CHN ISSN 1002-5529) **5396**
Waiguo Wenxue Yanjiu (Beijing)/Researches in Foreign Literature (CHN ISSN 1001-2885) **5396**
• Waiguo Wenxue Yanjiu (Wuhan) (CHN ISSN 1003-7519) **5396**
Waiguo Zhexue/Foreign Philosophy (CHN ISSN 1007-6719) **6960**
• Waiguoyu/Journal of Foreign Languages (Shanghai) (CHN ISSN 1004-5139) **5194**
• Waijiao Xueyuan Xuebao/Foreign Affairs College. Journal (CHN ISSN 1003-3386) **7272**
• Waikato District Crime Statistics (NZL ISSN 1178-1572) **2675**
Waikato District Statistics *see* Waikato District Crime Statistics **2675**
• ➤ Waikato Journal of Education/Hautaka Matauranga o Waikato (NZL ISSN 1173-6135) **2925**
• ➤ Waikato Law Review (NZL ISSN 1172-9597) **4810**
• Waikato Times (NZL ISSN 1170-0688) **3919**
• Waike Lilun yu Shijian/Journal of Surgery Concepts & Practice (CHN ISSN 1007-9610) **6262**
Waikiki News (USA) **8773**
• Waimakariri District Council. Annual Plan and Budget (NZL ISSN 1171-039X) **7505**
Waimakariri District Council. Draft Annual Plan and Budget *see* Waimakariri District Council. Long Term Council Community Plan **7505**
Waimakariri District Council. Long Term Council Community Plan (NZL) **7505**
Waimao Jingji, Guoji Maoyi (CHN ISSN 1001-3407) **1587**
Wairarapa News (NZL) **3919**
• Wairarapa Times-age (NZL ISSN 1170-0009) **3919**
Waishi Tiandi/Foreign Affairs World (CHN) **7272**
▼ • Waitemata District Crime Statistics (NZL ISSN 1178-1548) **2675**
Waitemata District Statistics *see* Waitemata District Crime Statistics **2675**
• Waitrose Food Illustrated (GBR ISSN 1472-409X) **3667**
• Waiyu Dianhua Jiaoxue/Audio-Visual Teaching of Foreign Languages (CHN ISSN 1001-5795) **3087**
• Waiyu Jiaoxue yu Yanjiu/Foreign Language Teaching & Research (CHN ISSN 1000-0429) **5194**
• Waiyu Xuekan/Journal of Foreign Languages (Heilongjiang) (CHN ISSN 1000-0100) **5194**
• Waiyujie/Foreign Language World (CHN ISSN 1004-5112) **5194**
Wajibu (KEN ISSN 1016-9717) **3902**
Wakan Iyakugaku Zasshi/Journal of Traditional Medicines *see* Journal of Traditional Medicines **6856**
Wakatlat al-Sudan Lil-Anba. Weekly Review *see* Sudan News Agency. Weekly Review **3790**
Wakayama Daigaku Kyoikugakubu Kiyo. Shizen Kagaku/Wakayama University. Faculty of Education. Bulletin: Natural Science (JPN ISSN 1342-4645) **7928**
Wakayama Economic Review *see* Keizai Riron **1770**
Wakayama Igaku *see* Wakayama Medicine **5729**
Wakayama Insect Society. Bulletin *see* Kinokuni **853**
Wakayama-ken Kisho Nenpo *see* Wakayama Prefecture. Annual Report of Meteorology **6397**
Wakayama Kenritsu Shizen Hakubutsukan Kanpo/Wakayama Prefectural Museum of Natural History. Annual Report (JPN) **6540**
Wakayama Medical Reports (JPN ISSN 0511-084X) **5729**
Wakayama Medicine/Wakayama Igaku (JPN ISSN 0043-0013) **5729**
Wakayama Prefectural Museum of Natural History. Annual Report *see* Wakayama Kenritsu Shizen Hakubutsukan Kanpo **6540**
Wakayama Prefecture. Annual Report of Meteorology/Wakayama-ken Kisho Nenpo (JPN ISSN 0910-4542) **6397**
Wakayama Prefecture. Monthly Report of Meteorology *see* Wakayamaken Kisho Geppo **6398**
Wakayama University. Faculty of Economics. Annals (JPN ISSN 1343-0637) **1193**
Wakayama University. Faculty of Education. Bulletin: Natural Science *see* Wakayama Daigaku Kyoikugakubu Kiyo. Shizen Kagaku **7928**
Wakayamaken Kisho Geppo/Wakayama Prefecture. Monthly Report of Meteorology (JPN ISSN 0043-0021) **6398**
Wake Boarding *see* WakeBoarding **8215**
Wake County Genealogical Society Updates *see* W C G S Updates **3787**
• Wake Forest Intellectual Property Law Journal (USA ISSN 1936-8666) **4810**
• Wake Forest Law Review (USA ISSN 0043-003X) **4810**
Wake Forest University School of Law. Continuing Legal Education. Annual Review, North Carolina (USA ISSN 0738-0798) **4810**
Wake-Robin (USA) **7928**
• Wake Treasures (USA ISSN 1055-7857) **3787**
Wakeboard Canada (CAN ISSN 1488-2132) **8215**
• WakeBoarding (USA ISSN 1079-0136) **8215**
Wakefield Court Rolls Series (GBR) **4278**
Wakesurfing (USA) **8340**
Wakili Bulletin (TZA ISSN 1821-5521) **4810**
Wakker Nieuws (NLD ISSN 1876-0635) **322**
Wakou (FRA ISSN 0998-2221) **2221**
Waksman Foundation of Japan. Report (JPN ISSN 0509-5832) **6885**
Wal-Mart Diabetes Digest (USA) **5901**
Walbauernverband Nordrhein-Westfalen. Mitteilungsblatt (DEU) **3707**
Wald in Oesterreich (AUT) **3707**
Wald und Holz (CHE ISSN 1423-2456) **3717**
Wald und Holz in der Schweiz. Jahrbuch (CHE ISSN 1424-1552) **3709**
Der Waldbesitzer (DEU ISSN 0178-367X) **3707**
Waldeckische Landeszeitung (DEU) **3859**
Waldeckischer Landeskalender (DEU) **4278**
Waldenburger Heimatbote (DEU) **4278**
Walden's A B C Guide (USA) **6739**
Walden's A B C Personnel Directory (USA) **6739**
Walden's North American Pulp & Paper Report (USA ISSN 1541-9959) **6739**
Walden's Paper Catalog (USA) **6739**
Walden's Paper Handbook (USA) **6739**
Walden's Paper Report (USA) **6739**
Waldenser-Magazin (DEU ISSN 1867-0644) **7693**
Das Waldviertel (AUT ISSN 0259-8957) **4278**
Waldviertel und Golf (AUT) **8340**
Der Waldwirt (DEU) **3707**
Wales Business Insider *see* Insider. Wales Business Insider **1124**
Wales Caterers Guide (GBR) **4400**

Wales Council for Voluntary Action Annual Report *see* W C V A Annual Report **8077**
Wales Council for Voluntary Action. Briefing Paper/Cyngor Gweithredu Gwirfoddol Cymru. Paparau Crynhoi (GBR) **8077**
Wales Council for Voluntary Action. Report Series/Cyngor Gweithredu Gwirfoddol Cymru Cyfres. Adroddiadau (GBR ISSN 1367-9198) **8077**
Wales Funding Handbook/Llawlyfr Cyllido Cymru - Diweddariad (GBR) **8077**
● Wales on Sunday (GBR ISSN 0961-1002) **3872**
The Wales Yearbook (Year) (GBR) **7193**
Walford's Guide to Reference Material (GBR) **638**
Walia (ETH ISSN 1026-3861) **3474**
WALIS News (Western Australian Land Information Service) (AUS ISSN 1320-3878) **208**
● Walk (London) (GBR ISSN 1752-7295) **2631**
Walker Art Gallery. Annual Report and Bulletin (GBR ISSN 0306-0888) **6540**
● The Walker Market Letter (USA) **1658**
Walkerana (USA ISSN 1053-637X) **967**
● Walkerton Herald-Times (CAN ISSN 0834-7298) **3819**
Walking (DEU) **6999**
Walking Horse Report (USA ISSN 0093-6928) **8300**
† ● Walking Together (AUS ISSN 1326-4869) **8998**
Walking World Ireland (IRL ISSN 0791-8801) **8340**
Wall Coverings (USA ISSN 1932-9385) **4552**
● Wall Street & Technology (USA ISSN 1060-989X) **1394**
Wall Street and Technology *see* Wall Street & Technology **1394**
Wall Street Boersen-Almanach *see* Stock Trader's Almanac **1654**
Wall Street Digest (USA ISSN 0899-0530) **1390**
Wall Street Journal *see* W S J **5086**
● Wall Street Journal (Central Edition) (USA ISSN 1092-0935) **1390**
● Wall Street Journal (Classroom Edition) (USA ISSN 1538-6732) **1193**
● Wall Street Journal (Eastern Edition) (USA ISSN 0099-9660) **1390**
● Wall Street Journal (Western Edition) (USA ISSN 0193-2241) **1390**
The Wall Street Journal Asia *see* The Asian Wall Street Journal **1309**
● The Wall Street Journal Europe (BEL ISSN 0921-9986) **1390**
● The Wall Street Journal Index (USA ISSN 1042-9840) **1274**
Wall Street Journal Online *see* Wall Street Journal (Eastern Edition) **1390**
Wall Street Journal Online *see* Wall Street Journal (Western Edition) **1390**
Wall Street Journal Online *see* Wall Street Journal Online (Media & Marketing Edition) **1847**
Wall Street Journal Online *see* Wall Street Journal (Central Edition) **1390**
● Wall Street Journal Online (Media & Marketing Edition) (USA) **1847**
Wall Street Lawyer (USA) **2567**
● Wall Street Letter (USA ISSN 0277-4992) **1658**
Wall Street Reporter (USA ISSN 1555-0966) **1658**
Wall Street Research Magazine (USA) **1658**
● The Wall Street Transcript (USA ISSN 0043-0102) **1658**
➤ Wallace Stevens Journal (USA ISSN 0148-7132) **5437**
● Wallaces Farmer (USA ISSN 0043-0129) **169**
Wallcoverings *see* Key Note Market Report: Wallcoverings and Ceramic Tiles **4544**
Walleye Guide (USA) **8340**
Walleye In-Sider (USA ISSN 1068-2112) **8340**
Wallis (CHE) **8773**
Walliser Bauernblatt (CHE) **169**
Wallonie (BEL ISSN 0379-3753) **1524**
▼ Walloomsack Review (USA ISSN 1943-9644) **4317**
Wallpaper (GBR ISSN 1364-4475) **4552**
● Wallraf-Richartz-Jahrbuch (DEU) **525**
● Walls & Ceilings (USA ISSN 0043-0161) **1042**
Walls, Windows & Floors (USA ISSN 1550-5707) **4552**
Walls, Windows and Floors *see* Walls, Windows & Floors **4552**
WallSt.net Digest (USA) **1390**
Walneck's Classic Cycle Trader (USA ISSN 1051-8088) **8270**
Walpole Society. Volume (GBR ISSN 0141-0016) **525**
● The Walrus (CAN ISSN 1708-4032) **3820**
● Walt Disney World (Year) (USA ISSN 8756-9779) **8773**
Walt Disney World & Orlando with Kids *see* Frommer's Walt Disney World & Orlando with Kids **8711**
Walt Disney World & Universal Orlando with Kids *see* Walt Disney World with Kids **8773**
Walt Disney World with Kids *see* Walt Disney World with Kids **8773**
Walt Disney World with Kids (USA ISSN 1945-9238) **8773**
Walt Disney's Donald Duck (NLD ISSN 0165-1293) **2221**
Walt Disney's Donald Duck Vakantieboek (NLD ISSN 1874-9313) **2221**
Walt Disney's Fantonald *see* Fantonald **2188**
Walt Disney's Kalle Anka & Co *see* Kalle Anka & Co **2196**
Walt Disney's Kalle Ankas Pocket *see* Kalle Ankas Pocket **2196**
Walt Disney's Katrien *see* Katrien **2196**
Walt Disney's Lustiges Taschenbuch (DEU) **2221**
● Walt Disney's Micky Maus (DEU ISSN 1437-2185) **2221**
Walt Disney's Mikke Mus *see* Mikke **2202**
Walt Disney's Musse Pigg och C:o *see* Musse Pigg och C:o **2203**
➤ Walt Whitman Quarterly Review (USA ISSN 0737-0679) **5396**
➤ Walter and Andree de Nottbeck Foundation. Scientific Reports (FIN ISSN 0358-6758) **898**
Walter Lynwood Fleming Lectures in Southern History (USA ISSN 0083-7121) **4317**
Walter Reuther Library Newsletter (USA) **1714**
Walter Roth Museum of Anthropology. Journal (GUY) **360**
† Walter Skinner's North Sea and Europe Offshore Yearbook and Buyers' Guide (GBR ISSN 0309-4758) **8998**
Walter van Gerven Lectures (NLD) **4810**
† Walter W.S. Cook Alumni Lecture (USA ISSN 0083-7148) **8998**
● ➤ Walters Art Museum. Journal (USA) **525**
The Walters Magazine (USA ISSN 1541-8863) **525**
Waltham Focus (American Edition) *see* Veterinary Focus **6816**
Waltham Focus (American Edition) *see* Waltham Focus (Japanese Edition) **6816**
Waltham Focus (Japanese Edition) (GBR ISSN 1355-5413) **6816**
Waltham International Focus (French Edition) *see* Veterinary Focus **6816**
Waltham International Focus (French Edition) *see* Waltham Focus (Japanese Edition) **6816**
Waltham International Focus (German Edition) *see* Veterinary Focus **6816**
Waltham International Focus (German Edition) *see* Waltham Focus (Japanese Edition) **6816**
Waltham International Focus (Greek Edition) *see* Veterinary Focus **6816**
Waltham International Focus (Greek Edition) *see* Waltham Focus (Japanese Edition) **6816**
Waltham International Focus (Italian Edition) *see* Veterinary Focus **6816**
Waltham International Focus (Italian Edition) *see* Waltham Focus (Japanese Edition) **6816**
Waltham International Focus (Spanish Edition) *see* Veterinary Focus **6816**
Waltham International Focus (Spanish Edition) *see* Waltham Focus (Japanese Edition) **6816**
Walthari (DEU ISSN 0930-0279) **5396**
Walther-Studien (DEU ISSN 1615-651X) **5396**
Walworth County Genealogical Society. Newsletter (USA ISSN 1088-5765) **3787**
● Wam (HRV ISSN 1332-019X) **6627**
Wamp (POL ISSN 1231-3270) **6301**
Wampiurs Wars (POL) **5448**
† Wampum Neskenonu (CZE) **8998**
Wan (JPN) **6816**
Wanasan (THA ISSN 0043-0196) **3707**
Wanbao Wencui/Extracts from Evening Papers (CHN ISSN 1002-8757) **3828**
Wanbli Ho/Eagle's Voice (USA) **3571**
Wander Revue (CHE) **8340**
● Wanderer (USA ISSN 1068-168X) **7822**
● Wanderer's World Daily (USA) **3992**
Wandering Volhynians (CAN ISSN 1180-2901) **3572**
Wandering Wolfs (USA ISSN 0887-3860) **3787**
Wanderlust (GBR ISSN 1351-4733) **8773**
Wandermagazin (DEU ISSN 0178-1677) **8340**
Wandern (CHE) **4984**
Wanderungen in die Erdgeschichte (DEU) **2774**
Wandsbeker Wochenblatt (DEU) **3859**
● Wanganui Chronicle (NZL ISSN 1170-067X) **3920**
Wanganui Midweek (NZL ISSN 1170-1447) **3920**
† ● Wangkuan Shidai/Broad Times (CHN ISSN 1673-5730) **8998**
Wangluo Chuanbo/Newmedia (CHN ISSN 1672-7967) **2504**
● Wangqiu Tiandi/Tennis World (CHN ISSN 1006-2300) **8251**
Wanita (MYS ISSN 0126-544X) **2263**
Wanju Kubao *see* Cool Toys **2183**
Wannahaves, the Magazine (NLD ISSN 1574-2970) **5086**
● Wannan Yixueyuan Xuebao/Acta Academiae Medicinae Wannan (CHN ISSN 1002-0217) **5729**
Wanpi Wawa/Naughty Baby (CHN ISSN 1003-4013) **2221**
Wanted (USA) **6301**
Wantok (PNG) **3926**
Want's Federal-State Court Directory *see* Federal-State Court Directory (Year) **4951**
Want's Your Nation's Courts Online *see* Your Nation's Courts Online **4967**
Wapahke (CAN ISSN 1480-7815) **6636**
Wapenveld (NLD ISSN 0167-1871) **7693**
Wapiti (FRA ISSN 0984-2314) **2221**
Waqa'i Dawlat al-Imarat/Emirates Events (UAE) **4326**
War and Literature *see* Krieg und Literatur **4238**
➤ War & Society (AUS ISSN 0729-2473) **4166**
† War and Society Newsletter (DEU ISSN 0344-3086) **8998**
● ➤ War Crimes, Genocide, and Crimes Against Humanity (USA ISSN 1551-322X) **4899**
War Cry *see* Salvationist.Ca **7741**
War Cry (GBR ISSN 0043-0226) **7779**
War Cry (NGA ISSN 0049-688X) **7717**
War Cry (NZL ISSN 0043-0242) **7779**
The War Cry (USA ISSN 0043-0234) **7779**
War Cry (ZAF ISSN 0043-0250) **7779**
● ➤ War in History (GBR ISSN 0968-3445) **6453**
War, Literature & the Arts *see* W L A **5396**
War Studies Journal (GBR ISSN 1363-1225) **6453**
War Studies Review *see* Michigan War Studies Review **6434**
War Technology and History (USA ISSN 1556-4924) **6453**
War Whoop (USA) **2309**
Warasan Loha, Watsadu lae Lae/Metals, Materials and Minerals Bulletin (THA ISSN 0857-6149) **6336**
Warasan Satharanasuk Sat/Journal of Public Health (THA ISSN 0125-1678) **7545**
Warasan Thammachat Witthaya haeng Chulalongkorn Mahawitthayalai *see* Chulalongkorn University. Natural History Journal **4135**
Warasarn Prachakornsatr *see* Journal of Demography **7286**
Warbirds International (USA ISSN 1523-0031) **74**
WarbirdTech Series (USA) **74**
Warbonnet (USA) **4350**
Warburg Institute. Colloquia (GBR ISSN 1352-9986) **4482**
Warburg Institute Studies and Texts (GBR ISSN 1471-5481) **4482**
Warburg Institute. Surveys and Texts (GBR ISSN 0266-1772) **4482**
Warcry (AUS) **7694**
● Ward 6 Review (USA ISSN 1934-3353) **5396**
Ward Foundation News (USA ISSN 1042-3311) **6540**
Ward - Phillips Lectures in English Language and Literature (USA ISSN 0083-7210) **5396**
Ward's Auto World *see* Ward's AutoWorld **8611**
● Ward's Automotive Reports (USA ISSN 0886-5175) **8611**
● Ward's Automotive Yearbook (USA ISSN 0083-7229) **8532**
● Ward's AutoWorld (USA ISSN 0043-0315) **8611**
Ward's Business Directory of Private and Public Companies in Canada and Mexico (USA ISSN 1542-3301) **2033**
● Ward's Business Directory of U S Private and Public Companies (USA ISSN 1048-8707) **2033**
● Ward's Dealer Business (USA ISSN 1086-1629) **8611**
Ward's Engine and Vehicle Technology Update (USA ISSN 1088-6869) **8611**
● De Ware Tijd (SUR ISSN 1606-5239) **3954**
Ware tyd *see* De Ware Tijd **3954**
Warehouse (CAN ISSN 1708-5888) **460**
▼ ● Warehouse & Greenhouse (ZAF ISSN 1995-736X) **4369**
Warehouse Computing (GBR ISSN 0269-2996) **1855**
Warehouse Journal (USA) **2309**
Warehousing - Distribution Directory (USA ISSN 1075-0282) **8678**
Warehousing Forum *see* Ackerman Warehousing Forum **1723**
● Warenursprung und Praeferenzen in der Taeglichen Praxis (DEU) **1587**
Warenwetgeving Info (BEL ISSN 1374-8637) **6671**
Wares New Zealand (NZL ISSN 1177-4231) **5461**
● ➤ Warfare (GBR ISSN 0308-0676) **6453**
Wargamers Information (USA) **8215**
Wargames Illustrated (GBR ISSN 0957-6444) **8215**
Warhammer Monthly (GBR ISSN 1461-2089) **5448**
Warm Earth (AUS ISSN 1320-3940) **3753**
Warm Line (USA) **7743**
† Warman's Baseball Card Field Guide (USA ISSN 1931-020X) **8998**
Warman's Coins & Paper Money (USA ISSN 1933-561X) **6653**
Warman's Depression Glass (USA ISSN 1938-4491) **369**
Warmblood News (USA ISSN 1079-4433) **8300**
Warme und Versorgungstechnik *see* T G A-Fachplaner **4127**
Warmer Bulletin (GBR ISSN 1362-654X) **3513**
● Warning Letter Bulletin (USA ISSN 1069-4218) **5729**
Das Warnkreuz (DEU ISSN 0343-1525) **6688**
Warp Four (USA) **5448**
Warranty Dollars and Sense for Ford Dealers *see* Warranty Dollars & Sense for Ford Dealers **8611**
Warranty Dollars & Sense for Ford Dealers (USA ISSN 1088-1743) **8611**
Warranty Dollars & Sense for GM Dealers (USA ISSN 1088-1735) **8611**
Warranty Dollars and Sense for GM Dealers *see* Warranty Dollars & Sense for GM Dealers **8611**
Warren County Reflections (USA) **4317**
Warren, Gorham and Lamont Tax Journal Digest *see* W G & L Tax Journal Digest **1954**
Warren Miller Snoworld (USA) **8340**
Warren Miller'S Ski World *see* Warren Miller Snoworld **8340**
● Warren's Consumer Electronics Daily (USA ISSN 1537-3088) **8445**
Warren's Consumer Electronics Daily *see* Consumer Electronics Daily **3091**
Warren's Farm & Ranch Directory (CAN ISSN 1197-3625) **169**
Warren's Forms of Agreement: Fern's Desk Edition (USA) **4810**
● Warren's Forms of Agreements (USA) **4883**
● Warren's Heaton on Surrogates' Court Practice (USA) **4967**
Warren's Movie Poster Price Guide (USA) **4350**
● Warren's Negligence in New York Courts (USA) **4844**
Warren's Telecom A M *see* Telecom A.M. **2340**
● Warren's Weed New York Real Property (USA) **7615**
➤ Warrington Papers in Leisure and Sport Research (GBR) **4984**
Warrior (CAN ISSN 1910-3662) **3820**
Warrior (IND) **8773**
Warrior Magazine *see* Warrior **3820**
▼ The Warrior Nation (USA ISSN 1933-5369) **8251**
Warrnambool Standard *see* The Standard (Warrnambool) **8990**
Warsaw Agricultural University. S G G W. Annals. Agricultural Economics and Rural Sociology (POL) **208**
Warsaw Agricultural University. S G G W. Annals. Agriculture (POL) **169**
Warsaw Agricultural University. S G G W. Annals. Animal Science (POL) **303**
Warsaw Agricultural University. S G G W. Annals. Food Technology and Nutrition (POL) **3667**
Warsaw Agricultural University. S G G W. Annals. Forestry and Wood Technology (POL) **3717**
Warsaw Agricultural University. S G G W. Annals. Horticulture (POL) **3753**
Warsaw Agricultural University. S G G W. Annals. Land Reclamation (POL) **258**
Warsaw Agricultural University. Treatises and Monographs *see* Szkola Glowna Gospodarstwa Wiejskiego. Rozprawy Naukowe i Monografie **160**
Warsaw Book of Lists (Year) (POL) **1193**
● Warsaw Business Journal (POL ISSN 1233-7889) **1193**
Warsaw Convention *see* Montreal Convention **8504**
Warsaw In Your Pocket (POL) **8773**
Warsaw University ot Technology. Institute of Heat Engineering. Bulletin *see* Politechnika Warszawska. Instytut Techniki Cieplnej. Biuletyn **7056**
● Warsaw Voice (POL ISSN 0860-7591) **3930**
Warsaw Voice Business & Economy Yearbook (POL) **1193**
The Warsaw Voice I S O Almanac (Year) (POL ISSN 1506-4883) **2033**
The Warsaw Voice Tourism Guide (POL ISSN 1506-4891) **8773**
Warship (GBR ISSN 0142-6222) **6453**
Warship International (USA ISSN 0043-0374) **6453**
● Warship Technology (GBR ISSN 0957-5537) **8664**
Warship World (GBR) **6453**
Warships Forecast *see* Market Intelligence Reports: Warships Forecast **6434**
Warships of the World *see* Weyers Flottentaschenbuch **6454**
Warsteiner (DEU) **3859**
● Warta Demografi (IDN ISSN 0125-9679) **7295**
Warta Geologi/Geological Society of Malaysia Newsletter (MYS ISSN 0126-5539) **2774**
Warta K O W A N I *see* K O W A N I News **8870**
Warta Konsumen (IDN ISSN 0126-3455) **2642**
Wartime (AUS ISSN 1328-2727) **6453**
Der Wartturm (DEU ISSN 0723-7553) **4278**
Warunki Srodowiskowe Polskiej Strefy Poludniowego Baltyku - Materialy Oddzialu Morskiego *see* Instytut Meteorologii i Gospodarki Wodnej. Oddzial Morski w Gdyni. Materialy. Warunki Srodowiskowe Polskiej Strefy Poludniowego Baltyku **2807**
● Warwick Business School Research Papers (GBR ISSN 1363-0520) **1193**
Warwick Papers on Education Policy (GBR ISSN 1362-6558) **2925**
Warwick Studies in European Philosophy (GBR) **6960**
Warwick Studies in the Humanities (GBR) **4482**
Warwickshire Farmer (GBR ISSN 0955-0283) **169**
† Warzones (USA ISSN 1540-2207) **8998**
Was Lefft (DEU ISSN 1618-4831) **5244**
Was und Wie? (DEU ISSN 0341-7158) **7694**
Wasada Journal of Human Sciences *see* Ningen Kagaku Kenkyuu **350**
● Wasafiri: Caribbean, African, Asian and Associated Literatures in English (GBR ISSN 0269-0055) **5396**
● Wasaga Sun (CAN ISSN 1197-995X) **3820**
Wasahington Hiking *see* Foghorn Outdoors. Washington Hiking **8314**
The Wasatch Letter (USA ISSN 1068-1477) **1390**
➤ Wascana Review (CAN ISSN 0043-0412) **5397**
Waseda Architectural News (JPN) **460**
Waseda Architecture (JPN) **460**
Waseda Biology *see* Waseda Seibutsu **711**
● Waseda Bulletin of Comparative Law (JPN ISSN 0285-9211) **4944**
Waseda Bungaku (JPN) **5397**
Waseda Business and Economic Studies (JPN ISSN 0388-1008) **1193**
Waseda Commercial Review *see* Waseda Shogaku **1434**
Waseda Daigaku Daigakuin Rikogaku Kenkyu Iho/Waseda University. Graduate School of Science and Engineering. Synopses of Science and Engineering Papers (JPN ISSN 0507-9683) **3234**
Waseda Daigaku Kyoikugakubu Gakujutsu Kenkyu. Seibutsugaku, Chigaku Hen/Waseda University. School of Education. Scientific Researches: Biology, Earth Sciences (JPN ISSN 0913-0187) **711**

Title

11018 WASEDA DAIGAKU KYOIKUGAKUBU GAKUJUTSU KENKYU. SUGAKU ULRICH'S PERIODICALS

Waseda Daigaku Kyoikugakubu Gakujutsu Kenkyu. Sugaku Hen/Waseda University. School of Education. Scientific Researches: Mathematics (JPN ISSN 0913-0195) **5546**
Waseda Daigaku Ningen Kagaku Kenkyu/Waseda Studies in Human Sciences *see* Ningen Kagaku Kenkyuu **350**
Waseda Journal of Asian Studies (JPN ISSN 0388-3906) **4190**
Waseda Journal of Political Science and Economics *see* Waseda Seiji Keizaigaku Zasshi **7193**
Waseda Political Studies (JPN ISSN 0511-196X) **7193**
Waseda Seibutsu/Waseda Biology (JPN ISSN 0511-1978) **711**
Waseda Seiji Keizaigaku Zasshi/Waseda Journal of Political Science and Economics (JPN ISSN 0287-7007) **7193**
Waseda Shogaku/Waseda Commercial Review (JPN ISSN 0387-3404) **1434**
Waseda University. Graduate School of Science and Engineering. Synopses of Science and Engineering Papers *see* Waseda Daigaku Daigakuin Rikogaku Kenkyu Iho **3234**
Waseda University. Kagami Memorial Laboratory for Materials Science and Technology *see* Zaiken **6337**
Waseda University. School of Education. Scientific Researches: Biology, Earth Sciences *see* Waseda Daigaku Kyoikugakubu Gakujutsu Kenkyu. Seibutsugaku, Chigaku Hen **711**
Waseda University. School of Education. Scientific Researches: Mathematics *see* Waseda Daigaku Kyoikugakubu Gakujutsu Kenkyu. Sugaku Hen **5546**
Wash P I R G Reports *see* Washington Public Interest Research Group Reports **2642**
Wash Wader Ringing Group. Report (GBR ISSN 0963-3111) **916**
• Washburn Law Journal (USA ISSN 0043-0420) **4810**
Washington *see* Washington Afro-American Newspaper **3572**
Washington (Marietta) (USA ISSN 1047-6628) **3787**
Washington (State). Affirmative Action Information *see* Washington (State). Employment Security Department. Affirmative Action Information **1274**
Washington (State) Department of Community, Trade, and Economic Development. Biennial Energy Report (USA ISSN 1930-9910) **3150**
Washington (State). Department of Fish and Wildlife. Annual Report (USA ISSN 0097-3939) **3611**
• Washington (State). Department of Natural Resources. Annual Report (USA) **3474**
Washington (State). Department of Natural Resources. Division of Geology and Earth Resources. Bulletin (USA ISSN 1045-2982) **2774**
Washington (State). Department of Natural Resources. Division of Geology and Earth Resources. Information Circular (USA ISSN 0147-1783) **2774**
Washington (State). Department of Natural Resources. Division of Geology and Earth Resources. Report of Investigations (USA) **2774**
Washington (State). Department of Revenue. Forest Tax Section. Forest Tax Annual Report (USA) **1954**
Washington (State). Department of Revenue. Quarterly Business Review (USA ISSN 0149-7618) **1193**
Washington (State). Department of Revenue. Research Division. Comparative State - Local Taxes (USA) **1954**
Washington (State). Department of Revenue. Research Division. Property Tax Statistics (USA) **1274**
Washington (State). Department of Revenue. Research Division. Tax Statistics (USA) **1274**
Washington (State). Employment Security Department. Affirmative Action Information (USA) **1274**
Washington (State). Employment Security Department. Annual Demographic Information (USA) **6705**
Washington (State). Employment Security Department. Area Wage Surveys (USA) **1714**
Washington (State). Employment Security Department. County Labor Market and Economic Profiles (USA) **1714**
Washington (State). Employment Security Department. Monthly Job Service Statistics (USA) **6707**
Washington (State). Employment Security Department. Occupational Profiles (USA) **6707**
Washington (State). Employment Security Department. Occupational Projections (USA) **1714**
Washington (State). Employment Security Department. Studies in Industry and Employment (USA) **1714**
Washington (State). Employment Security Department. Weekly Insured Unemployment Report (USA) **4530**
Washington (State) Legislature. Pictorial Directory (USA ISSN 0091-8253) **7193**
Washington (State) Patrol. Annual Report (USA) **2671**
Washington (Year) (USA ISSN 0083-7393) **1193**
➤ Washington Academy of Sciences. Journal (USA ISSN 0043-0439) **7928**
• Washington Administrative Law Practice Manual (USA) **4853**
Washington Afro-American and the Washington Tribune *see* Washington Afro-American Newspaper **3572**
Washington Afro-American Newspaper (USA) **3572**
Washington Agricultural Record (USA ISSN 0195-0673) **169**
• Washington Agricultural Statistics (USA ISSN 0095-4330) **189**
Washington: All-Industries *see* Harris Directory. Washington All-Industries **2003**
Washington & Jefferson College Magazine *see* W & J Magazine **2308**
• Washington and Lee Journal of Civil Rights and Social Justice (USA ISSN 1942-5732) **4844**
• Washington and Lee Law Review (USA ISSN 0043-0463) **4810**
Washington and Lee University Magazine *see* W & L Magazine **2308**
Washington Appellate Reports (USA ISSN 0093-1810) **4967**
Washington Basin Outlook Report (USA) **8836**
• The Washington Blade (USA ISSN 0278-9892) **4380**
Washington Bride *see* Modern Bride Washington **5560**
Washington Buddhist (USA) **7703**
• Washington Bulletin (USA) **6796**
• Washington Business Directory (USA ISSN 1043-9781) **2033**
Washington Business Forward (USA ISSN 1522-8290) **1193**
• Washington Business Journal (USA ISSN 0737-3147) **1193**
▼ Washington Business Law (USA ISSN 1944-0561) **4883**
• Washington C E O (Chief Executive Officer) (USA ISSN 1048-4981) **1800**
Washington Chinese News (USA) **3572**
• Washington Cities & Counties Graphic Performance Analysis (USA ISSN 1935-5637) **7485**
Washington: Compass American Guides *see* Compass American Guides: Washington **8694**
• Washington Consumers' Checkbook (USA ISSN 0272-0469) **2642**
Washington Corporations, Associations, Partnerships, and Related Laws Annotated (USA) **4883**
Washington Counseletter (USA ISSN 0740-8501) **6705**
• Washington Counts in the 21st Century (USA) **7295**
Washington Criminal Law and Procedure Annotated (USA) **4899**
• Washington Criminal Practice in Courts of Limited Jurisdiction (USA) **4899**
Washington Crossing Card Collectors Club Newsletter (USA ISSN 0885-9027) **4350**
Washington Curiosities (USA ISSN 1933-9739) **8773**
Washington D.C.: All-Industries *see* Harris Directory. Washington D.C. All-Industries **2003**
• Washington D.C. Area Business Directory (USA ISSN 1048-7077) **2033**
Washington D.C. Beverage Journal (USA ISSN 1058-9341) **612**
Washington D.C. Council on Environmental Quality. Environmental Quality (USA ISSN 0095-2044) **3474**
Washington D.C., Maryland, Northern Virginia Office Buildings (USA) **7615**
Washington D C - Small Business News *see* Small Business News - Washington D.C. **1967**
Washington, D.C. Style *see* D C Style **5069**
Washington D.C. Super Lawyers (USA ISSN 1939-697X) **4811**
Washington, D.C. with Kids *see* Fodor's Family Washington, D.C. with Kids **8705**
Washington Diocese *see* Washington Window **7779**
Washington. Division of Geology and Earth Resources. Mines and Minerals of Washington. Annual Report (USA) **6483**
Washington. Division of Mines and Geology. Bulletin (USA) **2774**
Washington Drug Letter *see* Washington Drug Letter (Washington, 1979) **6885**
• Washington Drug Letter (Washington, 1979) (USA ISSN 0194-1291) **6885**
Washington Education Directory (USA) **2925**
Washington Educational Telecommunications Association Magazine *see* W E T A Magazine **2398**
• Washington Employment Law Letter (USA ISSN 1072-0588) **4810**
Washington Environmental Regulations and Liability (USA) **4899**
Washington Facts (USA ISSN 1044-9078) **3122**
Washington Federal Science Newsletter (USA ISSN 0740-0535) **7928**
Washington Feedline (USA) **275**
Washington Flyer Magazine (USA ISSN 1046-3089) **8773**
Washington Gardener (USA ISSN 1555-8959) **3753**
Washington. General Secretariat Organization of American States. Summary of the Decisions Taken at the Meetings and Texts of the Resolutions Approved (USA ISSN 0250-6319) **7476**
Washington Geological Survey. Annual Report (USA) **2774**
Washington Geological Survey. Bulletin (USA) **2774**
• Washington Guardianship Law (USA) **4967**
Washington Healthcare Summit (USA ISSN 1935-5599) **4810**
Washington Hispanic (USA) **3572**
➤ Washington History (USA ISSN 1042-9719) **4317**
• Washington Information Directory (Year) (USA ISSN 0887-8064) **7193**
• Washington Informer (USA ISSN 0741-9414) **3572**
Washington Inquirer (USA ISSN 0749-1050) **7218**
Washington Institute for Near East Policy. Policy Conference. Proceedings (USA) **7193**
Washington Institute for Near East Policy. Policy Focus (USA) **7193**
Washington Institute for Near East Policy. Policy Papers (USA) **7193**
• Washington Insurance Law (USA) **4527**
Washington Insurance Law Letter (USA ISSN 1064-1378) **4810**
• Washington International (USA ISSN 1051-0257) **8773**
• Washington International Business Report (USA ISSN 0049-691X) **1587**
Washington - Japan Journal (USA) **7272**
• Washington Jewish Week (USA ISSN 0746-9373) **7731**
Washington Job Source (USA ISSN 1067-0769) **6705**
Washington Journal (USA) **3572**
Washington Journal of Modern China (USA ISSN 1064-3028) **7272**
Washington Journey (USA ISSN 1096-8660) **8773**
Washington Labor Market (USA) **1274**
Washington Law & Politics (USA ISSN 1095-7359) **4810**
• ➤ Washington Law Review (USA ISSN 0043-0617) **4811**
• Washington Lawyer (USA ISSN 0890-8761) **4811**
Washington Letter (USA) **5245**
Washington Letter of Oceanography (USA) **2821**
• Washington Literary Review (Online) (USA ISSN 2150-3125) **5437**
Washington Literary Review (Print) *see* Washington Literary Review (Online) **5437**
Washington Living (USA ISSN 0744-6373) **3572**
• Washington Manufacturers Directory (USA ISSN 1525-4100) **2033**
• Washington Manufacturers Register (USA ISSN 0148-5687) **2033**
Washington: Manufacturing *see* Harris Directory. Washington Manufacturing **2003**
Washington Maryland Virginia Home & Design (USA ISSN 1551-0247) **4552**
Washington Masonic Tribune (USA ISSN 1060-393X) **2270**
Washington Memo *see* American Public Welfare Association. W - Memo **8025**
Washington Memo (Akron) (USA) **7743**
Washington Mining Bureau. Annual Report (USA) **6483**
• The Washington Monthly (USA ISSN 0043-0633) **7193**
Washington Morning Update *see* Frontrunner **7137**
➤ Washington Native Plant Society. Occasional Papers (USA ISSN 1097-2714) **822**
Washington Newsletter *see* N M O A - Mail Order Digest **1835**
Washington Newspaper (USA ISSN 0043-0684) **4585**
Washington Notary Law Primer (USA ISSN 1098-6510) **4811**
Washington Notes on Africa (USA ISSN 0512-610X) **7272**
• The Washington Nurse (USA ISSN 0734-5666) **5983**
Washington Opera Magazine (USA ISSN 0196-3236) **6627**
Washington - Oregon Game & Fish (USA ISSN 1056-0106) **8340**
The Washington Pacific Report (USA ISSN 0748-6359) **7193**
Washington Papers (USA ISSN 0278-937X) **7272**
Washington Park Arboretum Bulletin (USA ISSN 1046-8749) **3753**
Washington Peace Letter (USA ISSN 1050-2823) **7273**
Washington Performing Arts Society Museletter *see* W P A S Museletter **6627**
Washington Perspective (USA) **1390**
The Washington Pharmacist (USA ISSN 0745-7413) **6885**
• The Washington Post Index (USA ISSN 1041-1534) **4588**
The Washington Post Presents: Metrolife (USA) **3992**
• Washington Practice Series (USA) **4811**
• Washington Public Affairs Digest (USA) **7476**
Washington Public Interest Research Group Reports (USA) **2642**
• ➤ The Washington Quarterly (USA ISSN 0163-660X) **7273**
Washington Recreation and Park Association. Syllabus (USA) **7476**
• Washington Remote Sensing Letter (USA ISSN 0739-6538) **74**
• Washington Report (New York) (USA) **1607**
• Washington Report (Washington, 1977) (USA) **7505**
• Washington Report on Middle East Affairs (USA ISSN 8755-4917) **7273**
Washington Report on the Hemisphere (USA ISSN 0275-5599) **7273**
Washington Report to Presbyterians (USA) **7779**
Washington Reports. 2d Series (USA ISSN 0889-8162) **4967**
Washington Representatives (USA ISSN 0192-060X) **7476**
Washington Review (USA ISSN 0163-903X) **525**
Washington School Directory *see* M D R's School Directory. Washington **2960**
Washington Sea Grant Program. Publication (USA) **3611**
Washington Sea Grant Program. Report (USA) **3611**
Washington Sea Grant Program. Technical Report (USA) **3611**
Washington Semesters and Internships (USA ISSN 1522-6786) **2925**
Washington Smart C E O *see* Washington SmartC E O **1801**
Washington SmartC E O (Chief Executive Officer) (USA ISSN 1554-6993) **1801**
Washington Spectator (USA ISSN 0887-428X) **7193**
Washington Square (USA) **2309**
• Washington Square News (USA ISSN 1549-9383) **2309**
Washington Star (GBR) **3872**
Washington State Bar Association. Administrative Law Section. Newsletter (USA) **4811**
Washington State Bar Association. Business and Law Section. Newsletter (USA) **4811**
Washington State Bar Association. Corporate Law Department Newsletter (USA) **4883**
Washington State Bar Association. Creditor - Debtor Law Section Newsletter (USA) **1390**
Washington State Bar Association. Criminal Law Section Newsletter (USA) **4899**
Washington State Bar Association. Family Law Section. Newsletter (USA) **4915**
Washington State Bar Association. Intellectual and Industrial Property Section. Newsletter (USA) **6760**
Washington State Bar Association. International Practice Law Section. Newsletter *see* International Practice Law Newsletter **4932**
Washington State Bar Association. Real Property, Probate and Trust Section. Newsletter (USA) **7615**
• Washington State Bar News (USA ISSN 0886-5213) **4811**
Washington State Case Management Resource Directory (USA) **8077**
Washington State Charitable Trust Directory (USA) **8078**
Washington State Dental Association Membership Directory & Resource Guide *see* W S D A Membership Directory & Resource Guide **5869**
Washington State Dental Association News *see* W S D A News **5869**
• Washington State Environmental Policy Act (USA) **4811**
The Washington State Genealogist (USA ISSN 1932-1635) **3787**
Washington State Grange News (USA ISSN 1070-4442) **169**
Washington State International Trade Directory (USA) **2033**
▼ • ➤ Washington State Journal of Public Health Practice (USA ISSN 1934-6360) **7545**
Washington State Labor Market and Economic Report (Year) (USA) **1714**
Washington State Lodging & Travel Guide *see* Washington State Visitors' Guide **8773**
Washington State University. College of Agriculture and Home Economics. Research Bulletin (USA ISSN 1059-8022) **169**
Washington State University. Cooperative Extension. Circular (USA ISSN 0884-3406) **169**
Washington State University. Cooperative Extension. Extension Bulletin (USA ISSN 0748-125X) **169**
Washington State University. Cooperative Extension. WREP (USA ISSN 1057-2465) **169**
➤ Washington State University. Mathematics Notes (USA ISSN 0043-082X) **5546**
Washington State Visitors' Guide (USA) **8773**
Washington State Youth Soccer News (USA) **8251**
• Washington Summary (USA ISSN 0886-0807) **7201**
Washington Super Lawyers (USA ISSN 1933-4907) **4811**
Washington Tariff & Trade Letter (USA ISSN 0276-8275) **4944**
Washington Tax Decisions (USA) **1954**
† Washington Taxes (USA) **8998**
• Washington Technology (USA ISSN 1058-9163) **7486**
† • Washington Techway (USA ISSN 1528-7815) **8998**
Washington Telecom Directory (USA ISSN 8755-2876) **2373**
• Washington Telecom Newswire (USA ISSN 1087-433X) **3992**
• The Washington Times Index (USA ISSN 1042-5128) **4588**
• Washington Trade Daily (USA ISSN 1522-3671) **1587**
Washington Tribune *see* Washington Afro-American Newspaper **3572**
Washington Trooper (USA ISSN 0883-5799) **2671**
• Washington University. Global Studies Law Review (USA ISSN 1546-6981) **4944**
• Washington University. Journal of Law and Policy (USA ISSN 1533-4686) **4811**
• Washington University. Law Review (USA) **4811**

▼ *new title*　　† *ceased*　　● *electronic media*　　➤ *refereed*

11020 WATER SOFTWARE SYSTEMS RESEARCH REPORTS ULRICH'S PERIODICALS

Water Software Systems Research Reports (GBR) **3334**
Water Software Systems Research Series *see* W S S Research Series **3334**
▼ • Water Solutions (Online) (AUS) **8840**
Water Solutions (Print) *see* Water Solutions (Online) **8840**
Water Statistics *see* The U K Water Industry: Water Statistics (Year) **8843**
Water Stewards (USA) **8840**
Water Stone (USA ISSN 1520-457X) **5397**
• Water Strategist (USA ISSN 1545-8113) **8841**
➤ Water Studies (GBR ISSN 1462-6071) **3365**
Water Supply and Sanitation Collaborative Council Catalogue of Documents and Publications *see* W S S C C Catalogue of Documents and Publications **8835**
† Water Supply and Wastewater Disposal - International Almanac (NLD ISSN 0169-2577) **8998**
Water Supply Outlook for the Northeastern United States (USA ISSN 0732-5312) **8841**
Water Supply Outlook for the Western United States (USA) **8841**
Water Technology (USA ISSN 0192-3633) **8841**
Water Technology Directory Issue *see* Water Technology **8841**
Water Transport Statistics of India (IND) **8532**
Water Transportation Management *see* Shuiyun Guanli **8662**
Water Treatment in China (USA ISSN 1944-3234) **2096**
Water Twenty One *see* Water 21 **3492**
Water Utilities Market Report *see* Key Note Market Report: Water Utilities **1896**
• Water Utility Management International (GBR ISSN 1747-7751) **8841**
• Water Week (AUS ISSN 1833-5047) **8841**
Water Well Journal (USA ISSN 0043-1443) **8841**
• Water Wheel (ZAF ISSN 1816-7969) **8841**
Water, Woods & Wildlife (USA ISSN 0161-3561) **822**
Water World *see* Waterworld **8841**
Water Writes (USA) **8841**
Wateralmanak (NLD ISSN 1872-0900) **8284**
• ➤ Waterbirds (USA ISSN 1524-4695) **916**
• Waterborne & High Solids Coatings Bulletin (GBR ISSN 0140-8798) **6721**
Waterborne Commerce of the United States (USA ISSN 0083-7725) **8664**
Waterbury Inquirer *see* Inquiring News **3539**
Watercare Services. Annual Report (Year) (NZL) **8841**
• Watercolor Artist (USA ISSN 1941-5451) **526**
Watercolor Magic *see* Watercolor Artist **526**
Watercolour Challenge (GBR) **526**
Watercolour News (CAN) **526**
Watercraft Philately (CAN ISSN 1074-5890) **6901**
• WaterCraft World (USA ISSN 1073-3191) **8284**
Waterford Chamber of Commerce. News Letter (IRL) **1411**
Waterford News & Star (IRL ISSN 1649-2781) **3895**
Waterfowl (GBR) **916**
Waterfowl and Retriever *see* Waterfowl & Retriever **8340**
• Waterfowl & Retriever (USA ISSN 1931-6240) **8340**
Waterfowl Hunter (USA) **8340**
• Waterfront Home and Design (USA ISSN 1933-7728) **461**
Waterfront News (USA ISSN 8756-0038) **8284**
Waterfront World Spotlight (USA ISSN 0733-0677) **4431**
Waterkampioen (NLD ISSN 0043-1451) **8284**
Waterkampioen 2eHands (NLD) **8284**
De Waterkwaliteit ter Hoogte van Zwemgelegenheden in het IJsselmmer, Markermeer en de Randmeren (NLD ISSN 1574-5996) **8841**
Waterlife (GBR ISSN 1752-7392) **916**
• Waterline (AUS ISSN 1324-4043) **8665**
Waterline (GBR ISSN 0954-7711) **8841**
• ➤ Waterlines (GBR ISSN 0262-8104) **8841**
Waterlog (GBR ISSN 1365-7585) **8340**
Waterloo Chronicle (CAN ISSN 0832-3410) **3820**
Waterloo Computer Systems Group News *see* WatCom News **2599**
➤ Waterloo Historical Society (CAN ISSN 0315-5021) **4317**
• The Waterlow Stock Exchange Yearbook (GBR ISSN 1477-7185) **1659**
Waterlow's Solicitors' and Barristers' Diary (GBR ISSN 1356-6261) **4811**
• Waterlow's Solicitors' and Barristers' Directory (GBR ISSN 1356-6253) **4811**
Waterlow's Unquoted Companies (Year) (GBR ISSN 1471-5716) **2034**
• Watermark (CAN ISSN 1912-838X) **3611**
• Watermark (Beacon) (USA ISSN 1933-9275) **2631**
The Watermark (Boston) (USA ISSN 1934-7448) **5397**
The Watermark (New York) (USA ISSN 1553-7641) **5054**
• Watermarks (USA ISSN 0894-511X) **8841**
Waterpoint (PHL ISSN 0117-536X) **8841**
Waterpower (USA ISSN 1057-1841) **3287**
Waters (CAN) **967**
• Waters (GBR) **1394**
• Waters and Water Rights (USA) **8841**
Water's Edge (USA ISSN 1529-6288) **5086**
Het Waterschap (NLD ISSN 1380-4251) **8841**
Waterschap Zuiderzeeland. Jaarrapportage Watersysteembeheer (NLD ISSN 1871-6490) **8841**
WaterShapes (USA ISSN 1522-6581) **461**
Watershed (USA) **2631**
▼ Watershed (Bloomsburg) (USA ISSN 1943-9687) **5397**
Watershed and Wet Weather Technical Bulletin (USA ISSN 1558-5999) **8841**
Watershed Focus (USA) **3493**
Watershed Protection Techniques (USA ISSN 1073-9610) **8841**
Watershed Sentinel (CAN ISSN 1188-360X) **2631**
Waterski *see* Waterski & Wakeboard Magazine **8215**
• WaterSki (USA ISSN 0883-7813) **8340**
Waterski & Wakeboard Magazine (NLD ISSN 1871-2851) **8215**
▼ Waterstand (NLD ISSN 1876-1984) **8841**
Waterstone's Books Quarterly (GBR ISSN 1474-4260) **5245**
Waterway Guide - Mid-Atlantic (USA ISSN 0509-917X) **8284**
Waterway Guide - Northern (USA ISSN 0090-712X) **8284**
Waterway Guide - Southern (USA ISSN 0511-3806) **8284**
• Waterways (GBR ISSN 0969-0654) **8284**
Waterways (USA ISSN 0197-4777) **5437**
• Waterways Journal (USA ISSN 0043-1524) **8665**
Waterways World (GBR ISSN 0309-1422) **8284**
Waterweek *see* A W W A Streamlines **8817**
Waterwheel (USA ISSN 0898-6606) **8904**
• Waterworld (USA ISSN 1083-0723) **8841**
Watford and District Industrial History Society. Journal (GBR ISSN 0307-5281) **4278**
Watford & Hemel Hempstead Business Directory *see* Commerce Business Directories. Watford & Hemel Hempstead **1980**
Al-Watha'iq al-Filastiniyyah/Palestinian Documents (UAE) **4326**
Watha'iq Dawlat al-Imarat/Emirates Documents (UAE) **4326**
➤ Al-Watha'iq wal-Makhtutat/Documents and Manuscripts (LBY) **4326**
Al-Wathiqa (BHR) **4326**
Watra *see* Vatra **3570**
Watrous Manitou (CAN) **3820**
➤ Watsonia (GBR ISSN 0043-1532) **822**
Watt *see* Watt Elettroforniture **3334**
• Watt Elettroforniture (ITA ISSN 1825-5116) **3334**
• Watt Poultry Global E-news (USA) **303**
Watt Poultry Statistical Yearbook: International Edition (USA) **189**
Watt Poultry U S A *see* Poultry U S A **297**
Wattenmeer International (DEU ISSN 0256-7059) **2631**
Wattnow (ZAF ISSN 1991-0452) **3334**
Watt's Manual of Criminal Jury Instructions (CAN ISSN 1910-4537) **4811**
Watt's On (GBR) **2309**
• Al-Watwan/Journal des Comores (COM ISSN 1013-6843) **5245**
Wave Front (IND ISSN 0973-4708) **7046**
• ➤ Wave Motion (NLD ISSN 0165-2125) **7046**
Wave South Florida (USA) **8285**
• Wavelength (GBR ISSN 0967-2079) **8340**
Wavelength (Newport Beach) (USA) **4527**
Wavelength Magazine *see* Wavelength **8340**
• ➤ Wavelength Magazine (GBR ISSN 1359-1193) **7928**
WaveLength Paddling Magazine (CAN ISSN 1188-5432) **8215**
Wavelengths *see* Journal of Laser Dentistry **5852**
Waveney District Council. Planning & Building Control. Information Notes (GBR) **4431**
Waves (AUS) **8340**
• ➤ Waves in Random and Complex Media (GBR ISSN 1745-5030) **7046**
• Waves in Random and Complex Media (Online) (GBR ISSN 1745-5049) **7046**
Waves in Random Media (Online) *see* Waves in Random and Complex Media (Online) **7046**
Wavriensia (BEL ISSN 0043-1567) **4278**
• Wawa Huabao/Illustrated Periodical for Kindergarteners (CHN ISSN 1004-0072) **2221**
Wawa Leyuan (CHN ISSN 1005-5452) **2221**
Wawatay News (CAN ISSN 0703-9387) **3572**
Wax (GBR ISSN 1362-5519) **6627**
Waxmann Studies (DEU ISSN 1431-4452) **8014**
• ➤ The Way (GBR ISSN 0043-1575) **7694**
The Way *see* Cels **7630**
The Way (Philadelphia)/Shliakh (USA ISSN 0043-1583) **7822**
Way Dickie Magazine (USA) **5437**
The Way Forward *see* Nouvelles sur les Prochaines Etapes **7457**
• The Way Forward News/Nouvelles sur les Prochaines Etapes (CAN ISSN 1718-4886) **7476**
The Way Fourth (USA) **7694**
➤ Way North (NOR) **360**
Way of Life (GBR ISSN 0043-1605) **7694**
Way of St. Francis (USA ISSN 0273-8295) **7822**
➤ Way Station Magazine (USA) **5397**
Way We Work and Live *see* E E O Trust Work & Life Awards (Series) **1676**
Waybill (USA ISSN 0897-7577) **8627**
▼ • The Wayfarer (AUS ISSN 1834-4070) **5437**
• Waymark (GBR) **7743**
Wayn-E-Gram Magazine (USA) **276**
Wayne County Historian (USA ISSN 1047-0093) **4317**
• Wayne E. Sabbe Arkansas Soil Fertility Studies (USA ISSN 1941-1545) **258**
• The Wayne Law Review (USA ISSN 0043-1621) **4811**
Wayne State Magazine (USA) **2309**
Wayne State University Alumni News (USA ISSN 0043-163X) **2309**
Wayne State University Law School. Comparative Criminal Law Project. Publications Series (USA) **4899**
• Waypoint Online Newsletter (AUS ISSN 1833-8569) **2821**
Ways of Knowing in Science Series (USA) **3087**
Ways to a Successful Composition *see* Zuowen Chenggong zhi Lu **2929**
• WaySouth (USA) **3992**
We (THA) **5561**
We Are One World (DEU) **2221**
We Love Science *see* Women Ai Kexue **2222**
We Magazine (New York) (USA) **4070**
• We Magazine for Women (USA ISSN 1937-9900) **8888**
We Need Not Walk Alone (USA) **7414**
We Proceeded On (USA ISSN 0275-6706) **4317**
We Remember Dean International (USA) **6516**
Weal (CAN) **2309**
Wealth (GBR ISSN 1742-1748) **1390**
▼ Wealth (IRL ISSN 1649-9360) **1659**
Wealth *see* Caifu **1078**
• Wealth Asia (IND) **3474**
The Wealth Connection (GBR) **1659**
The Wealth Liberty Institute Report (CAN ISSN 1712-7491) **1659**
Wealth Management Resource Guide (USA) **1390**
Wealth Manager (USA ISSN 1522-6565) **1659**
A Wealth of Resources (CAN ISSN 1718-2336) **8078**
• WealthStrategies 202.com eNewsletter (USA ISSN 1559-5447) **1969**
• WealthStrategies for Translators eNewsletter (USA ISSN 1559-5439) **1969**
Weaping Willow (ITA ISSN 1970-5379) **5448**
• Weapons Complex Monitor (USA ISSN 1047-8957) **3514**
Weapons Journal *see* Wingman **6454**
▼ Weapons of Mass Destruction and Terrorism (USA ISSN 1935-8431) **7273**
Weapons Offences Manual (CAN) **4900**
WeAr (AUT ISSN 1813-7768) **2263**
• ➤ Wear (NLD ISSN 0043-1648) **3399**
We'ar Different *see* W A D **2220**
We'ar Different Hors-Serie *see* W A D. Hors-Serie **2220**
Wear Valley Mercury (GBR ISSN 1751-5300) **3968**
• Wearables Business (USA ISSN 1096-3766) **2250**
• ➤ Weather (GBR ISSN 0043-1656) **6398**
† Weather Almanac (USA ISSN 0731-5627) **8998**
➤ Weather and Climate (NZL ISSN 0111-5499) **6398**
• ➤ Weather and Forecasting (USA ISSN 0882-8156) **6398**
▼ • Weather and Society Watch (USA ISSN 1948-2450) **6398**
Weather Service Bulletin *see* Sokko Jiho **6395**
• Weather Zine (USA) **6398**
Weatherguide *see* Minnesota WeatherGuide Calendar **6391**
• Weathervane (USA) **6398**
• Weatherwise (USA ISSN 0043-1672) **6398**
• ➤ The Weaver (AUS ISSN 1329-881X) **2925**
Weaver's Digest (English Edition) (CHE ISSN 1424-5752) **8462**
Weaver's Digest (French Edition) (CHE ISSN 1424-5736) **8462**
Weaver's Digest (German Edition) (CHE ISSN 1424-5728) **8462**
Weaver's Digest (Italian Edition) (CHE ISSN 1424-5744) **8462**
Weaver's Digest (Spanish Edition) (CHE ISSN 1424-5760) **8462**
• Weavings (USA ISSN 0890-6491) **7780**
• Web 2.0 Journal (USA) **2567**
Web Ad Monthly (USA ISSN 1541-5392) **2567**
Web Advertising (Year) (USA ISSN 1098-7754) **2568**
Web & Publishing *see* Henshu Kaigi **7562**
Web Bound Special Edition: Top 12,000 Sports Websites (USA) **2568**
• Web Commerce Today (USA ISSN 1094-9011) **1193**
Web Content Report (USA ISSN 1099-7202) **2568**
• Web del Sol (USA) **5397**
Web Design Index (NLD ISSN 1871-8299) **2568**
Web Designer (GBR ISSN 1745-3534) **2568**
▼ Web Designer (NLD ISSN 1875-8525) **2568**
Web Designer Magazine (ITA ISSN 1724-4692) **2568**
• Web Designers Gazette (USA) **2568**
Web Developer's & Designer's Journal (USA) **2490**
• Web Developer's Journal (GBR) **2568**
• The Web Developer's Journal (USA) **2568**
• Web Developer's Virtual Library (USA) **2568**
• Web Ecology (DNK ISSN 1399-1183) **3474**
• ➤ Web Exclusives (USA ISSN 1544-5208) **7545**
• WEB - F U (Wiener Elektronische Beitraege des Instituts fuer Finno Ugristik) (AUT ISSN 1609-882X) **5194**
• Web Feet (Online) (USA) **2568**
• Web Feet K - 8 (USA ISSN 1533-2543) **3087**
• Web Gold (USA) **2568**
Web Guide (USA ISSN 1524-2609) **2568**
• Web Informant (Port Washington) (USA ISSN 1524-6353) **2568**
• Web Intelligence and Agent Systems (NLD ISSN 1570-1263) **2457**
• ➤ Web Journal of Current Legal Issues (USA ISSN 1360-1326) **4811**
• Web Journal of Formal, Computational & Cognitive Linguistics (RUS) **5194**
• ➤ Web Journal of Mass Communication Research (USA) **2344**
• ➤ Web Journal of Modern Language Linguistics (GBR ISSN 1461-4499) **5194**
• Web Journal on Cultural Patrimony (ITA ISSN 1827-8868) **423**
Web M & M *see* A H R Q Web M&M **7505**
▼ Web Magasin (NOR ISSN 1890-3738) **2568**
† • Web Magazine (FRA ISSN 1295-697X) **8998**
• Web Marketing Today (USA ISSN 1094-8112) **1847**
Web Marketing Update (USA ISSN 1091-1405) **1847**
Web - Online Services (Year) (USA ISSN 1549-3288) **2568**
Web Pages Made Easy (GBR ISSN 1464-7427) **2568**
• The Web Philippines (PHL) **2568**
• Web Review (USA) **2568**
• The Web - Savvy Writer (USA ISSN 1933-1509) **1848**
Web Semantics *see* Journal of Web Semantics **2563**
• Web Services Strategies (USA ISSN 1542-3336) **2510**
Web Sight Directory Magazine (USA) **2568**
• The Web Singapore (SGP) **2568**
Web Site Source Book (Year) (USA ISSN 1089-4861) **2568**
• Web Solutions (USA) **2568**
• Web Surfer Travel Journal (USA) **8773**
• Web Times (CAN) **2568**
Web Times (International Edition) *see* Web Times **2568**
web trade *see* Webtrade **2569**
Web User (GBR) **2568**
Web Wire *see* Union Wire **4604**
• Web Wit (USA ISSN 1559-6532) **2568**
• Web - Zine (USA) **2568**
Web3D (Year) Symposium. Proceedings (USA ISSN 1552-9886) **2490**
Web3D Symposium *see* Web3D (Year) Symposium. Proceedings **2490**
Web3D - V R M L Symposium. Proceedings *see* Web3D (Year) Symposium. Proceedings **2490**
• WebActive (USA) **3992**
Webb Society Quarterly Journal *see* The Deep-Sky Observer **574**
➤ Webbia (ITA ISSN 0083-7792) **822**
• The WebBiz Telegram (USA) **1848**
• Webcreate (GBR) **2568**
• WebDesign & Review (USA) **2568**
• Webdo (CHE ISSN 1422-2728) **2568**
• Webdo Mag (CHE ISSN 1423-8705) **2568**
Weben (DEU ISSN 0947-3386) **8462**
• ➤ Weber Studies: Voices and Viewpoints of the Contemporary West (USA) **4482**
• Webgeist (USA) **5397**
• WebLogic Developer's Journal (USA ISSN 1535-9581) **2510**
▼ Webmagazinet.dk (DNK ISSN 1902-7834) **2504**
• The Webmaster Tribune (USA) **2569**
• Webmasters Ezine (USA) **2569**
WebMD Little Blue Book (Year) (USA) **5729**
WebMD Little Yellow Book (Year) (USA) **5729**
• WebMD the Magazine (USA ISSN 1553-9946) **5729**
• Webnewz (SGP) **2569**
• ➤ Webology (IRN ISSN 1735-188X) **5054**
• ➤ Webpondo.org (COL) **1193**
• Webprofessions Monthly Update (USA) **2569**
• Webreference Update (USA) **2569**
▼ Webs (USA ISSN 1948-5069) **5397**
Webselling (DEU) **2569**
• Website Magazine (USA ISSN 1942-0633) **2569**
Website Services *see* Website Magazine **2569**
• Website Success Monthly (USA ISSN 1529-0409) **2569**
• WebSite Weekly (GBR) **2569**
Websphere Advisor *see* Databased Advisor Magazine **2554**
• WebSphere Journal (USA ISSN 1940-3348) **2510**
• Webspherepower Magazine (USA ISSN 1554-5598) **2599**
The Webster Agricultural Letter *see* Agri-Pulse Newsletter **82**
• Webster's Real Estate Law in North Carolina (USA) **7615**
Webster's Wagon Wheel (USA ISSN 1067-523X) **3787**
• Websurfers Biweekly Earth Science Review (USA) **2569**
• WebTrack (USA) **2569**
• Webtrade (DEU) **2569**
WebWUUrks (USA) **5397**
Wechselwirkung (NLD ISSN 0172-1623) **8445**
Wechselwirkungen (CHE ISSN 1424-7674) **5397**
Wechselwirkungen (DEU ISSN 0724-3324) **3010**
Wedding (GBR ISSN 1750-2551) **5561**
Wedding and Home *see* Wedding **5561**
Wedding & Portrait Photographers International Monthly *see* W P P I Monthly **6978**
Wedding Belle (IRL ISSN 1649-8895) **5561**
Wedding Bells *see* Weddingbells (Regional Ontario Edition) **5562**

Link to your serials resources and content with ulrichsweb.com

Title

Weifang University. Journal see Weifang Xueyuan Xuebao **8014**
- Weifang Xueyuan Xuebao/Weifang University. Journal (CHN ISSN 1671-4288) **8014**
- Weifang Yixueyuan Xuebao/Acta Academiae Medicinae Weifang (CHN ISSN 1004-3101) **5729**
Weifen Fangcheng Niankan see Annals of Differential Equations **5471**
Weighing & Measurement (USA ISSN 0095-537X) **6407**
Weight in America see Information Plus Reference Series. Weight in America **6989**
Weight Loss Doctor (CAN ISSN 1712-7076) **7000**
Weight Watchers (DEU) **6671**
Weight Watchers (Sydney) (AUS ISSN 1327-5267) **6671**
Weight Watchers Magazine (GBR ISSN 0309-8095) **7000**
- Weight Watchers Magazine (USA ISSN 0043-2180) **6671**
Weightlifting U S A (USA) **7000**
Der Weihenstephaner (DEU ISSN 0171-5089) **612**
- Weijisuanji Xinxi/Control & Automation (CHN ISSN 1008-0570) **2573**
- Weijisuanji Yingyong/Microcomputer Applications (CHN ISSN 1003-1944) **2573**
Weile Haizi/For the Children (CHN ISSN 1000-4319) **2171**
- Weiliang Yuansu yu Jiankang Yanjiu/Studies of Trace Elements and Health (CHN ISSN 1005-5320) **5729**
Weill Cornell Medicine (USA ISSN 1551-4455) **5729**
Weil's Arkansas Government Register (USA ISSN 1531-2208) **7476**
Weil's Connecticut Government Register (USA) **7476**
Weil's Georgia Government Register (USA) **7476**
Weil's Hawaii Government Register (USA ISSN 1097-8550) **7476**
Weil's Wyoming Government Register (USA ISSN 1083-0359) **7476**
- ➤ Weimar and Now: German Cultural Criticism (USA ISSN 1549-1870) **5397**
Weimar Kultur Journal (DEU) **4278**
Weimaraner Magazine (USA ISSN 0162-315X) **6816**
Weimarer Beitraege (AUT ISSN 0043-2199) **5397**
Weimarer Monographien zur Ur- und Fruehgeschichte (DEU ISSN 0232-265X) **423**
Weimarer Studien zur Kulturpolitik und Kulturoekonomie (DEU ISSN 1860-8639) **8014**
Weimian yu Ganran Zazhi see Journal of Microbiology, Immunology and Infection **889**
Wein & Speisen (DEU) **612**
Wein Gourmet (DEU) **612**
Wein und Markt (DEU ISSN 1439-6440) **612**
Weinberg & Blank on Takeovers & Mergers (GBR) **4811**
Weini Shishang (Guoji Zhongwen Ban) see ViVi (Chinese Edition) **8888**
† Weinig Info (DEU) **8998**
- Weinig PartnerNews (DEU) **3717**
Weinrecht (DEU) **1587**
- Weinstein, Korn and Miller C P L R Manual (Civil Practice Law and Rules) (USA) **4844**
- Weinstein's Evidence Manual (USA ISSN 1556-6471) **4812**
- Weinwelt (DEU ISSN 1437-7276) **612**
Weinwirtschaft (DEU ISSN 1430-8762) **612**
- Weiqi Tiandi/Weiqi World (CHN ISSN 1002-8706) **8215**
Weiqi World see Weiqi Tiandi **8215**
Weir Bulletin (GBR) **3226**
Weird N J (New Jersey) (USA) **8774**
- The Weird Side Ezine (BEL) **6301**
Weird Tales (USA) **5448**
Weirdbook Encores (USA) **5448**
Weirdo (USA) **5245**
Weirdology (USA) **6744**
- Weisheng Dulixue Zazhi/Journal of Hygiene Research (CHN ISSN 1002-3127) **5729**
- Weisheng Jingji Yanjiu/Health Economics Research (CHN ISSN 1004-7778) **1193**
- Weisheng Yanjiu/Journal of Hygiene Research (CHN ISSN 1000-8020) **7000**
- Weisheng Zhiye Jiaoyu/Health Vocational Education (CHN ISSN 1671-1246) **2925**
- ➤ Weishengwu Xuebao/Acta Microbiologica Sinica (CHN ISSN 0001-6209) **898**
- Weishengwuxue Mianyixue Jinzhan/Progess in Microbiology and Immunology (CHN ISSN 1005-5673) **898**
- Weishengwuxue Tongbao/Microbiology (CHN ISSN 0253-2654) **898**
- Weishengwuxue Zazhi/Journal of Microbiology (CHN ISSN 1005-7021) **898**
Weiss Ratings Consumer Guide to Elder Care Choices see TheStreet.com Ratings' Consumer Guide to Elder Care Choices **8074**
Weiss Ratings' Consumer Guide to Homeowners Insurance see TheStreet.com Ratings' Consumer Guide to Homeowners Insurance **4525**
Weiss Ratings' Consumer Guide to Long-term Care Insurance see TheStreet.com Ratings' Consumer Guide to Long-term Care Insurance **4525**
Weiss Ratings' Consumer Guide to Medicare Prescription Drug Coverage see TheStreet.com Ratings' Consumer Guide to Medicare Prescription Drug Coverage **4525**

Weiss Ratings' Consumer Guide to Medicare Supplement Insurance see TheStreet.com Ratings' Consumer Guide to Medicare Supplement Insurance **4525**
Weiss Ratings' Consumer Guide to Term Life Insurance see TheStreet.com Ratings' Consumer Guide to Term Life Insurance **4525**
Weiss Ratings Consumer Guide to Variable Annuities see TheStreet.com Ratings' Consumer Guide to Variable Annuities **1655**
Weiss Ratings Guide to Banks and Thrifts see TheStreet.com Ratings' Guide to Banks and Thrifts **1386**
Weiss Ratings' Guide to Bond and Money Market Mutual Funds see TheStreet.com Ratings' Guide to Bond and Money Market Mutual Funds **1655**
Weiss Ratings' Guide to Brokerage Firms (USA ISSN 1532-1835) **1659**
Weiss Ratings' Guide to Closed-End Mutual Funds see TheStreet.com Ratings' Guide to Exchange-Traded Funds **1655**
Weiss Ratings' Guide to Common Stocks see TheStreet.com Ratings' Guide to Common Stocks **1655**
Weiss Ratings' Guide to Life, Health, and Annuity Insurers see TheStreet.com Ratings' Guide to Life and Annuity Insurers **4525**
Weiss Ratings' Guide to Stock Mutual Funds see TheStreet.com Ratings' Guide to Stock Mutual Funds **1655**
Weiss Ratings' Ultimate Guided Tour of Stock Investing see TheStreet.com Ratings' Ultimate Guided Tour of Stock Investing **1655**
Weissbuch zur Lage und Entwicklung der Bundeswehr (DEU ISSN 0938-2631) **6454**
Die Weisse Rose (AUT) **7193**
Weissenberger's Federal Civil Procedure (Year) Litigation Manual (USA) **4844**
Weissenberger's Federal Civil Procedure Litigation Manual see Weissenberger's Federal Civil Procedure (Year) Litigation Manual **4844**
- Weissenberger's Federal Civil Procedure Litigation Manual (USA) **4844**
- Weissenberger's Federal Evidence (USA) **4967**
Weissenberger's Federal Evidence Courtroom Manual see Federal Evidence Courtroom Manual **4951**
Weissenberger's Indiana Evidence Courtroom Manual see Indiana Evidence Courtroom Manual **4953**
Weissenberger's Michigan Civil Procedure Litigation Manual see Michigan Civil Procedure **4837**
Weissenberger's Ohio Civil Procedure (Year) Litigation Manual (USA ISSN 1938-999X) **4844**
Weisses Kreuz (DEU) **7780**
Weisses Minarett (DEU) **7717**
- Weissmann Travel Reports (USA) **8774**
Weissrussland und Unternehmen see Delo (Minsk) **1090**
Weite Welt (DEU) **7694**
- ➤ Weiterbildung (DEU ISSN 1861-0501) **2925**
Weitersehen (DEU) **4086**
- ➤ Weiti Gushengwu Xuebao/Acta Micropalaeontologica Sinica (CHN ISSN 1000-0674) **898**
- Weixi Jiagong Jishu/Microfabrication Technology (CHN ISSN 1003-8213) **3116**
Weixing Xiaoshuo Xuankan (CHN ISSN 1005-3840) **5397**
- Weixing yu Wangluo/Satellite & Network (CHN ISSN 1672-965X) **2344**
Weixingji Xinxi/Microcomputer Information see Weijisuanji Xinxi **2573**
- Weixunhuanxue Zazhi/Chinese Journal of Microcirculation (CHN ISSN 1005-1740) **5801**
- Weizmann Institute of Science, Rehovot, Israel. Scientific Activities (ISR ISSN 0083-7849) **7928**
De Wekker (NLD ISSN 0167-1227) **7780**
Wela (TZA) **3961**
- Welara Journal (USA) **8300**
Welcome! (DEU) **8774**
Welcome see Failte **8703**
Welcome see Odini **7810**
Welcome see Ahlan wa-Sahlan **8782**
Welcome Back Student Magazine (CAN) **2309**
Welcome Home (Des Moines) (USA ISSN 1545-7656) **4552**
Welcome Home Magazine of Denver (USA) **3992**
Welcome Home Magazine of Las Vegas see Welcome Home Magazine of Denver **3992**
Welcome Homeowner (USA) **7615**
Welcome to America's Heartland (GBR) **8774**
Welcome to Bucharest (ROM ISSN 1582-2648) **8774**
- Welcome to Costa Rica (CRI) **8774**
Welcome to Finland see Welcome to Finland **8774**
Welcome to Finland (FIN ISSN 1797-2620) **8774**
Welcome to Greater Louisville (USA) **8774**
Welcome to Miami and the Beaches (USA ISSN 0192-4257) **8786**
Welcome to Nigeria ...The Land of Hospitality, Cultural Diversity and Scenic Beauty see Nigeria Tourism Development Corporation. Official Tourist Guide **8741**
Welcome to Planet Earth (USA ISSN 0747-8968) **567**
Welcome to the C I H R - Rx & D Progress Report (Year)/Rapport d'Etape d I R S C/Rx & D (Canadian Institutes of Health Research) (CAN ISSN 1701-9583) **6885**
Welcome to the Family (DEU) **2171**
- Welcome to the World of... (GBR) **8078**

Weld County Genealogical Society. Quarterly (USA ISSN 0896-1875) **3787**
- Weldasearch Select (GBR) **6342**
Welded Steel Tube and Pipe Monthly (GBR ISSN 1749-3765) **6336**
† The Welder (GBR ISSN 0043-2237) **8998**
Welding see Zvaranie **6345**
Welding and Allied Processes see Literaturschau: Schweissen und Verwandte Verfahren **6340**
Welding and Cutting (DEU ISSN 1612-3433) **6344**
Welding & Joining see Hanjie **6342**
Welding and Metal Fabrication (GBR ISSN 0043-2245) **6344**
Welding & Metal Fabrication Buyers Guide (GBR ISSN 1357-7328) **6345**
Welding Design & Fabrication see Penton's Welding Magazine **6343**
Welding Fumes see Litigation Watch. Welding Fume **4724**
- ➤ Welding in the World/Soudage dans le Monde (FRA ISSN 0043-2288) **6345**
- Welding Innovation (USA) **6345**
- Welding International (GBR ISSN 0950-7116) **6345**
- ➤ Welding Journal (USA ISSN 0043-2296) **6345**
Welding News see Yosetu Nyusu **6345**
Welding Research (USA ISSN 0096-7629) **6345**
Welding Research Abroad (USA ISSN 0043-2318) **6345**
Welding Research Council Bulletin (USA ISSN 0043-2326) **6345**
Welding Research Council Progress Reports see W R C Progress Reports **6344**
Welding Research Institute Journal see W R I Journal **6344**
Welding Research News (USA ISSN 0511-4381) **6345**
The Welding Review see Yosetu Gijutsu **6345**
- Welding Review International (GBR) **6345**
Weleda Korrespondenzblaetter fuer Aerzte (CHE ISSN 0379-7031) **5729**
Welfare Benefits (GBR ISSN 1353-1123) **4969**
Welfare Benefits and Immigration Law (GBR ISSN 1465-6841) **4969**
Welfare Benefits Guide (USA) **1714**
Welfare Benefits Handbook (GBR ISSN 1467-2081) **8078**
Welfare Bulletin (USA ISSN 1091-4056) **4826**
Welfare in Australia (Print) see Practice Reflexions **8062**
Welfare News (USA) **8078**
Welfare Rights Bulletin (GBR ISSN 0263-2098) **8078**
Welfare to Work (USA ISSN 1060-5622) **8078**
- Welfare World (GBR ISSN 1365-9820) **8078**
Welfengarten see Weltengarten **5245**
- The Well (AUS ISSN 1441-7472) **37**
- The Well (USA) **5397**
Well Being Journal (USA ISSN 1559-4955) **7000**
- The Well-Connected Attorney (USA) **4812**
Well Done (DNK) **4400**
Well Inventory Series. Metric Units (GBR ISSN 0308-5368) **2774**
Well Log see Water Well Journal **8841**
Well Logging Technology see Cejing Jishu **6765**
Well Magazine (USA) **7000**
Well Read see Bolan Qunshu **5265**
Well Said (AUS ISSN 1833-9697) **646**
The Well Service Market Report (USA ISSN 1058-0646) **6797**
Well Servicing (USA ISSN 0043-2393) **6797**
Well Testing see Youqijing Ceshi **6798**
The Well Workplace Newsletter (USA) **7545**
Welland Historical Museum Newsletter (CAN) **6540**
- Welland Tribune (CAN ISSN 0841-632X) **3820**
▼ Wellard's N H S Guide (Year) (National Health Service) (GBR) **6885**
▼ Wellbeing (Year) (USA) **8848**
Wellbeing Astrolog (AUS ISSN 1445-8837) **567**
WellBeing Magazine (AUS ISSN 1328-7540) **7000**
- Wellcome History (GBR ISSN 1477-4860) **5729**
- Wellcome News (GBR ISSN 1461-0949) **5729**
Wellcome Trust Annual Review (GBR) **5730**
Wellcome Unit for the History of Medicine. Research Publications (GBR ISSN 0143-7984) **5730**
Wellcome Witnesses to Twentieth Century Medicine (GBR) **5730**
Wellensittich Magazin (DEU ISSN 0178-7373) **916**
Wellensittich-Papageien Magazin see WP-Magazin **6817**
Wellesley College Friends of Art Newsletter (USA) **6540**
Wellesley Magazine (USA) **2309**
Wellesley Studies in Critical Theory, Literary History and Culture (GBR) **5397**
Wellfit see Freundin Wellfit **8845**
Wellington Contact see The Wellingtonian **3920**
Wellington County History (CAN ISSN 1186-6195) **4317**
- Wellington District Crime Statistics (NZL ISSN 1178-1610) **2675**
Wellington District Statistics see Wellington District Crime Statistics **2675**
Wellington Letter see Bert Dohmen's Wellington Letter **1612**
Wellington Occasional Papers in Applied Linguistics (NZL ISSN 1174-6610) **5194**
Wellington Orchid Society, Incorporated. Bulletin (NZL ISSN 1177-0864) **3754**
Wellington Orchid Society. Journal see Wellington Orchid Society, Incorporated. Bulletin **3754**

Wellington Regional Outlook (NZL ISSN 1176-9416) **1524**
Wellington Times see Times (Wellington) **3818**
Wellington Weekly News (GBR ISSN 0961-4370) **3873**
Wellington Working Papers in Linguistics (NZL ISSN 1170-1978) **5194**
The Wellingtonian (NZL) **3920**
Wellness (DEU) **7000**
- Wellness (HUN ISSN 1588-3531) **8848**
† Wellness & Fitness Entrepreneur (USA ISSN 1931-5430) **8998**
Wellness and Fitness Entrepreneur see Wellness & Fitness Entrepreneur **8998**
Wellness & Organic Ingredients Directory see Prepared Foods. Wellness and Organic Ingredients Directory **3660**
Wellness Bound (USA) **5086**
Wellness en Bouwen aan de Toekomst (NLD) **461**
Wellness Foods see Food Processing **3640**
Wellness Foods Europe (DEU ISSN 1612-247X) **6671**
Wellness Letter see University of California, Berkeley. Wellness Letter **6999**
Wellness Magazine (NLD ISSN 1871-0697) **315**
- Wellness Networker (CAN ISSN 1914-5861) **315**
Wellness Program Management Advisor (USA ISSN 1085-7125) **7000**
- WellnessOptions (CAN ISSN 1496-1008) **7545**
The Wells College Express (USA ISSN 1062-1636) **2309**
Wellsian (GBR ISSN 0263-1776) **5397**
- WellSpring (CAN ISSN 1187-7472) **7000**
Wellsprings/Ma'yanot (USA ISSN 0887-011X) **7731**
▼ Welser Universitaere Schriften (AUT) **8014**
Welsh Advisory Committee on Telecommunications. Report (GBR) **2353**
Welsh Agricultural Statistics see Welsh Agricultural Statistics **190**
Welsh Agricultural Statistics (GBR ISSN 0262-8325) **190**
Welsh-American Genealogical Society Newsletter (USA ISSN 1520-8249) **3787**
Welsh Birds (GBR ISSN 1359-1649) **916**
Welsh Black Cattle Society Herd Book (GBR) **304**
Welsh Black Cattle Society Journal (GBR) **304**
Welsh Book Studies see Y Llyfr Yng Nghymru **7566**
Welsh Development Agency. Annual Report/Awdurdod Datblygu Cymru. Adroddiad Blynyddol (GBR) **1607**
Welsh Economic Review (GBR ISSN 0963-0864) **1524**
Welsh Economic Trends (GBR ISSN 0262-8309) **1274**
Welsh Education Statistics Bulletins (GBR ISSN 0951-3191) **2937**
- Welsh Enterprise Institute. Working Papers Series (GBR) **1193**
Welsh Farmer/Y Tir (GBR ISSN 0040-8050) **169**
Welsh Governance Centre. Working Paper (GBR ISSN 1471-9681) **7193**
Welsh Historian/Hanesydd Cymreig (GBR) **4278**
- ➤ Welsh History Review/Cylchgrawn Hanes Cymru (GBR ISSN 0043-2431) **4166**
Welsh House Condition Survey (GBR ISSN 0263-9629) **4437**
Welsh Housing Quarterly (GBR ISSN 0962-9602) **4431**
Welsh Housing Statistics (GBR ISSN 0262-8333) **4437**
Welsh Inter Censal Survey (GBR ISSN 0956-0793) **7317**
- ➤ Welsh Journal of Education (GBR ISSN 0957-297X) **2925**
Welsh Local Government Financial Statistics (GBR ISSN 0140-4482) **7485**
Welsh Music/Cerddoriaeth Cymru (GBR ISSN 0043-244X) **6628**
Welsh Music History Journal (GBR ISSN 1362-0681) **6628**
† Welsh Office. Social Services Inspectorate. Training Support Programme for the Personal Social Services. Progress Report (GBR) **8998**
Welsh Pony and Cob Society Journal (GBR) **8300**
Welsh Pony and Cob Society. Journal (ZAF ISSN 1815-9117) **8300**
Welsh Soils Discussion Group. Report (GBR ISSN 0083-7938) **259**
De Welsh Springer (NLD ISSN 1383-3960) **6816**
➤ Welsh Studies (USA ISSN 1543-7892) **8014**
Welsh Transport Statistics (GBR ISSN 0267-8160) **8532**
Welsh Writing in English (GBR ISSN 1356-0301) **5397**
Die Welt (DEU ISSN 0173-8437) **3859**
Welt am Sonntag (DEU ISSN 0949-7188) **3859**
Welt der Farben (DEU) **6721**
Welt der Frau (AUT) **2263**
† Welt der Frau (DEU) **8998**
Welt der Frau Frisuren (DEU) **592**
Welt der Milch see Die Molkerei-Zeitung Welt der Milch **267**
Die Welt der Slaven (DEU ISSN 0043-2520) **5195**
▼ Welt der Stars (DEU) **8888**
Welt der Wunder (DEU) **7928**
- Die Welt des Islams/World of Islam (NLD ISSN 0043-2539) **7717**
Welt des Kindes (DEU ISSN 0373-5885) **7823**
➤ Die Welt des Orients (DEU ISSN 0043-2547) **4167**
Welt Konjunktur (CHE) **1659**
Welt-Spirale (DEU ISSN 0943-092X) **6648**

DIRECTORY 2010 WEST CENTRAL BUSINESS JOURNAL 11023

Welt und Umwelt der Bibel (DEU ISSN 1431-2379) **7694**
Weltarbeitsgruppe fur Greifvogel und Eulen. Rundbrief (DEU ISSN 1013-8013) **916**
Weltbund der Partnerstadte. Mitteilungsblatt *see* United Towns News. Newsletter **7504**
▼ Welten der Philosophie (DEU) **6960**
Welten Ostasiens/Worlds of East Asia (CHE ISSN 1660-9131) **563**
Weltenbummler (DEU) **3859**
➤ Weltengarten (DEU ISSN 1613-012X) **5245**
Weltentwicklungsbericht *see* World Development Report **1608**
Weltentwicklungsbericht *see* Rapport sur le Developpement dans le Monde **1604**
Welternaehrungsbericht *see* World Food Report **3668**
Welthandel/World Trade (DEU ISSN 0720-3683) **1587**
Weltkunst (DEU ISSN 0043-261X) **369**
Weltraum-Philatelie (DEU ISSN 0948-6097) **6901**
Weltrundschau (CHE) **3959**
➤ WeltTrends (DEU ISSN 0944-8101) **7273**
WeltTrends-Lehrtexte (DEU ISSN 1861-5139) **7273**
▼ WeltTrends-Papiere (DEU ISSN 1864-0656) **7273**
▼ WeltTrends-Thesis (DEU ISSN 1866-0738) **7273**
Weltweit Verbunden (DEU ISSN 1866-3109) **7780**
Weltwirtschaftliches Archiv *see* Review of World Economics **1166**
Weltwissen Sachunterricht (DEU) **7928**
Die Weltwoche (CHE ISSN 0043-2660) **3959**
Weltwunder der Kinematographie (DEU ISSN 1430-7987) **6516**
Wembley & Kingsbury Chronicle (GBR) **3873**
Wembley History Society Journal (GBR) **4278**
Wembly Observer *see* Harrow Observer **3866**
• WeMedia Magazine (USA ISSN 1092-9533) **4070**
• Wen Bo/Journal of Museums & Archaeology (CHN ISSN 1000-7954) **6540**
Wen Hsueh Taiwan/Literary Taiwan (TWN ISSN 1023-9898) **5397**
• Wen Shi Zhe/Journal of Literature, History and Philosophy (CHN ISSN 0511-4721) **4482**
• Wenatchee Business Journal (USA ISSN 0043-3365) **1193**
Wend (USA ISSN 1933-3056) **8774**
Wendezeit (CHE) **6648**
Wendy (DEU) **2221**
Wendy (DNK ISSN 1902-5572) **2221**
Wendy (NOR ISSN 0805-1615) **2221**
Wendy (SWE ISSN 1402-5655) **2221**
▼ Wenhua Chanye/China Cultural Industry (CHN ISSN 1674-3520) **4190**
Wenhua Guangchang (CHN) **3828**
Wenhua Yanjiu/Cultural Research (CHN ISSN 1001-2788) **8014**
Wenhua Yicong *see* Shijie Wenhua **5371**
Wenhua Yuekan/Culture Monthly (CHN ISSN 1004-6631) **5397**
• Wenhua Yule/Relish of Culture (CHN ISSN 1000-2928) **4984**
➤ Wenhua Zichan Baocun Xuekan/Journal of Cultural Property Conservation (TWN ISSN 1995-0268) **4190**
• Wenhui Bao/Wenhui Daily (CHN) **3828**
Wenhui Book Review *see* Wenhui Dushu Zhoubao **5397**
Wenhui Daily *see* Wenhui Bao **3828**
Wenhui Dushu Zhoubao/Wenhui Book Review (CHN) **5397**
• Wenjiao Ziliao/Data of Culture and Education (CHN ISSN 1004-8359) **8014**
Wenke Aihaozhe/Liberal Arts Fans (CHN ISSN 1671-1270) **4482**
Wenlun Yuekan/Criticism Monthly (CHN) **5245**
Wenner-Gren International Series *see* Wenner - Gren International Symposium Series **7928**
➤ Wenner - Gren International Symposium Series (GBR ISSN 1475-536X) **7928**
• Wenshan Shifan Gaodeng Zhuanke Xuexiao Xuebao/Wenshan Teachers College. Journal (CHN ISSN 1671-3303) **3010**
Wenshan Teachers College. Journal *see* Wenshan Shifan Gaodeng Zhuanke Xuexiao Xuebao **3010**
• Wenshi Jinghua/Gems of Culture and History (CHN ISSN 1005-4154) **4167**
Wenshi Zhexue Bao *see* Guoli Taiwan Daxue. Wenshi Zhexue Bao **4182**
Wenshi Zhishi/Knowledge of Literature and History (CHN ISSN 1002-9869) **8014**
Wenshizhe *see* Wen Shi Zhe **4482**
Wenskrant (NLD ISSN 1874-6845) **3035**
• ➤ Wenti yu Yanjiu/Issues and Studies (TWN ISSN 0591-2539) **7273**
Wentorfer Courier (DEU) **7193**
Wentworth Bygones (CAN ISSN 0083-8004) **4317**
• Wentworth Courier (AUS) **3797**
Wentzville Union and St. Charles County Record *see* St. Charles County Business Record **1179**
• Wenwu/Cultural Relics (CHN ISSN 0511-4772) **423**
• Wenwu Baohu yu Kaogu Kexue/Sciences of Conservation and Archaeology (CHN ISSN 1005-1538) **423**
• Wenwu Chunqiu/Stories of Relics (CHN ISSN 1003-6555) **423**
Wenwu Tiandi/Cultural Relics World (CHN ISSN 1000-0194) **423**
Wenxian/Documents (CHN ISSN 1000-0437) **639**
Wenxue Bao/Literature Press (CHN) **5397**
• Wenxue Daguan/Music Fashion Humanism Inauguarate Cinema Youth Culture Photo Art (CHN ISSN 1005-4626) **5397**
Wenxue Gang/Literature Port Magazine (CHN ISSN 1003-6830) **5397**
Wenxue Jiaoyu/Literature Education (CHN) **2925**
• Wenxue Pinglun/Literary Review (CHN ISSN 0511-4683) **5397**
Wenxue Pinglunjia/Literary Critics (CHN) **5397**
Wenxue Qingnian/Youth Literature Journal (CHN) **5397**
Wenxue Shaonian/Adolescent Literature (CHN ISSN 1003-7640) **5398**
• Wenxue Yichan/Literary Heritage (CHN ISSN 0257-5914) **5398**
• Wenxue Ziyou Tan (CHN ISSN 1003-2789) **5245**
• Wenyi Bao/Literature and Art News (CHN ISSN 0258-8226) **5398**
Wenyi Lilun/Literary and Art Theories (CHN ISSN 1001-2761) **5245**
Wenyi Lilun Wenzhai Ka/Literature and Art Theories Abstracts on Cards (CHN) **530**
• Wenyi Lilun Yanjiu/Theoretical Studies In Literature and Art (CHN ISSN 0257-0254) **5398**
• Wenyi Pinglun/Literary and Art Review (CHN ISSN 1003-5672) **5245**
• Wenyi Pinglun yu Piping/Theory and Criticism of Literature and Art (CHN ISSN 1002-9583) **5245**
Wenyi Xuexi/Art Studies (CHN ISSN 0510-0380) **526**
• Wenyi Yanjiu/Literature and Art Studies (CHN ISSN 0257-5876) **5398**
• Wenyi Zhengming (CHN ISSN 1003-9538) **5245**
Wenyuan/Literary World *see* Piya Beijing - Wenyuan **5351**
• Wenzhai Zhoubao (CHN) **3828**
• Wenzhai Zhoukan (Hefei)/Weekly Digest (Hefei) (CHN) **3828**
Wenzhai Zhoukan (Kunming)/Weekly Digest (Kunming) (CHN) **3828**
Wenzhaibao/Press Digest (CHN) **3829**
Wenzhou Daily *see* Wenzhou Ribao **3829**
• ➤ Wenzhou Daxue Xuebao (Shehui Kexue Ban)/Wenzhou University. Journal (Social Sciences) (CHN ISSN 1674-3555) **8014**
• ➤ Wenzhou Daxue Xuebao (Ziran Kexue Ban)/Wenzhou University. Journal (Natural Sciences) (CHN ISSN 1674-3563) **7928**
Wenzhou Medical College. Journal *see* Wenzhou Yixueyuan Xuebao **5730**
• Wenzhou Ribao/Wenzhou Daily (CHN) **3829**
Wenzhou Shifan Xueyuan Xuebao/Wenzhou Normal College. Journal *see* Wenzhou Daxue Xuebao (Ziran Kexue Ban) **7928**
Wenzhou University. Journal (Natural Sciences) *see* Wenzhou Daxue Xuebao (Ziran Kexue Ban) **7928**
Wenzhou University. Journal (Social Sciences) *see* Wenzhou Daxue Xuebao (Shehui Kexue Ban) **8014**
Wenzhou Vocational and Technical College. Journal *see* Wenzhou Zhiye Jishu Xueyuan Xuebao **8014**
• Wenzhou Yixueyuan Xuebao/Wenzhou Medical College. Journal (CHN ISSN 1000-2138) **5730**
• Wenzhou Zhiye Jishu Xueyuan Xuebao/Wenzhou Vocational and Technical College. Journal (CHN ISSN 1671-4326) **8014**
• Weon'ye Gwahag Gi'sulji/Korean Journal of Horticultural Science and Technology (KOR ISSN 1226-8763) **822**
• Wer Baut Maschinen in Deutschland (DEU ISSN 0943-3260) **3399**
• Wer Gehoert zu Wem (Online) (DEU) **2034**
• Wer Ist Wer? (DEU ISSN 0172-911X) **646**
Wer Ist Wer in der Schweiz und im Fuerstenstum Liechtenstein? *see* Swiss Biographical Index of Prominent Persons **646**
• Wer Liefert Was? (DEU) **2034**
• Wer Liefert Was? CD - Marketing (DEU) **2034**
• Wer Liefert Was? Central Europe (DEU) **2034**
• Wer Liefert Was? Euro CD Book (DEU) **2034**
Wer und Was - Backgewerbe (DEU ISSN 1618-0526) **2034**
Wer und Was - Fleisch-, Fisch-, Feinkost-Industrie (DEU ISSN 1619-3288) **304**
Wer und Was - Getraenke-Industrie (DEU ISSN 1610-2150) **612**
Wer und Was in der Deutschen Getraenke - Industrie *see* Wer und Was - Getraenke-Industrie **612**
Wer und Was - Koerperpflege-, Wasch- und Reinigungsmittel-Industrie (DEU ISSN 1618-4807) **596**
Wer und Was - Milchwirtschaft (DEU) **2034**
Wer und Was - Obst-, Gemuese-, Kartoffel- und Naehrmittel-Industrie (DEU ISSN 1619-9081) **2034**
Wer und Was - Pharmazeutische Industrie (DEU ISSN 1618-9795) **6885**
Wer und Was - Suesswaren-Industrie (DEU) **2034**
Wer und Was - Tiefkuehl- und Convenience-Indusrie (DEU ISSN 1618-4793) **2034**
Wer - Was - Wo im Studentenwerk (DEU) **2309**
Wer? Wo? Was? in der Hoergeschaedigtenpaedagogik (DEU) **4071**
Werbe Woche (CHE) **37**
• Werbealmanach (AUT ISSN 1817-1060) **37**
Werbeartikel Nachrichten (DEU ISSN 1439-3026) **37**
Werben und Verkaufen *see* W & V **37**
Werben und Verkaufen. Media (DEU ISSN 1866-7058) **1848**
WerbePraxis Aktuell (DEU) **37**
Werbetechnik (DEU ISSN 1437-4935) **37**
Werbung in Deutschland (Year) (DEU) **37**
Werden (DEU ISSN 0508-3133) **1714**
Werder Bremen (DEU) **8251**
De Wereld Achter de Cijfers *see* Fact (Rotterdam) **1288**
Wereld en Zending (NLD ISSN 0165-988X) **7694**
De Wereld Morgen (BEL ISSN 1370-2378) **1607**
➤ De Wereld van het Jonge Kind (NLD ISSN 0165-4772) **2925**
Werelddelen (NLD ISSN 1871-9570) **8078**
De Wereldfietser (NLD ISSN 1382-7278) **8270**
WereldOuders. Nieuwsbrief (NLD ISSN 1874-4958) **4944**
Wereldvisie *see* Reeks Wereldvisie **4939**
Wereldwijd (BEL ISSN 0779-665X) **7273**
Werk! (NLD ISSN 1874-6462) **6705**
• Werk - Bauen & Wohnen (CHE ISSN 0257-9332) **461**
Werk en Handicap (NLD ISSN 1572-8331) **1714**
Werk in Uitvoering *see* Lumpsum Nieuwsbrief **2884**
Werk und Zeit (DEU ISSN 1617-058X) **461**
Werk und Zeit. Brief *see* Werk und Zeit **461**
Werkblad (NLD ISSN 1574-4450) **1714**
Werkblatt (AUT ISSN 0257-3601) **7414**
• Werken (CHL ISSN 0717-5639) **423**
Werken Gelre *see* Vereeniging tot Beofening van Geldersche Geschiedenis, Oudheidkunde en Recht. Werken **4276**
Werken in het Buitenland (NLD ISSN 1872-5198) **1714**
Werken, Uitgegeven door Gelre *see* Vereeniging tot Beofening van Geldersche Geschiedenis, Oudheidkunde en Recht. Werken **4276**
Werken und Wohnen (DEU ISSN 0083-8047) **3624**
Werken van het Oud-Vaderlandsch Recht (NLD) **4167**
Werkgelegenheid en Werkloosheid. Enquete naar de Arbeidskrachten *see* Belgium. Nationaal Instituut voor de Statistiek. Werkgelegenheid en Werkloosheid. Enquete naar de Arbeidskrachten (Year) **1214**
Werkgelegenheid in de Nederlandse Zeehavens (NLD ISSN 1386-7903) **1274**
Werkgelegenheid in Haaglanden *see* Monitor Werkgelegenheid Haaglanden **1698**
Werkgeven (NLD ISSN 1573-644X) **1714**
Werkgever Alert (NLD ISSN 1872-4612) **1714**
Werkgroep Elites. Bulletin (NLD) **4278**
Werkgroep Vlinderfaunistiek. Nieuwsbrief *see* European Invertebrate Survey-Nederland. Nieuwsbrief **942**
Werklocaties (NLD ISSN 1871-8817) **1714**
Werkloosheidswet en Wet op de Arbeidsongschiktheidsverzekering (NLD ISSN 1574-4000) **4527**
Werkmeister/Contremaitre (CHE) **8445**
Werkmeister Studies (NLD) **6960**
Werkplaats voor de Leefomgeving (NLD ISSN 1574-2083) **169**
Die Werkstatt (DEU) **2688**
Werkstatt 3 - Programm (DEU) **7273**
Werkstatt fuer Liturgie und Predigt (DEU ISSN 0938-0868) **7780**
➤ Werkstatt Geschichte (DEU ISSN 0942-704X) **8014**
Werkstatt: Praxis (DEU ISSN 1436-0063) **4431**
Werkstatt und Betrieb (DEU ISSN 0043-2792) **5461**
Werkstatt und Montagepraxis (DEU ISSN 0179-5589) **4127**
Werkstattberichte aus der Betrieblichen Umweltinformatik (DEU ISSN 1860-059X) **1801**
Werkstoff Forschung und Technik *see* W F T **3226**
Werkstoff- und Materialpruefung *see* Informationsdienst F I Z Technik. Werkstoff- und Materialpruefung **3231**
Werkstoffe - in der Fertigung (DEU ISSN 0939-2629) **8445**
Werkstoffe und Konstruktion (DEU ISSN 0932-2450) **3359**
† Werkverkehr und Verlader (BRD ISSN 0175-3061) **8998**
Werkvloer (NLD ISSN 1572-5251) **169**
Werkwijs *see* Infra Actie **3270**
Werkze (NLD) **2947**
Werkzeug Technik (FRA ISSN 0997-6981) **5461**
Werkzeug & Formenbau (DEU ISSN 0934-0912) **5461**
Werkzeuge (DEU ISSN 0939-5342) **5461**
Werlmagazin (DEU) **3859**
Wermlandiana (SWE ISSN 1100-0635) **5398**
➤ Wertheim Publications in Industrial Relations (USA) **1714**
Wertpapier (DEU ISSN 0049-7169) **1659**
Wertpapier-Mitteilungen Allgemeine Verlosungstabelle *see* W M Allgemeine Verlosungstabelle **1389**
Wertpapier-Mitteilungen Teil II: Nachrichten ueber Deutsche Festverzinsliche Werte *see* W M Teil II: Nachrichten ueber Deutsche Festverzinsliche Werte **1389**
Wertpapier-Mitteilungen Teil IIb: Sammelliste Gekuendigter und Verloster Wertpapiere *see* W M Teil IIb: Sammelliste Gekuendigter und Verloster Wertpapiere **1389**
Wertpapier-Mitteilungen Teil III: Nachrichten ueber Deutsche Aktien, Anteile, Genussscheine, Kuxe und Optionsscheine *see* W M Teil III: Nachrichten ueber Deutsche Aktien, Anteile, Genussscheine, Kuxe und Optionsscheine **1389**
Wertpapier-Mitteilungen Teil IV: Zeitschrift fuer Wirtschafts- und Bankrecht *see* W M Teil IV: Zeitschrift fuer Wirtschafts- und Bankrecht **4810**
Wertpapier-Mitteilungen Teil Va: Nachrichten ueber Auslaendische Aktien, Anteile, Optionsscheine und Aktienaehnliche Werte *see* W M Teil Va: Nachrichten ueber Auslaendische Aktien, Anteile, Optionsscheine und Aktienaehnliche Werte **1389**
Wertpapier Mitteilungen Teil Vb: Nachrichten ueber Auslaendische Festverzinsliche Wertpapiere *see* W M Teil Vb: Nachrichten ueber Auslaendische Festverzinsliche Wertpapiere **1389**
Wertpapier Mitteilungen Teil VI: Nachrichten ueber Optionen und Futures *see* W M Teil VI: Nachrichten ueber Optionen und Futures **1390**
Wes-Kaap. Offisiele Koerant/Western Cape. Official Gazette (ZAF) **7476**
Weser-Kurier (DEU) **3859**
Wesley Historical Society. Proceedings (GBR ISSN 0043-2873) **7780**
Wesleyan Advocate *see* Wesleyan Life **7780**
Wesleyan Christian Advocate (USA ISSN 0190-6097) **7780**
Wesleyan Life (USA) **7780**
➤ Wesleyan Poetry Program (USA ISSN 0511-4934) **5437**
Wesleyan Theological Journal (USA ISSN 0092-4245) **7780**
Wesleyan University Alumni Magazine (USA) **3010**
The Wesleyan Woman (USA ISSN 1040-1415) **6960**
Wesleyan World (USA ISSN 0739-0440) **7694**
Wesnuus/West News (ZAF) **3950**
Wespennest (AUT ISSN 1012-7313) **5245**
Wessex Cave Club Journal (GBR) **2774**
Wessex Institute of Technology Transactions on Biomedicine and Health *see* W I T Transactions on Biomedicine and Health **5729**
Wessex Institute of Technology Transactions on Ecology and the Environment *see* W I T Transactions on Ecology and the Environment **3474**
Wessex Institute of Technology Transactions on Engineering Sciences *see* W I T Transactions on Engineering Sciences **3226**
Wessex Institute of Technology Transactions on Information and Communication Technologies *see* W I T Transactions on Information and Communication Technologies **2353**
Wessex Institute of Technology Transactions on Modelling and Simulation *see* W I T Transactions on Modelling and Simulation **2518**
Wessex Institute of Technology Transactions on the Built Environment *see* W I T Transactions on the Built Environment **3287**
Wessex Scene (GBR) **3873**
Wessex Studies in Special Education (GBR ISSN 0144-5359) **3049**
West *see* Xibu **5402**
▼ West 10th (USA ISSN 1941-4374) **5398**
West 47 (IRL ISSN 1649-0126) **5398**
West Africa Annual (NGA ISSN 0083-8144) **4179**
▼ • West Africa Monthly Bulletin of Cereal Prices (USA ISSN 1946-8881) **208**
• ➤ West Africa Review (USA ISSN 1525-4488) **4179**
West Africa Rice Development Association. Annual Report (CIV) **259**
West African Journal of Archaeology (NGA ISSN 0331-3158) **423**
West African Journal of Biological and Applied Chemistry (NGA ISSN 0043-2989) **746**
West African Journal of Education (NGA ISSN 0043-2997) **2925**
➤ West African Journal of Educational and Vocational Measurement (NGA ISSN 0331-0515) **2925**
• West African Journal of Medicine (NGA ISSN 0189-160X) **5730**
West African Journal of Modern Languages/Revue Ouest Africaine des Langues Vivantes (NGA ISSN 0331-0531) **5195**
➤ West African Journal of Nursing (NGA ISSN 1117-9686) **5983**
• ➤ West African Journal of Pharmacology and Drug Research (NGA ISSN 0303-691X) **6885**
West African Journal of Sociology and Political Science (NGA ISSN 0308-4450) **8146**
West African Religion (NGA ISSN 0083-8187) **7694**
West African Science Association. Journal (NGA ISSN 0043-3020) **7929**
West & East/Chung-Mei Yueh-K'an (TWN ISSN 0043-3047) **7273**
West Asia and Africa *see* Xiya Feizhou **8016**
• West Australian Business News (AUS) **1587**
• West Australian Nut and Tree Crop Association. Yearbook (AUS ISSN 0810-6681) **259**
West Bengal (IND ISSN 0049-7193) **7476**
West Bengal. Annual Financial Statement (Budget) (IND) **1274**
West Bengal. Bureau of Applied Economics and Statistics. Statistical Handbook (IND ISSN 0511-5493) **1274**
West Bengal Labour Gazette (IND ISSN 0043-3071) **1714**
West-Brabant Business (NLD ISSN 1574-9894) **1721**
➤ West Branch (USA ISSN 0149-6441) **5438**
• West By Northwest (USA) **5398**
• West Caribbean Business Forecast Report (GBR ISSN 1745-0772) **1524**
West Central Business Journal (USA) **1193**

Title

11024 WEST CENTRAL KENTUCKY FAMILY RESEARCH ASSOCIATION ULRICH'S PERIODICALS

West Central Kentucky Family Research Association. Bulletin (USA) **3787**
West Central Kentucky Family Research Association. Family Records Series (USA) **3787**
West-China Exploration Engineering *see* Xibu Tankuang Gongcheng **6484**
West China Journal of Pharmaceutical Sciences *see* Huaxi Yaoxue Zazhi **6846**
West China Journal of Stomatology *see* Huaxi Kouqiang Yixue Zazhi **5846**
West China Medical Journal *see* Huaxi Yixue **5630**
The West Cities & Counties Graphic Performance Analysis (USA ISSN 1935-5602) **7485**
The West Cities and Counties Graphic Performance Analysis *see* The West Cities & Counties Graphic Performance Analysis **7485**
West Coast *see* America's Favorite Inns, B & Bs & Small Hotels: The West Coast **4381**
• West Coast Conference on Formal Linguistics. Proceedings (USA ISSN 1042-1068) **5195**
▼ • West Coast Leaf (USA ISSN 1945-2101) **2700**
West Coast Libertarian (CAN) **5245**
• ➤ West Coast Line (CAN ISSN 1182-4271) **5398**
West Coast Lock Collectors (USA) **369**
West Coast Peddler (USA ISSN 0199-3356) **369**
West Coast Railway Association News *see* W C R A News **8627**
† West Coast Reliability Symposium (USA ISSN 0083-8217) **8998**
West Coast Sailors (USA ISSN 0273-4699) **8665**
West Coast Woman (USA) **8889**
West Country Business Review (GBR) **1434**
• West Encyclopedia of American Law (USA) **4812**
• ➤ West European Politics (GBR ISSN 0140-2382) **7273**
West Federal Reporter and West's Federal Appendix (USA ISSN 1543-5539) **4967**
West Federal Taxation: Advanced Business Entity Taxation (USA ISSN 1544-3582) **4883**
West Federal Taxation. Comprehensive Volume *see* West's Federal Taxation. Comprehensive Volume **1954**
West Federal Taxation: Taxation of Business Entities (USA ISSN 1544-3590) **4883**
West Forty Seven *see* West 47 **5398**
West-Friese Kroniek (NLD ISSN 1874-9690) **3624**
West Highland Free Press (GBR) **3873**
West Indian Law Journal (JAM ISSN 0253-7370) **4812**
➤ West Indian Medical Journal (JAM ISSN 0043-3144) **5730**
West Indian Medical Journal. Supplement *see* West Indian Medical Journal **5730**
• West Indian Reports (GBR) **4853**
West J E M *see* Western Journal of Emergency Medicine **6075**
West Japan Society of Naval Architects. Abstracts from Research Report *see* Seibu Zosenkai Ronbun Kogai **8530**
West Japan Whales Society. News *see* Kujira **953**
West Kent Property Observer *see* Property Observer **7605**
West Los Angeles Living (USA) **4552**
▼ West Marin Review (USA ISSN 1936-8844) **5054**
West Mercia Business Directory (GBR) **1411**
West Midland Bird Club. Annual Report (GBR ISSN 0963-312X) **916**
West Midland Bird Club. Bulletin (GBR ISSN 1477-6111) **916**
West Midlands Auto Trader *see* Midland Auto Trader **8590**
West Midlands Chamber of Commerce Directory (GBR) **1411**
West Midlands Fire and Civil Defence Authority. Best Value Perfomance Plan (GBR) **3582**
West Midlands Salary Survey (GBR) **1714**
West Nebraska Register (USA) **7823**
West News *see* Wesnuus **3950**
• West Niagara News (CAN) **3820**
West Nile Virus Program (Year): Planning Document for Municipalities (CAN ISSN 1910-6319) **7545**
West Pasco Press (USA) **4812**
West Rand Times (ZAF) **3950**
West Riding Farmer (GBR ISSN 0955-0291) **169**
West River Catholic (USA) **7823**
West Shore Magazine (USA ISSN 1941-8884) **5086**
West Side Story (USA) **2925**
• West Sussex County Times (Horsham Edition) (GBR ISSN 0963-228X) **3968**
• West Sussex County Times (South Downs Edition) (GBR ISSN 0963-2271) **3968**
West Sussex Gazette (GBR ISSN 0963-3898) **3873**
• West Tennessee Historical Society. Papers (USA ISSN 0361-6215) **4317**
West Tenth *see* West 10th **5398**
West Texas Angelus (USA ISSN 0273-7345) **7823**
West Texas Catholic (USA ISSN 0745-516X) **7823**
West Texas Geological Society. Bulletin (USA ISSN 0739-5957) **2774**
West Texas Geological Society. Fieldtrip Guidebooks (USA) **2774**
West Texas Geological Society. Special Publications (USA) **2774**
➤ West Texas Historical Association Yearbook (USA ISSN 0886-6155) **4317**
The West University Buzz (USA) **3992**
• West University of Timisoara. Annals. Series of Chemistry (ROM ISSN 1224-9513) **2084**
West Virginia A F L - C I O Observer (USA ISSN 0190-3268) **4605**
➤ West Virginia Academy of Science. Proceedings (USA ISSN 0096-4263) **7929**
West Virginia. Agricultural and Forestry Experiment Station. Annual Report (USA) **169**
West Virginia. Agricultural and Forestry Experiment Station. Bulletin (USA) **169**
West Virginia. Agricultural and Forestry Experiment Station. Current Report (USA) **169**
West Virginia: All-Industries *see* Harris Directory. West Virginia All-Industries **2003**
West Virginia: An Economic-Statistical Profile (USA) **1411**
West Virginia and Regional History Collection Newsletter (USA ISSN 1041-8695) **4167**
West Virginia Association of College English Teachers. Bulletin (USA ISSN 0887-4409) **5398**
West Virginia Beverage Journal (USA ISSN 1054-6553) **612**
• West Virginia Business Directory (USA ISSN 1047-9007) **2034**
West Virginia Business Index (USA ISSN 0195-4644) **1193**
West Virginia C.P.A. (USA ISSN 0043-3217) **1303**
• West Virginia Children, Youth and Family Laws Annotated (USA ISSN 1541-6704) **4915**
West Virginia Cities & Counties Graphic Performance Analysis (USA ISSN 1935-5424) **7485**
West Virginia Coal Facts (USA ISSN 0091-5513) **6488**
West Virginia. Commission on Aging. Annual Progress Report (USA ISSN 0083-8438) **4057**
West Virginia Construction News (USA) **1043**
West Virginia Corporations, Partnerships and Associations Law Annotated (USA) **4883**
• West Virginia Criminal and Traffic Law Manual (USA ISSN 1525-1098) **4900**
West Virginia Dental Association News *see* W V D A News **5869**
West Virginia. Department of Agriculture. Market Bulletin (USA ISSN 0025-3545) **170**
West Virginia Domestic Relations Annotated *see* West Virginia Children, Youth and Family Laws Annotated **4915**
West Virginia Economic Summary (USA) **1714**
West Virginia Education Directory (USA ISSN 0085-8099) **2926**
West Virginia Employment and Earnings Trends: Annual Summary (USA) **1714**
• West Virginia Employment Law Letter (USA ISSN 1083-0049) **4812**
West Virginia Forestry Notes (USA ISSN 0197-1387) **3707**
West Virginia Fourth Estatesman (USA) **2309**
West Virginia Game & Fish (USA ISSN 0897-9162) **8341**
West Virginia. Geological and Economic Survey. Annual Report (USA ISSN 0161-1011) **2774**
West Virginia Geological and Economic Survey. Bulletin (USA ISSN 0363-1052) **2774**
• West Virginia History (USA ISSN 0043-325X) **4317**
West Virginia. Human Rights Commission. Report (USA ISSN 0083-8594) **7218**
• West Virginia Law Review (USA ISSN 0043-3268) **4812**
West Virginia Lawyer (USA) **4812**
West Virginia Legionnaire (USA ISSN 0745-2799) **6454**
West Virginia. Legislature. Commission on Special Investigations. Report to the West Virginia Legislature (USA) **7193**
West Virginia Libraries (USA ISSN 0043-3276) **5054**
• West Virginia Manufacturers Register (USA ISSN 0893-2824) **2034**
West Virginia: Manufacturing *see* Harris Directory. West Virginia Manufacturing **2003**
➤ West Virginia Medical Journal (USA ISSN 0043-3284) **5730**
West Virginia Mineral Industries Directory (USA) **6483**
• West Virginia Motor Vehicle Laws (USA) **8520**
• West Virginia Nurse (USA ISSN 1074-8091) **5984**
West Virginia. Office of Miner's Health, Safety & Training. Report & Digest Directory (USA) **6483**
West Virginia Practice Handbook (USA) **4812**
West Virginia Probate & Related Laws Annotated (USA) **4906**
West Virginia Probate and Related Laws Annotated *see* West Virginia Probate & Related Laws Annotated **4906**
West Virginia Research League. Statistical Handbook (USA ISSN 0893-4568) **7485**
West Virginia Rules of Court *see* Court Rules Pamphlet(s). West Virginia Rules of Court, State and Federal **4949**
West Virginia School Directory *see* M D R's School Directory. West Virginia **2960**
West Virginia School Journal (USA ISSN 0274-8606) **2926**
West Virginia Shakespeare and Renaissance Association. Selected Papers (USA ISSN 0885-9574) **5398**
West Virginia Tax Calendar (USA) **1954**
West Virginia Transporter (USA) **8678**
West Virginia Union List of Serials (USA ISSN 0512-4743) **639**
West Virginia University. Agricultural and Forestry Experiment Station. Circular (USA ISSN 0889-8065) **170**
West Virginia University Alumni Magazine (USA) **2309**
West Virginia University Alumni News (USA) **2309**
• West Virginia University. Philological Papers (Morgantown, 1947) (USA ISSN 0363-3470) **5195**
West Wimmera Landcare News (AUS ISSN 1449-1796) **3474**
West Word (CAN ISSN 1184-678X) **5398**
Westar Institute. Seminar Papers (USA) **7694**
• Westbridge Art Market Report (CAN ISSN 1191-3371) **526**
Westchester Bar Journal (USA ISSN 0746-1844) **4812**
Westchester Business Review (USA) **1193**
Westchester Commerce (USA ISSN 0888-3459) **1411**
Westchester - Connecticut Office Buildings (USA) **7615**
Westchester Connections (USA ISSN 1059-4272) **3787**
Westchester Country Club News (USA) **2271**
• Westchester County Business Journal (USA ISSN 1057-686X) **1524**
• Westchester County Weekly (USA) **3992**
• Westchester Family (USA ISSN 1043-6774) **2171**
Westchester Health & Life (USA) **5086**
Westchester Health and Life *see* Westchester Health & Life **5086**
Westchester Historian (USA ISSN 0049-7266) **4317**
Westchester Law Journal (USA ISSN 0049-7274) **4812**
Westchester Life (USA ISSN 1541-4019) **3992**
Westchester Magazine (USA) **3992**
Westchester Parent (USA) **2171**
Westchester Planning (USA ISSN 0363-356X) **7476**
Westchester Realtor (USA ISSN 0043-339X) **7615**
▼ The Westchester Review (USA ISSN 1938-6486) **5245**
Westchester Spotlight *see* Westchester Magazine **3992**
The Westchester WAG *see* The WAG **3992**
Westcoast Fisherman (CAN ISSN 0836-8600) **3611**
Westcoast Mariner (CAN ISSN 0844-5567) **8665**
The Westcoast Reader (CAN ISSN 0822-7225) **2947**
Westcoast Speculator (CAN) **1659**
• Westdeutsche Allgemeine Zeitung (DEU) **3860**
Westdeutsche Gesellschaft fuer Familienkunde. Mitteilungen (DEU ISSN 0172-1879) **3787**
Westdeutsche Kegler Rundschau (DEU) **8251**
Westdeutsche Zeitung (DEU) **3860**
Westdeutscher Tuermer (DEU) **7615**
Westender (GBR) **3873**
Westerheem (NLD ISSN 0166-4301) **423**
➤ Westerly (AUS ISSN 0043-342X) **5398**
Westermarck-Seura. Transactions (FIN ISSN 0357-1823) **8146**
Western Alcohol and Drugs Education Society (W A D E S) Herald *see* W A D E S Herald **2700**
Western Alumni Gazette (CAN ISSN 1189-6272) **2309**
• ➤ Western American Literature (USA ISSN 0043-3462) **5398**
Western & South Wales Auto Trader (GBR ISSN 0958-4005) **8611**
• Western Appeal Cases (CAN) **4812**
▼ Western Art & Architecture (USA ISSN 1942-3012) **526**
▼ Western Art Collector (USA ISSN 1936-7546) **526**
Western Association for Art Conservation Newsletter *see* W A A C Newsletter **525**
Western Association of Fish and Wildlife Agencies. Proceedings (USA ISSN 0198-6600) **2631**
Western Association of Graduate Schools. Proceedings of the Annual Meeting (USA ISSN 0511-6848) **3010**
Western Association of Map Libraries. Information Bulletin (USA ISSN 0049-7282) **5055**
Western Association of Map Libraries. Occasional Papers (USA) **5055**
• Western Australia. Agriculture Protection Board. Annual Report (Years) (AUS ISSN 0511-6872) **170**
Western Australia. Anti-Corruption Commission. Annual Report *see* Western Australia. Corruption and Crime Commission. Annual Report **4900**
• Western Australia. Corruption and Crime Commission. Annual Report (AUS ISSN 1832-9713) **4900**
• Western Australia. Department of Agriculture. Annual Report (AUS) **170**
Western Australia. Department of Agriculture. Bulletin *see* Western Australia. Department of Agriculture. Bulletin **170**
• Western Australia. Department of Agriculture. Bulletin (AUS ISSN 1833-7236) **170**
• Western Australia. Department of Agriculture. Farmnote (AUS ISSN 0726-934X) **170**
Western Australia. Department of Agriculture. Primary Focus (AUS) **170**
• Western Australia. Department of Agriculture. Resource Management Technical Reports (AUS ISSN 1039-7205) **259**
Western Australia. Department of Conservation and Land Management. Annual Report *see* Western Australia. Department of Environment and Conservation. Annual Report **2631**
Western Australia. Department of Corrective Services. Annual Report (AUS) **2671**
• Western Australia. Department of Environment and Conservation. Annual Report (AUS ISSN 1835-1131) **2631**
Western Australia. Department of Environment. Annual Report *see* Western Australia. Department of Environment and Conservation. Annual Report **2631**
Western Australia. Department of Environment. Technical Series (AUS ISSN 1449-9622) **3474**
• Western Australia. Department of Fisheries. Annual Report (AUS ISSN 1031-6930) **3611**
• Western Australia. Department of Transport. Annual Report (AUS ISSN 1035-1671) **8520**
• Western Australia. Environmental Protection Authority. Annual Report (AUS) **2631**
• Western Australia. Fisheries Department. Fisheries Management Paper (AUS ISSN 0819-4327) **3611**
• Western Australia. Fisheries Department. Fisheries Management Report (AUS ISSN 1329-7902) **3611**
• Western Australia. Fisheries Department. Fisheries Research Reports (AUS ISSN 1035-4549) **3611**
• Western Australia. Fisheries Department. Occasional Publications (AUS ISSN 1447-2058) **3611**
Western Australia. Geological Survey. 1: 250,000 Geological Series. Explanatory Notes (AUS ISSN 0729-3720) **2774**
• Western Australia. Geological Survey. Annual Review (AUS ISSN 1324-504X) **2774**
• Western Australia. Geological Survey. Bulletin (AUS ISSN 0085-8137) **2774**
• Western Australia. Geological Survey. Records (AUS ISSN 0728-2311) **2774**
• Western Australia. Geological Survey. Report (AUS ISSN 0508-4741) **2774**
• Western Australia. Government Gazette (AUS ISSN 0043-3489) **7476**
• Western Australia. Industrial Gazette (AUS) **1434**
Western Australia Law Almanac (AUS ISSN 0085-8161) **4812**
Western Australia - Northern Territory Nursery Register (AUS) **3754**
• Western Australia. Office of the Public Sector Standards Commissioner. Annual Report (AUS ISSN 1832-9411) **7477**
Western Australia Organic Life *see* W A Organic Life **3753**
Western Australia. Recreational Fishing Advisory Committee. Paper (AUS ISSN 1443-4814) **8341**
Western Australia Reports (AUS) **4967**
• Western Australia. Water Corporation. Development Services Branch. Information Sheet (AUS ISSN 1833-8283) **8841**
Western Australia Wildlife Management Program (AUS ISSN 0816-9713) **967**
Western Australian Department of Training. Community Relations Section. Handbook (AUS) **3010**
Western Australian Economic Review (Online) *see* Economic Compass **1479**
The Western Australian Fishing Magazine (AUS ISSN 1832-3251) **8341**
Western Australian Government Business Migration Update *see* Western Australian Government State Migration Update **1969**
• Western Australian Government State Migration Update (AUS ISSN 1833-9301) **1969**
Western Australian Land Information Service News *see* WALIS News **208**
• Western Australian Museum. Annual Report (Online) (AUS) **6540**
Western Australian Museum. Annual Report (Print) *see* Western Australian Museum. Annual Report (Online) **6540**
➤ Western Australian Museum. Records (AUS ISSN 0312-3162) **6540**
➤ Western Australian Museum. Records. Supplement (AUS ISSN 0313-122X) **6540**
➤ The Western Australian Naturalist (AUS ISSN 0726-9609) **7929**
• Western Australian Prospect (AUS ISSN 1037-4590) **1659**
Western Australian Research Activities (AUS ISSN 1323-6229) **2821**
• Western Australian Resource Development Services. Directory (AUS ISSN 0816-2271) **2034**
Western Australian Statistical Indicators (Online) *see* Australia. Bureau of Statistics. Western Australian Office. Western Australian Statistical Indicators (Online) **8355**
Western Australia's Best Kitchens and Bathrooms *see* W A's Best Kitchens and Bathrooms **4552**
Western Australia's Young People *see* Australia. Bureau of Statistics. Western Australian Office. Western Australia's Young People **7617**
Western Banking (USA) **1390**
Western Beef Producer (USA ISSN 1074-0031) **304**
Western-Bestseller (CZE ISSN 1212-916X) **5413**
➤ Western Birds (USA ISSN 0160-1121) **916**
Western Blue Chip Economic Forecast (USA ISSN 1042-6795) **1524**
Western Buddhist (GBR ISSN 0144-9818) **7703**
• Western Builder (USA ISSN 0043-3535) **1043**
Western Builder. Annual Buyers Guide & Directory (USA) **1043**
Western Builder. Annual Buyers Guide and Directory *see* Western Builder. Annual Buyers Guide & Directory **1043**
Western Canada and Alaska *see* CampBook: Western Canada and Alaska **8691**

Link to your serials resources and content with ulrichsweb.com

Western Canada and Alaska - Alberta, British Columbia, Manitoba, Northwest Territories, Saskatchewan, Yukon Territory and Alaska TourBook *see* TourBook: Western Canada and Alaska **8762**
Western Canada Highway News Magazine (CAN) **8678**
Western Canada Stallion Directory *see* Western Canadian Stallion Edition **8300**
Western Canada Stallion Edition *see* Western Canadian Stallion Edition **8300**
Western Canadian (CAN) **3820**
Western Canadian Aerospace Industry Capabilities Guide (CAN ISSN 1499-2396) **75**
Western Canadian Dairy Seminar. Proceedings *see* Advances in Dairy Technology **261**
Western Canadian Stallion Edition (CAN ISSN 1914-0835) **8300**
Western Cape Business (ZAF ISSN 1816-370X) **1193**
Western Cape Business Register (ZAF) **2034**
Western Cape. Official Gazette *see* Wes-Kaap. Offisiele Koerant **7476**
• Western Cape Provincial Legislation Library (ZAF ISSN 1683-2701) **4812**
Western Carolinian (USA) **2309**
Western Catholic Reporter (CAN ISSN 0512-5235) **7823**
Western Caver (AUS) **2774**
• Western City (USA ISSN 0279-5337) **7505**
Western Civilization *see* The Best Test Preparation for the C L E P. Western Civilization II **4132**
Western Cleaner and Launderer (USA ISSN 0049-741X) **2244**
Western Clippings (USA) **6516**
Western Concept (USA) **2309**
Western Courier (USA) **2309**
• ➤ Western Criminology Review (USA ISSN 1096-4886) **2671**
• Western Daily Press (GBR ISSN 0307-2738) **3873**
Western Dairy Business (USA ISSN 1528-4360) **269**
Western Dairy Farmer Quarterly Magazine (CAN ISSN 1194-9511) **269**
Western District Farmer (AUS) **170**
Western District Holiday News (AUS) **8774**
Western Dry Kiln Association. Proceedings (USA) **3717**
• Western Economic Developments (USA) **1524**
Western Economic Diversification Canada. Sustainable Development Strategy/ Diversification de l'Economie de l'Ouest Strategie pour un Developpement Durable (CAN ISSN 1912-774X) **1908**
Western Edition of Notices to Mariners *see* Notices to Mariners Publication (Western Edition) (Print) **8655**
Western Energy (USA ISSN 1062-4147) **3150**
Western - English Industry Report (USA) **2250**
Western Europe (Year) (GBR ISSN 0953-6906) **7193**
Western Europe (Year) (USA ISSN 1056-4373) **8774**
Western European Food Industry (Year) (GBR) **3667**
Western European Food Report (GBR) **3667**
Western European Market & Media Fact (GBR ISSN 1469-6614) **2349**
Western European Stages (USA ISSN 1050-1991) **8484**
Western European Union. Institute for Security Studies. Occasional Papers *see* European Union Institute for Security Studies. Occasional Papers **7234**
• Western Farm Press (USA ISSN 1525-1217) **170**
• Western Farm Press Daily (USA) **259**
• The Western Farmer - Stockman (USA ISSN 1542-2054) **304**
Western Fisheries (AUS ISSN 1320-3924) **3611**
The Western Flyer (AUS ISSN 0817-5802) **5413**
• Western Folklore (USA ISSN 0043-373X) **3624**
Western Football *see* Athlon's Western Football **8221**
Western Foundation of Vertebrate Zoology. Occasional Papers (USA ISSN 0511-7542) **967**
Western Foundation of Vertebrate Zoology. Proceedings (USA ISSN 0511-7550) **967**
Western Frontier Library (USA ISSN 0083-887X) **4317**
Western Frontiersmen Series (USA ISSN 0083-8888) **4317**
Western Fruit and Vegetable (USA) **208**
• Western Fruit Grower (USA ISSN 0164-6001) **259**
Western Geographer (AUS ISSN 0313-8860) **4034**
Western Geography (CAN ISSN 1187-1121) **4034**
Western Grocer Magazine (CAN ISSN 0705-906X) **3682**
• Western Grower and Shipper (USA ISSN 0043-3799) **259**
Western H V A C R News *see* H V A C R Business **4120**
Western Herald (USA) **2309**
• The Western Historical Quarterly (USA ISSN 0043-3810) **4317**
Western Hog Journal (CAN ISSN 0225-3488) **304**
Western Horizons (CAN ISSN 0043-3829) **6885**
Western Horse (DEU ISSN 0933-9345) **8300**
The Western Horse (USA ISSN 1062-3914) **8300**
Western Horse Breeders Annual (AUS ISSN 1449-7581) **8300**
• Western Horseman (USA ISSN 0043-3837) **8300**
Western - Hotelier (CAN ISSN 1483-4715) **4400**
Western Hotelier Magazine (CAN) **4400**
➤ Western Humanities Review (USA ISSN 0043-3845) **5398**
Western Institute for the Deaf and Hard of Hearing. Quarterly Newsletter *see* The W I D H H Wave **4077**
Western Institute for the Deaf & Hard of Hearing Wave *see* The W I D H H Wave **4077**
• Western Interiors and Design (USA ISSN 1543-2807) **4552**
The Western Investor (CAN) **7615**
Western Japanese Research Society for Spine. Journal *see* Nishinihon Sekitsui Kenkyukaishi **6068**
• ➤ Western Journal of Applied Forestry (USA ISSN 0885-6095) **3707**
• ➤ The Western Journal of Black Studies (USA ISSN 0197-4327) **3572**
• ➤ Western Journal of Communication (GBR ISSN 1057-0314) **5195**
• Western Journal of Emergency Medicine (USA ISSN 1936-900X) **6075**
➤ The Western Journal of Graduate Research (CAN ISSN 0843-9699) **3010**
• ➤ Western Journal of Nursing Research (USA ISSN 0193-9459) **5984**
Western Kentucky Catholic (USA) **7823**
Western Kentucky Journal (USA ISSN 1072-6756) **3787**
Western Lands and Waters Series (USA ISSN 0083-8934) **2632**
Western Leader (NZL ISSN 1170-1145) **3920**
• Western Legal History (USA ISSN 0896-2189) **4812**
Western Legislature (USA) **7193**
Western Livestock Journal Weekly (USA ISSN 0094-6710) **304**
Western Livestock Reporter (USA) **304**
Western Living (Vancouver Edition) (CAN ISSN 0824-0604) **3820**
Western Living Travels (CAN ISSN 1910-1236) **8774**
• Western Lumber (Year) Buyers Manual (USA) **3717**
• Western Lumber Facts (USA) **3709**
Western Lumber Production Statistics for Analysis *see* Western Wood Products Association. Statistics for Analysis **3717**
Western Magazin (DEU) **4317**
• Western Mail (DEU ISSN 0944-0658) **6628**
Western Maryland Genealogy (USA ISSN 0747-7805) **3787**
Western Massachusetts Business Magazine (USA) **1193**
Western Massachusetts Law Review (USA) **4812**
Western Michigan Business Revire *see* Business Review Western Michigan **1075**
Western Mining Directory (USA ISSN 0162-9026) **6483**
Western Montana Genealogical Society Bulletin (USA ISSN 0748-2515) **3787**
Western Native News (CAN ISSN 0845-7220) **3572**
• Western New England Law Review (USA ISSN 0190-6593) **4812**
Western New York (USA ISSN 1552-6097) **8774**
• Western New York Catholic (USA ISSN 1079-1205) **7823**
Western New York Family (USA) **2171**
Western New York Genealogical Society Journal (USA ISSN 0890-6858) **3787**
Western New York Heritage (USA ISSN 1097-0568) **4317**
Western New York Library Resources Council Watch Newsletter *see* W N Y L R C Watch Newsletter **5054**
Western New York Motorist (USA ISSN 0043-3977) **8611**
Western Nigeria Illustrated (NGA) **3921**
• Western North American Naturalist (USA ISSN 1527-0904) **967**
• Western North American Naturalist. Monographs (USA ISSN 1545-0228) **967**
Western North Carolina Business Journal *see* W N C Business Journal **1193**
Western Ontario Series *see* The Western Ontario Series in Philosophy of Science **6960**
➤ The Western Ontario Series in Philosophy of Science (NLD ISSN 1566-659X) **6960**
Western Outdoor News (USA ISSN 0049-7479) **8341**
Western Outdoors (USA ISSN 0043-4000) **8341**
Western Pacific Information *see* W E S T P A C Information **2820**
Western Pennsylvania Bluegrass Committee. Newsletter (USA) **6628**
Western Pennsylvania History (USA ISSN 1525-4755) **4318**
Western People (CAN) **3820**
Western People (IRL ISSN 1393-595X) **3895**
† • Western Pferde Journal (DEU) **8998**
➤ Western Pharmacology Society. Proceedings (USA ISSN 0083-8969) **6885**
Western Places (USA ISSN 1092-8782) **4318**
Western Policies (IRL) **7193**
Western Potato and Onion Report (USA) **208**
Western Poultry Disease Conference. Proceedings (USA) **304**
• Western Power Corporation. Annual Report (AUS) **3150**
Western Press (USA) **2309**
▼ • Western Price Summary (USA ISSN 1934-9793) **3717**
• Western Producer (CAN ISSN 0043-4094) **170**
Western Publications Association News - E-mail *see* W P A News - E-mail **7576**
Western Railroader (USA) **8627**
Western Real Estate Business (USA ISSN 1547-965X) **7616**
Western Real Estate News (USA ISSN 0043-4124) **7616**
Western Recorder (USA ISSN 0043-4132) **7780**
Western Regional Industrial Directory (USA) **3372**
Western Regions Studies *see* Xiyu Yanjiu **8016**
Western Reserve Historical Society News (USA ISSN 0882-3154) **4318**
Western Restaurant News (CAN) **4400**
Western Retailer (USA ISSN 1044-7768) **215**
Western Roofing - Insulation - Siding (USA ISSN 0164-5803) **1043**
The Western Sahara *see* L' Ouest Saharien **4468**
• Western Sahara Weekly News (ESH) **3790**
The Western Scholar (USA ISSN 1550-5731) **4482**
▼ • Western Shooting Horse (USA ISSN 1937-6405) **8300**
Western Show News (USA) **4062**
Western Slope Fence Post (USA) **170**
Western Snow Conference. Proceedings (USA ISSN 0161-0589) **2799**
† • Western Society for French History. Proceedings of the Annual Meeting (USA ISSN 0099-0329) **8998**
Western Society of Malacologists. Annual Report (USA ISSN 0361-1175) **967**
Western Society of Periodontology. Journal. Periodontal Abstracts (USA ISSN 0148-4893) **5751**
Western Society of Weed Science. Proceedings (USA ISSN 0091-4487) **822**
Western Society of Weed Science. Research Progress Report (USA ISSN 0090-8142) **822**
Western Spectrum (CAN ISSN 0317-333X) **3010**
Western Sportsman (CAN ISSN 0709-1532) **8341**
• Western Standard (CAN ISSN 1710-1026) **3820**
• Western Star (CAN ISSN 0839-3664) **3820**
Western State College Top O' the World (USA) **2309**
• Western State University Law Review (USA ISSN 0362-8892) **4812**
Western States Jewish History (USA ISSN 0749-5471) **7731**
Western States Petroleum Industry (USA) **6797**
Western Style Travelogue (USA) **3992**
Western Sun (USA) **2309**
Western Sunday Independent (GBR) **3873**
Western Sweden Chamber of Commerce. Membership Directory (SWE) **1411**
• Western Teacher (AUS ISSN 0310-5369) **2926**
Western Texan (USA) **2309**
Western Viking (USA ISSN 1520-5061) **3572**
Western Water (USA ISSN 0735-5424) **8842**
▼ Western Wealth Management Business (USA ISSN 1942-5007) **1659**
• Western Weekly Reports (CAN ISSN 0049-7525) **4812**
• Western Wood Products Association. Coast Index Grade Price Average (USA) **3717**
• Western Wood Products Association. Export Report (USA ISSN 0730-5176) **3709**
• Western Wood Products Association. Import Report (USA ISSN 1536-2078) **3717**
• Western Wood Products Association. Inland Index Grade Price Average (USA) **3717**
Western Wood Products Association. Quarterly Injury & Illness Incidence Report (USA ISSN 0195-9344) **6691**
Western Wood Products Association. Statistical Yearbook (USA ISSN 0195-931X) **3709**
Western Wood Products Association. Statistics for Analysis (USA ISSN 1523-3960) **3717**
Western Woodland (CAN) **3717**
† Western World (CZE ISSN 1213-5119) **8998**
Western Writers Series (USA ISSN 0886-7348) **5245**
The Westerner (USA ISSN 0279-3628) **2309**
Westernliving Travels *see* Western Living Travels **8774**
Westernlore Ghost Town Series (USA ISSN 0083-9019) **4318**
Westerns & Serials (USA) **6516**
Westerville Magazine (USA) **5086**
Westfaelische Beitraege zur Niederdeutschen Philologie (DEU ISSN 1615-2549) **5195**
Westfaelische Forschungen (DEU ISSN 0083-9027) **4278**
• Westfaelische Nachrichten (DEU) **3860**
Westfaelische Quellen und Archivpublikationen (DEU ISSN 0946-0594) **4278**
Westfaelische Rundschau (DEU) **3860**
Westfaelische Wilhelms-Universitaet. Journal *see* Forschungs-Journal **7855**
Westfaelische Wilhelms-Universitaet Muenster. Institut fuer Allgemeine Sprachwissenschaft. Arbeitshefte (DEU ISSN 0175-5382) **5195**
Westfaelische Wilhelms-Universitaet Muenster. Lehrstuhl fuer Betriebswirtschaftslehre, insb. Distribution und Handel. Arbeitspapiere *see* Arbeitspapiere - Distribution & Handel **1879**
Westfaelischen Museum fuer Naturkunde. Abhandlungen (DEU ISSN 0175-3495) **7929**
Westfaelischer Anzeiger (DEU ISSN 0177-5804) **3860**
Westfaelisches Aerzteblatt (DEU ISSN 0340-5257) **5730**
Westfaelisches Freilichtmuseum Detmold. Schriften (DEU ISSN 0930-9144) **360**
Westfalen-Blatt (DEU) **3860**
Westfalen Tennis (DEU) **8251**
Westfalenpost (DEU) **3860**
Westfalenspiegel (DEU ISSN 0508-5942) **4278**
Westfalia Sacra (DEU) **7694**
• Westfield Center. Newsletter (Email) (USA) **6628**
Westfield Publications in Medieval and Renaissance Studies (BEL) **4278**
▼ Westheimer Life Magazine (USA ISSN 1941-5028) **5086**
Westie Imprint (USA) **6816**
Westinghouse Savannah River Co. Technical Report (USA) **3175**
• Westlaw (USA) **4812**
• Westlaw Edge for Associates (USA) **4812**
• WestlawPRO (USA) **4812**
Westlife (GBR) **6628**
Westlife Official *see* Westlife **6628**
Westmeath Examiner (IRL ISSN 1393-5623) **3895**
Westmeath Independent (IRL ISSN 1393-046X) **3895**
The Westminster College Library of Biblical Symbolism (USA ISSN 1079-5723) **7694**
Westminster Confidential (GBR ISSN 1355-9753) **7193**
Westminster Letter (GBR ISSN 0964-1637) **7477**
➤ Westminster Magazine (USA ISSN 1062-6700) **2309**
• ➤ Westminster Papers in Communication and Culture (GBR ISSN 1744-6708) **2344**
The Westminster Tanner-McMurrin Lectures on the History and Philosophy of Religion at Westminster College (USA ISSN 1049-9792) **2926**
• Westminster Theological Journal (USA ISSN 0043-4388) **7694**
Westmont (USA) **2309**
Westmount Examiner (CAN ISSN 0834-7557) **3820**
Westmount Historian (CAN ISSN 1496-4066) **4167**
Westmuensterland (DEU) **3860**
Westostpassagen (DEU ISSN 1860-4692) **5398**
Westport (USA) **3992**
Der Westpreusse (DEU ISSN 0043-4418) **3860**
• Westpreussen - Jahrbuch (DEU ISSN 0511-8484) **4278**
▼ West's 50 State Surveys: Family Law (USA ISSN 1942-0315) **4915**
West's Alabama Reporter (USA ISSN 1076-268X) **4812**
• West's Alaska Reporter (USA ISSN 1076-2671) **4812**
West's Annotated California Codes (USA) **4812**
West's Annotated Indiana Code (USA) **4812**
West's Arkansas Civil Procedure Laws *see* Arkansas Civil Procedure Laws **4827**
West's Atlantic Reporter (USA ISSN 1048-3810) **4812**
• West's Bankruptcy Code, Rules and Forms (USA ISSN 1079-381X) **4813**
West's Bankruptcy Digest (USA ISSN 0272-5991) **4813**
West's Bankruptcy Reporter (USA ISSN 0199-5782) **1390**
West's Bankruptcy Series (USA) **4813**
West's California Code Forms (USA) **4967**
• West's California Reporter (USA ISSN 8750-2623) **4813**
▼ West's Code of Federal Regulations Annotated. Title 20, Employees' Benefits (USA ISSN 1942-0234) **1714**
▼ West's Code of Federal Regulations Annotated. Title 37, Patents, Trademarks, and Copyrights (USA ISSN 1942-0250) **6760**
West's Code of Federal Regulations Annotated. Title 42, Public Health (USA ISSN 1942-0242) **7545**
West's Colorado Civil Procedure Law (USA ISSN 1932-2194) **4844**
West's Delaware Report *see* Delaware Reporter **4655**
West's Education Law Reporter (USA ISSN 0744-8716) **4813**
West's Federal Appendix (USA ISSN 1537-7032) **4967**
West's Federal Case News (USA ISSN 0162-2005) **4967**
• West's Federal Reporter (USA ISSN 1048-3888) **4844**
West's Federal Rules Decisions *see* National Reporter System. Federal Rules Decisions **4739**
West's Federal Supplement (USA ISSN 1047-7306) **4813**
West's Federal Taxation: Advanced Taxation *see* West Federal Taxation: Advanced Business Entity Taxation **4883**
West's Federal Taxation. Comprehensive Volume (USA ISSN 0741-5184) **1954**
West's Federal Taxation: Introduction to Business Entities *see* West Federal Taxation: Taxation of Business Entities **4883**
West's Fifty State Surveys: Family Law *see* West's 50 State Surveys: Family Law **4915**
West's Florida Statutes Annotated (USA) **4813**
West's General Digest (USA ISSN 0511-8522) **4813**
West's Hawaii Reports (USA ISSN 1079-1957) **4967**
• West's Illinois Family Law and Court Rules (USA) **4915**
West's Jury Verdicts. Arizona Reports (USA ISSN 1559-8950) **4813**
West's Jury Verdicts. Colorado Reports (USA ISSN 1933-7515) **4813**
West's Jury Verdicts. Connecticut Reports (USA ISSN 1933-7531) **4813**

Title

▼ new title　　　† ceased　　　• electronic media　　　➤ refereed

DIRECTORY 2010 WISCONSIN. DEPARTMENT OF FINANCIAL INSTITUTIONS. ANNUAL 11031

Winnipeg Men (CAN ISSN 1719-6663) **6302**
• Winnipeg Sun (CAN ISSN 0711-3773) **3820**
Winona Courier (USA) **7823**
Winona Courier see Courier (Winona) **7794**
Winq (NLD ISSN 1871-7985) **4380**
Winsford & Middlewich Guradian see Middlewich Guardian **3968**
Winston-Salem Magazine (USA ISSN 8755-9587) **3993**
Winter Bird Highlights (USA ISSN 1933-1061) **917**
Winter Holidays Market Report see Key Note Market Report: Winter Holidays **8727**
• Winter Simulation Conference. Proceedings (USA ISSN 0891-7736) **2518**
Der Wintergarten (DEU ISSN 1860-2657) **3754**
Der Wintergarten (DEU) **4552**
Wintergreen (USA) **5247**
Winterhuder Wochenblatt (DEU) **3860**
Wintersalon. 19e eeuw see Wintersalon. Negentiende eeuw **526**
Wintersalon. 20e eeuw see Wintersalon. Twintigste eeuw **526**
Wintersalon. Negentiende eeuw (NLD ISSN 1871-5508) **526**
Wintersalon. Twintigste eeuw (NLD ISSN 1871-5516) **526**
Winterthur Magazine (USA ISSN 1070-2156) **526**
• ➤ Winterthur Portfolio (USA ISSN 0084-0416) **526**
Winx (ESP ISSN 1698-5370) **2222**
▼ Winx Club (DEU) **2222**
Winx Club (SWE ISSN 1652-800X) **2222**
WinxClub (NLD ISSN 1871-0522) **2222**
Der Winzer (AUT ISSN 0043-5953) **259**
Die Winzer Zeitschrift (DEU ISSN 0935-5723) **613**
Wipes and Non-Wovens Innovation News see Wipes Innovation News **2244**
• Wipes Innovation News (GBR ISSN 1751-5483) **2244**
Wir (DEU) **8775**
Wir (Minden) (DEU) **2222**
Wir Brueckenbauer see Migros-Magazin **1024**
Wir Eltern (CHE ISSN 0258-3739) **2171**
Wir Frauen (DEU ISSN 0178-6083) **8889**
Wir Fuehrhundhalter (DEU) **4086**
Wir im Sport (DEU ISSN 1611-3640) **8215**
Wir Kaufleute (CHE) **1434**
Wir Lernen Deutsch see Deyu Xuexi **5111**
Wir Senioren (AUT) **4057**
Wir Staedtischen (CHE) **7505**
Wir Steuerzahler (AUT) **1955**
Wir vom Bau (DEU) **1043**
Wir von Maingas (DEU) **3150**
Wir Walser (CHE) **3624**
Wire (DEU ISSN 0043-5996) **6336**
• The Wire (GBR ISSN 0952-0686) **6628**
The Wire (Glasgow) (GBR) **2672**
• The Wire (London, 1963) (GBR ISSN 1472-443X) **7273**
The Wire (Maresfield) (GBR ISSN 1462-9259) **2344**
Wire & Cable Asia (GBR) **3372**
Wire & Cable Connector see Wire & Cable Technology International **2399**
▼ Wire & Cable International Overview (USA) **2399**
Wire & Cable Technology Buyer's Guide (USA) **2399**
Wire & Cable Technology International (USA ISSN 1097-7155) **2399**
Wire Association International. Annual Convention Proceedings (USA ISSN 0731-4191) **3334**
Wire Industry (GBR ISSN 0043-6011) **6336**
Wire Industry News (USA) **6336**
Wire Industry Yearbook see Equip4wire.Com **6311**
• Wire Journal International (USA ISSN 0277-4275) **3334**
Wire Journal International Reference Guide (USA) **3334**
Wire Line (Dallas) see Wireline (Dallas) **5869**
Wire Rope News and Sling Technology (USA ISSN 0740-1809) **6715**
• The Wire Worker (USA) **541**
• Wired (USA ISSN 1059-1028) **8147**
Wired (UK Edition) see Wired **8147**
• Wired Art From Wired Hearts (USA ISSN 1537-0453) **5399**
• Wired Librarian's Newsletter (USA ISSN 0884-593X) **5064**
• Wired West (CAN ISSN 1483-9288) **5055**
WireGrass Times & Alabama News (USA) **3572**
Wireless America Magazine (GBR) **2344**
Wireless Application Protocol Magazin see W A P Magazin **2344**
• Wireless Asia (USA ISSN 1681-1399) **2344**
• Wireless Broadband (USA) **2373**
• Wireless Business & Technology (USA ISSN 1533-6735) **2344**
Wireless Business and Technology see Wireless Business & Technology **2344**
• Wireless Business Forecast (Online) (USA) **2535**
• ➤ Wireless Communications and Mobile Computing (GBR ISSN 1530-8669) **2344**
Wireless Communications and Networking Conference. Proceedings see I E E E Wireless Communications and Networking Conference. Proceedings **2324**
Wireless Communications Magazine see I E E E Wireless Communications Magazine **2324**
Wireless Comunicaciones (BRA) **2344**
Wireless Design & Development see Wireless Design and Development **3334**
• Wireless Design and Development (USA ISSN 1076-4240) **3334**
Wireless Design & Development (Asian Edition) see Wireless Design and Development **3334**
Wireless Design & Development (European Edition) see Wireless Design and Development **3334**
Wireless Design & Development Buyer's Guide see Wireless Design and Development **3334**
• Wireless Evolution (GBR ISSN 1472-7226) **2504**
Wireless Fidelity see xChange **2374**
• Wireless International (HKG) **2344**
• Wireless L A N (USA) **2344**
Wireless Market see Global Mobile Communications Market **8959**
• ➤ Wireless Networks (USA ISSN 1022-0038) **2344**
• Wireless P C S - G S M (Personal Communications System) (USA) **2353**
Wireless P C S - G S M Newsletter see Wireless P C S - G S M **2353**
• ➤ Wireless Personal Communications (USA ISSN 0929-6212) **2365**
• Wireless Personal Multimedia Communications Symposia. Proceedings (AUS) **2345**
Wireless Review see Telephony **2373**
Wireless Satellite and Broadcasting Newsletter see Wireless Satellite and Broadcasting Telecommunications **2345**
• Wireless Satellite and Broadcasting Telecommunications (USA) **2345**
Wireless Telecom (CAN ISSN 1201-8538) **2345**
• Wireless Telecom Investor (USA ISSN 1075-413X) **2374**
Wireless Telecommunications see Wireless L A N **2344**
• Wireless Telecommunications Regulation (USA) **2374**
Wireless Telecommunications Symposium (USA ISSN 1934-5070) **2345**
Wireless Wave (USA ISSN 1949-002X) **2374**
• Wireless Week (USA ISSN 1085-0473) **2345**
Wireless, Wi-Fi, R F I D & Cellular Industry Almanac see Plunkett's Wireless, Wi-Fi, R F I D & Cellular Industry Almanac **2371**
Wireless World (SGP) **2374**
Wireline (Alexandria) (USA) **1908**
Wireline (Dallas) (USA ISSN 1062-8746) **5869**
Wiretap Report (USA) **4967**
Wiretapping & Eavesdropping (USA) **7218**
Wirkendes Wort (DEU ISSN 0935-879X) **5195**
Die Wirtschaft (AUT) **1194**
Die Wirtschaft (DEU ISSN 0176-9162) **1194**
Wirtschaft (DEU) **1411**
Wirtschaft (Braunschweig) (DEU ISSN 0176-7011) **1411**
Wirtschaft (Giessen) (DEU) **1411**
Wirtschaft Aktiv (AUT) **1194**
Wirtschaft am Bayerischen Untermain (DEU ISSN 0173-329X) **1411**
Wirtschaft an Strom und Meer (DEU ISSN 1616-6434) **1412**
Die Wirtschaft Chiles (CHL) **1412**
Wirtschaft Elbe Weser (DEU) **1412**
Wirtschaft Heute (AUT) **1390**
Wirtschaft im Dialog (DEU) **1412**
Wirtschaft im Revier (DEU ISSN 0724-4142) **1412**
Wirtschaft im Saarland (DEU) **1412**
Wirtschaft im Suedoestlichen Westfalen (DEU ISSN 0949-5541) **1412**
Wirtschaft im Suedwesten (DEU ISSN 0936-5885) **1194**
Wirtschaft in Bremen (DEU ISSN 0931-2196) **1412**
Wirtschaft in der TechnologieRegion Karlsruhe (DEU ISSN 1439-2593) **1412**
Wirtschaft in Mainfranken (DEU ISSN 0946-7378) **1194**
Wirtschaft in Mittelfranken (DEU ISSN 1437-7071) **1412**
Wirtschaft in Mittelnassau (DEU ISSN 1616-7554) **1412**
Wirtschaft in Ostwuerttemberg (DEU ISSN 0938-8230) **1412**
Wirtschaft in Suedwestsachsen (DEU) **1412**
Wirtschaft, Information, Fortbildung see W I F - Wirtschaft, Information, Fortbildung **1389**
Wirtschaft Konkret (DEU) **1412**
Wirtschaft Lahn Dill (DEU ISSN 1617-0792) **1412**
Wirtschaft Neckar-Alb (DEU) **1412**
Wirtschaft Nordhessen (DEU ISSN 0940-4449) **1412**
Wirtschaft Osnabrueck-Emsland (DEU ISSN 1617-1152) **1412**
Wirtschaft Ostfriesland und Papenburg (DEU) **1412**
• Wirtschaft Regional (LIE ISSN 1819-0618) **1525**
Wirtschaft Regional (Bielefeld) (DEU) **1412**
Wirtschaft Studieren (DEU) **2963**
➤ Wirtschaft und Berufserziehung (DEU ISSN 0341-339X) **6705**
Wirtschaft und Energie (CHE) **2642**
Wirtschaft und Erziehung (DEU ISSN 0174-6170) **1550**
Wirtschaft und Gesellschaft (AUT ISSN 0378-5130) **1194**
Wirtschaft und Handel in det Tschechischen see Czech Business and Trade **1561**
Wirtschaft und Markt (DEU ISSN 0863-5323) **1194**
Wirtschaft und Recht in Osteuropa (DEU ISSN 0941-6293) **4944**
• Wirtschaft und Statistik (DEU ISSN 0043-6143) **1194**
Wirtschaft und Unterricht (DEU) **1194**
Wirtschaft und Verwaltung see Gewerbearchiv **4868**
Wirtschaft und Weiterbildung (DEU ISSN 0942-4946) **2947**
Wirtschaft und Wettbewerb (DEU ISSN 0043-6151) **1908**
Wirtschaft und Wissenschaft (DEU ISSN 0943-5123) **7929**
Wirtschaft Zwischen Alb und Bodensee (DEU) **1412**
Wirtschaft Zwischen Nord- und Ostsee (DEU ISSN 0049-7703) **1412**
Wirtschaft Zwischen Ostsee und Elbe (DEU ISSN 1616-0746) **1412**
Wirtschaftliche Lage in der Bundesrepublik Deutschland see Schlaglichter der Wirtschaftspolitik **1516**
Wirtschaftlichkeit in Konstruktion und Fertigung im Maschinen- und Anlagenbau see Informationsdienst F I Z Technik. Wirtschaftlichkeit in Konstruktion und Fertigung im Maschinen- und Anlagenbau **3231**
Wirtschafts Ausblick see O E C D Economic Outlook **1502**
Wirtschafts Ausblick see Perspectives Economiques de l'O E C D **1159**
Wirtschafts-Kurier (DEU ISSN 0170-3390) **1194**
Wirtschafts-Nachrichten (DEU ISSN 0931-2552) **1194**
Wirtschafts-News (DEU) **1525**
Wirtschafts- und Sozialhistorische Studien (DEU) **1194**
Wirtschafts- und Sozialpolitische see W I S O **8014**
Wirtschafts- und Sozialpolitische Dokumente see W I S O - Dokumente **8014**
Wirtschafts- und Sozialpolitische Zeitschrift des I S W see W I S O **8014**
Wirtschafts- und Sozialwissenschaftliches Institut Mitteilungen see W S I Mitteilungen **8014**
• Wirtschafts und Steuer Hefte (DEU ISSN 0722-3358) **1194**
➤ Wirtschafts- und Verwaltungsrechtliche Studien (AUT ISSN 0937-6844) **4815**
Wirtschaftsanalysen (DEU) **1525**
Wirtschaftsbericht Berlin (DEU) **1525**
WirtschaftsBild (DEU ISSN 0344-3035) **1525**
• WirtschaftsBlatt (AUT) **1194**
• Wirtschaftsblatt (BGR ISSN 0861-8445) **1434**
Wirtschaftsbrief fuer den Frauenarzt see Wirtschaftsmagazin fuer den Frauenarzt **5731**
Wirtschaftsbrief fuer den Nervenarzt see Wirtschaftsmagazin fuer den Nervenarzt **6189**
Wirtschaftsbrief fuer den Orthopaeden see Wirtschaftsmagazin fuer den Orthopaeden **6075**
Wirtschaftsbrief fuer den Urologen see Wirtschaftsmagazin fuer den Urologen **6277**
• ➤ Wirtschaftsdienst (DEU ISSN 0043-6275) **1194**
Wirtschaftsdienst (Dresden) (DEU) **1412**
Wirtschaftsdienst fuer Ingenieure und Architekten (DEU ISSN 1433-8300) **3227**
Wirtschaftsdienst fuer Versicherungs- und Bausparkaufleute (DEU ISSN 0720-9657) **4528**
Wirtschaftsdienst fuer Versicherungsmakler (DEU ISSN 1436-0721) **4528**
† Das Wirtschaftseigene Futter (DEU ISSN 0049-7711) **8998**
Wirtschaftsfuehrer fuer Rechtsreferendare (DEU) **4815**
Wirtschaftsgeographische Studien (AUT ISSN 1017-0510) **4034**
Wirtschaftshandbuch Asien, Pazifik see Asien-Pazifik. Wirtschaftshandbuch **1438**
Wirtschaftshandbuch Asien-Pazifik (DEU) **1525**
• ➤ Wirtschaftsinformatik (DEU ISSN 0937-6429) **2538**
Wirtschaftsjournal (DEU ISSN 1617-6669) **1194**
• Wirtschaftsjournalist (AUT) **4585**
Wirtschaftskompass (DEU) **1412**
Wirtschaftskybernetik und Systemanalyse (DEU ISSN 0720-6992) **1421**
Wirtschaftsmagazin (AUT) **1194**
Wirtschaftsmagazin fuer den Allgemeinarzt (DEU ISSN 1617-3058) **5731**
Wirtschaftsmagazin fuer den Arzt see Wirtschaftsmagazin fuer den Allgemeinarzt **5731**
Wirtschaftsmagazin fuer den Frauenarzt (DEU ISSN 1616-3885) **5731**
Wirtschaftsmagazin fuer den Hautarzt (DEU ISSN 1616-3869) **5883**
Wirtschaftsmagazin fuer den Kinderarzt (DEU ISSN 1611-2644) **6105**
Wirtschaftsmagazin fuer den Nervenarzt (DEU ISSN 1611-4272) **6189**
Wirtschaftsmagazin fuer den Orthopaeden (DEU ISSN 1616-3877) **6075**
Wirtschaftsmagazin fuer den Urologen (DEU ISSN 1616-3850) **6277**
Wirtschaftsmagazin Pfalz (DEU) **1412**
Wirtschaftsmagazin Rhein-Neckar (DEU ISSN 1434-1573) **1412**
Wirtschaftspaedagogische Studien zur Individuellen und Kollektiven Entwicklung (DEU ISSN 1437-1693) **1195**
Wirtschaftspolitik in Forschung und Praxis (DEU ISSN 1619-8867) **1525**
Wirtschaftspolitische Blaetter (AUT ISSN 0043-6291) **1412**
Wirtschaftspolitische Kolloquien der Adolf-Weber-Stiftung (DEU ISSN 0720-6879) **1195**
Wirtschaftspolitische Studien (USA ISSN 0172-5963) **1550**
Wirtschaftspruefer-Kompendium. Band 1: Wirtschaftliches Pruefungswesen (DEU) **1303**
Wirtschaftsprueferkammer Magazin see W P K Magazin **1303**
Wirtschaftsprueferkammer. Mitteilungen see W P K Magazin **1303**
➤ Wirtschaftspsychologie (DEU ISSN 1615-7729) **7415**
Wirtschaftspsychologie Aktuell (DEU ISSN 1618-9507) **7415**
Wirtschaftspsychologische Schriften (DEU ISSN 0721-0213) **7415**
Wirtschaftsraum Hanau Kinzigtal (DEU) **1412**
Wirtschaftsrechtliche Blaetter see Juristische Blaetter **4707**
Wirtschaftsrechtliche Forschungsergebnisse (DEU ISSN 1435-683X) **1195**
Wirtschaftsreport Rheinhessen (DEU ISSN 1435-8425) **1413**
Wirtschaftsreport Siegen-Olpe-Wittgenstein (DEU) **1195**
Wirtschaftsrundschau (AUT) **1413**
Wirtschaftsrundschau Italia - Oesterreich (AUT) **1413**
WirtschaftsSpiegel (DEU ISSN 1439-0000) **1195**
Wirtschaftsspiegel (DEU) **1195**
Wirtschaftsspiegel Credit-Curier (DEU) **1525**
Wirtschaftsspiegel Gelbe Hefte (DEU) **1525**
Wirtschaftsspiegel Sachsen-Anhalt (DEU ISSN 1860-8558) **1525**
Wirtschaftsspiegel Thueringen (DEU) **1525**
Das Wirtschaftsstudium - W I S U (DEU ISSN 0340-3084) **2926**
WirtschaftsTip fuer Dermatologen - Allergologen (DEU ISSN 1866-2935) **5883**
WirtschaftsTip fuer Diabetologen (DEU ISSN 1866-2838) **5901**
WirtschaftsTip fuer Gynaekologen (DEU ISSN 1866-2927) **6006**
WirtschaftsTip fuer Orthopaeden - Rheumatologen (DEU ISSN 1866-2846) **6075**
WirtschaftsTip fuer Paediater (DEU ISSN 1866-2919) **6105**
WirtschaftsTip fuer Urologen (DEU ISSN 1866-2900) **6277**
Wirtschaftstrends zum Jahreswechsel (DEU) **4279**
Der Wirtschaftstreuhaender (AUT ISSN 0043-6321) **1303**
➤ Wirtschaftsuniversitaet Wien. Forschungsinstitut fuer Europa-Fragen. Schriftenreihe/Research Institute for European Affairs. Publication Series (AUT) **4815**
Wirtschaftsvereinigung Gross- und Aussenhandel Hamburg e.V. Geschaeftsbericht see W G A Geschaeftsbericht **1586**
Wirtschaftswissenschaftliche Abhandlungen (DEU ISSN 0510-5587) **1195**
Wirtschaftswissenschaftliche Veroeffentlichungen see Freie Universitaet Berlin. Osteuropa-Institut. Wirtschaftswissenschaftliche Veroeffentlichungen **1112**
• Wirtschaftswoche (DEU ISSN 0042-8582) **1525**
Wirtschaftswoche e-Business see e-Business **2555**
Wirtschaftswissenschaftliches Studium (DEU ISSN 0340-1650) **1195**
Wisconsin Academy of Sciences, Arts and Letters. Transactions (USA ISSN 0084-0505) **7929**
Wisconsin Academy Review see Wisconsin People & Ideas **5245**
• Wisconsin Administrative Code (USA) **7477**
• Wisconsin Administrative Code (CD-ROM Edition) (USA) **7477**
Wisconsin Adult Jail Population (Year) (USA) **2672**
• Wisconsin Agriculturist (USA ISSN 0043-6356) **170**
Wisconsin AIDS Update (USA) **5828**
Wisconsin: All-Industries see Harris Directory. Wisconsin All-Industries **2003**
➤ The Wisconsin Archeologist (USA ISSN 0043-6364) **424**
Wisconsin Architect (USA) **461**
• Wisconsin Astrophysics (USA ISSN 0363-3675) **583**
Wisconsin Badger Builder (USA) **1043**
Wisconsin Banking News (USA) **1390**
Wisconsin Beverage Journal (USA ISSN 0043-6399) **613**
Wisconsin Blue Book (USA) **7477**
Wisconsin Bookwatch (USA) **639**
• Wisconsin Business Directory (USA ISSN 1048-7433) **2035**
The Wisconsin C P A see On Balance **1298**
Wisconsin Center for Education Research Research Highlights see W C E R Research Highlights **3087**
Wisconsin Center for Pushkin Studies. Publications (USA) **5399**
Wisconsin Cities & Counties Graphic Performance Analysis (USA ISSN 1935-5629) **7485**
Wisconsin Counties (USA ISSN 0749-6818) **7505**
Wisconsin Court Rules and Procedure see Court Rules Pamphlet(s). Wisconsin Court Rules and Procedure, State and Federal **4949**
Wisconsin Crime and Arrests (Year) (USA) **2675**
Wisconsin Criminal Law see West's Wisconsin Criminal Law **4900**
Wisconsin Deer & Turkey Show Preview (USA) **8342**
Wisconsin Dental Association Journal see W D A Journal **5869**
Wisconsin. Department of Administration. Annual Fiscal Report (USA ISSN 0085-8226) **7477**
Wisconsin. Department of Financial Institutions. Annual Report (USA) **1659**

Title

Wisconsin. Department of Financial Institutions. Division of Securities. Securities Bulletin (USA) **1659**

Wisconsin. Department of Natural Resources. Research - Management Findings Series (USA) **2633**

Wisconsin. Department of Natural Resources. Research Report (USA ISSN 0084-0556) **3475**

Wisconsin. Department of Natural Resources. Research Report Series (USA) **2633**

Wisconsin. Department of Natural Resources. Technical Bulletin Series (USA ISSN 0084-0564) **2633**

Wisconsin. Department of Transportation. Division of Planning and Budget. Highway Mileage Data (USA ISSN 0084-0572) **8532**

Wisconsin. Department of Veterans Affairs. Biennial Report (USA) **6454**

Wisconsin. Department of Veterans Affairs. Update (USA) **6454**

Wisconsin. Division of Corrections. Office of Information Management. Admissions to Juvenile Institutions (USA) **2675**

Wisconsin. Division of Corrections. Office of Information Management. Releases from Juvenile Institutions (USA) **2675**

Wisconsin Economy Studies (USA ISSN 0084-0599) **1195**

Wisconsin Educational Communications Board. Biennial Report (USA ISSN 0361-2120) **3035**

Wisconsin Electronic Sales and Service Association Newsletter *see* W E S A Newsletter **1969**

● Wisconsin Employment Law Letter (USA ISSN 1059-5066) **4815**

Wisconsin Energy Cooperative News (USA) **3993**

Wisconsin Engineer (USA ISSN 0043-6453) **3227**

Wisconsin English Journal (USA ISSN 0512-1213) **3088**

† ● Wisconsin Environmental Law Journal (USA ISSN 1077-9299) **8998**

Wisconsin Facts (USA ISSN 1046-8331) **3122**

Wisconsin Fire Journal (USA ISSN 0744-8201) **3582**

Wisconsin Genealogical Council Newsletter *see* W I Genealogical Council Newsletter **3787**

Wisconsin Geological and Natural History Survey. Bulletin (USA ISSN 0375-8265) **2774**

Wisconsin Geological and Natural History Survey. Educational Series (USA) **2775**

Wisconsin Geological and Natural History Survey. Field Trip Guide Books (USA ISSN 0271-8502) **2775**

Wisconsin Geological and Natural History Survey. Information Circulars (USA ISSN 0512-0640) **2775**

Wisconsin. Geological and Natural History Survey. Special Report (USA ISSN 0512-0659) **2775**

Wisconsin Golf Directory of Courses (USA) **8251**

Wisconsin Golfer (USA ISSN 1528-5421) **8251**

Wisconsin Grocer (USA) **3667**

Wisconsin In Step (USA) **4380**

Wisconsin Independent Agent (USA) **4528**

● Wisconsin International Law Journal (USA ISSN 0743-7951) **4944**

Wisconsin Introductions to Scandinavia 1 *see* W I T S: 1 **3571**

Wisconsin Introductions to Scandinavia 2 *see* W I T S: 2 **3571**

Wisconsin Jewish Chronicle (USA ISSN 0043-6488) **7731**

Wisconsin Journal of Family Law (USA) **4915**

● Wisconsin Journal of Law, Gender & Society (USA ISSN 1943-1600) **4815**

● Wisconsin Law Journal (USA ISSN 1534-1917) **4815**

Wisconsin Law Reporter (USA ISSN 0199-9095) **4815**

● ➤ Wisconsin Law Review (USA ISSN 0043-650X) **4815**

Wisconsin Lawyer (USA ISSN 1043-0490) **4815**

Wisconsin Legislative Council Rules Clearinghouse. Annual Report (USA) **4815**

Wisconsin Library Association Newsletter *see* W L A Newsletter **5054**

Wisconsin Library Service Record (USA ISSN 0361-2848) **2947**

● Wisconsin Light (USA) **4380**

Wisconsin Lutheran Quarterly (USA ISSN 0362-5648) **7780**

● Wisconsin Magazine of History (USA ISSN 0043-6534) **4318**

● Wisconsin Manufacturers Register (USA ISSN 0738-0070) **2035**

Wisconsin: Manufacturing *see* Harris Directory. Wisconsin Manufacturing **2003**

● ➤ Wisconsin Medical Journal (USA ISSN 1098-1861) **5731**

Wisconsin Meetings (USA) **6283**

● Wisconsin Natural Resources (USA ISSN 0736-2277) **2633**

Wisconsin Newmonth (USA ISSN 1059-0935) **3993**

Wisconsin, Off the Beaten Path *see* Off the Beaten Path: Wisconsin **8744**

† Wisconsin Outdoor Journal (USA ISSN 0893-5769) **8998**

● Wisconsin Outdoor News (USA ISSN 1076-0067) **8342**

The Wisconsin P-H-C Contractor (USA) **4128**

● Wisconsin Parent Teacher (USA) **2926**

Wisconsin Pastoral Handbook (USA) **7823**

● Wisconsin People & Ideas (USA ISSN 1558-9633) **5245**

Wisconsin Population Projections (USA ISSN 0091-5254) **7295**

Wisconsin Preservation (USA ISSN 0276-4156) **4318**

Wisconsin Public Documents (USA ISSN 0364-507X) **7485**

Wisconsin R E C News *see* Wisconsin Energy Cooperative News **3993**

Wisconsin Real Estate and Construction Law Statutes Annotated (USA ISSN 1944-849X) **7616**

Wisconsin Reports *see* West's Jury Verdicts. Wisconsin Reports **4967**

Wisconsin Restaurateur (USA ISSN 0274-7472) **4400**

Wisconsin Review (USA ISSN 0043-6631) **5438**

Wisconsin School Directory *see* M D R's School Directory. Wisconsin **2960**

Wisconsin School Musician (USA ISSN 0043-6658) **6628**

Wisconsin School News (USA) **3035**

Wisconsin Session Laws (USA ISSN 0145-6628) **7477**

Wisconsin Sheriff and Deputy (USA) **2672**

Wisconsin Snowmobile News (USA ISSN 0745-161X) **8342**

Wisconsin South Asian Area Center News Report (USA) **2310**

Wisconsin Sportsman (USA ISSN 0361-9451) **8342**

Wisconsin. State Elections Board. Biennial Report (USA) **7193**

Wisconsin State Farmer (USA) **170**

Wisconsin State Genealogical Society Newsletter (USA ISSN 1094-9445) **3788**

The Wisconsin Statutes and Annotations (USA) **4815**

Wisconsin Studies in Autobiography (USA) **5399**

The Wisconsin Taxpayer (USA ISSN 0043-6720) **7477**

Wisconsin Trails (USA ISSN 0095-4314) **3993**

Wisconsin Vocational Association Views & Visions *see* W V A Views & Visions **2947**

Wisconsin Water Quality Assessment (USA) **3493**

Wisconsin West Magazine (USA) **4318**

Wisconsin Women's Law Journal *see* Wisconsin Journal of Law, Gender & Society **4815**

● Wisconsin's Forest Resources in (Year) (USA ISSN 1930-8809) **3707**

Wisden Asia Cricket *see* Cricinfo **8226**

The Wisden Cricket Monthly *see* The Wisden Cricketer **8251**

The Wisden Cricketer (GBR) **8251**

The Wisden Cricketer (South African Edition) (ZAF ISSN 1813-0011) **8251**

Wisden Cricketers' Almanack (Year) (GBR ISSN 0142-9213) **8252**

Wisdom *see* Kinaadman **554**

Wisdom (USA ISSN 1547-1403) **3572**

Wisdom (Digest Edition) *see* Xin Zhihui (Wezhai Ban) **5246**

Wisdom (Literature Edition) *see* Xin Zhihui (Gushi Ban) **5402**

Wisdom (Wealth Edition) *see* Xin Zhihui (Caifu Ban) **1196**

Wisdom of Persia (IRN) **4326**

Wise Planning (USA) **7694**

The Wise Woman (USA ISSN 0883-119X) **8889**

Wise Words (USA) **8848**

Wiser *see* W I S E R **8998**

Wish (CAN) **8889**

Wish to Import (CAN) **1587**

Wish U Were Here (USA) **5438**

Wish You Happiness *see* Zhuni Xingfu (Zonghe Ban) **8893**

Wish You Happiness (Afternoon Edition) *see* Zhuni Xingfu (Wuhou Ban) **3830**

The Wishing Well (USA ISSN 1525-3902) **4380**

WISO *see* W I S O **8014**

WISO-Dokumente *see* W I S O - Dokumente **8014**

▼ Wissen Kompakt (DEU ISSN 1863-2637) **5869**

Wissen und Lernen in Organisationen (DEU ISSN 1613-3544) **2926**

WissenHeute (DEU ISSN 1613-4389) **2374**

Wissenplus (AUT ISSN 1817-4019) **3088**

Wissenplus (DEU) **3860**

Wissenschaft Ohne Grenzen (DEU ISSN 0948-9096) **7929**

Wissenschaft, Politik und Gesellschaft (DEU ISSN 1863-7655) **8015**

Wissenschaft und Forschung (DEU ISSN 0935-6908) **7929**

Wissenschaft und Frieden (DEU) **7929**

Wissenschaft und Glaube (AUT ISSN 1012-3067) **7823**

Wissenschaft und Weisheit (DEU ISSN 0043-678X) **7823**

Wissenschaft vom Menschen (DEU) **8015**

Wissenschaftliche Abhandlungen (CAN ISSN 1942-9126) **6628**

Wissenschaftliche Abhandlungen und Reden zur Philosophie, Politik und Geistesgeschichte (DEU ISSN 0935-5200) **6961**

Wissenschaftliche Alpenvereinshefte (DEU ISSN 0084-0912) **4034**

† Wissenschaftliche Beitraege zur Informatik (DEU ISSN 0863-0798) **8998**

Wissenschaftliche Beitraege zur Sozialen Arbeit (DEU ISSN 1862-7889) **8078**

Wissenschaftliche Berichte F Z K A - P F T (Forschungszentrum Karlsruhe - Projekttraeger Fertigungstechnik) (DEU ISSN 0948-1427) **3475**

Wissenschaftliche Monographien zum Alten und Neuen Testament (DEU ISSN 0512-1582) **7694**

Wissenschaftliche Paperbacks. Sozial- und Wirtschaftsgeschichte (DEU ISSN 0170-3579) **1551**

Wissenschaftliche Untersuchungen zum Neuen Testament (DEU ISSN 0512-1604) **7694**

Wissenschaftliche Vereinigung fuer Augenoptik und Optometrie. Fachvortraege des W V A O Jahreskongresses (DEU ISSN 0171-6433) **6053**

Wissenschaftliche Vereinigung fuer Internationales Verfahrensrecht. Veroeffentlichungen (DEU) **4944**

† Wissenschaftlicher Ergebnisbericht (DEU ISSN 0931-8364) **8998**

Wissenschaftlicher Verlag Trier Handbuch zum Literaturwissenschaftlichen Studium *see* W V T Handbuch zum Literaturwissenschaftlichen Studium **5396**

Wissenschaftliches Arbeiten (DEU) **3088**

Wissenschaftliches Forum fuer Internationale Sicherheit Aktuell *see* W I F I S Aktuell **7272**

Wissenschaftliches Forum fuer Internationale Sicherheit. Schriftenreihe (DEU ISSN 1864-6131) **7273**

Wissenschaftsethik und Technikfolgenbeurteilung (DEU) **7929**

Wissenschaftskultur um 1900 (DEU ISSN 1613-673X) **7929**

Wissenschaftskultur um Neunzehnhundert *see* Wissenschaftskultur um 1900 **7929**

Wissenschaftsmanagement (DEU ISSN 0947-9546) **7929**

Wissenschaftsmanagement Special (DEU) **7929**

Wissenschaftspolitik und Wissenschaftsrecht (DEU) **3010**

● Wissenschaftsrecht (DEU ISSN 0948-0218) **4815**

Wissenschaftszentrum Berlin fuer Sozialforschung Forschung *see* W Z B Forschung **8021**

Wissenschaftszentrum Berlin fuer Sozialforschung Mitteilungen *see* W Z B - Mitteilungen **8014**

Wissenschaftszentrum Berlin fuer Sozialforschung Papers *see* W Z B Papers **8014**

Wissensliteratur im Mittelalter (DEU) **5399**

Wissensmanagement (DEU ISSN 1438-4426) **1801**

Wisteria (USA ISSN 1931-986X) **5438**

Wistra (DEU ISSN 0721-6890) **4815**

Wit & Humor *see* Youmo Dashi **5246**

Wita (DEU) **1195**

WITCH *see* W.I.T.C.H. **2220**

WITCH *see* W.I.T.C.H. **2220**

WITCH *see* W.I.T.C.H. **2220**

WITCH *see* W.I.T.C.H. **2220**

WITCH *see* W.I.T.C.H. **2220**

WITCH *see* W.I.T.C.H. **2220**

WITCH *see* W.I.T.C.H. **2220**

WITCH *see* W.I.T.C.H. **2220**

WITCH *see* W.I.T.C.H. **2220**

Witch *see* W.I.T.C.H. **2220**

WITCH *see* W.I.T.C.H. **2220**

WITCH *see* W.I.T.C.H. **2220**

Witch Mag *see* W I T C H Mag **2220**

With (JPN) **8889**

With/Yushishang (Guoji Zhongwen Ban) (TWN ISSN 1812-4062) **8889**

With Marriage in Mind (GBR ISSN 0968-7165) **5562**

With New York Firefighters *see* W N Y F **3582**

Witherloese (DNK ISSN 1600-6526) **4279**

Without Prejudice (CAN ISSN 0833-1278) **4528**

Witness *see* Victorian Baptist Witness **7779**

➤ Witness (USA ISSN 0891-1371) **5245**

Witness (ZAF ISSN 1814-7542) **3950**

The Witness (Diocesan) Newspaper (USA ISSN 0745-0427) **7823**

Witt Weiden Kundenjournal (DEU) **8889**

▼ De Witte Bison (NLD ISSN 1874-625X) **5399**

De Witte Raaf (BEL ISSN 0774-8523) **526**

Wittenberg Review of Literature and Art (USA ISSN 0147-0868) **5399**

† The Wittington Door (USA ISSN 1554-2459) **8998**

Witterung in Oesterreich. Monatsuebersicht (AUT ISSN 0043-7077) **6398**

† Witterungs-Report. Daten (DEU ISSN 1436-6797) **8998**

† ● Witterungs-Report. Express (Online) (DEU ISSN 1863-3757) **8998**

Wittgenstein (USA ISSN 0043-7093) **4279**

Wittgenstein Gesellschaft. Schriftenreihe *see* Austrian Ludwig Wittgenstein Society. Publications **6906**

† Wittgenstein-Jahrbuch (DEU ISSN 1439-765X) **8998**

➤ Wittgenstein, Ludwig: Wiener Ausgabe (AUT) **6961**

Wittgenstein Studien *see* Wittgenstein Studien. Neue Folge **6961**

● Wittgenstein Studien. Neue Folge (DEU ISSN 1868-7431) **6961**

The Wittliff Gallery Series (USA) **6978**

WittyWorld (USA ISSN 0892-9807) **527**

Witwatersrand Bird Club News *see* W B C News **916**

Wiwar (NOR ISSN 0333-3566) **4279**

WiWi-Press (DEU) **2310**

● Wizard (USA ISSN 1065-6499) **4350**

▼ Wjerklank (NLD ISSN 1875-4287) **6961**

Wlokna Naturalne *see* Natural Fibres **8455**

Wo Bekomme Ich Mein Baby? (DEU) **6105**

Wo de Gushi/My Story (CHN) **5399**

Wo Geht's Lang? (DEU) **3010**

Woche Aktuell *see* Woche der Frau Aktuell **8889**

● Woche Bildpost (AUT) **3798**

Woche der Frau *see* Woche der Frau Aktuell **8889**

▼ Woche der Frau Aktuell (DEU) **8889**

▼ Woche Gesund (AUT) **7000**

▼ Woche Heute (DEU ISSN 1866-9123) **8889**

Die Woche in Australien (AUS ISSN 0726-4860) **3572**

Wochen Rundschau (AUT) **3798**

Wochenblatt fuer Kaiserslautern (DEU) **3860**

Wochenblatt fuer Landau (DEU) **3860**

Wochenblatt fuer Ludwigshafen (DEU) **3860**

Wochenblatt fuer Mannheim (DEU) **3860**

Wochenblatt fuer Neustadt (DEU) **3860**

● Wochenblatt fuer Papierfabrikation (DEU ISSN 0043-7131) **6739**

Wochenblatt fuer Speyer (DEU) **3860**

Wochenblattmagazin (DEU) **170**

● Wochenschau (HUN ISSN 1218-8700) **3877**

Wochenschau fuer Politische Erziehung, Sozial- und Gemeinschaftskunde. Ausgabe fuer Sekundarstufe I (DEU ISSN 0342-8990) **8015**

Wochenschau fuer Politische Erziehung, Sozial- und Gemeinschaftskunde. Ausgabe fuer Sekundarstufe II (DEU ISSN 0342-8974) **8015**

Woddis News (USA) **2271**

Woerkshop/Workshop (DEU ISSN 0934-585X) **37**

Woerterbuch der Mittelhochdeutschen Urkundensprache (DEU) **5195**

Wohl Fuehlen *see* Sueddeutsche Zeitung **3857**

Wohlau-Steinauer Heimatblatt (DEU) **3860**

Wohn Design *see* Wohn!Design **4552**

Wohn! Design (DEU) **461**

Wohnart (DEU ISSN 0935-8854) **4552**

Wohnbaden (DEU ISSN 0178-2509) **4563**

Wohnbauforschung in Oesterreich *see* W B F O **4431**

Wohn!Design (DEU) **4552**

Wohneigentum (CHE) **7616**

Wohnen (AUT) **4552**

Das Wohnen (CHE) **1043**

Wohnen (DEU) **7616**

Wohnen (Munchen) *see* Wohnen-Zeitschrift fuer das Wohnungswesen in Bayern **1955**

● Wohnen in Berlin - Brandenburg (DEU) **4431**

Wohnen in Wien (AUT) **7616**

Wohnen Plus (AUT) **4431**

Wohnen Traeume (DEU) **4552**

Wohnen & Garten (DEU) **4552**

Wohnen-Zeitschrift fuer das Wohnungswesen in Bayern (DEU ISSN 0942-7228) **1955**

Wohnentraeume *see* Wohnen Traeume **4552**

Wohnidee (DEU ISSN 0179-4140) **4552**

Wohnkultur (AUT) **4552**

Wohnmagazin (DEU) **4563**

Wohnmedizin (DEU ISSN 0342-5967) **7545**

Wohnmobil & Reisen (DEU) **8342**

Wohnmobil, Wohnwagen-Markt (DEU) **8342**

Wohnmobil, Wohnwagen-Markt International *see* Wohnmobil, Wohnwagen-Markt **8342**

Wohnmobile und Wohnwagen bis 20,000 Euro (DEU) **8342**

● ➤ Wohnrechtliche Blaetter (AUT ISSN 0933-2766) **4815**

Wohnrevue (CHE) **4553**

Wohntex (AUT) **4553**

Wohnung & Gesundheit (DEU ISSN 0176-0513) **461**

➤ Der Wohnungseigentuemer (DEU ISSN 0344-8738) **1043**

Wohnungseigentum *see* Wohnungseigentum, Mietrecht **1043**

Wohnungseigentum, Mietrecht (DEU ISSN 1861-020X) **1043**

● Wohnungseigentum (DEU) **7616**

Wohnungslos (DEU ISSN 0948-7441) **8078**

Die Wohnungswirtschaft (DEU ISSN 0939-625X) **7616**

Wohnwirtschaft (CHE) **7616**

Wojskowa Akademia Techniczna. Biuletyn (POL ISSN 1234-5865) **6454**

Wokol Plytek Ceramicznych (POL ISSN 1429-9089) **2046**

WOLF! Magazine (USA) **968**

Wolf Moon Journal (USA ISSN 1545-4258) **5438**

Wolf Park News (USA) **968**

Wolf Tales (USA) **2310**

Wolfenbuetteler Abhandlungen zur Renaissanceforschung (DEU ISSN 0724-956X) **4279**

Wolfenbuetteler Arbeiten zur Barockforschung (DEU ISSN 0724-472X) **4279**

Wolfenbuetteler Barock - Nachrichten (DEU ISSN 0340-6318) **5055**

Wolfenbuetteler Beitraege (DEU ISSN 0300-2012) **5055**

Wolfenbuetteler Bibliotheks - Informationen (DEU ISSN 0931-4032) **4167**

Wolfenbuetteler Forschungen (DEU ISSN 0724-9594) **4279**

Wolfenbuetteler Hefte (DEU) **4279**

Wolfenbuetteler Mittelalter Studien (DEU ISSN 0937-5724) **4279**

Wolfenbuetteler Notizen zur Buchgeschichte (DEU ISSN 0341-2253) **7576**

Wolfenbuetteler Renaissance Mitteilungen (DEU ISSN 0342-4340) **4279**

Wolfenbuetteler Schriften zur Geschichte des Buchwesens (DEU ISSN 0724-9586) **7329**

Wolfenbuetteler Studien zur Aufklaerung. Schriftenreihe (DEU ISSN 0342-5940) **4167**

Title

11034 WOMEN'S LEAGUE OUTLOOK ULRICH'S PERIODICALS

• Women's League Outlook (USA ISSN 0043-7557) 7731
Women's Life see Funu Shenghuo 8864
Women's Literature see Nuzi Wenxue 5344
Women's Mental Health & Development (USA) 8849
Women's Money Magazine (AUS ISSN 1447-1426) 8891
Women's Monthly see Rajam 8881
Women's Music Plus (USA) 6628
Women's Network (USA) 8891
Women's News (NCL ISSN 1017-3900) 8891
Women's News (USA) 8891
Women's Newsletter see Women's News 8891
Women's Organisations in the United Kingdom (GBR) 8891
Women's Organizations: A New York City Directory (USA) 8891
Women's Philanthropy Institute News (USA ISSN 1522-144X) 8078
Women's Physique World (USA ISSN 1069-4927) 8849
➤ Women's Policy Journal of Harvard (USA ISSN 1534-0473) 8905
Women's Policy Research Conference. Proceedings see Institute for Women's Policy Research. Conference Proceedings 8899
Women's Pro Rodeo News (USA ISSN 1093-9202) 8300
Women's Public Opinion/Fujin Koron (JPN) 8891
Women's Psychology (USA ISSN 1931-0021) 7415
Women's Resource & Action Center. Newsletter (USA) 8891
Women's Resources International see Women's Studies International (Baltimore) 8906
Women's Resources International (BiblioLine) see Women's Studies International (Baltimore) 8906
Women's Resources International (BiblioLine) see Women Studies Abstracts 8906
• The Women's Review of Books (USA ISSN 0738-1433) 5245
• Women's Rights Law Reporter (USA ISSN 0085-8269) 4815
▼ Women's Roles in American History (USA ISSN 1553-507X) 4318
• Women's Roles Through History (USA ISSN 1553-5088) 4167
Women's Self Defense (USA) 8891
Women's Skiing see Skiing Magazine 8333
Women's Sports Experience (USA ISSN 1061-1568) 8216
Women's Studies see Funu Yanjiu 8897
• ➤ Women's Studies (USA ISSN 0049-7878) 8905
➤ Women's Studies (Lewiston) (USA ISSN 1044-5676) 8905
Women's Studies Association (N.Z.). Newsletter (NZL) 8905
Women's Studies Forum see Gender Studies and Policy Review 8898
• ➤ Women's Studies in Communication (USA ISSN 0749-1409) 8905
Women's Studies International (USA ISSN 1041-9527) 8905
• Women's Studies International (Baltimore) (USA) 8906
• ➤ Women's Studies International Forum (GBR ISSN 0277-5395) 8905
† • ➤ Women's Studies Journal (NZL ISSN 0112-4099) 8999
• ➤ Women's Studies Journal (Online) (NZL) 8905
Women's Studies Newsletter (USA) 8905
• ➤ Women's Studies Quarterly (USA ISSN 0732-1562) 8905
Women's Studies Review see Irish Feminist Review 8899
Women's Voice see Yeo'seong 8906
(Year) Women's Volleyball Media Guide (USA) 8252
Women's Watch (USA) 7218
Women's Wear Daily see W W D 2250
Women's World see Nuzi Shijie 8878
• Women's World (UGA ISSN 1019-1534) 8892
Women's World (VNM) 8891
• ➤ Women's Writing (GBR ISSN 0969-9082) 8905
Women's Yellow Pages (USA) 8892
Women's Zionist Organization of South Africa. News and Views (ZAF) 7732
• Women'space (Online Edition) (CAN) 8905
• Women@Work (AUS) 4605
• Womuunweb W & R (Women & Religion) (USA ISSN 1946-8717) 7694
Womyn's Words (USA ISSN 1084-3760) 8905
Wonder Time (USA ISSN 1558-7495) 2171
Wonderful West Virginia (USA ISSN 0030-7157) 2633
Wonderful World of Flying (USA ISSN 1064-4997) 75
Wonderland (AUT ISSN 1818-2070) 461
Wonderland (GBR ISSN 1747-8448) 527
Wondertime see Wonder Time 2171
Woningwet (NLD ISSN 1871-5788) 4431
Wonjaryok Hakhoeji see Nuclear Engineering and Technology 7069
Wonka Vision (USA) 6628
Wood/Bois (CAN ISSN 1183-6652) 3717
Wood see Puu 1051
Wood see Drewno 1050
Wood see Drevo 1050
Wood see Better Homes and Gardens Wood 4437
➤ Wood and Fiber Science (USA ISSN 0735-6161) 3717
Wood & Vale Express (GBR ISSN 1479-3717) 3873
• Wood & Wood Products (USA ISSN 0043-7662) 3717
• Wood Based Panels International (GBR ISSN 0144-7238) 3717
Wood Carbonization Research see Mokushitsu Tanka Gakkaishi 3714
Wood Carving Illustrated (USA ISSN 1096-2816) 541
▼ • Wood Coin (USA ISSN 1946-4320) 5400
Wood Design & Building (CAN ISSN 1206-677X) 3718
Wood Design Focus (USA ISSN 1066-5757) 3718
• Wood Digest (USA ISSN 1045-7348) 3718
Wood Digest's Finishing see Finishing 4557
Wood Duck (CAN ISSN 0049-7886) 7929
Wood Finishing Quarterly (USA) 1052
Wood Flooring (USA ISSN 1940-5316) 1049
Wood in Archaeology (GBR ISSN 1369-6963) 424
Wood Industries of New Mexico (USA) 3718
Wood Industry/Mokuzai Kogyo (JPN ISSN 0026-8917) 3718
Wood Machinery Manufacturers of America. Buyer's Guide and Directory (USA) 3718
Wood Machining News (USA ISSN 0743-5231) 3718
Wood Magazine see Better Homes and Gardens Wood 4437
• ➤ Wood Material Science and Engineering (GBR ISSN 1748-0272) 3718
Wood News see WoodNews 3718
Wood Processing Industry see Derevoobrabatyvayushchaya Promyshlennost' 3711
• Wood Processing Newsletter (NZL ISSN 0113-6224) 3718
• Wood Products: International Trade and Foreign Markets (USA) 208
Wood Products Review (USA ISSN 1078-831X) 3718
➤ Wood Research (SVK ISSN 1336-4561) 3718
• ➤ Wood Science and Technology (DEU ISSN 0043-7719) 3718
Wood Southern Africa & Timber Times (ZAF ISSN 1022-8209) 3707
Wood Surfer (FRA ISSN 1628-9706) 461
Woodall's Camperways (USA ISSN 0744-8120) 8775
Woodall's Campground Directory. Eastern Edition see Woodall's Eastern America Campground Directory 8342
Woodall's Campground Directory. Western Edition see Woodall's Western Campground Directory 8342
Woodall's Campground Guide: Frontier West/Great Plains and Mountain Region see Woodall's Campground Guide: Frontier West/Great Plains & Mountain Region 8775
Woodall's Campground Guide: Frontier West/Great Plains & Mountain Region (USA ISSN 1548-4181) 8775
Woodall's Campground Management (USA ISSN 0162-3796) 8342
▼ Woodall's Camping Life Magazine (USA) 8342
Woodall's Eastern America Campground Directory (USA ISSN 1545-8997) 8342
Woodall's Florida R V Traveler (USA) 8637
Woodall's Midwest R V Traveler (USA) 8637
• Woodall's North America Campground Directory (USA ISSN 1547-6340) 8342
Woodall's Northeast Outdoors (USA ISSN 1093-4189) 8342
Woodall's Plan It - Pack It - Go see Woodall's Camping Life Magazine 8342
Woodall's R V Buyer's Guide (USA ISSN 0162-7368) 8520
Woodall's Southern R V (USA) 8342
Woodall's Tenting Directory see Woodall's Camping Life Magazine 8342
Woodall's Western Campground Directory (USA ISSN 0162-7414) 8342
The Woodbridge Club (CAN ISSN 1712-7289) 1195
Woodbridge Lectures, Columbia University (USA) 6961
Woodcarving (GBR ISSN 0965-9463) 1052
Woodcraft see Woodcraft et Pourquoi Pas? 2271
Woodcraft et Pourquoi Pas? (FRA ISSN 1955-8864) 2271
Woodcraft Magazine (USA ISSN 1553-2461) 1052
Wooden Bell (USA) 8078
The Wooden O Symposium. Journal (USA ISSN 1539-5758) 8484
The Woodenboat (USA ISSN 0095-067X) 8285
Woodfall: Landlord & Tenant (GBR) 7616
Woodland Report (USA) 3707
Woodmen see W f m 4527
Woodmen of the World Fraternal Magazine m see W f m 4527
• WoodNews (IND ISSN 0971-6734) 3718
Woodpecker see Zhuomuniao 5405
Woodrow Wilson Birthplace Newsletter (USA) 6540
Woodrow Wilson International Center for Scholars. Annual Report (USA ISSN 0271-3195) 3016
Woodrow Wilson National Fellowship Foundation. Annual Report (USA ISSN 0084-1145) 3010
Woodrow Wilson National Fellowship Foundation. Newsletter (USA ISSN 0084-1137) 3010
Woodrow Wilson School of Public and International Affairs. Discussion Papers in Economics (USA ISSN 0735-9411) 1195
Woods Hole Currents (USA) 2821
Woods Hole Folk Music Society Newsletter (USA) 2688
Woods Hole Oceanographic Institution - Annual Report (USA ISSN 1062-2152) 2821
Woods Hole Oceanographic Institution. Technical Report (USA ISSN 0730-9694) 2821
• Woods of the World (GBR) 3718
Woods, Water & Wildlife (USA) 2633
Woods, Water and Wildlife see Woods, Water & Wildlife 2633
Woodshop News (USA ISSN 0894-5403) 1052
Woodsman Newsletter (UGA) 3707
Woodsmith (USA ISSN 0164-4114) 1052
The Woodson Review (USA ISSN 1932-832X) 3572
Woodturning (GBR ISSN 0958-9457) 1052
Woodturning Design (USA ISSN 1550-8412) 541
Woodwatch (FIN ISSN 1457-3946) 3718
The Woodwind Quarterly see The Journal of Musical Instrument Technology 6581
Woodwork (USA ISSN 1045-3040) 4439
The Woodworker (GBR) 1052
The Woodworker & Woodturner see The Woodworker 1052
• Woodworker's Journal (USA ISSN 0199-1892) 4439
Woodworker's Journal eZine see Woodworker's Journal 4439
• Woodworkers West (USA ISSN 1080-0042) 1052
• Woodworking (CAN ISSN 0838-4185) 1053
Woodworking see Woodworking Magazine 1053
• Woodworking at Home (USA) 1053
Woodworking D B M (DEU) 3718
Woodworking International (DEU ISSN 0177-7114) 3718
Woodworking Magazine (USA ISSN 1941-5834) 1053
Woofin' (JPN) 6628
Wool & Wattles (USA ISSN 0749-9957) 304
Wool and Woolens of India (IND ISSN 0043-7808) 8462
Wool & Woollen (IND ISSN 0970-504X) 8462
Wool Gathering (USA) 6643
Wool Market News see National Wool Market Review 294
• Wool Market Review (AUS ISSN 1441-9440) 8462
Wool News (IND ISSN 0043-7824) 8462
Wool News see Wolnuus 8462
Wool Record see Twist 8461
• Wool Record Weekly Market Report (Email) (GBR) 8462
Wool Record Weekly Market Report (Print) see Wool Record Weekly Market Report (Email) 8462
† Wool Research Organisation of New Zealand Reports (NZL ISSN 0112-2851) 8999
Wool Research Organisation of New Zealand Special Publications (NZL ISSN 0112-2754) 8462
Wool Statistics (BEL ISSN 0260-2016) 8464
Wool Technology and Sheep Breeding (Print) see International Journal of Sheep and Wool Science 290
Wool Textile Journal see Maofang Keji 8454
• Wool Trade Directory of the World (GBR ISSN 0268-3601) 2035
➤ Woolf Studies Annual (USA ISSN 1080-9317) 5400
• Woolgatherings (CAN) 4350
Woolhope Naturalists' Field Club, Herefordshire. Transactions (GBR ISSN 0084-1226) 424
Woollen Exporters Directory (IND) 8462
The Woolly Times (USA) 8462
Woolner Indological Series (IND ISSN 0084-1242) 6961
• Woolworths Australian Parents (AUS) 2171
Woolworths Taste see Taste 4368
Woon Journaal (NLD ISSN 1570-6338) 4563
Woon Recht see W R 7615
Woonboot Magazine (NLD ISSN 0928-4702) 8285
Woonconsument see Eigen Huis Magazine 1006
Wooninnovatie Reeks (NLD ISSN 1573-9902) 1043
WoonKwaliteit (NLD ISSN 1574-9908) 1043
Woord en Daad see Wereldelen 8078
• Woord & Daad/Word & Action (ZAF ISSN 0257-8921) 7780
Woord en Dienst (NLD ISSN 0165-2443) 7780
Woord en Gebaar (NLD ISSN 0167-8930) 4077
• Woorilla (AUS ISSN 1038-9725) 5400
Wooster (USA ISSN 0894-8798) 2310
Worcester Business Journal (USA ISSN 1063-6595) 1434
Worcester Medicine (USA ISSN 1055-6370) 5731
Worcester Polytechnic Institute Journal see W P I Journal 3226
Worcester Polytechnic Institute - Studies in Science, Technology and Culture (USA ISSN 0897-926X) 7929
Worcester Public Library Staff Newsletter (USA) 5055
Worcester Quarterly (USA) 3993
• ➤ The Worcester Review (USA ISSN 8756-5277) 5438
Worcestershire Archaeological Society. Transactions (GBR ISSN 0143-2389) 424
Worcestershire Archaeology Society. Recorder (GBR ISSN 1362-0657) 424
Worcestershire Farmer & Record (GBR ISSN 0955-0305) 170
Worcestershire Naturalists' Club. Transactions (GBR ISSN 0264-7702) 2633
• Word (CAN) 5245
Word (IND ISSN 0043-7948) 2345
Word see Captivate 8030
The Word (Chicago) (USA) 3116
➤ Word (New York, 1945) (USA ISSN 0043-7956) 5195
The Word (Rochester, NY) (USA ISSN 0740-6754) 6648
Word (Waldport) (USA ISSN 1524-5624) 5400
Word 4 the Urban Teenage Girl of Faith see Esther 2188
• The Word Among Us (USA ISSN 0742-4639) 7823
Word & Action see Woord & Daad 7780
Word & Deed (USA) 5828
• ➤ Word & Image (GBR ISSN 0266-6286) 5246
Word & Image Interactions (NLD ISSN 1388-3569) 5400
• Word and Music Studies (NLD ISSN 1566-0958) 6628
Word & Sense see Slovo a Smysl 5374
Word and Speech see Slovo a Slovesnost 5175
Word and Way (USA ISSN 0049-7959) 7780
• Word & Witness (USA ISSN 1047-2339) 7780
Word and Work (USA) 7694
Word & World (USA ISSN 0275-5270) 7780
Word & World. Supplement see Word & World 7780
Word Art see Umjetnost Rijeci 5391
Word at Work (GBR) 7780
• Word for Today (USA) 7780
Word for Word (NZL ISSN 1176-3612) 5195
Word from Washington (San Antonio) (USA) 1715
Word from Washington (Washington, D.C.) (USA ISSN 0738-8012) 4070
Word in Action (GBR) 7694
• Word in Season (USA ISSN 0279-6007) 7695
Word is Out Poetry Journal (AUS ISSN 1833-8917) 5438
The Word Magazine (IRL ISSN 1649-1297) 7695
➤ Word Matters (GBR ISSN 1757-9384) 8484
The Word Newsource (USA) 1195
• Word of Faith (USA) 7695
Word of Life Quarterly (USA) 7695
• Word of Mouth (San Antonio) (USA ISSN 1048-3950) 3049
Word of Salvation (AUS ISSN 0813-7951) 7695
Word One (USA) 7695
Word Progress (USA ISSN 1055-3983) 4845
Word Salad (USA) 5438
Word Smart (USA ISSN 1559-8659) 3010
Word Smart 2 see Word Smart Second 3010
Word Smart for the G R E (Graduate Record Exam) (USA ISSN 1559-8233) 3010
Word Smart Second (USA ISSN 1559-8241) 3010
▼ • Word Structure (GBR ISSN 1750-1245) 5195
Word, The, see The Word Newsource 1195
Word Tips see Wordtips 2601
Word Up! (Paramus) (USA ISSN 1056-4691) 6628
Word Warrior (USA) 4070
• Word Ways (USA ISSN 0043-7980) 5195
Word Works (CAN ISSN 0843-1329) 5400
Word Wrap (CAN ISSN 0848-0397) 5400
Word Wrights see WordWrights 5400
• Wordgun (USA) 5246
Wordly Remains (USA) 6629
• WordPerfect Suite Newsletter Online (USA) 2600
• Words & Music (CAN ISSN 1195-8316) 6629
Words and Phrases, Legal Maxims see Sanagan's Encyclopedia of Words and Phrases, Legal Maxims 4778
Words and Phrases Legally Defined (CAN) 4815
Words and Pictures see Ord & Bild 5232
Words for Today (GBR ISSN 1476-3893) 7780
Words from Inside (CAN ISSN 0316-8670) 5400
• Words-Myth (USA ISSN 1931-6143) 5438
Words of L I F E (Living in Freedom Eternally, Inc.) (USA) 7695
Words of Life (CAN ISSN 1480-0675) 7823
Words on Cassette (Year) see Books Out Loud 620
• Words Without Borders (USA ISSN 1936-1459) 5400
▼ Words Without Music (USA ISSN 1938-4556) 6629
Wordsearch World (GBR ISSN 1369-622X) 4350
Wordsearches see Take a Break's Wordsearches 4348
Wordsearches Collection see Take a Break's Wordsearches Collection 4348
WordStar Scroll (USA ISSN 0890-524X) 2601
• ➤ Wordsworth Circle (USA ISSN 0043-8006) 5400
Wordt Vervolgd (NLD ISSN 0165-4241) 7218
• Wordtips (USA ISSN 1522-3744) 2601
WordWrights (USA) 5400
• ➤ Work (NLD ISSN 1051-9815) 6688
Work America (USA ISSN 0740-4077) 1525
• Work and Family Life (USA ISSN 1040-0958) 2926
• ➤ Work and Occupations (USA ISSN 0730-8884) 8147
Work and Progress (NZL ISSN 1174-9970) 3049
Work and Society see Travail & Societe 8011
• ➤ Work and Stress (GBR ISSN 0267-8373) 7415
Work at Home Moms see W A H M 8888
▼ • The Work-at-Home Parent Magazine (USA ISSN 1943-930X) 1969
• Work at Home Parents E-Zine (USA ISSN 1529-3009) 1969
Work-at-Home Sourcebook (USA) 6705
• ➤ Work Based Learning in Primary Care (GBR ISSN 1740-3715) 5731
Work Boat World (AUS ISSN 1037-3748) 8665
• The Work Doctor Magazine (USA) 1715
• ➤ Work, Employment & Society (GBR ISSN 0950-0170) 8147

DIRECTORY 2010 WORLD AFFAIRS (WASHINGTON) 11035

• Work Experience of the Population (USA ISSN 0162-0592) **6707**
• Work + Family Newsbrief (USA ISSN 1084-1377) **8147**
Work - Health - Safety *see* Tyo, Terveys, Turvallisuus **6688**
† Work Health Safety (FIN ISSN 0783-6899) **8999**
Work in America Institute: Highlights of the Literature (USA ISSN 0149-8703) **1274**
Work in America Institute Studies in Productivity (USA ISSN 0149-869X) **1274**
• Work in Progress (USA) **4605**
Work Life in Transition *see* Arbetsliv i Omvandling **1664**
Work - Life Today (USA ISSN 1546-9859) **1877**
• Work Organisation, Labour & Globalisation (GBR ISSN 1745-641X) **1715**
Work Organization, Labor & Globalization *see* Work Organisation, Labour & Globalisation **1715**
Work Programs Special Interest Section Quarterly (USA ISSN 1093-7145) **6705**
Work Research Foundation Comment *see* W R F Comment **7693**
▼ • Work Truck Magazine (USA) **8679**
WorkAmerica *see* Work America **1525**
Workamper News (USA ISSN 0895-3678) **6705**
• Workbench (USA ISSN 0043-8057) **4439**
• WorkBoat (USA ISSN 0043-8014) **8665**
Workboats *see* Work Boat World **8665**
Workbox (GBR ISSN 1360-0699) **6643**
The Worker (GMB ISSN 0796-0158) **3843**
Worker *see* Mfanyakazi **3961**
Workers *see* Kulloja **4597**
Workers' Challenge (ZMB) **7823**
† Workers' Charter (NZL ISSN 1177-343X) **8999**
Workers' Comp Advisor (New York) (USA) **4528**
• Workers' Comp Bottom Line (USA ISSN 1553-8974) **4528**
• Workers' Comp Executive (USA ISSN 1074-0988) **1715**
• Workers' Comp. Florida (USA ISSN 1932-9857) **1715**
• Workers' Comp. Illinois (USA ISSN 1932-9636) **1715**
† • Workers' Comp Managed Care (USA ISSN 1066-2669) **8999**
• Workers' Comp. New York (USA ISSN 1932-9652) **1715**
• Workers' Comp. Ohio (USA ISSN 1932-9679) **1715**
• Workers' Comp. Pennsylvania (USA ISSN 1932-9695) **1715**
Worker's Comp Quarterly (USA) **4528**
• Workers' Comp. Texas (USA ISSN 1932-9717) **1715**
• Workers Compensation (USA) **4528**
Workers' Compensation Appeal Tribunal. Annual Report (CAN ISSN 1912-5836) **1715**
• Workers' Compensation Board Insight (CAN ISSN 1488-4631) **4528**
Workers' Compensation Board of British Columbia. Annual Report (CAN ISSN 0704-0946) **4528**
Workers' Compensation Board of Nova Scotia. Annual Report (CAN ISSN 1184-0137) **4528**
Workers' Compensation - Business Management Guide Newsletter (USA) **4528**
Workers Compensation Coverage (USA ISSN 1939-7763) **4528**
• Worker's Compensation Guide (USA) **1877**
Workers' Compensation Insurance (USA) **4528**
Workers' Compensation Journal of Ohio (USA ISSN 0886-9162) **7477**
• Workers' Compensation Law Bulletin (USA ISSN 0748-7878) **1715**
• Workers Compensation Law Manual N S W (AUS) **4528**
Workers Compensation Law Manual New South Wales *see* Workers Compensation Law Manual N S W **4528**
Workers' Compensation Law of Maryland Annotated *see* Maryland Workers' Compensation Law **1696**
Workers' Compensation Law Reporter *see* Michigan Workers' Compensation Law Reporter **4515**
Workers' Compensation Law Reporter *see* Pennsylvania Workers' Compensation Law Reporter **4518**
• Workers' Compensation Laws of California (USA ISSN 0748-4135) **4816**
† • Workers' Compensation Monitor (USA ISSN 1096-7850) **8999**
• Workers Compensation N S W (AUS) **1715**
Workers' Compensation News and Four-Forty Report (USA) **1715**
• Workers' Compensation Outlook (USA ISSN 1052-6358) **4528**
• Workers Compensation Report (AUS ISSN 0816-2107) **1715**
• Workers' Compensation Report (USA ISSN 1051-4775) **1715**
Worker's Daily *see* Gongren Ribao **1488**
Workers Defense League, Inc. News *see* W D L News **1714**
Workers Education Journal (IND) **1715**
Workers Hammer (GBR ISSN 0267-8721) **7194**
Workers' Health International Newsletter (GBR ISSN 1351-4792) **6689**
Worker's Herald *see* Ergatiko Vima **1680**
Workers Life (Pretoria) (ZAF) **6689**
• Workers News (AUS) **4605**
• Workers Online (AUS ISSN 1442-6617) **4605**
Workers Press (GBR) **1715**
Workers Solidarity (USA) **1715**
Workers Vanguard (USA ISSN 0276-0746) **7194**
Worker's Voice (ATG) **4605**
Worker's Voice *see* Ergatiki Phoni **1680**
Worker's Voice *see* Sawt al-Ummal **4602**
Workers Voice (ZMB) **4605**
Workers World (USA ISSN 0043-809X) **7194**
Workflow Handbook *see* B P M and Workflow Handbook **4590**
Workflow Handbook Including Business Process Management *see* B P M and Workflow Handbook **4590**
• Workforce (AUS ISSN 0811-9023) **1715**
Workforce *see* Workforce Management **1877**
Workforce Diversity for Engineering and I T Professionals (USA) **1877**
Workforce. Industrial Relations Index *see* Workforce **1715**
• Workforce Management (USA ISSN 1547-5565) **1877**
• Workforce N T Report (Northern Territory) (AUS ISSN 1832-2891) **1715**
Workforce Northern Territory Report *see* Workforce N T Report **1715**
Workforce Performance Solutions *see* Talent Management **1876**
Workforce Professional (USA ISSN 1524-1033) **1716**
Workforce Tools *see* Workforce Management **1877**
Workforce Trends of Licensed Practical Nurses in Canada *see* Tendances de la Main-d'Oeuvre des Infirmieres et Infirmiers Autorises au Canada (Print) **5982**
Workforce Trends of Licensed Practical Nurses in Canada (Online) *see* Tendances de la Main-d'Oeuvre des Infirmieres et Infirmiers Autorises au Canada (Online) **5982**
• Workforce Trends of Registered Nurses in Canada (CAN ISSN 1709-7541) **5984**
• Workforce Trends of Registered Psychiatric Nurses in Canada (CAN ISSN 1711-2613) **5984**
• Workgroup Computing Report (USA ISSN 1068-9699) **2538**
• Workindex (USA) **1716**
▼ • Workinfo.com Human Resources Magazine (ZAF ISSN 1993-0798) **1877**
Working Abroad (London) (GBR) **8775**
Working America (USA ISSN 1524-3257) **4605**
Working at Office *see* working@office **1878**
The Working Border Collie (USA ISSN 1059-6267) **6817**
The Working Class (IND ISSN 0377-6611) **4605**
Working Class Hero (USA) **2271**
Working Class Opposition/Oposicion Obrera (USA) **7194**
The Working Communicator (USA ISSN 1099-7245) **1801**
• Working Conference on Reverse Engineering. Proceedings (USA ISSN 1095-1350) **2600**
▼ Working Education (USA ISSN 1947-2234) **2947**
Working for Yourself (GBR) **1969**
Working Group on Migratory Birds of the Western Paleoarctic Region. Newsletter *see* O M P O. Newsletter **2623**
Working Group on Software Newsletter *see* W G S Newsletter **2599**
Working Journalist (IND) **4585**
Working Kelpie Council. National Stud Book (AUS ISSN 0312-3480) **304**
Working Kelpie Council News Bulletin *see* W K C News Bulletin **6816**
Working Life Research in Europe. Report (SWE ISSN 1404-790X) **1716**
Working Moms and Dads (USA) **2171**
• Working Money (Online) (USA) **1659**
• Working Mother (USA ISSN 0278-193X) **8892**
Working Nights (USA) **6705**
Working Paper Series in Business Administration *see* S S E/E F I Working Paper Series in Business Administration **1170**
• Working Paper Series on Electronic Voting and Participation (AUT ISSN 1992-6014) **7194**
Working Papers *see* Twenty-First Century Papers **4479**
• Working Papers for Philosophy and Economics (NLD ISSN 1871-6482) **6961**
Working Papers in Accounting and Finance *see* Cardiff Business School. Working Papers in Accounting and Finance **1284**
Working Papers in African Studies (USA ISSN 0281-6814) **8015**
• Working Papers in Art and Design (Online) (GBR ISSN 1466-4917) **527**
Working Papers in Coastal Zone Management Series (GBR ISSN 1350-2867) **8842**
• ➤ Working Papers in Communication Research (NZL ISSN 1177-3707) **8147**
• Working Papers in Composition & T E S O L (Teachers of English to Speakers of Other Languages) (USA ISSN 1948-0741) **5195**
▼ • Working Papers in Economics and Statistics (AUT ISSN 1993-4378) **1195**
Working Papers in Educational Linguistics (USA ISSN 1548-3134) **5195**
• Working Papers in Functional Grammar (NLD ISSN 0924-1205) **5196**
Working Papers in International Journalism *see* Arbeitshefte Internationaler Journalismus **4571**
Working Papers in Irish Studies (USA ISSN 0732-2674) **3572**
Working Papers in Linguistics *see* Arbeitspapiere zur Linguistik **5096**
Working Papers in Linguistics (ITA ISSN 1720-2310) **5196**
Working Papers in Linguistics *see* Working Papers ISK **5196**
• Working Papers in Linguistics (Online) (USA ISSN 1931-8952) **5196**
• Working Papers in Social Insurance (SWE ISSN 1653-1353) **4528**
• Working Papers in Trade and Development (AUS ISSN 0816-5181) **1587**
Working Papers in Trade and Development *see* Asia Pacific School of Economics and Management Working Papers. Southeast Asia **1591**
Working Papers ISK (Institutt for Spraak og Kommunikasjonsstudier) (NOR ISSN 1503-9390) **5196**
Working Papers on Caribbean Society. Series A: New Perspectives in Theory and Analysis (TTO) **8147**
Working Papers on Caribbean Society. Series C: Research Findings (TTO) **8147**
Working Papers on Contemporary France (GBR ISSN 1466-5573) **5196**
Working Papers on Culture, Education and Human Development *see* Papeles de Trabajo sobre Cultura, Educacion y Desarrollo Humano **7389**
Working Papers on Literacy (CAN) **5196**
• ➤ Working Papers on the Web (GBR ISSN 1478-3703) **5400**
Working Papers on Women in International Development (USA ISSN 0888-5354) **1607**
Working Papers Political Science (NLD ISSN 1569-3546) **7194**
Working Party Reports (BEL) **7274**
• Working People's Advocate (USA ISSN 1949-2308) **7194**
Working Press of the Nation *see* Bowker's News Media Directory **8937**
Working Results (IND) **190**
Working Smart (USA ISSN 1049-4855) **1801**
Working Smarter with Microsoft Access (USA ISSN 1530-4353) **2600**
Working Smarter with Microsoft Excel (USA ISSN 1530-4337) **2600**
Working Smarter with Microsoft Office (USA) **2601**
† Working Smarter with Microsoft PowerPoint (USA ISSN 1530-4345) **8999**
Working Smarter with Microsoft Word (USA ISSN 1530-4299) **2601**
Working Smarter with Office 2000 (USA ISSN 1530-4329) **2600**
Working Smarter with Outlook (USA ISSN 1534-7001) **2600**
Working Smarter with WordPerfect (USA ISSN 1530-4280) **2601**
Working the Screen *see* RealTime **8477**
Working Together (USA ISSN 1525-0857) **1877**
Working Together (Seattle) (USA ISSN 1064-8585) **2672**
Working Together for Children in Need. Conference Report (GBR) **2171**
Working Together in Rural Canada *see* Canada. Rural Secretariat. Annual Report to Parliament **7427**
Working Together to Improve Community Safety Through the Reduction of Crime *see* B C Crime Prevention Pages. Directory of Services **2644**
• ➤ Working U S A (USA ISSN 1089-7011) **1716**
• ➤ Working With English (GBR ISSN 1740-8547) **5400**
• Working with Older People (GBR ISSN 1366-3666) **8078**
Working with Parents (GBR ISSN 1472-5177) **3088**
Working with Victims of Crime *see* Guide de Traitement des Victimes d'Actes Criminels **2654**
Working with Your State: A Guide for Regional Councils (USA) **7477**
Working Women (KOR) **8906**
• Working Writers Newsletter (USA) **5400**
• working@office (DEU ISSN 1438-471X) **1878**
WorkingUSA *see* Working U S A **1716**
• Worklife (Kingston) (CAN ISSN 0700-3102) **1716**
† Workman Branches (USA ISSN 1071-1554) **8999**
Workmen's Benefit Fund of the United States of America In Action *see* W B F In Action **4527**
The Workmen's Circle - Arbiter Ring Call (USA ISSN 0043-8111) **3572**
• WorkOutWire (USA) **1391**
Workpapers in Papua New Guinea Languages *see* Data Papers on Papua New Guinea Languages **5110**
Workplace (GBR) **4553**
• Workplace (USA) **3088**
Workplace Assistance & Benefits (USA ISSN 1945-3469) **1878**
Workplace Diversity and Discrimination Briefing (GBR ISSN 1741-9751) **1878**
• Workplace Equity Guide (CAN) **1716**
Workplace Ergonomics News (USA ISSN 1528-8013) **6689**
Workplace Gazette (CAN ISSN 1480-6886) **1716**
• Workplace H R & Safety (Online) (USA) **1878**
Workplace H R & Safety (Print) *see* Workplace H R & Safety (Online) **1878**
Workplace Hazardous Materials Information System at Work *see* W H M I S at Work **6688**
Workplace Hazardous Materials Information Systems Compliance Manual *see* W H M I S Compliance Manual **6688**
▼ • Workplace Immigration Report (USA ISSN 1940-1973) **1716**
• Workplace Injuries and Illnesses in (Year) (USA ISSN 1932-085X) **6691**
† Workplace Intelligence (AUS) **8999**
Workplace Law (ZAF) **1716**
Workplace News (CAN ISSN 1204-4229) **4605**
• Workplace Relations Australia (AUS) **4883**
• Workplace Report (GBR ISSN 1740-6307) **1716**
Workplace Safety Advisor *see* Keller's Workplace Safety Advisor **6680**
Workplace Safety and Insurance Appeals Tribunal in Focus *see* W S I A T in Focus **1714**
† • Workplace Substance Abuse Advisor (USA ISSN 1091-823X) **8999**
• Workplace Today (CAN ISSN 1487-9107) **1878**
Workpower *see* F N V Infopocket. Solliciteren **1681**
Workpower *see* F N V Infopocket. Stage **1681**
Workpower *see* F N V Infopocket. Bijbaan en Vakantiewerk **1681**
Workpower *see* F N V Infopocket. Geld **1681**
Workpower *see* F N V Infopocket. Rechten en Plichten **1681**
Works (CHE) **1878**
Works (GBR ISSN 0954-3902) **5449**
The Works (GBR ISSN 1466-1500) **6629**
➤ Works and Days (USA ISSN 0886-2060) **5400**
Works by Japanese Composers (Year) (JPN) **6629**
Works + Conversations (USA ISSN 1095-5224) **527**
Works Issued by the Hakluyt Society *see* Hakluyt Society **4141**
• Works Management (GBR ISSN 0374-4795) **1801**
Works Management Special Report for Smaller Companies (GBR) **1969**
Works of Art (USA) **6517**
• The Works of Dante (GBR) **2569**
The Works: Your Source for Abundant Living (USA) **7695**
• WorkSafe Magazine (CAN ISSN 1494-7412) **6689**
WorkSafe Newsletter for O S H Professionals *see* SafetyLine Newsletter for O S H Professionals **6686**
WorkSafe Newsletter for Safety and Health Representatives *see* SafetyLine Newsletter for Safety and Health Representatives **6686**
Workshop *see* Woerkshop **37**
Workshop and Maintenance Guide *see* Guia de Oficinas e Manutencao **57**
• Workshop di Archeologia Classica (ITA ISSN 1724-9120) **424**
Workshop for Oil & Acrylic Painters (USA ISSN 1930-4668) **527**
▼ Workshop Internacional (ARG ISSN 1851-6661) **7274**
Workshop of Peace/Muntada as-Salaam (BHR) **3016**
• Workshop on Computers in Power Electronics. Proceedings (USA ISSN 1541-5848) **2474**
Workshop on Computers in Power Electronics. Record *see* Workshop on Computers in Power Electronics. Proceedings **2474**
Workshop on Enabling Technologies: Infrastructure for Collaborative Enterprises, Proceedings *see* I E E E International Workshops on Enabling Technologies: Infrastructure for Collaborative Enterprises. Proceedings **3312**
• Workshop on Future Trends of Distributed Computing Systems. Proceedings (USA ISSN 1071-0485) **2525**
• Workshop on Hot Topics in Operating Systems (USA ISSN 1530-1621) **2600**
• Workshop on Interaction Between Compilers and Computer Architectures. Proceedings (USA ISSN 1550-6207) **2468**
• Workshop on Mobile Computing Systems and Applications (USA ISSN 1550-6193) **2457**
• Workshop on Multimedia Signal Processing (USA) **2535**
• Workshop on New Paradigms in Information Visualization and Manipulation (USA ISSN 1544-8118) **2518**
• Workshop on Parallel and Distributed Simulation. Proceedings (USA ISSN 1087-4097) **2468**
Workshop on Robot Motion and Control (USA) **2587**
• WorkSite (Online) (AUS) **4605**
Worksite News (CAN ISSN 1203-3774) **6689**
Worksite Wellness Works *see* The Well Workplace Newsletter **7545**
Worksop Trader (GBR) **3873**
• Workspan (USA ISSN 1529-9465) **1716**
The Workstation Report (USA ISSN 1062-7650) **1855**
Workvessel *see* Sagyosen **8659**
• Workwise Work Related Death Prevention: the Coronial Approach (AUS ISSN 1834-2213) **6689**
† World (FRA ISSN 1287-406X) **8999**
World *see* Sekai **7182**
• World (USA ISSN 0888-157X) **3993**
The World (New York) (USA ISSN 0043-8154) **5438**
• ➤ World Academy of Science, Engineering and Technology. Proceedings (TUR ISSN 2070-3740) **7929**
World Accounting (USA) **1304**
• World Accounting Report (GBR ISSN 1469-2716) **1304**
• World Aerospace & Defense Intelligence (Online) (USA) **75**
• World Aerospace Database (USA) **75**
World Aerospace Database. Buyer's Guide (USA) **8553**
World Affairs *see* Shijie Zhishi **7265**
• World Affairs (IND ISSN 0971-8052) **7274**
• ➤ World Affairs (Washington) (USA ISSN 0043-8200) **7274**

Title

11036 WORLD AFFAIRS PICTORIAL ULRICH'S PERIODICALS

World Affairs Pictorial *see* Shijie Zhishi Huabao **3828**
• World Affairs Report (USA ISSN 0090-7103) **7274**
World Ag Expo (USA) **170**
World Ag Expo V I P Preview (Very Important Producers) (USA) **170**
• World Agricultural Economics and Rural Sociology Abstracts (GBR ISSN 0043-8219) **190**
• World Agricultural Production (USA ISSN 1052-0279) **170**
• World Agricultural Supply and Demand Estimates (USA ISSN 0277-3139) **208**
World Agriculture *see* Shijie Nongye **156**
World Agriculture, Forestry and Fisheries *see* Sekai no Norinsuisan **155**
† WorldAIDS (GBR ISSN 0954-6510) **8999**
World Air Forces *see* Jane's World Air Forces **6428**
• World Air Transport Statistics (CAN ISSN 0084-1366) **8532**
World Aircraft Accident Summary (GBR ISSN 1366-6800) **8553**
World Aircraft Information Files (GBR ISSN 1369-6483) **75**
World Airline Fleets News (GBR ISSN 0951-8673) **8553**
World Airline Maintenance Forecast: Fleet Planning and Forecasts *see* Market Intelligence Reports: World Airline Maintenance Forecast **8972**
World Airline Report (USA) **8520**
World Airnews (ZAF ISSN 0261-2399) **75**
World Airport Guide (GBR) **8553**
World Airshow News (USA ISSN 0888-5265) **75**
World Alert *see* T M A World Alert **8487**
▼ • The World Allergy Organization Journal (USA ISSN 1939-4551) **5767**
World Alliance of Reformed Churches. Update (CHE) **7780**
World Alliance of Y M C A's Directory (CHE ISSN 0513-6032) **2271**
• The World Almanac and Book of Facts (USA ISSN 0084-1382) **3123**
The World Almanac Book of Records (USA ISSN 1939-0017) **3123**
The World Almanac for Kids (USA ISSN 1087-1764) **2222**
World Aluminium Databook (GBR) **6337**
World Amateur Boxing Magazine (CHE) **8216**
World Amateur Golf Council. Record Book (USA) **8252**
• World Anaesthesia News (GBR ISSN 1471-8820) **5774**
The World & Chongqing *see* Chongqing yu Shijie **3823**
• The World & I Online (USA) **3993**
World and Press (DEU ISSN 0509-1632) **4585**
World and United States Aviation and Space Records (USA ISSN 0890-510X) **75**
• World Animal Health in (Year) (FRA ISSN 1017-3102) **8815**
World Animal Review (Multilingual Edition)/Revista Mondial de Zootecnia/Revue Mondiale de Zootechnie (ITA ISSN 1014-6954) **304**
➤ World Animal Science (NLD) **968**
➤ World Applied Sciences Journal (PAK ISSN 1818-4952) **7930**
World Aquaculture (USA ISSN 1041-5602) **2821**
• ➤ World Aquaculture Society. Journal (USA ISSN 0893-8849) **2821**
World Aquaculture Society. Workshop Series (USA) **2821**
World Arab Trade (UAE) **1587**
† World Arbitration & Mediation Report (USA ISSN 0960-0949) **8999**
World Arbitration & Mediation Report *see* The World Arbitration and Mediation Review **4816**
• The World Arbitration and Mediation Review (USA ISSN 1934-3310) **4816**
• World Arbitration Reporter (USA) **4944**
World Archaeological Bulletin (GBR) **424**
World Archaeological Society Newsletter *see* W A S Newsletter **423**
World Archaeological Society. Special Publication (USA ISSN 1060-2887) **424**
• ➤ World Archaeology (GBR ISSN 0043-8243) **424**
World Architecture Herald *see* Shijie Jianzhu Daobao **457**
World Ark (USA) **8078**
World Armies *see* Jane's World Armies **6428**
• World Around You (USA ISSN 0199-8293) **3049**
World Around You. Teacher's Edition (USA ISSN 1059-9894) **4077**
World Art *see* Shijie Meishu **517**
World Art Glass Quarterly (USA ISSN 1934-8665) **2046**
▼ • World Articles in Ear Nose and Throat (USA ISSN 1948-9579) **6086**
World Assembly of Muslim Youth. European Newsletter (GBR) **7717**
World Association for Animal Production Book of the Year *see* W A A P Book of the Year **303**
World Association for Educational Research. Congress Reports (BEL) **2926**
World Association of Document Examiners Journal *see* W A D E Journal **2671**
▼ World at War (USA ISSN 1943-9806) **6454**
World at Work Journal *see* WorldatWork Journal **1878**
World Atlas of Hydropower & Dams *see* The International Journal on Hydropower & Dams **3163**
World Author Series *see* Twayne's World Authors Series **5391**
• World Authors (USA ISSN 1093-6564) **648**
• World Automotive Manufacturing (GBR ISSN 1463-1857) **8612**
World Automotive Statistics (FRA) **8532**
A World Awaits You (USA) **3016**
• World Badminton (MYS ISSN 0255-4429) **8216**
World Bamboo and Rattan *see* Shijie Zhuteng Tongxun **3702**
World Bank. Annual Conference on Development in Latin America and the Caribbean (USA ISSN 1020-6140) **1607**
• World Bank. Annual Report (USA ISSN 0252-2942) **1607**
World Bank Atlas *see* The Atlas of Global Development **1591**
World Bank Country Study (USA ISSN 0253-2123) **1608**
World Bank Directory (USA) **2035**
World Bank. E D I Development Study (USA ISSN 1020-105X) **1608**
• ➤ The World Bank Economic Review (USA ISSN 0258-6770) **1525**
World Bank Environment Paper (USA ISSN 1026-115X) **1608**
World Bank. Global Environment Facility. Working Paper (USA ISSN 1020-0894) **1608**
World Bank Implementation Unit Project News *see* N U C Project News **2994**
The World Bank Legal Review (NLD) **4816**
World Bank. Monthly Operational Summary of Bank and I D A Proposed Projects (USA ISSN 1931-3683) **1608**
World Bank. Monthly Operational Summary of Proposed Projects *see* World Bank. Monthly Operational Summary of Bank and I D A Proposed Projects **1608**
• World Bank Operations Evaluation Study (USA ISSN 1011-0984) **1195**
• World Bank Policy Paper (USA ISSN 0258-2120) **1608**
• World Bank. Policy Research Working Papers (Online) (USA ISSN 1564-6378) **1195**
† • World Bank. Policy Research Working Papers (Print) (USA ISSN 1020-0525) **8999**
† World Bank. Publications Update (USA ISSN 1014-5842) **8999**
World Bank Regional and Sectoral Studies (USA ISSN 1564-7838) **1608**
World Bank. Reprint Series (USA ISSN 0253-2131) **1391**
• ➤ World Bank Research Observer (GBR ISSN 0257-3032) **1391**
World Bank Research Program (USA ISSN 0258-3143) **1274**
World Bank Series on Evaluation and Development (USA) **1608**
• World Bank Working Paper (USA ISSN 1726-5878) **1608**
• World Banking Abstracts (GBR ISSN 0265-9484) **1391**
World Banking Abstracts. Index *see* World Banking Abstracts **1391**
World Baseball (CHE ISSN 1040-5216) **8252**
World Bibliography of Bibliographies of Bibliographies (AUS) **639**
• World Biodiversity Database Series (FRA) **711**
World Birdwatch (GBR) **917**
World Books *see* Shijie Tushu **8988**
World Broadcast Engineering *see* Broadcast Engineering (World Edition) **2376**
World Buiatrics Congress (BEL) **8815**
World Bulk Trades (NOR ISSN 0801-4086) **8665**
World Bureau of Metal Statistics. Annual Report (GBR) **6342**
† World Business (GBR ISSN 1749-9275) **8999**
World Business (PRT) **1195**
• World Business Conference (CAN) **1587**
World Business Directory (USA ISSN 1062-1172) **2035**
World Business Review (USA ISSN 1081-3284) **1587**
World Cargo Economist (GBR) **8520**
† World Cartography (USA ISSN 0084-1471) **8999**
World Casualty Statistics (GBR ISSN 1364-9876) **8533**
World Catalogue of Insects (DNK ISSN 1398-8700) **861**
World Catalysts (USA ISSN 1945-1873) **2084**
• World Cement (GBR ISSN 0263-6050) **1043**
World Cement & Concrete Additives (USA ISSN 1932-7730) **1908**
World Cement Directory (BEL ISSN 1013-9532) **1043**
World Ceramics Abstracts (GBR ISSN 0957-8897) **2047**
World Ceramics & Refractories (GBR ISSN 0959-6127) **2047**
World Chamber of Commerce Directory (USA ISSN 1048-2849) **1413**
World Children *see* Shijie Ertong **2168**
World Chinese Journal of Digestology *see* Shijie Huaren Xiaohua Zazhi **5931**
World Choral Census (USA) **6629**
World Cinema *see* Shijie Dianying **6513**
World Cinema (GBR ISSN 0269-2600) **6517**
World Class Weddings (USA) **5562**
▼ • World Climate Change Report (USA ISSN 1943-4650) **3475**
• World Climate News (CHE) **6398**
World Climate Review (USA) **3475**
World Clinical Drugs *see* Shijie Linchuang Yaowu **6880**
World Clothing Manufacturer *see* Fashion Business International **2247**
World Cocoa Directory *see* I C C O World Cocoa Directory **3646**
World Coffee and Tea Yearbook (Year) (GBR) **3668**
World Cogeneration (USA ISSN 1053-5802) **3150**
• World Coin News (USA ISSN 0145-9090) **6653**
World Coinage Report *see* United States Mint. World Coinage Report **6653**
World Coins *see* Standard Catalog of World Coins. 1901-2000 **6653**
▼ World Commerce Review (GBR ISSN 1751-0023) **1587**
World Commercial Aircraft - Engine Orders & Options *see* Market Intelligence Reports: World Commercial Aircraft - Engine Orders & Options **65**
World Commercial Refrigeration Equipment (USA ISSN 1937-948X) **4128**
World Commercial Vehicles (Online) *see* Commercial Vehicles Monthly Digest **8575**
• World Commodity Forecasts: Food Feedstuffs and Beverages (USA ISSN 1351-8968) **1195**
• World Commodity Forecasts. Industrial Raw Materials (USA ISSN 1351-8976) **1195**
World Commodity Perspective (USA) **1660**
World Commodity Profiles (USA) **1587**
World Commodity Survey (CHE ISSN 1020-7813) **1587**
World Communication Report (FRA) **2345**
• World Communications Regulation Report (GBR ISSN 1750-1784) **2345**
World Community Studies Weekly (USA ISSN 1556-3553) **2926**
• World Competition (NLD ISSN 1011-4548) **4944**
The World Competitiveness Yearbook (CHE ISSN 1026-2628) **1525**
World Conference on Animal Production. Proceedings (ITA ISSN 0084-1552) **304**
World Congress of Food Science and Technology. Proceedings (CAN) **3668**
World Congress of Gerontology *see* Australasian Journal on Ageing **4041**
World Congress of Jewish Studies. Proceedings *see* World Union of Jewish Studies. Proceedings **8999**
World Congress of Pain. Proceedings *see* Pain Research and Clinical Management **5692**
World Congress of Psychiatry. Proceedings (CHE ISSN 0084-1609) **6189**
World Congress of the W F D. Proceedings (World Federation of the Deaf) (ITA ISSN 0510-8292) **4077**
World Congress on Fertility and Sterility. Proceedings (USA ISSN 0084-1641) **6006**
World Congress on the Prevention of Occupational Accidents and Diseases. Proceedings (CHE ISSN 0084-165X) **6689**
World Conservation (CHE ISSN 1027-0965) **2633**
World Conservation Congress. Proceedings (CHE) **2633**
World Consumer Income and Expenditure Patterns *see* World Income Distribution **2036**
World Consumer Lifestyles Databook: Key Trends (GBR) **2035**
• World Consumer Markets (GBR) **2035**
World Consumer Spending (GBR) **2035**
World Consumption & Production *see* T M A World Consumption & Production **8487**
World Copper Databook (GBR ISSN 0950-2262) **6483**
World Cosmetics and Toiletries Marketing Directory (GBR) **596**
World Cost of Living Survey (USA ISSN 1092-1702) **1195**
World Cotton Markets Review (PAK) **8462**
World Council for Curriculum and Instruction. Newsletter (USA) **3088**
• World Council for Gifted and Talented Children. Biennial Conference. Proceedings (CAN) **3049**
World Council of Churches. Faith and Order Papers *see* Faith and Order Papers **7642**
World Council of Churches Focus *see* W C C Focus **7693**
World Council of Churches. General Assembly. Assembly - Reports (CHE ISSN 0084-1676) **7695**
World Council of Churches. Minutes and Reports of the Central Committee Meeting (CHE ISSN 0084-1684) **7695**
World Council of Churches News *see* W C C News **7693**
World Council of Churches. Office of Education. Education Newsletter (CHE) **7695**
World Council of Churches Publications *see* W C C Publications **7693**
World Council of Comparative Education Societies. Newsletter/Conseil Mondial des Societes d'Education Comparee. Bulletin d'Information (GBR) **2926**
World Council of Credit Unions. Annual and Statistical Report (USA) **1391**
➤ World Council of Enterostomal Therapists Journal (AUS ISSN 0819-4610) **5932**
World Council of Service Clubs. Minutes of the General Meeting (NZL) **8078**
World Court Digest (DEU ISSN 0943-9145) **4816**
World Crane Guide (GBR) **1043**
• ➤ World Crop Pests (NLD ISSN 1572-4379) **259**
World Cruise Industry Review (GBR ISSN 0954-1500) **8665**
• World Cultural Psychiatry Research Review (USA ISSN 1932-6270) **7415**
World Culture *see* Shijie Wenhua **5371**
World Culture Report (FRA) **4482**
• World Cultures (CD-ROM) (USA ISSN 1931-3748) **8015**
World Cultures (Print) *see* World Cultures (CD-ROM) **8015**
World Customs Organization. Annual Report (BEL) **7477**
World Customs Organization News *see* W C O News **7476**
• World Data Center A for Glaciology (Snow and Ice). New Accessions List (USA) **2721**
World Data Center C2 for Aurora. Data Catalogue (JPN) **6398**
World Data Center for Ionosphere. Catalogue of Data (JPN ISSN 1347-1546) **2791**
World Data Center for Marine Environmental Sciences Reports *see* W D C - M A R E Reports **3492**
• World Data Protection Report (USA ISSN 1473-3579) **2569**
• World Database of Business Information Sources (GBR) **1274**
World Database of Business Information Sources on the Internet *see* World Database of Business Information Sources **1274**
World Defence Industry *see* Jane's World Defence Industry **1131**
• World Defence Systems (GBR) **7274**
• World Dentistry (USA ISSN 1534-2530) **5869**
• ➤ World Development (GBR ISSN 0305-750X) **1608**
• World Development Indicators (USA ISSN 1029-4325) **1587**
World Development Movement in Action *see* W D M in Action **1607**
• World Development Report (USA ISSN 0163-5085) **1608**
World Development Report (Arabic Edition) *see* World Development Report **1608**
World Development Report (Arabic Edition) *see* Rapport sur le Developpement dans le Monde **1604**
• World Diabetes/Diabete Mondial (CHE ISSN 1564-0795) **5801**
▼ ➤ World Digital Libraries (IND) **5064**
World Directory of Business Information Libraries (GBR) **5055**
World Directory of Business Information Websites (GBR) **2569**
World Directory of Collections of Cultures of Microorganisms (JPN) **823**
World Directory of Crematoria (GBR ISSN 1356-9244) **3720**
World Directory of Crustacea Copepoda of Inland Waters (NLD) **968**
• World Directory of Crystallographers and of Other Scientists Employing Crystallographic Methods (NLD ISSN 0512-2724) **2112**
World Directory of Crystallographers and Other Persons Working with Crystallographic Methods *see* World Directory of Crystallographers and of Other Scientists Employing Crystallographic Methods **2112**
World Directory of Diplomatic Representation (GBR ISSN 0965-3783) **7274**
• World Directory of Environmental Organizations Online (USA) **2633**
World Directory of Fertilizer Manufacturers (GBR) **259**
World Directory of Fertilizer Products (GBR) **259**
World Directory of Historians of Mathematics (CAN ISSN 0315-1700) **5546**
• World Directory of Human Rights Research and Training Institutions (FRA) **7218**
• World Directory of Leisure Aviation (GBR ISSN 1368-485X) **75**
World Directory of Liner Shipping Agents (Year) (GBR) **2035**
World Directory of Marketing Information Sources (GBR) **1848**
World Directory of Mathematicians (USA ISSN 0512-2740) **5546**
World Directory of Medical Schools (CHE ISSN 0512-2759) **5731**
World Directory of National Science and Technology Policy-Making Bodies (FRA) **8445**
World Directory of Non-Official Statistical Sources (GBR) **1274**
World Directory of Parliaments (CHE ISSN 1013-0365) **7194**
† World Directory of Renewable Energy Suppliers and Services (GBR ISSN 1361-7524) **8999**
World Directory of Teacher-Training Institutions (FRA) **3010**
World Directory of Trade and Business Associations (GBR) **2035**
World Disasters Report (CHE ISSN 0929-0850) **7545**
• World Disease Weekly (USA ISSN 1553-6963) **5731**
World Distilleries Guide *see* F.O. Licht's World Distilleries Guide (Years) **603**
World Dredging Conference. Proceedings (USA) **3287**
World Dredging Mining & Construction (USA ISSN 1045-0343) **3287**
World Drink Trends (GBR ISSN 0969-8159) **614**

DIRECTORY 2010 WORLD JOURNAL OF UROLOGY 11037

World Drinks Databook (GBR) 614
World Drinks Marketing Directory (GBR) 614
• World Drinks Report (GBR ISSN 1360-7995) 614
World Drug Alerts. Consolidated Title (GBR ISSN 1353-7881) 6885
World Drug Alerts. Immune System (GBR ISSN 1353-7822) 6885
• World Drug Market Manual. Company (GBR ISSN 0140-4806) 6885
• World Drug Market Manual. Country Markets (GBR) 1195
World Drywall & Building Plasters (USA ISSN 1944-3226) 1049
World Dyes and Organic Pigments see World Dyes & Organic Pigments 2244
• World Dyes & Organic Pigments (USA ISSN 1940-5235) 2244
World Earthquake Engineering see Shijie Dizhen Gongcheng 3282
World Economic and Financial Surveys see International Monetary Fund. World Economic and Financial Surveys 1358
• World Economic and Social Survey (USA) 1525
World Economic Factbook (GBR) 1274
World Economic Outlook see International Monetary Fund. World Economic Outlook 1493
World Economic Papers see Shijie Jingji Wenhui 1173
World Economic Processing Zones Association Newsletter see W E P Z A Newsletter 1586
• World Economic Prospects (GBR ISSN 1461-9601) 1525
World Economics see Shijie Jingjixue 1721
• World Economics (GBR ISSN 1468-1838) 1195
• ➤ The World Economy (GBR ISSN 0378-5920) 1196
World Economy Study see Shijie Jingji Yanjiu 1517
World Education Report (FRA ISSN 1020-0479) 2926
World Education Reports (USA ISSN 0300-7006) 8147
World Electric Vehicle Association Journal see W E V A Journal 8611
World Employment (Year) (CHE ISSN 1020-3079) 1716
• World Energy (USA ISSN 1550-7769) 3150
• World Energy (Online Edition) (AUS ISSN 1832-7494) 3150
World Energy Conference. Directory of Energy Information Centres in the World (FRA) 2035
• World Energy Monthly Review (USA ISSN 1556-2689) 3150
World Energy Yearbook (GBR ISSN 1461-4693) 3150
World Engineering Industries and Automation (USA ISSN 1020-1300) 3359
• ➤ World Englishes (GBR ISSN 0883-2919) 5196
▼ • World Enterprise (HKG ISSN 1993-5463) 1587
World Environment see Shijie Huanjing 3466
World Ethanol & Biofuels Report see F.O. Licht's World Ethanol & Biofuels Report 732
World Ethno-National Studies see Shijie Minzu 355
• World Ethylene and Derivatives (USA) 2084
World Evangelical Alliance Theological News see W E A Theological News 7693
• World Executive's Digest - China Edition/Jingliren Wenzhai (HKG ISSN 1022-7784) 1801
World Explorer (USA ISSN 1061-0103) 8776
World Expo see Shijie Bolan 3828
World Expo (GBR) 6797
World Export Credit Guide see The Citi World Official Agency Guide 1327
World Expro (GBR ISSN 0968-2996) 6797
• World Factbook (USA ISSN 0277-1527) 7274
World Fairs Guide (IND) 1848
World Fast Ferry Market (AUS ISSN 1327-9408) 8665
World Federalist Newsletter (USA ISSN 0196-2574) 7274
World Federation (IND ISSN 0043-8448) 7274
• World Federation for Mental Health. Annual Report (USA) 7415
• World Federation for Mental Health. Newsletter (USA) 7415
World Federation of Democratic Youth News see W F D Y News 2220
World Federation of Hemophilia. Proceedings of Congress (CAN ISSN 0084-1765) 5942
World Fellowship of Buddhists. Book Series (THA ISSN 0084-1781) 7703
World Fellowship of Buddhists Review see W F B Review 7703
World Fence News (USA ISSN 1054-5115) 1043
World Fertility Survey. Summaries of Country Reports (Print Edition) see World Fertility Survey. Summary of Country Reports (CD-ROM Edition) 8999
† • World Fertility Survey. Summary of Country Reports (CD-ROM Edition) (NLD) 8999
World Fertilizer Plant List and Atlas (GBR ISSN 0512-2953) 259
World Financial Markets (USA ISSN 0190-2083) 1391
World Fine Art (USA) 527
World Fish Report see WorldFish Report 3612
World Fishing (GBR ISSN 0043-8480) 3611
• World Flat Glass (USA ISSN 1940-5251) 1587
World Fleet Statistics (GBR) 8533
World Flight see Huanqiu Feixing 58
• World Focus (GBR) 6262
World Focus (IND) 7194
World Food Aid Needs and Availabilities. Food Needs Assessment (USA) 1608
• World Food Aid Needs and Availabilities. Food Security Assessment (USA) 1608
World Food Data & Statistics (GBR) 3668
• World Food Law Monthly (GBR ISSN 1462-6489) 4945
World Food Marketing Directory (GBR) 3668
World Food Programme. Annual Report (ITA ISSN 1020-3753) 1608
World Food Programme Journal (ITA ISSN 1010-9099) 6671
• World Food Regulation Review (GBR ISSN 0963-4894) 3668
World Food Report (USA ISSN 1010-1039) 3668
World Footwear (CAN ISSN 0894-3079) 7942
World Free Internet (USA) 6648
• World Furniture (Online) (ITA) 4563
• ➤ World Future Review (USA ISSN 1946-7567) 7930
• ➤ World Futures (USA ISSN 0260-4027) 6961
• World Gas Intelligence (USA ISSN 1052-8776) 6797
World Gas Yearbook (GBR ISSN 1461-4707) 6797
World Gastroenterology News (NLD ISSN 1567-7753) 5932
World Geophysical News (USA ISSN 1053-9859) 6797
World Glassware Industry Directory (ITA ISSN 1129-3969) 2036
World Gold (GBR ISSN 1463-9319) 6337
World Gold Analyst (GBR ISSN 1463-9327) 6337
World Goodwill Commentary (USA ISSN 0161-2360) 7274
World Goodwill Newsletter (USA ISSN 0818-4984) 8079
• World Grain (USA ISSN 0745-8991) 276
• World Grain Markets Report (GBR ISSN 1745-2899) 276
World Grain Markets Report Online see World Grain Markets Report 276
World Grain Statistics (Year) see International Grains Council. World Grain Statistics (Year) 182
World Guide see Guia del Mundo 3120
World Guide to Covered Bridges (USA) 4318
World Guide to Higher Education (FRA) 3010
• World Guide to Libraries (DEU ISSN 0936-0085) 5055
World Guide to Libraries Plus see World Guide to Libraries 5055
World Guide to Scientific Associations and Learned Societies (DEU) 7930
World Guide to Special Libraries (DEU ISSN 0724-8717) 5055
† • (Year) World Guide to Television (USA ISSN 1084-9475) 8999
World Guide to Trade Associations see Internationales Verzeichnis der Wirtschaftsverbaende 2009
World Harp Congress Review (USA ISSN 1542-9415) 6629
▼ World Health Design (SWE ISSN 1654-9694) 4112
World Health Organization. Basic Documents (CHE ISSN 0512-3003) 4945
• ➤ World Health Organization. Bulletin (CHE ISSN 0042-9686) 5731
World Health Organization Drug Information see W H O Drug Information 7545
• World Health Organization. Fact Sheet (CHE) 7545
World Health Organization Food Additives Series see W H O Food Additives Series 3667
World Health Organization. Handbook of Resolutions and Decisions of the World Health Assembly and the Executive Board. (CHE ISSN 0301-0740) 7545
World Health Organization Pharmaceuticals Newsletter see W H O Pharmaceuticals Newsletter 6885
• World Health Organization. Press Release (CHE) 7545
• World Health Organization. Regional Office for the Eastern Mediterranean. Annual Report of the Regional Director (EGY) 7545
• World Health Organization Regional Publications. European Series (DNK ISSN 0378-2255) 7545
World Health Organization Technical Report Series see W H O Technical Report Series 5729
World Health Organization. Technical Reports (CHE) 5828
• The World Health Report (CHE ISSN 1020-3311) 7545
• World Heart Journal (USA ISSN 1556-4002) 5801
World Helicopter Resource see Rotor & Wing 69
World Heritage Review (FRA ISSN 1020-4202) 4167
World Heritage Series (FRA) 4167
World Highways/Routes du Monde (GBR ISSN 0964-4598) 8637
World History see Shijieshi 4161
World History see Shijie Lishi 4161
World History Bulletin (USA ISSN 0886-117X) 4167
• World History Connected (USA ISSN 1931-8642) 4167
† • World Hockey (Online) (GBR) 8999
• World Hospitality and Tourism Trends (GBR ISSN 1471-8553) 8776
• ➤ World Hospitals and Health Services (GBR ISSN 1029-0540) 4113
World Hotel and Convention Directory (JPN) 4400
• World Hotel D B (Database) (JPN) 4400
World I P Contacts Handbook (Year) (GBR) 6760
† World Immigration Policy Report (AUS ISSN 1445-677X) 8999
World in (Year) (GBR ISSN 0954-3074) 1196
The World in English see I Love English 2193
World Income Distribution (GBR) 2036
World Index of Yarns and Fibres (GBR ISSN 1746-6903) 2036
• World Indigenous Nations Higher Education Consortium. Journal (NZL ISSN 1177-1364) 3010
• World Industrial Reporter (USA ISSN 0043-8561) 5461
World Industry (TWN) 1196
World Information see Shijie Xinxi Bao 3828
• World Information Report (FRA) 5055
World Information Service on Energy/Nuclear Information and Resource Service Nuclear Monitor see W I S E/N I R S Nuclear Monitor 3175
World Informo (IND ISSN 0043-857X) 7274
World Insurance Corporate Report (GBR ISSN 0955-4823) 4528
World Insurance Policy Guide (GBR ISSN 1467-8764) 4528
• World Insurance Report (GBR ISSN 0306-3445) 4528
World Intellectual Property Organization Magazine see W I P O Magazine 6760
• World Intellectual Property Report (GBR ISSN 0952-7613) 6760
World Interior Design (JPN) 4553
• World Investment Prospects (USA) 1660
World Investment Report (CHE ISSN 1020-2218) 1660
World Investor (USA ISSN 1080-9201) 1660
World Iron & Steel see Shijie Gangtie 6332
World Issues (GBR) 8079
World Jewelery Machinery Directory & Yearbook (Year) (GBR) 4570
World Jewelogue (Year) (HKG) 4570
World Jewish Directory (CAN) 3572
World Journal (CAN) 3820
World Journal see Shijie Ribao (New York) 3564
World Journal (Los Angeles) see Shijie Ribao (Monterey Park) 3564
World Journal (San Francisco Edition) see Shijie Ribao (San Francisco) 3564
▼ • World Journal for Pediatric and Congenital Heart Surgery (USA ISSN 2150-1351) 6262
➤ World Journal for Tourism Development and Marketing (ZAF ISSN 1819-8538) 1848
• World Journal of Acupuncture - Moxibustion (CHN ISSN 1003-5257) 315
World Journal of Acupuncture - Moxibustion (Italian Edition) (ITA ISSN 1972-019X) 315
World Journal of Africa Development (ZAF ISSN 1990-8660) 1608
World Journal of Africa Renaissance (ZAF ISSN 1990-8679) 1551
➤ World Journal of Agricultural Development (ZAF ISSN 1990-8687) 209
• ➤ World Journal of Agricultural Sciences (PAK ISSN 1817-3047) 170
➤ World Journal of Arts (ZAF ISSN 1991-105X) 527
➤ World Journal of Banking (ZAF ISSN 1990-8695) 1391
• The World Journal of Biological Psychiatry (GBR ISSN 1562-2975) 6189
• World Journal of Business Management (ZAF ISSN 1819-8589) 1801
• ➤ World Journal of Chemical Engineering (ZAF ISSN 1991-1076) 3257
World Journal of Civil Engineering (ZAF ISSN 1991-1084) 3287
World Journal of Community Development (ZAF ISSN 1819-8635) 8147
World Journal of Conflict Resolution (ZAF ISSN 1819-8600) 7274
➤ World Journal of Corporate Affairs (ZAF ISSN 1990-8717) 1196
➤ World Journal of Defence and Military Sciences (ZAF ISSN 1991-1262) 6454
World Journal of Democracy and Transformation (ZAF ISSN 1991-1092) 7194
World Journal of Design and Innovation (ZAF ISSN 1991-1106) 1801
➤ World Journal of Diversity and Nations (ZAF ISSN 1990-8709) 7194
World Journal of E-Tourism (ZAF ISSN 1990-8814) 8776
World Journal of Economic Development (ZAF ISSN 1990-8725) 1608
➤ World Journal of Ecotourism (ZAF ISSN 1990-8733) 8776
➤ World Journal of Education and Development (ZAF ISSN 1990-8741) 2926
➤ World Journal of Electrical Engineering (ZAF ISSN 1991-1114) 3334
• World Journal of Emergency Surgery (GBR ISSN 1749-7922) 6262
World Journal of Engineering (CAN ISSN 1708-5284) 3227
➤ World Journal of Entrepreneurship (ZAF ISSN 1990-875X) 1801
➤ World Journal of Environmental Management and Urbanization (ZAF ISSN 1990-8768) 2633
World Journal of Events and Sports Tourism (ZAF ISSN 1819-8546) 8776
World Journal of Financial Management (ZAF ISSN 1991-1122) 1391
• World Journal of Gastroenterology (CHN ISSN 1007-9327) 5932
World Journal of Geography (ZAF ISSN 1991-1130) 4034
World Journal of Governmental Studies (ZAF ISSN 1991-1149) 7194
World Journal of Health Sciences (ZAF ISSN 1991-1157) 5731
World Journal of History and Anthropology (ZAF ISSN 1990-8776) 4167
World Journal of HIV and AIDS (ZAF ISSN 1990-8822) 5828
➤ World Journal of Hotel and Restaurant Management (ZAF ISSN 1991-1165) 4400
World Journal of Human Resources (ZAF ISSN 1991-1173) 1878
World Journal of Integrated Traditional and Western Medicine see Shijie ZhongXiyi Jiehe Zazhi 5713
➤ World Journal of International Relations (ZAF ISSN 1819-8619) 7274
➤ World Journal of International Trade (ZAF ISSN 1991-1181) 1587
➤ World Journal of Investment (ZAF ISSN 1990-8784) 1660
➤ World Journal of Jewish Studies (ZAF ISSN 1991-119X) 7732
World Journal of Labour Relations (ZAF ISSN 1991-1203) 1716
▼ ➤ World Journal of Laparoscopic Surgery (IND ISSN 0974-5092) 6262
➤ World Journal of Leadership (ZAF ISSN 1991-1068) 1801
World Journal of Linguistics and Communications (ZAF ISSN 1991-122X) 5196
• ➤ World Journal of Management and Economics (ZAF ISSN 1819-8643) 1196
• ➤ World Journal of Managing Events (ZAF ISSN 1991-1238) 1801
➤ World Journal of Marketing Management (ZAF ISSN 1991-1246) 1848
World Journal of Mechanical Engineering (ZAF ISSN 1991-1254) 3399
• ➤ World Journal of Medical Sciences (PAK ISSN 1817-3055) 5731
• ➤ World Journal of Microbiology and Biotechnology (NLD ISSN 0959-3993) 771
World Journal of Modelling and Simulation (GBR ISSN 1746-7233) 2518
World Journal of Natural Resources (ZAF ISSN 1991-1270) 711
World Journal of Nuclear Economics (ZAF ISSN 1991-1289) 3175
World Journal of Nuclear Energy (ZAF ISSN 1991-1297) 3175
• World Journal of Nuclear Medicine (CYP ISSN 1450-1147) 6210
• World Journal of Organizational Dynamics (ZAF ISSN 1994-7674) 1801
• World Journal of Orthodontics (USA ISSN 1530-5678) 5869
➤ World Journal of Peace and Security (ZAF ISSN 1991-1300) 7274
World Journal of Peace through Tourism (ZAF ISSN 1819-8562) 8776
• ➤ World Journal of Pediatrics (CHN ISSN 1708-8569) 6105
➤ World Journal of Planning and Development (ZAF ISSN 1991-1319) 7194
World Journal of Political Economy (ZAF ISSN 1991-1211) 1551
➤ World Journal of Political Studies (ZAF ISSN 1991-1327) 7194
World Journal of Project Management (ZAF ISSN 1990-8792) 1801
World Journal of Public Administration and Management (ZAF ISSN 1819-866X) 7477
World Journal of Public Health (ZAF ISSN 1991-1335) 7545
World Journal of Public Policy (ZAF ISSN 1819-8597) 7194
World Journal of Public Relations (ZAF ISSN 1990-8806) 37
World Journal of Research and Sciences (ZAF ISSN 1991-1343) 7930
▼ • World Journal of Retail Business Management (ZAF ISSN 1994-2915) 1848
➤ World Journal of Sciences and Educational Administration (ZAF ISSN 1819-8627) 3035
World Journal of Sports Management (ZAF ISSN 1991-1351) 8216
➤ World Journal of Strategic Management (ZAF ISSN 1991-136X) 1801
• ➤ World Journal of Surgery (USA ISSN 0364-2313) 6262
• ➤ World Journal of Surgical Oncology (GBR ISSN 1477-7819) 6036
➤ World Journal of Sustainable Development (ZAF ISSN 1819-8651) 3475
➤ World Journal of Terrorism and Nations (ZAF ISSN 1991-1378) 7274
➤ World Journal of Tourism Administration (ZAF ISSN 1990-8652) 8776
➤ World Journal of Tourism and Hospitality Management (ZAF ISSN 1819-8554) 8776
• ➤ World Journal of Tourism, Leisure and Sports (ZAF ISSN 1819-8570) 8776
➤ World Journal of Tourism Operations and Transport (ZAF ISSN 1991-1386) 8776
• World Journal of Tourism Small Business Management (ZAF ISSN 1991-1394) 8776
• ➤ World Journal of Urology (DEU ISSN 0724-4983) 6277

Title

DIRECTORY 2010 WORLD POKER TOUR POKER 11039

World of Information Business Intelligence Reports. French Polynesia (GBR) **1528**
• World of Information Business Intelligence Reports. Gabon (GBR ISSN 1364-3266) **1528**
World of Information Business Intelligence Reports. Georgia (GBR) **1528**
• World of Information Business Intelligence Reports. Germany (GBR ISSN 1364-3274) **1528**
• World of Information Business Intelligence Reports. Ghana (GBR ISSN 1364-3282) **1528**
World of Information Business Intelligence Reports. Gibraltar (GBR) **1528**
• World of Information Business Intelligence Reports. Greece (GBR ISSN 1364-3290) **1528**
World of Information Business Intelligence Reports. Greenland (GBR) **1528**
World of Information Business Intelligence Reports. Grenada (GBR) **1528**
World of Information Business Intelligence Reports. Guadeloupe (GBR) **1528**
World of Information Business Intelligence Reports. Guam (GBR) **1528**
• World of Information Business Intelligence Reports. Guatemala (GBR ISSN 1364-3304) **1528**
World of Information Business Intelligence Reports. Guinea (GBR) **1528**
World of Information Business Intelligence Reports. Guinea-Bissau (GBR) **1528**
• World of Information Business Intelligence Reports. Guyana (GBR ISSN 1364-3312) **1528**
• World of Information Business Intelligence Reports. Haiti (GBR ISSN 1364-3320) **1528**
• World of Information Business Intelligence Reports. Honduras (GBR ISSN 1364-3339) **1528**
• World of Information Business Intelligence Reports. Hong Kong (GBR ISSN 1364-3347) **1529**
• World of Information Business Intelligence Reports. Hungary (GBR ISSN 1363-9129) **1588**
World of Information Business Intelligence Reports. Iceland (GBR) **1529**
• World of Information Business Intelligence Reports. India (GBR ISSN 1364-3355) **1529**
• World of Information Business Intelligence Reports. Indonesia (GBR ISSN 1364-3363) **1529**
• World of Information Business Intelligence Reports. Iran (GBR ISSN 1364-3371) **1529**
• World of Information Business Intelligence Reports. Iraq (GBR ISSN 1364-338X) **1529**
• World of Information Business Intelligence Reports. Ireland (GBR ISSN 1364-3398) **1529**
• World of Information Business Intelligence Reports. Israel (GBR ISSN 1364-3401) **1529**
• World of Information Business Intelligence Reports. Italy (GBR ISSN 1364-341X) **1529**
• World of Information Business Intelligence Reports. Jamaica (GBR ISSN 1364-3428) **1529**
• World of Information Business Intelligence Reports. Japan (GBR ISSN 1364-3436) **1529**
• World of Information Business Intelligence Reports. Jordan (GBR ISSN 1364-3444) **1529**
• World of Information Business Intelligence Reports. Kazakhstan (GBR ISSN 1364-1050) **1529**
• World of Information Business Intelligence Reports. Kenya (GBR ISSN 1364-3452) **1529**
World of Information Business Intelligence Reports. Kiribati (GBR) **1529**
• World of Information Business Intelligence Reports. Korea (GBR ISSN 1364-3460) **1529**
• World of Information Business Intelligence Reports. Kuwait (GBR ISSN 1364-3479) **1529**
• World of Information Business Intelligence Reports. Kyrghyzstan (GBR ISSN 1364-1069) **1529**
World of Information Business Intelligence Reports. Laos (GBR) **1529**
• World of Information Business Intelligence Reports. Latvia (GBR ISSN 1364-1077) **1529**
• World of Information Business Intelligence Reports. Lebanon (GBR ISSN 1364-3487) **1529**
World of Information Business Intelligence Reports. Lesotho (GBR) **1529**
World of Information Business Intelligence Reports. Liberia (GBR) **1529**
• World of Information Business Intelligence Reports. Libya (GBR ISSN 1364-3495) **1529**
World of Information Business Intelligence Reports. Liechtenstein (GBR) **1529**
• World of Information Business Intelligence Reports. Lithuania (GBR ISSN 1364-1085) **1530**
• World of Information Business Intelligence Reports. Luxembourg (GBR ISSN 1364-4556) **1530**
World of Information Business Intelligence Reports. Macao (GBR) **1530**
• World of Information Business Intelligence Reports. Macedonia (GBR ISSN 1474-4368) **1530**
World of Information Business Intelligence Reports. Madagascar (GBR) **1530**
World of Information Business Intelligence Reports. Malawi (GBR) **1530**
• World of Information Business Intelligence Reports. Malaysia (GBR ISSN 1364-4564) **1530**
World of Information Business Intelligence Reports. Maldives (GBR) **1530**
World of Information Business Intelligence Reports. Mali (GBR) **1530**
World of Information Business Intelligence Reports. Malta (GBR) **1530**
World of Information Business Intelligence Reports. Marshall Islands (GBR) **1530**
World of Information Business Intelligence Reports. Martinique (GBR) **1530**
World of Information Business Intelligence Reports. Mauritania (GBR) **1530**
World of Information Business Intelligence Reports. Mauritius (GBR) **1530**
• World of Information Business Intelligence Reports. Mexico (GBR ISSN 1364-4572) **1530**
• World of Information Business Intelligence Reports. Moldova (GBR ISSN 1364-1093) **1530**
World of Information Business Intelligence Reports. Monaco (GBR) **1530**
World of Information Business Intelligence Reports. Mongolia (GBR) **1530**
World of Information Business Intelligence Reports. Montserrat (GBR) **1530**
• World of Information Business Intelligence Reports. Morocco (GBR ISSN 1364-4580) **1530**
• World of Information Business Intelligence Reports. Mozambique (GBR ISSN 1364-4599) **1530**
World of Information Business Intelligence Reports. Myanmar (GBR) **1530**
World of Information Business Intelligence Reports. Namibia (GBR) **1530**
World of Information Business Intelligence Reports. Nauru (GBR) **1530**
World of Information Business Intelligence Reports. Nepal (GBR) **1530**
• World of Information Business Intelligence Reports. Netherlands (GBR ISSN 1364-4602) **1530**
World of Information Business Intelligence Reports. New Caledonia (GBR) **1530**
• World of Information Business Intelligence Reports. New Zealand (GBR ISSN 1364-4610) **1530**
• World of Information Business Intelligence Reports. Nicaragua (GBR ISSN 1364-4629) **1531**
World of Information Business Intelligence Reports. Niger (GBR) **1531**
• World of Information Business Intelligence Reports. Nigeria (GBR ISSN 1364-4637) **1531**
World of Information Business Intelligence Reports. Niue (GBR) **1531**
World of Information Business Intelligence Reports. Norfolk Island (GBR) **1531**
World of Information Business Intelligence Reports. North Korea (GBR) **1531**
• World of Information Business Intelligence Reports. Norway (GBR ISSN 1364-4645) **1531**
• World of Information Business Intelligence Reports. Oman (GBR ISSN 1364-4653) **1531**
• World of Information Business Intelligence Reports. Pakistan (GBR ISSN 1364-4661) **1531**
World of Information Business Intelligence Reports. Palestine (GBR) **1531**
• World of Information Business Intelligence Reports. Panama (GBR ISSN 1364-467X) **1531**
• World of Information Business Intelligence Reports. Papua New Guinea (GBR ISSN 1364-4688) **1531**
• World of Information Business Intelligence Reports. Paraguay (GBR ISSN 1364-4696) **1531**
• World of Information Business Intelligence Reports. Peru (GBR ISSN 1364-470X) **1531**
• World of Information Business Intelligence Reports. Philippines (GBR ISSN 1364-4718) **1531**
World of Information Business Intelligence Reports. Pitcairn Island (GBR) **1531**
• World of Information Business Intelligence Reports. Poland (GBR ISSN 1363-7290) **1531**
• World of Information Business Intelligence Reports. Portugal (GBR ISSN 1364-4726) **1531**
• World of Information Business Intelligence Reports. Puerto Rico (GBR ISSN 1364-4734) **1531**
World of Information Business Intelligence Reports. Qatar (GBR) **1531**
World of Information Business Intelligence Reports. Reunion (GBR) **1531**
• World of Information Business Intelligence Reports. Romania (GBR ISSN 1363-9137) **1531**
• World of Information Business Intelligence Reports. Russia (GBR ISSN 1364-1107) **1531**
World of Information Business Intelligence Reports. Rwanda (GBR) **1531**
World of Information Business Intelligence Reports. Samoa (GBR) **1531**
World of Information Business Intelligence Reports. San Marino (GBR) **1531**
World of Information Business Intelligence Reports. Sao Tome e Principe (GBR) **1532**
• World of Information Business Intelligence Reports. Saudi Arabia (GBR ISSN 1364-4742) **1532**
• World of Information Business Intelligence Reports. Senegal (GBR ISSN 1364-4750) **1532**
• World of Information Business Intelligence Reports. Serbia (GBR ISSN 1364-1115) **1532**
World of Information Business Intelligence Reports. Serbia and Montenegro (GBR ISSN 1744-6317) **1532**
World of Information Business Intelligence Reports. Seychelles (GBR) **1532**
World of Information Business Intelligence Reports. Sierra Leone (GBR) **1532**
• World of Information Business Intelligence Reports. Singapore (GBR ISSN 1364-4769) **1532**
• World of Information Business Intelligence Reports. Slovakia (GBR ISSN 1364-1123) **1532**
• World of Information Business Intelligence Reports. Slovenia (GBR ISSN 1364-1131) **1532**
World of Information Business Intelligence Reports. Solomon Islands (GBR) **1532**
World of Information Business Intelligence Reports. Somalia (GBR) **1532**
• World of Information Business Intelligence Reports. South Africa (GBR ISSN 1364-4777) **1532**
World of Information Business Intelligence Reports. South Georgia (GBR) **1532**
• World of Information Business Intelligence Reports. Spain (GBR ISSN 1364-4785) **1532**
• World of Information Business Intelligence Reports. Sri Lanka (GBR ISSN 1364-4793) **1532**
World of Information Business Intelligence Reports. St Helena (GBR) **1532**
World of Information Business Intelligence Reports. St Kitts and Nevis (GBR) **1532**
World of Information Business Intelligence Reports. St Lucia (GBR) **1532**
World of Information Business Intelligence Reports. St Vincent and the Grenadines (GBR) **1532**
• World of Information Business Intelligence Reports. Sudan (GBR ISSN 1364-6257) **1532**
World of Information Business Intelligence Reports. Suriname (GBR) **1532**
World of Information Business Intelligence Reports. Swaziland (GBR) **1532**
• World of Information Business Intelligence Reports. Sweden (GBR ISSN 1364-114X) **1532**
• World of Information Business Intelligence Reports. Switzerland (GBR ISSN 1364-6265) **1532**
• World of Information Business Intelligence Reports. Syria (GBR ISSN 1364-6273) **1532**
• World of Information Business Intelligence Reports. Taiwan (GBR ISSN 1364-6281) **1533**
• World of Information Business Intelligence Reports. Tajikistan (GBR ISSN 1364-1158) **1533**
• World of Information Business Intelligence Reports. Tanzania (GBR ISSN 1364-629X) **1533**
World of Information Business Intelligence Reports. Terres Australes (GBR) **1533**
• World of Information Business Intelligence Reports. Thailand (GBR ISSN 1364-6303) **1533**
World of Information Business Intelligence Reports. The Gambia (GBR) **1533**
World of Information Business Intelligence Reports. The Netherlands Antilles (GBR) **1533**
World of Information Business Intelligence Reports. Timor-Leste (GBR) **1533**
World of Information Business Intelligence Reports. Togo (GBR) **1533**
World of Information Business Intelligence Reports. Tokelau (GBR) **1533**
World of Information Business Intelligence Reports. Tonga (GBR) **1533**
• World of Information Business Intelligence Reports. Trinidad and Tobago (GBR ISSN 1474-4384) **1533**
• World of Information Business Intelligence Reports. Tunisia (GBR ISSN 1364-6311) **1533**
• World of Information Business Intelligence Reports. Turkey (GBR ISSN 1364-632X) **1533**
• World of Information Business Intelligence Reports. Turkmenistan (GBR ISSN 1364-1166) **1533**
World of Information Business Intelligence Reports. Turks and Caicos Islands (GBR) **1533**
World of Information Business Intelligence Reports. Tuvalu (GBR) **1533**
• World of Information Business Intelligence Reports. Uganda (GBR ISSN 1364-6338) **1533**
• World of Information Business Intelligence Reports. Ukraine (GBR ISSN 1364-1174) **1533**
• World of Information Business Intelligence Reports. United Arab Emirates (GBR ISSN 1364-6354) **1533**
• World of Information Business Intelligence Reports. United Kingdom (GBR ISSN 1364-6346) **1533**
• World of Information Business Intelligence Reports. United States (GBR ISSN 1364-6370) **1533**
• World of Information Business Intelligence Reports. Uruguay (GBR ISSN 1364-6362) **1533**
World of Information Business Intelligence Reports. US Virgin Islands (GBR) **1533**
• World of Information Business Intelligence Reports. Uzbekistan (GBR ISSN 1364-1182) **1533**
World of Information Business Intelligence Reports. Vanuatu (GBR) **1533**
World of Information Business Intelligence Reports. Vatican City (GBR) **1534**
• World of Information Business Intelligence Reports. Venezuela (GBR ISSN 1364-1190) **1534**
• World of Information Business Intelligence Reports. Vietnam (GBR ISSN 1364-6389) **1534**
World of Information Business Intelligence Reports. Wallis and Futuna (GBR) **1534**
World of Information Business Intelligence Reports. Yemen (GBR) **1534**
• World of Information Business Intelligence Reports. Zambia (GBR ISSN 1364-6400) **1534**
• World of Information Business Intelligence Reports. Zimbabwe (GBR ISSN 1364-6419) **1534**
• World of Information Regional Development Series (GBR) **1534**
The World of Interiors (GBR ISSN 0264-083X) **4553**
The World of Internet (GRC) **2569**
The World of Irish Nursing *see* The World of Irish Nursing & Midwifery **5984**
The World of Irish Nursing & Midwifery (IRL) **5984**
World of Islam *see* Die Welt des Islams **7717**
• World of Learning (Year) (GBR ISSN 0084-2117) **2963**
World of Light *see* Guang de Shijie **7075**
The World of Literature *see* Svet Literatury **5383**
The World of Lubavitch (CAN ISSN 1719-5322) **3573**
• World of Metallurgy - Erzmetall (DEU ISSN 1613-2394) **6337**
World of Mining - Surface & Underground (DEU ISSN 1613-2408) **6483**
The World of Music *see* Yinyue Tiandi **6630**
World of Music *see* Yinyue Shijie **6629**
➤ The World of Music (DEU ISSN 0043-8774) **6629**
World of Music Journal *see* W O M Journal **6627**
The World of National Art *see* Minzu Yilin **506**
The World of Newfoundlands (Years) (NLD) **6817**
World of Obstetrics and Gynecology *see* Sanfujinka no Sekai **6004**
The World of Parliaments (CHE) **7196**
World of Physics (USA ISSN 1531-0809) **7046**
World of Politics (USA ISSN 0094-2316) **7196**
World of Polymers *see* Svet Polimera **7100**
• World of Powerboats (GBR ISSN 1756-0594) **8285**
World of Print (DEU ISSN 1618-8381) **7576**
World of Property Magazine (GBR) **7616**
World of Re-Unicycling *see* Re-Unicycling the Past **368**
World of Seeds *see* Zhongzi Shijie **260**
World of Soul *see* Kosmos tis Psychis **6742**
• World of Special Finance (USA) **1391**
World of Sport (DEU) **8216**
World of Stones *see* Mir Kamnya **6473**
The World of Survey and Research *see* Diao-yan Shijie **8366**
World of Tennis (GBR ISSN 0305-6325) **8252**
World of Tennis *see* Cosmos tou Tennis **8225**
World of the Bible *see* Mir Biblii **7663**
World of the Creation *see* Sozo no Sekai **3467**
World of the Elderly *see* Laoren Shijie **4050**
• The World of Welding (USA ISSN 1545-9691) **6345**
World of Wheels (CAN ISSN 0824-5487) **8612**
World of Wine (GBR ISSN 1473-3897) **614**
➤ World of Wood (USA ISSN 1068-7300) **3718**
• World of Work (International Labour Organization) (CHE ISSN 1020-0010) **8079**
• World Oil (USA ISSN 0043-8790) **6797**
World Oil & Gas Technologies (GBR) **6797**
World Oil Tanker Trends (GBR) **8665**
• World Oil Trade (GBR ISSN 0950-1029) **6797**
• World Online Gambling Law Report (GBR ISSN 1477-2922) **8216**
World Opinion Update (USA ISSN 0193-3329) **7274**
World Optometry *see* World Focus **6262**
World Order (USA ISSN 0043-8804) **7695**
World Order Studies Program. Occasional Papers *see* Princeton University. Center of International Studies. World Order Studies Program. Occasional Papers **7260**
World Outlook (CAN ISSN 0843-4328) **1534**
World Outlook (GBR) **7780**
World Outlook (TWN) **7196**
World Outlook (USA ISSN 0895-7452) **7274**
• ➤ World Patent Information (GBR ISSN 0172-2190) **6760**
World Patent Law and Practice (USA) **6760**
World Peacemakers Quarterly (USA ISSN 0893-0228) **7274**
World Pesticides *see* Shijie Nongyao **252**
• World Petroleum Arrangements (Year) (USA) **6797**
World Petroleum Congress. Proceedings (GBR ISSN 0084-2176) **6797**
World Petroleum Trends (GBR ISSN 0963-5807) **6797**
World Pharmaceutical Frontiers (GBR ISSN 1742-3791) **6886**
• World Pharmaceutical Markets (GBR ISSN 1460-0781) **1534**
World Pheasant Association. Annual Review (GBR) **917**
World Pheasant Association News *see* W P A News **916**
World Philosophy *see* Shijie Zhexue **6952**
World Phytomedicines *see* Guowai Yiyao (Zhiwuyao Fence) **6845**
World Plastics *see* Guowai Suliao **7092**
World Ploughing Contest. Official Handbook (GBR) **215**
World Plumbing Review *see* W P R **1042**
World Poetry Letter (USA) **5438**
World Poker Tour Poker *see* W P T Poker **8215**

▼ *new title* † *ceased* • *electronic media* ➤ *refereed*

Title

World Wildlife Fund. Conservation Issues (USA ISSN 1074-1283) **2633**
World Wildlife Fund Journal *see* W W F Journal **2631**
World Wildlife Fund News *see* W W F News **2631**
The World Wireless Beacon (USA) **2374**
The World Women's Polo Championship Magazine (GBR) **8300**
The World Working Group on Birds of Prey and Owls. Newsletter (GBR ISSN 1013-8005) **917**
World Wrestling Entertainment, Inc. Divas (Year) *see* W W E Divas (Year) **6301**
World Wrestling Entertainment, Inc. Kids Magazine *see* W W E Kids Magazine **2221**
World Wrestling Entertainment, Inc. Magazine *see* W W Magazine **8215**
World Writing *see* Viswa Rachana **5395**
World Wrought Copper Statistics (GBR ISSN 0266-7347) **6342**
World Yearbook of Education (GBR ISSN 0084-2508) **2926**
World Youth/Jeunesse du Monde/Juventud del Mundo (HUN ISSN 0043-9274) **2222**
• World Youth Report (USA) **2171**
World Zionist Organization. Zionist Congress *see* Ha-Kongres Ha-Tsiyoni. Hahlatot **7139**
† World Zionist Press Service (ISR) **8999**
• WorldatWork Journal (USA ISSN 1529-9457) **1878**
WorldFish Center. Annual Report (MYS) **3611**
WorldFish Center. Bibliographies (MYS ISSN 0115-5997) **3614**
WorldFish Center. Conference Proceedings (MYS ISSN 0115-4435) **968**
WorldFish Center. Contribution (MYS ISSN 1047-9694) **3611**
WorldFish Center. Education Series (MYS ISSN 0116-5720) **3612**
WorldFish Center. Software (MYS ISSN 0116-6964) **2600**
WorldFish Center. Studies and Reviews (MYS ISSN 0115-4389) **3612**
WorldFish Center. Technical Reports (MYS ISSN 0115-5547) **3612**
WorldFish Center. Translations (MYS ISSN 0115-4141) **3612**
• WorldFish Report (GBR ISSN 1360-7391) **3612**
• WorldLaw Business (GBR ISSN 1466-6820) **4883**
WorldLinks U S A *see* Inky Trail News **4337**
Worldlit (CAN ISSN 0820-6686) **2947**
Worldly Remains (USA ISSN 1529-6725) **3993**
• Worldmark Encyclopedia of Cultures and Daily Life (USA) **8147**
Worldmark Encyclopedia of the Nations (USA ISSN 1531-1635) **4034**
Worldmark Encyclopedia of the States (USA ISSN 1531-1627) **4034**
• Worldmark Yearbook (USA ISSN 1527-6503) **7197**
Worldorama (USA ISSN 1058-4463) **7743**
WorldOrganics News *see* Eurofood **3634**
• The WorldPaper (USA ISSN 1065-0997) **7275**
• Worldpower and Energy (GBR ISSN 1464-6269) **3150**
• Worldprofit Online Magazine (USA) **1969**
Worldradio (USA) **2365**
World's Best *see* Travel & Leisure the Best of the World's Greatest Hotels, Resorts + Spas **8766**
• World's Best Money Managers (USA ISSN 1081-2539) **1660**
World's Children (GBR ISSN 0043-9290) **2171**
World's Fair (GBR ISSN 0043-9304) **1849**
World's Major Multinationals *see* World Leading Global Brand Owners **2036**
Wor(l)ds of Change: Latin American and Iberian Literature (USA ISSN 1072-334X) **5400**
Worlds of East Asia *see* Welten Ostasiens **563**
World's Poultry Science Association. Proceedings of World's Poultry Congress (NLD) **304**
• ➤ World's Poultry Science Journal (GBR ISSN 0043-9339) **304**
The World's Top 100 Retailers *see* The Retail Directory. The World's Top 100 Retailers **2026**
World's Watch Complications and Manufacturers *see* Grand Complications **4566**
The World's Water (USA ISSN 1528-7165) **8842**
World's Woman's Christian Temperance Union. Triennial Report (USA) **2700**
• Worldsteel Newsletter (BEL) **6337**
• WorldView Magazine (USA ISSN 1047-5338) **7275**
• ➤ Worldviews (NLD ISSN 1363-5247) **3475**
• ➤ Worldviews on Evidence-Based Nursing (USA ISSN 1545-102X) **5984**
Worldwatch *see* World Watch **3475**
• Worldwatch Database Disk (USA) **3475**
Worldwatch Environmental Alert Series (USA) **3475**
Worldwatch Papers *see* Worldwatch Report **3475**
Worldwatch Reader (USA) **3475**
• Worldwatch Report (USA) **3475**
• Worldwide (USA) **4529**
• Worldwide Biotech (USA) **771**
Worldwide Business Collaborations - Consultants News and Business Opportunities (IND) **1588**
• Worldwide Business Cost Comparisons (USA) **1588**
Worldwide Business Practices Report (USA ISSN 1069-4447) **1588**
Worldwide Challenge (USA ISSN 0746-9241) **7695**
▼ Worldwide Coins (USA ISSN 1935-4622) **6653**
• Worldwide Computer Products News (GBR ISSN 1363-9889) **2441**
• Worldwide Cost of Living (USA) **1955**
• Worldwide Databases (USA) **2532**
• Worldwide Directory of Agrobiologicals on CD-ROM (GBR ISSN 1369-2062) **170**
• Worldwide Directory of Consultants and Contractors (USA ISSN 1058-5818) **2036**
• Worldwide Directory of Defense Authorities (USA ISSN 1073-5097) **6454**
Worldwide Directory of Film and Video Festivals and Events (USA) **6517**
Worldwide Directory of Multichip Module Vendors and Related Companies (USA) **2036**
The Worldwide Directory of Securities Lending and Repo (Year) (GBR ISSN 1356-8930) **1660**
The Worldwide Electric Power Industry (USA) **3162**
• Worldwide Energy (USA) **3150**
▼ • Worldwide Forum on Education and Culture. Journal (USA ISSN 1949-2774) **2926**
• Worldwide Government Directory (USA ISSN 0894-1521) **7477**
Worldwide Government Directory, with International Organizations *see* Worldwide Government Directory **7477**
Worldwide Guide To Homeschooling (USA ISSN 1932-2674) **2926**
▼ • ➤ Worldwide Hospitality and Tourism Themes (GBR ISSN 1755-4217) **8776**
Worldwide Marketing Opportunities Digest (GBR ISSN 0309-4960) **1849**
Worldwide Military and Police Award (IRL) **6454**
• Worldwide Monitor Market Tracker (USA) **3116**
Worldwide Motor, Fire, Marine and Air Cargo Insurance Surveyors and Claims Settling Agents (IRL) **4529**
Worldwide News (USA) **7780**
† • Worldwide Offshore Rig Owners & Personnel Directory (USA ISSN 1073-8037) **8999**
Worldwide Offshore Rig Owners and Personnel Directory *see* Worldwide Offshore Rig Owners & Personnel Directory **8999**
Worldwide Offshore Rig Owners and Personnel Directory, Including Worldwide Marine Rig Register *see* Worldwide Offshore Rig Owners & Personnel Directory **8999**
Worldwide Offshore Rigowners and Personnel Directory *see* Worldwide Offshore Rig Owners & Personnel Directory **8999**
Worldwide Pig Progress *see* Pig Progress **296**
Worldwide Political Science Abstracts *see* C S A Worldwide Political Science Abstracts **7199**
Worldwide Register of Adult Education (USA ISSN 0084-2486) **2947**
• Worldwide Regulatory Update (USA) **1588**
Worldwide Rubber Statistics (USA) **7828**
Worldwide Survey of International Assignment Policies and Practices. European Edition (GBR) **1878**
Worldwide Survey of L I M S Users (Laboratory Information Management Systems) (USA ISSN 1944-4192) **6689**
• Worldwide Tax Treaties on CD-ROM (USA ISSN 1089-8921) **1955**
• Worldwide Telecom (USA) **2374**
Worldwide Uranium Producer Profiles (USA) **3176**
• Worldwide Videotex Update (USA ISSN 0731-7891) **2569**
Worldwide W A M M (Women Against Military Madness) (USA) **8892**
• Worldwide Yellow Pages (USA) **2036**
Worldwide Yellow Pages Markets (Year) *see* Worldwide Yellow Pages **2036**
• Worldwoman (GBR) **8892**
• Worm Digest (USA ISSN 1090-560X) **968**
Der Wormsgau (DEU ISSN 0084-2613) **4279**
Der Wormsgau. Beiheft (DEU ISSN 0342-426X) **4279**
Wormsloe Foundation. Publications (USA ISSN 0084-2621) **4318**
Woroni (AUS ISSN 1326-2793) **2310**
• ➤ Worship (USA ISSN 0043-941X) **7695**
Worship Facilities (USA ISSN 1559-6923) **7695**
▼ Worship Kidstyle (Children's Edition) (USA ISSN 1935-4959) **7780**
▼ Worship Kidstyle (Preschool Edition) (USA ISSN 1935-4975) **7781**
Worship KidStyle: Children All-In-One Pack *see* Worship Kidstyle (Children's Edition) **7780**
Worship KidStyle: Preschool All-In-One Pack *see* Worship Kidstyle (Preschool Edition) **7781**
Worship Leader Magazine (USA ISSN 1066-1247) **7695**
Worshipful Company of Butchers Newsletter and Bulletin *see* W C B Newsletter and Bulletin **3667**
• Worshipful Company of Goldsmith's. Technical Report (GBR ISSN 1745-2961) **4570**
Wort fuer die Woche (DEU) **7781**
Das Wort fuer Heute (DEU ISSN 0930-3995) **7781**
Wort-Suchspiel (DEU ISSN 0942-6590) **8216**
Wort und Antwort (DEU ISSN 0342-6378) **7695**
Wort und Dienst (DEU ISSN 0342-3085) **7781**
• Worth (USA ISSN 1931-9908) **1660**
Worth Avenue (USA) **3993**
Worthing Guardian (GBR) **3873**
Worthington Living (USA) **5087**
WorthStyle (USA) **2263**
Worthwhile *see* Motto **1150**
• Wortlaut.de (DEU ISSN 1437-2002) **5400**
• Wostok (DEU ISSN 0942-1262) **5246**
WOt-Studies (Wettelijke Onderzoekstaken) (NLD ISSN 1871-0298) **3476**
Wota Saiensu Kenkyukai Semina Yokoshu/Water Science Institute. Seminar Proceedings (JPN) **8842**
• Wotanging Ikche/Native American News (USA) **6636**
Wotanin Wowapi (USA) **3573**
• Would That It Were (USA) **5449**
➤ Wound Ballistics Review (USA ISSN 1055-0305) **5917**
▼ Wound Care Handbook (Years) (GBR ISSN 1757-7519) **6075**
Wound Care Times (ITA ISSN 1722-7895) **5731**
Wound Management *see* Leczenie Ran **6066**
➤ Wound Practice & Research (AUS) **6075**
• ➤ Wound Repair and Regeneration (USA ISSN 1067-1927) **6075**
• ➤ Wounds (USA ISSN 1044-7946) **6075**
• ➤ Wounds U K (GBR ISSN 1746-6814) **6075**
WOW! (DEU) **7781**
woxx (LUX) **3906**
WP-Magazin (DEU ISSN 0947-3092) **6817**
WPg - Die Wirtschaftspruefung (DEU ISSN 0340-9031) **1304**
• Wprost (POL ISSN 0209-1747) **3931**
WR *see* W R **5396**
WR News Senior Edition *see* W R News. Senior Edition **2220**
Wraf! (NLD ISSN 1872-5775) **6817**
Wrangell-Institut fuer Umweltgerechte Produktionsautomatisierung. Berichte (DEU ISSN 1615-2557) **3359**
Wrangler (USA ISSN 0512-4077) **4318**
Wrangler's Roost (GBR ISSN 0043-9452) **6517**
Wrap-Up *see* Approaching Crime Prevention **2644**
Wreck Bay Aboriginal Community Council. Annual Report (AUS ISSN 1832-5181) **3476**
WREP *see* Washington State University. Cooperative Extension. WREP **169**
The Wrestler (USA ISSN 1052-0899) **8216**
Wrestling *see* Brydning **8937**
† Wrestling All Stars Heroes and Villains (USA ISSN 0885-8551) **8999**
The Wrestling Analyst (USA ISSN 1097-4725) **8216**
Wrestling Case Book and Manual (USA) **8216**
Wrestling Chatterbox (USA) **8216**
• Wrestling Digest (USA ISSN 1524-0371) **8216**
The Wrestling News (USA ISSN 0891-0707) **8216**
Wrestling Observer Newsletter (USA ISSN 1083-9593) **8216**
Wrestling Perspective (USA) **8216**
† Wrestling Power (ITA ISSN 1826-4344) **8999**
Wrestling Rules Book (USA) **8216**
Wrestling - Then & Now (USA) **8216**
• Wrestling U S A (Missoula) (USA ISSN 0199-6258) **8216**
Wright Angles (USA ISSN 1059-4396) **461**
Wright Family Workbook (USA ISSN 8756-7229) **3788**
• Wright's Anesthesia and Critical Care Resources on the Internet (USA ISSN 1090-3577) **5774**
• Wrightsville Beach Magazine (USA ISSN 1937-9978) **5087**
▼ Wrigley Season Ticket (USA ISSN 1942-2369) **8252**
Write it Right (USA) **2672**
• Write Now! (USA ISSN 1555-502X) **527**
Write On *see* Victorian Writer **7575**
• The Write Stuff (AUS ISSN 1323-7721) **5400**
Write-Up (USA) **7415**
The Write Way (USA) **5400**
• The Writer (USA ISSN 0043-9517) **5400**
Writer (Penzance) (GBR ISSN 0260-2776) **5401**
Writer Literature Monthly *see* Zuojia Zazhi **5405**
Writer Magazine *see* Zuojia Zazhi **5405**
• Writer On Line (USA) **5401**
Writers and Artists Services International *see* W A S I **525**
• Writers' and Artists' Yearbook (GBR ISSN 0084-2664) **7576**
Writers' and Poets' Yearbook (GBR) **5401**
Writers Ask (USA ISSN 1522-9920) **5401**
Writers' Bloc (USA) **5438**
• Writer's Block (CAN ISSN 1488-4801) **5401**
• The Writer's Block (Austin) (USA) **5401**
• Writer's Block Magazine (CAN ISSN 1483-3492) **5401**
• Writer's Carousel (USA) **5401**
The Writer's Chronicle (USA ISSN 1529-5443) **4585**
• Writer's Digest (USA ISSN 0043-9525) **4585**
• The Writers Directory (USA ISSN 0084-2699) **7576**
† Writer's Forum (Cincinnati) (USA ISSN 1057-0756) **8999**
† Writers' Forum (Niwot) (USA ISSN 0163-9072) **8999**
• Writer's Gazette (CAN) **7576**
Writers Gazette (USA ISSN 1520-3484) **5401**
Writer's Guidelines and News (USA ISSN 1539-2198) **5401**
Writer's Guidelines Magazine (USA ISSN 1053-1793) **4585**
Writers Guild of America, East. Newsletter (USA) **5401**
Writer's Handbook (USA ISSN 0084-2710) **5401**
• Writers in Paradise (USA ISSN 1522-6751) **5401**
Writers Information Network Informer *see* The W I N Informer **7575**
Writers Ink (USA) **7576**
Writers' Journal (USA ISSN 0891-8759) **5438**
Writer's Lifeline (CAN ISSN 0225-610X) **7576**
• Writer's Market (USA ISSN 0084-2729) **7576**
Writer's N W (USA ISSN 0895-898X) **7576**
Writers News (GBR ISSN 0957-3577) **5401**
• Writer's Nook News (USA) **4585**
Writer's Northwest Handbook (USA ISSN 0896-7946) **7576**
• ➤ Writers Notes Magazine (USA ISSN 1548-2774) **5438**
Writer's Notes Magazine *see* Writers Notes Magazine **5438**
Writers of Wales (GBR ISSN 0141-5050) **5401**
Writers' Potpourri (USA) **5401**
▼ The Writers Studio Journal (USA ISSN 1942-6860) **5401**
Writers' Trust of Canada. Newsletter (CAN ISSN 1914-0754) **5401**
Writers Union of Free Afghanistan *see* W U F A **4190**
The Writers Voice Annual (USA ISSN 1941-4617) **5401**
Writer's Voice the Magazine of Emerging Writers *see* W V, the Magazine of Emerging Writers **5396**
Writers Workshop Literary Reader (IND) **5401**
Writer's World (USA ISSN 1057-0772) **5401**
Writer's Yearbook (USA ISSN 0084-2737) **7576**
Writing *see* Xiezuo **5402**
† • Writing (USA ISSN 0279-7208) **8999**
Writing *see* W R **5396**
Writing about Women: Feminist Literary Studies (USA ISSN 1053-7937) **5401**
Writing Across the Curriculum Journal *see* The W A C Journal **3087**
▼ • ➤ Writing & Pedagogy (GBR ISSN 1756-5839) **5401**
➤ The Writing Center Journal (USA ISSN 0889-6143) **2926**
Writing Edge *see* Writing Edge Magazine **5087**
• Writing Edge Magazine (AUS ISSN 1833-1734) **5087**
• Writing for Money (Online Edition) (USA) **4585**
• The Writing Forum (USA) **5438**
• ➤ The Writing Instructor (Online Edition) (USA) **2926**
Writing Lab Newsletter (USA ISSN 1040-3779) **3088**
Writing Magazine (GBR) **5401**
Writing Matters (GBR) **527**
Writing on the Edge (USA ISSN 1064-6051) **5401**
Writing Program Administration (USA ISSN 0196-4682) **3010**
Writing Research (USA) **5401**
Writing Science (USA) **4585**
Writing Studies (USA ISSN 1045-7992) **5401**
• ➤ Writing Systems Research (GBR ISSN 1758-6801) **5196**
▼ • ➤ Writing Technologies (GBR ISSN 1754-9035) **4585**
Writing That Works (USA) **4585**
Writing Ulster (GBR ISSN 0969-4846) **5401**
Writings from the Ancient World (NLD ISSN 1570-7008) **7695**
➤ Writings from the Greco-Roman World (NLD ISSN 1569-3600) **7695**
Writings on Irish History (IRL ISSN 0791-9824) **4171**
Written (USA ISSN 1931-9029) **5087**
• Written By (USA ISSN 1092-468X) **5401**
• ➤ Written Communication (USA ISSN 0741-0883) **2345**
• ➤ Written Language and Literacy (NLD ISSN 1387-6732) **5196**
Written Magazine *see* Written **5087**
Wroclaw In Your Pocket (POL) **8776**
Wroclawska Gazeta Polska (POL ISSN 1232-8170) **5246**
Wroclawska Stomatologia *see* Dental and Medical Problems **5839**
Wroclawski Przeglad Teologiczny (POL ISSN 1231-1731) **7823**
Wroclawski Rocznik Ekonomiczny (POL ISSN 0084-2974) **1196**
Wroclawskie Towarzystwo Naukowe. Komisja Historii Sztuki. Rozprawy (POL ISSN 0084-2982) **527**
Wroclawskie Towarzystwo Naukowe. Komisja Jezykowa. Rozprawy (POL ISSN 0084-2990) **5196**
Wroclawskie Towarzystwo Naukowe. Prace. Seria A. Humanistyka (POL ISSN 0084-3016) **4482**
Wroclawskie Towarzystwo Naukowe. Prace. Seria B. Nauki Scisle (POL ISSN 0084-3024) **4482**
Wroclawskie Towarzystwo Naukowe. Sprawozdania. Seria A (POL ISSN 0371-4756) **7930**
Wrongful Dismissal (CAN) **4816**
Wrongful Dismissal Law (CAN) **4816**
• Wrongful Dismissal Notice Searcher (CAN) **1716**
Wrongful Dismissal Practice Manual (CAN) **1716**
Wrozki *see* Wrozki Dzwoneczek **2222**
Wrozki Dzwoneczek (POL ISSN 1899-7783) **2222**
Wskazniki, Stawki, Dokumenty (POL ISSN 1641-0777) **1304**
• Wspolczesna Onkologia/Contemporary Oncology (POL ISSN 1428-2526) **6036**
Wspolnota (POL ISSN 0867-0935) **7505**
➤ Wszechswiat/Universe (POL ISSN 0043-9592) **7930**
W!tness *see* Victorian Baptist Witness **7779**
• Wu-tan Zhuangbei/Equipment for Geophysical Prospecting (CHN ISSN 1671-0657) **6798**
Wuce Yiwen *see* Geo-Spatial Information Science **4007**
• Wudang (CHN ISSN 1004-5821) **8216**
• Wudao/Dancing (CHN ISSN 0512-4204) **2688**
Wudao Luncong/Forum of Dancing (CHN) **2688**
Wudao Yishu/Art of Dancing (CHN ISSN 1003-3777) **2688**
Wuerttemberg Tennis (DEU) **8252**

Title

X-ology (USA) **8445**
X P Essentials *see* Windows X P Made Easy **2583**
X P How To (GBR ISSN 1745-266X) **2441**
X R S *see* X-Ray Spectrometry **2107**
X-Ray (USA) **5402**
X-Ray Magazine (Online) (USA) **7580**
X-Ray Magazine (Print) *see* X-Ray Magazine (Online) **7580**
▼ • ➤ X-Ray Optics and Instrumentation (USA ISSN 1687-7632) **7085**
• ➤ X-Ray Spectrometry (GBR ISSN 0049-8246) **2107**
X S (USA) **3993**
X S P Advisor (USA) **2441**
• X Sen Bunseki no Shinpo/Advances in X-Ray Chemical Analysis (JPN ISSN 0911-7806) **2107**
X Sen Bunseki Toronkai Koen Yoshishu/Abstracts of Annual Conference on X-Ray Chemical Analysis (JPN) **2096**
x-tra (USA ISSN 1937-5069) **527**
X-treme Magazine (GBR) **5087**
X X L (USA ISSN 1093-0647) **6629**
X X L Basketball (GBR ISSN 1365-8077) **8252**
X X L Presents: Scratch (USA) **6629**
• X X vs. X Y (USA ISSN 1541-4272) **4057**
• X Y: Men, Masculinities and Gender Politcs (AUS) **6302**
X Y Z (CAN ISSN 0828-5608) **5402**
X Y Z (FRA ISSN 0290-9057) **4034**
• X Y Z Z Y News (USA) **5449**
X3 (DEU) **2482**
▼ X360 (BRA) **2482**
X360 (GBR) **2482**
Xalteva (NIC) **3920**
Xama (ARG ISSN 0327-1250) **361**
Xanadu (USA ISSN 0146-0463) **5438**
• Xander Mellish (USA) **5449**
Xantener Berichte. Grabung, Forschung, Praesentation (DEU) **424**
Xantippe (USA ISSN 1542-6963) **5402**
Xantypa (CZE ISSN 1211-7587) **3833**
Xareli (SEN) **7197**
Xaverian Missions Newsletter (USA) **7823**
Xaverian Weekly (CAN ISSN 0043-9886) **2310**
Xavier (USA ISSN 1075-1017) **2310**
Xavier Catholic Review (USA) **7823**
Xavier Review (USA ISSN 0887-6681) **5402**
XBox *see* X3 **2482**
Xbox 360 (AUS ISSN 1833-3257) **2482**
Xbox 360 (BRA ISSN 1980-5241) **2482**
XBox 360 *see* X3 **2482**
Xbox 360 (FRA) **2482**
Xbox 360 (GBR ISSN 1747-6992) **2482**
Xbox 360 (ITA ISSN 1826-5804) **2482**
Xbox 360 (SWE ISSN 1653-9583) **2482**
Xbox Games (DEU) **2482**
Xbox Life (SWE) **2482**
XBox Magazin *see* X B M **2482**
Xbox Magazine *see* Xbox 360 **2482**
Xbox Magazine *see* Official Xbox Magazine **2479**
• Xbox Nation (USA ISSN 1538-9723) **2482**
Xbox World *see* Xbox World 360 **8217**
Xbox World 360 (GBR ISSN 1752-718X) **8217**
• Xcell Journal (USA) **2510**
Xcellent (NLD ISSN 1872-6631) **1721**
Xcentric (DEU) **3860**
• xChange (USA ISSN 1095-3647) **2374**
• ➤ Xchanges (USA ISSN 1558-6456) **4482**
Xenharmonikon (USA ISSN 0098-3330) **6629**
Xenia Antiqua (ITA ISSN 1121-9688) **2242**
• ➤ Xenobiotica (GBR ISSN 0049-8254) **746**
Xenophora (FRA ISSN 0755-8198) **968**
• ➤ Xenotransplantation (DNK ISSN 0908-665X) **6262**
Xenotransplantation.. Supplement *see* Xenotransplantation **6262**
Xeografica (ESP ISSN 1578-5637) **4034**
• Xergi (NOR ISSN 1500-371X) **3150**
Xerography Debt (USA) **5246**
Xerolage (USA ISSN 1557-0983) **5438**
Xerox Debt *see* Xerography Debt **5246**
Xes (USA) **6302**
Xi Psi Phi Fraternity Quarterly (USA ISSN 1531-118X) **5869**
Xia Wa *see* Eve **8861**
▼ Xiamen Academy of International Law. Collected Courses (NLD ISSN 1875-4678) **4945**
• Xiamen Daxue Xuebao (Zhexue Shehui Kexue Ban)/Xiamen University. Journal: A Bimonthly for Studies in Arts & Social Sciences (CHN ISSN 0438-0460) **8015**
• Xiamen Daxue Xuebao (Ziran Kexue Ban)/Xiamen University. Journal (Natural Science Edition) (CHN ISSN 0438-0479) **7930**
Xiamen Economic Daily *see* Xiamen Shangbao **1196**
• Xiamen Ligong Xueyuan Xuebao/Xiamen University of Technology. Journal (CHN ISSN 1673-4432) **7930**
Xiamen Literature *see* Xiamen Wenxue **5402**
Xiamen Shangbao/Xiamen Economic Daily (CHN) **1196**
Xiamen University. Journal (Natural Science Edition) *see* Xiamen Daxue Xuebao (Ziran Kexue Ban) **7930**
Xiamen University. Journal (Natural Science) *see* Xiamen Daxue Xuebao (Zhexue Shehui Kexue Ban) **8015**
Xiamen University. Journal: A Bimonthly for Studies in Arts & Social Sciences *see* Xiamen Daxue Xuebao (Zhexue Shehui Kexue Ban) **8015**
Xiamen University of Technology. Journal *see* Xiamen Ligong Xueyuan Xuebao **7930**
• Xiamen Wenxue/Xiamen Literature (CHN ISSN 1004-0765) **5402**
• Xi'an Caijing Xueyuan Xuebao/Xi'an Institute of Finance & Economics. Journal (CHN ISSN 1672-2817) **1196**
Xi'an Dianzi Keji Daxue Xuebao *see* Xi'an Dianzi Keji Daxue Xuebao (Shehui Kexue Ban) **8015**
• Xi'an Dianzi Keji Daxue Xuebao (Shehui Kexue Ban)/Xidian University. Journal (Social Science Edition) (CHN ISSN 1008-472X) **8015**
• Xi'an Dianzi Keji Daxue Xuebao (Ziran Kexue Ban)/Xidian University. Journal (Natural Science Edition) (CHN) **3116**
• ➤ Xi'an Gongcheng Keji Xueyuan Xuebao/Xi'an University of Engineering Science and Technology. Journal (CHN ISSN 1671-850X) **8462**
Xi'an Gonglu Jiaotong Daxue Xuebao *see* Chang'an Daxue Xuebao. Ziran Kexue Ban **8630**
• Xi'an Gongye Daxue Xuebao/Xian Technological University. Journal (CHN) **7930**
Xi'an Gongye Xueyuan Xuebao/Xi'an Institute of Technology. Journal *see* Xi'an Gongye Daxue Xuebao **7930**
Xi'an Highway University. Journal *see* Chang'an Daxue Xuebao. Ziran Kexue Ban **8630**
Xi'an Institute of Finance & Economics. Journal *see* Xi'an Caijing Xueyuan Xuebao **1196**
Xi'an Institute of Physical Education. Journal *see* Xi'an Tiyu Xueyuan Xuebao **7000**
• Xi'an Jianzhu Keji Daxue Xuebao (Shehui Kexue Ban)/Xi'an University of Architecture & Technology. Journal (Social Science Edition) (CHN ISSN 1008-7192) **8015**
• Xi'an Jianzhu Keji Daxue Xuebao (Ziran Kexue Ban)/Xi'an University of Architecture and Technology. Journal (Natural Science Edition) (CHN ISSN 1006-7930) **461**
• Xi'an Jiaotong Daxue Xuebao/Xi'an Jiaotong University. Journal (CHN ISSN 0253-987X) **7931**
• Xi'an Jiaotong Daxue Xuebao (Shehui Kexue Ban)/Xi'an Jiaotong University. Journal (Social Sciences) (CHN ISSN 1008-245X) **8015**
• Xi'an Jiaotong Daxue Xuebao (Yixue Ban)/Xi'an Jiaotong University. Journal (Medical Edition) (CHN ISSN 1671-8259) **5732**
Xi'an Jiaotong University. Journal *see* Xi'an Jiaotong Daxue Xuebao **7931**
Xi'an Jiaotong University. Journal (Medical Edition) *see* Xi'an Jiaotong Daxue Xuebao (Yixue Ban) **5732**
Xi'an Jiaotong University. Journal (Social Sciences) *see* Xi'an Jiaotong Daxue Xuebao (Shehui Kexue Ban) **8015**
Xi'an Jiaoyu Xueyuan Xuebao/Xi'an College of Education. Journal *see* Xi'an Wenli Xueyuan Xuebao (Ziran Kexue Ban) **7931**
• Xi'an Jiatong University. Academic Journal (CHN ISSN 1671-8267) **7931**
Xi'an Ke-Ji Xueyuan Xuebao *see* Xi'an Keji Daxue Xuebao **7931**
• Xi'an Keji Daxue Xuebao/Xi'an University of Science and Technology. Journal (CHN ISSN 1672-9315) **7931**
• Xi'an Ligong Daxue Xuebao/Xi'an University of Technology. Journal (CHN ISSN 1006-4710) **8445**
Xi'an Petroleum University. Journal (Natural Science Edition) *see* Xi'an Shiyou Daxue Xuebao (Ziran Kexue Ban) **7931**
• Xi'an Shiyou Daxue Xuebao (Shehui Kexue Ban)/Xi'an Shiyou University. Journal (Social Sciences) (CHN) **8015**
• ➤ Xi'an Shiyou Daxue Xuebao (Ziran Kexue Ban)/Xi'an Petroleum University. Journal (Natural Science Edition) (CHN ISSN 1673-064X) **7931**
Xi'an Shiyou University. Journal (Social Sciences) *see* Xi'an Shiyou Daxue Xuebao (Shehui Kexue Ban) **8015**
Xian Technological University. Journal *see* Xi'an Gongye Daxue Xuebao **7930**
• ➤ Xi'an Tiyu Xueyuan Xuebao/Xi'an Institute of Physical Education. Journal (CHN ISSN 1001-747X) **7000**
Xi'an University of Architecture and Technology. Journal (Natural Science Edition) *see* Xi'an Jianzhu Keji Daxue Xuebao (Ziran Kexue Ban) **461**
Xi'an University of Architecture & Technology. Journal (Social Science Edition) *see* Xi'an Jianzhu Keji Daxue Xuebao (Shehui Kexue Ban) **8015**
Xi'an University of Engineering Science and Technology. Journal *see* Xi'an Gongcheng Keji Xueyuan Xuebao **8462**
Xi'an University of Post and Telecom. Journal *see* Xi'an Youdian Xueyuan Xuebao **2345**
Xi'an University of Science and Technology. Journal *see* Xi'an Keji Daxue Xuebao **7931**
Xi'an University of Technology. Journal *see* Xi'an Ligong Daxue Xuebao **8445**
• Xi'an Waiguoyu Xueyuan Xuebao (CHN ISSN 1008-4703) **5196**
• Xi'an Wenli Xueyuan Xuebao (Ziran Kexue Ban) (CHN) **7931**
• Xi'an Youdian Xueyuan Xuebao/Xi'an University of Post and Telecom. Journal (CHN ISSN 1007-3264) **2345**
Xiandai Bingqi/Modern Weaponry (CHN ISSN 1000-7385) **6454**
Xiandai Chengshi Guidao Jiaotong/Modern Urban Transit (CHN ISSN 1672-7533) **8628**
Xiandai Chuanbo/Modern Communication (CHN ISSN 1007-8770) **2345**
Xiandai Chuban Xue - 21 Shiji Xinwen yu Chuanboxue Xilie Jiaocai/Modern Publishing - 21 Century Journalism & Communication Studies (CHN ISSN 1673-3959) **7576**
• Xiandai Dianli/Modern Electric Power (CHN ISSN 1007-2322) **3162**
• Xiandai Dianshenglixue Zazhi/Journal of Modern Electrophysiology (CHN ISSN 1672-0458) **928**
• ➤ Xiandai Dizhi/Geoscience (CHN ISSN 1000-8527) **2775**
• Xiandai Fangyu Jishu/Modern Defence Technology (CHN ISSN 1009-086X) **6454**
• Xiandai Fangzhi Jishu/Advanced Textile Technology (CHN ISSN 1009-265X) **8462**
• Xiandai Faxue/Modern Law Science (CHN ISSN 1001-2397) **4816**
• Xiandai Fuchanke Jinzhan/Progress in Obstetrics and Gynecology (CHN ISSN 1004-7379) **5732**
• Xiandai Funu/Modern Women (CHN ISSN 1007-4244) **8892**
• ➤ Xiandai Guoji Guanxi (CHN ISSN 1000-6192) **7275**
Xiandai Huabao/Modern Pictorial (CHN) **3829**
• Xiandai Huli/Modern Nursing (CHN ISSN 1009-9689) **5984**
Xiandai Jiadian/Modern Household Appliances (CHN ISSN 1672-5239) **3116**
• Xiandai Jianyan Yixue Zazhi/Journal of Modern Medical Inspection & Testing (CHN ISSN 1671-7414) **5911**
• Xiandai Jiaoyu Jishu/Modern Educational Technology (CHN ISSN 1009-8097) **2927**
• Xiandai Jiating/Modern Family (CHN ISSN 1000-4300) **4369**
• Xiandai Jingji Tantao/Modern Economic Research (CHN ISSN 1009-2382) **1551**
Xiandai Jisuanji *see* Xiandai Jisuanji (Puji Ban) **2441**
Xiandai Jisuanji *see* Xiandai Jisuanji (Zhuanye Ban) **2441**
• Xiandai Jisuanji (Puji Ban)/Modern Computer (Regular Edition) (CHN) **2441**
• Xiandai Jisuanji (Zhuanye Ban)/Modern Computer (Professional Edition) (CHN) **2441**
• Xiandai Jixie/Modern Machinery (CHN ISSN 1002-6886) **5461**
• Xiandai Kouqiang Yixue Zazhi/Journal of Modern Stomatology (CHN ISSN 1003-7632) **5932**
Xiandai Kuaibao (CHN) **3829**
• Xiandai Leida/Modern Radar (CHN ISSN 1004-7859) **7073**
• Xiandai Linchuang Huli/Modern Clinical Nursing (CHN ISSN 1671-8283) **5984**
• Xiandai Linchuang Yixue Shengwu Gongchengxue Zazhi/Moderen Clinical Medical Bioengineering (CHN ISSN 1008-634X) **751**
Xiandai Lingdao/Modern Leadership (CHN ISSN 1000-4513) **7197**
• Xiandai Mianyixue/Courrent Immunlolgy (CHN ISSN 1001-2478) **5767**
• Xiandai Nongcunbao/Modern Rural News (CHN) **3829**
Xiandai Qiche *see* China Automotive Journal **8574**
• Xiandai Qiye/Modern Enterprise (CHN ISSN 1000-9671) **1196**
• Xiandai Qiye Wenhua/Modern Enterprise Culture (CHN ISSN 1674-1145) **1196**
• ➤ Xiandai Riben Jingji/Contemporary Japanese Economics (CHN ISSN 1000-355X) **1196**
• Xiandai Shangmao Gongye/Modern Business Trade Industry (CHN ISSN 1672-3198) **1196**
Xiandai Sheying/Inphoto (CHN) **6978**
• ➤ Xiandai Shipin Keji/Modern Food Science & Technology (CHN ISSN 1673-9078) **3668**
Xiandai Shipin yu Yaopin Zazhi/Journal of Modern Food and Pharmaceuticals *see* Jinri Yaoxue **6851**
• Xiandai Shiyong Yixue/Modern Practical Medicine (CHN ISSN 1671-0800) **5732**
Xiandai Suidao Jishu/Modern Tunnelling Technology (CHN ISSN 1009-6582) **1043**
▼ Xiandai Suzhou/Modern Suzhou (CHN ISSN 1674-1196) **3829**
• Xiandai Tongxin/Communications Today (CHN ISSN 1000-6559) **2355**
• Xiandai Tushu Qingbao Jishu/New Technology of Library and Information Service (CHN ISSN 1003-3513) **5064**
• Xiandai Waiyu/Modern Foreign Languages (CHN ISSN 1003-6105) **5196**
• Xiandai Wuli Zhishi/Modern Physics (CHN ISSN 1001-0610) **7047**
• Xiandai Yangsheng/Health Care Today (CHN ISSN 1671-0223) **5732**
• ➤ Xiandai Yixue/Modern Medical Journal (CHN ISSN 1671-7562) **5732**
• Xiandai Yiyao Weisheng/Modern Medicine & Health (CHN ISSN 1009-5519) **5732**
• Xiandai Yiyong Yingxiangxue/Modern Medical Imagelogy (CHN ISSN 1006-7035) **6210**
• Xiandai Yiyuan Guanli/Modern Hospital Management (CHN ISSN 1672-4232) **4113**
• Xiandai Yuancheng Jiaoyu Yanjiu/Modern Distance Education Study (CHN ISSN 1009-5195) **2399**
• Xiandai Yuer Bao (CHN) **2927**
• Xiandai Yufang Yixue/Modern Preventive Medicine (CHN ISSN 1003-8507) **5732**
Xiandai Yuwen *see* Xiandai Yuwen (Yuyan Yanjiu) **5196**
Xiandai Yuwen *see* Xiandai Yuwen (Jiaoyu Yanjiu) **5196**
Xiandai Yuwen *see* Xiandai Yuwen (Wenxue Yanjiu) **5196**
• Xiandai Yuwen (Jiaoyu Yanjiu)/Modern Chinese (Education Research) (CHN) **5196**
• Xiandai Yuwen (Wenxue Yanjiu)/Modern Chinese (Literarary Research) (CHN) **5196**
• Xiandai Yuwen (Yuyan Yanjiu)/Modern Chinese (Linguistics Research) (CHN) **5196**
• Xiandai Yuye Xinxi/Modern Fisheries Information (CHN ISSN 1004-8340) **3612**
• ➤ Xiandai Zhenduan yu Zhiliao/Modern Diagnosis & Treatment (CHN ISSN 1001-8174) **5732**
• Xiandai Zhexue/Modern Philosophy (CHN ISSN 1000-7660) **6961**
Xiandai Zhong-xiaoxue Jiaoyu/Modern Primary and Secondary Education (CHN ISSN 1002-1477) **2927**
Xiandai Zhongliu Yixue/Journal of Modern Oncology (CHN ISSN 1672-4992) **6036**
Xiandai Zhongwen Wenxue Xuebao *see* Journal of Modern Literature in Chinese **5315**
• Xiandai Zhongxiyijiehe Zazhi/Modern Journal of Integrated Chinese Traditional and Western Medicine (CHN ISSN 1008-8849) **5732**
Xiandai Zhuangshi/Modern Decoration (CHN) **4553**
Xiandai Zuojia/Modern Writers *see* Xingxing Shikan **5438**
• Xiandaihua Nongye/Modernizing Agriculture (CHN ISSN 1001-0254) **171**
Xiandangdai Wenxue Wenzhai Ka/Contemporary Literature Abstracts on Cards (CHN ISSN 1671-3451) **5408**
Xianfaxue, Xingzheng Faxue/Studies of Constitutions, Studies of Administrative Law (CHN ISSN 1007-0575) **7477**
Xiangfan University. Journal *see* Xiangfan Xueyuan Xuebao **8015**
• Xiangfan Xueyuan Xuebao/Xiangfan University. Journal (CHN ISSN 1009-2854) **8015**
• Xianggang (Year) (HKG ISSN 0072-629X) **7295**
Xianggang Dianzi Lingjian *see* Hong Kong Electronic Components and Parts **3101**
Xianggang Fangshe Jishi Zazhi/Hong Kong Radiographers Journal (HKG ISSN 1028-1460) **6210**
Xianggang Fengqing/Hong Kong Customs (CHN) **8147**
Xianggang Huli Zazhi *see* Hong Kong Nursing Journal **5960**
Xianggang Jianzhu Zhinan (Zhongguo Ban) *see* Hong Kong Builder Directory (Hong Kong Edition) **1012**
Xianggang Nanbao *see* Xianggang (Year) **7295**
Xianggang Shehui Kexue Xuebao *see* Hong Kong Journal of Social Sciences **7969**
• Xianggang Tebie Xingzhengqu Zhengfu Xianbao/Government of the Hong Kong Special Administrative Region Gazette (HKG) **7477**
Xianggang Uankeyixueyuan Yuekan *see* Hong Kong Practitioner **5629**
Xianggang Zhongshen Fayuan Anli Huibao *see* The Hong Kong Court of Final Appeal Reports **4687**
Xiangjian Xiaolu/Country Road (TWN ISSN 1015-8367) **171**
• Xiangjiao Gongye/China Rubber Industry (CHN ISSN 1000-890X) **7827**
Xiangnan University. Journal *see* Xiangnan Xueyuan Xuebao **8015**
• Xiangnan Xueyuan Xuebao/Xiangnan University. Journal (CHN ISSN 1672-8173) **8015**
Xiangqi Yanjiu/Chinese Chess Studies (CHN ISSN 1002-1906) **8217**
• Xiangsu Jishu yu Zhuangbei/China Rubber / Plastics Technology & Equipment (CHN ISSN 1009-797X) **7100**
• Xiangtan Daxue Xuebao (Zhexue Shehui Kexue Ban)/Xiangtan University. Journal (Philosophy and Social Sciences Edition) (CHN) **8015**
• Xiangtan Daxue Ziran Kexue Xuebao/Natural Science Journal of Xiangtan University (CHN ISSN 1000-5900) **7931**
Xiangtan Gongxueyuan Xuebao (Shehui Kexue Ban)/Social Science Journal of Xiangtan Polytechnic University *see* Hunan Keji Daxue Xuebao (Shehui Kexue Ban) **7971**
Xiangtan Kuangye Xueyuan Xuebao/Xiangtan Mining Institute. Journal *see* Hunan Keji Daxue Xuebao (Ziran Kexue Ban) **6464**
Xiangtan Normal University. Journal (Social Science Edition) *see* Xiangtan Shifan Xueyuan Xuebao (Shehui Kexue Ban) **8015**
• Xiangtan Shifan Xueyuan Xuebao (Shehui Kexue Ban)/Xiangtan Normal University. Journal (Social Science Edition) (CHN ISSN 1009-4482) **8015**
• Xiangtan Shifan Xueyuan Xuebao (Ziran Kexue Ban) (CHN ISSN 1671-0231) **7931**
Xiangtan Shifan Xueyuan Xuebao/Xiangtan Teachers College. Journal *see* Xiangtan Shifan Xueyuan Xuebao (Ziran Kexue Ban) **7931**
Xiangtan University. Journal (Philosophy and Social Sciences Edition) *see* Xiangtan Daxue Xuebao (Zhexue Shehui Kexue Ban) **8015**
Xiangtu/Local Colour: A Literary Monthly (CHN ISSN 1003-8299) **3829**

Title

Title

Title

Title

11052 Z F V - ZEITSCHRIFT FUER GEODAESIE, GEOINFORMATION ULRICH'S PERIODICALS

➤ Z f V - Zeitschrift fuer Geodaesie, Geoinformation und Landmanagement (DEU ISSN 1618-8950) **3287**
Z f W T *see* Zeitschrift fuer die Welt der Tuerken **4483**
Z F W - Zeitschrift fuer Wasserrecht (DEU ISSN 0722-8910) **8842**
Z G A P Mitteilungen (Zoologische Gesellschaft fuer Arten- und Populationsschutz e.V.) (DEU ISSN 1616-9956) **2633**
Z G M R *see* Zeitschrift fuer das Gesamte Medizin- und Gesundheitsrecht **5734**
Z Grodu Szczukow (POL) **3931**
Z I B *see* Zeitschrift fuer Internationale Beziehungen **7275**
Z I E Year Book *see* Zimbabwe Institution of Engineers. Year Book **3228**
Z I International (Ziegelindustrie) (DEU ISSN 0341-0552) **2047**
Z I Jahrbuch (Ziegelindustrie International) (DEU ISSN 0933-5293) **3287**
Z J E R *see* Zimbabwe Journal of Educational Research **2929**
Z K J *see* Zeitschrift fuer Kindschaftsrecht und Jugendhilfe **4915**
Z K N - Mitteilungen (Zahnaerztekammer Niedersachsen) (DEU) **5869**
Z L R - Zeitschrift fuer das Gesamte Lebensmittelrecht (DEU ISSN 0342-3476) **4818**
Z M (GBR) **6302**
Z M E *see* Zeitschrift fuer Medizinische Ethik **5734**
Z M K *see* Zahnheilkunde, Management, Kultur **5870**
Z M Magazine (Zorg Management) (NLD ISSN 1381-0901) **4113**
Z M P Agrarmarkt (Zentrale Markt und Preisberichtstelle GmbH) (DEU ISSN 0946-6614) **171**
Z M P Bilanz Dairy Review *see* Z M P Marktbilanz Dairy Review **270**
Z M P Bilanz Eier und Gefluegel *see* Z M P Marktbilanz Eier und Gefluegel **305**
Z M P Bilanz Forst und Holz *see* Z M P Marktbilanz Forst und Holz **3708**
Z M P Bilanz Gemuese *see* Z M P Marktbilanz Gemuese **259**
Z M P Bilanz Getreide, Oelsaaten, Futtermittel *see* Z M P Marktbilanz Getreide, Oelsaaten, Futtermittel **276**
Z M P Bilanz Kartoffeln *see* Z M P Marktbilanz Kartoffeln **260**
Z M P Bilanz Milch *see* Z M P Marktbilanz Milch **270**
Z M P Bilanz Obst *see* Z M P Marktbilanz Obst **260**
Z M P Bilanz Vieh und Fleisch *see* Z M P Marktbilanz Vieh und Fleisch **305**
Z M P D Kwartalny Biuletyn Informacyjny (Zrzeszenie Miedzynarodowych Przewoznikow Drogowych) (POL ISSN 0514-809X) **8679**
Z M P Marktbericht. Der Markt Obst und Gemuese (Zentrale Markt und Preisberichtstelle GmbH) (DEU) **259**
Z M P Marktbericht. Europamarkt Dauermilch (Zentrale Markt und Preisberichtstelle GmbH) (DEU ISSN 0946-6525) **269**
Z M P Marktbericht. Europamarkt Milch - Butter - Kaese (Zentrale Markt und Preisberichtstelle GmbH) (DEU ISSN 0946-6517) **270**
Z M P Marktbericht. Fruehkartoffeln (Zentrale Markt und Preisberichtstelle GmbH) (DEU ISSN 0946-6576) **259**
Z M P Marktbericht. Gefluegel (Zentrale Markt und Preisberichtstelle GmbH) (DEU ISSN 0946-6533) **305**
• Z M P Marktbericht. Getreide - Oelsaaten - Futtermittel (Zentrale Markt und Preisberichtstelle GmbH) (DEU) **276**
Z M P Marktbericht. Kartoffeln (Zentrale Markt und Preisberichtstelle GmbH) (DEU) **259**
Z M P Marktbericht. Marktjournal Eier (Zentrale Markt und Preisberichtstelle GmbH) (DEU) **305**
Z M P Marktbericht. Milchwirtschaftliche Vorschau (Zentrale Markt und Preisberichtstelle GmbH) (DEU ISSN 1432-7236) **270**
Z M P Marktbericht. Obst und Gemuese - Suedwest (Zentrale Markt und Preisberichtstelle GmbH) (DEU) **259**
Z M P Marktbericht. Oelsaaten Spezialinfo (Zentrale Markt und Preisberichtstelle GmbH) (DEU) **276**
Z M P Marktbericht. Vieh und Fleisch (Zentrale Markt und Preisberichtstelle GmbH) (DEU ISSN 0946-6509) **305**
Z M P Marktbilanz Dairy Review (Zentrale Markt und Preisberichtstelle GmbH) (DEU) **270**
• Z M P Marktbilanz Eier und Gefluegel (Zentrale Markt und Preisberichtstelle GmbH) (DEU) **305**
• Z M P Marktbilanz Forst und Holz (Zentrale Markt und Preisberichtstelle GmbH) (DEU) **3708**
• Z M P Marktbilanz Gemuese (Zentrale Markt und Preisberichtstelle GmbH) (DEU) **259**
• Z M P Marktbilanz Getreide, Oelsaaten, Futtermittel (Zentrale Markt und Preisberichtstelle GmbH) (DEU) **276**
• Z M P Marktbilanz Kartoffeln (Zentrale Markt und Preisberichtstelle GmbH) (DEU) **260**
• Z M P Marktbilanz Milch (Zentrale Markt und Preisberichtstelle GmbH) (DEU) **270**
• Z M P Marktbilanz Obst (Zentrale Markt und Preisberichtstelle GmbH) (DEU) **260**
• Z M P Marktbilanz Vieh und Fleisch (Zentrale Markt und Preisberichtstelle GmbH) (DEU) **305**
Z M P Nachrichten (Zentrale Markt und Preisberichtstelle GmbH) (DEU ISSN 0946-6630) **171**
Z M R *see* Zeitschrift fuer Miet- und Raumrecht **7616**
Z M T Contributions (Zentrum fuer Marine Tropenoekologie) (DEU ISSN 0944-0143) **711**
Z M - Zahnaerztliche Mitteilungen (DEU ISSN 0342-0264) **5869**
Z M - Zahnaerztliche Mitteilungen. Ausgabe A *see* Z M - Zahnaerztliche Mitteilungen **5869**
• Z Magazine (USA ISSN 1056-5507) **7197**
Z N C C Directory *see* Zimbabwe National Chamber of Commerce Directory **2036**
Z N C C Newsletter (Zimbabwe National Chamber of Commerce) (ZWE) **1413**
Z N N - Zahnaerztliche Nachrichten Niedersachsen *see* Z K N - Mitteilungen **5869**
Z N R *see* Zeitschrift fuer Neuere Rechtsgeschichte **4819**
Z N S & Schmerz (Zentrales Nerven System) (DEU ISSN 1439-2623) **6190**
➤ Z N S - Zentrales Nervensystem (DEU ISSN 0931-7015) **6190**
Z N T - Zeitschrift fuer Neues Testament (DEU ISSN 1435-2249) **7696**
Z O (Zelfstandig Ondernemen) (BEL ISSN 0779-3804) **1969**
Z O K U Info (CHE) **8079**
Z O O - B U M (RUS) **2224**
Z O V (Zeitschrift fuer Offene Vermoegensfragen) (DEU ISSN 0943-3147) **4432**
Z P A - Zeitschrift fuer Praktische Augenheilkunde und Augenaerztliche Fortbildung (DEU ISSN 1436-0322) **6053**
Z P P M *see* Zeitschrift fuer Psychotraumatologie und Psychologische Medizin **7416**
Z R F G *see* Risk, Fraud and Compliance **2667**
Z R P *see* Zeitschrift fuer Rechtspolitik **4819**
Z S B Bezugsquellen (DEU) **3668**
Z S E *see* Zeitschrift fuer Staats- und Europawissenschaften **7276**
Z St *see* Zeitschrift zum Stiftungswesen **1660**
Z T (Zahntechnik) (DEU ISSN 0949-6092) **5869**
Z T E Communications (Zhongxing Telecommunication Equipment) (CHN ISSN 1673-5188) **2374**
Z T R - Zeitschrift fuer Tarif-, Arbeits- und Sozialrecht des Oeffentlichen Dienstes (Zeitschrift fuer Tarifrecht) (DEU ISSN 1439-5908) **1955**
Z T - Zahntechnik Zeitung (DEU) **5869**
• ➤ Z U M A - Nachrichten (Zentrum fuer Umfragen Methoden und Analysen e.V.) (DEU ISSN 0944-1670) **8151**
Z U M - R D *see* Zeitschrift fuer Urheber- und Medienrecht - Rechtsprechungsdienst **4819**
Z V E I Electro & Electronics Buyers' Guide *see* Z V E I Elektro und Elektronik - Einkaufsfuehrer **3293**
• Z V E I Elektro und Elektronik - Einkaufsfuehrer (DEU ISSN 0933-0194) **3293**
Z V E I Guia de Equipos Electricos et Electronicos *see* Z V E I Elektro und Elektronik - Einkaufsfuehrer **3293**
Z V E I Guide de l'Equipement Electrique et Electronique *see* Z V E I Elektro und Elektronik - Einkaufsfuehrer **3293**
Z V E I Mitteilungen (Zentralverband Elektrotechnik- und Elektronikindustrie e.V.) (DEU ISSN 0172-715X) **3334**
Z V Information (Zentralverband) (CHE) **7505**
Z V Informationen (Zentralverband des Deutschen Getreide-, Futter- und Duengemittelhandels e.V.) (DEU) **276**
Z V R *see* Zeitschrift fuer Verkehrsrecht **4819**
Z V S - Info (Zentralstelle fuer die Vergabe von Studienplaetzen) (DEU) **3011**
Z W E *see* Zeitschrift fuer Wohnungseigentumsrecht **7616**
Z W F (Zeitschrift fuer Wirtschaftlichen Fabrikbetrieb) (DEU ISSN 0947-0085) **5461**
Z W L *see* Zahntechnik Wirtschaft Labor **5870**
Z W P *see* Zahnarzt Wirtschaft Praxis **5870**
Z W P Spezial (Zahnarzt Wirtschaft Praxis) (DEU) **5869**
• Z W R (Zahnaerztliche Welt Rundschau) (DEU ISSN 0044-166X) **5869**
Z Z A - Zoologischer Zentral-Anzeiger (DEU ISSN 1438-5384) **968**
Z Z G Nieuws (Zeister Zendingsgenootschap) (NLD ISSN 1569-5956) **7696**
Z Z P *see* Zeitschrift fuer Zivilprozess **4844**
Z Zagadnien Nauk Sadowych (POL ISSN 1230-7483) **4967**
Za Bezopasnost' Dvizheniya (RUS ISSN 0201-7776) **2228**
▼ • Za Kulturou.cz (CZE ISSN 1802-4076) **3833**
• Za Obe Shchechki (RUS) **6105**
• Za Rulem (RUS ISSN 0321-4249) **8613**
De Zaaier (NLD ISSN 1873-992X) **171**
Zaama (FRA ISSN 1296-8366) **8079**
Zabaikal'skii Rabochii (RUS) **3943**
† Zabaveno (CZE ISSN 1214-911X) **8999**
Zabawy i Marzenia z Barbie (POL ISSN 1506-2546) **2224**
Zabergaeu-Leintal Anzeiger (DEU) **3860**
Zabolevaniya, Peredavaemye Polovym Putem (RUS) **5734**
Zabs Review *see* Z A B S Review **6407**
Zacchia (ITA ISSN 0044-1570) **5917**
Zack (DEU ISSN 1438-2792) **2224**
Zack (LUX ISSN 1016-2399) **2224**
Zack Magazine (AUS ISSN 1832-4991) **3797**
Zadarska Smotra (HRV ISSN 1330-4577) **5246**
Zadok Centre Reading Guides (AUS ISSN 0156-7500) **7696**
• Zadok Papers (AUS ISSN 1322-0705) **7696**
• Zadok Perspectives (AUS ISSN 0810-9796) **7696**
Zadra (POL ISSN 1508-6976) **8892**
Zaduzbina (SRB ISSN 0353-2739) **5404**
Zaetost i Bezrabotitsa/Employment and Unemployment (BGR ISSN 1311-2309) **8414**
• ➤ Zagadnienia Ekonomiki Rolnej (POL ISSN 0044-1600) **209**
Zagadnienia Eksploatacji Maszyn/Exploitation Problems of Machines (POL ISSN 0137-5474) **3399**
➤ Zagadnienia Filozoficzne w Nauce (POL ISSN 0867-8286) **6961**
Zagadnienia Informacji Naukowej (POL ISSN 0324-8194) **5055**
Zagadnienia Metodologiczne Nauk Praktycznych (POL) **7933**
Zagadnienia Naukoznawstwa (POL ISSN 0044-1619) **7933**
Zagadnienia Rodzajow Literackich/Problemes des Genres Litteraires (POL ISSN 0084-4446) **5404**
Zagadnienia Wychowawcze a Zdrowie Psychiczne (POL ISSN 0324-8526) **6190**
Zagazig Journal of Agricultural Research/Magallat al-Bihu? al-Ziraa'iyyat Koliyyat al-Ziraa'at al-Zaqaaziq (EGY ISSN 1110-0338) **171**
▼ • ➤ Zagazig Journal of Occupational Health and Safety/Magalat al-Zaqaziq li-l-Sihhat wa-al-Salamat al-Mihaniyyat/Majalat al-Zaqaziq li-l-Sihhat wa-al-Salamat al-Mihaniyyat (EGY ISSN 1687-8671) **6689**
Zagazig Journal of Pharmaceutical Sciences (EGY ISSN 1110-5089) **6886**
Zagazig Medical Association Journal *see* Zagazig University Medical Journal **5734**
Zagazig University. Faculty of Science. Bulletin (EGY ISSN 1110-1555) **7933**
Zagazig University. Journal of Commercial Research *see* Gami'at al-Zagazig. Magallat al-Buhuth al-Tigariyyat **1113**
Zagazig University Medical Journal (EGY ISSN 1110-1431) **5734**
Zagazig Veterinary Journal (EGY ISSN 1110-1458) **8815**
Zagle (POL ISSN 0860-2670) **8286**
Zagmag (IND) **2224**
Zagorodnaya Zhizn' *see* Homes & Gardens **4558**
Zagotovitel'nye Proizvodstva v Mashinostroenii (RUS ISSN 1684-1107) **5461**
Zagreb In Your Pocket (HRV) **8777**
Zagreb International Review of Economics & Business (HRV ISSN 1331-5609) **1197**
➤ Zagreber Germanistische Beitraege (HRV ISSN 1330-0946) **5404**
Zagvozd (HRV ISSN 1332-0483) **4279**
Al-Zahf al-Akhdar (LBY) **3905**
Zahlen zur Kohlenwirtschaft (DEU ISSN 0723-0036) **6484**
Zahlungsbilanz der Schweiz (CHE) **1955**
Zahn Magazin (DEU ISSN 0933-1786) **5869**
Zahnaerzte Wirtschaftsdienst (DEU ISSN 0724-0376) **5869**
Zahnaerzteblatt Baden-Wuerttemberg (DEU ISSN 0340-3017) **5870**
Zahnaerzteblatt Brandenburg (DEU) **5870**
Zahnaerzteblatt Niedersachsen (DEU ISSN 1860-9961) **5870**
Zahnaerzteblatt Sachsen (DEU ISSN 0938-8486) **5870**
Zahnaerzteblatt Westfalen-Lippe (DEU ISSN 0344-211X) **5870**
Zahnaerztekammer Niedersachsen Mitteilungen *see* Z K N - Mitteilungen **5869**
Zahnaerztliche Welt Rundschau *see* Z W R **5869**
Zahnaerztlicher Anzeiger (DEU ISSN 0027-3198) **5870**
Zahnaerztlicher Gesundheitsdienst (DEU ISSN 0340-5478) **5870**
Zahnaerztliches Fortbildungszentrum Niedersachsen Seminarprogramm *see* Z F N Seminarprogramm **5869**
• ZahnArzt (AUT ISSN 1862-7560) **5870**
Zahnarzt und Praxis (DEU ISSN 1863-7965) **5870**
Zahnarzt und Praxis International *see* Zahnarzt und Praxis **5870**
Der Zahnarzt und Sein Recht (DEU ISSN 1436-6029) **5870**
Zahnarzt Wirtschaft Praxis (DEU ISSN 1617-5077) **5870**
Zahnarzt Wirtschaft Praxis Spezial *see* Z W P Spezial **5869**
Die Zahnarzt Woche (DEU) **5870**
Die Zahnarzthelferin *see* Die Zahnmedizinische Fachangestellte **5870**
Zahnheilkunde, Management, Kultur (DEU ISSN 1862-0914) **5870**
▼ • Zahnmedizin up2date (DEU ISSN 1865-0457) **5870**
Die Zahnmedizinische Fachangestellte (DEU ISSN 1618-9469) **5870**
Zahnraeder und Zahnradgetriebe *see* Informationsdienst F I Z Technik. Zahnraeder und Zahnradgetriebe **3231**
ZahnRat (DEU ISSN 1435-2508) **5870**
Zahntechnik *see* Z T **5869**
Zahntechnik Wirtschaft Labor (DEU ISSN 1617-5085) **5870**
Zahora (ESP ISSN 1132-7030) **5198**
Zahoroda (POL) **3573**
• Zahradaweb (CZE ISSN 1214-763X) **3754**
Zahradkar (CZE ISSN 0139-7761) **3754**
• Zahradkar (SVK ISSN 0862-5565) **3754**
Zahradnictvi (CZE ISSN 1213-7596) **3754**
Zahranicna Politika (SVK ISSN 1336-7218) **7275**
Zahranicni Politika Ceske Republiky. Dokumenty (CZE ISSN 1210-5600) **7275**
Zahrat al-Khalij (UAE) **8892**
Zaidan Hojin Toyo Bunko *see* Oriental Library. Research Department. Memoirs **4187**
• Zaihaixue/Journal of Catastrophology (CHN ISSN 1000-811X) **2228**
Zaikai/Financial World (JPN) **1391**
Zaiken/Waseda University. Kagami Memorial Laboratory for Materials Science and Technology (JPN ISSN 0919-8423) **6337**
Zainak (ESP ISSN 1137-439X) **361**
Zaire Business (COD) **1534**
Zaire. Conseil Legislatif National. Compte Rendu Analytique (COD) **4818**
Zaire. Direction Generale des Finances. Bulletin des Finances (COD) **1955**
Zaire. Institut National de la Statistique. Bulletin Trimestriel des Statistiques Generales (COD) **8414**
Zairyo (JPN ISSN 0514-5163) **3360**
Zairyo Kagaku *see* Zairyou no Kagaku to Kougaku **3360**
Zairyo Kenkyu Rengo Koenkai Ronbunshu *see* Japan Congress on Materials Research. Proceedings **3348**
Zairyo no Hiro ni Kansuru Kenkyu no Susei *see* Bibliography of Materials Fatigue **3228**
Zairyo Rikigaku Koenkai Koen Ronbunshu/ Conference on Materials and Mechanics. Proceedings (JPN) **3399**
Zairyo Shisutemu/Materials System (JPN ISSN 0286-6013) **3228**
Zairyo to Kankyo/Corrosion Engineering (JPN ISSN 0917-0480) **6337**
➤ Zairyo to Purosesu/Current Advances in Materials and Processes (JPN ISSN 0914-6628) **6337**
Zairyou no Kagaku to Kougaku/Materials Science and Technology (JPN ISSN 1347-4774) **3360**
Zaisheng Ziyuan Yanjiu/Recycling Research *see* Zaisheng Ziyuan yu Xunhuan Jingji **3476**
• Zaisheng Ziyuan yu Xunhuan Jingji/Renewable Resources and Recycling Economy (CHN ISSN 1674-0912) **3476**
Zajednicar (USA) **3573**
Zaji yu Moshu/Acrobatics and Magic (CHN) **4351**
• Zajiao Shuidao/Journal of Hybrid Rice (CHN ISSN 1005-3956) **260**
Zakar *see* Zakar Magazine **8892**
▼ • Zakar Magazine (USA ISSN 1946-6420) **8892**
Zakavkazskie Voennye Vedomosti (GEO) **6455**
Zakazenia (POL ISSN 1428-1287) **5734**
Zakboek Arbowet (NLD ISSN 1574-4027) **1716**
Zakboek Bijstand en Belastingen (NLD ISSN 1872-4175) **1955**
Zakboek Handhaving Ruimtelijke Regelgeving (NLD ISSN 1871-4153) **4432**
Zakboek Mediation (NLD ISSN 1574-4019) **4818**
Zakboek Onderwijsstatistieken *see* Jaarboek Onderwijs **2934**
Zakboek Proces-Verbaal *see* Zakboek Proces-Verbaal en Bewijsrecht **2672**
Zakboek Proces-Verbaal en Bewijsrecht (NLD ISSN 1876-2409) **2672**
Zakboek Sociale Zekerheid M K B *see* Zakboek Sociale Zekerheid Midden- en Klein Bedrijf **1716**
Zakboek Sociale Zekerheid Midden- en Klein Bedrijf (NLD ISSN 1574-5643) **1716**
• Zakboek Strafvordering voor de Hulpofficier van Justitie (NLD ISSN 1389-4528) **4900**
Zakboek Uitvaartwezen *see* Uitvaartwezen Compact **3720**
Zakboekje Beslagrecht *see* Memo Beslagrecht **4837**
† Zakboekje Jaarrekening Kleinbedrijf (NLD ISSN 1872-4213) **8999**
Zakboekje Sociale Zekerheid (NLD ISSN 1872-4221) **4529**
Zakelijk *see* Zakelijk (Regio Eindhoven-Helmond) **1802**
Zakelijk *see* Zakelijk (Regio den Bosch) **1802**
▼ Zakelijk (Regio Breda-Tilburg) (NLD ISSN 1875-0613) **1802**
▼ Zakelijk (Regio den Bosch) (NLD ISSN 1875-0524) **1802**
▼ Zakelijk (Regio Eindhoven-Helmond) (NLD ISSN 1875-0532) **1802**
Zakenauto (NLD ISSN 0169-4723) **8613**
Zakenblad Regio Valkenswaard (NLD ISSN 1872-0331) **1721**
Zakenpunt (NLD ISSN 1574-762X) **1197**
Zakenreis Magazine (NLD) **8777**
Zakka Catalog (JPN) **4553**
• Zakladani (CZE ISSN 1212-1711) **1044**
Zakmira (DEU) **424**
Zakon (RUS ISSN 0869-4400) **4818**
Zakon i Armiya (RUS) **6455**
Zakonnost' (RUS ISSN 0869-4486) **2672**
Zakonodatel'naya i Prikladnaya Metrologiya (RUS) **6407**
Zakonodatel'stvo i Ekonomika (RUS) **1197**
Zakony (SVK ISSN 1335-6127) **4818**
Zalai Gyujtemeny (HUN ISSN 0133-5499) **4279**
Zalai Hirlap (HUN ISSN 0133-0500) **3877**
Zalioji Lietuva (LTU) **3476**

Zaman (DEU ISSN 1860-0581) **3860**
Zaman *see* Today's Zaman **3963**
Zaman - Azerbaidzhan (AZE) **3799**
Zamana (MUS) **3573**
• ➤ Zambezia (ZWE ISSN 0379-0622) **8018**
Zambia *see* The P R S Group. Country Reports: Zambia **1510**
Zambia Bureau of Standards Review *see* Z A B S Review **6407**
Zambia. Central Statistical Office. Agricultural and Pastoral Production (Commercial and Non-Commercial) (ZMB) **190**
Zambia. Central Statistical Office. Agricultural and Pastoral Production (Commercial Farms) (ZMB) **190**
Zambia. Central Statistical Office. Agricultural and Pastoral Production (Non-Commercial) (ZMB) **190**
Zambia. Central Statistical Office. Annual Statement of External Trade (ZMB ISSN 0084-4489) **1275**
Zambia. Central Statistical Office. Balance of Payments Statistics (ZMB) **1275**
Zambia. Central Statistical Office. Consumer Price Statistics (ZMB) **1275**
Zambia. Central Statistical Office. Employment and Earnings (ZMB ISSN 0084-4500) **1275**
Zambia. Central Statistical Office. Financial Statistics of Government Sector (Economic and Functional Analysis) (ZMB) **7485**
Zambia. Central Statistical Office. Financial Statistics of Public Corporations (ZMB ISSN 0084-4519) **1275**
Zambia. Central Statistical Office. Fisheries Statistics (Natural Waters) (ZMB ISSN 0514-8731) **3614**
Zambia. Central Statistical Office. Industry Monographs (ZMB) **1275**
Zambia. Central Statistical Office. Manpower Survey (ZMB) **1275**
Zambia. Central Statistical Office. Migration Statistics (ZMB ISSN 0084-4543) **7317**
Zambia. Central Statistical Office. Migration Statistics: Immigrants and Visitors *see* Zambia. Central Statistical Office. Migration Statistics **7317**
Zambia. Central Statistical Office. Monthly Digest of Statistics (ZMB ISSN 0027-0377) **8414**
Zambia. Central Statistical Office. National Accounts (ZMB) **7485**
Zambia. Central Statistical Office. Quarterly Agricultural Statistical Bulletin (ZMB) **190**
Zambia. Central Statistical Office. Registered Births, Marriages and Deaths (Vital Statistics) *see* Zambia. Central Statistical Office. Vital Statistics **7317**
Zambia. Central Statistical Office. Statistical Year Book (ZMB ISSN 0084-4551) **8414**
Zambia. Central Statistical Office. Transport Statistics (ZMB ISSN 0514-5392) **8533**
Zambia. Central Statistical Office. Vital Statistics (ZMB ISSN 0084-456X) **7317**
Zambia. Commission for Investigations. Annual Report (ZMB) **7478**
Zambia. Commission for the Preservation of Natural and Historical Monuments and Relics. Annual Report (ZMB ISSN 0084-4586) **2633**
Zambia Consolidated Copper Mines Ltd. Annual Report and Accounts (ZMB) **6484**
• Zambia Daily Mail (ZMB) **3996**
Zambia. Department of Agriculture. Research and Specialist Services. Annual Report (ZMB) **260**
Zambia. Department of Civil Aviation. Annual Report (ZMB) **8553**
Zambia. Department of Customs and Excise. Annual Report of the Controller of Customs and Excise (ZMB) **1955**
Zambia. Department of Fisheries. Annual Report (ZMB) **3612**
Zambia. Department of Fisheries. Research Division. Annual Report (ZMB) **3612**
Zambia. Department of Forestry. Report (ZMB ISSN 0084-4616) **3708**
Zambia. Department of Labour. Report (ZMB ISSN 0084-4632) **1717**
Zambia. Department of Legal Aid. Annual Report (ZMB ISSN 0304-6931) **4818**
Zambia. Department of Social Development. Report (ZMB) **8079**
Zambia. Department of Taxes. Annual Report of the Commissioner of Taxes (ZMB ISSN 0084-4675) **1955**
Zambia. Department of the Administrator-General and Official Receiver. Report (ZMB ISSN 0084-4683) **1955**
Zambia. Department of Veterinary and Tsetse Control Services. Annual Report (ZMB) **8815**
Zambia. Department of Water Affairs. Report (ZMB ISSN 0084-4705) **8842**
Zambia. Educational and Occupational Assessment Service. Annual Report (ZMB ISSN 0514-5457) **6706**
Zambia Educational Journal *see* Zambia Journal of Education **3011**
Zambia Electricity Supply Corporation. Annual Report (ZMB) **3334**
• Zambia Food Security Outlook (USA ISSN 2150-0746) **1608**
Zambia Food Security Update *see* Zambia Food Security Outlook **1608**
Zambia. Geological Survey. Annual Reports (ZMB ISSN 0084-473X) **2776**
Zambia. Geological Survey. Economic Reports (ZMB ISSN 0084-4748) **2776**
Zambia. Geological Survey. Occasional Papers (ZMB ISSN 0084-4756) **2776**
Zambia. Geological Survey. Reports (ZMB ISSN 0084-4764) **2776**
Zambia. Geological Survey. Technical Reports (ZMB) **2776**
Zambia Heritage (ZMB) **2633**
Zambia. High Court. Law Directory and Legal Calendar (ZMB) **4818**
Zambia. Immigration Department. Report (ZMB ISSN 0084-4802) **7296**
Zambia Industrial and Mining Corporation. Annual Report (ZMB) **6484**
Zambia Journal of Applied Earth Sciences (ZMB ISSN 1010-5913) **2718**
Zambia Journal of Education (ZMB ISSN 1996-3645) **3011**
➤ Zambia Law Journal (ZMB ISSN 1027-7862) **4818**
• Zambia Law Reports (ZAF ISSN 1028-9208) **4818**
The Zambia Lowdown (ZMB) **3996**
Zambia. Meteorological Department. Totals of Monthly and Annual Rainfall (ZMB ISSN 0302-5047) **6400**
Zambia Mining Yearbook (ZMB ISSN 0377-8118) **6484**
Zambia. Ministry of Agriculture and Water Development. Land Use Branch. Soil Survey Report (ZMB) **260**
Zambia. Ministry of Agriculture, Food and Fisheries. Annual Agricultural Statistical Bulletin (ZMB) **190**
Zambia. Ministry of Cooperatives. Annual Report (ZMB) **1425**
Zambia. Ministry of Decentralisation. District Councils Revenue and Capital Estimates (ZMB) **1197**
Zambia. Ministry of Education. Annual Report (ZMB ISSN 0084-487X) **2928**
Zambia. Ministry of Legal Affairs. Annual Report (ZMB) **1197**
Zambia. Ministry of Planning and Finance. Annual Report (ZMB) **1909**
Zambia. Ministry of Youth and Sport. Department of Youth Development. Annual Report (ZMB) **2174**
Zambia. Ministry of Youth and Sport. Report (ZMB) **8217**
Zambia Museums Journal (ZMB ISSN 1682-7570) **361**
Zambia. National Commission for Development Planning. Economic Report (ZMB) **1534**
Zambia. National Council for Scientific Research. Annual Report (ZMB ISSN 0084-4950) **7933**
Zambia. National Council for Scientific Research. N C S R Bibliography (ZMB) **7939**
Zambia. National Food and Nutrition Commission. Annual Report (ZMB ISSN 0084-4969) **3668**
Zambia. National Heritage Conservation Commission. Annual Report (ZMB) **2633**
Zambia. National Museums Board. Report (ZMB ISSN 0084-4977) **6540**
Zambia. Natural Resources Department. Annual Report (ZMB) **2633**
Zambia Nieuwsbrief (NLD ISSN 1380-8915) **4179**
Zambia. Office of the Auditor-General. Report of the Auditor-General (ZMB ISSN 0303-2760) **1955**
Zambia. Posts and Telecommunications Corporation. Annual Report (ZMB) **2355**
Zambia. Prisons Department. Report (ZMB ISSN 0084-4659) **2672**
Zambia. Public Service Commission. Report (ZMB ISSN 0084-5035) **8079**
Zambia Science Abstracts (ZMB) **7939**
Zambia State Insurance Corporation. Report and Accounts (ZMB) **4529**
Zambia. Survey Department. Report (ZMB ISSN 0084-5078) **4034**
Zambia. Teaching Service Commission. Annual Report (ZMB ISSN 0556-9001) **2928**
Zambia Trade Directory (ZAF) **2036**
Zambian Climatological Summary; Surface and Upper Air Data (ZMB) **6400**
• The Zambian Marketer (ZMB ISSN 1817-2717) **1849**
Zambian Ornithological Society. Newsletter (ZMB ISSN 0378-4533) **917**
Zambian Ornithological Society. Occasional Papers (ZMB) **917**
➤ Zambian Papers (ZMB ISSN 1028-2351) **4179**
Zamecky Roman (CZE ISSN 1801-0490) **5413**
Zamestitel' Glavnogo Vracha (RUS) **7546**
Zamojski Informator Diecezjalny (POL ISSN 1425-7777) **7823**
Zamojski Kwartalnik Kulturalny (POL ISSN 0239-8710) **5246**
Zamzam (IRN ISSN 1024-9656) **7717**
Zan-e Ruz (IRN ISSN 1023-7178) **8892**
Zan Zhene Zaman (KAZ) **4818**
• Zanco Journal of Medical Sciences (IRQ ISSN 1995-5588) **5734**
Zandera (DEU ISSN 0940-9920) **3755**
Zanders Magazine (NLD ISSN 1873-7455) **1955**
▼ Het Zandkasteel Vakantie! (NLD ISSN 1876-3510) **2224**
Zane Grey Review (USA ISSN 1083-7140) **5413**
Zango/Forum (ZMB) **3996**
Zanmai (CAN) **7703**
• Zany Zine (IND) **2569**
• Zaochuan Jishu/Marine Technology (CHN ISSN 1000-3878) **8665**
• Zaoqi Jiaoyu (Jiajiao Ban)/Early Education (Home School Edition) (CHN) **2928**
• Zaoqi Jiaoyu (Jiaoshi Ban)/Early Education (Teacher's Edition) (CHN ISSN 1005-6017) **2928**
• Zaoqi Jiaoyu (Meishu Ban)/Early Education (Art Edition) (CHN) **2928**
Zaoxing Yishu/Plastic Art (CHN ISSN 1009-7635) **528**
• Zaozhi Huaxuepin/Paper Chemicals (CHN ISSN 1007-2225) **6740**
• Zaozhi Kexue yu Jishu/Paper Science & Technology (CHN ISSN 1671-4571) **6740**
Zaozhi Xinxi/China Papermaking News (CHN ISSN 1006-8791) **6740**
Zap (BEL ISSN 0778-2322) **2224**
Zap! Fernsehen und Buecher (DEU) **2399**
Zapadne Slovensko (SVK) **4279**
• ➤ Zapadoceska Univerzita v Plzni. Fakulta Pedagogicka. Sbornik. Dejepis (CZE ISSN 1213-7812) **4279**
Zapadoceske Muzeum v Plzni. Sbornik. Historie (CZE ISSN 0862-3597) **4279**
Zapadoceske Muzeum v Plzni. Sbornik. Priroda (CZE ISSN 0232-0738) **6540**
Zapateri (ESP ISSN 1131-933X) **861**
Zapiski *see* Association of Russian - American Scholars in the U S A. Transactions **3520**
➤ Zapiski Historyczne (POL ISSN 0044-1791) **4168**
Zapiski Otdela Rukopisei *see* Rossiiskaya Gosudarstvennaya Biblioteka. Nauchno-Issledovatel'skii Otdel Rukopisei. Zapiski **5044**
Zapolyarnaya Pravda (RUS) **3943**
Zaposlena Zena (HRV ISSN 1330-6642) **8892**
Zapp! (NLD) **4086**
Zapp dele Clic al Mundo *see* Zapp Jorden Rundt **7275**
Zapp Jorden Rundt/Zapp dele Clic al Mundo/Zapp Magazine (DNK ISSN 0908-0686) **7275**
Zapp Magazine *see* Zapp Jorden Rundt **7275**
Zapresicki Godisnjak (HRV ISSN 1332-277X) **5404**
Zaqaziq Journal of Occupational Health and Safety *see* Zagazig Journal of Occupational Health and Safety **6689**
Zaraat (PAK) **171**
Zarai Taraqiati Bank Ltd. Annual Report (PAK) **209**
Zaranie Slaskie (POL ISSN 0044-183X) **4279**
Zarin's Radiology Liability Alert (USA ISSN 1938-6559) **4818**
➤ Zariya Veterinarian (NGA ISSN 0794-5086) **8815**
Zariya Veterinarian *see* Zariya Veterinarian **8815**
Zarja/Dawn (USA ISSN 0044-1848) **3573**
➤ Zarqa Journal for Research and Studies (JOR) **7933**
Zartonk (LBN) **3573**
Zarubezhnaya Elektronnaya Tekhnika (RUS ISSN 0130-1462) **3116**
Zarubezhnaya Periodicheskaya Pechat' na Russkom Yazyke (USA ISSN 1066-4858) **18**
Zarubezhnaya Radioelektronika *see* Zarubezhnaya Radioelektronika. Uspekhi Sovremennoi Elektroniki **3116**
Zarubezhnaya Radioelektronika. Uspekhi Sovremennoi Elektroniki (RUS) **3116**
• Zarubezhnoe Voennoe Obozrenie (RUS ISSN 0134-921X) **6455**
Zarzadzanie na Swiecie (POL ISSN 1230-3747) **1802**
Zarzadzanie Zasobami Ludzkimi (POL ISSN 1641-0874) **1878**
Zashchita i Karantin Rastenii (RUS ISSN 1026-8634) **260**
Zashchita Informatsii-Konfident (RUS) **2228**
Zashchita Metallov *see* Fizikokhimiya Poverkhnosti i Zashchita Materialov **6312**
Zashchita Okruzhayushchei Sredy v Neftegazovom Komplekse (RUS) **6798**
Zashchita Rastenii (RUS) **260**
Zasshi Shinbun so Katarogu (CD-ROM)/Japan's Serials Directory (CD-ROM Edition) *see* Kikan Shoshi Nabi **628**
• Zasshi Shinbun Sokatarogu/Periodicals in Print in Japan (JPN ISSN 0387-7000) **639**
Zasso Kenkyu/Weed Research (JPN ISSN 0372-798X) **823**
Zastita Materijala/Materials Protection (SRB ISSN 0351-9465) **6721**
Zastita Prirode (SRB ISSN 0514-5899) **3476**
Zastita Rada (SRB ISSN 0044-1880) **6689**
† Zav-Zav (ISR ISSN 0792-9307) **8999**
Zavarivanje (HRV ISSN 0044-1902) **6345**
Zavod za Hrvatsku Povijest. Radovi (HRV ISSN 0351-2142) **4279**
Zavod za Povijest Hrvatske Knjizevnosti, Kazalista i Glazbe. Kronika (HRV ISSN 1330-6731) **5246**
➤ Zavodskaya Laboratoriya. Diagnostika Materialov/Industrial Laboratory. Diagnostics of Materials (RUS ISSN 1028-6861) **2107**
• Zavtra (RUS) **5246**
Zavtra Rossii (RUS) **7197**
• Zawen Yuekan/Monthly of Essays (CHN ISSN 1009-2218) **5246**
Zaza Mimosa (FRA ISSN 1771-8252) **2224**
ZaZen (ZAF ISSN 1819-298X) **316**
Zbior Dokumentow - Polski Instytut Spraw Miedzynarodowych *see* Akademia Dyplomatyczna. Zbior Dokumentow **7220**
Zbirnyk Uryadovykh Normatyvnykh Aktiv Ukrainy (UKR) **7478**
Zbornik Drustva za Povjesnicu Klana *see* Drustvo za Povjesnicu Klana. Zbornik **4215**
• Zbornik Gozdarstva in Lesarstva (SVN ISSN 0351-3114) **3708**
Zbornik Istorije Knjizevnosti/Recueil des Travaux de l'Histoire de la Litterature (SRB ISSN 0084-5183) **5404**
Zbornik Istrazivackih Radova iz Oblasti Materijala i Konstrukcija u Gradjevinarstvu (BIH ISSN 0353-4146) **3287**
➤ Zbornik Matice Srpske za Drustvene Nauke (SRB ISSN 0352-5732) **8018**
➤ Zbornik Matice Srpske za Filologiju i Lingvistiku (SRB ISSN 0352-5724) **5198**
➤ Zbornik Matice Srpske za Istoriju (SRB ISSN 0352-5716) **4280**
➤ Zbornik Matice Srpske za Knjizevnost i Jezik (SRB ISSN 0543-1220) **5198**
➤ Zbornik Matice Srpske za Likovne Umetnosti (SRB ISSN 0352-6844) **528**
➤ Zbornik Matice Srpske za Prirodne Nauke (SRB ISSN 0352-4906) **7933**
➤ Zbornik Matice Srpske za Scenske Umetnosti i Muziku/Matica Srpska Review of Stage Art and Music (SRB ISSN 0352-9738) **8485**
• ➤ Zbornik Matice Srpske za Slavistiku/Review of Slavic Studies (SRB ISSN 0352-5007) **5198**
Zbornik Narodne in Univerzitetne Knjiznice *see* Narodna in Univerzitetna Knjiznica. Zbornik **5034**
Zbornik Narodnog Muzeja o Beogradu. Istoriya Umetnosti (SRB) **528**
Zbornik Narodnog Muzeja u Beogradu. Arheologiya (SRB ISSN 0352-2474) **424**
Zbornik o Zagori (HRV ISSN 1331-6370) **4280**
Zbornik Pravnog Fakulteta u Zagrebu *see* Univerzitet u Zagrebu. Pravni Fakultet. Zbornik **4805**
Zbornik Radova. Journal of Information and Organizational Sciences *see* Journal of Information and Organizational Sciences **2548**
Zbornik Vedeckych Prac Drevarskej Fakulty Vysokej Skoly Lenickej a Drevarskej vo Zvolene *see* Vysoka Skola Lesnicka a Drevarska vo Zvolene. Drevarska Fakulta. Zbornik Vedeckych Prac **3707**
Zbornik za Istoriju, Jezik i Knjizevnost Srpskog Naroda. Fontes Rerum Slavorum Meridionalium (SRB ISSN 0084-5191) **4280**
Zbornik za Istoriju, Jezik i Knjizevnost Srpskog Naroda. Spomenici na Srpskom Jeziku (SRB ISSN 0084-5205) **5404**
Zbornik za Istoriju, Jezik i Knjizevnost Srpskog Naroda. Spomenici na Tudjim Jezicima (SRB ISSN 0084-5213) **4280**
Zbrane & Naboje (CZE ISSN 1212-5210) **8343**
ZCG *see* Zeitschrift fuer Corporate Governance **1802**
• ZCommerce (USA) **2569**
Zdanie (POL ISSN 0137-3242) **7197**
ZDF-WISO Magazin *see* Z D F - W I S O Magazin **8999**
➤ Zdobutky Khimichnoi i Eksperymental'noi Medytsyny/Achievements of Clinical and Experimental Medicine (UKR ISSN 1811-2471) **5912**
Zdorov (CAN ISSN 1206-3673) **3966**
• Zdorov'e (RUS ISSN 0044-1945) **7546**
Zdorov'e Naseleniya i Sreda Obitaniya (RUS) **7546**
Zdorov'ya Zhinky *see* Zdorov'ye Zhenshchiny **8850**
Zdorov'ye Detei (RUS) **7001**
Zdorov'ye Muzhchiny/Zrorov'ya Cholovika (UKR) **6277**
➤ Zdorov'ye Zhenshchiny/Zdorov'ya Zhinky (UKR) **8850**
Zdorovyi Obraz Zhizni (RUS) **8217**
Zdraveopazvane (BGR ISSN 0324-1920) **8414**
Zdravi Zivot (HRV ISSN 1330-6081) **7546**
• Zdravie (SVK ISSN 0044-1953) **7001**
• Zdravie.sk (SVK ISSN 1336-8745) **7001**
• Zdravniski Vestnik (SVN ISSN 1318-0347) **5734**
Zdravookhranenie (BLR ISSN 1027-7218) **7546**
Zdravookhranenie (RUS ISSN 1028-9771) **7546**
Zdravookhranenie Rossiiskoi Federatsii/Public Healthcare of the Russian Federation (RUS ISSN 0044-197X) **7546**
Zdravookhranenie v Rossii (Year) (RUS) **7550**
Zdravotni Pojisteni a Revizni Lekarstvi *see* Revizni a Posudkove Lekarstvi **4110**
Zdravotnicke Listy *see* E-mail Noviny Zdravotnicke Listy **5608**
• Zdravotnicke Noviny (CZE ISSN 0044-1996) **7546**
Zdravotnicke Noviny (SVK ISSN 1335-4477) **7546**
† Zdravotnicke Pravo v Praxi (CZE ISSN 1214-2883) **8999**
Zdravstvuite! (RUS) **3943**
Zdravyi Smysl (BLR) **3801**
Zdrowie (POL ISSN 0137-8066) **7001**
➤ Zdrowie Psychiczne (POL ISSN 0044-2003) **6190**
Zdrowie Publiczne (POL ISSN 0044-2011) **7546**
Zdrowie Seniora (POL ISSN 1642-9478) **4057**
Ze Carioca (BRA ISSN 0104-3404) **2224**
Ze T *see* Zeitschrift fuer Tagesmuetter und -vaeter **2173**
Zeal (USA ISSN 0514-2482) **7823**
Zeba (USA ISSN 1931-759X) **3573**
• ➤ Zebrafish (USA ISSN 1545-8547) **968**
The Zebra's Voice (BWA) **6540**
ZebrasOmag *see* ZebrasO'Mag **6817**
▼ ZebrasO'Mag (FRA ISSN 1957-2840) **6817**
Zee (BEL) **8628**
Het Zee-Aquarium (NLD ISSN 0166-8706) **968**
Zeebrugge and Ostend Ports. Annual *see* Havens Zeebrugge en Oostende. Jaarboek **8645**
Zeehavens Amsterdam/Amsterdam Seaports (NLD ISSN 1569-7304) **8665**

Title

▼ *new title*   † *ceased*   ● *electronic media*   ➤ *refereed*

- • Zhongguo Huanbao Chanye/China Environmental Protection Industry (CHN ISSN 1006-5377) **3476**
- • Zhongguo Huangjin Zhubao/Jewelry & Gold (CHN ISSN 1009-6841) **4570**
- • Zhongguo Huanjing Guanli Ganbu Xueyuan Xuebao/Environmental Management College of China. Journal (CHN ISSN 1008-813X) **3476**
- • ➤ Zhongguo Huanjing Kexue/China Environmental Science (CHN ISSN 1000-6923) **3476**
- Zhongguo Huazhuangpin/China Cosmetics Review (CHN ISSN 1004-5163) **596**
- Zhongguo Huizhan/China Conference & Exhibition (CHN ISSN 1674-3598) **6283**
- • Zhongguo Huxi yu Weizhong Jianhu Zazhi/Chinese Journal of Respiratory and Critical Care Medicine (CHN ISSN 1671-6205) **6221**
- Zhongguo Jiaju/China Furniture (CHN) **4563**
- • Zhongguo Jiancai Bao/China Building Materials News (CHN) **1044**
- • ➤ Zhongguo Jianchuan Yanjiu/Chinese Journal of Ship Research (CHN ISSN 1673-3185) **8666**
- • Zhongguo Jiankang Yuekan/China Health (CHN ISSN 1005-0515) **7001**
- Zhongguo Jianshe Bao/China Construction News (CHN) **1044**
- • Zhongguo Jianzai (CHN ISSN 1002-4549) **2228**
- Zhongguo Jianzhu *see* Chinese Architecture **437**
- Zhongguo Jianzhuye Nianjian/China Building Industry Almanac (CHN) **1044**
- • Zhongguo Jiaodian/China Focus (CAN ISSN 1912-0168) **3573**
- Zhongguo Jiaotong Nianjian/China Communications and Transportation Yearbook (CHN ISSN 1002-8617) **2345**
- • Zhongguo Jiaoxing Waike Zazhi/Orthopedic Journal of China (CHN ISSN 1005-8478) **6076**
- Zhongguo Jiaoxue Cankao/Reference for Middle School Education (CHN ISSN 1674-6058) **2928**
- Zhongguo Jiaoyu Bao/Chinese Education Daily (CHN) **2928**
- Zhongguo Jiaoyu Nianjian/China Education Yearbook (CHN) **2928**
- • Zhongguo Jiaoyu Xuekan/China Education Association. Journal (CHN ISSN 1002-4808) **2928**
- • Zhongguo Jiceng Yiyao/Chinese Journal of Primary Medicine and Pharmacy (CHN ISSN 1008-6706) **5736**
- • Zhongguo Jidian Gongye/China Machinery & Electronics Industry (CHN ISSN 1002-977X) **1198**
- • Zhongguo Jieru Yingxiang yu Zhiliaoxue/Chinese Journal of Interventional Imaging and Therapy (CHN ISSN 1672-8475) **6210**
- • Zhongguo Jiguang/Chinese Journal of Lasers (CHN ISSN 0258-7025) **7085**
- • Zhongguo Jiguang Yixue Zazhi/Chinese Journal of Laser Medicine & Surgery (CHN ISSN 1003-9430) **5736**
- • Zhongguo Jihua Mianyi/Chinese Journal of Vaccines and Immunization (CHN ISSN 1006-916X) **5767**
- • Zhongguo Jihua Zhengyuxue Zazhi/Chinese Journal of Family Planning (CHN ISSN 1004-8189) **973**
- • ➤ Zhongguo Jijiu Yixue/Chinese Journal of Critical Care Medicine (CHN ISSN 1002-1949) **5736**
- • Zhongguo Jiliang Xueyuan Xuebao/China Jiliang University. Journal (CHN ISSN 1004-1540) **7934**
- Zhongguo Jindaishi/Modern History of China (CHN ISSN 1001-2621) **4191**
- • Zhongguo Jing Ji Ping Lun/China Business Review (USA ISSN 1536-9056) **1588**
- Zhongguo Jingji Daobao/China Economic Herald (CHN) **1534**
- Zhongguo Jingji Jingqi Yuebao/China Monthly Economic Indicators (CHN ISSN 1009-3834) **1535**
- Zhongguo Jingji Kuaixun/China Economic News Weekly *see* Zhongguo Jingji Zhoukan **1198**
- Zhongguo Jingji Nianjian/Almanac of China's Economy (CHN ISSN 1006-561X) **1803**
- • Zhongguo Jingji Tizhi Gaige Nianjian/China Economic Systems Reform Yearbook (CHN ISSN 1005-703X) **1535**
- Zhongguo Jingji Wenti (CHN ISSN 1000-4181) **1722**
- Zhongguo Jingji Xinwen/China Economic News (HKG ISSN 1000-9094) **1535**
- Zhongguo Jingji Xinxi/Chinese Economic Information (CHN ISSN 1003-5974) **1198**
- Zhongguo Jingji Zhoukan/China Economic Weekly (CHN ISSN 1672-7150) **1198**
- • Zhongguo Jingjishi Yanjiu/Researches in Chinese Economic History (CHN ISSN 1002-8005) **1551**
- • ➤ Zhongguo Jingkuangyan/China Well and Rock Salt (CHN ISSN 1001-0335) **6484**
- • Zhongguo Jingmao Daokan/China Economic & Trade Herald (CHN ISSN 1007-9777) **1198**
- • Zhongguo Jingying Bao/China Business Journal (CHN) **1198**
- • Zhongguo Jinrong/China Finance (CHN ISSN 0578-1485) **1392**
- Zhongguo Jinrong Nianjian/China Finance Year Book (CHN ISSN 1001-5841) **1392**
- • Zhongguo Jishengchongxue yu Jishengchongbing Zazhi/Chinese Journal of Parasitology and Parasitic Diseases (CHN ISSN 1000-7423) **898**
- • Zhongguo Jisuanji Yonghu/The Journal of China Computer Users (CHN ISSN 1003-031X) **2441**
- Zhongguo Jiuye/China Employment (CHN ISSN 1006-8120) **1878**
- • Zhongguo Jixie Gongcheng/China Mechanical Engineering (CHN ISSN 1004-132X) **3400**
- Zhongguo Jiyou/China Philately (CHN ISSN 1002-6789) **6901**
- Zhongguo Jiyou Bao/China Philately News (CHN) **6901**
- • Zhongguo Jizhe/Chinese Journalist (CHN ISSN 1003-1146) **4586**
- • Zhongguo Jizhu Jisui Zazhi/Chinese Journal of Spine and Spinal Cord (CHN ISSN 1004-406X) **6076**
- • Zhongguo Kangfu/Chinese Journal of Rehabilitation (CHN ISSN 1001-2001) **7001**
- • Zhongguo Kangfu Lilun Yu Shijian/Chinese Journal of Rehabilitation Theory & Practice (CHN ISSN 1006-9771) **6117**
- • ➤ Zhongguo Kangfu Yixue Zazhi/Chinese Journal of Rehabilitation Medicine (CHN ISSN 1001-1242) **5736**
- Zhongguo Kangganran Hualiao Zazhi/Chinese Journal of Infection and Chemotherapy *see* Zhongguo Ganran Kongzhi Zazhi **5829**
- • Zhongguo Kangshengsu Zazhi/Chinese Journal of Antibiotics (CHN ISSN 1001-8689) **6887**
- Zhongguo Katong/Cartoon of China (CHN ISSN 1007-094X) **528**
- • Zhongguo Keji Chanye/Science & Technology Industry of China (CHN ISSN 1002-0608) **1803**
- • Zhongguo Keji Luntan/Forum on Science and Technology in China (CHN ISSN 1002-6711) **7934**
- • ➤ Zhongguo Keji Lunwen Zaixian/Sciencepaper Online (CHN ISSN 1673-7180) **7934**
- • Zhongguo Keji Qikan Yanjiu/Chinese Journal of Scientific and Technical Periodical (CHN ISSN 1001-7143) **7576**
- Zhongguo Keji Shiliao *see* Zhongguo Kejishi Zazhi **7934**
- Zhongguo Keji Shiliao/China Historical Materials of Science and Technology (CHN) **7934**
- • Zhongguo Keji Shuyu/China Terminology (CHN) **5199**
- Zhongguo Keji Tongji Nianjian/China Statistical Yearbook on Science and Technology (CHN) **7939**
- • Zhongguo Keji Ziyuan Daokan/China Science & Technology Resources Review (CHN ISSN 1674-1544) **5056**
- • Zhongguo Kejishi Zazhi/Historical Material of Chinese Science and Technology (CHN) **7934**
- Zhongguo Kexue. A Ji (Shuxue, Wulixue, Tianwenxue, Jishu kexue) *see* Zhongguo Kexue. G Ji: Wulixue, Tianwenxue **7047**
- • ➤ Zhongguo Kexue. A Ji: Shuxue (CHN ISSN 1006-9232) **5547**
- Zhongguo Kexue. A Ji: Shuxue, Wulixue, Tianwenxue, Jishu Kexue *see* Zhongguo Kexue. A Ji: Shuxue **5547**
- • ➤ Zhongguo Kexue. B Ji: Huaxue (CHN ISSN 1006-9240) **7934**
- Zhongguo Kexue. B Ji: Huaxue, Shengwuxue, Nongxue, Yixue, Dixue *see* Zhongguo Kexue. B Ji: Huaxue **7934**
- Zhongguo Kexue Bao *see* Kexue Shibao **7876**
- • ➤ Zhongguo Kexue. C Ji: Shengming Kexue (CHN ISSN 1006-9259) **7934**
- • Zhongguo Kexue. D Ji: Diqiu Kexue (CHN ISSN 1006-9267) **7934**
- • ➤ Zhongguo Kexue. E Ji: Jishu Kexue (CHN ISSN 1006-9275) **7934**
- • Zhongguo Kexue. F Ji: Xinxi Kexue (CHN ISSN 1674-5973) **2551**
- • ➤ Zhongguo Kexue. G Ji: Wulixue, Tianwenxue (CHN ISSN 1672-1780) **7047**
- • Zhongguo Kexue Jijin/Science Foundation in China (CHN ISSN 1000-8217) **7934**
- • Zhongguo Kexue Jishu Daxue Xuebao/University of Science and Technology of China. Journal (CHN ISSN 0253-2778) **7934**
- Zhongguo Kexue Wenzhai A *see* Chinese Science Abstracts. Part A **7936**
- Zhongguo Kexue Wenzhai B *see* Chinese Science Abstracts. Part B **7936**
- • Zhongguo Kexueyuan Yuankan/Chinese Academy of Sciences. Bulletin (CHN ISSN 1000-3045) **7934**
- Zhongguo Konggang/China Airports Magazines (HKG ISSN 1009-993X) **3876**
- • ➤ Zhongguo Kongjian Kexue Jishu/Chinese Space Science and Technology (CHN ISSN 1000-758X) **76**
- • Zhongguo Kouqiang Hemian Waike Zazhi/China Journal of Oral and Maxillofacial Surgery (CHN ISSN 1672-3244) **6263**
- • Zhongguo Kouqiang Zhongzhixue Zazhi/Chinese Journal of Oral Implantology (CHN ISSN 1007-3957) **5870**
- • Zhongguo Kuangye/China Mining Magazine (CHN ISSN 1004-4051) **6484**
- • Zhongguo Kuangye Daxue Xuebao/China University of Mining and Technology. Journal (CHN ISSN 1000-1964) **6484**
- • Zhongguo Kuangye Daxue Xuebao (Shehui Kexue Ban)/China University of Mining & Technology. Journal (Social Sciences) (CHN ISSN 1009-105X) **8018**
- • Zhongguo Laodong/China Labour (CHN ISSN 1007-8746) **1717**
- • Zhongguo Laodong Guanxi Xueyuan Xuebao/China Institute Relations of Industry. Bulletin (CHN) **4606**
- Zhongguo Laonian/Elderly Chinese (CHN ISSN 1002-5278) **4058**
- Zhongguo Laonian Bao/China Elderly Journal (CHN) **4058**
- • Zhongguo Laonianxue Zazhi/Chinese Journal of Gerontology (CHN ISSN 1005-9202) **4058**
- • Zhongguo Liangyou Xuebao/Chinese Cereals and Oils Association. Journal (CHN ISSN 1003-0174) **276**
- Zhongguo Lianhuanhua/China Picture-Story (CHN ISSN 1003-210X) **528**
- • Zhongguo Linchuang Jiepouxue Zazhi/Chinese Journal of Clinical Anatomy (CHN ISSN 1001-165X) **928**
- Zhongguo Linchuang Kangfu *see* Zhongguo Zuzhi Gongcheng yu Linchuang Kangfu **6117**
- • Zhongguo Linchuang Shenjing Kexue/Chinese Journal of Clinical Neurosciences (CHN ISSN 1008-0678) **6191**
- • Zhongguo Linchuang Xinlixue Zazhi/Chinese Journal of Clinical Psychology (CHN ISSN 1005-3611) **6191**
- • Zhongguo Linchuang Yaolixue yu Zhiliaoxue/Chinese Journal of Clinical Pharmacology and Therapeutics (CHN ISSN 1009-2501) **6887**
- • Zhongguo Linchuang Yaolixue Zazhi/The Chinese Journal of Clinical Pharmacology (CHN ISSN 1001-6821) **6887**
- • Zhongguo Linchuang Yaoxue Zazhi/Chinese Journal of Clinical Pharmacy (CHN ISSN 1007-4406) **6887**
- • Zhongguo Linchuang Yingyang Zazhi/Chinese Journal of Clinical Nutrition (CHN ISSN 1008-5882) **6671**
- • Zhongguo Linchuang Yisheng/Journal of Chinese Physician (CHN ISSN 1008-1089) **5736**
- • Zhongguo Linchuang Yixue/Chinese Journal of Clinical Medicine (CHN ISSN 1008-6358) **5736**
- • Zhongguo Linchuang Yixue Yingxiang Zazhi/Journal of China Clinic Medical Imaging (CHN ISSN 1008-1062) **6210**
- • Zhongguo Linye/Forestry in China (CHN ISSN 1000-0623) **3708**
- • Zhongguo Linye Jiaoyu/China Forestry Education (CHN ISSN 1001-7232) **3708**
- Zhongguo Luse Shibao/Chinese Green Times (CHN) **3476**
- • Zhongguo Lushi/Chinese Lawyer (CHN ISSN 1002-9745) **4820**
- Zhongguo Lushi Bao/China Lawyer News (CHN) **4820**
- Zhongguo Luyou *see* China Tourism **8693**
- Zhongguo Luyou Bao/China Tourism News (CHN) **8777**
- • Zhongguo Luyou Zazhi/China Tourism (CHN ISSN 1005-331X) **8777**
- Zhongguo Lyou Yanjiu *see* Journal of China Tourism Research **8725**
- • Zhongguo Mafeng Pifubing Zazhi/China Journal of Leprosy and Skin Diseases (CHN ISSN 1009-1157) **5736**
- Zhongguo Mafeng Zazhi/China Leprosy Journal *see* Zhongguo Mafeng Pifubing Zazhi **5736**
- • Zhongguo Malingshu/Chinese Potato Journal (CHN) **260**
- Zhongguo Manhua/China Cartoons (CHN ISSN 1005-6955) **528**
- Zhongguo Maoyi Bao/China Trade News (CHN) **1588**
- • Zhongguo Maye/Plant Fibers and Products (CHN ISSN 1671-3532) **260**
- • Zhongguo Meijie Shengwuxue ji Kongzhi Zazhi/Chinese Journal of Vector Biology and Control (CHN ISSN 1003-8280) **5767**
- • Zhongguo Meirong Yixue/Chinese Journal of Aesthetic Medicine (CHN ISSN 1008-6455) **5736**
- • Zhongguo Meirong Zhengxing Waike Zazhi/Chinese Journal of Aesthetic and Plastic Surgery (CHN ISSN 1673-7040) **6263**
- • Zhongguo Meishu Xueyuan Bao/China Academy of Art Newspaper (CHN) **528**
- • Zhongguo Meitan (CHN ISSN 1006-530X) **6484**
- Zhongguo Meitan Bao/China Coal News (CHN) **3150**
- • Zhongguo Meitan Dizhi/Coal Geology of China (CHN ISSN 1674-1803) **6484**
- Zhongguo Meitan Gongye Nianjian (CHN ISSN 1008-6528) **6484**
- • Zhongguo Meitan Gongye Yixue Zazhi/Chinese Journal of Coal Industry Medicine (CHN ISSN 1007-9564) **5736**
- • ➤ Zhongguo Mianyixue Zazhi/Chinese Journal of Immunology (CHN ISSN 1000-484X) **5767**
- • Zhongguo Minbing/China Militia (CHN ISSN 1002-5081) **6455**
- Zhongguo Mingpai/China Top Brands (CHN ISSN 1004-9525) **1849**
- Zhongguo Minhang/C A A C Inflight Magazine (HKG ISSN 1003-6253) **8789**
- Zhongguo Minhang Bao/Civil Aviation Administration of China. Journal (CHN ISSN 1001-2079) **8777**
- • ➤ Zhongguo Minhang Daxue Xuebao/Civil Aviation University of China. Journal (CHN ISSN 1674-5590) **76**
- Zhongguo Minhang Xueyuan Xuebao/Civil Aviation Institute of China. Journal *see* Zhongguo Minhang Daxue Xuebao **76**
- • Zhongguo Minjian Liaofa/China's Naturopathy (CHN ISSN 1007-5798) **316**
- • Zhongguo Minkang Yixue/Medical Journal of Chinese People Health (CHN ISSN 1672-0369) **7547**
- • Zhongguo Minying Keji yu Jingji/China Non-Governmental Sciencetechnology and Economy (CHN ISSN 1007-3280) **1434**
- • Zhongguo Minyong Hangkong/Civil Aviation Economics and Technology (CHN ISSN 1009-8739) **76**
- • Zhongguo Minzheng/China Civil Affairs (CHN ISSN 1002-4441) **7198**
- Zhongguo Minzheng Yixue Zazhi/Medical Journal of Chinese Civil Administration *see* Zhongguo Minkang Yixue **7547**
- • Zhongguo Minzu/China Ethnicity (CHN ISSN 1009-8887) **3573**
- • Zhongguo Minzu Jiaoyu/Nationalities Education of China (CHN ISSN 1002-5952) **2928**
- • Zhongguo Minzu Yiyao Zazhi/Journal of Medicine & Pharmacy of Chinese Minorities (MNG ISSN 1006-6810) **5736**
- • Zhongguo Musilin/China Muslim (CHN ISSN 1004-3578) **7717**
- Zhongguo Musilin (Weiwen) *see* Zhongguo Musilin **7717**
- • Zhongguo Nanfang Guoshu/South China Fruits (CHN ISSN 1007-1431) **172**
- • Zhongguo Nankexue Zazhi/Chinese Journal of Andrology (CHN ISSN 1008-0848) **6285**
- • Zhongguo Naoxueguanbing Zazhi/Chinese Journal of Cerebrovascular Diseases (CHN ISSN 1672-5921) **5802**
- • Zhongguo Neijing Zazhi/China Journal of Endoscopy (CHN ISSN 1007-1989) **5736**
- • Zhongguo Nengyuan/Energy of China (CHN ISSN 1003-2355) **3150**
- Zhongguo Nianjian (CHN ISSN 1000-9647) **3123**
- Zhongguo Nongcun/Rural China (CHN ISSN 1004-8111) **8018**
- • Zhongguo Nongcun Guancha/China Rural Survey (CHN ISSN 1006-4583) **209**
- • Zhongguo Nongcun Jingji/Chinese Rural Economy (CHN ISSN 1002-8870) **209**
- Zhongguo Nongcun Jinrong/China Rural Finance (CHN) **1392**
- • ➤ Zhongguo Nongji Tuiguang/China Agro-Technology Extension (CHN ISSN 1002-381X) **172**
- • Zhongguo Nongshi/Agricultural History of China (CHN ISSN 1000-4459) **172**
- • Zhongguo Nongye Daxue Xuebao/China Agricultural University. Journal (CHN ISSN 1007-4333) **172**
- • Zhongguo Nongye Jiaoyu/China Agricultural Education (CHN ISSN 1009-1173) **172**
- • Zhongguo Nongye Keji Daobao/Review of China Agricultural Science and Technology (CHN ISSN 1008-0864) **172**
- • Zhongguo Nongye Kexue/Scientia Agricultura Sinica (CHN ISSN 0578-1752) **172**
- Zhongguo Nongye Nianjian (CHN ISSN 1009-6558) **172**
- • Zhongguo Nongye Qixiang/Chinese Journal of Agrometeorology (CHN ISSN 1000-6362) **6400**
- Zhongguo Nongye Wenzhai - Nongye Gongcheng/Chinese Agricultural Abstracts - Agricultural Engineering (CHN ISSN 1002-5103) **190**
- • Zhongguo Nongye Ziyuan yu Quhua/China Agricultural Resources and Regional Planning (CHN ISSN 1005-9121) **173**
- Zhongguo Nuxing (Zhongwen Haiwai Ban) *see* Women of China **8904**
- • Zhongguo Pengren/Chinese Cookery (CHN ISSN 1000-1115) **4369**
- • Zhongguo Pifu Xingbingxue Zazhi (CHN ISSN 1001-7089) **5883**
- Zhongguo Pige Xinxi/China Leather News (CHN ISSN 1006-625X) **4975**
- Zhongguo Pinpai yu Fangwei/China Brand and Anti-Counterfeition (CHN) **6760**
- • Zhongguo Pu-wai Jichu yu Linchuang Zazhi/Chinese Journal of Bases and Clinics in General Surgery (CHN ISSN 1007-9424) **6263**
- • Zhongguo Putong Waike Zazhi/Chinese Journal of General Surgery (CHN ISSN 1005-6947) **6263**
- • Zhongguo Qianbi/China Numismatics (CHN ISSN 1001-8638) **6653**
- Zhongguo Qiche *see* China Auto **8523**
- Zhongguo Qiche Bao/China Automotive News (CHN) **8613**
- Zhongguo Qigong (CHN ISSN 1000-8268) **7001**
- Zhongguo Qinggongye Nianjian/China Light Industry Yearbook (CHN ISSN 1004-3675) **1198**
- Zhongguo Qingnian/China Youth (CHN ISSN 1002-9532) **2224**
- • Zhongguo Qingnian Bao/Chinese Youth Daily (CHN) **2224**
- Zhongguo Qingnian Bao Hedingben *see* Zhongguo Qingnian Bao **2224**
- • Zhongguo Qingnian Yanjiu/China Youth Study (CHN ISSN 1002-9931) **2173**
- • Zhongguo Qixiang Kexue Yanjiuyuan Nianbao/Academy of Meteorological Science. Annual Report (CHN ISSN 1001-7496) **6400**
- • Zhongguo Qiyejia/Chinese Entrepreneur (CHN ISSN 1003-5087) **1969**
- • Zhongguo Quanke Yixue/Chinese General Practice (CHN ISSN 1007-9572) **5736**

Title

11060 ZHONGGUO QUYU DIZHI/REGIONAL GEOLOGY OF CHINA ULRICH'S PERIODICALS

Zhongguo Quyu Dizhi/Regional Geology of China *see* Dizhi Tongbao **2732**
• Zhongguo Redai Yixue/China Tropical Medicine (CHN ISSN 1009-9727) **5736**
• Zhongguo Rencai/Chinese Talent (CHN ISSN 1003-4072) **1878**
• Zhongguo Renkou Ziyuan yu Huanjing/China Population Resources and Environment (CHN ISSN 1002-2104) **7296**
• Zhongguo Renli Ziyuan Kaifa/Human Resource Development of China (CHN ISSN 1004-4124) **1878**
• Zhongguo Renmin Daxue Xuebao/China People's University. Journal (CHN ISSN 1000-5420) **8019**
• Zhongguo Renmin Jingguan Daxue Xuebao (Ziran Kexue Ban)/Chinese People's Public Security University. Journal (Science and Technology) (CHN ISSN 1007-1784) **7934**
Zhongguo Renshi Bao/Chinese Personnel Gazette (CHN) **1878**
• ➤ Zhongguo Renshou Gonghuanbing Zazhi/Chinese Journal of Zoonoses (CHN ISSN 1002-2694) **898**
Zhongguo Ribao *see* China Daily **3823**
• Zhongguo Ruankexue/China Soft Science (CHN ISSN 1005-0566) **7934**
• Zhongguo Rupin Gongye/China Dairy Industry (CHN ISSN 1001-2230) **270**
• Zhongguo Senlin Bingchong/Forest Pest and Disease (CHN ISSN 1671-0886) **861**
• Zhongguo Shamo/Journal of China Desert Research (CHN ISSN 1000-694X) **2718**
• Zhongguo Shangcan Yixue/Chinese Journal of Trauma and Disability Medicine (CHN ISSN 1673-6567) **6076**
Zhongguo Shangwu Nianjian *see* China Commerce Yearbook **1082**
Zhongguo Shangye Nianjian/Almanac of China's Commerce (CHN ISSN 1673-1158) **1434**
Zhongguo Shangye Nianjian/Almanac of China's Commerce *see* Zhongguo Shangye Nianjian **1434**
Zhongguo Shaonian Bao/China Youngster News (CHN) **2224**
• ➤ Zhongguo Shaoshang Chuangshang Zazhi/Chinese Journal of Burns, Wounds & Surface Ulcers (CHN ISSN 1001-0726) **6076**
• Zhongguo Shebei Gongcheng/China Plant Engineering (CHN ISSN 1671-0711) **3372**
Zhongguo Shehui Bao/China Social News (CHN) **8019**
• Zhongguo Shehui Daokan/China Society Periodical (CHN ISSN 1008-7206) **8019**
• Zhongguo Shehui Jingjishi Yanjiu/Journal of Chinese Social and Economic History (CHN ISSN 1000-422X) **4191**
• ➤ Zhongguo Shehui Kexue/Social Sciences in China (CHN ISSN 1002-4921) **8019**
• Zhongguo Shehui Kexueyuan Yanjiu Shengyuan Xuebao/Chinese Academy of Social Sciences. Graduate School. Journal (CHN ISSN 1000-2952) **8019**
Zhongguo Shehui Xuekan/Chinese Journal of Sociology *see* Taiwan Shehui Xuekan **8142**
• Zhongguo Shenghua Yaowu Zazhi (CHN ISSN 1005-1678) **6887**
Zhongguo Shenglixue Zazhi *see* Chinese Journal of Physiology **921**
• Zhongguo Shengtai Nongye Xuebao/Chinese Journal of Eco-Agriculture (CHN ISSN 1671-3990) **173**
• ➤ Zhongguo Shengwu Fangzhi/Chinese Journal of Biological Control (CHN ISSN 1005-9261) **712**
• Zhongguo Shengwu Gongcheng Zazhi/China Biotechnology (CHN ISSN 1671-8135) **771**
• ➤ Zhongguo Shengwu Huaxue yu Fenzi Shengwu Xuebao/Chinese Journal of Biochemistry and Molecular Biology (CHN ISSN 1007-7626) **746**
• Zhongguo Shengwu Yixue Gongcheng Xuebao (CHN ISSN 0258-8021) **5736**
• Zhongguo Shengwuxue Wenzhai/Chinese Biological Abstracts (CHN ISSN 1001-1900) **720**
• Zhongguo Shengwuzhipinxue Zazhi/Chinese Journal of Biologicals (CHN ISSN 1004-5503) **712**
• Zhongguo Shengyu Jiankang Zazhi/Chinese Journal for Health of Women in Childbirth (CHN ISSN 1671-878X) **973**
• Zhongguo Shenji/Auditing in China (CHN ISSN 1002-5049) **1304**
Zhongguo Shenjing Kexue Zazhi/Chinese Journal of Neuroscience *see* Neuroscience Bulletin **6169**
• Zhongguo Shenjing Mianyixue he Shenjingbingxue Zazhi/Chinese Journal of Neuroimmunology and Neurology (CHN ISSN 1006-2963) **6191**
• Zhongguo Shenxue Yanjiuyuan Qikan/China Graduate School of Theology Journal (HKG ISSN 1812-3651) **7697**
• Zhongguo Shequ Yishi/Chinese Community Doctors (CHN) **5736**
Zhongguo Sheying/Chinese Photography (CHN ISSN 0529-6420) **6979**
• Zhongguo Shichang/China Market (CHN ISSN 1005-6432) **1198**
• Zhongguo Shipin/China Food (CHN ISSN 1000-1085) **4369**
• Zhongguo Shipin Bao/China's Food News (CHN) **3668**
• Zhongguo Shipin Gongye/Food and Beverage Industry (CHN ISSN 1006-6195) **3668**
• Zhongguo Shipin Tianjiaji/China Food Additives (CHN ISSN 1006-2513) **3668**
Zhongguo Shipin Xuebao/Chinese Institute of Food Science and Technology. Journal (CHN ISSN 1009-7848) **3668**
• Zhongguo Shipin Zhiliang Bao/China Food Quality News (CHN) **3668**
Zhongguo Shiyan Dongwu Xuebao/Acta Laboratorium Animalis Scientia Sinica (CHN ISSN 1005-4847) **969**
• Zhongguo Shiyan Fangjixue Zazhi/Chinese Journal of Experimental Traditional Medical Formulae (CHN ISSN 1005-9903) **6887**
• Zhongguo Shiyan Xueyexue Zazhi/Journal of Experimental Hematology (CHN ISSN 1009-2137) **5942**
• ➤ Zhongguo Shiyong Erke Zazhi/Chinese Journal of Practical Pediatrics (CHN ISSN 1005-2224) **6105**
• ➤ Zhongguo Shiyong Fuke yu Chanke Zazhi/Chinese Journal of Practical Gynecology and Obstetrics (CHN ISSN 1005-2216) **6006**
• ➤ Zhongguo Shiyong Neike Zazhi/Chinese Journal of Practical Internal Medicine (CHN ISSN 1005-2194) **5949**
Zhongguo Shiyong Shenjing Jibing Zazhi/Chinese Journal of Practical Nervous Diseases (CHN ISSN 1673-5110) **6191**
• ➤ Zhongguo Shiyong Waike Zazhi/Chinese Journal of Practical Surgery (CHN ISSN 1005-2208) **6263**
• Zhongguo Shiyong Xiangcun Yisheng Zazhi/Chinese Practical Journal of Rural Doctor (CHN ISSN 1672-7185) **5736**
• Zhongguo Shiyong Yanke Zazhi/Chinese Journal of Practical Ophthalmology (CHN ISSN 1006-4443) **6053**
• Zhongguo Shiyongjun/Edible Fungi of China (CHN ISSN 1003-8310) **824**
Zhongguo Shiyou Bao/Chinese Petroleum Gazette (CHN) **6798**
• Zhongguo Shiyou Daxue Xuebao (Ziran Kexue Ban)/China University of Petroleum. Journal (Natural Science Edition) (CHN ISSN 1673-5005) **6798**
• Zhongguo Shiyou he Huagong/China Petroleum and Chemical Industry (CHN ISSN 1008-1852) **6798**
• Zhongguo Shiyou Kantan/China Petroleum Exploration (CHN ISSN 1672-7703) **6798**
Zhongguo Shouyi Keji/Chinese Journal of Veterinary Science and Technology *see* Zhongguo Shouyi Kexue **8815**
• Zhongguo Shouyi Kexue/Veterinary Science in China (CHN) **8815**
• Zhongguo Shouyi Xuebao/Chinese Journal of Veterinary Science (CHN ISSN 1005-4545) **8815**
• Zhongguo Shouyi Zazhi/Chinese Journal of Veterinary Medicine (CHN ISSN 0529-6005) **8815**
Zhongguo Shucai/Chinese Vegetables (CHN ISSN 1000-6346) **260**
• Zhongguo Shufa/Chinese Calligraphy (CHN ISSN 1003-1782) **528**
• Zhongguo Shuhua/Chinese Painting & Calligraphy (CHN ISSN 1672-2329) **528**
• Zhongguo Shuichan/Chinese Fisheries (CHN ISSN 1002-6681) **3612**
• Zhongguo Shuichan Kexue/Journal of Fishery Sciences of China (CHN ISSN 1005-8737) **3612**
Zhongguo Shuichan Wenzhai/Chinese Fisheries Abstracts (CHN ISSN 1002-1612) **3614**
• ➤ Zhongguo Shuidao Kexue/Chinese Journal of Rice Science (CHN ISSN 1001-7216) **276**
Zhongguo Shuidao Yanjiu Tongbao *see* Rice Science **275**
Zhongguo Shuili Bao/China Water Resources News (CHN) **8842**
• Zhongguo Shuili Shuidian Kexue Yanjiuyuan Xuebao/China Institute of Water Resources and Hydropower Research. Journal (CHN ISSN 1672-3031) **8842**
• Zhongguo Shuitu Baochi (CHN ISSN 1000-0941) **260**
• Zhongguo Shuitu Baochi Kexue/Science of Soil and Water Conservation (CHN ISSN 1672-3007) **2634**
• Zhongguo Shuiwu/China Taxation (CHN ISSN 1003-4471) **1955**
Zhongguo Shuiwu Bao/China Taxation News (CHN) **1955**
Zhongguo Shuxue Wenzhai/Chinese Mathematics Abstracts (CHN ISSN 1001-1919) **5549**
• Zhongguo Sifa/Judicature of China (CHN ISSN 1009-329X) **4820**
Zhongguo Sifa Baodao (CHN) **4820**
• Zhongguo Sifa Jianding/Chinese Journal of Forensic Sciences (CHN ISSN 1671-2072) **5917**
• Zhongguo Siliao/China Feed (CHN ISSN 1004-3314) **305**
• Zhongguo Tangliao/Sugar Crops of China (CHN ISSN 1007-2624) **173**
• Zhongguo Tangniaobing Zazhi/Chinese Journal of Diabetes (CHN ISSN 1006-6187) **5901**
• Zhongguo Taoci/Chinese Ceramics (CHN ISSN 1001-9642) **2047**
Zhongguo Techan Bao/China Special Native Products (CHN) **1909**
• Zhongguo Tengtong Yixue Zazhi/Chinese Journal of Pain Medicine (CHN ISSN 1006-9852) **5736**
• Zhongguo Teshu Jiaoyu/Chinese Journal of Special Education (CHN ISSN 1007-3728) **3049**
• Zhongguo Tiancai Tangye/China Beet & Sugar (CHN ISSN 1002-0551) **173**
• Zhongguo Tianran Yaowu/Chinese Journal of Natrual Medicines (CHN ISSN 1672-3651) **316**
Zhongguo Tianzhujiao/Catholic Church in China (CHN) **7823**
• Zhongguo Tiaoweipin/China Condiment (CHN ISSN 1000-9973) **3668**
• Zhongguo Tiedao Kexue/China Railway Science (CHN ISSN 1001-4632) **8628**
Zhongguo Tiedao Kexue Yanjiuyuan Yuankan *see* Tiedao Keyanbao **8626**
• Zhongguo Tielu (CHN ISSN 1001-683X) **8628**
• Zhongguo Tishixue yu Tuxiang Fenxi/Chinese Journal of Stereology and Image Analysis (CHN ISSN 1007-1482) **6979**
Zhongguo Tiyu *see* China Sports **8166**
Zhongguo Tiyu Bao/Chinese's Sports News (CHN) **8217**
• Zhongguo Tongji/China Statistics (CHN ISSN 1002-4557) **8414**
Zhongguo Tongji Nianjian *see* China Statistical Yearbook **8363**
Zhongguo Tongji Xuebao (TWN ISSN 0529-6528) **8414**
• Zhongguo Tongyi Zhanxian (CHN ISSN 1005-5819) **6455**
Zhongguo Toushi *see* China Monitor - Europe **1083**
Zhongguo Tuliao Gongye *see* China Coatings Journal **6716**
Zhongguo Tumu Shuili Gongcheng Xuekan/Chinese Institute of Civil and Hydraulic Engineering. Journal (TWN ISSN 1015-5856) **3288**
• Zhongguo Tushu Pinglun/China Book Review (CHN ISSN 1002-235X) **7576**
Zhongguo Tushu Shangbao/China Book Business Report (CHN) **7576**
• Zhongguo Tushuguan Xuebao/Journal of the Library Science in China (CHN ISSN 1001-8867) **5056**
Zhongguo Tushuguan Xuehui Huiwu Tongxun *see* Library Association of China. Newsletter **5027**
Zhongguo Waijiao/Chinese Foreign Affairs (CHN ISSN 1001-2842) **7276**
• Zhongguo Wei Qinxi Shenjing Waike Zazhi/Chinese Journal of Minimally Invasive Neurosurgery (CHN ISSN 1009-122X) **6263**
• Zhongguo Weichuang Waike Zazhi/Chinese Journal of Minimally Invasive Surgery (CHN ISSN 1009-6604) **6263**
Zhongguo Weijingmao *see* China International Business **1555**
• Zhongguo Weisheng Jianyan/Chinese Journal of Health Laboratory Technology (CHN ISSN 1004-8685) **5912**
Zhongguo Weisheng Nianjian/China Health Yearbook (CHN) **5736**
• Zhongguo Weisheng Tongji/Chinese Journal of Health Statistics (CHN ISSN 1002-3674) **7002**
• Zhongguo Weisheng Ziyuan/Chinese Health Resources (CHN ISSN 1007-953X) **7547**
Zhongguo Weishengtaixue Zazhi/Chinese Journal of Microecology (CHN ISSN 1005-376X) **712**
• Zhongguo Weizhongbing Jijiu Yixue/Chinese Critical Care Medicine (CHN ISSN 1003-0603) **5736**
Zhongguo Wenfang Sibao/Chinese Four Treasures of the Study (CHN) **1855**
Zhongguo Wenhua Bao/China Culture News (CHN) **3830**
• Zhongguo Wenhua Yanjiu/Chinese Culture Research (CHN ISSN 1005-3247) **4483**
Zhongguo Wenhua Yanjiusuo Xuebao/Journal of Chinese Studies (HKG ISSN 1016-4464) **564**
Zhongguo Wenhua Yichan/China Cultural Heritage (CHN ISSN 1672-7819) **4168**
Zhongguo Wenwu Bao/China Cultural Relic News (CHN) **425**
• Zhongguo Wenxue Yanjiu/Research of Chinese Literature (CHN ISSN 1003-7535) **5404**
Zhongguo Wuji Fenxi Huaxue Wenzhai/Chinese Inorganic Analytical Chemistry Abstracts (CHN) **2096**
• Zhongguo Wujia/China Price (CHN ISSN 1003-398X) **1198**
Zhongguo Wuli B *see* Chinese Physics B **7008**
Zhongguo Wuli Kuaibao *see* Chinese Physics Letters **7008**
Zhongguo Wuli Wenzhai/Chinese Physics Abstracts (CHN ISSN 1000-8802) **7050**
Zhongguo Wuli Xuekan *see* Chinese Journal of Physics **7008**
• Zhongguo Wuliu yu Caigou/China Logistics and Purchasing (CHN ISSN 1671-6663) **1198**
• Zhongguo Wuxiandian Dianzixue Wenzhai/Chinese Radio Electronics Digest (CHN ISSN 1003-1928) **2365**
• Zhongguo Wuzhenxue Zazhi/Chinese Journal of Misdiagnosis (CHN ISSN 1009-6647) **5736**
Zhongguo Wuzi Bao/China Materials News (CHN) **3360**
Zhongguo Wuzi Jingji/Chinese Commodity Economics (CHN) **1198**
Zhongguo Wuzi Liutong *see* Zhongguo Wuliu yu Caigou **1198**
Zhongguo Xiandai, Dangdai Wenxue Yanjiu/Researches in Modern and Contemporary Chinese Literature (CHN ISSN 1001-2907) **5404**
• Zhongguo Xiandai Putong Waike Jinzhan/Chinese Journal of Current Advances in General Surgery (CHN ISSN 1009-9905) **6263**
• Zhongguo Xiandai Shoushuxue Zazhi/Chinese Journal of Modern Operative Surgery (CHN ISSN 1009-2188) **6263**
• Zhongguo Xiandai Yingyong Yaoxue/Chinese Journal of Modern Applied Pharmacy (CHN ISSN 1007-7693) **6887**
• Zhongguo Xiandai Yixue/China Journal of Modern Medicine (CHN ISSN 1005-8982) **5737**
Zhongguo Xiandaishi/Contemporary History of China (CHN ISSN 1001-2672) **4191**
Zhongguo Xiangcun Yisheng/Chinese Rural Doctors *see* Zhongguo Shequ Yishi **5736**
Zhongguo Xiangjiao/China Rubber (CHN ISSN 1009-5640) **7100**
• Zhongguo Xiangzhen Qiye/China's Township Enterprises News (CHN ISSN 1002-4905) **1969**
• ➤ Zhongguo Xiaoduxue Zazhi/Chinese Journal of Disinfection Science (CHN ISSN 1001-7658) **5737**
• Zhongguo Xiaoer Jijiu Yixue/Chinese Pediatric Emergency Medicine (CHN) **6105**
Zhongguo Xiaofang/Fire Protection in China (CHN ISSN 1000-1107) **3582**
Zhongguo Xiaofeizhe Bao/China Consumer News (CHN) **2642**
• Zhongguo Xiju/Chinese Theatre (CHN ISSN 1001-8018) **8485**
Zhongguo Xinan/Southwest China (CHN ISSN 1004-9835) **1198**
Zhongguo Xing *see* China Journey **8693**
Zhongguo Xingbing Aizibing Fangzhi/Chinese Journal of Prevention and Control of STD & AIDS *see* Zhongguo Aizibing Xingbing **5828**
• Zhongguo Xingshifa Zazhi/Chinese Criminal Science (CHN ISSN 1007-9017) **2672**
• Zhongguo Xingzheng Guanli/Chinese Public Administration (CHN ISSN 1006-0863) **7478**
• ➤ Zhongguo Xinli Weisheng Zazhi/Chinese Mental Health Journal (CHN ISSN 1000-6729) **7416**
• Zhongguo Xinwen Chuban Bao/China Press and Publishing Journal (CHN) **4586**
Zhongguo Xinwen Zhoukan (CHN) **3830**
Zhongguo Xinxi Daobao/China Information Review *see* Zhongguo Keji Ziyuan Daokan **5056**
• Zhongguo Xinxi Jishu Jiaoyu/China Information Technology Education (CHN ISSN 1674-2117) **2928**
Zhongguo Xinxihua/iChina (CHN ISSN 1672-5158) **3830**
• Zhongguo Xinxueguanbing Yanjiu/Chinese Journal of Cardiovascular Review (CHN ISSN 1672-5301) **5802**
Zhongguo Xinxun *see* China Mail **1555**
• ➤ Zhongguo Xinyao Yu Linchuang Zazhi/Chinese Journal of New Drugs and Clinical Remedies (CHN ISSN 1007-7669) **6887**
• Zhongguo Xinyao Zazhi/Chinese New Drugs Journal (CHN ISSN 1003-3734) **6887**
• Zhongguo Xinyongka/China Credit Card (CHN ISSN 1009-2056) **1392**
• Zhongguo Xinzang Qibo yu Xindian Shengli Zazhi/Chinese Journal of Cardiac Pacing and Electrophysiology (CHN ISSN 1007-2659) **5802**
• ➤ Zhongguo Xiongxin Xueguan Waike Linchuang Zazhi (CHN ISSN 1007-4848) **5802**
Zhongguo Xitu Xuebao *see* Journal of Rare Earths **6319**
• Zhongguo Xiuchuan/China Shiprepair (CHN ISSN 1001-8328) **8666**
• ➤ Zhongguo Xiufu Chongjian Waike Zazhi/Chinese Journal of Reparative and Reconstructive Surgery (CHN ISSN 1002-1892) **6263**
• Zhongguo Xizang (CHN ISSN 1002-9591) **3830**
Zhongguo Xueshu Qikan Wenzhai/Academic Periodical Abstracts of China (CHN ISSN 1005-8923) **18**
• Zhongguo Xuexiao Weisheng/Journal of Chinese School Health (CHN ISSN 1000-9817) **7001**
• Zhongguo Xuexichongbing Fangzhi Zazhi/Chinese Journal of Schistosomiasis Control (CHN ISSN 1005-6661) **5737**
• Zhongguo Xueye Jinghua/Chinese Journal of Blood Purification (CHN ISSN 1671-4091) **5942**
• Zhongguo Xumu Shouyi/China Animal Husbandry & Veterinary Medicine (CHN ISSN 1671-7236) **305**
Zhongguo Xumu Xuehui Huizhi/Chinese Society of Animal Science. Journal (TWN ISSN 0253-9187) **969**
• Zhongguo Xumu Zazhi/Chinese Journal of Animal Science (CHN ISSN 0258-7033) **305**
• Zhongguo Xunzheng Yixue Zazhi/Chinese Journal of Evidence-Based Medicine (CHN ISSN 1672-2531) **5737**
• Zhongguo Yancao Kexue/Chinese Tobacco Science (CHN ISSN 1007-5119) **8489**
• Zhongguo Yangfeng/Apiculture of China (CHN ISSN 0412-4367) **173**
Zhongguo Yanjiusheng/China Postgraduate (CHN ISSN 1671-9042) **3011**
• ➤ Zhongguo Yanrong/Carsologica Sinica (CHN ISSN 1001-4810) **2776**

Link to your serials resources and content with ulrichsweb.com

Title

11062 ZHONGHUA MINGUO TAIWAN DIQU. JINRONG TONGJI YUEBAO/FINANCIAL ULRICH'S PERIODICALS

Zhonghua Minguo Taiwan Diqu. Jinrong Tongji Yuebao/Financial Statistics Monthly, Taiwan District, Republic of China *see* Zhonghua Minguo Jinrong Tongji Yuebao **1275**

Zhonghua Minguo Wuli Xuehui Tongxun *see* Wuli Shuanyuekan **7046**

Zhonghua Minguo Xiaohua Xiyi Xuehui Zazhi *see* Taiwan Xiaohua Xiyi Xuehui Zazhi **5931**

Zhonghua Minguo Xinzang Xuehui Zazhi (TWN ISSN 1011-6842) **5802**

Zhonghua Minguo Yingyang Xuehui Zazhi/Chinese Nutrition Society. Journal (TWN ISSN 1011-6958) **6671**

• Zhonghua Miniao Waike Zazhi/Chinese Journal of Urology (CHN ISSN 1000-6702) **6277**

• Zhonghua Nankexue/National Journal of Andrology (CHN ISSN 1009-3591) **6285**

• Zhonghua Neifenmi Daixie Zazhi/Chinese Journal of Endocrinology and Metabolism (CHN ISSN 1000-6699) **5901**

• Zhonghua Neike Zazhi/Chinese Journal of Internal Medicine (CHN ISSN 0578-1426) **5949**

➤ Zhonghua Nongxue Huibao/Chung Hua Nung Hsueh Hui Pao (TWN ISSN 0578-1434) **173**

Zhonghua Nongye Yanjiu/Journal of Agricultural Research of China *see* Taiwan Nongye Yanjiu **160**

• Zhonghua Nuzi Xueyuan Shandong Fenyuan Xuebao/Women's Academy at Shandong. Journal (CHN ISSN 1008-6838) **8906**

• Zhonghua Nuzi Xueyuan Xuebao/China Women's University. Journal (CHN ISSN 1007-3698) **8906**

Zhonghua Pifuke Yixue Zazhi/Dermatologica Sinica (TWN ISSN 1027-8117) **5883**

• Zhonghua Pifuke Zazhi/Chinese Journal of Dermatology (CHN ISSN 0412-4030) **5883**

• Zhonghua Putong Waike Zazhi/Chinese Journal of General Surgery (CHN ISSN 1007-631X) **5738**

Zhonghua Qigong *see* Zhonghua Yangsheng Baojian **7001**

• Zhonghua Qiguan Yizhi Zazhi/Chinese Journal of Organ Transplantation (CHN ISSN 0254-1785) **6264**

• Zhonghua Quanke Yishi Zazhi/Chinese Journal of General Practitioners (CHN ISSN 1671-7368) **5738**

Zhonghua Renmin Gongheguo. Duiwai Maoyi Jingji Hezuobu. Tongbao/People's Republic of China. Ministry of Foreign Trade & Economic Cooperation. Bulletin (CHN) **1589**

Zhonghua Renmin Gongheguo. Duiwai Maoyi Jingji Hezuobu. Xinwen Gongbao/People's Republic of China. Ministry of Foreign Trade & Economic Cooperation. Bulletin (CHN ISSN 1004-7247) **1589**

Zhonghua Renmin Gongheguo Fadian/Code of the People's Republic of China (CHN) **4968**

▼ Zhonghua Renmin Gongheguo Guojia Fazhan he Gaige Weiyuanhui Wengao/National Development and Reform Commission of the People's Republic of China. Gazette (CHN ISSN 1674-2028) **7478**

• Zhonghua Renmin Gongheguo Guowuyuan Gongbao/China, People's Republic. State Council. Gazette (CHN ISSN 1004-3438) **7478**

Zhonghua Renmin Gongheguo Hongkong Tebei Xingzhengqu. Zhengfu Tongjichu. Hong Kong Baiozhun Xingye Fenlei. Diyece *see* Hong Kong Special Administrative Region of China. Census and Statistics Department. Hong Kong Standard Industrial Classification. Volume One **1238**

• Zhonghua Renmin Gongheguo Quanguo Renmin Daibiao Dahui Changwu Weiyuanhui Gongbao/People's Republic of China. National People's Congress. Standing Committee. Gazette (CHN ISSN 1000-0070) **7478**

• Zhonghua Renmin Gongheguo Shuishou Fagui Gonggao/Tax Laws and Regulations of People's Republic of China (CHN ISSN 1007-6174) **1956**

Zhonghua Renmin Gongheguo Zuigao Renmin Fayuan Gongbao/Supreme People's Court of the People's Republic of China. Bulletin (CHN ISSN 1002-4611) **4820**

Zhonghua Renmin Gongheguo. Zuigao Renmin Jianchayuan Gongbao/China, People's Republic. Supreme People's Procurate Post. Bulletin (CHN ISSN 1001-067X) **7478**

Zhonghua Sanwen/Chinese Prose *see* Wo de Gushi **5399**

Zhonghua Shaonian/China Juveniles (CHN ISSN 1004-2377) **2224**

• Zhonghua Shaoshang Zazhi/Chinese Journal of Burns (CHN ISSN 1009-2587) **5883**

• Zhonghua Shenjing Waike Jibing Yanjiu Zazhi/Chinese Journal of Neurosurgical Disease Research (CHN ISSN 1671-2897) **6191**

• ➤ Zhonghua Shenjing Waike Zazhi/Chinese Journal of Neurosurgery (CHN ISSN 1001-2346) **6264**

• Zhonghua Shenjing Yixue Zazhi/Chinese Journal of Neuromedicine (CHN ISSN 1671-8925) **6191**

• ➤ Zhonghua Shenjingke Zazhi/Chinese Journal of Neurology (CHN ISSN 1006-7876) **6191**

• Zhonghua Shenzangbing Zazhi/Chinese Journal of Nephrology (CHN ISSN 1001-7097) **5901**

Zhonghua Shexue yu Yixue (USA ISSN 1930-4579) **316**

• Zhonghua Shiyan he Linchuang Bingduxue Zazhi/Chinese Journal of Experimental and Clinical Virology (CHN ISSN 1003-9279) **5829**

• Zhonghua Shiyong Zhenduan yu Zhiliao Zazhi/Journal of Chinese Practical Diagnosis and Therapy (CHN ISSN 1674-3474) **5738**

Zhonghua Shiyong Zhongxiyi Zazhi *see* Chinese Journal of the Practical Chinese with Modern Medicine **5594**

• Zhonghua Shouwaike Zazhi/Chinese Journal of Hand Surgery (CHN ISSN 1005-054X) **6264**

• Zhonghua Waike Zazhi/Chinese Journal of Surgery (CHN ISSN 0529-5815) **6264**

• Zhonghua Wei-chang Waike Zazhi/Chinese Journal of Gastrointestinal Surgery (CHN ISSN 1671-0274) **6264**

• Zhonghua Weichan Yixue Zazhi/Chinese Journal of Perinatal Medicine (CHN ISSN 1007-9408) **6006**

• Zhonghua Weishengwuxue he Mianyixue Zazhi/Chinese Journal of Microbiology and Immunology (CHN ISSN 0254-5101) **5767**

• ➤ Zhonghua Wuli Yixue yu Kangfu Zazhi/Chinese Journal of Physical Medicine and Rehabilitation (CHN) **6117**

• Zhonghua Wushu/Chinese Martial Arts (CHN ISSN 1000-3525) **8217**

Zhonghua Xiandai Linchuang Yixue Zazhi/Chinese Journal of Current Clinical Medicine (CHN ISSN 1726-7587) **5738**

• Zhonghua Xiaoer Waike Zazhi/Chinese Journal of Pediatric Surgery (CHN ISSN 0253-3006) **6105**

• Zhonghua Xiaohua Neijing Zazhi/Chinese Journal of Digestive Endoscopy (CHN ISSN 1007-5232) **5901**

• ➤ Zhonghua Xiaohua Waike Zazhi/Chinese Journal of Digestive Surgery (CHN ISSN 1673-9752) **5933**

• Zhonghua Xiaohua Zazhi/Chinese Journal of Digestion (CHN ISSN 0254-1432) **5933**

• Zhonghua Xin-Xueguanbing Zazhi/Chinese Journal of Cardiology (CHN ISSN 0253-3758) **5802**

• Zhonghua Xinlu Shichangxue Zazhi/China Journal of Cardiac Arrhythmia (CHN ISSN 1007-6638) **5803**

• Zhonghua Xiong-xin Xueguan Waike Zazhi/Chinese Journal of Thoracic and Cardiovascular Surgery (CHN ISSN 1001-4497) **5803**

• Zhonghua Xueyexue Zazhi/Chinese Journal of Hematology (CHN ISSN 0253-2727) **5942**

• ➤ Zhonghua Yandibing Zazhi/Chinese Journal of Ocular Fundus Diseases (CHN ISSN 1005-1015) **6053**

• Zhonghua Yangsheng Baojian/Chinese Breath Exercise (CHN ISSN 1009-8011) **7001**

• Zhonghua Yanke Zazhi/Chinese Journal of Ophthalmology (CHN ISSN 0412-4081) **6053**

Zhonghua Yaoxue Zazhi (Taipei)/Chinese Pharmaceutical Journal (Taibei) (TWN ISSN 1016-1015) **6888**

Zhonghua Yayixue Zazhi *see* Chunghua Yaihsueh Tsachih **5837**

Zhonghua Yingcai/China's Talents (CHN ISSN 1001-0688) **3830**

• Zhonghua Yishi Zazhi/Chinese Journal of Medical History (CHN ISSN 0255-7053) **5738**

• Zhonghua Yixue Chaosheng Zazhi/Chinese Journal of Medical Ultrasound (Electronic Version) (CHN ISSN 1672-6448) **6211**

Zhonghua Yixue Gongcheng Xuekan *see* Journal of Medical and Biological Engineering **5651**

Zhonghua Yixue Gongcheng Xuekan/Chinese Journal of Medical and Biological Engineering *see* Journal of Medical and Biological Engineering **5651**

Zhonghua Yixue Jianyan Zazhi/Chinese Journal of Medical Laboratory Technology *see* Zhonghua Jianyan Yixue Zazhi **5912**

Zhonghua Yixue Jiaoyu Zazhi/Chinese Journal of Medical Education (CHN ISSN 1673-677X) **5738**

• Zhonghua Yixue Meirong Zazhi/Chinese Journal of Medical Aethetics and Cosmetology (CHN ISSN 1671-0290) **596**

• ➤ Zhonghua Yixue Tushu Qingbao Zazhi/Chinese Journal of Medical Library and Information Science (CHN ISSN 1671-3982) **5056**

• Zhonghua Yixue Yichuanxue Zazhi/Chinese Journal of Medical Genetics (CHN ISSN 1003-9406) **879**

• Zhonghua Yixue Zazhi/National Medical Journal of China (CHN ISSN 0376-2491) **5738**

Zhonghua Yixue Zazhi Yingwen Ban *see* Chinese Medical Journal **5594**

• Zhonghua Yiyuan Guanli Zazhi/Chinese Journal of Hospital Administration (CHN ISSN 1000-6672) **4113**

• Zhonghua Yufang Yixue Zazhi/Chinese Journal of Preventive Medicine (CHN ISSN 0253-9624) **5738**

• Zhonghua Zhengxing Waike Zazhi/Chinese Journal of Plastic Surgery (CHN ISSN 1009-4598) **6264**

• Zhonghua Zhiye/China Pulp & Paper Industry (CHN ISSN 1007-9211) **6740**

• Zhonghua Zhongliu Fangzhi Zazhi/Chinese Journal of Cancer Prevention and Treatment (CHN ISSN 1673-5269) **6037**

• Zhonghua Zhongliu Zazhi/Chinese Journal of Oncology (CHN ISSN 0253-3766) **6037**

• Zhonghua Zhongxiyi Zazhi (CHN ISSN 1606-8106) **5738**

• Zhonghua Zhongyiyao Xuekan/Chinese Archives of Traditional Chinese Medicine (CHN ISSN 1673-7717) **5738**

• Zhonghua Zhongyiyao Zazhi/China Journal of Traditional Chinese Medicine and Pharmacy (CHN ISSN 1673-1727) **6888**

Zhongkao Jinkan (CHN) **2929**

• Zhongliu/Tumor (CHN ISSN 1000-7431) **6037**

• Zhongliu Fangzhi Yanjiu/Cancer Research on Prevention and Treatment (CHN ISSN 1000-8578) **6037**

Zhongliu Fangzhi Zazhi/China Journal of Cancer Prevention and Treatment *see* Zhonghua Zhongliu Fangzhi Zazhi **6037**

• Zhongliu Jichu yu Linchuang/Journal of Basic and Clinical Oncology (CHN ISSN 1673-5412) **6037**

• ➤ Zhongliu Yanjiu yu Linchuang/Cancer Research and Clinic (CHN ISSN 1006-9801) **6037**

• Zhongliu Yufang yu Zhiliao/Journal of Cancer Control and Treatment (CHN ISSN 1674-0904) **6037**

• ➤ Zhongnan Caijing Daxue Xuebao/Central-South University of Finance and Economics. Journal (CHN ISSN 1003-5230) **1551**

• Zhongnan Daxue Xuebao (Shehui Kexue Ban)/Central South University. Journal (Social Science) (CHN ISSN 1672-3104) **8019**

• Zhongnan Daxue Xuebao (Yixue Ban)/Central South University. Journal (Medical Sciences) (CHN ISSN 1672-7347) **5738**

• ➤ Zhongnan Daxue Xuebao (Ziran Kexue Ban)/Central South University. Journal (Science and Technology) (CHN ISSN 1672-7207) **6484**

Zhongnan Gongye Daxue Xuebao (Shehui Kexue Ban) *see* Zhongnan Daxue Xuebao (Shehui Kexue Ban) **8019**

• Zhongnan Linxueyuan Xuebao/Central South Forestry University. Journal (CHN ISSN 1000-2502) **3708**

• Zhongnan Minzu Daxue Xuebao (Renwen Shehui Kexue Ban)/South-Central University for Nationalities. Journal (Humanities and Social Sciences) (CHN ISSN 1672-433X) **4483**

• Zhongnan Minzu Daxue Xuebao (Ziran Kexue Ban)/South-Central University for Nationalities. Journal (Natural Science Edition) (CHN ISSN 1672-4321) **7935**

• Zhongnan Yaoxue/Central South Pharmacy (CHN ISSN 1672-2981) **6888**

Zhongnan Zhengfa Xueyuan Xuebao/South Central Institute of Political Science and Law. Journal *see* Fashang Yanjiu **4671**

Zhongnanren *see* Zhongnian Zuzhe **3830**

Zhongnian Zuzhe/The Middle-Aged (CHN) **3830**

Zhongpian Xiaoshuo/Novelette (CHN) **5405**

Zhongpian Xiaoshuo Xuankan/Selected Novellas (CHN) **5405**

• Zhongri Youhao Yiyuan Xuebao/Journal of China-Japan Friendship Hospital (CHN ISSN 1001-0025) **5738**

Zhongshan (CHN ISSN 1005-7595) **5405**

• Zhongshan Daxue Xuebao (Shehui Kexue Ban)/Sun Yat-sen University. Journal (Social Science Edition) (CHN ISSN 1000-9639) **8019**

• Zhongshan Daxue Xuebao (Yixue Kexue Ban)/Sun Yat-sen University. Journal (Medical Sciences Edition) (CHN ISSN 1672-3554) **5739**

• Zhongshan Daxue Xuebao (Ziran Kexue Ban)/Acta Scientiarum Naturalium Universitatis Sunyatseni (CHN ISSN 0529-6579) **7935**

• Zhongshan Daxue Xuebao Luncong/Sun Yatsen University Forum (CHN ISSN 1007-1792) **8019**

Zhongshan Renwen Xuebao/Sun Yat-sen Journal of Humanities (TWN ISSN 1024-3631) **4483**

Zhongshan Yike Daxue Xuebao/Sun Yat-Sen University of Medical Sciences. Academic Journal *see* Zhongshan Daxue Xuebao (Yixue Kexue Ban) **5739**

† Zhongua Minguo Taiwan Diqu Jingji Tongji Tubiao/Graphical Survey of the Economy of Taiwan District, Republic of China (TWN ISSN 1017-9631) **9000**

† Zhongwai Dianshi Yuekan/Chinese & Overseas T V Monthly (CHN ISSN 1005-0965) **9000**

• Zhongwai Faxue/Peking University Law Journal (CHN ISSN 1002-4875) **4820**

Zhongwai Funu Wenzhai (CHN) **8893**

Zhongwai Fuzhuang/China Garment (CHN ISSN 1002-1914) **2263**

• Zhongwai Gonglu/Journal of China & Foreign Highway (CHN ISSN 1671-2579) **8637**

Zhongwai Gushi/Chinese and Foreign Stories (CHN) **5405**

† Zhongwai Gushi Chuanqi (CHN ISSN 1004-7972) **9000**

Zhongwai Jingmao Xinxi/Information on China and Foreign Trade (CHN ISSN 1005-4448) **1589**

Zhongwai Junshi Yingshi/Chinese and Foreign Military Films and T V Programme (CHN ISSN 1007-5305) **6517**

† Zhongwai Keji Xinxi/Science & Technology International (CHN ISSN 1007-7618) **9000**

• ➤ Zhongwai Nengyuan/Sino-Global Energy (CHN ISSN 1673-579X) **3150**

Zhongwai Qiye Wenhua - Baoxian Wenhua *see* Baoxian Wenhua **4494**

Zhongwai Qiye Wenhua/Chinese and Foreign Corporation Culture *see* Baoxian Wenhua **4494**

Zhongwai Shaonian (CHN) **2173**

Zhongwai Shuzhai/Digest of Chinese and Foreign Books (CHN ISSN 1000-6095) **7576**

Zhongwai Tonghua Huakan/Chinese and Foreign Fairy Tales Pictorial (CHN) **2224**

Zhongwai Wenhua Jiaoliu *see* China & The World Cultural Exchange **3012**

Zhongwai Wenhua Jiaoliu *see* China & The World Cultural Exchange **3012**

Zhongwai Wenxue/Chinese and Foreign Literature (CHN) **5405**

▼ • Zhongwai Yiliao/China Foreign Medical Treatment (CHN ISSN 1674-0742) **5739**

Zhongwai Zazhi *see* Kaleidoscope **5222**

Zhongwen Falu Lunwen Suoyin *see* Index to Chinese Legal Periodicals **4822**

• Zhongwen Keji Ziliao Mulu (Yiyao Weisheng)/Chinese Science and Technology Catalogue (Medical Health) (CHN ISSN 1003-0379) **5752**

• Zhongwen Xinxi/Chinese Information Processing (CHN ISSN 1003-9082) **5056**

Zhongwen Zixiu/Chinese Self-Study (CHN ISSN 1000-7245) **5199**

Zhongwen Zixue Zhidao/Teach Yourself Chinese (CHN ISSN 1008-2484) **5199**

• Zhongxi Wenhua Yanjiu/Study of Sino-Western Culture (MAC ISSN 1683-6804) **5405**

Zhongxiao Qiye Fazhan Jikan/Journal for S M E Development (TWN ISSN 1991-8550) **1198**

• Zhongxiaoxue Guanli/Administration of Elementary and Secondary School (CHN ISSN 1002-2384) **3035**

Zhongxiaoxue Jiaoyu/Middle and Primary School Education (CHN ISSN 1001-2982) **2929**

Zhongxiaoxue Xueyuan Guanli/Primary and Secondary School Management (CHN ISSN 1009-7686) **2929**

Zhongxiaoxue Yingyu Jiaoxue yu Yanjiu *see* English Teaching and Research for Elementary and Secondary Schools **5115**

Zhongxiaoxue Yinyue Jiaoyu/Music Education for Elementary and High Schools (CHN ISSN 1002-7580) **6630**

Zhongxiaoxue Zuowen Jiaoxue *see* Jiaoshi **2872**

Zhongxing Telecommunication Equipment Communications *see* Z T E Communications **2374**

• Zhongxiyi Jiehe Ganbing Zazhi/Chinese Journal of Integrated Traditional and Western Medicine on Liver Disease (CHN ISSN 1005-0264) **5901**

• ➤ Zhongxiyi Jiehe Xuebao/Journal of Chinese Integrative Medicine (CHN ISSN 1672-1977) **5739**

Zhongxiyi Jiehe Yanke Zazhi *see* Yanshi Guangxue Zazhi **6053**

Zhongxue Huaxue Jiaoyuxue/Teaching and Learning of Chemistry in Middle School (CHN ISSN 1009-2935) **2084**

Zhongxue Jiaoyu/Secondary School Education (CHN ISSN 0412-3921) **2929**

Zhongxue Keji/Middle School Science & Technology (CHN ISSN 1006-0545) **2929**

Zhongxue Like *see* Zhongguo Jiaoxue Cankao **2928**

Zhongxue Lishi Dili Jiaoxue *see* Zhongxue Lishi, Dili Jiaoxue **2929**

Zhongxue Lishi, Dili Jiaoxue/Teaching of History and Geography in Middle School (CHN ISSN 1009-2978) **2929**

• Zhongxue Shengwuxue/Middle School Biology (CHN ISSN 1003-7586) **2929**

• Zhongxue Shishi Bao/Middle School Times (CHN) **2224**

• Zhongxue Shuxue Jiaoxue/High School Mathematics Teaching (CHN ISSN 1002-4123) **2929**

Zhongxue Shuxue Jiaoyuxue/Teaching and Learning of Mathematics in Middle School (CHN ISSN 1009-2919) **5547**

Zhongxue Waiyu Jiaoyuxue/Teaching and Learning of Foreign Language in Middle School (CHN ISSN 1009-2943) **5199**

Zhongxue Wuli Jiaoyuxue/Teaching and Learning of Physics in Middle School (CHN ISSN 1009-2927) **7047**

Zhongxue Yingyu zhi You (Chuer Ban) *see* Zhongxue Yingyu zhi You (Chuzhong Ban) **5200**

Zhongxue Yingyu zhi You (Chusan Ban) *see* Zhongxue Yingyu zhi You (Chuzhong Ban) **5200**

Zhongxue Yingyu zhi You (Chuyi Ban) *see* Zhongxue Yingyu zhi You (Chuzhong Ban) **5200**

▼ Zhongxue Yingyu zhi You (Chuzhong Ban)/A School Friend of English (Junior High School Edition) (MNG ISSN 1674-2567) **5200**

Zhongxue Yingyu zhi You (Gaozhong Ban)/A School Friend of English (High School Edition) (MNG ISSN 1674-2575) **5200**

Zhongxue Yuwen Jiaoyuxue/Teaching and Learning of Chinese in Middle School (CHN ISSN 1009-2986) **5200**

Zhongxue Yuwen Yuandi/School Garden of Chinese (CHN ISSN 1007-628X) **5200**

Zhongxue Zhengzhi ji Qida Geke Jiaoxue *see* Zhongxue Zhengzhi Ji Qita Geke Jiaoxue **2929**

Zhongxue Zhengzhi Ji Qita Geke Jiaoxue/Teaching and Learning of Politics and Other Subjects in Middle School (CHN ISSN 1009-296X) **2929**

Zhongxuesheng/Middle School Student (CHN ISSN 1003-0204) **2929**

Zhongxuesheng Kexue Jiaoyu/Middle School Student Science Education (CHN) **2929**

• Zhongxuesheng Shu Li Hua (Chuzhong Ban Ba-Nan Ji)/School Journal of Mathematics, Physics and Chemistry (Junior High School Edition) (CHN) **5548**

Title

▼ *new title*   † *ceased*   ● *electronic media*   ➤ *refereed*

▼ *new title*   † *ceased*   ● *electronic media*   ➤ *refereed*

Producer Listing/ Serials on CD-ROM

This section is an alphabetical listing of identified producers of serials on CD-ROM. Entries include the producer address and contact information, and an alphabetical listing of all serial titles known to be available. Page numbers refer to the title's complete entry in the CLASSIFIED LIST OF SERIALS.

R.R. Bowker LLC (Subsidiary of: ProQuest LLC (Ann Arbor)) 630 Central Ave, New Providence, NJ 07974 TEL 908-219-0291, 908-286-1090, 800-526-9537, FAX 908-219-0182, info@bowker.com, http://www.bowker.com
Books in Print on Disc (USA) **620**
Books in Print with Book Reviews on Disc (USA) **620**
Bowker's Global Books in Print on Disc (USA) **621**
Canadian Books in Print on Disc (USA) **622**

Chadwyck-Healey Inc. (Subsidiary of: ProQuest LLC (Ann Arbor)) 789 E Eisenhower Pkwy, Ann Arbor, MI 48106-1346 TEL 800-521-0600, info@proquest.com, http://www.proquest.com/en-US/products/brands/pl_ch.shtml
Actualidad Economica (ESP) **1435**
Actualidad Economica en CD-ROM (USA) **1056**
Annual Bibliography of English Language and Literature (GBR) **5406**
B N B on CD-ROM (GBR) **616**
Bibliografia Nacional Portuguesa em CD-ROM (USA) **617**
Bibliografia Nazionale Italiana. Monografie (ITA) **7577**
Catalogue of British Official Publications Not Published by H.M.S.O. (USA) **622**
Daily Mail (GBR) **3863**
Daily Telegraph (GBR) **3864**
Economist. Annual Index (GBR) **1481**
The Economist on CD-ROM (USA) **1481**
Expansion de la Actualidad Economica Diaria (ESP) **1108**
Expansion en CD-ROM (USA) **1108**
Film Index International (USA) **6518**
Financial Times (Frankfurt Edition) (DEU) **1346**
Financial Times (London, 1888) (GBR) **1346**
Financial Times (North American Edition) (USA) **1346**
Financial Times on CD-ROM (USA) **1346**
Great Britain. House of Lords. Parliamentary Debates (GBR) **7139**
Great Britain. House of Lords. Parliamentary Debates (CD-ROM Edition) (USA) **7139**
The Guardian on CD-ROM (USA) **3866**
The Independent (GBR) **3867**
The Independent on CD-ROM (USA) **3867**
The Independent on Sunday (GBR) **3867**
Index to House of Commons Parliamentary Papers (USA) **7200**
The Leadership Library (USA) **2012**
The Mail on CD-ROM (USA) **3868**
The Mail on Sunday (GBR) **3868**
News Media Yellow Book (USA) **2021**
Nineteenth Century Bibliographic Records (USA) **632**
The Observer (GBR) **3869**
La Recherche (FRA) **7902**
Il Sole 24 Ore su CD-ROM (ITA) *CD-ROM edition of* Il Sole 24 Ore. **3898**
Sunday Telegraph (GBR) **3871**
The Sunday Times (GBR) **3871**
The Telegraph on CD-ROM (USA) **3872**
The Times (GBR) **3872**

The Times and the Sunday Times Compact Disc Edition (USA) **3872**
Times Educational Supplement (GBR) **2920**
Times Higher Education (GBR) **3005**

The Dialog Corporation (Subsidiary of: ProQuest LLC (Ann Arbor)) 11000 Regency Pkwy, Ste 10, Cary, NC 27518 TEL 919-462-8600, 800-334-2564, FAX 919-468-9890, customer@dialog.com, http://www.dialog.com
American Banker (USA) **1307**
Analytical Abstracts On CD-ROM (GBR) *CD-ROM edition of* Analytical Abstracts. **2085**
Australian Education Index (Online) (AUS) **2930**
Biotechnology and Bioengineering (Print) (USA) **760**
British Education Index (GBR) **2931**
Business India Intelligence (USA) **1073**
Chemical Hazards in Industry (GBR) **6690**
China Hand (USA) **1083**
Daily Journal of Commerce (Portland) (USA) **1427**
Dialog on Disc Chemical Business News Base (GBR) *CD-ROM edition of* Chemical Business NewsBase. **2093**
Dialog on Disc Chemical Engineering and Biotechnology Abstracts (DEU) *CD-ROM edition of* Chemical Engineering and Biotechnology Abstracts (Online). **3229**
Dialog OnDisc Environmental Chemistry, Health and Safety (GBR) **3495**
Directory of Research Grants (USA) **2978**
Directory of United States Exporters (USA) **1561**
Directory of United States Importers (USA) **1561**
Energy Science and Technology Database (USA) **3133**
Environmental Chemistry, Health & Safety (GBR) *CD-ROM edition of* Chemical Safety NewsBase. **6690**
Environmental Sciences and Pollution Management (USA) **3479**
Health Devices Alerts (USA) **5747**
I N I S Atomindex (Online Edition) (AUT) **7048**
International Aerospace Abstracts (USA) **76**
International Pharmaceutical Abstracts (USA) **6889**
Key Abstracts - Business Automation (GBR) **2443**
Laboratory Hazards Bulletin (GBR) **6690**
Management and Marketing Abstracts (GBR) **1251**
Medline C D (USA) *CD-ROM edition of* MEDLINE. **5749**
Metals Abstracts Index (USA) **6341**
New England Water Works Association. Journal (USA) **8830**
Packaging Month (GBR) **6715**
Paperbase Abstracts (GBR) **6740**
Petroleum Abstracts (USA) **6801**
Pollution Abstracts (USA) **3480**
Process and Chemical Engineering (GBR) **3233**
Profiles of Worldwide Government Leaders (GBR) **7173**
Resources in Education (USA) **2935**
Standard & Poor's Register of Corporations, Directors and Executives (USA) **1794**
Theoretical Chemical Engineering (GBR) **3234**
ThomasNet.com (USA) **2030**
Toxicology Abstracts (USA) **3481**
Traffic World (USA) **8513**

World Surface Coating Abstracts (GBR) **6722**
Worldwide Directory of Defense Authorities (USA) **6454**
Worldwide Government Directory (USA) **7477**

Justis Publishing Ltd. Grand Union House, 20 Kentish Town Rd., London NW1 9NR, United Kingdom TEL 44-20-72848080, FAX 44-20-72671133, customerservices@justis.com, http://www.justis.com
Common Market Law Reports (GBR) **4646**
Criminal Appeal Reports (GBR) **2649**
Justis Celex (GBR) **4823**
Justis European Commentaries (BEL) *CD-ROM edition of* European Update. **1922**
Justis Family Law (GBR) *CD-ROM edition of* Family Law Reports. **4910**
Justis Industrial Cases (GBR) *CD-ROM edition of* Industrial Cases Reports. **4870**
Justis Parliament (GBR) **4823**
Justis U K Statutes (GBR) **4954**
Justis U K Statutory Instruments (GBR) *CD-ROM edition of* Great Britain. H.M.S.O. Statutory Instruments List. **625**
JUSTIS Weekly Law Reports (GBR) *CD-ROM edition of* Weekly Law Reports. **4811**
Lloyd's Electronic Law Reports (GBR) *CD-ROM edition of* Lloyd's Law Reports. **4724**
Lloyd's Electronic Law Reports on CD-ROM (GBR) **4724**
The Times Electronic Law Reports (GBR) *CD-ROM edition of* Times Law Reports. **4796**

N I S C International, Inc. Wyman Towers, 3100 St Paul St, Baltimore, MD 21218 TEL 410-243-0797, FAX 410-243-0982, sales@nisc.com, http://www.nisc.com
A S T I S Occasional Publications (CAN) **2718**
African HealthLine (USA) **5739**
Alternative Press Index (USA) **4571**
Arctic & Antarctic Regions (USA) **2719**
Avery Index to Architectural Periodicals (USA) **462**
B H A Bibliography of the History of Art (USA) **529**
Bibliography of Economic Geology (USA) **2719**
Bibliography on Cold Regions Science & Technology (USA) **3228**
Cabo (ZAF) **4174**
Ceramic Abstracts (USA) **2047**
Ceramic Abstracts / World Ceramic Abstracts (USA) **2047**
Derwent Biotechnology Abstracts (USA) **715**
Earthquake Engineering Abstracts (USA) **3229**
Earthquakes and the Built Environment Index (USA) **3229**
Estuaries and Coastal Waters of the British Isles (USA) **3229**
Family & Society Studies Worldwide (USA) **5562**
Family Relations (USA) **2856**
Fish & Fisheries Worldwide (USA) **716**
Geoscience Documentation (GBR) **2720**
Geosources (GBR) **2720**
Geotitles (GBR) **2720**
Hispanic American Periodicals Index (USA) **4170**
Hydrotitles (GBR) **2720**
Index to South African Periodicals (ZAF) **8**
Info - A S E A N & Pacific Rim (USA) **1242**

Info - C I S (USA) **1242**
Info - S A A R C (USA) **1242**
The Investors' Guide (ZAF) **1634**
Journal of Marriage and Family (USA) **8114**
Latin American Studies. Volume 1 (USA) **4170**
Latin American Studies. Volume 2 (USA) **4171**
Libros en Venta en Hispanoamerica y Espana (USA) **629**
Linguistics and Language Behavior Abstracts (USA) **5201**
M U S E, MUsic SEarch (USA) **6631**
Marine Literature Review (GBR) *CD-ROM edition of* Oceanographic Literature Review. **2720**
Marine Pollution Research Titles (GBR) **3488**
A Matter of Fact: Statements Containing Statistics on Current Social, Economic and Political Issues (USA) **4152**
Microbiology Abstracts: Section A. Industrial & Applied Microbiology (USA) **717**
Microbiology Abstracts: Section C. Algology, Mycology and Protozoology (USA) **717**
N E L M Index Series (ZAF) **5408**
NotiCen (USA) **1502**
NotiSur (USA) **7160**
Oceanic Abstracts (USA) **2720**
Pollution Abstracts (USA) **3480**
Popline (USA) **7289**
Resources in Education (USA) **2935**
Sociofile (USA) **8150**
SourceMex (USA) **1518**
South African National Bibliography (Online) (ZAF) **635**
Water Resources Abstracts (USA) **8843**
Water Resources Worldwide (ZAF) **8843**
Wildlife Review Abstracts (USA) **2634**
Wildlife Worldwide (USA) **720**
Women's Studies International (Baltimore) (USA) **8906**

Ovid Technologies, Inc. (Subsidiary of: Wolters Kluwer N.V.) 333 Seventh Ave, New York, NY 10001 TEL 646-674-6300, 800-950-2035, FAX 646-674-6301, sales@ovid.com, http://www.ovid.com
A O R N Journal (USA) **5949**
Advances in Nursing Science (USA) **5950**
American Academy of Child and Adolescent Psychiatry. Journal (USA) **6121**
American Board of Family Medicine. Journal (USA) **5571**
The American Journal of Cardiology (USA) **5776**
American Journal of Health-System Pharmacy (USA) **6819**
American Journal of Infection Control (USA) **5809**
The American Journal of Medicine (USA) **5572**
American Journal of Nursing (USA) **5951**
American Journal of Obstetrics and Gynecology (USA) **5985**
American Journal of Psychiatry (USA) **6122**
American Journal of Public Health (USA) **7507**
The American Journal of Surgery (USA) **6235**
Anesthesia and Analgesia (USA) **5769**
Anesthesiology (USA) **5769**
Annals of Internal Medicine (USA) **5943**
Annals of the Rheumatic Diseases (GBR) **6221**

Annual Review of Psychology (USA) 7335
Archives of Disease in Childhood (GBR) 6088
Arteriosclerosis, Thrombosis, and Vascular Biology (USA) 5777
British Journal of Haematology (GBR) 5935
British Journal of Psychiatry (GBR) 6128
British Journal of Surgery (GBR) 6238
C A B C D (GBR) *CD-ROM edition of* C A B Abstracts. 176
C I N: Computers, Informatics, Nursing (USA) 5829
C M A J (CAN) 5590
Cancer Nursing (USA) 5954
Chest (USA) 6212
Circulation (Baltimore) (USA) 5782
Circulation Research (USA) 5782
Critical Care Medicine (USA) 5601
Dermatology Nursing (USA) 5875
Diabetes (USA) 5886
Diabetes Care (USA) 5887
EMBASE. Drugs & Pharmacology (NLD) 6889
Environmental Sciences and Pollution Management (USA) 3479
F R A N C I S (FRA) 4484
Fertility and Sterility (USA) 5990
GeoRef (USA) 2719
Gut (GBR) 5925
Heart (GBR) 5787
Heart & Lung (USA) 5959
Hypertension (USA) 5789
I B S S CD-ROM (USA) 8020
Journal for Nurses in Staff Development (USA) 5963
Journal of Advanced Nursing (GBR) 5964
Journal of Bone and Joint Surgery: American Volume (USA) 6063
Journal of Bone and Joint Surgery: British Volume on CD-ROM (GBR) *CD-ROM edition of* Journal of Bone and Joint Surgery: British Volume. 6063
Journal of Clinical Investigation (USA) 5647
Journal of Clinical Nursing (GBR) 5964
Journal of Clinical Pathology (GBR) 5647
Journal of Clinical Psychopharmacology (USA) 6853
Journal of Emergency Nursing (USA) 5964
Journal of Infusion Nursing (USA) 5965
Journal of Medical Genetics (GBR) 874
Journal of Neurology, Neurosurgery and Psychiatry (GBR) 6154
The Journal of Nursing Administration (USA) 5965
Journal of Nursing Scholarship (USA) 5966
Journal of Obstetric, Gynecologic, and Neonatal Nursing (USA) 5966
The Journal of Pediatrics (USA) 6095
Journal of Trauma (USA) 6066
The Journal of Urology (USA) 6270
M C N: American Journal of Maternal Child Nursing (USA) 5969
Mayo Clinic Proceedings (USA) 5665
Medicine (Baltimore) (USA) 5674
Nature (GBR) 7889
New England Journal of Medicine (USA) 5685
Nurse Educator (USA) 5972
Nurse Researcher (GBR) 5972
Nursing Education Perspectives (USA) 5973
Nursing for Women's Health (USA) 8847
Nursing Management (GBR) 5974
Nursing Research (USA) 5975
Nursing Standard (GBR) 5975
Obstetrical & Gynecological Survey (USA) 6000
Occupational and Environmental Medicine (GBR) 6682
Pediatrics (English Edition) (USA) 6102
Professional Case Management (USA) 5978
Psychological Medicine (GBR) 6178
Psychosomatic Medicine (USA) 6179
Q J M (GBR) 5701
R N (USA) 5979
Science (USA) 7908
Sexually Transmitted Infections (GBR) 5881
Sociological Abstracts (USA) 8150
Stroke (USA) 5800
Thorax (GBR) 6220
Year Book of Psychiatry and Applied Mental Health (USA) 6190

ProQuest LLC (Ann Arbor) (Subsidiary of: Cambridge Information Group) 789 E Eisenhower Pkwy, PO Box 1346, Ann Arbor, MI 48106-1346 TEL 734-761-4700, 800-521-0600, FAX 734-997-4040, 800-864-0019, info@proquest.com, http://www.proquest.com
African Journal of International Affairs & Development (NGA) 7219
America (USA) 7782
American Craft (USA) 531
American Doctoral Dissertations (USA) 2966
Archives of Environmental and Occupational Health (USA) 3404
Arts Education Policy Review (USA) 475
Asian Affairs: An American Review (USA) 7222
The Atlantic (USA) 5207
Audubon (USA) 2603
Behavioral Medicine (USA) 7339
Bulletin of the Atomic Scientists (USA) 7224
Change (USA) 2971
The Christian Century (USA) 7631
The Clearing House (USA) 2837
College Teaching (USA) 2973
Commonweal (USA) 5211
Critique (Washington) (USA) 5280
Current (Washington, 1960) (USA) 2840
Current Health 2 (USA) 3055
Defense Counsel Journal (USA) 4830
Dissertation Abstracts International. Section A: Humanities and Social Sciences (USA) 4484
Dissertation Abstracts International. Section B: Physical Sciences and Engineering (USA) 7937
Dissertation Abstracts International. Section C: Worldwide (USA) 4484
Dissertation Abstracts on Disc (USA) 4484
Ebony (USA) 3531
The Education Digest (USA) 2847
Environment (USA) 3420
The Explicator (USA) 5294
Family Process (USA) 7357
Film Comment (USA) 6498
Foreign Affairs (USA) 7235
The Geographical Journal (GBR) 4010
The Germanic Review (USA) 5122
Greek Orthodox Theological Review (USA) 7704
Harper's (USA) 5219
The Hemingway Review (USA) 5305
Historical Methods (USA) 8149
History (Washington) (USA) 4145
History Today (GBR) 4230
Hospital Topics (USA) 4101
Jet (USA) 3979
The Journal of American College Health (USA) 6990
Journal of Arts Management, Law, and Society (USA) 4700
The Journal of Economic Education (USA) 1134
Journal of Education for Business (USA) 1136
The Journal of Educational Research (USA) 2875
The Journal of Environmental Education (USA) 3445
The Journal of Experimental Education (USA) 3067
The Journal of General Psychology (USA) 7374
The Journal of Genetic Psychology (USA) 873
Journal of Group Psychotherapy, Psychodrama and Sociometry (USA) 7374
Journal of Higher Education (USA) 2990
Journal of Money, Credit & Banking (USA) 1362
Journal of Motor Behavior (USA) 7376
Journal of Popular Film and Television (USA) 6505
Journal of Sport Behavior (USA) 8182
Kiplinger's Personal Finance (USA) 1364
Maclean's (CAN) 3812
Masters Abstracts International (USA) 2934
Money (New York) (USA) 1368
Mother Jones (USA) 5228
Motor Trend (USA) 8593
Multinational Business Review (USA) 1578
The Nation (USA) 5229
Natural History (USA) 7888
The New Republic (USA) 5230
Nieman Reports (USA) 4581
Outdoor Life (USA) 8327
Parents (USA) 2164
Perspectives on Political Science (USA) 7165
Ploughshares (USA) 5352
Popular Mechanics (USA) 8435
Popular Science (USA) 8435
Preventing School Failure (USA) 3045
Psychology Today (USA) 7400
Rocks and Minerals (USA) 6478
Rolling Stone (USA) 6613
Sacramento Business Journal (USA) 1170
Science Activities (USA) 7908
Seventeen (USA) 8883
Il Sole 24 Ore su CD-ROM (ITA) *CD-ROM edition of* Il Sole 24 Ore. 3898
Techniques (USA) 2918
Time (USA) 3990
U S News & World Report (USA) 3991
Weatherwise (USA) 6398

R M I T, Publishing A'Beckett St, PO Box 12058, Melbourne, VIC 8006, Australia TEL 61-3-99258100, FAX 61-3-99258134, info@rmitpublishing.com.au, http://www.rmitpublishing.com.au/
Australian Architecture Database (AUS) 462
N U C O S on Disk (AUS) 631
The Whole Story (AUS) 639

K.G. Saur Verlag (Subsidiary of: Walter de Gruyter GmbH & Co. KG) Ortlerstrasse 8, Munich, Germany TEL 49-89-769020, FAX 49-89-76902150, saur.info@thomson.com, http://www.saur.de/
Bonner Katalog (DEU) 6631
Catalogo dei Libri in Commercio (CD-ROM) (ITA) 622
International Bibliography of Printed Music, Music Manuscripts and Recordings (DEU) 6631
International Directory of Arts & Museums of the World CD-ROM (DEU) 496
International Guide to Microform Masters (DEU) 627
Marburger Index (DEU) 530
Music Manuscripts After 1600 (DEU) 6632
Publishers' International I S B N Directory (Year) (DEU) 7570
Publishers' International I S B N Directory Plus (DEU) 7571
Russian National Bibliography (DEU) 634
Verzeichnis Lieferbarer Buecher (DEU) 638
World Guide to Libraries Plus (DEU) *CD-ROM edition of* World Guide to Libraries. 5055
Yearbook Plus (DEU) 7275

SilverPlatter Information, Incorporated (Subsidiary of: Ovid Technologies, Inc.) 333 Seventh Ave, 20th Fl, New York, NY 10001 TEL 646-674-6300, 800-950-2035, FAX 646-674-6301, sales@ovid.com, http://www.ovid.com
AgeLine (USA) 4058
Agris (ITA) 86
American Journal of Critical Care (USA) 5951
Analytical Abstracts On CD-ROM (GBR) *CD-ROM edition of* Analytical Abstracts. 2085
Applied Science & Technology Abstracts (USA) 3228
Applied Science & Technology Index (USA) 3228
Art Index (USA) 529
Bibliography of Bioethics (USA) 5741
Biography Index (USA) 648
Biological Abstracts (USA) 713
Biological Abstracts - R R M (Online Edition) (USA) 713
Biological & Agricultural Index (USA) 713
Biomedical and Environmental Sciences (GBR) 5585
Book Review Digest (USA) 5209
Booklist (USA) 7554
Books in Print with Book Reviews on Disc (USA) 620
Business Periodicals Index (USA) 1216
China Hand (USA) 1083
Choice (USA) 7558
Country Commerce. Venezuela (USA) 1560
Country Forecast. Europe (USA) 7121
Country Forecast. Germany (USA) 7121
Country Forecast. Global Outlook (USA) 7121
Country Report. Fiji (USA) 1454
Country Risk Service. Cyprus (USA) 1472
Country Risk Service. Greece (USA) 1472
Country Risk Service. Portugal (USA) 1474
Country Risk Service. Singapore (USA) 1474
Country Risk Service. South Korea (USA) 1474
Country Risk Service. Spain (USA) 1474
Country Risk Service. Sri Lanka (USA) 1474
Country Risk Service. Taiwan (USA) 1475
Country Risk Service. Thailand (USA) 1475
Country Risk Service. Turkey (USA) 1475
Criminal Justice Abstracts (USA) 2673
Cumulative Index to Nursing & Allied Health Literature (USA) 5743
Current Biography (USA) 642
The Dictionary of Substances and Their Effects (GBR) 3495
Drug Information Fulltext (USA) *CD-ROM edition of* A H F S Drug Information. 6817
E I N E C S Plus C D (USA) 2060
E I U Country Reports on Disc: Western Europe (USA) 1478
Education Index (USA) 2932
Electric Utility Week (USA) 3302
Electric Utility Week's Energy Services & Telecom Report (USA) 3157
EMBASE Alert (USA) 5744
EMBASE C D (NLD) *CD-ROM edition of* Excerpta Medica. Abstract Journals. 715
Encyclopedia of Associations (USA) 3119
Essay and General Literature Index (USA) 5407
Exceptional Child Education Resources (Online) (USA) 2933
Excerpta Medica. Section 1: Anatomy, Anthropology, Embryology & Histology (NLD) 715
Excerpta Medica. Section 10: Obstetrics and Gynecology (NLD) 5744
Excerpta Medica. Section 11: Otorhinolaryngology (NLD) 5744
Excerpta Medica. Section 12: Ophthalmology (NLD) 5744
Excerpta Medica. Section 13: Dermatology and Venereology (NLD) 5744
Excerpta Medica. Section 14: Radiology (NLD) 5744
Excerpta Medica. Section 15: Chest Diseases, Thoracic Surgery and Tuberculosis (NLD) 5745
Excerpta Medica. Section 16: Cancer (NLD) 5745
Excerpta Medica. Section 17: Public Health, Social Medicine and Epidemiology (NLD) 7547
Excerpta Medica. Section 18: Cardiovascular Diseases and Cardiovascular Surgery (NLD) 5745
Excerpta Medica. Section 19: Rehabilitation and Physical Medicine (NLD) 5745
Excerpta Medica. Section 2: Physiology (NLD) 5745
Excerpta Medica. Section 20: Gerontology and Geriatrics (NLD) 4058
Excerpta Medica. Section 21: Developmental Biology and Teratology (NLD) 715
Excerpta Medica. Section 22: Human Genetics (NLD) 715
Excerpta Medica. Section 23: Nuclear Medicine (NLD) 5745
Excerpta Medica. Section 24: Anesthesiology (NLD) 5745
Excerpta Medica. Section 25: Hematology (NLD) 5745
Excerpta Medica. Section 26: Immunology, Serology and Transplantation (NLD) 5745
Excerpta Medica. Section 27: Biophysics, Bio-Engineering and Medical Instrumentation (NLD) 715
Excerpta Medica. Section 28: Urology and Nephrology (NLD) 5745
Excerpta Medica. Section 29: Clinical and Experimental Biochemistry (NLD) 715
Excerpta Medica. Section 3: Endocrinology (NLD) 5745
Excerpta Medica. Section 30: Clinical and Experimental Pharmacology (NLD) 6889
Excerpta Medica. Section 31: Arthritis and Rheumatism (NLD) 5745
Excerpta Medica. Section 32: Psychiatry (NLD) 5746
Excerpta Medica. Section 33: Orthopedic Surgery (NLD) 5746
Excerpta Medica. Section 35: Occupational Health and Industrial Medicine (NLD) 5746
Excerpta Medica. Section 36: Health Policy, Economics and Management (NLD) 4113
Excerpta Medica. Section 38: Adverse Reactions Titles (NLD) 6889
Excerpta Medica. Section 4: Microbiology: Bacteriology, Mycology, Parasitology and Virology (NLD) 715
Excerpta Medica. Section 40: Drug Dependence, Alcohol Abuse and Alcoholism (NLD) 2701
Excerpta Medica. Section 46: Environmental Health and Pollution Control (NLD) 3479
Excerpta Medica. Section 48: Gastroenterology (NLD) 5746
Excerpta Medica. Section 49: Forensic Science Abstracts (NLD) 5746
Excerpta Medica. Section 5: General Pathology and Pathological Anatomy (NLD) 716
Excerpta Medica. Section 50: Epilepsy Abstracts (NLD) 5746
Excerpta Medica. Section 52: Toxicology (NLD) 3479
Excerpta Medica. Section 6: Internal Medicine (NLD) 5746
Excerpta Medica. Section 7: Pediatrics and Pediatric Surgery (NLD) 5746
Excerpta Medica. Section 8: Neurology and Neurosurgery (NLD) 5746
Excerpta Medica. Section 9: Surgery (NLD) 5746
Film & Video Finder (USA) 2347
Food Science and Technology Abstracts (GBR) 3669
Gale Directory of Databases (USA) 2530
General Science Index (USA) 7937
Global Power Report (USA) 3136
Humanities Abstracts (USA) 4484
Humanities Abstracts Full Text (USA) 4484
I B S S CD-ROM (USA) 8020
I N I S Atomindex (Online Edition) (AUT) 7048
Index to Foreign Legal Periodicals (USA) 4822
Index to Legal Periodicals & Books (USA) 4822
Information Research Watch International (GBR) 5016
Inside Energy (USA) 3138
Inside F E R C (USA) 3138
Inside F E R C's Gas Market Report (USA) 6773
Inside N R C (USA) 3168
International Pharmaceutical Abstracts (USA) 6889
International Political Science Abstracts (FRA) 7200
Journal of Economic Literature (USA) 1247
Journal of Punjab Studies (IND) 7979
Library Literature & Information Science (USA) 5059
Linguistics and Language Behavior Abstracts (USA) 5201
MathSci Disc (USA) *CD-ROM edition of* Mathematical Reviews. 5548
MathSci Disc (USA) *CD-ROM edition of* MathSciNet. 5548
MathSci Disc (USA) *CD-ROM edition of* Current Mathematical Publications. 5548
A Matter of Fact: Statements Containing Statistics on Current Social, Economic and Political Issues (USA) 4152
Medline C D (USA) *CD-ROM edition of* MEDLINE. 5749
Meyler's Side Effects of Drugs (NLD) 6861
Microbiology Abstracts: Section A. Industrial & Applied Microbiology (USA) 717
Microbiology Abstracts: Section B. Bacteriology (USA) 717
Microbiology Abstracts: Section C. Algology, Mycology and Protozoology (USA) 717
Monthly Catalog of United States Government Publications (USA) 7482
N I O S H T I C (USA) 6681
N T I S Bibliographic Database (USA) 7938
NuclearFuel (USA) 3172
Nucleonics Week (USA) 3143
P A I S International on SilverPlatter (USA) *CD-ROM edition of* P A I S International in Print (Monthly). 7200
Peterson's Graduate and Professional Programs: An Overview (USA) 2961
Peterson's Graduate and Professional Programs: Business, Education, Health, Information Studies, Law, and Social Work (USA) 2961
Peterson's Graduate Programs in Engineering & Applied Sciences (USA) 3214
Peterson's Graduate Programs in the Biological Sciences (USA) 2961
Peterson's Graduate Programs in the Humanities, Arts, and Social Sciences (USA) 4469
Peterson's Graduate Programs in the Physical Sciences, Mathematics, Agricultural Sciences, the Environment & Natural Resources (USA) 7898
Pharmacoeconomics and Outcomes News (NZL) 6890
Pollution Abstracts (USA) 3480
R T E C S (USA) 3500
Reactions Weekly (NZL) 6890
Readers' Guide to Periodical Literature (USA) 13
Resources in Education (USA) 2935
Schweizerische Zeitschrift fuer Volkswirtschaft und Statistik (CHE) 1171
Side Effects of Drugs Annual (NLD) 6881
Social Sciences Full Text (WilsonDisc) (USA) *CD-ROM edition of* Social Sciences Full Text (WilsonWeb). 8021
Social Sciences Index (WilsonDisc) (USA) *CD-ROM edition of* Social Sciences Index. 8021

Sociological Abstracts (USA) **8150**
South Asian Survey (IND) **4188**
T R I S Electronic Bibliographic Data Base (USA) **8530**
Toxicology Abstracts (USA) **3481**
The Ulster Medical Journal (GBR) **5725**
Virology and AIDS Abstracts (USA) **720**
Wilson Business Abstracts (USA) **1274**
Wilson Business Full Text (USA) **1274**
Wilson OmniFile Full Text Mega Edition (USA) **18**
Year Book of Cardiology (USA) **5802**
Zoological Record on Compact Disc (USA) *CD-ROM edition of* Zoological Record. **720**

Thomson Reuters, Scientific (Subsidiary of: Thomson Reuters Corp.) 1500 Spring Garden, 4th Fl, Philadelphia, PA 19130 TEL 215-386-0100, 800-336-4474, FAX 215-386-2911, general.info@thomson.com, service@tsdoc.com, http://science.thomsonreuters.com/, http://scientific.thomson.com/products/ds/
Arts & Humanities Citation Index (Online) (USA) **529**
Biochemistry and Biophysics Citation Index (USA) **713**
Biotechnology Citation Index (USA) **713**
Chemistry Citation Index (USA) **2093**
Current Contents: Agriculture, Biology & Environmental Sciences (USA) **178**

Current Contents: Arts & Humanities (USA) **4484**
Current Contents: Clinical Medicine (USA) **5743**
Current Contents. Engineering, Computing & Technology with Abstracts (USA) *CD-ROM edition of* Current Contents: Engineering, Computing & Technology. **3229**
Current Contents: Life Sciences (USA) **715**
Current Contents: Physical, Chemical & Earth Sciences (USA) **2094**
Index to Scientific & Technical Proceedings CD-ROM (USA) *CD-ROM edition of* Index to Scientific & Technical Proceedings. **7937**
Index to Social Sciences & Humanities Proceedings (USA) **8020**
Materials Science Citation Index (USA) **3232**
Neuroscience Citation Index (USA) **5749**
Science Citation Index (USA) **7938**
Social Sciences Citation Index (USA) **8021**

Tsinghua Tongfang Optical Disc Co., Ltd. Room 1300, Huaye Building, Tsing Hua University, PO BOX 84-48, Beijing 100084, China TEL 86-1-62791819, FAX 86-1-62791944, Beijing@cnki.net, http://www.cnki.net
Chinese Academic Journals Full-Text Database. Agriculture (CHN) **101**
Chinese Academic Journals Full-Text Database. Economics, Politics & Laws (CHN) **7954**

Chinese Academic Journals Full-Text Database. Education & Social Sciences (CHN) **2836**
Chinese Academic Journals Full-Text Database. Literature, History & Philosophy (CHN) **4447**
Chinese Academic Journals Full-Text Database. Medicine & Hygiene (CHN) **5594**
Chinese Academic Journals Full-Text Database. Science & Engineering, Series A (CHN) **7845**
Chinese Academic Journals Full-Text Database. Science & Engineering, Series B (CHN) **7845**
Chinese Academic Journals Full-Text Database. Science & Engineering, Series C (CHN) **7845**

H.W. Wilson 950 University Ave, Bronx, NY 10452-4224 TEL 718-588-8400, 800-367-6770, FAX 718-681-1511, custserv@hwwilson.com, http://www.hwwilson.com
Applied Science & Technology Abstracts (USA) **3228**
Applied Science & Technology Index (USA) **3228**
Art Abstracts (USA) **529**
Art Index (USA) **529**
Art Index Retrospective (USA) **529**
Biography Index (USA) **648**
Biological & Agricultural Index (USA) **713**
Book Review Digest (USA) **5209**
Business Periodicals Index (USA) **1216**
Canadian Journal of History (CAN) **4134**

Current Biography (USA) **642**
Current Biography Yearbook (USA) **642**
Education Index (USA) **2932**
Essay and General Literature Index (USA) **5407**
General Science Index (USA) **7937**
Humanities Abstracts (USA) **4484**
Humanities Abstracts Full Text (USA) **4484**
Humanities Abstracts Full Text (USA) **4484**
Humanities Index (USA) **4484**
Index to Legal Periodicals & Books (USA) **4822**
Library Literature & Information Science (USA) **5059**
Monthly Catalog of United States Government Publications (USA) **7482**
Ploughshares (USA) **5352**
Readers' Guide to Periodical Literature (USA) **13**
Social Policy (USA) **8003**
Social Sciences Full Text (WilsonDisc) (USA) *CD-ROM edition of* Social Sciences Full Text (WilsonWeb). **8021**
Social Sciences Index (WilsonDisc) (USA) *CD-ROM edition of* Social Sciences Index. **8021**
The Structurist (CAN) **519**
Wilson Business Abstracts (USA) **1274**
Wilson Business Full Text (USA) **1274**
Wilson OmniFile Full Text Mega Edition (USA) **18**

Producer

Online Service Listing/ Serials Online

This section is an alphabetical listing of identified providers of online serials. Entries include the provider address and contact information, and an alphabetical listing of all serial titles known to be available. Page numbers refer to the title's complete entry in the CLASSIFIED LIST OF SERIALS.

African Journals Online 19 Worcester St, PO Box 377, Grahamstown 6140, South Africa TEL 27-46-6229698, FAX 27-46-6229550, info@ajol.info, http://www.ajol.info
Acta Academica (ZAF) **4440**
Acta Commercii (ZAF) **1723**
Acta Criminologica (ZAF) **2643**
Africa Development (SEN) **1589**
Africa Insight (ZAF) **4172**
Africa Online, INASP London (NGA) *see* I F E PsychologIA. **7361**
The African Anthropologist (CMR) **323**
African Health Sciences (UGA) **5569**
African Journal for Physical, Health Education, Recreation and Dance (ZAF) **6981**
African Journal of AIDS Research (ZAF) **5808**
African Journal of Aquatic Science (ZAF) **651**
African Journal of Biotechnology (USA) **755**
African Journal of Clinical and Experimental Microbiology (NGA) **880**
African Journal of Economic Policy (NGA) **1057**
African Journal of Finance and Management (TZA) **1057**
African Journal of Food, Agriculture, Nutrition and Development (KEN) **6654**
African Journal of Food and Nutritional Security (KEN) **6654**
African Journal of Health Sciences (KEN) **5569**
African Journal of International Affairs (SEN) **7219**
African Journal of Library, Archives and Information Science (NGA) **4987**
African Journal of Livestock Extension (NGA) **277**
African Journal of Political Science (ZAF) **7103**
African Journal of Range & Forage Science (ZAF) **216**
African Journal of Reproductive Health (NGA) **8843**
African Journal of Urology (FRA) **6264**
African Journal on Conflict Resolution (ZAF) **7220**
African Plant Protection (ZAF) **774**
African Sociological Review (SEN) **8086**
Africanus (ZAF) **7103**
Agronomie Africaine (CIV) **88**
Akroterion (ZAF) **2229**
Annales Aequatoria (BEL) **324**
Annals of African Medicine (NGA) **5575**
Botswana Journal of Technology (BWA) **8417**
C O D E S R I A Bulletin (SEN) **4174**
Central African Journal of Medicine (ZWE) **5593**
Chemical Society of Ethiopia. Bulletin (ETH) **2055**
Codicillus (ZAF) **4644**
Conflict Trends Magazine (ZAF) **8035**
E S A R B I C A Journal (ZAF) **5007**
East African Agricultural and Forestry Journal (KEN) **106**
East and Central African Journal of Pharmaceutical Sciences (KEN) **6837**
Eastern Africa Social Science Research Review (ETH) **7960**
Ecquid Novi: African Journalism Studies (ZAF) **4574**
Egyptian Journal of Biology (EGY) **670**
Egyptian Journal of Medical Laboratory Sciences (EGY) **5905**
Egyptian Journal of Natural History (EGY) **670**

The Ethiopian Journal of Health Development (ETH) **7516**
Ghana Journal of Agricultural Science (GHA) **115**
Ghana Science Association. Journal (GHA) **7858**
Global Journal of Agricultural Sciences (NGA) **115**
Global Journal of Engineering Research (NGA) **3194**
Global Journal of Environmental Sciences (NGA) **3434**
Global Journal of Geological Sciences (NGA) **2745**
Global Journal of Humanities (NGA) **4454**
Global Journal of Mathematical Sciences (NGA) **5490**
Global Journal of Medical Sciences (NGA) **5620**
Global Journal of Pure and Applied Sciences (NGA) **7858**
Global Journal of Social Sciences (NGA) **7967**
Health S A Gesondheid (ZAF) **5626**
Humanities Review Journal (NGA) **4456**
I S S N Portal (FRA) **626**
Innovation (ZAF) **5017**
Institute of African Studies Research Review (GHA) **7973**
International Journal of Agriculture and Rural Development (NGA) **123**
International Journal of Tropical Insect Science (KEN) **850**
Journal for Studies in Economics and Econometrics (ZAF) **1544**
Journal for the Study of Religion (ZAF) **7653**
Journal of Agriculture and Social Research (NGA) **126**
Journal of Applied Science and Technology (GHA) **8429**
Journal of Applied Science in Southern Africa (ZWE) **7871**
Journal of Applied Sciences and Environmental Management (NGA) **3488**
Journal of Aquatic Sciences (NGA) **3599**
Journal of Child and Adolescent Mental Health (ZAF) **6150**
Journal of Cultural Studies (NGA) **7978**
Journal of Environmental Extension (NGA) **3445**
The Journal of Food Technology in Africa (KEN) **3651**
Journal of Humanities (MWI) **4460**
Journal of Librarianship and Information Science in Africa (NGA) **5021**
Journal of Medicine and Biomedical Research (NGA) **5652**
Journal of Medicine and Medical Sciences (NGA) **5652**
Journal of Mining and Geology (NGA) **6467**
Journal of Modeling, Design and Management of Engineering Systems (NGA) **3206**
Journal of Psychology in Africa (ZAF) **7379**
Journal of Social Development in Africa (ZWE) **8051**
L B S Management Review (NGA) **1771**
Mary Slessor Journal of Medicine (NGA) **5822**
Mathematics Connection (GHA) **5515**
Muziki (ZAF) **6597**
Nigeria Journal of Pure and Applied Physics (NGA) **7028**
Nigeria Veterinary Journal (NGA) **8803**

Nigerian Agricultural Journal (NGA) **140**
Nigerian Infection Control Association. Journal (NGA) **5823**
Nigerian Journal of Clinical and Counselling Psychology (NGA) **7388**
Nigerian Journal of Clinical Practice (NGA) **5686**
Nigerian Journal of Health and Biomedical Sciences (NGA) **5686**
Nigerian Journal of Horticultural Science (NGA) **3745**
Nigerian Journal of Ophthalmology (NGA) **6046**
Nigerian Journal of Surgical Research (NGA) **6253**
Nigerian Libraries (NGA) **5036**
Nigerian Quarterly Journal of Hospital Medicine (NGA) **5686**
Ostrich (ZAF) **913**
Philosophical Papers (ZAF) **6941**
Quaestiones Mathematicae (ZAF) **5527**
Review of Southern African Studies (LSO) **7996**
Revue de l'Information Scientifique et Technique (DZA) **2907**
S A Journal of Industrial Psychology (ZAF) **7406**
Sahara J (ZAF) **5826**
Sahel Medical Journal (NGA) **5708**
Scientific Medical Journal (EGY) **5711**
Sinet (ETH) **7916**
South African Actuarial Journal (ZAF) **4524**
South African Computer Journal (ZAF) **2438**
South African Journal of Agricultural Extension (ZAF) **157**
South African Journal of Anaesthesiology and Analgesia (ZAF) **5774**
South African Journal of Animal Science (ZAF) **301**
South African Journal of Botany (NLD) **818**
South African Journal of Chemistry (ZAF) **2081**
South African Journal of Education (ZAF) **2914**
South African Journal of Higher Education (ZAF) **3002**
South African Journal of Industrial Engineering (ZAF) **3371**
South African Journal of Musicology (ZAF) **6618**
South African Journal of Wildlife Research (ZAF) **2627**
Southern African Feminist Review (ZWE) **8903**
Southern African Linguistics and Applied Language Studies (ZAF) **5176**
Southern Forests (ZAF) **3703**
Suid-Afrikaanse Tydskrif vir Navorsing in Sport, Liggaamlike Opvoedkunde en Ontspanning (ZAF) **6997**
Tanzania Journal of Health Research (TZA) **5720**
Technologies Avancees (DZA) **2439**
Tropical Freshwater Biology (NGA) **3610**
Tropical Journal of Pharmaceutical Research (NGA) **6883**
Tropical Veterinarian (NGA) **8809**
Tydskrif vir Letterkunde (ZAF) **5391**
Tydskrif vir Taalonderrig (ZAF) **5189**
The Uganda Journal (UGA) **4178**
UniSwa Journal of Agriculture (SWZ) **165**
Universite de Lome. Journal de la Recherche Scientifique (TGO) **7926**
University of Dar es Salaam Library Journal (TZA) **5053**

University of Stellenbosch. Bureau for Economic Research. Economic Prospects (ZAF) **1523**
Water Wheel (ZAF) **8841**
West African Journal of Medicine (NGA) **5730**
West African Journal of Pharmacology and Drug Research (NGA) **6885**
Zambezia (ZWE) **8018**
Zimbabwe Journal of Educational Research (ZWE) **2929**
The Zimbabwe Science News (ZWE) **7935**
Zimbabwe Scientific Association. Transactions (ZWE) **7935**
Zimbabwe Veterinary Journal (ZWE) **8816**
Allen Press Inc. PO Box 368, Lawrence, KS 66044 810 E 10th St, Lawrence, KS 66044-3018 TEL 785-843-1234, 800-627-0326, FAX 785-843-1244, OnlineJournals@allenpress.com, http://www.allenpress.com
Ambio Journal Online (SWE) *see* Ambio. **3402**
American Fisheries Society. Transactions (USA) **3584**
American Journal on Intellectual and Developmental Disabilities (USA) **6122**
American Meteorological Society. Bulletin (USA) **6346**
Angle Orthodontist (USA) **5834**
Archives of Pathology & Laboratory Medicine (USA) **5902**
Avian Diseases (USA) **8794**
Cell Stress & Chaperones (NLD) **5592**
Cleft Palate - Craniofacial Journal (CAN) **6239**
Earth Interactions (USA) **2706**
Ecological Applications (USA) **3416**
Ecological Monographs (USA) **3417**
Ecology (USA) **3417**
Environmental Toxicology and Chemistry (USA) **3497**
Evolution (USA) **866**
Fisheries (USA) **3592**
Frontiers in Ecology and the Environment (USA) **674**
G S A Today (USA) **2734**
Geological Society of America Bulletin (USA) **2738**
Geology (Boulder) (USA) **2742**
In Vitro Cellular & Developmental Biology - Animal (DEU) **5633**
Inquiry (Rochester) (USA) **5635**
Intellectual and Developmental Disabilities (USA) **3041**
International Journal of Leprosy and Other Mycobacterial Diseases (USA) **5818**
Journal of Applied Meteorology and Climatology (USA) **6358**
Journal of Aquatic Animal Health (USA) **3599**
Journal of Atmospheric and Oceanic Technology (USA) **6358**
Journal of Climate (USA) **6358**
Journal of Coastal Research (USA) **2809**
Journal of Endovascular Therapy (USA) **6247**
Journal of Hydrometeorology (USA) **2796**
Journal of Mammalogy (USA) **951**
Journal of Oral Implantology (USA) **5852**
Journal of Paleontology (USA) **6726**
Journal of Physical Oceanography (USA) **2810**

11074 AMERICAN CHEMICAL SOCIETY ULRICH'S PERIODICALS

Journal of School Nursing (USA) **5967**
Journal of Strength and Conditioning Research (USA) **6231**
Journal of the Atmospheric Sciences (USA) **6359**
Journal of Veterinary Internal Medicine (USA) **8801**
Mammalian Species (Online) (USA) **955**
Monthly Weather Review (USA) **6391**
N A S N School Nurse (USA) **5970**
North American Benthological Society. Journal (USA) **694**
North American Journal of Aquaculture (USA) **3603**
North American Journal of Fisheries Management (USA) **3603**
Nursing Education Perspectives (USA) **5973**
The Ochsner Journal (USA) **5689**
P L o S Biology (USA) **696**
P L o S Computational Biology (USA) **826**
P L o S Genetics (USA) **877**
P L o S Medicine (USA) **5692**
P L o S Pathogens (USA) **894**
Paleobiology (USA) **6728**
Photochemistry and Photobiology (USA) **2139**
Phycologia (USA) **808**
Rangeland Ecology & Management (USA) **699**
Rangelands (USA) **297**
Strength and Conditioning Journal (USA) **6997**
Weather and Forecasting (USA) **6398**
Weed Science (USA) **258**
Weed Technology (USA) **258**
Wilderness and Environmental Medicine (USA) **5730**

American Chemical Society PO 3337, Columbus, OH 43210 TEL 614-447-3776, 888-338-0012, FAX 614-447-3671, help@acs.org, http://pubs.acs.org
A C S Chemical Biology (USA) **2047**
Accounts of Chemical Research (USA) **2048**
American Chemical Society. Journal (USA) **2049**
Analytical Chemistry (USA) **2098**
Biochemistry (USA) **725**
Bioconjugate Chemistry (USA) **726**
Biomacromolecules (USA) **2120**
Biotechnology Progress (USA) **761**
Chemical Research in Toxicology (USA) **3495**
Chemical Reviews (USA) **2054**
Chemistry of Materials (USA) **3240**
Crystal Growth & Design (USA) **2109**
Energy & Fuels (USA) **3130**
Environmental Science & Technology (Washington) (USA) **3429**
Industrial & Engineering Chemistry Research (USA) **3246**
Inorganic Chemistry (USA) **2116**
Journal of Agricultural and Food Chemistry (USA) **238**
Journal of Chemical and Engineering Data (USA) **2067**
Journal of Chemical Education (USA) **2067**
Journal of Chemical Information and Modeling (USA) **2108**
Journal of Chemical Theory and Computation (USA) **2067**
Journal of Combinatorial Chemistry (USA) **2102**
Journal of Medicinal Chemistry (USA) **6854**
Journal of Natural Products (USA) **6854**
The Journal of Organic Chemistry (USA) **2124**
The Journal of Physical Chemistry Part A: Molecules, Spectroscopy, Kinetics, Environment and General Theory (USA) **2137**
The Journal of Physical Chemistry Part B: Condensed Matter, Materials, Surfaces, Interfaces & Biophysical (USA) **2137**
Journal of Proteome Research (USA) **737**
Langmuir (USA) **2138**
Macromolecules (USA) **2126**
Molecular Pharmaceutics (USA) **2073**
Nano Letters (USA) **3355**
Organic Letters (USA) **2128**
Organic Process Research and Development (GBR) **2128**
Organometallics (USA) **2128**

American Institute of Physics, Scitation Ste 1NO1, 2 Huntington Quadrangle, Melville, NY 11747-4502 TEL 516-576-2664, 800-874-6383, FAX 516-576-2604, subs@aip.org, http://scitation.aip.org/
A I P Conference Proceedings (USA) **7002**
Acoustical Physics (RUS) **7086**
Acoustical Society of America. Journal (USA) **7086**
American Journal of Physics (USA) **7004**
Applied Mechanics Reviews (USA) **3228**
Applied Physics Letters (USA) **7006**
Astronomy Letters (RUS) **571**
Astronomy Reports (RUS) **571**
Chaos (USA) **7008**
Computing in Science & Engineering (USA) **7050**
Crystallography Reports (RUS) **2110**
Doklady Physics (RUS) **7010**
Earthquake Spectra (USA) **2780**
Electrochemical and Solid-State Letters (USA) **2061**
Electrochemical Society. Journal (USA) **2113**
Electronics Letters (GBR) **3097**
Geochemical Transactions (GBR) **2708**
Geophysics (USA) **2782**
I E T Circuits, Devices and Systems (GBR) **3316**
I E T Communications (GBR) **3316**
I E T Computers and Digital Techniques (GBR) **2540**
I E T Control Theory and Applications (GBR) **2460**
I E T Electric Power Applications (GBR) **3317**
I E T Generation, Transmission and Distribution (GBR) **3317**
I E T Intelligent Transport Systems (GBR) **8498**
I E T Microwaves Antennas & Propagation (GBR) **3317**
I E T Nanobiotechnology (GBR) **765**
I E T Optoelectronics (GBR) **7076**
I E T Radar, Sonar and Navigation (GBR) **3317**
I E T Science, Measurement and Technology (GBR) **3318**
I E T Software (GBR) **2590**
I E T Systems Biology (GBR) **825**
International Journal of Geomechanics (USA) **2748**
J E T P Letters Online (USA) *see* J E T P Letters. **7019**
Journal of Aerospace Engineering (USA) **3274**
Journal of Applied Mechanics (USA) **3385**
Journal of Applied Physics (USA) **7019**
Journal of Architectural Engineering (USA) **447**
Journal of Biomechanical Engineering (USA) **5646**
Journal of Biomedical Optics (USA) **7078**
Journal of Bridge Engineering (USA) **1018**
Journal of Chemical Physics (USA) **7019**
Journal of Cold Regions Engineering (USA) **3274**
Journal of Composites for Construction (USA) **3274**
Journal of Computational and Nonlinear Dynamics (USA) **3385**
Journal of Computing and Information Science in Engineering (USA) **3385**
Journal of Computing in Civil Engineering (USA) **3292**
Journal of Construction Engineering and Management (USA) **3274**
Journal of Dynamic Systems, Measurement and Control (USA) **3349**
Journal of Electronic Imaging (USA) **6970**
Journal of Electronic Packaging (USA) **3106**
Journal of Energy Engineering (USA) **3275**
Journal of Energy Resources Technology (USA) **3140**
Journal of Engineering for Gas Turbines and Power (USA) **3385**
Journal of Engineering Materials and Technology (USA) **3349**
Journal of Engineering Mechanics (USA) **3275**
Journal of Environmental Engineering (USA) **3445**
Journal of Experimental and Theoretical Physics (USA) **7020**
Journal of Fluids Engineering (USA) **3363**
Journal of Fuel Cell Science and Technology (USA) **3385**
Journal of Geotechnical and Geoenvironmental Engineering (USA) **3275**
Journal of Heat Transfer (USA) **3385**
Journal of Hydraulic Engineering (New York) (USA) **3275**
Journal of Hydrologic Engineering (USA) **3275**
The Journal of Imaging Science and Technology (USA) **6970**
Journal of Infrastructure Systems (USA) **3275**
Journal of Irrigation and Drainage Engineering (USA) **3275**
Journal of Laser Applications (GBR) **7078**
Journal of Management in Engineering (USA) **3205**
Journal of Manufacturing Science and Engineering (USA) **3385**
Journal of Materials in Civil Engineering (USA) **3276**
Journal of Mathematical Physics (USA) **7021**
Journal of Mechanical Design (USA) **3386**
Journal of Micro/Nanolithography, M E M S, and M O E M S (USA) **7078**
Journal of Offshore Mechanics and Arctic Engineering (USA) **3386**
Journal of Performance of Constructed Facilities (USA) **3276**
Journal of Physical and Chemical Reference Data (USA) **2068**
Journal of Pressure Vessel Technology (USA) **3386**
Journal of Professional Issues in Engineering Education and Practice (USA) **3276**
Journal of Rheology (USA) **7060**
Journal of Solar Energy Engineering (USA) **3176**
Journal of Structural Engineering (USA) **3276**
Journal of Surveying Engineering (USA) **3276**
Journal of Transportation Engineering (USA) **8501**
Journal of Tribology (USA) **6776**
Journal of Turbomachinery (USA) **3387**
Journal of Urban Planning and Development (USA) **4418**
Journal of Vacuum Science & Technology. A: International Journal Devoted to Vacuum, Surfaces, and Films (USA) **7023**
Journal of Vacuum Science and Technology. Part B. Microelectronics and Nanometer Structures (USA) **7023**
Journal of Vibration and Acoustics (USA) **3387**
Journal of Water Resources Planning and Management (USA) **8827**
Journal of Waterway, Port, Coastal, and Ocean Engineering (USA) **8649**
Leadership and Management in Engineering (USA) **3278**
The Leading Edge (Tulsa) (USA) **2786**
Low Temperature Physics (USA) **7055**
Medical & Biological Engineering & Computing (DEU) **826**
Medical Physics (USA) **5670**
Natural Hazards Review (USA) **3455**
Noise-Con Proceedings (USA) **3489**
Optical Engineering (USA) **7081**
Optics and Spectroscopy (RUS) **7083**
Physics of Atomic Nuclei (RUS) **7071**
Physics of Fluids (USA) **7033**
Physics of Plasmas (USA) **7033**
Physics of the Solid State (USA) **7033**
The Physics Teacher (USA) **7034**
Plasma Physics Reports (RUS) **7035**
Powder Diffraction (USA) **3215**
Practice Periodical of Hazardous, Toxic and Radioactive Waste Management (USA) **3510**
Practice Periodical on Structural Design and Construction (USA) **3281**
Progress in Biomedical Optics and Imaging (USA) **7084**
Review of Scientific Instruments (USA) **4489**
Semiconductors (USA) **7039**
Society for Information Display. Journal (USA) **2490**
Society of Exploration Geophysicists. S E G Technical Program Expanded Abstracts (USA) **2790**
Surface Science Spectra (USA) **7042**
Technical Physics (USA) **7042**
Technical Physics Letters (USA) **7042**
Tire Science and Technology (USA) **7827**

American Psychological Association PsycARTICLES, 750 First St, NE, Washington, DC 20002-4242 TEL 202-336-5650, 800-374-2722, FAX 202-336-5633, psycinfo@apa.org, http://www.apa.org/psycarticles
American Journal of Orthopsychiatry (USA) **7333**
American Psychologist (USA) **7333**
Behavioral Neuroscience (USA) **7339**
Canadian Journal of Behavioural Science (CAN) **7343**
Canadian Journal of Experimental Psychology (CAN) **7343**
Canadian Psychology (CAN) **7344**
Clinician's Research Digest (USA) **7417**
Consulting Psychology Journal (USA) **7348**
Crisis (Kirkland) (USA) **7350**
Cultural Diversity & Ethnic Minority Psychology (USA) **8097**
Developmental Psychology (USA) **7351**
Emotion (USA) **7354**
European Journal of Psychological Assessment (USA) **7356**
European Psychologist (USA) **7356**
Experimental and Clinical Psychopharmacology (USA) **7356**
Experimental Psychology (USA) **7357**
Families, Systems, & Health (USA) **5613**
Group Dynamics (USA) **7359**
Health Psychology (USA) **7360**
History of Psychology (USA) **7360**
International Journal of Stress Management (USA) **5640**
Journal of Abnormal Psychology (USA) **7368**
Journal of Applied Psychology (USA) **7369**
Journal of Comparative Psychology (USA) **7371**
Journal of Consulting and Clinical Psychology (USA) **7371**
Journal of Counseling Psychology (USA) **7372**
Journal of Educational Psychology (USA) **2875**
Journal of Experimental Psychology: Animal Behavior Processes (USA) **7373**
Journal of Experimental Psychology: Applied (USA) **7373**
Journal of Experimental Psychology: General (USA) **7373**
Journal of Experimental Psychology: Human Perception and Performance (USA) **7373**
Journal of Experimental Psychology: Learning, Memory, and Cognition (USA) **7373**
Journal of Family Psychology (USA) **7374**
Journal of Individual Differences (USA) **7375**
Journal of Occupational Health Psychology (USA) **6680**
Journal of Personality and Social Psychology (USA) **7377**
Journal of Psychophysiology (USA) **7379**
Journal of Psychotherapy Integration (USA) **6156**
Methodology (USA) **7385**
Neuropsychology (USA) **6168**
Professional Psychology: Research and Practice (USA) **7392**
Psychoanalytic Psychology (USA) **7395**
Psychological Assessment (USA) **7396**
Psychological Bulletin (USA) **7396**
Psychological Methods (USA) **7396**
Psychological Review (USA) **7397**
Psychological Services (USA) **7397**
Psychology and Aging (USA) **4053**
Psychology of Addictive Behaviors (USA) **2698**
Psychology of Men & Masculinity (USA) **7399**
Psychology, Public Policy, and Law (USA) **7400**
Psychotherapy (USA) **7401**
Rehabilitation Psychology (USA) **7402**
Review of General Psychology (USA) **7403**
Swiss Journal of Psychology (CHE) **7411**

American Theological Library Association 300 South Wacker Dr, Ste 2100, Chicago, IL 60606-6701 TEL 312-454-5100, 888-665-2852, FAX 312-454-5505, atla@atla.com, http://www.atla.com
A F E R (KEN) **7781**
American Academy of Religion. Journal (USA) **7620**
American Theological Library Association. Conference. Summary of Proceedings (USA) **4989**
Arts (New Brighton) (USA) **474**
Asian Ethnology (JPN) **329**
Bibliotheca Sacra (USA) **7748**
Brethren Life and Thought (USA) **7749**
Calvin Theological Journal (USA) **7749**
Canadian Church Historical Society Journal (CAN) **7749**
Catholic Biblical Quarterly (USA) **7788**
The Christian Century (USA) **7631**
Christianity Today (USA) **7632**
Church History (USA) **7633**
Cross Currents (New York) (USA) **2976**
Currents in Theology and Mission (USA) **7753**
Dialogue & Alliance (USA) **7638**
Direction (Winnipeg) (CAN) **7734**
Eastern Buddhist (JPN) **7701**
Ecumenical Review (CHE) **7639**
Evangelical Theological Society. Journal (USA) **7756**
Family and Community Ministries (USA) **7758**
First Things (USA) **7643**
Greek Orthodox Theological Review (USA) **7704**
Hebrew Union College Annual (USA) **7721**
Homiletic (Online) (USA) **7760**
Horizons (Villanova) (USA) **7800**
International Bulletin of Missionary Research (USA) **7762**
The International Journal for the Psychology of Religion (USA) **7650**
International Review of Mission (CHE) **7651**
Interpretation (Richmond) (USA) **7651**
Japanese Journal of Religious Studies (JPN) **7737**
Journal for Preachers (USA) **7762**
Journal for the Scientific Study of Religion (USA) **7653**
Journal for the Study of the New Testament (GBR) **7653**
Journal for the Study of the Old Testament (GBR) **7653**
Journal of Biblical Literature (USA) **7654**
Journal of Chinese Religions (USA) **7737**
Journal of Ecumenical Studies (USA) **7655**
Journal of Feminist Studies in Religion (USA) **7655**
Journal of Pastoral Care and Counseling (USA) **7655**
Journal of Pastoral Theology (USA) **7655**
Journal of Religious Ethics (USA) **7656**
Journal of Ritual Studies (USA) **345**
Journal of Theology for Southern Africa (ZAF) **7657**
Latin American Indian Literatures Journal (USA) **5320**
The Living Pulpit (USA) **7661**
Missiology (USA) **7739**
Mission Studies (NLD) **7664**
Modern Theology (GBR) **7664**
Muslim World (USA) **7715**
Near Eastern Archaeology (USA) **407**
Novum Testamentum (NLD) **7666**
Numen (NLD) **7667**
Perspectives in Religious Studies (USA) **7770**
Pneuma (NLD) **7770**
Religion in the News (USA) **4583**
Religious Education (USA) **7676**
Religious Studies Review (USA) **7699**
Review and Expositor (USA) **7773**
St. Vladimir's Theological Quarterly (USA) **7706**
Semeia Studies (NLD) **7680**
Society of Christian Ethics. Journal (USA) **7682**
Sociology of Religion (USA) **8139**
Theological Education (USA) **7689**
Theological Studies (USA) **7689**
Theology Today (USA) **7690**
Vetus Testamentum (NLD) **7731**
Worship (USA) **7695**
Zygon (USA) **7697**

Annual Reviews 4139 El Camino Way, PO Box 10139, Palo Alto, CA 94303-0139 TEL 650-493-4400, 800-523-8635, FAX 650-855-9815, 650-424-0910, service@annualreviews.org, http://www.annualreviews.org/
Annual Review of Astronomy and Astrophysics (USA) **568**
Annual Review of Clinical Psychology (USA) **7335**
Annual Review of Ecology, Evolution and Systematics (USA) **3403**
Annual Review of Environment and the Resources (USA) **3124**
Annual Review of Materials Research (USA) **3341**
Annual Review of Pathology: Mechanisms of Disease (USA) **5576**
Annual Review of Plant Biology (USA) **775**
Annual Review of Political Science (USA) **7106**

Ashley Publications Ltd. (Subsidiary of: P J B Publications Ltd.) Unitec House 3rd Fl, 2 Albert Pl, Finchley Central, London N3 1QB, United Kingdom TEL 44-20-83433883, FAX 44-20-83432313, info@ashley-pub.com, http://www.ashley-pub.com
Aging Health (GBR) **4039**
Expert Opinion on Biological Therapy (GBR) **5612**
Expert Opinion on Drug Delivery (GBR) **6839**
Expert Opinion on Drug Metabolism & Toxicology (GBR) **6839**
Expert Opinion on Drug Safety (GBR) **6839**
Expert Opinion on Emerging Drugs (GBR) **6839**
Expert Opinion on Investigational Drugs (GBR) **6839**
Expert Opinion on Pharmacotherapy (GBR) **6839**
Expert Opinion on Therapeutic Patents (GBR) **6839**
Expert Opinion On Therapeutic Targets (GBR) **6840**
Expert Review of Anti-infective Therapy (GBR) **6109**
Expert Review of Anticancer Therapy (GBR) **6840**
Expert Review of Cardiovascular Therapy (GBR) **5787**
Expert Review of Clinical Immunology (GBR) **5758**
Expert Review of Medical Devices (GBR) **5905**
Expert Review of Molecular Diagnostics (GBR) **6840**
Expert Review of Neurotherapeutics (GBR) **6840**
Expert Review of Pharmacoeconomics & Outcomes Research (GBR) **6840**

Link to your serials resources and content with ulrichsweb.com

Expert Review of Proteomics (GBR) 732
Expert Review of Vaccines (GBR) 5758
Future Cardiology (GBR) 5787
Future Neurology (GBR) 6142
Future Oncology (GBR) 6020
Future Virology (GBR) 886
International Journal of Clinical Rheumatology (GBR) 6224
Personalized Medicine (GBR) 5695
Pharmacogenomics (GBR) 6871
Regenerative Medicine (GBR) 5702
Therapy (GBR) 5911
Women's Health (London, 2005) (GBR) 8849

Association For Computing Machinery, Inc., A C M Digital Library 2 Penn Plaza, Ste 701, New York, NY 10121-0701 TEL 212-626-0500, 800-342-6626, FAX 212-944-1318, acm@helpacm.org, http://portal.acm.org/dl.cfm
A C M Computing Surveys (USA) 2405
A C M Journal of Computer Documentation (USA) 2541
A C M Journal on Emerging Technologies in Computing Systems (USA) 2569
A C M Queue (USA) 2587
A C M / S I G P L A N Notices (USA) 2504
A C M Transactions on Algorithms (USA) 5549
A C M Transactions on Asian Language Information Processing (USA) 5202
A C M Transactions on Computational Logic (USA) 2405
A C M Transactions on Computer - Human Interaction (USA) 2470
A C M Transactions on Computer Systems (USA) 2519
A C M Transactions on Database Systems (USA) 2529
A C M Transactions on Embedded Computing Systems (USA) 2405
A C M Transactions on Graphics (USA) 2483
A C M Transactions on Information and System Security (USA) 2511
A C M Transactions on Information Systems (USA) 1413
A C M Transactions on Internet Technology (USA) 2552
A C M Transactions on Mathematical Software (USA) 2587
A C M Transactions on Modeling and Computer Simulation (USA) 2405
A C M Transactions on Multimedia Computing Communications and Applications (USA) 2532
A C M Transactions on Programming Languages and Systems (USA) 2504
A C M Transactions on Sensor Networks (USA) 2495
A C M Transactions on Software Engineering and Methodology (USA) 2587
A C M Transactions on Speech and Language Processing (USA) 2505
A C M Transactions on Storage (USA) 2519
Accessibility and Computing (USA) 4071
Annual A C M Symposium on the Theory of Computing. Proceedings (USA) 2600
Association for Computing Machinery. Communications (USA) 2533
Association for Computing Machinery. Journal (USA) 2407
Automated Software Engineering (USA) 2446
Computational Linguistics (Online) (USA) 5202
Computers in Entertainment (USA) 2413
Crossroads (ITA) 1089
Data Mining and Knowledge Discovery (USA) 2530
eLearn Magazine (USA) 2469
I E E E - A C M Transactions on Computational Biology and Bioinformatics (USA) 825
I E E E - A C M Transactions on Networking (USA) 2497
Intelligence (Kidlington) (GBR) 7363
Interactions (New York) (USA) 2507
International Journal of Network Management (GBR) 2327
Journal of Experimental Algorithmics (USA) 2508
Journal of Multiple-Valued Logic and Soft Computing (USA) 5506
Linux Journal (USA) 2594
Mobile Networks and Applications (NLD) 2501
Personal and Ubiquitous Computing (GBR) 2435
S I G A C T News (USA) 2464
S I G I T E Newsletter (USA) 3079
Simulation Digest (USA) 2518
Transactions on Design Automation of Electronic Systems (USA) 3293
Ubiquity (USA) 8444
Wireless Networks (NLD) 2344

Bioline International, Bioline.International@utoronto.ca, http://www.bioline.org.br
African Crop Science Journal (UGA) 216
African Health Sciences (UGA) 5569
African Journal of Biomedical Research (NGA) 5569
African Journal of Biotechnology (USA) 755
African Journal of Food and Nutritional Security (KEN) 6654
African Journal of Reproductive Health (NGA) 8843
African Journal of Traditional, Complementary and Alternative Medicines (NGA) 5570
Annals of African Medicine (NGA) 5575
Archivos Latinoamericanos de Produccion Animal (VEN) 279
AusBiotech Journal (AUS) 756
Biokemistri (NGA) 726
Brazilian Journal of Oral Sciences (BRA) 5836
Caderno de Pesquisa. Serie Biologia (BRA) 663
Chilean Journal of Agricultural Research (Online) (CHL) *see* Chilean Journal of Agricultural Research (Print). 101
Chinese Academic Journals Full-Text Database. Science & Engineering, Series A (CHN) 7845
Colombia Medica (Online Edition) (COL) 5599
Dongwuxue Yanjiu (CHN) 940
Electronic Journal of Biotechnology (CHL) 763
Entomotropica (VEN) 847
Etude de la Population Africaine (SEN) 7283
European Journal of General Medicine (TUR) 5611
Indian Association of Pediatric Surgeons. Journal (IND) 6092
Indian Journal of Cancer (IND) 6022
Indian Journal of Critical Care Medicine (IND) 5633
Indian Journal of Dermatology, Venereology and Leprology (IND) 5877
Indian Journal of Human Genetics (IND) 872
Indian Journal of Medical Microbiology (IND) 5760
Indian Journal of Medical Sciences (IND) 5634
Indian Journal of Occupational and Environmental Medicine (IND) 5634
Indian Journal of Pharmacology (IND) 6848
Indian Journal of Plastic Surgery (IND) 6245
Indian Journal of Surgery (IND) 6245
Instituto Oswaldo Cruz, Rio de Janeiro. Memorias (BRA) 678
J L B Smith Institute of Ichthyology. Ichthyological Bulletin (ZAF) 949
Journal of Applied Sciences and Environmental Management (NGA) 3488
Journal of Cancer Research and Therapeutics (IND) 6024
Journal of Culture Collections (BGR) 889
The Journal of Food Technology in Africa (KEN) 3651
Journal of Health Population and Nutrition (BGD) 5748
Journal of Medicine and Biomedical Research (NGA) 5652
Journal of Minimal Access Surgery (IND) 6249
Journal of Postgraduate Medicine (IND) 5654
Malaysian Journal of Medical Science (MYS) 5664
Medical Journal of the Islamic Republic of Iran (IRN) 5669
Medicina (HRV) 5673
Middle East Fertility Society Journal (EGY) 5998
Neurology India (IND) 6166
Nigerian Journal of Physiological Sciences (NGA) 5948
Nigerian Journal of Surgical Research (NGA) 6253
Smithiana Bulletin (ZAF) 963
Smithiana. Special Publication (ZAF) 963
Systematic and Applied Acarology (GBR) 860
Tropical Journal of Pharmaceutical Research (NGA) 6883
Vitae (VEN) 5728
Zhiwu Xuebao (CHN) 824
Zootecnia Tropical (VEN) 305

BioOne 21 Dupont Circle, Ste 800, Washington, DC 20036 TEL 202-296-2296, 800-843-8482, FAX 202-872-0884, http://www.bioone.org/
Academy of Natural Sciences of Philadelphia. Proceedings (USA) 7831
Ambio Journal Online (SWE) *see* Ambio. 3402
The American Biology Teacher (USA) 652
American Fern Journal (USA) 774
American Midland Naturalist (USA) 7834
American Museum Novitates (USA) 931
American Museum of Natural History. Bulletin (USA) 931
Applied Vegetation Science (DNK) 776
The Arabidopsis Book (USA) 776
Arctic, Antarctic, and Alpine Research (USA) 7836
Arizona-Nevada Academy of Science. Journal (USA) 7837
The Auk (USA) 901
Avian Diseases (USA) 8794
Biology of Reproduction (USA) 660
Bios (USA) 661
BioScience (USA) 661
Biotropica (USA) 662
The Botanical Review (USA) 781
Brittonia (USA) 782
Bryologist (USA) 782
Castanea (USA) 783
Cell Stress & Chaperones (NLD) 5592
The Coleopterists Bulletin (USA) 842
Comparative Parasitology (USA) 938
The Condor (USA) 905
Copeia (USA) 939
Economic Botany (USA) 786
Entomologica Americana (USA) 844
Entomological Society of America. Annals (USA) 845
Environmental Entomology (USA) 847
Evolution (USA) 866
Florida Entomologist (USA) 847
Herpetologica (USA) 946
Herpetological Monographs (USA) 946
In Vitro Cellular & Developmental Biology - Animal (DEU) 5633
In Vitro Cellular & Developmental Biology - Plant (DEU) 793
Integrative & Comparative Biology (GBR) 947
Journal of Arachnology (USA) 950
Journal of Avian Medicine and Surgery (USA) 8800
Journal of Coastal Conservation (NLD) 2809
Journal of Coastal Research (USA) 2809
Journal of Crustacean Biology (USA) 950
Journal of Economic Entomology (USA) 851
The Journal of Eukaryotic Microbiology (USA) 889
Journal of Field Ornithology (USA) 909
Journal of Herpetology (USA) 951
Journal of Insect Science (USA) 852
Journal of Mammalogy (USA) 951
Journal of Medical Entomology (USA) 852
Journal of Orthoptera Research (USA) 852
Journal of Paleontology (USA) 6726
The Journal of Parasitology (SUN) 5821
Journal of Vegetation Science (SWE) 799
Journal of Vertebrate Paleontology (USA) 6726
The Journal of Wildlife Management (USA) 2616
Journal of Zoo and Wildlife Medicine (USA) 8802
Kansas Academy of Science. Transactions (Print) (USA) 7874
Mammalian Species (Online) (USA) 955
Micropaleontology (USA) 6726
Mountain Research and Development (CHE) 2713
North American Benthological Society. Journal (USA) 694
Northeastern Naturalist (USA) 805
Northwestern Naturalist (USA) 959
Palaios (USA) 6728
Paleobiology (USA) 6728
Palynology (USA) 6729
Photochemistry and Photobiology (USA) 2139
Radiation Research (USA) 7072
Rangeland Ecology & Management (USA) 699
Rangelands (USA) 297
Society of Wetland Scientists. Bulletin (USA) 8832
Southeastern Naturalist (USA) 818
Southwestern Naturalist (USA) 7919
Systematic Botany (USA) 819
Ursus (USA) 966
Waterbirds (USA) 916
Weed Science (USA) 258
Weed Technology (USA) 258
Wetlands (USA) 8842
The Wilson Journal of Ornithology (USA) 917

The Bureau of National Affairs, Inc. 1231 25th St, NW, Washington, DC 20037 TEL 202-452-4200, 800-372-1033, FAX 202-452-4226, customercare@bna.com, http://www.bna.com/
A B A / B N A Lawyers' Manual on Professional Conduct (USA) *see* A B A / B N A Lawyers' Manual on Professional Conduct Current Reports. 4606
Affirmative Action Compliance Manual for Federal Contractors (USA) 1662
Americans with Disabilities Cases (USA) 4615
Antitrust & Trade Regulation Daily (USA) 1879
Antitrust & Trade Regulation Report (USA) 4855
B N A's Americans with Disabilities Act Manual. Newsletter (USA) 4968
B N A's Banking Report (Online) (USA) 1310
B N A's Corporate Counsel Weekly (USA) 1727
B N A's Eastern Europe Reporter (USA) 1439
B N A's Employment Discrimination Report (USA) 1856
B N A's Environmental Compliance Bulletin (USA) 4625
B N A's Environmental Due Diligence Guide (USA) 4625
B N A's Federal Environment & Safety Regulatory Monitoring Report (USA) 3405
B N A's Health Care Daily Report (USA) 4088
B N A's Health Care Fraud Report (USA) 4088
B N A's Health Care Policy Report (USA) 7509
B N A's Health Law & Business Series (USA) 4088
B N A's Health Law Reporter (Online) (USA) 4625
B N A's Medicare Report (USA) 5583
B N A's Patent, Trademark & Copyright Journal (USA) 6746
B N A's SafetyNet (USA) 6674
B N A's State Environment & Safety Regulatory Monitoring Report (USA) 3405
B N A's State H I P A A and Privacy Monitoring Report (USA) 4494
Banking Daily (USA) 1317
Bankruptcy Law Daily (USA) 4626
Benefits & Compensation Management Update (USA) 1667
Biotech Watch (USA) 759
Broker/Dealer Compliance Report (Online) (USA) 1614
Bulletin to Management (USA) 1857
Canadian Environment and Safety Library (USA) 3409
Chemical Regulation Daily (USA) 3484
Chemical Regulation Reporter (USA) 3484
Class Action Litigation Report (USA) 4643
Collective Bargaining Negotiations and Contracts (USA) 4592
Computer Technology Law Report (USA) 4648
Construction Labor Report (USA) 1673
Corporate Accountability Report (USA) 4651
Corporate Governance Report (USA) 4651
Corporate Law Daily (USA) 4864
Corporate Practice Series (USA) 4865
Criminal Law Reporter (USA) 4887
Daily Environment Report (Online) (USA) 3413
Daily Labor Report (USA) 1674
Daily Report for Executives (USA) 1737
Daily Tax Report (USA) 1919
E-Commerce Law Daily (USA) 4662
E-Commerce Tax Report (Online) (USA) 1921
E H S Global Alert (USA) 6676
Electronic Commerce & Law Report (USA) 4830
Employee Benefit Cases (USA) 1677
Employment Discrimination Verdicts and Settlements (USA) 1678
Employment Guide (USA) 1678
Environment Reporter (USA) 3422
Expert Evidence Report (USA) 4670
Fair Employment Practice Cases (USA) 1681
The Family Law Reporter (USA) 4910
Federal Contracts Daily (USA) 7436
Federal Contracts Report (USA) 7436
Government Employee Relations Report (USA) 1684
H R Department Benchmarks and Analysis (USA) 1862
Health Care Program Compliance Guide Monthly Focus (USA) 4095
Health Law & Business Library (USA) 4096
Homeland Security Briefing (USA) 2654
Human Resources Library (USA) 1865
Human Resources Report (USA) 1685
I R S Practice Adviser Report (USA) 1928
Intellectual Property Library (USA) 4694
International Business & Finance Daily (USA) 1126
International Environment Daily (USA) 3441
International Environment Reporter (USA) 3441
International Tax Monitor (USA) 1930
International Trade Daily (USA) 1571
International Trade Reporter (USA) 1572
International Trade Reporter Decisions (USA) 1572
International Trade Reporter Export Reference Manual (USA) 1572
International Trade Reporter. Import Reference Manual (USA) 1572
Labor and Employment Law Library (USA) 5024
Labor Relations Reference Manual (USA) 1693
Labor Relations Reporter (USA) 1693
Labor Relations Reporter. Wage and Hour Cases (USA) 1693
Labor Relations Week (USA) 1693
Media Law Reporter (USA) 2332
Medical Research Law and Policy Report (USA) 5671
Mergers & Acquistions Law Report (USA) 4876
Money & Politics Report (USA) 7453
Occupational Safety & Health Daily (USA) 6683
Occupational Safety & Health Reporter (USA) 6683
On The Line (Washington, D.C.) (USA) 4600
Patent, Trademark & Copyright Law Daily (USA) 6756
Payroll Administration Guide Newsletter (USA) 1702
Payroll Library on C D (USA) 1158
Pension & Benefits Daily (USA) 1702
Pension & Benefits Reporter (USA) 1702
Pharmaceutical Law & Industry Report (USA) 6869
Prevention of Corporate Liability: Current Report (USA) 4879
Product Liability Daily (USA) 1901
Product Safety and Liability Reporter (USA) 7536
Right-to-Know Planning Guide Report (USA) 3463
Safety Library (USA) 6686
Securities Law Daily (USA) 1650
Securities Regulation & Law Report (USA) 4781
State Environment Daily (USA) 3467
State Health Care Regulatory Developments (USA) 4111
Tax Management Compensation Planning Journal (USA) 1797
Tax Management Estates, Gifts and Trusts Journal (USA) 1655
Tax Management Financial Planning Journal (USA) 1386
Tax Management International Forum (GBR) 1948
Tax Management International Journal (USA) 1948
Tax Management Memorandum (USA) 1948
Tax Management Primary Sources (USA) 1948
Tax Management Real Estate Journal (USA) 7613
Tax Management Tax Practice Series Bulletin (USA) 1948
Tax Management Transfer Pricing Portfolio Series (USA) 1948
Tax Management Transfer Pricing Report (USA) 1948
Tax Management Weekly Report (USA) 1948
Tax Management Weekly State Tax Report (USA) 1949
Tax Management's Multistate Tax Portfolio Series (USA) 1949
Tax Planning International (GBR) 1949
Tax Planning International European Tax Service (GBR) 1949
Tax Practice Plus (DVD) (USA) 1949
TaxCore (USA) 1951
Telecommunications Monitor (USA) 2341
Toxics Law Daily (USA) 3513
Toxics Law Reporter (USA) 3513
Transportation Watch (USA) 8517
Union Labor Report Newsletter (USA) 4604
United States Law Week (USA) 4801
United States Patents Quarterly (USA) 6759
W T O Reporter (USA) 1587
Workers' Compensation Report (USA) 1715
World Data Protection Report (USA) 2569
World Intellectual Property Report (GBR) 6760
World Securities Law Report (GBR) 1660

C S A (Subsidiary of: ProQuest LLC (Bethesda)) 7200 Wisconsin Ave, Ste 601, Bethesda, MD 20814 TEL 301-961-6700, FAX 301-961-6720, http://www.csa.com
Academy of Marketing Science. Journal (USA) 1803
Academy of Natural Sciences of Philadelphia. Proceedings (USA) 7831
Acta Sociologica (NOR) 8085
Action Research (GBR) 5567
Active Learning in Higher Education (GBR) 2965
Administration & Society (USA) 7418

11076 CAMBRIDGE UNIVERSITY PRESS ULRICH'S PERIODICALS

Adult Education Quarterly (USA) **2938**
Advances in Developing Human Resources (USA) **1855**
Ambio Journal Online (SWE) *see* Ambio. **3402**
American Academy of Political and Social Science. Annals (USA) **7104**
American Behavioral Scientist (USA) **7946**
The American Biology Teacher (USA) **652**
American Fern Journal (USA) **774**
American Journal of Orthopsychiatry (USA) **7333**
American Midland Naturalist (USA) **7834**
American Museum Novitates (USA) **931**
American Museum of Natural History. Bulletin (USA) **931**
American Politics Research (USA) **7105**
American Psychologist (USA) **7333**
American Review of Public Administration (USA) **7419**
Applied Psychological Measurement (USA) **7336**
Applied Vegetation Science (DNK) **776**
The Arabidopsis Book (USA) **776**
Arctic, Antarctic, and Alpine Research (USA) **7836**
Arizona-Nevada Academy of Science. Journal (USA) **7837**
Arts and Humanities in Higher Education (GBR) **4443**
Asia Pacific Journal of Human Resources (GBR) **1856**
Assessment (USA) **7337**
The Auk (USA) **901**
Autism (GBR) **6125**
Avian Diseases (USA) **8794**
Behavior Modification (USA) **7339**
Behavioral Neuroscience (USA) **7339**
Biological Research for Nursing (USA) **5953**
Biology of Reproduction (USA) **660**
Bios (USA) **661**
BioScience (USA) **661**
Biotropica (USA) **662**
Body & Society (GBR) **7951**
The Botanical Review (USA) **781**
Brittonia (USA) **782**
Bryologist (USA) **782**
Business & Society (USA) **1070**
C S A Human Population & Natural Resource Management (USA) **7304**
C S A Sustainability Science Abstracts (USA) **3477**
Canadian Journal of Behavioural Science (CAN) **7343**
Canadian Journal of Experimental Psychology (CAN) **7343**
Canadian Psychology (CAN) **7344**
Castanea (USA) **783**
Cell Stress & Chaperones (NLD) **5592**
Child Maltreatment (USA) **2148**
Childhood (GBR) **2148**
Clinical Child Psychology & Psychiatry (GBR) **2149**
Clinical Nursing Research (USA) **5955**
Clinician's Research Digest (USA) **7417**
The Coleopterists Bulletin (USA) **842**
Communication Research (USA) **8094**
Comparative Parasitology (USA) **938**
Comparative Political Studies (USA) **7117**
Compensation and Benefits Review (USA) **1671**
The Condor (USA) **905**
Consulting Psychology Journal (USA) **7348**
Cooperation and Conflict (GBR) **7228**
Copeia (USA) **939**
Cornell Hospitality Quarterly (USA) **4384**
The Counseling Psychologist (USA) **7349**
Crime & Delinquency (USA) **2648**
Crime, Media, Culture (GBR) **2648**
Criminal Justice & Behavior (USA) **2649**
Criminal Justice Policy Review (USA) **4886**
Criminal Justice Review (USA) **4887**
Criminology & Criminal Justice (Print) (GBR) **2650**
Crisis (Kirkland) (USA) **7350**
Cultural Diversity & Ethnic Minority Psychology (USA) **8097**
Culture & Psychology (GBR) **7350**
Current Sociology (GBR) **8098**
Dementia (GBR) **6135**
Developmental Psychology (USA) **7351**
Discourse & Society (GBR) **7352**
Discourse Studies (GBR) **5112**
East European Politics & Societies (USA) **7131**
Economic and Industrial Democracy (GBR) **7131**
Economic Botany (USA) **786**
Economic Development Quarterly (USA) **1539**
Education and Urban Society (USA) **2847**
Educational Administration Quarterly (USA) **3021**
Educational and Psychological Measurement (USA) **7353**
Educational Management, Administration & Leadership (Online) (GBR) *see* Educational Management, Administration & Leadership (Print). **3021**
Educational Policy (USA) **3022**
Emotion (USA) **7354**
Emotional and Behavioural Difficulties (GBR) **3039**
Entomologica Americana (USA) **844**
Entomological Society of America. Annals (USA) **845**
Environment and Behavior (USA) **8100**
Environment and Urbanization (GBR) **3421**
Environmental Entomology (USA) **847**
Ethnography (GBR) **337**
European Journal of Communication (GBR) **8101**
European Journal of Criminology (GBR) **2651**
European Journal of Industrial Relations (GBR) **1681**
European Journal of International Relations (GBR) **7234**
European Journal of Political Theory (GBR) **7134**
European Journal of Psychological Assessment (USA) **7356**
European Journal of Social Theory (GBR) **8101**
European Physical Education Review (GBR) **3061**
European Psychologist (USA) **7356**
European Union Politics (GBR) **7234**
European Urban and Regional Studies (GBR) **7963**
Evaluation and the Health Professions (USA) **5612**
Evolution (USA) **866**
Experimental and Clinical Psychopharmacology (USA) **7356**
Experimental Psychology (USA) **7357**
F R A N C I S (FRA) **4484**
Families, Systems, & Health (USA) **5613**
Family & Consumer Sciences Research Journal (USA) **4357**
The Family Journal (USA) **7357**
Feminism & Psychology (GBR) **7357**
First Language (GBR) **5119**
Florida Entomologist (USA) **847**
Gender & Society (USA) **8104**
Group Analysis (GBR) **7359**
Group & Organization Management (USA) **2861**
Group Dynamics (USA) **7359**
Group Processes & Intergroup Relations (GBR) **8105**
Health (GBR) **7520**
Health Education & Behavior (USA) **7522**
Health Promotion Practice (USA) **7523**
Health Psychology (USA) **7360**
Herpetologica (USA) **946**
Herpetological Monographs (USA) **946**
High Performance Polymers (GBR) **2123**
Hispanic Journal of Behavioral Sciences (USA) **7360**
History of Psychology (USA) **7360**
Home Health Care Management and Practice (USA) **4098**
Homicide Studies (USA) **2654**
Human Resource Development Review (USA) **1864**
Improving Schools (GBR) **3024**
In Vitro Cellular & Developmental Biology - Animal (DEU) **5633**
In Vitro Cellular & Developmental Biology - Plant (DEU) **793**
Integrative & Comparative Biology (GBR) **947**
The International Communication Gazette (Online) (GBR) **2326**
International Criminal Justice Review (USA) **4891**
International Journal of Behavioral Development (GBR) **7364**
International Journal of Cross Cultural Management (GBR) **1867**
International Journal of Damage Mechanics (GBR) **3346**
International Journal of Music Education (GBR) **6577**
International Journal of Offender Therapy and Comparative Criminology (USA) **2655**
International Journal of Press / Politics (USA) **4577**
International Journal of Social Psychiatry (GBR) **6147**
International Journal of Stress Management (USA) **5640**
International Political Science Review (GBR) **7244**
International Regional Science Review (USA) **7975**
International Relations (GBR) **7245**
International Review for the Sociology of Sport (GBR) **8110**
International Review of Administrative Sciences (GBR) **7447**
International Small Business Journal (GBR) **1962**
International Sociology (GBR) **8110**
Journal of Abnormal Psychology (USA) **7368**
Journal of Adolescent Research (USA) **7368**
Journal of Aging and Health (USA) **4048**
The Journal of Applied Behavioral Science (USA) **7368**
Journal of Applied Psychology (USA) **7369**
Journal of Arachnology (USA) **950**
Journal of Attention Disorders (USA) **6149**
Journal of Avian Medicine and Surgery (USA) **8800**
Journal of Bioactive and Compatible Polymers (GBR) **734**
Journal of Biomaterials Applications (GBR) **6247**
Journal of Black Psychology (USA) **7369**
Journal of Business and Technical Communication (USA) **1133**
Journal of Career Assessment (USA) **7369**
Journal of Cases in Educational Leadership (USA) **3025**
Journal of Cellular Plastics (GBR) **7093**
Journal of Child Health Care (GBR) **6094**
Journal of Coastal Conservation (NLD) **2809**
Journal of Coastal Research (USA) **2809**
Journal of Communication Inquiry (USA) **8112**
Journal of Comparative Psychology (USA) **7371**
Journal of Composite Materials (GBR) **3349**
Journal of Conflict Resolution (USA) **7978**
Journal of Consulting and Clinical Psychology (USA) **7371**
Journal of Contemporary Criminal Justice (USA) **4892**
Journal of Contemporary Ethnography (USA) **8112**
Journal of Counseling Psychology (USA) **7372**
Journal of Cross-Cultural Psychology (USA) **7372**
Journal of Crustacean Biology (USA) **950**
Journal of Early Adolescence (USA) **2156**
Journal of Early Childhood Literacy (GBR) **2875**
Journal of Early Childhood Research (GBR) **6094**
Journal of Economic Entomology (USA) **851**
Journal of Educational Psychology (USA) **2875**
Journal of Elastomers and Plastics (GBR) **7093**
The Journal of Eukaryotic Microbiology (USA) **889**
Journal of Experimental Psychology: Animal Behavior Processes (USA) **7373**
Journal of Experimental Psychology: Applied (USA) **7373**
Journal of Experimental Psychology: General (USA) **7373**
Journal of Experimental Psychology: Human Perception and Performance (USA) **7373**
Journal of Experimental Psychology: Learning, Memory, and Cognition (USA) **7373**
Journal of Family Issues (USA) **8113**
Journal of Family Nursing (USA) **5965**
Journal of Family Psychology (USA) **7374**
Journal of Field Ornithology (USA) **909**
Journal of Health Psychology (GBR) **7374**
Journal of Herpetology (USA) **951**
Journal of Hispanic Higher Education (USA) **2991**
Journal of Holistic Nursing (USA) **5965**
Journal of Hospitality & Tourism Research (USA) **4392**
Journal of Humanistic Psychology (USA) **7375**
Journal of Individual Differences (USA) **7375**
Journal of Industrial Textiles (GBR) **8454**
Journal of Insect Science (USA) **852**
Journal of Intellectual Disabilities (GBR) **3042**
Journal of Intelligent Material Systems and Structures (GBR) **3349**
Journal of Interpersonal Violence (USA) **2657**
Journal of Language and Social Psychology (USA) **7375**
Journal of Macromarketing (USA) **1825**
Journal of Mammalogy (USA) **951**
Journal of Management (GBR) **1767**
Journal of Management Education (USA) **1768**
Journal of Management Inquiry (USA) **1768**
Journal of Marketing Education (USA) **1825**
Journal of Medical Entomology (USA) **852**
Journal of Occupational Health Psychology (USA) **6680**
Journal of Orthoptera Research (USA) **852**
Journal of Paleontology (USA) **6726**
The Journal of Parasitology (SUN) **5821**
Journal of Peace Research (GBR) **7249**
Journal of Personality and Social Psychology (USA) **7377**
Journal of Planning Education and Research (USA) **4417**
Journal of Planning History (USA) **4417**
Journal of Planning Literature (USA) **4417**
Journal of Plastic Film and Sheeting (GBR) **7093**
Journal of Psychophysiology (USA) **7379**
Journal of Psychotherapy Integration (USA) **6156**
Journal of Reinforced Plastics & Composites (GBR) **3351**
Journal of Research in Crime and Delinquency (USA) **2658**
Journal of Research in International Education (GBR) **3014**
Journal of Research in Nursing (GBR) **5967**
Journal of Sandwich Structures & Materials (GBR) **3351**
Journal of Service Research (USA) **1826**
Journal of Social and Personal Relationships (GBR) **7380**
Journal of Sociology (GBR) **8116**
Journal of Sport and Social Issues (USA) **8182**
Journal of Studies in International Education (USA) **3014**
Journal of Teacher Education (USA) **2878**
Journal of Theoretical Politics (GBR) **7148**
Journal of Thermoplastic Composite Materials (GBR) **7094**
Journal of Transcultural Nursing (USA) **5967**
Journal of Transformative Education (USA) **2879**
Journal of Urban History (USA) **4150**
Journal of Vegetation Science (SWE) **799**
Journal of Vertebrate Paleontology (USA) **6726**
The Journal of Wildlife Management (USA) **2616**
Journal of Zoo and Wildlife Medicine (USA) **8802**
Journalism (GBR) **4577**
Kansas Academy of Science. Transactions (Print) (USA) **7874**
Leadership (GBR) **4463**
M L A International Bibliography (USA) **5407**
Mammalian Species (Online) (USA) **955**
Management Communication Quarterly (USA) **1775**
Management Learning (GBR) **1776**
Marketing Theory (GBR) **1833**
Mathematics and Mechanics of Solids (GBR) **7026**
Media, Culture & Society (GBR) **8120**
Medical Care Research and Review (USA) **7548**
Men and Masculinities (USA) **6303**
Methodology (USA) **7385**
Micropaleontology (USA) **6726**
Mountain Research and Development (CHE) **2713**
Neuropsychology (USA) **6168**
New Media & Society (GBR) **8123**
Nonprofit and Voluntary Sector Quarterly (USA) **8059**
North American Benthological Society. Journal (USA) **694**
Northeastern Naturalist (USA) **805**
Northwestern Naturalist (USA) **959**
Nursing Science Quarterly (USA) **5975**
Organization (GBR) **1784**
Organization & Environment (USA) **6684**
Organization Studies (DEU) **7990**
Organizational Research Methods (USA) **1784**
Palaios (USA) **6728**
Paleobiology (USA) **6728**
Palynology (USA) **6729**
Party Politics (GBR) **7164**
Personality and Social Psychology Bulletin (USA) **7390**
Photochemistry and Photobiology (USA) **2139**
Planning Theory (GBR) **4423**
Police Quarterly (USA) **4896**
Policy, Politics & Nursing Practice (USA) **5978**
Political Theory (USA) **7169**
Politics and Society (USA) **7170**
Politics, Philosophy & Economics (GBR) **7171**
The Prison Journal (USA) **2666**
Probation Journal (GBR) **2666**
Professional Psychology: Research and Practice (USA) **7392**
Psychoanalytic Psychology (USA) **7395**
Psychological Assessment (USA) **7396**
Psychological Bulletin (USA) **7396**
Psychological Methods (USA) **7396**
Psychological Review (USA) **7397**
Psychological Services (USA) **7397**
Psychology and Aging (USA) **4053**
Psychology of Addictive Behaviors (USA) **2698**
Psychology of Men & Masculinity (USA) **7399**
Psychology of Music (GBR) **6608**
Psychology, Public Policy, and Law (USA) **7400**
Psychotherapy (USA) **7401**
Public Works Management & Policy (USA) **7463**
Punishment & Society (GBR) **2666**
Qualitative Health Research (USA) **5701**
Race & Class (GBR) **3560**
Radiation Research (USA) **7072**
Rangeland Ecology & Management (USA) **699**
Rangelands (USA) **297**
Rationality and Society (GBR) **7995**
Rehabilitation Psychology (USA) **7402**
Research on Aging (USA) **4054**
Review of General Psychology (USA) **7403**
Review of Radical Political Economics (USA) **1548**
School Psychology International (GBR) **3080**
Science Communication (USA) **8131**
Security Dialogue (GBR) **7265**
Sexualities (GBR) **7408**
Simulation & Gaming (USA) **2518**
Small Group Research (USA) **7408**
Social Compass (GBR) **8132**
Social Science Information (GBR) **8003**
Social Studies of Science (GBR) **7917**
Society of Wetland Scientists. Bulletin (USA) **8832**
Sociological Methods & Research (USA) **8137**
Sociology (GBR) **8138**
Southeastern Naturalist (USA) **818**
Southwestern Naturalist (USA) **7919**
Space & Culture (USA) **4029**
Strategic Organization (GBR) **1795**
Structural Health Monitoring (GBR) **8439**
Swiss Journal of Psychology (CHE) **7411**
Systematic Botany (USA) **819**
Television & New Media (USA) **2396**
Theoretical Criminology (GBR) **2670**
Theory & Psychology (GBR) **7412**
Theory and Research in Education (Online) (GBR) *see* Theory and Research in Education (Print). **2919**
Theory, Culture & Society (GBR) **8143**
Thesis Eleven (GBR) **7188**
Time & Society (GBR) **8144**
Transcultural Psychiatry (GBR) **6188**
Trauma, Violence & Abuse (USA) **6074**
Urban Affairs Review (USA) **4429**
Urban Education (USA) **2924**
Ursus (USA) **966**
Violence Against Women (USA) **8146**
Visual Communication (GBR) **2343**
Waterbirds (USA) **916**
Weed Science (USA) **258**
Weed Technology (USA) **258**
Western Journal of Nursing Research (USA) **5984**
Wetlands (USA) **8842**
The Wilson Journal of Ornithology (USA) **917**
Work and Occupations (USA) **8147**
Work, Employment & Society (GBR) **8147**
Written Communication (USA) **2345**
Youth & Society (USA) **2172**

Cambridge University Press The Edinburgh Bldg, Shaftesbury Rd, Cambridge CB2 2RU, United Kingdom TEL 44-1223-326070, FAX 44-1223-325150, journals@cambridge.org, http://journals.cambridge.org/
A J S Review (GBR) **7717**
A R Q: Architectural Research Quarterly (GBR) **426**
Acta Numerica (GBR) **5465**
Ageing and Society (GBR) **4039**
American Political Science Review (GBR) **7105**
Ancient Mesoamerica (GBR) **4283**
Anglo-Saxon England (GBR) **4198**
Animal Conservation (GBR) **2602**
Annals of Human Genetics (GBR) **862**
Annual Review of Applied Linguistics (GBR) **5094**
Antarctic Science (GBR) **653**
Applied Psycholinguistics (GBR) **5095**
Arabic Sciences and Philosophy (GBR) **4131**
Archaeological Dialogues (GBR) **376**
Archives Europeennes de Sociologie (GBR) **8088**
Artificial Intelligence for Engineering Design, Analysis and Manufacturing (GBR) **2446**
Behavioral and Brain Sciences (GBR) **7339**
Behavioural and Cognitive Psychotherapy (GBR) **7340**

Link to your serials resources and content with ulrichsweb.com

Bilingualism (GBR) **5100**
Biological Reviews (GBR) **658**
BioSocieties (GBR) **7950**
Bird Conservation International (GBR) **902**
British Journal for the History of Science (GBR) **7842**
British Journal of Anaesthetic & Recovery Nursing (GBR) **5953**
British Journal of Music Education (GBR) **6551**
British Journal of Political Science (GBR) **7110**
Cambridge Archaeological Journal (GBR) **386**
The Cambridge Law Journal (GBR) **4637**
Cambridge Opera Journal (GBR) **6553**
Cambridge Philosophical Society. Mathematical Proceedings (GBR) **5477**
Cambridge Quarterly of Healthcare Ethics (GBR) **5591**
Canadian Journal of Political Science (GBR) **7113**
Cardiology in the Young (GBR) **5780**
China Quarterly (GBR) **546**
Classical Quarterly (GBR) **2232**
Classical Review (GBR) **2233**
Combinatorics, Probability & Computing (GBR) **5551**
Comparative Studies in Society and History (GBR) **8095**
Compositio Mathematica (GBR) **5480**
Contemporary European History (GBR) **4212**
Continuity and Change (GBR) **7280**
Development and Psychopathology (GBR) **7351**
Developmental Medicine and Child Neurology (GBR) **6091**
Du Bois Review (GBR) **7960**
Early Music History (GBR) **6563**
Econometric Theory (GBR) **1539**
Economics and Philosophy (GBR) **1481**
Edinburgh Journal of Botany (GBR) **786**
Edinburgh Mathematical Society. Proceedings (GBR) **5485**
Eighteenth-Century Music (GBR) **6564**
English Language and Linguistics (GBR) **5115**
English Today (GBR) **5115**
Environment and Development Economics (GBR) **3420**
Environmental Conservation (GBR) **3423**
Environmental Practice (GBR) **3427**
Epidemiology and Infection (GBR) **885**
Ergodic Theory and Dynamical Systems (GBR) **5486**
European Business Organization Law Review (NLD) **4668**
European Constitutional Law Review (NLD) **4848**
European Journal of Anaesthesiology (GBR) **5771**
European Journal of Applied Mathematics (GBR) **5486**
European Journal of Phycology (GBR) **787**
European Review (GBR) **7853**
European Review of Economic History (GBR) **1541**
Experimental Agriculture (GBR) **109**
Experimental Physiology (GBR) **922**
Expert Reviews in Molecular Medicine (GBR) **5945**
Fetal and Maternal Medicine Review (GBR) **5990**
Financial History Review (GBR) **1344**
Foreign Policy Bulletin (GBR) **7235**
Fungal Biology Reviews (GBR) **790**
Genetics Research (GBR) **870**
Geological Magazine (GBR) **2738**
Glasgow Mathematical Journal (GBR) **5490**
Greece and Rome (GBR) **2234**
Harvard Theological Review (GBR) **7646**
Health Economics, Policy and Law (GBR) **5625**
Historical Journal (GBR) **4143**
Institute of Mathematics of Jussieu. Journal (GBR) **5494**
International Astronomical Union. Proceedings (GBR) **576**
International Journal of Asian Studies (GBR) **551**
International Journal of Astrobiology (GBR) **678**
International Journal of Cultural Property (GBR) **497**
International Journal of Law in Context (GBR) **4695**
International Journal of Middle East Studies (GBR) **552**
International Journal of Neuropsychopharmacology (GBR) **6850**
International Journal of Technology Assessment in Health Care (GBR) **5906**
International Labor and Working-Class History (GBR) **1689**
International Neuropsychological Society. Journal (GBR) **6147**
International Organization (GBR) **7244**
International Phonetic Association. Journal (GBR) **5130**
International Psychogeriatrics (GBR) **6148**
International Review of Social History (GBR) **4147**
Japanese Journal of Political Science (GBR) **7145**
Journal of Advertising Research (USA) **27**
The Journal of African History (GBR) **4176**
Journal of African Law (GBR) **4700**
The Journal of Agricultural Science (GBR) **126**
Journal of American Studies (GBR) **4299**
Journal of Biosocial Science (GBR) **8112**
Journal of Child Language (GBR) **2156**
Journal of Dairy Research (GBR) **266**
Journal of Ecclesiastical History (GBR) **7654**
The Journal of Economic History (GBR) **1544**
Journal of Fluid Mechanics (GBR) **3363**
Journal of French Language Studies (GBR) **5133**
Journal of Functional Programming (GBR) **2508**
Journal of Germanic Linguistics (GBR) **5133**
Journal of Global History (GBR) **4149**
Journal of Institutional Economics (GBR) **1137**
Journal of Laryngology and Otology (GBR) **6081**
Journal of Latin American Studies (GBR) **4299**
Journal of Linguistics (GBR) **5134**
Journal of Modern African Studies (GBR) **7147**
Journal of Navigation (GBR) **8648**
Journal of Pension Economics and Finance (GBR) **1868**
Journal of Plasma Physics (GBR) **7022**
Journal of Psychiatric Intensive Care (GBR) **6156**
Journal of Public Policy (GBR) **7979**
Journal of Radiotherapy in Practice (GBR) **6201**
Journal of Social Policy (GBR) **8051**
Journal of Southeast Asian Studies (GBR) **4185**
Journal of Systematic Palaeontology (GBR) **2751**
Journal of Tropical Ecology (GBR) **3448**
Journal of Zoology (GBR) **953**
Knowledge Engineering Review (GBR) **2454**
Language in Society (GBR) **5140**
Language Teaching (GBR) **5201**
Language Variation and Change (GBR) **5142**
Laser and Particle Beams (GBR) **7079**
Legal Information Management (GBR) **5025**
Legal Theory (GBR) **4721**
Leiden Journal of International Law (GBR) **4935**
The Lichenologist (GBR) **800**
London Mathematical Society. Bulletin (GBR) **5509**
London Mathematical Society. Journal (GBR) **5509**
London Mathematical Society. Proceedings (GBR) **5510**
Macroeconomic Dynamics (GBR) **1720**
Marine Biological Association of the United Kingdom. Journal (GBR) **688**
Mathematical Structures in Computer Science (GBR) **5554**
Meteorological Applications (GBR) **6390**
Microscopy and Microanalysis (USA) **900**
Modern Asian Studies (GBR) **556**
Modern Intellectual History (GBR) **5228**
Mycological Research (GBR) **803**
N T Q. New Theatre Quarterly (GBR) **8474**
Natural Language Engineering (GBR) **2509**
Netherlands International Law Review (NLD) **4936**
Netherlands Yearbook of International Law (NLD) **4936**
Neuron Glia Biology (Online) (GBR) **6167**
New Testament Studies (GBR) **7666**
Nordic Journal of Linguistics (GBR) **5155**
Organised Sound (GBR) **6603**
Oryx (GBR) **959**
P S: Political Science & Politics (GBR) **7163**
Palliative & Supportive Care (USA) **5692**
Parasitology (Cambridge) (GBR) **5824**
Perspectives on Politics (GBR) **7165**
Philosophy (GBR) **6942**
Phonology (GBR) **5161**
Plainsong & Medieval Music (GBR) **6606**
Polar Record (GBR) **4024**
Politics & Gender (GBR) **7170**
Popular Music (GBR) **6607**
Probability in the Engineering and Informational Sciences (GBR) **3233**
Psychological Medicine (GBR) **6178**
Psychophysiology (GBR) **6179**
Quarterly Reviews of Biophysics (GBR) **754**
ReCall (GBR) **2469**
Religious Studies (GBR) **7676**
Review of International Studies (GBR) **7262**
Reviews in Clinical Gerontology (GBR) **4054**
Robotica (GBR) **2586**
Royal Asiatic Society. Journal (GBR) **560**
Royal Historical Society. Transactions (GBR) **4260**
Rural History (GBR) **4260**
Science in Context (GBR) **7909**
Scottish Journal of Theology (GBR) **7680**
Social Anthropology (GBR) **355**
Social Philosophy and Policy (GBR) **6952**
Social Policy and Society (GBR) **8133**
Sociology (GBR) **8138**
Studies in American Political Development (GBR) **7186**
Studies in Second Language Acquisition (GBR) **5183**
Systematics and Biodiversity (GBR) **707**
Tempo (London, 1939) (GBR) **6622**
Theatre Research International (GBR) **8483**
Theatre Survey (GBR) **8483**
Theory and Practice of Logic Programming (GBR) **2510**
Twentieth Century Music (GBR) **6625**
University of London. School of Oriental and African Studies. Bulletin (GBR) **4480**
Urban History (GBR) **4276**
Utilitas (GBR) **6959**
Victorian Literature and Culture (GBR) **5395**
Visual Neuroscience (GBR) **6189**
World Trade Review (GBR) **1588**
Zygote (GBR) **879**

CanWest Interactive Inc., FPInfomart 1450 Don Mills Rd, Toronto, ON M3B 2X7, Canada TEL 416-442-2121, 800-661-7678, FAX 416-442-2968, Helpdesk@canwest.com, http://www.fpinfomart.ca
Les Affaires (CAN) **1306**
Calgary Herald (CAN) **3806**
Canada. Statistics Canada. Inter-Corporate Ownership (CAN) **1426**
Canadian Forest Industries (CAN) **3710**
Canadian Mining Journal (CAN) **6459**
Canadian Underwriter (CAN) **4498**
Le Devoir (CAN) **3808**
Ecoweek.ca (CAN) **3478**
Financial Post Directory of Directors (CAN) **1746**
Gazette (Montreal) (CAN) **3810**
Maclean's (CAN) **3812**
Nickle's New Technology Magazine (CAN) **6780**
The Northern Miner (CAN) **6475**
Pulp & Paper Canada (CAN) **6737**

CEDOCAR (Subsidiary of: Ministere de la Defense Nationale) 9 Boulevard Liedot, Angouleme 16021, France TEL 33-5-45371963, FAX 33-5-45371916, clt08@cedocar.dga.defense.gouv.fr, http://www.cedocar.defense.gouv.fr
Alloys Index (USA) **6338**
Applied Spectroscopy (USA) **2098**
Computer & Control Abstracts (GBR) **2442**
Electrical & Electronics Abstracts (GBR) **3229**
Key Abstracts - Business Automation (GBR) **2443**
Metals Abstracts (USA) **6340**
Physics Abstracts (GBR) **7048**

Chadwyck-Healey Inc. (Subsidiary of: ProQuest LLC (Ann Arbor)) 789 E Eisenhower Pkwy, Ann Arbor, MI 48106-1346 TEL 800-521-0600, info@proquest.com, http://www.proquest.com/en-US/products/brands/pl_ch.shtml
A M E Church Review (USA) **7743**
A N Q: A Quarterly Journal of Short Articles, Notes and Reviews (USA) **5248**
A R S C Journal (USA) **8151**
A S E A N Economic Bulletin (SGP) **1055**
A T Q (USA) **5248**
The Accounting Review (USA) **1278**
Acoustic Guitar (USA) **6542**
Acta Classica (ZAF) **2229**
Adolescence (USA) **2143**
Aegyptus (ITA) **371**
Aevum (ITA) **5091**
Affilia (USA) **8024**
Africa (GBR) **4172**
Africa Today (USA) **7102**
African American Review (USA) **3516**
African Arts (USA) **464**
African Business (GBR) **1589**
African Journal of Legal Studies (CAN) **4611**
Afro-Hispanic Review (USA) **3517**
Agricultural History (USA) **83**
Ahfad Journal (SDN) **8893**
American Behavioral Scientist (USA) **7946**
American Choral Review (USA) **6543**
American Cinematographer (USA) **6489**
American Drama (USA) **8465**
American Imago (USA) **6121**
American Indian Quarterly (USA) **6634**
American Jewish History (USA) **7718**
American Journal of Community Psychology (USA) **8086**
The American Journal of Psychoanalysis (USA) **7333**
American Journal of Psychology (USA) **7333**
The American Journal of Semiotics (USA) **4442**
American Literary History (USA) **5252**
American Music (USA) **6544**
American Music Teacher (USA) **6544**
American Musical Instrument Society. Journal (USA) **6544**
American Musicological Society. Journal (USA) **6544**
American Poetry Review (USA) **5416**
American Quarterly (USA) **4442**
American Record Guide (USA) **6544**
American Recorder (USA) **6544**
American Scholar (USA) **5206**
American String Teacher (USA) **6544**
American Theatre (USA) **8465**
Anales Cervantinos (ESP) **5093**
Analyse & Kritik (DEU) **7947**
AnMal Electronica (ESP) *see* Analecta Malacitana. **5093**
Annual Organ Handbook (USA) **6545**
Annual Review of Jazz Studies (USA) **6545**
Anthropologica (CAN) **325**
Anthropological Quarterly (USA) **325**
Antioch Review (USA) **5206**
Anuario de Estudios Americanos (ESP) **7947**
Anuario de Estudios Medievales (ESP) **4199**
Anuario Filosofico (ESP) **6904**
Anuario Musical (ESP) **6545**
Applied Linguistics (GBR) **5095**
Arabica (NLD) **542**
Arbeiten aus Anglistik und Amerikanistik (DEU) **5256**
Arcadia (DEU) **5256**
Archeologia Medievale (ITA) **379**
Archives (GBR) **4200**
Archivo Espanol de Arqueologia (ESP) **380**
Archivo Espanol de Arte (ESP) **467**
Archivum Historicum Societatis Iesu (ITA) **7784**
Arethusa (USA) **2230**
Arizona Quarterly (USA) **5207**
Ars Lyrica (BEL) **6546**
The Art Bulletin (USA) **468**
Art Journal (USA) **470**
Arthuriana (USA) **4201**
Arts Education Policy Review (USA) **475**
Asian Affairs: An American Review (USA) **7222**
Asian Music (USA) **6546**
Asian Theatre Journal (USA) **8466**
Attitude: The Dancers' Magazine (USA) **2682**
Australasian Drama Studies (AUS) **8466**
Australasian Journal of Philosophy (GBR) **6906**
Australian Bureau of Agricultural and Resource Economics. Australian Commodities (AUS) **194**
The Australian Journal of Anthropology (AUS) **330**
Australian Music Research (AUS) **6546**
Bandwagon (USA) **8466**
Bass Player (USA) **6548**
Bayreuth African Studies Series (DEU) **3522**
Billboard.com (USA) *see* Billboard (New York). **6549**
Biography (Honolulu) (USA) **640**
Black Camera (USA) **6490**
The Black Collegian (USA) **6693**
Black Collegian Online (USA) **6693**
Black Enterprise.com (USA) *see* Black Enterprise. **1068**
Black History Bulletin (USA) **3522**
Black Issues Book Review (USA) **3522**
Black Masks (USA) **8467**
Black Renaissance (USA) **3523**
Black Scholar (USA) **3523**
The British Journal for the Philosophy of Science (GBR) **7842**
British Journal of Aesthetics (GBR) **6908**
The British Journal of Criminology (GBR) **2645**
British Journal of Psychology (GBR) **7342**
The British Journal of Social Work (GBR) **8028**
Bulletin of Hispanic Studies (Online Edition, Liverpool, 2002) (GBR) **5267**
Bulletin of Spanish Studies (GBR) **5267**
Bulletin of the Comediantes (USA) **5267**
Bulletin of the History of Medicine (USA) **5589**
Business History Review (USA) **1072**
California Management Review (USA) **1732**
Callaloo (USA) **5269**
Cambridge Journal of Economics (GBR) **1079**
The Cambridge Quarterly (GBR) **5269**
Canadian Journal for Traditional Music (CAN) **6554**
Canadian Journal of Film Studies (CAN) **6492**
Canadian Journal of History (CAN) **4134**
Canadian Journal of Philosophy (CAN) **6909**
Canadian Journal of Philosophy. Supplementary Volume Series (CAN) **6909**
Canadian Literature (CAN) **5270**
Canadian Music Educator (CAN) **6554**
Canadian Musician (CAN) **6554**
Caribbean Quarterly (JAM) **5210**
Central European History (GBR) **4209**
Challenge (Atlanta) (USA) **3526**
Chicago Review (USA) **5273**
Children's Literature (Baltimore) (USA) **5273**
Choral Journal (USA) **6555**
Christianity and Literature (USA) **5210**
Church History (USA) **7633**
Cineaste (USA) **6493**
Cinema Journal (USA) **6493**
Classical Antiquity (USA) **2232**
Classical Bulletin (USA) **2232**
Classical World (USA) **2233**
Clio (Ft. Wayne) (USA) **4135**
Clues (USA) **5275**
College Composition and Communication (USA) **3055**
College English (USA) **3055**
College Literature (USA) **5276**
Colloquia Germanica (DEU) **5107**
Columbia Journalism Review (USA) **4573**
Commentary (USA) **7720**
Commonweal (USA) **5211**
Community Development Journal (GBR) **8034**
Comparative Drama (USA) **5277**
Comparative Literature (USA) **5277**
Comparative Political Studies (USA) **7117**
Configurations (USA) **5277**
Conflict Resolution Quarterly (USA) **7348**
Confrontation (USA) **5277**
Conradiana (USA) **5278**
The Contemporary Review (GBR) **5212**
Contributions to Music Education (USA) **6559**
Contributions to Political Economy (GBR) **1448**
Crime, Law and Social Change (NLD) **2648**
Criminal Justice Ethics (USA) **6912**
The Crisis (USA) **3528**
Critical Inquiry (USA) **5212**
Critical Review (Columbus) (USA) **5212**
Critical Sociology (GBR) **5212**
Criticism (USA) **5280**
Critique (Washington) (USA) **5280**
Current History (USA) **7229**
Current Musicology (USA) **6560**
D H Lawrence Review (USA) **5282**
Daedalus (USA) **4449**
Dance Chronicle (USA) **2683**
Dance Research Journal (USA) **2684**
Dance Teacher (USA) **2685**
DanceView (USA) **2685**
Deutsche Vierteljahrsschrift fuer Literaturwissenschaft und Geistesgeschichte (DEU) **4449**
Deutsche Zeitschrift fuer Philosophie (DEU) **6913**
Diacritics (USA) **5284**
The Diapason (USA) **6561**
Dickens Quarterly (USA) **5284**
Dirty Linen (USA) **6562**
Discourse (Detroit, 1979) (USA) **4450**
Diverse Issues in Higher Education (USA) **2978**
Down Beat (USA) **6562**
E L H (USA) **5286**
Early American Literature (USA) **5287**
Early Music (GBR) **6563**
Early Music America (USA) **6563**
Economic Development and Cultural Change (USA) **1595**
Economic Inquiry (GBR) **1100**
Eighteenth-Century Studies (USA) **4138**
Emerita (ESP) **5114**
The Emily Dickinson Journal (USA) **5421**
eMusician.com (USA) *see* Electronic Musician. **6564**
The English Historical Review (GBR) **4217**
English Literature in Transition, 1880-1920 (USA) **5290**

English Studies in Africa (GBR) **4451**
Environment and Behavior (USA) **8100**
Erkenntnis (NLD) **6916**
Essays on Canadian Writing (CAN) **5291**
Estudios Geograficos (ESP) **4005**
Ethnohistory (USA) **337**
Ethnology (USA) **337**
Ethnomusicology (USA) **6565**
Etudes Anglaises (FRA) **5292**
Etudes de Linguistique Appliquee (FRA) **5117**
European Sociological Review (GBR) **8101**
The Explicator (USA) **5294**
Explorations in Economic History (USA) **1541**
Extrapolation (USA) **5442**
Fabula (DEU) **3617**
Fanfare (Tenafly) (USA) **6566**
The Faulkner Journal (USA) **5295**
Feminist Review (GBR) **8896**
Feminist Studies (USA) **8896**
Feministische Studien (DEU) **8897**
Film & History (USA) **6498**
Film Comment (USA) **6498**
Film Criticism (USA) **6498**
Film History (USA) **6499**
Film Quarterly (USA) **6499**
Film Score Monthly (USA) **6566**
Film Studies (GBR) **6499**
Filmmaker (USA) **6500**
Folk Music Journal (GBR) **6567**
Folklore (GBR) **3617**
Foreign Affairs (USA) **7235**
Forum for Modern Language Studies (GBR) **5120**
Forum Modernes Theater (DEU) **8470**
Framework (USA) **6501**
French Historical Studies (USA) **4222**
French History (GBR) **4222**
The Galpin Society Journal (GBR) **6569**
Geographische Zeitschrift (DEU) **4012**
German History (GBR) **4223**
The German Quarterly (USA) **5122**
The Germanic Review (USA) **5122**
Goldmine (USA) **6570**
Gothic Studies (GBR) **5301**
Greek, Roman and Byzantine Studies (USA) **2234**
Griot (USA) **3536**
Harper's (USA) **5219**
The Harvard Review (USA) **4454**
Health & Social Work (USA) **8044**
Health Policy and Planning (GBR) **7522**
The Hemingway Review (USA) **5305**
The Henry James Review (USA) **5305**
Hermes (DEU) **2235**
Hispania (ESP) **4227**
Hispanic Review (USA) **5125**
The Historian (East Lansing) (USA) **4143**
Historical Journal of Film, Radio and Television (GBR) **4143**
Historical Methods (USA) **8149**
History & Memory (USA) **4145**
History of Religions (USA) **7647**
History of Science (GBR) **7862**
History Today (GBR) **4230**
History Workshop Journal (GBR) **4146**
Hitchcock Annual (USA) **6502**
Holocaust and Genocide Studies (USA) **4230**
The Horn Call (USA) **6573**
Hotel Amerika (USA) **5219**
Howard Law Journal (USA) **4688**
Hudson Review (USA) **5220**
Human Biology (Detroit) (USA) **871**
Human Communication Research (USA) **7360**
Human Resource Management (USA) **1864**
Human Rights Quarterly (USA) **7208**
Huntington Library Quarterly (USA) **5307**
Hypatia (USA) **8898**
I A J R C Journal (CAN) **6574**
In Theory Only (USA) **6575**
The Independent (New York) (USA) **6503**
Indiana Review (USA) **5308**
Industrial and Labor Relations Review (USA) **1687**
Inter-American Music Review (USA) **6576**
International Bulletin of Missionary Research (USA) **7762**
International Council for Traditional Music. Bulletin (AUS) **6576**
International Journal for Philosophy of Religion (NLD) **7650**
International Journal of African Historical Studies (USA) **4175**
International Journal of Africana Studies (USA) **3540**
International Journal of Comparative Sociology (NLD) **8108**
International Journal of Music Education (GBR) **6577**
International Monetary Fund. Staff Papers (USA) **1358**
International Musician (USA) **6577**
International Review of African American Art (USA) **497**
Interview (New York) (USA) **3979**
The Iowa Review (USA) **5310**
Iranica Antiqua (BEL) **399**
Isegoria (ESP) **6927**
Italica (USA) **5311**
Ius Canonicum (ESP) **7652**
Jazziz (USA) **6579**
Jewish Social Studies (USA) **7724**
Journal for the Study of Judaism (NLD) **7725**
Journal of Abnormal Child Psychology (USA) **7368**
Journal of Adolescence (GBR) **2156**
Journal of African American History (USA) **3544**
Journal of African American Studies (USA) **6302**
Journal of American Culture (USA) **4459**
Journal of American Ethnic History (USA) **3544**
Journal of American Folklore (USA) **3619**
Journal of Arabic Literature (NLD) **5314**
Journal of Arts Management, Law, and Society (USA) **4700**
Journal of Asian and African Studies (GBR) **8112**
Journal of Asian Studies (USA) **553**
Journal of Biblical Literature (USA) **7654**
Journal of Black Psychology (USA) **7369**
Journal of Black Studies (USA) **7978**
Journal of Blacks in Higher Education (USA) **2989**
Journal of British Studies (USA) **4235**
Journal of Business Ethics (NLD) **1134**
Journal of Communication (USA) **8112**
Journal of Community Health (USA) **5647**
Journal of Contemporary Asia (GBR) **4184**
Journal of Contemporary Ethnography (USA) **8112**
Journal of Contemporary History (GBR) **4149**
Journal of Cultural Economics (USA) **1544**
Journal of Developing Societies (Online) (GBR) **7978**
Journal of Early Christian Studies (USA) **7802**
The Journal of Economic Education (USA) **1134**
Journal of Economics (AUT) **1135**
The Journal of Educational Research (USA) **2875**
Journal of European Studies (Chalfont Saint Giles) (GBR) **4235**
The Journal of Experimental Education (USA) **3067**
Journal of Family History (USA) **8113**
Journal of Family Issues (USA) **8113**
Journal of Film and Video (USA) **6505**
Journal of Folklore Research (USA) **3619**
The Journal of General Psychology (USA) **7374**
The Journal of Genetic Psychology (USA) **873**
Journal of Geography (USA) **4017**
Journal of Health Care for the Poor and Underserved (USA) **5649**
Journal of Historical Geography (GBR) **4017**
Journal of Indian Philosophy (NLD) **6928**
Journal of Individual Psychology (USA) **7375**
Journal of International Affairs (USA) **7248**
Journal of Jewish Music and Liturgy (USA) **6580**
Journal of Marketing (USA) **1825**
Journal of Marketing Research (USA) **1825**
Journal of Memory and Language (USA) **5134**
Journal of Military History (USA) **6429**
Journal of Modern Greek Studies (USA) **4236**
Journal of Modern Literature (USA) **5315**
Journal of Multicultural Counseling and Development (USA) **7376**
Journal of Music Teacher Education (Online) (USA) **6580**
Journal of Music Therapy (USA) **6111**
Journal of Negro Education (USA) **2877**
Journal of Phenomenological Psychology (NLD) **7378**
Journal of Philosophical Logic (NLD) **6929**
Journal of Policy Analysis and Management (USA) **7448**
Journal of Popular Culture (USA) **5315**
Journal of Popular Film and Television (USA) **6505**
The Journal of Psychology (USA) **7378**
Journal of Regulatory Economics (USA) **1546**
Journal of Religion in Africa (NLD) **7737**
The Journal of Religious Thought (USA) **7656**
Journal of Research in Music Education (USA) **6581**
Journal of Semitic Studies (GBR) **5135**
Journal of Singing (USA) **6581**
Journal of Social History (USA) **8115**
The Journal of Social Psychology (USA) **7380**
Journal of Southern African Studies (GBR) **7980**
Journal of the Economic and Social History of the Orient (NLD) **4322**
Journal of the History of Ideas (USA) **4461**
Journal of the History of Medicine and Allied Sciences (GBR) **5655**
Journal of the History of Philosophy (USA) **6930**
Journal of Theological Studies (GBR) **7657**
Journal of Urban History (USA) **4150**
The Journal of Value Inquiry (NLD) **6930**
The Journal of Voice (USA) **6082**
Journal of West Indian Literature (BRB) **5316**
Journal of Women's History (USA) **8900**
Jump Cut (USA) **6505**
Kant Studien (DEU) **6930**
The Kenyon Review (USA) **5425**
Keyboard (USA) **6582**
Klio (DEU) **2236**
Langston Hughes Review (USA) **5320**
Latin American Music Review (USA) **6584**
Latin American Research Review (USA) **7982**
Law and Literature (USA) **4713**
Law & Society Review (USA) **4714**
Legacy (Lincoln) (USA) **5320**
The Lion and the Unicorn (USA) **5323**
The Literary Review (USA) **5324**
Literature & History (GBR) **5325**
Literature and Medicine (USA) **5325**
Literature and Theology (GBR) **5325**
Literature Film Quarterly (USA) **6506**
Live Design (USA) **8473**
M E L U S (USA) **5328**
M I T Sloan Management Review (USA) **1773**
M L N (USA) **5149**
Marvels & Tales (USA) **3620**
Massachusetts Review (USA) **5227**
Medical History (GBR) **5669**
Medieval and Renaissance Drama in England (USA) **8473**
Medium Aevum (GBR) **5332**
Meridians (USA) **8901**
Method & Theory in the Study of Religion (NLD) **7663**
Michigan Quarterly Review (USA) **5227**
Middle East Journal (USA) **7252**
Millennium Film Journal (USA) **6507**
Millimeter (USA) **6507**
Milton Studies (USA) **5334**
Minnesota Review (USA) **5334**
The Mississippi Quarterly (USA) **5227**
Mix Magazine (USA) **8154**
Mnemosyne (NLD) **2237**
Modern Age (USA) **5228**
Modern Drummer (USA) **6588**
M F S Modern Fiction Studies (USA) **5335**
Modern Language Review (GBR) **5335**
Modernism/Modernity (USA) **4153**
Mosaic (Winnipeg, 1967) (CAN) **5336**
Music and Letters (GBR) **6589**
Music Clubs Magazine (USA) **6590**
Music Educators Journal (USA) **6590**
Music Library Association. Notes (USA) **5033**
Music Perception (USA) **6591**
Music Theory Spectrum (USA) **6592**
Music Therapy Perspectives (USA) **6592**
Musical Opinion (GBR) **6593**
The Musical Quarterly (USA) **6594**
Musical Times (GBR) **6594**
N W S A Journal (USA) **8901**
Nabokov Studies (USA) **5337**
The National Black Law Journal (USA) **4738**
National Political Science Review (USA) **7156**
Natural Language and Linguistic Theory (NLD) **5154**
Negro Educational Review (USA) **2890**
Neophilologus (NLD) **5339**
Neue Zeitschrift fuer Systematische Theologie und Religionsphilosophie (DEU) **7665**
New African (GBR) **1602**
The New England Quarterly (USA) **5340**
New England Review (USA) **5340**
New England Theatre Journal (USA) **8474**
New Literary History (USA) **5340**
New York History (USA) **4305**
The New Yorker (USA) **5230**
Nineteenth-Century Literature (Berkeley) (USA) **5342**
Nineteenth Century Music (USA) **6599**
The North American Review (USA) **5230**
Notes and Queries (GBR) **5343**
Nottingham Medieval Studies (BEL) **4249**
Novel: A Forum on Fiction (USA) **5344**
Novum Testamentum (NLD) **7666**
Numen (NLD) **7667**
O E C D Observer (FRA) **1504**
Obsidian III: Literature in the African Diaspora (USA) **5345**
Oceania (AUS) **350**
Opera - Canada (CAN) **6601**
Opera Journal (USA) **6602**
Opera News (USA) **6602**
The Opera Quarterly (GBR) **6602**
The Organ (GBR) **6602**
Orientalistische Literaturzeitung (DEU) **558**
Oxford Art Journal (GBR) **510**
Oxford Review of Economic Policy (GBR) **1158**
P N Review (GBR) **5429**
Pacific Affairs (CAN) **7257**
Pacific Historical Review (USA) **4307**
Papers on Language and Literature (USA) **5348**
The Paris Review (USA) **5349**
Parliamentary History (GBR) **4155**
Parnassus: Poetry in Review (USA) **5429**
Pastoral Music (USA) **6604**
Il Pensiero Politico (Florence) (ITA) **7164**
Performing Arts and Entertainment in Canada (CAN) **8475**
Performing Arts Resources (USA) **8476**
Persona y Derecho (ESP) **4757**
Perspectives of New Music (USA) **6605**
Perspectives on Political Science (USA) **7165**
Philological Quarterly (USA) **5160**
Philologus (DEU) **2239**
Philosophical Studies (NLD) **6941**
Philosophy and Literature (USA) **6942**
Philosophy East and West (USA) **6943**
Philosophy of Music Education Review (USA) **6605**
Philosophy of the Social Sciences (USA) **7992**
Philosophy Today (USA) **6944**
Phronesis (NLD) **6944**
Piano Today (USA) **6605**
Ploughshares (USA) **5352**
Poet Lore (USA) **5430**
Poetry (Chicago) (USA) **5430**
Policing (Bingley) (GBR) **2664**
Policy Review (USA) **7166**
Policy Sciences (NLD) **7166**
Policy Studies Journal (USA) **7167**
Political Research Quarterly (USA) **7169**
Popular Music & Society (GBR) **6607**
Population and Environment (USA) **7391**
Population Research and Policy Review (NLD) **7290**
Portuguese Studies (GBR) **5353**
Post Script (Commerce) (USA) **4470**
Prairie Schooner (USA) **5353**
Prooftexts (USA) **5354**
Psychology & Marketing (USA) **7398**
Psychology of Music (GBR) **6608**
Psychomusicology (CAN) **6608**
Publishing History (GBR) **7571**
Puppetry Journal (USA) **8477**
Al- Qantara (ESP) **5164**
R I L C E (ESP) **5165**
R S A Journal (GBR) **514**
R U S I Journal (GBR) **6442**
Raritan (USA) **5357**
Religious Education (USA) **7676**
Renaissance Drama (USA) **8477**
Renaissance Quarterly (USA) **5359**
Renaissance Studies (GBR) **4158**
Renascence (USA) **5359**
Representations (USA) **4472**
Research in African Literatures (USA) **5360**
Research in Phenomenology (NLD) **6947**
Review of African Political Economy (GBR) **7262**
The Review of Black Political Economy (USA) **1165**
The Review of Contemporary Fiction (USA) **5360**
The Review of English Studies (GBR) **5360**
Review of Financial Economics (GBR) **1166**
The Review of Higher Education (USA) **3000**
The Review of Metaphysics (USA) **6948**
The Review of Politics (GBR) **7178**
Revista de Filologia Espanola (ESP) **5167**
Revista de Filosofia (ESP) **6948**
Revista de Indias (ESP) **4311**
Revista Internacional de Sociologia (ESP) **8129**
Revue de Litterature Comparee (FRA) **5362**
Revue de Philologie, de Litterature et d'Histoire Anciennes (FRA) **2239**
Revue d'Histoire Moderne et Contemporaine (FRA) **4159**
Revue Francaise de Sociologie (FRA) **8129**
Rhetoric Society Quarterly (USA) **5362**
Rhetorica (USA) **5168**
Rinascimento (ITA) **4473**
Rock & Rap Confidential (USA) **6612**
Rolling Stone (USA) **6613**
Romanic Review (USA) **5364**
Romanische Forschungen (DEU) **5169**
Royal Anthropological Institute. Journal (GBR) **354**
Royal Musical Association. Journal (GBR) **6613**
Sacred Music (USA) **6614**
Salmagundi (USA) **4474**
Scandinavian Review (USA) **3563**
Scandinavian Studies (Provo) (USA) **5367**
The Scottish Historical Review (GBR) **4160**
Sefarad (ESP) **4325**
The Seventeenth Century (GBR) **5369**
Seventeenth - Century News (USA) **5369**
The Sewanee Review (USA) **5370**
Sex Roles (USA) **7407**
Shakespeare Quarterly (USA) **5370**
Shakespeare Studies (USA) **5370**
Sight and Sound (GBR) **6513**
Signs (USA) **8903**
Sing Out! (USA) **6616**
Slavonic and East European Review (GBR) **5373**
Small Axe (USA) **5239**
Social and Economic Studies (JAM) **8002**
Social Forces (USA) **8133**
Social Indicators Research (NLD) **8150**
Social Research (USA) **8003**
Social Science Quarterly (USA) **8004**
Social Security Bulletin (USA) **4523**
Social Service Review (USA) **8069**
The Social Studies (USA) **8005**
Social Theory and Practice (USA) **6952**
The Sociological Quarterly (USA) **8137**
The Sondheim Review (USA) **8479**
Southeast Asian Affairs (SGP) **7184**
Southern Cultures (USA) **4475**
Southern Literary Journal (USA) **5375**
Southern Quarterly (USA) **4476**
The Southern Review (USA) **5375**
Spectator (Los Angeles, 1987) (USA) **6513**
Stereo Review's Sound & Vision Online (USA) *see* Sound & Vision. **8155**
Strings (USA) **6620**
Studi Romani (ITA) **4162**
Studies in American Fiction (USA) **5380**
Studies in American Indian Literatures (USA) **5380**
Studies in English Literature 1500-1900 (USA) **5381**
Studies in Philology (USA) **5183**
Studies in Romanticism (USA) **5381**
Studies in the Literary Imagination (USA) **5382**
Studies in the Novel (USA) **5382**
Style (DeKalb) (USA) **5382**
Survival (Abingdon) (GBR) **7268**
Symploke (USA) **4477**
Symposium (USA) **5384**
Synthese (NLD) **6956**
T D & T (USA) **8480**
Teaching English in the Two-Year College (USA) **3004**
Teaching Music (USA) **6622**
Technology and Culture (USA) **8442**
Texas Studies in Literature and Language (USA) **5386**
Theatre Annual (USA) **8482**
Theatre History Studies (USA) **8482**
Theatre Journal (Baltimore) (USA) **8482**
Theatre Survey (GBR) **8483**
Theatre Topics (USA) **8483**
TheatreForum (USA) **8483**
Theological Studies (USA) **7689**
Theory and Decision (NLD) **8009**
Thomas Wolfe Review (USA) **5388**
T'oung Pao (NLD) **562**
Town Planning Review (GBR) **4428**
Trabajos de Prehistoria. Nueva Serie (ESP) **421**
The Tracker (USA) **6624**
TriQuarterly (USA) **5243**
Twentieth Century Literature (USA) **5391**
Unitarian Historical Society, London. Transactions (GBR) **7743**
University of Chicago Law Review (USA) **4803**

Update (Online) (USA) **6626**
Urban History Review (CAN) **4316**
Variety (USA) **8484**
The Velvet Light Trap (USA) **6516**
Viator (BEL) **4166**
Victorian Poetry (USA) **5437**
Victorian Studies (USA) **4481**
Vigiliae Christianae (NLD) **7692**
Virginia Quarterly Review (USA) **5244**
Visual Culture in Britain (GBR) **525**
Vivarium (NLD) **4277**
Western Folklore (USA) **3624**
The Western Journal of Black Studies (USA) **3572**
White Tops (USA) **8484**
Women and Music (USA) **6628**
World Literature Today (USA) **5400**
Yearbook for Traditional Music (USA) **6629**
Yearbook of English Studies (GBR) **5403**
The Year's Work in Critical and Cultural Theory (GBR) **4483**
Year's Work in Modern Language Studies (GBR) **5202**
Yeats Eliot Review (USA) **5438**
Youth & Society (USA) **2172**
Zeitschrift fuer Dialektologie und Linguistik (DEU) **5198**
Zeitschrift fuer Germanistische Linguistik (DEU) **5199**
Zeitschrift fuer Literaturwissenschaft und Linguistik (DEU) **5199**
Zeitschrift fuer Philosophische Forschung (DEU) **6962**
Zeitschrift fuer Religions- und Geistesgeschichte (NLD) **7697**

D I M D I/German Institute of Medical Documentation and Information
Weisshausstrasse 36-38a, Cologne D-50676, Germany TEL 49-221-47241, FAX 49-221-4724444, http://www.dimdi.de

Abstracts on Hygiene and Communicable Diseases (GBR) **5739**
AgBiotechNet (GBR) *see* AgBiotech News and Information. **712**
Agricultural Engineering Abstracts (GBR) **174**
Agroforestry Abstracts (Online) (GBR) **174**
Animal Breeding Abstracts (GBR) **174**
Biocontrol News and Information (GBR) **176**
Biological Abstracts (USA) **713**
Biological Abstracts - R R M (Online Edition) (USA) **713**
Bulletin of Entomological Research (GBR) **841**
Crop Physiology Abstracts (GBR) **178**
Dairy Science Abstracts (GBR) **179**
EMBASE (NLD) *see* Excerpta Medica. Abstract Journals. **715**
Excerpta Medica. Section 1: Anatomy, Anthropology, Embryology & Histology (NLD) **715**
Excerpta Medica. Section 10: Obstetrics and Gynecology (NLD) **5744**
Excerpta Medica. Section 11: Otorhinolaryngology (NLD) **5744**
Excerpta Medica. Section 12: Ophthalmology (NLD) **5744**
Excerpta Medica. Section 13: Dermatology and Venereology (NLD) **5744**
Excerpta Medica. Section 14: Radiology (NLD) **5744**
Excerpta Medica. Section 15: Chest Diseases, Thoracic Surgery and Tuberculosis (NLD) **5745**
Excerpta Medica. Section 16: Cancer (NLD) **5745**
Excerpta Medica. Section 17: Public Health, Social Medicine and Epidemiology (NLD) **7547**
Excerpta Medica. Section 18: Cardiovascular Diseases and Cardiovascular Surgery (NLD) **5745**
Excerpta Medica. Section 19: Rehabilitation and Physical Medicine (NLD) **5745**
Excerpta Medica. Section 2: Physiology (NLD) **5745**
Excerpta Medica. Section 20: Gerontology and Geriatrics (NLD) **4058**
Excerpta Medica. Section 21: Developmental Biology and Teratology (NLD) **715**
Excerpta Medica. Section 22: Human Genetics (NLD) **715**
Excerpta Medica. Section 23: Nuclear Medicine (NLD) **5745**
Excerpta Medica. Section 24: Anesthesiology (NLD) **5745**
Excerpta Medica. Section 25: Hematology (NLD) **5745**
Excerpta Medica. Section 26: Immunology, Serology and Transplantation (NLD) **5745**
Excerpta Medica. Section 27: Biophysics, Bio-Engineering and Medical Instrumentation (NLD) **715**
Excerpta Medica. Section 28: Urology and Nephrology (NLD) **5745**
Excerpta Medica. Section 29: Clinical and Experimental Biochemistry (NLD) **715**
Excerpta Medica. Section 3: Endocrinology (NLD) **5745**
Excerpta Medica. Section 30: Clinical and Experimental Pharmacology (NLD) **6889**
Excerpta Medica. Section 31: Arthritis and Rheumatism (NLD) **5745**
Excerpta Medica. Section 32: Psychiatry (NLD) **5746**
Excerpta Medica. Section 33: Orthopedic Surgery (NLD) **5746**
Excerpta Medica. Section 35: Occupational Health and Industrial Medicine (NLD) **5746**
Excerpta Medica. Section 36: Health Policy, Economics and Management (NLD) **4113**
Excerpta Medica. Section 4: Microbiology: Bacteriology, Mycology, Parasitology and Virology (NLD) **715**
Excerpta Medica. Section 40: Drug Dependence, Alcohol Abuse and Alcoholism (NLD) **2701**
Excerpta Medica. Section 46: Environmental Health and Pollution Control (NLD) **3479**
Excerpta Medica. Section 48: Gastroenterology (NLD) **5746**
Excerpta Medica. Section 49: Forensic Science Abstracts (NLD) **5746**
Excerpta Medica. Section 5: General Pathology and Pathological Anatomy (NLD) **716**
Excerpta Medica. Section 50: Epilepsy Abstracts (NLD) **5746**
Excerpta Medica. Section 52: Toxicology (NLD) **3479**
Excerpta Medica. Section 6: Internal Medicine (NLD) **5746**
Excerpta Medica. Section 7: Pediatrics and Pediatric Surgery (NLD) **5746**
Excerpta Medica. Section 8: Neurology and Neurosurgery (NLD) **5746**
Excerpta Medica. Section 9: Surgery (NLD) **5746**
Field Crop Abstracts (GBR) **180**
Food Science and Technology Abstracts (GBR) **3669**
Forest Products Abstracts (GBR) **3709**
Forestry Abstracts (GBR) **3709**
Grasslands and Forage Abstracts (GBR) **181**
Helminthological Abstracts (GBR) **716**
Horticultural Science Abstracts (GBR) **3755**
Index of Fungi (GBR) **716**
Index Veterinarius (GBR) **8816**
Informationsdienst Krankenhauswesen (DEU) **4102**
International Biodeterioration and Biodegradation (GBR) **765**
International Pharmaceutical Abstracts (USA) **6889**
Irrigation and Drainage Abstracts (GBR) **182**
Leisure Tourism Database (GBR) *see* Leisure, Recreation and Tourism Abstracts. **8779**
Maize Abstracts Online (GBR) **183**
Nematological Abstracts (GBR) **717**
Nutrition Abstracts and Reviews. Series A: Human and Experimental (GBR) **6671**
Nutrition Abstracts and Reviews. Series B: Livestock Feeds and Feeding (GBR) **184**
Ornamental Horticulture (GBR) **3755**
Pig News & Information (GBR) **184**
Plant Breeding Abstracts (GBR) **185**
Plant Growth Regulator Abstracts (GBR) **185**
Potato Abstracts (GBR) **185**
Poultry Abstracts (GBR) **185**
Protozoological Abstracts (GBR) **718**
PsycINFO (USA) **7417**
Review of Agricultural Entomology (GBR) **185**
Review of Medical and Veterinary Entomology (GBR) **5750**
Review of Medical and Veterinary Mycology (GBR) **720**
Review of Plant Pathology (GBR) **720**
Rice Abstracts (GBR) **186**
Rural Development Abstracts (GBR) **4436**
Salud Publica de Mexico (MEX) **7540**
Science Citation Index (USA) **7938**
Seed Abstracts (GBR) **720**
Social Sciences Citation Index (USA) **8021**
Sociological Abstracts (USA) **8150**
Soils and Fertilizers (GBR) **186**
Soybean Abstracts (Online) (GBR) **720**
Tropical Diseases Bulletin (GBR) **5751**
Veterinary Science Database (GBR) *see* Veterinary Bulletin. **8816**
Weed Abstracts (GBR) **190**
Wheat, Barley and Triticale Abstracts (GBR) **190**
World Agricultural Economics and Rural Sociology Abstracts (GBR) **190**

DataStar (Subsidiary of: The Dialog Corporation)
11000 Regency Pkwy, Ste 10, Cary, NC 27511 TEL 919-462-8600, 800-334-2564, FAX 919-468-9890 Data Center, Laupenstrasse 18a, Berne 38008, Switzerland TEL 41-31-3849511, FAX 43-31-3849675, customer@dialog.com, http://www.datastarweb.com/

A B B Review (CHE) **3293**
A B C Europ Production (DEU) **1551**
A B I - INFORM (USA) **1199**
A H F S Drug Information (USA) **6817**
A M E D (GBR) **316**
Abstracts in New Technologies and Engineering (USA) **8446**
Adhesives Abstracts (GBR) **2085**
Agricultural Supply Industry (GBR) **85**
Agrow (GBR) **89**
AIDS Weekly (USA) **5809**
Air Safety Week (Online) (USA) **44**
Airline Business (GBR) **8536**
Alcoholism & Drug Abuse Weekly (USA) **2691**
Alloys Index (USA) **6338**
American Banker (USA) **1307**
American Doctoral Dissertations (USA) **2966**
Analytic Separations News (USA) **2097**
Analytical Abstracts Online (GBR) *see* Analytical Abstracts. **2085**
Animal Pharm (GBR) **8792**
Asset Securitization Report (USA) **1610**
Audiotex Update (USA) **2349**
The Autoparts Report (USA) **8566**
B D I Deutschland Liefert (DEU) **1553**
B T Today (GBR) **2365**
Battery & E V Technology News (USA) **3296**
Biological Abstracts (USA) **713**
Biological Abstracts - R R M (Online Edition) (USA) **713**
Biotech Business (USA) **759**
Blood Weekly (USA) **5934**
The Boston Business Journal (USA) **1068**
The Business Journal (Minneapolis - St. Paul) (USA) **1073**
Business Travel News (USA) **8689**
Cancer Weekly (USA) **6014**
Chemical Engineering and Biotechnology Abstracts (Online) (DEU) **3229**
Chemical Hazards in Industry (GBR) **6690**
Chemical Safety NewsBase (GBR) **6690**
Clinica (GBR) **5595**
Communications Daily (USA) **2378**
The Composites and Adhesives Newsletter (USA) **7091**
Computer & Control Abstracts (GBR) **2442**
Computer Database (USA) **2529**
Computer Fraud & Security (GBR) **2512**
Computer Protocols (USA) **2496**
Country Forecasts (Syracuse) (USA) **1088**
Cumulative Index to Nursing & Allied Health Literature (USA) **5743**
The Cyprus Review (CYP) **7958**
Development Business (New York, 1978) (USA) **1593**
Dissertation Abstracts International. Section A: Humanities and Social Sciences (USA) **4484**
Dissertation Abstracts International. Section B: Physical Sciences and Engineering (USA) **7937**
Dissertation Abstracts International. Section C: Worldwide (USA) **4484**
Dissertation Abstracts on Disc (USA) **4484**
Drug G M P Report (USA) **6835**
Electrical & Electronics Abstracts (GBR) **3229**
EMBASE (NLD) *see* Excerpta Medica. Abstract Journals. **715**
The Energy Daily (USA) **3130**
Environment Abstracts (USA) **2634**
Environment Abstracts Annual (USA) **3478**
EURALex (GBR) **6838**
Excerpta Medica. Section 1: Anatomy, Anthropology, Embryology & Histology (NLD) **715**
Excerpta Medica. Section 10: Obstetrics and Gynecology (NLD) **5744**
Excerpta Medica. Section 11: Otorhinolaryngology (NLD) **5744**
Excerpta Medica. Section 12: Ophthalmology (NLD) **5744**
Excerpta Medica. Section 13: Dermatology and Venereology (NLD) **5744**
Excerpta Medica. Section 14: Radiology (NLD) **5744**
Excerpta Medica. Section 15: Chest Diseases, Thoracic Surgery and Tuberculosis (NLD) **5745**
Excerpta Medica. Section 16: Cancer (NLD) **5745**
Excerpta Medica. Section 17: Public Health, Social Medicine and Epidemiology (NLD) **7547**
Excerpta Medica. Section 18: Cardiovascular Diseases and Cardiovascular Surgery (NLD) **5745**
Excerpta Medica. Section 19: Rehabilitation and Physical Medicine (NLD) **5745**
Excerpta Medica. Section 2: Physiology (NLD) **5745**
Excerpta Medica. Section 20: Gerontology and Geriatrics (NLD) **4058**
Excerpta Medica. Section 21: Developmental Biology and Teratology (NLD) **715**
Excerpta Medica. Section 22: Human Genetics (NLD) **715**
Excerpta Medica. Section 23: Nuclear Medicine (NLD) **5745**
Excerpta Medica. Section 24: Anesthesiology (NLD) **5745**
Excerpta Medica. Section 25: Hematology (NLD) **5745**
Excerpta Medica. Section 26: Immunology, Serology and Transplantation (NLD) **5745**
Excerpta Medica. Section 27: Biophysics, Bio-Engineering and Medical Instrumentation (NLD) **715**
Excerpta Medica. Section 28: Urology and Nephrology (NLD) **5745**
Excerpta Medica. Section 29: Clinical and Experimental Biochemistry (NLD) **715**
Excerpta Medica. Section 3: Endocrinology (NLD) **5745**
Excerpta Medica. Section 30: Clinical and Experimental Pharmacology (NLD) **6889**
Excerpta Medica. Section 31: Arthritis and Rheumatism (NLD) **5745**
Excerpta Medica. Section 32: Psychiatry (NLD) **5746**
Excerpta Medica. Section 33: Orthopedic Surgery (NLD) **5746**
Excerpta Medica. Section 35: Occupational Health and Industrial Medicine (NLD) **5746**
Excerpta Medica. Section 36: Health Policy, Economics and Management (NLD) **4113**
Excerpta Medica. Section 4: Microbiology: Bacteriology, Mycology, Parasitology and Virology (NLD) **715**
Excerpta Medica. Section 40: Drug Dependence, Alcohol Abuse and Alcoholism (NLD) **2701**
Excerpta Medica. Section 46: Environmental Health and Pollution Control (NLD) **3479**
Excerpta Medica. Section 48: Gastroenterology (NLD) **5746**
Excerpta Medica. Section 49: Forensic Science Abstracts (NLD) **5746**
Excerpta Medica. Section 5: General Pathology and Pathological Anatomy (NLD) **716**
Excerpta Medica. Section 50: Epilepsy Abstracts (NLD) **5746**
Excerpta Medica. Section 52: Toxicology (NLD) **3479**
Excerpta Medica. Section 6: Internal Medicine (NLD) **5746**
Excerpta Medica. Section 7: Pediatrics and Pediatric Surgery (NLD) **5746**
Excerpta Medica. Section 8: Neurology and Neurosurgery (NLD) **5746**
Excerpta Medica. Section 9: Surgery (NLD) **5746**
Financial Regulation International (GBR) **1345**
Firmendatenbank Ostdeutschland (DEU) **1885**
Flight International (GBR) **55**
Food Chemical News (USA) **3638**
Food Science and Technology Abstracts (GBR) **3669**
Foreign Policy Bulletin (GBR) **7235**
G P (GBR) **5617**
Gale Directory of Databases (USA) **2530**
Generic Line (USA) **6844**
Global Environmental Change (GBR) **3434**
The Gray Sheet (USA) **5620**
Handbuch der Grossunternehmen (DEU) **1887**
Harvard Business Review (USA) **1117**
Haznews (GBR) **3507**
Health News Daily (USA) **5625**
Holland Exports (NLD) **1568**
I E E E International S O I Conference Proceedings (USA) **3312**
Imaging Abstracts (GBR) **6979**
Improved Recovery Week (USA) **3137**
Industrial Health & Hazards Update (USA) **6678**
Industrial Specialties News (CAN) **6465**
Information Management Report (GBR) **2545**
Inspec (GBR) **3232**
International Country Risk Guide (USA) **1492**
International Pharmaceutical Abstracts (USA) **6889**
International Product Alert (USA) **1822**
International Tax Report (GBR) **1930**
Key Abstracts - Business Automation (GBR) **2443**
L A N Product News (USA) **2500**
Laboratory Hazards Bulletin (GBR) **6690**
Mainframe Computing (USA) **2431**
Management and Marketing Abstracts (GBR) **1251**
Market: Africa - Mid-East (USA) **1577**
Market: Asia Pacific (USA) **1577**
Market: Europe (USA) **1577**
Martindale: the Complete Drug Reference (GBR) **6860**
Materials Business File (USA) **6340**
Medeconomics (GBR) **5666**
Membrane and Separation Technology News (USA) **768**
Metals Abstracts (USA) **6340**
Meyler's Side Effects of Drugs (NLD) **6861**
Mittelstaendische Unternehmen (DEU) **1899**
Modem User News (USA) **2501**
N T I S Bibliographic Database (USA) **7938**
Nederlands A B C (NLD) **2019**
Networks Update (USA) **2502**
New Product Focus (GBR) **6863**
North Sea Rig Forecast (GBR) **3143**
Octane Week (USA) **6782**
Online Libraries and Microcomputers (USA) **5063**
Online Newsletter (USA) **2565**
P C Business Products (USA) **1393**
The P R S Group. Country Reports: Algeria (USA) **1505**
The P R S Group. Country Reports: Argentina (USA) **1505**
The P R S Group. Country Reports: Australia (USA) **1505**
The P R S Group. Country Reports: Austria (USA) **1505**
The P R S Group. Country Reports: Belgium (USA) **1505**
The P R S Group. Country Reports: Bolivia (USA) **1506**
The P R S Group. Country Reports: Brazil (USA) **1506**
The P R S Group. Country Reports: Bulgaria (USA) **1506**
The P R S Group. Country Reports: Cameroon (USA) **1506**
The P R S Group. Country Reports: Canada (USA) **1506**
The P R S Group. Country Reports: Chile (USA) **1506**
The P R S Group. Country Reports: China (USA) **1506**
The P R S Group. Country Reports: Colombia (USA) **1506**
The P R S Group. Country Reports: Congo (Kinshasa) (USA) **1506**
The P R S Group. Country Reports: Costa Rica (USA) **1506**
The P R S Group. Country Reports: Cote d'Ivoire (USA) **1506**
The P R S Group. Country Reports: Czech Republic (USA) **1506**
The P R S Group. Country Reports: Denmark (USA) **1506**
The P R S Group. Country Reports: Dominican Republic (USA) **1506**
The P R S Group. Country Reports: Ecuador (USA) **1506**
The P R S Group. Country Reports: Egypt (USA) **1506**
The P R S Group. Country Reports: El Salvador (USA) **1506**

Online Service

Dangdai Yuyanxue (CHN) **5110**
Dangdai Zuojia Pinglun (CHN) **5282**
Dangshi Bolan (CHN) **7128**
Dangshi Tiandi (CHN) **7128**
Dangshi Yuye (CHN) **3590**
Daodan yu Hangtian Yunzai Jishu (CHN) **52**
Daode yu Wenming (CHN) **7128**
Daqing Shehui Kexue (CHN) **7958**
Daqing Shiyou Xueyuan Xuebao (CHN) **6766**
Datong Yixue Zhuanke Xuexiao Xuebao (CHN) **5603**
Dawutai (CHN) **8468**
Daxue Huaxue (CHN) **2059**
Daxue Tushuguan Xuebao (CHN) **5005**
Daxue Wuli (CHN) **7010**
Dazhong Dianying (CHN) **6495**
Daziran Tansuo (CHN) **7849**
Deyu Xuexi (CHN) **5111**
Di-Er Jun-Yi Daxue Xuebao (CHN) **5604**
Di-San Junyi Daxue Xuebao (CHN) **5604**
Di Si Junyi Daxue Xuebao (CHN) **5604**
Di Yi Junyi Daxue Xuebao (CHN) **5604**
Dialog (RUS) **7130**
Dian Huaxue (CHN) **2113**
Diance yu Yibiao (CHN) **4486**
Dianchi (Changsha) (CHN) **3127**
Diandu yu Huanbao (CHN) **3485**
Diandu yu Jingshi (CHN) **2113**
Diandu yu Tushi (CHN) **2113**
Diangong Dianneng Xinjishu (CHN) **3299**
Diangong Jishu Xuebao (CHN) **3300**
Diangong Jishu Zazhi (CHN) **3092**
Dianji yu Kongzhi Xuebao (CHN) **3300**
Dianli Kexue yu Jishu Xuebao (CHN) **7850**
Dianli Xitong Baohu yu Kongzhi (CHN) **3300**
Dianli Xitong Jiqi Zidong Huaxue Bao (CHN) **7850**
Dianli Xitong Zidonghua (CHN) **3156**
Dianli Xuebao (CHN) **3156**
Dianli Zidonghua Shebei (CHN) **3300**
Diannao Jishu (CHN) **2416**
Diannao Kaifa yu Yingyong (CHN) **2416**
Dianpo Kexue Xuebao (CHN) **2358**
Dianqi Chuandong (CHN) **3300**
Dianwang Jishu (CHN) **3300**
Dianxin Jishu (CHN) **2367**
Dianxin Kexue (CHN) **2319**
Dianying Chuangzuo (CHN) **6496**
Dianying Yishu (CHN) **6496**
Dianyuan Jishu (CHN) **3300**
Dianzi Celiang yu Yiqi Xuebao (CHN) **6401**
Dianzi Jishu (CHN) **3092**
Dianzi Jishu Yingyong (CHN) **3092**
Dianzi Keji Daxue Xuebao (CHN) **8420**
Dianzi Xianwei Xuebao (CHN) **7010**
Dianzi Xuebao (CHN) **3092**
Dianzi yu Zidonghua (CHN) **3093**
Dianzi Yuanjian yu Cailiao (CHN) **3093**
Dianzi Zhishi Chanquan (CHN) **6749**
Dicengxue Zazhi (CHN) **2731**
Difangbing Tongbao (CHN) **5812**
Dili Kexue (CHN) **4004**
Dili Kexue Jinzhan (CHN) **4004**
Dili Xuebao (CHN) **4004**
Dili Yanjiu (CHN) **4004**
Dili yu Dili Xinxi Kexue (CHN) **2731**
Diqiu Huaxue (CHN) **2731**
Diqiu Kexue (CHN) **2705**
Diqiu Kexue Jinzhan (CHN) **2705**
Diqiu Wuli Xuebao (CHN) **2779**
Diqiu Wulixue Jinzhan (CHN) **2705**
Diqiu Xuebao (CHN) **2731**
Disiji Yanjiu (CHN) **2731**
Distance Education Journal (CHN) **2842**
Ditu (CHN) **4004**
Diwen Wuli Xuebao (CHN) **7054**
Dixue Qianyuan (CHN) **2705**
Diya Dianqi (CHN) **3300**
Dizhen (CHN) **2779**
Dizhen Dici Guance yu Yanjiu (CHN) **2779**
Dizhen Dizhi (CHN) **2779**
Dizhen Gongcheng yu Gongcheng Zhendong (CHN) **2779**
Dizhen Xuebao (CHN) **2780**
Dizhen Yanjiu (CHN) **2731**
Dizhi Diqiu Huaxue (CHN) **2731**
Dizhi Jishu Jingji Guanli (CHN) **1092**
Dizhi Keji Qingbao (CHN) **2731**
Dizhi Kexue (CHN) **2731**
Dizhi Tongbao (CHN) **2732**
Dizhi yu Kantan (CHN) **2732**
Dizhi Zaihai yu Huanjing Baohu (CHN) **3414**
Dizhi Zhaokuang Luncong (CHN) **2732**
Dongbei Daxue Xuebao (Shehui Kexue Ban) (CHN) **7959**
Dongbei Daxue Xuebao (Ziran Kexue Ban) (CHN) **8420**
Dongbei Dianli Xueyuan Xuebao (CHN) **3156**
Dongbei Linye Daxue Xuebao (CHN) **3687**
Dongbei Nongye Daxue Xuebao (CHN) **105**
Dongbei Shi-Daxuebao (Zhexue Shehui Kexue Ban) (CHN) **7960**
Dongbei Shi-Daxuebao (Ziran Kexue Ban) (CHN) **7851**
Donghai Haiyang (CHN) **2803**
Donghua Daxue Xuebao (Ziran Ban) (CHN) **7851**
Donghua Ligong Xueyuan Xuebao (CHN) **2732**
Dongjiang Xuekan (Zhexue Shehui Kexue Ban) (CHN) **7960**
Dongli Gongcheng (CHN) **3376**
Dongnan Daxue Xuebao (Yixue Ban) (CHN) **5606**
Dongnan Daxue Xuebao (Ziran Kexue Ban) (CHN) **7851**
Dongnan Wenhua (CHN) **391**
Dongnan Xueshu (CHN) **7960**
Dongnanya (CHN) **548**
Dongnanya Yanjiu (CHN) **548**
Dongnanya Zongheng (CHN) **7960**
Dongwu Fenlei Xuebao (CHN) **940**
Dongwu Yixue Jinzhan (CHN) **8796**
Dongwuxue Yanjiu (CHN) **940**
Dongwuxue Zazhi (CHN) **940**
Dongyue Luncong (CHN) **7960**
Druzhba Narodov (RUS) **5214**
Duanya Jishu (CHN) **6310**
Dufu Yanjiu Xuekan (CHN) **5214**
Duilian - Minjian Duilian Gushi (CHN) **5286**
Duiwai Jingmao Shiwu (CHN) **1562**
Dunhuang Yanjiu (CHN) **391**
Dushu (CHN) **5286**
East China Normal University. Journal. (Social Science Edition) (CHN) **7960**
Ekonomika i Matematicheskie Metody (RUS) **1103**
Electricity (CHN) **3157**
Eluosi Wenyi (CHN) **5289**
Erke Yaoxue Zazhi (CHN) **6091**
Ertong Dashijie (CHN) **2187**
Etnograficheskoe Obozrenie (RUS) **338**
Eyu Xuexi (CHN) **5118**
Ezhenedel'nyi Zhurnal (Online Edition) (RUS) **3935**
Faguang Xuebao (CHN) **7075**
Faguo Yanjiu (CHN) **7964**
Falu Kexue (CHN) **4671**
Falu Shiyong (CHN) **4671**
Falu yu Shenghuo (CHN) **4671**
Fangshe Mianyixue Zazhi (CHN) **5758**
Fangshexue Shijian (CHN) **6197**
Fangyan (CHN) **5118**
Fangzhi Gaoxiao Jichu Kexue Xuebao (CHN) **8450**
Fangzhi Xuebao (CHN) **8450**
Fanzui Yanjiu (CHN) **4889**
Far Eastern Affairs (USA) **5215**
Farmatsiya (RUS) **6842**
Fashang Yanjiu (CHN) **4671**
Faxue (Shanghai) (CHN) **4671**
Faxue Pinlun (CHN) **4671**
Faxue Yanjiu (CHN) **4671**
Faxue Zazhi (CHN) **4671**
Fayin (CHN) **7701**
Fayixue Zazhi (CHN) **5913**
Fayu Xuexi (CHN) **5118**
Fazhan Yanjiu (CHN) **1109**
Fazhi yu Shehui Fazhan (CHN) **4671**
Feidie Tansuo (CHN) **55**
Feihang Daodan (CHN) **55**
Feixing Lixue (CHN) **55**
Fengji Jishu (CHN) **3178**
Fenmo Yejin Gongye (CHN) **6311**
Fenmo Yejin Jishu (CHN) **6311**
Fenxi Huaxue (CHN) **2100**
Fenxi Kexue Xuebao (CHN) **7854**
Fenxi Shiyanshi (CHN) **7012**
Fenxi Yiqi (CHN) **4486**
Fenzi Cuihua (CHN) **7012**
Filosofkie Issledovaniya (RUS) **6920**
Focus on Geography (USA) **4006**
Fojiao Wenhua (CHN) **7701**
Forestry Studies in China (CHN) **3690**
Foshan Kexue Jishu Xueyuan Xuebao (Ziran Kexue Ban) (CHN) **7855**
Fubu Waike (CHN) **6244**
Fudan Xuebao (Shehui Kexue Ban) (CHN) **7965**
Fudan Xuebao (Yixue Ban) (CHN) **5616**
Fudan Xuebao (Ziran Kexue Ban) (CHN) **7856**
Fuhe Cailiao Xuebao (CHN) **3345**
Fujian Chaye (CHN) **232**
Fujian Dizhi (CHN) **2734**
Fujian Guoshu (CHN) **232**
Fujian Jianzhu (CHN) **443**
Fujian Jinrong (CHN) **1348**
Fujian Linxueyuan Xuebao (CHN) **3691**
Fujian Luntan (Renwen Shehui Kexue Ban) (CHN) **4453**
Fujian Luntan (She-ke Jiaoyu Ban) (CHN) **1112**
Fujian Nongye (CHN) **114**
Fujian Nongye Keji (CHN) **114**
Fujian Nongye Xuebao (CHN) **114**
Fujian Qingfang (CHN) **7965**
Fujian Shifan Daxue Xuebao (Shehui Kexue Ban) (CHN) **7965**
Fujian Shifan Daxue Xuebao (Ziran Kexue Ban) (CHN) **7856**
Fujian Shuichan (CHN) **3595**
Fujian Tiyu Keji (CHN) **8174**
Fujian Xumu Shouyi (CHN) **8797**
Fujian Yike Daxue Xuebao (CHN) **5616**
Fujian Yishu (CHN) **8471**
Fujian Yiyao Zazhi (CHN) **6843**
Fujian Zhongyi Xueyuan Xuebao (CHN) **5616**
Fujian Zhongyi Yao (CHN) **309**
Funu Yanjiu Luncong (CHN) **8897**
Fushe Fanghu (CHN) **7066**
Fushe Yanjiu yu Fushe Gongyi Xuebao (CHN) **3167**
Fushi Kexue yu Fanghu Jishu (CHN) **6313**
Fushi yu Fanghu (CHN) **2113**
Fuyang Shifan Xueyuan Xuebao (Shehui Kexueban) (CHN) **7965**
Fuzhou Daxue Xuebao (Zhexue Shehui Kexue Ban) (CHN) **7965**
Fuzhou Daxue Xuebao (Ziran Kexue Ban) (CHN) **7856**
Gaige (CHN) **7965**
Gaige yu Zhanlue (CHN) **7966**
Gandan Waike Zazhi (CHN) **5923**
Gandanyi Waike Zazhi (CHN) **5924**
Gang Ao Jingji (CHN) **1113**
Gangtie (CHN) **6313**
Gangtie Yanjiu Xuebao (CHN) **6313**
Ganhanqu Dili (CHN) **4007**
Ganhanqu Yanjiu (CHN) **6353**
Gannan Yixueyuan Xuebao (CHN) **5617**
Gansu Kexue Xuebao (CHN) **7857**
Gansu Lianhe Daxue Xuebao (Ziran Kexue Ban) (CHN) **7857**
Gansu Nongye Daxue Xuebao (CHN) **115**
Gansu Shehui Kexue (CHN) **7966**
Ganzang (CHN) **5924**
Gaodeng Xuexiao Huaxue Gongcheng Xuebao (CHN) **3244**
Gaodeng Xuexiao Huaxue Xuebao (CHN) **2062**
Gaodianya Jishu (CHN) **3309**
Gaofenzi Cailiao Kexue yu Gongcheng (CHN) **3244**
Gaofenzi Tongbao (CHN) **2062**
Gaofenzi Xuebao (CHN) **2135**
Gaojishu Tongxun (CHN) **8422**
Gaokeji yu Chanyehua (CHN) **8423**
Gaoxiao Dizhi Xuebao (CHN) **2735**
Gaoxiao Lilun Zhanxian (CHN) **2982**
Gaoxiao Yingyong Shuxue Xuebao (CHN) **5489**
Gaoya Dianqi (CHN) **7051**
Gaoya Wuli Xuebao (CHN) **7059**
Gaoyuan Qixiang (CHN) **6353**
Gaoyuan Yixue Zazhi (CHN) **5617**
Geo-Spatial Information Science (CHN) **4007**
Geren Diannao (CHN) **2419**
Gong Lu (CHN) **8631**
Gong'an Yanjiu (CHN) **2677**
Gongcheng Baopo (CHN) **3194**
Gongcheng Dizhi Xuebao (CHN) **2745**
Gongcheng Jixie (CHN) **1009**
Gongcheng Jixie yu Weixiu (CHN) **5452**
Gongcheng Lixue (CHN) **3345**
Gongcheng Rewuli Xuebao (CHN) **7054**
Gongcheng Sheji Xuebao (CHN) **3194**
Gongcheng Shuxue Xuebao (CHN) **3194**
Gongcheng Suoliao Yingyong (CHN) **7092**
Gongguan Shijie (CHN) **25**
Gonghui Bolan (CHN) **4595**
Gongkuang Zidonghua (CHN) **6463**
Gongneng Cailiao (CHN) **3345**
Gongneng Cailiao yu Qijian Xuebao (CHN) **6314**
Gongneng Gaofenzi Xuebao (CHN) **3244**
Gongye Cuihua (CHN) **3367**
Gongye Gongcheng (CHN) **3367**
Gongye Gongcheng yu Guanli (CHN) **3367**
Gongye Jianzhu (CHN) **1009**
Gongye Jiare (CHN) **4119**
Gongye Kongzhi Jisuanji (CHN) **2460**
Gongye Lu (CHN) **3345**
Gongye Shui Chuli (CHN) **3486**
Gongye Weisheng yu Zhiyebin (CHN) **6677**
Gongye Weishengwu (CHN) **765**
Gongye Yongshui yu Feishui (CHN) **3506**
Gosudarstvo i Pravo (RUS) **4682**
Guang Tongxin Jishu (CHN) **2322**
Guangdian Gongcheng (CHN) **3309**
Guangdianzi - Jiguang (CHN) **7075**
Guangdong Dianli (CHN) **3158**
Guangdong Haiyang Daxue Xuebao (CHN) **2709**
Guangdong Huagong (CHN) **2062**
Guangdong Qixiang (CHN) **6353**
Guangdong Shehui Kexue (CHN) **7967**
Guangdong Tongxin Jishu (CHN) **2322**
Guangdong Weiliang Yuansu Kexue (CHN) **6197**
Guangdong Yaoxueyuan Xuebao (CHN) **6845**
Guangdong Yixue (CHN) **5621**
Guangdong Yixueyuan Xuebao (CHN) **5621**
Guangming Zhongyi (CHN) **5621**
Guangpan Jishu (CHN) **2419**
Guangpu Shiyanshi (CHN) **7014**
Guangpuxue yu Guangpu Fenxi (CHN) **7075**
Guangxi Daxue Xuebao (Zhexue Shehui Kexue Ban) (CHN) **7967**
Guangxi Daxue Xuebao (Ziran Kexue Ban) (CHN) **7858**
Guangxi Gongxueyuan Xuebao (CHN) **8423**
Guangxi Kexue (CHN) **7858**
Guangxi Kexueyuan Xuebao (CHN) **7859**
Guangxi Linye Kexue (CHN) **3692**
Guangxi Minzu Xueyuan Xuebao (Ziran Kexue Ban) (CHN) **7859**
Guangxi Nongxuebao (CHN) **117**
Guangxi Qixiang (CHN) **6353**
Guangxi Shifan Daxue Xuebao (Zhexue Shehui Kexue Ban) (CHN) **7967**
Guangxi Shifan Daxue Xuebao (Ziran Kexue Ban) (CHN) **7859**
Guangxi Wuli (CHN) **7014**
Guangxi Yike Daxue Xuebao (CHN) **5621**
Guangxi Yixue (CHN) **5621**
Guangxi Zhiwu (CHN) **791**
Guangxi Zhongyiyao (CHN) **309**
Guangxian yu Dianlan (CHN) **3309**
Guangxue Jingmi Gongcheng (CHN) **3194**
Guangxue Jishu (CHN) **7075**
Guangxue Xuebao (CHN) **7076**
Guangxue Yiqi (CHN) **4487**
Guangzhou Huagong (CHN) **3244**
Guangzhou Tiyu Xueyuan Xuebao (CHN) **2861**
Guangzhou Yiyao (CHN) **6845**
Guangzhou Zhongyiyao Daxue Xuebao (CHN) **5621**
Guangzi Xuebao (CHN) **7076**
Guanli Gongcheng Xuebao (CHN) **3194**
Guanli Shijie (CHN) **1749**
Guanzi Xuekan (CHN) **4454**
Gugong Bowuyuan Yuankan (CHN) **4454**
Guhanyu Yanjiu (CHN) **5124**
Guijinshu (CHN) **6314**
Guilin Dianzi Gongye Xueyuan Xuebao (CHN) **3100**
Guilin Gongxueyuan Xuebao (CHN) **8423**
Guisuanyan Tongbao (CHN) **2116**
Guisuanyan Xuebao (CHN) **2116**
Guiyang Yixueyuan Xuebao (CHN) **5621**
Guizhou Daxue Xuebao (Ziran Kexue Ban) (CHN) **7859**
Guizhou Kexue (CHN) **7859**
Guizhou Minzu Yanjiu (CHN) **550**
Guizhou Nongye Kexue (CHN) **117**
Guizhou Shehui Kexue (CHN) **7967**
Guizhou Shifan Daxue Xuebao (Shehui Kexue Ban) (CHN) **7967**
Guizhou Shifan Daxue Xuebao (Ziran Kexueban) (CHN) **7859**
Guizhou Yiyao (CHN) **5621**
Guji Zhengli Yanjiu Xuekan (CHN) **5011**
Gujian Yuanlin Jishu (CHN) **444**
Gujizhui Dongwu Xuebao (CHN) **945**
Guo Moruo Xuekan (CHN) **643**
Guocheng Gongcheng Xuebao (CHN) **3244**
Guofang Keji Daxue Xuebao (CHN) **6423**
Guoji Bingduxue Zazhi (CHN) **5913**
Guoji Bingli Kexue yu Linchuang Zazhi (CHN) **5622**
Guoji Dizhen Dongtai (CHN) **2783**
Guoji Guancha (CHN) **7239**
Guoji Guanxi Xueyuan Xuebao (CHN) **7239**
Guoji Hangkong (CHN) **57**
Guoji Jianyan Yixue Zazhi (CHN) **5622**
Guoji Jingji Hezuo (CHN) **1596**
Guoji Jingmao Tansuo (CHN) **1567**
Guoji Maoyi (CHN) **1567**
Guoji Maoyi Wenti (CHN) **1567**
Guoji Rencai Jiaoliu (CHN) **3012**
Guoji Shengzhi Jiankang / Jihua Shengyu Zazhi (CHN) **972**
Guoji Shichang (CHN) **1568**
Guoji Wenti Yanjiu (CHN) **7239**
Guoji Xinwenjie (CHN) **26**
Guoji Yaoxue Yanjiu Zazhi (CHN) **6845**
Guoji Yixue Fangshexue Zazhi (CHN) **6197**
Guoji Yiyao Weisheng Daobao (CHN) **5622**
Guoji Zaozhi (CHN) **6733**
Guoji Zhongliuxue Zazhi (CHN) **6020**
Guoshu Xuebao (CHN) **3735**
Guotu Ziyuan Keji Guanli (CHN) **1749**
Guotu Ziyuan Yaogan (CHN) **2709**
Guowai Dianzi Yuanqijian (CHN) **3100**
Guowai Shehui Kexue (CHN) **7968**
Guowai Yixue (Er Bi Yanhou Kexue Fence) (CHN) **6080**
Guowai Yixue (Erkexue Fence) (CHN) **6092**
Guowai Yixue (Fangshe Yixue Heyixue Fence) (CHN) **6197**
Guowai Yixue (Fu-you Baojian Fence) (CHN) **5991**
Guowai Yixue (Gukexue Fence) (CHN) **6061**
Guowai Yixue (Hulixue Fence) (CHN) **5959**
Guowai Yixue (Huxi Xitong Fence) (CHN) **6214**
Guowai Yixue (Jingshenbingxue Fence) (CHN) **6143**
Guowai Yixue (Jishengbing Fence) (CHN) **886**
Guowai Yixue (Kouqiang Yixue Fence) (CHN) **5925**
Guowai Yixue (Liuxingbingxue Chuanranbingxue Fence) (CHN) **5814**
Guowai Yixue (Mazuixue yu Fusu Fence) (CHN) **5771**
Guowai Yixue (Mianyixue Fence) (CHN) **5758**
Guowai Yixue (Miniao Xitong Fence) (CHN) **6268**
Guowai Yixue (Naoxieguan Jibing) (CHN) **6143**
Guowai Yixue (Neifenmixue Fence) (CHN) **5893**
Guowai Yixue (Neikexue Fence) (CHN) **5945**
Guowai Yixue (Shehui Yixue Fence) (CHN) **5622**
Guowai Yixue (Shengwu Yixue Gongcheng Fence) (CHN) **748**
Guowai Yixue (Shenjingbingxue Shenjing Waikexue Fence) (CHN) **6143**
Guowai Yixue (Waikexue Fence) (CHN) **6244**
Guowai Yixue (Weisheng Jingji Fence) (CHN) **7520**
Guowai Yixue (Weishengxue Fence) (CHN) **6987**
Guowai Yixue (Wuli Yixue yu Kangfuxue Fence) (CHN) **6109**
Guowai Yixue (Xiaohuaxi Jibing Fence) (CHN) **5925**
Guowai Yixue (Xinxueguan Jibing Fence) (CHN) **5787**
Guowai Yixue (Yankexue Fence) (CHN) **6043**
Guowai Yixue (Yichuanxue Fence) (CHN) **871**
Guowai Yixue (Yixue Dili Fence) (CHN) **5622**
Guowai Yixue (Yufang, Zhenduan, Zhiliao Yong Shengwu Zhipin Fence) (CHN) **5622**
Guowai Yiyao (Kangshengsu Fence) (CHN) **6845**
Guoyi Luntan (CHN) **6845**
Gushengwu Xuebao (CHN) **6725**
Guti Dianzixue Yanjiu yu Jinzhan (CHN) **3100**
Guti Huojian Jishu (CHN) **57**
Guti Lixue Xuebao (CHN) **7059**
H N - Hospodarske Noviny (CZE) **1116**
Haerbin Gongye Daxue Xuebao (Shehui Kexue Ban) (CHN) **7968**
Haerbin Ligong Daxue Xuebao (CHN) **7859**
Ha'erbin Yike Daxue Xuebao (CHN) **5622**
Ha'erbin Yiyao (CHN) **6845**
Haian Gongcheng (CHN) **2805**
Haijun Gongcheng Daxue Xuebao (CHN) **3194**
Hainan Daxue Xuebao (Renwen Shehui Kexueban) (CHN) **4454**
Hainan Daxue Xuebao (Ziran Kexue Ban) (CHN) **7859**
Hainan Jinrong (CHN) **1350**
Hainan Yixue (CHN) **5623**
Hainan Yixueyuan Xuebao (CHN) **5623**
Haixia Keji yu Chanye (CHN) **1116**
Haixia Yufang Yixue Zazhi (CHN) **5623**

Online Service

Online Service

Renmin Zhujiang (CHN) **3364**
Renwen Zazhi (CHN) **4472**
Reproduction and Contraception (SGP) **973**
Research in Astronomy and Astrophysics (GBR) **580**
Riben Wenti Yanjiu (CHN) **559**
Riben Xuekan (CHN) **1515**
Riben Yixue Jieshao (CHN) **5706**
Ribenxue Luntan (CHN) **7998**
Riyong Huaxue Gongye (CHN) **2244**
Riyu Xuexi yu Yanjiu (CHN) **5169**
Riyu Zhishi (CHN) **5169**
Rossiiskaya Akademiya Nauk. Izvestiya. Seriya Literatury i Yazyka (RUS) **5365**
Rossiiskaya Arkheologiya (RUS) **415**
Rossiiskaya Yustitsiya (RUS) **4776**
Roulei Yanjiu (CHN) **3662**
Ruan Kexue (CHN) **7906**
Ruanjian Gongchengshi (CHN) **2596**
Ruanjian Shijie (CHN) **2596**
Ruanjian Xuebao (CHN) **2596**
Runhua yu Mifeng (CHN) **3395**
Russkaya Literatura (RUS) **5365**
Russkaya Rech' (RUS) **5170**
S.Sh.A. Ekonomika, Politika, Ideologiya (RUS) **4311**
Sanyuefeng (CHN) **2338**
Science Foundation in China (CHN) **7909**
Science in China. Series A: Mathematics (CHN) **5533**
Science in China. Series B: Chemistry (CHN) **2080**
Science in China. Series C: Life Sciences (CHN) **703**
Science in China. Series D: Earth Sciences (CHN) **2716**
Science in China. Series E: Technological Sciences (CHN) **8437**
Science in China. Series F: Information Sciences (CHN) **2437**
Science in China. Series G: Physics, Mechanics & Astronomy (CHN) **7039**
Science in Russia (RUS) **7910**
Scientia Geologica Sinica (CHN) **2766**
Seedling (ESP) **770**
Senlin Fanghuo (CHN) **3581**
Senlin Gongcheng (CHN) **3715**
Senlin yu Renlei (CHN) **3702**
Sepu (CHN) **7084**
Shaanxi Keji Daxue Xuebao (Ziran Kexue Ban) (CHN) **7914**
Shaanxi Shifan Daxue Xuebao (Zhexue Shehui Kexue Ban) (CHN) **6951**
Shaanxi Shifan Daxue Xuebao (Ziran Kexue Ban) (CHN) **7914**
Shaanxi Yixue Zazhi (CHN) **5712**
Shaanxi Zhongyi Xueyuan Xuebao (CHN) **5712**
Shandi Xuebao (CHN) **2767**
Shandong Daxue Jichuyixueyuan Xuebao (CHN) **5712**
Shandong Daxue Xuebao (Lixue Ban) (CHN) **7914**
Shandong Daxue Xuebao (Yixue Ban) (CHN) **5712**
Shandong Daxue Xuebao (Zhexue Shehui Kexue Ban) (CHN) **8000**
Shandong Gongshang Xueyuan Xuebao (CHN) **1173**
Shandong Gongye Daxue Xuebao (Shehui Kexue Ban) (CHN) **8000**
Shandong Jianzhu Gongcheng Xueyuan Xuebao (CHN) **457**
Shandong Jingji (CHN) **1173**
Shandong Jingji Zhanlue Yanjiu (CHN) **1721**
Shandong Keji Daxue Xuebao (Ziran Kexue Ban) (CHN) **6479**
Shandong Qinggongye Xueyuan Xuebao (CHN) **7914**
Shandong Shehui Kexue (CHN) **8000**
Shandong Shifan Daxue Xuebao (Renwen Shehui Kexue Ban) (CHN) **8000**
Shandong Shifan Daxue Xuebao (Ziran Kexue Ban) (CHN) **7914**
Shandong Tiyu Xueyuan Xuebao (CHN) **3081**
Shandong Wenxue (CHN) **5371**
Shandong Yike Daxue Xuebao (Shehui Kexue Ban) (CHN) **8000**
Shandong Yixue Gaodeng Zhuanke Xuexiao Xuebao (CHN) **5712**
Shandong Yiyao (CHN) **5713**
Shanghai Baoxian (CHN) **4523**
Shanghai Baozhuang (CHN) **6715**
Shanghai Dang'an (CHN) **5047**
Shanghai Daxue Xuebao (Ziran Kexue Ban) (CHN) **7914**
Shanghai Di-er Gongye Daxue Xuebao (CHN) **7914**
Shanghai Dianli Xueyuan Xuebao (CHN) **3161**
Shanghai Fangzhi Keji (CHN) **8457**
Shanghai Haishi Daxue Xuebao (CHN) **8660**
Shanghai Hangtian (CHN) **70**
Shanghai Huagong (CHN) **3255**
Shanghai Huanjing Kexue (CHN) **3466**
Shanghai Jianshe Keji (CHN) **1035**
Shanghai Jiaotong Daxue Xuebao (CHN) **8438**
Shanghai Jiaotong University. Journal (CHN) **8438**
Shanghai Jingji Yanjiu (CHN) **1173**
Shanghai Jinrong (CHN) **1383**
Shanghai Jiyou (CHN) **6899**
Shanghai Keji Fanyi (CHN) **5173**
Shanghai Kouqiang Yixue (CHN) **5931**
Shanghai Kuaiji (CHN) **1301**
Shanghai Ligong Daxue Xuebao (CHN) **8438**
Shanghai Nongye Xuebao (CHN) **155**
Shanghai Qiye (CHN) **1432**
Shanghai Shifan Daxue Xuebao (Zhexue Shehui Kexue Ban) (CHN) **8000**
Shanghai Shuichan Daxue Xuebao (CHN) **3608**
Shanghai Tiyu Xueyuan Xuebao (CHN) **2911**
Shanghai Tongji (CHN) **8399**
Shanghai Tuke (CHN) **6720**
Shanghai University. Journal (CHN) **7914**
Shanghai Wenxue (CHN) **5371**
Shanghai Xumu Shouyi Tongxun (CHN) **8807**
Shanghai Yixue (CHN) **5713**
Shanghai Yixue Jianyan Zazhi (CHN) **5911**
Shanghai Yiyao (CHN) **5713**
Shanghai Yufang Yixue (CHN) **5713**
Shanghai Zhenjiu Zazhi (CHN) **315**
Shanghai Zonghe Jingji (CHN) **1721**
Shangqiu Shifan Xueyuan Xuebao (CHN) **3002**
Shangye Jingji yu Guanli (CHN) **1793**
Shangye Yanjiu (CHN) **1173**
Shantou Daxue Xuebao (Renwen Kexue Ban) (CHN) **4475**
Shantou Daxue Xuebao (Ziran Kexue Ban) (CHN) **7914**
Shantou Daxue Yixueyuan Xuebao (CHN) **5713**
Shanxi Agriculture (CHN) **155**
Shanxi Chengren Jiaoyu (CHN) **2946**
Shanxi Daxue Xuebao (Shehui Kexue Ban) (CHN) **8000**
Shanxi Daxue Xuebao (Ziran Kexue Ban) (CHN) **7914**
Shanxi Dizhen (CHN) **2789**
Shanxi Guoshu (CHN) **155**
Shanxi Jiaoyu (CHN) **2911**
Shanxi Nongye Daxue Xuebao (Ziran Kexue Ban) (CHN) **7914**
Shanxi Qixiang (CHN) **6395**
Shanxi Shi-da Xuebao (Shehui Kexue Ban) (CHN) **8000**
Shanxi Yike Daxue Xuebao (CHN) **5713**
Shanxi Yiyao Zazhi (CHN) **6880**
Shanxi Zhongyi (CHN) **315**
Shaonian Ertong Yanjiu (CHN) **2168**
Shchit i Mech (RUS) **8200**
Shehui (CHN) **8000**
Shehui Kexue Jikan (CHN) **8001**
Shehui Kexue Yanjiu (CHN) **8001**
Shehui Kexue Zhanxian (CHN) **8001**
Shehuixue Yanjiu (CHN) **8132**
Shehuizhuyi Yanjiu (Wuhan) (CHN) **7182**
Shengjingjibing yu Jingshen Weisheng (CHN) **6185**
Shengli Kexue Jinzhan (CHN) **928**
Shengming Kexue (CHN) **704**
Shengming Kexue Yanjiu (CHN) **704**
Shengming Shijie (CHN) **817**
Shengtai Duli Xuebao (CHN) **3466**
Shengtai Xuebao (CHN) **3466**
Shengtai yu Nongcun Huanjing Xuebao (CHN) **3466**
Shengtaixue Zazhi (CHN) **3466**
Shengwu Duoyangxing (CHN) **704**
Shengwu Gongcheng Xuebao (CHN) **770**
Shengwu Huaxue yu Shengwu Wuli Jinzhan (CHN) **745**
Shengwu Jishu (CHN) **770**
Shengwu Shuxue Xuebao (CHN) **704**
Shengwu Yixue Gongcheng yu Linchuang (CHN) **5713**
Shengwu Yixue Gongchengxue Zazhi (CHN) **5713**
Shengwuxue Tongbao (CHN) **704**
Shengxue Jishu (CHN) **7089**
Shengxue Xuebao (CHN) **7089**
Shengzhi Yixue Zazhi (CHN) **6004**
Shengzhi yu Biyun (CHN) **973**
Shenji Yanjiu (CHN) **1301**
Shenji Yuekan (CHN) **1301**
Shenjing Jiepouxue Zazhi (CHN) **6185**
Shenyang Gongye Daxue Xuebao (CHN) **7915**
Shenyang Huagong Xueyuan Xuebao (CHN) **7915**
Shenyang Jianzhu Daxue Xuebao (Ziran Kexue Ban) (CHN) **7915**
Shenyang Ligong Daxue Xuebao (CHN) **7915**
Shenyang Nongye Daxue Xuebao (CHN) **155**
Shenyang Shifan Daxue Xuebao (Shehui Kexue Ban) (CHN) **8001**
Shenyang Shifan Daxue Xuebao (Ziran Kexue Ban) (CHN) **7915**
Shenyang Tiyu Xueyuan Xuebao (CHN) **2912**
Shenyang Yaoke Daxue Xuebao (CHN) **6880**
Shenzangbing yu Touxi Shenyizhi Zazhi (CHN) **6274**
Shenzhen Daxue Xuebao (Ligong Ban) (CHN) **7915**
Shenzhen Daxue Xuebao (Renwen Sheke Ban) (CHN) **2912**
Shenzhen Zhiye Jiezhu Xueyuan Xuebao (CHN) **7915**
Shenzhen Zhongxiyi Jiehe Zazhi (CHN) **5713**
Shenzhou Xueren (CHN) **3002**
Shezhi (CHN) **5713**
Shi (CHN) **2261**
Shichang Zhoukan (CHN) **1173**
Shidai Jianzhu (CHN) **3282**
Shidi Kexue (CHN) **3466**
Shigong Jishu (CHN) **457**
Shigong Qiye Guanli (CHN) **1793**
Shihua Jishu Yu Yingyong (CHN) **6792**
Shijiazhuang Tiedao Xueyuan Xuebao (CHN) **8511**
Shijie Dianxin (CHN) **2338**
Shijie Dianying (CHN) **6513**
Shijie Hanxue (CHN) **3564**
Shijie Hanyu Jiaoxue (CHN) **5173**
Shijie Hexin Yixue Qikan Wenzhai (Erkexue Fence) (CHN) **5713**
Shijie Hexin Yixue Qikan Wenzhai (Fuchang Kexue Fence) (CHN) **6004**
Shijie Hexin Yixue Qikan Wenzhai (Pifubingxue Fence) (CHN) **5882**
Shijie Hexin Yixue Qikan Wenzhai (Shengjingbingxue Fence) (CHN) **6185**
Shijie Hexin Yixue Qikan Wenzhai (Weichangbingxue Fence) (CHN) **5931**
Shijie Hexin Yixue Qikan Wenzhai (Xinzangbeingxue Fence) (CHN) **5799**
Shijie Hexin Yixue Qikan Wenzhai (Yankexue Fence) (CHN) **6051**
Shijie Huanjing (CHN) **3466**
Shijie Huaren Xiaohua Zazhi (CHN) **5931**
Shijie Jianzhu Daobao (CHN) **457**
Shijie Jingji Yanjiu (CHN) **1517**
Shijie Kexue Jishu (CHN) **7915**
Shijie Linchuang Yaowu (CHN) **6880**
Shijie Lishi (CHN) **4161**
Shijie Meishu (CHN) **517**
Shijie Nongye (CHN) **156**
Shijie Wenhua (CHN) **5371**
Shijie Zhexue (CHN) **6952**
Shijie Zongjiao Wenhua (CHN) **7681**
Shijie Zongjiao Yanjiu (CHN) **7681**
Shilin (CHN) **5434**
Shinei Sheji (CHN) **4550**
Shinei Sheji yu Zhuangxiu (CHN) **4550**
Shipin Gongye (Shanghai) (CHN) **3663**
Shipin Gongye Keji (CHN) **3663**
Shipin Keji (CHN) **6669**
Shipin Kexue (CHN) **3663**
Shipin yu Jixie (CHN) **3663**
Shiping yu Faxiao Gongye (CHN) **3663**
Shishi Qiushi (CHN) **7182**
Shixue Jikan (CHN) **4161**
Shixue Lilun Yanjiu (CHN) **4161**
Shixue Yuekan (CHN) **4161**
Shixueshi Yanjiu (CHN) **4161**
Shiyan Liuti Lixue (CHN) **7063**
Shiyan Lixue (CHN) **7063**
Shiyan yu Jianyan Yixue (CHN) **5911**
Shiyong Aizheng Zazhi (CHN) **6034**
Shiyong Erke Linchuang Zazhi (CHN) **6104**
Shiyong Fangshexue Zazhi (CHN) **6208**
Shiyong Fuchanke Zazhi (CHN) **6004**
Shiyong Guke Zazhi (CHN) **6073**
Shiyong Kouqiang Yixue Zazhi (CHN) **5931**
Shiyong Laonian Yixue (CHN) **4056**
Shiyong Linchuang Yixue (CHN) **5714**
Shiyong Linchuang Yiyao Zazhi (CHN) **5714**
Shiyong Shouwaike Zazhi (CHN) **6258**
Shiyong Xinnaofei Xueguanbing Zazhi (CHN) **5799**
Shiyong Yaowu yu Linchuang (CHN) **5714**
Shiyong Yixue Zazhi (CHN) **5714**
Shiyong Yiyao Zazhi (CHN) **5714**
Shiyong Yufang Yixue (CHN) **5714**
Shiyong Zhongliu Zazhi (CHN) **6034**
Shiyong Zhongxiyi Jiehe Linchuang (CHN) **5714**
Shiyongjun Xuebao (CHN) **817**
Shiyou Dili Wuli Kantan (CHN) **2767**
Shiyou Gongcheng Jianshe (CHN) **6792**
Shiyou Huagong (CHN) **6792**
Shiyou Huagong Zidonghua (CHN) **6792**
Shiyou Kantan yu Kaifa (CHN) **6792**
Shiyou Kuangchang Jixie (CHN) **5459**
Shiyou Lianzhi yu Huagong (CHN) **6792**
Shiyou Tianranqi Xuebao (CHN) **6792**
Shiyou Wutan (CHN) **6792**
Shiyou Xuebao (CHN) **6792**
Shiyou Xuebao. Shiyou Jiagong (CHN) **6792**
Shiyou yu Tianranqi Dizhi (CHN) **2767**
Shiyou Zuancai Gongyi (CHN) **6792**
Shiyou Zuantan Jishu (CHN) **6793**
Shizhen Guoyi Guoyao (CHN) **6881**
Shoudu Shifan Daxue Xuebao (Shehui Kexue Ban) (CHN) **8001**
Shoudu Shifan Daxue Xuebao (Ziran Kexue Ban) (CHN) **7916**
Shoudu Yike Daxue Xuebao (CHN) **5714**
Shoudu Yiyao (CHN) **5714**
Shoulei Xuebao (CHN) **963**
Shucai (CHN) **252**
Shuhua Yishu (CHN) **517**
Shui Kexue Jinzhan (CHN) **2798**
Shuichan Keji Qingbao (CHN) **3608**
Shuichan Kexue (CHN) **3608**
Shuichan Xuebao (CHN) **3608**
Shuidian Nengyuan Kexue (CHN) **3163**
Shuili Fadian (CHN) **8831**
Shuili Fadian Xuebao (CHN) **3163**
Shuili Keji yu Jingji (CHN) **2627**
Shuili Shuidian Jishu (CHN) **3364**
Shuili Shuiyun Gongcheng Xuebao (CHN) **3163**
Shuili Xuebao (CHN) **3364**
Shuini Jishu (CHN) **1035**
Shuisheng Shengwu Xuebao (CHN) **704**
Shuitu Baochi Tongbao (CHN) **252**
Shuitu Baochi Xuebao (CHN) **252**
Shuitu Baochi Yanjiu (CHN) **252**
Shuiwen (CHN) **2798**
Shuiwen Dizhi Gongcheng Dizhi (CHN) **2798**
Shuiwu Yanjiu (CHN) **1943**
Shuiwu yu Jingji (CHN) **1383**
Shuiyun Guanli (CHN) **8662**
Shuju Caiji Yu Chuli (CHN) **2338**
Shuli Yiyaoxue Zazhi (CHN) **6881**
Shuliang Jingji Jishu Jingji Yanjiu (CHN) **1174**
Shuxue de Shijian yu Renshi (CHN) **5535**
Shuxue Jiaoxue (CHN) **3082**
Shuxue Jiaoyu Xuebao (CHN) **2912**
Shuxue Jikan (CHN) **5535**
Shuxue Jinzhan (CHN) **5535**
Shuxue Lilun yu Yingyong (CHN) **5535**
Shuxue Tongbao (CHN) **5535**
Shuxue Tongxun (CHN) **5535**
Shuxue Wuli Xuebao (A Ji) (CHN) **5536**
Shuxue Xuebao (CHN) **5536**
Shuxue Yanjiu (CHN) **5536**
Shuxue Yanjiu yu Pinglun (CHN) **5536**
Shuxue Zazhi (CHN) **5536**
Shuyou Shiyan Dizhi (CHN) **2767**
Shuzhi Jisuan yu Jisuanji Yingyong (CHN) **7940**
Shuzi Tongxin (CHN) **3113**
Shuzi Yu Suowei Yingxiang (CHN) **6980**
Sichou (CHN) **8457**
Sichou zhi Lu (CHN) **8756**
Sichuan Dang'an (CHN) **4188**
Sichuan Daxue Xuebao (Gongcheng Kexue Ban) (CHN) **7916**
Sichuan Daxue Xuebao (Yixue Ban) (CHN) **5714**
Sichuan Daxue Xuebao (Zhexue Shehui Kexue Ban) (CHN) **8001**
Sichuan Daxue Xuebao (Ziran Kexue Ban) (CHN) **7916**
Sichuan Dizhi Xuebao (CHN) **2767**
Sichuan Huanjing (CHN) **3466**
Sichuan Jianzhu (CHN) **457**
Sichuan Jiaoyu (CHN) **2912**
Sichuan Kuaiji (CHN) **1301**
Sichuan Nongye Daxue Xuebao (CHN) **156**
Sichuan Pengren (CHN) **4367**
Sichuan Shifan Daxue Xuebao (Shehui Kexue Ban) (CHN) **8001**
Sichuan Shifan Daxue Xuebao (Ziran Kexue Ban) (CHN) **7916**
Sichuan Sichou (CHN) **8457**
Sichuan Tushuguan Xuebao (CHN) **5047**
Sichuan Weiyue Xueyuan Xuebao (CHN) **7265**
Sichuan Wenwu (CHN) **416**
Sichuan Xiju (CHN) **517**
Sichuan Yixue (CHN) **5715**
Sichuan Zhongyi (CHN) **315**
Siliao Bolan (CHN) **275**
Siwang Yinshua (CHN) **7328**
Siwei yu Zhihui (CHN) **8002**
Sixiang Zhanxian (CHN) **8002**
Sixiang Zhengzhi Gongzuo Yanjiu (CHN) **7183**
Sixiang Zhengzhike Jiaoxue (CHN) **2913**
Slavyanovedenie (RUS) **4264**
Social Sciences (USA) **8004**
Social Sciences in China (USA) **8004**
Songliao Xuekan (Ziran Kexue Ban) (CHN) **7918**
Sotsiologicheskie Issledovaniya (RUS) **8139**
Southeast University. Journal (CHN) **7919**
Southwest Jiaotong University. Journal (CHN) **7919**
The Sowetan (ZAF) **3950**
Der Spiegel (DEU) **3857**
Sueddeutsche Zeitung (DEU) **3857**
Suxing Gongcheng Xuebao (CHN) **3256**
Suzhou Daxue Xuebao (Gongke Ban) (CHN) **8457**
Suzhou Daxue Xuebao (Yixue Ban) (CHN) **5719**
Suzhou Daxue Xuebao (Zhexue Shehui Kexue Ban) (CHN) **8008**
Suzhou Daxue Xuebao (Ziran Kexue Ban) (CHN) **7921**
Tai Sheng (CHN) **3567**
Taishan Yixueyuan Xuebao (CHN) **5720**
Taiwan Haixia (CHN) **2818**
Taiyang Neng Xuebao (CHN) **3178**
Taiyangneng (CHN) **3178**
Taiyuan Keji Daxue Xuebao (CHN) **7922**
Tankuang Gongcheng (Yantu Zuanjue Gongcheng) (CHN) **6480**
Tanxingti (CHN) **3256**
Taoci Yanjiu (CHN) **2046**
Telecom Product World (CHN) **2341**
Tequ Jingji (CHN) **1182**
Teshu Gang (CHN) **6335**
Tezhong Youqicang (CHN) **6795**
Tezhong Zhuzao Ji Youse Hejin (CHN) **6335**
Tianfu Xinlun (CHN) **8010**
Tianjin Daxue Xuebao (Shehui Kexue Ban) (CHN) **8010**
Tianjin Daxue Xuebao (Ziran Kexue Ban) (CHN) **7923**
Tianjin Gongye Daxue Xuebao (CHN) **8461**
Tianjin Keji Daxue Xuebao (CHN) **3223**
Tianjin Ligong Daxue Xuebao (CHN) **8443**
Tianjin Nongye Kexue (CHN) **162**
Tianjin Shangye Daxue Xuebao (CHN) **1183**
Tianjin Shehui Kexue (CHN) **8010**
Tianjin Shifan Daxue Xuebao (Jichu Jiaoyu Ban) (CHN) **2919**
Tianjin Shifan Daxue Xuebao (Shehui Kexue Ban) (CHN) **8010**
Tianjin Shifan Daxue Xuebao (Ziran Kexue Ban) (CHN) **7923**
Tianjin Tiyu Xueyuan Xuebao (CHN) **6998**
Tianjin Tongxin Jishu (CHN) **2342**
Tianjin Yaoxue (CHN) **6883**
Tianjin Yike Daxue Xuebao (CHN) **5721**
Tianjin Yiyao (CHN) **6883**
Tianjing (CHN) **8337**
Tianran Chanwu Yanjiu yu Kaifa (CHN) **2082**
Tianranqi Diqiou Kexue (CHN) **6795**
Tianranqi Gongye (CHN) **6795**
Tianranqi Huagong (CHN) **6795**
Tianwen Aihaozhe (CHN) **583**
Tianwen Xuebao (CHN) **583**
Tianwenxue Jinzhan (CHN) **583**
Tianzhong Xuekan (CHN) **8010**
Tiedao Jianzhu (CHN) **8626**
Tiedao Yunshu yu Jingji (CHN) **8626**
Tinglixue ji Yanyu Jibing Zazhi (CHN) **6085**
Tiyu Keyan (CHN) **6234**
Tiyu Xuekan (CHN) **6998**
Tongji Daxue Xuebao (Shehui Kexue Ban) (CHN) **8010**
Tongji Daxue Xuebao (Yixue Ban) (CHN) **5723**

Tongji Daxue Xuebao (Ziran Kexue Ban) (CHN) **7924**
Tongweisu (CHN) **7072**
Tongxin Xuebao (CHN) **2342**
Tongye Gongcheng (CHN) **6335**
Tongyi Luntan (CHN) **8010**
Touzi Yanjiu (CHN) **1952**
Tuijin Jishu (CHN) **73**
Tuliao Gongye (CHN) **6721**
Tumu Gongcheng Xuebao (CHN) **3286**
Turang (CHN) **2717**
Turang Feiliao (CHN) **256**
Turang Xuebao (CHN) **2717**
Turkish Daily News (TUR) **3963**
Tushu Qingbao Zhishi (CHN) **5051**
Tushuguan Gongzuo yu Yanjiu (CHN) **5051**
Tushuguan Jianshe (CHN) **5051**
Tushuguan Jie (CHN) **5051**
Tushuguan Qingbao Gongzuo (CHN) **5051**
Tushuguan Xuebao (CHN) **5051**
Ukrains'kyi Istorychnyi Zhurnal (UKR) **4165**
University of Science and Technology Beijing. Journal (CHN) **6483**
Vechernyaya Moskva (RUS) **3942**
Vestnik Drevnei Istorii (RUS) **4166**
Vidomosti Verkhovnoi Rady Ukrainy (UKR) **7476**
Virologica Sinica (DEU) **897**
Voennaya Mysl' (RUS) **6452**
Voice of Friendship (CHN) **7272**
Voprosy Ekonomiki (RUS) **1192**
Voprosy Filologii (RUS) **5194**
Voprosy Filosofii (RUS) **6960**
Voprosy Istorii (RUS) **4166**
Voprosy Istorii Estestvoznaniya i Tekhniki (RUS) **7928**
Voprosy Literatury (RUS) **5396**
Voprosy Yazykoznaniya (RUS) **5194**
Vostok (RUS) **563**
Vrach (RUS) **5729**
Waiguo Jiaoyu Yanjiu (CHN) **2925**
Waiguo Jingji yu Guanli (CHN) **1800**
Waiguo Wenxue (CHN) **5396**
Waiguo Wenxue Yanjiu (Wuhan) (CHN) **5396**
Waiguoyu (CHN) **5194**
Waijiao Xueyuan Xuebao (CHN) **7272**
Waike Lilun yu Shijian (CHN) **6262**
Waiyu Dianhua Jiaoxue (CHN) **3087**
Waiyu Jiaoxue yu Yanjiu (CHN) **5194**
Waiyu Xuekan (CHN) **5194**
Waiyujie (CHN) **5194**
Wangqiu Tiandi (CHN) **8251**
Wannan Yixueyuan Xuebao (CHN) **5729**
Weibo Xuebao (CHN) **3116**
Weichangbingxue (CHN) **5932**
Weichangbingxue he Ganbingxue Zazhi (CHN) **5932**
Weidiannao Shijie (CHN) **2441**
Weidianzixue (CHN) **2466**
Weifang Yixueyuan Xuebao (CHN) **5729**
Weijisuanji Xinxi (CHN) **2573**
Weijisuanji Yingyong (CHN) **2573**
Weiliang Yuansu yu Jiankang Yanjiu (CHN) **5729**
Weisheng Dulixue Zazhi (CHN) **5729**
Weisheng Jingji Yanjiu (CHN) **1193**
Weisheng Yanjiu (CHN) **7000**
Weishengwuxue Mianyixue Jinzhan (CHN) **898**
Weishengwuxue Tongbao (CHN) **898**
Weishengwuxue Zazhi (CHN) **898**
Weiti Gushengwu Xuebao (CHN) **898**
Weixi Jiagong Jishu (CHN) **3116**
Weixunhuanxue Zazhi (CHN) **5801**
Wen Bo (CHN) **6540**
Wen Shi Zhe (CHN) **4482**
Wenshi Jinghua (CHN) **4167**
Wenwu (CHN) **423**
Wenwu Baohu yu Kaogu Kexue (CHN) **423**
Wenwu Chunqiu (CHN) **423**
Wenxue Pinglun (CHN) **5397**
Wenxue Yichan (CHN) **5398**
Wenxue Ziyou Tan (CHN) **5245**
Wenyi Lilun Yanjiu (CHN) **5398**
Wenyi Pinglun (CHN) **5245**
Wenyi Pinglun yu Piping (CHN) **5245**
Wenyi Yanjiu (CHN) **5398**
Wenyi Zhengming (CHN) **5245**
Wenzhou Yixueyuan Xuebao (CHN) **5730**
Women of China (CHN) **8246**
World Journal of Acupuncture - Moxibustion (CHN) **315**
Wudang (CHN) **8216**
Wudao (CHN) **2688**
Wuhan Daxue Xuebao (Gongxue Ban) (CHN) **3365**
Wuhan Daxue Xuebao (Lixue Ban) (CHN) **7930**
Wuhan Daxue Xuebao (Xinxi Kexue Ban) (CHN) **4034**
Wuhan Daxue Xuebao (Yixue Ban) (CHN) **5731**
Wuhan Daxue Xuebao (Zhexue Shehui Kexue Ban) (CHN) **8015**
Wuhan Gongcheng Daxue Xuebao (CHN) **3257**
Wuhan Gongye Xueyuan Xuebao (CHN) **7930**
Wuhan KeJi Daxue Xuebao (Shehui Kexue Ban) (CHN) **8015**
Wuhan Keji Daxue Xuebao (Ziran Kexue Ban) (CHN) **7930**
Wuhan Keji Xueyuan Xuebao (CHN) **7930**
Wuhan Ligong Daxue Xuebao (CHN) **7930**
Wuhan Ligong Daxue Xuebao (Jiaotong Kexue yu Gongcheng Ban) (CHN) **3287**
Wuhan Ligong DaxueXuebao (Xinxi yu Guanligongcheng Ban) (CHN) **2551**
Wuhan Tiyuan Xuebao (CHN) **2926**
Wuhan University Journal of Natural Sciences (CHN) **7930**
Wuhan University of Technology. Journal (Material Science Edition) (CHN) **8445**
Wuhan Wenshi Ziliao (CHN) **4190**
Wuhan Zhiwuxue Yanjiu (CHN) **823**
Wuji Cailiao Xuebao (CHN) **2119**
Wuji Huaxue Xuebao (CHN) **2119**
Wujing Yixue (CHN) **5732**
Wujiyan Gongye (CHN) **3257**
Wuli (CHN) **7046**
Wuli Huaxue Xuebao (CHN) **2142**
Wuli Xuebao (CHN) **7046**
Wuli yu Gongcheng (CHN) **7047**
Wuran Fangzhi Jishu (CHN) **3493**
Wutaishan Yanjiu (CHN) **4167**
Wutan Huatan Jisuan Jishu (CHN) **2718**
Wutan yu Huatan (CHN) **6484**
Wuxi Qinggong Daxue Xuebao (CHN) **8445**
Wuxiandian Gongcheng (CHN) **2365**
Wuxiandian Tongxin Jishu (CHN) **2365**
Wuyi Daxue Xuebao (Ziran Kexue Ban) (CHN) **7930**
Wuyi Kexue (CHN) **711**
Xiamen Daxue Xuebao (Zhexue Shehui Kexue Ban) (CHN) **8015**
Xiamen Daxue Xuebao (Ziran Kexue Ban) (CHN) **7930**
Xi'an Dianzi Keji Daxue Xuebao (Ziran Kexue Ban) (CHN) **3116**
Xi'an Gongcheng Keji Xueyuan Xuebao (CHN) **8462**
Xi'an Jianzhu Keji Daxue Xuebao (Ziran Kexue Ban) (CHN) **461**
Xi'an Jiaotong Daxue Xuebao (CHN) **7931**
Xi'an Jiaotong Daxue Xuebao (Yixue Ban) (CHN) **5732**
Xi'an Ligong Daxue Xuebao (CHN) **8445**
Xi'an Shiyou Daxue Xuebao (Shehui Kexue Ban) (CHN) **8015**
Xi'an Shiyou Daxue Xuebao (Ziran Kexue Ban) (CHN) **7931**
Xi'an Tiyu Xueyuan Xuebao (CHN) **7000**
Xiandai Dianli (CHN) **3162**
Xiandai Dianshenglixue Zazhi (CHN) **928**
Xiandai Dizhi (CHN) **2775**
Xiandai Fangyu Jishu (CHN) **6454**
Xiandai Faxue (CHN) **4816**
Xiandai Funu (CHN) **8892**
Xiandai Guoji Guanxi (CHN) **7275**
Xiandai Huli (CHN) **5984**
Xiandai Jianyan Yixue Zazhi (CHN) **5911**
Xiandai Jingji Tantao (CHN) **1551**
Xiandai Jixie (CHN) **5461**
Xiandai Kouqiang Yixue Zazhi (CHN) **5932**
Xiandai Mianyixue (CHN) **5767**
Xiandai Riben Jingji (CHN) **1196**
Xiandai Shiyong Yixue (CHN) **5732**
Xiandai Tongxin (CHN) **2355**
Xiandai Tushu Qingbao Jishu (CHN) **5064**
Xiandai Waiyu (CHN) **5196**
Xiandai Wuli Zhishi (CHN) **7047**
Xiandai Yixue (CHN) **5732**
Xiandai Yiyao Weisheng (CHN) **5732**
Xiandai Yiyong Yingxiangxue (CHN) **6210**
Xiandai Yuancheng Jiaoyu Yanjiu (CHN) **2399**
Xiandai Yufang Yixue (CHN) **5732**
Xiandai Yuye Xinxi (CHN) **3612**
Xiandai Zhenduan yu Zhiliao (CHN) **5732**
Xiandai Zhexue (CHN) **6961**
Xiandai Zhongxiyijiehe Zazhi (CHN) **5732**
Xiangjiao Gongye (CHN) **7827**
Xiangtan Daxue Xuebao (Zhexue Shehui Kexue Ban) (CHN) **8015**
Xiangtan Daxue Ziran Kexue Xuebao (CHN) **7931**
Xianning Xueyuan Xuebao (Yixue Ban) (CHN) **8015**
Xianweisu Kexue yu Jishu (CHN) **6740**
Xiaofang Kexue yu Jishu (CHN) **3582**
Xiaoshuo Jie (CHN) **5402**
Xiaoshuo Pinglun (CHN) **5402**
Xiaoxing Neiranji (CHN) **3399**
Xiaoxing Weixing Jisuanji Xitong (CHN) **2574**
Xiaoxue Yuwen Jiaoxue (CHN) **3088**
Xiaoxuesheng Yuwen Xuexi (CHN) **5196**
Xibao yu Fenzi Mianyixue Zazhi (CHN) **5767**
Xibei Daxue Xuebao (Shehui Kexue Ban) (CHN) **8015**
Xibei Daxue Xuebao (Ziran Kexue Ban) (CHN) **7931**
Xibei Gongye Daxue Xuebao (CHN) **8445**
Xibei Guofang Yixue Zazhi (CHN) **5732**
Xibei Linxueyuan Xuebao (CHN) **3707**
Xibei Mingzu (CHN) **4190**
Xibei Minzu Daxue Xuebao (Zhexue Shehui Kexue Ban) (CHN) **8015**
Xibei Minzu Yanjiu (CHN) **563**
Xibei Nongye Xuebao (CHN) **171**
Xibei Shi-Da Xuebao (Shehui Kexue Ban) (CHN) **8016**
Xibei Shifan Daxue Xuebao (Ziran Kexue Ban) (CHN) **7931**
Xibei Yaoxue Zazhi (CHN) **6886**
Xibei Yixue Jiaoyu (CHN) **2927**
Xibei Zhiwu Xuebao (CHN) **823**
Xibu Tankuang Gongcheng (CHN) **6484**
Xihua Daxue Xuebao (Ziran Kexue Ban) (CHN) **7931**
Xihua Shifan Xueyuan Xuebao (Zhexue Shehui Kexue Ban) (CHN) **8016**
Xihua Shifan Xueyuan Xuebao (Ziran Kexue Ban) (CHN) **7931**
Xiju (CHN) **8484**
Xin Wenxue Shiliao (CHN) **5402**
Xi'nan Daxue Xuebao (Shehui Kexue Ban) (CHN) **8016**
Xinan Jiaotong Daxue Xuebao (CHN) **7931**
Xi'nan Jinrong (CHN) **1391**
Xinan Minzu Daxue Xuebao (Zhexue Shehui Kexue Ban) (CHN) **8016**
Xinan Minzu Daxue Xuebao (Ziran Kexue Ban) (CHN) **7931**
Xinan Nongye Daxue Xuebao (Ziran Kexue Ban) (CHN) **7931**
Xi'nan Shifan Daxue Xuebao (Ziran Kexue Ban) (CHN) **7931**
Xinan Shiyou Xueyuan Xuebao (CHN) **6798**
Xindianxue Zazhi (CHN) **5802**
Xinfeixueguanbing Zazhi (CHN) **5802**
Xingshi Jishu (CHN) **5917**
Xinjiang Daxue Xuebao (Ziran Kexue Ban) (CHN) **7931**
Xinjiang Dizhi (CHN) **2775**
Xinjiang Shehui Kexue (Hanwen Ban) (CHN) **8016**
Xinjiang Yike Daxue Xuebao (CHN) **5732**
Xinli Kexue (CHN) **7415**
Xinli Xuebao (CHN) **7415**
Xinsheng Erke Zazhi (CHN) **6105**
Xinshiye (CHN) **7197**
Xintiyu (CHN) **8217**
Xinwen Daxue (CHN) **4586**
Xinwen Jizhe (CHN) **4586**
Xinwen Qianshao (CHN) **4586**
Xinwen yu Chengcai (CHN) **4586**
Xinwen yu Chuanbo Yanjiu (CHN) **4586**
Xinwen yu Xiezuo (CHN) **4586**
Xinwen Zhanxian (CHN) **4586**
Xinwenjie (CHN) **4586**
Xinxi Xitong Gongcheng (CHN) **2345**
Xinxi yu Kongzhi (CHN) **2464**
Xinxiang Yixueyuan Xuebao (CHN) **5732**
Xinxibu (CHN) **1534**
Xinxing Tancailiao (CHN) **3257**
Xinxueguan Kangfu Yixue Zazhi (CHN) **5802**
Xinxueguanbingxue Jinzhan (CHN) **5802**
Xinyang Shifan Xueyuan Xuebao (Zhexue Shehui Kexueban) (CHN) **8016**
Xinyang Shifan Xueyuan Xuebao (Ziran Kexueban) (CHN) **7932**
Xinyixue (CHN) **5732**
Xinzhongyi (CHN) **315**
Xitong Fangzhen Xuebao (CHN) **75**
Xitong Gongcheng Lilun Fangfa Yingyong (CHN) **2474**
Xitong Gongcheng Lilun yu Shijian (CHN) **2525**
Xitong Gongcheng Xuebao (CHN) **3227**
Xitong Gongcheng yu Dianzi Jishu (CHN) **3227**
Xitong Kexue yu Shuxue (CHN) **2525**
Xiuci Xuexi (CHN) **5196**
Xiya Feizhou (CHN) **8016**
Xiyou Jinshu Cailiao yu Gongcheng (CHN) **1197**
Xiyu Yanjiu (CHN) **8016**
Xizang Daxue Xuebao (CHN) **8016**
Xizang Wenxue (CHN) **5402**
Xizang Yanjiu (CHN) **563**
Xizang Yishu Yanjiu (CHN) **527**
Xizang Yiyao Zazhi (CHN) **5732**
Xuanmei Jishu (CHN) **6484**
Xue Hai (CHN) **8016**
Xueqian Jiaoyu (CHN) **2927**
Xueshu Luntan (CHN) **8016**
Xueshu Yanjiu (CHN) **8016**
Xuewei yu Yanjiusheng Jiaoyu (CHN) **3011**
Xuexi yu Tansuo (CHN) **8017**
Xumu Shouyi Xuebao (CHN) **8815**
Xuzhou Shifan Daxue Xuebao (Ziran Kexue Ban) (CHN) **7932**
Xuzhou Yixueyuan Xuebao (CHN) **5732**
Ya-tai Jingji (CHN) **1197**
Yadian yu Shengguang (CHN) **3334**
Yan'an Daxue Xuebao (Shehui Kexueban) (CHN) **8017**
Yanbian Daxue Xuebao (Ziran Kexue Ban) (CHN) **7932**
Yanbian Daxue Yixue Xuebao (CHN) **5733**
Yancheng Shifan Xueyuan Xuebao (Renwen Shehui Kexue Ban) (CHN) **8017**
Yangsheng Yuekan (CHN) **7000**
Yangzhou Daxue Xuebao (Gao Jiao Yanjiu Ban) (CHN) **3011**
Yangzhou Daxue Xuebao (Nongye yu Shengming Kexue Ban) (CHN) **171**
Yangzhou Daxue Xuebao (Ziran Kexue Ban) (CHN) **7932**
Yanhe (CHN) **5403**
Yanhuang Chunqiu (CHN) **4190**
Yanjiu yu Fazhan Guanli (CHN) **1802**
Yanke (CHN) **6053**
Yanke Xin Jinzhan (CHN) **6053**
Yanke Xuebao (CHN) **6053**
Yanke Yanjiu (CHN) **6053**
Yankuang Ceshi (CHN) **2775**
Yanshi Guangxue Zazhi (CHN) **6053**
Yanshi Kuangwuxue Zazhi (CHN) **6798**
Yanshi Lixue yu Gongcheng Xuebao (CHN) **7064**
Yanshi Xuebao (CHN) **2775**
Yantai Daxue Xuebao (Shehui Kexue Ban) (CHN) **8017**
Yantai Daxue Xuebao (Ziran Kexue yu Gongcheng Ban) (CHN) **7932**
Yantu Gongcheng Xuebao (CHN) **3287**
Yantu Lixue (CHN) **2791**
Yanwaishang Zhiye Yanbing Zazhi (CHN) **6053**
Yaogan Jishu yu Yingyong (CHN) **2718**
Yaogan Xinxi (CHN) **4034**
Yaogan Xuebao (CHN) **4034**
Yaopin Pingjia (CHN) **6886**
Yaowu Fenxi Zazhi (CHN) **6886**
Yaoxue Fuwu yu Yanjiu (CHN) **6886**
Yaoxue Xuebao (CHN) **6886**
Yaredai Zhiwu Kexue (CHN) **823**
Yati Yasui Yazhoubingxue Zazhi (CHN) **5869**
Yejin Fenxi (CHN) **6337**
Yejin Nengyuan (CHN) **6337**
Yejin Shebei (CHN) **6337**
Yejing yu Xianshi (CHN) **7085**
Yibiao Jishu (CHN) **4490**
Yibiao Jishu yu Chuanganqi (CHN) **4490**
Yichuan (CHN) **879**
Yilin (CHN) **5403**
Yin Ran (CHN) **8462**
Yindu Xuekan (CHN) **4190**
Yingguo Yixue Zazhi (Chinese Edition) (CHN) **5733**
Yingxiang Jishu (CHN) **6978**
Yingxiang Kexue yu Guanghuaxue (CHN) **6978**
Yingxiang Shijue (CHN) **6978**
Yingxiang Zhenduan yu Jieru Fangshexue (CHN) **6210**
Yingyang Xuebao (CHN) **6671**
Yingyong Fanhan Fenxi Xuebao (CHN) **7073**
Yingyong Gailu Tongji (CHN) **5547**
Yingyong Huaxue (CHN) **2084**
Yingyong Jichu yu Gongcheng Kexue Xuebao (CHN) **7932**
Yingyong Jiguang (CHN) **7085**
Yingyong Kexue Xuebao (CHN) **7932**
Yingyong Lixue Xuebao (CHN) **3399**
Yingyong Qixiang Xuebao (CHN) **6400**
Yingyong Shengtai Xuebao (CHN) **3476**
Yingyong Shengxue (CHN) **7090**
Yingyong Shuxue (CHN) **5547**
Yingyong Shuxue he Lixue (CHN) **5547**
Yingyong Shuxue Xuebao (CHN) **5547**
Yingyong Shuxue yu Jisuan Shuxue Xuebao (CHN) **5547**
Yingyong Yu Huanjing Shengwu Xuebao (CHN) **711**
Yingyong Yufang Yixue (CHN) **5733**
Yinmu Neiwai D V D (CHN) **6517**
Yinshua Jishu (CHN) **7329**
Yinshua Zazhi (CHN) **7329**
Yinyue Tansuo (CHN) **6630**
Yinyue Tiandi (CHN) **6630**
Yinyue Yanjiu (CHN) **6630**
Yinyue Yishu (CHN) **6630**
Yiqi Yibiao Xuebao (CHN) **4490**
Yishu Baijia (CHN) **528**
Yishu Shenghuo (CHN) **528**
Yixi Gongye (CHN) **6798**
Yixue Linchuang Yanjiu (CHN) **5733**
Yixue Xinxixue Zazhi (CHN) **5832**
Yixue yu Shehui (CHN) **5733**
Yixue yu Zhexue (CHN) **6961**
Yiyao Gongcheng Sheji (CHN) **6886**
Yiyong Shengwu Lixue (CHN) **5733**
Youji Huaxue (CHN) **2132**
Youjiang Minzu Yixueyuan Xuebao (CHN) **5734**
Youkuang Dizhi (CHN) **2775**
Youkuangye (CHN) **6484**
Youqijing Ceshi (CHN) **6798**
Youqitian Huanjing Baohu (CHN) **3476**
Youse Jinshu (CHN) **6337**
Youtian Huaxue (CHN) **6798**
Youyong (CHN) **8217**
Yuanyi Xuebao (CHN) **3754**
Yuanzi Hewuli Pinglun (CHN) **7073**
Yuanzi yu Fenzi Wuli Xuebao (CHN) **7073**
Yuanzineng Kexue Jishu (CHN) **3176**
Yuedu yu Xiezuo (CHN) **5403**
Yuefu Xin Sheng (CHN) **6630**
Yuhang Cailiao Gongyi (CHN) **75**
Yuhang Jice Jishu (CHN) **76**
Yuhang Xuebao (CHN) **76**
Yuhua (CHN) **5403**
Yumi Kexue (CHN) **276**
Yunan Daxue Xuebao(Ziran Kexue Ban) (CHN) **7933**
Yunchouxue Xuebao (CHN) **7933**
Yunnan Dili Huanjing Yanjiu (CHN) **4034**
Yunnan Minzu Daxue Xuebao (Zhexue Shehui Kexue Ban) (CHN) **8017**
Yunnan Minzu Daxue Xuebao (Ziran Kexue Ban) (CHN) **7933**
Yunnan Nongye Daxue Xuebao (CHN) **171**
Yunnan Shehui Kexue (CHN) **8018**
Yunnan Tianwentai Taikan (CHN) **584**
Yunnan Zhiwu Yanjiu (CHN) **823**
Yunnan Zhongyi Xueyuan Xuebao (CHN) **5734**
Yunnan Zhongyi Zhongyao Zazhi (CHN) **315**
Yunyang Yixueyuan Xuebao (CHN) **5734**
Yuwen Jianshe (CHN) **5197**
Yuwen Jiaoxue Tongxun (CHN) **5197**
Yuwen Jiaoxue yu Yanjiu (Dazhong Ban) (CHN) **5197**
Yuwen Jiaoxue yu Yanjiu (Jiaoshi Ban) (CHN) **5197**
Yuwen Jiaoxue yu Yanjiu (Xuesheng Ban) (CHN) **5197**
Yuwen Yanjiu (CHN) **5197**
Yuyan Jiaoxue yu Yanjiu (CHN) **5198**
Yuyan Wenzi Yingyong (CHN) **5198**
Yuye Xiandaihua (CHN) **3612**
Zaihaixue (CHN) **2228**
Zajiao Shuidao (CHN) **260**
Zaochuan Jishu (CHN) **8665**
Zaoqi Jiaoyu (Jiaoshi Ban) (CHN) **2928**
Zaozhi Huaxuepin (CHN) **6740**
Zarubezhnoe Voennoe Obozrenie (RUS) **6455**
Zhanghui Xiaoshuo (CHN) **5404**
Zhanlue yu Guanli (CHN) **1802**
Zhaoming Gongcheng Xuebao (CHN) **7085**
Zhaoxiangji (CHN) **6978**
Zhejiang Chuangshang Waike (CHN) **6075**

Advances in Anatomic Pathology (USA) **5568**
Advances in Anesthesia (USA) **5768**
Advances in Applied Ceramics (Online) (GBR) **2047**
Advances in Applied Mathematics (USA) **5466**
Advances in Applied Probability (GBR) **5466**
Advances in Art & Urban Futures (GBR) **8085**
Advances in Atmospheric Sciences (CHN) **6346**
Advances in Cement Research (GBR) **975**
Advances in Chronic Kidney Disease (USA) **6264**
Advances in Colloid and Interface Science (NLD) **2132**
Advances in Competitiveness Research (USA) **1551**
Advances in Complex Systems (SGP) **7833**
Advances in Computational Mathematics (NLD) **5549**
Advances in Consumer Research (USA) **1804**
Advances in Dental Research (USA) **5833**
Advances in Dermatology (USA) **5871**
Advances in Developing Human Resources (USA) **1855**
Advances in Difference Equations (USA) **5466**
Advances in Engineering Software (GBR) **3288**
Advances in Enzyme Regulation (GBR) **721**
Advances in Geometry (DEU) **5466**
Advances in Health Sciences Education (NLD) **5568**
Advances in Mathematics (USA) **5466**
Advances in Neonatal Care (USA) **6087**
Advances in Nursing Science (USA) **5950**
Advances in Pediatrics (USA) **6087**
Advances in Physics (GBR) **7004**
Advances in Physiology Education (USA) **918**
Advances in Physiotherapy (SWE) **6106**
Advances in Polymer Technology (USA) **7090**
Advances in Psychiatric Treatment (Online) (GBR) *see* Advances in Psychiatric Treatment. **6120**
Advances in Skin and Wound Care (USA) **5871**
Advances in Space Research (GBR) **41**
Advances in Structural Engineering (GBR) **3258**
Advances in Surgery (USA) **6235**
Advances in Theoretical and Mathematical Physics (USA) **5467**
Advances in Therapy (GBR) **5568**
Advances in Water Resources (GBR) **8817**
Adverse Drug Reaction Bulletin (Italian Edition) (ITA) **6819**
Advertising Age (USA) **20**
Advertising & Society Review (USA) **20**
The Advertising Forecast (GBR) **20**
Advisor Today (USA) **4491**
The Advocate (Los Angeles, 1967) (USA) **4370**
Adweek (USA) **20**
Aegypten und Levante (AUT) **371**
Aequationes Mathematicae (CHE) **5467**
Aerobiologia (NLD) **651**
Aerosol Science and Technology (USA) **2049**
Aerospace Daily & Defense Report (USA) **43**
Aerospace Science and Technology (FRA) **43**
Aerztliche Praxis. Dermatologie, Allergologie (DEU) **5871**
Aesthetic Plastic Surgery (USA) **6235**
Aesthetic Surgery Journal (USA) **6235**
Affilia (USA) **8024**
Africa (GBR) **4172**
Africa Confidential (GBR) **7102**
Africa Monitor. North Africa (GBR) **1435**
Africa Monitor. Southern Africa (GBR) **1435**
Africa Monitor. West & Central Africa (GBR) **1435**
Africa Research Bulletin. Economic, Financial and Technical Series (GBR) **1435**
Africa Research Bulletin. Political, Social and Cultural Series (GBR) **7102**
Africa Today (USA) **7102**
African Affairs (GBR) **7103**
African American Review (USA) **3516**
African and Asian Studies (NLD) **8086**
African Archaeological Review (USA) **371**
African Arts (USA) **464**
African Business (GBR) **1589**
African Development Review (GBR) **1590**
African Health Sciences (UGA) **5569**
African Identities (GBR) **3516**
African Journal of AIDS Research (ZAF) **5808**
African Journal of Aquatic Science (ZAF) **651**
African Journal of Ecology Online (GBR) **651**
African Journal of Marine Science (ZAF) **3583**
African Journal of Range & Forage Science (ZAF) **216**
African Security Review (ZAF) **6408**
African Studies (GBR) **323**
African Studies Review (USA) **3516**
African Zoology (ZAF) **931**
Afro-Hispanic Review (USA) **3517**
Afterimage (USA) **6963**
Aftermarket Business (USA) **8555**
AgBiotech Reporter (USA) **80**
Age (NLD) **4038**
Age and Ageing (GBR) **4038**
Ageing and Society (GBR) **4039**
Ageing International (USA) **4039**
Ageing Research Reviews (IRL) **4039**
Aggiornamento Medico (ITA) **5570**
Aggression and Violent Behavior (GBR) **7332**
Aggressive Behavior (USA) **7332**
Aging & Mental Health (GBR) **4039**
Aging Cell (GBR) **827**
Aging Clinical and Experimental Research (ITA) **4039**
Aging Health (GBR) **4039**
The Aging Male (GBR) **6283**
Agni (USA) **5250**
Agra Europe (GBR) **191**
Agribusiness (New York) (USA) **191**
Agricultural and Forest Entomology (GBR) **837**
Agricultural and Forest Meteorology (NLD) **6346**
Agricultural Economics (USA) **192**
Agricultural History (USA) **83**
Agricultural Research (USA) **217**
Agricultural Systems (NLD) **85**
Agricultural Water Management (NLD) **217**
Agriculture and Human Values (NLD) **85**
Agriculture, Ecosystems & Environment (NLD) **85**
Agro Food Industry Hi-Tech (ITA) **86**
Agroforestry Systems (NLD) **87**
Agrokemia es Talajtan (HUN) **87**
Agronomy for Sustainable Development (FRA) **217**
Agronomy Journal (USA) **88**
Ahfad Journal (SDN) **8893**
AIDS (USA) **5808**
AIDS Alert (USA) **5808**
AIDS & Behavior (USA) **5752**
AIDS Clinical Care (USA) **5808**
AIDS Education and Prevention (USA) **7506**
AIDS Patient Care and S T Ds (USA) **5809**
AIDS Research and Human Retroviruses (USA) **5809**
AIDS Research and Therapy (GBR) **5752**
AIDS Treatment News (USA) **5809**
Air & Space Law (NLD) **8534**
The Air & Space Power Journal (USA) **6408**
Air & Waste Management Association. Journal (USA) **3503**
Air Cargo World (USA) **8534**
Air Conditioning, Heating & Refrigeration News (USA) **4116**
Air Force Comptroller (USA) **6409**
Air Force Journal of Logistics (USA) **6409**
Air Force Law Review (USA) **4971**
Air Medical Journal (USA) **5570**
The Air Pollution Consultant (USA) **3482**
Air Power History (USA) **44**
Air Safety Week (Online) (USA) **44**
Air Transport World (USA) **45**
Aircraft Economics (GBR) **8535**
Aircraft Engineering and Aerospace Technology (GBR) **45**
Airfinance Journal (GBR) **8535**
AirForceTimes.com (USA) *see* Air Force Times (U.S. Edition). **6409**
Airline Business (GBR) **8536**
Airman (USA) **6409**
Airport Business (USA) **46**
Akademiai Ertesito (HUN) **3016**
Akroterion (ZAF) **2229**
Aktuelle Dermatologie (DEU) **5871**
Aktuelle Ernaehrungsmedizin (DEU) **6654**
Aktuelle Neurologie (DEU) **6120**
Aktuelle Rheumatologie (DEU) **6221**
Aktuelle Urologie (DEU) **6264**
The Alabama Review (USA) **4282**
Albany Law Review (USA) **4612**
Alberta Sweetgrass (CAN) **3517**
Alces (CAN) **931**
Alcohol (New York) (USA) **2690**
Alcohol and Alcoholism (GBR) **2690**
Alcohol Research & Health (USA) **2691**
Alcoholism & Drug Abuse Weekly (USA) **2691**
Alcoholism: Clinical and Experimental Research (USA) **2691**
Alcoholism Treatment Quarterly (USA) **2691**
Algebra and Logic (USA) **5467**
Algebra Colloquium (SGP) **5468**
Algebra Universalis (CHE) **5468**
Algebras and Representation Theory (NLD) **5468**
Algorithmica (USA) **2406**
Alimentary Pharmacology and Therapeutics (GBR) **5920**
Alive (CAN) **6981**
All Hands (USA) **6410**
Allen's Trademark Digest (USA) **4613**
Allergology International (JPN) **5753**
Allergy (GBR) **5753**
Allergy and Asthma Proceedings (USA) **5753**
Allured's Cosmetics and Toiletries (USA) **592**
Alternate Routes (CAN) **7946**
Alternative & Complementary Therapies (USA) **306**
Alternative Medicine Alert (USA) **306**
Alternative Medicine Review (USA) **306**
Alternative Therapies in Health and Medicine (USA) **306**
Alternative Therapies in Women's Health (USA) **306**
Alternatives (USA) **7220**
Alternatives (TUR) **7220**
Alternatives Journal (CAN) **3402**
Alternatives to the High Cost of Litigation (USA) **4613**
AlterTexto (MEX) **5251**
Aluminium International Today (GBR) **6304**
Alzheimer Disease and Associated Disorders (USA) **6121**
Alzheimer's & Dementia (USA) **6121**
Alzheimer's Care Today (USA) **6121**
Ambio Journal Online (SWE) *see* Ambio. **3402**
Ambix (GBR) **2049**
America (USA) **7782**
The American (Washington, D.C.) (USA) **7104**
American Academy of Audiology. Journal (USA) **6077**
American Academy of Business, Cambridge. Journal (USA) **1058**
American Academy of Child and Adolescent Psychiatry. Journal (USA) **6121**
American Academy of Dermatology. Journal (USA) **5871**
American Academy of Nurse Practitioners. Journal (USA) **5951**
American Academy of Orthopaedic Surgeons. Journal (USA) **6055**
American Academy of Orthopaedic Surgeons. Journal (Spanish Edition) (ESP) **6055**
American Academy of Political and Social Science. Annals (USA) **7104**
American Academy of Psychiatry and the Law. Journal (USA) **6121**
American Academy of Psychoanalysis and Dynamic Psychiatry. Journal (USA) **7332**
American Academy of Religion. Journal (USA) **7620**
The American Acupuncturist (USA) **306**
American Animal Hospital Association. Journal (Online Edition) (USA) **8791**
American Annals of the Deaf (USA) **4071**
American Art (USA) **465**
American Artist (USA) **465**
American Association for Laboratory Animal Science. Journal (USA) **5902**
American Association for Pediatric Ophthalmology and Strabismus. Journal (USA) **6038**
American Association of Occupational Health Nurses Journal (USA) **5951**
American Banker (USA) **1307**
American Banker's Financial Modernization Report (USA) **1307**
American Bankruptcy Law Journal (USA) **4614**
American Behavioral Scientist (USA) **7946**
American Board of Family Medicine. Journal (Online Edition) (USA) *see* American Board of Family Medicine. Journal. **5571**
American Book Review (USA) **5205**
American Business Law Journal (USA) **4854**
American Ceramic Society. Bulletin (USA) **2037**
American Ceramic Society. Journal (USA) **2037**
American Cheerleader (USA) **8158**
American Chemical Society. Journal (USA) **2049**
American Chiropractic Association. Journal (USA) **5803**
The American Chiropractor (USA) **5803**
American City & County (USA) **7487**
American Coin-Op (USA) **2242**
American College of Cardiology. Journal (USA) **5776**
American College of Nutrition. Journal (USA) **6654**
American College of Radiology. Journal (USA) **6192**
American College of Surgeons. Journal (USA) **6235**
American Communist History (GBR) **4282**
American Dental Association. Journal (USA) **5834**
American Dietetic Association. Journal (USA) **6654**
American Drycleaner (USA) **2242**
The American Economic Review (USA) **1436**
American Economist (USA) **1436**
American Family Physician (USA) **5571**
American Fisheries Society. Transactions (USA) **3584**
American Fitness (USA) **6981**
American Foreign Policy Interests (USA) **7220**
American Forests (USA) **3683**
American Gas (USA) **6762**
American Geriatrics Society. Journal (USA) **4040**
American Heart Journal (USA) **5776**
American Heritage (USA) **4282**
American Historical Review (USA) **4129**
American History (Leesburg) (USA) **4282**
American Imago (USA) **6121**
American Indian and Alaska Native Mental Health Research (Online Edition) (USA) **6634**
American Indian Quarterly (USA) **6634**
American Jails (USA) **2643**
American Jewish History (USA) **7718**
American Journal of Agricultural Economics (USA) **193**
American Journal of Audiology (USA) **4072**
The American Journal of Bioethics (USA) **862**
American Journal of Botany (USA) **774**
American Journal of Business (USA) **1059**
The American Journal of Cardiology (USA) **5776**
American Journal of Cardiovascular Drugs (NZL) **5776**
The American Journal of Chinese Medicine (SGP) **5740**
American Journal of Clinical Dermatology (NZL) **5871**
American Journal of Clinical Nutrition (USA) **6655**
American Journal of Clinical Oncology (USA) **6007**
American Journal of Clinical Pathology (USA) **5572**
American Journal of Community Psychology (USA) **8086**
American Journal of Criminal Justice (USA) **2643**
American Journal of Criminal Law (USA) **2643**
American Journal of Critical Care (USA) **5951**
American Journal of Dance Therapy (USA) **2682**
American Journal of Dermatopathology (USA) **5572**
American Journal of Distance Education (USA) **2938**
American Journal of Drug and Alcohol Abuse (USA) **2691**
American Journal of Economics and Sociology (USA) **1059**
American Journal of Education (USA) **2826**
American Journal of Electroneurodiagnostic Technology (USA) **6121**
American Journal of Emergency Medicine (USA) **6055**
American Journal of Enology and Viticulture (USA) **597**
American Journal of Epidemiology (USA) **5572**
American Journal of Evaluation (USA) **7946**
American Journal of Family Law (USA) **4906**
American Journal of Family Therapy (USA) **7333**
American Journal of Forensic Medicine and Pathology (USA) **5912**
American Journal of Gastroenterology (USA) **5920**
The American Journal of Geriatric Pharmacotherapy (USA) **6819**
American Journal of Geriatric Psychiatry (USA) **4040**
American Journal of Health Behavior (USA) **6981**
American Journal of Health Studies (Online) (USA) **6982**
American Journal of Health-System Pharmacy (USA) **6819**
American Journal of Hematology (USA) **5933**
American Journal of Homeopathic Medicine (USA) **5803**
American Journal of Human Biology (USA) **652**
American Journal of Human Genetics (USA) **862**
American Journal of Hypertension (USA) **5776**
American Journal of Industrial Medicine (USA) **6672**
American Journal of Infection Control (USA) **5809**
American Journal of Kidney Diseases (USA) **6265**
American Journal of Law & Medicine (USA) **4614**
American Journal of Mathematics (USA) **5468**
American Journal of Medical Genetics. Part A (USA) **862**
American Journal of Medical Genetics. Part B: Neuropsychiatric Genetics (USA) **862**
American Journal of Medical Genetics. Part C: Seminars in Medical Genetics (USA) **862**
American Journal of Medical Quality (USA) **5572**
The American Journal of Medicine (USA) **5572**
The American Journal of Medicine. Supplement (USA) **5573**
American Journal of Nephrology (CHE) **6265**
American Journal of Neuroradiology (USA) **6192**
American Journal of Nursing (USA) **5951**
American Journal of Obstetrics and Gynecology (USA) **5985**
American Journal of Occupational Therapy (USA) **6672**
American Journal of Ophthalmology (USA) **6038**
American Journal of Orthodontics and Dentofacial Orthopedics (USA) **5834**
American Journal of Orthopsychiatry (USA) **7333**
American Journal of Otolaryngology (USA) **6077**
The American Journal of Pathology (USA) **5573**
American Journal of Perinatology (USA) **5985**
American Journal of Philology (USA) **5092**
American Journal of Physical Anthropology (USA) **324**
American Journal of Physical Medicine and Rehabilitation (USA) **6106**
American Journal of Physics (USA) **7004**
American Journal of Political Science (USA) **7105**
American Journal of Preventive Medicine (USA) **5573**
American Journal of Primatology (USA) **931**
American Journal of Psychiatric Rehabilitation (USA) **6121**
American Journal of Psychiatry (USA) **6122**
The American Journal of Psychoanalysis (USA) **7333**
American Journal of Psychology (USA) **7333**
American Journal of Psychotherapy (USA) **6122**
American Journal of Public Health (USA) **7507**
American Journal of Reproductive Immunology Online (DNK) **5754**
American Journal of Respiratory and Critical Care Medicine (USA) **6211**
American Journal of Respiratory Cell and Molecular Biology (USA) **6211**
American Journal of Rhinology & Allergy (USA) **6077**
American Journal of Roentgenology (USA) **6192**
American Journal of Sexuality Education (USA) **6982**
American Journal of Sociology (USA) **8087**
American Journal of Speech - Language Pathology (USA) **4072**
American Journal of Sports Medicine (USA) **6228**
The American Journal of Surgery (USA) **6235**
American Journal of Surgical Pathology (USA) **5573**
American Journal of the Medical Sciences (USA) **5573**
American Journal of Therapeutics (GBR) **5573**
American Journal of Transplantation (Online) (DNK) **6236**
American Journal of Tropical Medicine and Hygiene (USA) **5810**
American Journal on Addictions (USA) **2691**
American Journal on Intellectual and Developmental Disabilities (USA) **6122**
American Journalism (USA) **4571**
American Laundry News (USA) **2242**
American Law and Economics Review (GBR) **4614**
American Letters & Commentary (USA) **5205**
American Libraries (USA) **4988**
American Literary History (USA) **5252**
American Literary Scholarship (USA) **5252**
American Literature (USA) **5252**
American Machinist (USA) **1879**
American Mathematical Society. Bulletin. New Series (USA) **5469**
American Mathematical Society. Journal (USA) **5469**
American Mathematical Society. Notices (USA) **5469**
American Mathematical Society. Proceedings (USA) **5469**
American Mathematical Society. Transactions (USA) **5469**
American Medical Directors Association. Journal (USA) **4087**

Online Service

DIRECTORY 2010 EBSCO HOST 11093

B J U International (Online) (GBR) **6265**
B M B Reports (KOR) **724**
B M C Anesthesiology (GBR) **5770**
B M C Biochemistry (GBR) **724**
B M C Bioinformatics (GBR) **824**
B M C Biology (GBR) **655**
B M C Biotechnology (GBR) **756**
B M C Blood Disorders (GBR) **5934**
B M C Cancer (GBR) **6009**
B M C Cardiovascular Disorders (GBR) **5778**
B M C Cell Biology (GBR) **827**
B M C Chemical Biology (GBR) **724**
B M C Clinical Pathology (GBR) **5934**
B M C Clinical Pharmacology (GBR) **6824**
B M C Complementary and Alternative Medicine (GBR) **307**
B M C Dermatology (GBR) **5872**
B M C Developmental Biology (GBR) **655**
B M C Ear, Nose and Throat Disorders (GBR) **6078**
B M C Ecology (GBR) **655**
B M C Emergency Medicine (GBR) **6056**
B M C Endocrine Disorders (GBR) **5884**
B M C Evolutionary Biology (GBR) **863**
B M C Family Practice (GBR) **5582**
B M C Gastroenterology (GBR) **5920**
B M C Genetics (GBR) **863**
B M C Genomics (GBR) **863**
B M C Geriatrics (GBR) **4041**
B M C Health Services Research (GBR) **5582**
B M C Immunology (GBR) **5755**
B M C Infectious Diseases (GBR) **5810**
B M C International Health and Human Rights (GBR) **7509**
B M C Medical Education (GBR) **5582**
B M C Medical Ethics (GBR) **5582**
B M C Medical Genetics (GBR) **863**
B M C Medical Imaging (GBR) **6193**
B M C Medical Informatics and Decision Making (GBR) **5829**
B M C Medical Physics (GBR) **6193**
B M C Medical Research Methodology (GBR) **5582**
B M C Medicine (GBR) **5582**
B M C Microbiology (GBR) **882**
B M C Molecular Biology (GBR) **655**
B M C Musculoskeletal Disorders (GBR) **6056**
B M C Nephrology (GBR) **6265**
B M C Neurology (GBR) **6125**
B M C Neuroscience (GBR) **920**
B M C Nursing (GBR) **5952**
B M C Ophthalmology (GBR) **6039**
B M C Oral Health (GBR) **5836**
B M C Palliative Care (GBR) **5582**
B M C Pediatrics (GBR) **6088**
B M C Pharmacology (GBR) **6824**
B M C Physiology (GBR) **920**
B M C Plant Biology (GBR) **778**
B M C Pregnancy and Childbirth (GBR) **5986**
B M C Psychiatry (GBR) **6126**
B M C Public Health (GBR) **7509**
B M C Pulmonary Medicine (GBR) **6212**
B M C Structural Biology (GBR) **655**
B M C Surgery (GBR) **6237**
B M C Urology (GBR) **6265**
B M C Veterinary Research (GBR) **8794**
B M C Women's Health (GBR) **8844**
B M J (Clinical Research Edition) (GBR) **5582**
B M X Plus (USA) **8254**
B T Technology Journal (NLD) **2313**
B to B (USA) **1806**
B Y U Journal of Public Law (USA) **4625**
Babel (NLD) **5098**
Baby Talk (USA) **2144**
Bach Perspectives (USA) **6547**
Background Notes (USA) **4000**
Backpacker (USA) **8305**
Backyard Flyer (USA) **4328**
Balint-Journal (DEU) **6126**
Baltic Security and Defence Review (Online Edition) (EST) *see* Baltic Security and Defence Review. **2225**
Bamboo Ridge (USA) **5260**
Banach Center Publications (POL) **5475**
Bandolier Journal (GBR) **5583**
Bank Accounting & Finance (USA) **1281**
Bank Investment Consultant (USA) **1611**
Bank Loan Report (USA) **1313**
Bank of Canada. Review (CAN) **1313**
Bank of England Quarterly Bulletin (GBR) **1441**
Bank Technology News (USA) **1316**
Banking & Financial Services Policy Report (USA) **1317**
Baseball Digest (USA) **8222**
Baseline (New York) (USA) **2408**
Bases (FRA) **5060**
Basic and Applied Ecology (DEU) **3405**
Basic and Applied Social Psychology (USA) **7338**
Basic & Clinical Pharmacology & Toxicology Online (GBR) **6824**
Basic Research in Cardiology (DEU) **5778**
Basin Research (Online) (GBR) **2702**
Bauphysik (DEU) **980**
Bautechnik (DEU) **981**
Bauwelt (DEU) **435**
Bay Nature (USA) **3406**
Bay Windows (USA) **4371**
Baylor Business Review (USA) **1065**
The Beaver (CAN) **4285**
Beef (USA) **280**
Before Farming (GBR) **383**
Behavior Analysis Digest (USA) **7338**
The Behavior Analyst Today (USA) **7338**
Behavior and Philosophy (USA) **7338**
Behavior and Social Issues (USA) **7339**
Behavior Genetics (USA) **863**
Behavior Modification (USA) **7339**
Behavior Research Methods (USA) **7339**
Behavior Therapy (USA) **7339**
Behavioral and Brain Functions (GBR) **6126**
Behavioral and Brain Sciences (GBR) **7339**
Behavioral & Social Sciences Librarian (USA) **4994**
Behavioral Ecology (USA) **656**
Behavioral Ecology and Sociobiology (DEU) **3406**
Behavioral Interventions (GBR) **6126**
Behavioral Medicine (USA) **7339**
Behavioral Neuroscience (USA) **7339**
Behavioral Research in Accounting (USA) **1281**
Behavioral Sciences & the Law (GBR) **7339**
Behavioral Sleep Medicine (USA) **7339**
Behaviour (NLD) **935**
Behaviour and Information Technology (GBR) **7340**
Behaviour Research and Therapy (GBR) **7340**
Behavioural and Cognitive Psychotherapy (GBR) **7340**
Behavioural Brain Research (NLD) **6126**
Behavioural Neurology (NLD) **6126**
Behavioural Pharmacology (USA) **6825**
Behavioural Processes (NLD) **6126**
Beilstein Journal of Organic Chemistry (DEU) **2119**
Le Bel Age (CAN) **4041**
Belgian Journal of Linguistics (NLD) **5099**
Bell Labs Technical Journal (USA) **2365**
Belle (AUS) **4533**
Bellingham Review (USA) **5261**
Beloit Poetry Journal (USA) **5417**
Benchmarking (GBR) **1727**
Benefits Canada (CAN) **1667**
Benefits Law Journal (USA) **4968**
Benefits Quarterly (USA) **1856**
Berichte zur Wissenschaftsgeschichte (DEU) **7840**
Berkeley Journal of Employment and Labor Law (USA) **1667**
Berkeley Journal of Gender, Law & Justice (USA) **4629**
Berkeley Journal of International Law (USA) **4918**
Berkeley La Raza Law Journal (USA) **4629**
Berkeley Technology Law Journal (USA) **4629**
Berliner und Muenchener Tieraerztliche Wochenschrift (DEU) **8794**
Bernoulli (NLD) **5475**
Best of New Orleans (USA) *see* New Orleans Magazine. **3983**
Best Practice (AUS) **5584**
Best Practice & Research: Clinical Anaesthesiology (GBR) **5770**
Best Practice & Research: Clinical Endocrinology & Metabolism (GBR) **5884**
Best Practice & Research: Clinical Gastroenterology (GBR) **5920**
Best Practice & Research: Clinical Haematology (GBR) **5934**
Best Practice & Research: Clinical Obstetrics & Gynaecology (GBR) **5986**
Best Practice & Research: Clinical Rheumatology (GBR) **6222**
Best Practice Measurement Strategies (GBR) **2313**
Best Practices in Mental Health (USA) **6126**
Best's Review. Insurance Issues and Analysis (USA) **4495**
Beton- und Stahlbetonbau (DEU) **982**
Better Nutrition (USA) **6656**
Beverage Industry (USA) **599**
Beverage World (USA) **599**
Biblical Interpretation (NLD) **7627**
Bibliotheca Sacra (USA) **7748**
Bibliothek Forschung und Praxis (DEU) **4996**
Bibliotheksdienst (DEU) **4996**
Bicycle Retailer and Industry News (USA) **8254**
Bicycling (USA) **8254**
Bijdragen (BEL) **6907**
Bilingual Review (USA) **2831**
Bilingualism (GBR) **5100**
Billboard.com (USA) *see* Billboard (New York). **6549**
Bio - I T World (USA) **757**
Bio-Medical Materials and Engineering (NLD) **747**
Biocatalysis and Biotransformation (CHE) **757**
Biochemical and Biophysical Research Communications (USA) **724**
Biochemical Engineering Journal (NLD) **724**
Biochemical Genetics (USA) **863**
Biochemical Journal (GBR) **724**
Biochemical Pharmacology (USA) **6825**
Biochemical Society Transactions (GBR) **725**
Biochemical Systematics and Ecology (GBR) **725**
Biochemistry (USA) **725**
Biochemistry (Moscow) (RUS) **725**
Biochemistry and Cell Biology (CAN) **725**
Biochemistry and Molecular Biology Education (USA) **725**
Biochimica et Biophysica Acta (NLD) **726**
Biochimica et Biophysica Acta. Gene Regulatory Mechanisms (NLD) **864**
Biochimie (FRA) **726**
Bioconjugate Chemistry (USA) **726**
BioControl (NLD) **841**
Biocontrol Science and Technology (GBR) **221**
BioCycle (USA) **3504**
Biodegradation (NLD) **3504**
Biodiversity and Conservation (NLD) **2604**
BioDrugs (NZL) **6825**
Bioelectromagnetics (USA) **752**
BioEssays (GBR) **657**
Bioethics (GBR) **6907**
BioFactors (USA) **726**
Biofouling (CHE) **3494**
Biogenic Amines (SVK) **726**
Biogeochemistry (NLD) **726**
Biogerontology (NLD) **4041**
Biography (Honolulu) (USA) **640**
Biography (New York) (USA) **2375**
Bioinformatics (Online) (GBR) **825**
Bioinformation (IND) **657**
Biologia Plantarum (NLD) **779**
Biological and Cultural Tests for Control of Plant Diseases (USA) **779**
Biological & Pharmaceutical Bulletin (JPN) **6825**
Biological Bulletin (USA) **658**
Biological Chemistry (DEU) **727**
Biological Conservation (NLD) **2604**
Biological Control (USA) **658**
Biological Cybernetics (DEU) **825**
Biological Invasions (NLD) **658**
Biological Psychiatry (USA) **6126**
Biological Psychology (NLD) **7340**
Biological Research for Nursing (USA) **5953**
Biological Reviews (GBR) **658**
Biological Rhythm Research (NLD) **658**
Biological Therapies in Dentistry (CAN) **5836**
Biological Therapies in Psychiatry Newsletter (USA) **6127**
Biological Trace Element Research (USA) **727**
Biologicals (GBR) **659**
Biologie Aujourd'hui (FRA) **659**
Biologie in Unserer Zeit (DEU) **659**
Biologist (GBR) **659**
Biology and Environment (IRL) **660**
Biology and Fertility of Soils (DEU) **221**
Biology and Philosophy (NLD) **660**
Biology Direct (GBR) **660**
Biology of Blood and Marrow Transplantation (USA) **5934**
Biology of Reproduction (USA) **660**
Biology of the Cell (GBR) **828**
Biomacromolecules (USA) **2120**
BioMagnetic Research and Technology (GBR) **727**
Biomarkers (GBR) **5585**
Biomass & Bioenergy (GBR) **3124**
Biomaterials (NLD) **5585**
Biomechanics and Modeling in Mechanobiology (DEU) **748**
Biomedical Business & Technology (USA) **5585**
Biomedical Chromatography (GBR) **2098**
Biomedical Digital Libraries (GBR) **5585**
Biomedical Engineering (USA) **5585**
BioMedical Engineering OnLine (GBR) **5586**
Biomedical Microdevices (USA) **5586**
Biomedical Safety & Standards (USA) **5586**
Biomedicine & Pharmacotherapy (FRA) **5587**
BioMetals (NLD) **727**
Biometric Technology Today (GBR) **3090**
Biometrical Journal (DEU) **660**
Biometrics (GBR) **8358**
Biometrika (GBR) **713**
Bioorganic & Medicinal Chemistry (GBR) **2120**
Bioorganic & Medicinal Chemistry Letters (GBR) **2120**
Bioorganic Chemistry (USA) **2120**
BioPharm International (USA) **6825**
Biopharmaceutics & Drug Disposition (GBR) **6825**
Biophysical Chemistry (NLD) **752**
Biophysical Journal (USA) **752**
Biophysical Reviews and Letters (SGP) **7006**
Biopolymers (USA) **2120**
Biopreservation and Biobanking (USA) **828**
Bioprocess and Biosystems Engineering (DEU) **758**
Bioquimia (MEX) **2051**
Bioremediation Journal (USA) **3483**
Bioresource Technology (NLD) **758**
Biorheology (NLD) **752**
BioScience (USA) **661**
Bioscience, Biotechnology, and Biochemistry (JPN) **758**
Bioscience Reports (GBR) **828**
Biosecurity and Bioterrorism (USA) **758**
Biosensors and Bioelectronics (NLD) **759**
BioSocieties (GBR) **7950**
Biostatistics (GBR) **5587**
BioSystems (IRL) **662**
Biosystems Engineering (GBR) **222**
Biotech Business (USA) **759**
Biotechnic and Histochemistry (GBR) **898**
BioTechniques (USA) **759**
Biotechnology Advances (USA) **760**
Biotechnology and Applied Biochemistry (GBR) **760**
Biotechnology and Bioengineering (Online) (USA) *see* Biotechnology and Bioengineering (Print). **760**
Biotechnology Journal (DEU) **761**
Biotechnology Law Report (USA) **761**
Biotechnology Letters (NLD) **761**
Biotechnology Progress (USA) **761**
Biotecnologia Aplicada (CUB) **761**
Biotropica (USA) **662**
Bipolar Disorders Online (DNK) **6127**
Bird Behavior (USA) **902**
Bird Conservation International (GBR) **902**
Bird Study (GBR) **903**
Birder's World (USA) **903**
Birth (USA) **5986**
Birth Defects Research. Part A: Clinical and Molecular Teratology (USA) **662**
Birth Defects Research. Part B: Developmental and Reproductive Toxicology (USA) **5587**
The Birth Gazette (USA) **5987**
The Birthkit (USA) **5987**
Bit (Lisse) (NLD) **2505**
BizEd (USA) **2969**
Blacfax (USA) **3522**
The Black Collegian (USA) **6693**
Black Collegian Online (USA) **6693**
Black Enterprise.com (USA) *see* Black Enterprise. **1068**
Black History Bulletin (USA) **3522**
Black Issues Book Review (USA) **3522**
Black Masks (USA) **8467**
Black Scholar (USA) **3523**
Black Theology (GBR) **7628**
Blood (USA) **5934**
Blood Cells, Molecules and Diseases (USA) **5934**
Blood Coagulation and Fibrinolysis (USA) **5934**
Blood Pressure (NOR) **5778**
Blood Pressure Monitoring (USA) **5778**
Blood Purification (CHE) **5934**
Blood Reviews (GBR) **5934**
Blueprint (Washington, D.C.) (USA) **7110**
Board Leadership (USA) **1728**
Boating World (USA) **8273**
Bochumer Philosophisches Jahrbuch fuer Antike und Mittelalter (NLD) **6908**
Body & Society (GBR) **7951**
Body Image (NLD) **7341**
Body, Movement and Dance in Psychotherapy (GBR) **2683**
Boersenblatt (DEU) **7553**
Bollettino di Storia delle Scienze Matematiche (ITA) **5476**
The Bond Buyer (USA) **1613**
Bone (USA) **6056**
Bone Marrow Transplantation (GBR) **5903**
Bonplandia (ARG) **780**
Book History (USA) **7554**
Book Links (USA) **2146**
Book Publishing Report (USA) **7554**
Booklist (USA) **7554**
The Bookseller (GBR) **7555**
Border Crossings (CAN) **479**
Boreas (DNK) **2726**
Borneo Research Bulletin (USA) **331**
The Boston Business Journal (USA) **1068**
Boston College Environmental Affairs Law Review (USA) **3407**
Boston Review (USA) **5209**
Botanica Helvetica (CHE) **780**
Botanica Lithuanica (LTU) **780**
Botanica Marina (DEU) **780**
Botanische Jahrbuecher fuer Systematik, Pflanzengeschichte und Pflanzengeographie (DEU) **781**
Botany (CAN) **781**
The Bottom Line (GBR) **4998**
Boulevard (USA) **5265**
Boundary 2 (USA) **5265**
Boundary-Layer Meteorology (NLD) **6347**
Boundary Value Problems (USA) **5476**
Bowhunter (USA) **8306**
Boys' Life (USA) **2180**
Boys' Quest (USA) **2180**
Brachytherapy (USA) **6009**
Brahms Studies (USA) **6551**
The Braille Forum (USA) **4080**
Brain (GBR) **6127**
Brain and Cognition (USA) **7341**
Brain & Development (NLD) **6127**
Brain and Language (USA) **7341**
Brain, Behavior and Evolution (CHE) **6127**
Brain, Behavior, and Immunity (USA) **5755**
Brain Impairment (AUS) **6127**
Brain Injury (GBR) **6127**
Brain Pathology (USA) **6127**
Brain Research (NLD) **6128**
Brain Research Bulletin (USA) **6128**
Brain Research Reviews (NLD) **6128**
Brain Structure and Function (Online Edition) (DEU) *see* Brain Structure and Function (Print Edition). **920**
Brain Topography (USA) **6128**
Brand Strategy (GBR) **22**
Brandweek (USA) **22**
Brazil Business Forecast Report (GBR) **1443**
The Breast (GBR) **5987**
Breast Cancer Research (Online Edition) (GBR) **6010**
Breast Cancer Research and Treatment (USA) **6010**
Breast Care (CHE) **5987**
Breast Disease (NLD) **5987**
Breast Diseases: A Year Book Quarterly (USA) **5987**
The Breast Journal (USA) **5987**
Bridge Structures (GBR) **3260**
Bridges (USA) **8894**
Briefings in Bioinformatics (GBR) **825**
Briefings in Entrepreneurial Finance (GBR) **1729**
Briefings in Functional Genomics & Proteomics (GBR) **864**
Briefings In Real Estate Finance (GBR) **7584**
Briefings on Patient Safety (USA) **4089**
Brigham Young University Law Review (USA) **4632**
The British Accounting Review (GBR) **1282**
British Actuarial Journal (GBR) **4496**
British Archaeological Association. Journal (GBR) **384**
British Association of Psychotherapists. Journal (GBR) **7341**
British Astronomical Association. Journal (GBR) **572**
British Columbia Magazine (CAN) **8688**
British Educational Research Journal (GBR) **2832**
British Food Journal (GBR) **3628**
British Heritage (USA) **4206**
British Journal for the History of Philosophy (GBR) **6908**

Online Service

British Journal for the History of Science (GBR) **7842**
The British Journal for the Philosophy of Science (GBR) **7842**
British Journal of Aesthetics (GBR) **6908**
British Journal of Anaesthesia (GBR) **5770**
British Journal of Anaesthetic & Recovery Nursing (GBR) **5953**
British Journal of Cancer (GBR) **6010**
The British Journal of Cardiology (GBR) **5778**
British Journal of Clinical Pharmacology (GBR) **6826**
British Journal of Clinical Psychology (GBR) **7341**
British Journal of Community Nursing (GBR) **5953**
The British Journal of Criminology (GBR) **2645**
British Journal of Dermatology (GBR) **5872**
British Journal of Developmental Psychology (GBR) **7341**
British Journal of Educational Psychology (GBR) **7341**
British Journal of Educational Studies (GBR) **2832**
British Journal of Educational Technology (GBR) **3053**
British Journal of General Practice (GBR) **5588**
British Journal of Guidance and Counselling (GBR) **6693**
British Journal of Haematology (GBR) **5935**
British Journal of Health Psychology (GBR) **7342**
British Journal of Hospital Medicine (London, 2005) (GBR) **5588**
British Journal of Industrial Relations (GBR) **1668**
British Journal of Learning Disabilities (GBR) **6128**
British Journal of Management (GBR) **1729**
British Journal of Mathematical and Statistical Psychology (GBR) **7342**
British Journal of Middle Eastern Studies (GBR) **4320**
British Journal of Midwifery (GBR) **5987**
British Journal of Music Education (GBR) **6551**
British Journal of Neurosurgery (GBR) **6238**
The British Journal of Nutrition (GBR) **6656**
British Journal of Occupational Therapy (GBR) **5589**
British Journal of Oral and Maxillofacial Surgery (GBR) **6238**
British Journal of Pharmacology (GBR) **6826**
British Journal of Phytotherapy (GBR) **307**
British Journal of Political Science (GBR) **7110**
The British Journal of Politics and International Relations (GBR) **7110**
British Journal of Psychiatry (GBR) **6128**
British Journal of Psychology (GBR) **7342**
British Journal of Radiology (GBR) **6193**
British Journal of Religious Education (GBR) **7628**
British Journal of Social Psychology (GBR) **7342**
The British Journal of Social Work (GBR) **8028**
British Journal of Sociology (GBR) **8091**
British Journal of Sociology of Education (GBR) **2832**
British Journal of Special Education (GBR) **3037**
British Journal of Surgery (GBR) **6238**
British Journal of Visual Impairment (GBR) **4080**
British Journalism Review (GBR) **4572**
British Medical Bulletin (GBR) **5589**
British Poultry Science (GBR) **281**
British Rate and Data (GBR) **621**
British Review of New Zealand Studies (GBR) **4191**
Broadcast (GBR) **2376**
Broadcast Engineering (USA) **2376**
Broadcast Engineering (World Edition) (USA) **2376**
Broadcasting & Cable (USA) **2376**
Broadcasting & Cable T V Fax (USA) **2376**
Broadcasting and Telecommunications (CAN) **2346**
Bronte Studies (GBR) **5266**
Brookings Papers on Economic Activity (USA) **1536**
Brookings Papers on Education Policy (Year) (USA) **3018**
Brookings Trade Forum (USA) **1553**
Brookings-Wharton Papers on Financial Services (USA) **1321**
Brookings-Wharton Papers on Urban Affairs (Year) (USA) **8091**
Brown Journal of World Affairs (USA) **3971**
Brown University Child and Adolescent Behavior Letter (USA) **2146**
Brown University Child & Adolescent Psychopharmacology Update (USA) **6089**
Brown University Digest of Addiction Theory & Application (USA) **2692**
The Brown University Geriatric Psychopharmacology Update (USA) **4042**
Bruce Hopkins' Nonprofit Counsel (USA) **4632**
Budapest Business Journal (HUN) **1069**
The Budapest Sun (HUN) **3876**
Buddhist - Christian Studies (USA) **7700**
Builders Merchants Journal (GBR) **984**
Building (GBR) **435**
Building Acoustics (GBR) **7087**
Building and Environment (GBR) **984**
Building Design (GBR) **436**
Building Design + Construction (USA) **985**
Building Research and Information (GBR) **986**
Building Services Engineering Research & Technology (GBR) **986**
Buildings (USA) **987**
Built Environment (GBR) **436**
Bulk Transporter (USA) **8669**
Bulletin des Sciences Mathematiques (FRA) **5476**
Bulletin du Cancer (Online) (FRA) **6010**
Bulletin of Earthquake Engineering (NLD) **2778**
Bulletin of Economic Research (GBR) **1070**
Bulletin of Engineering Geology and the Environment (DEU) **3261**
Bulletin of Entomological Research (GBR) **841**
Bulletin of Environmental Contamination and Toxicology (USA) **3494**
Bulletin of Experimental Biology and Medicine (USA) **663**
The Bulletin of Good Practice in Popular Education (AUS) **2833**
Bulletin of Hispanic Studies (Online Edition, Liverpool, 2002) (GBR) **5267**
Bulletin of Indonesian Economic Studies (AUS) **1443**
Bulletin of Latin American Research (GBR) **7951**
Bulletin of Marine Science (USA) **2801**
Bulletin of Mathematical Biology (USA) **663**
Bulletin of Science, Technology & Society (USA) **7842**
Bulletin of Spanish Studies (GBR) **5267**
The Bulletin of Symbolic Logic (USA) **5476**
Bulletin of the Atomic Scientists (USA) **7224**
Bulletin of the History of Medicine (USA) **5589**
Bulletin of Volcanology (DEU) **2778**
Bundesgesundheitsblatt - Gesundheitsforschung - Gesundheitsschutz (DEU) **7510**
Burns (GBR) **6057**
Business and Commercial Aviation (USA) **50**
Business & Economic Review (USA) **1070**
Business and Politics (Online) (USA) **1070**
Business & Society (USA) **1070**
Business and Society Review (USA) **1070**
Business Communication Quarterly (USA) **1729**
The Business Communicator (GBR) **1071**
Business Credit (USA) **1322**
Business Economics (USA) **1071**
Business Ethics (GBR) **1072**
Business Ethics Quarterly (USA) **6909**
Business Franchise (GBR) **1957**
Business History (GBR) **1072**
Business Horizons (USA) **1072**
Business India Intelligence (HKG) **1073**
Business Information Review (GBR) **1730**
Business Insurance (USA) **4496**
The Business Journal (Fresno) (USA) **1073**
Business Law Review (NLD) **4859**
Business N H Magazine (USA) **1426**
Business North Carolina (USA) **1957**
Business Perspectives (USA) **1075**
Business Process Management Journal (GBR) **1730**
Business Strategy and the Environment (GBR) **3407**
Business Strategy Review (GBR) **1730**
The Business Torts Reporter (USA) **4859**
Business Travel News (USA) **8689**
Business Travel World (GBR) **8689**
BusinessWeek Online (USA) *see* BusinessWeek. **1077**
BusinessWest (USA) **1077**
Buyouts (USA) **1614**
Byzantine and Modern Greek Studies (GBR) **4208**
C A (USA) **6010**
C A Magazine (CAN) **1282**
C A S W Bulletin (CAN) **8029**
C D Computing News (USA) **2491**
C E D (USA) **2377**
C E S - I F O Economic Studies (GBR) **1078**
C F O (USA) **1078**
C I D O B d'Afers Internationals (ESP) **7224**
C I N: Computers, Informatics, Nursing (USA) **5829**
C I O (USA) **1414**
C I O Insight (USA) **1414**
C J E M (CAN) **6057**
C L C Web: Comparative Literature and Culture (USA) **5268**
C M A Management (CAN) **1283**
C M I G Extra: Cases (USA) **5829**
C M Magazine (CAN) **7557**
C N S & Neurological Disorders (NLD) **6129**
C N S Drugs (NZL) **6827**
C O B R A Advisory (USA) **4089**
C O P D (USA) **6212**
The C P A Letter (Online) (USA) **1283**
C P A Managing Partner Report (USA) **1283**
C P A Marketing Report (USA) **1809**
C P A Personnel Report (USA) **1857**
The C P A Technology Advisor (USA) **1415**
C P C U eJournal (USA) **4497**
C P Online (USA) *see* Current Psychology (New York). **7350**
C Q Researcher (USA) **7111**
C Q Weekly (USA) **7112**
C R M Magazine (USA) **1731**
C S L A Journal (USA) **4999**
C U 360 Newsletter (USA) **1323**
C V D Prevention and Control (NLD) **5779**
Cabinet Maker (GBR) **4554**
Cabling Installation and Maintenance (USA) **2378**
CADalyst (USA) **3289**
Cahiers de Biologie Marine (FRA) **664**
Cahiers de Nutrition et de Dietetique (FRA) **6656**
Cahiers d'Etudes et de Recherches Francophones. Agricultures (FRA) **99**
Calcified Tissue International (USA) **5884**
Calcolo (ITA) **5477**
Calculus of Variations and Partial Differential Equations (DEU) **5477**
California C P A (USA) **1284**
California Construction (USA) **989**
California Journal of Oriental Medicine (USA) **307**
California Law Review (USA) **4636**
California Management Review (USA) **1732**
Callaloo (USA) **5269**
Calliope (Peru) (USA) **4134**
CALPHAD (GBR) **2107**
Cambridge Archaeological Journal (GBR) **386**
Cambridge Journal of Economics (GBR) **1079**
Cambridge Journal of Education (GBR) **2970**
The Cambridge Law Journal (GBR) **4637**
Cambridge Opera Journal (GBR) **6553**
Cambridge Philosophical Society. Mathematical Proceedings (GBR) **5477**
The Cambridge Quarterly (GBR) **5269**
Cambridge Quarterly of Healthcare Ethics (GBR) **5591**
Cambridge Review of International Affairs (GBR) **7225**
Camden Fifth Series (GBR) **4209**
Camera Obscura (USA) **6491**
Campaign (London, 1968) (GBR) **22**
Camping Magazine (USA) **2146**
Campus Wide Information Systems (GBR) **2495**
Canada Communicable Disease Report (CAN) **7511**
Canada. Statistics Canada. Canadian Social Trends (CAN) **7304**
Canada. Statistics Canada. Education in Canada (CAN) **2931**
Canada. Statistics Canada. Education Quarterly Review (CAN) **2834**
Canada. Statistics Canada. Retail Trade (CAN) **1218**
Canada - United States Law Journal (USA) **4919**
Canadian Applied Mathematics Quarterly (CAN) **5477**
Canadian Architect (CAN) **436**
Canadian Association of Radiologists Journal (CAN) **6193**
Canadian Banker (Online Edition) (CAN) **1324**
Canadian Banker (Print Edition) (CAN) **1324**
Canadian Bar Review (CAN) **4638**
Canadian Business (CAN) **1079**
Canadian Chiropractic Association. Journal (CAN) **5803**
Canadian Church Historical Society Journal (CAN) **7749**
Canadian Consulting Engineer (CAN) **3184**
Canadian Dimension (CAN) **7113**
Canadian Economic Observer (CAN) **1220**
Canadian Entomologist (CAN) **842**
Canadian Ethnic Studies (CAN) **3525**
Canadian Family Physician (CAN) **5591**
Canadian Gas Price Reporter (CAN) **6765**
The Canadian Geographer (USA) **4001**
Canadian Geographic (CAN) **4001**
Canadian Geotechnical Journal (CAN) **2703**
Canadian Historical Review (CAN) **4134**
Canadian Investment Review (CAN) **1615**
Canadian Journal of Administrative Sciences (GBR) **1080**
Canadian Journal of Agricultural Economics (USA) **195**
Canadian Journal of Anaesthesia (USA) **5770**
Canadian Journal of Animal Science (CAN) **283**
Canadian Journal of Archaeology (CAN) **386**
Canadian Journal of Behavioural Science (CAN) **7343**
Canadian Journal of Cardiology (CAN) **5779**
Canadian Journal of Chemical Engineering (USA) **3237**
Canadian Journal of Chemistry (CAN) **2052**
Canadian Journal of Civil Engineering (CAN) **3261**
Canadian Journal of Clinical Pharmacology (CAN) **6827**
Canadian Journal of Communication (CAN) **8092**
Canadian Journal of Criminology and Criminal Justice (CAN) **2646**
Canadian Journal of Earth Sciences (CAN) **2703**
Canadian Journal of Economics (USA) **1080**
Canadian Journal of Experimental Psychology (CAN) **7343**
Canadian Journal of Fisheries and Aquatic Sciences (CAN) **3588**
Canadian Journal of Forest Research (CAN) **3685**
Canadian Journal of Gastroenterology (CAN) **5921**
Canadian Journal of Higher Education (CAN) **2971**
Canadian Journal of History (CAN) **4134**
Canadian Journal of Human Sexuality (CAN) **7343**
Canadian Journal of Infectious Diseases & Medical Microbiology (CAN) **5811**
Canadian Journal of Information and Library Science (CAN) **5000**
Canadian Journal of Linguistics (CAN) **5104**
Canadian Journal of Mathematics (CAN) **5477**
Canadian Journal of Microbiology (CAN) **882**
Canadian Journal of Neurological Sciences (CAN) **6129**
The Canadian Journal of Nursing Research (CAN) **5954**
Canadian Journal of Philosophy (CAN) **6909**
Canadian Journal of Physics (CAN) **7007**
Canadian Journal of Physiology and Pharmacology (CAN) **920**
Canadian Journal of Plant Pathology (CAN) **783**
Canadian Journal of Plant Science (CAN) **783**
Canadian Journal of Plastic Surgery (CAN) **6238**
Canadian Journal of Political Science (GBR) **7113**
Canadian Journal of Program Evaluation (CAN) **7428**
Canadian Journal of Remote Sensing (CD-ROM) (CAN) **50**
The Canadian Journal of Rural Medicine (CAN) **5592**
Canadian Journal of Science, Mathematics and Technology Education (USA) **7844**
Canadian Journal of Soil Science (CAN) **223**
Canadian Journal of Statistics (USA) **8362**
Canadian Journal of Surgery (CAN) **6238**
Canadian Journal of Urban Research (CAN) **4406**
Canadian Journal of Women and the Law (CAN) **4639**
Canadian Journal of Zoology (CAN) **937**
Canadian Journal on Aging (GBR) **4042**
Canadian Literature (CAN) **5270**
Canadian Living (CAN) **5067**
Canadian Manager (CAN) **1732**
Canadian Mathematical Bulletin (CAN) **5477**
Canadian Metallurgical Quarterly (CAN) **6308**
Canadian Mineralogist (CAN) **2727**
Canadian Mining Journal (CAN) **6459**
Canadian Modern Language Review (CAN) **5104**
Canadian Musician (CAN) **6554**
Canadian Plastics (CAN) **7091**
Canadian Psychology (CAN) **7344**
Canadian Respiratory Journal (CAN) **6212**
Canadian Review of American Studies (CAN) **4287**
Canadian Review of Sociology (CAN) **8092**
Canadian Sailings (CAN) **8640**
Canadian Theatre Review (CAN) **8467**
Canadian Transportation Logistics (CAN) **8493**
Canadian Underwriter (CAN) **4498**
Canadian Water Resources Journal (CAN) **8819**
Cancer (USA) **6010**
Cancer and Metastasis Reviews (USA) **6011**
Cancer Biomarkers (NLD) **6011**
Cancer Biotherapy & Radiopharmaceuticals (USA) **6011**
Cancer Causes & Control (NLD) **6011**
Cancer Cell (USA) **6011**
Cancer Cell International (GBR) **6011**
Cancer Chemotherapy and Pharmacology (DEU) **6011**
Cancer Control (USA) **6011**
Cancer Epidemiology (USA) **6012**
Cancer Epidemiology, Biomarkers & Prevention (USA) **6012**
Cancer Gene Therapy (USA) **6012**
Cancer Genetics and Cytogenetics (USA) **6012**
Cancer Imaging (GBR) **6012**
Cancer Immunology, Immunotherapy (DEU) **6012**
Cancer Investigation (USA) **6013**
The Cancer Journal (USA) **6013**
The Cancer Journal (Online Edition) (FRA) **5592**
Cancer Letters (IRL) **6013**
Cancer Nursing (USA) **5954**
Cancer Radiotherapie (FRA) **6013**
Cancer Research (USA) **6014**
Cancer Science (JPN) **6014**
Cancer Treatment Reviews (GBR) **6014**
Cancerologia (MEX) **6015**
Candy Industry (USA) **3672**
Canzona (NZL) **6554**
Capital and Class (GBR) **1536**
Capital Sante (CAN) **6983**
Capitalism, Nature, Socialism (GBR) **7114**
Carbohydrate Polymers (GBR) **2120**
Carbohydrate Research (GBR) **2120**
Carbon (GBR) **2121**
Carcinogenesis (GBR) **6015**
Card Technology Today (GBR) **3090**
Il Cardiologo (ITA) **5779**
Cardiology (CHE) **5779**
Cardiology in Review (USA) **5780**
Cardiology in the Young (GBR) **5780**
Cardiovascular & Hematological Agents in Current Medicinal (NLD) **5780**
Cardiovascular & Hematological Disorders - Drug Targets (NLD) **5780**
Cardiovascular and Interventional Radiology (USA) **6193**
Cardiovascular Device Update (USA) **5780**
Cardiovascular Diabetology (GBR) **5884**
Cardiovascular Drugs and Therapy (USA) **5781**
Cardiovascular Engineering (USA) **5781**
Cardiovascular Pathology (USA) **5781**
Cardiovascular Research (NLD) **5781**
Cardiovascular Revascularization Medicine (USA) **5781**
Cardiovascular Toxicology (USA) **5781**
Cardiovascular Ultrasound (GBR) **6193**
Cards & Payments (USA) **1325**
Care Management Journals (USA) **5954**
Career Development for Exceptional Individuals (USA) **3037**
Career Development International (GBR) **6694**
The Career Development Quarterly (USA) **6694**
Career World (USA) **6695**
Careers & Colleges (Online) (USA) **6695**
Caribbean Business (PRI) **1081**
Caries Research (CHE) **5837**
The Carolina Quarterly (USA) **5271**
The Cartographic Journal (GBR) **4037**
Cartographica (CAN) **4002**
Cartography and Geographic Information Science (USA) **4002**
Case Management Advisor (USA) **5592**
The Case Manager (USA) **5592**
Case Western Reserve Journal of International Law (USA) **4920**
Case Western Reserve Law Review (USA) **4641**
Cataloging & Classification Quarterly (USA) **5001**
Catalysis Communications (NLD) **2052**
Catalysis Letters (NLD) **2052**
Catalysis Reviews: Science and Engineering (USA) **2133**
Catalysis Surveys from Asia (NLD) **2133**
Catalysis Today (NLD) **3237**
Catalyst (Dublin) (USA) **1284**
Catalysts & Catalysed Reactions (GBR) **2093**
Catedra Corona (COL) **1732**
CATENA (NLD) **2728**

Link to your serials resources and content with ulrichsweb.com

Danse (Paris, 2001) (FRA) 2685
Daphnis (NLD) 5283
Darwiniana (ARG) 785
Data & Knowledge Engineering (NLD) 2416
Data Base for Advances in Information Systems (USA) 2529
Data Communications Management (USA) 2533
Data Mining and Knowledge Discovery (USA) 2530
Data Security Management (USA) 2513
Daughters (USA) 2150
DavarLogos (ARG) 7637
Dead Sea Discoveries (NLD) 7720
Deakin Law Review (AUS) 4655
DealerNews (USA) 8257
Death Studies (USA) 7351
Debate Feminista (MEX) 8895
Debatte (GBR) 4213
Decision (IND) 1738
Decision Analysis (USA) 1738
Decision Sciences (USA) 1738
Decision Sciences Journal of Innovative Education (USA) 2841
Decision Support Systems (NLD) 1738
Decisions in Economics and Finance (ITA) 5482
Decisions Marketing (FRA) 1813
Decormag (CAN) 4537
Deep-Sea Research. Part 1: Oceanographic Research Papers (GBR) 2803
Deep-Sea Research. Part 2: Topical Studies in Oceanography (GBR) 2803
Defence and Peace Economics (GBR) 6417
Defence and Security Analysis (GBR) 6417
Defence Studies (GBR) 6418
Defense A T & L (USA) 2520
Defense Counsel Journal (USA) 4830
Defense Daily (USA) 52
Defense Monitor (USA) 6419
The Delaware Journal of Corporate Law (USA) 4865
Delicious Living (USA) 5069
Delta Kappa Gamma Bulletin (USA) 2977
Delta Pi Epsilon Journal (USA) 2977
Dementia (GBR) 6135
Dementia and Geriatric Cognitive Disorders (CHE) 6136
Democracy and Security (USA) 7129
Democratization (GBR) 7230
Demography (USA) 7281
Demokratizatsiya (USA) 7129
Dendrochronologia (DEU) 785
Dental Implantology Update (USA) 5840
Dental Materials (USA) 5840
Dental Traumatology Online (GBR) 5841
Dentistry Today (USA) 5842
Dentomaxillofacial Radiology (GBR) 6195
Depression and Anxiety (Hoboken) (USA) 7351
Dermatitis (CAN) 5874
Dermatologia (MEX) 5874
Dermatologic Surgery Online (USA) 6241
Dermatologic Therapy (DNK) 5874
Dermatologie in Beruf und Umwelt (DEU) 5875
Dermatology (CHE) 5875
Dermatology Nursing (USA) 5875
Dermatology Times (USA) 5875
Des Moines Business Record (USA) 1091
Desalination (NLD) 8820
Desarrollo y Sociedad (COL) 1476
Design Automation for Embedded Systems (NLD) 2460
Design - Build (USA) 3264
Design Issues (USA) 486
Design News Online (USA) *see* Design News. 8420
Design Studies (GBR) 440
Design Week (GBR) 486
Designed Monomers and Polymers (Online) (NLD) 3242
Designs, Codes and Cryptography (USA) 5482
Deutsche Apotheker Zeitung (DEU) 6832
Deutsche Gesellschaft fuer Geowissenschaften. Zeitschrift (DEU) 2730
Deutsche Medizinische Wochenschrift (DEU) 5604
Deutsche Zeitschrift fuer Onkologie (DEU) 6018
Deutsche Zeitschrift fuer Wirtschaftsrecht und Insolvenzrecht (DEU) 4657
Deutsches Aerzteblatt. Ausgabe A (DEU) 5604
Developing World Bioethics (GBR) 6913
Development (Basingstoke) (GBR) 1593
Development (Cambridge) (GBR) 668
Development and Change (GBR) 1593
Development and Learning in Organizations (GBR) 1859
Development and Psychopathology (GBR) 7351
Development, Genes and Evolution (DEU) 668
Development, Growth and Differentiation (AUS) 668
Development in Practice (GBR) 1594
Development Policy Review (GBR) 1594
Development Southern Africa (GBR) 1594
Developmental & Comparative Immunology (GBR) 5757
Developmental Biology (USA) 668
Developmental Cell (USA) 832
Developmental Disabilities Research Reviews (USA) 6136
Developmental Dynamics (USA) 668
Developmental Medicine and Child Neurology (GBR) 6091
Developmental Neurobiology (USA) 921
Developmental Neuropsychology (USA) 7351
Developmental Neurorehabilitation (Online) (GBR) *see* Developmental Neurorehabilitation. 6108
Developmental Neuroscience (CHE) 6136
Developmental Psychobiology (USA) 668
Developmental Psychology (USA) 7351
Developmental Review (USA) 7352
Developmental Science (GBR) 7352
Deviant Behavior (USA) 8098
Il Diabete (ITA) 5886
Diabetes (USA) 5886
Diabetes & Metabolism (FRA) 5886
Diabetes Care (USA) 5887
The Diabetes Educator (USA) 5887
Diabetes-Journal (DEU) 5888
Diabetes - Metabolism: Research and Reviews (Online) (GBR) 5888
Diabetes, Obesity and Metabolism Online (GBR) 5888
Diabetes Research and Clinical Practice (IRL) 5888
Diabetes Spectrum (USA) 5888
Diabetes Technology & Therapeutics (USA) 5889
Diabetic Medicine Online (GBR) 5889
Der Diabetologe (DEU) 5889
Diabetologia (DEU) 5890
Diachronica (NLD) 5111
Diacritics (USA) 5284
Diagnostic and Therapeutic Endoscopy (CHE) 5905
Diagnostic Cytopathology (USA) 832
Diagnostic Histopathology (Oxford) (GBR) 5944
Diagnostic Microbiology and Infectious Disease (USA) 884
Diagnostic Molecular Pathology (USA) 5605
Diagnostica (DEU) 7352
Dialectica (USA) 6914
Dialectical Anthropology (NLD) 335
Dialog (St Paul) (USA) 7637
Dialogue (Salt Lake City) (USA) 7734
Dialogue and Universalism (POL) 6914
Diamond and Related Materials (CHE) 2110
Dianoia (MEX) 6914
Diaspora (CAN) 7959
Differences (USA) 8895
Differential Equations (RUS) 5482
Differential Geometry and Its Applications (NLD) 5482
Differentiation (GBR) 669
Dig (USA) 390
Digest of Middle East Studies (USA) 548
Digestion (CHE) 5922
Digestive and Liver Disease (GBR) 5922
Digestive Diseases (CHE) 5922
Digestive Diseases and Sciences (USA) 5922
Digestive Endoscopy (AUS) 5922
Digestive Surgery (CHE) 6241
Digital Content Producer (USA) 2401
Digital Creativity (GBR) 2485
Digital Investigation (GBR) 5913
Digital Media: A Seybold Report (USA) 2571
Digital Signal Processing (USA) 3093
Digital Software Magazine (USA) 2589
Dimensions in Critical Care Nursing (USA) 5957
Diogenes (English Edition) (GBR) 7959
Diplomacy & Statecraft (GBR) 4137
Diplomatic History (USA) 4137
Direct (New York, 1988) (USA) 1813
Direct Marketing (Online Edition) (USA) 1813
Director (GBR) 1739
Directorship (USA) 1739
Diritto e Pratica del Lavoro (ITA) 4866
Dirt Bike (USA) 8258
Disability and Rehabilitation (GBR) 4065
Disability and Rehabilitation: Assistive Technology (USA) 6108
Disability & Society (GBR) 4077
Disability Studies Quarterly (USA) 4065
Disaster Management & Response (USA) 5957
Disaster Prevention and Management (GBR) 7514
Disasters (GBR) 1594
DisClosure (Lexington) (USA) 7959
Discourse (Abingdon) (GBR) 3020
Discourse (Detroit, 1979) (USA) 4450
Discourse & Society (GBR) 7352
Discourse Processes (USA) 7959
Discourse Studies (GBR) 5112
Discover (USA) 7851
Discovery Medicine (USA) 763
Discrete & Computational Geometry (USA) 5483
Discrete and Continuous Dynamical Systems. Series A (USA) 5483
Discrete and Continuous Dynamical Systems. Series B (USA) 5483
Discrete Applied Mathematics (NLD) 5483
Discrete Dynamics in Nature and Society (USA) 7851
Discrete Event Dynamic Systems (USA) 2517
Discrete Mathematics (NLD) 5483
Discrete Mathematics and Applications (DEU) 5483
Discrete Mathematics and Theoretical Computer Science (Online Edition) (FRA) 5483
Discrete Optimization (NLD) 5552
Disease-A-Month (USA) 5605
Disease Management & Health Outcomes (NZL) 5605
Disease Markers (NLD) 6018
Diseases of Aquatic Organisms (Online) (DEU) 884
Diseases of the Colon and Rectum (USA) 6241
Diseases of the Esophagus (AUS) 6079
Display & Design Ideas (USA) 4538
Displays (NLD) 2485
Dispute Resolution Journal (USA) 1675
Dissent (New York) (USA) 7130
Dissertationes Mathematicae (POL) 5484
Distance Education (AUS) 2940
Distance Education Report (USA) 2978
Distributed and Parallel Databases (USA) 2530
Distributed Computing (DEU) 2417
District Administration (USA) 3058
Diverse Issues in Higher Education (USA) 2978
Diversity and Distributions (GBR) 669
Diversity in Health and Care (GBR) 8037
Diversity Suppliers & Business Magazine (USA) 1814
DiversityInc (USA) 4866
Division of Labor and Transaction Costs (SGP) 1676
Doctor (GBR) 5606
Documenta Ophthalmologica (NLD) 6041
La Documentation Catholique (FRA) 7795
Dog World (USA) 6807
Doklady Biochemistry and Biophysics (RUS) 731
Doklady Biological Sciences (RUS) 669
Doklady Chemistry (RUS) 2060
Doklady Physical Chemistry (RUS) 2134
Doklady Physics (RUS) 7010
Doll Reader (USA) 4333
Dollars & Sense (Cambridge) (USA) 1477
Dolly (AUS) 2186
Domestic Animal Endocrinology (USA) 8796
Dose-Response (USA) 5606
Douleurs (FRA) 5607
Dow Theory Forecasts (USA) 1621
Dr. Dobb's Journal (USA) 2589
Dramatherapy (GBR) 7352
The Dramatist (USA) 8469
Dredging & Port Construction (GBR) 8642
Dress (USA) 2253
Drip Investor (USA) 1621
Droit Nucleaire (FRA) 3166
Drug and Alcohol Dependence (IRL) 2693
Drug and Alcohol Review (GBR) 2693
Drug and Chemical Toxicology (USA) 6833
Drug Data Report (ESP) 6833
Drug Delivery (USA) 6834
Drug Development and Industrial Pharmacy (USA) 6834
Drug Development Research (USA) 6834
Drug Discovery & Development (USA) 6834
Drug Discovery Today (GBR) 6834
Drug Discovery Today: BIOSILICO (GBR) 6834
Drug Discovery Today: Disease Mechanisms (GBR) 6834
Drug Discovery Today: Disease Models (GBR) 6835
Drug Discovery Today: Technologies (GBR) 6835
Drug Discovery Today: Therapeutic Strategies (GBR) 6835
Drug Formulary Review (USA) 6835
Drug Information Journal (USA) 6835
Drug Metabolism and Disposition (USA) 6835
Drug Metabolism Reviews (USA) 5607
Drug News & Perspectives (ESP) 6836
Drug Resistance Updates (GBR) 5607
Drug Safety (NZL) 6836
Drug Store News (USA) 1814
Drugs (GBR) 2693
Drugs (NZL) 6836
Drugs & Aging (NZL) 6836
Drugs & Therapy Perspectives (NZL) 6836
Drugs in R & D (NZL) 6837
Drugs of the Future (ESP) 6837
Drugs of Today (ESP) 6837
Drying Technology (USA) 2134
Dth (NLD) 7353
Du Bois Review (GBR) 7960
Duke Law Journal (USA) 4661
Duke Mathematical Journal (USA) 5484
Dyes and Pigments (GBR) 2060
Dynamic Medicine (GBR) 5607
Dynamical Systems (Online) (GBR) 2417
Dynamics of Atmospheres and Oceans (NLD) 6352
Dyslexia (GBR) 3038
Dysphagia (USA) 6079
E (USA) 3414
e A D C - F & N (GBR) *see* Archives of Disease in Childhood. Fetal and Neonatal Edition. 5986
E A S Publications Series (FRA) 574
E A U - E B U Update Series (NLD) 6267
E C & M (USA) 3300
e C M A J (CAN) *see* C M A J. 5590
E C Tax Review (NLD) 1921
E D N Access (USA) *see* E D N World. 3093
E D N Europe (USA) 3093
E D Nursing (USA) 5957
E D P A C S (USA) 2513
E D P Auditing (USA) 2536
E H S Today (USA) 6676
E I U Country Forecasts: Eastern Europe (USA) *see* Country Forecast. Poland. 7122
E I U Country Forecasts: Eastern Europe (USA) *see* Country Forecast. Hungary. 7121
E I U Country Forecasts: Eastern Europe (USA) *see* Country Report. Ukraine. 1463
E I U Country Forecasts: Eastern Europe (USA) *see* Country Report. Russia. 1460
E I U Country Forecasts: Eastern Europe (USA) *see* Country Report. Kazakhstan. 1456
E I U Country Forecasts: Eastern Europe (USA) *see* Country Forecast. Slovakia. 7122
E I U Country Forecasts: Eastern Europe (USA) *see* Country Forecast. Romania. 7122
E I U Country Forecasts: Eastern Europe (USA) *see* Country Forecast. Bulgaria. 7120
E I U Country Forecasts: Eastern Europe (USA) *see* Country Forecast. Eastern Europe. 7121
E I U Country Forecasts: Eastern Europe (USA) *see* Country Forecast. Czech Republic. 7120
E I U Country Forecasts: Eastern Europe (USA) *see* Country Forecast. Russia. 7122
E I U Country Reports: Asia-Pacific (USA) *see* Country Report. Myanmar. 1458
E I U Country Reports: Asia-Pacific (USA) *see* Country Report. Vietnam. 1464
E I U Country Reports: Asia-Pacific (USA) *see* Country Report. Thailand. 1462
E I U Country Reports: Asia-Pacific (USA) *see* Country Report. Bangladesh. 1450
E I U Country Reports: Asia-Pacific (USA) *see* Country Report. Philippines. 1460
E I U Country Reports: Asia-Pacific (USA) *see* Country Report. Papua New Guinea, Timor-Leste. 1459
E I U Country Reports: Asia-Pacific (USA) *see* Country Report. Singapore. 1461
E I U Country Reports: Asia-Pacific (USA) *see* Country Report. Hong Kong. 1455
E I U Country Reports: Asia-Pacific (USA) *see* Country Report. China. 1452
E I U Country Reports: Asia-Pacific (USA) *see* Country Report. Australia. 1449
E I U Country Reports: Asia-Pacific (USA) *see* Country Report. Pakistan. 1459
E I U Country Reports: Asia-Pacific (USA) *see* Country Report. Cambodia. 1451
E I U Country Reports: Asia-Pacific (USA) *see* Country Report. India. 1456
E I U Country Reports: Asia-Pacific (USA) *see* Country Report. New Zealand. 1459
E I U Country Reports: Asia-Pacific (USA) *see* Country Report. Sri Lanka. 1461
E I U Country Reports: Asia-Pacific (USA) *see* Country Report. Taiwan. 1462
E I U Country Reports: Asia-Pacific (USA) *see* Country Report. South Korea. 1461
E I U Country Reports: Asia-Pacific (USA) *see* Country Report. Japan. 1456
E I U Country Reports on Disc: Western Europe (USA) 1478
E I U International Business Newsletters (USA) *see* Business Africa. 1443
E I U International Business Newsletters (USA) *see* Business Europe. 1444
E I U International Business Newsletters (USA) *see* Business China. 1444
E I U International Business Newsletters (USA) *see* Country Monitor. 1449
E I U International Business Newsletters (USA) *see* Business Middle East. 1444
E I U International Business Newsletters (USA) *see* Business Eastern Europe. 1444
E I U International Business Newsletters (USA) *see* Business Asia. 1443
E I U International Business Newsletters (USA) *see* Business Latin America. 1444
e j m p & e p (TUR) 3366
E J V E S Extra (GBR) 5785
E L H (USA) 5286
E L T Journal (GBR) 5113
E-Learning (GBR) 3058
E.Learning Age (GBR) 1416
E M (USA) 3505
The E M B O Journal (GBR) 731
E M B O Reports (GBR) 866
E M B Online (GBR) *see* Evidence - Based Medicine. 5612
E M C - Psychiatrie (Online) (FRA) 6137
E M J Online (GBR) *see* Emergency Medicine Journal. 6059
E M S Insider (USA) 6058
The E N D S Report (GBR) 3415
E N R (USA) 3265
E P P O Bulletin (GBR) 228
E R I S A Litigation Alert (USA) 1676
E S A I M: Mathematical Modelling and Numerical Analysis (FRA) 5485
E S A I M: Probability & Statistics (FRA) 5485
E S A I M: Proceedings (FRA) 5485
The E S H R E Monographs (GBR) 921
E S R Review (USA) 1336
e-Service Journal (USA) 2543
E U R O S L A Yearbook (NLD) 5113
Ear and Hearing (USA) 6079
Ear, Nose & Throat Journal (USA) 6079
Early American Literature (USA) 5287
Early American Studies (USA) 4291
Early Child Development and Care (GBR) 2151
Early Childhood Education Journal (USA) 2844
Early Childhood Research Quarterly (GBR) 2844
Early Childhood Today (Online) (USA) 3058
Early Education and Development (USA) 2844
Early Human Development (IRL) 5989
Early Medieval Europe (GBR) 4216
Early Music (GBR) 6563
Early Music History (GBR) 6563
Early Popular Visual Culture (GBR) 8099
Early Science and Medicine (NLD) 5608
Early Theatre (CAN) 8470
Early Years (GBR) 3058
Earth and Planetary Science Letters (NLD) 2706
Earth Interactions (USA) 2706
Earth Island Journal (USA) 3415
Earth, Moon, and Planets (NLD) 574
Earth, Planets and Space (JPN) 2706
Earth - Science Reviews (NLD) 2706
Earth Surface Processes and Landforms (GBR) 2732
Earthquake Engineering & Structural Dynamics (GBR) 3266
Earthquake Spectra (USA) 2780
Earthwatch (USA) 7852

Link to your serials resources and content with ulrichsweb.com

DIRECTORY 2010 EBSCO HOST 11101

Excerpta e Dissertationibus in Philosophia (ESP) 6919
Excerpta e Dissertationibus in Sacra Theologica (ESP) 7797
Exchange (NLD) 7642
Executive Housekeeping Today (USA) 4385
Exemplaria (GBR) 5294
Exercise and Sport Sciences Reviews (USA) 6229
Existential Analysis (GBR) 6919
Expansion Management (USA) 1744
Expedition (USA) 339
Experimental Aging Research (USA) 7356
Experimental Agriculture (GBR) 109
Experimental & Applied Acarology (NLD) 942
Experimental and Clinical Cardiology (CAN) 5787
Experimental and Clinical Endocrinology and Diabetes (DEU) 5892
Experimental and Clinical Psychopharmacology (USA) 7356
Experimental and Molecular Pathology (USA) 5612
Experimental and Toxicologic Pathology (DEU) 5612
Experimental Astronomy (NLD) 574
Experimental Biology and Medicine (Maywood) (USA) 672
Experimental Brain Research (DEU) 6140
Experimental Cell Research (USA) 832
Experimental Dermatology Online (GBR) 5876
Experimental Diabesity Research (USA) 5758
Experimental Economics (USA) 1541
Experimental Eye Research (GBR) 6041
Experimental Gerontology (USA) 4044
Experimental Heat Transfer (USA) 7054
Experimental Hematology (USA) 5936
Experimental Lung Research (USA) 6214
Experimental Mechanics (USA) 3344
Experimental Neurology (USA) 6140
Experimental Parasitology (USA) 5813
Experimental Physiology (GBR) 922
Experimental Psychology (USA) 7357
Experimental Techniques (USA) 3344
Experimental Thermal and Fluid Science (USA) 3192
Experiments in Fluids (DEU) 3377
Expert Opinion on Biological Therapy (GBR) 5612
Expert Opinion on Drug Delivery (GBR) 6839
Expert Opinion on Drug Metabolism & Toxicology (GBR) 6839
Expert Opinion on Drug Safety (GBR) 6839
Expert Opinion on Emerging Drugs (GBR) 6839
Expert Opinion on Investigational Drugs (GBR) 6839
Expert Opinion on Pharmacotherapy (GBR) 6839
Expert Opinion on Therapeutic Patents (GBR) 6839
Expert Opinion On Therapeutic Targets (GBR) 6840
Expert Review of Anti-infective Therapy (GBR) 6109
Expert Review of Anticancer Therapy (GBR) 6840
Expert Review of Cardiovascular Therapy (GBR) 5787
Expert Review of Clinical Immunology (GBR) 5758
Expert Review of Medical Devices (GBR) 5905
Expert Review of Molecular Diagnostics (GBR) 6840
Expert Review of Neurotherapeutics (GBR) 6840
Expert Review of Pharmacoeconomics & Outcomes Research (GBR) 6840
Expert Review of Proteomics (GBR) 732
Expert Review of Vaccines (GBR) 5758
Expert Reviews in Molecular Medicine (GBR) 5945
Expert Systems (GBR) 2448
Expert Systems with Applications (GBR) 2448
The Explicator (USA) 5294
Explorations in Economic History (USA) 1541
Explore: The Journal of Science & Healing (USA) 7854
Expo (Overland Park) (USA) 1744
Export Today's Global Business (USA) 1564
Export Wise (CAN) 1108
Expositiones Mathematicae (DEU) 5487
Expository Times (GBR) 7642
Expresion Grafica Arquitectonica. Revista (ESP) 442
Extrapolation (USA) 5442
Extremes (USA) 8369
Extremophiles (JPN) 764
Eye (London, 1880) (GBR) 6042
Eye and Contact Lens (USA) 6042
The F A S E B Journal (USA) 672
F & W - Fuehren und Wirtschaften im Krankenhaus (DEU) 4093
F B I Law Enforcement Bulletin (USA) 2652
F D C C Quarterly (USA) 4867
The F E B S Journal (Online) (GBR) 732
F E B S Letters (NLD) 732
F E M S Immunology and Medical Microbiology (GBR) 885
F E M S Microbiology Ecology (GBR) 885
F E M S Microbiology Letters (GBR) 885
F E M S Microbiology Reviews (GBR) 885
F I U Hospitality Review (USA) 4385
F M (USA) 1744
Fabula (DEU) 3617
Faces (USA) 2188
Facial Plastic Surgery (USA) 6243
Facies (DEU) 2707
Facilities (GBR) 1007
Facultad de Ciencias Humanas. Anuario (ARG) 7964
Fair Employment Practices Guidelines (USA) 4670
Fairfield County Business Journal (USA) 1485
Fairplay (GBR) 8643
Familial Cancer (NLD) 6019
Families in Society (USA) 8039
Families, Systems, & Health (USA) 5613
Family and Community Health (USA) 7517
Family & Community History (GBR) 4139
Family and Community Ministries (USA) 7758
Family & Consumer Sciences Research Journal (USA) 4357
Family Business Review (USA) 1960
Family Court Review (USA) 4909
Family Economics and Nutrition Review (USA) 4358
The Family Journal (USA) 7357
Family Matters (AUS) 8102
Family Medicine (USA) 5613
Family Practice (GBR) 5613
Family Practice Management (USA) 5613
Family Process (USA) 7357
Family Relations (USA) 2856
Fancy Food & Culinary Products (USA) 3677
Fantasy & Science Fiction (USA) 5442
Far Eastern Affairs (USA) 5215
Faraday Discussions (Online) (GBR) *see* Faraday Discussions. 2135
Farm Industry News (USA) 111
Farmers Weekly (GBR) 112
Fashion Theory (GBR) 489
Fathering (USA) 8102
Fatigue & Fracture of Engineering Materials and Structures (GBR) 3192
The Faulkner Journal (USA) 5295
Feddes Repertorium (DEU) 787
Federal Probation (USA) 2652
Federal Reserve Bank of Atlanta. Economic Review (USA) 1485
Federal Reserve Bank of Atlanta. Financial Update (USA) 1342
Federal Reserve Bank of Boston. Regional Review (USA) 1486
Federal Reserve Bank of Boston. Research Review (USA) 1486
Federal Reserve Bank of Kansas City. Economic Review (USA) 1486
Federal Reserve Bank of New York. Economic Policy Review (USA) 1486
Federal Reserve Bank of Philadelphia. Business Review (USA) 1486
Federal Reserve Bank of Richmond. Economic Quarterly (USA) 1486
Federal Reserve Bank of St. Louis. Review (USA) 1486
Federal Reserve Bank of San Francisco. Economic Letter (USA) 1486
Federal Reserve Bank of San Francisco. Economic Review (USA) 1486
Federal Reserve Bulletin (USA) 1342
Federal Scientific Activities (CAN) 7854
Federal Sentencing Reporter (USA) 2652
Federal Staff Directory (USA) 7437
Federal Times (USA) 7437
Federation of European Microbiological Societies Yeast Research Online (GBR) *see* F E M S Yeast Research. 886
Fedgazette: Federal Reserve Bank of Minneapolis Regional Business & Economics Newspaper (USA) 1487
Feed International (USA) 272
Feedstuffs (USA) 272
Feliciter (CAN) 5009
Feminism & Psychology (GBR) 7357
Feminist Criminology (USA) 2652
Feminist Economics (GBR) 1109
Feminist Legal Studies (NLD) 4673
Feminist Media Studies (GBR) 8896
Feminist Review (GBR) 8896
Feminist Studies (USA) 8896
Feminist Theology (GBR) 8896
Feminist Theory (GBR) 8897
Fennia (FIN) 4006
Ferroelectrics (CHE) 7012
Ferroelectrics Letters Section (USA) 3308
Fertility and Sterility (USA) 5990
Fertility Weekly (USA) 5990
Fetal and Maternal Medicine Review (GBR) 5990
Fetal and Pediatric Pathology (Online Edition) (GBR) 6092
Fetal Diagnosis and Therapy (CHE) 5990
Feuillets de Radiologie (FRA) 6197
Few-Body Systems (AUT) 7012
Fiber and Integrated Optics (USA) 7075
Fibre Chemistry (USA) 8451
Fiction International (USA) 5296
Fidelium Iura (ESP) 4674
Field Crops Research (NLD) 231
Field Methods (USA) 339
FierceTelecom (USA) 2367
Film & History (USA) 6498
Film Comment (USA) 6498
Film Criticism (USA) 6498
Film History (USA) 6499
Film Journal International (USA) 6499
Film Quarterly (USA) 6499
Films in Review (Online Edition) (USA) 6501
Filtration Industry Analyst (GBR) 3367
Filtration + Separation (GBR) 3244
Finance and Stochastics (DEU) 1343
Finance Controle Strategie (FRA) 1745
Finance Research Letters (USA) 1343
Finance Week (ZAF) 1343
Financial Accountability & Management (GBR) 1924
Financial Analysts Journal (USA) 1623
Financial & Insurance Meetings (USA) 4502
Financial Director (GBR) 1344
Financial Executive (USA) 1745
Financial History Review (GBR) 1344
Financial Mail Interactive (ZAF) *see* Financial Mail. 1344
Financial Management (GBR) 1288
Financial Markets and Portfolio Management (USA) 1623
Financial Markets, Institutions and Instruments (USA) 1344
Financial Planning (USA) 1745
The Financial Review (Statesboro) (USA) 1345
Financial Services Review (GBR) 1345
Financial Statistics (GBR) 1230
Finanzarchiv (DEU) 1925
Fine Madness (USA) 5422
Finishing (USA) 4557
Finite Elements in Analysis and Design (NLD) 3291
Finite Fields and Their Applications (USA) 5488
Fire and Materials (GBR) 3344
Fire Chief (USA) 3577
Fire Engineering (USA) 3577
Fire Management Today (USA) 3688
Fire Safety Engineering (GBR) 3578
Fire Safety Journal (GBR) 3578
Fire Technology (USA) 3578
First Break Online (NLD) 2780
First Draft (USA) 7561
First Language (GBR) 5119
First Things (USA) 7643
Fiscal Studies (GBR) 1925
Fish and Fisheries (GBR) 943
Fish and Shellfish Immunology (GBR) 943
Fish Physiology & Biochemistry (NLD) 943
Fisheries Management & Ecology Online (GBR) 3592
Fisheries Oceanography Online (GBR) 3592
Fisheries Research (NLD) 3592
Fisheries Science (AUS) 3593
Fisioterapia (ESP) 5959
Fit Pregnancy (USA) 5990
Fitness Business Canada (CAN) 5614
Fitoterapia (ITA) 788
Five Fingers Review (USA) 5296
Fixed Point Theory and Applications (USA) 5488
Fizika Napivprovidnikiv Kvantova ta Optoelektronika (UKR) 7051
Fizika Tverdogo Tela (RUS) 7013
Flannery O'Connor Review (USA) 5296
Flare (Toronto) (CAN) 2255
Flavour and Fragrance Journal (GBR) 2123
Fleet Equipment (USA) 8670
Fleet Owner (USA) 8670
Fleurs, Plantes et Jardins (CAN) 3729
Flex (USA) 6986
Flexible Services and Manufacturing Journal (USA) 3344
Flight International (GBR) 55
Flora (DEU) 788
Flora de Veracruz (MEX) 788
Flora del Bajio y de Regiones Adyacentes (MEX) 788
The Florida Bar Journal (USA) 4675
Florida Entomologist (USA) 847
Florida Libraries (USA) 5009
Florida Nurse (USA) 5959
Florida Shipper (USA) 8644
Flow Control (USA) 7058
Flow Measurement and Instrumentation (GBR) 4486
Flow, Turbulence and Combustion (NLD) 7855
Fluctuation and Noise Letters (SGP) 8372
Fluid Dynamics (RUS) 7058
Fluid Dynamics Research (NLD) 3361
Fluid Phase Equilibria (NLD) 2135
Fly Fisherman (USA) 8314
Flying Safety (USA) 56
Focus on Autism and Other Developmental Disabilities (USA) 6141
Focus on Catalysts (USA) 2094
Focus on Exceptional Children (USA) 3040
Focus on Geography (USA) 4006
Focus on Pigments (USA) 6722
Focus on Powder Coatings (USA) 6722
Focus on Surfactants (USA) 2094
Folia Geobotanica (NLD) 790
Folia Linguistica (DEU) 5119
Folia Phoniatrica et Logopaedica (CHE) 6080
Folia Primatologica (CHE) 944
Folio: (USA) 7561
Folk Music Journal (GBR) 6567
Folklore (GBR) 3617
Fontes Artis Musicae (USA) 6631
Food Additives & Contaminants: Part A - Chemistry, Analysis, Control, Exposure & Risk Assessment (GBR) 6842
Food and Agricultural Immunology (GBR) 673
Food & Beverage Packaging (USA) 6710
Food and Bioproducts Processing (GBR) 764
Food and Chemical Toxicology (GBR) 3497
Food and Foodways (USA) 6659
Food Biophysics (USA) 753
Food Biotechnology (USA) 764
Food Chemistry (GBR) 2061
Food Control (GBR) 3638
Food Engineering (USA) 3638
Food Engineering & Ingredients (USA) 3638
Food Hydrocolloids (NLD) 3639
Food in Canada (CAN) 3639
Food Logistics (USA) 3640
Food Magazine (AUS) 3640
Food Management (USA) 3640
Food Manufacture (GBR) 3640
Food Microbiology (GBR) 886
Food Policy (GBR) 198
Food Quality and Preference (GBR) 3641
Food Research International (GBR) 3641
Food Reviews International (USA) 3641
Food Science & Technology Bulletin (GBR) 3642
Food Science and Technology International (USA) 3642
Food Technology (USA) 3643
Foodborne Pathogens and Disease (USA) 5814
FoodService Director (USA) 3643
Foodservice Equipment & Supplies (USA) 4386
The Foot (GBR) 6060
Foot and Ankle Surgery (GBR) 6244
Footwear News (USA) 7940
Forage and Grazinglands (USA) 790
Forbes.com (USA) *see* Forbes. 1746
Forbes Global (USA) 1110
Ford Foundation Report (USA) 7964
Fordham Journal of Corporate & Financial Law (USA) 4868
Foreign Affairs (USA) 7235
Foreign Policy (Washington) (USA) 7235
Foreign Policy Analysis (USA) 7235
Foreign Policy Bulletin (GBR) 7235
Forensic Echo (USA) 5913
The Forensic of Pi Kappa Delta (USA) 2321
Forensic Science International (IRL) 5913
Forensic Science, Medicine, and Pathology (USA) 5913
Foresight (Cambridge) (GBR) 8422
Forest Ecology and Management (NLD) 3688
Forest Pathology Online (DEU) 3689
Forest Policy and Economics (NLD) 3689
Forest Products Journal (USA) 3711
Forest Science (USA) 3689
Forestry (GBR) 3690
Forestry Chronicle (CAN) 3690
Forging (USA) 6312
Formacion Medica Continuada en Atencion Primaria (ESP) 5615
Formal Aspects of Computing (GBR) 2418
Formal Methods in System Design (USA) 2520
Formulary (USA) 6843
Foro Hispanico (NLD) 5297
Forschende Komplementaermedizin (CHE) 309
Forschung (DEU) 7855
Forschung im Ingenieurwesen (DEU) 3192
Fortschritte der Neurologie, Psychiatrie (DEU) 6141
Fortschritte der Physik (DEU) 7013
Fortune.com (USA) *see* Fortune. 1746
Fortune International (NLD) 1111
Fortune Small Business (USA) 1961
The Forum (USA) 7136
Forum der Psychoanalyse (DEU) 7357
Forum for Modern Language Studies (GBR) 5120
Forum: for Promoting 3-19 Comprehensive Education (GBR) 3023
Forum Mathematicum (DEU) 5488
Forum Philosophicum (POL) 6920
Forum Psychotherapeutische Praxis (DEU) 7357
Forum Qualitative Sozialforschung (DEU) 7965
Foundation News & Commentary (USA) 8041
Foundations of Chemistry (NLD) 2062
Foundations of Computational Mathematics (USA) 5552
Foundations of Physics (USA) 7013
Foundations of Science (NLD) 7856
Foundry Management & Technology (USA) 6312
Fourth Genre (USA) 5297
Fractals (SGP) 5552
Framework (USA) 6501
France Today (USA) 5216
Franchising World (USA) 1817
Franklin Institute. Journal (GBR) 7013
Fraser Forum (CAN) 1487
The Free Press (USA) 5216
Free Radical Biology & Medicine (USA) 673
Free Radical Research (CHE) 732
French Colonial History (USA) 4221
French Cultural Studies (GBR) 4221
French Forum (USA) 5217
French Historical Studies (USA) 4222
French History (GBR) 4222
French Politics (GBR) 7137
French Politics, Culture & Society (USA) 7137
French Studies (GBR) 5298
French Studies Bulletin (GBR) 5298
Freshwater Biology Online (GBR) 674
Frieze (GBR) 490
Frontera Norte (MEX) 4007
Frontier Perspectives (USA) 5616
Frontiers (Lincoln) (USA) 8897
Frontiers in Bioscience (Landmark Edition) (USA) 5616
Frontiers in Ecology and the Environment (USA) 674
Frontiers in Medicinal Chemistry (NLD) 5616
Frontiers in Neuroendocrinology (USA) 5893
Frontiers in Zoology (GBR) 944
Frontiers of Health Services Management (USA) 4093
Frozen Food Age (USA) 3644
Fruits (FRA) 3730
Ft. Worth Business Press (USA) 1112
Fuel (GBR) 6769
Fuel and Energy Abstracts (GBR) 6800
Fuel Cells (DEU) 3135
Fuel Cells Bulletin (GBR) 3135
Fuel Processing Technology (NLD) 6769
Fullerenes, Nanotubes, and Carbon Nanostructures (USA) 2135
Fun for Kidz (USA) 2189
Functional Analysis and Its Applications (USA) 5488
Functional & Integrative Genomics (DEU) 867
Functional Ecology (GBR) 2612
Functional Ingredients (USA) 6659
Functional Plant Biology (AUS) 790

Online Service

Heat Transfer - Asian Research (Online Edition) (USA) **3379**
Heat Transfer Engineering (USA) **3245**
Heat Transfer Research (USA) **3379**
Hebrew Union College Annual (USA) **7721**
Hecate (AUS) **8898**
The Hedgehog Review (USA) **4454**
Helgoland Marine Research (DEU) **2806**
Helicobacter (Oxford) (USA) **887**
Helvetica Chimica Acta (CHE) **2063**
Hematological Oncology (GBR) **5937**
Hematologie (FRA) **5937**
Hematology (GBR) **5937**
The Hematology Journal (GBR) **5789**
The Hemingway Review (USA) **5305**
Hemisphere (USA) **7240**
Hemodialysis International (USA) **5938**
Hemoglobin (GBR) **5938**
The Henry James Review (USA) **5305**
Hepato - Gastro (FRA) **5926**
Hepatology (USA) **5926**
Hepatology Research (GBR) **5926**
Herb, Spice and Medicinal Plant Digest (USA) **3736**
HerbalGram (USA) **792**
Hereditas (USA) **871**
Heredity (GBR) **871**
Heritage New Zealand (NZL) **4192**
Herizons (CAN) **8867**
Hermaphrodites with Attitudes (USA) **4374**
Hernia (DEU) **6245**
Hers (USA) **6988**
Herz (DEU) **5789**
Herzschrittmachertherapie und Elektrophysiologie (DEU) **5789**
Hesperia (GRC) **396**
Heteroatom Chemistry (USA) **2116**
Heterocycles (JPN) **2123**
The Heythrop Journal (GBR) **7647**
High Ability Studies (GBR) **3041**
High Altitude Medicine and Biology (USA) **5628**
High Country News (USA) **3436**
High Energy Chemistry (RUS) **2135**
High Energy Density Physics (GBR) **7051**
High Performance Polymers (GBR) **2123**
High Pressure Research (GBR) **7059**
The High School Journal (USA) **2863**
High Temperature (RUS) **7054**
High Temperature Material Processes (USA) **2135**
High Temperatures - High Pressures (USA) **7054**
High Yield Report (USA) **1351**
Higher Education (NLD) **2984**
Higher Education in Europe (GBR) **2984**
Higher Education Management and Policy (FRA) **2984**
Higher Education Policy (GBR) **2984**
Higher Education Quarterly (GBR) **2984**
Higher Education Research and Development (GBR) **2985**
Higher-Order and Symbolic Computation (USA) **2486**
Highlights for Children (USA) **2192**
Hip International (ITA) **5628**
The Hippocampus (USA) **5628**
Hiram Poetry Review (USA) **5423**
Hispanic (USA) **3537**
Hispanic American Historical Review (USA) **4295**
Hispanic Engineer & Information Technology (USA) **3195**
Hispanic Journal of Behavioral Sciences (USA) **7360**
Hispanic Research Journal (GBR) **5305**
Hispanic Review (USA) **5125**
Histochemistry and Cell Biology (DEU) **833**
Histoire, Economie et Societe (FRA) **1542**
Histology and Histopathology (ESP) **833**
Histopathology (GBR) **6021**
Historia (CHL) **4295**
Historia Critica (COL) **4295**
Historia Mathematica (USA) **5491**
The Historian (East Lansing) (USA) **4143**
Historical Biology (CHE) **6725**
Historical Journal (GBR) **4143**
Historical Journal of Film, Radio and Television (GBR) **4143**
Historical Materialism (NLD) **1542**
Historical Methods (USA) **8149**
Historical Records of Australian Science (AUS) **7861**
Historical Research (GBR) **4143**
Historical Society. Journal (USA) **4143**
Historical Studies in the Natural Sciences (USA) **7862**
Historiographia Linguistica (NLD) **5125**
History (Washington) (USA) **4145**
History and Anthropology (GBR) **341**
History & Memory (USA) **4145**
History and Philosophy of Logic (GBR) **6923**
History and Philosophy of the Life Sciences (GBR) **676**
History and Technology (GBR) **4145**
History and Theory (USA) **4145**
History Australia (Online) (AUS) **4192**
History in Africa (USA) **4175**
History of Education (GBR) **2863**
History of Education Quarterly (USA) **2864**
History of European Ideas (GBR) **6923**
History of Photography (GBR) **6969**
History of Political Economy (USA) **1542**
History of Political Thought (GBR) **7140**
History of Psychiatry (GBR) **6144**
History of Psychology (USA) **7360**
History of Religions (USA) **7647**
History of Science (GBR) **7862**
The History of the Family (GBR) **7969**
History of the Human Sciences (GBR) **7969**
History Online (GBR) *see* History. **4145**
History Review (GBR) **4145**
The History Teacher (USA) **4145**
History Today (GBR) **4230**
History Workshop Journal (GBR) **4146**
HIV Clinical Trials (USA) **5906**
HIV Medicine (GBR) **5815**
Holistic Nursing Practice (USA) **5960**
Hollins Critic (USA) **5219**
Hollywood Reporter: Premier Edition (USA) *see* The Hollywood Reporter. **6502**
Hollywood Scriptwriter (USA) **6502**
Holocaust and Genocide Studies (USA) **4230**
Holocaust Studies (GBR) **4146**
The Holocene (GBR) **3437**
Holy Land Studies (GBR) **7648**
Holzforschung (DEU) **3712**
Home Channel News (USA) **1118**
Home Cultures (GBR) **7969**
Home Furnishings (GBR) **4558**
Home Health Care Management and Practice (USA) **4098**
Home Health Care Services Quarterly (USA) **4098**
Home Media Magazine (USA) **2401**
Home Textiles Today (USA) **8451**
HomeCare Magazine (USA) **5960**
Homemaker's (CAN) **4360**
Homeopathy (Online) (GBR) *see* Homeopathy (Print). **5805**
HomePlanners Outdoor Living (USA) **3736**
Homicide Studies (USA) **2654**
Homiletic (Online) (USA) **7760**
Homily Service (USA) **7648**
HOMO (DEU) **341**
Homoeopathic Links (DEU) **5805**
Hong Kong Journal of Social Work (SGP) **8045**
Hopscotch (Bluffton) (USA) **2193**
Horizons (Villanova) (USA) **7800**
Hormone and Metabolic Research (DEU) **5893**
Hormone Research in Paediatrics (Online) (CHE) *see* Hormone Research in Paediatrics. **5894**
Hormones and Behavior (USA) **5894**
The Horn Book Magazine (USA) **7562**
Horse & Rider (USA) **8292**
Horticulture (USA) **3737**
Hospice Management Advisor (USA) **4099**
Hospital Access Management (USA) **4099**
The Hospital Accounts Receivable Analysis (USA) **4099**
Hospital Case Management (USA) **4100**
Hospital Development (GBR) **4100**
Hospital Employee Health (USA) **4100**
Hospital Home Health (USA) **4100**
Hospital Infantil de Mexico. Boletin Medico (MEX) **4100**
Hospital Infantil del Estado de Sonora. Boletin Clinico (MEX) **5629**
Hospital Infection Control & Prevention (USA) **5816**
Hospital Peer Review (USA) **4101**
Hospital Pharmacy (USA) **6846**
Hospital Topics (USA) **4101**
Hospitalidad E S D A I (MEX) **8719**
Hospitality Design (USA) **4542**
Hotel and Motel Management (USA) **4389**
Hotel Business (USA) **4389**
Hotels (USA) **4390**
House Beautiful (USA) **4542**
Houses (AUS) **445**
Housewares Magazine (GBR) **4559**
Housing Finance International (BEL) **1351**
Housing Studies (GBR) **4414**
Housing, Theory and Society (NOR) **4414**
Houston Journal of Mathematics (USA) **5491**
Howard Journal of Communications (USA) **2323**
The Howard Journal of Criminal Justice (GBR) **2654**
HRfocus (USA) **1863**
Hudson Review (USA) **5220**
Hudson Valley Business Journal (USA) **1119**
Human and Ecological Risk Assessment (USA) **3437**
Human & Experimental Toxicology (GBR) **3497**
Human Antibodies (NLD) **5758**
Human Biology (Detroit) (USA) **871**
Human Brain Mapping (USA) **6145**
Human Communication Research (USA) **7360**
Human - Computer Interaction (Mahwah) (USA) **2420**
Human Development (CHE) **5630**
Human Dimensions of Wildlife (USA) **3438**
Human Ecology (Ithaca) (USA) **7970**
Human Ecology (New York) (USA) **341**
Human Factors (USA) **3195**
Human Factors and Ergonomics in Manufacturing (USA) **3367**
Human Fertility (GBR) **5993**
Human Gene Therapy (USA) **871**
Human Genetics (DEU) **871**
Human Genomics (Online) (GBR) **872**
Human Heredity (CHE) **872**
Human Immunology (USA) **5759**
Human Life Review (USA) **8106**
Human Molecular Genetics (GBR) **872**
Human Movement Science (NLD) **5630**
Human Mutation (USA) **872**
Human Nature (USA) **7970**
Human Organization (USA) **341**
Human Pathology (USA) **5631**
Human Performance (USA) **7361**
Human Physiology (RUS) **5631**
Human Psychopharmacology: Clinical and Experimental (GBR) **6145**
Human Reproduction (GBR) **5993**
Human Reproduction Update (GBR) **716**
Human Resource Development International (GBR) **1863**
Human Resource Development Quarterly (USA) **1863**
Human Resource Development Review (USA) **1864**
Human Resource Management (USA) **1864**
Human Resource Management International Digest (GBR) **1864**
Human Resource Management Journal (GBR) **1864**
Human Resource Management Review (GBR) **1864**
Human Resources for Health (GBR) **5631**
Human Rights (Chicago) (USA) **7208**
Human Rights Law Review (GBR) **7208**
Human Rights Quarterly (USA) **7208**
Human Rights Review (NLD) **7209**
Human Studies (NLD) **6923**
Human Systems Management (NLD) **1750**
Human Vaccines (USA) **6846**
The Humanist (USA) **6923**
The Humanistic Psychologist (USA) **7361**
Humanitas (CHL) **342**
Humanitas (USA) **4455**
Humanities (USA) **4455**
Humanities International Index (USA) **4484**
Humanities Review Journal (NGA) **4456**
Humor (DEU) **8106**
Humpty Dumpty's Magazine (USA) **2193**
Hungarian Studies (HUN) **4456**
Hungary Business Forecast Report (GBR) **1489**
Huntington Library Quarterly (USA) **5307**
Hurricane Alice (USA) **8868**
Husserl Studies (NLD) **6924**
Hybridoma (Online) (USA) **733**
Hydraulics & Pneumatics (USA) **3361**
Hydrobiologia (NLD) **677**
Hydrobiological Journal (USA) **677**
Hydrocarbon Processing (USA) **6772**
Hydrocarbon Processing International Edition (USA) **6772**
Hydrogeology Journal (DEU) **2794**
Hydrological Processes (GBR) **2794**
Hydrological Sciences Journal (GBR) **2794**
Hydrology Research (GBR) **2795**
Hydrometallurgy (NLD) **6315**
Hypatia (USA) **8898**
Hyperfine Interactions (NLD) **7015**
Hypertension (USA) **5789**
Hypertension in Pregnancy (USA) **5789**
I A N Inside Products (USA) **4487**
I C E S Journal of Marine Science (GBR) **2806**
I C H F Newsletter (USA) **7524**
I C M A Public Management Magazine (USA) **7494**
I C R U Journal (GBR) **7066**
i-com (DEU) **2350**
I D S Bulletin (GBR) **1597**
I D S Employment Law Brief (GBR) **1685**
I D S H R Studies (GBR) **1686**
I D S Pay Benchmark (GBR) **1686**
I E E E - A C M Transactions on Computational Biology and Bioinformatics (USA) **825**
I E E E - A C M Transactions on Networking (USA) **2497**
I E E E - A S M E Transactions on Mechatronics (USA) **3367**
I E E E Aerospace and Electronic Systems Magazine (USA) **3101**
I E E E Annals of the History of Computing (USA) **2420**
I E E E Antennas and Propagation Magazine (USA) **3310**
I E E E Antennas and Wireless Propagation Letters (USA) **2323**
I E E E Circuits and Systems Magazine (USA) **2465**
I E E E Communications Letters (USA) **2323**
I E E E Communications Magazine (USA) **3311**
I E E E Computer Graphics and Applications (USA) **2486**
I E E E Design & Test of Computers (USA) **2471**
I E E E Distributed Systems Online (USA) **2520**
I E E E Electrical Insulation Magazine (USA) **3311**
I E E E Electron Device Letters (USA) **3101**
I E E E Engineering in Medicine and Biology Magazine (USA) **748**
I E E E Engineering Management Review (USA) **3196**
I E E E Geoscience and Remote Sensing Letters (USA) **3311**
I E E E Industry Applications Magazine (USA) **3311**
I E E E Instrumentation and Measurement Magazine (USA) **6402**
I E E E Intelligent Systems (USA) **2471**
I E E E Internet Computing (USA) **2557**
I E E E Journal of Microelectromechanical Systems (USA) **3312**
I E E E Journal of Oceanic Engineering (USA) **3312**
I E E E Journal of Quantum Electronics (USA) **3102**
I E E E Journal of Solid State Circuits (USA) **3312**
I E E E Journal on Selected Areas in Communications (USA) **2323**
I E E E Journal on Selected Topics in Quantum Electronics (USA) **3102**
I E E E Micro (USA) **2571**
I E E E Microwave and Wireless Components Letters (USA) **3312**
I E E E Microwave Magazine (USA) **3312**
I E E E MultiMedia Magazine (USA) **2486**
I E E E Network (USA) **2498**
I E E E Pervasive Computing (USA) **2420**
I E E E Photonics Technology Letters (USA) **7076**
I E E E Potentials (USA) **3313**
I E E E Power & Energy Magazine (USA) **7015**
I E E E Power Electronics Letters (USA) **7015**
I E E E Robotics and Automation Magazine (USA) **2584**
I E E E Sensors Journal (USA) **4487**
I E E E Signal Processing Letters (USA) **3313**
I E E E - Signal Processing Magazine (USA) **7087**
I E E E Software (USA) **2590**
I E E E Spectrum (USA) **3313**
I E E E Technology and Society Magazine (USA) **8424**
I E E E Transactions on Advanced Packaging (USA) **3314**
I E E E Transactions on Aerospace and Electronic Systems (USA) **3314**
I E E E Transactions on Antennas and Propagation (USA) **3314**
I E E E Transactions on Applied Superconductivity (USA) **3102**
I E E E Transactions on Audio, Speech and Language Processing (USA) **2351**
I E E E Transactions on Automatic Control (USA) **3314**
I E E E Transactions on Automation Science and Engineering (USA) **3314**
I E E E Transactions on Biomedical Engineering (USA) **749**
I E E E Transactions on Broadcasting (USA) **2382**
I E E E Transactions on Circuits and Systems for Video Technology (USA) **3102**
I E E E Transactions on Circuits and Systems Part 1: Regular Papers (USA) **3102**
I E E E Transactions on Circuits and Systems. Part 2: Express Briefs (USA) **3102**
I E E E Transactions on Communications (USA) **2324**
I E E E Transactions on Components and Packaging Technology (USA) **3314**
I E E E Transactions on Computer - Aided Design of Integrated Circuits and Systems (USA) **3117**
I E E E Transactions on Computers (USA) **2421**
I E E E Transactions on Consumer Electronics (USA) **3102**
I E E E Transactions on Control Systems Technology (USA) **3314**
I E E E Transactions on Dependable and Secure Computing (USA) **2513**
I E E E Transactions on Dielectrics and Electrical Insulation (USA) **3314**
I E E E Transactions on Education (USA) **3314**
I E E E Transactions on Electromagnetic Compatibility (USA) **3103**
I E E E Transactions on Electron Devices (USA) **3103**
I E E E Transactions on Electronics Packaging Manufacturing (USA) **3315**
I E E E Transactions on Energy Conversion (USA) **3159**
I E E E Transactions on Engineering Management (USA) **3315**
I E E E Transactions on Evolutionary Computation (USA) **2421**
I E E E Transactions on Fuzzy Systems (USA) **2449**
I E E E Transactions on Geoscience and Remote Sensing (USA) **3315**
I E E E Transactions on Image Processing (USA) **2486**
I E E E Transactions on Industrial Electronics (USA) **3103**
I E E E Transactions on Industry Applications (USA) **3315**
I E E E Transactions on Information Technology in Biomedicine (USA) **765**
I E E E Transactions on Information Theory (USA) **2544**
I E E E Transactions on Instrumentation and Measurement (USA) **6402**
I E E E Transactions on Intelligent Transportation Systems (USA) **8498**
I E E E Transactions on Knowledge & Data Engineering (USA) **3315**
I E E E Transactions on Magnetics (USA) **3315**
I E E E Transactions on Medical Imaging (USA) **6198**
I E E E Transactions on Microwave Theory and Techniques (USA) **3315**
I E E E Transactions on Mobile Computing (USA) **2421**
I E E E Transactions on Multimedia (USA) **2576**
I E E E Transactions on NanoBioscience (USA) **749**
I E E E Transactions on Nanotechnology (USA) **2571**
I E E E Transactions on Neural Networks (USA) **2449**
I E E E Transactions on Neural Systems and Rehabilitation Engineering (USA) **749**
I E E E Transactions on Nuclear Science (USA) **3315**
I E E E Transactions on Parallel and Distributed Systems (USA) **2467**
I E E E Transactions on Pattern Analysis and Machine Intelligence (USA) **2449**
I E E E Transactions on Plasma Science (USA) **7015**
I E E E Transactions on Power Delivery (USA) **3315**
I E E E Transactions on Power Electronics (USA) **3103**
I E E E Transactions on Power Systems (USA) **3159**

Online Service

International Journal of Pressure Vessels and Piping (GBR) 3383
International Journal of Primatology (USA) 948
International Journal of Prisoner Health (USA) 7527
International Journal of Product Development (GBR) 1760
International Journal of Production Economics (NLD) 3369
International Journal of Production Research (GBR) 1889
International Journal of Productivity and Performance Management (GBR) 1760
International Journal of Project Management (GBR) 1419
International Journal of Prosthodontics (USA) 5849
International Journal of Psychiatry in Clinical Practice (GBR) 6147
The International Journal of Psychiatry in Medicine (USA) 6147
The International Journal of Psychoanalysis (GBR) 7365
International Journal of Psychology (GBR) 7365
International Journal of Psychophysiology (NLD) 7365
International Journal of Public Administration (USA) 7447
International Journal of Public Health (CHE) 5639
International Journal of Public Opinion Research (GBR) 7144
International Journal of Public Sector Management (GBR) 1761
International Journal of Qualitative Methods (CAN) 7974
International Journal of Qualitative Studies in Education (GBR) 2870
International Journal of Quality & Reliability Management (GBR) 1761
International Journal of Quantum Chemistry (USA) 2065
International Journal of Quantum Information (SGP) 7017
International Journal of R F and Microwave Computer-Aided Engineering (Online) (USA) *see* International Journal of R F and Microwave Computer-Aided Engineering (Print). 3292
International Journal of Radiation Biology (GBR) 6023
International Journal of Radiation: Oncology - Biology - Physics (USA) 6199
International Journal of Reality Therapy (USA) 7366
International Journal of Refractory Metals and Hard Materials (GBR) 6317
International Journal of Refrigeration (GBR) 4122
International Journal of Refugee Law (GBR) 7243
International Journal of Rehabilitation Research (USA) 6110
International Journal of Reliability, Quality & Safety Engineering (SGP) 3202
International Journal of Remote Sensing (GBR) 2710
International Journal of Research and Method in Education (Online) (GBR) 2870
International Journal of Research in Marketing (NLD) 1822
International Journal of Retail & Distribution Management (GBR) 1822
International Journal of Rheumatic Diseases (AUS) 6224
The International Journal of Risk and Safety in Medicine (NLD) 4509
International Journal of Risk Assessment and Management (GBR) 1761
International Journal of River Basin Management (ESP) 3362
International Journal of Robotics Research (GBR) 2585
International Journal of Robust and Nonlinear Control (GBR) 3321
International Journal of Rock Mechanics and Mining Sciences (GBR) 6466
International Journal of Rotating Machinery (USA) 5453
International Journal of Rural Management (IND) 4016
International Journal of S T D & AIDS (GBR) 5818
International Journal of Satellite Communications and Networking (GBR) 2383
International Journal of Science and Mathematics Education (NLD) 7868
International Journal of Science Education (GBR) 2871
International Journal of Selection and Assessment (GBR) 1867
International Journal of Self-Help and Self-Care (USA) 7366
International Journal of Services and Standards (GBR) 1129
International Journal of Services Technology and Management (GBR) 1419
International Journal of Sexual Health (Online) (USA) *see* International Journal of Sexual Health. 7366
International Journal of Shaping Modeling (SGP) 2487
International Journal of Six Sigma and Competitive Advantage (GBR) 3369
International Journal of Social Economics (GBR) 1129
International Journal of Social Psychiatry (GBR) 6147
International Journal of Social Research Methodology (GBR) 7974
International Journal of Social Welfare (GBR) 8047
International Journal of Sociology (USA) 8109
International Journal of Sociology and Social Policy (GBR) 8109
International Journal of Sociology of Agriculture and Food (JPN) 8109
International Journal of Software Engineering and Knowledge Engineering (SGP) 2592
International Journal of Solids and Structures (GBR) 7059
International Journal of Space Structures (GBR) 1016
International Journal of Speech-Language Pathology (GBR) 5129
International Journal of Speech Technology (NLD) 5203
International Journal of Sport and Exercise Psychology (USA) 7366
International Journal of Sport Nutrition & Exercise Metabolism (USA) 6661
International Journal of Sports Management and Marketing (GBR) 1761
International Journal of Sports Medicine (DEU) 6230
International Journal of Strategic Property Management (LTU) 7596
International Journal of Stress Management (USA) 5640
International Journal of Stroke (AUS) 5790
International Journal of Structural Stability and Dynamics (SGP) 3383
International Journal of Surgery (GBR) 6246
International Journal of Surgical Pathology (USA) 6246
International Journal of Sustainability in Higher Education (Online) (GBR) 2988
International Journal of Sustainable Development (GBR) 3443
International Journal of Sustainable Development and World Ecology (GBR) 3443
International Journal of Sustainable Energy (GBR) 3176
International Journal of Systematic and Evolutionary Microbiology (GBR) 888
International Journal of Systematic Theology (GBR) 7651
International Journal of Systems Science (GBR) 3203
International Journal of Technology and Design Education (NLD) 3065
International Journal of Technology and Globalisation (GBR) 8427
International Journal of Technology Assessment in Health Care (GBR) 5906
International Journal of Technology Intelligence and Planning (GBR) 8427
International Journal of Technology Management (GBR) 8427
International Journal of Technology Management & Sustainable Development (GBR) 8427
International Journal of Technology Policy and Management (GBR) 8427
International Journal of Technology Transfer and Commercialisation (GBR) 8428
International Journal of Testing (USA) 7366
International Journal of the Classical Tradition (NLD) 2236
International Journal of the Economics of Business (GBR) 1129
The International Journal of the History of Sport (GBR) 4147
International Journal of the Legal Profession (GBR) 4695
International Journal of the Sociology of Language (DEU) 5130
International Journal of Theoretical and Applied Finance (SGP) 1357
International Journal of Theoretical Physics (USA) 7018
International Journal of Therapy and Rehabilitation (GBR) 6110
International Journal of Thermal Sciences (FRA) 7055
International Journal of Thermophysics (USA) 7055
International Journal of Tourism Research (GBR) 8723
International Journal of Toxicology (GBR) 3498
International Journal of Training & Development (GBR) 1867
The International Journal of Transgenderism (USA) 7366
International Journal of Tropical Insect Science (KEN) 850
International Journal of Tuberculosis and Lung Disease (FRA) 6215
International Journal of Uncertainty, Fuzziness and Knowledge-Based Systems (SGP) 2452
International Journal of Urban and Regional Research (GBR) 4416
International Journal of Urology (AUS) 6269
International Journal of Vegetable Science (USA) 237
International Journal of Vehicle Autonomous Systems (GBR) 8499
International Journal of Vehicle Design (GBR) 8499
International Journal of Vehicle Noise and Vibration (GBR) 8500
International Journal of Ventilation (GBR) 4122
International Journal of Water (GBR) 8826
International Journal of Water Resources Development (GBR) 8826
International Journal of Wavelets, Multiresolution and Information Processing (SGP) 5497
International Journal of Web Based Communities (GBR) 2559
International Journal of Web Engineering and Technology (GBR) 2547
International Journal of Wildland Fire (AUS) 3579
International Journal of Wireless Information Networks (USA) 2327
International Journal of Yoga Therapy (USA) 6990
International Journal on Algae (USA) 795
International Journal on Artificial Intelligence Tools (SGP) 2452
International Journal on Digital Libraries (DEU) 5062
International Journal on Document Analysis and Recognition (DEU) 2427
International Journal on E-learning (USA) 2560
International Journal on Minority and Group Rights (NLD) 7210
International Journal on Semantic Web and Information Systems (USA) 2547
International Journal on Software Tools for Technology Transfer (DEU) 2592
International Journal on World Peace (USA) 7244
International Justice Tribune (French Edition) (FRA) 4931
International Labor and Working-Class History (GBR) 1689
International Labour Review (GBR) 1689
International Law Update (USA) 4931
International Marketing Review (GBR) 1822
International Materials Reviews (GBR) 3348
International Mathematics Research Notices (USA) 5498
International Mathematics Research Surveys (GBR) 5498
International Microbiology (ESP) 888
International Migration (GBR) 7285
International Migration Review (USA) 7285
International Monetary Fund. Staff Papers (USA) 1358
International Money Marketing (GBR) 1358
International Negotiation (NLD) 7244
International Neuropsychological Society. Journal (GBR) 6147
International Nursing Review Online (GBR) 5962
International Ophthalmology (NLD) 6044
International Ophthalmology Clinics (USA) 6044
International Organization (GBR) 7244
International Organizations Law Review (NLD) 4932
International Orthodontics (FRA) 5849
International Orthopaedics (DEU) 6062
International Peacekeeping (GBR) 7244
International Perspectives on Sexual and Reproductive Health (USA) 5994
International Phonetic Association. Journal (GBR) 5130
International Planning Studies (GBR) 4416
International Political Science Review (GBR) 7244
International Politics (GBR) 7244
International Polymer Science and Technology (GBR) 7093
International Psychogeriatrics (GBR) 6148
International Public Management Journal (GBR) 7447
International Quarterly of Community Health Education (USA) 7527
International Regional Science Review (USA) 7975
International Relations (GBR) 7245
International Relations of the Asia-Pacific (GBR) 7245
International Research in Geographical and Environmental Education (GBR) 4016
International Review for Environmental Strategies (JPN) 3443
International Review for the Sociology of Sport (GBR) 8110
International Review of Administrative Sciences (GBR) 7447
International Review of Applied Economics (GBR) 1129
International Review of Economics & Finance (GBR) 1493
International Review of Education (DEU) 2871
International Review of Finance (GBR) 1358
International Review of Financial Analysis (GBR) 1359
International Review of Hydrobiology (DEU) 679
International Review of Law and Economics (USA) 4696
International Review of Law, Computers & Technology (GBR) 4845
International Review of Mission (CHE) 7651
International Review of Psychiatry (GBR) 6148
The International Review of Retail, Distribution and Consumer Research (GBR) 1822
International Review of Social History (GBR) 4147
International Review of Sociology (GBR) 8110
International Reviews in Physical Chemistry (GBR) 2136
International Reviews of Immunology (CHE) 5761
International Securities Finance (GBR) 1359
International Security (USA) 7245
International Seminars in Paediatric Gastroenterology and Nutrition (CAN) 5927
International Seminars in Surgical Oncology (GBR) 6023
International Shipbuilding Progress (NLD) 8647
International Small Business Journal (GBR) 1962
International Social Science Journal (GBR) 7975
International Social Science Review (USA) 7975
International Social Security Review (GBR) 4509
International Social Work (GBR) 8048
International Sociology (GBR) 8110
International SportMed Journal (ZAF) 6230
International Statistical Review (GBR) 8379
International Studies (IND) 7245
International Studies in Educational Administration (CYP) 3013
International Studies in Sociology of Education (GBR) 3066
International Studies in the Philosophy of Science (GBR) 6926
International Studies of Management and Organization (USA) 1762
International Studies Perspectives (USA) 7245
International Studies Quarterly (USA) 7245
International Studies Review (USA) 7245
International Tax and Public Finance (USA) 1930
International Tax Journal (USA) 1930
International Tax Review (GBR) 1571
International Trade Forum (CHE) 1571
The International Trade Journal (USA) 1572
International Transactions in Operational Research (GBR) 2427
International Union of Crystallography. Newsletter (USA) 2110
International Urogynecology Journal (GBR) 5994
International Urology and Nephrology (NLD) 6269
International Water Power and Dam Construction (GBR) 3163
International Wound Journal (GBR) 6062
The Internet and Higher Education (GBR) 2560
Internet Archaeology (GBR) 399
Internet Business (GBR) 2560
The Internet Journal of Academic Physician Assistants (USA) 5640
The Internet Journal of Advanced Nursing Practice (USA) 5962
The Internet Journal of Anesthesiology (USA) 5771
The Internet Journal of Asthma, Allergy and Immunology (USA) 5761
The Internet Journal of Cardiology (USA) 5790
The Internet Journal of Dermatology (USA) 5878
The Internet Journal of Emergency and Intensive Care Medicine (USA) 6062
The Internet Journal of Epidemiology (USA) 7527
The Internet Journal of Family Practice (USA) 5946
The Internet Journal of Gastroenterology (USA) 5927
The Internet Journal of Genomics and Proteomics (USA) 766
The Internet Journal of Gynecology and Obstetrics (USA) 5994
The Internet Journal of Health (USA) 7527
The Internet Journal of Healthcare Administration (USA) 4102
The Internet Journal of Hematology (USA) 5939
The Internet Journal of Infectious Diseases (USA) 5640
The Internet Journal of Internal Medicine (USA) 5946
The Internet Journal of Law, Healthcare and Ethics (USA) 5914
The Internet Journal of Medical Simulation (USA) 5640
The Internet Journal of Mental Health (USA) 7366
The Internet Journal of Nephrology (USA) 6269
The Internet Journal of Neurology (USA) 6148
The Internet Journal of Neuromonitoring (USA) 6148
The Internet Journal of Neurosurgery (USA) 6246
The Internet Journal of Nuclear Medicine (USA) 6199
The Internet Journal of Oncology (USA) 6023
The Internet Journal of Ophthalmology and Visual Science (USA) 6044
The Internet Journal of Orthopedic Surgery (USA) 6062
The Internet Journal of Otorhinolaryngology (USA) 6081
The Internet Journal of Pain, Symptom Control and Palliative Care (USA) 5771
The Internet Journal of Pathology (USA) 5640
The Internet Journal of Pediatrics and Neonatology (USA) 6093
The Internet Journal of Perfusionists (USA) 5790
The Internet Journal of Pharmacology (USA) 6850
The Internet Journal of Plastic Surgery (USA) 6246
The Internet Journal of Pulmonary Medicine (USA) 6215
The Internet Journal of Radiology (USA) 6199
The Internet Journal of Rescue and Disaster Medicine (USA) 6062
The Internet Journal of Rheumatology (USA) 6224
The Internet Journal of Surgery (USA) 6246
The Internet Journal of Third World Medicine (USA) 5640
The Internet Journal of Thoracic and Cardiovascular Surgery (USA) 6247
The Internet Journal of Tropical Medicine (USA) 5819
The Internet Journal of Urology (USA) 6269
The Internet Journal of World Health and Societal Politics (USA) 7527
Internet Reference Services Quarterly (USA) 5019
Internet Research (GBR) 2561
Internet Tax Advisor (USA) 1393
InternetTelephony (USA) *see* Telephony. 2373
Der Internist (DEU) 5946
Interpretation (Richmond) (USA) 7651
Interpreting (NLD) 5130
Intersections (AUS) 8899
Intertax (NLD) 1572
Intervencion Psicosocial (ESP) 7366
Intervention in School and Clinic (USA) 3042
Intervention Research (NLD) 7975

Online Service

Journal of Automation & Information Sciences (USA) **2462**
Journal of Avian Biology (DNK) **909**
Journal of Baccalaureate Social Work (USA) **8048**
Journal of Back and Musculoskeletal Rehabilitation (NLD) **6063**
Journal of Bacteriology (USA) **888**
Journal of Balkan and Near Eastern Studies (GBR) **4235**
Journal of Baltic Science Education (LTU) **2874**
Journal of Bamboo and Rattan (IND) **796**
Journal of Banking & Finance (NLD) **1360**
Journal of Banking Regulation (GBR) **1360**
Journal of Basic Microbiology (DEU) **888**
Journal of Basic Writing (USA) **5314**
Journal of Behavior Therapy and Experimental Psychiatry (GBR) **6149**
Journal of Behavioral Decision Making (GBR) **1763**
Journal of Behavioral Education (USA) **2874**
The Journal of Behavioral Finance (USA) **7369**
Journal of Behavioral Health Services and Research (USA) **7528**
Journal of Behavioral Medicine (USA) **6149**
Journal of Beliefs and Values (GBR) **2874**
Journal of Biblical Literature (USA) **7654**
Journal of Bioactive and Compatible Polymers (GBR) **734**
Journal of Biochemical and Molecular Toxicology (Online Edition) (USA) **681**
Journal of Biochemistry (GBR) **735**
The Journal of Biocommunication (USA) **5646**
Journal of Bioeconomics (USA) **681**
Journal of Bioenergetics and Biomembranes (USA) **735**
Journal of Biogeography (GBR) **4017**
Journal of Bioinformatics and Computational Biology (GBR) **681**
The Journal of Biolaw and Business (USA) **766**
Journal of Biological Chemistry (USA) **735**
Journal of Biological Education (GBR) **681**
Journal of Biological Inorganic Chemistry (DEU) **2117**
Journal of Biological Physics (NLD) **753**
Journal of Biological Rhythms (USA) **6149**
Journal of Biological Systems (SGP) **681**
Journal of Biology (GBR) **681**
Journal of Biomaterials Applications (GBR) **6247**
Journal of Biomaterials Science. Polymer Edition (NLD) **766**
Journal of Biomechanical Engineering (USA) **5646**
Journal of Biomechanics (GBR) **5646**
Journal of Biomedical Informatics (USA) **5832**
Journal of Biomedical Materials Research. Part A (USA) **766**
Journal of Biomedical Materials Research. Part B: Applied Biomaterials (USA) **766**
Journal of Biomedical Optics (USA) **7078**
Journal of Biomedical Science (GBR) **5646**
Journal of Biomedical Therapy (USA) **5646**
Journal of Biomedicine and Biotechnology (USA) **5646**
Journal of Biomolecular N M R (NLD) **735**
Journal of Biomolecular Screening (USA) **735**
Journal of Biomolecular Structure & Dynamics (USA) **735**
Journal of Biomolecular Techniques (USA) **767**
Journal of Biopharmaceutical Statistics (USA) **6889**
Journal of Bioscience and Bioengineering (JPN) **750**
Journal of Biosocial Science (GBR) **8112**
Journal of Biotechnology (NLD) **767**
Journal of Bisexuality (USA) **4375**
Journal of Black Psychology (USA) **7369**
Journal of Black Studies (USA) **7978**
Journal of Bodywork and Movement Therapies (GBR) **6111**
Journal of Bone and Joint Surgery: American Volume (USA) **6063**
Journal of Bone and Joint Surgery: British Volume (GBR) **6063**
Journal of Bone and Mineral Metabolism (JPN) **5895**
Journal of Bone and Mineral Research (USA) **6063**
The Journal of Brand Management (GBR) **1823**
Journal of Bridge Engineering (USA) **1018**
Journal of British Studies (USA) **4235**
Journal of Broadcasting and Electronic Media (USA) **2383**
Journal of Bronchology & Interventional Pulmonology (USA) **6215**
Journal of Bryology (GBR) **796**
Journal of Building Appraisal (GBR) **1018**
Journal of Building Physics (GBR) **3204**
Journal of Burn Care & Research (USA) **5646**
Journal of Business (Spokane) (USA) **1360**
Journal of Business and Economic Statistics (USA) **1247**
Journal of Business and Economic Studies (USA) **1133**
Journal of Business & Finance Librarianship (USA) **5020**
Journal of Business & Industrial Marketing (GBR) **1823**
Journal of Business and Management (USA) **1764**
Journal of Business & Psychology (USA) **7369**
Journal of Business and Public Affairs (Murray) (USA) **1133**
Journal of Business and Technical Communication (USA) **1133**
Journal of Business Chemistry (DEU) **2067**
Journal of Business Communication (USA) **1764**
Journal of Business Ethics (NLD) **1134**
Journal of Business Finance & Accounting (GBR) **1294**
The Journal of Business Forecasting (USA) **1134**
Journal of Business Logistics (USA) **1764**
Journal of Business Research (USA) **1764**
Journal of Business Strategies (USA) **1764**
Journal of Business Strategy (USA) **1764**
Journal of Business-to-Business Marketing (USA) **1823**
Journal of Business Venturing (USA) **1134**
Journal of Canadian Studies (CAN) **4460**
Journal of Cancer Education (USA) **6023**
Journal of Cancer Research and Clinical Oncology (DEU) **6024**
Journal of Cancer Research and Therapeutics (IND) **6024**
Journal of Carbohydrate Chemistry (USA) **2067**
Journal of Carcinogenesis (IND) **6024**
Journal of Cardiac Failure (USA) **5791**
Journal of Cardiac Surgery (USA) **5792**
Journal of Cardiopulmonary Rehabilitation and Prevention (USA) **5792**
Journal of Cardiothoracic and Vascular Anesthesia (USA) **5792**
Journal of Cardiovascular Electrophysiology (USA) **5792**
Journal of Cardiovascular Magnetic Resonance (GBR) **5792**
Journal of Cardiovascular Management (USA) **5792**
Journal of Cardiovascular Medicine (Hagerstown) (USA) **5792**
The Journal of Cardiovascular Nursing (USA) **5792**
Journal of Cardiovascular Pharmacology (USA) **6852**
The Journal of Cardiovascular Surgery (ITA) **5792**
Journal of Career Assessment (USA) **7369**
Journal of Career Development (USA) **6700**
Journal of Caribbean Literatures (USA) **5314**
Journal of Cases in Educational Leadership (USA) **3025**
Journal of Catalysis (USA) **2136**
Journal of Cataract & Refractive Surgery (USA) **6044**
The Journal of Cell Biology (USA) **833**
Journal of Cell Science (GBR) **833**
Journal of Cellular Biochemistry (USA) **735**
Journal of Cellular Physiology (USA) **923**
Journal of Cellular Plastics (GBR) **7093**
Journal of Cereal Science (GBR) **273**
Journal of Cerebral Blood Flow and Metabolism (USA) **6150**
The Journal of Change Management (GBR) **1764**
Journal of Chemical and Engineering Data (USA) **2067**
Journal of Chemical Crystallography (USA) **2111**
Journal of Chemical Ecology (USA) **3444**
Journal of Chemical Education (USA) **2067**
Journal of Chemical Health and Safety (USA) **3498**
Journal of Chemical Information and Modeling (USA) **2108**
Journal of Chemical Neuroanatomy (NLD) **6150**
Journal of Chemical Physics (USA) **7019**
Journal of Chemical Research (Online Edition) (GBR) *see* Journal of Chemical Research (Print Edition). **2067**
Journal of Chemical Technology and Biotechnology (GBR) **767**
Journal of Chemical Theory and Computation (USA) **2067**
The Journal of Chemical Thermodynamics (GBR) **2136**
Journal of Chemometrics (GBR) **2101**
Journal of Child and Adolescent Mental Health (ZAF) **6150**
Journal of Child and Adolescent Psychiatric Nursing (USA) **5964**
Journal of Child and Adolescent Psychopharmacology (USA) **6150**
Journal of Child & Adolescent Substance Abuse (USA) **2695**
Journal of Child and Family Studies (USA) **7370**
Journal of Child Custody (USA) **2156**
Journal of Child Health Care (GBR) **6094**
Journal of Child Language (GBR) **2156**
Journal of Child Neurology (USA) **6150**
Journal of Child Psychology and Psychiatry (GBR) **7370**
Journal of Child Psychotherapy (GBR) **7370**
Journal of Child Sexual Abuse (USA) **8049**
Journal of Children & Poverty (USA) **8049**
Journal of Chinese Economics and Business Studies (GBR) **1494**
Journal of Chinese Philosophy (USA) **6928**
Journal of Chinese Political Science (NLD) **7146**
Journal of Chinese Religions (USA) **7737**
Journal of Chiropractic Medicine (USA) **5806**
Journal of Chromatographic Science (USA) **2101**
Journal of Chromatography A (NLD) **2101**
Journal of Chromatography. B, Analytical Technologies in the Biomedical and Life Sciences (NLD) **2067**
Journal of Church and State (USA) **7654**
Journal of Circadian Rhythms (GBR) **5646**
Journal of Circuits, Systems and Computers (SGP) **2466**
Journal of Civil Society (GBR) **7146**
Journal of Classical Sociology (GBR) **8112**
Journal of Classification (USA) **5020**
Journal of Cleaner Production (NLD) **3369**
Journal of Climate (USA) **6358**
Journal of Clinical Anesthesia (USA) **5772**
Journal of Clinical Apheresis (USA) **5939**
Journal of Clinical Child and Adolescent Psychology (USA) **7370**
Journal of Clinical Densitometry (NLD) **5647**
Journal of Clinical Endocrinology and Metabolism (USA) **5895**
Journal of Clinical Engineering (USA) **750**
Journal of Clinical Epidemiology (USA) **5647**
The Journal of Clinical Ethics (USA) **5647**
Journal of Clinical Forensic and Legal Medicine (GBR) **5914**
Journal of Clinical Gastroenterology (USA) **5927**
Journal of Clinical Immunology (USA) **5762**
Journal of Clinical Investigation (USA) **5647**
Journal of Clinical Laboratory Analysis (USA) **5907**
Journal of Clinical Microbiology (USA) **5647**
Journal of Clinical Monitoring and Computing (NLD) **5647**
Journal of Clinical Neuromuscular Disease (USA) **5647**
Journal of Clinical Neurophysiology (USA) **6150**
Journal of Clinical Neuroscience (GBR) **6150**
Journal of Clinical Nursing (GBR) **5964**
Journal of Clinical Oncology (USA) **6024**
Journal of Clinical Orthodontics (USA) **5850**
Journal of Clinical Outcomes Management (USA) **4103**
Journal of Clinical Pediatric Dentistry (USA) **5851**
Journal of Clinical Periodontology (DNK) **5851**
The Journal of Clinical Pharmacology (USA) **6852**
Journal of Clinical Pharmacy and Therapeutics (GBR) **6852**
Journal of Clinical Psychiatry (USA) **6150**
Journal of Clinical Psychology (USA) **7370**
Journal of Clinical Psychology in Medical Settings (USA) **7370**
Journal of Clinical Psychopharmacology (USA) **6853**
Journal of Clinical Rheumatology (USA) **6224**
Journal of Clinical Ultrasound (USA) **6200**
Journal of Clinical Virology (NLD) **5819**
Journal of Cluster Science (USA) **2067**
Journal of Coastal Conservation (NLD) **2809**
Journal of Coastal Research (USA) **2809**
Journal of Cognition and Culture (NLD) **7370**
Journal of Cognition and Development (USA) **7370**
Journal of Cognitive Neuroscience (USA) **6151**
Journal of Cognitive Psychotherapy (USA) **7371**
Journal of Cognitive Rehabilitation (USA) **6111**
Journal of Cold Regions Engineering (USA) **3274**
Journal of Cold War Studies (USA) **7247**
Journal of Collective Negotiations (USA) **4596**
Journal of College Admission (USA) **2989**
Journal of College and University Student Housing (USA) **2989**
Journal of College Counseling (USA) **2989**
Journal of College Science Teaching (USA) **7872**
Journal of College Student Development (USA) **2989**
Journal of College Student Psychotherapy (USA) **7371**
Journal of College Student Retention: Research, Theory & Practice (USA) **2989**
Journal of Colloid and Interface Science (USA) **2136**
Journal of Colonialism & Colonial History (USA) **4149**
Journal of Combinatorial Chemistry (USA) **2102**
Journal of Combinatorial Designs (USA) **5501**
Journal of Combinatorial Optimization (NLD) **5553**
Journal of Combinatorial Theory, Series A (USA) **5501**
Journal of Combinatorial Theory. Series B (USA) **5501**
The Journal of Commerce (USA) **1430**
Journal of Commercial Biotechnology (GBR) **767**
Journal of Common Market Studies (GBR) **7146**
Journal of Commonwealth Literature (GBR) **5314**
Journal of Communication (USA) **8112**
The Journal of Communication and Religion (USA) **7654**
Journal of Communication Disorders (USA) **7371**
Journal of Communication Inquiry (USA) **8112**
Journal of Communication Management (GBR) **1765**
Journal of Communications and Networks (KOR) **2500**
Journal of Communist Studies and Transition Politics (GBR) **7247**
Journal of Community & Applied Social Psychology (GBR) **7371**
Journal of Community Health (USA) **5647**
Journal of Community Health Nursing (USA) **5964**
Journal of Community Practice (USA) **8049**
Journal of Community Psychology (USA) **7371**
Journal of Comparative Economics (USA) **1134**
Journal of Comparative Family Studies (CAN) **8112**
The Journal of Comparative Germanic Linguistics (NLD) **5133**
The Journal of Comparative Neurology (USA) **6151**
Journal of Comparative Pathology (GBR) **682**
Journal of Comparative Physiology A (DEU) **924**
Journal of Comparative Physiology B (DEU) **924**
Journal of Comparative Policy Analysis (USA) **7448**
Journal of Comparative Psychology (USA) **7371**
Journal of Compensation & Benefits (USA) **1868**
Journal of Competition Law and Economics (GBR) **4700**
Journal of Complexity (USA) **5553**
Journal of Composite Materials (GBR) **3349**
Journal of Composites for Construction (USA) **3274**
Journal of Computational Acoustics (SGP) **7050**
Journal of Computational Analysis and Applications (USA) **5501**
Journal of Computational and Applied Mathematics (NLD) **5502**
Journal of Computational and Graphical Statistics (USA) **5502**
Journal of Computational and Theoretical Nanoscience (USA) **7019**
Journal of Computational Biology (Online) (USA) **682**
Journal of Computational Chemistry (USA) **2068**
Journal of Computational Electronics (USA) **2428**
Journal of Computational Mathematics (CHN) **5502**
Journal of Computational Neuroscience (NLD) **6151**
Journal of Computational Physics (USA) **7050**
Journal of Computer - Aided Molecular Design (NLD) **2108**
Journal of Computer and System Sciences (USA) **2523**
Journal of Computer Assisted Learning (GBR) **2469**
Journal of Computer Assisted Tomography (USA) **6200**
Journal of Computer Information Systems (USA) **2523**
Journal of Computer-Mediated Communication (USA) **2351**
Journal of Computer Science and Technology (USA) **2468**
Journal of Computer Security (NLD) **2515**
Journal of Computers in Mathematics and Science Teaching (USA) **5553**
Journal of Computing and Information Science in Engineering (USA) **3385**
Journal of Computing in Civil Engineering (USA) **3292**
Journal of Conflict and Security Law (GBR) **4933**
Journal of Conflict Resolution (USA) **7978**
Journal of Consciousness Studies (GBR) **7371**
Journal of Construction Engineering and Management (USA) **3274**
Journal of Construction Research (SGP) **1018**
Journal of Constructional Steel Research (GBR) **3275**
Journal of Constructivist Psychology (USA) **7371**
Journal of Consulting and Clinical Psychology (USA) **7371**
Journal of Consumer Affairs (USA) **2639**
Journal of Consumer Behaviour (GBR) **2639**
Journal of Consumer Culture (GBR) **2639**
Journal of Consumer Health on the Internet (USA) **2562**
Journal of Consumer Marketing (GBR) **1823**
Journal of Consumer Policy (NLD) **2639**
Journal of Consumer Psychology (USA) **27**
Journal of Consumer Research (USA) **1823**
Journal of Contaminant Hydrology (NLD) **3488**
Journal of Contemporary African Studies (GBR) **7978**
Journal of Contemporary Asia (GBR) **4184**
Journal of Contemporary China (GBR) **4184**
Journal of Contemporary Criminal Justice (USA) **4892**
Journal of Contemporary Ethnography (USA) **8112**
Journal of Contemporary European Studies (Online Edition) (GBR) **7146**
Journal of Contemporary History (GBR) **4149**
Journal of Contemporary Psychotherapy (USA) **7372**
Journal of Contemporary Religion (GBR) **7654**
Journal of Contingencies and Crisis Management (GBR) **1765**
Journal of Continuing Education in Nursing (USA) **5964**
Journal of Continuing Education in the Health Professions (USA) **5648**
Journal of Controlled Release (NLD) **6853**
Journal of Convention & Event Tourism (USA) **6280**
Journal of Convex Analysis (DEU) **5502**
Journal of Cooperative Education and Internships (USA) **2874**
Journal of Coordination Chemistry (CHE) **2068**
Journal of Coptic Studies (BEL) **4322**
Journal of Corporate Accounting and Finance (USA) **1294**
The Journal of Corporate Citizenship (GBR) **1765**
Journal of Corporate Finance (NLD) **1360**
The Journal of Corporate Law Studies (GBR) **4872**
Journal of Corporate Real Estate (GBR) **7596**
The Journal of Corporation Law (USA) **4872**
Journal of Correctional Education (USA) **2656**
Journal of Cosmetic and Laser Therapy (Online) (GBR) **5878**
Journal of Cosmetic Dermatology (GBR) **5878**
Journal of Cosmology and Astroparticle Physics (GBR) **7020**
Journal of Counseling & Development (USA) **7372**
Journal of Counseling Psychology (USA) **7372**
Journal of Couple & Relationship Therapy (USA) **7372**
Journal of Cranio-Maxillofacial Surgery (GBR) **6247**
Journal of Craniofacial Surgery (USA) **6247**
Journal of Criminal Justice (GBR) **4892**
Journal of Criminal Justice Education (GBR) **2656**
The Journal of Criminal Law (GBR) **4892**
Journal of Criminal Law & Criminology (USA) **2657**
Journal of Critical Care (USA) **6063**
Journal of Critical Realism (GBR) **6928**
Journal of Crop Improvement (USA) **239**
Journal of Cross-Cultural Gerontology (NLD) **4049**
Journal of Cross-Cultural Psychology (USA) **7372**
Journal of Cryptology (USA) **5502**
Journal of Crystal Growth (NLD) **2111**
Journal of Culinary Science & Technology (USA) **6661**
Journal of Cultural Diversity (USA) **5964**
Journal of Cultural Economics (USA) **1544**

Online Service

Journal of Cultural Geography (USA) **4017**
Journal of Cultural Heritage (FRA) **344**
Journal of Cuneiform Studies (USA) **400**
Journal of Current Issues & Research in Advertising (USA) **27**
Journal of Curriculum Studies (GBR) **3067**
Journal of Customer Behavior (GBR) **1824**
Journal of Cutaneous Medicine and Surgery (CAN) **5878**
Journal of Cutaneous Pathology (DNK) **5878**
Journal of Cystic Fibrosis (NLD) **5927**
Journal of Dairy Research (GBR) **266**
Journal of Dairy Science (USA) **266**
Journal of Dance Education (USA) **2686**
Journal of Dance Medicine & Science (USA) **6111**
Journal of Database Management (USA) **2531**
The Journal of Database Marketing & Customer Strategy Management (Online Edition) (GBR) **1419**
The Journal of Deaf Studies and Deaf Education (USA) **4075**
Journal of Deferred Compensation (USA) **1690**
Journal of Democracy (USA) **7146**
Journal of Dental Education (USA) **2990**
Journal of Dental Hygiene (USA) **5851**
Journal of Dental Research (USA) **5851**
Journal of Dentistry (GBR) **5851**
The Journal of Derivatives (USA) **1360**
Journal of Derivatives & Hedge Funds (GBR) **1635**
Journal of Dermatological Science (IRL) **5878**
Journal of Dermatological Science. Supplement (IRL) **5879**
Journal of Dermatological Treatment (GBR) **5879**
Journal of Dermatology (GBR) **5879**
Journal of Design History (GBR) **498**
Journal of Developing Areas (USA) **1599**
Journal of Developing Societies (Online) (GBR) **7978**
Journal of Development Economics (NLD) **1600**
The Journal of Development Studies (GBR) **1600**
Journal of Developmental and Behavioral Pediatrics (USA) **6094**
Journal of Developmental and Physical Disabilities (USA) **4067**
Journal of Developmental Education (USA) **2990**
Journal of Developmental Entrepreneurship (SGP) **1962**
Journal of Diabetes and its Complications (USA) **5895**
Journal of Diagnostic Medical Sonography (USA) **6200**
Journal of Dietary Supplements (USA) **6853**
Journal of Difference Equations and Applications (CHE) **5502**
Journal of Differential Equations (USA) **5502**
Journal of Differential Geometry (USA) **5502**
Journal of Digestive Diseases (Online) (AUS) **5927**
Journal of Digital Asset Management (GBR) **1765**
Journal of Digital Imaging (USA) **6200**
Journal of Digital Information (USA) **2548**
Journal of Digital Information Management (IND) **2548**
Journal of Direct, Data and Digital Marketing Practice (Online) (GBR) **1824**
Journal of Disability Policy Studies (USA) **4067**
Journal of Dispersion Science and Technology (USA) **2136**
Journal of Display Technology (USA) **3106**
Journal of Divorce & Remarriage (USA) **5559**
Journal of Documentation (GBR) **5020**
Journal of Drug Education (USA) **2695**
Journal of Drug Issues (USA) **2695**
Journal of Drug Targeting (CHE) **6853**
Journal of Dual Diagnosis (USA) **2696**
Journal of Dynamic Systems, Measurement and Control (USA) **3349**
Journal of Dynamical and Control Systems (USA) **3369**
Journal of Dynamics and Differential Equations (USA) **5503**
Journal of Early Adolescence (USA) **2156**
Journal of Early Childhood Literacy (GBR) **2875**
Journal of Early Childhood Research (GBR) **6094**
Journal of Early Childhood Teacher Education (GBR) **2990**
Journal of Early Christian Studies (USA) **7802**
Journal of Early Modern History (NLD) **4149**
Journal of Earthquake Engineering (GBR) **3275**
Journal of East Asian Linguistics (NLD) **5133**
Journal of East Asian Studies (USA) **553**
Journal of East - West Business (USA) **1544**
The Journal of Eastern Christian Studies (BEL) **7737**
Journal of Ecclesiastical History (GBR) **7654**
Journal of Ecology (GBR) **682**
Journal of Econometrics (NLD) **1544**
Journal of Economic and Social Measurement (NLD) **8382**
Journal of Economic and Social Research (TUR) **1544**
Journal of Economic Behavior & Organization (NLD) **1134**
Journal of Economic Cooperation and Development (TUR) **1134**
Journal of Economic Dynamics and Control (NLD) **1544**
The Journal of Economic Education (USA) **1134**
Journal of Economic Entomology (USA) **851**
Journal of Economic Geography (GBR) **1494**
Journal of Economic Growth (USA) **1544**
The Journal of Economic History (GBR) **1544**
The Journal of Economic Inequality (USA) **1494**
Journal of Economic Integration (KOR) **1135**
Journal of Economic Literature (USA) **1247**
Journal of Economic Methodology (GBR) **1135**
Journal of Economic Perspectives (USA) **1545**
Journal of Economic Policy Reform (Online) (GBR) **1765**
Journal of Economic Psychology (NLD) **1824**
Journal of Economic Studies (GBR) **1135**
Journal of Economic Surveys (GBR) **1135**
Journal of Economic Theory (USA) **1545**
Journal of Economics (AUT) **1135**
Journal of Economics and Business (USA) **1135**
Journal of Economics and Finance (USA) **1135**
Journal of Economics & Management Strategy (USA) **1545**
Journal of Ecotourism (GBR) **8725**
Journal of Ecumenical Studies (USA) **7655**
Journal of Education (USA) **2875**
Journal of Education & Christian Belief (GBR) **7655**
Journal of Education and Work (GBR) **3067**
Journal of Education for Business (USA) **1136**
Journal of Education for Students Placed at Risk (USA) **3067**
Journal of Education for Teaching (GBR) **2875**
Journal of Education Policy (GBR) **3026**
Journal of Educational Administration (GBR) **3026**
Journal of Educational Administration and History (GBR) **3026**
Journal of Educational and Psychological Consultation (USA) **2875**
Journal of Educational Change (NLD) **2875**
Journal of Educational Computing Research (USA) **2949**
Journal of Educational Multimedia and Hypermedia (USA) **2469**
Journal of Educational Psychology (USA) **2875**
The Journal of Educational Research (USA) **2875**
Journal of Educational Technology Systems (USA) **2949**
Journal of Elasticity (NLD) **3349**
Journal of Elastomers and Plastics (GBR) **7093**
Journal of Elder Abuse & Neglect (USA) **4049**
Journal of Elections, Public Opinion, and Parties (GBR) **7147**
Journal of Electroanalytical Chemistry (CHE) **2102**
Journal of Electrocardiology (USA) **5793**
Journal of Electroceramics (USA) **3349**
The Journal of Electroconvulsive Therapy (USA) **6151**
Journal of Electromagnetic Waves and Applications (NLD) **7020**
Journal of Electromyography & Kinesiology (GBR) **754**
Journal of Electron Microscopy (JPN) **899**
Journal of Electron Spectroscopy and Related Phenomena (NLD) **7078**
Journal of Electronic Commerce Research (Online Edition) (USA) **3106**
Journal of Electronic Imaging (USA) **6970**
Journal of Electronic Materials (USA) **3106**
Journal of Electronic Packaging (USA) **3106**
Journal of Electronic Resources in Medical Libraries (USA) **5020**
Journal of Electronic Resources Librarianship (USA) **5020**
Journal of Electronic Testing (USA) **3322**
Journal of Electrostatics (NLD) **3322**
The Journal of Emergency Medicine (New York) (USA) **6064**
Journal of Emergency Nursing (USA) **5964**
Journal of Emerging Market Finance (IND) **1635**
Journal of Emerging Technologies in Accounting (USA) **1294**
Journal of Emotional and Behavioral Disorders (USA) **6151**
Journal of Empirical Finance (NLD) **1361**
Journal of Empirical Legal Studies (USA) **4701**
Journal of Empirical Theology (NLD) **7655**
Journal of Employment Counseling (USA) **7372**
Journal of Endocrinological Investigation (ITA) **5896**
Journal of Endocrinology (GBR) **5896**
The Journal of Endodontics (USA) **5851**
Journal of Endourology (USA) **6270**
Journal of Endovascular Therapy (USA) **6247**
Journal of Energetic Materials (USA) **7020**
Journal of Energy Engineering (USA) **3275**
The Journal of Energy Literature (GBR) **3153**
Journal of Energy Resources Technology (USA) **3140**
Journal of Engineering and Technology Management (NLD) **1765**
Journal of Engineering Design (GBR) **3205**
Journal of Engineering for Gas Turbines and Power (USA) **3385**
Journal of Engineering Materials and Technology (USA) **3349**
Journal of Engineering Mathematics (NLD) **3205**
Journal of Engineering Mechanics (USA) **3275**
Journal of Engineering Physics and Thermophysics (USA) **3205**
Journal of English for Academic Purposes (GBR) **3067**
Journal of English Linguistics (USA) **5133**
Journal of Enhanced Heat Transfer (GBR) **3385**
Journal of Enterprise Information Management (GBR) **5021**
Journal of Enterprising Culture (SGP) **1136**
Journal of Entrepreneurship (IND) **1765**
Journal of Environment & Development (USA) **3444**
Journal of Environmental Assessment Policy and Management (GBR) **3445**
Journal of Environmental Economics and Management (USA) **3445**
The Journal of Environmental Education (USA) **3445**
Journal of Environmental Engineering (USA) **3445**
Journal of Environmental Engineering and Science (Online) (CAN) **3445**
Journal of Environmental Health (USA) **3445**
Journal of Environmental Hydrology (USA) **2796**
Journal of Environmental Law (GBR) **3445**
Journal of Environmental Management (GBR) **3446**
Journal of Environmental Monitoring (GBR) **2102**
Journal of Environmental Pathology, Toxicology and Oncology (USA) **3499**
Journal of Environmental Planning and Management (GBR) **3446**
Journal of Environmental Policy and Planning (GBR) **3446**
Journal of Environmental Psychology (GBR) **7373**
Journal of Environmental Quality (USA) **3446**
Journal of Environmental Radioactivity (GBR) **3446**
Journal of Environmental Science and Health. Part A: Toxic Hazardous Substances and Environmental Engineering (USA) **3499**
Journal of Environmental Science and Health. Part B: Pesticides, Food Contaminants, and Agricultural Wastes (USA) **3447**
Journal of Environmental Science and Health. Part C: Environmental Carcinogenesis & Ecotoxicology Reviews (USA) **3499**
Journal of Environmental Sciences (NLD) **3447**
Journal of Environmental Systems (USA) **3447**
Journal of Enzyme Inhibition and Medicinal Chemistry (CHE) **736**
The Journal of Equine Veterinary Science (USA) **8800**
Journal of Essential Oil Research (USA) **595**
Journal of Esthetic and Restorative Dentistry (GBR) **5852**
The Journal of Ethics (NLD) **6928**
Journal of Ethnic & Cultural Diversity in Social Work (USA) **8049**
Journal of Ethnic and Migration Studies (GBR) **3544**
Journal of Ethnicity in Criminal Justice (USA) **2657**
Journal of Ethnicity in Substance Abuse (USA) **2696**
Journal of Ethnobiology and Ethnomedicine (GBR) **5648**
Journal of Ethnopharmacology (IRL) **6853**
Journal of Ethology (JPN) **950**
The Journal of Eukaryotic Microbiology (USA) **889**
Journal of Euromarketing (USA) **1824**
Journal of European Industrial Training (GBR) **1765**
Journal of European Public Policy (GBR) **7147**
Journal of European Social Policy (GBR) **7248**
Journal of European Studies (Chalfont Saint Giles) (GBR) **4235**
Journal of Evaluation in Clinical Practice Online (GBR) **5649**
Journal of Evidence-Based Dental Practice (USA) **5852**
Journal of Evidence-Based Social Work (USA) **8049**
Journal of Evolution Equations (CHE) **5503**
Journal of Evolutionary Biochemistry and Physiology (RUS) **736**
Journal of Evolutionary Biology (GBR) **873**
Journal of Evolutionary Economics (DEU) **1545**
Journal of Evolutionary Psychology (HUN) **7373**
Journal of Exotic Pet Medicine (USA) **8800**
Journal of Experiential Education (USA) **3067**
Journal of Experimental Algorithmics (USA) **2508**
Journal of Experimental & Clinical Assisted Reproduction (GBR) **5995**
Journal of Experimental & Theoretical Artificial Intelligence (GBR) **2453**
Journal of Experimental and Theoretical Physics (USA) **7020**
Journal of Experimental Animal Science (DEU) **5907**
The Journal of Experimental Biology (GBR) **682**
Journal of Experimental Botany (GBR) **796**
Journal of Experimental Child Psychology (USA) **7373**
Journal of Experimental Criminology (NLD) **2657**
The Journal of Experimental Education (USA) **3067**
Journal of Experimental Marine Biology and Ecology (NLD) **683**
The Journal of Experimental Medicine (USA) **5762**
Journal of Experimental Nanoscience (GBR) **2068**
Journal of Experimental Psychology: Animal Behavior Processes (USA) **7373**
Journal of Experimental Psychology: Applied (USA) **7373**
Journal of Experimental Psychology: General (USA) **7373**
Journal of Experimental Psychology: Human Perception and Performance (USA) **7373**
Journal of Experimental Psychology: Learning, Memory, and Cognition (USA) **7373**
Journal of Experimental Social Psychology (USA) **7373**
Journal of Experimental Therapeutics and Oncology Online (USA) **6024**
Journal of Experimental Zoology. Part A: Ecological Genetics and Physiology (Online Edition) (USA) **950**
Journal of Experimental Zoology. Part B: Molecular and Developmental Evolution (USA) **951**
Journal of Exposure Science and Environmental Epidemiology (GBR) **3447**
Journal of Facilities Management (GBR) **1766**
Journal of Failure Analysis and Prevention (USA) **6319**
Journal of Family and Economic Issues (USA) **7373**
Journal of Family Communication (USA) **8113**
Journal of Family History (USA) **8113**
Journal of Family Issues (USA) **8113**
Journal of Family Nursing (USA) **5965**
Journal of Family Planning and Reproductive Health Care (GBR) **973**
The Journal of Family Practice (USA) **5649**
Journal of Family Psychology (USA) **7374**
Journal of Family Psychotherapy (USA) **7374**
Journal of Family Social Work (USA) **8049**
Journal of Family Therapy (GBR) **6151**
Journal of Family Violence (USA) **2657**
Journal of Fashion Marketing and Management (GBR) **1824**
Journal of Feline Medicine and Surgery (GBR) **8800**
Journal of Feminist Family Therapy (USA) **8899**
Journal of Feminist Studies in Religion (USA) **7655**
Journal of Field Ornithology (USA) **909**
Journal of Field Robotics (USA) **2585**
Journal of Film and Video (USA) **6505**
The Journal of Finance (USA) **1361**
Journal of Financial and Quantitative Analysis (USA) **1361**
Journal of Financial Crime (GBR) **4892**
Journal of Financial Econometrics (GBR) **1361**
Journal of Financial Economics (CHE) **1136**
Journal of Financial Intermediation (USA) **1545**
Journal of Financial Management and Analysis (IND) **1361**
Journal of Financial Markets (NLD) **1361**
Journal of Financial Planning (USA) **1635**
Journal of Financial Regulation and Compliance (GBR) **1361**
Journal of Financial Research (USA) **1136**
Journal of Financial Service Professionals (USA) **1361**
Journal of Financial Services Marketing (GBR) **1824**
Journal of Financial Services Research (USA) **1361**
Journal of Financial Stability (USA) **1136**
Journal of Fire Protection Engineering (GBR) **3579**
Journal of Fire Sciences (GBR) **3349**
Journal of Fish Biology (GBR) **951**
Journal of Fish Diseases Online (GBR) **3599**
The Journal of Fixed Income (USA) **1635**
Journal of Flow Visualization and Image Processing (USA) **3385**
Journal of Fluency Disorders (USA) **7374**
Journal of Fluid Mechanics (GBR) **3363**
Journal of Fluids and Structures (GBR) **3205**
Journal of Fluids Engineering (USA) **3363**
Journal of Fluorescence (USA) **2117**
Journal of Fluorine Chemistry (CHE) **2117**
Journal of Folklore Research (USA) **3619**
Journal of Food Biochemistry (USA) **3650**
Journal of Food Composition and Analysis (USA) **3650**
Journal of Food Distribution Research (USA) **3650**
Journal of Food Engineering (GBR) **3650**
Journal of Food Lipids (USA) **3650**
Journal of Food Process Engineering (USA) **3650**
Journal of Food Processing and Preservation (USA) **3650**
Journal of Food Products Marketing (USA) **3650**
Journal of Food Protection (USA) **3650**
Journal of Food Quality (USA) **3651**
Journal of Food Safety (USA) **3651**
Journal of Food Science (USA) **3651**
Journal of Foodservice Business Research (USA) **4392**
The Journal of Foot & Ankle Surgery (USA) **6248**
Journal of Forecasting (GBR) **1766**
The Journal of Forensic Psychiatry & Psychology (Online) (GBR) **6151**
Journal of Forensic Psychology Practice (USA) **7374**
Journal of Forensic Sciences (USA) **5915**
Journal of Forest Economics (DEU) **3694**
Journal of Forest Research (JPN) **3694**
Journal of Forestry (USA) **3695**
Journal of Fourier Analysis and Applications (USA) **5503**
Journal of French Language Studies (GBR) **5133**
Journal of Fuel Cell Science and Technology (USA) **3385**
Journal of Functional Analysis (USA) **5503**
Journal of Functional and Logic Programming (USA) **2508**
Journal of Functional Programming (GBR) **2508**
Journal of Further and Higher Education (GBR) **2990**
Journal of Fusion Energy (USA) **3170**
The Journal of Futures Markets (USA) **1635**
Journal of G L B T Family Studies (USA) **4375**
Journal of Gambling Studies (USA) **6152**
Journal of Gastroenterology (JPN) **5927**
Journal of Gastroenterology and Hepatology (AUS) **5928**
Journal of Gastrointestinal Cancer (USA) **5896**
Journal of Gastrointestinal Surgery (USA) **6248**
Journal of Gay & Lesbian Mental Health (USA) **7374**
Journal of Gay & Lesbian Social Services (USA) **8049**
Journal of Gender Studies (GBR) **8899**
Journal of Gene Medicine (USA) **873**
Journal of General Education (USA) **2876**
Journal of General Internal Medicine (USA) **5946**
Journal of General Management (GBR) **1766**
Journal of General Physiology (USA) **924**
Journal of General Plant Pathology (JPN) **797**
The Journal of General Psychology (USA) **7374**
Journal of Generic Medicines (GBR) **6853**
Journal of Genetic Counseling (USA) **7374**
The Journal of Genetic Psychology (USA) **873**

Link to your serials resources and content with ulrichsweb.com

Link to your serials resources and content with ulrichsweb.com

Link to your serials resources and content with ulrichsweb.com

Online Service

Plant Pathology (GBR) **811**
Plant Physiology (USA) **812**
Plant Physiology and Biochemistry (FRA) **812**
Plant Science (IRL) **812**
Plant Science Bulletin (USA) **812**
Plant Species Biology (AUS) **812**
Plant Systematics and Evolution (AUT) **813**
Planta (DEU) **813**
Planta Medica (DEU) **6875**
Plasma Chemistry & Plasma Processing (USA) **3252**
Plasma Devices and Operations (CHE) **7035**
Plasma Physics and Controlled Fusion (GBR) **7035**
Plasma Physics Reports (RUS) **7035**
Plasma Processes and Polymers (DEU) **7035**
Plasma Sources Science and Technology (GBR) **7035**
Plasmid (USA) **698**
Plastic and Reconstructive Surgery (USA) **6255**
Plastic Surgical Nursing (USA) **5978**
Plastics, Additives and Compounding (GBR) **7096**
Plastics, Rubber and Composites (GBR) **7097**
Plastics Technology (USA) **7098**
PlasticsNews.com (USA) *see* Plastics News. **7097**
Platelets (London) (GBR) **5940**
Platinum Metals Review (Online) (GBR) **6329**
Plays (USA) **8476**
Playthings (USA) **4061**
Pleine Marge (BEL) **5352**
Ploughshares (USA) **5352**
Pneuma (NLD) **7770**
Der Pneumologe (DEU) **6217**
Pneumologie (DEU) **6217**
Poetics (NLD) **5352**
Poetics Today (USA) **5234**
Poetry (Chicago) (USA) **5430**
Poiesis & Praxis (DEU) **8434**
Point of Care (USA) **5697**
Point of Contact (USA) **5352**
Pointe (USA) **2687**
Poland Business Forecast Report (GBR) **1511**
Polar Biology (DEU) **698**
Polar Geography (USA) **4024**
Polar Record (GBR) **4024**
Police Chief (USA) **2663**
The Police Journal (GBR) **2663**
Police Practice and Research (GBR) **2664**
Police Quarterly (USA) **4896**
Policing (Bingley) (GBR) **2664**
Policing and Society (GBR) **2664**
Policy (AUS) **1160**
Policy and Management Review (USA) **7460**
Policy and Politics (GBR) **7166**
Policy & Practice (USA) **8062**
Policy and Practice in Health and Safety (GBR) **6684**
Policy Futures in Education (GBR) **3030**
Policy, Politics & Nursing Practice (USA) **5978**
Policy Review (USA) **7166**
Policy Sciences (NLD) **7166**
Policy Studies (GBR) **7166**
Policy Studies Journal (USA) **7167**
Polis (GBR) **7167**
Polish Academy of Sciences. Bulletin. Mathematics (POL) **5524**
Polish Journal of Environmental Studies (POL) **3460**
Politica y Gobierno (MEX) **7460**
Political Analysis (GBR) **7168**
Political Behavior (USA) **7168**
Political Communication (USA) **7168**
Political Geography (GBR) **7168**
Political Psychology (USA) **7168**
The Political Quarterly (GBR) **7169**
Political Science Quarterly (USA) **7169**
Political Science Reviewer (USA) **7169**
Political Studies (GBR) **7169**
Political Studies Review (GBR) **7169**
Political Theology (GBR) **7670**
Political Theory (USA) **7169**
Politicka Misao (HRV) **7170**
Politics (USA) **7170**
Politics (Oxford) (GBR) **7170**
Politics & Gender (GBR) **7170**
Politics & Policy (USA) **7170**
Politics and Society (USA) **7170**
Politics and the Life Sciences (USA) **7170**
Politics, Philosophy & Economics (GBR) **7171**
Politikon (GBR) **7171**
Politique Internationale (FRA) **7260**
Polity (GBR) **7172**
Pollution Engineering (USA) **3490**
Polycyclic Aromatic Compounds (CHE) **2129**
Polyhedron (GBR) **2117**
Polymer (GBR) **2076**
Polymer Bulletin (DEU) **2076**
Polymer Composites (USA) **7098**
Polymer Contents (USA) **3233**
Polymer Degradation and Stability (GBR) **2129**
Polymer Engineering and Science (USA) **3252**
Polymer International (GBR) **7099**
Polymer-Plastics Technology and Engineering (USA) **2129**
Polymer Reviews (USA) **2129**
Polymer Testing (GBR) **7099**
Polymers and Polymer Composites (GBR) **7099**
Polymers for Advanced Technologies (GBR) **7099**
The Pomegranate (GBR) **7670**
PopSci.com (USA) *see* Popular Science. **8435**
Popular Communication (USA) **2336**
Popular Government (USA) **7172**
Popular Mechanics PMZone (USA) *see* Popular Mechanics. **8435**
Popular Music (GBR) **6607**
Popular Music & Society (GBR) **6607**
Popular Music History (GBR) **6607**
Population and Development Review (USA) **7289**
Population and Environment (USA) **7391**
Population Ecology (JPN) **7290**
Population Health Management (USA) **5697**
Population Health Metrics (GBR) **7536**
Population Reports (English Edition) (USA) **7290**
Population Research and Policy Review (NLD) **7290**
Population Review (Online) (THA) **7290**
Population, Space and Place (GBR) **7290**
Population Studies (GBR) **7291**
Population Trends (GBR) **7291**
Portable Design (USA) **3215**
Portal (USA) **5039**
Portuguese Economic Journal (DEU) **1511**
Portuguese Journal of Social Science (GBR) **7993**
Portuguese Studies (GBR) **5353**
positions (USA) **559**
Positive Health (GBR) **6995**
Positivity (NLD) **5525**
Post-Communist Economies (GBR) **1547**
Post-Medieval Archaeology (GBR) **411**
Post-Soviet Affairs (USA) **1512**
Postcolonial Studies (GBR) **4156**
Postgraduate Medicine (USA) **5698**
Postharvest Biology and Technology (NLD) **769**
Postmodern Culture (USA) **4156**
Potential Analysis (NLD) **5525**
Pottery Making Illustrated (USA) **2044**
Poultry International (USA) **296**
Poultry Science (USA) **297**
Poultry World (GBR) **297**
Powder Diffraction (USA) **3215**
Powder Metallurgy (GBR) **6329**
Powder Metallurgy and Metal Ceramics (USA) **6329**
Powder Technology (CHE) **3253**
Power (Houston) (USA) **3393**
Power Electronics Technology (USA) **3111**
Power Engineering (USA) **3328**
Power Technology and Engineering (NLD) **3281**
Practica Pediatrica (MEX) **6103**
Practical Accountant (USA) **1299**
Practical Diabetes International (GBR) **5899**
Practical Horseman (USA) **8296**
Practical Neurology (GBR) **6174**
Practice (Abingdon) (GBR) **8062**
Practice Development in Health Care (GBR) **5698**
Practice Nurse (GBR) **5978**
Practice Periodical of Hazardous, Toxic and Radioactive Waste Management (USA) **3510**
Practice Periodical on Structural Design and Construction (USA) **3281**
The Practicing C P A (USA) **1299**
Praehistorische Zeitschrift (DEU) **412**
Praevention und Gesundheitsfoerderung (DEU) **7536**
Pragmatics & Cognition (NLD) **5204**
Prairie Schooner (USA) **5353**
Le Praticien en Anesthesie Reanimation (FRA) **5773**
Pratiques Psychologiques (FRA) **7391**
Praxis (CHE) **5699**
Precambrian Research (NLD) **2762**
Precision Agriculture (USA) **148**
Precision Engineering (USA) **3216**
Precision Marketing (GBR) **1838**
Prehospital and Disaster Medicine (USA) **6071**
Prehospital Emergency Care (GBR) **6071**
Prenatal Diagnosis (GBR) **6002**
Preparative Biochemistry and Biotechnology (USA) **742**
Prepared Foods (USA) **3660**
Presence (USA) **2489**
Presentations (USA) **32**
The Presidency (USA) **2998**
Presidential Studies Quarterly (USA) **7173**
La Presse Medicale (FRA) **5699**
Preventing School Failure (USA) **3045**
Prevention (USA) **6995**
Prevention Science (USA) **5825**
Preventive Medicine (USA) **5699**
Preventive Veterinary Medicine (NLD) **8805**
The Primary and Middle Years Educator (AUS) **2899**
Primary Care & Community Psychiatry (Online) (GBR) **6174**
Primary Care Companion to the Journal of Clinical Psychiatry (USA) **6174**
Primary Care Reports (USA) **6103**
Primary Care Respiratory Journal (GBR) **6217**
Primary Dental Care (GBR) **5861**
Primary Geographer (GBR) **4025**
Primary Health Care (GBR) **8063**
Primary Health Care Research and Development (GBR) **5699**
Primates (JPN) **960**
Print (USA) **2489**
Printed Circuit Design & Manufacture (USA) **2466**
Prisma (URY) **4470**
The Prison Journal (USA) **2666**
Private Equity Week (USA) **1376**
Private Placement Report (USA) **1376**
Probabilistic Engineering Mechanics (GBR) **3393**
Probability in the Engineering and Informational Sciences (GBR) **3233**
Probability Theory and Related Fields (DEU) **5526**
Probation Journal (GBR) **2666**
Problems & Perspectives in Management (UKR) **1786**
Problems of Economic Transition (USA) **1161**
Problems of Information Transmission (RUS) **2534**
Problems of Post-Communism (USA) **7173**
Probus (DEU) **5163**
Proceedings in Applied Mathematics and Mechanics (DEU) **5526**
Process Biochemistry (GBR) **769**
Process Cooling and Equipment (USA) **3371**
Process Engineering (GBR) **3253**
Process Safety and Environmental Protection (GBR) **3253**
Process Safety Progress (USA) **3253**
Processing (USA) **3253**
Product Design and Development (USA) **3216**
Production and Operations Management (USA) **1786**
Production Machining (USA) **5458**
Production Planning & Control (GBR) **3293**
Productivity Software (USA) **2596**
Products Finishing (USA) **6720**
El Profesional de la Informacion (ESP) **5063**
Professional Boatbuilder (USA) **8280**
Professional Builder (USA) **1030**
Professional Case Management (USA) **5978**
Professional Development in Education (GBR) **3077**
The Professional Educator (USA) **2900**
Professional Engineering (GBR) **3393**
The Professional Geographer (USA) **4025**
Professional Psychology: Research and Practice (USA) **7392**
Professional Remodeler (USA) **1030**
Professional Safety (USA) **6684**
Professional School Counseling (USA) **2900**
Profit (CAN) **1162**
Program (GBR) **5063**
Programming and Computer Software (RUS) **2596**
Progresos de Obstetricia y Ginecologia (ESP) **6002**
Progress in Aerospace Sciences (GBR) **68**
Progress in Agricultural Engineering Sciences (HUN) **213**
Progress in Biophysics & Molecular Biology (GBR) **754**
Progress in Cardiovascular Diseases (USA) **5798**
Progress in Computational Fluid Dynamics (GBR) **7050**
Progress in Crystal Growth and Characterization of Materials (GBR) **2112**
Progress in Development Studies (IND) **8126**
Progress in Energy and Combustion Science (GBR) **3145**
Progress in Histochemistry and Cytochemistry (DEU) **742**
Progress in Human Geography (GBR) **4025**
Progress in Industrial Ecology (GBR) **3461**
Progress in Lipid Research (GBR) **2130**
Progress in Materials Science (GBR) **3356**
Progress in Natural Science (USA) **7900**
Progress in Neuro-Psychopharmacology & Biological Psychiatry (USA) **6876**
Progress in Neurobiology (GBR) **927**
Progress in Nuclear Energy (USA) **3173**
Progress in Nuclear Magnetic Resonance Spectroscopy (NLD) **2104**
Progress in Oceanography (GBR) **2816**
Progress in Organic Coatings (NLD) **6720**
Progress in Orthodontics Online (DNK) **5862**
Progress in Palliative Care (GBR) **6032**
Progress in Particle and Nuclear Physics (GBR) **7071**
Progress in Pediatric Cardiology (IRL) **5798**
Progress in Photovoltaics (GBR) **3145**
Progress in Physical Geography (GBR) **4025**
Progress in Planning (GBR) **4424**
Progress in Polymer Science (GBR) **2130**
Progress in Quantum Electronics (GBR) **3111**
Progress in Reaction Kinetics and Mechanism (GBR) **2139**
Progress in Retinal and Eye Research (GBR) **6050**
Progress in Solid State Chemistry (GBR) **2140**
Progress in Surface Science (GBR) **7036**
Progress of Theoretical Physics (JPN) **7036**
The Progressive (Madison) (USA) **7173**
Progressive Grocer (New York, 2002) (USA) **3681**
Project Finance and Infrastructure Finance (GBR) **1376**
Project Finance International (GBR) **1376**
Project Management Journal (USA) **1787**
Prometheus (Abingdon) (GBR) **2336**
Promo (USA) **33**
Proofs (USA) **5862**
Prooftexts (USA) **5354**
Propellants, Explosives, Pyrotechnics (DEU) **3254**
Property Management (GBR) **7605**
Prose Studies (GBR) **5354**
Prospects (NLD) **2900**
Prostaglandins & Other Lipid Mediators (USA) **5899**
Prostaglandins, Leukotrienes & Essential Fatty Acids (GBR) **5899**
The Prostate (USA) **6273**
Prostate Cancer and Prostatic Diseases (GBR) **6033**
Prosthetics and Orthotics International (GBR) **6071**
Protection of Metals and Physical Chemistry of Surfaces (RUS) **6330**
Protein and Peptide Letters (NLD) **742**
Protein Engineering Design and Selection (Online) (GBR) **743**
Protein Expression and Purification (USA) **743**
The Protein Journal (USA) **743**
Protein Science (USA) **743**
Proteins: Structure, Function, and Bioinformatics (USA) **743**
Proteome Science (GBR) **743**
Proteomics (DEU) **743**
Protist (DEU) **698**
Protoplasma (AUT) **836**
Provincetown Arts (USA) **513**
Provincial China (GBR) **7261**
Psicoanalisis (ARG) **7392**
Psicologia Educativa (ESP) **7393**
Psikhe (CHL) **7394**
Psych. Pflege Heute (DEU) **6175**
Psychiatric Genetics (USA) **877**
Psychiatric News (USA) **6176**
Psychiatric Quarterly (USA) **6176**
Psychiatric Rehabilitation Journal (USA) **6176**
Psychiatric Services (USA) **6176**
Psychiatrische Praxis (DEU) **6177**
The Psychiatrist (GBR) **6177**
Psychiatry (Abingdon) (GBR) **6177**
Psychiatry (New York) (USA) **6177**
Psychiatry and Clinical Neurosciences (AUS) **6177**
Psychiatry Psychology and Law (GBR) **6177**
Psychiatry Research (IRL) **6178**
Psychiatry Research: Neuroimaging (IRL) **6178**
Psycho-Oncologie (FRA) **6033**
Psycho-Oncology (GBR) **6033**
Psychoanalysis, Culture & Society (GBR) **7395**
Psychoanalytic Dialogues (USA) **7395**
Psychoanalytic Inquiry (USA) **7395**
Psychoanalytic Psychology (USA) **7395**
Psychoanalytic Psychotherapy (GBR) **7395**
The Psychoanalytic Review (USA) **7395**
Psychoanalytic Social Work (USA) **8063**
Psychodynamic Practice (Online) (GBR) **6178**
Psychogeriatrics (AUS) **7396**
Psychological Assessment (USA) **7396**
Psychological Bulletin (USA) **7396**
Psychological Inquiry (USA) **7396**
Psychological Medicine (GBR) **6178**
Psychological Methods (USA) **7396**
Psychological Perspectives (USA) **7396**
The Psychological Record (USA) **7396**
Psychological Reports (USA) **7396**
Psychological Research (DEU) **7396**
Psychological Review (USA) **7397**
Psychological Science (GBR) **7397**
Psychological Science in the Public Interest (GBR) **7397**
Psychological Services (USA) **7397**
Psychologie du Travail et des Organisations (FRA) **7397**
Psychologie Francaise (FRA) **7397**
Psychologische Rundschau (DEU) **7398**
The Psychologist-Manager Journal (USA) **7398**
Psychology and Aging (USA) **4053**
Psychology and Developing Societies (IND) **7398**
Psychology & Health (GBR) **7398**
Psychology & Marketing (USA) **7398**
Psychology & Psychotherapy (GBR) **7399**
Psychology, Crime and Law (GBR) **7399**
Psychology, Health & Medicine (GBR) **7399**
Psychology in the Schools (USA) **7399**
Psychology of Addictive Behaviors (USA) **2698**
Psychology of Men & Masculinity (USA) **7399**
Psychology of Music (GBR) **6608**
Psychology of Sport and Exercise (NLD) **7399**
Psychology of Women Quarterly (USA) **7400**
Psychology, Public Policy, and Law (USA) **7400**
Psychology Today (USA) **7400**
Psychometrika (USA) **7400**
Psychoneuroendocrinology (GBR) **6178**
Psychonomic Bulletin & Review (USA) **7400**
Psychopathology (CHE) **6179**
Psychopharm Review (USA) **6179**
Psychopharmacology (DEU) **6876**
Psychopharmacology Update (USA) **6877**
Psychophysiology (GBR) **6179**
Psychopraxis (AUT) **7400**
Psychosomatic Medicine (USA) **6179**
Psychosomatics (USA) **6179**
Psychotherapeut (DEU) **6179**
Psychotherapie im Dialog (DEU) **6179**
Psychotherapy (USA) **7401**
Psychotherapy and Politics International (GBR) **6179**
Psychotherapy and Psychosomatics (CHE) **6180**
Psychotherapy Research (GBR) **7401**
Public Accounting Report (USA) **1299**
Public Administration (GBR) **7461**
Public Administration and Development (GBR) **1604**
Public Administration Quarterly (USA) **7461**
Public Administration Review (USA) **7461**
Public Budgeting and Finance (USA) **7462**
Public Choice (NLD) **1162**
Public Culture (USA) **5235**
Public Finance and Management (USA) **1940**
Public Finance Review (USA) **1941**
Public Health (GBR) **5700**
Public Health Genomics (CHE) **877**
Public Health Nursing (USA) **5979**
Public Health Nutrition (GBR) **6668**
Public Health Reports (USA) **7537**
The Public Historian (USA) **4157**
Public Integrity (USA) **7462**
Public Library Quarterly (USA) **5041**
Public Management Review (Online) (GBR) **1787**
Public Money and Management (GBR) **7462**
Public Opinion Quarterly (USA) **7174**
Public Organization Review (USA) **1787**
Public Performance and Management Review (USA) **7462**
Public Personnel Management (USA) **1873**
Public Policy Research (Online) (GBR) **1547**
Public-Private Finance (GBR) **1377**
Public Relations Quarterly (USA) **33**
Public Relations Review (GBR) **33**

Link to your serials resources and content with ulrichsweb.com

Public Relations Strategist (USA) **33**
Public Relations Tactics (USA) **33**
Public Roads (USA) **3281**
Public Services Quarterly (USA) **5041**
Public Understanding of Science (GBR) **7900**
Public Utilities Fortnightly (USA) **3510**
Public Works Management & Policy (USA) **7463**
Publicaciones de Biologia. Serie Botanica (ESP) **814**
Publications of Astronomical Society of Japan (JPN) **580**
Publishers Weekly (USA) **7571**
Publishing Research Quarterly (USA) **7571**
Publius (USA) **7174**
Pulmonary Pharmacology and Therapeutics (GBR) **6218**
Pulse (London, 1959) (GBR) **5700**
Pump Industry Analyst (GBR) **5459**
Punishment & Society (GBR) **2666**
Puppetry Journal (USA) **8477**
Purchasing (Newton) (USA) **1839**
Pure and Applied Chemistry (GBR) **2077**
Pure and Applied Geophysics (CHE) **2788**
Purinergic Signalling (NLD) **699**
Q J M (GBR) **5701**
Q S A R & Combinatorial Science (DEU) **6877**
Q S H C Online (GBR) *see* Quality and Safety in Health Care. **5701**
Quaderni Urbinati di Cultura Classica (ITA) **2239**
Quaerendo (NLD) **7571**
Quaestiones Mathematicae (ZAF) **5527**
Quaker Studies (GBR) **7740**
Qualified Remodeler (USA) **1031**
Qualitaet und Zuverlaessigkeit (DEU) **6405**
Qualitative Health Research (USA) **5701**
Qualitative Inquiry (USA) **7994**
Qualitative Market Research (GBR) **1839**
Qualitative Research (GBR) **7994**
Qualitative Research in Accounting & Management (GBR) **1299**
Qualitative Research in Psychology (GBR) **7402**
Qualitative Research Reports in Communication (GBR) **2336**
Qualitative Social Work (GBR) **8064**
Qualitative Sociology (USA) **8127**
Quality and Quantity (NLD) **8150**
Quality and Reliability Engineering International (GBR) **3328**
Quality Assurance in Education (GBR) **2901**
Quality Assurance Institute. Journal (USA) **6405**
The Quality Assurance Journal (GBR) **5701**
Quality Engineering (USA) **3216**
Quality in Higher Education (GBR) **2999**
Quality in Primary Care (Online) (GBR) **5701**
Quality Magazine (USA) **1788**
Quality Management in Health Care (USA) **4110**
Quality of Life Research (NLD) **5702**
Quantitative Finance (GBR) **1377**
Quantitative Marketing and Economics (USA) **1163**
Quantum Electronics (RUS) **7036**
Quantum Information Processing (USA) **2456**
The Quarterly Journal of Austrian Economics (USA) **1547**
The Quarterly Journal of Economics (USA) **1547**
Quarterly Journal of Engineering Geology and Hydrogeology (GBR) **3281**
The Quarterly Journal of Experimental Psychology (GBR) **7402**
Quarterly Journal of Finance and Accounting (USA) **1163**
Quarterly Journal of Mathematics (GBR) **5527**
Quarterly Journal of Mechanics and Applied Mathematics (GBR) **5527**
The Quarterly Journal of Nuclear Medicine and Molecular Imaging (ITA) **6205**
Quarterly Journal of Political Science (USA) **7175**
Quarterly Journal of Speech (USA) **2901**
Quarterly National Accounts (FRA) **1941**
Quarterly of Applied Mathematics (USA) **5527**
The Quarterly Review of Biology (USA) **699**
Quarterly Review of Distance Education (USA) **3078**
The Quarterly Review of Economics and Finance (GBR) **1163**
Quarterly Review of Film and Video (USA) **6510**
Quarterly Reviews of Biophysics (GBR) **754**
Quarterly Survey of Advertising Expenditure (GBR) **33**
Quaternary International (GBR) **2763**
Quaternary Research (USA) **2763**
Quaternary Science Reviews (GBR) **2763**
Quest (Champaign) (USA) **3078**
Questions Liturgiques (BEL) **7673**
Queueing Systems (NLD) **3328**
Quill (Greencastle) (USA) **4582**
Quintessence International (USA) **5862**
R A I R O - Operations Research (FRA) **2528**
R A I R O - Theoretical Informatics and Applications (FRA) **2528**
R A P R A Review Reports (GBR) **7101**
R A. Revista de Arquitectura (ESP) **454**
R & D Directions (USA) **6877**
R & D Magazine (USA) **8436**
R & D Management (GBR) **1788**
R B M News (FRA) **770**
R B. Revue Banque (FRA) **1377**
R C M Midwives (GBR) **6002**
R C. Respiratory Care (USA) **6218**
R D H (USA) **5862**
R E L C Journal (GBR) **5164**
R F Design (USA) **3111**
R N A (GBR) **877**
R N Web (USA) *see* R N. **5979**
R S I (USA) **1031**
R U S I Journal (GBR) **6442**
Ra Ximhai (MEX) **7994**
Rabels Zeitschrift fuer Auslaendisches und Internationales Privatrecht (DEU) **4938**
Race & Class (GBR) **3560**
Race Equality Teaching (GBR) **3015**
Race, Ethnicity and Education (GBR) **2902**
Race, Gender & Class (USA) **3560**
Race Relations Abstracts (USA) **8150**
Radiation and Environmental Biophysics (DEU) **754**
Radiation Effects and Defects in Solids (CHE) **7071**
Radiation Measurements (GBR) **7071**
Radiation Physics and Chemistry (GBR) **7071**
Radiation Protection Dosimetry (GBR) **7072**
Radiation Research (USA) **7072**
Radical History Review (USA) **4157**
Radical Teacher (USA) **7175**
The Radio Journal (GBR) **2362**
Radio Science (USA) **2788**
Radiocarbon (USA) **7901**
Radiochemistry (RUS) **2140**
Radiochimica Acta (DEU) **2140**
RadioGraphics (USA) **6206**
Radiography (GBR) **6206**
Der Radiologe (DEU) **6206**
La Radiologia Medica (ITA) **6206**
Radiologic Technology (USA) **6206**
Radiology (USA) **6206**
Radiophysics and Quantum Electronics (USA) **3112**
Radioprotection (FRA) **3174**
Radiotherapy & Oncology (IRL) **6207**
Radwaste Solutions (USA) **3510**
Ragan Report (USA) **1789**
Rail Business Intelligence (GBR) **8622**
Railway Age (USA) **8623**
Railway Gazette International (GBR) **8623**
Ralph (AUS) **6299**
The Ramanujan Journal (NLD) **5527**
RAND Journal of Economics (USA) **1164**
Random Operators and Stochastic Equations (DEU) **5528**
Random Structures & Algorithms (USA) **5528**
Rangeland Ecology & Management (USA) **699**
The Rangeland Journal (AUS) **2625**
Ranger Rick (USA) **2210**
Rapid Communications in Mass Spectrometry (GBR) **2104**
Rapid Prototyping Journal (GBR) **3394**
Raritan (USA) **5357**
Ratio (GBR) **6946**
Ratio Juris (GBR) **4765**
Rationality and Society (GBR) **7995**
Raven's Eye (CAN) **3560**
Reaction Kinetics and Catalysis Letters (HUN) **2140**
Reactions (GBR) **4520**
Reactions Weekly (NZL) **6890**
Reactive and Functional Polymers (NLD) **3254**
Read Magazine (USA) **3078**
Reading and Writing (NLD) **5165**
Reading and Writing Quarterly (USA) **3045**
Reading Improvement (USA) **3045**
Reading Online (USA) **2903**
Reading Psychology (USA) **2903**
Reading Research Quarterly (USA) **2903**
The Reading Teacher (USA) **2903**
Reading Time (AUS) **5358**
Reading Today (USA) **2903**
Real Analysis Exchange (USA) **5528**
Real Estate Economics (USA) **7608**
Real Estate Finance (USA) **7608**
Real Estate Issues (USA) **7609**
Real Estate Review (USA) **7609**
Real Living with Multiple Sclerosis (USA) **6180**
Real Simple (USA) **8881**
Real-Time Systems (USA) **2524**
Reanimation (FRA) **5773**
Reason (USA) **5236**
ReCall (GBR) **2469**
The Receivables Report (USA) **1299**
La Recherche (FRA) **7902**
Recherche et Applications en Marketing (FRA) **1839**
Recherches de Theologie et Philosophie Medievales (BEL) **7673**
Rechtsmedizin (DEU) **5916**
Reclaiming Children and Youth (USA) **7402**
Records Management Journal (GBR) **1789**
Recruitment and Retention in Higher Education (USA) **2999**
Red Cedar Review (USA) **5236**
Redbook (USA) **8882**
Redherring.com (USA) *see* The Red Herring (San Francisco). **8436**
Redox Report (Online) (GBR) **6878**
Reeves Journal (USA) **4125**
Reference and Research Book News (USA) **634**
Reference and User Services Quarterly (USA) **5042**
The Reference Librarian (USA) **5042**
Reference Reviews (GBR) **5042**
Reference Services Review (GBR) **5042**
Reflections (Cambridge) (USA) **1789**
Reflective Practice (GBR) **6947**
Reformation and Renaissance Review (GBR) **7673**
Refractories and Industrial Ceramics (USA) **2045**
Refrigerated Transporter (USA) **8675**
Refugee Survey Quarterly (GBR) **7314**
Regenerative Medicine (GBR) **5702**
The Region Magazine (USA) **1378**
Regional & Federal Studies (GBR) **7261**
Regional Anesthesia and Pain Medicine (USA) **5773**
Regional Environmental Change (DEU) **3462**
Regional Outlook: Southeast Asia (SGP) **1514**
Regional Science and Urban Economics (NLD) **4425**
Regional Studies (GBR) **4425**
Registered Nurse (USA) **5979**
Regular and Chaotic Dynamics (RUS) **5528**
Regulation (Washington, 1977) (USA) **7176**
Regulatory Peptides (NLD) **744**
Regulatory Toxicology and Pharmacology (USA) **3500**
Rehabilitacion (ESP) **6115**
Die Rehabilitation (DEU) **6115**
Rehabilitation Counseling Bulletin (USA) **4069**
Rehabilitation Psychology (USA) **7402**
Reimbursement Advisor (USA) **4110**
Reinardus (NLD) **5359**
Reinforced Plastics (GBR) **7099**
Rejuvenation Research (USA) **4054**
Relation (AUT) **8127**
Relations Industrielles (CAN) **1705**
Reliability Engineering & System Safety (GBR) **3217**
Reliable Computing (NLD) **2436**
Religion (GBR) **7674**
Religion and American Culture (USA) **7674**
Religion and the Arts (NLD) **7674**
Religion and Theology (NLD) **7674**
Religion East & West (USA) **7674**
Religion in Eastern Europe (USA) **7675**
Religion, State and Society (GBR) **7675**
Religious Education (USA) **7676**
Religious Studies (GBR) **7676**
Religious Studies Review (USA) **7699**
Remedial and Special Education (USA) **3046**
Remediation (USA) **3511**
Remote Sensing of Environment (USA) **4026**
Renaissance and Reformation (CAN) **5359**
Renaissance Papers (Year) (USA) **5359**
Renaissance Studies (GBR) **4158**
Renal Failure (USA) **6273**
Renascence (USA) **5359**
Renewable Agriculture and Food Systems (Online) (GBR) **150**
Renewable & Sustainable Energy Reviews (GBR) **3146**
Renewable Energy (GBR) **3146**
Renewable Energy Focus (GBR) **3146**
Rental Equipment Register (USA) **1839**
Reports on Mathematical Physics (GBR) **7037**
Reports on Progress in Physics (GBR) **7037**
Representation Theory (USA) **5528**
Representations (USA) **4472**
Reproduction (GBR) **700**
Reproduction, Fertility and Development (AUS) **700**
Reproduction in Domestic Animals Online (DEU) **8805**
Reproductive Biology and Endocrinology (GBR) **5899**
Reproductive BioMedicine Online (GBR) **6002**
Reproductive Health (GBR) **5703**
Reproductive Health Matters (NLD) **8848**
Reproductive Medicine and Biology (JPN) **5703**
Reproductive Sciences (USA) **6003**
Reproductive Toxicology (USA) **927**
Requirements Engineering (GBR) **3293**
Res Publica (NLD) **6947**
Research and Information in Complementary Medicine (GBR) **5703**
Research and Practice for Persons with Severe Disabilities (USA) **4069**
Research and Theory for Nursing Practice (USA) **5979**
Research Evaluation (GBR) **7902**
Research in African Literatures (USA) **5360**
Research in Comparative and International Education (GBR) **3015**
Research in Dance Education (GBR) **2687**
Research in Developmental Disabilities (GBR) **6180**
Research in Drama Education (GBR) **8477**
Research in Education (Manchester) (GBR) **2904**
Research in Engineering Design (GBR) **3217**
Research in Healthcare Financial Management (USA) **4110**
Research in Higher Education (USA) **2999**
Research in Human Development (USA) **7403**
Research in International Business and Finance (USA) **1581**
Research in Microbiology (FRA) **895**
Research in Nondestructive Evaluation (USA) **3217**
Research in Nursing & Health (USA) **5980**
Research in Phenomenology (NLD) **6947**
Research in Post-Compulsory Education (GBR) **3000**
Research in Science & Technological Education (GBR) **2904**
Research in Science Education (NLD) **2904**
Research in Social and Administrative Pharmacy (USA) **6878**
Research in Sports Medicine (USA) **6232**
Research in the Teaching of English (USA) **3078**
Research in Veterinary Science (GBR) **8805**
Research on Aging (USA) **4054**
Research on Chemical Intermediates (NLD) **2078**
Research on Language and Computation (NLD) **5166**
Research on Language and Social Interaction (USA) **5166**
Research on Social Work Practice (USA) **8128**
Research Papers in Education (GBR) **2905**
Research Policy (NLD) **7903**
Research Technology Management (USA) **1790**
Reserve Bank of New Zealand Bulletin (NZL) **1379**
Residential Treatment for Children & Youth (USA) **2167**
Resource and Energy Economics (NLD) **3146**
Resource Sharing & Information Networks (USA) **5043**
Resources, Conservation and Recycling (NLD) **3511**
Resources for American Literary Study (USA) **5360**
Resources Policy (GBR) **3146**
Respiration (CHE) **6218**
Respiratory Medicine C M E (GBR) **6218**
Respiratory Physiology & Neurobiology (NLD) **927**
Respiratory Research (GBR) **6219**
Respirology (AUS) **6219**
Response Magazine (USA) **34**
Restaurant Business (USA) **4396**
Restaurant Hospitality (USA) **4397**
Restaurants & Institutions (USA) **4397**
Restoration Ecology (USA) **3463**
Restorative Neurology and Neuroscience (NLD) **6181**
Resuscitation (IRL) **6219**
The Retail Digest (GBR) **1903**
Retail Merchandiser (USA) **1840**
Retail Traffic (USA) **1841**
Retail Week (GBR) **1841**
Retailing Today (USA) **1841**
Rethinking History (GBR) **4158**
Rethinking Marxism (GBR) **7177**
Retina (USA) **6050**
Retirement Income Reporter (USA) **1647**
Retrovirology (GBR) **5825**
Reumatologia Clinica (ESP) **6226**
Review (New York, 1968) (USA) **5360**
Review and Expositor (USA) **7773**
Review of Accounting Studies (USA) **1300**
Review of African Political Economy (GBR) **7262**
The Review of Austrian Economics (USA) **1548**
Review of Automotive Engineering (NLD) **8601**
Review of Biblical Literature (Cumulative Edition) (USA) **7677**
The Review of Black Political Economy (USA) **1165**
Review of Business (USA) **1165**
Review of Central and East European Law (NLD) **4769**
Review of Cognitive Linguistics (NLD) **5166**
The Review of Communication (USA) **2337**
The Review of Contemporary Fiction (USA) **5360**
Review of Derivatives Research (USA) **1379**
Review of Development Economics (GBR) **1604**
Review of Economic Design (DEU) **1548**
Review of Economic Dynamics (USA) **1514**
The Review of Economic Studies (GBR) **1166**
The Review of Economics and Statistics (USA) **1166**
Review of Economics of the Household (USA) **1166**
The Review of Education - Pedagogy - Cultural Studies (USA) **2935**
The Review of English Studies (GBR) **5360**
Review of European Community and International Environmental Law (GBR) **3463**
Review of Finance (Print) (GBR) **1379**
Review of Financial Economics (GBR) **1166**
The Review of Financial Studies (USA) **1379**
Review of General Psychology (USA) **7403**
The Review of Higher Education (USA) **3000**
Review of Human Factor Studies (USA) **353**
Review of Income and Wealth (GBR) **1721**
Review of Industrial Organization (NLD) **1548**
Review of International Economics (GBR) **1166**
Review of International Political Economy (GBR) **1514**
Review of International Studies (GBR) **7262**
Review of Law & Economics (USA) **4879**
The Review of Litigation (USA) **4769**
Review of Marketing Science (USA) **1841**
Review of Middle East Economics and Finance (Online) (USA) **1166**
Review of Ophthalmology (USA) **6051**
Review of Optometry (USA) **6051**
Review of Pacific Basin Financial Markets and Policies (SGP) **1380**
Review of Palaeobotany and Palynology (NLD) **6730**
Review of Plant Pathology (GBR) **720**
The Review of Policy Research (USA) **7177**
Review of Political Economy (GBR) **7178**
The Review of Politics (GBR) **7178**
Review of Public Personnel Administration (USA) **7466**
Review of Quantitative Finance and Accounting (USA) **1300**
Review of Rabbinic Judaism (NLD) **7728**
Review of Radical Political Economics (USA) **1548**
Review of Regional Studies (USA) **4425**
Review of Religious Research (USA) **7677**
Review of Scientific Instruments (USA) **4489**
Review of Social Economy (GBR) **1166**
Review of Urban & Regional Development Studies (GBR) **1604**
Review of World Economics (DEU) **1166**
Reviews in American History (USA) **4310**
Reviews in Analgesia (USA) **5773**
Reviews in Anthropology (USA) **353**
Reviews in Clinical Gerontology (GBR) **4054**
Reviews in Endocrine & Metabolic Disorders (USA) **5899**
Reviews in Environmental Science and Biotechnology (NLD) **770**
Reviews in Fish Biology and Fisheries (NLD) **961**
Reviews in Fisheries Science (USA) **3605**
Reviews in Mathematical Physics (SGP) **7037**
Reviews in Medical Microbiology (USA) **5703**
Reviews in Medical Virology (GBR) **895**
Reviews in Religion and Theology (GBR) **7677**

Online Service

Online Service

The Southern Journal of Philosophy (USA) 6953
Southern Literary Journal (USA) 5375
Southern Medical Journal (USA) 5717
The Southern Review (USA) 5375
Southern Sporting Journal (USA) 8335
Southern Theatre (USA) 8479
Southwest Contractor (USA) 1036
Southwest Farm Press (USA) 158
The Southwest Review (USA) 5240
Southwestern American Literature (USA) 5376
Southwestern Historical Quarterly (USA) 4313
Souvenirs, Gifts, and Novelties (USA) 4061
Space & Culture (USA) 4029
Space and Polity (GBR) 7185
Space Communications (NLD) 71
Space Policy (GBR) 71
Space Research Today (GBR) 71
Space Science Reviews (NLD) 582
Spanish Economic Review (DEU) 1519
Spanish in Context (NLD) 5376
Spatial Cognition and Computation (NLD) 7409
Special Children (GBR) 3047
Speciality Chemicals (GBR) 3255
Spectrochimica Acta Part A: Molecular and Biomolecular Spectroscopy (NLD) 2105
Spectrochimica Acta Part B: Atomic Spectroscopy (NLD) 2105
Spectroscopy (USA) 2105
Spectroscopy (NLD) 745
Spectroscopy Letters (USA) 7085
Speech Communication (NLD) 5177
Spektrum der Wissenschaft (DEU) 7919
Spider (USA) 2214
Spiegel der Letteren (BEL) 5376
Spinal Cord (GBR) 6186
Spine (Philadelphia, 1976) (USA) 6073
The Spine Journal (NLD) 6073
Spiritus (FRA) 7683
Sport, Education and Society (GBR) 8203
Sport in History (GBR) 8204
Sport in Society (GBR) 8204
Sport Management Review (GBR) 1794
Sport Marketing Quarterly (USA) 8204
The Sport Psychologist (USA) 7409
Sport Sciences for Health (ITA) 6997
The Sporting Goods Dealer (USA) 8206
The Sporting News (USA) 8206
Sports Afield (USA) 8335
Sports Engineering (GBR) 8207
Sports Medicine (NZL) 6233
Sports Medicine and Arthroscopy Review (USA) 6073
Sportverletzung - Sportschaden (DEU) 5717
Sprache - Stimme - Gehoer (DEU) 3047
Sprachkunst (AUT) 5377
Spring Report (SVN) 1721
The St. Louis Journalism Review (USA) 4584
Stage Directions (USA) 8479
Stahlbau (DEU) 3283
Standort (DEU) 4030
Stanford Social Innovation Review (USA) 1179
Starch (DEU) 2130
State and Local Government Review (USA) 7503
State Health Watch (USA) 7542
State News (Lexington) (USA) 7470
State Politics & Policy Quarterly (USA) 7186
Statistica Neerlandica (GBR) 8403
Statistica Sinica (TWN) 8403
Statistical Abstract of the United States (Year) (USA) 7316
Statistical Inference for Stochastic Processes (NLD) 5538
Statistical Methodology (NLD) 5538
Statistical Methods and Applications (DEU) 8404
Statistical Methods in Medical Research (GBR) 8404
Statistical Modelling (IND) 5538
Statistical Papers (DEU) 8404
Statistical Science (USA) 8404
Statistics (CHE) 8405
Statistics and Computing (USA) 2444
Statistics and Decisions (DEU) 5538
Statistics & Probability Letters (NLD) 8406
Statistics in Medicine (GBR) 5751
Statute Law Review (GBR) 4788
Statutes and Decisions: The Laws of the U S S R & Its Successor States (USA) 4788
Steel Times International (GBR) 6334
Stem Cell Reviews (USA) 878
Stem Cells (USA) 706
Stem Cells and Development (USA) 5941
Stereotactic and Functional Neurosurgery (CHE) 6259
Steroids (USA) 745
Stimulus (NZL) 7683
Stochastic Analysis and Applications (USA) 5538
Stochastic Environmental Research and Risk Assessment (DEU) 3364
Stochastic Models (USA) 8407
Stochastic Processes and Their Applications (NLD) 5538
Stochastics (GBR) 5538
Stochastics and Dynamics (SGP) 8407
The Stockade (NZL) 4194
Stone Soup (USA) 2215
Stone World (USA) 6480
StoryQuarterly (USA) 5378
Storytelling, Self, Society (USA) 5378
Strabismus (London) (NLD) 6052
The Strad (GBR) 6620
Strahlentherapie und Onkologie (DEU) 6209
Strain (GBR) 3358
Strategic Commentary Online (USA) *see* Start-Up. 5717
Strategic Communication Management (GBR) 1795
Strategic Direction (GBR) 1179
Strategic Finance (USA) 1302
Strategic H R Review (GBR) 1875
Strategic Management Journal (GBR) 1795
Strategic Organization (GBR) 1795
Strategic Planning for Energy and the Environment (USA) 3148
Strategic Survey (GBR) 7267
Strategy (CAN) 1844
Strategy & Leadership (GBR) 1795
Street & Smith's SportsBusiness Journal (USA) 8209
Street Machine (AUS) 8511
Strength and Conditioning Journal (USA) 6997
Strength, Fracture and Complexity (NLD) 7063
Strength of Materials (USA) 3358
Stress (CHE) 5718
Stress and Health (Online) (GBR) 6187
Stroke (USA) 5800
Structural and Demographic Business Statistics (Online) (FRA) 1268
Structural and Multidisciplinary Optimization (DEU) 3293
Structural Change and Economic Dynamics (NLD) 1549
Structural Chemistry (USA) 2081
Structural Concrete (GBR) 3283
Structural Control and Health Monitoring (GBR) 7041
The Structural Design of Tall and Special Buildings (GBR) 3284
Structural Engineering and Mechanics (KOR) 3396
Structural Engineering International (CHE) 3284
Structural Equation Modeling (USA) 7410
Structural Health Monitoring (GBR) 8439
Structural Safety (NLD) 3284
Structural Survey (GBR) 1038
Structure (GBR) 706
Structure & Infrastructure Engineering (GBR) 3220
Studia Geophysica et Geodaetica (USA) 2790
Studia Iranica (BEL) 561
Studia Linguistica (GBR) 5180
Studia Logica (NLD) 6954
Studia Mathematica (POL) 5538
Studia Musicologica (HUN) 6620
Studia Neophilologica (SWE) 5180
Studia Scientiarum Mathematicarum Hungarica (HUN) 5538
Studia Slavica Academiae Scientiarum Hungaricae (HUN) 5181
Studia Theologica (NOR) 7684
Studies in American Indian Literatures (USA) 5380
Studies in American Naturalism (USA) 5380
Studies in American Political Development (GBR) 7186
Studies in Applied Mathematics (Malden) (USA) 5539
Studies in Bibliography (USA) 636
Studies in Christian Ethics (GBR) 7685
Studies in Comparative International Development (USA) 8008
Studies in Conflict and Terrorism (USA) 7267
Studies in Continuing Education (GBR) 2946
Studies in East European Thought (NLD) 7187
Studies in Educational Evaluation (GBR) 3083
Studies in English Literature 1500-1900 (USA) 5381
Studies in European Cinema (GBR) 6514
Studies in Family Planning (USA) 7294
Studies in French Cinema (GBR) 6514
Studies in Gender and Sexuality (USA) 8142
Studies in Higher Education (GBR) 3003
Studies in Hispanic Cinemas (GBR) 6514
Studies in History (New Delhi) (IND) 4189
Studies in History and Philosophy of Science Part A (GBR) 7920
Studies in History and Philosophy of Science Part B: Studies in History and Philosophy of Modern Physics (GBR) 7041
Studies in History and Philosophy of Science Part C: Studies in History and Philosophy of Biological and Biomedical Sciences (GBR) 706
Studies in Interreligious Dialogue (BEL) 7685
Studies in Language (NLD) 5182
Studies in Latin American Popular Culture (USA) 3989
Studies in Philology (USA) 5183
Studies in Philosophy and Education (NLD) 2916
Studies in Political Economy (CAN) 7187
Studies in Second Language Acquisition (GBR) 5183
Studies in Spirituality (BEL) 7685
Studies in the Education of Adults (GBR) 2946
Studies in the Literary Imagination (USA) 5382
Studies in the Novel (USA) 5382
Studies in Theatre and Performance (GBR) 8480
Studies in World Christianity (GBR) 7686
Studies in World Christianity and Interreligious Relations (NLD) 7686
Studies on Neotropical Fauna and Environment (GBR) 964
Studying Teacher Education (GBR) 2916
Style (DeKalb) (USA) 5382
Style at Home (CAN) 4428
Sub-Stance (USA) 5383
Substance Abuse (USA) 2699
Substance Abuse Treatment, Prevention, and Policy (GBR) 2699
Substance Use and Misuse (USA) 2699
Successful Meetings (USA) 1844
Suchtmedizin in Forschung und Praxis (DEU) 2699
Suchttherapie (DEU) 2699
Suicide and Life-Threatening Behavior (USA) 7411
Suid-Afrikaanse Argiefblad (ZAF) 5049
Superconductor Science & Technology (GBR) 7042
Superlattices and Microstructures (GBR) 2081
Supermarket News (USA) 3681
Supervision (USA) 1709
Supplier Selection & Management Report (USA) 1845
Supply & Demand Chain Executive (USA) 1796
Supply Chain Europe (GBR) 1845
Supply Chain Forum (FRA) 8511
Supply Chain Management (GBR) 1796
Supply Chain Management Review (USA) 1796
Supply House Times (USA) 4127
Support for Learning (GBR) 3047
Supportive Cancer Therapy (USA) 6034
Supportive Care in Cancer (DEU) 6034
Supramolecular Chemistry (CHE) 2081
Supreme Court Debates (USA) 4852
Supreme Court Economic Review (USA) 4965
The Supreme Court Review (USA) 4965
Surface and Coatings Technology (CHE) 2106
Surface and Interface Analysis (GBR) 2106
Surface Engineering (GBR) 6334
Surface Fabrication (USA) 4551
Surface Review and Letters (SGP) 3358
Surface Science (NLD) 7042
Surface Science Reports (NLD) 7042
Surface Science Spectra (USA) 7042
The Surgeon (GBR) 6259
Surgery (GBR) 6259
Surgery (USA) 6259
Surgery for Obesity and Related Diseases (USA) 6259
Surgery Today (JPN) 6259
Surgical and Radiologic Anatomy (FRA) 5718
Surgical Endoscopy (USA) 6259
Surgical Infections (USA) 6260
Surgical Laparoscopy, Endoscopy and Percutaneous Techniques (USA) 6260
Surgical Neurology (USA) 6260
Surgical Oncology (GBR) 6035
Surgical Practice (AUS) 6260
Survey of Anesthesiology (USA) 5751
Survey of Current Business (USA) 1521
Survey of Ophthalmology (USA) 5751
Surveys in Geophysics (NLD) 2790
Survival (Abingdon) (GBR) 7268
Sustainability: Science, Practice, & Policy (USA) 7921
Sustainable Development (GBR) 3468
Sustainable Facility (USA) 3148
Swim Magazine (Online) (USA) 8210
Swiss Journal of Geosciences (CHE) 2770
Swiss Journal of Psychology (CHE) 7411
Swiss Medical Forum (CHE) 5719
Symbolae Osloenses (GBR) 2241
Symbolic Interaction (USA) 8008
Symploke (USA) 4477
Symposium (USA) 5384
Synapse (New York) (USA) 6187
Synchrotron Radiation News (GBR) 7072
Synlett (DEU) 2131
Syntax (GBR) 5184
Synthese (NLD) 6956
Synthesis (DEU) 2131
Synthesis and Reactivity in Inorganic, Metal-Organic, and Nano-Metal Chemistry (USA) 2141
Synthetic Communications (USA) 2131
Synthetic Metals (CHE) 3358
Syracuse Journal of International Law & Commerce (USA) 4942
System (GBR) 3083
System Dynamics Review (GBR) 1796
System Inews (USA) 2541
Systematic and Applied Microbiology (DEU) 896
Systematic Biology (USA) 707
Systematic Botany (USA) 819
Systematic Entomology Online (GBR) 860
Systematic Parasitology (NLD) 707
Systematics and Biodiversity (GBR) 707
Systemic Practice and Action Research (USA) 1797
Systems and Computers in Japan (USA) 2439
Systems & Control Letters (NLD) 2464
Systems Biology in Reproductive Medicine (USA) 5719
Systems Development Management (USA) 2525
Systems Engineering (USA) 3396
Systems Research and Behavioral Science (GBR) 2525
T C (USA) 7687
t c e - online (GBR) *see* The Chemical Engineer. 3238
T+ D (USA) 1876
T D & T (USA) 8480
T D R (USA) 8480
T E L E M A S P Bulletin (USA) 2675
T E S O L Quarterly (USA) 5185
T H E Journal (USA) 2951
T L S (GBR) 5384
The T Q M Journal (GBR) 1797
T T J (GBR) 3716
T W I C E (USA) 3114
Taiwan Journal of Anthropology (TWN) 3567
Talanta (NLD) 2106
Talking Points (Urbana) (USA) 3083
Tamara (USA) 8009
The Tan Sheet (USA) 6882
Target (NLD) 5185
Targeted Oncology (FRA) 6035
Tarsadalomkutatas (HUN) 8143
The Tax Adviser (USA) 1947
The Tax Executive (USA) 1947
Tax Policy and the Economy (USA) 1949
Taxon (AUT) 819
Te Reo (NZL) 5185
Teacher Development (GBR) 3084
Teacher Librarian (USA) 2918
Teacher Magazine (USA) 3084
Teachers and Teaching (GBR) 3084
Teachers College Record (USA) 2918
Teaching and Learning (USA) 3084
Teaching and Learning in Medicine (USA) 5720
Teaching and Teacher Education (GBR) 3084
The Teaching Artist Journal (USA) 521
Teaching Education (USA) 2918
Teaching English in the Two-Year College (USA) 3004
Teaching Exceptional Children Plus (USA) 3048
Teaching for Success (USA) 3085
Teaching Geography (GBR) 4030
Teaching History (GBR) 3085
Teaching in Higher Education (GBR) 3004
Teaching Mathematics and Its Applications (GBR) 5541
Teaching Music (USA) 6622
Teaching of Psychology (USA) 7411
The Teaching Professor (USA) 3004
Teaching Science (AUS) 2918
Teaching Sociology (USA) 8143
Teaching Statistics (GBR) 2936
Teaching Theology and Religion (GBR) 7687
Teaching Thinking Magazine (GBR) 3085
Team in Practice (GBR) 5867
Team Performance Management (GBR) 1797
Tech Decisions for Insurance (USA) 4531
Tech Directions (USA) 3085
Technical Communication (USA) 2340
Technical Communication Quarterly (USA) 3085
Technical Physics (USA) 7042
Technical Physics Letters (USA) 7042
Technical Services Quarterly (USA) 5050
Techniques (USA) 2918
Techniques in Coloproctology (Online) (ITA) 5931
Techniques in Foot & Ankle Surgery (USA) 6260
Techniques in Gastrointestinal Endoscopy (USA) 5931
Techniques in Hand & Upper Extremity Surgery (USA) 6261
Techniques in Knee Surgery (USA) 6261
Techniques in Orthopaedics (USA) 6073
Techniques in Regional Anesthesia and Pain Management (USA) 5774
Techniques in Shoulder and Elbow Surgery (USA) 6261
Techniques in Vascular and Interventional Radiology (USA) 6209
Technisches Messen - T M (DEU) 4490
Technoetic Arts (GBR) 8441
Technological Forecasting and Social Change (USA) 8441
Technologies Internationales (FRA) 8442
Technology Analysis & Strategic Management (GBR) 8442
Technology and Culture (USA) 8442
Technology and Disability (NLD) 4070
Technology and Health Care (NLD) 5720
Technology in Cancer Research and Treatment (USA) 6035
Technology in Society (GBR) 8143
Technology, Instruction, Cognition and Learning (CHE) 7411
Technology Meetings (USA) 8442
Technology, Pedagogy and Education (GBR) 3085
Technology Review (USA) 7922
The Technology Teacher (USA) 3085
Technometrics (USA) 3222
Technovation (GBR) 8443
TechTrends (USA) 2951
Tecnica Pecuaria en Mexico (MEX) 302
Tecnicas Quirurgicas en Ortopedia y Traumatologia (ESP) 6073
Tecnologia Militar (DEU) 6448
Tecnologia Quimica (CUB) 2082
Tectonics (USA) 2791
Tectonophysics (NLD) 2791
Teddy Bear and Friends (USA) 4348
Teen Tribute (CAN) 2216
Telecom Asia (USA) 2372
Telecommunication Systems (NLD) 2372
Telecommunications and Radio Engineering (USA) 2341
Telecommunications Policy (GBR) 2341
Telecommunications Reports (USA) 2341
Teledetection (FRA) 4030
Telematics and Informatics (GBR) 2342
Telemedicine and e-Health (USA) 5832
Television & New Media (USA) 2396
Television Broadcast Europe (GBR) 2397
Television Quarterly (USA) 2397
Televisual (GBR) 2397
Teller Vision (USA) *E-mail edition.* 1386
Tellus. Series A: Dynamic Meteorology and Oceanography (USA) 6396
Tellus. Series B: Chemical and Physical Meteorology (USA) 6396
Telos (USA) 6956
Tempo (London, 1939) (GBR) 6622
Tennessee Bar Journal (USA) 4793
Tennis (USA) 8248
Teorema (ESP) 6956
Terminology (NLD) 5186

Terminus (USA) 5386
Terra Incognita (ESP) 5241
Terra Nova Online (GBR) 2717
Terrorism and Political Violence (GBR) 7268
Tertiary Education and Management (GBR) 3005
Test & Measurement World (USA) 3332
Tetrahedron (GBR) 2131
Tetrahedron: Asymmetry (GBR) 2131
Tetrahedron Letters (GBR) 2131
Texas Books in Review (USA) 636
Texas Business Review (USA) 1182
Texas Construction (USA) 1040
Texas Fish & Game (USA) 8337
Texas Heart Institute Journal (USA) 5800
Texas Hispanic Journal of Law and Policy (USA) 4794
Texas Intellectual Property Law Journal (USA) 4794
Texas Journal of Women and the Law (USA) 4794
Texas Journal on Civil Liberties and Civil Rights (USA) 4843
Texas Law Review (USA) 4794
Texas Poetry Journal (USA) 5436
Texas Review (USA) 5386
Texas Review of Entertainment and Sports Law (USA) 4795
Texas Review of Law & Politics (USA) 4795
Texas Speech Communication Journal (USA) 5187
Texas Studies in Literature and Language (USA) 5386
Text and Performance Quarterly (GBR) 5386
Text & Talk (DEU) 4477
Textile (GBR) 8459
Textile History (GBR) 8459
Textile Institute. Journal (GBR) 8460
Textile Progress (GBR) 8460
Textile Research Journal (GBR) 8460
Textile World (USA) 8461
Textiles Panamericanos (USA) 8461
Textual Practice (GBR) 5387
Textual Studies in Canada (CAN) 5241
Texture, Stress and Microstructure (USA) 2771
Textus (ITA) 5387
The Thailand Business Forecast Report (GBR) 1522
Thamyris / Intersecting (NLD) 8009
Theater (New Haven) (USA) 8481
Theatre Annual (USA) 8482
Theatre History Studies (USA) 8482
Theatre Journal (Baltimore) (USA) 8482
Theatre Research International (GBR) 8483
Theatre Survey (GBR) 8483
Theatre Topics (USA) 8483
TheatreForum (USA) 8483
Theological Review (LBN) 7689
Theological Studies (USA) 7689
Theology and Science (GBR) 7689
Theology and Sexuality (GBR) 7690
Theoretical and Applied Climatology (AUT) 6396
Theoretical and Applied Fracture Mechanics (NLD) 7063
Theoretical and Applied Genetics (DEU) 878
Theoretical and Computational Fluid Dynamics (DEU) 7063
Theoretical and Experimental Chemistry (USA) 2082
Theoretical and Mathematical Physics (USA) 7043
Theoretical Biology and Medical Modelling (GBR) 707
Theoretical Chemistry Accounts (DEU) 2082
Theoretical Computer Science (NLD) 2601
Theoretical Criminology (GBR) 2670
Theoretical Foundations of Chemical Engineering (RUS) 3256
Theoretical Issues in Ergonomics Science (GBR) 3223
Theoretical Linguistics (DEU) 5187
Theoretical Medicine and Bioethics (NLD) 5721
Theoretical Population Biology (USA) 707
Theoria (USA) 4477
Theory and Decision (NLD) 8009
Theory & Event (USA) 7188
Theory and Practice of Logic Programming (GBR) 2510
Theory & Psychology (GBR) 7412
Theory and Research in Education (Online) (GBR) *see* Theory and Research in Education (Print). 2919
Theory and Society (NLD) 8143
Theory, Culture & Society (GBR) 8143
Theory in Biosciences (DEU) 707
Theory into Practice (USA) 2919
Theory of Computing Systems (USA) 2601
Therapeutic Apheresis and Dialysis (JPN) 6275
Therapeutic Drug Monitoring (USA) 6882
Therapeutics and Clinical Risk Management (Online) (GBR) 6882
Therapie (FRA) 5721
Therapy (GBR) 5911
Therapy Today (GBR) 7412
Theriogenology (USA) 8808
Thermochimica Acta (NLD) 2141
Thesis Eleven (GBR) 7188
Thin Solid Films (CHE) 7043
Thin-Walled Structures (GBR) 3397
Thinking & Reasoning (GBR) 7412
Third Text (GBR) 522
Third World Quarterly (GBR) 1606
This Old House (USA) 1040
Thomas Wolfe Review (USA) 5388
Thomist (USA) 7820
The Thoracic and Cardiovascular Surgeon (DEU) 6261
Thorax (GBR) 6220
Thoreau Society Bulletin (USA) 5388
Thrombosis and Haemostasis (DEU) 5800
Thrombosis Journal (GBR) 5800
Thrombosis Research (GBR) 5800
Thunderbird International Business Review (USA) 1183
Thyroid (USA) 5900
The Tibet Journal (IND) 562
Tiempo de Paz (ESP) 7268
Tijdschrift voor Economische en Sociale Geografie (GBR) 4031
Tijdschrift voor Geneeskunde (BEL) 5722
Tijdschrift voor Rechtsgeschiedenis (NLD) 4796
Tikkun Magazine (USA) 5242
Time (USA) 3990
Time & Society (GBR) 8144
Time for Kids News Scoop (USA) 2217
Time for Kids World Report (USA) 2217
Time South Pacific (AUS) 3796
Times Higher Education (GBR) 3005
Tire Science and Technology (USA) 7827
TireBusiness.com (USA) *see* Tire Business. 8607
Tissue and Cell (GBR) 836
Tissue Antigens (DNK) 5722
Tissue Engineering. Part A. Tissue Engineering (USA) 751
The Tizard Learning Disability Review (GBR) 6188
Tlalocan (MEX) 358
Tobacco Europe (GBR) 8488
Tobacco Journal International (DEU) 8488
Tobbacco Control Online (GBR) *see* Tobacco Control. 8488
Today's Chiropractic Lifestyle (USA) 5807
Tolkien Studies (USA) 5389
Tooling & Production (USA) 5460
Topia (CAN) 4478
Topics in Catalysis (NLD) 2082
Topics in Clinical Nutrition (USA) 6670
Topics in Companion Animal Medicine (USA) 8808
Topics in Early Childhood Special Education (USA) 3048
Topics in Geriatric Rehabilitation (USA) 4057
Topics in Language Disorders (USA) 3048
Topics in Magnetic Resonance Imaging (USA) 6209
Topics in Pain Management (USA) 5723
Topics in Spinal Cord Injury Rehabilitation (USA) 6116
Topics in Stroke Rehabilitation (USA) 5801
Topoi (NLD) 6957
Topology (GBR) 5542
Topology and Its Applications (NLD) 5542
Topology Proceedings (USA) 5542
Total Health (USA) 6670
Total Quality Management & Business Excellence (Online) (GBR) 1798
Total Telecom (GBR) 2343
Totalitarian Movements and Political Religions (GBR) 7268
T'oung Pao (NLD) 562
Tourism (HRV) 8763
Tourism Analysis (USA) 8763
Tourism and Hospitality Planning & Development (GBR) 1798
Tourism and Hospitality Research (GBR) 8763
Tourism, Culture & Communication (USA) 8763
Tourism Economics (GBR) 8763
Tourism Geographies (GBR) 8763
Tourism Management (GBR) 8763
Tourism Review (GBR) 8764
Tourist Attractions and Parks (USA) 4983
Tourist Studies (GBR) 8764
Town & Country (New York) (USA) 3991
Town Planning Review (GBR) 4428
Townsend Letter (USA) 315
Toxicologic Pathology (USA) 3501
Toxicological and Environmental Chemistry (CHE) 3502
Toxicological Sciences (GBR) 3502
Toxicology (IRL) 3502
Toxicology and Applied Pharmacology (USA) 3502
Toxicology and Industrial Health (GBR) 3502
Toxicology in Vitro (GBR) 3502
Toxicology Letters (IRL) 3502
Toxicology Mechanisms and Methods (USA) 3503
Toxicon (GBR) 6883
Toxin Reviews (USA) 6883
Trade Finance (GBR) 1387
Trademark World (GBR) 6759
Traders Magazine (USA) 1387
Traffic (DNK) 837
Traffic Engineering & Control (GBR) 8635
Traffic Injury Prevention (USA) 3397
Traffic World (USA) 8513
Trailer / Body Builders (USA) 8676
Training (USA) 1798
Training & Coaching Today (GBR) 1876
Training Journal (GBR) 1876
Trains (USA) 8626
Trames (EST) 8010
Transactions in G I S (GBR) 4031
Transactions on Design Automation of Electronic Systems (USA) 3293
Transboundary and Emerging Diseases (Online) (DEU) *see* Transboundary and Emerging Diseases. 8809
Transcultural Psychiatry (GBR) 6188
Transformation (ZAF) 8010
Transformation (GBR) 7690
Transformation Groups (USA) 5542
Transfusion (USA) 5723
Transfusion and Apheresis Science (GBR) 5941
Transfusion Clinique et Biologique (FRA) 5942
Transfusion Medicine (GBR) 5942
Transfusion Medicine and Hemotherapy (CHE) 5723
Transfusion Medicine Reviews (USA) 5942
Transgender Tapestry (USA) 7413
Transgenic Research (NLD) 879
Transgenics (Lausanne. Online) (CHE) *see* Transgenics. 879
Transition (USA) 5242
Transition Metal Chemistry (NLD) 6335
Transition Studies Review (AUT) 8011
Translation and Literature (GBR) 5188
Translational Research (USA) 5911
Transmission & Distribution World (USA) 3161
Transplant Immunology (GBR) 5766
Transplant Infectious Disease Online (DNK) 6261
Transplant International (DEU) 5724
Transplantation (USA) 6261
Transplantation Proceedings (USA) 6261
Transplantation Reviews (USA) 6261
Transplantationsmedizin (DEU) 6262
Transport in Porous Media (NLD) 2083
Transport Policy (GBR) 8515
Transport Reviews (GBR) 8515
Transport Theory and Statistical Physics (USA) 7044
Transportation (NLD) 8515
Transportation Alternatives (USA) 8636
Transportation Journal (USA) 8516
Transportation Planning and Technology (CHE) 8516
Transportation Quarterly (USA) 8516
Transportation Research. Part A: Policy & Practice (GBR) 8516
Transportation Research. Part B: Methodological (GBR) 8517
Transportation Research. Part C: Emerging Technologies (GBR) 8517
Transportation Research. Part D: Transport & Environment (GBR) 8517
Transportation Research. Part E: Logistics and Transportation Review (GBR) 8517
Transportation Research. Part F: Traffic Psychology and Behaviour (GBR) 8517
Transportation Science (USA) 8517
Transworld Skateboarding (USA) 8338
Trauma (GBR) 6074
Trauma Reports (USA) 6074
Trauma und Berufskrankheit (DEU) 6074
Trauma, Violence & Abuse (USA) 6074
Traumatology (Online) (USA) 6074
Travel Agent (USA) 8765
Travel Medicine and Infectious Disease (USA) 5724
Travel Retailer International (GBR) 1846
Travel Trade Gazette U K & Ireland (GBR) 8768
Travel Weekly (GBR) 8768
Treasury Affairs (NLD) 1303
Treasury & Risk (USA) 1656
Treatment Guidelines from The Medical Letter (USA) 5724
Tree Genetics & Genomes (DEU) 820
Tree Physiology (CAN) 820
Trees (DEU) 820
Trends in Analytical Chemistry (NLD) 2107
Trends in Biochemical Sciences (GBR) 746
Trends in Biotechnology (GBR) 771
Trends in Cardiovascular Medicine (USA) 5801
Trends in Cell Biology (GBR) 837
Trends in Cognitive Sciences (GBR) 7413
Trends in Ecology & Evolution (GBR) 708
Trends in Endocrinology and Metabolism (GBR) 5900
Trends in Food Science & Technology (GBR) 3666
Trends in Genetics (GBR) 879
Trends in Immunology (GBR) 5766
Trends in Microbiology (GBR) 896
Trends in Molecular Medicine (GBR) 5724
Trends in Neurosciences (GBR) 6189
Trends in Organized Crime (USA) 2670
Trends in Parasitology (GBR) 897
Trends in Pharmacological Sciences (GBR) 6883
Trends in Plant Science (GBR) 820
Trials (GBR) 5801
Tribal College (USA) 3005
Tribology International (GBR) 3398
Tribology Letters (NLD) 3359
Tribology Transactions (USA) 3257
El Trimestre Economico (MEX) 1184
Trinity Seminary Review (USA) 3005
Tropical Animal Health and Production (NLD) 8809
Tropical Doctor (GBR) 5827
Tropical Medicine & International Health (GBR) 5827
Truck & Driver Magazine (GBR) 8676
Trustee (USA) 4112
Tsinghua Science & Technology (CHN) 7925
Tuberculosis (GBR) 6220
Tufts University Health & Nutrition Letter (USA) 6670
Tumor Biology (CHE) 6035
Tumordiagnostik & Therapie (DEU) 6035
Tunnelling and Underground Space Technology (GBR) 3224
Tunnels & Tunnelling International (GBR) 3286
Turcica (BEL) 562
Turkey Business Forecast Report (GBR) 1522
Turkish Journal of Agriculture and Forestry (TUR) 163
Turkish Journal of Biology (TUR) 708
Turkish Journal of Botany (TUR) 821
Turkish Journal of Cancer (TUR) 6036
Turkish Journal of Chemistry (TUR) 2083
Turkish Journal of Earth Sciences (TUR) 2717
Turkish Journal of Electrical Engineering and Computer Sciences (TUR) 2440
Turkish Journal of Engineering and Environmental Sciences (TUR) 3224
Turkish Journal of Mathematics (TUR) 5542
Turkish Journal of Medical Sciences (TUR) 5725
Turkish Journal of Physics (TUR) 7044
Turkish Journal of Veterinary and Animal Sciences (TUR) 8809
Turkish Journal of Zoology (TUR) 965
Turkish Studies (GBR) 7269
Turtle Magazine for Preschool Kids (USA) 2218
Twentieth Century British History (GBR) 4274
Twentieth Century Literature (USA) 5391
Twentieth Century Music (GBR) 6625
Twin Research and Human Genetics (GBR) 879
The U A E Business Forecast Report (GBR) 1522
U M T R I Research Review (USA) 8518
U N Chronicle (USA) 7269
U N L V Gaming Research & Review Journal (USA) 8213
U S A Today (Valley Stream) (USA) 2921
U.S. Air Force. Office of the Judge General. The Reporter (USA) 4972
U S B E and Information Technology (USA) 3224
U S Banker (USA) 1657
U.S. Bureau of Alcohol, Tobacco and Firearms. Quarterly Bulletin (USA) 2670
U.S. Bureau of Labor Statistics. C P I Detailed Report (Online) (USA) 1522
U S Catholic (USA) 7821
U.S. Congress. Congressional Directory (USA) 7190
U.S. Department of Energy. Energy Information Administration. Monthly Energy Review (Online) (USA) 3162
U.S. Department of Energy. Energy Information Administration. Natural Gas Monthly (Online) (USA) 6796
U.S. Marine Corps. Division of Public Affairs, Media Branch. Marines (USA) 6450
U S Naval Institute. Proceedings (USA) 6450
U.S. News & World Report Digital Edition (USA) *see* U S News & World Report. 3991
U. S. Stamp News (USA) 6901
Ubiquity (USA) 8444
Ukrainian Mathematical Journal (USA) 5543
Ultimate Home Plan Collection (USA) 1041
Ultramicroscopy (NLD) 7044
Ultraschall in der Medizin (DEU) 5725
Ultrasonic Imaging (USA) 6209
Ultrasonics (NLD) 7089
Ultrasonics Sonochemistry (NLD) 7089
Ultrasound (GBR) 6209
Ultrasound in Medicine & Biology (USA) 709
Ultrasound in Obstetrics and Gynecology (GBR) 6005
Ultrasound Quarterly (USA) 6210
Ultrastructural Pathology (USA) 6036
Umweltmedizin in Forschung und Praxis (DEU) 5726
Umweltwissenschaften und Schadstoff-Forschung (DEU) 3492
Underground Construction (USA) 6796
Undersea & Hyperbaric Medicine (USA) 5726
Der Unfallchirurg (DEU) 6074
United Nations. Economic Commission for Europe. Economic Studies (CHE) 1523
United Nations Statistical Office. Monthly Bulletin of Statistics (USA) 8412
United States Government Manual (USA) 7190
Universal Access in the Information Society (DEU) 2353
Universidad Nacional Autonoma de Mexico. Facultad de Medicina. Revista (MEX) 5726
Universidad Nacional de Cuyo. Facultad de Ciencias Agrarias. Revista (ARG) 165
University Affairs (CAN) 3008
The University Bookman (USA) 7575
University Business (USA) 3008
University of Ankara. Faculty of Science. Communications. Series A2-A3: Physics, Engineering Physics, Electronic Engineering and Astronomy (TUR) 3225
University of Ankara. Faculty of Science. Communications. Series B: Chemistry and Chemical Engineering (TUR) 2083
University of Ankara. Faculty of Science. Communications. Series C: Biology, Geological Engineering and Geophysical Engineering (TUR) 2772
University of California, Berkeley. Wellness Letter (USA) 6999
University of London. School of Oriental and African Studies. Bulletin (GBR) 4480
University of Tartu. Faculty of Economics and Business Administration. Working Paper Series (EST) 1189
University of Toronto Law Journal (CAN) 4805
University of Toronto Quarterly (CAN) 4481
Update (Online) (USA) 6626
Urban Affairs Review (USA) 4429
Urban Design International (GBR) 4430
Urban Ecosystems (USA) 4430
Urban Education (USA) 2924
Urban Forestry & Urban Greening (DEU) 3707
Urban Forum (NLD) 4430
Urban Geography (USA) 4430
Urban History (GBR) 4276
Urban Policy and Research (AUS) 4430
The Urban Review (USA) 3035
Urban Studies (GBR) 4430
Urban Water Journal (USA) 8834

Emerald Group Publishing Limited Howard House, Wagon Ln, Bingley BD16 1WA, United Kingdom TEL 44-1274-777700, FAX 44-1274-785201, http://www.emeraldinsight.com/
Accounting, Auditing and Accountability Journal (GBR) 1277

Link to your serials resources and content with ulrichsweb.com

Quill (Greencastle) (USA) 4582
R & D Directions (USA) 6877
The R M A Journal (USA) 1377
R N Web (USA) *see* R N. 5979
R V Business (USA) 8219
Race & Class (GBR) 3560
Radical Teacher (USA) 7175
Radiologic Technology (USA) 6206
Railway Age (USA) 8623
Railway Track & Structures (USA) 8624
RAND Journal of Economics (USA) 1164
Reactions (GBR) 4520
Reading Improvement (USA) 3045
Reading Research Quarterly (USA) 2903
The Reading Teacher (USA) 2903
Real Estate Finance and Investment (USA) 7608
Real Estate Issues (USA) 7609
Reason (USA) 5236
Reclaiming Children and Youth (USA) 7402
Recycling Today (USA) 3511
Redherring.com (USA) *see* The Red Herring (San Francisco). 8436
Reeves Journal (USA) 4125
Reference and User Services Quarterly (USA) 5042
Refrigerated and Frozen Foods (USA) 3662
Refrigerated Transporter (USA) 8675
Refuge (CAN) 7291
Regional Aviation News (Online) (USA) 8551
Regional Studies (GBR) 4425
Regulation (Washington, 1977) (USA) 7176
Rehabilitation Counseling Bulletin (USA) 4069
Relations Industrielles (CAN) 1705
Religion and American Culture (USA) 7674
Religious Conference Manager (USA) 7675
Religious Studies (GBR) 7676
Remedial and Special Education (USA) 3046
Remodeling Online (USA) *see* Remodeling. 1032
Renaissance Quarterly (USA) 5359
Renascence (USA) 5359
Rental Equipment Register (USA) 1839
Repair Shop Product News (USA) 8601
Research (San Francisco) (USA) 1647
Research in Healthcare Financial Management (USA) 4110
Research on Aging (USA) 4054
Research Quarterly for Exercise and Sport (USA) 6995
Research Technology Management (USA) 1790
Residential Architect (USA) 455
Resource (Niles) (USA) 250
Resource Links (CAN) 2210
Resources for Feminist Research (CAN) 8902
Response Magazine (USA) 34
Restaurant Business (USA) 4396
Restaurant Hospitality (USA) 4397
Restaurants & Institutions (USA) 4397
Retail Merchandiser (USA) 1840
Retailing Today (USA) 1841
Retirement Income Reporter (USA) 1647
The Review of Black Political Economy (USA) 1165
Review of Business (USA) 1165
The Review of Contemporary Fiction (USA) 5360
The Review of Economics and Statistics (USA) 1166
The Review of English Studies (GBR) 5360
Review of Financial Economics (GBR) 1166
The Review of Metaphysics (USA) 6948
The Review of Politics (GBR) 7178
Review of Social Economy (GBR) 1166
Reviews in American History (USA) 4310
Rhetorica (USA) 5168
Risk & Insurance (USA) 4521
Risk Management (USA) 4521
Rocks and Minerals (USA) 6478
Roeper Review (USA) 3079
Rolling Stone (USA) 6613
Romanic Review (USA) 5364
Roofing Contractor (USA) 1034
Royal Anthropological Institute. Journal (GBR) 354
Royal Australian Historical Society. Journal (AUS) 4194
Rubber World Online (USA) *see* Rubber World. 7827
Runner's World (USA) 8198
Rural Cooperatives (USA) 153
Rural Telecommunications (USA) 2371
Russian Life (USA) 8753
Russian Telecom Newsletter (USA) 2337
Rutgers Computer & Technology Law Journal (USA) 4845
S G B (USA) 8198
S T I Online (GBR) *see* Sexually Transmitted Infections. 5881
Sacramento Business Journal (USA) 1170
Safety Compliance Letter (USA) 6685
Safety Now (USA) 6686
St. Louis Business Journal (USA) 1170
Sales & Marketing Management (USA) 1842
San Antonio Business Journal (USA) 1170
San Diego Business Journal (USA) 1170
San Fernando Valley Business Journal (USA) 1170
San Francisco Business Times (USA) 1432
Sarasota Magazine (USA) 3987
Saturday Evening Post (USA) 3988
School Arts (USA) 3080
School Library Journal (USA) 5046
School Planning and Management (USA) 3032
School Psychology Review (USA) 7406
School Science and Mathematics (USA) 3081
Science (USA) 7908
Science Activities (USA) 7908
Science and Government Report (USA) 7468
Science News (USA) 7910
Science Progress (GBR) 7910
Science, Technology & Human Values (USA) 7911
Scientific American (USA) 7912
Scientific Computing (USA) 7940
The Scientist (USA) 7913
Scuba Diving (USA) 8332
Searcher (Medford) (USA) 2532
Security Distributing & Marketing (USA) 1843
Security Management Online (USA) *see* Security Management. 1792
Sensors (Online) (USA) 4490
Sex Roles (USA) 7407
Sexuality & Culture (USA) 8132
Shakespeare Studies (USA) 5370
Shofar (Ashland) (USA) 7729
Shoot (USA) 35
Shooting Industry (USA) 8200
SI.com (USA) *see* Sports Illustrated. 8207
Sierra (USA) 2627
Signs (USA) 8903
Skeptic (USA) 6743
Skeptical Inquirer (USA) 6743
Smithsonian Magazine Web (USA) *see* Smithsonian. 8002
Snack Food & Wholesale Bakery (USA) 3675
Snips (USA) 4126
Soap and Cosmetics (USA) 596
Soap, Perfumery & Cosmetics (GBR) 596
Social Education (USA) 3082
Social Forces (USA) 8133
Social Justice (USA) 7265
Social Policy (USA) 8003
Social Problems (USA) 8134
Social Research (USA) 8003
The Social Science Journal (USA) 8004
Social Science Quarterly (USA) 8004
Social Security Bulletin (USA) 4523
Social Service Review (USA) 8069
The Social Studies (USA) 8005
Social Theory and Practice (USA) 6952
Social Work (USA) 8070
Social Work Research (USA) 8071
Society (USA) 8005
Sociological Perspectives (USA) 8137
The Sociological Quarterly (USA) 8137
Sociology (GBR) 8138
Sociology of Religion (USA) 8139
Sojourn (SGP) 8139
Sojourners Magazine (USA) 7682
Solid State Technology (USA) 3114
Sound & Video Contractor (USA) 8155
South Carolina Academy of Science. Bulletin (USA) 7919
South Dakota Business Review (USA) 1177
South Florida Business Journal (USA) 1177
Southerly (AUS) 5375
Southern California Academy of Sciences. Bulletin (USA) 7919
Southern Cultures (USA) 4475
Southern Economic Journal (USA) 1178
Southern Literary Journal (USA) 5375
The Southern Review (USA) 5375
Southscan (GBR) 7184
The Southwest Review (USA) 5240
Space & Missile Defense Report (Email) (USA) 6447
Special Events Magazine (USA) 4398
Speciality Chemicals (GBR) 3255
The Spectator (GBR) 5240
Spectroscopy (USA) 2105
The Sporting Goods Dealer (USA) 8206
The St. Louis Journalism Review (USA) 4584
Stanford Law Review (USA) 4787
State Legislatures (USA) 7186
Stateways (USA) 610
Stone World (USA) 6480
Storyworks (USA) 3082
Strategic Finance (USA) 1302
Strategy & Leadership (GBR) 1795
Student B M J (GBR) 5718
Studies in American Fiction (USA) 5380
Studies in Comparative International Development (USA) 8008
Studies in Family Planning (USA) 7294
Studies in Romanticism (USA) 5381
Studies in the Literary Imagination (USA) 5382
Studies in the Novel (USA) 5382
Style (DeKalb) (USA) 5382
Style 1900 (USA) 369
Successful Meetings (USA) 1844
Supermarket News (USA) 3681
Supervision (USA) 1709
Supplier Selection & Management Report (USA) 1845
Supply Chain Management Review (USA) 1796
Supply House Times (USA) 4127
Survey of Current Business (USA) 1521
Sustainable Facility (USA) 3148
Swiss News (CHE) 8759
Symploke (USA) 4477
Symposium (USA) 5384
Synthesis - Regeneration: A Magazine of Green Social Thought (USA) 3469
Systems Research and Behavioral Science (GBR) 2525
T B & Outbreaks Week (USA) 5827
T+ D (USA) 1876
T D R (USA) 8480
T H E Journal (USA) 2951
T V International (GBR) 2393
Target Marketing (USA) 1845
The Tax Adviser (USA) 1947
The Tax Executive (USA) 1947
Teacher Librarian (USA) 2918
Teaching Children Mathematics (USA) 3085
Teaching History: A Journal of Methods (USA) 3085
Technical Communication (USA) 2340
Techniques (USA) 2918
Technology Access Report (USA) 8442
Technology and Learning (USA) 2951
Technology Review (USA) 7922
Telecommunications Reports (USA) *E-mail edition.* 2341
Teller Vision (USA) *E-mail edition.* 1386
Tennessee Academy of Science. Journal (USA) 7922
Test & Measurement World (USA) 3332
Texas Business Review (USA) 1182
Texas Journal of Science (USA) 7923
Texas Studies in Literature and Language (USA) 5386
Textile World (USA) 8461
Textual Studies in Canada (CAN) 5241
Theatre History Studies (USA) 8482
Theatre Journal (Baltimore) (USA) 8482
Theatre Research International (GBR) 8483
Theological Studies (USA) 7689
Theory into Practice (USA) 2919
TheStandard.com (USA) 2567
Thorax (GBR) 6220
Tikkun Magazine (USA) 5242
Time.com (USA) *see* Time. 3990
Tobacco Retailer (USA) 8488
Tobbacco Control Online (GBR) *see* Tobacco Control. 8488
Today's Refinery (USA) 6795
Tooling & Production (USA) 5460
Topics in Clinical Nutrition (USA) 6670
Topics in Early Childhood Special Education (USA) 3048
Topics in Geriatric Rehabilitation (USA) 4057
Topics in Language Disorders (USA) 3048
Tourist Attractions and Parks (USA) 4983
Townsend Letter (USA) 315
Trade Finance (GBR) 1387
Traders Magazine (USA) 1387
Tradeshow Week (USA) 36
Traffic World (USA) 8513
Training (USA) 1798
Training Media Review (USA) 6704
Transmission & Distribution World (USA) 3161
Transportation Journal (USA) 8516
Travel Retailer International (GBR) 1846
Travel Weekly (GBR) 8768
Trends in Amplification (USA) 6085
Trial (USA) 4966
TriQuarterly (USA) 5243
Truck & S U V Performance (USA) 8677
Trucking Technology (USA) 8678
Trusts & Estates (USA) 1656
Tufts University Health & Nutrition Letter (USA) 6670
TurfGrass Trends (USA) 3752
Twentieth Century Literature (USA) 5391
U C L A Journal of Environmental Law and Policy (USA) 3471
U N Chronicle (USA) 7269
U S A Today (Valley Stream) (USA) 2921
U.S. Department of Energy. Energy Information Administration. Monthly Energy Review (Online) (USA) 3162
U.S. Department of Energy. Energy Information Administration. Natural Gas Monthly (Online) (USA) 6796
U.S. Internal Revenue Service. Statistics of Income Bulletin (USA) 1272
U.S. Marine Corps. Division of Public Affairs, Media Branch. Marines (USA) 6450
U.S. News & World Report Digital Edition (USA) *see* U S News & World Report. 3991
U S Rail News (USA) 8627
University of California, Berkeley. Wellness Letter (USA) 6999
Update (Online) (USA) 6626
Urban Affairs Review (USA) 4429
Urban Studies (GBR) 4430
Urgent Communications (USA) 2364
Urologic Nursing (USA) 6276
Urology Times: The Urology Times Clinical Edition (USA) 6276
Utah Business (USA) 1190
Utopian Studies (USA) 6959
Vaccine Weekly (USA) 6884
Validation Times (USA) 6884
Valuation Insights and Perspectives (USA) 7614
Vanderbilt Journal of Transnational Law (USA) 4944
Variety (USA) 8484
Vascular and Endovascular Surgery (USA) 6262
The Velvet Light Trap (USA) 6516
Venture Capital Journal (USA) 1658
Vermont Business Magazine (USA) 1191
Victorian Poetry (USA) 5437
Video Age International (USA) 2398
Vision Systems Design (USA) 3226
Vital Speeches of the Day (USA) 4585
W H O Drug Information (CHE) 7545
W I N News (USA) 8904
W W D (USA) 2250
Wall Street & Technology (USA) 1394
Wall Street Letter (USA) 1658
Walls & Ceilings (USA) 1042
Ward's AutoWorld (USA) 8611
Washington Business Journal (USA) 1193
The Washington Monthly (USA) 7193
The Washington Quarterly (USA) 7273
Washington Report on Middle East Affairs (USA) 7273
Waste & Recycling News (USA) 3513
Wearables Business (USA) 2250
Weatherwise (USA) 6398
Web Commerce Today (USA) 1193
Web Marketing Today (USA) 1847
West European Politics (GBR) 7273
Westchester County Business Journal (USA) 1524
Western Farm Press (USA) 170
The Western Journal of Black Studies (USA) 3572
Western Journal of Communication (USA) 5195
Western Journal of Nursing Research (USA) 5984
White House Studies (Hauppauge) (USA) 4318
White House Weekly (USA) 7477
Wichita Business Journal (USA) 1194
William and Mary Law Review (USA) 4814
The Wilson Journal of Ornithology (USA) 917
The Wilson Quarterly (USA) 5245
Wines and Vines (USA) 613
Winterthur Portfolio (USA) 526
Wireless Design and Development (USA) 3334
Women and Language (USA) 5195
Women and Music (USA) 6628
Women in Action (PHL) 8890
Women in German Yearbook (USA) 8904
Women in Judaism (CAN) 7731
Women's Studies (CHE) 8905
Women's Studies in Communication (USA) 8905
Wood & Wood Products (USA) 3717
Wordsworth Circle (USA) 5400
Work and Occupations (USA) 8147
WorkBoat (USA) 8665
Workforce Management (USA) 1877
World Affairs (Washington) (USA) 7274
The World & I Online (USA) 3993
World Gas Intelligence (USA) 6797
World Health Organization. Bulletin (CHE) 5731
World Literature Today (USA) 5400
World Mining Equipment (GBR) 6483
World Oil (USA) 6797
World Policy Journal (USA) 7274
World Tobacco (GBR) 8489
World Trade: WT100 (USA) 1588
World War II (Leesburg) (USA) 4318
World Watch (USA) 3475
The Writer (USA) 5400
Written Communication (USA) 2345
The Yale Law Journal (USA) 4817
Yellow Pages & Directory Report (USA) 2036
Yomiuri Shimbun (Satellite Edition) (USA) 3901
Youth & Society (USA) 2172
401(k) Advisor (USA) 1661

G B I - Genios Deutsche Wirtschaftsdatenbank GmbH/GENIOS German Business Information Freischuetzstr 96, Munich 81927, Germany TEL 49-89-9928790, FAX 49-89-99287999, info@genios.de, http://www.genios.de/
Hamburger Wirtschaft (DEU) 1404
Handbuch der Grossunternehmen (DEU) 1887
Management and Marketing Abstracts (GBR) 1251
Mittelstaendische Unternehmen (DEU) 1899
Seibt Industriekatalog (DEU) 2027
Seibt Medizinische Technik (DEU) 5711
Seibt Oberflaechentechnik (DEU) 7062
Verbaende, Behoerden, Organisationen der Wirtschaft (DEU) 1524
Wer Liefert Was? (DEU) 2034

Gale (Subsidiary of: Cengage Learning) 27500 Drake Rd, Farmington Hills, MI 48331 TEL 248-699-4253, FAX 877-363-4253, gale.customerservice@cengage.com, http://www.gale.cengage.com
A A A S Report: Research and Development (USA) 7829
A B A Bank Marketing (USA) 1304
A B A Banking Journal (USA) 1304
A B Europe (GBR) 4975
A B N F Journal (USA) 5949
A C M Computing Surveys (USA) 2405
A C M Transactions on Computer Systems (USA) 2519
A C M Transactions on Database Systems (USA) 2529
A C M Transactions on Information Systems (USA) 1413
A C M Transactions on Mathematical Software (USA) 2587
A C M Transactions on Programming Languages and Systems (USA) 2504
A C O G Clinical Review (USA) 5739
A D H D Report (USA) 6117
A E R (AUS) 2822
A E Ue: International Journal of Electronics and Communication (DEU) 2310
A I Communications (NLD) 2444
A I D S Care (GBR) 5807
The A I D S Reader (USA) 5807
A I L A Review (NLD) 5088
A I Magazine (USA) 2445
A J R NewsLink (USA) *see* American Journalism Review. 4571
A L A TechSource (USA) *see* Library Technology Reports. 5029
A L T - J (GBR) 2964
A M T (USA) 8533
A N Q: A Quarterly Journal of Short Articles, Notes and Reviews (USA) 5248
A N S O M (USA) 2245

Online Service

DIRECTORY 2010 GALE 11139

Critique (Washington) (USA) **5280**
Crop Protection (NLD) **3242**
Crop Science (USA) **226**
Crops (GBR) **227**
Cross Country Skier (USA) **8310**
Cross Cultural Management (GBR) **1737**
Cross Currents (New York) (USA) **2976**
CrossCurrents (Toronto) (CAN) **2692**
Cruise Travel (USA) **8696**
Cruising World (USA) **8275**
Crustaceana (NLD) **939**
Cryo-Letters (GBR) **921**
Cryobiology (USA) **753**
Cryogenics (GBR) **7053**
Cryptogamie Algologie (FRA) **784**
Cryptogamie Bryologie (FRA) **784**
Cryptogamie Mycologie (FRA) **785**
Crystallography Reviews (GBR) **2110**
Cuadernos de Economia (CHL) **1089**
Cuadernos de Historia (CHL) **4290**
Cuadernos de Historia de Espana (ARG) **4213**
Cuadernos de Teologia (ARG) **7636**
CubaNews (USA) **1089**
Cultura y Educacion (ESP) **2840**
Cultural & Social History (GBR) **8097**
Cultural Geographies (GBR) **3413**
Cultural Politics (GBR) **7127**
Cultural Studies (GBR) **8097**
Cultural Studies - Critical Methodologies (USA) **5281**
Cultural Studies Review (AUS) **7957**
Cultural Trends (GBR) **484**
Culture and Religion (GBR) **7636**
Culture, Health and Sexuality (GBR) **8097**
Culture, Medicine and Psychiatry (NLD) **335**
Culture, Theory and Critique (GBR) **7957**
Cultures and Organizations (GBR) **7957**
Current Alzheimer Research (NLD) **6134**
Current Analytical Chemistry (NLD) **2099**
Current Anthropology (USA) **335**
Current Applied Physics (NLD) **7009**
Current Bioactive Compounds (NLD) **2059**
Current Biology (GBR) **667**
Current Cancer Drug Targets (NLD) **6017**
Current Cancer Therapy Reviews (NLD) **6017**
Current Cardiology Reviews (NLD) **5784**
Current Clinical Pharmacology (NLD) **6830**
Current Competition (USA) **3156**
Current Computer-Aided Drug Design (NLD) **5830**
Current Diabetes Reviews (NLD) **5885**
Current Directions in Psychological Science (USA) **7350**
Current Drug Delivery (NLD) **6830**
Current Drug Discovery Technologies (NLD) **6830**
Current Drug Metabolism (NLD) **6830**
Current Drug Safety (NLD) **6831**
Current Drug Targets (NLD) **6831**
Current Drug Therapy (NLD) **6831**
Current Enzyme Inhibition (NLD) **6831**
Current Events (USA) **2184**
Current Eye Research (GBR) **6040**
Current Gene Therapy (NLD) **865**
Current Genomics (NLD) **865**
Current H I V Research (NLD) **5812**
Current Health 2 (USA) **3055**
Current Hypertension Reviews (NLD) **5784**
Current Immunology Reviews (NLD) **5757**
Current Issues in Language Planning (GBR) **5110**
Current Issues in Tourism (GBR) **8696**
Current Medical Imaging Reviews (NLD) **6194**
Current Medical Research and Opinion (GBR) **5602**
Current Medicinal Chemistry (NLD) **2059**
Current Molecular Medicine (NLD) **884**
Current Nanoscience (NLD) **3186**
Current Neuropharmacology (NLD) **6134**
Current Neurovascular Research (NLD) **6134**
Current Nutrition & Food Science (NLD) **6657**
Current Opinion in Biotechnology (GBR) **762**
Current Opinion in Cell Biology (GBR) **831**
Current Opinion in Chemical Biology (GBR) **730**
Current Opinion in Colloid & Interface Science (GBR) **2134**
Current Opinion in Genetics & Development (GBR) **865**
Current Opinion in Immunology (GBR) **5743**
Current Opinion in Microbiology (GBR) **884**
Current Opinion in Neurobiology (GBR) **6134**
Current Opinion in Pharmacology (GBR) **6831**
Current Opinion in Plant Biology (GBR) **785**
Current Opinion in Solid State & Materials Science (GBR) **3298**
Current Opinion in Structural Biology (GBR) **730**
Current Organic Chemistry (NLD) **2122**
Current Organic Synthesis (NLD) **2122**
Current Pediatric Reviews (NLD) **6091**
Current Pharmaceutical Analysis (NLD) **6831**
Current Pharmaceutical Biotechnology (NLD) **763**
Current Pharmaceutical Design (NLD) **6831**
Current Pharmacogenomics and Personalized Medicine (NLD) **6831**
Current Protein and Peptide Science (NLD) **730**
Current Proteomics (NLD) **730**
Current Psychiatry Reviews (NLD) **6135**
Current Respiratory Medicine Reviews (NLD) **6213**
Current Rheumatology Reviews (NLD) **6223**
Current Science (USA) **2184**
Current Signal Transduction Therapy (NLD) **5812**
Current Stem Cell Research & Therapy (NLD) **730**
Current Therapeutic Research (USA) **6832**
Current Topics in Medicinal Chemistry (NLD) **5603**
Current Vascular Pharmacology (NLD) **5785**
Current Women's Health Reviews (NLD) **5989**
Currents in Theology and Mission (USA) **7753**
Curriculum Inquiry (USA) **3057**
Curriculum Journal (GBR) **3057**
Curriculum Review (USA) **3057**
Curtis's Botanical Magazine (GBR) **785**
Curve (USA) **4372**
Custom Home (USA) **1000**
Customer Inter@ction Solutions (USA) **2318**
Customer Loyalty Today (USA) **1812**
Customer Management Insight (Online) (USA) **1812**
Cyber Humanitatis (CHL) **4449**
Cybernetics & Human Knowing (GBR) **2526**
Cybernetics and Systems (USA) **2526**
Cybernetics and Systems Analysis (USA) **2526**
CyberPsychology & Behavior (USA) **2554**
Cytokine (GBR) **865**
Cytokine & Growth Factor Reviews (GBR) **730**
Cytopathology (GBR) **832**
Cytotechnology (NLD) **832**
Cytotherapy (GBR) **5936**
Czech Music (CZE) **6560**
Czechoslovak Mathematical Journal (DEU) **5481**
D A V Magazine (USA) **6417**
D & O Advisor (USA) **4865**
D C Plan News & Analysis (USA) **1334**
D I S A M Journal (USA) *see* The Management of Security Assistance. **7251**
D I Y Week (GBR) **4438**
D N A and Cell Biology (USA) **730**
D N A Repair (NLD) **731**
D N R (USA) **8449**
D Q R Studies in Literature (NLD) **5282**
D V (USA) **2379**
D V D Intelligence (GBR) **2400**
D V M (USA) **8796**
Daedalus (USA) **4449**
Daily Business Review (Broward Edition) (USA) **1090**
Daily Business Review (Online Edition) (USA) **1090**
Daily Business Review (Palm Beach Edition) (USA) **1090**
Daily Compilation of Presidential Documents (USA) **7128**
Daily Mail (GBR) **3863**
Daily NewsFax (USA) **4384**
Daily Record (GBR) **3967**
Daily Report (Atlanta) (USA) **4654**
Daily Variety (Los Angeles) (USA) **2379**
Dairy Farmer (GBR) **263**
Dairy Foods (USA) **3633**
Dairy Industries International (GBR) **3633**
Dairy Markets (GBR) **263**
Dairy Today (USA) **263**
Dallas Business Journal (USA) **1090**
Dance Magazine (USA) **2684**
Daphnis (NLD) **5283**
Data & Knowledge Engineering (NLD) **2416**
Data Mining and Knowledge Discovery (USA) **2530**
Database and Network Journal (GBR) **2496**
Databased Advisor Magazine (USA) **2554**
Daughters (USA) **2150**
Dead Sea Discoveries (NLD) **7720**
DealerNews (USA) **8257**
Dealerscope (USA) **3091**
Death Studies (USA) **7351**
Debate (PER) **5213**
Debatte (GBR) **4213**
Decision Analysis (USA) **1738**
Decision Sciences (USA) **1738**
Decision Support Systems (NLD) **1738**
Deep-Sea Research. Part 1: Oceanographic Research Papers (GBR) **2803**
Deep-Sea Research. Part 2: Topical Studies in Oceanography (GBR) **2803**
Defence and Peace Economics (GBR) **6417**
Defence and Security Analysis (GBR) **6417**
Defence Studies (GBR) **6418**
Defense A R Journal (USA) **6418**
Defense A T & L (USA) **2520**
Defense Counsel Journal (USA) **4830**
Defense Daily (USA) **52**
Defense Transportation Journal (USA) **6419**
Delaware Law Weekly (USA) **4655**
Dementia (GBR) **6135**
Democratization (GBR) **7230**
Demokratizatsiya (USA) **7129**
Dendrochronologia (DEU) **785**
The Dental Assistant (USA) **5839**
Dental Implantology Update (USA) **5840**
Dental Lab Products (USA) **5840**
Dental Materials (USA) **5840**
Dental Traumatology Online (GBR) **5841**
Dentomaxillofacial Radiology (GBR) **6195**
The Denver Business Journal (USA) **1091**
Denver Journal of International Law and Policy (USA) **4922**
Derivatives Week (USA) **1620**
Dermatologic Surgery Online (USA) **6241**
Dermatologic Therapy (DNK) **5874**
Dermatology Nursing (USA) **5875**
Dermatology Times (USA) **5875**
Des Moines Business Record (USA) **1091**
Desalination (NLD) **8820**
Design Automation for Embedded Systems (NLD) **2460**
Design Issues (USA) **486**
Design News Online (USA) *see* Design News. **8420**
Design Studies (GBR) **440**
Design Week (GBR) **486**
Designed Monomers and Polymers (Online) (NLD) **3242**
Designs, Codes and Cryptography (USA) **5482**
Detroiter (USA) **1401**
Deutsche Gesellschaft fuer Geowissenschaften. Zeitschrift (DEU) **2730**
Developing World Bioethics (GBR) **6913**
Development (Basingstoke) (GBR) **1593**
Development and Change (GBR) **1593**
Development and Learning in Organizations (GBR) **1859**
Development, Growth and Differentiation (AUS) **668**
Development in Practice (GBR) **1594**
Development Policy Review (GBR) **1594**
Development Southern Africa (GBR) **1594**
Developmental & Comparative Immunology (GBR) **5757**
Developmental Biology (USA) **668**
Developmental Cell (USA) **832**
Developmental Neuropsychology (USA) **7351**
Developmental Neurorehabilitation (Online) (GBR) *see* Developmental Neurorehabilitation. **6108**
Developmental Review (USA) **7352**
Developmental Science (GBR) **7352**
Deviant Behavior (USA) **8098**
Diabetes (USA) **5886**
Diabetes and Primary Care (GBR) **5886**
Diabetes Care (USA) **5887**
The Diabetes Educator (USA) **5887**
Diabetes Forecast (USA) **5887**
Diabetes, Obesity and Metabolism Online (GBR) **5888**
Diabetes Research and Clinical Practice (IRL) **5888**
Diabetes Spectrum (USA) **5888**
Diabetes Technology & Therapeutics (USA) **5889**
The Diabetic Foot (GBR) **5889**
Diabetic Medicine Online (GBR) **5889**
Diachronica (NLD) **5111**
Diagnostic Imaging (USA) **6195**
Diagnostic Microbiology and Infectious Disease (USA) **884**
Dialectica (USA) **6914**
Dialectical Anthropology (NLD) **335**
Dialog (St Paul) (USA) **7637**
Diamond and Related Materials (CHE) **2110**
Dianoia (MEX) **6914**
Dieciocho (USA) **5285**
Diesel Progress North American Edition (USA) **3376**
Differences (USA) **8895**
Differential Equations (RUS) **5482**
Differential Geometry and Its Applications (NLD) **5482**
Differentiation (GBR) **669**
Dig (USA) **390**
Digestive Diseases and Sciences (USA) **5922**
Digestive Endoscopy (AUS) **5922**
Digital Cinematography (USA) **6496**
Digital Content Producer (USA) **2401**
Digital Creativity (GBR) **2485**
Digital Imaging Techniques (USA) **2485**
Digital Media: A Seybold Report (USA) **2571**
Digital Signal Processing (USA) **3093**
Digital Software Magazine (USA) **2589**
Diogenes (English Edition) (GBR) **7959**
Diplomacy & Statecraft (GBR) **4137**
Diplomatic History (USA) **4137**
Direct (New York, 1988) (USA) **1813**
Direct Marketing (Online Edition) (USA) **1813**
Directors & Boards (USA) **1739**
Dirt Rider Magazine (USA) **8258**
Disability and Rehabilitation (GBR) **4065**
Disability & Society (GBR) **4077**
Disaster Prevention and Management (GBR) **7514**
Disasters (GBR) **1594**
Discourse (Abingdon) (GBR) **3020**
Discourse (Detroit, 1979) (USA) **4450**
Discourse Processes (USA) **7959**
Discover (USA) **7851**
Discrete Applied Mathematics (NLD) **5483**
Discrete Event Dynamic Systems (USA) **2517**
Discrete Mathematics (NLD) **5483**
Discrete Mathematics and Applications (DEU) **5483**
Disease Management & Health Outcomes (NZL) **5605**
Disease Markers (NLD) **6018**
Diseases of the Esophagus (AUS) **6079**
Display & Design Ideas (USA) **4538**
Display Development News (USA) **3093**
Displays (NLD) **2485**
Distance Education (AUS) **2940**
Distributed and Parallel Databases (USA) **2530**
District Administration (USA) **3058**
Diverse Issues in Higher Education (USA) **2978**
Diversity and Distributions (GBR) **669**
Diversity in Health and Care (GBR) **8037**
Diversity Suppliers & Business Magazine (USA) **1814**
Dixie Contractor (USA) **1002**
Doctor (GBR) **5606**
Doctor Ebiz (USA) **1959**
Document & Image Automation (USA) **5007**
Document Imaging Report (USA) **2533**
Documenta Ophthalmologica (NLD) **6041**
Documents International (GBR) **7319**
Doklady Biochemistry and Biophysics (RUS) **731**
Doklady Biological Sciences (RUS) **669**
Doklady Chemistry (RUS) **2060**
Doklady Physical Chemistry (RUS) **2134**
Dolan's Virginia Business Observer (USA) **4660**
Dollars & Sense (Cambridge) (USA) **1477**
Domestic Animal Endocrinology (USA) **8796**
Doors and Hardware (USA) **1053**
Dose-Response (USA) **5606**
Down Beat (USA) **6562**
Dream World Cruise Destinations (GBR) **8642**
Droit Nucleaire (FRA) **3166**
Drug and Alcohol Dependence (IRL) **2693**
Drug and Alcohol Review (GBR) **2693**
Drug Benefit Trends (USA) **6833**
Drug Cost Management Report (USA) **6833**
Drug Delivery (USA) **6834**
Drug Discovery & Development (USA) **6834**
Drug Discovery Today (GBR) **6834**
Drug Formulary Review (USA) **6835**
Drug Metabolism Reviews (USA) **5607**
Drug Resistance Updates (GBR) **5607**
Drug Safety (NZL) **6836**
Drug Store News (USA) **1814**
Drug Topics (USA) **6836**
Drug Week (USA) **6836**
Drugs (GBR) **2693**
Drugs (NZL) **6836**
Drugs & Aging (NZL) **6836**
Drugs & Therapy Perspectives (NZL) **6836**
Drugs in Context (International Edition) (GBR) **5812**
Drugs in R & D (NZL) **6837**
Drying Technology (USA) **2134**
Duke Environmental Law & Policy Forum (USA) **4661**
Duke Journal of Comparative and International Law (USA) **4923**
Duke Journal of Gender Law & Policy (USA) **7205**
Duke Law Journal (USA) **4661**
Duty Free News International (GBR) **8783**
Dyes and Pigments (GBR) **2060**
Dynamical Systems (Online) (GBR) **2417**
Dynamics of Atmospheres and Oceans (NLD) **6352**
Dyslexia (GBR) **3038**
E (USA) **3414**
e A D C - F & N (GBR) *see* Archives of Disease in Childhood. Fetal and Neonatal Edition. **5986**
E C & M (USA) **3300**
e C M A J (CAN) *see* C M A J. **5590**
E D Legal Letter (USA) **4662**
E D N Access (USA) *see* E D N World. **3093**
E D N Europe (USA) **3093**
E E: Evaluation Engineering (USA) **3093**
E E T Online (USA) *see* E E Times. **3094**
E E Times U K (GBR) **3094**
E H S Today (USA) **6676**
E L H (USA) **5286**
E L T Journal (GBR) **5113**
E M B O Reports (GBR) **866**
E M J Online (GBR) *see* Emergency Medicine Journal. **6059**
E M S Product News (USA) **7514**
E N T (Online) (USA) **2589**
E P P O Bulletin (GBR) **228**
E R I S A Litigation Alert (USA) **1676**
E R T Weekly (GBR) **2358**
e-Service Journal (USA) **2543**
The E-Tactics Letter (USA) **1815**
E U R O S L A Yearbook (NLD) **5113**
Ear, Nose & Throat Journal (USA) **6079**
Early American Literature (USA) **5287**
Early Child Development and Care (GBR) **2151**
Early Childhood Education Journal (USA) **2844**
Early Childhood Research & Practice (USA) **2844**
Early Childhood Research Quarterly (GBR) **2844**
Early Human Development (IRL) **5989**
Early Medieval Europe (GBR) **4216**
Early Modern Literary Studies (GBR) **5421**
Early Music (GBR) **6563**
Early Science and Medicine (NLD) **5608**
Early Years (GBR) **3058**
Earth and Planetary Science Letters (NLD) **2706**
Earth Island Journal (USA) **3415**
Earth, Moon, and Planets (NLD) **574**
Earth - Science Reviews (NLD) **2706**
East Asia (USA) **4181**
East European Insurance Report (GBR) **4501**
East European Jewish Affairs (GBR) **4216**
Eastern European Economics (USA) **1097**
Eating Behaviors (GBR) **7353**
Eating Disorders (USA) **7353**
Ebony (USA) **3531**
Echocardiography (USA) **5785**
Ecography (DNK) **3416**
Ecological Applications (USA) **3416**
Ecological Economics (NLD) **3416**
Ecological Engineering (NLD) **3417**
Ecological Entomology Online (GBR) **843**
Ecological Indicators (NLD) **3417**
Ecological Management & Restoration (AUS) **3417**
Ecological Modelling (NLD) **3481**
Ecological Monographs (USA) **3417**
Ecological Psychology (USA) **7353**
Ecological Research (AUS) **670**
Ecological Restoration (USA) **2609**
The Ecologist (Online) (GBR) **3417**
Ecology (USA) **3417**
Ecology Letters (GBR) **670**
Ecology of Food and Nutrition (USA) **6657**
Ecology of Freshwater Fish (DNK) **941**
Econometrica (GBR) **1097**
The Econometrics Journal (GBR) **1097**
Economic Affairs (GBR) **1098**
Economic and Financial Review (Dallas) (USA) **1336**
Economic Change and Restructuring (NLD) **1479**
Economic Commentary (USA) **1099**
Economic Development and Cultural Change (USA) **1595**
Economic Development Quarterly (USA) **1539**
Economic Geography (USA) **4005**
The Economic History Review (GBR) **1539**
Economic Indicators (Washington) (USA) **1480**
Economic Inquiry (GBR) **1100**

Online Service

Link to your serials resources and content with ulrichsweb.com

Genetica (NLD) 869
Geneva Papers on Risk and Insurance - Issues and Practice (GBR) 4503
The Geneva Risk and Insurance Review (USA) 4503
Genome (CAN) 870
Genomics (USA) 870
Genomics & Genetics Weekly (USA) 871
Genomics & Proteomics (USA) 764
GEO (Godmanchester) (GBR) 4037
Geobiology (GBR) 2735
Geobios (FRA) 6725
Geochemistry: Exploration, Environment, Analysis (GBR) 2735
Geochimica et Cosmochimica Acta (GBR) 2735
Geoderma (NLD) 232
Geodinamica Acta (FRA) 2736
Geofluids Online (GBR) 2736
Geoforum (GBR) 4008
Geografiska Annaler. Series A. Physical Geography (GBR) 4009
Geografiska Annaler. Series B. Human Geography (GBR) 340
Geographical (GBR) 4010
Geographical Analysis (USA) 4010
The Geographical Journal (GBR) 4010
Geographical Research (AUS) 4011
Geographie, Economie, Societe (FRA) 4011
Geography Review (GBR) 4012
Geoinformatica (USA) 2722
GeoJournal (NLD) 4012
Geological Society. Journal (GBR) 2738
Geologists' Association. Proceedings (GBR) 2742
Geology Today Online (GBR) 2742
Geomechanics Abstracts (GBR) 2719
Geometriae Dedicata (NLD) 5490
Geomicrobiology Journal (USA) 886
Geomorphology (NLD) 2743
Geophysical and Astrophysical Fluid Dynamics (CHE) 2781
Geophysical Journal International (GBR) 2782
Geophysical Prospecting (GBR) 2782
Geoplace.com (USA) *see* Geo World. 4037
Geopolitics (GBR) 7237
George Wells' Washington Beverage Insight (USA) 604
Georgetown Journal of International Law (USA) 4926
Georgia Journal of Science (USA) 7857
Georgia Trend (USA) 1349
Georgian Mathematical Journal (DEU) 5490
Geoscience Canada (CAN) 2743
Geotechnical and Geological Engineering (NLD) 6463
Geotextiles and Geomembranes (GBR) 8451
Geothermics (GBR) 2708
Geriatrics (USA) 4045
Geriatrics & Gerontology International (AUS) 4045
German Economic Review (GBR) 1488
German History (GBR) 4223
German Life and Letters (GBR) 5300
German Monitor (NLD) 5217
German Policy Studies (USA) 7439
German Politics (GBR) 7237
German Politics and Society (USA) 7138
The Germanic Review (USA) 5122
Germano-Slavica (CAN) 5300
Gerodontology (DNK) 5845
Gestalt Review (USA) 7358
Gesture (NLD) 8104
Gesunde Pflanzen (DEU) 3433
Getting Paid in Behavioral Healthcare (USA) 6143
Gifted Child Today (USA) 3040
Gifts & Decorative Accessories (USA) 4060
Girls' Life (USA) 2191
GIScience and Remote Sensing (USA) 4013
Glass (Redhill) (GBR) 2041
Glass and Ceramics (USA) 2041
Glass International (GBR) 2042
Glass Physics and Chemistry (RUS) 2042
Global and Planetary Change (NLD) 2744
Global Business and Organizational Excellence (USA) 1748
Global Change Biology (GBR) 675
Global Change, Peace & Security (Online) (GBR) 7237
Global Cosmetic Industry (USA) 594
Global Crime (GBR) 7237
Global Ecology and Biogeography (GBR) 3433
Global Environmental Change (GBR) 3434
Global Environmental Politics (USA) 3434
Global Finance Journal (NLD) 1349
Global Governance (USA) 7238
Global Investor (GBR) 1349
Global Mobile (GBR) 2322
Global Money Management (USA) 1626
Global Networks (Oxford) (USA) 8104
Global Private Power (GBR) 3158
Global Society (GBR) 7238
Global Telecoms Business (GBR) 2322
Global Virtue Ethics Review (USA) 7439
Global Water Report (GBR) 8824
Globalisation, Societies and Education (GBR) 2860
Globalizations (GBR) 7858
The Globe and Mail (CAN) 3810
Globe & Mail Report on Business Magazine (CAN) *see* Report on Business Magazine. 1165
Glycobiology (GBR) 733
Glycoconjugate Journal (USA) 733
Gold Bulletin (GBR) 6338
Golf Magazine (USA) 8232
Golf World (USA) 8233
Golf World Business (USA) 8233
GolfDigest.com (USA) *see* Golf Digest. 8231
Good Housekeeping (USA) 4359
Gourmet Retailer (USA) 3645
Governance (USA) 7138
Government and Opposition (GBR) 7138
Government Finance Review (USA) 1927
Government Information Quarterly (GBR) 7440
Government Procurement (USA) 7440
Government Product News (USA) 7440
Government Security (USA) 2677
Government Video (USA) 2401
Grain: World Markets and Trade (USA) 1997
Grana (NOR) 791
Grand Rounds (GBR) 5814
Graphic Arts Monthly (USA) 7322
Graphical Models (USA) 2485
Grass and Forage Science (GBR) 116
Grassroots Development (USA) 1596
Grazer Philosophische Studien (NLD) 6922
The Greater Baton Rouge Business Report (USA) 1488
Greece and Rome (GBR) 2234
The Green Sheet (GBR) 1236
Greener Management International (GBR) 3435
Grey Room (USA) 444
Grit (USA) 3977
The Grocer (GBR) 3679
Grocery Headquarters (USA) 3679
Ground Handling International (GBR) 8497
Ground Support Worldwide (USA) 57
Ground Water (USA) 2794
Group (New York) (USA) 7359
Group & Organization Management (USA) 2861
Group Decision and Negotiation (NLD) 1748
Groupwork (GBR) 8043
Growth and Change (USA) 1887
Growth Factors (CHE) 922
Gulf Shipper (USA) 8645
Guns & Ammo (USA) 8316
Guns Magazine (USA) 8176
Gut Online (GBR) *see* Gut. 5925
The Guttmacher Report on Public Policy (USA) 972
Gynecologic Oncology (USA) 5992
Gynecological Endocrinology (GBR) 5893
Gynecologie Obstetrique et Fertilite (FRA) 5992
H & H N Online (USA) *see* Hospital & Health Networks. 4099
H E C Forum (NLD) 4094
H F M Magazine (USA) 4094
H F N (USA) 4558
H K Staff (HKG) 1862
H M Treasury Economic Briefing (GBR) 1489
H P A C Engineering (USA) 4119
H P B (GBR) 5926
H R Magazine (USA) 1862
Habitat Australia (AUS) 2613
Habitat International (GBR) 4411
Habitation (USA) 3645
Haemophilia Online (GBR) 5937
Hairdressers' Journal International (GBR) 588
Handbook of Practice Management (GBR) 5623
Handguns (USA) 8317
Hardware Retailing (Indianapolis) (USA) 4438
Harmful Algae (NLD) 886
Harper's (USA) 5219
Harper's Bazaar (USA) 2256
Hart's Diesel Fuel News (USA) 6772
Harvard Business Review (USA) 1117
The Harvard Health Letter (USA) 6987
Harvard Heart Letter (USA) 5787
Harvard International Review (USA) 7239
Harvard Journal of African American Public Policy (USA) 7443
Harvard Journal of Law and Public Policy (USA) 4684
Harvard Law Review (USA) 4685
Harvard Men's Health Watch (USA) 6284
The Harvard Mental Health Letter (USA) 6144
The Harvard Review (USA) 4454
Harvard Review of Psychiatry (GBR) 6144
Harvard Theological Review (GBR) 7646
Harvard Women's Health Watch (USA) 8845
Hastings Center Report (USA) 5623
Hawaii Business (USA) 1489
Hawwa (NLD) 8898
Hay & Forage Grower (USA) 273
Hazardous Waste Consultant (USA) 3507
Haznews (GBR) 3507
Headache & Pain (USA) 6144
Headache Online (USA) 6144
Health (USA) 6987
Health Affairs (USA) 7520
Health & Medicine Week (USA) 5624
Health & Place (GBR) 4014
Health and Social Care in the Community (Online) (GBR) 7521
Health & Social Work (USA) 8044
Health Care Analysis (NLD) 5624
Health Care Financing Review (USA) 5624
Health Care for Women International (USA) 8846
Health Care Management Review (USA) 4095
Health Care Management Science (NLD) 4095
The Health Care Manager (USA) 4095
Health Communication (USA) 7521
Health Data Management (New York) (USA) 4096
Health Education (GBR) 6988
Health Education & Behavior (USA) 7522
Health Education Research (GBR) 8044
Health Expectations (GBR) 7522
Health Facilities Management (USA) 4096
Health Informatics Journal (GBR) 5830
Health Information and Libraries Journal (Online) (GBR) 5012
Health Law Journal (CAN) 4686
Health Law Review (CAN) 4686
Health Management Technology (USA) 5830
Health Plan Week (USA) 4505
Health Policy (IRL) 7522
Health Policy and Planning (GBR) 7522
Health Promotion International (GBR) 7523
Health, Risk & Society (GBR) 7523
Health Science (USA) 6660
Health Services and Outcomes Research Methodology (USA) 5626
Health Services Management Research (GBR) 5626
Health Services Research (USA) 4096
Healthcare Benchmarks and Quality Improvement (USA) 4097
Healthcare Purchasing News (USA) 4097
Healthcare Review (Northern New England Edition) (USA) 4098
Healthcare Risk Management (USA) 4098
Healthcare Traveler (USA) 4098
HealthFacts (USA) 5627
Hearing Journal (USA) 4074
Hearing Research (NLD) 6080
Heart Disease Weekly (USA) 5788
Heart Failure Reviews (USA) 5788
Heart Online (GBR) *see* Heart. 5787
Heat Transfer Engineering (USA) 3245
Hecate (AUS) 8898
The Hedgehog Review (USA) 4454
Heir Lines (USA) 3770
Helicobacter (Oxford) (USA) 887
Helios (USA) 5304
Hematology (GBR) 5937
The Hemingway Review (USA) 5305
Hemisphere (USA) 7240
Hemodialysis International (USA) 5938
Hepatitis Weekly (USA) 5815
Hepatology Research (GBR) 5926
The Herald (Conroe) (USA) 3770
Hereditas (USA) 871
Herizons (CAN) 8867
Herpetological Journal (GBR) 946
Hers (USA) 6988
Hesperia (GRC) 396
The Heythrop Journal (GBR) 7647
High Ability Studies (GBR) 3041
High Altitude Medicine and Biology (USA) 5628
High Energy Chemistry (RUS) 2135
High Performance Computing and Communications Week (USA) 2576
High Performance Plastics (GBR) 7092
High Pressure Research (GBR) 7059
The High School Journal (USA) 2863
High Temperature (RUS) 7054
High Yield Report (USA) 1351
Higher Education (NLD) 2984
Higher Education in Europe (GBR) 2984
Higher Education Management and Policy (FRA) 2984
Higher Education Policy (GBR) 2984
Higher Education Quarterly (GBR) 2984
Higher Education Research and Development (GBR) 2985
Higher-Order and Symbolic Computation (USA) 2486
Highlights for Children (USA) 2192
Hindsight G C S E Modern History Review (GBR) 4141
Hindu Business Line (IND) 1351
Hindu International Edition (IND) 3882
Hispanic American Historical Review (USA) 4295
Hispanic Journal of Behavioral Sciences (USA) 7360
Hispanic Research Journal (GBR) 5305
Histopathology (GBR) 6021
Historia Mathematica (USA) 5491
The Historian (East Lansing) (USA) 4143
Historical Biology (CHE) 6725
Historical Journal of Film, Radio and Television (GBR) 4143
Historical Materialism (NLD) 1542
Historical Methods (USA) 8149
Historical Records of Australian Science (AUS) 7861
Historical Research (GBR) 4143
Historical Society. Journal (USA) 4143
Historical Studies (CAN) 7800
Historiographia Linguistica (NLD) 5125
History (Washington) (USA) 4145
History and Anthropology (GBR) 341
History & Memory (USA) 4145
History and Philosophy of Logic (GBR) 6923
History and Philosophy of the Life Sciences (GBR) 676
History and Technology (GBR) 4145
History and Theory (USA) 4145
History of Education (GBR) 2863
History of European Ideas (GBR) 6923
History of Photography (GBR) 6969
History of Political Economy (USA) 1542
History of Political Thought (GBR) 7140
History of Religions (USA) 7647
The History of the Family (GBR) 7969
History Online (GBR) *see* History. 4145
History Review (GBR) 4145
History Today (GBR) 4230
History Workshop Journal (GBR) 4146
HIV Medicine (GBR) 5815
HIV Treatment ALERTS! (USA) 5758
Hoist (GBR) 1011
Hola (ESP) 3952
Holistic Nursing Practice (USA) 5960
Hollins Critic (USA) 5219
Hollywood Reporter: Premier Edition (USA) *see* The Hollywood Reporter. 6502
Holocaust and Genocide Studies (USA) 4230
The Holocene (GBR) 3437
Holography News (USA) 7076
Home Accents Today (USA) 4541
Home Channel News (USA) 1118
Home Channel News NewsFax (USA) 1011
Home Cultures (GBR) 7969
Home Energy (USA) 3137
Home Furnishings (GBR) 4558
Home Health Care Management and Practice (USA) 4098
Home Media Magazine (USA) 2401
Home Textiles Today (USA) 8451
HomeCare Magazine (USA) 5960
Homily Service (USA) 7648
HOMO (DEU) 341
Hopscotch (Bluffton) (USA) 2193
Hormones and Behavior (USA) 5894
The Horn Book Magazine (USA) 7562
Horse & Rider (USA) 8292
Horticulture (USA) 3737
Hospice Management Advisor (USA) 4099
Hospital Access Management (USA) 4099
Hospital Case Management (USA) 4100
Hospital Employee Health (USA) 4100
Hospital Home Health (USA) 4100
Hospital Infection Control & Prevention (USA) 5816
Hospital Law's Regan Report (USA) 4100
Hospital Materials Management (USA) 4100
Hospital Peer Review (USA) 4101
Hospital Pharmacist Report (USA) 6846
Hospital Topics (USA) 4101
Hospitality Design (USA) 4542
Hot Rod (USA) 8584
Hotel and Motel Management (USA) 4389
Hotels (USA) 4390
House Beautiful (USA) 4542
Household & Personal Products Industry (USA) 1819
Houses (AUS) 445
Housewares Magazine (GBR) 4559
Housing Studies (GBR) 4414
Housing, Theory and Society (NOR) 4414
Houston Business Journal (USA) 1489
Houston Journal of International Law (USA) 4688
Howard Journal of Communications (USA) 2323
The Howard Journal of Criminal Justice (GBR) 2654
HRfocus (USA) 1863
Huellas (COL) 4297
Human and Ecological Risk Assessment (USA) 3437
Human & Experimental Toxicology (GBR) 3497
Human Antibodies (NLD) 5758
Human Biology (Detroit) (USA) 871
Human Communication Research (USA) 7360
Human - Computer Interaction (Mahwah) (USA) 2420
Human Dimensions of Wildlife (USA) 3438
Human Ecology (Ithaca) (USA) 7970
Human Ecology (New York) (USA) 341
Human Factors (USA) 3195
Human Fertility (GBR) 5993
Human Gene Therapy (USA) 871
Human Genomics (Online) (GBR) 872
Human Immunology (USA) 5759
Human Molecular Genetics (GBR) 872
Human Movement Science (NLD) 5630
Human Performance (USA) 7361
Human Physiology (RUS) 5631
Human Reproduction (GBR) 5993
Human Reproduction Update (GBR) 716
Human Resource Development International (GBR) 1863
Human Resource Management International Digest (GBR) 1864
Human Resource Management Journal (GBR) 1864
Human Resource Management Review (GBR) 1864
Human Rights Quarterly (USA) 7208
Human Rights Review (NLD) 7209
Human Rights Watch World Report (USA) 7209
Human Studies (NLD) 6923
Human Systems Management (NLD) 1750
The Humanist (USA) 6923
Humanist Perspectives (CAN) 6924
Humanitas (USA) 4455
Humpty Dumpty's Magazine (USA) 2193
Husserl Studies (NLD) 6924
Hybridoma (Online) (USA) 733
Hydraulics & Pneumatics (USA) 3361
Hydrobiologia (NLD) 677
Hydrocarbon Processing International Edition (USA) 6772
Hydrometallurgy (NLD) 6315
Hypatia (USA) 8898
Hyperfine Interactions (NLD) 7015
I A N Inside Products (USA) 4487
I B M System User (GBR) 2520
I C E S Journal of Marine Science (GBR) 2806
I C M A Public Management Magazine (USA) 7494
I C S Cleaning Specialist (USA) 4559
I D E A Fitness Journal (USA) 6989
I D S Bulletin (GBR) 1597
I I E Transactions (USA) 3367
I M A Journal of Applied Mathematics (GBR) 5492
I M A Journal of Management Mathematics (GBR) 5492
I M A Journal of Mathematical Control & Information (GBR) 5492

Link to your serials resources and content with ulrichsweb.com

Online Service

The International Journal of Architectural Computing (GBR) **462**
International Journal of Art & Design Education (GBR) **3065**
International Journal of Audiology (NOR) **6081**
International Journal of Auditing (GBR) **1292**
The International Journal of Aviation Psychology (USA) **8546**
International Journal of Bank Marketing (GBR) **1356**
International Journal of Behavioral Development (GBR) **7364**
International Journal of Behavioral Medicine (USA) **7364**
International Journal of Bifurcation and Chaos in Applied Sciences and Engineering (SGP) **3200**
International Journal of Bilingual Education and Bilingualism (GBR) **2868**
International Journal of Bilingualism (GBR) **5129**
The International Journal of Biochemistry & Cell Biology (GBR) **734**
The International Journal of Biodiversity Science & Management (GBR) **2615**
International Journal of Biological Macromolecules (NLD) **734**
International Journal of Call Centre Management (GBR) **1755**
International Journal of Canadian Studies (CAN) **8108**
International Journal of Cardiology (IRL) **5790**
International Journal of Cardiovascular Imaging (NLD) **5790**
International Journal of Children's Spirituality (GBR) **7364**
International Journal of Clinical and Experimental Hypnosis (GBR) **5943**
The International Journal of Clinical Leadership (GBR) **5638**
International Journal of Clinical Practice (GBR) **5638**
International Journal of Clothing Science and Technology (GBR) **2247**
International Journal of Coal Geology (NLD) **2748**
International Journal of Coal Preparation and Utilization (USA) **6466**
International Journal of Commerce and Management (GBR) **1756**
International Journal of Comparative Criminology (CAN) **2655**
The International Journal of Comparative Labour Law and Industrial Relations (NLD) **4695**
International Journal of Comparative Sociology (NLD) **8108**
International Journal of Computational Fluid Dynamics (CHE) **7059**
International Journal of Computer Integrated Manufacturing (GBR) **3292**
International Journal of Computer Mathematics (CHE) **5552**
International Journal of Computer Vision (USA) **2451**
International Journal of Computers for Mathematical Learning (NLD) **5553**
International Journal of Constitutional Law (GBR) **4849**
International Journal of Consumer Studies (GBR) **2638**
International Journal of Contemporary Hospitality Management (GBR) **4391**
International Journal of Control (GBR) **3200**
International Journal of Corpus Linguistics (NLD) **5129**
International Journal of Cosmetic Science (GBR) **594**
The International Journal of Cultural Policy (GBR) **7974**
International Journal of Cultural Property (GBR) **497**
International Journal of Customer Relationship Management (GBR) **1756**
International Journal of Dairy Technology Online (GBR) **1127**
International Journal of Damage Mechanics (GBR) **3346**
International Journal of Dermatology (GBR) **5877**
International Journal of Developmental Neuroscience (GBR) **6146**
International Journal of Disability, Development and Education (GBR) **3041**
International Journal of Disaster Medicine (GBR) **5638**
International Journal of Disclosure and Governance (GBR) **1756**
International Journal of Drug Policy (NLD) **2695**
International Journal of E-business Strategy Management (GBR) **1756**
International Journal of Early Years Education (GBR) **2869**
International Journal of Educational Advancement (Online) (GBR) **2869**
International Journal of Educational Development (GBR) **2869**
International Journal of Educational Management (GBR) **1756**
International Journal of Educational Research (GBR) **2869**
International Journal of Electrical Power & Energy Systems (GBR) **3321**
International Journal of Electronic Commerce (USA) **1418**
International Journal of Electronics (GBR) **3105**
International Journal of Engine Research (GBR) **3382**
International Journal of Engineering Science (GBR) **3201**
International Journal of Entrepreneurial Behaviour & Research (GBR) **1962**
International Journal of Entrepreneurship and Innovation (GBR) **1128**
International Journal of Environmental Analytical Chemistry (GBR) **2101**
International Journal of Environmental Health Research (GBR) **3442**
International Journal of Epidemiology (GBR) **5638**
International Journal of Ethics (USA) **7143**
International Journal of Evidence-Based Healthcare (AUS) **5638**
International Journal of Experimental Pathology (GBR) **5638**
International Journal of Fatigue (GBR) **3346**
International Journal of Food Microbiology (NLD) **887**
International Journal of Food Science & Technology Online (GBR) **3648**
International Journal of Food Sciences and Nutrition (GBR) **6660**
International Journal of Forecasting (NLD) **1493**
International Journal of Fracture (NLD) **3347**
International Journal of General Systems (CHE) **2522**
International Journal of Geographical Information Science (GBR) **4037**
International Journal of Gynecological Cancer (USA) **5993**
International Journal of Gynecology & Obstetrics (IRL) **5994**
International Journal of Health Care Finance and Economics (USA) **7526**
International Journal of Health Care Quality Assurance (GBR) **5639**
International Journal of Heat and Fluid Flow (USA) **7054**
International Journal of Heat and Mass Transfer (GBR) **3382**
International Journal of Hematology (JPN) **5938**
International Journal of Heritage Studies (GBR) **4147**
International Journal of High Performance Computing Applications (USA) **2592**
International Journal of Historical Archaeology (USA) **398**
International Journal of Hospitality Management (GBR) **4391**
International Journal of Human-Computer Interaction (USA) **8151**
International Journal of Human-Computer Studies (GBR) **2527**
International Journal of Human Resource Management (GBR) **1867**
The International Journal of Human Rights (GBR) **7210**
The International Journal of Humanities and Peace (USA) **4457**
International Journal of Hydrogen Energy (GBR) **3139**
International Journal of Hygiene and Environmental Health (DEU) **7526**
International Journal of Hyperthermia (GBR) **6023**
International Journal of Immunogenetics (GBR) **873**
International Journal of Impact Engineering (GBR) **3201**
International Journal of Inclusive Education (GBR) **2870**
International Journal of Industrial Ergonomics (NLD) **3201**
International Journal of Industrial Organization (NLD) **1757**
International Journal of Information Management (GBR) **2547**
International Journal of Injury Control and Safety Promotion (GBR) **2638**
International Journal of Instructional Media (USA) **3065**
International Journal of Intelligence and Counterintelligence (USA) **7243**
International Journal of Intercultural Relations (GBR) **8109**
International Journal of Japanese Sociology (AUS) **8109**
International Journal of Kurdish Studies (USA) **4321**
International Journal of Laboratory Hematology (Online) (GBR) **5938**
International Journal of Language and Communication Disorders (GBR) **6081**
International Journal of Law and Information Technology (GBR) **4695**
International Journal of Law and Management (GBR) **1689**
International Journal of Law and Psychiatry (GBR) **4695**
International Journal of Law Crime and Justice (GBR) **4695**
International Journal of Law, Policy and the Family (GBR) **4911**
International Journal of Leadership in Education (GBR) **2870**
International Journal of Lexicography (GBR) **5129**
International Journal of Lifelong Education (GBR) **2942**
International Journal of Logistics (GBR) **1128**
International Journal of Lower Extremity Wounds (USA) **5639**
International Journal of Machine Tools and Manufacture (GBR) **3369**
International Journal of Management Reviews (GBR) **1759**
International Journal of Manpower (GBR) **1689**
International Journal of Market Research (GBR) **1821**
International Journal of Mass Spectrometry (NLD) **7077**
International Journal of Mathematical Education in Science and Technology (GBR) **5496**
International Journal of Mechanical Sciences (GBR) **3347**
International Journal of Medical Informatics (IRL) **5831**
International Journal of Medical Microbiology (DEU) **5818**
International Journal of Men's Health (USA) **6284**
International Journal of Mental Health Nursing (AUS) **6146**
International Journal of Methods in Psychiatric Research (GBR) **6147**
International Journal of Mineral Processing (NLD) **6466**
International Journal of Mining, Reclamation and Environment (GBR) **6466**
International Journal of Modern Physics B (SGP) **7017**
International Journal of Morphology (CHL) **5639**
The International Journal of Multilingualism (GBR) **5129**
International Journal of Multiphase Flow (GBR) **3382**
International Journal of Nautical Archaeology (GBR) **398**
International Journal of Neural Systems (SGP) **2452**
International Journal of Neuroscience (CHE) **6147**
International Journal of New Product Development & Innovation Management (GBR) **1760**
International Journal of Non-Linear Mechanics (GBR) **3347**
International Journal of Nonprofit and Voluntary Sector Marketing (GBR) **1822**
International Journal of Numerical Methods for Heat and Fluid Flow (GBR) **3272**
International Journal of Nursing Practice (AUS) **5962**
International Journal of Nursing Studies (GBR) **5962**
The International Journal of Nursing Terminologies and Classifications (USA) **5962**
International Journal of Operations and Production Management (GBR) **1760**
International Journal of Paediatric Dentistry (Online) (GBR) **5849**
International Journal of Parallel, Emergent and Distributed Systems (CHE) **2507**
International Journal of Parallel Programming (USA) **2507**
The International Journal of Pavement Engineering (GBR) **3272**
International Journal of Peace Studies (TWN) **7143**
International Journal of Pediatric Otorhinolaryngology (IRL) **6081**
International Journal of Peptide Research and Therapeutics (NLD) **734**
International Journal of Performance Analysis in Sport (GBR) **8180**
International Journal of Pest Management (GBR) **237**
International Journal of Pharmaceutics (NLD) **6850**
International Journal of Pharmacy Practice (GBR) **6850**
International Journal of Philosophical Studies Online (GBR) *see* International Journal of Philosophical Studies. **6926**
International Journal of Physical Distribution & Logistics Management (GBR) **8671**
International Journal of Phytoremediation (USA) **3443**
International Journal of Plant Sciences (USA) **795**
International Journal of Plasticity (GBR) **3348**
International Journal of Politics, Culture, and Society (USA) **7243**
International Journal of Polymer Analysis & Characterization (USA) **3247**
International Journal of Polymeric Materials (CHE) **3247**
International Journal of Press / Politics (USA) **4577**
International Journal of Pressure Vessels and Piping (GBR) **3383**
International Journal of Primatology (USA) **948**
International Journal of Production Economics (NLD) **3369**
International Journal of Production Research (GBR) **1889**
International Journal of Productivity and Performance Management (GBR) **1760**
International Journal of Project Management (GBR) **1419**
International Journal of Psychiatry in Clinical Practice (GBR) **6147**
The International Journal of Psychoanalysis (GBR) **7365**
International Journal of Psychology (GBR) **7365**
International Journal of Psychophysiology (NLD) **7365**
International Journal of Public Opinion Research (GBR) **7144**
International Journal of Public Sector Management (GBR) **1761**
International Journal of Qualitative Studies in Education (GBR) **2870**
International Journal of Quality & Reliability Management (GBR) **1761**
International Journal of Radiation Biology (GBR) **6023**
International Journal of Radiation: Oncology - Biology - Physics (USA) **6199**
International Journal of Refractory Metals and Hard Materials (GBR) **6317**
International Journal of Refrigeration (GBR) **4122**
International Journal of Refugee Law (GBR) **7243**
International Journal of Remote Sensing (GBR) **2710**
International Journal of Research and Method in Education (Online) (GBR) **2870**
International Journal of Research in Marketing (NLD) **1822**
International Journal of Retail & Distribution Management (GBR) **1822**
International Journal of Rheumatic Diseases (AUS) **6224**
International Journal of Robotics Research (GBR) **2585**
International Journal of Rock Mechanics and Mining Sciences (GBR) **6466**
International Journal of Rotating Machinery (USA) **5453**
International Journal of S T D & AIDS (GBR) **5818**
International Journal of Science and Mathematics Education (NLD) **7868**
International Journal of Science Education (GBR) **2871**
International Journal of Selection and Assessment (GBR) **1867**
International Journal of Social Economics (GBR) **1129**
International Journal of Social Research Methodology (GBR) **7974**
International Journal of Social Welfare (GBR) **8047**
International Journal of Sociology and Social Policy (GBR) **8109**
International Journal of Solids and Structures (GBR) **7059**
International Journal of Space Structures (GBR) **1016**
International Journal of Speech-Language Pathology (GBR) **5129**
International Journal of Speech Technology (NLD) **5203**
International Journal of Sports Marketing & Sponsorship (GBR) **8180**
International Journal of Stress Management (USA) **5640**
International Journal of Surgical Pathology (USA) **6246**
International Journal of Sustainability in Higher Education (Online) (GBR) **2988**
International Journal of Sustainable Development and World Ecology (GBR) **3443**
International Journal of Sustainable Energy (GBR) **3176**
International Journal of Systematic Theology (GBR) **7651**
International Journal of Systems Science (GBR) **3203**
International Journal of Technology and Design Education (NLD) **3065**
International Journal of Testing (USA) **7366**
International Journal of the Economics of Business (GBR) **1129**
The International Journal of the History of Sport (GBR) **4147**
International Journal of the Legal Profession (GBR) **4695**
International Journal of Theoretical and Applied Finance (SGP) **1357**
International Journal of Theoretical Physics (USA) **7018**
International Journal of Thermal Sciences (FRA) **7055**
International Journal of Thermophysics (USA) **7055**
International Journal of Toxicology (GBR) **3498**
International Journal of Training & Development (GBR) **1867**
International Journal of Tropical Insect Science (KEN) **850**
International Journal of Tuberculosis and Lung Disease (FRA) **6215**
International Journal of Urban and Regional Research (GBR) **4416**
International Journal of Urology (AUS) **6269**
International Journal of Water Resources Development (GBR) **8826**
International Journal of Wildland Fire (AUS) **3579**
International Journal of Wireless Information Networks (USA) **2327**
International Journal on E-learning (USA) **2560**
International Journal on World Peace (USA) **7244**
International Labour Review (GBR) **1689**
International Law Update (USA) **4931**
International Marketing Review (GBR) **1822**
International Materials Reviews (GBR) **3348**
International Midwifery (NLD) **5994**
International Migration (GBR) **7285**
International Migration Review (USA) **7285**
International Milling Directory (GBR) **273**
International Monetary Fund. Staff Papers (USA) **1358**
International Monetary Fund. World Economic Outlook (USA) **1493**
International Money Marketing (GBR) **1358**
International Nursing Review Online (GBR) **5962**
International Ophthalmology (NLD) **6044**
International Organization (GBR) **7244**
International Peacekeeping (GBR) **7244**
International Perspectives on Sexual and Reproductive Health (USA) **5994**
International Petroleum Finance (USA) **6774**
International Planning Studies (GBR) **4416**

Link to your serials resources and content with ulrichsweb.com

International Politics (GBR) **7244**
International Polymer Science and Technology (GBR) **7093**
International Product Alert (USA) **1822**
International Public Management Journal (GBR) **7447**
International Railway Journal (USA) **8619**
International Regional Science Review (USA) **7975**
International Relations of the Asia-Pacific (GBR) **7245**
International Research in Geographical and Environmental Education (GBR) **4016**
International Review for the Sociology of Sport (GBR) **8110**
International Review of Applied Economics (GBR) **1129**
International Review of Economics & Finance (GBR) **1493**
International Review of Education (DEU) **2871**
International Review of Finance (GBR) **1358**
International Review of Financial Analysis (GBR) **1359**
International Review of Law and Economics (USA) **4696**
International Review of Law, Computers & Technology (GBR) **4845**
International Review of Mission (CHE) **7651**
International Review of Psychiatry (GBR) **6148**
The International Review of Retail, Distribution and Consumer Research (GBR) **1822**
International Review of Sociology (GBR) **8110**
International Review of Women and Leadership (AUS) **8899**
International Reviews in Physical Chemistry (GBR) **2136**
International Reviews of Immunology (CHE) **5761**
International Securities Finance (GBR) **1359**
International Security (USA) **7245**
International Small Business Journal (GBR) **1962**
International Social Science Journal (GBR) **7975**
International Social Science Review (USA) **7975**
International Social Security Review (GBR) **4509**
International Studies in the Philosophy of Science (GBR) **6926**
International Studies Perspectives (USA) **7245**
International Studies Quarterly (USA) **7245**
International Studies Review (USA) **7245**
International Tax and Public Finance (USA) **1930**
International Tax Journal (USA) **1930**
International Tax Review (GBR) **1571**
International Trade Forum (CHE) **1571**
The International Trade Journal (USA) **1572**
International Transactions in Operational Research (GBR) **2427**
International Travel News (USA) **8724**
International Urology and Nephrology (NLD) **6269**
International Water Power and Dam Construction (GBR) **3163**
International Wound Journal (GBR) **6062**
Internet and Electronic Commerce Strategies (USA) **2560**
The Internet and Higher Education (GBR) **2560**
Internet Business News (GBR) **2560**
Internet Business Newsletter (USA) **2368**
The Internet Journal of Advanced Nursing Practice (USA) **5962**
The Internet Journal of Anesthesiology (USA) **5771**
The Internet Journal of Asthma, Allergy and Immunology (USA) **5761**
The Internet Journal of Dermatology (USA) **5878**
The Internet Journal of Endocrinology (USA) **5895**
The Internet Journal of Epidemiology (USA) **7527**
The Internet Journal of Family Practice (USA) **5946**
The Internet Journal of Gastroenterology (USA) **5927**
The Internet Journal of Genomics and Proteomics (USA) **766**
The Internet Journal of Gynecology and Obstetrics (USA) **5994**
The Internet Journal of Health (USA) **7527**
The Internet Journal of Healthcare Administration (USA) **4102**
The Internet Journal of Hematology (USA) **5939**
The Internet Journal of Internal Medicine (USA) **5946**
The Internet Journal of Law, Healthcare and Ethics (USA) **5914**
The Internet Journal of Medical Simulation (USA) **5640**
The Internet Journal of Mental Health (USA) **7366**
The Internet Journal of Nephrology (USA) **6269**
The Internet Journal of Neurology (USA) **6148**
The Internet Journal of Neuromonitoring (USA) **6148**
The Internet Journal of Nuclear Medicine (USA) **6199**
The Internet Journal of Oncology (USA) **6023**
The Internet Journal of Ophthalmology and Visual Science (USA) **6044**
The Internet Journal of Otorhinolaryngology (USA) **6081**
The Internet Journal of Pathology (USA) **5640**
The Internet Journal of Plastic Surgery (USA) **6246**
The Internet Journal of Radiology (USA) **6199**
The Internet Journal of Rescue and Disaster Medicine (USA) **6062**
The Internet Journal of Rheumatology (USA) **6224**
The Internet Journal of Surgery (USA) **6246**
The Internet Journal of Third World Medicine (USA) **5640**
The Internet Journal of Thoracic and Cardiovascular Surgery (USA) **6247**
The Internet Journal of Toxicology (USA) **6850**
The Internet Journal of Tropical Medicine (USA) **5819**
Internet Research (GBR) **2561**
Internet Tax Advisor (USA) **1393**
InternetTelephony (USA) *see* Telephony. **2373**
Interpretation (Richmond) (USA) **7651**
Interpreting (NLD) **5130**
Intertax (NLD) **1572**
Intertexts (USA) **5310**
Intervention in School and Clinic (USA) **3042**
Interventions (GBR) **5310**
Interview (New York) (USA) **3979**
Intra (GBR) **4544**
Inventory Management Report (USA) **1851**
Inverse Problems (GBR) **5553**
Inverse Problems in Science and Engineering (GBR) **3203**
Invertebrate Biology (USA) **948**
Invertebrate Systematics (AUS) **949**
Investigacion & Desarrollo (COL) **7975**
Investigational New Drugs (USA) **6851**
Investigations in Mathematics Learning (USA) **5498**
Investment Adviser (GBR) **1632**
Investment Dealers' Digest (USA) **1632**
Investment International (GBR) **1632**
The Investment Lawyer (USA) **1632**
Investment Management Weekly (USA) **1632**
Investment News (USA) **1633**
Investor's Business Daily (USA) **1633**
Investors Chronicle (London, 1860) (GBR) **1634**
Iowa Law Review (USA) **4696**
Iran and the Caucasus (NLD) **552**
Iranian Studies (GBR) **552**
Iris: A Journal about Women (USA) **8869**
Irish Educational Studies (GBR) **2871**
Irish Literary Supplement (USA) **5311**
Irish Political Studies (GBR) **7144**
Irish Studies Review (GBR) **5221**
Irish University Review (IRL) **5311**
Ironmaking & Steelmaking (GBR) **3348**
Irrigation and Drainage Systems (NLD) **212**
Isis (USA) **7868**
Islam and Christian - Muslim Relations (GBR) **7711**
Islam & Science (CAN) **7712**
Islamic Law and Society (NLD) **7712**
The Island Arc (AUS) **2748**
Isokinetics and Exercise Science (NLD) **6230**
Isotopes in Environmental and Health Studies (GBR) **2066**
Israel Affairs (GBR) **7246**
Israel Faxx (USA) **3541**
Israel Studies (USA) **7976**
Issues in Accounting Education (USA) **1293**
Issues in Comprehensive Pediatric Nursing (USA) **5963**
Issues in Law and Medicine (USA) **5642**
Issues in Mental Health Nursing (USA) **5963**
Issues in Science and Technology (USA) **7869**
Issues in Teacher Education (USA) **3066**
Italian Culture (GBR) **5311**
Italian Studies (GBR) **5311**
The Italianist (GBR) **4234**
Italica (USA) **5311**
ITNOW (Online) (GBR) **2427**
Ivey Business Journal (Online Edition) (CAN) **1762**
J A A P A (USA) **5642**
J A H Online (USA) *see* Journal of Adolescent Health. **5645**
J A M A: The Journal of the American Medical Association (USA) **5642**
J C K (USA) **4567**
J C P Online (GBR) *see* Journal of Clinical Pathology. **5647**
J C T (USA) **3066**
J C T CoatingsTech (USA) **6718**
J D D G (Online Edition) (DEU) *see* J D D G (Print Edition). **5878**
J E C H Online (GBR) *see* Journal of Epidemiology & Community Health. **5648**
J E G P (USA) **5312**
J E I (USA) **1543**
J E M (USA) **2872**
J M B Online (GBR) *see* Journal of Molecular Biology. **736**
J M E Online (GBR) *see* Journal of Medical Ethics. **5651**
J M G Online (GBR) *see* Journal of Medical Genetics. **874**
J M M (USA) **2328**
J N N P Online (GBR) *see* Journal of Neurology, Neurosurgery and Psychiatry. **6154**
J O M (USA) **6318**
Jack and Jill (Inkprint Edition) (USA) **2194**
Jakarta Post (IDN) **3891**
Japan and the World Economy (NLD) **1543**
Japan Chemical Week (JPN) **3248**
Japan Forum (GBR) **7247**
J@pan Inc. (JPN) **2562**
Japan Journal (English Edition) (JPN) **1599**
Japan Journal of Nursing Science (JPN) **5963**
Japan Telecom (USA) **2328**
The Japanese Economic Review (AUS) **1131**
Japanese Journal of Clinical Oncology (GBR) **6023**
Japanese Journal of Ophthalmology (NLD) **6044**
Japanese Psychological Research (JPN) **7367**
Japanese Studies (GBR) **8111**
Java Developer's Journal (USA) **2507**
Jet (USA) **3979**
Jewish History (ISR) **7723**
Jewish Social Studies (USA) **7724**
Jewish Studies Quarterly (DEU) **7724**
JobWatch (USA) **6852**
Joint Bone Spine (FRA) **6062**
Joint Commission Benchmark (USA) **4103**
The Joint Commission Journal on Quality and Patient Safety (USA) **4103**
Joint Commission Perspectives (USA) **7528**
Joint Commission Perspectives on Patient Safety (USA) **4103**
Joint Commission: The Source (USA) **4103**
Joint Force Quarterly (USA) **6429**
Journal de Mathematiques Pures et Appliquees (FRA) **5499**
Journal de Pediatrie et de Puericulture (FRA) **5645**
Journal for Cultural Research (GBR) **4459**
Journal for General Philosophy of Science (NLD) **7871**
Journal for Nature Conservation (DEU) **3444**
Journal for Specialists in Group Work (USA) **7367**
Journal for Specialists in Pediatric Nursing (USA) **5963**
Journal for the Scientific Study of Religion (USA) **7653**
Journal for the Study of Judaism (NLD) **7725**
Journal for the Study of the New Testament (GBR) **7653**
Journal for the Study of the Old Testament (GBR) **7653**
Journal for the Theory of Social Behaviour (GBR) **7367**
Journal for Vascular Ultrasound (Online Edition) (USA) **5791**
Journal of Abnormal Child Psychology (USA) **7368**
Journal of Academic Ethics (NLD) **2989**
The Journal of Academic Librarianship (GBR) **5020**
Journal of Access Policy & Practice (GBR) **2943**
Journal of Accountancy (USA) **1293**
Journal of Accounting and Economics (NLD) **1293**
Journal of Accounting and Public Policy (USA) **1293**
Journal of Accounting Education (GBR) **1293**
Journal of Accounting Research (USA) **1294**
Journal of Addictions & Offender Counseling (USA) **7368**
Journal of Addictions Nursing (GBR) **5964**
Journal of Adhesion (CHE) **7019**
Journal of Adhesion Science and Technology (NLD) **7093**
Journal of Adolescence (GBR) **2156**
Journal of Adolescent & Adult Literacy (USA) **3025**
Journal of Adult & Continuing Education (GBR) **2943**
Journal of Adult Development (USA) **7368**
The Journal of Adult Protection (GBR) **4700**
Journal of Advanced Academics (USA) **3042**
Journal of Advanced Nursing (GBR) **5964**
Journal of Advertising (USA) **27**
Journal of Advertising Research (USA) **27**
Journal of Aerosol Medicine and Pulmonary Drug Delivery (USA) **6215**
Journal of Aerosol Science (GBR) **6711**
Journal of Aesthetics and Art Criticism (USA) **498**
Journal of Affective Disorders (NLD) **6149**
Journal of African American History (USA) **3544**
Journal of African American Studies (USA) **6302**
Journal of African Cultural Studies (GBR) **4459**
Journal of African Earth Sciences (GBR) **2749**
Journal of African Economies (GBR) **1494**
The Journal of African History (GBR) **4176**
Journal of Aging Studies (GBR) **4048**
Journal of Agrarian Change (GBR) **201**
Journal of Agricultural and Environmental Ethics (NLD) **6927**
Journal of Agricultural, Biological, and Environmental Statistics (USA) **716**
Journal of Agricultural Economics (GBR) **202**
Journal of Agronomy and Crop Science Online (DEU) **239**
Journal of Air Transport Management (GBR) **1763**
Journal of Alcohol and Drug Education (USA) **2695**
Journal of Algebra (USA) **5500**
Journal of Algebraic Combinatorics (USA) **5500**
Journal of Algorithms (USA) **5553**
Journal of Allied Health (USA) **7528**
Journal of Alloys and Compounds (CHE) **6319**
Journal of Alternative & Complementary Medicine (USA) **311**
The Journal of Alternative Investments (USA) **1634**
Journal of Alzheimer's Disease (NLD) **6149**
Journal of Ambulatory Care Management (USA) **4103**
The Journal of American College Health (USA) **6990**
Journal of American Culture (USA) **4459**
Journal of American Ethnic History (USA) **3544**
Journal of Analytical and Applied Pyrolysis (NLD) **2066**
Journal of Analytical Chemistry (RUS) **2101**
Journal of Analytical Psychology (GBR) **7368**
Journal of Analytical Toxicology (USA) **3498**
Journal of Anatomy (GBR) **680**
Journal of Ancient Near Eastern Religions (NLD) **7737**
Journal of Animal Breeding and Genetics Online (DEU) **291**
Journal of Animal Ecology (GBR) **680**
Journal of Animal Physiology and Animal Nutrition Online (DEU) **923**
Journal of Anthropological Archaeology (USA) **344**
Journal of Antimicrobial Chemotherapy (GBR) **5819**
Journal of Anxiety Disorders (GBR) **7368**
Journal of Apicultural Research & Bee World (GBR) **127**
Journal of Appellate Practice and Process (USA) **4700**
Journal of Applied Animal Welfare Science (USA) **320**
Journal of Applied Biobehavioral Research (USA) **7369**
Journal of Applied Communication Research (USA) **2329**
Journal of Applied Corporate Finance (USA) **1360**
Journal of Applied Crystallography (DNK) **2111**
Journal of Applied Developmental Psychology (GBR) **7369**
Journal of Applied Ecology (GBR) **680**
Journal of Applied Electrochemistry (NLD) **2114**
Journal of Applied Entomology (Online) (DEU) **851**
Journal of Applied Geophysics (NLD) **2784**
Journal of Applied Gerontology (USA) **4049**
Journal of Applied Ichthyology Online (DEU) **950**
Journal of Applied Mathematics and Decision Sciences (USA) **5501**
Journal of Applied Mathematics and Mechanics (GBR) **3349**
Journal of Applied Mechanics and Technical Physics (RUS) **3349**
Journal of Applied Microbiology (GBR) **888**
Journal of Applied Philosophy (GBR) **6928**
Journal of Applied Phycology (NLD) **796**
Journal of Applied Research in Intellectual Disabilities (GBR) **6149**
Journal of Applied Social Psychology (USA) **7369**
Journal of Applied Spectroscopy (USA) **7077**
Journal of Applied Sport Psychology (USA) **6230**
Journal of Applied Statistics (GBR) **8382**
Journal of Approximation Theory (USA) **5501**
Journal of Arabic Literature (NLD) **5314**
Journal of Archaeological Method and Theory (USA) **400**
Journal of Archaeological Research (USA) **400**
Journal of Archaeological Science (GBR) **400**
Journal of Architectural Education (USA) **447**
The Journal of Architecture (GBR) **447**
Journal of Arid Environments (GBR) **4016**
Journal of Articles in Support of the Null Hypothesis (USA) **7872**
Journal of Arts Management, Law, and Society (USA) **4700**
Journal of Asian and African Studies (GBR) **8112**
Journal of Asian Earth Sciences (GBR) **2749**
Journal of Asian Economics (NLD) **1494**
Journal of Asian Natural Products Research (GBR) **311**
Journal of Asian Pacific Communication (NLD) **5132**
The Journal of Asset Management (GBR) **1635**
Journal of Assisted Reproduction and Genetics (USA) **5995**
Journal of Asthma (USA) **6215**
Journal of Atmospheric and Solar - Terrestrial Physics (GBR) **2784**
Journal of Atmospheric Chemistry (NLD) **2066**
Journal of Australian Studies (AUS) **4192**
Journal of Autism and Developmental Disorders (USA) **3042**
Journal of Autoimmunity (GBR) **5762**
Journal of Automated Methods & Management in Chemistry (USA) **2101**
Journal of Automated Reasoning (NLD) **2453**
Journal of Avian Biology (DNK) **909**
Journal of Back and Musculoskeletal Rehabilitation (NLD) **6063**
Journal of Balkan and Near Eastern Studies (GBR) **4235**
Journal of Bamboo and Rattan (IND) **796**
Journal of Banking & Finance (NLD) **1360**
Journal of Behavior Therapy and Experimental Psychiatry (GBR) **6149**
Journal of Behavioral Education (USA) **2874**
The Journal of Behavioral Finance (USA) **7369**
Journal of Behavioral Health Services and Research (USA) **7528**
Journal of Behavioral Medicine (USA) **6149**
Journal of Beliefs and Values (GBR) **2874**
Journal of Bioactive and Compatible Polymers (GBR) **734**
Journal of Biochemistry (GBR) **735**
Journal of Bioeconomics (USA) **681**
Journal of Bioenergetics and Biomembranes (USA) **735**
Journal of Biogeography (GBR) **4017**
Journal of Biological Physics (NLD) **753**
Journal of Biological Rhythms (USA) **6149**
Journal of Biomaterials Science. Polymer Edition (NLD) **766**
Journal of Biomechanics (GBR) **5646**
Journal of Biomedical Informatics (USA) **5832**
Journal of Biomedical Nanotechnology (USA) **766**
Journal of Biomedicine and Biotechnology (USA) **5646**
Journal of Biomolecular N M R (NLD) **735**
Journal of Biomolecular Screening (USA) **735**
Journal of Bioscience and Bioengineering (JPN) **750**
Journal of Biotechnology (NLD) **767**
Journal of Black Studies (USA) **7978**
Journal of Bone and Joint Surgery: British Volume (GBR) **6063**
The Journal of Brand Management (GBR) **1823**
Journal of British Studies (USA) **4235**
Journal of Broadcasting and Electronic Media (USA) **2383**
Journal of Bryology (GBR) **796**
Journal of Building Physics (GBR) **3204**
Journal of Business Administration and Policy Analysis (CAN) **1764**
Journal of Business and Economic Statistics (USA) **1247**

Online Service

Journal of Business & Industrial Marketing (GBR) **1823**
Journal of Business & Psychology (USA) **7369**
Journal of Business Communication (USA) **1764**
Journal of Business Ethics (NLD) **1134**
Journal of Business Finance & Accounting (GBR) **1294**
Journal of Business Research (USA) **1764**
Journal of Business Strategies (USA) **1764**
Journal of Business Strategy (USA) **1764**
Journal of Business Venturing (USA) **1134**
Journal of Cancer Education (USA) **6023**
Journal of Carbohydrate Chemistry (USA) **2067**
Journal of Cardiac Surgery (USA) **5792**
Journal of Cardiovascular Electrophysiology (USA) **5792**
The Journal of Cardiovascular Nursing (USA) **5792**
Journal of Cardiovascular Pharmacology and Therapeutics (USA) **6852**
Journal of Career Development (USA) **6700**
Journal of Catalysis (USA) **2136**
Journal of Cataract & Refractive Surgery (USA) **6044**
Journal of Celtic Linguistics (GBR) **5133**
Journal of Cereal Science (GBR) **273**
The Journal of Change Management (GBR) **1764**
Journal of Chemical Crystallography (USA) **2111**
Journal of Chemical Ecology (USA) **3444**
Journal of Chemical Health and Safety (USA) **3498**
Journal of Chemical Neuroanatomy (NLD) **6150**
Journal of Chemical Research (Online Edition) (GBR) *see* Journal of Chemical Research (Print Edition). **2067**
Journal of Chemical Technology and Biotechnology (GBR) **767**
The Journal of Chemical Thermodynamics (GBR) **2136**
Journal of Child and Adolescent Mental Health (ZAF) **6150**
Journal of Child and Adolescent Psychiatric Nursing (USA) **5964**
Journal of Child and Adolescent Psychopharmacology (USA) **6150**
Journal of Child and Family Studies (USA) **7370**
Journal of Child Psychology and Psychiatry (GBR) **7370**
Journal of Child Psychotherapy (GBR) **7370**
Journal of Children & Poverty (USA) **8049**
Journal of Chinese Economics and Business Studies (GBR) **1494**
Journal of Chinese Philosophy (USA) **6928**
Journal of Chromatographic Science (USA) **2101**
Journal of Chromatography A (NLD) **2101**
Journal of Chromatography. B, Analytical Technologies in the Biomedical and Life Sciences (NLD) **2067**
Journal of Church and State (USA) **7654**
Journal of Cleaner Production (NLD) **3369**
Journal of Clinical Anesthesia (USA) **5772**
Journal of Clinical Child and Adolescent Psychology (USA) **7370**
Journal of Clinical Densitometry (NLD) **5647**
Journal of Clinical Engineering (USA) **750**
Journal of Clinical Epidemiology (USA) **5647**
Journal of Clinical Immunology (USA) **5762**
Journal of Clinical Ligand Assay (USA) **5762**
Journal of Clinical Monitoring and Computing (NLD) **5647**
Journal of Clinical Nursing (GBR) **5964**
Journal of Clinical Periodontology (DNK) **5851**
The Journal of Clinical Pharmacology (USA) **6852**
Journal of Clinical Pharmacy and Therapeutics (GBR) **6852**
Journal of Clinical Psychology in Medical Settings (USA) **7370**
Journal of Clinical Virology (NLD) **5819**
Journal of Cluster Science (USA) **2067**
Journal of Coastal Research (USA) **2809**
Journal of Coatings Technology and Research (USA) **6718**
Journal of Cognition and Culture (NLD) **7370**
Journal of Cognition and Development (USA) **7370**
Journal of Cognitive Neuroscience (USA) **6151**
Journal of Cold War Studies (USA) **7247**
Journal of College Counseling (USA) **2989**
Journal of College Reading and Learning (USA) **2989**
Journal of College Science Teaching (USA) **7872**
Journal of Colloid and Interface Science (USA) **2136**
Journal of Combinatorial Optimization (NLD) **5553**
Journal of Combinatorial Theory, Series A (USA) **5501**
Journal of Combinatorial Theory. Series B (USA) **5501**
The Journal of Commerce (USA) **1430**
Journal of Commercial Biotechnology (GBR) **767**
Journal of Common Market Studies (GBR) **7146**
Journal of Communication (USA) **8112**
Journal of Communication Disorders (USA) **7371**
Journal of Communication Inquiry (USA) **8112**
Journal of Communication Management (GBR) **1765**
Journal of Communist Studies and Transition Politics (GBR) **7247**
Journal of Community Health (USA) **5647**
Journal of Community Health Nursing (USA) **5964**
Journal of Comparative Economics (USA) **1134**
Journal of Comparative Family Studies (CAN) **8112**
The Journal of Comparative Germanic Linguistics (NLD) **5133**
Journal of Comparative International Management (CAN) **1765**
Journal of Comparative Policy Analysis (USA) **7448**
Journal of Complexity (USA) **5553**
Journal of Computational Analysis and Applications (USA) **5501**
Journal of Computational and Applied Mathematics (NLD) **5502**
Journal of Computational and Graphical Statistics (USA) **5502**
Journal of Computational and Theoretical Nanoscience (USA) **7019**
Journal of Computational Biology (Online) (USA) **682**
Journal of Computational Electronics (USA) **2428**
Journal of Computational Neuroscience (NLD) **6151**
Journal of Computational Physics (USA) **7050**
Journal of Computer - Aided Molecular Design (NLD) **2108**
Journal of Computer and System Sciences (USA) **2523**
Journal of Computer Assisted Learning (GBR) **2469**
Journal of Computer Security (NLD) **2515**
Journal of Computers in Mathematics and Science Teaching (USA) **5553**
Journal of Conflict and Security Law (GBR) **4933**
Journal of Conflict Resolution (USA) **7978**
Journal of Consciousness Studies (GBR) **7371**
Journal of Constructional Steel Research (GBR) **3275**
Journal of Constructivist Psychology (USA) **7371**
Journal of Consumer Affairs (USA) **2639**
Journal of Consumer Behaviour (GBR) **2639**
Journal of Consumer Marketing (GBR) **1823**
Journal of Consumer Policy (NLD) **2639**
Journal of Consumer Psychology (USA) **27**
Journal of Consumer Research (USA) **1823**
Journal of Contaminant Hydrology (NLD) **3488**
Journal of Contemporary African Studies (GBR) **7978**
Journal of Contemporary Asia (GBR) **4184**
Journal of Contemporary China (GBR) **4184**
Journal of Contemporary Ethnography (USA) **8112**
Journal of Contemporary European Studies (Online Edition) (GBR) **7146**
Journal of Contemporary Psychotherapy (USA) **7372**
Journal of Contemporary Religion (GBR) **7654**
Journal of Contingencies and Crisis Management (GBR) **1765**
Journal of Controlled Release (NLD) **6853**
Journal of Coordination Chemistry (CHE) **2068**
The Journal of Corporate Citizenship (GBR) **1765**
Journal of Corporate Finance (NLD) **1360**
Journal of Corporate Real Estate (GBR) **7596**
Journal of Cosmetic and Laser Therapy (Online) (GBR) **5878**
Journal of Cosmetic Dermatology (GBR) **5878**
Journal of Counseling & Development (USA) **7372**
Journal of Criminal Justice (GBR) **4892**
Journal of Criminal Law & Criminology (USA) **2657**
Journal of Critical Realism (GBR) **6928**
Journal of Cross-Cultural Gerontology (NLD) **4049**
Journal of Cross-Cultural Psychology (USA) **7372**
Journal of Crystal Growth (NLD) **2111**
Journal of Cultural Diversity (USA) **5964**
Journal of Cultural Economics (USA) **1544**
Journal of Cultural Geography (USA) **4017**
Journal of Cultural Heritage (FRA) **344**
Journal of Curriculum Studies (GBR) **3067**
Journal of Customer Behavior (GBR) **1824**
Journal of Cutaneous Pathology (DNK) **5878**
Journal of Cystic Fibrosis (NLD) **5927**
Journal of Database Management (USA) **2531**
The Journal of Database Marketing & Customer Strategy Management (Online Edition) (GBR) **1419**
The Journal of Deaf Studies and Deaf Education (USA) **4075**
Journal of Deferred Compensation (USA) **1690**
Journal of Dental Hygiene (USA) **5851**
Journal of Dentistry (GBR) **5851**
The Journal of Derivatives (USA) **1360**
Journal of Derivatives & Hedge Funds (GBR) **1635**
Journal of Dermatological Science (IRL) **5878**
Journal of Dermatological Treatment (GBR) **5879**
Journal of Design History (GBR) **498**
Journal of Development Economics (NLD) **1600**
The Journal of Development Studies (GBR) **1600**
Journal of Developmental and Behavioral Pediatrics (USA) **6094**
Journal of Developmental and Physical Disabilities (USA) **4067**
Journal of Diabetes and its Complications (USA) **5895**
Journal of Diabetes Nursing (GBR) **5964**
Journal of Diagnostic Medical Sonography (USA) **6200**
Journal of Difference Equations and Applications (CHE) **5502**
Journal of Differential Equations (USA) **5502**
Journal of Digestive Diseases (Online) (AUS) **5927**
Journal of Digital Asset Management (GBR) **1765**
Journal of Direct, Data and Digital Marketing Practice (Online) (GBR) **1824**
Journal of Disability Policy Studies (USA) **4067**
Journal of Documentation (GBR) **5020**
Journal of Drug Targeting (CHE) **6853**
Journal of Drugs in Dermatology (USA) **5879**
Journal of Dynamical and Control Systems (USA) **3369**
Journal of Dynamics and Differential Equations (USA) **5503**
Journal of Early Childhood Teacher Education (GBR) **2990**
Journal of Early Modern History (NLD) **4149**
Journal of East Asian Linguistics (NLD) **5133**
Journal of East Asian Studies (USA) **553**
Journal of Eastern Townships Studies (CAN) **4299**
Journal of Ecclesiastical History (GBR) **7654**
Journal of Ecology (GBR) **682**
Journal of Econometrics (NLD) **1544**
Journal of Economic Behavior & Organization (NLD) **1134**
Journal of Economic Dynamics and Control (NLD) **1544**
The Journal of Economic Education (USA) **1134**
Journal of Economic Entomology (USA) **851**
Journal of Economic Geography (GBR) **1494**
Journal of Economic Growth (USA) **1544**
The Journal of Economic Inequality (USA) **1494**
Journal of Economic Literature (USA) **1247**
Journal of Economic Methodology (GBR) **1135**
Journal of Economic Perspectives (USA) **1545**
Journal of Economic Policy Reform (Online) (GBR) **1765**
Journal of Economic Psychology (NLD) **1824**
Journal of Economic Studies (GBR) **1135**
Journal of Economic Surveys (GBR) **1135**
Journal of Economic Theory (USA) **1545**
Journal of Economics and Business (USA) **1135**
Journal of Economics & Management Strategy (USA) **1545**
Journal of Ecotourism (GBR) **8725**
Journal of Ecumenical Studies (USA) **7655**
Journal of Education and Work (GBR) **3067**
Journal of Education for Business (USA) **1136**
Journal of Education for Students Placed at Risk (USA) **3067**
Journal of Education for Teaching (GBR) **2875**
Journal of Education Policy (GBR) **3026**
Journal of Educational Administration (GBR) **3026**
Journal of Educational Administration and History (GBR) **3026**
Journal of Educational and Psychological Consultation (USA) **2875**
Journal of Educational Change (NLD) **2875**
Journal of Educational Multimedia and Hypermedia (USA) **2469**
The Journal of Educational Research (USA) **2875**
Journal of Elasticity (NLD) **3349**
Journal of Electroanalytical Chemistry (CHE) **2102**
Journal of Electroceramics (USA) **3349**
Journal of Electromagnetic Waves and Applications (NLD) **7020**
Journal of Electromyography & Kinesiology (GBR) **754**
Journal of Electron Spectroscopy and Related Phenomena (NLD) **7078**
Journal of Electronic Materials (USA) **3106**
Journal of Electronic Testing (USA) **3322**
Journal of Electrostatics (NLD) **3322**
Journal of Elementary Science Education (USA) **3067**
The Journal of Emergency Medicine (New York) (USA) **6064**
Journal of Emotional and Behavioral Disorders (USA) **6151**
Journal of Empirical Finance (NLD) **1361**
Journal of Empirical Legal Studies (USA) **4701**
Journal of Empirical Theology (NLD) **7655**
Journal of Employee Assistance (USA) **6700**
Journal of Employment Counseling (USA) **7372**
Journal of Endourology (USA) **6270**
Journal of Energetic Materials (USA) **7020**
The Journal of Energy Literature (GBR) **3153**
Journal of Engineering and Technology Management (NLD) **1765**
Journal of Engineering Design (GBR) **3205**
Journal of Engineering Mathematics (NLD) **3205**
Journal of Engineering Physics and Thermophysics (USA) **3205**
Journal of English for Academic Purposes (GBR) **3067**
Journal of English Linguistics (USA) **5133**
Journal of Enhanced Heat Transfer (GBR) **3385**
Journal of Enterprise Information Management (GBR) **5021**
Journal of Environment & Development (USA) **3444**
Journal of Environmental Economics and Management (USA) **3445**
The Journal of Environmental Education (USA) **3445**
Journal of Environmental Engineering and Science (Online) (CAN) **3445**
Journal of Environmental Health (USA) **3445**
Journal of Environmental Law (GBR) **3445**
Journal of Environmental Management (GBR) **3446**
Journal of Environmental Planning and Management (GBR) **3446**
Journal of Environmental Policy and Planning (GBR) **3446**
Journal of Environmental Psychology (GBR) **7373**
Journal of Environmental Radioactivity (GBR) **3446**
Journal of Enzyme Inhibition and Medicinal Chemistry (CHE) **736**
The Journal of Ethics (NLD) **6928**
Journal of Ethnic and Migration Studies (GBR) **3544**
Journal of Ethnopharmacology (IRL) **6853**
Journal of European Industrial Training (GBR) **1765**
Journal of European Public Policy (GBR) **7147**
Journal of European Studies (Chalfont Saint Giles) (GBR) **4235**
Journal of Evaluation in Clinical Practice Online (GBR) **5649**
Journal of Evolutionary Biochemistry and Physiology (RUS) **736**
Journal of Evolutionary Biology (GBR) **873**
Journal of Evolutionary Psychology (USA) **7373**
Journal of Experimental & Theoretical Artificial Intelligence (GBR) **2453**
Journal of Experimental Botany (GBR) **796**
Journal of Experimental Child Psychology (USA) **7373**
The Journal of Experimental Education (USA) **3067**
Journal of Experimental Marine Biology and Ecology (NLD) **683**
Journal of Experimental Social Psychology (USA) **7373**
Journal of Experimental Therapeutics and Oncology Online (USA) **6024**
Journal of Facilities Management (GBR) **1766**
Journal of Failure Analysis and Prevention (USA) **6319**
Journal of Family and Economic Issues (USA) **7373**
Journal of Family Communication (USA) **8113**
Journal of Family History (USA) **8113**
Journal of Family Issues (USA) **8113**
Journal of Family Planning and Reproductive Health Care (GBR) **973**
The Journal of Family Practice (USA) **5649**
Journal of Family Therapy (GBR) **6151**
Journal of Family Violence (USA) **2657**
Journal of Fashion Marketing and Management (GBR) **1824**
Journal of Feminist Studies in Religion (USA) **7655**
The Journal of Finance (USA) **1361**
Journal of Financial Econometrics (GBR) **1361**
Journal of Financial Economics (CHE) **1136**
Journal of Financial Intermediation (USA) **1545**
Journal of Financial Markets (NLD) **1361**
Journal of Financial Regulation and Compliance (GBR) **1361**
Journal of Financial Research (USA) **1136**
Journal of Financial Services Marketing (GBR) **1824**
Journal of Financial Services Research (USA) **1361**
Journal of Fire Protection Engineering (GBR) **3579**
Journal of Fire Sciences (GBR) **3349**
Journal of Fish Biology (GBR) **951**
Journal of Fish Diseases Online (GBR) **3599**
The Journal of Fixed Income (USA) **1635**
Journal of Fluency Disorders (USA) **7374**
Journal of Fluids and Structures (GBR) **3205**
Journal of Fluorescence (USA) **2117**
Journal of Fluorine Chemistry (CHE) **2117**
Journal of Folklore Research (USA) **3619**
Journal of Food Composition and Analysis (USA) **3650**
Journal of Food Engineering (GBR) **3650**
Journal of Food Protection (USA) **3650**
Journal of Forensic Economics (USA) **1545**
The Journal of Forensic Psychiatry & Psychology (Online) (GBR) **6151**
Journal of Forest Economics (DEU) **3694**
Journal of Forestry (USA) **3695**
Journal of Functional Analysis (USA) **5503**
Journal of Further and Higher Education (GBR) **2990**
Journal of Fusion Energy (USA) **3170**
Journal of Gambling Studies (USA) **6152**
Journal of Gastroenterology and Hepatology (AUS) **5928**
Journal of Gastrointestinal Cancer (USA) **5896**
Journal of Gastrointestinal Surgery (USA) **6248**
The Journal of Gender, Race & Justice (USA) **3544**
Journal of Gender Studies (GBR) **8899**
Journal of General Internal Medicine (USA) **5946**
The Journal of General Psychology (USA) **7374**
Journal of Generic Medicines (GBR) **6853**
Journal of Genetic Counseling (USA) **7374**
The Journal of Genetic Psychology (USA) **873**
Journal of Genocide Research (GBR) **7147**
Journal of Genome Science and Technology (Online Edition) (USA) **874**
Journal of Geochemical Exploration (NLD) **2711**
Journal of Geodynamics (GBR) **2785**
Journal of Geography in Higher Education (GBR) **4017**
The Journal of Geology (USA) **2750**
Journal of Geometry and Physics (NLD) **5503**
Journal of Geriatric Psychiatry and Neurology (USA) **4049**
The Journal of Gift Planning (USA) **8050**
Journal of Glaciology (GBR) **2750**
Journal of Global Information Management (USA) **1766**
Journal of Global Optimization (NLD) **7940**
Journal of Greek Linguistics (NLD) **5133**
Journal of Grid Computing (NLD) **2508**
Journal of Group Psychotherapy, Psychodrama and Sociometry (USA) **7374**
Journal of Guidance, Control, and Dynamics (USA) **63**
Journal of Gynecologic Surgery (USA) **5995**
Journal of Happiness Studies (NLD) **7374**
Journal of Hazardous Materials (NLD) **3508**
Journal of Head Trauma Rehabilitation (USA) **6064**
Journal of Health and Social Behavior (USA) **8113**
Journal of Health Care Finance (USA) **4104**
Journal of Health Communication (USA) **5649**
Journal of Health Economics (NLD) **4104**
Journal of Health, Organization and Management (GBR) **4104**
Journal of Health Politics, Policy and Law (USA) **5649**
Journal of Health Services Research & Policy (GBR) **5650**
Journal of Healthcare Management (USA) **4104**
The Journal of Heart and Lung Transplantation (USA) **6248**

Journal of Heart-Centered Therapies (USA) **5650**
Journal of Helminthology (GBR) **5820**
Journal of Hepatology (DNK) **5928**
Journal of Heredity (GBR) **874**
Journal of Heuristics (USA) **2453**
Journal of High Speed Networks (NLD) **2500**
The Journal of High Technology Management Research (GBR) **1419**
Journal of Higher Education (USA) **2990**
Journal of Higher Education Policy and Management (GBR) **2990**
Journal of Historical Geography (GBR) **4017**
Journal of Historical Pragmatics (NLD) **5133**
Journal of Historical Sociology (GBR) **8113**
Journal of Holography and Speckle (USA) **7078**
Journal of Horticultural Science and Biotechnology (GBR) **3740**
Journal of Hospitality and Tourism Management (Online) (AUS) **8725**
Journal of Hospitality & Tourism Research (USA) **4392**
Journal of Housing and the Built Environment (NLD) **4417**
Journal of Housing Economics (USA) **4417**
Journal of Human Development and Capabilities (GBR) **345**
Journal of Human Evolution (GBR) **874**
Journal of Human Lactation (USA) **5995**
Journal of Human Nutrition and Dietetics (GBR) **6661**
The Journal of Human Resources (USA) **1868**
Journal of Human Rights (GBR) **7211**
Journal of Humanistic Counseling, Education and Development (USA) **7375**
Journal of Humanistic Psychology (USA) **7375**
Journal of Hydrology (NLD) **2796**
Journal of Iberian and Latin American Studies (GBR) **4299**
Journal of Immigrant and Minority Health (USA) **5650**
Journal of Immunological Methods (NLD) **5762**
Journal of Immunotoxicology (USA) **5763**
The Journal of Imperial and Commonwealth History (GBR) **4149**
Journal of Inclusion Phenomena and Macrocyclic Chemistry (NLD) **2136**
Journal of Income Distribution (USA) **1545**
Journal of Indian Philosophy (NLD) **6928**
Journal of Industrial Ecology (USA) **3447**
The Journal of Industrial Economics (GBR) **1136**
Journal of Industrial Relations (GBR) **1690**
Journal of Industrial Textiles (GBR) **8454**
Journal of Industry, Competition and Trade (USA) **1137**
Journal of Inequalities and Applications (USA) **5504**
Journal of Infant, Child and Adolescent Psychotherapy (USA) **7375**
The Journal of Infectious Diseases (USA) **5820**
Journal of Information Science (GBR) **5021**
The Journal of Information Systems (USA) **2548**
Journal of Information Technology (GBR) **5021**
Journal of Infrared, Millimeter and Terahertz Waves (Online) (USA) *see* Journal of Infrared, Millimeter and Terahertz Waves. **7078**
Journal of Inherited Metabolic Disease (NLD) **6094**
Journal of Inorganic and Organometallic Polymers and Materials (USA) **2124**
Journal of Inorganic Biochemistry (USA) **736**
Journal of Insect Behavior (USA) **852**
Journal of Insect Conservation (GBR) **852**
Journal of Insect Physiology (GBR) **852**
Journal of Institutional and Theoretical Economics (DEU) **7147**
Journal of Instructional Psychology (USA) **2876**
Journal of Integrative Environmental Sciences (GBR) **8114**
Journal of Integrative Plant Biology (GBR) **797**
Journal of Intellectual and Developmental Disability (GBR) **6152**
Journal of Intellectual Capital (GBR) **1766**
Journal of Intellectual Disability Research (GBR) **6152**
Journal of Intelligent and Fuzzy Systems (NLD) **5504**
Journal of Intelligent and Robotic Systems (NLD) **2453**
Journal of Intelligent Information Systems (USA) **2453**
Journal of Intelligent Manufacturing (GBR) **2453**
Journal of Intelligent Material Systems and Structures (GBR) **3349**
Journal of Intelligent Transportation Systems (USA) **2329**
Journal of Intensive Care Medicine (USA) **5650**
Journal of Interactive Learning Research (USA) **2950**
Journal of Intercultural Studies (GBR) **3544**
Journal of Interdisciplinary History (USA) **4149**
Journal of Interferon & Cytokine Research (USA) **5763**
Journal of Internal Medicine (GBR) **5946**
Journal of International Accounting, Auditing and Taxation (GBR) **1295**
Journal of International Accounting Research (USA) **1295**
Journal of International Affairs (USA) **7248**
Journal of International Arbitration (NLD) **4597**
Journal of International Business Studies (GBR) **1137**
Journal of International Criminal Justice (GBR) **2657**
Journal of International Economic Law (GBR) **4933**
Journal of International Economics (NLD) **1137**
Journal of International Entrepreneurship (USA) **1574**
Journal of International Financial Management and Accounting (GBR) **1362**
Journal of International Financial Markets, Institutions & Money (GBR) **1362**
Journal of International Management (USA) **1767**
Journal of International Money and Finance (GBR) **1362**
Journal of International Relations and Development (GBR) **7248**
The Journal of International Trade and Economic Development (GBR) **1600**
Journal of International Wildlife Law and Policy (USA) **3448**
Journal of International Women's Studies (USA) **8899**
Journal of Internet Law (USA) **4701**
Journal of Interpersonal Violence (USA) **2657**
Journal of Interprofessional Care (GBR) **5650**
Journal of Interventional Cardiac Electrophysiology (NLD) **5793**
Journal of Interventional Cardiology (USA) **5793**
Journal of Inverse and Ill-Posed Problems (DEU) **5504**
Journal of Invertebrate Pathology (USA) **951**
The Journal of Investigative Dermatology (USA) **5879**
The Journal of Investigative Dermatology Symposium Proceedings (USA) **5879**
Journal of Investigative Surgery (USA) **6248**
The Journal of Investing (USA) **1635**
Journal of Investment Compliance (GBR) **1635**
Journal of Islamic Studies (GBR) **7713**
The Journal of Israeli History (GBR) **4322**
The Journal of Jewish Thought and Philosophy (NLD) **7725**
Journal of Knowledge Management (GBR) **1767**
Journal of Labor Economics (USA) **1691**
Journal of Labor Research (USA) **1691**
Journal of Language, Identity, and Education (USA) **2876**
Journal of Laparoendoscopic & Advanced Surgical Techniques (USA) **6248**
Journal of Laryngology and Otology (GBR) **6081**
Journal of Latin American Cultural Studies (GBR) **4299**
Journal of Latin American Studies (GBR) **4299**
Journal of Latinos and Education (USA) **2877**
Journal of Law and Health (USA) **4702**
Journal of Law and Society (GBR) **4702**
Journal of Law, Economics, & Organization (GBR) **4702**
The Journal of Law, Medicine & Ethics (USA) **4703**
Journal of Leadership and Organizational Studies (USA) **1767**
Journal of Learning Disabilities (USA) **3042**
The Journal of Legal History (GBR) **4149**
The Journal of Legal Medicine (USA) **5651**
The Journal of Legislative Studies (GBR) **7249**
Journal of Leisure Research (USA) **4978**
Journal of Librarianship and Information Science (GBR) **5021**
The Journal of Light Construction (National Edition) (USA) **1018**
Journal of Light Construction (New England Edition) (USA) **1018**
Journal of Literary Studies (ZAF) **5315**
The Journal of Logic and Algebraic Programming (USA) **2508**
Journal of Logic and Computation (GBR) **2429**
Journal of Logic, Language and Information (NLD) **5134**
Journal of Loss & Trauma (USA) **7376**
Journal of Loss Prevention in the Process Industries (GBR) **3248**
Journal of Low Frequency Noise Vibration and Active Control (GBR) **7088**
Journal of Low Power Electronics (USA) **3106**
Journal of Low Temperature Physics (USA) **7055**
Journal of Lower Genital Tract Disease (Online) (USA) **5995**
Journal of Luminescence (NLD) **7078**
Journal of Machine Learning Research (Online) (USA) **2454**
Journal of Macroeconomics (NLD) **1719**
Journal of Magnetic Resonance (USA) **7020**
Journal of Magnetism and Magnetic Materials (NLD) **7020**
Journal of Mammalian Evolution (USA) **951**
Journal of Mammary Gland Biology and Neoplasia (USA) **924**
Journal of Management (GBR) **1767**
Journal of Management Accounting Research (USA) **1295**
Journal of Management & Governance (USA) **1767**
Journal of Management Development (GBR) **1767**
Journal of Management Information Systems (USA) **2548**
Journal of Management Studies (GBR) **1768**
Journal of Managerial Issues (USA) **1768**
Journal of Managerial Psychology (GBR) **1768**
Journal of Manufacturing Technology Management (GBR) **3292**
Journal of Marine Research (USA) **2809**
Journal of Marine Systems (NLD) **2809**
Journal of Marketing (USA) **1825**
Journal of Marketing Communications (GBR) **1825**
Journal of Marketing Management (GBR) **1825**
Journal of Marketing Research (USA) **1825**
Journal of Marriage and Family (USA) **8114**
Journal of Materials Engineering and Performance (USA) **3350**
Journal of Materials Processing Technology (CHE) **3386**
Journal of Materials Science (NLD) **3350**
Journal of Materials Science: Materials in Electronics (NLD) **3350**
Journal of Materials Science: Materials in Medicine (USA) **3350**
The Journal of Maternal - Fetal & Neonatal Medicine (GBR) **5995**
Journal of Mathematical Analysis and Applications (USA) **5505**
The Journal of Mathematical Behavior (USA) **5505**
Journal of Mathematical Chemistry (NLD) **5505**
Journal of Mathematical Economics (CHE) **1545**
Journal of Mathematical Imaging and Vision (USA) **5553**
Journal of Mathematical Modelling and Algorithms (NLD) **5505**
Journal of Mathematical Psychology (USA) **7376**
Journal of Mathematical Sciences (USA) **5505**
Journal of Mathematical Sociology (USA) **8149**
Journal of Mathematics Teacher Education (NLD) **5506**
Journal of Media and Religion (USA) **2329**
Journal of Media Economics (USA) **2329**
Journal of Medical Engineering & Technology (GBR) **5651**
Journal of Medical Entomology (USA) **852**
Journal of Medical Humanities (USA) **5651**
Journal of Medical Imaging and Radiation Oncology (AUS) **6200**
Journal of Medical Marketing (Online) (GBR) **6854**
Journal of Medical Primatology (DNK) **952**
Journal of Medical Screening (GBR) **5820**
Journal of Medical Speech - Language Pathology (USA) **6082**
Journal of Medical Systems (USA) **5832**
Journal of Medicinal Food (USA) **5652**
The Journal of Medicine and Philosophy (NLD) **5652**
Journal of Medieval and Early Modern Studies (USA) **4460**
Journal of Medieval History (NLD) **4236**
Journal of Membrane Science (NLD) **2137**
Journal of Memory and Language (USA) **5134**
Journal of Men's Health (NLD) **6284**
Journal of Men's Studies (USA) **6302**
Journal of Mental Health (GBR) **6152**
Journal of Mental Health Counseling (USA) **7376**
Journal of Metamorphic Geology (USA) **2750**
Journal of Microbiological Methods (NLD) **889**
Journal of Microencapsulation (GBR) **6854**
Journal of Micromechatronics (NLD) **3322**
Journal of Micropalaeontology (GBR) **6725**
Journal of Microscopy (GBR) **899**
Journal of Middle East Women's Studies (USA) **8900**
Journal of Midwifery & Women's Health (USA) **5995**
Journal of Military Ethics (NOR) **6429**
Journal of Minimal Access Surgery (IND) **6249**
Journal of Minimally Invasive Gynecology (USA) **5995**
Journal of Mining Science (USA) **6467**
The Journal of Modern History (USA) **4149**
Journal of Modern Italian Studies (GBR) **5315**
Journal of Modern Jewish Studies (GBR) **4460**
Journal of Modern Literature (USA) **5315**
Journal of Modern Optics (GBR) **7078**
Journal of Molecular and Cellular Cardiology (GBR) **5794**
Journal of Molecular Catalysis A: Chemical (NLD) **2137**
Journal of Molecular Catalysis B: Enzymatic (NLD) **736**
The Journal of Molecular Diagnostics (USA) **5653**
Journal of Molecular Graphics and Modelling (USA) **2108**
Journal of Molecular Histology (NLD) **834**
Journal of Molecular Liquids (NLD) **2137**
Journal of Molecular Neuroscience (USA) **6153**
Journal of Molecular Spectroscopy (USA) **7078**
Journal of Molecular Structure (NLD) **2068**
Journal of Molecular Structure: THEOCHEM (NLD) **2068**
Journal of Molluscan Studies (GBR) **952**
Journal of Monetary Economics (NLD) **1362**
Journal of Money, Credit & Banking (USA) **1362**
Journal of Moral Education (GBR) **2877**
Journal of Motor Behavior (USA) **7376**
Journal of Multicultural Counseling and Development (USA) **7376**
Journal of Multilingual & Multicultural Development (GBR) **3013**
Journal of Multinational Financial Management (NLD) **1769**
Journal of Multiple-Valued Logic and Soft Computing (USA) **5506**
Journal of Multivariate Analysis (USA) **5506**
Journal of Muscle Foods (USA) **3651**
Journal of Muscle Research and Cell Motility (NLD) **6064**
The Journal of Musculoskeletal Medicine (USA) **6064**
Journal of Music Teacher Education (Online) (USA) **6580**
Journal of Musicological Research (USA) **6581**
Journal of Muslim Minority Affairs (GBR) **7713**
Journal of Nanoparticle Research (NLD) **7021**
Journal of Nanoscience and Nanotechnology (USA) **7021**
Journal of Natural History (GBR) **684**
Journal of Near-Death Studies (USA) **6929**
Journal of Near Eastern Studies (USA) **401**
Journal of Network and Computer Applications (GBR) **2500**
Journal of Network and Systems Management (USA) **2500**
Journal of Neuro-Oncology (USA) **6025**
Journal of Neurochemistry (USA) **736**
Journal of Neuroendocrinology (GBR) **6153**
Journal of Neurogenetics (USA) **6153**
Journal of Neuroimaging (USA) **6153**
Journal of Neuroimmunology (NLD) **6154**
Journal of Neurolinguistics (GBR) **6154**
Journal of Neuroscience Methods (NLD) **6155**
Journal of Neuroscience Nursing (USA) **5965**
Journal of Neurotrauma (USA) **6064**
Journal of NeuroVirology (GBR) **6155**
Journal of Neutron Research (GBR) **7067**
Journal of New Music Research (GBR) **2495**
Journal of Non-Crystalline Solids (NLD) **7021**
Journal of Non-Newtonian Fluid Mechanics (NLD) **7059**
Journal of Nondestructive Evaluation (USA) **3350**
Journal of Nonparametric Statistics (CHE) **8383**
Journal of Nonverbal Behavior (USA) **7376**
The Journal of North African Studies (GBR) **4176**
Journal of Nuclear Materials (NLD) **7067**
Journal of Number Theory (USA) **5506**
Journal of Numerical Mathematics (DEU) **5553**
Journal of Nursing Care Quality (USA) **5966**
Journal of Nursing Management (GBR) **5966**
Journal of Nursing Scholarship (USA) **5966**
Journal of Nutritional & Environmental Medicine (GBR) **6662**
The Journal of Nutritional Biochemistry (USA) **6662**
Journal of Obstetrics and Gynaecology (GBR) **5996**
Journal of Obstetrics and Gynaecology Research (JPN) **5996**
Journal of Occupational and Environmental Hygiene (Online) (USA) **6680**
Journal of Occupational and Organizational Psychology (GBR) **7377**
Journal of Occupational Psychology, Employment and Disability (Online) (GBR) **7377**
Journal of Occupational Rehabilitation (USA) **6680**
Journal of Oceanography (NLD) **2809**
Journal of Ocular Pharmacology and Therapeutics (USA) **6045**
Journal of Oncology Pharmacy Practice (GBR) **6855**
Journal of Operations Management (NLD) **3369**
Journal of Optics (Online) (GBR) *see* Journal of Optics (Print). **7079**
Journal of Optimization Theory and Applications (USA) **5506**
Journal of Oral Pathology & Medicine (GBR) **5852**
Journal of Oral Rehabilitation (GBR) **5852**
Journal of Organizational and End User Computing (Online) (USA) *see* Journal of Organizational and End User Computing. **2571**
Journal of Organizational Change Management (GBR) **1769**
Journal of Organizational Computing and Electronic Commerce (USA) **1420**
Journal of Organometallic Chemistry (CHE) **2125**
Journal of Ornithology (Online Edition) (DEU) *see* Journal of Ornithology. **909**
Journal of Orthopaedic Research (USA) **6064**
The Journal of Pacific History (GBR) **4192**
Journal of Paediatrics and Child Health (GBR) **6094**
Journal of Pain and Symptom Management (USA) **6155**
Journal of Paleolimnology (NLD) **6726**
Journal of Palliative Medicine (USA) **5653**
Journal of Parallel and Distributed Computing (USA) **2429**
Journal of Parapsychology (USA) **6742**
The Journal of Pastoral Counseling (USA) **7655**
Journal of Pathology (GBR) **5653**
Journal of Peace Education (GBR) **7249**
The Journal of Peasant Studies (GBR) **8115**
Journal of Pediatric and Adolescent Gynecology (NLD) **6095**
Journal of Pediatric Oncology Nursing (USA) **6025**
Journal of Pediatric Psychology (GBR) **7377**
Journal of Pension Benefits (USA) **1691**
Journal of Pension Planning and Compliance (USA) **1931**
Journal of Perinatal and Neonatal Nursing (USA) **5967**
Journal of Perinatal Education (USA) **5996**
Journal of Periodontal Research (DNK) **5853**
Journal of Personal Selling and Sales Management (USA) **1826**
Journal of Personality (USA) **7377**
Journal of Personality Assessment (USA) **7377**
Journal of Personality Disorders (USA) **7378**
Journal of Pest Science (DEU) **852**
Journal of Petroleum Geology (GBR) **6776**
Journal of Petroleum Science and Engineering (NLD) **6776**
Journal of Petrology (GBR) **2750**
Journal of Pharmaceutical and Biomedical Analysis (NLD) **6855**
Journal of Pharmacokinetics and Pharmacodynamics (USA) **6855**
Journal of Pharmacological and Toxicological Methods (USA) **3499**
Journal of Pharmacy and Pharmacology (GBR) **6856**
Journal of Pharmacy Practice (USA) **6856**

Lakes and Reservoirs: Research and Management (AUS) **8828**
Lambda Book Report (USA) **4376**
The Lancet (North American Edition) (GBR) **5660**
The Lancet Infectious Diseases (GBR) **5821**
The Lancet Neurology (GBR) **6158**
The Lancet Oncology (GBR) **6026**
Land Economics (USA) **202**
Land Use Policy (GBR) **4418**
Landscape & Irrigation (USA) **241**
Landscape and Urban Planning (NLD) **2617**
Landscape Ecology (NLD) **3450**
Landscape Journal (USA) **448**
Landscape Management (USA) **3741**
Landscape Research (GBR) **448**
Language Acquisition (USA) **5139**
Language and Cognitive Processes (GBR) **5139**
Language & Communication (GBR) **5139**
Language and Computers (NLD) **5203**
Language and Education (GBR) **5139**
Language and Intercultural Communication (GBR) **5139**
Language and Literature (GBR) **5139**
Language and Speech (GBR) **5139**
Language Awareness (GBR) **5140**
Language, Culture and Curriculum (GBR) **5140**
Language Learning (USA) **5141**
Language Learning & Technology (USA) **5203**
Language Policy (NLD) **5141**
Language Problems and Language Planning (NLD) **5141**
Language Resources and Evaluation (NLD) **4485**
Language Sciences (GBR) **5141**
Language Teaching Research (GBR) **5141**
Language Testing (GBR) **5141**
Languages in Contrast (NLD) **5142**
Laser Chemistry (USA) **7079**
Laser Focus World (USA) **7080**
Lasers in Engineering (CHE) **7080**
LatAm Energy (GBR) **3141**
Laterality (GBR) **6158**
Latin American Antiquity (USA) **403**
Latin American Law and Business Report (USA) **4874**
Latin American Music Review (USA) **6584**
Latin American Perspectives (USA) **7982**
Latin American Politics and Society (USA) **7250**
Latin American Power Watch (USA) **3160**
Latin American Research Review (USA) **7982**
Latin American Telecom (USA) **2331**
Latin Beat Magazine (USA) **6584**
Latin Trade (USA) **1575**
LatinFinance (USA) **1365**
Latino Leaders (MEX) **3547**
Latino Studies (GBR) **8118**
Law and Contemporary Problems (USA) **4713**
Law and Critique (NLD) **4713**
Law and Human Behavior (USA) **4713**
Law and Philosophy (NLD) **4713**
Law & Policy (GBR) **4714**
Law and Social Inquiry (USA) **4714**
Law & Society Review (USA) **4714**
Law, Culture & the Humanities (GBR) **4714**
Law Enforcement Product News (USA) **2659**
Law Enforcement Technology (USA) **2659**
Law Firm Inc. (USA) **4874**
Law of the Sea Bulletin (USA) **4970**
Law, Probability and Risk (GBR) **4716**
Law Technology News (USA) **4717**
LawNow (CAN) **4717**
LawyersU S A (USA) **4718**
Leadership (Carol Stream) (USA) **7659**
Leadership (Sacramento) (USA) **2882**
Leadership & Organization Development Journal (GBR) **1772**
Leadership and Policy in Schools (USA) **3026**
Leadership for the Front Lines (USA) **1772**
Leadership in Health Services (GBR) **4105**
The Leadership Quarterly (USA) **1772**
Learned Publishing (GBR) **7565**
Learning & Behavior (USA) **7383**
Learning and Individual Differences (GBR) **2882**
Learning and Instruction (GBR) **2882**
Learning and Leading with Technology (USA) **2950**
Learning and Motivation (USA) **2882**
Learning Disabilities Research and Practice (USA) **3043**
Learning Disability Practice (GBR) **3043**
Learning Disability Quarterly (USA) **3043**
Learning Environments Research (NLD) **2882**
Learning in Health and Social Care (GBR) **5660**
Learning, Media & Technology (Online) (GBR) **3070**
The Learning Organization (GBR) **1869**
Leather International (GBR) **4974**
Lectura y Vida (USA) **5143**
Legacy (Lincoln) (USA) **5320**
Legal and Criminological Psychology (GBR) **7383**
Legal Information Alert (USA) **5025**
The Legal Intelligencer (USA) **4720**
The Legal Issues of Economic Integration (NLD) **4934**
Legal Medicine (NLD) **5915**
The Legal Publisher (USA) **4720**
Leisure Report (GBR) **4980**
Leisure Sciences (USA) **4980**
Leisure Studies (GBR) **4980**
Lenguas Modernas (CHL) **5143**
Leonardo: Art Science and Technology (USA) **502**
Leonardo Music Journal (USA) **6584**
Lethaia (NOR) **6726**
Letras Libres (MEX) **5224**
Letters in Applied Microbiology (GBR) **890**
Letters in Drug Design & Discovery (NLD) **6858**
Letters in Mathematical Physics (NLD) **7025**
Letters in Organic Chemistry (NLD) **2126**
Leukemia and Lymphoma (CHE) **5940**
Leukemia Research (GBR) **5940**
Leviathan (Malden) (USA) **5322**
Liberal Education (USA) **2992**
Libraries & the Cultural Record (USA) **5026**
Library & Information History (Online) (GBR) *see* Library & Information History. **5026**
Library & Information Science Research (GBR) **5027**
Library Collections, Acquisitions, and Technical Services (GBR) **5027**
Library Hi Tech (GBR) **5062**
Library Hi Tech News (GBR) **5062**
Library Journal (USA) **5028**
Library Management (GBR) **5028**
Library Media Connection (USA) **5028**
Library Philosophy and Practice (USA) **5029**
The Library Quarterly (USA) **5029**
Library Resources & Technical Services (USA) **5029**
Library Review (GBR) **5029**
Library Trends (USA) **5029**
License! Global (USA) **1829**
The Licensing Journal (USA) **6754**
The Licensing Letter (USA) **6754**
The Lichenologist (GBR) **800**
Lier en Boog (NLD) **503**
Life Insurance International (IRL) **4512**
Life Science Today (GBR) **6858**
Life Sciences (USA) **7880**
Lifetime Data Analysis (NLD) **8385**
Light (USA) **5323**
Light Truck and S U V (USA) **1829**
Lighting Research and Technology (GBR) **3324**
Lightwave (USA) **2331**
Lignes Directrices pour les Essais de Produits Chimiques (FRA) **3500**
Linear Algebra and Its Applications (USA) **5509**
Linear and Multilinear Algebra (CHE) **5509**
Lingua (NLD) **5144**
Linguistic Inquiry (USA) **5145**
Linguistic Variations Yearbook (NLD) **5146**
Linguistics (DEU) **5147**
Linguistics and Education (GBR) **5147**
Linguistics and Philosophy (NLD) **5147**
Linguistics in the Netherlands (NLD) **5147**
Lingvisticae Investigationes (NLD) **5147**
Linnean Society. Biological Journal (GBR) **687**
Linnean Society. Botanical Journal (GBR) **800**
Linnean Society. Zoological Journal (GBR) **953**
Liquid Crystals (GBR) **2111**
Liquid Crystals Today (Online) (GBR) **2111**
Literary and Linguistic Computing (GBR) **5203**
The Literary Review (USA) **5324**
Literator (ZAF) **5148**
Literature and Theology (GBR) **5325**
Literature Film Quarterly (USA) **6506**
Lithology and Mineral Resources (RUS) **2752**
Lithos (NLD) **2752**
Lithuanian Mathematical Journal (USA) **5509**
Liturgy (USA) **7660**
Live Design (USA) **8473**
Liver International (DNK) **5928**
Liverpool Law Review (NLD) **4724**
Livestock Science (NLD) **292**
Llen Cymru (GBR) **5327**
Local Economy (GBR) **1145**
Local Environment (GBR) **4419**
Local Government Studies (GBR) **7497**
Locksmith Ledger International (USA) **1054**
Lodging Hospitality (USA) **4393**
Logistics Management (USA) **8503**
Logopedics Phoniatrics Vocology (GBR) **6082**
Lolapress (DEU) **8900**
London Review of Education (GBR) **2884**
Long Island Business News (USA) **1145**
Long Range Planning (GBR) **1773**
Long-Term Living (USA) **5969**
Los Angeles Business Journal (USA) **1497**
Los Angeles Magazine (USA) **3980**
Loss Prevention Bulletin (GBR) **3250**
Louisiana Academy of Sciences. Proceedings (USA) **7880**
Loyalist Gazette (CAN) **4302**
Ludus (NLD) **8473**
Lung Cancer (IRL) **6026**
Lupus (GBR) **6224**
Lustre (USA) **1021**
Lymphatic Research and Biology (USA) **6026**
M A C L A S Latin American Essays (USA) **5328**
M A R G I N (AUS) **5328**
M E L U S (USA) **5328**
M H Online (GBR) **5663**
M I R: Management International Review (DEU) **1773**
M I S Quarterly (USA) **2523**
M I T Sloan Management Review (USA) **1773**
M L A International Bibliography (USA) **5407**
M L N (USA) **5149**
M M R (USA) **1774**
M M W R (USA) **7530**
Machine Design (USA) **3388**
Machine Learning (USA) **2454**
Machine Translation (NLD) **5204**
Maclean's (CAN) **3812**
Macroeconomics Annual (USA) **1720**
MacWorld (USA) **2577**
The Magazine Antiques (USA) **367**
Magnetic Resonance Imaging (USA) **6202**
Magnetic Resonance Materials in Physics, Biology and Medicine (GBR) **7068**
Main Group Chemistry (GBR) **2072**
Maintenance Management (USA) **1774**
Maintenance Supplies (USA) **1021**
Major Projects Association (GBR) **1146**
Malaria Weekly (USA) **5822**
Malaysian Business (MYS) **1146**
Mammal Review Online (GBR) **954**
Mammalian Biology (DEU) **954**
Manage (Online) (USA) **1774**
Managed Care Weekly Digest (USA) **5664**
Managed Healthcare Executive (USA) **4106**
Management Accounting Research (GBR) **1296**
Management & Organization Review (AUS) **1775**
Management Consultant International (IRL) **1775**
Management Decision (GBR) **1775**
Management of Environmental Quality (GBR) **3451**
Management Quarterly (USA) **1776**
Management Research Review (GBR) **1776**
Management Science (USA) **1776**
Management Today (GBR) **1777**
Managerial Auditing Journal (GBR) **1778**
Managerial Finance (GBR) **1778**
Managing Intellectual Property (GBR) **6754**
Managing Leisure (GBR) **4980**
Managing Service Quality (GBR) **1778**
The Manchester School (GBR) **1546**
Manitoba Business Magazine (CAN) **1498**
Manitoba History (CAN) **4302**
Manufacturers' Monthly (AUS) **1898**
Manufacturing and Service Operations Management (USA) **1778**
Manufacturing and Technology News (USA) **1898**
Manufacturing Business Technology (USA) **1898**
Manufacturing Chemist (GBR) **3250**
Manushi (IND) **8900**
Marie Claire (USA) **8873**
Marine and Freshwater Behaviour and Physiology (GBR) **687**
Marine & Freshwater Research (AUS) **2811**
Marine and Petroleum Geology (GBR) **2754**
Marine Chemistry (NLD) **2712**
Marine Ecology (DEU) **688**
Marine Environmental Research (GBR) **3488**
Marine Fisheries Review (USA) **3601**
Marine Geodesy (USA) **4019**
Marine Geology (NLD) **2812**
Marine Geophysical Researches (NLD) **2812**
Marine Georesources and Geotechnology (USA) **2812**
Marine Log (USA) **8651**
Marine Micropaleontology (NLD) **6726**
Marine Policy (GBR) **2812**
Marine Pollution Bulletin (GBR) **3488**
Marine Structures (GBR) **3388**
Marine Technology and S N A M E News (USA) **8652**
Maritime Economics & Logistics (GBR) **8652**
Maritime Policy and Management (GBR) **8652**
Market: Africa - Mid-East (USA) **1577**
Market: Asia Pacific (USA) **1577**
Market: Europe (USA) **1577**
Marketing (GBR) **1831**
Marketing Health Services (USA) **1832**
Marketing Intelligence & Planning (GBR) **1832**
Marketing Letters (USA) **1832**
Marketing News (USA) **1832**
Marketing Research (USA) **1833**
The Marketing Review (GBR) **1833**
Marketing Science (USA) **1833**
Marketing to the Emerging Majorities (USA) **1833**
Marketing to Women (USA) **1833**
Marketing Week (GBR) **1834**
Marquette Elder's Advisor (USA) **4904**
Marvels & Tales (USA) **3620**
Al- Masaq (GBR) **7714**
Masonry Construction (USA) **1022**
Mass Storage News (USA) **2540**
Mass Transit (USA) **8503**
Massachusetts Lawyers Weekly (USA) **4729**
The Masthead (Harrisburg) (USA) **4579**
Matatu (NLD) **5331**
Material Handling Management (USA) **5456**
Material Handling Product News (USA) **2462**
Material Religion (GBR) **7662**
Materials & Design (GBR) **3352**
Materials & Manufacturing Processes (USA) **3389**
Materials Characterization (USA) **6322**
Materials Chemistry and Physics (CHE) **3352**
Materials Letters (NLD) **7025**
Materials Management in Health Care (USA) **4106**
Materials Research Bulletin (GBR) **2111**
Materials Science (USA) **3353**
Materials Science and Engineering A: Structural Materials: Properties, Microstructures and Processing (CHE) **3353**
Materials Science and Engineering B: Advanced Functional Solid-state Materials (CHE) **3353**
Materials Science and Engineering C: Materials for Biological Applications (CHE) **3353**
Materials Science and Engineering R: Reports (CHE) **3353**
Materials Science and Technology (GBR) **3353**
Materials Science in Semiconductor Processing (GBR) **3108**
Materials Today (NLD) **2072**
Maternal and Child Health Journal (USA) **5998**
Maternal and Child Nutrition (GBR) **6663**
Mathematical and Computer Modelling (GBR) **5512**
Mathematical and Computer Modelling of Dynamical Systems (GBR) **5554**
Mathematical Biosciences (USA) **5512**
Mathematical Finance (USA) **1367**
Mathematical Geosciences (Online) (USA) *see* Mathematical Geosciences. **2754**
Mathematical Medicine and Biology (Online) (GBR) **5513**
Mathematical Physics, Analysis and Geometry (NLD) **7026**
Mathematical Population Studies (USA) **7287**
Mathematical Problems in Engineering (USA) **3209**
Mathematical Programming (DEU) **5554**
Mathematical Social Sciences (NLD) **5514**
Mathematical Thinking and Learning (USA) **5515**
Mathematics and Computers in Simulation (NLD) **2517**
Mathematics and Mechanics of Solids (GBR) **7026**
Mathematics of Operations Research (USA) **2431**
Matrix Biology (NLD) **5665**
Maturitas (IRL) **5998**
Max Weber Studies (GBR) **7984**
Maximum P C (USA) **2577**
McGill Law Journal (CAN) **4730**
The McKinsey Quarterly (USA) **1779**
McKnight's Long-Term Care News (USA) **4051**
Mealey's Litigation Report: E R I S A (USA) **4836**
Meanjin (AUS) **5227**
Measurement (NLD) **6403**
Measurement (USA) **5517**
Measurement and Evaluation in Counseling and Development (USA) **2886**
Measurement in Physical Education and Exercise Science (USA) **6992**
Measurement Techniques (USA) **6404**
Measuring Business Excellence (GBR) **1779**
Meat & Deli Retailer (USA) **3655**
Meat Science (NLD) **3656**
Mecanique & Industries (FRA) **3389**
Meccanica (NLD) **7060**
Mech (USA) **6434**
Mechanical Engineering (USA) **3389**
Mechanical Systems and Signal Processing (GBR) **3389**
Mechanics of Advanced Materials and Structures (USA) **3354**
Mechanics of Composite Materials (USA) **3250**
Mechanics of Materials (NLD) **3354**
Mechanics of Time Dependent Materials (NLD) **7061**
Mechanics Research Communications (GBR) **3354**
Mechanism and Machine Theory (GBR) **3389**
Mechanisms of Ageing and Development (IRL) **4051**
Mechanisms of Development (IRL) **834**
Mechatronics (GBR) **3390**
Med Ad News (USA) **1834**
Medecine et Droit (FRA) **5915**
Media History (GBR) **8120**
Media Industry Newsletter (USA) **29**
Media International Australia Incorporating Culture and Policy (AUS) **8120**
Media Psychology (USA) **7384**
Mediators of Inflammation (USA) **5666**
MediaWeek (USA) **30**
Medical & Veterinary Entomology Online (GBR) **5667**
Medical Anthropology (USA) **347**
Medical Benefits (USA) **4514**
Medical Decision Making (USA) **5667**
Medical Design (USA) **3210**
Medical Design Technology (Online) (USA) **5667**
Medical Device Technology (GBR) **5668**
Medical Dosimetry (USA) **6203**
Medical Economics (USA) **5668**
Medical Education (GBR) **5668**
Medical Engineering & Physics (GBR) **5668**
Medical Equipment Designer (USA) **4489**
Medical Ethics Advisor (USA) **5668**
Medical Hypotheses (GBR) **5669**
Medical Image Analysis (GBR) **6203**
Medical Laboratory Observer (USA) **5909**
Medical Laser Application (DEU) **5909**
Medical Law Review (GBR) **4731**
Medical Law's Regan Report (USA) **5669**
Medical Letter on the C D C & F D A (USA) **4106**
Medical Marketing & Media (USA) **6860**
Medical Meetings (USA) **6281**
Medical Mycology (GBR) **5822**
Medical Teacher (GBR) **5672**
Medical Textiles (GBR) **5672**
Medical Update (Chicago) (USA) **5672**
Medicinal Chemistry (NLD) **5673**
Medicine (Baltimore) (USA) **5674**
Medicine, Conflict and Survival (GBR) **5674**
Medicine, Healthcare and Philosophy (NLD) **5674**
Medieval and Renaissance Drama in England (USA) **8473**
Medieval Archaeology (GBR) **405**
Medieval Encounters (NLD) **7726**
Mediterranean Historical Review (GBR) **4323**
Mediterranean Politics (GBR) **7252**
Mediterranean Quarterly (USA) **7252**
Medium Aevum (GBR) **5332**
MedSurg Nursing (USA) **6252**
Meetings and Conventions (USA) **6281**
Melbourne Journal of International Law (AUS) **4935**
Melbourne Journal of Politics (AUS) **7154**
Melbourne University Law Review (AUS) **4732**
Melville Society Extracts (USA) **5332**
Membrane and Separation Technology News (USA) **768**
Membrane Technology (GBR) **2072**
Memory (GBR) **7384**
Memory and Cognition (USA) **7384**
Menninger Clinic. Bulletin (USA) **6159**
Menopause International (GBR) **5998**

Online Service

Link to your serials resources and content with ulrichsweb.com

Menopause News (USA) **8847**
Men's Fitness (USA) **6284**
Men's Health (United States Edition) (USA) **6285**
Mensaje (CHL) **7806**
Mensajero (ESP) **7662**
Mental Health in Family Medicine (GBR) **6160**
Mental Health Practice (GBR) **6160**
Mental Health, Religion & Culture (GBR) **7385**
Mental Health Weekly (USA) **7385**
Mentoring & Tutoring (GBR) **3072**
Mercator Media Forum (GBR) **2385**
Mergers & Acquisitions (New York, 1965) (USA) **1148**
Mergers & Acquisitions Report (USA) **1148**
Meridians (USA) **8901**
Merrill - Palmer Quarterly (USA) **7385**
Metabolic Brain Disease (USA) **5678**
Metabolic Engineering (USA) **750**
Metabolic Syndrome and Related Disorders (USA) **5897**
Metal Center News (USA) **6323**
Metal Finishing (USA) **6323**
Metal Powder Report (GBR) **6340**
Metal Producing & Processing (USA) **6323**
Metal Science and Heat Treatment (USA) **6323**
Metallurgical and Materials Transactions A - Physical Metallurgy and Materials Science (USA) **6324**
Metallurgical and Materials Transactions B - Process Metallurgy and Materials Processing Science (USA) **6324**
Metallurgist (USA) **6325**
Metalworking Insiders' Report (USA) **5457**
Metalworking Production (GBR) **6326**
Metaphilosophy (GBR) **6934**
Metaphor and Symbol (USA) **5151**
Metascience (GBR) **7882**
Meteoritics and Planetary Science (USA) **578**
Meteorologische Zeitschrift (DEU) **6391**
Method & Theory in the Study of Religion (NLD) **7663**
Methodology and Computing in Applied Probability (USA) **5517**
Methods (USA) **738**
Metro (AUS) **6507**
Metro Magazine (USA) **8504**
Metroeconomica (GBR) **1149**
Metrologia (FRA) **6404**
Miami Daily Business Review (USA) **1149**
Michigan Academician (USA) **4465**
Michigan Historical Review (Mt. Pleasant) (USA) **4303**
Michigan Lawyers Weekly (USA) **4733**
Microbes and Infection (FRA) **891**
Microbial Drug Resistance (USA) **5679**
Microbial Ecology in Health & Disease (GBR) **5822**
Microbial Pathogenesis (GBR) **5823**
Microbial Update International (USA) **3656**
Microbiological Research (DEU) **891**
Microbiology (RUS) **891**
Microchemical Journal (USA) **899**
Microcirculation (GBR) **5679**
Microelectronic Engineering (NLD) **3108**
Microelectronics International (GBR) **3109**
Microelectronics Journal (GBR) **3109**
Microelectronics Reliability (GBR) **3109**
Microlithography World (USA) **3109**
Micron (GBR) **899**
Microporous and Mesoporous Materials (NLD) **2138**
Microprocessor Report (USA) **2468**
Microprocessors and Microsystems (NLD) **2572**
Microscope (GBR) **2572**
Microvascular Research (USA) **5795**
Microwave Engineering (GBR) **3109**
Microwave Journal (International Edition) (USA) **3325**
Microwaves & R F (USA) **3325**
Midcontinental Journal of Archaeology (USA) **406**
The Middle East (GBR) **5227**
Middle East Critique (GBR) **555**
Middle East Economic Digest (GBR) **1499**
Middle East Journal (USA) **7252**
Middle East Policy (USA) **7252**
Middle East Quarterly (USA) **7253**
The Middle East Women's Studies Review (USA) **8901**
Middle Eastern Literatures (Online) (GBR) **5333**
Middle Eastern Studies (GBR) **4323**
Midstream (USA) **7727**
Midwest Contractor Magazine (USA) **1024**
Midwest Quarterly (USA) **4465**
Midwest Real Estate News (USA) **7599**
Midwest Studies in Philosophy (USA) **6934**
Midwifery Today (USA) **5998**
The Milbank Quarterly (USA) **7154**
Military & Aerospace Electronics (USA) **66**
The Military Balance (Year) (GBR) **6435**
Military History (USA) **4303**
Military Intelligence (USA) **6435**
Military Medicine (USA) **5679**
Military News Agency (RUS) **6436**
Military Police (USA) **6436**
Military Psychology (USA) **7385**
Military Review (English Edition) (USA) **6436**
Military Robotics Newsletter (USA) **2586**
Millennium (GBR) **7253**
Millimeter (USA) **6507**
Milling & Baking News (USA) **3674**
Milton Quarterly (USA) **5334**
Mind (GBR) **6934**
Mind & Language (GBR) **6934**
Mind and Matter (GBR) **7985**
Mind, Culture, and Activity (USA) **7986**
Minds and Machines (NLD) **2454**
Mineral Processing and Extractive Metallurgy Review (USA) **6326**
Mineralogical Magazine (GBR) **6471**
The Mineralogical Record (USA) **4340**
Minerals & Energy (GBR) **1601**
Minerals Engineering (GBR) **6471**
Minerva (NLD) **7882**
Minerva Journal of Women and War (USA) **6437**
Mini - Reviews in Medicinal Chemistry (NLD) **2073**
Mini - Reviews in Organic Chemistry (NLD) **2127**
Minimally Invasive Therapy and Allied Technologies (GBR) **5679**
Mining Journal (GBR) **6473**
Mining Magazine (GBR) **6473**
Minnesota Lawyer (USA) **4734**
Minority Health Today (USA) **5680**
Minority Nurse Newsletter (USA) **5970**
Mission Studies (NLD) **7664**
Mississippi (USA) **3982**
Mississippi Academy of Science. Journal (USA) **7882**
Mississippi Business Journal (USA) **1964**
The Mississippi Quarterly (USA) **5227**
Missouri Academy of Science. Transactions (USA) **7882**
Missouri Lawyers Weekly (USA) **4735**
Mitigation and Adaptation Strategies for Global Change (NLD) **3453**
Mitochondrial D N A (GBR) **738**
Mitochondrion (NLD) **893**
Mnemosyne (NLD) **2237**
Mobile Communications Europe (GBR) **2333**
Mobile Media (GBR) **2564**
Mobile Networks and Applications (NLD) **2501**
Model Railroader (USA) **4341**
Modern Age (USA) **5228**
Modern and Contemporary France (GBR) **4245**
Modern Applications News (USA) **6326**
Modern Brewery Age (USA) **607**
Modern Casting (USA) **6326**
Modern China (USA) **4186**
Modern Drama (CAN) **5335**
Modern Healthcare (USA) **4107**
Modern Italy (GBR) **4245**
Modern Jeweler (USA) **4568**
Modern Judaism (GBR) **3551**
Modern Language Journal (USA) **5151**
Modern Language Quarterly (USA) **5335**
Modern Language Review (GBR) **5335**
The Modern Law Review (GBR) **4735**
Modern Machine Shop (USA) **5457**
Modern Materials Handling (USA) **5457**
Modern Philology (USA) **5152**
Modern Physician (USA) **5680**
Modern Power Systems (GBR) **3142**
Modern Theology (GBR) **7664**
Modern Tire Dealer (USA) **7825**
The Modernism Magazine (USA) **450**
Molecular and Biochemical Parasitology (NLD) **738**
Molecular and Cellular Biochemistry (USA) **738**
Molecular and Cellular Endocrinology (IRL) **5897**
Molecular and Cellular Neuroscience (USA) **6161**
Molecular and Cellular Probes (GBR) **5909**
Molecular Aspects of Medicine (GBR) **5680**
Molecular Biology (RUS) **739**
Molecular Biology and Evolution (USA) **689**
Molecular Biology Reports (NLD) **739**
Molecular Breeding (NLD) **801**
Molecular Cell (USA) **835**
Molecular Crystals and Liquid Crystals (CHE) **2111**
Molecular Diversity (NLD) **7068**
Molecular Ecology (GBR) **893**
Molecular Ecology Resources (GBR) **893**
Molecular Genetics and Metabolism (USA) **739**
Molecular Human Reproduction (GBR) **5999**
Molecular Imaging (CAN) **835**
Molecular Imaging and Biology (NLD) **6203**
Molecular Immunology (GBR) **739**
Molecular Membrane Biology (GBR) **739**
Molecular Microbiology (GBR) **893**
Molecular Neurobiology (USA) **739**
Molecular Phylogenetics and Evolution (USA) **875**
Molecular Physics (GBR) **2138**
Molecular Plant Pathology (GBR) **802**
Molecular Simulation (CHE) **2073**
Molecular Therapy (GBR) **6028**
Molluscan Research (NZL) **955**
Momentum (New York) (USA) **6161**
Money Laundering Alert (USA) **2660**
Money Management (AUS) **1368**
Money Management (GBR) **1368**
Money Management Executive (USA) **1640**
Money Management Letter (USA) **1640**
Money Marketing (GBR) **1368**
Monist (USA) **6935**
Montalban (VEN) **4465**
Montana Business Quarterly (USA) **1150**
Monte Carlo Methods and Applications (DEU) **5555**
Monthly Climatic Data for the World (USA) **6391**
Monthly Prescribing Reference (USA) **6862**
Monthly Review (USA) **7155**
Mortality (GBR) **7532**
Mortgage Banking (USA) **1369**
Mortgage Servicing News (USA) **1369**
Mortgage Technology (USA) **7600**
Mosaic (Winnipeg, 1967) (CAN) **5336**
Mother Earth News (USA) **3982**
Mothering (USA) **8847**
MotherJones.com (USA) *see* Mother Jones. **5228**
Motion System Design (USA) **3390**
Motivation and Emotion (USA) **7386**
Motor Age (USA) **8592**
Motor Boating (USA) **8278**
Motor Transport (GBR) **8673**
Motor Trend (USA) **8593**
Motor Trend's Truck Trend (USA) **8593**
Motorcyclist (USA) **8263**
MotorHome (USA) **8323**
Mountain Bike (USA) **8265**
MoXie (Berkeley) (USA) **8876**
Mpls. - Saint Paul Magazine (USA) **3982**
Multi-Housing News (USA) **1025**
Multibody System Dynamics (NLD) **7061**
Multichannel Merchant (USA) **30**
Multichannel News (USA) **2385**
Multicultural Education (USA) **3073**
Multicultural Perspectives (USA) **3073**
Multidimensional Systems and Signal Processing (USA) **2524**
MultiMedia & Internet@Schools (USA) **2950**
Multimedia Information & Technology (GBR) **5032**
Multimedia Tools and Applications (NLD) **2488**
Multinational Monitor (USA) **1578**
Multiple Sclerosis (GBR) **6162**
Multivariate Behavioral Research (USA) **7386**
Municipal Finance Journal (USA) **1935**
Mural (MEX) **3909**
Muscle & Fitness (USA) **6993**
Museum International (English Edition) (GBR) **6531**
Museum Management and Curatorship (GBR) **6531**
Music Analysis (GBR) **6589**
Music and Letters (GBR) **6589**
Music Education Research (GBR) **6590**
Music Educators Journal (USA) **6590**
Music Library Association. Notes (USA) **5033**
Music Theory Spectrum (USA) **6592**
The Music Trades (USA) **6592**
Music Week (GBR) **6592**
The Musical Quarterly (USA) **6594**
Muslim World (USA) **7715**
Mustang Monthly (USA) **8594**
Mutagenesis (GBR) **875**
Mutation Research - Genetic Toxicology and Environmental Mutagenesis (NLD) **875**
Mutation Research - Reviews (NLD) **876**
Mycopathologia (NLD) **803**
Mycoses (DEU) **5681**
Mythlore (USA) **5445**
N A C L A Report on the Americas (USA) **7253**
N A F T A Report (USA) **2018**
N B E R Reporter OnLine (USA) *see* N B E R Reporter. **1546**
N C A H F Newsletter (USA) **7532**
N D T & E International (GBR) **3355**
N E A News (FRA) **3171**
N E A Today (USA) **2888**
N M A Online (GBR) *see* New Media Age. **2335**
N P A (USA) **1297**
N W S A Journal (USA) **8901**
N Z Business (NZL) **1151**
N Z Marketing Magazine (NZL) **1835**
Nan Nu (NLD) **557**
NanoBioTechnology (USA) **768**
Nanoparticle News (USA) **7027**
Nanoscale & Microscale Thermophysical Engineering (Online) (USA) **7056**
Nanotechnology (GBR) **7027**
Narrative (USA) **5338**
Narrative Inquiry (NLD) **5338**
Nashim (ISR) **8901**
Nashville Business and Lifestyles (USA) **1152**
The Nation (USA) **5229**
National Cancer Institute. Journal (Online) (GBR) **6028**
National Catholic Reporter (USA) **7808**
National Civic Review (USA) **7499**
National Committee on Planned Giving. Conference Proceedings (USA) **8056**
National Defense (USA) **6438**
National Driller (USA) **8829**
National Fisherman (USA) **3602**
National Floor Trends (USA) **4547**
National Geographic Adventure (USA) **8323**
National Geographic Espanol (ESP) **4020**
National Geographic Explorer (USA) **4020**
National Geographic Kids (USA) **4021**
National Geographic Online (USA) *see* National Geographic. **4020**
National Geographic Traveler (USA) **8740**
National Hog Farmer (USA) **294**
National Identities (GBR) **7156**
National Institute Economic Review (GBR) **1152**
National Institute of Standards and Technology. Journal of Research (USA) **6405**
The National Interest (USA) **7254**
National Jeweler (USA) **4568**
National Journal (USA) **7156**
The National Law Journal (USA) **4739**
National Mortgage News Daily (USA) *see* National Mortgage News. **1370**
National Observer (AUS) **7254**
National Parks (USA) **4981**
National Pastime (USA) **8239**
National Petroleum News (USA) **6779**
National Real Estate Investor (USA) **7601**
National Review (USA) **7156**
National Right to Life News (USA) **8057**
National Tax Journal (USA) **1936**
National Underwriter. Life & Health (USA) **4516**
National Underwriter. P & C (USA) **4516**
National Voter (USA) **7156**
National Weather Digest (USA) **6392**
National Wildlife (USA) **2620**
National Wildlife (World Edition) (USA) **2620**
National Women's Health Report (USA) **8847**
Nationalism & Ethnic Politics (GBR) **7254**
Nationalities Papers (GBR) **7987**
Nations and Nationalism (GBR) **7157**
Nation's Cities Weekly (USA) **7499**
Nation's Restaurant News (USA) **4394**
Native American Connections (USA) **4304**
Native Plants Journal (USA) **804**
Natural Computing (NLD) **2432**
Natural Foods Merchandiser (USA) **1835**
Natural Gas Information (FRA) **6779**
Natural Gas Week (USA) **6780**
Natural Hazards (NLD) **2713**
Natural Health (USA) **313**
Natural History (USA) **7888**
Natural Language and Linguistic Theory (NLD) **5154**
Natural Language Semantics (NLD) **5154**
Natural Life (CAN) **3813**
Natural Product Research (CHE) **2074**
Natural Resources Forum (GBR) **4021**
Natural Resources Research (USA) **6474**
Nature Canada (CAN) **2621**
Natures - Sciences - Societes (FRA) **2714**
Naval Aviation News (USA) **67**
Naval Engineers Journal (USA) **3212**
Naval War College Review (USA) **6438**
Navy Supply Corps Newsletter (USA) **6439**
Nebraska Academy of Sciences and Affiliated Societies. Transactions (USA) **7891**
Negotiation Journal (USA) **7254**
Nematology (NLD) **958**
Neohelicon (HUN) **5339**
Neophilologus (NLD) **5339**
NeoPlasia (USA) **6029**
Nephrology (AUS) **6272**
Nephrology, Dialysis, Transplantation (GBR) **6272**
Nephrology Nursing Journal (USA) **5971**
Netherlands Journal of Geosciences (NLD) **2757**
Netherlands Journal of Medicine (NLD) **5947**
Netnomics (NLD) **2501**
Network (London, 1990) (GBR) **6163**
Network Briefing (GBR) **2370**
Network News (Bluffton) (USA) **7768**
Network Security (GBR) **2501**
Network World (USA) **2502**
Networks and Spatial Economics (USA) **2518**
Neues Jahrbuch fuer Mineralogie. Abhandlungen (DEU) **6474**
Neural Computation (USA) **2455**
Neural Networks (GBR) **2455**
Neural Processing Letters (USA) **2455**
Neuro-Oncology (USA) **6029**
Neuro-Ophthalmology (GBR) **6163**
Neurobiology of Aging (USA) **925**
Neurobiology of Disease (USA) **6164**
Neurobiology of Learning and Memory (USA) **6164**
Neurocase (GBR) **6164**
Neurochemical Research (USA) **6164**
Neurochemistry International (GBR) **6164**
Neurocomputing (NLD) **2455**
Neurogastroenterology and Motility Online (GBR) **5929**
NeuroImage (USA) **6165**
NeuroInformatics (USA) **925**
Neurologic Clinics (USA) **6165**
Neurological Research (GBR) **6165**
Neurology Alert (USA) **6166**
Neurology India (IND) **6166**
Neurology, Neurophysiology and Neuroscience (Online) (USA) **6166**
Neuromodulation (USA) **6166**
NeuroMolecular Medicine (USA) **6167**
Neuromuscular Disorders (GBR) **6167**
Neuron (USA) **6167**
Neuropathology (AUS) **6167**
Neuropathology and Applied Neurobiology (GBR) **6167**
Neuropharmacology (GBR) **6863**
Neurophysiologie Clinique (FRA) **6167**
Neurophysiology (USA) **6167**
Neuropsychiatrie de l'Enfance et de l'Adolescence (FRA) **6097**
Neuropsychologia (GBR) **6168**
Neuropsychological Rehabilitation (GBR) **6168**
Neuropsychology, Development and Cognition. Section A: Journal of Clinical and Experimental Neuropsychology (NLD) **7387**
Neuropsychology, Development and Cognition. Section B: Aging, Neuropsychology and Cognition (GBR) **7387**
Neuropsychology, Development, and Cognition. Section C: Child Neuropsychology (NLD) **7387**
Neuropsychology, Development and Cognition. Section D: The Clinical Neuropsychologist (GBR) **7387**
Neuropsychology Review (USA) **6168**
Neuropsychopharmacology (USA) **6168**
NeuroRehabilitation (NLD) **6168**
Neurorehabilitation and Neural Repair (USA) **6168**
Neuroscience (GBR) **6169**
Neuroscience and Behavioral Physiology (USA) **6169**
Neuroscience & Biobehavioral Reviews (GBR) **6169**
Neuroscience Letters (IRL) **6169**
Neuroscience Research (IRL) **6169**
The Neuroscientist (USA) **6169**
NeuroToxicology (NLD) **6170**
Neurotoxicology and Teratology (USA) **6170**
Neutron News (USA) **7069**
New African (GBR) **1602**
The New American (Appleton) (USA) **7157**

Link to your serials resources and content with ulrichsweb.com

New Astronomy (NLD) 578
New Astronomy Reviews (GBR) 578
New Biotechnology (NLD) 769
New Blackfriars (GBR) 7809
New Coin Poetry (ZAF) 5427
New Criterion (USA) 5229
New England Construction (USA) 1026
New Equipment Digest (USA) 8433
New Forests (NLD) 3698
New Formations (GBR) 5229
New Genetics and Society (GBR) 876
New Hampshire Business Review (USA) 1431
New Ideas in Psychology (GBR) 7387
New Internationalist (GBR) 7255
New Jersey Academy of Science. Bulletin (USA) 7891
New Jersey Law Journal (USA) 4743
New Labor Forum (USA) 4599
New Library World (GBR) 5035
New Literary History (USA) 5340
New Materials Asia (GBR) 3355
New Media Creative (GBR) 2335
New Media Investor (GBR) 1642
New Media Markets (GBR) 2386
New Moon Girls (USA) 2204
New Orleans CityBusiness (USA) 1964
New Perspectives Quarterly (USA) 7158
New Phytologist (GBR) 804
New Political Economy (GBR) 1547
New Political Science (GBR) 7158
New Products Online (USA) 3658
The New Republic (USA) 5230
The New Review of Academic Librarianship (GBR) 5035
The New Review of Children's Literature and Librarianship (GBR) 5341
The New Review of Film and Television Studies (GBR) 2386
New Review of Hypermedia and Multimedia (GBR) 2488
The New Review of Information Networking (GBR) 2502
New Scientist: Planet Science (GBR) *see* New Scientist. 7891
New Scientist: Planet Science (GBR) *see* New Scientist on CD-ROM. 7892
New Statesman (GBR) 5230
New T V Strategies (GBR) 2386
New Technology, Work & Employment (GBR) 1699
New York Diamonds (USA) 4568
New York Law Journal (USA) 4745
The New York State Conservationist (USA) 2622
New York Times Book Review (USA) 7568
New York Times Magazine (USA) 3983
The New York Times Upfront (Student Edition) (USA) 2205
The New Yorker (USA) 5230
New Zealand Economic Papers (AUS) 1153
New Zealand Herald (NZL) 3918
New Zealand International Review (NZL) 7255
New Zealand Journal of Psychology (NZL) 7388
New Zealand Management (NZL) 1781
New Zealand Veterinary Journal (NZL) 8803
News of the World (GBR) 3869
NewsInc. (USA) 7568
Newsletter on Newsletters (USA) 4581
Newsletters on Stratigraphy (DEU) 2759
Newspaper Research Journal (USA) 4581
Newsweek (USA) 3983
Newsweek International (GBR) 3869
Nexos (MEX) 7989
Nicotine & Tobacco Research (GBR) 8486
Nieman Reports (USA) 4581
Nine (USA) 8240
Nineteenth-Century Contexts (GBR) 5341
Nineteenth Century French Studies (USA) 5342
Nineteenth-Century Literature (Berkeley) (USA) 5342
Nitric Oxide: Biology and Chemistry (USA) 741
Nitron + Syngas (GBR) 243
Nivedini (LKA) 8901
Noise & Health (IND) 6083
Noise & Vibration Worldwide (GBR) 7089
Noise Notes (GBR) 7089
Nomadias (CHL) 7989
Nomadic Peoples (GBR) 350
Nondestructive Testing and Evaluation (GBR) 3355
Nonlinear Analysis: Real World Applications (GBR) 5520
Nonlinear Analysis: Theory, Methods & Applications (GBR) 3212
Nonlinear Dynamics (NLD) 3391
Nonlinear Dynamics, Psychology, and Life Sciences (USA) 7388
Nonlinear Optics, Quantum Optics (CHE) 7081
Nonlinear Oscillations (Online) (USA) 5521
Nonlinearity (GBR) 5521
Nonprofit Times (USA) 1781
Nonwovens Industry (USA) 8455
Nora (NOR) 8901
Nordic Journal of Linguistics (GBR) 5155
Nordic Journal of Psychiatry (GBR) 6171
Norges Bank. Economic Bulletin (NOR) 1501
Norsk Geografisk Tidsskrift (NOR) 4022
Norsk Geologisk Tidsskrift (NOR) 2759
The North American Journal of Economics and Finance (GBR) 1502
The North American Review (USA) 5230
North Carolina Lawyers Weekly (USA) 4748
North Dakota Academy of Science. Proceedings (USA) 7893
North Sea Letter (GBR) 6781
North Sea Rig Forecast (GBR) 3143
Northern History (GBR) 4249
Northern Journal of Applied Forestry (USA) 3698
The Northern Miner (CAN) 6475
Northern Ontario Business (CAN) 1155
Northern Review (CAN) 4467
Northwest Public Power Association. Bulletin (USA) 3143
Norwegian Archaeological Review (NOR) 408
Notes and Abstracts in American and International Education (USA) 2934
Notes and Queries (GBR) 5343
Nous (USA) 6937
Nova Hedwigia (DEU) 806
Nova Religio (USA) 7739
Novum Testamentum (NLD) 7666
Nuclear Data Sheets (USA) 3171
Nuclear Engineering and Design (CHE) 3355
Nuclear Engineering International (GBR) 3171
Nuclear Instruments & Methods in Physics Research. Section A: Accelerators, Spectrometers, Detectors, and Associated Equipment (NLD) 7069
Nuclear Instruments & Methods in Physics Research. Section B: Beam Interactions with Materials and Atoms (Online) (NLD) *see* Nuclear Instruments & Methods in Physics Research. Section B: Beam Interactions with Materials and Atoms. 7069
Nuclear Medicine and Biology (USA) 6204
Nuclear Physics, Section A (NLD) 7069
Nuclear Physics, Section B (NLD) 7070
Nuclear Physics, Section B, Proceedings Supplements (NLD) 7070
Nucleic Acids Research (GBR) 741
Nucleosides, Nucleotides and Nucleic Acids (USA) 741
Numen (NLD) 7667
Numerical Algorithms (NLD) 5522
Numerical Heat Transfer Part A: Applications (USA) 3391
Numerical Heat Transfer Part B: Fundamentals (USA) 3392
Nurse Education Today (GBR) 5971
Nurse Researcher (GBR) 5972
Nursing (Year) (USA) 5972
Nursing Administration Quarterly (USA) 5973
Nursing and Health Sciences (AUS) 5973
Nursing Economics (USA) 5973
Nursing Education Perspectives (USA) 5973
Nursing Ethics (GBR) 5973
Nursing Forum (USA) 5973
Nursing in Critical Care (GBR) 5974
Nursing Inquiry (AUS) 5974
Nursing Law's Regan Report (USA) 5974
Nursing Management (GBR) 5974
Nursing Older People (GBR) 4052
Nursing Philosophy (GBR) 5975
Nursing Science Quarterly (USA) 5975
Nursing Standard (GBR) 5975
Nutraceuticals International (GBR) 6864
Nutraceuticals World (USA) 6664
Nutrient Cycling in Agroecosystems (NLD) 244
Nutrition (USA) 6665
Nutrition Action Health Letter (USA) 6665
Nutrition and Cancer (USA) 6665
Nutrition and Dietetics (AUS) 6665
Nutrition & Food Science (GBR) 6665
Nutrition Bulletin (GBR) 6665
Nutrition Clinique et Metabolisme (FRA) 5898
Nutrition Forum (USA) 6665
Nutrition Health Review (USA) 6666
Nutrition Research (USA) 6666
Nutrition Research Newsletter (USA) 6666
Nutrition Reviews (USA) 6666
Nutrition Society. Proceedings (GBR) 6667
Nutrition Today (USA) 6667
Nutritional Neuroscience (Online) (GBR) 6171
O C D E. Etudes Economiques (FRA) 1502
O C L C Systems & Services (GBR) 5037
O E C D Agriculture Statistics (FRA) 184
O E C D Banking Statistics (FRA) 1256
O E C D Economic Outlook: Statistics and Projections (FRA) 1256
O E C D Economic Surveys: Austria (FRA) 1503
O E C D Economic Surveys: Belgium (FRA) 1503
O E C D Economic Surveys: Denmark (FRA) 1503
O E C D Economic Surveys: Germany (FRA) 1503
O E C D Economic Surveys: Greece (FRA) 1503
O E C D Economic Surveys: Iceland (FRA) 1503
O E C D Economic Surveys: Spain (FRA) 1504
O E C D Economic Surveys: Switzerland (FRA) 1504
O E C D Economic Surveys: Turkey (FRA) 1504
O E C D Economic Surveys: United States (FRA) 1504
O E C D Employment and Labour Market Statistics (FRA) 1256
O E C D International Trade by Commodities Statistics (FRA) 1257
O E C D Journal on Development (FRA) 1602
O E C D Main Science and Technology Indicators (FRA) 8433
O E C D Observer (FRA) 1504
O E M Off-Highway (USA) 213
O E M Online (GBR) *see* Occupational and Environmental Medicine. 6682
O M I C S: A Journal of Integrative Biology (USA) 876
O M T. Barometro del Turismo Mundial (ESP) 8780
O P E C Energy Review (GBR) 6782
O R - M S Today (USA) 7894
O T C LatinA (GBR) 6865
O T C News and Market Report (GBR) 6865
O: The Oprah Magazine (USA) 8878
Ob/Gyn Clinical Alert (USA) 6000
Ob-Gyn News (USA) 6000
Obesity, Fitness, and Wellness Week (USA) 6994
Obesity Reviews (GBR) 6667
Obesity Surgery (USA) 6254
The Observer (GBR) 3869
Obstetrics and Gynecology (USA) 6001
Occupational Ergonomics (USA) 6682
Occupational Health (GBR) 5976
Occupational Health Management (USA) 6683
Occupational Medicine (GBR) 6683
Occupational Outlook Quarterly (USA) 6707
Ocean & Coastal Management (GBR) 2814
Ocean Development and International Law (USA) 2814
Ocean Engineering (GBR) 2814
Ocean Modelling (USA) 2814
Oceania (AUS) 350
Oceanic Linguistics (USA) 5157
Oceanographic Literature Review (GBR) 2720
Oceanus (USA) 2815
Octane Week (USA) 6782
October (USA) 509
Ocular Immunology and Inflammation (GBR) 6047
Odyssey (Peru) (USA) 2205
Of Counsel (USA) 4751
Off Our Backs (USA) 8902
Office Nurse (USA) 5976
Office Products International (GBR) 1853
Office Solutions (USA) 1853
The Officer (USA) 6440
Official Board Markets (USA) 6712
Offshore (Tulsa) (USA) 6782
The Ohio Journal of Science (USA) 7895
Oikos (DNK) 3458
Oil and Gas Investor (USA) 6783
Oil and Gas Investor This Week (USA) 6783
Oil and Gas Investor's A & D Watch (USA) 6783
Oil & Gas Journal (USA) 6783
Oil Daily (Online) (USA) 6784
Oil Express (USA) 6784
Oil, Gas & Petrochem Equipment (USA) 6784
Oil Information (FRA) 6784
Oil Spill Intelligence Report (USA) 3490
Oils & Fats International (GBR) 3658
Oligonucleotides (USA) 877
Omega (GBR) 1782
On Wall Street (USA) 1643
Oncology (USA) 6030
Oncology News International (USA) 6030
Oncology Research (USA) 6031
One Country (USA) 3458
One Up (GBR) 7667
OnEarth (USA) 3458
Onfilm (NZL) 6509
Online (USA) 2565
Online Hotline News Service - Archive Edition (USA) 2565
Online Information Review (GBR) 5038
Online Libraries and Microcomputers (USA) 5063
Open Economies Review (NLD) 1547
Open Learning (GBR) 2997
Open Systems and Information Dynamics (NLD) 2524
Opera - Canada (CAN) 6601
Opera News (USA) 6602
The Opera Quarterly (GBR) 6602
Operational Research Society. Journal (GBR) 2433
Operations Research (USA) 2433
Operations Research Letters (NLD) 7896
Operations Research Society of Japan. Journal (JPN) 1783
Ophthalmic and Physiological Optics (GBR) 6047
Ophthalmic Epidemiology (GBR) 6047
Ophthalmic Genetics (GBR) 6047
Ophthalmology (USA) 6048
Ophthalmology Times (USA) 6048
Oproelectronics Report (Online) (USA) *E-mail edition.* 7081
Optical and Quantum Electronics (NLD) 7081
Optical Fiber Technology (USA) 7082
Optical Materials (NLD) 7082
Optician (GBR) 6049
Optics & Laser Technology (GBR) 7082
Optics and Lasers in Engineering (GBR) 7082
Optics Communications (NLD) 7083
Optik (DEU) 7083
Optimization (CHE) 5523
Optimization and Engineering (USA) 3214
Optimization Methods and Software (GBR) 5555
Optimum Online (CAN) 7458
Option Bio (FRA) 696
Oral Diseases (GBR) 5859
Oral History Review (USA) 4155
Oral Microbiology and Immunology (DNK) 894
Oral Oncology Extra (GBR) *see* Oral Oncology. 6032
Orange County Business Journal (USA) 1505
Orbis (Kidlington) (GBR) 7256
Orbis Litterarum (DNK) 5346
Orbit (GBR) 6050
Order (NLD) 5523
Ore Geology Reviews (NLD) 2761
Oregon Business Magazine (USA) 1157
Oregon Historical Quarterly (USA) 4307
Organic Electronics (NLD) 3327
Organic Gardening (USA) 3746
Organic Geochemistry (GBR) 2128
Organisms Diversity & Evolution (DEU) 696
Organization Science (USA) 1784
Organization Studies (DEU) 7990
Organizational Behavior and Human Decision Processes (USA) 1784
Organizational Dynamics (USA) 1784
The Original Internist (USA) 5806
Origination News (USA) 1373
Origins of Life and Evolution of Biospheres (NLD) 696
Orlando Business Journal (USA) 1157
Orthodontics & Craniofacial Research (DNK) 5860
Oryx (GBR) 959
Osiris (Chicago) (USA) 7896
Ostrich (ZAF) 913
Outdoor Life (USA) 8327
Outdoor Power Equipment (USA) 3746
Outlook on Agriculture (GBR) 145
Outlook on Science Policy (GBR) 7896
Outsourced Logistics (USA) 8507
Owner Operator / Company Driver (USA) 8674
Oxford Art Journal (GBR) 510
Oxford Bulletin of Economics and Statistics (GBR) 1157
Oxford Development Studies (GBR) 1603
Oxford Economic Papers (GBR) 1158
Oxford German Studies (GBR) 5347
Oxford Journal of Archaeology (GBR) 410
Oxford Journal of Legal Studies (GBR) 4754
Oxford Review of Economic Policy (GBR) 1158
Oxford Review of Education (GBR) 2894
The Oxfordian (USA) 5428
Oxidation of Metals (USA) 2139
Ozone: Science and Engineering (USA) 3251
P A C E - Process & Control Engineering (AUS) 3251
P A J (USA) 8475
The P C I A Washington Bulletin (USA) 2335
P C Magazine (Online) (USA) 2434
P C Semanal (MEX) 2580
P C World (USA) 2581
P D R Family Guide to Prescription Drugs (USA) 6866
P I M A's Asia Pacific Papermaker (USA) 6735
P J E, Peabody Journal of Education (USA) 2894
P M A Magazine (USA) 6972
P M Engineer (USA) 4124
P M J Online (GBR) *see* Postgraduate Medical Journal. 5698
P M L A (USA) 5347
P M Online (GBR) *see* People Management. 2897
P N (USA) 4078
P O V Magazine (CAN) 2259
P P C J (GBR) 6719
P R News (USA) 31
P R O (Fort Atkinson) (USA) 3746
P R Week (UK Edition) (GBR) 32
P R Week (US Edition) (USA) 32
P S (USA) 5458
P S A Journal (USA) 6972
P S: Political Science & Politics (GBR) 7163
Pacific Affairs (CAN) 7257
Pacific-Basin Finance Journal (NLD) 1373
Pacific Builder and Engineer (USA) 1029
Pacific Business News (USA) 1158
Pacific Economic Review (AUS) 1510
Pacific Historical Review (USA) 4307
Pacific Philosophical Quarterly (GBR) 6938
The Pacific Review (GBR) 7257
Pacific Science (USA) 7896
Pacific Shipper (USA) 8656
Pacing and Clinical Electrophysiology (USA) 5797
PackagePrinting (USA) 7325
Packaging Digest (USA) 6713
Packaging Strategies (USA) 6713
Packaging Technology and Engineering (Online) (USA) 6713
Packaging Technology and Science (GBR) 6713
Packaging Today (GBR) 6714
Packaging, Transport, Storage & Security of Radioactive Material (GBR) 8508
Paedagogica Historica (GBR) 2895
Paediatric Anaesthesia Online (GBR) 5773
Paediatric and Perinatal Epidemiology (Online) (GBR) 6098
Paediatric Drugs (NZL) 6866
Paediatric Nursing (GBR) 5977
Paediatrics and Child Health (GBR) 6098
Pain (NLD) 6172
Pain & Central Nervous System Week (USA) 6172
The Pain Clinic (GBR) 5773
Pain Medicine (USA) 6172
Pain Practice (USA) 6173
Pain Reviews (GBR) 5692
Paint & Coatings Industry (USA) 6719
Paint and Resin Times (GBR) 6719
Palabra (Saltillo) (MEX) 3910
Palaeogeography, Palaeoclimatology, Palaeoecology (NLD) 6727
Palaeontology (GBR) 6728
Palaestra (USA) 3045
Palestine Exploration Quarterly (GBR) 410
Palliative Medicine (GBR) 5693
Paper, Film and Foil Converter (USA) 6714
Paperboard Packaging (USA) 6714
Papers: Explorations into Children's Literature (AUS) 5348
Papers on Language and Literature (USA) 5348
Parabola (USA) 3621
Parachute (CAN) 511
Parallax (GBR) 5349
Parallel Computing (NLD) 2468
Parameters (Carlisle) (USA) 6441

Online Service

Link to your serials resources and content with ulrichsweb.com

Progress in Biophysics & Molecular Biology (GBR) 754
Progress in Crystal Growth and Characterization of Materials (GBR) 2112
Progress in Development Studies (IND) 8126
Progress in Energy and Combustion Science (GBR) 3145
Progress in Human Geography (GBR) 4025
Progress in Lipid Research (GBR) 2130
Progress in Materials Science (GBR) 3356
Progress in Natural Science (USA) 7900
Progress in Neuro-Psychopharmacology & Biological Psychiatry (USA) 6876
Progress in Neurobiology (GBR) 927
Progress in Nuclear Energy (USA) 3173
Progress in Nuclear Magnetic Resonance Spectroscopy (NLD) 2104
Progress in Oceanography (GBR) 2816
Progress in Organic Coatings (NLD) 6720
Progress in Orthodontics Online (DNK) 5862
Progress in Palliative Care (GBR) 6032
Progress in Particle and Nuclear Physics (GBR) 7071
Progress in Pediatric Cardiology (IRL) 5798
Progress in Physical Geography (GBR) 4025
Progress in Physics (USA) 7036
Progress in Planning (GBR) 4424
Progress in Polymer Science (GBR) 2130
Progress in Quantum Electronics (GBR) 3111
Progress in Reaction Kinetics and Mechanism (GBR) 2139
Progress in Retinal and Eye Research (GBR) 6050
Progress in Solid State Chemistry (GBR) 2140
Progress in Surface Science (GBR) 7036
The Progressive (Madison) (USA) 7173
Progressive Grocer (New York, 2002) (USA) 3681
Prohistoria (ARG) 4309
Project Finance and Infrastructure Finance (GBR) 1376
Prometheus (Abingdon) (GBR) 2336
Promo (USA) 33
Promotions and Incentives (GBR) 1838
Prooftexts (USA) 5354
Property Management (GBR) 7605
Property Week (GBR) 7605
ProSales (USA) 1030
Prose Studies (GBR) 5354
Prospects (NLD) 2900
Prostaglandins & Other Lipid Mediators (USA) 5899
Protection of Metals and Physical Chemistry of Surfaces (RUS) 6330
Protein and Peptide Letters (NLD) 742
Protein Engineering Design and Selection (Online) (GBR) 743
Protein Expression and Purification (USA) 743
The Protein Journal (USA) 743
Protist (DEU) 698
Providence Business News (USA) 1162
Psicologia desde el Caribe (COL) 7393
Psicologica (ESP) 7393
Psychiatric Quarterly (USA) 6176
Psychiatric Times (USA) 6176
Psychiatry (New York) (USA) 6177
Psychiatry and Clinical Neurosciences (AUS) 6177
Psychiatry Psychology and Law (GBR) 6177
Psychiatry Research (IRL) 6178
Psychiatry Research: Neuroimaging (IRL) 6178
Psychoanalysis, Culture & Society (GBR) 7395
Psychoanalytic Dialogues (USA) 7395
Psychoanalytic Inquiry (USA) 7395
Psychoanalytic Psychotherapy (GBR) 7395
The Psychoanalytic Review (USA) 7395
Psychodynamic Practice (Online) (GBR) 6178
Psychologica Belgica (BEL) 7396
Psychological Inquiry (USA) 7396
The Psychological Record (USA) 7396
Psychological Science (GBR) 7397
Psychological Science in the Public Interest (GBR) 7397
Psychology & Health (GBR) 7398
Psychology & Psychotherapy (GBR) 7399
Psychology, Crime and Law (GBR) 7399
Psychology, Health & Medicine (GBR) 7399
Psychology of Sport and Exercise (NLD) 7399
Psychology of Women Quarterly (USA) 7400
Psychology Review (GBR) 7400
Psychology Today (USA) 7400
Psychoneuroendocrinology (GBR) 6178
Psychonomic Bulletin & Review (USA) 7400
Psychopharmacology Educational Update (USA) 6877
Psychopharmacology Update (USA) 6877
Psychophysiology (GBR) 6179
Psychotherapy Research (GBR) 7401
Public Administration (GBR) 7461
Public Administration Review (USA) 7461
Public Broadcasting Report (USA) 2388
Public Budgeting and Finance (USA) 7462
Public Choice (NLD) 1162
Public Culture (USA) 5235
Public Finance Review (USA) 1941
Public Health Nursing (USA) 5979
Public Health Nutrition (GBR) 6668
Public Health Reports (USA) 7537
The Public Historian (USA) 4157
Public Management Review (Online) (GBR) 1787
The Public Manager (USA) 7462
Public Money and Management (GBR) 7462
Public Opinion Quarterly (USA) 7174
Public Organization Review (USA) 1787
Public Personnel Management (USA) 1873
Public Policy Research (Online) (GBR) 1547
Public-Private Finance (GBR) 1377
Public Relations Journal (Online) (USA) 33
Public Relations Quarterly (USA) 33
Public Relations Review (GBR) 33
Public Roads (USA) 3281
Public Understanding of Science (GBR) 7900
Public Utilities Fortnightly (USA) 3510
Public Works (USA) 7501
Publishers Weekly (USA) 7571
Publishing Executive (USA) 7571
Publishing Research Quarterly (USA) 7571
Publius (USA) 7174
Puget Sound Business Journal (USA) 1162
Pulmonary Pharmacology and Therapeutics (GBR) 6218
Pulp & Paper Canada (CAN) 6737
Pulp & Paper International (USA) 6737
Pulse (London, 1959) (GBR) 5700
Pump Industry Analyst (GBR) 5459
Purchasing (Newton) (USA) 1839
Purchasing Management Bulletin (USA) 1839
Q J M (GBR) 5701
Q S H C Online (GBR) *see* Quality and Safety in Health Care. 5701
Quadrant (AUS) 5235
Quaerendo (NLD) 7571
Quaestiones Mathematicae (ZAF) 5527
Qualified Remodeler (USA) 1031
Qualitative Inquiry (USA) 7994
Qualitative Market Research (GBR) 1839
Qualitative Research in Psychology (GBR) 7402
Qualitative Sociology (USA) 8127
Quality (New York) (USA) 7291
Quality and Quantity (NLD) 8150
Quality Assurance in Education (GBR) 2901
Quality Engineering (USA) 3216
Quality in Higher Education (GBR) 2999
Quality in Primary Care (Online) (GBR) 5701
Quality Magazine (USA) 1788
Quality Management in Health Care (USA) 4110
Quality of Life Research (NLD) 5702
Quantitative Finance (GBR) 1377
Quantitative Marketing and Economics (USA) 1163
Quantum Information Processing (USA) 2456
The Quarterly Journal of Economics (USA) 1547
Quarterly Journal of Engineering Geology and Hydrogeology (GBR) 3281
Quarterly Journal of Finance and Accounting (USA) 1163
Quarterly Journal of Mathematics (GBR) 5527
Quarterly Journal of Mechanics and Applied Mathematics (GBR) 5527
Quarterly National Accounts (FRA) 1941
The Quarterly Review of Biology (USA) 699
The Quarterly Review of Economics and Finance (GBR) 1163
Quarterly Review of Film and Video (USA) 6510
Quaternary International (GBR) 2763
Quaternary Research (USA) 2763
Quaternary Science Reviews (GBR) 2763
Quebec Studies (USA) 5356
Queen's Quarterly (CAN) 3816
Queueing Systems (NLD) 3328
Quick Frozen Foods International (USA) 3661
Quick Printing (USA) 7327
Quill (Greencastle) (USA) 4582
Quill and Quire (CAN) 7572
R A P R A Review Reports (GBR) 7101
R & D Directions (USA) 6877
R & D Focus Drug News (GBR) 6877
R & D Magazine (USA) 8436
R & D Management (GBR) 1788
R B M News (FRA) 770
R C M Midwives (GBR) 6002
R F Design (USA) 3111
R I B A Journal (GBR) 455
R L A (CHL) 5165
The R M A Journal (USA) 1377
R N Web (USA) *see* R N. 5979
R U S I Journal (GBR) 6442
R V Business (USA) 8219
Rabels Zeitschrift fuer Auslaendisches und Internationales Privatrecht (DEU) 4938
Race & Class (GBR) 3560
Race, Ethnicity and Education (GBR) 2902
Radiance Online (USA) 8881
Radiation Effects and Defects in Solids (CHE) 7071
Radiation Measurements (GBR) 7071
Radiation Physics and Chemistry (GBR) 7071
Radiation Protection Dosimetry (GBR) 7072
Radical History Review (USA) 4157
Radical Teacher (USA) 7175
Radio (USA) 2362
Radiocarbon (USA) 7901
Radiochemistry (RUS) 2140
Radiologic Technology (USA) 6206
Radiophysics and Quantum Electronics (USA) 3112
Radiotherapy & Oncology (IRL) 6207
Railway Age (USA) 8623
Railway Gazette International (GBR) 8623
Railway Track & Structures (USA) 8624
The Ramanujan Journal (NLD) 5527
RAND Journal of Economics (USA) 1164
Random Operators and Stochastic Equations (DEU) 5528
Ranger Rick (USA) 2210
Rapid Prototyping Journal (GBR) 3394
Ratio (GBR) 6946
Ratio Juris (GBR) 4765
Reaction Kinetics and Catalysis Letters (HUN) 2140
Reactions (GBR) 4520
Reactions Weekly (NZL) 6890
Reactive and Functional Polymers (NLD) 3254
Reading and Writing (NLD) 5165
Reading and Writing Quarterly (USA) 3045
Reading Improvement (USA) 3045
Reading Psychology (USA) 2903
Reading Research Quarterly (USA) 2903
The Reading Teacher (USA) 2903
Reading Today (USA) 2903
Real Estate Alert (USA) 7608
Real Estate Economics (USA) 7608
Real Estate Finance (USA) 7608
Real Estate Finance and Investment (USA) 7608
Real Estate Issues (USA) 7609
Real Estate Weekly (USA) 7610
Real Lives (GBR) 973
Real Living with Diabetes (USA) 5899
Real Simple (USA) 8881
Real-Time Systems (USA) 2524
Realtor Magazine (USA) 7610
Reanimation (FRA) 5773
Reason (USA) 5236
Recent Patents on Anti-Cancer Drug Discovery (NLD) 6033
Recent Patents on Anti-Infective Drug Discovery (NLD) 5765
Recent Patents on Cardiovascular Drug Discovery (NLD) 5798
Reclaiming Children and Youth (USA) 7402
The Recorder (San Francisco) (USA) 4767
Records Management Journal (GBR) 1789
Recycling Today (USA) 3511
Redbook (USA) 8882
Redherring.com (USA) *see* The Red Herring (San Francisco). 8436
Redox Report (Online) (GBR) 6878
Reeves Journal (USA) 4125
Reference and Research Book News (USA) 634
Reference and User Services Quarterly (USA) 5042
Reference Services Review (GBR) 5042
Reflections (Cambridge) (USA) 1789
Reflective Practice (GBR) 6947
reforma.com (MEX) *see* Reforma. 3910
Refractories and Industrial Ceramics (USA) 2045
Refrigerated and Frozen Foods (USA) 3662
Refrigerated Transporter (USA) 8675
Refuge (CAN) 7291
Refugee Survey Quarterly (GBR) 7314
Regional & Federal Studies (GBR) 7261
Regional Aviation News (Online) (USA) 8551
Regional Science and Urban Economics (NLD) 4425
Regional Studies (GBR) 4425
Registered Rep (USA) 1647
Regulation (Washington, 1977) (USA) 7176
Regulatory Peptides (NLD) 744
Regulatory Toxicology and Pharmacology (USA) 3500
Rehabilitation Counseling Bulletin (USA) 4069
Reinardus (NLD) 5359
Reinforced Plastics (GBR) 7099
Rejuvenation Research (USA) 4054
Relaciones Internacionales (MEX) 7262
Relations Industrielles (CAN) 1705
Release 2.0 (USA) 2436
Reliability Engineering & System Safety (GBR) 3217
Reliable Computing (NLD) 2436
Religion (GBR) 7674
Religion and the Arts (NLD) 7674
Religion, State and Society (GBR) 7675
Religious Conference Manager (USA) 7675
Religious Education (USA) 7676
Religious Studies (GBR) 7676
Remedial and Special Education (USA) 3046
Remodeling Online (USA) *see* Remodeling. 1032
Remote Sensing of Environment (USA) 4026
Renaissance Quarterly (USA) 5359
Renaissance Studies (GBR) 4158
Renascence (USA) 5359
Renewable Agriculture and Food Systems (Online) (GBR) 150
Renewable & Sustainable Energy Reviews (GBR) 3146
Renewable Energy (GBR) 3146
Renewable Energy Focus (GBR) 3146
Rent Review and Lease Renewal (GBR) 7611
Rental and Staging Systems (USA) 2025
Rental Equipment Register (USA) 1839
Rental Product News (USA) 1902
Repair Shop Product News (USA) 8601
Report on Electronic Commerce (USA) 2566
Report on Medicare Compliance (USA) 4768
Reports on Mathematical Physics (GBR) 7037
Reports on Progress in Physics (GBR) 7037
Reproduction in Domestic Animals Online (DEU) 8805
Reproductive BioMedicine Online (GBR) 6002
Reproductive Health Matters (NLD) 8848
Reproductive Medicine and Biology (JPN) 5703
Reproductive Sciences (USA) 6003
Reproductive Toxicology (USA) 927
Res Publica (NLD) 6947
Research (San Francisco) (USA) 1647
Research Alert (New York) (USA) 1839
Research Centre for German and Austrian Exile Studies. Yearbook (NLD) 4257
Research Evaluation (GBR) 7902
Research in African Literatures (USA) 5360
Research in Dance Education (GBR) 2687
Research in Developmental Disabilities (GBR) 6180
Research in Drama Education (GBR) 8477
Research in Healthcare Financial Management (USA) 4110
Research in Higher Education (USA) 2999
Research in Microbiology (FRA) 895
Research in Nondestructive Evaluation (USA) 3217
Research in Phenomenology (NLD) 6947
Research in Science & Technological Education (GBR) 2904
Research in Science Education (NLD) 2904
Research in Sports Medicine (USA) 6232
Research Initiative / Treatment Action! (USA) 5765
Research on Aging (USA) 4054
Research on Chemical Intermediates (NLD) 2078
Research on Language and Computation (NLD) 5166
Research on Language and Social Interaction (USA) 5166
Research Papers in Education (GBR) 2905
Research Policy (NLD) 7903
Research Practitioner (USA) 5910
Research Quarterly for Exercise and Sport (USA) 6995
Research Technology Management (USA) 1790
Reserve Bank of New Zealand Bulletin (NZL) 1379
Residential Architect (USA) 455
Residential Design and Build (USA) 1033
Residential Systems (USA) 3112
Resource (Niles) (USA) 250
Resource and Energy Economics (NLD) 3146
Resource Links (CAN) 2210
Resources, Conservation and Recycling (NLD) 3511
Resources for Feminist Research (CAN) 8902
Resources Policy (GBR) 3146
Respiratory Physiology & Neurobiology (NLD) 927
Respirology (AUS) 6219
Response Magazine (USA) 34
Restaurant Business (USA) 4396
Restaurant Hospitality (USA) 4397
Restaurants & Institutions (USA) 4397
Restoration Ecology (USA) 3463
Restorative Neurology and Neuroscience (NLD) 6181
Resuscitation (IRL) 6219
Retail Banker International (IRL) 1379
The Retail Digest (GBR) 1903
Retail Finance Strategies (GBR) 1379
Retail Merchandiser (USA) 1840
Retail Traffic (USA) 1841
Retailing Today (USA) 1841
Rethink I T (GBR) 2550
Rethinking History (GBR) 4158
Rethinking Marxism (GBR) 7177
Retirement Income Reporter (USA) 1647
Review (New York, 1968) (USA) 5360
Review of Accounting Studies (USA) 1300
Review of African Political Economy (GBR) 7262
The Review of Austrian Economics (USA) 1548
Review of Automotive Engineering (NLD) 8601
The Review of Black Political Economy (USA) 1165
Review of Business (USA) 1165
Review of Central and East European Law (NLD) 4769
Review of Cognitive Linguistics (NLD) 5166
The Review of Contemporary Fiction (USA) 5360
Review of Derivatives Research (USA) 1379
Review of Development Economics (GBR) 1604
Review of Economic Dynamics (USA) 1514
The Review of Economic Studies (GBR) 1166
The Review of Economics and Statistics (USA) 1166
Review of Economics of the Household (USA) 1166
The Review of Education - Pedagogy - Cultural Studies (USA) 2935
The Review of English Studies (GBR) 5360
Review of European Community and International Environmental Law (GBR) 3463
Review of Finance (Print) (GBR) 1379
Review of Financial Economics (GBR) 1166
The Review of Financial Studies (USA) 1379
Review of Income and Wealth (GBR) 1721
Review of Industrial Organization (NLD) 1548
Review of International Economics (GBR) 1166
Review of International Political Economy (GBR) 1514
The Review of Metaphysics (USA) 6948
Review of Middle East Economics and Finance (Online) (USA) 1166
Review of Optometry (USA) 6051
Review of Palaeobotany and Palynology (NLD) 6730
The Review of Policy Research (USA) 7177
Review of Political Economy (GBR) 7178
The Review of Politics (GBR) 7178
Review of Quantitative Finance and Accounting (USA) 1300
Review of Rabbinic Judaism (NLD) 7728
Review of Radical Political Economics (USA) 1548
Review of Social Economy (GBR) 1166
Review of Urban & Regional Development Studies (GBR) 1604
Reviews in American History (USA) 4310
Reviews in Analgesia (USA) 5773
Reviews in Endocrine & Metabolic Disorders (USA) 5899
Reviews in Environmental Science and Biotechnology (NLD) 770
Reviews in Fish Biology and Fisheries (NLD) 961
Reviews in Fisheries Science (USA) 3605
Reviews in Medical Virology (GBR) 895
Reviews in Religion and Theology (GBR) 7677
Reviews on Recent Clinical Trials (NLD) 5704
Revista C E N I P E C (VEN) 2667
Revista Cartografica (MEX) 4026
Revista Chilena de Humanidades (CHL) 7996

Online Service

Link to your serials resources and content with ulrichsweb.com

Revista Chilena de Literatura (CHL) 5361
Revista de Arqueologia Americana (MEX) 413
Revista de Biologia Tropical (CRI) 701
Revista de Ciencias Sociales (CRI) 7996
Revista de Economia Mundial (ESP) 1515
Revista de Educacion (CRI) 2906
Revista de Filologia y Linguistica (CRI) 5167
Revista de Filosofia (CRI) 6948
Revista de Filosofia (Santiago, 1949) (CHL) 6948
Revista de Historia (CRI) 4310
Revista de Historia de America (MEX) 4310
Revista de Psicologia Social (ESP) 7404
Revista Geofisica (MEX) 2788
Revista Geologica de America Central (CRI) 2764
Revista Internacional del Trabajo (GBR) 1705
Revista Latinoamericana de Estudios Urbano Regionales (CHL) 4425
Revista Panamericana de Salud Publica (USA) 7539
Revolution (London) (GBR) 1421
Revolutionary Russia (GBR) 4257
La Revue de Medecine Interne (FRA) 5948
Revue du Rhumatisme (French Edition) (FRA) 6226
Revue Francaise d'Allergologie (FRA) 5765
Revue Francophone des Laboratoires (FRA) 701
Revue Internationale du Travail (GBR) 1705
Revue Romane (NLD) 5168
Rhetoric Review (USA) 5362
Rheumatology (Online) (GBR) 6227
Rhode Island Lawyers Weekly (USA) 4775
Rider (USA) 8267
Risk Analysis (USA) 5530
Risk & Insurance (USA) 4521
Risk Management (USA) 4521
Risk Management and Insurance Review (USA) 4521
Road & Track Road Gear (Online) (USA) 8602
Roads & Bridges (USA) 3282
Robotics and Autonomous Systems (NLD) 2586
Robotics and Computer-Integrated Manufacturing (GBR) 2586
Rock Products (USA) 1033
Rocks and Minerals (USA) 6478
Roeper Review (USA) 3079
Romance Studies (GBR) 5364
Romanic Review (USA) 5364
Roofing Contractor (USA) 1034
Rotor & Wing (USA) 69
Rotunda (CAN) 515
The Round Table (GBR) 7263
Royal Anthropological Institute. Journal (GBR) 354
Royal Astronomical Society. Monthly Notices (GBR) 580
Royal Australian Historical Society. Journal (AUS) 4194
Royal College of Surgeons of England. Annals (GBR) 6257
Royal College of Surgeons of England. Bulletin (GBR) 6257
Royal Meteorological Society. Quarterly Journal (GBR) 6394
Royal Musical Association. Journal (GBR) 6613
Royal Society of Edinburgh. Proceedings. Section A (Mathematics) (GBR) 5530
Royal Society of Edinburgh. Transactions. Earth and Environmental Science (GBR) 2716
Royal Society of London. Philosophical Transactions. Biological Sciences (GBR) 702
Royal Society of London. Philosophical Transactions. Mathematical, Physical and Engineering Sciences (GBR) 7038
Royal Society of London. Proceedings. Biological Sciences (GBR) 702
Royal Society of London. Proceedings. Mathematical, Physical and Engineering Sciences (GBR) 5530
Royal Society of Medicine. Journal (GBR) 5707
Royal Statistical Society. Journal. Series A: Statistics in Society (GBR) 8397
Royal Statistical Society. Journal. Series B: Statistical Methodology (GBR) 8397
Royal Statistical Society. Journal. Series C: Applied Statistics (GBR) 8397
Rubber & Plastics News (USA) 7826
Rubber World Online (USA) *see* Rubber World. 7827
Runner's World (USA) 8198
Running & FitNews (USA) 6996
Rural Cooperatives (USA) 153
Rural Society (AUS) 8130
Rural Telecommunications (USA) 2371
Russian Academy of Sciences. Biology Bulletin (RUS) 702
Russian Academy of Sciences. Colloid Journal (RUS) 2140
Russian Academy of Sciences. Mathematical Notes (RUS) 5530
Russian Chemical Bulletin (USA) 2079
Russian Journal of Applied Chemistry (RUS) 3255
Russian Journal of Bioorganic Chemistry (RUS) 2130
Russian Journal of Coordination Chemistry (RUS) 2079
Russian Journal of Developmental Biology (RUS) 702
Russian Journal of Ecology (RUS) 3464
Russian Journal of Electrochemistry (RUS) 2114
Russian Journal of General Chemistry (RUS) 2079
Russian Journal of Genetics (RUS) 878
Russian Journal of Marine Biology (RUS) 702
Russian Journal of Nondestructive Testing (RUS) 3357
Russian Journal of Numerical Analysis and Mathematical Modelling (DEU) 5530
Russian Journal of Organic Chemistry (RUS) 2130
Russian Journal of Plant Physiology (RUS) 816
Russian Life (USA) 8753
Russian Linguistics (NLD) 5170
Russian Microelectronics (RUS) 3112
Russian Physics Journal (USA) 7038
The Russian Review (USA) 4260
Russian Telecom Newsletter (USA) 2337
Rutgers Computer & Technology Law Journal (USA) 4845
S A M Advanced Management Journal (USA) 1792
S A Q: The South Atlantic Quarterly (USA) 5237
S A R and Q S A R in Environmental Research (CHE) 3464
S G B (USA) 8198
S M T Trends (USA) 3112
S P C Asia (GBR) 596
S T I Online (GBR) *see* Sexually Transmitted Infections. 5881
Sabretache (AUS) 6444
Sacramento Business Journal (USA) 1170
The Safety & Health Practitioner (GBR) 7540
Safety at Sea International (GBR) 8659
Safety Compliance Letter (USA) 6685
Safety Now (USA) 6686
Safety Science (NLD) 6686
Saigon Times Daily (VNM) 3994
Sailing World (USA) 8281
St. Louis Business Journal (USA) 1170
Sales & Marketing Management (USA) 1842
Same-Day Surgery (USA) 6257
Samuel Beckett Today - Aujourd'hui (NLD) 5366
San Antonio Business Journal (USA) 1170
San Diego Business Journal (USA) 1170
San Fernando Valley Business Journal (USA) 1170
San Francisco Business Times (USA) 1432
Santa Clara Computer and High Technology Law Journal (USA) 4779
Sarasota Magazine (USA) 3987
Sarcoma (USA) 6034
Sartre Studies International (GBR) 6951
SaskBusiness (CAN) 1171
Satellite News (Online) (USA) 2389
Satellite Week (USA) 2389
Saturday Evening Post (USA) 3988
Scandinavian Actuarial Journal (NOR) 4522
Scandinavian Cardiovascular Journal (NOR) 6257
Scandinavian Journal of Caring Sciences (NOR) 5710
Scandinavian Journal of Clinical & Laboratory Investigation (NOR) 5910
Scandinavian Journal of Economics (GBR) 1171
Scandinavian Journal of Educational Research (GBR) 2909
Scandinavian Journal of Forest Research (NOR) 3701
Scandinavian Journal of Gastroenterology (NOR) 5930
Scandinavian Journal of History (NOR) 4160
Scandinavian Journal of Hospitality and Tourism (GBR) 8754
Scandinavian Journal of Immunology (GBR) 5765
Scandinavian Journal of Infectious Diseases (NOR) 5826
Scandinavian Journal of Management (GBR) 1792
Scandinavian Journal of Medicine & Science in Sports (DNK) 6232
Scandinavian Journal of Occupational Therapy (NOR) 5710
Scandinavian Journal of Plastic and Reconstructive Surgery and Hand Surgery (NOR) 6257
Scandinavian Journal of Primary Health Care (NOR) 5710
Scandinavian Journal of Psychology (GBR) 7406
Scandinavian Journal of Public Health (GBR) 5710
Scandinavian Journal of Rheumatology (NOR) 6227
Scandinavian Journal of Statistics (GBR) 8398
Scandinavian Journal of the Old Testament (NOR) 7679
Scandinavian Journal of Urology and Nephrology (NOR) 6274
Scandinavian Political Studies (GBR) 7181
Scandinavian Studies (Provo) (USA) 5367
Scando-Slavica (NOR) 5172
Schizophrenia Research (NLD) 6184
Scholastic Choices (USA) 3080
School Administrator (USA) 3031
School Arts (USA) 3080
School Effectiveness and School Improvement (NLD) 2909
School Leadership & Management (Online) (GBR) 3032
School Library Journal (USA) 5046
School Planning and Management (USA) 3032
School Psychology Quarterly (USA) 7406
School Psychology Review (USA) 7406
School Science and Mathematics (USA) 3081
Schweizerische Mineralogische und Petrographische Mitteilungen (CHE) 6479
Schweizerische Zeitschrift fuer Politikwissenschaft (CHE) 7181
Science (USA) 7908
Science Activities (USA) 7908
Science and Children (USA) 7908
Science & Education (NLD) 7908
Science and Global Security (USA) 7908
Science and Government Report (USA) 7468
Science and Public Policy (GBR) 7181
Science & Sports (FRA) 6232
Science and Technology of Advanced Materials (GBR) 3357
Science and Technology of Welding and Joining (Online) (GBR) 6344
Science as Culture (GBR) 7909
Science News (USA) 7910
Science of Computer Programming (NLD) 2510
Science of the Total Environment (NLD) 3465
Science Progress (GBR) 7910
Science Scope (USA) 7910
The Science Teacher (USA) 3081
Science, Technology & Human Values (USA) 7911
Science Weekly. Level E (USA) 2212
Science Weekly. Level Pre-A (USA) 2212
Science World (USA) 3081
Scientia Horticulturae (NLD) 3750
Scientific Computing (USA) 7940
Scientific Programming (NLD) 2597
Scientific Studies of Reading (USA) 2910
The Scientist (USA) 7913
Scientometrics (HUN) 7913
SciTech Book News (USA) 635
Scottish Journal of Geology (GBR) 2766
Scottish Journal of Political Economy (GBR) 1172
Scouting (USA) 2168
Screen Education (AUS) 3081
Screen Finance (GBR) 6512
Scripta Materialia (GBR) 6331
Sea & Shore (USA) 7541
Seafood Business (USA) 3607
Seafood International (GBR) 3607
Sealing Technology (GBR) 6720
Searcher (Medford) (USA) 2532
Second Language Research (GBR) 5172
Securities Industry News (USA) 1650
Security (USA) 2680
Security Dealer & Integrator (USA) 1854
Security Distributing & Marketing (USA) 1843
Security Management Online (USA) *see* Security Management. 1792
Security Studies (Quarterly) (USA) 7265
Security Technology Executive (USA) 2680
Sedimentary Geology (NLD) 2766
Sedimentology Online (GBR) 2766
Seed Science Research (GBR) 251
Seed World (CAN) 252
Seeing and Perceiving (NLD) 5555
SELECT Journal (USA) 2532
Self and Identity (GBR) 7407
Selling (USA) 1793
Semana (ESP) 3953
Semeia Studies (NLD) 7680
Semiconductor International (USA) 3113
Semiconductor Science and Technology (GBR) 3113
Seminars in Cancer Biology (GBR) 928
Seminars in Cell and Developmental Biology (GBR) 836
Seminars in Dialysis (USA) 6274
Seminars in Immunology (GBR) 5766
Seminars in Ophthalmology (GBR) 6051
Sensing and Imaging (USA) 4489
Sensor Letters (USA) 3330
Sensor Review (GBR) 5459
Sensor Technology (USA) 2528
Sensors (Online) (USA) 4490
Sensors and Actuators A: Physical (CHE) 7052
Sensors and Actuators B: Chemical (CHE) 2114
Separation and Purification Technology (GBR) 3255
Sequential Analysis (USA) 8399
Serials Review (GBR) 5047
The Service Industries Journal (GBR) 1172
Set-Aside Alert (USA) 7468
Set-Valued and Variational Analysis (NLD) 5535
Sex Education (GBR) 2911
Sex Roles (USA) 7407
Sexual Abuse (USA) 7407
Sexual Addiction & Compulsivity (USA) 7407
Sexual and Relationship Therapy (GBR) 7407
Sexual Health (AUS) 5826
Sexuality & Culture (USA) 8132
Sexuality and Disability (USA) 5712
Shakespeare Bulletin (USA) 8478
Shakespeare in Southern Africa (ZAF) 5370
Shakespeare Newsletter (USA) 5370
Shakespeare Oxford Newsletter (USA) 5370
Shakespeare Studies (USA) 5370
Shape (USA) 8848
Shipping Digest (USA) 8661
Shock and Vibration (NLD) 7089
The Shock and Vibration Digest (USA) 3357
Shofar (Ashland) (USA) 7729
Shoot (USA) 35
Shooting Industry (USA) 8200
SI.com (USA) *see* Sports Illustrated. 8207
Siberian Mathematical Journal (USA) 5536
Sibirica (USA) 4028
Siempre! (MEX) 5239
Sierra (USA) 2627
Sign Language and Linguistics (Online) (NLD) 5173
Signal Processing (NLD) 2464
Signal Processing: Image Communication (NLD) 2535
Significance (GBR) 8399
Signs (USA) 8903
Silicon Chemistry (NLD) 2118
Silicon Valley - San Jose Business Journal (USA) 1174
Simone de Beauvoir Institute. Review (CAN) 8903
Simulation & Gaming (USA) 2518
Simulation Modelling Practice and Theory (NLD) 2518
Sinet (ETH) 7916
Sing Out! (USA) 6616
Singapore Journal of Tropical Geography (GBR) 4028
Singapore Management Review (SGP) 1793
Situation & Outlook Report. Feed Outlook (USA) 275
Situation & Outlook Report. Livestock, Dairy and Poultry (USA) 300
Situation & Outlook Report. Oil Crops Outlook (USA) 252
Situation & Outlook Report. Rice Outlook (USA) 252
Situation & Outlook Report. Sugar & Sweetener (USA) 206
Situation & Outlook Report. Vegetables & Specialties (USA) 252
Situation & Outlook Report. Wheat Outlook (USA) 252
Skeptic (USA) 6743
Skeptical Inquirer (USA) 6743
Ski (USA) 8333
Skiing Magazine (USA) 8333
Skin & Allergy News (USA) 5882
Skin Research and Technology (DNK) 5882
Skipping Stones (USA) 2213
Sky & Telescope (USA) 581
SkyWatch (USA) 581
Slavery and Abolition (GBR) 4161
Slavonic and East European Review (GBR) 5373
Slavonica (GBR) 5373
Sleep and Biological Rhythm (AUS) 5715
Sleep Medicine (NLD) 6186
Small Axe (USA) 5239
Small Business Economics (NLD) 1967
Small Ruminant Research (NLD) 300
Small Wars and Insurgencies (GBR) 7265
Smart Materials and Structures (GBR) 7040
Smithsonian Magazine Web (USA) *see* Smithsonian. 8002
Snack Food & Wholesale Bakery (USA) 3675
Snips (USA) 4126
Snow Goer (USA) 8334
Snow Week (USA) 8334
Soap and Cosmetics (USA) 596
Soap, Perfumery & Cosmetics (GBR) 596
Soccer and Society (GBR) 8245
Social Analysis (USA) 355
Social & Cultural Geography (GBR) 8002
Social Development (GBR) 8133
Social Education (USA) 3082
Social Epistemology (GBR) 6952
Social Forces (USA) 8133
Social History (GBR) 8003
Social History of Medicine (GBR) 5715
Social Identities (GBR) 3565
Social Indicators Research (NLD) 8150
Social Justice (USA) 7265
Social Justice Research (USA) 8133
Social Marketing Quarterly (USA) 1844
Social Movement Studies (GBR) 8003
Social Networks (NLD) 8003
Social Policy (USA) 8003
Social Policy and Administration (GBR) 8069
Social Policy Journal of New Zealand (NZL) 7183
Social Politics (GBR) 8903
Social Problems (USA) 8134
Social Psychology of Education (NLD) 2913
Social Psychology Quarterly (USA) 8134
Social Research (USA) 8003
Social Science & Medicine (GBR) 5715
Social Science History (USA) 8003
Social Science Japan Journal (GBR) 8004
The Social Science Journal (USA) 8004
Social Science Quarterly (USA) 8004
Social Science Research (USA) 8004
Social Security Bulletin (USA) 4523
Social Semiotics (GBR) 6952
Social Service Review (USA) 8069
The Social Studies (USA) 8005
Social Studies of Science (GBR) 7917
Social Text (USA) 8134
Social Theory & Health (GBR) 8134
Social Theory and Practice (USA) 6952
Social Work (USA) 8070
Social Work and Social Sciences Review (GBR) 8070
Social Work Education (GBR) 8070
Social Work Research (USA) 8071
Society (USA) 8005
Society and Animals (GBR) 321
Society and Economy (HUN) 1176
Society and Natural Resources (GBR) 3466
Society for Research in Child Development. Monographs (USA) 7409
Society of Archivists. Journal (GBR) 5048
Socio-Economic Planning Sciences (GBR) 7468
Socio-Economic Review (GBR) 1517
Sociologia Ruralis (GBR) 8136
Sociological Forum (USA) 8136
Sociological Inquiry (USA) 8136
Sociological Methodology (USA) 8136
The Sociological Quarterly (USA) 8137
The Sociological Review (GBR) 8137
Sociological Spectrum (USA) 8137
Sociological Theory (USA) 8137
Sociologie du Travail (FRA) 1707
Sociology of Education (USA) 2913
Sociology of Health and Illness (GBR) 8138
Sociology of Religion (USA) 8139
Sociology Review (GBR) 8139
Soft - Letter (USA) 2597
Software Futures (GBR) 2597
Software Industry Report (USA) 2597

Women Envision (PHL) **8904**
Women in Action (PHL) **8890**
Women in German Yearbook (USA) **8904**
Women in Higher Education (USA) **3010**
Women in Judaism (CAN) **7731**
The Women's Health Activist (USA) **8849**
Women's Health Issues (USA) **8849**
Women's Health Letter (USA) **8849**
Women's Health Weekly (USA) **8849**
The Women's Review of Books (USA) **5245**
Women's Studies (CHE) **8905**
Women's Studies in Communication (USA) **8905**
Women's Studies International Forum (GBR) **8905**
Wood & Wood Products (USA) **3717**
Wood Based Panels International (GBR) **3717**
Wood Digest (USA) **3718**
Word and Music Studies (NLD) **6628**
Word Ways (USA) **5195**
Wordsworth Circle (USA) **5400**
Work (NLD) **6688**
Work and Occupations (USA) **8147**
Work and Stress (GBR) **7415**
Work Based Learning in Primary Care (GBR) **5731**
Work + Family Newsbrief (USA) **8147**
WorkBoat (USA) **8665**
Workforce Management (USA) **1877**
Working U S A (USA) **1716**
Worklife (Kingston) (CAN) **1716**
World Affairs (Washington) (USA) **7274**
The World & I Online (USA) **3993**
World Archaeology (GBR) **424**
The World Bank Economic Review (USA) **1525**
World Bank Operations Evaluation Study (USA) **1195**
World Bank Research Observer (USA) **1391**
World Bank Working Paper (USA) **1608**
World Cement (GBR) **1043**
World Competition (NLD) **4944**
World Development (GBR) **1608**
World Economics (GBR) **1195**
The World Economy (GBR) **1196**
World Englishes (GBR) **5196**
World Futures (USA) **6961**
World Gas Intelligence (USA) **6797**
World Health Organization. Bulletin (CHE) **5731**
World Health Organization Regional Publications. European Series (DNK) **7545**
The World Health Report (CHE) **7545**
World Insurance Report (GBR) **4528**
World Journal of Microbiology and Biotechnology (GBR) **771**
World Literature Today (USA) **5400**
World Mining Equipment (GBR) **6483**
The World of Hibernia (USA) **3573**
World of Information Business Intelligence Reports. Albania (GBR) **1525**
World of Information Business Intelligence Reports. Algeria (GBR) **1587**
World of Information Business Intelligence Reports. Angola (GBR) **1525**
World of Information Business Intelligence Reports. Argentina (GBR) **1525**
World of Information Business Intelligence Reports. Australia (GBR) **1526**
World of Information Business Intelligence Reports. Austria (GBR) **1526**
World of Information Business Intelligence Reports. Azerbaijan (GBR) **1526**
World of Information Business Intelligence Reports. Bahamas (GBR) **1526**
World of Information Business Intelligence Reports. Bangladesh (GBR) **1526**
World of Information Business Intelligence Reports. Belarus (GBR) **1526**
World of Information Business Intelligence Reports. Belgium (GBR) **1526**
World of Information Business Intelligence Reports. Bolivia (GBR) **1526**
World of Information Business Intelligence Reports. Bosnia (GBR) **1526**
World of Information Business Intelligence Reports. Botswana (GBR) **1526**
World of Information Business Intelligence Reports. Brazil (GBR) **1526**
World of Information Business Intelligence Reports. Brunei (GBR) **1526**
World of Information Business Intelligence Reports. Bulgaria (GBR) **1587**
World of Information Business Intelligence Reports. Cameroon (GBR) **1526**
World of Information Business Intelligence Reports. Canada (GBR) **1527**
World of Information Business Intelligence Reports. Chile (GBR) **1527**
World of Information Business Intelligence Reports. China (GBR) **1527**
World of Information Business Intelligence Reports. Colombia (GBR) **1527**
World of Information Business Intelligence Reports. Cote d'Ivoire (GBR) **1527**
World of Information Business Intelligence Reports. Croatia (GBR) **1527**
World of Information Business Intelligence Reports. Cuba (GBR) **1527**
World of Information Business Intelligence Reports. Czech Republic (GBR) **1587**
World of Information Business Intelligence Reports. Democratic Republic of Congo (GBR) **1527**
World of Information Business Intelligence Reports. Denmark (GBR) **1527**
World of Information Business Intelligence Reports. Ecuador (GBR) **1527**
World of Information Business Intelligence Reports. Egypt (GBR) **1527**
World of Information Business Intelligence Reports. El Salvador (GBR) **1527**
World of Information Business Intelligence Reports. Estonia (GBR) **1528**
World of Information Business Intelligence Reports. Finland (GBR) **1528**
World of Information Business Intelligence Reports. Gabon (GBR) **1528**
World of Information Business Intelligence Reports. Germany (GBR) **1528**
World of Information Business Intelligence Reports. Ghana (GBR) **1528**
World of Information Business Intelligence Reports. Greece (GBR) **1528**
World of Information Business Intelligence Reports. Guatemala (GBR) **1528**
World of Information Business Intelligence Reports. Guyana (GBR) **1528**
World of Information Business Intelligence Reports. Haiti (GBR) **1528**
World of Information Business Intelligence Reports. Hong Kong (GBR) **1529**
World of Information Business Intelligence Reports. Hungary (GBR) **1588**
World of Information Business Intelligence Reports. India (GBR) **1529**
World of Information Business Intelligence Reports. Indonesia (GBR) **1529**
World of Information Business Intelligence Reports. Iran (GBR) **1529**
World of Information Business Intelligence Reports. Iraq (GBR) **1529**
World of Information Business Intelligence Reports. Ireland (GBR) **1529**
World of Information Business Intelligence Reports. Israel (GBR) **1529**
World of Information Business Intelligence Reports. Italy (GBR) **1529**
World of Information Business Intelligence Reports. Jamaica (GBR) **1529**
World of Information Business Intelligence Reports. Japan (GBR) **1529**
World of Information Business Intelligence Reports. Jordan (GBR) **1529**
World of Information Business Intelligence Reports. Kazakhstan (GBR) **1529**
World of Information Business Intelligence Reports. Kenya (GBR) **1529**
World of Information Business Intelligence Reports. Korea (GBR) **1529**
World of Information Business Intelligence Reports. Kuwait (GBR) **1529**
World of Information Business Intelligence Reports. Kyrghyzstan (GBR) **1529**
World of Information Business Intelligence Reports. Lebanon (GBR) **1529**
World of Information Business Intelligence Reports. Libya (GBR) **1529**
World of Information Business Intelligence Reports. Lithuania (GBR) **1530**
World of Information Business Intelligence Reports. Luxembourg (GBR) **1530**
World of Information Business Intelligence Reports. Macedonia (GBR) **1530**
World of Information Business Intelligence Reports. Malaysia (GBR) **1530**
World of Information Business Intelligence Reports. Mexico (GBR) **1530**
World of Information Business Intelligence Reports. Moldova (GBR) **1530**
World of Information Business Intelligence Reports. Morocco (GBR) **1530**
World of Information Business Intelligence Reports. Mozambique (GBR) **1530**
World of Information Business Intelligence Reports. Netherlands (GBR) **1530**
World of Information Business Intelligence Reports. New Zealand (GBR) **1530**
World of Information Business Intelligence Reports. Nigeria (GBR) **1531**
World of Information Business Intelligence Reports. Norway (GBR) **1531**
World of Information Business Intelligence Reports. Oman (GBR) **1531**
World of Information Business Intelligence Reports. Pakistan (GBR) **1531**
World of Information Business Intelligence Reports. Panama (GBR) **1531**
World of Information Business Intelligence Reports. Papua New Guinea (GBR) **1531**
World of Information Business Intelligence Reports. Paraguay (GBR) **1531**
World of Information Business Intelligence Reports. Peru (GBR) **1531**
World of Information Business Intelligence Reports. Philippines (GBR) **1531**
World of Information Business Intelligence Reports. Poland (GBR) **1531**
World of Information Business Intelligence Reports. Portugal (GBR) **1531**
World of Information Business Intelligence Reports. Romania (GBR) **1531**
World of Information Business Intelligence Reports. Russia (GBR) **1531**
World of Information Business Intelligence Reports. Saudi Arabia (GBR) **1532**
World of Information Business Intelligence Reports. Senegal (GBR) **1532**
World of Information Business Intelligence Reports. Serbia (GBR) **1532**
World of Information Business Intelligence Reports. Singapore (GBR) **1532**
World of Information Business Intelligence Reports. Slovakia (GBR) **1532**
World of Information Business Intelligence Reports. Slovenia (GBR) **1532**
World of Information Business Intelligence Reports. South Africa (GBR) **1532**
World of Information Business Intelligence Reports. Spain (GBR) **1532**
World of Information Business Intelligence Reports. Sri Lanka (GBR) **1532**
World of Information Business Intelligence Reports. Sudan (GBR) **1532**
World of Information Business Intelligence Reports. Sweden (GBR) **1532**
World of Information Business Intelligence Reports. Switzerland (GBR) **1532**
World of Information Business Intelligence Reports. Syria (GBR) **1532**
World of Information Business Intelligence Reports. Taiwan (GBR) **1533**
World of Information Business Intelligence Reports. Tajikistan (GBR) **1533**
World of Information Business Intelligence Reports. Tanzania (GBR) **1533**
World of Information Business Intelligence Reports. Thailand (GBR) **1533**
World of Information Business Intelligence Reports. Trinidad and Tobago (GBR) **1533**
World of Information Business Intelligence Reports. Tunisia (GBR) **1533**
World of Information Business Intelligence Reports. Turkey (GBR) **1533**
World of Information Business Intelligence Reports. Turkmenistan (GBR) **1533**
World of Information Business Intelligence Reports. Uganda (GBR) **1533**
World of Information Business Intelligence Reports. Ukraine (GBR) **1533**
World of Information Business Intelligence Reports. United Arab Emirates (GBR) **1533**
World of Information Business Intelligence Reports. United Kingdom (GBR) **1533**
World of Information Business Intelligence Reports. United States (GBR) **1533**
World of Information Business Intelligence Reports. Uruguay (GBR) **1533**
World of Information Business Intelligence Reports. Uzbekistan (GBR) **1533**
World of Information Business Intelligence Reports. Venezuela (GBR) **1534**
World of Information Business Intelligence Reports. Vietnam (GBR) **1534**
World of Information Business Intelligence Reports. Zambia (GBR) **1534**
World of Information Business Intelligence Reports. Zimbabwe (GBR) **1534**
World Oil (USA) **6797**
World Patent Information (GBR) **6760**
World Policy Journal (USA) **7274**
World Politics (USA) **7274**
World Pumps (GBR) **3399**
World Tobacco (GBR) **8489**
World Trade and Arbitration Materials (NLD) **1588**
World Trade: WT100 (USA) **1588**
World War II (Leesburg) (USA) **4318**
World Watch (USA) **3475**
World Wide Web (New York) (NLD) **2569**
World's Poultry Science Journal (GBR) **304**
Worldviews (NLD) **3475**
Worldviews on Evidence-Based Nursing (USA) **5984**
Worldwide Computer Products News (GBR) **2441**
Worldwide Videotex Update (USA) **2569**
Wound Repair and Regeneration (USA) **6075**
Wrestling Digest (USA) **8216**
The Writer (USA) **5400**
Written Communication (USA) **2345**
Written Language and Literacy (NLD) **5196**
X D S L Newsletter (USA) **2374**
Xenobiotica (GBR) **746**
Xenotransplantation (DNK) **6262**
Yachting (USA) **8285**
Yale Human Rights and Development Law Journal (USA) **4816**
Yale Journal of Biology and Medicine (USA) **5733**
The Yale Law Journal (USA) **4817**
The Yale Review (USA) **5246**
Yard and Garden (USA) **3754**
Yearbook of English Studies (GBR) **5403**
Yellow Pages & Directory Report (USA) **2036**
Yomiuri Shimbun (Satellite Edition) (USA) **3901**
Your Church (USA) **1969**
Youth & Society (USA) **2172**
Youth Markets Alert (USA) **1849**
Youth Studies Australia (AUS) **2172**
Zebrafish (USA) **968**
Zeitschrift fuer Kristallographie (DEU) **2112**
Zeitschrift fuer Religions- und Geistesgeschichte (NLD) **7697**
Zona Proxima (COL) **2929**
Zoologica Scripta (GBR) **969**
Zoologischer Anzeiger (DEU) **970**
Zoology (DEU) **970**
Zoonoses and Public Health (DEU) **8816**
Zygon (USA) **7697**
2.5 G-3 G (USA) **2346**
III - Vs Review (GBR) **3116**
3 D (GBR) **2490**
20th Century History Review (GBR) **4168**
401(k) Advisor (USA) **1661**

William S. Hein & Co., Inc. 1285 Main St, Buffalo, NY 14209-1987 TEL 716-882-2600, 800-828-7571, FAX 716-883-8100, mail@wshein.com, http://www.wshein.com

A B A Journal (USA) **4606**
Administrative Law Review (Chicago) (USA) **4610**
African Journal of Legal Studies (CAN) **4611**
Akron Law Review (USA) **4612**
Akron Tax Journal (USA) **1909**
Alabama Law Review (USA) **4612**
Alaska Law Review (USA) **4612**
Albany Law Review (USA) **4612**
Alberta Law Review (CAN) **4613**
American Bankruptcy Institute Law Review (USA) **1307**
American Bankruptcy Law Journal (USA) **4614**
American Indian Law Review (USA) **4614**
American Journal of Comparative Law (USA) **4916**
American Journal of Criminal Law (USA) **2643**
American Journal of International Law (USA) **4916**
American Journal of Jurisprudence (USA) **4614**
American University International Law Review (USA) **4916**
The American University Journal of Gender, Social Policy & the Law (USA) **4615**
American University Law Review (USA) **4615**
Animal Law (USA) **317**
Annals of Health Law (USA) **4617**
Antitrust Law Journal (USA) **4856**
Arab Law Quarterly (NLD) **4619**
Arizona Journal of International & Comparative Law (USA) **4917**
Arizona Law Review (USA) **4621**
Arizona State Law Journal (USA) **4621**
Arkansas Law Review (USA) **4621**
Asian-Pacific Law & Policy Journal (USA) **4622**
Auckland University Law Review (NZL) **4623**
Ave Maria Law Review (USA) **4624**
B Y U Journal of Public Law (USA) **4625**
The Banking Law Journal (USA) **1317**
Baylor Law Review (USA) **4628**
Berkeley Journal of Employment and Labor Law (USA) **1667**
Berkeley Journal of Gender, Law & Justice (USA) **4629**
Berkeley Journal of International Law (USA) **4918**
Berkeley La Raza Law Journal (USA) **4629**
Berkeley Technology Law Journal (USA) **4629**
Boston College Environmental Affairs Law Review (USA) **3407**
Boston College International and Comparative Law Review (USA) **4918**
Boston College Law Review (USA) **4631**
Boston College Third World Law Journal (USA) **4918**
Boston University International Law Journal (USA) **4918**
Boston University Law Review (USA) **4631**
Brigham Young University Law Review (USA) **4632**
The British Journal of Criminology (GBR) **2645**
British Year Book of International Law (GBR) **4919**
Brooklyn Journal of International Law (USA) **4919**
Brooklyn Law Review (USA) **4632**
Buffalo Environmental Law Journal (USA) **4633**
Buffalo Human Rights Law Review (USA) *see* Buffalo Human Rights Law Review. **4633**
Buffalo Law Review (USA) **4633**
The Buffalo Public Interest Law Journal (USA) **4633**
California Law Review (USA) **4636**
California Western International Law Journal (USA) **4919**
California Western Law Review (USA) **4637**
Cambrian Law Review (GBR) **4637**
Campbell Law Review (USA) **4637**
Canadian Journal of Family Law (CAN) **4639**
Canadian Journal of Law and Jurisprudence (CAN) **4639**
Canadian Journal of Law and Society (CAN) **4639**
Canadian Journal of Women and the Law (CAN) **4639**
Canadian Law Libraries (CAN) **5000**
Canterbury Law Review (NZL) **4640**
Capital University Law Review (USA) **2646**
Cardozo Arts & Entertainment Law Journal (USA) **4640**
Cardozo Journal of International and Comparative Law (USA) **4920**
Cardozo Journal of Law and Gender (USA) **4640**
Cardozo Law Review (USA) **4640**
Case Western Reserve Journal of International Law (USA) **4920**
Case Western Reserve Law Review (USA) **4641**
Catholic University Law Review (USA) **7790**
Chicago Journal of International Law (USA) **4920**
Children's Legal Rights Journal (USA) **4908**
Chinese Journal of International Law (GBR) **4920**
Cleveland State Law Review (USA) **4643**
Clinical Law Review (USA) **4643**
Columbia Business Law Review (USA) **4645**
Columbia Human Rights Law Review (USA) **4645**
Columbia Journal of Asian Law (USA) **4645**
Columbia Journal of Environmental Law (USA) **4645**
Columbia Journal of Gender and the Law (USA) **4645**
Columbia Journal of Law & the Arts (USA) **482**
Columbia Journal of Transnational Law (USA) **4921**
Columbia Law Review (USA) **4645**
CommLaw Conspectus (USA) **2315**
Common Law World Review (GBR) **4921**
Comparative Labor Law & Policy Journal (USA) **1671**
Connecticut Insurance Law Review (USA) **4500**

Online Service

Connecticut Journal of International Law (USA) **4922**
Connecticut Law Review (USA) **4648**
Constitutional Commentary (USA) **4847**
Cornell International Law Journal (USA) **4922**
Cornell Journal of Law and Public Policy (USA) **4651**
Cornell Law Review (USA) **4651**
Creighton Law Review (USA) **4652**
Criminal Justice Review (USA) **4887**
Cumberland Law Review (USA) **4653**
Current Issues in Criminal Justice (AUS) **2650**
Daily Compilation of Presidential Documents (USA) **7128**
Dalhousie Journal of Legal Studies (CAN) **4654**
Deakin Law Review (AUS) **4655**
Defense Counsel Journal (USA) **4830**
The Delaware Journal of Corporate Law (USA) **4865**
Denver Journal of International Law and Policy (USA) **4922**
Denver University Law Review (USA) **4656**
DePaul Business and Commercial Law Journal (USA) **4656**
DePaul Journal of Art, Technology & Intellectual Property Law (USA) **4656**
DePaul Journal of Health Care Law (USA) **4656**
DePaul Law Review (USA) **4656**
The Drake Journal of Agricultural Law (USA) **4661**
Drake Law Review (USA) **4661**
Duke Environmental Law & Policy Forum (USA) **4661**
Duke Journal of Comparative and International Law (USA) **4923**
Duke Law Journal (USA) **4661**
Duquesne Law Review (USA) **4662**
E C M I Journal on Ethnopolitics and Minority Issues in Europe (DEU) **3530**
Ecology Law Quarterly (USA) **4663**
Emory Bankruptcy Developments Journal (USA) **4830**
Emory International Law Review (USA) **4924**
Emory Law Journal (USA) **4664**
Energy Law Journal (USA) **4665**
European Journal of Health Law (NLD) **5611**
European Journal of International Law (GBR) **4925**
European Journal of Law Reform (NLD) **4669**
European Journal of Migration and Law (NLD) **4925**
Family Law Quarterly (USA) **4910**
Federal Communications Law Journal (USA) **4672**
Federal Law Review (AUS) **4951**
Federal Probation (USA) **2652**
Federal Register (USA) **4673**
Federal Reserve Bulletin (USA) **1342**
Federal Sentencing Reporter (USA) **2652**
Fletcher Forum of World Affairs (USA) **7235**
Florida Journal of International Law (USA) **4926**
Florida Law Review (USA) **4675**
Florida State University Law Review (USA) **4675**
The Florida Tax Review (USA) **4676**
Food and Drug Law Journal (USA) **4676**
Fordham Environmental Law Review (USA) **3431**
Fordham Intellectual Property, Media & Entertainment Law Journal (USA) **4676**
Fordham International Law Journal (USA) **4926**
Fordham Journal of Corporate & Financial Law (USA) **4868**
Fordham Law Review (USA) **4676**
Fordham Urban Law Journal (USA) **4676**
Foreign Affairs (USA) **7235**
George Mason Law Review (USA) **4679**
George Mason University. Civil Rights Law Journal (USA) **4831**
The George Washington International Law Review (USA) **4926**
George Washington Law Review (USA) **4679**
Georgetown Immigration Law Journal (USA) **4679**
Georgetown International Environmental Law Review (USA) **3433**
The Georgetown Journal of Gender and the Law (USA) **4679**
Georgetown Journal of International Affairs (USA) **7237**
Georgetown Journal of International Law (USA) **4926**
Georgetown Journal of Law & Public Policy (USA) **4679**
Georgetown Journal of Legal Ethics (USA) **4680**
Georgetown Journal on Poverty Law and Policy (USA) **8042**
Georgetown Law Journal (USA) **4680**
Georgia Law Review (USA) **4680**
Georgia State University Law Review (USA) **4680**
Global Governance (USA) **7238**
Golden Gate University Law Review (USA) **4681**
Gonzaga Law Review (USA) **4682**
The Green Bag (USA) **4682**
Hamline Journal of Public Law and Policy (USA) **4684**
Hamline Law Review (USA) **4684**
Harvard BlackLetter Law Journal (USA) **4832**
Harvard Environmental Law Review (USA) **4684**
Harvard Human Rights Journal (USA) **7207**
Harvard International Law Journal (USA) **4927**
Harvard Journal of Law & Gender (USA) **4684**
Harvard Journal of Law and Technology (USA) **4684**
Harvard Journal on Legislation (USA) **4685**
Harvard Law Review (USA) **4685**
Hastings Constitutional Law Quarterly (USA) **4849**
Hastings International and Comparative Law Review (USA) **4927**
Hastings Law Journal (USA) **4685**
Health Matrix: Journal of Law-Medicine (USA) **4686**
Hofstra Labor & Employment Law Journal (USA) **4687**
Hofstra Law Review (USA) **4687**
Houston Journal of Health Law & Policy (USA) **4101**
Houston Journal of International Law (USA) **4688**
Houston Law Review (USA) **4688**
Howard Law Journal (USA) **4688**
Human Rights Law Review (GBR) **7208**
Human Rights Quarterly (USA) **7208**
Idaho Law Review (USA) **4690**
Indiana Journal of Global Legal Studies (USA) **4691**
Indiana Law Journal (USA) **4691**
Indiana Law Review (USA) **4692**
Inter-American Law Review (USA) **4929**
International and Comparative Law Quarterly (GBR) **4929**
International Criminal Justice Review (USA) **4891**
International Financial Law Review (GBR) **4930**
International Journal of Communications Law and Policy (GBR) **2424**
International Journal of Law, Policy and the Family (GBR) **4911**
International Journal of Legal Information (USA) **5019**
The International Journal of Marine and Coastal Law (NLD) **4969**
International Journal of Refugee Law (GBR) **7243**
International Journal on Minority and Group Rights (NLD) **7210**
International Labour Review (GBR) **1689**
International Legal Materials (USA) **4932**
International Tax Review (GBR) **1571**
Iowa Law Review (USA) **4696**
Islamic Law and Society (NLD) **7712**
Israel Law Review (ISR) **4697**
Issues in Law and Medicine (USA) **5642**
Journal of Appellate Practice and Process (USA) **4700**
Journal of Broadcasting and Electronic Media (USA) **2383**
The Journal of Contemporary Health Law and Policy (USA) **5648**
The Journal of Contemporary Legal Issues (USA) **4700**
Journal of Criminal Justice Education (GBR) **2656**
Journal of Criminal Law & Criminology (USA) **2657**
Journal of Dispute Resolution (USA) **4701**
Journal of Environmental Law (GBR) **3445**
Journal of Environmental Law and Litigation (USA) **3446**
Journal of International Economic Law (GBR) **4933**
Journal of Land, Resources, & Environmental Law (USA) **3140**
Journal of Law & Commerce (USA) **4872**
Journal of Law and Health (USA) **4702**
Journal of Law and Policy (USA) **4702**
Journal of Law and Politics (USA) **4702**
Journal of Law & Public Policy (USA) **4702**
Journal of Law and Religion (USA) **4702**
Journal of Law and Social Policy (CAN) **4968**
Journal of Law, Economics, & Organization (GBR) **4702**
The Journal of Law in Society (USA) **4703**
Journal of Legal Aspects of Sport (USA) **4703**
Journal of Legal Economics (USA) **1545**
Journal of Legal Education (USA) **4703**
Journal of Legal Pluralism and Unofficial Law (GBR) **4703**
Journal of Legislation (USA) **4703**
Journal of Maritime Law and Commerce (USA) **4970**
Journal of Natural Resources & Environmental Law (USA) **3448**
Journal of Pharmacy & Law (USA) **4704**
Journal of Refugee Studies (GBR) **7249**
The Journal of Southern Legal History (USA) **4704**
Judicature (USA) **4953**
Jurimetrics (USA) **4706**
Justice Quarterly (GBR) **2658**
Juvenile and Family Court Journal (USA) **4912**
Juvenile Justice (Online) (USA) **2157**
Kansas Journal of Law & Public Policy (USA) **4709**
Kentucky Law Journal (USA) **4709**
Labor Lawyer (USA) **4711**
Law and Contemporary Problems (USA) **4713**
Law and History Review (GBR) **4713**
Law and Literature (USA) **4713**
Law & Sexuality (USA) **7211**
Law and Social Inquiry (USA) **4714**
Law Library Journal (USA) **5024**
Legal Studies (GBR) **4720**
Legal Studies Forum (USA) **4720**
Lewis & Clark Law Review (USA) **4723**
Lincoln Law Review (USA) **4724**
Litigation (Chicago) (USA) **4724**
Louisiana Law Review (USA) **4725**
Loyola Law Review (USA) **4726**
Loyola of Los Angeles Entertainment Law Review (USA) **4726**
Loyola of Los Angeles International and Comparative Law Review (USA) **4726**
Loyola of Los Angeles Law Review (USA) **4726**
Loyola University Chicago Law Journal (USA) **4726**
Macquarie Law Journal (AUS) **4726**
Managing Intellectual Property (GBR) **6754**
Manchester Journal of International Economic Law (GBR) **1577**
Marquette Intellectual Property Law Review (USA) **4875**
Marquette Law Review (USA) **4728**
McGeorge Law Review (USA) **4730**
McGill Law Journal (CAN) **4730**
Medical Law Review (GBR) **4731**
Melbourne Journal of International Law (AUS) **4935**
Melbourne University Law Review (AUS) **4732**
Mercer Law Review (USA) **4732**
Michigan Journal of Gender & Law (USA) **4733**
Michigan Journal of International Law (USA) **4935**
Michigan State Law Review (USA) **4733**
Michigan Telecommunications & Technology Law Review (USA) **4734**
Military Law Review (USA) **4971**
Minnesota Law Review (USA) **4734**
Mississippi College Law Review (USA) **4735**
Mississippi Law Journal (USA) **4735**
Missouri Law Review (USA) **4735**
Monash University Law Review (AUS) **4736**
Montana Law Review (USA) **4736**
National Association of Administrative Law Judiciary. Journal (USA) **4738**
Natural Resources & Environment (USA) **3455**
The Natural Resources Journal (USA) **2621**
Naval Law Review (USA) **4972**
Nebraska Law Review (USA) **4740**
New Criminal Law Review (USA) **4894**
New England Journal on Criminal and Civil Confinement (USA) **4741**
New England Law Review (USA) **4741**
New Mexico Law Review (USA) **4744**
New York Law School Law Review (USA) **4745**
New York University Annual Survey of American Law (USA) **4746**
New York University Environmental Law Journal (USA) **3456**
New York University Journal of International Law and Politics (USA) **4936**
New York University Journal of Legislation and Public Policy (USA) **7455**
New Zealand Armed Forces Law Review (NZL) **4972**
New Zealand Journal of Environmental Law (NZL) **4746**
Newcastle Law Review (AUS) **4746**
Nordic Journal of International Law (NLD) **4936**
North Carolina Central Law Journal (USA) **4748**
North Carolina Journal of International Law and Commercial Regulation (USA) **4937**
North Carolina Journal of Law & Technology (USA) **4748**
North Carolina Law Review (USA) **4748**
North Dakota Law Review (USA) **4748**
Northern Illinois University Law Review (USA) **4748**
Northern Ireland Legal Quarterly (GBR) **4749**
Northern Kentucky Law Review (USA) **4749**
Northwestern University Law Review (USA) **4749**
Notre Dame Journal of Law, Ethics & Public Policy (USA) **7457**
Nova Law Review (USA) **4749**
Ocean & Coastal Law Journal (USA) **4750**
Ohio Northern University Law Review (USA) **4752**
Ohio State Journal on Dispute Resolution (USA) **4752**
Ohio State Law Journal (USA) **4752**
Oklahoma City University Law Review (USA) **4752**
Oklahoma Law Review (USA) **4752**
Oregon Law Review (USA) **4754**
Osgoode Hall Law Journal (CAN) **4754**
Ottawa Law Review (CAN) **4754**
Oxford Journal of Legal Studies (GBR) **4754**
Pace Environmental Law Review (USA) **4755**
Pace Law Review (USA) **4755**
Patent and Trademark Office Society. Journal (USA) **6755**
Penn State International Law Review (USA) **4937**
Penn State Law Review (USA) **4756**
PENNumbra (USA) *see* University of Pennsylvania. Law Review. **4805**
Pepperdine Dispute Resolution Law Journal (USA) **4757**
Pepperdine Law Review (USA) **4757**
Pierce Law Review (USA) **4758**
Policing (Bingley) (GBR) **2664**
Public Contract Law Journal (USA) **4763**
Public Interest Law Journal (USA) **4763**
Queen's Law Journal (CAN) **4764**
Quinnipiac Law Review (USA) **4764**
Real Property, Trust and Estate Law Journal (USA) **4905**
Regent University Law Review (USA) **4767**
Review of Central and East European Law (NLD) **4769**
Roger Williams University Law Review (USA) **4776**
Rutgers Law Journal (USA) **4777**
Rutgers Law Review (USA) **4777**
Rutgers Race and the Law Review (USA) **4777**
S M U Law Review (USA) **4777**
Saint John's Journal of Legal Commentary (USA) **4778**
Saint John's Law Review (USA) **4778**
Saint Louis University. Law Journal (USA) **4778**
Saint Louis University. Public Law Review (USA) **4778**
St. Mary's Law Journal (USA) **4778**
Saint Thomas Law Review (USA) **4778**
San Diego Law Review (USA) **4778**
Santa Clara Computer and High Technology Law Journal (USA) **4779**
Santa Clara Law Review (USA) **4779**
Saskatchewan Law Review (CAN) **4779**
Scribes Journal of Legal Writing (USA) **4781**
Seattle University. Law Review (USA) **4781**
Security and Human Rights (NLD) **7215**
Seton Hall Journal of Sports and Entertainment Law (USA) **4782**
Seton Hall Law Review (USA) **4782**
Seton Hall Legislative Journal (USA) **4782**
Singapore Journal of Legal Studies (SGP) **4784**
Social Forces (USA) **8133**
Social Security Bulletin (USA) **4523**
South African Journal on Human Rights (ZAF) **7215**
South African Law Journal (ZAF) **4785**
South Carolina Law Review (USA) **4785**
South Dakota Law Review (USA) **4785**
South Texas Law Review (USA) **4785**
Southeastern Environmental Law Journal (USA) **4785**
Southern California Interdisciplinary Law Journal (USA) **4786**
Southern California Law Review (USA) **4786**
Southern California Review of Law and Social Justice (USA) **8903**
Southern Illinois University Law Journal (USA) **4786**
Southern University Law Review (USA) **4786**
Southwestern Law Review (USA) **4786**
Stanford Environmental Law Journal (USA) **4787**
Stanford Journal of International Law (USA) **4941**
Stanford Law & Policy Review (USA) **4787**
Stanford Law Review (USA) **4787**
Stetson Law Review (USA) **4789**
Suffolk University Law Review (USA) **4791**
Supreme Court Economic Review (USA) **4965**
The Supreme Court Review (USA) **4965**
The Sydney Law Review (AUS) **4792**
Syracuse Journal of International Law & Commerce (USA) **4942**
Syracuse Law Review (USA) **4792**
Tax Law Review (USA) **4792**
Temple International and Comparative Law Journal (USA) **4942**
Temple Law Review (USA) **4793**
Temple Political & Civil Rights Law Review (USA) **4852**
Tennessee Law Review (USA) **4794**
Texas Intellectual Property Law Journal (USA) **4794**
Texas Journal of Women and the Law (USA) **4794**
Texas Law Review (USA) **4794**
Texas Review of Entertainment and Sports Law (USA) **4795**
Texas Tech Law Review (USA) **4795**
Texas Wesleyan Law Review (USA) **4795**
Third World Legal Studies (Year) (USA) **4942**
Thomas Jefferson Law Review (USA) **4899**
Thomas M. Cooley Law Review (USA) **4796**
Thurgood Marshall Law Review (USA) **4796**
Tort Trial & Insurance Practice Law Journal (USA) **4843**
Touro Law Review (USA) **4797**
Transnational Law & Contemporary Problems (USA) **4798**
Transportation Law Journal (USA) **4798**
Tulane Environmental Law Journal (USA) **3471**
Tulane European and Civil Law Forum (USA) **4843**
Tulane Journal of International and Comparative Law (USA) **4942**
Tulane Law Review (USA) **4798**
Tulane Maritime Law Journal (USA) **4971**
Tulsa Law Review (USA) **4798**
U C Davis Law Review (USA) **4799**
U C L A Journal of Environmental Law and Policy (USA) **3471**
U C L A Journal of International Law and Foreign Affairs (USA) **4943**
U C L A Law Review (USA) **4799**
U C L A Pacific Basin Law Journal (USA) **4799**
U C L A Women's Law Journal (USA) **4799**
U M K C Law Review (USA) **4799**
U N B Law Journal (CAN) **4799**
University of Arkansas at Little Rock Law Review (USA) **4803**
University of Baltimore Journal of Environmental Law (USA) **4803**
University of Baltimore Law Review (USA) **4803**
University of British Columbia Law Review (CAN) **4803**
University of Chicago Law Review (USA) **4803**
University of Chicago Legal Forum (USA) **4803**
University of Cincinnati Law Review (USA) **4803**
University of Colorado Law Review (USA) **4803**
University of Dayton Law Review (USA) **4803**
University of Detroit Mercy Law Review (USA) **4804**
University of Illinois Law Review (USA) **4804**
University of Kansas Law Review (USA) **4804**
University of La Verne Law Review (USA) **4915**
University of Maryland Law Journal of Race, Religion, Gender and Class (USA) **4804**
University of Memphis Law Review (USA) **4804**
University of Miami Law Review (USA) **4804**
University of Michigan Journal of Law Reform (USA) **4804**
University of North Carolina School of Law Banking Institute (USA) **4804**
University of Ottawa Law & Technology Journal (CAN) **4804**
University of Pennsylvania. Journal of Constitutional Law (USA) **4853**
University of Pennsylvania. Journal of International Law (USA) **4944**
University of Pittsburgh Law Review (USA) **4805**
University of Queensland Law Journal (AUS) **4805**
University of Richmond Law Review (USA) **4805**
University of San Francisco Law Review (USA) **4805**
University of San Francisco Maritime Law Journal (USA) **4971**

Link to your serials resources and content with ulrichsweb.com

Journal of Obstetric, Gynecologic, and Neonatal Nursing (USA) **5966**
Journal of Oncology Pharmacy Practice (GBR) **6855**
The Journal of Orthodontics (Online Edition) (GBR) **5853**
Journal of Paleontology (USA) **6726**
Journal of Parenteral and Enteral Nutrition (USA) **6662**
Journal of Peace Research (GBR) **7249**
Journal of Pediatric Oncology Nursing (USA) **6025**
Journal of Pediatric Psychology (GBR) **7377**
Journal of Pentecostal Theology (NLD) **7762**
Journal of Petrology (GBR) **2750**
The Journal of Pharmacology and Experimental Therapeutics (USA) **6855**
Journal of Pharmacy Practice (USA) **6856**
Journal of Phycology (USA) **797**
The Journal of Physiology (GBR) **925**
Journal of Plankton Research (GBR) **684**
Journal of Planning Education and Research (USA) **4417**
Journal of Planning History (USA) **4417**
Journal of Planning Literature (USA) **4417**
Journal of Plastic Film and Sheeting (GBR) **7093**
Journal of Psychoeducational Assessment (USA) **2877**
Journal of Psychopharmacology (GBR) **6856**
Journal of Public Administration Research and Theory (GBR) **7448**
Journal of Public Health (Online) (GBR) **8050**
Journal of Refugee Studies (GBR) **7249**
Journal of Reinforced Plastics & Composites (GBR) **3351**
Journal of Research in Crime and Delinquency (USA) **2658**
Journal of Research in International Education (GBR) **3014**
Journal of Research in Nursing (GBR) **5967**
Journal of Sandwich Structures & Materials (GBR) **3351**
Journal of Sedimentary Research (USA) **2711**
Journal of Semantics (GBR) **5203**
Journal of Semitic Studies (GBR) **5135**
Journal of Service Research (USA) **1826**
Journal of Social and Personal Relationships (GBR) **7380**
Journal of Social Archaeology (GBR) **401**
Journal of Social Work (GBR) **8051**
Journal of Sociology (GBR) **8116**
Journal of South Asian Development (IND) **1600**
Journal of Speech, Language, and Hearing Research (USA) **4075**
Journal of Sport and Social Issues (USA) **8182**
Journal of Sports Economics (USA) **1138**
Journal of Studies in International Education (USA) **3014**
Journal of Teacher Education (USA) **2878**
Journal of the History of Collections (GBR) **6526**
Journal of the History of Medicine and Allied Sciences (GBR) **5655**
Journal of Theological Studies (GBR) **7657**
Journal of Theoretical Politics (GBR) **7148**
Journal of Thermoplastic Composite Materials (GBR) **7094**
The Journal of Thoracic and Cardiovascular Surgery (USA) **6250**
Journal of Transcultural Nursing (USA) **5967**
Journal of Transformative Education (USA) **2879**
Journal of Travel Research (USA) **8726**
Journal of Tropical Pediatrics (GBR) **6095**
Journal of Ultrasound in Medicine (USA) **6201**
Journal of Urban Health (USA) **5655**
Journal of Urban History (USA) **4150**
Journal of Vacation Marketing (GBR) **8726**
Journal of Vascular and Interventional Radiology (USA) **6201**
Journal of Veterinary Diagnostic Investigation (USA) **8801**
Journal of Veterinary Medical Education (CAN) **8801**
Journal of Vibration and Control (GBR) **7088**
Journal of Virology (USA) **890**
Journal of Visual Culture (GBR) **4461**
Journal Watch Cardiology (USA) **5748**
Journal Watch Dermatology (USA) **5879**
Journal Watch Emergency Medicine (USA) **6066**
Journal Watch Gastroenterology (USA) **5748**
Journal Watch Infectious Diseases (USA) **5748**
Journal Watch Neurology (USA) **5748**
Journal Watch Oncology and Hematology (USA) **6025**
Journal Watch Online (USA) *see* Journal Watch General Medicine. **5748**
Journal Watch Pediatrics & Adolescent Medicine (USA) **6095**
Journal Watch Psychiatry (USA) **5748**
Journalism (GBR) **4577**
Journals of Gerontology. Series A: Biological Sciences & Medical Sciences (USA) **4050**
Journals of Gerontology. Series B: Psychological Sciences & Social Sciences (USA) **4050**
Labor: Studies in Working-Class History of the Americas (USA) **1693**
Laboratory Investigation (USA) **5908**
Language and Literature (GBR) **5139**
Language, Speech and Hearing Services in Schools (USA) **6082**
Language Teaching Research (GBR) **5141**
Language Testing (GBR) **5141**
Latin American Perspectives (USA) **7982**
Law, Culture & the Humanities (GBR) **4714**
Law, Probability and Risk (GBR) **4716**
Leadership (GBR) **4463**
The Leading Edge (Tulsa) (USA) **2786**
Learning & Memory (Online) (USA) **6158**
The Library (GBR) **5026**
Lighting Research and Technology (GBR) **3324**
Literary and Linguistic Computing (GBR) **5203**
Literature and Theology (GBR) **5325**
Lupus (GBR) **6224**
M H Online (GBR) **5663**
Management & Organizational History (GBR) **1775**
Management Communication Quarterly (USA) **1775**
Management Learning (GBR) **1776**
Management Science (USA) **1776**
Manufacturing and Service Operations Management (USA) **1778**
Marketing Science (USA) **1833**
Marketing Theory (GBR) **1833**
Mathematical Medicine and Biology (Online) (GBR) **5513**
Mathematics and Mechanics of Solids (GBR) **7026**
Mathematics of Operations Research (USA) **2431**
Media, Culture & Society (GBR) **8120**
Medical Care Research and Review (USA) **7548**
Medical Decision Making (USA) **5667**
Medical Law Review (GBR) **4731**
The Medieval History Journal (IND) **4152**
Mediterranean Quarterly (USA) **7252**
Men and Masculinities (USA) **6303**
Microbiology (GBR) **892**
Microbiology and Molecular Biology Reviews (USA) **892**
Micropaleontology (USA) **6726**
Mind (GBR) **6934**
Mineralogical Magazine (GBR) **6471**
Modern China (USA) **4186**
Modern Judaism (GBR) **3551**
Modern Language Quarterly (USA) **5335**
Modern Pathology (GBR) **5680**
Molecular and Cellular Biology (USA) **739**
Molecular and Cellular Proteomics (USA) **739**
Molecular Biology and Evolution (USA) **689**
Molecular Biology of the Cell (USA) **834**
Molecular Cancer Research (USA) **6027**
Molecular Endocrinology (USA) **5897**
Molecular Human Reproduction (GBR) **5999**
Molecular Interventions (USA) **6862**
Molecular Pharmacology (USA) **6862**
Multiple Sclerosis (GBR) **6162**
Music and Letters (GBR) **6589**
The Musical Quarterly (USA) **6594**
Mutagenesis (GBR) **875**
N A S S P Bulletin (USA) **3027**
National Academy of Sciences. Proceedings (USA) **7886**
National Cancer Institute. Journal (Online) (GBR) **6028**
National Cancer Institute. Journal. Monographs (USA) **6028**
National Institute Economic Review (GBR) **1152**
NeoReviews.org (USA) **6097**
Nephrology, Dialysis, Transplantation (GBR) **6272**
Neural Computation (USA) **2455**
Neuro-Oncology (USA) **6029**
Neurology (USA) **6166**
Neurorehabilitation and Neural Repair (USA) **6168**
The Neuroscientist (USA) **6169**
Neurotherapeutics (USA) **6170**
New England Journal of Medicine (USA) **5685**
New German Critique (USA) **4466**
New Media & Society (GBR) **8123**
New York Academy of Sciences. Annals (USA) **7892**
Nonprofit and Voluntary Sector Quarterly (USA) **8059**
Notes and Queries (GBR) **5343**
Nucleic Acids Research (GBR) **741**
Nucleic Acids Symposium Series (GBR) **741**
Nursing Ethics (GBR) **5973**
Nursing for Women's Health (USA) **8847**
Nursing Science Quarterly (USA) **5975**
Nutrition in Clinical Practice (USA) **6666**
O E M Online (GBR) *see* Occupational and Environmental Medicine. **6682**
Obesity (USA) **5688**
Obstetrics and Gynecology (USA) **6001**
Occupational Medicine (GBR) **6683**
The Oncologist (USA) **6030**
The Opera Quarterly (GBR) **6602**
Operations Research (USA) **2433**
Ophthalmology (USA) **6048**
Organization (GBR) **1784**
Organization & Environment (USA) **6684**
Organization Science (USA) **1784**
Organization Studies (DEU) **7990**
Organizational Research Methods (USA) **1784**
Oxford Art Journal (GBR) **510**
Oxford Economic Papers (GBR) **1158**
Oxford Journal of Legal Studies (GBR) **4754**
Oxford Review of Economic Policy (GBR) **1158**
P M J Online (GBR) *see* Postgraduate Medical Journal. **5698**
Palaios (USA) **6728**
Paleobiology (USA) **6728**
Palliative Medicine (GBR) **5693**
Palynology (USA) **6729**
Parliamentary Affairs (GBR) **7163**
Party Politics (GBR) **7164**
Past & Present (GBR) **4155**
Pedagogy (USA) **3076**
Pediatric Asthma, Allergy & Immunology (USA) **6100**
Pediatric Research (USA) **6101**
Pediatrics (English Edition) (USA) **6102**
Pediatrics in Review (USA) **6102**
Perfusion (GBR) **5797**
Peritoneal Dialysis International (CAN) **5695**
Personality and Social Psychology Bulletin (USA) **7390**
Perspectives in Public Health (GBR) **8061**
Perspectives in Vascular Surgery and Endovascular Therapy (USA) **6255**
Pharmacological Reviews (USA) **6872**
Philosophia Mathematica (GBR) **6940**
Philosophical Review (USA) **6941**
Philosophy & Social Criticism (GBR) **6943**
Philosophy of the Social Sciences (USA) **7992**
Physical Therapy (USA) **6113**
Physician's First Watch (USA) **5696**
Physiological Genomics (USA) **742**
Physiological Reviews (USA) **926**
Physiology (USA) **926**
Planning Theory (GBR) **4423**
Plant and Cell Physiology (GBR) **835**
The Plant Cell (USA) **810**
Plant Physiology (USA) **812**
Poetics Today (USA) **5234**
Police Quarterly (USA) **4896**
Policy, Politics & Nursing Practice (USA) **5978**
Political Analysis (GBR) **7168**
Political Theory (USA) **7169**
Politics and Society (USA) **7170**
Politics, Philosophy & Economics (GBR) **7171**
positions (USA) **559**
Practical Neurology (GBR) **6174**
The Prison Journal (USA) **2666**
Probation Journal (GBR) **2666**
Progress in Development Studies (IND) **8126**
Progress in Human Geography (GBR) **4025**
Progress in Physical Geography (GBR) **4025**
Protein Engineering Design and Selection (Online) (GBR) **743**
Protein Science (USA) **743**
Psychiatric News (USA) **6176**
Psychiatric Services (USA) **6176**
The Psychiatrist (GBR) **6177**
Psychology and Developing Societies (IND) **7398**
Psychology of Music (GBR) **6608**
Psychosomatic Medicine (USA) **6179**
Psychosomatics (USA) **6179**
Psychotherapy Research (GBR) **7401**
Public Culture (USA) **5235**
Public Finance Review (USA) **1941**
Public Health Reports (USA) **7537**
Public Opinion Quarterly (USA) **7174**
Public Policy and Administration (GBR) **7462**
Public Understanding of Science (GBR) **7900**
Public Works Management & Policy (USA) **7463**
Publius (USA) **7174**
Punishment & Society (GBR) **2666**
Q J M (GBR) **5701**
Q S H C Online (GBR) *see* Quality and Safety in Health Care. **5701**
Qualitative Health Research (USA) **5701**
Qualitative Inquiry (USA) **7994**
Qualitative Research (GBR) **7994**
Qualitative Social Work (GBR) **8064**
Quarterly Journal of Engineering Geology and Hydrogeology (GBR) **3281**
Quarterly Journal of Mathematics (GBR) **5527**
Quarterly Journal of Mechanics and Applied Mathematics (GBR) **5527**
R E L C Journal (GBR) **5164**
R N A (GBR) **877**
Race & Class (GBR) **3560**
Race Relations Abstracts (USA) **8150**
Radical History Review (USA) **4157**
RadioGraphics (USA) **6206**
Radiologic Technology (USA) **6206**
Radiology (USA) **6206**
Rationality and Society (GBR) **7995**
Refugee Survey Quarterly (GBR) **7314**
Reproduction (GBR) **700**
Research on Aging (USA) **4054**
Research on Social Work Practice (USA) **8128**
The Review of English Studies (GBR) **5360**
Review of Finance (Print) (GBR) **1379**
The Review of Financial Studies (USA) **1379**
Review of Public Personnel Administration (USA) **7466**
Review of Radical Political Economics (USA) **1548**
Reviews in Mineralogy and Geochemistry (USA) **6477**
Rheumatology (Online) (GBR) **6227**
Rocky Mountain Geology (USA) **2765**
Royal Musical Association. Journal (GBR) **6613**
Royal Society of Medicine. Journal (GBR) **5707**
S A Q: The South Atlantic Quarterly (USA) **5237**
S T I Online (GBR) *see* Sexually Transmitted Infections. **5881**
Schizophrenia Bulletin (USA) **6184**
School Psychology International (GBR) **3080**
Science (USA) **7908**
Science Communication (USA) **8131**
Science Now (USA) **6394**
Science, Technology & Human Values (USA) **7911**
Science, Technology & Society (IND) **7911**
Screen (Oxford) (GBR) **2390**
Second Language Research (GBR) **5172**
Security Dialogue (GBR) **7265**
Seismological Society of America. Bulletin (USA) **2789**
Seminars in Cardiothoracic and Vascular Anesthesia (USA) **5799**
Sexualities (GBR) **7408**
The Shock and Vibration Digest (USA) **3357**
Simulation (GBR) **3220**
Simulation & Gaming (USA) **2518**
Small Group Research (USA) **7408**
Social & Legal Studies (GBR) **8132**
Social Cognitive and Affective Neuroscience (Online) (GBR) **6186**
Social Compass (GBR) **8132**
Social History of Medicine (GBR) **5715**
Social Politics (GBR) **8903**
Social Science Computer Review (USA) **2951**
Social Science History (USA) **8003**
Social Science Information (GBR) **8003**
Social Science Japan Journal (GBR) **8004**
Social Studies of Science (GBR) **7917**
Social Text (USA) **8134**
Societe Geologique de France. Bulletin (FRA) **2767**
Socio-Economic Review (GBR) **1517**
Sociological Methods & Research (USA) **8137**
Sociology (GBR) **8138**
Soil Science Society of America. Journal (USA) **253**
South African Journal of Geology (ZAF) **2768**
South Asia Economic Journal (IND) **1518**
South Asia Research (IND) **560**
South Asian Survey (IND) **4188**
Space & Culture (USA) **4029**
Statistical Methods in Medical Research (GBR) **8404**
Statistical Modelling (IND) **5538**
Statute Law Review (GBR) **4788**
Stem Cells (USA) **706**
Strategic Organization (GBR) **1795**
Stroke (USA) **5800**
Structural Health Monitoring (GBR) **8439**
Studies in Christian Ethics (GBR) **7685**
Studies in History (New Delhi) (IND) **4189**
Surgical Innovation (USA) **6260**
Survival (Abingdon) (GBR) **7268**
Teaching Mathematics and Its Applications (GBR) **5541**
Television & New Media (USA) **2396**
Textile Research Journal (GBR) **8460**
Theater (New Haven) (USA) **8481**
Theology and Sexuality (GBR) **7690**
Theoretical Criminology (GBR) **2670**
Theory & Psychology (GBR) **7412**
Theory and Research in Education (Online) (GBR) *see* Theory and Research in Education (Print). **2919**
Theory, Culture & Society (GBR) **8143**
Thesis Eleven (GBR) **7188**
Thorax (GBR) **6220**
Time & Society (GBR) **8144**
Tobbacco Control Online (GBR) *see* Tobacco Control. **8488**
Tourist Studies (GBR) **8764**
Toxicological Sciences (GBR) **3502**
Toxicology and Industrial Health (GBR) **3502**
Transcultural Psychiatry (GBR) **6188**
Transfusion (USA) **5723**
Transportation Science (USA) **8517**
Trauma (GBR) **6074**
Trauma, Violence & Abuse (USA) **6074**
Traumatology (Online) (USA) **6074**
Trusts & Trustees (GBR) **4906**
Twentieth Century British History (GBR) **4274**
Urban Affairs Review (USA) **4429**
Urban Education (USA) **2924**
Vadose Zone Journal (USA) **3473**
Vascular and Endovascular Surgery (USA) **6262**
Vascular Medicine (GBR) **5801**
Veterinary Pathology (USA) **8813**
The Veterinary Record (GBR) **8814**
Video Journal of Orthopaedics (USA) **6075**
Violence Against Women (USA) **8146**
Visual Communication (GBR) **2343**
War in History (GBR) **6453**
Waste Management and Research (GBR) **3513**
Western Journal of Nursing Research (USA) **5984**
Work and Occupations (USA) **8147**
Work, Employment & Society (GBR) **8147**
The World Bank Economic Review (USA) **1525**
World Bank Research Observer (USA) **1391**
Written Communication (USA) **2345**
The Year's Work in Critical and Cultural Theory (GBR) **4483**
The Year's Work in English Studies (GBR) **5403**
Young (IND) **2172**
Youth & Society (USA) **2172**
Youth Justice (GBR) **2672**
Youth Violence and Juvenile Justice (USA) **2672**

I E E E 3 Park Ave, 17th Fl, New York, NY 10016-5997 TEL 212-419-7900, FAX 212-752-4929, ieeeusa@ieee.org, http://www.ieee.org/ 445 Hoes Ln, Box 1331, Piscataway, NJ 08855-1331 TEL 732-981-0600, 800-678-4333, FAX 732-981-9667

A C M / I E E E Design Automation Conference. Proceedings (USA) **2457**
A C M / I E E E Joint Conference on Digital Libraries. Proceedings (USA) **4985**
American Control Conference. Proceedings (USA) **3295**
Annual Conference Computer Security Applications. Proceedings (USA) **2511**
Annual Hawaii International Conference on System Sciences. Proceedings (USA) **2519**
Annual I E E E Symposium on Field-Programmable Custom Computing Machines (USA) **2538**
Applied Imagery Pattern Recognition Workshop. Proceedings (USA) **2535**
Asia Pacific Software Engineering Conference. Proceedings (USA) **2587**
Asian Test Symposium. Proceedings (USA) **2539**

Online Service

DIRECTORY 2010 INGENTACONNECT 11163

I E T Microwaves Antennas & Propagation (GBR) **3317**
I E T Nanobiotechnology (GBR) **765**
I E T Optoelectronics (GBR) **7076**
I E T Radar, Sonar and Navigation (GBR) **3317**
I E T Science, Measurement and Technology (GBR) **3318**
I E T Software (GBR) **2590**
I E T Systems Biology (GBR) **825**
I P D P S Proceedings (USA) **2471**
I T I (HRV) **2421**
I T Professional (USA) **2421**
Industry Applications Society. I E E E - I A S Annual Meeting. Conference Record (USA) **3318**
Institute of Electrical and Electronics Engineers. Proceedings (USA) **3319**
Integration of Speech and Image Understanding. Proceedings (USA) **2351**
International Computer Performance and Dependability Symposium (USA) **2591**
International Conference of the Chilean Computer Science Society. Proceedings (USA) **2424**
International Conference on 3-D Digital Imaging and Modeling. Proceedings (USA) **2517**
International Conference on Advanced Information Networking and Applications. Proceedings (USA) **2498**
International Conference on Application of Concurrency to System Design. Proceedings (USA) **2521**
International Conference on Application-Specific Systems, Architecture and Processors. Proceedings (USA) **2471**
International Conference on Computer Animation and Social Agents. Proceedings (USA) **2487**
International Conference on Computer Communications and Networks. Proceedings (USA) **2498**
International Conference on Cooperative Information Systems. Proceedings (USA) **2498**
International Conference on Data Engineering. Proceedings (USA) **2471**
International Conference on Distributed Computing Systems. Proceedings (USA) **2467**
International Conference on Embedded and Real-Time Computing Systems and Applications. Proceedings (USA) **2521**
International Conference on G R I D Computing. Proceedings (USA) **2499**
International Conference on High-Performance Computing. Proceedings (USA) **2467**
International Conference on Image Processing. Proceedings (USA) **2487**
International Conference on Indium Phosphide and Related Materials. Proceedings (USA) **7077**
International Conference on Micro Electro Mechanical Systems (USA) **3320**
International Conference on Microelectronic Systems Education. Proceedings (USA) **2540**
International Conference on Network Protocols. Proceedings (USA) **2499**
International Conference on Neural Networks. Proceedings (USA) **2450**
International Conference on Parallel and Distributed Systems. Proceedings (USA) **2467**
International Conference on Parallel Architecture and Compilation Techniques. Proceedings (USA) **2467**
International Conference on Parallel Interconnects. Proceedings (USA) **2472**
International Conference on Parallel Processing. Proceedings (USA) **2467**
International Conference on Parallel Processing Workshop. Proceedings (USA) **2467**
International Conference on Pattern Recognition (USA) **2450**
International Conference on Scientific and Statistical Database Management. Proceedings (USA) **2591**
International Conference on Software Engineering. Proceedings (USA) **2591**
International Conference on Thermoelectrics (USA) **7052**
International Conference on V L S I Design. Proceedings (USA) **2540**
International Database Engineering and Applications Symposium (USA) **2521**
International Electron Devices Meeting. I E D M (Year) (USA) **3105**
International Enterprise Distributed Object Computing Conference. Proceedings (USA) **2521**
International Multimedia Modelling Conference. Proceedings (USA) **2534**
International Parallel Processing Symposium. Proceedings (USA) **2467**
International Power Modulator Symposium and High-Voltage Workshop. Proceedings (USA) **3321**
International Requirements Engineering Conference. Proceedings (USA) **2592**
International Symposium on Advanced Research in Asynchronous Circuits and Systems (USA) **3105**
International Symposium on Agent Systems and Applications. Proceedings (USA) **2522**
International Symposium on Defect and Fault - Tolerance in V L S I Systems. Proceedings (USA) **2540**
International Symposium on Discharges and Electrical Insulation in Vacuum. Proceedings (USA) **3321**
International Symposium on High-Performance Computer Architecture. Proceedings (USA) **2467**
International Symposium on High Performance Computing Systems and Applications. Proceedings (USA) **2522**
International Symposium on High-Performance Distributed Computing. Proceedings (USA) **2467**
International Symposium on Microarchitecture. Proceedings (USA) **2467**
International Symposium on Modeling, Analysis, and Simulation of Computer and Telecommunication Systems. Proceedings (USA) **2472**
International Symposium on Multiple-Valued Logic (USA) **2472**
International Symposium on Parallel Architectures, Algorithms, and Networks (USA) **2522**
International Symposium on Power Semiconductor Devices and ICs (USA) **3105**
International Symposium on Software Engineering Standards (USA) **2592**
International Symposium on Software Metrics (USA) **2592**
International Symposium on Software Reliability Engineering. Proceedings (USA) **2593**
International Symposium on System Synthesis. Proceedings (USA) **2593**
International Symposium on Uncertainty Modeling and Analysis. Proceedings (USA) **3321**
International Symposium on Wearable Computers. Digest of Papers (USA) **2427**
International Test Conference. Proceedings (USA) **2427**
International Verilog H D L Conference. Proceedings (USA) **2472**
International Workshop in Rapid System Prototyping. Proceedings (USA) **2593**
International Workshop on Database and Expert Systems Applications (USA) **2523**
International Workshop on Distributed Interactive Simulation and Real - Time Applications (USA) **2523**
International Workshop on Frontiers in Handwriting Recognition. Proceedings (USA) **2537**
International Workshop on Object Oriented Real Time Dependable Systems. Proceedings (USA) **2531**
International Workshop on Petri Nets and Performance Models (USA) **2452**
International Workshop on Principles of Software Evaluation. Proceedings (USA) **2593**
International Workshop on Program Comprehension. Proceedings (USA) **2427**
International Workshop on Recognition, Analysis, and Tracking of Faces and Gestures in Real-Time Systems. Proceedings (USA) **2427**
International Workshop on Research Issues in Data Engineering. Proceedings (USA) **2547**
International Workshop on Software Technology and Engineering Practice. Proceedings (USA) **2593**
International Workshop on Temporal Representation and Reasoning. Proceedings (USA) **2452**
International Workshop on Web Site Evaluation. Proceedings (USA) **2560**
Journal of Display Technology (USA) **3106**
Journal of Lightwave Technology (USA) **7078**
Machine Learning for Signal Processing (USA) **2454**
Midwest Symposium on Circuits and Systems. Conference Proceedings (USA) **2466**
N A S A - D O D Conference on Evolvable Hardware. Proceedings (USA) **2468**
Pacific Conference on Computer Graphics and Applications. Proceedings (USA) **2489**
Petroleum and Chemical Industry Conference. Record of Conference Papers (USA) **3252**
Pulp and Paper Industry Technical Conference. Conference Record (USA) **6737**
Real-Time Systems Symposium (USA) **2524**
Reliability and Maintainability Symposium. Proceedings (USA) **3329**
Simulation Symposium. Proceedings (USA) **2518**
Southcon Conference Record (USA) **3395**
Southeastern Symposium on System Theory. Proceedings (USA) **2525**
Southern Biomedical Engineering Conference. Proceedings (USA) **706**
Supercomputing Proceedings (USA) **2525**
Symposium on Computer Architecture and High Performance Computing. Proceedings (USA) **2551**
Symposium on Computer Arithmetic. Proceedings (USA) **2528**
Symposium on Foundations of Computer Science. Annual Proceedings (USA) **2438**
Symposium on Logic in Computer Science (USA) **2464**
Symposium on Reliable Distributed Systems. Proceedings (USA) **2525**
Symposium on the Frontiers of Massively Parallel Processing. Proceedings (USA) **2599**
Technology of Object Oriented Languages and Systems (USA) **2532**
Trends in Optics and Photonics Series (USA) **7085**
University - Government - Industry - Micro-Nano Symposium. Proceedings (USA) **3115**
User Interfaces to Data Intensive Systems. Proceedings (USA) **2532**
Working Conference on Reverse Engineering. Proceedings (USA) **2600**
Workshop on Computers in Power Electronics. Proceedings (USA) **2474**
Workshop on Future Trends of Distributed Computing Systems. Proceedings (USA) **2525**
Workshop on Hot Topics in Operating Systems (USA) **2600**
Workshop on Interaction Between Compilers and Computer Architectures. Proceedings (USA) **2468**
Workshop on Mobile Computing Systems and Applications (USA) **2457**
Workshop on Parallel and Distributed Simulation. Proceedings (USA) **2468**

IngentaConnect (Subsidiary of: Publishing Technology Plc.) 1 Riverside Court, Lower Bristol Rd., Bath BA2 3DZ, United Kingdom TEL 44-1225-361000, FAX 44-1225-361155 875; Massachusetts Ave., 7th Fl., Cambridge, MA 02139 TEL 617-497-6514, FAX 617-354-6875, info@ingenta.com, http://www.ingentaconnect.com/
A C O G Clinical Review (USA) **5739**
A E Ue: International Journal of Electronics and Communication (DEU) **2310**
A I & Society (GBR) **2444**
A I Communications (NLD) **2444**
A I D S Care (GBR) **5807**
A I L A Review (NLD) **5088**
A L T - J (GBR) **2964**
A N Z Journal of Surgery (AUS) **6234**
A Q Online (USA) *see* Academic Questions. **2965**
A St A - Advances in Statistical Analysis (DEU) **8343**
A St A - Wirtschafts- und Sozialstatistisches Archiv (DEU) **8343**
Abacus (GBR) **1275**
Abdominal Imaging (USA) **5919**
Academic Emergency Medicine (USA) **6054**
Academic Radiology (NLD) **6191**
Academie des Sciences. Comptes Rendus. Biologies (FRA) **649**
Academie des Sciences. Comptes Rendus. Chimie (FRA) **2048**
Academie des Sciences. Comptes Rendus. Geoscience (FRA) **7830**
Academie des Sciences. Comptes Rendus. Mathematique (FRA) **5464**
Academie des Sciences. Comptes Rendus. Mecanique (FRA) **3372**
Academie des Sciences. Comptes Rendus. Palevol (FRA) **6722**
Academie des Sciences. Comptes Rendus. Physique (FRA) **2132**
Accident Analysis & Prevention (GBR) **7506**
Accountability in Research (USA) **7831**
Accounting and Finance (GBR) **1277**
Accounting, Auditing and Accountability Journal (GBR) **1277**
Accounting, Business and Financial History (GBR) **1056**
Accounting Education (GBR) **1277**
Accounting, Organizations and Society (GBR) **1278**
Accreditation and Quality Assurance (DEU) **2096**
Acoustical Physics (RUS) **7086**
Across Languages and Cultures (HUN) **5089**
Acta Agriculturae Scandinavica. Section A. Animal Science (NOR) **277**
Acta Agriculturae Scandinavica. Section B. Soil and Plant Science (SWE) **216**
Acta Agriculturae Scandinavica. Section C. Food Economics (NOR) **190**
Acta Anaesthesiologica Scandinavica (DNK) **5768**
Acta Applicandae Mathematicae (NLD) **5464**
Acta Archaeologica (DNK) **370**
Acta Astronautica (GBR) **41**
Acta Biochimica et Biophysica Sinica (USA) **721**
Acta Biotheoretica (NLD) **649**
Acta Borealia (NOR) **7945**
Acta Chiropterologica (POL) **929**
Acta Crystallographica. Section A: Foundations of Crystallography. Online (DNK) *see* Acta Crystallographica. Section A: Foundations of Crystallography. **2108**
Acta Crystallographica. Section B: Structural Science. Online (DNK) *see* Acta Crystallographica. Section B: Structural Science. **2109**
Acta Crystallographica. Section C: Crystal Structure Communications (DNK) **2109**
Acta Crystallographica. Section D: Biological Crystallography (DNK) **2109**
Acta Crystallographica. Section E: Structure Reports Online (DNK) **2109**
Acta Diabetologica (DEU) **5883**
Acta Ethologica Online (DEU) **649**
Acta Geotechnica (DEU) **2776**
Acta Histochemica (DEU) **721**
Acta Ichthyologica et Piscatoria (POL) **929**
Acta Informatica (DEU) **2541**
Acta Juridica Hungarica (HUN) **4609**
Acta Linguistica Hungarica (HUN) **5090**
Acta Materialia (GBR) **6303**
Acta Mathematica Hungarica (NLD) **5464**
Acta Mathematica Sinica (DEU) **5464**
Acta Mathematicae Applicatae Sinica (DEU) **5465**
Acta Mechanica (AUT) **3372**
Acta Mechanica Sinica (DEU) **7057**
Acta Neurochirurgica (AUT) **6234**
Acta Neurologica Scandinavica (DNK) **6118**
Acta Neurologica Scandinavica. Supplementum (DNK) **6118**
Acta Neuropathologica (DEU) **6118**
Acta Neuropsychiatrica (DNK) **6118**
Acta Obstetricia et Gynecologica Scandinavica (GBR) **5985**
Acta Odontologica Scandinavica (NOR) **5833**
Acta Oecologica (FRA) **650**
Acta Oeconomica (HUN) **1056**
Acta Oncologica (SWE) **6007**
Acta Ophthamologica (Online) (DNK) **6037**
Acta Orientalia Academiae Scientiarum Hungaricae (HUN) **541**
Acta Ornithologica (POL) **901**
Acta Orthopaedica (Online) (GBR) **6054**
Acta Oto-Laryngologica (SWE) **6076**
Acta Paediatrica (GBR) **6086**
Acta Pathologica Microbiologica et Immunologica Scandinavica (DNK) **650**
Acta Pharmacologica Sinica (USA) **6818**
Acta Physiologiae Plantarum (DEU) **773**
Acta Physiologica (Online) (GBR) **918**
Acta Phytopathologica et Entomologica Hungarica (HUN) **773**
Acta Politica (GBR) **7101**
Acta Psychiatrica Scandinavica (GBR) **6119**
Acta Psychologica (NLD) **7330**
Acta Radiologica (GBR) **6192**
Acta Sociologica (NOR) **8085**
Acta Theriologica (POL) **930**
Acta Tropica (NLD) **5808**
Acta Veterinaria Hungarica (HUN) **8790**
Acta Zoologica Cracoviensia (POL) **930**
Acta Zoologica Online (GBR) **930**
Action Learning (GBR) **2824**
Active and Passive Electronic Components (GBR) **3294**
Acustica United with Acta Acustica (DEU) **7086**
Acute Cardiac Care (Online Edition) (GBR) **5775**
Acute Pain (NLD) **5567**
Ad Hoc Networks (NLD) **2495**
Addiction (GBR) **2689**
Addiction Biology (GBR) **2689**
Addiction Research and Theory (GBR) **2689**
Addictive Behaviors (GBR) **2690**
Additives for Polymers (GBR) **7090**
Adelphi Series (GBR) **7219**
Administration and Policy in Mental Health and Mental Health Services Research (USA) **5567**
Adoption and Fostering (GBR) **8023**
Adsorption (USA) **3235**
Adsorption Science and Technology (GBR) **3235**
Advanced Composite Materials (NLD) **3335**
Advanced Drug Delivery Reviews (NLD) **6819**
Advanced Engineering Informatics (GBR) **2445**
Advanced Powder Technology (NLD) **3235**
Advanced Robotics (NLD) **2584**
Advanced Science Letters (Valencia) (USA) **7833**
Advances in Applied Ceramics (Online) (GBR) **2047**
Advances in Applied Clifford Algebras (CHE) **2049**
Advances in Applied Mathematics (USA) **5466**
Advances in Colloid and Interface Science (NLD) **2132**
Advances in Computational Mathematics (NLD) **5549**
Advances in Data Analysis and Classification (DEU) **2541**
Advances in Engineering Software (GBR) **3288**
Advances in Enzyme Regulation (GBR) **721**
Advances in Health Sciences Education (NLD) **5568**
Advances in Mathematics (USA) **5466**
Advances in Organic Synthesis (NLD) **2119**
Advances in Physics (GBR) **7004**
Advances in Physiotherapy (SWE) **6106**
Advances in Space Research (GBR) **41**
Advances in Structural Engineering (GBR) **3258**
Advances in Therapy (GBR) **5568**
Advances in Water Resources (GBR) **8817**
Aequationes Mathematicae (CHE) **5467**
Aerobiologia (NLD) **651**
Aerosol Science and Technology (USA) **2049**
Aerospace Science and Technology (FRA) **43**
Aesthetic Plastic Surgery (USA) **6235**
Africa Research Bulletin. Economic, Financial and Technical Series (GBR) **1435**
Africa Research Bulletin. Political, Social and Cultural Series (GBR) **7102**
African Affairs (GBR) **7103**
African and Asian Studies (NLD) **8086**
African and Black Diaspora (USA) **3516**
African Archaeological Review (USA) **371**
African Development Review (GBR) **1590**
African Diaspora (NLD) **7945**
African Identities (GBR) **3516**
African Journal of AIDS Research (ZAF) **5808**
African Journal of Aquatic Science (ZAF) **651**
African Journal of Ecology Online (GBR) **651**
African Journal of Marine Science (ZAF) **3583**
African Journal of Range & Forage Science (ZAF) **216**
African Journal of Reproductive Health (NGA) **8843**
African Studies (GBR) **323**
Afro-Asian Journal of Finance and Accounting (GBR) **1279**
Age and Ageing (GBR) **4038**
Ageing Research Reviews (IRL) **4039**
Aggression and Violent Behavior (GBR) **7332**
Aging & Mental Health (GBR) **4039**
Aging Cell (GBR) **827**
Aging Health (GBR) **4039**
The Aging Male (GBR) **6283**
Agricultural and Food Science (Online) (FIN) *see* Agricultural and Food Science (Print). **83**
Agricultural and Forest Entomology (GBR) **837**
Agricultural and Forest Meteorology (NLD) **6346**
Agricultural Economics (USA) **192**
Agricultural Systems (NLD) **85**
Agricultural Water Management (NLD) **217**
Agriculture and Human Values (NLD) **85**

Online Service

Link to your serials resources and content with ulrichsweb.com

International Journal of Electrical Power & Energy Systems (GBR) **3321**
International Journal of Electronic Banking (GBR) **1357**
International Journal of Electronic Business (GBR) **1418**
International Journal of Electronic Customer Relationship Management (GBR) **1756**
International Journal of Electronic Democracy (GBR) **7143**
International Journal of Electronic Finance (GBR) **1357**
International Journal of Electronic Governance (GBR) **7446**
International Journal of Electronic Healthcare (GBR) **4102**
International Journal of Electronic Marketing and Retailing (GBR) **1821**
International Journal of Electronic Security and Digital Forensics (GBR) **2514**
International Journal of Electronics (GBR) **3105**
International Journal of Embedded Systems (GBR) **2425**
International Journal of Emergency Management (GBR) **1757**
International Journal of Emergency Medicine (Online) (USA) **6062**
International Journal of Emerging Markets (GBR) **1571**
International Journal of Energy Technology and Policy (CHE) **3139**
International Journal of Engineering Education (IRL) **3201**
International Journal of Engineering Science (GBR) **3201**
International Journal of Engineering Systems Modelling and Simulation (GBR) **3292**
International Journal of Enterprise Network Management (GBR) **1757**
International Journal of Entrepreneurial Behaviour & Research (GBR) **1962**
International Journal of Entrepreneurial Venturing (GBR) **1757**
International Journal of Entrepreneurship and Innovation (GBR) **1128**
International Journal of Entrepreneurship and Innovation Management (GBR) **1757**
International Journal of Entrepreneurship and Small Business (GBR) **1757**
International Journal of Environment and Health (GBR) **3441**
International Journal of Environment and Pollution (GBR) **3487**
International Journal of Environment and Sustainable Development (GBR) **3441**
International Journal of Environment and Waste Management (GBR) **3507**
International Journal of Environment, Workplace and Employment (GBR) **1689**
International Journal of Environmental Analytical Chemistry (GBR) **2101**
International Journal of Environmental Health Research (GBR) **3442**
International Journal of Environmental Technology and Management (GBR) **3442**
International Journal of Epidemiology (GBR) **5638**
International Journal of Evidence-Based Healthcare (AUS) **5638**
International Journal of Exergy (GBR) **3201**
International Journal of Experimental and Computational Biomechanics (GBR) **749**
International Journal of Experimental Pathology (GBR) **5638**
International Journal of Fatigue (GBR) **3346**
International Journal of Financial Services Management (GBR) **1357**
International Journal of Food Microbiology (NLD) **887**
International Journal of Food Safety, Nutrition and Public Health (GBR) **3648**
International Journal of Food Science & Technology Online (GBR) **3648**
International Journal of Food Sciences and Nutrition (GBR) **6660**
International Journal of Forecasting (NLD) **1493**
International Journal of Foresight and Innovation Policy (GBR) **7446**
International Journal of Fracture (NLD) **3347**
International Journal of Functional Informatics and Personalised Medicine (GBR) **5638**
International Journal of Game Theory (DEU) **5496**
International Journal of General Systems (CHE) **2522**
International Journal of Geographical Information Science (GBR) **4037**
International Journal of Global Energy Issues (GBR) **3139**
International Journal of Global Environmental Issues (GBR) **3442**
International Journal of Globalisation and Small Business (GBR) **1962**
International Journal of Green Economics (GBR) **1128**
International Journal of Grid and Utility Computing (GBR) **3155**
International Journal of Gynecological Cancer (USA) **5993**
International Journal of Gynecology & Obstetrics (IRL) **5994**
International Journal of Health Care Finance and Economics (USA) **7526**
International Journal of Health Care Quality Assurance (GBR) **5639**
International Journal of Healthcare Technology and Management (GBR) **5831**
International Journal of Heat and Fluid Flow (USA) **7054**
International Journal of Heat and Mass Transfer (GBR) **3382**
International Journal of Heavy Vehicle Systems (GBR) **8499**
International Journal of Hematology (JPN) **5938**
International Journal of Heritage Studies (GBR) **4147**
International Journal of High Performance Computing and Networking (GBR) **2499**
International Journal of High Performance Systems Architecture (GBR) **2467**
International Journal of Historical Archaeology (USA) **398**
International Journal of Hospitality Management (GBR) **4391**
International Journal of Human-Computer Studies (GBR) **2527**
International Journal of Human Factors Modelling and Simulation (GBR) **3292**
International Journal of Human Resource Management (GBR) **1867**
International Journal of Human Resources Development and Management (GBR) **1867**
The International Journal of Human Rights (GBR) **7210**
International Journal of Hydrogen Energy (GBR) **3139**
International Journal of Hygiene and Environmental Health (DEU) **7526**
International Journal of Hyperthermia (GBR) **6023**
International Journal of Immunogenetics (GBR) **873**
International Journal of Impact Engineering (GBR) **3201**
The International Journal of Inclusive Democracy (GBR) **7143**
International Journal of Inclusive Education (GBR) **2870**
International Journal of Indian Culture and Business Management (GBR) **1757**
International Journal of Industrial and Systems Engineering (GBR) **3368**
International Journal of Industrial Ergonomics (NLD) **3201**
International Journal of Industrial Organization (NLD) **1757**
International Journal of Infectious Diseases (GBR) **5818**
International Journal of Information and Communication Technology (GBR) **2559**
International Journal of Information and Computer Security (GBR) **2514**
International Journal of Information and Decision Sciences (GBR) **1757**
International Journal of Information and Operations Management Education (GBR) **1757**
International Journal of Information Management (GBR) **2547**
International Journal of Information Quality (GBR) **2547**
International Journal of Information Security (DEU) **2514**
International Journal of Information Systems and Change Management (GBR) **1758**
International Journal of Information Technology and Management (GBR) **2537**
International Journal of Injury Control and Safety Promotion (GBR) **2638**
International Journal of Innovation and Learning (GBR) **1758**
International Journal of Innovation and Regional Development (GBR) **1599**
International Journal of Innovation and Sustainable Development (GBR) **1758**
International Journal of Innovative Computing and Applications (GBR) **2451**
International Journal of Integrated Supply Management (GBR) **1821**
International Journal of Intellectual Property Management (GBR) **6753**
International Journal of Intelligence and Counterintelligence (USA) **7243**
International Journal of Intelligent Defence Support Systems (GBR) **2426**
International Journal of Intelligent Enterprise (GBR) **1128**
International Journal of Intelligent Information and Database Systems (GBR) **2531**
International Journal of Intelligent Systems Technologies and Applications (GBR) **2451**
International Journal of Intercultural Information Management (GBR) **2547**
International Journal of Intercultural Relations (GBR) **8109**
International Journal of Internet and Enterprise Management (GBR) **1758**
International Journal of Internet Manufacturing and Services (GBR) **2559**
International Journal of Internet Marketing and Advertising (GBR) **2559**
International Journal of Internet Protocol Technology (GBR) **2559**
International Journal of Internet Technology and Secured Transactions (GBR) **2559**
International Journal of Inventory Research (GBR) **1758**
International Journal of Japanese Sociology (AUS) **8109**
International Journal of Knowledge and Learning (GBR) **1758**
International Journal of Knowledge Engineering and Soft Data Paradigms (GBR) **2452**
International Journal of Knowledge Management Studies (GBR) **1758**
International Journal of Laboratory Hematology (Online) (GBR) **5938**
International Journal of Language and Communication Disorders (GBR) **6081**
International Journal of Law and Information Technology (GBR) **4695**
International Journal of Law and Management (GBR) **1689**
International Journal of Law and Psychiatry (GBR) **4695**
International Journal of Law Crime and Justice (GBR) **4695**
International Journal of Law, Policy and the Family (GBR) **4911**
International Journal of Leadership in Education (GBR) **2870**
The International Journal of Leadership in Public Service (GBR) **7447**
International Journal of Learning and Change (GBR) **1758**
International Journal of Learning and Intellectual Capital (GBR) **1867**
International Journal of Learning Technology (GBR) **8427**
International Journal of Leisure and Tourism Marketing (GBR) **8723**
International Journal of Lexicography (GBR) **5129**
International Journal of Liability and Scientific Enquiry (GBR) **7867**
International Journal of Lifelong Education (GBR) **2942**
International Journal of Logistics (GBR) **1128**
International Journal of Logistics Economics and Globalisation (GBR) **8499**
The International Journal of Logistics Management (GBR) **1758**
International Journal of Logistics Systems and Management (GBR) **1758**
International Journal of Low-Carbon Technologies (GBR) **3443**
International Journal of Low Radiation (GBR) **3443**
International Journal of Machine Tools and Manufacture (GBR) **3369**
International Journal of Machining and Machinability of Materials (GBR) **5453**
International Journal of Management and Decision Making (GBR) **1759**
International Journal of Management and Enterprise Development (GBR) **1759**
International Journal of Management and Network Economics (GBR) **1759**
International Journal of Management Concepts and Philosophy (GBR) **1759**
International Journal of Management in Education (GBR) **3013**
International Journal of Management Practice (GBR) **1759**
International Journal of Management Reviews (GBR) **1759**
International Journal of Managerial and Financial Accounting (GBR) **1292**
International Journal of Managerial Finance (GBR) **1357**
International Journal of Managing Projects in Business (GBR) **1759**
International Journal of Manpower (GBR) **1689**
International Journal of Manufacturing Research (GBR) **3382**
International Journal of Manufacturing Technology and Management (GBR) **3382**
The International Journal of Marine and Coastal Law (NLD) **4969**
International Journal of Mass Customisation (GBR) **1889**
International Journal of Mass Spectrometry (NLD) **7077**
International Journal of Materials and Product Technology (GBR) **3347**
International Journal of Materials and Structural Integrity (GBR) **3202**
International Journal of Mathematical Education in Science and Technology (GBR) **5496**
International Journal of Mathematics in Operational Research (GBR) **5497**
International Journal of Mechanical Engineering Education (GBR) **3202**
International Journal of Mechanical Sciences (GBR) **3347**
International Journal of Mechanics and Materials in Design (NLD) **3347**
International Journal of Mechatronics and Manufacturing Systems (GBR) **3382**
International Journal of Medical Engineering and Informatics (GBR) **5831**
International Journal of Medical Informatics (IRL) **5831**
International Journal of Medical Microbiology (DEU) **5818**
International Journal of Mental Health and Addiction (USA) **7365**
International Journal of Mental Health Nursing (AUS) **6146**
The International Journal of Mental Health Promotion (GBR) **7526**
International Journal of Metadata, Semantics and Ontologies (GBR) **2559**
International Journal of Methods in Psychiatric Research (GBR) **6147**
International Journal of Micro Air Vehicles (GBR) **61**
International Journal of Microstructure and Materials Properties (GBR) **3347**
International Journal of Mineral Processing (NLD) **6466**
International Journal of Mining and Mineral Engineering (GBR) **6466**
International Journal of Mining, Reclamation and Environment (GBR) **6466**
International Journal of Mobile Communications (GBR) **2327**
International Journal of Mobile Learning and Organisation (GBR) **1759**
International Journal of Mobile Network Design and Innovation (GBR) **2351**
International Journal of Modelling, Identification and Control (GBR) **2462**
International Journal of Monetary Economics and Finance (GBR) **1357**
International Journal of Multiphase Flow (GBR) **3382**
The International Journal of Multiphysics (GBR) **7017**
International Journal of Myriapodology (NLD) **850**
International Journal of Nano and Biomaterials (GBR) **7867**
International Journal of Nanomanufacturing (GBR) **3382**
International Journal of Nanoparticles (GBR) **766**
International Journal of Nanotechnology (GBR) **3347**
International Journal of Nautical Archaeology (GBR) **398**
International Journal of Networking and Virtual Organisations (GBR) **2499**
International Journal of Neuroscience (CHE) **6147**
International Journal of Non-Linear Mechanics (GBR) **3347**
International Journal of Nonprofit and Voluntary Sector Marketing (GBR) **1822**
International Journal of Nuclear Desalination (GBR) **8826**
International Journal of Nuclear Energy Science and Technology (GBR) **3169**
International Journal of Nuclear Governance, Economy and Ecology (GBR) **3169**
International Journal of Nuclear Hydrogen Production and Applications (GBR) **3169**
International Journal of Nuclear Knowledge Management (GBR) **3169**
International Journal of Nuclear Law (GBR) **4695**
International Journal of Numerical Methods for Heat and Fluid Flow (GBR) **3272**
International Journal of Nursing Practice (AUS) **5962**
International Journal of Nursing Studies (GBR) **5962**
The International Journal of Nursing Terminologies and Classifications (USA) **5962**
International Journal of Ocean Systems Management (GBR) **8647**
International Journal of Oil, Gas and Coal Technology (GBR) **6774**
International Journal of Older People Nursing (GBR) **5962**
International Journal of Operational Research (GBR) **1760**
International Journal of Operations and Production Management (GBR) **1760**
International Journal of Organizational Analysis (GBR) **1760**
International Journal of Paediatric Dentistry (Online) (GBR) **5849**
International Journal of Parallel, Emergent and Distributed Systems (CHE) **2507**
International Journal of Parallel Programming (USA) **2507**
The International Journal of Pavement Engineering (GBR) **3272**
International Journal of Pediatric Otorhinolaryngology (IRL) **6081**
International Journal of Peptide Research and Therapeutics (NLD) **734**
International Journal of Performance Analysis in Sport (GBR) **8180**
International Journal of Pest Management (GBR) **237**
International Journal of Pharmaceutics (NLD) **6850**
International Journal of Pharmacy Practice (GBR) **6850**
International Journal of Philosophical Studies Online (GBR) *see* International Journal of Philosophical Studies. **6926**
International Journal of Physical Distribution & Logistics Management (GBR) **8671**
International Journal of Phytoremediation (USA) **3443**
International Journal of Plasticity (GBR) **3348**
International Journal of Politics, Culture, and Society (USA) **7243**
International Journal of Polymer Analysis & Characterization (USA) **3247**
International Journal of Polymeric Materials (CHE) **3247**
International Journal of Postharvest Technology and Innovation (GBR) **201**
International Journal of Power and Energy Conversion (GBR) **3159**
International Journal of Power Electronics (GBR) **3105**
International Journal of Precision Technology (GBR) **3202**

Online Service

Link to your serials resources and content with ulrichsweb.com

International Journal of Pressure Vessels and Piping (GBR) **3383**
International Journal of Primatology (USA) **948**
International Journal of Private Law (GBR) **4695**
International Journal of Process Management and Benchmarking (GBR) **1760**
International Journal of Procurement Management (GBR) **1760**
International Journal of Product Development (GBR) **1760**
International Journal of Product Lifecycle Management (GBR) **1822**
International Journal of Production Economics (NLD) **3369**
International Journal of Production Research (GBR) **1889**
International Journal of Productivity and Performance Management (GBR) **1760**
International Journal of Productivity and Quality Management (GBR) **1760**
International Journal of Project Management (GBR) **1419**
International Journal of Project Organisation and Management (GBR) **1760**
International Journal of Psychiatry in Clinical Practice (GBR) **6147**
The International Journal of Psychoanalysis (GBR) **7365**
International Journal of Psychoanalytic Self Psychology (USA) **7365**
International Journal of Psychology (GBR) **7365**
International Journal of Psychophysiology (NLD) **7365**
International Journal of Public Administration (USA) **7447**
International Journal of Public Health (CHE) **5639**
International Journal of Public Opinion Research (GBR) **7144**
International Journal of Public Policy (GBR) **7447**
International Journal of Public Sector Management (GBR) **1761**
International Journal of Public Sector Performance Management (GBR) **7447**
International Journal of Public Theology (NLD) **7650**
International Journal of Qualitative Studies in Education (GBR) **2870**
International Journal of Quality & Reliability Management (GBR) **1761**
International Journal of Radiation Biology (GBR) **6023**
International Journal of Radiation: Oncology - Biology - Physics (USA) **6199**
International Journal of Radio Frequency Identification Technology and Applications (GBR) **2359**
International Journal of Refractory Metals and Hard Materials (GBR) **6317**
International Journal of Refrigeration (GBR) **4122**
International Journal of Refugee Law (GBR) **7243**
International Journal of Reliability and Safety (GBR) **3202**
International Journal of Remote Sensing (GBR) **2710**
International Journal of Research and Method in Education (Online) (GBR) **2870**
International Journal of Research in Marketing (NLD) **1822**
International Journal of Retail & Distribution Management (GBR) **1822**
International Journal of Revenue Management (GBR) **1357**
International Journal of Rheumatic Diseases (AUS) **6224**
International Journal of Risk Assessment and Management (GBR) **1761**
International Journal of Rock Mechanics and Mining Sciences (GBR) **6466**
International Journal of Science and Mathematics Education (NLD) **7868**
International Journal of Science Education (GBR) **2871**
International Journal of Security and Networks (GBR) **2499**
International Journal of Selection and Assessment (GBR) **1867**
International Journal of Sensor Networks (GBR) **2499**
International Journal of Services and Operations Management (GBR) **1761**
International Journal of Services and Standards (GBR) **1129**
International Journal of Services, Economics and Management (GBR) **1761**
International Journal of Services Operations and Informatics (GBR) **1761**
International Journal of Services Sciences (GBR) **1761**
International Journal of Services Technology and Management (GBR) **1419**
International Journal of Shipping and Transport Logistics (GBR) **8647**
International Journal of Signal and Imaging Systems Engineering (GBR) **3321**
International Journal of Simulation and Process Modelling (GBR) **1419**
International Journal of Six Sigma and Competitive Advantage (GBR) **3369**
International Journal of Social Economics (GBR) **1129**
International Journal of Social Humanistic Computing (GBR) **7974**
International Journal of Social Research Methodology (GBR) **7974**
International Journal of Social Welfare (GBR) **8047**
International Journal of Society Systems Science (GBR) **7975**
International Journal of Sociology and Social Policy (GBR) **8109**
International Journal of Solids and Structures (GBR) **7059**
International Journal of Space Structures (GBR) **1016**
International Journal of Speech-Language Pathology (GBR) **5129**
International Journal of Speech Technology (NLD) **5203**
International Journal of Sports Management and Marketing (GBR) **1761**
International Journal of Sports Science and Coaching (GBR) **8180**
International Journal of Strategic Business Alliances (GBR) **1129**
International Journal of Strategic Change Management (GBR) **1761**
International Journal of Stress Management (USA) **5640**
International Journal of Stroke (AUS) **5790**
International Journal of Surface Science and Engineering (GBR) **3348**
International Journal of Sustainability in Higher Education (Online) (GBR) **2988**
International Journal of Sustainable Design (GBR) **1129**
International Journal of Sustainable Development (GBR) **3443**
International Journal of Sustainable Development and World Ecology (GBR) **3443**
International Journal of Sustainable Economy (GBR) **1129**
International Journal of Sustainable Energy (GBR) **3176**
International Journal of Sustainable Society (GBR) **8110**
International Journal of Sustainable Strategic Management (GBR) **1761**
International Journal of System of Systems Engineering (GBR) **3202**
International Journal of Systematic Theology (GBR) **7651**
International Journal of Systems, Control and Communications (GBR) **2522**
International Journal of Systems Science (GBR) **3203**
International Journal of Teaching and Case Studies (GBR) **2871**
International Journal of Technoentrepreneurship (GBR) **1761**
International Journal of Technological Learning, Innovation and Development (GBR) **8427**
International Journal of Technology and Design Education (NLD) **3065**
International Journal of Technology and Globalisation (GBR) **8427**
International Journal of Technology Enhanced Learning (GBR) **3065**
International Journal of Technology Intelligence and Planning (GBR) **8427**
International Journal of Technology Management (GBR) **8427**
International Journal of Technology Marketing (GBR) **1822**
International Journal of Technology Policy and Management (GBR) **8427**
International Journal of Technology Transfer and Commercialisation (GBR) **8428**
International Journal of the Economics of Business (GBR) **1129**
The International Journal of the History of Sport (GBR) **4147**
International Journal of the Legal Profession (GBR) **4695**
International Journal of the Platonic Tradition (NLD) **6926**
International Journal of Theoretical and Applied Multiscale Mechanics (GBR) **3348**
International Journal of Theoretical Physics (USA) **7018**
International Journal of Thermal Sciences (FRA) **7055**
International Journal of Thermophysics (USA) **7055**
International Journal of Tourism Policy (GBR) **8723**
International Journal of Toxicology (GBR) **3498**
International Journal of Trade and Global Markets (GBR) **1762**
International Journal of Training & Development (GBR) **1867**
International Journal of Tropical Insect Science (KEN) **850**
International Journal of Tuberculosis and Lung Disease (FRA) **6215**
International Journal of Urban and Regional Research (GBR) **4416**
International Journal of Urological Nursing (GBR) **5962**
International Journal of Urology (AUS) **6269**
International Journal of Value Chain Management (GBR) **1762**
International Journal of Vehicle Autonomous Systems (GBR) **8499**
International Journal of Vehicle Design (GBR) **8499**
International Journal of Vehicle Information and Communication Systems (GBR) **8500**
International Journal of Vehicle Noise and Vibration (GBR) **8500**
International Journal of Vehicle Safety (GBR) **8500**
International Journal of Vehicle Systems Modelling and Testing (GBR) **8586**
International Journal of Virtual Technology and Multimedia (GBR) **2351**
International Journal of Water (GBR) **8826**
International Journal of Water Resources Development (GBR) **8826**
International Journal of Web and Grid Services (GBR) **2559**
International Journal of Web Based Communities (GBR) **2559**
International Journal of Web Engineering and Technology (GBR) **2547**
International Journal of Web Information Systems (GBR) **2560**
International Journal of Wireless and Mobile Computing (GBR) **2351**
International Journal of Wireless Information Networks (USA) **2327**
International Journal of Work Organisation and Emotion (GBR) **1867**
International Journal of Workplace Health Management (GBR) **6679**
International Journal on Digital Libraries (DEU) **5062**
International Journal on Document Analysis and Recognition (DEU) **2427**
International Journal on Minority and Group Rights (NLD) **7210**
International Journal on Software Tools for Technology Transfer (DEU) **2592**
International Labour Review (GBR) **1689**
International Marketing Review (GBR) **1822**
International Materials Reviews (GBR) **3348**
International Migration (GBR) **7285**
International Migration Review (USA) **7285**
International Monetary Fund. Economic Issues (USA) **1571**
International Monetary Fund. Research Bulletin (USA) **1358**
International Musculoskeletal Medicine (GBR) **6062**
International Negotiation (NLD) **7244**
International Nursing Review Online (GBR) **5962**
International Ophthalmology (NLD) **6044**
International Organizations Law Review (NLD) **4932**
International Orthopaedics (DEU) **6062**
International Peacekeeping (GBR) **7244**
International Planning Studies (GBR) **4416**
International Political Sociology (GBR) **8110**
International Politics (GBR) **7244**
International Public Management Journal (GBR) **7447**
International Relations of the Asia-Pacific (GBR) **7245**
International Review of Applied Economics (GBR) **1129**
International Review of Economics (DEU) **1130**
International Review of Economics & Finance (GBR) **1493**
International Review of Education (DEU) **2871**
International Review of Finance (GBR) **1358**
International Review of Financial Analysis (GBR) **1359**
International Review of Law and Economics (USA) **4696**
International Review of Law, Computers & Technology (GBR) **4845**
International Review of Psychiatry (GBR) **6148**
The International Review of Retail, Distribution and Consumer Research (GBR) **1822**
International Review of Sociology (GBR) **8110**
International Reviews in Physical Chemistry (GBR) **2136**
International Reviews of Immunology (CHE) **5761**
International Social Science Journal (GBR) **7975**
International Social Security Review (GBR) **4509**
The International Spectator (GBR) **7245**
International Statistical Review (GBR) **8379**
International Studies in Sociology of Education (GBR) **3066**
International Studies in the Philosophy of Science (GBR) **6926**
International Studies Perspectives (USA) **7245**
International Studies Quarterly (USA) **7245**
International Studies Review (USA) **7245**
International Tax and Public Finance (USA) **1930**
International Trade by Commodities Statistics (FRA) **1244**
The International Trade Journal (USA) **1572**
International Transactions in Operational Research (GBR) **2427**
International Urogynecology Journal (GBR) **5994**
International Urology and Nephrology (NLD) **6269**
International Wound Journal (GBR) **6062**
International Zoo Yearbook (GBR) **948**
Internationale Revue fuer Soziale Sicherheit (GBR) **7975**
The Internet and Higher Education (GBR) **2560**
Internet Research (GBR) **2561**
Der Internist (DEU) **5946**
Interpreting (NLD) **5130**
Interventions (GBR) **5310**
Inventiones Mathematicae (DEU) **5498**
Inverse Problems (GBR) **5553**
Inverse Problems in Science and Engineering (GBR) **3203**
Invertebrate Biology (USA) **948**
Invertebrate Neuroscience (DEU) **949**
Investigational New Drugs (USA) **6851**
Ionics (DEU) **7018**
Iran and the Caucasus (NLD) **552**
Iranian Studies (GBR) **552**
Irish Economic and Social History (IRL) **4232**
Irish Educational Studies (GBR) **2871**
Irish Journal of Medical Science (GBR) **5641**
Irish Political Studies (GBR) **7144**
The Irish Review (IRL) **3541**
Irish Studies Review (GBR) **5221**
Ironmaking & Steelmaking (GBR) **3348**
Irrigation and Drainage Systems (NLD) **212**
Irrigation Science (DEU) **124**
Islam and Christian - Muslim Relations (GBR) **7711**
Islamic Law and Society (NLD) **7712**
The Island Arc (AUS) **2748**
Isokinetics and Exercise Science (NLD) **6230**
Isotopes in Environmental and Health Studies (GBR) **2066**
Israel Affairs (GBR) **7246**
Israel Journal of Mathematics (USA) **5498**
Israel Studies Forum (USA) **4322**
Issues in Comprehensive Pediatric Nursing (USA) **5963**
Issues in Mental Health Nursing (USA) **5963**
Italian Studies (GBR) **5311**
The Italianist (GBR) **4234**
ITNOW (Online) (GBR) **2427**
J A H Online (USA) *see* Journal of Adolescent Health. **5645**
J A O C S (USA) **2124**
J A R O (USA) **6081**
J D D G (Online Edition) (DEU) *see* J D D G (Print Edition). **5878**
J E M (USA) **2872**
J E T P Letters Online (USA) *see* J E T P Letters. **7019**
J M B Online (GBR) *see* Journal of Molecular Biology. **736**
J O M (USA) **6318**
Jahrbuch fuer Regionalwissenschaft (DEU) **7869**
Japan and the World Economy (NLD) **1543**
Japan Forum (GBR) **7247**
Japan Journal of Nursing Science (JPN) **5963**
The Japanese Economic Review (AUS) **1131**
Japanese Journal of Clinical Oncology (GBR) **6023**
Japanese Journal of Ophthalmology (NLD) **6044**
Japanese Journal of Radiology (JPN) **6199**
Japanese Psychological Research (JPN) **7367**
Japanese Studies (GBR) **8111**
Jewish History (ISR) **7723**
Jewish Studies Quarterly (DEU) **7724**
Joint Bone Spine (FRA) **6062**
Joint Commission Benchmark (USA) **4103**
The Joint Commission Journal on Quality and Patient Safety (USA) **4103**
Joint Commission Perspectives (USA) **7528**
Joint Commission Perspectives on Patient Safety (USA) **4103**
Joint Commission: The Source (USA) **4103**
Journal de Mathematiques Pures et Appliquees (FRA) **5499**
Journal for Cultural Research (GBR) **4459**
Journal for Eighteenth-Century Studies (GBR) **4459**
Journal for European Environmental & Planning Law (NLD) **4699**
Journal for General Philosophy of Science (NLD) **7871**
Journal for Global Business Advancement (GBR) **1763**
Journal for International Business and Entrepreneurship Development (GBR) **1573**
Journal for Nature Conservation (DEU) **3444**
Journal for Specialists in Group Work (USA) **7367**
Journal for Specialists in Pediatric Nursing (USA) **5963**
Journal for the History of Astronomy (GBR) **576**
Journal for the Scientific Study of Religion (USA) **7653**
Journal for the Study of Judaism (NLD) **7725**
Journal for the Study of the Historical Jesus (NLD) **7653**
Journal for the Theory of Social Behaviour (GBR) **7367**
Journal for Vascular Ultrasound (Online Edition) (USA) **5791**
Journal fuer Betriebswirtschaft (DEU) **1763**
Journal fuer Rechtspolitik (AUT) **4699**
Journal fuer Verbraucherschutz und Lebensmittelsicherheit (CHE) **7528**
Journal in Computer Virology (FRA) **2515**
Journal of Abnormal Child Psychology (USA) **7368**
Journal of Academic Ethics (NLD) **2989**
The Journal of Academic Librarianship (GBR) **5020**
Journal of Access Policy & Practice (GBR) **2943**
Journal of Accounting and Economics (NLD) **1293**
Journal of Accounting & Organizational Change (GBR) **1293**
Journal of Accounting and Public Policy (USA) **1293**
Journal of Accounting Education (GBR) **1293**
Journal of Accounting Research (USA) **1294**
Journal of Addictions Nursing (GBR) **5964**
Journal of Adhesion (CHE) **7019**
Journal of Adhesion Science and Technology (NLD) **7093**
Journal of Adolescence (GBR) **2156**
Journal of Adult & Continuing Education (GBR) **2943**
Journal of Adult Development (USA) **7368**
The Journal of Adult Protection (GBR) **4700**
Journal of Advanced Nursing (GBR) **5964**
Journal of Advanced Transportation (CAN) **8500**
Journal of Aerosol Science (GBR) **6711**
Journal of Aesthetics and Art Criticism (USA) **498**

Journal of Affective Disorders (NLD) 6149
Journal of African Cultural Studies (GBR) 4459
Journal of African Earth Sciences (GBR) 2749
Journal of African Economies (GBR) 1494
Journal of Aging Studies (GBR) 4048
Journal of Agrarian Change (GBR) 201
Journal of Agricultural and Environmental Ethics (NLD) 6927
Journal of Agricultural Economics (GBR) 202
Journal of Agricultural Education and Extension (GBR) 126
Journal of Agronomy and Crop Science Online (DEU) 239
Journal of Air Transport Management (GBR) 1763
Journal of Algebra (USA) 5500
Journal of Algebraic Combinatorics (USA) 5500
Journal of Algorithms (USA) 5553
Journal of Algorithms & Computational Technology (GBR) 5500
Journal of Allied Health (USA) 7528
Journal of Alloys and Compounds (CHE) 6319
Journal of Alzheimer's Disease (NLD) 6149
Journal of American Culture (USA) 4459
Journal of Analytical and Applied Pyrolysis (NLD) 2066
Journal of Analytical Chemistry (RUS) 2101
Journal of Analytical Psychology (GBR) 7368
Journal of Analytical Toxicology (USA) 3498
Journal of Anatomy (GBR) 680
Journal of Ancient Near Eastern Religions (NLD) 7737
Journal of Anesthesia (JPN) 5772
Journal of Animal Breeding and Genetics Online (DEU) 291
Journal of Animal Ecology (GBR) 680
Journal of Animal Physiology and Animal Nutrition Online (DEU) 923
Journal of Anthropological Archaeology (USA) 344
Journal of Antimicrobial Chemotherapy (GBR) 5819
Journal of Anxiety Disorders (GBR) 7368
Journal of Applied and Industrial Mathematics (RUS) 5500
Journal of Applied Communication Research (USA) 2329
Journal of Applied Corporate Finance (USA) 1360
Journal of Applied Crystallography (DNK) 2111
Journal of Applied Developmental Psychology (GBR) 7369
Journal of Applied Ecology (GBR) 680
Journal of Applied Electrochemistry (NLD) 2114
Journal of Applied Entomology (Online) (DEU) 851
Journal of Applied Geophysics (NLD) 2784
Journal of Applied Ichthyology Online (DEU) 950
Journal of Applied Logic (NLD) 6928
Journal of Applied Mathematics and Mechanics (GBR) 3349
Journal of Applied Mechanics and Technical Physics (RUS) 3349
Journal of Applied Microbiology (GBR) 888
Journal of Applied Philosophy (GBR) 6928
Journal of Applied Phycology (NLD) 796
Journal of Applied Research in Intellectual Disabilities (GBR) 6149
Journal of Applied Social Psychology (USA) 7369
Journal of Applied Spectroscopy (USA) 7077
Journal of Applied Sport Psychology (USA) 6230
Journal of Applied Statistics (GBR) 8382
Journal of Approximation Theory (USA) 5501
Journal of Arabic Literature (NLD) 5314
Journal of Archaeological Method and Theory (USA) 400
Journal of Archaeological Research (USA) 400
Journal of Archaeological Science (GBR) 400
Journal of Architectural Education (USA) 447
The Journal of Architecture (GBR) 447
Journal of Arid Environments (GBR) 4016
Journal of Artificial Organs (JPN) 5906
Journal of Asian Earth Sciences (GBR) 2749
Journal of Asian Economics (NLD) 1494
Journal of Asian Natural Products Research (GBR) 311
Journal of Asian Pacific Communication (NLD) 5132
The Journal of Asset Management (GBR) 1635
Journal of Assisted Reproduction and Genetics (USA) 5995
Journal of Asthma (USA) 6215
Journal of Astrophysics and Astronomy (IND) 576
Journal of Atmospheric and Solar - Terrestrial Physics (GBR) 2784
Journal of Atmospheric Chemistry (NLD) 2066
Journal of Autism and Developmental Disorders (USA) 3042
Journal of Autoimmunity (GBR) 5762
Journal of Automated Methods & Management in Chemistry (USA) 2101
Journal of Automated Reasoning (NLD) 2453
Journal of Avian Biology (DNK) 909
Journal of Back and Musculoskeletal Rehabilitation (NLD) 6063
Journal of Balkan and Near Eastern Studies (GBR) 4235
Journal of Baltic Studies (USA) 4235
Journal of Bamboo and Rattan (IND) 796
Journal of Banking & Finance (NLD) 1360
Journal of Banking Regulation (GBR) 1360
Journal of Behavior Therapy and Experimental Psychiatry (GBR) 6149
Journal of Behavioral Education (USA) 2874
The Journal of Behavioral Finance (USA) 7369
Journal of Behavioral Health Services and Research (USA) 7528
Journal of Behavioral Medicine (USA) 6149
Journal of Beliefs and Values (GBR) 2874
Journal of Biobased Materials and Bioenergy (USA) 766
Journal of Biochemistry (GBR) 735
Journal of Bioeconomics (USA) 681
Journal of Bioenergetics and Biomembranes (USA) 735
Journal of Biogeography (GBR) 4017
Journal of Biological Inorganic Chemistry (DEU) 2117
Journal of Biological Physics (NLD) 753
Journal of Biomaterials Science. Polymer Edition (NLD) 766
Journal of Biomechanics (GBR) 5646
Journal of Biomedical Informatics (USA) 5832
Journal of Biomedical Nanotechnology (USA) 766
Journal of Biomedical Science (GBR) 5646
Journal of Biomolecular N M R (NLD) 735
Journal of Bionanoscience (USA) 750
Journal of Biopharmaceutical Statistics (USA) 6889
Journal of Bioscience and Bioengineering (JPN) 750
Journal of Biosciences (IND) 682
Journal of Biotechnology (NLD) 767
Journal of Bone and Mineral Metabolism (JPN) 5895
The Journal of Brand Management (GBR) 1823
Journal of Bryology (GBR) 796
Journal of Building Appraisal (GBR) 1018
Journal of Business & Industrial Marketing (GBR) 1823
Journal of Business & Psychology (USA) 7369
Journal of Business Ethics (NLD) 1134
Journal of Business Finance & Accounting (GBR) 1294
Journal of Business Research (USA) 1764
Journal of Business Strategy (USA) 1764
Journal of Business Venturing (USA) 1134
Journal of Cancer Research and Clinical Oncology (DEU) 6024
Journal of Carbohydrate Chemistry (USA) 2067
Journal of Cardiac Surgery (USA) 5792
Journal of Cardiovascular Electrophysiology (USA) 5792
Journal of Cardiovascular Magnetic Resonance (GBR) 5792
Journal of Career Development (USA) 6700
Journal of Catalysis (USA) 2136
Journal of Cataract & Refractive Surgery (USA) 6044
Journal of Cellular and Molecular Medicine (GBR) 5646
Journal of Celtic Linguistics (GBR) 5133
Journal of Cereal Science (GBR) 273
The Journal of Change Management (GBR) 1764
Journal of Chemical Crystallography (USA) 2111
Journal of Chemical Ecology (USA) 3444
Journal of Chemical Health and Safety (USA) 3498
Journal of Chemical Neuroanatomy (NLD) 6150
Journal of Chemical Research (Online Edition) (GBR) *see* Journal of Chemical Research (Print Edition). 2067
Journal of Chemical Sciences (Bangalore) (IND) 2067
Journal of Chemical Technology and Biotechnology (GBR) 767
The Journal of Chemical Thermodynamics (GBR) 2136
Journal of Child and Adolescent Mental Health (ZAF) 6150
Journal of Child and Adolescent Psychiatric Nursing (USA) 5964
Journal of Child and Family Studies (USA) 7370
Journal of Child Psychology and Psychiatry (GBR) 7370
Journal of Child Psychotherapy (GBR) 7370
Journal of Children & Poverty (USA) 8049
Journal of Children's Orthopaedics (DEU) 6063
Journal of Chinese Economics and Business Studies (GBR) 1494
Journal of Chinese Philosophy (USA) 6928
Journal of Chromatographic Science (USA) 2101
Journal of Chromatography A (NLD) 2101
Journal of Chromatography. B, Analytical Technologies in the Biomedical and Life Sciences (NLD) 2067
Journal of Civil Society (GBR) 7146
Journal of Classification (USA) 5020
Journal of Cleaner Production (NLD) 3369
Journal of Clinical Anesthesia (USA) 5772
Journal of Clinical Densitometry (NLD) 5647
Journal of Clinical Epidemiology (USA) 5647
Journal of Clinical Hypertension (USA) 5793
Journal of Clinical Immunology (USA) 5762
Journal of Clinical Ligand Assay (USA) 5762
Journal of Clinical Monitoring and Computing (NLD) 5647
Journal of Clinical Nursing (GBR) 5964
Journal of Clinical Periodontology (DNK) 5851
Journal of Clinical Pharmacy and Therapeutics (GBR) 6852
Journal of Clinical Psychology in Medical Settings (USA) 7370
Journal of Clinical Virology (NLD) 5819
Journal of Cluster Science (USA) 2067
Journal of Co-operative Studies (GBR) 1424
Journal of Coatings Technology and Research (USA) 6718
Journal of Cognition and Culture (NLD) 7370
Journal of Cognitive Education and Psychology (USA) 3067
Journal of Cognitive Engineering and Decision Making (USA) 7371
Journal of Cognitive Psychotherapy (USA) 7371
Journal of Colloid and Interface Science (USA) 2136
Journal of Combinatorial Optimization (NLD) 5553
Journal of Combinatorial Theory, Series A (USA) 5501
Journal of Combinatorial Theory. Series B (USA) 5501
Journal of Commercial Biotechnology (GBR) 767
Journal of Common Market Studies (GBR) 7146
Journal of Communication (USA) 8112
Journal of Communication Disorders (USA) 7371
Journal of Communication Management (GBR) 1765
Journal of Communications Technology and Electronics (RUS) 2329
Journal of Communist Studies and Transition Politics (GBR) 7247
Journal of Community Health (USA) 5647
Journal of Comparative Economics (USA) 1134
The Journal of Comparative Germanic Linguistics (NLD) 5133
Journal of Comparative Physiology A (DEU) 924
Journal of Comparative Physiology B (DEU) 924
Journal of Comparative Policy Analysis (USA) 7448
Journal of Complexity (USA) 5553
Journal of Computational Analysis and Applications (USA) 5501
Journal of Computational and Applied Mathematics (NLD) 5502
Journal of Computational and Theoretical Nanoscience (USA) 7019
Journal of Computational Electronics (USA) 2428
The Journal of Computational Multiphase Flows (GBR) 5553
Journal of Computational Neuroscience (NLD) 6151
Journal of Computational Physics (USA) 7050
Journal of Computer - Aided Molecular Design (NLD) 2108
Journal of Computer and System Sciences (USA) 2523
Journal of Computer and System Sciences International (RUS) 2527
Journal of Computer Assisted Learning (GBR) 2469
Journal of Computer-Mediated Communication (USA) 2351
Journal of Computer Science and Technology (USA) 2468
Journal of Computer Security (NLD) 2515
Journal of Conflict and Security Law (GBR) 4933
Journal of Consciousness Studies (GBR) 7371
Journal of Constructional Steel Research (GBR) 3275
Journal of Constructivist Psychology (USA) 7371
Journal of Consumer Affairs (USA) 2639
Journal of Consumer Behaviour (GBR) 2639
Journal of Consumer Marketing (GBR) 1823
Journal of Consumer Policy (NLD) 2639
Journal of Contaminant Hydrology (NLD) 3488
Journal of Contemporary African Studies (GBR) 7978
Journal of Contemporary Asia (GBR) 4184
Journal of Contemporary China (GBR) 4184
Journal of Contemporary European Studies (Online Edition) (GBR) 7146
Journal of Contemporary Psychotherapy (USA) 7372
Journal of Contemporary Religion (GBR) 7654
Journal of Contingencies and Crisis Management (GBR) 1765
Journal of Controlled Release (NLD) 6853
Journal of Coordination Chemistry (CHE) 2068
Journal of Corporate Finance (NLD) 1360
The Journal of Corporate Law Studies (GBR) 4872
Journal of Corporate Real Estate (GBR) 7596
Journal of Cosmetic and Laser Therapy (Online) (GBR) 5878
Journal of Cosmetic Dermatology (GBR) 5878
Journal of Criminal Justice (GBR) 4892
Journal of Criminal Justice Education (GBR) 2656
Journal of Critical Realism (GBR) 6928
Journal of Cross-Cultural Gerontology (NLD) 4049
Journal of Cryptology (USA) 5502
Journal of Crystal Growth (NLD) 2111
Journal of Cultural Economics (USA) 1544
Journal of Cultural Heritage (FRA) 344
Journal of Curriculum Studies (GBR) 3067
Journal of Customer Behavior (GBR) 1824
Journal of Cutaneous Medicine and Surgery (CAN) 5878
Journal of Cutaneous Pathology (DNK) 5878
Journal of Cystic Fibrosis (NLD) 5927
The Journal of Database Marketing & Customer Strategy Management (Online Edition) (GBR) 1419
The Journal of Deaf Studies and Deaf Education (USA) 4075
Journal of Dental Hygiene (USA) 5851
Journal of Dentistry (GBR) 5851
Journal of Dentistry for Children (Online Edition) (USA) 5851
Journal of Derivatives & Hedge Funds (GBR) 1635
Journal of Dermatological Science (IRL) 5878
Journal of Dermatological Treatment (GBR) 5879
Journal of Dermatology (GBR) 5879
Journal of Design History (GBR) 498
Journal of Design Research (GBR) 8429
Journal of Development Economics (NLD) 1600
The Journal of Development Studies (GBR) 1600
Journal of Developmental and Physical Disabilities (USA) 4067
Journal of Diabetes and its Complications (USA) 5895
Journal of Difference Equations and Applications (CHE) 5502
Journal of Differential Equations (USA) 5502
Journal of Digestive Diseases (Online) (AUS) 5927
Journal of Digital Asset Management (GBR) 1765
Journal of Digital Imaging (USA) 6200
Journal of Direct, Data and Digital Marketing Practice (Online) (GBR) 1824
Journal of Dispersion Science and Technology (USA) 2136
Journal of Documentation (GBR) 5020
Journal of Drug Targeting (CHE) 6853
Journal of Dynamical and Control Systems (USA) 3369
Journal of Dynamics and Differential Equations (USA) 5503
Journal of E M D R Practice and Research (USA) 6151
Journal of Early Childhood Teacher Education (GBR) 2990
Journal of Early Modern History (NLD) 4149
Journal of Earth System Science (IND) 2711
Journal of East Asian Linguistics (NLD) 5133
Journal of Ecology (GBR) 682
Journal of Econometrics (NLD) 1544
Journal of Economic Behavior & Organization (NLD) 1134
Journal of Economic Dynamics and Control (NLD) 1544
Journal of Economic Entomology (USA) 851
Journal of Economic Geography (GBR) 1494
Journal of Economic Growth (USA) 1544
The Journal of Economic Inequality (USA) 1494
Journal of Economic Interaction and Coordination (DEU) 1135
Journal of Economic Literature (USA) 1247
Journal of Economic Methodology (GBR) 1135
Journal of Economic Perspectives (USA) 1545
Journal of Economic Policy Reform (Online) (GBR) 1765
Journal of Economic Psychology (NLD) 1824
Journal of Economic Studies (GBR) 1135
Journal of Economic Surveys (GBR) 1135
Journal of Economic Theory (USA) 1545
Journal of Economics (AUT) 1135
Journal of Economics and Business (USA) 1135
Journal of Economics & Management Strategy (USA) 1545
Journal of Education and Work (GBR) 3067
Journal of Education for Teaching (GBR) 2875
Journal of Education Policy (GBR) 3026
Journal of Educational Administration (GBR) 3026
Journal of Educational Administration and History (GBR) 3026
Journal of Educational Change (NLD) 2875
Journal of Egyptian History (NLD) 4176
Journal of Elasticity (NLD) 3349
Journal of Electroanalytical Chemistry (CHE) 2102
Journal of Electroceramics (USA) 3349
Journal of Electromagnetic Waves and Applications (NLD) 7020
Journal of Electromyography & Kinesiology (GBR) 754
Journal of Electron Microscopy (JPN) 899
Journal of Electron Spectroscopy and Related Phenomena (NLD) 7078
Journal of Electronic Materials (USA) 3106
Journal of Electronic Testing (USA) 3322
Journal of Electrostatics (NLD) 3322
The Journal of Emergency Medicine (New York) (USA) 6064
Journal of Empirical Finance (NLD) 1361
Journal of Empirical Legal Studies (USA) 4701
Journal of Empirical Theology (NLD) 7655
Journal of Energetic Materials (USA) 7020
The Journal of Energy Literature (GBR) 3153
Journal of Engineering and Technology Management (NLD) 1765
Journal of Engineering Design (GBR) 3205
Journal of Engineering, Design and Technology (GBR) 3205
Journal of Engineering Mathematics (NLD) 3205
Journal of Engineering Physics and Thermophysics (USA) 3205
Journal of Engineering Thermophysics (RUS) 7020
Journal of English for Academic Purposes (GBR) 3067
Journal of Enhanced Heat Transfer (GBR) 3385
Journal of Enterprise Information Management (GBR) 5021
Journal of Environmental Economics and Management (USA) 3445
Journal of Environmental Engineering and Science (Online) (CAN) 3445
Journal of Environmental Law (GBR) 3445
Journal of Environmental Management (GBR) 3446
Journal of Environmental Planning and Management (GBR) 3446
Journal of Environmental Policy and Planning (GBR) 3446
Journal of Environmental Psychology (GBR) 7373
Journal of Environmental Radioactivity (GBR) 3446
Journal of Environmental Science and Health. Part B: Pesticides, Food Contaminants, and Agricultural Wastes (USA) 3447
Journal of Enzyme Inhibition and Medicinal Chemistry (CHE) 736
Journal of Esthetic and Restorative Dentistry (GBR) 5852
The Journal of Ethics (NLD) 6928
Journal of Ethnic and Migration Studies (GBR) 3544
Journal of Ethnopharmacology (IRL) 6853

Online Service

DIRECTORY 2010 INGENTACONNECT 11177

Music Analysis (GBR) **6589**
Music and Letters (GBR) **6589**
Music Education Research (GBR) **6590**
The Musical Quarterly (USA) **6594**
Muslim World (USA) **7715**
Mutagenesis (GBR) **875**
Mutation Research - Fundamental and Molecular Mechanisms of Mutagenesis (NLD) **875**
Mutation Research - Genetic Toxicology and Environmental Mutagenesis (NLD) **875**
Mutation Research - Reviews (NLD) **876**
Mycological Progress (DEU) **803**
Mycopathologia (NLD) **803**
Mycorrhiza (DEU) **803**
Mycoscience (JPN) **803**
Mycoses (DEU) **5681**
N D T & E International (GBR) **3355**
N E A News (FRA) **3171**
N T M Journal of History of Sciences, Technology, and Medicine (CHE) **7885**
Names (GBR) **5154**
Nan Nu (NLD) **557**
NanoBioTechnology (USA) **768**
NanoEthics (NLD) **8432**
Nanomedicine (GBR) **5683**
Nanoscale & Microscale Thermophysical Engineering (Online) (USA) **7056**
Nanoscale Research Letters (USA) **2074**
Nanoscience and Nanotechnology Letters (USA) **3326**
Nanotechnology (GBR) **7027**
Narrative Inquiry (NLD) **5338**
National Cancer Institute. Journal (Online) (GBR) **6028**
National Committee on Planned Giving. Conference Proceedings (USA) **8056**
National Gallery, London. Technical Bulletin (GBR) **508**
National Identities (GBR) **7156**
National Society for the Study of Education. Yearbook (USA) **2890**
Nationalism & Ethnic Politics (GBR) **7254**
Nationalities Papers (GBR) **7987**
Nations and Nationalism (GBR) **7157**
Natur und Recht (DEU) **4739**
Natural Computing (NLD) **2432**
Natural Gas Information (FRA) **6779**
Natural Hazards (NLD) **2713**
Natural Language and Linguistic Theory (NLD) **5154**
Natural Language Semantics (NLD) **5154**
Natural Product Research (CHE) **2074**
Natural Resource Modeling (USA) **5520**
Natural Resources Forum (GBR) **4021**
Natural Resources Research (USA) **6474**
Nature and Culture (USA) **692**
Natures - Sciences - Societes (FRA) **2714**
Naturwissenschaften (DEU) **7890**
Naunyn-Schmiedeberg's Archives of Pharmacology (DEU) **6863**
Naval Engineers Journal (USA) **3212**
Negotiation and Conflict Management Research (GBR) **8122**
Negotiation Journal (USA) **7254**
Nematology (NLD) **958**
Neohelicon (HUN) **5339**
Neophilologus (NLD) **5339**
Der Nephrologe (DEU) **6272**
Nephrology (AUS) **6272**
Nephrology, Dialysis, Transplantation (GBR) **6272**
Der Nervenarzt (DEU) **6163**
Netherlands Journal of Geosciences (NLD) **2757**
Netherlands Journal of Medicine (NLD) **5947**
Netnomics (NLD) **2501**
Network (London, 1990) (GBR) **6163**
Network Security (GBR) **2501**
Networks and Spatial Economics (USA) **2518**
Neues Jahrbuch fuer Geologie und Palaeontologie. Abhandlungen (DEU) **2757**
Neues Jahrbuch fuer Mineralogie. Abhandlungen (DEU) **6474**
Neural Computing and Applications (GBR) **2455**
Neural Networks (GBR) **2455**
Neural Processing Letters (USA) **2455**
Neuro-Ophthalmology (GBR) **6163**
Neurobiology of Aging (USA) **925**
Neurobiology of Disease (USA) **6164**
Neurobiology of Learning and Memory (USA) **6164**
Neurocase (GBR) **6164**
Neurochemical Research (USA) **6164**
Neurochemistry International (GBR) **6164**
Neurocomputing (NLD) **2455**
Neurocritical Care (USA) **5685**
Neurogastroenterology and Motility Online (GBR) **5929**
Neurogenetics (DEU) **876**
NeuroImage (USA) **6165**
NeuroInformatics (USA) **925**
Neurologic Clinics (USA) **6165**
Neurological Research (GBR) **6165**
Neurological Sciences (ITA) **6165**
Neuromodulation (USA) **6166**
NeuroMolecular Medicine (USA) **6167**
Neuromuscular Disorders (GBR) **6167**
Neuron (USA) **6167**
Neuropathology (AUS) **6167**
Neuropathology and Applied Neurobiology (GBR) **6167**
Neuropharmacology (GBR) **6863**
Neurophysiologie Clinique (FRA) **6167**
Neurophysiology (USA) **6167**
Neuropsychiatrie de l'Enfance et de l'Adolescence (FRA) **6097**
Neuropsychologia (GBR) **6168**
Neuropsychological Rehabilitation (GBR) **6168**
Neuropsychology, Development and Cognition. Section A: Journal of Clinical and Experimental Neuropsychology (NLD) **7387**
Neuropsychology, Development and Cognition. Section B: Aging, Neuropsychology and Cognition (GBR) **7387**
Neuropsychology, Development, and Cognition. Section C: Child Neuropsychology (NLD) **7387**
Neuropsychology, Development and Cognition. Section D: The Clinical Neuropsychologist (GBR) **7387**
Neuropsychology Review (USA) **6168**
Neuropsychopharmacology (USA) **6168**
Neuroradiology (DEU) **6204**
NeuroRehabilitation (NLD) **6168**
Neuroscience (GBR) **6169**
Neuroscience and Behavioral Physiology (USA) **6169**
Neuroscience & Biobehavioral Reviews (GBR) **6169**
Neuroscience Letters (IRL) **6169**
Neuroscience Research (IRL) **6169**
Neurosurgical Review (DEU) **6253**
Neurotoxicity Research (USA) **6170**
NeuroToxicology (NLD) **6170**
Neurotoxicology and Teratology (USA) **6170**
Neutron News (USA) **7069**
New Astronomy (NLD) **578**
New Astronomy Reviews (GBR) **578**
New Biotechnology (NLD) **769**
New Blackfriars (GBR) **7809**
The New Educator (USA) **2890**
New Forests (NLD) **3698**
New Formations (GBR) **5229**
New Genetics and Society (GBR) **876**
New Ideas in Psychology (GBR) **7387**
New Labor Forum (USA) **4599**
New Library World (GBR) **5035**
New Phytologist (GBR) **804**
New Political Economy (GBR) **1547**
New Political Science (GBR) **7158**
The New Review of Academic Librarianship (GBR) **5035**
The New Review of Children's Literature and Librarianship (GBR) **5341**
The New Review of Film and Television Studies (GBR) **2386**
New Review of Hypermedia and Multimedia (GBR) **2488**
The New Review of Information Networking (GBR) **2502**
New Technology, Work & Employment (GBR) **1699**
New York Academy of Sciences. Annals (USA) **7892**
New Zealand Geographer (AUS) **4022**
New Zealand Veterinary Journal (NZL) **8803**
Newsletters on Stratigraphy (DEU) **2759**
Nexus Network Journal (CHE) **451**
Nicotine & Tobacco Research (GBR) **8486**
Nineteenth-Century Contexts (GBR) **5341**
Nineteenth Century Theatre and Film (GBR) **8474**
Nitric Oxide: Biology and Chemistry (USA) **741**
No D E A - Nonlinear Differential Equations and Applications (CHE) **5520**
Noise & Health (IND) **6083**
Noise & Vibration Worldwide (GBR) **7089**
Noise Notes (GBR) **7089**
Nomadic Peoples (GBR) **350**
Nondestructive Testing and Evaluation (GBR) **3355**
Nonlinear Analysis: Real World Applications (GBR) **5520**
Nonlinear Analysis: Theory, Methods & Applications (GBR) **3212**
Nonlinear Dynamics (NLD) **3391**
Nonlinear Dynamics, Psychology, and Life Sciences (USA) **7388**
Nonlinear Optics, Quantum Optics (CHE) **7081**
Nonlinear Oscillations (Online) (USA) **5521**
Nonlinearity (GBR) **5521**
Nora (NOR) **8901**
Nordic Journal of Botany (DNK) **805**
Nordic Journal of International Law (NLD) **4936**
Nordic Journal of Linguistics (GBR) **5155**
Nordic Journal of Psychiatry (GBR) **6171**
Norsk Geografisk Tidsskrift (NOR) **4022**
Norsk Geologisk Tidsskrift (NOR) **2759**
The North American Journal of Economics and Finance (GBR) **1502**
Northern History (GBR) **4249**
Northern Journal of Applied Forestry (USA) **3698**
Norwegian Archaeological Review (NOR) **408**
Notes and Queries (GBR) **5343**
Notfall und Rettungsmedizin (DEU) **6068**
Nous (USA) **6937**
Nova Hedwigia (DEU) **806**
Novum Testamentum (NLD) **7666**
Nuclear Data Sheets (USA) **3171**
Nuclear Engineering and Design (CHE) **3355**
Nuclear Instruments & Methods in Physics Research. Section A: Accelerators, Spectrometers, Detectors, and Associated Equipment (NLD) **7069**
Nuclear Instruments & Methods in Physics Research. Section B: Beam Interactions with Materials and Atoms (Online) (NLD) *see* Nuclear Instruments & Methods in Physics Research. Section B: Beam Interactions with Materials and Atoms. **7069**
Nuclear Law Bulletin (FRA) **3172**
Nuclear Medicine and Biology (USA) **6204**
Nuclear Physics News (GBR) **7069**
Nuclear Physics, Section A (NLD) **7069**
Nuclear Physics, Section B (NLD) **7070**
Nuclear Physics, Section B, Proceedings Supplements (NLD) **7070**
Nucleic Acids Research (GBR) **741**
Nucleosides, Nucleotides and Nucleic Acids (USA) **741**
Numen (NLD) **7667**
Numerical Algorithms (NLD) **5522**
Numerical Functional Analysis and Optimization (USA) **5522**
Numerical Heat Transfer Part A: Applications (USA) **3391**
Numerical Heat Transfer Part B: Fundamentals (USA) **3392**
Numerische Mathematik (DEU) **5555**
Nurse Education Today (GBR) **5971**
Nursing and Health Sciences (AUS) **5973**
Nursing for Women's Health (USA) **8847**
Nursing Forum (USA) **5973**
Nursing History Review (USA) **5973**
Nursing in Critical Care (GBR) **5974**
Nursing Inquiry (AUS) **5974**
Nursing Philosophy (GBR) **5975**
Nutrient Cycling in Agroecosystems (NLD) **244**
Nutrition (USA) **6665**
Nutrition and Cancer (USA) **6665**
Nutrition and Dietetics (AUS) **6665**
Nutrition & Food Science (GBR) **6665**
Nutrition Bulletin (GBR) **6665**
Nutrition Clinique et Metabolisme (FRA) **5898**
Nutrition Research (USA) **6666**
Nutrition Reviews (USA) **6666**
Nutritional Neuroscience (Online) (GBR) **6171**
O C D E. Etudes Economiques (FRA) **1502**
O C L C Systems & Services (GBR) **5037**
O E C D Agriculture Statistics (FRA) **184**
O E C D Banking Statistics (FRA) **1256**
O E C D Economic Outlook (FRA) **1502**
O E C D Economic Outlook: Statistics and Projections (FRA) **1256**
O E C D Economic Surveys (FRA) **1502**
O E C D Education Statistics (FRA) **2935**
O E C D Employment and Labour Market Statistics (FRA) **1256**
O E C D Guidelines for the Testing of Chemicals (Online) (FRA) **3500**
O E C D International Development Statistics (Online) (FRA) **1256**
O E C D International Direct Investment Statistics (Online) (FRA) **1256**
O E C D International Migration Statistics (FRA) **1256**
O E C D International Trade by Commodities Statistics (FRA) **1257**
O E C D Main Economic Indicators (FRA) **1504**
O E C D Main Science and Technology Indicators (FRA) **8433**
O E C D Observer (FRA) **1504**
O E C D Science, Technology and R & D Statistics (FRA) **3233**
O E C D Statistics on International Trade in Services (FRA) **1257**
O E C D Telecommunications and Internet Statistics (FRA) **2348**
O P E C Energy Review (GBR) **6782**
O R Spectrum (DEU) **2433**
Obesite (FRA) **6667**
Obesity Reviews (GBR) **6667**
Obesity Surgery (USA) **6254**
Obstetrics and Gynecology (USA) **6001**
Occupational Ergonomics (USA) **6682**
Occupational Medicine (GBR) **6683**
Ocean & Coastal Management (GBR) **2814**
Ocean Development and International Law (USA) **2814**
Ocean Dynamics (DEU) **2814**
Ocean Engineering (GBR) **2814**
Ocean Modelling (USA) **2814**
Ocular Immunology and Inflammation (GBR) **6047**
The Ocular Surface (USA) **6047**
Odontology (JPN) **5858**
Oecologia (DEU) **695**
Oesterreichische Wasser- und Abfallwirtschaft (AUT) **8830**
Oikos (DNK) **3458**
Oil and Energy Trends (GBR) **3143**
Oil, Gas, Coal & Electricity Quarterly Statistics (FRA) **6801**
Oil Information (FRA) **6784**
Omega (GBR) **1782**
On the Horizon (USA) **2996**
Oncologie (FRA) **6030**
Oncology Research (USA) **6031**
Der Onkologe (DEU) **6031**
Online Information Review (GBR) **5038**
Open Economies Review (NLD) **1547**
Open Learning (GBR) **2997**
Open Systems and Information Dynamics (NLD) **2524**
The Opera Quarterly (GBR) **6602**
Operational Research Society. Journal (GBR) **2433**
Operations Research Letters (NLD) **7896**
Operations Research Society of Japan. Journal (JPN) **1783**
Operative Orthopaedie und Traumatologie (DEU) **6068**
Ophthalmic and Physiological Optics (GBR) **6047**
Ophthalmic Epidemiology (GBR) **6047**
Ophthalmic Genetics (GBR) **6047**
Der Ophthalmologe (DEU) **6048**
Ophthalmology (USA) **6048**
Optical and Quantum Electronics (NLD) **7081**
Optical Fiber Technology (USA) **7082**
Optical Materials (NLD) **7082**
Optical Review (JPN) **7082**
Optics & Laser Technology (GBR) **7082**
Optics and Lasers in Engineering (GBR) **7082**
Optics and Spectroscopy (RUS) **7083**
Optics Communications (NLD) **7083**
Optik (DEU) **7083**
Optimization (CHE) **5523**
Optimization and Engineering (USA) **3214**
Optimization Letters (DEU) **5523**
Optimization Methods and Software (GBR) **5555**
Option Bio (FRA) **696**
Optometry Today (GBR) **6050**
Oral and Maxillofacial Surgery (DEU) **6083**
Oral Diseases (GBR) **5859**
Oral Microbiology and Immunology (DNK) **894**
Oral Oncology Extra (GBR) *see* Oral Oncology. **6032**
Orbis (Kidlington) (GBR) **7256**
Orbis Litterarum (DNK) **5346**
Orbit (GBR) **6050**
Order (NLD) **5523**
Ore Geology Reviews (NLD) **2761**
Organic Electronics (NLD) **3327**
Organic Geochemistry (GBR) **2128**
Organisms Diversity & Evolution (DEU) **696**
Organizational Behavior and Human Decision Processes (USA) **1784**
Organizational Dynamics (USA) **1784**
Origins of Life and Evolution of Biospheres (NLD) **696**
Der Orthopaede (DEU) **6069**
Osteoporosis International (GBR) **5691**
Ostrich (ZAF) **913**
Otolaryngology - Head and Neck Surgery (USA) **6083**
Oud - Holland (NLD) **510**
Outlook on Agriculture (GBR) **145**
Outlook on Science Policy (GBR) **7896**
Outlooks on Pest Management (Online) (GBR) **245**
Oxford Art Journal (GBR) **510**
Oxford Bulletin of Economics and Statistics (GBR) **1157**
Oxford Development Studies (GBR) **1603**
Oxford Economic Papers (GBR) **1158**
Oxford German Studies (GBR) **5347**
Oxford Journal of Archaeology (GBR) **410**
Oxford Journal of Legal Studies (GBR) **4754**
Oxford Review of Economic Policy (GBR) **1158**
Oxford Review of Education (GBR) **2894**
Oxford University Commonwealth Law Journal (GBR) **4754**
Oxidation of Metals (USA) **2139**
Ozone: Science and Engineering (USA) **3251**
P L A Notes (GBR) **145**
Pacific Affairs (CAN) **7257**
Pacific-Basin Finance Journal (NLD) **1373**
Pacific Economic Review (AUS) **1510**
Pacific Focus (AUS) **7257**
Pacific Philosophical Quarterly (GBR) **6938**
The Pacific Review (GBR) **7257**
Pacing and Clinical Electrophysiology (USA) **5797**
Packaging Technology and Science (GBR) **6713**
Packaging, Transport, Storage & Security of Radioactive Material (GBR) **8508**
Paddy and Water Environment (DEU) **245**
Paedagogica Historica (GBR) **2895**
Paediatric Anaesthesia Online (GBR) **5773**
Paediatric and Perinatal Epidemiology (Online) (GBR) **6098**
Paediatric Drugs (NZL) **6866**
Paediatrie und Paedologie (AUT) **6098**
Pain (NLD) **6172**
The Pain Clinic (GBR) **5773**
Pain Medicine (USA) **6172**
Pain Practice (USA) **6173**
Pain Reviews (GBR) **5692**
Palaeogeography, Palaeoclimatology, Palaeoecology (NLD) **6727**
Palaeontology (GBR) **6728**
Paleontological Journal (RUS) **6729**
Palestine Exploration Quarterly (GBR) **410**
Papers in Regional Science (DEU) **7991**
Parallax (GBR) **5349**
Parallel Computing (NLD) **2468**
Parasite Immunology (GBR) **5824**
Parasitology International (NLD) **5824**
Parasitology Research (DEU) **894**
Parkinsonism & Related Disorders (GBR) **6173**
Parliamentary Affairs (GBR) **7163**
Parliamentary History (GBR) **4155**
Particulate Science and Technology (USA) **3251**
Past & Present (GBR) **4155**
Pastoral Care in Education (GBR) **2896**
Pastoral Psychology (USA) **7389**
Der Pathologe (DEU) **5693**
Pathologie et Biologie (FRA) **5693**
Pathology (GBR) **5693**
Pathology International (AUS) **5694**
Pathology, Research and Practice (DEU) **5694**
Pathophysiology (NLD) **926**
The Patient (NZL) **5694**
Patient Education and Counseling (IRL) **7535**
Pattern Analysis and Applications (GBR) **2455**
Pattern Recognition (GBR) **2456**
Pattern Recognition and Image Analysis (RUS) **5524**
Pattern Recognition Letters (NLD) **2456**
Patterns of Prejudice (GBR) **3557**
Peace & Change (USA) **7258**
Peace Review (GBR) **7259**
Pediatric Allergy and Immunology (GBR) **6099**

Online Service

Link to your serials resources and content with ulrichsweb.com

Online Service

The Tohoku Journal of Experimental Medicine (JPN) **5911**
Tokyo Dental College. Bulletin (JPN) **5868**
Tropical Medicine and Health (JPN) **5827**
Uchu Seibutsu Kagaku (JPN) **708**
Uirusu (JPN) **897**
Yakugaku Zasshi (JPN) **6886**
Yosetsu Gakkai Ronbunshu (JPN) **6345**
Zoological Science (JPN) **969**

JSTOR (Web-based Journal Archive) 149 Fifth Ave, 8th Fl, New York, NY 10010 TEL 212-358-6400, FAX 212-358-6499, support@jstor.org, http://www.jstor.org
A J S Review (GBR) **7717**
Academy of Management Journal (USA) **1723**
Academy of Management Review (USA) **1723**
The Accounting Review (USA) **1278**
Acta Musicologica (DEU) **6542**
Administrative Science Quarterly (USA) **7419**
Advances in Applied Probability (GBR) **5466**
Africa (GBR) **4172**
African Affairs (GBR) **7103**
African American Review (USA) **3516**
African Studies Review (USA) **3516**
Alif (EGY) **5416**
American Academy of Political and Social Science. Annals (USA) **7104**
American Academy of Religion. Journal (USA) **7620**
American Anthropologist (USA) **324**
American Antiquity (USA) **372**
American Art (USA) **465**
The American Economic Review (USA) **1436**
American Educational Research Journal (USA) **2825**
American Ethnologist (USA) **324**
American Fern Journal (USA) **774**
American Historical Review (USA) **4129**
American Indian Quarterly (USA) **6634**
American Institute for Conservation of Historic & Artistic Works. Journal (USA) **465**
American Journal of Agricultural Economics (USA) **193**
American Journal of Archaeology (USA) **372**
American Journal of Botany (USA) **774**
American Journal of Comparative Law (USA) **4916**
American Journal of Education (USA) **2826**
American Journal of International Law (USA) **4916**
American Journal of Mathematics (USA) **5468**
American Journal of Philology (USA) **5092**
American Journal of Political Science (USA) **7105**
American Journal of Psychology (USA) **7333**
American Journal of Sociology (USA) **8087**
American Literary History (USA) **5252**
American Literature (USA) **5252**
American Mathematical Monthly (USA) **5468**
American Mathematical Society. Journal (USA) **5469**
American Mathematical Society. Proceedings (USA) **5469**
American Mathematical Society. Transactions (USA) **5469**
American Midland Naturalist (USA) **7834**
American Music (USA) **6544**
American Musicological Society. Journal (USA) **6544**
The American Naturalist (USA) **652**
American Oriental Society. Journal (USA) **542**
American Philological Association. Transactions (USA) **2229**
American Philosophical Association. Proceedings and Addresses (USA) **6903**
American Philosophical Society. Proceedings (USA) **4442**
American Philosophical Society. Transactions (USA) **4442**
American Political Science Review (GBR) **7105**
American Quarterly (USA) **4442**
American Schools of Oriental Research. Bulletin (USA) **542**
American Sociological Review (USA) **8087**
American Speech (USA) **5092**
American Statistical Association. Journal (USA) **8344**
The American Statistician (USA) **8344**
The Americas (USA) **4283**
Annals of Applied Probability (USA) **5470**
Annals of Mathematics (USA) **5471**
Annals of Probability (USA) **5471**
Annals of Statistics (USA) **8345**
Annual Review of Ecology, Evolution and Systematics (USA) **3403**
Anthropology & Education Quarterly (USA) **326**
Anthropology Today (GBR) **327**
Applied Economic Perspectives and Policy (USA) **193**
Applied Vegetation Science (DNK) **776**
Archaeological Reports (London) (GBR) **376**
Architectural History (GBR) **429**
Archiv fuer Musikwissenschaft (DEU) **6545**
Archives of American Art Journal (USA) **467**
Arctic, Antarctic, and Alpine Research (USA) **7836**
The Art Bulletin (USA) **468**
Art Education (USA) **469**
Art Journal (USA) **470**
Artibus Asiae (CHE) **473**
Artibus Asiae Supplementum (CHE) **473**
Artibus et Historiae (POL) **473**
Asian Ethnology (JPN) **329**
Asian Music (USA) **6546**
Asian Survey (USA) **7107**
Asian Theatre Journal (USA) **8466**
Association for Preservation Technology International. Bulletin (USA) **434**
Association of American Geographers. Annals (USA) **3999**
Association of Teachers of Japanese. Newsletter (USA) **5097**
Avian Diseases (USA) **8794**
Biogeochemistry (NLD) **726**
Biological Bulletin (USA) **658**
Biometrics (GBR) **8358**
Biometrika (GBR) **713**
BioScience (USA) **661**
Biotropica (USA) **662**
Black Music Research Journal (USA) **6549**
Boundary 2 (USA) **5265**
Britannia (GBR) **2231**
British Educational Research Journal (GBR) **2832**
The British Journal for the Philosophy of Science (GBR) **7842**
British Journal of Educational Studies (GBR) **2832**
British Journal of Middle Eastern Studies (GBR) **4320**
British Journal of Political Science (GBR) **7110**
British Journal of Sociology (GBR) **8091**
British Journal of Sociology of Education (GBR) **2832**
Brittonia (USA) **782**
Brookings Papers on Economic Activity (USA) **1536**
Bryologist (USA) **782**
Buddhist - Christian Studies (USA) **7700**
The Bulletin of Symbolic Logic (USA) **5476**
Burlington Magazine (GBR) **480**
Business History Review (USA) **1072**
Callaloo (USA) **5269**
Cambridge Opera Journal (GBR) **6553**
Canadian Journal of African Studies (CAN) **7952**
Canadian Journal of Economics (USA) **1080**
Canadian Journal of Education (CAN) **3019**
Canadian Journal of Political Science (GBR) **7113**
Cell Stress & Chaperones (NLD) **5592**
Child Development (USA) **2147**
The China Journal (AUS) **546**
China Quarterly (GBR) **546**
Chinese Literature, Essays, Articles, Reviews (USA) **5273**
Church History (USA) **7633**
Cinema Journal (USA) **6493**
Classical Journal (USA) **2232**
Classical Philology (USA) **2232**
Classical Quarterly (GBR) **2232**
Classical Review (GBR) **2233**
Cognition and Instruction (USA) **7346**
College Composition and Communication (USA) **3055**
College English (USA) **3055**
College Mathematics Journal (USA) **5478**
Columbia Law Review (USA) **4645**
Comparative Education (GBR) **2838**
Comparative Education Review (USA) **2838**
Comparative Literature (USA) **5277**
Comparative Politics (USA) **7117**
Comparative Studies in Society and History (GBR) **8095**
The Condor (USA) **905**
Conservation Biology (USA) **2607**
Contemporary Literature (USA) **5278**
Contemporary Sociology (USA) **8095**
Copeia (USA) **939**
Crime and Justice (USA) **2648**
Critical Inquiry (USA) **5212**
Cultural Anthropology (USA) **334**
Cultural Critique (USA) **334**
Current Anthropology (USA) **335**
Curriculum Inquiry (USA) **3057**
Dance Chronicle (USA) **2683**
Dance Research (GBR) **2684**
Dance Research Journal (USA) **2684**
Demography (USA) **7281**
Design Issues (USA) **486**
Diacritics (USA) **5284**
Diversity and Distributions (GBR) **669**
Duke Law Journal (USA) **4661**
Dumbarton Oaks Papers (USA) **391**
E L H (USA) **5286**
E R Online (USA) *see* Educational Researcher. **2851**
Early Music (GBR) **6563**
Early Music History (GBR) **6563**
Ecological Applications (USA) **3416**
Ecological Monographs (USA) **3417**
Ecology (USA) **3417**
Econometrica (GBR) **1097**
Economic Development and Cultural Change (USA) **1595**
Economic Geography (USA) **4005**
The Economic History Review (GBR) **1539**
The Economic Journal (GBR) **1100**
Economic Policy (GBR) **1100**
Economica (GBR) **1101**
Educational Evaluation & Policy Analysis (USA) **3021**
Eighteenth-Century Studies (USA) **4138**
The Electronic Sixteenth Century Journal (USA) *see* Sixteenth Century Journal. **4475**
Electronic Transactions (GBR) *see* Institute of British Geographers. Transactions. **4015**
The Elementary School Journal (USA) **2852**
The English Historical Review (GBR) **4217**
English Journal (USA) **3061**
Estuaries and Coasts (USA) **671**
Ethics (USA) **6917**
Ethnohistory (USA) **337**
Ethnomusicology (USA) **6565**
Ethnomusicology Forum (GBR) **6565**
Ethos (Malden) (USA) **337**
Europe - Asia Studies (GBR) **1106**
European Journal of Education (GBR) **2855**
European Sociological Review (GBR) **8101**
Evolution (USA) **866**
Family Relations (USA) **2856**
Feminist Review (GBR) **8896**
Feminist Studies (USA) **8896**
Film Quarterly (USA) **6499**
Folklore (GBR) **3617**
Foreign Policy (Washington) (USA) **7235**
French Historical Studies (USA) **4222**
French Review (USA) **3062**
Functional Ecology (GBR) **2612**
The Future of Children (USA) **2153**
The Galpin Society Journal (GBR) **6569**
Garden History (GBR) **3731**
Gender & Society (USA) **8104**
Geografiska Annaler. Series A. Physical Geography (GBR) **4009**
Geografiska Annaler. Series B. Human Geography (GBR) **340**
The Geographical Journal (GBR) **4010**
The German Quarterly (USA) **5122**
German Studies Review (USA) **4223**
Gesta (USA) **491**
Global Ecology and Biogeography (GBR) **3433**
Greece and Rome (GBR) **2234**
Grey Room (USA) **444**
Harvard Journal of Asiatic Studies (USA) **551**
Harvard Law Review (USA) **4685**
Harvard Studies in Classical Philology (USA) **2235**
Harvard Theological Review (GBR) **7646**
Herpetological Monographs (USA) **946**
Hesperia (GRC) **396**
Hispania (USA) **5124**
Hispanic American Historical Review (USA) **4295**
Hispanic Review (USA) **5125**
Historical Journal (GBR) **4143**
History and Theory (USA) **4145**
History in Africa (USA) **4175**
History of Education Quarterly (USA) **2864**
History of Religions (USA) **7647**
The History Teacher (USA) **4145**
Human Rights Quarterly (USA) **7208**
Imago Mundi (GBR) **4146**
Industrial and Labor Relations Review (USA) **1687**
International Affairs (London) (GBR) **7243**
International and Comparative Law Quarterly (GBR) **4929**
International Economic Review (USA) **1126**
International Institute for Conservation of Historic and Artistic Works. Bulletin of the American Group (USA) **497**
International Journal of African Historical Studies (USA) **4175**
International Journal of American Linguistics (USA) **5129**
International Journal of Middle East Studies (GBR) **552**
International Journal of Plant Sciences (USA) **795**
International Migration Review (USA) **7285**
International Organization (GBR) **7244**
International Perspectives on Sexual and Reproductive Health (USA) **5994**
International Political Science Review (GBR) **7244**
International Review of the Aesthetics and Sociology of Music (HRV) **6577**
International Security (USA) **7245**
International Statistical Review (GBR) **8379**
International Studies Quarterly (USA) **7245**
International Studies Review (USA) **7245**
Invertebrate Biology (USA) **948**
Isis (USA) **7868**
Italica (USA) **5311**
J E M (USA) **2872**
Japanese Language and Literature (USA) **5131**
The Jewish Quarterly Review (USA) **7723**
Journal for Research in Mathematics Education (USA) **3066**
Journal for Research in Mathematics Education. Monograph (USA) **3067**
Journal for the Scientific Study of Religion (USA) **7653**
Journal of Accounting Research (USA) **1294**
Journal of Aesthetics and Art Criticism (USA) **498**
Journal of African American History (USA) **3544**
Journal of African Cultural Studies (GBR) **4459**
The Journal of African History (GBR) **4176**
Journal of African Law (GBR) **4700**
Journal of Agricultural, Biological, and Environmental Statistics (USA) **716**
Journal of American Folklore (USA) **3619**
Journal of American History (USA) **4298**
Journal of Animal Ecology (GBR) **680**
Journal of Applied Ecology (GBR) **680**
Journal of Applied Econometrics (GBR) **1544**
Journal of Applied Probability (GBR) **5501**
Journal of Architectural Education (USA) **447**
Journal of Asian Studies (USA) **553**
Journal of Biblical Literature (USA) **7654**
Journal of Biogeography (GBR) **4017**
Journal of Black Studies (USA) **7978**
Journal of Blacks in Higher Education (USA) **2989**
Journal of British Studies (USA) **4235**
Journal of Business and Economic Statistics (USA) **1247**
The Journal of Cell Biology (USA) **833**
Journal of Computational and Graphical Statistics (USA) **5502**
Journal of Conflict Resolution (USA) **7978**
Journal of Consumer Psychology (USA) **27**
Journal of Consumer Research (USA) **1823**
Journal of Contemporary History (GBR) **4149**
Journal of Criminal Law & Criminology (USA) **2657**
Journal of Crustacean Biology (USA) **950**
Journal of Cuneiform Studies (USA) **400**
Journal of Decorative and Propaganda Arts (USA) **498**
Journal of Design History (GBR) **498**
Journal of Ecology (GBR) **682**
The Journal of Economic Education (USA) **1134**
The Journal of Economic History (GBR) **1544**
Journal of Economic Literature (USA) **1247**
Journal of Economic Perspectives (USA) **1545**
Journal of Educational and Behavioral Statistics (USA) **2934**
Journal of Field Archaeology (USA) **400**
The Journal of Finance (USA) **1361**
Journal of Financial and Quantitative Analysis (USA) **1361**
Journal of Health and Social Behavior (USA) **8113**
Journal of Hellenic Studies (GBR) **2236**
Journal of Herpetology (USA) **951**
Journal of Higher Education (USA) **2990**
The Journal of Human Resources (USA) **1868**
The Journal of Industrial Economics (GBR) **1136**
Journal of Interdisciplinary History (USA) **4149**
Journal of International Business Studies (GBR) **1137**
Journal of Japanese Studies (USA) **553**
Journal of Labor Economics (USA) **1691**
Journal of Latin American Studies (GBR) **4299**
The Journal of Law and Economics (USA) **4702**
Journal of Law and Religion (USA) **4702**
Journal of Law and Society (GBR) **4702**
Journal of Law, Economics, & Organization (GBR) **4702**
The Journal of Legal Studies (Chicago) (USA) **4703**
Journal of Mammalogy (USA) **951**
Journal of Marketing (USA) **1825**
Journal of Marketing Research (USA) **1825**
Journal of Marriage and Family (USA) **8114**
Journal of Military History (USA) **6429**
Journal of Modern African Studies (GBR) **7147**
The Journal of Modern History (USA) **4149**
Journal of Money, Credit & Banking (USA) **1362**
Journal of Music Theory (USA) **6580**
Journal of Musicology (USA) **6581**
Journal of Near Eastern Studies (USA) **401**
Journal of Negro Education (USA) **2877**
Journal of Organizational Behavior (GBR) **7377**
Journal of Paleontology (USA) **6726**
Journal of Palestine Studies (USA) **4322**
The Journal of Parasitology (SUN) **5821**
Journal of Peace Research (GBR) **7249**
Journal of Philosophy (USA) **6929**
Journal of Political Economy (USA) **1138**
The Journal of Politics (USA) **7148**
Journal of Public Administration Research and Theory (GBR) **7448**
The Journal of Religion (USA) **7655**
Journal of Religion in Africa (NLD) **7737**
Journal of Risk and Insurance (USA) **4510**
Journal of Roman Studies (GBR) **2236**
Journal of Southern African Studies (GBR) **7980**
Journal of Southern History (USA) **4300**
The Journal of Symbolic Logic (USA) **5507**
Journal of the Early Republic (USA) **4300**
Journal of the History of Ideas (USA) **4461**
Journal of the Learning Sciences (USA) **2879**
Journal of the Warburg and Courtauld Institutes (GBR) **4461**
Journal of Tropical Ecology (GBR) **3448**
Journal of Vegetation Science (SWE) **799**
Koninklijke Vereniging voor Nederlandse Muziekgeschiedenis. Tijdschrift (NLD) **6583**
Land Economics (USA) **202**
Language (Washington) (USA) **5139**
Latin American Antiquity (USA) **403**
Latin American Music Review (USA) **6584**
Latin American Perspectives (USA) **7982**
Latin American Politics and Society (USA) **7250**
Latin American Research Review (USA) **7982**
Law and Contemporary Problems (USA) **4713**
Law and History Review (GBR) **4713**
Law and Human Behavior (USA) **4713**
Law and Literature (USA) **4713**
Law and Social Inquiry (USA) **4714**
Law & Society Review (USA) **4714**
Learning Disability Quarterly (USA) **3043**
Legislative Studies Quarterly (USA) **7151**
Leonardo: Art Science and Technology (USA) **502**
Leonardo Music Journal (USA) **6584**
Lied und Populaere Kultur (DEU) **6584**
Limnology and Oceanography (USA) **2797**
M E L U S (USA) **5328**
M I S Quarterly (USA) **2523**
M L N (USA) **5149**
Management Science (USA) **1776**
Managerial and Decision Economics (GBR) **1777**
Marburger Jahrbuch fuer Kunstwissenschaft (DEU) **504**
Marketing Science (USA) **1833**
Master Drawings (USA) **504**
Mathematics Magazine (USA) **5515**
Mathematics of Computation (USA) **5516**
Medical Anthropology Quarterly (USA) **347**
Metropolitan Museum Journal (BEL) **6529**
Metropolitan Museum of Art Bulletin (USA) **6529**
Mexican Studies (USA) **4464**
Micropaleontology (USA) **6726**
Middle East Report (USA) **4323**
Midwest Modern Language Association. Journal (USA) **5334**
Mind (GBR) **6934**

Online Service

DIRECTORY 2010 NATIONAL LIBRARY OF MEDICINE 11189

Micro (CAN) **1149**
Midland Penetanguishene Mirror (CAN) **3813**
Mississauga News (CAN) **3813**
Model Airplane News (USA) **4340**
Model Railroader (USA) **4341**
Modern Drama (CAN) **5335**
Monday Report on Retailers (CAN) **1835**
Money Digest (CAN) **1640**
MoneySense (CAN) **1150**
The Moose Jaw Times Herald (CAN) **3813**
Morning Star (CAN) **3813**
Mosaic (Winnipeg, 1967) (CAN) **5336**
Motor Trend (USA) **8593**
Motor Truck (CAN) **8673**
Municipal World (CAN) **7498**
National Journal of Constitutional Law (CAN) **4851**
National Post (Toronto) (CAN) **3813**
National Post Business (CAN) **1370**
National Wildlife (World Edition) (USA) **2620**
Natural Life (CAN) **3813**
Nature Canada (CAN) **2621**
Nature Matters (CAN) **2621**
Nelson Daily News (CAN) **3813**
Network (Winnipeg) (CAN) **8847**
New Internationalist (GBR) **7255**
News (Abbotsford) (CAN) **3814**
News (Esquimalt) (CAN) **3814**
News Advertiser (CAN) **3814**
Newsweek (USA) **3983**
Newsweek International (GBR) **3869**
Niagara Falls Review (CAN) **3814**
North Bay Nugget (North Bay, 1989) (CAN) **3814**
North Island Gazette (CAN) **3814**
North Island Weekender (CAN) **3814**
North Shore News (CAN) **3814**
North Shore Outlook (CAN) **3814**
North Thompson Star / Journal (CAN) **3814**
The North York Mirror (CAN) **3814**
Northern Daily News (CAN) **3814**
Northern Ontario Business (CAN) **1155**
Northern Sentinel (CAN) **3814**
Northumberland News (CAN) **3814**
Nursing B C (CAN) **5973**
O H S Canada Magazine (CAN) **6682**
Oakville Beaver (CAN) **3815**
Observer (CAN) **3815**
Octane (CAN) **6782**
Oilweek Magazine (CAN) **6785**
Ontario Out of Doors (CAN) **8326**
Ontario Secondary School Teachers' Federation. Update (CAN) **2893**
Opera - Canada (CAN) **6601**
Oral Health Magazine (CAN) **5859**
Orbit (CAN) **2894**
Orillia Today (CAN) **3815**
Ottawa Citizen (CAN) **3815**
Ottawa Letter (CAN) **7459**
Our Schools, Our Selves (CAN) **2894**
Our Times Magazine (CAN) **4600**
Outdoor Canada (CAN) **8327**
Pacific Affairs (CAN) **7257**
Packet & Times (CAN) **3815**
Patient Care (CAN) **5694**
Peace Arch News (CAN) **3815**
Peace Magazine (CAN) **7258**
Peace Research (CAN) **7258**
Peacekeeping & International Relations (CAN) **7259**
Performing Arts and Entertainment in Canada (CAN) **8475**
Perspectives on Labour and Income (CAN) **1258**
Peterborough Examiner (CAN) **3815**
Peterborough This Week (CAN) **3815**
Pharmacy Post (CAN) **6873**
Pharmacy Practice (CAN) **6873**
Phoenix (Toronto, 1946) (CAN) **2239**
Phycologia (USA) **808**
Physical & Health Education Journal (CAN) **7002**
Plant (CAN) **1785**
Plastics in Canada (CAN) **7097**
Playback (CAN) **2387**
PopSci.com (USA) *see* Popular Science. **8435**
Popular Mechanics PMZone (USA) *see* Popular Mechanics. **8435**
Presbyterian Record (CAN) **7771**
Prince Albert Daily Herald (CAN) **3816**
Prince George Free Press (CAN) **3816**
Prince Rupert Daily News (CAN) **3816**
Professional Sound (CAN) **6607**
Profit (CAN) **1162**
Propane - Canada (CAN) **6790**
Psychology Today (USA) **7400**
Pulp & Paper Canada (CAN) **6737**
Purchasing b2b (CAN) **1839**
Queen's Quarterly (CAN) **3816**
Quesnel Cariboo Observer (CAN) **3816**
Quill and Quire (CAN) **7572**
Ranger Rick (USA) **2210**
RealScreen (CAN) **1164**
The Record (CAN) **3816**
Regina Sun (CAN) **3816**
Relations Industrielles (CAN) **1705**
Religious Studies and Theology (GBR) **7676**
Reproductive BioMedicine Online (GBR) **6002**
Rescol (CAN) **2950**
Research Money (CAN) **1378**
Resource Links (CAN) **2210**
Resources for Feminist Research (CAN) **8902**
Review (Richmond) (CAN) **3816**
Richmond Hill Liberal (CAN) **3817**
Rolling Stone (USA) **6613**
Rotunda (CAN) **515**
S S G M. Service Station & Garage Management (CAN) **8603**
Saanich News (CAN) **3817**
Saskatchewan Registered Nurses' Association. Newsbulletin (CAN) **5980**
Saskatoon Sun (CAN) **3817**
SaskBusiness (CAN) **1171**
Sault Star (Sault Ste. Marie, 1975) (CAN) **3817**
Scarborough Mirror (CAN) **3817**
School Libraries in Canada Online (CAN) **5045**
SchoolNet Magazine (CAN) **2951**
Science News (USA) **7910**
Seventeen (USA) **8883**
Shareowner (CAN) **1651**
Shopping Centre News (CAN) **1433**
SI.com (USA) *see* Sports Illustrated. **8207**
Smithsonian Magazine Web (USA) *see* Smithsonian. **8002**
Solid Waste and Recycling (CAN) **3512**
Spectator (Ontario) (CAN) **3817**
Standard (Hope) (CAN) **3817**
The Standard (St. Catharines) (CAN) **3817**
Standard Freeholder (CAN) **3817**
Star-Phoenix (CAN) **3817**
Stoney Creek News (CAN) **3818**
Strategy (CAN) **1844**
Strategy (Ottawa) (CAN) **5718**
Studia Canonica (CAN) **7818**
Studies in Canadian Literature (CAN) **5380**
Sudbury Star (CAN) **3818**
Summit (CAN) **7471**
Sun Times (CAN) **3818**
Teacher Librarian (USA) **2918**
The Telegram (CAN) **3818**
Telesis (Ottawa) (CAN) **2373**
Terrace Standard (CAN) **3818**
This Magazine (CAN) **7188**
Time Lines (CAN) **4315**
Today's Parent, Baby & Toddler (CAN) **2169**
Today's Parent, Pregnancy & Birth (CAN) **6005**
Toronto Life (CAN) **3818**
Toronto Star (CAN) **3818**
Transportation Research. Part E: Logistics and Transportation Review (GBR) **8517**
Tri-City News (CAN) **3819**
Tribune (Welland) (CAN) **3819**
Truck News (CAN) **8677**
Truck West (CAN) **8677**
Truro Daily News (CAN) **3819**
U.S. News & World Report Digital Edition (USA) *see* U S News & World Report. **3991**
University of Toronto Quarterly (CAN) **4481**
Urban History Review (CAN) **4316**
Uxbridge Times-Journal (CAN) **3819**
The Vancouver Courier (CAN) **3819**
The Vancouver Sun (CAN) **3819**
Victoria News (CAN) **3819**
Walkerton Herald-Times (CAN) **3819**
West Coast Line (CAN) **5398**
Western Standard (CAN) **3820**
Westworld Magazine (British Columbia Edition) (CAN) **8611**
Windsor Review (CAN) **5245**
Windspeaker (CAN) **3572**
Women & Environments International Magazine (CAN) **8904**
Words & Music (CAN) **6629**
Worklife (Kingston) (CAN) **1716**

N I S C International, Inc. Wyman Towers, 3100 St Paul St, Baltimore, MD 21218 TEL 410-243-0797, FAX 410-243-0982, sales@nisc.com, http://www.nisc.com
Agricola (USA) **173**
AgroBase (USA) **174**
AIDSearch (USA) **5740**
Child Abuse, Child Welfare & Adoption (USA) **2173**
Derwent Biotechnology Abstracts (GBR) **715**
Ecology Abstracts (Bethesda) (USA) **3478**
Energy Science and Technology Database (USA) **3133**
Entomology Abstracts (USA) **715**
Family & Society Studies Worldwide (USA) **5562**
Federal Research in Progress Database (USA) **3192**
Fish & Fisheries Worldwide (USA) **716**
Index to South African Periodicals (ZAF) **8**
Info - A S E A N & Pacific Rim (USA) **1242**
Info - C I S (USA) **1242**
Info - Latinoamerica (USA) **1242**
The Investors' Guide (ZAF) **1634**
Libros en Venta en Hispanoamerica y Espana (USA) **629**
M U S E, MUsic SEarch (USA) **6631**
A Matter of Fact: Statements Containing Statistics on Current Social, Economic and Political Issues (USA) **4152**
N I O S H T I C (USA) **6681**
N T I S Bibliographic Database (USA) **7938**
Popline (USA) **7289**
PsycINFO (USA) **7417**
R I L M Abstracts of Music Literature (USA) **6632**
R T E C S (USA) **3500**
Resources in Education (USA) **2935**
SoftBase (USA) **2444**
South African Studies (ZAF) **4171**
Water Resources Abstracts (USA) **8843**
Water Resources Abstracts (Online, Bethesda) (USA) **8843**
Water Resources Worldwide (USA) **8843**
Wildlife Review Abstracts (USA) **2634**
Wildlife Worldwide (USA) **720**
Women's Resources International (BiblioLine) (USA) *see* Women Studies Abstracts. **8906**
Women's Resources International (BiblioLine) (USA) *see* Women's Studies International (Baltimore). **8906**

National Library of Medicine 8600 Rockville Pike, Bethesda, MD 20209 TEL 301-594-5983, 888-346-3656, FAX 301-496-4000, custserv@nlm.nih.gov, http://www.nlm.nih.gov
AIDS Research and Therapy (GBR) **5752**
American Journal of Human Genetics (USA) **862**
American Medical Informatics Association. Journal (USA) **5829**
American Ophthalmological Society. Transactions (USA) **6038**
Amphibian & Reptile Conservation (USA) **932**
Annals of Clinical Microbiology and Antimicrobials (GBR) **881**
Annals of General Psychiatry (GBR) **6123**
Antimicrobial Agents and Chemotherapy (USA) **881**
Applied and Environmental Microbiology (USA) **881**
Arthritis Research & Therapy (GBR) **5578**
Australia and New Zealand Health Policy (GBR) **7508**
B M C Anesthesiology (GBR) **5770**
B M C Biochemistry (GBR) **724**
B M C Bioinformatics (GBR) **824**
B M C Biology (GBR) **655**
B M C Biotechnology (GBR) **756**
B M C Blood Disorders (GBR) **5934**
B M C Cancer (GBR) **6009**
B M C Cardiovascular Disorders (GBR) **5778**
B M C Cell Biology (GBR) **827**
B M C Chemical Biology (GBR) **724**
B M C Clinical Pathology (GBR) **5934**
B M C Clinical Pharmacology (GBR) **6824**
B M C Complementary and Alternative Medicine (GBR) **307**
B M C Dermatology (GBR) **5872**
B M C Developmental Biology (GBR) **655**
B M C Ear, Nose and Throat Disorders (GBR) **6078**
B M C Ecology (GBR) **655**
B M C Emergency Medicine (GBR) **6056**
B M C Endocrine Disorders (GBR) **5884**
B M C Evolutionary Biology (GBR) **863**
B M C Family Practice (GBR) **5582**
B M C Gastroenterology (GBR) **5920**
B M C Genetics (GBR) **863**
B M C Genomics (GBR) **863**
B M C Geriatrics (GBR) **4041**
B M C Health Services Research (GBR) **5582**
B M C Immunology (GBR) **5755**
B M C Infectious Diseases (GBR) **5810**
B M C International Health and Human Rights (GBR) **7509**
B M C Medical Education (GBR) **5582**
B M C Medical Ethics (GBR) **5582**
B M C Medical Genetics (GBR) **863**
B M C Medical Imaging (GBR) **6193**
B M C Medical Informatics and Decision Making (GBR) **5829**
B M C Medical Physics (GBR) **6193**
B M C Medical Research Methodology (GBR) **5582**
B M C Medicine (GBR) **5582**
B M C Microbiology (GBR) **882**
B M C Molecular Biology (GBR) **655**
B M C Musculoskeletal Disorders (GBR) **6056**
B M C Nephrology (GBR) **6265**
B M C Neurology (GBR) **6125**
B M C Neuroscience (GBR) **920**
B M C Nursing (GBR) **5952**
B M C Ophthalmology (GBR) **6039**
B M C Oral Health (GBR) **5836**
B M C Palliative Care (GBR) **5582**
B M C Pediatrics (GBR) **6088**
B M C Pharmacology (GBR) **6824**
B M C Physiology (GBR) **920**
B M C Plant Biology (GBR) **778**
B M C Pregnancy and Childbirth (GBR) **5986**
B M C Psychiatry (GBR) **6126**
B M C Public Health (GBR) **7509**
B M C Pulmonary Medicine (GBR) **6212**
B M C Structural Biology (GBR) **655**
B M C Surgery (GBR) **6237**
B M C Urology (GBR) **6265**
B M C Veterinary Research (GBR) **8794**
B M C Women's Health (GBR) **8844**
B M J (Clinical Research Edition) (GBR) **5582**
Baylor University Medical Center Proceedings (USA) **5584**
Behavioral and Brain Functions (GBR) **6126**
Beilstein Journal of Organic Chemistry (DEU) **2119**
Biochemical Journal (GBR) **724**
Biology Direct (GBR) **660**
BioMagnetic Research and Technology (GBR) **727**
Biomedical Digital Libraries (GBR) **5585**
BioMedical Engineering OnLine (GBR) **5586**
Biophysical Journal (USA) **752**
Breast Cancer Research (Online Edition) (GBR) **6010**
C B E Life Sciences Education (USA) **828**
Canadian Journal of Veterinary Research (CAN) **8795**
Canadian Veterinary Journal (CAN) **8795**
Cancer Cell International (GBR) **6011**
Cardiovascular Diabetology (GBR) **5884**
Cardiovascular Ultrasound (GBR) **6193**
Cell & Chromosome (GBR) **828**
Cell Communication and Signaling (GBR) **665**
Cell Stress & Chaperones (NLD) **5592**
Cerebrospinal Fluid Research (GBR) **6130**
Chiropractic and Osteopathy (GBR) **5803**
Clinical and Molecular Allergy (GBR) **5756**
Clinical and Vaccine Immunology (Online) (USA) **5756**
Clinical Biochemist Reviews (AUS) **729**
Clinical Medicine & Research (USA) **5597**
Clinical Microbiology Reviews (USA) **883**
Clinical Practice and Epidemiology in Mental Health (GBR) **7345**
Comparative Hepatology (GBR) **5921**
Cost Effectiveness and Resource Allocation (GBR) **4091**
Cough (GBR) **6213**
Critical Care (Online Edition) (GBR) **5601**
CytoJournal (IND) **831**
Dynamic Medicine (GBR) **5607**
e C M A J (CAN) *see* C M A J. **5590**
The E M B O Journal (GBR) **731**
E M B O Reports (GBR) **866**
eHealth International (USA) **5830**
Emerging Themes in Epidemiology (GBR) **7515**
Environmental Health: A Global Access Science Source (GBR) **7515**
Environmental Health Perspectives (USA) **3425**
Epidemiologic Perspectives & Innovations (GBR) **7516**
Epilepsy Currents (USA) **6138**
Eukaryotic Cell (Online) (USA) **885**
Evidence - Based Complementary and Alternative Medicine (GBR) **309**
Frontiers in Zoology (GBR) **944**
Genes & Development (USA) **867**
Genetic Vaccines and Therapy (GBR) **869**
Genome Biology (Online) (GBR) **675**
Genome Research (USA) **870**
Globalization and Health (GBR) **7519**
Harm Reduction Journal (GBR) **7520**
Head & Face Medicine (GBR) **5624**
Health and Quality of Life Outcomes (GBR) **7521**
Health Research Policy and Systems (GBR) **7523**
Health Services Research (USA) **4096**
Human Resources for Health (GBR) **5631**
Immunity & Ageing (GBR) **5759**
Immunome Research (GBR) **887**
Infection and Immunity (USA) **5816**
International Journal for Equity in Health (GBR) **7526**
The International Journal of Behavioral Nutrition and Physical Activity (GBR) **7364**
International Journal of Biological Sciences (AUS) **678**
International Journal of Health Geographics (GBR) **7526**
International Journal of Medical Sciences (AUS) **5639**
International Seminars in Surgical Oncology (GBR) **6023**
J C P Online (GBR) *see* Journal of Clinical Pathology. **5647**
Journal of Applied Behavior Analysis (USA) **7368**
Journal of Athletic Training (USA) **6230**
Journal of Autoimmune Diseases (GBR) **873**
Journal of Bacteriology (USA) **888**
Journal of Biology (GBR) **681**
Journal of Biomedicine and Biotechnology (USA) **5646**
Journal of Carcinogenesis (IND) **6024**
Journal of Circadian Rhythms (GBR) **5646**
Journal of Clinical Investigation (USA) **5647**
Journal of Clinical Microbiology (USA) **5647**
Journal of Ethnobiology and Ethnomedicine (GBR) **5648**
Journal of Experimental & Clinical Assisted Reproduction (GBR) **5995**
Journal of Immune Based Therapies and Vaccines (GBR) **5762**
Journal of Inflammation (GBR) **6248**
Journal of Insect Science (USA) **852**
Journal of Nanobiotechnology (GBR) **767**
Journal of Negative Results in BioMedicine (GBR) **684**
Journal of NeuroEngineering and Rehabilitation (GBR) **6153**
Journal of Neuroinflammation (GBR) **6154**
Journal of Psychiatry and Neuroscience (CAN) **6156**
Journal of the Experimental Analysis of Behavior (USA) **7381**
Journal of Translational Medicine (GBR) **5655**
Journal of Virology (USA) **890**
Learning & Memory (Online) (USA) **6158**
Lipids in Health and Disease (GBR) **738**
Malaria Journal (GBR) **5822**
Medical History (GBR) **5669**
Medical Library Association. Journal (USA) **5669**
Medscape Journal of Medicine (USA) **5677**
Microbial Cell Factories (GBR) **834**
Microbiology and Molecular Biology Reviews (USA) **892**
Molecular and Cellular Biology (USA) **739**
Molecular Biology of the Cell (USA) **834**
Molecular Cancer (GBR) **6027**
Molecular Pain (GBR) **5680**
National Academy of Sciences. Proceedings (USA) **7886**
Neurotherapeutics (USA) **6170**
Nucleic Acids Research (GBR) **741**
Nutrition & Metabolism (GBR) **5688**
Nutrition Journal (GBR) **6666**
P L o S Biology (USA) **696**
P L o S Computational Biology (USA) **826**
P L o S Genetics (USA) **877**
P L o S Medicine (USA) **5692**
P L o S Pathogens (USA) **894**

Online Service

11190 NEWSBANK, INC. ULRICH'S PERIODICALS

Particle and Fibre Toxicology (GBR) **3500**
The Plant Cell (USA) **810**
Plant Methods (GBR) **811**
Plant Physiology (USA) **812**
Population Health Metrics (GBR) **7536**
Preventing Chronic Diseases (USA) **5699**
Primary Care Companion to the Journal of Clinical Psychiatry (USA) **6174**
Proteome Science (GBR) **743**
R N A (GBR) **877**
Reproductive Biology and Endocrinology (GBR) **5899**
Reproductive Health (GBR) **5703**
Respiratory Research (GBR) **6219**
Retrovirology (GBR) **5825**
Royal Society of Medicine. Journal (GBR) **5707**
Saline Systems (GBR) **896**
Skull Base (USA) **6258**
Texas Heart Institute Journal (USA) **5800**
Theoretical Biology and Medical Modelling (GBR) **707**
Thrombosis Journal (GBR) **5800**
Trials (GBR) **5801**
Virology Journal (GBR) **5728**
World Journal of Surgical Oncology (GBR) **6036**
Zhejiang University. Journal (Science A) (CHN) **7933**

Newsbank, Inc. 4501 Tamiami Trail N., Ste. 316, Naples, FL 34103 TEL 802-875-2910, 800-762-8182, FAX 239-263-3004, sales@newsbank.com, http://www.newsbank.com
Asahi Shimbun Japan Access (JPN) **3899**
The Australian (AUS) **3793**
Bangkok Post (THA) **3961**
Belfast Telegraph (GBR) **3861**
The Capital (Rhinebeck) (USA) **3761**
China Daily Web Edition (CHN) *see* China Daily (North American Edition). **3823**
Colorado Springs Business Journal (USA) **1084**
Daily Journal of Commerce (Portland) (USA) **1427**
Daily Mail (GBR) **3863**
Economic Times (IND) **1337**
The Economist (GBR) **1481**
The Economist on CD-ROM (USA) **1481**
Electronic Telegraph (GBR) *see* Daily Telegraph. **3864**
Financial Express (IND) **1344**
The Guardian (GBR) **3865**
The Guardian on CD-ROM (GBR) **3866**
The Hindu (Chennai) (IND) **3882**
Idaho Business Review (USA) **1121**
The Independent on Sunday (GBR) **3867**
Investor's Business Daily (USA) **1633**
Jakarta Post (IDN) **3891**
Japan Times Online (JPN) *see* The Japan Times. **3900**
Jersey Journal (USA) **290**
Journal Record (Oklahoma City) (USA) **1138**
Korea Herald (KOR) **3903**
Korea Times (KOR) **3903**
Kuwait Times (KWT) **3903**
Long Island Business News (USA) **1145**
Manila Standard (PHL) **3928**
Minnesota Lawyer (USA) **4734**
The New York Sun (USA) **3983**
New York Times Book Review (USA) **7568**
New York Times Magazine (USA) **3983**
New Zealand Herald (NZL) **3918**
News of the World (GBR) **3869**
Pacific Daily News (GUM) **3874**
Saigon Times Daily (VNM) **3994**
The Scotsman (GBR) **3870**
South China Morning Post (HKG) **3875**
Sportsman (AUS) **8298**
Sunday Mercury (GBR) **3871**
Sunday Star Times (NZL) **3919**
Turkish Daily News (TUR) **3963**
Turkish Probe (TUR) **3963**
U.S. Air Force. Office of the Judge General. The Reporter (USA) **4972**
Vancouver Business Journal (USA) **1191**
The Vancouver Sun (CAN) **3819**
The Washington Blade (USA) **4380**
Western Daily Press (GBR) **3873**
Wisconsin Law Journal (USA) **4815**

Northern Light Technology, Inc. Ten Canal Park, Cambridge, MA 02141 TEL 617-674-2074, FAX 617-674-2076, http://www.northernlight.com
A B A Bank Marketing (USA) **1304**
A I D S Care (GBR) **5807**
A J R NewsLink (USA) *see* American Journalism Review. **4571**
A L A TechSource (USA) *see* Library Technology Reports. **5029**
A S H A Leader (USA) **4071**
A T Q (USA) **5248**
Abya Yala News (USA) **3515**
Academe (USA) **2965**
Academic Psychiatry (USA) **6118**
Academie des Lettres et des Sciences Humaines. Presentations (CAN) **7945**
The Academy of Management Perspectives (USA) **1723**
Academy of Management Review (USA) **1723**
Accountancy (GBR) **1276**
The Accountant (KEN) **1276**
The Accountant (IRL) **1276**
De Accountant (NLD) **1276**
Accounting Education News (USA) **1277**
Accounting Historians Journal (USA) **1278**
Accounting History (AUS) **1278**
Accounting Horizons (USA) **1278**
Accounting Technology (USA) **1279**
Accounting Today (USA) **1279**
Addiction (GBR) **2689**
Addiction Biology (GBR) **2689**
Administrative Assistant's Update (CAN) **1855**
Administrative Science Quarterly (USA) **7419**
Adolescence (FRA) **6119**
Adolescent Psychiatry (USA) **6119**
Adult Basic Education and Literacy Journal (USA) **2937**
Adult Learning (USA) **2938**
Advanced Battery Technology (USA) **3294**
Advanced Ceramics Report (GBR) **2037**
Advanced Composites Bulletin (GBR) **7090**
Advanced Imaging (USA) **2349**
Advances in Textiles Technology (GBR) **8447**
Advertising Age (USA) **20**
Aerospace Daily & Defense Report (USA) **43**
Africa (ITA) **4172**
Africa (BRA) **4172**
Africa (GBR) **4172**
African Affairs (GBR) **7103**
African American Review (USA) **3516**
African Arts (USA) **464**
African Business (GBR) **1589**
Afro-Hispanic Review (USA) **3517**
Afterimage (USA) **6963**
Aftermarket Business (USA) **8555**
Agency Sales (USA) **1804**
Agra Europe (GBR) **191**
Agricultural History (USA) **83**
Agricultural Research (USA) **217**
Agriculture Online (USA) *see* Successful Farming. **159**
Ahfad Journal (SDN) **8893**
AIDS Alert (USA) **5808**
The Air & Space Power Journal (USA) **6408**
Air Cargo World (USA) **8534**
Air Classics (USA) **44**
Air Force Comptroller (USA) **6409**
Air Force Law Review (USA) **4971**
Air Power History (USA) **44**
Air Safety Week (Online) (USA) **44**
Air Transport World (USA) **45**
Airman (USA) **6409**
Airports (USA) **8537**
The Alabama Review (USA) **4282**
Alaska (USA) **3969**
Alaska Business Monthly (USA) **1058**
Alcoholism (HRV) **2691**
Alcoholism & Drug Abuse Weekly (USA) **2691**
All Hands (USA) **6410**
Alternatives Journal (CAN) **3402**
America (USA) **7782**
America (DEU) **8682**
The American (Washington, D.C.) (USA) **7104**
American Annals of the Deaf (USA) **4071**
American Antiquity (USA) **372**
American Banker (USA) **1307**
American Bankruptcy Institute Law Review (USA) **1307**
American Bankruptcy Law Journal (USA) **4614**
American Business Law Journal (USA) **4854**
American City & County (USA) **7487**
American Craft (USA) **531**
American Criminal Law Review (USA) **2643**
American Economist (USA) **1436**
American Family Physician (USA) **5571**
American Fitness (USA) **6981**
American Forests (USA) **3683**
American Fruit Grower (USA) **3722**
American Gas (USA) **6762**
The American Genealogist (USA) **3758**
American Hunter (USA) **8303**
American Indian Quarterly (USA) **6634**
American Jewish History (USA) **7718**
American Journal of Agricultural Economics (USA) **193**
American Journal of Community Psychology (USA) **8086**
American Journal of Critical Care (USA) **5951**
American Journal of Family Therapy (USA) **7333**
American Journal of Geriatric Psychiatry (USA) **4040**
American Journal of Health Studies (Online) (USA) **6982**
American Journal of International Law (USA) **4916**
American Journal of Law & Medicine (USA) **4614**
American Journal of Nephrology (CHE) **6265**
American Journal of Ophthalmology (USA) **6038**
American Journal of Pharmaceutical Education (USA) **6820**
American Journal of Psychiatry (USA) **6122**
The American Journal of Psychoanalysis (USA) **7333**
American Journal of Psychology (USA) **7333**
American Journal of Psychotherapy (USA) **6122**
American Journal of Public Health (USA) **7507**
American Journal of Sports Medicine (USA) **6228**
American Journal of Theology & Philosophy (USA) **7621**
American Literature (USA) **5252**
American Machinist (USA) **1879**
American Mathematical Monthly (USA) **5468**
American Metal Market (USA) **1805**
American Midland Naturalist (USA) **7834**
American Music (USA) **6544**
American Music Teacher (USA) **6544**
The American Nurse (USA) **5951**
American Philosophical Quarterly (USA) **6903**
American Poetry Review (USA) **5416**
American Printer (USA) **7318**
The American Prospect (USA) **7105**
American Record Guide (USA) **6544**
American Rifleman (USA) **8158**
American Salesman (USA) **1805**
American Salon (USA) **585**
American School & University (USA) **3017**
American Scientist (USA) **7835**
American Shipper (USA) **8638**
The American Spectator (USA) **5206**
American Speech (USA) **5092**
The American Statistician (USA) **8344**
American Surgeon (USA) **6236**
American Theatre (USA) **8465**
American Vegetable Grower (USA) **218**
The Americas (USA) **4283**
Analytic Separations News (USA) **2097**
Angiology (USA) **5777**
Anglican Theological Review (USA) **7746**
Annals of Vascular Surgery (USA) **6237**
Annual Review of Genetics (USA) **862**
Annual Review of Microbiology (USA) **881**
Annual Review of Psychology (USA) **7335**
Annual Review of Sex Research (USA) **7335**
Annual Review of Sociology (USA) **8088**
Anthropological Quarterly (USA) **325**
Antioch Review (USA) **5206**
Antiques & Collecting Magazine (USA) **363**
Antiquity (GBR) **374**
Antitrust Bulletin (USA) **4855**
Apparel (USA) **2245**
Appliance Design (USA) **3295**
Applied Economics (GBR) **1060**
Appraisal Journal (USA) **7582**
Approach (JPN) **427**
Architectural Record (USA) **430**
The Architectural Review (GBR) **430**
Archives of Environmental and Occupational Health (USA) **3404**
Archives of Pathology & Laboratory Medicine (USA) **5902**
Area Development Site & Facility Planning (USA) **4403**
Argumentation & Advocacy (USA) **5096**
Arizona Business Gazette (USA) **1061**
Arizona Nurse (USA) **5952**
Armada International (CHE) **47**
Armed Forces Comptroller (USA) **6410**
Armenian Reporter (USA) **3519**
Armor (USA) **6411**
Armor (FRA) **3840**
Arms Control Today (USA) **4917**
The Army Lawyer (USA) **4971**
Army Reserve Magazine (USA) **6412**
The Art Bulletin (USA) **468**
Art Education (USA) **469**
Art in America (USA) **469**
Artforum International (USA) **472**
Arts Education Policy Review (USA) **475**
Asian Affairs: An American Review (USA) **7222**
Asian Ethnology (JPN) **329**
Asian Perspectives (USA) **381**
Asian Philosophy (GBR) **6906**
Asian Survey (USA) **7107**
Asian Theatre Journal (USA) **8466**
Asian Women (KOR) **8894**
AsianWeek (USA) **3520**
Assessment & Evaluation in Higher Education (GBR) **2967**
Asset Securitization Report (USA) **1610**
Association for Heritage Interpretation. Interpretation Journal (GBR) **8089**
Association Now (USA) **1726**
Astronomy (USA) **570**
Atlantic Economic Journal (USA) **1063**
Audubon (USA) **2603**
The Auk (USA) **901**
Australian Accounting Review (AUS) **1281**
Australian Bulletin of Labour (AUS) **1666**
The Australian Journal of Anthropology (AUS) **330**
Australian Journal of Dairy Technology (AUS) **261**
Australian Journal of International Affairs (GBR) **7222**
Australian Journal of Management (AUS) **1727**
Australian Journal of Political Science (GBR) **7108**
Australian Nursing Journal (AUS) **5952**
Australian Tax Forum (AUS) **1911**
Automatic Merchandiser (USA) **1806**
Automotive News (USA) **8565**
The Autoparts Report (USA) **8566**
AutoWeek (BEL) **8567**
AutoWeek Online (USA) *see* AutoWeek. **8567**
Avian Pathology (GBR) **8794**
Aviation Daily (USA) **8538**
B J O Online (GBR) *see* British Journal of Ophthalmology. **6039**
Backpacker (USA) **8305**
Baltimore Business Journal (USA) **1065**
Baltimore Jewish Times (USA) **7718**
Banca Nazionale del Lavoro. Quarterly Review (ITA) **1310**
Bank Investment Consultant (USA) **1611**
Bank Marketing International (IRL) **1313**
Bank News (USA) **1313**
Bank of England Quarterly Bulletin (GBR) **1441**
Bank Systems & Technology (USA) **1316**
Bank Technology News (USA) **1316**
Batteries International (GBR) **3296**
Bee Culture (USA) **95**
Behavioral Medicine (USA) **7339**
Benefits Quarterly (USA) **1856**
Best of New Orleans (USA) *see* New Orleans Magazine. **3983**
Beverage Industry (USA) **599**
BioCycle (USA) **3504**
Biological Bulletin (USA) **658**
Biomedical Market Newsletter (USA) **1807**
BioPharm International (USA) **6825**
Biophysical Journal (USA) **752**
BioScience (USA) **661**
Bitamin (JPN) **6826**
Black Collegian Online (USA) **6693**
Black Enterprise.com (USA) *see* Black Enterprise. **1068**
Black History Bulletin (USA) **3522**
Black Masks (USA) **8467**
Black Scholar (USA) **3523**
Blood Weekly (USA) **5934**
Boating Industry (USA) **8273**
BodyShop Business (USA) **8570**
The Bond Buyer (USA) **1613**
Bone Marrow Transplantation (GBR) **5903**
Book Links (USA) **2146**
Bookbird (USA) **2180**
Booklist (USA) **7554**
Boston College Environmental Affairs Law Review (USA) **3407**
The Botanical Review (USA) **781**
The Bottom Line (CAN) **1069**
The Bottom Line (GBR) **4998**
Boundary 2 (USA) **5265**
Brain (GBR) **6127**
Brake & Front End (USA) **8570**
Brand Strategy (GBR) **22**
Brandweek (USA) **22**
Brazzil (Online) (USA) **3523**
Brigham Young University Law Review (USA) **4632**
British Columbia Magazine (CAN) **8688**
British Educational Research Journal (GBR) **2832**
The British Journal for the Philosophy of Science (GBR) **7842**
British Journal of Aesthetics (GBR) **6908**
British Journal of Biomedical Science (GBR) **5903**
British Journal of Clinical Psychology (GBR) **7341**
The British Journal of Criminology (GBR) **2645**
British Journal of Developmental Psychology (GBR) **7341**
British Journal of Educational Psychology (GBR) **7341**
British Journal of Middle Eastern Studies (GBR) **4320**
British Journal of Neurosurgery (GBR) **6238**
British Journal of Nursing (GBR) **5953**
British Journal of Psychology (GBR) **7342**
British Journal of Social Psychology (GBR) **7342**
British Journal of Sociology of Education (GBR) **2832**
British Poultry Science (GBR) **281**
Broadband Business Forecast (Online Edition) (USA) **2495**
Broadcasting & Cable (USA) **2376**
Broadcasting & Cable T V Fax (USA) **2376**
Brookings Papers on Economic Activity (USA) **1536**
Building Design + Construction (USA) **985**
Buildings (USA) **987**
Bulletin of the Atomic Scientists (USA) **7224**
Business & Economic Review (USA) **1070**
Business Communication Quarterly (USA) **1729**
Business Credit (USA) **1322**
Business Economics (USA) **1071**
Business History (GBR) **1072**
Business History Review (USA) **1072**
Business Horizons (USA) **1072**
Business Insurance (USA) **4496**
The Business Journal (Tampa) (USA) **1444**
The Business Lawyer (USA) **4859**
Business Leader (USA) **1730**
Business North Carolina (USA) **1957**
Business Perspectives (USA) **1075**
The Business Report & Journal (USA) **1075**
Business Times (USA) **1444**
Business Times (THA) **1076**
Business Times (NGA) **1076**
Business Travel News (USA) **8689**
Business Weekly (TWN) **1076**
BusinessWeek Online (USA) *see* BusinessWeek. **1077**
C R N (USA) **2510**
Cabinet Maker (GBR) **4554**
CADalyst (USA) **3289**
California Law Review (USA) **4636**
California Management Review (USA) **1732**
Cambridge Journal of Education (GBR) **2970**
Campaign (London, 1968) (GBR) **22**
Camping Magazine (USA) **2146**
Canadian Architect (CAN) **436**
Canadian Banker (Online Edition) (CAN) **1324**
Canadian Business (CAN) **1079**
Canadian Business Economics (CAN) **1079**
Canadian Communications Reports (CAN) **2378**
Canadian Dimension (CAN) **7113**
Canadian Electronics (CAN) **3297**
The Canadian Geographer (USA) **4001**
Canadian Geographic (CAN) **4001**
Canadian Insurance (CAN) **4498**
Canadian Journal of Administrative Sciences (GBR) **1080**
Canadian Journal of Criminology and Criminal Justice (CAN) **2646**
Canadian Journal of Experimental Psychology (CAN) **7343**
Canadian Journal of History (CAN) **4134**
Canadian Journal of Native Education (CAN) **2834**
Canadian Journal of Public Health (CAN) **7511**
Canadian Manager (CAN) **1732**

11192 NORTHERN LIGHT TECHNOLOGY, INC. ULRICH'S PERIODICALS

Headache Online (USA) **6144**
Health Affairs (USA) **7520**
Health & Social Work (USA) **8044**
Health Care Financing Review (USA) **5624**
Health Management Technology (USA) **5830**
Health Progress (USA) **4096**
Health Services Research (USA) **4096**
Healthcare Executive (USA) **4097**
Healthcare Risk Management (USA) **4098**
HealthFacts (USA) **5627**
Heart Online (GBR) *see* Heart. **5787**
Hecate (AUS) **8898**
The Hemingway Review (USA) **5305**
Hepatitis Weekly (USA) **5815**
Herizons (CAN) **8867**
Herpetological Review (USA) **946**
High Ability Studies (GBR) **3041**
High Performance Plastics (GBR) **7092**
The High School Journal (USA) **2863**
Highlights for Children (USA) **2192**
Hinduism Today (USA) **7707**
Hispanic (USA) **3537**
Hispanic American Historical Review (USA) **4295**
Hispanic Outlook in Higher Education (USA) **2985**
Hispanic Review (USA) **5125**
The Historian (GBR) **4142**
Historical Methods (USA) **8149**
History (Washington) (USA) **4145**
History of Political Economy (USA) **1542**
History Today (GBR) **4230**
Hollywood Reporter: Premier Edition (USA) *see* The Hollywood Reporter. **6502**
Home Media Magazine (USA) **2401**
Horizontes (BRA) **341**
Horizontes (PRI) **4455**
The Horn Book Magazine (USA) **7562**
Hospice Management Advisor (USA) **4099**
Hospital Access Management (USA) **4099**
Hospital Development (GBR) **4100**
Hospital Employee Health (USA) **4100**
Hospital Home Health (USA) **4100**
Hospital Materials Management (USA) **4100**
Hospital Topics (USA) **4101**
Hospitality (GBR) **4388**
Hospitality (NZL) **4388**
Hospitality Design (USA) **4542**
House Beautiful (GBR) **4559**
House Beautiful (USA) **4542**
Housing Studies (GBR) **4414**
How (USA) **26**
Huaxue Jiaoyu (CHN) **2063**
Human (NLD) **6923**
Human Ecology (Ithaca) (USA) **7970**
Human Factors (USA) **3195**
Human Life Review (USA) **8106**
Human Organization (USA) **341**
Human Quest (USA) **6923**
Human Resource Development Quarterly (USA) **1863**
Human Resource Management Journal (GBR) **1864**
Humanist (DNK) **2986**
The Humanist (USA) **6923**
Humanist (NOR) **6923**
Humanitas (ITA) **5220**
Humanities (USA) **4455**
Humpty Dumpty's Magazine (USA) **2193**
Hunger News & Hope (USA) **8045**
Huntington Library Quarterly (USA) **5307**
Hydraulics & Pneumatics (USA) **3361**
Hydrocarbon Processing (USA) **6772**
Hypertension (USA) **5789**
I C M A Public Management Magazine (USA) **7494**
Ice Cream Reporter (USA) **3674**
Implement & Tractor (USA) **211**
Improved Recovery Week (USA) **3137**
In-Plant Graphics (USA) **7323**
In School (USA) *see* Instructor (New York). **2867**
In Vitro Cellular & Developmental Biology - Animal (DEU) **5633**
Independent Banker (USA) **1353**
Independent Provisioner (USA) **3646**
India Abroad (USA) **3539**
India Currents (USA) **3539**
Indian Journal of Agricultural Economics (IND) **200**
Indiana Business Magazine (USA) **1490**
Indiana Business Review (USA) **1122**
Indianapolis Business Journal (USA) **1429**
Indonesia (USA) **551**
Indonesian Commercial Newsletter (IDN) **1429**
Industrial Distribution (USA) **1820**
Industrial Health & Hazards Update (USA) **6678**
Industrial Heating (USA) **3368**
Industrial Management (USA) **1752**
Industrial Specialties News (CAN) **6465**
IndustryWeek (USA) **1752**
Infantry (USA) **6424**
Infection Control & Hospital Epidemiology (USA) **5817**
Infonomics (USA) **2544**
The Information Advisor (USA) **5061**
Information Outlook (USA) **5016**
Information Technology for Development (USA) **1598**
Information Today (USA) **5062**
Information Week (German Edition) (DEU) **2558**
Information Week Online (USA) *see* Information Week (US Edition). **2531**
Information World Review (GBR) **2351**
Innovation (English Edition) (DEU) **7077**
Inside Public Accounting (USA) **1290**
Insight Magazine (NGA) **6645**
Institutional Investor Platinum (GBR) *see* Institutional Investor (America's Edition). **1630**
Integrative & Comparative Biology (GBR) **947**
Intercollegiate Review (USA) **5221**
Intereconomics (DEU) **1570**
Interior Design (USA) **4543**
Internal Auditor (USA) **1291**
Internal Medicine Alert (USA) **5945**
International Angiology (ITA) **5790**
International Bulletin of Missionary Research (USA) **7762**
International Economy (USA) **1570**
International Examiner (USA) **3540**
International Gaming & Wagering Business (USA) **8180**
International Herald Tribune (FRA) **3841**
International Immunology (GBR) **5761**
International Insurance Monitor (USA) **4509**
International Journal of Childbirth Education (USA) **5993**
International Journal of Comparative Sociology (NLD) **8108**
International Journal of Conflict Management (GBR) **1756**
International Journal of Early Childhood (HKG) **2155**
International Journal of Engineering Education (IRL) **3201**
International Journal of Epidemiology (GBR) **5638**
International Journal of Government Auditing (Online Edition) (USA) **7446**
International Journal of Group Psychotherapy (USA) **7365**
International Journal of Instructional Media (USA) **3065**
The International Journal of Logistics Management (GBR) **1758**
The International Journal of Nursing Terminologies and Classifications (USA) **5962**
International Journal of Organizational Analysis (GBR) **1760**
International Journal of Social Psychiatry (GBR) **6147**
International Journal of Surgical Pathology (USA) **6246**
International Journal of the Economics of Business (GBR) **1129**
International Journal on World Peace (USA) **7244**
International Labour Review (GBR) **1689**
International Monetary Fund. World Economic Outlook (USA) **1493**
International Money Marketing (GBR) **1358**
International Perspectives on Sexual and Reproductive Health (USA) **5994**
International Planning Studies (GBR) **4416**
International Review of Applied Economics (GBR) **1129**
International Review of Mission (CHE) **7651**
International Review of Psychiatry (GBR) **6148**
International Small Business Journal (GBR) **1962**
International Trade Finance (GBR) **1359**
International Trade Forum (CHE) **1571**
International Travel News (USA) **8724**
Intervirology (CHE) **888**
Iris: A Journal about Women (USA) **8869**
Irish Marketing Review (IRL) **1823**
The Irish Times (IRL) **3893**
Irish Voice (USA) **3541**
Issues in Accounting Education (USA) **1293**
J C P Online (GBR) *see* Journal of Clinical Pathology. **5647**
J E C H Online (GBR) *see* Journal of Epidemiology & Community Health. **5648**
J M E Online (GBR) *see* Journal of Medical Ethics. **5651**
J M G Online (GBR) *see* Journal of Medical Genetics. **874**
Jane's International Defence Review (GBR) **6427**
Japan Chemical Week (JPN) **3248**
Japan Echo (JPN) **4184**
JavaWorld (USA) **2507**
Jet (USA) **3979**
Jewish Advocate (USA) **7722**
Jewish Exponent (USA) **7722**
Jewish News of Greater Phoenix (USA) **7723**
The Jewish News Weekly of Northern California (USA) **7723**
The Jewish Week (USA) **7724**
Journal for Research in Mathematics Education (USA) **3066**
Journal of Abnormal Child Psychology (USA) **7368**
Journal of Accountancy (USA) **1293**
Journal of Accounting Literature (USA) **1294**
Journal of Accounting Research (USA) **1294**
Journal of Addictions & Offender Counseling (USA) **7368**
Journal of Advertising (USA) **27**
Journal of Advertising Research (USA) **27**
Journal of Aesthetic Education (USA) **2874**
The Journal of American College Health (USA) **6990**
Journal of American Culture (USA) **4459**
Journal of American Ethnic History (USA) **3544**
Journal of American History (USA) **4298**
Journal of Animal Science (USA) **291**
Journal of Applied Communication Research (USA) **2329**
Journal of Applied Meteorology and Climatology (USA) **6358**
Journal of Applied Rehabilitation Counseling (USA) **8048**
Journal of Applied Statistics (GBR) **8382**
Journal of Asian Studies (USA) **553**
Journal of Athletic Training (USA) **6230**
Journal of Blacks in Higher Education (USA) **2989**
Journal of Business Communication (USA) **1764**
Journal of Business Logistics (USA) **1764**
Journal of Business Strategy (USA) **1764**
Journal of California Law Enforcement (USA) **2656**
Journal of Canadian Studies (CAN) **4460**
The Journal of Cardiovascular Surgery (ITA) **5792**
Journal of Career Assessment (USA) **7369**
Journal of Chemical Education (USA) **2067**
Journal of Child Neurology (USA) **6150**
Journal of Climate (USA) **6358**
Journal of Clinical Psychiatry (USA) **6150**
Journal of Commerce (CAN) **1430**
Journal of Commerce (THA) **1494**
Journal of Communication (USA) **8112**
Journal of Community Health (USA) **5647**
Journal of Comparative Family Studies (CAN) **8112**
Journal of Computer Information Systems (USA) **2523**
Journal of Consumer Affairs (USA) **2639**
Journal of Contemporary Asia (GBR) **4184**
Journal of Contemporary China (GBR) **4184**
Journal of Contemporary History (GBR) **4149**
Journal of Continuing Education in Nursing (USA) **5964**
The Journal of Corporation Law (USA) **4872**
Journal of Criminal Law & Criminology (USA) **2657**
Journal of Cultural Diversity (USA) **5964**
Journal of Cuneiform Studies (USA) **400**
Journal of Dental Hygiene (USA) **5851**
Journal of Dental Research (USA) **5851**
The Journal of Development Studies (GBR) **1600**
Journal of Developmental Education (USA) **2990**
Journal of Drug Issues (USA) **2695**
The Journal of Economic Education (USA) **1134**
Journal of Education for Business (USA) **1136**
Journal of Education for Teaching (GBR) **2875**
Journal of Electrocardiology (USA) **5793**
Journal of Employment Counseling (USA) **7372**
Journal of Engineering Design (GBR) **3205**
Journal of Engineering Education (USA) **3205**
The Journal of Environmental Education (USA) **3445**
Journal of Environmental Health (USA) **3445**
Journal of Environmental Quality (USA) **3446**
Journal of Esthetic and Restorative Dentistry (GBR) **5852**
Journal of European Studies (PAK) **4235**
Journal of Experiential Education (USA) **3067**
The Journal of Family Practice (USA) **5649**
Journal of Financial Research (USA) **1136**
Journal of Forensic Identification (USA) **5914**
Journal of Forestry (USA) **3695**
Journal of Gay & Lesbian Social Services (USA) **8049**
Journal of Gender Studies (GBR) **8899**
The Journal of General Psychology (USA) **7374**
The Journal of Genetic Psychology (USA) **873**
Journal of Geography in Higher Education (GBR) **4017**
Journal of Gerontological Nursing (USA) **4049**
The Journal of Government Financial Management (USA) **1295**
Journal of Herpetology (USA) **951**
Journal of Higher Education (USA) **2990**
Journal of Higher Education (IND) **2990**
The Journal of Imaging Services (USA) **2487**
Journal of Indo-European Studies (USA) **7979**
Journal of Insurance Regulation (USA) **4510**
Journal of International Affairs (USA) **7248**
Journal of International Business Studies (GBR) **1137**
Journal of International Marketing (USA) **1825**
Journal of Interprofessional Care (GBR) **5650**
Journal of Investigative Medicine (USA) **5915**
Journal of Knee Surgery (USA) **6248**
Journal of Labor Research (USA) **1691**
Journal of Legal Economics (USA) **1545**
Journal of Leisure Research (USA) **4978**
Journal of Macroeconomics (NLD) **1719**
Journal of Macromarketing (USA) **1825**
Journal of Mammalogy (USA) **951**
Journal of Management (GBR) **1767**
Journal of Management Accounting Research (USA) **1295**
Journal of Management Information Systems (USA) **2548**
Journal of Managerial Issues (USA) **1768**
Journal of Manufacturing Systems (GBR) **3386**
Journal of Marketing (USA) **1825**
Journal of Mental Health (GBR) **6152**
Journal of Mental Health Counseling (USA) **7376**
Journal of Military History (USA) **6429**
Journal of Moral Education (GBR) **2877**
Journal of Motor Behavior (USA) **7376**
Journal of Musicology (USA) **6581**
Journal of Muslim Minority Affairs (GBR) **7713**
Journal of Negro Education (USA) **2877**
Journal of Neuroscience Nursing (USA) **5965**
Journal of Neurosurgical Sciences (ITA) **6249**
Journal of Nuclear Medicine Technology (USA) **6201**
Journal of Nursing Education (USA) **5966**
The Journal of Nutrition (USA) **6661**
Journal of Nutrition Education and Behavior (USA) **6662**
Journal of Nutritional & Environmental Medicine (GBR) **6662**
Journal of Orthopaedic Research (USA) **6064**
Journal of Otolaryngology - Head & Neck Surgery (CAN) **6082**
Journal of Paleontology (USA) **6726**
Journal of Palestine Studies (USA) **4322**
Journal of Palliative Care (CAN) **5653**
Journal of Parapsychology (USA) **6742**
Journal of Performance Management (USA) **1362**
Journal of Perioperative Practice (GBR) **5967**
Journal of Personality Disorders (USA) **7378**
Journal of Phase Equilibria and Diffusion (USA) **6319**
Journal of Phenomenological Psychology (NLD) **7378**
Journal of Physical Oceanography (USA) **2810**
Journal of Political Ideologies (GBR) **7147**
Journal of Popular Culture (USA) **5315**
Journal of Post Keynesian Economics (USA) **1545**
Journal of Property Management (USA) **7596**
Journal of Property Tax Assessment and Administration (USA) **7597**
Journal of Psychoactive Drugs (USA) **2696**
Journal of Public Policy & Marketing (USA) **1826**
Journal of Real Estate Literature (USA) **7597**
The Journal of Real Estate Portfolio Management (USA) **7597**
Journal of Real Estate Research (USA) **7597**
Journal of Rehabilitation (USA) **6111**
The Journal of Religious Thought (USA) **7656**
Journal of Research on Technology in Education (USA) **2950**
Journal of Retailing (GBR) **1826**
Journal of School Health (USA) **7529**
Journal of Sex Research (USA) **7380**
Journal of Small Business Management (USA) **1962**
Journal of Social History (USA) **8115**
The Journal of Social Psychology (USA) **7380**
Journal of Social Studies Research (USA) **7980**
Journal of Social Work Education (USA) **8051**
Journal of Social Work Practice (GBR) **8051**
Journal of Socio-Economics (GBR) **1546**
Journal of Southeast Asian Studies (GBR) **4185**
Journal of Southern African Studies (GBR) **7980**
Journal of Studies on Alcohol and Drugs (USA) **2696**
Journal of the Atmospheric Sciences (USA) **6359**
Journal of the Early Republic (USA) **4300**
Journal of the History of Philosophy (USA) **6930**
Journal of Theological Studies (GBR) **7657**
Journal of Thermal Spray Technology (USA) **7055**
Journal of Third World Studies (USA) **4150**
Journal of Trauma Nursing (USA) **5967**
Journal of Travel Medicine (USA) **5655**
Journal of Travel Research (USA) **8726**
Journal of Ukrainian Studies (CAN) **5316**
Journal of Urban Design (GBR) **4418**
Journal of Vascular Research (CHE) **5794**
Journal of Wine Research (GBR) **240**
Journal of Women's History (USA) **8900**
Journal of World History (USA) **4150**
Journal Record (Oklahoma City) (USA) **1138**
Journalism History (USA) **4578**
The Kansas Banker (USA) **1363**
Kansas Nurse (USA) **5968**
Kentucky Banker (USA) **1363**
The Kenyon Review (USA) **5425**
Kiplinger's Personal Finance (USA) **1364**
Knowledge Quest (USA) **5023**
Korea Observer (KOR) **554**
Korea Times (KOR) **3903**
Labor History (GBR) **1692**
Lafayette Business Digest (USA) **1496**
Lambda Book Report (USA) **4376**
The Lancet (GBR) **5660**
Land Economics (USA) **202**
Landscape Management (USA) **3741**
Landscape Research (GBR) **448**
The Lane Report (USA) **1143**
Las Vegas Business Press (USA) **1143**
Laser Focus World (USA) **7080**
Latin American Literary Review (USA) **5320**
Latin American Research Review (USA) **7982**
Latin Trade (USA) **1575**
Law & Society Review (USA) **4714**
Law Reporter (USA) **4716**
Leadership Excellence (USA) **1869**
League Sentinel (GBR) **5224**
Learning, Media & Technology (Online) (GBR) **3070**
Leatherneck (USA) **6431**
Legal Assistant Today (USA) **4719**
The Legal Publisher (USA) **4720**
Liaison (Vanier) (CAN) **503**
Liberal Education (USA) **2992**
Library Administrator's Digest (USA) **5026**
Library Trends (USA) **5029**
The Licensing Letter (USA) **6754**
Life Science Today (GBR) **6858**
Liguorian (USA) **7804**
Listen (DEU) **7566**
Listen (USA) **2696**
The Literary Review (USA) **5324**
Lodging Hospitality (USA) **4393**
Logistics Spectrum (USA) **8431**
Long Island Business News (USA) **1145**
Long-Term Living (USA) **5969**
Los Angeles Business Journal (USA) **1497**
The Lutheran (USA) **7765**
Lutheran Theological Journal (AUS) **7766**
M I R: Management International Review (DEU) **1773**
M I T Sloan Management Review (USA) **1773**
Machine Design (USA) **3388**
Machine Design (JPN) **3388**
Maclean's (CAN) **3812**
MacWorld (USA) **2577**
Macworld (GBR) **2577**
Macworld Sweden (SWE) **2577**
The Magazine Antiques (USA) **367**

Link to your serials resources and content with ulrichsweb.com

DIRECTORY 2010 NORTHERN LIGHT TECHNOLOGY, INC. 11193

Maintenance Solutions (USA) 1021
Malaysian Business (MYS) 1146
Management Quarterly (USA) 1776
Management Review (USA) 1776
Management Services (GBR) 1777
Management Today (GBR) 1777
Management Today (MEX) 1777
Manitoba History (CAN) 4302
Mankind Quarterly (USA) 347
Manufacturing Engineering (USA) 3209
Manushi (IND) 8900
Marine Corps Gazette (USA) 6432
Marine Technology Society Journal (USA) 2812
Marketing (DEU) 1831
Marketing (GBR) 1831
Marketing Management (USA) 1832
Marketing News (USA) 1832
Marketing to the Emerging Majorities (USA) 1833
Marketing to Women (USA) 1833
Marketplace (Menasha) (USA) 1147
Mass Transit (USA) 8503
Massachusetts Review (USA) 5227
The Masthead (Harrisburg) (USA) 4579
Materials Performance (USA) 3353
Mathematics Magazine (USA) 5515
Mathematics Teacher (USA) 3072
Mathematics Teaching in the Middle School (USA) 3072
Mayo Clinic Proceedings (USA) 5665
The McKinsey Quarterly (USA) 1779
Med Ad News (USA) 1834
Media Asia (SGP) 7567
Media Report to Women (USA) 8120
MediaWeek (USA) 30
Medical Decision Making (USA) 5667
Medical Economics (USA) 5668
Medical Ethics Advisor (USA) 5668
Medical History (GBR) 5669
Medical Marketing & Media (USA) 6860
Medical Teacher (GBR) 5672
Medical Textiles (GBR) 5672
Medium Aevum (GBR) 5332
MedSurg Nursing (USA) 6252
Membrane and Separation Technology News (USA) 768
Memphis Business Journal (USA) 1148
Menopause News (USA) 8847
Mergers & Acquisitions (New York, 1965) (USA) 1148
Metal Center News (USA) 6323
Metal Producing & Processing (USA) 6323
Metro Reporter (USA) 3550
Miami Times (USA) 3550
Michigan Banker (USA) 1499
Michigan Citizen (USA) 3550
Microprocessor Report (USA) 2468
MicroStation World (USA) 2493
Microwave Engineering (GBR) 3109
Mid-America Commerce & Industry (USA) 1499
The Middle East (GBR) 5227
Middle East Journal (USA) 7252
Middle Eastern Studies (GBR) 4323
Midwest Quarterly (USA) 4465
The Milbank Quarterly (USA) 7154
Military Images (USA) 6435
Military Medicine (USA) 5679
Military Review (English Edition) (USA) 6436
Military Technology (DEU) 6436
Milling & Baking News (USA) 3674
Mind (GBR) 6934
The Mineralogical Record (USA) 4340
Minerva Biotecnologica (ITA) 768
Mining Magazine (GBR) 6473
Minority Business Entrepreneur (USA) 1963
Minority Nurse Newsletter (USA) 5970
The Mississippi Quarterly (USA) 5227
Model Airplane News (USA) 4340
Model Railroader (USA) 4341
Modern Age (USA) 5228
Modern Brewery Age (USA) 607
Modern Casting (USA) 6326
Modern Language Quarterly (USA) 5335
Modern Machine Shop (USA) 5457
Modern Materials Handling (USA) 5457
Modern Power Systems (GBR) 3142
Modern Tire Dealer (USA) 7825
Moment (USA) 3551
Money Marketing (GBR) 1368
Montana Business Quarterly (USA) 1150
Monthly Review (USA) 7155
Monthly Weather Review (USA) 6391
Mortgage Banking (USA) 1369
Mother Earth News (USA) 3982
Mothering (USA) 8847
MotherJones.com (USA) see Mother Jones. 5228
MOTOR (USA) 8591
Motor (SWE) 8591
Motor (NOR) 8592
Motor (RUS) 8591
Motor (DNK) 8592
Motor (IND) 8591
Motor (NLD) 8262
Motor Age (USA) 8592
Motor Boating (USA) 8278
Motor Truck (CAN) 8673
Multichannel News (USA) 2385
Multicultural Education (USA) 3073
Multicultural Education Abstracts (Print) (GBR) 2934
MultiMedia & Internet@Schools (USA) 2950
Multinational Finance Journal (USA) 1393
Multinational Monitor (USA) 1578
Mundo Hispanico (USA) 3551
Museum (USA) 6531
The Music Trades (USA) 6592
Musical Opinion (GBR) 6593
Musical Times (GBR) 6594
Muslim World (PAK) 7156
Muslim World (USA) 7715
Nails (USA) 590
Narrative (USA) 5338
Nashville Business Journal (USA) 1152
The Nation (GMB) 3843
The Nation (CAN) 3552
The Nation (USA) 5229
The National Black Law Journal (USA) 4738
National Catholic Reporter (USA) 7808
National Civic Review (USA) 7499
National Contract Management Journal (USA) 1780
National Defense (USA) 6438
National Guard (USA) 6438
National Institute Economic Review (GBR) 1152
The National Interest (USA) 7254
National Mortgage News Daily (USA) see National Mortgage News. 1370
National Parks (USA) 4981
National Petroleum News (USA) 6779
National Post (Vancouver) (CAN) 5229
National Review (USA) 7156
National Tax Journal (USA) 1936
National Voter (USA) 7156
National Wildlife (USA) 2620
National Wildlife (World Edition) (USA) 2620
National Women's Health Report (USA) 8847
Nationalities Papers (GBR) 7987
Nation's Cities Weekly (USA) 7499
The Nation's Health (USA) 7533
Nation's Restaurant News (USA) 4394
Native Americas (USA) 6635
Natural History (USA) 7888
Naval Aviation News (USA) 67
Naval Forces (DEU) 6438
Naval War College Review (USA) 6438
Navy Medicine (USA) 5684
Nephron Physiology (CHE) see The Nephron Journals. 6272
Network Briefing (GBR) 2370
Network News (GBR) 2501
Network World (USA) 2502
Networkletter (CAN) 2370
Neuroendocrinology (CHE) 5898
Neuroepidemiology (CHE) 6164
Neurological Research (GBR) 6165
Neuropsychobiology (CHE) 6168
New Accountant (USA) 1297
New African (GBR) 1602
New England Economic Indicators (USA) 1501
The New England Quarterly (USA) 5340
New England Review (USA) 5340
New Hampshire Business Review (USA) 1431
New Internationalist (GBR) 7255
New Jersey Business (USA) 1899
New Media Markets (GBR) 2386
New Oxford Review (USA) 7809
New Perspectives Quarterly (USA) 7158
New Pittsburgh Courier (USA) 3554
New Political Economy (GBR) 1547
The New Republic (USA) 5230
New Statesman (GBR) 5230
New York Amsterdam News (USA) 3554
New York Review of Books (USA) 7568
The New York State Dental Journal (USA) 5857
New Zealand Journal of Employment Relations (Online) (NZL) 1700
New Zealand Journal of Psychology (NZL) 7388
News India-Times (USA) 3554
News Photographer (USA) 6971
Newspaper Research Journal (USA) 4581
Nieman Reports (USA) 4581
Nonlinear Studies (USA) 5521
Nonwovens Industry (USA) 8455
The North American Review (USA) 5230
North Sea Letter (GBR) 6781
Northeastern Naturalist (USA) 805
The Northern Colorado Business Report (USA) 1431
The Northern Miner (CAN) 6475
Northwestern Financial Review (USA) 1372
Novel: A Forum on Fiction (USA) 5344
Nucleonics Week (USA) 3143
The Nurse Practitioner (USA) 5972
Nurse Researcher (GBR) 5972
Nursing (PRT) 5972
Nursing Economics (USA) 5973
Nursing Forum (USA) 5973
Nursing Law's Regan Report (USA) 5974
Nursing Management (GBR) 5974
Nursing Management (USA) 5974
Nursing Standard (GBR) 5975
Nutrition Forum (CAN) 6665
Nutrition Forum (USA) 6665
Nutrition Health Review (USA) 6666
Nutrition in Clinical Practice (USA) 6666
Nutrition Research Newsletter (USA) 6666
Nutrition Reviews (USA) 6666
Nutrition Today (USA) 6667
The Observer (GBR) 3869
Occupational Health & Safety (USA) 6682
Occupational Outlook Handbook (USA) 6707
Occupational Outlook Quarterly (USA) 6707
Occupational Therapy International (GBR) 6683
Ocean News & Technology (USA) 2815
Oceania (AUS) 350
Oceanus (USA) 2815
Off Our Backs (USA) 8902
Off Road (DEU) 8596
Office World News (USA) 1853
The Officer (USA) 6440
Oil & Gas Journal (USA) 6783
Oil Daily (Online) (USA) 6784
Old Testament Abstracts (USA) 7699
On Campus with Women (USA) 2996
Onderstepoort Journal of Veterinary Research (ZAF) 8804
One Country (USA) 3458
OnEarth (USA) 3458
Online Information Review (GBR) 5038
Opera News (USA) 6602
Ophthalmology Times (USA) 6048
Optimum Online (CAN) 7458
Optometric Management (USA) 6049
Oral History Review (USA) 4155
Orange County Business Journal (USA) 1505
Orbis (Kidlington) (GBR) 7256
Orbis (Nuneaton) (GBR) 5428
Organization Development Journal (USA) 1784
Organization Studies (DEU) 7990
Organizational Dynamics (USA) 1784
Ornamental Outlook (USA) 3757
Orthopedics (USA) 6070
Outdoor Life (USA) 8327
Outlook (CAN) 4754
Outsourced Logistics (USA) 8507
Oxford Economic Papers (GBR) 1158
Oxford Review of Education (GBR) 2894
P M A Magazine (USA) 6972
P M J Online (GBR) see Postgraduate Medical Journal. 5698
P M Online (GBR) see People Management. 2897
P N (USA) 4078
Pacific Affairs (CAN) 7257
Pacific Science (USA) 7896
Packaging Digest (USA) 6713
Packaging Strategies (USA) 6713
Paint & Coatings Industry (USA) 6719
Palaestra (USA) 3045
Paperboard Packaging (USA) 6714
Parabola (USA) 3621
The Paris Review (USA) 5349
Parliamentary Affairs (GBR) 7163
Parnassus: Poetry in Review (USA) 5429
Pathobiology (CHE) 5764
Patient Care (CAN) 5694
Peace Review (GBR) 7259
Peacekeeping & International Relations (CAN) 7259
Peacework (USA) 7164
Pediatric Annals (USA) 6100
Pediatric Emergency Medicine Reports (USA) 6070
Pediatric Nursing (USA) 5977
Pediatrics (Italian Edition) (ITA) 6102
Pediatrics for Parents (USA) 6102
Pensions & Investments (USA) 1644
People & Strategy (USA) 1871
People's Medical Society Newsletter (USA) 2640
Personnel Psychology (USA) 7390
Perspective (CHE) 1055
Perspective (GBR) 453
Perspective (Toronto, 1967) (CAN) 6939
Perspectives in Psychiatric Care (USA) 5977
Perspectives of New Music (USA) 6605
Perspectives on Sexual and Reproductive Health (USA) 6001
Pest Management Professional (USA) 246
Pesticide & Toxic Chemical News (USA) 3659
Petroleum Economist (GBR) 6787
Pharma Japan (JPN) 6867
Pharmaceutical Executive (USA) 6869
Pharmaceutical Technology (USA) 6870
Phi Delta Kappan (USA) 2898
Philadelphia Tribune (USA) 3557
Philological Quarterly (USA) 5160
Philosophical Psychology (GBR) 7391
Philosophy Today (USA) 6944
Phycologia (USA) 808
Physical Educator (USA) 3076
Physical Therapy (USA) 6113
Physician Executive (USA) 4109
Physiological Reviews (USA) 926
Physiotherapy Research International (GBR) 6114
Pipeline & Gas Journal (USA) 6788
PipeLine and Gas Technology (USA) 6789
Pit & Quarry (USA) 6476
Plains Anthropologist (USA) 351
Planning (USA) 4423
Plant Engineering (USA) 3215
Plastic Surgical Nursing (USA) 5978
Plastics Engineering (USA) 7097
Plastics News (IND) 7097
Plastics Technology (USA) 7098
PlasticsNews.com (USA) see Plastics News. 7097
Platt's Metals Week (USA) 6476
Plays (USA) 8476
Playthings (USA) 4061
Plumbing & Mechanical (USA) 4125
Poetics Today (USA) 5234
Poetry (IND) 5430
Police (GBR) 2663
Police (USA) 2663
Policy & Practice (USA) 8062
Policy Review (USA) 7166
Policy Studies Journal (USA) 7167
Polish American Journal (USA) 3558
Political Research Quarterly (USA) 7169
Political Science Quarterly (USA) 7169
Political Science Reviewer (USA) 7169
Polymer Composites (USA) 7098
PopSci.com (USA) see Popular Science. 8435
Popular Electronics India (IND) 3111
Popular Mechanics PMZone (USA) see Popular Mechanics. 8435
Popular Music & Society (GBR) 6607
Postgraduate Medicine (USA) 5698
Power Engineering (USA) 3328
Power Generation Technology & Markets (USA) 3145
Practical Accountant (USA) 1299
The Practical Lawyer (USA) 4759
The Practical Litigator (USA) 4759
The Practical Real Estate Lawyer (USA) 4759
Practical Summaries in Acute Care (USA) 6071
The Practical Tax Lawyer (USA) 1939
Precision Marketing (GBR) 1838
Precision Toolmaker (GBR) 6329
Premise Wiring (USA) 2352
Prepared Foods (USA) 3660
Presentations (USA) 32
Presidential Studies Quarterly (USA) 7173
The Priest (USA) 7813
Principal's Report (USA) 1786
Print (USA) 2489
Print (GBR) 7325
Printing Impressions (USA) 7326
Privacy Journal (USA) 2515
Process Engineering (GBR) 3253
Process Heating (USA) 3371
Process Safety Progress (USA) 3253
Products Finishing (USA) 6720
Professional Builder (USA) 1030
Professional Safety (USA) 6684
Professional School Counseling (USA) 2900
Profit (CAN) 1162
Progress in Cardiovascular Nursing (USA) 5798
Progressive Grocer (New York, 2002) (USA) 3681
Psychiatric Annals (USA) 6176
Psychiatry (New York) (USA) 6177
The Psychoanalytic Review (USA) 7395
The Psychological Record (USA) 7396
The Psychologist (GBR) 7398
Psychology & Psychotherapy (GBR) 7399
Psychology Today (USA) 7400
Psychopathology (CHE) 6179
Psychosomatics (USA) 6179
Psychotherapy Research (GBR) 7401
Public Administration Quarterly (USA) 7461
Public Administration Review (PAK) 7461
Public Administration Review (USA) 7461
Public Broadcasting Report (USA) 2388
Public Health Reports (USA) 7537
Public Management Review (Online) (GBR) 1787
Public Personnel Management (USA) 1873
Public Relations Journal (Online) (USA) 33
Public Relations Quarterly (USA) 33
Public Relations Review (GBR) 33
Public Relations Tactics (USA) 33
Public Roads (USA) 3281
Public Utilities Fortnightly (USA) 3510
Public Works (USA) 7501
Publius (USA) 7174
Pulp & Paper Canada (CAN) 6737
Pulp & Paper International (USA) 6737
Purchasing (IND) 1838
QST (USA) 2361
Qualitative Health Research (USA) 5701
Quality (NGA) 3921
Quality Magazine (USA) 1788
Quarterly Journal of Speech (USA) 2901
Quick Frozen Foods International (USA) 3661
Radical Teacher (USA) 7175
Radio Control Boat Modeler (USA) 4344
Radio Control Car Action (USA) 4345
Radiologic Technology (USA) 6206
Railway Age (USA) 8623
Ranger Rick (USA) 2210
Raritan (USA) 5357
Reactions (GBR) 4520
Reading Research Quarterly (USA) 2903
The Reading Teacher (USA) 2903
Reading Today (USA) 2903
Real Estate Economics (USA) 7608
Real Estate Issues (USA) 7609
Reason (USA) 5236
Redbook (USA) 8882
Reeves Journal (USA) 4125
Region Focus (USA) 1513
Regional Studies (GBR) 4425
Rehabilitation Nursing (USA) 5979
Religious Education (USA) 7676
Renaissance Quarterly (USA) 5359
Renascence (USA) 5359
Report on Microsoft (USA) 2493
Research in Drama Education (GBR) 8477
Research in Education (Manchester) (GBR) 2904
Research in Phenomenology (NLD) 6947
Research in Science & Technological Education (GBR) 2904
Research into Higher Education Abstracts (GBR) 2935
Research Money (CAN) 1378
The Resource (GBR) 3462
Resource Links (CAN) 2210
Restaurant Business (USA) 4396
Restaurant Hospitality (USA) 4397
Retail Merchandiser (USA) 1840
Retail Traffic (USA) 1841
Retailing Today (USA) 1841
Rethinking Marxism (GBR) 7177
Review of Business (USA) 1165
The Review of Contemporary Fiction (USA) 5360
The Review of Economic Studies (GBR) 1166

Online Service

Link to your serials resources and content with ulrichsweb.com

11194 O C L C ONLINE COMPUTER LIBRARY CENTER, INC. ULRICH'S PERIODICALS

Review of Educational Research (USA) 2905
The Review of English Studies (GBR) 5360
The Review of Litigation (USA) 4769
The Review of Metaphysics (USA) 6948
Review of Political Economy (GBR) 7178
The Review of Politics (GBR) 7178
Review of Public Personnel Administration (USA) 7466
Review of Social Economy (GBR) 1166
Rheumatology (CHE) 6226
Rheumatology (Online) (GBR) 6227
Risk Management (GBR) 4521
Risk Management (USA) 4521
Rock Products (USA) 1033
Roeper Review (USA) 3079
Rolling Stone (USA) 6613
Rolling Stone (AUS) 6613
Romanic Review (USA) 5364
Rough Notes (USA) 4522
The Round Table (GBR) 7263
Rubber & Plastics News (USA) 7826
Rubber World Online (USA) *see* Rubber World. 7827
Runner's World (USA) 8198
Runner's World (DEU) 8198
Runner's World (GBR) 8198
Rural Sociology (USA) 8130
Rural Telecommunications (USA) 2371
Russian Life (USA) 8753
Russian Social Science Review (USA) 7181
S B S Digital Design (USA) 7580
S M E Resource Guide (USA) 6478
Sacramento Business Journal (USA) 1170
Sacramento Observer (USA) 3562
Saint Anthony Messenger (USA) 7816
Saint John's Law Review (USA) 4778
Salmagundi (USA) 4474
San Diego Business Journal (USA) 1170
San Francisco Business Times (USA) 1432
Sanitary Maintenance (USA) 1842
Sarasota Magazine (USA) 3987
SaskBusiness (CAN) 1171
Satellite News (Online) (USA) 2389
Satellite Week (USA) 2389
Saturday Evening Post (USA) 3988
Scale Ship Modeler (USA) 4346
Scandinavian Journal of Educational Research (GBR) 2909
Scandinavian Review (USA) 3563
Schizophrenia Bulletin (USA) 6184
Scholastic Action (USA) 3079
Scholastic Art (USA) 3079
Scholastic Scope (USA) 3080
School Administrator (USA) 3031
School Leadership & Management (Online) (GBR) 3032
School Psychology Quarterly (USA) 7406
School Psychology Review (USA) 7406
Science Activities (USA) 7908
Science & Society (USA) 7182
Science News (USA) 7910
Science World (USA) 3081
Sciences (FRA) 7911
Sea Power (USA) 6445
Sea Technology (USA) 3219
Searcher (CAN) 4602
The Searcher (GBR) 4346
Seattle (USA) 5082
Secured Lender (USA) 1382
Security Management Online (USA) *see* Security Management. 1792
Seminole Tribune (USA) 3563
Seoul Journal of Economics (KOR) 1172
The Service Industries Journal (GBR) 1172
Sewanee Theological Review (USA) 7774
The Seybold Report (USA) 7580
Shakespeare Quarterly (USA) 5370
Shakespeare Studies (JPN) 5370
Shakespeare Studies (USA) 5370
Shape (USA) 8848
Shareowner (CAN) 1651
Shooting Industry (USA) 8200
Sierra (USA) 2627
Signal (CAN) 6687
Signal (DEU) 6034
Simulation & Gaming (USA) 2518
Singapore Management Review (SGP) 1793
Single Mother (USA) 8884
Sister Namibia (NAM) 8884
The Skeptic (AUS) 6743
Skeptic (USA) 6743
Skeptical Inquirer (USA) 6743
Skipping Stones (USA) 2213
Sky & Telescope (USA) 581
Smith College Studies in Social Work (USA) 8068
Social Cognition (USA) 7408
Social Education (USA) 3082
Social Forces (USA) 8133
Social Justice (USA) 7265
Social Policy (USA) 8003
Social Problems (USA) 8134
Social Science History (USA) 8003
The Social Science Journal (USA) 8004
Social Security Bulletin (USA) 4523
The Social Studies (USA) 8005
Social Work (ZAF) 8070
Social Work (USA) 8070
Social Work Research (USA) 8071
Society (CAN) 8135
Society (USA) 8005
Sociological Perspectives (USA) 8137
Sociology (GBR) 8138
Sociology of Religion (USA) 8139
Soft - Letter (USA) 2597
Software Industry Report (USA) 2597
Sojourners Magazine (USA) 7682
Soldiers (USA) 6446
Solid State Technology (USA) 3114
South America Report (USA) 1582
South China Morning Post (HKG) 3875
South Dakota Business Review (USA) 1177
Southern Communication Journal (USA) 2339
Southern Economic Journal (USA) 1178
Southern Literary Journal (USA) 5375
Southern Living (USA) 3988
The Southern Review (USA) 5375
Southern Review (AUS) 8140
The Southwest Review (USA) 5240
Special Delivery (USA) 6005
Special Educational Needs Abstracts (GBR) 2936
Special Warfare (USA) 6447
The Spectator (GBR) 5240
Spectroscopy (USA) 2105
Spectroscopy (NLD) 745
Spiritual Life (USA) 7683
The Sporting News (USA) 8206
Springfield Business Journal (USA) 1178
St. Louis Commerce Magazine (USA) 1410
The St. Louis Journalism Review (USA) 4584
Stamps (USA) 6900
State Legislatures (USA) 7186
State Tax Review (USA) 1945
Stone World (USA) 6480
Storyworks (USA) 3082
Strategy & Leadership (GBR) 1795
Stress (CHE) 5718
Strings (USA) 6620
Stroke (USA) 5800
Studies in American Fiction (USA) 5380
Studies in Art Education (USA) 520
Studies in Comparative International Development (USA) 8008
Studies in Family Planning (USA) 7294
Studies in Higher Education (GBR) 3003
Studies in Philology (USA) 5183
Studies in Romanticism (USA) 5381
Studies in the Literary Imagination (USA) 5382
Studies in the Novel (USA) 5382
Style (CAN) 2261
Successful Meetings (USA) 1844
Sulphur (GBR) 3256
Sun Reporter (USA) 3567
Sunset (USA) 3989
Supermarket News (USA) 3681
Supervision (DEU) 1709
Supervision (USA) 1709
Supplier Selection & Management Report (USA) 1845
Survey of Current Business (USA) 1521
Sustainable Facility (USA) 3148
Swedish Press (CAN) 3567
Swimming Technique (Online) (USA) 8210
Symposium (BRA) 4477
Symposium (USA) 5384
Target Marketing (USA) 1845
The Tax Executive (USA) 1947
Tax Management Compensation Planning Journal (USA) 1797
Tax Management Financial Planning Journal (USA) 1386
Tax Management International Journal (USA) 1948
Tax Management Memorandum (USA) 1948
Tax Management Real Estate Journal (USA) 7613
Teaching Children Mathematics (USA) 3085
Teaching Exceptional Children Plus (USA) 3048
Teaching History (AUS) 3085
Teaching History (GBR) 3085
Teaching in Higher Education (GBR) 3004
Tech Directions (USA) 3085
Technical Communication (USA) 2340
Technicalities (USA) 5050
Technology Access Report (USA) 8442
Technology Analysis & Strategic Management (GBR) 8442
Technology Review (USA) 7922
The Technology Teacher (USA) 3085
Technometrics (USA) 3222
Telco Business Report (USA) 2371
Telecom Markets (GBR) 1905
Tennessee Tribune (USA) 3568
Texas Banking (USA) 1386
Texas Business Review (USA) 1182
Texas Law Review (USA) 4794
Theatre Research International (GBR) 8483
Theatre Survey (GBR) 8483
Theological Studies (USA) 7689
Theology Today (USA) 7690
Theory into Practice (USA) 2919
Therapeutic Recreation Journal (USA) 6998
Third World Quarterly (GBR) 1606
Thorax (GBR) 6220
TireBusiness.com (USA) *see* Tire Business. 8607
Today's Catholic Teacher (USA) 2920
Tooling & Production (USA) 5460
Total Health (USA) 6670
Total Quality Management & Business Excellence (Online) (GBR) 1798
Traders Magazine (USA) 1387
Traffic World (USA) 8513
Trailer Boats (USA) 8283
Trailer Life (USA) 8338
Trains (USA) 8626
Transition (GUY) 8011
Transition (CAN) 8144
Transition (USA) 5242
Transpacific (USA) 3568
Transport Europe (BEL) 8514
Transportation Journal (USA) 8516
Travel Agent (USA) 8765
Trial (USA) 4966
Tribology & Lubrication Technology (USA) 3398
Tribune (GBR) 4603
The Tribune (New York) (USA) 8886
Tribune Business Weekly (USA) 1184
Trinity Journal (USA) 7691
TriQuarterly (USA) 5243
Trustee (USA) 4112
Twentieth Century Literature (USA) 5391
Undersea & Hyperbaric Medicine (USA) 5726
Unitas (PHL) 523
Units (USA) 4429
University of Chicago Law Review (USA) 4803
University of Queensland Law Journal (AUS) 4805
Urban Studies (GBR) 4430
Urologic Nursing (USA) 6276
Urology Times (USA) 6276
Vaccine Weekly (USA) 6884
Vanderbilt Law Review (USA) 4807
Vegetarian Times (USA) 6670
Vermont Business Magazine (USA) 1191
Veterinary Economics (USA) 1969
Veterinary Medicine (USA) 8813
Vibrant Life (USA) 6999
Video Age International (USA) 2398
Videography (USA) 2404
Virginia Quarterly Review (USA) 5244
Vital Speeches of the Day (USA) 4585
Vocational Education & Training Abstracts (GBR) 2937
Voice (CAN) 2308
The Voice (GBR) 3571
Voice (ESP) 6627
Vox Sanguinis (CHE) 5767
W T Online (USA) *see* Washington Technology. 7486
Waikato Times (NZL) 3919
Wall Street Letter (USA) 1658
Wallaces Farmer (USA) 169
Ward's AutoWorld (USA) 8611
Ward's Dealer Business (USA) 8611
Warning Letter Bulletin (USA) 5729
The Washington Monthly (USA) 7193
Water Environment & Technology (USA) 3492
Water Environment Research (USA) 3493
Weatherwise (USA) 6398
The Week (GBR) 4585
Weekly Epidemiological Record (CHE) 7545
The Weekly of Business Aviation (USA) 8552
West European Politics (GBR) 7273
Westchester County Business Journal (USA) 1524
Western Folklore (USA) 3624
Western Fruit Grower (USA) 259
The Western Journal of Black Studies (USA) 3572
Western Journal of Communication (USA) 5195
What's New in Electronics (AUS) 3116
The Wilson Journal of Ornithology (USA) 917
The Wilson Quarterly (USA) 5245
Wine Business Insider (USA) 613
Wings (AUS) 75
Wings (CAN) 8552
Wings of Gold (USA) 75
Wireless Business Forecast (Online) (USA) 2535
Wireless Week (USA) 2345
Woman Engineer (USA) 3227
The Woman Engineer (GBR) 3227
Women & Therapy (USA) 7415
Women in Action (PHL) 8890
Women in Business (USA) 1195
WomenPolice (USA) 2672
The Women's Review of Books (USA) 5245
Women's Studies (CHE) 8905
Women's Studies in Communication (USA) 8905
Wood & Wood Products (USA) 3717
Woodworking (CAN) 1053
Workbench (USA) 4439
Workforce (AUS) *E-mail edition.* 1715
Worklife (Kingston) (CAN) 1716
Works Management (GBR) 1801
The World & I Online (USA) 3993
The World Bank Economic Review (USA) 1525
World Bank Research Observer (USA) 1391
World Literature Today (USA) 5400
World Mining Equipment (GBR) 6483
World Oil (USA) 6797
World Policy Journal (USA) 7274
World Today (GBR) 7275
World Trade (IND) 1588
World Watch (USA) 3475
Yachting (USA) 8285
The Yale Journal on Regulation (USA) 4817
The Yale Law Journal (USA) 4817
Yellow Pages & Directory Report (USA) 2036
Youth Markets Alert (USA) 1849

O C L C Online Computer Library Center, Inc.
6565 Kilgour Pl, Dublin, OH 43017 TEL 614-764-6000, 800-848-5878, FAX 614-764-6096, oclc@oclc.org, http://www.oclc.org
A A C E International Transactions (USA) 3179
A A R P: The Magazine (USA) 5064
A B A Bank Compliance (USA) 1304
A B A Bank Marketing (USA) 1304
A B A Banking Journal (USA) 1304
A B A Journal (USA) 4606
A B Europe (GBR) 4975
A C I Structural Journal (USA) 974
A C M Computing Surveys (USA) 2405
A D H D Report (USA) 6117
A E Ue: International Journal of Electronics and Communication (DEU) 2310
A F E R (KEN) 7781
A F P Exchange (USA) 1305
A I Communications (NLD) 2444
A I D S Care (GBR) 5807
A I Magazine (USA) 2445
A J P Online (USA) *see* American Journal of Physiology (Consolidated). 918
A J R NewsLink (USA) *see* American Journalism Review. 4571
A J S Review (GBR) 7717
A L A TechSource (USA) *see* Library Technology Reports. 5029
A L A Washington News (USA) 4985
A L C T S Newsletter Online (USA) 4985
A L T - J (GBR) 2964
A N Q: A Quarterly Journal of Short Articles, Notes and Reviews (USA) 5248
A N Z Journal of Surgery (AUS) 6234
A Q Online (USA) *see* Academic Questions. 2965
A R D Online (GBR) *see* Annals of the Rheumatic Diseases. 6221
A R I E L (CAN) 5248
A R L (USA) 4986
A R Q: Architectural Research Quarterly (GBR) 426
A S A Bulletin (NLD) 4915
A S E A N Economic Bulletin (SGP) 1055
A S E E Prism (USA) 3179
A S H E Higher Education Report Series (USA) 2964
A S H R A E Journal (USA) 4115
A T Q (USA) 5248
Abacus (GBR) 1275
About Campus (USA) 2965
Abya Yala News (USA) 3515
Academe (USA) 2965
Academic Leader (USA) 2965
Academic Pediatrics (USA) 6086
Academy of Management Journal (USA) 1723
The Academy of Management Perspectives (USA) 1723
Academy of Management Review (USA) 1723
Academy of Marketing Science. Journal (USA) 1803
Academy of Natural Sciences of Philadelphia. Proceedings (USA) 7831
Access Control & Security Systems (USA) 2676
Accountability in Research (USA) 7831
Accountancy (GBR) 1276
The Accountant (IRL) 1276
Accounting and Business Research (GBR) 1277
Accounting and Finance (GBR) 1277
Accounting, Auditing and Accountability Journal (GBR) 1277
Accounting, Business and Financial History (GBR) 1056
Accounting Department Management Report (USA) 1277
Accounting Education (GBR) 1277
Accounting Forum (GBR) 1277
Accounting History (AUS) 1278
Accounting Horizons (USA) 1278
The Accounting Review (USA) 1278
Accounting Technology (USA) 1279
Accounting Today (USA) 1279
Acta Agriculturae Scandinavica. Section A. Animal Science (NOR) 277
Acta Agriculturae Scandinavica. Section B. Soil and Plant Science (SWE) 216
Acta Agriculturae Scandinavica. Section C. Food Economics (NOR) 190
Acta Anaesthesiologica Scandinavica (DNK) 5768
Acta Applicandae Mathematicae (NLD) 5464
Acta Biochimica et Biophysica Sinica (USA) 721
Acta Biotheoretica (NLD) 649
Acta Borealia (NOR) 7945
Acta Crystallographica. Section A: Foundations of Crystallography. Online (DNK) *see* Acta Crystallographica. Section A: Foundations of Crystallography. 2108
Acta Crystallographica. Section B: Structural Science. Online (DNK) *see* Acta Crystallographica. Section B: Structural Science. 2109
Acta Crystallographica. Section C: Crystal Structure Communications (DNK) 2109
Acta Crystallographica. Section D: Biological Crystallography (DNK) 2109
Acta Crystallographica. Section E: Structure Reports Online (DNK) 2109
Acta Crystallographica. Section F: Structural Biology and Crystallization Communications Online (DNK) 2109
Acta Diabetologica (DEU) 5883
Acta Haematologica (CHE) 5933
Acta Histochemica (DEU) 721
Acta Juridica Hungarica (HUN) 4609
Acta Linguistica Hungarica (HUN) 5090
Acta Mathematica Hungarica (NLD) 5464
Acta Neurologica Scandinavica (DNK) 6118
Acta Neuropsychiatrica (DNK) 6118
Acta Numerica (GBR) 5465
Acta Obstetricia et Gynecologica Scandinavica (GBR) 5985
Acta Odontologica Scandinavica (NOR) 5833
Acta Oncologica (SWE) 6007
Acta Ophthamologica (Online) (DNK) 6037
Acta Orthopaedica (Online) (GBR) 6054
Acta Oto-Laryngologica (SWE) 6076
Acta Paediatrica (GBR) 6086

Acta Pathologica Microbiologica et Immunologica Scandinavica (DNK) **650**
Acta Pharmacologica Sinica (USA) **6818**
Acta Physiologica (Online) (GBR) **918**
Acta Politica (GBR) **7101**
Acta Psychiatrica Scandinavica (GBR) **6119**
Acta Radiologica (GBR) **6192**
Acta Sociologica (NOR) **8085**
Acta Zoologica Online (GBR) **930**
Action in Teacher Education (USA) **2824**
Action Learning (GBR) **2824**
Action Research (GBR) **5567**
Active and Passive Electronic Components (GBR) **3294**
Active Learning in Higher Education (GBR) **2965**
Activities, Adaptation & Aging (USA) **4038**
Actualite Economique (CAN) **1056**
Acute Cardiac Care (Online Edition) (GBR) **5775**
Ad Astra (USA) **41**
Adaptive Behavior (GBR) **2445**
Addiction (GBR) **2689**
Addiction Biology (GBR) **2689**
Addiction Research and Theory (GBR) **2689**
Adelphi Series (GBR) **7219**
Adelphia Law Journal (USA) **4609**
Adhesives & Sealants Industry (USA) **3235**
Administration and Policy in Mental Health and Mental Health Services Research (USA) **5567**
Administration & Society (USA) **7418**
Administration in Social Work (USA) **8023**
Administrative Science Quarterly (USA) **7419**
Administrative Theory & Praxis (USA) **7419**
Adolescence (USA) **2143**
Adoption Quarterly (USA) **8023**
Adsorption (USA) **3235**
Adult Education Quarterly (USA) **2938**
Adult Learning (USA) **2938**
Advanced Composite Materials (NLD) **3335**
Advanced Imaging (USA) **2349**
Advanced Materials & Processes (USA) **3335**
Advanced Packaging (USA) **3089**
Advanced Powder Technology (NLD) **3235**
Advanced Robotics (NLD) **2584**
Advanced Technology Libraries (USA) **4987**
Advances in Applied Mathematics (USA) **5466**
Advances in Competitiveness Research (USA) **1551**
Advances in Complex Systems (SGP) **7833**
Advances in Computational Mathematics (NLD) **5549**
Advances in Developing Human Resources (USA) **1855**
Advances in Geometry (DEU) **5466**
Advances in Health Sciences Education (NLD) **5568**
Advances in Mathematics (USA) **5466**
Advances in Physics (GBR) **7004**
Advances in Physiotherapy (SWE) **6106**
Advertising Age (USA) **20**
Advertising & Society Review (USA) **20**
Advisor Today (USA) **4491**
The Advocate (Los Angeles, 1967) (USA) **4370**
Adweek (USA) **20**
Aerobiologia (NLD) **651**
Aerosol Science and Technology (USA) **2049**
Aesthetic Surgery Journal (USA) **6235**
Affilia (USA) **8024**
Africa (GBR) **4172**
Africa Confidential (GBR) **7102**
Africa Link (KEN) **971**
Africa Research Bulletin. Economic, Financial and Technical Series (GBR) **1435**
Africa Research Bulletin. Political, Social and Cultural Series (GBR) **7102**
Africa Today (USA) **7102**
African Affairs (GBR) **7103**
African American Review (USA) **3516**
African and Asian Studies (NLD) **8086**
African Archaeological Review (USA) **371**
African Arts (USA) **464**
African Business (GBR) **1589**
African Development Review (GBR) **1590**
African Identities (GBR) **3516**
African Journal of Ecology Online (GBR) **651**
African Journal of Library, Archives and Information Science (NGA) **4987**
African Studies (GBR) **323**
Afterimage (USA) **6963**
Aftermarket Business (USA) **8555**
Age and Ageing (GBR) **4038**
Ageing and Society (GBR) **4039**
Ageing International (USA) **4039**
Agency Sales (USA) **1804**
Aging & Mental Health (GBR) **4039**
Aging Cell (GBR) **827**
The Aging Male (GBR) **6283**
Agni (USA) **5250**
Agricultural and Forest Entomology (GBR) **837**
Agricultural Economics (USA) **192**
The Agricultural Education Magazine (USA) **83**
Agricultural History (USA) **83**
Agricultural Research (USA) **217**
Agriculture and Human Values (NLD) **85**
Agriculture Online (USA) *see* Successful Farming. **159**
AgriMarketing (USA) **193**
Agroforestry Systems (NLD) **87**
Agronomy Journal (USA) **88**
Ahfad Journal (SDN) **8893**
AIDS (USA) **5808**
AIDS & Behavior (USA) **5752**
AIDS Education and Prevention (USA) **7506**
AIDS Patient Care and S T Ds (USA) **5809**
AIDS Research and Human Retroviruses (USA) **5809**
AIDS Weekly (USA) **5809**
Air & Space Law (NLD) **8534**
The Air & Space Power Journal (USA) **6408**
Air & Waste Management Association. Journal (USA) **3503**
Air Conditioning, Heating & Refrigeration News (USA) **4116**
Air & Cosmos (FRA) **44**
Air Force Comptroller (USA) **6409**
Air Force Journal of Logistics (USA) **6409**
Air Force Law Review (USA) **4971**
Air Power History (USA) **44**
Air Traffic Management (GBR) **8534**
Air Transport World (USA) **45**
Aircraft Economics (GBR) **8535**
Aircraft Engineering and Aerospace Technology (GBR) **45**
Aircraft Value News (USA) **8535**
Airfinance Journal (GBR) **8535**
Airline Business (GBR) **8536**
Airman (USA) **6409**
Airports International Magazine (GBR) **46**
Akron Law Review (USA) **4612**
Akron Tax Journal (USA) **1909**
Alabama Heritage (USA) **4282**
Alabama Librarian (USA) **4988**
Alaska (USA) **3969**
Alaska Business Monthly (USA) **1058**
Alcohol and Alcoholism (GBR) **2690**
Alcohol Research & Health (USA) **2691**
Alcoholism Treatment Quarterly (USA) **2691**
Algebra and Logic (USA) **5467**
Algebra Colloquium (SGP) **5468**
Algebras and Representation Theory (NLD) **5468**
Alimentary Pharmacology and Therapeutics (GBR) **5920**
Alki (USA) **4988**
All About R O I (USA) **1804**
Allergology International (JPN) **5753**
Allergy (GBR) **5753**
Allured's Cosmetics and Toiletries (USA) **592**
Alternative & Complementary Therapies (USA) **306**
Alternative Law Journal (AUS) **4613**
Amber Waves (USA) **90**
Ambio Journal Online (SWE) *see* Ambio. **3402**
America (USA) **7782**
The American (Washington, D.C.) (USA) **7104**
American Academy of Business, Cambridge. Journal (USA) **1058**
American Academy of Child and Adolescent Psychiatry. Journal (USA) **6121**
American Academy of Dermatology. Journal (USA) **5871**
American Academy of Matrimonial Lawyers. Journal (USA) **4906**
American Academy of Nurse Practitioners. Journal (USA) **5951**
American Academy of Political and Social Science. Annals (USA) **7104**
American Academy of Psychoanalysis and Dynamic Psychiatry. Journal (USA) **7332**
American Academy of Religion. Journal (USA) **7620**
American Agent and Broker (USA) **4492**
American Annals of the Deaf (USA) **4071**
American Anthropologist (USA) **324**
American Artist (USA) **465**
American Association for Pediatric Ophthalmology and Strabismus. Journal (USA) **6038**
American Banker (USA) **1307**
American Banker's Financial Modernization Report (USA) **1307**
American Bankruptcy Law Journal (USA) **4614**
American Behavioral Scientist (USA) **7946**
The American Biology Teacher (USA) **652**
American Book Review (USA) **5205**
American Business Law Journal (USA) **4854**
American Ceramic Society. Bulletin (USA) **2037**
American Ceramic Society. Journal (USA) **2037**
American Chamber of Commerce in Japan. Journal (JPN) **1395**
American Cinematographer (USA) **6489**
American City & County (USA) **7487**
American Communist History (GBR) **4282**
American Craft (USA) **531**
American Criminal Law Review (USA) **2643**
American Dietetic Association. Journal (USA) **6654**
American Drama (USA) **8465**
The American Economic Review (USA) **1436**
American Economist (USA) **1436**
American Educational Research Journal (USA) **2825**
American Ethnologist (USA) **324**
American Family Physician (USA) **5571**
American Fern Journal (USA) **774**
American Fitness (USA) **6981**
American Foreign Policy Interests (USA) **7220**
American Forests (USA) **3683**
American Gas (USA) **6762**
American Geriatrics Society. Journal (USA) **4040**
American Heart Journal (USA) **5776**
American Heritage (USA) **4282**
American Historical Review (USA) **4129**
American History (Leesburg) (USA) **4282**
American Hunter (USA) **8303**
American Imago (USA) **6121**
American Indian Culture and Research Journal (USA) **6634**
American Indian Quarterly (USA) **6634**
American Jewish History (USA) **7718**
American Journal of Agricultural Economics (USA) **193**
American Journal of Audiology (USA) **4072**
The American Journal of Bioethics (USA) **862**
American Journal of Botany (USA) **774**
American Journal of Business (USA) **1059**
American Journal of Cardiovascular Drugs (NZL) **5776**
The American Journal of Chinese Medicine (SGP) **5740**
American Journal of Clinical Dermatology (NZL) **5871**
American Journal of Clinical Nutrition (USA) **6655**
American Journal of Community Psychology (USA) **8086**
American Journal of Criminal Law (USA) **2643**
American Journal of Dance Therapy (USA) **2682**
American Journal of Distance Education (USA) **2938**
American Journal of Drug and Alcohol Abuse (USA) **2691**
American Journal of Economics and Sociology (USA) **1059**
American Journal of Education (USA) **2826**
American Journal of Emergency Medicine (USA) **6055**
American Journal of Epidemiology (USA) **5572**
American Journal of Family Therapy (USA) **7333**
American Journal of Gastroenterology (USA) **5920**
American Journal of Health Studies (Online) (USA) **6982**
American Journal of Infection Control (USA) **5809**
American Journal of International Law (USA) **4916**
American Journal of Jurisprudence (USA) **4614**
American Journal of Kidney Diseases (USA) **6265**
American Journal of Law & Medicine (USA) **4614**
American Journal of Mathematics (USA) **5468**
American Journal of Nephrology (CHE) **6265**
American Journal of Nursing (USA) **5951**
American Journal of Obstetrics and Gynecology (USA) **5985**
American Journal of Orthodontics and Dentofacial Orthopedics (USA) **5834**
American Journal of Orthopsychiatry (USA) **7333**
American Journal of Otolaryngology (USA) **6077**
American Journal of Perinatology (USA) **5985**
American Journal of Philology (USA) **5092**
American Journal of Political Science (USA) **7105**
American Journal of Psychiatric Rehabilitation (USA) **6121**
American Journal of Psychiatry (USA) **6122**
The American Journal of Psychoanalysis (USA) **7333**
American Journal of Psychology (USA) **7333**
American Journal of Psychotherapy (USA) **6122**
American Journal of Public Health (USA) **7507**
American Journal of Reproductive Immunology Online (DNK) **5754**
American Journal of Sports Medicine (USA) **6228**
American Journal of Tax Policy (USA) **1910**
American Journal of Therapeutics (GBR) **5573**
American Journal of Transplantation (Online) (DNK) **6236**
American Journal on Addictions (USA) **2691**
American Journal on Intellectual and Developmental Disabilities (USA) **6122**
American Journalism (USA) **4571**
American Law and Economics Review (GBR) **4614**
The American Legion (USA) **2264**
American Libraries (USA) **4988**
American Literary History (USA) **5252**
American Literary Scholarship (USA) **5252**
American Literature (USA) **5252**
American Machinist (USA) **1879**
American Mathematical Monthly (USA) **5468**
American Mathematical Society. Bulletin. New Series (USA) **5469**
American Mathematical Society. Journal (USA) **5469**
American Mathematical Society. Proceedings (USA) **5469**
American Mathematical Society. Transactions (USA) **5469**
American Metal Market (USA) **1805**
American Meteorological Society. Bulletin (USA) **6346**
American Midland Naturalist (USA) **7834**
American Museum Novitates (USA) **931**
American Museum of Natural History. Bulletin (USA) **931**
American Music (USA) **6544**
American Music Teacher (USA) **6544**
American Musicological Society. Journal (USA) **6544**
American Nineteenth Century History (GBR) **4282**
American Oriental Society. Journal (USA) **542**
American Periodicals (USA) **5252**
American Philological Association. Transactions (USA) **2229**
American Philosophical Society. Proceedings (USA) **4442**
American Philosophical Society. Transactions (USA) **4442**
American Photo (USA) **6963**
American Planning Association. Journal (USA) **4403**
American Poetry Review (USA) **5416**
American Political Science Review (GBR) **7105**
American Politics Research (USA) **7105**
American Printer (USA) **7318**
The American Prospect (USA) **7105**
American Psychiatric Nurses Association. Journal (USA) **5951**
American Psychologist (USA) **7333**
American Quarterly (USA) **4442**
American Record Guide (USA) **6544**
American Review of Public Administration (USA) **7419**
American Rifleman (USA) **8158**
American Salesman (USA) **1805**
American Scholar (USA) **5206**
American School & University (USA) **3017**
American Schools of Oriental Research. Bulletin (USA) **542**
American Scientist (USA) **7835**
American Secondary Education (USA) **3017**
American Society for Information Science and Technology. Bulletin (USA) **4989**
American Society of Echocardiography. Journal (USA) **5776**
American Society of International Law. Proceedings of the Annual Meeting (USA) **4916**
American Sociological Review (USA) **8087**
The American Sociologist (USA) **8087**
The American Spectator (USA) **5206**
American Speech (USA) **5092**
The American Statistician (USA) **8344**
American Taxation Association. Journal (USA) **1910**
American Teacher (USA) **4589**
American Theatre (USA) **8465**
American Theological Library Association. Conference. Summary of Proceedings (USA) **4989**
American University International Law Review (USA) **4916**
The American University Journal of Gender, Social Policy & the Law (USA) **4615**
The Americas (USA) **4283**
Americas (English Edition) (USA) **4442**
Amphibia - Reptilia (NLD) **932**
Amyloid (GBR) **6221**
Amyotrophic Lateral Sclerosis (GBR) **6122**
Anaerobe (GBR) **880**
Anaesthesia (Oxford) (GBR) **5768**
Analog Integrated Circuits and Signal Processing (USA) **2465**
Analog Science Fiction & Fact (USA) **5439**
Analyse & Kritik (DEU) **7947**
Analyses of Social Issues and Public Policy (USA) **8087**
Analysis (GBR) **6904**
Analysis and Applications (SGP) **5469**
Analysis in Theory and Applications (NLD) **5470**
Analysis Mathematica (HUN) **5470**
The Analyst (Online) (GBR) *see* The Analyst. **2097**
Analytical Biochemistry (USA) **722**
Analytical Letters (USA) **2098**
Analytische Psychologie (CHE) **7334**
Anatomia, Histologia, Embryologia Online (DEU) **8792**
Anatomical Science International (JPN) **653**
Ancient Civilizations from Scythia to Siberia (NLD) **4179**
Ancient Mesoamerica (GBR) **4283**
Andrologia (DEU) **5574**
Angelaki (GBR) **4443**
Angiogenesis (GBR) **6008**
Anglo-Saxon England (GBR) **4198**
Animal Behaviour (GBR) **932**
Animal Biology (NLD) **932**
Animal Biotechnology (Online Edition) (USA) *see* Animal Biotechnology (Print Edition). **755**
Animal Conservation (GBR) **2602**
Animal Genetics (GBR) **862**
Animal Production Science (AUS) **218**
Animal Science Journal (AUS) **278**
Animation Magazine (USA) **466**
Annals of Applied Biology (GBR) **653**
Annals of Behavioral Medicine (USA) **5575**
Annals of Biomedical Engineering (USA) **5575**
Annals of Botany (GBR) **775**
Annals of Clinical Biochemistry (GBR) **722**
Annals of Clinical Psychiatry (USA) **6123**
Annals of Diagnostic Pathology (USA) **5575**
Annals of Dyslexia (USA) **3036**
Annals of Emergency Medicine (USA) **6055**
Annals of Global Analysis and Geometry (NLD) **5471**
Annals of Health Law (USA) **4617**
Annals of Human Biology (GBR) **653**
Annals of Human Genetics (GBR) **862**
Annals of Mathematics and Artificial Intelligence (NLD) **2445**
Annals of Medicine (SWE) **5902**
Annals of Noninvasive Electrocardiology (USA) **5777**
Annals of Nutrition and Metabolism (CHE) **6655**
Annals of Occupational Hygiene (GBR) **6672**
Annals of Oncology (GBR) **6008**
Annals of Operations Research (NLD) **2406**
Annals of Ophthalmology (USA) **6038**
Annals of Physics (USA) **7005**
Annals of Public and Cooperative Economics (GBR) **1422**
Annals of Science (GBR) **7835**
Annals of Tropical Medicine & Parasitology (GBR) **5810**
Annals of Tropical Paediatrics (GBR) **6087**
Annual Bulletin of Historical Literature (GBR) **4199**
Annual Review of Applied Linguistics (GBR) **5094**
Annual Review of Astronomy and Astrophysics (USA) **568**
Annual Review of Ecology, Evolution and Systematics (USA) **3403**
Annual Review of O C L C Research (Online Edition) (USA) **4989**
Annual Review of Plant Biology (USA) **775**
Annual Review of Sex Research (USA) **7335**
Antarctic Science (GBR) **653**
Anthropological Forum (AUS) **325**
Anthropological Literature (USA) **361**

Online Service

11196 O C L C ONLINE COMPUTER LIBRARY CENTER, INC. ULRICH'S PERIODICALS

Anthropological Quarterly (USA) **325**
Anthropological Theory (GBR) **326**
Anthropology and Archeology of Eurasia (USA) **326**
Anthropology & Education Quarterly (USA) **326**
Anthropology & Medicine (GBR) **327**
Anthropology Today (GBR) **327**
Anti-Cancer Drugs (USA) **6008**
Anti-Corrosion Methods and Materials (GBR) **6305**
Antioch Review (USA) **5206**
Antioxidants & Redox Signaling (USA) **5576**
Antipode (USA) **3998**
Antiques & Collecting Magazine (USA) **363**
Antiquity (GBR) **374**
Antitrust Bulletin (USA) **4855**
Antonie van Leeuwenhoek (NLD) **756**
Anxiety, Stress and Coping (GBR) **7335**
Aperture (USA) **6964**
Aphasiology (GBR) **6123**
Apoptosis (USA) **827**
Apparel (USA) **2245**
Appetite (GBR) **6655**
Appliance Design (USA) **3295**
Applicable Analysis (CHE) **5471**
Applications of Mathematics (New York, 1956) (USA) **5471**
Applied and Computational Harmonic Analysis (USA) **5472**
Applied Artificial Intelligence (USA) **2445**
Applied Arts (CAN) **467**
Applied Biochemistry and Biotechnology (USA) **723**
Applied Biochemistry and Microbiology (RUS) **723**
Applied Categorical Structures (NLD) **5550**
Applied Composite Materials (NLD) **3341**
Applied Developmental Science (USA) **7335**
Applied Economic Perspectives and Policy (USA) **193**
Applied Economics (GBR) **1060**
Applied Economics Letters (GBR) **1060**
Applied Environmental Education and Communication (USA) **3403**
Applied Financial Economics (GBR) **1437**
Applied Intelligence (USA) **2446**
Applied Linguistics (GBR) **5095**
Applied Mathematical Finance (GBR) **5472**
Applied Mathematics and Mechanics (NLD) **5472**
Applied Measurement in Education (USA) **2827**
Applied Neuropsychology (USA) **6123**
Applied Nursing Research (USA) **5952**
Applied Psycholinguistics (GBR) **5095**
Applied Psychological Measurement (USA) **7336**
Applied Psychology (GBR) **7336**
Applied Psychophysiology and Biofeedback (USA) **7336**
Applied Spectroscopy (USA) **2098**
Applied Spectroscopy Reviews (USA) **7074**
Applied Vegetation Science (DNK) **776**
Appraisal Journal (USA) **7582**
Aquaculture Economics & Management (GBR) **3585**
Aquaculture International (NLD) **3585**
Aquaculture Nutrition (GBR) **3585**
Aquaculture Research (GBR) **3585**
Aquatic Ecology (NLD) **654**
Aquatic Ecosystem Health & Management (USA) **776**
Aquatic Geochemistry (NLD) **2701**
Aquatic Insects (NLD) **839**
Arab Law Quarterly (NLD) **4619**
Arabian Archaeology and Epigraphy Online (DNK) **374**
Arabic Sciences and Philosophy (GBR) **4131**
Arabica (NLD) **542**
Arbitration International (NLD) **4917**
Arboriculture & Urban Forestry (USA) **3723**
Archaeological Dialogues (GBR) **376**
Archaeometry (GBR) **378**
Architectural Digest (USA) **4531**
The Architectural Review (GBR) **430**
Archiv fuer Acker- und Pflanzenbau und Bodenkunde (GBR) **218**
Archiv fuer Geschichte der Philosophie (DEU) **6905**
Archiv fuer Phytopathologie und Pflanzenschutz (GBR) **92**
Archival Issues (USA) **4990**
Archival Science (NLD) **4990**
Archives Europeennes de Sociologie (GBR) **8088**
Archives of Animal Nutrition (GBR) **8793**
Archives of Biochemistry and Biophysics (USA) **723**
Archives of Disease in Childhood (GBR) **6088**
Archives of Environmental and Occupational Health (USA) **3404**
Archives of General Psychiatry (USA) **6124**
Archives of Internal Medicine (USA) **5944**
Archives of Neurology (USA) **6124**
Archives of Ophthalmology (USA) **6038**
Archives of Otolaryngology - Head & Neck Surgery (USA) **6077**
Archives of Pediatrics & Adolescent Medicine (USA) **6088**
Archives of Physical Medicine and Rehabilitation (USA) **6106**
Archives of Physiology and Biochemistry (NLD) **919**
Archives of Psychiatric Nursing (USA) **5952**
Archives of Sexual Behavior (USA) **5577**
Archives of Suicide Research (USA) **7336**
Archives of Surgery (USA) **6237**
Archivo Espanol de Arte (ESP) **467**
Arctic, Antarctic, and Alpine Research (USA) **7836**
Area (GBR) **3999**
Arethusa (USA) **2230**
Argumentation (NLD) **6905**
Argumentation & Advocacy (USA) **5096**
Argus (Montreal) (CAN) **4990**
Argus Gas Connections (GBR) **6762**
Argus Global Markets (GBR) **6762**
Arid Land Research and Management (USA) **219**
Aries (NLD) **6643**
Aristotelian Society. Proceedings (Online) (GBR) **6905**
Aristotelian Society. Proceedings. Supplementary Volume (GBR) **6906**
Arizona Quarterly (USA) **5207**
Arkansas Business and Economic Review (USA) **1061**
Arkansas Business Journal (USA) **1061**
Arkansas Libraries (USA) **4991**
Armada International (CHE) **47**
Armed Forces and Society (USA) **6410**
Armed Forces Comptroller (USA) **6410**
Armor (USA) **6411**
Arms Control Today (USA) **4917**
The Army Lawyer (USA) **4971**
Army Logistician (USA) **6412**
Arrows for Change (MYS) **8852**
Ars Orientalis (USA) **543**
Art & Antiques (USA) **364**
Art, Antiquity, and Law (NLD) **468**
The Art Book (GBR) **468**
The Art Bulletin (USA) **468**
Art Bulletin of Nationalmuseum Stockholm (SWE) **6519**
Art Business News (USA) **468**
Art Criticism (USA) **469**
Art, Design & Communication in Higher Education (GBR) **469**
Art Documentation (CAN) **4991**
Art Education (USA) **469**
Art History (GBR) **469**
Art in America (USA) **469**
Art Journal (USA) **470**
Art Monthly (GBR) **470**
Art New England (USA) **470**
Art Nexus (English Edition) (COL) **470**
Art Nexus (Spanish Edition) (COL) **470**
Art Papers Magazine (USA) **471**
Art Press (FRA) **471**
Art U S (USA) **471**
Arte Veneta (ITA) **472**
Arthroscopy: The Journal of Arthroscopy and Related Surgery (USA) **6056**
Arthur Frommer's Budget Travel (USA) **8684**
Artichoke (CAN) **473**
Artificial Cells, Blood Substitutes, and Biotechnology (USA) **5902**
Artificial Intelligence and Law (NLD) **4622**
Artificial Intelligence for Engineering Design, Analysis and Manufacturing (GBR) **2446**
Artificial Intelligence Review (NLD) **2446**
Artificial Life (USA) **2446**
Artificial Organs (USA) **5903**
Artnews (USA) **474**
ArtReview:Digital (GBR) *see* Art Review (London). **471**
Arts (New Brighton) (USA) **474**
Arts and Activities (USA) **3051**
Arts and Humanities in Higher Education (GBR) **4443**
Arts Education Policy Review (USA) **475**
ArtUS (USA) **475**
Artweek (USA) **476**
Asia Cover (GBR) **4493**
Asia Pacific Business Review (GBR) **1061**
Asia Pacific Family Medicine (Online) (GBR) **5579**
Asia - Pacific Financial Markets (NLD) **1392**
The Asia Pacific Journal of Anthropology (AUS) **329**
Asia Pacific Journal of Clinical Nutrition (AUS) **6655**
Asia Pacific Journal of Clinical Oncology (GBR) **6009**
Asia Pacific Journal of Environmental Law (NLD) **3404**
Asia Pacific Journal of Human Resources (GBR) **1856**
Asia Pacific Journal of Management (SGP) **1725**
Asia Pacific Journal of Marketing and Logistics (GBR) **1805**
Asia Pacific Journal of Operational Research (SGP) **2407**
Asia - Pacific Journal of Teacher Education (AUS) **3051**
Asia Pacific Journal of Tourism Research (GBR) **8684**
Asia - Pacific Journal on Human Rights and the Law (NLD) **7202**
Asia Pacific Law Review (USA) **4622**
Asia - Pacific Review (GBR) **7222**
Asia - Pacific Telecom Newsletter (USA) **2365**
Asia Pacific Viewpoint (AUS) **1591**
AsiaMoney (CHN) **1308**
Asian Affairs (GBR) **543**
Asian Affairs: An American Review (USA) **7222**
Asian Business & Management (GBR) **1726**
Asian Case Research Journal (SGP) **1062**
Asian Communications (GBR) **2365**
Asian Development Review (PHL) **1591**
Asian Economic Journal (AUS) **1535**
Asian Economic Papers (USA) **1062**
Asian Ethnicity (GBR) **3520**
Asian Ethnology (JPN) **329**
Asian Journal of Andrology (USA) **5579**
Asian Journal of Communication (GBR) **2312**
Asian Journal of Social Psychology (AUS) **7337**
Asian Journal of Social Science (NLD) **7948**
Asian Music (USA) **6546**
Asian - Pacific Economic Literature (AUS) **1200**
Asian Perspectives (USA) **381**
Asian Philosophy (GBR) **6906**
Asian Review of Business and Technology (GBR) **8416**
Asian Studies Review (GBR) **4180**
Asian Survey (USA) **7107**
Asian Theatre Journal (USA) **8466**
Aslib Proceedings (GBR) **4991**
ASSAY and Drug Development Technologies (USA) **6823**
Assembly (Oak Brook) (USA) **3182**
Assembly Automation (GBR) **2457**
Assessment (USA) **7337**
Assessment & Evaluation in Higher Education (GBR) **2967**
Assessment in Education: Principles, Policy and Practice (GBR) **2827**
Assessment Update (USA) **2967**
Asset Securitization Report (USA) **1610**
Association for Computing Machinery. Communications (USA) **2533**
Association for Computing Machinery. Journal (USA) **2407**
Association Meetings (USA) **6278**
Association Now (USA) **1726**
Association of American Geographers. Annals (USA) **3999**
Association of Nurses in AIDS Care. Journal (USA) **5810**
Association of Pacific Coast Geographers. Yearbook (USA) **4035**
Association of the Bar of the City of New York. Record (USA) **4622**
Associazione Italiana Biblioteche. Bollettino (ITA) **4992**
Assurances et Gestion des Risques (CAN) **4493**
Astrobiology (USA) **654**
Astronomical and Astrophysical Transactions (IND) **569**
Astronomical Society of Australia. Publications (Online) (AUS) **569**
Astronomy (USA) **570**
Astronomy & Geophysics (GBR) **571**
Astrophysics (USA) **572**
Astrophysics and Space Science (NLD) **572**
Astropolitics (GBR) **572**
Asymptotic Analysis (NLD) **5474**
Atlanta Business Journal (USA) *see* Atlanta Business Chronicle. **1438**
Atlanta Magazine (USA) **3969**
The Atlantic (USA) **5207**
Atlantic Journal of Communication (USA) **8089**
Atlantic Studies (GBR) **5207**
Atlantis (ESP) **5097**
Atmospheric Science Letters (GBR) **6347**
Atomic Data and Nuclear Data Tables (USA) **7065**
Atomic Energy (USA) **3164**
Attachment and Human Development (GBR) **7337**
Attention, Perception & Psychophysics (USA) **7337**
Audience Development (USA) **7552**
Audiological Medicine (GBR) **6078**
Audiology and Neurotology (CHE) **6078**
Auditing (USA) **1280**
Audubon (USA) **2603**
Augmentative and Alternative Communication (GBR) **5580**
The Auk (USA) **901**
Austin Business Journal (USA) **1063**
Austral Ecology (AUS) **655**
Australasian Journal of Dermatology (AUS) **5872**
Australasian Journal of Philosophy (GBR) **6906**
Australasian Journal on Ageing (AUS) **4041**
Australasian Plant Pathology (AUS) **777**
Australasian Psychiatry (GBR) **6125**
Australasian Public Libraries and Information Services (AUS) **4993**
Australian Academic & Research Libraries (AUS) **4993**
Australian and New Zealand Journal of Family Therapy (GBR) **8089**
The Australian and New Zealand Journal of Obstetrics and Gynecology (AUS) **5986**
Australian & New Zealand Journal of Psychiatry (AUS) **6125**
Australian and New Zealand Journal of Public Health (AUS) **7508**
Australian & New Zealand Journal of Statistics (GBR) **8356**
Australian Bulletin of Labour (AUS) **1666**
Australian Business Law Review (AUS) **4857**
Australian Economic History Review (GBR) **1536**
Australian Economic Papers (GBR) **1064**
The Australian Economic Review (GBR) **1064**
Australian Feminist Studies (GBR) **8894**
Australian Geographer (GBR) **3999**
Australian Health Review (AUS) **4088**
The Australian Journal of Agricultural and Resource Economics (GBR) **194**
The Australian Journal of Anthropology (AUS) **330**
Australian Journal of Botany (AUS) **777**
Australian Journal of Chemistry (AUS) **2051**
Australian Journal of Earth Sciences (AUS) **2726**
Australian Journal of Education (AUS) **2829**
Australian Journal of Entomology (AUS) **840**
Australian Journal of International Affairs (GBR) **7222**
Australian Journal of Linguistics (AUS) **5097**
Australian Journal of Management (AUS) **1727**
Australian Journal of Political Science (GBR) **7108**
Australian Journal of Politics and History (GBR) **7108**
Australian Journal of Psychology (GBR) **7338**
Australian Journal of Public Administration (AUS) **7421**
Australian Journal of Rural Health (AUS) **7509**
Australian Journal of Soil Research (AUS) **220**
Australian Journal of Zoology (AUS) **934**
Australian Occupational Therapy Journal (AUS) **6107**
Australian Psychologist (GBR) **7338**
Australian Social Work (AUS) **8027**
Australian Systematic Botany (AUS) **777**
Australian Tax Review (AUS) **1911**
Autism (GBR) **6125**
Autoimmunity (GBR) **5755**
Automated Software Engineering (USA) **2446**
Automation and Remote Control (RUS) **2458**
Automotive Design & Production (USA) **8564**
Automotive Engineer (GBR) **8564**
Automotive Industries (USA) **8565**
Automotive News (USA) **8565**
Autonomic & Autacoid Pharmacology Online (GBR) **6824**
Autonomous Agents and Multi-Agent Systems (USA) **2447**
Autonomous Robots (NLD) **2584**
Avery Index to Architectural Periodicals (USA) **462**
Avian Diseases (USA) **8794**
Avian Pathology (GBR) **8794**
Aviation Week & Space Technology (USA) **49**
Axiomathes (Online) (NLD) **6907**
B C Business (CAN) **1064**
B J O G (GBR) **5986**
B J O Online (GBR) *see* British Journal of Ophthalmology. **6039**
B J S M Online (GBR) *see* British Journal of Sports Medicine. **6229**
B J U International (Online) (GBR) **6265**
B M J (Clinical Research Edition) (GBR) **5582**
B T Technology Journal (NLD) **2313**
B to B (USA) **1806**
B Y U Journal of Public Law (USA) **4625**
Baby Talk (USA) **2144**
Backpacker (USA) **8305**
Baltimore Business Journal (USA) **1065**
Bank Accounting & Finance (USA) **1281**
Bank Investment Consultant (USA) **1611**
Bank Loan Report (USA) **1313**
Bank Marketing International (IRL) **1313**
Bank of Canada. Review (CAN) **1313**
Bank Systems & Technology (USA) **1316**
Bank Technology News (USA) **1316**
The Banker (GBR) **1316**
Banking and Finance Law Review (CAN) **1317**
Banking Strategies (Online) (USA) **1318**
Barron's (USA) **1611**
Baseline (New York) (USA) **2408**
Basic and Applied Ecology (DEU) **3405**
Basic and Applied Social Psychology (USA) **7338**
Basic & Clinical Pharmacology & Toxicology Online (GBR) **6824**
Basin Research (Online) (GBR) **2702**
Battery Industry Guide (GBR) **1880**
Baumeister (DEU) **435**
Baylor Business Review (USA) **1065**
Baylor Law Review (USA) **4628**
Beaux Arts Magazine (FRA) **477**
Beef (USA) **280**
Behavior Genetics (USA) **863**
Behavior Modification (USA) **7339**
Behavioral and Brain Sciences (GBR) **7339**
Behavioral & Social Sciences Librarian (USA) **4994**
Behavioral Ecology (USA) **656**
Behavioral Healthcare (USA) **2692**
Behavioral Medicine (USA) **7339**
Behavioral Neuroscience (USA) **7339**
Behavioral Research in Accounting (USA) **1281**
Behavioral Sleep Medicine (USA) **7339**
Behaviour (NLD) **935**
Behaviour and Information Technology (GBR) **7340**
Behavioural and Cognitive Psychotherapy (GBR) **7340**
Behavioural Neurology (NLD) **6126**
Behavioural Pharmacology (USA) **6825**
Behind the Headlines (CAN) **7223**
Bell Labs Technical Journal (USA) **2365**
Bench & Bar of Minnesota (USA) **4628**
Benchmarking (GBR) **1727**
Benefits & Compensation International (GBR) **4495**
Benefits Canada (CAN) **1667**
Benefits Quarterly (USA) **1856**
Bernoulli (NLD) **5475**
Best of New Orleans (USA) *see* New Orleans Magazine. **3983**
Best Practice & Research: Clinical Anaesthesiology (GBR) **5770**
Best Practice & Research: Clinical Endocrinology & Metabolism (GBR) **5884**
Best Practice & Research: Clinical Gastroenterology (GBR) **5920**
Best Practice & Research: Clinical Haematology (GBR) **5934**
Best Practice & Research: Clinical Obstetrics & Gynaecology (GBR) **5986**
Best Practice & Research: Clinical Rheumatology (GBR) **6222**
Best's Review. Insurance Issues and Analysis (USA) **4495**
Better Homes and Gardens (USA) **4533**
Better Nutrition (USA) **6656**
Beverage Industry (USA) **599**
Beverage World (USA) **599**
Biblical Interpretation (NLD) **7627**
Bibliotekarz (POL) **4995**

11198 O C L C ONLINE COMPUTER LIBRARY CENTER, INC. ULRICH'S PERIODICALS

Cell Communication & Adhesion (Online Edition) (USA) 664
Cell Death & Differentiation (GBR) 829
Cell Proliferation (GBR) 830
Cell Stress & Chaperones (NLD) 5592
Cells, Tissues, Organs (CHE) 5593
Cellular & Molecular Neurobiology (USA) 6130
Cellular Immunology (USA) 5755
Cellular Microbiology Online (GBR) 830
Cellular Oncology (NLD) 830
Cellular Physiology and Biochemistry (CHE) 830
Cellulose (NLD) 2121
Centaurus (Copenhagen) (DNK) 7844
Center for Children's Books. Bulletin (USA) 2147
Central Asian Survey (GBR) 7115
Central European History (GBR) 4209
Central European Journal of Physics (POL) 7007
Central Penn Business Journal (USA) 1081
Cephalalgia (GBR) 6130
Ceramic Industry (USA) 2038
Ceramic Review (GBR) 2039
Ceramics Art and Perception (AUS) 2039
Ceramics Monthly (USA) 2039
Ceramics Technical (AUS) 2040
The Cerebellum (USA) 6130
Cerebral Cortex (USA) 6130
Cerebrovascular Diseases (CHE) 6130
Chain Drug Review (USA) 1732
Chain Leader (USA) 4383
Chain Store Age (USA) 1809
Chain Store Age Executive Fax (USA) 1082
Challenge (Armonk) (USA) 1082
Change (USA) 2971
Changing English (GBR) 2835
Charlotte Business Journal (USA) 1082
Chaucer Review (USA) 5272
Chemical and Petroleum Engineering (USA) 3238
Chemical Biology & Drug Design (Online) (DNK) 728
Chemical Communications (GBR) 2053
Chemical Engineering (USA) 3238
Chemical Engineering Communications (GBR) 3238
Chemical Engineering Research & Design (GBR) 3239
Chemical Senses (GBR) 920
Chemical Society Reviews (GBR) 2055
Chemical Week (USA) 3240
Chemie der Erde / Geochemistry (DEU) 2728
Cheminformatics (NLD) 2107
Chemist & Druggist (GBR) 6828
Chemistry & Biology (GBR) 2056
Chemistry and Ecology (CHE) 2056
Chemistry & Industry (GBR) 2057
Chemistry and Technology of Fuels and Oils (USA) 6765
Chemistry of Heterocyclic Compounds (New York, 1965) (USA) 2121
Chemistry of Natural Compounds (USA) 2121
Chemotherapy (CHE) 6828
Chicago Fed Letter (USA) 1446
Chicago Journal of International Law (USA) 4920
Chicago Magazine (USA) 8693
Chicago Review (USA) 5273
Chief Executive Magazine (USA) 1733
Child and Adolescent Mental Health (Online) (GBR) *see* Child and Adolescent Mental Health. 7344
Child and Adolescent Psychopharmacology News (USA) 6131
Child and Adolescent Social Work Journal (USA) 8093
Child & Family Behavior Therapy (USA) 7344
Child & Family Social Work Online (GBR) 8032
Child and Youth Care Forum (USA) 2147
Child & Youth Services (USA) 8032
Child: Care, Health and Development (GBR) 6089
Child Care in Practice (GBR) 2147
Child Development (USA) 2147
Child Health Alert (USA) 6089
Child Language Teaching and Therapy (GBR) 3037
Child Maltreatment (USA) 2148
Child Psychiatry and Human Development (USA) 6131
Child Study Journal (USA) 2836
Child Welfare (USA) 8032
Childhood (GBR) 2148
Childhood Education (USA) 3054
Children and Libraries (USA) 5001
Children & Schools (USA) 8033
Children's Geographies (GBR) 7344
Children's Health Care (USA) 8033
Children's Literature (Baltimore) (USA) 5273
Children's Literature Association Quarterly (USA) 5001
Children's Literature in Education (USA) 2149
China: An International Journal (SGP) 7954
China Business Review (USA) 1555
China Chemical Reporter (CHN) 3241
China Information (GBR) 546
The China Journal (AUS) 546
China Law & Practice (HKG) 4642
China Quarterly (GBR) 546
China Review International (USA) 3823
Chinese Annals of Mathematics. Series B (DEU) 5478
The Chinese Economy (USA) 1083
Chinese Education and Society (USA) 2836
Chinese Journal of Polymer Science (SGP) 2121
Chinese Law and Government (USA) 4642
Chinese Sociology and Anthropology (USA) 8093
Chinese Studies in History (USA) 4135
Christian Bioethics (NLD) 5595
The Christian Century (USA) 7631
Christian Higher Education (USA) 7632
Christian Scholar's Review (USA) 7632
Christianity and Literature (USA) 5210
Christianity Today (USA) 7632
Chromosome Research (NLD) 728
Chronic Respiratory Disease (GBR) 6212
The Chronicle of Higher Education (USA) 2972
Chronobiology International (USA) 666
Church & State (USA) 7633
Church History (USA) 7633
Ciencia da Informacao (BRA) 5002
Cincinnati Magazine (USA) 3972
Cineaste (USA) 6493
Cinema Journal (USA) 6493
Circuit World (GBR) 8418
Citizenship Studies (GBR) 7116
City (GBR) 4407
City & Community (USA) 8033
Civil Engineering (Reston) (USA) 3262
Civil Engineering and Environmental Systems (CHE) 3262
Civil War History (USA) 4288
Civil Wars (GBR) 7227
Cladistics (GBR) 666
Classical and Modern Literature (USA) 5274
Classical Antiquity (USA) 2232
Classical Journal (USA) 2232
Classical Philology (USA) 2232
Classical Quarterly (GBR) 2232
Classical Review (GBR) 2233
Classical World (USA) 2233
Clay Minerals (GBR) 2704
Cleanroom Technology (GBR) 3184
CleanRooms (USA) 3366
The Clearing House (USA) 2837
Cleft Palate - Craniofacial Journal (CAN) 6239
Cleveland Magazine (USA) 3973
Climacteric (GBR) 8844
Climatic Change (NLD) 6349
Climbing (USA) 8309
Clin-Alert (USA) 6889
Clinical and Experimental Allergy (GBR) 5756
Clinical and Experimental Allergy Reviews (GBR) 5756
Clinical and Experimental Dermatology (GBR) 5873
Clinical and Experimental Hypertension (USA) 5782
Clinical and Experimental Immunology (GBR) 5756
Clinical and Experimental Metastasis (NLD) 6015
Clinical and Experimental Ophthalmology (AUS) 6040
Clinical and Experimental Pharmacology & Physiology (AUS) 921
Clinical Autonomic Research (USA) 5596
Clinical Case Studies (USA) 6131
Clinical Chemistry and Laboratory Medicine (DEU) 729
Clinical Child and Family Psychology Review (USA) 7345
Clinical Child Psychology & Psychiatry (GBR) 2149
Clinical Drug Investigation (NZL) 6828
Clinical Dysmorphology (USA) 666
Clinical Endocrinology (GBR) 5885
Clinical Genetics (DNK) 864
Clinical Gerontologist (USA) 4043
Clinical Governance (GBR) 5596
Clinical Hemorheology and Microcirculation (NLD) 5935
Clinical Immunology (USA) 5756
Clinical Intensive Care (GBR) 5944
Clinical Law Review (USA) 4643
Clinical Linguistics & Phonetics (GBR) 6132
Clinical Microbiology and Infection (GBR) 5597
Clinical Nursing Research (USA) 5955
Clinical Nutrition (NLD) 6656
Clinical Oral Implants Research (DNK) 5838
Clinical Otolaryngology (GBR) 6078
Clinical Pharmacokinetics (NZL) 6829
Clinical Pharmacology and Therapeutics (USA) 6829
Clinical Physiology and Functional Imaging (GBR) 5597
Clinical Proteomics (USA) 729
Clinical Psychologist (GBR) 7345
Clinical Psychology (USA) 7345
Clinical Radiology (GBR) 6194
Clinical Rehabilitation (GBR) 6107
Clinical Research and Regulatory Affairs (GBR) 6829
Clinical Reviews in Allergy & Immunology (USA) 5756
Clinical Reviews in Bone and Mineral Metabolism (USA) 6016
Clinical Risk (GBR) 5597
Clinical Social Work Journal (USA) 8034
The Clinical Supervisor (USA) 8034
The Clinical Teacher (GBR) 5597
Clinical Toxicology (USA) 6829
Clinical Transplantation (DNK) 6240
Clinical Trials (GBR) 5904
Clio (Ft. Wayne) (USA) 4135
Cloning and Stem Cells (USA) 864
Club Industry's Fitness Business Pro (USA) 6984
Club Management (USA) 2265
Cluster Computing (NLD) 2496
CNN/Money (USA) *see* Money (New York). 1368
Coach and Athletic Director (USA) 8166
Coal U.K. (GBR) 3126
Coast Business (USA) 1083
Coastal Engineering Journal (SGP) 3263
Coastal Management (USA) 2802
Coatings World (USA) 6716
Cogeneration and Distributed Generation Journal (USA) 3126
Cognition and Emotion (GBR) 7346
Cognition and Instruction (USA) 7346
Cognitive Behaviour Therapy (GBR) 7346
Cognitive Linguistics (DEU) 5106
Cognitive Neuropsychiatry (GBR) 7347
Cognitive Neuropsychology (GBR) 6133
Cognitive Psychology (USA) 7347
Cognitive Science (USA) 7347
Cognitive Therapy and Research (USA) 7347
Cold War History (GBR) 4135
The Coleopterists Bulletin (USA) 842
Collection Building (GBR) 5002
Collection Management (USA) 5002
Collections and Credit Risk (USA) 1327
College & Research Libraries (USA) 5002
College & Research Libraries News (USA) 5003
College & Undergraduate Libraries (USA) 5003
College & University Media Review (USA) 2972
College English (USA) 3055
College Literature (USA) 5276
College Mathematics Journal (USA) 5478
College Student Journal (USA) 2973
College Teaching (USA) 2973
Colonial Latin American Review (GBR) 4289
Colorado Journal of International Environmental Law and Policy (USA) 4920
Colorado Libraries (USA) 5003
Colorado Springs Business Journal (USA) 1084
ColoradoBiz (USA) 1447
Colorectal Disease Online (GBR) 5921
ColorLines (USA) 7117
Columbia Journal of Asian Law (USA) 4645
Columbia Journal of Transnational Law (USA) 4921
Columbia Journalism Review (USA) 4573
Columbus Business First (USA) 1084
Combinatorics, Probability & Computing (GBR) 5551
Combustion, Explosion and Shock Waves (USA) 3241
Combustion Science and Technology (CHE) 2134
Commentary (USA) 7720
Comments on Inorganic Chemistry (USA) 2115
Commercial Carrier Journal (USA) 8669
Commercial Law Bulletin (USA) 4646
Commercial Lending Review (USA) 1328
Commercial Motor (GBR) 8669
Commercial Property News (USA) 7587
Common Ground (Washington, DC) (USA) 388
Common Knowledge (USA) 6911
Common Market Law Review (NLD) 4921
Commonweal (USA) 5211
Commonwealth and Comparative Politics (GBR) 7227
Communication Abstracts Online (USA) *see* Communication Abstracts. 2347
Communication and Critical/Cultural Studies (USA) 2315
Communication and Medicine (GBR) 5599
Communication Booknotes Quarterly (USA) 2347
Communication Education (USA) 3055
Communication Law and Policy (USA) 4646
Communication Monographs (USA) 2837
Communication Quarterly (USA) 8094
Communication Research (USA) 8094
The Communication Review (USA) 2315
Communication Studies (USA) 8094
Communication Systems Design (Online) (USA) 2316
Communication Teacher (Online) (GBR) 2838
Communication Theory (USA) 5107
Communication World (USA) 1734
Communications (DEU) 2316
Communications in Algebra (USA) 5479
Communications in Contemporary Mathematics (SGP) 5479
Communications in Partial Differential Equations (USA) 5480
Communications in Soil Science and Plant Analysis (USA) 225
Communications in Statistics: Simulation and Computation (USA) 2442
Communications in Statistics: Theory and Methods (USA) 8364
Communications News (USA) 2316
Communications Technology (USA) 2379
Community & Junior College Libraries (USA) 5003
Community Banker (Washington, 1880) (USA) 1328
Community Care (Sutton) (GBR) 8034
The Community College Enterprise (USA) 2973
Community College Journal of Research and Practice (USA) 2974
Community College Review (USA) 2974
Community Dentistry and Oral Epidemiology Online (DNK) 5838
Community Development Journal (GBR) 8034
Community Mental Health Journal (USA) 8035
Community, Work & Family (GBR) 7955
Comparative American Studies (GBR) 7956
Comparative Drama (USA) 5277
Comparative Economic Studies (USA) 1537
Comparative Education (GBR) 2838
Comparative European Politics (GBR) 7227
Comparative Labor Law & Policy Journal (USA) 1671
Comparative Literature (USA) 5277
Comparative Literature Studies (USA) 5277
Comparative Parasitology (USA) 938
Comparative Political Studies (USA) 7117
Comparative Sociology (NLD) 8095
Comparative Strategy (USA) 7118
Comparative Studies in Society and History (GBR) 8095
Comparative Studies of South Asia, Africa and the Middle East (USA) 4181
Comparative Technology Transfer and Society (USA) 8418
Compare (GBR) 2838
Compel (GBR) 5551
Compensation and Benefits Review (USA) 1671
Competition & Change (GBR) 1085
Competition and Regulation in Network Industries (BEL) 4862
Competitiveness Review (GBR) 1556
Complementary Health Practice Review (USA) 308
Complementary Therapies in Clinical Practice (GBR) 5956
Complex Variables and Elliptic Equations (CHE) 5480
ComPlexUs (CHE) 666
Composite Interfaces (Online) (NLD) 7009
Compositio Mathematica (GBR) 5480
Comprehensive Psychiatry (USA) 6133
Comprehensive Therapy (USA) 5599
Computational and Mathematical Methods in Medicine (GBR) 5599
Computational & Mathematical Organization Theory (USA) 5551
Computational Economics (NLD) 1415
Computational Geosciences (NLD) 2721
Computational Intelligence (USA) 2410
Computational Linguistics (Online) (USA) 5202
Computational Mathematics and Modeling (USA) 5551
Computational Optimization and Applications (USA) 5551
Computer-Aided Civil and Infrastructure Engineering (USA) 3289
Computer Assisted Language Learning (NLD) 2468
Computer Business Review (GBR) 2491
Computer Graphics Forum (GBR) 2484
Computer Graphics World (USA) 2484
The Computer Journal (GBR) 2412
Computer Methods in Biomechanics and Biomedical Engineering (GBR) 825
Computer Music Journal (USA) 6632
Computer Science Education (NLD) 2948
Computer Speech and Language (GBR) 2506
Computer Supported Cooperative Work (NLD) 2412
Computer Technology News (USA) *see* Computer Technology Review. 2412
Computer Vision and Image Understanding (USA) 2447
Computer Weekly (GBR) 2413
Computergram International (GBR) 2413
Computers in Libraries (GBR) 2570
Computers in the Schools (USA) 2948
Computerworld (USA) 2570
Concrete Construction (USA) 992
Concrete Products (USA) 993
Concurrent Engineering: Research and Applications (GBR) 2470
The Condor (USA) 905
The Conference Board Review (USA) 1735
Configurations (USA) 5277
Conflict Management and Peace Science (GBR) 7227
Conflict Resolution Quarterly (USA) 7348
Conflict, Security & Development (GBR) 7227
Conformal Geometry and Dynamics (USA) 5481
Confrontation (USA) 5277
Congenital Anomalies (AUS) 5600
Congress & the Presidency (USA) 7118
Connecticut Bar Journal (USA) 4648
Connecting Industry.com / Automation (GBR) 2584
Connection Science (GBR) 2447
Connective Tissue Research (GBR) 831
Conscience (USA) 7793
Consciousness and Cognition (USA) 7348
Conservation Biology (USA) 2607
Conservation Genetics (NLD) 865
Constellations (GBR) 7119
Constitutional Political Economy (USA) 4847
Constraints (USA) 2447
Construction Equipment (USA) 995
Construction Innovation (GBR) 996
Construction Management and Economics (GBR) 997
Construction Review (USA) 1045
Consulting Psychology Journal (USA) 7348
Consulting - Specifying Engineer (USA) 3185
Consulting to Management (USA) 1735
Consumption, Markets & Culture (GBR) 1718
Contact Dermatitis (DNK) 5873
Contact Lens & Anterior Eye (GBR) 6040
Contemporary Accounting Research (CAN) 1285
Contemporary British History (GBR) 4212
Contemporary Buddhism (GBR) 7701
Contemporary Chinese Thought (USA) 6911
Contemporary Economic Policy (GBR) 1086
Contemporary Educational Psychology (USA) 2839
Contemporary European History (GBR) 4212
Contemporary Family Therapy (USA) 7349
Contemporary French and Francophone Studies (CHE) 5278
Contemporary Justice Review (GBR) 4650
Contemporary Literature (USA) 5278
Contemporary Longterm Care (USA) 4091
Contemporary Music Review (GBR) 6558
The Contemporary Pacific (USA) 3792
Contemporary Physics (GBR) 7009
Contemporary Political Theory (GBR) 7119
Contemporary Politics (GBR) 7119
The Contemporary Review (GBR) 5212
Contemporary Security Policy (GBR) 7228

11200 O C L C ONLINE COMPUTER LIBRARY CENTER, INC. ULRICH'S PERIODICALS

East European Jewish Affairs (GBR) **4216**
East European Politics & Societies (USA) **7131**
Eastern Africa Social Science Research Review (ETH) **7960**
Eastern Buddhist (JPN) **7701**
Eastern Economic Journal (USA) **1097**
Eastern European Economics (USA) **1097**
Eastern Pennsylvania Business Journal (USA) **1097**
Eating Disorders (USA) **7353**
Ebony (USA) **3531**
Echocardiography (USA) **5785**
Ecography (DNK) **3416**
Ecological Entomology Online (GBR) **843**
Ecological Management & Restoration (AUS) **3417**
Ecological Monographs (USA) **3417**
Ecological Psychology (USA) **7353**
Ecological Research (AUS) **670**
The Ecologist (Online) (GBR) **3417**
Ecology (USA) **3417**
Ecology Letters (GBR) **670**
Ecology of Food and Nutrition (USA) **6657**
Ecology of Freshwater Fish (DNK) **941**
Econometric Reviews (USA) **1478**
Econometric Theory (GBR) **1539**
Econometrica (GBR) **1097**
The Econometrics Journal (GBR) **1097**
Economia (Washington, D.C.) (USA) **1427**
Economic Affairs (GBR) **1098**
Economic and Financial Review (Dallas) (USA) **1336**
Economic and Industrial Democracy (GBR) **7131**
Economic Botany (USA) **786**
Economic Change and Restructuring (NLD) **1479**
Economic Commentary (USA) **1099**
Economic Development Quarterly (USA) **1539**
Economic Development Review (USA) **1884**
Economic Geography (USA) **4005**
The Economic History Review (GBR) **1539**
Economic Indicators (Washington) (USA) **1480**
Economic Inquiry (GBR) **1100**
The Economic Journal (GBR) **1100**
Economic Notes (GBR) **1100**
Economic Outlook (GBR) **1480**
Economic Perspectives (Chicago) (USA) **1480**
Economic Policy (GBR) **1100**
The Economic Record (AUS) **1100**
Economic Review (USA) **1337**
Economic Systems Research (GBR) **1540**
Economic Times (IND) **1337**
Economica (GBR) **1101**
Economics and Philosophy (GBR) **1481**
Economics & Politics (GBR) **1540**
Economics of Innovation and New Technology (GBR) **8420**
The Economics of Transition (GBR) **1540**
The Economist (GBR) **1481**
De Economist (NLD) **1102**
The Economist on CD-ROM (USA) **1481**
Economy and Society (GBR) **7961**
EContent (USA) **2556**
EContent Xtra (USA) **2556**
Ecotoxicology (USA) **3496**
Ecotoxicology and Environmental Safety (USA) **3496**
Ecumenical Review (CHE) **7639**
eDefense (USA) **6420**
Edinburgh Journal of Botany (GBR) **786**
Edinburgh Mathematical Society. Proceedings (GBR) **5485**
Editor & Publisher (USA) **4574**
Education (USA) **2846**
Education and Information Technologies (USA) **3059**
Education and the Law (GBR) **4663**
Education & Training (GBR) **2940**
Education and Training in Developmental Disabilities (USA) **3039**
Education & Treatment of Children (USA) **2847**
Education and Urban Society (USA) **2847**
Education Canada (CAN) **2847**
The Education Digest (USA) **2847**
Education Economics (GBR) **3021**
Education for Information (NLD) **5008**
Education for Primary Care (GBR) **5608**
Education Libraries (Online Edition) (USA) **5008**
Education Next (USA) **3021**
Education Week (USA) **2849**
Educational Administration Abstracts (USA) **2932**
Educational Administration Quarterly (USA) **3021**
Educational and Psychological Measurement (USA) **7353**
Educational Assessment (USA) **2849**
Educational Assessment, Evaluation and Accountability (Online) (NLD) *see* Educational Assessment, Evaluation and Accountability (Print). **2849**
Educational Evaluation & Policy Analysis (USA) **3021**
The Educational Forum (USA) **2979**
Educational Foundations (USA) **3059**
Educational Gerontology (USA) **4044**
Educational Horizons (USA) **2850**
Educational Leadership (USA) **3059**
Educational Management, Administration & Leadership (Online) (GBR) *see* Educational Management, Administration & Leadership (Print). **3021**
Educational Measurement: Issues and Practice (USA) **2850**
Educational Media International (GBR) **3059**
Educational Philosophy and Theory (GBR) **2850**
Educational Policy (USA) **3022**
Educational Psychologist (USA) **7353**
Educational Psychology (GBR) **2850**
Educational Psychology in Practice (GBR) **2850**
Educational Psychology Review (USA) **2850**
Educational Research (GBR) **2851**
Educational Research and Evaluation (NLD) **2851**
Educational Research for Policy and Practice (NLD) **2851**
Educational Research Quarterly (USA) **2851**
Educational Review (GBR) **2851**
Educational Studies (GBR) **2851**
Educational Studies (USA) **2851**
Educational Studies in Mathematics (NLD) **5485**
Educational Technology Research & Development (USA) **3059**
Educational Theory (USA) **2852**
EduExec (USA) **3022**
Eighteenth-Century Life (USA) **4217**
Eighteenth-Century Music (GBR) **6564**
Eighteenth-Century Studies (USA) **4138**
Eire - Ireland (USA) **4450**
Ekistics (GRC) **4409**
Election Law Journal (USA) **4848**
Electric Light and Power (USA) **3302**
Electric Perspectives (USA) **3302**
Electric Power Components & Systems (USA) **3302**
Electrical Apparatus (USA) **3302**
Electrical Wholesaling (USA) **1815**
The Electricity Journal (USA) **3157**
Electromagnetic Biology and Medicine (USA) **753**
Electromagnetics (USA) **3304**
Electronic Commerce Research (USA) **2556**
Electronic Communication Law Review (NLD) **2533**
Electronic Design (USA) **3095**
Electronic Engineering Design (GBR) **3095**
Electronic Green Journal (USA) **3419**
Electronic Journal of Science Education (USA) **2852**
The Electronic Library (GBR) **5061**
Electronic Markets (CHE) **1815**
Electronic Payments International (IRL) **1392**
The Electronic Sixteenth Century Journal (USA) *see* Sixteenth Century Journal. **4475**
Electronic Transactions (GBR) *see* Institute of British Geographers. Transactions. **4015**
Electronics Weekly (GBR) **3097**
Emerging Infectious Diseases (Online) (USA) **7515**
Emerging Markets Finance & Trade (USA) **1563**
The Emily Dickinson Journal (USA) **5421**
Emory Bankruptcy Developments Journal (USA) **4830**
Emory International Law Review (USA) **4924**
Emory Law Journal (USA) **4664**
Emotion (USA) **7354**
Emotional and Behavioural Difficulties (GBR) **3039**
Empirica (USA) **1483**
Empirical Software Engineering (USA) **2589**
Employee Benefit News (USA) **1677**
Employee Benefit Plan Review (USA) **1860**
Employee Benefits (GBR) **1860**
Employee Relations (GBR) **1677**
Employee Relations Law Journal (USA) **4664**
Employee Responsibilities and Rights Journal (USA) **1677**
Emu (AUS) **906**
eMusician.com (USA) *see* Electronic Musician. **6564**
Endangered Species Update (USA) **2610**
Endocrine (USA) **5890**
Endocrine Pathology (USA) **5891**
Endocrine Research (GBR) **5891**
Endodontic Topics (DNK) **5843**
Endothelium (GBR) **671**
Energy & Mineral Law Institute (USA) **4665**
Energy Economist (GBR) **3131**
Energy Engineering (USA) **3131**
Energy Institute. Journal (GBR) **3132**
The Energy Journal (USA) **3132**
Energy Law Journal (USA) **4665**
Energy Resource & Environmental Sustainable Management (GBR) **3133**
Energy Sources. Part A. Recovery, Utilization, and Environmental Effects (Online Edition) (USA) *see* Energy Sources. Part A. Recovery, Utilization, and Environmental Effects. **3133**
The Engineer (GBR) **3188**
Engineered Systems (USA) **4118**
Engineering (GBR) **3188**
Engineering Computations (GBR) **3291**
Engineering, Construction and Architectural Management (GBR) **1006**
The Engineering Economist (USA) **3189**
Engineering Management Journal (USA) **3190**
Engineering Optimization (CHE) **3190**
The English Historical Review (GBR) **4217**
English Journal (USA) **3061**
English Language and Linguistics (GBR) **5115**
English Language Notes (USA) **5290**
English Literary Renaissance (GBR) **5290**
English Today (GBR) **5115**
Enterprise and Society (USA) **1105**
Entertainment Marketing Letter (USA) **1815**
Entomologia Experimentalis et Applicata (NLD) **844**
Entomologica Americana (USA) **844**
Entomological Science (AUS) **845**
Entomological Society of America. Annals (USA) **845**
Entrepreneurship & Regional Development (GBR) **1105**
Entrepreneurship: Theory and Practice (USA) **1960**
Environment (USA) **3420**
Environment and Behavior (USA) **8100**
Environment and Development Economics (GBR) **3420**
Environment, Development and Sustainability (NLD) **3421**
Environmental and Ecological Statistics (USA) **3478**
Environmental and Resource Economics (NLD) **3422**
Environmental Biology of Fishes (NLD) **941**
Environmental Chemistry (Online) (AUS) **3423**
Environmental Claims Journal (USA) **4666**
Environmental Conservation (GBR) **3423**
Environmental Design + Construction (USA) **1007**
Environmental Education Research (GBR) **3424**
Environmental Engineering Science (Online) (USA) **3424**
Environmental Entomology (USA) **847**
Environmental Fluid Mechanics (Dordrecht, 2001) (NLD) **2707**
Environmental Forensics (USA) **3506**
Environmental Geochemistry and Health (NLD) **3424**
Environmental Geosciences (USA) **3424**
Environmental Health Perspectives (USA) **3425**
Environmental History (USA) **4138**
Environmental Microbiology (GBR) **884**
Environmental Modeling & Assessment (NLD) **3482**
Environmental Monitoring and Assessment (NLD) **3426**
Environmental Politics (GBR) **7232**
Environmental Practice (GBR) **3427**
Environmental Quality Management (USA) **3428**
Environmental Research (USA) **3428**
Environmental Reviews (CAN) **3428**
Environmental Studies: Sections A & B (NLD) *see* International Journal of Environmental Studies. **3442**
Environmental Values (GBR) **3429**
The Environmentalist (USA) **3429**
Epidemiologic Reviews (USA) **5609**
Epidemiology and Infection (GBR) **885**
Epilepsia (USA) **6138**
Epilepsy & Behavior (USA) **5610**
Epilepsy Currents (USA) **6138**
Equal Opportunities Review (GBR) **1680**
Equality, Diversity and Inclusion (GBR) **8895**
Equity & Excellence in Education (USA) **2853**
Ergodic Theory and Dynamical Systems (GBR) **5486**
Ergonomics (GBR) **3191**
Erkenntnis (NLD) **6916**
Esquire (USA) **6289**
Essays in Criticism (GBR) **5291**
Essays in Medieval Studies (USA) **4218**
Essays on Canadian Writing (CAN) **5291**
Essence (New York) (USA) **8861**
Estates Gazette (GBR) **7589**
Estuarine, Coastal and Shelf Science (GBR) **2804**
Etc. (Fort Worth) (USA) **5117**
Ethical Theory and Moral Practice (NLD) **6917**
Ethics & Behavior (USA) **7355**
Ethics and Information Technology (NLD) **5008**
Ethics & International Affairs (USA) **7232**
Ethics & the Environment (GBR) **6917**
Ethics, Place and Environment (GBR) **6917**
Ethnic and Racial Studies (GBR) **7962**
Ethnicities (GBR) **7962**
Ethnicity and Health (GBR) **7516**
Ethnography (GBR) **337**
Ethnohistory (USA) **337**
Ethnologies (CAN) **3616**
Ethnology (USA) **337**
Ethnomusicology (USA) **6565**
Ethnomusicology Forum (GBR) **6565**
Ethnos (GBR) **337**
Ethology Online (DEU) **942**
Euphytica (NLD) **229**
Euro-East (BEL) **7233**
Euromoney Online (GBR) *see* Euromoney. **1338**
Europace (GBR) **5786**
Europe - Asia Studies (GBR) **1106**
Europe Energy (BEL) **3134**
Europe Information Social (English Edition) (BEL) **7233**
European Academy of Dermatology and Venereology. Journal (BEL) **5876**
The European Accounting Review (GBR) **1287**
European Addiction Research (CHE) **2694**
European Banker (IRL) **1339**
European Business Forum (GBR) **1106**
European Business Law Review (NLD) **4668**
European Business Organization Law Review (NLD) **4668**
European Business Review (Bingley) (GBR) **1107**
European Cosmetic Markets (GBR) **594**
European Economic Association. Journal (USA) **1563**
European Economic Review (NLD) **1107**
European Education (USA) **2855**
European Employment Review (GBR) **1680**
European Energy and Environmental Law Review (NLD) **4669**
European Financial Management (GBR) **1339**
European Foreign Affairs Review (NLD) **7233**
European Heart Journal (Online) (GBR) **5786**
European History Quarterly (GBR) **4219**
European Journal of American Culture (GBR) **4452**
European Journal of Anaesthesiology (GBR) **5771**
European Journal of Applied Mathematics (GBR) **5486**
European Journal of Archaeology (GBR) **393**
European Journal of Cancer Care Online (GBR) **6019**
European Journal of Cancer Prevention (USA) **6019**
European Journal of Cardiovascular Prevention & Rehabilitation (USA) **5786**
European Journal of Cell Biology (DEU) **832**
European Journal of Clinical Investigation (GBR) **5611**
European Journal of Clinical Nutrition (GBR) **6658**
European Journal of Cognitive Psychology (GBR) **7355**
European Journal of Combinatorics (GBR) **5487**
European Journal of Communication (GBR) **8101**
The European Journal of Contraception and Reproductive Health Care (GBR) **972**
European Journal of Crime, Criminal Law and Criminal Justice (NLD) **4889**
European Journal of Criminology (GBR) **2651**
European Journal of Cultural Studies (GBR) **8101**
European Journal of Dental Education Online (DNK) **5843**
The European Journal of Development Research (GBR) **1595**
European Journal of Developmental Psychology (GBR) **7355**
European Journal of East Asian Studies (NLD) **549**
European Journal of Echocardiography (GBR) **5786**
European Journal of Education (GBR) **2855**
European Journal of Emergency Medicine (GBR) **6060**
European Journal of Engineering Education (GBR) **3192**
European Journal of English Studies (NLD) **5293**
European Journal of Epidemiology (NLD) **5611**
The European Journal of Finance (GBR) **1339**
European Journal of Forest Research (DEU) **3688**
European Journal of Gastroenterology and Hepatology (USA) **5923**
European Journal of Haematology (DNK) **5936**
European Journal of Health Law (NLD) **5611**
European Journal of Housing Policy (GBR) **4410**
European Journal of Human Genetics (GBR) **866**
European Journal of Industrial Relations (GBR) **1681**
European Journal of Information Systems (GBR) **2543**
European Journal of Innovation Management (GBR) **1742**
European Journal of International Law (GBR) **4925**
European Journal of International Relations (GBR) **7234**
European Journal of Law and Economics (USA) **1107**
European Journal of Law Reform (NLD) **4669**
European Journal of Marketing (GBR) **1816**
European Journal of Migration and Law (NLD) **4925**
European Journal of Neurology (USA) **6139**
European Journal of Neuroscience (GBR) **6139**
European Journal of Oncology Nursing (GBR) **5958**
European Journal of Oral Sciences Online (DNK) **5844**
European Journal of Orthodontics (GBR) **5844**
European Journal of Paediatric Neurology (GBR) **6091**
European Journal of Pain (GBR) **5611**
European Journal of Philosophy (GBR) **6918**
European Journal of Phycology (GBR) **787**
European Journal of Plant Pathology (NLD) **787**
European Journal of Political Research (NLD) **7134**
European Journal of Political Theory (GBR) **7134**
European Journal of Population (NLD) **7306**
European Journal of Protistology (DEU) **6724**
European Journal of Psychological Assessment (USA) **7356**
European Journal of Psychotherapy and Counselling (GBR) **6139**
European Journal of Public Health (GBR) **7516**
European Journal of Social Security (BEL) **4502**
European Journal of Social Theory (GBR) **8101**
European Journal of Social Work (GBR) **8039**
European Journal of Soil Science (GBR) **229**
European Journal of Special Needs Education (GBR) **3039**
European Journal of Surgical Oncology (GBR) **6019**
European Journal of Teacher Education (GBR) **2855**
European Journal of the History of Economic Thought (GBR) **1541**
European Journal of Vascular and Endovascular Surgery (GBR) **5786**
European Journal of Women's Studies (GBR) **8896**
European Journal of Work and Organizational Psychology (GBR) **7356**
European Journal on Criminal Policy and Research (NLD) **2651**
European Law Journal (GBR) **4925**
The European Legacy (USA) **6918**
European Management Journal (GBR) **1742**
European Management Review (GBR) **1743**
European Neurology (CHE) **6140**
European Photography (DEU) **6967**
European Physical Education Review (GBR) **3061**
European Planning Studies (GBR) **4410**
European Psychologist (USA) **7356**
European Public Law (NLD) **4925**
The European Respiratory Journal (CHE) **6214**
European Review (GBR) **7853**
European Review of Agricultural Economics (GBR) **197**
European Review of Economic History (GBR) **1541**
European Review of History (GBR) **4219**
European Review of Private Law (NLD) **4925**
European Review of Social Psychology (Online Edition) (GBR) **7356**
European Romantic Review (GBR) **5293**
European Rubber Journal (GBR) **7824**

11204 O C L C ONLINE COMPUTER LIBRARY CENTER, INC. ULRICH'S PERIODICALS

International Journal of Intelligence and Counterintelligence (USA) **7243**
International Journal of Japanese Sociology (AUS) **8109**
International Journal of Knowledge-Based and Intelligent Engineering Systems (NLD) **2451**
International Journal of Laboratory Hematology (Online) (GBR) **5938**
International Journal of Language and Communication Disorders (GBR) **6081**
International Journal of Law and Information Technology (GBR) **4695**
International Journal of Law and Management (GBR) **1689**
International Journal of Law Crime and Justice (GBR) **4695**
International Journal of Law, Policy and the Family (GBR) **4911**
International Journal of Leadership in Education (GBR) **2870**
International Journal of Lexicography (GBR) **5129**
International Journal of Lifelong Education (GBR) **2942**
International Journal of Logistics (GBR) **1128**
The International Journal of Logistics Management (GBR) **1758**
International Journal of Lower Extremity Wounds (USA) **5639**
International Journal of Management (GBR) **1759**
International Journal of Management Reviews (GBR) **1759**
International Journal of Manpower (GBR) **1689**
The International Journal of Marine and Coastal Law (NLD) **4969**
International Journal of Market Research (GBR) **1821**
International Journal of Mathematical Education in Science and Technology (GBR) **5496**
International Journal of Mathematics (SGP) **5497**
International Journal of Mechanical Engineering Education (GBR) **3202**
International Journal of Mechanics and Materials in Design (NLD) **3347**
International Journal of Medical Microbiology (DEU) **5818**
International Journal of Mental Health (USA) **7365**
International Journal of Mental Health Nursing (AUS) **6146**
International Journal of Middle East Studies (GBR) **552**
International Journal of Mining, Reclamation and Environment (GBR) **6466**
International Journal of Modern Physics A (SGP) **7017**
International Journal of Modern Physics B (SGP) **7017**
International Journal of Modern Physics C: Physics and Computers (SGP) **7017**
International Journal of Modern Physics D: Gravitation, Astrophysics and Cosmology (SGP) **7017**
International Journal of Modern Physics E (SGP) **7067**
International Journal of Nanoscience (SGP) **2571**
International Journal of Nautical Archaeology (GBR) **398**
International Journal of Neural Systems (SGP) **2452**
International Journal of Neuropsychopharmacology (GBR) **6850**
International Journal of Neuroscience (CHE) **6147**
International Journal of Nonprofit and Voluntary Sector Marketing (GBR) **1822**
International Journal of Number Theory (SGP) **5497**
International Journal of Numerical Methods for Heat and Fluid Flow (GBR) **3272**
International Journal of Nursing Practice (AUS) **5962**
The International Journal of Nursing Terminologies and Classifications (USA) **5962**
International Journal of Obesity (GBR) **6660**
International Journal of Obstetric Anesthesia (GBR) **5994**
International Journal of Offender Therapy and Comparative Criminology (USA) **2655**
International Journal of Operations and Production Management (GBR) **1760**
International Journal of Oral and Maxillofacial Surgery (GBR) **5849**
International Journal of Organization Theory and Behavior (USA) **7447**
International Journal of Organizational Analysis (GBR) **1760**
International Journal of Paediatric Dentistry (Online) (GBR) **5849**
International Journal of Parallel, Emergent and Distributed Systems (CHE) **2507**
International Journal of Parallel Programming (USA) **2507**
International Journal of Pattern Recognition and Artificial Intelligence (SGP) **2452**
The International Journal of Pavement Engineering (GBR) **3272**
International Journal of Peptide Research and Therapeutics (NLD) **734**
International Journal of Pest Management (GBR) **237**
International Journal of Philosophical Studies Online (GBR) *see* International Journal of Philosophical Studies. **6926**
International Journal of Physical Distribution & Logistics Management (GBR) **8671**
International Journal of Physical Education (DEU) **3065**
International Journal of Phytoremediation (USA) **3443**
International Journal of Plant Sciences (USA) **795**
International Journal of Political Economy (USA) **7144**
International Journal of Politics, Culture, and Society (USA) **7243**
International Journal of Polymer Analysis & Characterization (USA) **3247**
International Journal of Polymeric Materials (CHE) **3247**
International Journal of Press / Politics (USA) **4577**
International Journal of Primatology (USA) **948**
International Journal of Production Research (GBR) **1889**
International Journal of Productivity and Performance Management (GBR) **1760**
International Journal of Psychiatry in Clinical Practice (GBR) **6147**
International Journal of Psychology (GBR) **7365**
International Journal of Public Administration (USA) **7447**
International Journal of Public Opinion Research (GBR) **7144**
International Journal of Public Sector Management (GBR) **1761**
International Journal of Qualitative Studies in Education (GBR) **2870**
International Journal of Quality & Reliability Management (GBR) **1761**
International Journal of Quantum Information (SGP) **7017**
International Journal of Radiation Biology (GBR) **6023**
International Journal of Refugee Law (GBR) **7243**
International Journal of Rehabilitation Research (USA) **6110**
International Journal of Reliability, Quality & Safety Engineering (SGP) **3202**
International Journal of Remote Sensing (GBR) **2710**
International Journal of Research and Method in Education (Online) (GBR) **2870**
International Journal of Retail & Distribution Management (GBR) **1822**
International Journal of Rheumatic Diseases (AUS) **6224**
The International Journal of Risk and Safety in Medicine (NLD) **4509**
International Journal of Robotics Research (GBR) **2585**
International Journal of Rotating Machinery (USA) **5453**
International Journal of S T D & AIDS (GBR) **5818**
International Journal of Science and Mathematics Education (NLD) **7868**
International Journal of Science Education (GBR) **2871**
International Journal of Selection and Assessment (GBR) **1867**
International Journal of Sexual Health (Online) (USA) *see* International Journal of Sexual Health. **7366**
International Journal of Social Economics (GBR) **1129**
International Journal of Social Education (USA) **7974**
International Journal of Social Psychiatry (GBR) **6147**
International Journal of Social Research Methodology (GBR) **7974**
International Journal of Social Welfare (GBR) **8047**
International Journal of Sociology (USA) **8109**
International Journal of Sociology and Social Policy (GBR) **8109**
International Journal of Software Engineering and Knowledge Engineering (SGP) **2592**
International Journal of Speech-Language Pathology (GBR) **5129**
International Journal of Speech Technology (NLD) **5203**
International Journal of Strategic Property Management (LTU) **7596**
International Journal of Stress Management (USA) **5640**
International Journal of Structural Stability and Dynamics (SGP) **3383**
International Journal of Sustainability in Higher Education (Online) (GBR) **2988**
International Journal of Sustainable Energy (GBR) **3176**
International Journal of Systematic Theology (GBR) **7651**
International Journal of Systems Science (GBR) **3203**
International Journal of Technology and Design Education (NLD) **3065**
International Journal of Technology Assessment in Health Care (GBR) **5906**
International Journal of Technology Management & Sustainable Development (GBR) **8427**
International Journal of Testing (USA) **7366**
International Journal of the Classical Tradition (NLD) **2236**
International Journal of the Economics of Business (GBR) **1129**
The International Journal of the History of Sport (GBR) **4147**
International Journal of the Legal Profession (GBR) **4695**
International Journal of the Sociology of Language (DEU) **5130**
International Journal of Theoretical and Applied Finance (SGP) **1357**
International Journal of Theoretical Physics (USA) **7018**
International Journal of Thermophysics (USA) **7055**
International Journal of Toxicology (GBR) **3498**
International Journal of Training & Development (GBR) **1867**
The International Journal of Transgenderism (USA) **7366**
International Journal of Uncertainty, Fuzziness and Knowledge-Based Systems (SGP) **2452**
International Journal of Urban and Regional Research (GBR) **4416**
International Journal of Urology (AUS) **6269**
International Journal of Vegetable Science (USA) **237**
International Journal of Water Resources Development (GBR) **8826**
International Journal of Wavelets, Multiresolution and Information Processing (SGP) **5497**
International Journal of Web Services Research (USA) **2560**
International Journal of Wildland Fire (AUS) **3579**
International Journal of Wine Business Research (GBR) **605**
International Journal of Wireless Information Networks (USA) **2327**
International Journal on Artificial Intelligence Tools (SGP) **2452**
International Journal on E-learning (USA) **2560**
International Journal on Minority and Group Rights (NLD) **7210**
International Journal on World Peace (USA) **7244**
International Labor and Working-Class History (GBR) **1689**
International Labour Review (GBR) **1689**
International Marketing Review (GBR) **1822**
International Midwifery (NLD) **5994**
International Migration (GBR) **7285**
International Migration Review (USA) **7285**
International Monetary Fund. Staff Papers (USA) **1358**
International Money Marketing (GBR) **1358**
International Negotiation (NLD) **7244**
International Neuropsychological Society. Journal (GBR) **6147**
International Nursing Review Online (GBR) **5962**
International Ophthalmology (NLD) **6044**
International Organization (GBR) **7244**
International Peacekeeping (GBR) **7244**
International Perspectives on Sexual and Reproductive Health (USA) **5994**
International Philosophical Quarterly (USA) **6926**
International Phonetic Association. Journal (GBR) **5130**
International Planning Studies (GBR) **4416**
International Political Science Review (GBR) **7244**
International Politics (GBR) **7244**
International Product Alert (USA) **1822**
International Psychogeriatrics (GBR) **6148**
International Regional Science Review (USA) **7975**
International Relations (GBR) **7245**
International Relations of the Asia-Pacific (GBR) **7245**
International Review for the Sociology of Sport (GBR) **8110**
International Review of Administrative Sciences (GBR) **7447**
International Review of African American Art (USA) **497**
International Review of Applied Economics (GBR) **1129**
International Review of Education (DEU) **2871**
International Review of Finance (GBR) **1358**
International Review of Law, Computers & Technology (GBR) **4845**
International Review of Mission (CHE) **7651**
International Review of Psychiatry (GBR) **6148**
The International Review of Retail, Distribution and Consumer Research (GBR) **1822**
International Review of Social History (GBR) **4147**
International Review of Sociology (GBR) **8110**
International Review of Women and Leadership (AUS) **8899**
International Reviews in Physical Chemistry (GBR) **2136**
International Reviews of Immunology (CHE) **5761**
International Securities Finance (GBR) **1359**
International Security (USA) **7245**
International Small Business Journal (GBR) **1962**
International Social Science Journal (GBR) **7975**
International Social Security Review (GBR) **4509**
International Social Work (GBR) **8048**
International Sociology (GBR) **8110**
International Studies in the Philosophy of Science (GBR) **6926**
International Studies of Management and Organization (USA) **1762**
International Studies Perspectives (USA) **7245**
International Studies Quarterly (USA) **7245**
International Studies Review (USA) **7245**
International Tax and Public Finance (USA) **1930**
International Tax Review (GBR) **1571**
International Trade Forum (CHE) **1571**
The International Trade Journal (USA) **1572**
International Transactions in Operational Research (GBR) **2427**
International Urology and Nephrology (NLD) **6269**
International Water Power and Dam Construction (GBR) **3163**
International Wound Journal (GBR) **6062**
Internet Reference Services Quarterly (USA) **5019**
Internet Research (GBR) **2561**
InternetTelephony (USA) *see* Telephony. **2373**
Interpretation (Richmond) (USA) **7651**
Intertax (NLD) **1572**
Intervention in School and Clinic (USA) **3042**
Intervention Research (NLD) **7975**
Interventions (GBR) **5310**
Interview (New York) (USA) **3979**
Intervirology (CHE) **888**
Intheblack (AUS) **1293**
Inventory Management Report (USA) **1851**
Inverse Problems in Science and Engineering (GBR) **3203**
Invertebrate Biology (USA) **948**
Invertebrate Systematics (AUS) **949**
Investigational New Drugs (USA) **6851**
Investment Dealers' Digest (USA) **1632**
Investment News (USA) **1633**
Investors Chronicle (London, 1860) (GBR) **1634**
Iran and the Caucasus (NLD) **552**
Iranian Studies (GBR) **552**
Iris: A Journal about Women (USA) **8869**
Irish Accounting Review (GBR) **1293**
Irish Arts Review (IRL) **497**
Irish Journal of Management (IRL) **1130**
Irish Marketing Review (IRL) **1823**
Irish Political Studies (GBR) **7144**
Irish Studies Review (GBR) **5221**
Irrigation and Drainage Systems (NLD) **212**
Islam and Christian - Muslim Relations (GBR) **7711**
Islamic Horizons (USA) **7712**
Islamic Law and Society (NLD) **7712**
The Island Arc (AUS) **2748**
Isokinetics and Exercise Science (NLD) **6230**
Isotopes in Environmental and Health Studies (GBR) **2066**
Israel Affairs (GBR) **7246**
Israel Studies (USA) **7976**
Issues and Letters (PHL) **7976**
Issues in Accounting Education (USA) **1293**
Issues in Comprehensive Pediatric Nursing (USA) **5963**
Issues in Law and Medicine (USA) **5642**
Issues in Mental Health Nursing (USA) **5963**
Issues in Science and Technology (USA) **7869**
Issues in Writing (USA) **4577**
ITNOW (Online) (GBR) **2427**
Ivey Business Journal (Online Edition) (CAN) **1762**
J A O C S (USA) **2124**
J C K (USA) **4567**
J C P Online (GBR) *see* Journal of Clinical Pathology. **5647**
J C T (USA) **3066**
J C T CoatingsTech (USA) **6718**
J D D G (Online Edition) (DEU) *see* J D D G (Print Edition). **5878**
J E C H Online (GBR) *see* Journal of Epidemiology & Community Health. **5648**
J E G P (USA) **5312**
J E I (USA) **1543**
J E M (USA) **2872**
J E T: Journal of Educational Thought (CAN) **2872**
J I T T A (HKG) **2547**
J M B Online (GBR) *see* Journal of Molecular Biology. **736**
J M E Online (GBR) *see* Journal of Medical Ethics. **5651**
J M G Online (GBR) *see* Journal of Medical Genetics. **874**
J M M (USA) **2328**
J N N P Online (GBR) *see* Journal of Neurology, Neurosurgery and Psychiatry. **6154**
James Cook University Law Review (AUS) **4698**
Japan Chemical Week (JPN) **3248**
Japan Forum (GBR) **7247**
Japan Journal of Nursing Science (JPN) **5963**
The Japan Times International (JPN) **3900**
The Japanese Economic Review (AUS) **1131**
The Japanese Economy (USA) **1131**
Japanese Journal of Clinical Oncology (GBR) **6023**
Japanese Journal of Political Science (GBR) **7145**
Japanese Journal of Religious Studies (JPN) **7737**
Japanese Psychological Research (JPN) **7367**
Japanese Studies (GBR) **8111**
Jet (USA) **3979**
Jewish History (ISR) **7723**
The Jewish Quarterly Review (USA) **7723**
Jewish Social Studies (USA) **7724**
Jiaoyu Ziliao yu Tushuguanxue (TWN) **5019**
Journal for Cultural Research (GBR) **4459**
Journal for Early Modern Cultural Studies (USA) **7977**
Journal for General Philosophy of Science (NLD) **7871**
Journal for Nature Conservation (DEU) **3444**
Journal for Preachers (USA) **7762**
Journal for Quality and Participation (USA) **1867**
Journal for Research in Mathematics Education (USA) **3066**
Journal for Specialists in Group Work (USA) **7367**
Journal for Specialists in Pediatric Nursing (USA) **5963**
Journal for the Education of the Gifted (USA) **3042**
Journal for the Scientific Study of Religion (USA) **7653**
Journal for the Study of Judaism (NLD) **7725**
Journal for the Study of the New Testament (GBR) **7653**
Journal for the Study of the Old Testament (GBR) **7653**

Journal for the Theory of Social Behaviour (GBR) 7367
Journal fuer die Reine und Angewandte Mathematik (DEU) 5500
Journal of Abnormal Child Psychology (USA) 7368
Journal of Abnormal Psychology (USA) 7368
Journal of Academic Ethics (NLD) 2989
The Journal of Academic Librarianship (GBR) 5020
Journal of Access Services (USA) 5062
Journal of Accountancy (USA) 1293
Journal of Accounting Research (USA) 1294
Journal of Addictions & Offender Counseling (USA) 7368
Journal of Addictions Nursing (GBR) 5964
Journal of Addictive Diseases (USA) 2695
Journal of Adhesion (CHE) 7019
Journal of Adhesion Science and Technology (NLD) 7093
Journal of Adolescence (GBR) 2156
Journal of Adolescent & Adult Literacy (USA) 3025
Journal of Adolescent Research (USA) 7368
Journal of Adult Development (USA) 7368
The Journal of Adult Protection (GBR) 4700
Journal of Advanced Academics (USA) 3042
Journal of Advanced Manufacturing Systems (SGP) 1890
Journal of Advanced Nursing (GBR) 5964
Journal of Advertising (USA) 27
Journal of Advertising Research (USA) 27
Journal of Aerosol Medicine and Pulmonary Drug Delivery (USA) 6215
Journal of Aesthetic Education (USA) 2874
Journal of Aesthetics and Art Criticism (USA) 498
Journal of African American Studies (USA) 6302
Journal of African Business (USA) 1133
Journal of African Cultural Studies (GBR) 4459
Journal of African Economies (GBR) 1494
The Journal of African History (GBR) 4176
Journal of African Languages and Linguistics (DEU) 5132
Journal of African Law (GBR) 4700
Journal of Aggression, Maltreatment & Trauma (USA) 7368
Journal of Aging and Health (USA) 4048
Journal of Aging & Social Policy (USA) 4048
Journal of Aging Studies (GBR) 4048
Journal of Agrarian Change (GBR) 201
Journal of Agricultural and Environmental Ethics (NLD) 6927
Journal of Agricultural & Food Information (USA) 126
The Journal of Agricultural Science (GBR) 126
Journal of Agromedicine (USA) 6679
Journal of Agronomy and Crop Science Online (DEU) 239
Journal of Air Law and Commerce (USA) 4700
Journal of Alcohol and Drug Education (USA) 2695
Journal of Algebra (USA) 5500
Journal of Algebra and its Applications (SGP) 5500
Journal of Algebraic Combinatorics (USA) 5500
Journal of Algorithms (USA) 5553
Journal of Allergy and Clinical Immunology (USA) 5762
Journal of Alternative & Complementary Medicine (USA) 311
The Journal of Alternative Investments (USA) 1634
Journal of Alzheimer's Disease (NLD) 6149
The Journal of American College Health (USA) 6990
Journal of American Culture (USA) 4459
Journal of American Ethnic History (USA) 3544
Journal of American Folklore (USA) 3619
Journal of American History (USA) 4298
Journal of American Indian Education (USA) 6635
Journal of American Studies (GBR) 4299
Journal of Analytical Atomic Spectrometry (GBR) 2101
Journal of Analytical Chemistry (RUS) 2101
Journal of Analytical Psychology (GBR) 7368
Journal of Anatomy (GBR) 680
Journal of Ancient Near Eastern Religions (NLD) 7737
Journal of Animal Breeding and Genetics Online (DEU) 291
Journal of Animal Ecology (GBR) 680
Journal of Animal Physiology and Animal Nutrition Online (DEU) 923
Journal of Animal Science (USA) 291
Journal of Anthropological Archaeology (USA) 344
Journal of Antimicrobial Chemotherapy (GBR) 5819
Journal of Applied Animal Welfare Science (USA) 320
Journal of Applied Aquaculture (USA) 3599
Journal of Applied Behavior Analysis (USA) 7368
The Journal of Applied Behavioral Science (USA) 7368
Journal of Applied Business Research (USA) 1133
Journal of Applied Communication Research (USA) 2329
Journal of Applied Corporate Finance (USA) 1360
Journal of Applied Crystallography (DNK) 2111
Journal of Applied Ecology (GBR) 680
Journal of Applied Electrochemistry (NLD) 2114
Journal of Applied Entomology (Online) (DEU) 851
Journal of Applied Finance (USA) 1360
Journal of Applied Gerontology (USA) 4049
Journal of Applied Ichthyology Online (DEU) 950
Journal of Applied Mathematics and Decision Sciences (USA) 5501
Journal of Applied Mechanics and Technical Physics (RUS) 3349
Journal of Applied Meteorology and Climatology (USA) 6358
Journal of Applied Microbiology (GBR) 888
Journal of Applied Philosophy (GBR) 6928
Journal of Applied Phycology (NLD) 796
Journal of Applied Psychology (USA) 7369
Journal of Applied Research in Intellectual Disabilities (GBR) 6149
Journal of Applied School Psychology (USA) 3042
Journal of Applied Security Research (USA) 2874
Journal of Applied Spectroscopy (USA) 7077
Journal of Applied Sport Psychology (USA) 6230
Journal of Applied Statistics (GBR) 8382
Journal of Approximation Theory (USA) 5501
Journal of Aquatic Food Product Technology (USA) 3649
Journal of Arabic Literature (NLD) 5314
Journal of Arachnology (USA) 950
Journal of Archaeological Method and Theory (USA) 400
Journal of Archaeological Research (USA) 400
Journal of Archaeological Science (GBR) 400
Journal of Architectural and Planning Research (USA) 447
Journal of Architectural Education (USA) 447
The Journal of Architecture (GBR) 447
Journal of Archival Organization (USA) 5020
Journal of Arid Environments (GBR) 4016
Journal of Arthroplasty (USA) 6063
Journal of Artists' Books (USA) 498
Journal of Arts Management, Law, and Society (USA) 4700
Journal of Asia - Pacific Business (USA) 1573
Journal of Asian American Studies (USA) 8111
Journal of Asian and African Studies (GBR) 8112
Journal of Asian Natural Products Research (GBR) 311
Journal of Asian Studies (USA) 553
The Journal of Asset Management (GBR) 1635
Journal of Assisted Reproduction and Genetics (USA) 5995
Journal of Asthma (USA) 6215
Journal of Athletic Training (USA) 6230
Journal of Atmospheric and Oceanic Technology (USA) 6358
Journal of Atmospheric Chemistry (NLD) 2066
Journal of Autism and Developmental Disorders (USA) 3042
Journal of Autoimmunity (GBR) 5762
Journal of Automated Methods & Management in Chemistry (USA) 2101
Journal of Automated Reasoning (NLD) 2453
Journal of Avian Biology (DNK) 909
Journal of Avian Medicine and Surgery (USA) 8800
Journal of Back and Musculoskeletal Rehabilitation (NLD) 6063
Journal of Balkan and Near Eastern Studies (GBR) 4235
Journal of Bamboo and Rattan (IND) 796
Journal of Banking Regulation (GBR) 1360
Journal of Basic Writing (USA) 5314
Journal of Behavioral Education (USA) 2874
The Journal of Behavioral Finance (USA) 7369
Journal of Behavioral Health Services and Research (USA) 7528
Journal of Behavioral Medicine (USA) 6149
Journal of Beliefs and Values (GBR) 2874
Journal of Biblical Literature (USA) 7654
Journal of Bioactive and Compatible Polymers (GBR) 734
Journal of Bioeconomics (USA) 681
Journal of Bioenergetics and Biomembranes (USA) 735
Journal of Biogeography (GBR) 4017
Journal of Bioinformatics and Computational Biology (GBR) 681
Journal of Biological Education (GBR) 681
Journal of Biological Physics (NLD) 753
Journal of Biological Rhythms (USA) 6149
Journal of Biological Systems (SGP) 681
Journal of Biomaterials Applications (GBR) 6247
Journal of Biomaterials Science. Polymer Edition (NLD) 766
Journal of Biomedical Informatics (USA) 5832
Journal of Biomedical Science (GBR) 5646
Journal of Biomolecular N M R (NLD) 735
Journal of Biomolecular Screening (USA) 735
Journal of Biopharmaceutical Statistics (USA) 6889
Journal of Biosocial Science (GBR) 8112
Journal of Bisexuality (USA) 4375
Journal of Black Psychology (USA) 7369
Journal of Black Studies (USA) 7978
Journal of Bodywork and Movement Therapies (GBR) 6111
Journal of Bone and Mineral Metabolism (JPN) 5895
The Journal of Brand Management (GBR) 1823
Journal of Broadcasting and Electronic Media (USA) 2383
Journal of Building Physics (GBR) 3204
Journal of Business (Spokane) (USA) 1360
Journal of Business and Economic Studies (USA) 1133
Journal of Business & Finance Librarianship (USA) 5020
Journal of Business & Industrial Marketing (GBR) 1823
Journal of Business and Management (USA) 1764
Journal of Business & Psychology (USA) 7369
Journal of Business and Technical Communication (USA) 1133
Journal of Business Communication (USA) 1764
Journal of Business Ethics (NLD) 1134
Journal of Business Finance & Accounting (GBR) 1294
The Journal of Business Forecasting (USA) 1134
Journal of Business Logistics (USA) 1764
Journal of Business Strategies (USA) 1764
Journal of Business Strategy (USA) 1764
Journal of Business-to-Business Marketing (USA) 1823
The Journal of Canadian Art History (CAN) 498
Journal of Canadian Studies (CAN) 4460
Journal of Cancer Education (USA) 6023
Journal of Carbohydrate Chemistry (USA) 2067
Journal of Cardiac Failure (USA) 5791
Journal of Cardiac Surgery (USA) 5792
Journal of Cardiothoracic and Vascular Anesthesia (USA) 5792
Journal of Cardiovascular Electrophysiology (USA) 5792
Journal of Cardiovascular Magnetic Resonance (GBR) 5792
Journal of Career Assessment (USA) 7369
Journal of Career Development (USA) 6700
Journal of Cases in Educational Leadership (USA) 3025
Journal of Catalysis (USA) 2136
Journal of Cellular Plastics (GBR) 7093
Journal of Cereal Science (GBR) 273
Journal of Cerebral Blood Flow and Metabolism (USA) 6150
The Journal of Change Management (GBR) 1764
Journal of Chemical Crystallography (USA) 2111
Journal of Chemical Ecology (USA) 3444
Journal of Chemical Education (USA) 2067
Journal of Chemical Research (Online Edition) (GBR) *see* Journal of Chemical Research (Print Edition). 2067
The Journal of Chemical Thermodynamics (GBR) 2136
Journal of Child and Adolescent Psychiatric Nursing (USA) 5964
Journal of Child and Adolescent Psychopharmacology (USA) 6150
Journal of Child & Adolescent Substance Abuse (USA) 2695
Journal of Child and Family Studies (USA) 7370
Journal of Child Custody (USA) 2156
Journal of Child Health Care (GBR) 6094
Journal of Child Language (GBR) 2156
Journal of Child Psychology and Psychiatry (GBR) 7370
Journal of Child Psychotherapy (GBR) 7370
Journal of Child Sexual Abuse (USA) 8049
Journal of Children & Poverty (USA) 8049
Journal of Children's Literature (USA) 2156
Journal of Chinese Economics and Business Studies (GBR) 1494
Journal of Chinese Philosophy (USA) 6928
Journal of Chinese Religions (USA) 7737
Journal of Church and State (USA) 7654
Journal of Circuits, Systems and Computers (SGP) 2466
Journal of Classical Sociology (GBR) 8112
Journal of Classroom Interaction (USA) 2874
Journal of Climate (USA) 6358
Journal of Clinical Child and Adolescent Psychology (USA) 7370
Journal of Clinical Densitometry (NLD) 5647
Journal of Clinical Forensic and Legal Medicine (GBR) 5914
Journal of Clinical Immunology (USA) 5762
Journal of Clinical Monitoring and Computing (NLD) 5647
Journal of Clinical Neuroscience (GBR) 6150
Journal of Clinical Nursing (GBR) 5964
Journal of Clinical Periodontology (DNK) 5851
The Journal of Clinical Pharmacology (USA) 6852
Journal of Clinical Pharmacy and Therapeutics (GBR) 6852
Journal of Clinical Psychology (USA) 7370
Journal of Clinical Psychology in Medical Settings (USA) 7370
Journal of Cluster Science (USA) 2067
Journal of Coastal Research (USA) 2809
Journal of Coatings Technology and Research (USA) 6718
Journal of Cognition and Culture (NLD) 7370
Journal of Cognition and Development (USA) 7370
Journal of Cognitive Neuroscience (USA) 6151
Journal of Cold War Studies (USA) 7247
Journal of College Admission (USA) 2989
Journal of College Counseling (USA) 2989
Journal of College Reading and Learning (USA) 2989
Journal of College Science Teaching (USA) 7872
Journal of College Student Development (USA) 2989
Journal of College Student Psychotherapy (USA) 7371
Journal of Colloid and Interface Science (USA) 2136
Journal of Colonialism & Colonial History (USA) 4149
Journal of Combinatorial Optimization (NLD) 5553
Journal of Combinatorial Theory, Series A (USA) 5501
Journal of Combinatorial Theory. Series B (USA) 5501
The Journal of Commerce (USA) 1430
Journal of Commercial Biotechnology (GBR) 767
Journal of Common Market Studies (GBR) 7146
Journal of Commonwealth Literature (GBR) 5314
Journal of Communication (USA) 8112
Journal of Communication Inquiry (USA) 8112
Journal of Communication Management (GBR) 1765
Journal of Communist Studies and Transition Politics (GBR) 7247
Journal of Community Health (USA) 5647
Journal of Community Health Nursing (USA) 5964
Journal of Community Practice (USA) 8049
Journal of Comparative Economics (USA) 1134
Journal of Comparative Family Studies (CAN) 8112
The Journal of Comparative Germanic Linguistics (NLD) 5133
Journal of Comparative International Management (CAN) 1765
Journal of Comparative Pathology (GBR) 682
Journal of Comparative Policy Analysis (USA) 7448
Journal of Comparative Psychology (USA) 7371
Journal of Complexity (USA) 5553
Journal of Composite Materials (GBR) 3349
Journal of Computational Acoustics (SGP) 7050
Journal of Computational Analysis and Applications (USA) 5501
Journal of Computational Biology (Online) (USA) 682
Journal of Computational Electronics (USA) 2428
Journal of Computational Methods in Sciences and Engineering (NLD) 5502
Journal of Computational Neuroscience (NLD) 6151
Journal of Computational Physics (USA) 7050
Journal of Computer - Aided Molecular Design (NLD) 2108
Journal of Computer and System Sciences (USA) 2523
Journal of Computer Assisted Learning (GBR) 2469
Journal of Computer Security (NLD) 2515
Journal of Computers in Mathematics and Science Teaching (USA) 5553
Journal of Conflict and Security Law (GBR) 4933
Journal of Conflict Resolution (USA) 7978
Journal of Consciousness Studies (GBR) 7371
Journal of Construction Research (SGP) 1018
Journal of Constructivist Psychology (USA) 7371
Journal of Consulting and Clinical Psychology (USA) 7371
Journal of Consumer Affairs (USA) 2639
Journal of Consumer Behaviour (GBR) 2639
Journal of Consumer Culture (GBR) 2639
Journal of Consumer Health on the Internet (USA) 2562
Journal of Consumer Marketing (GBR) 1823
Journal of Consumer Policy (NLD) 2639
Journal of Consumer Psychology (USA) 27
Journal of Consumer Satisfaction, Dissatisfaction and Complaining Behavior (USA) 1824
Journal of Contemporary African Studies (GBR) 7978
Journal of Contemporary Asia (GBR) 4184
Journal of Contemporary China (GBR) 4184
Journal of Contemporary Criminal Justice (USA) 4892
Journal of Contemporary Ethnography (USA) 8112
Journal of Contemporary European Studies (Online Edition) (GBR) 7146
Journal of Contemporary History (GBR) 4149
Journal of Contemporary Psychotherapy (USA) 7372
Journal of Contemporary Religion (GBR) 7654
Journal of Contingencies and Crisis Management (GBR) 1765
Journal of Continuing Education in Nursing (USA) 5964
Journal of Convention & Event Tourism (USA) 6280
Journal of Coordination Chemistry (CHE) 2068
The Journal of Corporate Citizenship (GBR) 1765
Journal of Corporate Real Estate (GBR) 7596
The Journal of Corporation Law (USA) 4872
Journal of Correctional Education (USA) 2656
Journal of Cosmetic and Laser Therapy (Online) (GBR) 5878
Journal of Cosmetic Dermatology (GBR) 5878
Journal of Counseling & Development (USA) 7372
Journal of Counseling Psychology (USA) 7372
Journal of Couple & Relationship Therapy (USA) 7372
Journal of Cranio-Maxillofacial Surgery (GBR) 6247
Journal of Criminal Law & Criminology (USA) 2657
Journal of Critical Realism (GBR) 6928
Journal of Crop Improvement (USA) 239
Journal of Cross-Cultural Gerontology (NLD) 4049
Journal of Cross-Cultural Psychology (USA) 7372
Journal of Crustacean Biology (USA) 950
Journal of Cultural Economics (USA) 1544
Journal of Cultural Research in Art Education (USA) 498
Journal of Curriculum Studies (GBR) 3067
Journal of Cutaneous Pathology (DNK) 5878
Journal of Dairy Research (GBR) 266
Journal of Database Management (USA) 2531
The Journal of Database Marketing & Customer Strategy Management (Online Edition) (GBR) 1419
The Journal of Deaf Studies and Deaf Education (USA) 4075
Journal of Democracy (USA) 7146
The Journal of Derivatives (USA) 1360
Journal of Derivatives & Hedge Funds (GBR) 1635
Journal of Dermatological Treatment (GBR) 5879
Journal of Design History (GBR) 498
Journal of Design Manufacturing and Automation (USA) 3204
Journal of Developing Areas (USA) 1599
Journal of Developing Societies (Online) (GBR) 7978
The Journal of Development Studies (GBR) 1600

Online Service

Journal of Interferon & Cytokine Research (USA) **5763**
Journal of Intergenerational Relationships (USA) **8114**
Journal of Interlibrary Loan, Document Supply & Electronic Reserve (USA) **5021**
Journal of Internal Medicine (GBR) **5946**
Journal of International Accounting Research (USA) **1295**
Journal of International Affairs (USA) **7248**
Journal of International and Area Studies (KOR) **1573**
Journal of International Arbitration (NLD) **4597**
Journal of International Biotechnology Law (DEU) **4701**
Journal of International Business Studies (GBR) **1137**
Journal of International Consumer Marketing (USA) **1825**
Journal of International Criminal Justice (GBR) **2657**
Journal of International Economic Law (GBR) **4933**
Journal of International Entrepreneurship (USA) **1574**
Journal of International Financial Management and Accounting (GBR) **1362**
Journal of International Food & Agribusiness Marketing (USA) **202**
Journal of International Marketing (USA) **1825**
Journal of International Peacekeeping (NLD) **7248**
Journal of International Relations and Development (GBR) **7248**
The Journal of International Trade and Economic Development (GBR) **1600**
Journal of International Wildlife Law and Policy (USA) **3448**
Journal of Internet Commerce (USA) **1420**
Journal of Interpersonal Violence (USA) **2657**
Journal of Interprofessional Care (GBR) **5650**
Journal of Interventional Cardiac Electrophysiology (NLD) **5793**
Journal of Interventional Cardiology (USA) **5793**
Journal of Inverse and Ill-Posed Problems (DEU) **5504**
Journal of Invertebrate Pathology (USA) **951**
The Journal of Investigative Dermatology (USA) **5879**
The Journal of Investigative Dermatology Symposium Proceedings (USA) **5879**
Journal of Investigative Surgery (USA) **6248**
The Journal of Investing (USA) **1635**
Journal of Investment Compliance (GBR) **1635**
Journal of Islamic Studies (GBR) **7713**
The Journal of Israeli History (GBR) **4322**
Journal of Japanese Studies (USA) **553**
Journal of Jewish Education (USA) **2876**
The Journal of Jewish Thought and Philosophy (NLD) **7725**
Journal of Knot Theory and Its Ramifications (SGP) **5504**
Journal of Knowledge Management (GBR) **1767**
Journal of L G B T Youth (USA) **2876**
Journal of Labor Economics (USA) **1691**
Journal of Labor Research (USA) **1691**
Journal of Language and Social Psychology (USA) **7375**
Journal of Language, Identity, and Education (USA) **2876**
Journal of Laparoendoscopic & Advanced Surgical Techniques (USA) **6248**
Journal of Laryngology and Otology (GBR) **6081**
Journal of Laser Applications (GBR) **7078**
Journal of Latin American and Caribbean Anthropology (USA) **345**
Journal of Latin American Cultural Studies (GBR) **4299**
Journal of Latin American Geography (USA) **4017**
Journal of Latin American Studies (GBR) **4299**
Journal of Latinos and Education (USA) **2877**
Journal of Law & Commerce (USA) **4872**
Journal of Law and Education (USA) **4702**
Journal of Law & Public Policy (USA) **4702**
Journal of Law and Society (GBR) **4702**
Journal of Law, Economics, & Organization (GBR) **4702**
The Journal of Law, Medicine & Ethics (USA) **4703**
Journal of Leadership and Organizational Studies (USA) **1767**
Journal of Learning Disabilities (USA) **3042**
Journal of Legal Economics (USA) **1545**
The Journal of Legal Medicine (USA) **5651**
Journal of Legal Studies Education (USA) **4703**
The Journal of Legislative Studies (GBR) **7249**
Journal of Leisure Research (USA) **4978**
Journal of Lesbian Studies (USA) **4375**
Journal of Librarianship and Information Science (GBR) **5021**
Journal of Library Administration (USA) **5022**
Journal of Library & Information Services in Distance Learning (USA) **5022**
Journal of Library Metadata (USA) **2563**
Journal of Linguistics (GBR) **5134**
Journal of Liposome Research (USA) **6854**
Journal of Liquid Chromatography & Related Technologies (USA) **2068**
Journal of Literary Semantics (DEU) **5134**
Journal of Logic and Computation (GBR) **2429**
Journal of Logic, Language and Information (NLD) **5134**
Journal of Loss & Trauma (USA) **7376**
Journal of Low Temperature Physics (USA) **7055**
Journal of Lower Genital Tract Disease (Online) (USA) **5995**
Journal of Machine Learning Research (Online) (USA) **2454**
Journal of Macromarketing (USA) **1825**
Journal of Macromolecular Science: Part A - Pure and Applied Chemistry (USA) **2124**
Journal of Macromolecular Science: Part B - Physics (USA) **7020**
Journal of Magnetic Resonance (USA) **7020**
Journal of Mammalian Evolution (USA) **951**
Journal of Mammalogy (USA) **951**
Journal of Mammary Gland Biology and Neoplasia (USA) **924**
Journal of Management (GBR) **1767**
Journal of Management Accounting Research (USA) **1295**
Journal of Management & Governance (USA) **1767**
Journal of Management & Organization (AUS) **1767**
Journal of Management Development (GBR) **1767**
Journal of Management Education (USA) **1768**
Journal of Management Information Systems (USA) **2548**
Journal of Management Inquiry (USA) **1768**
Journal of Management Studies (GBR) **1768**
Journal of Managerial Issues (USA) **1768**
Journal of Managerial Psychology (GBR) **1768**
Journal of Manipulative and Physiological Therapeutics (USA) **5806**
Journal of Manufacturing Processes (GBR) **1890**
Journal of Manufacturing Systems (GBR) **3386**
Journal of Manufacturing Technology Management (GBR) **3292**
Journal of Map & Geography Libraries (USA) **5022**
Journal of Marital and Family Therapy (USA) **7376**
Journal of Maritime Law and Commerce (USA) **4970**
Journal of Marketing (USA) **1825**
Journal of Marketing Channels (USA) **1825**
Journal of Marketing Communications (GBR) **1825**
Journal of Marketing Education (USA) **1825**
Journal of Marketing for Higher Education (USA) **2991**
Journal of Marketing Research (USA) **1825**
Journal of Marketing Theory and Practice (USA) **1826**
Journal of Marriage and Family (USA) **8114**
Journal of Mass Media Ethics (USA) **8114**
Journal of Material Culture (GBR) **8114**
Journal of Materials Chemistry (GBR) **2068**
Journal of Materials Science (NLD) **3350**
Journal of Materials Science: Materials in Electronics (NLD) **3350**
Journal of Materials Science: Materials in Medicine (USA) **3350**
The Journal of Maternal - Fetal & Neonatal Medicine (GBR) **5995**
Journal of Mathematical Analysis and Applications (USA) **5505**
Journal of Mathematical Chemistry (NLD) **5505**
Journal of Mathematical Imaging and Vision (USA) **5553**
Journal of Mathematical Logic (SGP) **5505**
Journal of Mathematical Modelling and Algorithms (NLD) **5505**
Journal of Mathematical Psychology (USA) **7376**
Journal of Mathematical Sciences (USA) **5505**
Journal of Mathematical Sociology (USA) **8149**
Journal of Mathematics Teacher Education (NLD) **5506**
Journal of Mechanics in Medicine and Biology (SGP) **683**
Journal of Media and Religion (USA) **2329**
Journal of Media Economics (USA) **2329**
Journal of Media Practice (GBR) **2329**
Journal of Medical Engineering & Technology (GBR) **5651**
Journal of Medical Entomology (USA) **852**
Journal of Medical Humanities (USA) **5651**
Journal of Medical Imaging and Radiation Oncology (AUS) **6200**
Journal of Medical Marketing (Online) (GBR) **6854**
Journal of Medical Microbiology (GBR) **889**
Journal of Medical Primatology (DNK) **952**
Journal of Medical Screening (GBR) **5820**
Journal of Medical Systems (USA) **5832**
Journal of Medicinal Food (USA) **5652**
The Journal of Medicine and Philosophy (NLD) **5652**
Journal of Medieval and Early Modern Studies (USA) **4460**
Journal of Memory and Language (USA) **5134**
Journal of Men's Studies (USA) **6302**
Journal of Mental Health (GBR) **6152**
Journal of Metamorphic Geology (USA) **2750**
Journal of Microencapsulation (GBR) **6854**
Journal of Micromechatronics (NLD) **3322**
Journal of Microscopy (GBR) **899**
Journal of Middle East Women's Studies (USA) **8900**
Journal of Military Ethics (NOR) **6429**
Journal of Military History (USA) **6429**
Journal of Mining Science (USA) **6467**
Journal of Modern African Studies (GBR) **7147**
Journal of Modern Greek Studies (USA) **4236**
Journal of Modern Italian Studies (GBR) **5315**
Journal of Modern Jewish Studies (GBR) **4460**
Journal of Modern Literature (USA) **5315**
Journal of Modern Optics (GBR) **7078**
Journal of Molecular and Cellular Cardiology (GBR) **5794**
Journal of Molecular Histology (NLD) **834**
Journal of Molecular Microbiology and Biotechnology (GBR) **890**
Journal of Molecular Neuroscience (USA) **6153**
Journal of Molecular Spectroscopy (USA) **7078**
Journal of Molluscan Studies (GBR) **952**
Journal of Money, Credit & Banking (USA) **1362**
Journal of Moral Education (GBR) **2877**
Journal of Motor Behavior (USA) **7376**
Journal of Multicultural Counseling and Development (USA) **7376**
Journal of Multiple-Valued Logic and Soft Computing (USA) **5506**
Journal of Multivariate Analysis (USA) **5506**
Journal of Muscle Foods (USA) **3651**
Journal of Muscle Research and Cell Motility (NLD) **6064**
Journal of Musculoskeletal Pain (USA) **6064**
Journal of Musculoskeletal Research (SGP) **6064**
Journal of Music Teacher Education (Online) (USA) **6580**
Journal of Music Therapy (USA) **6111**
Journal of Musicological Research (USA) **6581**
Journal of Musicology (USA) **6581**
Journal of Muslim Minority Affairs (GBR) **7713**
Journal of Nanoparticle Research (NLD) **7021**
Journal of Narrative Theory (USA) **5315**
Journal of Natural Fibers (USA) **273**
Journal of Natural History (GBR) **684**
Journal of Navigation (GBR) **8648**
Journal of Near-Death Studies (USA) **6929**
Journal of Near Eastern Studies (USA) **401**
Journal of Negro Education (USA) **2877**
Journal of Network and Computer Applications (GBR) **2500**
Journal of Network and Systems Management (USA) **2500**
Journal of Neuro-Oncology (USA) **6025**
Journal of Neurochemistry (USA) **736**
Journal of Neuroendocrinology (GBR) **6153**
Journal of Neurogenetics (USA) **6153**
Journal of Neuroimaging (USA) **6153**
Journal of Neurotherapy (USA) **6155**
Journal of Neurotrauma (USA) **6064**
Journal of NeuroVirology (GBR) **6155**
Journal of Neutron Research (GBR) **7067**
Journal of New Music Research (GBR) **2495**
Journal of New Seeds (USA) **239**
Journal of Nietzsche Studies (USA) **6929**
Journal of Non-Equilibrium Thermodynamics (DEU) **7055**
Journal of Nondestructive Evaluation (USA) **3350**
Journal of Nonlinear Optical Physics and Materials (SGP) **7079**
Journal of Nonparametric Statistics (CHE) **8383**
Journal of Nonprofit & Public Sector Marketing (USA) **1826**
Journal of Nonverbal Behavior (USA) **7376**
Journal of Nuclear Cardiology (USA) **6201**
Journal of Number Theory (USA) **5506**
Journal of Numerical Mathematics (DEU) **5553**
Journal of Nursing Education (USA) **5966**
Journal of Nursing Management (GBR) **5966**
Journal of Nursing Scholarship (USA) **5966**
The Journal of Nutrition (USA) **6661**
Journal of Nutrition Education and Behavior (USA) **6662**
Journal of Nutrition for the Elderly (USA) **4049**
Journal of Nutritional & Environmental Medicine (GBR) **6662**
Journal of Obstetric, Gynecologic, and Neonatal Nursing (USA) **5966**
Journal of Obstetrics and Gynaecology (GBR) **5996**
Journal of Obstetrics and Gynaecology Research (JPN) **5996**
Journal of Occupational and Environmental Hygiene (Online) (USA) **6680**
Journal of Occupational and Organizational Psychology (GBR) **7377**
Journal of Occupational Health Psychology (USA) **6680**
Journal of Occupational Rehabilitation (USA) **6680**
Journal of Oceanography (NLD) **2809**
Journal of Ocular Pharmacology and Therapeutics (USA) **6045**
Journal of Offender Rehabilitation (USA) **2657**
Journal of Oncology Pharmacy Practice (GBR) **6855**
Journal of Optimization Theory and Applications (USA) **5506**
Journal of Oral and Maxillofacial Surgery (USA) **5852**
Journal of Oral Implantology (USA) **5852**
Journal of Oral Pathology & Medicine (GBR) **5852**
Journal of Oral Rehabilitation (GBR) **5852**
Journal of Organisational Transformation and Social Change (GBR) **8115**
Journal of Organizational and End User Computing (Online) (USA) *see* Journal of Organizational and End User Computing. **2571**
Journal of Organizational Behavior Management (USA) **7377**
Journal of Organizational Change Management (GBR) **1769**
Journal of Organizational Computing and Electronic Commerce (USA) **1420**
Journal of Ornithology (Online Edition) (DEU) *see* Journal of Ornithology. **909**
The Journal of Orthodontics (Online Edition) (GBR) **5853**
Journal of Orthopaedic Nursing (GBR) **5966**
Journal of Orthoptera Research (USA) **852**
The Journal of Pacific History (GBR) **4192**
Journal of Paediatrics and Child Health (GBR) **6094**
The Journal of Pain (USA) **6155**
Journal of Pain & Palliative Care Pharmacotherapy (USA) **6855**
Journal of Paleolimnology (NLD) **6726**
Journal of Paleontology (USA) **6726**
Journal of Palestine Studies (USA) **4322**
Journal of Palliative Medicine (USA) **5653**
Journal of Parallel and Distributed Computing (USA) **2429**
Journal of Parapsychology (USA) **6742**
The Journal of Parasitology (SUN) **5821**
Journal of Pastoral Care and Counseling (USA) **7655**
Journal of Pastoral Theology (USA) **7655**
Journal of Peace Education (GBR) **7249**
Journal of Peace Research (GBR) **7249**
The Journal of Peasant Studies (GBR) **8115**
Journal of Pediatric and Adolescent Gynecology (NLD) **6095**
Journal of Pediatric Health Care (USA) **6095**
Journal of Pediatric Neurology (NLD) **6095**
Journal of Pediatric Nursing (USA) **5966**
Journal of Pediatric Oncology Nursing (USA) **6025**
Journal of Pediatric Psychology (GBR) **7377**
Journal of Pediatric Surgery (USA) **6249**
The Journal of Pediatrics (USA) **6095**
Journal of Pension Economics and Finance (GBR) **1868**
Journal of PeriAnesthesia Nursing (USA) **5967**
Journal of Perinatal Medicine (DEU) **5996**
Journal of Perinatology (GBR) **5996**
Journal of Periodontal Research (DNK) **5853**
Journal of Personal Selling and Sales Management (USA) **1826**
Journal of Personality (USA) **7377**
Journal of Personality and Social Psychology (USA) **7377**
Journal of Personality Assessment (USA) **7377**
Journal of Personality Disorders (USA) **7378**
Journal of Pest Science (DEU) **852**
Journal of Petrology (GBR) **2750**
Journal of Pharmacokinetics and Pharmacodynamics (USA) **6855**
Journal of Pharmacy Practice (USA) **6856**
Journal of Phenomenological Psychology (NLD) **7378**
Journal of Philosophical Logic (NLD) **6929**
Journal of Philosophy of Education (GBR) **6929**
Journal of Phonetics (GBR) **5135**
Journal of Phycology (USA) **797**
Journal of Physical Education, Recreation and Dance (USA) **3068**
Journal of Physical Oceanography (USA) **2810**
The Journal of Physiology (GBR) **925**
Journal of Phytopathology (DEU) **797**
Journal of Pineal Research (DNK) **6156**
Journal of Plankton Research (GBR) **684**
Journal of Planning Education and Research (USA) **4417**
Journal of Planning History (USA) **4417**
Journal of Planning Literature (USA) **4417**
Journal of Plant Nutrition (USA) **798**
Journal of Plant Physiology (DEU) **798**
Journal of Plasma Physics (GBR) **7022**
Journal of Plastic Film and Sheeting (GBR) **7093**
Journal of Plastic, Reconstructive & Aesthetic Surgery (Online Edition) (GBR) **6249**
Journal of Poetry Therapy (USA) **7378**
Journal of Police Crisis Negotiations (USA) **4892**
Journal of Policy and Practice in Intellectual Disabilities (USA) **4067**
Journal of Policy History (USA) **7147**
Journal of Policy Practice (Online) (USA) *see* Journal of Policy Practice. **8050**
Journal of Political and Military Sociology (USA) **8115**
Journal of Political Ideologies (GBR) **7147**
Journal of Political Marketing (USA) **7148**
Journal of Political Philosophy (GBR) **6929**
The Journal of Politics (USA) **7148**
Journal of Polymer Research (NLD) **7093**
Journal of Polymers and the Environment (USA) **2125**
Journal of Popular Culture (USA) **5315**
Journal of Popular Film and Television (USA) **6505**
Journal of Popular Music Studies (USA) **6581**
Journal of Porous Materials (USA) **3350**
The Journal of Portfolio Management (USA) **1635**
Journal of Positive Behavior Interventions (USA) **7378**
Journal of Post Keynesian Economics (USA) **1545**
Journal of Poverty (USA) **8050**
Journal of Prevention and Intervention in the Community (USA) **7417**
The Journal of Primary Prevention (USA) **7378**
The Journal of Private Equity (USA) **1635**
Journal of Product and Brand Management (GBR) **1826**
Journal of Product Innovation Management (USA) **1890**
Journal of Productivity Analysis (USA) **1769**
Journal of Professional Nursing (USA) **5967**
Journal of Progressive Human Services (USA) **8050**
Journal of Promotion Management (USA) **27**
Journal of Property Investment & Finance (GBR) **7596**
Journal of Property Management (USA) **7596**
Journal of Property Research (GBR) **4417**
Journal of Property Tax Assessment and Administration (USA) **7597**
Journal of Prosthetic Dentistry (USA) **5853**
Journal of Prosthodontics (USA) **5853**

Online Service

11208 O C L C ONLINE COMPUTER LIBRARY CENTER, INC. ULRICH'S PERIODICALS

Journal of Psychiatric and Mental Health Nursing Online (GBR) 6156
Journal of Psycholinguistic Research (USA) 5135
The Journal of Psychology (USA) 7378
Journal of Psychopathology and Behavioral Assessment (USA) 7379
Journal of Psychopharmacology (GBR) 6856
Journal of Psychophysiology (USA) 7379
Journal of Psychosocial Oncology (USA) 6025
Journal of Psychosomatic Obstetrics and Gynecology (GBR) 5997
Journal of Psychotherapy Integration (USA) 6156
Journal of Public Administration Research and Theory (GBR) 7448
Journal of Public Affairs (GBR) 7448
Journal of Public Budgeting, Accounting & Financial Management (USA) 7448
Journal of Public Economic Theory (USA) 1545
Journal of Public Health (Online) (GBR) 8050
Journal of Public Policy (GBR) 7979
Journal of Public Policy & Marketing (USA) 1826
Journal of Public Procurement (USA) 7449
Journal of Public Relations Research (USA) 27
Journal of Quality Assurance in Hospitality & Tourism (USA) 4392
Journal of Quality in Maintenance Engineering (GBR) 3369
Journal of Quality Technology (USA) 3351
Journal of Quantitative Criminology (USA) 2658
Journal of Quantitative Linguistics (NLD) 5203
Journal of Radio & Audio Media (USA) 2359
Journal of Radioanalytical and Nuclear Chemistry (HUN) 2102
Journal of Radiotherapy in Practice (GBR) 6201
Journal of Rapid Methods and Automation in Microbiology (USA) 890
Journal of Rational - Emotive and Cognitive - Behavior Therapy (USA) 7379
Journal of Real Estate Finance and Economics (USA) 7597
Journal of Real Estate Literature (USA) 7597
The Journal of Real Estate Portfolio Management (USA) 7597
Journal of Real Estate Practice and Education (USA) 7597
Journal of Real Estate Research (USA) 7597
Journal of Receptors and Signal Transduction (USA) 684
Journal of Refugee Studies (GBR) 7249
Journal of Regional Science (USA) 4417
Journal of Regulatory Economics (USA) 1546
Journal of Rehabilitation (USA) 6111
Journal of Rehabilitation Medicine (NOR) 8051
Journal of Rehabilitation Research and Development (USA) 6065
Journal of Reinforced Plastics & Composites (GBR) 3351
Journal of Relationship Marketing (USA) 1138
The Journal of Religion (USA) 7655
Journal of Religion and Health (USA) 7656
Journal of Religion and Spirituality in Social Work (USA) 8051
Journal of Religion, Disability & Health (USA) 7656
Journal of Religion in Africa (NLD) 7737
Journal of Religion, Spirituality & Aging (USA) 4049
Journal of Religious & Theological Information (USA) 7656
Journal of Religious Ethics (USA) 7656
Journal of Religious History (AUS) 7656
The Journal of Religious Thought (USA) 7656
Journal of Renal Nutrition (USA) 6662
Journal of Reproductive and Infant Psychology (GBR) 7379
The Journal of Research Administration (USA) 1769
Journal of Research in Childhood Education (USA) 2878
Journal of Research in Crime and Delinquency (USA) 2658
Journal of Research in International Education (GBR) 3014
Journal of Research in Music Education (USA) 6581
Journal of Research in Personality (USA) 7379
Journal of Research in Reading (GBR) 2878
The Journal of Research in Special Educational Needs (GBR) 3042
Journal of Research on Adolescence (USA) 2156
Journal of Research on Christian Education (USA) 2878
Journal of Research on Technology in Education (USA) 2950
Journal of Retail & Leisure Property (GBR) 7597
Journal of Retailing (GBR) 1826
Journal of Revenue and Pricing Management (GBR) 1295
Journal of Risk and Insurance (USA) 4510
Journal of Risk and Uncertainty (USA) 1546
The Journal of Risk Finance (GBR) 1636
Journal of Risk Research (GBR) 3448
Journal of Ritual Studies (USA) 345
Journal of Russian and East European Psychology (USA) 7379
Journal of Russian Laser Research (USA) 3206
Journal of S T E M Education (Online) (USA) 7872
Journal of Sandwich Structures & Materials (GBR) 3351
Journal of Scandinavian Studies in Criminology and Crime Prevention (NOR) 2658
Journal of Scheduling (USA) 2593
Journal of Scholarly Publishing (CAN) 7564
Journal of School Health (USA) 7529
Journal of School Nursing (USA) 5967
Journal of School Violence (USA) 2878
Journal of Science Education and Technology (USA) 7873
Journal of Science Teacher Education (NLD) 2878
Journal of Scientific Computing (USA) 7940
Journal of Seismology (NLD) 2785
Journal of Semantics (GBR) 5203
Journal of Semitic Studies (GBR) 5135
Journal of Sensory Studies (USA) 6157
Journal of Service Management (GBR) 1769
Journal of Service Research (USA) 1826
Journal of Services Marketing (GBR) 1827
Journal of Sex & Marital Therapy (USA) 7380
Journal of Sex Research (USA) 7380
Journal of Sexual Aggression (GBR) 7380
Journal of Sexual Medicine (GBR) 5654
Journal of Shoulder and Elbow Surgery (USA) 6250
Journal of Signal Processing Systems (USA) 2534
Journal of Sleep Research Online (GBR) 5654
Journal of Small Business and Enterprise Development (GBR) 1962
Journal of Small Business Management (USA) 1962
Journal of Social and Clinical Psychology (USA) 7380
Journal of Social and Personal Relationships (GBR) 7380
Journal of Social Archaeology (GBR) 401
Journal of Social History (USA) 8115
Journal of Social Issues (USA) 7380
Journal of Social Philosophy (USA) 6929
Journal of Social Policy (GBR) 8051
Journal of Social, Political and Economic Studies (USA) 7148
The Journal of Social Psychology (USA) 7380
Journal of Social Service Research (USA) 8051
Journal of Social Studies Research (USA) 7980
The Journal of Social Welfare and Family Law (GBR) 4911
Journal of Social Work (GBR) 8051
Journal of Social Work Education (USA) 8051
Journal of Social Work in Disability & Rehabilitation (USA) 8051
Journal of Social Work in End-of-Life & Palliative Care (USA) 7380
Journal of Social Work Practice (GBR) 8051
Journal of Social Work Practice in the Addictions (USA) 8051
Journal of Sociolinguistics (GBR) 5135
Journal of Sociology (GBR) 8116
Journal of Sociology and Social Welfare (USA) 8116
Journal of Soil and Water Conservation (USA) 2616
Journal of Sol-Gel Science and Technology (NLD) 3351
Journal of Solid State Chemistry (USA) 2138
Journal of Solution Chemistry (USA) 2138
Journal of Sound and Vibration (GBR) 7088
Journal of Southeast Asian Studies (GBR) 4185
Journal of Southeast European and Black Sea Studies (GBR) 7249
Journal of Southern African Studies (GBR) 7980
The Journal of Southern Legal History (USA) 4704
Journal of Spanish Cultural Studies (GBR) 3545
Journal of Special Education (USA) 3043
Journal of Special Education Technology (USA) 3043
Journal of Speculative Philosophy (USA) 6930
Journal of Speech, Language, and Hearing Research (USA) 4075
Journal of Spirituality in Mental Health (USA) 7381
Journal of Sport and Social Issues (USA) 8182
Journal of Sport and Tourism (GBR) 4978
Journal of Sports Economics (USA) 1138
The Journal of Sports Medicine and Physical Fitness (ITA) 6231
Journal of Sports Sciences (GBR) 8183
Journal of Staff Development (USA) 1868
Journal of Statistical Computation and Simulation (GBR) 2443
Journal of Statistical Physics (USA) 7022
Journal of Strain Analysis for Engineering Design (GBR) 3351
Journal of Strategic Marketing (GBR) 1827
The Journal of Strategic Studies (GBR) 7249
Journal of Strength and Conditioning Research (USA) 6231
Journal of Stroke & Cerebrovascular Diseases (USA) 5794
Journal of Structural and Functional Genomics (NLD) 874
Journal of Structural Biology (USA) 684
Journal of Structural Chemistry (USA) 2069
The Journal of Structured Finance (USA) 1363
Journal of Studies in International Education (USA) 3014
Journal of Studies on Alcohol and Drugs (USA) 2696
Journal of Substance Use (GBR) 2696
Journal of Sulfur Chemistry (GBR) 2069
Journal of Supercomputing (USA) 2430
Journal of Superconductivity and Novel Magnetism (USA) 7023
Journal of Supply Chain Management (USA) 1827
Journal of Supreme Court History (USA) 4953
Journal of Surfactants and Detergents (DEU) 2125
Journal of Surgical Research (USA) 6250
Journal of Sustainable Agriculture (USA) 128
Journal of Sustainable Forestry (USA) 3695
Journal of Symbolic Computation (GBR) 5553
Journal of Synchrotron Radiation (DNK) 7068
Journal of Systematic Palaeontology (GBR) 2751
Journal of Systemic Therapies (USA) 7381
Journal of Targeting, Measurement and Analysis for Marketing (GBR) 1890
Journal of Taxation and Regulation of Financial Institutions (USA) 1363
Journal of Teacher Education (USA) 2878
Journal of Teaching in International Business (USA) 1574
Journal of Teaching in Social Work (USA) 3068
Journal of Teaching in the Addictions (USA) 3068
Journal of Teaching in Travel & Tourism (USA) 3068
Journal of Technology and Teacher Education (USA) 2950
Journal of Technology in Human Services (USA) 8151
Journal of Technology Transfer (USA) 8429
Journal of Telemedicine and Telecare (GBR) 5655
Journal of Texture Studies (USA) 3652
Journal of the Asia Pacific Economy (GBR) 1495
Journal of the Atmospheric Sciences (USA) 6359
Journal of the Early Republic (USA) 4300
Journal of the Economic and Social History of the Orient (NLD) 4322
Journal of the History of Biology (NLD) 685
Journal of the History of Collections (GBR) 6526
Journal of the History of Economic Thought (GBR) 1546
Journal of the History of Ideas (USA) 4461
Journal of the History of International Law (NLD) 4933
Journal of the History of Medicine and Allied Sciences (GBR) 5655
Journal of the History of Philosophy (USA) 6930
Journal of the History of Sexuality (USA) 8116
Journal of the History of the Neurosciences (GBR) 6157
Journal of the Japanese and International Economies (USA) 1574
Journal of the Learning Sciences (USA) 2879
Journal of the Peripheral Nervous System Online (USA) 6157
Journal of the Royal Society. Interface (GBR) 7873
Journal of the Southwest (USA) 4300
Journal of Theological Studies (GBR) 7657
Journal of Theology for Southern Africa (ZAF) 7657
Journal of Theoretical and Computational Chemistry (SGP) 2108
Journal of Theoretical Biology (GBR) 685
Journal of Theoretical Politics (GBR) 7148
Journal of Theoretical Probability (USA) 5507
Journal of Thermal Analysis and Calorimetry (HUN) 2138
Journal of Thermal Stresses (USA) 3387
Journal of Thermoplastic Composite Materials (GBR) 7094
Journal of Third World Studies (USA) 4150
The Journal of Thoracic and Cardiovascular Surgery (USA) 6250
Journal of Thought (USA) 7980
Journal of Thrombosis and Thrombolysis (USA) 5794
Journal of Time Series Analysis (GBR) 8383
Journal of Toxicology and Environmental Health. Part A (USA) 3499
Journal of Toxicology and Environmental Health. Part B: Critical Reviews (USA) 3499
Journal of Traffic Safety Education (USA) 8587
Journal of Transcultural Nursing (USA) 5967
Journal of Transformative Education (USA) 2879
Journal of Transnational Management (USA) 1574
Journal of Trauma and Dissociation (USA) 7381
Journal of Traumatic Stress (USA) 7381
Journal of Travel & Tourism Marketing (USA) 8726
Journal of Travel Research (USA) 8726
Journal of Tropical Ecology (GBR) 3448
Journal of Tropical Pediatrics (GBR) 6095
Journal of Urban Affairs (USA) 4417
Journal of Urban Design (GBR) 4418
Journal of Urban Economics (USA) 1138
Journal of Urban Health (USA) 5655
Journal of Urban History (USA) 4150
Journal of Urban Technology (GBR) 8429
Journal of Vacation Marketing (GBR) 8726
The Journal of Value Inquiry (NLD) 6930
Journal of Vascular Nursing (USA) 5967
Journal of Vascular Research (CHE) 5794
Journal of Vascular Surgery (USA) 6250
Journal of Vegetation Science (SWE) 799
Journal of Vertebrate Paleontology (USA) 6726
Journal of Vestibular Research: Equilibrium and Orientation (NLD) 925
Journal of Veterinary Emergency and Critical Care (GBR) 8801
Journal of Veterinary Pharmacology and Therapeutics Online (GBR) 6857
Journal of Vibration and Control (GBR) 7088
Journal of Viral Hepatitis (GBR) 5928
Journal of Visual Art Practice (GBR) 499
Journal of Visual Communication and Image Representation (USA) 2488
Journal of Visual Communication in Medicine (Online) (GBR) 5655
Journal of Visual Culture (GBR) 4461
Journal of Visual Impairment & Blindness (USA) 4082
Journal of Visual Languages and Computing (GBR) 5203
Journal of Vocational Behavior (USA) 7381
Journal of Vocational Rehabilitation (NLD) 7381
Journal of W O C N (USA) 6250
Journal of Water Supply Research and Technology. Aqua Online (GBR) *see* Journal of Water Supply: Research and Technology. AQUA. 8828
The Journal of Wealth Management (USA) 1636
Journal of Wine Research (GBR) 240
Journal of Women and Aging (USA) 8900
Journal of Women, Politics & Policy (USA) 7148
Journal of Women's Health (USA) 8846
Journal of Women's History (USA) 8900
Journal of Wood Chemistry and Technology (USA) 2069
Journal of Workplace Behavioral Health (USA) 1868
Journal of Workplace Learning (GBR) 1868
Journal of World Business (GBR) 1574
Journal of World History (USA) 4150
Journal of World Prehistory (USA) 401
Journal of World Trade (NLD) 4934
Journal of X-Ray Science and Technology (NLD) 7023
Journal of Youth and Adolescence (USA) 2157
Journal of Youth Studies (GBR) 2157
Journal of Zoo and Wildlife Medicine (USA) 8802
Journal of Zoological Systematics and Evolutionary Research Online (DEU) 953
Journal of Zoology (GBR) 953
Journalism (GBR) 4577
Journalism and Communication Monographs (USA) 4577
Journalism and Mass Communication Educator (USA) 4577
Journalism and Mass Communication Quarterly (USA) 4578
Journalism History (USA) 4578
Journalism Studies (GBR) 4578
Journals of Cases on Information Technology (USA) 1770
Journals of Gerontology. Series A: Biological Sciences & Medical Sciences (USA) 4050
Journals of Gerontology. Series B: Psychological Sciences & Social Sciences (USA) 4050
Judaica Librarianship (USA) 5022
Judaism (USA) 7725
Judicature (USA) 4953
Jump Cut (USA) 6505
K M World (USA) 2537
K - Theory (NLD) 5507
Ka Ho 'Oilina (USA) 5136
Kansas Academy of Science. Transactions (Print) (USA) 7874
Kansas Journal of Law & Public Policy (USA) 4709
Kant Studien (DEU) 6930
Kappa Delta Pi Record (USA) 3069
Kennedy Institute of Ethics Journal (USA) 5657
Kentucky Libraries (USA) 5022
The Kenyon Review (USA) 5425
Key Words (Port Aransas) (USA) 5058
Kidney and Blood Pressure Research (CHE) 6270
Kidney International (USA) 6271
Kids Marketing Report (GBR) 1828
Kinetics and Catalysis (RUS) 2138
Kiplinger Tax Letter (USA) 1932
Kiplinger's Personal Finance (USA) 1364
Kiplinger's Retirement Report (USA) 1636
Kitchen & Bath Business (USA) 1019
Knowledge Engineering Review (GBR) 2454
Knowledge Management Research & Practice (GBR) 2430
Knowledge Management Review (GBR) 1771
Knowledge Quest (USA) 5023
Knowledge, Technology and Policy (NLD) 7981
Konsthistorisk Tidskrift (GBR) 500
Konyvtari Figyelo (HUN) 5023
Korean Studies (USA) 554
Koreana (KOR) 554
Kreisarchiv Soest. Schriften (DEU) 4238
Kritika (Bloomington) (USA) 4238
KronoScope (Online) (NLD) 577
Kunsthistorische Sammlungen in Wien. Jahrbuch (AUT) 501
Kybernetes (GBR) 2527
Kyklos (GBR) 8117
L I M R A's MarketFacts Quarterly (USA) 4512
L I T: Literature Interpretation Theory (USA) 5319
L P G World (GBR) 6776
L P - Gas (USA) 6776
L S A (FRA) 1829
L W F Documentation (CHE) 7764
L W F Studies (CHE) 7764
L W T - Food Science and Technology (GBR) *see* L W T- Food Science and Technology. 3653
L1 Educational Studies in Language and Literature (NLD) 2881
Lab On a Chip (GBR) 2071
Label & Narrow Web (USA) 2563
Labor History (GBR) 1692
Labor Law Journal (USA) 4711
Labor Studies Journal (USA) 1693
Laboratoriums-Medizin (DEU) 5908
Laboratory Animals (GBR) 953
Laboratory Investigation (USA) 5908
Labour (GBR) 1693
Lafayette Business Digest (USA) 1496
Lakes and Reservoirs: Research and Management (AUS) 8828
Lambda Book Report (USA) 4376
The Lancet (GBR) 5660
The Lancet (North American Edition) (GBR) 5660
Land Economics (USA) 202
Landscape Ecology (NLD) 3450
Landscape Management (USA) 3741
Landscape Research (GBR) 448
Language (Washington) (USA) 5139
Language Acquisition (USA) 5139
Language and Cognitive Processes (GBR) 5139
Language and Literature (GBR) 5139
Language Arts (USA) 3070
Language Assessment Quarterly (USA) 5140

DIRECTORY 2010 O C L C ONLINE COMPUTER LIBRARY CENTER, INC. 11209

Language in Society (GBR) **5140**
Language Learning (USA) **5141**
Language Learning and Development (USA) **5141**
Language Policy (NLD) **5141**
Language Resources and Evaluation (NLD) **4485**
Language, Speech and Hearing Services in Schools (USA) **6082**
Language Teaching (GBR) **5201**
Language Teaching Research (GBR) **5141**
Language Testing (GBR) **5141**
Language Variation and Change (GBR) **5142**
Las Vegas Business Press (USA) **1143**
Laser and Particle Beams (GBR) **7079**
Laser Focus World (USA) **7080**
Lasers in Engineering (CHE) **7080**
LatAm Energy (GBR) **3141**
Late Imperial China (USA) **4185**
Laterality (GBR) **6158**
Latin American Business Review (USA) **1575**
Latin American Indian Literatures Journal (USA) **5320**
Latin American Literary Review (USA) **5320**
Latin American Music Review (USA) **6584**
Latin American Perspectives (USA) **7982**
Latin American Politics and Society (USA) **7250**
Latin American Power Watch (USA) **3160**
Latin American Research Review (USA) **7982**
Latin Insurance (GBR) **4512**
Latin Trade (USA) **1575**
LatinFinance (USA) **1365**
Latino Studies (GBR) **8118**
Law & Business Review of the Americas (USA) **4934**
Law and Contemporary Problems (USA) **4713**
Law and Critique (NLD) **4713**
Law and Human Behavior (USA) **4713**
Law and Literature (USA) **4713**
Law and Philosophy (NLD) **4713**
Law & Policy (GBR) **4714**
The Law and Practice of International Courts and Tribunals (NLD) **4934**
Law & Society Review (USA) **4714**
Law Library Journal (USA) **5024**
Law, Probability and Risk (GBR) **4716**
The Lawyer (GBR) **4717**
Leader to Leader (USA) **1772**
Leadership (Sacramento) (USA) **2882**
Leadership & Organization Development Journal (GBR) **1772**
Leadership and Policy in Schools (USA) **3026**
Leadership Excellence (USA) **1869**
Leadership in Action (USA) **1772**
Leadership in Health Services (GBR) **4105**
Learning and Leading with Technology (USA) **2950**
Learning and Motivation (USA) **2882**
Learning and Teaching (GBR) **7983**
Learning Disabilities Research and Practice (USA) **3043**
Learning Disability Quarterly (USA) **3043**
Learning Environments Research (NLD) **2882**
Learning in Health and Social Care (GBR) **5660**
Learning, Media & Technology (Online) (GBR) **3070**
The Learning Organization (GBR) **1869**
Leather International (GBR) **4974**
Legacy (Lincoln) (USA) **5320**
Legal and Criminological Psychology (GBR) **7383**
Legal Assistant Today (USA) **4719**
Legal Issues of Economic Integration (NLD) **4934**
Legal Reference Services Quarterly (USA) **5025**
Legal Studies Forum (USA) **4720**
Legal Theory (GBR) **4721**
Leiden Journal of International Law (GBR) **4935**
Leisure Report (GBR) **4980**
Leisure Sciences (USA) **4980**
Leisure Studies (GBR) **4980**
Leonardo: Art Science and Technology (USA) **502**
Leonardo Music Journal (USA) **6584**
Lethaia (NOR) **6726**
Letter Arts Review (USA) **502**
Letters in Applied Microbiology (GBR) **890**
Letters in Mathematical Physics (NLD) **7025**
Leukemia (GBR) **5939**
Leukemia and Lymphoma (CHE) **5940**
Leukos (USA) **3208**
Lewis & Clark Law Review (USA) **4723**
Libraries & the Cultural Record (USA) **5026**
Library & Archival Security (USA) **5026**
Library Hi Tech (GBR) **5062**
Library Hi Tech News (GBR) **5062**
Library Journal (USA) **5028**
Library Leadership & Management (USA) **5028**
Library Management (GBR) **5028**
Library Media Connection (USA) **5028**
Library Personnel News (USA) **5028**
The Library Quarterly (USA) **5029**
Library Resources & Technical Services (USA) **5029**
Library Review (GBR) **5029**
Library Trends (USA) **5029**
The Licensing Letter (USA) **6754**
The Lichenologist (GBR) **800**
Life Insurance International (IRL) **4512**
Lifetime Data Analysis (NLD) **8385**
Lighting Design + Application (USA) **3324**
Lighting Research and Technology (GBR) **3324**
Lightwave (USA) **2331**
Limnology and Oceanography (USA) **2797**
Linear and Multilinear Algebra (CHE) **5509**
Linguistic Inquiry (USA) **5145**
The Linguistic Review (DEU) **5146**
Linguistic Typology (DEU) **5146**
Linguistics (DEU) **5147**
Linguistics and Philosophy (NLD) **5147**
Linnean Society. Biological Journal (GBR) **687**
Linnean Society. Botanical Journal (GBR) **800**
Linnean Society. Zoological Journal (GBR) **953**
The Lion and the Unicorn (USA) **5323**
Liquid Crystals (GBR) **2111**
Liquid Crystals Today (Online) (GBR) **2111**
Literacy (Oxford) (GBR) **2883**
Literacy Research and Instruction (USA) **3070**
Literary and Linguistic Computing (GBR) **5203**
The Literary Review (USA) **5324**
Literature and Medicine (USA) **5325**
Literature and Theology (GBR) **5325**
Literature Film Quarterly (USA) **6506**
Lithology and Mineral Resources (RUS) **2752**
Lithuanian Mathematical Journal (USA) **5509**
Liturgy (USA) **7660**
Live Design (USA) **8473**
Liver International (DNK) **5928**
Liver Transplantation (USA) **5929**
Liverpool Law Review (NLD) **4724**
The Living Pulpit (USA) **7661**
Local Economy (GBR) **1145**
Local Environment (GBR) **4419**
Local Government Studies (GBR) **7497**
Lodging Hospitality (USA) **4393**
Logistics Management (USA) **8503**
Logistics Spectrum (USA) **8431**
Logopedics Phoniatrics Vocology (GBR) **6082**
Logos (NLD) **7566**
Logos (St. Paul) (USA) **7805**
Lolapress (DEU) **8900**
London Mathematical Society. Bulletin (GBR) **5509**
London Mathematical Society. Journal (GBR) **5509**
London Mathematical Society. Proceedings (GBR) **5510**
London Review of Education (GBR) **2884**
Long Island Business News (USA) **1145**
Long-Term Living (USA) **5969**
Los Angeles Magazine (USA) **3980**
Loss Prevention Bulletin (GBR) **3250**
Louisiana Law Review (USA) **4725**
Louisiana Libraries (USA) **5030**
Louisville Magazine (USA) **3980**
Loyola Law Review (USA) **4726**
Loyola of Los Angeles International and Comparative Law Review (USA) **4726**
Loyola University Chicago Law Journal (USA) **4726**
Lupus (GBR) **6224**
Luso - Brazilian Review (USA) **5225**
Lutheran Education (USA) **7765**
Lymphatic Research and Biology (USA) **6026**
M E L U S (USA) **5328**
M H Online (GBR) **5663**
M I R: Management International Review (DEU) **1773**
M I S Quarterly (USA) **2523**
M I T Sloan Management Review (USA) **1773**
M L A International Bibliography (USA) **5407**
M L N (USA) **5149**
M M R (USA) **1774**
Machine Design (USA) **3388**
Machine Learning (USA) **2454**
Machine Translation (NLD) **5204**
Machining Science and Technology (USA) **3352**
Maclean's (CAN) **3812**
Macroeconomic Dynamics (GBR) **1720**
Macroeconomics Annual (USA) **1720**
MacWorld (USA) **2577**
The Magazine Antiques (USA) **367**
Magna's Campus Legal Monthly (USA) **2993**
Magnetic Resonance Materials in Physics, Biology and Medicine (GBR) **7068**
Maine Bar Journal (USA) **4727**
Maine Law Review (USA) **4727**
Malaysian Journal of Library and Information Science (MYS) **5031**
Mammal Review Online (GBR) **954**
Mammalian Biology (DEU) **954**
Mammalian Species (Online) (USA) **955**
Manage (Online) (USA) **1774**
Managed Healthcare Executive (USA) **4106**
Management Accounting Research (GBR) **1296**
Management & Organization Review (AUS) **1775**
Management Communication Quarterly (USA) **1775**
Management Decision (GBR) **1775**
Management Learning (GBR) **1776**
Management of Environmental Quality (GBR) **3451**
Management Quarterly (USA) **1776**
Management Research (USA) **1776**
Management Research Review (GBR) **1776**
Management Science (USA) **1776**
Management Services (GBR) **1777**
Management Today (GBR) **1777**
Manager (GBR) **1777**
Managerial Auditing Journal (GBR) **1778**
Managerial Finance (GBR) **1778**
Managing Intellectual Property (GBR) **6754**
Managing Leisure (GBR) **4980**
Managing Service Quality (GBR) **1778**
The Manchester School (GBR) **1546**
Manitoba Business Magazine (CAN) **1498**
Manoa (USA) **5330**
Manual Therapy (GBR) **6112**
Manufacturing and Service Operations Management (USA) **1778**
Manufacturing Business Technology (USA) **1898**
Manufacturing Chemist (GBR) **3250**
Manufacturing Engineering (USA) **3209**
Marg (Mumbai) (IND) **449**
Marine and Freshwater Behaviour and Physiology (GBR) **687**
Marine & Freshwater Research (AUS) **2811**
Marine Biological Association of the United Kingdom. Journal (GBR) **688**
Marine Corps Gazette (USA) **6432**
Marine Ecology (DEU) **688**
Marine Fisheries Review (USA) **3601**
Marine Geodesy (USA) **4019**
Marine Geophysical Researches (NLD) **2812**
Marine Georesources and Geotechnology (USA) **2812**
Marine Technology Society Journal (USA) **2812**
Maritime Economics & Logistics (GBR) **8652**
Maritime Policy and Management (GBR) **8652**
Market: Africa - Mid-East (USA) **1577**
Market: Asia Pacific (USA) **1577**
Market: Europe (USA) **1577**
Marketing (GBR) **1831**
Marketing Health Services (USA) **1832**
Marketing Intelligence & Planning (GBR) **1832**
Marketing Letters (USA) **1832**
Marketing Management (USA) **1832**
Marketing News (USA) **1832**
Marketing Online (CAN) *see* Marketing Magazine. **1832**
Marketing Research (USA) **1833**
Marketing Science (USA) **1833**
Marketing Theory (GBR) **1833**
Marketing to the Emerging Majorities (USA) **1833**
Marketing to Women (USA) **1833**
Marketing Week (GBR) **1834**
Marketplace (Menasha) (USA) **1147**
Marquette Law Review (USA) **4728**
Marriage & Family Review (USA) **8119**
Marvels & Tales (USA) **3620**
Maryland Bar Journal (USA) **4728**
Al- Masaq (GBR) **7714**
Masonry Construction (USA) **1022**
Mass Communication and Society (USA) **8119**
Mass High Tech (USA) **8431**
Mass Transit (USA) **8503**
Massachusetts Review (USA) **5227**
The Masthead (Harrisburg) (USA) **4579**
Material Handling Management (USA) **5456**
Material Handling Product News (USA) **2462**
Materials & Manufacturing Processes (USA) **3389**
Materials Management in Health Care (USA) **4106**
Materials Science (USA) **3353**
Materials World (GBR) **6322**
Maternal and Child Health Journal (USA) **5998**
Maternal and Child Nutrition (GBR) **6663**
Mathematical and Computer Modelling of Dynamical Systems (GBR) **5554**
Mathematical Finance (USA) **1367**
Mathematical Geosciences (Online) (USA) *see* Mathematical Geosciences. **2754**
Mathematical Medicine and Biology (Online) (GBR) **5513**
Mathematical Models and Methods in Applied Sciences (SGP) **5513**
Mathematical Physics, Analysis and Geometry (NLD) **7026**
Mathematical Population Studies (USA) **7287**
Mathematical Problems in Engineering (USA) **3209**
Mathematical Structures in Computer Science (GBR) **5554**
Mathematical Thinking and Learning (USA) **5515**
Mathematics and Computer Education (USA) **5515**
Mathematics and Mechanics of Solids (GBR) **7026**
Mathematics in School (GBR) **5515**
Mathematics Magazine (USA) **5515**
Mathematics of Computation (USA) **5516**
Mathematics of Operations Research (USA) **2431**
Mathematics Teacher (USA) **3072**
Mathematics Teaching (GBR) **5516**
Mathematics Teaching in the Middle School (USA) **3072**
McGill Journal of Education (CAN) **2885**
McGill Law Journal (CAN) **4730**
Measurement (USA) **5517**
Measurement and Evaluation in Counseling and Development (USA) **2886**
Measurement in Physical Education and Exercise Science (USA) **6992**
Measurement Techniques (USA) **6404**
Measuring Business Excellence (GBR) **1779**
Meat & Deli Retailer (USA) **3655**
Meccanica (NLD) **7060**
Mechanical Engineering (USA) **3389**
Mechanical Systems and Signal Processing (GBR) **3389**
Mechanics Based Design of Structures and Machines (USA) **3389**
Mechanics of Advanced Materials and Structures (USA) **3354**
Mechanics of Composite Materials (USA) **3250**
Mechanics of Time Dependent Materials (NLD) **7061**
Med Ad News (USA) **1834**
Media (HKG) **29**
Media, Culture & Society (GBR) **8120**
Media History (GBR) **8120**
Media Industry Newsletter (USA) **29**
Media Psychology (USA) **7384**
Media Report to Women (USA) **8120**
Mediators of Inflammation (USA) **5666**
MediaWeek (USA) **30**
Medical & Veterinary Entomology Online (GBR) **5667**
Medical Anthropology (USA) **347**
Medical Anthropology Quarterly (USA) **347**
Medical Care Research and Review (USA) **7548**
Medical Decision Making (USA) **5667**
Medical Design Technology (Online) (USA) **5667**
Medical Device Technology (GBR) **5668**
Medical Economics (USA) **5668**
Medical Education (GBR) **5668**
Medical Hypotheses (GBR) **5669**
Medical Image Analysis (GBR) **6203**
Medical Laboratory Observer (USA) **5909**
Medical Laser Application (DEU) **5909**
Medical Law Review (GBR) **4731**
The Medical Letter on Drugs and Therapeutics (English Edition) (USA) **6860**
Medical Letter on the C D C & F D A (USA) **4106**
Medical Library Association. Journal (USA) **5669**
Medical Marketing & Media (USA) **6860**
Medical Meetings (USA) **6281**
Medical Mycology (GBR) **5822**
Medical Oncology (GBR) **6027**
Medical Principles and Practice (CHE) **5670**
Medical Reference Services Quarterly (USA) **5031**
Medical Teacher (GBR) **5672**
Medicine and Science in Sports and Exercise (USA) **6231**
Medicine, Conflict and Survival (GBR) **5674**
Medicine, Healthcare and Philosophy (NLD) **5674**
Medieval Encounters (NLD) **7726**
Mediterranean Historical Review (GBR) **4323**
Mediterranean Politics (GBR) **7252**
Mediterranean Quarterly (USA) **7252**
Medium Aevum (GBR) **5332**
Meetings and Conventions (USA) **6281**
Melanoma Research (GBR) **6027**
Melbourne Journal of International Law (AUS) **4935**
Melbourne University Law Review (AUS) **4732**
Memory (GBR) **7384**
Memphis Business Journal (USA) **1148**
Men and Masculinities (USA) **6303**
Mendeleev Communications (RUS) **2072**
Menninger Clinic. Bulletin (USA) **6159**
Menopause International (GBR) **5998**
Men's Health (United States Edition) (USA) **6285**
Mental Health in Family Medicine (GBR) **6160**
Mental Health, Religion & Culture (GBR) **7385**
The Mental Health Review (GBR) **6160**
Mentoring & Tutoring (GBR) **3072**
Mercer Business Magazine (USA) **1407**
Mergers & Acquisitions (New York, 1965) (USA) **1148**
Mergers & Acquisitions Report (USA) **1148**
Meridians (USA) **8901**
Merrill - Palmer Quarterly (USA) **7385**
Metabolic Brain Disease (USA) **5678**
Metabolic Engineering (USA) **750**
Metabolic Syndrome and Related Disorders (USA) **5897**
Metabolism (USA) **5897**
Metal Bulletin (GBR) **6322**
Metal Center News (USA) **6323**
Metal Producing & Processing (USA) **6323**
Metal Science and Heat Treatment (USA) **6323**
Metallurgical and Materials Transactions A - Physical Metallurgy and Materials Science (USA) **6324**
Metallurgist (USA) **6325**
Metalsmith (USA) **537**
Metalworking Production (GBR) **6326**
Metaphilosophy (GBR) **6934**
Metaphor and Symbol (USA) **5151**
Metascience (GBR) **7882**
Meteorological Applications (GBR) **6390**
Method & Theory in the Study of Religion (NLD) **7663**
Methodology (USA) **7385**
Methodology and Computing in Applied Probability (USA) **5517**
Methods (USA) **738**
Metroeconomica (GBR) **1149**
Metropolitan Home (USA) **4546**
Mexican Studies (USA) **4464**
Michigan Feminist Studies (USA) **8875**
Michigan Quarterly Review (USA) **5227**
Microbial Drug Resistance (USA) **5679**
Microbial Ecology in Health & Disease (GBR) **5822**
Microbial Pathogenesis (GBR) **5823**
Microbiological Research (DEU) **891**
Microbiology (RUS) **891**
Microchemical Journal (USA) **899**
Microcirculation (GBR) **5679**
Microelectronics International (GBR) **3109**
Micropaleontology (USA) **6726**
Microscopy and Microanalysis (USA) **900**
Microvascular Research (USA) **5795**
Microwave Engineering (GBR) **3109**
Microwave Journal (International Edition) (USA) **3325**
Microwaves & R F (USA) **3325**
Mid-America Commerce & Industry (USA) **1499**
The Middle East (GBR) **5227**
Middle East Critique (GBR) **555**
Middle East Economic Digest (GBR) **1499**
Middle East Journal (USA) **7252**
Middle East Policy (USA) **7252**
Middle East Report (USA) **4323**
Middle Eastern Literatures (Online) (GBR) **5333**
Middle Eastern Studies (GBR) **4323**
The Middle Way (GBR) **7702**
Midwest Quarterly (USA) **4465**
Midwest Studies in Philosophy (USA) **6934**
Midwifery (GBR) **5998**
Midwifery Today (USA) **5998**
The Milbank Quarterly (USA) **7154**
Military & Aerospace Electronics (USA) **66**
The Military Balance (Year) (GBR) **6435**
Military History (USA) **4303**
Military Intelligence (USA) **6435**

Online Service

Link to your serials resources and content with ulrichsweb.com

11210 O C L C ONLINE COMPUTER LIBRARY CENTER, INC. ULRICH'S PERIODICALS

Military Law Review (USA) **4971**
Military Psychology (USA) **7385**
Military Review (English Edition) (USA) **6436**
Military Technology (DEU) **6436**
Millimeter (USA) **6507**
Milton Quarterly (USA) **5334**
Mind (GBR) **6934**
Mind & Language (GBR) **6934**
Mind, Culture, and Activity (USA) **7986**
Minds and Machines (NLD) **2454**
Mineral Processing and Extractive Metallurgy Review (USA) **6326**
Mineralogical Magazine (GBR) **6471**
The Mineralogical Record (USA) **4340**
Minerals & Energy (GBR) **1601**
Minerva (NLD) **7882**
Minerva Journal of Women and War (USA) **6437**
Minimally Invasive Therapy and Allied Technologies (GBR) **5679**
Minnesota Law Review (USA) **4734**
Minnesota Review (USA) **5334**
Missiology (USA) **7739**
Mission Studies (NLD) **7664**
Mississippi Business Journal (USA) **1964**
Mississippi Libraries (USA) **5032**
The Mississippi Quarterly (USA) **5227**
Missouri Bar. Journal (USA) **4735**
The Missouri Review (USA) **5335**
Mitigation and Adaptation Strategies for Global Change (NLD) **3453**
Mitochondrial D N A (GBR) **738**
Mix Magazine (USA) **8154**
Mnemosyne (NLD) **2237**
Mobile Communications Europe (GBR) **2333**
Mobile Networks and Applications (NLD) **2501**
Model Airplane News (USA) **4340**
Model Railroader (USA) **4341**
Modern Age (USA) **5228**
Modern and Contemporary France (GBR) **4245**
Modern Applications News (USA) **6326**
Modern Asian Studies (GBR) **556**
Modern Brewery Age (USA) **607**
Modern Casting (USA) **6326**
Modern China (USA) **4186**
Modern Drama (CAN) **5335**
M F S Modern Fiction Studies (USA) **5335**
Modern Healthcare (USA) **4107**
Modern Intellectual History (GBR) **5228**
Modern Italy (GBR) **4245**
Modern Judaism (GBR) **3551**
Modern Language Journal (USA) **5151**
Modern Language Quarterly (USA) **5335**
The Modern Law Review (GBR) **4735**
Modern Machine Shop (USA) **5457**
Modern Materials Handling (USA) **5457**
Modern Metals (USA) **6326**
Modern Painters (USA) **506**
Modern Pathology (GBR) **5680**
Modern Philology (USA) **5152**
Modern Physics Letters A (SGP) **7068**
Modern Physics Letters B (SGP) **7068**
Modern Power Systems (GBR) **3142**
Modern Theology (GBR) **7664**
Modernism/Modernity (USA) **4153**
Molecular and Cellular Biochemistry (USA) **738**
Molecular and Cellular Neuroscience (USA) **6161**
Molecular and Cellular Probes (GBR) **5909**
Molecular Biology (RUS) **739**
Molecular Biology and Evolution (USA) **689**
Molecular Biology Reports (NLD) **739**
Molecular Biotechnology (USA) **768**
Molecular Breeding (NLD) **801**
Molecular Crystals and Liquid Crystals (CHE) **2111**
Molecular Diversity (NLD) **7068**
Molecular Ecology (GBR) **893**
Molecular Ecology Resources (GBR) **893**
Molecular Genetics and Metabolism (USA) **739**
Molecular Human Reproduction (GBR) **5999**
Molecular Imaging (CAN) **835**
Molecular Medicine (USA) **6862**
Molecular Membrane Biology (GBR) **739**
Molecular Microbiology (GBR) **893**
Molecular Neurobiology (USA) **739**
Molecular Phylogenetics and Evolution (USA) **875**
Molecular Physics (GBR) **2138**
Molecular Plant Pathology (GBR) **802**
Molecular Psychiatry (Online) (GBR) *see* Molecular Psychiatry. **6161**
Molecular Simulation (CHE) **2073**
Molecular Systems Biology (GBR) **690**
Molecular Therapy (GBR) **6028**
Molluscan Research (NZL) **955**
Momentum (New York) (USA) **6161**
Momentum (Washington) (USA) **2887**
Money Management Executive (USA) **1640**
Money Management Letter (USA) **1640**
Money Marketing (GBR) **1368**
Monist (USA) **6935**
Montana Business Quarterly (USA) **1150**
Monte Carlo Methods and Applications (DEU) **5555**
Montessori Life (USA) **3073**
Monthly Review (USA) **7155**
Monthly Weather Review (USA) **6391**
Monumenta Nipponica (JPN) **556**
Mortality (GBR) **7532**
Mortgage Banking (USA) **1369**
Mortgage Servicing News (USA) **1369**
Mortgage Technology (USA) **7600**
Mosaic (Winnipeg, 1967) (CAN) **5336**
Mother Earth News (USA) **3982**
Mothering (USA) **8847**
MotherJones.com (USA) *see* Mother Jones. **5228**
Motion System Design (USA) **3390**
Motivation and Emotion (USA) **7386**
Motor Boating (USA) **8278**
Motor Trend (USA) **8593**
Mountain Bike (USA) **8265**
Mountain Research and Development (CHE) **2713**
Mousaion (ZAF) **5032**
The Moving Image (USA) **6508**
MoXie (Berkeley) (USA) **8876**
Mpls. - Saint Paul Magazine (USA) **3982**
Ms. (USA) **8901**
Multi-Housing News (USA) **1025**
Multibody System Dynamics (NLD) **7061**
Multichannel Merchant (USA) **30**
Multichannel News (USA) **2385**
Multicultural Education (USA) **3073**
Multicultural Perspectives (USA) **3073**
Multidimensional Systems and Signal Processing (USA) **2524**
Multilingua (DEU) **5153**
MultiMedia & Internet@Schools (USA) **2950**
Multimedia Tools and Applications (NLD) **2488**
Multinational Business Review (USA) **1578**
Multinational Finance Journal (USA) **1393**
Multinational Monitor (USA) **1578**
Multiple Sclerosis (GBR) **6162**
Multivariate Behavioral Research (USA) **7386**
Muscle & Fitness (USA) **6993**
Museum International (English Edition) (GBR) **6531**
Music Analysis (GBR) **6589**
Music & Copyright (GBR) **6589**
Music and Letters (GBR) **6589**
Music Education Research (GBR) **6590**
Music Educators Journal (USA) **6590**
Music Library Association. Notes (USA) **5033**
Music Perception (USA) **6591**
Music Reference Services Quarterly (USA) **5033**
Music Theory Spectrum (USA) **6592**
Music Week (GBR) **6592**
The Musical Quarterly (USA) **6594**
Musical Times (GBR) **6594**
Muslim World (USA) **7715**
Mutagenesis (GBR) **875**
Mycological Research (GBR) **803**
Mycopathologia (NLD) **803**
Mycoses (DEU) **5681**
N A C E Journal (USA) **1698**
N A C L A Report on the Americas (USA) **7253**
N A S P A Journal (Online) (USA) **2994**
N A S S P Bulletin (USA) **3027**
N A S S P Leadership for Student Activities (USA) **3027**
N E A News (FRA) **3171**
N E A Today (USA) **2888**
N F P A Journal (USA) **3580**
N J Biz (USA) **1151**
N M A Online (GBR) *see* New Media Age. **2335**
N P A (USA) **1297**
N T Q. New Theatre Quarterly (GBR) **8474**
N W S A Journal (USA) **8901**
Nabokov Studies (USA) **5337**
Nan Nu (NLD) **557**
NanoBioTechnology (USA) **768**
Nanoscale & Microscale Thermophysical Engineering (Online) (USA) **7056**
Narrative (USA) **5338**
Nashim (ISR) **8901**
Nashville Business Journal (USA) **1152**
The Nation (USA) **5229**
The National Black Law Journal (USA) **4738**
National Cancer Institute. Journal (Online) (GBR) **6028**
National Catholic Reporter (USA) **7808**
National Civic Review (USA) **7499**
National Contract Management Journal (USA) **1780**
National Council of Teachers of Mathematics. Yearbook (USA) **3074**
National Defense (USA) **6438**
National Dragster (USA) **8595**
National Floor Trends (USA) **4547**
National Geographic Kids (USA) **4021**
National Geographic Online (USA) *see* National Geographic. **4020**
National Guard (USA) **6438**
National Hog Farmer (USA) **294**
National Identities (GBR) **7156**
National Institute Economic Review (GBR) **1152**
National Institute of Standards and Technology. Journal of Research (USA) **6405**
The National Interest (USA) **7254**
National Jeweler (USA) **4568**
National Journal (USA) **7156**
National Mortgage News Daily (USA) *see* National Mortgage News. **1370**
National On-Campus Report (USA) **2293**
National Parks (USA) **4981**
National Petroleum News (USA) **6779**
National Real Estate Investor (USA) **7601**
National Review (USA) **7156**
National Society for the Study of Education. Yearbook (USA) **2890**
National Tax Association. Proceedings of the Annual Conference on Taxation and Minutes of the Annual Meeting (USA) **1936**
National Tax Journal (USA) **1936**
National Underwriter. Life & Health (USA) **4516**
National Underwriter. P & C (USA) **4516**
National Voter (USA) **7156**
National Wildlife (USA) **2620**
National Wildlife (World Edition) (USA) **2620**
National Women's Health Report (USA) **8847**
Nationalism & Ethnic Politics (GBR) **7254**
Nationalities Papers (GBR) **7987**
Nations and Nationalism (GBR) **7157**
The Nation's Health (USA) **7533**
Nation's Restaurant News (USA) **4394**
Native Peoples (USA) **6635**
Native Plants Journal (USA) **804**
Natural Computing (NLD) **2432**
Natural Foods Merchandiser (USA) **1835**
Natural Hazards (NLD) **2713**
Natural History (USA) **7888**
Natural Language and Linguistic Theory (NLD) **5154**
Natural Language Engineering (GBR) **2509**
Natural Language Semantics (NLD) **5154**
Natural Product Reports (GBR) **2127**
Natural Product Research (CHE) **2074**
Natural Resources Forum (GBR) **4021**
The Natural Resources Journal (USA) **2621**
Natural Resources Research (USA) **6474**
Naval Forces (DEU) **6438**
Naval War College Review (USA) **6438**
Near Eastern Archaeology (USA) **407**
Nebraska Library Association. Quarterly (USA) **5035**
Nebraska Life (USA) **3982**
Negotiation Journal (USA) **7254**
Negro Educational Review (USA) **2890**
Nematology (NLD) **958**
Neohelicon (HUN) **5339**
Neonatology (CHE) **5999**
Neophilologus (NLD) **5339**
NeoPlasia (USA) **6029**
Nephrology (AUS) **6272**
Nephrology, Dialysis, Transplantation (GBR) **6272**
Nephron Clinical Practice (CHE) **6252**
Nephron Experimental Nephrology (CHE) **6252**
Nephron Physiology (CHE) *see* The Nephron Journals. **6272**
Netherlands International Law Review (NLD) **4936**
Netherlands Journal of Geosciences (NLD) **2757**
Netherlands Quarterly of Human Rights (BEL) **4838**
Netnomics (NLD) **2501**
Network World (USA) **2502**
Networks and Spatial Economics (USA) **2518**
Neue Zeitschrift fuer Systematische Theologie und Religionsphilosophie (DEU) **7665**
Neural Computation (USA) **2455**
Neural Processing Letters (USA) **2455**
Neuro-Ophthalmology (GBR) **6163**
Neurobiology of Disease (USA) **6164**
Neurobiology of Learning and Memory (USA) **6164**
Neurocase (GBR) **6164**
Neurochemical Research (USA) **6164**
Neurocritical Care (USA) **5685**
Neurodegenerative Diseases (CHE) **5929**
Neuroembryology and Aging (CHE) **6164**
Neuroendocrinology (CHE) **5898**
Neuroepidemiology (CHE) **6164**
Neurogastroenterology and Motility Online (GBR) **5929**
NeuroImage (USA) **6165**
Neuroimmunomodulation (CHE) **5764**
NeuroInformatics (USA) **925**
Neurology, Neurophysiology and Neuroscience (Online) (USA) **6166**
Neuromodulation (USA) **6166**
NeuroMolecular Medicine (USA) **6167**
Neuron Glia Biology (Online) (GBR) **6167**
Neuropathology (AUS) **6167**
Neuropathology and Applied Neurobiology (GBR) **6167**
Neuropeptides (Edinburgh) (GBR) **740**
Neurophysiology (USA) **6167**
Neuropsychobiology (CHE) **6168**
Neuropsychological Rehabilitation (GBR) **6168**
Neuropsychology (USA) **6168**
Neuropsychology, Development and Cognition. Section A: Journal of Clinical and Experimental Neuropsychology (NLD) **7387**
Neuropsychology, Development and Cognition. Section B: Aging, Neuropsychology and Cognition (GBR) **7387**
Neuropsychology, Development, and Cognition. Section C: Child Neuropsychology (NLD) **7387**
Neuropsychology, Development and Cognition. Section D: The Clinical Neuropsychologist (GBR) **7387**
Neuropsychology Review (USA) **6168**
Neuropsychopharmacology (USA) **6168**
NeuroRehabilitation (NLD) **6168**
Neurorehabilitation and Neural Repair (USA) **6168**
NeuroReport (USA) **6169**
Neuroscience and Behavioral Physiology (USA) **6169**
The Neuroscientist (USA) **6169**
NeuroSignals (Print) (CHE) **740**
Neurotoxicity Research (USA) **6170**
The New American (Appleton) (USA) **7157**
New Blackfriars (GBR) **7809**
New Centennial Review (USA) **4466**
New Cinemas: Journal of Contemporary Film (GBR) **6508**
New Criterion (USA) **5229**
New Directions for Adult and Continuing Education (USA) **2944**
New Directions for Child and Adolescent Development (USA) **7387**
New Directions for Community Colleges (USA) **2995**
New Directions for Evaluation (USA) **7988**
New Directions for Higher Education (USA) **2995**
New Directions for Institutional Research (USA) **2995**
New Directions for Student Services (USA) **2995**
New Directions for Teaching and Learning (USA) **2995**
New Directions for Youth Development (USA) **2162**
The New England Journal of Higher Education (USA) **2995**
The New England Quarterly (USA) **5340**
New England Reading Association. Journal (USA) **2890**
New England Review (USA) **5340**
New Forests (NLD) **3698**
New Genetics and Society (GBR) **876**
New Hampshire Business Review (USA) **1431**
New Hibernia Review (USA) **350**
New Jersey Business (USA) **1899**
New Journal of Chemistry (GBR) **2074**
New Labor Forum (USA) **4599**
New Library World (GBR) **5035**
New Literary History (USA) **5340**
New Mathematics and Natural Computation (SGP) **5520**
New Media & Society (GBR) **8123**
New Media Investor (GBR) **1642**
New Media Markets (GBR) **2386**
New Mexico Law Review (USA) **4744**
New Moon Girls (USA) **2204**
New Orleans CityBusiness (USA) **1964**
New Perspectives Quarterly (USA) **7158**
New Phytologist (GBR) **804**
New Political Economy (GBR) **1547**
New Political Science (GBR) **7158**
The New Republic (USA) **5230**
The New Review of Academic Librarianship (GBR) **5035**
The New Review of Children's Literature and Librarianship (GBR) **5341**
The New Review of Film and Television Studies (GBR) **2386**
New Review of Hypermedia and Multimedia (GBR) **2488**
The New Review of Information Networking (GBR) **2502**
New Scientist: Planet Science (GBR) *see* New Scientist. **7891**
New Scientist: Planet Science (GBR) *see* New Scientist on CD-ROM. **7892**
New Statesman (GBR) **5230**
New Technology, Work & Employment (GBR) **1699**
New Testament Studies (GBR) **7666**
New York Diamonds (USA) **4568**
New York Law School Law Review (USA) **4745**
New York Magazine (USA) **3983**
New York Review of Books (USA) **7568**
The New York State Conservationist (USA) **2622**
The New York Times Upfront (Student Edition) (USA) **2205**
New Zealand Geographer (AUS) **4022**
New Zealand Journal of Environmental Law (NZL) **4746**
New Zealand Management (NZL) **1781**
Newcastle Law Review (AUS) **4746**
News Media and the Law (USA) **4580**
News Photographer (USA) **6971**
Newsletter on Intellectual Freedom (USA) **5036**
Newspaper Research Journal (USA) **4581**
Newsweek (USA) **3983**
Nicotine & Tobacco Research (GBR) **8486**
Nieman Reports (USA) **4581**
Nietzsche-Studien (DEU) **6936**
Nine (USA) **8240**
Nineteenth-Century Art Worldwide (USA) **509**
Nineteenth-Century Contexts (GBR) **5341**
Nineteenth Century French Studies (USA) **5342**
Nineteenth-Century Literature (Berkeley) (USA) **5342**
Nineteenth Century Music (USA) **6599**
Nitric Oxide: Biology and Chemistry (USA) **741**
Nivedini (LKA) **8901**
Nka (USA) **509**
Nondestructive Testing and Evaluation (GBR) **3355**
Nonlinear Dynamics (NLD) **3391**
Nonlinear Dynamics, Psychology, and Life Sciences (USA) **7388**
Nonlinear Optics, Quantum Optics (CHE) **7081**
Nonlinear Oscillations (Online) (USA) **5521**
Nonlinear Studies (USA) **5521**
Nonprofit and Voluntary Sector Quarterly (USA) **8059**
Nonprofit Management and Leadership (USA) **1781**
Nonprofit World (USA) **8059**
Nonwovens Industry (USA) **8455**
Nora (NOR) **8901**
Nordic Journal of International Law (NLD) **4936**
Nordic Journal of Linguistics (GBR) **5155**
Nordic Journal of Psychiatry (GBR) **6171**
Norges Bank. Economic Bulletin (NOR) **1501**
Norsk Geografisk Tidsskrift (NOR) **4022**
Norsk Geologisk Tidsskrift (NOR) **2759**
North American Actuarial Journal (USA) **4517**
The North American Review (USA) **5230**
North Carolina Central Law Journal (USA) **4748**
North Carolina Journal of International Law and Commercial Regulation (USA) **4937**
North Carolina Libraries (USA) **5036**
North Sea Letter (GBR) **6781**
North Sea Rig Forecast (GBR) **3143**
Northeast African Studies (USA) **3555**
Northeast Pennsylvania Business Journal (USA) **1155**
Northeastern Naturalist (USA) **805**
Northern Kentucky Law Review (USA) **4749**
The Northern Miner (CAN) **6475**
Northern Ontario Business (CAN) **1155**

Link to your serials resources and content with ulrichsweb.com

Online Service

11212 O C L C ONLINE COMPUTER LIBRARY CENTER, INC. ULRICH'S PERIODICALS

Plant Biotechnology Journal (GBR) 810
Plant Breeding Online (DEU) 810
Plant, Cell and Environment (GBR) 697
Plant Cell, Tissue and Organ Culture (NLD) 835
Plant Ecology (NLD) 811
Plant Engineering (USA) 3215
Plant Foods for Human Nutrition (USA) 6668
Plant Growth Regulation (NLD) 811
The Plant Journal (GBR) 811
Plant Molecular Biology (NLD) 697
Plant Molecular Biology Reporter (NLD) 742
Plant Pathology (GBR) 811
Plant Species Biology (AUS) 812
Plasma Chemistry & Plasma Processing (USA) 3252
Plasma Devices and Operations (CHE) 7035
Plasmid (USA) 698
Plastics and Rubber Asia (GBR) 7096
PlasticsNews.com (USA) *see* Plastics News. 7097
Platelets (London) (GBR) 5940
Platt's Metals Week (USA) 6476
Playthings (USA) 4061
Ploughshares (USA) 5352
PlugIn Datamation (USA) 2538
Plumbing & Mechanical (USA) 4125
Pneuma (NLD) 7770
Poetics Today (USA) 5234
Poetry (Chicago) (USA) 5430
Poets & Writers Online (USA) *see* Poets & Writers Magazine. 5432
Pointe (USA) 2687
Polar Record (GBR) 4024
Police Practice and Research (GBR) 2664
Police Quarterly (USA) 4896
Policing (Bingley) (GBR) 2664
Policing and Society (GBR) 2664
Policy & Practice (USA) 8062
Policy, Politics & Nursing Practice (USA) 5978
Policy Review (USA) 7166
Policy Sciences (NLD) 7166
Policy Studies (GBR) 7166
Policy Studies Journal (USA) 7167
Polis (GBR) 7167
Political Analysis (GBR) 7168
Political Behavior (USA) 7168
Political Communication (USA) 7168
Political Psychology (USA) 7168
The Political Quarterly (GBR) 7169
Political Research Quarterly (USA) 7169
Political Science Quarterly (USA) 7169
Political Studies (GBR) 7169
Political Studies Review (GBR) 7169
Political Theory (USA) 7169
Politics (USA) 7170
Politics (Oxford) (GBR) 7170
Politics and Society (USA) 7170
Politics and the Life Sciences (USA) 7170
Politics, Philosophy & Economics (GBR) 7171
Politikon (GBR) 7171
Polity (GBR) 7172
Pollution Engineering (USA) 3490
Polycyclic Aromatic Compounds (CHE) 2129
Polymer Engineering and Science (USA) 3252
Polymer-Plastics Technology and Engineering (USA) 2129
Polymer Reviews (USA) 2129
PopSci.com (USA) *see* Popular Science. 8435
Popular Communication (USA) 2336
Popular Mechanics PMZone (USA) *see* Popular Mechanics. 8435
Popular Music (GBR) 6607
Popular Music & Society (GBR) 6607
Popular Photography (USA) 6975
Population and Development Review (USA) 7289
Population and Environment (USA) 7391
Population Briefs (USA) 7289
Population Bulletin (USA) 7289
Population Health Management (USA) 5697
Population Research and Policy Review (NLD) 7290
Population Review (Online) (THA) 7290
Population Studies (GBR) 7291
Portable Design (USA) 3215
Portal (USA) 5039
Portuguese Journal of Social Science (GBR) 7993
positions (USA) 559
Positivity (NLD) 5525
Post-Communist Economies (GBR) 1547
Postcolonial Studies (GBR) 4156
Postmodern Culture (USA) 4156
Potential Analysis (NLD) 5525
Pottery Making Illustrated (USA) 2044
Poultry World (GBR) 297
Powder Metallurgy and Metal Ceramics (USA) 6329
Power Electronics Technology (USA) 3111
Power Engineering (USA) 3328
Power Engineering International (USA) 3328
Power Finance and Risk (USA) 1375
Power in Europe (GBR) 3160
Power in Latin America (GBR) 3160
Power Technology and Engineering (NLD) 3281
Power U K (GBR) 3160
Practical Accountant (USA) 1299
Practical Neurology (GBR) 6174
Practical Tax Strategies (USA) 1939
Practice (Abingdon) (GBR) 8062
Practice Nurse (GBR) 5978
The Practitioner (GBR) 5698
Prairie Schooner (USA) 5353
Precision Agriculture (USA) 148
Precision Marketing (GBR) 1838
Preparative Biochemistry and Biotechnology (USA) 742
Prepared Foods (USA) 3660
Presence (USA) 2489
Presentations (USA) 32
The Presidency (USA) 2998
Presidential Studies Quarterly (USA) 7173
Preventing School Failure (USA) 3045
Prevention (USA) 6995
Prevention Science (USA) 5825
Preventive Medicine (USA) 5699
Primary Care & Community Psychiatry (Online) (GBR) 6174
Primary Health Care Research and Development (GBR) 5699
Princeton University Art Museum. Record (USA) 6536
Principal (Alexandria) (USA) 3030
Principal Leadership (High School Edition) (USA) 2899
Principal Leadership (Middle School Edition) (USA) 2899
Print (USA) 2489
Print Professional (USA) 7326
Printed Circuit Design & Manufacture (USA) 2466
Printing Impressions (USA) 7326
The Prison Journal (USA) 2666
Private Asset Management (USA) 1645
Private Banker International (IRL) 1376
Private Equity Week (USA) 1376
Private Label Buyer (USA) 6714
Private Placement Letter (USA) 1376
Private Placement Report (USA) 1376
Pro Sound News (USA) 8154
Probability in the Engineering and Informational Sciences (GBR) 3233
Probation Journal (GBR) 2666
Problems of Economic Transition (USA) 1161
Problems of Information Transmission (RUS) 2534
Problems of Post-Communism (USA) 7173
Probus (DEU) 5163
Process Engineering (GBR) 3253
Process Heating (USA) 3371
Process Safety and Environmental Protection (GBR) 3253
Product Alert (USA) 3661
Product Design and Development (USA) 3216
Production and Operations Management (USA) 1786
Production Planning & Control (GBR) 3293
El Profesional de la Informacion (ESP) 5063
Professional Builder (USA) 1030
Professional Candy Buyer (USA) 3661
The Professional Geographer (USA) 4025
Professional Psychology: Research and Practice (USA) 7392
Professional Remodeler (USA) 1030
Professional Safety (USA) 6684
Professional School Counseling (USA) 2900
Profit-Building Strategies for Business Owners (USA) 1162
Program (GBR) 5063
Programming and Computer Software (RUS) 2596
Progress in Development Studies (IND) 8126
Progress in Human Geography (GBR) 4025
Progress in Orthodontics Online (DNK) 5862
Progress in Physical Geography (GBR) 4025
The Progressive (Madison) (USA) 7173
The Progressive Christian (USA) 7771
Progressive Grocer (New York, 2002) (USA) 3681
Progressive Librarian (USA) 5040
Project Finance and Infrastructure Finance (GBR) 1376
Project Management Journal (USA) 1787
Prologue (College Park) (USA) 4309
Prometheus (Abingdon) (GBR) 2336
Promo (USA) 33
Promotions and Incentives (GBR) 1838
Prooftexts (USA) 5354
Property Management (GBR) 7605
Property Week (GBR) 7605
Prospects (NLD) 2900
Prostaglandins, Leukotrienes & Essential Fatty Acids (GBR) 5899
Prostate Cancer and Prostatic Diseases (GBR) 6033
Protection of Metals and Physical Chemistry of Surfaces (RUS) 6330
Protein Engineering Design and Selection (Online) (GBR) 743
Protein Expression and Purification (USA) 743
The Protein Journal (USA) 743
Protein Science (USA) 743
Protist (DEU) 698
Provincial China (GBR) 7261
Psychiatric Genetics (USA) 877
Psychiatric Quarterly (USA) 6176
Psychiatric Times (USA) 6176
Psychiatry (New York) (USA) 6177
Psychiatry and Clinical Neurosciences (AUS) 6177
Psychoanalysis, Culture & Society (GBR) 7395
Psychoanalytic Dialogues (USA) 7395
Psychoanalytic Inquiry (USA) 7395
Psychoanalytic Psychology (USA) 7395
Psychoanalytic Psychotherapy (GBR) 7395
The Psychoanalytic Review (USA) 7395
Psychoanalytic Social Work (USA) 8063
Psychodynamic Practice (Online) (GBR) 6178
Psychogeriatrics (AUS) 7396
Psychological Assessment (USA) 7396
Psychological Bulletin (USA) 7396
Psychological Inquiry (USA) 7396
Psychological Medicine (GBR) 6178
Psychological Methods (USA) 7396
The Psychological Record (USA) 7396
Psychological Review (USA) 7397
Psychological Science (GBR) 7397
Psychological Science in the Public Interest (GBR) 7397
Psychological Services (USA) 7397
The Psychologist-Manager Journal (USA) 7398
Psychology and Aging (USA) 4053
Psychology & Health (GBR) 7398
Psychology & Psychotherapy (GBR) 7399
Psychology, Crime and Law (GBR) 7399
Psychology, Health & Medicine (GBR) 7399
Psychology of Addictive Behaviors (USA) 2698
Psychology of Men & Masculinity (USA) 7399
Psychology of Music (GBR) 6608
Psychology of Women Quarterly (USA) 7400
Psychology, Public Policy, and Law (USA) 7400
Psychology Today (USA) 7400
Psychonomic Bulletin & Review (USA) 7400
Psychopathology (CHE) 6179
Psychophysiology (GBR) 6179
Psychotherapy (USA) 7401
Psychotherapy and Psychosomatics (CHE) 6180
Psychotherapy Research (GBR) 7401
Public Administration (GBR) 7461
Public Administration Quarterly (USA) 7461
Public Administration Review (USA) 7461
Public Art Review (USA) 513
Public Budgeting and Finance (USA) 7462
Public Choice (NLD) 1162
Public Culture (USA) 5235
Public Finance Review (USA) 1941
Public Health (GBR) 5700
Public Health Genomics (CHE) 877
Public Health Nursing (USA) 5979
Public Health Reports (USA) 7537
The Public Historian (USA) 4157
Public Integrity (USA) 7462
Public Land & Resources Law Review (USA) 4763
Public Libraries (USA) 5040
Public Library Quarterly (USA) 5041
Public Management Review (Online) (GBR) 1787
Public Money and Management (GBR) 7462
Public Opinion Quarterly (USA) 7174
Public Organization Review (USA) 1787
Public Performance and Management Review (USA) 7462
Public Personnel Management (USA) 1873
Public Policy Research (Online) (GBR) 1547
Public-Private Finance (GBR) 1377
Public Relations Journal (Online) (USA) 33
Public Relations Quarterly (USA) 33
Public Relations Review (GBR) 33
Public Roads (USA) 3281
Public Understanding of Science (GBR) 7900
Public Utilities Fortnightly (USA) 3510
Public Works (USA) 7501
Public Works Management & Policy (USA) 7463
Publishers Weekly (USA) 7571
Publishing Executive (USA) 7571
Publishing Research Quarterly (USA) 7571
Publius (USA) 7174
Puget Sound Business Journal (USA) 1162
Pulmonary Pharmacology and Therapeutics (GBR) 6218
Pulp & Paper Canada (CAN) 6737
Pulp & Paper International (USA) 6737
Punishment & Society (GBR) 2666
Purchasing (Newton) (USA) 1839
Pure and Applied Chemistry (GBR) 2077
Q J M (GBR) 5701
Q S H C Online (GBR) *see* Quality and Safety in Health Care. 5701
QST (USA) 2361
Quaerendo (NLD) 7571
Qualitative Health Research (USA) 5701
Qualitative Inquiry (USA) 7994
Qualitative Market Research (GBR) 1839
Qualitative Research (GBR) 7994
Qualitative Research in Psychology (GBR) 7402
Qualitative Social Work (GBR) 8064
Qualitative Sociology (USA) 8127
Quality (New York) (USA) 7291
Quality and Quantity (NLD) 8150
Quality Assurance in Education (GBR) 2901
Quality Engineering (USA) 3216
Quality in Ageing (GBR) 4054
Quality in Higher Education (GBR) 2999
Quality in Primary Care (Online) (GBR) 5701
Quality Magazine (USA) 1788
Quality Management Journal (USA) 1788
Quality of Life Research (NLD) 5702
Quality Progress (USA) 1788
Quantitative Marketing and Economics (USA) 1163
Quantum Information Processing (USA) 2456
Quarterly Economic Commentary (IRL) 1163
The Quarterly Journal of Austrian Economics (USA) 1547
The Quarterly Journal of Economics (USA) 1547
Quarterly Journal of Mathematics (GBR) 5527
Quarterly Journal of Mechanics and Applied Mathematics (GBR) 5527
Quarterly Journal of Speech (USA) 2901
Quarterly National Accounts (FRA) 1941
Quarterly Review of Distance Education (USA) 3078
The Quarterly Review of Economics and Finance (GBR) 1163
Quarterly Review of Film and Video (USA) 6510
Quarterly Reviews of Biophysics (GBR) 754
Quaternary Research (USA) 2763
Queen's Law Journal (CAN) 4764
Queueing Systems (NLD) 3328
Quill (Greencastle) (USA) 4582
R & D Directions (USA) 6877
R & D Magazine (USA) 8436
R & D Management (GBR) 1788
R B M: A Journal of Rare Books, Manuscripts and Cultural Heritage (USA) 5041
R F Design (USA) 3111
The R M A Journal (USA) 1377
R N A (GBR) 877
R N Web (USA) *see* R N. 5979
R P S Journal (GBR) 6976
R U S I Journal (GBR) 6442
Race & Class (GBR) 3560
Race, Ethnicity and Education (GBR) 2902
Race Relations Abstracts (USA) 8150
Radiance Online (USA) 8881
Radiation Effects and Defects in Solids (CHE) 7071
Radiation Protection Dosimetry (GBR) 7072
Radiation Research (USA) 7072
Radical History Review (USA) 4157
Radical Teacher (USA) 7175
Radio (USA) 2362
The Radio Journal (GBR) 2362
Radiochemistry (RUS) 2140
Radiography (GBR) 6206
Radiophysics and Quantum Electronics (USA) 3112
Railway Age (USA) 8623
The Ramanujan Journal (NLD) 5527
RAND Journal of Economics (USA) 1164
Random Operators and Stochastic Equations (DEU) 5528
Rapid Prototyping Journal (GBR) 3394
Raritan (USA) 5357
Ratio (GBR) 6946
Ratio Juris (GBR) 4765
Rationality and Society (GBR) 7995
Reaction Kinetics and Catalysis Letters (HUN) 2140
Reactions (GBR) 4520
Reading and Writing (NLD) 5165
Reading and Writing Quarterly (USA) 3045
Reading Horizons (USA) 3045
Reading Improvement (USA) 3045
Reading Psychology (USA) 2903
The Reading Teacher (USA) 2903
Reading Today (USA) 2903
Real Estate Economics (USA) 7608
Real Estate Finance (USA) 7608
Real Estate Finance and Investment (USA) 7608
Real Estate Forum (USA) 7608
Real Estate Issues (USA) 7609
Real Lives (GBR) 973
Real Simple (USA) 8881
Real-Time Systems (USA) 2524
Reason (USA) 5236
ReCall (GBR) 2469
Reclaiming Children and Youth (USA) 7402
Records Management Journal (GBR) 1789
Recruitment and Retention in Higher Education (USA) 2999
Recycling Today (USA) 3511
Red Cedar Review (USA) 5236
Redbook (USA) 8882
Redherring.com (USA) *see* The Red Herring (San Francisco). 8436
Reeves Journal (USA) 4125
Reference and User Services Quarterly (USA) 5042
The Reference Librarian (USA) 5042
Reference Reviews (GBR) 5042
Reference Services Review (GBR) 5042
Reflections (Cambridge) (USA) 1789
Reflective Practice (GBR) 6947
Refractories and Industrial Ceramics (USA) 2045
Refrigerated and Frozen Foods (USA) 3662
Refrigerated Transporter (USA) 8675
Refugee Survey Quarterly (GBR) 7314
Regent University Law Review (USA) 4767
The Region Magazine (USA) 1378
Regional Anesthesia and Pain Medicine (USA) 5773
Regional Aviation News (Online) (USA) 8551
Regional Outlook: Southeast Asia (SGP) 1514
Regional Studies (GBR) 4425
Registered Rep (USA) 1647
Regulation (Washington, 1977) (USA) 7176
Regulatory Toxicology and Pharmacology (USA) 3500
Rehabilitation Counseling Bulletin (USA) 4069
Rehabilitation Psychology (USA) 7402
Rejuvenation Research (USA) 4054
Relations Industrielles (CAN) 1705
Reliable Computing (NLD) 2436
Religion (GBR) 7674
Religion and American Culture (USA) 7674
Religion and the Arts (NLD) 7674
Religion in the News (USA) 4583
Religion, State and Society (GBR) 7675
Religious Conference Manager (USA) 7675
Religious Education (USA) 7676
Religious Studies (GBR) 7676
Religious Studies Review (USA) 7699
Remedial and Special Education (USA) 3046
Renaissance Quarterly (USA) 5359
Renaissance Studies (GBR) 4158
Renal Failure (USA) 6273
Renascence (USA) 5359
Rent Review and Lease Renewal (GBR) 7611
Rental Equipment Register (USA) 1839
Representation Theory (USA) 5528
Representations (USA) 4472
Reproduction, Fertility and Development (AUS) 700
Reproduction in Domestic Animals Online (DEU) 8805
Reproductive Health Matters (NLD) 8848

11214 O C L C ONLINE COMPUTER LIBRARY CENTER, INC. ULRICH'S PERIODICALS

Skin Research and Technology (DNK) **5882**
Skull Base (USA) **6258**
Sky & Telescope (USA) **581**
Slavic & East European Information Resources (USA) **5048**
Slavic and East European Journal (USA) **5174**
Sleep and Biological Rhythm (AUS) **5715**
Sleep Medicine Reviews (FRA) **6186**
Small Axe (USA) **5239**
Small Business Economic Trends (USA) **1517**
Small Business Economics (NLD) **1967**
Small Group Research (USA) **7408**
Smart Business Cleveland (USA) **1175**
Smart Business Columbus (USA) **1175**
Smart Business Pittsburgh (USA) **1175**
Smith College Studies in Social Work (USA) **8068**
Smithsonian Magazine Web (USA) *see* Smithsonian. **8002**
Snack Food & Wholesale Bakery (USA) **3675**
Soap and Cosmetics (USA) **596**
Soap, Perfumery & Cosmetics (GBR) **596**
Social & Cultural Geography (GBR) **8002**
Social & Legal Studies (GBR) **8132**
Social Anthropology (GBR) **355**
Social Cognition (USA) **7408**
Social Compass (GBR) **8132**
Social Development (GBR) **8133**
Social Education (USA) **3082**
Social Epistemology (GBR) **6952**
Social Forces (USA) **8133**
Social History (GBR) **8003**
Social History of Medicine (GBR) **5715**
Social Identities (GBR) **3565**
Social Indicators Research (NLD) **8150**
Social Justice (USA) **7265**
Social Justice Research (USA) **8133**
Social Marketing Quarterly (USA) **1844**
Social Movement Studies (GBR) **8003**
Social Philosophy and Policy (GBR) **6952**
Social Policy (USA) **8003**
Social Policy and Administration (GBR) **8069**
Social Policy and Society (GBR) **8133**
Social Politics (GBR) **8903**
Social Problems (USA) **8134**
Social Psychology of Education (NLD) **2913**
Social Psychology Quarterly (USA) **8134**
Social Research (USA) **8003**
Social Science Computer Review (USA) **2951**
Social Science History (USA) **8003**
Social Science Information (GBR) **8003**
Social Science Japan Journal (GBR) **8004**
The Social Science Journal (USA) **8004**
Social Science Quarterly (USA) **8004**
Social Science Research (USA) **8004**
Social Sciences (USA) **8004**
Social Security Bulletin (USA) **4523**
Social Semiotics (GBR) **6952**
The Social Studies (USA) **8005**
Social Studies of Science (GBR) **7917**
Social Studies Review (USA) **8005**
Social Text (USA) **8134**
Social Theory & Health (GBR) **8134**
Social Theory and Practice (USA) **6952**
Social Work (USA) **8070**
Social Work Education (GBR) **8070**
Social Work in Health Care (USA) **8070**
Social Work in Mental Health (USA) **8071**
Social Work in Public Health (USA) **8071**
Social Work with Groups (USA) **8071**
Society (USA) **8005**
Society and Animals (GBR) **321**
Society and Natural Resources (GBR) **3466**
Society for Research in Child Development. Monographs (USA) **7409**
Society of Architectural Historians. Journal (USA) **457**
Society of Archivists. Journal (GBR) **5048**
Society of Christian Ethics. Journal (USA) **7682**
Society of Wetland Scientists. Bulletin (USA) **8832**
Socio-Economic Review (GBR) **1517**
Sociologia Ruralis (GBR) **8136**
Sociological Forum (USA) **8136**
Sociological Inquiry (USA) **8136**
Sociological Methodology (USA) **8136**
Sociological Methods & Research (USA) **8137**
Sociological Perspectives (USA) **8137**
The Sociological Quarterly (USA) **8137**
Sociological Research (USA) **8137**
The Sociological Review (GBR) **8137**
Sociological Spectrum (USA) **8137**
Sociological Theory (USA) **8137**
Sociology (GBR) **8138**
Sociology of Education (USA) **2913**
Sociology of Health and Illness (GBR) **8138**
Sociology of Religion (USA) **8139**
Soft Materials (USA) **7918**
Software Quality Journal (USA) **2598**
Software Quality Professional (USA) **2598**
Soil & Sediment Contamination (USA) **3491**
Soil Mechanics and Foundation Engineering (USA) **3283**
Soil Science (USA) **253**
Sojourners Magazine (USA) **7682**
Solar Physics (NLD) **581**
Solar System Research (RUS) **581**
Soldering & Surface Mount Technology (GBR) **6344**
Soldiers (USA) **6446**
Solid State Nuclear Magnetic Resonance (GBR) **2105**
Solid State Technology (USA) **3114**
Solvent Extraction and Ion Exchange (USA) **2105**
Somatosensory and Motor Research (GBR) **928**
Somnologie (DEU) **5716**
Souls (USA) **8140**
Sound and Vibration (USA) **3395**
Sound & Video Contractor (USA) **8155**
South African Journal of Economics (AUS) **1177**
South Asia (AUS) **4188**
South Asia Research (IND) **560**
South Asian Popular Culture (GBR) **356**
South Carolina Business Journal (USA) **1177**
South Central Review (USA) **5375**
South Dakota Business Review (USA) **1177**
South Dakota Law Review (USA) **4785**
South Dakota Magazine (USA) **4313**
South Florida Business Journal (USA) **1177**
Southeast Farm Press (USA) **158**
Southeastern Librarian (USA) **5048**
Southeastern Naturalist (USA) **818**
Southern Communication Journal (USA) **2339**
Southern Cultures (USA) **4475**
Southern Economic Journal (USA) **1178**
Southern Illinois University Law Journal (USA) **4786**
Southern Literary Journal (USA) **5375**
Southern Living (USA) **3988**
Southern Quarterly (USA) **4476**
The Southern Review (USA) **5375**
Southern University Law Review (USA) **4786**
Southwest Farm Press (USA) **158**
Southwest Journal of Business and Economics (USA) **1178**
The Southwest Review (USA) **5240**
Space & Culture (USA) **4029**
Space and Polity (GBR) **7185**
Space Communications (NLD) **71**
Space Science Reviews (NLD) **582**
Spaceflight (GBR) **72**
Spatial Cognition and Computation (NLD) **7409**
Special Events Magazine (USA) **4398**
The Spectator (GBR) **5240**
Spectroscopy (NLD) **745**
Spectroscopy Letters (USA) **7085**
Spinal Cord (GBR) **6186**
Spiritus (USA) **7683**
Sport, Education and Society (GBR) **8203**
Sport in Society (GBR) **8204**
The Sporting News (USA) **8206**
Sports Afield (USA) **8335**
Sports Engineering (GBR) **8207**
Sports Medicine (NZL) **6233**
Stage Directions (USA) **8479**
Stained Glass (USA) **540**
Stamps (USA) **6900**
Stanford Environmental Law Journal (USA) **4787**
Stanford Journal of Law, Business & Finance (USA) **4787**
State & Local Government Computer News (USA) **7486**
The State Journal (USA) **1179**
State Legislatures (USA) **7186**
Statistica Neerlandica (GBR) **8403**
Statistical Inference for Stochastic Processes (NLD) **5538**
Statistical Methods in Medical Research (GBR) **8404**
Statistical Modelling (IND) **5538**
Statistics (CHE) **8405**
Statistics and Computing (USA) **2444**
Statute Law Review (GBR) **4788**
Statutes and Decisions: The Laws of the U S S R & Its Successor States (USA) **4788**
Stem Cell Reviews (USA) **878**
Stem Cells and Development (USA) **5941**
Stereo Review's Sound & Vision Online (USA) *see* Sound & Vision. **8155**
Stereotactic and Functional Neurosurgery (CHE) **6259**
Stitches (USA) **2250**
Stochastic Analysis and Applications (USA) **5538**
Stochastic Models (USA) **8407**
Stochastics (GBR) **5538**
Stochastics and Dynamics (SGP) **8407**
Stone World (USA) **6480**
Stores (USA) **1844**
Storia dell'Arte (ITA) **519**
Strabismus (London) (NLD) **6052**
Strain (GBR) **3358**
Strategic Direction (GBR) **1179**
Strategic Finance (USA) **1302**
Strategic H R Review (GBR) **1875**
Strategic Management Journal (GBR) **1795**
Strategic Organization (GBR) **1795**
Strategic Planning for Energy and the Environment (USA) **3148**
Strategy & Leadership (GBR) **1795**
Strength and Conditioning Journal (USA) **6997**
Strength, Fracture and Complexity (NLD) **7063**
Strength of Materials (USA) **3358**
Stress (CHE) **5718**
Structural Chemistry (USA) **2081**
Structural Equation Modeling (USA) **7410**
Structural Health Monitoring (GBR) **8439**
Structural Survey (GBR) **1038**
Structure (GBR) **706**
The Structurist (CAN) **519**
Studia Geophysica et Geodaetica (USA) **2790**
Studia Linguistica (GBR) **5180**
Studia Logica (NLD) **6954**
Studia Neophilologica (SWE) **5180**
Studia Theologica (NOR) **7684**
Studies in American Fiction (USA) **5380**
Studies in American Indian Literatures (USA) **5380**
Studies in American Political Development (GBR) **7186**
Studies in Applied Mathematics (Malden) (USA) **5539**
Studies in Art Education (USA) **520**
Studies in Bibliography (USA) **636**
Studies in Comparative International Development (USA) **8008**
Studies in Conflict and Terrorism (USA) **7267**
Studies in Continuing Education (GBR) **2946**
Studies in East European Thought (NLD) **7187**
Studies in Economics and Finance (GBR) **1385**
Studies in English Literature 1500-1900 (USA) **5381**
Studies in European Cinema (GBR) **6514**
Studies in Family Planning (USA) **7294**
Studies in French Cinema (GBR) **6514**
Studies in Higher Education (GBR) **3003**
Studies in Hispanic Cinemas (GBR) **6514**
Studies in Iconography (USA) **520**
Studies in Philology (USA) **5183**
Studies in Philosophy and Education (NLD) **2916**
Studies in Romanticism (USA) **5381**
Studies in Second Language Acquisition (GBR) **5183**
Studies in the Education of Adults (GBR) **2946**
Studies in the Literary Imagination (USA) **5382**
Studies in the Novel (USA) **5382**
Studies in Theatre and Performance (GBR) **8480**
Studies in Twentieth and Twenty-First Century Literature (USA) **5382**
Studies on Neotropical Fauna and Environment (GBR) **964**
Studio Potter (USA) **540**
Style (DeKalb) (USA) **5382**
Sub-Stance (USA) **5383**
Substance Abuse (USA) **2699**
Substance Use and Misuse (USA) **2699**
Successful Meetings (USA) **1844**
Suicide and Life-Threatening Behavior (USA) **7411**
Summit (CAN) **7471**
Sunset (USA) **3989**
Superlattices and Microstructures (GBR) **2081**
Supermarket News (USA) **3681**
Supervision (USA) **1709**
Supplier Selection & Management Report (USA) **1845**
Supply Chain Management (GBR) **1796**
Supply Chain Management Review (USA) **1796**
Supply House Times (USA) **4127**
Supply Management (GBR) **1845**
Support for Learning (GBR) **3047**
Supramolecular Chemistry (CHE) **2081**
Surface Design (USA) **520**
Surface Review and Letters (SGP) **3358**
Surgery (USA) **6259**
Surgical Infections (USA) **6260**
Surgical Practice (AUS) **6260**
Survey of Current Business (USA) **1521**
Surveying and Land Information Science (USA) **4030**
Surveys in Geophysics (NLD) **2790**
Survival (Abingdon) (GBR) **7268**
Sustainable Facility (USA) **3148**
Swiss Journal of Psychology (CHE) **7411**
Symbolae Osloenses (GBR) **2241**
Symbolic Interaction (USA) **8008**
Symploke (USA) **4477**
Symposium (USA) **5384**
Synlett (DEU) **2131**
Syntax (GBR) **5184**
Synthese (NLD) **6956**
Synthesis (DEU) **2131**
Synthesis and Reactivity in Inorganic, Metal-Organic, and Nano-Metal Chemistry (USA) **2141**
Synthetic Communications (USA) **2131**
Syracuse Journal of International Law & Commerce (USA) **4942**
Systematic and Applied Microbiology (DEU) **896**
Systematic Biology (USA) **707**
Systematic Botany (USA) **819**
Systematic Entomology Online (GBR) **860**
Systematic Parasitology (NLD) **707**
Systematics and Biodiversity (GBR) **707**
Systemic Practice and Action Research (USA) **1797**
Systems Biology in Reproductive Medicine (USA) **5719**
T+ D (USA) **1876**
T D & T (USA) **8480**
T D R (USA) **8480**
T H E Journal (USA) **2951**
The T Q M Journal (GBR) **1797**
T T J (GBR) **3716**
T W I C E (USA) **3114**
The Take - Charge Assistant (USA) **1797**
Target Marketing (USA) **1845**
The Tax Adviser (USA) **1947**
The Tax Executive (USA) **1947**
Tax Management Estates, Gifts and Trusts Journal (USA) **1655**
Tax Management International Journal (USA) **1948**
Tax Policy and the Economy (USA) **1949**
Teacher Education and Special Education (USA) **3048**
Teacher Education Quarterly (USA) **3084**
The Teacher Educator (USA) **3004**
Teacher Librarian (USA) **2918**
Teacher Magazine (USA) **3084**
Teachers and Teaching (GBR) **3084**
Teachers College Record (USA) **2918**
Teaching and Learning in Medicine (USA) **5720**
The Teaching Artist Journal (USA) **521**
Teaching Children Mathematics (USA) **3085**
Teaching Education (USA) **2918**
Teaching Exceptional Children Plus (USA) **3048**
Teaching History (GBR) **3085**
Teaching in Higher Education (GBR) **3004**
Teaching Mathematics and Its Applications (GBR) **5541**
Teaching of Psychology (USA) **7411**
Teaching Statistics (GBR) **2936**
Teaching Theology and Religion (GBR) **7687**
Team Performance Management (GBR) **1797**
Tech Capital (USA) **1394**
Tech Directions (USA) **3085**
Technical Communication (USA) **2340**
Technical Communication Quarterly (USA) **3085**
Technical Services Quarterly (USA) **5050**
Technicalities (USA) **5050**
Techniques (USA) **2918**
Technoetic Arts (GBR) **8441**
Technology Analysis & Strategic Management (GBR) **8442**
Technology and Culture (USA) **8442**
Technology and Disability (NLD) **4070**
Technology and Health Care (NLD) **5720**
Technology and Learning (USA) **2951**
Technology Meetings (USA) **8442**
Technology Review (USA) **7922**
The Technology Teacher (USA) **3085**
Technovation (GBR) **8443**
TechTrends (USA) **2951**
Teknillinen Korkeakoulu. Radiotieteen ja -tekniikan Laitos. Oppimateriaalisarja (FIN) **7052**
Telecom Markets (GBR) **1905**
Telecommunication Systems (NLD) **2372**
Telemedicine and e-Health (USA) **5832**
Telesis (Ottawa) (CAN) **2373**
Television & New Media (USA) **2396**
Television Broadcast Europe (GBR) **2397**
Television Business International (GBR) **2397**
Television Quarterly (USA) **2397**
Televisual (GBR) **2397**
Tellus. Series A: Dynamic Meteorology and Oceanography (USA) **6396**
Tellus. Series B: Chemical and Physical Meteorology (USA) **6396**
Temple International and Comparative Law Journal (USA) **4942**
Temple Law Review (USA) **4793**
Tempo (London, 1939) (GBR) **6622**
Tennessee Law Review (USA) **4794**
Tennessee Libraries (Online) (USA) **5050**
Tennis (USA) **8248**
Terra Nova Online (GBR) **2717**
Tertiary Education and Management (GBR) **3005**
Test & Measurement World (USA) **3332**
Texas Banking (USA) **1386**
Texas Business Review (USA) **1182**
Texas Intellectual Property Law Journal (USA) **4794**
Texas Law Review (USA) **4794**
Texas Library Journal (USA) **5050**
Texas Studies in Literature and Language (USA) **5386**
Text and Performance Quarterly (GBR) **5386**
Text & Talk (DEU) **4477**
Textile Research Journal (GBR) **8460**
Textile World (USA) **8461**
Textual Practice (GBR) **5387**
Texture, Stress and Microstructure (USA) **2771**
Theater (New Haven) (USA) **8481**
Theatre History Studies (USA) **8482**
Theatre Journal (Baltimore) (USA) **8482**
Theatre Research International (GBR) **8483**
Theatre Survey (GBR) **8483**
Theatre Topics (USA) **8483**
Theological Education (USA) **7689**
Theological Studies (USA) **7689**
Theology and Science (GBR) **7689**
Theology Today (USA) **7690**
Theoretical and Experimental Chemistry (USA) **2082**
Theoretical and Mathematical Physics (USA) **7043**
Theoretical Criminology (GBR) **2670**
Theoretical Foundations of Chemical Engineering (RUS) **3256**
Theoretical Inquiries in Law (ISR) **4795**
Theoretical Issues in Ergonomics Science (GBR) **3223**
Theoretical Medicine and Bioethics (NLD) **5721**
Theoretical Population Biology (USA) **707**
Theory and Decision (NLD) **8009**
Theory & Event (USA) **7188**
Theory and Practice of Logic Programming (GBR) **2510**
Theory & Psychology (GBR) **7412**
Theory and Research in Education (Online) (GBR) *see* Theory and Research in Education (Print). **2919**
Theory and Society (NLD) **8143**
Theory, Culture & Society (GBR) **8143**
Theory in Biosciences (DEU) **707**
Theory into Practice (USA) **2919**
Therapeutic Apheresis and Dialysis (JPN) **6275**
Therapie (FRA) **5721**
Thesis Eleven (GBR) **7188**
Thinking (USA) **6957**
Thinking & Reasoning (GBR) **7412**
Third Text (GBR) **522**
Third World Quarterly (GBR) **1606**
This Old House (USA) **1040**
Thomas Jefferson Law Review (USA) **4899**
Thomas M Cooley Journal of Practical and Clinical Law (USA) **4795**
Thorax (GBR) **6220**
Thyroid (USA) **5900**
Tijdschrift voor Economische en Sociale Geografie (GBR) **4031**

Tijdschrift voor Rechtsgeschiedenis (NLD) **4796**
Tikkun Magazine (USA) **5242**
Time (USA) **3990**
Time & Society (GBR) **8144**
Time for Kids News Scoop (USA) **2217**
Time for Kids World Report (USA) **2217**
Tissue and Cell (GBR) **836**
Tissue Antigens (DNK) **5722**
Tissue Engineering. Part A. Tissue Engineering (USA) **751**
The Tizard Learning Disability Review (GBR) **6188**
Tobacco Retailer (USA) **8488**
Today's Catholic Teacher (USA) **2920**
Tok Blong Pasifik (CAN) **8010**
Tolkien Studies (USA) **5389**
Tooling & Production (USA) **5460**
Topics in Catalysis (NLD) **2082**
Topics in Early Childhood Special Education (USA) **3048**
Topoi (NLD) **6957**
Total Health (USA) **6670**
Total Quality Management & Business Excellence (Online) (GBR) **1798**
T'oung Pao (NLD) **562**
Tourism and Hospitality Planning & Development (GBR) **1798**
Tourism and Hospitality Research (GBR) **8763**
Tourism Geographies (GBR) **8763**
Tourist Studies (GBR) **8764**
Touro Law Review (USA) **4797**
Town & Country (New York) (USA) **3991**
Town Planning Review (GBR) **4428**
Toxicologic Pathology (USA) **3501**
Toxicological and Environmental Chemistry (CHE) **3502**
Toxicological Sciences (GBR) **3502**
Toxicology and Applied Pharmacology (USA) **3502**
Toxicology and Industrial Health (GBR) **3502**
Toxicology Mechanisms and Methods (USA) **3503**
Toxin Reviews (USA) **6883**
Trade Finance (GBR) **1387**
Traders Magazine (USA) **1387**
Tradeshow Week (USA) **36**
Traffic (DNK) **837**
Traffic Injury Prevention (USA) **3397**
Traffic World (USA) **8513**
Trailer Boats (USA) **8283**
Trailer / Body Builders (USA) **8676**
Trailer Life (USA) **8338**
Training (USA) **1798**
Training & Coaching Today (GBR) **1876**
Training & Management Development Methods (GBR) **1798**
Training Media Review (USA) **6704**
Trains (USA) **8626**
Transactions in G I S (GBR) **4031**
Transboundary and Emerging Diseases (Online) (DEU) *see* Transboundary and Emerging Diseases. **8809**
Transcultural Psychiatry (GBR) **6188**
Transformation (ZAF) **8010**
Transformations (Wayne) (USA) **8144**
Transfusion (USA) **5723**
Transfusion Medicine (GBR) **5942**
Transfusion Medicine and Hemotherapy (CHE) **5723**
Transgenic Research (NLD) **879**
Transition (USA) **5242**
Transition Metal Chemistry (NLD) **6335**
Translational Research (USA) **5911**
Transmission & Distribution World (USA) **3161**
Transplant Immunology (GBR) **5766**
Transplant Infectious Disease Online (DNK) **6261**
Transplant International (DEU) **5724**
Transport in Porous Media (NLD) **2083**
Transport Reviews (GBR) **8515**
Transport Theory and Statistical Physics (USA) **7044**
Transportation (NLD) **8515**
Transportation Journal (USA) **8516**
Transportation Planning and Technology (CHE) **8516**
Transportation Quarterly (USA) **8516**
Transportation Research. Part E: Logistics and Transportation Review (GBR) **8517**
Trauma (GBR) **6074**
Trauma, Violence & Abuse (USA) **6074**
Travel Agent (USA) **8765**
Travel Retailer International (GBR) **1846**
Travel Trade Gazette U K & Ireland (GBR) **8768**
TravelAge West (USA) **8768**
Treasury & Risk (USA) **1656**
Treasury Bulletin (USA) **1387**
Trends in Organized Crime (USA) **2670**
Trial (USA) **4966**
Triangle Business Journal (Greensboro) (USA) **1184**
Triangle Business Journal (Raleigh) (USA) **1184**
Tribal Art (USA) **6538**
Tribology & Lubrication Technology (USA) **3398**
Tribology Letters (NLD) **3359**
Tribology Transactions (USA) **3257**
The Tribune (New York) (USA) **8886**
Tribune Business Weekly (USA) **1184**
Tricycle (USA) **7702**
TriQuarterly (USA) **5243**
Tropical Animal Health and Production (NLD) **8809**
Tropical Doctor (GBR) **5827**
Tropical Medicine & International Health (GBR) **5827**
Trustee (USA) **4112**
Trusts & Estates (USA) **1656**
Tuberculosis (GBR) **6220**
Tufts University Health & Nutrition Letter (USA) **6670**
Tulsa Journal of Comparative & International Law (USA) **4942**
Tumor Biology (CHE) **6035**
Tunnels & Tunnelling International (GBR) **3286**
Twentieth Century British History (GBR) **4274**
Twentieth Century Literature (USA) **5391**
Twentieth Century Music (GBR) **6625**
Twin Research and Human Genetics (GBR) **879**
U K Gas Report (GBR) **3148**
U M A P Journal (USA) **5542**
U M K C Law Review (USA) **4799**
U N Chronicle (USA) **7269**
U N L V Gaming Research & Review Journal (USA) **8213**
U S A Today (Valley Stream) (USA) **2921**
U S Banker (USA) **1657**
U S Catholic (USA) **7821**
U.S. Department of Energy. Energy Information Administration. Monthly Energy Review (Online) (USA) **3162**
U.S. Library of Congress. Information Bulletin (USA) **5052**
U S Naval Institute. Proceedings (USA) **6450**
U.S. News & World Report Digital Edition (USA) *see* U S News & World Report. **3991**
Ukrainian Mathematical Journal (USA) **5543**
Ultrasonic Imaging (USA) **6209**
Ultrasound in Obstetrics and Gynecology (GBR) **6005**
Ultrastructural Pathology (USA) **6036**
Universidad de Granada. Cuadernos de Arte (ESP) **523**
Universite de Sherbrooke. Revue de Droit (CAN) **4802**
The University of Baltimore Intellectual Property Law Journal (USA) **6759**
University of Baltimore Journal of Environmental Law (USA) **4803**
University of Chicago Law Review (USA) **4803**
University of Colorado Law Review (USA) **4803**
University of Detroit Mercy Law Review (USA) **4804**
University of Kansas Law Review (USA) **4804**
University of La Verne Law Review (USA) **4915**
University of London. School of Oriental and African Studies. Bulletin (GBR) **4480**
University of Miami Law Review (USA) **4804**
University of New South Wales Law Journal (AUS) **4804**
University of Pittsburgh Law Review (USA) **4805**
University of San Francisco Law Review (USA) **4805**
University of Toronto Faculty of Law Review (CAN) **4805**
University of Toronto Law Journal (CAN) **4805**
University of Toronto Quarterly (CAN) **4481**
Update (Online) (USA) **6626**
The Upstart Crow (USA) **5394**
Urban Affairs Review (USA) **4429**
Urban Design International (GBR) **4430**
Urban Ecosystems (USA) **4430**
Urban Education (USA) **2924**
Urban Forestry & Urban Greening (DEU) **3707**
Urban Forum (NLD) **4430**
Urban History (GBR) **4276**
Urban Policy and Research (AUS) **4430**
The Urban Review (USA) **3035**
Urban Studies (GBR) **4430**
Urgent Communications (USA) **2364**
Urologia Internationalis (CHE) **6275**
Us Weekly (USA) **3991**
User Modeling and User-Adapted Interaction (NLD) **2951**
Utah Bar Journal (USA) **4806**
Utility Automation & Engineering T&D (USA) **3149**
Utility Week (GBR) **3149**
Utne Reader (USA) **3991**
Utopian Studies (USA) **6959**
V F W Magazine (USA) **6451**
V I N E (London, Online) (GBR) *see* V I N E. **5064**
V L S I Design (USA) **2474**
Valparaiso University Law Review (USA) **4806**
Value in Health (USA) **6884**
Vanderbilt Journal of Transnational Law (USA) **4944**
Vanderbilt Law Review (USA) **4807**
Variety (USA) **8484**
Vascular Medicine (GBR) **5801**
Vector Borne and Zoonotic Diseases (USA) **5728**
Vegetarian Journal (USA) **6670**
Vegetarian Times (USA) **6670**
Vehicle System Dynamics (NLD) **3399**
The Velvet Light Trap (USA) **6516**
Venture Capital (GBR) **1389**
Venture Capital Journal (USA) **1658**
Verhaltenstherapie (CHE) **6189**
Vermont Business Magazine (USA) **1191**
Vermont Law Review (USA) **4808**
Veterinary Anaesthesia and Analgesia (GBR) **8811**
Veterinary and Comparative Oncology (GBR) **8811**
Veterinary Dermatology (GBR) **8812**
The Veterinary Journal (GBR) **8812**
Veterinary Medicine (USA) **8813**
Veterinary Ophthalmology (GBR) **8813**
Veterinary Radiology & Ultrasound (USA) **8813**
Veterinary Research Communications (NLD) **8814**
Veterinary Surgery (USA) **8814**
Vetus Testamentum (NLD) **7731**
Victoria University of Wellington Law Review (NZL) **4808**
Victorian Literature and Culture (GBR) **5395**
Victorian Periodicals Review (USA) **5395**
Victorian Poetry (USA) **5437**
Victorian Studies (USA) **4481**
Video Business (USA) **2403**
Videography (USA) **2404**
Vietnam Investment Review (VNM) **1192**
Vigiliae Christianae (NLD) **7692**
Violence Against Women (USA) **8146**
Viral Immunology (USA) **5766**
Virginia Journal of Social Policy & the Law (USA) **4809**
Virginia Libraries (USA) **5054**
Virginia Magazine of History and Biography (USA) **4317**
Virginia Quarterly Review (USA) **5244**
Virology (USA) **897**
Virus Genes (USA) **897**
Visible Language (USA) **5194**
Vision Systems Design (USA) **3226**
Visual Anthropology (USA) **360**
Visual Cognition (GBR) **7414**
Visual Communication (GBR) **2343**
Visual Impairment Research (GBR) **4086**
Visual Neuroscience (GBR) **6189**
Visual Resources (GBR) **525**
Visual Studies (GBR) **8146**
Viszeralmedizin (CHE) **5932**
Vital Speeches of the Day (USA) **4585**
Vivarium (NLD) **4277**
Voennaya Mysl' (RUS) **6452**
Voice of Youth Advocates (USA) **2171**
The Volta Review (USA) **4076**
Voluntas (USA) **8077**
Vox Sanguinis (CHE) **5767**
W & V (DEU) **37**
W E F Highlights (USA) **3474**
W I N News (USA) **8904**
W T Online (USA) *see* Washington Technology. **7486**
W W D (USA) **2250**
Wall Street & Technology (USA) **1394**
The Wall Street Journal Europe (BEL) **1390**
Wall Street Journal Online (USA) *see* Wall Street Journal (Central Edition). **1390**
Wall Street Journal Online (USA) *see* Wall Street Journal (Eastern Edition). **1390**
Wall Street Journal Online (USA) *see* Wall Street Journal (Western Edition). **1390**
Wall Street Letter (USA) **1658**
Wallraf-Richartz-Jahrbuch (DEU) **525**
Walls & Ceilings (USA) **1042**
Walters Art Museum. Journal (USA) **525**
War in History (GBR) **6453**
Ward's AutoWorld (USA) **8611**
Ward's Dealer Business (USA) **8611**
Washington and Lee Law Review (USA) **4810**
Washington Business Journal (USA) **1193**
The Washington Monthly (USA) **7193**
The Washington Quarterly (USA) **7273**
Washington Report on Middle East Affairs (USA) **7273**
Washington University. Journal of Law and Policy (USA) **4811**
Washington University. Law Review (USA) **4811**
Washingtonian (USA) **3992**
Waste Age (USA) **3513**
Waste & Recycling News (USA) **3513**
Waste Management and Research (GBR) **3513**
Water, Air and Soil Pollution (NLD) **3492**
Water, Air & Soil Pollution: Focus (NLD) **3492**
Water Environment & Technology (USA) **3492**
Water Environment Research (USA) **3493**
Water Quality Research Journal of Canada (CAN) **3493**
Water Resources (RUS) **8838**
Water Resources Management (NLD) **8840**
Waterworld (USA) **8841**
Wearables Business (USA) **2250**
Weather and Forecasting (USA) **6398**
Weatherwise (USA) **6398**
Web Intelligence and Agent Systems (NLD) **2457**
Weed Biology and Management (AUS) **258**
Weed Research (GBR) **258**
Weed Science (USA) **258**
Weed Technology (USA) **258**
Weekly Epidemiological Record (CHE) **7545**
Welding Journal (USA) **6345**
Die Welt des Islams (NLD) **7717**
WeMedia Magazine (USA) **4070**
Werk - Bauen & Wohnen (CHE) **461**
Westchester County Business Journal (USA) **1524**
Western Farm Press (USA) **170**
Western Folklore (USA) **3624**
Western Journal of Communication (USA) **5195**
Western Journal of Nursing Research (USA) **5984**
Western New England Law Review (USA) **4812**
Wetlands (USA) **8842**
Wetlands Ecology and Management (NLD) **8842**
Wicazo Sa Review (USA) **6636**
Wichita Business Journal (USA) **1194**
Widener Law Journal (USA) **4853**
Wiener Medizinische Wochenschrift (AUT) **5730**
Wilderness and Environmental Medicine (USA) **5730**
Wildfire (Chicago) (USA) **3582**
Wildlife Research (AUS) **968**
William Mitchell Law Review (USA) **4814**
The Wilson Journal of Ornithology (USA) **917**
The Wilson Quarterly (USA) **5245**
Wire Journal International (USA) **3334**
Wireless Business Forecast (Online) (USA) **2535**
Wireless Design and Development (USA) **3334**
Wireless Networks (NLD) **2344**
Wireless Personal Communications (NLD) **2365**
Wireless Satellite and Broadcasting Telecommunications (USA) **2345**
Wireless Week (USA) **2345**
Wisconsin International Law Journal (USA) **4944**
Wisconsin Journal of Law, Gender & Society (USA) **4815**
Wisconsin Law Review (USA) **4815**
Woman's Art Journal (USA) **527**
Woman's Day (USA) **4369**
Women (GBR) **8904**
Women & Criminal Justice (USA) **4900**
Women & Environments International Magazine (CAN) **8904**
Women & Health (USA) **8849**
Women and Language (USA) **5195**
Women and Music (USA) **6628**
Women & Therapy (USA) **7415**
Women Artists News Book Review (USA) **527**
Women Envision (PHL) **8904**
Women in Business (USA) **1195**
Women in German Yearbook (USA) **8904**
Women in Higher Education (USA) **3010**
Women in Judaism (CAN) **7731**
The Women's Health Activist (USA) **8849**
Women's Health Letter (USA) **8849**
The Women's Review of Books (USA) **5245**
Women's Studies (CHE) **8905**
Women's Studies in Communication (USA) **8905**
Wood & Wood Products (USA) **3717**
Work (NLD) **6688**
Work and Occupations (USA) **8147**
Work and Stress (GBR) **7415**
Work Based Learning in Primary Care (GBR) **5731**
Work, Employment & Society (GBR) **8147**
Workbench (USA) **4439**
Workforce Management (USA) **1877**
Working U S A (USA) **1716**
Working with Older People (GBR) **8078**
Worklife (Kingston) (CAN) **1716**
Works Management (GBR) **1801**
World Affairs (Washington) (USA) **7274**
World Archaeology (GBR) **424**
The World Bank Economic Review (USA) **1525**
The World Bank Operations Evaluation Study (USA) **1195**
World Bank Research Observer (USA) **1391**
World Bank Working Paper (USA) **1608**
World Competition (NLD) **4944**
The World Economy (GBR) **1196**
World Englishes (GBR) **5196**
World Futures (USA) **6961**
World Health Organization. Bulletin (CHE) **5731**
World Health Organization Regional Publications. European Series (DNK) **7545**
World Insurance Report (GBR) **4528**
World Journal of Microbiology and Biotechnology (GBR) **771**
World Literature Today (USA) **5400**
World Oil (USA) **6797**
World Policy Journal (USA) **7274**
World Politics (USA) **7274**
World Today (GBR) **7275**
World Trade and Arbitration Materials (NLD) **1588**
World Trade Review (GBR) **1588**
World Trade: WT100 (USA) **1588**
World Watch (USA) **3475**
World Wide Web (New York) (NLD) **2569**
Worldviews (NLD) **3475**
Worldviews on Evidence-Based Nursing (USA) **5984**
Worship (USA) **7695**
Wound Repair and Regeneration (USA) **6075**
The Writer (USA) **5400**
Writer's Digest (USA) **4585**
The Writing Instructor (Online Edition) (USA) **2926**
Written Communication (USA) **2345**
Xenobiotica (GBR) **746**
Xenotransplantation (DNK) **6262**
Y C - Young Children (USA) **3088**
Yale Journal of Law & the Humanities (USA) **4483**
The Yale Journal on Regulation (USA) **4817**
The Yale Law Journal (USA) **4817**
The Yale Review (USA) **5246**
Yankee (USA) **3993**
Yearbook of Educational Law (USA) **4817**
Yearbook of New Zealand Jurisprudence (NZL) **4817**
Young (IND) **2172**
Young Adult Library Services (USA) **5055**
Youth & Society (USA) **2172**
Youth Markets Alert (USA) **1849**
Youth Violence and Juvenile Justice (USA) **2672**
Zebrafish (USA) **968**
Zeitschrift fuer Antikes Christentum (DEU) **7696**
Zeitschrift fuer die Alttestamentliche Wissenschaft (DEU) **7696**
Zeitschrift fuer die Neutestamentliche Wissenschaft und die Kunde der Aelteren Kirche (DEU) **7696**
Zeitschrift fuer Germanistische Linguistik (DEU) **5199**
Zeitschrift fuer Religions- und Geistesgeschichte (NLD) **7697**
Zeitschrift fuer Unternehmens- und Gesellschaftsrecht (DEU) **4819**
Zero - Un Informatique (Hebdomadaire) (FRA) **2551**
Zoologica Scripta (GBR) **969**
Zoologischer Anzeiger (DEU) **970**
Zoology (DEU) **970**
Zoonoses and Public Health (DEU) **8816**
Zygon (USA) **7697**
Zygote (GBR) **879**

Online Service

OhioLINK Ste 300, 2455 North Star Rd, Columbus, OH 43221 TEL 614-728-3600, FAX 614-728-3610, info@ohiolink.edu, http://www.ohiolink.edu/

A C M Communications in Computer Algebra (USA) **5549**
A C M Computing Surveys (USA) **2405**
A C M Journal of Computer Documentation (USA) **2541**
A C M Queue (USA) **2587**
A C M / S I G P L A N Notices (USA) **2504**
A C M S I GAda Ada Letters (USA) **2504**
A C M Transactions on Applied Perception (USA) **2405**
A C M Transactions on Architecture and Code Optimization (USA) **2466**
A C M Transactions on Asian Language Information Processing (USA) **5202**
A C M Transactions on Computational Logic (USA) **2405**
A C M Transactions on Computer - Human Interaction (USA) **2470**
A C M Transactions on Computer Systems (USA) **2519**
A C M Transactions on Computing Education (USA) **2822**
A C M Transactions on Database Systems (USA) **2529**
A C M Transactions on Embedded Computing Systems (USA) **2405**
A C M Transactions on Graphics (USA) **2483**
A C M Transactions on Information and System Security (USA) **2511**
A C M Transactions on Information Systems (USA) **1413**
A C M Transactions on Internet Technology (USA) **2552**
A C M Transactions on Mathematical Software (USA) **2587**
A C M Transactions on Modeling and Computer Simulation (USA) **2405**
A C M Transactions on Programming Languages and Systems (USA) **2504**
A C M Transactions on Software Engineering and Methodology (USA) **2587**
A C O G Clinical Review (USA) **5739**
A E Ue: International Journal of Electronics and Communication (DEU) **2310**
A I & Society (GBR) **2444**
A I Ch E Journal (USA) **3234**
A J S Review (GBR) **7717**
A N Z Journal of Surgery (AUS) **6234**
A P L Quote Quad (USA) **2574**
A Q Online (USA) *see* Academic Questions. **2965**
A R Q: Architectural Research Quarterly (GBR) **426**
A S A Bulletin (NLD) **4915**
A S H E Higher Education Report Series (USA) **2964**
Abacus (GBR) **1275**
Abdominal Imaging (USA) **5919**
About Campus (USA) **2965**
Academic Radiology (NLD) **6191**
Academie des Sciences. Comptes Rendus. Biologies (FRA) **649**
Academie des Sciences. Comptes Rendus. Chimie (FRA) **2048**
Academie des Sciences. Comptes Rendus. Geoscience (FRA) **7830**
Academie des Sciences. Comptes Rendus. Mathematique (FRA) **5464**
Academie des Sciences. Comptes Rendus. Mecanique (FRA) **3372**
Academie des Sciences. Comptes Rendus. Palevol (FRA) **6722**
Academie des Sciences. Comptes Rendus. Physique (FRA) **2132**
Academy of Natural Sciences of Philadelphia. Proceedings (USA) **7831**
Accessibility and Computing (USA) **4071**
Accident Analysis & Prevention (GBR) **7506**
Accounting and Finance (GBR) **1277**
Accounting, Auditing and Accountability Journal (GBR) **1277**
Accounting Forum (GBR) **1277**
Accounting, Organizations and Society (GBR) **1278**
Accounts of Chemical Research (USA) **2048**
Accreditation and Quality Assurance (DEU) **2096**
Acoustical Physics (RUS) **7086**
Acoustical Society of America. Journal (USA) **7086**
Acta Anaesthesiologica Scandinavica (DNK) **5768**
Acta Applicandae Mathematicae (NLD) **5464**
Acta Astronautica (GBR) **41**
Acta Biotheoretica (NLD) **649**
Acta Diabetologica (DEU) **5883**
Acta Ethologica Online (DEU) **649**
Acta Histochemica (DEU) **721**
Acta Informatica (DEU) **2541**
Acta Juridica Hungarica (HUN) **4609**
Acta Linguistica Hungarica (HUN) **5090**
Acta Materialia (GBR) **6303**
Acta Mathematica Hungarica (NLD) **5464**
Acta Mathematica Sinica (DEU) **5464**
Acta Mathematicae Applicatae Sinica (DEU) **5465**
Acta Mechanica (AUT) **3372**
Acta Mechanica Solida Sinica (CHN) **7057**
Acta Neurochirurgica (AUT) **6234**
Acta Neurologica Scandinavica (DNK) **6118**
Acta Neuropathologica (DEU) **6118**
Acta Neuropsychiatrica (DNK) **6118**
Acta Numerica (GBR) **5465**
Acta Obstetricia et Gynecologica Scandinavica (GBR) **5985**
Acta Oecologica (FRA) **650**
Acta Ophthamologica (Online) (DNK) **6037**
Acta Pathologica Microbiologica et Immunologica Scandinavica (DNK) **650**
Acta Physiologica (Online) (GBR) **918**
Acta Psychiatrica Scandinavica (GBR) **6119**
Acta Psychiatrica Scandinavica. Supplementum (DNK) **6119**
Acta Psychologica (NLD) **7330**
Acta Radiologica (GBR) **6192**
Acta Sociologica (NOR) **8085**
Acta Tropica (NLD) **5808**
Acta Zoologica Online (GBR) **930**
Action Research (GBR) **5567**
Active Learning in Higher Education (GBR) **2965**
Acute Pain (NLD) **5567**
Ad Hoc Networks (NLD) **2495**
Addiction (GBR) **2689**
Addictive Behaviors (GBR) **2690**
Additives for Polymers (GBR) **7090**
Administration and Policy in Mental Health and Mental Health Services Research (USA) **5567**
Administration & Society (USA) **7418**
Adsorption (USA) **3235**
Adult Education Quarterly (USA) **2938**
Advanced Ceramics Report (GBR) **2037**
Advanced Composites Bulletin (GBR) **7090**
Advanced Drug Delivery Reviews (NLD) **6819**
Advanced Engineering Informatics (GBR) **2445**
Advanced Engineering Materials (DEU) **3180**
Advanced Functional Materials (DEU) **2112**
Advanced Materials (DEU) **3335**
Advanced Micro- and Nanosystems (DEU) **2445**
Advanced Synthesis & Catalysis (DEU) **2048**
Advances in Applied Mathematics (USA) **5466**
Advances in Colloid and Interface Science (NLD) **2132**
Advances in Computational Mathematics (NLD) **5549**
Advances in Engineering Software (GBR) **3288**
Advances in Enzyme Regulation (GBR) **721**
Advances in Health Sciences Education (NLD) **5568**
Advances in Mathematics (USA) **5466**
Advances in Polymer Technology (USA) **7090**
Advances in Space Research (GBR) **41**
Advances in Textiles Technology (GBR) **8447**
Advances in Water Resources (GBR) **8817**
Advertising & Society Review (USA) **20**
Aequationes Mathematicae (CHE) **5467**
Aerobiologia (NLD) **651**
Aerosol Science and Technology (USA) **2049**
Aerospace Science and Technology (FRA) **43**
Aesthetic Plastic Surgery (USA) **6235**
Africa Confidential (GBR) **7102**
Africa Research Bulletin. Economic, Financial and Technical Series (GBR) **1435**
Africa Research Bulletin. Political, Social and Cultural Series (GBR) **7102**
Africa Today (USA) **7102**
African Affairs (GBR) **7103**
African and Asian Studies (NLD) **8086**
African Archaeological Review (USA) **371**
African Development Review (GBR) **1590**
African Journal of Ecology Online (GBR) **651**
Age and Ageing (GBR) **4038**
Ageing and Society (GBR) **4039**
Ageing International (USA) **4039**
Ageing Research Reviews (IRL) **4039**
Aggression and Violent Behavior (GBR) **7332**
Aggressive Behavior (USA) **7332**
Aging Cell (GBR) **827**
Agribusiness (New York) (USA) **191**
Agricultural and Forest Entomology (GBR) **837**
Agricultural and Forest Meteorology (NLD) **6346**
Agricultural Economics (USA) **192**
Agricultural Systems (NLD) **85**
Agricultural Water Management (NLD) **217**
Agriculture and Human Values (NLD) **85**
Agriculture, Ecosystems & Environment (NLD) **85**
Agroforestry Systems (NLD) **87**
Agronomy for Sustainable Development (FRA) **217**
Agronomy Journal (USA) **88**
AIDS & Behavior (USA) **5752**
Air & Space Law (NLD) **8534**
The Air Pollution Consultant (USA) **3482**
Aircraft Engineering and Aerospace Technology (GBR) **45**
Alcohol (New York) (USA) **2690**
Alcohol and Alcoholism (GBR) **2690**
Algebra and Logic (USA) **5467**
Algebra Colloquium (SGP) **5468**
Algebra Universalis (CHE) **5468**
Algebras and Representation Theory (NLD) **5468**
Algorithmica (USA) **2406**
Alimentary Pharmacology and Therapeutics (GBR) **5920**
Alimentary Pharmacology and Therapeutics. Supplement (GBR) **5920**
Allergology International (JPN) **5753**
Allergy (GBR) **5753**
Allergy. Supplement (GBR) **5754**
Alternatives to the High Cost of Litigation (USA) **4613**
Ambio Journal Online (SWE) *see* Ambio. **3402**
American Academy of Political and Social Science. Annals (USA) **7104**
American Annals of the Deaf (USA) **4071**
American Behavioral Scientist (USA) **7946**
The American Biology Teacher (USA) **652**
American Chemical Society. Journal (USA) **2049**
American College of Cardiology. Journal (USA) **5776**
American College of Radiology. Journal (USA) **6192**
American College of Surgeons. Journal (USA) **6235**
American Dietetic Association. Journal (USA) **6654**
American Fern Journal (USA) **774**
American Geriatrics Society. Journal (USA) **4040**
American Imago (USA) **6121**
American Indian Quarterly (USA) **6634**
American Jewish History (USA) **7718**
American Journal of Agricultural Economics (USA) **193**
The American Journal of Bioethics (USA) **862**
The American Journal of Cardiology (USA) **5776**
American Journal of Cardiovascular Drugs (NZL) **5776**
American Journal of Clinical Dermatology (NZL) **5871**
American Journal of Community Psychology (USA) **8086**
American Journal of Dance Therapy (USA) **2682**
American Journal of Distance Education (USA) **2938**
American Journal of Economics and Sociology (USA) **1059**
American Journal of Epidemiology (USA) **5572**
American Journal of Evaluation (USA) **7946**
American Journal of Gastroenterology (USA) **5920**
The American Journal of Geriatric Pharmacotherapy (USA) **6819**
American Journal of Hematology (USA) **5933**
American Journal of Human Biology (USA) **652**
American Journal of Hypertension (USA) **5776**
American Journal of Industrial Medicine (USA) **6672**
American Journal of Mathematics (USA) **5468**
American Journal of Medical Genetics. Part A (USA) **862**
American Journal of Medical Genetics. Part B: Neuropsychiatric Genetics (USA) **862**
American Journal of Medical Genetics. Part C: Seminars in Medical Genetics (USA) **862**
The American Journal of Medicine (USA) **5572**
The American Journal of Medicine. Supplement (USA) **5573**
American Journal of Ophthalmology (USA) **6038**
American Journal of Orthopsychiatry (USA) **7333**
American Journal of Perinatology (USA) **5985**
American Journal of Philology (USA) **5092**
American Journal of Physical Anthropology (USA) **324**
American Journal of Physics (USA) **7004**
American Journal of Political Science (USA) **7105**
American Journal of Preventive Medicine (USA) **5573**
American Journal of Primatology (USA) **931**
The American Journal of Psychoanalysis (USA) **7333**
American Journal of Reproductive Immunology Online (DNK) **5754**
The American Journal of Surgery (USA) **6235**
American Journal of Transplantation (Online) (DNK) **6236**
American Law and Economics Review (GBR) **4614**
American Literary History (USA) **5252**
American Literary Scholarship (USA) **5252**
American Literature (USA) **5252**
American Midland Naturalist (USA) **7834**
American Museum Novitates (USA) **931**
American Museum of Natural History. Bulletin (USA) **931**
American Philological Association. Transactions (USA) **2229**
American Political Science Review (GBR) **7105**
American Politics Research (USA) **7105**
American Psychologist (USA) **7333**
American Quarterly (USA) **4442**
American Review of Public Administration (USA) **7419**
American Society for Information Science and Technology. Journal (USA) **4989**
American Society for Mass Spectrometry. Journal (USA) **7073**
The American Sociologist (USA) **8087**
American Speech (USA) **5092**
The Americas (USA) **4283**
Amino Acids (AUT) **722**
Amphibia - Reptilia (NLD) **932**
Amsterdamer Beitraege zur Neueren Germanistik (NLD) **5253**
Anaerobe (GBR) **880**
Anaesthesia (Oxford) (GBR) **5768**
Der Anaesthesist (DEU) **5769**
Analog Integrated Circuits and Signal Processing (USA) **2465**
Analyses of Social Issues and Public Policy (USA) **8087**
Analysis (GBR) **6904**
Analysis in Theory and Applications (NLD) **5470**
Analysis Mathematica (HUN) **5470**
The Analyst (Online) (GBR) *see* The Analyst. **2097**
Analytica Chimica Acta (NLD) **2097**
Analytical and Bioanalytical Chemistry (DEU) **2097**
Analytical Biochemistry (USA) **722**
Analytical Chemistry (USA) **2098**
Anatomia, Histologia, Embryologia Online (DEU) **8792**
The Anatomical Record (USA) **652**
Anatomical Science International (JPN) **653**
Ancient Civilizations from Scythia to Siberia (NLD) **4179**
Ancient Mesoamerica (GBR) **4283**
Andrologia (DEU) **5574**
Anesthesia Progress (USA) **5834**
Angewandte Chemie (DEU) **2050**
Angewandte Chemie (International Edition) (DEU) **2050**
Angiogenesis (GBR) **6008**
Anglo-Saxon England (GBR) **4198**
Animal Behaviour (GBR) **932**
Animal Biology (NLD) **932**
Animal Cognition (DEU) **7334**
Animal Conservation (GBR) **2602**
Animal Feed Science and Technology (NLD) **270**
Animal Genetics (GBR) **862**
Animal Health Research Reviews (GBR) **8792**
Animal Reproduction Science (NLD) **278**
Animal Science Journal (AUS) **278**
Annalen der Physik (DEU) **7005**
Annales de Biologie Clinique (FRA) **653**
Annales de Cardiologie et d'Angeiologie (FRA) **5777**
Annales de Chimie, Science des Materiaux (FRA) **2050**
Annales de Chirurgie Plastique Esthetique (FRA) **6236**
Annales de Paleontologie (FRA) **6723**
Annales Francaises d'Anesthesie et de Reanimation (FRA) **5770**
Annales Geophysicae (DEU) **2777**
Annales Henri Poincare (CHE) **7005**
Annales Medico-Psychologiques, Revue Psychiatrique (FRA) *see* Annales Medico-Psychologiques. **7334**
Annales Scientifiques de l'Ecole Normale Superieure (FRA) **5470**
Annali di Matematica Pura ed Applicata (DEU) **5470**
Annals of Behavioral Medicine (USA) **5575**
Annals of Biomedical Engineering (USA) **5575**
Annals of Botany (GBR) **775**
Annals of Clinical Biochemistry (GBR) **722**
Annals of Clinical Microbiology and Antimicrobials (GBR) **881**
Annals of Clinical Psychiatry (USA) **6123**
Annals of Combinatorics (CHE) **5470**
Annals of Epidemiology (USA) **7507**
Annals of Finance (DEU) **1307**
Annals of Forest Science Online (FRA) *see* Annals of Forest Science. **3683**
Annals of General Psychiatry (GBR) **6123**
Annals of Global Analysis and Geometry (NLD) **5471**
Annals of Hematology (DEU) **5933**
Annals of Human Genetics (GBR) **862**
Annals of Mathematics and Artificial Intelligence (NLD) **2445**
Annals of Neurology (USA) **6123**
Annals of Noninvasive Electrocardiology (USA) **5777**
Annals of Nuclear Energy (GBR) **3164**
Annals of Occupational Hygiene (GBR) **6672**
Annals of Oncology (GBR) **6008**
Annals of Operations Research (NLD) **2406**
Annals of Physical and Rehabilitation Medicine (FRA) **6106**
Annals of Physics (USA) **7005**
Annals of Public and Cooperative Economics (GBR) **1422**
Annals of Pure and Applied Logic (NLD) **5471**
The Annals of Regional Science (DEU) **1060**
The Annals of Thoracic Surgery (USA) **6237**
Annals of Tourism Research (GBR) **8683**
Annals of Vascular Surgery (USA) **6237**
Annual Bulletin of Historical Literature (GBR) **4199**
Annual Review of Applied Linguistics (GBR) **5094**
Annual Reviews in Control (GBR) **2505**
Antarctic Science (GBR) **653**
Anthropological Quarterly (USA) **325**
L' Anthropologie (FRA) **326**
Anthropology Today (GBR) **327**
Anti-Corrosion Methods and Materials (GBR) **6305**
Antipode (USA) **3998**
Antiviral Research (NLD) **881**
Antonie van Leeuwenhoek (NLD) **756**
Apoptosis (USA) **827**
Appetite (GBR) **6655**
Applicable Algebra in Engineering, Communication and Computing (DEU) **5550**
Applications of Mathematics (New York, 1956) (USA) **5471**
Applied Acoustics (GBR) **7086**
Applied and Computational Harmonic Analysis (USA) **5472**
Applied and Preventive Psychology (GBR) **7335**
Applied Animal Behaviour Science (NLD) **933**
Applied Biochemistry and Biotechnology (USA) **723**
Applied Biochemistry and Microbiology (RUS) **723**
Applied Catalysis A: General (NLD) **3236**
Applied Catalysis B: Environmental (NLD) **3236**
Applied Categorical Structures (NLD) **5550**
Applied Clay Science (NLD) **2724**
Applied Cognitive Psychology (GBR) **7335**
Applied Composite Materials (NLD) **3341**
Applied Developmental Science (USA) **7335**
Applied Economic Perspectives and Policy (USA) **193**
Applied Energy (GBR) **3124**
Applied Ergonomics (GBR) **3181**
Applied Geochemistry (GBR) **2724**
Applied Geography (GBR) **3998**
Applied Intelligence (USA) **2446**
Applied Linguistics (GBR) **5095**
Applied Mathematical Modelling (USA) **5550**
Applied Mathematics and Computation (USA) **5472**
Applied Mathematics and Mechanics (NLD) **5472**
Applied Mathematics and Optimization (USA) **5472**
Applied Mathematics Letters (GBR) **5472**
Applied Measurement in Education (USA) **2827**
Applied Microbiology and Biotechnology (DEU) **756**
Applied Neuropsychology (USA) **6123**
Applied Numerical Mathematics (NLD) **5550**

Online Service

Link to your serials resources and content with ulrichsweb.com

Energy & Fuels (USA) **3130**
Energy Conversion and Management (GBR) **3130**
Energy Economics (NLD) **3130**
Energy Exploration & Exploitation (GBR) **3131**
Energy Policy (GBR) **3132**
Engineering Analysis with Boundary Elements (GBR) **3377**
Engineering Applications of Artificial Intelligence (GBR) **2448**
Engineering Computations (GBR) **3291**
Engineering, Construction and Architectural Management (GBR) **1006**
Engineering Failure Analysis (GBR) **3344**
Engineering Fracture Mechanics (GBR) **3344**
Engineering Geology (NLD) **3266**
Engineering in Life Sciences (DEU) **763**
Engineering Structures (GBR) **3266**
Engineering with Computers (GBR) **3291**
English for Specific Purposes (GBR) **5114**
The English Historical Review (GBR) **4217**
English Language and Linguistics (GBR) **5115**
English Literary Renaissance (GBR) **5290**
English Today (GBR) **5115**
Enterprise and Society (USA) **1105**
Entomologia Experimentalis et Applicata (NLD) **844**
Entomologica Americana (USA) **844**
Entomological Society of America. Annals (USA) **845**
Entrepreneurship: Theory and Practice (USA) **1960**
Environment and Behavior (USA) **8100**
Environment and Development Economics (GBR) **3420**
Environment, Development and Sustainability (NLD) **3421**
Environment International (GBR) **3421**
Environmental and Ecological Statistics (USA) **3478**
Environmental and Experimental Botany (NLD) **786**
Environmental and Molecular Mutagenesis (USA) **866**
Environmental and Resource Economics (NLD) **3422**
Environmental Biology of Fishes (NLD) **941**
Environmental Chemistry Letters (DEU) **2061**
Environmental Conservation (GBR) **3423**
Environmental Entomology (USA) **847**
Environmental Fluid Mechanics (Dordrecht, 2001) (NLD) **2707**
Environmental Forensics (USA) **3506**
Environmental Geochemistry and Health (NLD) **3424**
Environmental Geology (DEU) **2733**
Environmental Geosciences (USA) **3424**
Environmental Hazards (GBR) **3425**
Environmental Health: A Global Access Science Source (GBR) **7515**
Environmental Impact Assessment Review (USA) **3425**
Environmental Law and Management (GBR) **4667**
Environmental Management (New York) (USA) **3426**
Environmental Microbiology (GBR) **884**
Environmental Modeling & Assessment (NLD) **3482**
Environmental Modelling & Software (GBR) **3482**
Environmental Monitoring and Assessment (NLD) **3426**
Environmental Policy and Governance (Online) (GBR) *see* Environmental Policy and Governance. **3427**
Environmental Pollution (GBR) **3486**
Environmental Progress & Sustainable Energy (USA) **3427**
Environmental Quality Management (USA) **3428**
Environmental Research (USA) **3428**
Environmental Science & Policy (USA) **3428**
Environmental Science & Technology (Washington) (USA) **3429**
Environmental Toxicology (Online Edition) (USA) *see* Environmental Toxicology (Print Edition). **3496**
Environmental Toxicology and Chemistry (USA) **3497**
Environmental Toxicology and Pharmacology (NLD) **3497**
The Environmentalist (USA) **3429**
Environmetrics (GBR) **3430**
Enzyme and Microbial Technology (USA) **763**
Epidemiologic Perspectives & Innovations (GBR) **7516**
Epidemiology and Infection (GBR) **885**
Epilepsia (USA) **6138**
Epilepsy & Behavior (USA) **5610**
Epilepsy Currents (USA) **6138**
Epilepsy Research (NLD) **6138**
Equality, Diversity and Inclusion (GBR) **8895**
Ergodic Theory and Dynamical Systems (GBR) **5486**
Erkenntnis (NLD) **6916**
Erwerbs - Obstbau (DEU) **108**
Esophagus (JPN) **5923**
Essays in Criticism (GBR) **5291**
Essays in Medieval Studies (USA) **4218**
Estuarine, Coastal and Shelf Science (GBR) **2804**
Ethical Theory and Moral Practice (NLD) **6917**
Ethics & Behavior (USA) **7355**
Ethics and Information Technology (NLD) **5008**
Ethics & the Environment (GBR) **6917**
Ethik in der Medizin (DEU) **6918**
Ethnography (GBR) **337**
Ethnohistory (USA) **337**
Ethology Online (DEU) **942**
Euphytica (NLD) **229**
Eurasip Journal on Advances in Signal Processing (USA) **2470**
European Academy of Dermatology and Venereology. Journal (BEL) **5876**
European Academy of Dermatology and Venereology. Journal. Supplement (GBR) **5876**
European Archives of Oto-Rhino-Laryngology (DEU) **6079**
European Archives of Psychiatry and Clinical Neuroscience (DEU) **6139**
European Biophysics Journal (DEU) **753**
European Business Law Review (NLD) **4668**
European Business Organization Law Review (NLD) **4668**
European Business Review (Bingley) (GBR) **1107**
European Ceramic Society. Journal (GBR) **2040**
European Child & Adolescent Psychiatry (DEU) **6139**
European Eating Disorders Review (GBR) **7355**
European Economic Review (NLD) **1107**
European Electronics Markets Forecasts (GBR) **3099**
European Energy and Environmental Law Review (NLD) **4669**
European Financial Management (GBR) **1339**
European Food Research and Technology (DEU) **3669**
European Foreign Affairs Review (NLD) **7233**
European Heart Journal (Online) (GBR) **5786**
European Heart Journal Supplements (GBR) **5786**
European Journal of Agronomy (NLD) **229**
European Journal of Anaesthesiology (GBR) **5771**
European Journal of Applied Mathematics (GBR) **5486**
European Journal of Applied Physiology (DEU) **922**
European Journal of Cancer (GBR) **6019**
European Journal of Cancer Care Online (GBR) **6019**
European Journal of Cardio-Thoracic Surgery (NLD) **5786**
European Journal of Cardiovascular Nursing (NLD) **5958**
European Journal of Cell Biology (DEU) **832**
European Journal of Clinical Investigation (GBR) **5611**
European Journal of Clinical Microbiology & Infectious Diseases (DEU) **885**
European Journal of Clinical Pharmacology (DEU) **6838**
European Journal of Combinatorics (GBR) **5487**
European Journal of Communication (GBR) **8101**
European Journal of Crime, Criminal Law and Criminal Justice (NLD) **4889**
European Journal of Dental Education Online (DNK) **5843**
European Journal of East Asian Studies (NLD) **549**
European Journal of Education (GBR) **2855**
European Journal of Epidemiology (NLD) **5611**
European Journal of Forest Research (DEU) **3688**
European Journal of Haematology (DNK) **5936**
The European Journal of Health Economics (DEU) **5611**
European Journal of Health Law (NLD) **5611**
European Journal of Heart Failure (NLD) **5786**
European Journal of Immunology (DEU) **5758**
European Journal of Innovation Management (GBR) **1742**
European Journal of Inorganic Chemistry (DEU) **2115**
European Journal of Internal Medicine (USA) **5945**
European Journal of International Law (GBR) **4925**
European Journal of International Relations (GBR) **7234**
European Journal of Law and Economics (USA) **1107**
European Journal of Law Reform (NLD) **4669**
European Journal of Lipid Science and Technology (DEU) **3243**
European Journal of Marketing (GBR) **1816**
European Journal of Mechanics A - Solids (FRA) **7058**
European Journal of Mechanics B - Fluids (FRA) **7058**
European Journal of Medical Genetics (FRA) **866**
European Journal of Medicinal Chemistry (FRA) **731**
European Journal of Migration and Law (NLD) **4925**
European Journal of Neurology (USA) **6139**
European Journal of Neuroscience (GBR) **6139**
European Journal of Nuclear Medicine and Molecular Imaging (DEU) **6196**
European Journal of Nutrition (DEU) **6658**
European Journal of Obstetrics & Gynecology and Reproductive Biology (IRL) **5990**
European Journal of Operational Research (NLD) **1742**
European Journal of Organic Chemistry (DEU) **2122**
European Journal of Orthodontics (GBR) **5844**
European Journal of Orthopaedic Surgery & Traumatology (FRA) **6060**
European Journal of Pediatric Surgery (DEU) **6243**
European Journal of Pediatrics (DEU) **6091**
European Journal of Personality (GBR) **7355**
European Journal of Pharmaceutical Sciences (NLD) **6838**
European Journal of Pharmaceutics and Biopharmaceutics (NLD) **6838**
European Journal of Pharmacology (NLD) **6838**
European Journal of Philosophy (GBR) **6918**
European Journal of Phycology (GBR) **787**
European Journal of Physics (GBR) **7011**
European Journal of Plant Pathology (NLD) **787**
European Journal of Plastic Surgery (DEU) **6243**
European Journal of Political Economy (NLD) **7134**
European Journal of Political Research (NLD) **7134**
European Journal of Political Theory (GBR) **7134**
European Journal of Population (NLD) **7306**
European Journal of Protistology (DEU) **6724**
European Journal of Psychological Assessment (USA) **7356**
European Journal of Public Health (GBR) **7516**
European Journal of Radiology (IRL) **6196**
European Journal of Radiology Extra (USA) **6196**
European Journal of Social Psychology (GBR) **7356**
European Journal of Social Security (BEL) **4502**
European Journal of Social Theory (GBR) **8101**
European Journal of Soil Biology (FRA) **672**
European Journal of Soil Science (GBR) **229**
European Journal of Trauma and Emergency Surgery (DEU) **6060**
European Journal of Ultrasound (IRL) **6196**
European Journal of Wildlife Research (DEU) **319**
European Journal of Wood and Wood Industries (Online) (DEU) *see* European Journal of Wood and Wood Industries (Print). **3711**
European Journal on Criminal Policy and Research (NLD) **2651**
European Law Journal (GBR) **4925**
European Management Journal (GBR) **1742**
European Mathematical Society. Journal (DEU) **5487**
European Neuropsychopharmacology (NLD) **6140**
European Physical Education Review (GBR) **3061**
European Physical Journal A. Hadrons and Nuclei (DEU) **7065**
European Physical Journal B. Condensed Matter and Complex Systems (DEU) **7011**
European Physical Journal C. Particles and Fields (DEU) **7011**
European Physical Journal D. Atomic, Molecular, Optical and Plasma Physics (FRA) **7011**
European Physical Journal E. Soft Matter (FRA) **7011**
European Polymer Journal (GBR) **2123**
European Psychiatry (FRA) **6140**
European Psychologist (USA) **7356**
European Public Law (NLD) **4925**
European Radiology (DEU) **6196**
European Review (GBR) **7853**
European Review of Agricultural Economics (GBR) **197**
European Review of Economic History (GBR) **1541**
European Review of Private Law (NLD) **4925**
European Sociological Review (GBR) **8101**
European Spine Journal (DEU) **6243**
European Studies (NLD) **7234**
European Surgery Online (AUT) **6243**
European Transactions on Electrical Power (GBR) **3308**
European Union Politics (GBR) **7234**
European Urology (CHE) **6268**
European Urology Supplements (NLD) **6268**
Europhysics News (FRA) **7012**
Evaluation and Program Planning (GBR) **7963**
Evolution (USA) **866**
Evolution & Development Online (USA) **672**
Evolution and Human Behavior (USA) **942**
L' Evolution Psychiatrique (FRA) **6140**
Evolutionary Anthropology (USA) **339**
Evolutionary Ecology (NLD) **3431**
Exceptionality (USA) **3040**
Excerpta Medica. Section 35: Occupational Health and Industrial Medicine (NLD) **5746**
Experimental Agriculture (GBR) **109**
Experimental & Applied Acarology (NLD) **942**
Experimental and Clinical Endocrinology and Diabetes (DEU) **5892**
Experimental and Clinical Psychopharmacology (USA) **7356**
Experimental and Molecular Pathology (USA) **5612**
Experimental Astronomy (NLD) **574**
Experimental Brain Research (DEU) **6140**
Experimental Cell Research (USA) **832**
Experimental Dermatology Online (GBR) **5876**
Experimental Economics (USA) **1541**
Experimental Eye Research (GBR) **6041**
Experimental Gerontology (USA) **4044**
Experimental Hematology (USA) **5936**
Experimental Neurology (USA) **6140**
Experimental Parasitology (USA) **5813**
Experimental Physiology (GBR) **922**
Experimental Psychology (USA) **7357**
Experimental Thermal and Fluid Science (USA) **3192**
Experiments in Fluids (DEU) **3377**
Expert Reviews in Molecular Medicine (GBR) **5945**
Expert Systems (GBR) **2448**
Expert Systems with Applications (GBR) **2448**
Exploration & Mining Geology (CAN) **2733**
Explorations in Economic History (USA) **1541**
Extremes (USA) **8369**
Extremophiles (JPN) **764**
The F E B S Journal (Online) (GBR) **732**
F E B S Letters (NLD) **732**
F E M S Immunology and Medical Microbiology (GBR) **885**
F E M S Microbiology Ecology (GBR) **885**
F E M S Microbiology Letters (GBR) **885**
F E M S Microbiology Reviews (GBR) **885**
Facial Plastic Surgery (USA) **6243**
Facies (DEU) **2707**
Facilities (GBR) **1007**
Familial Cancer (NLD) **6019**
Families, Systems, & Health (USA) **5613**
Family & Consumer Sciences Research Journal (USA) **4357**
The Family Journal (USA) **7357**
Family Practice (GBR) **5613**
Faraday Discussions (Online) (GBR) *see* Faraday Discussions. **2135**
Fatigue & Fracture of Engineering Materials and Structures (GBR) **3192**
Feddes Repertorium (DEU) **787**
Federation of European Microbiological Societies Yeast Research Online (GBR) *see* F E M S Yeast Research. **886**
Feminism & Psychology (GBR) **7357**
Feminist Legal Studies (NLD) **4673**
Fertility and Sterility (USA) **5990**
Fetal and Maternal Medicine Review (GBR) **5990**
Few-Body Systems (AUT) **7012**
Fibre Chemistry (USA) **8451**
Field Crops Research (NLD) **231**
Film & History (USA) **6498**
Filtration Industry Analyst (GBR) **3367**
Filtration + Separation (GBR) **3244**
Finance and Stochastics (DEU) **1343**
Finance Research Letters (USA) **1343**
Financial Accountability & Management (GBR) **1924**
Financial History Review (GBR) **1344**
Financial Markets, Institutions and Instruments (USA) **1344**
The Financial Review (Statesboro) (USA) **1345**
Financial Services Review (GBR) **1345**
Finite Elements in Analysis and Design (NLD) **3291**
Finite Fields and Their Applications (USA) **5488**
Fire and Materials (GBR) **3344**
Fire Safety Journal (GBR) **3578**
Fire Technology (USA) **3578**
First Break Online (NLD) **2780**
First Language (GBR) **5119**
Fish and Fisheries (GBR) **943**
Fish and Shellfish Immunology (GBR) **943**
Fish Physiology & Biochemistry (NLD) **943**
Fisheries Management & Ecology Online (GBR) **3592**
Fisheries Oceanography Online (GBR) **3592**
Fisheries Research (NLD) **3592**
Fisheries Science (AUS) **3593**
Fitoterapia (ITA) **788**
Flavour and Fragrance Journal (GBR) **2123**
Flexible Services and Manufacturing Journal (USA) **3344**
Florida Entomologist (USA) **847**
Flow Measurement and Instrumentation (GBR) **4486**
Flow, Turbulence and Combustion (NLD) **7855**
Fluid Dynamics (RUS) **7058**
Fluid Dynamics Research (NLD) **3361**
Fluid Phase Equilibria (NLD) **2135**
Focus on Catalysts (USA) **2094**
Focus on Pigments (USA) **6722**
Focus on Powder Coatings (USA) **6722**
Focus on Surfactants (USA) **2094**
Food and Chemical Toxicology (GBR) **3497**
Food Chemistry (GBR) **2061**
Food Control (GBR) **3638**
Food, Cosmetics and Drug Packaging (GBR) **6710**
Food Hydrocolloids (NLD) **3639**
Food Microbiology (GBR) **886**
Food Policy (GBR) **198**
Food Quality and Preference (GBR) **3641**
Food Research International (GBR) **3641**
Foot and Ankle Surgery (GBR) **6244**
Forensic Science International (IRL) **5913**
Foresight (Cambridge) (GBR) **8422**
Forest Ecology and Management (NLD) **3688**
Forest Pathology Online (DEU) **3689**
Forest Policy and Economics (NLD) **3689**
Forestry (GBR) **3690**
Formal Aspects of Computing (GBR) **2418**
Formal Methods in System Design (USA) **2520**
Forschung (DEU) **7855**
Forschung im Ingenieurwesen (DEU) **3192**
Fortran Forum (USA) **2506**
Fortschritte der Physik (DEU) **7013**
The Forum (USA) **7136**
Forum der Psychoanalyse (DEU) **7357**
Forum for Modern Language Studies (GBR) **5120**
Foundations of Chemistry (NLD) **2062**
Foundations of Computational Mathematics (USA) **5552**
Foundations of Physics (USA) **7013**
Foundations of Science (NLD) **7856**
Fourth Genre (USA) **5297**
Franklin Institute. Journal (GBR) **7013**
Free Radical Biology & Medicine (USA) **673**
French Colonial History (USA) **4221**
French Forum (USA) **5217**
French Historical Studies (USA) **4222**
French History (GBR) **4222**
French Literature Series (NLD) **5407**
French Studies (GBR) **5298**
Freshwater Biology Online (GBR) **674**
Frontiers (Lincoln) (USA) **8897**
Frontiers in Neuroendocrinology (USA) **5893**
Frontiers in Zoology (GBR) **944**
Fruits (FRA) **3730**
Fuel (GBR) **6769**
Fuel and Energy Abstracts (GBR) **6800**
Fuel Cells (DEU) **3135**
Fuel Cells Bulletin (GBR) **3135**
Fuel Processing Technology (NLD) **6769**
Functional Analysis and Its Applications (USA) **5488**
Functional & Integrative Genomics (DEU) **867**
Functional Ecology (GBR) **2612**
Fundamental and Clinical Pharmacology (FRA) **6843**
Fungal Biology Reviews (GBR) **790**
Fungal Genetics and Biology (USA) **790**

Link to your serials resources and content with ulrichsweb.com

Journal of French Language Studies (GBR) **5133**
Journal of Functional Analysis (USA) **5503**
Journal of Functional Programming (GBR) **2508**
Journal of Fusion Energy (USA) **3170**
The Journal of Futures Markets (USA) **1635**
Journal of Gambling Studies (USA) **6152**
Journal of Gastroenterology (JPN) **5927**
Journal of Gastroenterology and Hepatology (AUS) **5928**
Journal of Gastrointestinal Cancer (USA) **5896**
Journal of Gastrointestinal Surgery (USA) **6248**
Journal of Gene Medicine (USA) **873**
Journal of General Education (USA) **2876**
Journal of General Internal Medicine (USA) **5946**
Journal of General Plant Pathology (JPN) **797**
Journal of Genetic Counseling (USA) **7374**
Journal of Geochemical Exploration (NLD) **2711**
Journal of Geodesy (DEU) **2785**
Journal of Geodynamics (GBR) **2785**
Journal of Geographical Systems (DEU) **4037**
Journal of Geometry (CHE) **5503**
Journal of Geometry and Physics (NLD) **5503**
Journal of Geophysics and Engineering (GBR) **2785**
Journal of Germanic Linguistics (GBR) **5133**
Journal of Global Optimization (NLD) **7940**
Journal of Graph Theory (USA) **5504**
Journal of Grid Computing (NLD) **2508**
Journal of Happiness Studies (NLD) **7374**
Journal of Hazardous Materials (NLD) **3508**
The Journal of Headache and Pain Online (ITA) **6152**
Journal of Health Care for the Poor and Underserved (USA) **5649**
Journal of Health Economics (NLD) **4104**
Journal of Health, Organization and Management (GBR) **4104**
Journal of Health Politics, Policy and Law (USA) **5649**
Journal of Health Services Research & Policy (GBR) **5650**
The Journal of Heart and Lung Transplantation (USA) **6248**
Journal of Helminthology (GBR) **5820**
Journal of Hepato - Biliary - Pancreatic Sciences (JPN) **6248**
Journal of Hepatology (DNK) **5928**
Journal of Heredity (GBR) **874**
Journal of Herpetology (USA) **951**
Journal of Heuristics (USA) **2453**
The Journal of High Energy Physics (Online) (GBR) **7020**
The Journal of High Technology Management Research (GBR) **1419**
Journal of Higher Education (USA) **2990**
Journal of Hispanic Higher Education (USA) **2991**
Journal of Historical Geography (GBR) **4017**
Journal of Historical Sociology (GBR) **8113**
Journal of Homeland Security and Emergency Management (USA) **2678**
Journal of Hospitality and Tourism Management (Online) (AUS) **8725**
Journal of Housing and the Built Environment (NLD) **4417**
Journal of Housing Economics (USA) **4417**
Journal of Human Evolution (GBR) **874**
Journal of Human Genetics (JPN) **874**
Journal of Human Nutrition and Dietetics (GBR) **6661**
Journal of Humanistic Psychology (USA) **7375**
Journal of Hydrology (NLD) **2796**
Journal of Immigrant and Minority Health (USA) **5650**
Journal of Immune Based Therapies and Vaccines (GBR) **5762**
Journal of Immunological Methods (NLD) **5762**
Journal of Inclusion Phenomena and Macrocyclic Chemistry (NLD) **2136**
Journal of Income Distribution (USA) **1545**
Journal of Indian Philosophy (NLD) **6928**
The Journal of Industrial Economics (GBR) **1136**
Journal of Industrial Microbiology and Biotechnology (GBR) **767**
Journal of Industrial Relations (GBR) **1690**
Journal of Industry, Competition and Trade (USA) **1137**
Journal of Infection and Chemotherapy (JPN) **6853**
Journal of Inflammation (GBR) **6248**
Journal of Infrared, Millimeter and Terahertz Waves (Online) (USA) *see* Journal of Infrared, Millimeter and Terahertz Waves. **7078**
Journal of Inherited Metabolic Disease (NLD) **6094**
Journal of Inorganic and Organometallic Polymers and Materials (USA) **2124**
Journal of Inorganic Biochemistry (USA) **736**
Journal of Insect Behavior (USA) **852**
Journal of Insect Conservation (GBR) **852**
Journal of Insect Physiology (GBR) **852**
Journal of Insect Science (USA) **852**
Journal of Intellectual Capital (GBR) **1766**
Journal of Intellectual Disability Research (GBR) **6152**
Journal of Intelligent and Robotic Systems (NLD) **2453**
Journal of Intelligent Information Systems (USA) **2453**
Journal of Intelligent Manufacturing (GBR) **2453**
Journal of Intensive Care Medicine (USA) **5650**
Journal of Interactive Marketing (USA) **1824**
Journal of Interdisciplinary History (USA) **4149**
Journal of Internal Medicine (GBR) **5946**
Journal of International Accounting, Auditing and Taxation (GBR) **1295**
Journal of International Arbitration (NLD) **4597**
Journal of International Development (GBR) **1600**
Journal of International Economic Law (GBR) **4933**
Journal of International Economics (NLD) **1137**
Journal of International Entrepreneurship (USA) **1574**
Journal of International Financial Management and Accounting (GBR) **1362**
Journal of International Financial Markets, Institutions & Money (GBR) **1362**
Journal of International Management (USA) **1767**
Journal of International Money and Finance (GBR) **1362**
Journal of International Peacekeeping (NLD) **7248**
Journal of International Wildlife Law and Policy (USA) **3448**
Journal of Interpersonal Violence (USA) **2657**
Journal of Interventional Cardiac Electrophysiology (NLD) **5793**
Journal of Interventional Cardiology (USA) **5793**
Journal of Invertebrate Pathology (USA) **951**
The Journal of Investigative Dermatology (USA) **5879**
Journal of Investigative Psychology and Offender Profiling (GBR) **7375**
Journal of Islamic Studies (GBR) **7713**
Journal of Japanese Studies (USA) **553**
Journal of Knowledge Management (GBR) **1767**
Journal of Labelled Compounds and Radiopharmaceuticals (GBR) **2102**
Journal of Language and Social Psychology (USA) **7375**
Journal of Language, Identity, and Education (USA) **2876**
Journal of Laryngology and Otology (GBR) **6081**
Journal of Latin American Geography (USA) **4017**
Journal of Latin American Studies (GBR) **4299**
Journal of Latinos and Education (USA) **2877**
Journal of Law and Society (GBR) **4702**
Journal of Law, Economics, & Organization (GBR) **4702**
Journal of Linguistics (GBR) **5134**
The Journal of Logic and Algebraic Programming (USA) **2508**
Journal of Logic and Computation (GBR) **2429**
Journal of Logic, Language and Information (NLD) **5134**
Journal of Loss Prevention in the Process Industries (GBR) **3248**
Journal of Low Temperature Physics (USA) **7055**
Journal of Lower Genital Tract Disease (Online) (USA) **5995**
Journal of Luminescence (NLD) **7078**
Journal of Machine Learning Research (Online) (USA) **2454**
Journal of Macroeconomics (NLD) **1719**
Journal of Magnetic Resonance (USA) **7020**
Journal of Magnetic Resonance Imaging (USA) **6200**
Journal of Magnetism and Magnetic Materials (NLD) **7020**
Journal of Mammalian Evolution (USA) **951**
Journal of Mammalogy (USA) **951**
Journal of Mammary Gland Biology and Neoplasia (USA) **924**
Journal of Management (GBR) **1767**
Journal of Management & Governance (USA) **1767**
Journal of Management Development (GBR) **1767**
Journal of Management Studies (GBR) **1768**
Journal of Managerial Psychology (GBR) **1768**
Journal of Manufacturing Systems (GBR) **3386**
Journal of Manufacturing Technology Management (GBR) **3292**
Journal of Marine Science and Technology (JPN) **2809**
Journal of Marine Systems (NLD) **2809**
Journal of Mass Media Ethics (USA) **8114**
Journal of Mass Spectrometry (GBR) **2102**
The Journal of Material Cycles and Waste Management (JPN) **3508**
Journal of Materials Chemistry (GBR) **2068**
Journal of Materials Processing Technology (CHE) **3386**
Journal of Materials Science (NLD) **3350**
Journal of Materials Science: Materials in Electronics (NLD) **3350**
Journal of Materials Science: Materials in Medicine (USA) **3350**
Journal of Mathematical Analysis and Applications (USA) **5505**
The Journal of Mathematical Behavior (USA) **5505**
Journal of Mathematical Biology (DEU) **683**
Journal of Mathematical Chemistry (NLD) **5505**
Journal of Mathematical Economics (CHE) **1545**
Journal of Mathematical Fluid Mechanics (CHE) **7021**
Journal of Mathematical Imaging and Vision (USA) **5553**
Journal of Mathematical Modelling and Algorithms (NLD) **5505**
Journal of Mathematical Physics (USA) **7021**
Journal of Mathematical Psychology (USA) **7376**
Journal of Mathematical Sciences (USA) **5505**
Journal of Mathematics Teacher Education (NLD) **5506**
Journal of Media and Religion (USA) **2329**
Journal of Media Economics (USA) **2329**
Journal of Medical Entomology (USA) **852**
Journal of Medical Humanities (USA) **5651**
Journal of Medical Imaging and Radiation Oncology (AUS) **6200**
Journal of Medical Primatology (DNK) **952**
Journal of Medical Systems (USA) **5832**
Journal of Medical Ultrasonics (JPN) **7088**
Journal of Medical Virology (USA) **5652**
Journal of Medicinal Chemistry (USA) **6854**
Journal of Medieval and Early Modern Studies (USA) **4460**
Journal of Medieval History (NLD) **4236**
Journal of Membrane Biology (USA) **834**
Journal of Membrane Science (NLD) **2137**
Journal of Memory and Language (USA) **5134**
Journal of Men's Health (NLD) **6284**
Journal of Mental Health Policy and Economics (Online Edition) (ITA) *see* Journal of Mental Health Policy and Economics (Print Edition). **7376**
Journal of Metamorphic Geology (USA) **2750**
Journal of Microbiological Methods (NLD) **889**
Journal of Microscopy (GBR) **899**
Journal of Midwifery & Women's Health (USA) **5995**
Journal of Military History (USA) **6429**
Journal of Mining Science (USA) **6467**
Journal of Modern African Studies (GBR) **7147**
Journal of Modern Greek Studies (USA) **4236**
Journal of Modern Literature (USA) **5315**
Journal of Molecular and Cellular Cardiology (GBR) **5794**
Journal of Molecular Catalysis A: Chemical (NLD) **2137**
Journal of Molecular Catalysis B: Enzymatic (NLD) **736**
Journal of Molecular Evolution (USA) **874**
Journal of Molecular Graphics and Modelling (USA) **2108**
Journal of Molecular Histology (NLD) **834**
Journal of Molecular Liquids (NLD) **2137**
Journal of Molecular Medicine (DEU) **5653**
Journal of Molecular Modeling (DEU) **2137**
Journal of Molecular Neuroscience (USA) **6153**
Journal of Molecular Recognition (GBR) **2124**
Journal of Molecular Spectroscopy (USA) **7078**
Journal of Molecular Structure (NLD) **2068**
Journal of Molecular Structure: THEOCHEM (NLD) **2068**
Journal of Molluscan Studies (GBR) **952**
Journal of Monetary Economics (NLD) **1362**
Journal of Money, Credit & Banking (USA) **1362**
Journal of Morphology (USA) **683**
Journal of Multi-Criteria Decision Analysis (GBR) **1769**
Journal of Multinational Financial Management (NLD) **1769**
Journal of Multivariate Analysis (USA) **5506**
Journal of Muscle Research and Cell Motility (NLD) **6064**
Journal of Nanobiotechnology (GBR) **767**
Journal of Nanoparticle Research (NLD) **7021**
Journal of Narrative Theory (USA) **5315**
Journal of Natural Products (USA) **6854**
Journal of Navigation (GBR) **8648**
Journal of Near-Death Studies (USA) **6929**
Journal of Negative Results in BioMedicine (GBR) **684**
Journal of Network and Computer Applications (GBR) **2500**
Journal of Network and Systems Management (USA) **2500**
Journal of Neural Engineering (GBR) **2454**
Journal of Neural Transmission (AUT) **6153**
Journal of Neuro-Oncology (USA) **6025**
Journal of Neurochemistry (USA) **736**
Journal of Neuroendocrinology (GBR) **6153**
Journal of NeuroEngineering and Rehabilitation (GBR) **6153**
Journal of Neuroimmunology (NLD) **6154**
Journal of Neuroinflammation (GBR) **6154**
Journal of Neurolinguistics (GBR) **6154**
Journal of Neurology (DEU) **6154**
Journal of Neuroscience Methods (NLD) **6155**
Journal of Neuroscience Research (USA) **6155**
Journal of Nietzsche Studies (USA) **6929**
Journal of Non-Crystalline Solids (NLD) **7021**
Journal of Non-Newtonian Fluid Mechanics (NLD) **7059**
Journal of Nondestructive Evaluation (USA) **3350**
Journal of Nonlinear Science (USA) **7021**
Journal of Nonverbal Behavior (USA) **7376**
Journal of Nuclear Materials (NLD) **7067**
Journal of Number Theory (USA) **5506**
Journal of Nursing Management (GBR) **5966**
The Journal of Nutritional Biochemistry (USA) **6662**
Journal of Obstetrics and Gynaecology Research (JPN) **5996**
Journal of Occupational and Environmental Hygiene (Online) (USA) **6680**
Journal of Occupational and Organizational Psychology (GBR) **7377**
Journal of Occupational Health Psychology (USA) **6680**
Journal of Occupational Rehabilitation (USA) **6680**
Journal of Oceanography (NLD) **2809**
Journal of Operations Management (NLD) **3369**
Journal of Optical Technology (USA) **7079**
Journal of Optics (Online) (GBR) *see* Journal of Optics (Print). **7079**
Journal of Optimization Theory and Applications (USA) **5506**
Journal of Oral Pathology & Medicine (GBR) **5852**
Journal of Oral Rehabilitation (GBR) **5852**
The Journal of Organic Chemistry (USA) **2124**
Journal of Organizational Behavior (GBR) **7377**
Journal of Organizational Change Management (GBR) **1769**
Journal of Organizational Computing and Electronic Commerce (USA) **1420**
Journal of Organometallic Chemistry (CHE) **2125**
Journal of Ornithology (Online Edition) (DEU) *see* Journal of Ornithology. **909**
Journal of Orofacial Orthopedics (DEU) **6064**
The Journal of Orthodontics (Online Edition) (GBR) **5853**
Journal of Orthopaedic Research (USA) **6064**
Journal of Orthopaedic Science (JPN) **6065**
Journal of Orthopaedics and Traumatology (ITA) **6065**
Journal of Orthoptera Research (USA) **852**
Journal of Paediatrics and Child Health (GBR) **6094**
Journal of Pain and Symptom Management (USA) **6155**
Journal of Paleolimnology (NLD) **6726**
Journal of Paleontology (USA) **6726**
Journal of Parallel and Distributed Computing (USA) **2429**
The Journal of Parasitology (SUN) **5821**
Journal of Pathology (GBR) **5653**
Journal of Peace Research (GBR) **7249**
Journal of Pediatric and Adolescent Gynecology (NLD) **6095**
Journal of Pediatric Psychology (GBR) **7377**
Journal of Pension Economics and Finance (GBR) **1868**
Journal of Peptide Science (GBR) **2125**
Journal of Periodontal Research (DNK) **5853**
Journal of Personality (USA) **7377**
Journal of Personality and Social Psychology (USA) **7377**
Journal of Personality Assessment (USA) **7377**
Journal of Pest Science (DEU) **852**
Journal of Petroleum Science and Engineering (NLD) **6776**
Journal of Petrology (GBR) **2750**
Journal of Pharmaceutical and Biomedical Analysis (NLD) **6855**
Journal of Pharmaceutical Sciences (USA) **6855**
Journal of Pharmacokinetics and Pharmacodynamics (USA) **6855**
Journal of Pharmacological and Toxicological Methods (USA) **3499**
Journal of Phenomenological Psychology (NLD) **7378**
Journal of Philosophical Logic (NLD) **6929**
Journal of Philosophy of Education (GBR) **6929**
Journal of Phonetics (GBR) **5135**
Journal of Photochemistry and Photobiology, A: Chemistry (CHE) **2137**
Journal of Photochemistry and Photobiology, B: Biology (CHE) **737**
Journal of Photochemistry and Photobiology, C: Photochemistry Reviews (CHE) **2137**
Journal of Phycology (USA) **797**
Journal of Physical and Chemical Reference Data (USA) **2068**
The Journal of Physical Chemistry Part A: Molecules, Spectroscopy, Kinetics, Environment and General Theory (USA) **2137**
The Journal of Physical Chemistry Part B: Condensed Matter, Materials, Surfaces, Interfaces & Biophysical (USA) **2137**
Journal of Physical Organic Chemistry (GBR) **2137**
Journal of Physics A: Mathematical and Theoretical (GBR) **7022**
Journal of Physics and Chemistry of Solids (GBR) **7022**
Journal of Physics B: Atomic, Molecular and Optical Physics (GBR) **7022**
Journal of Physics: Condensed Matter (GBR) **7022**
Journal of Physics: Conference Series (Online) (GBR) **7022**
Journal of Physics D: Applied Physics (GBR) **7022**
Journal of Physics G: Nuclear and Particle Physics (GBR) **7067**
The Journal of Physiology (GBR) **925**
Journal of Physiology (Paris) (FRA) **6156**
Journal of Phytopathology (DEU) **797**
Journal of Pineal Research (DNK) **6156**
Journal of Plankton Research (GBR) **684**
Journal of Plant Growth Regulation (USA) **798**
Journal of Plant Nutrition and Soil Science (DEU) **716**
Journal of Plant Physiology (DEU) **798**
Journal of Plant Research (JPN) **798**
Journal of Plasma Physics (GBR) **7022**
Journal of Plastic, Reconstructive & Aesthetic Surgery (Online Edition) (GBR) **6249**
Journal of Poetry Therapy (USA) **7378**
Journal of Policy Analysis and Management (USA) **7448**
Journal of Policy History (USA) **7147**
Journal of Policy Modeling (USA) **7147**
Journal of Political Philosophy (GBR) **6929**
The Journal of Politics (USA) **7148**
Journal of Polymer Research (NLD) **7093**
Journal of Polymer Science. Part A, Polymer Chemistry (USA) **2125**
Journal of Polymer Science. Part B, Polymer Physics (USA) **2125**
Journal of Polymers and the Environment (USA) **2125**
Journal of Popular Culture (USA) **5315**
Journal of Population Economics (DEU) **7286**
Journal of Porous Materials (USA) **3350**
Journal of Porphyrins and Phthalocyanines (SGP) **2068**
Journal of Power Sources (CHE) **3322**
Journal of Pragmatics (NLD) **5203**

Oecologia (DEU) **695**
Oikos (DNK) **3458**
Oilfield Review (GBR) **6785**
Omega (GBR) **1782**
On the Horizon (USA) **2996**
Oncologie (FRA) **6030**
Oncology Research (USA) **6031**
Der Onkologe (DEU) **6031**
Online Information Review (GBR) **5038**
Open Economies Review (NLD) **1547**
Open Systems and Information Dynamics (NLD) **2524**
The Opera Quarterly (GBR) **6602**
Operating Systems Review (USA) **2595**
Operations Research Letters (NLD) **7896**
Operations Research Society of Japan. Journal (JPN) **1783**
Operative Orthopaedie und Traumatologie (DEU) **6068**
Operative Techniques in General Surgery (USA) **6254**
Operative Techniques in Orthopaedics (USA) **6068**
Ophthalmic and Physiological Optics (GBR) **6047**
Der Ophthalmologe (DEU) **6048**
Ophthalmology (USA) **6048**
Optical and Quantum Electronics (NLD) **7081**
Optical Fiber Technology (USA) **7082**
Optical Materials (NLD) **7082**
Optical Society of America. Journal A: Optics, Image Science, and Vision (USA) **7082**
Optical Society of America. Journal B: Optical Physics (USA) **7082**
Optics & Laser Technology (GBR) **7082**
Optics and Lasers in Engineering (GBR) **7082**
Optics & Photonics News (USA) **7083**
Optics Communications (NLD) **7083**
Optics Letters (USA) **7083**
Optik (DEU) **7083**
Optimal Control Applications and Methods (GBR) **2463**
Optimization and Engineering (USA) **3214**
Option Bio (FRA) **696**
Oral and Maxillofacial Surgery (DEU) **6083**
Oral Diseases (GBR) **5859**
Oral Microbiology and Immunology (DNK) **894**
Oral Oncology Extra (GBR) *see* Oral Oncology. **6032**
Oral Radiology (JPN) **5859**
Oral Tradition (Online) (USA) **3621**
Orbis (Kidlington) (GBR) **7256**
Order (NLD) **5523**
Ore Geology Reviews (NLD) **2761**
Organic & Biomolecular Chemistry (GBR) **2127**
Organic Electronics (NLD) **3327**
Organic Geochemistry (GBR) **2128**
Organic Letters (USA) **2128**
Organic Process Research and Development (GBR) **2128**
Organised Sound (GBR) **6603**
Organisms Diversity & Evolution (DEU) **696**
Organizational Behavior and Human Decision Processes (USA) **1784**
Organizational Dynamics (USA) **1784**
Organometallics (USA) **2128**
Origins of Life and Evolution of Biospheres (NLD) **696**
Orthodontics & Craniofacial Research (DNK) **5860**
Der Orthopaede (DEU) **6069**
Oryx (GBR) **959**
Osteoarthritis and Cartilage (GBR) **6225**
Osteoporosis International (GBR) **5691**
Osteosynthesis and Trauma Care (DEU) **5806**
Otolaryngology - Head and Neck Surgery (USA) **6083**
Outlooks on Pest Management (Online) (GBR) **245**
Oxford Bulletin of Economics and Statistics (GBR) **1157**
Oxford Economic Papers (GBR) **1158**
Oxford Journal of Archaeology (GBR) **410**
Oxford Journal of Legal Studies (GBR) **4754**
Oxford Review of Economic Policy (GBR) **1158**
Oxidation of Metals (USA) **2139**
P A J (USA) **8475**
P C C P Online (GBR) *see* Physical Chemistry Chemical Physics. **2139**
P J E, Peabody Journal of Education (USA) **2894**
P S: Political Science & Politics (GBR) **7163**
Pacific-Basin Finance Journal (NLD) **1373**
Pacific Economic Review (AUS) **1510**
Pacific Philosophical Quarterly (GBR) **6938**
Pacific Science (USA) **7896**
Pacing and Clinical Electrophysiology (USA) **5797**
Packaging Technology and Science (GBR) **6713**
Paddy and Water Environment (DEU) **245**
Paediatric Anaesthesia Online (GBR) **5773**
Paediatric and Perinatal Epidemiology (Online) (GBR) **6098**
Paediatric Drugs (NZL) **6866**
Pain (NLD) **6172**
Pain Medicine (USA) **6172**
Pain Practice (USA) **6173**
Pain Reviews (GBR) **5692**
Palaeogeography, Palaeoclimatology, Palaeoecology (NLD) **6727**
Palaeontology (GBR) **6728**
Palaios (USA) **6728**
Paleobiology (USA) **6728**
Palliative & Supportive Care (USA) **5692**
Palliative Medicine (GBR) **5693**
Papers in Regional Science (DEU) **7991**
Parallel Computing (NLD) **2468**
Parasite Immunology (GBR) **5824**
Parasitology (Cambridge) (GBR) **5824**
Parasitology International (NLD) **5824**
Parasitology Research (DEU) **894**
Parenting (Philadelphia) (USA) **8125**
Parkinsonism & Related Disorders (GBR) **6173**
Parliamentary Affairs (GBR) **7163**
Particle & Particle Systems Characterization (DEU) **7029**
Party Politics (GBR) **7164**
Pastoral Care in Education (GBR) **2896**
Pastoral Psychology (USA) **7389**
Der Pathologe (DEU) **5693**
Pathologica (ITA) **5693**
Pathologie et Biologie (FRA) **5693**
Pathology International (AUS) **5694**
Pathology, Research and Practice (DEU) **5694**
Pathophysiology (NLD) **926**
Patient Education and Counseling (IRL) **7535**
Pattern Analysis and Applications (GBR) **2455**
Pattern Recognition (GBR) **2456**
Pattern Recognition Letters (NLD) **2456**
Peace & Change (USA) **7258**
Peace and Conflict (USA) **7389**
Pedagogy (USA) **3076**
Pediatric Allergy and Immunology (GBR) **6099**
Pediatric Allergy and Immunology. Supplementum (GBR) **6099**
Pediatric and Developmental Pathology (USA) **6100**
Pediatric Blood & Cancer (USA) **6032**
Pediatric Cardiology (USA) **5797**
Pediatric Clinics of North America (USA) **6100**
Pediatric Dermatology (USA) **5880**
Pediatric Nephrology (DEU) **6273**
Pediatric Neurology (USA) **6101**
Pediatric Pulmonology (USA) **6101**
Pediatric Radiology (DEU) **6205**
Pediatric Surgery International (DEU) **6255**
Pediatric Transplantation (DNK) **6101**
Pediatrics International (AUS) **6102**
Pedobiologia (DEU) **246**
Peptides (USA) **741**
Performance Evaluation (NLD) **2435**
Performance Measurement and Metrics (GBR) **5039**
Perfusion (GBR) **5797**
Periodica Mathematica Hungarica (NLD) **5524**
Periodontology 2000 Online (DNK) **5861**
Permafrost and Periglacial Processes (GBR) **2762**
Personal and Ubiquitous Computing (GBR) **2435**
Personal Relationships (USA) **7417**
Personality and Individual Differences (GBR) **7390**
Personality and Social Psychology Bulletin (USA) **7390**
Personality and Social Psychology Review (USA) **7390**
Personnel Review (GBR) **1872**
Perspectives in Biology and Medicine (USA) **5695**
Perspectives in Vascular Surgery and Endovascular Therapy (USA) **6255**
Perspectives on European Politics and Society (GBR) **7259**
Perspectives on Global Development and Technology (NLD) **7991**
Perspectives on Politics (GBR) **7165**
Perspectives on Science (USA) **7897**
Perspektiven der Wirtschaftspolitik (GBR) **1511**
Pest Management Science (GBR) **246**
Pesticide Biochemistry and Physiology (USA) **246**
Petroleum Chemistry (RUS) **6787**
Pfluegers Archiv (DEU) **5695**
Pharmaceutical Chemistry Journal (USA) **6868**
Pharmaceutical Research (USA) **6870**
Pharmaceutical Statistics (GBR) **6870**
PharmacoEconomics (NZL) **6871**
Pharmacoeconomics and Outcomes News (NZL) **6890**
Pharmacoepidemiology and Drug Safety (GBR) **6871**
Pharmacological Research (GBR) **6872**
Pharmacology & Therapeutics (USA) **6872**
Pharmacology, Biochemistry and Behavior (USA) **6872**
Pharmacopsychiatry (DEU) **6173**
Pharmacopsychiatry. Supplement (DEU) **6174**
Pharmacy World and Science (NLD) **6874**
Pharmazie in Unserer Zeit (DEU) **6875**
Phenomenology and the Cognitive Sciences (NLD) **6939**
Philological Society. Transactions (GBR) **5161**
Philosophical Books (GBR) **6963**
Philosophical Forum (USA) **6940**
Philosophical Investigations (GBR) **6940**
The Philosophical Quarterly (GBR) **6941**
Philosophical Studies (NLD) **6941**
Philosophy (GBR) **6942**
Philosophy and Literature (USA) **6942**
Philosophy and Public Affairs (USA) **7165**
Philosophy and Rhetoric (USA) **6943**
Philosophy East and West (USA) **6943**
Philosophy of Music Education Review (USA) **6605**
Philosophy, Psychiatry & Psychology (USA) **6943**
Phlebology (GBR) **5797**
Phonology (GBR) **5161**
Photochemical & Photobiological Sciences (GBR) **2075**
Photochemistry and Photobiology (USA) **2139**
Photodermatology, Photoimmunology & Photomedicine Online (DNK) **5880**
Photodiagnosis and Photodynamic Therapy (NLD) **6032**
The Photogrammetric Record (GBR) **4024**
Photonic Network Communications (USA) **7030**
Photonics and Nanostructures (NLD) **7030**
Photosynthesis Research (NLD) **742**
Photosynthetica (NLD) **807**
Phronesis (NLD) **6944**
Phycological Research (AUS) **808**
Physica A: Statistical Mechanics and its Applications (NLD) **7030**
Physica B: Condensed Matter (NLD) **7030**
Physica C: Superconductivity and its Applications (NLD) **7031**
Physica D: Nonlinear Phenomena (NLD) **7031**
Physica E: Low-Dimensional Systems and Nanostructures (FRA) **7031**
Physica Status Solidi. A: Applications and Materials Science (Online) (DEU) **7031**
Physica Status Solidi. B: Basic Research (DEU) **7031**
Physica Status Solidi. C: Current Topics in Solid State Physics (DEU) **7031**
Physical Biology (GBR) **7032**
Physical Oceanography (Online) (USA) **2816**
Physical Review A (Atomic, Molecular and Optical Physics) (USA) **7032**
Physical Review B (Condensed Matter and Materials Physics) (USA) **7032**
Physical Review C (Nuclear Physics) (USA) **7070**
Physical Review D (Particles, Fields, Gravitation and Cosmology) (USA) **7070**
Physical Review E (Statistical, Nonlinear, and Soft Matter Physics) (USA) **7032**
Physical Review Letters (USA) **7032**
Physics and Chemistry of Minerals (DEU) **6476**
Physics and Chemistry of the Earth (Online) (GBR) *see* Physics and Chemistry of the Earth (Print). **2714**
Physics Education (GBR) **7033**
Physics in Medicine and Biology (GBR) **7033**
Physics in Perspective (CHE) **7033**
Physics Letters. Section A: General, Atomic and Solid State Physics (NLD) **7070**
Physics Letters. Section B: Nuclear, Elementary Particle and High-Energy Physics (NLD) **7071**
Physics of Atomic Nuclei (RUS) **7071**
Physics of Fluids (USA) **7033**
Physics of Life Reviews (NLD) **697**
Physics of Plasmas (USA) **7033**
Physics of the Earth and Planetary Interiors (NLD) **2787**
Physics of the Solid State (USA) **7033**
Physics Reports (NLD) **7034**
Physics World (GBR) **7034**
Physik in Unserer Zeit (DEU) **7034**
Physiologia Plantarum (DNK) **808**
Physiological and Molecular Plant Pathology (GBR) **808**
Physiological Entomology Online (GBR) **857**
Physiological Measurement (GBR) **5696**
Physiology & Behavior (USA) **927**
Physiotherapy (GBR) **6114**
Phytochemical Analysis (GBR) **808**
Phytochemistry (GBR) **808**
Phytochemistry Reviews (NLD) **808**
Phytomedicine (DEU) **5696**
Phytotherapie (FRA) **6114**
Phytotherapy Research (GBR) **810**
Pigment & Resin Technology (GBR) **6720**
Pigment Cell & Melanoma Research (DNK) **835**
Pituitary (NLD) **5898**
Plainsong & Medieval Music (GBR) **6606**
Planetary and Space Science (GBR) **579**
Plant and Cell Physiology (GBR) **835**
Plant and Soil (NLD) **810**
Plant Biology (GBR) **810**
Plant Biotechnology Journal (GBR) **810**
Plant Breeding Online (DEU) **810**
Plant, Cell and Environment (GBR) **697**
Plant Cell Reports (DEU) **811**
Plant Cell, Tissue and Organ Culture (NLD) **835**
Plant Ecology (NLD) **811**
Plant Foods for Human Nutrition (USA) **6668**
Plant Growth Regulation (NLD) **811**
The Plant Journal (GBR) **811**
Plant Molecular Biology (NLD) **697**
Plant Molecular Biology Reporter (NLD) **742**
Plant Pathology (GBR) **811**
Plant Physiology and Biochemistry (FRA) **812**
Plant Science (IRL) **812**
Plant Species Biology (AUS) **812**
Plant Systematics and Evolution (AUT) **813**
Planta (DEU) **813**
Planta Medica (DEU) **6875**
Plasma Chemistry & Plasma Processing (USA) **3252**
Plasma Physics and Controlled Fusion (GBR) **7035**
Plasma Physics Reports (RUS) **7035**
Plasma Processes and Polymers (DEU) **7035**
Plasma Sources Science and Technology (GBR) **7035**
Plasmid (USA) **698**
Plastics, Additives and Compounding (GBR) **7096**
Plastics, Rubber and Composites (GBR) **7097**
Pneuma (NLD) **7770**
Der Pneumologe (DEU) **6217**
Poetics (NLD) **5352**
Poetics Today (USA) **5234**
Poiesis & Praxis (DEU) **8434**
Polar Biology (DEU) **698**
Polar Record (GBR) **4024**
Police Quarterly (USA) **4896**
Policing (Bingley) (GBR) **2664**
Policy Sciences (NLD) **7166**
Policy Studies Journal (USA) **7167**
Political Analysis (GBR) **7168**
Political Behavior (USA) **7168**
Political Geography (GBR) **7168**
Political Psychology (USA) **7168**
The Political Quarterly (GBR) **7169**
Political Studies (GBR) **7169**
Political Studies Review (GBR) **7169**
Political Theory (USA) **7169**
Politics (Oxford) (GBR) **7170**
Politics and Society (USA) **7170**
Politics, Philosophy & Economics (GBR) **7171**
Polyhedron (GBR) **2117**
Polymer (GBR) **2076**
Polymer Bulletin (DEU) **2076**
Polymer Composites (USA) **7098**
Polymer Contents (USA) **3233**
Polymer Degradation and Stability (GBR) **2129**
Polymer Engineering and Science (USA) **3252**
Polymer International (GBR) **7099**
Polymer Testing (GBR) **7099**
Polymers for Advanced Technologies (GBR) **7099**
Popular Communication (USA) **2336**
Popular Music (GBR) **6607**
Population and Environment (USA) **7391**
Population Ecology (JPN) **7290**
Population Health Metrics (GBR) **7536**
Population Research and Policy Review (NLD) **7290**
Population Review (Online) (THA) **7290**
Population, Space and Place (GBR) **7290**
Portal (USA) **5039**
Portuguese Economic Journal (DEU) **1511**
positions (USA) **559**
Positivity (NLD) **5525**
Postharvest Biology and Technology (NLD) **769**
Postmodern Culture (USA) **4156**
Potential Analysis (NLD) **5525**
Powder Metallurgy and Metal Ceramics (USA) **6329**
Powder Technology (CHE) **3253**
Power Technology and Engineering (NLD) **3281**
Practical Diabetes International (GBR) **5899**
Practical Neurology (GBR) **6174**
Prairie Schooner (USA) **5353**
Pratiques Psychologiques (FRA) **7391**
Precambrian Research (NLD) **2762**
Precision Agriculture (USA) **148**
Precision Engineering (USA) **3216**
Prenatal Diagnosis (GBR) **6002**
Presidential Studies Quarterly (USA) **7173**
Prevention Science (USA) **5825**
Preventive Medicine (USA) **5699**
Preventive Veterinary Medicine (NLD) **8805**
Primary Care Respiratory Journal (GBR) **6217**
Primary Health Care Research and Development (GBR) **5699**
Primates (JPN) **960**
The Prison Journal (USA) **2666**
Probabilistic Engineering Mechanics (GBR) **3393**
Probability in the Engineering and Informational Sciences (GBR) **3233**
Probability Theory and Related Fields (DEU) **5526**
Probation Journal (GBR) **2666**
Problems of Information Transmission (RUS) **2534**
Proceedings in Applied Mathematics and Mechanics (DEU) **5526**
Process Biochemistry (GBR) **769**
Process Safety Progress (USA) **3253**
The Professional Geographer (USA) **4025**
Professional Psychology: Research and Practice (USA) **7392**
Program (GBR) **5063**
Programming and Computer Software (RUS) **2596**
Progress in Aerospace Sciences (GBR) **68**
Progress in Biophysics & Molecular Biology (GBR) **754**
Progress in Crystal Growth and Characterization of Materials (GBR) **2112**
Progress in Development Studies (IND) **8126**
Progress in Energy and Combustion Science (GBR) **3145**
Progress in Human Geography (GBR) **4025**
Progress in Lipid Research (GBR) **2130**
Progress in Materials Science (GBR) **3356**
Progress in Neuro-Psychopharmacology & Biological Psychiatry (USA) **6876**
Progress in Neurobiology (GBR) **927**
Progress in Nuclear Energy (USA) **3173**
Progress in Nuclear Magnetic Resonance Spectroscopy (NLD) **2104**
Progress in Oceanography (GBR) **2816**
Progress in Organic Coatings (NLD) **6720**
Progress in Particle and Nuclear Physics (GBR) **7071**
Progress in Pediatric Cardiology (IRL) **5798**
Progress in Photovoltaics (GBR) **3145**
Progress in Physical Geography (GBR) **4025**
Progress in Planning (GBR) **4424**
Progress in Polymer Science (GBR) **2130**
Progress in Quantum Electronics (GBR) **3111**
Progress in Reaction Kinetics and Mechanism (GBR) **2139**
Progress in Retinal and Eye Research (GBR) **6050**
Progress in Solid State Chemistry (GBR) **2140**
Progress in Surface Science (GBR) **7036**
Prooftexts (USA) **5354**
Propellants, Explosives, Pyrotechnics (DEU) **3254**
Property Management (GBR) **7605**
Prospects (NLD) **2900**
Prostaglandins & Other Lipid Mediators (USA) **5899**
The Prostate (USA) **6273**
Protection of Metals and Physical Chemistry of Surfaces (RUS) **6330**
Protein Engineering Design and Selection (Online) (GBR) **743**

Link to your serials resources and content with ulrichsweb.com

Protein Expression and Purification (USA) 743
The Protein Journal (USA) 743
Protein Science (USA) 743
Proteins: Structure, Function, and Bioinformatics (USA) 743
Proteome Science (GBR) 743
Proteomics (DEU) 743
Protist (DEU) 698
Protoplasma (AUT) 836
Psychiatric Quarterly (USA) 6176
Psychiatry and Clinical Neurosciences (AUS) 6177
Psychiatry Research (IRL) 6178
Psychiatry Research: Neuroimaging (IRL) 6178
Psycho-Oncologie (FRA) 6033
Psycho-Oncology (GBR) 6033
Psychoanalysis, Culture & Society (GBR) 7395
Psychoanalytic Psychology (USA) 7395
Psychogeriatrics (AUS) 7396
Psychological Assessment (USA) 7396
Psychological Bulletin (USA) 7396
Psychological Inquiry (USA) 7396
Psychological Medicine (GBR) 6178
Psychological Methods (USA) 7396
Psychological Research (DEU) 7396
Psychological Review (USA) 7397
Psychological Science (GBR) 7397
Psychological Science in the Public Interest (GBR) 7397
Psychologie du Travail et des Organisations (FRA) 7397
Psychologie Francaise (FRA) 7397
Psychology and Aging (USA) 4053
Psychology & Marketing (USA) 7398
Psychology & Psychotherapy (GBR) 7399
Psychology in the Schools (USA) 7399
Psychology of Addictive Behaviors (USA) 2698
Psychology of Men & Masculinity (USA) 7399
Psychology of Music (GBR) 6608
Psychology of Sport and Exercise (NLD) 7399
Psychology of Women Quarterly (USA) 7400
Psychology, Public Policy, and Law (USA) 7400
Psychoneuroendocrinology (GBR) 6178
Psychopharmacology (DEU) 6876
Psychophysiology (GBR) 6179
Psychotherapeut (DEU) 6179
Psychotherapy (USA) 7401
Psychotherapy Research (GBR) 7401
Public Administration (GBR) 7461
Public Administration and Development (GBR) 1604
Public Administration Review (USA) 7461
Public Budgeting and Finance (USA) 7462
Public Choice (NLD) 1162
Public Culture (USA) 5235
Public Health Nursing (USA) 5979
Public Health Nutrition (GBR) 6668
Public Health Reports (USA) 7537
Public Money and Management (GBR) 7462
Public Organization Review (USA) 1787
Public Policy Research (Online) (GBR) 1547
Public Relations Review (GBR) 33
Public Understanding of Science (GBR) 7900
Public Works Management & Policy (USA) 7463
Publishing Research Quarterly (USA) 7571
Pulmonary Pharmacology and Therapeutics (GBR) 6218
Pump Industry Analyst (GBR) 5459
Punishment & Society (GBR) 2666
Pure and Applied Geophysics (CHE) 2788
Q J M (GBR) 5701
Q S A R & Combinatorial Science (DEU) 6877
Quaerendo (NLD) 7571
Qualitative Market Research (GBR) 1839
Qualitative Sociology (USA) 8127
Quality and Quantity (NLD) 8150
Quality and Reliability Engineering International (GBR) 3328
Quality Assurance in Education (GBR) 2901
The Quality Assurance Journal (GBR) 5701
Quality of Life Research (NLD) 5702
Quantitative Finance (GBR) 1377
Quantitative Marketing and Economics (USA) 1163
Quantum Information Processing (USA) 2456
The Quarterly Journal of Austrian Economics (USA) 1547
Quarterly Journal of Mathematics (GBR) 5527
Quarterly Journal of Mechanics and Applied Mathematics (GBR) 5527
The Quarterly Review of Economics and Finance (GBR) 1163
Quarterly Reviews of Biophysics (GBR) 754
Quaternary International (GBR) 2763
Quaternary Perspective (IRL) 2763
Quaternary Research (USA) 2763
Quaternary Science Reviews (GBR) 2763
Queueing Systems (NLD) 3328
R A I R O - Operations Research (FRA) 2528
R A I R O - Theoretical Informatics and Applications (FRA) 2528
R & D Management (GBR) 1788
R B M News (FRA) 770
R C R A Regulations and Keyword Index (USA) 3461
R N A (GBR) 877
Race & Class (GBR) 3560
Radiation and Environmental Biophysics (DEU) 754
Radiation Measurements (GBR) 7071
Radiation Physics and Chemistry (GBR) 7071
Radiation Research (USA) 7072
Radical History Review (USA) 4157
Radiochemistry (RUS) 2140
Der Radiologe (DEU) 6206
Radiophysics and Quantum Electronics (USA) 3112
Radiotherapy & Oncology (IRL) 6207
The Ramanujan Journal (NLD) 5527
Random Structures & Algorithms (USA) 5528
Rapid Communications in Mass Spectrometry (GBR) 2104
Rapid Prototyping Journal (GBR) 3394
Ratio (GBR) 6946
Ratio Juris (GBR) 4765
Rationality and Society (GBR) 7995
Reaction Kinetics and Catalysis Letters (HUN) 2140
Reactions Weekly (NZL) 6890
Reactive and Functional Polymers (NLD) 3254
Reading and Writing (NLD) 5165
Real Estate Economics (USA) 7608
Real-Time Systems (USA) 2524
Reanimation (FRA) 5773
ReCall (GBR) 2469
Rechtsmedizin (DEU) 5916
Records Management Journal (GBR) 1789
Reference Reviews (GBR) 5042
Reference Services Review (GBR) 5042
Refractories and Industrial Ceramics (USA) 2045
Regional Environmental Change (DEU) 3462
Regional Science and Urban Economics (NLD) 4425
Regulatory Peptides (NLD) 744
Regulatory Toxicology and Pharmacology (USA) 3500
Rehabilitation Psychology (USA) 7402
Reinforced Plastics (GBR) 7099
Reliability Engineering & System Safety (GBR) 3217
Reliable Computing (NLD) 2436
Religion (GBR) 7674
Religion and the Arts (NLD) 7674
Religious Studies (GBR) 7676
Remediation (USA) 3511
Remote Sensing of Environment (USA) 4026
Renaissance Studies (GBR) 4158
Renewable Agriculture and Food Systems (Online) (GBR) 150
Renewable & Sustainable Energy Reviews (GBR) 3146
Renewable Energy (GBR) 3146
Renewable Energy Focus (GBR) 3146
Reports on Mathematical Physics (GBR) 7037
Reports on Progress in Physics (GBR) 7037
Reproduction in Domestic Animals Online (DEU) 8805
Reproductive Biology and Endocrinology (GBR) 5899
Reproductive Health (GBR) 5703
Reproductive Health Matters (NLD) 8848
Reproductive Medicine and Biology (JPN) 5703
Reproductive Sciences (USA) 6003
Reproductive Toxicology (USA) 927
Requirements Engineering (GBR) 3293
Res Publica (NLD) 6947
Research in African Literatures (USA) 5360
Research in Developmental Disabilities (GBR) 6180
Research in Engineering Design (GBR) 3217
Research in Higher Education (USA) 2999
Research in Human Development (USA) 7403
Research in Microbiology (FRA) 895
Research in Nondestructive Evaluation (USA) 3217
Research in Nursing & Health (USA) 5980
Research in Phenomenology (NLD) 6947
Research in Science Education (NLD) 2904
Research on Aging (USA) 4054
Research on Language and Computation (NLD) 5166
Research on Language and Social Interaction (USA) 5166
Research Policy (NLD) 7903
Resource and Energy Economics (NLD) 3146
Resources, Conservation and Recycling (NLD) 3511
Resources for American Literary Study (USA) 5360
Resources Policy (GBR) 3146
Respiratory Physiology & Neurobiology (NLD) 927
Respiratory Research (GBR) 6219
Respirology (AUS) 6219
Restoration Ecology (USA) 3463
Restorative Neurology and Neuroscience (NLD) 6181
Resuscitation (IRL) 6219
Retrovirology (GBR) 5825
Review of Accounting Studies (USA) 1300
The Review of Austrian Economics (USA) 1548
Review of Automotive Engineering (NLD) 8601
The Review of Black Political Economy (USA) 1165
Review of Central and East European Law (NLD) 4769
Review of Derivatives Research (USA) 1379
Review of Development Economics (GBR) 1604
Review of Economic Design (DEU) 1548
Review of Economic Dynamics (USA) 1514
The Review of Economic Studies (GBR) 1166
The Review of Economics and Statistics (USA) 1166
Review of Economics of the Household (USA) 1166
The Review of English Studies (GBR) 5360
Review of European Community and International Environmental Law (GBR) 3463
Review of Finance (Print) (GBR) 1379
Review of Financial Economics (GBR) 1166
The Review of Financial Studies (USA) 1379
Review of General Psychology (USA) 7403
The Review of Higher Education (USA) 3000
Review of Income and Wealth (GBR) 1721
Review of Industrial Organization (NLD) 1548
Review of International Economics (GBR) 1166
Review of International Studies (GBR) 7262
Review of Marketing Science (USA) 1841
Review of Palaeobotany and Palynology (NLD) 6730
The Review of Policy Research (USA) 7177
Review of Quantitative Finance and Accounting (USA) 1300
Review of Rabbinic Judaism (NLD) 7728
Review of Radical Political Economics (USA) 1548
Review of Scientific Instruments (USA) 4489
Review of Urban & Regional Development Studies (GBR) 1604
Reviews in American History (USA) 4310
Reviews in Clinical Gerontology (GBR) 4054
Reviews in Endocrine & Metabolic Disorders (USA) 5899
Reviews in Environmental Science and Biotechnology (NLD) 770
Reviews in Fish Biology and Fisheries (NLD) 961
Reviews in Medical Virology (GBR) 895
Reviews in Religion and Theology (GBR) 7677
Reviews of Modern Physics (USA) 7037
Reviews of Physiology, Biochemistry and Pharmacology (USA) 927
La Revue de Medecine Interne (FRA) 5948
Revue de Micropaleontologie (FRA) 6730
Revue du Rhumatisme (French Edition) (FRA) 6226
Revue Europeene de Psychologie Appliquee (NLD) 7405
Revue Francaise d'Allergologie (FRA) 5765
Revue Francophone des Laboratoires (FRA) 701
Revue Romane (NLD) 5168
Rheologica Acta (DEU) 7062
Rhetoric & Public Affairs (USA) 5362
Rhetoric Review (USA) 5362
Rheumatology (Online) (GBR) 6227
Rheumatology International (DEU) 6227
Risk Analysis (USA) 5530
Risk Management and Insurance Review (USA) 4521
River Research and Applications (GBR) 8831
River Teeth (USA) 5363
Robotica (GBR) 2586
Robotics and Autonomous Systems (NLD) 2586
Robotics and Computer-Integrated Manufacturing (GBR) 2586
Rock Mechanics and Rock Engineering (AUT) 2764
Royal Anthropological Institute. Journal (GBR) 354
Royal Asiatic Society. Journal (GBR) 560
Royal Astronomical Society. Monthly Notices (GBR) 580
Royal Historical Society. Transactions (GBR) 4260
Royal Musical Association. Journal (GBR) 6613
Royal Society of Chemistry. Annual Reports on the Progress of Chemistry. Section A: Inorganic Chemistry (GBR) 2118
Royal Society of Chemistry. Annual Reports on the Progress of Chemistry. Section B: Organic Chemistry (GBR) 2130
Royal Society of Chemistry. Annual Reports on the Progress of Chemistry. Section C: Physical Chemistry (GBR) 2140
Royal Society of London. Philosophical Transactions. Biological Sciences (GBR) 702
Royal Society of London. Philosophical Transactions. Mathematical, Physical and Engineering Sciences (GBR) 7038
Royal Society of London. Proceedings. Biological Sciences (GBR) 702
Royal Society of London. Proceedings. Mathematical, Physical and Engineering Sciences (GBR) 5530
Royal Society of Tropical Medicine and Hygiene. Transactions (GBR) 5825
Royal Statistical Society. Journal. Series A: Statistics in Society (GBR) 8397
Royal Statistical Society. Journal. Series B: Statistical Methodology (GBR) 8397
Royal Statistical Society. Journal. Series C: Applied Statistics (GBR) 8397
Rural History (GBR) 4260
Russian Academy of Sciences. Biology Bulletin (RUS) 702
Russian Academy of Sciences. Colloid Journal (RUS) 2140
Russian Academy of Sciences. Mathematical Notes (RUS) 5530
Russian Chemical Bulletin (USA) 2079
Russian Chemical Reviews (RUS) 2079
Russian Journal of Applied Chemistry (RUS) 3255
Russian Journal of Bioorganic Chemistry (RUS) 2130
Russian Journal of Coordination Chemistry (RUS) 2079
Russian Journal of Developmental Biology (RUS) 702
Russian Journal of Ecology (RUS) 3464
Russian Journal of Electrochemistry (RUS) 2114
Russian Journal of General Chemistry (RUS) 2079
Russian Journal of Genetics (RUS) 878
Russian Journal of Marine Biology (RUS) 702
Russian Journal of Nondestructive Testing (RUS) 3357
Russian Journal of Organic Chemistry (RUS) 2130
Russian Journal of Plant Physiology (RUS) 816
Russian Linguistics (NLD) 5170
Russian Literature (NLD) 5365
Russian Microelectronics (RUS) 3112
Russian Physics Journal (USA) 7038
The Russian Review (USA) 4260
S A I S Review (USA) 7264
S A Q: The South Atlantic Quarterly (USA) 5237
S I G A C T News (USA) 2464
S I G A R C H Computer Architecture News (USA) 2468
S I G C H I Bulletin (USA) 8151
S I G C S E Bulletin Inroads (USA) 2951
S I G D A Newsletter (Online) (USA) 2464
S I G Group Bulletin (USA) 2524
S I G I R Forum (USA) 2550
S I G M E T R I C S Performance Evaluation Review (USA) 2474
S I G M O D Record (USA) 2532
Safety Science (NLD) 6686
Samuel Beckett Today - Aujourd'hui (NLD) 5366
Scandinavian Journal of Caring Sciences (NOR) 5710
Scandinavian Journal of Economics (GBR) 1171
Scandinavian Journal of Immunology (GBR) 5765
Scandinavian Journal of Management (GBR) 1792
Scandinavian Journal of Medicine & Science in Sports (DNK) 6232
Scandinavian Journal of Psychology (GBR) 7406
Scandinavian Journal of Statistics (GBR) 8398
Scandinavian Political Studies (GBR) 7181
Schizophrenia Research (NLD) 6184
Der Schmerz (DEU) 5710
School Psychology International (GBR) 3080
Science & Education (NLD) 7908
Science & Sports (FRA) 6232
Science and Technology of Advanced Materials (GBR) 3357
Science Communication (USA) 8131
Science Education (USA) 7909
Science in China. Series A: Mathematics (CHN) 5533
Science in China. Series B: Chemistry (CHN) 2080
Science in China. Series C: Life Sciences (CHN) 703
Science in China. Series D: Earth Sciences (CHN) 2716
Science in China. Series E: Technological Sciences (CHN) 8437
Science in Context (GBR) 7909
Science of Computer Programming (NLD) 2510
Science of the Total Environment (NLD) 3465
Scientia Horticulturae (NLD) 3750
Scientific Studies of Reading (USA) 2910
Scientometrics (HUN) 7913
Scottish Journal of Political Economy (GBR) 1172
Scottish Journal of Theology (GBR) 7680
Scripta Materialia (GBR) 6331
Sealing Technology (GBR) 6720
Second Language Research (GBR) 5172
Security and Human Rights (NLD) 7215
Security Dialogue (GBR) 7265
Security Journal (GBR) 2680
Sedimentary Geology (NLD) 2766
Sedimentology Online (GBR) 2766
Seed Science Research (GBR) 251
Selecta Mathematica (CHE) 5533
Semiconductor Science and Technology (GBR) 3113
Semiconductors (USA) 7039
Semigroup Forum (USA) 5533
Seminars in Cancer Biology (GBR) 928
Seminars in Cell and Developmental Biology (GBR) 836
Seminars in Dialysis (USA) 6274
Seminars in Hearing (USA) 6085
Seminars in Immunology (GBR) 5766
Seminars in Immunopathology (DEU) 5766
Seminars in Interventional Radiology (USA) 6208
Seminars in Liver Disease (USA) 5931
Seminars in Musculoskeletal Radiology (USA) 6208
Seminars in Neurology (USA) 6184
Seminars in Plastic Surgery (USA) 6258
Seminars in Reproductive Medicine (USA) 5900
Seminars in Respiratory and Critical Care Medicine (USA) 6219
Seminars in Speech and Language (USA) 6085
Seminars in Thrombosis and Hemostasis (USA) 5941
Sensing and Imaging (USA) 4489
Sensor Review (GBR) 5459
Sensors and Actuators A: Physical (CHE) 7052
Sensors and Actuators B: Chemical (CHE) 2114
Separation and Purification Technology (GBR) 3255
Serials Review (GBR) 5047
Set-Valued and Variational Analysis (NLD) 5535
Sex Roles (USA) 7407
Sexual Abuse (USA) 7407
Sexual Plant Reproduction (DEU) 817
Sexualities (GBR) 7408
Sexuality and Disability (USA) 5712
Sexuality, Reproduction & Menopause (USA) 6004
Shakespeare Quarterly (USA) 5370
Shaw (USA) 5371
Shock Waves (DEU) 7063
Shofar (Ashland) (USA) 7729
Siberian Mathematical Journal (USA) 5536
Sign Language Studies (USA) 5174
Signal Processing (NLD) 2464
Signal Processing: Image Communication (NLD) 2535
Signal Transduction (DEU) 836
Significance (GBR) 8399
Silicon Chemistry (NLD) 2118
Simulation Digest (USA) 2518
Simulation Modelling Practice and Theory (NLD) 2518
Singapore Journal of Tropical Geography (GBR) 4028
Skeletal Radiology (DEU) 6208
Skin Research and Technology (DNK) 5882
Skull Base (USA) 6258

Link to your serials resources and content with ulrichsweb.com

Online Service

Ovid Technologies, Inc. (Subsidiary of: Wolters Kluwer N.V.) 333 Seventh Ave, New York, NY 10001 TEL 646-674-6300, 800-950-2035, FAX 646-674-6301, sales@ovid.com, http://www.ovid.com

Clinical Diabetes (Alexandria) (USA) **5884**
Clinical Drug Investigation (NZL) **6828**
Clinical Dysmorphology (USA) **666**
Clinical Endocrinology (GBR) **5885**
Clinical Genetics (DNK) **864**
Clinical Journal of Pain (USA) **6131**
Clinical Journal of Sport Medicine (USA) **6229**
Clinical Medicine (GBR) **5597**
Clinical Microbiology and Infection (GBR) **5597**
Clinical Neuropharmacology (USA) **6829**
Clinical Nuclear Medicine (USA) **6194**
Clinical Nurse Specialist (USA) **5955**
Clinical Nutrition Insight (USA) **6656**
Clinical Obstetrics and Gynecology (USA) **5988**
Clinical Oral Implants Research (DNK) **5838**
Clinical Orthopaedics and Related Research (USA) **6057**
Clinical Otolaryngology (GBR) **6078**
Clinical Pediatrics (USA) **6090**
Clinical Pharmacokinetics (NZL) **6829**
Clinical Pharmacology and Therapeutics (USA) **6829**
Clinical Physiology and Functional Imaging (GBR) **5597**
Clinical Proteomics (USA) **729**
Clinical Pulmonary Medicine (USA) **6213**
Clinical Reviews in Allergy & Immunology (USA) **5756**
Clinical Reviews in Bone and Mineral Metabolism (USA) **6016**
Clinical Social Work Journal (USA) **8034**
The Clinical Teacher (GBR) **5597**
Clinical Transplantation (DNK) **6240**
Clinician's Research Digest (USA) **7417**
Clinics in Colon & Rectal Surgery (USA) **6240**
Cognitive and Behavioral Neurology (USA) **6132**
Cognitive Therapy and Research (USA) **7347**
Colorectal Disease Online (GBR) **5921**
Community Dentistry and Oral Epidemiology Online (DNK) **5838**
Community Mental Health Journal (USA) **8035**
Comparative Exercise Physiology (GBR) **8289**
Comprehensive Therapy (USA) **5599**
Computational Geosciences (NLD) **2721**
Computational Optimization and Applications (USA) **5551**
Conservation Biology (USA) **2607**
Conservation Genetics (NLD) **865**
Constraints (USA) **2447**
Consulting Psychology Journal (USA) **7348**
Contact Dermatitis (DNK) **5873**
Contemporary Critical Care (USA) **6058**
Contemporary Family Therapy (USA) **7349**
Contemporary Hypnosis (GBR) **5942**
Contemporary Neurosurgery (USA) **6240**
Contemporary Ophthalmology (USA) **6040**
Contemporary Optometry (Hagerstown) (USA) **6040**
Contemporary Spine Surgery (USA) **6240**
Continuing Education in Anaesthesia, Critical Care & Pain (GBR) **5770**
Continuum (Baltimore) (USA) **6133**
Cornea (USA) **6040**
Coronary Artery Disease (USA) **5783**
Crime, Law and Social Change (NLD) **2648**
Criminal Behaviour and Mental Health (GBR) **6133**
Crisis (Kirkland) (USA) **7350**
Critical Care Medicine (USA) **5601**
Critical Care Nursing Quarterly (USA) **5956**
Critical Pathways in Cardiology (USA) **5784**
Cross Currents (New York) (USA) **2976**
Cultural Diversity & Ethnic Minority Psychology (USA) **8097**
Culture, Medicine and Psychiatry (NLD) **335**
Current Opinion in Allergy and Clinical Immunology (USA) **5757**
Current Opinion in Anaesthesiology (USA) **5771**
Current Opinion in Cardiology (USA) **5784**
Current Opinion in Clinical Nutrition and Metabolic Care (USA) **6657**
Current Opinion in Critical Care (USA) **6058**
Current Opinion in Endocrinology, Diabetes and Obesity (USA) **5885**
Current Opinion in Gastroenterology (USA) **5922**
Current Opinion in Hematology (USA) **5935**
Current Opinion in HIV and AIDS (USA) **5812**
Current Opinion in Infectious Diseases (USA) **5812**
Current Opinion in Lipidology (GBR) **5784**
Current Opinion in Nephrology & Hypertension (USA) **6266**
Current Opinion in Neurology (USA) **6135**
Current Opinion in Obstetrics & Gynecology (USA) **5988**
Current Opinion in Oncology (USA) **6018**
Current Opinion in Ophthalmology (USA) **6041**
Current Opinion in Organ Transplantation (USA) **5602**
Current Opinion in Otolaryngology & Head and Neck Surgery (USA) **6079**
Current Opinion in Pediatrics (USA) **6090**
Current Opinion in Psychiatry (USA) **6135**
Current Opinion in Rheumatology (USA) **6223**
Current Opinion in Urology (USA) **6267**
Current Orthopaedic Practice (USA) **6058**
Currents in Theology and Mission (USA) **7753**
Cybernetics and Systems Analysis (USA) **2526**
Cytopathology (GBR) **832**
Cytotechnology (NLD) **832**
Dental Traumatology Online (GBR) **5841**
Dermatologic Therapy (DNK) **5874**
Dermatology Nursing (USA) **5875**
Design Automation for Embedded Systems (NLD) **2460**
Developing World Bioethics (GBR) **6913**
Developmental Psychology (USA) **7351**
Diabetes (USA) **5886**
Diabetes Care (USA) **5887**
Diabetes, Obesity and Metabolism Online (GBR) **5888**
Diabetic Medicine Online (GBR) **5889**
Diagnostic Molecular Pathology (USA) **5605**
Dialogue & Alliance (USA) **7638**
Differentiation (GBR) **669**
Digestive Diseases and Sciences (USA) **5922**
Digestive Endoscopy (AUS) **5922**
Dimensions in Critical Care Nursing (USA) **5957**
Direction (Winnipeg) (CAN) **7734**
Discrete Event Dynamic Systems (USA) **2517**
Disease Management & Health Outcomes (NZL) **5605**
Diseases of the Esophagus (AUS) **6079**
Distributed and Parallel Databases (USA) **2530**
Diversity in Health and Care (GBR) **8037**
Doklady Biochemistry and Biophysics (RUS) **731**
Doklady Biological Sciences (RUS) **669**
Drug Safety (NZL) **6836**
Drugs (NZL) **6836**
Drugs & Aging (NZL) **6836**
Drugs & Therapy Perspectives (NZL) **6836**
Drugs in R & D (NZL) **6837**
e A D C - F & N (GBR) *see* Archives of Disease in Childhood. Fetal and Neonatal Edition. **5986**
e C M A J (CAN) *see* C M A J. **5590**
E M B Online (GBR) *see* Evidence - Based Medicine. **5612**
E M J Online (GBR) *see* Emergency Medicine Journal. **6059**
Ear and Hearing (USA) **6079**
Early Childhood Education Journal (USA) **2844**
Earth, Moon, and Planets (NLD) **574**
Eastern Buddhist (JPN) **7701**
Echocardiography (USA) **5785**
Ecography (DNK) **3416**
Ecotoxicology (USA) **3496**
Ecumenical Review (CHE) **7639**
Education for Primary Care (GBR) **5608**
Emergency Medicine Australasia (Online) (AUS) **6059**
Emotion (USA) **7354**
Empirical Software Engineering (USA) **2589**
Endocrine (USA) **5890**
Endocrine Pathology (USA) **5891**
Endocrine Reviews (USA) **5891**
The Endocrinologist (USA) **5891**
Endocrinology (USA) **5891**
Endodontic Topics (DNK) **5843**
Environmental Microbiology (GBR) **884**
Environmental Reviews (CAN) **3428**
Epidemiologic Reviews (USA) **5609**
Epidemiology (USA) **7516**
Epidemiology and Infection (GBR) **885**
Epilepsia (USA) **6138**
Euphytica (NLD) **229**
Europace (GBR) **5786**
European Academy of Dermatology and Venereology. Journal (BEL) **5876**
European Heart Journal (Online) (GBR) **5786**
European Journal of American Culture (GBR) **4452**
European Journal of Cancer Care Online (GBR) **6019**
European Journal of Cancer Prevention (USA) **6019**
European Journal of Cardiovascular Prevention & Rehabilitation (USA) **5786**
European Journal of Clinical Investigation (GBR) **5611**
European Journal of Clinical Nutrition (GBR) **6658**
European Journal of Dental Education Online (DNK) **5843**
European Journal of Emergency Medicine (GBR) **6060**
European Journal of Epidemiology (NLD) **5611**
European Journal of Gastroenterology and Hepatology (USA) **5923**
European Journal of Haematology (DNK) **5936**
European Journal of Neurology (USA) **6139**
European Journal of Neuroscience (GBR) **6139**
European Journal of Oral Sciences Online (DNK) **5844**
European Journal of Orthodontics (GBR) **5844**
European Journal of Plant Pathology (NLD) **787**
European Journal of Psychological Assessment (USA) **7356**
European Journal of Public Health (GBR) **7516**
European Psychologist (USA) **7356**
Evangelical Theological Society. Journal (USA) **7756**
Evidence - Based Dentistry (GBR) **5844**
Evidence - Based Mental Health (GBR) **6140**
Evidence - Based Nursing (GBR) **5958**
Evidence - Based Ophthalmology (USA) **6041**
Exercise and Sport Sciences Reviews (USA) **6229**
Experimental & Applied Acarology (NLD) **942**
Experimental and Clinical Psychopharmacology (USA) **7356**
Experimental Dermatology Online (GBR) **5876**
Experimental Psychology (USA) **7357**
Eye and Contact Lens (USA) **6042**
The F E B S Journal (Online) (GBR) **732**
F I A F International FilmArchive Database (BEL) *see* International Index to Film Periodicals. **6518**
Facial Plastic Surgery (USA) **6243**
Families, Systems, & Health (USA) **5613**
Family and Community Health (USA) **7517**
Family and Community Ministries (USA) **7758**
Family Practice (GBR) **5613**
Fetal and Maternal Medicine Review (GBR) **5990**
First Things (USA) **7643**
Fish Physiology & Biochemistry (NLD) **943**
Forensic Science, Medicine, and Pathology (USA) **5913**
Formal Methods in System Design (USA) **2520**
Foundations of Physics (USA) **7013**
Fundamental and Clinical Pharmacology (FRA) **6843**
Gastroenterology Nursing (USA) **5925**
Gene Therapy (Basingstoke) (GBR) **5618**
Gene Therapy and Regulation (SGP) **867**
General Relativity and Gravitation (USA) **7014**
Genes and Immunity (GBR) **868**
Genes, Brain and Behavior (DNK) **868**
Genes to Cells (GBR) **868**
Genetic Resources and Crop Evolution (NLD) **869**
Genetica (NLD) **869**
Genetics In Medicine (USA) **870**
Genetics Research (GBR) **870**
Genome (CAN) **870**
Geoinformatica (USA) **2722**
GeoJournal (NLD) **4012**
Geotechnical and Geological Engineering (NLD) **6463**
Geriatric Nursing (USA) **4045**
Geriatrics & Gerontology International (AUS) **4045**
Glycobiology (GBR) **733**
Glycoconjugate Journal (USA) **733**
Greek Orthodox Theological Review (USA) **7704**
Group Dynamics (USA) **7359**
Gut Online (GBR) *see* Gut. **5925**
Haemophilia Online (GBR) **5937**
Headache Online (USA) **6144**
Health and Social Care in the Community (Online) (GBR) **7521**
Health Care Analysis (NLD) **5624**
Health Care Management Review (USA) **4095**
Health Care Management Science (NLD) **4095**
The Health Care Manager (USA) **4095**
Health Data Matrix (USA) **5624**
Health Education Research (GBR) **8044**
Health Expectations (GBR) **7522**
Health Information and Libraries Journal (Online) (GBR) **5012**
Health Physics (USA) **5626**
Health Policy and Planning (GBR) **7522**
Health Promotion International (GBR) **7523**
Health Psychology (USA) **7360**
Health Services and Outcomes Research Methodology (USA) **5626**
Health Services Research (USA) **4096**
Heart & Lung (USA) **5959**
Heart Failure Reviews (USA) **5788**
Heart Online (GBR) *see* Heart. **5787**
Hebrew Union College Annual (USA) **7721**
Helicobacter (Oxford) (USA) **887**
High Temperature (RUS) **7054**
Higher-Order and Symbolic Computation (USA) **2486**
Histopathology (GBR) **6021**
History of Psychology (USA) **7360**
Holistic Nursing Practice (USA) **5960**
Homiletic (Online) (USA) **7760**
Horizons (Villanova) (USA) **7800**
Hospital Pharmacy (USA) **6846**
Hospital Topics (USA) **4101**
Human Ecology (New York) (USA) **341**
Human Molecular Genetics (GBR) **872**
Human Physiology (RUS) **5631**
Human Reproduction (GBR) **5993**
Human Reproduction Update (GBR) **716**
Hyperfine Interactions (NLD) **7015**
Hypertension (USA) **5789**
Imaging Decisions M R I (DEU) **6198**
Immunologic Research (USA) **5759**
Immunological Reviews (DNK) **5759**
Immunology (GBR) **5760**
Immunology and Cell Biology (AUS) **5760**
Implant Dentistry (USA) **5847**
In Vitro Cellular & Developmental Biology - Plant (DEU) **793**
Indian Journal of Heredity (IND) **872**
Indoor Air Online (DNK) **7525**
Infants and Young Children (USA) **6093**
Infection Control & Hospital Epidemiology (USA) **5817**
Infectious Diseases in Clinical Practice (USA) **5634**
Inflammation (USA) **5635**
Inflammatory Bowel Diseases (USA) **5927**
Inflammopharmacology (CHE) **6848**
Informatics In Primary Care (GBR) **5831**
Injury Prevention (GBR) **6093**
Innovations (Philadelphia) (USA) **5790**
Inspec (GBR) **3232**
Instructional Science (NLD) **3065**
Instruments and Experimental Techniques (RUS) **4488**
Internal Medicine Journal (Online) (AUS) **5946**
International Anesthesiology Clinics (USA) **5771**
International Bulletin of Missionary Research (USA) **7762**
International Clinical Psychopharmacology (USA) **7363**
International Immunology (GBR) **5761**
International Journal for Quality in Health Care (GBR) **5637**
The International Journal for the Psychology of Religion (USA) **7650**
International Journal of Andrology (GBR) **6269**
International Journal of Cardiovascular Imaging (NLD) **5790**
The International Journal of Clinical Leadership (GBR) **5638**
International Journal of Clinical Practice (GBR) **5638**
International Journal of Computer Vision (USA) **2451**
International Journal of Cosmetic Science (GBR) **594**
International Journal of Dental Hygiene (DNK) **5848**
International Journal of Dermatology (GBR) **5877**
International Journal of Education Through Art (GBR) **2869**
International Journal of Epidemiology (GBR) **5638**
International Journal of Experimental Pathology (GBR) **5638**
International Journal of Food Science & Technology Online (GBR) **3648**
International Journal of Francophone Studies (GBR) **7974**
International Journal of Gynecological Cancer (USA) **5993**
International Journal of Gynecological Pathology (USA) **5993**
International Journal of Health Care Finance and Economics (USA) **7526**
International Journal of Iberian Studies (GBR) **4232**
International Journal of Immunogenetics (GBR) **873**
International Journal of Impotence Research (GBR) **6269**
International Journal of Laboratory Hematology (Online) (GBR) **5938**
International Journal of Mental Health Nursing (AUS) **6146**
International Journal of Methods in Psychiatric Research (GBR) **6147**
International Journal of Nursing Practice (AUS) **5962**
International Journal of Obesity (GBR) **6660**
International Journal of Paediatric Dentistry (Online) (GBR) **5849**
International Journal of Parallel Programming (USA) **2507**
International Journal of Performance Arts and Digital Media (GBR) **8471**
The International Journal of Psychoanalysis (GBR) **7365**
International Journal of Rehabilitation Research (USA) **6110**
International Journal of Rheumatic Diseases (AUS) **6224**
International Journal of S T D & AIDS (GBR) **5818**
International Journal of Social Welfare (GBR) **8047**
International Journal of Stress Management (USA) **5640**
International Journal of Surgical Pathology (USA) **6246**
International Journal of Technology Management & Sustainable Development (GBR) **8427**
International Journal of Theoretical Physics (USA) **7018**
International Journal of Thermophysics (USA) **7055**
International Journal of Tropical Insect Science (KEN) **850**
International Journal of Urology (AUS) **6269**
International Journal of Wireless Information Networks (USA) **2327**
International Nursing Review Online (GBR) **5962**
International Ophthalmology Clinics (USA) **6044**
International Review of Mission (CHE) **7651**
International Urology and Nephrology (NLD) **6269**
Interpretation (Richmond) (USA) **7651**
Investigational New Drugs (USA) **6851**
Investigative Radiology (USA) **6199**
J A I D S (USA) **5819**
J A M A: The Journal of the American Medical Association (USA) **5642**
J C P Online (GBR) *see* Journal of Clinical Pathology. **5647**
J E C H Online (GBR) *see* Journal of Epidemiology & Community Health. **5648**
J M E Online (GBR) *see* Journal of Medical Ethics. **5651**
J M G Online (GBR) *see* Journal of Medical Genetics. **874**
J N N P Online (GBR) *see* Journal of Neurology, Neurosurgery and Psychiatry. **6154**
J O N A's Healthcare Law, Ethics, and Regulation (USA) **5963**
Japanese Journal of Clinical Oncology (GBR) **6023**
Japanese Journal of Religious Studies (JPN) **7737**
Journal for Nurses in Staff Development (USA) **5963**
Journal for Preachers (USA) **7762**
Journal for the Scientific Study of Religion (USA) **7653**
Journal for the Study of the New Testament (GBR) **7653**
Journal for the Study of the Old Testament (GBR) **7653**
Journal of Abnormal Child Psychology (USA) **7368**
Journal of Abnormal Psychology (USA) **7368**
Journal of Advanced Nursing (GBR) **5964**
Journal of Agricultural and Environmental Ethics (NLD) **6927**
Journal of Allergy and Clinical Immunology (USA) **5762**
Journal of Ambulatory Care Management (USA) **4103**
Journal of Analytical Psychology (GBR) **7368**
Journal of Anatomy (GBR) **680**
Journal of Antimicrobial Chemotherapy (GBR) **5819**
Journal of Applied Microbiology (GBR) **888**
Journal of Applied Psychology (USA) **7369**
Journal of Applied Research in Intellectual Disabilities (GBR) **6149**
Journal of Applied Spectroscopy (USA) **7077**

Online Service

11232 OVID TECHNOLOGIES, INC. ULRICH'S PERIODICALS

Journal of Assisted Reproduction and Genetics (USA) **5995**
Journal of Atmospheric Chemistry (NLD) **2066**
Journal of Autism and Developmental Disorders (USA) **3042**
Journal of Automated Reasoning (NLD) **2453**
Journal of Behavioral Health Services and Research (USA) **7528**
Journal of Behavioral Medicine (USA) **6149**
Journal of Biblical Literature (USA) **7654**
Journal of Bioenergetics and Biomembranes (USA) **735**
Journal of Biological Physics (NLD) **753**
Journal of Biomolecular N M R (NLD) **735**
Journal of Bone and Joint Surgery: American Volume (USA) **6063**
Journal of Bone and Joint Surgery: British Volume (GBR) **6063**
Journal of Bronchology & Interventional Pulmonology (USA) **6215**
Journal of Burn Care & Research (USA) **5646**
Journal of Business & Psychology (USA) **7369**
Journal of Cardiac Surgery (USA) **5792**
Journal of Cardiopulmonary Rehabilitation and Prevention (USA) **5792**
Journal of Cardiovascular Electrophysiology (USA) **5792**
Journal of Cardiovascular Medicine (Hagerstown) (USA) **5792**
The Journal of Cardiovascular Nursing (USA) **5792**
Journal of Cardiovascular Pharmacology (USA) **6852**
Journal of Cardiovascular Pharmacology and Therapeutics (USA) **6852**
Journal of Child and Adolescent Psychiatric Nursing (USA) **5964**
Journal of Child and Family Studies (USA) **7370**
Journal of Child Psychology and Psychiatry (GBR) **7370**
Journal of Chinese Religions (USA) **7737**
Journal of Clinical Densitometry (NLD) **5647**
Journal of Clinical Endocrinology and Metabolism (USA) **5895**
Journal of Clinical Engineering (USA) **750**
Journal of Clinical Gastroenterology (USA) **5927**
Journal of Clinical Immunology (USA) **5762**
Journal of Clinical Investigation (USA) **5647**
Journal of Clinical Neuromuscular Disease (USA) **5647**
Journal of Clinical Neurophysiology (USA) **6150**
Journal of Clinical Nursing (GBR) **5964**
Journal of Clinical Oncology (USA) **6024**
Journal of Clinical Periodontology (DNK) **5851**
Journal of Clinical Pharmacy and Therapeutics (GBR) **6852**
Journal of Clinical Psychology in Medical Settings (USA) **7370**
Journal of Clinical Psychopharmacology (USA) **6853**
Journal of Clinical Rheumatology (USA) **6224**
Journal of Combinatorial Optimization (NLD) **5553**
Journal of Community Health (USA) **5647**
Journal of Comparative Psychology (USA) **7371**
Journal of Computational Neuroscience (NLD) **6151**
Journal of Computer Assisted Tomography (USA) **6200**
Journal of Consulting and Clinical Psychology (USA) **7371**
Journal of Contemporary Psychotherapy (USA) **7372**
Journal of Continuing Education in Nursing (USA) **5964**
Journal of Cosmetic Dermatology (GBR) **5878**
Journal of Counseling Psychology (USA) **7372**
Journal of Craniofacial Surgery (USA) **6247**
Journal of Critical Care (USA) **6063**
Journal of Cross-Cultural Gerontology (NLD) **4049**
Journal of Cutaneous Pathology (DNK) **5878**
Journal of Developmental and Behavioral Pediatrics (USA) **6094**
Journal of Digestive Diseases (Online) (AUS) **5927**
Journal of Ecumenical Studies (USA) **7655**
Journal of Educational Psychology (USA) **2875**
The Journal of Electroconvulsive Therapy (USA) **6151**
Journal of Electronic Testing (USA) **3322**
Journal of Emergency Nursing (USA) **5964**
The Journal of Endodontics (USA) **5851**
Journal of Engineering Physics and Thermophysics (USA) **3205**
Journal of Environmental Engineering and Science (Online) (CAN) **3445**
Journal of Evaluation in Clinical Practice Online (GBR) **5649**
Journal of Evolutionary Biochemistry and Physiology (RUS) **736**
Journal of Evolutionary Biology (GBR) **873**
Journal of Experimental Botany (GBR) **796**
Journal of Experimental Psychology: Animal Behavior Processes (USA) **7373**
Journal of Experimental Psychology: Applied (USA) **7373**
Journal of Experimental Psychology: General (USA) **7373**
Journal of Experimental Psychology: Human Perception and Performance (USA) **7373**
Journal of Experimental Psychology: Learning, Memory, and Cognition (USA) **7373**
Journal of Exposure Science and Environmental Epidemiology (GBR) **3447**
The Journal of Family Practice (USA) **5649**
Journal of Family Psychology (USA) **7374**
Journal of Family Therapy (GBR) **6151**
Journal of Family Violence (USA) **2657**
Journal of Feminist Studies in Religion (USA) **7655**
Journal of Gastroenterology and Hepatology (AUS) **5928**
Journal of Gastrointestinal Cancer (USA) **5896**
Journal of General Internal Medicine (USA) **5946**
Journal of Genetic Counseling (USA) **7374**
Journal of Gerontological Nursing (USA) **4049**
Journal of Glaucoma (USA) **6044**
Journal of Head Trauma Rehabilitation (USA) **6064**
Journal of Health Care Finance (USA) **4104**
Journal of Helminthology (GBR) **5820**
Journal of Hospice and Palliative Nursing (USA) **5965**
Journal of Human Hypertension (GBR) **5793**
Journal of Human Nutrition and Dietetics (GBR) **6661**
Journal of Hypertension (USA) **5793**
Journal of Immigrant and Minority Health (USA) **5650**
Journal of Immunotherapy (USA) **5763**
Journal of Inclusion Phenomena and Macrocyclic Chemistry (NLD) **2136**
Journal of Individual Differences (USA) **7375**
Journal of Infrared, Millimeter and Terahertz Waves (Online) (USA) *see* Journal of Infrared, Millimeter and Terahertz Waves. **7078**
Journal of Infusion Nursing (USA) **5965**
Journal of Inherited Metabolic Disease (NLD) **6094**
Journal of Insect Behavior (USA) **852**
Journal of Intellectual Disability Research (GBR) **6152**
Journal of Intelligent and Robotic Systems (NLD) **2453**
Journal of Intelligent Manufacturing (GBR) **2453**
Journal of Internal Medicine (GBR) **5946**
Journal of Interventional Cardiac Electrophysiology (NLD) **5793**
Journal of Interventional Cardiology (USA) **5793**
The Journal of Investigative Dermatology (USA) **5879**
Journal of Low Temperature Physics (USA) **7055**
Journal of Lower Genital Tract Disease (Online) (USA) **5995**
Journal of Mammary Gland Biology and Neoplasia (USA) **924**
Journal of Materials Science: Materials in Electronics (NLD) **3350**
Journal of Media Practice (GBR) **2329**
Journal of Medical Imaging and Radiation Oncology (AUS) **6200**
Journal of Medical Microbiology (GBR) **889**
Journal of Medical Primatology (DNK) **952**
Journal of Medical Systems (USA) **5832**
Journal of Microscopy (GBR) **899**
Journal of Molecular Histology (NLD) **834**
Journal of Molecular Neuroscience (USA) **6153**
Journal of Molluscan Studies (GBR) **952**
Journal of Muscle Research and Cell Motility (NLD) **6064**
Journal of Nervous and Mental Disease (USA) **6153**
Journal of Network and Systems Management (USA) **2500**
Journal of Neuro-Oncology (USA) **6025**
Journal of Neuro-Ophthalmology (USA) **6045**
Journal of Neurochemistry (USA) **736**
Journal of Neuroendocrinology (GBR) **6153**
Journal of Neuropathology and Experimental Neurology (USA) **6154**
Journal of Neuropsychiatry and Clinical Neurosciences (USA) **6154**
Journal of Neurosurgical Anesthesiology (USA) **5772**
The Journal of Nursing Administration (USA) **5965**
Journal of Nursing Care Quality (USA) **5966**
Journal of Nursing Education (USA) **5966**
Journal of Nursing Management (GBR) **5966**
Journal of Nursing Scholarship (USA) **5966**
Journal of Obstetric, Gynecologic, and Neonatal Nursing (USA) **5966**
Journal of Occupational and Environmental Medicine (USA) **5653**
Journal of Occupational and Organizational Psychology (GBR) **7377**
Journal of Occupational Health Psychology (USA) **6680**
Journal of Occupational Rehabilitation (USA) **6680**
Journal of Oral Pathology & Medicine (GBR) **5852**
Journal of Oral Rehabilitation (GBR) **5852**
Journal of Organisational Transformation and Social Change (GBR) **8115**
Journal of Orthopaedic Trauma (USA) **6065**
Journal of Paediatrics and Child Health (GBR) **6094**
Journal of Pastoral Care and Counseling (USA) **7655**
Journal of Pastoral Theology (USA) **7655**
Journal of Patient Safety (USA) **7529**
Journal of Pediatric Gastroenterology and Nutrition (USA) **6662**
Journal of Pediatric Hematology / Oncology (USA) **6025**
Journal of Pediatric Nursing (USA) **5966**
Journal of Pediatric Ophthalmology and Strabismus (USA) **6045**
Journal of Pediatric Orthopaedics (USA) **6065**
Journal of Pediatric Orthopaedics. Part B (USA) **6065**
Journal of Pediatric Psychology (GBR) **7377**
The Journal of Pediatrics (USA) **6095**
Journal of Pelvic Medicine and Surgery (USA) **6249**
Journal of PeriAnesthesia Nursing (USA) **5967**
Journal of Perinatal and Neonatal Nursing (USA) **5967**
Journal of Perinatal Medicine (DEU) **5996**
Journal of Perinatology (GBR) **5996**
Journal of Periodontal Research (DNK) **5853**
Journal of Personality and Social Psychology (USA) **7377**
Journal of Pharmacokinetics and Pharmacodynamics (USA) **6855**
Journal of Pineal Research (DNK) **6156**
Journal of Plankton Research (GBR) **684**
The Journal of Primary Prevention (USA) **7378**
Journal of Prosthetics and Orthotics (USA) **6065**
Journal of Psychiatric and Mental Health Nursing Online (GBR) **6156**
Journal of Psychiatric Practice (USA) **6156**
Journal of Psychiatry and Neuroscience (CAN) **6156**
Journal of Psycholinguistic Research (USA) **5135**
Journal of Psychopathology and Behavioral Assessment (USA) **7379**
Journal of Psychophysiology (USA) **7379**
Journal of Psychosocial Nursing and Mental Health Services (USA) **5967**
Journal of Psychotherapy Integration (USA) **6156**
Journal of Public Health (Online) (GBR) **8050**
Journal of Public Health Management and Practice (USA) **7529**
Journal of Quantitative Criminology (USA) **2658**
Journal of Radioanalytical and Nuclear Chemistry (HUN) **2102**
Journal of Reconstructive Microsurgery (USA) **6249**
Journal of Refractive Surgery (USA) **6249**
Journal of Religious Ethics (USA) **7656**
Journal of Research on Adolescence (USA) **2156**
Journal of Risk and Uncertainty (USA) **1546**
Journal of Ritual Studies (USA) **345**
The Journal of Rural Health (USA) **5654**
Journal of Seismology (NLD) **2785**
Journal of Signal Processing Systems (USA) **2534**
Journal of Sleep Research Online (GBR) **5654**
Journal of Spinal Disorders & Techniques (Online) (USA) **6065**
Journal of Statistical Physics (USA) **7022**
Journal of Supercomputing (USA) **2430**
Journal of Superconductivity and Novel Magnetism (USA) **7023**
Journal of the History of Medicine and Allied Sciences (GBR) **5655**
Journal of the Peripheral Nervous System Online (USA) **6157**
Journal of Theology for Southern Africa (ZAF) **7657**
The Journal of Thoracic and Cardiovascular Surgery (USA) **6250**
Journal of Thoracic Imaging (USA) **6201**
Journal of Thoracic Oncology (USA) **6025**
Journal of Thrombosis and Thrombolysis (USA) **5794**
Journal of Trauma (USA) **6066**
Journal of Tropical Pediatrics (GBR) **6095**
Journal of Urban Health (USA) **5655**
The Journal of Urology (USA) **6270**
Journal of Vascular and Interventional Radiology (USA) **6201**
Journal of Vascular Surgery (USA) **6250**
Journal of Viral Hepatitis (GBR) **5928**
Journal of Visual Art Practice (GBR) **499**
Journal of W O C N (USA) **6250**
Journal of Youth and Adolescence (USA) **2157**
Kidney International (USA) **6271**
Kinetics and Catalysis (RUS) **2138**
L P N (Year) (USA) **5968**
The Laryngoscope (USA) **6082**
Latin American Indian Literatures Journal (USA) **5320**
Law and Human Behavior (USA) **4713**
Learning Disabilities Research and Practice (USA) **3043**
Learning in Health and Social Care (GBR) **5660**
Legal and Criminological Psychology (GBR) **7383**
Letters in Applied Microbiology (GBR) **890**
Letters in Mathematical Physics (NLD) **7025**
Leukemia (GBR) **5939**
Lippincott's Bone and Joint Newsletter (USA) **6066**
Liver International (DNK) **5928**
The Living Pulpit (USA) **7661**
M C N: American Journal of Maternal Child Nursing (USA) **5969**
Machine Learning (USA) **2454**
Machine Translation (NLD) **5204**
Marine Geophysical Researches (NLD) **2812**
Mathematical Geosciences (Online) (USA) *see* Mathematical Geosciences. **2754**
Mayo Clinic Proceedings (USA) **5665**
Measurement Techniques (USA) **6404**
Medical Care (USA) **5667**
Medical Education (GBR) **5668**
Medical Law Review (GBR) **4731**
Medical Oncology (GBR) **6027**
Medical Physics (USA) **5670**
Medicine (Baltimore) (USA) **5674**
Medicine and Science in Sports and Exercise (USA) **6231**
MedSurg Nursing (USA) **6252**
Melanoma Research (GBR) **6027**
Menopause (USA) **5998**
Mental Health in Family Medicine (GBR) **6160**
Metabolic Brain Disease (USA) **5678**
Methodology (USA) **7385**
Microbiology (RUS) **891**
The Milbank Quarterly (USA) **7154**
Minds and Machines (NLD) **2454**
Missiology (USA) **7739**
Mission Studies (NLD) **7664**
Mobile Networks and Applications (NLD) **2501**
Modern Theology (GBR) **7664**
Molecular and Cellular Biochemistry (USA) **738**
Molecular Biology (RUS) **739**
Molecular Biology and Evolution (USA) **689**
Molecular Biology Reports (NLD) **739**
Molecular Biotechnology (USA) **768**
Molecular Breeding (NLD) **801**
Molecular Diversity (NLD) **7068**
Molecular Endocrinology (USA) **5897**
Molecular Human Reproduction (GBR) **5999**
Molecular Microbiology (GBR) **893**
Molecular Neurobiology (USA) **739**
Molecular Psychiatry (Online) (GBR) *see* Molecular Psychiatry. **6161**
Motivation and Emotion (USA) **7386**
Multidimensional Systems and Signal Processing (USA) **2524**
Muslim World (USA) **7715**
Mutagenesis (GBR) **875**
Mycoses (DEU) **5681**
NanoBioTechnology (USA) **768**
National Cancer Institute. Journal (Online) (GBR) **6028**
Nature (GBR) **7889**
Nature Clinical Practice Cardiovascular Medicine (GBR) **5796**
Nature Clinical Practice Endocrinology & Metabolism (GBR) **5898**
Nature Clinical Practice Gastroenterology & Hepatology (GBR) **5929**
Nature Clinical Practice Oncology (GBR) **6028**
Nature Reviews. Urology (GBR) **6271**
Near Eastern Archaeology (USA) **407**
Nephrology (AUS) **6272**
Nephrology, Dialysis, Transplantation (GBR) **6272**
Nephrology Nursing Journal (USA) **5971**
Neural Processing Letters (USA) **2455**
Neurochemical Research (USA) **6164**
Neurocritical Care (USA) **5685**
Neurogastroenterology and Motility Online (GBR) **5929**
NeuroInformatics (USA) **925**
The Neurologist (USA) **6166**
Neurology (USA) **6166**
Neurology Now (USA) **6166**
Neurology Today (USA) **6166**
Neuromodulation (USA) **6166**
NeuroMolecular Medicine (USA) **6167**
Neuropathology (AUS) **6167**
Neuropathology and Applied Neurobiology (GBR) **6167**
Neuropsychology (USA) **6168**
Neuropsychology Review (USA) **6168**
NeuroReport (USA) **6169**
Neurosurgery (Baltimore) (USA) **6170**
Neurosurgery Quarterly (USA) **6253**
New Cinemas: Journal of Contemporary Film (GBR) **6508**
New England Journal of Medicine (USA) **5685**
New Forests (NLD) **3698**
New York Academy of Sciences. Annals (USA) **7892**
Novum Testamentum (NLD) **7666**
Nuclear Medicine Communications (USA) **6204**
Nucleic Acids Research (GBR) **741**
Numen (NLD) **7667**
Nurse Educator (USA) **5972**
The Nurse Practitioner (USA) **5972**
Nurse Researcher (GBR) **5972**
Nursing (Year) (USA) **5972**
Nursing (Year) Critical Care (USA) **5972**
Nursing Administration Quarterly (USA) **5973**
Nursing and Health Sciences (AUS) **5973**
Nursing Economics (USA) **5973**
Nursing Education Perspectives (USA) **5973**
Nursing for Women's Health (USA) **8847**
Nursing Forum (USA) **5973**
Nursing Inquiry (AUS) **5974**
Nursing Made Incredibly Easy! (USA) **5974**
Nursing Management (GBR) **5974**
Nursing Research (USA) **5975**
Nursing Standard (GBR) **5975**
Nutrient Cycling in Agroecosystems (NLD) **244**
Nutrition Bulletin (GBR) **6665**
Nutrition Research Reviews (GBR) **6666**
Nutrition Society. Proceedings (GBR) **6667**
Nutrition Today (USA) **6667**
O E M Online (GBR) *see* Occupational and Environmental Medicine. **6682**
Obesity Reviews (GBR) **6667**
Obstetric Anesthesia Digest (USA) **5772**
Obstetrical & Gynecological Survey (USA) **6000**
Obstetrics and Gynecology (USA) **6001**
Occupational Medicine (GBR) **6683**
Occupational Therapy International (GBR) **6683**
Oikos (DNK) **3458**
Oncogene (GBR) **6029**
Ophthalmic and Physiological Optics (GBR) **6047**
Ophthalmic Plastic and Reconstructive Surgery (USA) **6048**
Ophthalmic Surgery, Lasers and Imaging (USA) **6254**
Optical and Quantum Electronics (NLD) **7081**
Optometry and Vision Science (USA) **6049**
Oral Diseases (GBR) **5859**
Oral Microbiology and Immunology (DNK) **894**
Oral Surgery, Oral Medicine, Oral Pathology, Oral Radiology and Endodontology (USA) **5859**
Orthopaedic Nursing Journal (USA) **5977**
Otolaryngology - Head and Neck Surgery (USA) **6083**
Otology & Neurotology (USA) **6084**

11234 PROJECT MUSE ULRICH'S PERIODICALS

Plant and Cell Physiology (GBR) 835
Political Analysis (GBR) 7168
Protein Engineering Design and Selection (Online) (GBR) 743
Public Opinion Quarterly (USA) 7174
Publius (USA) 7174
Q J M (GBR) 5701
Quarterly Journal of Mathematics (GBR) 5527
Quarterly Journal of Mechanics and Applied Mathematics (GBR) 5527
Radiation Protection Dosimetry (GBR) 7072
Refugee Survey Quarterly (GBR) 7314
The Review of English Studies (GBR) 5360
The Review of Financial Studies (USA) 1379
Rheumatology (Online) (GBR) 6227
Royal Musical Association. Journal (GBR) 6613
Schizophrenia Bulletin (USA) 6184
Social History of Medicine (GBR) 5715
Social Politics (GBR) 8903
Social Science Japan Journal (GBR) 8004
Socio-Economic Review (GBR) 1517
Statute Law Review (GBR) 4788
Teaching Mathematics and Its Applications (GBR) 5541
Toxicological Sciences (GBR) 3502
Twentieth Century British History (GBR) 4274
The World Bank Economic Review (USA) 1525
World Bank Research Observer (USA) 1391
The Year's Work in Critical and Cultural Theory (GBR) 4483
The Year's Work in English Studies (GBR) 5403

Project MUSE (Subsidiary of: The Johns Hopkins University Press) 2715 N Charles St, Baltimore, MD 21218-4319 TEL 410-516-6989, FAX 410-516-6968, muse@muse.jhu.edu, http://muse.jhu.edu
Advertising & Society Review (USA) 20
Africa Today (USA) 7102
African Studies Review (USA) 3516
American Annals of the Deaf (USA) 4071
American Imago (USA) 6121
American Indian Quarterly (USA) 6634
American Jewish History (USA) 7718
The American Journal of Bioethics (USA) 862
American Journal of Mathematics (USA) 5468
American Journal of Philology (USA) 5092
American Literary History (USA) 5252
American Literary Realism (USA) 5406
American Literary Scholarship (USA) 5252
American Literature (USA) 5252
American Periodicals (USA) 5252
American Philological Association. Transactions (USA) 2229
American Quarterly (USA) 4442
American Speech (USA) 5092
The Americas (USA) 4283
Anthropological Quarterly (USA) 325
Arethusa (USA) 2230
Arizona Quarterly (USA) 5207
Asian Music (USA) 6546
Asian Perspectives (USA) 381
Asian Theatre Journal (USA) 8466
Association of Pacific Coast Geographers. Yearbook (USA) 4035
Biography (Honolulu) (USA) 640
Book History (USA) 7554
Boundary 2 (USA) 5265
Bridges (USA) 8894
Brookings Papers on Economic Activity (USA) 1536
Brookings Papers on Education Policy (Year) (USA) 3018
Brookings Trade Forum (USA) 1553
Brookings-Wharton Papers on Financial Services (USA) 1321
Brookings-Wharton Papers on Urban Affairs (Year) (USA) 8091
Buddhist - Christian Studies (USA) 7700
Buildings & Landscapes (USA) 436
Bulletin of the History of Medicine (USA) 5589
Callaloo (USA) 5269
Camera Obscura (USA) 6491
Canadian Historical Review (CAN) 4134
Canadian Journal of Linguistics (CAN) 5104
Canadian Journal on Aging (GBR) 4042
Canadian Modern Language Review (CAN) 5104
Canadian Review of American Studies (CAN) 4287
The Catholic Historical Review (USA) 7789
Center for Children's Books. Bulletin (USA) 2147
Chaucer Review (USA) 5272
Children's Literature (Baltimore) (USA) 5273
Children's Literature Association Quarterly (USA) 5001
China: An International Journal (SGP) 7954
China Review International (USA) 3823
Cinema Journal (USA) 6493
Civil War History (USA) 4288
Classical World (USA) 2233
College Literature (USA) 5276
Common Knowledge (USA) 6911
The Comparatist (USA) 5276
Comparative Literature Studies (USA) 5277
Comparative Studies of South Asia, Africa and the Middle East (USA) 4181
Comparative Technology Transfer and Society (USA) 8418
Computer Music Journal (USA) 6632
Configurations (USA) 5277
Contemporary Literature (USA) 5278
The Contemporary Pacific (USA) 3792
Criticism (USA) 5280
Cuban Studies (USA) 4290
Cultural Critique (USA) 334
Dance Research Journal (USA) 2684
Demography (USA) 7281
Diacritics (USA) 5284
Differences (USA) 8895
Discourse (Detroit, 1979) (USA) 4450
E L H (USA) 5286
e-Service Journal (USA) 2543
Early American Literature (USA) 5287
Early Music (GBR) 6563
Eastern Africa Social Science Research Review (ETH) 7960
Economia (Washington, D.C.) (USA) 1427
Eighteenth-Century Life (USA) 4217
Eighteenth-Century Studies (USA) 4138
Eire - Ireland (USA) 4450
The Emily Dickinson Journal (USA) 5421
Enterprise and Society (USA) 1105
Essays in Medieval Studies (USA) 4218
Ethics & the Environment (GBR) 6917
Ethnohistory (USA) 337
Film & History (USA) 6498
Film History (USA) 6499
Fourth Genre (USA) 5297
Framework (USA) 6501
French Colonial History (USA) 4221
French Forum (USA) 5217
French Historical Studies (USA) 4222
Frontiers (Lincoln) (USA) 8897
The Future of Children (USA) 2153
G L Q (USA) 4373
Geographical Analysis (USA) 4010
Global Environmental Politics (USA) 3434
The Good Society (USA) 7138
Hastings Center Report (USA) 5623
The Hemingway Review (USA) 5305
The Henry James Review (USA) 5305
Hesperia (GRC) 396
The High School Journal (USA) 2863
Hispanic American Historical Review (USA) 4295
Hispanic Review (USA) 5125
History & Memory (USA) 4145
History in Africa (USA) 4175
History of Political Economy (USA) 1542
History Workshop Journal (GBR) 4146
Holocaust and Genocide Studies (USA) 4230
Human Biology (Detroit) (USA) 871
Human Rights Quarterly (USA) 7208
Hypatia (USA) 8898
Imagine (Baltimore) (USA) 3041
Indiana Journal of Global Legal Studies (USA) 4691
International Journal of Press / Politics (USA) 4577
International Organization (GBR) 7244
International Security (USA) 7245
Israel Studies (USA) 7976
The Jewish Quarterly Review (USA) 7723
Jewish Social Studies (USA) 7724
Journal for Early Modern Cultural Studies (USA) 7977
Journal of Aesthetic Education (USA) 2874
Journal of American Folklore (USA) 3619
Journal of Asian American Studies (USA) 8111
Journal of Chinese Overseas (NLD) 7978
Journal of Cold War Studies (USA) 7247
Journal of College Student Development (USA) 2989
Journal of Colonialism & Colonial History (USA) 4149
Journal of Democracy (USA) 7146
Journal of Developing Areas (USA) 1599
Journal of Early Christian Studies (USA) 7802
Journal of Feminist Studies in Religion (USA) 7655
Journal of Folklore Research (USA) 3619
Journal of General Education (USA) 2876
Journal of Health Care for the Poor and Underserved (USA) 5649
Journal of Health Politics, Policy and Law (USA) 5649
Journal of Higher Education (USA) 2990
Journal of Interdisciplinary History (USA) 4149
Journal of Japanese Studies (USA) 553
Journal of Latin American Geography (USA) 4017
Journal of Medieval and Early Modern Studies (USA) 4460
Journal of Middle East Women's Studies (USA) 8900
Journal of Military History (USA) 6429
Journal of Modern Greek Studies (USA) 4236
Journal of Modern Literature (USA) 5315
Journal of Money, Credit & Banking (USA) 1362
Journal of Narrative Theory (USA) 5315
Journal of Nietzsche Studies (USA) 6929
Journal of Policy History (USA) 7147
Journal of Scholarly Publishing (CAN) 7564
Journal of Social History (USA) 8115
Journal of Speculative Philosophy (USA) 6930
Journal of the Early Republic (USA) 4300
Journal of the History of Ideas (USA) 4461
Journal of the History of Medicine and Allied Sciences (GBR) 5655
Journal of the History of Philosophy (USA) 6930
Journal of the History of Sexuality (USA) 8116
Journal of Women's History (USA) 8900
Journal of World History (USA) 4150
Ka Ho 'Oilina (USA) 5136
Kennedy Institute of Ethics Journal (USA) 5657
Korean Studies (USA) 554
Kritika (Bloomington) (USA) 4238
Labor Studies Journal (USA) 1693
Language (Washington) (USA) 5139
Late Imperial China (USA) 4185
Latin American Music Review (USA) 6584
Latin American Politics and Society (USA) 7250
Latin American Research Review (USA) 7982
Legacy (Lincoln) (USA) 5320
Leonardo: Art Science and Technology (USA) 502
Leonardo Music Journal (USA) 6584
Libraries & the Cultural Record (USA) 5026
Library Trends (USA) 5029
Linguistic Inquiry (USA) 5145
The Lion and the Unicorn (USA) 5323
Literature and Medicine (USA) 5325
Logos (St. Paul) (USA) 7805
Luso - Brazilian Review (USA) 5225
M L N (USA) 5149
Manoa (USA) 5330
Marvels & Tales (USA) 3620
Mediterranean Quarterly (USA) 7252
Meridians (USA) 8901
Merrill - Palmer Quarterly (USA) 7385
Milton Quarterly (USA) 5334
The Missouri Review (USA) 5335
Modern Drama (CAN) 5335
M F S Modern Fiction Studies (USA) 5335
Modern Judaism (GBR) 3551
Modern Language Quarterly (USA) 5335
Modernism/Modernity (USA) 4153
Monumenta Nipponica (JPN) 556
The Moving Image (USA) 6508
Music and Letters (GBR) 6589
Music Library Association. Notes (USA) 5033
N W S A Journal (USA) 8901
Nabokov Studies (USA) 5337
Narrative (USA) 5338
Nashim (ISR) 8901
Native Plants Journal (USA) 804
New Centennial Review (USA) 4466
New Hibernia Review (USA) 350
New Literary History (USA) 5340
Nine (USA) 8240
Nineteenth Century French Studies (USA) 5342
Northeast African Studies (USA) 3555
Oceanic Linguistics (USA) 5157
The Opera Quarterly (GBR) 6602
Oral Tradition (Online) (USA) 3621
P A J (USA) 8475
Pacific Science (USA) 7896
Parergon (AUS) 4468
Past & Present (GBR) 4155
Pedagogy (USA) 3076
Perspectives in Biology and Medicine (USA) 5695
Perspectives on Science (USA) 7897
Philosophy and Literature (USA) 6942
Philosophy and Public Affairs (USA) 7165
Philosophy and Rhetoric (USA) 6943
Philosophy East and West (USA) 6943
Philosophy of Music Education Review (USA) 6605
Philosophy, Psychiatry & Psychology (USA) 6943
Poetics Today (USA) 5234
Population Review (Online) (THA) 7290
Portal (USA) 5039
positions (USA) 559
Postmodern Culture (USA) 4156
Prairie Schooner (USA) 5353
Prooftexts (USA) 5354
Psychoanalysis, Culture & Society (GBR) 7395
Public Culture (USA) 5235
Radical History Review (USA) 4157
Red Cedar Review (USA) 5236
Research in African Literatures (USA) 5360
Resources for American Literary Study (USA) 5360
The Review of Higher Education (USA) 3000
Reviews in American History (USA) 4310
Rhetoric & Public Affairs (USA) 5362
River Teeth (USA) 5363
Royal Musical Association. Journal (GBR) 6613
S A I S Review (USA) 7264
S A Q: The South Atlantic Quarterly (USA) 5237
Shakespeare Quarterly (USA) 5370
Shaw (USA) 5371
Shofar (Ashland) (USA) 7729
Sign Language Studies (USA) 5174
Sirena (Baltimore) (USA) 5434
Small Axe (USA) 5239
Social Forces (USA) 8133
Social Politics (GBR) 8903
Social Science History (USA) 8003
Social Text (USA) 8134
South Central Review (USA) 5375
Southern Cultures (USA) 4475
Southern Literary Journal (USA) 5375
Spiritus (USA) 7683
Studies in American Indian Literatures (USA) 5380
Studies in Bibliography (USA) 636
Studies in English Literature 1500-1900 (USA) 5381
Studies in Philology (USA) 5183
Sub-Stance (USA) 5383
Symploke (USA) 4477
T D R (USA) 8480
Technology and Culture (USA) 8442
Texas Studies in Literature and Language (USA) 5386
Theater (New Haven) (USA) 8481
Theatre Journal (Baltimore) (USA) 8482
Theatre Topics (USA) 8483
Theory & Event (USA) 7188
Theory into Practice (USA) 2919
Tolkien Studies (USA) 5389
Transformation (ZAF) 8010
Transition (USA) 5242
University of Toronto Law Journal (CAN) 4805
University of Toronto Quarterly (CAN) 4481
The Velvet Light Trap (USA) 6516
Victorian Periodicals Review (USA) 5395
Victorian Poetry (USA) 5437
Victorian Studies (USA) 4481
The Washington Quarterly (USA) 7273
Wicazo Sa Review (USA) 6636
Women and Music (USA) 6628
World Politics (USA) 7274

ProQuest K-12 Learning Solutions (Subsidiary of: ProQuest LLC (Ann Arbor)) 789 E Eisenhower Pkwy, PO Box 1346, Ann Arbor, MI 48106 TEL 734-761-4700, 800-521-0600, info@il.proquest.com, http://www.proquestk12.com/
A A R P Bulletin (USA) 4037
A I D S Care (GBR) 5807
A I Magazine (USA) 2445
A J R NewsLink (USA) *see* American Journalism Review. 4571
A L A TechSource (USA) *see* Library Technology Reports. 5029
A N Q: A Quarterly Journal of Short Articles, Notes and Reviews (USA) 5248
A R D Online (GBR) *see* Annals of the Rheumatic Diseases. 6221
A T Q (USA) 5248
Accounting Education News (USA) 1277
Accounting Today (USA) 1279
Addiction (GBR) 2689
Adhesives & Sealants Industry (USA) 3235
Adolescence (USA) 2143
Adolescent Medicine (Elk Grove) (USA) 6087
Adolescent Psychiatry (USA) 6119
Advanced Battery Technology (USA) 3294
Advanced Emergency Nursing Journal (USA) 6055
African Affairs (GBR) 7103
African American Review (USA) 3516
African Arts (USA) 464
African Business (GBR) 1589
Afterimage (USA) 6963
Aftermarket Business (USA) 8555
Age and Ageing (GBR) 4038
Agricultural Research (USA) 217
Agronomy Journal (USA) 88
AIDS Education and Prevention (USA) 7506
The Air & Space Power Journal (USA) 6408
Air Classics (USA) 44
Air Power History (USA) 44
Air Transport World (USA) 45
Aircraft Engineering and Aerospace Technology (GBR) 45
Airline Business (GBR) 8536
Airman (USA) 6409
Airpower (USA) 46
Alabama Heritage (USA) 4282
Alaska (USA) 3969
Alberta Sweetgrass (CAN) 3517
All Hands (USA) 6410
Alternative Therapies in Health and Medicine (USA) 306
Alternatives Journal (CAN) 3402
Alzheimer's Care Today (USA) 6121
Amber Waves (USA) 90
America (USA) 7782
The American (Washington, D.C.) (USA) 7104
American Academy of Psychoanalysis and Dynamic Psychiatry. Journal (USA) 7332
American Animal Hospital Association. Journal (Online Edition) (USA) 8791
American Annals of the Deaf (USA) 4071
American Anthropologist (USA) 324
American Artist (USA) 465
American Artist. Watercolor (USA) 465
The American Biology Teacher (USA) 652
American Business Law Journal (USA) 4854
American Cheerleader (USA) 8158
American Craft (USA) 531
American Dietetic Association. Journal (USA) 6654
American Drama (USA) 8465
American Educational Research Journal (USA) 2825
American Family Physician (USA) 5571
American Fitness (USA) 6981
American Forests (USA) 3683
American Heritage (USA) 4282
American History (Leesburg) (USA) 4282
American Indian Quarterly (USA) 6634
American Jewish History (USA) 7718
American Journal of Audiology (USA) 4072
American Journal of Clinical Nutrition (USA) 6655
American Journal of Community Psychology (USA) 8086
American Journal of Critical Care (USA) 5951
American Journal of Education (USA) 2826
American Journal of Family Law (USA) 4906
American Journal of Health Behavior (USA) 6981
American Journal of Health Studies (Online) (USA) 6982
American Journal of Law & Medicine (USA) 4614
American Journal of Mathematics (USA) 5468
American Journal of Nephrology (CHE) 6265
The American Journal of Pathology (USA) 5573
American Journal of Psychiatry (USA) 6122
The American Journal of Psychoanalysis (USA) 7333
American Journal of Psychology (USA) 7333
American Journal of Psychotherapy (USA) 6122
American Journal of Public Health (USA) 7507
American Journal of Respiratory Cell and Molecular Biology (USA) 6211
American Journal of Sociology (USA) 8087
American Journal of Speech - Language Pathology (USA) 4072
American Journal of Sports Medicine (USA) 6228
American Libraries (USA) 4988
American Literature (USA) 5252
American Machinist (USA) 1879

Link to your serials resources and content with ulrichsweb.com

DIRECTORY 2010 PROQUEST K-12 LEARNING SOLUTIONS 11235

American Mathematical Monthly (USA) 5468
American Medical Informatics Association. Journal (USA) 5829
American Medical News (USA) 5573
American Meteorological Society. Bulletin (USA) 6346
American Midland Naturalist (USA) 7834
American Music (USA) 6544
The American Nurse (USA) 5951
American Oriental Society. Journal (USA) 542
American Planning Association. Journal (USA) 4403
American Poetry Review (USA) 5416
American Printer (USA) 7318
American Record Guide (USA) 6544
American Rifleman (USA) 8158
American Scientist (USA) 7835
American Sociological Review (USA) 8087
The American Spectator (USA) 5206
American Statistical Association. Journal (USA) 8344
The American Statistician (USA) 8344
American Surgeon (USA) 6236
American Theatre (USA) 8465
American Woodworker (USA) 4437
America's Civil War (USA) 4283
Anaesthesia and Intensive Care (AUS) 5768
Analog Science Fiction & Fact (USA) 5439
Analytic Separations News (USA) 2097
Annals of Allergy, Asthma, & Immunology (USA) 5754
Annals of Anatomy (DEU) 5575
Annals of Clinical Biochemistry (GBR) 722
Annals of Dyslexia (USA) 3036
Annals of Nutrition and Metabolism (CHE) 6655
Annals of Otology, Rhinology and Laryngology (USA) 6077
Annals of Tropical Paediatrics (GBR) 6087
Annual Review of Astronomy and Astrophysics (USA) 568
Annual Review of Ecology, Evolution and Systematics (USA) 3403
Annual Review of Environment and the Resources (USA) 3124
Annual Review of Materials Research (USA) 3341
Annual Review of Plant Biology (USA) 775
Anthropological Quarterly (USA) 325
Anthropology & Education Quarterly (USA) 326
Anti-Corrosion Methods and Materials (GBR) 6305
Antioch Review (USA) 5206
Antiquity (GBR) 374
AppleSeeds (USA) 2176
Appraisal Journal (USA) 7582
Appropriate Technology (GBR) 194
Archives of Dermatology (USA) 5872
Archives of Disease in Childhood (GBR) 6088
Archives of Environmental and Occupational Health (USA) 3404
Archives of General Psychiatry (USA) 6124
Archives of Internal Medicine (USA) 5944
Archives of Neurology (USA) 6124
Archives of Ophthalmology (USA) 6038
Archives of Pathology & Laboratory Medicine (USA) 5902
Archives of Pediatrics & Adolescent Medicine (USA) 6088
Archives of Surgery (USA) 6237
Archivum Historicum Societatis Iesu (ITA) 7784
Argumentation & Advocacy (USA) 5096
Arkansas Business Journal (USA) 1061
Arkansas Historical Quarterly (USA) 4284
Armor (USA) 6411
Arms Control Today (USA) 4917
Army (USA) 6411
Army Reserve Magazine (USA) 6412
Art Business News (USA) 468
Arteriosclerosis, Thrombosis, and Vascular Biology (USA) 5777
Artforum International (USA) 472
The Artist's Magazine (USA) 473
Arts and Activities (USA) 3051
Arts Education Policy Review (USA) 475
Asian Ethnology (JPN) 329
Asian Perspectives (USA) 381
Asian Theatre Journal (USA) 8466
Ask (USA) 2176
Association Meetings (USA) 6278
Astronomy (USA) 570
The Atlantic (USA) 5207
Atlantic Economic Journal (USA) 1063
Audience Development (USA) 7552
Audiotex Update (USA) 2349
The Auk (USA) 901
Australian Accounting Review (AUS) 1281
Australian Geographer (GBR) 3999
The Australian Journal of Anthropology (AUS) 330
Automotive News (USA) 8565
Aviation History (USA) 48
Aviation Week & Space Technology (USA) 49
Azerbaijan International (USA) 7222
B J S M Online (GBR) *see* British Journal of Sports Medicine. 6229
Backpacker (USA) 8305
Bank Loan Report (USA) 1313
Barron's (USA) 1611
Baseline (New York) (USA) 2408
Bass Player (USA) 6548
Baylor Business Review (USA) 1065
Beef (USA) 280
Behavior Modification (USA) 7339
Behavioral Disorders (USA) 3037
Behavioral Medicine (USA) 7339
Behind the Headlines (CAN) 7223
Best of New Orleans (USA) *see* New Orleans Magazine. 3983
Best's Review. Insurance Issues and Analysis (USA) 4495
Better Investing (USA) 1612
Better Nutrition (USA) 6656
Bicycling (USA) 8254
Billboard.com (USA) *see* Billboard (New York). 6549
Biochemistry and Cell Biology (CAN) 725
BioCycle (USA) 3504
Biography (Honolulu) (USA) 640
Biological Bulletin (USA) 658
Biomedical Safety & Standards (USA) 5586
Biometrics (GBR) 8358
BioPharm International (USA) 6825
Biophysical Journal (USA) 752
BioScience (USA) 661
Biotech Business (USA) 759
Bioterrorism Week (Online) (USA) *see* Bioterrorism Week. 7223
The Black Collegian (USA) 6693
Black Collegian Online (USA) 6693
Black Enterprise.com (USA) *see* Black Enterprise. 1068
Black History Bulletin (USA) 3522
Black Issues Book Review (USA) 3522
Black Scholar (USA) 3523
Book Publishing Report (USA) 7554
Bookbird (USA) 2180
Booklist (USA) 7554
Botany (CAN) 781
Boundary 2 (USA) 5265
Bowhunter (USA) 8306
Boys' Life (USA) 2180
Brain, Behavior and Evolution (CHE) 6127
Brandweek (USA) 22
Briefings in Bioinformatics (GBR) 825
British Heritage (USA) 4206
British Journal for the History of Science (GBR) 7842
British Journal of Biomedical Science (GBR) 5903
British Journal of Clinical Psychology (GBR) 7341
British Journal of Developmental Psychology (GBR) 7341
British Journal of Health Psychology (GBR) 7342
British Journal of Mathematical and Statistical Psychology (GBR) 7342
British Journal of Psychology (GBR) 7342
British Journal of Social Psychology (GBR) 7342
Broadcast Engineering (USA) 2376
Builder (Washington) (USA) 984
Buildings (USA) 987
Bulk Transporter (USA) 8669
Bulletin of the Atomic Scientists (USA) 7224
Business Economics (USA) 1071
Business Leader (USA) 1730
Business Travel News (USA) 8689
C D Computing News (USA) 2491
C R N (USA) 2510
CabinetMaker (USA) 4554
Calgary Herald (CAN) 3806
California C P A (USA) 1284
Callaloo (USA) 5269
Canada. Statistics Canada. Juristat (CAN) 4821
Canadian Business (CAN) 1079
Canadian Electronics (CAN) 3297
Canadian Ethnic Studies (CAN) 3525
Canadian Gardening (CAN) 3726
The Canadian Geographer (USA) 4001
Canadian Geographic (CAN) 4001
Canadian Geotechnical Journal (CAN) 2703
Canadian Issues (CAN) 4446
Canadian Journal of Administrative Sciences (GBR) 1080
Canadian Journal of Chemistry (CAN) 2052
Canadian Journal of Civil Engineering (CAN) 3261
Canadian Journal of Dietetic Practice and Research (CAN) 6656
Canadian Journal of Earth Sciences (CAN) 2703
Canadian Journal of Experimental Psychology (CAN) 7343
Canadian Journal of Fisheries and Aquatic Sciences (CAN) 3588
Canadian Journal of Forest Research (CAN) 3685
Canadian Journal of History (CAN) 4134
Canadian Journal of Human Sexuality (CAN) 7343
Canadian Journal of Microbiology (CAN) 882
Canadian Journal of Physics (CAN) 7007
Canadian Journal of Physiology and Pharmacology (CAN) 920
The Canadian Journal of Rural Medicine (CAN) 5592
Canadian Journal of Zoology (CAN) 937
Canadian Literature (CAN) 5270
Canadian Musician (CAN) 6554
Canadian Psychology (CAN) 7344
Canadian Review of Sociology (CAN) 8092
Cardiovascular Week (USA) 5781
Career World (USA) 6695
Carnegie (USA) 481
Casual Living (USA) 4555
Catechist (USA) 7787
The Catholic Historical Review (USA) 7789
Cement Americas (USA) 990
Ceramic Engineering and Science Proceedings (USA) 2038
Chemical Engineering (USA) 3238
Chemical Engineering Progress (USA) 3239
Chemical Week (USA) 3240
Chesapeake and Ohio Historical Magazine (USA) 8616
Chicago Review (USA) 5273
Child Health Alert (USA) 6089
Childhood Education (USA) 3054
Children's Literature (Baltimore) (USA) 5273
The Christian Century (USA) 7631
Christian Scholar's Review (USA) 7632
Christianity Today (USA) 7632
Chronicle (Radford) (USA) 5440
Church History (USA) 7633
Cineaste (USA) 6493
Cinema Journal (USA) 6493
Civil Engineering (Reston) (USA) 3262
Civil War History (USA) 4288
Civil War Times (USA) 4288
Classical Bulletin (USA) 2232
The Clearing House (USA) 2837
Click (USA) 2182
Climbing (USA) 8309
Clinical and Investigative Medicine (Online) (CAN) 5596
Clinical Diabetes (Alexandria) (USA) 5884
Clinical Laboratory Science (USA) 5904
Clinical Pediatrics (USA) 6090
Clio (FRA) 8895
Clio (Ft. Wayne) (USA) 4135
Club Management (USA) 2265
Coach and Athletic Director (USA) 8166
Cobblestone (USA) 2183
College Literature (USA) 5276
College Mathematics Journal (USA) 5478
College Student Affairs Journal (Online Edition) (USA) 2278
College Student Journal (USA) 2973
College Teaching (USA) 2973
ColorLines (USA) 7117
Columbia Journalism Review (USA) 4573
The Combat Edge (USA) 51
Commonweal (USA) 5211
Communication Quarterly (USA) 8094
Communication Studies (USA) 8094
Communication World (USA) 1734
Communications Daily (USA) 2378
Communications News (USA) 2316
Community College Review (USA) 2974
Comparative Drama (USA) 5277
Comparative Education Review (USA) 2838
Comparative Literature (USA) 5277
The Computer & Internet Lawyer (USA) 4648
Computer Protocols (USA) 2496
Computer Technology News (USA) *see* Computer Technology Review. 2412
Computer Weekly (GBR) 2413
Computer Workstations (USA) 2573
Computers in Libraries (GBR) 2570
Computerworld (USA) 2570
Computerworld (CAN) 2511
Concrete Products (USA) 993
The Condor (USA) 905
The Conference Board Review (USA) 1735
Consumer Alert Comments (USA) 2636
Contemporary Economic Policy (GBR) 1086
The Contemporary Review (GBR) 5212
Contemporary South Asia (GBR) 7119
Contracting Business (USA) 4117
Contractor (USA) 999
Converting Magazine (USA) 6733
Corn and Soybean Digest (USA) 225
Corrosion (USA) 3375
Counseling and Human Development (USA) 2839
Country Living (New York) (USA) 4536
Crain's Chicago Business (USA) 1959
Crain's Cleveland Business (USA) 1476
Crain's New York Business (USA) 1088
Crainsdetroit.com (USA) *see* Crain's Detroit Business. 1088
Cranes Today (GBR) 5451
Criminal Justice Ethics (USA) 6912
Criminology (USA) 2650
The Crisis (USA) 3528
Critical Reviews in Environmental Science & Technology (USA) 3485
Critical Reviews in Food Science and Nutrition (USA) 3632
Critical Reviews in Plant Sciences (USA) 226
Critical Reviews in Toxicology (USA) 3495
Criticism (USA) 5280
Critique (Washington) (USA) 5280
Crop Science (USA) 226
Cross Currents (New York) (USA) 2976
Cryptologia (GBR) 2512
Cultural Anthropology (USA) 334
Current Anthropology (USA) 335
Current Events (USA) 2184
Current Health 1 (USA) 3055
Current Health 2 (USA) 3055
Current History (USA) 7229
Current Medical Literature. Psychiatry (GBR) 6134
Current Medical Research and Opinion (GBR) 5602
Current Musicology (USA) 6560
Current Science (USA) 2184
Cutis (USA) 5874
Cytogenetic and Genome Research (Online) (CHE) *see* Cytogenetic and Genome Research. 865
D V D News (USA) 2400
Daily Compilation of Presidential Documents (USA) 7128
Daily News (Halifax) (CAN) 3808
Dairy Industries International (GBR) 3633
Dance Magazine (USA) 2684
Dance Spirit (USA) 2685
Dance Teacher (USA) 2685
Daughters (USA) 2150
Decision Sciences (USA) 1738
Defense Counsel Journal (USA) 4830
Defense Daily (USA) 52
Delta Farm Press (USA) 104
Dementia and Geriatric Cognitive Disorders (CHE) 6136
Demography (USA) 7281
Dermatology Times (USA) 5875
Design News Online (USA) *see* Design News. 8420
Developmental Medicine and Child Neurology (GBR) 6091
Diabetes (USA) 5886
Diabetes Care (USA) 5887
Diabetes Forecast (USA) 5887
Diabetes Spectrum (USA) 5888
Diabetes Week (USA) 5889
Diagnostic Imaging (USA) 6195
Digital Cinematography (USA) 6496
Digital Content Producer (USA) 2401
Display Development News (USA) 3093
Dissent (New York) (USA) 7130
Diverse Issues in Higher Education (USA) 2978
Drug Discovery & Development (USA) 6834
Drug Information Journal (USA) 6835
Drug Week (USA) 6836
E (USA) 3414
e C M A J (CAN) *see* C M A J. 5590
E D N Access (USA) *see* E D N World. 3093
E E T Online (USA) *see* E E Times. 3094
E H S Today (USA) 6676
E N R (USA) 3265
E Q (New York) (USA) 8152
Early American Industries Association. Chronicle (USA) 1884
Early American Literature (USA) 5287
Early Childhood Today (Online) (USA) 3058
Earth Island Journal (USA) 3415
Ebony (USA) 3531
The Ecologist (Online) (GBR) 3417
Ecology (USA) 3417
Economic Geography (USA) 4005
Economic Inquiry (GBR) 1100
Economic Outlook (GBR) 1480
EContent (USA) 2556
EContent Xtra (USA) 2556
Ecumenical Review (CHE) 7639
eDefense (USA) 6420
The Edmonton Journal (CAN) 3809
Education Daily (USA) 2847
The Education Digest (USA) 2847
Education Grants Alert (USA) 3021
Education Week (USA) 2849
Ekistics (GRC) 4409
Electric Perspectives (USA) 3302
Electrical Wholesaling (USA) 1815
Electro Manufacturing (USA) 3291
Electronic Design (USA) 3095
The Electronic Library (GBR) 5061
Electronic Materials Update (USA) 3096
Emergency Medicine (USA) 6059
The Emily Dickinson Journal (USA) 5421
eMusician.com (USA) *see* Electronic Musician. 6564
Endangered Species Update (USA) 2610
Energy Engineering (USA) 3131
The Energy Journal (USA) 3132
Engineer (Fort Leonard Wood) (USA) 3188
Engineered Systems (USA) 4118
The English Historical Review (GBR) 4217
English Studies in Africa (GBR) 4451
Enterprise and Society (USA) 1105
Environment (USA) 3420
Environmental Design + Construction (USA) 1007
Environmental History (USA) 4138
Environmental Progress & Sustainable Energy (USA) 3427
Environmental Reviews (CAN) 3428
Ethics (USA) 6917
Ethics & Medicine (USA) 5610
Ethics & the Environment (GBR) 6917
Ethikos (USA) 6918
Ethnohistory (USA) 337
Ethnology (USA) 337
Euromoney Online (GBR) *see* Euromoney. 1338
European Automotive Design (GBR) 8579
European Journal of Cell Biology (DEU) 832
European Journal of Physical and Rehabilitation Medicine (ITA) 6109
European Neurology (CHE) 6140
European Planning Studies (GBR) 4410
European Review of History (GBR) 4219
Europolitics (BEL) 1340
EuroWeek (GBR) 1340
Event D V (USA) 2557
EW.com (USA) *see* Entertainment Weekly. 3975
eWEEK (USA) 2557
Exceptional Children (USA) 3040
Experimental & Applied Acarology (NLD) 942
Experimental Techniques (USA) 3344
The Explicator (USA) 5294
Extrapolation (USA) 5442
F A S Worldwide (USA) 197
F B I Law Enforcement Bulletin (USA) 2652
F C C Report (USA) 2320
Faces (USA) 2188
Family Economics and Nutrition Review (USA) 4358
Family Practice Management (USA) 5613
Family Process (USA) 7357
Family Relations (USA) 2856
Farm Industry News (USA) 111
Fathering (USA) 8102
The Faulkner Journal (USA) 5295
Federal Reserve Bank of Atlanta. Economic Review (USA) 1485

Online Service

Link to your serials resources and content with ulrichsweb.com

DIRECTORY 2010 PROQUEST K-12 LEARNING SOLUTIONS 11237

Library Administrator's Digest (USA) 5026
Library Hi Tech News (GBR) 5062
The Library Quarterly (USA) 5029
Library Trends (USA) 5029
The Lion and the Unicorn (USA) 5323
Listen (USA) 2696
The Literary Review (USA) 5324
Literature Film Quarterly (USA) 6506
Live Design (USA) 8473
Long-Term Living (USA) 5969
The Lutheran (USA) 7765
Lutheran Theological Journal (AUS) 7766
M E L U S (USA) 5328
m i n's b2b (USA) 7567
M I T Sloan Management Review (USA) 1773
Machine Design (USA) 3388
Maclean's (CAN) 3812
MacWorld (USA) 2577
The Magazine Antiques (USA) 367
Magazine of History (USA) 4152
Managed Healthcare Executive (USA) 4106
Management Today (GBR) 1777
Manitoba Business Magazine (CAN) 1498
Mankind Quarterly (USA) 347
Manufacturing Engineering (USA) 3209
Marine Corps Gazette (USA) 6432
Marketing Week (GBR) 1834
Marketplace (Menasha) (USA) 1147
Materials Performance (USA) 3353
Materials Science and Technology (GBR) 3353
Mathematics and Computer Education (USA) 5515
Mathematics and Mechanics of Solids (GBR) 7026
Mathematics Magazine (USA) 5515
Mayo Clinic Proceedings (USA) 5665
Mechanical Engineering (USA) 3389
Medical Anthropology Quarterly (USA) 347
Medical Decision Making (USA) 5667
Medical Device Technology (GBR) 5668
Medical History (GBR) 5669
Medical Journal of Australia (AUS) 5669
Medical Meetings (USA) 6281
Medical Update (Chicago) (USA) 5672
Mental Health Weekly Digest (USA) 6160
Metallurgical and Materials Transactions A - Physical Metallurgy and Materials Science (USA) 6324
Metallurgical and Materials Transactions B - Process Metallurgy and Materials Processing Science (USA) 6324
Metro Magazine (USA) 8504
Microbiological Research (DEU) 891
Microelectronics International (GBR) 3109
Midcontinental Journal of Archaeology (USA) 406
The Middle East (GBR) 5227
Middle East Journal (USA) 7252
Middle East Policy (USA) 7252
Military History (USA) 4303
Military Images (USA) 6435
Military Intelligence (USA) 6435
Military Medicine (USA) 5679
Military Review (English Edition) (USA) 6436
Military Technology (DEU) 6436
Millimeter (USA) 6507
The Mineralogical Record (USA) 4340
Minerals and Metallurgical Processing (USA) 6471
Minerva Biotecnologica (ITA) 768
Minority Business Entrepreneur (USA) 1963
The Mississippi Quarterly (USA) 5227
Mix Magazine (USA) 8154
Model Airplane News (USA) 4340
Model Railroader (USA) 4341
Modern Age (USA) 5228
Modern Drama (CAN) 5335
Modern Language Quarterly (USA) 5335
Momentum (New York) (USA) 6161
Money Marketing (GBR) 1368
Montessori Life (USA) 3073
Monthly Weather Review (USA) 6391
Mosaic (Winnipeg, 1967) (CAN) 5336
Mother Earth News (USA) 3982
MotherJones.com (USA) *see* Mother Jones. 5228
MOTOR (USA) 8591
Motor Boating (USA) 8278
Mountain Bike (USA) 8265
Ms. (USA) 8901
Multichannel Merchant (USA) 30
MultiMedia & Internet@Schools (USA) 2950
Music Week (GBR) 6592
Musical Opinion (GBR) 6593
Musical Times (GBR) 6594
N A S A Tech Briefs (USA) 66
N A S S P Leadership for Student Activities (USA) 3027
N A T O's Nations and Partners for Peace (DEU) 7254
The Nation (USA) 5229
National Cancer Institute. Journal (Online) (GBR) 6028
National Catholic Reporter (USA) 7808
National Defense (USA) 6438
National Dragster (USA) 8595
National Geographic Explorer (USA) 4020
National Geographic Kids (USA) 4021
National Geographic Online (USA) *see* National Geographic. 4020
National Geographic Traveler (USA) 8740
National Guard (USA) 6438
National Hog Farmer (USA) 294
National Institute of Standards and Technology. Journal of Research (USA) 6405
National Journal (USA) 7156
National Medical Association. Journal (USA) 5683
National N O W Times (USA) 8877
National Parks (USA) 4981
National Real Estate Investor (USA) 7601
National Review (USA) 7156
National Wildlife (USA) 2620
National Wildlife (World Edition) (USA) 2620
National Women's Health Report (USA) 8847
Nationalities Papers (GBR) 7987
The Nation's Health (USA) 7533
Native American Connections (USA) 4304
Natural History (USA) 7888
Natural Life (CAN) 3813
Nature Matters (CAN) 2621
Naval Aviation News (USA) 67
Naval Forces (DEU) 6438
Naval History (USA) 6438
Naval War College Review (USA) 6438
Navy Medicine (USA) 5684
Near Eastern Archaeology (USA) 407
Neuroendocrinology (CHE) 5898
Neuroepidemiology (CHE) 6164
Neurological Research (GBR) 6165
Neuropsychobiology (CHE) 6168
The New American (Appleton) (USA) 7157
New England Review (USA) 5340
New Equipment Digest (USA) 8433
New Hampshire Business Review (USA) 1431
New Jersey Business (USA) 1899
New Moon Girls (USA) 2204
New Oxford Review (USA) 7809
New Perspectives Quarterly (USA) 7158
New Statesman (GBR) 5230
The New York Times Upfront (Student Edition) (USA) 2205
The New Yorker (USA) 5230
News Media and the Law (USA) 4580
News Photographer (USA) 6971
Newsletter on Intellectual Freedom (USA) 5036
Newspaper Research Journal (USA) 4581
Newsweek International (GBR) 3869
Nonlinear Studies (USA) 5521
Nottingham Medieval Studies (BEL) 4249
Nuclear Engineering International (GBR) 3171
Nuclear Plant Journal (USA) 3172
NuclearFuel (USA) 3172
Nucleonics Week (USA) 3143
Nursing (Year) (USA) 5972
Nursing Older People (GBR) 4052
Nutrition Action Health Letter (USA) 6665
Nutrition Health Review (USA) 6666
Nutrition Reviews (USA) 6666
O T J R: Occupation, Participation and Health (USA) 5688
Occupational Health & Safety (USA) 6682
Occupational Outlook Quarterly (USA) 6707
Ocean News & Technology (USA) 2815
Oceania (AUS) 350
Odyssey (Peru) (USA) 2205
Onderstepoort Journal of Veterinary Research (ZAF) 8804
OnEarth (USA) 3458
Online Libraries and Microcomputers (USA) 5063
Opera News (USA) 6602
Ophthalmic Surgery, Lasers and Imaging (USA) 6254
Ophthalmology Times (USA) 6048
Orthopedics (USA) 6070
Outdoor Canada (CAN) 8327
Outdoor Life (USA) 8327
Oxford Economic Papers (GBR) 1158
Oxford Review of Education (GBR) 2894
P C Magazine (Online) (USA) 2434
P C World (USA) 2581
P M J Online (GBR) *see* Postgraduate Medical Journal. 5698
P R I M U S (USA) 5524
P R News (USA) 31
P S A Journal (USA) 6972
P T - Magazine of Physical Therapy (USA) 6113
Pacific Affairs (CAN) 7257
Pacific Science (USA) 7896
Parnassus: Poetry in Review (USA) 5429
Pathobiology (CHE) 5764
Pathology, Research and Practice (DEU) 5694
Peace Review (GBR) 7259
Peacework (USA) 7164
Pediatric Annals (USA) 6100
Pediatric Nursing (USA) 5977
Pediatrics (English Edition) (USA) 6102
Pediatrics for Parents (USA) 6102
Pedobiologia (DEU) 246
Peer Review (USA) 2997
The People (Mountain View) (USA) 7164
People en Espanol (USA) 3985
People's Medical Society Newsletter (USA) 2640
Perspectives in Biology and Medicine (USA) 5695
Perspectives in Psychiatric Care (USA) 5977
Perspectives of New Music (USA) 6605
Perspectives on Political Science (USA) 7165
Perspectives on Sexual and Reproductive Health (USA) 6001
Pest Management Professional (USA) 246
Pharmaceutical Technology (USA) 6870
Phi Delta Kappan (USA) 2898
Philosophy East and West (USA) 6943
Philosophy of Music Education Review (USA) 6605
Philosophy of Science (USA) 7898
Philosophy Today (USA) 6944
Photochemistry and Photobiology (USA) 2139
Phycologia (USA) 808
The Physician and Sportsmedicine (USA) 6232
Physiotherapy Research International (GBR) 6114
Phytomedicine (DEU) 5696
Pigment & Resin Technology (GBR) 6720
The Plant Cell (USA) 810
Plant Engineering (USA) 3215
Plant Physiology (USA) 812
Plastic Surgical Nursing (USA) 5978
Plastics Engineering (USA) 7097
Plastics Technology (USA) 7098
Plays (USA) 8476
Ploughshares (USA) 5352
Poetry (Chicago) (USA) 5430
The Point! (USA) 1408
Policy Studies Journal (USA) 7167
Political Research Quarterly (USA) 7169
Political Science Quarterly (USA) 7169
Pollution Engineering (USA) 3490
Polymer Composites (USA) 7098
Polymer Engineering and Science (USA) 3252
PopSci.com (USA) *see* Popular Science. 8435
Popular Mechanics PMZone (USA) *see* Popular Mechanics. 8435
Popular Music & Society (GBR) 6607
Population Bulletin (USA) 7289
Postgraduate Medicine (USA) 5698
Powder Metallurgy (GBR) 6329
Power Engineering (USA) 3328
Practical Horseman (USA) 8296
Prehospital Emergency Care (GBR) 6071
Presidential Studies Quarterly (USA) 7173
Preventing School Failure (USA) 3045
Prevention (USA) 6995
Privacy Journal (USA) 2515
Problems of Post-Communism (USA) 7173
Productivity Software (USA) 2596
Professional Animal Scientist (USA) 8805
Professional Engineering (GBR) 3393
Progress in Histochemistry and Cytochemistry (DEU) 742
The Progressive (Madison) (USA) 7173
Progressive Librarian (USA) 5040
The Province (CAN) 3816
Psychiatric Annals (USA) 6176
Psychiatric Rehabilitation Journal (USA) 6176
Psychiatry (New York) (USA) 6177
The Psychoanalytic Review (USA) 7395
The Psychological Record (USA) 7396
The Psychologist (GBR) 7398
Psychology & Psychotherapy (GBR) 7399
Psychology Today (USA) 7400
Psychopathology (CHE) 6179
Psychosomatics (USA) 6179
Psychotherapy and Psychosomatics (CHE) 6180
Psychotherapy Research (GBR) 7401
Public Broadcasting Report (USA) 2388
Public Libraries (USA) 5040
Public Opinion Quarterly (USA) 7174
Public Personnel Management (USA) 1873
Public Relations Quarterly (USA) 33
Publishers Weekly (USA) 7571
Publius (USA) 7174
Qualitative Inquiry (USA) 7994
Queen's Quarterly (CAN) 3816
Quill (Greencastle) (USA) 4582
Radio Control Car Action (USA) 4345
Railway Age (USA) 8623
Ranger Rick (USA) 2210
Read Magazine (USA) 3078
Real Living with Multiple Sclerosis (USA) 6180
Real Simple (USA) 8881
RealScreen (CAN) 1164
Reason (USA) 5236
Refrigerated Transporter (USA) 8675
The Region Magazine (USA) 1378
Regional Anesthesia and Pain Medicine (USA) 5773
Regulation (Washington, 1977) (USA) 7176
Religious Conference Manager (USA) 7675
Religious Studies and Theology (GBR) 7676
Remix (USA) 6610
Renaissance Quarterly (USA) 5359
Renascence (USA) 5359
Rental Equipment Register (USA) 1839
Research in African Literatures (USA) 5360
Research in Phenomenology (NLD) 6947
Research Money (CAN) 1378
Research on Aging (USA) 4054
Research Quarterly for Exercise and Sport (USA) 6995
Research Technology Management (USA) 1790
Resource Links (CAN) 2210
Restaurant Business (USA) 4396
Retail Traffic (USA) 1841
Rethinking Marxism (GBR) 7177
Review of African Political Economy (GBR) 7262
The Review of Contemporary Fiction (USA) 5360
The Review of Economic Studies (GBR) 1166
The Review of Metaphysics (USA) 6948
The Review of Politics (GBR) 7178
Rhetoric Society Quarterly (USA) 5362
Rinascimento (ITA) 4473
Rocks and Minerals (USA) 6478
Roll Call (USA) 7180
Rolling Stone (USA) 6613
Romance Quarterly (USA) 5364
Royal Anthropological Institute. Journal (GBR) 354
Royal Society of Medicine. Journal (GBR) 5707
Rubber Chemistry and Technology (USA) 7826
Rural Sociology (USA) 8130
Russian Life (USA) 8753
S T I Online (GBR) *see* Sexually Transmitted Infections. 5881
The Safety & Health Practitioner (GBR) 7540
Saint Anthony Messenger (USA) 7816
Sales & Marketing Management (USA) 1842
Sarasota Magazine (USA) 3987
Saskatchewan Sage (CAN) 3562
SaskBusiness (CAN) 1171
Satellite News (Online) (USA) 2389
Satellite Week (USA) 2389
Saturday Evening Post (USA) 3988
Scandinavian Review (USA) 3563
Scandinavian Studies (Provo) (USA) 5367
Schizophrenia Bulletin (USA) 6184
Scholastic Action (USA) 3079
Scholastic Art (USA) 3079
Scholastic Choices (USA) 3080
Scholastic Dynamath (USA) 3080
Scholastic Math (USA) 3080
School Library Journal (USA) 5046
School Talk (USA) 3081
Science (USA) 7908
Science Activities (USA) 7908
Science & Society (USA) 7182
Science Communication (USA) 8131
Science Letter (USA) 7910
Science News (USA) 7910
Science, Technology & Human Values (USA) 7911
Science World (USA) 3081
Sciences (FRA) 7911
Scientific American (USA) 7912
Scientific American Special (USA) 7912
Scientific Computing (USA) 7940
The Scientist (USA) 7913
The Scottish Historical Review (GBR) 4160
Screen Education (AUS) 3081
Sea Classics (USA) 8660
Sea Power (USA) 6445
Sea Technology (USA) 3219
Shakespeare Quarterly (USA) 5370
Shakespeare Studies (USA) 5370
SI.com (USA) *see* Sports Illustrated. 8207
Signs (USA) 8903
Simulation (GBR) 3220
Skeptical Inquirer (USA) 6743
Ski (USA) 8333
Skiing Magazine (USA) 8333
Skipping Stones (USA) 2213
Sky & Telescope (USA) 581
Smithsonian Magazine Web (USA) *see* Smithsonian. 8002
Social Behavior and Personality (NZL) 7408
Social Education (USA) 3082
Social Forces (USA) 8133
Social Justice (USA) 7265
Social Psychology Quarterly (USA) 8134
Social Research (USA) 8003
Social Science Computer Review (USA) 2951
Social Security Bulletin (USA) 4523
The Social Studies (USA) 8005
Social Theory and Practice (USA) 6952
Social Work (USA) 8070
Social Work Research (USA) 8071
Society (USA) 8005
Sociological Methodology (USA) 8136
Sociological Methods & Research (USA) 8137
Sociological Theory (USA) 8137
Sociology of Religion (USA) 8139
Soil & Sediment Contamination (USA) 3491
Soil Science Society of America. Journal (USA) 253
Sojourners Magazine (USA) 7682
Soldiers (USA) 6446
South Carolina Business Journal (USA) 1177
The South Carolina Historical Magazine (USA) 4313
South Dakota Business Review (USA) 1177
Southeast Farm Press (USA) 158
Southern Economic Journal (USA) 1178
Southern Journal of Applied Forestry (USA) 3703
Southern Literary Journal (USA) 5375
Southern Living (USA) 3988
The Southern Review (USA) 5375
Southwest Art (USA) 518
Southwest Farm Press (USA) 158
The Southwest Review (USA) 5240
Special Warfare (USA) 6447
The Spectator (GBR) 5240
Spectroscopy (USA) 2105
Spiritual Life (USA) 7683
Sports Afield (USA) 8335
Stage Directions (USA) 8479
State Legislatures (USA) 7186
State Telephone Regulation Report (USA) 2371
Strings (USA) 6620
Stroke (USA) 5800
Student Aid News (USA) 3003
Student B M J (GBR) 5718
Studies in Art Education (USA) 520
Studies in Comparative International Development (USA) 8008
Studies in Philology (USA) 5183
Studies in Romanticism (USA) 5381
Studies in the Literary Imagination (USA) 5382
Studies in the Novel (USA) 5382
Style (CAN) 2261
Style (DeKalb) (USA) 5382
Sunset (USA) 3989
Supervision (USA) 1709
Surgical Products (USA) 5718
Survey of Current Business (USA) 1521
Swim Magazine (Online) (USA) 8210
Symposium (USA) 5384
Systematic and Applied Microbiology (DEU) 896
Systematic Biology (USA) 707
T+ D (USA) 1876
Target Marketing (USA) 1845
Taxes - The Tax Magazine (USA) 1951
Teacher Librarian (USA) 2918

Link to your serials resources and content with ulrichsweb.com

Online Service

11238 PROQUEST LLC (ANN ARBOR) ULRICH'S PERIODICALS

Teaching Exceptional Children Plus (USA) **3048**
Teaching Mathematics and Its Applications (GBR) **5541**
Teaching Music (USA) **6622**
Tech Directions (USA) **3085**
Technology Meetings (USA) **8442**
Technology Review (USA) **7922**
The Technology Teacher (USA) **3085**
TechTrends (USA) **2951**
Telco Business Report (USA) **8461**
Telecom Policy Report (Online) (USA) **2341**
Test & Measurement World (USA) **3332**
Texas Business Review (USA) **1182**
Texas Law Review (USA) **4794**
Textile Research Journal (GBR) **8460**
Textile World (USA) **8461**
Theatre Survey (GBR) **8483**
Theological Studies (USA) **7689**
Theology Today (USA) **7690**
Theory into Practice (USA) **2919**
Therapeutic Recreation Journal (USA) **6998**
Third World Quarterly (GBR) **1606**
Tikkun Magazine (USA) **5242**
Time (USA) **3990**
Time for Kids News Scoop (USA) **2217**
Time for Kids World Report (USA) **2217**
The Tizard Learning Disability Review (GBR) **6188**
Topics in Early Childhood Special Education (USA) **3048**
Topics in Language Disorders (USA) **3048**
Topics in Stroke Rehabilitation (USA) **5801**
Toronto Life (CAN) **3818**
Torrey Botanical Society. Journal (USA) **820**
Total Health (USA) **6670**
Trailer / Body Builders (USA) **8676**
Trailer Life (USA) **8338**
Training (USA) **1798**
Trains (USA) **8626**
Transforming Anthropology (USA) **358**
Transport Europe (BEL) **8514**
Tribology & Lubrication Technology (USA) **3398**
Tribune (Welland) (CAN) **3819**
Trinity Journal (USA) **7691**
TriQuarterly (USA) **5243**
Twentieth Century Literature (USA) **5391**
U N Chronicle (USA) **7269**
U S B E and Information Technology (USA) **3224**
U.S. News & World Report Digital Edition (USA) *see* U S News & World Report. **3991**
Undersea & Hyperbaric Medicine (USA) **5726**
Urban Studies (GBR) **4430**
Urgent Communications (USA) **2364**
Urology Times (USA) **6276**
Urology Times: The Urology Times Clinical Edition (USA) **6276**
Us Weekly (USA) **3991**
Utne Reader (USA) **3991**
Variety (USA) **8484**
Vascular and Endovascular Surgery (USA) **6262**
Vegetarian Times (USA) **6670**
Venture Capital Journal (USA) **1658**
Vermont Business Magazine (USA) **1191**
Veterinary Medicine (USA) **8813**
Via Satellite (USA) **2343**
Vibrant Life (USA) **6999**
Victoria (USA) **3992**
Victorian Studies (USA) **4481**
Video Librarian (USA) **5054**
Virginia Quarterly Review (USA) **5244**
Visible Language (USA) **5194**
Vital Speeches of the Day (USA) **4585**
W H O Drug Information (CHE) **7545**
Wall Street & Technology (USA) **1394**
Wall Street Journal Online (USA) *see* Wall Street Journal (Central Edition). **1390**
Wall Street Journal Online (USA) *see* Wall Street Journal (Eastern Edition). **1390**
Wall Street Journal Online (USA) *see* Wall Street Journal (Western Edition). **1390**
Ward's AutoWorld (USA) **8611**
Ward's Dealer Business (USA) **8611**
Waste Age (USA) **3513**
Water Environment & Technology (USA) **3492**
Water Environment Research (USA) **3493**
Wearables Business (USA) **2250**
Weather and Forecasting (USA) **6398**
Weatherwise (USA) **6398**
Weekly Epidemiological Record (CHE) **7545**
Westchester County Business Journal (USA) **1524**
Western Farm Press (USA) **170**
Western Folklore (USA) **3624**
The Western Journal of Black Studies (USA) **3572**
What Works in Teaching and Learning (USA) **3087**
Whispering Wind (USA) **3572**
Wild West (USA) **4318**
The Wilson Journal of Ornithology (USA) **917**
The Wilson Quarterly (USA) **5245**
Windsor Star (CAN) **3820**
Windspeaker (CAN) **3572**
Wings of Gold (USA) **75**
Wireless Business Forecast (Online) (USA) **2535**
Wireless Week (USA) **2345**
Women and Language (USA) **5195**
Women in Business (USA) **1195**
Women's Health Weekly (USA) **8849**
Women's Studies in Communication (USA) **8905**
Woodworking (CAN) **1053**
Workforce Management (USA) **1877**
The World & I Online (USA) **3993**
World Archaeology (GBR) **424**
World Health Organization. Bulletin (CHE) **5731**
World Literature Today (USA) **5400**
World Policy Journal (USA) **7274**
World Today (GBR) **7275**
World Trade: WT100 (USA) **1588**
World War II (Leesburg) (USA) **4318**
World Watch (USA) **3475**
Worldwide Computer Products News (GBR) **2441**
Worldwide Videotex Update (USA) **2569**
The Writer (USA) **5400**
Writer's Digest (USA) **4585**
Xbox Nation (USA) **2482**
Yachting (USA) **8285**
Yankee (USA) **3993**
Yearbook of English Studies (GBR) **5403**
Young Adult Library Services (USA) **5055**
Youth Today (USA) **2172**

ProQuest LLC (Ann Arbor) (Subsidiary of: Cambridge Information Group) 789 E Eisenhower Pkwy, PO Box 1346, Ann Arbor, MI 48106-1346 TEL 734-761-4700, 800-521-0600, FAX 734-997-4040, 800-864-0019, info@proquest.com, http://www.proquest.com
A A C E International Transactions (USA) **3179**
A A N A Journal (USA) **5949**
A A R P: The Magazine (USA) **5064**
A B A Bank Compliance (USA) **1304**
A B A Bank Directors Briefing (USA) **1304**
A B A Bank Marketing (USA) **1304**
A B A Banking Journal (USA) **1304**
A B A Journal (USA) **4606**
A B A Trust & Investments (USA) **1304**
A B N F Journal (USA) **5949**
A C I Structural Journal (USA) **974**
A C M Computing Surveys (USA) **2405**
A C M Queue (USA) **2587**
A C M Transactions on Computer Systems (USA) **2519**
A D C Times (USA) **3514**
A D H D Report (USA) **6117**
A D L on the Frontline (USA) **7201**
A F P Exchange (USA) **1305**
A H A News (Chicago) (USA) **4086**
A I & Society (GBR) **2444**
A I Ch E Journal (USA) **3234**
A I D S Care (GBR) **5807**
A I M S Journal (GBR) **5985**
A I Magazine (USA) **2445**
A J R NewsLink (USA) *see* American Journalism Review. **4571**
A K C Gazette (USA) **6802**
The A L A N Review (USA) **3049**
A L A TechSource (USA) *see* Library Technology Reports. **5029**
A M T (USA) **8533**
A N Q: A Quarterly Journal of Short Articles, Notes and Reviews (USA) **5248**
A N S O M (USA) **2245**
A O R N Journal (USA) **5949**
A P I Account (USA) **1275**
A R D Online (GBR) *see* Annals of the Rheumatic Diseases. **6221**
A S E A N Economic Bulletin (SGP) **1055**
A S E E Prism (USA) **3179**
A S H A Leader (USA) **4071**
A S H R A E Journal (USA) **4115**
A S H R A E Transactions (USA) **4116**
A T M Global (USA) **41**
A T Q (USA) **5248**
Abdominal Imaging (USA) **5919**
Aboriginal Nurse (CAN) **5950**
About...Time (USA) **3515**
Abya Yala News (USA) **3515**
Academe (USA) **2965**
Academic Emergency Medicine (USA) **6054**
Academic Pediatrics (USA) **6086**
Academic Psychiatry (USA) **6118**
Academy of Management Journal (USA) **1723**
The Academy of Management Perspectives (USA) **1723**
Academy of Management Review (USA) **1723**
Academy of Marketing Science. Journal (USA) **1803**
Academy of Marketing Science Review (USA) **1803**
Accountancy (GBR) **1276**
Accountancy Age (GBR) **1276**
Accountancy Ireland (IRL) **1276**
Accountancy S A (ZAF) **1276**
The Accountant (IRL) **1276**
Accounting, Auditing and Accountability Journal (GBR) **1277**
Accounting Department Management Report (USA) **1277**
Accounting Education News (USA) **1277**
Accounting Historians Journal (USA) **1278**
Accounting History (AUS) **1278**
Accounting Horizons (USA) **1278**
Accounting Office Management & Administration Report (USA) **1278**
Accounting Perspectives (CAN) **1278**
The Accounting Review (USA) **1278**
Accounting Technology (USA) **1279**
Accounting Today (USA) **1279**
Acoustic Guitar (USA) **6542**
Acta Applicandae Mathematicae (NLD) **5464**
Acta Diabetologica (DEU) **5883**
Acta Ethologica Online (DEU) **649**
Acta Histochemica (DEU) **721**
Acta Informatica (DEU) **2541**
Acta Mechanica (AUT) **3372**
Acta Meteorologica Sinica (CHN) **6345**
Acta Neuropathologica (DEU) **6118**
Acta Pediatrica Espanola (ESP) **6087**
Acta Politica (GBR) **7101**
Active Living (CAN) **4063**
L' Actualite (CAN) **3805**
Actualite Economique (CAN) **1056**
L' Actualite Pharmaceutique (CAN) **6818**
Addiction (GBR) **2689**
Adelphi Series (GBR) **7219**
Adhesives & Sealants Industry (USA) **3235**
AdMedia (NZL) **19**
Administration and Policy in Mental Health and Mental Health Services Research (USA) **5567**
Administration & Society (USA) **7418**
Administrative Assistant's Update (CAN) **1855**
Administrative Science Quarterly (USA) **7419**
Administrative Theory & Praxis (USA) **7419**
Adolescence (USA) **2143**
Adolescent Medicine (Elk Grove) (USA) **6087**
Adolescent Psychiatry (USA) **6119**
Adult Basic Education and Literacy Journal (USA) **2937**
Adult Learning (USA) **2938**
Advanced Battery Technology (USA) **3294**
Advanced Emergency Nursing Journal (USA) **6055**
Advanced Imaging (USA) **2349**
Advanced Packaging (USA) **3089**
Advances in Competitiveness Research (USA) **1551**
Advances in Developing Human Resources (USA) **1855**
Advances in Skin and Wound Care (USA) **5871**
Advertiser (Adelaide) (AUS) **3793**
Advertising Age (USA) **20**
Advertising - Communications Times (USA) **20**
Advisor Today (USA) **4491**
Advisor's Edge (CAN) **1609**
The Advocate (Los Angeles, 1967) (USA) **4370**
Adweek (USA) **20**
Aequationes Mathematicae (CHE) **5467**
Africa (GBR) **4172**
Africa Analysis (GBR) **1435**
Africa Today (USA) **7102**
African Affairs (GBR) **7103**
African American Review (USA) **3516**
African Arts (USA) **464**
African Business (GBR) **1589**
African Journal of Legal Studies (CAN) **4611**
African Studies Review (USA) **3516**
Afro-Americans in New York Life and History (USA) **3517**
Afro-Hispanic Review (USA) **3517**
Afterimage (USA) **6963**
Aftermarket Business (USA) **8555**
Against the Current (USA) **7103**
Age and Ageing (GBR) **4038**
Agency Sales (USA) **1804**
Aging & Elder Health Week (USA) **4039**
The Aging Male (GBR) **6283**
Aging Today (USA) **4039**
Agribusiness (New York) (USA) **191**
Agricultural and Resource Economics Review (USA) **191**
The Agricultural Education Magazine (USA) **83**
Agricultural History (USA) **83**
Agricultural Research (USA) **217**
Agriculture and Human Values (NLD) **85**
Agriculture Online (USA) *see* Successful Farming. **159**
Agronomy Journal (USA) **88**
Ahfad Journal (SDN) **8893**
AIDS & Behavior (USA) **5752**
AIDS & Hepatitis Digest (GBR) **5808**
AIDS Education and Prevention (USA) **7506**
AIDS Vaccine Week (USA) **5809**
AIDS Weekly (USA) **5809**
AIDS Weekly & Law (USA) **4612**
Air Cargo World (USA) **8534**
Air Classics (USA) **44**
Air Conditioning, Heating & Refrigeration News (USA) **4116**
Air Force Comptroller (USA) **6409**
Air Force Journal of Logistics (USA) **6409**
Air Force Law Review (USA) **4971**
Air Power History (USA) **44**
Air Safety Week (Online) (USA) **44**
Air Transport World (USA) **45**
Aircraft Economics (GBR) **8535**
Aircraft Engineering and Aerospace Technology (GBR) **45**
Aircraft Value News (USA) **8535**
Airfinance Journal (GBR) **8535**
Airline Business (GBR) **8536**
Airman (USA) **6409**
Airport Business (USA) **46**
Airports (USA) **8537**
Alabama Heritage (USA) **4282**
Alabama Nurse (USA) **5950**
The Alabama Review (USA) **4282**
Alaska (USA) **3969**
Alaska Business Monthly (USA) **1058**
Alberta Journal of Educational Research (CAN) **2825**
Alberta R N (CAN) **5950**
Alberta Sweetgrass (CAN) **3517**
Alcohol and Alcoholism (GBR) **2690**
Alcohol Research & Health (USA) **2691**
Alice Magazine (USA) **8850**
All Hands (USA) **6410**
Allure (USA) **8851**
Alternative Therapies in Health and Medicine (USA) **306**
Alternatives Journal (CAN) **3402**
Alzheimer's Care Today (USA) **6121**
Ambio Journal Online (SWE) *see* Ambio. **3402**
America (USA) **7782**
The American (Washington, D.C.) (USA) **7104**
American Academy of Advertising. Proceedings of the Conference (USA) **20**
American Academy of Audiology. Journal (USA) **6077**
American Academy of Business, Cambridge. Journal (USA) **1058**
American Academy of Nurse Practitioners. Journal (USA) **5951**
American Academy of Psychoanalysis and Dynamic Psychiatry. Journal (USA) **7332**
American Academy of Religion. Journal (USA) **7620**
American Agent and Broker (USA) **4492**
American Animal Hospital Association. Journal (Online Edition) (USA) **8791**
American Annals of the Deaf (USA) **4071**
American Anthropologist (USA) **324**
American Artist (USA) **465**
American Artist. Watercolor (USA) **465**
American Association of Occupational Health Nurses Journal (USA) **5951**
American Banker (USA) **1307**
American Banker's Financial Modernization Report (USA) **1307**
American Bankruptcy Law Journal (USA) **4614**
American Behavioral Scientist (USA) **7946**
The American Biology Teacher (USA) **652**
American Business Law Journal (USA) **4854**
American Ceramic Society. Bulletin (USA) **2037**
American Ceramic Society. Journal (USA) **2037**
American Cheerleader (USA) **8158**
American Chiropractic Association. Journal (USA) **5803**
American City & County (USA) **7487**
American Craft (USA) **531**
American Criminal Law Review (USA) **2643**
American Dietetic Association. Journal (USA) **6654**
American Drama (USA) **8465**
The American Economic Review (USA) **1436**
American Economist (USA) **1436**
American Educational History Journal (USA) **2825**
American Educational Research Journal (USA) **2825**
American Family Physician (USA) **5571**
American Fastener Journal (USA) **3373**
American Forests (USA) **3683**
American Fruit Grower (USA) **3722**
American Gas (USA) **6762**
American Heritage (USA) **4282**
American Historical Review (USA) **4129**
American History (Leesburg) (USA) **4282**
American Imago (USA) **6121**
American Indian and Alaska Native Mental Health Research (Online Edition) (USA) **6634**
American Indian Quarterly (USA) **6634**
American Institute of Certified Public Accountants. Tax Division Newsletter (USA) **1910**
American Jewish History (USA) **7718**
American Journal of Audiology (USA) **4072**
American Journal of Business (USA) **1059**
American Journal of Clinical Hypnosis (USA) **5942**
American Journal of Clinical Nutrition (USA) **6655**
American Journal of Community Psychology (USA) **8086**
American Journal of Criminal Justice (USA) **2643**
American Journal of Criminal Law (USA) **2643**
American Journal of Critical Care (USA) **5951**
American Journal of Education (USA) **2826**
American Journal of Epidemiology (USA) **5572**
American Journal of Family Law (USA) **4906**
American Journal of Family Therapy (USA) **7333**
American Journal of Geriatric Psychiatry (USA) **4040**
American Journal of Health Behavior (USA) **6981**
American Journal of Health Education (USA) **3050**
American Journal of Health Studies (Online) (USA) **6982**
American Journal of Human Genetics (USA) **862**
American Journal of International Law (USA) **4916**
American Journal of Law & Medicine (USA) **4614**
American Journal of Mathematics (USA) **5468**
American Journal of Nephrology (CHE) **6265**
American Journal of Orthopsychiatry (USA) **7333**
The American Journal of Pathology (USA) **5573**
American Journal of Pharmaceutical Education (USA) **6820**
American Journal of Philology (USA) **5092**
American Journal of Political Science (USA) **7105**
American Journal of Potato Research (USA) **218**
American Journal of Psychiatry (USA) **6122**
The American Journal of Psychoanalysis (USA) **7333**
American Journal of Psychology (USA) **7333**
American Journal of Psychotherapy (USA) **6122**
American Journal of Public Health (USA) **7507**
American Journal of Respiratory and Critical Care Medicine (USA) **6211**
American Journal of Respiratory Cell and Molecular Biology (USA) **6211**
The American Journal of Semiotics (USA) **4442**
American Journal of Sociology (USA) **8087**
American Journal of Speech - Language Pathology (USA) **4072**
American Journal of Theology & Philosophy (USA) **7621**
American Law and Economics Review (GBR) **4614**
American Libraries (USA) **4988**
American Literary History (USA) **5252**
American Literature (USA) **5252**
American Machinist (USA) **1879**
American Mathematical Monthly (USA) **5468**
American Medical Informatics Association. Journal (USA) **5829**

American Meteorological Society. Bulletin (USA) **6346**
American Midland Naturalist (USA) **7834**
American Music (USA) **6544**
American Music Teacher (USA) **6544**
American Musicological Society. Journal (USA) **6544**
The American Naturalist (USA) **652**
The American Nurse (USA) **5951**
American Oriental Society. Journal (USA) **542**
American Philological Association. Transactions (USA) **2229**
American Philosophical Society. Proceedings (USA) **4442**
American Philosophical Society. Transactions (USA) **4442**
American Planning Association. Journal (USA) **4403**
American Poetry Review (USA) **5416**
American Political Science Review (GBR) **7105**
American Pomological Society. Journal (USA) **3722**
American Printer (USA) **7318**
The American Prospect (USA) **7105**
American Psychologist (USA) **7333**
American Quarterly (USA) **4442**
American Record Guide (USA) **6544**
American Salesman (USA) **1805**
American Salon (USA) **585**
American Scholar (USA) **5206**
American School & University (USA) **3017**
American Schools of Oriental Research. Bulletin (USA) **542**
American Scientist (USA) **7835**
American Secondary Education (USA) **3017**
American Society for Information Science and Technology. Bulletin (USA) **4989**
American Society for Information Science and Technology. Journal (USA) **4989**
American Society of International Law. Proceedings of the Annual Meeting (USA) **4916**
American Sociological Review (USA) **8087**
The American Spectator (USA) **5206**
American Statistical Association. Journal (USA) **8344**
The American Statistician (USA) **8344**
American Surgeon (USA) **6236**
American Taxation Association. Journal (USA) **1910**
American Teacher (USA) **4589**
American Theatre (USA) **8465**
American Vegetable Grower (USA) **218**
American Water Resources Association. Journal (USA) **8817**
American Water Works Association. E-Journal (USA) *see* American Water Works Association. Journal. **8817**
American Woodworker (USA) **4437**
The Americas (USA) **4283**
Americas (English Edition) (USA) **4442**
America's Civil War (USA) **4283**
Amyloid (GBR) **6221**
Anaesthesia and Intensive Care (AUS) **5768**
Analog Science Fiction & Fact (USA) **5439**
Analyse & Kritik (DEU) **7947**
El Andar (Online Edition) (USA) **3518**
Andean Report (PER) **1436**
Anesthesia Progress (USA) **5834**
Angiogenesis (GBR) **6008**
Angiogenesis Weekly (USA) **6820**
Angiology (USA) **5777**
Anglican and Episcopal History (USA) **7745**
Anglican Theological Review (USA) **7746**
Annals of Anatomy (DEU) **5575**
Annals of Botany (GBR) **775**
Annals of Clinical Biochemistry (GBR) **722**
Annals of Clinical Microbiology and Antimicrobials (GBR) **881**
Annals of Clinical Psychiatry (USA) **6123**
Annals of Dyslexia (USA) **3036**
Annals of Global Analysis and Geometry (NLD) **5471**
Annals of Internal Medicine (USA) **5943**
Annals of Nutrition and Metabolism (CHE) **6655**
Annals of Operations Research (NLD) **2406**
Annals of Otology, Rhinology and Laryngology (USA) **6077**
The Annals of Regional Science (DEU) **1060**
Annals of Surgical Oncology (USA) **6236**
Annals of Tropical Paediatrics (GBR) **6087**
Annals of Vascular Surgery (USA) **6237**
Annual of Psychoanalysis (USA) **7334**
Annual Organ Handbook (USA) **6545**
Annual Review of Astronomy and Astrophysics (USA) **568**
Annual Review of Clinical Psychology (USA) **7335**
Annual Review of Ecology, Evolution and Systematics (USA) **3403**
Annual Review of Environment and the Resources (USA) **3124**
Annual Review of Gerontology & Geriatrics (USA) **4040**
Annual Review of Nursing Research (USA) **5951**
Annual Review of Plant Biology (USA) **775**
Annual Review of Sex Research (USA) **7335**
Anthropological Quarterly (USA) **325**
Anthropology & Education Quarterly (USA) **326**
Anti-Corrosion Methods and Materials (GBR) **6305**
Anti-Infectives Week (USA) **5810**
The Antigonish Review (CAN) **5255**
Antike und Abendland (DEU) **2230**
Antioch Review (USA) **5206**
Antiques & Collecting Magazine (USA) **363**
Antiquity (GBR) **374**
Antitrust Bulletin (USA) **4855**
Apparel (USA) **2245**
AppleSeeds (USA) **2176**
Applied Linguistics (GBR) **5095**
Applied Mathematics and Optimization (USA) **5472**
Applied Psychophysiology and Biofeedback (USA) **7336**
Applied Radiology (USA) **6192**
Appraisal Journal (USA) **7582**
Approach (USA) **47**
Appropriate Technology (GBR) **194**
Aquatic Mammals (USA) **933**
Arbeit (DEU) **7948**
Arcadia (DEU) **5256**
Architectural Lighting (USA) **429**
Architectural Record (USA) **430**
The Architectural Review (GBR) **430**
Archival Science (NLD) **4990**
Archive for Mathematical Logic (DEU) **5473**
Archives of Dermatological Research (DEU) **5871**
Archives of Disease in Childhood (GBR) **6088**
Archives of Environmental and Occupational Health (USA) **3404**
Archives of Pathology & Laboratory Medicine (USA) **5902**
Archives of Sexual Behavior (USA) **5577**
Archives of Virology (AUT) **881**
Archives of Women's Mental Health (AUT) **8843**
Arctic (CAN) **7836**
Area Development Site & Facility Planning (USA) **4403**
Arethusa (USA) **2230**
Argumentation & Advocacy (USA) **5096**
Arizona Nurse (USA) **5952**
Arizona Quarterly (USA) **5207**
Arkansas Business and Economic Review (USA) **1061**
Arkansas Business Journal (USA) **1061**
Arkansas Historical Quarterly (USA) **4284**
Armada International (CHE) **47**
Armed Forces and Society (USA) **6410**
Armed Forces Comptroller (USA) **6410**
Armenian International Magazine (USA) **3519**
Armenian Reporter (USA) **3519**
Armor (USA) **6411**
Arms Control Today (USA) **4917**
Army (USA) **6411**
Army A L & T (USA) **6411**
The Army Lawyer (USA) **4971**
Army Logistician (USA) **6412**
Army Reserve Magazine (USA) **6412**
The Art Bulletin (USA) **468**
Art Business News (USA) **468**
Art Education (USA) **469**
Art in America (USA) **469**
Art Journal (USA) **470**
Artforum International (USA) **472**
Arthur Frommer's Budget Travel (USA) **8684**
Artificial Intelligence and Law (NLD) **4622**
Artificial Intelligence Review (NLD) **2446**
The Artist's Magazine (USA) **473**
Arts and Activities (USA) **3051**
Arts Education Policy Review (USA) **475**
Asia Computer Weekly (SGP) **2407**
Asia Inc (CHN) **1061**
Asia - Pacific Financial Markets (NLD) **1392**
Asia Pacific Journal of Management (SGP) **1725**
Asia Pacific Journal of Operational Research (SGP) **2407**
Asia - Pacific Journal of Teacher Education (AUS) **3051**
Asia - Pacific Telecom Newsletter (USA) **2365**
Asia Weekly Financial Alert (GBR) **1438**
AsiaLaw (HKG) **4856**
AsiaMoney (CHN) **1308**
Asian Affairs: An American Review (USA) **7222**
Asian Business & Management (GBR) **1726**
Asian Development Review (PHL) **1591**
Asian Ethnology (JPN) **329**
Asian Journal of Women's Studies (KOR) **8893**
Asian Music (USA) **6546**
Asian Pages (USA) **543**
Asian Perspectives (USA) **381**
Asian Philosophy (GBR) **6906**
The Asian Reporter (USA) **3520**
Asian Review of Business and Technology (GBR) **8416**
Asian Survey (USA) **7107**
Asian Theatre Journal (USA) **8466**
The Asian Wall Street Journal (CHN) **1309**
AsianWeek (USA) **3520**
Ask (USA) **2176**
Aslib Proceedings (GBR) **4991**
Asphalt Contractor (USA) **976**
Assembly (Oak Brook) (USA) **3182**
Assembly Automation (GBR) **2457**
Assessment & Evaluation in Higher Education (GBR) **2967**
Assessment in Education: Principles, Policy and Practice (GBR) **2827**
Asset-Backed Alert (USA) **1610**
Asset Securitization Report (USA) **1610**
Association for Computing Machinery. Communications (USA) **2533**
Association for Computing Machinery. Journal (USA) **2407**
Association Now (USA) **1726**
Assurances et Gestion des Risques (CAN) **4493**
Astronomy (USA) **570**
The Astronomy and Astrophysics Review (DEU) **571**
At-Home Dad (USA) **6286**
Atlanta Business Journal (USA) *see* Atlanta Business Chronicle. **1438**
Atlanta Tribune: The Magazine (USA) **3521**
The Atlantic (USA) **5207**
Atlantic Economic Journal (USA) **1063**
Attention, Perception & Psychophysics (USA) **7337**
Attorney - C P A (USA) **4856**
Audiology and Neurotology (CHE) **6078**
Audiotex Update (USA) **2349**
Auditing (USA) **1280**
Augmentative and Alternative Communication (GBR) **5580**
The Auk (USA) **901**
Aussenwirtschaft (CHE) **1552**
Austin Business Journal (USA) **1063**
Australasian Journal of Philosophy (GBR) **6906**
Australasian Marketing Journal (AUS) **1806**
Australasian Science (AUS) **7838**
The Australian (AUS) **3793**
Australian Accounting Review (AUS) **1281**
Australian and New Zealand Journal of Public Health (AUS) **7508**
Australian Bulletin of Labour (AUS) **1666**
Australian Business Law Review (AUS) **4857**
Australian Doctor (AUS) **5581**
Australian Geographer (GBR) **3999**
Australian Health Review (AUS) **4088**
The Australian Journal of Anthropology (AUS) **330**
Australian Journal of Clinical Hypnotherapy and Hypnosis (AUS) **5942**
Australian Journal of Dairy Technology (AUS) **261**
Australian Journal of International Affairs (GBR) **7222**
Australian Journal of Management (AUS) **1727**
Australian Journal of Political Science (GBR) **7108**
Australian Journal of Social Issues (AUS) **8026**
Australian Nursing Journal (AUS) **5952**
Australian Tax Forum (AUS) **1911**
Australian Tax Review (AUS) **1911**
Auto/Biography Studies (USA) **640**
Automatic Merchandiser (USA) **1806**
Automotive Body Repair News (USA) **8564**
Automotive Components Analyst (GBR) **8564**
Automotive Industries (USA) **8565**
Automotive News (USA) **8565**
AutoWeek Online (USA) *see* AutoWeek. **8567**
Avian Pathology (GBR) **8794**
Aviation Daily (USA) **8538**
Aviation History (USA) **48**
Aviation Week & Space Technology (USA) **49**
Azerbaijan International (USA) **7222**
Azizah (USA) **7709**
B & T (AUS) **21**
B C Studies (CAN) **7949**
B D J Online (GBR) *see* British Dental Journal. **5836**
B F u P - Betriebswirtschaftliche Forschung und Praxis (DEU) **1727**
B J O Online (GBR) *see* British Journal of Ophthalmology. **6039**
B J S M Online (GBR) *see* British Journal of Sports Medicine. **6229**
B M C Ear, Nose and Throat Disorders (GBR) **6078**
B M C Geriatrics (GBR) **4041**
B M C Oral Health (GBR) **5836**
B M C Pulmonary Medicine (GBR) **6212**
B T Technology Journal (NLD) **2313**
B to B (USA) **1806**
The B V A Bulletin (USA) **4079**
Baby Talk (USA) **2144**
Background Notes (USA) **4000**
Backpacker (USA) **8305**
Baking Management (USA) **3671**
Balance (Alexandria) (USA) **4041**
Baltimore Business Journal (USA) **1065**
Baltimore Jewish Times (USA) **7718**
Banca Nazionale del Lavoro. Quarterly Review (ITA) **1310**
Bank Accounting & Finance (USA) **1281**
Bank Auditing & Accounting Report (USA) **1312**
Bank Director (USA) **1312**
Bank Marketing International (IRL) **1313**
Bank News (USA) **1313**
Bank of Canada. Review (CAN) **1313**
Bank of England Quarterly Bulletin (GBR) **1441**
Bank Systems & Technology (USA) **1316**
Bank Technology News (USA) **1316**
The Banker (GBR) **1316**
Banking and Finance Law Review (CAN) **1317**
Banking & Financial Services Policy Report (USA) **1317**
Banking Technology (GBR) **1318**
Barron's (USA) **1611**
Basic Research in Cardiology (DEU) **5778**
Bass Player (USA) **6548**
Batteries International (GBR) **3296**
Baylor Business Review (USA) **1065**
Bee Culture (USA) **95**
Beef (USA) **280**
Beef Today (USA) **280**
Behavior and Philosophy (USA) **7338**
Behavior and Social Issues (USA) **7339**
Behavior Genetics (USA) **863**
Behavior Research Methods (USA) **7339**
Behavioral Disorders (USA) **3037**
Behavioral Ecology (USA) **656**
Behavioral Medicine (USA) **7339**
Behavioral Neuroscience (USA) **7339**
Behavioral Research in Accounting (USA) **1281**
Behaviour Change (AUS) **7340**
Belfast Telegraph (GBR) **3861**
Bell Labs Technical Journal (USA) **2365**
The Beltane Papers (USA) **8853**
Benchmarking (GBR) **1727**
Benefits Canada (CAN) **1667**
Benefits Law Journal (USA) **4968**
Benefits Quarterly (USA) **1856**
Best of New Orleans (USA) *see* New Orleans Magazine. **3983**
Best's Review. Insurance Issues and Analysis (USA) **4495**
Bestuursdinamika (ZAF) **1728**
Better Homes and Gardens (USA) **4533**
Better Investing (USA) **1612**
Beverage Industry (USA) **599**
Beverage World (USA) **599**
Biblical Archaeology Review (USA) **383**
Bicycle Retailer and Industry News (USA) **8254**
Bicycling (USA) **8254**
Billboard.com (USA) *see* Billboard (New York). **6549**
Biochemistry and Cell Biology (CAN) **725**
Biocontrol Science and Technology (GBR) **221**
BioCycle (USA) **3504**
Biodemography and Social Biology (USA) **864**
Biofeedback (Wheat Ridge) (USA) **7340**
Biography (Honolulu) (USA) **640**
Bioinformatics (Online) (GBR) **825**
Biological Bulletin (USA) **658**
Biological Therapies in Dentistry (CAN) **5836**
Biomedical Engineering (USA) **5585**
Biomedical Instrumentation & Technology (USA) **5586**
Biomedical Microdevices (USA) **5586**
Biomedical Safety & Standards (USA) **5586**
Biometrics (GBR) **8358**
Biometrika (GBR) **713**
BioPharm International (USA) **6825**
Biophysical Journal (USA) **752**
Bioremediation Journal (USA) **3483**
BioScience (USA) **661**
Biostatistics (GBR) **5587**
Biotech Business (USA) **759**
Biotech Business Week (USA) **759**
Biotech Law Weekly (USA) **4630**
Biotech Week (USA) **759**
Bird Study (GBR) **903**
Birmingham Business Journal (USA) **1067**
The Birth Gazette (USA) **5987**
The Birthkit (USA) **5987**
Bitch (USA) **8894**
The Black Collegian (USA) **6693**
Black Collegian Online (USA) **6693**
Black Enterprise.com (USA) *see* Black Enterprise. **1068**
Black Issues Book Review (USA) **3522**
Black Masks (USA) **8467**
Black Renaissance (USA) **3523**
Black Scholar (USA) **3523**
Blood Weekly (USA) **5934**
Boards (CAN) **2313**
BodyShop Business (USA) **8570**
The Bond Buyer (USA) **1613**
Bone Marrow Transplantation (GBR) **5903**
Book Links (USA) **2146**
Bookbird (USA) **2180**
Booklist (USA) **7554**
Borneo Review (MYS) **1068**
The Boston Business Journal (USA) **1068**
Boston College Environmental Affairs Law Review (USA) **3407**
The Boston Irish Reporter (USA) **3523**
Botany (CAN) **781**
The Bottom Line (GBR) **4998**
The Bottomline (USA) **1281**
The Boulder County Business Report (USA) **1425**
Boundary 2 (USA) **5265**
Bowhunter (USA) **8306**
Boys' Life (USA) **2180**
Brain (GBR) **6127**
Brain, Behavior and Evolution (CHE) **6127**
Brain Structure and Function (Online Edition) (DEU) *see* Brain Structure and Function (Print Edition). **920**
Brain Topography (USA) **6128**
Brake & Front End (USA) **8570**
Brand Strategy (GBR) **22**
Brandweek (USA) **22**
Breast Cancer Research and Treatment (USA) **6010**
Briefings in Bioinformatics (GBR) **825**
Briefings in Entrepreneurial Finance (GBR) **1729**
Briefings in Functional Genomics & Proteomics (GBR) **864**
Briefings In Real Estate Finance (GBR) **7584**
Brigham Young University Law Review (USA) **4632**
British Educational Research Journal (GBR) **2832**
British Food Journal (GBR) **3628**
British Heritage (USA) **4206**
British Journal for the History of Science (GBR) **7842**
The British Journal for the Philosophy of Science (GBR) **7842**
British Journal of Aesthetics (GBR) **6908**
British Journal of Anaesthesia (GBR) **5770**
British Journal of Biomedical Science (GBR) **5903**
British Journal of Cancer (GBR) **6010**
British Journal of Clinical Psychology (GBR) **7341**
The British Journal of Criminology (GBR) **2645**
British Journal of Developmental Psychology (GBR) **7341**
British Journal of Educational Psychology (GBR) **7341**
The British Journal of Forensic Practice (GBR) **5912**
British Journal of Guidance and Counselling (GBR) **6693**
British Journal of Health Psychology (GBR) **7342**
British Journal of Mathematical and Statistical Psychology (GBR) **7342**

Online Service

Link to your serials resources and content with ulrichsweb.com

British Journal of Middle Eastern Studies (GBR) **4320**
British Journal of Neurosurgery (GBR) **6238**
British Journal of Nursing (GBR) **5953**
British Journal of Pharmacology (GBR) **6826**
British Journal of Psychology (GBR) **7342**
British Journal of Social Psychology (GBR) **7342**
The British Journal of Social Work (GBR) **8028**
British Journal of Sociology of Education (GBR) **2832**
British Medical Bulletin (GBR) **5589**
British Poultry Science (GBR) **281**
British Psychological Society. Proceedings (GBR) **7342**
Broadcast Engineering (USA) **2376**
Broadcast Engineering (World Edition) (USA) **2376**
Broadcast Engineering News (AUS) **2376**
Broadcasting & Cable (USA) **2376**
Broadcasting & Cable T V Fax (USA) **2376**
Brookings Papers on Economic Activity (USA) **1536**
Bruce Hopkins' Nonprofit Counsel (USA) **4632**
Buddhist - Christian Studies (USA) **7700**
Builder (Washington) (USA) **984**
Builders Merchants Journal (GBR) **984**
Building (CAN) **984**
Building Design (GBR) **436**
Building Design + Construction (USA) **985**
Building Operating Management (USA) **986**
Building Services Engineering Research & Technology (GBR) **986**
Buildings (USA) **987**
Le Bulletin des Agriculteurs (CAN) **98**
Bulletin of Experimental Biology and Medicine (USA) **663**
Bulletin of Hispanic Studies (Online Edition, Liverpool, 2002) (GBR) **5267**
Bulletin of the Atomic Scientists (USA) **7224**
Bulletin of the Comediantes (USA) **5267**
Bulletin of the History of Medicine (USA) **5589**
Business and Commercial Aviation (USA) **50**
Business & Economic Review (USA) **1070**
Business & Society (USA) **1070**
The Business Communicator (GBR) **1071**
Business Courier (USA) **1071**
Business Credit (USA) **1322**
Business Economics (USA) **1071**
Business Entities (USA) **1913**
Business First (Buffalo) (USA) **1072**
Business First (Louisville) (USA) **1072**
Business Forum (Los Angeles) (USA) **1072**
Business History Review (USA) **1072**
Business in Broward (USA) **1957**
Business Insurance (USA) **4496**
Business Intelligence Journal (USA) **1730**
The Business Journal (Kansas City) (USA) **1073**
The Business Journal (Phoenix) (USA) **1073**
Business Journal (Portland) (USA) **1444**
Business Journal Serving Greater Milwaukee (USA) **1073**
The Business Lawyer (USA) **4859**
Business Leader (USA) **1730**
Business North Carolina (USA) **1957**
Business People (USA) **1074**
Business Perspectives (USA) **1075**
The Business Press (USA) **1075**
Business Process Management Journal (GBR) **1730**
The Business Review (USA) **1075**
Business Strategy and the Environment (GBR) **3407**
Business Times (USA) **1444**
The Business Torts Reporter (USA) **4859**
Business Travel News (USA) **8689**
Business World (PHL) **1881**
BusinessWest (USA) **1077**
Buyouts (USA) **1614**
C A Magazine (CAN) **1282**
C A N N T Journal (CAN) **5953**
C D Computing News (USA) **2491**
C E D (USA) **2377**
C E S - I F O Economic Studies (GBR) **1078**
C E S - I F O Forum (DEU) **1078**
C F O (USA) **1078**
C I M Magazine (CAN) **6459**
C I O (USA) **1414**
C I O Insight (USA) **1414**
C J E M (CAN) **6057**
C M A Management (CAN) **1283**
C M A Today (USA) **5954**
C P A Government and Nonprofit Report (USA) **1283**
The C P A Journal (USA) **1283**
The C P A Letter (Online) (USA) **1283**
The C P A Technology Advisor (USA) **1415**
C P C U eJournal (USA) **4497**
C P Online (USA) *see* Current Psychology (New York). **7350**
C R M Magazine (USA) **1731**
Cabinet Maker (GBR) **4554**
CabinetMaker (USA) **4554**
Cable and Satellite Europe (GBR) **2377**
Cable Optics (USA) **2314**
Cabling Installation and Maintenance (USA) **2378**
CADalyst (USA) **3289**
The Cairns Post (AUS) **3793**
Calcified Tissue International (USA) **5884**
Calcolo (ITA) **5477**
Calculus of Variations and Partial Differential Equations (DEU) **5477**
California Builder & Engineer (USA) **989**
California C P A (USA) **1284**
California Management Review (USA) **1732**
Callaloo (USA) **5269**
Calliope (Peru) (USA) **4134**
Cambridge Journal of Economics (GBR) **1079**
Cambridge Journal of Education (GBR) **2970**
The Cambridge Quarterly (GBR) **5269**
Camera Obscura (USA) **6491**
Campaign (London, 1968) (GBR) **22**
Camping Magazine (USA) **2146**
Campus Wide Information Systems (GBR) **2495**
Canadian - American Public Policy (USA) **7225**
Canadian Architect (CAN) **436**
Canadian Association of Radiologists Journal (CAN) **6193**
Canadian Business (CAN) **1079**
Canadian Business Conditions (CAN) **1079**
Canadian Business Economics (CAN) **1079**
Canadian Chiropractic Association. Journal (CAN) **5803**
Canadian Contractor (CAN) **990**
Canadian Criminal Law Review (CAN) **4885**
Canadian Dimension (CAN) **7113**
Canadian Entomologist (CAN) **842**
Canadian Ethnic Studies (CAN) **3525**
Canadian Family Law Quarterly (CAN) **4907**
Canadian Foreign Policy (CAN) **7225**
The Canadian Geographer (USA) **4001**
Canadian Geographic (CAN) **4001**
Canadian Geotechnical Journal (CAN) **2703**
Canadian Grocer (CAN) **3676**
Canadian H R Reporter (CAN) **1857**
Canadian Healthcare Manager (CAN) **4090**
Canadian Investment Review (CAN) **1615**
Canadian Jeweller (CAN) **4564**
Canadian Journal of Administrative Law and Practice (CAN) **4639**
Canadian Journal of Administrative Sciences (GBR) **1080**
Canadian Journal of Behavioural Science (CAN) **7343**
Canadian Journal of Chemistry (CAN) **2052**
Canadian Journal of Civil Engineering (CAN) **3261**
Canadian Journal of Criminology and Criminal Justice (CAN) **2646**
Canadian Journal of Dietetic Practice and Research (CAN) **6656**
Canadian Journal of Earth Sciences (CAN) **2703**
Canadian Journal of Education (CAN) **3019**
Canadian Journal of Experimental Psychology (CAN) **7343**
Canadian Journal of Family Law (CAN) **4639**
Canadian Journal of Film Studies (CAN) **6492**
Canadian Journal of Fisheries and Aquatic Sciences (CAN) **3588**
Canadian Journal of Forest Research (CAN) **3685**
Canadian Journal of History (CAN) **4134**
Canadian Journal of Human Sexuality (CAN) **7343**
Canadian Journal of Microbiology (CAN) **882**
Canadian Journal of Native Education (CAN) **2834**
Canadian Journal of Occupational Therapy (CAN) **6107**
Canadian Journal of Philosophy (CAN) **6909**
Canadian Journal of Physics (CAN) **7007**
Canadian Journal of Physiology and Pharmacology (CAN) **920**
Canadian Journal of Public Health (CAN) **7511**
The Canadian Journal of Rural Medicine (CAN) **5592**
Canadian Journal of Surgery (CAN) **6238**
Canadian Journal of Urban Research (CAN) **4406**
Canadian Journal of Zoology (CAN) **937**
Canadian Literature (CAN) **5270**
Canadian Manager (CAN) **1732**
Canadian Mining Journal (CAN) **6459**
Canadian Nurse (CAN) **5954**
Canadian Operating Room Nursing Journal (CAN) **5954**
Canadian Packaging (CAN) **6708**
Canadian Plastics (CAN) **7091**
Canadian Printer (CAN) **7319**
Canadian Property Valuation (CAN) **7586**
Canadian Psychology (CAN) **7344**
Canadian Review of Sociology (CAN) **8092**
Canadian Slavonic Papers (CAN) **4446**
Canadian Social Studies (CAN) **3054**
Canadian Tax Journal (CAN) **1915**
Canadian Today's Parent (CAN) **2146**
Canadian Transportation Logistics (CAN) **8493**
Canadian Treasury Management Review (CAN) **1324**
Canadian Underwriter (CAN) **4498**
Cancer and Metastasis Reviews (USA) **6011**
Cancer Biotherapy & Radiopharmaceuticals (USA) **6011**
Cancer Causes & Control (NLD) **6011**
Cancer Cell International (GBR) **6011**
Cancer Chemotherapy and Pharmacology (DEU) **6011**
Cancer Gene Therapy (USA) **6012**
Cancer Gene Therapy Week (USA) **6012**
Cancer Immunology, Immunotherapy (DEU) **6012**
The Cancer Journal (USA) **6013**
Cancer Vaccine Week (USA) **6014**
Cancer Weekly (USA) **6014**
Candy Industry (USA) **3672**
Capital and Class (GBR) **1536**
Capitalism, Nature, Socialism (GBR) **7114**
Carcinogenesis (GBR) **6015**
Cardiology (CHE) **5779**
Cardiopulmonary Physical Therapy Journal (USA) **6107**
Cardiovascular Business Week (USA) **1080**
Cardiovascular Device Liability Week (USA) **5780**
Cardiovascular Diabetology (GBR) **5884**
Cardiovascular Drugs and Therapy (USA) **5781**
Cardiovascular Engineering (USA) **5781**
Cardiovascular Week (USA) **5781**
Cards & Payments (USA) **1325**
Cards International (IRL) **1392**
Care Management Journals (USA) **5954**
Career Development for Exceptional Individuals (USA) **3037**
Career Development International (GBR) **6694**
The Career Development Quarterly (USA) **6694**
Career World (USA) **6695**
Caribbean Update (USA) **1554**
Caries Research (CHE) **5837**
Carpet & Flooring Review (GBR) **4554**
Case Western Reserve Journal of International Law (USA) **4920**
Castanea (USA) **783**
Casual Living (USA) **4555**
Catalyst (Dublin) (USA) **1284**
The Catalyst (Portland) (USA) **2939**
Catalyst Chicago (USA) **3019**
Catechist (USA) **7787**
Catholic Biblical Quarterly (USA) **7788**
The Catholic Historical Review (USA) **7789**
Catholic Woman (USA) **8855**
The Cato Journal (USA) **7114**
Cattleman (USA) **283**
Cell and Tissue Banking (NLD) **828**
Cell and Tissue Research (DEU) **829**
Cell Communication and Signaling (GBR) **665**
Cell Death & Differentiation (GBR) **829**
Cell Stress & Chaperones (NLD) **5592**
Cells, Tissues, Organs (CHE) **5593**
Cellular Polymers (GBR) **7091**
Cement Americas (USA) **990**
Center for Children's Books. Bulletin (USA) **2147**
Central Asian Survey (GBR) **7115**
Central European Journal of Operations Research (DEU) **2409**
Central Penn Business Journal (USA) **1081**
Ceramic Engineering and Science Proceedings (USA) **2038**
Ceramic Industry (USA) **2038**
Ceramics Monthly (USA) **2039**
Cereal Chemistry (USA) **3630**
Cereal Foods World (USA) **3630**
Cerebral Cortex (USA) **6130**
Cerebrovascular Diseases (CHE) **6130**
Chain Leader (USA) **4383**
Chain Store Age (USA) **1809**
Challenge (ISR) **7226**
Challenge (Armonk) (USA) **1082**
The Chamber Voice (USA) **1399**
Change (USA) **2971**
Charles S. Peirce Society. Transactions (USA) **6910**
Charlotte Business Journal (USA) **1082**
Chart (USA) **5955**
Chasqui (USA) **5272**
Chatelaine (English Edition) (CAN) **8855**
Chem.info (USA) **3237**
Chemical Engineering (USA) **3238**
Chemical Engineering Progress (USA) **3239**
Chemical Senses (GBR) **920**
Chemical Week (USA) **3240**
Chemist & Druggist (GBR) **6828**
Chemotherapy (CHE) **6828**
Cherokee Observer (USA) **3526**
Cherokee Phoenix and Indian Advocate (USA) **3526**
Cherokee Voice (USA) **8032**
Chesapeake and Ohio Historical Magazine (USA) **8616**
Chest (USA) **6212**
Chicago Enterprise (USA) **1082**
Chicago Fed Letter (USA) **1446**
Chicago Jewish Star (USA) **7720**
Chicago Journal of International Law (USA) **4920**
Chicago Reader (USA) **3972**
Chicago Review (USA) **5273**
Chief Executive Magazine (USA) **1733**
Child and Adolescent Psychopharmacology News (USA) **6131**
Child Health Alert (USA) **6089**
Child Language Teaching and Therapy (GBR) **3037**
Child Welfare (USA) **8032**
Childhood Education (USA) **3054**
Children & Schools (USA) **8033**
Children's Literature (Baltimore) (USA) **5273**
Children's Literature Association Quarterly (USA) **5001**
Children's Voice (USA) **8033**
China Business Review (USA) **1555**
China Daily Web Edition (CHN) *see* China Daily (North American Edition). **3823**
The China Journal (AUS) **546**
The China Review (HKG) **3823**
China Telecom Newsletter (USA) **2315**
Chinese Journal of International Law (GBR) **4920**
The Chiropractic Journal (USA) **5804**
Choice (USA) **7558**
The Christian Century (USA) **7631**
Christian Education Journal (USA) **7631**
Christian Scholar's Review (USA) **7632**
Christianity and Literature (USA) **5210**
Christianity Today (USA) **7632**
Chronicle (Radford) (USA) **5440**
The Chronicle of Higher Education (USA) **2972**
Chronique Internationale de l'I R E S (FRA) **1083**
Church & State (USA) **7633**
Church History (USA) **7633**
Cineaste (USA) **6493**
Cinema Journal (USA) **6493**
The Circle (USA) **6634**
Circuit World (GBR) **8418**
Circuitree Magazine (USA) **3090**
Circuits Assembly (USA) **3091**
Cistercian Studies Quarterly (USA) **7633**
Citizen Airman (USA) **51**
City Limits (Online) (USA) **7955**
Civil Engineering (ZAF) **3262**
Civil Engineering (Reston) (USA) **3262**
Civil War History (USA) **4288**
Civil War Times (USA) **4288**
Classical Antiquity (USA) **2232**
Classical Bulletin (USA) **2232**
Classical Philology (USA) **2232**
Classical Quarterly (GBR) **2232**
Clean Technologies and Environmental Policy (DEU) **3411**
CleanRooms (USA) **3366**
The Clearing House (USA) **2837**
Cleft Palate - Craniofacial Journal (CAN) **6239**
Cleveland Jewish News (USA) **3527**
Click (USA) **2182**
Clifford the Big Red Dog (USA) **2183**
Climacteric (GBR) **8844**
Climbing (USA) **8309**
Clinical and Experimental Medicine (ITA) **5596**
Clinical and Experimental Metastasis (NLD) **6015**
Clinical and Experimental Nephrology (JPN) **6266**
Clinical and Investigative Medicine (Online) (CAN) **5596**
Clinical Autonomic Research (USA) **5596**
Clinical Chemistry Online (USA) *see* Clinical Chemistry (Washington, DC). **5904**
Clinical Diabetes (Alexandria) (USA) **5884**
Clinical E E G and Neuroscience (USA) **6131**
Clinical Excellence for Nurse Practitioners (USA) **5955**
Clinical Governance (GBR) **5596**
Clinical Governance Bulletin (GBR) **4090**
Clinical Infectious Diseases (USA) **5811**
Clinical Journal of Oncology Nursing (USA) **5955**
Clinical Kinesiology (Online Edition) (USA) **6107**
Clinical Laboratory Science (USA) **5904**
Clinical Microbiology and Infection (GBR) **5597**
Clinical Oncology Week (USA) **6016**
Clinical Oral Investigations (DEU) **5838**
Clinical Pediatrics (USA) **6090**
Clinical Psychology (USA) **7345**
Clinical Rehabilitation (GBR) **6107**
Clinical Risk (GBR) **5597**
Clinical Social Work Journal (USA) **8034**
Clinical Trials (GBR) **5904**
Clinical Trials Week (USA) **5904**
Clio (Ft. Wayne) (USA) **4135**
Club Industry's Fitness Business Pro (USA) **6984**
Club Management (USA) **2265**
Clues (USA) **5275**
CNN/Money (USA) *see* Money (New York). **1368**
Coach and Athletic Director (USA) **8166**
Coal Outlook (USA) **6460**
Coast Business (USA) **1083**
Coatings (CAN) **6716**
Cobblestone (USA) **2183**
Cognition, Technology and Work (GBR) **7346**
Cognitive, Affective, & Behavioral Neuroscience (USA) **7346**
Cognitive Therapy and Research (USA) **7347**
Collection Building (GBR) **5002**
Collection of Czechoslovak Chemical Communications (CZE) **2058**
Collections and Credit Risk (USA) **1327**
College and University (USA) **2972**
College Composition and Communication (USA) **3055**
College English (USA) **3055**
College Literature (USA) **5276**
College Mathematics Journal (USA) **5478**
College Student Affairs Journal (Online Edition) (USA) **2278**
College Student Journal (USA) **2973**
College Teaching (USA) **2973**
Colorado Construction (USA) **992**
Colorado Springs Business Journal (USA) **1084**
ColorLines (USA) **7117**
Columbia Journal of Gender and the Law (USA) **4645**
Columbia Journalism Review (USA) **4573**
Columbus Business First (USA) **1084**
The Combat Edge (USA) **51**
Commentary (USA) **7720**
Commerce Comments (CAN) **1400**
Commercial Law Bulletin (USA) **4646**
Commercial Lending Review (USA) **1328**
Commercial Mortgage Alert (USA) **7587**
Commercial Motor (GBR) **8669**
Commercial Property News (USA) **7587**
Common Market Law Review (NLD) **4921**
Commonweal (USA) **5211**
Communication Disorders Quarterly (USA) **3038**
Communication Quarterly (USA) **8094**
Communication Reports (GBR) **5107**
Communication Studies (USA) **8094**
Communication Systems Design (Online) (USA) **2316**
Communication Theory (USA) **5107**
Communication World (USA) **1734**
Communications News (USA) **2316**
Communications Standards News (GBR) **2496**
Communications Technology's Pipeline (USA) **2316**
Communities (USA) **1422**
Community Banker (Washington, 1880) (USA) **1328**
Community Care (Sutton) (GBR) **8034**
The Community College Enterprise (USA) **2973**
Community College Journal (USA) **2973**

Online Service

The George Washington International Law Review (USA) **4926**
Georgetown International Environmental Law Review (USA) **3433**
Georgetown Journal of International Affairs (USA) **7237**
Georgetown Journal of International Law (USA) **4926**
Georgetown Journal of Legal Ethics (USA) **4680**
Georgetown Law Journal (USA) **4680**
Georgia Journal of Science (USA) **7857**
Georgia Nursing (USA) **5959**
Georgia Trend (USA) **1349**
Geriatrics (USA) **4045**
German History (GBR) **4223**
German Life (USA) **3535**
The German Quarterly (USA) **5122**
The Germanic Review (USA) **5122**
The Gerontologist (USA) **4046**
Gerontology (CHE) **4046**
Gestion (CAN) **1113**
Gifted Child Quarterly (USA) **3040**
Gifted Child Today (USA) **3040**
Gigabit / A T M (USA) **2497**
Girls' Life (USA) **2191**
Global Business and Organizational Excellence (USA) **1748**
Global Cosmetic Industry (USA) **594**
Global Finance (USA) **1349**
Global Governance (USA) **7238**
Global Health Promotion (GBR) **7519**
Global Investor (GBR) **1349**
Global Justice Report (CAN) **7238**
Global Outlook (Toronto) (CAN) **1488**
Global Pesticide Campaigner (USA) **3497**
Global Power Report (USA) **3136**
Global Society (GBR) **7238**
Global Telecoms Business (GBR) **2322**
Glow (CAN) **6987**
Glycobiology (GBR) **733**
Gold Coast Bulletin (AUS) **3794**
Golf Course Industry (USA) **8231**
Golf Magazine (USA) **8232**
Good Housekeeping (USA) **4359**
Gourmet News (USA) **3678**
Government Executive (USA) **7440**
Government Finance Review (USA) **1927**
Government Procurement (USA) **7440**
Government Product News (USA) **7440**
Government Video (USA) **2401**
Graefe's Archive for Clinical and Experimental Ophthalmology (DEU) **6043**
Grand Rapids Business Journal (USA) **1428**
Granular Matter (DEU) **3194**
Graphic Arts Monthly (USA) **7322**
Graphis Advertising Annual (USA) **25**
Graphis Design Annual (USA) **492**
Graphs and Combinatorics (JPN) **5552**
Grassroots Economic Organizing Newsletter (USA) **6698**
The Greater Baton Rouge Business Report (USA) **1488**
Greece and Rome (GBR) **2234**
Greek Orthodox Theological Review (USA) **7704**
Greek, Roman and Byzantine Studies (USA) **2234**
Green Teacher (CAN) **3063**
Greener Management International (GBR) **3435**
Greenhouse Grower (USA) **3734**
The Grocer (GBR) **3679**
Ground Support Worldwide (USA) **57**
Ground Water (USA) **2794**
Group (Loveland) (USA) **2154**
Group & Organization Management (USA) **2861**
Group Decision and Negotiation (NLD) **1748**
Group Dynamics (USA) **7359**
Group Facilitation (USA) **7359**
The Guardian (GBR) **3865**
The Guardian on CD-ROM (GBR) **3866**
The Guild Practitioner (USA) **4832**
Gut Online (GBR) *see* Gut. **5925**
Gynecologic and Obstetric Investigation (CHE) **5992**
Gynecological Endocrinology (GBR) **5893**
H & H N Online (USA) *see* Hospital & Health Networks. **4099**
H E C Forum (NLD) **4094**
H F M Magazine (USA) **4094**
H F N (USA) **4558**
H M E News (USA) **4047**
H P A C Engineering (USA) **4119**
H R Magazine (USA) **1862**
H V A C & R Research (USA) **4120**
Haiti Observateur (HTI) **3874**
Hampton Roads International Security Quarterly (USA) **7239**
Hardware Merchandising (CAN) **1054**
Harper's (USA) **5219**
Harper's Bazaar (USA) **2256**
Hart's Diesel Fuel News (USA) **6772**
Harvard Asia Pacific Review (USA) **7140**
Harvard Educational Review (USA) **2862**
Harvard International Review (USA) **7239**
Harvard Journal of Law and Public Policy (USA) **4684**
The Harvard Review (USA) **4454**
Harvard Ukrainian Studies (USA) **4226**
Hastings Center Report (USA) **5623**
Hawaii Business (USA) **1489**
Hazardous Waste Consultant (USA) **3507**
Health Affairs (USA) **7520**
Health & Hygiene (GBR) **7520**
Health & Medicine Week (USA) **5624**
Health & Social Work (USA) **8044**
Health at Every Size (USA) **6660**
Health Business Week (USA) **7521**
Health Care Financing Review (USA) **5624**
Health Care Management Review (USA) **4095**
Health Care Management Science (NLD) **4095**
The Health Care Manager (USA) **4095**
Health Data Management (New York) (USA) **4096**
Health Education (GBR) **6988**
Health Education Research (GBR) **8044**
Health Facilities Management (USA) **4096**
Health Insurance Law Weekly (USA) **4504**
Health Insurance Week (USA) **4505**
Health Law Journal (CAN) **4686**
Health Law Review (CAN) **4686**
Health Management Technology (USA) **5830**
Health Marketing Quarterly (USA) **7522**
Health Progress (USA) **4096**
Health Promotion International (GBR) **7523**
Health Psychology (USA) **7360**
Health Risk Factor Week (USA) **7523**
Health Services and Outcomes Research Methodology (USA) **5626**
Health Services Management Research (GBR) **5626**
Healthcare Executive (USA) **4097**
Healthcare Finance, Tax & Law Weekly (USA) **1351**
Healthcare Mergers, Acquisition and Ventures Week (USA) **4097**
Healthcare Purchasing News (USA) **4097**
Healthcare Traveler (USA) **4098**
HealthFacts (USA) **5627**
Heart and Vessels (JPN) **5788**
Heart Disease Weekly (USA) **5788**
Heart Failure Reviews (USA) **5788**
Heart Online (GBR) *see* Heart. **5787**
Heating, Plumbing, Air Conditioning (CAN) **4120**
Hecate (AUS) **8898**
Hellenic Times (USA) **3537**
Hematology Week (USA) **5938**
The Hemingway Review (USA) **5305**
The Henry James Review (USA) **5305**
Heredity (GBR) **871**
Herpetological Review (USA) **946**
Herz (DEU) **5789**
Hesperia (GRC) **396**
High Ability Studies (GBR) **3041**
High Country News (USA) **3436**
The High School Journal (USA) **2863**
Higher Education Policy (GBR) **2984**
Highlights for Children (USA) **2192**
Hinduism Today (USA) **7707**
Hispanic (USA) **3537**
Hispanic American Historical Review (USA) **4295**
Hispanic Engineer & Information Technology (USA) **3195**
Hispanic Enterprise (USA) **3537**
Hispanic Health Care International (USA) **5960**
Hispanic Outlook in Higher Education (USA) **2985**
Hispanic Review (USA) **5125**
Histochemistry and Cell Biology (DEU) **833**
The Historian (GBR) **4142**
Historical Journal of Film, Radio and Television (GBR) **4143**
Historical Methods (USA) **8149**
Historical Studies in the Natural Sciences (USA) **7862**
History (Washington) (USA) **4145**
History & Memory (USA) **4145**
History in Africa (USA) **4175**
History of Education Quarterly (USA) **2864**
History of Political Economy (USA) **1542**
History of Psychology (USA) **7360**
History of Religions (USA) **7647**
History Review (GBR) **4145**
History Today (GBR) **4230**
Hockey Weekly (USA) **8178**
Holistic Nursing Practice (USA) **5960**
Hollywood Reporter: Premier Edition (USA) *see* The Hollywood Reporter. **6502**
Holocaust and Genocide Studies (USA) **4230**
The Holocene (GBR) **3437**
Home Channel News (USA) **1118**
Home Furnishings (GBR) **4558**
Home Health Digest (USA) **5629**
Home Media Magazine (USA) **2401**
Home Textiles Today (USA) **8451**
HomeCare Magazine (USA) **5960**
Horn Book Guide to Children's and Young Adult Books (USA) **7562**
The Horn Book Magazine (USA) **7562**
Horse & Rider (USA) **8292**
Horticulture Week (GBR) **3737**
Hospital & Nursing Home Week (USA) **4099**
Hospital Business Week (USA) **4100**
Hospital Materials Management (USA) **4100**
Hospital Topics (USA) **4101**
Hospitality (GBR) **4388**
Hospitality Design (USA) **4542**
Hot Rod (USA) **8584**
Hotel Amerika (USA) **5219**
Hotel and Motel Management (USA) **4389**
Hotels (USA) **4390**
House Beautiful (USA) **4542**
Housewares Magazine (GBR) **4559**
Housing, Care and Support (GBR) **8045**
Housing Studies (GBR) **4414**
How (USA) **26**
HRfocus (USA) **1863**
Hudson Review (USA) **5220**
Human and Ecological Risk Assessment (USA) **3437**
Human & Experimental Toxicology (GBR) **3497**
Human Biology (Detroit) (USA) **871**
Human Communication Research (USA) **7360**
Human Development (CHE) **5630**
Human Ecology (Ithaca) (USA) **7970**
Human Ecology (New York) (USA) **341**
Human Factors (USA) **3195**
Human Factors and Ergonomics Society Annual Meeting. Proceedings (USA) **3195**
Human Genetics (DEU) **871**
Human Genomics (Online) (GBR) **872**
Human Heredity (CHE) **872**
Human Life Review (USA) **8106**
Human Molecular Genetics (GBR) **872**
Human Mutation (USA) **872**
Human Organization (USA) **341**
Human Reproduction (GBR) **5993**
Human Reproduction Update (GBR) **716**
Human Resource Development Quarterly (USA) **1863**
Human Resource Development Review (USA) **1864**
Human Resource Management (USA) **1864**
Human Resource Management International Digest (GBR) **1864**
Human Resource Management Journal (GBR) **1864**
Human Rights (Chicago) (USA) **7208**
Human Rights Quarterly (USA) **7208**
Human Rights Tribune (Online) (CAN) **7209**
Human Systems Management (NLD) **1750**
The Humanist (USA) **6923**
Humanitas (USA) **4455**
Humanities (USA) **4455**
Humanomics (GBR) **1543**
Humpty Dumpty's Magazine (USA) **2193**
Huntington Library Quarterly (USA) **5307**
Hurricane Alice (USA) **8868**
Hydraulics & Pneumatics (USA) **3361**
Hydrocarbon Processing International Edition (USA) **6772**
Hypatia (USA) **8898**
I A N Inside Products (USA) **4487**
I C M A Public Management Magazine (USA) **7494**
I.D. (USA) **4542**
I F O Dresden Berichtet (DEU) **1120**
I F O Schnelldienst (DEU) **1120**
I I E Transactions (USA) **3367**
I M A Journal of Applied Mathematics (GBR) **5492**
I M A Journal of Management Mathematics (GBR) **5492**
I M A Journal of Mathematical Control & Information (GBR) **5492**
I M A Journal of Numerical Analysis (GBR) **5492**
I N F O R Journal (CAN) **2536**
I N F O R M S Journal on Computing (USA) **2421**
I O M A's Complete Guide to Best Practices in Performance Management (USA) **1865**
I O M A's Payroll Manager's Report (USA) **1290**
I O M A's Report on Compensation & Benefits for Law Offices (USA) **1865**
I O M A's Report on Financial Analysis, Planning & Reporting (USA) **1751**
I O M A's Report on Managing 401k Plans (USA) **1865**
I O M A's Report on Managing Benefits Plans (USA) **1865**
I O M A's Report on Managing Credit, Receivables and Collections (USA) **1352**
I O M A's Report on Salary Surveys (USA) **1866**
The I P Litigator (USA) **6751**
I R A L. International Review of Applied Linguistics in Language Teaching (DEU) **5126**
I R B: A Review of Human Subjects Research (USA) **5906**
I R E Journal (USA) **4576**
I R E S. Revue (FRA) **1121**
I T Cost Management Strategies (USA) **2536**
I T E Journal (USA) **8631**
I T Training (GBR) **1866**
Idaho Business Review (USA) **1121**
Illinois State Historical Society. Journal (USA) **4297**
Illuminating Engineering Society. Journal (USA) **3318**
Imagination, Cognition and Personality (USA) **7362**
Immunobiology (DEU) **5759**
Immunotherapy Weekly (USA) **5760**
Impact (Strawberry Hills) (AUS) **8046**
Impressions (Dallas) (USA) **2256**
In M F G (USA) **8425**
In-Plant Graphics (USA) **7323**
In-Plant Printer (USA) **7323**
In School (USA) *see* Instructor (New York). **2867**
In-Store (GBR) **1820**
In the Family (USA) **4375**
In Vitro Cellular & Developmental Biology - Animal (DEU) **5633**
In Vitro Cellular & Developmental Biology - Plant (DEU) **793**
Inc. (USA) **1962**
Incentive (USA) **1820**
The Independent (GBR) **3867**
The Independent (New York) (USA) **6503**
Independent Banker (USA) **1353**
Independent Provisioner (USA) **3646**
The Independent Review (USA) **7142**
India Abroad (USA) **3539**
India Telecom (USA) **2325**
India - West (USA) **3539**
Indian Country Today (USA) **3539**
Indian Journal of Agricultural Economics (IND) **200**
Indian Journal of Cancer (IND) **6022**
Indian Journal of Dermatology, Venereology and Leprology (IND) **5877**
Indian Journal of Human Genetics (IND) **872**
The Indian Journal of Medical Research (IND) **5633**
Indian Journal of Pharmacology (IND) **6848**
Indian Journal of Plastic Surgery (IND) **6245**
Indian Journal of Surgery (IND) **6245**
Indiana Business Magazine (USA) **1490**
Indiana Business Review (USA) **1122**
Indiana Journal of Global Legal Studies (USA) **4691**
Indiana Review (USA) **5308**
Indianapolis Business Journal (USA) **1429**
Indogermanische Forschungen (DEU) **5127**
Indonesia (USA) **551**
Indonesian Commercial Newsletter (IDN) **1429**
Industrial and Commercial Training (GBR) **1866**
Industrial and Corporate Change (GBR) **1543**
Industrial and Labor Relations Review (USA) **1687**
Industrial Distribution (USA) **1820**
Industrial Engineer (USA) **3197**
The Industrial Geographer (USA) **4015**
Industrial Heating (USA) **3368**
Industrial Laser Solutions for Manufacturing (USA) **3197**
Industrial Law Journal (GBR) **1687**
Industrial Lubrication & Tribology (GBR) **3379**
Industrial Maintenance & Plant Operation (USA) **3368**
Industrial Management (USA) **1752**
Industrial Management + Data Systems (GBR) **1418**
Industrial Robot (GBR) **2584**
Industrial Worker (USA) **1688**
Industrielle Beziehungen (DEU) **1688**
Industry and Innovation (GBR) **1123**
IndustryWeek (USA) **1752**
Infantry (USA) **6424**
Infants and Young Children (USA) **6093**
Infection (DEU) **5634**
Infection Control & Hospital Epidemiology (USA) **5817**
Infectious Diseases in Obstetrics and Gynecology (USA) **5993**
Inflammation (USA) **5635**
Inflammation Research (CHE) **6848**
Info (Bingley) (GBR) **2325**
Infonomics (USA) **2544**
Inform (Champaign) (USA) **2065**
Information and Communications Technology Law (GBR) **2325**
Information Executive (USA) **2521**
Information Management (New York, 1998) (USA) **2545**
Information Management & Computer Security (GBR) **1752**
Information Outlook (USA) **5016**
Information Resources Management Journal (USA) **1753**
Information Retrieval (USA) **2545**
Information Security Journal (Online) (USA) *see* Information Security Journal. **2514**
Information Systems and e-Business Management (DEU) **2558**
Information Systems Frontiers (USA) **2545**
Information Systems Management (USA) **5061**
Information Systems Research (USA) **2545**
Information Technology and Libraries (USA) **5017**
Information Technology & Management (NLD) **1851**
Information Technology and People (GBR) **5062**
Information Technology for Development (USA) **1598**
Information Technology, Learning, and Performance Journal (USA) **2423**
Information Technology Management (USA) **1753**
Information Technology Newsletter (USA) **2546**
Information Today (USA) **5062**
Information Visualization (GBR) **2450**
Information Week Online (USA) *see* Information Week (US Edition). **2531**
Information World Review (GBR) **2351**
InfoStor (USA) **2546**
Injury Prevention (GBR) **6093**
Innovation (Abingdon) (GBR) **7972**
Innovations in Education and Teaching International (Online) (GBR) **3064**
Inquiry (Rochester) (USA) **5635**
Inroads (CAN) **7972**
Inside (Philadelphia) (USA) **3539**
Inside Auto C A D (USA) **2591**
Inside Energy (USA) **3138**
Inside F E R C's Gas Market Report (USA) **6773**
Inside Microsoft Access (USA) **2591**
Inside Microsoft Excel (USA) **2591**
Inside Microsoft Office (USA) **2507**
Inside Microsoft PowerPoint (USA) **2591**
Inside Microsoft Word (USA) **2591**
Inside N I S T (USA) **2326**
Inside Photoshop (USA) **2487**
Inside Public Accounting (USA) **1290**
Inside R & D (USA) **8426**
Insights (New York) (USA) **4870**
Instant & Small Commercial Printer (USA) **7324**
Institute of Environmental Sciences and Technology. Journal (USA) **3440**
Institute of Measurement and Control. Transactions (GBR) **4487**
Institute of Public Affairs. Review (AUS) **1125**
Institute of Statistical Mathematics. Annals (NLD) **5494**
Institution of Mechanical Engineers. Proceedings. Part A: Journal of Power and Energy (GBR) **3380**
Institution of Mechanical Engineers. Proceedings. Part B: Journal of Engineering Manufacture (GBR) **3380**

Online Service

Journal of Bone and Joint Surgery: American Volume (USA) **6063**
Journal of Bone and Joint Surgery: British Volume (GBR) **6063**
The Journal of Brand Management (GBR) **1823**
Journal of British Studies (USA) **4235**
Journal of Business (Spokane) (USA) **1360**
Journal of Business and Economic Statistics (USA) **1247**
Journal of Business and Economic Studies (USA) **1133**
Journal of Business & Industrial Marketing (GBR) **1823**
Journal of Business and Management (USA) **1764**
Journal of Business & Psychology (USA) **7369**
Journal of Business and Technical Communication (USA) **1133**
Journal of Business Ethics (NLD) **1134**
Journal of Business Logistics (USA) **1764**
Journal of Business Strategies (USA) **1764**
Journal of Business Strategy (USA) **1764**
Journal of California Law Enforcement (USA) **2656**
Journal of Canadian Studies (CAN) **4460**
Journal of Cancer Research and Clinical Oncology (DEU) **6024**
The Journal of Cardiovascular Nursing (USA) **5792**
The Journal of Cardiovascular Surgery (ITA) **5792**
Journal of Career Development (USA) **6700**
Journal of Cellular and Molecular Medicine (GBR) **5646**
Journal of Cerebral Blood Flow and Metabolism (USA) **6150**
The Journal of Change Management (GBR) **1764**
Journal of Chemical Education (USA) **2067**
Journal of Child and Adolescent Psychiatric Nursing (USA) **5964**
Journal of Child and Adolescent Psychopharmacology (USA) **6150**
Journal of Child Neurology (USA) **6150**
Journal of Child Sexual Abuse (USA) **8049**
Journal of Church and State (USA) **7654**
Journal of Classroom Interaction (USA) **2874**
Journal of Climate (USA) **6358**
Journal of Clinical Immunology (USA) **5762**
Journal of Clinical Investigation (USA) **5647**
Journal of Clinical Monitoring and Computing (NLD) **5647**
Journal of Coastal Research (USA) **2809**
Journal of Coatings Technology and Research (USA) **6718**
Journal of Cognitive Psychotherapy (USA) **7371**
Journal of College Admission (USA) **2989**
Journal of College Counseling (USA) **2989**
Journal of College Science Teaching (USA) **7872**
Journal of College Student Development (USA) **2989**
Journal of College Student Retention: Research, Theory & Practice (USA) **2989**
Journal of Commercial Biotechnology (GBR) **767**
Journal of Communication (USA) **8112**
Journal of Communication Management (GBR) **1765**
Journal of Community Health (USA) **5647**
Journal of Community Nursing (GBR) **5964**
Journal of Comparative Family Studies (CAN) **8112**
Journal of Comparative Policy Analysis (USA) **7448**
Journal of Comparative Psychology (USA) **7371**
Journal of Computational Neuroscience (NLD) **6151**
Journal of Computer Information Systems (USA) **2523**
Journal of Computers in Mathematics and Science Teaching (USA) **5553**
Journal of Conflict and Security Law (GBR) **4933**
Journal of Conflict Resolution (USA) **7978**
Journal of Construction Accounting and Taxation (USA) **1294**
Journal of Consulting and Clinical Psychology (USA) **7371**
Journal of Consumer Affairs (USA) **2639**
Journal of Consumer Marketing (GBR) **1823**
Journal of Consumer Policy (NLD) **2639**
Journal of Consumer Research (USA) **1823**
Journal of Consumer Satisfaction, Dissatisfaction and Complaining Behavior (USA) **1824**
Journal of Contemporary Asia (GBR) **4184**
Journal of Contemporary China (GBR) **4184**
Journal of Contemporary Psychotherapy (USA) **7372**
Journal of Continuing Education in Nursing (USA) **5964**
Journal of Continuing Education in the Health Professions (USA) **5648**
Journal of Cooperative Education and Internships (USA) **2874**
Journal of Corporate Accounting and Finance (USA) **1294**
The Journal of Corporate Citizenship (GBR) **1765**
Journal of Corporate Real Estate (GBR) **7596**
The Journal of Corporation Law (USA) **4872**
Journal of Correctional Education (USA) **2656**
Journal of Counseling & Development (USA) **7372**
Journal of Counseling Psychology (USA) **7372**
Journal of Criminal Justice Education (GBR) **2656**
Journal of Criminal Law & Criminology (USA) **2657**
Journal of Cultural Diversity (USA) **5964**
Journal of Cultural Economics (USA) **1544**
Journal of Cuneiform Studies (USA) **400**
Journal of Cutaneous Medicine and Surgery (CAN) **5878**
Journal of Dairy Science (USA) **266**
Journal of Database Management (USA) **2531**
The Journal of Database Marketing & Customer Strategy Management (Online Edition) (GBR) **1419**
The Journal of Deaf Studies and Deaf Education (USA) **4075**
Journal of Deferred Compensation (USA) **1690**
Journal of Democracy (USA) **7146**
Journal of Dental Research (USA) **5851**
The Journal of Derivatives (USA) **1360**
Journal of Derivatives & Hedge Funds (GBR) **1635**
The Journal of Development Studies (GBR) **1600**
Journal of Developmental Education (USA) **2990**
Journal of Developmental Entrepreneurship (SGP) **1962**
Journal of Digital Imaging (USA) **6200**
Journal of Direct, Data and Digital Marketing Practice (Online) (GBR) **1824**
Journal of Disability Policy Studies (USA) **4067**
Journal of Distance Education (CAN) **2943**
Journal of Divorce & Remarriage (USA) **5559**
Journal of Documentation (GBR) **5020**
Journal of Drug Issues (USA) **2695**
Journal of Early Christian Studies (USA) **7802**
Journal of Eastern Caribbean Studies (BRB) **7978**
Journal of Ecological Anthropology (USA) **344**
The Journal of Economic Education (USA) **1134**
Journal of Economic Geography (GBR) **1494**
Journal of Economic Growth (USA) **1544**
The Journal of Economic Inequality (USA) **1494**
Journal of Economic Literature (USA) **1247**
Journal of Economic Perspectives (USA) **1545**
Journal of Economic Studies (GBR) **1135**
Journal of Economics (AUT) **1135**
Journal of Economics and Finance (USA) **1135**
Journal of Education for Business (USA) **1136**
Journal of Education for Teaching (GBR) **2875**
Journal of Educational Administration (GBR) **3026**
Journal of Educational and Behavioral Statistics (USA) **2934**
Journal of Educational Multimedia and Hypermedia (USA) **2469**
Journal of Educational Psychology (USA) **2875**
The Journal of Educational Research (USA) **2875**
Journal of Elder Abuse & Neglect (USA) **4049**
Journal of Electrocardiology (USA) **5793**
Journal of Electron Microscopy (JPN) **899**
Journal of Electronic Commerce in Organizations (USA) **1419**
Journal of Electronic Materials (USA) **3106**
Journal of Emotional and Behavioral Disorders (USA) **6151**
Journal of Employment Counseling (USA) **7372**
Journal of Endovascular Therapy (USA) **6247**
Journal of Engineering Design (GBR) **3205**
Journal of Engineering Education (USA) **3205**
Journal of Engineering Technology (USA) **3205**
Journal of Enterprise Information Management (GBR) **5021**
The Journal of Environmental Education (USA) **3445**
Journal of Environmental Health (USA) **3445**
Journal of Environmental Law (GBR) **3445**
Journal of Environmental Law and Practice (CAN) **3446**
Journal of Environmental Planning and Management (GBR) **3446**
Journal of Environmental Quality (USA) **3446**
The Journal of Equipment Lease Financing (USA) **1136**
Journal of Essential Oil Research (USA) **595**
Journal of Esthetic and Restorative Dentistry (GBR) **5852**
Journal of Euromarketing (USA) **1824**
Journal of European Industrial Training (GBR) **1765**
Journal of Evolutionary Economics (DEU) **1545**
Journal of Experiential Education (USA) **3067**
Journal of Experimental Botany (GBR) **796**
The Journal of Experimental Education (USA) **3067**
Journal of Experimental Psychology: Animal Behavior Processes (USA) **7373**
Journal of Experimental Psychology: Applied (USA) **7373**
Journal of Experimental Psychology: General (USA) **7373**
Journal of Experimental Psychology: Human Perception and Performance (USA) **7373**
Journal of Experimental Psychology: Learning, Memory, and Cognition (USA) **7373**
Journal of Exposure Science and Environmental Epidemiology (GBR) **3447**
Journal of Facilities Management (GBR) **1766**
Journal of Family and Consumer Sciences (USA) **4361**
Journal of Family and Economic Issues (USA) **7373**
Journal of Family Psychology (USA) **7374**
Journal of Family Violence (USA) **2657**
Journal of Fashion Marketing and Management (GBR) **1824**
Journal of Feminist Family Therapy (USA) **8899**
Journal of Feminist Studies in Religion (USA) **7655**
Journal of Film and Video (USA) **6505**
Journal of Financial and Quantitative Analysis (USA) **1361**
Journal of Financial Crime (GBR) **4892**
Journal of Financial Management and Analysis (IND) **1361**
Journal of Financial Planning (USA) **1635**
Journal of Financial Regulation and Compliance (GBR) **1361**
Journal of Financial Service Professionals (USA) **1361**
Journal of Financial Services Marketing (GBR) **1824**
Journal of Financial Services Research (USA) **1361**
The Journal of Fixed Income (USA) **1635**
Journal of Folklore Research (USA) **3619**
Journal of Forecasting (GBR) **1766**
Journal of Forensic Identification (USA) **5914**
Journal of Forestry (USA) **3695**
The Journal of Futures Markets (USA) **1635**
Journal of Gambling Studies (USA) **6152**
Journal of Gastroenterology (JPN) **5927**
Journal of Gay & Lesbian Mental Health (USA) **7374**
Journal of Gay & Lesbian Social Services (USA) **8049**
Journal of Gender Studies (GBR) **8899**
Journal of Gene Medicine (USA) **873**
Journal of General Plant Pathology (JPN) **797**
The Journal of General Psychology (USA) **7374**
Journal of Generic Medicines (GBR) **6853**
Journal of Genetic Counseling (USA) **7374**
The Journal of Genetic Psychology (USA) **873**
Journal of Geographical Systems (DEU) **4037**
Journal of Geography (USA) **4017**
Journal of Geography in Higher Education (GBR) **4017**
The Journal of Geology (USA) **2750**
Journal of Geosciences (CZE) **2750**
Journal of Geriatric Physical Therapy (USA) **4049**
Journal of Gerontological Nursing (USA) **4049**
Journal of Global Information Management (USA) **1766**
Journal of Global Information Technology Management (USA) **2429**
Journal of Global Optimization (NLD) **7940**
The Journal of Government Financial Management (USA) **1295**
Journal of Group Psychotherapy, Psychodrama and Sociometry (USA) **7374**
Journal of Hand Surgery (American Volume) (USA) **6248**
Journal of Hand Therapy (USA) **6111**
Journal of Head Trauma Rehabilitation (USA) **6064**
Journal of Health and Human Services Administration (USA) **4104**
Journal of Health and Social Behavior (USA) **8113**
Journal of Health Care Compliance (USA) **5649**
Journal of Health Care Finance (USA) **4104**
Journal of Health Care for the Poor and Underserved (USA) **5649**
Journal of Health, Organization and Management (GBR) **4104**
Journal of Health Politics, Policy and Law (USA) **5649**
Journal of Health Services Research & Policy (GBR) **5650**
Journal of Healthcare Management (USA) **4104**
Journal of Heredity (GBR) **874**
Journal of Herpetology (USA) **951**
Journal of Heuristics (USA) **2453**
Journal of Higher Education (USA) **2990**
Journal of Higher Education Policy and Management (GBR) **2990**
Journal of Homosexuality (USA) **4375**
Journal of Housing and Community Development (USA) **4417**
Journal of Housing and the Built Environment (NLD) **4417**
Journal of Human Hypertension (GBR) **5793**
The Journal of Human Resources (USA) **1868**
Journal of Humanistic Counseling, Education and Development (USA) **7375**
Journal of Immigrant and Minority Health (USA) **5650**
Journal of Indian Philosophy (NLD) **6928**
Journal of Individual Differences (USA) **7375**
Journal of Industry, Competition and Trade (USA) **1137**
Journal of Infant, Child and Adolescent Psychotherapy (USA) **7375**
The Journal of Infectious Diseases (USA) **5820**
Journal of Information Privacy & Security (USA) **2515**
Journal of Information Science and Technology (USA) **5021**
The Journal of Information Systems (USA) **2548**
Journal of Information Systems Education (USA) **2950**
Journal of Information Technology (GBR) **5021**
Journal of Inherited Metabolic Disease (NLD) **6094**
Journal of Instructional Psychology (USA) **2876**
Journal of Insurance Issues (USA) **4510**
Journal of Insurance Regulation (USA) **4510**
Journal of Integrated Care (GBR) **8050**
Journal of Intellectual Capital (GBR) **1766**
Journal of Intelligent Information Systems (USA) **2453**
Journal of Intelligent Manufacturing (GBR) **2453**
Journal of Interactive Learning Research (USA) **2950**
Journal of Interactive Marketing (USA) **1824**
Journal of Interdisciplinary Studies (Pasadena) (USA) **4460**
Journal of Interferon & Cytokine Research (USA) **5763**
Journal of International Accounting Research (USA) **1295**
Journal of International Affairs (USA) **7248**
Journal of International and Area Studies (KOR) **1573**
Journal of International Business Studies (GBR) **1137**
Journal of International Consumer Marketing (USA) **1825**
Journal of International Development (GBR) **1600**
Journal of International Economic Law (GBR) **4933**
Journal of International Marketing (USA) **1825**
Journal of International Taxation (USA) **1931**
Journal of Internet Law (USA) **4701**
Journal of Interprofessional Care (GBR) **5650**
Journal of Interventional Cardiac Electrophysiology (NLD) **5793**
The Journal of Investigative Dermatology (USA) **5879**
The Journal of Investing (USA) **1635**
Journal of Islamic Studies (GBR) **7713**
Journal of Knee Surgery (USA) **6248**
Journal of Knowledge Management (GBR) **1767**
Journal of Labor Economics (USA) **1691**
Journal of Language for International Business (USA) **5134**
Journal of Laryngology and Otology (GBR) **6081**
Journal of Latin American and Caribbean Anthropology (USA) **345**
Journal of Law and Education (USA) **4702**
Journal of Law, Economics, & Organization (GBR) **4702**
The Journal of Law, Medicine & Ethics (USA) **4703**
Journal of Leadership and Organizational Studies (USA) **1767**
Journal of Learning Disabilities (USA) **3042**
Journal of Legal Economics (USA) **1545**
Journal of Legal Studies Education (USA) **4703**
Journal of Leisure Research (USA) **4978**
Journal of Lesbian Studies (USA) **4375**
Journal of Literacy Research (USA) **2877**
Journal of Logic and Computation (GBR) **2429**
Journal of Mammalogy (USA) **951**
Journal of Mammary Gland Biology and Neoplasia (USA) **924**
Journal of Management Accounting Research (USA) **1295**
Journal of Management & Governance (USA) **1767**
Journal of Management & Organization (AUS) **1767**
Journal of Management Development (GBR) **1767**
Journal of Management Education (USA) **1768**
Journal of Management Information Systems (USA) **2548**
Journal of Management Inquiry (USA) **1768**
Journal of Managerial Issues (USA) **1768**
Journal of Managerial Psychology (GBR) **1768**
Journal of Manufacturing Processes (GBR) **1890**
Journal of Manufacturing Systems (GBR) **3386**
Journal of Manufacturing Technology Management (GBR) **3292**
Journal of Marital and Family Therapy (USA) **7376**
Journal of Maritime Law and Commerce (USA) **4970**
Journal of Marketing (USA) **1825**
Journal of Marketing Education (USA) **1825**
Journal of Marketing Research (USA) **1825**
Journal of Marketing Theory and Practice (USA) **1826**
Journal of Marriage and Family (USA) **8114**
The Journal of Maternal - Fetal & Neonatal Medicine (GBR) **5995**
Journal of Medical Biography (GBR) **643**
Journal of Medical Marketing (Online) (GBR) **6854**
Journal of Medical Screening (GBR) **5820**
Journal of Medieval and Early Modern Studies (USA) **4460**
Journal of Membrane Biology (USA) **834**
Journal of Men's Studies (USA) **6302**
Journal of Mental Health (GBR) **6152**
Journal of Mental Health Counseling (USA) **7376**
Journal of Middle East Women's Studies (USA) **8900**
Journal of Military History (USA) **6429**
Journal of Minimal Access Surgery (IND) **6249**
Journal of Modern Greek Studies (USA) **4236**
The Journal of Modern History (USA) **4149**
Journal of Modern Literature (USA) **5315**
Journal of Molecular Medicine (DEU) **5653**
Journal of Molluscan Studies (GBR) **952**
Journal of Money, Credit & Banking (USA) **1362**
Journal of Money Laundering Control (GBR) **1362**
Journal of Moral Education (GBR) **2877**
Journal of Motor Behavior (USA) **7376**
Journal of Multi-Criteria Decision Analysis (GBR) **1769**
Journal of Multicultural Counseling and Development (USA) **7376**
Journal of Music Teacher Education (Online) (USA) **6580**
Journal of Music Therapy (USA) **6111**
Journal of Musicology (USA) **6581**
Journal of Muslim Minority Affairs (GBR) **7713**
Journal of Natural Resources and Life Sciences Education (USA) **684**
Journal of Near Eastern Studies (USA) **401**
Journal of Negro Education (USA) **2877**
Journal of Network and Systems Management (USA) **2500**
Journal of Neural Transmission (AUT) **6153**
Journal of Neuro-Oncology (USA) **6025**
Journal of Neurology (DEU) **6154**
Journal of Neuropathology and Experimental Neurology (USA) **6154**
Journal of Neuropsychiatry and Clinical Neurosciences (USA) **6154**
Journal of Neuroscience Nursing (USA) **5965**
Journal of Neurosurgical Sciences (ITA) **6249**
Journal of Neurotrauma (USA) **6064**
Journal of Nonverbal Behavior (USA) **7376**
Journal of Nuclear Medicine Technology (USA) **6201**
Journal of Nursing Care Quality (USA) **5966**
Journal of Nursing Education (USA) **5966**

Link to your serials resources and content with ulrichsweb.com

Journal of Nursing Law (USA) **5966**
Journal of Nursing Measurement (USA) **5966**
Journal of Nursing Scholarship (USA) **5966**
The Journal of Nutrition (USA) **6661**
Journal of Nutrition Education and Behavior (USA) **6662**
Journal of Nutritional & Environmental Medicine (GBR) **6662**
Journal of Obstetrics and Gynaecology (GBR) **5996**
Journal of Occupational and Environmental Hygiene (Online) (USA) **6680**
Journal of Occupational and Organizational Psychology (GBR) **7377**
Journal of Occupational Health Psychology (USA) **6680**
Journal of Occupational Rehabilitation (USA) **6680**
Journal of Oncology Pharmacy Practice (GBR) **6855**
Journal of Optimization Theory and Applications (USA) **5506**
Journal of Oral Implantology (USA) **5852**
Journal of Organizational and End User Computing (Online) (USA) *see* Journal of Organizational and End User Computing. **2571**
Journal of Organizational Behavior (GBR) **7377**
Journal of Organizational Behavior Management (USA) **7377**
Journal of Organizational Change Management (GBR) **1769**
The Journal of Orthodontics (Online Edition) (GBR) **5853**
Journal of Orthopaedic Research (USA) **6064**
Journal of Orthopaedic Surgery (HKG) **6065**
Journal of Otolaryngology - Head & Neck Surgery (CAN) **6082**
Journal of Paleontology (USA) **6726**
Journal of Palestine Studies (USA) **4322**
Journal of Palliative Care (CAN) **5653**
Journal of Parapsychology (USA) **6742**
Journal of Parenteral and Enteral Nutrition (USA) **6662**
The Journal of Pastoral Counseling (USA) **7655**
Journal of Pediatric Neurology (NLD) **6095**
Journal of Pediatric Ophthalmology and Strabismus (USA) **6045**
Journal of Pension Benefits (USA) **1691**
Journal of Pension Planning and Compliance (USA) **1931**
Journal of Perinatal and Neonatal Nursing (USA) **5967**
Journal of Perinatal Education (USA) **5996**
Journal of Perinatology (GBR) **5996**
Journal of Perioperative Practice (GBR) **5967**
Journal of Personal Selling and Sales Management (USA) **1826**
Journal of Personality and Social Psychology (USA) **7377**
Journal of Personality Disorders (USA) **7378**
Journal of Petrology (GBR) **2750**
Journal of Phenomenological Psychology (NLD) **7378**
Journal of Philosophical Logic (NLD) **6929**
Journal of Physical Education, Recreation and Dance (USA) **3068**
Journal of Physical Oceanography (USA) **2810**
Journal of Physical Therapy Education (USA) **6111**
Journal of Plankton Research (GBR) **684**
Journal of Plant Physiology (DEU) **798**
Journal of Policy Analysis and Management (USA) **7448**
Journal of Political and Military Sociology (USA) **8115**
Journal of Political Economy (USA) **1138**
Journal of Political Ideologies (GBR) **7147**
Journal of Popular Culture (USA) **5315**
Journal of Popular Film and Television (USA) **6505**
Journal of Population Economics (DEU) **7286**
The Journal of Portfolio Management (USA) **1635**
Journal of Positive Behavior Interventions (USA) **7378**
Journal of Post Keynesian Economics (USA) **1545**
Journal of Postgraduate Medicine (IND) **5654**
Journal of Practical Nursing (USA) **5967**
The Journal of Primary Prevention (USA) **7378**
Journal of Product and Brand Management (GBR) **1826**
Journal of Productivity Analysis (USA) **1769**
Journal of Professional Counseling, Practice, Theory & Research (USA) **2877**
Journal of Property Investment & Finance (GBR) **7596**
Journal of Property Management (USA) **7596**
Journal of Property Tax Assessment and Administration (USA) **7597**
Journal of Psychiatry and Neuroscience (CAN) **6156**
Journal of Psychoactive Drugs (USA) **2696**
Journal of Psychohistory (USA) **7378**
Journal of Psycholinguistic Research (USA) **5135**
The Journal of Psychology (USA) **7378**
Journal of Psychology and Theology (USA) **7379**
Journal of Psychophysiology (USA) **7379**
Journal of Psychosocial Nursing and Mental Health Services (USA) **5967**
Journal of Psychosomatic Obstetrics and Gynecology (GBR) **5997**
Journal of Psychotherapy Integration (USA) **6156**
Journal of Public Administration Research and Theory (GBR) **7448**
Journal of Public Affairs (GBR) **7448**
Journal of Public Budgeting, Accounting & Financial Management (USA) **7448**
Journal of Public Health (Online) (GBR) **8050**
Journal of Public Health Management and Practice (USA) **7529**
Journal of Public Health Policy (GBR) **7529**
Journal of Public Policy & Marketing (USA) **1826**
Journal of Public Procurement (USA) **7449**
Journal of Quality in Maintenance Engineering (GBR) **3369**
Journal of Quality Technology (USA) **3351**
Journal of Quantitative Criminology (USA) **2658**
Journal of Rational - Emotive and Cognitive - Behavior Therapy (USA) **7379**
Journal of Real Estate Finance and Economics (USA) **7597**
Journal of Real Estate Literature (USA) **7597**
The Journal of Real Estate Portfolio Management (USA) **7597**
Journal of Real Estate Practice and Education (USA) **7597**
Journal of Real Estate Research (USA) **7597**
Journal of Recreational Mathematics (USA) **5507**
Journal of Refractive Surgery (USA) **6249**
Journal of Refugee Studies (GBR) **7249**
Journal of Regulatory Economics (USA) **1546**
Journal of Rehabilitation (USA) **6111**
Journal of Rehabilitation Research and Development (USA) **6065**
The Journal of Religion (USA) **7655**
The Journal of Religious Thought (USA) **7656**
Journal of Reproductive and Infant Psychology (GBR) **7379**
The Journal of Research Administration (USA) **1769**
Journal of Research in Childhood Education (USA) **2878**
Journal of Research in Music Education (USA) **6581**
Journal of Research on Christian Education (USA) **2878**
Journal of Research on Technology in Education (USA) **2950**
Journal of Retail & Leisure Property (GBR) **7597**
Journal of Revenue and Pricing Management (GBR) **1295**
Journal of Risk and Insurance (USA) **4510**
Journal of Risk and Uncertainty (USA) **1546**
The Journal of Risk Finance (GBR) **1636**
Journal of S T E M Education (Online) (USA) **7872**
Journal of Scheduling (USA) **2593**
Journal of School Health (USA) **7529**
Journal of School Nursing (USA) **5967**
Journal of Science Education (COL) **7873**
Journal of Security Administration (USA) **2678**
Journal of Semantics (GBR) **5203**
Journal of Semitic Studies (GBR) **5135**
Journal of Service Management (GBR) **1769**
Journal of Service Research (USA) **1826**
Journal of Services Marketing (GBR) **1827**
Journal of Sex Research (USA) **7380**
Journal of Small Business and Enterprise Development (GBR) **1962**
Journal of Small Business Management (USA) **1962**
Journal of Social and Clinical Psychology (USA) **7380**
Journal of Social History (USA) **8115**
Journal of Social, Political and Economic Studies (USA) **7148**
The Journal of Social Psychology (USA) **7380**
Journal of Social Studies Research (USA) **7980**
Journal of Social Theory in Art Education (USA) **499**
Journal of Social Work Education (USA) **8051**
Journal of Soil and Water Conservation (USA) **2616**
Journal of Southern African Studies (GBR) **7980**
Journal of Southern History (USA) **4300**
Journal of Special Education (USA) **3043**
Journal of Special Education Technology (USA) **3043**
Journal of Speech, Language, and Hearing Research (USA) **4075**
The Journal of Sports Medicine and Physical Fitness (ITA) **6231**
Journal of Staff Development (USA) **1868**
Journal of State Taxation (USA) **1932**
Journal of Strength and Conditioning Research (USA) **6231**
Journal of Sugar Beet Research (USA) **3652**
Journal of Supply Chain Management (USA) **1827**
Journal of Surfactants and Detergents (DEU) **2125**
Journal of Systemic Therapies (USA) **7381**
Journal of Targeting, Measurement and Analysis for Marketing (GBR) **1890**
Journal of Taxation (USA) **1932**
Journal of Technology and Teacher Education (USA) **2950**
Journal of Technology Studies (USA) **8429**
Journal of Technology Transfer (USA) **8429**
Journal of Telemedicine and Telecare (GBR) **5655**
Journal of the Atmospheric Sciences (USA) **6359**
Journal of the Early Republic (USA) **4300**
Journal of the Experimental Analysis of Behavior (USA) **7381**
Journal of the History of Ideas (USA) **4461**
Journal of the History of Medicine and Allied Sciences (GBR) **5655**
Journal of the History of Philosophy (USA) **6930**
Journal of the History of Sexuality (USA) **8116**
Journal of the Southwest (USA) **4300**
Journal of Theological Studies (GBR) **7657**
Journal of Theology for Southern Africa (ZAF) **7657**
Journal of Theory Construction and Testing (USA) **5967**
Journal of Third World Studies (USA) **4150**
Journal of Thought (USA) **7980**
Journal of Thrombosis and Thrombolysis (USA) **5794**
Journal of Trace Elements in Medicine and Biology (DEU) **685**
Journal of Transpersonal Psychology (USA) **7381**
The Journal of Transport History (GBR) **8501**
Journal of Trauma Nursing (USA) **5967**
Journal of Traumatic Stress (USA) **7381**
Journal of Travel Medicine (USA) **5655**
Journal of Tropical Pediatrics (GBR) **6095**
Journal of Ukrainian Studies (CAN) **5316**
Journal of Urban Design (GBR) **4418**
Journal of Vacation Marketing (GBR) **8726**
The Journal of Value Inquiry (NLD) **6930**
Journal of Vascular Research (CHE) **5794**
Journal of Visual Communication in Medicine (Online) (GBR) **5655**
Journal of Visual Impairment & Blindness (USA) **4082**
The Journal of Wildlife Management (USA) **2616**
Journal of Wine Research (GBR) **240**
Journal of Women and Aging (USA) **8900**
Journal of Women, Politics & Policy (USA) **7148**
Journal of Women's History (USA) **8900**
Journal of Workplace Learning (GBR) **1868**
Journal of World History (USA) **4150**
Journal of World Trade (NLD) **4934**
Journal of Youth and Adolescence (USA) **2157**
Journal Record (Oklahoma City) (USA) **1138**
Journalism and Communication Monographs (USA) **4577**
Journalism and Mass Communication Educator (USA) **4577**
Journalism and Mass Communication Quarterly (USA) **4578**
Journalism History (USA) **4578**
Journals of Cases on Information Technology (USA) **1770**
Journals of Gerontology. Series A: Biological Sciences & Medical Sciences (USA) **4050**
Journals of Gerontology. Series B: Psychological Sciences & Social Sciences (USA) **4050**
Judaism (USA) **7725**
Judicature (USA) **4953**
Junior Scholastic (USA) **3069**
Justice Quarterly (GBR) **2658**
Justice System Journal (USA) **4954**
Juvenile Justice Digest (USA) **2658**
K M World (USA) **2537**
Kadin / Woman 2000 (CYP) **8900**
The Kansas Banker (USA) **1363**
Kansas Nurse (USA) **5968**
Kant Studien (DEU) **6930**
Kappa Delta Pi Record (USA) **3069**
Kennedy Institute of Ethics Journal (USA) **5657**
Kentucky Banker (USA) **1363**
Kentucky Nurse (USA) **5968**
The Kenyon Review (USA) **5425**
Kew Bulletin (GBR) **799**
Keyboard (USA) **6582**
Kidney and Blood Pressure Research (CHE) **6270**
Kidney International (USA) **6271**
KidScreen (CAN) **1828**
Kiplinger Agriculture Letter (USA) **131**
Kiplinger California Letter (USA) **1636**
The Kiplinger Letter (USA) **1636**
Kiplinger Tax Letter (USA) **1932**
Kiplinger's Personal Finance (USA) **1364**
Kiplinger's Personal Finance Mutual Funds (USA) **1636**
Kiplinger's Retirement Report (USA) **1636**
Kitchen & Bath Business (USA) **1019**
Kitchen & Bath Design News (USA) **4544**
Klinik Psikofarmakoloji Bulteni (TUR) **6157**
Knowledge and Information Systems (GBR) **2549**
Knowledge and Process Management (Online) (GBR) **1770**
Knowledge Management Research & Practice (GBR) **2430**
Knowledge Management Review (GBR) **1771**
Knowledge Quest (USA) **5023**
Korea Observer (KOR) **554**
Korean Studies (USA) **554**
Kuram ve Uygulamada Edytym Bylymlery (TUR) **2881**
Kybernetes (GBR) **2527**
L I M R A's MarketFacts Quarterly (USA) **4512**
L P - Gas (USA) **6776**
L S E Gender Institute. New Working Paper Series (GBR) **8900**
Lab Business Week (USA) **1143**
Labor History (GBR) **1692**
Labor Law Journal (USA) **4711**
Labor Notes (USA) **1692**
Laboratory Animals (GBR) **953**
Laboratory Equipment (USA) **5908**
Laboratory Investigation (USA) **5908**
Labour, Capital and Society (CAN) **1601**
Lafayette Business Digest (USA) **1496**
Lakewood Report on Positive Employee Practices (USA) **1771**
Lambda Book Report (USA) **4376**
The Lancet (GBR) **5660**
The Lancet (North American Edition) (GBR) **5660**
Land Economics (USA) **202**
Landscape Management (USA) **3741**
Landscape Research (GBR) **448**
Language and Speech (GBR) **5139**
Language Arts (USA) **3070**
Language, Speech and Hearing Services in Schools (USA) **6082**
Language Teaching Research (GBR) **5141**
Language Testing (GBR) **5141**
Las Vegas Business Press (USA) **1143**
Laser Focus World (USA) **7080**
Lasers in Medical Science (GBR) **5660**
Late Imperial China (USA) **4185**
Latin American Literary Review (USA) **5320**
Latin American Music Review (USA) **6584**
Latin American Politics and Society (USA) **7250**
Latin American Research Review (USA) **7982**
Latin American Telecom (USA) **2331**
Latin Trade (USA) **1575**
LatinFinance (USA) **1365**
Latino Studies (GBR) **8118**
Law & Health Weekly (USA) **4713**
Law and Human Behavior (USA) **4713**
Law and Literature (USA) **4713**
Law and Order Magazine (USA) **2659**
Law and Social Inquiry (USA) **4714**
Law & Society Review (USA) **4714**
Law Enforcement Product News (USA) **2659**
Law Enforcement Technology (USA) **2659**
Law Office Management & Administration Report (USA) **4715**
Law - Technology (USA) **4845**
The Lawyer (GBR) **4717**
LawyersU S A (USA) **4718**
Leader to Leader (USA) **1772**
Leadership (Sacramento) (USA) **2882**
Leadership & Organization Development Journal (GBR) **1772**
Leadership in Action (USA) **1772**
Leadership in Health Services (GBR) **4105**
Learning & Behavior (USA) **7383**
Learning Disability Quarterly (USA) **3043**
Learning, Media & Technology (Online) (GBR) **3070**
The Learning Organization (GBR) **1869**
Leather International (GBR) **4974**
Leatherneck (USA) **6431**
Leaven (Schaumburg) (USA) **2159**
Left Business Observer (USA) **1144**
Left Curve (USA) **5224**
Legal and Criminological Psychology (GBR) **7383**
Legal Assistant Today (USA) **4719**
Leukemia (GBR) **5939**
Leukos (USA) **3208**
Liberal Education (USA) **2992**
Librarians at Liberty (USA) **5025**
Libraries & the Cultural Record (USA) **5026**
Library Administrator's Digest (USA) **5026**
Library Hi Tech (GBR) **5062**
Library Hi Tech News (GBR) **5062**
Library Journal (USA) **5028**
Library Leadership & Management (USA) **5028**
Library Management (GBR) **5028**
The Library Quarterly (USA) **5029**
Library Review (GBR) **5029**
Library Trends (USA) **5029**
A Life in the Day (GBR) **8054**
Life Insurance International (IRL) **4512**
Lifetime Data Analysis (NLD) **8385**
Light and Medium Truck (USA) **8672**
Lighting Design + Application (USA) **3324**
Lightwave (USA) **2331**
Liguorian (USA) **7804**
Lilith (USA) **7726**
Link (Baltimore) (USA) **503**
The Lion and the Unicorn (USA) **5323**
Lipids (DEU) **738**
Listen (USA) **2696**
Literacy Research and Instruction (USA) **3070**
Literary and Linguistic Computing (GBR) **5203**
The Literary Review (USA) **5324**
Literature and Medicine (USA) **5325**
Literature and Theology (GBR) **5325**
Literature Film Quarterly (USA) **6506**
Little India (USA) **3548**
Live Design (USA) **8473**
Locksmith Ledger International (USA) **1054**
Lodging Hospitality (USA) **4393**
Logistics Management (USA) **8503**
Logistics Spectrum (USA) **8431**
Lolapress (DEU) **8900**
Long Island Business News (USA) **1145**
Long-Term Living (USA) **5969**
Los Angeles Business Journal (USA) **1497**
Los Angeles Sentinel (USA) **3548**
Louisville Magazine (USA) **3980**
Lung (USA) **6216**
Lupus (GBR) **6224**
Lustre (USA) **1021**
The Lutheran (USA) **7765**
Lutheran Theological Journal (AUS) **7766**
Lutheran Theological Seminary Bulletin (USA) **7766**
The M & A Tax Report (USA) **1933**
M D Week (USA) **5662**
M E L U S (USA) **5328**
M G M A Connexion (USA) **5663**
M H Q (USA) **4302**
M I R: Management International Review (DEU) **1773**
M I S Quarterly (USA) **2523**
M I T Sloan Management Review (USA) **1773**
M L A International Bibliography (USA) **5407**
M L N (USA) **5149**
M M W R (USA) **7530**
The MacAuthority (USA) **2577**
Machine Design (USA) **3388**
Maclean's (CAN) **3812**
MacWorld (USA) **2577**
The Magazine Antiques (USA) **367**
Magazine of History (USA) **4152**
Magistra (USA) **8900**
Magnetic Resonance Materials in Physics, Biology and Medicine (GBR) **7068**

The Maine Nurse (USA) **5969**
Maintenance Solutions (USA) **1021**
Maintenance Supplies (USA) **1021**
Making Waves (CAN) **8054**
Malaysian Business (MYS) **1146**
Mammalian Species (Online) (USA) **955**
Manage (Online) (USA) **1774**
Managed Care Business Week (USA) **1146**
Managed Care Law Weekly (USA) **4727**
Managed Care Weekly Digest (USA) **5664**
Managed Healthcare Executive (USA) **4106**
Management Communication Quarterly (USA) **1775**
Management Decision (GBR) **1775**
Management International (CAN) **1776**
Management Learning (GBR) **1776**
Management of Environmental Quality (GBR) **3451**
Management Quarterly (USA) **1776**
Management Report (Online Edition) (USA) **1696**
Management Research Review (GBR) **1776**
Management Revue (DEU) **1776**
Management Science (USA) **1776**
Management Services (GBR) **1777**
Management Today (GBR) **1777**
Manager (GBR) **1777**
Managerial and Decision Economics (GBR) **1777**
Managerial Auditing Journal (GBR) **1778**
Managerial Finance (GBR) **1778**
Managing Intellectual Property (GBR) **6754**
Managing Service Quality (GBR) **1778**
Manawatu Standard (NZL) **3917**
Mandala (USA) **7702**
Manitoba Business Magazine (CAN) **1498**
Manitoba History (CAN) **4302**
Mankind Quarterly (USA) **347**
Manufacturers' Monthly (AUS) **1898**
Manufacturing and Service Operations Management (USA) **1778**
Manufacturing Business Technology (USA) **1898**
Manufacturing Engineering (USA) **3209**
Marie Claire (USA) **8873**
Marine Biology (DEU) **688**
Marine Corps Gazette (USA) **6432**
Marine Log (USA) **8651**
Marine Technology and S N A M E News (USA) **8652**
Marine Technology Society Journal (USA) **2812**
Marketing (GBR) **1831**
Marketing Health Services (USA) **1832**
Marketing Intelligence & Planning (GBR) **1832**
Marketing Letters (USA) **1832**
Marketing Management (USA) **1832**
Marketing News (USA) **1832**
Marketing Online (CAN) *see* Marketing Magazine. **1832**
Marketing Research (USA) **1833**
Marketing Science (USA) **1833**
Marketing to Women (USA) **1833**
Marketing Week (GBR) **1834**
Marketplace (Menasha) (USA) **1147**
Marriage & Family Review (USA) **8119**
Marvels & Tales (USA) **3620**
Mass High Tech (USA) **8431**
Mass Storage News (USA) **2540**
Mass Transit (USA) **8503**
Massachusetts Review (USA) **5227**
The Masthead (Harrisburg) (USA) **4579**
Material Handling Management (USA) **5456**
Material Handling Product News (USA) **2462**
Materials Management & Distribution (CAN) **8503**
Materials Management in Health Care (USA) **4106**
Materials Performance (USA) **3353**
Materials Science and Technology (GBR) **3353**
Materials World (GBR) **6322**
Maternal and Child Health Journal (USA) **5998**
Mathematical Medicine and Biology (Online) (GBR) **5513**
Mathematical Methods of Operations Research (DEU) **1779**
Mathematical Programming (DEU) **5554**
Mathematics and Computer Education (USA) **5515**
Mathematics Magazine (USA) **5515**
Mathematics of Control, Signals and Systems (GBR) **3370**
Mathematics of Operations Research (USA) **2431**
Mathematics Teacher (USA) **3072**
Mathematics Teaching (GBR) **5516**
Mathematics Teaching in the Middle School (USA) **3072**
Mayo Clinic Proceedings (USA) **5665**
McGill Journal of Education (CAN) **2885**
McGraw-Hill's Power Markets Week (USA) **3160**
Measurement and Evaluation in Counseling and Development (USA) **2886**
Measuring Business Excellence (GBR) **1779**
Mechanical Engineering (USA) **3389**
Med Ad News (USA) **1834**
Media (HKG) **29**
Media Asia (SGP) **7567**
Media Industry Newsletter (USA) **29**
Media Report to Women (USA) **8120**
MediaWeek (USA) **30**
Medical Anthropology Quarterly (USA) **347**
Medical Benefits (USA) **4514**
Medical Design (USA) **3210**
Medical Design Technology (Online) (USA) **5667**
Medical Device Business Week (USA) **1148**
Medical Device Law Weekly (USA) **5668**
Medical Device Technology (GBR) **5668**
Medical Devices & Surgical Technology Week (USA) **5668**
Medical History (GBR) **5669**
Medical Imaging Business Week (USA) **1148**
Medical Imaging Law Weekly (USA) **6203**
Medical Imaging Week (USA) **6203**
Medical Journal of Australia (AUS) **5669**
Medical Laboratory Observer (USA) **5909**
Medical Laser Application (DEU) **5909**
Medical Law Review (GBR) **4731**
Medical Library Association. Journal (USA) **5669**
Medical Marketing & Media (USA) **6860**
Medical Microbiology and Immunology (DEU) **5763**
Medical Molecular Morphology (JPN) **899**
Medical Patent Business Week (USA) **6754**
Medical Patent Week (USA) **6755**
The Medical Post (CAN) **5670**
Medical Teacher (GBR) **5672**
Medical Verdicts & Law Weekly (USA) **4732**
Medicine and Health - Rhode Island (USA) **5674**
Medicine, Healthcare and Philosophy (NLD) **5674**
Medium Aevum (GBR) **5332**
Medizinhistorisches Journal (DEU) **5677**
MedSurg Nursing (USA) **6252**
Meeting News (USA) **6281**
Meetings & Incentive Travel (CAN) **6281**
Memory and Cognition (USA) **7384**
Memphis Business Journal (USA) **1148**
Menninger Clinic. Bulletin (USA) **6159**
Menopause News (USA) **8847**
Men's Health (United States Edition) (USA) **6285**
Mental Health Business Week (USA) **6160**
Mental Health Nursing Journal (GBR) **6160**
The Mental Health Review (GBR) **6160**
Mental Health Today (GBR) **6160**
Mental Health Weekly Digest (USA) **6160**
Mercer Business Magazine (USA) **1407**
The Mercury (AUS) **3795**
Mergers & Acquisitions (New York, 1965) (USA) **1148**
Mergers & Acquisitions Report (USA) **1148**
Meridians (USA) **8901**
Merrill - Palmer Quarterly (USA) **7385**
Metabolic Brain Disease (USA) **5678**
Metal Bulletin Monthly (GBR) **6323**
Metal Center News (USA) **6323**
Metallurgical and Materials Transactions A - Physical Metallurgy and Materials Science (USA) **6324**
Metallurgical and Materials Transactions B - Process Metallurgy and Materials Processing Science (USA) **6324**
Metalworking Production (GBR) **6326**
Meteorology and Atmospheric Physics (AUT) **6391**
Methodology and Computing in Applied Probability (USA) **5517**
Metis (San Francisco) (USA) **8874**
Metro Magazine (USA) **8504**
Metropolitan Universities (USA) **2993**
Mexican Studies (USA) **4464**
Miami Daily Business Review (USA) **1149**
Miami Times (USA) **3550**
Michigan Banker (USA) **1499**
Michigan Contractor & Builder (USA) **1024**
Michigan Quarterly Review (USA) **5227**
Microbial Drug Resistance (USA) **5679**
Microbiological Research (DEU) **891**
Microelectronics International (GBR) **3109**
Microscope (GBR) **2572**
MicroStation World (USA) **2493**
Microwave Journal (International Edition) (USA) **3325**
Microwaves & R F (USA) **3325**
Mid-America Commerce & Industry (USA) **1499**
Mid-Atlantic Construction (USA) **1024**
Midcontinental Journal of Archaeology (USA) **406**
The Middle East (GBR) **5227**
Middle East Journal (USA) **7252**
Middle East Policy (USA) **7252**
Middle Eastern Studies (GBR) **4323**
Midwest Construction (USA) **1024**
Midwest Contractor Magazine (USA) **1024**
Midwest Quarterly (USA) **4465**
Midwifery Matters (GBR) **5970**
Midwifery Today (USA) **5998**
Military History (USA) **4303**
Military Images (USA) **6435**
Military Medicine (USA) **5679**
Military Review (English Edition) (USA) **6436**
Military Technology (DEU) **6436**
Millennium Film Journal (USA) **6507**
Millimeter (USA) **6507**
Mind (GBR) **6934**
The Mineralogical Record (USA) **4340**
Mineralogy and Petrology (AUT) **6471**
Minerals and Metallurgical Processing (USA) **6471**
Minerva Biotecnologica (ITA) **768**
Minerva Journal of Women and War (USA) **6437**
Minnesota Review (USA) **5334**
Minority Business Entrepreneur (USA) **1963**
Minority Nurse Newsletter (USA) **5970**
Mississippi Business Journal (USA) **1964**
The Mississippi Quarterly (USA) **5227**
Mobile Communications Europe (GBR) **2333**
Mobile Communications International (GBR) **2333**
Mobile Networks and Applications (NLD) **2501**
Model Airplane News (USA) **4340**
Model Railroader (USA) **4341**
Modern Age (USA) **5228**
Modern Baking (USA) **3675**
Modern Casting (USA) **6326**
Modern Drama (CAN) **5335**
M F S Modern Fiction Studies (USA) **5335**
Modern Healthcare (USA) **4107**
Modern Jeweler (USA) **4568**
Modern Language Quarterly (USA) **5335**
Modern Machine Shop (USA) **5457**
Modern Materials Handling (USA) **5457**
Modern Pathology (GBR) **5680**
Modern Philology (USA) **5152**
Modern Power Systems (GBR) **3142**
Modern Psychoanalysis (USA) **7386**
Modern Rheumatology (JPN) **6225**
Modern Tire Dealer (USA) **7825**
Modernism/Modernity (USA) **4153**
Molecular Human Reproduction (GBR) **5999**
Molecular Plant - Microbe Interactions (USA) **740**
Molecular Psychiatry (Online) (GBR) *see* Molecular Psychiatry. **6161**
Moment (USA) **3551**
Momentum (New York) (USA) **6161**
Momentum (Washington) (USA) **2887**
Monday Report on Retailers (CAN) **1835**
Money Management (AUS) **1368**
Money Management Executive (USA) **1640**
MoneySense (CAN) **1150**
Montana Business Quarterly (USA) **1150**
Montessori Life (USA) **3073**
Monthly Review (USA) **7155**
Monthly Weather Review (USA) **6391**
Mortality (GBR) **7532**
Mortgage Banking (USA) **1369**
Mortgage Servicing News (USA) **1369**
Mortgage Technology (USA) **7600**
Mosaic (Winnipeg, 1967) (CAN) **5336**
Mosaic Literary Magazine (USA) **7568**
Mother Earth News (USA) **3982**
MotherJones.com (USA) *see* Mother Jones. **5228**
Motion System Design (USA) **3390**
MOTOR (USA) **8591**
Motor Age (USA) **8592**
Motor Business Japan (USA) **8592**
Motor Transport (GBR) **8673**
Motor Trend (USA) **8593**
Motor Truck (CAN) **8673**
Mountain Bike (USA) **8265**
Mountain Research and Development (CHE) **2713**
Ms. (USA) **8901**
Multi-Housing News (USA) **1025**
Multichannel Merchant (USA) **30**
Multichannel News (USA) **2385**
Multicultural Education (USA) **3073**
Multicultural Education Abstracts (Print) (GBR) **2934**
MultiMedia & Internet@Schools (USA) **2950**
Multinational Business Review (USA) **1578**
Multinational Finance Journal (USA) **1393**
Multinational Monitor (USA) **1578**
Multiple Sclerosis (GBR) **6162**
Municipal Finance Journal (USA) **1935**
Mural (MEX) **3909**
Muscle & Fitness (USA) **6993**
Muse (Chicago) (USA) **2203**
Music and Letters (GBR) **6589**
Music Educators Journal (USA) **6590**
Music Library Association. Notes (USA) **5033**
Music Perception (USA) **6591**
Music Theory Spectrum (USA) **6592**
Music Therapy Perspectives (USA) **6592**
Music Week (GBR) **6592**
Musical Opinion (GBR) **6593**
The Musical Quarterly (USA) **6594**
Musical Times (GBR) **6594**
Muslim World (USA) **7715**
Mutagenesis (GBR) **875**
Mycopathologia (NLD) **803**
N A C E Journal (USA) **1698**
N A C L A Report on the Americas (USA) **7253**
N A C T A Journal (USA) **138**
N A J A News (USA) **4580**
N A S A Tech Briefs (USA) **66**
N A S N School Nurse (USA) **5970**
N A S P A Journal (Online) (USA) **2994**
N A S S P Bulletin (USA) **3027**
N A S S P Leadership for Student Activities (USA) **3027**
N A T O's Nations and Partners for Peace (DEU) **7254**
N C A H F Newsletter (USA) **7532**
N C J R S Abstracts Database (USA) **4824**
N C J W Journal (USA) **7727**
N E A Today (USA) **2888**
N F P A Journal (USA) **3580**
N I A S Nytt (DNK) **556**
N J Biz (USA) **1151**
N M A Online (GBR) *see* New Media Age. **2335**
N P A (USA) **1297**
N W H P Network (USA) **8901**
N W S A Journal (USA) **8901**
N Z Business (NZL) **1151**
N Z Marketing Magazine (NZL) **1835**
Nails (USA) **590**
Narcotics Enforcement & Prevention Digest (USA) **2661**
Nase Gospodarstvo (SVN) **1152**
Nashim (ISR) **8901**
Nashville Business and Lifestyles (USA) **1152**
Nashville Business Journal (USA) **1152**
The Nation (USA) **5229**
The National Black Law Journal (USA) **4738**
National Cancer Institute. Journal (Online) (GBR) **6028**
National Catholic Reporter (USA) **7808**
National Contract Management Journal (USA) **1780**
National Defense (USA) **6438**
National Dragster (USA) **8595**
National Driller (USA) **8829**
National Fisherman (USA) **3602**
National Floor Trends (USA) **4547**
National Geographic Adventure (USA) **8323**
National Geographic Explorer (USA) **4020**
National Geographic Kids (USA) **4021**
National Geographic Online (USA) *see* National Geographic. **4020**
National Geographic Traveler (USA) **8740**
National Guard (USA) **6438**
National Hog Farmer (USA) **294**
National Institute of Standards and Technology. Journal of Research (USA) **6405**
The National Interest (USA) **7254**
National Jeweler (USA) **4568**
National Journal (USA) **7156**
National Journal of Constitutional Law (CAN) **4851**
National Medical Association. Journal (USA) **5683**
National Mortgage News Daily (USA) *see* National Mortgage News. **1370**
National N O W Times (USA) **8877**
National Parks (USA) **4981**
National Petroleum News (USA) **6779**
National Post (Toronto) (CAN) **3813**
National Real Estate Investor (USA) **7601**
National Review (USA) **7156**
National Tax Association. Proceedings of the Annual Conference on Taxation and Minutes of the Annual Meeting (USA) **1936**
National Tax Journal (USA) **1936**
National Underwriter. Life & Health (USA) **4516**
National Underwriter. P & C (USA) **4516**
National Wildlife (USA) **2620**
National Wildlife (World Edition) (USA) **2620**
National Women's Health Report (USA) **8847**
Nationalities Papers (GBR) **7987**
The Nation's Health (USA) **7533**
Nation's Restaurant News (USA) **4394**
Native Americas (USA) **6635**
Native Plants Journal (USA) **804**
Natural Foods Merchandiser (USA) **1835**
Natural Gas & Electricity (USA) **6779**
Natural Gas Week (USA) **6780**
Natural History (USA) **7888**
Natural Language and Linguistic Theory (NLD) **5154**
Nature (GBR) **7889**
Nature Biotechnology (USA) **768**
Nature Cell Biology (GBR) **835**
Nature Genetics (USA) **876**
Nature Materials (GBR) **3355**
Nature Medicine (GBR) **5684**
Nature Methods (GBR) **7889**
Nature Reviews. Drug Discovery (GBR) **6863**
Nature Reviews. Genetics (GBR) **876**
Nature Reviews. Microbiology (GBR) **893**
Nature Reviews. Neuroscience (GBR) **6162**
Nature, Society, and Thought (USA) **7157**
Nature Structural and Molecular Biology (USA) **693**
Naval Aviation News (USA) **67**
Naval Forces (DEU) **6438**
Naval History (USA) **6438**
Naval War College Review (USA) **6438**
Navy Medicine (USA) **5684**
Navy Supply Corps Newsletter (USA) **6439**
Near Eastern Archaeology (USA) **407**
Negotiation Journal (USA) **7254**
Negro Educational Review (USA) **2890**
Neonatology (CHE) **5999**
Neophilologus (NLD) **5339**
Nephrology, Dialysis, Transplantation (GBR) **6272**
Nephrology Nursing Journal (USA) **5971**
Nephron Physiology (CHE) *see* The Nephron Journals. **6272**
Network (Winnipeg) (CAN) **8847**
The Network Journal (USA) **3553**
Network World (USA) **2502**
Networks and Spatial Economics (USA) **2518**
Neue Zeitschrift fuer Systematische Theologie und Religionsphilosophie (DEU) **7665**
Neurocase (GBR) **6164**
Neurochemical Research (USA) **6164**
Neuroendocrinology (CHE) **5898**
Neuroepidemiology (CHE) **6164**
Neurogenetics (DEU) **876**
Neurological Research (GBR) **6165**
Neurological Sciences (ITA) **6165**
Neurology India (IND) **6166**
Neurophysiology (USA) **6167**
Neuropsychobiology (CHE) **6168**
Neuropsychology (USA) **6168**
Neuropsychology Review (USA) **6168**
Neuropsychopharmacology (USA) **6168**
Neuroradiology (DEU) **6204**
Neuroscience and Behavioral Physiology (USA) **6169**
Nevada R N Formation (USA) **5971**
New Accountant (USA) **1297**
New African (GBR) **1602**
The New American (Appleton) (USA) **7157**
New Beginnings (Schaumburg) (USA) **2162**
New Centennial Review (USA) **4466**
New England Construction (USA) **1026**
New England Economic Indicators (USA) **1501**
The New England Journal of Higher Education (USA) **2995**
New England Journal of Medicine (USA) **5685**
The New England Quarterly (USA) **5340**
New England Reading Association. Journal (USA) **2890**
New England Review (USA) **5340**
New Equipment Digest (USA) **8433**
New Genetics and Society (GBR) **876**
New German Critique (USA) **4466**
New Hampshire Business Review (USA) **1431**
New Internationalist (GBR) **7255**
New Jersey Business (USA) **1899**

Online Service

New Jersey Nurse (USA) **5971**
New Labor Forum (USA) **4599**
New Lebanese American Journal (USA) **4154**
New Library World (GBR) **5035**
New Literary History (USA) **5340**
New Mexico Woman (USA) **8877**
New Moon Girls (USA) **2204**
New Orleans CityBusiness (USA) **1964**
New Oxford Review (USA) **7809**
New Political Economy (GBR) **1547**
New Politics (USA) **7158**
The New Republic (USA) **5230**
New Scientist: Planet Science (GBR) *see* New Scientist. **7891**
New Scientist: Planet Science (GBR) *see* New Scientist on CD-ROM. **7892**
New Statesman (GBR) **5230**
New York Construction (USA) **1027**
New York Magazine (USA) **3983**
The New York State Conservationist (USA) **2622**
The New York State Dental Journal (USA) **5857**
New York Times Book Review (USA) **7568**
New York Times Magazine (USA) **3983**
The New York Times Upfront (Student Edition) (USA) **2205**
The New Yorker (USA) **5230**
New Zealand Journal of Psychology (NZL) **7388**
New Zealand Management (NZL) **1781**
News from Native California (USA) **6636**
News India-Times (USA) **3554**
News Media and the Law (USA) **4580**
Newsletter on Intellectual Freedom (USA) **5036**
Newspaper Financial Executives Quarterly (USA) **1781**
Newspaper Research Journal (USA) **4581**
NewsReport Online (USA) *see* The National Academies In Focus. **7886**
Newsweek (USA) **3983**
Newsweek International (GBR) **3869**
The Next American City (USA) **4421**
Nieman Reports (USA) **4581**
Nine (USA) **8240**
Nineteenth-Century Literature (Berkeley) (USA) **5342**
Nineteenth Century Music (USA) **6599**
Nonlinear Studies (USA) **5521**
Nonprofit World (USA) **8059**
Nordic Reach (USA) **3555**
Norges Bank. Economic Bulletin (NOR) **1501**
North American Actuarial Journal (USA) **4517**
North American Birds (USA) **911**
North American Post (USA) **3555**
Northeast African Studies (USA) **3555**
Northeast Pennsylvania Business Journal (USA) **1155**
Northeastern Naturalist (USA) **805**
Northern Journal of Applied Forestry (USA) **3698**
The Northern Miner (CAN) **6475**
Northern New Jersey Business (USA) **1502**
Northern Ontario Business (CAN) **1155**
Northwest Public Power Association. Bulletin (USA) **3143**
Northwestern Financial Review (USA) **1372**
Northwestern Journal of International Law & Business (USA) **4937**
Northwestern University Law Review (USA) **4749**
Notes and Queries (GBR) **5343**
Nova Religio (USA) **7739**
Novel: A Forum on Fiction (USA) **5344**
Nuclear Engineering International (GBR) **3171**
Nuclear Plant Journal (USA) **3172**
Nuclear Resister (USA) **7160**
NuclearFuel (USA) **3172**
Nucleic Acids Research (GBR) **741**
Nucleonics Week (USA) **3143**
El Nuevo Dia Interactivo (PRI) *see* El Nuevo Dia. **3931**
Nurse Author and Editor (Online) (GBR) **4581**
The Nurse Practitioner (USA) **5972**
Nurse Researcher (GBR) **5972**
Nursing (Year) (USA) **5972**
Nursing Administration Quarterly (USA) **5973**
Nursing B C (CAN) **5973**
Nursing Economics (USA) **5973**
Nursing Education Perspectives (USA) **5973**
Nursing Ethics (GBR) **5973**
Nursing Forum (USA) **5973**
Nursing History Review (USA) **5973**
Nursing Home & Elder Business Week (USA) **5974**
Nursing Journal of India (IND) **5974**
Nursing Management (USA) **5974**
Nursing Management (GBR) **5974**
Nursing Older People (GBR) **4052**
Nursing Standard (GBR) **5975**
Nutrition Action Health Letter (USA) **6665**
Nutrition & Food Science (GBR) **6665**
Nutrition Forum (USA) **6665**
Nutrition Health Review (USA) **6666**
Nutrition in Clinical Practice (USA) **6666**
Nutrition Journal (GBR) **6666**
Nutrition Reviews (USA) **6666**
O A H Newsletter (USA) **4306**
O B G Y N & Reproduction Week (USA) **6000**
O C L C Systems & Services (GBR) **5037**
O E C D Observer (FRA) **1504**
O E M Off-Highway (USA) **213**
O E M Online (GBR) *see* Occupational and Environmental Medicine. **6682**
O H S Canada Magazine (CAN) **6682**
O N S Connect (USA) **6029**
O R L (CHE) **6083**
O R Manager (USA) **4108**
O R Spectrum (DEU) **2433**
O T J R: Occupation, Participation and Health (USA) **5688**
O: The Oprah Magazine (USA) **8878**
Obesity & Diabetes Week (USA) **5898**
Obesity, Fitness, and Wellness Week (USA) **6994**
The Observer (GBR) **3869**
Occupational Health (GBR) **5976**
Occupational Health & Safety (USA) **6682**
Occupational Medicine (GBR) **6683**
Occupational Outlook Handbook (USA) **6707**
Occupational Outlook Quarterly (USA) **6707**
Occupational Therapy International (GBR) **6683**
Ocean Dynamics (DEU) **2814**
Ocean News & Technology (USA) **2815**
Oceania (AUS) **350**
Oceanus (USA) **2815**
Octane Week (USA) **6782**
Odontology (JPN) **5858**
Odyssey (Peru) (USA) **2205**
Of Counsel (USA) **4751**
Off Our Backs (USA) **8902**
Office Products International (GBR) **1853**
Office Solutions (USA) **1853**
Office World News (USA) **1853**
The Officer (USA) **6440**
Official Board Markets (USA) **6712**
Offshore (Tulsa) (USA) **6782**
Ohio (USA) **3984**
Ohio Libraries (USA) **5038**
Ohio Reading Teacher (USA) **3075**
Oil and Gas Investor (USA) **6783**
Oil and Gas Investor's A & D Watch (USA) **6783**
Oil & Gas Journal (USA) **6783**
Oil, Gas & Petrochem Equipment (USA) **6784**
Oil Spill Intelligence Report (USA) **3490**
Oklahoma Business Bulletin (USA) **1257**
Oligonucleotides (USA) **877**
On Campus with Women (USA) **2996**
On the Horizon (USA) **2996**
On Wall Street (USA) **1643**
Oncogene (GBR) **6029**
Oncology (CHE) **6030**
Oncology Business Week (USA) **6030**
Oncology Nursing Forum (USA) **5976**
Onderstepoort Journal of Veterinary Research (ZAF) **8804**
One Up (GBR) **7667**
OnEarth (USA) **3458**
Online (USA) **2565**
Online Information Review (GBR) **5038**
Online Journal of Issues in Nursing (USA) **5976**
Online Libraries and Microcomputers (USA) **5063**
Online Newsletter (USA) **2565**
Ontario Out of Doors (CAN) **8326**
Open Economies Review (NLD) **1547**
Opera - Canada (CAN) **6601**
Opera News (USA) **6602**
The Opera Quarterly (GBR) **6602**
Operational Research Society. Journal (GBR) **2433**
Operations Research (USA) **2433**
Ophthalmic Research (CHE) **6048**
Ophthalmic Surgery, Lasers and Imaging (USA) **6254**
Ophthalmologica (CHE) **6048**
Ophthalmology Times (USA) **6048**
Optician (GBR) **6049**
OptiMSt (CAN) **8879**
Optometric Management (USA) **6049**
Oral History Review (USA) **4155**
Orange County Business Journal (USA) **1505**
Oregon Business Magazine (USA) **1157**
Organic Gardening (USA) **3746**
Organization (GBR) **1784**
Organization & Environment (USA) **6684**
Organization Development Journal (USA) **1784**
Organization Science (USA) **1784**
Organizational Research Methods (USA) **1784**
Organized Crime Digest (USA) **2662**
Origination News (USA) **1373**
Orlando Business Journal (USA) **1157**
Orthopaedic Nursing Journal (USA) **5977**
Orthopedics (USA) **6070**
Osteoporosis International (GBR) **5691**
Ottawa Citizen (CAN) **3815**
Our Times Magazine (CAN) **4600**
Outdoor Life (USA) **8327**
Outsourced Logistics (USA) **8507**
Outstate Business (USA) **1505**
Overhaul & Maintenance (USA) **67**
Oxford Art Journal (GBR) **510**
Oxford Economic Papers (GBR) **1158**
Oxford Journal of Legal Studies (GBR) **4754**
Oxford Review of Economic Policy (GBR) **1158**
Oxford Review of Education (GBR) **2894**
P C Magazine (Online) (USA) **2434**
P C World (USA) **2581**
P M Engineer (USA) **4124**
P M J Online (GBR) *see* Postgraduate Medical Journal. **5698**
P M L A (USA) **5347**
P M Network (USA) **1785**
P M Online (GBR) *see* People Management. **2897**
P R I M U S (USA) **5524**
P R News (USA) **31**
P R O (Fort Atkinson) (USA) **3746**
P R Week (US Edition) (USA) **32**
P S A Journal (USA) **6972**
P S: Political Science & Politics (GBR) **7163**
P T - Magazine of Physical Therapy (USA) **6113**
Pacific Accounting Review (GBR) **1373**
Pacific Affairs (CAN) **7257**
Pacific and Asian Journal of Energy (IND) **3144**
Pacific Builder and Engineer (USA) **1029**
Pacific Business News (USA) **1158**
Pacific Historical Review (USA) **4307**
Pacific Science (USA) **7896**
PackagePrinting (USA) **7325**
Packaging Digest (USA) **6713**
Paediatric Nursing (GBR) **5977**
Pain & Central Nervous System Week (USA) **6172**
Pain Reviews (GBR) **5692**
Paint & Coatings Industry (USA) **6719**
Painting and Wallcovering Contractor (USA) **6719**
Palaestra (USA) **3045**
Paleobiology (USA) **6728**
Palestine - Israel Journal of Politics, Economics and Culture (ISR) **7163**
Palliative Medicine (GBR) **5693**
Pancreatology (CHE) **5898**
Paper, Film and Foil Converter (USA) **6714**
Paperboard Packaging (USA) **6714**
Papers in Regional Science (DEU) **7991**
Papers on Language and Literature (USA) **5348**
Parameters (Carlisle) (USA) **6441**
Parent & Child (USA) **2164**
Parents (USA) **2164**
The Paris Review (USA) **5349**
Parks and Recreation (USA) **4981**
Parliamentary Affairs (GBR) **7163**
Parnassus: Poetry in Review (USA) **5429**
Partner's Report (New York, 1987) (USA) **4878**
Partner's Report (New York, 1989) (USA) **1298**
Past & Present (GBR) **4155**
Pathobiology (CHE) **5764**
Pathology, Research and Practice (DEU) **5694**
Patient Care (CAN) **5694**
Pavement (Fort Atkinson) (USA) **3280**
Payroll Manager's Letter (USA) **1938**
Payroll Practitioner's Monthly (USA) **4756**
Payroll Practitioner's State Tax Alert (USA) **1938**
Peace and Freedom (USA) **7258**
Peace Research (CAN) **7258**
Peace Review (GBR) **7259**
Peacekeeping & International Relations (CAN) **7259**
Peacework (USA) **7164**
Pediatric and Developmental Pathology (USA) **6100**
Pediatric Annals (USA) **6100**
Pediatric Neurosurgery (CHE) **6173**
Pediatric Nursing (USA) **5977**
Pediatrics (English Edition) (USA) **6102**
Pediatrics for Parents (USA) **6102**
Pedobiologia (DEU) **246**
Peer Review (USA) **2997**
Pennsylvania C P A Journal (USA) **1298**
Pension Benefits (USA) **1702**
Pensions (GBR) **1871**
Pensions & Investments (USA) **1644**
Pensions Management (GBR) **1871**
Penton's Welding Magazine (USA) **6343**
People & Strategy (USA) **1871**
People's Medical Society Newsletter (USA) **2640**
Performance Chemicals Europe (GBR) **2075**
Performance Improvement (USA) **3076**
Performance Improvement Quarterly (USA) **3076**
Performance Measurement and Metrics (GBR) **5039**
Performing Arts and Entertainment in Canada (CAN) **8475**
Perfusion (GBR) **5797**
Personal and Ubiquitous Computing (GBR) **2435**
Personnel Psychology (USA) **7390**
Personnel Review (GBR) **1872**
Perspectives (CZE) **7259**
Perspectives (Baltimore, 1999) (USA) **8125**
Perspectives in Biology and Medicine (USA) **5695**
Perspectives in Psychiatric Care (USA) **5977**
Perspectives in Public Health (GBR) **8061**
Perspectives of New Music (USA) **6605**
Perspectives on Political Science (USA) **7165**
Perspectives on Sexual and Reproductive Health (USA) **6001**
Pest Management Professional (USA) **246**
Petroleum Economist (GBR) **6787**
Pharmaceutical Executive (USA) **6869**
Pharmaceutical Research (USA) **6870**
Pharmaceutical Technology (USA) **6870**
The Pharmacogenomics Journal (GBR) **6871**
Pharmacy News (AUS) **6873**
Pharmacy Post (CAN) **6873**
Pharmacy Practice (CAN) **6873**
Pharmacy World and Science (NLD) **6874**
Phi Delta Kappan (USA) **2898**
Philadelphia Business Journal (USA) **1511**
Philological Quarterly (USA) **5160**
Philosophical Psychology (GBR) **7391**
Philosophical Studies (NLD) **6941**
Philosophy and Literature (USA) **6942**
Philosophy and Public Affairs (USA) **7165**
Philosophy East and West (USA) **6943**
Philosophy of Music Education Review (USA) **6605**
Philosophy of Science (USA) **7898**
Philosophy, Psychiatry & Psychology (USA) **6943**
Philosophy Today (USA) **6944**
Phlebology (GBR) **5797**
Phoenix (Toronto, 1946) (CAN) **2239**
Photo District News (USA) **6973**
Photo Trade News (USA) **6973**
Photochemistry and Photobiology (USA) **2139**
Phycologia (USA) **808**
Phylon (USA) **8125**
Physical Educator (USA) **3076**
Physical Medicine and Rehabilitation Clinics of North America (USA) **6113**
Physical Therapy (USA) **6113**
The Physician and Sportsmedicine (USA) **6232**
Physician Business Week (USA) **5696**
Physician Law Weekly (USA) **4758**
Physiological Research (CZE) **926**
Physiotherapy Research International (GBR) **6114**
Phytomedicine (DEU) **5696**
Phytopathology (USA) **809**
Phytopathology News (USA) **809**
Pigment & Resin Technology (GBR) **6720**
Pipeline & Gas Journal (USA) **6788**
PipeLine and Gas Technology (USA) **6789**
Pit & Quarry (USA) **6476**
Pittsburgh Business Times (USA) **1159**
Pituitary (NLD) **5898**
Plains Anthropologist (USA) **351**
Plane and Pilot (USA) **68**
Planner (USA) **1298**
Planning (USA) **4423**
Planning (GBR) **4423**
Planning & Changing (USA) **3029**
Planning & Environmental Law (USA) **7604**
Plant (CAN) **1785**
Plant and Cell Physiology (GBR) **835**
The Plant Cell (USA) **810**
Plant Disease (USA) **247**
Plant Engineering (USA) **3215**
Plant Physiology (USA) **812**
Plastic Surgical Nursing (USA) **5978**
Plastics Engineering (USA) **7097**
Plastics in Canada (CAN) **7097**
Plastics Technology (USA) **7098**
Platt's Metals Week (USA) **6476**
Platt's Oilgram News (USA) **6789**
Playback (CAN) **2387**
Ploughshares (USA) **5352**
PlugIn Datamation (USA) **2538**
Plumbing & Mechanical (USA) **4125**
Poetics Today (USA) **5234**
Poetry (Chicago) (USA) **5430**
Poets & Writers Online (USA) *see* Poets & Writers Magazine. **5432**
Pointe (USA) **2687**
Police (USA) **2663**
Police Department Disciplinary Bulletin (USA) **2663**
Police Fleet Manager (USA) **2663**
Policing (Bingley) (GBR) **2664**
Policy Review (USA) **7166**
Policy Sciences (NLD) **7166**
Policy Studies Journal (USA) **7167**
Political Analysis (GBR) **7168**
Political Research Quarterly (USA) **7169**
Political Science Quarterly (USA) **7169**
Politics (USA) **7170**
Pollution Engineering (USA) **3490**
Polymer Composites (USA) **7098**
Polymer Engineering and Science (USA) **3252**
Polymers and Polymer Composites (GBR) **7099**
PopSci.com (USA) *see* Popular Science. **8435**
Popular Mechanics PMZone (USA) *see* Popular Mechanics. **8435**
Popular Music & Society (GBR) **6607**
Population and Environment (USA) **7391**
Population Bulletin (USA) **7289**
Population Ecology (JPN) **7290**
Population et Societes (FRA) **7290**
Population Research and Policy Review (NLD) **7290**
Portable Design (USA) **3215**
Portal (USA) **5039**
Portuguese Economic Journal (DEU) **1511**
Positivity (NLD) **5525**
Post-Communist Economies (GBR) **1547**
Postgraduate Medicine (USA) **5698**
Pottery Making Illustrated (USA) **2044**
Poultry Science (USA) **297**
Poultry World (GBR) **297**
Poverty & Race (USA) **8126**
Powder / Bulk Solids (USA) **3253**
Power (Houston) (USA) **3393**
Power Engineering (USA) **3328**
Power Engineering International (USA) **3328**
Power Finance and Risk (USA) **1375**
Practical Accountant (USA) **1299**
Practical Horseman (USA) **8296**
The Practical Lawyer (USA) **4759**
The Practical Litigator (USA) **4759**
The Practical Real Estate Lawyer (USA) **4759**
The Practical Tax Lawyer (USA) **1939**
Practice Nurse (GBR) **5978**
The Practicing C P A (USA) **1299**
The Practitioner (GBR) **5698**
Precision Marketing (GBR) **1838**
El Pregonero (USA) **7813**
Prehospital Emergency Care (GBR) **6071**
Presentations (USA) **32**
The Presidency (USA) **2998**
Presidential Studies Quarterly (USA) **7173**
Preventing School Failure (USA) **3045**
Prevention (USA) **6995**
Prevention Science (USA) **5825**
Preventive Medicine Week (USA) **5699**
Pride (London) (GBR) **8881**
Primary Health Care Research and Development (GBR) **5699**
Primates (JPN) **960**
Principal Leadership (High School Edition) (USA) **2899**
Principal Leadership (Middle School Edition) (USA) **2899**
Principal's Report (USA) **1786**
Print (USA) **2489**
Print Professional (USA) **7326**
Printed Circuit Design & Manufacture (USA) **2466**

DIRECTORY 2010 PROQUEST LLC (ANN ARBOR) 11249

Printing Impressions (USA) **7326**
Printing News (USA) **7327**
Privacy Journal (USA) **2515**
Private Banker International (IRL) **1376**
Pro Sound News (USA) **8154**
Probability Theory and Related Fields (DEU) **5526**
Problems of Post-Communism (USA) **7173**
Process Engineering (GBR) **3253**
Process Heating (USA) **3371**
Process Safety Progress (USA) **3253**
Product Design and Development (USA) **3216**
Production and Operations Management (USA) **1786**
Productivity Software (USA) **2596**
Products Finishing (USA) **6720**
Professional Animal Scientist (USA) **8805**
Professional Builder (USA) **1030**
Professional Distributor (USA) **3393**
Professional Engineering (GBR) **3393**
Professional Psychology: Research and Practice (USA) **7392**
Professional Remodeler (USA) **1030**
Professional Safety (USA) **6684**
Professional School Counseling (USA) **2900**
Professional Tool and Equipment News (USA) **8599**
Profit (CAN) **1162**
Profit-Building Strategies for Business Owners (USA) **1162**
Progress in Cardiovascular Nursing (USA) **5798**
Progress in Development Studies (IND) **8126**
Progress in Histochemistry and Cytochemistry (DEU) **742**
Progress in Human Geography (GBR) **4025**
Progress in Physical Geography (GBR) **4025**
Progress in Rubber, Plastics and Recycling Technology (GBR) **3254**
Progress in Transplantation (USA) **6256**
The Progressive (Madison) (USA) **7173**
Progressive Grocer (New York, 2002) (USA) **3681**
Progressive Librarian (USA) **5040**
Project Finance and Infrastructure Finance (GBR) **1376**
Project Management Journal (USA) **1787**
Promotions and Incentives (GBR) **1838**
Proofs (USA) **5862**
Propane - Canada (CAN) **6790**
Property Management (GBR) **7605**
Prostate Cancer and Prostatic Diseases (GBR) **6033**
Protein Engineering Design and Selection (Online) (GBR) **743**
Proteome Science (GBR) **743**
Proteomics Weekly (USA) **744**
Protist (DEU) **698**
Psychiatric Annals (USA) **6176**
Psychiatric Quarterly (USA) **6176**
Psychiatric Rehabilitation Journal (USA) **6176**
Psychiatric Times (USA) **6176**
Psychiatry (New York) (USA) **6177**
Psychoanalytic Dialogues (USA) **7395**
Psychoanalytic Inquiry (USA) **7395**
Psychoanalytic Psychology (USA) **7395**
The Psychoanalytic Review (USA) **7395**
Psychological Assessment (USA) **7396**
Psychological Bulletin (USA) **7396**
Psychological Methods (USA) **7396**
The Psychological Record (USA) **7396**
Psychological Research (DEU) **7396**
Psychological Review (USA) **7397**
Psychological Services (USA) **7397**
The Psychologist (GBR) **7398**
Psychology and Aging (USA) **4053**
Psychology & Marketing (USA) **7398**
Psychology & Psychotherapy (GBR) **7399**
Psychology, Health & Medicine (GBR) **7399**
Psychology of Addictive Behaviors (USA) **2698**
Psychology of Men & Masculinity (USA) **7399**
Psychology, Public Policy, and Law (USA) **7400**
Psychology Science Quarterly (DEU) **7400**
Psychology Today (USA) **7400**
Psychometrika (USA) **7400**
Psychomusicology (CAN) **6608**
Psychonomic Bulletin & Review (USA) **7400**
Psychopathology (CHE) **6179**
Psychopharmacology (DEU) **6876**
Psychopharmacology Bulletin (USA) **6877**
Psychosomatics (USA) **6179**
Psychotherapy (USA) **7401**
Psychotherapy and Psychosomatics (CHE) **6180**
Psychotherapy Networker (USA) **7401**
Psychotherapy Research (GBR) **7401**
Public Administration and Development (GBR) **1604**
Public Administration Quarterly (USA) **7461**
Public Administration Review (USA) **7461**
Public Choice (NLD) **1162**
The Public Eye (Somerville) (USA) **7174**
The Public Finance (GBR) **7501**
Public Health Genomics (CHE) **877**
Public Health Reports (USA) **7537**
The Public Historian (USA) **4157**
Public Libraries (USA) **5040**
The Public Manager (USA) **7462**
Public Opinion Quarterly (USA) **7174**
Public Organization Review (USA) **1787**
Public Personnel Management (USA) **1873**
Public Relations Journal (Online) (USA) **33**
Public Relations Quarterly (USA) **33**
Public Relations Strategist (USA) **33**
Public Relations Tactics (USA) **33**
Public Roads (USA) **3281**
Public Utilities Fortnightly (USA) **3510**
Public Works (USA) **7501**
Publishers Weekly (USA) **7571**
Publishing Research Quarterly (USA) **7571**
Publius (USA) **7174**
Puget Sound Business Journal (USA) **1162**
Pulp & Paper Canada (CAN) **6737**
Pulp & Paper International (USA) **6737**
Pulse (London, 1959) (GBR) **5700**
Purchasing (Newton) (USA) **1839**
Purchasing b2b (CAN) **1839**
Q S H C Online (GBR) *see* Quality and Safety in Health Care. **5701**
QST (USA) **2361**
Qualified Remodeler (USA) **1031**
Qualitative Market Research (GBR) **1839**
Qualitative Research in Psychology (GBR) **7402**
Quality Assurance in Education (GBR) **2901**
Quality in Ageing (GBR) **4054**
Quality Magazine (USA) **1788**
Quality Management in Health Care (USA) **4110**
Quality Management Journal (USA) **1788**
Quality Progress (USA) **1788**
Quarterly Economic Commentary (IRL) **1163**
Quarterly Journal of Finance and Accounting (USA) **1163**
Quarterly Journal of Mathematics (GBR) **5527**
Quarterly Journal of Mechanics and Applied Mathematics (GBR) **5527**
The Quarterly Journal of Nuclear Medicine and Molecular Imaging (ITA) **6205**
Quarterly Review of Distance Education (USA) **3078**
Queueing Systems (NLD) **3328**
Quick Printing (USA) **7327**
Quill (Greencastle) (USA) **4582**
R & D Directions (USA) **6877**
R D H (USA) **5862**
R F Design (USA) **3111**
The R M A Journal (USA) **1377**
R S I (USA) **1031**
R U S I Journal (GBR) **6442**
R V Trade Digest (USA) **8674**
Race, Gender & Class (USA) **3560**
Radiance Online (USA) **8881**
Radical Teacher (USA) **7175**
Radio (USA) **2362**
Radio Control Car Action (USA) **4345**
Ragged Edge (Online) (USA) **4084**
Railway Age (USA) **8623**
Railway Gazette International (GBR) **8623**
Railway Track & Structures (USA) **8624**
Ranch & Rural Living Magazine (USA) **297**
RAND Journal of Economics (USA) **1164**
Rangeland Ecology & Management (USA) **699**
Rangelands (USA) **297**
Ranger Rick (USA) **2210**
Rapid Prototyping Journal (GBR) **3394**
Raritan (USA) **5357**
Raven's Eye (CAN) **3560**
Reactions (GBR) **4520**
Read Magazine (USA) **3078**
Reading Horizons (USA) **3045**
Reading Improvement (USA) **3045**
The Reading Teacher (USA) **2903**
Reading Today (USA) **2903**
Real Analysis Exchange (USA) **5528**
Real Estate Alert (USA) **7608**
Real Estate Economics (USA) **7608**
Real Estate Finance (USA) **7608**
Real Estate Forum (USA) **7608**
Real Estate Issues (USA) **7609**
Real Estate Taxation (USA) **7610**
Real Property, Trust and Estate Law Journal (USA) **4905**
Real Simple (USA) **8881**
Realites Industrielles (FRA) **6477**
RealScreen (CAN) **1164**
Reason (USA) **5236**
Recherche et Applications en Marketing (FRA) **1839**
Reclaiming Children and Youth (USA) **7402**
Records Management Journal (GBR) **1789**
Red Cedar Review (USA) **5236**
Redbook (USA) **8882**
Reeves Journal (USA) **4125**
Reference and User Services Quarterly (USA) **5042**
Reference Reviews (GBR) **5042**
Reference Services Review (GBR) **5042**
Refrigerated Transporter (USA) **8675**
Region Focus (USA) **1513**
The Region Magazine (USA) **1378**
Regional Anesthesia and Pain Medicine (USA) **5773**
Regional Outlook: Southeast Asia (SGP) **1514**
Regional Studies (GBR) **4425**
Registered Rep (USA) **1647**
Regulation (Washington, 1977) (USA) **7176**
Rehabilitation Counseling Bulletin (USA) **4069**
Rehabilitation Nursing (USA) **5979**
Rehabilitation Psychology (USA) **7402**
Relations Industrielles (CAN) **1705**
Religion and American Culture (USA) **7674**
Religion, State and Society (GBR) **7675**
Religious Education (USA) **7676**
Religious Studies and Theology (GBR) **7676**
Remedial and Special Education (USA) **3046**
Renaissance Quarterly (USA) **5359**
Renascence (USA) **5359**
Rental and Staging Systems (USA) **2025**
Rental Product News (USA) **1902**
Report on Healthcare Information Management (USA) **5703**
Representations (USA) **4472**
Reproductive BioMedicine Online (GBR) **6002**
Research and Teaching in Developmental Education (USA) **2904**
Research and Theory for Nursing Practice (USA) **5979**
Research in African Literatures (USA) **5360**
Research in Drama Education (GBR) **8477**
Research in Education (Manchester) (GBR) **2904**
Research in Healthcare Financial Management (USA) **4110**
Research in Phenomenology (NLD) **6947**
Research in Science & Technological Education (GBR) **2904**
Research in the Teaching of English (USA) **3078**
Research into Higher Education Abstracts (GBR) **2935**
Research Money (CAN) **1378**
Research Quarterly for Exercise and Sport (USA) **6995**
Research Technology Management (USA) **1790**
Residential Systems (USA) **3112**
Resource (Niles) (USA) **250**
Resource Links (CAN) **2210**
Respiration (CHE) **6218**
Respiratory Therapeutics Week (USA) **6219**
Restaurant Business (USA) **4396**
Restaurant Hospitality (USA) **4397**
Restaurants & Institutions (USA) **4397**
Retail Banker International (IRL) **1379**
Retail Merchandiser (USA) **1840**
Retail Traffic (USA) **1841**
Retailing Today (USA) **1841**
Review of Accounting and Finance (GBR) **1300**
Review of Accounting Studies (USA) **1300**
Review of African Political Economy (GBR) **7262**
The Review of Austrian Economics (USA) **1548**
The Review of Banking & Financial Services (USA) **1379**
The Review of Black Political Economy (USA) **1165**
Review of Business (USA) **1165**
The Review of Contemporary Fiction (USA) **5360**
Review of Derivatives Research (USA) **1379**
Review of Economic Design (DEU) **1548**
The Review of Economic Studies (GBR) **1166**
Review of Economics of the Household (USA) **1166**
Review of Educational Research (USA) **2905**
The Review of English Studies (GBR) **5360**
Review of Finance (Print) (GBR) **1379**
The Review of Financial Studies (USA) **1379**
Review of General Psychology (USA) **7403**
The Review of Higher Education (USA) **3000**
Review of Industrial Organization (NLD) **1548**
The Review of Litigation (USA) **4769**
The Review of Metaphysics (USA) **6948**
Review of Political Economy (GBR) **7178**
The Review of Politics (GBR) **7178**
Review of Quantitative Finance and Accounting (USA) **1300**
Reviews in American History (USA) **4310**
Reviews in Endocrine & Metabolic Disorders (USA) **5899**
Reviews in Fisheries Science (USA) **3605**
Reviews in Medical Virology (GBR) **895**
Revista Cartografica (MEX) **4026**
Revista Geofisica (MEX) **2788**
Revolution (London) (GBR) **1421**
Revue de Gestion des Ressources Humaines (FRA) **1874**
Revue de Litterature Comparee (FRA) **5362**
Revue de Philologie, de Litterature et d'Histoire Anciennes (FRA) **2239**
La Revue des Sciences de Gestion (FRA) **1791**
Revue Francaise de Comptabilite (FRA) **1300**
Revue Francaise de Gestion (FRA) **1791**
Revue Francaise du Marketing (FRA) **1841**
Rhetoric & Public Affairs (USA) **5362**
Rhetoric Society Quarterly (USA) **5362**
Rhetorica (USA) **5168**
Rheumatology (Online) (GBR) **6227**
The Richmond Business Journal (USA) **1168**
Risk Management (USA) **4521**
Risk Management and Insurance Review (USA) **4521**
River Teeth (USA) **5363**
Rochester Business Journal (USA) **1515**
Rock Products (USA) **1033**
Rockrgrl (USA) **6612**
Rocks and Minerals (USA) **6478**
Roeper Review (USA) **3079**
Rolling Stone (USA) **6613**
Romance Quarterly (USA) **5364**
Romanic Review (USA) **5364**
Rough Notes (USA) **4522**
The Round Table (GBR) **7263**
Royal Musical Association. Journal (GBR) **6613**
Royal Society of Medicine. Journal (GBR) **5707**
Rubber Chemistry and Technology (USA) **7826**
Runner's World (USA) **8198**
Running & FitNews (USA) **6996**
Rural Cooperatives (USA) **153**
Rural Educator (USA) **2908**
Rural Sociology (USA) **8130**
Rural Special Education Quarterly (USA) **3046**
Rural Telecommunications (USA) **2371**
Russian Life (USA) **8753**
Russian Social Science Review (USA) **7181**
S A I S Review (USA) **7264**
S A M Advanced Management Journal (USA) **1792**
S A M Magazine (USA) **1841**
S A Q: The South Atlantic Quarterly (USA) **5237**
S C O R Report (USA) **1648**
S D Times (USA) **2596**
S E C Accounting Report (USA) **1301**
S E S I Journal (IND) **3177**
S G B (USA) **8198**
S M E Resource Guide (USA) **6478**
S M T Trends (USA) **3112**
S P C Asia (GBR) **596**
S Q L Server Magazine (USA) **2509**
S T I Online (GBR) *see* Sexually Transmitted Infections. **5881**
Sacramento Business Journal (USA) **1170**
The Safety & Health Practitioner (GBR) **7540**
Safety Compliance Letter (USA) **6685**
Safety Now (USA) **6686**
SageWoman (USA) **6647**
Saint Anthony Messenger (USA) **7816**
Saint John's Law Review (USA) **4778**
St. Louis Business Journal (USA) **1170**
Sales & Marketing Management (USA) **1842**
Salmagundi (USA) **4474**
San Antonio Business Journal (USA) **1170**
San Diego Business Journal (USA) **1170**
San Francisco Business Times (USA) **1432**
Sanitary Maintenance (USA) **1842**
Santa Clara Computer and High Technology Law Journal (USA) **4779**
Sarasota Magazine (USA) **3987**
Saskatchewan Registered Nurses' Association. Newsbulletin (CAN) **5980**
Saskatchewan Sage (CAN) **3562**
SaskBusiness (CAN) **1171**
Satellite News (Online) (USA) **2389**
Satellite Today (USA) **2338**
Saturday Evening Post (USA) **3988**
Scale Ship Modeler (USA) **4346**
Scandinavian Journal of Educational Research (GBR) **2909**
Scandinavian Press (CAN) **3562**
Scandinavian Review (USA) **3563**
Scandinavian Studies (Provo) (USA) **5367**
Schizophrenia Bulletin (USA) **6184**
Scholastic Action (USA) **3079**
Scholastic Administr@tor (USA) **3031**
Scholastic Art (USA) **3079**
Scholastic Choices (USA) **3080**
Scholastic Dynamath (USA) **3080**
Scholastic Math (USA) **3080**
Scholastic Scope (USA) **3080**
School Administrator (USA) **3031**
School Executive (USA) **3031**
School Leadership & Management (Online) (GBR) **3032**
School Libraries in Canada Online (CAN) **5045**
School Libraries Worldwide (USA) **5046**
School Library Journal (USA) **5046**
School Library Media Activities Monthly (USA) **5046**
School Planning and Management (USA) **3032**
School Psychology Quarterly (USA) **7406**
School Psychology Review (USA) **7406**
School Science and Mathematics (USA) **3081**
School Talk (USA) **3081**
Science (USA) **7908**
Science Activities (USA) **7908**
Science and Children (USA) **7908**
Science & Society (USA) **7182**
Science Educator (USA) **3081**
Science Letter (USA) **7910**
Science News (USA) **7910**
Science Scope (USA) **7910**
The Science Teacher (USA) **3081**
Science World (USA) **3081**
The Scientist (USA) **7913**
Scotland on Sunday (GBR) **3870**
The Scotsman (GBR) **3870**
Sea Classics (USA) **8660**
Sea Power (USA) **6445**
Sea Technology (USA) **3219**
Searcher (Medford) (USA) **2532**
Seattle (USA) **5082**
Second Language Research (GBR) **5172**
Secured Lender (USA) **1382**
Security (USA) **2680**
Security Dealer & Integrator (USA) **1854**
Security Distributing & Marketing (USA) **1843**
Security Management Online (USA) *see* Security Management. **1792**
Security Systems News (USA) **2680**
Security Technology Executive (USA) **2680**
Semeia Studies (NLD) **7680**
Semiconductor International (USA) **3113**
Seminars in Immunopathology (DEU) **5766**
Seminole Tribune (USA) **3563**
Sensing and Imaging (USA) **4489**
Sensor Review (GBR) **5459**
Seoul Journal of Economics (KOR) **1172**
The Service Industries Journal (GBR) **1172**
Service Management (GBR) **1173**
Services Marketing Quarterly (USA) **1843**
Seventeen (USA) **8883**
Seventeenth - Century News (USA) **5369**
Sewanee Theological Review (USA) **7774**
Sex Roles (USA) **7407**
Sexual and Relationship Therapy (GBR) **7407**
Sexuality and Disability (USA) **5712**
Shakespeare Quarterly (USA) **5370**
Shakespeare Studies (USA) **5370**
Shareowner (CAN) **1651**
Sheriff Magazine (USA) **2668**
Shofar (Ashland) (USA) **7729**
Shooting Industry (USA) **8200**
Shopping Centre News (CAN) **1433**
SI.com (USA) *see* Sports Illustrated. **8207**
Sierra (USA) **2627**
Sign Builder Illustrated (USA) **35**
Sign Language Studies (USA) **5174**
Signal Magazine (Fairfax) (USA) **2338**

Online Service

Signs (USA) **8903**
Silicon Valley - San Jose Business Journal (USA) **1174**
Singapore International Chamber of Commerce. Economic Bulletin (SGP) **1409**
Singapore Journal of Legal Studies (SGP) **4784**
Singapore Management Review (SGP) **1793**
Single Mother (USA) **8884**
Sinorama (USA) **3960**
Sister Namibia (NAM) **8884**
Six Sigma Forum (USA) **1904**
Skeptic (USA) **6743**
Skeptical Inquirer (USA) **6743**
Ski (USA) **8333**
Skiing Magazine (USA) **8333**
Skin Pharmacology and Physiology (CHE) **6881**
Skipping Stones (USA) **2213**
Sky & Telescope (USA) **581**
SkyWatch (USA) **581**
Sleep and Hypnosis (TUR) **6186**
Small Axe (USA) **5239**
Small Business Economic Trends (USA) **1517**
Small Business Economics (NLD) **1967**
Smart Business Now (USA) **1175**
Smith College Studies in Social Work (USA) **8068**
Smithsonian Magazine Web (USA) *see* Smithsonian. **8002**
Snips (USA) **4126**
Soap, Perfumery & Cosmetics (GBR) **596**
Social Anarchism (USA) **5239**
Social and Economic Studies (JAM) **8002**
Social Behavior and Personality (NZL) **7408**
Social Choice and Welfare (DEU) **8068**
Social Cognition (USA) **7408**
Social Education (USA) **3082**
Social Forces (USA) **8133**
Social Indicators Research (NLD) **8150**
Social Justice (USA) **7265**
Social Problems (USA) **8134**
Social Psychiatry and Psychiatric Epidemiology (DEU) **6186**
Social Psychology Quarterly (USA) **8134**
Social Research (USA) **8003**
Social Science History (USA) **8003**
Social Science Japan Journal (GBR) **8004**
Social Science Quarterly (USA) **8004**
Social Sciences (USA) **8004**
Social Security Bulletin (USA) **4523**
Social Service Review (USA) **8069**
The Social Studies (USA) **8005**
Social Studies Review (USA) **8005**
Social Theory & Health (GBR) **8134**
Social Theory and Practice (USA) **6952**
Social Work (USA) **8070**
Social Work Research (USA) **8071**
Socialism and Democracy (GBR) **7183**
Societal (FRA) **1517**
Society (USA) **8005**
Society of Archivists. Journal (GBR) **5048**
Sociological Methodology (USA) **8136**
Sociological Perspectives (USA) **8137**
The Sociological Quarterly (USA) **8137**
Sociological Theory (USA) **8137**
Sociology of Education (USA) **2913**
Sociology of Education Abstracts (GBR) **2935**
Sociology of Religion (USA) **8139**
Software and Systems Modeling (DEU) **2597**
Software Quality Journal (USA) **2598**
Software Quality Professional (USA) **2598**
Soil & Sediment Contamination (USA) **3491**
Soil Science Society of America. Journal (USA) **253**
Soldering & Surface Mount Technology (GBR) **6344**
Soldiers (USA) **6446**
Solid State Technology (USA) **3114**
Sound and Vibration (USA) **3395**
Sound & Video Contractor (USA) **8155**
Sound Business (USA) **1176**
South African Journal of Industrial Engineering (ZAF) **3371**
South Asian Journal of Management (IND) **1794**
South Carolina Business Journal (USA) **1177**
South Carolina Review (USA) **5375**
South Central Construction (USA) **1036**
South Dakota Business Review (USA) **1177**
South Florida Business Journal (USA) **1177**
Southeast Asian Affairs (SGP) **7184**
Southeast Asian Journal of Tropical Medicine and Public Health (THA) **5826**
Southeast Farm Press (USA) **158**
Southeastern Archaeology (USA) **418**
Southern African Feminist Review (ZWE) **8903**
Southern Communication Journal (USA) **2339**
Southern Cultures (USA) **4475**
Southern Economic Journal (USA) **1178**
Southern Journal of Applied Forestry (USA) **3703**
Southern Literary Journal (USA) **5375**
Southern Living (USA) **3988**
Southern Quarterly (USA) **4476**
The Southern Review (USA) **5375**
Southwest Art (USA) **518**
Southwest Farm Press (USA) **158**
Southwest Journal of Business and Economics (USA) **1178**
The Southwest Review (USA) **5240**
Special Educational Needs Abstracts (GBR) **2936**
Special Warfare (USA) **6447**
The Spectator (GBR) **5240**
Spectroscopy (USA) **2105**
Spinal Cord (GBR) **6186**
Spiritual Life (USA) **7683**
Spiritus (USA) **7683**
Sport, Education and Society (GBR) **8203**
The Sporting News (USA) **8206**
Sports Afield (USA) **8335**
Springfield Business Journal (USA) **1178**
St. Charles County Business Record (USA) **1179**
Stage Directions (USA) **8479**
Stamps (USA) **6900**
Stanford Law Review (USA) **4787**
Stanford Social Innovation Review (USA) **1179**
State & Local Health Law Weekly (USA) **4788**
The State Journal (USA) **1179**
State Legislatures (USA) **7186**
State Politics & Policy Quarterly (USA) **7186**
State Tax Review (USA) **1945**
Statistical Methods and Applications (DEU) **8404**
Statistical Methods in Medical Research (GBR) **8404**
Statistical Modelling (IND) **5538**
Statistical Papers (DEU) **8404**
Statistical Pocketbook of Indonesia (IDN) **8404**
Statute Law Review (GBR) **4788**
Stem Cell Week (USA) **5717**
Stitches (USA) **2250**
Stochastic Environmental Research and Risk Assessment (DEU) **3364**
Stone World (USA) **6480**
Storyworks (USA) **3082**
Strategic Direction (GBR) **1179**
Strategic Finance (USA) **1302**
Strategic H R Review (GBR) **1875**
Strategic Management Journal (GBR) **1795**
Strategies (Reston) (USA) **3083**
Strategy (CAN) **1844**
Strategy & Leadership (GBR) **1795**
Strength and Conditioning Journal (USA) **6997**
Strings (USA) **6620**
Structural Survey (GBR) **1038**
Student B M J (GBR) **5718**
Student Leader (USA) **2302**
Studies in American Indian Literatures (USA) **5380**
Studies in Art Education (USA) **520**
Studies in Comparative International Development (USA) **8008**
Studies in Economics and Finance (GBR) **1385**
Studies in English Literature 1500-1900 (USA) **5381**
Studies in Gender and Sexuality (USA) **8142**
Studies in Higher Education (GBR) **3003**
Studies in Philology (USA) **5183**
Studies in Romanticism (USA) **5381**
Studies in Science Education (GBR) **3083**
Studies in the Literary Imagination (USA) **5382**
Studies in the Novel (USA) **5382**
Studies on Women and Gender Abstracts (GBR) **8906**
Studio Photography (USA) **6977**
Style (DeKalb) (USA) **5382**
Succes d'Estime (USA) **8885**
Successful Meetings (USA) **1844**
Suicide and Life-Threatening Behavior (USA) **7411**
Sulphur (GBR) **3256**
Summit (CAN) **7471**
Sunday Mail (AUS) **3796**
Sunday Mail (Adelaide) (AUS) **3793**
Sunday Telegraph (GBR) **3871**
Sunday Territorian (AUS) **3796**
Sunday Times (AUS) **3796**
Sunset (USA) **3989**
Supermarket News (USA) **3681**
Supervision (USA) **1709**
Supplier Selection & Management Report (USA) **1845**
Supply & Demand Chain Executive (USA) **1796**
Supply Chain Management (GBR) **1796**
Supply Chain Management Review (USA) **1796**
Supply House Times (USA) **4127**
Supply Management (GBR) **1845**
The Supreme Court Review (USA) **4965**
Surgical Endoscopy (USA) **6259**
Surgical Products (USA) **5718**
Surround Professional (USA) **8155**
Survey of Current Business (USA) **1521**
Surveying and Land Information Science (USA) **4030**
Survival (Abingdon) (GBR) **7268**
Sustainable Development (GBR) **3468**
Swedish Press (CAN) **3567**
Swiss Journal of Psychology (CHE) **7411**
Symbolic Interaction (USA) **8008**
Symploke (USA) **4477**
Symposium (USA) **5384**
Synergy (GBR) **6209**
Synthese (NLD) **6956**
Syracuse Journal of International Law & Commerce (USA) **4942**
System Dynamics Review (GBR) **1796**
System Inews (USA) **2541**
Systematic and Applied Microbiology (DEU) **896**
Systematic Biology (USA) **707**
Systemes d'Information et Management (FRA) **1796**
Systemic Practice and Action Research (USA) **1797**
Systems Contractor News (USA) **3114**
Systems Research and Behavioral Science (GBR) **2525**
T B & Outbreaks Week (USA) **5827**
T+ D (USA) **1876**
T E L E M A S P Bulletin (USA) **2675**
T E Q (USA) **8440**
T H E Journal (USA) **2951**
The T Q M Journal (GBR) **1797**
T-Shirt Business Info Mapping Newsletter (USA) **1968**
T T J (GBR) **3716**
T W I C E (USA) **3114**
Taboo (USA) **2917**
Tactical Response (USA) **2669**
Take Pride! Community Magazine (USA) **3567**
Tamara (USA) **8009**
Target Marketing (USA) **1845**
The Tax Adviser (USA) **1947**
The Tax Executive (USA) **1947**
Tax Features (USA) **1947**
Tax Foundation. Special Reports (USA) **1947**
Tax Law Review (USA) **4792**
Tax Management Compensation Planning Journal (USA) **1797**
Tax Management Estates, Gifts and Trusts Journal (USA) **1655**
Tax Management Financial Planning Journal (USA) **1386**
Tax Management International Journal (USA) **1948**
Tax Management Memorandum (USA) **1948**
Tax Management Real Estate Journal (USA) **7613**
Taxes on Parade (USA) **1951**
Taxes - The Tax Magazine (USA) **1951**
Teacher Education Quarterly (USA) **3084**
The Teacher Educator (USA) **3004**
Teacher Librarian (USA) **2918**
Teacher Magazine (USA) **3084**
Teaching Business & Economics (GBR) **1181**
Teaching Children Mathematics (USA) **3085**
Teaching English in the Two-Year College (USA) **3004**
Teaching Exceptional Children Plus (USA) **3048**
Teaching History (GBR) **3085**
Teaching in Higher Education (GBR) **3004**
Teaching Mathematics and Its Applications (GBR) **5541**
Teaching Music (USA) **6622**
Teaching Science (AUS) **2918**
Teaching Sociology (USA) **8143**
Team Performance Management (GBR) **1797**
Tech Directions (USA) **3085**
Technical Communication (USA) **2340**
Technical Communication Quarterly (USA) **3085**
Technical Textiles International (GBR) **8458**
Technicalities (USA) **5050**
Techniques (USA) **2918**
Techniques in Coloproctology (Online) (ITA) **5931**
Technology Access Report (USA) **8442**
Technology Analysis & Strategic Management (GBR) **8442**
Technology and Culture (USA) **8442**
Technology and Learning (USA) **2951**
Technology Research News (USA) **8442**
Technology Review (USA) **7922**
The Technology Teacher (USA) **3085**
Technometrics (USA) **3222**
TechTrends (USA) **2951**
Telecom Markets (GBR) **1905**
Telecommunication Journal of Australia (AUS) **2341**
Telecommunication Systems (NLD) **2372**
Telecommunications Mergers and Acquisitions Newsletter (USA) **2372**
Telemedicine Business Week (USA) **5720**
Telemedicine Law Weekly (USA) **4793**
Telemedicine Week (USA) **1182**
Telesis (Ottawa) (CAN) **2373**
Television Business International (GBR) **2397**
Teller Vision (USA) *E-mail edition.* **1386**
Tempo (IDN) **3891**
Tennessee Tribune (USA) **3568**
Tertiary Education and Management (GBR) **3005**
Test & Measurement World (USA) **3332**
Texas Banking (USA) **1386**
Texas Business Review (USA) **1182**
Texas Construction (USA) **1040**
Texas Contractor (USA) **1040**
Texas Journal of Women and the Law (USA) **4794**
Texas Law Review (USA) **4794**
Texas Studies in Literature and Language (USA) **5386**
Textile Research Journal (GBR) **8460**
Textile World (USA) **8461**
Theatre History Studies (USA) **8482**
Theatre Journal (Baltimore) (USA) **8482**
Theatre Notebook (GBR) **8483**
Theatre Survey (GBR) **8483**
Theatre Topics (USA) **8483**
TheatreForum (USA) **8483**
Theological Studies (USA) **7689**
Theology Today (USA) **7690**
Theoretical and Applied Climatology (AUT) **6396**
Theoretical and Computational Fluid Dynamics (DEU) **7063**
Theoretical Inquiries in Law (ISR) **4795**
Theory and Decision (NLD) **8009**
Theory into Practice (USA) **2919**
Theory of Computing Systems (USA) **2601**
Therapeutic Recreation Journal (USA) **6998**
Third World Quarterly (GBR) **1606**
This Old House (USA) **1040**
Thomas Jefferson Law Review (USA) **4899**
Thorax (GBR) **6220**
Thunderbird International Business Review (USA) **1183**
Tikkun Magazine (USA) **5242**
Time (USA) **3990**
Time for Kids News Scoop (USA) **2217**
Time for Kids World Report (USA) **2217**
The Times (GBR) **3872**
Tissue Engineering. Part A. Tissue Engineering (USA) **751**
The Tizard Learning Disability Review (GBR) **6188**
Tobbacco Control Online (GBR) *see* Tobacco Control. **8488**
Today's Catholic Teacher (USA) **2920**
Today's Parent, Baby & Toddler (CAN) **2169**
Today's Parent, Pregnancy & Birth (CAN) **6005**
Tooling & Production (USA) **5460**
Top Producer (USA) **163**
Topics in Clinical Nutrition (USA) **6670**
Topics in Early Childhood Special Education (USA) **3048**
Topics in Geriatric Rehabilitation (USA) **4057**
Topics in Language Disorders (USA) **3048**
Toronto Star (CAN) **3818**
Torrey Botanical Society. Journal (USA) **820**
Total Health (USA) **6670**
Total Quality Management & Business Excellence (Online) (GBR) **1798**
Tourism and Hospitality Research (GBR) **8763**
Toward Freedom (USA) **7216**
Town & Country (New York) (USA) **3991**
Town Planning Review (GBR) **4428**
Townsville Bulletin (AUS) **3796**
Toxicology and Industrial Health (GBR) **3502**
Traders Magazine (USA) **1387**
Tradeshow Week (USA) **36**
Traffic World (USA) **8513**
Trailer Boats (USA) **8283**
Trailer / Body Builders (USA) **8676**
Trailer Life (USA) **8338**
Training (USA) **1798**
Training & Management Development Methods (GBR) **1798**
Training Journal (GBR) **1876**
Trains (USA) **8626**
Transformations (Wayne) (USA) **8144**
Transforming Anthropology (USA) **358**
Transition (USA) **5242**
Transitions (Minneapolis) (USA) **6303**
Transmission & Distribution World (USA) **3161**
Transplant International (DEU) **5724**
Transport Europe (BEL) **8514**
Transport Topics (USA) **8676**
Transportation (NLD) **8515**
Transportation Journal (USA) **8516**
Transportation Management & Engineering (USA) **8516**
Transportation Research. Part E: Logistics and Transportation Review (GBR) **8517**
Transportation Science (USA) **8517**
Trauma (GBR) **6074**
Travel Retailer International (GBR) **1846**
Travel Trade Gazette U K & Ireland (GBR) **8768**
Treasury Bulletin (USA) **1387**
Triangle Business Journal (Greensboro) (USA) **1184**
Triangle Business Journal (Raleigh) (USA) **1184**
Tribal College (USA) **3005**
Tribology & Lubrication Technology (USA) **3398**
Tribology Transactions (USA) **3257**
The Tribune (New York) (USA) **8886**
Tribune Business Weekly (USA) **1184**
Trikone Magazine (USA) **4379**
El Trimestre Economico (MEX) **1184**
Trinity Journal (USA) **7691**
TriQuarterly (USA) **5243**
Tropical Animal Health and Production (NLD) **8809**
Trustee (USA) **4112**
Trusts & Estates (USA) **1656**
Tuberculosis Week (USA) **6220**
Tufts University Health & Nutrition Letter (USA) **6670**
Tulsa Business Chronicle (USA) **1184**
Tumor Biology (CHE) **6035**
Turbomachinery International (USA) **3398**
Turkish Journal of Cancer (TUR) **6036**
Turning the Tide (USA) **7190**
Turtle Magazine for Preschool Kids (USA) **2218**
Twentieth Century British History (GBR) **4274**
Twentieth Century Literature (USA) **5391**
U M T R I Research Review (USA) **8518**
U N Chronicle (USA) **7269**
U N L V Gaming Research & Review Journal (USA) **8213**
U S A Today (Valley Stream) (USA) **2921**
U S B E and Information Technology (USA) **3224**
U S Banker (USA) **1657**
U.S. Bureau of Labor Statistics. C P I Detailed Report (Online) (USA) **1522**
U S Catholic (USA) **7821**
U.S. Department of Energy. Energy Information Administration. Monthly Energy Review (Online) (USA) **3162**
U.S. Internal Revenue Service. Bulletin (USA) **1953**
U.S. Internal Revenue Service. Statistics of Income Bulletin (USA) **1272**
U S Naval Institute. Proceedings (USA) **6450**
U.S. News & World Report Digital Edition (USA) *see* U S News & World Report. **3991**
U.S. Office of the Comptroller of the Currency. Quarterly Journal (Online) (USA) **1953**
U U World (USA) **7742**
Underhood Service (USA) **8609**
Undersea & Hyperbaric Medicine (USA) **5726**
Universal Access in the Information Society (DEU) **2353**
University of Chicago Law Review (USA) **4803**
University of Memphis Law Review (USA) **4804**
University of Queensland Law Journal (AUS) **4805**
Update (Online) (USA) **6626**
Upholstery Manufacturing (Mt. Morris) (USA) **4563**
The Upstart Crow (USA) **5394**
Urban Design International (GBR) **4430**
Urban History Review (CAN) **4316**
Urban Studies (GBR) **4430**
Urgent Communications (USA) **2364**

Urologic Nursing (USA) **6276**
Urology Times (USA) **6276**
User Modeling and User-Adapted Interaction (NLD) **2951**
Utility Automation & Engineering T&D (USA) **3149**
Utility Fleet Management (USA) **8678**
Utility Week (GBR) **3149**
V F W Magazine (USA) **6451**
V I N E (London, Online) (GBR) *see* V I N E. **5064**
Vaccine Weekly (USA) **6884**
Valuation Insights and Perspectives (USA) **7614**
The Vancouver Sun (CAN) **3819**
Vanderbilt Law Review (USA) **4807**
Vanity Fair (USA) **5244**
Variety (USA) **8484**
Vascular and Endovascular Surgery (USA) **6262**
Vascular Medicine (GBR) **5801**
Vegetarian Times (USA) **6670**
Venture Capital Journal (USA) **1658**
Veranda (USA) **4552**
Vermont Business Magazine (USA) **1191**
Veterinary Research Communications (NLD) **8814**
Via Satellite (USA) **2343**
Vibrant Life (USA) **6999**
Victoria (USA) **3992**
Victorian Studies (USA) **4481**
Video Business (USA) **2403**
Videography (USA) **2404**
Vietnam (USA) **6452**
Violence and Victims (USA) **8146**
Virginia Magazine of History and Biography (USA) **4317**
Virginia Quarterly Review (USA) **5244**
Virginia Tax Review (USA) **1954**
Virtual Reality (GBR) **2490**
Virus Genes (USA) **897**
Virus Weekly (USA) **5828**
Visible Language (USA) **5194**
Vision Systems Design (USA) **3226**
Vital (GBR) **5869**
Vital Speeches of the Day (USA) **4585**
Vocational Education & Training Abstracts (GBR) **2937**
Voennaya Mysl' (RUS) **6452**
Vogue (USA) **2262**
Voice Male (USA) **6301**
Voices from the Middle (USA) **3087**
The Volta Review (USA) **4076**
Volta Voices (USA) **4077**
Voluntas (USA) **8077**
W E F Highlights (USA) **3474**
W H O Drug Information (CHE) **7545**
W I N News (USA) **8904**
W T Online (USA) *see* Washington Technology. **7486**
W W D (USA) **2250**
Wall Street & Technology (USA) **1394**
Wall Street Journal Online (USA) *see* Wall Street Journal (Eastern Edition). **1390**
Wall Street Journal Online (USA) *see* Wall Street Journal (Central Edition). **1390**
Wall Street Journal Online (USA) *see* Wall Street Journal (Western Edition). **1390**
Wall Street Letter (USA) **1658**
Wallaces Farmer (USA) **169**
War in History (GBR) **6453**
Ward's AutoWorld (USA) **8611**
Ward's Dealer Business (USA) **8611**
Washington and Lee Law Review (USA) **4810**
Washington Business Journal (USA) **1193**
Washington Jewish Week (USA) **7731**
The Washington Monthly (USA) **7193**
Washington Report on Middle East Affairs (USA) **7273**
Waste Age (USA) **3513**
Water and Wastewater International (USA) **8837**
Water Environment & Technology (USA) **3492**
Water Environment Research (USA) **3493**
Wearables Business (USA) **2250**
Weather and Forecasting (USA) **6398**
Weatherwise (USA) **6398**
Weekly Epidemiological Record (CHE) **7545**
The Weekly Standard (USA) **7193**
Westchester County Business Journal (USA) **1524**
Western Builder (USA) **1043**
Western Farm Press (USA) **170**
Western Folklore (USA) **3624**
Western Fruit Grower (USA) **259**
Western Journal of Applied Forestry (USA) **3707**
The Western Journal of Black Studies (USA) **3572**
Western Journal of Communication (USA) **5195**
Westword (USA) **3992**
Whispering Wind (USA) **3572**
Whitireia Nursing Journal (NZL) **5984**
Wichita Business Journal (USA) **1194**
The Wide - Format Imaging (USA) **7329**
Wild West (USA) **4318**
Wilderness and Environmental Medicine (USA) **5730**
Wildlife Monographs (USA) **968**
The Wilson Journal of Ornithology (USA) **917**
The Wilson Quarterly (USA) **5245**
Windows I T Pro (USA) **2525**
Windspeaker (CAN) **3572**
Wings of Gold (USA) **75**
Wireless Design and Development (USA) **3334**
Wireless Networks (NLD) **2344**
Wireless Week (USA) **2345**
Woman and Earth (USA) **8889**
Woman Engineer (USA) **3227**
Women & Criminal Justice (USA) **4900**
Women & Environments International Magazine (CAN) **8904**
Women & Health (USA) **8849**
Women and Language (USA) **5195**
Women and Music (USA) **6628**
Women & Therapy (USA) **7415**
Women Artists News Book Review (USA) **527**
Women in Business (USA) **1195**
WomenPolice (USA) **2672**
The Women's Health Activist (USA) **8849**
Women's Health Law Weekly (USA) **5731**
Women's Health Weekly (USA) **8849**
Women's League Outlook (USA) **7731**
Women's Studies in Communication (USA) **8905**
Women's Studies Quarterly (USA) **8905**
Women's World (UGA) **8892**
Wood Based Panels International (GBR) **3717**
Wood Digest (USA) **3718**
The Word Among Us (USA) **7823**
Work and Family Life (USA) **2926**
Workforce Management (USA) **1877**
Working Mother (USA) **8892**
Working U S A (USA) **1716**
Working with Older People (GBR) **8078**
Worklife (Kingston) (CAN) **1716**
Works Management (GBR) **1801**
Workspan (USA) **1716**
World Accounting Report (GBR) **1304**
World Affairs (Washington) (USA) **7274**
The World & I Online (USA) **3993**
The World Bank Economic Review (USA) **1525**
World Bank Research Observer (USA) **1391**
World Disease Weekly (USA) **5731**
World Factbook (USA) **7274**
World Health Organization. Bulletin (CHE) **5731**
World Journal of Surgery (USA) **6262**
World Journal of Urology (DEU) **6277**
World Literature Today (USA) **5400**
World Oil (USA) **6797**
World Policy Journal (USA) **7274**
World Politics (USA) **7274**
World Today (GBR) **7275**
World Trade: WT100 (USA) **1588**
World War II (Leesburg) (USA) **4318**
World Watch (USA) **3475**
WorldatWork Journal (USA) **1878**
WorldView Magazine (USA) **7275**
Worldwide Videotex Update (USA) **2569**
The Writer (USA) **5400**
Writer's Digest (USA) **4585**
The Writing Instructor (Online Edition) (USA) **2926**
Xbox Nation (USA) **2482**
Y C - Young Children (USA) **3088**
Yachting (USA) **8285**
The Yale Journal on Regulation (USA) **4817**
The Yale Law Journal (USA) **4817**
Yankee (USA) **3993**
Yard and Garden (USA) **3754**
The Year's Work in Critical and Cultural Theory (GBR) **4483**
Yeats Eliot Review (USA) **5438**
Young Adult Library Services (USA) **5055**
Youth Today (USA) **2172**
Zeitschrift fuer die Alttestamentliche Wissenschaft (DEU) **7696**
Zeitschrift fuer die Neutestamentliche Wissenschaft und die Kunde der Aelteren Kirche (DEU) **7696**
Zeitschrift fuer Germanistische Linguistik (DEU) **5199**
Zeitschrift fuer Neuere Theologiegeschichte (DEU) **7696**
Zeitschrift fuer Personalforschung (DEU) **1878**
Zeitschrift fuer Soziologie (DEU) **8148**
Zeitschrift fuer Wirtschafts- und Unternehmensethik (DEU) **1197**
Zeitschrift fuer Wirtschaftspolitik (DEU) **1197**
401(k) Advisor (USA) **1661**

R M I T, Publishing A'Beckett St, PO Box 12058, Melbourne, VIC 8006, Australia TEL 61-3-99258265, 61-3-99258100, FAX 61-3-99258134, info@rmitpublishing.com.au, http://www.rmitpublishing.com.au/

A B R (AUS) **5204**
A C H: The Journal of the History of Culture in Australia (AUS) **4191**
Aboriginal History (AUS) **4191**
Adelaide Law Review (AUS) **4609**
Alternative Law Journal (AUS) **4613**
Anaesthesia and Intensive Care (AUS) **5768**
Anthropological Forum (AUS) **325**
Antipodes (USA) **5255**
Architecture Australia (AUS) **430**
Archives and Manuscripts (AUS) **4990**
Arena Journal (AUS) **7107**
Arena Magazine (AUS) **7107**
Art and Australia (AUS) **468**
Artefact (AUS) **381**
Asia - Pacific Defence Reporter (USA) **6412**
Asia Pacific Journal of Clinical Nutrition (AUS) **6655**
Asian Studies Review (GBR) **4180**
Australasian Canadian Studies (AUS) **329**
Australasian Catholic Record (AUS) **7785**
Australasian Drama Studies (AUS) **8466**
Australasian Psychiatry (GBR) **6125**
Australasian Public Libraries and Information Services (AUS) **4993**
Australian Aboriginal Studies (AUS) **330**
Australian Academic & Research Libraries (AUS) **4993**
Australian and New Zealand Journal of Family Therapy (GBR) **8089**
Australian and New Zealand Journal of Public Health (AUS) **7508**
Australian Archaeology (AUS) **382**
Australian Bar Review (AUS) **4623**
Australian Bulletin of Labour (AUS) **1666**
Australian Bureau of Agricultural and Resource Economics. Australian Commodities (AUS) **194**
Australian Catholic Historical Society. Journal (AUS) **7785**
Australian Defence Force Journal (AUS) **6413**
Australian Economic History Review (GBR) **1536**
The Australian Economic Review (GBR) **1064**
Australian Feminist Studies (GBR) **8894**
Australian Geographer (GBR) **3999**
Australian Historical Studies (AUS) **4132**
Australian Indigenous Law Review (AUS) **7202**
The Australian Journal of Anthropology (AUS) **330**
Australian Journal of Communication (AUS) **2313**
Australian Journal of Corporate Law (AUS) **4857**
Australian Journal of Early Childhood (AUS) **2144**
Australian Journal of Education (AUS) **2829**
Australian Journal of Family Law (AUS) **4907**
Australian Journal of Forensic Sciences (GBR) **5912**
Australian Journal of French Studies (AUS) **5259**
Australian Journal of Human Rights (AUS) **7203**
The Australian Journal of Indigenous Education (AUS) **2829**
Australian Journal of International Affairs (GBR) **7222**
Australian Journal of Labour Economics (AUS) **1666**
Australian Journal of Labour Law (AUS) **4857**
Australian Journal of Language and Literacy (AUS) **3017**
Australian Journal of Linguistics (AUS) **5097**
Australian Journal of Management (AUS) **1727**
Australian Journal of Physiotherapy (AUS) **6107**
Australian Journal of Political Science (GBR) **7108**
Australian Journal of Psychology (GBR) **7338**
Australian Journalism Review (AUS) **4572**
The Australian Library Journal (AUS) **4993**
Australian Literary Studies (AUS) **5259**
Australian Nursing Journal (AUS) **5952**
Australian Occupational Therapy Journal (AUS) **6107**
Australian Planner (AUS) **4404**
Australian Property Law Journal (AUS) **4827**
Australian Psychologist (GBR) **7338**
Australian Social Work (AUS) **8027**
Australian Tax Forum (AUS) **1911**
Australian Tax Review (AUS) **1911**
Babel (AUS) **3052**
Bond Law Review (AUS) **4631**
The British Journal of Criminology (GBR) **2645**
The Building Economist (AUS) **985**
Bulletin of Indonesian Economic Studies (AUS) **1443**
C E D A Growth Series (AUS) **1881**
Canberra Historical Journal (AUS) **4191**
Canberra Law Review (AUS) **4640**
Ceramics Art and Perception (AUS) **2039**
Chain Reaction (AUS) **3410**
Collegian (NLD) **5955**
Contemporary Nurse (AUS) **5956**
Continuum (AUS) **6495**
Current Issues in Criminal Justice (AUS) **2650**
Deakin Law Review (AUS) **4655**
Descent (AUS) **3764**
Distance Education (AUS) **2940**
Drug and Alcohol Review (GBR) **2693**
Economic Analysis and Policy (AUS) **1098**
The Economic Record (AUS) **1100**
Educational Philosophy and Theory (GBR) **2850**
English in Australia (AUS) **3061**
Family Matters (AUS) **8102**
Flinders Journal of History and Politics (AUS) **4191**
Flinders Journal of Law Reform (AUS) **4674**
Food Australia (AUS) **3638**
Geographical Education (AUS) **3063**
The Globe (AUS) **4013**
The Great Circle (AUS) **4141**
Habitat Australia (AUS) **2613**
Health Promotion Journal of Australia (AUS) **7523**
Hecate (AUS) **8898**
Historical Records of Australian Science (AUS) **7861**
History of Economics Review (AUS) **1118**
History of Education Review (AUS) **2864**
InCite (AUS) **5015**
Indigenous Law Bulletin (AUS) **4692**
Insurance Law Journal (AUS) **4693**
International Journal of Disability, Development and Education (GBR) **3041**
James Cook University Law Review (AUS) **4698**
Journal of Australian Political Economy (AUS) **1494**
Journal of Contract Law (AUS) **4700**
Journal of Family Studies (AUS) **5559**
Journal of Intercultural Studies (GBR) **3544**
Journal of Law and Information Science (AUS) **4702**
Journal of Northern Territory History (AUS) **4192**
The Journal of Occupational Health and Safety: Australia and New Zealand (AUS) **6680**
The Journal of Pacific History (GBR) **4192**
The Judicial Review (AUS) **4953**
The La Trobe Journal (AUS) **5024**
Labour History (AUS) **1694**
Landscape Architecture Australia (AUS) **3741**
Legal Education Review (AUS) **4719**
Legal History (AUS) **4720**
M A R G I N (AUS) **5328**
Magpies (AUS) **2160**
Management Today (AUS) **1777**
Meanjin (AUS) **5227**
Media and Arts Law Review (AUS) **4731**
Melbourne University Law Review (AUS) **4732**
Metro (AUS) **6507**
Monash Bioethics Review (AUS) **6935**
Musicology Australia (AUS) **6594**
New Doctor (AUS) **5685**
New Zealand Law Review (NZL) **4746**
Newcastle Law Review (AUS) **4746**
Oceania (AUS) **350**
Online Refereed Articles (AUS) **2997**
Overland Express (AUS) *see* Overland. **5232**
Parergon (AUS) **4468**
Pathology (GBR) **5693**
Photofile (AUS) **6974**
Policy (AUS) **1160**
Policy & Society (NLD) **7166**
Proctor (AUS) **4761**
Prometheus (Abingdon) (GBR) **2336**
Psychiatry Psychology and Law (GBR) **6177**
Queensland Archaeological Research (AUS) **413**
Queensland Review (AUS) **4194**
Ramus (AUS) **2239**
Reform (AUS) **4767**
Reproduction, Fertility and Development (AUS) **700**
Revenue Law Journal (AUS) **4769**
Rock Art Research (AUS) **354**
Royal Australian Historical Society. Journal (AUS) **4194**
Rural Society (AUS) **8130**
Script & Print (AUS) **7573**
Social Analysis (USA) **355**
Social Semiotics (GBR) **6952**
South Australian Geographical Journal (AUS) **4029**
Southern Review (AUS) **8140**
Studies in Conflict and Terrorism (USA) **7267**
The Sydney Law Review (AUS) **4792**
The Sydney Papers (AUS) **7187**
Taxation in Australia (AUS) **1950**
Telecommunication Journal of Australia (AUS) **2341**
Torts Law Journal (AUS) **4843**
University of New South Wales Law Journal (AUS) **4804**
University of Queensland Law Journal (AUS) **4805**
Urban Policy and Research (AUS) **4430**
Water (AUS) **8836**

SAGE Publications, Inc., SAGE Journals Online 2455 Teller Rd, Thousand Oaks, CA 91320 TEL 800-818-7243, http://online.sagepub.com/

Academy of Marketing Science. Journal (USA) **1803**
Acta Sociologica (NOR) **8085**
Action Research (GBR) **5567**
Active Learning in Higher Education (GBR) **2965**
Adaptive Behavior (GBR) **2445**
Administration & Society (USA) **7418**
Adult Education Quarterly (USA) **2938**
Advances in Developing Human Resources (USA) **1855**
Affilia (USA) **8024**
American Academy of Political and Social Science. Annals (USA) **7104**
American Behavioral Scientist (USA) **7946**
American Journal of Evaluation (USA) **7946**
American Journal of Medical Quality (USA) **5572**
American Journal of Sports Medicine (USA) **6228**
American Politics Research (USA) **7105**
American Psychiatric Nurses Association. Journal (USA) **5951**
American Review of Public Administration (USA) **7419**
Anthropological Theory (GBR) **326**
Applied Psychological Measurement (USA) **7336**
Aramaic Studies (NLD) **7622**
Arts and Humanities in Higher Education (GBR) **4443**
Asia Pacific Journal of Human Resources (GBR) **1856**
Asian Journal of Management Cases (IND) **1726**
Assessment (USA) **7337**
Autism (GBR) **6125**
Behavior Modification (USA) **7339**
Biological Research for Nursing (USA) **5953**
Body & Society (GBR) **7951**
British Journal of Visual Impairment (GBR) **4080**
British Journalism Review (GBR) **4572**
Bulletin of Science, Technology & Society (USA) **7842**
Business & Society (USA) **1070**
Business Communication Quarterly (USA) **1729**
Business Information Review (GBR) **1730**
Child Maltreatment (USA) **2148**
Childhood (GBR) **2148**
China Information (GBR) **546**
China Report (IND) **7226**
Clin-Alert (USA) **6889**
Clinical Case Studies (USA) **6131**
Clinical Child Psychology & Psychiatry (GBR) **2149**
Clinical Nursing Research (USA) **5955**
Communication Research (USA) **8094**
Comparative American Studies (GBR) **7956**
Comparative Political Studies (USA) **7117**
Compensation and Benefits Review (USA) **1671**
Complementary Health Practice Review (USA) **308**
Concurrent Engineering: Research and Applications (GBR) **2470**
Contributions to Indian Sociology - New Series (IND) **8096**
Cooperation and Conflict (GBR) **7228**
Cornell Hospitality Quarterly (USA) **4384**
The Counseling Psychologist (USA) **7349**
Crime & Delinquency (USA) **2648**
Crime, Media, Culture (GBR) **2648**
Criminal Justice & Behavior (USA) **2649**
Criminal Justice Policy Review (USA) **4886**
Criminal Justice Review (USA) **4887**
Criminology & Criminal Justice (Print) (GBR) **2650**
Critical Social Policy (GBR) **8036**

11252 SCIELO ULRICH'S PERIODICALS

Critique of Anthropology (GBR) **334**
Cross-Cultural Research (USA) **7957**
Cultural Dynamics (GBR) **6913**
Cultural Studies - Critical Methodologies (USA) **5281**
Culture & Psychology (GBR) **7350**
Current Sociology (GBR) **8098**
Currents in Biblical Research (GBR) **7636**
Dementia (GBR) **6135**
The Diabetes Educator (USA) **5887**
Diogenes (English Edition) (GBR) **7959**
Discourse & Society (GBR) **7352**
Discourse Studies (GBR) **5112**
East European Politics & Societies (USA) **7131**
Ecclesiology (NLD) **7639**
Economic and Industrial Democracy (GBR) **7131**
Economic Development Quarterly (USA) **1539**
Education and Urban Society (USA) **2847**
Educational Administration Quarterly (USA) **3021**
Educational and Psychological Measurement (USA) **7353**
Educational Management, Administration & Leadership (Online) (GBR) *see* Educational Management, Administration & Leadership (Print). **3021**
Educational Policy (USA) **3022**
Emotional and Behavioural Difficulties (GBR) **3039**
Environment and Behavior (USA) **8100**
Environment and Urbanization (GBR) **3421**
Ethnicities (GBR) **7962**
Ethnography (GBR) **337**
European History Quarterly (GBR) **4219**
European Journal of Archaeology (GBR) **393**
European Journal of Communication (GBR) **8101**
European Journal of Criminology (GBR) **2651**
European Journal of Cultural Studies (GBR) **8101**
European Journal of Industrial Relations (GBR) **1681**
European Journal of International Relations (GBR) **7234**
European Journal of Political Theory (GBR) **7134**
European Journal of Social Theory (GBR) **8101**
European Journal of Women's Studies (GBR) **8896**
European Physical Education Review (GBR) **3061**
European Union Politics (GBR) **7234**
European Urban and Regional Studies (GBR) **7963**
Evaluation (GBR) **7963**
Evaluation and the Health Professions (USA) **5612**
Evaluation Review (USA) **7963**
Experimental Mechanics (USA) **3344**
Expository Times (GBR) **7642**
Family & Consumer Sciences Research Journal (USA) **4357**
The Family Journal (USA) **7357**
Feminism & Psychology (GBR) **7357**
Feminist Theology (GBR) **8896**
Feminist Theory (GBR) **8897**
Field Methods (USA) **339**
First Language (GBR) **5119**
Food Science and Technology International (USA) **3642**
French Cultural Studies (GBR) **4221**
Gender & Society (USA) **8104**
Gender, Technology & Development (IND) **8898**
Global Business Review (IND) **1114**
Global Media and Communication (GBR) **2321**
Global Social Policy (GBR) **8042**
Group Analysis (GBR) **7359**
Group & Organization Management (USA) **2861**
Group Processes & Intergroup Relations (GBR) **8105**
Health (GBR) **7520**
Health Education & Behavior (USA) **7522**
Health Informatics Journal (GBR) **5830**
Health Promotion Practice (USA) **7523**
High Performance Polymers (GBR) **2123**
Hispanic Journal of Behavioral Sciences (USA) **7360**
History of Psychiatry (GBR) **6144**
History of the Human Sciences (GBR) **7969**
Home Health Care Management and Practice (USA) **4098**
Homicide Studies (USA) **2654**
Human Resource Development Review (USA) **1864**
I F L A Journal (GBR) **5013**
Improving Schools (GBR) **3024**
Indian Economic and Social History Review (IND) **7972**
Indian Journal of Gender Studies (IND) **8899**
Indoor and Built Environment (GBR) **5760**
Information Development (GBR) **5016**
Integrative Cancer Therapies (USA) **6022**
International Association of Physicians in AIDS Care. Journal (USA) **5818**
The International Communication Gazette (Online) (GBR) **2326**
International Criminal Justice Review (USA) **4891**
International Journal of Comparative Sociology (NLD) **8108**
International Journal of Cross Cultural Management (GBR) **1867**
International Journal of Cultural Studies (GBR) **8109**
International Journal of Damage Mechanics (GBR) **3346**
International Journal of High Performance Computing Applications (USA) **2592**
International Journal of Lower Extremity Wounds (USA) **5639**
International Journal of Music Education (GBR) **6577**
International Journal of Offender Therapy and Comparative Criminology (USA) **2655**
International Journal of Press / Politics (USA) **4577**
International Journal of Robotics Research (GBR) **2585**
International Journal of Social Psychiatry (GBR) **6147**
International Political Science Review (GBR) **7244**
International Regional Science Review (USA) **7975**
International Relations (GBR) **7245**
International Review for the Sociology of Sport (GBR) **8110**
International Review of Administrative Sciences (GBR) **7447**
International Small Business Journal (GBR) **1962**
International Social Work (GBR) **8048**
International Sociology (GBR) **8110**
International Studies (IND) **7245**
Journal for the Study of the Historical Jesus (NLD) **7653**
Journal for the Study of the New Testament (GBR) **7653**
Journal for the Study of the Old Testament (GBR) **7653**
Journal for the Study of the Pseudepigrapha (GBR) **7653**
Journal of Adolescent Research (USA) **7368**
Journal of Aging and Health (USA) **4048**
Journal of Anglican Studies (GBR) **7762**
The Journal of Applied Behavioral Science (USA) **7368**
Journal of Applied Gerontology (USA) **4049**
Journal of Asian and African Studies (GBR) **8112**
Journal of Attention Disorders (USA) **6149**
Journal of Bioactive and Compatible Polymers (GBR) **734**
Journal of Biological Rhythms (USA) **6149**
Journal of Biomaterials Applications (GBR) **6247**
Journal of Biomolecular Screening (USA) **735**
Journal of Black Psychology (USA) **7369**
Journal of Black Studies (USA) **7978**
Journal of Building Physics (GBR) **3204**
Journal of Business and Technical Communication (USA) **1133**
Journal of Business Communication (USA) **1764**
Journal of Career Assessment (USA) **7369**
Journal of Cellular Plastics (GBR) **7093**
Journal of Child Health Care (GBR) **6094**
Journal of Classical Sociology (GBR) **8112**
The Journal of Clinical Pharmacology (USA) **6852**
Journal of Commonwealth Literature (GBR) **5314**
Journal of Communication Inquiry (USA) **8112**
Journal of Composite Materials (GBR) **3349**
Journal of Conflict Resolution (USA) **7978**
Journal of Consumer Culture (GBR) **2639**
Journal of Contemporary Criminal Justice (USA) **4892**
Journal of Contemporary Ethnography (USA) **8112**
Journal of Contemporary History (GBR) **4149**
Journal of Cross-Cultural Psychology (USA) **7372**
Journal of Developing Societies (Online) (GBR) **7978**
Journal of Diagnostic Medical Sonography (USA) **6200**
Journal of Early Adolescence (USA) **2156**
Journal of Early Childhood Literacy (GBR) **2875**
Journal of Early Childhood Research (GBR) **6094**
Journal of Elastomers and Plastics (GBR) **7093**
Journal of Emerging Market Finance (IND) **1635**
Journal of English Linguistics (USA) **5133**
Journal of Entrepreneurship (IND) **1765**
Journal of Environment & Development (USA) **3444**
Journal of European Social Policy (GBR) **7248**
Journal of European Studies (Chalfont Saint Giles) (GBR) **4235**
Journal of Family History (USA) **8113**
Journal of Family Issues (USA) **8113**
Journal of Family Nursing (USA) **5965**
Journal of Fire Protection Engineering (GBR) **3579**
Journal of Fire Sciences (GBR) **3349**
Journal of Geriatric Psychiatry and Neurology (USA) **4049**
Journal of Hand Surgery (European Volume) (GBR) **6248**
Journal of Health Management (USA) **5649**
Journal of Health Psychology (GBR) **7374**
Journal of Hispanic Higher Education (USA) **2991**
Journal of Holistic Nursing (USA) **5965**
Journal of Human Lactation (USA) **5995**
Journal of Human Values (IND) **1766**
Journal of Humanistic Psychology (USA) **7375**
Journal of Industrial Textiles (GBR) **8454**
Journal of Information Science (GBR) **5021**
Journal of Intelligent Material Systems and Structures (GBR) **3349**
Journal of Intensive Care Medicine (USA) **5650**
Journal of Interpersonal Violence (USA) **2657**
Journal of Language and Social Psychology (USA) **7375**
Journal of Librarianship and Information Science (GBR) **5021**
Journal of Macromarketing (USA) **1825**
Journal of Management (GBR) **1767**
Journal of Management Education (USA) **1768**
Journal of Management Inquiry (USA) **1768**
Journal of Marketing Education (USA) **1825**
Journal of Material Culture (GBR) **8114**
Journal of Moral Philosophy (NLD) **6929**
Journal of Neuroimaging (USA) **6153**
Journal of Obstetric, Gynecologic, and Neonatal Nursing (USA) **5966**
Journal of Peace Research (GBR) **7249**
Journal of Pediatric Oncology Nursing (USA) **6025**
Journal of Pentecostal Theology (NLD) **7762**
Journal of Pharmacy Practice (USA) **6856**
Journal of Planning Education and Research (USA) **4417**
Journal of Planning History (USA) **4417**
Journal of Planning Literature (USA) **4417**
Journal of Plastic Film and Sheeting (GBR) **7093**
Journal of Psychopharmacology (GBR) **6856**
Journal of Reinforced Plastics & Composites (GBR) **3351**
Journal of Research in Crime and Delinquency (USA) **2658**
Journal of Research in International Education (GBR) **3014**
Journal of Research in Nursing (GBR) **5967**
Journal of Sandwich Structures & Materials (GBR) **3351**
Journal of Service Research (USA) **1826**
Journal of Social and Personal Relationships (GBR) **7380**
Journal of Social Archaeology (GBR) **401**
Journal of Social Work (GBR) **8051**
Journal of Sociology (GBR) **8116**
Journal of Sport and Social Issues (USA) **8182**
Journal of Sports Economics (USA) **1138**
Journal of Studies in International Education (USA) **3014**
Journal of Teacher Education (USA) **2878**
Journal of Theoretical Politics (GBR) **7148**
Journal of Thermoplastic Composite Materials (GBR) **7094**
Journal of Transcultural Nursing (USA) **5967**
Journal of Transformative Education (USA) **2879**
Journal of Travel Research (USA) **8726**
Journal of Urban History (USA) **4150**
Journal of Vacation Marketing (GBR) **8726**
Journal of Vibration and Control (GBR) **7088**
Journal of Visual Culture (GBR) **4461**
Journalism (GBR) **4577**
Language and Literature (GBR) **5139**
Latin American Perspectives (USA) **7982**
Leadership (GBR) **4463**
Management Communication Quarterly (USA) **1775**
Management Learning (GBR) **1776**
Marketing Theory (GBR) **1833**
Mathematics and Mechanics of Solids (GBR) **7026**
Media, Culture & Society (GBR) **8120**
Medical Care Research and Review (USA) **7548**
Medical Decision Making (USA) **5667**
The Medieval History Journal (IND) **4152**
Men and Masculinities (USA) **6303**
Modern China (USA) **4186**
National Institute Economic Review (GBR) **1152**
Neurorehabilitation and Neural Repair (USA) **6168**
The Neuroscientist (USA) **6169**
New Media & Society (GBR) **8123**
Nonprofit and Voluntary Sector Quarterly (USA) **8059**
Nursing for Women's Health (USA) **8847**
Nursing Science Quarterly (USA) **5975**
Organization (GBR) **1784**
Organization & Environment (USA) **6684**
Organization Studies (DEU) **7990**
Organizational Research Methods (USA) **1784**
Party Politics (GBR) **7164**
Personality and Social Psychology Bulletin (USA) **7390**
Philosophy & Social Criticism (GBR) **6943**
Philosophy of the Social Sciences (USA) **7992**
Planning Theory (GBR) **4423**
Police Quarterly (USA) **4896**
Policy, Politics & Nursing Practice (USA) **5978**
Political Theory (USA) **7169**
Politics and Society (USA) **7170**
Politics, Philosophy & Economics (GBR) **7171**
The Prison Journal (USA) **2666**
Probation Journal (GBR) **2666**
Psychology and Developing Societies (IND) **7398**
Psychology of Music (GBR) **6608**
Public Finance Review (USA) **1941**
Public Understanding of Science (GBR) **7900**
Public Works Management & Policy (USA) **7463**
Punishment & Society (GBR) **2666**
Qualitative Health Research (USA) **5701**
Qualitative Inquiry (USA) **7994**
Qualitative Research (GBR) **7994**
Qualitative Social Work (GBR) **8064**
R E L C Journal (GBR) **5164**
Race & Class (GBR) **3560**
Race Relations Abstracts (USA) **8150**
Rationality and Society (GBR) **7995**
Research on Aging (USA) **4054**
Research on Social Work Practice (USA) **8128**
Review of Public Personnel Administration (USA) **7466**
Review of Radical Political Economics (USA) **1548**
School Psychology International (GBR) **3080**
Science Communication (USA) **8131**
Science, Technology & Human Values (USA) **7911**
Science, Technology & Society (IND) **7911**
Security Dialogue (GBR) **7265**
Sexualities (GBR) **7408**
The Shock and Vibration Digest (USA) **3357**
Simulation (GBR) **3220**
Simulation & Gaming (USA) **2518**
Small Group Research (USA) **7408**
Social & Legal Studies (GBR) **8132**
Social Compass (GBR) **8132**
Social Science Computer Review (USA) **2951**
Social Science Information (GBR) **8003**
Social Studies of Science (GBR) **7917**
Sociological Methods & Research (USA) **8137**
Sociology (GBR) **8138**
South Asia Economic Journal (IND) **1518**
South Asia Research (IND) **560**
South Asian Survey (IND) **4188**
Space & Culture (USA) **4029**
Strategic Organization (GBR) **1795**
Structural Health Monitoring (GBR) **8439**
Studies in Christian Ethics (GBR) **7685**
Studies in History (New Delhi) (IND) **4189**
Television & New Media (USA) **2396**
Theology and Sexuality (GBR) **7690**
Theoretical Criminology (GBR) **2670**
Theory & Psychology (GBR) **7412**
Theory and Research in Education (Online) (GBR) *see* Theory and Research in Education (Print). **2919**
Theory, Culture & Society (GBR) **8143**
Thesis Eleven (GBR) **7188**
Time & Society (GBR) **8144**
Tourist Studies (GBR) **8764**
Transcultural Psychiatry (GBR) **6188**
Trauma, Violence & Abuse (USA) **6074**
Urban Affairs Review (USA) **4429**
Urban Education (USA) **2924**
Violence Against Women (USA) **8146**
Visual Communication (GBR) **2343**
Waste Management and Research (GBR) **3513**
Western Journal of Nursing Research (USA) **5984**
Work and Occupations (USA) **8147**
Work, Employment & Society (GBR) **8147**
Written Communication (USA) **2345**
Young (IND) **2172**
Youth & Society (USA) **2172**
Youth Violence and Juvenile Justice (USA) **2672**

SciELO CONICYT, Canada 308, Providencia, Santiago de Chile, Chile TEL 56-2-3654400, FAX 56-2-3654451, scielo@conicyt.cl, http://www.scielo.cl/ INFOMED, Calle 27 No 110 M y N, Vedado, Havana, Cuba TEL 537-55-3375, FAX 537-33-3063, webmaster@infomed.sld.cu, http://www.scielo.sld.cu/ FAPESP - BIREME, Rue Botucatu 862, Sao Paulo SP 04023-901, Brazil TEL 55-11-55769863, FAX 55-11-55758868, scielo@bireme.br, http://www.scielo.br, http://www.scielo.org
A R Q (CHL) **426**
Academia Brasileira de Ciencias. Anais (BRA) **7829**
Acimed (CUB) **5565**
Acta Cirurgica Brasileira (BRA) **6234**
Acta Literaria (CHL) **5249**
Acta Medica (CUB) **5566**
Acta Ortopedica Brasileira (BRA) **6054**
Akademos (VEN) **2825**
La Aljaba (ARG) **8893**
Anais Brasileiros de Dermatologia (BRA) **5871**
Andean Geology (CHL) **2724**
Archivos de Medicina Veterinaria (CHL) **8793**
Archivos del Instituto de Neurologia (URY) **6124**
Arquivo Brasileiro de Medicina Veterinaria e Zootecnia (BRA) **8793**
Arquivos Brasileiros de Cardiologia (BRA) **5777**
Arquivos de Neuro-Psiquiatria (BRA) **6124**
Asociacion Quimica Argentina. Anales (ARG) **2051**
Associacao Medica Brasileira. Revista (BRA) **5580**
Atenea (Year) (CHL) **4443**
Avances en Odontoestomatologia (ESP) **5836**
Avances en Periodoncia e Implantologia Oral (ESP) **5836**
Bioagro (VEN) **96**
Biocell (ARG) **827**
Biological Research (CHL) **658**
Bosque (CHL) **3685**
Bragantia (BRA) **97**
Brazilian Archives of Biology and Technology (BRA) **762**
Brazilian Chemical Society. Journal (BRA) **2051**
Brazilian Computer Society. Journal (BRA) **2408**
Brazilian Journal of Biology (BRA) **663**
Brazilian Journal of Chemical Engineering (BRA) **3236**
Brazilian Journal of Medical and Biological Research (BRA) **5588**
Brazilian Journal of Microbiology (BRA) **882**
Brazilian Journal of Physics (BRA) **7007**
Brazilian Journal of Veterinary Research and Animal Science (BRA) **8794**
Brazilian Oral Research (BRA) **5836**
Brazilian Society of Mechanical Sciences and Engineering. Journal (BRA) **3374**
C E D E S Cadernos (BRA) **2833**
Cadernos de Pesquisa (BRA) **2833**
Cadernos de Psicopedagogia (BRA) **2834**
Cadernos Pagu (BRA) **8091**
Ceramica (BRA) **2039**
The Chilean Chemical Society. Journal (CHL) **2058**
Chilean Journal of Agricultural Research (Online) (CHL) *see* Chilean Journal of Agricultural Research (Print). **101**
Chungara (Arica) (CHL) **387**
Ciencia da Informacao (BRA) **5002**
Ciencia del Suelo (ARG) **224**
Ciencia e Tecnologia de Alimentos (BRA) **3631**
Ciencia Rural (BRA) **101**
Ciencia y Enfermeria (CHL) **5955**
Circe de Clasicos y Modernos (ARG) **5274**
Clinics (BRA) **5598**
Computational and Applied Mathematics (BRA) **5551**
Cuadernos de Antropologia Social (ARG) **334**
Cuadernos de Cirugia (CHL) **6241**
Cuadernos de Economia (CHL) **1089**
Cuadernos de Historia de Espana (ARG) **4213**
Cuadernos de Medicina Forense (ESP) **5912**
Dados (BRA) **7958**

Link to your serials resources and content with ulrichsweb.com

Darwiniana (ARG) 785
Dermatologia Peruana (PER) 5874
Dikaiosyne (VEN) 4658
Documentacao de Estudos em Linguistica Teorica e Aplicada (BRA) 5112
Ecletica Quimica (BRA) 2060
Ecologia Austral (Online Edition) (ARG) 669
Educacao e Pesquisa (BRA) 2845
Educacao e Sociedade (BRA) 2845
Electronic Journal of Biotechnology (CHL) 763
Encuentro Educacional (VEN) 2853
Espacios (VEN) 7853
Estudios Filologicos (CHL) 5116
Estudos Afro-Asiaticos (BRA) 7962
Estudos de Psicologia (Campinas) (BRA) 7355
Folia Dermatologica Peruana (PER) 5876
Gayana (CHL) 944
Gayana: Botanica (CHL) 716
Genetics and Molecular Biology (BRA) 869
Genetics and Molecular Research (BRA) 869
Geoensenanza (VEN) 2859
Gestao & Producao (BRA) 1747
Gestion (CRI) 8042
Ginecologia y Obstetricia de Mexico (MEX) 5991
Historia (CHL) 4295
Historia, Ciencias, Saude - Manguinhos (BRA) 4142
El Hornero (ARG) 908
Hospital Nacional de Ninos Dr. Carlos Saez Herrera. Revista Medica (CRI) 6092
Imaginario (BRA) 7361
Informacion, Cultura y Sociedad (ARG) 5015
Instituto de Historia Argentina y Americana Doctor Emilio Ravignani. Boletin (ARG) 4298
Instituto de Medicina Tropical de Sao Paulo. Revista (BRA) 5818
Interdisciplinaria (ARG) 7363
International Journal of Morphology (CHL) 5639
Intersecciones en Antropologia (ARG) 343
Jornal Brasileiro de Patologia e Medicina Laboratorial (BRA) 5645
Journal of Applied Oral Science (BRA) 5850
Latin American Journal of Sedimentology and Basin Analysis (ARG) 2752
Literatura y Linguistica (CHL) 5148
Magallania (CHL) 7984
Mana (BRA) 347
Mastozoologia Neotropical (ARG) 955
Materials Research (BRA) 3353
Opiniao Publica (BRA) 7161
Pesquisa Agropecuaria Brasileira (BRA) 146
Pesquisa Veterinaria Brasileira (BRA) 8804
Polimeros (BRA) 7098
Proyecciones (CHL) 5526
Psicologia & Sociedade (BRA) 7993
Psicologia: Reflexao e Critica (BRA) 7393
Psicologia U S P (BRA) 7393
Quimica Nova (BRA) 2077
Quinto Sol (ARG) 4157
R L A (CHL) 5165
Revista Argentina de Cardiologia (ARG) 5798
Revista Brasileira de Botanica (BRA) 815
Revista Brasileira de Ciencia do Solo (BRA) 250
Revista Brasileira de Ciencias Sociais (BRA) 7996
Revista Brasileira de Cirurgia Cardiovascular (BRA) 5798
Revista Brasileira de Entomologia (BRA) 857
Revista Brasileira de Geociencias (BRA) 2715
Revista Brasileira de Geofisica (BRA) 2788
Revista Brasileira de Historia (BRA) 4310
Revista Brasileira de Medicina do Esporte (BRA) 6232
Revista Brasileira de Psiquiatria (BRA) 6181
Revista Chilena de Historia Natural (CHL) 700
Revista Chilena de Infectologia (CHL) 5825
Revista Chilena de Nutricion (CHL) 6668
Revista Chilena de Pediatria (CHL) 6103
Revista Colombiana de Cardiologia (COL) 5799
Revista Cubana de Cirugia (CUB) 6256
Revista Cubana de Educacion Medica Superior (CUB) 5704
Revista Cubana de Enfermeria (CUB) 5980
Revista Cubana de Estomatologia (CUB) 5863
Revista Cubana de Farmacia (CUB) 6878
Revista Cubana de Higiene y Epidemiologia (CUB) 7539
Revista Cubana de Investigaciones Biomedicas (CUB) 700
Revista Cubana de Medicina (CUB) 5704
Revista Cubana de Medicina General Integral (CUB) 5704
Revista Cubana de Medicina Militar (CUB) 5704
Revista Cubana de Medicina Tropical (CUB) 5825
Revista Cubana de Obstetricia y Ginecologia (CUB) 6003
Revista Cubana de Ortopedia y Traumatologia (CUB) 6072
Revista Cubana de Pediatria (CUB) 6103
Revista Cubana de Plantas Medicinales (CUB) 6878
Revista Cubana de Salud Publica (CUB) 7539
Revista da Escola de Minas (BRA) 3281
Revista de Antropologia (BRA) 353
Revista de Ciencia Politica (CHL) 7262
Revista de Direito Electronico (BRA) 4771
Revista de Estudios Historico Juridicos (CHL) 4959
Revista de Ingenieria de Construccion (CHL) 3282
Revista de Investigacion Clinica (MEX) 5705
Revista de Investigaciones Veterinarias del Peru (PER) 8806
Revista de Nutricao (BRA) 6668
Revista de Saude Publica (BRA) 7539
Revista Enfermagem (BRA) 5980
Revista Industrial y Agricola de Tucuman (ARG) 151

Revista Investigaciones Marinas (CHL) 701
Revista Latino-Americana de Enfermagem (BRA) 5980
Revista Latinoamericana de Estudios Urbano Regionales (CHL) 4425
Revista Medica de Chile (CHL) 5706
Revista Musical Chilena (CHL) 6611
Revista Panamericana de Salud Publica (USA) 7539
Revista Propiedad Intelectual (VEN) 4880
Revista Signos (CHL) 5361
Revista Uruguaya de Ciencia Politica (URY) 7179
Salud Publica de Mexico (MEX) 7540
Sao Paulo em Perspectiva (BRA) 7999
Sao Paulo Medical Journal (BRA) 5709
Scientia Agricola (BRA) 155
Sociedad Argentina de Botanica. Boletin (ARG) 817
Sociedad Venezolana de Microbiologia. Revista (VEN) 896
Sociedade Brasileira de Medicina Tropical. Revista (BRA) 5826
Temas Medievales (ARG) 4164
Teologia y Vida (CHL) 7820
Textos sobre Envelhecimento (BRA) 4057
Topicos (ARG) 6957
Union Matematica Argentina. Revista (ARG) 5543
Universidad Nacional Mayor de San Marcos. Facultad de Medicina. Anales (PER) 5726
Vision Gerencial (VEN) 1800

ScienceDirect (Subsidiary of: Elsevier Science & Technology) 360 Park Ave S, PO Box 945, New York, NY 10010-1710 TEL 212-633-3730, 888-437-4636, FAX 212-462-1974, usinfo@scidirect.com, http://www.sciencedirect.com/

A C O G Clinical Review (USA) 5739
A E Ue: International Journal of Electronics and Communication (DEU) 2310
A O R N Journal (USA) 5949
A S G E Clinical Update (USA) 5919
Academic Pediatrics (USA) 6086
Academic Radiology (NLD) 6191
Academie des Sciences. Comptes Rendus. Biologies (FRA) 649
Academie des Sciences. Comptes Rendus. Chimie (FRA) 2048
Academie des Sciences. Comptes Rendus. Geoscience (FRA) 7830
Academie des Sciences. Comptes Rendus. Mathematique (FRA) 5464
Academie des Sciences. Comptes Rendus. Mecanique (FRA) 3372
Academie des Sciences. Comptes Rendus. Palevol (FRA) 6722
Academie des Sciences. Comptes Rendus. Physique (FRA) 2132
Accident Analysis & Prevention (GBR) 7506
Accounting Forum (GBR) 1277
Accounting, Organizations and Society (GBR) 1278
Acta Astronautica (GBR) 41
Acta Biomaterialia (NLD) 755
Acta Histochemica (DEU) 721
Acta Materialia (GBR) 6303
Acta Mathematica Scientia (NLD) 5464
Acta Metallurgica Sinica (CHN) 6303
Acta Oecologica (FRA) 650
Acta Psychologica (NLD) 7330
Acta Tropica (NLD) 5808
Acute Pain (NLD) 5567
Ad Hoc Networks (NLD) 2495
Addictive Behaviors (GBR) 2690
Additives for Polymers (GBR) 7090
Advanced Drug Delivery Reviews (NLD) 6819
Advanced Engineering Informatics (GBR) 2445
Advances in Accounting (USA) 1279
Advances in Accounting Behavioral Research (GBR) 1279
Advances in Agronomy (USA) 79
Advances in Anesthesia (USA) 5768
Advances in Antiviral Drug Design (USA) 6819
Advances in Applied Business Strategy (USA) 1724
Advances in Applied Mathematics (USA) 5466
Advances in Applied Microbiology (USA) 880
Advances in Applied Microeconomics (USA) 1535
Advances in Austrian Economics (USA) 1057
Advances in Bioethics (USA) 6902
Advances in Botanical Research (USA) 773
Advances in Business Marketing and Purchasing (GBR) 1804
Advances in Cancer Research (USA) 6007
Advances in Carbohydrate Chemistry and Biochemistry (USA) 5568
Advances in Catalysis (USA) 2132
Advances in Cell Aging and Gerontology (NLD) 4038
Advances in Chemical Engineering (USA) 3235
Advances in Chronic Kidney Disease (USA) 6264
Advances in Clinical Chemistry (USA) 721
Advances in Colloid and Interface Science (NLD) 2132
Advances in Dermatology (USA) 5871
Advances in Developmental Biology (NLD) 651
Advances in DNA Sequence Specific Agents (USA) 721
Advances in Drug Research (USA) 6819
Advances in Early Education and Day Care (USA) 2824
Advances in Ecological Research (USA) 3401
Advances in Econometrics (USA) 1435
Advances in Educational Administration (USA) 3016
Advances in Engineering Software (GBR) 3288

Advances in Entrepreneurship, Firm Emergence and Growth (GBR) 1724
Advances in Enzyme Regulation (GBR) 721
Advances in Experimental Social Psychology (USA) 8085
Advances in Food and Nutrition Research (USA) 6654
Advances in Gender Research (USA) 8893
Advances in Genetics (USA) 861
Advances in Global Leadership (USA) 1057
Advances in Group Processes (USA) 8085
Advances in Health Care Management (GBR) 5568
Advances in Heterocyclic Chemistry (USA) 2119
Advances in Hospitality and Leisure (GBR) 8681
Advances in Human Factors - Ergonomics (NLD) 7331
Advances in Human Performance and Cognitive Engineering Research (USA) 7331
Advances in Immunology (USA) 5752
Advances in Industrial and Labor Relations (USA) 1662
Advances in Inorganic Chemistry (USA) 2115
Advances in Insect Physiology (USA) 837
Advances in Interdisciplinary Studies of Work Teams (USA) 1724
Advances in International Accounting (USA) 1279
Advances in International Management (GBR) 1551
Advances in International Marketing (USA) 1804
Advances in Learning and Behavioral Disabilities (GBR) 3036
Advances in Librarianship (USA) 4987
Advances in Library Administration and Organization (GBR) 4987
Advances in Magnetic and Optical Resonance (USA) 7004
Advances in Management Accounting (USA) 1279
Advances in Marine Biology (USA) 651
Advances in Mathematics (USA) 5466
Advances in Medical Sociology (GBR) 8085
Advances in Microbial Physiology (USA) 880
Advances in Molecular and Cell Biology (NLD) 826
Advances in Organometallic Chemistry (USA) 2119
Advances in Parallel Computing (NLD) 2466
Advances in Parasitology (USA) 880
Advances in Pediatrics (USA) 6087
Advances in Pharmaceutical Sciences (USA) 6819
Advances in Pharmacology (USA) 6819
Advances in Physical Organic Chemistry (USA) 2133
Advances in Planar Lipid Bilayers and Liposomes (USA) 651
Advances in Plant Pathology (USA) 773
Advances in Program Evaluation (GBR) 3050
Advances in Protein Chemistry (USA) 722
Advances in Psychology (NLD) 7331
Advances in Public Interest Accounting (USA) 1279
Advances in Quantum Chemistry (USA) 2049
Advances in Space Biology and Medicine (NLD) 41
Advances in Space Research (GBR) 41
Advances in Special Education (USA) 3036
Advances in Strategic Management (USA) 1724
Advances in Structural Biology (USA) 651
Advances in Surgery (USA) 6235
Advances in Taxation (USA) 1909
Advances in the Economic Analysis of Participatory and Labor-Managed Firms (USA) 1662
Advances in the Study of Behavior (USA) 7332
Advances in the Study of Entrepreneurship, Innovation, and Economic Growth (USA) 1435
Advances in Veterinary Medicine (USA) 8790
Advances in Virus Research (USA) 880
Advances in Water Resources (GBR) 8817
Aerospace Science and Technology (FRA) 43
Aesthetic Surgery Journal (USA) 6235
Ageing Research Reviews (IRL) 4039
Aggression and Violent Behavior (GBR) 7332
Agricultural and Forest Meteorology (NLD) 6346
Agricultural Economics (USA) 192
Agricultural Sciences in China (GBR) 85
Agricultural Systems (NLD) 85
Agricultural Water Management (NLD) 217
Agriculture, Ecosystems & Environment (NLD) 85
Air Medical Journal (USA) 5570
Alcohol (New York) (USA) 2690
Alkaloids: Chemical and Biological Perspectives (USA) 722
The Alkaloids: Chemistry and Biology (USA) 2119
Alpha Omegan (USA) 5834
Alzheimer's & Dementia (USA) 6121
American Academy of Dermatology. Journal (USA) 5871
American Association for Pediatric Ophthalmology and Strabismus. Journal (USA) 6038
American College of Cardiology. Journal (USA) 5776
American College of Radiology. Journal (USA) 6192
American College of Surgeons. Journal (USA) 6235
American Dietetic Association. Journal (USA) 6654
American Heart Journal (USA) 5776
The American Journal of Cardiology (USA) 5776
American Journal of Emergency Medicine (USA) 6055
American Journal of Evaluation (USA) 7946
American Journal of Gastroenterology (USA) 5920
The American Journal of Geriatric Pharmacotherapy (USA) 6819
American Journal of Human Genetics (USA) 862
American Journal of Hypertension (USA) 5776
American Journal of Infection Control (USA) 5809
American Journal of Kidney Diseases (USA) 6265
The American Journal of Medicine (USA) 5572

The American Journal of Medicine. Supplement (USA) 5573
American Journal of Obstetrics and Gynecology (USA) 5985
American Journal of Ophthalmology (USA) 6038
American Journal of Orthodontics and Dentofacial Orthopedics (USA) 5834
American Journal of Orthopsychiatry (USA) 7333
American Journal of Otolaryngology (USA) 6077
American Journal of Preventive Medicine (USA) 5573
The American Journal of Surgery (USA) 6235
American Medical Directors Association. Journal (USA) 4087
American Medical Informatics Association. Journal (USA) 5829
American Psychiatric Nurses Association. Journal (USA) 5951
American Psychologist (USA) 7333
American Society for Mass Spectrometry. Journal (USA) 7073
American Society for Surgery of the Hand. Journal (USA) 6236
American Society of Echocardiography. Journal (USA) 5776
American Society of Hypertension. Journal (USA) 5573
Anaerobe (GBR) 880
Anaesthesia and Intensive Care Medicine (GBR) 5768
Analytica Chimica Acta (NLD) 2097
Analytical Biochemistry (USA) 722
Analytical Spectroscopy Library (NLD) 2098
Anesthesiology Clinics (USA) 5770
Animal Behaviour (GBR) 932
Animal Feed Science and Technology (NLD) 270
Animal Reproduction Science (NLD) 278
Annales de Cardiologie et d'Angeiologie (FRA) 5777
Annales de Chimie, Science des Materiaux (FRA) 2050
Annales de Chirurgie Plastique Esthetique (FRA) 6236
Annales de Chirurgie Vasculaire (FRA) 6236
Annales de Dermatologie et de Venereologie (FRA) 5871
Annales de Paleontologie (FRA) 6723
Annales de Pathologie (FRA) 653
Annales d'Endocrinologie (FRA) 5883
Annales d'Oto-Laryngologie et de Chirurgie Cervico Faciale (FRA) 6077
Annales Francaises d'Anesthesie et de Reanimation (FRA) 5770
Annales Medico-Psychologiques, Revue Psychiatrique (FRA) see Annales Medico-Psychologiques. 7334
Annales Pharmaceutiques Francaises (FRA) 6820
Annales Scientifiques de l'Ecole Normale Superieure (FRA) 5470
Annals of Anatomy (DEU) 5575
Annals of Botany (GBR) 775
Annals of Diagnostic Pathology (USA) 5575
Annals of Discrete Mathematics (NLD) 5471
Annals of Emergency Medicine (USA) 6055
Annals of Epidemiology (USA) 7507
Annals of Nuclear Energy (GBR) 3164
Annals of Occupational Hygiene (GBR) 6672
Annals of Physical and Rehabilitation Medicine (FRA) 6106
Annals of Physics (USA) 7005
Annals of Pure and Applied Logic (NLD) 5471
The Annals of Thoracic Surgery (USA) 6237
Annals of Tourism Research (GBR) 8683
Annals of Vascular Surgery (USA) 6237
Annual Reports in Medicinal Chemistry (USA) 6821
Annual Reports on N M R Spectroscopy (USA) 7073
Annual Reviews in Control (GBR) 2505
L' Anthropologie (FRA) 326
Antibiotiques (FRA) 6821
Antiviral Research (NLD) 881
Appetite (GBR) 6655
Applied Acoustics (GBR) 7086
Applied and Computational Harmonic Analysis (USA) 5472
Applied and Preventive Psychology (GBR) 7335
Applied Animal Behaviour Science (NLD) 933
Applied Catalysis A: General (NLD) 3236
Applied Catalysis B: Environmental (NLD) 3236
Applied Clay Science (NLD) 2724
Applied Energy (GBR) 3124
Applied Ergonomics (GBR) 3181
Applied Geochemistry (GBR) 2724
Applied Geography (GBR) 3998
Applied Mathematical Modelling (USA) 5550
Applied Mathematics and Computation (USA) 5472
Applied Mathematics Letters (GBR) 5472
Applied Numerical Mathematics (NLD) 5550
Applied Nursing Research (USA) 5952
Applied Ocean Research (GBR) 2800
Applied Radiation and Isotopes (GBR) 7064
Applied Radiology (USA) 6192
Applied Soft Computing (NLD) 2587
Applied Soil Ecology (NLD) 218
Applied Surface Science (NLD) 6305
Applied Thermal Engineering (GBR) 7053
Aquacultural Engineering (NLD) 3584
Aquaculture (NLD) 3584
Aquatic Botany (NLD) 776
Aquatic Ecosystem Health & Management (USA) 776
Aquatic Living Resources (FRA) 3586
Aquatic Toxicology (NLD) 3493

Developments in Aquaculture and Fisheries Science (NLD) **940**
Developments in Atmospheric Science (NLD) **6352**
Developments in Crop Science (NLD) **228**
Developments in Earth Surface Processes (NLD) **2730**
Developments in Economic Geology (NLD) **2730**
Developments in Environmental Economics (NLD) **3413**
Developments in Environmental Modelling (NLD) **3481**
Developments in Environmental Science (GBR) **3414**
Developments in Food Science (NLD) **2122**
Developments in Geotechnical Engineering (NLD) **3264**
Developments in Geotectonics (NLD) **2730**
Developments in Marine Biology (NLD) **2803**
Developments in Mineral Processing (NLD) **2731**
Developments in Palaeontology and Stratigraphy (NLD) **6724**
Developments in Petroleum Science (NLD) **6767**
Developments in Petrology (NLD) **2731**
Developments in Plant Genetics and Breeding (NLD) **786**
Developments in Precambrian Geology (NLD) **2731**
Developments in Quaternary Science (NLD) **2731**
Developments in Sedimentology (NLD) **2731**
Developments in Water Science (NLD) **8820**
Diabetes & Metabolic Syndrome (USA) **5886**
Diabetes & Metabolism (FRA) **5886**
Diabetes Research and Clinical Practice (IRL) **5888**
Diagnostic Histopathology (Oxford) (GBR) **5944**
Diagnostic Microbiology and Infectious Disease (USA) **884**
Diamond and Related Materials (CHE) **2110**
Differential Geometry and Its Applications (NLD) **5482**
Digestive and Liver Disease (GBR) **5922**
Digital Investigation (GBR) **5913**
Digital Signal Processing (USA) **3093**
Disability and Health Journal (USA) **4064**
Disaster Management & Response (USA) **5957**
Discrete Applied Mathematics (NLD) **5483**
Discrete Mathematics (NLD) **5483**
Discrete Optimization (NLD) **5552**
Disease-A-Month (USA) **5605**
Dislocations in Solids (NLD) **7010**
Displays (NLD) **2485**
Domestic Animal Endocrinology (USA) **8796**
Douleurs (FRA) **5607**
Droit, Deontologie et Soin (FRA) **5607**
Drug and Alcohol Dependence (IRL) **2693**
Drug Discovery Today (GBR) **6834**
Drug Discovery Today: BIOSILICO (GBR) **6834**
Drug Discovery Today: Disease Mechanisms (GBR) **6834**
Drug Discovery Today: Disease Models (GBR) **6835**
Drug Discovery Today: Technologies (GBR) **6835**
Drug Discovery Today: Therapeutic Strategies (GBR) **6835**
Drug Resistance Updates (GBR) **5607**
Dyes and Pigments (GBR) **2060**
Dynamics of Atmospheres and Oceans (NLD) **6352**
E A U - E B U Update Series (NLD) **6267**
E J V E S Extra (GBR) **5785**
E M C - Neurologie (Online) (FRA) **6137**
E M C - Psychiatrie (Online) (FRA) **6137**
e - S P E N (NLD) **6657**
Early Childhood Research Quarterly (GBR) **2844**
Early Human Development (IRL) **5989**
Earth and Planetary Science Letters (NLD) **2706**
Earth - Science Reviews (NLD) **2706**
Eating Behaviors (GBR) **7353**
Ecological Complexity (NLD) **3416**
Ecological Economics (NLD) **3416**
Ecological Engineering (NLD) **3417**
Ecological Indicators (NLD) **3417**
Ecological Informatics (NLD) **3417**
Ecological Modelling (NLD) **3481**
Economic Modelling (NLD) **1539**
Economic Systems (NLD) **1562**
Economics and Human Biology (NLD) **7961**
Economics Letters (CHE) **1540**
Economics of Education Review (GBR) **3020**
Ecotoxicology and Environmental Safety (USA) **3496**
Edited Series on Advances in Nonlinear Science and Complexity (NLD) **5485**
Education for Chemical Engineers (GBR) **3242**
Educational Research Review (NLD) **2851**
Electoral Studies (GBR) **7132**
Electric Power Systems Research (CHE) **3302**
The Electricity Journal (USA) **3157**
Electrochemistry Communications (USA) **2113**
Electrochimica Acta (GBR) **2113**
Electronic Commerce Research and Applications (NLD) **2543**
Electronic Notes in Discrete Mathematics (NLD) **5486**
Electronic Notes in Theoretical Computer Science (NLD) **2600**
Elsevier Oceanography Series (NLD) **2804**
Emergency Medicine Clinics of North America (USA) **6059**
Emerging Markets Review (NLD) **1337**
Emotion (USA) **7354**
L' Encephale (FRA) **6137**
Endeavour (GBR) **7852**
Endocrinology & Metabolism Clinics of North America (USA) **5892**
Energy (GBR) **3130**
Energy and Buildings (CHE) **3130**
Energy Conversion and Management (GBR) **3130**
Energy Economics (NLD) **3130**
Energy Policy (GBR) **3132**
Engineering Analysis with Boundary Elements (GBR) **3377**
Engineering Applications of Artificial Intelligence (GBR) **2448**
Engineering Failure Analysis (GBR) **3344**
Engineering Fracture Mechanics (GBR) **3344**
Engineering Geology (NLD) **3266**
Engineering Structures (GBR) **3266**
English for Specific Purposes (GBR) **5114**
Environment International (GBR) **3421**
Environmental and Experimental Botany (NLD) **786**
Environmental Forensics (USA) **3506**
Environmental Hazards (GBR) **3425**
Environmental Impact Assessment Review (USA) **3425**
Environmental Modelling & Software (GBR) **3482**
Environmental Policy and Law (NLD) **3427**
Environmental Pollution (GBR) **3486**
Environmental Research (USA) **3428**
Environmental Science & Policy (USA) **3428**
Environmental Toxicology and Pharmacology (NLD) **3497**
The Environmentalist (USA) **3429**
Enzyme and Microbial Technology (USA) **763**
Epilepsy & Behavior (USA) **5610**
Epilepsy Research (NLD) **6138**
Estuarine, Coastal and Shelf Science (GBR) **2804**
Ethics & the Environment (GBR) **6917**
Ethique & Sante (FRA) **6985**
European Academy of Dermatology and Venereology. Journal (BEL) **5876**
European Ceramic Society. Journal (GBR) **2040**
European Economic Review (NLD) **1107**
European Journal of Agronomy (NLD) **229**
European Journal of Cancer (GBR) **6019**
European Journal of Cardio-Thoracic Surgery (NLD) **5786**
European Journal of Cardiovascular Nursing (NLD) **5958**
European Journal of Cell Biology (DEU) **832**
European Journal of Combinatorics (GBR) **5487**
European Journal of Heart Failure (NLD) **5786**
European Journal of Internal Medicine (USA) **5945**
European Journal of Mechanics A - Solids (FRA) **7058**
European Journal of Mechanics B - Fluids (FRA) **7058**
European Journal of Medical Genetics (FRA) **866**
European Journal of Medicinal Chemistry (FRA) **731**
European Journal of Obstetrics & Gynecology and Reproductive Biology (IRL) **5990**
European Journal of Oncology Nursing (GBR) **5958**
European Journal of Operational Research (NLD) **1742**
European Journal of Paediatric Neurology (GBR) **6091**
European Journal of Pain (GBR) **5611**
European Journal of Pharmaceutical Sciences (NLD) **6838**
European Journal of Pharmaceutics and Biopharmaceutics (NLD) **6838**
European Journal of Pharmacology (NLD) **6838**
European Journal of Political Economy (NLD) **7134**
European Journal of Protistology (DEU) **6724**
European Journal of Psychological Assessment (USA) **7356**
European Journal of Radiology (IRL) **6196**
European Journal of Radiology Extra (USA) **6196**
European Journal of Soil Biology (FRA) **672**
European Journal of Surgical Oncology (GBR) **6019**
European Journal of Ultrasound (IRL) **6196**
European Journal of Vascular and Endovascular Surgery (GBR) **5786**
European Management Journal (GBR) **1742**
European Neuropsychopharmacology (NLD) **6140**
European Polymer Journal (GBR) **2123**
European Psychiatry (FRA) **6140**
European Psychologist (USA) **7356**
European Urology (CHE) **6268**
European Urology Supplements (NLD) **6268**
Evaluation and Program Planning (GBR) **7963**
Evidence - Based Cardiovascular Medicine (GBR) **5787**
Evidence - Based Obstetrics & Gynaecology (GBR) **5990**
Evolution and Human Behavior (USA) **942**
L' Evolution Psychiatrique (FRA) **6140**
Experimental and Clinical Psychopharmacology (USA) **7356**
Experimental and Molecular Pathology (USA) **5612**
Experimental and Toxicologic Pathology (DEU) **5612**
Experimental Cell Research (USA) **832**
Experimental Eye Research (GBR) **6041**
Experimental Gerontology (USA) **4044**
Experimental Hematology (USA) **5936**
Experimental Neurology (USA) **6140**
Experimental Parasitology (USA) **5813**
Experimental Psychology (USA) **7357**
Experimental Thermal and Fluid Science (USA) **3192**
Expert Systems with Applications (GBR) **2448**
Explorations in Economic History (USA) **1541**
Explore: The Journal of Science & Healing (USA) **7854**
Expositiones Mathematicae (DEU) **5487**
F E B S Letters (NLD) **732**
F E M S Immunology and Medical Microbiology (GBR) **885**
F E M S Microbiology Ecology (GBR) **885**
F E M S Microbiology Letters (GBR) **885**
F E M S Microbiology Reviews (GBR) **885**
Facial Plastic Surgery Clinics of North America (USA) **6243**
Families, Systems, & Health (USA) **5613**
Federation of European Microbiological Societies Yeast Research Online (GBR) *see* F E M S Yeast Research. **886**
Fertility and Sterility (USA) **5990**
Feuillets de Radiologie (FRA) **6197**
Field Crops Research (NLD) **231**
Filtration Industry Analyst (GBR) **3367**
Filtration + Separation (GBR) **3244**
Finance Research Letters (USA) **1343**
Financial Services Review (GBR) **1345**
Finite Elements in Analysis and Design (NLD) **3291**
Finite Fields and Their Applications (USA) **5488**
Fire Safety Journal (GBR) **3578**
Fish and Shellfish Immunology (GBR) **943**
Fish Physiology (USA) **943**
Fisheries Research (NLD) **3592**
Fitoterapia (ITA) **788**
Flora (DEU) **788**
Flow Measurement and Instrumentation (GBR) **4486**
Fluid Dynamics Research (NLD) **3361**
Fluid Phase Equilibria (NLD) **2135**
Focus on Catalysts (USA) **2094**
Focus on Pigments (USA) **6722**
Focus on Powder Coatings (USA) **6722**
Focus on Surfactants (USA) **2094**
Food and Bioproducts Processing (GBR) **764**
Food and Chemical Toxicology (GBR) **3497**
Food Chemistry (GBR) **2061**
Food Control (GBR) **3638**
Food Hydrocolloids (NLD) **3639**
Food Microbiology (GBR) **886**
Food Policy (GBR) **198**
Food Quality and Preference (GBR) **3641**
Food Research International (GBR) **3641**
The Foot (GBR) **6060**
Foot and Ankle Clinics (USA) **6060**
Foot and Ankle Surgery (GBR) **6244**
Forensic Science International (IRL) **5913**
Forensic Science International: Genetics (NLD) **5913**
Forest Ecology and Management (NLD) **3688**
Forest Policy and Economics (NLD) **3689**
Formosan Medical Association. Journal (HKG) **5615**
The Foundation Years (GBR) **5616**
Franklin Institute. Journal (GBR) **7013**
Free Radical Biology & Medicine (USA) **673**
Frontiers in Neuroendocrinology (USA) **5893**
Fuel (GBR) **6769**
Fuel and Energy Abstracts (GBR) **6800**
Fuel Cells Bulletin (GBR) **3135**
Fuel Processing Technology (NLD) **6769**
Fungal Biology Reviews (GBR) **790**
Fungal Genetics and Biology (USA) **790**
Fusion Engineering and Design (CHE) **3378**
Fuss & Sprunggelenk (DEU) **6060**
Future Generation Computer Systems (NLD) **2520**
Futures (GBR) **1487**
Fuzzy Sets and Systems (NLD) **5489**
Gait & Posture (NLD) **5617**
Games and Economic Behavior (USA) **7358**
Gastroenterologie Clinique et Biologique (FRA) **5924**
Gastroenterology (USA) **5924**
Gastroenterology Clinics of North America (USA) **5924**
Gastrointestinal Endoscopy (USA) **5925**
Gastrointestinal Endoscopy Clinics of North America (USA) **5925**
Gender Medicine (USA) **5618**
Gene - C O M B I S (NLD) *see* Gene. **764**
Gene Expression Patterns (NLD) **867**
General and Comparative Endocrinology (USA) **5893**
General Hospital Psychiatry (USA) **6143**
Genomics (USA) **870**
Genomics Proteomics & Bioinformatics (GBR) **871**
Geobios (FRA) **6725**
Geochemical Society. Special Publication (USA) **2735**
Geochimica et Cosmochimica Acta (GBR) **2735**
Geoderma (NLD) **232**
Geodinamica Acta (FRA) **2736**
Geoforum (GBR) **4008**
Geographie, Economie, Societe (FRA) **4011**
Geomechanics Abstracts (GBR) **2719**
Geomorphology (NLD) **2743**
Geotextiles and Geomembranes (GBR) **8451**
Geothermics (GBR) **2708**
Geriatric Nursing (USA) **4045**
Global and Planetary Change (NLD) **2744**
Global Environmental Change (GBR) **3434**
Global Finance Journal (NLD) **1349**
Gondwana Research (NLD) **2709**
Government Information Quarterly (GBR) **7440**
Graphical Models (USA) **2485**
Group Dynamics (USA) **7359**
Growth Hormone & IGF Research (GBR) **5893**
Gynecologic Oncology (USA) **5992**
Gynecologie Obstetrique et Fertilite (FRA) **5992**
Habitat International (GBR) **4411**
Hand Clinics (USA) **6061**
Handbook of Analytical Separations (NLD) **2100**
Handbook of Behavioural Neuroscience (NLD) **6143**
Handbook of Biological Physics (NLD) **753**
Handbook of Chemical Neuroanatomy (NLD) **6144**
Handbook of Clinical Neurology (NLD) **6144**
Handbook of Exploration and Environmental Geochemistry (NLD) **2746**
Handbook of Geophysical Exploration (GBR) **2783**
Handbook of Numerical Analysis (NLD) **5491**
Handbook of Petroleum Exploration and Production (NLD) **6772**
Handbook of Powder Technology (NLD) **3268**
Handbook of Sensors and Actuators (NLD) **3100**
Handbook of Statistics (NLD) **8375**
Harmful Algae (NLD) **886**
Health & Place (GBR) **4014**
Health Policy (IRL) **7522**
Health Psychology (USA) **7360**
Hearing Research (NLD) **6080**
Heart & Lung (USA) **5959**
Heart Failure Clinics (USA) **5788**
Heart Rhythm (USA) **5788**
Hematology / Oncology Clinics of North America (USA) **6021**
Hepatology (USA) **5926**
Hepatology Research (GBR) **5926**
High Energy Density Physics (GBR) **7051**
Higher Education Policy (GBR) **2984**
Historia Mathematica (USA) **5491**
History of European Ideas (GBR) **6923**
History of Psychology (USA) **7360**
The History of the Family (GBR) **7969**
Homeopathy (Online) (GBR) *see* Homeopathy (Print). **5805**
HOMO (DEU) **341**
Hong Kong Journal of Nephrology (HKG) **6268**
Hong Kong Journal of Occupational Therapy (NLD) **6110**
Hong Kong Physiotherapy Journal (HKG) **6110**
Hormones and Behavior (USA) **5894**
Les Houches Summer School Proceedings (NLD) **7015**
Human and Ecological Risk Assessment (USA) **3437**
Human Factors in Information Technology (NLD) **2543**
Human Immunology (USA) **5759**
Human Movement Science (NLD) **5630**
Human Pathology (USA) **5631**
Human Resource Management Review (GBR) **1864**
Hydrometallurgy (NLD) **6315**
Hypatia (USA) **8898**
I R B M News (FRA) **765**
I S A Transactions (NLD) **3196**
I S P R S Journal of Photogrammetry and Remote Sensing (NLD) **4014**
Icarus (USA) **575**
Image and Vision Computing (NLD) **2487**
Imagerie de la Femme (FRA) **5633**
Immunity (USA) **5759**
Immunoanalyse et Biologie Specialisee (FRA) **677**
Immunobiology (DEU) **5759**
Immunology and Allergy Clinics of North America (USA) **5760**
Immunology Letters (NLD) **5760**
Indagationes Mathematicae (NLD) **5492**
Industrial Chemistry Library (NLD) **2065**
Industrial Crops and Products (NLD) **236**
Industrial Marketing Management (USA) **1820**
Industrial Safety Series (NLD) **6679**
Infant Behavior and Development (GBR) **7362**
Infection, Genetics and Evolution (NLD) **5634**
Infectious Disease Clinics of North America (USA) **5817**
Information and Computation (USA) **2422**
Information & Management (NLD) **2521**
Information and Organization (GBR) **1290**
Information and Software Technology (NLD) **2591**
Information Economics and Policy (NLD) **2325**
Information Fusion (NLD) **2467**
Information Processing & Management (GBR) **5016**
Information Processing Letters (NLD) **2537**
Information Sciences (USA) **2545**
Information Security Technical Report (GBR) **2514**
Information Systems (GBR) **2521**
Infosecurity (GBR) **2514**
Infrared Physics & Technology (NLD) **7076**
Injury (GBR) **6061**
Innovative Food Science and Emerging Technologies (NLD) **3647**
Inorganic Chemistry Communications (NLD) **2116**
Inorganica Chimica Acta (CHE) **2116**
Insect Biochemistry and Molecular Biology (GBR) **849**
Insight (Saint Louis) (USA) **6043**
l' Institut Henri Poincare. Annales (B). Probabilites et Statistiques (USA) **5493**
l' Institut Henri Poincare. Annales (C). Analyse Non Lineaire (FRA) **5493**
Insulin (USA) **5894**
Insurance: Mathematics and Economics (NLD) **4508**
Integration (NLD) **3319**
Intelligence (Kidlington) (GBR) **7363**
Intelligent Data Analysis (NLD) **2450**
Intensive and Critical Care Nursing (GBR) **5961**
Interacting with Computers (NLD) **2423**
Interactive Cardiovascular and Thoracic Surgery (CHE) **6246**
Intermetallics (GBR) **6316**
International Biodeterioration and Biodegradation (GBR) **765**
International Business Review (GBR) **1126**
International Commission on Radiological Protection. Annals (GBR) **6198**
International Communications in Heat and Mass Transfer (GBR) **3381**
International Dairy Journal (GBR) **265**

Online Service

Link to your serials resources and content with ulrichsweb.com

DIRECTORY 2010 SCIENCEDIRECT 11257

Journal of Molecular Graphics and Modelling (USA) **2108**
Journal of Molecular Liquids (NLD) **2137**
Journal of Molecular Spectroscopy (USA) **7078**
Journal of Molecular Structure (NLD) **2068**
Journal of Molecular Structure: THEOCHEM (NLD) **2068**
Journal of Monetary Economics (NLD) **1362**
Journal of Multinational Financial Management (NLD) **1769**
Journal of Multivariate Analysis (USA) **5506**
Journal of Natural Gas Chemistry (USA) **6775**
Journal of Neonatal Nursing (GBR) **5965**
Journal of Network and Computer Applications (GBR) **2500**
Journal of Neuroimmunology (NLD) **6154**
Journal of Neurolinguistics (GBR) **6154**
Journal of Neuroradiology (FRA) **6201**
Journal of Neuroscience Methods (NLD) **6155**
Journal of Non-Crystalline Solids (NLD) **7021**
Journal of Non-Newtonian Fluid Mechanics (NLD) **7059**
Journal of Nuclear Cardiology (USA) **6201**
Journal of Nuclear Materials (NLD) **7067**
Journal of Number Theory (USA) **5506**
Journal of Nutrition Education and Behavior (USA) **6662**
The Journal of Nutritional Biochemistry (USA) **6662**
Journal of Occupational Health Psychology (USA) **6680**
Journal of Operations Management (NLD) **3369**
Journal of Oral and Maxillofacial Surgery (USA) **5852**
Journal of Organometallic Chemistry (CHE) **2125**
Journal of Orthopaedic Nursing (GBR) **5966**
Journal of Orthopaedic Research (USA) **6064**
The Journal of Pain (USA) **6155**
Journal of Pain and Symptom Management (USA) **6155**
Journal of Parallel and Distributed Computing (USA) **2429**
Journal of Pediatric and Adolescent Gynecology (NLD) **6095**
Journal of Pediatric Health Care (USA) **6095**
Journal of Pediatric Nursing (USA) **5966**
Journal of Pediatric Oncology Nursing (USA) **6025**
Journal of Pediatric Surgery (USA) **6249**
Journal of Pediatric Urology (NLD) **6270**
The Journal of Pediatrics (USA) **6095**
Journal of PeriAnesthesia Nursing (USA) **5967**
Journal of Personality and Social Psychology (USA) **7377**
Journal of Petroleum Science and Engineering (NLD) **6776**
Journal of Pharmaceutical and Biomedical Analysis (NLD) **6855**
Journal of Pharmacological and Toxicological Methods (USA) **3499**
Journal of Phonetics (GBR) **5135**
Journal of Photochemistry and Photobiology, A: Chemistry (CHE) **2137**
Journal of Photochemistry and Photobiology, B: Biology (CHE) **737**
Journal of Photochemistry and Photobiology, C: Photochemistry Reviews (CHE) **2137**
Journal of Physics and Chemistry of Solids (GBR) **7022**
Journal of Physiology (Paris) (FRA) **6156**
Journal of Plant Physiology (DEU) **798**
Journal of Plastic, Reconstructive & Aesthetic Surgery (Online Edition) (GBR) **6249**
Journal of Policy Modeling (USA) **7147**
Journal of Power Sources (CHE) **3322**
Journal of Pragmatics (NLD) **5203**
Journal of Process Control (GBR) **2537**
Journal of Product Innovation Management (USA) **1890**
Journal of Professional Nursing (USA) **5967**
Journal of Prosthetic Dentistry (USA) **5853**
Journal of Proteomics (NLD) **737**
Journal of Psychiatric Research (GBR) **6156**
Journal of Psychophysiology (USA) **7379**
Journal of Psychosomatic Research (USA) **6156**
Journal of Psychotherapy Integration (USA) **6156**
Journal of Public Economics (CHE) **1545**
Journal of Purchasing & Supply Management (GBR) **1826**
Journal of Pure and Applied Algebra (NLD) **5506**
Journal of Quantitative Spectroscopy & Radiative Transfer (GBR) **7079**
Journal of Radiology Nursing (USA) **5967**
Journal of Rare Earths (NLD) **6319**
Journal of Renal Nutrition (USA) **6662**
Journal of Reproductive Immunology (IRL) **5763**
Journal of Research in Personality (USA) **7379**
Journal of Retailing (GBR) **1826**
Journal of Retailing and Consumer Services (GBR) **1826**
Journal of Rural Studies (GBR) **8115**
Journal of Safety Research (GBR) **6680**
Journal of School Psychology (GBR) **7380**
Journal of Science and Medicine in Sport (AUS) **6230**
Journal of Sea Research (NLD) **2810**
Journal of Second Language Writing (GBR) **5135**
Journal of Shoulder and Elbow Surgery (USA) **6250**
Journal of Socio-Economics (GBR) **1546**
Journal of Solid State Chemistry (USA) **2138**
Journal of Sound and Vibration (GBR) **7088**
Journal of South American Earth Sciences (GBR) **2711**
Journal of Statistical Planning and Inference (NLD) **8383**
The Journal of Steroid Biochemistry and Molecular Biology (GBR) **737**
Journal of Stored Products Research (GBR) **853**
The Journal of Strategic Information Systems (NLD) **2523**
Journal of Stroke & Cerebrovascular Diseases (USA) **5794**
Journal of Structural Biology (USA) **684**
Journal of Structural Geology (GBR) **2751**
Journal of Substance Abuse Treatment (USA) **2696**
The Journal of Supercritical Fluids (NLD) **2103**
Journal of Surgical Education (USA) **6250**
Journal of Surgical Research (USA) **6250**
Journal of Symbolic Computation (GBR) **5553**
Journal of Systems and Software (USA) **2593**
Journal of Systems Architecture (NLD) **2523**
Journal of Systems Engineering and Electronics (CHN) **64**
Journal of Terramechanics (GBR) **8501**
Journal of the Japanese and International Economies (USA) **1574**
Journal of the Mechanical Behavior of Biomedical Materials (NLD) **834**
Journal of the Mechanics and Physics of Solids (GBR) **7060**
Journal of the Neurological Sciences (NLD) **6157**
Journal of Theoretical Biology (GBR) **685**
Journal of Thermal Biology (GBR) **754**
The Journal of Thoracic and Cardiovascular Surgery (USA) **6250**
Journal of Tissue Viability (GBR) **5879**
Journal of Trace Elements in Medicine and Biology (DEU) **685**
Journal of Transport Geography (GBR) **4017**
Journal of Urban Economics (USA) **1138**
The Journal of Urology (USA) **6270**
Journal of Vascular and Interventional Radiology (USA) **6201**
Journal of Vascular Nursing (USA) **5967**
Journal of Vascular Surgery (USA) **6250**
Journal of Veterinary Behavior (USA) **8801**
Journal of Veterinary Cardiology (NLD) **8801**
Journal of Virological Methods (NLD) **890**
Journal of Visual Communication and Image Representation (USA) **2488**
Journal of Visual Languages and Computing (GBR) **5203**
Journal of Vocational Behavior (USA) **7381**
The Journal of Voice (USA) **6082**
Journal of Volcanology and Geothermal Research (NLD) **2785**
Journal of W O C N (USA) **6250**
Journal of Wind Engineering & Industrial Aerodynamics (NLD) **3387**
Journal of World Business (GBR) **1574**
Journal of X-Ray Science and Technology (NLD) **7023**
Kaohsiung Journal of Medical Sciences (TWN) **5656**
The Knee (NLD) **925**
Knowledge-Based Systems (NLD) **2454**
Korean Statistical Society. Journal (NLD) **8384**
Krankenhaus-Hygiene + Infektionsverhutung (DEU) **4105**
L W T - Food Science and Technology (GBR) *see* L W T- Food Science and Technology. **3653**
Laboratory Techniques in Biochemistry and Molecular Biology (NLD) **737**
Labour Economics (NLD) **1694**
The Lancet (GBR) **5660**
The Lancet Infectious Diseases (GBR) **5821**
The Lancet Neurology (GBR) **6158**
The Lancet Oncology (GBR) **6026**
Land Use Policy (GBR) **4418**
Landscape and Urban Planning (NLD) **2617**
Language & Communication (GBR) **5139**
Language Sciences (GBR) **5141**
The Leadership Quarterly (USA) **1772**
Learning and Individual Differences (GBR) **2882**
Learning and Instruction (GBR) **2882**
Learning and Motivation (USA) **2882**
Legal Medicine (NLD) **5915**
Leukemia Research (GBR) **5940**
Library & Information Science Research (GBR) **5027**
Library Collections, Acquisitions, and Technical Services (GBR) **5027**
The Lichenologist (GBR) **800**
Life Sciences (USA) **7880**
Limnologica (DEU) **2796**
Linear Algebra and Its Applications (USA) **5509**
Lingua (NLD) **5144**
Linguistics and Education (GBR) **5147**
Linnean Society. Biological Journal (GBR) **687**
Linnean Society. Botanical Journal (GBR) **800**
Linnean Society. Zoological Journal (GBR) **953**
Lithos (NLD) **2752**
Liver Transplantation (USA) **5929**
Livestock Science (NLD) **292**
Long Range Planning (GBR) **1773**
Lung Cancer (IRL) **6026**
Machine Intelligence and Pattern Recognition (NLD) **2454**
Magnetic Resonance Imaging (USA) **6202**
Magnetic Resonance Imaging Clinics of North America (USA) **6202**
Magnetic Resonance Materials in Physics, Biology and Medicine (GBR) **7068**
Mammalian Biology (DEU) **954**
Management Accounting Research (GBR) **1296**
Manual Therapy (GBR) **6112**
Manufacturing Research and Technology (NLD) **1898**
Marine and Petroleum Geology (GBR) **2754**
Marine Chemistry (NLD) **2712**
Marine Environmental Research (GBR) **3488**
Marine Geology (NLD) **2812**
Marine Micropaleontology (NLD) **6726**
Marine Policy (GBR) **2812**
Marine Pollution Bulletin (GBR) **3488**
Marine Structures (GBR) **3388**
Materials & Design (GBR) **3352**
Materials Characterization (USA) **6322**
Materials Chemistry and Physics (CHE) **3352**
Materials Letters (NLD) **7025**
Materials Research Bulletin (GBR) **2111**
Materials Science and Engineering A: Structural Materials: Properties, Microstructures and Processing (CHE) **3353**
Materials Science and Engineering B: Advanced Functional Solid-state Materials (CHE) **3353**
Materials Science and Engineering C: Materials for Biological Applications (CHE) **3353**
Materials Science and Engineering R: Reports (CHE) **3353**
Materials Science in Semiconductor Processing (GBR) **3108**
Materials Science Monographs (NLD) **3209**
Materials Today (NLD) **2072**
Mathematical and Computer Modelling (GBR) **5512**
Mathematical Biosciences (USA) **5512**
Mathematical Social Sciences (NLD) **5514**
Mathematics and Computers in Simulation (NLD) **2517**
Mathematics in Science and Engineering (USA) **5515**
Matrix Biology (NLD) **5665**
Maturitas (IRL) **5998**
Measurement (NLD) **6403**
Meat Science (NLD) **3656**
Mecanique & Industries (FRA) **3389**
Mechanical Systems and Signal Processing (GBR) **3389**
Mechanics of Materials (NLD) **3354**
Mechanics Research Communications (GBR) **3354**
Mechanism and Machine Theory (GBR) **3389**
Mechanisms of Ageing and Development (IRL) **4051**
Mechanisms of Development (IRL) **834**
Mechatronics (GBR) **3390**
Medecine des Maladies Metaboliques (FRA) **5897**
Medecine et Droit (FRA) **5915**
Medecine et Maladies Infectieuses (FRA) **5822**
Medecine Nucleaire (FRA) **6202**
Medecine Palliative (FRA) **5666**
Medical Clinics of North America (USA) **5667**
Medical Dosimetry (USA) **6203**
Medical Engineering & Physics (GBR) **5668**
Medical Hypotheses (GBR) **5669**
Medical Image Analysis (GBR) **6203**
Medical Laser Application (DEU) **5909**
Medicine (CD-ROM Edition) (GBR) **5674**
Medicine - U K Edition (GBR) **5674**
Membrane Science and Technology Series (NLD) **834**
Membrane Technology (GBR) **2072**
Mendeleev Communications (RUS) **2072**
Metabolic Engineering (USA) **750**
Metabolism (USA) **5897**
Metal Finishing (USA) **6323**
Metal Powder Report (GBR) **6340**
Metamaterials (NLD) **7061**
Methodology (USA) **7385**
Methods (USA) **738**
Methods in Cell Biology (USA) **834**
Methods in Enzymology (USA) **738**
Methods in Geochemistry and Geophysics (NLD) **2713**
Methods in Microbiology (USA) **891**
Methods in Neurosciences (USA) **6160**
Microbes and Infection (FRA) **891**
Microbial Pathogenesis (GBR) **5823**
Microbiological Research (DEU) **891**
Microchemical Journal (USA) **899**
Microelectronic Engineering (NLD) **3108**
Microelectronics Journal (GBR) **3109**
Microelectronics Reliability (GBR) **3109**
Micron (GBR) **899**
Microporous and Mesoporous Materials (NLD) **2138**
Microprocessors and Microsystems (NLD) **2572**
Microvascular Research (USA) **5795**
Midwifery (GBR) **5998**
Minerals Engineering (GBR) **6471**
Mitochondrion (NLD) **893**
Molecular and Biochemical Parasitology (NLD) **738**
Molecular and Cellular Endocrinology (IRL) **5897**
Molecular and Cellular Neuroscience (USA) **6161**
Molecular and Cellular Probes (GBR) **5909**
Molecular Aspects of Medicine (GBR) **5680**
Molecular Cell (USA) **835**
Molecular Genetics and Metabolism (USA) **739**
Molecular Imaging and Biology (NLD) **6203**
Molecular Immunology (GBR) **739**
Molecular Oncology (NLD) **6028**
Molecular Phylogenetics and Evolution (USA) **875**
Morphologie (FRA) **5680**
Motricite Cerebrale (FRA) **6161**
Museum Management and Curatorship (GBR) **6531**
Mutation Research - Fundamental and Molecular Mechanisms of Mutagenesis (NLD) **875**
Mutation Research - Genetic Toxicology and Environmental Mutagenesis (NLD) **875**
Mutation Research - Reviews (NLD) **876**
Mycological Research (GBR) **803**
N D T & E International (GBR) **3355**
N P G - Neurologie Psychiatrie Gerontologie (FRA) **6162**
Nanjing Medical University. Journal (CHN) **5682**
Nano Today (GBR) **750**
Nanomedicine: Nanotechnology, Biology and Medicine (USA) **5683**
Natures - Sciences - Societes (FRA) **2714**
Nephrologie & Therapeutique (FRA) **6272**
Netherlands Journal of Medicine (NLD) **5947**
Network Security (GBR) **2501**
Neural Networks (GBR) **2455**
Neurobiology of Aging (USA) **925**
Neurobiology of Disease (USA) **6164**
Neurobiology of Learning and Memory (USA) **6164**
Neurochemistry International (GBR) **6164**
Neurochirurgie (FRA) **6252**
Neurocomputing (NLD) **2455**
NeuroImage (USA) **6165**
Neuroimaging Clinics of North America (USA) **6203**
NeuroImmune Biology (NLD) **925**
Neurologic Clinics (USA) **6165**
Neuromuscular Disorders (GBR) **6167**
Neuron (USA) **6167**
Neuropeptides (Edinburgh) (GBR) **740**
Neuropharmacology (GBR) **6863**
Neurophysiologie Clinique (FRA) **6167**
Das Neurophysiologie - Labor (DEU) **5796**
Neuropsychiatrie de l'Enfance et de l'Adolescence (FRA) **6097**
Neuropsychologia (GBR) **6168**
Neuropsychology (USA) **6168**
Neuropsychopharmacology (USA) **6168**
Neuroscience (GBR) **6169**
Neuroscience & Biobehavioral Reviews (GBR) **6169**
Neuroscience Letters (IRL) **6169**
Neuroscience Research (IRL) **6169**
Neurosurgery Clinics of North America (USA) **6252**
Neurotherapeutics (USA) **6170**
NeuroToxicology (NLD) **6170**
Neurotoxicology and Teratology (USA) **6170**
New Astronomy (NLD) **578**
New Astronomy Reviews (GBR) **578**
New Biotechnology (NLD) **769**
New Carbon Materials (English Edition) (Online) (NLD) **3251**
New Comprehensive Biochemistry (NLD) **740**
New Ideas in Psychology (GBR) **7387**
New Scientist: Planet Science (GBR) *see* New Scientist on CD-ROM. **7892**
New Scientist: Planet Science (GBR) *see* New Scientist. **7891**
Newborn and Infant Nursing Reviews (USA) **5971**
Nitric Oxide: Biology and Chemistry (USA) **741**
Nonferrous Metals Society of China. Transactions (CHN) **6328**
Nonlinear Analysis: Hybrid Systems (GBR) **2433**
Nonlinear Analysis: Real World Applications (GBR) **5520**
Nonlinear Analysis: Theory, Methods & Applications (GBR) **3212**
The North American Journal of Economics and Finance (GBR) **1502**
North-Holland Mathematical Library (NLD) **5521**
North-Holland Mathematics Studies (NLD) **5521**
North-Holland Series in Applied Mathematics and Mechanics (NLD) **5521**
Norwegian Petroleum Society. Special Publication (NLD) **6781**
Nuclear Data Sheets (USA) **3171**
Nuclear Engineering and Design (CHE) **3355**
Nuclear Instruments & Methods in Physics Research. Section A: Accelerators, Spectrometers, Detectors, and Associated Equipment (NLD) **7069**
Nuclear Instruments & Methods in Physics Research. Section B: Beam Interactions with Materials and Atoms (Online) (NLD) *see* Nuclear Instruments & Methods in Physics Research. Section B: Beam Interactions with Materials and Atoms. **7069**
Nuclear Medicine and Biology (USA) **6204**
Nuclear Physics, Section A (NLD) **7069**
Nuclear Physics, Section B (NLD) **7070**
Nuclear Physics, Section B, Proceedings Supplements (NLD) **7070**
Nuclear Science and Techniques (NLD) **7070**
Nurse Education in Practice (GBR) **5971**
Nurse Education Today (GBR) **5971**
Nurse Leader (USA) **5972**
Nursing Clinics of North America (USA) **5973**
Nursing Outlook (USA) **5974**
Nutrition (USA) **6665**
Nutrition Clinique et Metabolisme (FRA) **5898**
Nutrition, Metabolism & Cardiovascular Diseases (GBR) **6666**
Nutrition Research (USA) **6666**
Obesity Research & Clinical Practice (NLD) **5689**
Obstetrics and Gynecology (USA) **6001**
Obstetrics and Gynecology Clinics of North America (USA) **6001**
Obstetrics, Gynecology and Reproductive Medicine (GBR) **6001**
Ocean & Coastal Management (GBR) **2814**
Ocean Engineering (GBR) **2814**
Ocean Modelling (USA) **2814**
Oceanographic Literature Review (GBR) **2720**
Omega (GBR) **1782**
Operations Research Letters (NLD) **7896**
Operative Techniques in General Surgery (USA) **6254**
Operative Techniques in Neurosurgery (USA) **6254**

Online Service

Online Service

11264 SWETSWISE ONLINE CONTENT ULRICH'S PERIODICALS

Academie des Sciences. Comptes Rendus. Chimie (FRA) **2048**
Academie des Sciences. Comptes Rendus. Geoscience (FRA) **7830**
Academie des Sciences. Comptes Rendus. Mathematique (FRA) **5464**
Academie des Sciences. Comptes Rendus. Mecanique (FRA) **3372**
Academie des Sciences. Comptes Rendus. Palevol (FRA) **6722**
Academie des Sciences. Comptes Rendus. Physique (FRA) **2132**
Academy of Marketing Science. Journal (USA) **1803**
Accident Analysis & Prevention (GBR) **7506**
Accountability in Research (USA) **7831**
Accounting and Finance (GBR) **1277**
Accounting, Auditing and Accountability Journal (GBR) **1277**
Accounting, Business and Financial History (GBR) **1056**
Accounting Education (GBR) **1277**
Accounting Forum (GBR) **1277**
Accounting, Organizations and Society (GBR) **1278**
Accounting Perspectives (CAN) **1278**
Accounts of Chemical Research (USA) **2048**
Accreditation and Quality Assurance (DEU) **2096**
Acoustical Physics (RUS) **7086**
Acoustical Society of America. Journal (USA) **7086**
Across Languages and Cultures (HUN) **5089**
Acta Agriculturae Scandinavica. Section A. Animal Science (NOR) **277**
Acta Agriculturae Scandinavica. Section B. Soil and Plant Science (SWE) **216**
Acta Agriculturae Scandinavica. Section C. Food Economics (NOR) **190**
Acta Agronomica Hungarica (HUN) **78**
Acta Alimentaria (HUN) **3625**
Acta Anaesthesiologica Scandinavica (DNK) **5768**
Acta Antiqua Academiae Scientiarum Hungaricae (HUN) **2229**
Acta Applicandae Mathematicae (NLD) **5464**
Acta Archaeologica (DNK) **370**
Acta Archaeologica Academiae Scientiarum Hungaricae (HUN) **370**
Acta Astronautica (GBR) **41**
Acta Biochimica et Biophysica Sinica (USA) **721**
Acta Biologica Hungarica (HUN) **649**
Acta Biomaterialia (NLD) **755**
Acta Biotheoretica (NLD) **649**
Acta Botanica Hungarica (HUN) **772**
Acta Crystallographica. Section A: Foundations of Crystallography. Online (DNK) *see* Acta Crystallographica. Section A: Foundations of Crystallography. **2108**
Acta Crystallographica. Section B: Structural Science. Online (DNK) *see* Acta Crystallographica. Section B: Structural Science. **2109**
Acta Crystallographica. Section C: Crystal Structure Communications (DNK) **2109**
Acta Crystallographica. Section D: Biological Crystallography (DNK) **2109**
Acta Crystallographica. Section E: Structure Reports Online (DNK) **2109**
Acta Crystallographica. Section F: Structural Biology and Crystallization Communications Online (DNK) **2109**
Acta Diabetologica (DEU) **5883**
Acta Ethnographica Hungarica (HUN) **322**
Acta Ethologica Online (DEU) **649**
Acta Geodaetica et Geophysica Hungarica (HUN) **2776**
Acta Haematologica (CHE) **5933**
Acta Histochemica (DEU) **721**
Acta Informatica (DEU) **2541**
Acta Juridica Hungarica (HUN) **4609**
Acta Linguistica Hungarica (HUN) **5090**
Acta Materialia (GBR) **6303**
Acta Mathematica Hungarica (NLD) **5464**
Acta Mathematica Sinica (DEU) **5464**
Acta Mathematicae Applicatae Sinica (DEU) **5465**
Acta Mechanica (AUT) **3372**
Acta Mechanica Sinica (DEU) **7057**
Acta Microbiologica et Immunologica Hungarica (HUN) **880**
Acta Neurochirurgica (AUT) **6234**
Acta Neurologica Scandinavica (DNK) **6118**
Acta Neurologica Scandinavica. Supplementum (DNK) **6118**
Acta Neuropathologica (DEU) **6118**
Acta Neuropsychiatrica (DNK) **6118**
Acta Numerica (GBR) **5465**
Acta Obstetricia et Gynecologica Scandinavica (GBR) **5985**
Acta Odontologica Scandinavica (NOR) **5833**
Acta Oecologica (FRA) **650**
Acta Oeconomica (HUN) **1056**
Acta Oncologica (SWE) **6007**
Acta Ophthalmologica. Supplementum (DNK) **6037**
Acta Ophthamologica (Online) (DNK) **6037**
Acta Orientalia Academiae Scientiarum Hungaricae (HUN) **541**
Acta Orthopaedica (Online) (GBR) **6054**
Acta Orthopaedica. Supplementum (Online Edition) (SWE) **6054**
Acta Oto-Laryngologica (SWE) **6076**
Acta Oto-Laryngologica. Supplement (NOR) **6076**
Acta Paediatrica (GBR) **6086**
Acta Pathologica Microbiologica et Immunologica Scandinavica (DNK) **650**
Acta Pharmacologica Sinica (USA) **6818**
Acta Physiologica (Online) (GBR) **918**
Acta Physiologica Hungarica (HUN) **918**
Acta Phytopathologica et Entomologica Hungarica (HUN) **773**
Acta Politica (GBR) **7101**
Acta Psychiatrica Scandinavica (GBR) **6119**
Acta Psychiatrica Scandinavica. Supplementum (DNK) **6119**
Acta Psychologica (NLD) **7330**
Acta Radiologica (GBR) **6192**
Acta Sociologica (NOR) **8085**
Acta Tropica (NLD) **5808**
Acta Veterinaria Hungarica (HUN) **8790**
Acta Zoologica Online (GBR) **930**
Action Learning (GBR) **2824**
Action Research (GBR) **5567**
Active and Passive Electronic Components (GBR) **3294**
Active Learning in Higher Education (GBR) **2965**
Activities, Adaptation & Aging (USA) **4038**
Acute Cardiac Care (Online Edition) (GBR) **5775**
Acute Pain (NLD) **5567**
Ad Hoc Networks (NLD) **2495**
Adaptive Behavior (GBR) **2445**
Addiction (GBR) **2689**
Addiction Biology (GBR) **2689**
Addiction Research and Theory (GBR) **2689**
Addictive Behaviors (GBR) **2690**
Addictive Disorders & Their Treatment (USA) **2690**
Additives for Polymers (GBR) **7090**
Adelphi Series (GBR) **7219**
Administration & Society (USA) **7418**
Administration in Social Work (USA) **8023**
Adoption Quarterly (USA) **8023**
Adsorption (USA) **3235**
Adsorption Science and Technology (GBR) **3235**
Adult Education Quarterly (USA) **2938**
Advanced Composite Materials (NLD) **3335**
Advanced Drug Delivery Reviews (NLD) **6819**
Advanced Engineering Informatics (GBR) **2445**
Advanced Engineering Materials (DEU) **3180**
Advanced Functional Materials (DEU) **2112**
Advanced Materials (DEU) **3335**
Advanced Micro- and Nanosystems (DEU) **2445**
Advanced Powder Technology (NLD) **3235**
Advanced Robotics (NLD) **2584**
Advanced Synthesis & Catalysis (DEU) **2048**
Advances in Anatomic Pathology (USA) **5568**
Advances in Anesthesia (USA) **5768**
Advances in Applied Ceramics (Online) (GBR) **2047**
Advances in Applied Clifford Algebras (CHE) **2049**
Advances in Applied Mathematics (USA) **5466**
Advances in Atmospheric Sciences (CHN) **6346**
Advances in Colloid and Interface Science (NLD) **2132**
Advances in Complex Systems (SGP) **7833**
Advances in Computational Mathematics (NLD) **5549**
Advances in Developing Human Resources (USA) **1855**
Advances in Difference Equations (USA) **5466**
Advances in Engineering Software (GBR) **3288**
Advances in Enzyme Regulation (GBR) **721**
Advances in Geometry (DEU) **5466**
Advances in Health Sciences Education (NLD) **5568**
Advances in Mathematics (USA) **5466**
Advances in Neonatal Care (USA) **6087**
Advances in Organic Synthesis (NLD) **2119**
Advances in Pediatrics (USA) **6087**
Advances in Physics (GBR) **7004**
Advances in Physiotherapy (SWE) **6106**
Advances in Polymer Technology (USA) **7090**
Advances in Skin and Wound Care (USA) **5871**
Advances in Space Research (GBR) **41**
Advances in Structural Engineering (GBR) **3258**
Advances in Water Resources (GBR) **8817**
Advertising & Society Review (USA) **20**
Aegypten und Levante (AUT) **371**
Aequationes Mathematicae (CHE) **5467**
Aerobiologia (NLD) **651**
Aerosol Science and Technology (USA) **2049**
Aerospace Science and Technology (FRA) **43**
Aesthetic Plastic Surgery (USA) **6235**
Aesthetic Surgery Journal (USA) **6235**
Affilia (USA) **8024**
Africa (GBR) **4172**
Africa Confidential (GBR) **7102**
Africa Research Bulletin. Economic, Financial and Technical Series (GBR) **1435**
Africa Research Bulletin. Political, Social and Cultural Series (GBR) **7102**
Africa Today (USA) **7102**
African Affairs (GBR) **7103**
African and Asian Studies (NLD) **8086**
African Archaeological Review (USA) **371**
African Development Review (GBR) **1590**
African Health Sciences (UGA) **5569**
African Identities (GBR) **3516**
African Journal of Ecology Online (GBR) **651**
African Studies (GBR) **323**
African Studies Review (USA) **3516**
Age (NLD) **4038**
Age and Ageing (GBR) **4038**
Ageing and Society (GBR) **4039**
Ageing International (USA) **4039**
Ageing Research Reviews (IRL) **4039**
Aggression and Violent Behavior (GBR) **7332**
Aggressive Behavior (USA) **7332**
Aging & Mental Health (GBR) **4039**
Aging Cell (GBR) **827**
The Aging Male (GBR) **6283**
Agribusiness (New York) (USA) **191**
Agricultural and Forest Entomology (GBR) **837**
Agricultural and Forest Meteorology (NLD) **6346**
Agricultural Economics (USA) **192**
Agricultural History (USA) **83**
Agricultural Systems (NLD) **85**
Agricultural Water Management (NLD) **217**
Agriculture and Human Values (NLD) **85**
Agriculture, Ecosystems & Environment (NLD) **85**
Agroforestry Systems (NLD) **87**
Agronomy for Sustainable Development (FRA) **217**
AIDS (USA) **5808**
AIDS & Behavior (USA) **5752**
AIDS Education and Prevention (USA) **7506**
AIDS Patient Care and S T Ds (USA) **5809**
AIDS Research and Human Retroviruses (USA) **5809**
AIDS Research and Therapy (GBR) **5752**
Air & Space Law (NLD) **8534**
Air Medical Journal (USA) **5570**
Aircraft Engineering and Aerospace Technology (GBR) **45**
Akademiai Ertesito (HUN) **3016**
Aktuelle Dermatologie (DEU) **5871**
Aktuelle Ernaehrungsmedizin (DEU) **6654**
Aktuelle Neurologie (DEU) **6120**
Aktuelle Rheumatologie (DEU) **6221**
Aktuelle Urologie (DEU) **6264**
Alcohol (New York) (USA) **2690**
Alcohol and Alcoholism (GBR) **2690**
Alcoholism & Drug Abuse Weekly (USA) **2691**
Alcoholism: Clinical and Experimental Research (USA) **2691**
Alcoholism Treatment Quarterly (USA) **2691**
Algebra and Logic (USA) **5467**
Algebra Colloquium (SGP) **5468**
Algebra Universalis (CHE) **5468**
Algebras and Representation Theory (NLD) **5468**
Algorithmica (USA) **2406**
Algorithms for Molecular Biology (GBR) **862**
Alimentary Pharmacology and Therapeutics (GBR) **5920**
Allergy (GBR) **5753**
Allergy. Supplement (GBR) **5754**
Alternative & Complementary Therapies (USA) **306**
Alternatives to the High Cost of Litigation (USA) **4613**
Alzheimer Disease and Associated Disorders (USA) **6121**
Ambix (GBR) **2049**
American Academy of Child and Adolescent Psychiatry. Journal (USA) **6121**
American Academy of Dermatology. Journal (USA) **5871**
American Academy of Nurse Practitioners. Journal (USA) **5951**
American Academy of Political and Social Science. Annals (USA) **7104**
American Academy of Psychoanalysis and Dynamic Psychiatry. Journal (USA) **7332**
American Academy of Religion. Journal (USA) **7620**
American Annals of the Deaf (USA) **4071**
American Association for Pediatric Ophthalmology and Strabismus. Journal (USA) **6038**
American Behavioral Scientist (USA) **7946**
American Business Law Journal (USA) **4854**
American Ceramic Society. Journal (USA) **2037**
American Chemical Society. Journal (USA) **2049**
American College of Cardiology. Journal (USA) **5776**
American College of Radiology. Journal (USA) **6192**
American College of Surgeons. Journal (USA) **6235**
American Communist History (GBR) **4282**
American Dietetic Association. Journal (USA) **6654**
American Foreign Policy Interests (USA) **7220**
American Geriatrics Society. Journal (USA) **4040**
American Heart Journal (USA) **5776**
American Imago (USA) **6121**
American Indian Quarterly (USA) **6634**
American Jewish History (USA) **7718**
American Journal of Agricultural Economics (USA) **193**
The American Journal of Bioethics (USA) **862**
The American Journal of Cardiology (USA) **5776**
American Journal of Cardiovascular Drugs (NZL) **5776**
The American Journal of Chinese Medicine (SGP) **5740**
American Journal of Clinical Dermatology (NZL) **5871**
American Journal of Clinical Oncology (USA) **6007**
American Journal of Community Psychology (USA) **8086**
American Journal of Dance Therapy (USA) **2682**
American Journal of Dermatopathology (USA) **5572**
American Journal of Distance Education (USA) **2938**
American Journal of Drug and Alcohol Abuse (USA) **2691**
American Journal of Economics and Sociology (USA) **1059**
American Journal of Emergency Medicine (USA) **6055**
American Journal of Epidemiology (USA) **5572**
American Journal of Evaluation (USA) **7946**
American Journal of Family Therapy (USA) **7333**
American Journal of Forensic Medicine and Pathology (USA) **5912**
American Journal of Gastroenterology (USA) **5920**
The American Journal of Geriatric Pharmacotherapy (USA) **6819**
American Journal of Geriatric Psychiatry (USA) **4040**
American Journal of Health Behavior (USA) **6981**
American Journal of Hematology (USA) **5933**
American Journal of Human Biology (USA) **652**
American Journal of Hypertension (USA) **5776**
American Journal of Industrial Medicine (USA) **6672**
American Journal of Infection Control (USA) **5809**
American Journal of Mathematics (USA) **5468**
American Journal of Medical Genetics. Part A (USA) **862**
American Journal of Medical Genetics. Part B: Neuropsychiatric Genetics (USA) **862**
American Journal of Medical Genetics. Part C: Seminars in Medical Genetics (USA) **862**
The American Journal of Medicine (USA) **5572**
American Journal of Nephrology (CHE) **6265**
American Journal of Nursing (USA) **5951**
American Journal of Obstetrics and Gynecology (USA) **5985**
American Journal of Ophthalmology (USA) **6038**
American Journal of Orthodontics and Dentofacial Orthopedics (USA) **5834**
American Journal of Otolaryngology (USA) **6077**
American Journal of Perinatology (USA) **5985**
American Journal of Philology (USA) **5092**
American Journal of Physical Anthropology (USA) **324**
American Journal of Physical Medicine and Rehabilitation (USA) **6106**
American Journal of Physics (USA) **7004**
American Journal of Political Science (USA) **7105**
American Journal of Preventive Medicine (USA) **5573**
American Journal of Primatology (USA) **931**
American Journal of Psychiatric Rehabilitation (USA) **6121**
American Journal of Psychiatry (USA) **6122**
The American Journal of Psychoanalysis (USA) **7333**
American Journal of Reproductive Immunology Online (DNK) **5754**
American Journal of Sexuality Education (USA) **6982**
American Journal of Sports Medicine (USA) **6228**
The American Journal of Surgery (USA) **6235**
American Journal of Surgical Pathology (USA) **5573**
American Journal of the Medical Sciences (USA) **5573**
American Journal of Therapeutics (GBR) **5573**
American Journal of Transplantation (Online) (DNK) **6236**
American Journal on Addictions (USA) **2691**
American Law and Economics Review (GBR) **4614**
American Literary History (USA) **5252**
American Literary Scholarship (USA) **5252**
American Literature (USA) **5252**
American Mathematical Society. Bulletin. New Series (USA) **5469**
American Mathematical Society. Journal (USA) **5469**
American Mathematical Society. Proceedings (USA) **5469**
American Mathematical Society. Transactions (USA) **5469**
American Medical Directors Association. Journal (USA) **4087**
American Musicological Society. Journal (USA) **6544**
American Nineteenth Century History (GBR) **4282**
American Periodicals (USA) **5252**
American Philological Association. Transactions (USA) **2229**
American Political Science Review (GBR) **7105**
American Politics Research (USA) **7105**
American Psychiatric Nurses Association. Journal (USA) **5951**
American Quarterly (USA) **4442**
American Review of Public Administration (USA) **7419**
American Society for Information Science and Technology. Journal (USA) **4989**
American Society for Mass Spectrometry. Journal (USA) **7073**
American Society for Surgery of the Hand. Journal (USA) **6236**
American Society of Echocardiography. Journal (USA) **5776**
The American Sociologist (USA) **8087**
American Speech (USA) **5092**
The Americas (USA) **4283**
Amino Acids (AUT) **722**
Amphibia - Reptilia (NLD) **932**
Amsterdamer Beitraege zur Aelteren Germanistik (NLD) **5253**
Amsterdamer Beitraege zur Neueren Germanistik (NLD) **5253**
Amyloid (GBR) **6221**
Amyotrophic Lateral Sclerosis (GBR) **6122**
Anaerobe (GBR) **880**
Anaesthesia (Oxford) (GBR) **5768**
Anaesthesia and Intensive Care Medicine (GBR) **5768**
Der Anaesthesist (DEU) **5769**
Analog Integrated Circuits and Signal Processing (USA) **2465**
Analyses of Social Issues and Public Policy (USA) **8087**
Analysis (GBR) **6904**
Analysis and Applications (SGP) **5469**
Analysis in Theory and Applications (NLD) **5470**
Analysis Mathematica (HUN) **5470**
The Analyst (Online) (GBR) *see* The Analyst. **2097**
Analytica Chimica Acta (NLD) **2097**
Analytical and Bioanalytical Chemistry (DEU) **2097**
Analytical Biochemistry (USA) **722**
Analytical Chemistry (USA) **2098**
Analytical Letters (USA) **2098**

DIRECTORY 2010 SWETSWISE ONLINE CONTENT 11267

Bulletin of Environmental Contamination and Toxicology (USA) **3494**
Bulletin of Experimental Biology and Medicine (USA) **663**
Bulletin of Indonesian Economic Studies (AUS) **1443**
Bulletin of Latin American Research (GBR) **7951**
Bulletin of Mathematical Biology (USA) **663**
Bulletin of Science, Technology & Society (USA) **7842**
Bulletin of Spanish Studies (GBR) **5267**
Bulletin of the History of Medicine (USA) **5589**
Bulletin of Volcanology (DEU) **2778**
Bundesgesundheitsblatt - Gesundheitsforschung - Gesundheitsschutz (DEU) **7510**
Burns (GBR) **6057**
Business and Politics (Online) (USA) **1070**
Business & Society (USA) **1070**
Business and Society Review (USA) **1070**
Business Communication Quarterly (USA) **1729**
Business Economics (USA) **1071**
Business Ethics (GBR) **1072**
Business History (GBR) **1072**
Business Horizons (USA) **1072**
Business Information Review (GBR) **1730**
Business Law Review (NLD) **4859**
Business Process Management Journal (GBR) **1730**
Business Strategy and the Environment (GBR) **3407**
Business Strategy Review (GBR) **1730**
Byzantine and Modern Greek Studies (GBR) **4208**
C I N: Computers, Informatics, Nursing (USA) **5829**
C M I G Extra: Cases (USA) **5829**
C N S & Neurological Disorders (NLD) **6129**
C N S Drugs (NZL) **6827**
C O P D (USA) **6212**
C P Online (USA) *see* Current Psychology (New York). **7350**
C R I N (NLD) **5268**
C S S E (NLD) **3053**
Calcified Tissue International (USA) **5884**
Calcolo (ITA) **5477**
Calculus of Variations and Partial Differential Equations (DEU) **5477**
Callaloo (USA) **5269**
CALPHAD (GBR) **2107**
Cambridge Archaeological Journal (GBR) **386**
Cambridge Journal of Economics (GBR) **1079**
Cambridge Journal of Education (GBR) **2970**
The Cambridge Law Journal (GBR) **4637**
Cambridge Opera Journal (GBR) **6553**
Cambridge Philosophical Society. Mathematical Proceedings (GBR) **5477**
The Cambridge Quarterly (GBR) **5269**
Cambridge Quarterly of Healthcare Ethics (GBR) **5591**
Cambridge Review of International Affairs (GBR) **7225**
Camden Fifth Series (GBR) **4209**
Camera Obscura (USA) **6491**
Campus Wide Information Systems (GBR) **2495**
The Canadian Geographer (USA) **4001**
Canadian Geotechnical Journal (CAN) **2703**
Canadian Historical Review (CAN) **4134**
Canadian Journal of Agricultural Economics (USA) **195**
Canadian Journal of Animal Science (CAN) **283**
Canadian Journal of Chemistry (CAN) **2052**
Canadian Journal of Civil Engineering (CAN) **3261**
Canadian Journal of Earth Sciences (CAN) **2703**
Canadian Journal of Economics (USA) **1080**
Canadian Journal of Fisheries and Aquatic Sciences (CAN) **3588**
Canadian Journal of Forest Research (CAN) **3685**
Canadian Journal of Linguistics (CAN) **5104**
Canadian Journal of Microbiology (CAN) **882**
Canadian Journal of Physics (CAN) **7007**
Canadian Journal of Physiology and Pharmacology (CAN) **920**
Canadian Journal of Plant Science (CAN) **783**
Canadian Journal of Political Science (GBR) **7113**
Canadian Journal of Soil Science (CAN) **223**
Canadian Journal of Zoology (CAN) **937**
Canadian Journal on Aging (GBR) **4042**
Canadian Mineralogist (CAN) **2727**
Cancer (USA) **6010**
Cancer and Metastasis Reviews (USA) **6011**
Cancer Biomarkers (NLD) **6011**
Cancer Biotherapy & Radiopharmaceuticals (USA) **6011**
Cancer Causes & Control (NLD) **6011**
Cancer Cell (USA) **6011**
Cancer Cell International (GBR) **6011**
Cancer Chemotherapy and Pharmacology (DEU) **6011**
Cancer Epidemiology (USA) **6012**
Cancer Gene Therapy (USA) **6012**
Cancer Genetics and Cytogenetics (USA) **6012**
Cancer Imaging (GBR) **6012**
Cancer Immunology, Immunotherapy (DEU) **6012**
Cancer Investigation (USA) **6013**
Cancer Letters (IRL) **6013**
Cancer Nursing (USA) **5954**
Cancer Radiotherapie (FRA) **6013**
Cancer Science (JPN) **6014**
Cancer Treatment Reviews (GBR) **6014**
Capitalism, Nature, Socialism (GBR) **7114**
Carbohydrate Polymers (GBR) **2120**
Carbohydrate Research (GBR) **2120**
Carbon (GBR) **2121**
Carcinogenesis (GBR) **6015**
Card Technology Today (GBR) **3090**
Cardiology (CHE) **5779**
Cardiology in Review (USA) **5780**
Cardiology in the Young (GBR) **5780**
Cardiovascular & Hematological Disorders - Drug Targets (NLD) **5780**
Cardiovascular and Interventional Radiology (USA) **6193**
Cardiovascular Diabetology (GBR) **5884**
Cardiovascular Drugs and Therapy (USA) **5781**
Cardiovascular Engineering (USA) **5781**
Cardiovascular Pathology (USA) **5781**
Cardiovascular Research (NLD) **5781**
Cardiovascular Revascularization Medicine (USA) **5781**
Cardiovascular Toxicology (USA) **5781**
Cardiovascular Ultrasound (GBR) **6193**
Career Development International (GBR) **6694**
Caries Research (CHE) **5837**
The Cartographic Journal (GBR) **4037**
The Case Manager (USA) **5592**
Cataloging & Classification Quarterly (USA) **5001**
Catalysis Communications (NLD) **2052**
Catalysis Letters (NLD) **2052**
Catalysis Reviews: Science and Engineering (USA) **2133**
Catalysis Surveys from Asia (NLD) **2133**
Catalysis Today (NLD) **3237**
CATENA (NLD) **2728**
Catheterization and Cardiovascular Interventions (USA) **5781**
The Catholic Historical Review (USA) **7789**
Celestial Mechanics and Dynamical Astronomy (NLD) **573**
Cell (USA) **828**
Cell & Chromosome (GBR) **828**
Cell and Tissue Banking (NLD) **828**
Cell and Tissue Research (DEU) **829**
Cell Biochemistry and Biophysics (USA) **829**
Cell Biochemistry & Function (GBR) **728**
Cell Biology and Toxicology (NLD) **3495**
Cell Biology International (GBR) **829**
Cell Calcium (GBR) **829**
Cell Communication & Adhesion (Online Edition) (USA) **664**
Cell Communication and Signaling (GBR) **665**
Cell Death & Differentiation (GBR) **829**
Cell Metabolism (USA) **829**
Cell Motility and the Cytoskeleton (USA) **829**
Cell Proliferation (GBR) **830**
Cell Research (GBR) **665**
Cell Stress & Chaperones (NLD) **5592**
Cells, Tissues, Organs (CHE) **5593**
Cellular and Molecular Life Sciences (CHE) **665**
Cellular & Molecular Neurobiology (USA) **6130**
Cellular Immunology (USA) **5755**
Cellular Microbiology Online (GBR) **830**
Cellular Oncology (NLD) **830**
Cellular Physiology and Biochemistry (CHE) **830**
Cellular Signalling (USA) **830**
Cellulose (NLD) **2121**
Cement and Concrete Composites (GBR) **990**
Cement and Concrete Research (GBR) **990**
Centaurus (Copenhagen) (DNK) **7844**
Center for Children's Books. Bulletin (USA) **2147**
Central Asian Survey (GBR) **7115**
Central Europe (GBR) **7953**
Central European Geology (HUN) **2728**
Central European History (GBR) **4209**
Central European Journal of Biology (POL) **665**
Central European Journal of Physics (POL) **7007**
Central European Neurosurgery (USA) **6130**
Central Nervous System Agents in Medicinal Chemistry (NLD) **6130**
Cephalalgia (GBR) **6130**
Ceramics International (GBR) **2039**
The Cerebellum (USA) **6130**
Cerebral Cortex (USA) **6130**
Cerebrospinal Fluid Research (GBR) **6130**
Cerebrovascular Diseases (CHE) **6130**
Challenge (Armonk) (USA) **1082**
Changing English (GBR) **2835**
Chaos (USA) **7008**
Chaos, Solitons & Fractals (GBR) **5478**
Chartered Institute of Building. Construction Information Quarterly (GBR) **1045**
Chaucer Review (USA) **5272**
ChemBioChem (DEU) **728**
Chemical and Petroleum Engineering (USA) **3238**
Chemical Biology & Drug Design (Online) (DNK) **728**
Chemical Communications (GBR) **2053**
Chemical Engineering and Processing (NLD) **3238**
Chemical Engineering and Technology (DEU) **3238**
Chemical Engineering Communications (GBR) **3238**
Chemical Engineering Journal (NLD) **3239**
Chemical Engineering Research & Design (GBR) **3239**
Chemical Engineering Science (GBR) **3239**
Chemical Geology (NLD) **2703**
Chemical Physics (NLD) **2133**
Chemical Physics Letters (NLD) **2133**
The Chemical Record (USA) **2054**
Chemical Research in Toxicology (USA) **3495**
Chemical Reviews (USA) **2054**
Chemical Senses (GBR) **920**
Chemical Society of Ethiopia. Bulletin (ETH) **2055**
Chemical Society Reviews (GBR) **2055**
Chemical Vapor Deposition (DEU) **2109**
Chemico-Biological Interactions (IRL) **3495**
Chemie der Erde / Geochemistry (DEU) **2728**
Chemie in Unserer Zeit (DEU) **2055**
Chemie-Ingenieur-Technik (DEU) **3240**
ChemInform (DEU) **2093**
Cheminformatics (NLD) **2107**
Chemistry: A European Journal (DEU) **2056**
Chemistry & Biodiversity (DEU) **2056**
Chemistry & Biology (GBR) **2056**
Chemistry and Ecology (CHE) **2056**
Chemistry and Physics of Lipids (IRL) **728**
Chemistry and Technology of Fuels and Oils (USA) **6765**
Chemistry of Heterocyclic Compounds (New York, 1965) (USA) **2121**
Chemistry of Materials (USA) **3240**
Chemistry of Natural Compounds (USA) **2121**
ChemKon - Chemie Konkret (DEU) **2057**
ChemMedChem (DEU) **6828**
Chemoecology (CHE) **2121**
Chemometrics and Intelligent Laboratory Systems (NLD) **2107**
Chemosphere (GBR) **3495**
Chemotherapy (CHE) **6828**
ChemPhysChem (DEU) **2133**
ChemSusChem (Online) (DEU) *see* ChemSusChem (Print). **2058**
Chicago Journal of Theoretical Computer Science (USA) **2409**
Child Abuse & Neglect (GBR) **2147**
Child Abuse Review (GBR) **8032**
Child and Adolescent Mental Health (Online) (GBR) *see* Child and Adolescent Mental Health. **7344**
Child and Adolescent Psychopharmacology News (USA) **6131**
Child and Adolescent Social Work Journal (USA) **8093**
Child & Family Behavior Therapy (USA) **7344**
Child & Family Social Work Online (GBR) **8032**
Child and Youth Care Forum (USA) **2147**
Child & Youth Services (USA) **8032**
Child: Care, Health and Development (GBR) **6089**
Child Care in Practice (GBR) **2147**
Child Development (USA) **2147**
Child Language Teaching and Therapy (GBR) **3037**
Child Maltreatment (USA) **2148**
Child Psychiatry and Human Development (USA) **6131**
Childhood (GBR) **2148**
Children & Society (GBR) **2148**
Children and Youth Services Review (GBR) **2148**
Children's Geographies (GBR) **7344**
Children's Health Care (USA) **8033**
Children's Literature (Baltimore) (USA) **5273**
Children's Literature Association Quarterly (USA) **5001**
Children's Literature in Education (USA) **2149**
Child's Nervous System (DEU) **6131**
China: An International Journal (SGP) **7954**
China & World Economy (GBR) **1082**
China Economic Review (Amsterdam) (NLD) **1447**
China Information (GBR) **546**
China Quarterly (GBR) **546**
China Report (IND) **7226**
China Review International (USA) **3823**
Chinese Annals of Mathematics. Series B (DEU) **5478**
Chinese Astronomy and Astrophysics (GBR) **573**
The Chinese Economy (USA) **1083**
Chinese Education and Society (USA) **2836**
The Chinese - German Journal of Clinical Oncology (DEU) **5594**
Chinese Journal of Agricultural Biotechnology (GBR) **101**
Chinese Journal of Chemistry (CHN) **2058**
Chinese Journal of Polymer Science (SGP) **2121**
Chinese Law and Government (USA) **4642**
Chinese Physics B (GBR) **7008**
Chinese Physics Letters (GBR) **7008**
Chinese Science Bulletin (CHN) **7845**
Chinese Sociology and Anthropology (USA) **8093**
Chinese Studies in History (USA) **4135**
Chirality (USA) **728**
Chiropractic and Osteopathy (GBR) **5803**
Der Chirurg (DEU) **6238**
Chirurgie de la Main (FRA) **6239**
Chloe (NLD) **5273**
Christian Bioethics (NLD) **5595**
Christian Higher Education (USA) **7632**
Chromatographia (DEU) **2099**
Chromosoma (DEU) **864**
Chromosome Research (NLD) **728**
Chronic Illness (GBR) **5595**
Chronic Respiratory Disease (GBR) **6212**
Chronobiology International (USA) **666**
Cinema Journal (USA) **6493**
Circuit World (GBR) **8418**
Circuits, Systems and Signal Processing (USA) **3297**
Circulation (Baltimore) (USA) **5782**
Circulation Research (USA) **5782**
Cities (GBR) **7489**
Citizenship Studies (GBR) **7116**
City (GBR) **4407**
City & Community (USA) **8033**
Civil Engineering and Environmental Systems (CHE) **3262**
Civil War History (USA) **4288**
Civil Wars (GBR) **7227**
Cladistics (GBR) **666**
Classical and Quantum Gravity (GBR) **7008**
Classical Antiquity (USA) **2232**
Classical Quarterly (GBR) **2232**
Classical Review (GBR) **2233**
Classical World (USA) **2233**
Clay Minerals (GBR) **2704**
CLEAN - Soil, Air, Water (Online Edition) (DEU) **8820**
Clean Technologies and Environmental Policy (DEU) **3411**
Climacteric (GBR) **8844**
Climate Dynamics (DEU) **6349**
Climate Policy (GBR) **2704**
Climatic Change (NLD) **6349**
Clin-Alert (USA) **6889**
Clinica Chimica Acta (NLD) **5595**
Clinical Anatomy (USA) **5596**
Clinical and Applied Immunology Reviews (USA) **5755**
Clinical and Experimental Allergy (GBR) **5756**
Clinical and Experimental Allergy Reviews (GBR) **5756**
Clinical and Experimental Dermatology (GBR) **5873**
Clinical and Experimental Hypertension (USA) **5782**
Clinical and Experimental Immunology (GBR) **5756**
Clinical and Experimental Medicine (ITA) **5596**
Clinical and Experimental Metastasis (NLD) **6015**
Clinical and Experimental Nephrology (JPN) **6266**
Clinical and Experimental Ophthalmology (AUS) **6040**
Clinical and Experimental Optometry (GBR) **6040**
Clinical and Experimental Pharmacology & Physiology (AUS) **921**
Clinical and Molecular Allergy (GBR) **5756**
Clinical Autonomic Research (USA) **5596**
Clinical Biochemistry (USA) **729**
Clinical Biomechanics (GBR) **5804**
Clinical Case Studies (USA) **6131**
Clinical Chemistry and Laboratory Medicine (DEU) **729**
Clinical Child and Family Psychology Review (USA) **7345**
Clinical Child Psychology & Psychiatry (GBR) **2149**
Clinical Chiropractic (GBR) **5804**
Clinical Cornerstone (USA) **4090**
Clinical Drug Investigation (NZL) **6828**
Clinical Dysmorphology (USA) **666**
Clinical Endocrinology (GBR) **5885**
Clinical Gastroenterology and Hepatology (USA) **5921**
Clinical Genetics (DNK) **864**
Clinical Gerontologist (USA) **4043**
Clinical Governance (GBR) **5596**
Clinical Hemorheology and Microcirculation (NLD) **5935**
Clinical Imaging (USA) **6193**
Clinical Immunology (USA) **5756**
Clinical Implant Dentistry and Related Research (GBR) **5838**
Clinical Intensive Care (GBR) **5944**
Clinical Journal of Pain (USA) **6131**
Clinical Journal of Sport Medicine (USA) **6229**
Clinical Linguistics & Phonetics (GBR) **6132**
Clinical Medicine (GBR) **5597**
Clinical Medicine & Research (USA) **5597**
Clinical Microbiology and Infection (GBR) **5597**
Clinical Microbiology Newsletter (USA) **883**
Clinical Neurology and Neurosurgery (NLD) **6132**
Clinical Neuropharmacology (USA) **6829**
Clinical Neurophysiology (IRL) **6132**
Clinical Neuroradiology (DEU) **6194**
Clinical Nuclear Medicine (USA) **6194**
Clinical Nurse Specialist (USA) **5955**
Clinical Nursing Research (USA) **5955**
Clinical Nutrition (NLD) **6656**
Clinical Obstetrics and Gynecology (USA) **5988**
Clinical Oncology (GBR) **6016**
Clinical Oral Implants Research (DNK) **5838**
Clinical Oral Investigations (DEU) **5838**
Clinical Orthopaedics and Related Research (USA) **6057**
Clinical Otolaryngology (GBR) **6078**
Clinical Pediatric Emergency Medicine (USA) **6090**
Clinical Pharmacokinetics (NZL) **6829**
Clinical Pharmacology and Therapeutics (USA) **6829**
Clinical Physiology and Functional Imaging (GBR) **5597**
Clinical Practice and Epidemiology in Mental Health (GBR) **7345**
Clinical Proteomics (USA) **729**
Clinical Psychologist (GBR) **7345**
The Clinical Psychologist (USA) **7345**
Clinical Psychology (USA) **7345**
Clinical Psychology & Psychotherapy (GBR) **7345**
Clinical Psychology Review (GBR) **7345**
Clinical Pulmonary Medicine (USA) **6213**
Clinical Radiology (GBR) **6194**
Clinical Rehabilitation (GBR) **6107**
Clinical Research and Regulatory Affairs (GBR) **6829**
Clinical Research in Cardiology (DEU) **5783**
Clinical Reviews in Allergy & Immunology (USA) **5756**
Clinical Reviews in Bone and Mineral Metabolism (USA) **6016**
Clinical Rheumatology (GBR) **6223**
Clinical Risk (GBR) **5597**
Clinical Science (GBR) **5597**
Clinical Social Work Journal (USA) **8034**
The Clinical Supervisor (USA) **8034**
The Clinical Teacher (GBR) **5597**
Clinical Techniques in Equine Practice (USA) **8795**
Clinical Therapeutics (USA) **6829**
Clinical Toxicology (USA) **6829**
Clinical Transplantation (DNK) **6240**
Clinical Trials (GBR) **5904**
Clinics in Colon & Rectal Surgery (USA) **6240**
Clinics in Dermatology (USA) **5873**

Online Service

Link to your serials resources and content with ulrichsweb.com

Online Service

European Journal of Sport Science (GBR) 8171
European Journal of Surgical Oncology (GBR) 6019
European Journal of Teacher Education (GBR) 2855
European Journal of the History of Economic Thought (GBR) 1541
European Journal of Trauma and Emergency Surgery (DEU) 6060
European Journal of Ultrasound (IRL) 6196
European Journal of Vascular and Endovascular Surgery (GBR) 5786
European Journal of Wildlife Research (DEU) 319
European Journal of Women's Studies (GBR) 8896
European Journal of Wood and Wood Industries (Online) (DEU) *see* European Journal of Wood and Wood Industries (Print). 3711
European Journal of Work and Organizational Psychology (GBR) 7356
European Journal on Criminal Policy and Research (NLD) 2651
European Joyce Studies (NLD) 5293
European Law Journal (GBR) 4925
The European Legacy (USA) 6918
European Management Journal (GBR) 1742
European Management Review (GBR) 1743
European Mathematical Society. Journal (DEU) 5487
European Neurology (CHE) 6140
European Neuropsychopharmacology (NLD) 6140
European Physical Education Review (GBR) 3061
European Physical Journal A. Hadrons and Nuclei (DEU) 7065
The European Physical Journal - Applied Physics (FRA) 7011
European Physical Journal B. Condensed Matter and Complex Systems (DEU) 7011
European Physical Journal C. Particles and Fields (DEU) 7011
European Physical Journal D. Atomic, Molecular, Optical and Plasma Physics (FRA) 7011
European Physical Journal Direct (DEU) 7011
European Physical Journal E. Soft Matter (FRA) 7011
European Physical Journal H (FRA) 7011
The European Physical Journal. Special Topics (Online) (DEU) *see* The European Physical Journal. Special Topics. 7012
European Planning Studies (GBR) 4410
European Political Science (GBR) 7134
European Polymer Journal (GBR) 2123
European Psychiatry (FRA) 6140
European Public Law (NLD) 4925
European Radiology (DEU) 6196
European Review (GBR) 7853
European Review of Agricultural Economics (GBR) 197
European Review of Contract Law (DEU) 4669
European Review of Economic History (GBR) 1541
European Review of History (GBR) 4219
European Review of Private Law (NLD) 4925
European Review of Social Psychology (Online Edition) (GBR) 7356
European Romantic Review (GBR) 5293
European Security (GBR) 7234
European Societies (GBR) 8101
European Society of Women in Theological Research. Journal (BEL) 7641
European Sociological Review (GBR) 8101
European Spine Journal (DEU) 6243
European Sport Management Quarterly (GBR) 8172
European Studies (NLD) 7234
European Surgery Online (AUT) 6243
European Surgical Research (CHE) 6243
European Taxation (NLD) 1922
European Transactions on Electrical Power (GBR) 3308
European Union Politics (GBR) 7234
European Urban and Regional Studies (GBR) 7963
European Urology (CHE) 6268
European Urology Supplements (NLD) 6268
Europhysics Letters (FRA) 7012
Europhysics News (FRA) 7012
Evaluation (GBR) 7963
Evaluation and Program Planning (GBR) 7963
Evaluation and Research in Education (GBR) 2855
Evaluation and the Health Professions (USA) 5612
Evaluation Review (USA) 7963
Event Management (USA) 8702
Evidence and Policy (GBR) 7964
Evidence - Based Cardiovascular Medicine (GBR) 5787
Evidence - Based Complementary and Alternative Medicine (GBR) 309
Evidence - Based Dentistry (GBR) 5844
Evidence - Based Obstetrics & Gynaecology (GBR) 5990
Evidence - Based Ophthalmology (USA) 6041
Evolution & Development Online (USA) 672
Evolution and Human Behavior (USA) 942
L' Evolution Psychiatrique (FRA) 6140
Evolutionary Anthropology (USA) 339
Evolutionary Computation (USA) 2418
Evolutionary Ecology (NLD) 3431
Exceptionality (USA) 3040
Exchange (NLD) 7642
Exercise and Sport Sciences Reviews (USA) 6229
Experimental Aging Research (USA) 7356
Experimental Agriculture (GBR) 109
Experimental & Applied Acarology (NLD) 942
Experimental and Clinical Endocrinology and Diabetes (DEU) 5892
Experimental and Molecular Pathology (USA) 5612
Experimental and Toxicologic Pathology (DEU) 5612
Experimental Astronomy (NLD) 574
Experimental Biology and Medicine (Maywood) (USA) 672
Experimental Brain Research (DEU) 6140
Experimental Cell Research (USA) 832
Experimental Dermatology Online (GBR) 5876
Experimental Diabesity Research (USA) 5758
Experimental Economics (USA) 1541
Experimental Eye Research (GBR) 6041
Experimental Gerontology (USA) 4044
Experimental Heat Transfer (USA) 7054
Experimental Hematology (USA) 5936
Experimental Lung Research (USA) 6214
Experimental Mechanics (USA) 3344
Experimental Neurology (USA) 6140
Experimental Parasitology (USA) 5813
Experimental Physiology (GBR) 922
Experimental Thermal and Fluid Science (USA) 3192
Experiments in Fluids (DEU) 3377
Expert Opinion on Biological Therapy (GBR) 5612
Expert Opinion on Drug Delivery (GBR) 6839
Expert Opinion on Drug Metabolism & Toxicology (GBR) 6839
Expert Opinion on Drug Safety (GBR) 6839
Expert Opinion on Emerging Drugs (GBR) 6839
Expert Opinion on Investigational Drugs (GBR) 6839
Expert Opinion on Pharmacotherapy (GBR) 6839
Expert Opinion on Therapeutic Patents (GBR) 6839
Expert Opinion On Therapeutic Targets (GBR) 6840
Expert Reviews in Molecular Medicine (GBR) 5945
Expert Systems (GBR) 2448
Expert Systems with Applications (GBR) 2448
Explorations in Economic History (USA) 1541
Explore: The Journal of Science & Healing (USA) 7854
Expositiones Mathematicae (DEU) 5487
Expository Times (GBR) 7642
Extremes (USA) 8369
Extremophiles (JPN) 764
Eye (London, 1880) (GBR) 6042
Eye and Contact Lens (USA) 6042
The F E B S Journal (Online) (GBR) 732
F E B S Letters (NLD) 732
F E M S Immunology and Medical Microbiology (GBR) 885
F E M S Microbiology Ecology (GBR) 885
F E M S Microbiology Letters (GBR) 885
F E M S Microbiology Reviews (GBR) 885
Fabula (DEU) 3617
Facial Plastic Surgery (USA) 6243
Facies (DEU) 2707
Facilities (GBR) 1007
Familial Cancer (NLD) 6019
Family & Consumer Sciences Research Journal (USA) 4357
Family Business Review (USA) 1960
Family Court Review (USA) 4909
The Family Journal (USA) 7357
Family Practice (GBR) 5613
Family Process (USA) 7357
Family Relations (USA) 2856
Faraday Discussions (Online) (GBR) *see* Faraday Discussions. 2135
Fatigue & Fracture of Engineering Materials and Structures (GBR) 3192
Feddes Repertorium (DEU) 787
Federal Sentencing Reporter (USA) 2652
Federation of European Microbiological Societies Yeast Research Online (GBR) *see* F E M S Yeast Research. 886
Feminism & Psychology (GBR) 7357
Feminist Criminology (USA) 2652
Feminist Economics (GBR) 1109
Feminist Legal Studies (NLD) 4673
Feminist Media Studies (GBR) 8896
Feminist Review (GBR) 8896
Feminist Theology (GBR) 8896
Feminist Theory (GBR) 8897
Ferroelectrics (CHE) 7012
Ferroelectrics Letters Section (USA) 3308
Fertility and Sterility (USA) 5990
Fetal and Maternal Medicine Review (GBR) 5990
Fetal and Pediatric Pathology (Online Edition) (GBR) 6092
Fetal Diagnosis and Therapy (CHE) 5990
Few-Body Systems (AUT) 7012
Fiber and Integrated Optics (USA) 7075
Fibre Chemistry (USA) 8451
Field Crops Research (NLD) 231
Field Methods (USA) 339
Film & History (USA) 6498
Film History (USA) 6499
Film Quarterly (USA) 6499
Film Studies (GBR) 6499
Filozofski Vestnik (SVN) 6920
Filtration Industry Analyst (GBR) 3367
Filtration + Separation (GBR) 3244
Finance and Stochastics (DEU) 1343
Finance Research Letters (USA) 1343
Financial Accountability & Management (GBR) 1924
Financial History Review (GBR) 1344
Financial Markets and Portfolio Management (USA) 1623
Financial Markets, Institutions and Instruments (USA) 1344
The Financial Review (Statesboro) (USA) 1345
Financial Services Review (GBR) 1345
Finite Elements in Analysis and Design (NLD) 3291
Finite Fields and Their Applications (USA) 5488
Fire and Materials (GBR) 3344
Fire Safety Journal (GBR) 3578
Fire Technology (USA) 3578
First Break Online (NLD) 2780
First Language (GBR) 5119
Fiscal Studies (GBR) 1925
Fish and Fisheries (GBR) 943
Fish and Shellfish Immunology (GBR) 943
Fish Physiology & Biochemistry (NLD) 943
Fisheries Management & Ecology Online (GBR) 3592
Fisheries Oceanography Online (GBR) 3592
Fisheries Research (NLD) 3592
Fisheries Science (AUS) 3593
Fitoterapia (ITA) 788
Fixed Point Theory and Applications (USA) 5488
Flavour and Fragrance Journal (GBR) 2123
Flexible Services and Manufacturing Journal (USA) 3344
Flora (DEU) 788
Flow Measurement and Instrumentation (GBR) 4486
Flow, Turbulence and Combustion (NLD) 7855
Fluctuation and Noise Letters (SGP) 8372
Fluid Dynamics (RUS) 7058
Fluid Dynamics Research (NLD) 3361
Fluid Phase Equilibria (NLD) 2135
Focus on Catalysts (USA) 2094
Focus on Pigments (USA) 6722
Focus on Powder Coatings (USA) 6722
Focus on Surfactants (USA) 2094
Folia Geobotanica (NLD) 790
Folia Linguistica (DEU) 5119
Folia Phoniatrica et Logopaedica (CHE) 6080
Folia Primatologica (CHE) 944
Folklore (GBR) 3617
Food Additives & Contaminants: Part A - Chemistry, Analysis, Control, Exposure & Risk Assessment (GBR) 6842
Food and Agricultural Immunology (GBR) 673
Food and Bioproducts Processing (GBR) 764
Food and Chemical Toxicology (GBR) 3497
Food and Foodways (USA) 6659
Food Biophysics (USA) 753
Food Biotechnology (USA) 764
Food Chemistry (GBR) 2061
Food Control (GBR) 3638
Food Hydrocolloids (NLD) 3639
Food Microbiology (GBR) 886
Food Policy (GBR) 198
Food Quality and Preference (GBR) 3641
Food Research International (GBR) 3641
Food Reviews International (USA) 3641
Food Science & Technology Bulletin (GBR) 3642
Food Science and Technology International (USA) 3642
Foodborne Pathogens and Disease (USA) 5814
The Foot (GBR) 6060
Foot and Ankle Surgery (GBR) 6244
Foreign Policy Analysis (USA) 7235
Foreign Policy Bulletin (GBR) 7235
Forensic Science International (IRL) 5913
Forensic Science, Medicine, and Pathology (USA) 5913
Forensic Toxicology (JPN) 5913
Foresight (Cambridge) (GBR) 8422
Forest Ecology and Management (NLD) 3688
Forest Pathology Online (DEU) 3689
Forest Policy and Economics (NLD) 3689
Forestry (GBR) 3690
Formal Aspects of Computing (GBR) 2418
Formal Methods in System Design (USA) 2520
Foro Hispanico (NLD) 5297
Forschende Komplementaermedizin (CHE) 309
Forschung (DEU) 7855
Forschung im Ingenieurwesen (DEU) 3192
Fortschritte der Neurologie, Psychiatrie (DEU) 6141
Fortschritte der Physik (DEU) 7013
Forum der Psychoanalyse (DEU) 7357
Forum for Modern Language Studies (GBR) 5120
Forum: for Promoting 3-19 Comprehensive Education (GBR) 3023
Forum Mathematicum (DEU) 5488
Foundations of Chemistry (NLD) 2062
Foundations of Computational Mathematics (USA) 5552
Foundations of Physics (USA) 7013
Foundations of Science (NLD) 7856
Fourth Genre (USA) 5297
Fractals (SGP) 5552
Framework (USA) 6501
Franklin Institute. Journal (GBR) 7013
Free Radical Biology & Medicine (USA) 673
Free Radical Research (CHE) 732
French Colonial History (USA) 4221
French Cultural Studies (GBR) 4221
French Forum (USA) 5217
French Historical Studies (USA) 4222
French History (GBR) 4222
French Literature Series (NLD) 5407
French Politics (GBR) 7137
French Studies (GBR) 5298
Freshwater Biology Online (GBR) 674
Frontiers (Lincoln) (USA) 8897
Frontiers in Drug Design and Discovery (NLD) 6843
Frontiers in Medicinal Chemistry (NLD) 5616
Frontiers in Neuroendocrinology (USA) 5893
Frontiers in Zoology (GBR) 944
Fruehmittelalterliche Studien (DEU) 4222
Fruits (FRA) 3730
Fuel (GBR) 6769
Fuel and Energy Abstracts (GBR) 6800
Fuel Cells (DEU) 3135
Fuel Cells Bulletin (GBR) 3135
Fuel Processing Technology (NLD) 6769
Fullerenes, Nanotubes, and Carbon Nanostructures (USA) 2135
Functional Analysis and Its Applications (USA) 5488
Functional & Integrative Genomics (DEU) 867
Functional Ecology (GBR) 2612
Functional Plant Biology (AUS) 790
Functions of Language (NLD) 5121
Fundamenta Informaticae (NLD) 5552
Fundamental and Applied Limnology (DEU) 674
Fundamental and Clinical Pharmacology (FRA) 6843
Fungal Biology Reviews (GBR) 790
Fungal Genetics and Biology (USA) 790
Fusion Engineering and Design (CHE) 3378
Fuss & Sprunggelenk (DEU) 6060
Future Generation Computer Systems (NLD) 2520
The Future of Children (USA) 2153
Futures (GBR) 1487
Fuzzy Optimization and Decision Making (USA) 2448
Fuzzy Sets and Systems (NLD) 5489
G L Q (USA) 4373
G P S Solutions (DEU) 4007
Gait & Posture (NLD) 5617
Games and Culture (USA) 8174
Games and Economic Behavior (USA) 7358
Gaming Law Review & Economics (USA) 4679
Gastric Cancer (JPN) 6020
Gastroenterologie up2date (DEU) 5924
Gastroenterology (USA) 5924
Gastroenterology Nursing (USA) 5925
Gastrointestinal Endoscopy (USA) 5925
Gastronomica (USA) 7966
Geburtshilfe und Frauenheilkunde (DEU) 5991
Gefaesschirurgie (DEU) 6244
Gender and Development (GBR) 8897
Gender and Education (GBR) 2859
Gender and History (GBR) 4140
Gender and Language (GBR) 5121
Gender & Society (USA) 8104
Gender in Management (GBR) 1747
Gender Issues (USA) 8898
Gender Medicine (USA) 5618
Gender, Place and Culture (GBR) 8898
Gender, Work and Organization (GBR) 1747
Gene - C O M B I S (NLD) *see* Gene. 764
Gene Expression Patterns (NLD) 867
Gene Therapy (Basingstoke) (GBR) 5618
Gene Therapy and Regulation (SGP) 867
General and Comparative Endocrinology (USA) 5893
General Hospital Psychiatry (USA) 6143
General Relativity and Gravitation (USA) 7014
Genes and Immunity (GBR) 868
Genes, Brain and Behavior (DNK) 868
Genes, Chromosomes & Cancer (USA) 868
Genes to Cells (GBR) 868
Genesis: The Journal of Genetics and Development (USA) 868
Genetic Epidemiology (USA) 869
Genetic Programming and Evolvable Machines (USA) 2448
Genetic Resources and Crop Evolution (NLD) 869
Genetic Testing and Molecular Biomarkers (Online) (USA) *see* Genetic Testing and Molecular Biomarkers. 869
Genetic Vaccines and Therapy (GBR) 869
Genetica (NLD) 869
Genetics In Medicine (USA) 870
Genetics Research (GBR) 870
Genetics Selection Evolution (GBR) 870
Geneva Papers on Risk and Insurance - Issues and Practice (GBR) 4503
The Geneva Risk and Insurance Review (USA) 4503
Genome (CAN) 870
Genome Biology (Online) (GBR) 675
Genomics (USA) 870
Gentse Bijdragen tot de Interieurgeschiedenis (BEL) 491
Geo-Marine Letters (DEU) 2735
Geoarchaeology (USA) 395
Geobiology (GBR) 2735
Geobios (FRA) 6725
Geochemical Transactions (GBR) 2708
Geochemistry: Exploration, Environment, Analysis (GBR) 2735
Geochemistry International (RUS) 2708
Geochimica et Cosmochimica Acta (GBR) 2735
Geoderma (NLD) 232
Geodinamica Acta (FRA) 2736
Geofluids Online (GBR) 2736
Geoforum (GBR) 4008
Geografiska Annaler. Series A. Physical Geography (GBR) 4009
Geografiska Annaler. Series B. Human Geography (GBR) 340
Geographical Analysis (USA) 4010
The Geographical Journal (GBR) 4010
Geographical Research (AUS) 4011
Geographie, Economie, Societe (FRA) 4011
Geoinformatica (USA) 2722
GeoJournal (NLD) 4011
Geological Journal (GBR) 2738
Geological Magazine (GBR) 2738
Geological Society. Journal (GBR) 2738
Geologists' Association. Proceedings (GBR) 2742
Geology of Ore Deposits (RUS) 6463
Geology Today Online (GBR) 2742
Geomagnetism and Aeronomy (RUS) 2781
Geometriae Dedicata (NLD) 5490
Geometric and Functional Analysis (CHE) 5490

Online Service

Link to your serials resources and content with ulrichsweb.com

DIRECTORY 2010 SWETSWISE ONLINE CONTENT 11273

Inflammation & Allergy - Drug Targets (NLD) 5761
Inflammation Research (CHE) 6848
Inflammatory Bowel Diseases (USA) 5927
Inflammopharmacology (CHE) 6848
Info (Bingley) (GBR) 2325
Informatica (LTU) 2461
Informatics for Health and Social Care (GBR) 5831
Informatics In Primary Care (GBR) 5831
Informatik-Spektrum (DEU) 3291
Information and Communications Technology Law (GBR) 2325
Information and Computation (USA) 2422
Information & Management (NLD) 2521
Information and Organization (GBR) 1290
Information and Software Technology (NLD) 2591
Information, Communication and Society (GBR) 2545
Information Development (GBR) 5016
Information Economics and Policy (NLD) 2325
Information Fusion (NLD) 2467
L' Information Grammaticale (BEL) 5127
Information - Knowledge - Systems Management (NLD) 2545
Information Management & Computer Security (GBR) 1752
Information Polity (NLD) 5061
Information Processing & Management (GBR) 5016
Information Processing Letters (NLD) 2537
Information Retrieval (USA) 2545
Information Sciences (USA) 2545
Information Security Technical Report (GBR) 2514
Information Services & Use (NLD) 2545
The Information Society (USA) 2545
Information Systems (GBR) 2521
Information Systems and e-Business Management (DEU) 2558
Information Systems Frontiers (USA) 2545
Information Systems Journal Online (GBR) 2521
Information Systems Research (USA) 2545
Information Technologies and International Development (USA) 2545
Information Technology & Management (NLD) 1851
Information Technology and People (GBR) 5062
Information Technology for Development (USA) 1598
Information Visualization (GBR) 2450
Informationen aus Orthodontie und Kieferorthopaedie (DEU) 5848
Infosecurity (GBR) 2514
Infrared Physics & Technology (NLD) 7076
Inhalation Toxicology (USA) 3498
Injury (GBR) 6061
Innate Immunity (GBR) 5894
Innovation (Abingdon) (GBR) 7972
Innovation Policy and the Economy (USA) 1124
Innovations in Education and Teaching International (Online) (GBR) 3064
Innovations in Systems and Software Engineering (GBR) 2591
Innovative Food Science and Emerging Technologies (NLD) 3647
Innovative Higher Education (USA) 2987
Inorganic Chemistry (USA) 2116
Inorganic Chemistry Communications (NLD) 2116
Inorganic Materials (RUS) 2116
Inorganic Reaction Mechanisms (USA) 2135
Inorganica Chimica Acta (CHE) 2116
Inquiry (NOR) 6925
Insect Biochemistry and Molecular Biology (GBR) 849
Insect Molecular Biology (GBR) 849
Insect Science (GBR) 849
Insectes Sociaux (CHE) 850
Insight (Northampton) (GBR) 3345
Insight (Saint Louis) (USA) 6043
Institut de Linguistique de Louvain. Cahiers (BEL) 5127
Institut des Hautes Etudes Scientifiques, Paris. Publications Mathematiques (DEU) 5493
Institut Dominicain d'Etudes Orientales du Caire. Melanges (BEL) 4321
l' Institut Henri Poincare. Annales (B). Probabilites et Statistiques (USA) 5493
l' Institut Henri Poincare. Annales (C). Analyse Non Lineaire (FRA) 5493
Institute of Materials, Minerals and Mining. Transactions. Section A: Mining Technology (GBR) 6465
Institute of Materials, Minerals and Mining. Transactions. Section B: Applied Earth Science (GBR) 6465
Institute of Materials, Minerals and Mining. Transactions. Section C: Mineral Processing & Extractive Metallurgy (GBR) 6465
Institute of Mathematics of Jussieu. Journal (GBR) 5494
Institute of Measurement and Control. Transactions (GBR) 4487
Institute of Metal Finishing. Transactions (GBR) 6316
Institute of Statistical Mathematics. Annals (NLD) 5494
Institution of Mechanical Engineers. Proceedings. Part A: Journal of Power and Energy (GBR) 3380
Institution of Mechanical Engineers. Proceedings. Part B: Journal of Engineering Manufacture (GBR) 3380
Institution of Mechanical Engineers. Proceedings. Part C: Journal of Mechanical Engineering Science (GBR) 3380
Institution of Mechanical Engineers. Proceedings. Part D: Journal of Automobile Engineering (GBR) 8585
Institution of Mechanical Engineers. Proceedings. Part E: Journal of Process Mechanical Engineering (GBR) 3380
Institution of Mechanical Engineers. Proceedings. Part F: Journal of Rail and Rapid Transit (GBR) 8619
Institution of Mechanical Engineers. Proceedings. Part G: Journal of Aerospace Engineering (GBR) 60
Institution of Mechanical Engineers. Proceedings. Part H: Journal of Engineering in Medicine (GBR) 749
Institution of Mechanical Engineers. Proceedings. Part I: Journal of Systems and Control Engineering (GBR) 3380
Institution of Mechanical Engineers. Proceedings. Part J: Journal of Engineering Tribology (GBR) 3381
Institution of Mechanical Engineers. Proceedings. Part K: Journal of Multi-Body Dynamics (GBR) 3381
Institution of Mechanical Engineers. Proceedings. Part L: Journal of Materials: Design and Applications (GBR) 3381
Institution of Mechanical Engineers. Proceedings. Part M: Journal of Engineering for the Maritime Environment (GBR) 8646
Institution of Mechanical Engineers. Proceedings. Part N: Journal of Nanoengineering and Nanosystems (GBR) 7016
Instructional Science (NLD) 3065
Instrumentation Science & Technology (USA) 2100
Instruments and Experimental Techniques (RUS) 4488
Insurance: Mathematics and Economics (NLD) 4508
Integral Equations and Operator Theory (CHE) 5494
Integral Transforms and Special Functions (GBR) 5494
Integrated Computer-Aided Engineering (NLD) 3291
Integrated Ferroelectrics (CHE) 3319
Integration (NLD) 3319
Integrative & Comparative Biology (GBR) 947
Integrative Cancer Therapies (USA) 6022
Integrative Psychological & Behavioral Science (USA) 6146
Intelligence (Kidlington) (GBR) 7363
Intelligence and National Security (GBR) 7242
Intelligent Service Robotics (DEU) 2585
Intelligent Systems in Accounting, Finance & Management (GBR) 1418
Intensiv (DEU) 5636
Intensive and Critical Care Nursing (GBR) 5961
Intensive Care Medicine (DEU) 5636
Intensivmedizin und Notfallmedizin (DEU) 5636
Intensivmedizin up2date (DEU) 5636
Inter-Asia Cultural Studies (GBR) 3540
Interacting with Computers (NLD) 2423
Interaction Studies (NLD) 5128
Interactive (GBR) 2949
Interactive Cardiovascular and Thoracic Surgery (CHE) 6246
Interactive Learning Environments (NLD) 2949
Interchange (NLD) 2867
Intercultural Education (GBR) 8108
Intercultural Pragmatics (DEU) 5128
Interdisciplinary Science Reviews (GBR) 7867
Intereconomics (DEU) 1570
Interest Group in Pure and Applied Logics. Logic Journal (GBR) 6925
Interfaces (Hanover) (USA) 1754
Interlending & Document Supply (GBR) 5018
Intermetallics (GBR) 6316
Internal Medicine Journal (Online) (AUS) 5946
International Advances in Economic Research (USA) 1126
International Affairs (London) (GBR) 7243
International and Comparative Corporate Law Journal (GBR) 4871
International and Comparative Law Quarterly (GBR) 4929
International Anesthesiology Clinics (USA) 5771
International Applied Mechanics (USA) 3346
International Archives of Allergy and Immunology (CHE) 5761
International Archives of Occupational and Environmental Health (DEU) 6679
International Association for Official Statistics. Statistical Journal (NLD) 8379
International Association of Physicians in AIDS Care. Journal (USA) 5818
International Astronomical Union. Proceedings (GBR) 576
International Biodeterioration and Biodegradation (GBR) 765
International Business Review (GBR) 1126
International Clinical Psychopharmacology (USA) 7363
International Commission on Radiological Protection. Annals (GBR) 6198
International Communications in Heat and Mass Transfer (GBR) 3381
International Corporate Rescue (GBR) 4871
International Criminal Law Review (NLD) 4891
International Dairy Journal (GBR) 265
International Economic Journal (KOR) 1493
International Economic Review (USA) 1126
International Economics and Economic Policy (DEU) 1570
International Emergency Nursing (GBR) 5961
International Endodontic Journal Online (GBR) 5848
The International Entrepreneurship and Management Journal (USA) 1754
International Environmental Agreements: Politics, Law and Economics (NLD) 3441
International Feminist Journal of Politics (GBR) 7143
International Finance (GBR) 1356
International Food and Agribusiness Management Review (GBR) 200
International Forestry Review (GBR) 3693
International Forum of Psychoanalysis (NOR) 7363
International Gambling Studies (GBR) 7363
International Game Theory Review (SGP) 8426
International Immunology (GBR) 5761
International Immunopharmacology (GBR) 6849
International Information and Library Review (GBR) 5018
International Insolvency Review (GBR) 1356
International Interactions (USA) 7243
International Journal for Academic Development (GBR) 2868
International Journal for Computational Methods in Engineering Science & Mechanics (USA) 5494
International Journal for Educational and Vocational Guidance (NLD) 2942
International Journal for Equity in Health (GBR) 7526
International Journal for Numerical and Analytical Methods in Geomechanics (GBR) 3272
International Journal for Numerical Methods in Engineering (GBR) 3200
International Journal for Numerical Methods in Fluids (GBR) 3362
International Journal for Parasitology (GBR) 5818
International Journal for Philosophy of Religion (NLD) 7650
International Journal for Quality in Health Care (GBR) 5637
International Journal for the Advancement of Counselling (NLD) 2868
The International Journal for the Psychology of Religion (USA) 7650
International Journal for the Semiotics of Law (NLD) 4694
International Journal for the Study of the Christian Church (GBR) 7650
The International Journal of Accounting (GBR) 1292
International Journal of Accounting Information Systems (GBR) 1292
International Journal of Adaptive Control and Signal Processing (GBR) 3320
International Journal of Adhesion and Adhesives (GBR) 7093
International Journal of Advanced Manufacturing Technology (GBR) 3381
International Journal of Aeroacoustics (GBR) 7088
International Journal of Agricultural Sustainability (GBR) 201
International Journal of Algebra and Computation (SGP) 5495
International Journal of Andrology (GBR) 6269
International Journal of Antimicrobial Agents (NLD) 887
International Journal of Applied Ceramic Technology (USA) 3246
International Journal of Applied Earth Observation and Geoinformation (NLD) 4016
The International Journal of Applied Electromagnetics and Mechanics (NLD) 3320
International Journal of Applied Linguistics (GBR) 5129
The International Journal of Applied Psychoanalytic Studies (GBR) 7364
International Journal of Approximate Reasoning (USA) 2450
The International Journal of Architectural Computing (GBR) 462
International Journal of Art & Design Education (GBR) 3065
International Journal of Art Therapy (GBR) 6110
International Journal of Artificial Intelligence in Education (NLD) 2450
International Journal of Asian Studies (GBR) 551
International Journal of Astrobiology (GBR) 678
International Journal of Audiology (NOR) 6081
International Journal of Auditing (GBR) 1292
International Journal of Automotive Technology and Management (GBR) 8586
The International Journal of Aviation Psychology (USA) 8546
International Journal of Bank Marketing (GBR) 1356
International Journal of Behavioral Development (GBR) 7364
International Journal of Behavioral Medicine (USA) 7364
The International Journal of Behavioral Nutrition and Physical Activity (GBR) 7364
International Journal of Bifurcation and Chaos in Applied Sciences and Engineering (SGP) 3200
International Journal of Bilingual Education and Bilingualism (GBR) 2868
International Journal of Bilingualism (GBR) 5129
The International Journal of Biochemistry & Cell Biology (GBR) 734
International Journal of Bioinformatics Research and Applications (GBR) 826
International Journal of Biological Macromolecules (NLD) 734
International Journal of Biomedical Imaging (USA) 5637
International Journal of Biometeorology (DEU) 6357
International Journal of Business Information Systems (GBR) 1755
International Journal of Cancer (USA) 6022
International Journal of Cardiology (IRL) 5790
International Journal of Cardiovascular Imaging (NLD) 5790
The International Journal of Cast Metals Research (GBR) 6316
International Journal of Chemical Kinetics (USA) 2136
The International Journal of Children's Rights (NLD) 7210
International Journal of Children's Spirituality (GBR) 7364
International Journal of Circuit Theory and Applications (GBR) 3320
International Journal of Climatology (GBR) 6357
International Journal of Clinical and Experimental Hypnosis (GBR) 5943
The International Journal of Clinical Leadership (GBR) 5638
International Journal of Clinical Oncology (Online) (JPN) 6023
International Journal of Clinical Practice (GBR) 5638
International Journal of Clothing Science and Technology (GBR) 2247
International Journal of Coal Geology (NLD) 2748
International Journal of Coal Preparation and Utilization (USA) 6466
International Journal of Colorectal Disease (DEU) 6246
International Journal of Communication Systems (GBR) 3320
International Journal of Comparative Criminology (CAN) 2655
International Journal of Comparative Sociology (NLD) 8108
International Journal of Computational Fluid Dynamics (CHE) 7059
International Journal of Computational Geometry and Applications (SGP) 5552
International Journal of Computational Intelligence and Applications (GBR) 2451
International Journal of Computational Methods (SGP) 5495
International Journal of Computational Science and Engineering (GBR) 2472
International Journal of Computer Applications in Technology (GBR) 2592
International Journal of Computer Integrated Manufacturing (GBR) 3292
International Journal of Computer Mathematics (CHE) 5552
International Journal of Computer Processing of Oriental Languages (SGP) 5202
International Journal of Computer-Supported Collaborative Learning (USA) 2949
International Journal of Computer Vision (USA) 2451
International Journal of Computers for Mathematical Learning (NLD) 5553
International Journal of Constitutional Law (GBR) 4849
International Journal of Consumer Studies (GBR) 2638
International Journal of Contemporary Hospitality Management (GBR) 4391
International Journal of Control (GBR) 3200
International Journal of Cooperative Information Systems (SGP) 2546
International Journal of Corpus Linguistics (NLD) 5129
International Journal of Cosmetic Science (GBR) 594
International Journal of Crashworthiness (GBR) 8499
International Journal of Critical Infrastructures (GBR) 3139
International Journal of Cross Cultural Management (GBR) 1867
The International Journal of Cultural Policy (GBR) 7974
International Journal of Cultural Property (GBR) 497
International Journal of Cultural Studies (GBR) 8109
International Journal of Dairy Technology Online (GBR) 1127
International Journal of Damage Mechanics (GBR) 3346
International Journal of Dental Hygiene (DNK) 5848
International Journal of Dermatology (GBR) 5877
International Journal of Developmental Neuroscience (GBR) 6146
International Journal of Disability, Development and Education (GBR) 3041
International Journal of Disaster Medicine (GBR) 5638
International Journal of Distributed Sensor Networks (USA) 2499
International Journal of Drug Policy (NLD) 2695
International Journal of Early Years Education (GBR) 2869
International Journal of Earth Sciences (DEU) 2748
International Journal of Eating Disorders (USA) 6660
International Journal of Economic Theory (GBR) 1543
International Journal of Education Through Art (GBR) 2869
International Journal of Educational Advancement (Online) (GBR) 2869
International Journal of Educational Development (GBR) 2869

Online Service

International Journal of Educational Management (GBR) 1756
International Journal of Educational Research (GBR) 2869
International Journal of Electrical Engineering Education (GBR) 3320
International Journal of Electrical Power & Energy Systems (GBR) 3321
International Journal of Electronic Business (GBR) 1418
International Journal of Electronic Commerce (USA) 1418
International Journal of Electronic Healthcare (GBR) 4102
International Journal of Electronics (GBR) 3105
International Journal of Emerging Markets (GBR) 1571
International Journal of Energy Research (GBR) 3139
International Journal of Energy Technology and Policy (CHE) 3139
International Journal of Engine Research (GBR) 3382
International Journal of Engineering Science (GBR) 3201
International Journal of Entrepreneurial Behaviour & Research (GBR) 1962
International Journal of Entrepreneurship and Innovation (GBR) 1128
International Journal of Entrepreneurship and Small Business (GBR) 1757
International Journal of Environment and Sustainable Development (GBR) 3441
International Journal of Environmental Analytical Chemistry (GBR) 2101
International Journal of Environmental Health Research (GBR) 3442
International Journal of Epidemiology (GBR) 5638
The International Journal of Essential Oil Therapeutics (GBR) 310
International Journal of Evidence & Proof (GBR) 4891
International Journal of Evidence-Based Healthcare (AUS) 5638
International Journal of Exergy (GBR) 3201
International Journal of Experimental Pathology (GBR) 5638
International Journal of Fatigue (GBR) 3346
International Journal of Finance & Economics (GBR) 1357
International Journal of Food Microbiology (NLD) 887
International Journal of Food Properties (USA) 679
International Journal of Food Science & Technology Online (GBR) 3648
International Journal of Food Sciences and Nutrition (GBR) 6660
International Journal of Forecasting (NLD) 1493
International Journal of Foundations of Computer Science (SGP) 2425
International Journal of Fracture (NLD) 3347
International Journal of Franchising Law (GBR) 4871
International Journal of Francophone Studies (GBR) 7974
International Journal of Fruit Science (USA) 237
International Journal of Game Theory (DEU) 5496
International Journal of General Systems (CHE) 2522
International Journal of Geographical Information Science (GBR) 4037
International Journal of Geomechanics (USA) 2748
International Journal of Geometric Methods in Modern Physics (SGP) 7016
International Journal of Geriatric Psychiatry (GBR) 4048
International Journal of Global Energy Issues (GBR) 3139
International Journal of Green Energy (USA) 3139
International Journal of Group Psychotherapy (USA) 7365
International Journal of Gynecological Cancer (USA) 5993
International Journal of Gynecological Pathology (USA) 5993
International Journal of Gynecology & Obstetrics (IRL) 5994
International Journal of Health Care Finance and Economics (USA) 7526
International Journal of Health Care Quality Assurance (GBR) 5639
International Journal of Health Geographics (GBR) 7526
International Journal of Health Planning and Management (GBR) 8047
International Journal of Healthcare Technology and Management (GBR) 5831
International Journal of Heat and Fluid Flow (USA) 7054
International Journal of Heat and Mass Transfer (GBR) 3382
International Journal of Hematology (JPN) 5938
International Journal of Heritage Studies (GBR) 4147
International Journal of High Performance Computing and Networking (GBR) 2499
International Journal of High Performance Computing Applications (USA) 2592
International Journal of High Speed Computing (SGP) 2507
International Journal of High Speed Electronics and Systems (SGP) 3105
International Journal of Historical Archaeology (USA) 398
International Journal of Hospitality and Tourism Administration (USA) 4391
International Journal of Hospitality Management (GBR) 4391
International Journal of Human-Computer Interaction (USA) 8151
International Journal of Human-Computer Studies (GBR) 2527
International Journal of Human Resource Management (GBR) 1867
International Journal of Human Resources Development and Management (GBR) 1867
The International Journal of Human Rights (GBR) 7210
International Journal of Humanoid Robotics (SGP) 2585
International Journal of Hybrid Intelligent Systems (NLD) 2451
International Journal of Hydrogen Energy (GBR) 3139
International Journal of Hygiene and Environmental Health (DEU) 7526
International Journal of Hyperthermia (GBR) 6023
International Journal of Iberian Studies (GBR) 4232
International Journal of Image and Graphics (SGP) 2487
International Journal of Imaging Systems and Technology (USA) 7017
International Journal of Immunogenetics (GBR) 873
International Journal of Impact Engineering (GBR) 3201
International Journal of Impotence Research (GBR) 6269
International Journal of Inclusive Education (GBR) 2870
International Journal of Industrial Ergonomics (NLD) 3201
International Journal of Industrial Organization (NLD) 1757
International Journal of Infectious Diseases (GBR) 5818
International Journal of Information Acquisition (SGP) 2426
International Journal of Information Management (GBR) 2547
International Journal of Information Security (DEU) 2514
International Journal of Information Systems and Change Management (GBR) 1758
International Journal of Information Technology and Decision Making (SGP) 2547
International Journal of Injury Control and Safety Promotion (GBR) 2638
International Journal of Innovation and Learning (GBR) 1758
International Journal of Innovation and Technology Management (SGP) 3201
International Journal of Innovation Management (GBR) 1758
International Journal of Integrated Supply Management (GBR) 1821
International Journal of Intelligence and Counterintelligence (USA) 7243
International Journal of Intelligent Systems (USA) 2451
International Journal of Intelligent Systems Technologies and Applications (GBR) 2451
International Journal of Intercultural Relations (GBR) 8109
International Journal of Internet and Enterprise Management (GBR) 1758
International Journal of Japanese Sociology (AUS) 8109
International Journal of Knowledge-Based and Intelligent Engineering Systems (NLD) 2451
International Journal of Laboratory Hematology (Online) (GBR) 5938
International Journal of Language and Communication Disorders (GBR) 6081
International Journal of Law and Information Technology (GBR) 4695
International Journal of Law and Management (GBR) 1689
International Journal of Law and Psychiatry (GBR) 4695
International Journal of Law Crime and Justice (GBR) 4695
International Journal of Law in Context (GBR) 4695
International Journal of Law, Policy and the Family (GBR) 4911
International Journal of Leadership in Education (GBR) 2870
International Journal of Learning Technology (GBR) 8427
International Journal of Lexicography (GBR) 5129
International Journal of Life Cycle Assessment (DEU) 3443
International Journal of Lifelong Education (GBR) 2942
International Journal of Logistics (GBR) 1128
International Journal of Lower Extremity Wounds (USA) 5639
International Journal of Machine Tools and Manufacture (GBR) 3369
International Journal of Management Concepts and Philosophy (GBR) 1759
International Journal of Management Reviews (GBR) 1759
International Journal of Manpower (GBR) 1689
The International Journal of Marine and Coastal Law (NLD) 4969
International Journal of Mass Customisation (GBR) 1889
International Journal of Mass Spectrometry (NLD) 7077
International Journal of Mathematical Education in Science and Technology (GBR) 5496
International Journal of Mathematics (SGP) 5497
International Journal of Mathematics and Mathematical Sciences (USA) 5497
International Journal of Mechanical Engineering Education (GBR) 3202
International Journal of Mechanical Sciences (GBR) 3347
International Journal of Mechanics and Materials in Design (NLD) 3347
International Journal of Media and Cultural Politics (GBR) 2327
International Journal of Medical Informatics (IRL) 5831
International Journal of Medical Microbiology (DEU) 5818
International Journal of Mental Health (USA) 7365
International Journal of Mental Health Nursing (AUS) 6146
International Journal of Methods in Psychiatric Research (GBR) 6147
International Journal of Middle East Studies (GBR) 552
International Journal of Mineral Processing (NLD) 6466
International Journal of Mining, Reclamation and Environment (GBR) 6466
International Journal of Mobile Communications (GBR) 2327
International Journal of Modelling, Identification and Control (GBR) 2462
International Journal of Modern Physics A (SGP) 7017
International Journal of Modern Physics B (SGP) 7017
International Journal of Modern Physics C: Physics and Computers (SGP) 7017
International Journal of Modern Physics D: Gravitation, Astrophysics and Cosmology (SGP) 7017
International Journal of Modern Physics E (SGP) 7067
The International Journal of Multilingualism (GBR) 5129
International Journal of Multiphase Flow (GBR) 3382
International Journal of Music Education (GBR) 6577
International Journal of Nanoscience (SGP) 2571
International Journal of Nautical Archaeology (GBR) 398
International Journal of Network Management (GBR) 2327
International Journal of Neural Systems (SGP) 2452
International Journal of Neuropsychopharmacology (GBR) 6850
International Journal of Neuroscience (CHE) 6147
International Journal of Non-Linear Mechanics (GBR) 3347
International Journal of Nonprofit and Voluntary Sector Marketing (GBR) 1822
International Journal of Nuclear Energy Science and Technology (GBR) 3169
International Journal of Nuclear Governance, Economy and Ecology (GBR) 3169
International Journal of Numerical Methods for Heat and Fluid Flow (GBR) 3272
International Journal of Numerical Modelling: Electronic Networks, Devices and Fields (GBR) 3292
International Journal of Nursing Practice (AUS) 5962
International Journal of Nursing Studies (GBR) 5962
The International Journal of Nursing Terminologies and Classifications (USA) 5962
International Journal of Obesity (GBR) 6660
International Journal of Obstetric Anesthesia (GBR) 5994
International Journal of Offender Therapy and Comparative Criminology (USA) 2655
International Journal of Older People Nursing (GBR) 5962
International Journal of Operations and Production Management (GBR) 1760
International Journal of Oral and Maxillofacial Surgery (GBR) 5849
International Journal of Organization Theory and Behavior (USA) 7447
International Journal of Osteoarchaeology (GBR) 343
International Journal of Osteopathic Medicine (GBR) 6062
International Journal of Paediatric Dentistry (Online) (GBR) 5849
International Journal of Palliative Nursing (GBR) 5962
International Journal of Parallel, Emergent and Distributed Systems (CHE) 2507
International Journal of Parallel Programming (USA) 2507
International Journal of Pattern Recognition and Artificial Intelligence (SGP) 2452
The International Journal of Pavement Engineering (GBR) 3272
International Journal of Pediatric Obesity (GBR) 6661
International Journal of Pediatric Otorhinolaryngology (IRL) 6081
International Journal of Peptide Research and Therapeutics (NLD) 734
International Journal of Performance Arts and Digital Media (GBR) 8471
International Journal of Pest Management (GBR) 237
International Journal of Pharmaceutics (NLD) 6850
International Journal of Pharmacy Practice (GBR) 6850
International Journal of Philosophical Studies Online (GBR) *see* International Journal of Philosophical Studies. 6926
International Journal of Physical Distribution & Logistics Management (GBR) 8671
International Journal of Phytoremediation (USA) 3443
International Journal of Plasticity (GBR) 3348
International Journal of Police Science and Management (GBR) 2655
International Journal of Political Economy (USA) 7144
International Journal of Politics, Culture, and Society (USA) 7243
International Journal of Polymer Analysis & Characterization (USA) 3247
International Journal of Polymeric Materials (CHE) 3247
International Journal of Practical Theology (DEU) 7650
International Journal of Press / Politics (USA) 4577
International Journal of Pressure Vessels and Piping (GBR) 3383
International Journal of Primatology (USA) 948
International Journal of Product Lifecycle Management (GBR) 1822
International Journal of Production Economics (NLD) 3369
International Journal of Production Research (GBR) 1889
International Journal of Productivity and Performance Management (GBR) 1760
International Journal of Productivity and Quality Management (GBR) 1760
International Journal of Project Management (GBR) 1419
International Journal of Psychiatry in Clinical Practice (GBR) 6147
The International Journal of Psychoanalysis (GBR) 7365
International Journal of Psychology (GBR) 7365
International Journal of Psychophysiology (NLD) 7365
International Journal of Public Administration (USA) 7447
International Journal of Public Health (CHE) 5639
International Journal of Public Opinion Research (GBR) 7144
International Journal of Public Policy (GBR) 7447
International Journal of Public Sector Management (GBR) 1761
International Journal of Qualitative Studies in Education (GBR) 2870
International Journal of Qualitative Studies on Health and Well-Being (GBR) 5639
International Journal of Quality & Reliability Management (GBR) 1761
International Journal of Quantum Chemistry (USA) 2065
International Journal of Quantum Information (SGP) 7017
International Journal of R F and Microwave Computer-Aided Engineering (Online) (USA) *see* International Journal of R F and Microwave Computer-Aided Engineering (Print). 3292
International Journal of Radiation Biology (GBR) 6023
International Journal of Radiation: Oncology - Biology - Physics (USA) 6199
International Journal of Refractory Metals and Hard Materials (GBR) 6317
International Journal of Refrigeration (GBR) 4122
International Journal of Refugee Law (GBR) 7243
International Journal of Rehabilitation Research (USA) 6110
International Journal of Reliability, Quality & Safety Engineering (SGP) 3202
International Journal of Remote Sensing (GBR) 2710
International Journal of Research and Method in Education (Online) (GBR) 2870
International Journal of Research in Marketing (NLD) 1822
International Journal of Retail & Distribution Management (GBR) 1822
International Journal of Rheumatic Diseases (AUS) 6224
The International Journal of Risk and Safety in Medicine (NLD) 4509
International Journal of River Basin Management (ESP) 3362
International Journal of Robotics Research (GBR) 2585
International Journal of Robust and Nonlinear Control (GBR) 3321
International Journal of Rock Mechanics and Mining Sciences (GBR) 6466
International Journal of Rotating Machinery (USA) 5453
International Journal of S T D & AIDS (GBR) 5818

Link to your serials resources and content with ulrichsweb.com

International Journal of Satellite Communications and Networking (GBR) **2383**
International Journal of Science and Mathematics Education (NLD) **7868**
International Journal of Science Education (GBR) **2871**
International Journal of Selection and Assessment (GBR) **1867**
International Journal of Services and Operations Management (GBR) **1761**
International Journal of Services and Standards (GBR) **1129**
International Journal of Sexual Health (Online) (USA) *see* International Journal of Sexual Health. **7366**
International Journal of Six Sigma and Competitive Advantage (GBR) **3369**
International Journal of Social Economics (GBR) **1129**
International Journal of Social Psychiatry (GBR) **6147**
International Journal of Social Research Methodology (GBR) **7974**
International Journal of Social Welfare (GBR) **8047**
International Journal of Sociology (USA) **8109**
International Journal of Sociology and Social Policy (GBR) **8109**
International Journal of Software Engineering and Knowledge Engineering (SGP) **2592**
International Journal of Solids and Structures (GBR) **7059**
International Journal of Space Structures (GBR) **1016**
International Journal of Speech, Language and the Law (GBR) **4695**
International Journal of Speech-Language Pathology (GBR) **5129**
International Journal of Speech Technology (NLD) **5203**
International Journal of Sports Medicine (DEU) **6230**
International Journal of Stress Management (USA) **5640**
International Journal of Stroke (AUS) **5790**
International Journal of Structural Stability and Dynamics (SGP) **3383**
International Journal of Surgery (GBR) **6246**
International Journal of Sustainability in Higher Education (Online) (GBR) **2988**
International Journal of Sustainable Energy (GBR) **3176**
International Journal of Systematic Theology (GBR) **7651**
International Journal of Systems Science (GBR) **3203**
International Journal of Technology and Design Education (NLD) **3065**
International Journal of Technology Assessment in Health Care (GBR) **5906**
International Journal of Technology Intelligence and Planning (GBR) **8427**
International Journal of Technology Management & Sustainable Development (GBR) **8427**
International Journal of Technology Marketing (GBR) **1822**
International Journal of Technology Policy and Management (GBR) **8427**
International Journal of Technology Transfer and Commercialisation (GBR) **8428**
International Journal of Testing (USA) **7366**
International Journal of the Classical Tradition (NLD) **2236**
International Journal of the Economics of Business (GBR) **1129**
The International Journal of the History of Sport (GBR) **4147**
International Journal of the Legal Profession (GBR) **4695**
International Journal of the Sociology of Language (DEU) **5130**
International Journal of Theoretical and Applied Finance (SGP) **1357**
International Journal of Theoretical Physics (USA) **7018**
International Journal of Thermal Sciences (FRA) **7055**
International Journal of Thermophysics (USA) **7055**
International Journal of Tourism Research (GBR) **8723**
International Journal of Toxicology (GBR) **3498**
International Journal of Training & Development (GBR) **1867**
The International Journal of Transgenderism (USA) **7366**
International Journal of Tropical Insect Science (KEN) **850**
International Journal of Uncertainty, Fuzziness and Knowledge-Based Systems (SGP) **2452**
International Journal of Urban and Regional Research (GBR) **4416**
International Journal of Urology (AUS) **6269**
International Journal of Vegetable Science (USA) **237**
International Journal of Vehicle Design (GBR) **8499**
International Journal of Vehicle Noise and Vibration (GBR) **8500**
International Journal of Vehicle Systems Modelling and Testing (GBR) **8586**
International Journal of Ventilation (GBR) **4122**
International Journal of Water Resources Development (GBR) **8826**
International Journal of Wavelets, Multiresolution and Information Processing (SGP) **5497**
International Journal of Web and Grid Services (GBR) **2559**
International Journal of Web Based Communities (GBR) **2559**
International Journal of Web Engineering and Technology (GBR) **2547**
International Journal of Wildland Fire (AUS) **3579**
International Journal of Wireless Information Networks (USA) **2327**
International Journal on Artificial Intelligence Tools (SGP) **2452**
International Journal on Digital Libraries (DEU) **5062**
International Journal on Document Analysis and Recognition (DEU) **2427**
International Journal on Minority and Group Rights (NLD) **7210**
International Journal on Software Tools for Technology Transfer (DEU) **2592**
International Labor and Working-Class History (GBR) **1689**
International Labour Review (GBR) **1689**
International Marketing Review (GBR) **1822**
International Materials Reviews (GBR) **3348**
International Mathematics Research Notices (USA) **5498**
International Mathematics Research Surveys (GBR) **5498**
International Microbiology (ESP) **888**
International Migration (GBR) **7285**
International Negotiation (NLD) **7244**
International Neuropsychological Society. Journal (GBR) **6147**
International Nursing Review Online (GBR) **5962**
International Ophthalmology (NLD) **6044**
International Ophthalmology Clinics (USA) **6044**
International Organization (GBR) **7244**
International Organizations Law Review (NLD) **4932**
International Orthopaedics (DEU) **6062**
International Peacekeeping (GBR) **7244**
International Phonetic Association. Journal (GBR) **5130**
International Planning Studies (GBR) **4416**
International Political Science Review (GBR) **7244**
International Politics (GBR) **7244**
International Psychogeriatrics (GBR) **6148**
International Regional Science Review (USA) **7975**
International Relations (GBR) **7245**
International Relations of the Asia-Pacific (GBR) **7245**
International Research in Geographical and Environmental Education (GBR) **4016**
International Review for the Sociology of Sport (GBR) **8110**
International Review of Administrative Sciences (GBR) **7447**
International Review of Applied Economics (GBR) **1129**
International Review of Economics & Finance (GBR) **1493**
International Review of Education (DEU) **2871**
International Review of Finance (GBR) **1358**
International Review of Financial Analysis (GBR) **1359**
International Review of Hydrobiology (DEU) **679**
International Review of Law and Economics (USA) **4696**
International Review of Law, Computers & Technology (GBR) **4845**
International Review of Psychiatry (GBR) **6148**
The International Review of Retail, Distribution and Consumer Research (GBR) **1822**
International Review of Social History (GBR) **4147**
International Review of Sociology (GBR) **8110**
International Reviews in Physical Chemistry (GBR) **2136**
International Reviews of Immunology (CHE) **5761**
International Security (USA) **7245**
International Seminars in Paediatric Gastroenterology and Nutrition (CAN) **5927**
International Seminars in Surgical Oncology (GBR) **6023**
International Small Business Journal (GBR) **1962**
International Social Science Journal (GBR) **7975**
International Social Security Review (GBR) **4509**
International Social Work (GBR) **8048**
International Sociology (GBR) **8110**
International Studies (IND) **7245**
International Studies in Sociology of Education (GBR) **3066**
International Studies in the Philosophy of Science (GBR) **6926**
International Studies of Management and Organization (USA) **1762**
International Studies Perspectives (USA) **7245**
International Studies Quarterly (USA) **7245**
International Studies Review (USA) **7245**
International Tax and Public Finance (USA) **1930**
The International Trade Journal (USA) **1572**
International Transactions in Operational Research (GBR) **2427**
International Transfer Pricing Journal (NLD) **1359**
International Urogynecology Journal (GBR) **5994**
International Urology and Nephrology (NLD) **6269**
International V A T Monitor (NLD) **1930**
International Wound Journal (GBR) **6062**
The Internet and Higher Education (GBR) **2560**
Internet Archaeology (GBR) **399**
Internet Reference Services Quarterly (USA) **5019**
Internet Research (GBR) **2561**
Der Internist (DEU) **5946**
Interplay (GBR) **2155**
Interpreting (NLD) **5130**
Intertax (NLD) **1572**
Intervention Research (NLD) **7975**
Interventions (GBR) **5310**
Intervirology (CHE) **888**
Inventiones Mathematicae (DEU) **5498**
Inverse Problems (GBR) **5553**
Inverse Problems in Science and Engineering (GBR) **3203**
Invertebrate Biology (USA) **948**
Invertebrate Neuroscience (DEU) **949**
Invertebrate Systematics (AUS) **949**
Investigational New Drugs (USA) **6851**
Investigative Radiology (USA) **6199**
Iran and the Caucasus (NLD) **552**
Iranian Studies (GBR) **552**
Iranica Antiqua (BEL) **399**
Irish Educational Studies (GBR) **2871**
Irish Political Studies (GBR) **7144**
Irish Studies Review (GBR) **5221**
Ironmaking & Steelmaking (GBR) **3348**
Irrigation and Drainage (GBR) **124**
Irrigation and Drainage Systems (NLD) **212**
Irrigation Science (DEU) **124**
Der Islam (DEU) **7711**
Islam and Christian - Muslim Relations (GBR) **7711**
Islamic Law and Society (NLD) **7712**
The Island Arc (AUS) **2748**
Isokinetics and Exercise Science (NLD) **6230**
Isotopes in Environmental and Health Studies (GBR) **2066**
Israel Affairs (GBR) **7246**
Israel Studies (USA) **7976**
Issues in Comprehensive Pediatric Nursing (USA) **5963**
Issues in Mental Health Nursing (USA) **5963**
Italian Studies (GBR) **5311**
The Italianist (GBR) **4234**
ITNOW (Online) (GBR) **2427**
Izvestiya: Mathematics (RUS) **5499**
J A H Online (USA) *see* Journal of Adolescent Health. **5645**
J A I D S (USA) **5819**
J A R O (USA) **6081**
J D D G (Online Edition) (DEU) *see* J D D G (Print Edition). **5878**
J E M (USA) **2872**
J E T P Letters Online (USA) *see* J E T P Letters. **7019**
J M B Online (GBR) *see* Journal of Molecular Biology. **736**
J M M (USA) **2328**
J O N A's Healthcare Law, Ethics, and Regulation (USA) **5963**
J3eA (FRA) **7869**
Jahrbuch der Oesterreichischen Byzantinistik (AUT) **4234**
Japan and the World Economy (NLD) **1543**
Japan Forum (GBR) **7247**
Japan Journal of Nursing Science (JPN) **5963**
The Japanese Economic Review (AUS) **1131**
The Japanese Economy (USA) **1131**
Japanese Journal of Clinical Oncology (GBR) **6023**
Japanese Journal of Ophthalmology (NLD) **6044**
Japanese Journal of Political Science (GBR) **7145**
Japanese Psychological Research (JPN) **7367**
Japanese Studies (GBR) **8111**
Jewish History (ISR) **7723**
Jewish Social Studies (USA) **7724**
Joint Bone Spine (FRA) **6062**
Journal Asiatique (BEL) **553**
Journal de Mathematiques Pures et Appliquees (FRA) **5499**
Journal de Pediatrie et de Puericulture (FRA) **5645**
Journal for Cultural Research (GBR) **4459**
Journal for Early Modern Cultural Studies (USA) **7977**
Journal for General Philosophy of Science (NLD) **7871**
Journal for International Business and Entrepreneurship Development (GBR) **1573**
Journal for Nature Conservation (DEU) **3444**
Journal for Nurse Practitioners (USA) **5963**
Journal for Nurses in Staff Development (USA) **5963**
Journal for Specialists in Group Work (USA) **7367**
Journal for Specialists in Pediatric Nursing (USA) **5963**
Journal for the Scientific Study of Religion (USA) **7653**
Journal for the Study of Judaism (NLD) **7725**
Journal for the Study of Religion, Nature and Culture (GBR) **7653**
Journal for the Study of the Historical Jesus (NLD) **7653**
Journal for the Study of the New Testament (GBR) **7653**
Journal for the Study of the Old Testament (GBR) **7653**
Journal for the Study of the Pseudepigrapha (GBR) **7653**
Journal for the Theory of Social Behaviour (GBR) **7367**
Journal fuer Betriebswirtschaft (DEU) **1763**
Journal fuer die Reine und Angewandte Mathematik (DEU) **5500**
Journal fuer Verbraucherschutz und Lebensmittelsicherheit (CHE) **7528**
Journal in Computer Virology (FRA) **2515**
Journal of Abnormal Child Psychology (USA) **7368**
Journal of Academic Ethics (NLD) **2989**
The Journal of Academic Librarianship (GBR) **5020**
Journal of Access Services (USA) **5062**
Journal of Accounting and Economics (NLD) **1293**
Journal of Accounting & Organizational Change (GBR) **1293**
Journal of Accounting and Public Policy (USA) **1293**
Journal of Accounting Education (GBR) **1293**
Journal of Accounting Research (USA) **1294**
Journal of Addictions Nursing (GBR) **5964**
Journal of Addictive Diseases (USA) **2695**
Journal of Adhesion (CHE) **7019**
Journal of Adhesion Science and Technology (NLD) **7093**
Journal of Adolescence (GBR) **2156**
Journal of Adolescent Research (USA) **7368**
Journal of Adult Development (USA) **7368**
Journal of Adult Theological Education (GBR) **7653**
Journal of Advanced Manufacturing Systems (SGP) **1890**
Journal of Advanced Nursing (GBR) **5964**
Journal of Advertising (USA) **27**
Journal of Advertising Research (USA) **27**
Journal of Aerosol Medicine and Pulmonary Drug Delivery (USA) **6215**
Journal of Aerosol Science (GBR) **6711**
Journal of Aerospace Engineering (USA) **3274**
Journal of Aesthetic Education (USA) **2874**
Journal of Aesthetics and Art Criticism (USA) **498**
Journal of Affective Disorders (NLD) **6149**
Journal of African Business (USA) **1133**
Journal of African Cultural Studies (GBR) **4459**
Journal of African Earth Sciences (GBR) **2749**
Journal of African Economies (GBR) **1494**
The Journal of African History (GBR) **4176**
Journal of African Languages and Linguistics (DEU) **5132**
Journal of African Law (GBR) **4700**
Journal of Aggression, Maltreatment & Trauma (USA) **7368**
Journal of Aging and Health (USA) **4048**
Journal of Aging & Social Policy (USA) **4048**
Journal of Aging Studies (GBR) **4048**
Journal of Agrarian Change (GBR) **201**
Journal of Agricultural and Environmental Ethics (NLD) **6927**
Journal of Agricultural and Food Chemistry (USA) **238**
Journal of Agricultural & Food Information (USA) **126**
Journal of Agricultural Economics (GBR) **202**
The Journal of Agricultural Science (GBR) **126**
Journal of Agromedicine (USA) **6679**
Journal of Agronomy and Crop Science Online (DEU) **239**
Journal of Air Transport Management (GBR) **1763**
Journal of Algebra (USA) **5500**
Journal of Algebra and its Applications (SGP) **5500**
Journal of Algebraic Combinatorics (USA) **5500**
Journal of Algorithms (USA) **5553**
Journal of Allergy and Clinical Immunology (USA) **5762**
Journal of Alloys and Compounds (CHE) **6319**
Journal of Alternative & Complementary Medicine (USA) **311**
Journal of Alzheimer's Disease (NLD) **6149**
Journal of American Culture (USA) **4459**
Journal of American Ethnic History (USA) **3544**
Journal of American Folklore (USA) **3619**
Journal of American Studies (GBR) **4299**
Journal of Analytical and Applied Pyrolysis (NLD) **2066**
Journal of Analytical Atomic Spectrometry (GBR) **2101**
Journal of Analytical Chemistry (RUS) **2101**
Journal of Analytical Psychology (GBR) **7368**
Journal of Analytical Toxicology (USA) **3498**
Journal of Anatomy (GBR) **680**
Journal of Ancient Near Eastern Religions (NLD) **7737**
Journal of Anesthesia (JPN) **5772**
Journal of Anglican Studies (GBR) **7762**
Journal of Animal Breeding and Genetics Online (DEU) **291**
Journal of Animal Ecology (GBR) **680**
Journal of Animal Physiology and Animal Nutrition Online (DEU) **923**
Journal of Anthropological Archaeology (USA) **344**
Journal of Antimicrobial Chemotherapy (GBR) **5819**
Journal of Anxiety Disorders (GBR) **7368**
Journal of Applied Animal Welfare Science (USA) **320**
Journal of Applied Aquaculture (USA) **3599**
The Journal of Applied Behavioral Science (USA) **7368**
Journal of Applied Communication Research (USA) **2329**
Journal of Applied Corporate Finance (USA) **1360**
Journal of Applied Crystallography (DNK) **2111**
Journal of Applied Developmental Psychology (GBR) **7369**
Journal of Applied Ecology (GBR) **680**
Journal of Applied Econometrics (GBR) **1544**
Journal of Applied Electrochemistry (NLD) **2114**
Journal of Applied Entomology (Online) (DEU) **851**
Journal of Applied Geophysics (NLD) **2784**
Journal of Applied Gerontology (USA) **4049**
Journal of Applied Ichthyology Online (DEU) **950**
Journal of Applied Linguistics (GBR) **5132**
Journal of Applied Logic (NLD) **6928**
Journal of Applied Mathematics (USA) **5501**
Journal of Applied Mathematics and Decision Sciences (USA) **5501**
Journal of Applied Mathematics and Mechanics (GBR) **3349**

Online Service

11276 SWETSWISE ONLINE CONTENT ULRICH'S PERIODICALS

Journal of Applied Mathematics and Stochastic Analysis (USA) **5501**
Journal of Applied Mechanics (USA) **3385**
Journal of Applied Mechanics and Technical Physics (RUS) **3349**
Journal of Applied Microbiology (GBR) **888**
Journal of Applied Philosophy (GBR) **6928**
Journal of Applied Phycology (NLD) **796**
Journal of Applied Physics (USA) **7019**
Journal of Applied Polymer Science (USA) **3248**
Journal of Applied Research in Intellectual Disabilities (GBR) **6149**
Journal of Applied School Psychology (USA) **3042**
Journal of Applied Security Research (USA) **2874**
Journal of Applied Social Psychology (USA) **7369**
Journal of Applied Spectroscopy (USA) **7077**
Journal of Applied Sport Psychology (USA) **6230**
Journal of Applied Statistics (GBR) **8382**
Journal of Applied Toxicology (GBR) **3498**
Journal of Approximation Theory (USA) **5501**
Journal of Aquatic Food Product Technology (USA) **3649**
Journal of Arabic Literature (NLD) **5314**
Journal of Archaeological Method and Theory (USA) **400**
Journal of Archaeological Research (USA) **400**
Journal of Archaeological Science (GBR) **400**
Journal of Architectural Education (USA) **447**
Journal of Architectural Engineering (USA) **447**
The Journal of Architecture (GBR) **447**
Journal of Archival Organization (USA) **5020**
Journal of Arid Environments (GBR) **4016**
Journal of Arthroplasty (USA) **6063**
Journal of Artificial Organs (JPN) **5906**
Journal of Asia - Pacific Business (USA) **1573**
Journal of Asian American Studies (USA) **8111**
Journal of Asian and African Studies (GBR) **8112**
Journal of Asian Earth Sciences (GBR) **2749**
Journal of Asian Economics (NLD) **1494**
Journal of Asian Natural Products Research (GBR) **311**
Journal of Asian Pacific Communication (NLD) **5132**
The Journal of Asset Management (GBR) **1635**
Journal of Assisted Reproduction and Genetics (USA) **5995**
Journal of Asthma (USA) **6215**
Journal of Atmospheric and Solar - Terrestrial Physics (GBR) **2784**
Journal of Atmospheric Chemistry (NLD) **2066**
Journal of Attention Disorders (USA) **6149**
Journal of Autism and Developmental Disorders (USA) **3042**
Journal of Autoimmune Diseases (GBR) **873**
Journal of Autoimmunity (GBR) **5762**
Journal of Automated Methods & Management in Chemistry (USA) **2101**
Journal of Automated Reasoning (NLD) **2453**
Journal of Avian Biology (DNK) **909**
Journal of Back and Musculoskeletal Rehabilitation (NLD) **6063**
Journal of Balkan and Near Eastern Studies (GBR) **4235**
Journal of Bamboo and Rattan (IND) **796**
Journal of Banking & Finance (NLD) **1360**
Journal of Basic Microbiology (DEU) **888**
Journal of Behavior Therapy and Experimental Psychiatry (GBR) **6149**
Journal of Behavioral Decision Making (GBR) **1763**
Journal of Behavioral Education (USA) **2874**
The Journal of Behavioral Finance (USA) **7369**
Journal of Behavioral Medicine (USA) **6149**
Journal of Beliefs and Values (GBR) **2874**
Journal of Bioactive and Compatible Polymers (GBR) **734**
Journal of Biochemical and Molecular Toxicology (Online Edition) (USA) **681**
Journal of Biochemistry (GBR) **735**
Journal of Bioeconomics (USA) **681**
Journal of Bioenergetics and Biomembranes (USA) **735**
Journal of Biogeography (GBR) **4017**
Journal of Bioinformatics and Computational Biology (GBR) **681**
Journal of Biological Inorganic Chemistry (DEU) **2117**
Journal of Biological Physics (NLD) **753**
Journal of Biological Rhythms (USA) **6149**
Journal of Biological Systems (SGP) **681**
Journal of Biology (GBR) **681**
Journal of Biomaterials Applications (GBR) **6247**
Journal of Biomaterials Science. Polymer Edition (NLD) **766**
Journal of Biomechanical Engineering (USA) **5646**
Journal of Biomechanics (GBR) **5646**
Journal of Biomedical Informatics (USA) **5832**
Journal of Biomedical Materials Research. Part A (USA) **766**
Journal of Biomedical Materials Research. Part B: Applied Biomaterials (USA) **766**
Journal of Biomedical Optics (USA) **7078**
Journal of Biomedical Science (GBR) **5646**
Journal of Biomedicine and Biotechnology (USA) **5646**
Journal of Biomolecular N M R (NLD) **735**
Journal of Biomolecular Screening (USA) **735**
Journal of Biopharmaceutical Statistics (USA) **6889**
Journal of Bioscience and Bioengineering (JPN) **750**
Journal of Biosocial Science (GBR) **8112**
Journal of Biotechnology (NLD) **767**
Journal of Bisexuality (USA) **4375**
Journal of Black Psychology (USA) **7369**
Journal of Black Studies (USA) **7978**
Journal of Bodywork and Movement Therapies (GBR) **6111**
Journal of Bone and Mineral Metabolism (JPN) **5895**
The Journal of Brand Management (GBR) **1823**
Journal of Bridge Engineering (USA) **1018**
Journal of Broadcasting and Electronic Media (USA) **2383**
Journal of Bronchology & Interventional Pulmonology (USA) **6215**
Journal of Bryology (GBR) **796**
Journal of Building Physics (GBR) **3204**
Journal of Burn Care & Research (USA) **5646**
Journal of Business & Finance Librarianship (USA) **5020**
Journal of Business & Industrial Marketing (GBR) **1823**
Journal of Business & Psychology (USA) **7369**
Journal of Business and Technical Communication (USA) **1133**
Journal of Business Communication (USA) **1764**
Journal of Business Ethics (NLD) **1134**
Journal of Business Finance & Accounting (GBR) **1294**
Journal of Business Research (USA) **1764**
Journal of Business Strategy (USA) **1764**
Journal of Business-to-Business Marketing (USA) **1823**
Journal of Business Venturing (USA) **1134**
Journal of Cancer Education (USA) **6023**
Journal of Cancer Research and Clinical Oncology (DEU) **6024**
Journal of Cancer Research and Therapeutics (IND) **6024**
Journal of Carbohydrate Chemistry (USA) **2067**
Journal of Carcinogenesis (IND) **6024**
Journal of Cardiac Failure (USA) **5791**
Journal of Cardiac Surgery (USA) **5792**
Journal of Cardiopulmonary Rehabilitation and Prevention (USA) **5792**
Journal of Cardiothoracic and Vascular Anesthesia (USA) **5792**
Journal of Cardiothoracic-Renal Research (GBR) **5792**
Journal of Cardiovascular Electrophysiology (USA) **5792**
Journal of Cardiovascular Magnetic Resonance (GBR) **5792**
Journal of Cardiovascular Pharmacology (USA) **6852**
Journal of Career Assessment (USA) **7369**
Journal of Career Development (USA) **6700**
Journal of Cases in Educational Leadership (USA) **3025**
Journal of Catalysis (USA) **2136**
Journal of Cataract & Refractive Surgery (USA) **6044**
Journal of Cellular Biochemistry (USA) **735**
Journal of Cellular Physiology (USA) **923**
Journal of Cellular Plastics (GBR) **7093**
Journal of Cereal Science (GBR) **273**
Journal of Cerebral Blood Flow and Metabolism (USA) **6150**
The Journal of Change Management (GBR) **1764**
Journal of Chemical and Engineering Data (USA) **2067**
Journal of Chemical Crystallography (USA) **2111**
Journal of Chemical Ecology (USA) **3444**
Journal of Chemical Information and Modeling (USA) **2108**
Journal of Chemical Neuroanatomy (NLD) **6150**
Journal of Chemical Physics (USA) **7019**
Journal of Chemical Research (Online Edition) (GBR) *see* Journal of Chemical Research (Print Edition). **2067**
Journal of Chemical Technology and Biotechnology (GBR) **767**
Journal of Chemical Theory and Computation (USA) **2067**
The Journal of Chemical Thermodynamics (GBR) **2136**
Journal of Chemometrics (GBR) **2101**
Journal of Child and Adolescent Psychiatric Nursing (USA) **5964**
Journal of Child and Adolescent Psychopharmacology (USA) **6150**
Journal of Child & Adolescent Substance Abuse (USA) **2695**
Journal of Child and Family Studies (USA) **7370**
Journal of Child Custody (USA) **2156**
Journal of Child Health Care (GBR) **6094**
Journal of Child Language (GBR) **2156**
Journal of Child Neurology (USA) **6150**
Journal of Child Psychology and Psychiatry (GBR) **7370**
Journal of Child Psychotherapy (GBR) **7370**
Journal of Child Sexual Abuse (USA) **8049**
Journal of Children & Poverty (USA) **8049**
Journal of Chinese Economics and Business Studies (GBR) **1494**
Journal of Chinese Philosophy (USA) **6928**
Journal of Chromatographic Science (USA) **2101**
Journal of Chromatography A (NLD) **2101**
Journal of Chromatography. B, Analytical Technologies in the Biomedical and Life Sciences (NLD) **2067**
Journal of Circadian Rhythms (GBR) **5646**
Journal of Circuits, Systems and Computers (SGP) **2466**
Journal of Classical Sociology (GBR) **8112**
Journal of Classification (USA) **5020**
Journal of Cleaner Production (NLD) **3369**
Journal of Clinical Anesthesia (USA) **5772**
Journal of Clinical Apheresis (USA) **5939**
Journal of Clinical Child and Adolescent Psychology (USA) **7370**
Journal of Clinical Densitometry (NLD) **5647**
Journal of Clinical Epidemiology (USA) **5647**
Journal of Clinical Forensic and Legal Medicine (GBR) **5914**
Journal of Clinical Gastroenterology (USA) **5927**
Journal of Clinical Immunology (USA) **5762**
Journal of Clinical Laboratory Analysis (USA) **5907**
Journal of Clinical Monitoring and Computing (NLD) **5647**
Journal of Clinical Neuromuscular Disease (USA) **5647**
Journal of Clinical Neurophysiology (USA) **6150**
Journal of Clinical Neuroscience (GBR) **6150**
Journal of Clinical Nursing (GBR) **5964**
Journal of Clinical Periodontology (DNK) **5851**
The Journal of Clinical Pharmacology (USA) **6852**
Journal of Clinical Pharmacy and Therapeutics (GBR) **6852**
Journal of Clinical Psychology (USA) **7370**
Journal of Clinical Psychology in Medical Settings (USA) **7370**
Journal of Clinical Psychopharmacology (USA) **6853**
Journal of Clinical Rheumatology (USA) **6224**
Journal of Clinical Ultrasound (USA) **6200**
Journal of Clinical Virology (NLD) **5819**
Journal of Cluster Science (USA) **2067**
Journal of Coastal Conservation (NLD) **2809**
Journal of Cognition and Culture (NLD) **7370**
Journal of Cognition and Development (USA) **7370**
Journal of Cognitive Neuroscience (USA) **6151**
Journal of Cold Regions Engineering (USA) **3274**
Journal of Cold War Studies (USA) **7247**
Journal of College Student Development (USA) **2989**
Journal of College Student Psychotherapy (USA) **7371**
Journal of Colloid and Interface Science (USA) **2136**
Journal of Colonialism & Colonial History (USA) **4149**
Journal of Combinatorial Chemistry (USA) **2102**
Journal of Combinatorial Designs (USA) **5501**
Journal of Combinatorial Optimization (NLD) **5553**
Journal of Combinatorial Theory, Series A (USA) **5501**
Journal of Combinatorial Theory. Series B (USA) **5501**
Journal of Commercial Biotechnology (GBR) **767**
Journal of Common Market Studies (GBR) **7146**
Journal of Commonwealth Literature (GBR) **5314**
Journal of Communication (USA) **8112**
Journal of Communication Disorders (USA) **7371**
Journal of Communication Inquiry (USA) **8112**
Journal of Communication Management (GBR) **1765**
Journal of Communications Technology and Electronics (RUS) **2329**
Journal of Communist Studies and Transition Politics (GBR) **7247**
Journal of Community & Applied Social Psychology (GBR) **7371**
Journal of Community Health (USA) **5647**
Journal of Community Health Nursing (USA) **5964**
Journal of Community Practice (USA) **8049**
Journal of Community Psychology (USA) **7371**
Journal of Comparative Economics (USA) **1134**
The Journal of Comparative Germanic Linguistics (NLD) **5133**
The Journal of Comparative Neurology (USA) **6151**
Journal of Comparative Pathology (GBR) **682**
Journal of Comparative Physiology A (DEU) **924**
Journal of Comparative Physiology B (DEU) **924**
Journal of Comparative Policy Analysis (USA) **7448**
Journal of Complexity (USA) **5553**
Journal of Composite Materials (GBR) **3349**
Journal of Composites for Construction (USA) **3274**
Journal of Computational Acoustics (SGP) **7050**
Journal of Computational Analysis and Applications (USA) **5501**
Journal of Computational and Applied Mathematics (NLD) **5502**
Journal of Computational Biology (Online) (USA) **682**
Journal of Computational Chemistry (USA) **2068**
Journal of Computational Electronics (USA) **2428**
Journal of Computational Methods in Sciences and Engineering (NLD) **5502**
Journal of Computational Neuroscience (NLD) **6151**
Journal of Computational Physics (USA) **7050**
Journal of Computer - Aided Molecular Design (NLD) **2108**
Journal of Computer and System Sciences (USA) **2523**
Journal of Computer Assisted Learning (GBR) **2469**
Journal of Computer Assisted Tomography (USA) **6200**
Journal of Computer Science and Technology (USA) **2468**
Journal of Computer Security (NLD) **2515**
Journal of Computing and Information Science in Engineering (USA) **3385**
Journal of Computing in Civil Engineering (USA) **3292**
Journal of Conflict and Security Law (GBR) **4933**
Journal of Conflict Resolution (USA) **7978**
Journal of Consciousness Studies (GBR) **7371**
Journal of Construction Engineering and Management (USA) **3274**
Journal of Construction Research (SGP) **1018**
Journal of Constructional Steel Research (GBR) **3275**
Journal of Constructivist Psychology (USA) **7371**
Journal of Consumer Affairs (USA) **2639**
Journal of Consumer Behaviour (GBR) **2639**
Journal of Consumer Culture (GBR) **2639**
Journal of Consumer Health on the Internet (USA) **2562**
Journal of Consumer Marketing (GBR) **1823**
Journal of Consumer Policy (NLD) **2639**
Journal of Consumer Psychology (USA) **27**
Journal of Contaminant Hydrology (NLD) **3488**
Journal of Contemporary African Studies (GBR) **7978**
Journal of Contemporary China (GBR) **4184**
Journal of Contemporary Criminal Justice (USA) **4892**
Journal of Contemporary Ethnography (USA) **8112**
Journal of Contemporary European Studies (Online Edition) (GBR) **7146**
Journal of Contemporary History (GBR) **4149**
Journal of Contemporary Psychotherapy (USA) **7372**
Journal of Contemporary Religion (GBR) **7654**
Journal of Contingencies and Crisis Management (GBR) **1765**
Journal of Continuing Education in the Health Professions (USA) **5648**
Journal of Controlled Release (NLD) **6853**
Journal of Convention & Event Tourism (USA) **6280**
Journal of Coordination Chemistry (CHE) **2068**
Journal of Coptic Studies (BEL) **4322**
Journal of Corporate Accounting and Finance (USA) **1294**
Journal of Corporate Finance (NLD) **1360**
Journal of Corporate Real Estate (GBR) **7596**
Journal of Cosmetic and Laser Therapy (Online) (GBR) **5878**
Journal of Cosmetic Dermatology (GBR) **5878**
Journal of Cosmology and Astroparticle Physics (GBR) **7020**
Journal of Couple & Relationship Therapy (USA) **7372**
Journal of Cranio-Maxillofacial Surgery (GBR) **6247**
Journal of Craniofacial Surgery (USA) **6247**
Journal of Criminal Justice (GBR) **4892**
Journal of Criminal Justice Education (GBR) **2656**
The Journal of Criminal Law (GBR) **4892**
Journal of Critical Care (USA) **6063**
Journal of Critical Realism (GBR) **6928**
Journal of Crop Improvement (USA) **239**
Journal of Cross-Cultural Gerontology (NLD) **4049**
Journal of Cross-Cultural Psychology (USA) **7372**
Journal of Cryptology (USA) **5502**
Journal of Crystal Growth (NLD) **2111**
Journal of Culinary Science & Technology (USA) **6661**
Journal of Cultural Economics (USA) **1544**
Journal of Cultural Heritage (FRA) **344**
Journal of Curriculum Studies (GBR) **3067**
Journal of Customer Behavior (GBR) **1824**
Journal of Cutaneous Medicine and Surgery (CAN) **5878**
Journal of Cutaneous Pathology (DNK) **5878**
Journal of Cystic Fibrosis (NLD) **5927**
Journal of Dairy Research (GBR) **266**
The Journal of Database Marketing & Customer Strategy Management (Online Edition) (GBR) **1419**
The Journal of Deaf Studies and Deaf Education (USA) **4075**
Journal of Democracy (USA) **7146**
Journal of Dentistry (GBR) **5851**
Journal of Dermatological Science (IRL) **5878**
Journal of Dermatological Treatment (GBR) **5879**
Journal of Design History (GBR) **498**
Journal of Design Manufacturing and Automation (USA) **3204**
Journal of Developing Areas (USA) **1599**
Journal of Developing Societies (Online) (GBR) **7978**
Journal of Development Economics (NLD) **1600**
The Journal of Development Studies (GBR) **1600**
Journal of Developmental and Behavioral Pediatrics (USA) **6094**
Journal of Developmental and Physical Disabilities (USA) **4067**
Journal of Diabetes and its Complications (USA) **5895**
Journal of Diagnostic Medical Sonography (USA) **6200**
Journal of Difference Equations and Applications (CHE) **5502**
Journal of Differential Equations (USA) **5502**
Journal of Digestive Diseases (Online) (AUS) **5927**
Journal of Digital Imaging (USA) **6200**
Journal of Dispersion Science and Technology (USA) **2136**
Journal of Divorce & Remarriage (USA) **5559**
Journal of Documentation (GBR) **5020**
Journal of Drug Targeting (CHE) **6853**
Journal of Dual Diagnosis (USA) **2696**
Journal of Dynamic Systems, Measurement and Control (USA) **3349**
Journal of Dynamical and Control Systems (USA) **3369**
Journal of Dynamics and Differential Equations (USA) **5503**
Journal of Early Adolescence (USA) **2156**
Journal of Early Childhood Literacy (GBR) **2875**
Journal of Early Childhood Research (GBR) **6094**

Journal of Early Childhood Teacher Education (GBR) 2990
Journal of Early Christian Studies (USA) 7802
Journal of Early Modern History (NLD) 4149
Journal of Earthquake Engineering (GBR) 3275
Journal of East Asian Linguistics (NLD) 5133
Journal of East - West Business (USA) 1544
The Journal of Eastern Christian Studies (BEL) 7737
Journal of Ecclesiastical History (GBR) 7654
Journal of Ecology (GBR) 682
Journal of Econometrics (NLD) 1544
Journal of Economic and Social Measurement (NLD) 8382
Journal of Economic Behavior & Organization (NLD) 1134
Journal of Economic Dynamics and Control (NLD) 1544
Journal of Economic Geography (GBR) 1494
Journal of Economic Growth (USA) 1544
The Journal of Economic History (GBR) 1544
The Journal of Economic Inequality (USA) 1494
Journal of Economic Methodology (GBR) 1135
Journal of Economic Policy Reform (Online) (GBR) 1765
Journal of Economic Psychology (NLD) 1824
Journal of Economic Studies (GBR) 1135
Journal of Economic Surveys (GBR) 1135
Journal of Economic Theory (USA) 1545
Journal of Economics (AUT) 1135
Journal of Economics and Business (USA) 1135
Journal of Economics & Management Strategy (USA) 1545
Journal of Ecotourism (GBR) 8725
Journal of Education and Work (GBR) 3067
Journal of Education for Students Placed at Risk (USA) 3067
Journal of Education for Teaching (GBR) 2875
Journal of Education Policy (GBR) 3026
Journal of Educational Administration (GBR) 3026
Journal of Educational Administration and History (GBR) 3026
Journal of Educational and Psychological Consultation (USA) 2875
Journal of Educational Change (NLD) 2875
Journal of Elasticity (NLD) 3349
Journal of Elastomers and Plastics (GBR) 7093
Journal of Elder Abuse & Neglect (USA) 4049
Journal of Elections, Public Opinion, and Parties (GBR) 7147
Journal of Electroanalytical Chemistry (CHE) 2102
Journal of Electrocardiology (USA) 5793
Journal of Electroceramics (USA) 3349
The Journal of Electroconvulsive Therapy (USA) 6151
Journal of Electromagnetic Waves and Applications (NLD) 7020
Journal of Electromyography & Kinesiology (GBR) 754
Journal of Electron Microscopy (JPN) 899
Journal of Electron Spectroscopy and Related Phenomena (NLD) 7078
Journal of Electronic Imaging (USA) 6970
Journal of Electronic Packaging (USA) 3106
Journal of Electronic Resources in Medical Libraries (USA) 5020
Journal of Electronic Resources Librarianship (USA) 5020
Journal of Electronic Testing (USA) 3322
Journal of Electrostatics (NLD) 3322
Journal of Emergency Nursing (USA) 5964
Journal of Emerging Market Finance (IND) 1635
Journal of Empirical Finance (NLD) 1361
Journal of Empirical Legal Studies (USA) 4701
Journal of Empirical Theology (NLD) 7655
Journal of Endocrinology (GBR) 5896
Journal of Endourology (USA) 6270
Journal of Energetic Materials (USA) 7020
Journal of Energy Engineering (USA) 3275
Journal of Energy Resources Technology (USA) 3140
Journal of Engineering and Technology Management (NLD) 1765
Journal of Engineering Design (GBR) 3205
Journal of Engineering for Gas Turbines and Power (USA) 3385
Journal of Engineering Materials and Technology (USA) 3349
Journal of Engineering Mathematics (NLD) 3205
Journal of Engineering Mechanics (USA) 3275
Journal of Engineering Physics and Thermophysics (USA) 3205
Journal of English for Academic Purposes (GBR) 3067
Journal of English Linguistics (USA) 5133
Journal of Enhanced Heat Transfer (GBR) 3385
Journal of Enterprise Information Management (GBR) 5021
Journal of Entrepreneurship (IND) 1765
Journal of Environment & Development (USA) 3444
Journal of Environmental Assessment Policy and Management (GBR) 3445
Journal of Environmental Economics and Management (USA) 3445
Journal of Environmental Engineering (USA) 3445
Journal of Environmental Engineering and Science (Online) (CAN) 3445
Journal of Environmental Law (GBR) 3445
Journal of Environmental Management (GBR) 3446
Journal of Environmental Monitoring (GBR) 2102
Journal of Environmental Planning and Management (GBR) 3446
Journal of Environmental Policy and Planning (GBR) 3446
Journal of Environmental Psychology (GBR) 7373
Journal of Environmental Radioactivity (GBR) 3446
Journal of Environmental Science and Health. Part A: Toxic Hazardous Substances and Environmental Engineering (USA) 3499
Journal of Environmental Science and Health. Part B: Pesticides, Food Contaminants, and Agricultural Wastes (USA) 3447
Journal of Environmental Science and Health. Part C: Environmental Carcinogenesis & Ecotoxicology Reviews (USA) 3499
Journal of Environmental Sciences (NLD) 3447
Journal of Enzyme Inhibition and Medicinal Chemistry (CHE) 736
The Journal of Equine Veterinary Science (USA) 8800
Journal of Esthetic and Restorative Dentistry (GBR) 5852
The Journal of Ethics (NLD) 6928
Journal of Ethnic & Cultural Diversity in Social Work (USA) 8049
Journal of Ethnic and Migration Studies (GBR) 3544
Journal of Ethnicity in Criminal Justice (USA) 2657
Journal of Ethnicity in Substance Abuse (USA) 2696
Journal of Ethnobiology and Ethnomedicine (GBR) 5648
Journal of Ethnopharmacology (IRL) 6853
Journal of Ethology (JPN) 950
The Journal of Eukaryotic Microbiology (USA) 889
Journal of Euromarketing (USA) 1824
Journal of European Industrial Training (GBR) 1765
Journal of European Public Policy (GBR) 7147
Journal of European Social Policy (GBR) 7248
Journal of European Studies (Chalfont Saint Giles) (GBR) 4235
Journal of Evaluation in Clinical Practice Online (GBR) 5649
Journal of Evidence-Based Dental Practice (USA) 5852
Journal of Evidence-Based Social Work (USA) 8049
Journal of Evolution Equations (CHE) 5503
Journal of Evolutionary Biochemistry and Physiology (RUS) 736
Journal of Evolutionary Biology (GBR) 873
Journal of Evolutionary Economics (DEU) 1545
Journal of Evolutionary Psychology (HUN) 7373
Journal of Exotic Pet Medicine (USA) 8800
Journal of Experimental & Clinical Assisted Reproduction (GBR) 5995
Journal of Experimental & Theoretical Artificial Intelligence (GBR) 2453
Journal of Experimental and Theoretical Physics (USA) 7020
Journal of Experimental Animal Science (DEU) 5907
Journal of Experimental Botany (GBR) 796
Journal of Experimental Child Psychology (USA) 7373
Journal of Experimental Criminology (NLD) 2657
Journal of Experimental Marine Biology and Ecology (NLD) 683
Journal of Experimental Nanoscience (GBR) 2068
Journal of Experimental Social Psychology (USA) 7373
Journal of Experimental Therapeutics and Oncology Online (USA) 6024
Journal of Experimental Zoology. Part A: Ecological Genetics and Physiology (Online Edition) (USA) 950
Journal of Experimental Zoology. Part B: Molecular and Developmental Evolution (USA) 951
Journal of Exposure Science and Environmental Epidemiology (GBR) 3447
Journal of Facilities Management (GBR) 1766
Journal of Family and Economic Issues (USA) 7373
Journal of Family Communication (USA) 8113
Journal of Family History (USA) 8113
Journal of Family Issues (USA) 8113
Journal of Family Nursing (USA) 5965
Journal of Family Psychotherapy (USA) 7374
Journal of Family Social Work (USA) 8049
Journal of Family Therapy (GBR) 6151
Journal of Family Violence (USA) 2657
Journal of Fashion Marketing and Management (GBR) 1824
Journal of Feline Medicine and Surgery (GBR) 8800
Journal of Feminist Family Therapy (USA) 8899
Journal of Feminist Studies in Religion (USA) 7655
Journal of Field Robotics (USA) 2585
The Journal of Finance (USA) 1361
Journal of Financial Crime (GBR) 4892
Journal of Financial Econometrics (GBR) 1361
Journal of Financial Economics (CHE) 1136
Journal of Financial Intermediation (USA) 1545
Journal of Financial Markets (NLD) 1361
Journal of Financial Regulation and Compliance (GBR) 1361
Journal of Financial Research (USA) 1136
Journal of Financial Services Marketing (GBR) 1824
Journal of Financial Services Research (USA) 1361
Journal of Financial Stability (USA) 1136
Journal of Fire Protection Engineering (GBR) 3579
Journal of Fire Sciences (GBR) 3349
Journal of Fish Biology (GBR) 951
Journal of Fish Diseases Online (GBR) 3599
Journal of Fluency Disorders (USA) 7374
Journal of Fluid Mechanics (GBR) 3363
Journal of Fluids and Structures (GBR) 3205
Journal of Fluids Engineering (USA) 3363
Journal of Fluorescence (USA) 2117
Journal of Fluorine Chemistry (CHE) 2117
Journal of Folklore Research (USA) 3619
Journal of Food Biochemistry (USA) 3650
Journal of Food Composition and Analysis (USA) 3650
Journal of Food Engineering (GBR) 3650
Journal of Food Lipids (USA) 3650
Journal of Food Process Engineering (USA) 3650
Journal of Food Processing and Preservation (USA) 3650
Journal of Food Products Marketing (USA) 3650
Journal of Food Quality (USA) 3651
Journal of Food Safety (USA) 3651
Journal of Foodservice Business Research (USA) 4392
The Journal of Foot & Ankle Surgery (USA) 6248
Journal of Forecasting (GBR) 1766
The Journal of Forensic Psychiatry & Psychology (Online) (GBR) 6151
Journal of Forensic Psychology Practice (USA) 7374
Journal of Forensic Sciences (USA) 5915
Journal of Forest Economics (DEU) 3694
Journal of Forest Research (JPN) 3694
Journal of Fourier Analysis and Applications (USA) 5503
Journal of French Language Studies (GBR) 5133
Journal of Fuel Cell Science and Technology (USA) 3385
Journal of Functional Analysis (USA) 5503
Journal of Functional Programming (GBR) 2508
Journal of Further and Higher Education (GBR) 2990
Journal of Fusion Energy (USA) 3170
The Journal of Futures Markets (USA) 1635
Journal of G L B T Family Studies (USA) 4375
Journal of Gambling Studies (USA) 6152
Journal of Gastroenterology (JPN) 5927
Journal of Gastroenterology and Hepatology (AUS) 5928
Journal of Gastrointestinal Cancer (USA) 5896
Journal of Gastrointestinal Surgery (USA) 6248
Journal of Gay & Lesbian Mental Health (USA) 7374
Journal of Gay & Lesbian Social Services (USA) 8049
Journal of Gender Studies (GBR) 8899
Journal of Gene Medicine (USA) 873
Journal of General Education (USA) 2876
Journal of General Internal Medicine (USA) 5946
Journal of General Plant Pathology (JPN) 797
Journal of Genetic Counseling (USA) 7374
Journal of Genocide Research (GBR) 7147
Journal of Geochemical Exploration (NLD) 2711
Journal of Geodesy (DEU) 2785
Journal of Geodynamics (GBR) 2785
Journal of Geographical Sciences (CHN) 4017
Journal of Geographical Systems (DEU) 4037
Journal of Geography in Higher Education (GBR) 4017
Journal of Geometry (CHE) 5503
Journal of Geometry and Physics (NLD) 5503
Journal of Geophysics and Engineering (GBR) 2785
Journal of Geotechnical and Geoenvironmental Engineering (USA) 3275
Journal of Geriatric Psychiatry and Neurology (USA) 4049
Journal of Germanic Linguistics (GBR) 5133
Journal of Gerontological Social Work (USA) 4049
Journal of Glaucoma (USA) 6044
Journal of Global Ethics (GBR) 7979
Journal of Global History (GBR) 4149
Journal of Global Marketing (USA) 1824
Journal of Global Optimization (NLD) 7940
Journal of Graph Theory (USA) 5504
Journal of Greek Linguistics (NLD) 5133
Journal of Grid Computing (NLD) 2508
Journal of Group Theory (DEU) 5504
Journal of Gynecologic Surgery (USA) 5995
Journal of Hand Surgery (American Volume) (USA) 6248
Journal of Hand Surgery (European Volume) (GBR) 6248
Journal of Happiness Studies (NLD) 7374
Journal of Hazardous Materials (NLD) 3508
The Journal of Headache and Pain Online (ITA) 6152
Journal of Health Care Chaplaincy (USA) 6991
Journal of Health Care for the Poor and Underserved (USA) 5649
Journal of Health Communication (USA) 5649
Journal of Health Economics (NLD) 4104
Journal of Health Management (USA) 5649
Journal of Health, Organization and Management (GBR) 4104
Journal of Health Politics, Policy and Law (USA) 5649
Journal of Health Psychology (GBR) 7374
Journal of Health Services Research & Policy (GBR) 5650
The Journal of Heart and Lung Transplantation (USA) 6248
Journal of Heat Transfer (USA) 3385
Journal of Helminthology (GBR) 5820
Journal of Hepato - Biliary - Pancreatic Sciences (JPN) 6248
Journal of Hepatology (DNK) 5928
Journal of Herbs, Spices & Medicinal Plants (USA) 3740
Journal of Heredity (GBR) 874
Journal of Heritage Tourism (GBR) 8725
Journal of Heuristics (USA) 2453
The Journal of High Energy Physics (Online) (GBR) 7020
Journal of High Speed Networks (NLD) 2500
The Journal of High Technology Management Research (GBR) 1419
Journal of Higher Education (USA) 2990
Journal of Higher Education Policy and Management (GBR) 2990
Journal of Hispanic Higher Education (USA) 2991
Journal of Historical Geography (GBR) 4017
Journal of Historical Pragmatics (NLD) 5133
Journal of Historical Sociology (GBR) 8113
Journal of HIV - AIDS & Social Services (USA) 8050
Journal of HIV - AIDS Prevention in Children & Youth (USA) 5820
Journal of Holistic Nursing (USA) 5965
Journal of Homosexuality (USA) 4375
Journal of Hospice and Palliative Nursing (USA) 5965
Journal of Hospital Infection (GBR) 5820
Journal of Hospital Librarianship (USA) 5021
Journal of Hospital Marketing & Public Relations (USA) 1824
Journal of Hospital Medicine (USA) 5650
Journal of Hospitality and Tourism Management (Online) (AUS) 8725
Journal of Hospitality Marketing and Management (USA) 4392
Journal of Housing and the Built Environment (NLD) 4417
Journal of Housing Economics (USA) 4417
Journal of Housing for the Elderly (USA) 4049
Journal of Human Behavior in the Social Environment (USA) 8050
Journal of Human Development and Capabilities (GBR) 345
Journal of Human Evolution (GBR) 874
Journal of Human Genetics (JPN) 874
Journal of Human Hypertension (GBR) 5793
Journal of Human Lactation (USA) 5995
Journal of Human Nutrition and Dietetics (GBR) 6661
Journal of Human Resources in Hospitality & Tourism (USA) 4392
Journal of Human Rights (GBR) 7211
Journal of Human Values (IND) 1766
Journal of Humanistic Psychology (USA) 7375
Journal of Hydraulic Engineering (New York) (USA) 3275
Journal of Hydraulic Research (ESP) 3363
Journal of Hydroinformatics (GBR) 3447
Journal of Hydrologic Engineering (USA) 3275
Journal of Hydrology (NLD) 2796
Journal of Hyperbolic Differential Equations (SGP) 5504
Journal of Hypertension (USA) 5793
Journal of Iberian and Latin American Studies (GBR) 4299
Journal of Ichthyology (RUS) 951
Journal of Immigrant and Minority Health (USA) 5650
Journal of Immigrant & Refugee Studies (Online) (USA) *see* Journal of Immigrant & Refugee Studies. 7248
Journal of Immune Based Therapies and Vaccines (GBR) 5762
Journal of Immunoassay and Immunochemistry (USA) 2102
Journal of Immunological Methods (NLD) 5762
Journal of Immunotherapy (USA) 5763
Journal of Immunotoxicology (USA) 5763
The Journal of Imperial and Commonwealth History (GBR) 4149
Journal of Inclusion Phenomena and Macrocyclic Chemistry (NLD) 2136
Journal of Income Distribution (USA) 1545
Journal of Indian Philosophy (NLD) 6928
Journal of Industrial Ecology (USA) 3447
The Journal of Industrial Economics (GBR) 1136
Journal of Industrial Microbiology and Biotechnology (GBR) 767
Journal of Industrial Relations (GBR) 1690
Journal of Industrial Textiles (GBR) 8454
Journal of Industry, Competition and Trade (USA) 1137
Journal of Inequalities and Applications (USA) 5504
Journal of Infection (GBR) 5820
Journal of Infection and Chemotherapy (JPN) 6853
Journal of Inflammation (GBR) 6248
Journal of Information & Knowledge Management (SGP) 5021
Journal of Information Science (GBR) 5021
Journal of Information Technology (GBR) 5021
Journal of Information Technology & Politics (Online) (USA) *see* Journal of Information Technology & Politics. 7448
Journal of Infrared, Millimeter and Terahertz Waves (Online) (USA) *see* Journal of Infrared, Millimeter and Terahertz Waves. 7078
Journal of Infrastructure Systems (USA) 3275
Journal of Infusion Nursing (USA) 5965
Journal of Inherited Metabolic Disease (NLD) 6094
Journal of Inorganic and Organometallic Polymers and Materials (USA) 2124
Journal of Inorganic Biochemistry (USA) 736
Journal of Insect Behavior (USA) 852
Journal of Insect Conservation (GBR) 852
Journal of Insect Physiology (GBR) 852
Journal of Institutional Economics (GBR) 1137
Journal of Integrated Design & Process Science (NLD) 3205
Journal of Integrative Environmental Sciences (GBR) 8114

Online Service

Journal of Paediatrics and Child Health (GBR) **6094**
The Journal of Pain (USA) **6155**
Journal of Pain & Palliative Care Pharmacotherapy (USA) **6855**
Journal of Pain and Symptom Management (USA) **6155**
Journal of Paleolimnology (NLD) **6726**
Journal of Palestine Studies (USA) **4322**
Journal of Palliative Medicine (USA) **5653**
Journal of Parallel and Distributed Computing (USA) **2429**
Journal of Pathology (GBR) **5653**
Journal of Peace Education (GBR) **7249**
Journal of Peace Research (GBR) **7249**
The Journal of Peasant Studies (GBR) **8115**
Journal of Pediatric and Adolescent Gynecology (NLD) **6095**
Journal of Pediatric Gastroenterology and Nutrition (USA) **6662**
Journal of Pediatric Health Care (USA) **6095**
Journal of Pediatric Hematology / Oncology (USA) **6025**
Journal of Pediatric Neurology (NLD) **6095**
Journal of Pediatric Nursing (USA) **5966**
Journal of Pediatric Oncology Nursing (USA) **6025**
Journal of Pediatric Orthopaedics (USA) **6065**
Journal of Pediatric Orthopaedics. Part B (USA) **6065**
Journal of Pediatric Psychology (GBR) **7377**
Journal of Pediatric Surgery (USA) **6249**
Journal of Pediatric Urology (NLD) **6270**
The Journal of Pediatrics (USA) **6095**
Journal of Pelvic Medicine and Surgery (USA) **6249**
Journal of Pension Economics and Finance (GBR) **1868**
Journal of Peptide Science (GBR) **2125**
Journal of Performance of Constructed Facilities (USA) **3276**
Journal of PeriAnesthesia Nursing (USA) **5967**
Journal of Perinatal Medicine (DEU) **5996**
Journal of Perinatology (GBR) **5996**
Journal of Periodontal Research (DNK) **5853**
Journal of Personal Selling and Sales Management (USA) **1826**
Journal of Personality (USA) **7377**
Journal of Personality Assessment (USA) **7377**
Journal of Personality Disorders (USA) **7378**
Journal of Pest Science (DEU) **852**
Journal of Petroleum Science and Engineering (NLD) **6776**
Journal of Petrology (GBR) **2750**
Journal of Pharmaceutical and Biomedical Analysis (NLD) **6855**
Journal of Pharmaceutical Sciences (USA) **6855**
Journal of Pharmacokinetics and Pharmacodynamics (USA) **6855**
Journal of Pharmacological and Toxicological Methods (USA) **3499**
Journal of Pharmacy and Pharmacology (GBR) **6856**
Journal of Pharmacy Practice (USA) **6856**
Journal of Phenomenological Psychology (NLD) **7378**
Journal of Philosophical Logic (NLD) **6929**
Journal of Philosophy of Education (GBR) **6929**
Journal of Phonetics (GBR) **5135**
Journal of Photochemistry and Photobiology, A: Chemistry (CHE) **2137**
Journal of Photochemistry and Photobiology, B: Biology (CHE) **737**
Journal of Photochemistry and Photobiology, C: Photochemistry Reviews (CHE) **2137**
Journal of Phycology (USA) **797**
Journal of Physical and Chemical Reference Data (USA) **2068**
The Journal of Physical Chemistry Part A: Molecules, Spectroscopy, Kinetics, Environment and General Theory (USA) **2137**
The Journal of Physical Chemistry Part B: Condensed Matter, Materials, Surfaces, Interfaces & Biophysical (USA) **2137**
Journal of Physical Organic Chemistry (GBR) **2137**
Journal of Physics A: Mathematical and Theoretical (GBR) **7022**
Journal of Physics and Chemistry of Solids (GBR) **7022**
Journal of Physics B: Atomic, Molecular and Optical Physics (GBR) **7022**
Journal of Physics: Condensed Matter (GBR) **7022**
Journal of Physics: Conference Series (Online) (GBR) **7022**
Journal of Physics D: Applied Physics (GBR) **7022**
Journal of Physics G: Nuclear and Particle Physics (GBR) **7067**
The Journal of Physiology (GBR) **925**
Journal of Physiology (Paris) (FRA) **6156**
Journal of Phytopathology (DEU) **797**
Journal of Pidgin and Creole Languages (NLD) **5135**
Journal of Pineal Research (DNK) **6156**
Journal of Plankton Research (GBR) **684**
Journal of Planning Education and Research (USA) **4417**
Journal of Planning History (USA) **4417**
Journal of Planning Literature (USA) **4417**
Journal of Plant Growth Regulation (USA) **798**
Journal of Plant Nutrition (USA) **798**
Journal of Plant Nutrition and Soil Science (DEU) **716**
Journal of Plant Physiology (DEU) **798**
Journal of Plant Research (JPN) **798**
Journal of Plasma Physics (GBR) **7022**
Journal of Plastic Film and Sheeting (GBR) **7093**
Journal of Plastic, Reconstructive & Aesthetic Surgery (Online Edition) (GBR) **6249**
Journal of Poetry Therapy (USA) **7378**
Journal of Police Crisis Negotiations (USA) **4892**
Journal of Policy Analysis and Management (USA) **7448**
Journal of Policy and Practice in Intellectual Disabilities (USA) **4067**
Journal of Policy History (USA) **7147**
Journal of Policy Modeling (USA) **7147**
Journal of Politeness Research (DEU) **5135**
Journal of Political Ideologies (GBR) **7147**
Journal of Political Marketing (USA) **7148**
Journal of Political Philosophy (GBR) **6929**
Journal of Political Science Education (USA) **7148**
The Journal of Politics (USA) **7148**
Journal of Polymer Research (NLD) **7093**
Journal of Polymer Science. Part A, Polymer Chemistry (USA) **2125**
Journal of Polymer Science. Part B, Polymer Physics (USA) **2125**
Journal of Polymers and the Environment (USA) **2125**
Journal of Popular Culture (USA) **5315**
Journal of Popular Music Studies (USA) **6581**
Journal of Population Economics (DEU) **7286**
Journal of Porous Materials (USA) **3350**
Journal of Porphyrins and Phthalocyanines (SGP) **2068**
The Journal of Positive Psychology (GBR) **7378**
Journal of Post Keynesian Economics (USA) **1545**
Journal of Postcolonial Writing (GBR) **5315**
Journal of Postgraduate Medicine (IND) **5654**
Journal of Poverty (USA) **8050**
The Journal of Poverty and Social Justice (Online) (GBR) *see* The Journal of Poverty and Social Justice. **8050**
Journal of Power Sources (CHE) **3322**
Journal of Practice Teaching in Health & Social Work (GBR) **8050**
Journal of Pragmatics (NLD) **5203**
Journal of Pressure Vessel Technology (USA) **3386**
Journal of Prevention and Intervention in the Community (USA) **7417**
The Journal of Primary Prevention (USA) **7378**
Journal of Process Control (GBR) **2537**
Journal of Product and Brand Management (GBR) **1826**
Journal of Product Innovation Management (USA) **1890**
Journal of Productivity Analysis (USA) **1769**
Journal of Professional Issues in Engineering Education and Practice (USA) **3276**
Journal of Professional Nursing (USA) **5967**
Journal of Progressive Human Services (USA) **8050**
Journal of Promotion Management (USA) **27**
Journal of Property Investment & Finance (GBR) **7596**
Journal of Property Research (GBR) **4417**
Journal of Prosthetic Dentistry (USA) **5853**
Journal of Prosthodontics (USA) **5853**
Journal of Proteome Research (USA) **737**
Journal of Proteomics (NLD) **737**
Journal of Psychiatric and Mental Health Nursing Online (GBR) **6156**
Journal of Psychiatric Practice (USA) **6156**
Journal of Psychiatric Research (GBR) **6156**
Journal of Psychoeducational Assessment (USA) **2877**
Journal of Psycholinguistic Research (USA) **5135**
Journal of Psychopathology and Behavioral Assessment (USA) **7379**
Journal of Psychopharmacology (GBR) **6856**
Journal of Psychosocial Oncology (USA) **6025**
Journal of Psychosomatic Obstetrics and Gynecology (GBR) **5997**
Journal of Psychosomatic Research (USA) **6156**
Journal of Psychotherapy Integration (USA) **6156**
Journal of Public Administration Research and Theory (GBR) **7448**
Journal of Public Affairs (GBR) **7448**
Journal of Public Economic Theory (USA) **1545**
Journal of Public Economics (CHE) **1545**
Journal of Public Health (Online) (GBR) **8050**
Journal of Public Health Policy (GBR) **7529**
Journal of Public Policy (GBR) **7979**
Journal of Public Relations Research (USA) **27**
Journal of Purchasing & Supply Management (GBR) **1826**
Journal of Pure and Applied Algebra (NLD) **5506**
Journal of Quality Assurance in Hospitality & Tourism (USA) **4392**
Journal of Quality in Maintenance Engineering (GBR) **3369**
Journal of Quantitative Criminology (USA) **2658**
Journal of Quantitative Linguistics (NLD) **5203**
Journal of Quantitative Spectroscopy & Radiative Transfer (GBR) **7079**
Journal of Quaternary Science (GBR) **2751**
Journal of Radio & Audio Media (USA) **2359**
Journal of Radioanalytical and Nuclear Chemistry (HUN) **2102**
Journal of Radiological Protection (GBR) **3170**
Journal of Radiology Nursing (USA) **5967**
Journal of Raman Spectroscopy (GBR) **2103**
Journal of Rapid Methods and Automation in Microbiology (USA) **890**
Journal of Rational - Emotive and Cognitive - Behavior Therapy (USA) **7379**
Journal of Real Estate Finance and Economics (USA) **7597**
Journal of Real Estate Literature (USA) **7597**
Journal of Receptors and Signal Transduction (USA) **684**
Journal of Reconstructive Microsurgery (USA) **6249**
Journal of Refugee Studies (GBR) **7249**
Journal of Regional Science (USA) **4417**
Journal of Regulatory Economics (USA) **1546**
Journal of Rehabilitation Medicine (NOR) **8051**
Journal of Reinforced Plastics & Composites (GBR) **3351**
Journal of Relationship Marketing (USA) **1138**
Journal of Religion and Health (USA) **7656**
Journal of Religion and Spirituality in Social Work (USA) **8051**
Journal of Religion, Disability & Health (USA) **7656**
Journal of Religion in Africa (NLD) **7737**
Journal of Religion, Spirituality & Aging (USA) **4049**
Journal of Religious & Theological Information (USA) **7656**
Journal of Religious Ethics (USA) **7656**
Journal of Religious History (AUS) **7656**
Journal of Renovascular Disease (GBR) **5794**
Journal of Reproductive and Infant Psychology (GBR) **7379**
Journal of Reproductive Immunology (IRL) **5763**
Journal of Research in Crime and Delinquency (USA) **2658**
Journal of Research in International Education (GBR) **3014**
Journal of Research in Nursing (GBR) **5967**
Journal of Research in Personality (USA) **7379**
Journal of Research in Reading (GBR) **2878**
Journal of Research in Science Teaching (USA) **7872**
The Journal of Research in Special Educational Needs (GBR) **3042**
Journal of Research on Adolescence (USA) **2156**
Journal of Retailing (GBR) **1826**
Journal of Retailing and Consumer Services (GBR) **1826**
Journal of Revenue and Pricing Management (GBR) **1295**
Journal of Risk and Insurance (USA) **4510**
Journal of Risk and Uncertainty (USA) **1546**
The Journal of Risk Finance (GBR) **1636**
Journal of Risk Research (GBR) **3448**
The Journal of Rural Health (USA) **5654**
Journal of Rural Studies (GBR) **8115**
Journal of Russian and East European Psychology (USA) **7379**
Journal of Russian Laser Research (USA) **3206**
Journal of Safety Research (GBR) **6680**
Journal of Sandwich Structures & Materials (GBR) **3351**
Journal of Scandinavian Studies in Criminology and Crime Prevention (NOR) **2658**
Journal of Scheduling (USA) **2593**
Journal of Scholarly Publishing (CAN) **7564**
Journal of School Health (USA) **7529**
Journal of School Psychology (GBR) **7380**
Journal of School Violence (USA) **2878**
Journal of Science Education and Technology (USA) **7873**
Journal of Science Teacher Education (NLD) **2878**
Journal of Scientific Computing (USA) **7940**
Journal of Sea Research (NLD) **2810**
Journal of Second Language Writing (GBR) **5135**
Journal of Seismology (NLD) **2785**
Journal of Semantics (GBR) **5203**
Journal of Semitic Studies (GBR) **5135**
Journal of Sensory Studies (USA) **6157**
Journal of Separation Science (DEU) **2103**
Journal of Service Management (GBR) **1769**
Journal of Service Research (USA) **1826**
Journal of Services Marketing (GBR) **1827**
Journal of Sex & Marital Therapy (USA) **7380**
Journal of Sexual Aggression (GBR) **7380**
Journal of Sexual Medicine (GBR) **5654**
Journal of Shoulder and Elbow Surgery (USA) **6250**
Journal of Signal Processing Systems (USA) **2534**
The Journal of Slavic Military Studies (GBR) **6429**
Journal of Sleep Research Online (GBR) **5654**
Journal of Small Business and Enterprise Development (GBR) **1962**
Journal of Small Business Management (USA) **1962**
Journal of Social and Clinical Psychology (USA) **7380**
Journal of Social and Personal Relationships (GBR) **7380**
Journal of Social Archaeology (GBR) **401**
Journal of Social Development in Africa (ZWE) **8051**
Journal of Social History (USA) **8115**
Journal of Social Issues (USA) **7380**
Journal of Social Philosophy (USA) **6929**
Journal of Social Policy (GBR) **8051**
Journal of Social Service Research (USA) **8051**
The Journal of Social Welfare and Family Law (GBR) **4911**
Journal of Social Work (GBR) **8051**
Journal of Social Work in Disability & Rehabilitation (USA) **8051**
Journal of Social Work in End-of-Life & Palliative Care (USA) **7380**
Journal of Social Work Practice (GBR) **8051**
Journal of Social Work Practice in the Addictions (USA) **8051**
Journal of Socio-Economics (GBR) **1546**
Journal of Sociolinguistics (GBR) **5135**
Journal of Sociology (GBR) **8116**
Journal of Software Maintenance and Evolution (GBR) **2593**
Journal of Sol-Gel Science and Technology (NLD) **3351**
Journal of Solar Energy Engineering (USA) **3176**
Journal of Solid State Chemistry (USA) **2138**
Journal of Solid State Electrochemistry (DEU) **2114**
Journal of Solution Chemistry (USA) **2138**
Journal of Sound and Vibration (GBR) **7088**
Journal of South American Earth Sciences (GBR) **2711**
Journal of Southeast Asian Studies (GBR) **4185**
Journal of Southeast European and Black Sea Studies (GBR) **7249**
Journal of Southern African Studies (GBR) **7980**
Journal of Spanish Cultural Studies (GBR) **3545**
Journal of Speculative Philosophy (USA) **6930**
Journal of Spinal Disorders & Techniques (Online) (USA) **6065**
Journal of Spirituality in Mental Health (USA) **7381**
Journal of Sport and Social Issues (USA) **8182**
Journal of Sport and Tourism (GBR) **4978**
Journal of Sports Economics (USA) **1138**
Journal of Sports Sciences (GBR) **8183**
Journal of Statistical Computation and Simulation (GBR) **2443**
Journal of Statistical Mechanics: Theory and Experiment (GBR) **7060**
Journal of Statistical Physics (USA) **7022**
Journal of Statistical Planning and Inference (NLD) **8383**
The Journal of Steroid Biochemistry and Molecular Biology (GBR) **737**
Journal of Stored Products Research (GBR) **853**
Journal of Strain Analysis for Engineering Design (GBR) **3351**
The Journal of Strategic Information Systems (NLD) **2523**
Journal of Strategic Marketing (GBR) **1827**
The Journal of Strategic Studies (GBR) **7249**
Journal of Stroke & Cerebrovascular Diseases (USA) **5794**
Journal of Structural and Functional Genomics (NLD) **874**
Journal of Structural Biology (USA) **684**
Journal of Structural Chemistry (USA) **2069**
Journal of Structural Engineering (USA) **3276**
Journal of Structural Geology (GBR) **2751**
Journal of Studies in International Education (USA) **3014**
Journal of Substance Abuse Treatment (USA) **2696**
Journal of Substance Use (GBR) **2696**
Journal of Supercomputing (USA) **2430**
Journal of Superconductivity and Novel Magnetism (USA) **7023**
The Journal of Supercritical Fluids (NLD) **2103**
Journal of Supply Chain Management (USA) **1827**
Journal of Supreme Court History (USA) **4953**
Journal of Surgical Education (USA) **6250**
Journal of Surgical Oncology (USA) **6250**
Journal of Surgical Research (USA) **6250**
Journal of Surveying Engineering (USA) **3276**
Journal of Sustainable Agriculture (USA) **128**
Journal of Sustainable Forestry (USA) **3695**
Journal of Sustainable Tourism (GBR) **8726**
Journal of Symbolic Computation (GBR) **5553**
Journal of Synchrotron Radiation (DNK) **7068**
Journal of Systematic Palaeontology (GBR) **2751**
Journal of Systemic Therapies (USA) **7381**
Journal of Systems and Software (USA) **2593**
Journal of Systems Architecture (NLD) **2523**
Journal of Systems Science and Systems Engineering (DEU) **2523**
Journal of Targeting, Measurement and Analysis for Marketing (GBR) **1890**
Journal of Teacher Education (USA) **2878**
Journal of Teaching in International Business (USA) **1574**
Journal of Teaching in Social Work (USA) **3068**
Journal of Teaching in the Addictions (USA) **3068**
Journal of Teaching in Travel & Tourism (USA) **3068**
Journal of Technology in Human Services (USA) **8151**
Journal of Technology Management in China (GBR) **8429**
Journal of Technology Transfer (USA) **8429**
Journal of Telemedicine and Telecare (GBR) **5655**
Journal of Terramechanics (GBR) **8501**
Journal of Testing and Evaluation (USA) **3351**
Journal of Texture Studies (USA) **3652**
Journal of the Asia Pacific Economy (GBR) **1495**
Journal of the Early Republic (USA) **4300**
Journal of the Economic and Social History of the Orient (NLD) **4322**
Journal of the History of Biology (NLD) **685**
Journal of the History of Collections (GBR) **6526**
Journal of the History of Economic Thought (GBR) **1546**
Journal of the History of Ideas (USA) **4461**
Journal of the History of International Law (NLD) **4933**
Journal of the History of Medicine and Allied Sciences (GBR) **5655**
Journal of the History of Philosophy (USA) **6930**
Journal of the History of Sexuality (USA) **8116**
Journal of the History of the Behavioral Sciences (USA) **7381**
Journal of the History of the Neurosciences (GBR) **6157**
Journal of the Japanese and International Economies (USA) **1574**
Journal of the Learning Sciences (USA) **2879**
Journal of the Mechanics and Physics of Solids (GBR) **7060**

Online Service

DIRECTORY 2010 SWETSWISE ONLINE CONTENT 11281

Al- Masaq (GBR) **7714**
Mass Communication and Society (USA) **8119**
Mass Spectrometry Reviews (USA) **7080**
Matatu (NLD) **5331**
Materials and Corrosion (DEU) **6321**
Materials & Design (GBR) **3352**
Materials & Manufacturing Processes (USA) **3389**
Materials and Structures (NLD) **1022**
Materials Characterization (USA) **6322**
Materials Chemistry and Physics (CHE) **3352**
Materials Letters (NLD) **7025**
Materials Research Bulletin (GBR) **2111**
Materials Research Innovations (GBR) **7881**
Materials Science (USA) **3353**
Materials Science and Engineering A: Structural Materials: Properties, Microstructures and Processing (CHE) **3353**
Materials Science and Engineering B: Advanced Functional Solid-state Materials (CHE) **3353**
Materials Science and Engineering C: Materials for Biological Applications (CHE) **3353**
Materials Science and Engineering R: Reports (CHE) **3353**
Materials Science and Technology (GBR) **3353**
Materials Science in Semiconductor Processing (GBR) **3108**
Materials Today (NLD) **2072**
Materialwissenschaft und Werkstofftechnik (DEU) **6322**
Materiaux et Techniques (FRA) **3354**
Maternal and Child Health Journal (USA) **5998**
Maternal and Child Nutrition (GBR) **6663**
Mathematical and Computer Modelling (GBR) **5512**
Mathematical and Computer Modelling of Dynamical Systems (GBR) **5554**
Mathematical Biosciences (USA) **5512**
Mathematical Finance (USA) **1367**
Mathematical Geosciences (Online) (USA) *see* Mathematical Geosciences. **2754**
Mathematical Logic Quarterly (DEU) **5513**
Mathematical Medicine and Biology (Online) (GBR) **5513**
Mathematical Methods in the Applied Sciences (GBR) **5513**
Mathematical Methods of Operations Research (DEU) **1779**
Mathematical Models and Methods in Applied Sciences (SGP) **5513**
Mathematical Physics, Analysis and Geometry (NLD) **7026**
Mathematical Population Studies (USA) **7287**
Mathematical Problems in Engineering (USA) **3209**
Mathematical Programming (DEU) **5554**
Mathematical Social Sciences (NLD) **5514**
Mathematical Structures in Computer Science (GBR) **5554**
Mathematical Thinking and Learning (USA) **5515**
Mathematics and Computers in Simulation (NLD) **2517**
Mathematics and Mechanics of Solids (GBR) **7026**
Mathematics of Computation (USA) **5516**
Mathematics of Control, Signals and Systems (GBR) **3370**
Mathematics of Operations Research (USA) **2431**
Mathematische Annalen (DEU) **5516**
Mathematische Nachrichten (DEU) **5517**
Mathematische Zeitschrift (DEU) **5517**
Matrix Biology (NLD) **5665**
Maturitas (IRL) **5998**
Das Mauerwerk (DEU) **1023**
Measurement (NLD) **6403**
Measurement (USA) **5517**
Measurement in Physical Education and Exercise Science (USA) **6992**
Measurement Techniques (USA) **6404**
Measuring Business Excellence (GBR) **1779**
Meat Science (NLD) **3656**
Mecanique & Industries (FRA) **3389**
Meccanica (NLD) **7060**
Mechanical Systems and Signal Processing (GBR) **3389**
Mechanics Based Design of Structures and Machines (USA) **3389**
Mechanics of Advanced Materials and Structures (USA) **3354**
Mechanics of Composite Materials (USA) **3250**
Mechanics of Materials (NLD) **3354**
Mechanics of Time Dependent Materials (NLD) **7061**
Mechanics Research Communications (GBR) **3354**
Mechanism and Machine Theory (GBR) **3389**
Mechanisms of Ageing and Development (IRL) **4051**
Mechanisms of Development (IRL) **834**
Mechatronics (GBR) **3390**
Medecine et Chirurgie du Pied (FRA) **6252**
Medecine et Droit (FRA) **5915**
Medecine et Maladies Infectieuses (FRA) **5822**
Media, Culture & Society (GBR) **8120**
Media History (GBR) **8120**
Media Psychology (USA) **7384**
Mediators of Inflammation (USA) **5666**
Medical & Biological Engineering & Computing (DEU) **826**
Medical & Veterinary Entomology Online (GBR) **5667**
Medical Anthropology (USA) **347**
Medical Care (USA) **5667**
Medical Care Research and Review (USA) **7548**
Medical Decision Making (USA) **5667**
Medical Dosimetry (USA) **6203**
Medical Education (GBR) **5668**
Medical Engineering & Physics (GBR) **5668**
Medical Hypotheses (GBR) **5669**
Medical Image Analysis (GBR) **6203**
Medical Laser Application (DEU) **5909**
Medical Law Review (GBR) **4731**
Medical Microbiology and Immunology (DEU) **5763**
Medical Molecular Morphology (JPN) **899**
Medical Mycology (GBR) **5822**
Medical Oncology (GBR) **6027**
Medical Physics (USA) **5670**
Medical Principles and Practice (CHE) **5670**
Medical Reference Services Quarterly (USA) **5031**
Medical Teacher (GBR) **5672**
Medicinal Chemistry (NLD) **5673**
Medicinal Chemistry Research (USA) **5673**
Medicinal Research Reviews (USA) **6861**
Medicine (Baltimore) (USA) **5674**
Medicine (CD-ROM Edition) (GBR) **5674**
Medicine and Science in Sports and Exercise (USA) **6231**
Medicine, Conflict and Survival (GBR) **5674**
Medicine, Healthcare and Philosophy (NLD) **5674**
Medicine - U K Edition (GBR) **5674**
Medieval Archaeology (GBR) **405**
Medieval Encounters (NLD) **7726**
The Medieval History Journal (IND) **4152**
Mediterranean Historical Review (GBR) **4323**
Mediterranean Journal of Mathematics (CHE) **5517**
Mediterranean Politics (GBR) **7252**
Mediterranean Quarterly (USA) **7252**
Medizinische Klinik (DEU) **5677**
Medizinrecht (DEU) **5915**
Melanoma Research (GBR) **6027**
Membrane Technology (GBR) **2072**
Memory (GBR) **7384**
Memory and Cognition (USA) **7384**
Men and Masculinities (USA) **6303**
Mendeleev Communications (RUS) **2072**
Menninger Clinic. Bulletin (USA) **6159**
Menopause (USA) **5998**
Menopause International (GBR) **5998**
Mental Health in Family Medicine (GBR) **6160**
Mental Health, Religion & Culture (GBR) **7385**
Mental Health Weekly (USA) **7385**
Mentalhigiene es Pszichoszomatika (HUN) **6160**
Mentoring & Tutoring (GBR) **3072**
Meridians (USA) **8901**
Merrill - Palmer Quarterly (USA) **7385**
Metabolic Brain Disease (USA) **5678**
Metabolic Engineering (USA) **750**
Metabolic Syndrome and Related Disorders (USA) **5897**
Metabolism (USA) **5897**
Metabolomics (USA) **925**
Metacognition and Learning (USA) **2886**
Metal Finishing (USA) **6323**
Metal Powder Report (GBR) **6340**
Metal Science and Heat Treatment (USA) **6323**
Metallurgist (USA) **6325**
Metaphilosophy (GBR) **6934**
Metaphor and Symbol (USA) **5151**
Metascience (GBR) **7882**
Meteorological Applications (GBR) **6390**
Meteorologische Zeitschrift (DEU) **6391**
Meteorology and Atmospheric Physics (AUT) **6391**
Method & Theory in the Study of Religion (NLD) **7663**
Methodology and Computing in Applied Probability (USA) **5517**
Methods (USA) **738**
Methods of Information in Medicine (DEU) **5678**
Metrika (DEU) **8388**
Metroeconomica (GBR) **1149**
Metrologia (FRA) **6404**
Mexican Studies (USA) **4464**
Microbes and Infection (FRA) **891**
Microbial Cell Factories (GBR) **834**
Microbial Drug Resistance (USA) **5679**
Microbial Ecology (USA) **891**
Microbial Ecology in Health & Disease (GBR) **5822**
Microbial Pathogenesis (GBR) **5823**
Microbiological Research (DEU) **891**
Microbiology (RUS) **891**
Microchemical Journal (USA) **899**
Microchimica Acta (AUT) **2103**
Microcirculation (GBR) **5679**
Microelectronic Engineering (NLD) **3108**
Microelectronics International (GBR) **3109**
Microelectronics Journal (GBR) **3109**
Microelectronics Reliability (GBR) **3109**
Microfluidics and Nanofluidics (DEU) **3390**
Micron (GBR) **899**
Microporous and Mesoporous Materials (NLD) **2138**
Microprocessors and Microsystems (NLD) **2572**
Microscopy and Microanalysis (USA) **900**
Microscopy Research and Technique (USA) **900**
Microsurgery (USA) **6252**
Microsystem Technologies (DEU) **2473**
Microvascular Research (USA) **5795**
Microwave & Optical Technology Letters (USA) **7080**
Middle East Critique (GBR) **555**
Middle East Policy (USA) **7252**
Middle Eastern Literatures (Online) (GBR) **5333**
Middle Eastern Studies (GBR) **4323**
Midwest Studies in Philosophy (USA) **6934**
Midwifery (GBR) **5998**
Milan Journal of Mathematics (CHE) **5518**
The Milbank Quarterly (USA) **7154**
The Military Balance (Year) (GBR) **6435**
Military Psychology (USA) **7385**
Milton Quarterly (USA) **5334**
Mind (GBR) **6934**
Mind & Language (GBR) **6934**
Mind & Society (DEU) **7985**
Mind, Culture, and Activity (USA) **7986**
Minds and Machines (NLD) **2454**
Mine Water and the Environment (DEU) **3489**
Mineral Processing and Extractive Metallurgy Review (USA) **6326**
Mineralium Deposita (DEU) **2755**
Mineralogical Magazine (GBR) **6471**
Mineralogy and Petrology (AUT) **6471**
Minerals & Energy (GBR) **1601**
Minerals Engineering (GBR) **6471**
Minerva (NLD) **7882**
Minerva Journal of Women and War (USA) **6437**
Mini - Reviews in Medicinal Chemistry (NLD) **2073**
Mini - Reviews in Organic Chemistry (NLD) **2127**
Minimally Invasive Neurosurgery (DEU) **6161**
Minimally Invasive Therapy and Allied Technologies (GBR) **5679**
Mission Studies (NLD) **7664**
The Missouri Review (USA) **5335**
Mitigation and Adaptation Strategies for Global Change (NLD) **3453**
Mitochondrial D N A (GBR) **738**
Mitochondrion (NLD) **893**
Mitteilungen aus dem Museum fuer Naturkunde in Berlin - Deutsche Entomologische Zeitschrift (DEU) **855**
Mitteilungen aus dem Museum fuer Naturkunde in Berlin - Geowissenschaftliche Reihe (DEU) **2713**
Mitteilungen zur Christlichen Archaeologie (AUT) **506**
Mnemosyne (NLD) **2237**
Mobile Networks and Applications (NLD) **2501**
Mobilities (GBR) **7287**
Modern and Contemporary France (GBR) **4245**
Modern Asian Studies (GBR) **556**
Modern China (USA) **4186**
Modern Drama (CAN) **5335**
M F S Modern Fiction Studies (USA) **5335**
Modern Intellectual History (GBR) **5228**
Modern Italy (GBR) **4245**
Modern Judaism (GBR) **3551**
Modern Language Journal (USA) **5151**
Modern Language Quarterly (USA) **5335**
The Modern Law Review (GBR) **4735**
Modern Pathology (GBR) **5680**
Modern Physics Letters A (SGP) **7068**
Modern Physics Letters B (SGP) **7068**
Modern Rheumatology (JPN) **6225**
Modern Theology (GBR) **7664**
Modernism/Modernity (USA) **4153**
Molecular and Biochemical Parasitology (NLD) **738**
Molecular and Cellular Biochemistry (USA) **738**
Molecular and Cellular Endocrinology (IRL) **5897**
Molecular and Cellular Neuroscience (USA) **6161**
Molecular and Cellular Probes (GBR) **5909**
Molecular Aspects of Medicine (GBR) **5680**
Molecular Biology (RUS) **739**
Molecular Biology and Evolution (USA) **689**
Molecular Biology Reports (NLD) **739**
Molecular BioSystems (GBR) **689**
Molecular Biotechnology (USA) **768**
Molecular Breeding (NLD) **801**
Molecular Cancer (GBR) **6027**
Molecular Carcinogenesis (USA) **6028**
Molecular Cell (USA) **835**
Molecular Crystals and Liquid Crystals (CHE) **2111**
Molecular Diagnosis and Therapy (NZL) **5680**
Molecular Diversity (NLD) **7068**
Molecular Ecology (GBR) **893**
Molecular Ecology Resources (GBR) **893**
Molecular Genetics and Genomics (DEU) **875**
Molecular Genetics and Metabolism (USA) **739**
Molecular Human Reproduction (GBR) **5999**
Molecular Imaging (CAN) **835**
Molecular Imaging and Biology (NLD) **6203**
Molecular Immunology (GBR) **739**
Molecular Medicine (USA) **6862**
Molecular Membrane Biology (GBR) **739**
Molecular Microbiology (GBR) **893**
Molecular Neurobiology (USA) **739**
Molecular Nutrition & Food Research (Online) (DEU) **6663**
Molecular Pain (GBR) **5680**
Molecular Pharmaceutics (USA) **2073**
Molecular Phylogenetics and Evolution (USA) **875**
Molecular Physics (GBR) **2138**
Molecular Plant Pathology (GBR) **802**
Molecular Psychiatry (Online) (GBR) *see* Molecular Psychiatry. **6161**
Molecular Reproduction and Development (USA) **740**
Molecular Simulation (CHE) **2073**
Molecular Systems Biology (GBR) **690**
Molecular Therapy (GBR) **6028**
Molluscan Research (NZL) **955**
Monatshefte fuer Chemie (AUT) **2073**
Monatshefte fuer Mathematik (AUT) **5518**
Monatsschrift Kinderheilkunde (DEU) **6097**
Monte Carlo Methods and Applications (DEU) **5555**
Monumenta Nipponica (JPN) **556**
Mortality (GBR) **7532**
Moscow Mathematical Society. Transactions (USA) **5518**
Motivation and Emotion (USA) **7386**
Movement Disorders (USA) **6162**
The Moving Image (USA) **6508**
Multibody System Dynamics (NLD) **7061**
Multicultural Perspectives (USA) **3073**
Multidimensional Systems and Signal Processing (USA) **2524**
Multilingua (DEU) **5153**
Multimedia Systems (DEU) **2488**
Multimedia Tools and Applications (NLD) **2488**
Multiple Sclerosis (GBR) **6162**
Multiscale Modeling & Simulation: a S I A M Interdisciplinary Journal (USA) **5519**
Multivariate Behavioral Research (USA) **7386**
Muscle & Nerve (USA) **5681**
Le Museon (BEL) **556**
Museum International (English Edition) (GBR) **6531**
Museum Management and Curatorship (GBR) **6531**
Music Analysis (GBR) **6589**
Music and Letters (GBR) **6589**
Music Education Research (GBR) **6590**
Music Library Association. Notes (USA) **5033**
Music Perception (USA) **6591**
Music Reference Services Quarterly (USA) **5033**
Music Theory Spectrum (USA) **6592**
The Musical Quarterly (USA) **6594**
Muslim World (USA) **7715**
Mutagenesis (GBR) **875**
Mutation Research - Genetic Toxicology and Environmental Mutagenesis (NLD) **875**
Mutation Research - Reviews (NLD) **876**
Mycological Progress (DEU) **803**
Mycological Research (GBR) **803**
Mycopathologia (NLD) **803**
Mycorrhiza (DEU) **803**
Mycoscience (JPN) **803**
Mycoses (DEU) **5681**
N D T & E International (GBR) **3355**
N E A News (FRA) **3171**
N M R in Biomedicine (GBR) **6203**
N T M Journal of History of Sciences, Technology, and Medicine (CHE) **7885**
N T Q. New Theatre Quarterly (GBR) **8474**
N W S A Journal (USA) **8901**
Naamkunde (BEL) **5154**
Nabokov Studies (USA) **5337**
Nan Nu (NLD) **557**
Nano Letters (USA) **3355**
NanoBioTechnology (USA) **768**
Nanomedicine: Nanotechnology, Biology and Medicine (USA) **5683**
Nanoscale & Microscale Thermophysical Engineering (Online) (USA) **7056**
Nanotechnology (GBR) **7027**
Narrative (USA) **5338**
Narrative Inquiry (NLD) **5338**
Nashim (ISR) **8901**
National Academy of Sciences. Proceedings (USA) **7886**
National Cancer Institute. Journal (Online) (GBR) **6028**
National Cancer Institute. Journal. Monographs (USA) **6028**
National Civic Review (USA) **7499**
National Identities (GBR) **7156**
National Institute Economic Review (GBR) **1152**
National Society for the Study of Education. Yearbook (USA) **2890**
Nationalism & Ethnic Politics (GBR) **7254**
Nationalities Papers (GBR) **7987**
Nations and Nationalism (GBR) **7157**
Native Plants Journal (USA) **804**
Natur und Recht (DEU) **4739**
Natural Computing (NLD) **2432**
Natural Gas & Electricity (USA) **6779**
Natural Hazards (NLD) **2713**
Natural Hazards Review (USA) **3455**
Natural Language and Linguistic Theory (NLD) **5154**
Natural Language Engineering (GBR) **2509**
Natural Language Semantics (NLD) **5154**
Natural Product Reports (GBR) **2127**
Natural Product Research (CHE) **2074**
Natural Resources Forum (GBR) **4021**
Natural Resources Research (USA) **6474**
Nature (GBR) **7889**
Nature Biotechnology (USA) **768**
Nature Cell Biology (GBR) **835**
Nature Chemical Biology (GBR) **2074**
Nature Clinical Practice Cardiovascular Medicine (GBR) **5796**
Nature Clinical Practice Endocrinology & Metabolism (GBR) **5898**
Nature Clinical Practice Gastroenterology & Hepatology (GBR) **5929**
Nature Clinical Practice Oncology (GBR) **6028**
Nature Genetics (USA) **876**
Nature Immunology (USA) **5764**
Nature Materials (GBR) **3355**
Nature Medicine (GBR) **5684**
Nature Methods (GBR) **7889**
Nature Neuroscience (USA) **6162**
Nature Physics (GBR) **7028**
Nature Reviews. Cancer (GBR) **6028**
Nature Reviews. Drug Discovery (GBR) **6863**
Nature Reviews. Genetics (GBR) **876**
Nature Reviews. Immunology (GBR) **5764**
Nature Reviews. Microbiology (GBR) **893**
Nature Reviews. Molecular Cell Biology (GBR) **893**
Nature Reviews. Neuroscience (GBR) **6162**
Nature Reviews. Urology (GBR) **6271**
Nature Structural and Molecular Biology (USA) **693**
Natures - Sciences - Societes (FRA) **2714**
Naturwissenschaften (DEU) **7890**
Naunyn-Schmiedeberg's Archives of Pharmacology (DEU) **6863**
Naval Research Logistics (USA) **6438**
Negotiation Journal (USA) **7254**
Nematology (NLD) **958**
Neohelicon (HUN) **5339**

Online Service

Link to your serials resources and content with ulrichsweb.com

Online Service

The Review of Economics and Statistics (USA) 1166
Review of Economics of the Household (USA) 1166
The Review of Education - Pedagogy - Cultural Studies (USA) 2935
The Review of English Studies (GBR) 5360
Review of European Community and International Environmental Law (GBR) 3463
Review of Finance (Print) (GBR) 1379
Review of Financial Economics (GBR) 1166
The Review of Financial Studies (USA) 1379
The Review of Higher Education (USA) 3000
Review of Income and Wealth (GBR) 1721
Review of Industrial Organization (NLD) 1548
Review of International Economics (GBR) 1166
Review of International Political Economy (GBR) 1514
Review of International Studies (GBR) 7262
Review of Marketing Research (USA) 1841
Review of Middle East Economics and Finance (Online) (USA) 1166
Review of Pacific Basin Financial Markets and Policies (SGP) 1380
Review of Palaeobotany and Palynology (NLD) 6730
The Review of Policy Research (USA) 7177
Review of Political Economy (GBR) 7178
Review of Public Personnel Administration (USA) 7466
Review of Quantitative Finance and Accounting (USA) 1300
Review of Rabbinic Judaism (NLD) 7728
Review of Radical Political Economics (USA) 1548
Review of Scientific Instruments (USA) 4489
Review of Social Economy (GBR) 1166
Review of Urban & Regional Development Studies (GBR) 1604
Review of World Economics (DEU) 1166
Reviews in American History (USA) 4310
Reviews in Anthropology (USA) 353
Reviews in Clinical Gerontology (GBR) 4054
Reviews in Endocrine & Metabolic Disorders (USA) 5899
Reviews in Environmental Science and Biotechnology (NLD) 770
Reviews in Fish Biology and Fisheries (NLD) 961
Reviews in Fisheries Science (USA) 3605
Reviews in Mathematical Physics (SGP) 7037
Reviews in Medical Microbiology (USA) 5703
Reviews in Medical Virology (GBR) 895
Reviews in Religion and Theology (GBR) 7677
Reviews of Physiology, Biochemistry and Pharmacology (USA) 927
Reviews on Recent Clinical Trials (NLD) 5704
Revista de Psicologia Social (ESP) 7404
Revista Internacional del Trabajo (GBR) 1705
Revolutionary Russia (GBR) 4257
La Revue de Medecine Interne (FRA) 5948
Revue de Metallurgie (FRA) 6330
Revue de Micropaleontologie (FRA) 6730
Revue d'Egyptologie (BEL) 414
Revue des Etudes Armeniennes. Nouvelle Serie (BEL) 4324
Revue des Etudes Juives (BEL) 7729
Revue d'Integration Europeenne (GBR) 7263
Revue du Rhumatisme (French Edition) (FRA) 6226
Revue Europeene de Psychologie Appliquee (NLD) 7405
Revue Francaise d'Allergologie (FRA) 5765
Revue Internationale du Travail (GBR) 1705
Revue Philosophique de Louvain (BEL) 6949
Revue Romane (NLD) 5168
Rheologica Acta (DEU) 7062
Rhetoric & Public Affairs (USA) 5362
Rhetoric Review (USA) 5362
Rhetorica (USA) 5168
Rheumatology (Online) (GBR) 6227
Rheumatology International (DEU) 6227
Risk Analysis (USA) 5530
Risk Management and Insurance Review (USA) 4521
River Research and Applications (GBR) 8831
River Teeth (USA) 5363
Robotica (GBR) 2586
Robotics and Autonomous Systems (NLD) 2586
Robotics and Computer-Integrated Manufacturing (GBR) 2586
Rock Mechanics and Rock Engineering (AUT) 2764
RoeFo. Fortschritte auf dem Gebiet der Roentgenstrahlen und der bildgebenden Verfahren (DEU) 6207
Roemische Historische Mitteilungen (AUT) 4259
Roentgenpraxis (DEU) 6208
Romance Studies (GBR) 5364
Romanistisches Jahrbuch (DEU) 5170
The Round Table (GBR) 7263
Royal Anthropological Institute. Journal (GBR) 354
Royal Asiatic Society. Journal (GBR) 560
Royal Astronomical Society. Monthly Notices (GBR) 580
Royal College of Surgeons of England. Annals (GBR) 6257
Royal College of Surgeons of England. Bulletin (GBR) 6257
Royal Historical Society. Transactions (GBR) 4260
Royal Musical Association. Journal (GBR) 6613
Royal Society of Chemistry. Annual Reports on the Progress of Chemistry. Section A: Inorganic Chemistry (GBR) 2118
Royal Society of Chemistry. Annual Reports on the Progress of Chemistry. Section B: Organic Chemistry (GBR) 2130
Royal Society of Chemistry. Annual Reports on the Progress of Chemistry. Section C: Physical Chemistry (GBR) 2140
Royal Society of London. Notes and Records (GBR) 7904
Royal Society of London. Philosophical Transactions. Biological Sciences (GBR) 702
Royal Society of London. Philosophical Transactions. Mathematical, Physical and Engineering Sciences (GBR) 7038
Royal Society of London. Proceedings. Biological Sciences (GBR) 702
Royal Society of London. Proceedings. Mathematical, Physical and Engineering Sciences (GBR) 5530
Royal Society of Medicine. Journal (GBR) 5707
Royal Society of Tropical Medicine and Hygiene. Transactions (GBR) 5825
Royal Statistical Society. Journal. Series A: Statistics in Society (GBR) 8397
Royal Statistical Society. Journal. Series B: Statistical Methodology (GBR) 8397
Royal Statistical Society. Journal. Series C: Applied Statistics (GBR) 8397
Rural History (GBR) 4260
Russian Academy of Sciences. Biology Bulletin (RUS) 702
Russian Academy of Sciences. Colloid Journal (RUS) 2140
Russian Academy of Sciences. Izvestiya. Atmospheric and Oceanic Physics (RUS) 6394
Russian Academy of Sciences. Izvestiya. Physics of the Solid Earth (RUS) 2789
Russian Academy of Sciences. Mathematical Notes (RUS) 5530
Russian Chemical Bulletin (USA) 2079
Russian Chemical Reviews (RUS) 2079
Russian Education and Society (USA) 2908
Russian Journal of Applied Chemistry (RUS) 3255
Russian Journal of Bioorganic Chemistry (RUS) 2130
Russian Journal of Coordination Chemistry (RUS) 2079
Russian Journal of Developmental Biology (RUS) 702
Russian Journal of Ecology (RUS) 3464
Russian Journal of Electrochemistry (RUS) 2114
Russian Journal of General Chemistry (RUS) 2079
Russian Journal of Genetics (RUS) 878
Russian Journal of Inorganic Chemistry (RUS) 2118
Russian Journal of Marine Biology (RUS) 702
Russian Journal of Nondestructive Testing (RUS) 3357
Russian Journal of Numerical Analysis and Mathematical Modelling (DEU) 5530
Russian Journal of Organic Chemistry (RUS) 2130
Russian Journal of Physical Chemistry A (RUS) 2141
Russian Journal of Plant Physiology (RUS) 816
Russian Linguistics (NLD) 5170
Russian Mathematical Surveys (RUS) 5530
Russian Microelectronics (RUS) 3112
Russian Physics Journal (USA) 7038
Russian Politics and Law (USA) 4777
The Russian Review (USA) 4260
Russian Social Science Review (USA) 7181
Russian Studies in History (USA) 4159
Russian Studies in Literature (USA) 5365
Russian Studies in Philosophy (USA) 6950
S A I S Review (USA) 7264
S A Q: The South Atlantic Quarterly (USA) 5237
S A R and Q S A R in Environmental Research (CHE) 3464
S I A M Journal on Applied Dynamical Systems (USA) 5531
S I A M Journal on Applied Mathematics (USA) 5531
S I A M Journal on Numerical Analysis (USA) 5531
S I A M Review (USA) 5532
S T U F - Sprachtypologie und Universalienforschung (DEU) 5171
Safety Science (NLD) 6686
St. Petersburg Mathematical Journal (USA) 5532
Saline Systems (GBR) 896
Samuel Beckett Today - Aujourd'hui (NLD) 5366
Sarcoma (USA) 6034
Sbornik: Mathematics (RUS) 5533
Scandinavian Actuarial Journal (NOR) 4522
Scandinavian Cardiovascular Journal (NOR) 6257
Scandinavian Cardiovascular Journal. Supplementum (NOR) 5799
Scandinavian Journal of Caring Sciences (NOR) 5710
Scandinavian Journal of Clinical & Laboratory Investigation (NOR) 5910
Scandinavian Journal of Clinical and Laboratory Investigation. Supplement (SWE) 5910
Scandinavian Journal of Disability Research (NOR) 4069
Scandinavian Journal of Economics (GBR) 1171
Scandinavian Journal of Educational Research (GBR) 2909
Scandinavian Journal of Forest Research (NOR) 3701
Scandinavian Journal of Gastroenterology (NOR) 5930
Scandinavian Journal of Gastroenterology. Supplement (NOR) 5930
Scandinavian Journal of History (NOR) 4160
Scandinavian Journal of Hospitality and Tourism (GBR) 8754
Scandinavian Journal of Immunology (GBR) 5765
Scandinavian Journal of Infectious Diseases (NOR) 5826
Scandinavian Journal of Management (GBR) 1792
Scandinavian Journal of Medicine & Science in Sports (DNK) 6232
Scandinavian Journal of Occupational Therapy (NOR) 5710
Scandinavian Journal of Plastic and Reconstructive Surgery and Hand Surgery (NOR) 6257
Scandinavian Journal of Primary Health Care (NOR) 5710
Scandinavian Journal of Psychology (GBR) 7406
Scandinavian Journal of Public Health (GBR) 5710
Scandinavian Journal of Public Health. Supplement (SWE) 5710
Scandinavian Journal of Rheumatology (NOR) 6227
Scandinavian Journal of Rheumatology. Supplement (SWE) 6227
Scandinavian Journal of Statistics (GBR) 8398
Scandinavian Journal of the Old Testament (NOR) 7679
Scandinavian Journal of Urology and Nephrology (NOR) 6274
Scandinavian Journal of Urology and Nephrology. Supplement (NOR) 6274
Scandinavian Political Studies (GBR) 7181
Scando-Slavica (NOR) 5172
Schizophrenia Bulletin (USA) 6184
Schizophrenia Research (NLD) 6184
Der Schmerz (DEU) 5710
School Effectiveness and School Improvement (NLD) 2909
School Leadership (GBR) 2909
School Leadership & Management (Online) (GBR) 3032
School Psychology International (GBR) 3080
School Psychology Quarterly (USA) 7406
Science & Education (NLD) 7908
Science and Global Security (USA) 7908
Science and Public Policy (GBR) 7181
Science & Society (USA) 7182
Science & Sports (FRA) 6232
Science & Technology Libraries (USA) 5046
Science and Technology of Advanced Materials (GBR) 3357
Science and Technology of Welding and Joining (Online) (GBR) 6344
Science as Culture (GBR) 7909
Science Communication (USA) 8131
Science Education (USA) 7909
Science in China. Series A: Mathematics (CHN) 5533
Science in China. Series B: Chemistry (CHN) 2080
Science in China. Series C: Life Sciences (CHN) 703
Science in China. Series D: Earth Sciences (CHN) 2716
Science in China. Series E: Technological Sciences (CHN) 8437
Science in China. Series F: Information Sciences (CHN) 2437
Science in China. Series G: Physics, Mechanics & Astronomy (CHN) 7039
Science in Context (GBR) 7909
Science of Computer Programming (NLD) 2510
Science of the Total Environment (NLD) 3465
Science, Technology & Human Values (USA) 7911
Science, Technology & Society (IND) 7911
Scientia Horticulturae (NLD) 3750
Scientific Programming (NLD) 2597
Scientific Studies of Reading (USA) 2910
The Scientific World Journal (GBR) 7913
Scientometrics (HUN) 7913
Scottish Journal of Geology (GBR) 2766
Scottish Journal of Political Economy (GBR) 1172
Scottish Journal of Theology (GBR) 7680
Scripta Materialia (GBR) 6331
Sealing Technology (GBR) 6720
Second Language Research (GBR) 5172
Security and Human Rights (NLD) 7215
Security Dialogue (GBR) 7265
Security Studies (Quarterly) (USA) 7265
Sedimentary Geology (NLD) 2766
Sedimentology Online (GBR) 2766
Seed Science Research (GBR) 251
Seeing and Perceiving (NLD) 5555
Seizure - European Journal of Epilepsy (GBR) 6184
Selecta Mathematica (CHE) 5533
Self and Identity (GBR) 7407
Semiconductor Science and Technology (GBR) 3113
Semiconductors (USA) 7039
Semigroup Forum (USA) 5533
Seminars in Anesthesia, Perioperative Medicine and Pain (USA) 5774
Seminars in Arthritis and Rheumatism (USA) 6227
Seminars in Cancer Biology (GBR) 928
Seminars in Cell and Developmental Biology (GBR) 836
Seminars in Cutaneous Medicine and Surgery (USA) 5881
Seminars in Dialysis (USA) 6274
Seminars in Fetal & Neonatal Medicine (GBR) 6004
Seminars in Hearing (USA) 6085
Seminars in Immunology (GBR) 5766
Seminars in Immunopathology (DEU) 5766
Seminars in Inflammatory Bowel Disease (CAN) 5931
Seminars in Integrative Medicine (USA) 5712
Seminars in Interventional Radiology (USA) 6208
Seminars in Liver Disease (USA) 5931
Seminars in Musculoskeletal Radiology (USA) 6208
Seminars in Neurology (USA) 6184
Seminars in Nuclear Medicine (USA) 6208
Seminars in Oncology Nursing (USA) 5981
Seminars in Ophthalmology (GBR) 6051
Seminars in Orthodontics (USA) 5865
Seminars in Pain Medicine (USA) 6185
Seminars in Pediatric Infectious Diseases (USA) 6104
Seminars in Pediatric Neurology (USA) 6185
Seminars in Perinatology (USA) 6104
Seminars in Plastic Surgery (USA) 6258
Seminars in Radiation Oncology (USA) 6034
Seminars in Reproductive Medicine (USA) 5900
Seminars in Respiratory and Critical Care Medicine (USA) 6219
Seminars in Roentgenology (USA) 6208
Seminars in Speech and Language (USA) 6085
Seminars in Thrombosis and Hemostasis (USA) 5941
Seminars in Ultrasound, C T and M R I (USA) 6208
Semiotica (DEU) 5173
Senologie (DEU) 8848
Sensing and Imaging (USA) 4489
Sensor Review (GBR) 5459
Sensors and Actuators A: Physical (CHE) 7052
Sensors and Actuators B: Chemical (CHE) 2114
Separation and Purification Reviews (Online) (USA) *see* Separation and Purification Reviews. 2105
Separation and Purification Technology (GBR) 3255
Separation Science and Technology (USA) 2105
Sequential Analysis (USA) 8399
Serials (Online) (GBR) 5047
The Serials Librarian (USA) 5047
Serials Review (GBR) 5047
The Service Industries Journal (GBR) 1172
Services Marketing Quarterly (USA) 1843
Set-Valued and Variational Analysis (NLD) 5535
The Seventeenth Century (GBR) 5369
Sex Education (GBR) 2911
Sex Roles (USA) 7407
Sexual Abuse (USA) 7407
Sexual Addiction & Compulsivity (USA) 7407
Sexual and Relationship Therapy (GBR) 7407
Sexual Health (AUS) 5826
Sexual Plant Reproduction (DEU) 817
Sexualities (GBR) 7408
Sexuality & Culture (USA) 8132
Sexuality and Disability (USA) 5712
Sexuality, Reproduction & Menopause (USA) 6004
Sexually Transmitted Diseases (USA) 5881
Shakespeare (GBR) 5370
Shakespeare Quarterly (USA) 5370
Shaw (USA) 5371
Ships and Offshore Structures (GBR) 8661
Shock (Philadelphia) (USA) 5714
Shock and Vibration (NLD) 7089
The Shock and Vibration Digest (USA) 3357
Shock Waves (DEU) 7063
Shofar (Ashland) (USA) 7729
Siberian Mathematical Journal (USA) 5536
Sibirica (USA) 4028
Sign Language and Linguistics (Online) (NLD) 5173
Sign Language Studies (USA) 5174
Signal Processing (NLD) 2464
Signal Processing: Image Communication (NLD) 2535
Signal Transduction (DEU) 836
Significance (GBR) 8399
Sikh Formations (GBR) 7741
Silicon Chemistry (NLD) 2118
Simulation (GBR) 3220
Simulation & Gaming (USA) 2518
Simulation Modelling Practice and Theory (NLD) 2518
Singapore Economic Review (SGP) 1174
Singapore Journal of Tropical Geography (GBR) 4028
Sirena (Baltimore) (USA) 5434
Skeletal Radiology (DEU) 6208
Skin Pharmacology and Physiology (CHE) 6881
Skin Research and Technology (DNK) 5882
Skull Base (USA) 6258
Slavery and Abolition (GBR) 4161
Slavic & East European Information Resources (USA) 5048
Slavonica (GBR) 5373
Sleep and Biological Rhythm (AUS) 5715
Sleep and Breathing (DEU) 6185
Sleep Medicine (NLD) 6186
Sleep Medicine Reviews (FRA) 6186
Small (DEU) 3357
Small Axe (USA) 5239
Small Business Economics (NLD) 1967
Small Group Research (USA) 7408
Small Ruminant Research (NLD) 300
Small Wars and Insurgencies (GBR) 7265
Smart Materials and Structures (GBR) 7040
Soccer and Society (GBR) 8245
Social & Cultural Geography (GBR) 8002
Social & Legal Studies (GBR) 8132
Social Anthropology (GBR) 355
Social Behavior and Personality (NZL) 7408
Social Choice and Welfare (DEU) 8068
Social Cognition (USA) 7408
Social Compass (GBR) 8132
Social Development (GBR) 8133
Social Epistemology (GBR) 6952
Social Forces (USA) 8133
Social History (GBR) 8003
Social History of Medicine (GBR) 5715
Social Identities (GBR) 3565
Social Indicators Research (NLD) 8150
Social Justice Research (USA) 8133

Online Service

Link to your serials resources and content with ulrichsweb.com

Online Service

11288 THOMSON WEST ULRICH'S PERIODICALS

Zeitschrift fuer Physikalische Chemie (DEU) **2142**
Zeitschrift fuer Phytotherapie (DEU) **5734**
Zeitschrift fuer Religions- und Geistesgeschichte (NLD) **7697**
Zeitschrift fuer Rheumatologie (DEU) **6228**
Zeitschrift fuer Sexualforschung (DEU) **5735**
Zeitschrift fuer Sprachwissenschaft (DEU) **5199**
Zeitschrift fuer Staats- und Europawissenschaften (DEU) **7276**
Zeitschrift fuer Unternehmens- und Gesellschaftsrecht (DEU) **4819**
Zentralblatt fuer Chirurgie (DEU) **6263**
Zentralblatt fuer Gynaekologie (DEU) **6006**
Zentralblatt MATH (DEU) **5549**
Zhejiang University. Journal (Science A) (CHN) **7933**
Zoo Biology (USA) **969**
Zoologica Scripta (GBR) **969**
Zoologischer Anzeiger (DEU) **970**
Zoology (DEU) **970**
Zoomorphology (DEU) **712**
Zoonoses and Public Health (DEU) **8816**
Zoosystematics and Evolution (DEU) **971**
Zygon (USA) **7697**
Zygote (GBR) **879**
III - Vs Review (GBR) **3116**
4 O R (DEU) **2441**

Thomson West (Subsidiary of: Thomson Reuters Corp.) 610 Opperman Dr, Eagan, MN 55123 TEL 651-687-8000, 651-687-7000, 800-344-5008, 800-328-4880, FAX 651-687-7302, 651-687-6674, west.support@thomson.com, http://west.thomson.com
A B A Journal (USA) **4606**
Alabama Law Review (USA) **4612**
The Alabama Lawyer (USA) **4612**
Albany Law Review (USA) **4612**
Alternatives to the High Cost of Litigation (USA) **4613**
American Criminal Law Review (USA) **2643**
American Indian Law Review (USA) **4614**
American Journal of Law & Medicine (USA) **4614**
American Journal of Tax Policy (USA) **1910**
American University Law Review (USA) **4615**
Americans with Disabilities Cases (USA) **4615**
Antitrust & Trade Regulation Report (USA) **4855**
Antitrust Law Journal (USA) **4856**
Antitrust Magazine (USA) **4856**
Arizona State Law Journal (USA) **4621**
The Army Lawyer (USA) **4971**
B N A's Americans with Disabilities Act Manual. Newsletter (USA) **4968**
B N A's Patent, Trademark & Copyright Journal (USA) **6746**
Banking Daily (USA) **1317**
Boston College Law Review (USA) **4631**
Boston University International Law Journal (USA) **4918**
Boston University Law Review (USA) **4631**
The Brief (Chicago) (USA) **4631**
Brigham Young University Law Review (USA) **4632**
Brooklyn Journal of International Law (USA) **4919**
Buffalo Law Review (USA) **4633**
The Business Lawyer (USA) **4859**
C B A Record (USA) **4635**
Campbell Law Review (USA) **4637**
Canadian Journal of Law and Jurisprudence (CAN) **4639**
Capital University Law Review (USA) **2646**
Chemical Regulation Reporter (USA) **3484**
Chicago - Kent Law Review (USA) **4642**
Chicano - Latino Law Review (USA) **4642**
Cleveland State Law Review (USA) **4643**
Columbia Journal of Law and Social Problems (USA) **4645**
Columbia Journal of Transnational Law (USA) **4921**
Columbia Law Review (USA) **4645**
The Computer & Internet Lawyer (USA) **4648**
Connecticut Law Review (USA) **4648**
Constitutional Commentary (USA) **4847**
Cornell International Law Journal (USA) **4922**
Cornell Journal of Law and Public Policy (USA) **4651**
Cornell Law Review (USA) **4651**
Creighton Law Review (USA) **4652**
Cumberland Law Review (USA) **4653**
Current Law Index (USA) **4822**
Daily Environment Report (Online) (USA) **3413**
Daily Labor Report (USA) **1674**
Daily Report for Executives (USA) **1737**
Daily Tax Report (USA) **1919**
Defense Counsel Journal (USA) **4830**
The Delaware Journal of Corporate Law (USA) **4865**
Denver Journal of International Law and Policy (USA) **4922**
Denver University Law Review (USA) **4656**
DePaul Business and Commercial Law Journal (USA) **4656**
Drake Law Review (USA) **4661**
Duke Law Journal (USA) **4661**
Duquesne Law Review (USA) **4662**
East Asian Executive Reports (USA) **1478**
Emory International Law Review (USA) **4924**
Emory Law Journal (USA) **4664**
Energy Law Journal (USA) **4665**
Environment Reporter (USA) **3422**
Environmental Law Reporter (USA) **3426**
Estate Planning (New York, 1973) (USA) **4902**
Family Advocate (USA) **4909**
Family Law Quarterly (USA) **4910**
Federal Contracts Report (USA) **7436**
The Federal Lawyer (USA) **4673**
Federal Register (USA) **4673**
Federal Sentencing Reporter (USA) **2652**
Fletcher Forum of World Affairs (USA) **7235**
The Florida Bar Journal (USA) **4675**
Florida Law Review (USA) **4675**
Florida State University Law Review (USA) **4675**
Fordham Intellectual Property, Media & Entertainment Law Journal (USA) **4676**
Fordham International Law Journal (USA) **4926**
Fordham Law Review (USA) **4676**
Fordham Urban Law Journal (USA) **4676**
Forensic Services Directory (USA) **4676**
George Mason Law Review (USA) **4679**
The George Washington International Law Review (USA) **4926**
George Washington Law Review (USA) **4679**
Georgetown Immigration Law Journal (USA) **4679**
Georgetown International Environmental Law Review (USA) **3433**
Georgetown Journal of International Law (USA) **4926**
Georgetown Law Journal (USA) **4680**
Georgia Journal of International and Comparative Law (USA) **4926**
Georgia Law Review (USA) **4680**
Golden Gate University Law Review (USA) **4681**
Government Employee Relations Report (USA) **1684**
Gower Federal Service - Mining (USA) **6464**
Gower Federal Service - Miscellaneous Land Decisions (USA) **6464**
Gower Federal Service - Oil and Gas (USA) **6771**
Gower Federal Service - Outer Continental Shelf (USA) **6771**
Hamline Law Review (USA) **4684**
Harvard Civil Rights - Civil Liberties Law Review (USA) **4832**
Harvard Environmental Law Review (USA) **4684**
Harvard International Law Journal (USA) **4927**
Harvard Journal of Law & Gender (USA) **4684**
Harvard Journal of Law and Public Policy (USA) **4684**
Harvard Journal on Legislation (USA) **4685**
Harvard Law Review (USA) **4685**
Hastings Communications and Entertainment Law Journal (USA) **4685**
Hastings Constitutional Law Quarterly (USA) **4849**
Hastings International and Comparative Law Review (USA) **4927**
Hastings Law Journal (USA) **4685**
Hastings Women's Law Journal (USA) **4685**
Hofstra Labor & Employment Law Journal (USA) **4687**
Hofstra Law Review (USA) **4687**
Houston Journal of International Law (USA) **4688**
Houston Law Review (USA) **4688**
Howard Law Journal (USA) **4688**
Human Rights (Chicago) (USA) **7208**
Idaho Law Review (USA) **4690**
Index to Legal Periodicals & Books (USA) **4822**
Indiana Law Journal (USA) **4691**
Indiana Law Review (USA) **4692**
Industrial and Labor Relations Review (USA) **1687**
Inside Counsel (USA) **4870**
Inter-American Law Review (USA) **4929**
The International Lawyer (USA) **4931**
International Trade Reporter (USA) **1572**
Iowa Law Review (USA) **4696**
Issues in Law and Medicine (USA) **5642**
John Marshall Law Review (USA) **4699**
Journal of Air Law and Commerce (USA) **4700**
The Journal of Corporation Law (USA) **4872**
Journal of Criminal Law & Criminology (USA) **2657**
Journal of Land, Resources, & Environmental Law (USA) **3140**
Journal of Law & Commerce (USA) **4872**
The Journal of Law and Economics (USA) **4702**
The Journal of Law, Medicine & Ethics (USA) **4703**
Journal of Taxation (USA) **1932**
Judicature (USA) **4953**
Judicial Conduct Reporter (USA) **4953**
Kentucky Law Journal (USA) **4709**
Labor Relations Reference Manual (USA) **1693**
Labor Relations Reporter (USA) **1693**
Labor Relations Reporter. Fair Employment Practices (USA) **1693**
Labor Relations Reporter. Labor Arbitration and Dispute Settlements (USA) **1693**
Labor Relations Reporter. Wage and Hour Manual (USA) **1693**
Law & Business Directory of Corporate Counsel (USA) **4874**
Law Practice (USA) **4716**
Litigation (Chicago) (USA) **4724**
Louisiana Law Review (USA) **4725**
Loyola Law Review (USA) **4726**
Loyola of Los Angeles International and Comparative Law Review (USA) **4726**
Loyola University Chicago Law Journal (USA) **4726**
Maine Law Review (USA) **4727**
Marquette Law Review (USA) **4728**
Maryland Law Review (USA) **4728**
McGeorge Law Review (USA) **4730**
Mealey's Daubert Report (USA) **4836**
Mealey's Emerging Drugs & Devices (USA) **4875**
Mealey's Emerging Insurance Disputes (USA) **4514**
Mealey's Emerging Toxic Torts (USA) **3509**
Mealey's International Arbitration Report (USA) **4935**
Mealey's Litigation Report: Asbestos (USA) **4836**
Mealey's Litigation Report: Fen-Phen - Redux (USA) **6860**
Mealey's Litigation Report: Insurance (USA) **4836**
Mealey's Litigation Report: Insurance Bad Faith (USA) **4836**
Mealey's Litigation Report: Insurance Fraud (USA) **4836**
Mealey's Litigation Report: Insurance Insolvency (USA) **4836**
Mealey's Litigation Report: Intellectual Property (USA) **6754**
Mealey's Litigation Report: Lead (USA) **4836**
Mealey's Litigation Report: Patents (USA) **6754**
Mealey's Litigation Report: Reinsurance (USA) **4837**
Mealey's Litigation Report: Tobacco (USA) **4837**
Mealey's Pollution Liability Report (USA) **4837**
Mealey's Year 2000 Report (USA) **4845**
Melbourne University Law Review (AUS) **4732**
Mercer Law Review (USA) **4732**
Michigan Bar Journal (USA) **4733**
Middle East Executive Reports (USA) **1577**
Military Law Review (USA) **4971**
Minnesota Law Review (USA) **4734**
Mississippi College Law Review (USA) **4735**
Mississippi Law Journal (USA) **4735**
Missouri Law Review (USA) **4735**
Natural Resources & Environment (USA) **3455**
Naval Law Review (USA) **4972**
Nebraska Law Review (USA) **4740**
Nevada Lawyer (USA) **4741**
New England Law Review (USA) **4741**
New Jersey Lawyer Magazine (New Brunswick) (USA) **4743**
New Mexico Law Review (USA) **4744**
New York State Bar Association. Journal (USA) **4745**
New York University Law Review (New York, 1950) (USA) **4746**
North Carolina Journal of International Law and Commercial Regulation (USA) **4937**
North Carolina Law Review (USA) **4748**
North Dakota Law Review (USA) **4748**
Northern Illinois University Law Review (USA) **4748**
Northwestern Journal of International Law & Business (USA) **4937**
Northwestern University Law Review (USA) **4749**
Notre Dame Law Review (USA) **4749**
Nova Law Review (USA) **4749**
Ohio Northern University Law Review (USA) **4752**
Ohio State Journal on Dispute Resolution (USA) **4752**
Ohio State Law Journal (USA) **4752**
Oklahoma City University Law Review (USA) **4752**
Oklahoma Law Review (USA) **4752**
Oregon Law Review (USA) **4754**
Oregon State Bar Bulletin (USA) **4754**
Patent and Trademark Office Society. Journal (USA) **6755**
Penn State International Law Review (USA) **4937**
Penn State Law Review (USA) **4756**
PENNumbra (USA) *see* University of Pennsylvania. Law Review. **4805**
Pension & Benefits Reporter (USA) **1702**
Pepperdine Law Review (USA) **4757**
Preview of United States Supreme Court Cases (USA) **4959**
Probate & Property (USA) **4905**
Public Contract Law Journal (USA) **4763**
Public Employment Law Notes (USA) **1704**
Public Utilities Fortnightly (USA) **3510**
Public Utilities Reports (USA) **3145**
Quinnipiac Law Review (USA) **4764**
Real Property, Trust and Estate Law Journal (USA) **4905**
S E C Docket (USA) **1648**
S E C News Digest (USA) **1648**
S M U Law Review (USA) **4777**
Saint Louis University. Public Law Review (USA) **4778**
Saint Thomas Law Review (USA) **4778**
San Diego Law Review (USA) **4778**
Santa Clara Computer and High Technology Law Journal (USA) **4779**
Santa Clara Law Review (USA) **4779**
The SciTech Lawyer (USA) **4780**
Seattle University. Law Review (USA) **4781**
Securities Regulation & Law Report (USA) **4781**
Seton Hall Legislative Journal (USA) **4782**
South Carolina Law Review (USA) **4785**
South Dakota Law Review (USA) **4785**
South Texas Law Review (USA) **4785**
Southern Illinois University Law Journal (USA) **4786**
Stanford Journal of International Law (USA) **4941**
Stanford Law & Policy Review (USA) **4787**
Stanford Law Review (USA) **4787**
Stetson Law Review (USA) **4789**
Suffolk Transnational Law Review (USA) **4941**
Suffolk University Law Review (USA) **4791**
Syracuse Journal of International Law & Commerce (USA) **4942**
Tax Law Review (USA) **4792**
The Tax Lawyer (USA) **4792**
Tax Management Compensation Planning Journal (USA) **1797**
Tax Management Estates, Gifts and Trusts Journal (USA) **1655**
Tax Management Foreign Income Portfolios (USA) **1948**
Tax Management Memorandum (USA) **1948**
Tax Management Real Estate Journal (USA) **7613**
Tax Management U S Income (USA) **1948**
Tax Management Weekly Report (USA) **1948**
Taxation and Revenue Policies - State Capitals (USA) **1950**
Temple Law Review (USA) **4793**
Tennessee Bar Journal (USA) **4793**
Tennessee Law Review (USA) **4794**
Texas Journal of Women and the Law (USA) **4794**
Texas Tech Law Review (USA) **4795**
Thurgood Marshall Law Review (USA) **4796**
Tort Trial & Insurance Practice Law Journal (USA) **4843**
Transportation Law Journal (USA) **4798**
Tulane Environmental Law Journal (USA) **3471**
Tulane European and Civil Law Forum (USA) **4843**
Tulane Law Review (USA) **4798**
Tulane Maritime Law Journal (USA) **4971**
Tulsa Law Review (USA) **4798**
U C Davis Law Review (USA) **4799**
U C L A Law Review (USA) **4799**
U N B Law Journal (CAN) **4799**
United States Law Week (USA) **4801**
United States Tax Court Reports (USA) **1954**
University of Baltimore Law Review (USA) **4803**
University of Chicago Legal Forum (USA) **4803**
University of Cincinnati Law Review (USA) **4803**
University of Colorado Law Review (USA) **4803**
University of Dayton Law Review (USA) **4803**
University of Illinois Law Review (USA) **4804**
University of Kansas Law Review (USA) **4804**
University of Pennsylvania. Journal of International Law (USA) **4944**
University of Pittsburgh Law Review (USA) **4805**
University of Richmond Law Review (USA) **4805**
University of San Francisco Law Review (USA) **4805**
Utah Law Review (USA) **4806**
Valparaiso University Law Review (USA) **4806**
Vanderbilt Journal of Transnational Law (USA) **4944**
Vanderbilt Law Review (USA) **4807**
Villanova Law Review (USA) **4808**
Virginia Environmental Law Journal (USA) **3473**
Virginia Journal of International Law (USA) **4944**
Virginia Law Review (USA) **4809**
Virginia Tax Review (USA) **1954**
Washington and Lee Law Review (USA) **4810**
Washington Law Review (USA) **4811**
Washington University. Law Review (USA) **4811**
The Wayne Law Review (USA) **4811**
Widener Law Review (USA) **4814**
Willamette Law Review (USA) **4814**
Wisconsin Law Review (USA) **4815**
Yale Journal of International Law (USA) **4945**

WanFang Data Corp. Rm 432, 15 Fu Xing Lu, Beijing 100038, China TEL 86-10-58882496, FAX 86-10-58882434, zjx@wanfangdata.com.cn, http://www.periodicals.net.cn/
Aba Shifan Gaodeng Zhuanke Xuexiao Xuebao (CHN) **7944**
Acta Geologica Sinica (AUS) **2723**
Acta Metallurgica Sinica (CHN) **6303**
Acta Seismologica Sinica (CHN) **2777**
Advances in Atmospheric Sciences (CHN) **6346**
Agricultural Science & Technology (CHN) **84**
Agricultural Sciences in China (GBR) **85**
Ahnui Gongye Daxue Xuebao (Ziran Kexue Ban) (CHN) **6304**
Aibian, Jibian, Tubian (CHN) **3401**
Aizheng (CHN) **6007**
Alabo Shijie (CHN) **5092**
An-Fang Keji (CHN) **2676**
Anhui Daxue Xuebao (Ziran Kexue Ban) (CHN) **7835**
Anhui Gongye Daxue Xuebao (Shehui Kexue Ban) (CHN) **7947**
Anhui Guangbo Dianshi Daxue Xuebao (CHN) **2375**
Anhui Huabao (CHN) **3822**
Anhui Huagong (CHN) **3236**
Anhui Jianzhu Gongye Xueyuan Xuebao (Ziran Kexue Ban) (CHN) **7835**
Anhui Jidian Xueyuan Xuebao (CHN) **3373**
Anhui Nongxueyuan Xuebao (CHN) **91**
Anhui Nongye Daxue Xuebao (CHN) **7835**
Anhui Nongye Daxue Xuebao (Shehui Kexue Ban) (CHN) **7947**
Anhui Shida Xuebao (CHN) **7835**
Anhui Shixue (CHN) **4179**
Anhui Weisheng Zhiye Jishu Xueyuan Xuebao (CHN) **5574**
Anhui Yike Daxue Xuebao (CHN) **5574**
Anhui Yixue (CHN) **5574**
Anhui Zhongyi Xueyuan Xuebao (CHN) **5574**
Anjisuan He Shengwu Ziyuan (CHN) **2050**
Ankang Shi-Zhuan Xuebao (CHN) **2826**
Anquan (CHN) **7508**
Anquan yu Huanjing Gongcheng (CHN) **3403**
Anquan yu Huanjing Xuebao (CHN) **3403**
Anquan yu Jiankang (CHN) **7508**
Anshu Keji (CHN) **776**
Anshun Shifan Gaodeng Zhuanke Xuexiao Xuebao (CHN) **2826**
Anyang Gongxueyuan Xuebao (CHN) **8416**
Anyang Shifan Xueyuan Xuebao (CHN) **5255**
Applied Geophysics (CHN) **2777**
Applied Mathematics. A Journal of Chinese Universities. Series B (CHN) **5472**
Applied Mathematics and Mechanics (NLD) **5472**
Bainianchao (CHN) **4180**
Baiqiuen Junyi Xueyuan Xuebao (CHN) **5583**
Baixuebing. Linbabing (CHN) **5934**
Bandaoti Guangdian (CHN) **7051**
Bandaoti Jishu (CHN) **3296**
Bangbu Yixueyuan Xuebao (CHN) **5583**
Bangongshi Yewu (CHN) **1849**
Banzhuren (CHN) **3052**
Bao Po (CHN) **3236**
Baoding Xueyuan Xuebao (CHN) **7839**

Baogang Keji (CHN) 6306
Baoji Wenli Xueyuan Xuebao (Ziran Kexue) (CHN) 7839
Baopo Qicai (CHN) 3236
Baoshan Shi-Zhuan Xuebao (CHN) 2830
Baoshi he Baoshixue Zazhi (CHN) 4564
Baotou Gangtie Xueyuan Xuebao (CHN) 6306
Baotou Yixueyuan Xuebao (CHN) 5583
Baoxian yu Jiagong (CHN) 94
Baozha yu Chongji (CHN) 7006
Baozhuang yu Shipin Jixie (CHN) 6708
Beifang Gongye Daxue Xuebao (CHN) 7839
Beifang Guoshu (CHN) 221
Beifang Jingmao (CHN) 1066
Beifang Shuidao (CHN) 270
Beifang Wenxue (CHN) 5261
Beihua Daxue Xuebao (Ziran Kexue Ban) (CHN) 7839
Beijing Caimao Zhiye Xueyuan Xuebao (CHN) 1066
Beijing Dang'an (CHN) 4994
Beijing Daxue Xuebao (Yixue Ban) (CHN) 5584
Beijing Di-er Waiguoyu Xueyuan Xuebao (CHN) 7223
Beijing Dianying Xueyuan Xuebao (CHN) 6490
Beijing Dizhi (CHN) 2726
Beijing Fuzhuang Xueyuan Xuebao (Ziran Kexue Ban) (CHN) 7839
Beijing Gongshang Daxue Xuebao (Shehui Kexue Ban) (CHN) 7949
Beijing Gongshang Daxue Xuebao (Ziran Kexue Ban) (CHN) 1066
Beijing Gongye Daxue Xuebao (Shehui Kexue Ban) (CHN) 7949
Beijing Hangkong Hangtian Daxue Xuebao (CHN) 49
Beijing Hangkong Hangtian Daxue Xuebao (Shehui Kexue Ban) (CHN) 7949
Beijing Huagong Daxue Xuebao (Shehui Kexue Ban) (CHN) 7949
Beijing Huagong Daxue Xuebao (Ziran Kexue Ban) (CHN) 7839
Beijing Institute of Technology. Journal (CHN) 7839
Beijing Jianzhu Gongcheng Xueyuan Xuebao (CHN) 3260
Beijing Jiaotong Daxue Xuebao (Shehui Kexue Ban) (CHN) 7950
Beijing Jiaoyu Xueyuan Xuebao (CHN) 2830
Beijing Jijie Gongye Xueyuan Xuebao (Zonghe Ban) (CHN) 5449
Beijing Keji Daxue Xuebao (CHN) 6458
Beijing Keji Daxue Xuebao (Shehui Kexue Ban) (CHN) 7950
Beijing Lianhe Daxue Xuebao (Renwen Shehui Kexue Ban) (CHN) 4444
Beijing Lianhe Daxue Xuebao (Ziran Kexue Ban) (CHN) 7840
Beijing Ligong Daxue Xuebao (CHN) 7840
Beijing Ligong Daxue Xuebao (Shehui Kexue Ban) (CHN) 7950
Beijing Linye Daxue Xuebao (CHN) 7840
Beijing Linye Daxue Xuebao (Shehui Kexue Ban) (CHN) 7950
Beijing Qingnian Zhengzhi Xueyuan Xuebao (CHN) 7109
Beijing Shehui Kexue (CHN) 7950
Beijing Shengwu Yixue Gongcheng (CHN) 5584
Beijing Shifan Daxue Xuebao (Ziran Kexue Ban) (CHN) 7840
Beijing Shiyou Huagong Xueyuan Xuebao (CHN) 3236
Beijing Shuiwu (CHN) 8818
Beijing University of Posts and Telecommunications. Journal (CHN) 2313
Beijing Wudao Xueyuan Xuebao (CHN) 2682
Beijing Yinshua Xueyuan Xuebao (CHN) 7318
Beijing Yixue (CHN) 5584
Beijing Youdian Daxue Xuebao (CHN) 2313
Beijing Youdian Daxue Xuebao (Shehui Kexue Ban) (CHN) 7950
Beijing Zhongyiyao Daxue Xuebao (CHN) 5584
Beijing Zhongyiyao Daxue Xuebao (Zhongyi Linchuang Ban) (CHN) 5584
Bianji Xuebao (CHN) 7552
Bianji Xuekan (CHN) 7552
Bianji zhi You (CHN) 7552
Bianjiang Jingji yu Wenhua (CHN) 1067
Bianyaqi (CHN) 3296
Biaoji Mianyi Fenxi yu Linchuang (CHN) 5755
Biaomian Gongcheng Zixun (CHN) 3183
Bijiao Jiaoyu Yanjiu (CHN) 2831
Bijie Xueyuan Xuebao (CHN) 2831
Bingchuan Dongtu (CHN) 2778
Bingdu Xuebao (CHN) 5585
Binggong Xuebao (CHN) 6413
Binggong Zidonghua (CHN) 6413
Bingqi Cailiao Kexue yu Gongcheng (CHN) 6413
Bingqi Zhishi (CHN) 6413
Binzhou Yixueyuan Xuebao (CHN) 5585
Biomedical and Environmental Sciences (GBR) 5585
Bohai Daxue Xuebao (Zhexue Shehui Kexue Ban) (CHN) 7951
Bohai Daxue Xuebao (Ziran Kexue Ban) (CHN) 7841
Boleigang / Fuhecailiao (CHN) 3236
Boli yu Tangci (CHN) 2038
Bopuxue Zazhi (CHN) 7074
Caijing Kexue (CHN) 1323
Caijing Luncong (CHN) 1079
Caikuai Xuexi (CHN) 1283
Cailiao Baohu (CHN) 3342
Cailiao Gongcheng (CHN) 50
Cailiao Kaifa yu Yingyong (CHN) 3342
Cailiao Kexue yu Gongcheng Xuebao (CHN) 3342
Cailiao Rechuli Xuebao (CHN) 6307
Cailiao Yanjiu Xuebao (CHN) 6307
Cailiao Yanjiu yu Yingyong (CHN) 6307
Cailiao yu Yejin Xuebao (CHN) 6307
Cangzhou Shifan Zhuanke Xuexiao Xuebao (CHN) 7953
Canxue Tongxun (CHN) 842
Caodi Xuebao (CHN) 100
Caoye yu Xumu (CHN) 283
Caoyuan yu Caoping (CHN) 783
Cehui Gongcheng (CHN) 4002
Cehui Kexue (CHN) 4002
Cehui Kexue Jishu Xuebao (CHN) 4002
Cehui Tongbao (CHN) 4002
Cehui Xinxi yu Gongcheng (CHN) 4002
Cehui Xuebao (CHN) 2778
Cehui yu Kongjian Dili Xinxi (CHN) 4002
Cejing Jishu (CHN) 6765
Cekong Jishu (CHN) 51
Central South University of Technology. Journal (CHN) 6460
Ceshi Jishu Xuebao (CHN) 7844
Chaidamu Kaifa Yanjiu (CHN) 7953
Chaiyouji (CHN) 3375
Chaiyouji Sheji yu Zhizao (CHN) 3375
Chang'an Daxue Xuebao. Ziran Kexue Ban (CHN) 8630
Changchun Daxue Xuebao (CHN) 2835
Changchun Gongcheng Xueyuan Xuebao (Shehui Kexue Ban) (CHN) 7953
Changchun Gongye Daxue Xuebao (Gaojiao Yanjiu Ban) (CHN) 2971
Changchun Gongye Daxue Xuebao (Shehui Kexue Ban) (CHN) 7953
Changchun Jinrong Gaodeng Zhuanke Xuexiao Xuebao (CHN) 1326
Changchun Ligong Daxue Xuebao (CHN) 7845
Changchun Zhongyiyao Daxue Xuebao (CHN) 5593
Changde Shifan Xueyuan Xuebao (Ziran Kexue Ban) (CHN) 7845
Changjiang Daxue Xuebao (Shehui Kexueban) (CHN) 8093
Changjiang Kexueyuan Yuanbao (CHN) 3360
Changjiang Liuyu Ziyuan yu Huanjing (CHN) 3410
Changjiang Luntan (CHN) 7115
Changsha Daxue Xuebao (CHN) 7953
Changsha Ligong Daxue Xuebao (Shehui Kexue Ban) (CHN) 7954
Changsha Ligong Daxue Xuebao (Ziran Kexue Ban) (CHN) 7845
Changshu Ligong Xueyuan Xuebao (CHN) 8418
Changwai yu Changnei Yingyang (CHN) 6656
Changzhi Yixueyuan Xuebao (CHN) 5593
Changzhou Gongxueyuan Xuebao (CHN) 7845
Changzhou Gongxueyuan Xuebao (Sheke Ban) (CHN) 7954
Changzhou Xinxi Zhiye Jishu Xueyuan Xuebao (CHN) 2542
Chanye yu Keji Luntan (CHN) 1082
Chanyeyong Fangzhipin (CHN) 8449
Chaye Kexue Jishu (CHN) 224
Cheliang yu Dongli Jishu (CHN) 8573
Chemical Research in Chinese Universities (CHN) 2054
Chengcai zhi Lu (CHN) 8573
Chengde Shiyou Gaodeng Zhuanke Xuexiao Xuebao (CHN) 6765
Chengde Yixueyuan Xuebao (CHN) 5593
Chengdu Daxue Xuebao (Shehui Kexue Ban) (CHN) 7954
Chengdu Daxue Xuebao (Ziran Kexue Ban) (CHN) 7845
Chengdu Fangzhi Gaodeng Zhuanke Xuexiao Xuebao (CHN) 8449
Chengdu Ligong Daxue Xuebao (Ziran Kexue Ban) (CHN) 8418
Chengdu Xinxi Gongcheng Xueyuan Xuebao (CHN) 6349
Chengdu Yixueyuan Xuebao (CHN) 5593
Chengdu Zhongyiyao Daxue Xuebao (CHN) 5593
Chengshi (CHN) 4406
Chengshi Cheliang (CHN) 8493
Chengshi Fazhan Yanjiu (CHN) 4406
Chengshi Guidao Jiaotong Yanjiu (CHN) 8493
Chengshi Guihua Huikan (CHN) 3262
Chengshi Huanjing Sheji (CHN) 4407
Chengshi Jianshe yu Shangye Wangdian (CHN) 4407
Chengshi Jianzhu (CHN) 4407
Chengshi Jiaotong (CHN) 8493
Chengshi Kance (CHN) 4407
Chengshi yu Jianzai (CHN) 3262
Chengxiang Jianshe (CHN) 4407
Chenji Xuebao (CHN) 2728
Cheyong Fadongji (CHN) 8573
China Petroleum Processing and Petrochemical Technology (CHN) 6766
China University of Geosciences. Journal (CHN) 2704
China Welding (CHN) 6342
China's Foreign Trade (CHN) 1555
Chinese Academic Journals Full-Text Database. Science & Engineering, Series A (CHN) 7845
Chinese Chemical Letters (GBR) 2058
Chinese Geographical Science (CHN) 2729
Chinese Journal of Cancer Research (CHN) 6015
Chinese Journal of Chemical Engineering (CHN) 3241
Chinese Journal of Chemistry (CHN) 2058
Chinese Journal of Electronics (CHN) 3090
Chinese Journal of Integrated Medicine (CHN) 5594
Chinese Journal of Mechanical Engineering (CHN) 3375
Chinese Journal of Oceanology and Limnology (CHN) 2801
Chinese Medical Journal (CHN) 5594
Chinese Medical Sciences Journal (GBR) 5594
Chinese Optics Letters (CHN) 7074
Chinese Science Bulletin (CHN) 7845
Chizhou Shi-Zhuan Xuebao (CHN) 2836
Chongqing Daxue Xuebao (Shehui Kexue Ban) (CHN) 7954
Chongqing Daxue Xuebao (Ziran Kexue Ban) (CHN) 7846
Chongqing Gongshang Daxue Xuebao (Shehui Kexue Ban) (CHN) 7954
Chongqing Gongshang Daxue Xuebao (Ziran Kexue Ban) (CHN) 7846
Chongqing Gongxueyuan Xuebao (Ziran Kexue Ban) (CHN) 7846
Chongqing Guangbo Dianshi Daxue Xuebao (CHN) 2357
Chongqing Jianzhu (CHN) 437
Chongqing Jianzhu Daxue Xuebao (CHN) 437
Chongqing Jianzhu Daxue Xuebao (Shehui Kexue Ban) (CHN) 7954
Chongqing Jiaotong Daxue Xuebao (Shehui Kexue Ban) (CHN) 7115
Chongqing Jiaotong Daxue Xuebao (Ziran Kexue Ban) (CHN) 8493
Chongqing Keji Xueyuan Xuebao (Shehui Kexue Ban) (CHN) 7954
Chongqing Keji Xueyuan Xuebao (Ziran Kexue Ban) (CHN) 7846
Chongqing Sanxia Xueyuan Xuebao (CHN) 7954
Chongqing Shifan Daxue Xuebao (Zhexue Shehui Kexue Ban) (CHN) 7954
Chongqing Shifan Daxue Xuebao (Ziran Kexue Ban) (CHN) 7846
Chongqing Wenli Xueyuan Xuebao (Shehui Kexue Ban) (CHN) 7954
Chongqing Yike Daxue Xuebao (CHN) 5594
Chongqing Yixue (CHN) 5594
Chongqing Youdian Daxue Xuebao (Ziran Kexue Ban) (CHN) 7846
Chuan-hai Gongcheng (CHN) 8641
Chuanbo Lixue (CHN) 8641
Chuandong Jishu (CHN) 3184
Chuan'ganqi Shijie (CHN) 3090
Chuangshang Waike Zazhi (CHN) 6239
Chuangxin Keji (CHN) 7846
Chuanmei Guancha (CHN) 4573
Chuanshan Xuekan (CHN) 4447
Chuban Cankao (CHN) 7558
Chuban yu Yinshua (CHN) 7558
Chuncui Shuxue yu Yingyong Shuxue (CHN) 5478
Chuxiong Shifan Xueyuan Xuebao (CHN) 7955
Communications in Theoretical Physics (GBR) 7008
Cuihua Xuebao (CHN) 2115
Dachang-Gangmenbing Waike Zazhi (CHN) 5603
Dadi Celiang yu Diqiu Donglixue (CHN) 2779
Dadi Gouzao yu Chengkuangxue (CHN) 2730
Daiqi Kexue (CHN) 6351
Dali Yixueyuan Xuebao (Yixue Ban) (CHN) 5603
Dalian Daxue Xuebao (CHN) 7958
Dalian Gongye Daxue Xuebao (CHN) 7849
Dalian Haishi Daxue Xuebao (CHN) 8642
Dalian Haishi Daxue Xuebao (Shehui Kexue Ban) (CHN) 7958
Dalian Jiaotong Daxue Xuebao (CHN) 7849
Dalian Ligong Daxue Xuebao (CHN) 7849
Dalian Ligong Daxue Xuebao (Shehui Kexue Ban) (CHN) 7958
Dalian Minzu Xueyuan Xuebao (CHN) 7849
Dalian Yike Daxue Xuebao (CHN) 5603
Dandao Xuebao (CHN) 6417
Dang De Jianshe (CHN) 7128
Dang De Shenghuo (Ha'erbin) (CHN) 7128
Dang'an Shikong (CHN) 5005
Dangan Tiandi (CHN) 5005
Dang'an Xue Yanjiu (CHN) 5005
Dangdai Faxue (CHN) 4655
Dangdai Huagong (CHN) 3242
Dangdai Hushi (CHN) 5957
Dangdai Jiaoshi Jiaoyu (CHN) 2940
Dangdai Jiaoyu Luntan (CHN) 2841
Dangdai Jingji (CHN) 1090
Dangdai Nong-ji (CHN) 210
Dangdai Qiche (CHN) 8577
Dangdai Wentan (CHN) 5282
Dangdai Xiju (CHN) 8468
Dangdai Ya-Tai (CHN) 547
Dangdai Yixue (CHN) 5603
Dangdai Yuyanxue (CHN) 5110
Dangdai Zuojia Pinglun (CHN) 5282
Dangdairen (CHN) 5282
Dangshi Bocai (CHN) 7128
Dangshi Bolan (CHN) 7128
Dangshi Tiandi (CHN) 7128
Dangshi Zonglan (CHN) 7128
Danjian yu Zhidao Xuebao (CHN) 52
Danpianji yu Qianrushi Xitong Yingyong (CHN) 2416
Daodan yu Hangtian Yunzai Jishu (CHN) 52
Daode yu Wenming (CHN) 7128
Daqing Shehui Kexue (CHN) 7958
Datong Yixue Zhuanke Xuexiao Xuebao (CHN) 5603
Daxing Zhuduanjian (CHN) 6310
Daxue Chuban (CHN) 7559
Daxue Jiaoyu Kexue (CHN) 2977
Daxue Shidai (CHN) 2281
Daxue Shuxue (CHN) 5482
Daxue Tushu Qingbao Xuekan (CHN) 5005
Daxue Wuli (CHN) 7010
Dazhong Keji (CHN) 8419
Dazhong Wenyi (CHN) 485
Daziran Tansuo (CHN) 7849
Deguo Yanjiu (CHN) 7230
Di-Er Jun-Yi Daxue Xuebao (CHN) 5604
Di-San Junyi Daxue Xuebao (CHN) 5604
Di Si Junyi Daxue Xuebao (CHN) 5604
Di-Yi Junyi Daxue Fenxiao Xuebao (CHN) 5604
Di Yi Junyi Daxue Xuebao (CHN) 5604
Dian Huaxue (CHN) 2113
Dianchi (Changsha) (CHN) 3127
Dianchi Gongye (CHN) 3156
Diandong Gongju (CHN) 5451
Diandu yu Jingshi (CHN) 2113
Diangong Cailiao (CHN) 3299
Diangong Dianneng Xinjishu (CHN) 3299
Dianguang yu Kongzhi (CHN) 7075
Dianhanji (CHN) 6342
Diani yu Fengzhuang (CHN) 6709
Dianji yu Kongzhi Xuebao (CHN) 3300
Dianli Dianrongqi yu Wugong Buchang (CHN) 3127
Dianli Dianzi Jishu (CHN) 3092
Dianli Jiche yu Chenggui Cheliang (CHN) 8616
Dianli Jishu Jingji (CHN) 1092
Dianli Kexue yu Gongcheng (CHN) 3156
Dianli Kexue yu Jishu Xuebao (CHN) 7850
Dianli Xitong Baohu yu Kongzhi (CHN) 3300
Dianli Xitong Zidonghua (CHN) 3156
Dianli Xuebao (CHN) 3156
Dianli Zidonghua Shebei (CHN) 3300
Diannao Biancheng Jiqiao yu Weihu (CHN) 2506
Dianpo Kexue Xuebao (CHN) 2358
Dianqi (CHN) 4356
Dianqi Chuandong (CHN) 3300
Dianqi Gongye (CHN) 3300
Dianqi Pingjie (CHN) 3092
Dianqi Shidai (CHN) 3156
Dianshi Yanjiu (CHN) 2380
Dianwang yu Qingjie Nengyuan (CHN) 3127
Dianying (CHN) 6496
Dianzi Celiang yu Yiqi Xuebao (CHN) 6401
Dianzi Gongcheng Zhuanji. China (SGP) 3187
Dianzi Gongcheng Zhuanji. Taiwan (SGP) 3187
Dianzi Keji (CHN) 3092
Dianzi Keji Daxue Xuebao (CHN) 8420
Dianzi Keji Daxue Xuebao (Shehui Kexue Xuebao) (CHN) 7959
Dianzi Qijian (CHN) 3092
Dianzi Shijie (CHN) 3092
Dianzi Xianwei Xuebao (CHN) 7010
Dianzi yu Diannao (CHN) 2416
Dianzi Yuanjian yu Cailiao (CHN) 3093
Dianzi Zhengwu (CHN) 7485
Dianzi Zhishi Chanquan (CHN) 6749
Dicengxue Zazhi (CHN) 2731
Difangbing Tongbao (CHN) 5812
Dili Kexue (CHN) 4004
Dili Kexue Jinzhan (CHN) 4004
Dili Yanjiu (CHN) 4004
Dili yu Dili Xinxi Kexue (CHN) 2731
Diqiu Huaxue (CHN) 2731
Diqiu Kexue (CHN) 2705
Diqiu Kexue Jinzhan (CHN) 2705
Diqiu Kexue yu Huanjing Xuebao (CHN) 2705
Diqiu Wuli Xuebao (CHN) 2779
Diqiu Wulixue Jinzhan (CHN) 2705
Diqiu Xinxi Kexue (CHN) 2705
Diqiu Xuebao (CHN) 2731
Disiji Yanjiu (CHN) 2731
Ditu (CHN) 4004
Diwen Gongcheng (CHN) 7054
Diwen Wuli Xuebao (CHN) 7054
Dixue Qianyuan (CHN) 2705
Dizhen (CHN) 2779
Dizhen Dici Guance yu Yanjiu (CHN) 2779
Dizhen Dizhi (CHN) 2779
Dizhen Gongcheng yu Gongcheng Zhendong (CHN) 2779
Dizhen Xuebao (CHN) 2780
Dizhen Yanjiu (CHN) 2731
Dizhi Diaocha yu Yanjiu (CHN) 2731
Dizhi Diqiu Huaxue (CHN) 2731
Dizhi Jishu Jingji Guanli (CHN) 1092
Dizhi Keji Qingbao (CHN) 2731
Dizhi Lixue Xuebao (CHN) 2780
Dizhi Lun-Ping (CHN) 2732
Dizhi Tongbao (CHN) 2732
Dizhi Xuebao (CHN) 2732
Dizhi yu Kantan (CHN) 2732
Dizhi Zaihai yu Huanjing Baohu (CHN) 3414
Dizhi Zhaokuang Luncong (CHN) 2732
Dizhi Zhuangbei (CHN) 4486
Dongbei Cai-Jing Daxue Xuebao (CHN) 1336
Dongbei Daxue Xuebao (Shehui Kexue Ban) (CHN) 7959
Dongbei Daxue Xuebao (Ziran Kexue Ban) (CHN) 8420
Dongbei Nongye Daxue Xuebao (CHN) 105
Dongbei Shi-Daxuebao (Zhexue Shehui Kexue Ban) (CHN) 7960
Dongbei Shi-Daxuebao (Ziran Kexue Ban) (CHN) 7851
Dongfang Jian (CHN) 5409
Dongfang Luntan (CHN) 548
Dongfang Qiyejia (CHN) 1093
Dongfang Yishu (CHN) 487
Donghai Haiyang (CHN) 2803
Donghua Daxue Xuebao (Shehui Kexue Ban) (CHN) 7960
Donghua Daxue Xuebao (Ziran Ban) (CHN) 7851

Online Service

Yanwaishang Zhiye Yanbing Zazhi (CHN) 6053
Yanye yu Huangong (CHN) 3257
Yaogan Jishu yu Yingyong (CHN) 2718
Yaogan Xinxi (CHN) 4034
Yaogan Xuebao (CHN) 4034
Yaopin Pingjia (CHN) 6886
Yaowu Buliang Fanying Zazhi (CHN) 6886
Yaowu Shengwu Jishu (CHN) 6886
Yaoxue Fuwu yu Yanjiu (CHN) 6886
Yaoxue Shijian Zazhi (CHN) 6886
Yaoxue Xuebao (CHN) 6886
Yaredai Zhiwu Kexue (CHN) 823
Yaredai Ziyuan yu Huanjing Xuebao (CHN) 3476
Yati Yasui Yazhoubingxue Zazhi (CHN) 5869
Yejin Zidonghua (CHN) 6337
Yejing yu Xianshi (CHN) 7085
Yeya Qidong yu Mifeng (CHN) 3365
Yichuan (CHN) 879
Yichun Xueyuan Xuebao (CHN) 8017
Yidong Tongxin (CHN) 2345
Yin Ran (CHN) 8462
Yinanbing Zazhi (CHN) 5733
Yingguo Yixue Zazhi (Chinese Edition) (CHN) 5733
Yingshan Xuekan (Shehui Kexue Ban) (MNG) 8017
Yingxiang Kexue yu Guanghuaxue (CHN) 6978
Yingxiang Shijue (CHN) 6978
Yingxiang Zhenduan yu Jieru Fangshexue (CHN) 6210
Yingyang Xuebao (CHN) 6671
Yingyong Fanhan Fenxi Xuebao (CHN) 7073
Yingyong Gailu Tongji (CHN) 5547
Yingyong Guangxue (CHN) 7085
Yingyong Huagong (CHN) 3257
Yingyong Jichu yu Gongcheng Kexue Xuebao (CHN) 7932
Yingyong Keji (CHN) 8445
Yingyong Lixue Xuebao (CHN) 3399
Yingyong Shengtai Xuebao (CHN) 3476
Yingyong Shengxue (CHN) 7090
Yingyong Shuxue he Lixue (CHN) 5547
Yingyong Shuxue yu Jisuan Shuxue Xuebao (CHN) 5547
Yingyong Yufang Yixue (CHN) 5733
Yinran Zhuji (CHN) 8463
Yinshua Jishu (CHN) 7329
Yinyue Shijie (CHN) 6629
Yinyue Yanjiu (CHN) 6630
Yishu Pinglun (CHN) 528
Yixue Fenzi Shengwuxue Zazhi (CHN) 898
Yixue Jiaoyu Tansuo (CHN) 5733
Yixue Linchuang Yanjiu (CHN) 5733
Yixue Xinxixue Zazhi (CHN) 5832
Yixue Yanjiu Tongxun (CHN) 5733
Yixue Yingxiangxue Zazhi (CHN) 6210
Yixue yu Shehui (CHN) 5733
Yiyao Gongcheng Sheji (CHN) 6886
Yiyong Shengwu Lixue (CHN) 5733
Youji Huaxue (CHN) 2132
Youjiang Minzu Yixueyuan Xuebao (CHN) 5734
Youkuang Dizhi (CHN) 2775
Youkuangye (CHN) 6484
Youqi Dizhi yu Caishoulu (CHN) 6798
Youqijing Ceshi (CHN) 6798
Youqitian Dimian Gongcheng (CHN) 6798
Youqitian Huanjing Baohu (CHN) 3476
Youse Jinshu (CHN) 6337
Youse Jinshu. Xuankuang Bufen (CHN) 6337
Youtian Huaxue (CHN) 6798
Yuanyi Xuebao (CHN) 3754
Yuanzi yu Fenzi Wuli Xuebao (CHN) 7073
Yueyang Zhigong Gaodeng Zhuanke Xuexiao Xuebao (CHN) 6706
Yuhang Cailiao Gongyi (CHN) 75
Yuhang Jice Jishu (CHN) 76
Yuhang Xuebao (CHN) 76
Yulei Jishu (CHN) 6455
Yumi Kexue (CHN) 276
Yunan Daxue Xuebao(Ziran Kexue Ban) (CHN) 7933
Yuncheng Xueyuan Xuebao (CHN) 8017
Yunchou yu Guanli (CHN) 1802
Yunmeng Xuekan (CHN) 4483
Yunnan Caijing Daxue Xuebao (CHN) 1197
Yunnan Daxue Xuebao (Shehui Kexue Ban) (CHN) 8017
Yunnan Jingguan Xueyuan Xuebao (CHN) 2672
Yunnan Minzu Daxue Xuebao (Zhexue Shehui Kexue Ban) (CHN) 8017
Yunnan Minzu Daxue Xuebao (Ziran Kexue Ban) (CHN) 7933
Yunnan Nongye Daxue Xuebao (CHN) 171
Yunnan Shifan Daxue Xuebao (Duiwai Hanyu Jiaoxue yu Yanjiu Ban) (CHN) 5197
Yunnan Shifan Daxue Xuebao (Ziran Kexue Ban) (CHN) 7933
Yunnan Tianwentai Taikan (CHN) 584
Yunnan Yishu Xueyuan Xuebao (CHN) 528
Yunnan Zhongyi Xueyuan Xuebao (CHN) 5734
Yunnan Zhongyi Zhongyao Zazhi (CHN) 315
Yunyang Shifan Gaodeng Zhuanke Xuexiao Xuebao (CHN) 2947
Yunyang Yixueyuan Xuebao (CHN) 5734
Yuye Xiandaihua (CHN) 3612
Zaihaixue (CHN) 2228
Zaisheng Ziyuan yu Xunhuan Jingji (CHN) 3476
Zajiao Shuidao (CHN) 260
Zaoqi Jiaoyu (Jiajiao Ban) (CHN) 2928
Zaoqi Jiaoyu (Jiaoshi Ban) (CHN) 2928
Zaoqi Jiaoyu (Meishu Ban) (CHN) 2928
Zaozhi Kexue yu Jishu (CHN) 6740
Zawen Yuekan (CHN) 5246
Zhangjiakou Zhiye Jishu Xueyuan Xuebao (CHN) 8445
Zhangzhou Shifan Xueyuan Xuebao (Ziran Kexue Ban) (CHN) 7933
Zhangzhou Zhiye Jishu Xueyuan Xuebao (CHN) 7933
Zhaoming Gongcheng Xuebao (CHN) 7085
Zhaoqing Xueyuan Xuebao (CHN) 8018
Zhaotong Shifan Gaodeng Zhuanke Xuexiao Xuebao (CHN) 2928
Zhejiang Chuangshang Waike (CHN) 6075
Zhejiang Daxue Xuebao (Gongxue Ban) (CHN) 3228
Zhejiang Daxue Xuebao (Lixue Ban) (CHN) 7933
Zhejiang Daxue Xuebao (Nongye yu Shengming Kexue Ban) (CHN) 172
Zhejiang Daxue Xuebao (Renwen Shehui Kexue Ban) (CHN) 8018
Zhejiang Daxue Xuebao (Yixue Ban) (CHN) 5735
Zhejiang Dianli (CHN) 3162
Zhejiang Fangzhi Fuzhuang Zhiye Jishu Xueyuan Xuebao (CHN) 2263
Zhejiang Gong-Mao Zhiye Jishu Xueyuan Xuebao (CHN) 2928
Zhejiang Gong-Shang Zhiye Jishu Xueyuan Xuebao (CHN) 1197
Zhejiang Gongshang Daxue Xuebao (CHN) 1197
Zhejiang Gongye Daxue Xuebao (CHN) 8446
Zhejiang Haiyang Xueyuan Xuebao (Renwen Shehui Kexue Ban) (CHN) 4483
Zhejiang Haiyang Xueyuan Xuebao (Ziran Kexue Ban) (CHN) 7933
Zhejiang Jiaoyu Xueyuan Xuebao (CHN) 2928
Zhejiang Keji Xueyuan Xuebao (CHN) 7933
Zhejiang Ligong Daxue Xuebao (CHN) 8463
Zhejiang Linchuang Yixue (CHN) 5735
Zhejiang Nongye Kexue (CHN) 172
Zhejiang Nongye Xuebao (CHN) 172
Zhejiang Shifan Daxue Xuebao (Ziran Kexue Ban) (CHN) 7933
Zhejiang Shiyong Yixue (CHN) 5735
Zhejiang Shuili Shuidian Zhuanke Xuexiao Xuebao (CHN) 8842
Zhejiang Shuren Daxue Xuebao (CHN) 2928
Zhejiang University. Journal (Science A) (CHN) 7933
Zhejiang Wanli Xueyuan Xuebao (CHN) 8018
Zhejiang Yishu Zhiye Xueyuan Xuebao (CHN) 8018
Zhejiang Yufang Yixue (CHN) 5735
Zhejiang Zhongxiyi Jiehe Zazhi (CHN) 5735
Zhejiang Zhongyi Zazhi (CHN) 316
Zhejiang Zhongyiyao Daxue Xuebao (CHN) 5735
Zhejiang Zhuanmei Xueyuan Xuebao (CHN) 2345
Zhendong Ceshi yu Zhenduan (CHN) 3399
Zhenduanxue Lilun yu Shijian (CHN) 5735
Zhengfa Xuekan (CHN) 4819
Zhengju Kexue (CHN) 4820
Zhengquan Shichang Daobao (CHN) 1660
Zhengzhou Daxue Xuebao (Gongxue Ban) (CHN) 3228
Zhengzhou Daxue Xuebao (Lixue Ban) (CHN) 7934
Zhengzhou Daxue Xuebao (Yixue Ban) (CHN) 5735
Zhengzhou Daxue Xuebao (Zhexue Shehui Kexue Ban) (CHN) 8018
Zhengzhou Gongye Daxue Xuebao (Shehui Kexue Ban) (CHN) 8018
Zhengzhou Hangkong Gongye Guanli Xueyuan Xuebao (Shehui Kexue Ban) (CHN) 8018
Zhengzhou Qinggongye Xueyuan Xuebao (Shehui Kexue Ban) (CHN) 8018
Zhenkong Kexue yu Jishu (CHN) 3400
Zhenzhi Gongye (CHN) 8463
Zhidao yu Yinxin (CHN) 6455
Zhishi Chuang (CHN) 7934
Zhishi Jiushi Liliang (CHN) 7934
Zhiwu Baohu (CHN) 823
Zhiwu Baohu Xuebao (CHN) 823
Zhiwu Bingli Xuebao (CHN) 823
Zhiwu Shenglixue Tongxun (CHN) 824
Zhiwu Yanjiu (CHN) 824
Zhiwu Ziyuan yu Huanjing (CHN) 824
Zhiwuxue Tongbao (CHN) 824
Zhiye Jishu (CHN) 8446
Zhiye Yixue (CHN) 5735
Zhiye yu Jiankang (CHN) 7546
Zhizaoye Zidonghua (CHN) 1909
Zhong-Gong Yili Zhou-Wei Dangxiao Xuebao (CHN) 7198
Zhong-xiao Qiye Keji (CHN) 1198
Zhongbei Daxue Xuebao (Shehui Kexue Ban) (CHN) 8018
Zhongbei Daxue Xuebao (Ziran Kexue Ban) (CHN) 8446
Zhongcaoyao (CHN) 5735
Zhongchenyao (CHN) 6887
Zhongfeng yu Shenjing Jibing Zazhi (CHN) 6191
Zhonggong Dangshi Yanjiu (CHN) 4190
Zhonggou Dongmai Yinghua Zazhi (CHN) 5735
Zhongguo Aizibing Xingbing (CHN) 5828
Zhongguo Baojian (CHN) 7546
Zhongguo Biaomian Gongcheng (CHN) 3228
Zhongguo Bing'an (CHN) 5735
Zhongguo Bingli Shengli Zazhi (CHN) 5735
Zhongguo Bingyuan Shengwuxue Zazhi (CHN) 5828
Zhongguo Ceshi Jishu (CHN) 6407
Zhongguo Chaosheng Yixue Zazhi (CHN) 6210
Zhongguo Chengshi Jinrong (CHN) 1198
Zhongguo Chengshi Linye (CHN) 3708
Zhongguo Chuanmei Daxue (Ziran Kexue Ban) (CHN) 7934
Zhongguo Chuji Weisheng Baojian (CHN) 5735
Zhongguo Dangdai Erke Zazhi (CHN) 6105
Zhongguo Daxue Jiaoxue (CHN) 3011
Zhongguo Dianji Gongcheng Xuebao (CHN) 3334
Zhongguo Dianzi Kexue Yanjiuyuan Xuebao (CHN) 3116
Zhongguo Dizhen (CHN) 2792
Zhongguo Dizhi Daxue Xuebao (Shehui Kexue Ban) (CHN) 8018
Zhongguo Dongwu Baojian (CHN) 8815
Zhongguo Er-Bi-Yanhou-Ludi Waike Zazhi (CHN) 6086
Zhongguo Er-Bi-Yanhou-Tou-Jing Waike (CHN) 6086
Zhongguo Ertong Baojian Zazhi (CHN) 6105
Zhongguo Fanglao Tongxun (CHN) 6221
Zhongguo Fangzhi (CHN) 8463
Zhongguo Feiyan Zazhi (CHN) 6221
Zhongguo Fenzi Xinzangbingxue Zazhi (CHN) 5802
Zhongguo Fuchanke Linchuang Zazhi (CHN) 6006
Zhongguo Funu (CHN) 8892
Zhongguo Fushe Weisheng (CHN) 6210
Zhongguo Fushi yu Fanghu Xuebao (CHN) 6721
Zhongguo Fuyou Baojian (CHN) 6006
Zhongguo Fuyun (CHN) 8906
Zhongguo Ganran Kongzhi Zazhi (CHN) 5829
Zhongguo Gaoxiao Keji yu Chanyehua (CHN) 8446
Zhongguo Geti Fanghu Zhuangbei (CHN) 6689
Zhongguo Gongcheng Zixun (CHN) 3228
Zhongguo Gonggong Weisheng (CHN) 7546
Zhongguo Gonggong Weisheng Guanli (CHN) 7546
Zhongguo Gonglu Xuebao (CHN) 8637
Zhongguo Gongwuyuan (CHN) 7478
Zhongguo Gongye Jingji (CHN) 1721
Zhongguo Gongye Yixue Zazhi (CHN) 6689
Zhongguo Gua-cai (CHN) 172
Zhongguo Guangxue yu Yingyong Guangxue Wenzhai (CHN) 7050
Zhongguo Guanli Kexue (CHN) 1803
Zhongguo Guanli Xinxihua (CHN) 2551
Zhongguo Guanxing Jishu Xuebao (CHN) 3228
Zhongguo Guojia Dili (CHN) 4035
Zhongguo Guoqing Guoli (CHN) 1534
Zhongguo Guotu Ziyuan Jingji (CHN) 3476
Zhongguo Gushang (CHN) 6076
Zhongguo Guzhi Shusong Zazhi (CHN) 4058
Zhongguo Haishang Youqi (CHN) 6798
Zhongguo Haiyang Daxue Xuebao (Shehui Kexue Ban) (CHN) 8018
Zhongguo Haiyang Daxue Xuebao (Ziran Kexue Ban) (CHN) 2821
Zhongguo Huagong Zhuangbei (CHN) 3258
Zhongguo Huangjin Zhubao (CHN) 4570
Zhongguo Huanjing Guanli Ganbu Xueyuan Xuebao (CHN) 3476
Zhongguo Huanjing Kexue (CHN) 3476
Zhongguo Huxi yu Weizhong Jianhu Zazhi (CHN) 6221
Zhongguo Jianchuan Yanjiu (CHN) 8666
Zhongguo Jiankang Yuekan (CHN) 7001
Zhongguo Jianzai (CHN) 2228
Zhongguo Jiaoxing Waike Zazhi (CHN) 6076
Zhongguo Jiceng Yiyao (CHN) 5736
Zhongguo Jidian Gongye (CHN) 1198
Zhongguo Jieru Yingxiang yu Zhiliaoxue (CHN) 6210
Zhongguo Jiguang (CHN) 7085
Zhongguo Jiguang Yixue Zazhi (CHN) 5736
Zhongguo Jihua Mianyi (CHN) 5767
Zhongguo Jiliang Xueyuan Xuebao (CHN) 7934
Zhongguo Jingji Tizhi Gaige Nianjian (CHN) 1535
Zhongguo Jingkuangyan (CHN) 6484
Zhongguo Jishengchongxue yu Jishengchongbing Zazhi (CHN) 898
Zhongguo Jisuanji Yonghu (CHN) 2441
Zhongguo Jizhu Jisui Zazhi (CHN) 6076
Zhongguo Kangfu Lilun Yu Shijian (CHN) 6117
Zhongguo Kangfu Yixue Zazhi (CHN) 5736
Zhongguo Kangshengsu Zazhi (CHN) 6887
Zhongguo Keji Chanye (CHN) 1803
Zhongguo Keji Luntan (CHN) 7934
Zhongguo Keji Qikan Yanjiu (CHN) 7576
Zhongguo Keji Shuyu (CHN) 5199
Zhongguo Keji Ziyuan Daokan (CHN) 5056
Zhongguo Kexue. A Ji: Shuxue (CHN) 5547
Zhongguo Kexue. B Ji: Huaxue (CHN) 7934
Zhongguo Kexue. C Ji: Shengming Kexue (CHN) 7934
Zhongguo Kexue. D Ji: Diqiu Kexue (CHN) 7934
Zhongguo Kexue. E Ji: Jishu Kexue (CHN) 7934
Zhongguo Kexue Jijin (CHN) 7934
Zhongguo Kexue Jishu Daxue Xuebao (CHN) 7934
Zhongguo Kongjian Kexue Jishu (CHN) 76
Zhongguo Kouqiang Hemian Waike Zazhi (CHN) 6263
Zhongguo Kouqiang Zhongzhixue Zazhi (CHN) 5870
Zhongguo Kuangye (CHN) 6484
Zhongguo Kuangye Daxue Xuebao (Shehui Kexue Ban) (CHN) 8018
Zhongguo Laodong (CHN) 1717
Zhongguo Laodong Guanxi Xueyuan Xuebao (CHN) 4606
Zhongguo Laonianxue Zazhi (CHN) 4058
Zhongguo Liangyou Xuebao (CHN) 276
Zhongguo Linchuang Jiepouxue Zazhi (CHN) 928
Zhongguo Linchuang Shenjing Kexue (CHN) 6191
Zhongguo Linchuang Yaolixue yu Zhiliaoxue (CHN) 6887
Zhongguo Linchuang Yaolixue Zazhi (CHN) 6887
Zhongguo Linchuang Yaoxue Zazhi (CHN) 6887
Zhongguo Linchuang Yingyang Zazhi (CHN) 6671
Zhongguo Linchuang Yisheng (CHN) 5736
Zhongguo Linchuang Yixue (CHN) 5736
Zhongguo Linchuang Yixue Yingxiang Zazhi (CHN) 6210
Zhongguo Malingshu (CHN) 260
Zhongguo Maye (CHN) 260
Zhongguo Meijie Shengwuxue ji Kongzhi Zazhi (CHN) 5767
Zhongguo Meirong Yixue (CHN) 5736
Zhongguo Meirong Zhengxing Waike Zazhi (CHN) 6263
Zhongguo Meitan Dizhi (CHN) 6484
Zhongguo Meitan Gongye Yixue Zazhi (CHN) 5736
Zhongguo Mianyixue Zazhi (CHN) 5767
Zhongguo Minhang Daxue Xuebao (CHN) 76
Zhongguo Minkang Yixue (CHN) 7547
Zhongguo Minying Keji yu Jingji (CHN) 1434
Zhongguo Minzheng (CHN) 7198
Zhongguo Minzu Yiyao Zazhi (MNG) 5736
Zhongguo Musilin (CHN) 7717
Zhongguo Nanfang Guoshu (CHN) 172
Zhongguo Nankexue Zazhi (CHN) 6285
Zhongguo Neijing Zazhi (CHN) 5736
Zhongguo Nengyuan (CHN) 3150
Zhongguo Nongji Tuiguang (CHN) 172
Zhongguo Nongshi (CHN) 172
Zhongguo Nongye Keji Daobao (CHN) 172
Zhongguo Nongye Kexue (CHN) 172
Zhongguo Nongye Qixiang (CHN) 6400
Zhongguo Nongye Ziyuan yu Quhua (CHN) 173
Zhongguo Pifu Xingbingxue Zazhi (CHN) 5883
Zhongguo Pu-wai Jichu yu Linchuang Zazhi (CHN) 6263
Zhongguo Putong Waike Zazhi (CHN) 6263
Zhongguo Qixiang Kexue Yanjiuyuan Nanbao (CHN) 6400
Zhongguo Quanke Yixue (CHN) 5736
Zhongguo Redai Yixue (CHN) 5736
Zhongguo Renkou Ziyuan yu Huanjing (CHN) 7296
Zhongguo Renli Ziyuan Kaifa (CHN) 1878
Zhongguo Renmin Jingguan Daxue Xuebao (Ziran Kexue Ban) (CHN) 7934
Zhongguo Renshou Gonghuanbing Zazhi (CHN) 898
Zhongguo Ruankexue (CHN) 7934
Zhongguo Senlin Bingchong (CHN) 861
Zhongguo Shamo (CHN) 2718
Zhongguo Shangcan Yixue (CHN) 6076
Zhongguo Shehui Daokan (CHN) 8019
Zhongguo Shehui Jingjishi Yanjiu (CHN) 4191
Zhongguo Shenghua Yaowu Zazhi (CHN) 6887
Zhongguo Shengtai Nongye Xuebao (CHN) 173
Zhongguo Shengwu Fangzhi (CHN) 712
Zhongguo Shengwu Gongcheng Zazhi (CHN) 771
Zhongguo Shengwu Huaxue yu Fenzi Shengwu Xuebao (CHN) 746
Zhongguo Shengwu Yixue Gongcheng Xuebao (CHN) 5736
Zhongguo Shengyu Jiankang Zazhi (CHN) 973
Zhongguo Shenjing Mianyixue he Shenjingbingxue Zazhi (CHN) 6191
Zhongguo Shequ Yishi (CHN) 5736
Zhongguo Shichang (CHN) 1198
Zhongguo Shipin Gongye (CHN) 3668
Zhongguo Shipin Tianjiaji (CHN) 3668
Zhongguo Shiyan Xueyexue Zazhi (CHN) 5942
Zhongguo Shiyong Erke Zazhi (CHN) 6105
Zhongguo Shiyong Fuke yu Chanke Zazhi (CHN) 6006
Zhongguo Shiyong Neike Zazhi (CHN) 5949
Zhongguo Shiyong Waike Zazhi (CHN) 6263
Zhongguo Shiyong Xiangcun Yisheng Zazhi (CHN) 5736
Zhongguo Shiyou he Huagong (CHN) 6798
Zhongguo Shiyou Kantan (CHN) 6798
Zhongguo Shouyi Kexue (CHN) 8815
Zhongguo Shouyi Xuebao (CHN) 8815
Zhongguo Shouyi Zazhi (CHN) 8815
Zhongguo Shuili Shuidian Kexue Yanjiuyuan Xuebao (CHN) 8842
Zhongguo Shuitu Baochi Kexue (CHN) 2634
Zhongguo Sifa Jianding (CHN) 5917
Zhongguo Tangliao (CHN) 173
Zhongguo Tangniaobing Zazhi (CHN) 5901
Zhongguo Tengtong Yixue Zazhi (CHN) 5736
Zhongguo Teshu Jiaoyu (CHN) 3049
Zhongguo Tiaoweipin (CHN) 3668
Zhongguo Tiedao Kexue (CHN) 8628
Zhongguo Tielu (CHN) 8628
Zhongguo Tishixue yu Tuxiang Fenxi (CHN) 6979
Zhongguo Tongji (CHN) 8414
Zhongguo Tongyi Zhanxian (CHN) 6455
Zhongguo Wei Qinxi Shenjing Waike Zazhi (CHN) 6263
Zhongguo Weichuang Waike Zazhi (CHN) 6263
Zhongguo Weisheng Jianyan (CHN) 5912
Zhongguo Weisheng Tongji (CHN) 7002
Zhongguo Weisheng Ziyuan (CHN) 7547
Zhongguo Wenhua Yanjiu (CHN) 4483
Zhongguo Wenxue Yanjiu (CHN) 5404
Zhongguo Wujia (CHN) 1198
Zhongguo Wuxiandian Dianzixue Wenzhai (CHN) 2365
Zhongguo Wuzhenxue Zazhi (CHN) 5736
Zhongguo Xiandai Putong Waike Jinzhan (CHN) 6263
Zhongguo Xiandai Shoushuxue Zazhi (CHN) 6263
Zhongguo Xiandai Yingyong Yaoxue (CHN) 6887
Zhongguo Xiandai Yixue (CHN) 5737
Zhongguo Xiangzhen Qiye (CHN) 1969
Zhongguo Xiaoer Jijiu Yixue (CHN) 6105
Zhongguo Xiju (CHN) 8485
Zhongguo Xingshifa Zazhi (CHN) 2672
Zhongguo Xinli Weisheng Zazhi (CHN) 7416
Zhongguo Xinxi Jishu Jiaoyu (CHN) 2928
Zhongguo Xinxueguanbing Yanjiu (CHN) 5802
Zhongguo Xinyao Yu Linchuang Zazhi (CHN) 6887

Online Service

DIRECTORY 2010 H.W. WILSON 11301

Botany (CAN) **781**
Brandweek (USA) **22**
The British Journal of Criminology (GBR) **2645**
British Journal of Educational Technology (GBR) **3053**
The British Journal of Nutrition (GBR) **6656**
British Journal of Psychology (GBR) **7342**
Broadcast Engineering (USA) **2376**
Broadcast Engineering (World Edition) (USA) **2376**
Broadcasting & Cable (USA) **2376**
Broadcasting & Cable T V Fax (USA) **2376**
Brookings Papers on Economic Activity (USA) **1536**
Buddhist - Christian Studies (USA) **7700**
Buffalo Human Rights Law Review (USA) *see* Buffalo Human Rights Law Review. **4633**
The Buffalo Public Interest Law Journal (USA) **4633**
Builder (Washington) (USA) **984**
Building Design + Construction (USA) **985**
Buildings (USA) **987**
Bulk Transporter (USA) **8669**
Bulletin of Entomological Research (GBR) **841**
Bulletin of Marine Science (USA) **2801**
Bulletin of the Atomic Scientists (USA) **7224**
Business & Economic Review (USA) **1070**
Business and Health (Online Edition) (USA) **4496**
Business and Society Review (USA) **1070**
Business Credit (USA) **1322**
Business Economics (USA) **1071**
Business Ethics Quarterly (USA) **6909**
Business History Review (USA) **1072**
Business Horizons (USA) **1072**
Business Insurance (USA) **4496**
Business Travel World (GBR) **8689**
C A Magazine (CAN) **1282**
C I O Insight (USA) **1414**
C P C U eJournal (USA) **4497**
C R M (Washington) (USA) **385**
California Western International Law Journal (USA) **4919**
California Western Law Review (USA) **4637**
Cambridge Journal of Economics (GBR) **1079**
Campbell Law Review (USA) **4637**
Canada - United States Law Journal (USA) **4919**
Canadian Banker (Online Edition) (CAN) **1324**
Canadian Banker (Print Edition) (CAN) **1324**
Canadian Business (CAN) **1079**
Canadian Ethnic Studies (CAN) **3525**
The Canadian Geographer (USA) **4001**
Canadian Geographic (CAN) **4001**
Canadian Geotechnical Journal (CAN) **2703**
Canadian Journal of Agricultural Economics (USA) **195**
Canadian Journal of Behavioural Science (CAN) **7343**
Canadian Journal of Chemistry (CAN) **2052**
Canadian Journal of Civil Engineering (CAN) **3261**
Canadian Journal of Earth Sciences (CAN) **2703**
Canadian Journal of Education (CAN) **3019**
Canadian Journal of Experimental Psychology (CAN) **7343**
Canadian Journal of Family Law (CAN) **4639**
Canadian Journal of Fisheries and Aquatic Sciences (CAN) **3588**
Canadian Journal of Forest Research (CAN) **3685**
Canadian Journal of Higher Education (CAN) **2971**
Canadian Journal of History (CAN) **4134**
Canadian Journal of Law and Jurisprudence (CAN) **4639**
Canadian Journal of Microbiology (CAN) **882**
Canadian Journal of Physics (CAN) **7007**
Canadian Journal of Physiology and Pharmacology (CAN) **920**
Canadian Journal of Zoology (CAN) **937**
Canadian Modern Language Review (CAN) **5104**
Canadian Psychology (CAN) **7344**
Canadian Review of Sociology (CAN) **8092**
Canadian Sailings (CAN) **8640**
Canadian Social Studies (CAN) **3054**
Canadian Woman Studies (CAN) **8894**
Capital and Class (GBR) **1536**
Capital University Law Review (USA) **2646**
Car and Driver (USA) **8571**
Cardozo Arts & Entertainment Law Journal (USA) **4640**
Career and Technical Education Research (USA) **2834**
The Career Development Quarterly (USA) **6694**
Career World (USA) **6695**
Caribbean Law Review (JAM) **4640**
Case Western Reserve Journal of International Law (USA) **4920**
Case Western Reserve Law Review (USA) **4641**
Catalogue & Index (GBR) **5057**
Catalyst for Change (USA) **3019**
Caterer & Hotelkeeper (GBR) **4383**
Catholic Biblical Quarterly (USA) **7788**
Catholic Education (USA) **2835**
The Catholic Historical Review (USA) **7789**
The Cato Journal (USA) **7114**
Center for Children's Books. Bulletin (USA) **2147**
Central European History (GBR) **4209**
Ceramic Review (GBR) **2039**
Ceramics Art and Perception (AUS) **2039**
Ceramics Monthly (USA) **2039**
Ceramics Technical (AUS) **2040**
Chain Store Age (USA) **1809**
Challenge (Armonk) (USA) **1082**
Change (USA) **2971**
Chemical Week (USA) **3240**
Chemistry & Industry (GBR) **2057**
Chicago Review (USA) **5273**
Child Study Journal (USA) **2836**
Childhood Education (USA) **3054**
Children and Libraries (USA) **5001**
China Business Review (USA) **1555**
Chinese Education and Society (USA) **2836**
Chinese Law and Government (USA) **4642**
Chinese Sociology and Anthropology (USA) **8093**
Chinese Studies in History (USA) **4135**
The Christian Century (USA) **7631**
Christianity and Literature (USA) **5210**
Christianity Today (USA) **7632**
The Chronicle of Higher Education (USA) **2972**
Church History (USA) **7633**
Ciencia da Informacao (BRA) **5002**
Ciencia Rural (BRA) **101**
Cincinnati Magazine (USA) **3972**
Cineaste (USA) **6493**
Cinema Journal (USA) **6493**
Civil War History (USA) **4288**
Classical and Modern Literature (USA) **5274**
Classical Antiquity (USA) **2232**
Classical Journal (USA) **2232**
Classical World (USA) **2233**
The Clearing House (USA) **2837**
Clinical Law Review (USA) **4643**
Clio (Ft. Wayne) (USA) **4135**
Club Industry's Fitness Business Pro (USA) **6984**
CNN/Money (USA) *see* Money (New York). **1368**
Coach and Athletic Director (USA) **8166**
College & Research Libraries (USA) **5002**
College & Research Libraries News (USA) **5003**
College & University Media Review (USA) **2972**
College Literature (USA) **5276**
College Student Journal (USA) **2973**
College Teaching (USA) **2973**
Colorado Journal of International Environmental Law and Policy (USA) **4920**
Colorado Libraries (USA) **5003**
Columbia Journal of Asian Law (USA) **4645**
Columbia Journal of Transnational Law (USA) **4921**
Columbia Journalism Review (USA) **4573**
Commentary (USA) **7720**
Commercial Motor (GBR) **8669**
Common Ground (Washington, DC) (USA) **388**
Commonweal (USA) **5211**
Communication Quarterly (USA) **8094**
Communications News (USA) **2316**
Community Banker (Washington, 1880) (USA) **1328**
Community Care (Sutton) (GBR) **8034**
Community College Review (USA) **2974**
Comparative Drama (USA) **5277**
Comparative Labor Law & Policy Journal (USA) **1671**
Comparative Literature (USA) **5277**
Compensation and Benefits Review (USA) **1671**
The Computer Journal (GBR) **2412**
Computer Weekly (GBR) **2413**
Computers in Libraries (GBR) **2570**
Computerworld (USA) **2570**
Concrete Construction (USA) **992**
The Concrete Producer (USA) **993**
Concrete Products (USA) **993**
The Conference Board Review (USA) **1735**
Confrontation (USA) **5277**
Connecticut Bar Journal (USA) **4648**
Construction Review (USA) **1045**
Contemporary Economic Policy (GBR) **1086**
Contemporary Literature (USA) **5278**
The Contemporary Review (GBR) **5212**
Contract (USA) **4535**
Contract Journal (GBR) **999**
Control Engineering Online (USA) *see* Control Engineering. **2459**
Convergence (CAN) **2940**
Converting Magazine (USA) **6733**
Corn and Soybean Digest (USA) **225**
Corporate Meetings & Incentives (USA) **6279**
Corporate Money (GBR) **1329**
Corrections Today (USA) **2648**
Counseling and Values (USA) **7794**
Counselor Education and Supervision (USA) **2839**
Court Review (USA) **4948**
Crafts (GBR) **533**
Crain's Chicago Business (USA) **1959**
Crain's Cleveland Business (USA) **1476**
Crain's New York Business (USA) **1088**
Crainsdetroit.com (USA) *see* Crain's Detroit Business. **1088**
Creative Review (GBR) **1812**
Creativity Plus (USA) **7126**
Creighton Law Review (USA) **4652**
Criminal Justice Ethics (USA) **6912**
Criminal Justice Review (USA) **4887**
Critical Reviews in Environmental Science & Technology (USA) **3485**
Critical Survey (GBR) **5212**
Criticism (USA) **5280**
Critique (Washington) (USA) **5280**
Crops (GBR) **227**
Cross-Cultural Research (USA) **7957**
Cross Currents (New York) (USA) **2976**
Cultural Anthropology (USA) **334**
Curator (USA) **6523**
Current Health 2 (USA) **3055**
Current Science (USA) **2184**
Current Studies in Librarianship (USA) **5004**
Curriculum Review (USA) **3057**
Customer Management Insight (Online) (USA) **1812**
CustomRetailer (USA) **1089**
Cycle World (USA) **8257**
D (USA) **3973**
D E S I D O C Journal of Library & Information Technology (IND) **5004**
D T T P (USA) **5005**
D V (USA) **2379**
D V M (USA) **8796**
Dance Magazine (USA) **2684**
Deakin Law Review (AUS) **4655**
Dealerscope (USA) **3091**
Defense Counsel Journal (USA) **4830**
Delaware Law Review (USA) **4655**
Delicious Living (USA) **5069**
Delta Farm Press (USA) **104**
Delta Kappa Gamma Bulletin (USA) **2977**
Delta Pi Epsilon Journal (USA) **2977**
Demography (USA) **7281**
Demokratizatsiya (USA) **7129**
Denver Journal of International Law and Policy (USA) **4922**
Denver University Law Review (USA) **4656**
DePaul Journal of Art, Technology & Intellectual Property Law (USA) **4656**
DePaul Journal of Health Care Law (USA) **4656**
Design Issues (USA) **486**
Design Management Review (USA) **1738**
Design News Online (USA) *see* Design News. **8420**
Design Week (GBR) **486**
Deutscher Verein fuer Kunstwissenschaft. Zeitschrift (DEU) **486**
Deutsches Archaeologisches Institut. Jahrbuch (DEU) **390**
Deutsches Archaeologisches Institut. Roemische Abteilung. Mitteilungen (DEU) **390**
Developmental Policy (USA) **7129**
Differences (USA) **8895**
Digital Content Producer (USA) **2401**
Digital Marketing (Toronto, 2000) (CAN) **1813**
Diogenes (English Edition) (GBR) **7959**
Direct (New York, 1988) (USA) **1813**
Discover (USA) **7851**
Dispute Resolution Journal (USA) **1675**
Dissent (New York) (USA) **7130**
Distance Education Report (USA) **2978**
Diverse Issues in Higher Education (USA) **2978**
Dress (USA) **2253**
Drug Discovery & Development (USA) **6834**
Drug Topics (USA) **6836**
E (USA) **3414**
E C & M (USA) **3300**
E D N Access (USA) *see* E D N World. **3093**
E E: Evaluation Engineering (USA) **3093**
E H S Today (USA) **6676**
E L T Journal (GBR) **5113**
E R Online (USA) *see* Educational Researcher. **2851**
e-Service Journal (USA) **2543**
Early American Literature (USA) **5287**
Early American Studies (USA) **4291**
Early Childhood Today (Online) (USA) **3058**
Early Music (GBR) **6563**
East European Politics & Societies (USA) **7131**
Ebony (USA) **3531**
The Ecologist (Online) (GBR) **3417**
Economic Botany (USA) **786**
Economic Indicators (Washington) (USA) **1480**
Economic Inquiry (GBR) **1100**
EContent (USA) **2556**
EContent Xtra (USA) **2556**
Ecumenical Review (CHE) **7639**
Editor & Publisher (USA) **4574**
Education (USA) **2846**
Education and Training in Developmental Disabilities (USA) **3039**
Education & Treatment of Children (USA) **2847**
Education Canada (CAN) **2847**
The Education Digest (USA) **2847**
Education Libraries (Online Edition) (USA) **5008**
Education Next (USA) **3021**
Educational and Psychological Measurement (USA) **7353**
Educational Considerations (USA) **2849**
Educational Evaluation & Policy Analysis (USA) **3021**
The Educational Forum (USA) **2979**
Educational Foundations (USA) **3059**
Educational Horizons (USA) **2850**
Educational Leadership (USA) **3059**
Educational Studies (USA) **2851**
Educational Technology Research & Development (USA) **3059**
Educause Review (USA) **2980**
EduExec (USA) **3022**
Eire - Ireland (USA) **4450**
The Elder Law Journal (USA) **4664**
Electric Perspectives (USA) **3302**
Electrical Wholesaling (USA) **1815**
Electronic Design (USA) **3095**
Electronic Green Journal (USA) **3419**
Electronic Journal of Science Education (USA) **2852**
The Electronic Sixteenth Century Journal (USA) *see* Sixteenth Century Journal. **4475**
Electronics Weekly (GBR) **3097**
Emerging Infectious Diseases (Online) (USA) **7515**
Emory Bankruptcy Developments Journal (USA) **4830**
Emory International Law Review (USA) **4924**
Emory Law Journal (USA) **4664**
Employee Benefits (GBR) **1860**
Employee Rights and Employment Policy Journal (USA) **1677**
eMusician.com (USA) *see* Electronic Musician. **6564**
Endeavour (GBR) **7852**
Energy & Mineral Law Institute (USA) **4665**
Energy Engineering (USA) **3131**
Energy Institute. Journal (GBR) **3132**
The Energy Journal (USA) **3132**
Energy Law Journal (USA) **4665**
The Engineer (GBR) **3188**
Engineering (GBR) **3188**
The Engineering Economist (USA) **3189**
The English Historical Review (GBR) **4217**
English Language Notes (USA) **5290**
Entrepreneurship: Theory and Practice (USA) **1960**
Environment (USA) **3420**
Environmental Health Perspectives (USA) **3425**
Environmental Values (GBR) **3429**
Esquire (USA) **6289**
Essays in Criticism (GBR) **5291**
Essays on Canadian Writing (CAN) **5291**
Estates Gazette (GBR) **7589**
Etc. (Fort Worth) (USA) **5117**
Ethics & International Affairs (USA) **7232**
Ethics & the Environment (GBR) **6917**
Ethnologies (CAN) **3616**
Euromoney Online (GBR) *see* Euromoney. **1338**
European Education (USA) **2855**
European Photography (DEU) **6967**
Event D V (USA) **2557**
Evolution (USA) **866**
EW.com (USA) *see* Entertainment Weekly. **3975**
eWEEK (USA) **2557**
Exceptional Children (USA) **3040**
Exceptional Parent (USA) **3040**
Experimental Mechanics (USA) **3344**
Experimental Techniques (USA) **3344**
The Explicator (USA) **5294**
Extra! (USA) **4575**
F A S Worldwide (USA) **197**
F B I Law Enforcement Bulletin (USA) **2652**
F D C C Quarterly (USA) **4867**
F M (USA) **1744**
Families in Society (USA) **8039**
Farm Industry News (USA) **111**
Farmers Weekly (GBR) **112**
Fashion Theory (GBR) **489**
Federal Communications Law Journal (USA) **4672**
Federal Law Review (AUS) **4951**
The Federal Lawyer (USA) **4673**
Federal Probation (USA) **2652**
Federal Reserve Bank of Atlanta. Regional Update (USA) **1486**
Federal Reserve Bank of Boston. Regional Review (USA) **1486**
Federal Reserve Bank of Boston. Research Review (USA) **1486**
Federal Reserve Bank of Kansas City. Economic Review (USA) **1486**
Federal Reserve Bank of Philadelphia. Business Review (USA) **1486**
Federal Reserve Bank of Richmond. Economic Quarterly (USA) **1486**
Federal Reserve Bank of St. Louis. Review (USA) **1486**
Federal Reserve Bank of San Francisco. Economic Review (USA) **1486**
Federal Reserve Bulletin (USA) **1342**
Feliciter (CAN) **5009**
Feminist Studies (USA) **8896**
Femspec (USA) **8863**
Fiberarts (USA) **8450**
FierceTelecom (USA) **2367**
Film Criticism (USA) **6498**
Film History (USA) **6499**
Film Quarterly (USA) **6499**
Films in Review (Online Edition) (USA) **6501**
Financial & Insurance Meetings (USA) **4502**
Financial Executive (USA) **1745**
Fire Chief (USA) **3577**
Fire Protection Engineering (USA) **3577**
First Things (USA) **7643**
Fishery Bulletin (USA) **3593**
Flash Art International (ITA) **489**
Fleet Owner (USA) **8670**
Flight International (GBR) **55**
The Florida Bar Journal (USA) **4675**
Florida Journal of International Law (USA) **4926**
Florida Libraries (USA) **5009**
Florida Shipper (USA) **8644**
The Florida Tax Review (USA) **4676**
Flying (USA) **56**
Focus on Autism and Other Developmental Disabilities (USA) **6141**
Focus on Exceptional Children (USA) **3040**
Focus on Geography (USA) **4006**
Folio: (USA) **7561**
Folk Music Journal (GBR) **6567**
Folklore (GBR) **3617**
Fontes Artis Musicae (USA) **6631**
Food Engineering (USA) **3638**
Fordham Law Review (USA) **4676**
Foreign Affairs (USA) **7235**
Foreign Policy (Washington) (USA) **7235**
Forging (USA) **6312**
Fortune.com (USA) *see* Fortune. **1746**
Franchising World (USA) **1817**
Furnaces International (GBR) **6313**
Futures (Chicago) (USA) **1626**
The Futurist (USA) **7856**
G Q (New York) (USA) **6291**
Game Developer (USA) **2476**
The Gay & Lesbian Review Worldwide (USA) **4374**
General Music Today (Online) (USA) **6569**
General Practice Update (GBR) **5619**
Generations (San Francisco) (USA) **4045**
Genome (CAN) **870**
Genome Research (USA) **870**
Genomics & Proteomics (USA) **764**

Online Service

DIRECTORY 2010 H.W. WILSON 11303

Journal of the Southwest (USA) 4300
Journal of Theological Studies (GBR) 7657
Journal of Third World Studies (USA) 4150
Journal of Travel Research (USA) 8726
Journal of Urban Affairs (USA) 4417
Journal of Visual Art Practice (GBR) 499
Journal of Visual Impairment & Blindness (USA) 4082
Journal of Women, Politics & Policy (USA) 7148
Journal of Women's History (USA) 8900
Journal of World Business (GBR) 1574
Journalism and Mass Communication Educator (USA) 4577
Journalism and Mass Communication Quarterly (USA) 4578
Journalism History (USA) 4578
Judaica Librarianship (USA) 5022
Judaism (USA) 7725
Judicature (USA) 4953
Jump Cut (USA) 6505
Kansas Journal of Law & Public Policy (USA) 4709
Kappa Delta Pi Record (USA) 3069
Kentucky Libraries (USA) 5022
The Kenyon Review (USA) 5425
Key Words (Port Aransas) (USA) 5058
Kiplinger Agriculture Letter (USA) 131
Kiplinger California Letter (USA) 1636
The Kiplinger Letter (USA) 1636
Kiplinger Tax Letter (USA) 1932
Kiplinger's Personal Finance (USA) 1364
Kiplinger's Personal Finance Mutual Funds (USA) 1636
Kiplinger's Retirement Report (USA) 1636
Knowledge Quest (USA) 5023
Konsthistorisk Tidskrift (GBR) 500
Konyvtari Figyelo (HUN) 5023
Koreana (KOR) 554
Kritika (Bloomington) (USA) 4238
Kunsthistorische Sammlungen in Wien. Jahrbuch (AUT) 501
Kyklos (GBR) 8117
Labor Law Journal (USA) 4711
Land Economics (USA) 202
Landscape Management (USA) 3741
Language Learning (USA) 5141
Language, Speech and Hearing Services in Schools (USA) 6082
Latin American Politics and Society (USA) 7250
Latin American Research Review (USA) 7982
LatinFinance (USA) 1365
Law and Contemporary Problems (USA) 4713
Law & Society Review (USA) 4714
Law Library Journal (USA) 5024
Leadership (Sacramento) (USA) 2882
Learning and Leading with Technology (USA) 2950
Learning and Motivation (USA) 2882
The Learning Assistance Review (USA) 3070
Learning Disability Quarterly (USA) 3043
Legal Studies Forum (USA) 4720
Leonardo: Art Science and Technology (USA) 502
Letter Arts Review (USA) 502
Leukos (USA) 3208
Lewis & Clark Law Review (USA) 4723
Libraries & the Cultural Record (USA) 5026
Library Journal (USA) 5028
Library Leadership & Management (USA) 5028
Library Media Connection (USA) 5028
Library Personnel News (USA) 5028
Library Resources & Technical Services (USA) 5029
Library Trends (USA) 5029
Lighting Design + Application (USA) 3324
Limnology and Oceanography (USA) 2797
Literacy Research and Instruction (USA) 3070
The Literary Review (USA) 5324
Literature Film Quarterly (USA) 6506
Live Design (USA) 8473
Lodging Hospitality (USA) 4393
Logistics Management (USA) 8503
Logos (NLD) 7566
Los Angeles Magazine (USA) 3980
Louisiana Law Review (USA) 4725
Louisiana Libraries (USA) 5030
Loyola Law Review (USA) 4726
Loyola of Los Angeles International and Comparative Law Review (USA) 4726
Loyola University Chicago Law Journal (USA) 4726
Lutheran Education (USA) 7765
M E L U S (USA) 5328
M I R: Management International Review (DEU) 1773
M I S Quarterly (USA) 2523
M I T Sloan Management Review (USA) 1773
Machine Design (USA) 3388
Maclean's (CAN) 3812
Macquarie Law Journal (AUS) 4726
The Magazine Antiques (USA) 367
Magna's Campus Legal Monthly (USA) 2993
Maine Bar Journal (USA) 4727
Maine Law Review (USA) 4727
Malaysian Journal of Library and Information Science (MYS) 5031
Managed Healthcare Executive (USA) 4106
Manufacturing Business Technology (USA) 1898
Manufacturing Engineering (USA) 3209
Marg (Mumbai) (IND) 449
Marine Fisheries Review (USA) 3601
Marine Technology and S N A M E News (USA) 8652
Marine Technology Society Journal (USA) 2812
Marketing Health Services (USA) 1832
Marketing Management (USA) 1832
Marketing News (USA) 1832
Marketing Online (CAN) *see* Marketing Magazine. 1832
Marketing Research (USA) 1833
Marketing Week (GBR) 1834
Marquette Law Review (USA) 4728
Maryland Bar Journal (USA) 4728
Masonry Construction (USA) 1022
Mass Transit (USA) 8503
Massachusetts Review (USA) 5227
Material Handling Management (USA) 5456
Mathematics and Computer Education (USA) 5515
Mathematics in School (GBR) 5515
Mathematics Teacher (USA) 3072
Mathematics Teaching (GBR) 5516
Mathematics Teaching in the Middle School (USA) 3072
McGill Journal of Education (CAN) 2885
McGill Law Journal (CAN) 4730
Measurement and Evaluation in Counseling and Development (USA) 2886
MediaWeek (USA) 30
Medical Anthropology Quarterly (USA) 347
Medical Economics (USA) 5668
Medical Laboratory Observer (USA) 5909
Medical Law Review (GBR) 4731
Medical Meetings (USA) 6281
Medicine and Science in Sports and Exercise (USA) 6231
Medium Aevum (GBR) 5332
Melbourne University Law Review (AUS) 4732
Men's Health (United States Edition) (USA) 6285
Mergers & Acquisitions (New York, 1965) (USA) 1148
Meridians (USA) 8901
Merrill - Palmer Quarterly (USA) 7385
Metal Producing & Processing (USA) 6323
Metalsmith (USA) 537
Metalworking Production (GBR) 6326
Mexican Studies (USA) 4464
Michigan Feminist Studies (USA) 8875
Michigan Quarterly Review (USA) 5227
Microwave Journal (International Edition) (USA) 3325
Microwaves & R F (USA) 3325
Middle East Economic Digest (GBR) 1499
The Middle Way (GBR) 7702
Midwest Quarterly (USA) 4465
Military Law Review (USA) 4971
Millennium Film Journal (USA) 6507
Millimeter (USA) 6507
The Mineralogical Record (USA) 4340
Minnesota Law Review (USA) 4734
Mississippi Libraries (USA) 5032
The Mississippi Quarterly (USA) 5227
Missouri Bar. Journal (USA) 4735
Mix Magazine (USA) 8154
Model Railroader (USA) 4341
Modern Age (USA) 5228
Modern Applications News (USA) 6326
Modern Casting (USA) 6326
Modern Healthcare (USA) 4107
Modern Judaism (GBR) 3551
Modern Language Journal (USA) 5151
Modern Machine Shop (USA) 5457
Modern Materials Handling (USA) 5457
Modern Metals (USA) 6326
Modern Painters (USA) 506
Momentum (Washington) (USA) 2887
Money Marketing (GBR) 1368
Monist (USA) 6935
Montessori Life (USA) 3073
Monthly Review (USA) 7155
Monthly Weather Review (USA) 6391
Mortgage Banking (USA) 1369
Mother Earth News (USA) 3982
MotherJones.com (USA) *see* Mother Jones. 5228
Motion System Design (USA) 3390
Motor Boating (USA) 8278
Motor Trend (USA) 8593
Mountain Bike (USA) 8265
Mousaion (ZAF) 5032
Multichannel Merchant (USA) 30
Multicultural Education (USA) 3073
MultiMedia & Internet@Schools (USA) 2950
Multinational Business Review (USA) 1578
Music and Letters (GBR) 6589
Music Educators Journal (USA) 6590
Music Library Association. Notes (USA) 5033
The Musical Quarterly (USA) 6594
Musical Times (GBR) 6594
Muslim World (USA) 7715
N A C L A Report on the Americas (USA) 7253
N A S P A Journal (Online) (USA) 2994
N A S S P Bulletin (USA) 3027
N M A Online (GBR) *see* New Media Age. 2335
N P A (USA) 1297
N W S A Journal (USA) 8901
Nashim (ISR) 8901
The Nation (USA) 5229
National Civic Review (USA) 7499
National Council of Teachers of Mathematics. Yearbook (USA) 3074
National Geographic Kids (USA) 4021
National Geographic Online (USA) *see* National Geographic. 4020
National Hog Farmer (USA) 294
National Institute Economic Review (GBR) 1152
National Institute of Standards and Technology. Journal of Research (USA) 6405
The National Interest (USA) 7254
National On-Campus Report (USA) 2293
National Parks (USA) 4981
National Petroleum News (USA) 6779
National Real Estate Investor (USA) 7601
National Review (USA) 7156
National Tax Association. Proceedings of the Annual Conference on Taxation and Minutes of the Annual Meeting (USA) 1936
National Tax Journal (USA) 1936
National Underwriter. Life & Health (USA) 4516
National Underwriter. P & C (USA) 4516
National Wildlife (USA) 2620
National Wildlife (World Edition) (USA) 2620
Nation's Restaurant News (USA) 4394
Native Peoples (USA) 6635
Native Plants Journal (USA) 804
Natural History (USA) 7888
The Natural Resources Journal (USA) 2621
Near Eastern Archaeology (USA) 407
Nebraska Library Association. Quarterly (USA) 5035
Nebraska Life (USA) 3982
Negro Educational Review (USA) 2890
New Criterion (USA) 5229
New Directions for Adult and Continuing Education (USA) 2944
New Directions for Community Colleges (USA) 2995
New Directions for Student Services (USA) 2995
New England Reading Association. Journal (USA) 2890
New England Review (USA) 5340
New Mexico Law Review (USA) 4744
New Perspectives Quarterly (USA) 7158
The New Republic (USA) 5230
New Scientist: Planet Science (GBR) *see* New Scientist. 7891
New Scientist: Planet Science (GBR) *see* New Scientist on CD-ROM. 7892
New Statesman (GBR) 5230
New York Diamonds (USA) 4568
New York Law School Law Review (USA) 4745
New York Review of Books (USA) 7568
The New York State Conservationist (USA) 2622
New York Times Magazine (USA) 3983
New Zealand Journal of Environmental Law (NZL) 4746
Newcastle Law Review (AUS) 4746
Newsletter on Intellectual Freedom (USA) 5036
Newspaper Research Journal (USA) 4581
Newsweek (USA) 3983
Nineteenth-Century Art Worldwide (USA) 509
Nineteenth Century French Studies (USA) 5342
Nineteenth-Century Literature (Berkeley) (USA) 5342
Nineteenth Century Music (USA) 6599
Nka (USA) 509
The North American Review (USA) 5230
North Carolina Central Law Journal (USA) 4748
North Carolina Journal of International Law and Commercial Regulation (USA) 4937
North Carolina Libraries (USA) 5036
Northern Kentucky Law Review (USA) 4749
Notes and Queries (GBR) 5343
Notre Dame Journal of Law, Ethics & Public Policy (USA) 7457
Notre Dame Law Review (USA) 4749
Novel: A Forum on Fiction (USA) 5344
Novyi Mir Iskusstva (RUS) 509
Nutrition Research Reviews (GBR) 6666
Nutrition Today (USA) 6667
O E C D Observer (FRA) 1504
O L A Quarterly (USA) 5037
Occupational Health (GBR) 5976
Occupational Outlook Quarterly (USA) 6707
Oceania (AUS) 350
Oceanus (USA) 2815
October (USA) 509
Office Solutions (USA) 1853
Ohio State Journal on Dispute Resolution (USA) 4752
Ohio State Law Journal (USA) 4752
Oilheating (USA) 6785
Online (USA) 2565
Online Cl@ssroom (USA) 2950
Opera News (USA) 6602
The Opera Quarterly (GBR) 6602
Optician (GBR) 6049
Oral History Review (USA) 4155
Oral Tradition (Online) (USA) 3621
Orbis (Kidlington) (GBR) 7256
Oregon Law Review (USA) 4754
Organic Gardening (USA) 3746
Organizational Dynamics (USA) 1784
Ornament (USA) 4568
Osgoode Hall Law Journal (CAN) 4754
Otago Law Review (NZL) 4754
Ottawa Law Review (CAN) 4754
Outdoor Life (USA) 8327
Outsourced Logistics (USA) 8507
Oxford Art Journal (GBR) 510
Oxford Economic Papers (GBR) 1158
Oxford Journal of Legal Studies (GBR) 4754
P C Magazine (Online) (USA) 2434
P C World (USA) 2581
P J E, Peabody Journal of Education (USA) 2894
P M Network (USA) 1785
P M Online (GBR) *see* People Management. 2897
P N L A Quarterly (CAN) 5038
P S: Political Science & Politics (GBR) 7163
Pacific Historical Review (USA) 4307
Pacific Shipper (USA) 8656
PackagePrinting (USA) 7325
Packaging Digest (USA) 6713
Pakistan Library & Information Science Journal (PAK) 5039
Paper, Film and Foil Converter (USA) 6714
Papers on Language and Literature (USA) 5348
Parabola (USA) 3621
Parachute (CAN) 511
Parameters (Carlisle) (USA) 6441
Parents (USA) 2164
Parliamentary Affairs (GBR) 7163
Parnassus: Poetry in Review (USA) 5429
Patent and Trademark Office Society. Journal (USA) 6755
Peace, Prosperity & Democracy (USA) 7164
Penn State International Law Review (USA) 4937
Penn State Law Review (USA) 4756
Pensions & Investments (USA) 1644
Penton's Welding Magazine (USA) 6343
People (New York) (USA) 3985
People & Strategy (USA) 1871
Perfumer & Flavorist (USA) 595
Personnel Today (GBR) 1872
Perspectives in Mexican American Studies (USA) 3557
Perspectives of New Music (USA) 6605
Perspectives on Political Science (USA) 7165
Petroleum Economist (GBR) 6787
Pharmaceutical Executive (USA) 6869
Phi Delta Kappan (USA) 2898
Philological Quarterly (USA) 5160
Philosophy East and West (USA) 6943
Philosophy of Music Education Review (USA) 6605
Physical Educator (USA) 3076
Piecework (USA) 6641
Pierce Law Review (USA) 4758
Pioneer America Society. Transactions (USA) 4308
Pipeline & Gas Journal (USA) 6788
Places (Brooklyn) (USA) 453
Planning for Higher Education (USA) 2998
Plant Engineering (USA) 3215
Plastics Technology (USA) 7098
Ploughshares (USA) 5352
PlugIn Datamation (USA) 2538
Poetry (Chicago) (USA) 5430
Policy & Practice (USA) 8062
Policy Review (USA) 7166
Policy Studies Journal (USA) 7167
Political Research Quarterly (USA) 7169
Political Science Quarterly (USA) 7169
Politics and the Life Sciences (USA) 7170
Pollution Engineering (USA) 3490
PopSci.com (USA) *see* Popular Science. 8435
Popular Mechanics PMZone (USA) *see* Popular Mechanics. 8435
Popular Music & Society (GBR) 6607
Popular Photography (USA) 6975
Population Bulletin (USA) 7289
Pottery Making Illustrated (USA) 2044
Poultry World (GBR) 297
Power Electronics Technology (USA) 3111
Practical Accountant (USA) 1299
Practice Nurse (GBR) 5978
Precision Marketing (GBR) 1838
Prepared Foods (USA) 3660
Presidential Studies Quarterly (USA) 7173
Preventing School Failure (USA) 3045
Prevention (USA) 6995
Princeton University Art Museum. Record (USA) 6536
Principal (Alexandria) (USA) 3030
Principal Leadership (High School Edition) (USA) 2899
Principal Leadership (Middle School Edition) (USA) 2899
Print (USA) 2489
Printing Impressions (USA) 7326
Problems of Economic Transition (USA) 1161
Process Engineering (GBR) 3253
Production Machining (USA) 5458
Products Finishing (USA) 6720
Professional Builder (USA) 1030
Professional Remodeler (USA) 1030
Professional Safety (USA) 6684
Professional School Counseling (USA) 2900
The Progressive (Madison) (USA) 7173
The Progressive Christian (USA) 7771
Progressive Grocer (New York, 2002) (USA) 3681
Progressive Librarian (USA) 5040
Project Management Journal (USA) 1787
Prologue (College Park) (USA) 4309
Promo (USA) 33
Prooftexts (USA) 5354
Psychiatric Times (USA) 6176
The Psychological Record (USA) 7396
Psychology Today (USA) 7400
Public Administration Review (USA) 7461
Public Art Review (USA) 513
Public Health Reports (USA) 7537
Public Land & Resources Law Review (USA) 4763
Public Libraries (USA) 5040
Public Performance and Management Review (USA) 7462
Public Personnel Management (USA) 1873
Public Relations Quarterly (USA) 33
Public Relations Review (GBR) 33
Public Works (USA) 7501
Publishers Weekly (USA) 7571
Publishing Executive (USA) 7571
Publius (USA) 7174
Purchasing (Newton) (USA) 1839
QST (USA) 2361
Quality Magazine (USA) 1788
Quality Progress (USA) 1788
The Quarterly Journal of Economics (USA) 1547

Online Service

Link to your serials resources and content with ulrichsweb.com

Index to Publications of International Organizations

This index is divided into four sections: publications of the European Union, International Congress proceedings, publications of International Organizations, and publications of the United Nations. Numbers in bold refer to the page in the CLASSIFIED LIST OF SERIALS where the full entry appears.

EUROPEAN UNION

INTERNATIONAL CONGRESS PROCEEDINGS

DIRECTORY 2010 INTERNATIONAL CONGRESS PROCEEDINGS 11307

Int'l Org

International Association of Plant Breeders for the Protection of Plant Varieties. Congress Reports **3739**
International Association of State Lotteries. (Reports of Congress) **1930**
International Association of Theoretical and Applied Limnology. Proceedings/Internationale Vereinigung fuer Theoretische und Angewandte Limnologie. Verhandlungen **2795**
International Astronomical Union. General Assembly. Highlights of Astronomy **576**
International Astronomical Union. Proceedings of Symposia **576**
International Astronomical Union. Transactions **576**
International Basketball Federation. Official Report of the World Congress **8236**
International Beekeeping Congress. Reports **122**
International Biophysics Congress. Abstracts **716**
International Botanical Congress. Abstracts of Papers **716**
International Botanical Congress. Proceedings **794**
International Bridge Conference. Proceedings **3272**
International Commission for Uniform Methods of Sugar Analysis. Report of the Proceedings of the Session (Year) **3648**
International Commission of Sugar Technology. Proceedings of the General Assembly **3648**
International Commission on Irrigation and Drainage. Congress Reports **8826**
International Commission on Large Dams. Transactions/Commission Internationale des Grands Barrages. Comptes Rendus **3272**
International Comparative Literature Association. Proceedings of the Congress **5309**
International Confederation for Agricultural Credit. Assembly and Congress Reports **200**
International Confederation of Free Trade Unions. World Congress Reports **4596**
International Confederation of Midwives. Congress Reports **5993**
International Conference of Agricultural Economists. Proceedings **200**
International Conference of Building Officials. Building Department Administration **1015**
International Conference of Building Officials. Code Changes Committee. Annual Report **1015**
International Conference of Building Officials. Plan Review Manual **1015**
International Conference of Ethiopian Studies. Proceedings **4175**
International Conference on Asphalt Pavements. Proceedings **8632**
International Conference on Assessment Administration. Proceedings **1126**
International Conference on Chemical Vapor Deposition. Proceedings **2065**
International Conference on Cloud Physics. Proceedings **6357**
International Conference on Computing Fixed Points with Applications. Proceedings **5494**
International Conference on Cosmic Rays. Proceedings **7067**
International Conference on Experimental Meson Spectroscopy. Proceedings **7077**
International Conference on Fluid Sealing. Papers Presented **3381**
International Conference on Lead. Proceedings **6316**
International Conference on Lighthouses and Other Aids to Navigation. Reports **8646**
International Conference on Liquefied Natural Gas. Papers **6774**
International Conference on Pressure Surges. Proceedings **3381**
International Conference on Social Welfare. Conference Proceedings **8047**
International Conference on Teaching Statistics. Proceedings **3065**
International Conference on the Physics of Electronic and Atomic Collisions. Abstracts of Contributed Papers and Invited Papers **7067**
International Conference on Vehicle Structural Mechanics. Proceedings **8585**
International Congress for Analytical Psychology. Proceedings **7363**
International Congress for Cybernetics. Proceedings/Congres International de Cybernetique. Actes **2527**
International Congress for Papyrology. Proceedings **398**
International Congress for Stereology. Proceedings **3346**
International Congress for the Study of Pre-Columbian Cultures of the Lesser Antilles. Proceedings **343**
International Congress of Electroencephalography and Clinical Neurophysiology (Proceedings) **6146**
International Congress of Entomology **850**
International Congress of Histochemistry and Cytochemistry. Proceedings **734**
International Congress of Linguists. Proceedings **5129**
International Congress of Occupational Therapy. Proceedings **6679**
International Congress of Ophthalmology. Abstracts **6043**
International Congress of Parasitology. Proceedings **948**
International Congress of Pharmaceutical Sciences. Proceedings **6849**
International Congress of Primatology. Proceedings **948**
International Congress of Psychology. Proceedings **7363**
International Congress of Radiology. Reports **6198**
International Congress of Sugarcane Technologists. Proceedings **3648**
International Congress on Alcoholism and Drug Dependence. Proceedings **2695**
International Congress on Animal Reproduction. Proceedings **8799**
International Congress on Archives. Proceedings **5018**
International Congress on Canned Foods. Texts of Papers Presented and Resolutions/Congres International de la Conserve. Textes des Communications **3648**
International Congress on Combustion Engines. Proceedings **3381**
International Congress on Experimental Mechanics. Proceedings (CD-ROM) **3346**
International Congress on Technology and Technology Exchange. Proceedings **3200**
International Congress on the History of Art. Proceedings **496**
International Council of Onomastic Sciences. Congress Proceedings **5129**
International Council on Large High Voltage Electric Systems. Proceedings **3320**
International Economic Association. Proceedings of the Conferences and Congresses **1126**
International Electron Devices Meeting. I E D M (Year) **3105**
International Energy Agency. Greenhouse Gas R & D Programme. Conference Proceedings. **3507**
International Eucharist Congress. Proceedings **7801**
International European Conference on High Energy Physics. Proceedings **7067**
International Federation for Psychotherapy. Congress Reports **6146**
International Federation of Asian and Western Pacific Contractors' Associations. Proceedings of the Annual Convention **6280**
International Federation of Catholic Universities. General Assembly. Report **2987**
International Federation of Operational Research Societies. Airline Group. Proceedings **8546**
International Foundry Congress. Papers and Communications **6316**
International Gas Union. Proceedings of World Gas Conferences **6774**
International Grains Council. Report for Fiscal Year **273**
International Grassland Congress. Proceedings **237**
International Horticultural Congress. Proceedings **3739**
International Hydrographic Conference. Reports of Proceedings **2808**
International Institute for Beet Research. Congress Proceedings **237**
International Institute of Administrative Sciences. Reports of the International Congress **7446**
International Institute of Ibero-American Literature. Congress Proceedings. Memoria **5310**
International Institute of Philosophy. Actes **6926**
International Institute of Synthetic Rubber Producers. Proceedings Annual General Meeting **7825**
International Iron and Steel Institute. Summaries of Conference Reports **6316**
International Joint Conference on Artificial Intelligence. Advance Papers of the Conference **2450**
International Joint Conference on Artificial Intelligence. Proceedings **2450**
International Law Association. Reports of Conferences **4931**
International Literary and Artistic Association. Proceedings and Reports of Congress **4458**
International Meeting of Animal Nutrition Experts. Proceedings **290**
International Metalworkers' Congress. Reports **6317**
International Mineralogical Association. Proceedings of Meetings **6467**
International Navigation Congress. Papers **8647**
International Ocean Institute. Pacem in Maribus. Proceedings **2808**
International Olympic Academy. Report of the Sessions **8181**
International Ornithological Congress. Proceedings **908**
International Pediatric Association. Proceedings of Congress **6093**
International Philatelic Federation. General Assembly. Proces-Verbal **6896**
International Political Science Association. World Congress **7144**
International Potash Institute. Congress Proceedings **238**
International Potash Institute. Proceedings of Colloquium, Congresses, Workshops, Seminars **238**
International Publishers Association. Proceedings of Congress **7563**
International Road Congresses. Proceedings **8632**
International Satellite Symposium on Acute Renal Failure. Proceedings **6269**
International School of Physics "Enrico Fermi." Proceedings **7018**
International Seaweed Symposium. Proceedings **795**
International Sedimentological Congress. Guidebook **2748**
International Skating Union. Minutes of Congress **8181**
International Social Security Association. Reports of the General Assemblies of the I S S A **4509**
International Society for Labour Law and Social Legislation. Proceedings of Congress **4696**
International Society for Mushroom Science. Symposia Proceedings **795**
International Society for Rock Mechanics. Congress. Proceedings **3273**
International Society for Terrain-Vehicle Systems. Proceedings of International Conference **3273**
International Statistical Institute. Bulletin. Proceedings of the Biennial Sessions **8379**
International Symposium on Chemical Reaction Engineering. Proceedings **3247**
International Symposium on Concrete Roads. Reports **3273**
International Symposium on Crop Protection. Proceedings **238**
International Symposium on Regional Development. Papers and Proceedings **4416**
International Symposium on the Aerodynamics and Ventilation of Vehicle Tunnels. Papers Presented **3273**
International Textile Manufacturers Federation. Annual Conference Report (Year) **8453**
International Thermal Spraying Conference. Preprint of Papers **6343**
International Trade Conference of Workers of the Building, Wood and Building Materials Industries. (Brochure) **1016**
International U V - E B Processing Conference and Exhibition. Proceedings **2065**
International Union Against Cancer. Proceedings of Congress **6023**
International Union for Quaternary Research. Congress Proceedings **2748**
International Union of Biological Sciences. General Assemblies. Proceedings **679**
International Union of Crystallography. Collected Abstracts of the Triennial Congress **2110**
International Union of Food, Agricultural, Hotel, Restaurant, Catering, Tobacco and Allied Workers' Associations. Meeting of the Executive Committee. I. Documents of the Secretariat. II. Summary Report **4596**
International Union of Geodesy and Geophysics. Proceedings of the General Assembly **2784**
International Union of Public Transport. Congress Reports **8500**
International Union of Radio Science. Records of General Assemblies **2359**
International Water Conference. Official Proceedings **8826**
Internationaler Weltkongress der U F O-Forscher. Dokumentarbericht **61**
Jet Cutting Technology **3384**
Kongresa Libro **6281**
Lymphology **5896**
Malaysian Rubber Board. Rubber Growers' Conference - Proceedings **7825**
Mathematics and Computers in Simulation **2517**
Microwave Heating Symposium. Proceedings **3325**
Mushroom Science **802**
N A D C A International Die Casting Congress. Transactions (North American Die Casting Association) **3354**
N A T O Annual Economic Colloquia. Proceedings/O T A N Colloques Annuels (North Atlantic Treaty Organization) **1578**
N A T O Challenges of Modern Society (North Atlantic Treaty Organization) **7884**
Nobel Symposium **4467**
North Atlantic Treaty Organization. Expert Panel on Air Pollution Modeling. Proceedings **3490**
Open Door International for the Emancipation of the Woman Worker. Report of Congress **1701**
P O A C. Proceedings (International Conference on Port and Ocean Engineering under Arctic Conditions) **3214**
Pacific Science Association. Congress and Inter-Congress Proceedings **7897**
Parapsychology Foundation. Proceedings of International Conferences **6743**
Progress in Protozoology **895**
Rencontres de Philosophie Medievale **6947**
Review of Population Reviews (Online) **7292**
Scandinavian Conference on Artificial Intelligence **2456**
Soil & Environment **3467**
The Study of Time **582**
Surfactants in Solution **3256**
Theoretical and Computational Acoustics **7050**
Trade Unions International of Chemical, Oil and Allied Workers. International Trade Conference. Documents **4603**
TropMed Seminars on Tropical Medicine. Proceedings **5828**
U I C C International Calendar of Meetings on Cancer (Union Internationale Contre le Cancer) **6283**
UNESCO Records of the General Conference. Proceedings **7270**
UNESCO Records of the General Conference. Resolutions **7270**
Union Academique Internationale. Compte Rendu de la Session Annuelle du Comite **4479**
Union of the Electricity Industry. Congress Proceedings **3333**
United Nations Issues Conference. Report **7271**
United Nations of the Next Decade Conference. Report **7271**
United Schools International. Documents of the Biennial Conference **3015**
Water Science and Technology **8840**
World Association for Educational Research. Congress Reports **2926**
World Buiatrics Congress **8815**
World Conference on Animal Production. Proceedings **304**
World Congress of Food Science and Technology. Proceedings **3668**
World Congress of Psychiatry. Proceedings **6189**
World Congress of the W F D. Proceedings (World Federation of the Deaf) **4077**
World Congress on Fertility and Sterility. Proceedings **6006**
World Congress on the Prevention of Occupational Accidents and Diseases. Proceedings **6689**
World Conservation Congress. Proceedings **2633**
World Council of Churches. General Assembly. Assembly - Reports **7695**
World Council of Churches. Minutes and Reports of the Central Committee Meeting **7695**
World Council of Service Clubs. Minutes of the General Meeting **8078**
World Federation of Hemophilia. Proceedings of Congress **5942**
World Mining Congress. Report **6483**

World Movement of Mothers. Reports of Meetings 8079
World Muslim Conference. Proceedings 7717
World Veterinary Congress. Proceedings 8815
World's Poultry Science Association. Proceedings of World's Poultry Congress 304
World's Woman's Christian Temperance Union. Triennial Report 2700

INTERNATIONAL ORGANIZATIONS

A C A R T S O D Monograph Series (African Centre for Applied Research and Training in Social Development) 1589
A C A R T S O D Newsletter (African Centre for Applied Research and Training in Social Development) 1589
A D B Review (Asian Development Bank) 1589
A I Communications (Artificial Intelligence) 2444
A I R I M P - Passenger (Air Reservations Interline Message Procedures) 8533
A P O Annual Report (Asian Productivity Organization) 1878
A P O News (Asian Productivity Organization) 1878
A S A I H L Seminar Reports (Association of Southeast Asian Institutions of Higher Learning) 2964
A S E A N Economic Info View (Association of South East Asian Nations) 1589
A S I F A Magazine (Association Internationale du Film d'Animation) 6488
Academy of European Law. The Collected Courses/Academie de Droit Europeen. Recueil des Cours 4916
Across the Oceans 2799
Acta Colloquii Didactici Classici 5089
Acta Crystallographica. Section A: Foundations of Crystallography 2108
Acta Crystallographica. Section B: Structural Science 2109
Acta Crystallographica. Section C: Crystal Structure Communications 2109
Acta Crystallographica. Section D: Biological Crystallography/Biological Crystallography 2109
Acta Cytologica 826
Acta Haematologica 5933
Acta Horticulturae 3721
Acta Musicologica 6542
Acta Oncologica 6007
Acta Radiologica 6192
The Activist 7202
Adelphi Series 7219
Advances in Limnology 2792
Advances in Natural and Technological Hazards Research 8415
Advances in Systems Science and Applications 2541
Aerospace U F O News 43
Africa Media Monograph Series 4571
Africa Media Review/Revue Africaine des Medias 8085
African Development Bank. Report by the Board of Directors/Banque Africaine de Developpement. Rapport Annuel/Banque Africaine de Developpement. Rapport du Conseil d'Administration 1590
African Development Fund. Annual Report/Fonds Africain de Developpement. Rapport Annuel 1590
African Journal of Plant Protection/Revue Africaine de la Protection des Vegetaux 216
African Livestock Research 277
Africom 2312
Agricultural Policies in O E C D Countries: Monitoring and Evaluation (Organisation for Economic Cooperation and Development) 1909
Agroforestry Systems 87
Airline Coding Directory 8536
Airline Economic Results and Prospects 8536
Airlines International 8536
Airport and Air Navigation Charges Manual 8537
Airport Handling Manual 8537
Alcoholism 2691
Aluminum Industry Abstracts 6338
America Cooperativa 1422
Americas (English Edition) 4442
Amnesty International Report 7221
Amphibia - Reptilia 932
Anales Galdosianos 5254
Anatomia, Histologia, Embryologia 8792
Anciens Pays et Assemblees d'Etats 7106
Andrologia 5574
Anesthesia and Analgesia 5769
Animals International 318
Annals of Oncology 6008
Annals of Public and Cooperative Economics 1422
L'Annee Hippique 8287
L'Annee Philologique 2242
Annotated Bibliography for English Studies 5406
Annotated Bibliography of Literature on Cooperative Movements in South-East Asia 615
Annotated Guide to Current National Bibliographies 5056
Annual Bibliography of the History of the Printed Book and Library 7577
Annual Egyptological Bibliography/Bibliographie Egyptologique Annuelle/Jaehrliche Aegyptologische Bibliographie 4169

Annual Report on the Environment and Natural Resources 3403
Annual Report on the Results of Treatment in Gynecological Cancer 6008
Anthos 427
Antiviral Research 881
Anuario Estadistico Centroamericano de Comercio Exterior 1200
Anuario Interamericano de Derechos Humanos/Inter-American Yearbook on Human Rights 4917
Apiacta 92
Applied Geochemistry 2724
Applied Numerical Mathematics 5550
Aquaculture Economics & Management 3585
Aquatic Mammals 933
Arab Journal of Language Studies/Al-Majallah al-'Arabiyyah lil-Dirasat al-Lughawiyyah 5095
Arab League Educational, Scientific, and Cultural Organization. Information Newsletter 2827
Arab Petroleum 6762
Archiv fuer Rechts- und Sozialphilosophie/Archives de Philosophie du Droit et de Philosophie Sociale/Archives for Philosophy of Law and Social Philosophy 6905
Archiv fuer Rechts- und Sozialphilosophie. Beihefte 6905
Archiv fuer Religionspsychologie/Archive for the Psychology of Religion 7622
Asia-Pacific Regional Co-operative Forums 1422
Asia-Pacific Scouting 2264
Asia - Pacific Tax Bulletin 1910
Asia-Pacific - Taxation & Investment Database 1911
Asian and Pacific Council. Food and Fertilizer Technology Center. Extension - Technical Bulletin 93
Asian and Pacific Labour 4590
Asian Development Bank. Annual Report 1308
Asian Development Bank. Board of Governors. Summary of Proceedings. 1591
Asian Development Bank. Key Indicators of Developing Asian and Pacific Countries 1308
Asian Development Bank. Statistical Report Series 1200
Asian Institute of Technology. Annual Research and Activities Report 8416
Asian News Sheet 4493
Asociacion 2143
Asociacion Interamericana de Bibliotecarios, Documentalistas y Especialistas en Informacion Agricola. Boletin Informativo 4992
Asociacion Interamericana de Bibliotecarios, Documentalistas y Especialistas en Informacion Agricola. Boletin Tecnico 93
Assemblee de l'Union de l'Europe Occidentale. Lettre de l'Assemblee 4918
Association Internationale de Geodesie. Commission des Marees Terrestres. Marees Terrestres Bulletin d'Information 2778
Association Internationale de Signalisation Maritime. Bulletin/I A L A Bulletin 8639
Association Internationale d'Etudes du Sud-Est Europeen. Bulletin 4201
Association Internationale d'Etudes Patristiques. Bulletin d'Information et de Liaison 7623
Association of Commonwealth Universities. Annual Report of the Council Together with the Accounts of the Association 2967
Association of Southeast Asian Institutions of Higher Learning. Newsletter 2968
Atherosclerosis 5778
Audiology and Neurotology 6078
Australian and New Zealand Journal of European Studies 7222
Automatica 2458
Automation in Construction 2458
Aviation Regulatory Watch Group Reports 8538
B I C - Code (Bureau International des Containers) 6708
B S P Data Interchange Specifications Handbook (Billing and Settlement Plans) 1310
Babel 5098
Bank for International Settlements. Annual Report 1313
Beche-de-Mer 3587
Behavioral Ecology 656
Benelux Economic Union. Conseil Central de l'Economie. Rapport du Secretaire sur l'Activite du Conseil 1880
Benelux Publikatieblad/Bulletin Benelux 7423
Bernoulli 5475
Bernoulli News 5475
Bibliographie de la Philosophie/Bibliography of Philosophy 6962
Bibliographie Internationale de l'Humanisme et de la Renaissance 4484
Bibliography on Irrigation, Drainage, River Training and Flood Control/Bibliographie de la C I I D. Irrigation, Drainage et Maitrise des Crues 8843
Big Official U C A S Guide to University and College Entrance (Universities and Colleges Admissions Service) 2969
Biochemistry and Molecular Biology Education 725
BioFactors 726
Biology and Fertility of Soils 221
Biorheology 752
Blutalkohol 2692
Boletim Tecnico Interamericano de Formacion Profesional 2832
Boletin Epidemiologico 7510
Boreas 2726

Brahmavidya 7733
Brain Pathology 6127
Building and Wood 4591
Building Research and Information 986
Bulletin de Philosophie Medievale 6909
Bulletin du Bibliophile 7556
Bulletin Eucarpia 782
Bulletin for International Taxation 1913
Bulletin of Volcanology 2778
Bureau International des Societes Gerant les Droits d'Enregistrement et de Reproduction Mecanique. Bulletin 7318
C A R A P H I N News (Caribbean Animal and Plant Health Information Network) 98
C C I A Background Information (Commission of the Churches on International Affairs) 7629
C D - Info (Christian Democrat International) 7111
C E R N Courier 7065
C E R N - H E R A Reports 7065
C E R N Reports 7065
C E R N School of Computing. Proceedings 7939
C I A T in Perspective (Distribucion de Publicaciones) 98
C I C A E Bulletin d'Information (Confederation Internationale des Cinemas d'Art et d'Essai) 6491
C I L E C T News (Centre International de Liaison des Ecoles de Cinema et de Television) 2377
C I N T E R F O R Estudios y Monografias (Centro Interamericano de Investigacion y Documentacion Sobre Formacion Profesional) 2833
C I R A Bulletin (Centre International de Recherches sur l'Anarchisme) 7111
C I R P Annals (College International pour la Recherche en Productique) 3375
C M A S Bulletin d'Information/C M A S Newsletter (Confederation Mondiale des Activites Subaquatiques) 2801
C M I Yearbooks & News Letters (Comite Maritime International) 8640
C O D E S R I A Book Series (Council for the Development of Economic and Social Research in Africa) 7111
C O N C A W E Review (Conservation of Clean Air and Water in Europe) 3408
Cahiers de Droit Fiscal International 4919
Les Cahiers de l' I P D/P A I D Reports (Institut Panafricain pour le Developpement) 1592
Call-Ej Online 3053
Canada - Taxation & Investment 1915
Capture Section Reports 3588
Cardiovascular Drugs and Therapy 5781
Caribbean - Taxation & Investment 1916
Catalogo de Publicaciones Latinoamericanas sobre Formacion Profesional 2835
Catalogus Musicus 6554
Catalogus Translationem et Commentatorium 5407
Cellular Oncology 830
Central/Eastern Europe - Taxation & Investment 1916
Centro de Estudios Monetarios Latinoamericanos. Ensayos 1326
Centro Interamericano de Investigacion y Documentacion sobre Formacion Profesional. Informes 3054
Centro Interamericano de Investigacion y Documentacion sobre Formacion Profesional. Serie Bibliografica 2931
Centro Latinoamericano de Economia Humana. Cuadernos 7953
Chaine/Keten 319
Chemical Disarmament 7115
Chemical Geology 2703
Chemistry International 2057
Chemoreception Abstracts (Online) 2093
Child Abuse & Neglect 2147
Child's Nervous System 6131
China - Taxation & Investment 1917
Chronica Horticulturae 3727
Chronicle of Parliamentary Elections 7116
Chronobiology International 666
Ciguatera 3589
Cites Unies/Ciudades Unidas/United Cities 7227
Clinical Hemorheology and Microcirculation 5935
Clinical Neurophysiology 6132
Clinical Neurophysiology. Supplement 6132
Coastline 2802
Cocoa Newsletter 3631
Colecciones Basicas C I N T E R F O R 3054
Collection of Documents for the Study of International Non-Governmental Relations 4920
Collezione di Monografie Preistoriche e Archeologiche 387
Colombo Plan Bureau. The Colombo Plan Council Report 1592
Colombo Plan Newsletter 1592
Comite International de Cooperation dans les Recherches Nationales en Demographie. Actes des Seminaires 7279
Comite International de Dachau. Bulletin 4211
Commission for the Geological Map of the World. Bulletin 2729
Commissioner for Human Rights. Annual Report to the Committee of Ministers and the Parliamentary Assembly 7204
Commonwealth Judicial Journal 4921

11310 INTERNATIONAL ORGANIZATIONS ULRICH'S PERIODICALS

Haemophilia 5937
Haemophilia. Supplement 5937
Health Policy 7522
Hegel-Studien. Beiheft 6922
Higher Education Management and Policy 2984
Higher Education Policy 2984
Histopathology 6021
History of European Ideas 6923
Horticultural Research International 3737
Hospital Management International 4100
Human Rights Bulletin (New York) 7208
Hydrographic Journal 2709
Hydrographic Society. International Headquarters. Special Publications 8825
Hydrological Sciences Journal/Journal des Sciences Hydrologiques 2794
Hygiea Internationalis 7524
Hypertension in Pregnancy 5789
I A B S E Report (International Association for Bridge and Structural Engineering) 3269
I A G A Bulletin (International Association of Geomagnetism and Aeronomy) 2783
I A G A News (International Association of Geomagnetism and Aeronomy) 2783
I A J R C Journal (International Association of Jazz Record Collectors) 6574
I A L News (International Association of Laryngectomees) 6080
I A M H I S T Newsletter (International Association for Media and History) 8106
I A S A Journal (International Association of Sound and Audiovisual Archives) 8153
I A S L Newsletter (International Association of School Librarianship) 5012
I A T A City Code Directory (International Air Transport Association) 8544
I A T A Environmental Review (Online) (International Air Transport Association) 3438
I A T A List of Ticket and Airport Taxes and Fees (Online) (International Air Transport Association) 8544
I A T A Ticketing Handbook (International Air Transport Association) 8544
I A W A Journal (International Association of Wood Anatomists) 793
I B N S Journal (International Bank Note Society) 6651
I C A C Recorder (International Cotton Advisory Committee) 8452
I C A Regional Bulletin (International Cooperative Alliance) 1423
I C A Regional Womens Forum (International Co-operative Alliance) 8899
I C A S A L S Newsletter (International Center for Arid and Semiarid Land Studies) 2614
I C A S E - L A R C Interdisciplinary Series in Science and Engineering (Institute for Computer Applications in Science and Engineering - Langley Research Center) 7864
I C C Annual Report (International Chamber of Commerce) 1404
I C C O Annual Report (International Cocoa Organization) 3646
I C C O World Cocoa Directory (International Cocoa Organization) 3646
I C E L References (International Council of Environmental Law) 3479
I C E S Cooperative Research Report/Conseil International pour l'Exploration de la Mer Rapport des Recherches Collectives (International Council for the Exploration of the Sea) 3597
I C E S Journal of Marine Science (International Council for the Exploration of the Sea) 2806
I C H A Buyers' Guide to Manufacturers (Year) (International Cargo Handling Co-ordination Association) 8646
I C H C A News and Cargo Today (International Cargo Handling Co-ordination Association) 8526
I C J Review (International Commission of Jurists) 4928
I C M A Newsletter (International City/County Management Association) 7494
I C O M News (English Edition) (International Council of Museums) 6525
I C R A - Agrimissio Information (International Catholic Rural Association) 7800
I C S U Newsletter (International Council for Science) 7864
I D B Projects (Inter-American Development Bank) 1352
I E A Clean Coal Centre. Newsletter (International Energy Agency) 3137
I E A Clean Coal Centre. Profiles (International Energy Agency) 3137
The I E A Journal of Ergonomics (International Ergonomics Association) 3196
I E C Bulletin (International Electrotechnical Commission) 3310
I E C Catalogue of Publications (International Electrotechnical Commission) 3101
I F A P Newsletter: World Farmer (Online) (International Federation of Agricultural Producers) 119
I F H O H Journal (International Federation of the Hard of Hearing) 4074
I F H P Newsletter (International Federation for Housing and Planning) 4414
I F L A Directory (International Federation of Library Associations and Institutions) 5013
I F L A Journal (International Federation of Library Associations and Institutions) 5013
I F L A Publications (International Federation of Library Associations) 5013
I F L A Series on Bibliographic Control (International Federation of Library Associations and Institutions) 5014
I G F - Journal (International Graphical Federation) 7323
I H F Management Handbooks (International Hospital Federation) 4102
I I A S A Annual Report (International Institute for Applied Systems Analysis) 3482
I I C Annual Report (Inter-American Investment Corporation) 1352
I I R A Bulletin (International Industrial Relations Association) 1686
I L C A Annual Report and Programme Highlights (International Livestock Centre for Africa) 288
I L C A Newsletter (International Livestock Centre for Africa) 288
I L C A Research Report (International Livestock Centre for Africa) 288
I L G A Bulletin (International Lesbian and Gay Association) 4375
I M F Heavily Indebted Poor Countries Country Documents (International Monetary Fund) 1597
I M F News (International Metalworkers Federation) 6315
I M F Working Paper (International Monetary Fund) 1490
I N A S P Newsletter (International Network for the Availability of Scientific Publications) 5014
I P I Global Journalist (International Press Institute) 4576
I P S F News Bulletin (International Pharmaceutical Students Federation) 6847
I P T C Spectrum (International Press Telecommunications Council) 2368
I R R I Program Report (International Rice Research Institute) 273
I S M S Newsletter (International Society for Mushroom Science) 793
I S O Focus (English Edition) (International Organization for Standardization) 6402
I S O Journal (International Society of Organbuilders) 6574
I S O Memento (International Organization for Standardization) 6402
I S P R S Journal of Photogrammetry and Remote Sensing (International Society for Photogrammetry and Remote Sensing) 4014
I S S F News (International Shooting Sport Federation) 8178
I S U Constitution and General Regulations (International Skating Union) 8178
I T M F Country Statements (International Textile Manufacturers Federation) 8452
I T M F Directory (International Textile Manufacturers Federation) 8452
I U B M B Life (International Union of Biochemistry and Molecular Biology) 733
I U C N Environmental Policy and Law Papers 3438
I U F R O World Congress. Congress Reports (International Union of Forestry Research Organizations) 3693
I U F R O World Series (International Union of Forestry Research Organizations) 3693
I U G G Year Book/Annuaire U G G I (International Union of Geodesy and Geophysics) 2783
I U O M A Magazine (International Union of Mail Artists) 494
I U P I W Views (International Union of Petroleum & Industrial Workers) 6773
I U S S P. Newsletter/U I E S P. Bulletin (International Union for the Scientific Study of Population) 7284
I W G I A Document (International Work Group for Indigenous Affairs) 342
Ice 2746
Immunology Letters 5760
Inclusion (English Edition) 7362
Index of African Social Science Periodical Articles 7200
Index to Plant Chromosome Numbers 716
Indicadores Economicos Centroamericanos 1490
Indigenous Affairs 342
Indologica Taurinensia 551
Infonomics 2544
Information & Management 2521
Information Europe 5016
Ingenieria Sanitaria 7525
Institut de Droit International. Annuaire 4929
Institut International du Froid. Bulletin/International Institute of Refrigeration. Bulletin 4121
Institut Panafricain pour le Developpement. Travaux d'Etudiants. Bulletin Analytique 1598
Institut Panafricain pour le Developpement. Travaux Manuscrits 200
Institut Syndical Europeen. Rapport d'Activites 4596
Insurance Statistics Yearbook 4530
Integrated Coastal Fisheries Management Project Technical Document 3598
Intensive Care Medicine 5636
Inter-American Bar Association. Newsletter 4694
Inter-American Center of Tax Administrators. Informativo - Newsletter 1929
Inter-American Council of Commerce and Production. Uruguayan Section. Publicaciones 1598
Inter-American Development Bank. Annual Report 1355
Inter-American Development Bank. Occasional Papers 1355
Inter-American Development Bank. Working Papers Series 1355
Inter-American Tropical Tuna Commission. Annual Report/Comision Interamericana del Atun Tropical. Informe Anual 3598
Inter-American Tropical Tuna Commission. Bulletin/Comision Interamericana del Atun Tropical. Boletin 3598
Inter-American Tropical Tuna Commission. Data Report 3598
Inter-Parliamentary Union. Series: Reports and Documents 7143
InterMedia 2383
International Abstracts in Operations Research 2443
International Academy of Legal Medicine. Newsletter 5914
International Angiology 5790
International Arthurian Society. Bibliographical Bulletin/Societe Internationale Arthurienne. Bulletin Bibliographique 5407
International Association for Byzantine Studies. Bulletin d'Information et de Coordination 4232
International Association for Educational and Vocational Information. Studies and Reports 2868
International Association for Shell and Spatial Structures. Journal 3272
International Association for the Exchange of Students for Technical Experience. Annual Report 3013
International Association of Agricultural Information Specialists. Quarterly Bulletin 5018
International Association of Geodesy. Central Bureau for Satellite Geodesy. Bibliography 4036
International Association of Geodesy. Central Bureau for Satellite Geodesy. Information Bulletin 4016
International Association of Geodesy Symposia 2783
International Association of Law Libraries. Directory 5018
International Association of Liberal Religious Women. Newsletter 7650
International Association of Logopedics and Phoniatrics. Reports of Congress 6146
International Association of Philatelic Journalists. Bulletin 6896
International Atomic Energy Agency. Safety Reports Series 3169
International Baccalaureate Organisation. Annual Report 2987
International Badminton Federation. Annual Statute Book 8180
International Cataloguing and Bibliographic Control 5018
International Centre for Settlement of Investment Disputes. Annual Report 1630
International Civil Defence Journal/Revista Internacional de Proteccion Civil/Revue Internationale de Protection Civile 2226
International College of Dentists. European Section. Newsletter 5848
International Commission on Irrigation and Drainage. Report 8826
International Commission on Large Dams. Bulletin 3272
International Commission on Radiological Protection. Annals 6198
International Committee for Historical Science. Bulletin d'Information 4147
International Committee of the Red Cross. Annual Report/Comite International de la Croix Rouge. Rapport Annuel 8047
International Committee of the Red Cross. Forum 8047
International Committee on Urgent Anthropological Research. Bulletin 343
International Confectionery Association. Statistical Bulletin Review (Year) 3674
International Confederation of Societies of Authors and Composers 6753
International Conference of Social Security Actuaries and Statisticians. Reports 4509
International Conference on Data Processing in the Field of Social Security. Reports 4509
International Congress Calendar 6280
International Congress Science Series 6280
International Cooperative Alliance. Cooperative Series 1423
International Cotton Industry Statistics 8463
International Council for Science. Year Book 7867
International Council for Traditional Music. Bulletin 6576
International Customs Journal/Bulletin International des Douanes 1930
International Dairy Federation. Bulletin/Federation Internationale de Laiterie. Bulletin 265
International Dairy Federation. Catalogue of I D F Publications/Federation Internationale Laitiere. Catalogue des Publications 182
International Dairy Federation. International Standard/Federation Internationale de Laiterie. Norme Internationale 265
International Dairy Federation. Newsletters/Federation Internationale de Laiterie. Newsletter 265
International Dental Journal 5848
International Directory of Antiquarian Booksellers/Repertoire International de la Librairie Ancienne 7563
International Earth Rotation Service. Annual Report 576
International Earth Rotation Service. Monthly Bulletin 576
International Energy Agency. Greenhouse Gas R & D Programme. Annual Report 3507
International Energy Agency. Greenhouse R&D Programme. Public Summary Reports 3507
International Federation for Housing and Planning. Membership List and Directory 4416
International Federation of Commercial Clerical, Professional and Technical Employees. Newsletter 4596
International Federation of Journalists and Travel Writers. Official List/Repertoire Officiel 8723
International Federation of Medical Students' Associations. Newsletter 5637
International Grains Council. Food Aid Shipments 1599
International Grains Council. Grain Market Report 201
International Grains Council. Ocean Freight Rates 8647
International Grains Council. World Grain Statistics (Year) 182

International Graphical Federation. Report of Activities 4596

International Gravimetrique Bureau. Bulletin d'Information 2783

International Handbook of Universities 2987

International Handbook on Commercial Arbitration 4931

International Humanist News 6925

International Hydrographic Organization. Yearbook 2808

International Index to Film Periodicals 6518

International Institute for Land Reclamation and Improvement. Publication 237

International Institute of Administrative Sciences Monographs 7446

International Institute of Seismology and Earthquake Engineering. Bulletin 2783

International Institute of Seismology and Earthquake Engineering. Individual Studies by Participants at I I S E E 2784

International Institute of Seismology and Earthquake Engineering. Year Book 2784

International Institute on the Prevention and Treatment of Dependencies. Selected Papers 2695

International Journal for Educational and Vocational Guidance 2942

International Journal for the Advancement of Counselling 2868

International Journal of Applied Earth Observation and Geoinformation 4016

International Journal of Biometeorology 6357

International Journal of Cancer/Journal International du Cancer 6022

International Journal of Continuing Engineering Education and Life-Long Learning 3200

International Journal of Dermatology 5877

International Journal of Developmental Neuroscience 6146

International Journal of Early Childhood 2155

International Journal of Environment and Pollution 3487

International Journal of Fertility and Women's Medicine 5638

International Journal of Food Microbiology 887

International Journal of Government Auditing (Online Edition) 7446

International Journal of Gynecology & Obstetrics 5994

International Journal of Hospitality Management 4391

International Journal of Humanities and Arts Computing 2426

International Journal of Hydrogen Energy 3139

International Journal of Industrial Ergonomics 3201

International Journal of Injury Control and Safety Promotion 2638

International Journal of Legal Information 5019

International Journal of Leprosy and Other Mycobacterial Diseases 5818

International Journal of Oral and Maxillofacial Surgery 5849

International Journal of Physical Education/Internationale Zeitschrift fuer Sportpaedagogik 3065

International Journal of Prosthodontics 5849

The International Journal of Psychoanalysis 7365

International Journal of Psychology/Journal International de Psychologie 7365

International Journal of Psychophysiology 7365

International Journal of Speleology 2748

International Journal of Sport Psychology 6230

International Journal of Systematic and Evolutionary Microbiology 888

International Journal of the Classical Tradition 2236

The International Journal on Hydropower & Dams 3163

International Linguistic Association. Special Publications 5130

International Monetary Fund. World Economic Outlook 1493

International Narcotics Control Board. Psychotropic Substances 6889

International Narcotics Control Board. Report for (Year) 6850

International Nursing Review 5962

International Ocean Institute. Occasional Papers 2808

International Organization 7244

International Organization for Cooperation in Health Care. General Assembly. Report 5640

International Organization for Migration. Annual Report 7285

International Orthopaedics 6062

International Pacific Halibut Commission. Annual Report 3598

International Pacific Halibut Commission. Scientific Report 3598

International Peace Update 7244

International Peat Journal 795

International Pharmacy Journal 6850

International Political Science Abstracts/Documentation Politique Internationale 7200

International Political Science Review/Revue Internationale de Science Politique 7244

International Psychologist 7366

International Quantum Electronics Conference 3321

International Railway Statistics (Year) 8526

International Rayon and Synthetic Fibres Committee. Statistical Yearbook 8463

International Reconciliation 7210

International Rehabilitation Review 5640

International Rescue Committee. Annual Report 8048

International Review for Business Education/Internationale Zeitschrift fuer Kaufmaennisches Bildungswesen/Revista Internacional para la Ensenanza Comercial/Revue Internationale pour l'Enseignement Commercial/Rivista Internazionale per la Cultura Commerciale 1129

International Review of Administrative Sciences 7447

International Review of Mission 7651

International Review of Social History 4147

International Review of the Red Cross 4932

International Seismological Centre. Bulletin 2784

International Silk Association. Monthly Newsletter 8453

International Skating Union. Special Regulations Ice Dancing 8181

International Social Security Association. Committee on Provident Funds. Reports and Summaries of Discussions 4509

International Social Security Review 4509

International Social Work 8048

International Society for Labour Law and Social Security. Bulletin 1689

International Society for Occupational Ergonomics and Safety. Newsletter 6679

International Society for Respiratory Protection. Journal 6215

International Society for Teacher Education. Journal 2871

International Society of Criminology. Bulletin 2656

International Society of Plant Morphologists. Yearbook 795

International Statistical Handbook of Urban Public Transport/Internationales Statistik-Handbuch fuer den Oeffentlichen Stadtverkehr/Recueil International de Statistiques des Transports Publics Urbains 8526

International Statistical Institute. Newsletter 5498

International Statistical Review/Revue Internationale de Statistique 8379

International Sugar Organization. Statistical Bulletin 3670

International Surgery 6246

International Textile Machinery Shipment Statistics 8463

International Tin Research Institute. Annual Report 6317

International Transactions in Operational Research 2427

The International Tsunami Information Center (Year) Annual 2710

International U S Surgeon 6246

International Union for Inland Navigation. Annual Report 8500

International Union of Alpine Associations. Bulletin/Union Internationale des Associations d'Alpinisme. Bulletin 8724

International Union of Food, Agricultural, Hotel, Restaurant, Catering, Tobacco and Allied Workers' Associations. News Bulletin 4596

International Union of Physiological Sciences. Newsletter (Online Edition) 923

International Union of Soil Sciences. Bulletin 238

International V A T Monitor (Value Added Taxation) 1930

International Whaling Commission. Annual Report 948

International Women's News 8868

Internationale Seilbahn-Rundschau/International Aerial Lift Review 8500

Internationale Stiftung Mozarteum. Mitteilungen 6577

Intervirology 888

Iron Production 6340

Irrigation and Drainage 124

Islamic Academy of Sciences. Medical Journal 7869

Isotope and Radiation Research/Buhuth al-Naza'ir Wa-al-Ish'a' 6199

J A C C Report (Joint Assessment of Commodity Chemicals) 3498

Jahrbuch fuer Liturgik und Hymnologie 7762

Jazzforschung/Jazz Research 6579

Jazzmen's Reference Book 6579

Journal of Adolescent & Adult Literacy 3025

Journal of Applied Crystallography 2111

Journal of Applied Electrochemistry 2114

Journal of Biomechanics 5646

Journal of Bronchology & Interventional Pulmonology 6215

The Journal of Cardiovascular Surgery 5792

Journal of Cerebral Blood Flow and Metabolism 6150

Journal of Coastal Conservation 2809

Journal of Communication 8112

Journal of Cranio-Maxillofacial Surgery 6247

Journal of Cross-Cultural Psychology 7372

Journal of Cryptology 5502

Journal of Energy and Natural Resources Law 4701

Journal of Environmental Pathology, Toxicology and Oncology 3499

Journal of Film Preservation 6505

Journal of Forensic Odonto-Stomatology (Online) 5915

Journal of Geochemical Exploration 2711

Journal of Geodesy 2785

Journal of Glaciology 2750

The Journal of Heart and Lung Transplantation 6248

Journal of Hepatology 5928

Journal of Hydraulic Research 3363

Journal of Hypertension 5793

Journal of Hypertension. Supplement 5793

Journal of Logic, Language and Information 5134

Journal of Magnetism and Magnetic Materials 7020

Journal of Marine Systems 2809

Journal of Molecular and Cellular Cardiology 5794

Journal of Near-Death Studies 6929

Journal of Neurochemistry 736

Journal of Neuroimmunology 6154

Journal of Neurology/Zeitschrift fuer Neurologie 6154

Journal of Oral Pathology & Medicine 5852

Journal of Orofacial Pain 5853

Journal of Psychosomatic Obstetrics and Gynecology 5997

Journal of Reproductive Immunology 5763

Journal of Rural Cooperation 1424

The Journal of Sports Medicine and Physical Fitness 6231

Journal of Systems Architecture 2523

Journal of Terramechanics 8501

Journal of the Neurological Sciences 6157

Journal of Tropical Ecology 3448

Journal of Water Supply: Research and Technology. AQUA 8828

Journal of Wind Engineering & Industrial Aerodynamics 3387

Justice 4850

Kidney International 6271

Kidney International. Supplement 6271

Knowledge Organization 5023

L W F Documentation/Lutherische Rundschau (Lutheran World Federation) 7764

Labor Magazine 4597

Laser Therapy 5660

Latin America - Taxation & Investment 1933

Legislative Information 1695

Leonardo: Art Science and Technology 502

Leonardo Music Journal 6584

Lethaia 6726

Office International de la Vigne et du Vin. La Lettre 606

Ligures 404

Linguistic Bibliography/Bibliographie Linguistique 5201

Live Reef Fish 3601

Livestock Science 292

Log of the Star Class 8277

Lung Cancer 6026

Materials Characterization 6322

Mathematica Balkanica 5512

Mathematical and Computer Modelling 5512

Maturitas 5998

Measurement 6403

Mechanism and Machine Theory 3389

Medailles 4339

Media Development 2332

Medical & Biological Engineering & Computing 826

Medical and Pediatric Oncology. Supplement 6027

Medical Mycology 5822

Medical Science Monitor 5671

Mergers and Acquisitions 1934

Messianic Jewish Life 7739

Metabolic, Pediatric and Systemic Ophthalmology 6046

Metrologia 6404

Mileage Manual 8548

The Military Balance (Year) 6435

Ministerial Formation 7663

Monthly Statistics of International Trade/Statistiques Mensuelles du Commerce International 1252

Multilateral Interline Traffic Agreements Manual 8548

Musikforum 6596

Muslim World 7156

N A T O Advanced Science Institutes Series G: Ecological Sciences (North Atlantic Treaty Organization) 3454

N A T O Advanced Science Institutes Series H: Cell Biology (North Atlantic Treaty Organization) 835

N A T O Advanced Science Institutes Series. Partnership Sub-Series 4: Science and Technology Policy (North Atlantic Treaty Organization) 7884

N A T O Data (North Atlantic Treaty Organization (NATO)) 6437

N A T O Final Communiques/O T A N Communiques (North Atlantic Treaty Organization) 7253

N A T O Handbook (North Atlantic Treaty Organization) 7253

N A T O Science Series. Series 1: Life and Behavioural Sciences (North Atlantic Treaty Organization) 4465

N A T O Science Series. Series III: Computer and Systems Sciences (North Atlantic Treaty Organization) 2524

N A T O Scientific Publications. Newsletter (North Atlantic Treaty Organization) 7885

N E A News (Nuclear Energy Agency) 3171

Names of Persons 5034

Narcotic Drugs: Estimated World Requirements for (Year) 6890

National Accounts of O E C D Countries. Volume 1 Main Aggregates/Comptes Nationaux des pays de l'O C D E. Volume I 1252

National Accounts of O E C D Countries. Volume 2 Detailed Tables 1252

National Accounts of O E C D Countries. Volume 3, Financial Accounts/Comptes Nationaux des pays de l'O C D E. Volume III - Comptes Financiers (Organization for Economic Cooperation and Development) 1369

National Accounts of O E C D Countries. Volume 4, General Government Accounts/Comptes Nationaux des pays de l'O C D E. Volume IV, Comptes des Administrations Publiques (Organization for Economic Cooperation and Development) 1936

Natural Hazards 2713

Natural Resources Research 6474

UNITED NATIONS

This User's Guide refers exclusively to the U.S. Newspaper Section of Volume 4, which contains a comprehensive listing of general-interest daily and weekly newspapers published in the United States. *Subject-oriented newspapers* from the United States, and *all* newspapers from the rest of the world are subject-classified and listed in the CLASSIFIED LIST OF SERIALS, Volumes 1-3 of **Ulrich's**.

This volume is arranged in several sections: DAILY NEWSPAPERS, detailed citations of daily newspapers filed alphabetically by state, city, and newspaper name; WEEKLY NEWSPAPERS, detailed citations of weekly newspapers filed alphabetically by state, city, name, and TITLE INDEX.

This User's Guide is separated into three divisions for ease of use: (1) Section Descriptions, (2) Full Entry Content Description, and (3) Alphabetizing Rules for Main Entry Title.

Section Descriptions

DAILY NEWSPAPERS

This section comprises active U.S. general-interest newspapers that are published four or more days per week. All titles are active and are arranged alphabetically by state, city, and newspaper name.

WEEKLY NEWSPAPERS

This section comprises active U.S. general-interest newspapers that are published three or less days per week. All titles are active and are arranged alphabetically by state, city, and newspaper name.

TITLE INDEX

The TITLE INDEX is a major point of access to the newspapers contained in Volume 4 of **Ulrich's**. Only U.S.-based general-interest daily and weekly newspaper titles listed in Volume 4 are included in this index; the titles of other types of serials, as well as titles of subject-specific newspapers from the U.S. and all categories of newspapers from the rest of the world, can be found in the main TITLE INDEX in Volume 4 of **Ulrich's**.

The TITLE INDEX lists all current newspapers in this directory. The city and state of publication appear in parentheses next to the newspaper title. Boldface type indicates the page number where the complete entry can be found in Volume 4.

Prior to consulting the TITLE INDEX, a user should become familiar with title alphabetizing rules as described in the "Alphabetizing Rules for Main Entry Title" paragraphs of this User's Guide on p. ii. Newspapers with identical titles are sorted alphabetically by their two-letter state abbreviation.

Full Entry Content Description

Basic Information

The following items are mandatory for listing and appear in all entries: main entry title, frequency of publication, address, and owner name. Other items listed are not mandatory and are also briefly described below.

Title

The main title is printed in boldfaced, uppercased lettering as the first item of an entry. Titles are listed alphabetically within their respective states and cities.

Address, Telephone and Fax Numbers, E-mail and Web Site Addresses, and Mailing Address

The location address, telephone and fax number, e-mail address and Uniform Resource Locator (URL), if available, are listed in each entry.

Year Established

The year first published is given if provided by the publisher.

Publication Frequency

The frequency of a publication is given in abbreviated form, such as "d." for daily, "w." for weekly. For newspapers published less than seven days per week, the days of the week the newspaper is published are given, if known. Abbreviations for frequency notations are listed in the "Abbreviations" on p. Iv.

Page Size

If known, the trim size of the newspaper is listed. The size, such as "tabloid" will be preceded by the words "Page size."

Subscription Rate

The price is listed in U.S. dollars. The price may be given for annual subscriptions, per copy, per month, in state, out of county, and so forth. There may be several price structures, depending on the information received from the publisher.

Advertising Rate

When provided by the publisher, an advertising display rate is listed. The price is preceded by the words "Adv. Rate."

Wire Services

If a newspaper is known to use one or more news or photo wire services, abbreviations or names of the services are listed in the entry. Such information is preceded by the boldfaced words "Wire Service(s)." Abbreviations for wire services used are listed in the " Abbreviations" on p.iv.

Circulation

All circulation figures used are approximate. Circulation is given only if provided by the publisher. Various types of circulations may be noted, such as "paid," "free," or "controlled." There may be more than one circulation figure and more than one type of circulation listed. If the type of circulation is not known, only the circulation figure will be listed. All circulation data are preceded by the notation "circulation." If the circulation figures are known to pertain to either Sunday, evening, or morning circulation, or a combination thereof, such information is noted.

Owner Information

The name of the owner of a newspaper is listed. The owner's address, telephone, and fax number are also listed if different from the newspaper contact information. Occasionally there will be more than one owner listed. This information is preceded by the boldfaced notation "Owner(s):."

Management

A publisher and/or advertising contact name is given when provided. This information is preceded by the boldfaced notation "Management." Advanced degrees and titles are omitted.

Editorial

Principal editorial staff names are provided, preceded by the boldfaced notation "Editorial." They may include the Editor-in-Chief, the Managing Editor, or other high-ranking editors. Advanced degrees and titles are omitted.

Alphabetizing Rules for Main Entry Title

Titles are filed in strict alphabetical order, without regard to acronyms, abbreviations, or hyphens. Spaces precede alphabetical order. For example:

> News Tribune
> News-Chronicle
> Newsday
> News-Dispatch
>
> St. Louis Post-Dispatch
> Standard Banner
> Ste. Genevieve Herald
> Stillwater Sun Gazette

Articles at the beginning of titles are omitted, or are bypassed in filing.

In an index, when two or more titles with the same name are listed, the titles will sort alphabetically on the two-letter state abbreviations.

SAMPLE ENTRY

❶ ALASKA

❷ KODIAK

❸ KODIAK DAILY MIRROR. ❹ 1419 Selig St., Kodiak, AK 99615. ❺ TEL 907-486-3227;
❻ FAX 907-486-3088. ❼ E-MAIL: nfreeman@dailymirror.com; URL: http://www.dailymirror.com
❽ Mailing Address: P.O Box 555, Kodiak, AK 99615-0555. ❾ Year Established: 1940.
❿ Pub. Frequency: d. (Mon.-Fri.). ⓫ Page Size: tabloid. ⓬ Materials: 02, 10, 32,33.
⓭ Subscrip. Rate: $.50 newsstand/cover; $8/mo. Home delivery local. ⓮ Adv. Rate: col. Inch
$12.50 ⓯ **Wire service(s):** AP. ⓰ Circulation: 3,000 evening (paid); 3,500 Sunday (paid).
⓱ **Owner(s):** Kodiac Publishing Co., Inc., see address and contact information above.
⓲ **Management:** Nancy Freeman, Publisher. Amy Willis, Advertising Manager. ⓳ **Editorial:** Andy Hall,
Editor.

KEY

❶ State
❷ City
❸ Title
❹ Address
❺ Telephone number
❻ Fax number
❼ E-mail, URL addresses
❽ Mailing Address
❾ Year first published
❿ Frequency of Publication
⓫ Size of Publication
⓬ Materials accepted/included
⓭ Price
⓮ Advertising Rate
⓯ Wire Service(s)
⓰ Circulation
⓱ Owner(s)
⓲ Management personnel
⓳ Editorial personnel

Abbreviations
General Abbreviations and Special Symbols

3/m.	3 times per month		CQ	Congressional Quarterly Service
3/yr.	3 times per year		CSM	Christian Science Monitor
a.	annual		CST	Chicago Sun-Times
abstr.	abstracts		Ct.	Court
adv.	advertising		CT-NYT	Chicago Tribune-New York Times
Affs.	Affairs		Ctr.	Center
aft.	Afternoon		cy.	county
AFP	Agence France Presse		d.	daily
AP	Associated Press		Dec.	December
approx.	approximately		deliv.	delivery
Apr.	April		Dept.	Department
Apt.	Apartment		Dgn.	Design
Assn.	Association		Dir.	Director
Asst.	Assistant		DJNS	Dow Jones Newswire
Aug.	August		Dr.	Drive
Ave.	Avenue		E.	East
Bd.	Board		ea.	each
Bhd.	Brotherhood		Ed.	Editor
bi-m.	every 2 months		Ent.	Entertainment
bi-w.	biweekly		exc.	except
bibl.	bibliography		Expy.	Expressway
Bldg.	Building		Feb.	February
Blvd.	Boulevard		Fl.	Floor
BPI	BPI Entertainment News Wire		fortn.	fortnightly
BPS	Black Press Service		Fri.	Friday
BUP	British United Press		Fwy.	Freeway
c/o	care of		Gen.	General
CanP	Canadian Press		GNS	Gannett News Service
CaNS	Catholic News Service		Govt.	Government
CEO	Chief Executive Officer		HHS	Hearst Headline Service
CFO	Chief Financial Officer		HNS	History News Service
CiNS	City News Service		Hwy.	Highway
Cir.	Circle		in.	inch
circ.	circulation		Int'l.	International
Clas.	Classified		IPN	International Photo News
CNS	Copley News Service		irreg.	irregular
col.	column		ITNA	Independent Television News Association
Comns.	Communications			
Comp.	Composer		Jan.	January
contr.	controlled		Jct.	Junction
COO	Chief Operating Officer		JTA	Jewish Telegraph Agency
Coord.	Coordinator		Jul.	July
COP	Congressional Observer Pubs.		Jun.	June
COXN	Cox Newspapers		KR	Knight Ridder

KRT	Knight Ridder Tribune		Rd.	Road
LAT	Los Angeles Times		rec.	recording
LAT-WP	Los Angeles Times-Washington Press		rev.	review
LDE	London Daily News		R.D.	Rural Delivery
lit.	literature		Rels.	Relations
Ln.	Lane		Rm.	Room
m.	monthly		RN	Reuters News Service
Mar.	March		RNS	Religious News Service
MCNS	McClatchy NS		Rte.	Route
Mgmt.	Management		s-a.	twice annually
Mgr.	Manager		s-m.	twice monthly
Mktg.	marketing		s-w.	twice weekly
Mng.	Managing		S.	South
MNS	Massachusetts News Service		Sat.	Saturday
mo.	month		SAU	Standard Advertising Unit
Mon.	Monday		SC	Southern News Service
morn.	morning		Sep.	September
Mt.	Mount		SHNS	Scripps-Howard News Service
mult.	multiple		sing.	Single
N	National News Service		S-MCNS	Scripps-McClatchy NS
N.	North		SNS	State News Service
Nat'l.	National		Sq.	Square
NEA	Newspaper Enterprises Association		St.	Street
NNS	Newhouse News Service		Sta.	Station
No.	Number		Ste.	Suite
Nov.	November		Sun.	Sunday
NWS	National Weather Service		Supvr.	Supervisor
NYT	New York Times News Service		Svcs.	Services
Oct.	October		TASS	Russian News Agency
ONS	Ottawa News Service		Terr.	Terrace
P	Pacific News Service		Thu.	Thursday
Pbcty.	Publicity		Tpke.	Turnpike
pg.	page		Tue.	Tuesday
Pk.	Park		UPI	United Press International
Pkwy.	Parkway		Utd.	United
Pl.	Place		W.	West
Plz.	Plaza		w.	weekly
PR	PR Newswire		wd.	word
Pres.	President		Wed.	Wednesday
prod.	product		WIP	Washington International Press
prodn.	production		wk.	week
promo.	promotion		WN	World News
pub.	publication		WNS	Women's News Service
Publ.	Publisher		WP	Washington Press
q.	quarterly		yr.	year
qtr.	quarter		†	denotes ceased title
			▼	denotes newly published title

United States Abbreviations

AK	Alaska		MT	Montana
AL	Alabama		NC	North Carolina
AR	Arkansas		ND	North Dakota
AZ	Arizona		NE	Nebraska
CA	California		NH	New Hampshire
CO	Colorado		NJ	New Jersey
CT	Connecticut		NM	New Mexico
DC	District of Columbia		NV	Nevada
DE	Delaware		NY	New York
FL	Florida		OH	Ohio
GA	Georgia		OK	Oklahoma
HI	Hawaii		OR	Oregon
IA	Iowa		PA	Pennsylvania
ID	Idaho		RI	Rhode Island
IL	Illinois		SC	South Carolina
IN	Indiana		SD	South Dakota
KS	Kansas		TN	Tennessee
KY	Kentucky		TX	Texas
LA	Louisiana		UT	Utah
MA	Massachusetts		VA	Virginia
MD	Maryland		VT	Vermont
ME	Maine		WA	Washington
MI	Michigan		WI	Wisconsin
MN	Minnesota		WV	West Virginia
MO	Missouri		WY	Wyoming
MS	Mississippi			

ALABAMA

ALEXANDER CITY

OUTLOOK (ALEXANDER CITY), THE. 548 Cherokee Rd, Alexander City, AL 35010. Telephone: 256-234-4281. FAX: 256-234-6550. E-MAIL: timreeves@alexcityoutlook.com. URL: http://www.alexcityoutlook.com. Mailing Address: P.O. Box 999, Alexander City, AL 35011. Year Established: 1892. Pub. Frequency: d. (Tue.-Sun.) Page Size: broadsheet. Subscrip. Rate: $.50 newsstand/cover; $1 newsstand/cover Sun.; $136/yr mailed in county; $148/yr mailed out of county. Wire Service(s): AP. Circulation: 5,500 morning (paid); 5,000 Sunday (paid). Owner(s): Boone Newspapers, Inc., 15222 Freemen's Bend Rd., Northport, AL 35475. Telephone: 205-330-4100. Management: Tim Reeves, Publisher. Editorial: Kevin Taylor, Managing Editor. Tommy Chandler, Sports Editor.

ANDALUSIA

ANDALUSIA STAR NEWS. 207 Dunson St., Andalusia, AL 36420. Telephone: 334-222-2402. FAX: 334-222-6597. E-MAIL: rhaynes@andalusiastarnews.com. URL: http://www.andalusiastarnews.com. Mailing Address: PO Drawer 430, Andalusia, AL 36420. Pub. Frequency: d. (Tue.-Sat.) Page Size: broadsheet. Subscrip. Rate: $.50 newsstand/cover; $8.64 home delivery/mo. in county; $95.04/yr home delivery; $9.72 mailed/mo. out of county; $116.64/yr mailed. Circulation: 4,000 morning (paid). Owner(s): Boone Newspapers, Inc., PO Box 2370, Tuscaloosa, AL 35403. Telephone: 205-752-3381. Management: Michele Gerlach, Publisher. Ruck Ashworth, Advertising Manager. Jeff Moore, Circulation Director. Sharron Smith, Classified Adv. Mgr.. Editorial: Michele Gerlach, Managing Editor. Mary Reeves, Lifestyle Editor. John Wallace, Sports Editor.

ANNISTON

ANNISTON STAR. 4305 McClellan Blvd., Anniston, AL 36201. Telephone: 256-236-1551. FAX: 256-241-1991. E-MAIL: news@annistonstar.com. URL: http://www.annistonstar.com. Mailing Address: 4305 McClellan Blvd, PO Box 189, Anniston, AL 36206. Year Established: 1883. Pub. Frequency: d. Page Size: broadsheet. Subscrip. Rate: $.50 newsstand/cover; $1 newsstand/cover Sun.; $12 carrier delivery/mo.. Freelance Pay: $25-$125/article. Wire Service(s): AP, NYT. Circulation: 30,000 morning (paid). Owner(s): Consolidated Publishing Co., See address and contact information above. Management: H. Brandt Ayers, Publisher. Ken Warren, Advertising Director. Dennis Dunn, Circulation Director. Editorial: Bob Davis, Editor. Anthony Cook, Managing Editor. Ben Cunningham, Metro Editor. Trent Penny, Photographer. Bran Strickland, Sports Editor.

ATHENS

NEWS-COURIER, THE.   ISSN 0739-1307
410 W. Green St., Athens, AL 35612. Telephone: 256-232-2720. FAX: 256-233-7753. URL: http://www.enewscourier.com. Mailing Address: PO Box 670, Athens, AL 35611. Year Established: 1880. Pub. Frequency: d. (Tue.-Fri. & Sun.) Page Size: broadsheet. Subscrip. Rate: $.50 newsstand/cover; $1 newsstand/cover Sun.; $91.80/yr carrier delivery in city; $160.65/yr mailed in county. Adv. Rate: col. inch $5.70 Wire Service(s): AP. Circulation: 7,500 morning (paid); 8,500 Sunday (paid). Owner(s): Community Newspaper Holdings, Inc., 3500 Colonnade Pkwy., Ste. 600, Birmingham, AL 35243. Telephone: 205-298-7100. FAX: 205-298-7101. Management: Ann Lawrence, Publisher. Teresa Gibbs, Advertising. Carmeal Jenkins, Circulation Manager. Venessa Byars, Business Manager. Editorial: Sonny Turner, Editor. Kelly Kazek, Managing Editor.

BIRMINGHAM

BIRMINGHAM NEWS.   ISSN 0899-0050
2200 Fourth Ave., N., Birmingham, AL 35203. Telephone: 205-325-2237. URL: http://www.bhamnews.com. Mailing Address: PO Box 2553, Birmingham, AL 35202. Year Established: 1888. Pub. Frequency: d. Page Size: broadsheet. Subscrip. Rate: $.35 newsstand/cover; $1.50 newsstand/cover Sun.; $148.80/yr home delivery local; $154.80/yr mailed in state. Wire Service(s): AP, LAT-WAT, MCT. Circulation: 181,620 morning (paid); 205,245 Sunday (paid). Owner(s): Newhouse Newspapers, See address and contact information above. Bureau(s): Newhouse News Service, Washington, DC 10036. Telephone: 202-383-7837. Contact: Michael Brumas, Reporter. Management: Victor Hanson III, General Manager. Victor H. Hanson III, Publisher. Carl A. Bates, Advertising Manager. Toby Pearson, Circulation Director. Haley M. Smith, Marketing Director. Editorial: Tom Scarritt, Editor. Alec Harvey, Lifestyle Editor.

CLANTON

CLANTON ADVERTISER.   ISSN 1050-2084
1109 Seventh St, Clanton, AL 35046. Telephone: 205-755-5747. URL: http://www.clantonadvertiser.com. Year Established: 1972. Pub. Frequency: d. (Tue.-Fri. & Sun.) Page Size: broadsheet. Subscrip. Rate: $.50 newsstand/cover; $70.20/yr domestic area deliv; $72.01/yr mailed in county; $77.41/yr mailed in state; $93.61/yr out of state. Adv. Rate: col. inch $10.10 Circulation: 4,700 morning (paid). Owner(s): Boone Newspapers, Inc., 15222 Freemen's Bend Rd., Northport, AL 35475. Management: Mike Kelley, President. Peggy Kelley, Office Manager. John Sanders, Advertising Director. Michelle Price, Circulation Director. Editorial: Brent Maze, Managing Editor. Scott Mimo, News Editor. Stephen Dawkens, Sports Editor.

CULLMAN

CULLMAN TIMES.   ISSN 1096-7877
300 Fourth Ave., S.E., Cullman, AL 35055. Telephone: 256-734-2131. FAX: 256-737-1006. URL: http://www.cullmantimes.com. Year Established: 1901. Pub. Frequency: d. Page Size: broadsheet. Subscrip. Rate: $.50 newsstand/cover; $1.50 newsstand/cover Sun.; $118/yr carrier delivery in county; $220/yr mailed out of county. Adv. Rate: col. inch $8.95 Wire Service(s): AP. Circulation: 20,000 morning (paid). Owner(s): Community Newspaper Holdings, Inc., 3500 Colonnade Pkwy., Ste. 600, Birmingham, AL 35243. Telephone: 205-298-7100. FAX: 205-298-7101. Management: Bill Mogan, Publisher. Kathy McLeroy, Advertising Manager. Sam Mazzara, Circulation Manager. Debbie Miller, Classified Adv. Mgr.. Editorial: Brian Lazy, Managing Editor.

DECATUR

DECATUR DAILY, THE. 201 First Ave., S.E., Decatur, AL 35601. Telephone: 256-353-4612. FAX: 256-340-2411. E-MAIL: webmaster@decaturdaily.com. URL: http://www.decaturdaily.com. Mailing Address: PO Box 2213, Decatur, AL 35609. Year Established: 1912. Pub. Frequency: d. Page Size: broadsheet. Subscrip. Rate: $.50 newsstand/cover; $1.25 newsstand/cover Sun.; $10 home delivery/mo.; $119.70/yr home delivery. Wire Service(s): AP, SH, NYT. Circulation: 26,595 evening (paid); 28,165 Sunday (paid). Owner(s): Tennessee Valley Printing Co., Inc., See address and contact information above. Management: Clint Shelton, General Manager. Barrett C. Shelton Jr., Publisher. Gary Lloyd, Photography Director. Editorial: Tom Wright, Executive Editor. Scott Morris, Managing Editor. Barry Sublett, Lifestyle Editor. Regina Wright, Metro Editor. Richard McCann, News Editor. Mark Edwards, Sports Editor.

DEMOPOLIS

DEMOPOLIS TIMES, THE. 315 E. Jefferson St., Demopolis, AL 36732. Telephone: 334-289-4017. FAX: 334-289-4019. E-MAIL: demtimes@westal.net. URL: http://www.demopolistimes.com. Mailing Address: PO Box 860, Demopolis, AL 36732. Year Established: 1905. Pub. Frequency: d. (Tue.-Sat.) Page Size: broadsheet. Subscrip. Rate: $22 in county for 3 mos.; $45/yr in county; $35 mailed out of county for 3 mos.; $92/yr mailed out of county. Circulation: 2,500 per issue (paid). Owner(s): Boone Newspapers, Inc., 15222 Freemen's Bend Rd., Northport, AL 35475. Telephone: 205-330-4100. Management: Sam R Hall, Publisher. Brandy Philips, Advertising Manager. Brandy Maddox, Classified Adv. Mgr.. Editorial: Sam R Hall, Editor. Gennie Phillips, Managing Editor.

DOTHAN

DOTHAN EAGLE.   ISSN 0745-855X
227 N. Oates St., Dothan, AL 36303. URL: http://www.dothaneagle.com/gulfcoasteast/dea/home.html. Mailing Address: PO Box 1968, Dothan, AL 36302. Year Established: 190?. Pub. Frequency: d. Owner(s): Media General, Inc., See address and contact information above.

ENTERPRISE

ENTERPRISE LEDGER, THE. 106 N. Edwards St., Enterprise, AL 36331. Telephone: 334-347-9533. FAX: 334-347-0825. E-MAIL: entledger@hotmail.com. URL: http://www.eprisenow.com. Mailing Address: PO Box 311130, Enterprise, AL 36331-1130. Year Established: 1898. Pub. Frequency: d. (Tue.-Fri. & Sun.) Page Size: broadsheet. Subscrip. Rate: $.50 newsstand/cover; $1.25 newsstand/cover Sun.; $154.80/yr carrier delivery. Freelance Pay: $0.75/column-inch. Circulation: 11,000 morning (paid); 12,250 Sunday (paid). **Owner(s):** Media General, Inc., 333 E. Franklin St., Richmond, VA 23219. Telephone: 804-649-6000. **Management:** Jim Whittum, Publisher. Julie Stewart, Advertising Director. Lynn Tipton, Classified Editor. **Editorial:** Jim Whittum, Editor. Nan Stinnett, Managing Editor. Norman Lewis, Circulation Editor. Steve Butterworth, Sports Editor.

FORT PAYNE

TIMES-JOURNAL (FORT PAYNE), THE. 811 Greenhill Blvd. N.W., Fort Payne, AL 35967. Telephone: 256-845-2550. FAX: 256-845-7459. E-MAIL: tjnews@times-journal.com. URL: http://www.times-journal.com. Mailing Address: PO Box 680349, Fort Payne, AL 35968. Year Established: 1879. Pub. Frequency: d. (Tue.-Sat.) Page Size: broadsheet. Subscrip. Rate: $.50 newsstand/cover; $.75 newsstand/cover Sat.; $71/yr local; $78/yr mailed. Freelance Pay: $0.20/column-inch. Circulation: 6,500 evening (paid). **Owner(s):** Southern Newspapers, Inc., 5701 Woodway Dr., Ste. 131, Houston, TX 77057-1589. **Management:** J D Davidson, Publisher. Gloria Jackson, Advertising Manager. Tammy Stevens, Circulation Manager. **Editorial:** Jared Felkins, Managing Editor. Lew Gilliland, Sports Editor.

HUNTSVILLE

HUNTSVILLE TIMES, THE. 2317 S. Memorial Pkwy., Huntsville, AL 35801. Telephone: 256-532-4000. FAX: 256-532-4420. E-MAIL: htimes@htimes.com. URL: http://www.htimes.com. Year Established: 1910. Pub. Frequency: d. Page Size: broadsheet. Subscrip. Rate: $.50 newsstand/cover; $1.25 newsstand/cover Sun.; $11 carrier delivery/mo.; $140/yr carrier delivery. **Wire Service(s):** AP, LAT-WAT. Circulation: 65,000 evening (paid); 83,000 Sunday (paid). **Owner(s):** Advance Publications, Inc., PO Box 1487, W Sta., Huntsville, AL 35807. Telephone: 256-532-4000. **Bureau(s):** Contact: David Brewer, Bureau Chief. **Management:** Bob Ludwig, Publisher. William Joyner Jr., Advertising Director. Steve Wilson, Advertising Manager. Frank Maier, Circulation Manager. Sheila Runnels, Classified Adv. Mgr.. **Editorial:** Melinda Gorham, Managing Editor. Jim Steele, Automotive Editor. Shelly Haskins, City Editor. John Ehinger, Editorial Page Editor. Challen Stephens, Education Editor. Debra Storey, Entertainment Editor. Joe Duncan, News Editor. John Anderson, Political Editor. Bill Bryant, Sports Editor.

JASPER

DAILY MOUNTAIN EAGLE. ISSN 0893-0759
1301 Viking Dr., Jasper, AL 35501. Telephone: 205-221-2840. FAX: 205-221-6203. E-MAIL: jasper@mountaineagle.com. URL: http://www.mountaineagle.com. Mailing Address: PO Box 1469, Jasper, AL 35502. Year Established: 1872. Pub. Frequency: d. Page Size: broadsheet. Subscrip. Rate: $.50 newsstand/cover; $1 newsstand/cover Sun.; $10.25/mo.; $123/yr. Adv. Rate: col. inch $16.66 **Wire Service(s):** AP. Circulation: 14,200 evening (paid); 14,200 Sunday (controlled and free). **Owner(s):** Cleveland Newspapers, Inc., 1505 25th St., N.W., Cleveland, TN 37311. Telephone: 423-472-5041. **Management:** Jerome Wassman Jr., President. J.H. Boshill, Circulation Manager. Jerry Geddings, Classified Adv. Mgr.. **Editorial:** Ron Harris, Managing Editor. Jonathan Bentley, Sports Editor.

LANETT

VALLEY TIMES-NEWS, THE. 220 N. 12th St., Lanett, AL 36863. Telephone: 334-644-1101. FAX: 334-644-5587. E-MAIL: vt-n@mindspring.com. URL: http://www.valleytimes-news.com. Mailing Address: PO Box 850, Lanett, AL 36863-0850. Year Established: 1950. Pub. Frequency: d. (Mon.-Fri.) Page Size: broadsheet. Subscrip. Rate: $.50 newsstand/cover; $7.25 home delivery/mo.; $78/yr home delivery. Adv. Rate: col. inch $8.50 **Wire Service(s):** AP. Circulation: 7,500 evening (paid). **Owner(s):** Valley Newspapers, Inc., See address and contact information above. **Management:** Cy Wood, Publisher. Phillip Jones, Advertising. Martha Milner, Classified Adv. Mgr.. **Editorial:** Cy Wood, Editor. Wayne Clark, Business Editor. Scott Sickler, Sports Editor.

MOBILE

PRESS - REGISTER. 401 N. Water St., Mobile, AL 36602. Telephone: 251-219-5400. FAX: 251-219-5799. URL: http://www.mobileregister.com/indexmain.html. Mailing Address: PO Box 2488, Mobile, AL 36652. Year Established: 1813. Pub. Frequency: d. Page Size: broadsheet. Subscrip. Rate: $13.50 home delivery/mo.. **Wire Service(s):** AP, SH, LAT-WAT. Circulation: 104,000 morning (paid); 117,000 Sunday (paid). **Owner(s):** Advance Publications, Inc., See address and contact information above. **Management:** Ricky Mathews, Publisher. Larry Wooley, Advertising Director. Steve Hall, Advertising Manager. George Markevicz, Circulation Manager. **Editorial:** Mike Marshall, Editor. Frances Coleman, Editorial Page Editor. Debbie Lord, Lifestyle Editor. Kathy Jumper, Real Estate Editor. Randy Kennedy, Sports Editor.

MONTGOMERY

MONTGOMERY ADVERTISER. ISSN 0892-4457
425 Molton St., Montgomery, AL 36104-1000. Telephone: 334-262-1611. FAX: 334-261-1505. URL: http://www.montgomeryadvertiser.com. Mailing Address: PO Box 1000, Montgomery, AL 36101-1000. Year Established: 1827. Pub. Frequency: d. Page Size: broadsheet. Subscrip. Rate: $.50 newsstand/cover; $1.75 Sun.; $15.16/mo.. **Wire Service(s):** AP, SH. Circulation: 50,500 morning (paid); 65,100 Sunday (paid). **Owner(s):** Gannett Company, Inc., 7950 Jones Branch Dr., McLean, VA 22107-0001. Telephone: 703-854-2000. **Management:** Scott M. Brown, Publisher. Ron Davidson, Advertising Director. Michael Walton, Circulation Director. **Editorial:** Wanda Lloyd, Executive Editor. Marilyn Mitchell, Managing Editor.

OPELIKA

OPELIKA-AUBURN NEWS. ISSN 1044-7539
3505 Pepperell Pkwy., Opelika, AL 36801. Telephone: 334-749-6271. FAX: 334-749-1228. E-MAIL: msneed@oanow.com. URL: http://www.oanow.com. Mailing Address: P.O. Drawer 2208, Opelika, AL 36803. Year Established: 1903. Pub. Frequency: d. Page Size: broadsheet. Subscrip. Rate: $.50 newsstand/cover; $1 newsstand/cover Sun.; $90/yr home delivery Sun; $141/yr home delivery daily. **Wire Service(s):** AP. Circulation: 16,000 morning (paid); 16,500 Sunday (paid). **Owner(s):** Media General, Inc., 333 E. Franklin St., Richmond, VA 23219. Telephone: 804-649-6000. **Management:** James Rainey, Publisher. Lamar Smitherman, Advertising Director. Jerry May, Circulation Director. Kathy Dodwell, Classified Adv. Mgr.. **Editorial:** Mitch Sneed, Managing Editor.

SCOTTSBORO

DAILY SENTINEL (SCOTTSBORO), THE. 701 Veterans Dr., Scottsboro, AL 35768. Telephone: 256-259-1020. FAX: 256-259-2707. E-MAIL: dsnews@thedailysentinel.com. URL: http://www.thedailysentinel.com. Year Established: 1887. Pub. Frequency: d. (Tue.-Fri. & Sun.) Page Size: broadsheet. Subscrip. Rate: $.50 newsstand/cover; $1 newsstand/cover Sun.; $72/yr home delivery; $64.50/yr home delivery to senior citizens; $74/yr mailed in county; $78/yr mailed elsewhere. Circulation: 6,500 evening (paid); 7,000 Sunday (paid). **Owner(s):** Scottsboro Newspapers, Inc., See address and contact information above. **Management:** Mike DeLapp, Publisher. Laurie Chapman, Advertising Director. Rebecca Long, Business Manager. **Editorial:** Mike DeLapp, Editor. Mazie Aldrich, Managing Editor. Travis Tubbs, Sports Editor.

SELMA

SELMA TIMES-JOURNAL. ISSN 1043-9129
1018 Water Ave., Selma, AL 36701. Telephone: 334-875-2110. FAX: 334-872-4588. E-MAIL: newsroom@selmatimesjournal.com. URL: http://www.selmatimesjournal.com. Mailing Address: PO Box 611, Selma, AL 36701-0611. Year Established: 1827. Pub. Frequency: d. (Sun.-Fri.) Page Size: broadsheet. Subscrip. Rate: $.50 newsstand/cover; $1.50 newsstand/cover Sun.; $155.40/yr home delivery in county; $174/yr mailed in zone 367; $174/yr mailed out of zone. **Wire Service(s):** AP. Circulation: 7,049 morning (paid); 6,669 Sunday (paid). **Owner(s):** Boone Newspapers, Inc., PO Box 2370, Tuscaloosa, AL 35403. Telephone: 205-752-3381. FAX: 205-752-3392. **Management:** Dennis Palmer, Publisher. Erica Slone, Advertising Director. Frank Harrison, Circulation Director. **Editorial:** Tammy Leytham, Managing Editor. Fred Scoty, Production Manager. Victor Ing, City Editor. George Jones, Sports.

TALLADEGA

DAILY HOME. ISSN 1059-6461
4 Sylacauga Hwy., Talladega, AL 35160. Telephone: 256-362-1000. FAX: 256-249-4315. E-MAIL: news@dailyhome.com. URL: http://www.dailyhome.com. Year Established: 1867. Pub. Frequency: d. (Tue.-Sun.) Page Size: standard. Subscrip. Rate: $.50 newsstand/cover; $10/mo. in county; $11/mo. out of county; $13/mo. out of state. **Wire Service(s):** AP. Circulation: 18,000 morning (paid and free); 18,000 Sunday (paid and free). **Owner(s):** Consolidated Publishing Co., PO Box 977, Talladega, AL 35161. Telephone: 256-362-1000. **Bureau(s):** 22 N. Broadway, Sylacauga, AL 35150. Telephone: 256-249-4311. FAX: 256-249-4314. Contact: Denise Sinclair, Manager. **Management:** Carol Pappas, Publisher. Pam Adamson, Advertising Director. Sandy Carden, Advertising Manager. Kandi George, Circulation Manager. Alta Bolding, Classified Adv. Mgr.. **Editorial:** Carol Pappas, Editor. Graham Hadley, Managing Editor. June Winters, Food Editor. Laura Nation, Lifestyle Editor. Bran Strickland, Sports.

ALASKA

ANCHORAGE

ANCHORAGE DAILY NEWS. ISSN 0194-6870
1001 Northway Dr., Anchorage, AK 99508. Telephone: 907-257-4200. FAX: 907-258-2157. URL: http://www.adn.com/. Mailing Address: PO Box 149001, Anchorage, AK 99514-9001. Year Established: 1946. Pub. Frequency: d. Page Size: broadsheet. Subscrip. Rate: $.05 newsstand/cover; $1.50 Sun.; $45.50 carrier delivery in city for 13 wks.; $46.50 carrier delivery for 13 wks. in MatSu. Adv. Rate: B&W page $545 **Wire Service(s):** AP, SH. Circulation: 89,423 Sunday (paid and controlled); 71,711 per issue (paid and controlled). **Owner(s):** The/McClatchy Company, 2100 Q St, Sacramento, CA 95816. Telephone: 916-321-1936. **Management:** Mike Sexton, Publisher. Pat Bridges, Advertising Director. Mike Wiley, Advertising Manager. Roger Weinfurter, Circulation Manager. Heather Davis, Classified Adv. Mgr.. **Editorial:** Patrick Dougherty, Editor.

FAIRBANKS

FAIRBANKS DAILY NEWS-MINER. ISSN 8750-5495
200 N. Cushman St., Fairbanks, AK 99701. Telephone: 907-456-6661. FAX: 907-452-5054. URL: http://www.newsminer.com. Mailing Address: PO Box 70710, Fairbanks, AK 99707. Year Established: 1903. Pub. Frequency: d. Page Size: broadsheet. Subscrip. Rate: $.75 newsstand/cover; $1.50 newsstand/cover Sun.; $175.80/yr home delivery; $87/yr home delivery Sat. & Sun. only; $306/yr mailed. **Wire Service(s):** AP, NYT. Circulation: 44,367 morning (paid). **Owner(s):** Fairbanks Publishing Co., 1560 Broadway, Ste. 2100, Denver, CO 80202. Telephone: 303-563-6360. FAX: 303-820-1929. **Management:** Marilyn Romano, Publisher. Kathryn Styrle, Finance Director. Paula Kothe, Advertising Manager. Alice Hansen, Classified Adv. Mgr.. Sam Harrell, Photography Director. Danita Swenson, Promotion Manager. **Editorial:** Kelly Bostian, Managing Editor. Rod Boyce, City Editor. Sam Bishop, Editorial Page Editor.

JUNEAU

JUNEAU EMPIRE. 3100 Channel Dr., Juneau, AK 99801. Telephone: 907-586-3740. FAX: 907-586-9097. URL: http://www.juneauempire.com. Year Established: 1912. Pub. Frequency: d. (Sun.-Fri.) Page Size: broadsheet. Subscrip. Rate: $.50 newsstand/cover; $1.25 newsstand/cover Sun.; $36.75 home delivery for 3 mos.; $70.35 home delivery for 6 mos.; $131.25/yr home delivery. **Wire Service(s):** AP, LAT-WAT, MCT. Circulation: 7,000 evening (paid); 8,000 Sunday (paid). **Owner(s):** Morris Multimedia, Inc., PO Box 936, Augusta, GA 30903-0936. Telephone: 706-724-0851. **Management:** Robert Hale, Publisher. Marie Toland, Advertising Manager. Mike Lockridge, Circulation Manager. Angie Walker, Classified Adv. Mgr.. **Editorial:** Lori Thompson, Managing Editor. Brandon Loomis, City Editor. Charles Bingham, Sports Editor.

KENAI

PENINSULA CLARION. 150 Trading Bay Rd., Kenai, AK 99611. Telephone: 907-283-7551. FAX: 907-283-3299. E-MAIL: pitlo@alaska.net. URL: http://www.peninsulaclarion.com. Mailing Address: PO Box 3009, Kenai, AK 99611. Year Established: 1970. Pub. Frequency: d. (Sun.-Fri.) Page Size: broadsheet. Subscrip. Rate: $.50 newsstand/cover; $.75 newsstand/cover Sun.; $93/yr carrier delivery local; $107/yr carrier delivery in county; $125/yr mailed in state; $145/yr mailed out of state. **Wire Service(s):** AP. Circulation: 6,500 evening (paid); 7,000 Sunday (paid). **Owner(s):** Morris Multimedia, Inc., PO Box 936, Augusta, GA 30930-0936. Telephone: 706-724-0851. **Management:** Stan Pitlo, Publisher. Evy Gebbart, Advertising Director. Doug Munn, Marketing Director. **Editorial:** Lori Evans, Executive Editor. Bob Honea, Production Manager.

KETCHIKAN

KETCHIKAN DAILY NEWS. ISSN 0274-581X
501 Dock St., Ketchikan, AK 99901. Telephone: 907-225-3157. FAX: 907-225-1096. E-MAIL: news@ketchikandailynews.com. URL: http://www.ketchikandailynews.com. Mailing Address: PO Box 7900, Ketchikan, AK 99901. Year Established: 1936. Pub. Frequency: d. (Mon.-Sat.) Page Size: broadsheet. Subscrip. Rate: $.75 newsstand/cover; $1.50 newsstand/cover Sat.; $137/yr local; $193/yr mailed. **Wire Service(s):** AP. Circulation: 5,670 evening (paid). **Owner(s):** Pioneer Printing Co., See address and contact information above. **Management:** Lew Williams III, Co-Publisher. Karolyn Hallman, Advertising. Nancy Kaste, Circulation Manager. Marley Glass, Classified Adv. Mgr. **Editorial:** Terry Miller, Managing Editor.

KODIAK

KODIAK DAILY MIRROR. ISSN 0740-2112
1419 Selig St., Kodiak, AK 99615. Telephone: 907-486-3227. FAX: 907-486-3088. URL: http://www.kodiakdailymirror.com. Year Established: 1940. Pub. Frequency: d. (Mon.-Fri.) Page Size: broadsheet. Subscrip. Rate: $.50 newsstand/cover; $10/mo. local. Freelance Pay: $1.50/column-inch. **Wire Service(s):** AP. **Owner(s):** Fairbanks Daily News-Minor, PO Box 70710, Fairbanks, AK 99707-0710. Telephone: 907-459-7512. **Management:** Amy Willis, Publisher. Lynn Devlin, Advertising Manager. Janet Baker, Circulation Manager. **Editorial:** Jacob Brooks, Managing Editor.

SITKA

DAILY SITKA SENTINEL. 112 Barracks St., Sitka, AK 99835. Telephone: 907-747-3219. FAX: 907-747-8898. URL: http://www.sitkasentinel.com. Year Established: 1939. Pub. Frequency: d. (Mon.-Fri.) Page Size: broadsheet. Subscrip. Rate: $.50 newsstand/cover; $85/yr local. **Wire Service(s):** AP. Circulation: 3,375 evening (paid). **Owner(s):** Verstovia Corp., See address and contact information above. **Management:** Sandy Poulson, Publisher. Catherine Bagley, Advertising Manager. Libby Mears, Circulation Manager. Cynthia Cassedy, Classified Adv. Mgr. Sandy Poulson, Business Manager. **Editorial:** Thad Poulson, Managing Editor. Sandy Poulson, City Editor.Readers: Sitka area residents

AMERICAN SAMOA

PAGO PAGO

SAMOA NEWS. PO Box 909, Pago Pago, AS 96799. Telephone: 684-633-5599. FAX: 684-633-4864. E-MAIL: letters@samoanews.com. URL: http://www.samoanews.com. Year Established: 1969. Pub. Frequency: d. (Mon.-Sat.) Page Size: tabloid. Subscrip. Rate: $350/yr in county; $600/yr out of county. Freelance Pay: $1.50/column-inch. **Wire Service(s):** AP. Circulation: 3,500 morning (paid). **Owner(s):** Samoa News, See address and contact information above. **Management:** Vera Annesley, Publisher.

UTULEI

NEWS BULLETIN. Office of Public Information, Utulei, AS 96799. Telephone: 684-633-5490. Pub. Frequency: d. (Mon.-Fri.) Page Size: standard. **Owner(s):** American Samoa Gov't, Office of Public Information, See address and contact information above. **Management:** Philip Swett, Publisher.

ARIZONA

BISBEE

BISBEE DAILY REVIEW. 12 Main St., Bisbee, AZ 85603-0127. Telephone: 520-432-2231. FAX: 520-432-2356. E-MAIL: svhnews@c2i2.com. URL: http://www.svherald.com. Mailing Address: PO Box 127, Bisbee, AZ 85603-0127. Pub. Frequency: d. (Sun.-Fri.) Page Size: broadsheet. Subscrip. Rate: $.50 newsstand/cover; $1.25 newsstand/cover Sun.; $107.80/yr home delivery local; $129.60/yr mailed in state; $141.60/yr mailed elsewhere. Circulation: 1,200 morning (paid). **Owner(s):** Wick Communications, Inc., 333 W. Wilcox Dr., Ste. 302, Sierra Vista, AZ 85635. Telephone: 928-458-0200. **Management:** Walter Wick, Publisher. Bob Brooks, Circulation Manager. **Editorial:** Keith Allen, Managing Editor.

BULLHEAD CITY

MOHAVE VALLEY DAILY NEWS. ISSN 1061-8589
2435 Miracle Mile, Bullhead City, AZ 86442. Telephone: 928-763-2505. FAX: 928-763-7820. URL: http://www.mohavedailynews.com. Mailing Address: PO Box 21209, Bullhead City, AZ 86439. Year Established: 1926. Pub. Frequency: d. (Sun.-Fri.) Page Size: broadsheet. Subscrip. Rate: $.50 newsstand/cover; $1 newsstand/cover Sun.; $107.93/yr home delivery; $187.20/yr mailed. **Wire Service(s):** AP. Circulation: 9,200 morning (paid); 10,000 Sunday (paid). **Owner(s):** Brehm Communications, Inc., 16644 W. Bernardo Dr., Ste. 300, San Diego, CA 92127. Telephone: 858-451-6200. **Management:** Paul Stubler, General Manager. Chuck Rathbun, Publisher. Maria Pynakker, Advertising Manager. Ed Clary, Circulation Manager. Kathy Jones, Classified Adv. Mgr. **Editorial:** Wayne Agner, Managing Editor.

CASA GRANDE

CASA GRANDE DISPATCH. 200 W Second St, Casa Grande, AZ 85222. Telephone: 520-836-7461. E-MAIL: dkramerjr@trivalleycentral.com. URL: http://www.trivalleycentral.com. Mailing Address: PO Box 15002, Casa Grande, AZ 85222-5002. Year Established: 1912. Pub. Frequency: d. (Mon.-Sat.) Page Size: broadsheet. Subscrip. Rate: $.50 newsstand/cover; $9.75, $117/yr carrier delivery in area; $126/yr motor route; $156/yr mailed in county. Adv. Rate: col. inch $12.47 **Wire Service(s):** AP. Circulation: 10,019 evening (paid). **Owner(s):** Casa Grande Valley Newspapers, Inc., See address and contact information above. **Management:** Donovan Kramer, Jr., Publisher. Kara Cooper, Advertising Director. Richard Rosales, Circulation Director. Kim Sumpter, Classified Adv. Mgr. **Editorial:** Donovan Kramer, Jr., Editor. Oscar Perez, Photographer. Edward Petruska, Sports Editor.

DOUGLAS

DAILY DISPATCH (DOUGLAS), THE. 530 11th St., Douglas, AZ 85607. Telephone: 520-364-3424. FAX: 520-364-6750. E-MAIL: publisher@douglasdispatch.com. URL: http://www.douglasdispatch.com. Mailing Address: PO Box H, Douglas, AZ 85608. Year Established: 1901. Pub. Frequency: d. (Tue.-Sat.) Page Size: broadsheet. Subscrip. Rate: $.50 newsstand/cover; $75/yr carrier delivery; $120/yr motor route. Adv. Rate: col. inch $7.15 **Wire Service(s):** AP. Circulation: 2,300 morning (paid); 2,900 Sunday (paid). **Owner(s):** Wick Communications, Inc., 333 W. Wilcox Dr., Ste. 302, Sierra Vista, AZ 85635. Telephone: 928-458-0200. **Management:** Larry Blaskey, Publisher. Ana Maria Santana, Advertising Manager. Karl Sproule, Circulation Manager. Marta Gallegos, Business Manager. **Editorial:** Larry Blaskey, Editor. April Martin, Managing Editor.

FLAGSTAFF

ARIZONA DAILY SUN. ISSN 1054-9536
1751 S. Thompson, Flagstaff, AZ 86001. Telephone: 928-774-4545. FAX: 928-773-1934. E-MAIL: azdsnews@azdailysun.com. URL: http://www.azdailysun.com. Mailing Address: PO Box 1849, Flagstaff, AZ 86002. Year Established: 1887. Pub. Frequency: d. Page Size: broadsheet. Subscrip. Rate: $.50 newsstand/cover; $1.50 newsstand/cover Sun.; $153/yr carrier delivery. **Wire Service(s):** AP. Circulation: 13,249 evening (paid); 15,554 Sunday (paid). **Owner(s):** Lee Enterprises, Inc., 900 N. Tucker Blvd., St. Louis, MO 63101. Telephone: 313-340-8000. **Management:** Don Rowley, Publisher. Ken Bohl, Circulation Manager. Brenda Hazelett, Classified Adv. Mgr. Kristi Hostler, Business Manager. **Editorial:** Randy Wilson, Managing Editor. Laura Clymer, City Editor. Amy Dohm, Feature Editor. Jake Bacon, Photographer. Chris Lang, Sports.

KINGMAN

KINGMAN DAILY MINER. ISSN 0742-485X
3015 Stockton Hill Rd., Kingman, AZ 86401-4162. Telephone: 928-753-6397. FAX: 928-753-5661. E-MAIL: edit@ctaz.com. URL: http://www.kingmandailyminer.com. Year Established: 1882. Pub. Frequency: d. (Sun.-Fri.) Page Size: broadsheet. Subscrip. Rate: $.50 newsstand/cover; $1 newsstand/cover Sun.; $36 in county for 12 wks.; $45 out of county for 12 wks. Adv. Rate: col. inch $13.50 **Wire Service(s):** AP. Circulation: 9,758 evening (paid); 9,891 Sunday (paid). **Owner(s):** Western News & Info., Inc., 1748 S. Arizona Ave., Yuma, AZ 85364-5727. **Management:** Debbie Hoel, President. Robin Mauser, Publisher. Shay Givens, Advertising Director. Jamie Lyman, Advertising Manager. Brett Weaver, Circulation Director. Kandy Cummins, Circulation Manager. **Editorial:** Mark Borgard, Editor.

LAKE HAVASU CITY

TODAY'S NEWS-HERALD. ISSN 1068-1876
2225 W. Acoma Blvd., Lake Havasu City, AZ 86403-1756. Telephone: 928-453-4237. FAX: 928-855-9892. E-MAIL: news@havasunews.com. URL: http://www.havasunews.com. Year Established: 1980. Pub. Frequency: d. Page Size: broadsheet. Subscrip. Rate: $.75 newsstand/cover; $1.25 newsstand/cover Sun.; $122.03/yr in city; $283.43/yr out of county. Adv. Rate: col. inch $13 Freelance Pay: $1/column-inch. **Wire Service(s):** AP. Circulation: 11,906 morning (paid); 13,711 Sunday (paid). **Owner(s):** River City Newspapers LLC, See address and contact information above. **Management:** Michael Quinn, Publisher. Steven Stevens, Advertising Manager. Jim Abdon, Circulation Manager. **Editorial:** Becky Maxedon, Managing Editor, Pam Ashley, Feature Editor.

MESA

TRIBUNE (MESA), THE. 120 W. First Ave., Mesa, AZ 85210. Telephone: 480-898-6500. FAX: 480-898-6362. URL: http://www.aztribune.com. Mailing Address: PO Box 1547, Mesa, AZ 85211-1547. Year Established: 1915. Pub. Frequency: d. Page Size: broadsheet. Subscrip. Rate: $.50 newsstand/cover; $1.75 newsstand/cover Sun.; $117/yr. **Wire Service(s):** AP, SH, NYT, LAT-WAT. Circulation: 112,963 morning (paid); 114,007 Sunday (paid). **Owner(s):** Freedom Communications, Inc., 17666 Fitch, Irvine, CA 92614. Telephone: 949-253-2300. **Management:** Karen Wittmer, Publisher. Todd Halvorsen, Circulation Director. Terry Alvarez, Classified Adv. Mgr. **Editorial:** Jim Ripley, Executive Editor. Tom Gibbons, Business Editor. Christa Gibbons, Metro Editor. Bob Satnan, News Editor.

PHOENIX

ARIZONA REPUBLIC. ISSN 0892-8711
200 E. Van Buren St., Phoenix, AZ 85002. Telephone: 602-444-8000. FAX: 602-444-8044. URL: http://www.arizonarepublic.com/. Mailing Address: PO Box 2245, Phoenix, AZ 85001. Year Established: 1930. Pub. Frequency: d. Page Size: standard. Subscrip. Rate: $.75 newsstand/cover; $2.50/wk. **Wire Service(s):** AP, NYT, LAT-WAT. Circulation: 432,284 per issue. **Owner(s):** Gannett Company, Inc., 7950 Jones Branch Dr, McLean, VA 22107. Telephone: 703-854-6000. **Management:** Sue Clark-Johnson, Publisher. Linda Greiwe, Advertising Director. Marjorie Cochran, Advertising Manager. **Editorial:** Ward Bushee, Editor. Randy Lovely, Managing Editor. David Fritze, Business Editor. James Abundis, Graphics Editor. Mike Meister, Photo Editor. Dave Lumia, Sports Editor.

SIERA VISTA

SIERRA VISTA HERALD. ISSN 8750-3891
102 Fab Ave., Siera Vista, AZ 85635. Telephone: 520-458-9440. FAX: 520-459-0120. E-MAIL: philipvega@svherald.com. URL: http://www.svherald.com. Year Established: 1955. Pub. Frequency: d. Page Size: broadsheet. Subscrip. Rate: $.50 newsstand/cover; $1.50 newsstand/cover Sun.; $11.50 home delivery/mo.; $69 home delivery for 6 mos.; $126/yr home delivery. **Wire Service(s):** AP, NYT. Circulation: 12,000 evening (paid); 12,000 Sunday (paid). **Owner(s):** Wick Communications, Inc., 333 W. Wilcox Dr., Ste. 302, Sierra Vista, AZ 85635-1357. **Management:** Walter Wick, Owner. Philip Vega, Publisher. **Editorial:** Keith Allen, Managing Editor. Kristi O'Brien, Lifestyle Editor. Ed Honda, Photographer. Matt Hickman, Sports Editor.

SUN CITY

DAILY NEWS-SUN. 10102 Santa Fe Dr., Sun City, AZ 85351. Telephone: 623-977-8351. FAX: 623-876-3695. URL: http://www.dailynews-sun.com. Mailing Address: PO Box 1779, Sun City, AZ 85372-1779. Year Established: 1957. Pub. Frequency: d. (Mon.-Sat.) Page Size: broadsheet. Subscrip. Rate: $.50 newsstand/cover; $84.24/yr home delivery; $135/yr mailed. Adv. Rate: col. inch $13.98 **Wire Service(s):** AP. Circulation: 21,200 evening (paid). **Owner(s):** Freedom Communications, Inc., 17666 Fitch, Irvine, CA 92614. Telephone: 949-253-2300. **Management:** Jason Joseph, Publisher. Tom Coakdey, Advertising Director. Cathy Carlson, Circulation Manager. Monica Dickey, Classified Adv. Mgr. **Editorial:** Maryanne Leyshon, Editor. Dan McCarthy, Executive Editor. Rich Bolas, Sports.

TUCSON

ARIZONA DAILY STAR. ISSN 0888-546X
4850 S. Park Ave., Tucson, AZ 85714-1637. Telephone: 520-573-4220. FAX: 520-573-4107. E-MAIL: bjbuel@azstarnet.com. URL: http://www.azstarnet.com/. Mailing Address: PO Box 26807, Tucson, AZ 85726-6807. Year Established: 1879. Pub. Frequency: d. Page Size: broadsheet. Subscrip. Rate: $.50 newsstand/cover; $1.50 newsstand/cover Sun.; $34.80 home delivery for 3 mos.; $150.80/yr home delivery; $81 mailed for 3 mos.; $351/yr mailed. Freelance Pay: $25-$75/article. **Wire Service(s):** AP, NYT. Circulation: 165,029 per issue. **Owner(s):** Lee Enterprises, Inc., 900 N. Tucker Blvd., St. Louis, MO 63101. Telephone: 314-340-8000. **Management:** Jane Amari, Publisher. Barbara Chodos, Advertising Director. **Editorial:** Dana Murray, Editor. Bobbie Jo Buel, Managing Editor. Valerie Vinyard, Book Review Editor. Jill Jorden Spitz, Business Editor. Jim Kiser, Editorial Page Editor. Maria Parham, Feature Editor. Edie Jarolim, Food Editor. Tim Konski, Metro Editor. George Campbell, News Editor. Sergey Shayevich, Photo Editor. Phil Villarreal, Radio-TV Editor. James Bennett, Sports Editor. Elena Chabolla, Travel Editor.

TUCSON CITIZEN (ONLINE). 4850 S. Park Ave., Tucson, AZ 85714. URL: http://tucsoncitizen.com/. Mailing Address: PO Box 26767, Tucson, AZ 85726. Pub. Frequency: d. **Owner(s):** Gannett Company, Inc., 7950 Jones Branch Dr, McLean, VA 22107.

YUMA

DAILY COURIER, THE. 1748 S. Arizona Ave., Yuma, AZ 85364. URL: http://www.prescottaz.com. Mailing Address: PO Box 312, Prescott, AZ 86302. Year Established: 1882. Pub. Frequency: d. (Sun.-Fri.) Page Size: broadsheet. Subscrip. Rate: $.50 newsstand/cover; $1.25 newsstand/cover Sun.; $132.60/yr mailed in county; $202.80/yr mailed out of county; $234/yr mailed out of state. Adv. Rate: col. inch $12.46 Freelance Pay: $10-$100/article. **Wire Service(s):** AP, LAT-WAT. Circulation: 17,900 evening (paid); 20,001 Sunday (paid). **Owner(s):** Western News & Info., Inc., 1958 Commerce Center Cir., Prescott, AZ 86301. Telephone: 928-445-3333. FAX: 928-759-5682. **Management:** Kit Atwell, Publisher. Gil Walter, Advertising Director. Roy Traham, Advertising Manager. John Harrell, Circulation Director. **Editorial:** Ben Hansen, Editor. Dan Beeson, Sports Editor.

SUN (YUMA), THE. ISSN 1538-0955
2055 S. Arizona Ave., Yuma, AZ 85364. Telephone: 928-783-3333. FAX: 928-343-1009. E-MAIL: jmoreno@yumasun.com. URL: http://www.yumasun.com. Mailing Address: PO Box 271, Yuma, AZ 85366. Year Established: 1872. Pub. Frequency: d. Page Size: broadsheet. Subscrip. Rate: $.50 newsstand/cover; $1.50 newsstand/cover Sun.; $11 carrier delivery/mo. local; $63 home delivery for 6 mos.; $180/yr mailed in state; $228/yr mailed out of state. Adv. Rate: col. inch $26.18 **Wire Service(s):** AP. Circulation: 18,605 morning (paid); 21,304 Sunday (paid). **Owner(s):** Freedom Communications, Inc., 17666 Fitch, Irvine, CA 92614. Telephone: 949-253-2300. **Management:** Julie Moreno, Publisher. Lisa Miller, Advertising Director. Bob Roeser, Circulation Director. Lori Stoft, Marketing Director. David Fornof, Production Director. Lee Knapp, Business Manager. **Editorial:** Terry L. Ross, Editor. Randy Hoeft, Managing Editor. Cathy Everette, Business Editor. John Vaughn, City Editor. Terry L. Ross, Editorial Page Editor. Joyce Lobeck, Farm Editor. Roxanne Lehmann, News Editor. Ross Priest, Sports Editor.

ARKANSAS

ARKADELPHIA

ARKADELPHIA DAILY SIFTINGS HERALD. 205 S 26th St, Arkadelphia, AR 71923. Telephone: 870-246-5525. FAX: 870-246-6556. E-MAIL: news@siftingsherald.com. URL: http://www.siftingsherald.com. Mailing Address: PO Box 10, Arkadelphia, AR 71923. Year Established: 1886. Pub. Frequency: d. (Mon.-Fri.) Page Size: broadsheet. Subscrip. Rate: $.50 newsstand/cover; $8 home delivery/mo.; $99/yr in county; $108/yr elsewhere. Circulation: 34,000 morning (paid). **Owner(s):** GateHouse Media, Inc, 350 WillowBrook Office Park, Fairport, NY 14450. Telephone: 585-598-0030. **Management:** George Jinks, Publisher. Sherry Kizziar, Advertising Manager. Donnie Hollis, Circulation Manager. **Editorial:** Donna Hilton, Lifestyle Editor.

BATESVILLE

BATESVILLE GUARD. ISSN 1076-4801
258 W. Main St., Batesville, AR 72501. Telephone: 870-793-2383. FAX: 870-793-9268. E-MAIL: batguard@intellinet.com. URL: http://www.guardonline.com. Mailing Address: PO Box 2036, Batesville, AR 72503. Year Established: 1876. Pub. Frequency: d. (Mon.-Fri.) Page Size: standard. Subscrip. Rate: $.50 newsstand/cover; $72/yr in county; $80/yr out of county. Adv. Rate: col. inch $7.52 Freelance Pay: $0.40/column-inch. **Wire Service(s):** AP. Circulation: 9,500 morning (paid). **Owner(s):** Batesville Guard-Record Co., Inc., See address and contact information above. **Management:** O.E. Jones, President. Pat Jones, Publisher. Mike Smith, Advertising Manager. Christine Brown, Circulation Manager. Shelly Garth, Classified Adv. Mgr.. **Editorial:** Angelia Roberts, Managing Editor. Paul Glover, Sports Editor.

BENTON

BENTON COURIER. 321 N Market St, Benton, AR 72015. Telephone: 501-315-8228. FAX: 501-315-1920. URL: http://www.bentoncourier.com. Mailing Address: PO Box 207, Benton, AR 72018-0207. Year Established: 1876. Pub. Frequency: d. Page Size: broadsheet. Subscrip. Rate: $.50 newsstand/cover; $1 newsstand/cover Sun.; $93/yr home delivery local; $118/yr mailed in county; $127/yr mailed out of county. **Wire Service(s):** AP. Circulation: 8,833 evening (paid); 8,833 Sunday (paid). **Owner(s):** Horizon Publications, Inc., 1120 N. Carbon St, Ste 100, Marion, IL 62959. **Management:** Jim Perry, Publisher. Barney Partridge, Advertising Director. Gerald Reed, Circulation Manager. **Editorial:** Whit Jones, Editor.

BENTONVILLE

BENTON COUNTY DAILY RECORD. 104 S W "A" St., Bentonville, AR 72712. Telephone: 479-271-3700. FAX: 479-271-3744. URL: http://www.nwanews.com. Mailing Address: P.O. Box 929, Bentonville, AR 72712. Year Established: 1886. Pub. Frequency: d. Page Size: broadsheet. Subscrip. Rate: $.50 newsstand/cover; $1.50 newsstand/cover Sun.; $29.75 home delivery for 3 mos.; $109/yr. Adv. Rate: col. inch $13.31 Circulation: 17,975 morning (paid); 19,635 Sunday (paid). **Owner(s):** Wehco Media, Inc., PO Box 2221, Little Rock, AR 72203. Telephone: 501-378-3400. **Management:** Kent Marts, President. Jeff Jeffus, Publisher. Jim Quillen, Advertising Director. Kaye Hunton, Classified Adv. Mgr.. **Editorial:** Mike Jones, Managing Editor.

BLYTHEVILLE

BLYTHEVILLE COURIER NEWS. 900 N. Broadway, Blytheville, AR 72316. Telephone: 870-763-4461. FAX: 870-763-6874. URL: http://www.blythevillecn.com. Mailing Address: PO Box 1108, Blytheville, AR 72316. Year Established: 1903. Pub. Frequency: d. (Sun.-Fri.) Page Size: broadsheet. Subscrip. Rate: $.50 newsstand/cover; $110/yr home delivery in city; $127/yr mailed. Freelance Pay: $0.25/column-inch. **Wire Service(s):** AP, NYT. Circulation: 6,000 evening (paid); 10,000 Sunday (paid). **Owner(s):** Tennyson Publishing, See address and contact information above. **Management:** David Tennyson, Publisher. Bess Ann Pease, Advertising Manager. Melissa Andrew, Circulation Manager. Sheila Gale, Classified Adv. Mgr.. **Editorial:** Sandra Tennyson, Editor. Andy Weld, Managing Editor. Mark Brassfield, Sports.

CAMDEN

CAMDEN NEWS. 113 Madison Ave, Camden, AR 71701. Telephone: 870-836-8192. FAX: 870-837-1414. E-MAIL: camnews@ipa.net. URL: http://www.camdenarknews.com. Year Established: 1921. Pub. Frequency: d. (Mon.-Fri.) Page Size: broadsheet. Subscrip. Rate: $.50 newsstand/cover; $24.75 home delivery for 3 mos.; $99/yr home delivery. Adv. Rate: col. inch $7.50 Circulation: 5,000 evening (paid). **Owner(s):** Wehco Media, Inc., PO Box 2221, Little Rock, AR 72203. Telephone: 501-378-3400. **Management:** Walter E. Hussman Jr., Publisher. Sue Silliman, Advertising Manager. LaDonna Foster, Circulation Manager. **Editorial:** Jim Edwards, Managing Editor. Kelly Blair, Sports Editor.

CONWAY

LOG CABIN DEMOCRAT. 1058 Front St., Conway, AR 72032-0969. Telephone: 501-505-1212. FAX: 501-327-6787. E-MAIL: dkeith@thecabin.net. URL: http://www.thecabin.net. Mailing Address: PO Box 969, Conway, AR 72033-0969. Year Established: 1879. Pub. Frequency: d. (Sun.-Fri.) Page Size: broadsheet. Subscrip. Rate: $.50 newsstand/cover; $1 newsstand/cover Sun.; $133/yr mailed out of county. **Wire Service(s):** AP, SH. Circulation: 11,000 evening (paid); 13,000 Sunday (paid). **Owner(s):** Morris Multimedia, Inc., PO Box 936, Augusta, GA 30903-0936. Telephone: 706-724-0851. **Management:** Scot Morrissey, Publisher. Donna Spears, Advertising Manager. Jeb Eustis, Circulation Manager. **Editorial:** David Keith, Managing Editor. Rob O'Connor, Business Editor. Becky Harris, City Editor. Mike Kemp, Photo Editor. David McCollum, Sports Editor.

DEQUEEN

DE QUEEN DAILY CITIZEN, THE. 404 DeQueen Ave., DeQueen, AR 71832. Telephone: 870-642-2111. FAX: 870-642-3138. E-MAIL: dqbee@ipa.net. URL: http://www.dequeen.com. Mailing Address: PO Box 1000, DeQueen, AR 71832-1000. Year Established: 1933. Pub. Frequency: d. (Mon.-Fri.) Page Size: broadsheet. Subscrip. Rate: $.50 newsstand/cover; $55/yr mailed local; $75/yr mailed out of area. **Wire Service(s):** AP. Circulation: 2,646 evening (paid). **Owner(s):** Anita Kimball Marshall, See address and contact information above. **Management:** Anita Marshall, President. Leoda Matthews, Advertising Manager. Melissa Blankenship, Circulation Manager. **Editorial:** Scott Smith, Editor. Rick Wright, Sports.

EL DORADO

EL DORADO NEWS-TIMES. 111 N Madison, El Dorado, AR 71730. Telephone: 870-862-6611. FAX: 870-862-9482. E-MAIL: editorial@eldoradonews.com. URL: http://www.eldoradonews.com. Mailing Address: PO Box 912, El Dorado, AR 71731-0912. Year Established: 1888. Pub. Frequency: d. Page Size: broadsheet. Subscrip. Rate: $.50 newsstand/cover; $1 newsstand/cover Sun.; $30.75 home delivery local for 3 mos.. Adv. Rate: col. inch $24.90 **Wire Service(s):** AP. Circulation: 10,000 morning (paid); 16,000 Sunday (paid). **Owner(s):** Wehco Media, Inc., PO Box 2221, Little Rock, AR 72203. Telephone: 501-378-3400. **Management:** Betty Chatham, General Manager. Walter E. Hussman Jr., Publisher. Nicole Patterson, Advertising Manager. Scott Bramlett, Circulation Manager. **Editorial:** Shea Wilson, Managing Editor. Tony Burns, Sports Editor.

FAYETTEVILLE

NORTHWEST ARKANSAS TIMES. ISSN 1066-3355
212 N East Ave, Fayetteville, AR 72702. Telephone: 479-442-1700. FAX: 479-442-5477. E-MAIL: nwads@nwanews.com. URL: http://www.nwanews.com/nwat. Mailing Address: P.O. Box 1607, Fayetteville, AR 72702. Year Established: 1860. Pub. Frequency: d. Page Size: broadsheet. Subscrip. Rate: $.50 newsstand/cover; $1.25 newsstand/cover Sun.; $109/yr in county; $228/yr mailed out of county. Adv. Rate: col. inch $15.79 Circulation: 21,000 morning (paid). **Owner(s):** Wehco Media, Inc., PO Box 2221, Little Rock, AR 72203. Telephone: 501-378-3400. **Management:** Jeff Jeffus, Publisher. Brian Parson, Advertising Manager. Kaye Hunton, Classified Adv. Mgr.. **Editorial:** Christie Swanson, Managing Editor.

FORREST CITY

TIMES-HERALD (FORREST CITY). 222 N. Izard St., Forrest City, AR 72335. Telephone: 870-633-3130. FAX: 870-633-0579. E-MAIL: addept@thnews.com. URL: http://www.thnews.com. Mailing Address: PO Box 1699, Forrest City, AR 72336-1699. Year Established: 1871. Pub. Frequency: d. (Mon.-Fri.) Page Size: broadsheet. Subscrip. Rate: $.50 newsstand/cover; $7 home delivery/mo. in county; $95.75/yr mailed in county; $121/yr mailed out of county. Adv. Rate: col. inch $10.38 **Wire Service(s):** AP. Circulation: 5,000 evening (paid). **Owner(s):** Times-Herald Publishing Co., Inc., See address and contact information above. **Management:** Weston M. Lewey, Publisher. Jim Wirski, Advertising Manager. Betty Bridges, Classified Adv. Mgr.. **Editorial:** Tamara Johnson, Managing Editor. Katherine Leftwich, Society Editor. Fred Conley, Sports.

FORT SMITH

SOUTHWEST TIMES RECORD. 3600 Wheeler Ave., Fort Smith, AR 72901. Telephone: 479-785-7700. FAX: 479-785-7741. URL: http://www.swtimes.com. Mailing Address: PO Box 1359, Fort Smith, AR 72902. Year Established: 1832. Pub. Frequency: d. Page Size: broadsheet. Subscrip. Rate: $.50 newsstand/cover; $1 newsstand/cover Sun.; $107.04/yr home delivery; $182/yr mailed in retail trading zone. **Wire Service(s):** AP. Circulation: 43,000 morning (paid); 45,700 Sunday (paid). **Owner(s):** Stephens Group, Inc., 1111 W. Bonanza Rd., Las Vegas, NV 89125-0070. Telephone: 702-383-0211. **Management:** Gene Kincy, Publisher. John Speck, Advertising Director. Dennis Arnoldssen, Circulation Manager. Julie Newman, Classified Adv. Mgr.. **Editorial:** Tina Dole, Feature Editor. Judi Hansen, Metro Editor.

HARRISON

HARRISON DAILY TIMES. ISSN 1074-0384
111 W. Rush Ave., Harrison, AR 72601. Telephone: 870-741-2325. FAX: 870-741-5632. URL: http://www.harrisondailytimes.com. Mailing Address: PO Box 40, Harrison, AR 72602. Year Established: 1876. Pub. Frequency: d. (Sun.-Fri.) Page Size: standard. Subscrip. Rate: $.50 newsstand/cover; $1 newsstand/cover Sun.; $99/yr home delivery in area; $102.75/yr mailed in county; $108.75/yr mailed in state. **Wire Service(s):** AP. Circulation: 10,000 evening (paid). **Owner(s):** Community Publishers, Inc., PO Box 1049, Bentonville, AR 72712. **Management:** D. Jeff Christenson, Publisher. Jason Overman, Advertising Manager. Dick Hudleson, Circulation Manager. **Editorial:** Dwain Lair, Editor. Donna Braymer, Business Editor. Yvonne Cone, Community Editor.

HELENA

DAILY WORLD, THE. ISSN 8750-5274
417 York St., Helena, AR 72342. Telephone: 870-338-9181. FAX: 870-338-9184. E-MAIL: thedailywor@ipa.net. URL: http://www.helena-arkansas.com/. Mailing Address: PO Box 340, Helena, AR 72342-0340. Year Established: 1871. Pub. Frequency: d. (Mon.-Fri.) Page Size: broadsheet. Subscrip. Rate: $.50 newsstand/cover; $27 home delivery local for 3 mos.; $108/yr home delivery in county; $110/yr mailed out of county. Freelance Pay: $5/article. Circulation: 5,200 evening (paid). **Owner(s):** GateHouse Media, Inc, 350 WillowBrook Office Park, Fairport, NY 14450. Telephone: 585-598-0030. FAX: 585-248-2631. **Management:** Clark Smith, Publisher. Ann Puckett, Advertising Manager. Donna Ginn, Circulation Manager. Kerri Dunlap-Davis, Classified Adv. Mgr.. **Editorial:** Randy Hogan, Managing Editor.

HOPE

HOPE STAR, THE. 522 W Third St, Hope, AR 71801. Telephone: 870-777-8841. FAX: 870-777-3311. E-MAIL: hopestar@iyahoo.net. URL: http://www.hopestar.com. Mailing Address: PO Box 648, Hope, AR 71802-0648. Year Established: 1899. Pub. Frequency: d. (Mon.-Fri.) Page Size: broadsheet. Subscrip. Rate: $.50 newsstand/cover; $79/yr. Freelance Pay: $0.25/column-inch. Circulation: 4,100 evening (paid). **Owner(s):** GateHouse Media, Inc, 350 WillowBrook Office Park, Fairport, NY 14450. Telephone: 585-598-0030. FAX: 585-248-2631. **Management:** George Jinks, Publisher. Richard Haycox, Advertising Manager. Donnie Hollis, Circulation Manager. **Editorial:** Pat Harris, Managing Editor.

HOT SPRINGS

SENTINEL-RECORD, THE. 300 Spring St, Hot Springs, AR 71901. Telephone: 501-623-7711. FAX: 501-623-2984. E-MAIL: hotsr@hotsr.com. URL: http://www.hotsr.com. Mailing Address: PO Box 580, Hot Springs, AR 71902-0580. Year Established: 1877. Pub. Frequency: d. Page Size: broadsheet. Subscrip. Rate: $.50 newsstand/cover; $1 newsstand/cover Sun.; $11 home delivery/mo.; $120/yr home delivery. Adv. Rate: col. inch $19.60 Circulation: 17,923 morning (paid); 19,168 Sunday (paid). **Owner(s):** Wehco Media, Inc., PO Box 2221, Little Rock, AR 72203. Telephone: 501-378-3400. **Management:** Floyd Emerson, General Manager. Walter E. Hussman Jr., Publisher. Penny Thornton, Advertising Director. Ed Dorsey, Circulation Director. **Editorial:** Melinda Gassaway, Executive Editor. Lynda Lampinen, Business Editor. Bob Wisiner, Sports Editor.

JONESBORO

JONESBORO SUN, THE. 518 Carson St., Jonesboro, AR 72401. Telephone: 870-935-5525. FAX: 870-935-5823. E-MAIL: sunop@jonesborosun.com. URL: http://www.jonesborosun.com. Mailing Address: PO Box 1249, Jonesboro, AR 72403. Year Established: 1903. Pub. Frequency: d. Page Size: broadsheet. Subscrip. Rate: $.50 newsstand/cover; $1.25 newsstand/cover Sun.; $12/mo.. **Wire Service(s):** AP. Circulation: 27,958 morning (paid); 30,791 Sunday (paid). **Owner(s):** Paxton Media Group Llc, 201 S. Fourth St., Paducah, KY 42003. Telephone: 270-575-8600. FAX: 270-442-8188. **Management:** David Mosesso, Publisher. Harry Porter, Advertising Manager. Randy Mitchell, Circulation Director. Lisia Nuhung, Classified Adv. Mgr.. **Editorial:** Roy Ockert, Editor-in-Chief. Larry Fugate, Managing Editor. Roger Brumley, Production Editor. Kevin Purbeville, Sports.

LITTLE ROCK

ARKANSAS DEMOCRAT-GAZETTE. ISSN 1060-4332
121 E Capitol Ave, Little Rock, AR 72201. Telephone: 501-378-3400. FAX: 501-372-4765. E-MAIL: news@ardemgaz.com. URL: http://www.arkansasonline.com. Year Established: 1870. Pub. Frequency: d. Page Size: broadsheet. Subscrip. Rate: $.50 newsstand/cover; $1.25 newsstand/cover Sun.; $10.75 home delivery/mo. local area; $129/yr out of area; $216/yr mailed in state; $240/yr mailed out of state. Circulation: 173,079 morning (paid); 284,553 Sunday (paid). **Owner(s):** Wehco Media, Inc., PO Box 2221, Little Rock, AR 72203. Telephone: 501-378-3400. **Management:** Paul Smith, General Manager. Walter E. Hussman Jr., Publisher. John Mobbs, Advertising Director. Larry Graham, Circulation Director. **Editorial:** David Bailey, Managing Editor. Wally Hall, Sports Editor.

MAGNOLIA

BANNER-NEWS. 134 S Washington, Magnolia, AR 71753. Telephone: 870-234-5130. FAX: 870-234-2551. URL: http://www.bannernews.net. Mailing Address: PO Box 100, Magnolia, AR 71754. Year Established: 1878. Pub. Frequency: d. (Sun.-Fri.) Page Size: broadsheet. Subscrip. Rate: $.50 newsstand/cover; $1 newsstand/cover Sun.; $8.75/mo.; $105/yr. Adv. Rate: col. inch $10.46 Circulation: 4,100 evening (paid); 17,000 Sunday (paid). **Owner(s):** Wehco Media, Inc., PO Box 2221, Little Rock, AR 72203. Telephone: 501-378-3400. **Management:** Susan Gill, General Manager. Walter E. Hussman Jr., Publisher. Susan Gill, Advertising Manager. Maebelle Green, Circulation Manager. **Editorial:** Mike McNeil, Managing Editor.

MALVERN

MALVERN DAILY RECORD. 219 Locust St., Malvern, AR 72104-0070. Telephone: 501-337-7523. FAX: 501-337-1226. E-MAIL: mdrecord@ipa.net. URL: http://www.malvern-online.com. Mailing Address: PO Box 70, Malvern, AR 72104-0070. Year Established: 1916. Pub. Frequency: d. (Tue.-Sat.) Page Size: standard. Subscrip. Rate: $.50 newsstand/cover; $84/yr home delivery local; $105/yr mailed. **Wire Service(s):** AP. Circulation: 8,628 evening (paid and free). **Owner(s):** Horizon Publications, Inc., 1120 N. Carbon St., Ste.100, Marion, IL 62959. Telephone: 618-993-1693. FAX: 618-997-4018. **Management:** Richard Folds, Publisher. Kathi Ledbetter, Circulation Manager. Gwen Robbins, Classified Adv. Mgr.. **Editorial:** Mark Bivens, Editor.

MOUNTAIN HOME

BAXTER BULLETIN. ISSN 0745-7707
16 W. Sixth St., Mountain Home, AR 72653. Telephone: 870-425-3133. FAX: 870-425-5091. URL: http://www.baxterbulletin.com. Mailing Address: PO Box 1750, Mountain Home, AR 72654-1750. Year Established: 1901. Pub. Frequency: d. (Mon.-Sat.) Page Size: broadsheet. Subscrip. Rate: $.35 newsstand/cover; $.50 newsstand/cover Sat.; $79.56/yr. Freelance Pay: $0.50/column-inch. **Wire Service(s):** AP, GNS. Circulation: 11,000 morning (paid). **Owner(s):** Gannett Company, Inc., 7950 Jones Branch Dr., McLean, VA 22107-0001. Telephone: 703-854-6000. **Management:** Betty Barker-Smith, Publisher. Kelly Frudensprung, Marketing Director. **Editorial:** Sheila Boggess, Managing Editor. Garrett Sonny, City Editor. Elliot Sonny, Sports Editor. Contact: Aimee Morrell, Editor.

PARAGOULD

PARAGOULD DAILY PRESS. 1401 W. Hunt St., Paragould, AR 72450. Telephone: 870-239-8562. FAX: 870-239-8565. E-MAIL: dnelson@paragoulddailypress.com. URL: http://www.paraguoulddailypress.com. Mailing Address: PO Box 38, Paragould, AR 72451. Year Established: 1883. Pub. Frequency: d. (Tue.-Sun.) Page Size: broadsheet. Subscrip. Rate: $.50 newsstand/cover; $1 newsstand/cover Sun.; $95/yr home delivery. Adv. Rate: col. inch $9.54 **Wire Service(s):** AP. Circulation: 6,000 morning (paid); 6,000 Sunday (paid). **Owner(s):** Paxton Media Group LLC, 201 S. Fourth St., Paducah, KY 42003. Telephone: 270-575-8600. FAX: 270-442-8188. **Management:** Donna Nelson, Publisher. Angela Fuller, Advertising Manager. **Editorial:** Travis Justice, Editor. Mike McKinney, Sports.

PINE BLUFF

PINE BLUFF COMMERCIAL. 300 Beech St., Pine Bluff, AR 71601. Telephone: 870-534-3400. FAX: 870-534-0113. URL: http://www.pbcommercial.com. Mailing Address: PO Box 6469, Pine Bluff, AR 71611. Year Established: 1881. Pub. Frequency: d. Page Size: broadsheet. Subscrip. Rate: $.50 newsstand/cover; $1 newsstand/cover Sun.; $111/yr local; $132/yr mailed in county; $148/yr mailed out of county. **Wire Service(s):** AP, MCT. Circulation: 18,500 morning (paid); 9,000 Sunday (paid). **Owner(s):** Stephens Group, Inc., 111 Center St., Little Rock, AR 72201. Telephone: 501-377-2000. **Management:** Charles Berry, Publisher. Jim Parker, Advertising Manager. Scott Melton, Circulation Manager. **Editorial:** Larry Sullivan, Executive Editor. Kelly Fenton, Sports.

RUSSELLVILLE

COURIER (RUSSELLVILLE), THE. ISSN 1075-1866
201 E. Second St., Russellville, AR 72811. Telephone: 479-968-5252. FAX: 479-968-4037. URL: http://www.couriernews.com. Mailing Address: PO Box 887, Russellville, AR 72811-0887. Year Established: 1874. Pub. Frequency: d. (Tue.-Sun.) Page Size: broadsheet. Subscrip. Rate: $.50 newsstand/cover; $1 newsstand/cover Sun.; $10.75/mo.. Freelance Pay: $10-$15/article. **Wire Service(s):** AP. Circulation: 10,500 morning (paid); 12,500 Sunday (paid). **Owner(s):** Paxton Media Group. Inc., 201 S. Fourth St., Paducah, KY 42003. Telephone: 270-575-8600. FAX: 270-442-8188. **Management:** Marvin Enderle, President. Michelle Harris, Advertising Director. Mike Geiss, Circulation Manager. Kelly Davis, Business Manager. **Editorial:** Rick Fahr, Editor. Henry Apple, Sports.

SEARCY

DAILY CITIZEN, THE. ISSN 0747-0401
3000 E. Race Ave., Searcy, AR 72143. Telephone: 501-268-8621. FAX: 501-268-6277. E-MAIL: citizen@cswnet.com. URL: http://www.thedailycitizen.com. Mailing Address: PO Box 1379, Searcy, AR 72145. Year Established: 1854. Pub. Frequency: d. (Tue.-Sun.) Page Size: broadsheet. Subscrip. Rate: $.50 newsstand/cover; $1 newsstand/cover Sun.; $9.25 home delivery/mo. local. Freelance Pay: $10-$25/article. **Wire Service(s):** AP. Circulation: 6,800 morning (paid); 7,200 Sunday (paid). **Owner(s):** Paxton Media Group LLC, 201 S. Fourth St., Paducah, KY 42003. Telephone: 270-575-8600. FAX: 270-442-8188. **Management:** Mike Murphy, Publisher. Kathy Smith, Advertising Director. Scott Bramlett, Circulation Manager. **Editorial:** Jay Straser, Editor. Warren Watkins, Managing Editor. Julie Hill, Lifestyle Editor. Kelly Fenton, Sports.

SPRINGDALE

MORNING NEWS OF NORTHWEST ARKANSAS. ISSN 1053-9689
2560 Lowell Rd., Springdale, AR 72765-0007. Telephone: 479-751-6200. FAX: 479-872-5055. E-MAIL: jmorriss@nwaonline.net. URL: http://www.nwaonline.net. Mailing Address: PO Box 7, Springdale, AR 72765-0007. Year Established: 1886. Pub. Frequency: d. Page Size: broadsheet. Subscrip. Rate: $.25 newsstand/cover; $1 newsstand/cover Sun.; $70/yr home delivery local area; $87/yr mailed in state; $156/yr mailed out of state. **Wire Service(s):** AP, LAT-WAT. Circulation: 35,000 morning (paid); 37,000 Sunday (paid). **Owner(s):** Stephens Media LLC, 1111 W. Bonanza Rd., Las Vegas, NV 89106. Telephone: 702-382-5020. **Management:** Tom Stallbaumer, Publisher. Kent Eikenberry, Advertising Director. Keith Sanford, Circulation Director. Toni Fenton, Classified Adv. Mgr.. Sandy Harmon, Business Manager. **Editorial:** Jim Morriss, Executive Editor. Lisa Thompson, Managing Editor. Al Gaspery, News Editor.

STUTTGART

STUTTGART DAILY LEADER. 111 W. Sixth St., Stuttgart, AR 72160-0531. Telephone: 870-673-8533. FAX: 870-673-3671. E-MAIL: daily-leader@arkansas-web.com. URL: http://www.stuttgartdailyleader.com. Year Established: 1889. Pub. Frequency: d. (Mon.-Fri.) Page Size: broadsheet. Subscrip. Rate: $.50 newsstand/cover; $108/yr carrier delivery in county; $114/yr mailed out of county. Circulation: 3,500 evening (paid). **Owner(s):** GateHouse Media, Inc, 350 WillowBrook Office Park, Fairport, NY 14450. Telephone: 585-598-0030. FAX: 585-248-2631. **Management:** Clark Smith, Publisher. Tony Cooper, Advertising Manager. Willene Boehn, Circulation Manager. Dannie Jo Bueker, Classified Adv. Mgr.. **Editorial:** Jeannie Nugent, Managing Editor. Josh Troy, Sports.

WEST MEMPHIS

EVENING TIMES (WEST MEMPHIS). 111 E. Bond, West Memphis, AR 72303. Telephone: 870-775-1010. FAX: 870-735-1020. E-MAIL: etnews@midsouth.rr.com. URL: http://www.theeveningtimes.com/. Mailing Address: PO Box 459, West Memphis, AR 72303. Year Established: 1931. Pub. Frequency: d. (Mon.-Fri.) Page Size: broadsheet. Subscrip. Rate: $.50 newsstand/cover; $75/yr in county; $85/yr out of county. **Wire Service(s):** AP. Circulation: 9,650 evening (paid). **Owner(s):** Crittenden Publishing Co., Inc., See address and contact information above. **Management:** Alexander P. Coulter, President. Robert Stewart, Advertising Director. Gwyn Woelfle, Classified Adv. Mgr.. Alice Raines, Business Manager. **Editorial:** Mike Bowie, News Editor. Ted Beasley, Sports.

CALIFORNIA

AUBURN

AUBURN JOURNAL. 1030 High St., Auburn, CA 95604. Telephone: 530-885-5656. FAX: 530-887-1231. E-MAIL: ajournal@goldcountrymedia.com. URL: http://www.auburnjournal.com. Mailing Address: PO Box 5910, Auburn, CA 95604. Year Established: 1872. Pub. Frequency: d. (Sun.-Fri.) Page Size: broadsheet. Subscrip. Rate: $.50 newsstand/cover; $1 newsstand/cover Sun.; $53.10/yr home delivery local for 3 mos.; $177.96/yr home delivery local. Adv. Rate: col. inch $21 **Wire Service(s):** AP. Circulation: 13,000 morning (paid); 14,000 Sunday (paid). **Owner(s):** Brehm Communications, Inc., 16644 W. Bernardo Dr., Ste. 300, San Diego, CA 92127. Telephone: 858-451-6200. **Management:** Deric Rothe, General Manager. Tony Hazarian, Publisher. Beth O'Brien, Advertising Director. Mike Spezia, Circulation Director. Steve Jameson, Classified Adv. Mgr.. **Editorial:** Deric Rothe, Senior Editor. Kristine Coman, News Editor. Ben Furtado, Photo Editor. Todd Mordhorst, Sports Editor.

BAKERSFIELD

BAKERSFIELD CALIFORNIAN. ISSN 0276-5837
1707 Eye St., Bakersfield, CA 93301. Telephone: 661-395-7519. URL: http://www.bakersfield.com. Mailing Address: PO Box 440, Bakersfield, CA 93302. Year Established: 1866. Pub. Frequency: d. Page Size: broadsheet. Subscrip. Rate: $.50 newsstand/cover; $1.50 newsstand/cover Sun.; $15.25/mo.. Freelance Pay: $25-$100/article. **Wire Service(s):** AP. Circulation: 71,987 morning (paid); 85,918 Sunday (paid). **Owner(s):** Bakersfield Californian Corp., See address and contact information above. **Management:** Richard Beene, President. Ginger Moorhouse, Publisher. Dee McCallister, Advertising Manager. Ellen Rink, Circulation Director. Sally Ellis, Classified Adv. Mgr.. **Editorial:** Mike Jenner, Executive Editor. Logan Molen, Managing Editor. Tony Lacara, Sports Editor.

BARSTOW

DESERT DISPATCH. ISSN 1086-1157
130 Coolwater Ln., Barstow, CA 92311-3289. Telephone: 760-256-2257. FAX: 760-256-0685. URL: http://www.desertdispatch.com. Year Established: 1910. Pub. Frequency: d. Page Size: broadsheet. Subscrip. Rate: $.50 newsstand/cover; $1.50 newsstand/cover Sun.; $9.75/mo.. **Wire Service(s):** AP. Circulation: 6,000 morning (paid); 3,500 Sunday (paid). **Owner(s):** Freedom Communications, Inc., 17666 Fitch, Irvine, CA 92614. Telephone: 714-553-9292. **Management:** Stephen Wingert, Publisher. Bea Lint, Advertising. Jackie Parsons, Circulation Director. **Editorial:** John Bennett, Editor-in-Chief. Jeff Galian, Sports.

BENICIA

BENICIA HERALD. 820 First St., Benicia, CA 94510. Telephone: 707-745-0733. FAX: 707-557-6380. E-MAIL: benheral@pacbell.net. Mailing Address: PO Box 65, Benicia, CA 94510. Year Established: 1877. Pub. Frequency: d. (Tue.-Fri. & Sun.) Page Size: broadsheet.Subscrip. Rate: $.50 newsstand/cover; $62/yr local Circulation: 10,000 morning (paid); 10,000 Sunday (paid). **Owner(s):** Gibson Publications, Inc., 544 Curtola Pkwy, Vallejo, CA 94590. Telephone: 707-643-2552. **Management:** David L. Payne, Publisher. Pam Poppe, Advertising Manager. Sam LiRon, Circulation Manager. **Editorial:** Les Mahler, Editor.

CHICO

CHICO ENTERPRISE-RECORD. ISSN 0746-5548
400 E. Park Ave., Chico, CA 95928. Telephone: 530-891-1234. FAX: 530-342-3617. URL: http://www.chicoer.com. Mailing Address: PO Box 9, Chico, CA 95927. Year Established: 1853. Pub. Frequency: d. Page Size: broadsheet. Subscrip. Rate: $.50 newsstand/cover; $1 newsstand/cover Sun.; $10.73/mo.; $128.70/yr; $11.80 motor route/mo.; $141.57/yr motor route. **Wire Service(s):** AP. Circulation: 33,635 morning (paid); 33,326 Sunday (paid). **Owner(s):** MediaNews Group, Inc., 101 W Colfax Ave, Ste 1100, Denver, CO 80202. FAX: 303-954-6320. **Management:** Wolf Rosenberg, Publisher. Azurae Shults, Advertising Director. Clay Eubank, Circulation Director. Rene Ridgell, Classified Adv. Mgr.. **Editorial:** David Little, Editor. Bill Husa, Photographer. John Johnson, Sports Editor.

COSTA MESA

DAILY PILOT, THE. 1375 Sunflower Ave., Costa Mesa, CA 92627. Telephone: 714-966-4600. FAX: 714-966-4679. E-MAIL: dpilot@latimes.com. URL: http://www.dailypilot.com. Year Established: 1907. Pub. Frequency: d. Page Size: broadsheet. Subscrip. Rate: $.25 newsstand/cover; $30 mailed/mo.. **Wire Service(s):** AP. Circulation: 35,000 morning (paid); 30,000 Sunday (paid). **Owner(s):** Tribune Company, 435 N Michigan Ave, Chicago, IL 60601. Telephone: 312.222.9100. **Management:** Tom Johnson, Publisher. Lisa Coserza, Advertising Manager. **Editorial:** Tony Dodero, Editor. Carol Chambers, City Editor. Rich Dunn, Sports Editor.

CRESCENT CITY

DAILY TRIPLICATE, THE. ISSN 1056-9510
312 H St., Crescent City, CA 95531. Telephone: 707-464-2141. FAX: 707-464-5102. URL: http://www.triplicate.com. Mailing Address: PO Box 277, Crescent City, CA 95531. Year Established: 1879. Pub. Frequency: d. (Tue.-Sat.) Page Size: broadsheet. Subscrip. Rate: $.35 newsstand/cover; $.50 newsstand/cover Sat.; $77.22/yr carrier delivery. Freelance Pay: $0.75/column-inch. **Wire Service(s):** AP. Circulation: 5,200 morning (paid). **Owner(s):** Western Communication, Inc., 1777 S.W. Chandler Ave., Bend, OR 97702. Telephone: 541-382-1811. FAX: 541-383-0372. **Management:** Michele Thomas, Publisher. Alan Turner, Advertising Director. Mike Gambrall, Circulation Manager. Barbara Jones, Business Manager. **Editorial:** Mike Schmeltzer, Editor. Aaron Finley, Sports Editor.

DANVILLE

SAN RAMON VALLEY TIMES, THE. 524 Hartz Ave, Danville, CA 94526. Telephone: 925-837-4267. FAX: 925-837-4334. URL: http://www.contracostatimes.com. Mailing Address: PO Box 68, Danville, CA 94526. Year Established: 1945. Pub. Frequency: d. Page Size: broadsheet. Subscrip. Rate: $.25 newsstand/cover; $1 Sun.; $11.85 carrier delivery/mo.; $159.64/yr carrier delivery. **Wire Service(s):** AP. Circulation: 40,000 morning (paid); 45,000 Sunday (paid). **Owner(s):** MediaNews Group, Inc., 101 W Colfax Ave, Ste 1100, Denver, CO 80202. FAX: 303-954-6320. **Management:** George E Armstrong, Publisher. **Editorial:** Jeanine Benca, Editor. Kevin Keane, Executive Editor. Tom Barnidge, Sports Editor.

DAVIS

DAVIS ENTERPRISE. 315 G St., Davis, CA 95616. Mailing Address: PO Box 1470, Davis, CA 95617-1470. Year Established: 1897. Pub. Frequency: d. (Sun.-Fri.) Page Size: broadsheet. Subscrip. Rate: $.50 newsstand/cover; $85/yr in area; $65/yr to senior citizens. Freelance Pay: $35/story. **Owner(s):** McNaughton Newspapers, PO Box 1078, Davis, CA 95617. Telephone: 916-756-0800. **Management:** Foy S. McNaughton, President. Burt McNaughton, Publisher. Nancy Hannell, Advertising Director. Vickie Owens, Classified Adv. Mgr.. Debbie Davis, Assistant Publisher. **Editorial:** Debbie Davis, Managing Editor. Kim Orender, Sports Editor.

EL CENTRO

IMPERIAL VALLEY PRESS. ISSN 1072-9283
205 N. Eighth St., El Centro, CA 92243. Telephone: 760-337-3400. FAX: 760-353-3003. URL: http://www.ivpressonline.com. Year Established: 1901. Pub. Frequency: d. (Sun.-Fri.) Page Size: broadsheet. Subscrip. Rate: $.50 newsstand/cover; $1.25 newsstand/cover Sun.; $27 carrier delivery/mo. local; $30 motor route/mo. local; $33 mailed/mo. in county; $42 mailed/mo. out of county. **Wire Service(s):** AP. Circulation: 18,500 evening (paid); 19,000 Sunday (paid). **Owner(s):** Schurz Communications, Inc., 225 W. Colfax Ave., South Bend, IN 46626. Telephone: 219-287-1001. **Management:** Dave Leone, Publisher. John Yanni, Advertising Director. Todd Benz, Circulation Manager. **Editorial:** Bret Kofford, Managing Editor. Eric Galvan, Sports Editor.

ESCONDIDO

NORTH COUNTY TIMES. ISSN 1059-5694
207 E. Pennsylvania Ave., Escondido, CA 92025. Telephone: 760-433-7333. FAX: 760-745-3769. URL: http://www.nctimes.com. Year Established: 1986. Pub. Frequency: d. Page Size: broadsheet. Subscrip. Rate: $.35 newsstand/cover; $1.25 newsstand/cover Sun.; $12.50/mo. local. **Wire Service(s):** AP. Circulation: 93,417 evening (paid); 93,083 Sunday (paid). **Owner(s):** Lee Enterprises, Inc., 201 N. Harrison St., Davenport, IA 52801. **Management:** Richard High, Publisher. Mark Henschen, Circulation Director. **Editorial:** Kent Davy, Editor. W. Russel Harris, Managing Editor. Gary Hyvonen, Sports Editor.

EUREKA

TIMES-STANDARD. 930 Sixth St., Eureka, CA 95501. Telephone: 707-441-0500. FAX: 707-441-0565. E-MAIL: dlippman@times-standard.com. URL: http://www.times-standard.com. Mailing Address: PO Box 3580, Eureka, CA 95502. Year Established: 1854. Pub. Frequency: d. Page Size: broadsheet. Subscrip. Rate: $.50 newsstand/cover; $1.50 newsstand/cover Sun.; $33.50 carrier delivery for 13 wks.; $13.50 mailed/mo.. Adv. Rate: col. inch $27.50 **Wire Service(s):** AP. Circulation: 20,000 morning (paid); 22,000 Sunday (paid). **Owner(s):** MediaNews Group, Inc., 101 W Colfax Ave, Ste 1100, Denver, CO 80202. FAX: 303-954-6320. **Management:** Greg Stevens, Publisher. David Lippman, Advertising Director. Kelly Leibold, Circulation Director. **Editorial:** Rich Somerville, Managing Editor. Kimberly Wear, City Editor. Heather Shelton, Lifestyle Editor. Ray Aspuria, Sports Editor.

FAIRFIELD

DAILY REPUBLIC (FAIRFIELD). ISSN 0746-5858
1250 Texas St., Fairfield, CA 94533. Telephone: 707-425-4646. FAX: 707-425-5924. E-MAIL: drnews@dailyrepublic.com. URL: http://www.dailyrepublic.com. Mailing Address: PO Box 47, Fairfield, CA 94533. Year Established: 1855. Pub. Frequency: d. Page Size: broadsheet. Subscrip. Rate: $.35 newsstand/cover; $1.25 newsstand/cover Sun.; $10.20 home delivery/mo. local; $9.39/mo. local to senior citizens. Freelance Pay: $0.50/column-inch. **Wire Service(s):** AP, SH, NYT. Circulation: 20,000 morning (paid); 22,000 Sunday (paid). **Owner(s):** McNaughton Newspapers, PO Box 1078, Davis, CA 95617. Telephone: 916-756-0800. **Management:** Foy McNaughton, Publisher. Sharon Guy, Advertising Director. **Editorial:** Bill James, Editor. Maureen Fissolo, News Editor. Gary Goldsmith, Photographer. Ted Sillanpaa, Sports.

FREMONT

ARGUS, THE. 39737 Paseo Padre Pkwy, Fremont, CA 94538. Telephone: 510-353-7012. FAX: 510-353-7029. URL: http://www.angnewspapers.com. Mailing Address: P O Box 5100, Fremont, CA 94537-5100. Year Established: 1960. Pub. Frequency: d. Page Size: broadsheet. Subscrip. Rate: $.50 newsstand/cover; $1.25 newsstand/cover Sun.; $64.95/yr. **Wire Service(s):** AP, SH, NYT, LAT-WAT, CNS. Circulation: 31,438 morning (paid); 31,714 Sunday (paid). **Owner(s):** MediaNews Group, Inc., 101 W Colfax Ave, Ste 1100, Denver, CO 80202. FAX: 303-954-6320. **Management:** Joe Kustelski, Advertising Manager. **Editorial:** Pete Wevurski, Editor. Jon Becker, Sports Editor.

FRESNO

FRESNO BEE, THE. ISSN 0889-6070
1626 E St., Fresno, CA 93786. Telephone: 559-441-6111. FAX: 559-441-6054. E-MAIL: staff@fresnobee.com. URL: http://www.fresnobee.com. Year Established: 1922. Pub. Frequency: d. Page Size: standard. Subscrip. Rate: $.50 newsstand/cover; $1.75 newsstand/cover Sun.; $1.93 home delivery/wk.; $6.98 mailed/wk.. **Wire Service(s):** RN, AP, SH, NYT. Circulation: 156,466 morning (paid); 193,062 Sunday (paid). **Owner(s):** The/McClatchy Company, 2100 Q St, Sacramento, CA 95816. Telephone: 916-321-1936. **Management:** Roy Steele, Publisher. Tim Ritchey, Advertising Director. Tom Cullinan, Circulation Director. Della Hemphill, Classified Adv. Mgr.. **Editorial:** Betsy Lumbye, Executive Editor. Lisa Bayles, Associate Editor. Robert Zizzo, Sports Editor.

GILROY

GILROY DISPATCH, THE. 6400 Monterey St, Gilroy, CA 95020. Telephone: 408-842-6400. FAX: 408-802-7105. URL: http://www.gilroydispatch.com. Mailing Address: PO Box 22365, Gilroy, CA 95021-2365. Year Established: 1868. Pub. Frequency: d. (Tue.-Sat.) Page Size: broadsheet. Subscrip. Rate: $.50 newsstand/cover; $29 carrier delivery for 6 mos.; $49/yr carrier delivery. Adv. Rate: col. inch $18.55 **Wire Service(s):** AP. Circulation: 5,671 morning (paid). **Owner(s):** Main Street Media Group, See address and contact information above. **Management:** Steve Staloch, Publisher. David Marin, VP Advertising. Walt Glines, Circulation Manager. Carrie Gault, Classified Adv. Mgr.. **Editorial:** Mark Derry, Editor.

HOLLISTER FREE LANCE. 6400 Monterey St, Gilroy, CA 95020. Telephone: 408-842-6400. FAX: 408-802-7105. URL: http://www.freelancenews.com. Mailing Address: PO Box 22365, Gilroy, CA 95021-2365. Year Established: 1873. Pub. Frequency: d. (Mon.-Fri.) Page Size: broadsheet. Subscrip. Rate: $.50 newsstand/cover; $97/yr in county; $197/yr out of county. Adv. Rate: col. inch $15.70 **Wire Service(s):** AP. Circulation: 4,600 morning (paid). **Owner(s):** Main Street Media Group, See address and contact information above. **Management:** Steve Staloch, Publisher. David Marin, VP Advertising. Scott Levander, Circulation Manager. Carrie Gault, Classified Adv. Mgr.. **Editorial:** Mike Schmeltzer, Editor.

GLENDALE

GLENDALE NEWS-PRESS. ISSN 0746-3340
111 W Wilson ave, Ste 3200, Glendale, CA 91204-1269. Telephone: 818-637-3200. FAX: 818-637-1975. URL: http://www.ourtimes.com/glendale. Mailing Address: PO Box 991, Glendale, CA 91209. Year Established: 1905. Pub. Frequency: d. (Mon.-Sat.) Page Size: broadsheet. Subscrip. Rate: $7.50/mo.. **Wire Service(s):** AP. Circulation: 20,149 morning (paid and free). **Owner(s):** Los Angeles Times Communications LLC, See address and contact information above. **Editorial:** Jeff Keating, Editor.

GRASS VALLEY

UNION (GRASS VALLEY), THE. 464 Sutton Way, Grass Valley, CA 95945. Telephone: 530-273-9561. FAX: 530-477-4292. E-MAIL: mail@theunion.com. URL: http://www.theunion.com. Year Established: 1864. Pub. Frequency: d. (Mon.-Sat.) Page Size: broadsheet. Subscrip. Rate: $.50 newsstand/cover; $9.25 carrier delivery/mo.; $14 mailed/mo. in county; $18 mailed/mo. out of county. **Wire Service(s):** AP. Circulation: 16,500 evening (paid). **Owner(s):** Swift Newspapers, Inc., 500 Double Eagle Ct., Reno, NV 89511. Telephone: 775-850-7676. FAX: 775-850-7677. **Management:** Craig Dennis, General Manager. Jeff Ackerman, Publisher. Craig Underwood, Circulation Director. Gayle Greco, Sales Manager. **Editorial:** Pat Butler, Editor.

HANFORD

SENTINEL (HANFORD), THE. 300 W. Sixth St., Hanford, CA 93230. Telephone: 559-582-0471. FAX: 559-582-8631. E-MAIL: dbohannan@sentilnews.net. URL: http://www.newzcentral.com. Mailing Address: PO Box 9, Hanford, CA 93232. Year Established: 1886. Pub. Frequency: d. Page Size: broadsheet. Subscrip. Rate: $.50 newsstand/cover; $1 newsstand/cover Sun.; $11 carrier delivery/mo.; $11.50 motor route/mo.. **Wire Service(s):** AP. Circulation: 13,800 evening (paid); 13,800 Sunday (paid). **Owner(s):** Lee Enterprises, Inc., 900 N. Tucker Blvd., St. Louis, MO 63101. Telephone: 314-340-8000. **Management:** Mark Daniel, Publisher. Greg Barkley, Circulation Director. Kevin Crawford, Classified Adv. Mgr.. Zelma Silva, Business Manager. **Editorial:** Denis Bohannan, Editor-in-Chief. Apolinar Fonseca, Photo Editor. Jon Matsune, Sports Editor.

HAYWOOD

DAILY REVIEW (HAYWOOD), THE. 22533 Foothill Blvd, Haywood, CA 94541. Telephone: 510-783-6111. FAX: 510-293-2490. URL: http://www.insidebayarea.com. Year Established: 1892. Pub. Frequency: d. Page Size: broadsheet. Subscrip. Rate: $.50 newsstand/cover; $1.50 newsstand/cover Sun.; $144.37/yr home delivery. **Wire Service(s):** AP, SH, NYT, LAT-WAT. Circulation: 41,900 morning (paid); 50,500 Sunday (paid). **Owner(s):** MediaNews Group, Inc., 101 W Colfax Ave, Ste 1100, Denver, CO 80202. **Management:** Kevin Keane, Publisher. Sharon Kinkade, Advertising Director. **Editorial:** Connie Rux, Editor. Norman Bell, Managing Editor. Drew Voros, Business Editor. Jon Becker, Sports Editor.

LAKEPORT

LAKE COUNTY RECORD-BEE. ISSN 0746-4304
P O Box 849, Lakeport, CA 95453. Telephone: 707-263-5636. FAX: 707-263-0600. E-MAIL: editorial@record-bee.com. URL: http://www.record-bee.com. Year Established: 1961. Pub. Frequency: d. (Tue.-Sat.) Page Size: broadsheet. Subscrip. Rate: $.50 newsstand/cover; $.75 newsstand/cover Sat.; $90.80/yr carrier delivery; $114.80/yr mailed in county; $116.10/yr mailed out of county. Circulation: 10,000 morning (paid). **Owner(s):** MediaNews Group, Inc., 101 W Colfax Ave, Ste 1100, Denver, CO 80202. FAX: 303-954-6320. **Management:** Gregg McConnell, Publisher. Shawn Garrison, Advertising. Mallory Albertson, Classified Adv. Mgr.. **Editorial:** Rick Kennedy, Managing Editor. Jim Davis, Circulation Editor. Brian Sumpter, Sports Editor.

LODI

LODI NEWS-SENTINEL. 125 N. Church St., Lodi, CA 95240. Telephone: 209-369-2761. FAX: 209-369-1084. E-MAIL: lodinews@mall.softcom.net. URL: http://www.lodinews.com. Mailing Address: PO Box 1360, Lodi, CA 95241-1360. Year Established: 1881. Pub. Frequency: d. (Mon.-Sat.) Page Size: broadsheet. Subscrip. Rate: $.35 newsstand/cover; $8.25/mo.. **Wire Service(s):** AP. Circulation: 18,000 morning (paid). **Owner(s):** Lodi News-Sentinel, See address and contact information above. **Management:** Fred Weybret, Owner. Marty Weybret, Publisher. Chuck Higgs, Advertising Manager. Gary Greider, Circulation Manager. Kimberly Anger, Classified Adv. Mgr.. **Editorial:** Richard Hanner, Editor. Jake Armstrong, Business Editor. Jennifer Bennett, City Editor. Scott Howell, Sports.

LOMPOC

LOMPOC RECORD, THE. 115 N. H St., Lompoc, CA 93436. Telephone: 805-736-2313. FAX: 805-735-5118. E-MAIL: advertising@lompocrecord.com. URL: http://www.lompocrecord.com. Mailing Address: PO Box 578, Lompoc, CA 93438. Year Established: 1875. Pub. Frequency: d. (Sun.-Fri.) Page Size: broadsheet. Subscrip. Rate: $.50 newsstand/cover; $1 newsstand/cover Sun.; $8.75/mo.; $100/yr. **Wire Service(s):** AP. Circulation: 7,950 evening (paid); 8,150 Sunday (paid). **Owner(s):** Lee Enterprises, Inc., 900 N. Tucker Blvd., St. Louis, MO 63101. Telephone: 314-340-8000. **Management:** Paula Patton, Publisher. Rich Macke, Advertising Manager. Tony Burkhammer, Circulation Manager. **Editorial:** Russ Stockton, Editor. Brenda Poe, Lifestyle Editor. Alan Hunt, Sports.

LONG BEACH

PRESS-TELEGRAM (LONG BEACH). 300 Oceangate, Long Beach, CA 90844. Telephone: 562-435-1161. FAX: 562-437-7892. E-MAIL: ptnews@presstelegram.com. URL: http://www.presstelegram.com. Mailing Address: PO Box 230, Long Beach, CA 90844-0230. Year Established: 1897. Pub. Frequency: d. Page Size: broadsheet. Subscrip. Rate: $.25 newsstand/cover; $1 newsstand/cover Sun.; $4.35 home delivery/wk.. **Wire Service(s):** AP. Circulation: 89,000 morning (paid); 99,000 Sunday (paid). **Owner(s):** MediaNews Group, Inc., 101 W Colfax Ave, Ste 1100, Denver, CO 80202. FAX: 303-954-6320. **Management:** Mark Ficarra, Publisher. Howard Young, Advertising Director. Dennis Schafer, Circulation Manager. **Editorial:** John Futch, Executive Editor.

LOS ANGELES

LOS ANGELES BULLETIN. 210 S. Spring St., Los Angeles, CA 90012-3710. Telephone: 213-346-0033. FAX: 213-687-3886. E-MAIL: news@metnews.com. URL: http://www.mnc.net. Mailing Address: PO Box 60859, Los Angeles, CA 90060. Pub. Frequency: d. (Mon.-Fri.) Page Size: tabloid. Subscrip. Rate: $.50 newsstand/cover; $69/yr mailed. **Wire Service(s):** AP. Circulation: 1,700 morning (paid). **Owner(s):** Metropolitan News Co., See address and contact information above. **Management:** Roger M. Grace, General Manager. Jo-Ann W. Grace, Publisher. **Editorial:** Roger M. Grace, Editor.

LOS ANGELES TIMES. ISSN 0458-3035
202 W. First St., Los Angeles, CA 90012. FAX: 213-237-4712. E-MAIL: letters@latimes.com. URL: http://www.latimes.com. Year Established: 1886. Pub. Frequency: d. Page Size: broadsheet. Subscrip. Rate: $.50, $1.50 newsstand/cover. **Wire Service(s):** RN, AP, UPI, LAT-WAT, CiNS, DJNS. Circulation: 955,211. **Owner(s):** Tribune Company, 435 N Michigan Ave, Chicago, IL 60601. Telephone: 312.222.9100. **Bureau(s):** Market Place Tower, Seattle, WA 98121. Telephone: 206-448-6949. **Management:** David D Hiller, Publisher. Mark H. Kurtich, Operations Manager. Steven U. Lee, Circulation Director. **Editorial:** Dean Baquet, Editor. Russ Stanton, Business Editor. Bill Sing, Economics Editor. Amy Wallace, Entertainment Editor. Frank Clifford, Environmental Editor. Pat Benson, News Editor.

MADERA

MADERA TRIBUNE. ISSN 8750-9571
100 E. Seventh St., Madera, CA 93638. Telephone: 559-674-2424. FAX: 559-673-6526. URL: http://www.maderatribune.com. Mailing Address: PO Box 269, Madera, CA 93639. Year Established: 1892. Pub. Frequency: d. (Mon.-Sat.) Page Size: broadsheet. Subscrip. Rate: $.50 newsstand/cover; $96/yr home delivery in area; $144/yr mailed in county; $179/yr mailed out of county. **Wire Service(s):** AP. Circulation: 4,600 morning (paid). **Owner(s):** Pacific-Sierra Publishing, Inc., See address and contact information above. **Management:** Charles Doud, Publisher. Shirley James, Advertising Manager. Keith Pendleton, Circulation Manager. **Editorial:** Charles Doud, Editor. Glenna Jarvis, News Editor. Paul Stanford, Sports Editor.

MANTECA

MANTECA BULLETIN. ISSN 0745-2748
531 E Yosemite Ave, Manteca, CA 95336. Telephone: 209-249-3500. FAX: 209-549-3559. URL: http://www.mantecabulletin.com. Year Established: 1908. Pub. Frequency: d. Page Size: broadsheet. Subscrip. Rate: $.50 newsstand/cover; $9.50 carrier delivery/mo.; $121.60/yr mailed. **Wire Service(s):** AP. Circulation: 7,500 morning (paid); 7,500 Sunday (paid). **Owner(s):** Morris Newspaper Corporation, 27 Abercorn St., Savannah, GA 31401. Telephone: 912-233-1281. FAX: 912-232-4639. **Management:** Randy McCants, Publisher. Dawn Barrett, Advertising. Brad Barnes, Circulation Manager. Chantel Hansen, Classified Adv. Mgr.. **Editorial:** Dennis Wyatt, Editor.

MARYSVILLE

APPEAL-DEMOCRAT. 1530 Ellis Lake Dr., Marysville, CA 95901. Telephone: 530-741-2345. FAX: 530-741-0140. E-MAIL: appeal@syix.com. URL: http://www.appeal-democrat.com. Mailing Address: PO Box 431, Marysville, CA 95901. Year Established: 1860. Pub. Frequency: d. Page Size: broadsheet. Subscrip. Rate: $.50 newsstand/cover; $1 newsstand/cover Sun.; $10 home delivery/mo. local. **Wire Service(s):** AP, NYT. Circulation: 22,000 morning (paid); 23,000 Sunday (paid). **Owner(s):** Freedom Communications, Inc., 17666 Fitch, Irvine, CA 92614. Telephone: 949-553-9292. **Management:** Glenn Goodman, Business Manager. **Editorial:** Larry Badger, Managing Editor. Jennifer Picard, Entertainment Editor. Leticia Gutierrez, Local News Editor. Dave Nielsen, Photo Editor. Eri Vodden, Sports Editor.

MERCED

MERCED SUN-STAR. 3033 N. G St., Merced, CA 95340. Telephone: 209-722-1511. FAX: 209-385-2460. E-MAIL: sunstar@mercedsun-star.com. URL: http://www.mercedsun-star.com. Mailing Address: PO Box 739, Merced, CA 95341. Year Established: 1869. Pub. Frequency: d. (Mon.-Sat.) Page Size: broadsheet. Subscrip. Rate: $.50 newsstand/cover; $1.25 newsstand/cover Sat.; $57 home delivery for 6 mos.; $114/yr home delivery. **Wire Service(s):** AP. Circulation: 17,000 morning (paid). **Owner(s):** The/McClatchy Company, PO Box 15779, Sacramento, CA 95852. **Management:** Hank VanderVeen, Publisher. Larry Dovichi, Advertising Director. **Editorial:** Joe Kieta, Editor. Mike Fitzgerald, City Editor.

MODESTO

MODESTO BEE, THE. 1325 H St., Modesto, CA 95354. E-MAIL: metro@modbee.com. URL: http://www.modbee.com. Mailing Address: PO Box 3928, Modesto, CA 95352. Year Established: 1884. Pub. Frequency: d. Page Size: broadsheet. Subscrip. Rate: $.50 newsstand/cover; $2.30/wk.; $12/mo.. **Wire Service(s):** AP, NYT. Circulation: 85,000 morning (paid); 94,000 Sunday (paid). **Owner(s):** The/McClatchy Company, 2100 Q St, Sacramento, CA 95816. Telephone: 916-321-1936. **Bureau(s): Management:** Margaret Randazzo, Publisher. Tim Ritchey, Advertising Director. Michael Miller, Circulation Director. Eric Johnston, Development Manager. **Editorial:** Mark S. Vasche, Editor. Bill Poindexter, Sports Editor.

MONTEREY

MONTEREY COUNTY HERALD, THE. ISSN 0889-3101
8 Upper Ragsdale Dr, Monterey, CA 93940-2013. Telephone: 831-372-3311. FAX: 831-372-8401. E-MAIL: mchnews@montereyherald.com. URL: http://www.montereyherald.com. Year Established: 1922. Pub. Frequency: d. Page Size: broadsheet. Subscrip. Rate: $.50 newsstand/cover; $1.50 Sun.; $180.18/yr mailed daily; $109.40/yr mailed Fri, Sat & Sun. **Wire Service(s):** AP, LAT-WAT. Circulation: 21,000 morning (paid); 23,000 Sunday (paid). **Owner(s):** MediaNews Group, Inc., 101 W Colfax Ave, Ste 1100, Denver, CO 80202. FAX: 303-954-6320. **Management:** Gary Omernick, President. Mazi Kovoosi, Circulation Manager. John Marino, Classified Adv. Mgr.. **Editorial:** Caroline Garcia, Executive Editor.

NAPA

NAPA VALLEY REGISTER. 1615 Second St., Napa, CA 94559. Telephone: 707-226-3711. FAX: 707-224-3963. E-MAIL: napanews@napanews.com. URL: http://www.napanews.com. Mailing Address: PO Box 150, Napa, CA 94559. Year Established: 1863. Pub. Frequency: d. Page Size: broadsheet. Subscrip. Rate: $.50 newsstand/cover; $1.25 Sun.; $12.50/mo.; $139/yr. Freelance Pay: $25/article. **Wire Service(s):** AP. Circulation: 18,969 evening (paid). **Owner(s):** Lee Enterprises, Inc., 900 N. Tucker Blvd., St. Louis, MO 63101. Telephone: 314-340-8000. **Management:** Mario Van Dongen, Publisher. Norma Kostecka, Advertising Director. Joe Brazil, Circulation Director. Nona Alessio, Classified Adv. Mgr.. **Editorial:** Bill Kisliuk, Executive Editor. Jeanne Claire, Business Editor. Chris Tribbey, City Editor. Sasha Paulsen, Feature Editor. Randy Johnson, Sports Editor.

NOVATO

MARIN INDEPENDENT JOURNAL. ISSN 0891-5164
150 Alameda Del Prado, Novato, CA 94949. Telephone: 415-884-1495. FAX: 415-883-5458. E-MAIL: opinion@marinijcom. URL: http://www.marinij.com. Mailing Address: P O Box 6150, Novato, CA 94948-6150. Year Established: 1861. Pub. Frequency: d. Page Size: broadsheet. Subscrip. Rate: $.50 newsstand/cover; $1.25 newsstand/cover Sun.; $189.62/yr home delivery local; $223.08/yr mailed elsewhere. **Wire Service(s):** AP, NYT, GNS. Circulation: 51,400 morning (paid); 52,000 Sunday (paid). **Owner(s):** MediaNews Group, Inc., 101 W Colfax Ave, Ste 1100, Denver, CO 80202. FAX: 303-954-6320. **Management:** Amy Ebbesen, Classified Adv. Mgr.. **Editorial:** Matthew Wilson, Executive Editor. Robert Sterling, City Editor. Dave Allen, Sports Editor.

OAKLAND

ALAMEDA TIMES-STAR. 401 13th St, Oakland, CA 94612. Telephone: 510-208-6300. FAX: 510-293-2383. URL: http://www.insidebayarea.com. Year Established: 1872. Pub. Frequency: d. Page Size: broadsheet. Subscrip. Rate: $.50 newsstand/cover; $1.25 Sun.; $19.94 home delivery/mo. local; $118/yr. **Wire Service(s):** AP, UPI, NYT, CNS. Circulation: 7,500 morning (paid); 7,500 Sunday (paid). **Owner(s):** MediaNews Group, Inc., 101 W Colfax Ave, Ste 1100, Denver, CO 80202. FAX: 303-954-6320. **Management:** John Schuela, Publisher. **Editorial:** Pete Wevurski, Editor. Martin Reynolds, Managing Editor. Drew Voros, Business Editor. Nick Lammers, Photo. Steve Herendeen, Sports Editor.

OAKLAND TRIBUNE, THE. 401 13th St, Oakland, CA 94612. Telephone: 510-208-6300. FAX: 510-293-2383. URL: http://www.oaklandtribune.com. Year Established: 1874. Pub. Frequency: d. Page Size: broadsheet. Subscrip. Rate: $.50 newsstand/cover; $1.50 newsstand/cover Sun.; $19.92 home delivery/mo. local; $64.95/yr home delivery. **Wire Service(s):** SH, LAT-WAT. Circulation: 68,426 morning (paid); 65,413 Sunday (paid). **Owner(s):** MediaNews Group, Inc., 101 W Colfax Ave, Ste 1100, Denver, CO 80202. FAX: 303-954-6320. **Management:** John Schuela, Publisher. **Editorial:** Pete Wevurski, Editor. Martin Reynolds, Managing Editor. Drew Voros, Business Editor. Jolene Thym, Food Editor. Nick Lammers, Photo. Steve Herendeen, Sports Editor.

ONTARIO

INLAND VALLEY DAILY BULLETIN. 2041 E Fourth St, Ontario, CA 91764. Telephone: 909-987-6397. FAX: 909-987-9038. E-MAIL: citydesk@dailybulletin.com. URL: http://www.dailybulletin.com. Mailing Address: P O Box 4000, Ontario, CA 91761. Year Established: 1885. Pub. Frequency: d. Page Size: broadsheet. Subscrip. Rate: $.50 newsstand/cover; $1 newsstand/cover Sun.; $3.35/wk.; $29.25 13 wks.. Adv. Rate: col. inch $35.60 **Wire Service(s):** AP. Circulation: 68,000 morning (paid); 75,000 Sunday (paid). **Owner(s):** MediaNews Group, Inc., 101 W Colfax Ave, Ste 1100, Denver, CO 80202. FAX: 303-954-6320. **Management:** Bob Blazer, Publisher. Peggy Del Toro, Advertising Director. Jim Parks, Circulation Director. **Editorial:** Steve Lambert, Editor. Jim Mahr, Sports Editor.

OROVILLE

OROVILLE MERCURY-REGISTER. 2081 Second St, Oroville, CA 95965. Telephone: 530-533-3131. FAX: 530-533-3127. E-MAIL: biano@cncnet.com. URL: http//www.orovillemr.com. Mailing Address: P O Box 651, Oroville, CA 95965. Year Established: 1873. Pub. Frequency: d. (Mon.-Sat.) Page Size: broadsheet. Subscrip. Rate: $.50 newsstand/cover; $1 newsstand/cover Sat.; $10.73 carrier delivery/mo.. **Wire Service(s):** AP. Circulation: 7,800 evening (paid). **Owner(s):** MediaNews Group, Inc., 101 W Colfax Ave, Ste 1100, Denver, CO 80202. FAX: 303-954-6320. **Management:** Carmen Biano, General Manager. Wolf Rosenberg, Publisher. Karen Eastham, Advertising Director. Darlene Stewart, Circulation Manager.

PALM SPRINGS

DESERT SUN, THE. 750 N. Gene Autry Trail, Palm Springs, CA 92262. Telephone: 760-322-8889. FAX: 760-778-4654. URL: http://www.desertsun.com. Mailing Address: PO Box 2734, Palm Springs, CA 92263. Year Established: 1927. Pub. Frequency: d. Page Size: broadsheet. Subscrip. Rate: $.50 newsstand/cover; $.75 newsstand/cover Sat.; $1.25 newsstand/cover Sun.; $142.88/yr. **Wire Service(s):** AP, NYT, GNS. Circulation: 63,500 morning (paid); 72,000 Sunday (paid). **Owner(s):** Gannett Company, Inc., 7950 Jones Branch Dr, McLean, VA 22107. Telephone: 703-854-6000. **Management:** Robert Dickey, Publisher. Greg Castro, Circulation Director. Michelle Krans, Marketing Director. **Editorial:** Bruce Fessier, Entertainment Editor. Jeff Hendrickson, Sports Editor.

PALMDALE

ANTELOPE VALLEY PRESS. ISSN 0744-5830
37404 Sierra Hwy, Palmdale, CA 93550-9343. Telephone: 661-273-2700. FAX: 661-947-4870. E-MAIL: editor@avpress.com. URL: http://www.avpress.com. Mailing Address: PO Box 4050, Palmdale, CA 93590-4050. Pub. Frequency: d. Page Size: broadsheet. Subscrip. Rate: $.50, $1.50 newsstand/cover; $161/yr carrier delivery in area; $321/yr mailed in county; $401.25/yr mailed in state. Adv. Rate: col. inch $21.99 Freelance Pay: $25-$50/article. **Wire Service(s):** AP, NYT. Circulation: 56,276 morning (paid); 58,775 Sunday (paid). **Owner(s):** Antelope Valley Press, See address and contact information above. **Editorial:** Dennis Anderson, Editor. Charles Bostwick, Managing Editor. William Wu, News Editor. Robert Johnson, Sports Editor.

PALO ALTO

PALO ALTO DAILY NEWS. 324 High St., Palo Alto, CA 94301. Telephone: 650-327-9090. FAX: 650-327-0676. E-MAIL: editorial@paloaltodailynews.com. URL: http://www.paloaltodailynews.com. Year Established: 1995. Pub. Frequency: d. Page Size: tabloid. Subscrip. Rate: $198/yr. Adv. Rate: col. inch $16.50 Circulation: 47,500 morning (free). **Owner(s):** Priceless LLC, See address and contact information above. **Management:** Michael Gelbman, General Manager. Jeanne Marie Kopaigorodski, Advertising. Mike Higgins, Circulation Manager. Michael Relay, Classified Adv. Mgr.. **Editorial:** Dario Dianda, Executive Editor. Jamie Casini, Managing Editor. Dylan Kruse, Sports Editor.

PASADENA

PASADENA STAR-NEWS, THE. ISSN 1069-2827
911 E. Colorado Blvd., Pasadena, CA 91106. Telephone: 626-578-6300. E-MAIL: starnews@earthlink.net. URL: http://www.pasadenastarnews.com. Year Established: 1886. Pub. Frequency: d. Page Size: broadsheet. Subscrip. Rate: $.50 newsstand/cover; $1 newsstand/cover Sun.; $39 newsstand/cover 13 wks.. **Wire Service(s):** AP, NYT. Circulation: 42,800 morning (paid); 42,800 Sunday (paid). **Owner(s):** MediaNews Group, Inc., 101 W Colfax Ave, Ste 1100, Denver, CO 80202. FAX: 303-954-6320. **Management:** Ron Wood, Publisher. Joe Robidoux, Circulation Manager. Michael Moreno, Sales Manager. **Editorial:** Larry Wilson, Editor. Steve O'Sullivan, Executive Editor. Steve Hunt, Managing Editor. Jennifer Errico, Entertainment Editor. Catherine Gaugh, Feature Editor. Tim Berger, Photo Editor. Doug Spoon, Sports Editor.

PLACERVILLE

MOUNTAIN DEMOCRAT. 1360 Broadway, Placerville, CA 95667. Telephone: 530-622-1255. FAX: 530-622-7894. E-MAIL: mtdemo@mtdemocrat.com. URL: http://www.mtdemocrat.com. Mailing Address: PO Box 1088, Placerville, CA 95667-1088. Year Established: 1851. Pub. Frequency: d. (Mon. & Wed.-Fri.) Page Size: broadsheet. Subscrip. Rate: $.50 newsstand/cover; $75/yr in county; $110/yr out of county; $67/yr in county Sr. Citizens. Adv. Rate: col. inch $17 Freelance Pay: $25/story. **Wire Service(s):** NYT. Circulation: 13,600 morning (paid). **Owner(s):** Mountain Democrat, Inc., See address and contact information above. **Management:** James C. Webb, Publisher. Suzanne Stevenson, Advertising Director. Gerry Ulm, Circulation Manager. Pat Hooper, Classified Adv. Mgr.. **Editorial:** Michael Raffety, Editor. Pat Lakey, Managing Editor. Noel Stack, City Editor.

PLEASANTON

TRI-VALLEY HERALD. ISSN 1051-5739
4770 Willow Rd, Pleasanton, CA 94588. Telephone: 925-734-8600. FAX: 925-416-4850. E-MAIL: apacciorini@angnewspapers.com. URL: http://www.trivalleyherald.com. Mailing Address: P O Box 10367, Pleasanton, CA 94588. Year Established: 1874. Pub. Frequency: d. Page Size: broadsheet. Subscrip. Rate: $.50 newsstand/cover; $1.50 newsstand/cover Sun.; $3.08 carrier delivery/wk.; $43.34 carrier delivery for 13 wks.. **Wire Service(s):** AP, SH, NYT, LAT-WAT. Circulation: 43,453 morning (paid); 43,199 Sunday (paid). **Owner(s):** MediaNews Group, Inc., 101 W Colfax Ave, Ste 1100, Denver, CO 80202. FAX: 303-954-6320. **Management:** Kevin Keane, Publisher. **Editorial:** Bob Goll, Editor. Drew Voros, Business Editor. Alexander DeFelice, City Editor. Tom Tuttle, Editorial Page Editor. Ron Reisterer, Photo Editor. Jon Becker, Sports Editor.

VALLEY TIMES. 127 Spring St. P, Pleasanton, CA 4566A. FAX: 925-847-2189. E-MAIL: contr@costatimes.com. URL: http://www.hotcoco.com. Mailing Address: PO Box 607, Pleasanton, CA 94566. Year Established: 1885. Pub. Frequency: d. Page Size: broadsheet. Subscrip. Rate: $.25 newsstand/cover; $53.50/yr home delivery. **Wire Service(s):** AP, NYT, LAT-WAT. Circulation: 43,891 evening (paid); 45,679 Sunday (paid). **Owner(s):** Knight Ridder, Inc., 50 W. San Fernando St., Ste. 1200, San Jose, CA 95113. Telephone: 831-938-7777. FAX: 831-938-7755. **Management:** John Armstrong, Publisher. Lynn Marleau, Advertising Manager. Frank Erias, Circulation Manager. **Editorial:** Kelly Gust, Editor. Marcus Thompson, Sports Editor.

PORTERVILLE

PORTERVILLE RECORDER, THE. 115 E. Oak Ave., Porterville, CA 93257. Telephone: 559-784-5000. FAX: 559-784-5245. URL: http://www.myopr.com. Mailing Address: PO Box 151, Porterville, CA 93258-0151. Year Established: 1908. Pub. Frequency: d. (Mon.-Sat.) Page Size: broadsheet. Subscrip. Rate: $.50 newsstand/cover; $.75 newsstand/cover Sat.; $18.40 carrier delivery for 2 mos.; $19.90 motor route for 2 mos.. **Wire Service(s):** AP. Circulation: 10,000 evening (paid). **Owner(s):** Freedom Communications, Inc., 17666 Fitch, Irvine, CA 92614. Telephone: 949-553-9292. FAX: 949-474-7675. **Management:** Paul Mauney, Publisher. Donna Schendel, Circulation Manager. Jan Parnell, Classified Adv. Mgr.. Sheila Seaman, Marketing Manager. **Editorial:** Glen Faison, Editor-in-Chief. Tom Price, Sports Editor.

RANCHO MIRAGE

BEVERLY HILLS TODAY & PALM SPRINGS TODAY. ISSN 0893-7990
6 Exeter Ct, Rancho Mirage, CA 92270. Telephone: 760-324-0801. FAX: 760-324-0068. E-MAIL: thenewstoday@yahoo.com. Year Established: 1945. Pub. Frequency: d. (Mon.-Fri.) Page Size: tabloid. Subscrip. Rate: $.50 newsstand/cover; $83/yr. Circulation: 11,500 morning (paid and controlled). **Owner(s):** California News Bureau, See address and contact information above. **Management:** Lee Soble, Publisher. Sam Gordon, Advertising Manager. Norman Blum, Circulation Director. **Editorial:** Lee Soble, Editor-in-Chief. Leonard Miller, Editorial Page Editor.

RED BLUFF

RED BLUFF DAILY NEWS. 545 Diamond Ave., Red Bluff, CA 96080. Telephone: 530-527-2151. FAX: 530-527-3719. E-MAIL: rbeditor@tehama.net. URL: http://www.redbluffdailynews.com. Mailing Address: PO Box 220, Red Bluff, CA 96080. Year Established: 1885. Pub. Frequency: d. (Mon.-Sat.) Page Size: standard. Subscrip. Rate: $.50 newsstand/cover; $8 carrier delivery/mo.; $25.89 motor route for 3 mos.. **Wire Service(s):** AP. Circulation: 8,000 evening (paid). **Owner(s):** MediaNews Group, Inc., 101 W Colfax Ave, Ste 1100, Denver, CO 80202. FAX: 303-954-6320. **Management:** Gayla Eckels, Advertising Director. **Editorial:** Michael Griffin, Editor. David Zimmerle, Sports Editor.

REDDING

RECORD SEARCHLIGHT. 1101 Twin View Blvd., Redding, CA 96003. Telephone: 530-243-2424. FAX: 530-225-8236. E-MAIL: tking@redding.com. URL: http://www.redding.com. Mailing Address: PO Box 492397, Redding, CA 96049-2397. Year Established: 1938. Pub. Frequency: d. Page Size: broadsheet. Subscrip. Rate: $.50 newsstand/cover; $1.50 newsstand/cover Sun.. **Wire Service(s):** AP, SH, NYT. Circulation: 35,239 morning (paid); 38,549 Sunday (paid). **Owner(s):** E.W. Scripps Co., 312 Walnut St., 28th Fl., Cincinnati, OH 45202. Telephone: 513-977-3000. **Management:** Shanna Cannon, Publisher. Rebecca Alexander, Advertising. Ian Balentine, Advertising Manager. Robbie Parham, Circulation Director. Michelle M. Streeby, Marketing Director. **Editorial:** Carole Ferguson, Managing Editor. Maline Hazle, City Editor. Bruce Ross, Editorial Page Editor. Laura Christman, Garden Editor. Lori Bredemeyer, News Editor.

REDLANDS

REDLANDS DAILY FACTS. 700 Brookside Ave, Redlands, CA 92373. Telephone: 909-793-3221. FAX: 909-793-9588. E-MAIL: rdfnews@aol.com. URL: http://www.redlandsdailyfacts.com. Year Established: 1890. Pub. Frequency: d. (Sun.-Fri.) Page Size: broadsheet. Subscrip. Rate: $.25 newsstand/cover; $1 newsstand/cover Sun.; $91.20/yr home delivery; $168/yr mailed. **Wire Service(s):** AP. Circulation: 8,000 evening (paid); 8,000 Sunday (paid). **Owner(s):** MediaNews Group, Inc., 101 W Colfax Ave, Ste 1100, Denver, CO 80202. FAX: 303-954-6320. **Management:** Fred Board, Publisher. Michael Jordan, Advertising Manager. Dan Hesley, Circulation Manager. **Editorial:** James Folmer, Editor.

RICHMOND

WEST COUNTY TIMES. ISSN 0746-6323
4301 Lakeside Dr, Richmond, CA 94806. Telephone: 510-262-2770. FAX: 510-262-2719. E-MAIL: wcletters@cctimes.com. URL: http://www.contracostatimes.com. Year Established: 1899. Pub. Frequency: d. Page Size: broadsheet. Subscrip. Rate: $.25 newsstand/cover; $1.50 newsstand/cover Sun.; $12.50 home delivery/mo.. **Wire Service(s):** AP, NYT, LAT-WAT. Circulation: 29,000 morning (paid); 29,000 Sunday (paid). **Owner(s):** MediaNews Group, Inc., 101 W Colfax Ave, Ste 1100, Denver, CO 80202. FAX: 303-954-6320. **Management:** John Armstrong, Publisher. **Editorial:** Todd Perlman, Editor. Kevin Keane, Executive Editor. Robert Jordan, Sports.

RIDGECREST

DAILY INDEPENDENT, THE. ISSN 1076-0059
224 E. Ridgecrest Blvd., Ridgecrest, CA 93555. Telephone: 760-375-4481. FAX: 760-375-4880. URL: http://www.ridgecrestca.com. Mailing Address: PO Box 7, Ridgecrest, CA 93556. Year Established: 1928. Pub. Frequency: d. (Tue.-Sat.) Page Size: broadsheet. Subscrip. Rate: $.55 newsstand/cover; $1.50 newsstand/cover Sat.; $8.66 carrier delivery/mo. local; $9.40 mailed/mo. in state; $10.40 mailed/mo. out of state. **Wire Service(s):** AP, SH. Circulation: 5,500 morning (paid and controlled); 7,600 evening (paid); 8,100 Sunday (paid). **Owner(s):** GateHouse Media, Inc, 350 WillowBrook Office Park, Fairport, NY 14450. Telephone: 585-598-0030. FAX: 585-248-2631. **Management:** John Watkins, Publisher. Karen Sanders, Advertising Director. Chris Bradley, Circulation Manager. **Editorial:** Nathan Ahle, Managing Editor.

RIVERSIDE

PRESS-ENTERPRISE, THE. ISSN 0746-4258
3450 14th St., Riverside, CA 92501. Telephone: 951-684-1200. FAX: 951-368-9021. E-MAIL: syepez@pe.com. URL: http://www.pe.com. Mailing Address: PO Box 792, Riverside, CA 92502. Year Established: 1878. Pub. Frequency: d. Page Size: broadsheet. Subscrip. Rate: $.25 newsstand/cover; $1.25 Sun.; $165.36/yr in county. **Wire Service(s):** AP, NYT. Circulation: 184,562 morning (paid); 189,095 Sunday (paid). **Owner(s):** Belo Corp., P.O. Box 655237, Dallas, TX 75265-5237. 400 S. Record St., Ste. 1300, Dallas, TX 75202. Telephone: 214-977-6606. **Management:** Shelly Yepez, Circulation Director. **Editorial:** John Gryka, Managing Editor. Mark Coast, Business Editor. Roger Ruvolo, News Editor. Dave Annenheuser, Sports Editor.

SACRAMENTO

FORT WORTH STAR-TELEGRAM. ISSN 0889-0013
2100 Q St, Sacramento, CA 95816. Telephone: 916-321-1936. FAX: 916-321-1869. E-MAIL: wes@star-telegram.com. URL: http://www.star-telegram.com. Mailing Address: PO Box 1870, Fort Worth, TX 76115. Year Established: 1906. Pub. Frequency: d. Page Size: broadsheet. Subscrip. Rate: $.50 newsstand/cover; $1.50 newsstand/cover Sun.; $16 carrier delivery/mo.. **Wire Service(s):** AP, LAT-WAT. Circulation: 245,332 morning (paid); 342,353 Sunday (paid). **Owner(s):** The/McClatchy Company, See address and contact information above. **Management:** Wesley Turner, Publisher. Mike Winter, VP Advertising. Weldon Whiteman, VP Circulation. **Editorial:** Jim Witt, Executive Editor. Patricia Rodriguez, Feature Editor.

SACRAMENTO BEE. ISSN 0890-5738
2100 Q St, Sacramento, CA 95816. Telephone: 916-321-1936. FAX: 916-321-1869. E-MAIL: rrodriguez@sacbee.com. URL: http://www.sacbee.com. Mailing Address: PO Box 15779, Sacramento, CA 95852-5779. Year Established: 1857. Pub. Frequency: d. Page Size: broadsheet. Subscrip. Rate: $.50 newsstand/cover; $1.50 newsstand/cover Sun.; $25 home delivery for 10 wks.. **Wire Service(s):** AP, SH. Circulation: 307,238 morning (paid); 358,087 Sunday (paid). **Owner(s):** The/McClatchy Company, See address and contact information above. **Management:** Steve Bernard, VP Advertising. Suzanne Deegan, Advertising Manager. **Editorial:** Rick Rodriguez, Executive Editor. Joyce Terhaar, Managing Editor. Bill Bradley, Sports Editor.

SALINAS

SALINAS CALIFORNIAN, THE. 123 W. Alisal St., Salinas, CA 93901. Telephone: 831-424-2221. FAX: 831-754-4104. E-MAIL: valleynews@aol.com. URL: http://www.thecalifornian.com. Mailing Address: PO Box 81091, Salinas, CA 93912. Year Established: 1871. Pub. Frequency: d. (Mon.-Sat.) Page Size: broadsheet. Subscrip. Rate: $.50 newsstand/cover; $1 newsstand/cover Sat.; $11/mo. in county. **Wire Service(s):** AP, GNS. Circulation: 17,966 morning (paid); 20,501 Saturday (paid). **Owner(s):** Gannett Company, Inc., 7950 Jones Branch Dr., McLean, VA 22102. Telephone: 703-854-6000. **Management:** Scott Faust, Publisher. Robert Powell, Advertising Director. Pam Watson, Advertising Manager. **Editorial:** Scott Faust, Executive Editor. Mike Nemeth, Senior Editor. Roberto Robledo, Community Editor. Richard Green, Photographer. Joey Delgado, Sports.

SAN BERNARDINO

SAN BERNARDINO COUNTY SUN. 399 N D St, San Bernardino, CA 92401. Telephone: 909-889-9666. FAX: 909-885-8741. URL: http://www.sbsun.com. Year Established: 1894. Pub. Frequency: d. Page Size: broadsheet. Subscrip. Rate: $.50 newsstand/cover; $1.50 newsstand/cover Sun.; $20 for 10 wks.; $127.17/yr. **Wire Service(s):** AP, NYT, GNS. Circulation: 77,672 morning (paid); 92,000 Sunday (paid). **Owner(s):** MediaNews Group, Inc., 101 W Colfax Ave, Ste 1100, Denver, CO 80202. FAX: 303-954-6320. **Management:** Gene Pearlman, Advertising Director. Susan Mosher, Classified Adv. Mgr.. **Editorial:** Steve Lambert, Editor. Paul Mohr, Sports Editor.

SAN DIEGO

SAN DIEGO UNION-TRIBUNE. ISSN 1063-102X
350 Camino De La Reina, San Diego, CA 92108. E-MAIL: nancy.wyld@uniontrib.com. URL: http://www.uniontrib.com. Mailing Address: PO Box 120191, San Diego, CA 92112-0191. Year Established: 1868. Pub. Frequency: d. Page Size: broadsheet. Subscrip. Rate: $.50 newsstand/cover; $1.50 Sun.; $49.99 local for 3 mos.. **Wire Service(s):** RN, AP, NYT, MCT, CNS, DJNS. Circulation: 385,000 morning (paid); 459,000 Sunday (paid). **Owner(s):** Union-Tribune Publishing Co., See address and contact information above. **Management:** Roy E. Bell, President. David Copley, Publisher. Scott Whitley, Advertising Director. Dexter Lapierre, Classified Adv. Mgr.. Michael Franklin, Photography Director. **Editorial:** Karin Winner, Editor. Nancy Wyld, Senior Editor. Jim Watters, Business Editor. Ellen Bevier, City Editor. Michele Parente, Feature Editor. Mitch Weinstock, National Editor. Bernie Jones, Opinion Editor. Chuck Scott, Sports Editor.

SAN FRANCISCO

SAN FRANCISCO CHRONICLE. ISSN 1932-8672
901 Mission St., San Francisco, CA 94103-2988. Telephone: 415-777-1111. FAX: 415-543-7708. E-MAIL: letters@sfchronicle.com. URL: http://www.sfchron.com. Year Established: 1865. Pub. Frequency: d. Page Size: broadsheet. Subscrip. Rate: $.25 newsstand/cover; $1 newsstand/cover Sun.; $15.80 home delivery/mo.; $138.84/yr home delivery. **Wire Service(s):** RN, AP, NYT, LAT-WAT. Circulation: 512,000 morning (paid); 520,000 Sunday (paid). **Owner(s):** Hearst Corp., The, 959 Eighth Ave., New York, NY 10019. Telephone: 212-649-2000. **Management:** Frank B Vega, President. BeverlyBart Best, Advertising Director. **Editorial:** Narda Zacchino, Executive Editor. Kenn Altine, Managing Editor. John P Curley, Asst. Managing Ed.. John Diaz, Editorial Page Editor. Andrew Ross, Foreign Editor. Linda Strean, News Editor.

SAN FRANCISCO EXAMINER. 450 Mission St., San Francisco, CA 94105. Telephone: 415-359-2600. FAX: 415-826-2766. E-MAIL: info@sfexaminer.com. URL: http://www.examiner.com. Year Established: 1887. Pub. Frequency: d. (Mon.-Sat.) Page Size: standard. **Wire Service(s):** RN, AP. Circulation: 116,620 evening (paid); 629,939 Sunday (paid). **Owner(s):** S F Newspaper Co., See address and contact information above. **Management:** Mark Hutt, Advertising. Eddy Alejandre, Circulation Manager. **Editorial:** Jim Pimentel, Managing Editor. Albert C. Pacciorini, Business Editor. Deidre Hussey, City Editor. Sonia Mansfield, Feature Editor.

SAN JOSE

SAN JOSE MERCURY NEWS. ISSN 0747-2099
750 Ridder Park Dr, San Jose, CA 95190. Telephone: 408-920-5254. FAX: 408-271-3792. E-MAIL: dyarnold@sjmercury.com. URL: http://www.mercurynews.com. Year Established: 1983. Pub. Frequency: d. Page Size: broadsheet. Subscrip. Rate: $.50 newsstand/cover in city; $1 newsstand/cover Sun. in city; $175.80/yr in city. **Wire Service(s):** AP, NYT, LAT-WAT. Circulation: 276,166 per issue (paid); 309,520 Sunday (paid). **Owner(s):** MediaNews Group, Inc., 101 W Colfax Ave, Ste 1100, Denver, CO 80202. FAX: 303-954-6320. **Management:** Chip Visci, Publisher. Harry Wold, Circulation Director. **Editorial:** David Yamold, Executive Editor. David Satterfield, Managing Editor. Consuelo Alba, Feature Editor. Craig Lancaster, Sports Editor.

SAN LUIS OBISPO

TRIBUNE (SAN LUIS OBISPO), THE. 3825 S Higuera St, San Luis Obispo, CA 93401. Telephone: 805-781-7800. FAX: 805-781-7870. E-MAIL: sduerr@thetribunenews.com. URL: http://www.sanluisobispo.com. Mailing Address: PO Box 112, San Luis Obispo, CA 93406-0112. Year Established: 1869. Pub. Frequency: d. Page Size: broadsheet. Subscrip. Rate: $.50 newsstand/cover; $1.25 newsstand/cover Sun.; $168/yr home delivery local. **Wire Service(s):** AP, SH. Circulation: 38,169 morning (paid). **Owner(s):** The/McClatchy Company, 2100 Q St, Sacramento, CA 95816. Telephone: 916-321-1936. **Editorial:** Sandra Duerr, Executive Editor. Ted Weber, Managing Editor. Matt Lozier, City Editor. Melissa Geisler, Sports Editor.

SAN MATEO

SAN MATEO COUNTY TIMES. 477 Ninth Ave, San Mateo, CA 94402. Telephone: 650-348-4321. FAX: 650-348-4446. E-MAIL: twinckler@angnewspapers.com. URL: http://www.sanmateocountytimes.com. Year Established: 1889. Pub. Frequency: d. (Mon.-Sat.) Page Size: broadsheet. Subscrip. Rate: $.50 newsstand/cover; $.75 newsstand/cover Sat.; $7.50 home delivery/mo.; $19.95 home delivery for 10 wks.; $15.98 mailed for 4 wks.; $60/yr home delivery. **Wire Service(s):** AP, SH, NYT. Circulation: 37,000 evening (paid). **Owner(s):** MediaNews Group, Inc., 101 W Colfax Ave, Ste 1100, Denver, CO 80202. FAX: 303-954-6320. **Management:** Roger Grossman, Publisher. Dan Cruey, Circulation Manager. **Editorial:** Terry Winckler, Editor. Glenn Rabinowitz, Executive Editor. Drew Voros, Business Editor. Mike Meena, City Editor. Tom Tuttle, Editorial Page Editor. Glenn Reeves, Sports Editor.

SANTA ANA

ORANGE COUNTY REGISTER, THE. ISSN 0886-4934
625 N Grand Ave, Santa Ana, CA 92701. Telephone: 714-796-7000. FAX: 714-796-3657. URL: http://www.ocregister.com. Mailing Address: PO Box 11626, Santa Ana, CA 92711. Year Established: 1952. Pub. Frequency: d. Page Size: broadsheet. Subscrip. Rate: $.50 newsstand/cover; $1.25 newsstand/cover Sun.. **Wire Service(s):** RN, AP, SH, NYT, MCT. Circulation: 302,864 morning (paid); 370,911 Sunday (paid). **Owner(s):** Freedom Communications, Inc., 17666 Fitch, Irvine, CA 92614. Telephone: 949-553-9292. **Management:** Christopher Anderson, Publisher. William Felder, Classified Adv. Mgr.. **Editorial:** Tonnie Katz, Editor. Ken Brusic, Executive Editor. Jim Wolcott, News Director. Cathy Lawhon, Feature Editor. Jonathan Lansner, Financial Editor.

SANTA BARBARA

SANTA BARBARA NEWS-PRESS. 715 Anacapa St., Santa Barbara, CA 93101-2203. Telephone: 805-564-5200. FAX: 805-564-5228. E-MAIL: tbolton@newspress.com. URL: http://www.newspress.com. Mailing Address: PO Box 1359, Santa Barbara, CA 93102-1359. Year Established: 1855. Pub. Frequency: d. Page Size: broadsheet. Subscrip. Rate: $.50 newsstand/cover; $1.50 newsstand/cover Sun.; $3.18 home delivery/wk.. **Wire Service(s):** AP, NYT. Circulation: 48,000 morning (paid); 51,000 Sunday (paid). **Owner(s):** Ampersand Publishing LLC, See address and contact information above. **Management:** Arthur vonWiesenberger, Co-Publisher. Jerry Roberts, Publisher. Kathy Knobbe, Circulation Director. Rachel Samson, Classified Adv. Mgr.. **Editorial:** Jerry Roberts, Editor. George Foulsham, Managing Editor. Travis Armstrong, Editorial Page Editor. Andrea Huebner, Lifestyle Editor. Jane Pulse, Metro Editor. Len Wood, Photo Editor. Gerry Spratt, Sports Editor.

Dailies

SANTA MARIA

SANTA MARIA TIMES. ISSN 0745-6166
3200 Skyway Dr., Santa Maria, CA 93455-1896. Telephone: 805-925-2691. FAX: 805-928-5657. URL: http://www.santamariatimes.com. Mailing Address: PO Box 400, Santa Maria, CA 93456-0400. Year Established: 1882. Pub. Frequency: d. Page Size: broadsheet. Subscrip. Rate: $.50 newsstand/cover; $1 newsstand/cover Sun.; $11 home delivery/mo.; $11 motor route/mo.; $11 mailed/mo. out of state. **Wire Service(s):** AP, SH. Circulation: 20,000 morning (paid); 22,000 Sunday (paid). **Owner(s):** Lee Enterprises, Inc., 900 N. Tucker Blvd., St. Louis, MO 63101. Telephone: 314-340-8000. **Management:** Cynthia Scheer, Publisher. Debbi Johnson, Business Manager. **Editorial:** Tom Bolton, Executive Editor. Kent Miller, Business Editor. Tom Bolton, Editorial Page Editor. Peter Moberly, News Editor. Elliott Stern, Sports Editor.

SCOTTS VALLEY

SANTA CRUZ COUNTY SENTINEL. ISSN 1072-446X
1800 Green Hills Rd, Ste 210, Scotts Valley, CA 950666. Telephone: 831-423-4242. FAX: 831-429-9620. E-MAIL: news@santacruzsentinel.com. URL: http://www.santacruzsentinel.com. Year Established: 1856. Pub. Frequency: d. Page Size: broadsheet. Subscrip. Rate: $.50 newsstand/cover; $1.50 newsstand/cover Sun.; $127/yr. **Wire Service(s):** AP, NYT. Circulation: 28,000 morning (paid); 30,021 Sunday (paid). **Owner(s):** MediaNews Group, Inc., 101 W Colfax Ave, Ste 1100, Denver, CO 80202. FAX: 303-954-6320. **Management:** Dave Regan, Publisher. Mardi Browning, Circulation Manager. **Editorial:** Don Miller, Editor. Julie Copeland, City Editor. Julie Jag, Sports Editor.

SONORA

UNION DEMOCRAT, THE. 84 S. Washington St., Sonora, CA 95370. Telephone: 209-532-7151. FAX: 209-532-6451. E-MAIL: newsroom@uniondemocrat.com. URL: http://www.uniondemocrat.com. Year Established: 1854. Pub. Frequency: d. (Mon.-Fri.) Page Size: broadsheet. Subscrip. Rate: $.50 newsstand/cover; $21 home delivery for 3 mos.; $78/yr home delivery; $32 mailed for 3 mos; $98/yr mailed. **Wire Service(s):** AP. Circulation: 13,000 evening (paid). **Owner(s):** Western Communication, Inc., 1777 S.W. Chandler Ave., Bend, OR 97702. Telephone: 541-382-1811. FAX: 541-383-0372. **Management:** Geoffrey White, Publisher. Gary Piech, Advertising Director. Don Robinson, Circulation Manager. Peggy Pietrowicz, Classified Adv. Mgr.. **Editorial:** Patty Fuller, Managing Editor. Kevin Sauls, Sports. Gary Linehan, Weekend Editor.

SOUTH LAKE TAHOE

TAHOE DAILY TRIBUNE. ISSN 8750-3948
3079 Harrison Ave., South Lake Tahoe, CA 96150. Telephone: 530-541-3880. FAX: 530-541-0373. E-MAIL: tribune@tahoe.com. URL: http://www.tahoe.com. Year Established: 1958. Pub. Frequency: d. (Mon.-Fri.) Page Size: broadsheet. Subscrip. Rate: $.50 newsstand/cover; $102/yr home delivery; $120/yr mailed. **Wire Service(s):** AP. Circulation: 8,500 morning (paid). **Owner(s):** Swift Newspapers, Inc., 500 Double Eagle Ct., Reno, NV 89511. Telephone: 775-850-7676. FAX: 775-850-7677. **Management:** Phillip E. Swift, President. Paul Middle Brook, Publisher. **Editorial:** Michele Weijel, Editor. Jeff Munson, City Editor. Tim Parsons, Editorial Page Editor. Nancy Oliver, Local News Editor. Steve Yingling, Sports Editor.

STOCKTON

RECORD (STOCKTON), THE. 530 E. Market St., Stockton, CA 95202. Telephone: 209-943-6568. FAX: 209-547-8186. E-MAIL: newsroom@recordnet.com. URL: http://www.recordnet.com. Mailing Address: PO Box 900, Stockton, CA 95201. Year Established: 1895. Pub. Frequency: d. Page Size: broadsheet. Subscrip. Rate: $.75 newsstand/cover; $1.50 newsstand/cover Sun.; $30 home delivery/mo. local 17 wks Stockton & Lodi. **Wire Service(s):** AP, NYT. Circulation: 56,360 morning (paid); 61,619 Sunday (paid); 55,996 Saturday (paid). **Owner(s):** World Newspapers, Inc., Landmark Ctr., 1299 Farnam St., 15th Fl., Omaha, NE 68102-1841. Telephone: 402-444-1000. **Bureau(s):** 925 L St., Ste. 308, Sacramento, CA 95814. Telephone: 916-441-4078. FAX: 916-441-0482. Contact: Will Shuck, Bureau Chief. **Management:** Roger Coover, President. Deitra Kenoly, Advertising. Peter Gutierrez, Circulation Manager. Peggy Takahashi, Controller. Sandi Johnson, Human Res. Mgr.. **Editorial:** Damian Glick, Production Manager.

TEMECULA

CALIFORNIAN, THE. ISSN 1045-5868
28765 Single Oak Dr., Ste. 100, Temecula, CA 92590. Telephone: 951-676-4315. FAX: 951-694-1215. E-MAIL: llockwood@nctimes.com. URL: http://www.nctimes.com. Mailing Address: PO Box 970, Temecula, CA 92593. Year Established: 1976. Pub. Frequency: d. Page Size: broadsheet. Subscrip. Rate: $.25 newsstand/cover; $1.25 newsstand/cover Sun.; $10.75/mo.; $32.25 for 3 mos. Adv. Rate: col. inch $11.25 **Wire Service(s):** AP. Circulation: 20,989 morning (paid); 21,235 Sunday (paid). **Owner(s):** Lee Enterprises, Inc., 215 N. Main St., Davenport, IA 52801. Telephone: 563-383-2100. **Management:** Claude Reinke, Publisher. Wayne Burton, Circulation Manager. **Editorial:** Wayne Halberg, Editor. James Curran, Entertainment Editor. David Carlson, Photographer. Landon Negri, Sports Editor.

TORRANCE

DAILY BREEZE. 5215 Torrance Blvd, Torrance, CA 90503. Telephone: 310-540-5511. FAX: 310-540-6272. E-MAIL: breezead@aol.com. URL: http://www.dailybreeze.com. Mailing Address: PO Box 2982, Torrace, CA 90509. Year Established: 1895. Pub. Frequency: d. Page Size: broadsheet. Subscrip. Rate: $.25 newsstand/cover; $1.25 newsstand/cover Sun.; $161.20/yr home delivery; $227.26/yr mailed. **Wire Service(s):** AP, NYT, CNS. Circulation: 83,800 morning (paid); 81,725 Sunday (paid). **Owner(s):** MediaNews Group, Inc., 101 W Colfax Ave, Ste 1100, Denver, CO 80202. FAX: 303-954-6320. **Management:** Mark Ficarra, Publisher. Gregg Bertness, Advertising Director. Cathy Hardt, Classified Adv. Mgr.. **Editorial:** Phillip Sanfield, Editor.

TRACY

TRACY PRESS. 145 W. Tenth St., Tracy, CA 95376. Telephone: 209-835-3030. FAX: 209-835-0655. URL: http://www.tracypress.com. Mailing Address: PO Box 419, Tracy, CA 95378-0419. Year Established: 1898. Pub. Frequency: d. (Mon.-Sat.) Page Size: broadsheet. Subscrip. Rate: $.25 newsstand/cover; $25/yr carrier delivery. **Wire Service(s):** AP, NYT. Circulation: 11,000 morning (paid). **Owner(s):** Tom, Bob & Sam Matthews, See address and contact information above. **Management:** Robert S. Matthews, General Manager. Tonya Luiz, Advertising Manager. Jackie D'Angelo, Circulation Manager. **Editorial:** Cheri Matthews, Editor. Eric Firpo, City Editor. Glen Moore, Photographer. Christopher Roberts, Sports Editor.

TULARE

TULARE ADVANCE-REGISTER. 388 E. Cross Ave., Tulare, CA 93274. Telephone: 559-688-0521. FAX: 559-688-5580. E-MAIL: tularenews@visaliatimesdelta.com. URL: http://www.tulareadvanceregister.com. Mailing Address: PO Box 30, Tulare, CA 93275. Year Established: 1882. Pub. Frequency: d. (Mon.-Sat.) Page Size: broadsheet. Subscrip. Rate: $.50 newsstand/cover; $26.25 carrier delivery for 3 mos.; $87.50/yr carrier delivery; $36 mailed for 3 mos.; $144/yr mailed. **Wire Service(s):** AP, SH, GNS. Circulation: 9,000 evening (paid). **Owner(s):** Gannett Company, Inc., 7950 Jones Branch Dr., McLean, VA 22107-0001. Telephone: 703-854-6000. **Management:** Amy L. Pack, President. Kanon Hauser, Advertising Director. Debra Davenport, Advertising Manager. Brett Neumann, Classified Adv. Mgr.. **Editorial:** Amee M Thompson, Editor. Linda Green, Executive Editor. Jim Houck, City Editor. Marty Burleson, Feature Editor. Kevin McCusker, Sports Editor.

UKIAH

UKIAH DAILY JOURNAL, THE. 590 S. School St., Ukiah, CA 95482. Telephone: 707-468-0123. FAX: 707-468-5780. E-MAIL: udj@saber.net. URL: http://www.ukiahdailyjournal.com. Mailing Address: PO Box 749, Ukiah, CA 95482. Year Established: 1862. Pub. Frequency: d. Page Size: broadsheet. Subscrip. Rate: $.50 newsstand/cover; $1 newsstand/cover Sun.; $120/yr home delivery; $144/yr mailed in county; $168/yr mailed out of county. **Wire Service(s):** AP. Circulation: 7,609 evening (paid); 7,727 Sunday (paid). **Owner(s):** MediaNews Group, Inc., 101 W Colfax Ave, Ste 1100, Denver, CO 80202. FAX: 303-954-6320. **Management:** Kevin McConnell, Publisher. Cindy Delk, Advertising Manager. Don Miller, Circulation Director. Cindy Delk, Classified Adv. Mgr.. **Editorial:** K.C. Meadows, Managing Editor. Jody Martinez, Assistant Editor. Laura Clark, Feature Editor. Jeff Casperses, Sports.

VACAVILLE

REPORTER (VACAVILLE), THE. ISSN 0746-4193
916 Cotting Ln, Vacaville, CA 95688. Telephone: 707-448-6401. FAX: 707-447-8411. URL: http://www.thereporter.com. Mailing Address: PO Box 1509, Vacaville, CA 95696. Year Established: 1883. Pub. Frequency: d. Page Size: broadsheet. Subscrip. Rate: $.50 newsstand/cover; $1.25 newsstand/cover Sun.; $171.26/yr home delivery in area; $61.14 mailed 13 wks. in city. **Wire Service(s):** AP. Circulation: 21,500 morning (paid); 22,500 Sunday (paid). **Owner(s):** MediaNews Group, Inc., 101 W Colfax Ave, Ste 1100, Denver, CO 80202. FAX: 303-954-6320. **Management:** Steve Huddleston, Publisher. Debi Tavey, Advertising Director. Jerry Schoenberg, Circulation Manager. **Editorial:** Diane Barney, Editor. Robin Miller, City Editor.

VALENCIA

SIGNAL (VALENCIA), THE. 24000 Creekside Rd, Valencia, CA 91355. Telephone: 661-259-1234. FAX: 661-259-8068. E-MAIL: info@the-signal.com. URL: http://www.the-signal.com. Year Established: 1919. Pub. Frequency: d. Page Size: broadsheet. Subscrip. Rate: $.50 newsstand/cover; $1 newsstand/cover Sun.; $25 home delivery for 13 wks.; $50 home delivery for 26 wks.; $130/yr carrier delivery; $575/yr mailed. **Wire Service(s):** AP. Circulation: 46,000 morning (paid); 50,000 Sunday (paid). **Owner(s):** Morris Newspaper Corporation, 27 Abercorn St., Savannah, GA 31401. Telephone: 912-233-1281. FAX: 912-232-4639. **Management:** Tim Whyte, General Manager. Richard Budman, Publisher. Russ Briely, Circulation Manager. **Editorial:** Leon Worden, City Editor. Michele Buttleman, Lifestyle Editor. Grant Gordon, Sports Editor.

VALLEJO

TIMES-HERALD (VALLEJO). 440 Curtola Pkwy, Vallejo, CA 94590. Telephone: 707-644-1141. FAX: 707-643-0128. URL: http://www.timesheraldonline.com. Mailing Address: P O Box 3188, Vallejo, CA 94590. Year Established: 1875. Pub. Frequency: d. Page Size: broadsheet. Subscrip. Rate: $.50 newsstand/cover; $1.50 Sun.; $10.12/mo.; $126/yr. **Wire Service(s):** AP. Circulation: 24,000 morning (paid). **Owner(s):** MediaNews Group, Inc., 101 W Colfax Ave, Ste 1100, Denver, CO 80202. FAX: 303-954-6320. **Management:** Ron Rhea, Publisher. Heidi Hoffman, Advertising Director. Robert Wilson, Circulation Manager. **Editorial:** Ted Vollmer, Editor. Jack Bungart, Managing Editor. Mary M Leahy, City Editor. J L Sousa, Photo.

VENTURA

VENTURA COUNTY STAR. 5250 Ralston St., Ventura, CA 93003. Telephone: 805-650-2900. FAX: 805-650-2950. E-MAIL: gallagher@staronline.com. URL: http://www.insidevc.com. Mailing Address: PO Box 6711, Ventura, CA 93006-6711. Year Established: 1883. Pub. Frequency: d. Page Size: broadsheet. Subscrip. Rate: $.50 newsstand/cover; $1.50 newsstand/cover Sun.; $169/yr carrier delivery; $130 mailed for 6 mos.; $260/yr mailed. Freelance Pay: $25-$35/article. **Wire Service(s):** AP, SH, NYT. Circulation: 97,000 morning (paid); 112,000 Sunday (paid). **Owner(s):** E.W. Scripps Co., 312 Walnut St., 28th Fl., Cincinnati, OH 45202. Telephone: 513-977-3000. **Management:** Tim Gallagher, President. Steve Smith, Circulation Manager. Tom Rosenthal, Classified Adv. Mgr.. **Editorial:** Tim Gallagher, Editor. Joe Howry, Managing Editor. Frank Moraga, Business Editor. Colleen Cason, Columnist. Marianne Ratcliff, Editorial Page Editor. Mark Wycoff, Entertainment Editor. Lisa McKinnon, Fashion Editor. Jim Medina, Feature Editor. Frank Moraga, Financial Editor. Gary Phelps, Photographer. Amy Stroba, Real Estate Editor. Mike Blackwell, Sports Editor. Deann Justen, Weekend Editor.

VICTORVILLE

DAILY PRESS (VICTORVILLE). ISSN 1042-8496
13891 Park Ave., Victorville, CA 92392-1389. Telephone: 760-241-7744. FAX: 760-241-1860. E-MAIL: rmm@vvdailypress.com. URL: http://www.vvdailypress.com. Mailing Address: PO Box 1389, Victorville, CA 92393-1389. Year Established: 1937. Pub. Frequency: d. Page Size: broadsheet. Subscrip. Rate: $.50 newsstand/cover; $1.25 newsstand/cover Sun.; $143.40/yr home delivery; $90.77 mailed in state for 13 wks.; $84.24 mailed out of state for 13 wks. **Wire Service(s):** AP. Circulation: 35,000 morning (paid); 37,192 Sunday (paid). **Owner(s):** Freedom Communications, Inc., 17666 Fitch, Irvine, CA 92614. Telephone: 949-253-2300. **Management:** Stephen Wingert, Publisher. Susan Drake, Advertising Director. Jackie Parsons, Circulation Manager. Susan Drake, Classified Adv. Mgr.. **Editorial:** Don Holland, Executive Editor. Steven M. Williams, Editorial Page Editor. John Iddings, News Editor. Jason Vritis, Sports Editor.

VISALIA

VISALIA TIMES-DELTA. 330 N. West St., Visalia, CA 93291. Telephone: 559-735-3200. FAX: 559-735-3399. E-MAIL: sfaust@visalia.gannett.com. URL: http://www.visaliatimesdelta.com. Mailing Address: PO Box 31, Visalia, CA 93279. Year Established: 1859. Pub. Frequency: d. (Mon.-Sat.) Page Size: broadsheet. Subscrip. Rate: $.50 newsstand/cover; $1 newsstand/cover Sat.; $2.60 carrier delivery/wk.; $3.34 mailed/wk.. Freelance Pay: $28/article. **Wire Service(s):** AP, GNS. Circulation: 24,000 morning (paid). **Owner(s):** Gannett Company, Inc., 7950 Jones Branch Dr., McLean, VA 22107-0001. Telephone: 703-854-6000. **Management:** Amy L. Pack, Publisher. Kanon Hauser, Advertising Director. **Editorial:** Linda Green, Executive Editor. Jim Houck, City Editor. Marty Burleson, Feature Editor. Jamie Butow-Gonzales, News Editor. Kevin McCusker, Sports Editor.

WALNUT CREEK

CONTRA COSTA TIMES. ISSN 0192-0235
2640 Shadelands Dr, Walnut Creek, CA 94598. Telephone: 925-935-2525. FAX: 925-977-8457. URL: http://www.contracostatimes.com. Year Established: 1911. Pub. Frequency: d. Page Size: broadsheet. Subscrip. Rate: $.50 newsstand/cover; $14.29/mo.; $171.48/yr. **Wire Service(s):** AP, NYT, LAT-WAT. Circulation: 110,636 morning (paid); 119,338 Sunday (paid). **Owner(s):** MediaNews Group, Inc., P O Box 5088, Walnut Creek, CA 92393-1389. 101 W Colfax Ave, Ste 1100, Denver, CO 80202. FAX: 303-954-6320. **Management:** George E Armstrong, Publisher. **Editorial:** Kevin Keane, Executive Editor. Carolyn McMillan, News Editor. Tom Barnidge, Sports Editor.

WATSONVILLE

REGISTER-PAJARONIAN. 100 Westridge Dr., Watsonville, CA 95076. Telephone: 831-761-7300. FAX: 831-722-8386. E-MAIL: pajaro@cruzio.com. URL: http://www.register-pajaronian.com. Mailing Address: PO Box 50055, Watsonville, CA 95077. Year Established: 1868. Pub. Frequency: d. (Mon.-Sat.) Page Size: broadsheet. Subscrip. Rate: $.50 newsstand/cover; $1 newsstand/cover Sat.; $32.06 home delivery for 3 mos.; $64.13 home delivery for 6 mos.; $128.25/yr home delivery. Adv. Rate: col. inch $20.60 **Wire Service(s):** AP, LAT-WAT. Circulation: 7,200 morning (paid). **Owner(s):** News Media Corp., 228 Main St., Lingle, WY 82223. Telephone: 307-532-2184. **Management:** Douglas Leifheit, Publisher. Victoria Nelson, Advertising Manager. John Hernandez, Circulation Manager. Kelly Micholson, Classified Adv. Mgr.. **Editorial:** Jon Chown, Managing Editor. Daniel Hindin, Feature Editor. Tarmo Hannula, Photographer. Michael Oxendine, Sports Editor.

WEST COVINA

SAN GABRIEL VALLEY TRIBUNE. ISSN 8755-9595
1210 N.Azusa Canyon Rd., West Covina, CA 91790. Telephone: 626-962-8811. FAX: 626-962-8849. URL: http://www.sgvtribune.com. Mailing Address: PO Box 1259, West Covina, CA 91790. Year Established: 1955. Pub. Frequency: d. Page Size: broadsheet. Subscrip. Rate: $.50 newsstand/cover; $1 newsstand/cover Sun.; $31.20 home delivery for 8 wks.; $202.80/yr home delivery. **Wire Service(s):** AP, SH, NYT, CNS. Circulation: 48,541 morning (paid); 51,321 Sunday (paid). **Owner(s):** MediaNews Group, Inc., 101 W Colfax Ave, Ste 1100, Denver, CO 80202. FAX: 303-954-6320. **Management:** Ron Wood, Publisher. Tim Guesman, Advertising Director. Janice Jones, Advertising Manager. Joe Robidoux, Circulation Director. **Editorial:** Steve O'Sullivan, Executive Editor. Doug Spoon, Sports Editor.

WHITTIER

WHITTIER DAILY NEWS. ISSN 1069-2819
7612 Greenleaf Ave., Whittier, CA 90602. Telephone: 562-698-0955. FAX: 562-698-0450. E-MAIL: wdailynews@earthlink.net. URL: http://www.whittierdailynews.com. Year Established: 1900. Pub. Frequency: d. Page Size: broadsheet. Subscrip. Rate: $.50, $1.50 newsstand/cover; $39 home delivery for 13 wks.. **Wire Service(s):** AP, NYT, MCT, CiNS, DJNS. Circulation: 19,000 morning (paid); 19,000 Sunday (paid). **Owner(s):** MediaNews Group, Inc., 101 W Colfax Ave, Ste 1100, Denver, CO 80202. **Management:** Steve Lambert, Publisher. Jim Maurer, Advertising Director. **Editorial:** Steve Hunt, Executive Editor.

WOODLAND

DAILY DEMOCRAT. ISSN 0747-1890
711 Main St, Woodland, CA 95695. Telephone: 530-662-5421. FAX: 530-662-1288. E-MAIL: ddnews@dailydemocrat.com. URL: http://www.dailydemocrat.com. Mailing Address: P O Box 730, Woodland, CA 95776. Year Established: 1857. Pub. Frequency: d. Page Size: broadsheet. Subscrip. Rate: $.50 newsstand/cover; $1 newsstand/cover Sun.; $51 for 6 mos.; $102/yr. **Wire Service(s):** AP. Circulation: 10,800 evening (paid); 12,500 Sunday (paid). **Owner(s):** MediaNews Group, Inc., 101 W Colfax Ave, Ste 1100, Denver, CO 80202. FAX: 303-954-6320. **Management:** Kelly Leibold, Publisher. Marlene Harling, Advertising. Robert Mapalo, Circulation Manager. Sabrina Liams, Classified Adv. Mgr.. **Editorial:** Jim Smith, Managing Editor. Mary Goetz, Lifestyle Editor. Bruce Burton, Sports Editor.

WOODLAND HILLS

DAILY NEWS (WOODLAND HILLS), LA. 21221 Oxnard St, Woodland Hills, CA 91367. Telephone: 818-713-3000. FAX: 818-346-6397. URL: http://www.dailynews.com. Mailing Address: PO Box 4200, Woodland Hills, CA 91365. Year Established: 1911. Pub. Frequency: d. Page Size: broadsheet. Subscrip. Rate: $.50 newsstand/cover; $2 newsstand/cover Sun.; $3.75/wk.. Circulation: 178,204 morning (paid); 201,061 Sunday (paid). **Owner(s):** MediaNews Group, Inc., 101 W Colfax Ave, Ste 1100, Denver, CO 80202. FAX: 303-954-6320. **Management:** Melene Alfonso, Classified Adv. Mgr.. Art Williams, Sales Manager. **Editorial:** Ron Kaye, Editor. Melissa Lalum, Managing Editor.

YREKA

SISKIYOU DAILY NEWS. 309 S. Broadway, Yreka, CA 96097. Telephone: 530-842-5777. FAX: 530-842-6787. E-MAIL: publisher@siskiyoudaily.com. URL: http://www.siskiyoudaily.com. Mailing Address: PO Box 129, Yreka, CA 96097. Year Established: 1859. Pub. Frequency: d. (Mon.-Fri.) Page Size: broadsheet. Subscrip. Rate: $.50 newsstand/cover; $7.85/mo.; $94.50/yr. **Wire Service(s):** AP. Circulation: 9,800 morning (paid). **Owner(s):** GateHouse Media, Inc, 350 WillowBrook Office Park, Fairport, NY 14450. Telephone: 585-598-0030. FAX: 585-248-2631. **Management:** Rod Dowse, Publisher. David Nelmes, Advertising Manager. **Editorial:** Deborra Clayton, Managing Editor. Dan Murphy, Sports Editor.

COLORADO

ALAMOSA

VALLEY COURIER (ALAMOSA). ISSN 1047-1170
401 State St., Alamosa, CO 81101. Telephone: 719-589-2553. FAX: 719-589-6573. E-MAIL: krc@fone.net. URL: http://www.alamosanews.com. Mailing Address: PO Box 1099, Alamosa, CO 81101. Year Established: 1925. Pub. Frequency: d. (Tue.-Sat.) Page Size: broadsheet. Subscrip. Rate: $.50 newsstand/cover; $9.25/mo.. Adv. Rate: col. inch $11.25 **Wire Service(s):** AP. Circulation: 5,150 morning (paid). **Owner(s):** News Media Corp., PO Box 46, Rochelle, IL 61068. Telephone: 815-562-2061. **Management:** Keith R. Cerny, Publisher. Shasta Hunter, Circulation Manager. Tiffany Jaramillo, Classified Adv. Mgr.. **Editorial:** Hew Hallock, Editor. Michelle Boyd, Production Manager. Lloyd Engen, Sports Editor.

ASPEN

ASPEN DAILY NEWS. 517 E. Hopkins, Aspen, CO 81611. Telephone: 970-925-2220. FAX: 970-925-6397. E-MAIL: letters@aspendailynews.com. URL: http://www.aspendailynews.com. Mailing Address: PO Box DD, Aspen, CO 81612. Year Established: 1978. Pub. Frequency: d. Page Size: tabloid.Adv. Rate: col. inch $6.40 **Wire Service(s):** AP. Circulation: 13,000 morning (free). **Owner(s):** David Danforth, See address and contact information above. **Management:** David Cook, Publisher. Lynn Chaffier, Advertising Director. Kim Hood, Classified Adv. Mgr.. **Editorial:** Rick Carroll, Editor. Catherine Lutz, Managing Editor.

ASPEN TIMES, THE. 310 E. Main St., Aspen, CO 81611. Telephone: 970-925-3414. FAX: 970-925-6240. E-MAIL: mail@aspentimes.com. URL: http://www.aspentimes.com. Year Established: 1881. Pub. Frequency: d. (Mon.-Fri.) Page Size: tabloid. Subscrip. Rate: $32/yr out of town. **Wire Service(s):** AP. Circulation: 10,000 morning (paid and free). **Owner(s):** Swift Newspapers, Inc., 500 Double Eagle Ct., Reno, NV 89511. Telephone: 775-850-7676. FAX: 775-850-7677. **Management:** Jenna Weatherred, Publisher. Gunnilla Isreal, Advertising Manager. **Editorial:** Allyn Harney, Editor. Paul Conrad, Photographer. Bob Ward, Weekend Editor.

AVON

VAIL DAILY. 40780 US Hwy. 6 & 24, Avon, CO 81620. Telephone: 970-949-0555. FAX: 970-949-7096. E-MAIL: vaileditor@vaidaily.com. URL: http://www.vaildaily.com. Mailing Address: PO Box 81, Vail, CO 81658. Year Established: 1981. Pub. Frequency: d. Page Size: tabloid. Subscrip. Rate: $82 mailed for 6 mos. 1st class; $160/yr mailed. **Wire Service(s):** AP. Circulation: 13,111 morning (free); 12,030 Sunday (free). **Owner(s):** Swift Newspapers, Inc., 500 Double Eagle Ct., Reno, NV 89511. Telephone: 775-850-7676. **Management:** Steve Pope, Publisher. Andrea Palm-Porter, Advertising Manager. Mark Bircklin, Circulation Manager. **Editorial:** Andrea Palm-Porter, Editor. Ed Stoner, News Editor. Bret Hartman, Photo Editor.

BOULDER

DAILY CAMERA, THE. ISSN 0746-8733
1048 Pearl St., Boulder, CO 80302. Telephone: 303-442-1202. FAX: 303-449-9358. URL: http://www.dailycamera.com. Mailing Address: PO Box 591, Boulder, CO 80306. Year Established: 1891. Pub. Frequency: d. Page Size: broadsheet. Subscrip. Rate: $.50 newsstand/cover; $1 newsstand/cover Sun.; $32.50 home delivery for 13 weeks; $130/yr home delivery. **Wire Service(s):** AP, NYT, LAT-WAT. Circulation: 34,000 morning (paid); 41,037 Sunday (paid). **Owner(s):** E.W. Scripps Co., 312 Walnut St., 28th Fl., Cincinnati, OH 45202. Telephone: 513-977-3000. FAX: 513-977-3768. **Management:** Gregory Anderson, Publisher. **Editorial:** Sue Deans, Editor. Clay Evans, Associate Editor. Michael Cote, Business Editor. Kevin Kaufman, City Editor. Steve Millard, Editorial Page Editor. Greg Glasgow, Entertainment Editor. Cindy Sutter, Feature Editor. Carol Taylor, Librarian. Paul Aiken, Photo Editor. Gary Baines, Sports Editor.

CANON CITY

CANON CITY DAILY RECORD. ISSN 1054-3457
701 S. Ninth St., Canon City, CO 81212. Telephone: 719-275-7565. FAX: 719-275-1353. URL: http://www.canoncitydailyrecord.com. Year Established: 1896. Pub. Frequency: d. (Mon.-Sat.) Page Size: broadsheet. Subscrip. Rate: $.50 newsstand/cover; $7.50 carrier delivery/mo. in city; $8 motor route/mo.; $12 mailed/mo.. **Wire Service(s):** AP. Circulation: 8,120 evening (paid). **Owner(s):** Lehman Communications Corp., See address and contact information above. **Management:** Terry Cochran, General Manager. Dean Lehman, President. Ed Lehman, Publisher. Anita Kroh, Advertising Manager. Melissa Woolsey, Circulation Manager. Dolly Dempsey, Classified Adv. Mgr.. **Editorial:** Lee Spaulding, Editor. Michael Alcala, City Editor. Charlotte Burrous, Community Editor.

COLORADO SPRINGS

GAZETTE (COLORADO SPRINGS), THE. 30 S. Prospect St., Colorado Springs, CO 80903. Telephone: 719-632-5511. FAX: 719-636-0202. E-MAIL: editor@gazette.com. URL: http://www.gazette.com. Mailing Address: PO Box 1779, Colorado Springs, CO 80901. Year Established: 1872. Pub. Frequency: d. Page Size: broadsheet. Subscrip. Rate: $.75 newsstand/cover; $1.50 newsstand/cover Sun.. **Wire Service(s):** AP, SH, MCT. Circulation: 95,000 morning (paid); 100,000 Sunday (paid). **Owner(s):** Freedom Communications, Inc., 17666 Fitch, Irvine, CA 92614. Telephone: 714-553-9292. **Management:** Steven Pope, Publisher. Stuart Wong, Photography Director. **Editorial:** Jeff Thomas, Editor. Larry Ryckman, Managing Editor. Wayne Laugesen, Editorial Page Editor.

CRAIG

CRAIG DAILY PRESS. 466 Yampa Ave., Craig, CO 81625. Telephone: 970-824-7031. FAX: 970-824-6810. Mailing Address: PO Box 5, Craig, CO 81626. Year Established: 1965. Pub. Frequency: d. (Mon.-Sat.) Page Size: tabloid. Subscrip. Rate: $7.50 home delivery/mo.. **Wire Service(s):** AP. Circulation: 3,250 morning (free). **Owner(s):** WorldWest LLC, 609 New Hampshire, P.O. Box 688, Lawrence, KS 66044. Telephone: 785-843-1000. **Management:** Bryce Jacobson, Publisher. Renee Campbell, Advertising Manager. Amy Fontenot, Circulation Manager. **Editorial:** Jennifer Grubbs, Managing Editor. Melaney McDaniels, Sports Editor.

DENVER

DENVER POST. ISSN 1930-2193
101 W Colfax Ave, Ste 1100, Denver, CO 80202. FAX: 303-954-6320. E-MAIL: newsroom@denverpost.com. URL: http://www.denverpost.com. Year Established: 1895. Pub. Frequency: d. Page Size: broadsheet. Subscrip. Rate: $.25 newsstand/cover; $1 newsstand/cover Sun.; $7.25 home delivery/mo.. **Wire Service(s):** AP, UPI, NYT, LAT-WAT, MCT, DJNS. Circulation: 413,730 morning (paid); 558,560 Sunday (paid). **Owner(s):** MediaNews Group, Inc., See address and contact information above. **Management:** William Dean Singleton, Publisher. Judd Alvord, Circulation Manager. **Editorial:** Greg Moore, Editor-in-Chief. Don Knox, Business Editor. Frank Scandale, City Editor. Judith Howard, Feature Editor. Charles Meyers, Outdoor Editor. Joanne Davidson, Society Editor. Charles Meyers, Sports Editor.

DURANGO

DURANGO HERALD. 1275 Main Ave., Durango, CO 81301. Telephone: 970-247-3504. FAX: 970-259-5011. E-MAIL: herald@durangoherald.com. URL: http://www.durangoherald.com. Mailing Address: PO Drawer A, Durango, CO 81302. Year Established: 1881. Pub. Frequency: d. Page Size: broadsheet. Subscrip. Rate: $.50 newsstand/cover; $1 newsstand/cover Sun.; $25 mailed/mo. in state; $30 mailed/mo. out of state. **Wire Service(s):** AP. Circulation: 10,000 morning (paid); 10,672 Sunday (paid). **Owner(s):** Morley C. Ballentine, See address and contact information above. **Management:** Sharon Harmes, General Manager. Morley C Ballantine, President. Richard G Ballantine, Publisher. Dennis Hanson, Advertising Director. **Editorial:** Morley C Ballantine, Editor. David Buck, Managing Editor. Dale Strode, Sports Editor.

FORT COLLINS

FORT COLLINS COLORADOAN. ISSN 0164-9167
1212 Riverside Ave., Fort Collins, CO 80524. Telephone: 970-224-7730. FAX: 970-224-7899. E-MAIL: news@coloradoan.com. URL: http://www.coloradoan.com. Mailing Address: PO Box 1577, Fort Collins, CO 80522. Year Established: 1873. Pub. Frequency: d. Page Size: broadsheet. Subscrip. Rate: $.50 newsstand/cover; $1 newsstand/cover Sun.; $47.60 carrier delivery for 17 weeks. **Wire Service(s):** AP, LAT-WAT, GNS. Circulation: 29,004 morning (paid); 35,893 Sunday (paid). **Owner(s):** Gannett Company, Inc., 7950 Jones Branch Dr, McLean, VA 22107. Telephone: 703-854-6000. **Management:** Dorothy Bland, President. Dan Walker, Advertising Director. T. Mark McFann, Circulation Manager. Lisa Barclay, Marketing Director. Richard Haro, Photography Director. **Editorial:** David W. Greiling, Executive Editor. Bob Baun, Business Editor. Kathleen Duff, Editorial Page Editor. Maggie Hall Walsh, Lifestyle Editor. Jeff Eisele, News Editor.

FORT MORGAN

FORT MORGAN TIMES, THE. 329 Main St., Fort Morgan, CO 80701-4000. Telephone: 970-867-5651. FAX: 970-867-7448. E-MAIL: fmtimes@fmtimes.com. URL: http://www.fortmorgantimes.com. Mailing Address: PO Box 4000, Fort Morgan, CO 80701-4000. Year Established: 1884. Pub. Frequency: d. (Mon.-Sat.) Page Size: broadsheet. Subscrip. Rate: $.50 newsstand/cover; $108/yr in county; $130/yr out of county. Adv. Rate: col. inch $9.25 **Wire Service(s):** AP. Circulation: 4,390 evening (paid). **Owner(s):** MediaNews Group, Inc., 101 W Colfax Ave, Ste 1100, Denver, CO 80202. FAX: 303-954-6320. **Management:** William Holland, Publisher. Theresa Leake, Advertising Manager. **Editorial:** Wayne Wacker, Production Manager. Anthony Besetti, Business Editor. Bill Spencer, City Editor. John LaPorte, News Editor. Rich Headley, Sports Editor.

FRISCO

SUMMIT DAILY NEWS. 40 W. Main St., Frisco, CO 80443. Telephone: 970-668-3998. FAX: 970-668-3859. URL: http://www.summitdaily.com. Mailing Address: PO Box 329, Frisco, CO 80443. Year Established: 1989. Pub. Frequency: d. Page Size: tabloid. Subscrip. Rate: $3.50 mailed Sun. for 12 wks.. **Wire Service(s):** AP. Circulation: 10,500 morning (free). **Owner(s):** Swift Newspapers, Inc., 500 Double Eagle Ct., Reno, NV 89511. **Management:** James Morgan, Publisher. David Mercier, Advertising Director. Ed Pankevicius, Circulation Manager. **Editorial:** Jim Pokrandt, Editor. Ryan Slaybaugh, News Editor. Brad Odekirk, Photo Editor. Jason Starr, Sports Editor.

Dailies

GLENWOOD SPRINGS

GLENWOOD SPRINGS POST INDEPENDENT. 2014 Grand Ave., Glenwood Springs, CO 81601. Telephone: 970-945-8515. FAX: 970-945-8518. E-MAIL: glenpost@sopris.net. URL: http://www.postindependent.com. Mailing Address: PO Box 550, Glenwood Springs, CO 81602. Year Established: 1890. Pub. Frequency: d. (Sun.-Fri.) Page Size: tabloid. Subscrip. Rate: $85/yr home delivery in county; $142/yr mailed in county; $150/yr mailed elsewhere. **Wire Service(s):** AP. Circulation: 5,600 morning (paid and free). **Owner(s):** Swift Newspapers, Inc., 500 Double Eagle Ct., Reno, NV 89511. Telephone: 775-850-7676. FAX: 775-850-7677. **Management:** Michael Bennett, Publisher. Mark Michaud, Advertising Director. Jenny Peterson, Circulation Manager. Christine Holaday-Schriok, Classified Adv. Mgr.. Michelle Wurtsmith, Business Manager. **Editorial:** Heather McGregor, Managing Editor. Patti Bentley, Production Manager. Sean Kelly, Sports.

GRAND JUNCTION

DAILY SENTINEL (GRAND JUNCTION), THE. 734 S. Seventh St., Grand Junction, CO 81501-7786. Telephone: 970-242-5050. FAX: 970-241-6860. URL: http://www.gjsentinel.com. Mailing Address: PO Box 668, Grand Junction, CO 81502. Year Established: 1893. Pub. Frequency: d. Page Size: broadsheet. Subscrip. Rate: $.50 newsstand/cover; $1 newsstand/cover Sun.; $117/yr home delivery; $260/yr mailed. **Wire Service(s):** AP, SH, NYT, LAT-WAT. Circulation: 34,000 morning (paid); 36,000 Sunday (paid). **Owner(s):** Cox Newspapers, Inc., 6205 Peachtree Dunwoody Rd, Atlanta, GA 30328. Telephone: 404-843-5000. **Management:** George Orbanek, President. Dennis Mitchell, Advertising Director. Tracy McClaskey, Circulation Manager. Robert Fowler, Sales Manager. **Editorial:** Dennis Herzog, Managing Editor. Dave Haynes, City Editor. Bob Silbernagel, Editorial Page Editor. Todd Powell, Feature Editor. Brian Harvey, News Editor. Christopher Tomlinson, Photographer. Patti Arnold, Sports.

GRAND JUNCTION FREE PRESS. 145 N 4th St, Grand Junction, CO 81501. Telephone: 970-243-2200. FAX: 970-243-4224. URL: http://www.gjfreepress.com. Pub. Frequency: d. (Mon.-Fri.) Subscrip. Rate: $52/yr home delivery. **Owner(s):** Swift Newspapers, Inc., 500 Double Eagle Ct., Reno, NV 89511. Telephone: 775-850-7676. FAX: 775-850-7677. **Management:** Michael Bennett, Publisher. **Editorial:** Josh Nichols, Managing Editor.

GREELEY

GREELEY TRIBUNE. 501 8th Ave, Greeley, CO 80632. Telephone: 970-352-0211. FAX: 970-352-4059. E-MAIL: perkins@greeleytrib.com. URL: http://www.greeleytrib.com. Mailing Address: PO Box 1690, Greeley, CO 80632. Year Established: 1870. Pub. Frequency: d. Page Size: broadsheet. Subscrip. Rate: $8.50 home delivery/mo. local; $9.75 mailed/mo. in county; $16.25 mailed/mo. out of county. Freelance Pay: $1.15/column-inch. **Wire Service(s):** AP, LAT-WAT. Circulation: 25,374 evening (paid); 25,582 Sunday (paid). **Owner(s):** Swift Newspapers, Inc., 500 Double Eagle Ct., Reno, NV 89511. Telephone: 775-850-7676. FAX: 775-850-7677. **Management:** Bart Smith, Publisher. Stephanie Schafer, Advertising Director. **Editorial:** Randy Bangert, Editor. Nate Miller, Sports Editor.

WINDSOR TRIBUNE. 501 8th Ave, Greeley, CO 80632. Telephone: 970-352-0211. URL: http://www.windsortribune.com. Year Established: 2002. Pub. Frequency: d. Subscrip. Rate: $27.90/yr home delivery. **Owner(s):** Swift Newspapers, Inc., 500 Double Eagle Ct., Reno, NV 89511. Telephone: 775-850-7676. FAX: 775-850-7677. **Management:** Chris Cobler, Publisher. **Editorial:** Randy Bangert, Editor.

LA JUNTA

LAJUNTA TRIBUNE-DEMOCRAT. ISSN 1056-4616
422 Colorado, La Junta, CO 81050. Telephone: 719-384-4475. FAX: 719-384-5999. E-MAIL: mail@ljtd.com. URL: http://www.lajuntatribunedemocrat.com. Mailing Address: PO Box 480, La Junta, CO 81050-0480. Year Established: 1897. Pub. Frequency: d. (Mon.-Fri.) Page Size: tabloid. Subscrip. Rate: $.50 newsstand/cover; $75/yr carrier delivery in city; $118/yr carrier delivery out of area. Circulation: 4,000 evening (paid). **Owner(s):** GateHouse Media, Inc, 350 WillowBrook Office Park, Fairport, NY 14450. Telephone: 585-598-0030. FAX: 585-248-2631. **Management:** Pat Ptolemy, Publisher. Jessica Peck, Circulation Manager. Angela Hardy, Classified Adv. Mgr.. **Editorial:** Candi Miell, Editor.

LAMAR

LAMAR DAILY NEWS. 310 S Fifth St, Lamar, CO 81052. Telephone: 719-336-2266. FAX: 719-336-2526. E-MAIL: ldnews@ria.net. Mailing Address: PO Box 1217, Lamar, CO 81052. Year Established: 1907. Pub. Frequency: d. (Mon.-Fri.) Page Size: broadsheet. Subscrip. Rate: $.50 newsstand/cover; $84/yr home delivery local. **Wire Service(s):** AP. Circulation: 2,800 evening (paid). **Owner(s):** MediaNews Group, Inc., 101 W Colfax Ave, Ste 1100, Denver, CO 80202. FAX: 303-954-6320. **Management:** Brenda Brown, Publisher. Debbie Wilson, Circulation Manager. **Editorial:** Cindy Burton, Editor.

LONGMONT

DAILY TIMES-CALL. 350 Terry St., Longmont, CO 80501. Telephone: 303-776-2244. FAX: 303-678-8615. E-MAIL: news@times-call.com. URL: http://www.longmontfyi.com. Mailing Address: PO Box 299, Longmont, CO 80502-0299. Year Established: 1871. Pub. Frequency: d. Page Size: broadsheet. Subscrip. Rate: $.50 newsstand/cover; $1 newsstand/cover Sun.; $9.81 home delivery/mo.; $18 mailed/mo.. **Wire Service(s):** AP, LAT-WAT. Circulation: 20,938 evening (paid); 22,623 Sunday (paid). **Owner(s):** Times-Call Publishing Corp., See address and contact information above. **Management:** Edward Lehman, Publisher. Penny Dille, Advertising Director. Mary KinCannon, Advertising Manager. Kathy Pias, Circulation Manager. Andrea Willett, Classified Adv. Mgr.. **Editorial:** Dean G. Lehman, Editor. John Vahlenkamp, Managing Editor. Tony Kindelspire, Business Editor. K.J. Ritter, News Editor. Michael Kelly, Sports Editor.

LOVELAND

LOVELAND DAILY REPORTER-HERALD. 201 E. Fifth St., Loveland, CO 80537. Telephone: 970-669-5050. FAX: 970-667-1111. E-MAIL: news@reporter-herald.com. URL: http://www.reporterherald.com. Mailing Address: PO Box 59, Loveland, CO 80539-0059. Year Established: 1880. Pub. Frequency: d. Page Size: broadsheet. Subscrip. Rate: $.50 newsstand/cover; $1 newsstand/cover Sun.; $9.85 carrier delivery/mo.; $18 mailed/mo.. **Wire Service(s):** AP, LAT-WAT. Circulation: 18,000 morning (paid); 18,500 Sunday (paid). **Owner(s):** Loveland Publishing Co., See address and contact information above. **Management:** Dean Lehman, President. Edward Lehman, Publisher. Terry Emler, Advertising Director. Jenny Sparks, Photography Director. **Editorial:** Christine Kapperman, Managing Editor. Phyllis Walbye, Entertainment Editor.

MONTROSE

MONTROSE DAILY PRESS. 535 S. First St., Montrose, CO 81401. Telephone: 970-249-3444. FAX: 970-249-3331. E-MAIL: editor@montrosepress.com. URL: http://www.montrosepress.com. Mailing Address: PO Box 850, Montrose, CO 81402. Year Established: 1908. Pub. Frequency: d. (Sun.-Fri.) Page Size: broadsheet. Subscrip. Rate: $.50 newsstand/cover; $1 newsstand/cover Sun.; $96/yr home delivery in state; $175.50/yr mailed in state; $199.50/yr mailed out of state. Freelance Pay: $1/column-inch. **Wire Service(s):** AP. Circulation: 7,000 evening (paid). **Owner(s):** Wick Communications, Inc., 333 W. Wilcox Dr., Ste. 302, Sierra Vista, AZ 85635. Telephone: 928-458-0200. FAX: 928-458-6166. **Management:** Steven Woody, Publisher. Tim Frates, Advertising Manager. **Editorial:** Bill Swaim, Managing Editor. Elaine Hale-Jones, Lifestyle Editor. Katharhynn Heidenberg, News Editor. Johathan Maness, Sports.

PUEBLO

PUEBLO CHIEFTAIN. ISSN 0747-3559
825 W. Sixth St., Pueblo, CO 81003-4040. Telephone: 719-544-3520, 800-279-6397. FAX: 719-595-4334. E-MAIL: pueblo@chieftain.com. URL: http://www.chieftain.com. Mailing Address: PO Box 4040, Pueblo, CO 81003. Year Established: 1868. Pub. Frequency: d. Page Size: broadsheet. Subscrip. Rate: $.25 newsstand/cover; $.75 newsstand/cover Sun.; $9.95 carrier delivery/mo.; $119.40/yr carrier delivery; $183/yr mailed. Freelance Pay: $0.50/column-inch. **Wire Service(s):** AP. Circulation: 53,250 morning (paid); 55,000 Sunday (paid). **Owner(s):** Star Journal Publishing Corp., Inc., See address and contact information above. **Management:** Marvin Laut, General Manager. Robert H. Rawlings, Publisher. Lou Braden, Advertising Manager. Matt Butorac, Circulation Manager. Robert Hudson, Classified Adv. Mgr.. **Editorial:** Robert H. Rawlings, Editor-in-Chief. Steve Henson, Managing Editor. John Norton, Business Editor. Larry Lopez, News Editor.

ROCKY FORD

ROCKY FORD DAILY GAZETTE. 912 Elm Ave., Rocky Ford, CO 81067. Telephone: 719-254-3351. FAX: 719-254-3354. E-MAIL: news@rockyforddailygazette.com. URL: http://www.rockyforddailygazette.com. Mailing Address: PO Box 430, Rocky Ford, CO 81067-0430. Year Established: 1907. Pub. Frequency: d. (Mon.-Fri.) Page Size: broadsheet. Subscrip. Rate: $.50 newsstand/cover; $75/yr carrier delivery; $100/yr mailed. Circulation: 3,200 evening (paid). **Owner(s):** Rocky Ford Publishing Co., See address and contact information above. **Management:** J.R. Thompson, General Manager. Laura Thompson, Advertising Manager. Pamela Griego, Circulation Manager. Toby Jaramillo, Classified Adv. Mgr..

SALIDA

MOUNTAIN MAIL, THE. 125 E. Second St., Salida, CO 81201. Telephone: 719-539-6691. FAX: 719-539-6630. E-MAIL: mtnmail@rmii.com. URL: http://www.themountainmail.com. Mailing Address: PO Box 189, Salida, CO 81201-0189. Year Established: 1880. Pub. Frequency: d. (Mon.-Fri.) Page Size: tabloid. Subscrip. Rate: $.75 newsstand/cover; $57/yr home delivery; $46/yr home delivery to senior citizens. Freelance Pay: $0.65/column-inch. Circulation: 3,500 morning (paid). **Owner(s):** Arkansas Valley Publishing, See address and contact information above. **Management:** Merle Baranczyk, Publisher. Vickie Vigil, Advertising Director. Sandra Christensen, Circulation Manager. Annette Appel, Classified Adv. Mgr.. **Editorial:** Merle Baranczyk, Editor-in-Chief. Christopher Kolomitz, Managing Editor. Paul Goetz, News Editor. Denise Ronald, Sports.

STEAMBOAT SPRINGS

STEAMBOAT TODAY. 1901 Curve Plz., Steamboat Springs, CO 80477. Telephone: 970-879-1502. FAX: 970-879-2888. E-MAIL: editor@steamboatpilot.com. URL: http://www.steamboatpilot.com. Mailing Address: PO Box 4827, Steamboat Springs, CO 80477. Year Established: 1989. Pub. Frequency: d. (Mon.-Sat.) Page Size: tabloid **Wire Service(s):** AP. Circulation: 9,500 morning (free). **Owner(s):** WorldWest LLC, 609 New Hampshire, P.O. Box 688, Lawrence, KS 66044. Telephone: 785-843-1000. **Management:** Suzanne Schlicht, General Manager. Bryna Larsen, Publisher. Laura Soard, Classified Adv. Mgr.. **Editorial:** Scott Stanford, Editor. Melissa Roddy, City Editor.

STERLING

STERLING JOURNAL-ADVOCATE. 504 N Third St, Sterling, CO 80751. Telephone: 970-522-1990. FAX: 970-522-2320. E-MAIL: sjournal@ria.net. URL: http://www.journal-advocate.com. Mailing Address: P O Box 1272, Sterling, CO 80751. Year Established: 1885. Pub. Frequency: d. (Mon.-Sat.) Page Size: broadsheet. Subscrip. Rate: $.50 newsstand/cover; $78/yr carrier delivery; $87.25/yr motor route; $87.25/yr mailed in county; $116/yr mailed out of county. **Wire Service(s):** AP. Circulation: 5,300 evening (paid). **Owner(s):** MediaNews Group, Inc., 101 W Colfax Ave, Ste 1100, Denver, CO 80202. FAX: 303-954-6320. **Management:** David McClain, Publisher. Sharon Freidlander, Advertising Director. Deb McFarland, Circulation Manager. **Editorial:** Forrest Hershberger, Editor.

TELLURIDE

TELLURIDE DAILY PLANET. 307 E Colorado St, Telluride, CO 81435. Telephone: 970-728-9788. FAX: 970-728-9793. E-MAIL: editor@telluridenews.com. URL: http://www.telluridegateway.com. Year Established: 1993. Pub. Frequency: d. (Mon.-Fri.) Page Size: tabloid. Subscrip. Rate: $60/yr Fri. only. Adv. Rate: col. inch $9.50 Circulation: 6,500 morning (paid and free). **Owner(s):** GateHouse Media, Inc, 350 WillowBrook Office Park, Fairport, NY 14450. FAX: 585-248-2631. **Management:** Gary Dickson, Publisher. John Dourlet, Advertising Manager. Cheryl Thornton, Classified Adv. Mgr.. **Editorial:** Matt Beaudin, Editor. Contact: Andrew Wynne, Advertising.

TRINIDAD

CHRONICLE NEWS, THE. 200 W. Church St., Trinidad, CO 81082. Telephone: 719-846-3311. FAX: 719-846-3612. Mailing Address: PO Box 763, Trinidad, CO 81082. Year Established: 1876. Pub. Frequency: d. (Mon.-Fri.) Page Size: broadsheet. Subscrip. Rate: $.50 newsstand/cover; $60/yr home delivery in town; $84/yr home delivery out of town. Freelance Pay: $0.50/column-inch. **Wire Service(s):** AP. Circulation: 4,000 morning (paid). **Owner(s):** Lake Charles American Press, 327 Board St., Lake Charles, LA 70601. Telephone: 318-439-2781. **Management:** Thomas B Sherman III, President. Aileen Hood, Publisher. Sheila Hamlin, Production Director.

CONNECTICUT

BRIDGEPORT

CONNECTICUT POST. ISSN 1070-874X
410 State St, Bridgeport, CT 06604. Telephone: 203-333-0161. FAX: 203-367-8158. E-MAIL: edit@snet.net. URL: http://www.connpost.com. Year Established: 1883. Pub. Frequency: d. Page Size: broadsheet. Subscrip. Rate: $.50 newsstand/cover; $1.75 newsstand/cover Sun.; $4.50 home delivery/wk.; $234/yr home delivery. **Wire Service(s):** AP, UPI, MCT. Circulation: 77,000 morning (paid); 93,000 Sunday (paid). **Owner(s):** MediaNews Group, Inc., 101 W Colfax Ave, Ste 1100, Denver, CO 80202. FAX: 303-954-6320. **Management:** Robert Laska, Publisher. Brenda McDonald, Advertising Director. John Treutt, Circulation Director. **Editorial:** James Smith, Editor. Michael Daly, Managing Editor.

BRISTOL

BRISTOL PRESS, THE. ISSN 0891-5563
188 Main St., Bristol, CT 06010. Telephone: 860-584-0501. FAX: 860-585-9283. E-MAIL: editor@bristolpress.com. URL: http://www.bristolpress.com. Mailing Address: PO Box 2158, Bristol, CT 06011-2158. Year Established: 1871. Pub. Frequency: d. Page Size: broadsheet. Subscrip. Rate: $.50 newsstand/cover; $1.25 newsstand/cover Sun.; $46.80 home delivery for 3 mos.; $187.20/yr home delivery; $273/yr mailed. **Wire Service(s):** AP. Circulation: 12,091 evening (paid); 29,539 Sunday (paid). **Owner(s):** Journal Register Co., 50 W State St, 12th Fl, Trenton, NJ 08608. Telephone: 609-396-2200. **Management:** William E. Sheedy Jr., Publisher. Nancy Frede, Advertising Director. John Moise, Circulation Director. **Editorial:** William Sarno, Editor. Rob Connors, Sports Editor.

DANBURY

NEWS-TIMES, THE. ISSN 1044-4106
333 Main St, Danbury, CT 06810. Telephone: 203-744-5100. FAX: 203-792-8730. URL: http://www.newstimes.com. Year Established: 1883. Pub. Frequency: d. Page Size: broadsheet. Subscrip. Rate: $.50 newsstand/cover; $1.75 newsstand/cover Sun.; $199.50/yr home delivery in area. Adv. Rate: col. inch $21.54 **Wire Service(s):** AP, MCT. Circulation: 38,000 morning (paid); 43,600 Sunday (paid). **Owner(s):** MediaNews Group, Inc., 101 W Colfax Ave, Ste 1100, Denver, CO 80202. FAX: 303-954-6320. **Management:** John Brosz, Executive Director. John Dunster, Publisher. **Editorial:** Art Cummings, Editor.

GREENWICH

GREENWICH TIME. ISSN 0279-5213
20 E. Elm St., Greenwich, CT 06830. Telephone: 203-625-4400. FAX: 203-625-4419. URL: http://www.greenwichtime.com. Year Established: 1861. Pub. Frequency: d. Page Size: broadsheet. Subscrip. Rate: $.50 newsstand/cover; $1.50 newsstand/cover Sun.; $58.50 home delivery for 13 wks.; $85.80 mailed for 13 wks.. **Wire Service(s):** AP, LAT-WAT, MCT. Circulation: 13,000 evening (paid); 14,000 Sunday (paid). **Owner(s):** Tribune Company, 435 N Michigan Ave, Chicago, IL 60601. Telephone: 312.222.9100. **Management:** Durham Monsma, Publisher. Eileen Zaccagnino, Advertising Director. Bob Dance, Circulation Manager. Cindy Ross, Classified Adv. Mgr.. **Editorial:** Joseph F. Pisani, Editor. Bruce Hunter, Managing Editor. Jim Wolfe, Feature Editor. Mel Greer, Photographer.

MANCHESTER

JOURNAL INQUIRER. 306 Progress Dr., Manchester, CT 06040. Telephone: 860-643-8111. FAX: 860-643-1180. E-MAIL: news@journalinquirer.com. URL: http://www.journalinquirer.com. Mailing Address: PO Box 510, Manchester, CT 06045-0510. Year Established: 1968. Pub. Frequency: d. (Mon.-Sat.) Page Size: tabloid. Subscrip. Rate: $.50 newsstand/cover; $1 newsstand/cover Sat.; $140.40/yr carrier delivery. **Wire Service(s):** AP. Circulation: 44,000 evening (paid). **Owner(s):** Elizabeth S. Ellis, See address and contact information above. **Management:** Elizabeth S. Ellis, Publisher. Bill Sybert, Classified Adv. Mgr.. **Editorial:** Chris Powell, Managing Editor. Chris Dehnel, Business Editor. Keith Burris, Editorial Page Editor. Richard Tambling, Feature Editor. Ralph Williams, News Editor. Brian Coyne, Sports Editor.

MERIDEN

RECORD-JOURNAL. 11 Crown St., Meriden, CT 06450-5788. Telephone: 203-235-1661. FAX: 203-639-0210. E-MAIL: newsroom@record-journal.com. URL: http://www.record-journal.com. Mailing Address: PO Box 915, Meriden, CT 06450-5788. Year Established: 1867. Pub. Frequency: d. Page Size: broadsheet. Subscrip. Rate: $.75 newsstand/cover; $1.75 newsstand/cover Sun.; $5.25 home delivery/wk.; $273/yr mailed. **Wire Service(s):** AP, NYT. Circulation: 21,500 morning (paid); 22,000 Sunday (paid). **Owner(s):** Record-Journal Publishing Co., 11 Crown St., Meriden, CT 06450. Telephone: 203-235-1661. **Management:** Michael F Killian, General Manager. Eliot C. White, Publisher. Brian Monroe, Advertising Manager. **Editorial:** Ralph Tomaselli, Managing Editor.

MIDDLETOWN

MIDDLETOWN PRESS. 2 Main St., Middletown, CT 06457. Telephone: 860-347-3331. FAX: 860-347-3380. E-MAIL: editor@middletownpress.com. URL: http://www.middletownpress.com. Year Established: 1884. Pub. Frequency: d. Page Size: standard. Subscrip. Rate: $.50 newsstand/cover; $1 newsstand/cover Sun.; $3.50 home delivery in county wk for13 wks.. **Wire Service(s):** AP, NYT. Circulation: 12,360 morning (paid). **Owner(s):** Journal Register Co., 50 W State St, 12th Fl, Trenton, NJ 08608. Telephone: 609-396-2200. **Management:** Marc Romanow, Publisher. Susan Hyde, Advertising Manager. Larry Marciano, Circulation Manager. **Editorial:** Alice Clayton, Editor. Cassandra Day, Feature Editor. Paul Nichols, Sports Editor.

NEW BRITAIN

HERALD (NEW BRITAIN), THE. One Herald Sq., New Britain, CT 06050-2050. Telephone: 860-225-4601. FAX: 860-225-2601. E-MAIL: nbnews@etcentrol.com. URL: http://www.newbritainherald.com. Year Established: 1880. Pub. Frequency: d. Page Size: broadsheet. Subscrip. Rate: $.50 newsstand/cover; $1.25 newsstand/cover Sun.; $187.20/yr home delivery; $317.20/yr mailed. **Wire Service(s):** AP. Circulation: 34,000 evening (paid). **Owner(s):** Journal Register Co., 50 W State St, 12th Fl, Trenton, NJ 08608. Telephone: 609-396-2200. **Management:** Chris Chamberlain, Publisher. Bryan Canto, Advertising Director. Joseph Jr. Cannata, Circulation Director. **Editorial:** Brian Straight, Managing Editor. Lin Noble, News Editor. Jeremy Dominick, Sports Editor.

NEW HAVEN

NEW HAVEN REGISTER. 40 Sargent Dr., New Haven, CT 06511. Telephone: 203-789-5200. FAX: 203-865-7894. E-MAIL: news@nhregister.com. URL: http://www.newhavenregister.com. Year Established: 1812. Pub. Frequency: d. Page Size: broadsheet. Subscrip. Rate: $.50 newsstand/cover; $1.75 newsstand/cover Sun.; $68.25 home delivery for 13 wks.; $248/yr home delivery; $130 mailed for 13 wks.; $520/yr mailed. Freelance Pay: $15-$90/story. **Wire Service(s):** AP, LAT-WAT, MCT. Circulation: 100,410 morning (paid); 120,109 Sunday (paid). **Owner(s):** Journal Register Co., 50 W State St, 12th Fl, Trenton, NJ 08608. Telephone: 609-396-2200. **Bureau(s):** 58 River St., Milford, CT 06460. Telephone: 203-877-5168. **Management:** Kevin Walsh, Publisher. Dan Graziano, Advertising Director. Steve Earley, Circulation Manager. **Editorial:** Jack Kramer, Editor. Matt Pepin, Sports Editor.

NEW LONDON

DAY (NEW LONDON), THE. ISSN 0744-0499
47 Eugene O'Neil Dr, New London, CT 06320. Telephone: 800-542-3354. FAX: 860-447-1683. E-MAIL: g.farrugia@theday.com. URL: http://www.theday.com. Mailing Address: PO Box 1231, New London, CT 06320-1231. Year Established: 1881. Pub. Frequency: d. Page Size: broadsheet. Subscrip. Rate: $.50 newsstand/cover; $1.50 newsstand/cover Sun.; $192.92/yr home delivery. Freelance Pay: $25-$50/article. **Wire Service(s):** AP, NYT. Circulation: 100,410 morning (paid). **Owner(s):** The Day Publishing Co., See address and contact information above. **Bureau(s):** 457 W. Main St., Norwich, CT 06360. Telephone: 860-886-6883. **Management:** Gary Farrugia, Publisher. Shawn Palmer, Advertising Manager. Mark L. Barry, Circulation Director. **Editorial:** Gary Farrugia, Editor. Lance Johnson, Managing Editor. Morgan McGinley, Editorial Page Editor. Chuck Banning, Sports Editor.

NORWALK

HOUR, THE. 346 Main Ave., Norwalk, CT 06851. Telephone: 203-846-3281. FAX: 203-846-9897. URL: http://www.thehour.com. Mailing Address: PO Box 790, Norwalk, CT 06852-0790. Year Established: 1871. Pub. Frequency: d. Page Size: broadsheet. Subscrip. Rate: $.50 newsstand/cover; $1 newsstand/cover Sun.; $4 home delivery/wk.; $192/yr home delivery. **Wire Service(s):** AP, MCT. Circulation: 21,500 morning (paid). **Owner(s):** Estate of Nellie Thomas, See address and contact information above. **Management:** Chet Valiante, Publisher. Debra Hanson, Advertising Director. Mark Koch, Circulation Director. Nicole Mendoza, Circulation Manager. Linda Guckert, Classified Adv. Mgr.. **Editorial:** Donna Bertoli, Editor. David Lampe-Wilson, Feature Editor. Marty Auturoi, News Editor. Matt Doran, Sports Editor.

NORWALK REFLECTOR. ISSN 0745-4023
61 E. Monroe St., Norwalk, CT 44857. Telephone: 419-668-3771. FAX: 419-668-2424. E-MAIL: news@goreflector.com. URL: http://www.norwalkreflector.com. Year Established: 1830. Pub. Frequency: d. (Mon.-Sat.) Page Size: broadsheet. Subscrip. Rate: $.50 newsstand/cover; $109.20/yr carrier delivery; $120/yr mailed in county; $160/yr mailed out of county. Adv. Rate: col. inch $11.38 **Wire Service(s):** AP. Circulation: 9,100 morning (paid). **Owner(s):** Reflector Herald Inc., PO Box 71, Norwalk, OH 44857. **Management:** David A. Rau, President. Steve Trosley, Publisher. John Ringenberg, Advertising Director. Carol McLaughlin, Circulation Manager. Anne Seaman, Classified Adv. Mgr.. **Editorial:** Joe Centers, Editor. Matt Roche, News Editor. Peter Reda Lou, Photographer.

Dailies

NORWICH

NORWICH BULLETIN. 66 Franklin St, Norwich, CT 06360. Telephone: 860-887-9211. FAX: 860-887-9666. E-MAIL: news@norwichbulletin.com. URL: http://www.norwichbulletin.com. Year Established: 1791. Pub. Frequency: d. Page Size: broadsheet. Subscrip. Rate: $.75 newsstand/cover; $1.25 newsstand/cover Sun.. **Wire Service(s):** AP, GNS. Circulation: 32,000 morning (paid); 36,000 Sunday (paid). **Owner(s):** GateHouse Media, Inc, See address and contact information above. **Management:** Ellen Lind, Owner. Paul Provost, Advertising Director. Obuse E Iweriebor, Circulation Director. **Editorial:** Stuart Shinske, Editor. Jim Konrad, Executive Editor. Adam Bowles, City Editor. Khoy Ton, Photo Editor. Marc Allard, Sports.

STAMFORD

ADVOCATE (STAMFORD), THE. ISSN 0279-5167
75 Tresser Blvd., Stamford, CT 06904-9307. Telephone: 203-964-2200. FAX: 203-964-2345. E-MAIL: letters.advocate@scni.com. URL: http://www.stamfordadvocate.com. Mailing Address: PO Box 9307, Stamford, CT 06904-9307. Year Established: 1829. Pub. Frequency: d. Page Size: broadsheet. Subscrip. Rate: $.50 newsstand/cover; $1.50 newsstand/cover Sun.; $2.79 home delivery/wk. local. **Wire Service(s):** AP. Circulation: 128,316 morning (paid). **Owner(s):** Tribune Company, 435 N Michigan Ave, Chicago, IL 60601. Telephone: 312.222.9100. **Management:** Durham Monsma, Publisher. Cindy Ross, Advertising Director. Craig Allen, Circulation Director. Tim Stanton, Classified Adv. Mgr.. **Editorial:** Joseph Pisani, Editor. Joy Haenlein, Editorial Page Editor. Valerie Foster, Feature Editor. Terri Vanech, Lifestyle Editor. Robert Kennedy, Sports Editor.

TORRINGTON

REGISTER CITIZEN. ISSN 0746-8180
190 Water St., Torrington, CT 06790-0058. Telephone: 860-489-3121. FAX: 860-489-6790. E-MAIL: tcrossman@registercitizen.com. URL: http://www.registercitizen.com. Mailing Address: PO Box 58, Torrington, CT 06790. Year Established: 1874. Pub. Frequency: d. Page Size: broadsheet. Subscrip. Rate: $.50 newsstand/cover; $1.25 newsstand/cover Sun.; $149.76/yr home delivery; $286/yr mailed. **Wire Service(s):** AP, NYT. Circulation: 13,000 morning (paid). **Owner(s):** Journal Register Co., 50 W State St, 12th Fl, Trenton, NJ 08608. Telephone: 609-396-2200. **Management:** Tilda Crossman, Advertising Director. **Editorial:** Mary Dempsey, Editor. Albie Yuranich, City Editor. Garrett Dale, Sports Editor.

WATERBURY

WATERBURY REPUBLICAN-AMERICAN. 389 Meadow St., Waterbury, CT 06702. E-MAIL: releases@rep-am.com. URL: http://www.rep-am.com. Mailing Address: P.O.Box 2090, Waterbury, CT 06722-2090. Year Established: 1990. Pub. Frequency: d. Page Size: broadsheet. Subscrip. Rate: $.50 newsstand/cover; $1.50 newsstand/cover Sun.; $208/yr home delivery; $260/yr mailed. Freelance Pay: $80-$125/article. **Wire Service(s):** AP. Circulation: 58,326 morning (paid); 71,892 Sunday (paid). **Owner(s):** Republican-American, Inc., See address and contact information above. **Management:** William J. Pape II, Publisher. Edward Winters, Circulation Director. William B. Pape II, Business Manager. **Editorial:** Ed Goodman, Editor. Johnathan Kellogg, Executive Editor. Robert D. Veillette, Managing Editor. Alison Skratt, Business Editor. Debbie Aleksinas, Lifestyle Editor. Ann Karolyi, Metro Editor.

WILLIMANTIC

CHRONICLE (WILLIMANTIC), THE. One Chronicle Rd., Willimantic, CT 06226. Telephone: 860-423-8466. FAX: 860-423-6585. E-MAIL: chron@thechronicle.com. URL: http://www.thechronicle.com. Year Established: 1876. Pub. Frequency: d. (Mon.-Sat.) Page Size: broadsheet. Subscrip. Rate: $.50 newsstand/cover; $31.86 home delivery for 3 mos.. **Wire Service(s):** AP. Circulation: 13,000 evening (paid). **Owner(s):** Lucy Crosbie, See address and contact information above. **Management:** Kevin Crosbie, Publisher. Jean Beckley, Advertising Manager. **Editorial:** Ron Robillard, Editor. Mike Sypher, Sports Editor. Terese Karmel, Womens Interest Editor.

DELAWARE

DOVER

DELAWARE STATE NEWS. ISSN 0745-8096 110 Galaxy Dr., Dover, DE 19901. Telephone: 302-674-3600. FAX: 302-741-8261. E-MAIL: dsnews@intercom.net. URL: http://www.newszap.com. Year Established: 1953. Pub. Frequency: d. Page Size: broadsheet. Subscrip. Rate: $.50 newsstand/cover; $1.50 newsstand/cover Sun.; $2.80/wk.. **Wire Service(s):** LAT-WAT. Circulation: 25,000 morning (paid); 38,000 Sunday (paid). **Owner(s):** Independent Newspapers, Inc., PO Box 737, Dover, DE 19903. Telephone: 302-674-3600. FAX: 302-674-9510. **Management:** Ed Dulin, Publisher. Pat Lee, Advertising. Don Clendaniel, Circulation Manager. Jennifer Wright, Classified Adv. Mgr.. **Editorial:** Andy West, Managing Editor. Andy Walter, Sports Editor.

NEW CASTLE

NEWS JOURNAL (NEW CASTLE), THE. ISSN 1042-4121 950 W. Basin Rd., New Castle, DE 19720. Telephone: 302-324-2500. FAX: 302-324-5509. E-MAIL: njletter@newsjournal.com. URL: http://www.delawareonline.com. Mailing Address: PO Box 15505, Wilmington, DE 19850. Pub. Frequency: d. Page Size: broadsheet. Subscrip. Rate: $.50 newsstand/cover; $1.50 Sun.; $195/yr carrier delivery; $312/yr mailed. **Wire Service(s):** AP, SH, LAT-WAT, GNS. Circulation: 124,000 morning (paid); 144,000 Sunday (paid). **Owner(s):** Gannett Company, Inc., 7950 Jones Branch Dr, McLean, VA 22107. Telephone: 703-854-6000. **Management:** W. Curtis Riddle, Publisher. Mark Logson, Advertising Manager. Michael Kane, Circulation Manager. Bettyann Dobek, Classified Adv. Mgr.. Liz Claus, Photography Director. **Editorial:** Debra Henley, Executive Editor. Calvin Stovall, Managing Editor. Dave Hale, Chief News Editor. John H. Taylor Jr., Editorial Page Editor. Ron Fritz, Sports Editor.

DISTRICT OF COLUMBIA

WASHINGTON

WASHINGTON POST, THE. ISSN 0190-8286 1150 15th St, N W, Washington, DC 20071. Telephone: 202-334-6000. E-MAIL: webpost@washpost.com. URL: http://www.washingtonpost.com/. Year Established: 1877. Pub. Frequency: d. Page Size: broadsheet. Subscrip. Rate: $.35 newsstand/cover; $1.50 newsstand/cover Sun.; $187.20/yr home delivery. **Wire Service(s):** AP, UPI, NYT, LAT-WAT. Circulation: 732,872. **Owner(s):** Washington Post Co., See address and contact information above. **Management:** Stephen Hills, President. Boisfeuillet Jones Jr., Publisher. Susan O'Leary, Advertising Director. Joyce Richardson, Classified Adv. Mgr.. **Editorial:** Glenn Frankel, Editor. Steve Coll, Managing Editor. Marie Arana, Book Review Editor. Fred Hiatt, Editorial Page Editor. Shirley Carswell, Feature Editor. Phyllis Richman, Food Editor. Michael Abramowitz, Government Affrs. Ed.. Bell Elving, Home Editor. Mary Pat Flaherty, Metro Editor. Michael Abramowitz, National Editor. Leonard Downie, News Editor. Michael Hill, Radio-TV Editor. Effie Dawson, Sports Editor. K.C. Summers, Travel Editor.

FLORIDA

ARCADIA

DESOTO SUN. 108 S. Polk Ave., Arcadia, FL 33821. Telephone: 941-492-2434. E-MAIL: dcedit@sunline.net. URL: http://www.sun-herald.com. Pub. Frequency: d. Page Size: broadsheet. Subscrip. Rate: $.50 newsstand/cover; $1.50 Sun.; $45.48/quarter; $150.87/yr. Circulation: 3,000 morning (paid); 3,400 Sunday (paid). **Owner(s):** Derek Dunn-Rankin, See address and contact information above. **Management:** Richard Hitt, General Manager. Derek Dunn-Rankin, Publisher. Kathleen Fox, Advertising Manager. Richard Hitt, Circulation Manager. **Editorial:** Dawn Krebs, Editor.

BOCA RATON

BOCA RATON NEWS. 1141 S Rogers Cir, Boca Raton, FL 33487. Telephone: 561-893-6400. FAX: 561-893-6677. E-MAIL: wwagman@bocanews.com. URL: http://www.bocanews.com. Year Established: 1958. Pub. Frequency: d. Page Size: broadsheet. Subscrip. Rate: $.25 newsstand/cover; $.75 newsstand/cover Sun.; $65/yr home delivery. **Wire Service(s):** AP, LAT-WAT, MCT. Circulation: 15,000 morning (paid); 18,000 Sunday (paid). **Owner(s):** South Florida Media Group, See address and contact information above. **Management:** Craig Swill, Publisher. **Editorial:** John Johnston, Co-Editor.

BRADENTON

BRADENTON HERALD. 102 Manatee Ave, W, Bradenton, FL 34205-8810. Telephone: 941-748-0411. FAX: 941-745-7097. E-MAIL: hhaitz@bradentonherald.com. URL: http://www.bradenton.com. Mailing Address: PO Box 921, Bradenton, FL 34206-0921. Year Established: 1922. Pub. Frequency: d. Page Size: broadsheet. Subscrip. Rate: $.25 newsstand/cover; $1 newsstand/cover Sun.; $83.03/yr. **Wire Service(s):** AP, LAT-WAT. Circulation: 47,109 morning (paid); 53,904 Sunday (paid). **Owner(s):** The/McClatchy Company, 2100 Q St, Sacramento, CA 95816. Telephone: 916-321-1936. FAX: 916-321-1869. **Management:** William Fleet, Publisher. Steve Braver, Advertising Manager. Terry Tramell, Circulation Director. **Editorial:** Joan Krauter, Executive Editor. Jim Smith, Managing Editor.

BROOKSVILLE

HERNANDO TODAY. 15299 Cortez Blvd., Brooksville, FL 34613-6095. Telephone: 352-544-5200. FAX: 352-544-5249. URL: http://www.hernandotoday.com. Year Established: 1987. Pub. Frequency: d. Page Size: broadsheet. Subscrip. Rate: $.25 newsstand/cover; $.50 newsstand/cover Sun.; $27.56/yr home delivery. Freelance Pay: $10-$25/article. **Wire Service(s):** AP. Circulation: 25,600 morning (paid); 25,600 Sunday (paid). **Owner(s):** Media General, Inc., 333 E. Franklin St., Richmond, VA 23219-0001. Telephone: 804-649-6000. **Management:** Duane Chinchester, General Manager. Duane Chichester, Publisher. Mike Ripley, Circulation Manager. Tim Smolarick, Classified Adv. Mgr.. **Editorial:** Robert Nolte, Managing Editor. Sue Quigley, Associate Editor. Dave Casey, Photographer. Tony Castro, Sports Editor.

CAPE CORAL

CAPE CORAL DAILY BREEZE. ISSN 1072-6152 2510 Del Prado Blvd., Cape Coral, FL 33904. Telephone: 239-574-1110. FAX: 239-574-5693. E-MAIL: swsnews1@flguide.com. URL: http://www.cape-coral-daily-breeze.com. Mailing Address: PO Box 151306, Cape Coral, FL 33915-1305. Year Established: 1984. Pub. Frequency: d. Page Size: broadsheet. Subscrip. Rate: $.50 newsstand/cover; $10 mailed for 2 mos.. **Wire Service(s):** AP. Circulation: 3,000 morning (controlled and free). **Owner(s):** Ogden Newspapers of Minnesota, Inc., See address and contact information above. **Management:** Jack Glarrow, General Manager. Karen Pnazek, Advertising Manager. Scott Oliver, Circulation Manager. Henry Phillips, Associate Publisher. **Editorial:** Chris Strine, Editor. Valerie Harring, Executive Editor. Jim Linette, Sports Editor.

CHARLOTTE HARBOR

CHARLOTTE SUN HERALD. 23170 Harbor View Rd., Charlotte Harbor, FL 33980. Telephone: 941-206-1000. FAX: 941-629-2085. E-MAIL: jgouvellis@sunletter.com. URL: http://www.sun-herald.com. Year Established: 1893. Pub. Frequency: d. Page Size: broadsheet. Subscrip. Rate: $.50 newsstand/cover; $1.25 Sun.; $43.34/quarter; $173.36/yr. **Wire Service(s):** AP. Circulation: 34,570 morning (paid); 36,743 Sunday (paid). **Owner(s):** Sun Coast Media Group, Inc., See address and contact information above. **Management:** Derek Dunn-Rankin, Publisher. **Editorial:** Buddy Martin, Editor. Jim Gouvellis, Executive Editor. Chris Porter, Managing Editor. Lorraine Schneeberger, City Editor. Donna Davidson, Feature Editor.

CRYSTAL RIVER

CITRUS COUNTY CHRONICLE. 1624 N. Meadowcrest Blvd., Crystal River, FL 34429. Telephone: 352-563-6363. FAX: 352-563-5665. E-MAIL: citrus@infi.net. URL: http://www.chronicle-online.com. Mailing Address: PO Box 1899, Inverness, FL 34451. Year Established: 1890. Pub. Frequency: d. Page Size: broadsheet. Subscrip. Rate: $.25 newsstand/cover; $.75 newsstand/cover Sun.; $108.12/yr home delivery. **Wire Service(s):** AP. Circulation: 26,231 morning (paid); 29,349 Sunday (paid). **Owner(s):** Landmark Community Newspapers, Inc., 601 Taylorsville Rd, Shelbyville, KY 40065-0549. Telephone: 502-633-4334. PO Box 549, Shelbyville, KY 40065. **Management:** Gerard Mulligan, Publisher. John Provost, Advertising Director. John Murphy, Classified Adv. Mgr.. **Editorial:** Charlie Brennan, Editor. Mike Arnold, News Editor. Matt Beck, Photo Editor.

DAYTONA BEACH

NEWS-JOURNAL (DAYTONA BEACH), THE. 901 Sixth St., Daytona Beach, FL 32117. Telephone: 386-252-1511. FAX: 386-258-8465. E-MAIL: lori.kopp@new-jrnl.com. URL: http://www.news-journalonline.com. Year Established: 1904. Pub. Frequency: d. Page Size: broadsheet. Subscrip. Rate: $.50 newsstand/cover; $1.25 newsstand/cover Sun.; $10.18/mo.; $149.53/yr. Adv. Rate: col. inch $53.55 **Wire Service(s):** AP, NYT. Circulation: 99,631 morning (paid); 118,701 Sunday (paid). **Owner(s):** News-Journal Corp., See address and contact information above. **Bureau(s):** 111 S. Alabama Ave., DeLand, FL 32721. Telephone: 904-734-2070. FAX: 904-736-2714. Contact: Ronald Williamson, Editor. **Management:** Tippen Davidson, President. Georgia Kaney, Publisher. Kathy Coughlin, Advertising Director. Michael Redding, Classified Adv. Mgr.. **Editorial:** Donald Lindley, Executive Editor. Kathy Kelly, Asst. Managing Ed.. Cecil Brumley, Business Editor. David Wiggins, Editorial Page Editor. Cory Lancaster, Metro Editor. Troy Moore, News Editor. David Markowitz, Sports Editor. Denise O'Toole, Sunday Editor.

ENGLEWOOD

ENGLEWOOD SUN. 167 W. Dearborn St., Englewood, FL 34223. Telephone: 941-681-3000. FAX: 941-681-3008. E-MAIL: sbaumann@sun-herald.com. URL: http://www.sun-herald.com. Pub. Frequency: d. Page Size: broadsheet. Subscrip. Rate: $.50 newsstand/cover; $1.50 newsstand/cover Sun.; $32.17 carrier delivery/quarter in county; $144.45/yr carrier delivery in county. **Wire Service(s):** AP. Circulation: 35,000 morning (paid); 40,000 Sunday (paid). **Owner(s):** Sun Coast Media Group, Inc., 23170 Harbor View Rd., Charlotte Harbor, FL 33980. Telephone: 941-206-1000. FAX: 941-629-2085. **Management:** Derek Dunn-Rankin, Publisher. Lang Capasso, Advertising Director. Jeana Nottingham, Classified Adv. Mgr.. **Editorial:** Steve Baumann, Editor. Jim Gouvellis, Executive Editor. Roselle Zayes, Business Editor. John Hackworth, Editorial Page Editor. Donna Davidson, Feature Editor. John Fineran, Sports Editor.

FORT LAUDERDALE

SOUTH FLORIDA SUN-SENTINEL. ISSN 0744-8139
200 E. Las Olas Blvd., Fort Lauderdale, FL 33301-2293. Telephone: 954-356-4000. FAX: 954-356-4500. Pub. Frequency: d. Page Size: broadsheet. Subscrip. Rate: $.35 newsstand/cover; $1 newsstand/cover Sun.; $2.50/wk.. **Wire Service(s):** RN, AP, NYT, LAT-WAT, MCT, DJNS. Circulation: 337,526 per issue (paid and controlled). **Owner(s):** Tribune Company, 435 N Michigan Ave, Chicago, IL 60601. **Management:** Bob Gremillion, President. Sheldon L Greenberger, Advertising Director. Howard Greenberg, Circulation Director. **Editorial:** Earl Maucker, Editor. Ellen Soeteber, Managing Editor. Rick Robb, City Editor. Fred Turner, Sports Editor.

FORT MYERS

NEWS-PRESS, THE. 2442 Martin Luther King, Jr. Blvd., Fort Myers, FL 33901-2442. Telephone: 239-335-0200. FAX: 239-334-0708. URL: http://www.news-press.com. Mailing Address: PO Box 10, Fort Myers, FL 33902. Year Established: 1884. Pub. Frequency: d. Page Size: broadsheet. Subscrip. Rate: $.50 newsstand/cover; $1.50 Sun.; $15.90/mo.. Freelance Pay: $20-$50/article. **Wire Service(s):** AP, MCT, GNS. Circulation: 112,000 per issue (paid). **Owner(s):** Gannett Company, Inc., 7950 Jones Branch Dr., McLean, VA 22107-0001. Telephone: 703-854-6000. **Bureau(s):** 4720 S.E. 15th Ave., Ste. 112, Cape Coral, FL 33990. Telephone: 941-574-5777. **Management:** Carole Hudler, Publisher. Bob Carlson, Advertising Manager. Steve Ecken, Circulation Director. Greg Helton, Communications Dir.. **Editorial:** Ronnie Ramos, Managing Editor. Steve McQuilkin, Business Editor. Kate Marymonth, News Editor. Tom Hayden, Sports Editor.

FORT PIERCE

TRIBUNE (FORT PIERCE), THE. 600 Edwards Rd., Fort Pierce, FL 34982. Telephone: 772-461-2050. FAX: 772-461-4447. E-MAIL: tribedit@fptribune.com. URL: http://www.tcpalm.com. Year Established: 1903. Pub. Frequency: d. Page Size: standard. Subscrip. Rate: $.25 newsstand/cover; $1 Sun.; $109.27/yr home delivery; $234/yr mailed. **Wire Service(s):** AP, UPI. Circulation: 32,298 morning (paid); 35,097 Sunday (paid). **Owner(s):** E.W. Scripps Co., 1939 S.E. Federal Hwy., Stuart, FL 34994. Telephone: 772-287-1550. FAX: 772-221-4175. **Management:** Tom Weber, Publisher. Christine Stonecipher, Advertising Manager. Mary Gaylord, Circulation Manager. **Editorial:** Anthony Westbury, Editor. Gary Strassburg, Lifestyle Editor. Mike Graham, Sports Editor.

FORT WALTON BEACH

NORTHWEST FLORIDA DAILY NEWS. ISSN 0898-168X
200 Race Track Rd., N.W., Fort Walton Beach, FL 32547. Telephone: 850-863-1111. FAX: 850-862-5230. URL: http://www.nwfdailynews.com. Mailing Address: PO Box 2949, Fort Walton Beach, FL 32549. Year Established: 1946. Pub. Frequency: d. Page Size: broadsheet. Subscrip. Rate: $.50 newsstand/cover; $1.25 newsstand/cover Sun.; $13/mo.; $158/yr. **Wire Service(s):** AP. Circulation: 38,122 morning (paid); 49,086 Sunday (paid). **Owner(s):** Freedom Communications, Inc., 17666 Fitch, Irvine, CA 92714. Telephone: 714-553-9292. **Management:** Tom Conner, Publisher. John Whitehead, Advertising Director. Daryll Watson, Circulation Director. Joe Nacchia, Classified Adv. Mgr.. **Editorial:** Patrick Rice, Editor. Colin Lipnicky, Managing Editor. Morris Fraser, Business Editor. Jim Shoffner, Editorial Page Editor. Brenda Shoffner, Entertainment Editor. Jeffrey Willis, News Editor. Mark Kulaw, Photo Editor. Perry Ballard, Sports Editor.

JACKSONVILLE

FLORIDA TIMES-UNION, THE. ISSN 0740-2325
One Riverside Ave., Jacksonville, FL 32202-4904. Telephone: 904-359-4111. FAX: 904-359-4478. URL: http://www.jacksonville.com. Mailing Address: PO Box 1949, Jacksonville, FL 32231-0053. Year Established: 1864. Pub. Frequency: d. Page Size: broadsheet. Subscrip. Rate: $.50 newsstand/cover; $1.65 newsstand/cover Sun.; $182.50/yr. **Wire Service(s):** AP, NYT, LAT-WAT, DJNS. Circulation: 177,170 morning (paid); 240,069 Sunday (paid). **Owner(s):** Morris Multimedia, Inc., PO Box 936, Augusta, GA 30903-0936. Telephone: 706-724-0851. **Management:** Robert Martin, General Manager. Carl N. Cannon, Publisher. Mike Begue, Advertising Director. Andrew Gentry, Circulation Director. Geri Kotz, Classified Adv. Mgr.. **Editorial:** Pat Yak, Editor. Mike Richey, Managing Editor. Ted Crosby, Production Manager. John Burr, Asst. Managing Ed.. Joe Adams, Editorial Page Editor. Mike Marino, News Editor. Chet Fussman, Sports Editor.

KEY WEST

KEY WEST CITIZEN, THE. 3420 Northside Dr., Key West, FL 33040. Telephone: 305-292-7777. FAX: 305-294-0768. E-MAIL: citizen@keywest.com. URL: http://www.keysnews.com. Mailing Address: PO Box 1800, Key West, FL 33041. Year Established: 1876. Pub. Frequency: d. Page Size: broadsheet. Subscrip. Rate: $.50 newsstand/cover; $1 newsstand/cover Sun.; $102/yr carrier delivery; $244/yr mailed. **Wire Service(s):** AP. Circulation: 10,940 morning (paid); 11,470 Sunday (paid). **Owner(s):** Cooke Communications LLC, See address and contact information above. **Management:** John Kent Cooke Jr., Publisher. Kim Works, Advertising Manager. Bob Timmerman, Circulation Manager. **Editorial:** Tom Tuell, Managing Editor. Cheryl Smith, News Editor.

LADY LAKE

VILLAGES DAILY SUN, THE. 1100 Main St., Lady Lake, FL 32159-7721. Telephone: 352-753-1119. FAX: 352-753-2380. URL: http://www.thevillagesdailysun.com. Pub. Frequency: d. Page Size: standard. Subscrip. Rate: $.25 newsstand/cover; $.75 newsstand/cover Sun.; $48/yr. Circulation: 34,000 morning (paid). **Owner(s):** The Villages Lake/Sumter Inc., See address and contact information above. **Management:** Philip Markward, Publisher. Dan Sprung, Classified Adv. Mgr.. Bob Sattibene, Sales Manager. **Editorial:** Larry Croom, Editor. Matt Fry, Managing Editor. Bill Mitchell, Photo Editor.

LAKE CITY

LAKE CITY REPORTER. 180 E. Duval St., Lake City, FL 32055. Telephone: 386-752-1293. FAX: 386-752-9400. URL: http://www.lakecityreporter.com. Mailing Address: PO Box 1709, Lake City, FL 32056. Year Established: 1874. Pub. Frequency: d. (Tue.-Sun.) Page Size: broadsheet. Subscrip. Rate: $.50 newsstand/cover; $.75 newsstand/cover Sun.; $83.46/yr home delivery; $179.40/yr mailed. **Wire Service(s):** AP, NYT. Circulation: 10,500 morning (paid). **Owner(s):** Community Newspapers (Athens), Inc., PO Box 792, Athens, GA 30603. Telephone: 706-548-0010. FAX: 706-548-0808. **Management:** Michael Leonard, Publisher. Russell Waters, Circulation Manager. **Editorial:** Todd Wilson, Editor.

LEESBURG

DAILY COMMERCIAL. 212 E. Main St., Leesburg, FL 34748. Telephone: 352-365-8200. FAX: 352-365-1951. E-MAIL: reporter@dailycommercial.com. URL: http://www.dailycommercial.com. Mailing Address: PO Box 490007, Leesburg, FL 34749-007. Year Established: 1875. Pub. Frequency: d. Page Size: broadsheet. Subscrip. Rate: $.35 newsstand/cover; $1 Sun.; $8 carrier delivery/mo.; $63.67/yr home delivery; $112/yr mailed. **Wire Service(s):** AP. Circulation: 24,330 morning (paid); 25,023 Sunday (paid). **Owner(s):** HarborPoint Media, LLC, 125 Basin St., Ste. 200, Daytona Beach, FL 32114. Telephone: 386-252-9921. FAX: 386-252-9925. **Management:** Michael Redding, Owner. Ron Wallace, Publisher. Alan Ferguson, Advertising Director. Rick Copeland, Circulation Manager. Tina Reader, Classified Adv. Mgr.. Chris McGonigal, Photography Director. **Editorial:** Dan Fields, Managing Editor. Steve Otte, News Editor. Adam Minichino, Sports Editor.

MARIANNA

JACKSON COUNTY FLORIDAN. 4403 Constitution Ln., Marianna, FL 32448. Telephone: 850-526-3614. FAX: 850-482-4478. E-MAIL: floridan@wfeca.net. URL: http://www.jcfloridan.com. Mailing Address: PO Box 520, Marianna, FL 32447-0520. Year Established: 1927. Pub. Frequency: d. (Tue.-Fri. & Sun.) Page Size: broadsheet. Subscrip. Rate: $.50 newsstand/cover; $1 newsstand/cover Sun.; $119.40/yr home delivery; $154.80/yr mailed. **Wire Service(s):** AP. Circulation: 7,000 morning (paid); 7,200 Sunday (paid). **Owner(s):** Media General, Inc., 333 E. Franklin St., Richmond, VA 23219. Telephone: 804-649-6000. **Management:** Roger Underwood, Publisher. Valeria Roberts, Advertising Manager. Dave Frix, Circulation Manager. John David Adams, Production Director. **Editorial:** Douglas Grant, Editor. Dustin Kent, Sports Editor.

MELBOURNE

FLORIDA TODAY. ISSN 1051-8304
One Gannett Plz., Melbourne, FL 32940. Telephone: 321-242-3500. FAX: 321-255-9550. Mailing Address: PO Box 419000, Melbourne, FL 32941-9000. Year Established: 1966. Pub. Frequency: d. Page Size: broadsheet. Subscrip. Rate: $.50 newsstand/cover; $1.50 newsstand/cover Sun.; $13.78/mo.. **Wire Service(s):** AP, LAT-WAT, GNS. Circulation: 97,000 morning (paid); 100,000 Sunday (paid). **Owner(s):** Gannett Company, Inc., See address and contact information above. **Bureau(s):** Contact: Marilyn Meyers, Bureau Chief. **Management:** Michael J Coleman, Publisher. Barry Barlow, Advertising Director. Cedric Johnson, Circulation Manager. **Editorial:** Bob Stover, Managing Editor.

MIAMI

MIAMI HERALD, THE. ISSN 0898-865X
One Herald Plaza, Miami, FL 33132. Telephone: 305-350-2111. URL: http://herald.com. Year Established: 1910. Pub. Frequency: d. Page Size: broadsheet. Subscrip. Rate: $.35 newsstand/cover; $1 newsstand/cover Sun.; $90.69/yr. **Wire Service(s):** AP, UPI, LAT-WAT. Circulation: 280,496 per issue (paid); 381,375 Sunday (paid). **Owner(s):** The/McClatchy Company, 2100 Q St, Sacramento, CA 95816. Telephone: 916-321-1936. FAX: 916-321-1869. **Management:** Alexandra Villoch, VP Advertising. Terry Whitney, VP Circulation. **Editorial:** Anders Gyllenhaal, Executive Editor. Dave Wilson, Managing Editor.

NAPLES

NAPLES DAILY NEWS. 1075 Central Ave., Naples, FL 34102. Telephone: 239-262-3161. FAX: 239-435-3451. URL: http://www.naplesnews.com. Year Established: 1923. Pub. Frequency: d. Page Size: broadsheet. Subscrip. Rate: $.50 newsstand/cover; $1.50 Sun.; $211.71/yr in state; $220/yr elsewhere. Circulation: 59,000 morning (paid); 75,000 Sunday (paid). **Owner(s):** E.W. Scripps Co., 312 Walnut St., 28th Fl., Cincinnati, OH 45202. Telephone: 513-977-3000. **Management:** John W. Fish, General Manager. Bob Sandy, Advertising Director. Ken Tanner, Circulation Manager. **Editorial:** Phil Lewis, Editor. Bill Blanton, Managing Editor. Allen Bartlett, City Editor.

NEW SMYRNA BEACH

OBSERVER (NEW SMYRNA), THE. 823 S. Dixie Fwy., New Smyrna Beach, FL 32168. Telephone: 386-427-1000. FAX: 386-424-9858. E-MAIL: observernews@bellsouth.net. URL: http://www.nsb-observer.com. Mailing Address: PO Box 10, New Smyrna Beach, FL 32170. Year Established: 1918. Pub. Frequency: d. (Tue.-Sat.) Page Size: broadsheet. Subscrip. Rate: $.50 newsstand/cover; $70/yr mailed in county; $110/yr mailed in state; $103/yr mailed out of state. Adv. Rate: col. inch $6.50 **Wire Service(s):** AP. Circulation: 3,000 morning (paid); 200 morning (free). **Owner(s):** Horizon Publications, Inc., 1120 N. Carbon St, Ste 100, Marion, IL 62959. **Management:** Philip Jackson, Publisher. John Haglof, Circulation Manager. **Editorial:** Henry Frederick, Editor.

NORTH PORT

NORTH PORT SUN. 13644 S. Tamiami Trail, North Port, FL 34287. Telephone: 941-426-9544. FAX: 941-423-2318. E-MAIL: eallen@sun-herald.com. URL: http://www.northport-florida.com. Pub. Frequency: d. Page Size: broadsheet. Subscrip. Rate: $.50 newsstand/cover; $1.50 home delivery Sun.; $144.45/yr home delivery. Circulation: 4,000 morning (paid); 4,000 Sunday (paid). **Owner(s):** Sun Coast Media Group, Inc., 23170 Harbor View Rd., Charlotte Harbor, FL 33980. Telephone: 941-206-1000. FAX: 941-629-2085. **Management:** Steve Sachkar, General Manager. Derek Dunn-Rankin, Publisher. Marisa Sinclair, Advertising Director. **Editorial:** Elaine Allen, Editor.

OKEECHOBEE

OKEECHOBEE NEWS. 107 SW 17th St, Ste. D, Okeechobee, FL 34974. Telephone: 863-763-3134. FAX: 863-763-5901. E-MAIL: okeenews@okeechobee.com. URL: http://www.newsthatszap.com/okeechobee. Mailing Address: PO Box 639, Okeechobee, FL 34973. Year Established: 1910. Pub. Frequency: d. Page Size: broadsheet. Subscrip. Rate: $.50 newsstand/cover; $.75 newsstand/cover Sun.; $9.81 home delivery/mo. in county; $16.20 mailed/mo. out of county. **Wire Service(s):** AP. Circulation: 3,600 morning (paid); 11,000 Sunday (paid). **Owner(s):** Independent Newspapers, Inc., PO Box 737, Dover, DE 19903. Telephone: 302-674-3600. FAX: 302-674-9510. **Management:** Judy Kasten, Publisher. Janet Madrey, Circulation Manager. **Editorial:** Eric Kopp, Editor. Lorna Jablonski, Sports Editor.

PALATKA

PALATKA DAILY NEWS. ISSN 0163-5050
1825 St. Johns Ave., Palatka, FL 32177. Telephone: 386-312-5200. FAX: 386-312-5209. URL: http://www.palatkadailynews.com. Mailing Address: PO Box 777, Palatka, FL 32178. Year Established: 1885. Pub. Frequency: d. (Tue.-Sat.) Page Size: broadsheet. Subscrip. Rate: $.50 newsstand/cover; $96.30/yr. **Wire Service(s):** AP. Circulation: 11,500 evening (paid). **Owner(s):** Community Newspapers (Athens), Inc., PO Box 792, Athens, GA 30603. Telephone: 706-548-0010. **Management:** Robert R. Starr, Publisher. Mary Kaye Wells, Advertising Manager. John Allender, Circulation Director. **Editorial:** Larry Sullivan, Editor. Kirk Collier, City Editor. Trish Murphy, Food Editor.

PALM BEACH

PALM BEACH DAILY NEWS. 265 Royal Poinciana Way, Palm Beach, FL 33480-4041. Telephone: 561-820-3800. E-MAIL: jreingold@pddailynews.com. URL: http://www.palmbeachdailynews.com. Year Established: 1897. Pub. Frequency: d. (mid-May-mid-Sep; w.: Thu. & Sun., Sep-mid-May) Page Size: standard. Subscrip. Rate: $.50 newsstand/cover; $1.50 newsstand/cover Sun.; $135.16/yr home delivery in area. Adv. Rate: col. inch $47.28 Freelance Pay: $35/article. Circulation: 7,500 morning (paid); 8,500 Sunday (paid). **Owner(s):** Cox Newspapers, Inc., 6205 Peachtree Dunwoody Rd., Atlanta, GA 30328. Telephone: 678-645-0000. **Management:** Joyce Reingold, Publisher. Linda Goings, Advertising Director. **Editorial:** Joyce Reingold, Editor. Carol Carnivale, News Editor.

PANAMA CITY

NEWS HERALD. 501 W. 11th St., Panama City, FL 32401. Telephone: 850-747-5000. FAX: 850-763-4636. E-MAIL: nhborny@pbnh.com. URL: http://www.newsherald.com. Mailing Address: PO Box 1940, Panama City, FL 32402. Year Established: 1970. Pub. Frequency: d. Page Size: standard. Subscrip. Rate: $.50 newsstand/cover; $1.25 Sun.; $155.65/yr carrier delivery in county. **Wire Service(s):** AP, MCT. Circulation: 33,185 morning (paid); 38,954 Sunday (paid). **Owner(s):** Freedom Communications, Inc., 17666 Fitch, Irvine, CA 92614. Telephone: 949-253-2300. FAX: 949-474-7675. **Management:** Karen Hanes, Publisher. Pam Gregory, Advertising Manager. Rhoda Andriesse, Circulation Manager. **Editorial:** Phil Lucas, Executive Editor. Mike Cazalas, Managing Editor. Claude Duncan, Editorial Page Editor. Pat McCann, Sports Editor.

PENSACOLA

PENSACOLA NEWS JOURNAL. 101 E. Romana St., Pensacola, FL 32502. Telephone: 850-435-8500. FAX: 850-435-8633. E-MAIL: news@pnj.com. URL: http://www.pnj.com. Mailing Address: PO Box 12710, Pensacola, FL 32591. Year Established: 1889. Pub. Frequency: d. Page Size: broadsheet. Subscrip. Rate: $.75 newsstand/cover; $1.50 newsstand/cover Sun.; $19.43 home delivery/mo. daily & Sun.. **Wire Service(s):** AP, GNS. **Owner(s):** Gannett Company, Inc., 7950 Jones Branch Dr, McLean, VA 22107. Telephone: 703-854-6000. **Management:** Kevin Doyle, Publisher. Bobby Rice, Advertising Director. Pat Daugherty, Circulation Director. Becca Boles, Marketing Director. Cindy Hall, Manager. **Editorial:** Shannon Nickinson, Editor. Ginny Graybiel, Managing Editor. Gary McCracken, Photo Editor.

PORT ST. LUCIE

PORT ST. LUCIE NEWS. 695 NW Enterprise Dr., Port St. Lucie, FL 34986. Telephone: 772-408-5300. FAX: 772-221-4246. URL: http://www.tcpalm.com. Pub. Frequency: d. Page Size: broadsheet. Subscrip. Rate: $.50 newsstand/cover; $1 newsstand/cover Sun.; $33.55 home delivery for 3 mos.; $120.77/yr home delivery. **Wire Service(s):** AP, NYT. Circulation: 18,606 Sunday (paid); 14,128 morning (paid). **Owner(s):** E.W. Scripps Co., 312 Walnut St., 28th Fl., Cincinnati, OH 45202. Telephone: 513-977-3000. **Editorial:** Larry Reisman, Executive Editor. Dennis Durkee, Managing Editor. Gary Strassberg, Feature Editor. Joshua Pearl, News Editor. Mike Graham, Sports Editor. Ike Crumpler, Travel Editor.

ST. AUGUSTINE

ST. AUGUSTINE RECORD, THE. ISSN 1041-1577
One News Pl, St. Augustine, FL 32086. Telephone: 904-829-6562. FAX: 904-819-3557. E-MAIL: record@staugustine.com. URL: http://www.staugustine.com. Mailing Address: PO Box 1630, St. Augustine, FL 32085. Year Established: 1894. Pub. Frequency: d. Page Size: broadsheet. Subscrip. Rate: $.50 newsstand/cover; $1 newsstand/cover Sun.; $63.28 for 6 mos.; $126/yr carrier delivery. **Wire Service(s):** AP, LAT-WAT, MCT. Circulation: 17,000 evening (paid); 18,000 Sunday (paid). **Owner(s):** Morris Multimedia, Inc., PO Box 936, Augusta, GA 30903. Telephone: 706-724-0851. FAX: 706-722-0011. **Management:** Ronnie Hughes, Publisher. Cheryl Brunk, Advertising Manager. Bill Mitchell, Circulation Manager. Dawn Ginnane, Classified Adv. Mgr.. **Editorial:** Peter Ellis, Editor. Margo Pope, Associate Editor. Anne L. Heymen, Feature Editor. Justin Barney, Sports Editor.

ST. PETERSBURG

ST. PETERSBURG TIMES. 490 First Ave., S., St. Petersburg, FL 33701-1121. Telephone: 727-893-8111. FAX: 727-892-2328. URL: http://www.tampabay.com. Mailing Address: PO Box 1121, St. Petersburg, FL 33731-1121. Year Established: 1884. Pub. Frequency: d. Page Size: broadsheet. Subscrip. Rate: $.50 newsstand/cover; $1 newsstand/cover Sun.; $168.98/yr home delivery in county. **Wire Service(s):** AP, SH, NYT, LAT-WAT. Circulation: 316,007 morning (paid); 432,779 Sunday (paid). **Owner(s):** Times Publishing Co., See address and contact information above. **Management:** Paul Tash, Chief Executive Ofc. . Ben Hayes, Director. Joe DeLuca, Publisher. Paul Tash, Chairman. Jana Jones, CFO. Marty Petty, Executive VP. Andrew Corty, Vice President. Richard Reeves, VP Mktg. & Sales. Moya Neville, Sales Manager. Jerry Hill, Development Manager. Andrew Corty, Secretary. **Editorial:** Paul Tash, Editor. Neil Brown, Executive Editor.

STUART

PRESS JOURNAL (STUART). 1939 S.E. Federal Hwy., Stuart, FL 34994. URL: http://www.tcpalm.com. Year Established: 1919. Pub. Frequency: d. Page Size: broadsheet. Subscrip. Rate: $.50 newsstand/cover per issue; $1 newsstand/cover Sun.; $41.03 home delivery for 3 mos.; $154.52/yr home delivery. **Wire Service(s):** AP. Circulation: 32,000 morning (paid); 35,000 Sunday (paid). **Owner(s):** E.W. Scripps Co., 312 Walnut St., 28th Fl., Cincinnati, OH 45202. Telephone: 513-977-3000. FAX: 513-977-3689. **Management:** Kim Kerr, Publisher. **Editorial:** Mark Tomasik, Editor. Dennis Durkee, News Editor. Kelly Rogers, Photo Editor. Mike Graham, Sports Editor.

STUART NEWS. 1939 S. Federal Hwy., Stuart, FL 34994. Telephone: 772-287-1550. FAX: 772-221-4246. URL: http://www.tcpalm.com. Mailing Address: PO Box 9009, Stuart, FL 34995. Year Established: 1913. Pub. Frequency: d. Page Size: broadsheet. Subscrip. Rate: $.50 newsstand/cover; $1 newsstand/cover Sun.; $9.49/mo.; $212/yr. **Wire Service(s):** AP, SH, NYT. Circulation: 39,104 morning (paid); 47,214 Sunday (paid). **Owner(s):** E.W. Scripps Co., 312 Walnut St., Cincinnati, OH 45202. Telephone: 513-977-3000. **Management:** Thomas E. Weber, President. Bob Brunjes, Advertising Director. Becky Freeman, Business Manager. **Editorial:** Tom Webber, Editor. Jason Nuttle, Graphics Editor. Marjorie Bril, Librarian. Dan Lovely, Metro Editor.

TALLAHASSEE

TALLAHASSEE DEMOCRAT. ISSN 0738-5153
227 N Magnolia Dr, Tallahassee, FL 32301. Telephone: 850-599-2100. FAX: 850-599-2295. E-MAIL: bshaw@taldem.com. URL: http://www.tallahassee.com. Mailing Address: PO Box 990, Tallahassee, FL 32302. Year Established: 1905. Pub. Frequency: d. Page Size: broadsheet. Subscrip. Rate: $.50 newsstand/cover; $1.25 Sun.. **Wire Service(s):** AP, NYT, LAT-WAT, MCT. Circulation: 56,000 morning (paid); 77,000 Sunday (paid). **Owner(s):** Gannett Company, Inc., 7950 Jones Branch Dr., McLean, VA 22102. **Management:** Patrick Dorsey, Publisher. Barry Barlow, Advertising Director. **Editorial:** Robert Gabordi, Executive Editor. Africa Price, Managing Editor.

TAMPA

TAMPA TRIBUNE, THE. ISSN 1042-3761
202 S. Parker St., Tampa, FL 33606-2395. Telephone: 813-259-7711. FAX: 813-259-7676. URL: http://www.tampatrib.com. Mailing Address: PO Box 191, Tampa, FL 33601-0191. Year Established: 1895. Pub. Frequency: d. Page Size: broadsheet. Subscrip. Rate: $.50 newsstand/cover; $1.39 Sun.; $153.01/yr home delivery in county daily & Sun. **Wire Service(s):** AP. Circulation: 209,117 morning (paid); 277,420 Sunday (paid). **Owner(s):** Media General, Inc., 333 E. Franklin St., Richmond, VA 23219. Telephone: 804-649-6000. **Management:** Denise Palmer, President. Gil Thelen, Publisher. Janet Coats, Vice President. Graham Annett, VP Circulation. Kelly Mirt, Advertising Director. Todd Chappel, Photography Director. **Editorial:** Janet Coats, Editor. Richard "Duke" Maas, Managing Editor. Craig Gemoules, Asst. Managing Ed.. Mark Guidera Sr., Business Editor. Nick Publiese, Sports Editor.

WEST PALM BEACH

PALM BEACH POST. ISSN 1528-5758
2751 S. Dixie Hwy., West Palm Beach, FL 33405. Telephone: 561-820-4100. FAX: 561-820-4445. E-MAIL: metro@pbpost.com. URL: http://www.palmbeachpost.com. Mailing Address: PO Box 24700, West Palm Beach, FL 33416. Year Established: 1923. Pub. Frequency: d. Page Size: broadsheet. Subscrip. Rate: $.50 newsstand/cover; $1.50 newsstand/cover Sun.; $2.75 home delivery/wk.; $143/yr home delivery; $418/yr mailed. **Wire Service(s):** RN, AP, NYT, LAT-WAT. Circulation: 180,000 morning (paid); 220,000 Sunday (paid). **Owner(s):** Cox Newspapers, Inc., 6205 Peachtree Dunwoody Rd, Atlanta, GA 30328. **Bureau(s):** 2915 S. Congress Ave., Delray Beach, FL 33445. Telephone: 561-279-3450. **Management:** Tom Giuffrida, Publisher. Chuck Gerardi, Advertising Director. **Editorial:** John Bartosek, Managing Editor. Holly Baltz, Assistant Editor. Randy Schultz, Editorial Page Editor. Anne Smith, Feature Editor. Carolyn DiPaolo, Metro Editor. Eric Weiss, News Editor.

WINTER HAVEN

NEWS CHIEF, THE. 650 Sixth St., S.W., Winter Haven, FL 33880. Telephone: 863-294-7731. FAX: 863-294-2008. E-MAIL: news@newschief.com. URL: http://www.polkonline.com. Mailing Address: PO Box 1440, Winter Haven, FL 33882. Year Established: 1879. Pub. Frequency: d. Page Size: broadsheet. Subscrip. Rate: $.25 newsstand/cover; $.50 newsstand/cover Sun.; $92.60/yr. Adv. Rate: col. inch $15 **Wire Service(s):** AP. Circulation: 12,700 evening (paid); 13,700 Sunday (paid). **Owner(s):** Morris Multimedia, Inc., PO Box 936, Augusta, GA 30903. Telephone: 706-724-0851. **Management:** Wayne Ezell, Publisher. Mary Lynn, Advertising Manager. Dan Wroblewski, Circulation Manager. Denny Wilkson, Production Director. **Editorial:** Christie Gilpin, Editor. Paul Crate, Photographer. Contact: Jackie Unger-Pool, Classified Adv. Mgr.. Contact: Susan Holley, Advertising Director; Linda Mooney, Circulation Manager; Bill Megivern, Classified Adv. Mgr.; Christie Gilpin, Editor.

GEORGIA

ALBANY

ALBANY HERALD, THE. 126 N Washington St, Albany, GA 31701. Telephone: 229-888-9300. FAX: 229-888-9357. E-MAIL: albanyh@surfsouth.com. URL: http://www.albanyherald.com. Mailing Address: PO Box 48, Albany, GA 31702. Year Established: 1891. Pub. Frequency: d. Page Size: standard. Subscrip. Rate: $.50 newsstand/cover; $1.50 Sun.; $180/yr. **Wire Service(s):** AP. Circulation: 34,000 morning (paid); 40,000 Sunday (paid). **Owner(s):** Triple Crown Media, Inc., 546 E Main St, Lexington, KY 40508. Telephone: 859-226-4678. FAX: 859-226-4308. **Management:** Michael Gebhart, Publisher. Tami Abbott, Advertising Director. J. Michael Hill, Circulation Director. John Bush, Classified Adv. Mgr.. **Editorial:** Jim Hendricks, Editor. Danny Carter, Managing Editor.

AMERICUS

AMERICUS TIMES-RECORDER. 101 Hwy. 27 E., Americus, GA 31709. Telephone: 229-924-2751. FAX: 229-928-6344. URL: http://www.americustimesrecorder.com. Mailing Address: PO Box 1247, Americus, GA 31709-1247. Year Established: 1879. Pub. Frequency: d. (Tue.-Fri. & Sun.) Page Size: broadsheet. Subscrip. Rate: $.50 newsstand/cover; $8 home delivery/mo.; $104.65/yr home delivery. **Wire Service(s):** AP. Circulation: 7,400 morning (paid); 12,500 Sunday (paid). **Owner(s):** Community Newspaper Holdings, Inc., 3500 Colonnade Pkwy., Ste. 600, Birmingham, AL 35243. Telephone: 205-298-7100. FAX: 205-298-7101. **Management:** Dan Sutton, Publisher. Linda Barwick, Advertising Director. Laura Rogers, Advertising Manager. Linda Nobles, Circulation Director. **Editorial:** Beth Alston, Managing Editor.

ATHENS

ATHENS BANNER HERALD. ISSN 0898-3712
One Press Pl., Athens, GA 30601. Telephone: 706-549-0123. FAX: 706-543-5234. URL: http://www.onlineathens.com. Mailing Address: PO Box 912, Athens, GA 30603. Year Established: 1965. Pub. Frequency: d. Page Size: broadsheet. Subscrip. Rate: $.50 newsstand/cover; $1.50 newsstand/cover Sun.; $9.95 carrier delivery/mo.; $104/yr carrier delivery. **Wire Service(s):** AP, NYT, LAT-WAT. Circulation: 30,827 evening (paid); 32,687 Sunday (paid). **Owner(s):** Morris Multimedia, Inc., PO Box 936, Augusta, GA 30903. Telephone: 706-724-0851. **Management:** Jeff Wilson, Publisher. Ron Forrest, Circulation Director. Angela Smith, Classified Adv. Mgr.. Gary Cleveland, Production Director. **Editorial:** Don Nelson, Associate Editor. Roger Nielson, Metro Editor. Bill Stewart, News Editor. John Curry, Photographer. Andy Johanston, Sports Editor.

ATLANTA

ATLANTA JOURNAL - CONSTITUTION, THE. ISSN 1539-7459
6205 Peachtree Dunwoody Rd., Atlanta, GA 30328. Telephone: 678-645-0000. E-MAIL: constitution@ajc.com. URL: http://www.ajc.com/. Year Established: 2001. Pub. Frequency: d. Page Size: broadsheet. Subscrip. Rate: $.50 newsstand/cover; $2 newsstand/cover Sun.; $120/yr carrier delivery in city. Circulation: 382,421 per issue. **Owner(s):** Cox Newspapers, Inc., 72 Marietta St., N..W., Atlanta, GA 30303. Telephone: 404-526-5151. FAX: 404-526-5156. **Management:** John Mellott, Publisher. Mike Perricone, Advertising Director. **Editorial:** Julia Wallace, Editor. Hank Klibanoff, Managing Editor. Mark Braykovich, Business Editor. Howard Pousner, Entertainment Editor. Ron Feinberg, Lifestyle Editor.

AUGUSTA

AUGUSTA CHRONICLE, THE. ISSN 0747-1343
PO Box 1928, Augusta, GA 30903-1928. FAX: 706-722-7403. E-MAIL: newsroom@augustachronicle.com. URL: http://www.augustachronicle.com/. Pub. Frequency: d. Page Size: broadsheet. Subscrip. Rate: $.50 newsstand/cover; $1.25 newsstand/cover Sun.; $156/yr home delivery. **Wire Service(s):** AP, LAT-WAT. Circulation: 79,597 morning (paid); 922,917 Sunday (paid). **Owner(s):** Morris Multimedia, Inc., See address and contact information above. **Management:** Don Bailey, General Manager. William S. Morris IV, President. William S Morris III, Publisher. Markelly Core, Advertising Manager. Jeff Hartley, Circulation Manager. Mark Lane, Sales Manager. **Editorial:** Dennis Sodomka, Executive Editor. Elizabeth Adams, Managing Editor. Michael Ryan, Editorial Page Editor. Mike Wynn, Metro Editor. Johnathan Ernst, Photographer.

BRUNSWICK

BRUNSWICK NEWS, THE. ISSN 1090-3895
3011 Altama Ave., Brunswick, GA 31520-1557. Telephone: 912-265-8320. FAX: 912-264-4973. E-MAIL: brunswicknews@technonet.com. URL: http://www.thebrunswicknews.com. Year Established: 1902. Pub. Frequency: d. (Mon.-Sat.) Page Size: broadsheet. Subscrip. Rate: $.50 newsstand/cover; $6.81 carrier delivery/mo.; $88/yr carrier delivery. **Wire Service(s):** AP. Circulation: 17,000 morning (paid). **Owner(s):** Brunswick News Publishing Co., PO Box 1557, Brunswick, GA 31521-1557. Telephone: 912-265-8320. FAX: 912-264-4973. **Management:** Ron Maulden, General Manager. C. Howard Leavy IV, Publisher. Frank Hill, Circulation Manager. **Editorial:** C. Howard Leavy IV, Editor. Kerry Klumpe, Managing Editor. Kathy Arens, Feature Editor. Hank Rowland, Metro Editor. Bobbie Haven, Photographer. Bud Ellis, Sports Editor.

GEORGIA TIMES-UNION. 3675 Community Rd., Brunswick, GA 31520. Telephone: 912-264-0720. FAX: 912-264-1407. Pub. Frequency: d. Page Size: broadsheet. Subscrip. Rate: $.50 newsstand/cover; $1 newsstand/cover Sun.; $3.28 home delivery/wk. local; $143.51/yr. Circulation: 700,633 morning (paid). **Owner(s):** Morris Multimedia, Inc., PO Box 936, Augusta, GA 30903. Telephone: 706-724-9851. **Management:** Robert E. Martin, General Manager. Carl N. Cannon, Publisher. Geri Kotz, Classified Adv. Mgr.. **Editorial:** Greg Walsh, Editor.

CANTON

CHEROKEE TRIBUNE, THE. 521 E. Main St., Canton, GA 30114. Telephone: 770-479-1441. FAX: 770-479-3505. URL: http://cherokeetribune.com. Mailing Address: PO Box 966, Canton, GA 30114. Year Established: 1973. Pub. Frequency: d. (Wed.-Sun.) Page Size: broadsheet. Subscrip. Rate: $.50 newsstand/cover; $.75 newsstand/cover Sun.; $55/yr home delivery in county. Circulation: 32,000 morning (paid and free); 32,000 Sunday (paid and free). **Owner(s):** Marietta Daily Journal & Neighbor Newspapers, 580 Fairground St., Marietta, GA 30060. Telephone: 770-428-9411. FAX: 770-428-7945. **Management:** Otis Brumby Jr., Publisher. Carla Barnen, Advertising Manager. Rusty Powell, Circulation Manager. **Editorial:** Barbara Perry, News Editor. Chris Whitefield, Sports Editor.

CARROLTON

TIMES-GEORGIAN. ISSN 1049-9458
901 Hay's Mill Rd., Carrolton, GA 30117. Telephone: 770-834-6631. FAX: 770-834-9991. Mailing Address: PO Box 460, Carrollton, GA 30117. Year Established: 1872. Pub. Frequency: d. (Tue.-Sun.) Page Size: broadsheet. Subscrip. Rate: $.50 newsstand/cover; $1 newsstand/cover Sun.; $104/yr carrier delivery. **Wire Service(s):** AP. Circulation: 13,000 morning (paid). **Owner(s):** Paxton Media Group Llc, 201 S. Fourth St., Paducah, KY 42003. Telephone: 270-575-8600. FAX: 270-442-8188. **Management:** Thomas Overton, Publisher. Tim Holder, Advertising Director. Mik Floye, Circulation Director. Glenda Hicks, Classified Adv. Mgr.. **Editorial:** Bruce Browning, Editor. Chris Golterman, Sports Editor.

CARTERSVILLE

DAILY TRIBUNE NEWS, THE. ISSN 1049-6750
251 S. Tennessee St., Cartersville, GA 30120. Telephone: 770-382-4545. FAX: 770-382-2711. E-MAIL: news@daily-tribune.com. URL: http://www.daily-tribune.com. Mailing Address: PO Box 70, Cartersville, GA 30120-0070. Year Established: 1946. Pub. Frequency: d. (Sun.-Fri.) Page Size: broadsheet. Subscrip. Rate: $.50 newsstand/cover; $1 Sun.; $26.95 carrier delivery for 3 mos.; $89.95/yr. Adv. Rate: col. inch $8.55 **Wire Service(s):** AP. Circulation: 12,000 Sunday (paid); 11,000 per issue (paid). **Owner(s):** Cleveland Newspapers, Inc., 1505 25th St., N.W., Cleveland, TN 37311. Telephone: 423-472-5041. **Management:** Johnette Dawson, Publisher. Jennifer Moates, Advertising Director. Tony Henderson, Circulation Manager. **Editorial:** Johnette Dawson, Editor. Joe Hiett, Managing Editor. Elizabeth Cochran, Lifestyle Editor. Joseph Myers, Sports Editor.

COLUMBUS

COLUMBUS LEDGER-ENQUIRER. ISSN 0898-3860
17 W 12th St, Columbus, GA 31901. Telephone: 706-324-5526. FAX: 706-576-6290. E-MAIL: info@ledger-enquirer.com. URL: http://www.ledger-enquirer.com. Mailing Address: PO Box 711, Columbus, GA 31902-0711. Year Established: 1828. Pub. Frequency: d. Page Size: broadsheet. Subscrip. Rate: $.50, $1.50 newsstand/cover; $102 carrier delivery for 6 mos.; $182 mailed for 6 mos.. **Wire Service(s):** AP. Circulation: 48,146 morning (paid); 58,629 Sunday (paid). **Owner(s):** The/McClatchy Company, 2100 Q St, Sacramento, CA 95816. FAX: 916-321-1869. **Management:** Pam Siddall, Publisher. Jodi Bell, Advertising Director. John Kelly, Circulation Director. Lori Ziegelmann, Classified Adv. Mgr.. **Editorial:** Ben Holden, Executive Editor.

CONYERS

ROCKDALE CITIZEN. ISSN 1050-1401
969 S Main St, Conyers, GA 30012. Telephone: 770-483-7108. FAX: 770-483-5797. E-MAIL: jeff.johnson@rockdalecitizen.com. URL: http://www.rockdalecitizen.com. Mailing Address: PO Box 136, Conyers, GA 30012. Year Established: 1909. Pub. Frequency: d. Page Size: broadsheet. Subscrip. Rate: $.50 newsstand/cover; $1.50 newsstand/cover Sun.; $120.32/yr carrier delivery in county; $221/yr mailed out of county. Circulation: 17,000 morning (paid); 17,000 Sunday (paid). **Owner(s):** Triple Crown Media, Inc., 546 E Main St, Lexington, KY 40508. Telephone: 859-226-4678. FAX: 859-226-4308. **Management:** Alice Queen, Publisher. Brenda Bennett, Advertising Manager. **Editorial:** Colin Stewart, Editor. Bill Herbert, Circulation Editor.

CORDELE

CORDELE DISPATCH. 306 13th. Ave., W., Cordele, GA 31015. Telephone: 229-273-2277. FAX: 229-273-7239. URL: http://www.cordeledispatch.com. Mailing Address: PO Box 1058, Cordele, GA 31010. Year Established: 1908. Pub. Frequency: d. (Tue.-Fri. & Sun.) Page Size: broadsheet. Subscrip. Rate: $.50 newsstand/cover; $.75 newsstand/cover Sun.; $89.75/yr carrier delivery. **Wire Service(s):** AP. Circulation: 5,061 evening (paid). **Owner(s):** Community Newspaper Holdings, Inc., 3500 Colonnade Pkwy., Ste. 600, Birmingham, AL 35243. Telephone: 205-298-7100. **Management:** Peggy King, Publisher. Chris Mann, Advertising Director. Ashli Garrick, Circulation Manager. Cathy Baker, Classified Adv. Mgr.. **Editorial:** Carmen Lindsey, Managing Editor.

COVINGTON

NEWTON CITIZEN. 7121 Turner Lake Rd, Covington, GA 30014. URL: http://www.newtoncitizen.com. Pub. Frequency: w. (Mon.-Fri.) Page Size: broadsheet. Subscrip. Rate: $.50 newsstand/cover; $66/yr in county; $237.14/yr out of county. Circulation: 5,309 per issue (paid). **Owner(s):** Triple Crown Media, Inc., 546 E Main St, Lexington, KY 40508. **Management:** Alice Queen, Publisher. Brenda Bennett, Advertising Manager. **Editorial:** Colin Stewart, Editor. Bill Herbert, Circulation Editor.

DALTON

DAILY CITIZEN NEWS. 308 S. Thornton Ave., Dalton, GA 30720-1167. Telephone: 706-278-6397. FAX: 706-275-6641. E-MAIL: williambronson@daltoncitizen.com. URL: http://www.daltondailycitizen.com. Mailing Address: PO Box 1167, Dalton, GA 30722. Year Established: 1847. Pub. Frequency: d. Page Size: broadsheet. Subscrip. Rate: $.50 newsstand/cover; $1 newsstand/cover Sun.; $135.24/yr home delivery in area; $167.16/yr mailed elsewhere. Freelance Pay: $0.50/column-inch. **Wire Service(s):** AP. Circulation: 14,500 morning (paid); 15,500 Sunday (paid). **Owner(s):** Community Newspaper Holdings, Inc., 3500 Colonnade Pkwy., Ste. 600, Birmingham, AL 35243. Telephone: 205-298-7100. FAX: 205-298-7101. **Management:** William Bronson III, Publisher. Jeff Mutter, Advertising Director. Claudia Harrell, Circulation Director. **Editorial:** Jim Espy, Executive Editor.

DOUGLASVILLE

DOUGLAS COUNTY SENTINEL. 8501 Bowden St., Douglasville, GA 30134. Telephone: 770-942-6571. FAX: 770-949-7556. E-MAIL: news@douglascountysentianl.com. Mailing Address: PO Box 1586, Douglasville, GA 30133. Year Established: 1902. Pub. Frequency: d. (Tue.-Sun.) Page Size: broadsheet. Subscrip. Rate: $.50 newsstand/cover; $1 newsstand/cover Sun.; $100/yr carrier delivery. Freelance Pay: $25/story. **Wire Service(s):** AP. Circulation: 7,000 evening (paid); 7,000 Sunday (paid). **Owner(s):** Paxton Media Group Llc, 201 S. Fourth St., Paducah, KY 42003. Telephone: 270-575-8600. FAX: 270-442-8188. **Management:** Mitchell Lynch, Publisher. **Editorial:** Bill Fordham, Editor. Sheila Ervin, News Editor. Stephen Barrett, Photographer. Bill Evans, Sports Editor.

DUBLIN

COURIER-HERALD, THE. 115 S. Jefferson St., Dublin, GA 31040. Telephone: 478-272-5522. FAX: 478-272-2189. E-MAIL: press@courier-herald.com. URL: http://www.courier-herald.com. Year Established: 1913. Pub. Frequency: d. (Mon.-Sat.) Page Size: broadsheet. Subscrip. Rate: $.50 newsstand/cover; $112/yr home delivery; $159/yr mailed. **Wire Service(s):** AP. Circulation: 11,800 evening (paid). **Owner(s):** DuBose Porter & Griffin Lovett, 115 S. Jefferson St., Dublin, GA 31021. Telephone: 478-272-5522. **Management:** DuBose Porter, General Manager. Griffin Lovett, Publisher. Marsha Green, Advertising Director. Cheryl Gay, Circulation Manager. Donna Aldridge, Classified Adv. Mgr.. **Editorial:** DuBose Porter, Editor. Stacye Lee, Managing Editor. Brandy Mullis, Lifestyle Editor.

FAYETTEVILLE

FAYETTE DAILY NEWS. 210 Jeff Davis Pl., Fayetteville, GA 30214. Telephone: 770-461-6317. FAX: 770-460-8172. URL: http://www.fayettedailynews.com. Mailing Address: PO Box 96, Fayetteville, GA 30214. Year Established: 1886. Pub. Frequency: d. (Tue.-Sat) Page Size: broadsheet. Subscrip. Rate: $.50 newsstand/cover; $38.96/yr. **Wire Service(s):** AP. Circulation: 28,000 morning (paid). **Owner(s):** Trib Publications, Inc., PO Box 648, Manchester, GA 31816. Telephone: 706-846-4336. **Management:** Chuck Morley, Publisher. Geneva Weaver, Advertising Manager. **Editorial:** Chuck Morley, Editor-in-Chief. Cindy Morley, Managing Editor.

TODAY IN PEACHTREE CITY. 210 Jeff Davis Pl., Fayetteville, GA 30214. Telephone: 770-461-6317. FAX: 770-460-8172. URL: http://www.fayettevilledailynews.com. Mailing Address: PO Box 96, Fayetteville, GA 30214. Year Established: 1997. Pub. Frequency: d. (Tue.-Sat.) Page Size: broadsheet. Subscrip. Rate: $.50 newsstand/cover; $38.96/yr in county; $60.64/yr out of county. Adv. Rate: col. inch $9 Circulation: 4,500 morning (paid). **Owner(s):** Trib Publications, Inc., PO Box 648, Manchester, GA 31816. Telephone: 706-846-4336. **Management:** Robert Tribble, President. Chuck Morley, Publisher. Geneva Weaver, Advertising Manager. **Editorial:** Chuck Morley, Editor-in-Chief. Cindy Morley, Managing Editor.

GAINESVILLE

TIMES (GAINESVILLE), THE. 345 Green St, NW, Gainesville, GA 30501. Telephone: 770-532-1234. FAX: 770-535-2859. URL: http://www.gainesvilletimes.com. Mailing Address: PO Box 838, Gainesville, GA 30503. Pub. Frequency: d. Subscrip. Rate: $.50 newsstand/cover; $1.50 newsstand/cover Sun.; $169/yr home delivery local. **Wire Service(s):** AP. Circulation: 22,754 evening (paid); 26,693 Sunday (paid). **Owner(s):** Morris Newspaper Corporation, 27 Abercorn St., Savannah, GA 31401. Telephone: 912-233-1281. FAX: 912-232-4639. **Management:** Steven Reynolds, Publisher. Frank Bauer, Advertising Director.

GRIFFIN

GRIFFIN DAILY NEWS. ISSN 0746-3324
323 E. Solomon St., Griffin, GA 30224. Telephone: 770-227-3276. FAX: 770-412-1678. E-MAIL: editor@griffin-news.com. URL: http://www.griffindailynews.com. Mailing Address: P.O. Drawer M, Griffin, GA 30224. Pub. Frequency: d. Page Size: broadsheet. Subscrip. Rate: $.50 newsstand/cover; $1.50 newsstand/cover Sun.; $12 home delivery/mo.. Circulation: 13,000 morning (paid); 15,000 Sunday (paid). **Owner(s):** Paxton Media Group. Inc., 201 S. Fourth St., Paducah, KY 42003. Telephone: 270-575-8600. FAX: 270-442-8188. **Management:** David Clevenger, Publisher. Joy Gaddy, Advertising Manager. **Editorial:** Renee Carey, Editor. Regina Fisher, Asst. Managing Ed.. John Sullivan, Sports Editor.

JONESBORO

CLAYTON NEWS DAILY. 138 Church St., Jonesboro, GA 30237. Telephone: 770-478-5753. FAX: 770-473-9032. E-MAIL: cmartin@news-daily.com. URL: http://www.news-daily.com. Mailing Address: PO Box 368, Jonesboro, GA 30237. Year Established: 1970. Pub. Frequency: d. (Mon.-Sat.) Page Size: broadsheet. Subscrip. Rate: $.50 newsstand/cover; $90.95/yr home delivery; $151.08/yr mailed out of county; $169.52/yr mailed out of state. **Wire Service(s):** UPI. Circulation: 6,800 evening (paid). **Owner(s):** Triple Crown Media, Inc., 546 E Main St, Lexington, KY 40508. Telephone: 859-226-4678. FAX: 859-226-4308. **Management:** Bonnie Pratt, Publisher. Christy Collier, Advertising Director. Rita Camp, Classified Adv. Mgr.. **Editorial:** Chet Fuller, Managing Editor.

LA GRANGE

LA GRANGE DAILY NEWS. 105 Ashton St., La Grange, GA 30240. Telephone: 706-884-7311. FAX: 706-884-8712. E-MAIL: ldn@wp-lag.minespring.com. URL: http://www.lagrangenews.com. Mailing Address: PO Box 929, La Grange, GA 31240. Pub. Frequency: d. Page Size: broadsheet. Subscrip. Rate: $.50 newsstand/cover; $1.25 newsstand/cover Sun.; $132/yr home delivery. **Wire Service(s):** AP. Circulation: 11,289 (paid). **Owner(s):** Crescent Media Group, PO Box 1634, Spartanburg, SC 29304. Telephone: 864-583-2907. **Management:** Jennifer Bell, General Manager. Mike Pippin, Publisher. Lynne B. Holle, Advertising Manager. Judy Phillips, Business Manager. **Editorial:** Andrea LoveJoy, Editor. Roland Foiles, Production Manager. Dan Baker, News Editor.

LAWRENCEVILLE

GWINNETT DAILY POST. 725 Old Norcross Rd, Lawrenceville, GA 30045. Telephone: 770-963-9205. FAX: 770-339-8081. URL: http://www.gwinnettdailypost.com. Mailing Address: PO Box 603, Lawrenceville, GA 30046-0603. Year Established: 1970. Pub. Frequency: d. (Tue.-Sun.) Page Size: broadsheet. Subscrip. Rate: $.50 newsstand/cover; $1.50 newsstand/cover Sun.; $36/yr in county; $150/yr mailed out of county. **Wire Service(s):** AP. Circulation: 62,070 morning (paid); 104,941 Sunday (paid). **Owner(s):** Triple Crown Media, Inc., 546 E Main St, Lexington, KY 40508. Telephone: 859-226-4678. FAX: 859-226-4308. **Management:** J.K. Murphy, Publisher. Brenda Bohn, Advertising Director. David Graham, Circulation Manager. Kellie Moore, Classified Adv. Mgr.. **Editorial:** Todd Cline, Editor.

MACON

TELEGRAPH (MACON), THE. ISSN 1054-2485
120 Broadway, Macon, GA 31201. Telephone: 478-744-4200. FAX: 478-744-4385. URL: http://www.macontelegraph.com. Mailing Address: PO Box 4167, Macon, GA 31208-4167. Year Established: 1826. Pub. Frequency: d. Page Size: broadsheet. Subscrip. Rate: $.50 newsstand/cover; $1.50 newsstand/cover Sun.; $45.37 for 13 wks.. **Wire Service(s):** AP, NYT. Circulation: 70,000 morning (paid); 85,000 Sunday (paid). **Owner(s):** The/McClatchy Company, 2100 Q St, Sacramento, CA 95816. Telephone: 916-321-1936. FAX: 916-321-1869. **Management:** P.J. Browning, Publisher. Debbie Williams, VP Advertising. **Editorial:** Sherri Marshall, Executive Editor. Oby Brown, Feature Editor. Daniel Shirley, Sports Editor.

MARIETTA

MARIETTA DAILY JOURNAL. ISSN 8750-4618
580 Fairground St., Marietta, GA 30060. Telephone: 770-795-3000. FAX: 770-422-9533. URL: http://www.mdjonline.com. Mailing Address: PO Box 449, Marietta, GA 30061. Year Established: 1866. Pub. Frequency: d. Page Size: broadsheet. Subscrip. Rate: $.50 newsstand/cover; $.75 Sun.; $114.08/yr home delivery. **Wire Service(s):** AP, SH. Circulation: 21,800 morning (paid); 21,800 Sunday (paid). **Owner(s):** Otis A. Brumby, Jr., See address and contact information above. **Management:** Otis Brumby Jr., Publisher. Wade Stephens, Advertising Manager. Jay Whorton, Associate Publisher. **Editorial:** Billy Mitchell, Managing Editor. Joe Kirby, Editorial Page Editor. Chris Whitfield, Sports Editor.

MCDONOUGH

HENRY DAILY HERALD, THE. 38 Sloan St, McDonough, GA 30253. Telephone: 770-957-9161. FAX: 770-954-0282, URL: http://www.henryherald.com. Mailing Address: PO Box 278, McDonough, GA 30253-0278. Year Established: 1874. Pub. Frequency: d. (Mon.- Sat.) Page Size: broadsheet. Subscrip. Rate: $.50 newsstand/cover; $90.95/yr; $151.08/yr mailed out of county; $169.52/yr mailed out of state. Freelance Pay: $25/story. Circulation: 4,200 morning (paid). **Owner(s):** Triple Crown Media, Inc., 546 E Main St, Lexington, KY 40508. Telephone: 859-226-4678. FAX: 859-226-4308. **Management:** Bonnie Pratt, Publisher. Christy Collier, Advertising Director. **Editorial:** Chet Fuller, Managing Editor.

MILLEDGEVILLE

UNION-RECORDER, THE. 165 Garrett Way, Milledgeville, GA 31061-0520. Telephone: 478-452-0567. FAX: 478-453-4539. E-MAIL: ahood@cnhi.com. URL: http://www.unionrecorder.com. Mailing Address: PO Box 520, Milledgeville, GA 31059-0520. Year Established: 1820. Pub. Frequency: d. (Tue.-Sat.) Page Size: broadsheet. Subscrip. Rate: $.50 newsstand/cover; $22.75 home delivery for 13 wks.; $27.65 mailed for 13 wks.. **Wire Service(s):** AP, MCT. Circulation: 8,500 morning (paid). **Owner(s):** Community Newspaper Holdings, Inc., 3500 Colonnade Pkwy., Ste. 600, Birmingham, AL 35243. Telephone: 205-298-7100. FAX: 205-298-7101. **Management:** Keith Barlow, Publisher. Erin Simmons, Advertising Manager. Michael Evans, Circulation Manager. **Editorial:** Judy Bailey, Executive Editor.

MOULTRIE

MOULTRIE OBSERVER, THE. 25 N. Main St., Moultrie, GA 31768. Telephone: 229-985-4545. FAX: 292-985-3569. E-MAIL: moultrie.observer@gaflnews.com. URL: http://www.sgaonline.com. Mailing Address: PO Box 2349, Moultrie, GA 31776. Year Established: 1894. Pub. Frequency: d. (Tue.-Sun.) Page Size: broadsheet. Subscrip. Rate: $.50 newsstand/cover; $1 newsstand/cover Sun.; $10.40/mo.; $124/yr. **Wire Service(s):** AP, GNS. Circulation: 7,500 per issue (paid); 16,500 Sunday (paid). **Owner(s):** Community Newspaper Holdings, Inc., 3500 Colonnade Pkwy., Ste. 600, Birmingham, AL 35243. Telephone: 205-298-7100. FAX: 205-298-7101. **Management:** Dwain Waldon, Publisher. Cathy New, Advertising Director. Laura Rogers, Advertising Manager. Shawn Highsmith, Circulation Director. Cathy New, Classified Adv. Mgr.. **Editorial:** Dwain Waldon, Editor.

NEWNAN

TIMES-HERALD, THE. ISSN 0883-2536
16 Jefferson St., Newnan, GA 30263. Telephone: 770-253-1576. FAX: 770-253-2538. E-MAIL: webmaster@newnan.com. URL: http://times-herald.com. Mailing Address: PO Box 1052, Newnan, GA 30264. Year Established: 1865. Pub. Frequency: d. Page Size: broadsheet. Subscrip. Rate: $.50 newsstand/cover; $1.25 newsstand/cover Sun.; $124/yr home delivery in county; $245/yr mailed; $99/yr to senior citizens. Adv. Rate: col. inch $16.65 **Wire Service(s):** AP. Circulation: 10,033 morning (paid); 10,033 Sunday (paid). **Owner(s):** W. W. Thomasson, See address and contact information above. **Management:** William Thomasson, President. Sam Jones, Publisher. Marianne Thomasson, Vice President. Lamar Truitt, Advertising Manager. Naomi Jackson, Circulation Director. Colleen D Mitchell, Marketing Director. **Editorial:** Winston Skinner, Assistant Editor. Ellen Corker, News Editor. Tommy Camp, Sports Editor.

PERRY

HOUSTON HOME JOURNAL, THE. 1210 Washington St., Perry, GA 31069. Telephone: 478-987-1823. FAX: 478-988-9194. E-MAIL: hhjnews@evansnewspapers.com@home.net. URL: http://www.hhjnews.com. Mailing Address: PO Box 1910, Perry, GA 31069. Year Established: 1870. Pub. Frequency: d. (Tue. - Sat.) Page Size: broadsheet. Subscrip. Rate: $.50 newsstand/cover; $40/yr in county; $60/yr out of county. Circulation: 12,000 per issue (paid). **Owner(s):** Daniel Evans, See address and contact information above. **Management:** Daniel Evans, Publisher. Audrey Evans, Vice President. Julie Evans, Marketing. Cheri Adams, Assistant Publisher. **Editorial:** Randolph Murray, Managing Editor.

ROME

ROME NEWS-TRIBUNE. ISSN 1060-4049
305 E. Sixth Ave., Rome, GA 30161. E-MAIL: romenewstribune@RN-T.com. URL: http://www.romenews-tribune.com. Mailing Address: PO Box 1633, Rome, GA 30162-1633. Year Established: 1838. Pub. Frequency: d. (Sun.-Fri.) Page Size: broadsheet. Subscrip. Rate: $.50 newsstand/cover; $1.50 Sun.; $100.64/yr. **Wire Service(s):** AP. Circulation: 19,915 evening (paid); 21,567 Sunday (paid). **Owner(s):** News Publishing Co., See address and contact information above. **Management:** Burgett Mooney, Publisher. Trip Hapley, Advertising Director. Robert Ronco, Circulation Manager. Joe Morgan, Business Manager. **Editorial:** Charlotte Atkins, Editor. Meaghan Marr, Lifestyle Editor.

SAVANNAH

SAVANNAH MORNING NEWS. ISSN 1047-028X
111 W. Bay St., Savannah, GA 31402. Telephone: 912-236-9511. FAX: 912-234-6522. Mailing Address: PO Box 1088, Savannah, GA 31402. Year Established: 1850. Pub. Frequency: d. Page Size: broadsheet. Subscrip. Rate: $.50 newsstand/cover; $1.25 newsstand/cover Sun.; $102/yr home delivery. **Wire Service(s):** AP, LAT-WAT. Circulation: 69,090 morning (paid); 83,217 Sunday (paid). **Owner(s):** Morris Multimedia, Inc., 27 Abercorn St., Savannah, GA 31401. Telephone: 912-233-1281. **Management:** Frank Anderson, Publisher. **Editorial:** Rexanna Lester, Executive Editor. Daniel Suwyn, Managing Editor. Carl Elmore, Community Editor. Arlinda Broady, Lifestyle Editor. Larry Peterson, Political Editor. Tony Stastny, Sports Editor.

STATESBORO

STATESBORO HERALD. ISSN 0746-4665
#1 Proctor St, Herald Sq, Statesboro, GA 30459. Telephone: 912-764-9031. FAX: 912-489-8181. E-MAIL: randy@statesboroherald.net. URL: http://www.statesboroherald.net. Mailing Address: PO Box 888, Statesboro, GA 30459. Year Established: 1937. Pub. Frequency: d. Page Size: broadsheet. Subscrip. Rate: $.50 newsstand/cover; $1 newsstand/cover Sun.; $10.80 for 4 wks.; $35.10 for 13 wks.; $70.20 for 26 wks.; $140.40/yr. **Wire Service(s):** AP. Circulation: 7,637 morning (paid). **Owner(s):** Morris Newspaper Corporation, 27 Abercorn St., Savannah, GA 31401. Telephone: 912-233-1281. FAX: 912-232-4639. **Management:** Randy Morton, Publisher. Jan Melton, Advertising Manager. Darrell Elliott, Circulation Manager. Pam Pollard, Classified Adv. Mgr.. **Editorial:** Nancy Welch, Editor. James Healy, Executive Editor. Eddie Ledbetter, Managing Editor.

THOMASVILLE

THOMASVILLE TIMES-ENTERPRISE. ISSN 0746-4894
106 South St., Thomasville, GA 31792. Telephone: 229-226-2400. FAX: 912-228-5863. E-MAIL: southga.online@gaflnews.com. URL: http://www.sgaonline.com. Mailing Address: PO Box 650, Thomasville, GA 31799. Year Established: 1889. Pub. Frequency: d. (Tue.-Sun.) Page Size: broadsheet. Subscrip. Rate: $.50 newsstand/cover; $1 newsstand/cover Sun.; $126/yr home delivery; $144/yr mailed. **Wire Service(s):** AP. Circulation: 9,600 morning (paid); 9,700 Sunday (paid). **Owner(s):** Community Newspaper Holdings, Inc., 3500 Colonnade Pkwy., Ste. 600, Birmingham, AL 35243. Telephone: 205-298-7100. FAX: 205-298-7101. **Management:** Norman Bankston, Publisher. Christine White, Advertising Director. Laura Rogers, Advertising Manager. Thomas Clements, Circulation Manager. **Editorial:** Mark Lastinger, Managing Editor.

TIFTON

TIFTON GAZETTE, THE. ISSN 1065-2884
211 N. Tift Ave., Tifton, GA 31794. Telephone: 229-382-4321. FAX: 229-387-7322. E-MAIL: flo.rankin@gaflnews.com. URL: http://www.tiftongazette.com. Mailing Address: PO Box 708, Tifton, GA 31793. Year Established: 1888. Pub. Frequency: d. (Tue.-Sun.) Page Size: broadsheet. Subscrip. Rate: $.50 newsstand/cover; $1 newsstand/cover Sun.; $104.88/yr home delivery; $114.40/yr mailed. **Wire Service(s):** AP. Circulation: 9,500 morning (paid); 8,600 Sunday (paid). **Owner(s):** Community Newspaper Holdings, Inc., 3500 Colonnade Pkwy., Ste. 600, Birmingham, AL 35243. Telephone: 205-298-7100. FAX: 205-298-7101. **Management:** Frank Sayles, Publisher. Darrin Wilson, Advertising Manager. Brent Griffin, Circulation Manager. **Editorial:** Flo Rankin, Managing Editor. Dusty Vassey, City Editor. Steve Carter, Sports.

VALDOSTA

VALDOSTA DAILY TIMES, THE. 201 N. Troup St., Valdosta, GA 31601. Telephone: 229-244-1880. FAX: 292-244-2560. E-MAIL: jkillon@cnhi.com. URL: http://www.sgaonline.com. Mailing Address: PO Box 968, Valdosta, GA 31603. Year Established: 1867. Pub. Frequency: d. Page Size: broadsheet. Subscrip. Rate: $.50 newsstand/cover; $1 Sun.; $11.80 home delivery/mo.. **Wire Service(s):** AP. Circulation: 21,150 morning (paid); 21,150 Sunday (paid). **Owner(s):** Community Newspaper Holdings, Inc., 3500 Colonnade Pkwy., Ste. 600, Birmingham, AL 35243. Telephone: 205-298-7100. FAX: 205-298-7101. **Management:** Sandy Sanders, Publisher. Julie Killion, Advertising Director. Hal Welch, Advertising Manager. Samuil Kikolov, Circulation Director. Angela Lynch, Classified Adv. Mgr.. **Editorial:** Kay Harris, Managing Editor.

WAYCROSS

WAYCROSS JOURNAL HERALD. 400 Isabella St., Waycross, GA 31501. Telephone: 912-283-2244. FAX: 912-285-5255. E-MAIL: jack.williams@wjhnews.com. URL: http://www.wjhnews.com. Mailing Address: PO Box 219, Waycross, GA 31502. Year Established: 1875. Pub. Frequency: d. (Mon.-Sat.) Page Size: broadsheet. Subscrip. Rate: $.50 newsstand/cover; $9.25/mo. local; $111/yr local. Adv. Rate: col. inch $7.20 **Wire Service(s):** AP. Circulation: 11,000 evening (paid). **Owner(s):** Journal Herald Co., Inc., See address and contact information above. **Management:** Roger L. Williams, Publisher. David Tanner, Advertising Manager. Lori Fanucci, Circulation Manager. **Editorial:** Jack Williams III, Editor-in-Chief. Gary Griffin, Managing Editor. Myra Thrift, City Editor. Amy Roundtree, Feature Editor. Gary Griffin, Financial Editor.

HAWAII

HILO

HAWAII TRIBUNE-HERALD. 355 Kinoole St., Hilo, HI 96720. Telephone: 808-935-6621. FAX: 808-969-9100. URL: http://www.hawaiitribune-herald.com. Mailing Address: PO Box 767, Hilo, HI 96721-0767. Year Established: 1923. Pub. Frequency: d. (Sun.-Fri.) Page Size: broadsheet. Subscrip. Rate: $.50 newsstand/cover; $1 Sun.; $57.50 home delivery/mo. daily only; $71.50 mailed/mo. with Sun.; $24 mailed/mo. Sun. only. Freelance Pay: $20/article. **Wire Service(s):** AP. Circulation: 19,282 morning (paid); 23,075 Sunday (paid). **Owner(s):** Stephens Media LLC, 1111 W. Bonanza Rd., Las Vegas, NV 89106. Telephone: 702-383-0211. FAX: 702-383-4676. **Management:** David Bock, Managing Director. Ted Dixon, Publisher. Alice Sledge, Advertising Director. Bill Crawford, Circulation Director. **Editorial:** William Ing, Photographer. Bill O'Rear, Sports.

HONOLULU

HONOLULU ADVERTISER, THE. ISSN 1072-7191
605 Kapiolani Blvd., Honolulu, HI 96813. Telephone: 808-525-8000. FAX: 808-525-8037. URL: http://www.honoluluadvertiser.com. Mailing Address: PO Box 3110, Honolulu, HI 96802. Year Established: 1856. Pub. Frequency: d. Page Size: broadsheet. Subscrip. Rate: $.50 newsstand/cover; $1.75 newsstand/cover Sun.; $32.50 mailed for 4 wks.. Freelance Pay: $35-$150/article. **Wire Service(s):** AP, LAT-WAT, MCT. Circulation: 146,252 morning (paid); 168,213 Sunday (paid). **Owner(s):** Gannett Company, Inc., 7950 Jones Branch Dr., McLean, VA 22107-0001. Telephone: 703-854-6000. **Management:** Michael Fisch, Publisher. Jeff Green, Advertising Director. Michael Cusato Jr., Circulation Manager. **Editorial:** Saundra Keyes, Editor. Mark Platte, Managing Editor. David Butts, Business Editor. Fernando Pizarro, City Editor. Ken Kobayashi, Court Editor. Jeanne Mariani-Belding, Editorial Page Editor. Wayne Harada, Entertainment Editor. Steve Petranik, News Editor. Seth Jones, Photo Editor. Curtis Murayama, Sports Editor.

HONOLULU STAR-BULLETIN. 500 Alamoane Blvd.,, 7 Waterfront Plaza, Ste. 500, Honolulu, HI 96813. Telephone: 808-525-8640. FAX: 808-247-7246. E-MAIL: citydesk@starbulletin.com. URL: http://www.starbulletin.com. Year Established: 1882. Pub. Frequency: d. Page Size: broadsheet. Subscrip. Rate: $.50 newsstand/cover; $11.25/mo.; $33.75 for 3 mos.; $64.25 for 6 mos.; $85.80/yr. **Wire Service(s):** RN, AP, SH, NYT. Circulation: 61,976 evening (paid). **Owner(s):** David Black, See address and contact information above. **Management:** Dennis Francis, Publisher. Dave Kennedy, VP Circulation. **Editorial:** Frank Bridgewater, Editor. Lucy Young-Oda, Assistant Editor. Alan Vaughn, Business Editor. Ed Lynch, City Editor. Mary Poole, Editorial Page Editor. Nadine Kam, Lifestyle Editor. Paul Arnett, Sports Editor.

KAILUA KONA

WEST HAWAII TODAY. ISSN 0744-4591
75-5580 Kuakini Hwy., Kailua Kona, HI 96745-0789. Telephone: 808-329-9311. FAX: 808-329-4860. URL: http://www.westhawaiitoday.com. Mailing Address: PO Box 789, Kailua Kona, HI 96745-0789. Year Established: 1968. Pub. Frequency: d. Page Size: broadsheet. Subscrip. Rate: $.50 newsstand/cover; $1 newsstand/cover Sun.; $9 carrier delivery/mo. Koma area; $108/yr carrier delivery. **Wire Service(s):** AP, LAT-WAT. Circulation: 12,308 morning (paid); 16,386 Sunday (paid). **Owner(s):** Stephens Media LLC, 1111 W. Bonanza Rd., Las Vegas, NV 89106. Telephone: 702-382-5020. **Management:** Richard Asbach, Publisher. Tracey Fosso, Advertising Director. Gloria Fleming, Advertising Manager. John Shackelford, Circulation Director. **Editorial:** Reed Flickinger, Editor.

LIHUE

GARDEN ISLAND NEWSPAPER. ISSN 0744-4028
3-3137 Kuhio Hwy., Lihue, HI 96766. Telephone: 808-245-3681. FAX: 808-245-5286. E-MAIL: ccook@pulitzer.net. URL: http://www.kauaiworld.com. Mailing Address: PO Box 231, Lihue, HI 96766. Pub. Frequency: d. Page Size: broadsheet. Subscrip. Rate: $.50 newsstand/cover; $1.25 newsstand/cover Sun.; $9.75 home delivery/mo.; $52 home delivery for 6 mos.; $104/yr home delivery. Adv. Rate: col. inch $18.75 Circulation: 10,000 morning (paid); 10,000 Sunday (paid). **Owner(s):** Lee Enterprises, Inc., 900 N. Tucker Blvd., St. Louis, MO 63116. Telephone: 314-340-8000. **Management:** Shanna Pollard, Publisher. David Campbell, Circulation Director. **Editorial:** Chris Cook, Editor. Rita DeSilva, Food Editor. Kendyce Manguchei, Lifestyle Editor. Contact: Rita DeSilva, Food Editor.

WAILUKU

MAUI NEWS, THE. ISSN 8750-457X
100 Mahalani St., Wailuku, HI 96793. Telephone: 808-244-3981. FAX: 808-242-9087. E-MAIL: mauinews@maui.net. URL: http://www.maui.net/mauinews. Mailing Address: PO Box 550, Wailuku, HI 96793. Year Established: 1900. Pub. Frequency: d. (Sun.-Fri.) Page Size: broadsheet. Subscrip. Rate: $.50 newsstand/cover; $1.50 newsstand/cover Sun.; $118/yr home delivery; $62/yr home delivery sun only. **Wire Service(s):** AP. Circulation: 8,500 morning (paid). **Owner(s):** Ogden Newspapers of Minnesota, Inc., 1500 Main St., Wheeling, WV 26003. Telephone: 304-233-0100. FAX: 304-233-0327. **Management:** Joe Bradley, Publisher. Dawne Miguel, Advertising Manager. Chris Minford, Circulation Manager. **Editorial:** David Hoff, Editor-in-Chief. Edwin Tanji, City Editor. Lee Imada, News Editor.

IDAHO

BLACKFOOT

MORNING NEWS, THE. ISSN 0893-3812
34 N. Ash St., Blackfoot, ID 83221. Telephone: 208-785-1100. FAX: 208-785-4239. E-MAIL: dblack@am-news.com. URL: http://www.am-news.com. Mailing Address: PO Box 70, Blackfoot, ID 83221. Year Established: 1904. Pub. Frequency: d. (Mon.-Sat.) Page Size: broadsheet. Subscrip. Rate: $.50 newsstand/cover; $89/yr carrier delivery; $99/yr motor route in county; $101.50/yr mailed out of county. **Wire Service(s):** AP. Circulation: 40,000 morning (paid). **Owner(s):** Horizon Publications, Inc., 1120 N. Carbon St., Ste.100, Marion, IL 62959. Telephone: 618-993-1693. **Management:** Leonard Martin, Publisher. Wayne Ingram, Advertising Manager. Phil Ward, Circulation Manager. Jackie Graham, Classified Adv. Mgr.. **Editorial:** Chris O'Nan, Managing Editor.

BOISE

IDAHO STATESMAN, THE. 1200 N Curtis Rd, Boise, ID 83706. Telephone: 208-377-6200. FAX: 208-377-6309. E-MAIL: newsroom@idahostatesman.com. URL: http://www.idahostatesman.com. Mailing Address: PO Box 40, Boise, ID 83707. Year Established: 1864. Pub. Frequency: d. Page Size: broadsheet. Subscrip. Rate: $.50 newsstand/cover; $1.50 newsstand/cover Sun.; $200.20/yr home delivery. **Wire Service(s):** AP, NYT, GNS. Circulation: 143,098 morning (paid); 178,388 Sunday (paid). **Owner(s):** The/McClatchy Company, 2100 Q St, Sacramento, CA 95816. Telephone: 916-321-1936. FAX: 916-321-1869. **Management:** Mi-Ai Parrish, Publisher. Steve Howard, Advertising Manager. Frank Peak, Circulation Director. Athena Killeen, Classified Adv. Mgr.. **Editorial:** Vicki Gowler, Editor.

BURLEY

SOUTH IDAHO PRESS. 230 E. Main St., Burley, ID 83318. Telephone: 208-678-2201. FAX: 208-678-0412. E-MAIL: news@southidahopress.com. URL: http://www.southidahopress.com. Year Established: 1904. Pub. Frequency: d. (Sun.-Fri.) Page Size: broadsheet. Subscrip. Rate: $.50 newsstand/cover; $.75 newsstand/cover Sun.; $8.90/mo.. Adv. Rate: col. inch $10.95 Freelance Pay: $0.50/column-inch. **Wire Service(s):** AP. Circulation: 4,700 evening (paid); 4,700 Sunday (paid). **Owner(s):** GateHouse Media, Inc, 3000 Dundee Rd., Ste. 203, Northbrook, IL 60062. Telephone: 847-272-2244. FAX: 847-272-6244. **Management:** Steve Baker, Publisher. Meghan Grisham, Circulation Manager. Ann Harper, Business Manager. **Editorial:** Chip Thompson, Managing Editor. Mark Jones, Sports Editor.

COEUR D'ALENE

COEUR D'ALENE PRESS, THE. ISSN 1041-2883
201 Second St, Coeur d'Alene, ID 83814. URL: http://www.cdapress.com. Year Established: 1892. Pub. Frequency: d. Page Size: broadsheet. Subscrip. Rate: $.50 newsstand/cover; $1.50 newsstand/cover Sun.; $48.75 home delivery/quarter in county; $22.60 mailed/mo.. **Wire Service(s):** AP. Circulation: 30,000 morning (paid); 30,000 Sunday (paid). **Owner(s):** Hagadone Corp., 111 S. First St., Coeur d'Alene, ID 83814-1937. Telephone: 208-667-3431. **Management:** Jim Thompson, Publisher. Paul Burke, Advertising. Dan Phillips, Circulation Director. Jen Porter, Classified Adv. Mgr.. **Editorial:** Mike Patrick, Editor. Bill Buley, News Editor. Jason Hunt, Photographer. Mark Nelke, Sports Editor.

IDAHO FALLS

IDAHO FALLS POST REGISTER. 333 Northgate Mile, Idaho Falls, ID 83401. Telephone: 208-522-1800. FAX: 208-529-3142. E-MAIL: dmiller@idahonews.com.. URL: http://www.idahonews.com. Mailing Address: PO Box 1800, Idaho Falls, ID 83401. Year Established: 1881. Pub. Frequency: d. Page Size: broadsheet. Subscrip. Rate: $.50 newsstand/cover; $1.50 newsstand/cover Sun.. **Wire Service(s):** AP, MCT. Circulation: 29,000 evening (paid); 30,000 Sunday (paid). **Owner(s):** The Post Co., See address and contact information above. **Management:** Roger Plothow, Publisher. Ron Lee, Advertising Director. Stacy Simonet, Circulation Manager. Hilary Witt, Classified Adv. Mgr.. **Editorial:** Roger Plothow, Editor. Dean Miller, Managing Editor. Rob Thornberry, Outdoor Editor. Lance Hanlin, Sports.

Dailies

KELLOGG

SHOSHONE NEWS-PRESS. 401 Main St., Kellogg, ID 83837. Telephone: 208-783-1107. FAX: 208-784-6791. E-MAIL: clobfinger@cdapress.com. URL: http://www.shoshonenewspress.com. Year Established: 1926. Pub. Frequency: d. (Tue.-Sun.) Page Size: broadsheet. Subscrip. Rate: $.50 newsstand/cover; $1.50 newsstand/cover Sun.; $156/yr home delivery. **Wire Service(s):** AP. Circulation: 3,500 morning (paid); 3,300 Sunday (paid). **Owner(s):** Hagadone Corp., 111 S. First St., Coeur d'Alene, ID 83814-1937. Telephone: 208-667-3431. **Management:** Duane Hagadone, President. Dan Drewry, Publisher. Don Redding, Circulation Manager. **Editorial:** Lauren Tandy, Managing Editor. Suzanne Jacobson, Reporter. Jason Elliott, Sports Editor.

LEWISTON

LEWISTON TRIBUNE. PO Box 957, Lewiston, ID 83501. Telephone: 208-743-9411. E-MAIL: city@lmtribune.com. URL: http://www.lmtribune.com. Year Established: 1892. Pub. Frequency: d. Page Size: broadsheet. Subscrip. Rate: $.50 newsstand/cover; $1.50 newsstand/cover Sun.; $159/yr carrier delivery local; $168/yr motor route; $183/yr mailed. Adv. Rate: col. inch $18.45 **Wire Service(s):** AP, NYT. Circulation: 25,537 morning (paid); 27,287 Sunday (paid). **Owner(s):** Tribune Publishing Company, Inc., 505 C St, Lewiston, ID 83501-1843. Telephone: 208-743-9411. **Management:** A L Alford, Publisher. **Editorial:** Paul Emerson, Managing Editor.

MOSCOW

MOSCOW-PULLMAN DAILY NEWS. 409 S Jackson St, Moscow, ID 83843. Telephone: 208-882-5561. FAX: 208-883-8205. E-MAIL: editor@moscow.com. URL: http://www.dnews.com. Mailing Address: PO Box 8187, Moscow, ID 83843. Year Established: 1981. Pub. Frequency: d. (Mon.-Sat.) Page Size: broadsheet. Subscrip. Rate: $.50 newsstand/cover; $1.25 newsstand/cover Sat.; $110.25/yr carrier delivery; $120.75/yr motor route (effective 2006); $150/yr mailed. Freelance Pay: $25/story. **Wire Service(s):** AP, MCT. Circulation: 6,700 evening (paid). **Owner(s):** Tribune Publishing Company, Inc., PO Box 957, Lewiston, ID 83501. Telephone: 208-743-9411. **Management:** Nathan Alford, Publisher. **Editorial:** Nathan Alford, Editor. Steve McClure, Managing Editor.

NAMPA

IDAHO PRESS-TRIBUNE. 1618 N. Midland Blvd., Nampa, ID 83651. Telephone: 208-467-9251. FAX: 208-467-9562. E-MAIL: vholbrook@idahopress.com. URL: http://www.idahopress.com. Mailing Address: PO Box 9399, Nampa, ID 83652. Year Established: 1883. Pub. Frequency: d. Page Size: broadsheet. Subscrip. Rate: $.50 newsstand/cover; $1 newsstand/cover Sun.; $10.50 home delivery/mo. in city; $111/yr home delivery in city; $117/yr motor route in city. **Wire Service(s):** AP. Circulation: 22,000 evening (paid); 22,000 Sunday (paid). **Owner(s):** Pioneer Newspapers, 221 First Ave., W., Ste. 405, Seattle, WA 98119. Telephone: 206-284-4424. **Management:** Rick Weaver, Publisher. Brian Doane, Advertising Manager. Laura Stewart, Circulation Manager. Rhonda McMurtrie, Business Manager. **Editorial:** Vickie Holbrook, Managing Editor. Kaye Steffler, Church Editor. David Woolsey, City Editor.

POST FALLS

POST FALLS PRESS. 318 Spokane St., Post Falls, ID 83854. Telephone: 208-773-7502. FAX: 208-773-7002. E-MAIL: mfeiler@cdapress.com. URL: http://www.cdapress.com. Mailing Address: PO Box 39, Post Falls, ID 83877. Year Established: 1998. Pub. Frequency: d. Page Size: broadsheet. Subscrip. Rate: $.50 newsstand/cover; $1.50 Sun.; $48.75 for 13 wks.. **Wire Service(s):** AP. Circulation: 4,000 morning (paid); 4,200 Sunday (paid). **Owner(s):** Hagadone Corp., 111 S. First St., Coeur d'Alene, ID 83814-1937. **Management:** Jim Thompson, Publisher. Paul Burke, Advertising. Dan Phillips, Circulation Director. **Editorial:** Mike Patrick, Managing Editor. Mark Nelke, Sports Editor.

SANDPOINT

BONNER COUNTY DAILY BEE. ISSN 1047-6822
310 Church St., Sandpoint, ID 83864. Telephone: 208-263-9534. FAX: 208-263-9091. URL: http://www.bonnercountydailybee.com. Mailing Address: PO Box 159, Sandpoint, ID 83864. Year Established: 1965. Pub. Frequency: d. (Tue.-Sun.) Page Size: broadsheet. Subscrip. Rate: $.50 newsstand/cover; $1.25 Sun.; $38.40 local for 12 wks.; $24 mailed for 4 wks.. **Wire Service(s):** AP. Circulation: 6,800 evening (paid); 32,000 Sunday (paid). **Owner(s):** Hagadone Corp., 111 S. First St., Coeur d'Alene, ID 83814. **Management:** Duane Hagadone, President. David Keyes, Publisher. Kathy Hubbard, Advertising Manager. Heather Cunningham, Circulation Manager. **Editorial:** Caroline Lobsinger, Editor. Keith Kinndard, News Editor. Eric Plummer, Sports Editor.

TWIN FALLS

TIMES-NEWS (TWIN FALLS), THE. 132 Fairfield St., W., Twin Falls, ID 83301. Telephone: 208-733-0931. FAX: 208-734-5538. E-MAIL: twinews@mindspring.com. URL: http://www.magicvalley.com. Mailing Address: PO Box 548, Twin Falls, ID 83303. Year Established: 1905. Pub. Frequency: d. Page Size: broadsheet. Subscrip. Rate: $.50 newsstand/cover; $1.50 newsstand/cover Sun.; $17.40 home delivery for 4 wks.; $72 mailed in state for 12 wks.; $84 mailed out of state for 12 wks.. **Wire Service(s):** AP, LAT-WAT, MCT. Circulation: 22,200 Sunday (paid); 23,000 morning (paid). **Owner(s):** Lee Enterprises, Inc., 215 N. Main St., Davenport, IA 52801. Telephone: 563-383-2100. FAX: 563-323-9608. **Management:** Pat Schlauch, Publisher. Janet Goffin, Advertising Manager. Deby Johnson, Classified Adv. Mgr.. **Editorial:** Chris Steinback, Managing Editor. Virginia Hutchings, Business Editor. Joe Paisley, Sports Editor.

ILLINOIS

ALTON

TELEGRAPH (ALTON), THE. ISSN 0897-456X
111 E. Broadway, Alton, IL 62002. Telephone: 618-463-2500. FAX: 618-463-9829. E-MAIL: telegrapheditor@hotmail. URL: http://www.thetelegraph.com. Mailing Address: PO Box 278, Alton, IL 62002. Year Established: 1836. Pub. Frequency: d. Page Size: broadsheet. Subscrip. Rate: $.50 newsstand/cover per issue; $1.50 newsstand/cover Sun.; $14/mo.. Adv. Rate: col. inch $33.39 **Wire Service(s):** AP. Circulation: 27,091 morning (paid); 29,038 Sunday (paid). **Owner(s):** Freedom Communications, Inc., 17666 Fitch, Irvine, CA 92614. Telephone: 949-253-2300. **Bureau(s):** 200 Vandala St., Edwardville, IL 62035. Telephone: 618-656-7500. FAX: 618-656-7568. Contact: Sanford Schmidt, Court Editor. **Management:** James E Shrader, Publisher. Steve Herron, Advertising Manager. **Editorial:** Dan Brannan, Managing Editor. Dennis Grubaugh, City Editor. Vickie Kinney, News Editor. John Badman, Photographer. Pete Hays, Sports.

ARLINGTON HEIGHTS

DAILY HERALD (ARLINGTON HEIGHTS). 155 E. Algonquin Rd., Arlington Heights, IL 60005. Telephone: 847-427-4300. FAX: 847-427-1301. URL: http://www.dailyherald.com. Mailing Address: PO Box 280, Arlington Heights, IL 60006. Year Established: 1872. Pub. Frequency: d. Page Size: broadsheet. Subscrip. Rate: $.50 newsstand/cover; $1.50 Sun.; $189.80/yr carrier delivery local; $78/yr carrier delivery local Sunday deliv.. **Wire Service(s):** AP, UPI. Circulation: 141,331 morning (paid); 139,200 Sunday (paid). **Owner(s):** Paddock Publications, See address and contact information above. **Management:** Doug Ray, President. Daniel E. Baumann, Publisher. John Kelly, Advertising Director. Jim Galentano, Circulation Director. Michelle Huntley, Classified Adv. Mgr.. Mike Seeling, Photography Director. **Editorial:** John Lampinen, Executive Editor. Eileen Brown, Managing Editor. Diane Dungey, Feature Editor.

AURORA

BEACON NEWS, THE. 101 S. River St., Aurora, IL 60506. Telephone: 630-844-5844. FAX: 630-844-5818. URL: http://www.beaconnewsonline.com. Year Established: 1846. Pub. Frequency: d. Page Size: broadsheet. Subscrip. Rate: $.50 newsstand/cover; $1.50 newsstand/cover Sun.; $52/yr; $156/yr mailed. **Wire Service(s):** AP, CNS. Circulation: 40,000 morning (paid). **Owner(s):** Sun-Times Media Group, 350 N Orleans St, Ste 10-S, Chicago, IL 60654. **Management:** Rick Nagel, Publisher. Mike Bertok, Advertising Manager. Debra Ryan, Classified Adv. Mgr.. **Editorial:** Denise Crosby, Managing Editor. John Russell, Associate Editor.

BELLEVILLE

BELLEVILLE NEWS-DEMOCRAT. ISSN 8750-1058
120 S Illinois St, Belleville, IL 62220-2130. E-MAIL: gberkley@bnd.com. URL: http://www.belleville.com. Year Established: 1858. Pub. Frequency: d. Page Size: broadsheet. Subscrip. Rate: $.50 newsstand/cover; $1.25 newsstand/cover Sun.; $18/mo.; $216/yr. **Wire Service(s):** AP, NYT. Circulation: 53,881 morning (paid); 63,273 Sunday (paid). **Owner(s):** The/McClatchy Company, 2100 Q St, Sacramento, CA 95816. Telephone: 916-321-1936. FAX: 916-321-1869. **Management:** Jay Tebbe, Publisher. Brenda Fedak, Advertising Manager. John Grove, Classified Adv. Mgr.. **Editorial:** Jeff Couch, Editor. Candice Mount, News Editor.

BENTON

EVENING NEWS. 111-113 E. Church St., Benton, IL 62812. Telephone: 618-438-5611. FAX: 618-435-2413. E-MAIL: benton@intrnet.net. URL: http://www.bentoneveningnews.com. Mailing Address: PO Box 877, Benton, IL 62812. Pub. Frequency: d. (Mon.-Sat.) Page Size: broadsheet. Subscrip. Rate: $.50 newsstand/cover; $116/yr in county; $136/yr out of state. Circulation: 4,800 morning (paid); 4,800 Sunday (paid). **Owner(s):** GateHouse Media, Inc, 350 WillowBrook Office Park, Fairport, NY 14450. Telephone: 585-598-0030. FAX: 585-248-2631. **Management:** Terra Kerkemeyer, Publisher. Sheila McCune, Circulation Manager. Sandy Vukadinovich, Classified Adv. Mgr.. **Editorial:** Diana Winson, News Editor.

BLOOMINGTON

PANTAGRAPH, THE. 301 W. Washington St., Bloomington, IL 61701. Telephone: 309-829-9000. FAX: 309-829-7000. E-MAIL: mailbox@pantagraph.com. URL: http://www.pantagraph.com. Mailing Address: PO Box 2907, Bloomington, IL 61702-2907. Year Established: 1837. Pub. Frequency: d. Page Size: broadsheet. Subscrip. Rate: $.50 newsstand/cover; $1.75 newsstand/cover Sun.; $205/yr carrier delivery in county; $212/yr motor route in county. Freelance Pay: $50-$100/story. **Wire Service(s):** AP, MCT. Circulation: 48,076 morning (paid); 50,463 Sunday (paid). **Owner(s):** Lee Enterprises, Inc., 900 N. Tucker Blvd., St. Louis, MO 63101. Telephone: 314-340-8000. FAX: 314-340-3125. **Management:** Barry Winterland, General Manager. Linda Lindus, Publisher. Loretta Vance, Advertising Director. **Editorial:** Julie Gerke, Managing Editor. Chuck Blystone, Feature Editor. Robin Helenthal, Librarian. Bryan Bloodworth, Sports Editor.

CANTON

DAILY LEDGER (CANTON). 53 W. Elm St., Canton, IL 61520. Telephone: 309-647-5100. FAX: 309-647-4665. E-MAIL: dlyledger@theramp.net. URL: http://www.cantondailyledger.com. Mailing Address: PO Box 540, Canton, IL 61520. Year Established: 1849. Pub. Frequency: d. (Mon.-Sat.) Page Size: broadsheet. Subscrip. Rate: $.75 newsstand/cover; $128/yr carrier delivery in county; $151/yr out of county. **Wire Service(s):** AP. Circulation: 60,000 evening (paid). **Owner(s):** GateHouse Media, Inc, 350 WillowBrook Office Park, Fairport, NY 14450. Telephone: 585-598-0030. FAX: 585-248-2631. **Management:** Scott Koon, Publisher. Jackie Caulkins, Advertising Manager. Rick Bybee, Circulation Manager. **Editorial:** Linda Woods, Executive Editor. Stephen Shank, Sports.

CARBONDALE

SOUTHERN ILLINOISAN, THE. 710 N. Illinois Ave., Carbondale, IL 62901. Telephone: 618-529-5454. FAX: 618-457-2935. E-MAIL: sinews@midwest.com. URL: http://www.southernillinoisan.com. Mailing Address: PO Box 2108, Carbondale, IL 62902. Year Established: 1947. Pub. Frequency: d. Page Size: broadsheet. Subscrip. Rate: $.50 newsstand/cover; $1.50 newsstand/cover Sun.; $14/mo. local; $169/yr. **Wire Service(s):** AP. Circulation: 30,000 morning (paid); 38,000 Sunday (paid). **Owner(s):** Lee Enterprises, Inc., 215 N. Main St., Davenport, IA 52801. Telephone: 563-383-2100. FAX: 563-323-9608. **Management:** Dennis DeRossett, Publisher. Abby Hatfield, Advertising Manager. T.J. Gentry, Circulation Manager. Mark Dynis, Classified Adv. Mgr.. **Editorial:** Meta Minton, Editor.

CARMI

CARMI TIMES. 323 E. Main St., Carmi, IL 62821. Telephone: 618-382-4176. FAX: 618-384-2163. E-MAIL: carmitimes@midwest.net. URL: http://www.carmitimes.com. Mailing Address: PO Box 190, Carmi, IL 62821. Year Established: 1950. Pub. Frequency: d. (Mon.-Sat.) Page Size: broadsheet. Subscrip. Rate: $.50 newsstand/cover; $113/yr carrier delivery local; $117/yr motor route in county; $110/yr mailed out of county. **Wire Service(s):** AP. Circulation: 3,200 evening (paid). **Owner(s):** GateHouse Media, Inc, 350 WillowBrook Office Park, Fairport, NY 14450. Telephone: 585-598-0030. FAX: 585-248-2631. **Management:** Barry C. Cleveland, Publisher. Linda Devoy, Advertising Manager. Brenda Pennington, Circulation Manager. **Editorial:** Barry C. Cleveland, Editor. Ray Mitchell, News Editor. Toby Brown, Sports.

CENTRALIA

MORNING SENTINEL (CENTRALIA). 232 E. Broadway, Centralia, IL 62801. Telephone: 618-532-5604. FAX: 618-532-1212. E-MAIL: sentinel@accessus.net. URL: http://www.morningsentinel.com. Mailing Address: PO Box 672, Centralia, IL 62801. Year Established: 1863. Pub. Frequency: d. Page Size: broadsheet. Subscrip. Rate: $.50 newsstand/cover; $1 Sun.; $90/yr carrier delivery; $130/yr mailed in area. **Wire Service(s):** AP, LAT-WAT. Circulation: 16,250 morning (paid); 17,100 Sunday (paid). **Owner(s):** Centralia Press, Ltd., See address and contact information above. **Management:** Dan Nichols, General Manager. William Perrine, Publisher. Ray Albert, Advertising Manager. Chuck Koepke, Circulation Manager. Julie Copple, Classified Adv. Mgr.. **Editorial:** Bryan Hunt, Photographer. Randy List, Sports.

CHARLESTON

TIMES-COURIER (CHARLESTON). 2110 Woodfall Dr. # 10, Charleston, IL 61920. Telephone: 217-345-7085. FAX: 217-345-7090. URL: http://www.jg-tc.com. Year Established: 1840. Pub. Frequency: d. (Mon.-Sat.) Page Size: broadsheet. Subscrip. Rate: $.50 newsstand/cover; $.75 newsstand/cover Sat.; $32.25 carrier delivery for 13 wks.; $126.50/yr mailed. Adv. Rate: col. inch $6.50 **Wire Service(s):** AP. Circulation: 8,000 morning (paid). **Owner(s):** Lee Enterprises, Inc., 201 N. Harrison St, Ste 600, Davenport, IA 52801-1924. **Management:** Carl Walworth, Publisher. Chris Davis, Advertising Manager. Alan Baker, Circulation Manager. **Editorial:** Carl Walworth, Editor. Bill Lair, Managing Editor. Beth Heldebrandt, Feature Editor. Brian Nielsen, Sports Editor.

CHICAGO

CHICAGO DEFENDER. ISSN 0745-7014
200 S. Michigan Ave, Ste. 1700, Chicago, IL 60604. Telephone: 312-225-2400. FAX: 312-225-5659. E-MAIL: editorial@chicagodefender.com. URL: http://www.chicagodefender.com. Year Established: 1905. Pub. Frequency: d. (Mon.-Thu. & Sat.) Page Size: tabloid. Subscrip. Rate: $.35 newsstand/cover; $.50 newsstand/cover Sat.; $159.80/yr. **Wire Service(s):** AP. Circulation: 20,000 Saturday (paid); 15,005 morning (paid). **Owner(s):** Real Times Inc., See address and contact information above. **Management:** Lou Ransom, Publisher. Denise Campbell, Advertising Director. Carol Bell, Circulation Manager. **Editorial:** Lou Ransom, Executive Editor. Glenn Reedus, Managing Editor.

CHICAGO SUN-TIMES. 350 N Orleans St, Ste 10-S, Chicago, IL 60654. Telephone: 312-321-2299. URL: http://www.suntimes.com. Year Established: 1948. Pub. Frequency: d. Page Size: tabloid. Subscrip. Rate: $.50 newsstand/cover; $1.25 newsstand/cover Sun.; $4 carrier delivery/wk.. **Wire Service(s):** RN, AP, LAT-WAT, DJNS, GNS. Circulation: 482,234 morning (paid); 482,300 Sunday (paid). **Owner(s):** Sun-Times Media Group, See address and contact information above. **Management:** John Cruickshank, Publisher. Paul Davis, Advertising Director. Courtney Price, Circulation Director. Regina Brown, Classified Adv. Mgr.. **Editorial:** Michael Cooke, Editor-in-Chief. Don Hayner, Managing Editor. Zach Finken, News Editor.

DAILY PRESS (NEWPORT NEWS), THE. 435 N Michigan Ave, Chicago, IL 60601. Telephone: 312.222.9100. E-MAIL: bevans@dailypress.com. URL: http://www.hamptonroads.digitalcity.com. Year Established: 1896. Pub. Frequency: d. Page Size: broadsheet. Subscrip. Rate: $.50 newsstand/cover; $1.50 newsstand/cover Sun.; $3.05/wk.. **Wire Service(s):** AP, SH, LAT-WAT, MCT. Circulation: 95,400 morning (paid); 116,472 Sunday (paid). **Owner(s):** Tribune Company, See address and contact information above.

HARTFORD COURANT, THE. ISSN 1047-4153
435 N Michigan Ave, Chicago, IL 60601. Telephone: 312.222.9100. URL: http://www.courant.com. Year Established: 1764. Pub. Frequency: d. Page Size: broadsheet. Subscrip. Rate: $.50 newsstand/cover; $1.50 newsstand/cover Sun.; $4.20/wk.; $54.60/yr. **Wire Service(s):** RN, AP, LAT-WAT, DJNS. Circulation: 207,000 morning (paid); 358,889 Sunday (paid). **Owner(s):** Tribune Company, See address and contact information above. **Management:** Jack W Davis Jr., Publisher. David Bennett, Circulation Director. Mary Lou Stoneburner, Classified Adv. Mgr.. Tom Anischik, Production Director. **Editorial:** Brian Toolan, Editor. Clifford L. Teutsch, Managing Editor. George Gombossy, Business Editor.

ORLANDO SENTINEL. ISSN 0744-6055
435 N Michigan Ave, Chicago, IL 60601. Telephone: 312.222.9100. E-MAIL: oso@aol.com. URL: http://www.orlandosentinel.com. Pub. Frequency: d. Page Size: broadsheet. **Wire Service(s):** RN, AP, SH, NYT, LAT-WAT, MCT, DJNS. Circulation: 366,028 per issue. **Owner(s):** Tribune Company, See address and contact information above. **Management:** Kathy Waltz, Publisher. Gail Rayos, Business Manager. **Editorial:** Timothy Franklin, Editor. Bob Shaw, Managing Editor. Anne Hellmuth, Associate Editor. Jane Healy, Editorial Page Editor.

SUN (BALTIMORE), THE. ISSN 1930-8965
435 N Michigan Ave, Chicago, IL 60601. Telephone: 312.222.9100. URL: http://www.baltimoresun.com/. Year Established: 1837. Pub. Frequency: d. Page Size: broadsheet. Subscrip. Rate: $.50 newsstand/cover; $1.66 Sun.; $14.76 carrier delivery/mo.; $14.75 mailed/mo.. **Wire Service(s):** RN, AP, NYT, LAT-WAT. Circulation: 321,165 morning (paid); 475,075 Sunday (paid). **Owner(s):** Tribune Company, See address and contact information above. **Bureau(s):** 8131 Ritchie Hwy, Ste. 2-A, Pasadena, MD 21122. Telephone: 410-315-8920. FAX: 410-315-8912. Contact: Diane Fancher, Bureau Chief. **Management:** Denise E Palmer, Publisher. **Editorial:** Anthony Barbieri, Managing Editor. Michael Leary, National Editor.

CLINTON

CLINTON DAILY JOURNAL. Rte. 54 W., Clinton, IL 61727. Telephone: 217-935-3171. FAX: 217-935-6086. E-MAIL: cdjemail@aol.com. URL: http://www.clintondailyjournal.com. Mailing Address: PO Box 615, Clinton, IL 61727. Year Established: 1905. Pub. Frequency: d. (Mon.-Sat) Page Size: broadsheet. Subscrip. Rate: $.50 newsstand/cover; $99.25/yr. **Wire Service(s):** AP. Circulation: 4,000 evening (paid). **Owner(s):** New Media Corp., 401 N. Main, Rochelle, IL 61068. Telephone: 815-562-4171. **Management:** Randi Smith, Publisher. Marnie Hutchison, Circulation Manager. Brittany Thompson, Classified Adv. Mgr.. Alisha Boysen, Sales Manager. **Editorial:** Gordon Woods, Editor. Byron Painter, Sports.

CRYSTAL LAKE

NORTHWEST HERALD. ISSN 8750-0396
7717 S. Rte. 31, Crystal Lake, IL 60014. Telephone: 815-459-4040. FAX: 815-477-4960. E-MAIL: sobeditor@nwherald.com. URL: http://www.nwherald.com. Mailing Address: PO Box 250, Crystal Lake, IL 60039-0250. Year Established: 1875. Pub. Frequency: d. Page Size: broadsheet. Subscrip. Rate: $.50 newsstand/cover; $1.50 newsstand/cover Sun.; $4.15 home delivery/wk.; $53.95 home delivery for 13 wks.; $205.40/yr home delivery. Freelance Pay: $20-$50/article. **Wire Service(s):** AP. Circulation: 33,972 morning (paid); 35,754 Sunday (paid). **Owner(s):** Shaw Newspapers, PO Box 487, Dixon, IL 61021-0409. Telephone: 815-284-4000. **Bureau(s):** 41 N. Ayer St., Havard, IL 60033. Telephone: 815-943-4411. FAX: 815-943-4405. **Management:** John Rung, Publisher. Clin Schroeder, Advertising Director. Terry Wagner, Circulation Manager. Mary-Margaret Maule, Marketing. **Editorial:** Chris Krug, Editor. Kevin Polzin, Business Editor. Dick Peterson, Editorial Page Editor. Mary Sweetwood, Feature Editor. Melanie Balog, News Editor. Scott Dalzell, Photo Editor. Jason Schaumburg, Sports.

DANVILLE

COMMERCIAL-NEWS. ISSN 0742-8286
17 W. North St., Danville, IL 61832. Telephone: 217-446-1000. FAX: 217-446-9825. E-MAIL: info@dancomnews.com. URL: http://www.commercial-news.com. Year Established: 1866. Pub. Frequency: d. Page Size: broadsheet. Subscrip. Rate: $.50 newsstand/cover; $1.50 Sun.; $40.30 for 13 wks.; $148.20/yr. **Wire Service(s):** AP, GNS. Circulation: 19,999 evening (paid); 21,715 Sunday (paid). **Owner(s):** Community Newspaper Holdings, Inc., 3500 Colonnade Pkwy., Ste. 600, Birmingham, AL 35243. Telephone: 205-298-7100. FAX: 205-298-7101. **Management:** Carol Nichols, Publisher. Dave Conner, Advertising Director. Chuck Harbaugh, Circulation Manager. Cindy Decker, Classified Adv. Mgr.. **Editorial:** Larry Smith, Editor.

DE KALB

DAILY CHRONICLE. 1586 Barber Green Rd., De Kalb, IL 60115. Telephone: 815-756-4841. FAX: 815-758-5059. E-MAIL: jsecor@pulitzer.net. URL: http://www.daily-chronicle.com. Mailing Address: PO Box 587, De Kalb, IL 60115. Year Established: 1879. Pub. Frequency: d. Page Size: broadsheet. Subscrip. Rate: $.50 newsstand/cover; $1 Sun.; $62.95 for 6 mos. in city area; $114.35/yr. **Wire Service(s):** AP. Circulation: 12,599 evening (paid); 12,825 Sunday (paid). **Owner(s):** Lee Enterprises, Inc., 201 N. Harrison St, Ste 600, Davenport, IA 52801-1924. **Management:** Chris Doyle, Publisher. Christine Patrick, Classified Adv. Mgr.. **Editorial:** John Kelleher, Managing Editor. Chris Richert, Business Editor. Inger Koch, City Editor. Steven Nemeth, Sports Editor.

DECATUR

HERALD & REVIEW. 601 E. William, Decatur, IL 62523. Telephone: 217-429-5151. FAX: 217-421-7965. URL: http://www.herald-review.com. Mailing Address: PO Box 311, Decatur, IL 62525. Year Established: 1873. Pub. Frequency: d. Page Size: broadsheet. Subscrip. Rate: $.50 newsstand/cover; $1.75 newsstand/cover Sun.; $15.20 home delivery for 4 wks.. **Wire Service(s):** AP, MCT. Circulation: 44,000 morning (paid); 55,000 Sunday (paid). **Owner(s):** Lee Enterprises, Inc., 215 N. Main St., Davenport, IA 52801. Telephone: 563-383-2202. FAX: 563-323-9608. **Management:** Linda Lindus, Publisher. Jen Barkus, Advertising Director. Lori Ravallette, Classified Adv. Mgr.. **Editorial:** Gary Sawyer, Editor. David Dawson, Managing Editor. Scott Perry, Business Editor. Tim Cain, Entertainment Editor. Mike Albright, Sports Editor.

DIXON

TELEGRAPH (DIXON), THE. ISSN 0889-4612
PO Box 487, Dixon, IL 61021-0409. Telephone: 815-284-2222. FAX: 815-625-9390. E-MAIL: shawnews@essex1.com. URL: http://www.saukvalley.com. Mailing Address: PO Box 490, Sterling, IL 61081-0498. Year Established: 1851. Pub. Frequency: d. Page Size: broadsheet. Subscrip. Rate: $.50 newsstand/cover; $1.50 newsstand/cover Sun.; $12.55/mo. local; $147/yr local. Adv. Rate: col. inch $24.16 **Wire Service(s):** AP, CNS. Circulation: 10,300 evening (paid); 23,000 Sunday (paid). **Owner(s):** Shaw Newspapers, See address and contact information above. **Management:** James Nelson, General Manager. Thomas D. Shaw, President. William E. Shaw, Publisher. Dan Goetz, Advertising Director. Sheryl Gulbranson, Circulation Manager. **Editorial:** Jonie Larson, Executive Editor. Jim Dunn, Managing Editor. Tim O'Brien, Entertainment Editor. Andrea Mills, Lifestyle Editor. Brian Weidman, Sports Editor.

DU QUOIN

DU QUOIN EVENING CALL. 9 N. Division St., Du Quoin, IL 62832. Telephone: 618-542-2133. FAX: 618-542-2726. E-MAIL: duquoin@intrnet.net. URL: http://www.duquoin.com. Mailing Address: PO Box 184, Du Quoin, IL 62832. Year Established: 1895. Pub. Frequency: d. (Mon.-Sat.) Page Size: broadsheet. Subscrip. Rate: $.50 newsstand/cover; $102/yr carrier delivery in city; $108/yr motor route in county; $110/yr mailed out of county. **Wire Service(s):** AP. Circulation: 4,200 evening (paid). **Owner(s):** GateHouse Media, Inc, 350 WillowBrook Office Park, Fairport, NY 14450. Telephone: 585-598-0030. FAX: 585-248-2631. **Management:** John Croessman, Publisher. Terri Fisher, Advertising Manager. Patty Malinee, Circulation Manager. **Editorial:** John Croessman, Managing Editor. Craig Shrum, News Editor. Jeff Profitt, Sports Editor.

EDWARDSVILLE

EDWARDSVILLE INTELLIGENCER. ISSN 1074-1860
117 N. Second St., Edwardsville, IL 62025. Telephone: 618-656-4700. FAX: 618-656-7618. URL: http://www.goedwardsville.com. Mailing Address: PO Box 70, Edwardsville, IL 62025. Year Established: 1862. Pub. Frequency: d. (Mon.-Sat.) Page Size: broadsheet. Subscrip. Rate: $.50 newsstand/cover; $2.10 carrier delivery/wk.; $99.50 carrier delivery 48 wks.; $160.50 mailed 48 wks.. Adv. Rate: col. inch $19.73 **Wire Service(s):** AP. Circulation: 6,000 evening (paid). **Owner(s):** Hearst Corp., 959 Eighth Ave, New York, NY 10019. **Management:** Bruce Coury, Publisher. Linda Grysiewicz, Advertising Manager. Rose Mary Kebel, Circulation Manager. **Editorial:** Bill Tucker, Editor.

EFFINGHAM

EFFINGHAM DAILY NEWS. 201 N. Banker St., Effingham, IL 62401. Telephone: 217-347-7151. FAX: 217-342-9315. E-MAIL: ednnet@xelnet.comm. URL: http://www.effinghamdailynews.com. Mailing Address: PO Box 370, Effingham, IL 62401. Year Established: 1899. Pub. Frequency: d. (Mon.-Sat.) Page Size: broadsheet. Subscrip. Rate: $.50 newsstand/cover; $120/yr carrier delivery & mailed in state; $155/yr mailed out of state. **Wire Service(s):** AP. Circulation: 13,315 morning (paid). **Owner(s):** Community Newspaper Holdings, Inc., 3500 Colonnade Pkwy., Ste. 600, Birmingham, AL 35243. Telephone: 205-298-7100. **Management:** Steve Raymond, Publisher. Ken Goeckner, Advertising Director. Todd Buenker, Circulation Manager. Jean Voelker, Classified Adv. Mgr.. **Editorial:** Donna Riley-Gordon, Managing Editor. Cathy Thoele-Griffith, Feature Editor. Millie Lange, Sports.

ELDORADO

ELDORADO DAILY JOURNAL. 1200 Locust St., Eldorado, IL 62930. Telephone: 618-273-3379. FAX: 618-273-3738. Year Established: 1911. Pub. Frequency: d. (Mon.-Sat.) Page Size: broadsheet. Subscrip. Rate: $.50 newsstand/cover; $2.10/wk.; $54 for 6 mos.; $104/yr. **Wire Service(s):** AP. Circulation: 7,200 evening (paid). **Owner(s):** GateHouse Media, Inc, 350 WillowBrook Office Park, Fairport, NY 14450. Telephone: 585-598-0030. FAX: 585-248-2631. **Management:** George Wilson, Publisher. Bob Sirtak, Circulation Manager. Doris Wilson, Marketing Director. **Editorial:** Terry Geese, Managing Editor. Phil Knapper, Sports.

ELGIN

COURIER NEWS (ELGIN), THE. 300 Lake St., Elgin, IL 60120. Telephone: 847-888-7800. FAX: 847-888-7836. URL: http://www.suburbanchicagonewspapers.com. Mailing Address: PO Box 531, Elgin, IL 60121. Year Established: 1874. Pub. Frequency: d. Page Size: broadsheet. Subscrip. Rate: $.50 newsstand/cover; $1.25 newsstand/cover Sun.; $52/yr; $208/yr mailed in county. **Wire Service(s):** AP, CNS. Circulation: 14,735 evening (paid); 15,321 Sunday (paid). **Owner(s):** Sun-Times Media Group, 350 N Orleans St, Ste 10-S, Chicago, IL 60654. Telephone: 312-321-2299. **Management:** Robert Wall, Publisher. Joe Weber, Circulation Manager. Debbie Ryan, Classified Adv. Mgr.. **Editorial:** Mike Bailey, Managing Editor. Marty O'Mara, News Editor.

FLORA

DAILY CLAY COUNTY ADVOCATE-PRESS. 105 W. North Ave., Flora, IL 62839. Telephone: 618-662-2108. FAX: 618-662-2939. URL: http://www.advocatepress.com. Mailing Address: PO Box 519, Flora, IL 62839. Year Established: 1886. Pub. Frequency: d. (Mon.-Fri.) Page Size: broadsheet. Subscrip. Rate: $.50 newsstand/cover; $74/yr in county; $83/yr out of county. **Wire Service(s):** AP. Circulation: 3,500 evening (paid). **Owner(s):** GateHouse Media, Inc, 350 WillowBrook Office Park, Fairport, NY 14450. Telephone: 585-598-0030. FAX: 585-248-2631. **Management:** Bob Hiemenz, Publisher. Jennifer Lusk, Circulation Manager. Tiffany Bowles, Classified Adv. Mgr.. **Editorial:** Mark Lambird, Editor. Keith Gibson, Sports Editor.

FREEPORT

JOURNAL-STANDARD, THE. 27 S State Ave, Freeport, IL 61032. Telephone: 815-232-1171. FAX: 815-232-3601. URL: http://www.journalstandard.com. Mailing Address: PO Box 330, Freeport, IL 61032-0330. Year Established: 1847. Pub. Frequency: d. Page Size: broadsheet. Subscrip. Rate: $.50 newsstand/cover; $1.25 Sun.; $39.50 home delivery/quarter; $171.60/yr. Adv. Rate: col. inch $12 **Wire Service(s):** AP. Circulation: 17,000 evening (paid); 17,000 Sunday (paid). **Owner(s):** GateHouse Media, Inc, 350 WillowBrook Office Park, Fairport, NY 14450. Telephone: 585-598-0030. FAX: 585-248-2631. **Management:** Steve Trosley, Publisher. Ann Young, Advertising Manager. Lisa Ray, Circulation Manager. **Editorial:** Andrew Analore, Editor.

GALESBURG

REGISTER-MAIL, THE. 140 S Prairie St, Galesburg, IL 61401. Telephone: 309-343-7181. FAX: 309-343-2382. E-MAIL: twelty@galesburg.net. URL: http://www.register-mail.com. Mailing Address: PO Box 310, Galesbrug, IL 61401-0310. Year Established: 1872. Pub. Frequency: d. Page Size: broadsheet. Subscrip. Rate: $.50 newsstand/cover; $1.25 Sun.; $134.68/yr carrier delivery & motor rte.; $152.88/yr mailed in state; $247.52/yr mailed out of state. **Wire Service(s):** AP. Circulation: 17,000 evening (paid); 16,300 Sunday (paid). **Owner(s):** GateHouse Media, Inc, 350 WillowBrook Office Park, Fairport, NY 14450. Telephone: 585-598-0030. FAX: 585-248-2631. **Management:** Don Cooper, Publisher. Doris Medhurst, Advertising Manager. Loleta Berry, Classified Adv. Mgr.. **Editorial:** Tom Martin, Editor.

ULRICH'S PERIODICALS DIRECTORY 2010

HARRISBURG

HARRISBURG DAILY REGISTER. 35 S. Vine St., Harrisburg, IL 62946. Telephone: 618-253-7146. FAX: 618-252-0863. E-MAIL: register@internet.net. URL: http://www.dailyregister.com. Mailing Address: PO Box 248, Harrisburg, IL 62946. Year Established: 1869. Pub. Frequency: d. (Mon.-Sat.) Page Size: broadsheet. Subscrip. Rate: $.50 newsstand/cover; $133/yr in county & adj. cys.; $145.90/yr mailed in state; $158.70/yr mailed out of state. **Wire Service(s):** AP. Circulation: 6,200 evening (paid). **Owner(s):** GateHouse Media, Inc, 350 WillowBrook Office Park, Fairport, NY 14450. Telephone: 585-598-0030. FAX: 585-248-2631. **Management:** George Wilson, Publisher. Doris Wilson, Advertising Manager. Bob Sirtak, Circulation Manager. Becky Dale, Classified Adv. Mgr.. **Editorial:** Terry Geese, Managing Editor. Phil Knapper, Sports Editor.

JACKSONVILLE

JACKSONVILLE JOURNAL-COURIER. 235 W. State St., Jacksonville, IL 62651-1048. Telephone: 217-245-6121. FAX: 217-243-7659. URL: http://www.journal-courier.net. Year Established: 1830. Pub. Frequency: d. Page Size: broadsheet. Subscrip. Rate: $.50 newsstand/cover; $1.50 Sun.; $3.65 carrier delivery/wk.; $201.60/yr home delivery; $207.90/yr mailed. Adv. Rate: col. inch $12.80 **Wire Service(s):** AP. Circulation: 14,878 morning (paid); 14,447 Sunday (paid). **Owner(s):** Illinois Freedom Newspapers, Inc., See address and contact information above. **Management:** John R. Power, Publisher. Tom Linstromberg, Advertising Manager. Ron Hance, Circulation Manager. Jeanne Strubbe, Classified Adv. Mgr.. Bruce Shafer, Business Manager. **Editorial:** Ted Roth, Editor. Jeff Lonergan, Production Manager.

JERSEYVILLE

TELEGRAPH (COUNTY EDITION), THE. 201 N. State St., Jerseyville, IL 62052. Telephone: 618-498-5551. FAX: 618-498-3964. URL: http://www.thetelegraph.com. Mailing Address: PO Box 389, Jerseyville, IL 62052-0389. Year Established: 1919. Pub. Frequency: d. (Tue.-Sat.) Page Size: standard. Subscrip. Rate: $.50 newsstand/cover; $1.50 newsstand/cover Sun.; $49.14 home delivery for 13 wks.; $176.90/yr home delivery. Circulation: 9,660 per issue (paid). **Owner(s):** Freedom Communications, Inc., 17666 Fitch, Irvine, CA 92614. Telephone: 949-253-2300. FAX: 949-474-7675. **Management:** Jim Shrader, Publisher. Barbara Horstman, Circulation Manager. **Editorial:** Dan Brannon, Editor. Laura Pranaitis, Bureau Chief.

JOLIET

HERALD NEWS (JOLIET), THE. 300 Caterpillar Dr., Joliet, IL 60436-1097. Telephone: 815-729-6161. FAX: 815-729-6059. URL: http://www.suburbanchicagonews.com/heraldnews/. Year Established: 1839. Pub. Frequency: d. Page Size: broadsheet. Subscrip. Rate: $.50 newsstand/cover; $1.50 newsstand/cover Sun.; $52/yr in county; $166.40/yr mailed in county. **Wire Service(s):** AP, CNS. Circulation: 42,000 morning (paid); 48,000 Sunday (paid). **Owner(s):** Sun-Times Media Group, 350 N Orleans St, Ste 10-S, Chicago, IL 60654. Telephone: 312-321-2299. **Management:** Larry Randa, Publisher. Brian Garrigan, Advertising Manager. **Editorial:** Dave Monaghan, Managing Editor. Julie Todd, News Editor.

KANKAKEE

DAILY JOURNAL (KANKAKEE), THE. 8 Dearborn Sq., Kankakee, IL 60901. Telephone: 815-937-3300. FAX: 815-933-3301. E-MAIL: webmaster@daily-journal.com. URL: http://www.daily-journal.com. Year Established: 1903. Pub. Frequency: d. (Sun.-Fri.) Page Size: broadsheet. Subscrip. Rate: $.50 newsstand/cover; $1.75 Sun.; $150/yr home delivery local; $198/yr mailed adj. cys.. **Wire Service(s):** AP. Circulation: 31,914 evening (paid); 27,829 Sunday (paid). **Owner(s):** Small Newspaper Group, See address and contact information above. **Bureau(s):** 1183 National Press Bldg., Washington, DC 20045. Telephone: 202-662-7240. **Management:** Mario Sebastiani, General Manager. Len R. Small, Publisher. Douglas McAvoy, Circulation Director. **Editorial:** Len R. Small, Editor. Denise Renckens, Executive Editor. Phil Angelo, Managing Editor. Bob Thomas, Editorial Page Editor. John Stewart, Entertainment Editor. Kristin Szremski, Lifestyle Editor. Tim Ahrens, Sports Editor.

KEWANEE

STAR-COURIER. 105 E. Central Blvd., Kewanee, IL 61443. Telephone: 309-852-2181. FAX: 309-852-0010. E-MAIL: editor@starcourier.com. URL: http://www.starcourier.com. Mailing Address: PO Box A, Kewanee, IL 61443. Year Established: 1893. Pub. Frequency: d. (Mon.-Sat.) Page Size: broadsheet. Subscrip. Rate: $.50 newsstand/cover; $119.25/yr local. **Wire Service(s):** AP. Circulation: 5,500 evening (paid). **Owner(s):** GateHouse Media, Inc, 350 WillowBrook Office Park, Fairport, NY 14450. Telephone: 585-598-0030. FAX: 585-248-2631. **Management:** Susan Griffith, Publisher. Jolene Clark, Classified Adv. Mgr.. **Editorial:** Rocky Stuffelbeam, Managing Editor.

LA SALLE

NEWS TRIBUNE. 426 Second St., La Salle, IL 61301-2366. Telephone: 815-223-3200. FAX: 815-223-2543. E-MAIL: ntnews@newstrib.com. URL: http://www.newstrib.com. Year Established: 1891. Pub. Frequency: d. (Mon.-Sat.) Page Size: broadsheet. Subscrip. Rate: $.50 newsstand/cover; $98.90/yr home delivery local. **Wire Service(s):** AP. Circulation: 19,550 evening (paid). **Owner(s):** Daily News-Tribune, Inc., See address and contact information above. **Management:** Peter Miller III, President. Joyce McCullough, Publisher. Bill DeLorme, Circulation Manager. Robert Vickrey, Marketing Director. **Editorial:** Linda Kleczewski, Managing Editor. Cindy Rolando, Lifestyle Editor. Craig Sterrett, News Editor. Jackie Pokryfke, Sports Editor.

LAWRENCEVILLE

DAILY RECORD (LAWRENCEVILLE), THE. 1209 State St., Lawrenceville, IL 62439. Telephone: 618-943-2331. E-MAIL: lawnews@lawdailyrecord.com. URL: http://www.lawdailyrecord.com. Year Established: 1847. Pub. Frequency: d. (Mon.-Fri.) Page Size: broadsheet. Subscrip. Rate: $.50 newsstand/cover; $69/yr home delivery; $46/yr mailed in county; $69/yr mailed out of county. **Wire Service(s):** AP. Circulation: 4,200 evening (paid). **Owner(s):** Larry H. Lewis, See address and contact information above. **Management:** Larry H. Lewis, President. Sadie Young, Advertising Manager. Joyce Tredway, Circulation Manager. **Editorial:** Michael Van Dorn, Editor. Bill Richardson, Sports Editor.

LINCOLN

COURIER (LINCOLN), THE. 601 Pulaski St, Lincoln, IL 62656. Telephone: 217-732-2101. FAX: 217-732-7039. E-MAIL: courier@lincolncourier.com. URL: http://www.lincolncourier.com. Mailing Address: PO Box 740, Lincoln, IL 62656-0740. Year Established: 1856. Pub. Frequency: d. (Mon.-Sat.) Page Size: broadsheet. Subscrip. Rate: $.50 newsstand/cover; $147.16/yr home delivery in city; $159.64/yr out of city; $189.80/yr mailed in county; $222.04/yr mailed out of county. **Wire Service(s):** AP. Circulation: 6,800 evening (paid). **Owner(s):** GateHouse Media, Inc, 350 WillowBrook Office Park, Fairport, NY 14450. Telephone: 585-598-0030. FAX: 585-248-2631. **Management:** Tom Tillman, Publisher. Julie Danosky, Circulation Manager. **Editorial:** Jeff Nelson, Managing Editor.

LITCHFIELD

LITCHFIELD NEWS-HERALD. 112 E. Ryder St., Litchfield, IL 62056-0160. Telephone: 217-324-2121. FAX: 217-324-2122. E-MAIL: lfdnews@litchfieldil.com. Mailing Address: PO Box 160, Litchfield, IL 62056-0160. Year Established: 1856. Pub. Frequency: d. (Mon.-Fri.) Page Size: broadsheet. Subscrip. Rate: $.30 newsstand/cover; $62.40/yr home delivery. **Wire Service(s):** AP. **Owner(s):** Litchfield News-Herald, Inc., See address and contact information above. **Management:** John C. Hanafin, President. Fred W. Jones, Advertising Manager. **Editorial:** Micki Romanus, Managing Editor.

MACOMB

MACOMB JOURNAL. 203 N. Randolph, Macomb, IL 61455. Telephone: 309-833-2114. FAX: 309-833-2346. E-MAIL: news@macombjournal.com. URL: http://www.macombjournal.com. Year Established: 1855. Pub. Frequency: d. (Sun.-Fri.) Page Size: broadsheet. Subscrip. Rate: $.50 newsstand/cover; $1 Sun.; $99/yr in county & adj. cys.; $124/yr motor route in county. Adv. Rate: col. inch $10.38 **Wire Service(s):** AP. Circulation: 7,000 evening (paid); 7,800 Sunday (paid). **Owner(s):** GateHouse Media, Inc, 350 WillowBrook Office Park, Fairport, NY 14450. Telephone: 585-598-0030. FAX: 585-248-2631. **Management:** Pam McDowell, General Manager. Robert Wise, Circulation Manager. **Editorial:** Chuck Gysi, News Editor. Shelby Burgett, Sports Editor.

MARION

MARION DAILY REPUBLICAN. 502 W. Jackson St., Marion, IL 62959. Telephone: 618-993-2626. FAX: 618-993-8326. E-MAIL: editor@mariondaily.com. URL: http://www.mariondaily.com. Mailing Address: PO Box 490, Marion, IL 62959. Year Established: 1914. Pub. Frequency: d. (Mon.-Sat.) Page Size: broadsheet. Subscrip. Rate: $.50 newsstand/cover; $110/yr carrier delivery in county; $145/yr motor route in county; $142/yr mailed out of county. **Wire Service(s):** AP. Circulation: 3,600 evening (paid). **Owner(s):** GateHouse Media, Inc, 350 WillowBrook Office Park, Fairport, NY 14450. Telephone: 585-598-0030. FAX: 585-248-2631. **Management:** Tim Petrowich, Publisher. Dave Broy, Advertising Director. Jim Nobles, Circulation Manager. Betty Caraker, Classified Adv. Mgr.. **Editorial:** Tim Petrowich, Managing Editor. Justin Walker, Sports Editor.

MATTOON

JOURNAL GAZETTE. ISSN 0747-377X
100 Broadway Ave., Mattoon, IL 61938. Telephone: 217-235-5656. FAX: 217-238-6886. E-MAIL: editorial@jg-tc.com. URL: http://www.jg-tc.com. Year Established: 1905. Pub. Frequency: d. (Mon.-Sat.) Page Size: broadsheet. Subscrip. Rate: $.50 newsstand/cover; $.75 newsstand/cover Sat.; $21.13 carrier delivery for 13 weeks; $84.50/yr carrier delivery. Adv. Rate: col. inch $9.15 **Wire Service(s):** AP. Circulation: 11,423 evening (paid). **Owner(s):** Lee Enterprises, Inc., 201 N. Harrison St, Ste 600, Davenport, IA 52801-1924. **Management:** Carl Walworth, Publisher. Jen Barkus, Advertising Director. Kim Bowe, Circulation Manager. **Editorial:** Carl Walworth, Editor. Bill Lair, Managing Editor. Beth Hildebrandt, Entertainment Editor. Kevin Kilhoffer, Photographer. Brian Nielsen, Sports Editor.

MOLINE

DISPATCH (MOLINE), THE. 1720 Fifth Ave., Moline, IL 61265-7907. Telephone: 309-764-4344. FAX: 309-797-0311. E-MAIL: advertising@qconline.com. URL: http://www.qconline.com/. Year Established: 1878. Pub. Frequency: d. Page Size: broadsheet. Subscrip. Rate: $.50 newsstand/cover; $1.50 Sun.; $45.60 home delivery for 3 mos.; $48.60 motor route for 3 mos.. Adv. Rate: col. inch $28.95 Circulation: 41,800 evening (paid); 48,000 Sunday (paid). **Owner(s):** Small Newspaper Group, 8 Dearborn Sq., Kankakee, IL 60901. Telephone: 815-937-3300. **Management:** Gerald J Taylor, Publisher. Nick Norman, Advertising Director. John Newby, Circulation Director. Val Yazbec, Classified Adv. Mgr.. Nick Norman, Marketing Director. **Editorial:** Laura Fraembs, Associate Editor. Carolyn Hardin, Business Editor. Joe Beach, City Editor. Kenda Burrows, Editorial Page Editor. Sean Leary, Entertainment Editor. Lisa Mohr, Food Editor. Joe Payne, Lifestyle Editor. Mark Nesseler, Sports Editor.

MONMOUTH

DAILY REVIEW ATLAS. 400 S. Main St., Monmouth, IL 61462. Telephone: 309-734-3176. FAX: 309-734-7649. URL: http://www.reviewatlas.com. Mailing Address: PO Box 650, Monmouth, IL 61462. Pub. Frequency: d. (Mon.-Sat.) Page Size: broadsheet. Subscrip. Rate: $.50 newsstand/cover; $28.25 carrier delivery for 3 mos.; $99.50/yr carrier delivery. Adv. Rate: col. inch $7.40 **Wire Service(s):** AP. Circulation: 2,900 evening (paid). **Owner(s):** GateHouse Media, Inc, 350 WillowBrook Office Park, Fairport, NY 14450. Telephone: 585-598-0030. FAX: 585-248-2631. **Management:** Tony Scott, Publisher. Wendy Todd, Advertising Manager. Brian Elliott, Circulation Manager. **Editorial:** Stacey Creasy, Editor. Dan Worthington, Sports Editor.

MORRIS

MORRIS DAILY HERALD. 1804 N. Division St., Morris, IL 60450. Telephone: 815-942-3221. FAX: 815-942-0988. E-MAIL: news@morrisdailyherald.com. URL: http://www.morrisdailyherald.com. Mailing Address: PO Box 749, Morris, IL 60450. Year Established: 1855. Pub. Frequency: d. (Mon.-Fri.) Page Size: broadsheet. Subscrip. Rate: $.50 newsstand/cover; $93.60/yr home delivery; $98.28/yr motor route; $123.56/yr mailed in county; $135/yr out of county. Adv. Rate: col. inch $10 **Wire Service(s):** AP. Circulation: 8,000 evening (paid). **Owner(s):** Shaw Newspapers, 444 Pine Hill Dr., Dixon, IL 61021. Telephone: 815-284-2222. **Management:** Timothy J. West, Publisher. Jon Ringer, Advertising Manager. Lori Carlson, Circulation Manager. **Editorial:** Patrick Graziano, Managing Editor. T.G. Smith, Sports Editor.

MT. CARMEL

DAILY REPUBLICAN REGISTER. 117 E. Fourth St., Mt. Carmel, IL 62863-0550. Telephone: 618-262-5144. FAX: 618-263-4437. E-MAIL: news@mtcarmelregister.com. URL: http://www.tristate-media.com. Mailing Address: PO Box 550, Mt. Carmel, IL 62863. Year Established: 1839. Pub. Frequency: d. (Mon.-Fri.) Page Size: broadsheet. Subscrip. Rate: $.50 newsstand/cover; $73/yr carrier delivery; $66/yr mailed in county; $91/yr mailed out of county; $121/yr mailed elsewhere. Adv. Rate: col. inch $10.85 **Wire Service(s):** AP. Circulation: 4,250 morning (paid). **Owner(s):** Brehm Communications, Inc., 16644 W. Bernardo Dr., Ste. 300, San Diego, CA 92127. Telephone: 858-451-6200. FAX: 858-451-3814. **Management:** Phil Summers, Publisher. Sally Voigt, Advertising Manager. Dave Adkins, Circulation Manager. Brenna Crooks, Classified Adv. Mgr.. **Editorial:** Phil Gower, Editor. Tom Dunn, Society Editor. Bob Livingston, Sports.

MT. VERNON

REGISTER-NEWS (MT. VERNON), THE. 911 Broadway, Mt. Vernon, IL 62864. Telephone: 618-242-0113. FAX: 618-242-8286. URL: http://www.register-news.com. Mailing Address: PO Box 489, Mt. Vernon, IL 62864. Year Established: 1871. Pub. Frequency: d. (Mon.-Sat.) Page Size: broadsheet. Subscrip. Rate: $.50 newsstand/cover; $90/yr home delivery in area; $94/yr mailed out of area; $95/yr mailed out of state. **Wire Service(s):** AP. Circulation: 70,000 evening (paid). **Owner(s):** Community Newspaper Holdings, Inc., 3500 Colonnade Pkwy., Ste. 600, Birmingham, AL 25243. **Management:** Jeff Egbert, Advertising Director. Don Falcone, Circulation Manager. Amber Creed, Classified Adv. Mgr.. **Editorial:** MaryKay Davis, Editor. Gegory Norfleet, Associate Editor.

NAPERVILLE

NAPERVILLE SUN. 1500 W. Ogden Ave., Naperville, IL 60540. Telephone: 630-355-8014. FAX: 630-416-5163. E-MAIL: thesun@scn1.com. URL: http://www.suburbanchicagonews.com/napervillesun/. Year Established: 1935. Pub. Frequency: d. Page Size: tabloid. Subscrip. Rate: $.50 newsstand/cover; $1 newsstand/cover Sun.; $52/yr home delivery local. **Wire Service(s):** AP. Circulation: 19,677 Sunday (paid); 30,514 per issue (paid). **Owner(s):** Sun-Times Media Group, 350 N Orleans St, Ste 10-S, Chicago, IL 60654. Telephone: 312-321-2299. **Management:** Jim Lynch, Publisher. Lois Mayer, Advertising Manager. Debi Ryan, Classified Adv. Mgr.. **Editorial:** Ted Slowik, Managing Editor. Cynthia Goldberg, News Editor.

OLNEY

OLNEY DAILY MAIL. 206 Whittle Ave., Olney, IL 62450-0340. Telephone: 618-393-2931. FAX: 618-392-2953. E-MAIL: editor@wabash.net. URL: http://www.olneydailymail.com. Mailing Address: PO Box 340, Olney, IL 62450-0340. Year Established: 1898. Pub. Frequency: d. (Mon.-Fri.) Page Size: broadsheet. Subscrip. Rate: $.50 newsstand/cover; $110/yr home delivery local; $112/yr mailed. **Wire Service(s):** AP. Circulation: 5,000 evening (paid). **Owner(s):** GateHouse Media, Inc, 350 WillowBrook Office Park, Fairport, NY 14450. **Management:** Ray McGrew, Publisher. Joe Gardner, Circulation Manager. **Editorial:** Mark Allen, Editor.

OTTAWA

DAILY TIMES (OTTAWA). 110 W. Jefferson St., Ottawa, IL 61350. Telephone: 815-433-2000. URL: http://www.inottowa.com. Year Established: 1844. Pub. Frequency: d. (Mon.-Sat.) Page Size: broadsheet. Subscrip. Rate: $.50 newsstand/cover; $2.25/wk. local; $112.50/yr home delivery local; $127.50/yr motor route local. **Wire Service(s):** AP. Circulation: 13,879 evening (paid). **Owner(s):** Ottawa Publishing Co., See address and contact information above. **Bureau(s):** 174 W. Washington St., Marseilles, IL 61341. Telephone: 815-795-2023. FAX: 815-795-3446. **Management:** James Malley, General Manager. Sherry Patterson, Advertising Director. Cindy Liptak, Circulation Director. **Editorial:** Lonny Cain, Managing Editor. Paul Carpenter, News Editor.

TIMES (OTTAWA), THE. 110 W. Jefferson St., Ottawa, IL 61350. Telephone: 815-433-2000. FAX: 815-433-1626. E-MAIL: ccirculation@mywebtimes.com. URL: http://www.mywebtimes.com. Year Established: 1927. Pub. Frequency: d. (Mon.-Sat.) Page Size: broadsheet. Subscrip. Rate: $.75 newsstand/cover; $32.50 home delivery for 13 wks.; $125/yr home delivery; $36 motor route for 13 wks.; $140/yr motor route. **Wire Service(s):** AP. Circulation: 9,100 evening (paid). **Owner(s):** Small Newspaper Group, National Press Bldg., Washington, DC 20045. Telephone: 202-662-7240. FAX: 202-662-7242. 8 Dearborn Sq., Kankakee, IL 60901. Telephone: 815-937-3300. **Management:** Sherry Patterson, Advertising. Cathy Warren, Circulation Manager. **Editorial:** Lonny Cain, Managing Editor.

PARIS

PARIS BEACON NEWS. 218 N. Main St., Paris, IL 61944. Telephone: 217-465-6424. FAX: 217-463-1232. E-MAIL: advertising@parisbeacon.com. URL: http://www.parisbeacon.com. Year Established: 1848. Pub. Frequency: d. (Mon.-Sat.) Page Size: broadsheet. Subscrip. Rate: $.50 newsstand/cover; $100/yr carrier delivery. Adv. Rate: col. inch $7.50 Freelance Pay: $15-$20/story. **Wire Service(s):** AP. Circulation: 5,850 evening (paid). **Owner(s):** Ned Jenison, See address and contact information above. **Management:** Kevin Jenison, General Manager. Ned Jenison, President. Libby Brown, Advertising Manager. Dana Wooten, Circulation Manager. **Editorial:** Ned Jenison, Editor. Kathy Rhoads, Managing Editor. Jameson Morgan, Sports Editor.

PAXTON

PAXTON DAILY RECORD. 218 N. Market St., Paxton, IL 60957. Telephone: 217-379-2356. FAX: 217-379-3104. E-MAIL: advpaxtonrecord@illicom.net. Year Established: 1865. Pub. Frequency: d. (Mon.-Fri.) Page Size: broadsheet. Subscrip. Rate: $.35 newsstand/cover; $70/yr in county; $95/yr elsewhere. Adv. Rate: col. inch $8.65 Circulation: 1,100 evening (paid). **Owner(s):** Paxton Printing Co., See address and contact information above. **Management:** Pat Killion, Advertising Manager. Joyce Sage, Circulation Manager. Cathy Younker, Classified Adv. Mgr.. **Editorial:** David Hinton, Editor. Will Brumleve, Columnist.

PEKIN

PEKIN DAILY TIMES. ISSN 0745-7863
20 S. Fourth St., Pekin, IL 61554. Telephone: 309-346-1111. FAX: 309-346-9815. URL: http://www.pekintimes.com. Mailing Address: PO Box 430, Pekin, IL 61555. Year Established: 1880. Pub. Frequency: d. (Mon.-Sat.) Page Size: broadsheet. Subscrip. Rate: $.75 newsstand/cover; $127/yr. **Wire Service(s):** AP. Circulation: 14,000 evening (paid). **Owner(s):** GateHouse Media, Inc, 350 WillowBrook Office Park, Fairport, NY 14450. Telephone: 585-598-0030. FAX: 585-248-2631. **Management:** Greg Ratliff, Publisher. Michele Long, Advertising Director. Anthony Moreno, Circulation Manager. **Editorial:** Rick Wade, Editor.

PEORIA

PEORIA JOURNAL STAR. One News Plz, Peoria, IL 61643. Telephone: 309-686-3000. FAX: 309-686-3265. E-MAIL: janderson@pjstar.com. URL: http://www.pjstar.com. Year Established: 1855. Pub. Frequency: d. Page Size: broadsheet. Subscrip. Rate: $.75 newsstand/cover; $1 newsstand/cover Sat.; $2 newsstand/cover Sun.; $221/yr carrier delivery; $281/yr mailed. Adv. Rate: col. inch $64.75 **Wire Service(s):** AP, MCT. Circulation: 70,000 morning (paid); 90,350 Sunday (paid). **Owner(s):** GateHouse Media, Inc, 350 WillowBrook Office Park, Fairport, NY 14450. Telephone: 585-598-0030. FAX: 585-248-2631. **Management:** John McConnell, Publisher. Sue Patterson, Advertising Manager. Kiley Quinn, Classified Adv. Mgr.. **Editorial:** Paul Gordon, Business Editor.

PONTIAC

PONTIAC DAILY LEADER. 318 N. Main St., Pontiac, IL 61764. Telephone: 815-842-1153. FAX: 815-842-4388. URL: http://www.pontiacdailyleader.com. Mailing Address: PO Box 170, Pontiac, IL 61764. Year Established: 1880. Pub. Frequency: d. (Mon.-Sat.) Page Size: broadsheet. Subscrip. Rate: $.50 newsstand/cover; $13/mo.; $120/yr. **Wire Service(s):** AP. Circulation: 6,500 evening (paid). **Owner(s):** GateHouse Media, Inc, 350 WillowBrook Office Park, Fairport, NY 14450. Telephone: 585-598-0030. FAX: 585-248-2631. **Management:** Thomas E Hutson, Publisher. Gary DeVault, Advertising Manager. Roger Swearingen, Circulation Manager. **Editorial:** Erich Murphy, Managing Editor.

QUINCY

QUINCY HERALD-WHIG. ISSN 0746-6358
130 S. Fifth St., Quincy, IL 62301. Telephone: 217-223-5100. FAX: 217-221-3397. E-MAIL: whig@whig.com. URL: http://www.whig.com. Mailing Address: PO Box 909, Quincy, IL 62306. Year Established: 1835. Pub. Frequency: d. Page Size: broadsheet. Subscrip. Rate: $.50 newsstand/cover; $1.75 newsstand/cover Sun.; $159.55/yr; $96/yr Sun only. **Wire Service(s):** AP. Circulation: 23,605 evening (paid); 28,117 Sunday (paid). **Owner(s):** Quincy Newspapers, Inc., See address and contact information above. **Management:** Scott Ruff, General Manager. Thomas A. Oakley, President. Lincoln Lieber, Advertising Manager. Gene Armstrong, Classified Adv. Mgr.. Mary Winters, Asst. General Mgr.. **Editorial:** Michael Hilfrink, Editor. Don Crim, Managing Editor. Dave Adam, News Editor. Don O'Brien, Sports Editor.

ROBINSON

ROBINSON DAILY NEWS. 302 S. Cross St., Robinson, IL 62454. E-MAIL: news@robdailynews.com. URL: http://www.robdailynews.com. Mailing Address: P.O. Box 639, Robinson, IL 62454. Year Established: 1919. Pub. Frequency: d. (Mon.-Sat.) Page Size: broadsheet. Subscrip. Rate: $.50 newsstand/cover; $99/yr carrier delivery in county; $60/yr mailed in county & adj. cys.; $99/yr mailed elsewhere. **Wire Service(s):** AP, CNS. Circulation: 5,636 evening (paid). **Owner(s):** Lewis Newspapers, See address and contact information above. **Management:** Larry H. Lewis, President. Wally Dean, Advertising Manager. Robert Fox, Circulation Manager. Dinah Corder, Classified Adv. Mgr.. **Editorial:** Greg Bilbrey, Managing Editor. Greg Cummins, Production Manager. Tom Osborne, Copy Editor. Michelle Wagoner, Society Editor. Tim Brooks, Sports.

ROCK ISLAND

ROCK ISLAND ARGUS, THE. 1724 Fourth Ave., Rock Island, IL 61201. Telephone: 309-764-4344. FAX: 309-797-0321. E-MAIL: sysop@qconline.com. URL: http://www.rockislandargus.com. Year Established: 1878. Pub. Frequency: d. Page Size: broadsheet. Subscrip. Rate: $.50 newsstand/cover; $1.50 newsstand/cover Sun.; $3.80 home delivery/wk.; $45.60 home delivery for 3 mos.. Adv. Rate: col. inch $28.95 **Wire Service(s):** AP, NYT, MCT. Circulation: 46,820 evening (paid); 48,600 Sunday (paid). **Owner(s):** Small Newspaper Group, 8 Dearborn Sq., Kankakee, IL 60901. Telephone: 815-937-3300. **Management:** Len R. Small, President. Gerald J Taylor, Publisher. Nick Norman, Advertising Director. John Newby, Circulation Director. Nick Norman, Marketing Director. **Editorial:** Russell Scott, Managing Editor. Laura Fraembs, Associate Editor. Joe Payne, Beauty Editor. Carolyn Hardin, Business Editor. Joe Beach, City Editor. Kenda Burrows, Editorial Page Editor. Sean Leary, Entertainment Editor. Lisa Mohr, Food Editor. Joe Payne, Lifestyle Editor. Terry Herbig, Photo Editor. Leon Lagerstam, Religion Editor. Mark Nesseler, Sports Editor.

Dailies

ROCKFORD

REGISTER STAR. 99 E. State St., Rockford, IL 61104-1004. Telephone: 815-987-1200. FAX: 815-987-1365. URL: http://www.rrstar.com. Year Established: 1855. Pub. Frequency: d. Page Size: broadsheet. Subscrip. Rate: $.50 newsstand/cover; $1.50 newsstand/cover Sun.; $195/yr carrier delivery; $208/yr motor route. **Wire Service(s):** AP, GNS. Circulation: 65,968 morning (paid); 79,155 Sunday (paid). **Owner(s):** Gannett Company, Inc., 7950 Jones Branch Dr., McLean, VA 22107-0001. Telephone: 703-854-6000. **Management:** Fritz Jacobi, Publisher. Rick Szabrak, Circulation Director. Michele Massoth, Classified Adv. Mgr.. **Editorial:** Linda Cunningham, Executive Editor. Jeff Gauger, Managing Editor. Doug Gass, Asst. Managing Ed.. Adam Lowenstein, Business Editor.

SHELBYVILLE

SHELBYVILLE DAILY UNION. 100 W. Main St., Shelbyville, IL 62565. Telephone: 217-774-2161. FAX: 217-774-5732. URL: http://www.shelbyvilledailyunion.com. Year Established: 1887. Pub. Frequency: d. (Mon.-Fri.) Page Size: broadsheet. Subscrip. Rate: $.50 newsstand/cover; $75/yr carrier delivery area; $75/yr mailed in county & adj. cys.; $84.50/yr mailed elsewhere. **Wire Service(s):** AP. Circulation: 3,000 per issue (paid). **Owner(s):** Community Newspaper Holdings, Inc., 3500 Colonnade Pkwy., Ste. 600, Birmingham, AL 35243. Telephone: 205-298-7100. **Management:** Mindy Mars, Publisher. Deanna Sickles, Advertising. Traci Zientara, Circulation Manager. **Editorial:** Frank Mulholland, Managing Editor. John Curtis, Sports Editor.

SPRINGFIELD

STATE JOURNAL-REGISTER, THE. One Copley Plz, Springfield, IL 62705. Telephone: 217-788-1300. FAX: 217-788-1551. E-MAIL: sjr@sj-r.com. URL: http://www.sj-r.com. Mailing Address: PO Box 219, Springfield, IL 62705-0219. Year Established: 1831. Pub. Frequency: d. Page Size: broadsheet. Subscrip. Rate: $.50 newsstand/cover; $1.50 newsstand/cover Sun.; $19.46 home delivery/mo.. **Wire Service(s):** AP, SH. Circulation: 57,459 morning (paid); 66,215 Sunday (paid). **Owner(s):** GateHouse Media, Inc, 350 WillowBrook Office Park, Fairport, NY 14450. Telephone: 585-598-0030. FAX: 585-248-2631. **Management:** Mike Kreppert, General Manager. Scott Bowers, Publisher. Gary Tyler, Advertising Director. **Editorial:** Jon K Broadbooks, Executive Editor.

ST. CHARLES

KANE COUNTY CHRONICLE. 333 N. Randall Rd., St. Charles, IL 60174. Telephone: 630-845-5355. FAX: 630-444-1641. E-MAIL: editorial@kcchronicle.com. URL: http://www.kcchronicle.com. Year Established: 1881. Pub. Frequency: d. Page Size: broadsheet. Subscrip. Rate: $.50 newsstand/cover; $1 newsstand/cover Sat.; $99.50/yr home delivery; $156/yr mailed out of county. **Wire Service(s):** AP. Circulation: 15,000 morning (paid). **Owner(s):** Shaw Newspapers, 444 Pine Hill Dr., Dixon, IL 61021. Telephone: 815-284-2222. FAX: 815-254-9290. **Management:** Thomas D. Shaw, President. Bonnie Reicks, Advertising Manager. Kevin Elder, Production Director.

STERLING

DAILY GAZETTE (STERLING). 3200 E. Lincolnway, Sterling, IL 61081. Telephone: 815-625-3600. FAX: 815-625-9390. Mailing Address: PO Box 498, Sterling, IL 61081. Year Established: 1854. Pub. Frequency: d. Page Size: broadsheet. Subscrip. Rate: $.50 newsstand/cover; $1.25 Sun.; $134.40/yr home delivery local. **Wire Service(s):** AP, SH, CNS. Circulation: 2,400 evening (paid); 1,300 Sunday (paid). **Owner(s):** Shaw Newspapers, 444 Pine Hill Dr., Dixon, IL 61021. Telephone: 815-284-4000. **Bureau(s):** 222 W. Main St., Morrison, IL 61270. Telephone: 815-772-3458. FAX: 815-772-3458. Contact: Grace Whitten, Bureau Chief. **Management:** William E. Shaw, Publisher. **Editorial:** Jonie Larson, Executive Editor. Clark Kelly, Political Editor. Tim O'Brien, Radio-TV Editor. Josh Welge, Sports Editor.

TAYLORVILLE

TAYLORVILLE BREEZE-COURIER. PO Box 440, Taylorville, IL 62568. Telephone: 217-824-2233. FAX: 217-824-2026. E-MAIL: breezenews@ctitech.com. URL: http://www.breeze-courier.com. Year Established: 1894. Pub. Frequency: d. (Sun.-Fri.) Page Size: broadsheet. Subscrip. Rate: $.50 newsstand/cover; $1 Sun.; $99.10/yr carrier delivery domestic. Adv. Rate: col. inch $6.30 **Wire Service(s):** AP. Circulation: 6,900 evening (paid and free); 6,900 Sunday (paid and free). **Owner(s):** Marylee Cooper Lasswell, See address and contact information above. **Management:** Marylee Cooper Lasswell, General Manager. Jospeh Dorr, Advertising Manager. Marsha Harris, Circulation Manager. **Editorial:** J. Matthew Corso, Editor. Ed Nelson, Sports.

TINLEY PARK

SOUTHTOWN STAR. ISSN 1941-3483
6901 W 159th St, Tinley Park, IL 60477. Telephone: 708-802-8800. FAX: 708-633-4859. URL: http://www.southtownstar.com/index.html. Year Established: 2007. Pub. Frequency: d. **Owner(s):** Sun-Times Media Group, See address and contact information above. **Management:** Murdoch L. Davis, Publisher.

WATSEKA

IROQUOIS COUNTY TIMES-REPUBLIC. 1492 E Walnut St, Watseka, IL 60970. Telephone: 815-432-5227. FAX: 815-432-5159. URL: http://www.watsekatimesrepublic.com. Mailing Address: PO Box 250, Watseka, IL 60970. Year Established: 1870. Pub. Frequency: d. (Mon.-Fri.) Page Size: tabloid. Subscrip. Rate: $.50 newsstand/cover; $99/yr mailed in state; $114/yr mailed out of state. **Wire Service(s):** AP. Circulation: 2,593 evening (paid). **Owner(s):** Community Media Group, Inc, PO Box 10, West Frankfort, IL 62896. Telephone: 618-937-6412. **Management:** Don Hurd, Publisher. Roberta Kempen, Advertising Director. **Editorial:** Carla Waters, Editor. Brandon Netiuk, Sports.

WAUKEGAN

NEWS SUN (WAUKEGAN), THE. 2383 N. Delaney Rd., Waukegan, IL 60087-1836. Telephone: 847-336-7000. FAX: 847-249-7202. URL: http://www.suburbanchicagonewspapers.com. Year Established: 1892. Pub. Frequency: d. (Mon.-Sat.) Page Size: broadsheet. Subscrip. Rate: $.50 newsstand/cover; $1.50 newsstand/cover Sat.; $3.25 home delivery/wk. local; $156/yr home delivery. **Wire Service(s):** AP. Circulation: 40,000 evening (paid). **Owner(s):** Sun-Times Media Group, 350 N Orleans St, Ste 10-S, Chicago, IL 60654. Telephone: 312-321-2299. **Management:** Larry Lucas, Circulation Manager. **Editorial:** Chris Cashman, Managing Editor. Charles Selle, News Editor. Jeff Bonato, Sports Editor.

WEST FRANKFORT

DAILY AMERICAN (WEST FRANKFORT). 111 S. Emma St., West Frankfort, IL 62896. Telephone: 618-932-2146. FAX: 618-937-6006. URL: http://www.dailyamericannews.com. Mailing Address: PO Box 617, West Frankfort, IL 62896. Year Established: 1916. Pub. Frequency: d. (Mon.-Sat.) Page Size: broadsheet. Subscrip. Rate: $.50 newsstand/cover; $9.50 carrier delivery/mo. local; $10.50 motor route/mo.; $94.50/yr mailed in county; $104.50/yr mailed in state. **Wire Service(s):** AP. Circulation: 4,000 evening (paid). **Owner(s):** GateHouse Media, Inc, 350 WillowBrook Office Park, Fairport, NY 14450. Telephone: 585-598-0030. FAX: 585-248-2631. **Management:** Lynn Kidd, Publisher. Diann Walthes, Advertising Manager. Pat Hampton, Circulation Manager. Lindsey Leek, Classified Adv. Mgr.. **Editorial:** Allen Parker, Editor.

INDIANA

ANDERSON

HERALD BULLETIN, THE. 1133 Jackson St., Anderson, IN 46016. Telephone: 765-622-1212. FAX: 765-640-4815. URL: http://www.theheraldbulletin.com. Mailing Address: PO Box 1090, Anderson, IN 46015. Year Established: 1868. Pub. Frequency: d. Page Size: broadsheet. Subscrip. Rate: $.50 newsstand/cover; $1.50 newsstand/cover Sun.; $15.40 carrier delivery/mo. in area; $170/yr carrier delivery; $23.80 mailed/mo.. **Wire Service(s):** AP. Circulation: 35,000 morning (paid); 45,000 Sunday (paid). **Owner(s):** Community Newspaper Holdings, Inc., 3500 Colonnade Pkwy., Ste. 600, Birmingham, AL 35243. Telephone: 205-298-7100. FAX: 205-298-7101. **Management:** Mike Casuscelli, Publisher. Connie Alexander, Advertising Director. ReneeKen Newby, Circulation Manager. Annette Burcharts, Classified Adv. Mgr.. **Editorial:** Patrick Sanders, Managing Editor.

ANGOLA

HERALD-REPUBLICAN. 45 S. Public Sq., Angola, IN 46703. Telephone: 260-665-3117. FAX: 260-665-2322. E-MAIL: mikem@kpcnews.net. URL: http://www.kpcnews.com. Mailing Address: PO Box 180, Angola, IN 46703. Year Established: 1857. Pub. Frequency: d. Page Size: standard. Subscrip. Rate: $.50 newsstand/cover; $1 newsstand/cover Sun.; $160/yr home delivery. Adv. Rate: col. inch $7.45 **Wire Service(s):** CNS. Circulation: 5,000 morning (paid); 6,000 Sunday (paid). **Owner(s):** Kendallville Publishing Co, PO Box 39, Kendallville, IN 46755. Telephone: 260-347-0400. FAX: 260-347-7281. **Management:** Terry Housholder, Publisher. Richard Fisher, Advertising Manager. Sam Ashe, Circulation Manager. **Editorial:** Matt Getts, Editor. Michael Marturello, Managing Editor.

AUBURN

EVENING STAR, THE. 118 W. Ninth St., Auburn, IN 46706-0431. Telephone: 260-925-2611. FAX: 260-925-2625. E-MAIL: dkurtz@kpcnews.net. URL: http://www.kpcnews.com. Mailing Address: PO Box 431, Auburn, IN 46706-0431. Year Established: 1871. Pub. Frequency: d. (Mon.-Sun.) Page Size: broadsheet. Subscrip. Rate: $.50 newsstand/cover; $1 newsstand/cover Sun.; $85 home delivery for 6 mos.; $160/yr home delivery. **Wire Service(s):** AP. Circulation: 7,000 evening (paid). **Owner(s):** Kendallville Publishing Co., 112 N. Main St., Kendallville, IN 46755. Telephone: 219-347-0400. **Management:** Terry Housholder, General Manager. George O. Witwer, Owner. Terry Housholder, Publisher. Sam Ashe, Circulation Manager. **Editorial:** David Kurtz, Managing Editor. Jackie Musser, Lifestyle Editor. Mark Murdock, Sports Editor.

BEDFORD

TIMES-MAIL. 813 16th St., Bedford, IN 47421. Telephone: 812-275-3355. FAX: 812-275-4191. E-MAIL: tmnews@tmnews.com. URL: http://www.tmnews.com. Mailing Address: PO Box 849, Bedford, IN 47421. Year Established: 1884. Pub. Frequency: d. Page Size: broadsheet. Subscrip. Rate: $.50 newsstand/cover; $13.45 home delivery/mo. local; $156/yr home delivery. **Wire Service(s):** AP. Circulation: 14,000 evening (paid). **Owner(s):** Schurz Communications, Inc., 225 W. Colfax Ave., South Bend, IN 46626. Telephone: 219-287-1001. **Management:** Scott C. Schurz, President. Mayer Maloney, Publisher. Joe Green, Circulation Manager. Angie Blanton, Classified Adv. Mgr.. Ellen Ware, Marketing Director. **Editorial:** Mayer Maloney, Editor. Mike Lewis, Managing Editor. Sara Clifford, Lifestyle Editor. Dawn Duncan, Sports.

BLOOMINGTON

HERALD-TIMES. ISSN 1044-4246
1900 S. Walnut St., Bloomington, IN 47403. Telephone: 812-332-4401. FAX: 812-331-4285. E-MAIL: htnews@heraldt.com. URL: http://www.hoosiertimes.com. Mailing Address: PO Box 909, Bloomington, IN 47402. Year Established: 1877. Pub. Frequency: d. Page Size: broadsheet. Subscrip. Rate: $.50 newsstand/cover; $1.50 newsstand/cover Sun.; $89.70 home delivery for 6 mos.; $167.40/yr home delivery. Freelance Pay: $25-$50/article. **Wire Service(s):** AP, NYT. Circulation: 28,500 morning (paid); 44,000 Sunday (paid). **Owner(s):** Schurz Communications, Inc., 225 W. Colfax Ave., South Bend, IN 46626. Telephone: 219-287-1001. **Management:** E. Mayer Maloney, Publisher. Tim Smith, Circulation Manager. **Editorial:** Bob Zaltsberg, Editor. Brian Werth, Business Editor.

BLUFFTON

BLUFFTON NEWS-BANNER. 125 N Johnson St, Bluffton, IN 46714. Telephone: 260-824-0224. FAX: 260-824-0700. E-MAIL: email@newsbanner.com. URL: http://www.news-banner.com. Mailing Address: PO Box 436, Bluffton, IN 46714. Year Established: 1892. Pub. Frequency: d. (Mon.-Sat.) Page Size: broadsheet. Subscrip. Rate: $.50 newsstand/cover; $119/yr carrier delivery local; $128/yr motor route local; $166/yr mailed out of state. **Wire Service(s):** AP. Circulation: 5,378 evening (paid). **Owner(s):** News-Banner Publications, Inc., See address and contact information above. **Management:** Mark Miller, Publisher. Jean Bordner, Advertising Manager. Rhonda Hesher, Circulation Manager. Patty Elwell, Classified Adv. Mgr.. **Editorial:** Dave Schultz, Editor. Paul Beitler, Sports.

BRAZIL

BRAZIL TIMES. 100 N. Meridian, Brazil, IN 47834. Telephone: 812-446-2216. FAX: 812-446-0938. E-MAIL: btimes@indiana.net. URL: http://www.braziltimes.com. Mailing Address: PO Box 429, Brazil, IN 47834. Year Established: 1888. Pub. Frequency: d. (Mon.-Sat.) Page Size: broadsheet. Subscrip. Rate: $.50 newsstand/cover; $96/yr motor route; $102/yr mailed in state. **Wire Service(s):** AP. Circulation: 10,000 evening (paid and free). **Owner(s):** Rust Communications, Inc., 301 Broadway, Cape Girardeau, MO 63701. Telephone: 800-879-1210. **Management:** Randy List, Publisher. Lynne Llewellyn, Advertising Director. Earl Hutcheson, Circulation Manager. Jan Stapp, Classified Adv. Mgr.. **Editorial:** Frank Phillips, Editor.

CHESTERTON

CHESTERTON TRIBUNE. 193 S. Calumet Rd., Chesterton, IN 46304. Telephone: 219-926-1131. FAX: 219-926-6389. E-MAIL: chestertontrib@earthlink.net. URL: http://chestertribune.com. Year Established: 1884. Pub. Frequency: d. (Mon.-Fri.) Page Size: broadsheet. Subscrip. Rate: $.50 newsstand/cover; $6 carrier delivery/mo.; $8 mailed/mo.. Adv. Rate: col. inch $5.80 Circulation: 5,100 evening (paid). **Owner(s):** Warren Canright, See address and contact information above. **Management:** Warren Canright, Publisher. Harry Lewis, Advertising Manager. Alma Rabe, Circulation Manager. Betty Canright, Business Manager. **Editorial:** David Canright, Managing Editor.

CLINTON

DAILY CLINTONIAN. 422 S. Main St., Clinton, IN 47842-2414. Telephone: 765-832-2443. E-MAIL: gbcarey@aol.com. Mailing Address: PO Box 309, Clinton, IN 47842-0309. Year Established: 1912. Pub. Frequency: d. (Mon.-Fri.) Page Size: broadsheet. Subscrip. Rate: $.50 newsstand/cover; $1.85 home delivery/wk. in county; $2.10 motor route/wk. in county; $134.85/yr mailed in county; $141.50/yr mailed out of county. Adv. Rate: col. inch $7 **Wire Service(s):** AP. Circulation: 5,430 evening (paid). **Owner(s):** Clinton Color Crafters, Inc., See address and contact information above. **Management:** Diane E. Waugh, Owner. George B Carey, Publisher. Bev Falls, Advertising Manager. D Waugh, Circulation Manager. Diane E. Waugh, Business Manager. **Editorial:** Jinanne Carey, Editor. George B. Carey, Production Manager.

COLUMBIA CITY

POST & MAIL, THE. ISSN 0746-9950
927 W Connexion Way, Columbia City, IN 46725. Telephone: 260-244-5153. FAX: 260-244-7598. E-MAIL: postandmail@earthlink.net. URL: http://www.thepostandmail.com. Mailing Address: PO Box 837, Columbia City, IN 46725. Year Established: 1853. Pub. Frequency: d. (Mon.-Sat.) Page Size: broadsheet. Subscrip. Rate: $.50 newsstand/cover; $115.10/yr home delivery; $125/yr motor route & mailed. Freelance Pay: $0.50/column-inch. **Wire Service(s):** AP. Circulation: 4,700 evening (paid). **Owner(s):** Horizon Publications, Inc., 1120 N. Carbon St, Ste 100, Marion, IL 62959. **Management:** Doug Brown, Publisher. Mick Long, Advertising Manager. Sally Ballard, Circulation Manager. **Editorial:** Ruth Stanley, Managing Editor.

COLUMBUS

REPUBLIC, THE. 333 Second St., Columbus, IN 47201. Telephone: 812-372-7811. FAX: 812-379-5711. E-MAIL: advertise@therepublic.com. URL: http://www.therepublic.com. Year Established: 1872. Pub. Frequency: d. Page Size: broadsheet. Subscrip. Rate: $.50 newsstand/cover; $1.50 Sun.; $13 home delivery/mo.; $145.50/yr home delivery; $25 mailed/mo.; $192/yr mailed. Adv. Rate: col. inch $22.65 **Wire Service(s):** AP, SH, MCT. Circulation: 22,000 morning (paid); 26,000 Sunday (paid). **Owner(s):** Home News Enterprises, See address and contact information above. **Management:** Jeffrey N.. Brown, President. Howard Herron, Publisher. Pamela Wells-Lego, Advertising. Lynne Klamo, Circulation Manager. **Editorial:** John Harmon, Editor. Bob Gustin, Managing Editor. Harry McCawley, Associate Editor. Kirk Johannesen, Sports.

CONNERSVILLE

CONNERSVILLE NEWS-EXAMINER. 406 Central Ave., Connersville, IN 47331. Telephone: 765-825-0585. FAX: 765-825-4599. E-MAIL: newsexaminer@newsexaminer.com. URL: http://www.newsexaminer.com. Mailing Address: PO Box 287, Connersville, IN 47331. Year Established: 1888. Pub. Frequency: d. (Mon.-Sat.) Page Size: broadsheet. Subscrip. Rate: $.50 newsstand/cover; $11 home delivery/mo. in county; $11.50 motor route/mo. in county. **Wire Service(s):** AP. Circulation: 9,200 evening (paid). **Owner(s):** Paxton Media Group Llc, 201 S. Fourth St., Paducah, KY 42003. Telephone: 270-575-8600. FAX: 270-442-8188. **Management:** Patrick Keller, Publisher. Carole Byrd, Advertising Manager. Chris Foreman, Business Manager. **Editorial:** Rick Mullen, Editor. Gary Hufferd, Managing Editor.

CRAWFORDSVILLE

CRAWFORDSVILLE JOURNAL REVIEW. 119 N. Green St., Crawfordsville, IN 47933. Telephone: 765-362-1200. FAX: 765-364-5424. E-MAIL: jreview@link2000.net. URL: http://www.journalreview.com. Mailing Address: PO Box 512, Crawfordsville, IN 47933. Year Established: 1841. Pub. Frequency: d. (Mon.-Sat.) Page Size: broadsheet. Subscrip. Rate: $.50 newsstand/cover; $1.25 Sat.; $11 carrier delivery/mo.. **Wire Service(s):** AP, MCT. Circulation: 10,700 morning (paid). **Owner(s):** PTS, 221-A 35th St.,N.E., Fort Payne, AL 35967. Telephone: 256-845-4590. **Management:** Randy Pribble, Publisher. Mark Deacon, Advertising Director. **Editorial:** Maria Flora, Managing Editor. Joanne Hammer, Business Editor. Matt Wilson, Sports Editor.

DECATUR

DECATUR DAILY DEMOCRAT, THE. ISSN 0894-2307
141 S Secon St, Decatur, IN 46733. E-MAIL: dailydemo@decaturnet.com. URL: http://www.decaturdailydemocrat.com. Mailing Address: PO Box 1001, Decatur, IN 46733. Year Established: 1857. Pub. Frequency: d. (Mon.-Sat.) Page Size: broadsheet. Subscrip. Rate: $.50 newsstand/cover; $115/yr home delivery; $120/yr motor route; $135/yr mailed in county & adj. cys.. **Wire Service(s):** AP. Circulation: 6,100 evening (paid). **Owner(s):** Horizon Publications, Inc., 1120 N. Carbon St, Ste 100, Marion, IL 62959. **Management:** Gary Loftus, Publisher. Abigail Schoeff, Circulation Manager. Jamie Melching, Classified Adv. Mgr.. **Editorial:** Bob Shraluka, Editor.

ELKHART

TRUTH, THE. ISSN 0746-7516
421 S. Second St., Elkhart, IN 46516. Telephone: 574-294-1661. FAX: 574-293-3302. URL: http://www.elktruth.com. Mailing Address: PO Box 487, Elkhart, IN 46515. Year Established: 1889. Pub. Frequency: d. Page Size: broadsheet. Subscrip. Rate: $.50 newsstand/cover; $1.50 Sun.; $12.95 home delivery/mo.; $18 mailed/mo. out of county. **Wire Service(s):** AP, SH. Circulation: 28,500 morning (paid); 31,500 Sunday (paid). **Owner(s):** Truth Publishing Co., See address and contact information above. **Management:** Brandon Erlacher, General Manager. David Ogle, Publisher. Shane Forest, Circulation Manager. Mark Wolf, Classified Adv. Mgr.. Kay Luther, Sales Manager. **Editorial:** Bill Wilson, Editor. Greg Halling, Managing Editor. Fred Flury, Photographer. Bill Beck, Sports.

ELWOOD

CALL-LEADER. 317 S. Anderson St., Elwood, IN 46036. Telephone: 765-552-3355. FAX: 765-552-3358. E-MAIL: elpub@elwoodpublishing.com. Mailing Address: P.O. Box 85, Elwood, IN 46036-0085. Year Established: 1891. Pub. Frequency: d. (Mon.-Sat.) Page Size: broadsheet. Subscrip. Rate: $.50 newsstand/cover; $86.40/yr in county; $97.20/yr motor route in county; $125/yr mailed out of county. Adv. Rate: col. inch $7.75 **Wire Service(s):** AP. Circulation: 3,750 evening (paid). **Owner(s):** Elwood Publishing Co., Inc., See address and contact information above. **Management:** Dan Skinner, General Manager. Jack L. Barnes, President. Robert Nash, Publisher. Jay Puterbaugh, Classified Adv. Mgr.. **Editorial:** Sandy Burton, Managing Editor. Ed Hamilton, Sports.

EVANSVILLE

EVANSVILLE COURIER & PRESS. ISSN 1559-1581
300 E. Walnut St., Evansville, IN 47713. Telephone: 812-424-7711. FAX: 812-422-8196. E-MAIL: courierpress@evansville.net. URL: http://www.courierpress.com. Mailing Address: PO Box 268, Evansville, IN 47702-0268. Year Established: 1998. Pub. Frequency: d. Page Size: broadsheet. Subscrip. Rate: $.50 newsstand/cover; $2 newsstand/cover Sun.; $16.80 carrier delivery for 28 days; $17.40 motor route for 28 days. **Wire Service(s):** AP, SH, NYT, LAT-WAT. Circulation: 73,000 morning (paid); 107,000 Sunday (paid). **Owner(s):** E.W. Scripps Co., 312 Walnut St., 28th Fl., Cincinnati, OH 45202. Telephone: 513-977-3000. **Management:** Jack Pate, President. Pat Bridges, Advertising Director. Dan Mashburn, Circulation Manager. **Editorial:** G. Bruce Bauman, Executive Editor. Roger McBain, Art Editor. Alan Julian, Business Editor. Garret Mathews, Columnist. Linda Negro, Feature Editor. Anne Schleper, Food Editor. Roseann Derk, Librarian. Linda Negro, Lifestyle Editor. John Martin, Political Editor. Becky Coudret, Radio-TV Editor. Tim Ethridge, Sports Editor.

FORT WAYNE

JOURNAL-GAZETTE, THE. ISSN 0734-3701
600 W. Main, Fort Wayne, IN 46802. Telephone: 260-461-8516. FAX: 260-461-8648. E-MAIL: jgnews@jg.net. URL: http://www.journalgazette.net. Mailing Address: PO Box 88, Fort Wayne, IN 46801. Year Established: 1863. Pub. Frequency: d. Page Size: broadsheet. Subscrip. Rate: $.50 newsstand/cover; $1.75 Sun.; $11.50/mo.. **Wire Service(s):** AP, SH, LAT-WAT. Circulation: 60,000 morning (paid); 130,000 Sunday (paid). **Owner(s):** Richard G. Inskeep, See address and contact information above. **Management:** Julie Inskeep, Publisher. Henry Phillips, Advertising Director. **Editorial:** Craig Klugman, Editor. Sherry Skufca, Managing Editor. Tom Germuska, Metro Editor. Keith Elchert, News Editor. Mark Jaworski, Sports Editor.

FRANKFORT

FRANKFORT TIMES. 251 E. Clinton St., Frankfort, IN 46041. Telephone: 765-659-4622. FAX: 765-654-7031. E-MAIL: adv@ftimes.com. URL: http://www.ftimes.com. Mailing Address: PO Box 9, Frankfort, IN 46041-0009. Year Established: 1885. Pub. Frequency: d. (Mon.-Sat.) Page Size: standard. Subscrip. Rate: $.50 newsstand/cover; $11.75 carrier delivery/mo.. Adv. Rate: col. inch $18.79 **Wire Service(s):** AP. Circulation: 6,597 evening (paid). **Owner(s):** Paxton Media Group Llc, 201 S. Fourth St., Paducah, KY 42003. Telephone: 270-575-8600. FAX: 270-442-8188. **Management:** Rick Welch, President. Don Hurd, Advertising Director. Larry Harper, Circulation Manager. Kim Ray, Business Manager. **Editorial:** Jim Bush, Managing Editor. Janice Thornton, Feature Editor. Randy Rendfeld, News Editor. Brian Peloza, Sports Editor.

FRANKLIN

DAILY JOURNAL (FRANKLIN), THE. 2575 N. Morton St., Franklin, IN 46131. Telephone: 317-736-7101. FAX: 317-736-2713. URL: http://www.dailyjournal.net. Mailing Address: PO Box 699, Franklin, IN 46131. Year Established: 1962. Pub. Frequency: d. (Mon.-Sat.) Page Size: broadsheet. Subscrip. Rate: $.75 newsstand/cover; $1.50 newsstand/cover Sat. (effective 2009); $10.40 carrier delivery/mo.; $118.80/yr carrier delivery; $13 mailed/mo.; $49 mailed 4 mos.; $147/yr mailed. **Wire Service(s):** AP, SH. Circulation: 18,000 morning (paid). **Owner(s):** Home News Enterprises, 333 Second St., Columbus, IN 47201. Telephone: 812-372-7811. **Management:** Chuck Wells, Publisher. Christina Cosner, Advertising Director. **Editorial:** Scarlett Syse, Editor. Michelle Frye, Managing Editor. Rick Morwick, Sports Editor.

GOSHEN

GOSHEN NEWS, THE. ISSN 8750-3867
114 S Main St, Goshen, IN 46526. Telephone: 574-533-2157. FAX: 574-533-0839. E-MAIL: news@goshennews.com. URL: http://www.goshennews.com. Mailing Address: PO Box 569, Goshen, IN 46527. Year Established: 1837. Pub. Frequency: d. Page Size: broadsheet. Subscrip. Rate: $.50, $1.50 newsstand/cover; $140/yr local; $18 mailed/mo. in county. **Wire Service(s):** AP. Circulation: 18,000 evening (paid); 18,000 Sunday (paid). **Owner(s):** Community Newspaper Holdings, Inc., 3500 Colonnade Pkwy., Ste. 600, Birmingham, AL 35243. **Management:** Mary K. Beer, Advertising Director. Rick Carlson, Circulation Manager. Angie Kulczar, Classified Adv. Mgr.. **Editorial:** Gerry Hertzler, Editor.

GREENCASTLE

BANNER-GRAPHIC. 100 N. Jackson St., Greencastle, IN 46135. Telephone: 765-653-5151. FAX: 765-653-2063. URL: http://www.bannergraphic.com. Mailing Address: PO Box 509, Greencastle, IN 46135. Year Established: 1918. Pub. Frequency: d. (Mon.-Sat.) Page Size: broadsheet. Subscrip. Rate: $.75 newsstand/cover; $102/yr in state. **Wire Service(s):** AP. Circulation: 6,500 morning (paid). **Owner(s):** Rust Communications Inc., 301 Broadway, Cape Girardeau, MO 63701. Telephone: 573-335-6611. **Management:** Randy List, Publisher. john York, Advertising Manager. Becky Underwood, Circulation Manager. Denise Frazier, Business Manager. **Editorial:** Jamie Barrand, Editor. Eric Bernsee, Editorial Page Editor. Jarred Jernigan, Sports.

GREENFIELD

DAILY REPORTER (GREENFIELD). 22 W. New Rd., Greenfield, IN 46140. Telephone: 317-462-5528. FAX: 317-467-6017. URL: http://www.greenfieldreporter.com. Mailing Address: PO Box 279, Greenfield, IN 46140. Year Established: 1908. Pub. Frequency: d. (Mon.-Sat.) Page Size: broadsheet. Subscrip. Rate: $.50 newsstand/cover; $8.80 home delivery/mo.; $97/yr home delivery; $14.85 mailed/mo. in county; $120.75/yr mailed in county. **Wire Service(s):** AP. Circulation: 9,500 evening (paid). **Owner(s):** Home News Enterprises, 333 Second St., Columbus, IN 47201. Telephone: 812-372-7811. **Management:** Randall Shields, Publisher. Tina West, Advertising Manager. Kara Hansen, Circulation Manager. **Editorial:** Dave Hill, Editor. Karen Crawford, Managing Editor. Tom Russo, Photographer. Andrew Smith, Sports.

GREENSBURG

GREENSBURG DAILY NEWS. 135 S. Franklin St., Greensburg, IN 47240. Telephone: 812-663-3111. FAX: 812-663-2985. E-MAIL: greensburgdailynews@cnhiind.com. URL: http://www.greensburgdailynews.com. Mailing Address: PO Box 106, Greensburg, IN 47240. Year Established: 1894. Pub. Frequency: d. (Mon.-Sat.) Page Size: broadsheet. Subscrip. Rate: $.50 newsstand/cover; $118/yr carrier delivery; $135/yr mailed. **Wire Service(s):** AP. Circulation: 6,600 evening (paid). **Owner(s):** Community Newspaper Holdings, Inc., 3500 Colonnade Pkwy., Ste. 600, Birmingham, AL 35243. Telephone: 205-298-7100. **Management:** Peter VanBaalen, Publisher. Laura Welborn, Advertising Director. Lisa Huff, Circulation Manager. **Editorial:** Jim Cummings, Managing Editor. Aaron Kirchoff, Sports.

HARTFORD CITY

NEWS-TIMES (HARTFORD CITY). 123 S. Jefferson St., Hartford City, IN 47348. Telephone: 765-348-0110. FAX: 765-348-0112. E-MAIL: newstimes@skyenet.net. Mailing Address: PO Box 690, Hartford City, IN 47348. Year Established: 1892. Pub. Frequency: d. (Mon.-Sat.) Page Size: broadsheet. Subscrip. Rate: $.50 newsstand/cover; $2.20 home delivery/wk.; $127.79/yr home delivery; $137/yr mailed. **Wire Service(s):** AP. Circulation: 1,450 morning (paid). **Owner(s):** Community Media Group, Inc, PO Box 10, West Frankfort, IL 62896. Telephone: 618-937-6412. **Management:** Missy Shrock, Publisher. **Editorial:** Jenny West, Editor.

HUNTINGTON

HERALD-PRESS (HUNTINGTON). PO Box 860, Huntington, IN 46750-0860. Telephone: 260-356-6700. FAX: 260-356-9026. E-MAIL: hpads@fwi.com. URL: http://www.h-ponline.com. Year Established: 1848. Pub. Frequency: d. (Sun.-Fri.) Page Size: broadsheet. Subscrip. Rate: $.50 newsstand/cover; $1.50 newsstand/cover Sun.; $93.60/yr carrier delivery in city; $101.40/yr motor route in county; $171.60/yr mailed. **Wire Service(s):** AP. Circulation: 7,800 evening (paid); 9,000 Sunday (paid). **Owner(s):** Huntington Newspapers, Inc., See address and contact information above. **Management:** Steve Kimmel, General Manager. Marty Alexander, Advertising Manager. Bonnie Hall, Circulation Manager. Brenda Ross, Classified Adv. Mgr.. **Editorial:** Michael V Perkins, Editor. Cindy Klepper, City Editor. Paul Siegfried, Sports Editor.

INDIANAPOLIS

INDIANAPOLIS STAR & NEWS. 307 N. Pennsylvania St., Indianapolis, IN 46204-1899. Telephone: 317-444-4000. FAX: 317-444-6600. E-MAIL: lmannweiler@starnews.com. URL: http://www.starnews.com. Mailing Address: PO Box 145, Indianapolis, IN 46206-0145. Year Established: 1903. Pub. Frequency: d. Page Size: broadsheet. Subscrip. Rate: $.50 newsstand/cover; $1.75 newsstand/cover Sun.; $3.60 carrier delivery/wk.; $171.60/yr carrier delivery. **Wire Service(s):** AP, SH, NYT, LAT-WAT, MCT. Circulation: 235,000 morning (paid); 380,000 Sunday (paid). **Owner(s):** Gannett Company, Inc., 7950 Jones Branch Dr., McLean, VA 22107-0001. Telephone: 703-854-6000. **Bureau(s):** 1000 National Press Bldg., Washington, DC 20045. Telephone: 202-662-7262. **Management:** Linda Renner, Advertising Manager. Guin Taylor, Classified Adv. Mgr.. **Editorial:** Barbara Henry, Editor. Pam Fine, Managing Editor. Zach Dunkin, Art Editor. Charles Staff, Music Editor. Todd Moore, News Editor. Robert Goebel, Photo Editor. Jim Lefko, Sports Editor. David Mannweiler, Travel Editor.

JEFFERSONVILLE

EVENING NEWS (JEFFERSONVILLE), THE. 221 Spring St., Jeffersonville, IN 47130. Telephone: 812-283-6636. FAX: 812-284-7081. E-MAIL: enews@mis.net. URL: http://www.news-tribune.net. Mailing Address: PO Box 867, Jeffersonville, IN 47130. Year Established: 1872. Pub. Frequency: d. (Tue.-Sat.) Page Size: broadsheet. Subscrip. Rate: $.50 newsstand/cover; $1.25 newsstand/cover Sun.; $98/yr home delivery. **Wire Service(s):** AP, SH. Circulation: 25,000 evening (paid). **Owner(s):** Community Newspaper Holdings, Inc., 3500 Colonnade Pkwy., Ste. 600, Birmingham, AL 35243. Telephone: 205-298-7100. FAX: 205-298-7101. **Management:** John Tucker, Publisher. Mike Massek, Circulation Manager. Joann Galligan, Classified Adv. Mgr.. **Editorial:** Steve Kozarovich, Executive Editor. Jim Nichols, Managing Editor.

KENDALLVILLE

NEWS-SUN (KENDALLVILLE), THE. ISSN 8750-0876
112 N. Main St., Kendallville, IN 46755. Telephone: 260-347-0400. FAX: 260-347-2693. E-MAIL: kpc@kpcnews.net. URL: http://kpcnews.net. Pub. Frequency: d. Page Size: broadsheet. Subscrip. Rate: $.50 newsstand/cover; $1.50 newsstand/cover Sun.; $160/yr carrier delivery. Circulation: 8,000 evening (paid). **Owner(s):** Kendallville Publishing Co., See address and contact information above. **Management:** Terry Housholder, Publisher. Sam Ashe, Circulation Manager. **Editorial:** Matt Getts, Managing Editor. Dennis Nartker, Amusement Editor. Grace Housholder, Editorial Page Editor. Jan Richardson, Feature Editor. Terry Housholder, Political Editor.

KOKOMO

KOKOMO TRIBUNE. ISSN 0746-2034
300 N. Union St., Kokomo, IN 46901. Telephone: 765-457-2170. FAX: 765-457-3815. URL: http://www.kokomotribune.com. Mailing Address: PO Box 9014, Kokomo, IN 46904-9014. Year Established: 1850. Pub. Frequency: d. Page Size: broadsheet. Subscrip. Rate: $.50 newsstand/cover; $1.50 newsstand/cover Sun.; $162/yr carrier delivery. **Wire Service(s):** AP. Circulation: 25,000 evening (paid); 27,000 Sunday (paid). **Owner(s):** Community Newspaper Holdings, Inc., 3500 Colonnade Pkwy., Ste. 600, Birmingham, AL 35243. Telephone: 205-298-7100. **Management:** Robyn McCloskey, Publisher. Thomas Kelling, Advertising Director. Richard Schram, Circulation Manager. **Editorial:** Jeff Kovaleski, Managing Editor. Patrick Ethridge, City Editor. Tom Carey, Community Editor. David Kitchell, Sports Editor.

LA PORTE

LA PORTE HERALD-ARGUS. 701 State St., La Porte, IN 46350. Telephone: 219-362-2161. FAX: 219-362-2166. E-MAIL: ha@heraldargus.com. URL: http://www.heraldargus.com. Year Established: 1880. Pub. Frequency: d. (Mon.-Sat.) Page Size: broadsheet. Subscrip. Rate: $.50 newsstand/cover; $31.85 carrier delivery/quarter; $108/yr carrier delivery; $35.10 motor route/quarter; $108/yr motor route. Adv. Rate: col. inch $8.45 **Wire Service(s):** AP, SH. Circulation: 12,800 evening (paid). **Owner(s):** Small Newspaper Group, 8 Dearborn Sq., Kankakee, IL 60901. Telephone: 815-937-3300. **Management:** Jason Sethre, General Manager. Robert Hill, Publisher. Donna Maglio, Advertising Manager. Julie McKiel, Circulation Manager. Donna Maglio, Classified Adv. Mgr.. Rich Parcels, Business Manager. **Editorial:** Chris Schable, City Editor. Sondra Provan, Lifestyle Editor. Julie Kessler, News Editor. Bob Wellinski, Photographer. Chris Schable, Sports Editor.

LAFAYETTE

JOURNAL & COURIER. 217 N. Sixth St., Lafayette, IN 47901-1420. Telephone: 765-423-5511. FAX: 765-420-5246. E-MAIL: bangert@journal-courier.com. URL: http://www.jconline.com. Year Established: 1829. Pub. Frequency: d. Page Size: broadsheet. Subscrip. Rate: $.50 newsstand/cover; $1.50 newsstand/cover Sun.; $3.75 home delivery/wk.; $195/yr home delivery; $3.95 motor route/wk.; $5.10 mailed/wk. in state. **Wire Service(s):** AP, LAT-WAT, GNS. Circulation: 37,132 morning (paid); 44,892 Sunday (paid). **Owner(s):** Gannett Company, Inc., 7950 Jones Branch Dr., McLean, VA 22107-0001. Telephone: 703-854-6000. **Management:** Gary Suisman, Publisher. Jim Homes, Advertising Director. Mick Siemers, Circulation Director. **Editorial:** Julie Doll, Managing Editor. Julie McClure, Lifestyle Editor. Jim Stofford, Sports Editor.

LEBANON

LEBANON REPORTER, THE. 117 E. Washington St., Lebanon, IN 46052. Telephone: 765-482-4650. FAX: 765-482-4652. E-MAIL: gsanderson@reporter.net. URL: http://www.reporter.net. Year Established: 1891. Pub. Frequency: d. (Mon.-Sat.) Page Size: broadsheet. Subscrip. Rate: $.50 newsstand/cover; $89/yr home delivery in county; $135/yr motor route out of county. **Wire Service(s):** AP. Circulation: 7,000 morning (paid). **Owner(s):** Community Newspaper Holdings, Inc., 3500 Colonnade Pkwy., Ste. 600, Birmingham, AL 35243. Telephone: 205-298-7100. **Management:** Harold Allen, Publisher. Rick Whiteman, Advertising Manager. Cathy Armold, Circulation Manager. Mary Jo Denney, Classified Adv. Mgr.. **Editorial:** George Piper, Managing Editor. Rod Rose, Asst. Managing Ed..

LINTON

EVENING WORLD, THE. 79 S. Main St., Linton, IN 47441. E-MAIL: cpruett@dailycitizen.com. URL: http://www.dailycitizen.com. Mailing Address: PO Box 129, Linton, IN 47441. Year Established: 1930. Pub. Frequency: d. (Mon.-Fri.) Page Size: broadsheet. Subscrip. Rate: $.50 newsstand/cover; $7.25 carrier delivery/mo.. **Wire Service(s):** AP. Circulation: 3,200 evening (paid). **Owner(s):** Rust Communications, Inc., 301 Broadway, Cape Girardeau, MO 63701. Telephone: 573-335-6611. **Management:** Chris Pruett, General Manager. Kathleen Bland, Advertising Manager. **Editorial:** Chris Pruett, Editor. Mark Downey, Sports.

LINTON DAILY CITIZEN. 79 S. Main St., Linton, IN 47441. Telephone: 812-847-4487. FAX: 812-847-9513. E-MAIL: jerry.hargis@dailycitizen.com. URL: http://www.dailycitizen.com. Mailing Address: PO Box 129, Linton, IN 47441. Year Established: 1900. Pub. Frequency: d. (Mon.-Fri.) Page Size: broadsheet. Subscrip. Rate: $.50 newsstand/cover; $87/yr carrier delivery. Adv. Rate: col. inch $25 **Wire Service(s):** AP. Circulation: 9,500 evening (paid). **Owner(s):** Rust Communications, Inc., 301 Broadway, Cape Girardeau, MO 63701. Telephone: 573-335-6611. **Management:** Randy List, Publisher. Kathy Bland, Advertising Manager. Christy Lehman, Circulation Manager. Tina Miller, Classified Adv. Mgr.. **Editorial:** Chris Pruett, Editor.

LOGANSPORT

PHAROS-TRIBUNE. 517 E. Broadway, Logansport, IN 46947. Telephone: 574-722-5000. FAX: 574-732-5070. URL: http://www.pharostribune.com. Mailing Address: PO Box 210, Logansport, IN 46947. Year Established: 1844. Pub. Frequency: d. Page Size: broadsheet. Subscrip. Rate: $.50 newsstand/cover; $1.50 newsstand/cover Sun.; $155/yr carrier delivery in county & adj. cys.; $221/yr carrier delivery out of area. **Wire Service(s):** AP, MCT. Circulation: 13,500 evening (paid); 14,500 Sunday (paid). **Owner(s):** Community Newspaper Holdings, Inc., 3500 Colonnade Pkwy., Ste. 600, Birmingham, AL 35243. Telephone: 205-298-7100. **Management:** Robyn McCloskey, Publisher. Stefani Closson, Advertising Director. Robin Harper, Circulation Manager. Dawn Rictor, Classified Adv. Mgr.. **Editorial:** Kelly Hawes, Managing Editor. Chris Breach, Sports.

MADISON

MADISON COURIER. 310 Courier Sq., Madison, IN 47250. Telephone: 812-265-3641. E-MAIL: cjacobs@madisoncourier.com. URL: http://www.madisoncourier.com. Year Established: 1837. Pub. Frequency: d. (Mon.-Sat.) Page Size: broadsheet. Subscrip. Rate: $.50 newsstand/cover; $7.15 carrier delivery/mo.; $7.50 motor route/mo.; $90/yr mailed IN & KY. **Wire Service(s):** AP. Circulation: 9,100 evening (paid). **Owner(s):** Madison Courier, Inc., See address and contact information above. **Management:** Curt Jacobs, General Manager. Jane W. Jacobs, Owner. Curt Jacobs, Advertising Manager. Doug Patrick, Circulation Manager. **Editorial:** Elliot Tompkin, Editor. Jack Ulrey, Production Manager. Mark Campbell, News Editor.

MARION

CHRONICLE-TRIBUNE. 610 S. Adams St., Marion, IN 46953. Telephone: 765-664-5111. FAX: 765-668-4256. E-MAIL: cteditor@comtech.com. URL: http://www.chronicle-tribune.com. Mailing Address: PO Box 309, Marion, IN 46952. Year Established: 1886. Pub. Frequency: d. Page Size: broadsheet. Subscrip. Rate: $.50 newsstand/cover; $1.50 newsstand/cover Sun.; $44.20 carrier delivery for 13 wks.; $46.15 motor route local for 13 wks.; $63.30 mailed in state for 13 wks.. Circulation: 20,812 morning (paid); 25,050 Sunday (paid). **Owner(s):** Gannett Company, Inc., 7950 Jones Branch Dr., McLean, VA 22107-0001. Telephone: 703-854-6000. **Management:** Emmett Smelser, Publisher. Linda Kozlowski, Circulation Manager. **Editorial:** Tammy Pearson, Executive Editor. Mike Cline, Editorial Page Editor.

MARTINSVILLE

REPORTER-TIMES, THE. 60 S. Jefferson, Martinsville, IN 46151. Telephone: 765-342-3311. FAX: 765-342-1446. E-MAIL: reporter@reportert.com.net. URL: http://www.reporter-times.com. Mailing Address: PO Box 1636, Martinsville, IN 46151. Year Established: 1889. Pub. Frequency: d. Page Size: broadsheet. Subscrip. Rate: $.50 newsstand/cover; $1.50 newsstand/cover Sun.; $105.75/yr home delivery in county; $113.55/yr motor route in county; $174/yr mailed out of county. **Wire Service(s):** UPI. Circulation: 8,000 evening (paid). **Owner(s):** Schurz Communications, Inc., 225 W. Colfax Ave., South Bend, IN 46626. Telephone: 219-287-1001. **Management:** Jim Kroemer, General Manager. E. Mayer Maloney, Publisher. Shawn Everett, Advertising Manager. Eric Moore, Classified Adv. Mgr.. **Editorial:** Marilyn Brock, Lifestyle Editor. Rob Downey, Sports Editor.

MERRIVILLE

POST-TRIBUNE. ISSN 8750-3492
1433 E. 83rd, Merriville, IN 46410. Telephone: 219-648-3000. E-MAIL: drutter@post-trib.com. URL: http://www.post-trib.com. Year Established: 1907. Pub. Frequency: d. Page Size: broadsheet. Subscrip. Rate: $.50 newsstand/cover; $1 newsstand/cover Sun.; $52/yr home delivery; $234.60/yr mailed. Freelance Pay: $25/article. **Wire Service(s):** AP, LAT-WAT. Circulation: 67,228 morning (paid); 76,210 Sunday (paid). **Owner(s):** Sun-Times Media Group, 350 N Orleans St, Ste 10-S, Chicago, IL 60654. **Bureau(s): Management:** Murdoch L. Davis, Publisher. Rich Cains, Advertising Manager. Terry Weaver, Classified Adv. Mgr.. **Editorial:** Paulette Haddix, Executive Editor. Michelle Holmes, Managing Editor.

MICHIGAN CITY

MICHIGAN CITY NEWS-DISPATCH. ISSN 1047-6016
121 W. Michigan Blvd., Michigan City, IN 46360. Telephone: 219-874-7211. FAX: 219-872-8511. E-MAIL: ndnews@michigancityin.com. URL: http://www.michigancityin.com. Year Established: 1881. Pub. Frequency: d. Page Size: broadsheet. Subscrip. Rate: $.50 newsstand/cover; $1.50 newsstand/cover Sun.; $132.25/yr carrier delivery; $139/yr motor route; $258/yr mailed in state. **Wire Service(s):** AP. Circulation: 16,000 morning (paid); 16,500 Sunday (paid). **Owner(s):** Paxton Media Group Llc, 201 S. Fourth St., Paducah, KY 42003. Telephone: 270-575-8600. FAX: 270-442-8188. **Management:** Leonard Woolsey, Publisher. Isis Leon-Cains, Advertising Director. Steve Hahn, Circulation Director. Isis Leon-Cains, Classified Adv. Mgr.. Linda Lindsey, Business Manager. **Editorial:** Dave Hawk, Managing Editor. Rick Richards, City Editor. Andrew Tallackson, Entertainment Editor. Sue Humphrey, Lifestyle Editor.

MONTICELLO

HERALD-JOURNAL, THE. 114 S. Main St., Monticello, IN 47960. Telephone: 574-583-5121. FAX: 574-583-4241. E-MAIL: dmaroney@thehj.com. URL: http://www.thehj.com. Mailing Address: PO Box 409, Monticello, IN 47960. Year Established: 1862. Pub. Frequency: d. (Mon.-Sat.) Page Size: broadsheet. Subscrip. Rate: $.50 newsstand/cover; $13 home delivery/mo. local; $91.80/yr home delivery; $14 mailed/mo. in state. **Wire Service(s):** UPI. Circulation: 5,200 evening (paid). **Owner(s):** Home News Enterprises, PO Box 3011, Columbus, IN 47202. Telephone: 812-379-5658. **Management:** Kevin Lashbrook, Publisher. Karen Franscoviak, Advertising Director. Bonnie Kain, Business Manager. **Editorial:** Trent Wright, Editor. Christine Walsh, Managing Editor. Trent Wright, Sports Editor.

MUNCIE

STAR PRESS, THE. 345 S. High St., Muncie, IN 47305. Telephone: 765-747-5700. FAX: 765-213-5858. E-MAIL: news@thestarpress.com. URL: http://www.thestarpress.com. Mailing Address: PO Box 2408, Muncie, IN 47307-0408. Year Established: 1899. Pub. Frequency: d. Page Size: broadsheet. Subscrip. Rate: $.50 newsstand/cover; $1.75 newsstand/cover Sun.. **Wire Service(s):** AP, SH, MCT. Circulation: 33,000 morning (paid); 36,000 Sunday (paid). **Owner(s):** Gannett Company, Inc., 7950 Jones Branch Dr., McLean, VA 22107-0001. Telephone: 703-853-4600. **Management:** Emmett Smelser, Publisher. Jim Holm, Advertising Manager. Tim Alexander, Circulation Manager. Kim Scott, Classified Adv. Mgr.. **Editorial:** Evan Miller, Editor. Scott Underwood, Associate Editor. Larry Shores, Editorial Page Editor. Breena Wysong, Librarian. Kyle Evens, Photo Editor. Phil Beebe, Sports Editor.

MUNSTER

ILLINOIS TIMES, THE. 601 W. 45th Ave., Munster, IN 46321-2875. Telephone: 219-933-3200. FAX: 219-933-3249. Pub. Frequency: d. Page Size: broadsheet. Subscrip. Rate: $.50 newsstand/cover; $1.75 newsstand/cover Sun.; $117/yr. **Wire Service(s):** AP, NYT, MCT. Circulation: 13,000 morning (paid); 13,000 Sunday (paid). **Owner(s):** Lee Enterprises, Inc., 201 N. Harrison St., Davenport, IA 52801. **Management:** Bill Masterson Jr., Publisher. Lisa Dougherty, Advertising Director. **Editorial:** William Nangle, Executive Editor. Paul Mulaney, Managing Editor.

NEW ALBANY

TRIBUNE (NEW ALBANY), THE. 303 Scribner Dr., New Albany, IN 47150. Telephone: 812-944-6481. FAX: 812-206-4600. E-MAIL: editor@tribnews.com. URL: http://www.news-tribune.com. Mailing Address: PO Box 997, New Albany, IN 47150. Year Established: 1845. Pub. Frequency: d. (Tue.-Sun.) Page Size: broadsheet. Subscrip. Rate: $.50 newsstand/cover; $1.25 newsstand/cover Sun.; $115/yr home delivery. Freelance Pay: $0.30/column-inch. **Wire Service(s):** AP. Circulation: 9,000 evening (paid); 9,000 Sunday (paid). **Owner(s):** Community Newspaper Holdings, Inc., 3500 Colonnade Pkwy., Ste. 600, Birmingham, AL 35243. Telephone: 205-298-7100. FAX: 205-298-7101. **Management:** John Tucker, Publisher. Jim Grahm, Advertising Director. Joann Galligan, Classified Adv. Mgr.. **Editorial:** Steve Kozarovich, Executive Editor. Chris Morris, Managing Editor.

NEW CASTLE

COURIER-TIMES (NEW CASTLE), THE. 201 S. 14th St., New Castle, IN 47362. Telephone: 765-529-1111. FAX: 765-529-1731. E-MAIL: dradford@thecouriertimes.com. URL: http://www.newcastlein.com. Mailing Address: PO Box 369, New Castle, IN 47362. Year Established: 1841. Pub. Frequency: d. (Mon.-Sat.) Page Size: broadsheet. Subscrip. Rate: $.50 newsstand/cover; $13 carrier delivery/mo. in city; $150/yr carrier delivery; $13.20/mo. in county; $152.40/yr; $15.70 mailed/mo. in county $162/yr. **Wire Service(s):** AP. Circulation: 11,900 evening (paid). **Owner(s):** Paxton Media Group Llc, 201 S. Fourth St., Paducah, KY 42003. Telephone: 270-575-8600. FAX: 270-442-8188. **Management:** David Holgate, Publisher. Scott Hart, Advertising Director. Mark Ganote, Circulation Manager. Theresa Blake, Classified Adv. Mgr.. **Editorial:** Darrel Radford, Editor. Frankie Zile, Business Editor. Sharon Godsey, News Editor. John Guglielmi, Photographer. Donna Cronk, Society Editor. John Hodge, Sports Editor.

PERU

PERU TRIBUNE. 26 W. Third St., Peru, IN 46970. Telephone: 765-473-6641. FAX: 765-472-4438. E-MAIL: bboyce@miamicountylife.com. URL: http://www.miamicountylife.com. Mailing Address: PO Box 87, Peru, IN 46970. Year Established: 1921. Pub. Frequency: d. (Mon.-Sat.) Page Size: broadsheet. Subscrip. Rate: $.50 newsstand/cover; $1 newsstand/cover Sat.; $11/mo. in county; $15/mo. in state; $16/mo. elsewhere. **Wire Service(s):** AP. Circulation: 6,300 morning (paid). **Owner(s):** Paxton Media Group Llc, 201 S. Fourth St., Paducah, KY 42003. Telephone: 270-575-8600. FAX: 270-442-8188. **Management:** Paul Heidbreder, Publisher. Michelle Boswell, Advertising Manager. **Editorial:** Brian Boyce, Managing Editor. Tony Hare, Photo Editor.

PLYMOUTH

PILOT NEWS, THE. 214 N Michigan St, Plymouth, IN 46563. Telephone: 574-936-3101. FAX: 574-936-7491. E-MAIL: ads@thepilotnews.com. URL: http://www.thepilotnews.com. Mailing Address: PO Box 220, Plymouth, IN 46563. Year Established: 1851. Pub. Frequency: d. (Mon.-Sat.) Page Size: broadsheet. Subscrip. Rate: $.50 newsstand/cover; $90/yr carrier delivery in city; $96/yr motor route out of area; $114/yr mailed in state; $200/yr mailed out of state. Adv. Rate: col. inch $8.30 **Wire Service(s):** AP. Circulation: 6,500 evening (paid). **Owner(s):** Horizon Publications, Inc., 1120 N. Carbon St, Ste 100, Marion, IL 62959. **Management:** Jerry Bingle, General Manager. Rick A. Kreps, Publisher. Cindy Stockton, Advertising Manager. James Radican, Circulation Manager. **Editorial:** Maggie Nixon, Managing Editor.

PRINCETON

PRINCETON DAILY CLARION. 100 N. Gibson St., Princeton, IN 47670. Telephone: 812-385-2525. FAX: 812-386-6199. E-MAIL: andrea@pdclarion.com. URL: http://www.tristate-media.com. Mailing Address: PO Box 30, Princeton, IN 47670. Year Established: 1846. Pub. Frequency: d. (Mon.-Fri.) Page Size: broadsheet. Subscrip. Rate: $.50 newsstand/cover; $94.50/yr carrier delivery; $97.50/yr motor route; $97.50/yr mailed in county & adj. cys.. **Wire Service(s):** AP. Circulation: 6,800 morning (paid). **Owner(s):** Brehm Communications, Inc., 16644 W. Bernardo Dr., Ste. 300, San Diego, CA 92127. Telephone: 858-451-6200. **Management:** Gary Blackburn, Publisher. Debra Walker, Advertising Manager. Jim Hansen, Circulation Manager. Maggie Armstrong, Classified Adv. Mgr.. **Editorial:** Andrea Howe, Editor. Mike Linville, Sports Editor.

RENSSELAER

RENSSELAER REPUBLICAN. 117 N Van Rensselaer, Rensselaer, IN 47978. Telephone: 219-866-5111. FAX: 219-866-3775. E-MAIL: ads@rensselaerrepublican.com. URL: http://www.rensselaerrepublican.com. Mailing Address: PO Box 298, Rensselaer, IN 47978-0298. Year Established: 1865. Pub. Frequency: d. (Mon.-Sat.) Page Size: broadsheet. Subscrip. Rate: $.50 newsstand/cover; $110/yr mailed in Jasper & Newton cys.. **Wire Service(s):** AP. Circulation: 2,400 morning (paid). **Owner(s):** Community Media Group, Inc, PO Box 10, West Frankfort, IL 62896. Telephone: 618-937-6412. **Management:** Don Hurd, Publisher. **Editorial:** Clayton Doty, Editor. Harley Tomlinson, Sports Editor.

RICHMOND

PALLADIUM-ITEM. 1175 N. A St., Richmond, IN 47374. Telephone: 765-962-1575. FAX: 765-973-4570. E-MAIL: palitem@richmond.gannett.com. URL: http://www.pal-item.com. Mailing Address: PO Box 308, Richmond, IN 47375. Year Established: 1831. Pub. Frequency: d. Page Size: broadsheet. Subscrip. Rate: $.50 newsstand/cover; $1.50 newsstand/cover Sun.; $169/yr home delivery; $238/yr mailed in IN & OH. Freelance Pay: $10-$40/article. **Wire Service(s):** AP, GNS. Circulation: 17,833 evening (paid); 22,122 Sunday (paid). **Owner(s):** Gannett Company, Inc., 7950 Jones Branch Dr, McLean, VA 22107. Telephone: 703-854-6000. **Management:** Patrick Doyle, Publisher. Erin Humphrey, Advertising Director. Kevin Welsh, Circulation Manager. Johnny Martinez, Classified Adv. Mgr.. **Editorial:** Rich Jackson, Executive Editor.

ROCHESTER

ROCHESTER SENTINEL, THE. 118 E. Eighth St., Rochester, IN 46975-0260. Telephone: 574-223-2111. FAX: 574-223-5782. E-MAIL: news@rochsent.com. URL: http://www.rochsent.com. Mailing Address: PO Box 260, Rochester, IN 46975-0260. Year Established: 1858. Pub. Frequency: d. (Mon.-Sat.) Page Size: broadsheet. Subscrip. Rate: $.50 newsstand/cover; $159/yr carrier delivery; $195/yr motor route in county. Adv. Rate: col. inch $7.44 **Wire Service(s):** AP. Circulation: 4,000 evening (paid). **Owner(s):** Sentinel Corp., See address and contact information above. **Management:** Jack K. Overmyer, President. Sarah O. Wilson, Publisher. Karen Vojtasek, Advertising Manager. Gary Roe, Circulation Manager. Mitzi Anderson, Classified Adv. Mgr.. **Editorial:** William S. Wilson, Editor. Val Tsoutsouns, Sports Editor.

RUSHVILLE

RUSHVILLE REPUBLICAN. ISSN 8756-6443
306 N. Main St., Rushville, IN 46173. Telephone: 765-932-2222. FAX: 765-932-4358. E-MAIL: marilyn.land@cnhimedia.com. URL: http://www.rushvillerepublican.com. Mailing Address: PO Box 189, Rushville, IN 46173. Year Established: 1840. Pub. Frequency: d. (Mon.-Sat.) Page Size: broadsheet. Subscrip. Rate: $.50 newsstand/cover; $110/yr in county; $119/yr out of county. **Wire Service(s):** AP. Circulation: 4,150 evening (paid). **Owner(s):** Community Newspaper Holdings, Inc., 3500 Colonnade Pkwy., Ste. 600, Birmingham, AL 35243. Telephone: 205-298-7100. FAX: 205-298-7101. **Management:** Peter Van Baalen, Publisher. Laura Welborn, Advertising Director. Marilyn Land, Advertising Manager. Lisa Huff, Circulation Manager. **Editorial:** Kevin Green, Managing Editor.

SEYMOUR

TRIBUNE (SEYMOUR), THE. 100 St. Louis Ave, Seymour, IN 47274. Telephone: 812-522-4871. FAX: 812-522-7691. URL: http://www.tribtown.com. Mailing Address: PO Box 477, Seymour, IN 47274. Year Established: 1879. Pub. Frequency: d. (Mon.-Sat.) Page Size: broadsheet. Subscrip. Rate: $.50 newsstand/cover; $1 newsstand/cover Sat.; $174.48/yr mailed in state; $190.20/yr mailed out of state. Circulation: 8,923 evening (paid). **Owner(s):** Freedom Communications, Inc., 17666 Fitch St., Irvine, CA 92614-6022. Telephone: 714-553-9292. **Management:** Richard Davis, Publisher. Scott Embry, Advertising Director. Steve Herron, Advertising Manager. Tom Kisterson, Circulation Manager. Michelle Schaefer, Business Manager. **Editorial:** Dan Davis, Managing Editor. Joanne Persinger, Local News Editor. Dan Burch, Sports Editor.

Dailies

SHELBYVILLE

SHELBYVILLE NEWS. 123 E. Washington St., Shelbyville, IN 46176. Telephone: 317-398-6631. FAX: 317-398-0194. E-MAIL: bwalsh@shelbynews.com. URL: http://www.shelbynews.com. Mailing Address: PO Box 750, Shelbyville, IN 46176. Year Established: 1948. Pub. Frequency: d. (Mon.-Sat.) Page Size: broadsheet. Subscrip. Rate: $.50 newsstand/cover; $120/yr carrier delivery; $126/yr motor route; $181 mailed out of county 171/yr; $187/yr mailed out of state. **Wire Service(s):** RN, AP, SH, NYT. Circulation: 11,500 evening (paid). **Owner(s):** Paxton Media Group Llc, 201 S. Fourth St., Paducah, KY 42003. Telephone: 270-575-8600. FAX: 270-442-8188. **Management:** Paul Mahony, President. Dennis Bonner, Advertising Director. Gina Lemasters, Circulation Director. Karen Ragin, Classified Adv. Mgr.. **Editorial:** Bill Walsh, Editor. Leona Stieglitz, News Editor. Scott Roberson, Photographer. Jeff Brown, Sports Editor.

SOUTH BEND

SOUTH BEND TRIBUNE. 225 W. Colfax Ave., South Bend, IN 46626. Telephone: 574-235-6161. FAX: 574-239-2642. URL: http://www.southbendtribune.com. Year Established: 1872. Pub. Frequency: d. Page Size: broadsheet. Subscrip. Rate: $.50 newsstand/cover; $1.50 newsstand/cover Sun.; $162/yr home delivery. **Wire Service(s):** AP, SH, NYT. Circulation: 74,000 morning (paid); 101,500 Sunday (paid). **Owner(s):** Schurz Communications, Inc., See address and contact information above. **Management:** Tim Timmons, General Manager. David C. Ray, President. Carol Smith, Advertising Director. **Editorial:** David C. Ray, Editor. Gayle Dantzler, Editorial Page Editor. Chris Benninghoff, Feature Editor. Virginia Black, Metro Editor. Greg Swiercz, Photo Editor. Bill Bilinski, Sports Editor.

SPENCER

SPENCER EVENING WORLD. ISSN 0745-7227
114 E. Franklin St., Spencer, IN 47460. Telephone: 812-829-2255. FAX: 812-829-4666. E-MAIL: editor@spencereveningworld.com. URL: http://www.spencereveningworld.com. Mailing Address: P.O. Box 226, Spencer, IN 47460. Year Established: 1927. Pub. Frequency: d. (Mon.-Fri.) Page Size: broadsheet. Subscrip. Rate: $.50 newsstand/cover; $15 in county for 3 months; $27 for 6 mos.; $67/yr in state; $77/yr mailed out of state. Adv. Rate: col. inch $5.50 Circulation: 3,000 evening (paid). **Owner(s):** Spencer Evening World, Inc., See address and contact information above. **Management:** Tom Gillaspy, Director. John A. Gillaspy, General Manager. John T. Gillaspy, Publisher. Kim Bray, Circulation Director. Chris Harp, Classified Editor. **Editorial:** Travis Curry, Editor. Philip Gillaspy, Production Manager.

SULLIVAN

SULLIVAN DAILY TIMES. PO Box 130, Sullivan, IN 47882. Telephone: 812-268-6356. FAX: 812-268-3110. E-MAIL: sullivantimes@ticz.com. Year Established: 1905. Pub. Frequency: d. (Mon.-Fri.) Page Size: broadsheet. Subscrip. Rate: $.50 newsstand/cover; $63/yr in county; $69/yr out of county. **Wire Service(s):** AP. Circulation: 4,400 evening (paid). **Owner(s):** Pierce Oil Co., Inc., See address and contact information above. **Management:** Nancy Pierce Gettinger, Publisher. Tom Gettinger, Advertising Manager. **Editorial:** Jeff Salyers, Editor. Tom Gettinger, Managing Editor.

TERRE HAUTE

TRIBUNE-STAR, THE. ISSN 0745-9599
222 S. Seventh St., Terre Haute, IN 47807-0149. Telephone: 812-231-4200. FAX: 812-231-4321. E-MAIL: trevis.mayfield@tribstar.com. URL: http://www.tribstar.com. Mailing Address: PO Box 149, Terre Haute, IN 47808. Year Established: 1894. Pub. Frequency: d. Page Size: broadsheet. Subscrip. Rate: $.50 newsstand/cover; $1.50 newsstand/cover Sun.; $190/yr home delivery in area; $21.45 mailed/mo. out of area; $23.70 mailed/mo. out of IL or IN. **Wire Service(s):** AP. Circulation: 36,000 morning (paid); 43,000 Sunday (paid). **Owner(s):** Community Newspaper Holdings, Inc., 3500 Colonnade Pkwy., Ste. 600, Birmingham, AL 35243. Telephone: 205-298-7100. FAX: 205-298-7101. **Management:** David Thornberry, Publisher. Jeremiah Turner, Advertising Director. Tanya Wilhoyte, Advertising Manager. Tony McCarter, Circulation Director. Leslie Mikolajaczyk, Classified Adv. Mgr.. **Editorial:** Max Jones, Editor. Zach Taylor, News Editor.

VALPARAISO

VIDETTE-TIMES. 1111 Glendale Blvd., Valparaiso, IN 46383. Telephone: 219-462-5151. FAX: 219-465-7298. E-MAIL: comments@nwitimes.com. URL: http://www.thetimesonline.com. Mailing Address: PO Box 2350, Valparaiso, IN 46384. Year Established: 1927. Pub. Frequency: d. Page Size: broadsheet. Subscrip. Rate: $.50 newsstand/cover; $1.75 newsstand/cover Sun.; $195/yr home delivery. **Wire Service(s):** AP, SH, CNS. Circulation: 87,476 evening (paid); 94,565 Sunday (paid). **Owner(s):** Lee Enterprises, Inc., 201 N. Harrison St., Davenport, IA 52801-1924. **Management:** Don Asher, General Manager. Kevin Mowbray, Publisher. Varinda Missette, Advertising Director. **Editorial:** William Nangle, Executive Editor. Paul Mullaney, Managing Editor. Crista Zivanovic, News Editor. Paul Bowker, Sports Editor.

VINCENNES

VINCENNES SUN-COMMERCIAL. ISSN 1072-3609
702 Main St., Vincennes, IN 47591. Telephone: 812-886-9955. FAX: 812-885-2235. E-MAIL: suncomm@wvc.net. URL: http://www.suncommercial.com. Mailing Address: PO Box 396, Vincennes, IN 47591. Year Established: 1804. Pub. Frequency: d. (Sun.-Fri.) Page Size: broadsheet. Subscrip. Rate: $.50 newsstand/cover; $1.50 newsstand/cover Sun.; $115/yr home delivery; $126/yr motor route. **Wire Service(s):** AP. Circulation: 11,000 per issue (paid); 13,200 Sunday (paid). **Owner(s):** Paxton Media Group LLC, 201 S. Fourth St., Paducah, KY 42003. Telephone: 270-575-8600. FAX: 270-442-8188. **Management:** Vickie K Palmer, Publisher. Sarah Carie, Advertising Director. Ronda Willmont, Circulation Manager. **Editorial:** Bernard Schmitt, Managing Editor. Crystal Holmes, Associate Editor. Susan Wright, Lifestyle Editor. David Staver, Sports Editor.

WABASH

WABASH PLAIN DEALER. 123 W. Canal St., Wabash, IN 46992. Telephone: 260-563-2131. FAX: 260-563-0816. E-MAIL: wabashplaindealer@intranix.com. URL: http://www.wabashplaindealer.com. Mailing Address: PO Box 379, Wabash, IN 46992. Year Established: 1859. Pub. Frequency: d. (Mon.-Sat.) Page Size: broadsheet. Subscrip. Rate: $.50 newsstand/cover; $10 carrier delivery/mo.; $111/yr carrier delivery; $10.50 motor route/mo.; $117/yr motor route. **Wire Service(s):** UPI. Circulation: 6,000 per issue (paid). **Owner(s):** Paxton Media Group Llc, 201 S. Fourth St., Paducah, KY 42003. Telephone: 270-575-8600. FAX: 270-442-8188. **Management:** Paul Heidbreder, Publisher. Andy Eads, Advertising Manager. Rick Steg, Circulation Manager. Andy Eads, Classified Adv. Mgr.. **Editorial:** Joseph Slacian Jr., Managing Editor. Michael K. Plummer, Production Manager. Joseph Slacian Jr., Editorial Page Editor. Kathi Moyer, Entertainment Editor. Roy Church, News Editor. Greg Dannacher, Photographer. Darren Phillips, Sports Editor.

WARSAW

TIMES-UNION. Market & Indiana Sts., Warsaw, IN 46580. Telephone: 574-267-3111. FAX: 574-267-7784. E-MAIL: advertising@timesuniononline.com. URL: http://www.timeswrsw.com. Mailing Address: PO Box 1448, Warsaw, IN 46581-1448. Year Established: 1854. Pub. Frequency: d. (Mon.-Sat.) Page Size: broadsheet. Subscrip. Rate: $.50 newsstand/cover; $1 newsstand/cover Sat.; $11 motor route/mo.; $12 mailed/mo. in county & adj. cys.; $13 mailed/mo. elsewhere. Adv. Rate: col. inch $10.50 **Wire Service(s):** AP, NYT. Circulation: 12,000 evening (paid). **Owner(s):** Reub Williams & Sons, Inc., See address and contact information above. **Management:** Norman Hagg, General Manager. William Hays, Advertising Manager. Becky Walton, Circulation Manager. Laura Sowers, Classified Adv. Mgr.. **Editorial:** Norman Hagg, Editor-in-Chief. Gary Gerard, Managing Editor. Dale Hubler, Sports Editor.

WASHINGTON

WASHINGTON TIMES-HERALD. 102 E Van Trees St, Washington, IN 47501. Telephone: 812-254-0480. FAX: 812-254-7517. E-MAIL: mbrunson@washtimesherald.com. URL: http://www.washtimesherald.com. Mailing Address: PO Box 471, Washington, IN 47501. Year Established: 1867. Pub. Frequency: d. (Mon.-Sat.) Page Size: standard. Subscrip. Rate: $.75 newsstand/cover; $105/yr home delivery in county; $162/yr mailed out of county. **Wire Service(s):** AP. Circulation: 7,000 evening (paid). **Owner(s):** Community Newspaper Holdings, Inc., 3500 Colonnade Pkwy., Ste. 600, Birmingham, AL 35242. **Management:** Ron Smith, Publisher. Stacey Ramsey, Advertising Director. Laura Theine, Circulation Manager. **Editorial:** Melody Brunson, Editor. Pat Morrison, News Editor.

WINCHESTER

NEWS-GAZETTE, THE. 224 W. Franklin St., Winchester, IN 47394. Telephone: 765-584-4501. FAX: 765-584-3066. E-MAIL: ngeditor@infightbb.com. URL: http://www.winchesternewsgazette.com. Mailing Address: PO Box 429, Winchester, IN 47394. Year Established: 1847. Pub. Frequency: d. (Mon.-Sat.) Page Size: broadsheet. Subscrip. Rate: $.50 newsstand/cover; $146/yr in county; $178/yr mailed out of county. **Wire Service(s):** AP. Circulation: 2,700 per issue (paid). **Owner(s):** Community Media Group, Inc, PO Box 10, West Frankfort, IL 62896. Telephone: 618-937-6412. **Management:** Leesa Friend, Publisher. **Editorial:** Gene Moreland, Managing Editor. Rick Reed, Sports.

IOWA

AMES

TRIBUNE (AMES), THE. ISSN 0893-7915
317 Fifth St., Ames, IA 50010. Telephone: 515-232-2160. FAX: 515-323-2364. E-MAIL: dkraemer@amestrib.com. URL: http://www.amestrib.com. Year Established: 1867. Pub. Frequency: d. (Mon.-Sat.) Page Size: broadsheet. Subscrip. Rate: $.50 newsstand/cover; $1 newsstand/cover Sat.; $133.38/yr home delivery in county; $169.88/yr mailed in county; $212/yr mailed out of county. Adv. Rate: col. inch $12.75 Circulation: 15,300 Saturday (paid); 11,700 evening (paid). **Owner(s):** Iowa Newspapers, Inc., See address and contact information above. **Management:** Joe Craig, Publisher. Johnny Aguirre, Advertising Director. Dan Cronin, Circulation Manager. **Editorial:** David Kraemer, Editor. Scott Nulph, Sports.

ATLANTIC

ATLANTIC NEWS-TELEGRAPH. ISSN 8756-6400
410 Walnut St., Atlantic, IA 50022. Telephone: 712-243-2624. FAX: 712-243-4988. URL: http://www.atlanticnewstelegraph.com. Mailing Address: PO Box 230, Atlantic, IA 50022. Year Established: 1871. Pub. Frequency: d. (Mon.-Sat.) Page Size: broadsheet. Subscrip. Rate: $.50 newsstand/cover; $134/yr home delivery & mailed; $145/yr motor route. **Wire Service(s):** AP. Circulation: 4,500 evening (paid). **Owner(s):** Community Media Group, Inc, PO Box 10, West Frankfort, IL 62896. Telephone: 618-937-6412. **Management:** Ron Sohl, General Manager. Connie Collins, Advertising Manager. Deb Baker, Circulation Manager. **Editorial:** Jeff Lundquist, Managing Editor. Drew Herron, Sports Editor.

BOONE

BOONE NEWS-REPUBLICAN. ISSN 1050-4087
2136 E Mamie Eisenhower, Boone, IA 50036. Telephone: 515-432-6694. FAX: 515-432-7811. E-MAIL: news@newsrepublican.com. URL: http://www.newsrepublican.com. Mailing Address: PO Box 100, Boone, IA 50036-0100. Year Established: 1865. Pub. Frequency: d. ((Mon-Sat)) Page Size: broadsheet. Subscrip. Rate: $.50 newsstand/cover; $90/yr carrier delivery in county; $110/yr motor route in county; $154/yr mailed in county. **Wire Service(s):** AP. Circulation: 12,000 (paid). **Owner(s):** Iowa Newspapers, Inc., See address and contact information above. **Management:** Claudia Lovin, Publisher. Susan E Tolan, Advertising Manager. **Editorial:** Susan Hildreth, Editor. Mo Kelly, Sports.

CARROLL

DAILY TIMES HERALD. 508 N. Court St., Carroll, IA 51401. Telephone: 712-792-3573. FAX: 712-792-5218. E-MAIL: l.devine@carrollspaper.com. Year Established: 1928. Pub. Frequency: d. (Mon.-Fri.) Page Size: broadsheet. Subscrip. Rate: $.50 newsstand/cover; $88/yr home delivery. **Wire Service(s):** AP. Circulation: 6,411 evening (paid and free). **Owner(s):** James B. & Ann Wilson, See address and contact information above. **Management:** Ann Wilson, General Manager. James B. Wilson, President. Marsha Jensen, Advertising Manager. Tom Burns, Circulation Manager. Ann Wilson, Promotion Manager. **Editorial:** Larry Devine, Editor. Ashley Schable, Outdoor Editor. Jeff Storjohann, Photo Editor. Ashley Schable, Sports Editor.

CEDAR RAPIDS

GAZETTE (CEDAR RAPIDS), THE. ISSN 1066-0291
500 Third Ave., S.E., Cedar Rapids, IA 52401. Telephone: 319-398-8211. FAX: 319-398-5846. E-MAIL: dave.storey@gazettecommunications.com. URL: http://www.gazetteonline.com. Mailing Address: PO Box 511, Cedar Rapids, IA 52406. Year Established: 1883. Pub. Frequency: d. Page Size: broadsheet. Subscrip. Rate: $.75 newsstand/cover Mon.-Fri.; $.75 newsstand/cover Sat.; $2 newsstand/cover Sun.; $236.95/yr home delivery. Adv. Rate: col. inch $43.89 **Wire Service(s):** AP, LAT-WAT, MCT. Circulation: 68,700 morning (paid); 79,032 Sunday (paid). **Owner(s):** Gazette Communications, Inc., See address and contact information above. **Management:** Chuck Peters, Chief Executive Ofc. . Joseph Hladky III, Chairman. Dave Storey, Classified Adv. Mgr.. **Editorial:** Lyle Muller, Editor. Annette Schulfe, Book Review Editor. Jeff Tecklenberg, Editorial Page Editor. Cecilia Hanley, Food Editor. Mary Sharp, Local News Editor. Rollin Banderob, Photo Editor. Keith Gottschack, Religion Editor. J.R. Ogden, Sports Editor. Contact: Annette Schulfe, Travel Editor. Contact: Joe Jennison, Entertainment Editor.

CENTERVILLE

DAILY IOWEGIAN. 105 N Main St, Centerville, IA 52544. Telephone: 641-856-6336. FAX: 641-856-8118. E-MAIL: iowegian@lisco.com. URL: http://www.dailyiowegian.com. Mailing Address: PO Box 610, Centerville, IA 52544-0610. Year Established: 1883. Pub. Frequency: d. (Mon., Tue., Thu., Fri.) Page Size: broadsheet. Subscrip. Rate: $.50 newsstand/cover; $61/yr local; $77/yr mailed elsewhere. Adv. Rate: col. inch $6 **Wire Service(s):** AP. Circulation: 3,100 morning (paid). **Owner(s):** Community Newspaper Holdings, Inc., 3500 Colonnade Pkwy., Ste. 600, Birmingham, AL 35243-7017. **Management:** Becky Maxwell, Publisher. Jean Clark, Circulation Manager. Sheila Selix, Classified Adv. Mgr.. **Editorial:** Dan Ehl, Managing Editor. Patsy Cincotta, Lifestyle Editor. Jason McGrann, Sports Editor.

CHARLES CITY

CHARLES CITY PRESS. ISSN 1049-7242
801 Riverside Dr., Charles City, IA 50616. Telephone: 641-228-3211. FAX: 641-228-2641. E-MAIL: editor@charlescitypress.com. URL: http://www.charlescitypress.com. Mailing Address: PO Box 397, Charles City, IA 50616. Year Established: 1896. Pub. Frequency: d. (Mon.-Fri.) Page Size: broadsheet. Subscrip. Rate: $.50 newsstand/cover; $106/yr in county; $112/yr mailed in state; $125/yr mailed out of state. Adv. Rate: col. inch $8.49 **Wire Service(s):** AP. Circulation: 3,100 evening (paid). **Owner(s):** GateHouse Media, Inc, 350 WillowBrook Office Park, Fairport, NY 14450. Telephone: 585-598-0030. FAX: 585-248-2631. **Management:** Gene A. Hall, Publisher. **Editorial:** Mark Wicks, Managing Editor.

CHEROKEE

CHRONICLE TIMES. ISSN 0747-4776
111 S. Second St., Cherokee, IA 51012. Telephone: 712-225-5111. FAX: 712-225-2910. E-MAIL: ckedt@ncn.net. URL: http://www.cherokeedailytimes.com. Mailing Address: PO Box 281, Cherokee, IA 51012-0281. Year Established: 1870. Pub. Frequency: d. (Mon.-Fri.) Page Size: broadsheet. Subscrip. Rate: $.50 newsstand/cover; $75/yr in county; $119/yr out of county. **Wire Service(s):** AP. Circulation: 3,100 morning (paid). **Owner(s):** Rust Communications, Inc., 301 Broadway, Cape Girardeau, MO 03701. Telephone: 573-335-6611. **Management:** Paul Struck, Publisher. Troy Valentine, Advertising Manager. **Editorial:** Paul Struck, Editor.

Dailies

CLINTON

CLINTON HERALD. 221 Sixth Ave., S., Clinton, IA 52732. Telephone: 563-242-7142. FAX: 563-242-7147. URL: http://www.clintonherald.com. Mailing Address: PO Box 2961, Clinton, IA 52733-2961. Year Established: 1856. Pub. Frequency: d. (Mon.-Sat.) Page Size: broadsheet. Subscrip. Rate: $.50 newsstand/cover; $90/yr home delivery. **Wire Service(s):** AP. Circulation: 13,000 evening (paid). **Owner(s):** Community Newspaper Holdings, Inc., 3500 Colonnade Pkwy., Ste. 600, Birmingham, AL 35243. Telephone: 205-298-7100. FAX: 205-298-7101. **Management:** Harvey Brock, Publisher. Wayne Larkey, Advertising Director. Maureen Miller, Circulation Director. Sherri Enwright, Classified Adv. Mgr.. **Editorial:** Charlene Biehema, Editor. Ted Schultz, Sports Editor.

COUNCIL BLUFF

DAILY NONPAREIL. ISSN 1046-1833
535 W Broadway, Ste 300, Council Bluff, IA 51503. Telephone: 712-328-1811. FAX: 712-325-5813. URL: http://www.nonpareilonline.com. Mailing Address: PO Box 797, Council Bluff, IA 51502-0797. Year Established: 1857. Pub. Frequency: d. Page Size: broadsheet. Subscrip. Rate: $.50 newsstand/cover; $1.25 newsstand/cover Sun.; $10.50 home delivery/mo.; $119.80/yr home delivery. **Wire Service(s):** AP. Circulation: 17,800 evening (paid); 19,500 Sunday (paid). **Owner(s):** Omaha World-Herald Co., 1314 Douglas St, Omaha, NE 68102. Telephone: 402-444-1000. FAX: 402-345-0183. **Management:** Cindy Bunten, Advertising Manager. Mendy Showalter, Circulation Manager. Shelly Brisell, Classified Adv. Mgr.. **Editorial:** Jon Leu, Managing Editor. Marshall Hoffman, News Editor.

CRESTON

CRESTON NEWS ADVERTISER. 503 W. Adams St., Creston, IA 50801. Telephone: 641-782-2141. FAX: 641-782-6628. E-MAIL: cna@creston.heartland.net. URL: http://www.crestonnewsadvertiser.com. Mailing Address: PO Box 126, Creston, IA 50801-0126. Year Established: 1881. Pub. Frequency: d. (Mon.-Fri.) Page Size: broadsheet. Subscrip. Rate: $.50 newsstand/cover; $89/yr. Adv. Rate: col. inch $8.50 **Wire Service(s):** AP. Circulation: 5,250 evening (paid). **Owner(s):** Shaw Newspaper Co., 444 Pine Hill Dr., Dixon, IL 61021. Telephone: 815-284-4000. **Management:** Tom Shaw, President. Rich Paulsen, Publisher. Roger Lanning, Advertising Manager. Ron Bernard, Circulation Manager. **Editorial:** Stephanie Finley, Family Editor.

DAVENPORT

QUAD-CITY TIMES. ISSN 1064-2986
500 E. Third St., Davenport, IA 52802. Telephone: 563-333-2601. FAX: 563-333-2666. URL: http://www.qctimes.com/. Year Established: 1855. Pub. Frequency: d. Page Size: broadsheet. Subscrip. Rate: $.50 newsstand/cover; $2 newsstand/cover Sun.; $53.75 carrier delivery local for 13 wks.. **Wire Service(s):** AP. Circulation: 58,000 morning (paid); 82,000 Sunday (paid). **Owner(s):** Lee Enterprises, Inc., 201 N. Harrison St, Ste 600, Davenport, IA 52801-1924. **Management:** Michael Phelps, Publisher. Cheryl Riley, Advertising Manager. **Editorial:** John Humenik, Editor. Craig Brown, City Editor. Greg Swanson, Feature Editor. Don Doxsie, Sports Editor. Contact: Bob Craft, Circulation Manager.

DES MOINES

DES MOINES REGISTER. 715 Locust St., Des Moines, IA 50309. Telephone: 515-284-8000. FAX: 515-284-8287. URL: http://www.desmoinesregister.com. Mailing Address: PO Box 957, Des Moines, IA 50304. Year Established: 1849. Pub. Frequency: d. Page Size: broadsheet. Subscrip. Rate: $.50 newsstand/cover; $1.50 newsstand/cover Sun.; $16.25 home delivery/mo.. **Wire Service(s):** AP, LAT-WAT, DJNS, GNS. Circulation: 149,452 morning (paid); 240,502 Sunday (paid). **Owner(s):** Gannett Company, Inc., 7950 Jones Branch Dr., McLean, VA 22107-0001. Telephone: 703-854-6000. **Bureau(s): Management:** Mary Stier, Publisher. Rick Bell, VP Circulation. Brad Robertson, Advertising Director. Beth McDonald, Classified Adv. Mgr.. **Editorial:** Randy Brubaker, Managing Editor. Lynn Hicks, Business Editor. Bryce Miller, Sports Editor.

DUBUQUE

TELEGRAPH HERALD. ISSN 1041-293X
801 Bluff St., Dubuque, IA 52001. Telephone: 563-588-5611. FAX: 563-588-5745. URL: http://www.thonline.com. Year Established: 1836. Pub. Frequency: d. Page Size: broadsheet. Subscrip. Rate: $.75 newsstand/cover; $2 newsstand/cover Sun.; $4.15 home delivery/wk.; $215.40/yr home delivery. **Wire Service(s):** AP. Circulation: 29,860 morning (paid); 34,872 Sunday (paid). **Owner(s):** Woodward Communications Inc., PO Box 688, Dubuque, IA 52004-0688. Telephone: 363-588-5687. FAX: 363-588-5739. **Management:** Tom Yunt, President. James Normandin, Publisher. Steve Fisher, Advertising Director. Michael Newland, Circulation Manager. **Editorial:** Brian Cooper, Executive Editor. Ken Brown, City Editor. Jim Swenson, Feature Editor. Mark Hirsch, Photo Editor. Jim Leitner, Sports.

ESTHERVILLE

ESTHERVILLE DAILY NEWS. ISSN 0747-0754
10 N. Seventh St., Estherville, IA 51334. Telephone: 712-362-2622. FAX: 712-362-2624. URL: http://www.esthervilledailynews.com. Year Established: 1902. Pub. Frequency: d. (Mon.-Sat.) Page Size: broadsheet. Subscrip. Rate: $72/yr in county; $97/yr out of county. Circulation: 2,500 morning (paid). **Owner(s):** Ogden Newspapers of Minnesota, Inc., 1500 Main St., Wheeling, WV 26003. Telephone: 304-233-0100. **Management:** Glen Caron, Publisher. Dar Isaackson, Advertising Manager. Beverly Fisher, Circulation Manager. **Editorial:** David Swartz, Sports.

FAIRFIELD

FAIRFIELD LEDGER. ISSN 1061-4508
112 E. Broadway, Fairfield, IA 52556. Telephone: 641-472-4129. FAX: 641-472-1916. E-MAIL: fsledger@lisco.com. URL: http://www.fledger.com. Mailing Address: PO Box 110, Fairfield, IA 52556. Year Established: 1849. Pub. Frequency: d. (Mon.-Fri.) Page Size: broadsheet. Subscrip. Rate: $.50 newsstand/cover; $107/yr home delivery. **Wire Service(s):** AP. Circulation: 5,000 evening (paid). **Owner(s):** Inland Industries, Inc., PO Box 15999, Shawnee Mission, KS 66285. **Management:** Jeff Wilson, Publisher. Gene Luedtke, Advertising Manager. Dan Manley, Circulation Manager. **Editorial:** Vicki Tillis, Managing Editor. Chad Drury, Sports Editor.

FORT DODGE

FORT DODGE MESSENGER. ISSN 0740-6991
713 Central Ave., Fort Dodge, IA 50501-0659. Telephone: 515-573-2141. FAX: 515-573-2148. E-MAIL: editor@frontiernet.net. URL: http://www.messengernews.net. Mailing Address: PO Box 659, Fort Dodge, IA 50501-0659. Year Established: 1855. Pub. Frequency: d. Page Size: standard. Subscrip. Rate: $.50 newsstand/cover; $1.50 newsstand/cover Sun.; $135.20/yr. **Wire Service(s):** AP. Circulation: 18,390 morning (paid); 20,710 Sunday (paid). **Owner(s):** Ogden Newspapers of Minnesota, Inc., 1500 Main St., Wheeling, WV 26003. Telephone: 304-233-0100. **Management:** Larry D. Bushman, General Manager. Steve Baker, Advertising Manager. Grant Gibbons, Circulation Manager. Jean Browning, Classified Adv. Mgr.. **Editorial:** Bob Van Enkenwood, Editor. Barbara Wallace Hughes, Business Editor. Deanna Swartz, City Editor. Sandy Mickelson, Lifestyle Editor. Eric Pratt, Sports.

FORT MADISON

FORT MADISON DAILY DEMOCRAT. ISSN 0746-4266
1226 Ave. H, Fort Madison, IA 52627. Telephone: 319-372-6421. FAX: 319-372-3867. E-MAIL: democrat@interl.net. URL: http://www.dailydem.com. Mailing Address: PO Box 160, Fort Madison, IA 52627. Year Established: 1869. Pub. Frequency: d. (Mon.-Fri.) Page Size: broadsheet. Subscrip. Rate: $.50 newsstand/cover; $79.40/yr home delivery local; $88.22/yr motor route. **Wire Service(s):** AP. Circulation: 6,500 evening (paid). **Owner(s):** Brehm Communications, Inc., 16644 W. Bernardo Dr., Ste. 300, San Diego, CA 92127. Telephone: 858-451-6200. **Management:** Gary Milks, Publisher. Joni Keller, Advertising Manager. Brandi Coleman, Circulation Manager. **Editorial:** Robin Delaney, Managing Editor. Chris Faulkner, Sports.

IOWA CITY

IOWA CITY PRESS-CITIZEN. 1725 N. Dodge St., Iowa City, IA 52245. Telephone: 319-337-3181. FAX: 319-834-1083. E-MAIL: newsroom@press-citizen.com. URL: http://www.press-citizen.com. Mailing Address: PO Box 2480, Iowa City, IA 52244. Year Established: 1841. Pub. Frequency: d. Page Size: broadsheet. Subscrip. Rate: $.50 newsstand/cover; $.75 newsstand/cover Sat.; $1.50 newsstand/cover Sun.; $41.60 carrier delivery for 13 wks.; $44.85 motor route for 13 wks.. Freelance Pay: $25/story. **Wire Service(s):** AP, GNS. Circulation: 16,500 morning (paid); 19,000 Sunday (paid). **Owner(s):** Gannett Company, Inc., 7950 Jones Branch Dr., McLean, VA 22107-0001. Telephone: 703-854-6000. **Management:** Andrea Rhoades, Advertising Director. Victoria Gilpin, Advertising Manager. Jean Suckow, Circulation Director. Matt Forsyth, Classified Adv. Mgr.. **Editorial:** Jim Lewers, Managing Editor. Greg Smith, Assignment Editor. Tricia Newall, Lifestyle Editor. Teresa Thorpe, News Editor. Jason Cook, Photo Editor. Ryan Suchomel, Sports Editor. Contact: Jeff Schroeter, Advertising Director; Kim Wustrack, Circulation Manager; Matt Meyers, Manager.

KEOKUK

DAILY GATE CITY. 1016 Main St., Keokuk, IA 52632-0430. Telephone: 319-524-8300. FAX: 319-524-4363. E-MAIL: advertising@dailygate.com. URL: http://www.dailygate.com. Mailing Address: PO Box 430, Keokuk, IA 52632-0430. Year Established: 1847. Pub. Frequency: d. (Mon.-Fri.) Page Size: broadsheet. Subscrip. Rate: $.50 newsstand/cover; $83/yr carrier delivery local; $94/yr mailed in county; $101/yr mailed elsewhere. Adv. Rate: col. inch $9.45 **Wire Service(s):** AP. Circulation: 5,200 per issue (paid). **Owner(s):** Brehm Communications, Inc., 16644 W. Bernardo Dr., Ste. 300, San Diego, CA 92127. Telephone: 858-451-6200. **Management:** Mark Smidt, Publisher. Doug Shipman, Advertising Manager. Diane Bolton, Circulation Manager. **Editorial:** Steve Dunn, Managing Editor. Brad Cameron, Sports.

LE MARS

LE MARS DAILY SENTINEL. 41 First Ave., N.E., Le Mars, IA 51031. Telephone: 712-546-7031. FAX: 712-546-7035. E-MAIL: barnable@lemarscomm.net. URL: http://www.lemarsentinel.com. Mailing Address: PO Box 930, Le Mars, IA 51031. Year Established: 1870. Pub. Frequency: d. (Mon.-Fri.) Page Size: broadsheet. Subscrip. Rate: $.75 newsstand/cover (effective 2009); $99.75/yr carrier delivery local; $128.95/yr mailed local; $158.75/yr in state; $203.95/yr out of state. Circulation: 3,654 evening (paid). **Owner(s):** Rust Communications, Inc., 301 Broadway, Cape Girardeau, MO 63702. Telephone: 800-879-1212. **Management:** Tom Stangl, Publisher. Monte Jost, Advertising Manager. Christine Pape, Circulation Manager. Judy Barnable, Business Manager. **Editorial:** Magdalene Landegent, Editor.

MARSHALLTOWN

TIMES-REPUBLICAN (MARSHALLTOWN). ISSN 1074-147X
135 W. Main St., Marshalltown, IA 50158-1300. Telephone: 641-753-6611. FAX: 641-753-7221. E-MAIL: timesr@timesrepublican.com. URL: http://www.timesrepublican.com. Mailing Address: PO Box 1300, Marshalltown, IA 50158-1300. Year Established: 1858. Pub. Frequency: d. Page Size: broadsheet. Subscrip. Rate: $.50 newsstand/cover; $1 newsstand/cover Sun.; $125.20/yr carrier delivery; $143.20/yr mailed. **Wire Service(s):** AP. Circulation: 12,500 evening (paid); 12,500 Sunday (paid). **Owner(s):** Ogden Newspapers of Minnesota, Inc., 1500 Main St., Wheeling, WV 26003. Telephone: 304-233-0100. **Management:** Mike Schlesinger, Publisher. **Editorial:** Jim Stern, Editor. Bryan Schultz, Reporter. Ross Theded, Sports Editor.

MASON CITY

GLOBE-GAZETTE. 300 N. Washington Ave., Mason City, IA 50401-3222. Telephone: 641-421-0524. FAX: 641-421-0516. E-MAIL: news@globegazette.com. URL: http://www.globegazette.com. Year Established: 1893. Pub. Frequency: d. Page Size: broadsheet. Subscrip. Rate: $.50 newsstand/cover; $1.50 Sun.; $198/yr. **Wire Service(s):** AP, NYT. Circulation: 18,962 morning (paid); 23,121 Sunday (paid). **Owner(s):** Lee Enterprises, Inc., 201 N. Harrison St, Ste 600, Davenport, IA 52801-1924. **Management:** Howard Query, Publisher. Greg Wilderman, Advertising Manager. Jeff Binstock, Circulation Manager. **Editorial:** Bob Stenson, Managing Editor. Kris Buehner, Fashion Editor. Karen Jacobs, Lifestyle Editor. Jane Reynolds, News Editor.

MT. PLEASANT

MT. PLEASANT NEWS. 215 W. Monroe St., Mt. Pleasant, IA 52641. Telephone: 319-385-3131. FAX: 319-385-8048. E-MAIL: news@mpnews.net. URL: http://www.mpnews.net. Mailing Address: PO Box 240, Mt. Pleasant, IA 52641. Year Established: 1878. Pub. Frequency: d. (Mon.-Fri.) Page Size: broadsheet. Subscrip. Rate: \$.50 newsstand/cover; \$92/yr. **Wire Service(s):** AP. Circulation: 2,900 evening (paid). **Owner(s):** Mt. Pleasant News, Inc., See address and contact information above. **Management:** Darwin Sherman, President. Emery Styron, Publisher. Billie Allender, Advertising Manager. **Editorial:** Joe Benedict, Editor.

MUSCATINE

MUSCATINE JOURNAL. 301 E. Third St., Muscatine, IA 52761. Telephone: 563-263-2331. FAX: 563-262-8042. E-MAIL: news@muscatinejournal.com. URL: http://www.muscatinejournal.com. Year Established: 1888. Pub. Frequency: d. (Mon.-Sat.) Page Size: broadsheet. Subscrip. Rate: \$.50 newsstand/cover; \$121.75/yr in county. **Wire Service(s):** AP. Circulation: 10,000 evening (paid). **Owner(s):** Lee Enterprises, Inc., 201 N. Harrison St, Ste 600, Davenport, IA 52801-1924. **Management:** Lisa Sievers, Publisher. Cynthia Gyger, Advertising Director. Steve Waldorf, Circulation Manager. **Editorial:** Jeff Tecklenburg, Editor.

NEWTON

NEWTON DAILY NEWS.   ISSN 1040-1539
200 First Ave., E., Newton, IA 50208. Telephone: 641-792-3121. FAX: 641-792-5505. E-MAIL: ndnews@iowatelecom.net. URL: http://www.newtondailynews.com. Mailing Address: PO Box 967, Newton, IA 50208. Year Established: 1902. Pub. Frequency: d. (Mon.-Sat.) Page Size: broadsheet. Subscrip. Rate: \$.50 newsstand/cover; \$115.80/yr carrier delivery; \$142.20/yr motor route; \$159/yr mailed in county; \$180/yr mailed out of county. **Wire Service(s):** UPI. Circulation: 5,883 evening (controlled and free). **Owner(s):** Shaw Newspapers, 444 Pine Hill Dr., Dixon, IL 61021. Telephone: 815-284-2222. FAX: 815-254-9290. **Management:** John DeGrado, General Manager. Jim Nelson, Publisher. Shawn Wolfe, Advertising Director. Kelly Vest, Circulation Manager. **Editorial:** Pete Hussmann, Managing Editor. Doug Dornath, Sports Editor.

OELWEIN

OELWEIN DAILY REGISTER. 25 First St, SE, Oelwein, IA 50662. Telephone: 319-283-2144. FAX: 319-283-3268. E-MAIL: classifieds@oelweindailyregister.com. URL: http://www.oelweindailyregister.com. Mailing Address: PO Box 511, Oelwein, IA 50662-0511. Year Established: 1881. Pub. Frequency: d. (Mon.-Sat.) Page Size: broadsheet. Subscrip. Rate: \$.50 newsstand/cover; \$1 newsstand/cover Sat.; \$2.95 carrier delivery/wk. local; \$145/yr mailed in state; \$160/yr mailed elsewhere. **Wire Service(s):** AP. Circulation: 5,200 evening (paid). **Owner(s):** Community Media Group, Inc, PO Box 10, West Frankfort, IL 62896. Telephone: 815-432-5227. **Management:** John Perratto, Publisher. Tami Shannon, Advertising. Susan Hosto, Circulation Manager. Melissa Boeck, Classified Adv. Mgr.. **Editorial:** Jack Swanson, Managing Editor. John Jensen, Sports Editor.

OSKALOOSA

OSKALOOSA HERALD, THE.   ISSN 0898-2066
1901 A Ave., W., Oskaloosa, IA 52577. Telephone: 641-672-2581. FAX: 641-672-2294. E-MAIL: tkurtz@oskyherald.com. URL: http://www.oskaloosa.com. Mailing Address: PO Box 530, Oskaloosa, IA 52577. Year Established: 1850. Pub. Frequency: d. (Mon.-Fri.) Page Size: broadsheet. Subscrip. Rate: \$.50 newsstand/cover; \$88/yr in county; \$101.75/yr out of county; \$121/yr out of state. Circulation: 3,400 (paid). **Owner(s):** Community Newspaper Holdings, Inc., 3500 Colonnade Pkwy., Ste. 600, Birmingham, AL 35243. Telephone: 205-298-7100. FAX: 205-298-7101. **Management:** Tim Kurtz, Publisher. Deb Van Engelenhoven, Advertising Director. Connie Davis, Circulation Manager. Gayle Verploegh, Classified Adv. Mgr.. **Editorial:** Duane Nollen, Editor. Andy Goodell, City Editor. Jim Gries, Sports Editor.Readers: Mahaska County

OTTUMWA

OTTUMWA COURIER.   ISSN 0886-4209
213 E. Second St., Ottumwa, IA 52501. Telephone: 641-684-4611. FAX: 641-684-7326. E-MAIL: news@ottumwacourier.com. URL: http://www.ottumwacourier.com. Year Established: 1848. Pub. Frequency: d. (Mon.-Sat.) Page Size: broadsheet. Subscrip. Rate: \$.50 newsstand/cover; \$1 newsstand/cover Sat.; \$37.35 carrier delivery local for 13 wks.; \$45.75 mailed out of area for 13 wks.; \$59.90 mailed out of state for 13 wks.. **Wire Service(s):** AP. Circulation: 17,000 morning (paid). **Owner(s):** Community Newspaper Holdings, Inc., 3500 Colonnade Pkwy., Ste. 600, Birmingham, AL 35243. Telephone: 205-298-7100. FAX: 205-298-7108. **Management:** Tom Hawley, Publisher. Dan Canny, Advertising Director. Jason McNeely, Circulation Manager. **Editorial:** Judy Krieger, Editor. Jeff Hutton, Associate Editor.

SHENANDOAH

VALLEY NEWS TODAY. 702 W Sheridan St, Shenandoah, IA 51601. Telephone: 712-246-3097. FAX: 712-246-3099. E-MAIL: valleynews@shenessex.heartland.net. URL: http://www.valleynewstoday.com. Mailing Address: PO Box 369, Shenandoah, IA 51601-0369. Year Established: 1993. Pub. Frequency: d. (Tue.-Fri. & Sun.) Page Size: tabloid. Subscrip. Rate: \$.50 newsstand/cover; \$1 newsstand/cover Sun.; \$86/yr local. Circulation: 3,500 evening (paid); 3,500 Sunday (paid). **Owner(s):** Omaha World-Herald Co., 1314 Douglas St, Omaha, NE 68102. Telephone: 402-444-1000. FAX: 402-345-0183. **Management:** David Gustafson, Publisher. Carolyn Lewis, Circulation Manager. **Editorial:** Alan Cross, Editor.

SIOUX CITY

SIOUX CITY JOURNAL, THE. 515 Pavonia St., Sioux City, IA 51102. Telephone: 712-293-4250. FAX: 712-279-5059. E-MAIL: scj@siouxcityjournal.com. URL: http://siouxcityjournal.com. Mailing Address: PO Box 118, Sioux City, IA 51102. Year Established: 1854. Pub. Frequency: d. Page Size: broadsheet. Subscrip. Rate: \$.50 newsstand/cover; \$1.75 newsstand/cover Sun.; \$14.50 carrier delivery/mo.; \$208/yr carrier delivery. **Wire Service(s):** AP. Circulation: 50,000 morning (paid); 50,000 Sunday (paid). **Owner(s):** Lee Enterprises, Inc., 201 N. Harrison St, Ste 600, Davenport, IA 52801-1924. **Management:** Ron Peterson, Publisher. Bob Carruth, Advertising Director. Mark Lewis, Circulation Manager. **Editorial:** Larry Myhre, Editor. Karen Luken, Managing Editor. Dave Dreeszen, Business Editor. Bruce Miller, Lifestyle Editor. Jim Jenkins, News Editor. Tim Hynds, Photo Editor. Terry Hersom, Sports Editor.

SPENCER

SPENCER DAILY REPORTER.   ISSN 0746-0872
310 E. Milwaukee, Spencer, IA 51301. Telephone: 712-262-6610. FAX: 712-262-3044. Mailing Address: PO Box 197, Spencer, IA 51301. Year Established: 1875. Pub. Frequency: d. (Tue.-Sat.) Page Size: broadsheet. Subscrip. Rate: \$.50 newsstand/cover; \$70/yr carrier delivery. **Wire Service(s):** AP. Circulation: 4,000 morning (paid). **Owner(s):** Rust Communications, Inc., 301 Broadway, Cape Girardeau, MO 63701. Telephone: 573-335-6611. **Management:** Paula Buenger, Publisher. Janelle Madison, Advertising Director. Monica Kerns, Classified Adv. Mgr.. **Editorial:** Randy Cauthron, Editor.

VINTON

CEDAR VALLEY DAILY TIMES. 108 E. Fifth St., Vinton, IA 52349. Telephone: 319-472-2311. FAX: 319-472-4811. E-MAIL: angie.mcfarland@cedarvalleydailytimes.com. URL: http://www.cedarvalleydailytimes.com. Mailing Address: PO Box 468, Vinton, IA 52349. Year Established: 1889. Pub. Frequency: d. (Mon.-Fri.) Page Size: broadsheet. Subscrip. Rate: \$.50 newsstand/cover; \$89/yr in city; \$89/yr mailed in county & adj. cys.. **Wire Service(s):** LAT-WAT. Circulation: 2,000 evening (paid). **Owner(s):** Community Media Group, Inc, PO Box 10, West Frankfort, IL 62896. Telephone: 618-937-6412. **Management:** Larry Perotto, President. Scott Richter, Advertising Manager. Sue Hosto, Circulation Manager. **Editorial:** Dean Close, News Editor. Brett Meyers, Sports Editor.

WASHINGTON

WASHINGTON EVENING JOURNAL.   ISSN 0894-2552
111 N. Marion Ave., Washington, IA 52353. Telephone: 319-653-2191. FAX: 319-653-7524. E-MAIL: pub@washjrnl.com. URL: http://www.washjrnl.com. Mailing Address: PO Box 471, Washington, IA 52353. Year Established: 1893. Pub. Frequency: d. (Mon.-Fri.) Page Size: broadsheet. Subscrip. Rate: \$.50 newsstand/cover; \$10.75 carrier delivery/mo.; \$10.25 mailed/mo. in county; \$13 mailed/mo. in state. **Wire Service(s):** AP. Circulation: 3,600 evening (paid). **Owner(s):** Washington Publishing Co., Inc., See address and contact information above. **Management:** Darwin Sherman, President. Nicole Patterson, Advertising Manager. **Editorial:** Darwin Sherman, Editor. Chris Kruckeberg, Managing Editor.

WATERLOO

COURIER (WATERLOO, 1859).   ISSN 1555-5771
501 Commercial St., Waterloo, IA 50701. Telephone: 319-291-1400. FAX: 319-234-6405. URL: http://www.wcfcourier.com. Mailing Address: PO Box 540, Waterloo, IA 50704. Year Established: 1859. Pub. Frequency: d. (Sun.-Fri.) Page Size: broadsheet. Subscrip. Rate: \$.50 newsstand/cover; \$2 newsstand/cover Sun.; \$130/yr carrier delivery; \$150/yr mailed. **Wire Service(s):** AP, LAT-WAT. Circulation: 52,000 evening (paid); 56,000 Sunday (paid). **Owner(s):** Lee Enterprises, Inc., 201 N. Harrison St, Ste 600, Davenport, IA 52801-1924. **Bureau(s):** 109 W. Second St., Cedar Falls, IA 50613. Telephone: 319-266-7904. Contact: John Ericson, Bureau Chief. **Editorial:** Saul Shapiro, Editor. Nancy Newhoff, Managing Editor. Mike McClure, Circulation Editor. Doug Newhoff, Sports Editor.

WEBSTER CITY

DAILY FREEMAN JOURNAL. 720 Second St., Webster City, IA 50595. Telephone: 515-832-4350. FAX: 515-832-2314. E-MAIL: dfjwc@ncn.net. Mailing Address: PO Box 490, Webster City, IA 50595. Year Established: 1857. Pub. Frequency: d. (Mon.-Fri.) Page Size: broadsheet. Subscrip. Rate: \$.50 newsstand/cover; \$75.40/yr home delivery. Circulation: 5,500 morning (paid). **Owner(s):** Ogden Newspapers of Minnesota, Inc., 1500 Main St., Wheeling, WV 26003. **Management:** Mike Fertig, Publisher. **Editorial:** Lori Nilles, Editor. Troy Banning, Sports Editor.

KANSAS

ABILENE

ABILENE REFLECTOR-CHRONICLE.   ISSN 0890-345X
303 N. Broadway, Abilene, KS 67410. Telephone: 785-263-1000. FAX: 785-263-1645. E-MAIL: abreflector@access-one.com. URL: http://www.abilene-rc.com. Year Established: 1872. Pub. Frequency: d. (Mon.-Sat.) Page Size: broadsheet. Subscrip. Rate: \$.50 newsstand/cover; \$6.75/mo. in county; \$78/yr in county; \$87/yr mailed out of county. Freelance Pay: \$1/column-inch. **Wire Service(s):** AP. Circulation: 4,000 evening (paid). **Owner(s):** Reflector-Chronicle Publishing Corp., See address and contact information above. **Management:** Dave Bergmeier, Publisher. **Editorial:** Judy Dickson, Managing Editor. Dustin Kimmel, Sports.

ARKANSAS CITY

ARKANSAS CITY TRAVELER.   ISSN 0888-8485
200 E. Fifth Ave., Arkansas City, KS 67005-0988. Telephone: 620-442-4200. FAX: 620-442-7483. E-MAIL: news@arkcity.net. URL: http://www.arkcity.net/. Mailing Address: PO Box 988, Arkansas City, KS 67005-0988. Year Established: 1870. Pub. Frequency: d. (Mon.-Sat.) Page Size: broadsheet. Subscrip. Rate: \$.50 newsstand/cover; \$74.70/yr home delivery local; \$79.95/yr motor route; \$125.83/yr mailed in state. **Wire Service(s):** AP. Circulation: 6,000 evening (paid). **Owner(s):** Winfield Publishing Co., Inc., 201 E. Ninth Ave., Winfield, KS 67156. Telephone: 620-221-1050. FAX: 620-221-1101. **Management:** Lloyd Craig, General Manager. Dave Seaton, Publisher. Aaron Blake, Advertising Manager. Barbara Babcock, Circulation Manager. Susie Kinkaid, Business Manager. **Editorial:** James Jordon, Managing Editor. Jim Luksic, Sports Editor.

ATCHISON

ATCHISON DAILY GLOBE. 1015-25 Main St., Atchison, KS 66002. Telephone: 913-367-0583. FAX: 913-367-7531. E-MAIL: globe@npgco.com. URL: http://www.atchisondailyglobe.com. Mailing Address: PO Box 247, Atchison, KS 66002. Year Established: 1877. Pub. Frequency: d. (Mon.-Sat.) Page Size: broadsheet. Subscrip. Rate: \$.50 newsstand/cover; \$.75 newsstand/cover Sat.; \$99/yr carrier delivery in KS & MO; \$113.40/yr mailed in KS & MO. Adv. Rate: col. inch \$12.12 **Wire Service(s):** AP. Circulation: 3,700 evening (paid and free). **Owner(s):** St. Joseph News-Press & Gazette Co., PO Box 29, St. Joseph, MO 64502-0029. Telephone: 816-271-8500. **Management:** Chris Wessel, Publisher. Marilyn Andre, Office Manager. Christy McKibben, Advertising Manager. Terry Knopke, Circulation Manager. Jan Wessel, Classified Adv. Mgr.. **Editorial:** Michael Terry, Managing Editor. Rita Jones, Production Manager. Andy Brown, Sports Editor.

AUGUSTA

AUGUSTA DAILY GAZETTE. 204 E. Fifth St., Augusta, KS 67010-0009. Telephone: 316-775-2218. FAX: 316-775-3220. URL: http://www.augustagazette.com. Mailing Address: PO Box 9, Augusta, KS 67010-0009. Year Established: 1893. Pub. Frequency: d. (Mon.-Fri.) Page Size: broadsheet. Subscrip. Rate: $.50 newsstand/cover; $89.04/yr in city; $89.61/yr in county. **Wire Service(s):** AP. Circulation: 7,900 evening (paid). **Owner(s):** GateHouse Media, Inc, 350 WillowBrook Office Park, Fairport, NY 14450. Telephone: 585-598-0030. FAX: 585-248-2631. **Management:** Leca Weber, Publisher. Amber Jackson, Advertising Manager. Brenda Sutton, Classified Adv. Mgr.. **Editorial:** Michael McDermott, Editor. Kim Mangus, Sports Editor.

CLAY CENTER

CLAY CENTER DISPATCH. 805 Fifth St., Clay Center, KS 67432. Telephone: 785-632-2127. FAX: 785-632-6526. E-MAIL: dispatch@claycenter.com. URL: http://www.claycenter.com. Mailing Address: PO Box 519, Clay Center, KS 67432. Year Established: 1873. Pub. Frequency: d. (Mon.-Fri.) Page Size: broadsheet. Subscrip. Rate: $.50 newsstand/cover; $84/yr carrier delivery; $95/yr mailed in state; $108/yr mailed out of state. **Wire Service(s):** AP. Circulation: 3,100 per issue (paid). **Owner(s):** Clay Center Publishing Co., See address and contact information above. **Management:** Ned Valentine, Publisher. Kathy Pippenger, Advertising Manager. McKenna Porter, Circulation Manager. **Editorial:** Ned Valentine, Editor. Ryan Wilson, News Editor. Dave Berggren, Sports.

COFFEYVILLE

COFFEYVILLE JOURNAL, THE. ISSN 0746-8202
Eighth & Elm Sts., Coffeyville, KS 67337. Telephone: 620-251-3300. FAX: 620-251-1905. E-MAIL: edit@wwebservice.net. URL: http://www.cjournal.com. Mailing Address: PO Box 849, Coffeyville, KS 67337. Year Established: 1892. Pub. Frequency: d. (Tue.-Fri. & Sun.) Page Size: broadsheet. Subscrip. Rate: $.50 newsstand/cover; $1 newsstand/cover Sun.; $77.70/yr home delivery; $93.60/yr mailed in state; $95.33/yr mailed out of state. Freelance Pay: $0.15/column-inch. **Wire Service(s):** AP. Circulation: 5,000 evening (paid); 6,000 Sunday (paid). **Owner(s):** Community Newspaper Holdings, Inc., 3500 Colonnade Pkwy., Ste. 600, Birmingham, AL 35243. Telephone: 205-298-7100. FAX: 205-298-7101. **Management:** Tina Alvidrez, Advertising Manager. Anna Ellsworth, Circulation Manager. Lola Cowan, Classified Adv. Mgr.. **Editorial:** Daniel Walker, Managing Editor.

COLBY

COLBY FREE PRESS. 155 W Fifth St, Colby, KS 67701. Telephone: 785-462-3963. FAX: 785-462-7749. E-MAIL: kballard@nwkansas.com. URL: htttp://www.nwkansas.com. Year Established: 1888. Pub. Frequency: d. (Mon., Wed.-Fri.) Page Size: broadsheet. Subscrip. Rate: $.75 newsstand/cover; $85/yr carrier delivery. **Wire Service(s):** AP. Circulation: 2,500 evening (paid). **Owner(s):** NorWest Newspapers, Inc., 170 S Penn Ave, Oberlin, KS 67749. Telephone: 785-475-2206. FAX: 785-475-2800. **Management:** Steve Haynes, Publisher. Jasmine Stewart, Advertising Director. Kathryn Ballard, Circulation Manager. **Editorial:** Kevin Bottrell, Editor.

COLUMBUS

COLUMBUS DAILY ADVOCATE. ISSN 8756-6044
215 S. Kansas Ave., Columbus, KS 66725. Telephone: 620-429-2773. FAX: 620-429-3223. E-MAIL: coladv@columbus-ks.com. Mailing Address: PO Box 231, Columbus, KS 66725. Year Established: 1874. Pub. Frequency: d. (Mon.-Fri.) Page Size: broadsheet. Subscrip. Rate: $.50 newsstand/cover; $47.75/yr carrier delivery. **Wire Service(s):** AP. Circulation: 2,300 evening (paid). **Owner(s):** Sumner Media Group, See address and contact information above. **Management:** Don Sumner, General Manager. Darrell Sumner, President. Don Sumner, Publisher. Sonya Hale, Advertising Manager. Carla Britt, Circulation Manager. **Editorial:** Alan Storey, Editor.

CONCORDIA

CONCORDIA BLADE-EMPIRE. 510 Washington St., Concordia, KS 66901. Telephone: 785-243-2424. FAX: 785-243-4407. E-MAIL: bladeempire@cebridge.net. URL: http://www.bladeempire.com. Mailing Address: PO Box 309, Concordia, KS 66901-0309. Year Established: 1902. Pub. Frequency: d. (Mon.-Fri.) Page Size: broadsheet. Subscrip. Rate: $.50 newsstand/cover; $80.80/yr trade area; $80.58/yr carrier delivery; $97.43/yr mailed out of area. **Wire Service(s):** AP. Circulation: 2,450 evening (paid). **Owner(s):** Blade-Empire Publishing Co., Inc., See address and contact information above. **Management:** Brad Lowell, Publisher. Joni Regnier, Advertising Manager. Denise Lahodny, Circulation Manager. **Editorial:** Brad Lowell, Editor. Jim Lowell, Managing Editor. Sharon Coy, Lifestyle Editor.

COUNCIL GROVE

COUNCIL GROVE REPUBLICAN. 208 W. Main St., Council Grove, KS 66846-1705. Telephone: 620-767-5123. FAX: 620-767-5124. E-MAIL: cgnews@cgtelco.net. Year Established: 1872. Pub. Frequency: d. (Mon.-Fri.) Page Size: broadsheet. Subscrip. Rate: $.35 newsstand/cover; $65.40/yr carrier delivery local. Adv. Rate: col. inch $4.97 **Wire Service(s):** AP. Circulation: 2,200 evening (paid). **Owner(s):** Council Grove Publishing Co., Inc., See address and contact information above. **Management:** Craig A. McNeal, Publisher. Don A. McNeal, Advertising Manager. Christy Jimerson, Circulation Manager.

DERBY

DERBY REPORTER, THE. 201 S. Baltimore St., Derby, KS 67037. E-MAIL: clements@derbyreporter.com. URL: http://www.derbydailyrep.com. Mailing Address: PO Box 190, Derby, KS 67037. Pub. Frequency: d. (Mon.-Fri.) Page Size: standard. Subscrip. Rate: $.50 newsstand/cover; $74.28/yr carrier delivery in city; $99.32/yr mailed elsewhere. Circulation: 2,000 per issue (paid). **Owner(s):** GateHouse Media, Inc, 350 WillowBrook Office Park, Fairport, NY 14450. **Management:** Jim Clements, Publisher. Fred Bonner, Advertising. Lori Rubendall, Circulation Manager. **Editorial:** Julie Anderson, Editor.

DODGE CITY

DODGE CITY DAILY GLOBE. ISSN 0889-3489
705 Second Ave., Dodge City, KS 67801. Telephone: 620-225-4151. FAX: 620-225-4154. E-MAIL: dcnew@globenetworks.com. URL: http://www.dodgeglobe.com. Mailing Address: PO Box 820, Dodge City, KS 67801. Year Established: 1911. Pub. Frequency: d. (Mon.-Sat.) Page Size: broadsheet. Subscrip. Rate: $.50 newsstand/cover; $114.94/yr. **Wire Service(s):** AP. Circulation: 22,032 morning (paid). **Owner(s):** Morris Multimedia, Inc., PO Box 936, Augusta, GA. **Management:** Terry Cochran, Publisher. Darryl Adams, Advertising Manager. Wayne Simmons, Circulation Manager. Linda Berry, Business Manager. **Editorial:** Rick Druse, Assistant Editor.

EL DORADO

EL DORADO TIMES. ISSN 1053-9999
114 N. Vine, El Dorado, KS 67042. Telephone: 316-321-1120. FAX: 316-321-7722. E-MAIL: eldtimes@southwind.net. URL: http://www.eldoradotimes.com. Mailing Address: PO Box 694, El Dorado, KS 67042. Year Established: 1919. Pub. Frequency: d. (Mon.-Sat.) Page Size: broadsheet. Subscrip. Rate: $.50 newsstand/cover; $106.80/yr carrier delivery local; $121.88/yr mailed in state; $150.75/yr mailed out of state. **Wire Service(s):** AP. Circulation: 4,000 evening (paid). **Owner(s):** GateHouse Media, Inc, 350 WillowBrook Office Park, Fairport, NY 14450. Telephone: 585-598-0030. FAX: 585-248-2631. **Management:** Leca Weber, Publisher. Terry Preston, Advertising Manager. Dawanna Fangohr, Circulation Manager.

EMPORIA

EMPORIA GAZETTE. 517 Merchant St., Emporia, KS 66801. Telephone: 620-342-4800. FAX: 620-342-8108. E-MAIL: gazette@emporia.com. URL: http://www.emporiagazette.com. Year Established: 1890. Pub. Frequency: d. (Mon.-Sat.) Page Size: broadsheet. Subscrip. Rate: $.50 newsstand/cover; $8.28 carrier delivery/wk.; $8.75 motor route/wk.; $8.55 mailed/wk.. **Wire Service(s):** AP, NYT. Circulation: 10,000 evening (paid). **Owner(s):** White Corp., Inc., See address and contact information above. **Management:** Christopher White Walker, Publisher. Carolyn Hadding, Advertising Manager. **Editorial:** Christopher White Walker, Editor. John Lechliter, Executive Editor. Patrick Kelley, Editorial Page Editor. Gwen Larson, News Editor. David Doemland, Photographer. Stuart Goldman, Sports.

FORT SCOTT

FORT SCOTT TRIBUNE, THE. ISSN 8755-3171
6 E. Wall St., Fort Scott, KS 66701-0150. Telephone: 620-223-1460. FAX: 620-223-1469. URL: http://www.fstribune.com. Mailing Address: PO Box 150, Fort Scott, KS 66701-0150. Year Established: 1884. Pub. Frequency: d. (Mon.-Sat.) Page Size: broadsheet. Subscrip. Rate: $.50 newsstand/cover; $86/yr carrier delivery; $85/yr mailed. **Wire Service(s):** AP. Circulation: 3,200 evening (paid). **Owner(s):** Rust Communications, 301 Broadway, Cape Girardeau, MO 63701. Telephone: 573-335-6611. **Management:** Kathy Fleener, Advertising Manager. Janice Cagle, Circulation Manager. Rebecka Headrick, Classified Adv. Mgr.. **Editorial:** Robin Hixon, Editor. Tom Epling, Farm Editor. Scott Nuzum, Sports Editor.

GARDEN CITY

GARDEN CITY TELEGRAM. ISSN 1087-9722
310 N. Seventh St., Garden City, KS 67846. Telephone: 620-275-8500. FAX: 620-275-5165. E-MAIL: denas@gctelegram.com. URL: http://www.gctelegram.com. Mailing Address: PO Box 958, Garden City, KS 67846. Year Established: 1929. Pub. Frequency: d. (Mon.-Sat.) Page Size: broadsheet. Subscrip. Rate: $.50 newsstand/cover; $1 newsstand/cover Sat.; $102.12/yr carrier delivery. **Wire Service(s):** AP. Circulation: 11,408 evening (paid). **Owner(s):** Kansas Newspapers LLC, One N Main St, Hutchinson, KS 67501-5229. Telephone: 620-694-5830. **Management:** Dena Sattler, Publisher. Matt Gnoth, Circulation Manager. **Editorial:** Brett Riggs, Managing Editor. Tony Adame, Sports Editor.

GREAT BEND

GREAT BEND TRIBUNE. ISSN 0891-7078
2012 Forest Ave, Great Bend, KS 67530-0228. Telephone: 620-792-1211. E-MAIL: email@gbtribune.com. URL: http://www.gbtribune.com. Year Established: 1876. Pub. Frequency: d. (Tue-Fri, Sun) Page Size: broadsheet. Subscrip. Rate: $.50 newsstand/cover; $1.25 newsstand/cover Sun.; $29.55/yr carrier delivery in city for 3 mos.; $106.38/yr carrier delivery; $180/yr motor route. Adv. Rate: col. inch $9.90 **Wire Service(s):** AP. Circulation: 8,100 morning (paid); 8,400 Sunday (paid). **Owner(s):** Morris Newspaper Corporation, 27 Abercorn St., Savannah, GA 31401. **Management:** Judy Murphy, Publisher. **Editorial:** Dale Hogg, Managing Editor. Shawn Hein, Sports.

HAYS

HAYS DAILY NEWS. 507 Main St., P.O. Box 857, Hays, KS 67601. E-MAIL: advertising@dailynews.net. URL: http://www.hdnews.net. Mailing Address: PO Box 857, Hays, KS 67601-0857. Year Established: 1929. Pub. Frequency: d. (Sun.-Fri.) Page Size: standard. Subscrip. Rate: $.50 newsstand/cover; $1 newsstand/cover Sun.; $134.26/yr. Adv. Rate: col. inch $13.80 **Wire Service(s):** AP. Circulation: 13,500 evening (paid and free); 14,500 Sunday (paid and free). **Owner(s):** News Publishing Co., See address and contact information above. **Management:** Mary Karst, Advertising Manager. Robert Weigel, Circulation Manager. Janice Tinkel, Business Manager. **Editorial:** Mike Corn, Managing Editor. Steve Hausler, Photo Editor.

HUTCHINSON

HAWK EYE, THE. ISSN 1073-9297
One N Main St, Hutchinson, KS 67501-5229. Telephone: 620-694-5830. URL: http://www.thehawkeye.com. Mailing Address: PO Box 10, Burlington, IA 52601. Year Established: 1837. Pub. Frequency: d. Page Size: broadsheet. Subscrip. Rate: $.50 newsstand/cover; $1.50 newsstand/cover Sun.; $12 carrier delivery/mo.; $135/yr carrier delivery. **Wire Service(s):** AP. Circulation: 19,406 morning (paid); 20,954 Sunday (paid). **Owner(s):** Kansas Newspapers LLC, 800 S. Main St., Burlington, IA 52601. Telephone: 319-754-8461. FAX: 319-754-6824. **Management:** Steve Delaney, Publisher. Janet Stottmeister, Advertising Manager. Lauri Trautner, Classified Adv. Mgr.. LeDonna Kitsch, Business Manager. **Editorial:** Steve Delaney, Editor. Dale Alison, Managing Editor. Ron Fields, Business Editor. Criss Roberts, Lifestyle Editor. John Gaines, Photo Editor. John Bohnenkamp, Sports.

HUTCHINSON NEWS. 300 W Second Ave, Hutchinson, KS 67501-0190. Telephone: 620-694-5700. FAX: 620-662-4186. E-MAIL: letters@hutchnews.com. URL: http://www.hutchnews.com. Mailing Address: P O Box 190, Hutchinson, KS 67501-0190. Year Established: 1872. Pub. Frequency: d. Page Size: broadsheet. Subscrip. Rate: $.50 newsstand/cover; $1.50 newsstand/cover Sun.; $150.24/yr home delivery. **Wire Service(s):** AP, LAT-WAT. Circulation: 40,000 morning (paid); 42,000 Sunday (paid). **Owner(s):** Kansas Newspapers LLC, One N Main St, Hutchinson, KS 67501-5229. **Management:** Jim Bloom, Publisher. Leslie Shea, Advertising Director. Rex Christner, Business Manager. **Editorial:** Jim Bloom, Editor-in-Chief. Greg Halling, Managing Editor. Mary Rintoul, City Editor. Greg Halling, News Editor.

INDEPENDENCE

INDEPENDENCE DAILY REPORTER. 320 N. 6th St., Independence, KS 67301. Mailing Address: P.O. Box 869, Independence, KS 67301. Year Established: 1881. Pub. Frequency: d. Page Size: broadsheet. Subscrip. Rate: $.50 newsstand/cover; $1 newsstand/cover Sun.; $99/yr. **Wire Service(s):** AP. Circulation: 7,675 evening (paid); 7,675 Sunday (paid). **Owner(s):** Reporter Publishing Co., Inc., See address and contact information above. **Management:** Herbert A. Meyer III, President. Steve McBride, Advertising Manager. James Tracey, Circulation Manager. Steve McBride, Promotion Manager. **Editorial:** Herbert A. Meyer III, Editor. Georgia High, Managing Editor. Brian Thomas, Sports Editor.

Dailies

IOLA

IOLA REGISTER, INC., THE. 302 S. Washington, Iola, KS 66749. Telephone: 620-365-2111. FAX: 620-365-6289. E-MAIL: iolaregister@irkscoxmail.com. URL: http://www.iolaregister.com. Mailing Address: PO Box 767, Iola, KS 66749-0767. Year Established: 1867. Pub. Frequency: d. (Mon.-Sat.) Page Size: broadsheet. Subscrip. Rate: $.50 newsstand/cover; $89.04/yr carrier delivery; $103.44/yr motor route; $107.38/yr mailed in trade area. **Wire Service(s):** AP. Circulation: 4,250 evening (paid). **Owner(s):** Susan Lynn, See address and contact information above. **Management:** Susan Lynn, Publisher. Mark Hastings, Advertising Manager. Glenda Aikins, Business Manager. **Editorial:** Susan Lynn, Editor. Emerson Lynn, Associate Editor. Robert Johnson, City Editor. Jenelle Johnson, Family Editor. Bruce Symes, News Editor. Jocelyn Sheets, Sports Editor.

JUNCTION CITY

JUNCTION CITY DAILY UNION.   ISSN 0745-743X
222 W. Sixth St., Junction City, KS 66441. Telephone: 785-762-5000. FAX: 785-762-4584. URL: http://www.dailyu.com. Year Established: 1861. Pub. Frequency: d. Page Size: broadsheet. Subscrip. Rate: $.50 newsstand/cover; $1 newsstand/cover Sun.; $100/yr carrier delivery; $106/yr motor route; $116/yr motor route out of area. Adv. Rate: col. inch $8.85 **Wire Service(s):** AP, CNS. Circulation: 7,249 evening (paid); 8,047 Sunday (paid). **Owner(s):** Montgomery Communications, Inc., See address and contact information above. **Management:** John G. Montgomery, Publisher. Penny Nelson, Office Manager. Pat Keefe, Advertising Manager. David Auldridge, Circulation Manager. **Editorial:** Tim Thorne, Editor. Ron Maley, Production Manager. Jeff Theisen, Sports Editor.

KANSAS CITY

KANSAS CITY KANSAN. 8200 State St., Kansas City, KS 66112. Telephone: 913-371-4300. FAX: 913-342-8620. E-MAIL: kckdaily@discoverynet.com. URL: http://www.kansascitykansan.com. Mailing Address: PO Box 175002, Kansas City, KS 66117. Year Established: 1921. Pub. Frequency: d. (Tue.-Sat.) Page Size: broadsheet. Subscrip. Rate: $.50 newsstand/cover; $1.25 newsstand/cover Sat.; $84.79/yr mailed in county; $107.44/yr mailed out of county. **Wire Service(s):** AP. Circulation: 6,000 evening (paid). **Owner(s):** GateHouse Media, Inc, 350 WillowBrook Office Park, Fairport, NY 14450. Telephone: 585-598-0030. FAX: 585-248-2631. **Management:** Drew Savage, Publisher. Ken Yarnovich, Advertising. Drew Savage, Advertising Director. Sandy McMillian, Circulation Manager. **Editorial:** Matt Kelsey, Managing Editor. Jeremy Banks, Sports Editor.

LARNED

TILLER & TOILER.   ISSN 0888-1189
115 W. Fifth St., Larned, KS 67550. Telephone: 620-285-3111. FAX: 620-285-6062. E-MAIL: tiller@rurallink.net. Year Established: 1879. Pub. Frequency: d. (Mon.-Fri.) Page Size: broadsheet. Subscrip. Rate: $.50 newsstand/cover; $63.78/yr. Adv. Rate: col. inch $6.85 **Wire Service(s):** AP. Circulation: 3,000 evening (paid). **Owner(s):** Star Communications, Inc., See address and contact information above. **Management:** Marshall Settle, Publisher. Dennis Martin, Advertising Manager. **Editorial:** Dennis Martin, Managing Editor.

LAWRENCE

LAWRENCE JOURNAL-WORLD, THE. 609 New Hampshire St., Lawrence, KS 66044-0888. Telephone: 785-843-1000. FAX: 785-843-1922. E-MAIL: news@lsworld.com. URL: http://www.ljworld.com. Year Established: 1891. Pub. Frequency: d. Page Size: broadsheet. Subscrip. Rate: $.50 newsstand/cover; $1.25 newsstand/cover Sun.; $35.40 carrier delivery for 3 mos.; $36.90 motor route for 3 mos.; $159.90/yr motor route; $182/yr mailed. **Wire Service(s):** AP, LAT-WAT, MCT. Circulation: 20,000 morning (paid); 20,000 Sunday (paid). **Owner(s):** World Co., 609 New Hampshire St., Lawrence, KS 66044. Telephone: 913-843-1000. FAX: 913-832-7207. **Management:** Ralph Gage, General Manager. Dolph C. Simons III, President. Dolph C. Simons Jr., Chairman. Al Bonner, Advertising Manager. Joe Lewis, Circulation Manager. **Editorial:** Bill Snead, Senior Editor. Ann Gardner, Editorial Page Editor. Mindie Paget, Feature Editor. John Taylor, News Editor. Chuck Woodling, Sports.

LEAVENWORTH

LEAVENWORTH TIMES, THE. 422 Seneca St., Leavenworth, KS 66048. Telephone: 913-682-0305. FAX: 913-682-1114. E-MAIL: ltimesed@fdcglobal.net. URL: http://www.leavenworthtimes.com. Mailing Address: PO Box 144, Leavenworth, KS 66048. Year Established: 1857. Pub. Frequency: d. (Mon.-Sat.) Page Size: broadsheet. Subscrip. Rate: $.50 newsstand/cover; $1 newsstand/cover Sat.; $115.43/yr. **Wire Service(s):** AP. Circulation: 6,500 evening (paid); 7,000 Sunday (paid). **Owner(s):** GateHouse Media, Inc, 350 WillowBrook Office Park, Fairport, NY 14450. Telephone: 585-598-0030. FAX: 585-248-2631. **Management:** David Thompson, Publisher. Meredith Timmons, Advertising Manager. Barbara Daniels, Circulation Manager. Tanya Wilder, Classified Adv. Mgr.. **Editorial:** Scott Lowder, Managing Editor. Neil Fuller, Sports Editor.

LIBERAL

SOUTHWEST DAILY TIMES.   ISSN 0745-8916
16 S. Kansas Ave., Liberal, KS 67901. Telephone: 620-624-2541. FAX: 620-624-0735. E-MAIL: editor@swdtimes.com. URL: http://www.swdtimes.com. Mailing Address: PO Box 889, Liberal, KS 67905. Year Established: 1886. Pub. Frequency: d. (Sun.-Fri.) Page Size: broadsheet. Subscrip. Rate: $.50 newsstand/cover; $1 newsstand/cover Sun.; $110/yr home delivery. **Wire Service(s):** AP. Circulation: 5,200 evening (paid); 5,400 Sunday (paid). **Owner(s):** Liberal Publishing Co. LLC, PO Box 889, Liberal, KS 67905-0889. Telephone: 316-624-2541. FAX: 316-624-0735. **Management:** Earl Watt, Publisher. Joan Jackson, Business Manager. **Editorial:** Larry Phillips, Editor.

LYONS

LYONS DAILY NEWS.   ISSN 1040-1504
210 W. Commercial, Lyons, KS 67554. Telephone: 620-257-2368. FAX: 620-257-2369. E-MAIL: news@ldn.kscoxmail.com. Mailing Address: PO Box 768, Lyons, KS 67554-0768. Year Established: 1906. Pub. Frequency: d. (Mon.-Fri.) Page Size: broadsheet. Subscrip. Rate: $.50 newsstand/cover; $54.90/yr. **Wire Service(s):** AP. Circulation: 2,300 evening (paid). **Owner(s):** Lyons Publishing Co., Inc., See address and contact information above. **Management:** Jack Krier, Publisher. Doug Kepka, Advertising Manager. Christy Gautier, Circulation Manager. **Editorial:** Shane Schneider, Editor. Melissa McLoughlin, Assistant Editor.

MANHATTAN

MANHATTAN MERCURY. 318 N Fifth St, Manhattan, KS 66505. Telephone: 785-776-8808. FAX: 785-776-8807. E-MAIL: news@themercury.com. URL: http://www.themercury.com. Mailing Address: PO Box 787, Manhattan, KS 66505. Year Established: 1884. Pub. Frequency: d. (Sun.-Fri.) Page Size: broadsheet. Subscrip. Rate: $.50 newsstand/cover; $1 newsstand/cover Sun.; $120/yr in county. **Wire Service(s):** AP, NYT, LAT-WAT. Circulation: 11,000 evening (paid); 12,000 Sunday (paid). **Owner(s):** Seaton Publishing Co., See address and contact information above. **Management:** Ned Seaton, General Manager. Edward Seaton, Publisher. Steve Stallwitz, Advertising Manager. Bryan Sandmeier, Circulation Manager. Mary Phelps, Classified Adv. Mgr.. **Editorial:** Edward Seaton, Editor-in-Chief. Bill Felber, Executive Editor. Mark Janssen, Sports Editor.

MCPHERSON

MCPHERSON SENTINEL. 301 S. Main, McPherson, KS 67460. Telephone: 620-241-2422. FAX: 620-241-2425. E-MAIL: sentinel@sbcglobal.net. URL: http://www.mcphersonsentinel.com. Mailing Address: PO Box 926, McPherson, KS 67460. Year Established: 1887. Pub. Frequency: d. (Tue.-Sat.) Page Size: broadsheet. Subscrip. Rate: $.75 newsstand/cover; $165/yr mailed. Adv. Rate: col. inch $14 Freelance Pay: $20/article. **Wire Service(s):** AP. Circulation: 3,900 evening (paid). **Owner(s):** GateHouse Media, Inc, 350 WillowBrook Office Park, Fairport, NY 14450. Telephone: 585-598-0030. FAX: 585-248-2631. **Management:** Gary Mehl, Publisher. Joni Regnier, Advertising Manager. **Editorial:** Katie Stockstill, Editor.

NEWTON

NEWTON KANSAN, THE. 121 W. Sixth St., Newton, KS 67114-0268. Telephone: 316-283-1500. FAX: 316-283-2471. E-MAIL: news@thekansan.com. URL: http://www.thekansan.com. Mailing Address: PO Box 268, Newton, KS 67114-0268. Year Established: 1872. Pub. Frequency: d. (Mon.-Sat.) Page Size: broadsheet. Subscrip. Rate: $.50 newsstand/cover; $9 for 4 wks.. **Wire Service(s):** AP. Circulation: 8,015 evening (paid). **Owner(s):** Morris Multimedia, Inc., PO Box 936, Augusta, GA 30903-0936. Telephone: 706-724-0851. **Management:** Dave Phillips, Publisher. Darla Craig, Advertising Manager. Mike Jantzi, Circulation Manager. Janice Nesser, Business Manager. **Editorial:** Chris Strunk, Managing Editor. Ken Driskill, Production Manager.

OLATHE

OLATHE NEWS, THE. 514 S Kansas Ave, Olathe, KS 66061. Telephone: 913-764-2211. FAX: 913-764-3672. E-MAIL: odn@theolathenews.com. URL: http://www.theolathenews.com. Year Established: 1861. Pub. Frequency: 2/w. Page Size: tabloid. Subscrip. Rate: $.50 newsstand/cover. **Wire Service(s):** MCT. Circulation: 25,000 morning (paid). **Owner(s):** The/McClatchy Company, 2100 Q St, Sacramento, CA 95816. Telephone: 916-321-1936. FAX: 916-321-1869. **Management:** Sarah Harrington, Advertising Manager. **Editorial:** Rick Babson, Editor.

OTTAWA

OTTAWA HERALD. 104 S. Cedar, Ottawa, KS 66067. Telephone: 785-242-4700. FAX: 785-242-9420. E-MAIL: jsharp@ottawaherald.com. URL: http://www.ottawaherald.com. Year Established: 1896. Pub. Frequency: d. (Mon.-Sat.) Page Size: broadsheet. Subscrip. Rate: $.50 newsstand/cover; $105.95/yr home delivery local; $158/yr mailed. **Wire Service(s):** AP. Circulation: 6,000 evening (paid). **Owner(s):** Kansas Newspapers LLC, One N Main St, Hutchinson, KS 67501-5229. Telephone: 620-694-5830. **Management:** Jeanny J. Sharp, President. Linda Brown, Advertising Director. Bill Grey, Circulation Director. Bill Gray, Marketing Director. **Editorial:** Jeanny J. Sharp, Editor. Gordon Billingsley, Managing Editor. John Nowak, Photo Editor. Greg Mast, Sports Editor.

PARSONS

PARSONS SUN. 220 S. 18th St., Parsons, KS 67357-0836. Telephone: 620-421-2000. FAX: 620-421-2217. E-MAIL: editor@parsonssun.com. URL: http://www.parsonssun.com. Mailing Address: PO Box 836, Parsons, KS 67357-0836. Year Established: 1871. Pub. Frequency: d. (Tue.-Sat.) Page Size: broadsheet. Subscrip. Rate: $.50 newsstand/cover; $108.51/yr carrier delivery; $108.51/yr mailed in county; $141.41/yr mailed out of county. Adv. Rate: col. inch $9.25 **Wire Service(s):** AP. Circulation: 6,200 evening (paid). **Owner(s):** Kansas Newspapers LLC, One N Main St, Hutchinson, KS 67501-5229. **Management:** Ann K. Charles, Publisher. Amy Jensen, Circulation Manager. Shanna Guiot, Business Manager. **Editorial:** Kate Thompson, Editor. Ray Nolting, Managing Editor. Brian Holderman, Photographer.

PITTSBURG

PITTSBURG MORNING SUN. 701 N. Locust St., Pittsburg, KS 66762. Telephone: 620-231-2600. FAX: 620-231-0645. URL: http://www.morningsun.net. Mailing Address: P.O. Drawer H, Pittsburg, KS 66762. Year Established: 1887. Pub. Frequency: d. Page Size: broadsheet. Subscrip. Rate: $.50 newsstand/cover; $1 newsstand/cover Sun.; $109.55/yr home delivery. **Wire Service(s):** AP. Circulation: 12,000 morning (paid); 12,000 Sunday (paid). **Owner(s):** Morris Multimedia, Inc., PO Box 936, Augusta, GA 30903. Telephone: 706-724-0851. **Management:** Stephen Wade, Publisher. Cindy Clingan, Advertising Manager. Dylan Elliot, Circulation Manager. **Editorial:** Ted Kadau, Managing Editor. Bill McMillen, News Editor. Ray Brecheisen, Photographer.

PRATT

PRATT TRIBUNE.   ISSN 1048-3675
320 S. Main St., Pratt, KS 67124. Telephone: 620-672-5511. FAX: 620-672-5514. E-MAIL: bnavarrette@pratttribune.com. URL: http://www.pratttribune.com. Mailing Address: PO Box 909, Pratt, KS 67124. Year Established: 1917. Pub. Frequency: d. (Mon.-Fri.) Page Size: broadsheet. Subscrip. Rate: $.50 newsstand/cover; $109.19/yr carrier delivery; $111.33/yr motor route in county; $101/yr mailed out of area. **Wire Service(s):** AP. Circulation: 2,700 morning (paid). **Owner(s):** GateHouse Media, Inc, 350 WillowBrook Office Park, Fairport, NY 14450. Telephone: 585-598-0030. FAX: 585-248-2631. **Management:** Keith Lippoldt, Publisher. Laurie Anderson, Advertising Manager. Leslie Barnes, Circulation Manager. **Editorial:** Conrad Easterday, Managing Editor.

SALINA

SALINA JOURNAL.   ISSN 0745-127X
333 S Fourth St, Salina, KS 67401. Telephone: 785-823-6363. FAX: 785-827-6363. URL: http://www.saljournal.com. Mailing Address: P O Box 740, Salina, KS 67402. Year Established: 1871. Pub. Frequency: d. Page Size: broadsheet. Subscrip. Rate: $.50 newsstand/cover; $1.50 newsstand/cover Sun.; $44.18 carrier delivery for 13 wks.; $50.05 motor route for 13 wks.; $51.27 mailed in state for 13 wks.; $61.44 mailed out of state for 13 wks.. Adv. Rate: col. inch $26.50 **Wire Service(s):** AP. Circulation: 30,000 morning (paid); 31,000 Sunday (paid). **Owner(s):** Kansas Newspapers LLC, One N Main St, Hutchinson, KS 67501-5229. Telephone: 620-694-5830. **Management:** Tom Bell, Publisher. Kim Norwood, Advertising Director. Bob Spessard, Circulation Director. Jackie Ryba, Human Res. Mgr.. **Editorial:** Ben Wearing, Editor. Scott Seirer, Executive Editor. Jackie Ryba, Business Editor. Tom Dorsey, Photo Editor. Bob Davidson, Sports Editor.

TOPEKA

TOPEKA CAPITAL-JOURNAL. ISSN 1067-1994
616 S.E. Jefferson St., Topeka, KS 66607. Telephone: 785-295-1111. FAX: 785-295-1261. URL: http://www.cjonline.com. Year Established: 1879. Pub. Frequency: d. Page Size: broadsheet. Subscrip. Rate: $.50 newsstand/cover; $1.50 newsstand/cover Sun.; $151/yr carrier delivery. **Wire Service(s):** AP, LAT-WAT. Circulation: 62,000 morning (paid); 64,000 Sunday (paid). **Owner(s):** Morris Multimedia, Inc., PO Box 936, Augusta, GA 30903-0936. Telephone: 706-724-0851. **Management:** David Meadows, General Manager. John Fish, Publisher. Leslie Magalios, Advertising Director. Vicky Palmer, Advertising Manager. Terri Benson, Marketing Director. **Editorial:** Will Kennedy, Executive Editor. Wayne Stewart, Managing Editor. Ed Robertson, Production Manager. Michael Hooper, Business Editor. Fred Johnson, City Editor. Mike Hall, Editorial Page Editor. Thad Alton, Photographer. Eric Turner, Sports Editor.

WELLINGTON

WELLINGTON DAILY NEWS. 113 W. Harvey St., Wellington, KS 67152-0368. Telephone: 620-326-3326. FAX: 620-326-3260. E-MAIL: wdn@idir.net. URL: http://www.wgtndailynews.com. Mailing Address: PO Box 368, Wellington, KS 67152-0368. Year Established: 1901. Pub. Frequency: d. (Mon.-Fri.) Page Size: broadsheet. Subscrip. Rate: $.50 newsstand/cover; $86.91/yr carrier delivery in city; $95.59/yr mailed in county & adj. cys.; $123.07/yr mailed elsewhere. **Wire Service(s):** AP. Circulation: 3,500 evening (paid). **Owner(s):** GateHouse Media, Inc, 350 WillowBrook Office Park, Fairport, NY 14450. Telephone: 585-598-0030. FAX: 585-248-2631. **Management:** Richard A. Horn, Publisher. Trish Word, Advertising. Terry Herl, Circulation Manager. Paula Krier, Classified Adv. Mgr.. **Editorial:** Richard A. Horn, Editor. Ryan Metzen, Sports Editor.

WICHITA

WICHITA EAGLE, THE. ISSN 1046-3127
825 Douglas, Wichita, KS 67201. Telephone: 316-268-6000. FAX: 316-268-6627. URL: http://www.kansas.com. Mailing Address: PO Box 820, Wichita, KS 67201-0820. Year Established: 1872. Pub. Frequency: d. Page Size: broadsheet. Subscrip. Rate: $.75 newsstand/cover; $2 newsstand/cover Sun.. **Wire Service(s):** AP, NYT, MCT, CNS. Circulation: 92,000 morning (paid); 155,000 Sunday (paid). **Owner(s):** The/McClatchy Company, 2100 Q St, Sacramento, CA 95816. Telephone: 916-321-1936. FAX: 916-321-1869. **Management:** Pam Siddall, Publisher. Gene Hildebrandt, Advertising Manager. **Editorial:** Sherry Chisenhall, Editor. Jean Hays, Assistant Editor.

WINFIELD

WINFIELD DAILY COURIER. ISSN 0889-6747
201 E. Ninth Ave., Winfield, KS 67156. Telephone: 620-221-1050. FAX: 620-221-1101. URL: http://www.winfieldcourier.com. Year Established: 1873. Pub. Frequency: d. (Mon.-Sat.) Page Size: tabloid. Subscrip. Rate: $.50 newsstand/cover; $77.80/yr carrier delivery in town; $97.45/yr mailed in state; $102.20/yr mailed out of state. **Wire Service(s):** AP. Circulation: 6,000 evening (paid). **Owner(s):** Winfield Publishing Co., Inc., See address and contact information above. **Management:** Lloyd Craig, General Manager. F.D. Seaton, Publisher. Marsha Wesseler, Advertising Manager. Wes Townsley, Circulation Manager. **Editorial:** Roy Graber, Managing Editor. Judith Zaccaira, Lifestyle Editor.

KENTUCKY

ASHLAND

DAILY INDEPENDENT (ASHLAND), THE. ISSN 0744-6837
224 17th St, Ashland, KY 41101. E-MAIL: mreliford@dailyindependent.com. URL: http://www.dailyindependent.com. Mailing Address: PO Box 311, Ashland, KY 41105-0311. Year Established: 1896. Pub. Frequency: d. Page Size: broadsheet. Subscrip. Rate: $.50 newsstand/cover; $1.50 newsstand/cover Sun.; $187.20/yr carrier delivery; $189.80/yr motor route. **Wire Service(s):** AP, SH. Circulation: 24,889 morning (paid); 26,933 Sunday (paid). **Owner(s):** Community Newspaper Holdings, Inc., 3500 Colonnade Pkwy., Ste. 600, Birmingham, AL 35243-2304. **Management:** Eddie Blakley, Publisher. Nikki Clay, Advertising Manager. **Editorial:** Mike Reliford, Editor. Mark Maynard, Managing Editor. Rick Greene, Sports Editor.

BOWLING GREEN

DAILY NEWS (BOWLING GREEN). 813 College St., Bowling Green, KY 42101. Telephone: 270-781-1700. FAX: 270-783-3237. E-MAIL: dnews@bgn.mindspring.com. URL: http://www.bgdailynews.com. Mailing Address: PO Box 90012, Bowling Green, KY 42102-9012. Year Established: 1854. Pub. Frequency: d. Page Size: broadsheet. Subscrip. Rate: $.50 newsstand/cover; $1.50 newsstand/cover Sun.; $145/yr home delivery local; $172.25/yr mailed in state; $188.05/yr mailed out of state. **Wire Service(s):** AP. Circulation: 21,038 evening (paid); 27,575 Sunday (paid). **Owner(s):** News Publishing LLC, See address and contact information above. **Management:** Mark VanPatten, General Manager. John B. Gaines, President. Pipes Gaines, Publisher. Kent O'Toole, Advertising Director. Troy Warren, Circulation Director. Julie Dickens, Classified Adv. Mgr.. **Editorial:** Michael Alexieff, Managing Editor. Joe Imel, Photographer. O.J. Stapleton, Sports. Aaron Flicker, Weekend Editor.

CORBIN

TIMES-TRIBUNE. 201 N. Kentucky Ave., Corbin, KY 40701. Telephone: 606-528-2464. FAX: 606-528-9850. E-MAIL: newsroom@corbintimes.com. URL: http://www.corbintimes.com. Mailing Address: PO Box 516, Corbin, KY 40702-0516. Year Established: 1892. Pub. Frequency: d. (Mon.-Sat.) Page Size: broadsheet. Subscrip. Rate: $.50 newsstand/cover; $108/yr in county & adj. cys.; $180/yr mailed in state; $216/yr mailed out of state. **Wire Service(s):** AP. Circulation: 7,000 evening (paid). **Owner(s):** Community Newspaper Holdings, Inc., 3500 Colonnade Pkwy., Ste. 600, Birmingham, AL 35243. Telephone: 205-298-7100. FAX: 205-298-7101. **Management:** Bill Hanson, Publisher. Melissa Newman, Advertising Director. Anthony DeZarn, Circulation Manager. **Editorial:** Samantha Swindler, Managing Editor. Les Dixon, Sports.

COVINGTON

KENTUCKY POST, THE. 421 Madison Ave., Covington, KY 41011. Telephone: 859-292-2600. FAX: 859-291-2525. E-MAIL: kypost@fuse.net. URL: http://www.kypost.com. Mailing Address: PO Box 2678, Covington, KY 41012-2678. Year Established: 1890. Pub. Frequency: d. (Mon.-Sat.) Page Size: broadsheet. Subscrip. Rate: $.50 newsstand/cover; $1 newsstand/cover Sat.; $9.95 home delivery/mo.. **Wire Service(s):** AP. Circulation: 38,147 evening (paid). **Owner(s):** E.W. Scripps Co., 312 Walnut St., 28th Fl., Cincinnati, OH 45202. Telephone: 513-977-3000. **Management:** Bill Hunsberger, Circulation Director. **Editorial:** Mike Philipps, Editor. Mark Neikirk, Managing Editor. Mike Kaiser, Asst. Managing Ed.. Crystal Harden, Education Editor.

DANVILLE

ADVOCATE-MESSENGER. ISSN 0889-0056
330 S. Fourth St., Danville, KY 40422. Telephone: 859-236-2551. FAX: 859-236-9566. E-MAIL: advocate@amnews.com. URL: http://www.amnews.com. Mailing Address: PO Box 149, Danville, KY 40423. Year Established: 1865. Pub. Frequency: d. (Sun.-Fri.) Page Size: broadsheet. Subscrip. Rate: $.50 newsstand/cover; $1.50 newsstand/cover Sun.; $1.65 carrier delivery Sun.; $14 carrier delivery/mo.; $154.55/yr mailed. **Wire Service(s):** AP, MCT. Circulation: 13,000 evening (paid); 13,000 Sunday (paid). **Owner(s):** Schurz Communications, Inc., 223 W. Colfax, South Bend, IN 46601. **Management:** Mary Schurz, Publisher. Mike Elliott, Advertising Manager. **Editorial:** Mary Schurz, Editor. John Nelson, Managing Editor. Clay Jackson, Photographer.

ELIZABETHTOWN

NEWS-ENTERPRISE. 408 W. Dixie Ave., Elizabethtown, KY 42701. Telephone: 270-769-2312. FAX: 270-769-6965. E-MAIL: ne@mail.the-ne.com. URL: http://www.the-ne.com. Year Established: 1974. Pub. Frequency: d. (Sun.-Fri.) Page Size: broadsheet. Subscrip. Rate: $.50 newsstand/cover; $1 newsstand/cover Sun.; $114/yr in county; $170/yr mailed elsewhere. **Wire Service(s):** AP. Circulation: 16,800 morning (paid); 19,000 Sunday (paid). **Owner(s):** Landmark Communications, Inc., 150 W. Brambleton Ave., Norfolk, VA 23510. Telephone: 757-446-2010. **Management:** Chris Ordway, Publisher. Steve Wheatley, Advertising Manager. Bill Rice, Classified Adv. Mgr.. **Editorial:** Warren Wheat, Editor. Neal Cardin, Photographer. Jeff D'Alessio, Sports.

FRANKFORT

STATE JOURNAL. 1216 Wilkinson Blvd., Frankfort, KY 40601. Telephone: 502-227-4556. FAX: 502-227-2831. URL: http://www.state-journal.com. Mailing Address: PO Box 1418, Frankfort, KY 40602. Year Established: 1902. Pub. Frequency: d. (Sun.-Fri.) Page Size: broadsheet. Subscrip. Rate: $.50 newsstand/cover; $1.25 newsstand/cover Sun.; $120/yr home delivery local; $132.50/yr mailed out of area. Circulation: 10,500 evening (paid); 12,500 Sunday (paid). **Owner(s):** Dix Communications Group, 212 E. Liberty St., Wooster, OH 44691. Telephone: 330-264-1125. **Management:** Ann Dix Maenza, Publisher. Lloyd Lynch, Advertising Manager. Rick Kuiper, Circulation Manager. **Editorial:** Carlton West, Editor. Keren Henderson, News Editor. Phil Case, Sports Editor.

GLASGOW

GLASGOW DAILY TIMES. 100 Commerce Dr., Glasgow, KY 42141. Telephone: 270-678-5171. FAX: 270-678-5052. URL: http://www.glasgowdailytimes.com. Mailing Address: PO Box 1179, Glasgow, KY 42142. Year Established: 1865. Pub. Frequency: d. (Sun.-Fri.) Page Size: broadsheet. Subscrip. Rate: $.50 newsstand/cover; $1 newsstand/cover Sun.; $99/yr home delivery local; $132/yr mailed out of county & elsewhere. Circulation: 10,200 evening (paid); 10,200 Sunday (paid). **Owner(s):** Community Newspaper Holdings, Inc., 3500 Colonnade Pkwy., Ste. 600, Birmingham, AL 35243. Telephone: 205-298-7100. FAX: 205-298-7101. **Management:** Peter Mio, Publisher. Harold Spear, Advertising Manager. Dwayne Jones, Circulation Manager. **Editorial:** Kay Harris, Managing Editor. Daniel Pike, Sports.

HARLAN

HARLAN DAILY ENTERPRISE. 1548 US Hwy 421 S, Harlan, KY 40831. Telephone: 606-573-4510. FAX: 606-573-0042. URL: http://www.harlandaily.com/. Year Established: 1901. Pub. Frequency: d. (Mon.-Sat.) Page Size: broadsheet. Subscrip. Rate: $.50 newsstand/cover; $114/yr carrier delivery; $192/yr mailed. **Wire Service(s):** AP. Circulation: 7,000 morning (paid). **Owner(s):** Heartland Publications, LLC, 20 Research Pkwy, Ste G, Old Saybrook, CT 06475. Telephone: 860-388-3470. FAX: 860-388-3490. **Management:** Pat Lay, Publisher. Wylene Miniard, Advertising Director. Brenda Howard, Circulation Manager. Christy Freeman, Classified Adv. Mgr.. **Editorial:** John Henson, Managing Editor.

HENDERSON

GLEANER, THE. 455 Klutey Park Plz., Henderson, KY 42420. Telephone: 270-827-2000. FAX: 270-827-2765. E-MAIL: gleamer@henderson.com. URL: http://www.myinky.com. Mailing Address: PO Box 4, Henderson, KY 42419. Year Established: 1884. Pub. Frequency: d. (Tue.-Sun.) Page Size: broadsheet. Subscrip. Rate: $.50 newsstand/cover; $1.75 newsstand/cover Sun.; $11.95 home delivery/mo. .. **Wire Service(s):** AP. Circulation: 11,300 morning (paid); 13,200 Sunday (paid). **Owner(s):** E.W. Scripps Co., 312 Walnut St., 28th Fl., Cincinnati, OH 45202. Telephone: 513-977-3000. FAX: 513-977-3689. **Management:** Steve Austin, Publisher. Maureen Glidewell, Advertising Manager. Lori Bush, Circulation Manager. **Editorial:** Ron Jenkins, Editor. David Dixon, Managing Editor. Judy Jenkins, Columnist. Donna Stinnett, Entertainment Editor. Frank Boyette, Political Editor.

HOPKINSVILLE

KENTUCKY NEW ERA. 1618 E. Ninth St., Hopkinsville, KY 42240. Telephone: 270-886-4444. E-MAIL: editor@kentuckynewera.com. URL: http://www.kentuckynewera.com. Mailing Address: PO Box 729, Hopkinsville, KY 42241. Year Established: 1869. Pub. Frequency: d. (Mon.-Sat.) Page Size: broadsheet. Subscrip. Rate: $.75 newsstand/cover; $1.50 newsstand/cover Sat.; $150/yr home delivery local; $180/yr mailed in state. Adv. Rate: col. inch $22.65 **Wire Service(s):** AP. Circulation: 15,500 evening (paid). **Owner(s):** Kentucky New Era, Inc., See address and contact information above. **Management:** Charles Henderson, General Manager. Taylor W. Hayes, Publisher. Ted Jatczak, Advertising Manager. George McCouch, Circulation Manager. Nancy Reece, Classified Adv. Mgr.. **Editorial:** Laura Noeth, Editor. Melanie George, Feature Editor. Joe Wilson, Sports Editor.

Dailies

LEXINGTON

LEXINGTON HERALD-LEADER. ISSN 0745-4260
100 Midland Ave, Lexington, KY 40508-1999. Telephone: 859-231-3100. FAX: 859-254-9738. URL: http://www.kentucky.com. Year Established: 1888. Pub. Frequency: d. Page Size: broadsheet. Subscrip. Rate: $.50 newsstand/cover; $1.75 Sun.; $19.95 carrier delivery/mo. local; $10.40 mailed/mo. in state; $32.99 carrier delivery/mo. local; $90 for 6 mos. for 6 mos.. Wire Service(s): AP. Circulation: 110,000 morning (paid); 135,000 Sunday (paid). Owner(s): The/McClatchy Company, 2100 Q St, Sacramento, CA 95816. Telephone: 916-321-1936. FAX: 916-321-1869. Management: Mike Johnson, Director. Tim Kelly, President. Linda Austin, Vice President. Wayne Snow, VP Advertising. Bekki Franklin, Classified Adv. Mgr.. Editorial: Linda Austin, Editor. Tom Eblen, Managing Editor. Vanessa Gallman, Editorial Page Editor.

SUN HERALD (GULFPORT), THE. 100 Midland Ave, Lexington, KY 40508-1999. E-MAIL: salondon@sunherald.com. URL: http://www.sunherald.com. Mailing Address: PO Box 15779, Sacramento, CA 95852-5779. Year Established: 1884. Pub. Frequency: d. Page Size: broadsheet. Subscrip. Rate: $.50 newsstand/cover; $1.25 newsstand/cover Sun.; $42 for 3 mos.. Wire Service(s): AP, NYT. Circulation: 53,000 morning (paid); 63,000 Sunday (paid). Owner(s): The/McClatchy Company, 2100 Q St, Sacramento, CA 95816. Telephone: 916-321-1936. FAX: 916-321-1869. Management: Ricky Mathews, Publisher. J. Crowe, Advertising. Latisha Price, Classified Adv. Mgr.. Editorial: Stan Tiner, Executive Editor.

LOUISVILLE

COURIER-JOURNAL, THE. 525 W. Broadway, Louisville, KY 40202. Telephone: 502-582-4011. FAX: 502-582-4200. URL: http://www.courier-journal.com. Mailing Address: PO Box 740031, Louisville, KY 40201-7431. Year Established: 1868. Pub. Frequency: d. Page Size: broadsheet. Subscrip. Rate: $.75 newsstand/cover (effective 2009); $1.75 newsstand/cover Sun.; $16.50 home delivery/mo.; $9 home delivery/mo. Mon.-Fri.; $8.90 carrier delivery/mo. Sun. & holidays. Wire Service(s): AP, NYT, LAT-WAT, DJNS, GNS. Circulation: 192,896 morning (paid); 268,942 Sunday (paid). Owner(s): Gannett Company, Inc., 7950 Jones Branch Dr, McLean, VA 22107. Telephone: 703-854-6000. Management: Arnold Garson, President. Edward E. Manassah, Publisher. Anna St. Charles, Advertising Director. Mike Huot, Circulation Director. Elaine Huot, Marketing Director. Editorial: Bennie L. Ivory, Executive Editor. Chris Apel, Production Manager. David Daley, Art Editor. Keith Runyon, Book Review Editor. Joel Welin, Entertainment Editor. Jean Porter, Metro Editor. Harry Bryan, Sports Editor.

MADISONVILLE

MESSENGER (MADISONVILLE), THE. 221 S. Main St., Madisonville, KY 42431. Telephone: 270-824-3300. FAX: 270-821-6855. E-MAIL: newsroom@the-messenger.com. URL: http://www.the-messenger.com. Mailing Address: PO Box 529, Madisonville, KY 42431. Year Established: 1917. Pub. Frequency: d. (Tue.-Sun.) Page Size: broadsheet. Subscrip. Rate: $.50 newsstand/cover; $1 Sun.; $119.40/yr home delivery local. Wire Service(s): AP. Circulation: 9,800 evening (paid). Owner(s): Paxton Media Group Llc, 201 S. Fourth St., Paducah, KY 42003. Telephone: 270-575-8600. FAX: 270-442-8188. Management: Tony Maddox, Publisher. Debbie Littlepage, Advertising Manager. Bill Patterson, Circulation Manager. Editorial: Tom Clinton, Executive Editor. LaMar Brian, Managing Editor. Jeff Anderson, Sports.

MAYFIELD

MAYFIELD MESSENGER. 201 N. Eight St., Mayfield, KY 42066. Telephone: 270-247-5223. FAX: 270-247-6336. E-MAIL: mayfieldmessenger@newwavecomm.com. Mailing Address: P.O. Box 709, Mayfield, KY 42066-0709. Year Established: 1900. Pub. Frequency: d. (Mon.-Sat.) Page Size: broadsheet. Subscrip. Rate: $.50 newsstand/cover; $7 home delivery/mo.. Adv. Rate: col. inch $8.30 Wire Service(s): AP. Circulation: 6,000 evening (paid). Owner(s): Messenger Messenger Corp., See address and contact information above. Management: Eric Hoffman, Publisher. Susan B Seay, Advertising Director. Mike Clark, Circulation Manager. Zina Smith, Classified Adv. Mgr.. Carolyn Williams, Business Manager. Editorial: Jim Abernathy, Editor.Readers: Mayfield & Graves County

MAYSVILLE

LEDGER-INDEPENDENT. 41-43 W. Second St., Maysville, KY 41056. Telephone: 606-564-9091. FAX: 606-564-6893. E-MAIL: ponto@ntr.net. URL: http://www.maysville-online.com. Mailing Address: PO Box 518, Maysville, KY 41056. Year Established: 1968. Pub. Frequency: d. (Mon.-Sat.) Page Size: broadsheet. Subscrip. Rate: $.50 newsstand/cover; $.75 newsstand/cover Sat.; $35.65 for 13 wks.; $135/yr. Wire Service(s): AP. Circulation: 9,400 morning (paid). Owner(s): Lee Enterprises, Inc., 201 N. Harrison St, Ste 600, Davenport, IA 52801-1924. Management: Robert Hendrickson, Publisher. Patty Moore, Advertising Manager. Marsha Fritz, Circulation Manager. Becky Striplin, Classified Adv. Mgr.. Editorial: Mary Ann Kerns, Editor. Marla Toncray, News Editor.

MIDDLESBORO

MIDDLESBORO DAILY NEWS. ISSN 1041-7095
120 N. 11th St., Middlesboro, KY 40965. Telephone: 606-248-1010. FAX: 606-248-7614. URL: http://www.middlesborodailynews.com. Mailing Address: PO Box 579, Middlesboro, KY 40965. Year Established: 1911. Pub. Frequency: d. (Mon.-Sat.) Page Size: broadsheet. Subscrip. Rate: $.50 newsstand/cover; $119/yr home delivery local; $204/yr mailed. Wire Service(s): AP. Circulation: 7,200 evening (paid). Owner(s): Heartland Publications, LLC, 20 Research Pkwy, Ste G, Old Saybrook, CT 06475. Telephone: 860-388-3470. FAX: 860-388-3490. Management: Tom Spargur, Publisher. Patricia Cheek, Advertising Director. Lisa Gray, Circulation Manager. Mary Gordon, Classified Adv. Mgr.. Editorial: Marisa Anders, Managing Editor.

MURRAY

MURRAY LEDGER & TIMES. 1001 Whitnell St., Murray, KY 42071. Telephone: 270-753-1916. FAX: 270-753-1927. E-MAIL: mlt@murrayledger.com. URL: http://www.murrayledger.com. Mailing Address: P.O. Box 1040, Murray, KY 42071-1040. Year Established: 1879. Pub. Frequency: d. (Mon.-Sat.) Page Size: broadsheet. Subscrip. Rate: $.75 newsstand/cover; $105/yr home delivery. Wire Service(s): AP. Circulation: 7,100 evening (paid). Owner(s): Murray Newspapers, Inc., See address and contact information above. Management: Alice Rouse, Publisher. Richard Lanham, Circulation Manager. Editorial: Alice Rouse, Editor-in-Chief. Eric Walker, Assignment Editor. Jo Burkeen, Lifestyle Editor. Michael Dann, Outdoor Editor. Scott Nanney, Sports. Hawkins Teague, Writer.

OWENSBORO

MESSENGER-INQUIRER. 1401 Frederica St., Owensboro, KY 42301. Telephone: 270-926-0123. FAX: 270-686-7868. URL: http://www.messenger-inquirer.com. Mailing Address: PO Box 1480, Owensboro, KY 42302-1480. Year Established: 1874. Pub. Frequency: d. Page Size: broadsheet. Subscrip. Rate: $.50 newsstand/cover; $1.75 newsstand/cover Sun.; $179.80/yr carrier delivery; $201.60/yr mailed. Wire Service(s): AP, LAT-WAT, MCT. Circulation: 31,900 morning (paid); 34,700 Sunday (paid). Owner(s): Paxton Media Group Llc, 201 S. Fourth St., Paducah, KY 42003. Telephone: 270-575-8600. FAX: 270-442-8188. Bureau(s): 603 S. Main St., Hartford, KY 42347. Telephone: 502-298-7947. FAX: 502-298-7948. Contact: John Martin, Reporter. Management: Bob Childress, Publisher. Elaine Morgan, Advertising Director. Barry Carden, Circulation Director. Kathleen Hensley, Classified Adv. Mgr.. Editorial: Bob Ashley, Editor. Karen Owen, Church Editor. Dan Heckel, Editorial Page Editor. Robert Bruck, Photo Editor. Jim Pickens, Sports.

PADUCAH

PADUCAH SUN, THE. ISSN 1050-0030
201 S. Fourth St., Paducah, KY 42003. Telephone: 270-575-8600. FAX: 270-442-8188. URL: http://www.paducahsun.com. Mailing Address: PO Box 2300, Paducah, KY 42002. Year Established: 1929. Pub. Frequency: d. Page Size: broadsheet. Subscrip. Rate: $.75 newsstand/cover; $1.75 newsstand/cover Sun.. Wire Service(s): AP, NYT. Circulation: 30,570 morning (paid); 33,042 Sunday (paid). Owner(s): Paxton Media Group Llc, See address and contact information above. Management: Fred Paxton, President. Jim Paxton, Publisher. Rachel Rainey, Advertising Manager. Matt Jones, Circulation Director. Editorial: Karl Harrison, Editor. Ron Clark, City Editor. Barkley Thieleman, Photographer. Steve Millizer, Sports.

RICHMOND

RICHMOND REGISTER. 380 Big Hill Ave., Richmond, KY 40475. Telephone: 859-623-1669. FAX: 859-623-2337. E-MAIL: publisher@richmondregister.com. URL: http://www.richmondregister.com. Mailing Address: PO Box 99, Richmond, KY 40476. Year Established: 1917. Pub. Frequency: d. Page Size: broadsheet. Subscrip. Rate: $.50 newsstand/cover; $1 newsstand/cover Sun.; $120/yr carrier delivery local. Wire Service(s): AP. Circulation: 9,700 morning (paid); 9,800 Sunday (paid). Owner(s): Community Newspaper Holdings, Inc., 3500 Colonnade Pkwy., Ste. 600, Birmingham, AL 35243-2304. Telephone: 205-298-7100. FAX: 205-298-7108. Management: Nicholas Lewis, Publisher. Sherrie Hawn, Advertising Director. Cecil Foster, Circulation Manager. Mayme Foland, Classified Adv. Mgr.. Editorial: James Todd, Editor.

SOMERSET

COMMONWEALTH JOURNAL. ISSN 0899-1839
110-112 E. Mount Vernon St., Somerset, KY 42501. Telephone: 606-678-8191. FAX: 606-679-9225. URL: http://www.somerset-kentucky.com. Mailing Address: PO Box 859, Somerset, KY 42502. Year Established: 1912. Pub. Frequency: d. (Tue.-Sun.) Page Size: broadsheet. Subscrip. Rate: $.50 newsstand/cover; $1.25 newsstand/cover Sun.; $100/yr home delivery; $176/yr mailed. Wire Service(s): AP. Circulation: 13,000 evening (paid); 15,500 Sunday (paid). Owner(s): Community Newspaper Holdings, Inc., 3500 Colonnade Pkwy., Ste. 600, Birmingham, AL 35243. Telephone: 205-298-7100. FAX: 205-298-7101. Management: Jack McNeely, Publisher. Melanie Sander, Advertising Director. Jim Gridler, Circulation Manager. Courtney Chumbley, Classified Adv. Mgr.. Editorial: Ken Shmidheiser, Editor. Steve Cornelius, Sports Editor.

WINCHESTER

WINCHESTER SUN. 20 Wall St., Winchester, KY 40392-4300. Telephone: 859-744-3123. FAX: 859-745-0638. E-MAIL: bb@winchestersun.com. URL: http://www.winchestersun.com. Mailing Address: PO Box 4300, Winchester, KY 40392-4300. Year Established: 1878. Pub. Frequency: d. (Mon.-Sat.) Page Size: broadsheet. Subscrip. Rate: $.50 newsstand/cover; $111/yr. Wire Service(s): AP. Circulation: 7,280 evening (paid). Owner(s): Winchester Sun Co., Inc., 20 Wall St., Winchester, KY 40391. Telephone: 859-744-3123. FAX: 859-745-0638. Management: George Tatman Jr., President. Jim Kroemer, Publisher. Sean Lewis, Advertising Director. Bob Martin, Circulation Manager. Editorial: Randolph Patrick, Managing Editor. Betty R. Smith, Community Editor. Jessica Griffin, Photographer. Keith Taylor, Sports Editor.

LOUISIANA

ABBEVILLE

ABBEVILLE MERIDIONAL. 318 N. Main St., Abbeville, LA 70510. Telephone: 337-893-4223. FAX: 337-898-9022. E-MAIL: merid@acadian.net. Mailing Address: PO Box 400, Abbeville, LA 70511. Year Established: 1857. Pub. Frequency: d. (Tue.-Fri. & Sun.) Page Size: broadsheet. Subscrip. Rate: $.50 newsstand/cover; $1 newsstand/cover Sun.; $74.16/yr carrier delivery; $71.88/yr mailed in parish; $87.86/yr mailed in state; $84/yr mailed out of state. Wire Service(s): AP. Circulation: 6,000 morning (paid); 5,860 Sunday (paid). Owner(s): Louisiana State Newspapers, 600 Jefferson St., Lafayette, LA 70501. Management: Kathy Cormier, General Manager. Kevin Moody, President. Cindy Nicholas, Circulation Manager. Courtney Picou, Classified Adv. Mgr.. Editorial: Gwen Broussard, Managing Editor. Charlene Lege, Education Editor. Seth Johnson, Sports Editor.

ALEXANDRIA

TOWN TALK, THE. 1201 Third St., Alexandria, LA 71301. Telephone: 318-487-6397. FAX: 318-487-2950. URL: http://www.thetowntalk.com. Mailing Address: PO Box 7558, Alexandria, LA 71306. Year Established: 1883. Pub. Frequency: d. Page Size: broadsheet. Subscrip. Rate: $.50 newsstand/cover; $1.25 newsstand/cover Sun.; $156/yr home delivery local; $162/yr mailed local; $168/yr mailed out of area. Wire Service(s): AP, SH, NYT. Circulation: 39,000 morning (paid); 43,000 Sunday (paid). Owner(s): Gannett Company, Inc., 7950 Jones Branch Dr., McLean, VA 22107-0001. Telephone: 703-854-6000. Bureau(s): Capitol Station, Baton Rouge, LA. Telephone: 504-343-2445. Management: John E. Newhouse II, Publisher. Bill Heutzler, Advertising Director. Ron Nicklas, Advertising Manager. Bill Buschmann, Classified Adv. Mgr.. Editorial: Paul R Carty, Executive Editor. Ron Grant, Opinion Editor. Leandro Huebner, Photo Editor. John Marcase, Sports Editor.

BASTROP

BASTROP DAILY ENTERPRISE. 119 E. Hickory, Bastrop, LA 71220. Telephone: 318-281-4421. FAX: 318-283-1699. E-MAIL: news@bastropenterprise.com. URL: http://www.bastropenterprise.com. Mailing Address: PO Box 311, Bastrop, LA 71221. Year Established: 1899. Pub. Frequency: d. (Tue.-Sat.) Page Size: broadsheet. Subscrip. Rate: $.50 newsstand/cover; $85/yr home delivery in parish. **Wire Service(s):** AP, LAT-WAT. Circulation: 5,000 evening (paid). **Owner(s):** GateHouse Media, Inc, 350 WillowBrook Office Park, Fairport, NY 14450. Telephone: 585-598-0030. FAX: 585-248-2631. **Management:** Jerry Pye, Publisher. Lydia Crow, Advertising Manager. Ricky Shaw, Circulation Manager. **Editorial:** Marq Mitcham, Sports Editor. Ashley Adams, Writer.

BATON ROUGE

ADVOCATE (BATON ROUGE). ISSN 1061-3978 7290 Bluebonnet Blvd, Baton Rouge, LA 70810. Telephone: 225-388-0304. URL: http://www.2theadvocate.com. Mailing Address: Box 588, Baton Rouge, LA 70821-0588. Year Established: 1842. Pub. Frequency: d. Page Size: broadsheet. **Wire Service(s):** AP, MCT. Circulation: 209,792 morning (paid); 131,939 Sunday (paid). **Owner(s):** Capital City Press, See address and contact information above. **Management:** David Manship, Publisher. Dean Banchard, Circulation Manager. **Editorial:** Milford Fryer, Managing Editor. Bobby Lamb, Business Editor. John Wirt, Entertainment Editor. Chris Baughman, Metro Editor. Butch Muir, Sports. Art Adams, Sunday Editor. Ann Price, Theatrical Editor.

BOGALUSA

DAILY NEWS (BOGALUSA), THE. 525 Ave. V, Bogalusa, LA 70427. Telephone: 985-732-2565. FAX: 985-732-4006. Mailing Address: PO Box 820, Bogalusa, LA 70429-0820. Year Established: 1927. Pub. Frequency: d. (Sun.-Fri.) Page Size: broadsheet. Subscrip. Rate: $.50 newsstand/cover; $1.25 newsstand/cover Sun.; $10.50/mo. in parish; $160/yr mailed out of state. **Wire Service(s):** UPI. Circulation: 8,000 evening (paid); 9,000 Sunday (paid). **Owner(s):** Wick Communications, 333 W. Wilcox Dr., Ste. 302, Sierra Vista, AZ 85635. Telephone: 928-458-0200. FAX: 928-458-6166. **Management:** Joe Fannin, Publisher. Linda Clements, Advertising Director. Trich Spears, Circulation Manager. Debbie Doty, Classified Adv. Mgr.. **Editorial:** Sheila Morley, Managing Editor.

DE RIDDER

BEAUREGARD DAILY NEWS. 903 W. First St., De Ridder, LA 70634. Telephone: 337-462-0616. FAX: 337-463-5347. E-MAIL: bdnews@suddenlinkmail.com. URL: http://www.deridderdailynews.com. Mailing Address: PO Box 698, De Ridder, LA 70634. Pub. Frequency: d. (Tue.-Fri. & Sun.) Page Size: broadsheet. Subscrip. Rate: $.50 newsstand/cover; $.75 newsstand/cover Sun.; $23.25 home delivery for 3 mos.; $93/yr home delivery. **Wire Service(s):** AP. Circulation: 13,800 morning (paid); 13,800 Sunday (paid). **Owner(s):** GateHouse Media, Inc, 350 WillowBrook Office Park, Fairport, NY 14450. Telephone: 585-598-0030. FAX: 585-248-2631. **Management:** Beaux Victor, General Manager. Marie Perkins, Circulation Manager. **Editorial:** William C. Wadsack, Editor. George Mahl, Sports Editor.

FRANKLIN

FRANKLIN BANNER-TRIBUNE. 115 Wilson St., Franklin, LA 70538. Telephone: 337-828-3706. FAX: 337-828-2874. E-MAIL: pub@banner-tribune.com. URL: http://www.banner-tribune.com. Mailing Address: PO Box 566, Franklin, LA 70538-0566. Year Established: 1884. Pub. Frequency: d. (Mon.-Fri.) Page Size: broadsheet. Subscrip. Rate: $.50 newsstand/cover; $65.46/yr home delivery in parish; $125.81/yr mailed. **Wire Service(s):** AP. Circulation: 4,100 evening (paid). **Owner(s):** Shirley Newspapers LLC, 1014 Front St., Morgan City, LA 70381. Telephone: 985-384-8370. **Management:** Allan R. Von Werder, Publisher. Debbie Von Werder, Advertising Manager. Opal Killingsworth, Circulation Manager. Geraldine Williams, Classified Adv. Mgr.. **Editorial:** Allan R. Von Werder, Editor. Vanessa Pritchett, Managing Editor. Michelle Baker, Lifestyle Editor. Anthony Mitchell, Sports Editor.

HAMMOND

HAMMOND DAILY STAR. ISSN 1049-3395 725 S. Morrison Blvd., Hammond, LA 70403. Telephone: 985-345-2333. FAX: 985-542-5292. E-MAIL: star@i-55.com. URL: http://www.hammondstar.com. Mailing Address: PO Box 1149, Hammond, LA 70404. Year Established: 1959. Pub. Frequency: d. (Sun.-Fri.) Page Size: broadsheet. Subscrip. Rate: $.50 newsstand/cover; $1 newsstand/cover Sun.; $10.25 carrier delivery/mo.. **Wire Service(s):** AP. Circulation: 13,200 evening (paid); 14,227 Sunday (paid). **Owner(s):** Paxton Media Group Llc, 201 S. Fourth St., Paducah, KY 42003. Telephone: 270-575-8600. FAX: 270-442-8188. **Management:** Robert Morris, Publisher. Sheery Hatfield, Advertising Manager. Gwen Hoover, Circulation Manager. Joe Davis, Business Manager. **Editorial:** Lil Mirando, Editor. Art Graziano, Production Manager.

JENNINGS

JENNINGS DAILY NEWS. 238 Market St., Jennings, LA 70546. Telephone: 337-824-3011. FAX: 337-824-3019. URL: http://www.jenningsdailynews.net. Mailing Address: PO Box 910, Jennings, LA 70546. Year Established: 1896. Pub. Frequency: d. (Tue.-Fri. & Sun.) Page Size: broadsheet. Subscrip. Rate: $.50 newsstand/cover; $1 newsstand/cover Sun.; $108/yr home delivery in parish; $126/yr mailed in parish; $132/yr mailed out of parish. Adv. Rate: col. inch $8.05 **Wire Service(s):** AP. Circulation: 6,000 evening (paid); 6,000 Sunday (paid). **Owner(s):** Newspaper Service Co., Inc., See address and contact information above. **Management:** Marc Richard, President. Donna Smith, Publisher. Christine Touchet, Advertising Director. Sandra Miller, Circulation Manager. Brenda Oliver, Classified Adv. Mgr.. **Editorial:** Jessica Richard, Editor.

LAFAYETTE

CROWLEY POST-SIGNAL. 600 Jefferson St., Lafayette, LA 70501. Telephone: 337-266-2151. E-MAIL: cpsnews@bellsouth.net. URL: http://www.crowleytoday.com. Year Established: 1974. Pub. Frequency: d. (Tue.-Fri. & Sun.) Page Size: broadsheet. Subscrip. Rate: $.50 newsstand/cover; $1.25 newsstand/cover Sun.; $90/yr home delivery in parish; $106/yr out of parish; $119/yr out of state. **Wire Service(s):** AP. Circulation: 5,225 evening (paid); 5,572 Sunday (paid). **Owner(s):** Louisiana State Newspapers, See address and contact information above. **Management:** Harold Gonzales, General Manager. Becky Lafleur, Classified Adv. Mgr.. **Editorial:** Shantelle Breaux, Editor. Pam Venissat, Lifestyle Editor.

DAILY ADVERTISER, THE. 221 Jefferson St., Lafayette, LA 70501. Telephone: 337-289-6300. FAX: 337-289-6443. URL: http://www.theadvertiser.com. Mailing Address: PO Box 3268, Lafayette, LA 70502. Year Established: 1894. Pub. Frequency: d. Page Size: broadsheet. Subscrip. Rate: $.50 newsstand/cover; $1.25 newsstand/cover Sun.; $12.95 home delivery/mo. local; $14 mailed/mo. elsewhere. Circulation: 51,000 evening (paid); 51,000 Sunday (paid). **Owner(s):** Gannett Company, Inc., 7950 Jones Branch Dr., McLean, VA 22107-0001. Telephone: 703-854-6000. **Management:** Ted Power, Publisher. Craig Hatcher, Advertising Manager. Robert Binkley, Circulation Manager. **Editorial:** Juli Metzger, Editor. Kristy Bonner, Business Editor. Marc Gilbert, City Editor.

LAKE CHARLES

AMERICAN PRESS (LAKE CHARLES). ISSN 1931-9479 4900 Hwy. 90 E., Lake Charles, LA 70615. Telephone: 337-462-1213. FAX: 337-462-1221. E-MAIL: news@americanpress.com. URL: http://www.americanpress.com. Mailing Address: PO Box 2893, Lake Charles, LA 70602-2893. Year Established: 1895. Pub. Frequency: d. Page Size: broadsheet. Subscrip. Rate: $.50 newsstand/cover; $1.25 Sun.; $11.50/mo.; $133/yr. **Wire Service(s):** AP. Circulation: 38,000 morning (paid); 43,000 Sunday (paid). **Owner(s):** Shearman Corp., PO Box 2893, Lake Charles, LA 70602. Telephone: 318-433-3000. FAX: 318-494-4010. **Bureau(s):** 108 W. First St., DeRidder, LA 70634. Telephone: 337-494-4072. FAX: 337-494-4070. Contact: Shawn Martin, Bureau Chief. **Management:** Thomas B. Shearman III, President. Connie Perkins, Advertising Manager. Jeff Helms, Circulation Manager. **Editorial:** Brett Downer, Editor. Bobby Dower, Managing Editor. Hector San Miguel, City Editor. Gail Norris, Entertainment Editor. Pamela Seal, Lifestyle Editor. Linda Young, News Editor. John Felsher, Outdoor Editor. Scooter Hobbs, Sports Editor.

LEESVILLE

LEESVILLE DAILY LEADER. ISSN 1069-3548 206 E. Texas St., Leesville, LA 71446. Telephone: 337-239-3444. FAX: 337-238-1152. E-MAIL: ldleader@worldnet.att.net. URL: http://www.leesvilledailyleader.com. Mailing Address: PO Box 619, Leesville, LA 71446. Year Established: 1870. Pub. Frequency: d. (Tue.-Fri. & Sun.) Page Size: broadsheet. Subscrip. Rate: $.50 newsstand/cover; $.75 newsstand/cover Sun.; $93/yr carrier delivery; $100/yr mailed out of parish. **Wire Service(s):** AP. Circulation: 9,000 morning (paid); 13,800 Sunday (paid). **Owner(s):** GateHouse Media, Inc, 350 WillowBrook Office Park, Fairport, NY 14450. Telephone: 585-598-0030. FAX: 585-248-2631. **Management:** Brian Trahan, Publisher. Andrea O'Connor, Advertising Manager. Judy Olandese, Circulation Manager. Kim Lopez, Classified Adv. Mgr.. **Editorial:** Will Tubbs, Sports Editor.

MINDEN

MINDEN PRESS-HERALD. 203 Gleason St., Minden, LA 71055. Telephone: 318-377-1866. FAX: 318-377-1895. URL: http://www.press-herald.com. Mailing Address: PO Box 1339, Minden, LA 71058. Year Established: 1849. Pub. Frequency: d. (Mon.-Fri.) Page Size: broadsheet. Subscrip. Rate: $.50 newsstand/cover; $9 home delivery/mo.; $54 for 6 mos.; $108/yr; $11 mailed/mo. local. Adv. Rate: col. inch $7.50 **Wire Service(s):** AP. Circulation: 6,300 evening (paid). **Owner(s):** Specht Newspapers, Inc., See address and contact information above. **Management:** Nila Johnson, General Manager. Josh Beavers, Publisher. Shelly Moesch, Advertising Director. Lou Sandlin, Circulation Manager. Stacey Vallacchi, Classified Adv. Mgr.. **Editorial:** Christy Ritchie, Community Editor. Greg Parks, Sports.

MONROE

NEWS-STAR, THE. 411 N. Fourth St., Monroe, LA 71201. Telephone: 318-322-5161. FAX: 318-362-0311. E-MAIL: newstar@linknet.net. URL: http://www.thenewsstar.com. Mailing Address: PO Box 1502, Monroe, LA 71210. Pub. Frequency: d. Page Size: broadsheet. Subscrip. Rate: $.50 newsstand/cover; $1.50 newsstand/cover Sun.; $14.35 home delivery/mo.; $172.20/yr home delivery. **Wire Service(s):** AP. Circulation: 40,000 morning (paid); 46,000 Sunday (paid). **Owner(s):** Gannett Company, Inc., 7950 Jones Branch Dr, McLean, VA 22107. Telephone: 703-854-6000. **Management:** David Petty, Publisher. Roy Heatherly, Advertising Manager. **Editorial:** Kathy Spurlock, Executive Editor. Barry Johnson, Editorial Page Editor. Margaret Croft, Photographer.

MORGAN CITY

DAILY REVIEW (MORGAN CITY), THE. 1014 Front St., Morgan City, LA 70380-0948. Telephone: 985-384-8370. FAX: 985-384-4255. E-MAIL: news@daily-review.com. URL: http://www.daily-review.com. Mailing Address: P.O. Box 948, Morgan City, LA 70381. Year Established: 1872. Pub. Frequency: d. (Mon.-Fri.) Page Size: broadsheet. Subscrip. Rate: $.50 newsstand/cover; $72.25/yr carrier delivery; $120/yr mailed out of parish. Adv. Rate: col. inch $6.65 **Wire Service(s):** AP. Circulation: 6,037 evening (paid). **Owner(s):** Morgan City Newspapers, Inc., 1014 Front St., Morgan City, LA 70381. Telephone: 985-384-8370. FAX: 985-384-4255. **Management:** Steve Shirley, Publisher. Andy Shirley, Advertising Manager. Kathy Trahan, Classified Adv. Mgr.. Andy Shirley, Associate Publisher. **Editorial:** Steve Shirley, Editor. Ted McManus, Managing Editor.

NATCHITOCHES

NATCHITOCHES TIMES. 904 Hwy. 1 S., Natchitoches, LA 71457. Telephone: 318-352-3618. FAX: 318-352-7842. E-MAIL: nattimes@worldnetla.net. URL: http://www.natchitochestimes.com. Mailing Address: PO Box 448, Natchitoches, LA 71458. Year Established: 1903. Pub. Frequency: d. (Tue.-Sat.) Page Size: broadsheet. Subscrip. Rate: $.50 newsstand/cover; $72.80/yr in county; $175/yr out of county. Adv. Rate: col. inch $9.25 Freelance Pay: $25/story. **Wire Service(s):** AP. Circulation: 8,100 evening (paid). **Owner(s):** Lovan B. & Patricia W. Thomas, See address and contact information above. **Management:** Lovan B. Thomas, Publisher. Charles Norman, Advertising Manager. Jerry Hooper, Circulation Manager. **Editorial:** Carolyn Roy, Editor. Al Guidry, Sports.

NEW IBERIA

DAILY IBERIAN, THE. 926 E. Main St., New Iberia, LA 70560. Telephone: 337-365-6773. FAX: 337-367-9640. URL: http://www.iberiannet.com. Mailing Address: PO Box 9290, New Iberia, LA 70562-9290. Year Established: 1893. Pub. Frequency: d. (Sun.-Fri.) Page Size: broadsheet. Subscrip. Rate: $.50 newsstand/cover; $1.25 newsstand/cover Sun.; $120/yr home delivery local; $228/yr mailed. **Wire Service(s):** AP. Circulation: 16,500 evening (paid); 17,000 Sunday (paid). **Owner(s):** Wick Communications, Inc., 333 W. Wilcox Dr., Ste. 302, Sierra Vista, AZ 85635. Telephone: 928-728-4488. FAX: 928-728-6090. **Management:** Will Chapman, Publisher. John Poirier, Circulation Manager. **Editorial:** Don Shoopman, Outdoor Editor. Bill Smith, Photographer. Chris Landry, Sports.

NEW ORLEANS

TIMES-PICAYUNE. ISSN 1055-3053
3800 Howard Ave., New Orleans, LA 70125. Telephone: 504-826-3279. FAX: 504-826-3007. E-MAIL: tpletters@aol.com. URL: http://www.neworleans.net. Year Established: 1837. Pub. Frequency: d. Page Size: broadsheet. Subscrip. Rate: $.50 newsstand/cover; $1.50 newsstand/cover Sun.; $11/mo.. **Wire Service(s):** AP, CNS, DJNS. **Owner(s):** Advance Publications, Inc., 950 Fingerboard Rd., Staten Island, NY 10305. Telephone: 718-981-1234. **Bureau(s):** 1101 Connecticut Ave., N.W., Washington, DC 20036-4303. Telephone: 202-785-0101. FAX: 202-296-9537. Contact: John McQuaid, Bureau Editor. **Management:** Ashton Phelps Jr., Publisher. Greg Smith, Advertising Manager. Philip Ehrhardt, Circulation Manager. **Editorial:** Jim Amoss, Editor. Peter Kovacs, Managing Editor. Robert Scott, Business Editor. Jed Horne, City Editor. Dan Shea, Copy Editor. Terri Groncle, Editorial Page Editor. Chris Bynum, Health Editor. Bob Marshall, Outdoor Editor. Doug Parker, Photo Editor. Renee Peck, Radio-TV Editor. Bruce Nolan, Religion Editor. Nell Nolan, Society Editor. David Meeks, Sports Editor. Millie Ball, Travel Editor.

OPELOUSAS

DAILY WORLD. 5367 Interstate 49 Service Rd. S., Opelousas, LA 70570. Telephone: 337-942-4971. FAX: 337-948-6572. URL: http://www.dailyworld.com. Mailing Address: PO Box 2389, Opelousas, LA 70571-2389. Year Established: 1940. Pub. Frequency: d. (Sun.-Fri.) Page Size: broadsheet. Subscrip. Rate: $.50 newsstand/cover; $1 newsstand/cover Sun.; $116.40/yr home delivery in parish; $134.40/yr mailed. **Wire Service(s):** AP, NYT. Circulation: 13,000 evening (paid); 14,500 Sunday (paid). **Owner(s):** Gannett Company, Inc., 7950 Jones Branch Dr., McLean, VA 22107-0001. Telephone: 703-854-6000. **Management:** Ted Power, President. Bobby Binkley, Classified Adv. Mgr.. **Editorial:** Emily Eschalfano, Managing Editor. Fred Herpin, Photographer. Tom Dodge, Sports Editor.

RUSTON

RUSTON DAILY LEADER. ISSN 0891-8708
212 W. Park Ave., Ruston, LA 71270. Telephone: 318-255-4353. FAX: 318-255-4006. E-MAIL: rick@rustonleader.com. URL: http://www.rustonleader.com. Year Established: 1894. Pub. Frequency: d. (Sun.-Fri.) Page Size: broadsheet. Subscrip. Rate: $.50 newsstand/cover; $1.50 newsstand/cover Sun.; $2.75 home delivery/wk.; $4 mailed/wk.. Adv. Rate: col. inch $11.90 **Wire Service(s):** AP. Circulation: 5,200 evening (paid); 5,400 Sunday (paid). **Owner(s):** Ruston Newspapers, Inc., PO Box 520, Ruston, LA 71273. Telephone: 318-255-4353. **Management:** Rick Hohlt, Publisher. Jeanie McCartney, Advertising Manager. Caskey Schexnyder, Circulation Manager. Marion Hotard, Classified Adv. Mgr.. **Editorial:** Rick Hohlt, Editor. Cody Richard, Production Manager. O.K. "Buddy" Davis, Sports Editor.Readers: Lincoln Parish

SHREVEPORT

TIMES (SHREVEPORT), THE. 222 Lake St., Shreveport, LA 71101. Telephone: 318-459-3200. FAX: 318-459-3301. E-MAIL: mcalhoun@shrevepo.gannett.com. URL: http://www.shreveport.times.com. Mailing Address: PO Box 30222, Shreveport, LA 71130-0222. Year Established: 1871. Pub. Frequency: d. Page Size: broadsheet. Subscrip. Rate: $.50 newsstand/cover; $1.50 newsstand/cover Sun.; $16.40 carrier delivery/mo.; $22.45 mailed/mo.. Freelance Pay: $35/article. **Wire Service(s):** AP, GNS. Circulation: 63,211 morning (paid); 76,193 Sunday (paid). **Owner(s):** Gannett Company, Inc., 7950 Jones Branch Dr, McLean, VA 22107. Telephone: 703-854-6000. **Management:** Larry Whitaker, Publisher. Ellison Rhodes, Circulation Director. Dewayne Gray, Production Director. **Editorial:** Alan English, Editor. Kalhie Rowell, Drama Editor. Craig Durrett, Editorial Page Editor. Margaret Martin, Fashion Editor. Kathie Rowell, Lifestyle Editor. Mike Silva, Photo Editor.

SLIDELL

SLIDELL SENTRY-NEWS. 3648 Pontchartrain Dr., Slidell, LA 70459. Telephone: 985-643-4918. FAX: 985-643-4966. E-MAIL: dsentry@bellsouth.net. URL: http://www.slidellsentry.com. Mailing Address: PO Box 910, Slidell, LA 70458. Year Established: 1965. Pub. Frequency: d. (Tue.-Sun.) Page Size: broadsheet. Subscrip. Rate: $.50 newsstand/cover; $1.25 Sun.; $101/yr; $121.28/yr mailed. **Wire Service(s):** AP. Circulation: 5,100 morning (paid and free); 26,750 Sunday (paid and free). **Owner(s):** Wick Communications, Inc., 333 W. Wilcox Dr., Ste. 302, Sierra Vista, AZ 85635. Telephone: 928-728-4488. FAX: 928-728-6090. **Management:** Terry Maddox, Publisher. Debbie Simmons, Advertising Manager. Brett Bridges, Circulation Manager. **Editorial:** Kevin Chiri, Managing Editor. Betsy Sweson, Lifestyle Editor. Pat Phillips, Radio-TV Editor.

SULPHUR

SOUTHWEST DAILY NEWS. 716 E. Napoleon St., Sulphur, LA 70663. Telephone: 337-527-7075. FAX: 337-528-3044. URL: http://www.sulphurdailynews.com. Mailing Address: PO Box 1999, Sulphur, LA 70664-1999. Year Established: 1930. Pub. Frequency: d. (Tue.-Fri. & Sun.) Page Size: broadsheet. Subscrip. Rate: $.50 newsstand/cover; $.75 newsstand/cover Sun.; $83.40/yr home delivery in parish. **Wire Service(s):** AP. Circulation: 9,000 morning (paid). **Owner(s):** GateHouse Media, Inc, 350 WillowBrook Office Park, Fairport, NY 14450. Telephone: 585-598-0030. FAX: 585-248-2631. **Management:** Lewis Cain, Publisher. Susan Peveto, Advertising Manager. **Editorial:** Carla Bastos, Editor. David Folse, Sports Editor.

MAINE

AUGUSTA

KENNEBEC JOURNAL. ISSN 0745-2039
274 Western Ave., Augusta, ME 04330. Telephone: 207-623-3811. FAX: 207-623-2220. E-MAIL: kjedit@centralmaine.com. URL: http://www.kjonline.com/. Year Established: 1975. Pub. Frequency: d. Page Size: tabloid. Subscrip. Rate: $.50 newsstand/cover; $.75 newsstand/cover Sat.; $1.25 newsstand/cover Sun.; $132.93/yr carrier delivery Sat.& Sun.. **Wire Service(s):** AP. Circulation: 5,000. **Owner(s):** Blethen Maine Newspapers, 390 Congress St., Portland, ME 04101. Telephone: 207-791-6650. **Management:** John Christie, President. Michael Hersey, Classified Adv. Mgr.. **Editorial:** David B. Offer, Executive Editor. Patricia Ammons, City Editor.

BIDDEFORD

JOURNAL TRIBUNE, THE. 457 Alford St., Biddeford, ME 04005. Telephone: 207-282-1535. FAX: 207-282-3138. E-MAIL: news@journaltribune.com. URL: http://www.journaltribune.com. Mailing Address: PO Box 627, Biddeford, ME 04005. Year Established: 1884. Pub. Frequency: d. (Mon.-Sat.) Page Size: broadsheet. Subscrip. Rate: $.50 newsstand/cover; $1 newsstand/cover Sat.; $130/yr carrier delivery; $195/yr mailed. **Wire Service(s):** AP, MCT. Circulation: 10,500 evening (paid). **Owner(s):** Beacon Press, Inc., See address and contact information above. **Management:** Chris McKenny, Publisher. Mark Wilcox, Advertising Director. Charles Osbon, Circulation Director. **Editorial:** Drew McMullin, Editor. Eric Wicklund, Feature Editor. John Swinconeck, Photographer. Al Edwards, Sports Editor.

BRUNSWICK

TIMES-RECORD (BRUNSWICK), THE. ISSN 0747-1300
3 Business Pkwy, Brunswick, ME 04011-1302. Telephone: 208-729-3311. FAX: 208-729-5728. E-MAIL: news@timesrecord.com. URL: http://www.timesrecord.com. Mailing Address: PO Box 10, Brunswick, ME 04011. Year Established: 1967. Pub. Frequency: d. (Mon.-Fri.) Page Size: broadsheet. Subscrip. Rate: $.50 newsstand/cover; $.75 newsstand/cover Fri.; $111.15/yr carrier delivery; $115.20/yr mailed in area. Adv. Rate: col. inch $12.30 **Wire Service(s):** AP. Circulation: 11,000 evening (paid). **Owner(s):** Brunswick Publishing Co., See address and contact information above. **Management:** Douglas M. Niven, Publisher. John Bamford, Advertising Director. **Editorial:** Christopher Cousins, City Editor. Jonathan White, Feature Editor. Paul Cunningham, Photo Editor. George Almasi, Sports Editor.

LEWISTON

SUN JOURNAL, THE. 104 Park St., Lewiston, ME 04243-4400. E-MAIL: editor@sunjournal.com. URL: http://www.sunjournal.com. Mailing Address: PO Box 4400, Lewiston, ME 04243-4400. Year Established: 1893. Pub. Frequency: d. Page Size: broadsheet. Subscrip. Rate: $.60 newsstand/cover; $1.75 newsstand/cover Sun.; $50 home delivery for 3 mos.; $191/yr home delivery. **Wire Service(s):** AP, MCT. Circulation: 39,500 morning (paid); 42,700 Sunday (paid). **Owner(s):** James Costello, Sr., See address and contact information above. **Management:** James Costello Sr., Publisher. Steve Costello, Advertising Manager. Marianne Ireland, Classified Adv. Mgr.. Jeff Haggerty, Promotion Manager. **Editorial:** Judy Meyer, Editorial Director. Rex Rhoades, Executive Editor. Judy Meyer, Managing Editor. David Farmer, Asst. Managing Ed.. Karen Kreworuka, City Editor. Ursula Albert, Entertainment Editor. Sue Levasseur, Local News Editor. Heather McCarthy, News Editor. Russ Dillingham, Photographer. Kalle Oakes, Sports Editor.

PORTLAND

PORTLAND PRESS HERALD. 390 Congress St., Portland, ME 04101. Telephone: 207-791-6650. FAX: 207-791-6924. E-MAIL: letters@pressherald.com. URL: http://www.portland.com. Mailing Address: PO Box 1460, Portland, ME 04104. Year Established: 1921. Pub. Frequency: d. Page Size: broadsheet. Subscrip. Rate: $.60 newsstand/cover; $1.75 newsstand/cover Sun.; $179.95/yr carrier delivery local; $334.95/yr mailed in state. **Wire Service(s):** AP. Circulation: 56,335 morning (paid); 65,516 Sunday (paid). **Owner(s):** Blethen Maine Newspapers, See address and contact information above. **Management:** Charles Cochrane, Publisher. Susan Burtchell, Advertising Director. **Editorial:** David Warren, Editor. Eric Conrad, Managing Editor. Eric Blom, Business Editor. Andrew Russell, City Editor. John Porter, Editorial Page Editor. Linda Fullerton, Feature Editor. Rick Wakely, Graphics Editor. Dieter Bradbury, Metro Editor. Andrea Nemitz, Photo Editor. Dan Dinsmore, Sports Editor.

WATERVILLE

MORNING SENTINEL (WATERVILLE). 31 Front St., Waterville, ME 04901. Telephone: 207-873-3341. FAX: 207-861-9222. URL: http://www.onlinesentinel.com. Year Established: 1904. Pub. Frequency: d. Page Size: broadsheet. Subscrip. Rate: $.50 newsstand/cover; $.75 newsstand/cover Sat.; $1.25 newsstand/cover Sun.; $129.90/yr carrier delivery local Sat. & Sun; $189.90/yr carrier delivery local. **Wire Service(s):** AP, UPI. Circulation: 22,400 morning (paid); 18,900 Sunday (paid). **Owner(s):** Blethen Maine Newspapers, PO Box 1460, Portland, ME 04104. Telephone: 207-791-6650. **Management:** John Christie, President. Mary Kee, Advertising. Cindy Stevens, Advertising Director. Dick Boyer, Circulation Director. Michael Hersey, Classified Adv. Mgr.. **Editorial:** Glenn Turner, Editor. David B. Offer, Executive Editor. Ben Sturtevant, Sports Editor.

MARYLAND

ANNAPOLIS

CAPITAL (ANNAPOLIS), THE. 2000 Capital Dr., Annapolis, MD 21401. Telephone: 410-268-5000. FAX: 410-268-4543. URL: http://www.hometownannapolis.com. Mailing Address: PO Box 911, Annapolis, MD 21404. Year Established: 1727. Pub. Frequency: d. Page Size: broadsheet. Subscrip. Rate: $.50 newsstand/cover; $1 newsstand/cover Sun.; $172.67/yr home delivery local; $117/yr mailed in state Mon.-Fri.. Adv. Rate: page $2,700 **Wire Service(s):** AP, MCT. Circulation: 48,000 evening (paid); 50,000 Sunday (paid). **Owner(s):** Capital Gazette Newspapers, Inc., See address and contact information above. **Management:** James B. Brown, Publisher. Bernie Hoff, Advertising Director. Rob Pryor, Circulation Director. Doris Burges, Circulation Manager. **Editorial:** Tom Marquardt, Executive Editor. Loretta Haring, Managing Editor. Gerry Jackson, Sports Editor.

CAMBRIDGE

DAILY BANNER. 1000 Goodwill Rd., Cambridge, MD 21613. Telephone: 410-822-3827. FAX: 410-228-6547. E-MAIL: dafb@aol.com. URL: http://www.newszap.com. Mailing Address: PO Box 580, Cambridge, MD 21613. Year Established: 1897. Pub. Frequency: d. (Mon.-Sat.) Page Size: broadsheet. Subscrip. Rate: $.50 newsstand/cover; $78/yr carrier delivery; $95/yr mailed. **Wire Service(s):** LAT-WAT. Circulation: 6,705 evening (paid). **Owner(s):** Independent Newspapers, Inc., PO Box 737, Dover, DE 19903. Telephone: 302-674-3600. FAX: 302-674-9510. **Management:** Christie Miller, Advertising. Ray Brillhorn, Circulation Manager. **Editorial:** Andy West, Managing Editor.

CUMBERLAND

CUMBERLAND TIMES-NEWS. 19 Baltimore St., Cumberland, MD 21502. Telephone: 301-722-4600. FAX: 301-722-4870. E-MAIL: timesnews@mindspring.com. URL: http://www.times-news.com. Mailing Address: PO Box 1662, Cumberland, MD 21501-1662. Year Established: 1869. Pub. Frequency: d. Page Size: broadsheet. Subscrip. Rate: $.50 newsstand/cover; $1.25 newsstand/cover Sun.; $146.85/yr home delivery local; $162.30/yr mailed in state & PA, WV, DC, VA; $181.95/yr mailed elsewhere & PA, WV, DC, VA. **Wire Service(s):** AP. Circulation: 32,991 morning (paid); 35,598 Sunday (paid). **Owner(s):** Community Newspaper Holdings, Inc., 3500 Colonnade Pkwy., Ste. 600, Birmingham, AL 35243. Telephone: 205-298-7100. **Management:** Ronald Monahan, Publisher. Stephen Stouffer, Advertising Manager. George J. Griffin, Circulation Director. Cindy Hopkins, Classified Adv. Mgr.. **Editorial:** Jan Alderton, Managing Editor. Debra Haan, Community Editor. Mike Burke, Sports.

EASTON

STAR-DEMOCRAT, THE. ISSN 1065-2345
29088 Airpark Dr., Easton, MD 21601. FAX: 410-770-4019. E-MAIL: stardem@chespub.com. URL: http://www.stardem.com. Mailing Address: PO Box 600, Easton, MD 21601. Year Established: 1799. Pub. Frequency: d. (Sun.-Fri.) Page Size: broadsheet. Subscrip. Rate: $.50 newsstand/cover; $1.25 newsstand/cover Sun.; $110.95/yr; $200/yr mailed in state; $225/yr mailed elsewhere. Adv. Rate: col. inch $18.50 **Wire Service(s):** AP. Circulation: 16,863 morning (paid); 17,123 evening (paid). **Owner(s):** Chesapeake Publishing Corp., See address and contact information above. **Management:** Larry Effingham, Publisher. **Editorial:** Denise Riley, Editor. Barbara Sauers, Managing Editor. Christy Nichols, Business Editor. Peter Howell, Music Editor. Bill Haufe, Sports Editor.

ELKTON

CECIL WHIG. ISSN 1046-2058
601 Bridge St., Elkton, MD 21922. Telephone: 410-398-3311. FAX: 410-398-4044. E-MAIL: ehoffman@chespub.com. URL: http://www.cecilwhig.com. Mailing Address: PO Box 600, Elkton, MD 21922-0429. Year Established: 1841. Pub. Frequency: d. (Mon.-Fri.) Page Size: broadsheet. Subscrip. Rate: $.50 newsstand/cover; $87.50/yr carrier delivery. Adv. Rate: col. inch $20.50 Freelance Pay: $30-$40/article. **Wire Service(s):** AP. Circulation: 17,500 morning (paid). **Owner(s):** Chesapeake Publishing Corp., 29088 Airpark Dr., Easton, MD 21601. FAX: 410-770-4012. **Management:** Jeff Mezzatesta, Publisher. Ed Hoffman, Advertising Manager. Mary Ferguson, Circulation Manager. **Editorial:** Terry Peddicord, Managing Editor. David Healy, Feature Editor.

FREDERICK

FREDERICK NEWS-POST, THE. 200 E. Patrick St., Frederick, MD 21701-5632. Telephone: 301-662-1177. FAX: 301-662-1615. E-MAIL: letters@fredericknewspost.com. URL: http://www.fredericknewspost.com. Mailing Address: PO Box 578, Frederick, MD 21705-0578. Year Established: 1883. Pub. Frequency: d. Page Size: broadsheet. Subscrip. Rate: $.50 newsstand/cover; $1.25 newsstand/cover Sun.; $117.18/yr home delivery. **Wire Service(s):** AP. Circulation: 40,762 evening (paid). **Owner(s):** Randall Family LLC, See address and contact information above. **Management:** Myron W. Randall, President. Gina Posey, Advertising Manager. Phil Ferrara, Circulation Director. Dawn Whitson, Classified Adv. Mgr.. **Editorial:** Dave Elliott, Managing Editor. Nancy Luse, Asst. Managing Ed.. Edwin Waters, Business Editor. Teresa Bell-Stockman, Entertainment Editor. Linda Gregory, Lifestyle Editor. Sam Yu, Photographer. Stan Goldberg, Sports Editor.

HAGERSTOWN

HERALD MAIL, THE. 100 Summit Ave., Hagerstown, MD 21740. Telephone: 301-733-5131. FAX: 301-714-0245. E-MAIL: news@herald-mail.com. URL: http://www.herald-mail.com. Pub. Frequency: d. Page Size: broadsheet. Subscrip. Rate: $.50 newsstand/cover; $1.50 newsstand/cover Sun.; $75.29 carrier delivery for 6 mos.; $150.58 motor route 13 mos.. **Wire Service(s):** AP, MCT. Circulation: 13,322 evening (paid). **Owner(s):** Schurz Communications, Inc., 225 W. Colfax Ave., South Bend, IN 46626. Telephone: 219-287-1001. **Management:** John League, Publisher. Scott Stavrakas, Advertising Director. Mark Kukiela, Circulation Director. Ken Garber, Classified Adv. Mgr.. **Editorial:** Terry Headlee, Executive Editor. Tony Mulieri, Managing Editor. Dave Rhodes, Business Editor. Liz Thompson, City Editor. Bob Maginnis, Editorial Page Editor. Meg Partington, Entertainment Editor. Jake Womer, Lifestyle Editor. Mark Keller, Sports Editor.

SALISBURY

DAILY TIMES (SALISBURY), THE. 115 E. Carroll St., Salisbury, MD 21801-1937. Telephone: 410-749-7171. FAX: 410-543-8736. E-MAIL: newsroom@shore.intercom.net. URL: http://www.delmarvanow.com. Mailing Address: PO Box 1937, Salisbury, MD 21802-1937. Year Established: 1886. Pub. Frequency: d. Page Size: broadsheet. Subscrip. Rate: $.50 newsstand/cover; $1.25 newsstand/cover Sun.; $2.90 carrier delivery/wk.; $2.79 mailed/wk. for DE & VA. **Wire Service(s):** AP. Circulation: 27,326 morning (paid); 31,482 Sunday (paid). **Owner(s):** Gannett Company, Inc., 7950 Jones Branch Dr, McLean, VA 22107. Telephone: 703-854-6000. **Management:** Lawrence Jock, Publisher. Barbara Gallo, Circulation Director. Phyllis Miller, Classified Adv. Mgr.. **Editorial:** Greg Bassett, Managing Editor. Erick Sahler, Assoc. Managing Ed.. Susan Parker, Editorial Page Editor. Cindy Robinson, Lifestyle Editor. Shawn Yonkers, Sports Editor.

WESTMINSTER

CARROLL COUNTY TIMES. ISSN 0746-7494
201 Railroad Ave., Westminster, MD 21157. Telephone: 410-848-4400. FAX: 410-857-8749. E-MAIL: carolcty@cct.infi.net. URL: http://www.carrollcountyonline.com. Mailing Address: PO Box 346, Westminster, MD 21158. Year Established: 1911. Pub. Frequency: d. Page Size: broadsheet. Subscrip. Rate: $.50 newsstand/cover; $1 newsstand/cover Sun.; $124.95/yr. **Wire Service(s):** AP, SH, GNS. Circulation: 23,400 morning (paid); 23,637 Sunday (paid). **Owner(s):** Landmark Community Newspapers, Inc., PO Box 549, Shelbyville, KY 40065. Telephone: 502-633-4334. **Management:** Sarah Baker, Publisher. Charles Baker, Advertising Manager. Mike Memphis, Circulation Director. **Editorial:** Jim Lee, Editor. Ellen Cornelius, Feature Editor. Bob Blubaugh, Sports Editor.

MASSACHUSETTS

ATHOL

ATHOL DAILY NEWS. 225 Exchange St., Athol, MA 01331-1000. Telephone: 978-249-3535. FAX: 978-249-9630. E-MAIL: adn@atholdailynews.com. URL: http://www.atholdailynews.com. Year Established: 1934. Pub. Frequency: d. (Mon.-Sat.) Page Size: broadsheet. Subscrip. Rate: $.50 newsstand/cover; $2.70 carrier delivery/wk.; $135/yr carrier delivery; $156/yr mailed. Adv. Rate: col. inch $6 **Wire Service(s):** AP. Circulation: 5,000 evening (paid). **Owner(s):** Athol Press, Inc., 225 Exchange St., Athol, MA 01331. Telephone: 978-249-3535. **Management:** Richard J. Chase Jr., President. Dan Mahoney, Advertising Manager. **Editorial:** Barney Cummings, Editor.

ATTLEBORO

SUN CHRONICLE, THE. ISSN 1053-7805
34 S. Main St., Attleboro, MA 02703-0600. Telephone: 508-222-7000. FAX: 508-236-0462. URL: http://www.thesunchronicle.com. Mailing Address: PO Box 600, Attleboro, MA 02703. Year Established: 1971. Pub. Frequency: d. Page Size: broadsheet. Subscrip. Rate: $.50 newsstand/cover; $1.75 newsstand/cover Sun.; $195/yr. **Wire Service(s):** AP. Circulation: 30,000 evening (paid); 30,000 Sunday (paid). **Owner(s):** United Communications Corp., 5800 Seventh Ave., Kenosha, WI 53410. Telephone: 262-657-1000. **Management:** Roy Belcher, General Manager. Oreste D'Arconte, Publisher. Paul Morrissey, Advertising Director. Arleen McGlone, Circulation Manager. **Editorial:** Michael Kirby, Editor. Craig Borges, Business Editor. Ken Ross, Feature Editor. Dale Ransom, Sports Editor.

BEVERLY

SALEM NEWS (BEVERLY). 32 Durham Rd, Beverly, MA 01915. Telephone: 978-922-1234. FAX: 978-927-4524. E-MAIL: sen@ecnnews.com. URL: http://www.salemnews.com. Year Established: 1893. Pub. Frequency: d. (Mon.-Sat.) Page Size: broadsheet. Subscrip. Rate: $.50 newsstand/cover; $39.26 local for 26 wks.. Adv. Rate: col. inch $40.97 Freelance Pay: $0.50/column-inch. **Wire Service(s):** AP. Circulation: 30,672 evening (paid). **Owner(s):** Community Newspaper Holdings, Inc., 3500 Colonnade Pkwy., Ste. 600, Birmingham, AL 35243-7017. **Management:** Al Getler, Publisher. Ed Roberts, Advertising Manager. Steven Malone, Circulation Director. **Editorial:** Karen Andreas, Editor.

BOSTON

BOSTON GLOBE, THE. ISSN 0743-1791
135 Morrissey Blvd, Boston, MA 02107. Telephone: 617-929-2000. E-MAIL: news@globe.com. URL: http://www.boston.com/globe/. Year Established: 1872. Pub. Frequency: d. Page Size: broadsheet. Subscrip. Rate: $322.40/yr. **Wire Service(s):** RN, AP, UPI, LAT-WAT. Circulation: 450,538. **Owner(s):** New York Times Company, See address and contact information above. **Editorial:** Matthew V. Storin, Editor.

BOSTON HERALD. ISSN 0738-5854
One Herald Square, Boston, MA 02106-2096. URL: http://www.bostonherald.com. Mailing Address: PO Box 55843, Boston, MA 02205-0843. Year Established: 1982. Pub. Frequency: d. Page Size: tabloid. Subscrip. Rate: $.50 newsstand/cover; $2 Sun.; $162.76/yr home delivery in zip code area; $357.24/yr mailed. **Wire Service(s):** RN, AP, SH, LAT-WAT, CNS, DJNS, GNS. Circulation: 243,696 per issue. **Owner(s):** Herald Media, Inc., See address and contact information above. **Management:** John Hoarty, VP Circulation. Scott Whelan, Advertising Manager. Joseph Lopalato, Classified Adv. Mgr.. **Editorial:** Kenneth Chandler Jr., Editor. Kevin Convey, Managing Editor. Lisa Druke, City Editor. Linda Kincaid, Entertainment Editor. Jim Mahoney, Photo Editor. Henry Hryniewicz, Sports Editor.

CHRISTIAN SCIENCE MONITOR (TREELESS EDITION) (DAILY ONLINE), THE. ISSN 1540-4617
One Norway St, Boston, MA 02115. Telephone: 617-450-7929. URL: http://www.csmonitor.com. Year Established: 2002. Pub. Frequency: d. **Owner(s):** The Christian Science Publishing Society, See address and contact information above. **Management:** Larissa O'Donnell, Advertising. **Editorial:** Mary Trammel, Editor-in-Chief. Marshall Ingwerson, Managing Editor.

BROCTON

ENTERPRISE (BROCTON), THE. ISSN 0279-4683
60 Main St., Brocton, MA 02301. Telephone: 508-586-6200. FAX: 508-747-2148. E-MAIL: newsroom@enterprisenews.com. URL: http://www.southofboston.com. Mailing Address: P.O. Box 1450, Brocton, MA 02303-1450. Year Established: 1880. Pub. Frequency: d. Page Size: broadsheet. Subscrip. Rate: $.50 newsstand/cover; $2 newsstand/cover Sun.; $3.50 carrier delivery/wk.; $45.50 carrier delivery for 13 wks.; $212.16/yr carrier delivery. **Wire Service(s):** AP, SH, LAT-WAT. Circulation: 50,000 evening (paid); 60,000 Sunday (paid). **Owner(s):** GateHouse Media, Inc, See address and contact information above. **Management:** Greg Mellis, Publisher. Kay Flores, Classified Adv. Mgr.. **Editorial:** Chazy Dowaliby, Editor. Sarah Corbitt, Editor-in-Chief.

Dailies

FALL RIVER

HERALD NEWS (FALL RIVER), THE. ISSN 1074-052X
207 Pocasset St., Fall River, MA 02722. Telephone: 508-676-8211. FAX: 508-676-2566. URL: http://www.heraldnews.com. Year Established: 1872. Pub. Frequency: d. Page Size: broadsheet. Subscrip. Rate: $.50 newsstand/cover; $1.75 newsstand/cover Sun.; $215.80/yr carrier delivery; $286/yr mailed. **Wire Service(s):** AP. Circulation: 22,000 morning (paid); 23,000 Sunday (paid). **Owner(s):** Northeast Publishing Co., See address and contact information above. **Management:** Dan Goodrich, Publisher. **Editorial:** Lisa Strattan, Editor. Linda Murphy, Managing Editor. Mike Silva, Sports Editor.

FITCHBURG

SENTINEL & ENTERPRISE. ISSN 1049-1155
808 Main St., Fitchburg, MA 01420. Telephone: 978-343-6911. FAX: 978-342-1158. E-MAIL: afrantz@medianewsgroup.com. URL: http://www.sentinelandenterprise.com. Mailing Address: PO Box 730, Fitchburg, MA 01420. Year Established: 1838. Pub. Frequency: d. Page Size: broadsheet. Subscrip. Rate: $.50 newsstand/cover; $1 newsstand/cover Sun.; $156/yr. Adv. Rate: col. inch $31.50 **Wire Service(s):** AP. Circulation: 17,596 evening (paid); 17,498 Sunday (paid). **Owner(s):** MediaNews Group, Inc., 101 W Colfax Ave, Ste 1100, Denver, CO 80202. FAX: 303-954-6320. **Management:** Chuck Owens, Publisher. Holly Conroy, Advertising. Dennis West, Circulation Manager. **Editorial:** Jeff McMenemy, Executive Editor.

FRAMINGHAM

METROWEST DAILY NEWS. 33 New York Ave., Framingham, MA 01701. Telephone: 508-626-3800. FAX: 508-626-4400. E-MAIL: mnews@cnc.com. URL: http://www.townonline.com. Year Established: 1897. Pub. Frequency: d. Page Size: broadsheet. Subscrip. Rate: $.50 newsstand/cover; $1.75 newsstand/cover Sun.; $221/yr carrier delivery. Adv. Rate: col. inch $34 **Wire Service(s):** RN, AP. Circulation: 45,871 evening (paid); 44,040 Sunday (paid). **Owner(s):** GateHouse Media, Inc, 350 WillowBrook Office Park, Fairport, NY 14450. Telephone: 585-598-0030. FAX: 585-248-2631. **Management:** Patrick J. Purcell, Publisher. Mark Olivieri, Advertising Director. **Editorial:** Joe Dwinell, Editor. Richard Lodge, Editor-in-Chief. Greg Turner, Business Editor. Nancy Olesin, Feature Editor. Art Illman, Photo Editor. Craig Larson, Sports Editor.

GARDNER

GARDNER NEWS. ISSN 0740-0837
309 Central St., Gardner, MA 01440. Telephone: 978-632-8000. FAX: 978-630-5410. E-MAIL: editorialdept@thegardnernews.com. URL: http://www.thegardnernews.com. Year Established: 1869. Pub. Frequency: d. (Mon.-Sat.) Page Size: broadsheet. Subscrip. Rate: $.60 newsstand/cover; $156/yr carrier delivery local & motor rte; $228/yr mailed. Freelance Pay: $25/story. **Wire Service(s):** AP. Circulation: 8,000 evening (paid). **Owner(s):** Gardner News, Inc., The, See address and contact information above. **Management:** Alberta Bell, President. Nicole O'Malley, Advertising Manager. **Editorial:** Stu Norwood, Editor. Andres Caamano, Business Editor. Ernie King, Photographer. Tom Trainque, Sports Editor.

GLOUCESTER

GLOUCESTER DAILY TIMES. 36 Whittemore St, Gloucester, MA 01930. Telephone: 978-283-7000. FAX: 978-282-4397. URL: http://www.gloucestertimes.com. Year Established: 1856. Pub. Frequency: d. (Mon.-Sat.) Page Size: broadsheet. Subscrip. Rate: $.50 newsstand/cover; $39 for 26 wks.. Adv. Rate: col. inch $21.28 **Wire Service(s):** AP. Circulation: 10,377 evening (paid). **Owner(s):** Community Newspaper Holdings, Inc., 3500 Colonnade Pkwy., Ste. 600, Birmingham, AL 35243-2304. Telephone: 205-298-7100. FAX: 205-298-7108. **Management:** Al Getler, Publisher. Mary Beth Callahan, Advertising Manager. Joseph Wilson, Circulation Manager. **Editorial:** Dominick Nicastro, Editor.

GREENFIELD

RECORDER (GREENFIELD), THE. 14 Hope St., Greenfield, MA 01301. Telephone: 413-772-0261. FAX: 413-774-5020. E-MAIL: news@recorder.com. URL: http://www.recorder.com. Mailing Address: PO Box 1367, Greenfield, MA 01302. Year Established: 1792. Pub. Frequency: d. (Mon.-Sat.) Page Size: broadsheet. Subscrip. Rate: $.50 newsstand/cover; $140.40/yr home delivery in area; $187.20/yr mailed. **Wire Service(s):** AP, LAT-WAT. Circulation: 20,037 morning (paid). **Owner(s):** Newspapers of New England, Inc., PO Box 1177, Concord, NH 03302. **Management:** Kay Berenson, Publisher. Rich Fahey, Advertising Manager. John Rose, Circulation Manager. Jean Martin, Classified Adv. Mgr.. **Editorial:** Tim Blagg, Editor. George Forcier, Managing Editor. Tom D'Errico, Entertainment Editor. Gary Sanderson, Sports Editor.

HYANNIS

CAPE COD TIMES. ISSN 0747-1467
319 Main St., Hyannis, MA 02601. Telephone: 508-775-1200. FAX: 508-775-7337. URL: http://www.capecodonline.com. Year Established: 1936. Pub. Frequency: d. Page Size: standard. Subscrip. Rate: $.50 newsstand/cover; $1.75 Sun.; $245.70/yr home delivery. **Wire Service(s):** AP, NYT. Circulation: 50,521 weekly (paid); 58,454 Sunday (paid). **Owner(s):** Ottaway Newspapers, Inc., PO Box 401, Campbell Hall, NY 10916. Telephone: 914-294-8181. **Management:** Peter Meyer, Publisher. Doug Burke, Advertising Director. Lisa Maiden Mabile, Advertising Manager. Robert Sypeck, Circulation Manager. Jeff Rixon, Classified Adv. Mgr.. **Editorial:** Paul Pronovost, Editor-in-Chief. Alicia Blaisdell-Bannon, Managing Editor. Stacey Meyers, Business Editor. William Mills, Editorial Page Editor. Gwenn Fuss, Food Editor. Bill O'Neill, Lifestyle Editor. Susan Moeller, News Editor.

LOWELL

LOWELL SUN. 491 Dutton St, Lowell, MA 01852. Telephone: 978-458-7100. FAX: 978-970-4600. E-MAIL: advertising@lowellsun.com. URL: http://www.lowellsun.com. Mailing Address: PO Box 1477, Lowell, MA 01853. Year Established: 1878. Pub. Frequency: d. Page Size: broadsheet. Subscrip. Rate: $.50 newsstand/cover; $1.75 newsstand/cover Sun.; $3.60 carrier delivery/wk.. Adv. Rate: col. inch $23.80 **Wire Service(s):** AP, SH, LAT-WAT, CNS. Circulation: 54,000 evening (paid); 57,000 Sunday (paid). **Owner(s):** MediaNews Group, Inc., 101 W Colfax Ave, Ste 1100, Denver, CO 80202. FAX: 303-954-6320. **Management:** Mark O'Neil, Publisher. Paul Schwabe, Advertising Director. Mark Cox, Classified Adv. Mgr.. **Editorial:** James Campanini, Editor. Cheryl Miller, Photographer. Dennis Whitton, Sports Editor.

LYNN

DAILY ITEM (LYNN), THE. ISSN 8750-8249
38 Exchange St., Lynn, MA 01901. Telephone: 781-593-7700. FAX: 781-586-1113. E-MAIL: lynnitem@shore.net. URL: http://www.thedailyitemoflynn.com. Mailing Address: PO Box 951, Lynn, MA 01901. Year Established: 1877. Pub. Frequency: d. (Mon.-Sat.) Page Size: broadsheet. Subscrip. Rate: $.50 newsstand/cover; $130/yr home delivery; $195/yr mailed. **Wire Service(s):** AP, SH, CNS. Circulation: 21,548 evening (paid). **Owner(s):** Peter H. Gamage, See address and contact information above. **Management:** Peter Gamage, Publisher. Tara Cleary, Advertising Director. Edward Odey, Circulation Manager. **Editorial:** Allan Kort, Executive Editor. Henry Collins, Managing Editor. Sean Leonard, City Editor. Owen O'Rourke, Photographer. Steve Krause, Sports Editor.

MALDEN

MALDEN EVENING NEWS. 277 Commercial St., Malden, MA 02148. Telephone: 781-321-8000. FAX: 781-321-8008. E-MAIL: editor@maldennews.com. Pub. Frequency: d. (Mon.-Fri.) Page Size: broadsheet. Subscrip. Rate: $.50 newsstand/cover; $10 home delivery/mo. local. **Wire Service(s):** UPI. Circulation: 14,000 morning (paid). **Owner(s):** Daniel Horgan, See address and contact information above. **Management:** Daniel Horgan, Publisher. James Horgan, Advertising Director. Patrick Horgan, Circulation Manager. **Editorial:** Daniel Horgan, Editor-in-Chief. Stephan Freker, Executive Editor. Kevin Maccioli, Sports.

MEDFORD DAILY MERCURY. 277 Commercial St., Malden, MA 02148. E-MAIL: editor@maldennews.com. Year Established: 1908. Pub. Frequency: d. (Mon.-Fri.) Page Size: broadsheet. Subscrip. Rate: $.50 newsstand/cover; $7.40 home delivery/mo. domestic. **Wire Service(s):** UPI. Circulation: 13,800 evening (paid). **Owner(s):** Daniel Horgan, See address and contact information above. **Management:** Daniel Horgan, Publisher. **Editorial:** Stephan Freker, Editor. Daniel Horgan, Editor-in-Chief. Dave O'Connor, Sports.

MILFORD

MILFORD DAILY NEWS, THE. 159 S. Main St., Milford, MA 01757. Telephone: 508-634-7563. FAX: 508-634-7514. E-MAIL: milford@cnc.com. URL: http://www.townonline.com. Mailing Address: PO Box 160, Milford, MA 01757. Year Established: 1887. Pub. Frequency: d. Page Size: broadsheet. Subscrip. Rate: $.50 newsstand/cover; $1.75 Sun.; $27.69 home delivery for 13 wks.. Adv. Rate: col. inch $15.60 **Wire Service(s):** AP. Circulation 15,000 evening (paid). **Owner(s):** GateHouse Media, Inc, 350 WillowBrook Office Park, Fairport, NY 14450. Telephone: 585-598-0030. FAX: 585-248-2631. **Management:** Patrick J. Purcell, Publisher. Tom Sawyer, Advertising Director. **Editorial:** Al Becker, Editor. Kevin Convey, Editor-in-Chief. David Raines, Photographer.

NEEDHAM

DAILY NEWS TRANSCRIPT. ISSN 1542-2070
254 Second Ave., Needham, MA 02494. Telephone: 781-433-8200. FAX: 781-433-8202. E-MAIL: sharon@cnc.com. URL: http://www.dailynewstranscript.com. Pub. Frequency: d. (Mon.-Fri.) Page Size: broadsheet. Subscrip. Rate: $.50 newsstand/cover; $2.55/mo.; $33.15/yr. Adv. Rate: col. inch $13.65 Circulation: 6,100 morning (paid). **Owner(s):** GateHouse Media, Inc, 350 WillowBrook Office Park, Fairport, NY 14450. Telephone: 585-598-0030. FAX: 585-248-2631. **Management:** Patrick J. Purcell, Publisher. Mark Olivieri, Advertising Director. Brian Casalinova, Circulation Manager. **Editorial:** Richard Lodge, Editor-in-Chief. Al Becker, Managing Editor. Tom Fargo, Sports.

NEW BEDFORD

C V N, THE. ISSN 0279-9219
147 Auburn St, New Bedford, MA 02740. Telephone: 508-997-2300. E-MAIL: cvn@concast.net. URL: http://www.cvntv.com. Year Established: 1980. Pub. Frequency: d. Subscrip. Rate: $.25 newsstand/cover; $15/yr in state; $30/yr elsewhere. **Owner(s):** C V N, See address and contact information above.

STANDARD-TIMES (NEW BEDFORD), THE. ISSN 0745-3574
25 Elm St., New Bedford, MA 02740. Telephone: 508-979-4497. FAX: 508-997-7852. E-MAIL: newsroom@s-t.com. URL: http://www.SouthCoastToday.com. Mailing Address: PO Box 5912, New Bedford, MA 02742. Year Established: 1932. Pub. Frequency: d. Page Size: broadsheet. Subscrip. Rate: $.50 newsstand/cover; $2 newsstand/cover Sun.; $197.60/yr local. Freelance Pay: $10-$125/article. **Wire Service(s):** AP, NYT, DJNS. Circulation: 35,223 evening (paid); 38,774 Sunday (paid). **Owner(s):** Ottaway Newspapers, Inc., PO Box 401, Campbell Hall, NY 10916. Telephone: 845-294-8181. **Management:** William T Kennedy, Publisher. Tom Biermann, Circulation Manager. Sheila Parker, Marketing Director. **Editorial:** Bob Unger, Executive Editor. Dan Rosenfeld, Managing Editor. Anne Humphrey, Feature Editor. Josh Egerman, Sports Editor.

NEWBURYPORT

DAILY NEWS OF NEWBURYPORT, THE. 23 Liberty St, Newburyport, MA 01950-2750. Telephone: 978-462-6666. FAX: 978-463-9612. URL: http://www.newburyportnews.com. Year Established: 1793. Pub. Frequency: d. (Mon.-Sat.) Page Size: broadsheet. Subscrip. Rate: $.50 newsstand/cover; $39 home delivery/mo.. Adv. Rate: col. inch $21.28 **Wire Service(s):** UPI. Circulation: 13,170 evening (paid). **Owner(s):** Community Newspaper Holdings, Inc., 3500 Colonnade Pkwy., Ste. 600, Birmingham, AL 25243. **Management:** Al Getler, Publisher. Mark Zappella, Advertising Director. **Editorial:** John Macone, Editor.

NORTH ADAMS

NORTH ADAMS TRANSCRIPT. 124 American Legion Dr, North Adams, MA 01247. Telephone: 413-663-3741. FAX: 413-662-2792. E-MAIL: natrans@bcn.net. URL: http://www.thetranscript.com. Mailing Address: P O Box 1840, North Adams, MA 01247-1840. Year Established: 1896. Pub. Frequency: d. (Mon.-Sat.) Page Size: broadsheet. Subscrip. Rate: $.50 newsstand/cover; $130.10/yr home delivery. **Wire Service(s):** AP. Circulation: 8,500 morning (paid). **Owner(s):** MediaNews Group, Inc., 101 W Colfax Ave, Ste 1100, Denver, CO 80202. FAX: 303-954-6320. **Management:** Robert Chapman, Publisher. Jack Fleishman, Circulation Manager. **Editorial:** Glenn Drohan, Editor. Tammy Daniels, Managing Editor. Ryan Holmes, Sports Editor.

NORTH ANDOVER

EAGLE TRIBUNE, THE. ISSN 1084-4708
100 Turnpike St, North Andover, MA 01845-5096. Telephone: 978-946-2000. FAX: 978-685-1588. E-MAIL: rfranks@eagletribune.com. URL: http://www.eagletribune.com. Year Established: 1868. Pub. Frequency: d. Page Size: broadsheet. Subscrip. Rate: $.50 newsstand/cover; $1.75 Sun.; $111 carrier delivery for 6 mos.; $210/yr carrier delivery. Adv. Rate: col. inch $39.83 **Wire Service(s):** AP, SH. Circulation: 43,374 evening (paid); 51,267 Sunday (paid). **Owner(s):** Community Newspaper Holdings, Inc., 3500 Colonnade Pkwy., Ste. 600, Birmingham, AL 25243. **Management:** Al Getler, Publisher. Mark Zappella, Advertising Director. Steven Malone, Circulation Director. **Editorial:** Bill Ketter, Editor.

NORTHAMPTON

DAILY HAMPSHIRE GAZETTE. ISSN 0739-3504
115 Conz St., Northampton, MA 01060. Telephone: 413-584-5000. FAX: 413-585-5299. E-MAIL: news@gazettenet.com. URL: http://www.gazettenet.com. Mailing Address: PO Box 299, Northampton, MA 01061. Year Established: 1786. Pub. Frequency: d. (Mon.-Sat.) Page Size: broadsheet. Subscrip. Rate: $.50, $.75 newsstand/cover; $128.50/yr. **Wire Service(s):** AP, LAT-WAT. Circulation: 21,400 Saturday (paid); 19,500 evening (paid). **Owner(s):** H.S. Gere & Sons, Inc., See address and contact information above. **Management:** Peter L. DeRose, Publisher. Mark Elliot, Advertising Manager. Dennis Skoglund, Circulation Manager. **Editorial:** James Foudy, Editor. Lou Groccia, Managing Editor. Laurie Loisel, City Editor. Deborah Scherban, Lifestyle Editor. Stan Moulton, Sports.

PITTSFIELD

BERKSHIRE EAGLE. ISSN 0895-8793
75 S Church St, Pittsfield, MA 01201. Telephone: 413-447-7311. FAX: 413-499-3419. E-MAIL: eagle@berkshire.net. URL: http://www.berkshireeagle.com. Mailing Address: PO Box 1171, Pittsfield, MA 01201. Year Established: 1789. Pub. Frequency: d. Page Size: broadsheet. Subscrip. Rate: $.60 newsstand/cover; $1.75 newsstand/cover Sun.; $164.20/yr carrier delivery; $247.70/yr mailed. Freelance Pay: $25-$50/article. **Wire Service(s):** AP, NYT. Circulation: 30,500 morning (paid); 34,000 Sunday (paid). **Owner(s):** MediaNews Group, Inc., 101 W Colfax Ave, Ste 1100, Denver, CO 80202. FAX: 303-954-6320. **Management:** Don Watson, Advertising Manager. James Whittingham, Circulation Manager. Robbie Brassard, Classified Adv. Mgr.. **Editorial:** David Scribner, Editor. Tim Farkas, Executive Editor. Kevin Moran, Managing Editor.

QUINCY

PATRIOT LEDGER, THE. ISSN 0889-2253
400 Crown Colony Dr., Quincy, MA 02169. Telephone: 617-786-7000. E-MAIL: info@southofboston.com. URL: http://ledger.southofboston.com. Year Established: 1837. Pub. Frequency: d. (Mon.-Sat.) Page Size: broadsheet. Subscrip. Rate: $.75 newsstand/cover; $1.25 newsstand/cover Sat.; $104 home delivery local for 26 wks.; $187.20/yr home delivery local. Freelance Pay: $25-$100/story. **Wire Service(s):** AP, NYT. Circulation: 74,500 evening (paid). **Owner(s):** GateHouse Media, Inc, 350 WillowBrook Office Park, Fairport, NY 14450. Telephone: 585-598-0030. FAX: 585-248-2631. **Management:** Patrick J DeGiso, General Manager. James Plugh, Publisher. Dawn Waterman, Circulation Director. Linda Siemers, Classified Adv. Mgr.. **Editorial:** Chazy Dowaliby, Editor. Terry Ryan, Managing Editor. Jon Chestel, Business Editor. Ken Johnson, City Editor. Lisa McMannan, Feature Editor. Earl LaChance, Sports Editor.

SOUTHBRIDGE

SOUTHBRIDGE EVENING NEWS. 25 Elm St., Southbridge, MA 01550. Telephone: 508-764-4325. FAX: 508-764-8015. URL: http://www.stonebridgepress.com. Year Established: 1923. Pub. Frequency: d. (Mon.-Fri.) Page Size: tabloid. Subscrip. Rate: $.50 newsstand/cover; $88.60/yr carrier delivery; $137.60/yr mailed in county; $169.60/yr out of county. Freelance Pay: $20/story. **Wire Service(s):** AP. Circulation: 5,400 evening (paid). **Owner(s):** Stonebridge Press, Inc., See address and contact information above. **Management:** Frank Chilinski, President. Jean Ashton, Advertising Director. Kerri Johnson, Circulation Manager. **Editorial:** Lorraine Urbanski, Editor. Brennen Cipro, Photographer. David Forbes, Sports Editor.

SPRINGFIELD

UNION-NEWS/SUNDAY REPUBLICAN. ISSN 0894-2765
1860 Main St., Springfield, MA 01102. Telephone: 413-788-1000. FAX: 413-788-1301. E-MAIL: news@union-news.com. URL: http://www.masslive.com. Mailing Address: PO Box 2350, Springfield, MA 01102-2350. Year Established: 1976. Pub. Frequency: d. Page Size: standard. Subscrip. Rate: $.50 newsstand/cover; $1.50 newsstand/cover Sun.; $234/yr. **Wire Service(s):** AP, UPI. Circulation: 95,000 morning (paid); 143,000 Sunday (paid). **Owner(s):** Advance Publications, Inc., See address and contact information above. **Management:** Larry McDermott, Publisher. Joel Morse, Advertising Director. Fred Fedesco, Circulation Director. Maureen Thorpe, Classified Adv. Mgr.. **Editorial:** Wayne E. Phaneuf, Executive Editor. Marie Grady, Managing Editor. Ken Ross, Business Editor.

TAUNTON

TAUNTON DAILY GAZETTE. 5 Cohannet St., Taunton, MA 02780. Telephone: 508-880-9000. FAX: 508-880-9049. E-MAIL: newsroom@tauntongazette.com. URL: http://www.tauntongazette.com. Mailing Address: PO Box 111, Taunton, MA 02780. Year Established: 1848. Pub. Frequency: d. Page Size: broadsheet. Subscrip. Rate: $.50 newsstand/cover; $1.25 newsstand/cover Sun.; $85.80 home delivery for 26 wks.; $171.60/yr home delivery. **Wire Service(s):** AP. Circulation: 15,570 evening (paid). **Owner(s):** Journal Register Co., 50 W State St, 12th Fl, Trenton, NJ 08608. Telephone: 609-396-2200. **Management:** Jim O'Rouke, Publisher. Jordon Tessier, Advertising. Marc Precourt, Circulation Director. **Editorial:** Dino Celeberti, Editor. Dave Brown, Managing Editor. Laurie Los, Sports Editor.

WAKEFIELD

WAKEFIELD DAILY ITEM, THE. 26 Albion St., Wakefield, MA 01880. Telephone: 781-245-0080. FAX: 781-246-0061. E-MAIL: dailyitem@aol.com. URL: http://www.wakefielditem.com. Year Established: 1894. Pub. Frequency: d. (Mon.-Fri.) Page Size: broadsheet. Subscrip. Rate: $.50 newsstand/cover; $2.75 home delivery/wk.. **Wire Service(s):** AP. Circulation: 5,000 evening (paid). **Owner(s):** Wakefield Item Co., Inc., See address and contact information above. **Management:** Glenn Dolbeare, Publisher. Phil Solmonson, Advertising Manager. Marcia Perry, Classified Adv. Mgr.. **Editorial:** Peter Rossi, Editor. Robert Burgess, Assistant Editor. Jim Southmayd, Sports Editor.

WALTHAM

DAILY NEWS TRIBUNE, THE. 738-A Main St., Waltham, MA 02451. Telephone: 781-398-8001. FAX: 781-398-8010. E-MAIL: newstribune@cnc.com. URL: http://www.dailynewstribune.com. Pub. Frequency: d. (Mon.-Fri.) Page Size: broadsheet. Subscrip. Rate: $.50 newsstand/cover; $156/yr. Adv. Rate: col. inch $13.90 Circulation: 8,500 morning (paid). **Owner(s):** GateHouse Media, Inc, 350 WillowBrook Office Park, Fairport, NY 14450. Telephone: 585-598-0030. FAX: 585-248-2631. **Management:** Kirk Davis, Publisher. Mark Olivieri, Advertising Director. Phil Ouellett, Circulation Manager. **Editorial:** Brad Spiegel, Editor. Richard Lodge, Editor-in-Chief. Greg Turner, Business Editor. Scott Souza, Sports Editor.

WESTFIELD

WESTFIELD EVENING NEWS. 64 School St., Westfield, MA 01085. Telephone: 413-562-4181. FAX: 413-562-4185. Year Established: 1932. Pub. Frequency: d. (Mon.-Sat.) Page Size: broadsheet. Subscrip. Rate: $.50 newsstand/cover; $125/yr. **Wire Service(s):** UPI. Circulation: 5,900 evening (paid). **Owner(s):** Westfield News Publishing, Inc., PO Box 930, Westfield, MA 01086-0930. Telephone: 413-562-4181. **Management:** Marie Brazee, General Manager. E. Carol Mazza, Publisher. Marty Baillaigeron, Advertising Manager. Blanche Fischer, Circulation Manager. Diane DiSanto, Classified Adv. Mgr.. **Editorial:** Dave Canton, Editor. Chris Putz, Sports.

WOBURN

DAILY TIMES CHRONICLE. One Arrow Dr., Woburn, MA 01801-2090. Telephone: 781-933-3700. FAX: 781-932-3321. E-MAIL: news@woburnonline.com. URL: http://www.homenewshere.com. Year Established: 1901. Pub. Frequency: d. (Mon.-Fri.) Page Size: broadsheet. Subscrip. Rate: $1 newsstand/cover; $3.50/wk.; $216/yr in county; $320/yr out of county. Adv. Rate: col. inch $20.60 **Wire Service(s):** AP. Circulation: 14,000 evening (paid). **Owner(s):** Haggerty Family, One Arrow Dr., Woburn, MA 01801. Telephone: 781-933-3700. FAX: 781-932-3321. **Management:** Richard Haggerty, General Manager. Peter Haggerty, President. Joel Haggerty, Office Manager. Marcia Santarpio, Advertising. Peter A Curran, Circulation Manager. Joel Haggerty, Classified Adv. Mgr.. Thomas R. Kirk, Marketing Director. **Editorial:** Jaime Haggerty, Editor. James Haggerty III, Editor-in-Chief. Gordon Vincent, News Director. Patrick Blais, Education Editor. Mark Haggerty, Lifestyle Editor. Joe Brown, Photo Editor. William F. Sullivan, Political Editor. Gordon Vincent, Science Editor. Steve Algeri, Sports Editor.

MICHIGAN

ADRIAN

DAILY TELEGRAM (ADRIAN), THE. 133 N. Winter St., Adrian, MI 49221. Telephone: 517-265-5111. FAX: 517-263-4152. E-MAIL: telegram@lenconnect.com. URL: http://www.lenconnect.com. Mailing Address: PO Box 647, Adrian, MI 49221-0647. Year Established: 1892. Pub. Frequency: d. Page Size: broadsheet. Subscrip. Rate: $.50 newsstand/cover; $1.50 newsstand/cover Sun.; $176/yr carrier delivery; $188/yr motor route; $240/yr mailed. **Wire Service(s):** AP. Circulation: 14,000 evening (paid); 15,000 Sunday (paid). **Owner(s):** GateHouse Media, Inc, 350 WillowBrook Office Park, Fairport, NY 14450. Telephone: 585-598-0030. FAX: 585-248-2631. **Management:** Paul Heidbreder, Publisher. Deb Werner, Advertising Director. Jeff Stahl, Circulation Director. **Editorial:** Mark Lenz, Editor.

ALPENA

ALPENA NEWS, THE. 130 Park Pl., Alpena, MI 49707. Telephone: 989-354-3111. FAX: 989-354-2096. E-MAIL: newsroom@theapenanews.com. URL: http://www.oweb.com/upnorth. Mailing Address: PO Box 367, Alpena, MI 49707. Year Established: 1899. Pub. Frequency: d. (Mon.-Sat.) Page Size: broadsheet. Subscrip. Rate: $.50 newsstand/cover; $.75 newsstand/cover Sat.; $130/yr in county; $172/yr in state; $189/yr out of state. Adv. Rate: col. inch $15.83 **Wire Service(s):** AP. Circulation: 12,000 evening (paid). **Owner(s):** Ogden Newspapers of Minnesota, Inc., 1500 Main St., Wheeling, WV 26003. Telephone: 304-233-0100. FAX: 304-233-0327. **Management:** William B. Speer Jr., Publisher. Mike Buck, Advertising Manager. Ken Pokorzynski, Circulation Director. **Editorial:** William B. Speer Jr., Editor. Steve Murch, Managing Editor.

ANN ARBOR

ANNARBOR.COM. 340 E. Huron St., Ann Arbor, MI 48104-1147. Telephone: 734-994-6989. FAX: 734-994-6879. E-MAIL: share@annarbor.com. URL: http://annarbor.com/. Mailing Address: PO Box 1147, Ann Arbor, MI 48106-1147. Year Established: 1835. Pub. Frequency: s-w. (Tue & Sun.) Page Size: broadsheet.Adv. Rate: col. inch $28.64 **Wire Service(s):** AP, NYT, LAT-WAT. Circulation: 58,094 evening (paid); 75,221 Sunday (paid). **Owner(s):** Advance Publications, Inc., 950 Fingerboard Rd., Staten Island, NY 10305. **Management:** David Sharp, Publisher. Joe Grech, Advertising Director. Barbara Montgomery, Advertising Manager. Fred Jahnke, Circulation Manager. James Zamberlan, Classified Adv. Mgr.. **Editorial:** Ed Petykiewicz, Editor. Mary Morgan, Business Editor. Victor Scheffner, Editorial Page Editor. Bob Needham, Entertainment Editor. Judy McGovern, Feature Editor. Tom Krisher, Metro Editor. Michael Thompson, News Editor. Bruce Shields, Photo Editor. Jim Knight, Sports Editor.

BAD AXE

HURON DAILY TRIBUNE. 211 N. Heisterman St., Bad Axe, MI 48413. Telephone: 989-269-6461. FAX: 989-269-2691. E-MAIL: vicki@hdtinfo.com. URL: http://www.michiganstthumb.com. Year Established: 1876. Pub. Frequency: d. (Sun.-Fri.) Page Size: broadsheet. Subscrip. Rate: $.50 newsstand/cover; $1.25 newsstand/cover Sun.; $115.20/yr carrier delivery; $115.20/yr motor route; $141.12/yr mailed in county. **Wire Service(s):** AP. Circulation: 9,000 evening (paid); 18,000 Sunday (paid). **Owner(s):** Hearst Corp., 959 Eighth Ave, New York, NY 10019. **Management:** Vicki Yaroch, Advertising Director. Jan Stoeckle, Circulation Director. **Editorial:** Kelly Niebel, Editor. Mike Bogan, Sports Editor.

BALDWIN

PIONEER (BALDWIN), THE. ISSN 8750-5533
851 Michigan Ave., Baldwin, MI 49304. Telephone: 231-745-4635. FAX: 231-745-7733. E-MAIL: info@pioneergroup.net. URL: http://www.pioneergroup.net. Year Established: 1862. Pub. Frequency: d. (Mon.-Sat.) Page Size: broadsheet. Subscrip. Rate: $.50 newsstand/cover; $.75 newsstand/cover Sat.; $137.50/yr in county; $164.50/yr out of county; $213.20/yr out of state. **Wire Service(s):** AP, UPI. Circulation: 6,000 morning (paid). **Owner(s):** The Pioneer Group, See address and contact information above. **Management:** John A. Batdorff Sr., President. John Norton, Publisher. Sharon Frederick, Advertising Manager. Sue Vellanti, Circulation Manager. Sharon Doxsee, Business Manager. **Editorial:** Judy Hale, Managing Editor. Juanita Decater, Production Manager.

BATTLE CREEK

BATTLE CREEK ENQUIRER. 155 W. Van Buren St., Battle Creek, MI 49017. Telephone: 269-964-7161. FAX: 269-964-0299. E-MAIL: getpublished@battlecreekenquirer.com. URL: http://www.battlecreekenquirer.com. Year Established: 1900. Pub. Frequency: d. Page Size: broadsheet. Subscrip. Rate: $.50 newsstand/cover; $1.50 newsstand/cover Sun.; $3.25 carrier delivery/wk. local; $3.50 motor route/wk. out of area. **Wire Service(s):** AP, GNS. Circulation: 22,000 morning (paid); 28,000 Sunday (paid). **Owner(s):** Gannett Company, Inc., 7950 Jones Branch Dr., McLean, VA 22107-0001. Telephone: 703-854-6000. **Management:** Lesa Nye Sr., Advertising Manager. Merrie Shina, Circulation Director. Karen Burns, Human Res. Mgr.. **Editorial:** Eric Greene, Local News Editor. Bill Broderick, Sports Editor.

BAY CITY

BAY CITY TIMES, THE. 311 Fifth St., Bay City, MI 48708-5853. Telephone: 989-895-8551. FAX: 989-893-0649. E-MAIL: newsroom@bc-times.com. URL: http://www.mlive.com/bctimes/. Year Established: 1873. Pub. Frequency: d. Page Size: broadsheet. Subscrip. Rate: $.50 newsstand/cover; $1.50 newsstand/cover Sun.; $144/yr home delivery; $150/yr mailed. **Wire Service(s):** AP, NYT. Circulation: 37,373 morning (paid); 48,354 Sunday (paid). **Owner(s):** Advance Publications, Inc., 950 Fingerboard Rd., Staten Island, NY 10305. Telephone: 718-981-1234. FAX: 718-981-1456. **Management:** Kevin Dykema, Publisher. Cynthia Orr, Advertising Director. Mike Krygier, Circulation Manager. Denise Taglauer, Classified Adv. Mgr.. **Editorial:** Tony Dearing, Editor. Clark Huges, Editorial Page Editor. John Hiner, Metro Editor. David Vizard, News Editor. Mike Randolph, Photo Editor. Bruce Gunther, Sports Editor.

CADILLAC

CADILLAC EVENING NEWS. ISSN 0745-3655
130 N. Mitchell St., Cadillac, MI 49601-0640. Telephone: 231-775-6565. FAX: 231-775-8790. E-MAIL: customerservice@cadillacnews.com. URL: http://www.cadillacnews.com. Mailing Address: PO Box 640, Cadillac, MI 49602-0640. Year Established: 1872. Pub. Frequency: d. (Mon.-Sat.) Page Size: broadsheet. Subscrip. Rate: $.50 newsstand/cover; $1 newsstand/cover Sat.; $128/yr. **Wire Service(s):** AP, LAT-WAT, MCT. Circulation: 12,000 morning (paid). **Owner(s):** Chris Huckle, See address and contact information above. **Management:** Chris Huckle, Publisher. Charity England, Advertising. Tom Aldrich, Circulation Manager. Ronald Belleville, Business Manager. **Editorial:** Matt Seward, Managing Editor.

CHEBOYGAN

CHEBOYGAN DAILY TRIBUNE. ISSN 0746-665X
308 N. Main St., Cheboygan, MI 49721. Telephone: 231-627-7144. FAX: 231-627-5331. URL: http://www.cheboygannews.com. Year Established: 1875. Pub. Frequency: d. (Mon.-Fri.) Page Size: broadsheet. Subscrip. Rate: $.75 newsstand/cover; $140/yr home delivery local; $170/yr mailed out of area. Adv. Rate: col. inch $10.70 **Wire Service(s):** UPI. Circulation: 5,500 morning (paid). **Owner(s):** GateHouse Media, Inc, 350 WillowBrook Office Park, Fairport, NY 14450. Telephone: 585-598-0030. FAX: 585-248-2631. **Management:** Valerie Rose, Publisher. Nancy Kidder, Advertising Manager. Mary Whaley, Circulation Manager. Laurel Taylor, Classified Adv. Mgr.. **Editorial:** Rich Adams, Editor.

COLDWATER

DAILY REPORTER (COLDWATER), THE. ISSN 0745-6794
15 W. Pearl St., Coldwater, MI 49036. Telephone: 517-278-2318. FAX: 517-278-6041. E-MAIL: editor@thedailyreporter.com. URL: http://www.thedailyreporter.com. Year Established: 1896. Pub. Frequency: d. (Mon.-Sat.) Page Size: broadsheet. Subscrip. Rate: $.75 newsstand/cover; $111.30/yr carrier delivery; $120/yr motor route; $180/yr mailed. Freelance Pay: $0.60/column-inch. **Wire Service(s):** AP. Circulation: 6,000 morning (paid). **Owner(s):** GateHouse Media, Inc, 350 WillowBrook Office Park, Fairport, NY 14450. Telephone: 585-598-0030. FAX: 585-248-2631. **Management:** David Ferro, Publisher. Craig Sowers, Circulation Manager. **Editorial:** Heather Jeffrey, Executive Editor. James Fisher, Sports Editor.

DETROIT

DETROIT FREE PRESS. ISSN 1055-2758
600 W Fort St, Detroit, MI 48226. Telephone: 313-222-6400. FAX: 313-222-5981. URL: http://www.freep.com. Year Established: 1858. Pub. Frequency: d. Subscrip. Rate: $234/yr home delivery; $520/yr mailed in state. **Owner(s):** Detroit Free Press, Inc., See address and contact information above. **Management:** Mark Silverman, Publisher. Randall Brant, Advertising Director. **Editorial:** Carole Leigh Hutton, Managing Editor.

DETROIT NEWS. ISSN 1055-2715
615 W Lafayette, Detroit, MI 48226. Telephone: 313-222-2300. FAX: 313-222-2335. E-MAIL: metro@detnews.com. URL: http://www.detnews.com. Pub. Frequency: d. Page Size: broadsheet. Subscrip. Rate: $.35 newsstand/cover; $1.75 newsstand/cover Sun.; $156/yr home delivery; $520/yr mailed in state; $556.40/yr mailed out of state. **Wire Service(s):** AP, UPI, NYT, DJNS. Circulation: 232,434 evening (paid); 758,913 Sunday (paid). **Owner(s):** MediaNews Group, Inc., 101 W Colfax Ave, Ste 1100, Denver, CO 80202. FAX: 303-954-6320. **Management:** Jonathan Wolman, Publisher. Randall Brant, Advertising Director. Ed Humphrey, Circulation Director. **Editorial:** Jonathan Wolman, Editor. Ruben Luna, Sports Editor.

ESCANABA

DAILY PRESS (ESCANABA), THE. 600 Lundington St., Escanaba, MI 49829. Telephone: 906-786-2021. FAX: 906-786-9006. E-MAIL: mscott@dailypress.net. URL: http://www.dailypress.net. Mailing Address: PO Box 828, Escanaba, MI 49824. Pub. Frequency: d. (Mon.-Sat.) Page Size: broadsheet. Subscrip. Rate: $.50 newsstand/cover; $.75 newsstand/cover Sat.; $161.70/yr home delivery; $176.35/yr mailed in state. Adv. Rate: col. inch $17.97 Circulation: 13,000 evening (paid). **Owner(s):** Ogden Newspapers of Minnesota, Inc., 19260 San Carlos Blvd., Fort Myers Beach, FL 33931. Telephone: 239-463-4421. **Management:** Michael Scott, Publisher. Ann Troutman, Advertising Director. Dennis Bowen, Circulation Manager. **Editorial:** Rick Rudden, Editor. Brian Rowell, Managing Editor.

FLINT

FLINT JOURNAL, THE. 200 E. First St., Flint, MI 48502-1925. Telephone: 810-766-6100. FAX: 810-767-7518. E-MAIL: fj@flintjournal.com. URL: http://www.flintjournal.com. Year Established: 1876. Pub. Frequency: d. Page Size: broadsheet. Subscrip. Rate: $.50 newsstand/cover; $1.50 Sun.; $11.49 carrier delivery/mo.; $12.49 motor route/mo.. Adv. Rate: col. inch $57.12 **Wire Service(s):** AP, NYT, LAT-WAT. Circulation: 84,848 evening (paid); 102,394 Sunday (paid). **Owner(s):** Advance Publications, Inc., See address and contact information above. **Management:** David Sharp, Publisher. Thomas Eason, Advertising Director. Sam Harris, Circulation Director. Jerry Carlson, Circulation Manager. Tammy Reaves, Classified Adv. Mgr.. **Editorial:** Paul Keep, Editor. Brooke Rausch, Managing Editor. Carl Stoddard, Business Editor. Cookie Wascha, Feature Editor. Brian Masck, Photographer. Howard Thomas, Sports Editor.

GRAND HAVEN

GRAND HAVEN TRIBUNE. 101 N. Third St., Grand Haven, MI 49417. Telephone: 616-842-6400. FAX: 616-842-9584. URL: http://www.grandhaventribune.com. Year Established: 1885. Pub. Frequency: d. (Mon.-Sat.) Page Size: broadsheet. Subscrip. Rate: $.50 newsstand/cover; $28.60 carrier delivery local for 3 mos.; $29.90 motor route local for 3 mos.; $33 motor route in county for 3 mos.. **Wire Service(s):** AP. Circulation: 10,500 morning (paid). **Owner(s):** Grand Haven Publishing Corp., See address and contact information above. **Management:** Paul Bedient, Publisher. Rob Francis, Advertising Director. Ken Metzdorf, Circulation Manager. **Editorial:** Len Painter, Managing Editor. Becky Vargo, News Editor. Andy Loree, Photographer. Matt DeYoung, Sports Editor.

GRAND RAPIDS

GRAND RAPIDS PRESS, THE. 155 Michigan St., N.W., Grand Rapids, MI 49503. Telephone: 616-222-5400. FAX: 616-222-5409. URL: http://www.gr.mlive.com. Year Established: 1892. Pub. Frequency: d. Page Size: broadsheet. Subscrip. Rate: $.50 newsstand/cover; $1.75 newsstand/cover Sun.; $10 carrier delivery/mo.; $24.50 mailed/mo.. Adv. Rate: col. inch $62.10 **Wire Service(s):** AP, NYT. Circulation: 138,818 evening (paid); 191,518 Sunday (paid). **Owner(s):** Advance Publications, Inc., See address and contact information above. **Bureau(s):** 209 E. Eighth St., Holland, MI 49423. Telephone: 616-396-0353. FAX: 616-396-6429. Contact: Julie Hoogland, Bureau Chief. **Management:** Danny R. Gaydou, Publisher. Steven Westphal, Advertising Director. Martha Heins, Circulation Director. Michelle Covington, Classified Adv. Mgr.. **Editorial:** Michael Lloyd, Editor.

GREENVILLE

DAILY NEWS (GREENVILLE). ISSN 0899-6342
109 N. Lafayette St., Greenville, MI 48838. Telephone: 616-754-9301. FAX: 616-754-8559. URL: http://www.thedailynews.cc. Year Established: 1856. Pub. Frequency: d. (Mon.-Sat.) Page Size: broadsheet. Subscrip. Rate: $.50 newsstand/cover; $.75 newsstand/cover Sat.; $144/yr. **Wire Service(s):** AP. Circulation: 10,232 evening (paid). **Owner(s):** Rob Stafford, See address and contact information above. **Management:** John Frizzo, General Manager. Rob Stafford, President. Carol Pettengill, Circulation Manager. Kim Mathewson, Classified Adv. Mgr.. **Editorial:** John Frizzo, Editor. Darrin Clark, News Editor. John Raffel, Sports Editor.

HILLSDALE

HILLSDALE DAILY NEWS. 33 McCollum St, Hillsdale, MI 49242-1630. Telephone: 517-437-7351. FAX: 517-437-3963. E-MAIL: jwest@hillsdale.net. URL: http://www.hillsdale.net. Mailing Address: PO Box 287, Hillsdale, MI 49242-0287. Year Established: 1909. Pub. Frequency: d. (Mon.-Sat.) Page Size: broadsheet. Subscrip. Rate: $.50 newsstand/cover; $24.70 mailed for 3 mos.; $47.88 mailed for 6 mos.; $90.72/yr mailed. **Wire Service(s):** AP. Circulation: 8,100 evening (paid and free). **Owner(s):** Morris Multimedia, Inc., PO Box 936, Augusta, GA 30903. Telephone: 706-724-0851. **Management:** Kim Benedict, Publisher. Marleana McGraw, Advertising Manager. Cyndi Armstrong, Circulation Manager. Becky Hill, Sales Manager. Loann Godrey, Business Manager. **Editorial:** Jim Pruitt, Managing Editor. David Stanfield, Photographer.

HOLLAND

HOLLAND SENTINEL, THE. ISSN 1050-4044
54 W. Eighth St., Holland, MI 49423. Telephone: 616-392-2311. FAX: 616-392-3526. E-MAIL: hlldsntnl@sentinelnet.com. URL: http://www.thehollandsentinel.net. Year Established: 1896. Pub. Frequency: d. Page Size: broadsheet. Subscrip. Rate: $.50 newsstand/cover; $1.50 newsstand/cover Sun.; $45/yr. **Wire Service(s):** AP. Circulation: 20,000 morning (paid); 20,000 Sunday (paid). **Owner(s):** Morris Multimedia, Inc., PO Box 936, Augusta, GA 30903. Telephone: 706-724-0851. **Management:** Mike Hengel, Publisher. Steve Kenemer, Operations Manager. Barry Neal, Advertising Director. Janet Johnson, Classified Adv. Mgr.. Sharla Vander Yacht, Sales Manager. Christina Smith, Business Manager. **Editorial:** Jim Timmerman, Managing Editor. Randy Benson, City Editor. Jim Hayden, News Editor. Alan Babbitt, Sports Editor.

HOUGHTON

DAILY MINING GAZETTE. 206 Shelden Ave., Houghton, MI 49931. Telephone: 906-482-1500. FAX: 906-482-2726. E-MAIL: gazette@upgroup.com. URL: http://www.mininggazette.com. Mailing Address: PO Box 368, Houghton, MI 49931. Year Established: 1858. Pub. Frequency: d. (Mon.-Sat.) Page Size: broadsheet. Subscrip. Rate: $.50 newsstand/cover; $2.54 carrier delivery/wk.; $11 motor route/mo.. **Wire Service(s):** AP. Circulation: 12,000 evening (paid). **Owner(s):** Ogden Newspapers of Minnesota, Inc., 19260 San Carlos Blvd., Fort Myers Beach, FL 33931. Telephone: 239-463-4421. **Management:** John Elchert, General Manager. Mary Jo Stimac, Advertising Manager. **Editorial:** Bud Sargent, Managing Editor. Mary Ann Cancilla, Feature Editor. Nancy Barny, News Editor. Michele Jokinen, Photo Editor. Barry Happala, Sports Editor.

HOWELL

LIVINGSTON COUNTY DAILY PRESS & ARGUS. 323 E Grand River Ave, Howell, MI 48843. Telephone: 517-548-2000. FAX: 517-548-3005. URL: http://www.htnews.com. Mailing Address: PO Box 230, Howell, MI 48843-0230. Year Established: 2001. Pub. Frequency: d. (Sun.-Fri.) Page Size: broadsheet. Subscrip. Rate: $.50 newsstand/cover; $1 Sun.; $104/yr in county; $182/yr out of county. Circulation: 18,000 per issue (paid). **Owner(s):** Gannett Company, Inc., 7950 Jones Branch Dr., McLean, VA 22107-0001. Telephone: 703-853-4600. **Management:** Rich Perlberg, General Manager. Grace Perry, Advertising Director. Mary Scott, Circulation Manager. **Editorial:** Rich Perlberg, Executive Editor. Maria Stuart, Managing Editor. Mike Malott, News Editor.

IONIA

IONIA SENTINEL-STANDARD. ISSN 0745-2128
114 N. Depot St, Ionia, MI 48846. Telephone: 616-527-2100. FAX: 616-527-6860. E-MAIL: newsroom@sentinel-standard.com. URL: http://www.sentinel-standard.com. Year Established: 1866. Pub. Frequency: d. (Tue.-Sat.) Page Size: broadsheet. Subscrip. Rate: $.50 newsstand/cover; $99/yr in county; $120/yr out of county. **Wire Service(s):** AP. Circulation: 3,200 morning (paid); 25,000 Sunday (paid). **Owner(s):** GateHouse Media, Inc, 350 WillowBrook Office Park, Fairport, NY 14450. **Management:** Cindy Conrad, Publisher. Vicki Jockeck, Circulation Manager. **Editorial:** Amanda Cairo, Editor.

IRON MOUNTAIN

DAILY NEWS (IRON MOUNTAIN). 215 E. Ludington St., Iron Mountain, MI 49801. Telephone: 906-774-2772. FAX: 906-774-7660. E-MAIL: news@ironmountain.com. URL: http://www.ironmountaindailynews.com. Mailing Address: PO Box 460, Iron Mountain, MI 49801. Year Established: 1921. Pub. Frequency: d. (Mon.-Sat.) Page Size: broadsheet. Subscrip. Rate: $.50 newsstand/cover; $151.40/yr home delivery; $158.20/yr motor route; $16.60 mailed/mo. in state area. **Wire Service(s):** AP. Circulation: 11,500 evening (paid). **Owner(s):** Ogden Newspapers of Minnesota, Inc., 19260 San Carlos Blvd., Fort Myers Beach, FL 33931. Telephone: 239-463-4421. **Bureau(s):** 117 Genesee, Iron River, MI 49935. Telephone: 906-265-4210. Contact: Don Maki, Bureau Editor. **Management:** Robert Johnson, Publisher. Rebekah Rose, Circulation Manager. Kathy Dishaw, Classified Adv. Mgr.. **Editorial:** Blaine Hyska, Managing Editor. Jim Anderson, News Editor. Burt Angeli, Sports Editor.

IRONWOOD

IRONWOOD DAILY GLOBE. 118 E. McLeod Ave., Ironwood, MI 49938. Telephone: 906-932-2211. FAX: 906-932-5358. E-MAIL: globenews@charterinternet.com. URL: http://www.yourdailyglobe.com. Year Established: 1919. Pub. Frequency: d. (Mon.-Sat.) Page Size: broadsheet. Subscrip. Rate: $.75 newsstand/cover; $11.35 carrier delivery/mo.; $12.65 motor route/mo.; $15 mailed/mo.. **Wire Service(s):** AP. Circulation: 8,500 evening (paid). **Owner(s):** Daily Globe, Inc, See address and contact information above. **Management:** Joe Karius, Publisher. Kathy DiShaw, Circulation Manager. **Editorial:** Milt Lehto, Production Manager.

JACKSON

JACKSON CITIZEN PATRIOT. 214 S. Jackson St., Jackson, MI 49201-2282. Telephone: 517-787-2300. FAX: 517-787-4053. E-MAIL: prepress@citpat.com. URL: http://www.citpat.com. Year Established: 1837. Pub. Frequency: d. Page Size: broadsheet. Subscrip. Rate: $.50 newsstand/cover; $1.50 newsstand/cover Sun.; $12 carrier delivery/mo.; $57 mailed out of state for 3 mos.. **Wire Service(s):** AP, SH. Circulation: 37,500 evening (paid); 42,000 Sunday (paid). **Owner(s):** Advance Publications, Inc., See address and contact information above. **Management:** Sandra D. Petykiewicz, Publisher. Margaret Parshall, Advertising Director. Sandy Eisele, Circulation Manager. Margaret Parshall, Classified Adv. Mgr.. **Editorial:** Eileen Lehnert, Editor. Jerry Sova, News Editor. John Stewart, Photo Editor.

KALAMAZOO

KALAMAZOO GAZETTE. 401 S. Burdick, Kalamazoo, MI 49007. Telephone: 616-345-3511. E-MAIL: news@kalamazoogazette.com. URL: http://www.kalamazoo-gazette.com. Year Established: 1837. Pub. Frequency: d. Page Size: standard. Subscrip. Rate: $.50 newsstand/cover per issue; $1.25 newsstand/cover Sun.; $12.60 home delivery/mo. local; $20.75 mailed/mo. in state. **Wire Service(s):** AP, NYT. Circulation: 60,000 evening (paid); 76,000 Sunday (paid). **Owner(s):** Advance Publications, Inc., See address and contact information above. **Management:** George Arwady, Publisher. Linda Depta, Advertising Director. Ken Cogswell, Circulation Manager. **Editorial:** Rebecca Pierce, Editor. Al Jones, Business Editor. Charlotte Channing, Editorial Page Editor. Margaret DeRitter, Feature Editor. Paul Bowker, Sports Editor.

LANSING

LANSING STATE JOURNAL. ISSN 0274-9742
120 E. Lenawee, Lansing, MI 48919. Telephone: 517-377-1000. FAX: 517-377-1298. URL: http://www.lsj.com. Year Established: 1855. Pub. Frequency: d. Page Size: standard. Subscrip. Rate: $.50 newsstand/cover; $1.50 newsstand/cover Sun.; $3.75 carrier delivery/wk.; $195/yr carrier delivery; $4.05 motor route/wk.; $210.60/yr motor route. **Wire Service(s):** AP, LAT-WAT, GNS. Circulation: 72,000 morning (paid); 91,700 Sunday (paid). **Owner(s):** Gannett Company, Inc., 7950 Jones Branch Dr, McLean, VA 22107. Telephone: 703-854-6000. **Management:** Michael G. Kane, Publisher. Diana Kennedy, Circulation Director. **Editorial:** Michael "Mickey" Hirten, Executive Editor. Mark Nixon, Editorial Page Editor. Mike Hughes, Entertainment Editor.

LUDINGTON

LUDINGTON DAILY NEWS. 202 N. Rath Ave., Ludington, MI 49431-4011. Telephone: 231-845-5181. FAX: 231-843-4011. E-MAIL: ldn@ludingtondailynews.com. URL: http://www.ludingtondailynews.com. Mailing Address: PO Box 340, Ludington, MI 49431-0340. Year Established: 1873. Pub. Frequency: d. (Mon.-Sat.) Page Size: broadsheet. Subscrip. Rate: $.50 newsstand/cover; $1 newsstand/cover Sat.; $148/yr local; $203.10/yr mailed out of area. **Wire Service(s):** AP. Circulation: 8,638 evening (paid). **Owner(s):** Shoreline Media, Inc., See address and contact information above. **Management:** Jeffrey N. Evans, Publisher. Julie Payment, Circulation Manager. **Editorial:** Steve Begnoche, Managing Editor.

MANISTEE

MANISTEE NEWS ADVOCATE. 75 Maple St., Manistee, MI 49660-1554. Telephone: 231-723-3593. FAX: 231-723-4733. E-MAIL: advocate@pioneergroup.net. URL: http://www.bigrapidsnews.com. Mailing Address: PO Box 317, Manistee, MI 49666-1554. Year Established: 1894. Pub. Frequency: d. (Mon.-Sat.) Page Size: broadsheet. Subscrip. Rate: $.50 newsstand/cover; $.75 newsstand/cover Sat.; $30.25 mailed in county for 3 mos.; $34.40 mailed in state for 3 mos.; $45.50 mailed out of state for 3 mos.. **Wire Service(s):** AP. Circulation: 5,200 morning (paid). **Owner(s):** The Pioneer Group, 851 Michigan Ave., Baldwin, MI 49304. **Management:** Marilyn Barker, Publisher. Dawn Day, Circulation Manager. **Editorial:** David Barber, Editor. Greg Gielczyk, Sports Editor.

MARQUETTE

MINING JOURNAL, THE. ISSN 0898-4964
249 W. Washington St., Marquette, MI 49855. Telephone: 906-228-2500. FAX: 906-228-5556. E-MAIL: mmjournal@upgroup.com. URL: http://www.miningjournal.net. Mailing Address: PO Box 430, Marquette, MI 49855. Year Established: 1846. Pub. Frequency: d. Page Size: standard. Subscrip. Rate: $.50 newsstand/cover; $1.25 Sun.; $42.25 carrier delivery/quarter; $50.05 mailed/quarter local; $52 mailed/quarter out of area. **Wire Service(s):** AP. Circulation: 18,500 evening (paid); 20,000 Sunday (paid). **Owner(s):** Ogden Newspapers of Minnesota, Inc., 19260 San Carlos Blvd., Fort Myers Beach, FL 33931. Telephone: 239-463-4421. FAX: 239-463-1402. **Management:** James Reeves, Publisher. Gary Schneider, Advertising Director. **Editorial:** Dave Edwards, Managing Editor. Barbara Bannister, News Editor.

MIDLAND

MIDLAND DAILY NEWS. 124 S. McDonald St., Midland, MI 48640. Telephone: 989-835-7171. FAX: 989-835-6991. E-MAIL: circulation@mdn.net. URL: http://www.ourmidland.com. Mailing Address: PO Box 432, Midland, MI 48640. Year Established: 1937. Pub. Frequency: d. Page Size: broadsheet. Subscrip. Rate: $.50 newsstand/cover; $1.25 newsstand/cover Sun.; $137.76/yr home delivery local; $154.56/yr mailed in state; $171.36/yr mailed out of state. **Wire Service(s):** AP. Circulation: 16,265 evening (paid); 17,978 Sunday (paid). **Owner(s):** Hearst Corp., 959 Eighth Ave, New York, NY 10019. **Management:** Jenny Anderson, Publisher. Jack Starling, Advertising Director. Gary Wamsley, Circulation Director. Terry Kenny, Classified Adv. Mgr.. **Editorial:** John Telfer II, Editor. Ralph Wirtz, Managing Editor. Chris Stevens, Sports Editor.

MONROE

MONROE EVENING NEWS. 20 W. First St., Monroe, MI 48161. Telephone: 734-242-1100. FAX: 734-242-3175. E-MAIL: news1@monroenews.com. URL: http://www.monroenews.com. Mailing Address: PO Box 1176, Monroe, MI 48161-6176. Year Established: 1825. Pub. Frequency: d. Page Size: broadsheet. Subscrip. Rate: $.50 newsstand/cover; $1.25 newsstand/cover Sun.; $3.40 carrier delivery/wk.. Adv. Rate: col. inch $21.70 **Wire Service(s):** AP. Circulation: 21,776 evening (paid); 25,214 Sunday (paid). **Owner(s):** Monroe Publishing LLC, See address and contact information above. **Management:** Lonnie Peppler-Moyer, Publisher. Karen Hopkinson, Advertising. Jeff Pezzano, Sales Manager. Shirley Hyden, Business Manager. **Editorial:** Deborah Saul, Editor. Ron Montri, Sports Editor.

MT CLEMENS

MACOMB DAILY, THE. ISSN 1071-1406
100 Macomb Daily Dr, Mt Clemens, MI 48043. Telephone: 586-469-4510. FAX: 586-469-2892. E-MAIL: edit@macombdaily.com. URL: http://www.macombdaily.com. Mailing Address: P O Box 707, Mt Clemens, MI 48043. Year Established: 1860. Pub. Frequency: d. Page Size: broadsheet. Subscrip. Rate: $.50 newsstand/cover; $1.25 newsstand/cover Sun.; $3.60 carrier delivery/wk.; $275.60/yr carrier delivery. **Wire Service(s):** AP, SH. Circulation: 45,000 morning (paid); 69,000 Sunday (paid). **Owner(s):** Journal Register Co., 50 W State St, 12th Fl, Trenton, NJ 08608. **Management:** Kevin Haezebroeck, President. Justin Wilcox, Advertising Director. **Editorial:** Jason Schmitt, Sports Editor.

MT PLEASANT

MORNING SUN, THE. 711 W Pickard St, Mt Pleasant, MI 48804. Telephone: 989-779-6000. FAX: 989-779-6051. E-MAIL: cfox@michigannewspapers.com. URL: http://www.themorningsun.com. Year Established: 1977. Pub. Frequency: d. (Sun.-Fri.) Page Size: broadsheet. Subscrip. Rate: $.50 newsstand/cover; $1.50 newsstand/cover Sun.; $17 carrier delivery/mo. in county; $221/yr carrier delivery in county; $291.20/yr mailed elsewhere. **Wire Service(s):** AP. Circulation: 12,053 morning (paid); 13,545 Sunday (paid). **Owner(s):** Journal Register Co., 50 W State St, 12th Fl, Trenton, NJ 08608. **Management:** Albert Frattura, President. Don Negus, Advertising Director. Christine Fox-Martimer, Circulation Director. Donna Pung, Classified Adv. Mgr.. **Editorial:** Rick Mills, Executive Editor. Steve Coon, Managing Editor. Jim Lahde, Sports Editor.

MUSKEGON

MUSKEGON CHRONICLE, THE. 981 Third St., Muskegon, MI 49440. Telephone: 231-722-3161. FAX: 231-722-2552. URL: http://www.mlive.com. Mailing Address: PO Box 59, Muskegon, MI 49443-0059. Year Established: 1857. Pub. Frequency: d. Page Size: broadsheet. Subscrip. Rate: $.50 newsstand/cover; $1.50 newsstand/cover Sun.; $53 carrier delivery for 4 mos.; $12.50 mailed/mo. in state; $13.50/mo. out of state. **Wire Service(s):** AP, LAT-WAT. Circulation: 48,507 evening (paid); 53,248 Sunday (paid). **Owner(s):** Advance Publications, Inc., 950 Fingerboard Rd., Staten Island, NY 10305. **Bureau(s):** 217 N. Sycamore, Lansing, MI 48933. Telephone: 517-487-8888. FAX: 517-487-1227. Contact: Megan Holland, Bureau Chief. **Management:** Gary Ostrom, Publisher. Kevin Newton, Advertising Director. J.D. Wallace, Circulation Director. Linda Allard, Classified Adv. Mgr.. **Editorial:** D. Gunnar Carlson, Editor. David Alexander, Business Editor. Jerry Morlock, City Editor. David J. Kolb, Editorial Page Editor. John Stephenson, Metro Editor. Paula Holmes Greeley, News Editor. Greg Dorsett, Photo Editor. Cindy Fairfield, Sports Editor.

NILES

DOWAGIAC DAILY NEWS. 217 N. Fourth St., Niles, MI 49120. Telephone: 269-683-2101. E-MAIL: mcooper@leaderpub.com. URL: http://www.leaderpub.com. Year Established: 1897. Pub. Frequency: d. (Mon.-Fri.) Page Size: broadsheet. Subscrip. Rate: $.50 newsstand/cover; $81/yr carrier delivery; $117/yr mailed. **Wire Service(s):** UPI. Circulation: 2,915 evening (paid). **Owner(s):** Boone Newspapers, Inc., 15222 Freemen's Bend Rd., Northport, AL 35475. Telephone: 205-330-4100. **Management:** Jan Griffey, Publisher. Mary Cooper, Advertising Director. Linda Marks, Circulation Manager. Julie Korkos, Classified Adv. Mgr.. **Editorial:** Jan Griffey, Editor. John Eby, Managing Editor. Scott Novak, Sports Editor.

NILES DAILY STAR. 217 N. Fourth St., Niles, MI 49120. Telephone: 269-683-2101. FAX: 269-683-2175. E-MAIL: dailystar@leaderpub.com. URL: http://www.nilesstar.com. Year Established: 1886. Pub. Frequency: d. (Mon.-Sat.) Page Size: broadsheet. Subscrip. Rate: $.50 newsstand/cover; $90/yr carrier delivery; $126/yr mailed. **Wire Service(s):** UPI. Circulation: 5,000 evening (paid). **Owner(s):** Boone Newspapers, Inc., 15222 Freemen's Bend Rd., Northport, AL 35475. Telephone: 205-330-4100. **Management:** Jan Griffey, Publisher. Jane Means, Advertising Director. Andrew Heasley, Circulation Manager. Mary Cooper, Classified Adv. Mgr.. **Editorial:** Jan Griffey, Editor. Erika Pickles, Sports Editor.

OWOSSO

ARGUS-PRESS, THE. 201 E. Exchange St., Owosso, MI 48867. Telephone: 989-725-5136. FAX: 989-725-6376. E-MAIL: argus@chartermi.net. URL: http://www.argus-press.com. Year Established: 1854. Pub. Frequency: d. Page Size: broadsheet. Subscrip. Rate: $.50 newsstand/cover; $1.25 newsstand/cover Sun.; $9.75 carrier delivery/mo.; $99/yr. **Wire Service(s):** AP. Circulation: 12,000 evening (paid); 30,000 Sunday (paid). **Owner(s):** Argus-Press Co., See address and contact information above. **Management:** Thomas E. Campbell, Publisher. Michael Kruszkowski, Advertising Manager. Cathy Campbell, Marketing Director. **Editorial:** Richard Campbell, Executive Editor. Sarah Bazzetta, Managing Editor. Gary Webster, Feature Editor. Dan Basso, Sports Editor.

PETOSKEY

PETOSKEY NEWS-REVIEW. 319 State St., Petoskey, MI 49770-0528. Telephone: 231-347-2544. FAX: 231-347-6833. E-MAIL: kwint@petoskeynews.com. URL: http://www.petoskeynews.com. Mailing Address: PO Box 528, Petoskey, MI 49770-0528. Year Established: 1875. Pub. Frequency: d. (Mon.-Fri.) Page Size: broadsheet. Subscrip. Rate: $.50 newsstand/cover; $12.20/mo.; $142.75/yr. Adv. Rate: col. inch $30.08 **Wire Service(s):** AP. Circulation: 11,245 evening (paid). **Owner(s):** Northern Michigan Review, Inc., PO Box 528, Petoskey, MI 49770. Telephone: 231-347-2544. FAX: 231-347-6833. **Management:** Ken Winter, Publisher. Christy Bur, Advertising Manager. Carl Redder, Circulation Manager. Shirley Gibson, Classified Adv. Mgr.. **Editorial:** Ken Winter, Editor. Kendall Stanley, Managing Editor. B. Stenuis, Consumer Affrs. Ed.. Jerry Rosevear, Sports Editor.

Dailies

PONTIAC

OAKLAND PRESS, THE. 48 W Huron, Pontiac, MI 48342. URL: http://www.theoaklandpress.com. Mailing Address: P O Box 436009, Pontiac, MI 48343. Pub. Frequency: d. Page Size: standard. Subscrip. Rate: $.50 newsstand/cover; $1.50 newsstand/cover Sun.; $3 carrier delivery/wk.; $45.60 carrier delivery for 12 wks.. Freelance Pay: $10-$300/article. **Wire Service(s):** AP. Circulation: 25,251 morning (paid). **Owner(s):** Journal Register Co., 50 State St 12 fl, Trenton, NJ 08608-1298. Telephone: 609-396-2000. FAX: 609-396-2292. **Management:** Scott A Wright, Publisher. Tina Erb, Operations Manager. Teresa Goodrich, Advertising Director. Jeff Schell, Circulation Director. Deanna Sera, Classified Editor. **Editorial:** Neil Munro, Editor. Glenn Gilbert, Executive Editor. Susan Hood, Managing Editor. Gary Gosselin, Business Editor. Dolly Moiseeff, Feature Editor.

PORT HURON

TIMES HERALD (PORT HURON), THE. 911 Military St., Port Huron, MI 48060. Telephone: 810-985-7171. FAX: 810-989-6294. E-MAIL: tmshrld@ic.net2. URL: http://www.thetimesherald.com. Mailing Address: PO Box 5009, Port Huron, MI 48061-5009. Year Established: 1869. Pub. Frequency: d. Page Size: broadsheet. Subscrip. Rate: $.50 newsstand/cover; $1.50 newsstand/cover Sun.; $21 carrier delivery for 6 wks; $285.48/yr mailed. **Wire Service(s):** AP, GNS. Circulation: 30,905 evening (paid); 43,099 Sunday (paid). **Owner(s):** Gannett Company, Inc., 7950 Jones Branch Dr., McLean, VA 22107-0001. Telephone: 703-854-6000. **Management:** Charles T. Wanninger, President. Lori Driscoll, Advertising Director. Don Laskey, Circulation Director. **Editorial:** Denise Richter, Executive Editor.

ROYAL OAK

DAILY TRIBUNE (ROYAL OAK), THE. ISSN 1041-9977
210 E Third St, Royal Oak, MI 48067. Telephone: 248-541-3000. FAX: 248-541-7903. E-MAIL: woehmke@dailytribune.com. URL: http://www.dailytribune.com. Year Established: 1902. Pub. Frequency: d. (Sun.-Fri.) Page Size: broadsheet. Subscrip. Rate: $.50 newsstand/cover; $1.50 newsstand/cover Sun.; $2.75 carrier delivery/wk.. **Wire Service(s):** AP. Circulation: 14,377 evening (paid); 17,626 Sunday (paid). **Owner(s):** Journal Register Co., 50 W State St, 12th Fl, Trenton, NJ 08608. **Management:** Kevin Haezebroeck, President. Wayne Oehmke, Publisher. Jennifer Gorczany, Advertising Director. Betsy Karmeisool, Circulation Director. Deb Harper, Classified Adv. Mgr.. **Editorial:** Mike Beeson, Editor. Richard Hunt, Photo Editor.

SAGINAW

SAGINAW NEWS, THE. 203 S. Washington Ave., Saginaw, MI 48607. Telephone: 989-752-7171. FAX: 989-752-3115. URL: http://www.sa.mlive.com. Year Established: 1859. Pub. Frequency: d. Page Size: broadsheet. Subscrip. Rate: $.50 newsstand/cover; $1.50 newsstand/cover Sun.; $12.50 home delivery/mo. local; $13.50 motor route/mo.; $15.75 mailed/mo. in state. Adv. Rate: col. inch $34.91 **Wire Service(s):** AP. Circulation: 51,749 evening (paid); 61,827 Sunday (paid). **Owner(s):** Booth Newspapers, Inc., PO Box 2168, Grand Rapids, MI 49501. Telephone: 616-459-1400. **Management:** Renee Hampton, Publisher. Michael F Gallagher, Advertising Director. Jim Stevenson, Advertising Manager. Vincent Cone, Circulation Director. Jim Stevenson, Classified Adv. Mgr.. **Editorial:** Paul C Chaffee, Editor. Terence Smith, Editorial Page Editor. Ken Tabascko, Feature Editor. Rob Handeyside, Metro Editor. Brian Hlavaty, News Editor. Bernie Eng, Photo Editor. Paul Neumeyer, Sports Editor.

SAULT STE. MARIE

SAULT STE. MARIE EVENING NEWS. 109 Arlington St., Sault Ste. Marie, MI 49783. Telephone: 906-632-2235. FAX: 906-632-1222. E-MAIL: ensales@sooeveningnews.com. URL: http://www.sooeveningnews.com. Year Established: 1903. Pub. Frequency: d. (Sun.-Fri.) Page Size: broadsheet. Subscrip. Rate: $.75 newsstand/cover; $1.25 newsstand/cover Sun.; $197.50/yr carrier delivery; $209/yr mailed. Adv. Rate: col. inch $10.65 **Wire Service(s):** AP. Circulation: 7,000 evening (paid); 7,100 Sunday (paid). **Owner(s):** GateHouse Media, Inc, 350 WillowBrook Office Park, Fairport, NY 14450. Telephone: 585-598-0030. FAX: 585-248-2631. **Management:** Howard Kaiser, Publisher. Penny Joss, Advertising Manager. Mike Ferraro, Circulation Manager. Kathy Kaiser, Classified Adv. Mgr.. **Editorial:** Ken Filkins, Editor.

ST. JOSEPH

HERALD-PALLADIUM, THE. ISSN 0387-4400
3450 Hollywood Rd., St. Joseph, MI 49085. Telephone: 269-429-1396. FAX: 269-429-4398. E-MAIL: dbrown@heraldpalladium.com. URL: http://www.heraldpalladium.com. Mailing Address: PO Box 128, St. Joseph, MI 49085. Year Established: 1858. Pub. Frequency: d. Page Size: broadsheet. Subscrip. Rate: $.50 newsstand/cover; $1.50 newsstand/cover Sun.; $15 carrier delivery/mo. & motor rte; $18 mailed/mo. in area; $21.50 mailed/mo. out of area. **Wire Service(s):** AP. Circulation: 30,000 evening (paid); 30,000 Sunday (paid). **Owner(s):** Paxton Media Group Llc, 201 S. Fourth St., Paducah, KY 42003. Telephone: 270-575-8600. FAX: 270-442-8188. **Management:** Geoff Moser, Publisher. Rick Schmidt, Advertising Director. Tom O'Neill, Circulation Manager. **Editorial:** David Brown, Managing Editor. Dale Brewer, Editorial Page Editor. Sue Lorenz, Feature Editor. Steve Jewell, News Editor. John Madill, Photographer.

STURGIS

STURGIS JOURNAL. ISSN 0747-3230
209 John St., Sturgis, MI 49091. Telephone: 269-651-5407. FAX: 269-651-2296. E-MAIL: journal@voyager.net. URL: http://www.sturgisjournal.com. Mailing Address: PO Box 660, Sturgis, MI 49091. Year Established: 1859. Pub. Frequency: d. (Mon.-Sat.) Page Size: broadsheet. Subscrip. Rate: $.75 newsstand/cover; $118.20/yr. **Wire Service(s):** AP, GNS. Circulation: 7,500 evening (paid). **Owner(s):** GateHouse Media, Inc, 350 WillowBrook Office Park, Fairport, NY 14450. Telephone: 585-598-0030. FAX: 585-248-2631. **Management:** Dan Tollefson, Publisher. Brenda Kane, Advertising Manager. Laurie Blosser, Circulation Manager. **Editorial:** Candice Phelps, Editor.

THREE RIVERS

THREE RIVERS COMMERCIAL-NEWS. 124 N. Main St., Three Rivers, MI 49093. Telephone: 269-279-7488. FAX: 269-279-6007. E-MAIL: news@threeriversnews.com. URL: http://www.threeriversnews.com. Mailing Address: PO Box 130, Three Rivers, MI 49093. Year Established: 1895. Pub. Frequency: d. (Mon.-Sat.) Page Size: broadsheet. Subscrip. Rate: $.50 newsstand/cover; $8.50/mo.; $102/yr. **Wire Service(s):** AP. Circulation: 2,962 evening (paid). **Owner(s):** Milliman Communications, Inc., 4435 W. Saginaw, Ste. 204, Lansing, MI 48917. Telephone: 517-327-8407. **Management:** Dirk Milliman, Publisher. Tammy Chrisman, Advertising. Sharon Summers, Circulation Manager. **Editorial:** Dirk Milliman, Editor. Elena Hines, Managing Editor.

TRAVERSE CITY

TRAVERSE CITY RECORD-EAGLE. 120 W Front St, Traverse City, MI 49684. Telephone: 231-946-2000. FAX: 231-946-8632. E-MAIL: bthomas@record-eagle.com. URL: http://www.record-eagle.com. Mailing Address: PO Box 632, Traverse City, MI 49685. Year Established: 1904. Pub. Frequency: d. Page Size: broadsheet. Subscrip. Rate: $.50 newsstand/cover; $1.75 newsstand/cover Sun.. **Wire Service(s):** AP, MCT. Circulation: 29,000 morning (paid); 35,000 Sunday (paid). **Owner(s):** Community Newspaper Holdings, Inc., 3500 Colonnade Pkwy., Ste. 600, Birmingham, AL 35243-7017. **Management:** Michael Casuscelli, Publisher. Jacki Krolczyk, Advertising Director. Rich Roxbury, Circulation Manager. Jeana Daenzer, Classified Adv. Mgr.. **Editorial:** Bill Thomas, Editor.

MIDDLE PACIFIC

SAIPAN

GUAM VARIETY. PO Box 231, Saipan, MP 96950. Telephone: 670-234-6341. E-MAIL: younis@vzpacifica.net/gvgn@ite.net. Year Established: 1998. Pub. Frequency: d. (Mon.-Fri.) Page Size: tabloid. Subscrip. Rate: $.50 newsstand/cover; $72 for 6 mos.; $144/yr; $16.50 mailed/mo. foreign countries. **Wire Service(s):** RN, AP. Circulation: 4,000 morning (paid and free). **Owner(s):** Younis Art Studio, Inc., See address and contact information above. **Management:** Abed Younis, President. Paz Younis, Vice President. Abed Younis, Manager. **Editorial:** Zaldy Dandan, Editor.

MARIANAS VARIETY NEWS & VIEWS. PO Box 231, Saipan, MP 96950. Telephone: 670-234-6341. FAX: 680-488-4565. E-MAIL: younis@gtepacifica.net. URL: http://www.mvariety.com. Year Established: 1972. Pub. Frequency: d. (Mon.-Fri.) Page Size: tabloid. Subscrip. Rate: $.50 newsstand/cover; $150/yr carrier delivery hand deliv; $375/yr mailed area; $1,095/yr mailed elsewhere. **Wire Service(s):** RN, AP. Circulation: 5,000 morning (paid and free). **Owner(s):** Younis Art Studio, Inc., See address and contact information above. **Management:** Abed Younis, President. Paz Younis, Publisher. Abed Younis, Manager. **Editorial:** Zaldy Dandan, Editor.

MINNESOTA

ALBERT LEA

ALBERT LEA TRIBUNE. ISSN 1051-7421
808 W. Front St., Albert Lea, MN 56007-0060. Telephone: 507-373-1411. FAX: 507-373-0333. URL: http://www.albertleatribune.com. Mailing Address: PO Box 60, Albert Lea, MN 56007. Year Established: 1897. Pub. Frequency: d. (Sun.-Fri.) Page Size: broadsheet. Subscrip. Rate: $.50 newsstand/cover; $1.50 newsstand/cover Sun.; $43 home delivery local for 4 mos.; $129/yr home delivery; $198/yr mailed out of area. **Wire Service(s):** AP. Circulation: 7,500 evening (paid); 8,000 Sunday (paid). **Owner(s):** Boone Newspapers, Inc., 15222 Freemen's Bend Rd., Northport, AL 35475. Telephone: 205-330-4100. **Management:** Scott Schmeltzer, Publisher. Crystal Miller, Advertising Manager. Nancy Goodwin, Circulation Director. **Editorial:** Tim Engstrom, Managing Editor.

AUSTIN

AUSTIN DAILY HERALD. ISSN 0746-9713
310 N E Second St., Austin, MN 55912. Telephone: 507-433-8851. FAX: 507-437-8644. E-MAIL: newsroom@austindailyherald.com. URL: http://www.austindailyherald.com. Mailing Address: PO Box 578, Austin, MN 55912. Pub. Frequency: d. (Sun.-Fri.) Page Size: broadsheet. Subscrip. Rate: $.50 newsstand/cover; $1.50 newsstand/cover Sun.; $11.25 home delivery/mo.; $13 motor route/mo.; $16 mailed/mo.. **Wire Service(s):** AP. Circulation: 8,000 evening (paid); 8,000 Sunday (paid). **Owner(s):** Boone Newspapers, Inc., 15222 Freemen's Bend Rd., Northport, AL 35475. Telephone: 205-330-4100. **Management:** Kevin True, General Manager. **Editorial:** Bryan Clapper, Managing Editor. Katie Johnson, News Editor. Matt Steichen, Sports Editor.

BEMIDJI

PIONEER (BEMIDJI), THE. ISSN 0899-1812
1320 Nielson Ave., S. E., Bemidji, MN 56601. Telephone: 218-751-3740. FAX: 218-751-6914. E-MAIL: jmail@bemidjipioneer.com. URL: http://www.bemidjipioneer.com. Mailing Address: PO Box 455, Bemidji, MN 56619-0455. Year Established: 1896. Pub. Frequency: d. (Tue.-Sun.) Page Size: broadsheet. Subscrip. Rate: $.50 newsstand/cover; $1.50 Sun.; $11.75 carrier delivery/mo.. Adv. Rate: col. inch $7.30 **Wire Service(s):** AP. Circulation: 10,261 morning (paid); 11,187 Sunday (paid). **Owner(s):** Jeff Meyer, 101 Fifth St., N., Fargo, ND 58102. Telephone: 701-235-7311. **Management:** Dennis Doeden, General Manager. Jeff Halverson, Advertising Manager. Darla Vagle, Classified Adv. Mgr.. Tammie Richter, Business Manager. **Editorial:** Molly Miron, Editor. Monte Draper, Photographer. Contact: Molly Miron, Editor.

BRAINERD

BRAINERD DAILY DISPATCH, THE. 506 James St., Brainerd, MN 56401. Telephone: 218-829-4705. FAX: 218-829-7735. E-MAIL: dailyd@brainerd.net. URL: http://www.brainerddispatch.com. Mailing Address: PO Box 974, Brainerd, MN 56401. Year Established: 1881. Pub. Frequency: d. (Sun.-Fri.) Page Size: broadsheet. Subscrip. Rate: $.50 newsstand/cover; $1.50 Sun.; $110/yr carrier delivery; $119/yr motor route; $165/yr mailed out of state. **Wire Service(s):** AP. Circulation: 15,950 evening (paid); 19,200 Sunday (paid). **Owner(s):** Morris Multimedia, Inc., PO Box 936, Augusta, GA 30903. Telephone: 706-721-0851. **Management:** Will Morris, President. Terry McCollough, Publisher. Mary Panzer, Advertising. Greg Guenin, Circulation Manager. Keri Lake, Business Manager. **Editorial:** Roy Miller, Editor. Mike O'Rourke, City Editor. Vin Mayer, Outdoor Editor. Steve Kohls, Photographer. Mike Bialka, Sports Editor.

CROOKSTON

CROOKSTON DAILY TIMES. 124 S. Broadway, Crookston, MN 56716. Telephone: 218-281-2730. FAX: 218-281-7234. E-MAIL: editor@crookstontimes.com. URL: http://www.crookstontimes.com. Mailing Address: PO Box 615, Crookston, MN 56716. Year Established: 1885. Pub. Frequency: d. (Mon.-Fri.) Page Size: broadsheet. Subscrip. Rate: $.50 newsstand/cover; $107/yr carrier delivery; $94/yr mailed. **Wire Service(s):** AP. Circulation: 2,200 evening (paid). **Owner(s):** GateHouse Media, Inc, 350 WillowBrook Office Park, Fairport, NY 14450. Telephone: 585-598-0030. FAX: 585-248-2631. **Management:** Randal Hultgren, Publisher. Calvin Anderson, Advertising Manager. Carl Melbye, Circulation Manager. Janelle Brekken, Classified Adv. Mgr.. **Editorial:** Mike Christopherson, Managing Editor. Jason Ivanitz, Sports Editor.

FAIRMONT

FAIRMONT SENTINEL. ISSN 0893-3804
64 Downtown Plz., Fairmont, MN 56031-0681. Telephone: 507-235-3303. FAX: 507-235-3718. E-MAIL: news@fairmontsentinel.com. URL: http://www.fairmontsentinel.com. Mailing Address: PO Box 681, Fairmont, MN 56031-0681. Year Established: 1874. Pub. Frequency: d. (Mon.-Sat.) Page Size: broadsheet. Subscrip. Rate: $.50 newsstand/cover; $.75 newsstand/cover Sat.; $118.60/yr carrier delivery; $124.60/yr mailed in area; $156.80/yr out of area. **Wire Service(s):** AP. Circulation: 8,500 morning (paid). **Owner(s):** Ogden Newspapers of Minnesota, Inc., 19260 San Carlos Blvd., Fort Myers Beach, FL 33931. Telephone: 239-463-4421. **Management:** Gary Andersen, Publisher. Kathy Ratcliff, Advertising Manager. Debbie Foster, Business Manager. **Editorial:** Lee Smith, Editor. Chip Pearson, Photographer. Chuck Sorrells, Sports.

FARIBAULT

FARIBAULT DAILY NEWS. ISSN 0889-8898
514 Central Ave., Faribault, MN 55021. Telephone: 507-333-3111. FAX: 507-333-3102. E-MAIL: lschwarz@faribault.com. URL: http://www.faribault.com. Mailing Address: PO Box 249, Faribault, MN 55021. Year Established: 1914. Pub. Frequency: d. (Tue.-Sun.) Page Size: broadsheet. Subscrip. Rate: $.50 newsstand/cover; $138/yr carrier delivery local; $150/yr motor route local; $150/yr mailed in county; $177/yr mailed out of county. **Wire Service(s):** AP. Circulation: 7,800 evening (paid). **Owner(s):** Huckle Publishing, Inc., 6291 Peninsula Dr., Traverse City, MI 49684. Telephone: 616-929-3571. **Management:** Jim Huckle, President. Paula Patton, Publisher. Lisa Ebert, Circulation Manager. **Editorial:** Paula Patton, Editor. Kevira Murtha, News Editor. Robb Long, Photographer. Corey Voegele, Sports.

FERGUS FALLS

DAILY JOURNAL (FERGUS FALLS), THE. 914 E. Channing Ave., Fergus Falls, MN 56537. Telephone: 218-736-7511. FAX: 218-736-5919. E-MAIL: djournal@prtel.com. URL: http://www.fergusfallsjournal.com. Mailing Address: PO Box 506, Fergus Falls, MN 56538. Year Established: 1873. Pub. Frequency: d. (Mon.-Sat.) Page Size: broadsheet. Subscrip. Rate: $.75 newsstand/cover; $10.95 carrier delivery/mo. local; $13 motor route/mo. in city; $12 mailed/mo. in state; $13 mailed/mo. elsewhere. **Wire Service(s):** AP. Circulation: 8,000 evening (paid). **Owner(s):** Boone Newspapers, Inc., 15222 Freemen's Bend Rd., Northport, AL 35475. Telephone: 205-330-4100. **Management:** Joel Myhre, General Manager. David Churchill, Publisher. Connie Knapp, Circulation Manager. **Editorial:** Debbie Irmen, Managing Editor. Brian Hansel, Sports Editor.

HIBBING

DAILY TRIBUNE (HIBBING), THE. ISSN 1075-4040
2142 First Ave., Hibbing, MN 55746. Telephone: 218-262-1011. FAX: 218-262-4318. E-MAIL: tribune@hibbingmn.com. URL: http://www.hibbingmn.com. Mailing Address: PO Box 38, Hibbing, MN 55746. Year Established: 1894. Pub. Frequency: d. (Tue.-Sun.) Page Size: broadsheet. Subscrip. Rate: $.50 newsstand/cover; $1.25 Sun.; $145/yr carrier delivery local & motor rte; $152.88/yr mailed local. **Wire Service(s):** AP. Circulation: 9,000 evening (paid); 18,000 Sunday (paid). **Owner(s):** Superior Publishing Corp., 1105 Tower Ave, Superior, WI 54880. Telephone: 715-395-5725. FAX: 715-395-5729. **Management:** Terese Almquist, General Manager. Scott Schmeltzer, Advertising Director. **Editorial:** Patrick Ethridde, Editor. Gary Giombetti, Sports.

INTERNATIONAL FALLS

DAILY JOURNAL (INTERNATIONAL FALLS), THE. 1602 Hwy 71, International Falls, MN 56649. Telephone: 218-285-7411. FAX: 218-285-7206. E-MAIL: nspub@norshore.com. URL: http://www.ifallsdailyjournal.com. Year Established: 1920. Pub. Frequency: d. (Mon.-Fri.) Page Size: broadsheet. Subscrip. Rate: $.50 newsstand/cover; $107/yr carrier delivery local; $117/yr motor route; $128/yr mailed. **Wire Service(s):** AP. Circulation: 4,080 evening (paid). **Owner(s):** North Star Publishing Co., See address and contact information above. **Management:** Wayne Kasich, General Manager. Dana Hartje, Circulation Manager. Cyndie Beninger, Classified Adv. Mgr.. **Editorial:** David Knutsen, Managing Editor. Laurel Beager, City Editor.

MANKATO

FREE PRESS (MANKATO), THE. ISSN 0893-3715
418 S Second St, Mankato, MN 56001. Telephone: 507-625-4451. FAX: 507-388-4355. E-MAIL: editor@mankato-freepress.com. URL: http://www.mankato-freepress.com. Mailing Address: PO Box 3287, Mankato, MN 56002. Year Established: 1887. Pub. Frequency: d. (Mon.-Sat.) Page Size: broadsheet. Subscrip. Rate: $.50 newsstand/cover; $1.25 newsstand/cover Sun.; $166/yr carrier delivery; $175/yr motor route; $199/yr mailed. Freelance Pay: $20/article. **Wire Service(s):** AP, LAT-WAT. Circulation: 22,629 morning (paid). **Owner(s):** Community Newspaper Holdings, Inc., 3500 Colonnade Pkwy., Ste. 600, Birmingham, AL 35243-2304. Telephone: 205-298-7100. **Management:** Jim Santori, Publisher. David Habrat, Advertising Director. Kathy Connelly, Classified Adv. Mgr.. **Editorial:** Joe Spears, Managing Editor. Jim Rueda, Sports Editor.

MARSHALL

MARSHALL INDEPENDENT. 1500 Main St, Marshall, MN 56258. E-MAIL: news@marshallindependent.com. URL: http://www.marshallindependent.com. Mailing Address: PO Box 411, Marshall, MN 56258. Year Established: 1886. Pub. Frequency: d. (Mon.-Sat.) Page Size: broadsheet. Subscrip. Rate: $.50 newsstand/cover; $.75 newsstand/cover Sat.; $124.80/yr home delivery local; $179.40/yr mailed out of area. Adv. Rate: col. inch $20.89 **Wire Service(s):** AP. Circulation: 7,400 morning (paid). **Owner(s):** Ogden Newspapers of Minnesota, Inc., See address and contact information above. **Management:** Russ Labat, Publisher. Jane Sovell, Office Manager. Tara Brandl, Advertising Manager. Julie Dobrenski, Circulation Manager. Ruth Staeffler, Classified Adv. Mgr.. **Editorial:** Rae Kruger, Editor. Deb Johnson, Creative Director. Andy Rennecke, Sports.

MINNEAPOLIS

STAR TRIBUNE. ISSN 0895-2825
425 Portland Ave., Minneapolis, MN 55488. Telephone: 612-673-4000. FAX: 612-673-4359. E-MAIL: andersg@startribune.com. URL: http://www.startribune.com. Year Established: 1867. Pub. Frequency: d. Page Size: standard. Subscrip. Rate: $.50 newsstand/cover; $1.75 newsstand/cover Sun.; $3.10 carrier delivery/wk.; $161.20/yr mailed. **Wire Service(s):** AP, SH, NYT, LAT-WAT. Circulation: 415,497 morning (paid); 674,345 Sunday (paid). **Owner(s):** The/McClatchy Company, PO Box 15779, Sacramento, CA 95852. Telephone: 916-321-1936. **Bureau(s):** 500 Medical Arts Bldg., Duluth, MN 55802. Telephone: 218-727-7344. FAX: 218-727-7901. Contact: Larry Oakes, Bureau Chief. **Management:** Keith Moyer, President. Steve Alexander, Circulation Manager. Tom Mohr, Classified Adv. Mgr.. **Editorial:** Scott Gillespie, Managing Editor. Susan Allbright, Editorial Page Editor. Susie Hopper, Feature Editor. Bill Dunn, Graphics Editor. Sherri Marshall, News Editor. Steve Ronald, Production Editor. Glen Crevier, Sports Editor.

NEW ULM

JOURNAL (NEW ULM), THE. 303 N. Minnesota St., New Ulm, MN 56073-0487. Telephone: 507-359-2911. FAX: 507-359-7362. E-MAIL: editor@nujournal.com. URL: http://www.nujournal.com. Mailing Address: PO Box 487, New Ulm, MN 56073-0487. Year Established: 1898. Pub. Frequency: d. Page Size: broadsheet. Subscrip. Rate: $.50 newsstand/cover; $1 Sun.; $150/yr carrier delivery; $156/yr mailed in county; $222/yr elsewhere. **Wire Service(s):** AP. Circulation: 8,214 morning (paid); 8,793 Sunday (paid). **Owner(s):** Ogden Newspapers of Minnesota, Inc., 1500 Main St., Wheeling, WV 26003. Telephone: 304-233-0100. **Management:** Robert M Nutting, President. Bruce Fenske, Publisher. Debbie Dubberly, Office Manager. Tim Babel, Advertising Director. Steve Grosam, Circulation Manager. **Editorial:** Kevin Sweeney, Managing Editor. Donna Weber, News Editor. Steve Muscatello, Photographer. Jeremy Behnke, Sports Editor.

OWATONNA

OWATONNA PEOPLE'S PRESS. ISSN 0890-2860
135 W. Pearl, Owatonna, MN 55060. Telephone: 507-451-2840. FAX: 507-444-2382. E-MAIL: rensley@owatonna.com. URL: http://www.owatonna.com. Mailing Address: PO Box 346, Owatonna, MN 55060-0346. Year Established: 1874. Pub. Frequency: d. (Tue.-Sun.) Page Size: broadsheet. Subscrip. Rate: $.50 newsstand/cover; $138/yr home delivery local. **Wire Service(s):** AP. Circulation: 8,000 morning (paid); 8,200 Sunday (paid). **Owner(s):** Huckle Publishing, Inc., See address and contact information above. **Management:** Ron Ensley, Publisher. Debbie Ensley, Advertising Manager. Carol Harvey, Circulation Manager. **Editorial:** Jeffrey Jackson, Managing Editor.

RED WING

RED WING REPUBLICAN EAGLE. 2760 N. Service Dr., Red Wing, MN 55066-0015. Telephone: 651-388-8235. FAX: 651-388-3404. E-MAIL: news@republican-eagle.com. URL: http://www.republican-eagle.com. Mailing Address: PO Box 15, Red Wing, MN 55066-0015. Year Established: 1857. Pub. Frequency: d. (Mon.-Sat.) Page Size: broadsheet. Subscrip. Rate: $.50 newsstand/cover; $1 newsstand/cover Sat.; $118.95/yr carrier delivery; $132.95/yr motor route; $146.25/yr mailed. Adv. Rate: col. inch $10.99 **Wire Service(s):** AP. Circulation: 7,600 morning (paid). **Owner(s):** Jeff Meyer, 101 Fifth St., N., Fargo, ND 58102. Telephone: 701-235-7311. **Management:** Michael Kuehn, General Manager. Steve Messick, Publisher. Michael Kuehn, Advertising Manager. Marty Matousek, Circulation Manager. Michael Kuehn, Classified Adv. Mgr.. John Bueller, Business Manager. **Editorial:** Anne Jacobson, Editor-in-Chief. Ben Pearson, Sports.

ROCHESTER

POST-BULLETIN. 18 First Ave., S.E., Rochester, MN 55904. Telephone: 507-285-7600. FAX: 507-285-7772. E-MAIL: news@postbulletin.com. URL: http://www.postbulletin.com. Mailing Address: PO Box 6118, Rochester, MN 55903. Year Established: 1925. Pub. Frequency: d. (Mon.-Sat.) Page Size: broadsheet. Subscrip. Rate: $.50 newsstand/cover; $1.75 newsstand/cover Sat.; $39.65 in city for 13 wks.; $42.90 motor route for 13 wks. **Wire Service(s):** AP, NYT, MCT. Circulation: 42,307 evening (paid). **Owner(s):** Small Newspaper Group, 8 Dearborn Sq., Kankakee, IL 60901. Telephone: 815-937-3300. **Bureau(s):** 1183 National Press Bldg., Washington, DC 20045. Telephone: 202-262-7241. Contact: Edward Felker, Bureau Chief. **Management:** Gerry Rhea, Advertising Manager. Bill Lisser, Circulation Director. Sue Lovejoy, Classified Adv. Mgr.. **Editorial:** Jon Losness, Editor. Jay Furst, Managing Editor. Brian Sander, City Editor. Jay Johnson, Editorial Page Editor. Jerry Reising, Feature Editor. Jan McFarland, Lifestyle Editor. John Weiss, Outdoor Editor. Germiene Neimann, Photographer. Craig Swalboski, Sports Editor.

ST PAUL

ST. PAUL PIONEER PRESS. ISSN 1050-0405
345 Cedar St, St Paul, MN 55101. Telephone: 651-222-5011. FAX: 650228-5500. E-MAIL: letters@pioneerpress.com. URL: http://www.twincities.com. Year Established: 1849. Pub. Frequency: d. Page Size: broadsheet. Subscrip. Rate: $.25 newsstand/cover; $1 newsstand/cover Sun.; $34.84 for 13 wks.. **Wire Service(s):** AP, LAT-WAT. Circulation: 197,477 morning (paid); 258,429 Sunday (paid). **Owner(s):** MediaNews Group, Inc., 101 W Colfax Ave, Ste 1100, Denver, CO 80202. FAX: 303-954-6320. **Management:** Harold Higgins, President. **Editorial:** Vicki Gowler, Managing Editor. Chris Worthington, Business Editor.

ST. CLOUD

ST. CLOUD TIMES. ISSN 0899-5028
3000 N. Seventh St., St. Cloud, MN 56303. Telephone: 320-255-8700. FAX: 320-255-8775. E-MAIL: sctimes@cloudnet.com. URL: http://www.sctimes.com. Mailing Address: PO Box 768, St. Cloud, MN 56302. Year Established: 1861. Pub. Frequency: d. Page Size: broadsheet. Subscrip. Rate: $.50 newsstand/cover; $1.50 newsstand/cover Sun.; $42.25/yr carrier delivery; $46.15/yr motor route; $55.25/yr mailed in state. **Wire Service(s):** AP, GNS. Circulation: 28,399 morning (paid); 38,625 Sunday (paid). **Owner(s):** Gannett Company, Inc., 7950 Jones Branch Dr., McLean, VA 22102. Telephone: 703-854-6000. **Management:** Bill Albrecht, President. Mike Corbett, Advertising Director. Geary Yaeger, Circulation Director. **Editorial:** Susan Ihne, Executive Editor. John Bodette, Managing Editor. Randy Krebs, Editorial Page Editor. Rene Kaluza, Feature Editor.

STILLWATER

STILLWATER GAZETTE. 1931 Curve Crest Blvd., Stillwater, MN 55082. Telephone: 651-439-3130. FAX: 651-439-4713. E-MAIL: gazads@acnpapers.com. URL: http://www.stillwatergazette.com. Year Established: 1870. Pub. Frequency: d. (Mon.-Fri.) Page Size: broadsheet. Subscrip. Rate: $.50 newsstand/cover; $99/yr carrier delivery; $119/yr mailed in state. Adv. Rate: B&W page $1,115 **Wire Service(s):** AP. Circulation: 4,200 evening (paid and free). **Owner(s):** American Community Newspapers LLC, 10917 Valley View Rd, Eden Prairie, MN 55344. **Management:** Mark Berriman, Publisher. David Mooney, Circulation Manager. Jayne Miller, Classified Adv. Mgr.. **Editorial:** Kris Janisch, Managing Editor.

VIRGINIA

MESABI DAILY NEWS. ISSN 1930-9465
704 Seventh Ave., S., Virginia, MN 55792. Telephone: 218-741-5544. FAX: 218-741-1005. E-MAIL: mdnedit@virgiamn.com. URL: http://www.virginiamn.com. Mailing Address: PO Box 956, Virginia, MN 55792. Year Established: 1893. Pub. Frequency: d. Page Size: broadsheet. Subscrip. Rate: $.50 newsstand/cover; $1.50 Sun.; $48.75 carrier delivery for 13 wks.; $65 mailed for 13 wks. **Wire Service(s):** UPI. Circulation: 12,245 morning (paid); 22,166 Sunday (paid). **Owner(s):** Superior Publishing Corp., 1105 Tower Ave, Superior, WI 54880. Telephone: 715-395-5725. FAX: 715-395-5729. **Management:** Scott Ashbach, General Manager. Chris Knight, Advertising Manager. Larry Rogers, Circulation Manager. Nancy Novak, Business Manager. **Editorial:** Bill Hanna, Executive Editor. Linda Tyssen, Lifestyle Editor. Mark Sauer, Photographer. Jim Laine, Sports.

WILLMAR

WEST CENTRAL TRIBUNE. 2208 W. Trott Ave., Willmar, MN 56201-0839. Telephone: 320-235-1150. FAX: 320-235-6769. E-MAIL: feedback@wctrib.com. URL: http://www.wctrib.com. Mailing Address: PO Box 839, Willmar, MN 56201-0839. Year Established: 1895. Pub. Frequency: d. (Mon.-Sat.) Page Size: broadsheet. Subscrip. Rate: $.50 newsstand/cover; $131.10/yr carrier delivery; $139.25/yr mailed. **Wire Service(s):** AP. Circulation: 17,500 morning (paid). **Owner(s):** Jeff Meyer, 101 Fifth St., N., Fargo, ND 58102. Telephone: 701-235-7311. **Management:** Steve Ammermann, General Manager. William C. Marcil, President. Steve Ammermann, Publisher. Jan Queenan, Advertising Manager. Mark Herman, Circulation Manager. **Editorial:** Kelly Boldar, Editor. Dave Little, Farm Editor. William Zimmer, Photographer.

WINONA

WINONA DAILY NEWS. ISSN 0273-9941
601 Franklin St., Winona, MN 55987. Telephone: 507-453-3500. FAX: 507-454-1440. E-MAIL: wdn@luminet.net. URL: http://www.winonadailynews.com. Mailing Address: PO Box 5147, Winona, MN 55987. Year Established: 1855. Pub. Frequency: d. Page Size: standard. Subscrip. Rate: $.50 newsstand/cover; $1.25 newsstand/cover Sun.; $167.49/yr home delivery; $208/yr mailed. **Wire Service(s):** AP. Circulation: 14,000 morning (paid); 14,363 Sunday (paid). **Owner(s):** Lee Enterprises, Inc., 201 N. Harrison St, Ste 600, Davenport, IA 52801-1924. **Management:** Rusty Cunningham, Publisher. Tom Kelly, Advertising Manager. Dan Peterson, Circulation Manager. Vicky Peterson, Classified Adv. Mgr.. **Editorial:** Darrell Ehrlick, Editor. Chris Hubbuch, City Editor. Jim Kohner, Sports.

WORTHINGTON

DAILY GLOBE. ISSN 1045-487X
300 11th St., Worthington, MN 56187. Telephone: 507-376-9711. FAX: 507-376-5202. E-MAIL: dglobe@dglobe.com. URL: http://www.dglobe.com. Mailing Address: PO Box 639, Worthington, MN 56187-0639. Year Established: 1872. Pub. Frequency: d. (Mon.-Sat.) Page Size: broadsheet. Subscrip. Rate: $.50 newsstand/cover; $143/yr carrier delivery; $147.25/yr mailed local. Adv. Rate: col. inch $15.89 **Wire Service(s):** AP. Circulation: 9,900 morning (paid). **Owner(s):** Jeff Meyer, 101 Fifth St., N., Fargo, ND 58207. Telephone: 701-223-7311. **Management:** Joni Harms, Publisher. Dona Ellerbroek, Advertising Manager. Denise Erwin, Circulation Manager. Anita Holmes, Business Manager.

MISSISSIPPI

BROOKHAVEN

DAILY LEADER, THE. 128 N. Railroad Ave., Brookhaven, MS 39601. Telephone: 601-833-6961. FAX: 601-833-6714. E-MAIL: news@dailyleader.com. URL: http://www.dailyleader.com. Mailing Address: PO Box 551, Brookhaven, MS 39602. Year Established: 1883. Pub. Frequency: d. (Sun.-Fri.) Page Size: broadsheet. Subscrip. Rate: $.50 newsstand/cover; $1 newsstand/cover Sun.; $10/mo.; $112/yr. **Wire Service(s):** AP. Circulation: 7,500 evening (paid); 7,500 Sunday (paid). **Owner(s):** Southwest Publishers, Inc., See address and contact information above. **Management:** William O. Jacobs, Publisher. David Culpepper, Advertising Manager. Kevin Trantham, Circulation Manager. Carrie Bergeron, Classified Adv. Mgr.. **Editorial:** William O. Jacobs, Editor-in-Chief. Matt Coleman, Managing Editor. Tom Goetz, Sports.

CLARKSDALE

CLARKSDALE PRESS REGISTER. 128 Second St., Clarksdale, MS 38614. Telephone: 662-627-2201. FAX: 662-624-5125. E-MAIL: bkeller@pressregister.com. URL: http://www.pressregister.com. Mailing Address: PO Box 1119, Clarksdale, MS 38614. Year Established: 1865. Pub. Frequency: 3/w. (Wed., Fri., Sat.) Page Size: broadsheet. Subscrip. Rate: $.75 newsstand/cover; $5 home delivery/mo. in area; $52/yr. Adv. Rate: col. inch $11.55 Circulation: 3,500 morning (paid). **Owner(s):** Emmerich Newspapers, Inc., PO Box 16709, Jackson, MS 39236. Telephone: 601-957-1122. **Management:** Wyatt Emmerich, President. Brenda Keller, Advertising Director. Steve Smith, Circulation Manager.

CLEVELAND

BOLIVAR COMMERCIAL, THE. 821 N. Chrisman Ave., Cleveland, MS 38732. Telephone: 662-843-4241. FAX: 662-843-1830. E-MAIL: publisher@bolivarcommercial.com. URL: http://www.bolivarcom.com. Mailing Address: PO Box 1050, Cleveland, MS 38732. Year Established: 1917. Pub. Frequency: d. (Mon.-Fri.) Page Size: broadsheet. Subscrip. Rate: $.50 newsstand/cover; $26 home delivery local for 4 mos.; $26 mailed in county for 4 mos.; $30 mailed out of county for 4 mos.. **Wire Service(s):** AP. Circulation: 8,100 evening (paid). **Owner(s):** Walls Newspapers, Inc., 525 Office Park Dr., Birmingham, AL 35223. Telephone: 205-870-1684. **Management:** Mark Williams, Publisher. David Laster, Advertising Manager. Wayne Evrard, Circulation Manager. Renee Walker, Classified Adv. Mgr.. **Editorial:** Mark Williams, Editor. Denise Strub, Managing Editor. Aimee Robinette, Lifestyle Editor. Andy Collier, Sports.

COLUMBUS

COMMERCIAL DISPATCH, THE. ISSN 0746-7729
516 Main St., Columbus, MS 39701-0511. Telephone: 662-328-2427. FAX: 662-329-8937. E-MAIL: letters@cdispatch.com. URL: http://www.cdispatch.com. Mailing Address: PO Box 511, Columbus, MS 39703-0511. Year Established: 1879. Pub. Frequency: d. (Sun.-Fri.) Page Size: broadsheet. Subscrip. Rate: $.25 newsstand/cover; $1 newsstand/cover Sun.; $120/yr home delivery. Adv. Rate: col. inch $11.20 **Wire Service(s):** AP, LAT-WAT. Circulation: 14,003 evening (paid); 15,000 Sunday (paid). **Owner(s):** Commercial Dispatch, Inc., See address and contact information above. **Management:** Birney Imes, Publisher. Fay Dexter, Advertising Manager. Bobby Tingle, Circulation Manager. Leigh Nicholes, Classified Adv. Mgr.. **Editorial:** Birney Imes, Editor. Steve Rogers, City Editor. Sarah Annie Carter, News Editor. Henry Matuszak, Sports Editor.

CORINTH

DAILY CORINTHIAN. 1607 S. Harper Rd., Corinth, MS 38834. Telephone: 662-287-6111. FAX: 662-287-3525. E-MAIL: news@dailycorinthian.com. Mailing Address: PO Box 1800, Corinth, MS 38835. Year Established: 1895. Pub. Frequency: d. (Tue.-Sun.) Page Size: standard. Subscrip. Rate: $.50 newsstand/cover; $1 newsstand/cover Sun.; $31.80 carrier delivery & motor rte for 3 mos.. **Wire Service(s):** AP. Circulation: 7,165 morning (paid); 7,165 Sunday (paid). **Owner(s):** Paxton Media Group, LLC, 201 S. Fourth St., Paducah, KY 42003. Telephone: 270-575-8600. FAX: 270-442-8188. **Management:** Reece Terry, Publisher. Norman Isbell, Advertising Manager. Cindy Leatherwood, Circulation Manager. Paula Gunn, Business Manager. **Editorial:** Mark Boehler, Executive Editor. Mike McEwen, Photographer. Lee Smith, Sports Editor.

GREENVILLE

DELTA DEMOCRAT-TIMES. 988 N. Broadway, Greenville, MS 38701. Telephone: 662-335-1155. FAX: 662-335-2860. E-MAIL: danway@link.freedom.com. URL: http://www.ddtonline.com. Mailing Address: PO Box 1618, Greenville, MS 38702. Year Established: 1868. Pub. Frequency: d. (Sun.-Fri.) Page Size: standard. Subscrip. Rate: $.50 newsstand/cover; $1 newsstand/cover Sun.; $10/mo.. **Wire Service(s):** AP. Circulation: 13,100 evening (paid); 15,000 Sunday (paid). **Owner(s):** Emmerich Newspapers, Inc., PO Box 16709, Jackson, MS 39236. Telephone: 601-957-1122. **Management:** Wyatt Emmerich, President. John S Clark, Publisher. Alan Curran, Circulation Director. Katrina Shaw, Classified Adv. Mgr.. Beth Horn, Business Manager. **Editorial:** David Lush, Managing Editor. Sallie Gresham, Senior Editor.

GREENWOOD

GREENWOOD COMMONWEALTH. ISSN 0884-4569
329 Hwy. 82 W, Greenwood, MS 38930. Telephone: 662-453-5312. FAX: 662-453-2908. E-MAIL: tkalich@gwcommonwealth.com. URL: http://www.gwcommonwealth.com. Mailing Address: PO Box 8050, Greenwood, MS 38935-8050. Year Established: 1896. Pub. Frequency: d. (Sun.-Fri.) Page Size: broadsheet. Subscrip. Rate: $.50 newsstand/cover; $1 newsstand/cover Sun.; $32.75 home delivery in city for 3 mos.; $102/yr home delivery in city; $32.75 mailed in county for 3 mos.; $131/yr mailed in county. Adv. Rate: col. inch $10 **Wire Service(s):** AP, NYT. Circulation: 8,140 evening (paid); 8,465 Sunday (paid). **Owner(s):** Emmerich Newspapers, Inc., PO Box 16709, Jackson, MS 39236. Telephone: 601-957-1122. FAX: 601-957-1533. **Management:** Wyatt Emmerich, President. Tim Kalich, Publisher. Larry Alderman, Advertising Manager. Shirley Cooper, Circulation Manager. **Editorial:** Tim Kalich, Editor. Jenny Humphryes, Managing Editor. Jesse Barbosa, Production Manager.

GRENADA

DAILY STAR (GRENADA), THE. ISSN 1066-7512
50 Corporate Row, Grenada, MS 38901. Telephone: 662-226-4321. FAX: 662-226-8310. E-MAIL: dailystar@grenadastar.com. URL: http://www.grenadastar.com. Mailing Address: PO Box 907, Grenada, MS 38901. Year Established: 1854. Pub. Frequency: d. (Mon.-Fri.) Page Size: broadsheet. Subscrip. Rate: $.50 newsstand/cover; $7.75 carrier delivery/mo.; $93/yr. Adv. Rate: col. inch $8 **Wire Service(s):** AP. Circulation: 6,000 evening (paid). **Owner(s):** Grenada Newspapers, Inc., See address and contact information above. **Management:** Fred Adams, General Manager. Joe Lee III, Publisher. Wanda Roche, Advertising Director. Fred Adams, Circulation Manager. **Editorial:** Terri Ferguson, Managing Editor. Helen Thomas, Lifestyle Editor. Chuck Hathcock, Sports Editor.

HATTIESBURG

HATTIESBURG AMERICAN. 825 N. Main St., Hattiesburg, MS 39401. Telephone: 601-582-4321. FAX: 601-584-3130. E-MAIL: hattiesburgamerican@aol.com. URL: http://www.hattiesburgamerican.com. Mailing Address: PO Box 1111, Hattiesburg, MS 39403-1111. Year Established: 1885. Pub. Frequency: d. Page Size: broadsheet. Subscrip. Rate: $.50 newsstand/cover; $1.50 newsstand/cover Sun.; $36/yr carrier delivery; $144/yr mailed in state; $225/yr mailed out of state. Freelance Pay: $25/story. **Wire Service(s):** AP, GNS. Circulation: 22,290 evening (paid); 26,479 Sunday (paid). **Owner(s):** Gannett Company, Inc., 7950 Jones Branch Dr., McLean, VA 22107-0001. Telephone: 703-854-6000. **Management:** Skippy Haik, Publisher. Liz Cotten, Advertising Manager. Stephen May, Circulation Director. Rosalind Cooley, Circulation Manager. Mark Coleman, Classified Adv. Mgr.. **Editorial:** Jon Broadbooks, Executive Editor. Dan Davis, Managing Editor.

HERNANDO

DE SOTO TIMES TODAY. 315 Losher St., Hernando, MS 38632. Telephone: 662-429-6397. FAX: 662-429-5229. E-MAIL: destimes@aol.com. URL: http://www.desototimes.com. Mailing Address: P.O. Box 100, Hernando, MS 38632. Year Established: 1839. Pub. Frequency: d. (Tue.-Sat.) Page Size: standard. Subscrip. Rate: $.50 newsstand/cover; $54 for 6 mos.; $108/yr; $48 for 6 mos. for senior citizens; $96/yr for senior citizens. Adv. Rate: col. inch $8.05 **Wire Service(s):** AP. Circulation: 8,138 morning (paid). **Owner(s):** PH Publications LLC, See address and contact information above. **Management:** Ron Tate, Publisher. Sherry Ray, Circulation Manager. Diane Smith, Classified Adv. Mgr.. **Editorial:** Chris Sheffield, Managing Editor. Ron Caldwell, Sports Editor.

JACKSON

CLARION-LEDGER, THE. ISSN 0744-9526
201 S. Congress St., Jackson, MS 39201. Telephone: 601-961-7142. FAX: 601-961-7155. URL: http://www.clarionledger.com. Mailing Address: PO Box 40, Jackson, MS 39205. Year Established: 1837. Pub. Frequency: d. Page Size: broadsheet. Subscrip. Rate: $.50 newsstand/cover; $1.50 newsstand/cover Sun.; $14.50 carrier delivery/mo.; $23.50 mailed/mo. in state; $25 mailed/mo. out of state. **Wire Service(s):** AP, NYT, MCT, GNS. Circulation: 96,978 morning (paid); 110,731 Sunday (paid). **Owner(s):** Gannett Company, Inc., 7950 Jones Branch Dr, McLean, VA 22107. Telephone: 703-854-6000. **Management:** Bill Hunsberger, President. Tom Privett, Advertising Director. Lee Warmouth, Circulation Director. Helene McDonald, Classified Adv. Mgr.. Dave Hollingsworth, Marketing Director. Chris Todd, Photography Director. **Editorial:** David Hampton, Editorial Director. Ronnie Agnew, Executive Editor. Ralph Baldwin, News Editor.

LAUREL

LAUREL LEADER-CALL. 130 Beacon St., Laurel, MS 39440. Telephone: 601-428-0551. FAX: 601-426-3550. E-MAIL: publisher@laurelleadercall.com. URL: http://www.leadercall.com. Mailing Address: P.O. Drawer 728, Laurel, MS 39441. Year Established: 1911. Pub. Frequency: d. Page Size: broadsheet. Subscrip. Rate: $.50 newsstand/cover; $1 newsstand/cover Sun.; $9.95 home delivery/mo.; $108/yr home delivery. **Wire Service(s):** AP. Circulation: 8,300 evening (paid); 8,300 Sunday (paid). **Owner(s):** Community Newspaper Holdings, Inc., 3500 Colonnade Pkwy., Ste. 600, Birmingham, AL 35243. Telephone: 205-298-7100. FAX: 205-298-7101. **Management:** Chris Zimmerman, Publisher. Tammy Broome, Advertising Manager. Lisa Miller, Circulation Manager. Jack Hales, Classified Adv. Mgr.. **Editorial:** Amy Beets, Lifestyle Editor. Murray Bozeman, News Editor. Shawn Wansley, Sports Editor.

MCCOMB

ENTERPRISE-JOURNAL. 112 Oliver Emmerich Dr., McComb, MS 39648. Telephone: 601-684-2421. FAX: 601-684-0836. E-MAIL: news@enterprise-journal.com. URL: http://www.enterprise-journal.com. Mailing Address: PO Box 2009, McComb, MS 39649-2009. Year Established: 1889. Pub. Frequency: d. (Sun.-Fri.) Page Size: broadsheet. Subscrip. Rate: $.50 newsstand/cover; $1 newsstand/cover Sun.; $11.50/mo.. **Wire Service(s):** AP. Circulation: 12,000 evening (paid); 12,000 Sunday (paid). **Owner(s):** J.O. Emmerich Enterprises, Inc., See address and contact information above. **Management:** Wyatt Emmerich, President. Jack Ryan, Publisher. Lauren W. Devereaux, Advertising Manager. Freddie Deere, Circulation Manager. Vicky Deere, Classified Adv. Mgr.. **Editorial:** Matt Williamson, Managing Editor. Allyson Reynolds-Dixon, News Editor. Randy Hammons, Sports.

MERIDIAN

MERIDIAN STAR. ISSN 1064-9549
814 22nd Ave., Meridian, MS 39301. Telephone: 601-693-1551. FAX: 601-485-1275. URL: http://www.meridianstar.com. Mailing Address: PO Box 1591, Meridian, MS 39302. Year Established: 1896. Pub. Frequency: d. Page Size: standard. Subscrip. Rate: $.50 newsstand/cover; $1.25 newsstand/cover Sun.; $147/yr carrier delivery in county; $168/yr mailed in county & out of cy.. **Wire Service(s):** AP, MCT. Circulation: 19,000 evening (paid); 22,500 Sunday (paid). **Owner(s):** Community Newspaper Holdings, Inc., 3500 Colonnade Pkwy., Ste. 600, Birmingham, AL 35243. Telephone: 205-298-7101. **Management:** Crystal Dupre, Publisher. Richard Maloof, Advertising Manager. Ricky Bryant, Circulation Director. Susan Reede, Classified Adv. Mgr.. **Editorial:** Fredie Carmichael, Executive Editor. Steve Gillespie, Managing Editor.

NATCHEZ

NATCHEZ DEMOCRAT. ISSN 0888-8744
503 N. Canal St., Natchez, MS 39120. Telephone: 601-442-9101. FAX: 601-442-7315. E-MAIL: newsroom@natchezdemocrat.com. URL: http://www.natchezdemocrat.com. Mailing Address: PO Box 1447, Natchez, MS 39121. Year Established: 1865. Pub. Frequency: d. Page Size: broadsheet. Subscrip. Rate: $.50 newsstand/cover; $1.50 newsstand/cover Sun.; $15 home delivery/mo. local; $20 mailed/mo.; $9.75 mailed/mo. Sun only. **Wire Service(s):** AP. Circulation: 13,500 morning (paid); 14,000 Sunday (paid). **Owner(s):** Boone Newspapers, Inc., 15222 Freemen's Bend Rd., Northport, AL 35475. Telephone: 205-330-4100. **Management:** Todd Carpenter, President. Kevin Cooper, Advertising Director. Sam King, Circulation Manager. **Editorial:** Julie Finley, Editor. Katie Stallcup, City Editor. Joan Gandy, Community Editor. Bill Hillyer, Photo Editor. Marcus Fraizer, Sports Editor.

PASCAGOULA

MISSISSIPPI PRESS. ISSN 1059-7166
1225 Jackson Ave., Pascagoula, MS 39567. Telephone: 228-934-1419. FAX: 228-934-1454. E-MAIL: mspress@datysync.com. URL: http://www.gulflive.com. Mailing Address: PO Box 849, Pascagoula, MS 39568-0849. Year Established: 1964. Pub. Frequency: d. (Sun.-Fri.) Page Size: broadsheet. Subscrip. Rate: $.25 newsstand/cover; $1 newsstand/cover Sun.; $9 home delivery/mo.; $108/yr home delivery. **Wire Service(s):** AP. Circulation: 22,493 evening (paid); 23,700 Sunday (paid). **Owner(s):** Advance Publications, Inc., See address and contact information above. **Management:** Wanda H Jacobs, Publisher. Tommy Chelette, Advertising Director. Roy May, Advertising Manager. Monty Todd, Circulation Manager. **Editorial:** Steve Cox, Editor-in-Chief. Paul South, Managing Editor.

PICAYUNE

PICAYUNE ITEM. 17 Richardson Ozna Rd., Picayune, MS 39466. Telephone: 601-798-4766. FAX: 601-798-8602. URL: http://www.picayuneitem.com. Mailing Address: PO Box 580, Picayune, MS 39466-0580. Year Established: 1904. Pub. Frequency: d. (Tue.-Fri. & Sun.) Page Size: standard. Subscrip. Rate: $.50 newsstand/cover; $1 newsstand/cover Sun.; $79.80/yr home delivery; $108/yr mailed. Circulation: 7,307 morning (paid); 7,800 Sunday (paid). **Owner(s):** Community Newspaper Holdings, Inc., 3500 Colonnade Pkwy., Ste. 600, Birmingham, AL 35243. Telephone: 205-298-7100. FAX: 205-298-7101. **Management:** Tom Andrews, Publisher. Mary Ann Weems, Advertising Director. Annette Weber, Circulation Manager. **Editorial:** Will Sullivan, Editor. Curtis Rockwell, Sports Editor.

STARKVILLE

STARKVILLE DAILY NEWS. ISSN 1044-3657
316 University Dr., Starkville, MS 39759. Telephone: 662-323-1642. FAX: 662-323-6586. E-MAIL: dnews@netdoor.com. URL: http://www.starkvilledailynews.com. Mailing Address: P.O. Drawer 1068, Starkville, MS 39760. Year Established: 1901. Pub. Frequency: d. Page Size: broadsheet. Subscrip. Rate: $.50 newsstand/cover; $1 newsstand/cover Sun.; $106/yr home delivery local; $133/yr mailed. **Wire Service(s):** AP. Circulation: 7,950 morning (paid). **Owner(s):** Horizon Publications, Inc., 1120 N. Carbon St., Ste.100, Marion, IL 62959. Telephone: 618-993-1693. FAX: 618-997-4018. **Management:** Don Norman, Publisher. Lisa McReynolds, Classified Adv. Mgr.. **Editorial:** Brian Hawkins, Managing Editor.

TUPELO

NORTHEAST MISSISSIPPI DAILY JOURNAL. ISSN 0744-5431
1241 S Green St, Tupelo, MS 39902. Telephone: 662-842-2611. FAX: 662-842-2233. E-MAIL: classifieds@djournal.com. URL: http://www.djournal.com. Mailing Address: PO Box 909, Tupelo, MS 39902-0909. Year Established: 1870. Pub. Frequency: d. Page Size: broadsheet. Subscrip. Rate: $.50 newsstand/cover; $1.50 newsstand/cover Sun.; $11 carrier delivery/mo. in county; $120/yr carrier delivery in county; $45 mailed/mo. out of state. **Wire Service(s):** AP, MCT. Circulation: 35,447 morning (paid); 35,890 Sunday (paid). **Owner(s):** Journal Publishing Co., Inc., See address and contact information above. **Management:** Billy Crews, Publisher. Lisa Bryant, Advertising Director. Clay Foster, Circulation Manager. Cindy Carr, Classified Adv. Mgr.. **Editorial:** Lloyd Gray, Editor. Mike Tonos, Managing Editor.

VICKSBURG

VICKSBURG POST, THE. ISSN 0884-8912
1601-F N. Frontage Rd., Vicksburg, MS 39180. Telephone: 601-636-4545. FAX: 601-634-0897. E-MAIL: systemadmin@vicksburgpost.com. URL: http://www.vicksburgpost.com. Mailing Address: PO Box 821668, Vicksburg, MS 39182-0008. Year Established: 1883. Pub. Frequency: d. Page Size: broadsheet. Subscrip. Rate: $.50 newsstand/cover; $1.25 newsstand/cover Sun.; $13 home delivery/mo.; $156/yr home delivery. **Wire Service(s):** AP. Circulation: 14,073 evening (paid); 14,405 Sunday (paid). **Owner(s):** Vicksburg Printing & Publishing Co., See address and contact information above. **Management:** Pat Cashman, Publisher. David Gillis, Advertising Manager. Becky Chandler, Circulation Manager. Vickie Newman, Classified Adv. Mgr.. **Editorial:** Pat Cashman, Editor. Charles D. Mitchell, Executive Editor. Karen Gamble, Managing Editor. Sean Murphy, Sports Editor.

WEST POINT

DAILY TIMES LEADER. 227 Court St., West Point, MS 39773. Telephone: 662-494-1422. FAX: 662-494-1414. E-MAIL: dtlnews@dailytimesleader.com. URL: http://www.dailytimesleader.com. Mailing Address: PO Box 1176, West Point, MS 39773. Year Established: 1929. Pub. Frequency: d. (Tue.-Fri. & Sun.) Page Size: broadsheet. Subscrip. Rate: $.50 newsstand/cover; $84/yr carrier delivery; $92/yr mailed. Circulation: 4,000 morning (paid); 4,000 Sunday (paid). **Owner(s):** Horizon Publications, Inc., 1120 N. Carbon St., Ste.100, Marion, IL 62959. Telephone: 618-993-1693. **Management:** Don Norman, Publisher. Holley Manning, Advertising Manager. Don White, Circulation Manager. Renee Williams, Classified Editor. **Editorial:** Jeannetta Edwards, Editor.

MISSOURI

BLUE SPRINGS

BLUE SPRINGS EXAMINER. 500 W.R.D. Mize Rd., Blue Springs, MO 64015. Telephone: 816-229-9161. FAX: 816-229-6785. E-MAIL: shdavis@examiner.net. URL: http://www.examiner.net. Mailing Address: PO Box 1057, Blue Springs, MO 64013. Year Established: 1974. Pub. Frequency: d. (Mon.-Sat.) Page Size: broadsheet. Subscrip. Rate: $.50 newsstand/cover; $.75 Sat.; $94.80/yr carrier delivery; $130/yr mailed in county; $135/yr out of county; $150/yr out of state. **Wire Service(s):** AP. Circulation: 5,500 morning (paid). **Owner(s):** Morris Multimedia, Inc., PO Box 936, Augusta, GA 30903. Telephone: 706-724-0851. **Management:** Ben Weir Jr., Publisher. Sharon Dankenbring, Advertising Director. Kevin Quinn, Circulation Director. **Editorial:** Dale Brendel, Executive Editor. Sheila Davis, Managing Editor. Karl Zinke, Sports Editor.

BOONVILLE

BOONVILLE DAILY NEWS. 412 E High St., Boonville, MO 65233. Telephone: 660-882-5335. FAX: 660-882-2256. E-MAIL: bdn@mid-mo.net. URL: http://www.boonvilledailynews.com. Mailing Address: PO Box 47, Boonville, MO 65233. Year Established: 1919. Pub. Frequency: d. (Mon.-Fri.) Page Size: broadsheet. Subscrip. Rate: $.75 newsstand/cover; $104.73/yr in Cooper & Howard cys.; $115.34/yr elsewhere. **Wire Service(s):** AP. Circulation: 3,200 evening (paid). **Owner(s):** GateHouse Media, Inc, 350 WillowBrook Office Park, Fairport, NY 14450. Telephone: 585-598-0030. FAX: 585-248-2631. **Management:** Scott J. Jackson, Publisher. Deborah Marshall, Advertising Manager. Lisa Glasscock, Circulation Manager. **Editorial:** Theresa Schweitzer Krebs, Editor.

BROOKFIELD

DAILY NEWS-BULLETIN, THE. 107-109 N. Main St., Brookfield, MO 64628. Telephone: 660-258-7237. FAX: 660-258-7238. E-MAIL: bnb@shighway.com. URL: http://www.brookfieldtownnews.com. Mailing Address: PO Box 40, Brookfield, MO 64628. Year Established: 1879. Pub. Frequency: d. (Mon.-Fri.) Page Size: broadsheet. Subscrip. Rate: $.75 newsstand/cover; $23 carrier delivery/quarter; $71/yr in state; $81/yr mailed out of state. **Wire Service(s):** AP. Circulation: 3,300 evening (paid and free). **Owner(s):** GateHouse Media, Inc, 3000 Dundee Rd., Ste. 203, Northbrook, IL 60062. Telephone: 847-272-2244. **Management:** Rod Dixon, Publisher. Stacey Jackson, Advertising Manager. Larry Bradley, Circulation Manager. **Editorial:** Bryan Day, Editor. Gregory Orear, Sports.

CAMDENTON

LAKE SUN LEADER. ISSN 1063-7001
918 N State Hwy 5, Camdenton, MO 65020. Telephone: 573-346-2132. FAX: 573-346-4508. E-MAIL: lakesun@is.usmo.com. URL: http://www.lakesunleader.com. Year Established: 1879. Pub. Frequency: d. (Mon.-Fri.) Page Size: broadsheet. Subscrip. Rate: $.50 newsstand/cover; $102.95/yr mailed in county; $114.35/yr mailed out of area; $121.75/yr mailed out of state. **Wire Service(s):** AP. Circulation: 5,850 evening (paid). **Owner(s):** GateHouse Media, Inc, 350 WillowBrook Office Park, Fairport, NY 14450. Telephone: 585-598-0030. FAX: 585-248-2631. **Management:** Jules Molenda, Publisher. Lisa Miller, Advertising Manager. **Editorial:** David Schiefelbein, Editor. Matthew Wilson, Sports Editor.

Dailies

CAPE GIRARDEAU

SOUTHEAST MISSOURIAN. ISSN 0746-4452
301 Broadway, Cape Girardeau, MO 63701. FAX: 573-334-7288. E-MAIL: jsullivan@semissourian.com. URL: http://www.semissourian.com. Mailing Address: PO Box 699, Cape Girardeau, MO 63702-0699. Year Established: 1904. Pub. Frequency: d. Page Size: broadsheet. Subscrip. Rate: $.50 newsstand/cover; $1.50 newsstand/cover Sun.; $42 home delivery for 13 wks.. Circulation: 17,215 morning (paid); 20,300 Sunday (paid). **Owner(s):** Rust Communications, Inc., See address and contact information above. **Management:** Jon Rust, Publisher. Donna Denson, Advertising Director. Mark Kneer, Circulation Director. Donna Denson, Classified Adv. Mgr.. **Editorial:** Joe Sullivan, Editor.

CARTHAGE

CARTHAGE PRESS. 800 W Central, Carthage, MO 64836. Telephone: 417-358-2191. FAX: 417-358-7428. E-MAIL: advertising@carthagepress.com. URL: http://www.carthagepress.com. Mailing Address: PO Box 678, Carthage, MO 64836. Year Established: 1872. Pub. Frequency: d. (Sun.-Fri.) Page Size: broadsheet. Subscrip. Rate: $.50 newsstand/cover; $9.42/mo.; $108/yr. **Wire Service(s):** AP. Circulation: 4,500 evening (paid). **Owner(s):** GateHouse Media, Inc, 350 WillowBrook Office Park, Fairport, NY 14450. Telephone: 585-598-0030. FAX: 585-248-2631. **Management:** Buzz Ball, General Manager. Tammy Collins, Advertising. Amy Willis, Circulation Manager. Amber Carter, Classified Adv. Mgr.. **Editorial:** Buzz Ball, Editor. Dennis Sowers, City Editor. Cody Dyer, Sports.

CHILLICOTHE

CONSTITUTION-TRIBUNE. ISSN 0746-8555
818 Washington St., Chillicothe, MO 64601. Telephone: 660-646-2411. FAX: 660-646-2028. E-MAIL: ctribune@greenhills.net. URL: http://www.chillicothenews.com. Mailing Address: PO Box 707, Chillicothe, MO 64601. Year Established: 1860. Pub. Frequency: d. (Mon.-Fri.) Page Size: broadsheet. Subscrip. Rate: $.50 newsstand/cover; $110.44/yr in county & adj. cys.; $117.95/yr out of county; $112/yr mailed out of state. **Wire Service(s):** AP. Circulation: 4,700 evening (paid). **Owner(s):** GateHouse Media, Inc, 350 WillowBrook Office Park, Fairport, NY 14450. Telephone: 585-598-0030. FAX: 585-248-2631. **Management:** Andrea Graves, Advertising Director. Connie Jones, Classified Adv. Mgr.. **Editorial:** Catherine Stortz, News Editor. Paul Sturm, Sports Editor.

CLINTON

CLINTON DAILY DEMOCRAT. 212 S. Washington St., Clinton, MO 64735. Telephone: 660-885-2281. FAX: 660-885-2265. Mailing Address: PO Box 586, Clinton, MO 64735-0586. Year Established: 1868. Pub. Frequency: d. (Mon.-Fri.) Page Size: broadsheet. Subscrip. Rate: $.50 newsstand/cover; $69/yr in county; $79.50/yr out of county. Adv. Rate: col. inch $5.80 Circulation: 4,300 evening (paid). **Owner(s):** Democrat Publishing Co., See address and contact information above. **Management:** Daniel B. Miles Jr., General Manager. Kathleen Miles, Publisher. Katherine Miles, Advertising Manager. Mary Jo Witherspoon, Circulation Manager. Mike Gregory, Classified Adv. Mgr.. **Editorial:** Daniel B. Miles Jr., Managing Editor. Denise Smith, Society Editor. Gar Garman, Sports.

COLUMBIA

COLUMBIA DAILY TRIBUNE. ISSN 1543-6535
100 N. Fourth St., Columbia, MO 65201. Telephone: 573-815-1500. FAX: 573-815-1701. E-MAIL: editor@tribmail.com. URL: http://www.columbiatribune.com. Mailing Address: PO Box 798, Columbia, MO 65205. Year Established: 1901. Pub. Frequency: d. Page Size: broadsheet. Subscrip. Rate: $.50 newsstand/cover; $1.50 newsstand/cover Sun.; $151.01/yr. Adv. Rate: col. inch $14.10 Freelance Pay: $2.50/column-inch. **Wire Service(s):** AP, MCT. Circulation: 18,262 per issue (paid); 23,416 Sunday (paid). **Owner(s):** Tribune Publishing Company, Inc., See address and contact information above. **Management:** Henry J. Waters IV, General Manager. Jennifer Vanderpool, Advertising Director. Dirk Dunkle, Circulation Director. Pati McDonald, Classified Adv. Mgr.. Vicki Russell, Associate Publisher. **Editorial:** Jim Robertson, Managing Editor. Lynn Israel, Feature Editor. Joe Walljasper, Sports Editor.

COLUMBIA MISSOURIAN. ISSN 0747-1874
221 S. Eighth St., Columbia, MO 65201. Telephone: 573-882-5700. FAX: 573-882-5702. E-MAIL: reporter@digmo.com. URL: http://www.digmo.org. Year Established: 1908. Pub. Frequency: d. (Sun.-Fri.) Page Size: broadsheet. Subscrip. Rate: $.50 newsstand/cover; $.75 newsstand/cover Sun.; $85/yr mailed in county. **Wire Service(s):** AP, SH, NYT. Circulation: 7,200 morning (paid); 5,300 Sunday (paid). **Owner(s):** Missourian Publishing Co., PO Box 917, Columbia, MO 65205. Telephone: 573-882-5700. **Management:** Daniel S. Potter, General Manager. Dean Mills, Publisher. Jack Swartz, Advertising Manager. Patrick Fitzsimmons, Circulation Manager. **Editorial:** Tom Warhover, Executive Editor. Nina Johnson, Librarian.

DEXTER

DAILY STATESMAN. 133 S. Walnut, Dexter, MO 63841. Telephone: 573-624-4545. FAX: 573-624-7449. E-MAIL: publisher@dailystatesman.com. URL: http://www.dailystatesman.com. Mailing Address: PO Box 579, Dexter, MO 63841. Pub. Frequency: d. (Tue.- Fri. & Sun.) Page Size: broadsheet. Subscrip. Rate: $.50 newsstand/cover; $.75 newsstand/cover Sun.; $42.50 home delivery for 6 mos.; $80/yr home delivery. Circulation: 4,200 evening (paid); 4,200 Sunday (paid). **Owner(s):** Rust Communications, Inc., 301 Broadway, Cape Girardeau, MO 63701. Telephone: 573-335-6611. **Management:** Bud Hunt, Publisher. Elaine Pursell, Advertising Manager. **Editorial:** Annabeth Miller, Editor. Jos Hester, Sports Editor.

FULTON

FULTON SUN, THE. ISSN 8750-6696
115 E. Fifth St., Fulton, MO 65251. Telephone: 573-642-7272. FAX: 573-642-0656. Mailing Address: PO Box 550, Fulton, MO 65251. Year Established: 1876. Pub. Frequency: d. (Tue.-Fri. & Sun.) Page Size: broadsheet. Subscrip. Rate: $61/yr carrier delivery; $78/yr mailed in county; $81.82/yr in state; $86.32/yr out of state; $77.68/yr to senior citizens. **Wire Service(s):** AP. Circulation: 4,500 morning (paid); 4,500 Sunday (paid). **Owner(s):** Walter E. Hussman Jr., PO Box 420, Jefferson City, MO 65101. Telephone: 573-636-3131. **Management:** Betty H. Weldon, President. Tony Weldon, Publisher. Annessa Weiners, Circulation Manager. **Editorial:** Karen Atkins, Managing Editor. Ryan Boland, Sports Editor.

HANNIBAL

HANNIBAL COURIER-POST. 200 N. Third St., Hannibal, MO 63401. Telephone: 573-221-2800. FAX: 573-221-1568. E-MAIL: hcp@nemonet.com. URL: http://www.hannibal.net. Mailing Address: PO Box A, Hannibal, MO 63401. Year Established: 1838. Pub. Frequency: d. (Mon.-Sat.) Page Size: standard. Subscrip. Rate: $.50 newsstand/cover; $.75 newsstand/cover Sat.; $52.15 home delivery for 6 mos. local; $100.95/yr. Adv. Rate: col. inch $12.60 **Wire Service(s):** AP. Circulation: 9,500 morning (paid). **Owner(s):** Morris Multimedia, Inc., PO Box 936, Augusta, GA 30903. Telephone: 706-724-0851. **Management:** Jack Whitaker, Publisher. Tina Kopecky, Advertising Director. Ron Scott, Circulation Manager. Shirley Jackson, Classified Adv. Mgr.. **Editorial:** Mary Lou Montgomery, Managing Editor.

HOLLISTER

BRANSON DAILY NEWS. 200 Industrial Park Dr., Hollister, MO 65672. Telephone: 417-334-3161. FAX: 417-334-8275. URL: http://www.bransondailynews.com. Mailing Address: PO Box 1900, Branson, MO 65615. Year Established: 1898. Pub. Frequency: d. (Tue.-Sat.) Page Size: broadsheet. Subscrip. Rate: $.50 newsstand/cover; $125/yr in Stone & Taney counties; $185/yr out of area. Adv. Rate: col. inch $18 **Wire Service(s):** AP. Circulation: 9,000 morning (paid). **Owner(s):** Tri Lakes Newspapers, See address and contact information above. **Management:** Ted Delaney, Publisher. **Editorial:** Chad Hunter, News Editor. Pat Dailey, Sports Editor.

INDEPENDENCE

INDEPENDENCE EXAMINER, THE. 410 S. Liberty, Independence, MO 64050. Telephone: 816-254-8600. FAX: 816-836-3805. URL: http://www.examiner.net. Mailing Address: PO Box 459, Independence, MO 64051. Year Established: 1898. Pub. Frequency: d. (Mon.-Sat.) Page Size: broadsheet. Subscrip. Rate: $.50 newsstand/cover; $.75 newsstand/cover Sat.; $9/mo.; $27 for 3 mos.. Adv. Rate: col. inch $19.05 **Wire Service(s):** AP. Circulation: 10,068 evening (paid). **Owner(s):** Morris Multimedia, Inc., PO Box 936, Augusta, GA 30903. Telephone: 706-724-0851. **Management:** Ben F. Weir Jr., Publisher. Sharon Dankenbring, Advertising Director. Kevin Quinn, Circulation Manager. Luke Daniel, Classified Adv. Mgr.. Sharon Hall, Business Manager. **Editorial:** Dale Brendel, Executive Editor. Sheila Davis, News Editor. Paul Beaver, Photo Editor. Karl Zinke, Sports Editor.

JEFFERSON CITY

NEWS TRIBUNE (JEFFERSON CITY). 210 Monroe St., Jefferson City, MO 65101. Telephone: 573-636-3131. FAX: 573-636-7035. E-MAIL: jane@newstribune.com. URL: http://www.newstribune.com. Mailing Address: PO Box 420, Jefferson City, MO 65102. Pub. Frequency: d. (Tue.-Sun.) Page Size: broadsheet. Subscrip. Rate: $.50 newsstand/cover; $1 Sun.; $90/yr; $98/yr mailed in state. **Wire Service(s):** AP. Circulation: 19,500 morning (paid); 22,000 Sunday (paid). **Owner(s):** Walter E. Hussman Jr., See address and contact information above. **Management:** Mike Vivion, General Manager. Walter E Hussman Jr., Publisher. Jane Haslag, Advertising Director. Rob Siebeneck, Circulation Manager. **Editorial:** Richard McGonegal, Managing Editor. Tom Rackers, Sports Editor.

POST-TRIBUNE (JEFFERSON CITY). PO Box 420, Jefferson City, MO 65101. Telephone: 573-636-3131. FAX: 573-761-0235. E-MAIL: nt@newstribune.com. URL: http://www.newstribune.com. Year Established: 1865. Pub. Frequency: d. Page Size: standard. Subscrip. Rate: $.50 newsstand/cover; $1 Sun.; $8.50/mo.; $90/yr. **Wire Service(s):** AP, SH, NYT, CNS. Circulation: 18,000 evening (paid). **Owner(s):** Walter E. Hussman Jr., PO Box 420, Jefferson City, MO 65102. Telephone: 573-636-3131. FAX: 573-636-7035. **Management:** Jane Haslag, Advertising Director. John Tucker, Advertising Manager. Rob Siebeneck, Circulation Manager. Mike Vivion, Business Manager. **Editorial:** Doug Waggoner, Executive Editor. Richard McGonegal, Managing Editor. Don Norfleet, Business Editor. Michelle Reagan, Religion Editor. Tom Rackers, Sports.

JOPLIN

JOPLIN GLOBE, THE. 117 E. Fourth St., Joplin, MO 64801. Telephone: 417-623-3480. FAX: 417-623-8450. URL: http://www.joplinglobe.com. Mailing Address: PO Box 7, Joplin, MO 64802. Year Established: 1896. Pub. Frequency: d. Page Size: broadsheet. Subscrip. Rate: $.50 newsstand/cover; $1.50 Sun.; $172.40/yr carrier delivery in county; $242.86/yr mailed in state. **Wire Service(s):** AP. Circulation: 36,350 morning (paid); 46,000 Sunday (paid). **Owner(s):** Community Newspaper Holdings, Inc., 3500 Colonnade Pkwy., Ste. 600, Birmingham, AL 35243. Telephone: 205-298-7100. **Management:** Dan Chiodo, Publisher. Tim Holden, Advertising Director. Jack Kaminsky, Circulation Director. Janet Cooper, Classified Adv. Mgr.. **Editorial:** Carol Stark, Editor. Mike Pound, Entertainment Editor. Jim Fryar, Sports Editor.

KANSAS CITY

KANSAS CITY STAR, THE. ISSN 0745-1067
1729 Grand Blvd., Kansas City, MO 64108-1413. Telephone: 816-234-4636. FAX: 816-234-4926. URL: http://www.kcstar.com. Year Established: 1880. Pub. Frequency: d. Page Size: broadsheet. Subscrip. Rate: $.50 newsstand/cover; $1.25 Sun.; $53.26 home delivery for 26 wks.; $204/yr home delivery. Adv. Rate: col. inch $153.13 **Wire Service(s):** AP, NYT. Circulation: 275,735 morning (paid); 397,776 Sunday (paid). **Owner(s):** The/McClatchy Company, 2100 Q St, Sacramento, CA 95816. Telephone: 916-321-1936. FAX: 916-321-1869. **Management:** Mac Tully, Publisher. Marty Goodnight, Advertising Director. Mark Maassen, Sales Manager. **Editorial:** Mark Zieman, Editor. Jeff Goldsmith, News Editor.

KENNETT

DAILY DUNKLIN DEMOCRAT. ISSN 1047-7160
203 First St., Kennett, MO 63857. Telephone: 573-888-4505. FAX: 573-888-5114. URL: http://www.dddnews.com. Mailing Address: PO Box 669, Kennett, MO 63857-0669. Year Established: 1888. Pub. Frequency: d. (Tue.-Fri. & Sun.) Page Size: standard. Subscrip. Rate: $.50 newsstand/cover; $.75 newsstand/cover Sun.; $8 carrier delivery/mo.; $87/yr. Freelance Pay: $1/column-inch. **Wire Service(s):** AP. Circulation: 5,200 morning (paid). **Owner(s):** Delta Publishing Co., Inc., See address and contact information above. **Management:** Bud Hunt, Publisher. Diane McClain, Advertising Manager. Randy Hindmon, Circulation Manager. Christina Folkes, Classified Adv. Mgr.. **Editorial:** Jack Rollins, Managing Editor. Lyman Skyles, Associate Editor.

KIRKSVILLE

KIRKSVILLE DAILY EXPRESS. 110 E. McPherson St., Kirksville, MO 63501. Telephone: 660-665-2808. FAX: 660-665-2608. URL: http://www.kirksvilledailyexpress.com. Mailing Address: PO Box 809, Kirksville, MO 63501. Year Established: 1905. Pub. Frequency: d. (Sun.-Fri.) Page Size: broadsheet. Subscrip. Rate: $.75 newsstand/cover; $.75 Sun.; $165/yr in state. **Wire Service(s):** AP. Circulation: 6,700 evening (paid); 7,000 Sunday (paid). **Owner(s):** GateHouse Media, Inc, 350 WillowBrook Office Park, Fairport, NY 14450. Telephone: 585-598-0030. FAX: 585-248-2631. **Management:** Larry W. Freels, Publisher. George Wriedt, Advertising Manager. Carole Murphy, Classified Adv. Mgr.. **Editorial:** Greg Orear, Managing Editor. Jason Hunsicker, Sports.

LEBANON

LEBANON DAILY RECORD. 100 E. Commerce, Lebanon, MO 65536. Telephone: 417-532-9131. E-MAIL: editor@lebanondailyrecord.com. URL: http://www.lebpubco.com. Mailing Address: PO Box 192, Lebanon, MO 65536. Year Established: 1934. Pub. Frequency: d. (Sun.-Fri.) Page Size: broadsheet. Subscrip. Rate: $.50 newsstand/cover; $1 newsstand/cover Sun.; $136/yr in county & adj. cys.; $149.60/yr in state; $171.22/yr out of state. **Wire Service(s):** AP. Circulation: 4,500 evening (paid); 4,800 Sunday (paid). **Owner(s):** Dalton Wright, See address and contact information above. **Management:** Dalton Wright, Publisher. Rene Barker, Advertising Manager. Lawrence Damme, Circulation Manager. Beth Durreman, Classified Adv. Mgr.. Phyllis Wilson, Business Manager. **Editorial:** Chris Wrinkle, Editor. Israel Potoczny, Sports Editor.

MACON

MACON CHRONICLE-HERALD. 204 W. Bourke St., Macon, MO 63552. Telephone: 660-385-3121. FAX: 660-385-3082. E-MAIL: maconch@istmacon.net. URL: http://www.maconch.com. Mailing Address: PO Box 7, Macon, MO 63552. Year Established: 1910. Pub. Frequency: d. (Tue.-Fri.) Page Size: broadsheet. Subscrip. Rate: $.50 newsstand/cover; $12.91/mo.; $113.99/yr. **Wire Service(s):** AP. Circulation: 3,000 evening (paid). **Owner(s):** GateHouse Media, Inc, 350 WillowBrook Office Park, Fairport, NY 14450. Telephone: 585-598-0030. FAX: 585-248-2631. **Management:** Pat Quinly, Publisher. Chuck Kindle, Advertising Manager. Clinton House, Circulation Manager. Chandrea Growe, Classified Adv. Mgr.. **Editorial:** Terri Hackett, Editor.

MARSHALL

MARSHALL DEMOCRAT-NEWS. 121 N. Lafayette St., Marshall, MO 65340. Telephone: 660-886-2233. FAX: 660-886-8544. E-MAIL: marshalleditor@socket.net. URL: http://www.marshallnews.com. Mailing Address: PO Box 100, Marshall, MO 65340. Year Established: 1881. Pub. Frequency: d. (Mon.-Fri.) Page Size: broadsheet. Subscrip. Rate: $.50 newsstand/cover; $92.35/yr in county. **Wire Service(s):** AP. Circulation: 4,300 evening (paid). **Owner(s):** Rust Communications, Inc., 301 Broadway, Cape Girardeau, MO 63702. Telephone: 573-335-6611. **Management:** Shelly M. Arth, Publisher. Mike Davis, Advertising Manager. Pat Morrow, Circulation Manager. **Editorial:** Mark Lile, Managing Editor.

MARYVILLE

MARYVILLE DAILY FORUM. 111 E. Jenkins St., Maryville, MO 64468. Telephone: 660-562-2424. FAX: 660-562-2823. E-MAIL: adv@classicnet.net. URL: http://www.maryvilledailyforum.com. Mailing Address: PO Box 188, Maryville, MO 64468. Year Established: 1869. Pub. Frequency: d. (Mon.-Fri.) Page Size: broadsheet. Subscrip. Rate: $.75 newsstand/cover; $10/mo. in county; $90/yr in county; $120/yr out of county. **Wire Service(s):** AP. Circulation: 3,400 evening (paid); 3,600 Sunday (paid). **Owner(s):** GateHouse Media, Inc, 350 WillowBrook Office Park, Fairport, NY 14450. Telephone: 585-598-0030. FAX: 585-248-2631. **Management:** Mike Herring, Publisher. Phil Cobb, Advertising Manager. Rita Piveral, Classified Adv. Mgr.. **Editorial:** Mike Herring, Managing Editor. Charlie Slenker, Sports.

MEXICO

MEXICO LEDGER, THE. 300 N Washington St, Mexico, MO 65265. Telephone: 573-581-1111. FAX: 573-581-2029. E-MAIL: news@mexicoledger.com. URL: http://www.mexicoledger.com. Mailing Address: PO Box 8, Mexico, MO 65265-0008. Year Established: 1855. Pub. Frequency: d. (Mon.-Fri.) Page Size: broadsheet. Subscrip. Rate: $.75 newsstand/cover; $13 carrier delivery/mo. & motor rte.; $125/yr carrier delivery & motor rte.; $125/yr mailed. **Wire Service(s):** AP. Circulation: 7,085 evening (paid). **Owner(s):** GateHouse Media, Inc, 350 WillowBrook Office Park, Fairport, NY 14450. Telephone: 585-598-0030. FAX: 585-248-2631. **Management:** Joe May, Publisher. Martin Keller, Advertising Director. Leslie Chapman, Classified Adv. Mgr.. **Editorial:** Janeen Sims, Managing Editor. Brenda Fike, Assistant Editor. Jim Stanley, Sports.

MOBERLY

MOBERLY MONITOR INDEX. 218 N. Williams St., Moberly, MO 65270. Telephone: 660-263-4123. FAX: 660-263-3626. E-MAIL: moberlymonitor@missvalley.com. URL: http://www.moberlymonitor.com. Mailing Address: PO Box 697, Moberly, MO 65270. Year Established: 1869. Pub. Frequency: d. (Sun.-Fri.) Page Size: broadsheet. Subscrip. Rate: $.50 newsstand/cover; $1 newsstand/cover Sun.; $108/yr carrier delivery local; $120/yr mailed in state; $132/yr mailed out of state. Adv. Rate: col. inch $10.61 **Wire Service(s):** AP. Circulation: 6,200 evening (paid); 6,500 Sunday (paid). **Owner(s):** GateHouse Media, Inc, 350 WillowBrook Office Park, Fairport, NY 14450. Telephone: 585-598-0030. FAX: 585-248-2631. **Management:** Bob Cunningham, Publisher. Judy Orton, Advertising Director. Tammy Bradds, Circulation Manager. Nancy Bartolacci, Classified Adv. Mgr.. **Editorial:** Ruth Carr, Editor. Amy Compney, City Editor. Chuck Embree, Sports Editor.

MONETT

MONETT TIMES. 505 Broadway, Monett, MO 65708. Telephone: 417-235-3135. FAX: 417-235-8852. E-MAIL: news@monett-times.com. URL: http://www.monett-times.com. Mailing Address: PO Box 40, Monett, MO 65708. Year Established: 1888. Pub. Frequency: d. (Mon.-Fri.) Page Size: broadsheet. Subscrip. Rate: $.50 newsstand/cover; $40/yr carrier delivery local; $57/yr mailed in Barry & Lawrence cys.. Circulation: 4,100 evening (paid). **Owner(s):** Walls Newspapers, Inc., 525 Office Park Dr., Birmingham, AL 35223. Telephone: 205-870-1684. **Management:** Michael L. Stubbs, Publisher. Lisa Craft, Advertising Director. **Editorial:** Michael L. Stubbs, Editor. Murray Bishoff, Managing Editor.

NEOSHO

NEOSHO DAILY NEWS, THE. 1006 W. Harmony St., Neosho, MO 64850. Telephone: 417-451-1520. FAX: 417-451-6408. E-MAIL: editor@neoshodailynews.com. URL: http://www.neoshodailynews.com. Mailing Address: PO Box 848, Neosho, MO 64850. Year Established: 1905. Pub. Frequency: d. (Sun.-Fri.) Page Size: broadsheet. Subscrip. Rate: $.50 newsstand/cover; $1 Sun.; $101.40/yr carrier delivery & motor rte; $106.80/yr mailed in state; $111.55/yr mailed out of state. **Wire Service(s):** AP. Circulation: 4,600 evening (paid); 5,200 Sunday (paid). **Owner(s):** GateHouse Media, Inc, 350 WillowBrook Office Park, Fairport, NY 14450. Telephone: 585-598-0030. FAX: 585-248-2631. **Management:** Buzz Ball, General Manager. Rick Rogers, Publisher. Tommy Todd, Advertising Manager. Bill Lyttle, Circulation Director. Sharon Choate, Classified Adv. Mgr.. **Editorial:** John Ford, Associate Editor.

NEVADA

DAILY MAIL/HERALD MAIL, THE. ISSN 1056-3555
131 S. Cedar St., Nevada, MO 64772. Telephone: 417-667-3344. FAX: 417-667-8121. E-MAIL: dailym@mailcity.com. Mailing Address: PO Box 247, Nevada, MO 64772. Year Established: 1883. Pub. Frequency: d. (Tue.-Fri. & Sun.) Page Size: broadsheet. Subscrip. Rate: $.50 newsstand/cover; $8 home delivery/mo.; $79/yr home delivery. **Wire Service(s):** AP. Circulation: 3,000 evening (paid); 3,700 Sunday (paid). **Owner(s):** Rust Communications, Inc., 301 Broadway, Cape Girardeau, MO 62702. Telephone: 800-879-1212. **Management:** Carl Simpson, Publisher. Kelly Brock, Advertising.

PARK HILLS

DAILY JOURNAL. 1513 Saint Joe Dr., Park Hills, MO 63601. Telephone: 573-431-2010. FAX: 573-431-7640. Mailing Address: PO Box A, Park Hills, MO 63601. Pub. Frequency: d. Page Size: broadsheet. Subscrip. Rate: $.50 newsstand/cover; $1 newsstand/cover Sun.. **Wire Service(s):** AP. Circulation: 8,700 evening (paid); 8,500 Sunday (paid). **Owner(s):** Lee Enterprises, Inc., 900 N. Tucker Blvd., St. Louis, MO 63101. Telephone: 314-340-8000. **Management:** Don Rowley, Publisher. Denise McMillen, Advertising Director. Mark Cedeck, Circulation Manager. **Editorial:** Sherry Greminger, Managing Editor. Donn Adamson, Sports.

POPLAR BLUFF

DAILY AMERICAN REPUBLIC (POPLAR BLUFF). ISSN 1061-7116
208 Poplar St., Poplar Bluff, MO 63901. Telephone: 573-785-1414. FAX: 573-785-2706. URL: http://www.darnews.com. Mailing Address: PO Box 7, Poplar Bluff, MO 63902. Year Established: 1923. Pub. Frequency: d. (Sun.-Fri.) Page Size: broadsheet. Subscrip. Rate: $.50 newsstand/cover; $1 Sun.; $99/yr carrier delivery in county & mailed in state; $156/yr mailed out of state. **Wire Service(s):** AP. Circulation: 15,000 evening (paid); 22,000 Sunday (paid). **Owner(s):** Rust Communications, Inc., 301 Broadway, Cape Girardeau, MO 63701. Telephone: 573-335-6611. **Management:** Don Schrieber, Publisher. Joe Jordan, Advertising Manager. Gary Richard, Circulation Manager. Gayle Mobley, Business Manager. **Editorial:** Stan Berry, Editor.

RICHMOND

DAILY NEWS (RICHMOND). 204 W.N. Main St., Richmond, MO 64085. Telephone: 816-776-5454. FAX: 816-470-7108. E-MAIL: publisher@richmond-dailynews.com. URL: http://www.richmond-dailynews.com. Mailing Address: PO Box 100, Richmond, MO 64085. Year Established: 1914. Pub. Frequency: d. (Mon.-Fri.) Page Size: broadsheet. Subscrip. Rate: $.50 newsstand/cover; $66/yr carrier delivery local; $68/yr mailed. Adv. Rate: col. inch $6.75 Freelance Pay: $10/article. Circulation: 2,660 evening (paid). **Owner(s):** The Richmond News, Inc., See address and contact information above. **Management:** Brian Rice, Publisher. Karen Reynolds, Classified Adv. Mgr.. **Editorial:** Brian Rice, Managing Editor. Joseph Frederick, Sports.

ROLLA

ROLLA DAILY NEWS. 101 W. Seventh St., Rolla, MO 65401. Telephone: 573-364-2468. FAX: 573-341-5847. E-MAIL: news@therolladailynews.com. URL: http://www.therolladailynews.com. Mailing Address: PO Box 808, Rolla, MO 65402-0808. Year Established: 1942. Pub. Frequency: d. (Mon.-Sat.) Page Size: standard. Subscrip. Rate: $.50 newsstand/cover; $1 Sat.-Sun.; $99.65/yr home delivery; $160.70/yr mailed in county; $190.25/yr mailed out of county; $191/yr mailed out of state. **Wire Service(s):** UPI. Circulation: 5,300 evening (paid); 5,300 Sunday (paid). **Owner(s):** GateHouse Media, Inc, 350 WillowBrook Office Park, Fairport, NY 14450. Telephone: 585-598-0030. FAX: 585-248-2631. **Management:** Stephen E. Sowers, Publisher. Lonna Stephenson, Advertising Manager. Kelly Wallis, Circulation Manager. Kristin Douglas, Classified Adv. Mgr.. **Editorial:** Stephen E. Sowers, Editor. Alan Gerstenecker, Managing Editor. Seth Sowers, Sports.

SEDALIA

SEDALIA DEMOCRAT, THE. ISSN 1061-1762
700 S. Massachusetts Ave., Sedalia, MO 65301. Telephone: 660-826-1000. FAX: 660-826-2413. E-MAIL: democrat@ozarks.net. URL: http://www.sedaliademocrat.com. Mailing Address: PO Box 848, Sedalia, MO 65302. Year Established: 1868. Pub. Frequency: d. Page Size: broadsheet. Subscrip. Rate: $.50 newsstand/cover; $1.50 Sun.; $118/yr carrier delivery local & motor rte; $118/yr mailed in county; $154.20/yr mailed out of county. **Wire Service(s):** AP, MCT. Circulation: 13,000 evening (paid); 14,500 Sunday (paid). **Owner(s):** Freedom Communications, Inc., 17666 Fitch, Irvine, CA 92614. Telephone: 714-553-9292. **Management:** Charlie Fischer, Publisher. Lisa Lynn, Advertising Director. Brandon Grose, Circulation Manager. **Editorial:** Oliver Wiest, Editor. Kaye Fair, City Editor. Kyle Smith, Sports.

SIKESTON

STANDARD DEMOCRAT, THE. ISSN 1074-4460
205 S. New Madrid, Sikeston, MO 63801. Telephone: 573-471-1137. FAX: 573-471-6277. E-MAIL: standem@yahoo.com. URL: http://www.standarddemocrat.com. Year Established: 1913. Pub. Frequency: d. (Sun.-Fri.) Page Size: broadsheet. Subscrip. Rate: $1 newsstand/cover; $1.50 newsstand/cover Sun.; $85/yr carrier delivery; $99.80/yr mailed in state; $123/yr mailed out of state. Freelance Pay: $0.35/column-inch. **Wire Service(s):** AP. Circulation: 8,100 morning (paid); 10,200 Sunday (paid). **Owner(s):** D.A. Publishing LC, See address and contact information above. **Management:** Don Culbertson, General Manager. Michael Jensen, Publisher. DeAnna Nelson, Advertising Manager. Merlin Hagy, Circulation Manager. **Editorial:** Jill Bock, Managing Editor.

SPRINGFIELD

SPRINGFIELD NEWS-LEADER, THE. ISSN 0893-3448
651 Boonville Ave., Springfield, MO 65806. Telephone: 417-836-1100. FAX: 417-837-1381. URL: http://www.springfieldnews-leader.com. Mailing Address: PO Box 798, Springfield, MO 65801. Year Established: 1867. Pub. Frequency: d. Page Size: broadsheet. Subscrip. Rate: $.50 newsstand/cover; $1.75 newsstand/cover Sun.; $14.08 carrier delivery/mo.; $182/yr carrier delivery; $19.32 mailed/mo.; $266.24/yr mailed. **Wire Service(s):** AP, LAT-WAT, GNS. Circulation: 63,589 morning (paid); 95,000 Sunday (paid). **Owner(s):** Gannett Company, Inc., 7950 Jones Branch Dr, McLean, VA 22107. Telephone: 703-854-6000. **Bureau(s):** 209 Clay St., Jefferson City, MO 65101. Telephone: 314-636-4911. **Management:** Tom Bookstaver, President. Dee McCants, Advertising Manager. David Brown, Circulation Director. Cindy Butner, Marketing Director. **Editorial:** Cheryl Whitsitt, Managing Editor. Dean Curtis, Photographer.

ST. JOSEPH

ST. JOSEPH NEWS-PRESS. ISSN 1063-4312
825 Edmond, St. Joseph, MO 64501. Telephone: 816-271-8500. FAX: 816-271-8696. E-MAIL: davidb@npgco.com. URL: http://www.stjoelive.com. Mailing Address: PO Box 29, St. Joseph, MO 64502. Year Established: 1988. Pub. Frequency: d. Page Size: standard. Subscrip. Rate: $.50 newsstand/cover; $.75 Sat.; $1.50 Sun.; $184.40/yr home delivery. **Wire Service(s):** AP, NYT. Circulation: 41,817 morning (paid); 46,629 Sunday (paid). **Owner(s):** News-Press & Gazette Co., See address and contact information above. **Management:** Lee M. Sawyer, General Manager. David R. Bradley Jr., Publisher. Tim Weddle, Advertising Director. Kevin Smith, Circulation Director. **Editorial:** David R. Bradley Jr., Editor. Dennis Ellsworth, Executive Editor. Greg Kozol, Business Editor. Steve Booher, City Editor. Mark Sheehan, Editorial Page Editor. Jess DeHaven, Lifestyle Editor. Eric Keith, Photographer. Eddie Burns, Sports Editor.

ST. LOUIS

ST. LOUIS POST-DISPATCH. ISSN 1930-9600
900 N Tucker Blvd., St. Louis, MO 63101. Telephone: 314-340-8000. FAX: 314-340-3050. E-MAIL: letters@post-dispatch.com. URL: http://www.stltoday.com. Year Established: 1878. Pub. Frequency: d. Page Size: standard. Subscrip. Rate: $.50 newsstand/cover; $1.25 Sun.; $4.10 carrier delivery/wk.; $213.20/yr carrier delivery. **Wire Service(s):** RN, AP, SH, LAT-WAT, MCT. Circulation: 286,310 morning (paid); 449,845 Sunday (paid). **Owner(s):** Lee Enterprises, Inc., 201 N. Harrison St, Ste 600, Davenport, IA 52801-1924. **Management:** Kevin Mowbray, Publisher. Amy Owens, Advertising Director. **Editorial:** Arnie Robbins, Editor. Pam Maples, Managing Editor. Susan Hegger, Feature Editor. Adam Goodman, Metro Editor.

ST. ROBERT

DAILY GUIDE. 108 Holly Dr., St. Robert, MO 65584. Telephone: 573-336-3711. FAX: 573-336-4640. E-MAIL: dailyguide@jobe.net. URL: http://www.waynesvilledailyguide.com. Mailing Address: PO Box 578, Waynesville, MO 65583. Year Established: 1962. Pub. Frequency: d. (Tue.-Fri.) Page Size: broadsheet. Subscrip. Rate: $.50 newsstand/cover; $77.90/yr in county; $87.45/yr mailed in state; $105.95/yr mailed out of state. Circulation: 2,300 evening (paid). **Owner(s):** GateHouse Media, Inc, 350 WillowBrook Office Park, Fairport, NY 14450. Telephone: 585-598-0030. FAX: 585-248-2631. **Management:** Bill Mills, Publisher. Karen Hood, Advertising Manager. Linda Campbell, Circulation Manager. **Editorial:** Dan Hassett, Editor.

STE. GENEVIEVE

SUN TIMES NEWS ONLINE. 21851 White Sands Rd., Ste. Genevieve, MO 63670. Telephone: 573-883-2980. FAX: 573-883-2866. E-MAIL: news@suntimesnews.com. URL: http://www.suntimesnews.com. Mailing Address: PO Box 428, Ste. Genevieve, MO 63670.Year Established: 1989 Pub. Frequency: d. Circulation: 3,000 per issue (free). **Owner(s):** Donze Communications, 10 Perry Plz., Perryville, MO 63775. **Management:** Elmo Donze, Owner. Bob Scott, Advertising Manager. **Editorial:** Don Pritchard, Editor.

TRENTON

TRENTON REPUBLICAN TIMES. 514 Town & Country, Trenton, MO 64683. Telephone: 660-359-2212. FAX: 660-359-4414. E-MAIL: rtimes@lyn.net. URL: http://www.northwestmissouri.com. Year Established: 1864. Pub. Frequency: d. (Mon.-Fri.) Page Size: broadsheet. Subscrip. Rate: $.50 newsstand/cover; $53.36/yr in county. **Wire Service(s):** AP. Circulation: 3,100 evening (paid). **Owner(s):** Wendell J. Lenhart, See address and contact information above. **Management:** Wendell J. Lenhart, Publisher. Angela Dugan, Advertising Manager. Donna Wilson, Circulation Manager. **Editorial:** Wendell J. Lenhart, Managing Editor. Diane Raynes, Lifestyle Editor. Greg Dalrymple, Sports Editor.

WARRENSBURG

DAILY STAR-JOURNAL, THE. 135 E. Market, Warrensburg, MO 64093. Telephone: 660-747-8123. FAX: 660-747-8741. E-MAIL: dsjads@npgco.com. URL: http://www.dailystarjournal.com. Mailing Address: PO Box 68, Warrensburg, MO 64093-0068. Year Established: 1865. Pub. Frequency: d. (Mon.-Fri.) Page Size: broadsheet. Subscrip. Rate: $.50 newsstand/cover; $53.23/yr carrier delivery; $64.63/yr mailed out of state. **Wire Service(s):** AP. Circulation: 5,425 evening (paid). **Owner(s):** News Press Gazette, See address and contact information above. **Management:** Bill James, Publisher. D J Lowery, Advertising Manager. Kevin Quinn, Circulation Manager. **Editorial:** Sue Sterling, Court Editor. Skye Cobb, Feature Editor. Jack Miles, News Editor. Corey Edwards, Sports Editor.

WEST PLAINS

WEST PLAINS DAILY QUILL. 125 N Jefferson, West Plains, MO 65775. Telephone: 417-256-9191. FAX: 417-256-9196. E-MAIL: news@westplainsquill.com. URL: http://www.westplainsquill.com. Mailing Address: P.O. Box 110, West Plains, MO 65775-0110. Year Established: 1902. Pub. Frequency: d. (Mon.-Fri.) Page Size: broadsheet. Subscrip. Rate: $.50 newsstand/cover; $46.54/yr carrier delivery local; $39.95/yr mailed in county; $41/yr mailed out of county; $61/yr mailed elsewhere. **Wire Service(s):** AP. Circulation: 9,800 evening (paid). **Owner(s):** Quill Press Co., See address and contact information above. **Management:** Frank L. Martin III, Publisher. Carla Bean, Advertising Manager. Lea Hodo, Circulation Manager. Heather Gabriel, Classified Adv. Mgr.. Judy Collins, Business Manager. **Editorial:** Frank L. Martin III, Editor. Jerry P. Womack, Managing Editor. Carol Bruce, City Editor. Dennis Crider, Sports Editor.

MONTANA

BILLINGS

BILLINGS GAZETTE. 401 N. Broadway, Billings, MT 59101. Telephone: 406-657-1200. FAX: 406-657-1208. URL: http://www.billingsgazette.com. Mailing Address: PO Box 36300, Billings, MT 59107-6300. Year Established: 1885. Pub. Frequency: d. Page Size: broadsheet. Subscrip. Rate: $.75 newsstand/cover; $1.75 newsstand/cover Sun.; $18.90 home delivery local for 4 wks.; $237.30/yr home delivery. Freelance Pay: $50/article. **Wire Service(s):** AP, MCT. Circulation: 62,370 morning (paid); 64,064 Sunday (paid). **Owner(s):** Lee Enterprises, Inc., 201 N. Harrison St., Ste. 600, Davenport, IA 52801-1924. **Management:** Michael Gulledge, Publisher. Dave Worstell, Advertising Manager. Allen Wilson, Circulation Manager. Heather Davis, Classified Adv. Mgr.. **Editorial:** Steve Prosinski, Editor. Kristi Angel, Managing Editor. Chris Rubich, Feature Editor. Larry Mayer, Photo Editor. Mike Zimmer, Sports Editor.

BOZEMAN

BOZEMAN DAILY CHRONICLE. 2820 W. College, Bozeman, MT 59718. Telephone: 406-587-4491. FAX: 406-587-7995. URL: http://www.dailychronicle.com. Mailing Address: PO Box 1190, Bozeman, MT 59771. Year Established: 1883. Pub. Frequency: d. Page Size: broadsheet. Subscrip. Rate: $.50 newsstand/cover; $1.25 Sun.; $162/yr home delivery local; $174/yr motor route local. **Wire Service(s):** AP, LAT-WAT. Circulation: 18,000 morning (paid); 18,140 Sunday (paid). **Owner(s):** Big Sky Publishing LLC, See address and contact information above. **Management:** Stephanie Pressly, Publisher. Doug Weber, Advertising Director. Steve Buckner, Circulation Director. **Editorial:** Nick Ehli, Managing Editor. Karin Ronnow, Asst. Managing Ed.. Tim Dumas, Sports Editor.

BUTTE

MONTANA STANDARD, THE. 25 W. Granite St., Butte, MT 59701. Telephone: 406-496-5500. FAX: 406-496-5551. URL: http://www.mtstandard.com. Mailing Address: PO Box 627, Butte, MT 59701. Year Established: 1876. Pub. Frequency: d. Page Size: broadsheet. Subscrip. Rate: $.50 newsstand/cover; $.75 newsstand/cover Sat.; $1.50 newsstand/cover Sun.; $3.50 home delivery/wk. local; $4.20 mailed/wk. in state. **Wire Service(s):** AP, NYT. Circulation: 15,000 morning (paid); 15,500 Sunday (paid). **Owner(s):** Lee Enterprises, Inc., 201 N. Harrison St, Ste 600, Davenport, IA 52801-1924. **Management:** Janet Taylor, Publisher. Patti Arntson, Advertising Manager. Laurie Tripp, Circulation Manager. Karen Corbin, Classified Adv. Mgr.. **Editorial:** Gerry O'Brien, Editor. Carmen Winslow, Associate Editor.

GREAT FALLS

GREAT FALLS TRIBUNE. 205 River Dr., S., Great Falls, MT 59405. Telephone: 406-791-1444. FAX: 406-791-1431. URL: http://www.greatfallstribune.com. Mailing Address: PO Box 5468, Great Falls, MT 59403. Year Established: 1884. Pub. Frequency: d. Page Size: broadsheet. Subscrip. Rate: $.50 newsstand/cover; $1.50 newsstand/cover Sun.; $187.20/yr carrier delivery; $195/yr motor route. **Wire Service(s):** AP, SH, NYT, GNS. Circulation: 34,000 morning (paid); 39,000 Sunday (paid). **Owner(s):** Gannett Company, Inc., 7950 Jones Branch Dr, McLean, VA 22107. Telephone: 703-854-6000. **Management:** Jim Strauss, Publisher. Max Smith, Advertising Manager. Katy Kurrtz, Classified Adv. Mgr.. **Editorial:** Jim Strauss, Executive Editor. Gary Moseman, Managing Editor. Wendy Raney, Business Editor. Robin Loznak, Photo Editor. George Geise, Sports Editor.

HAMILTON

RAVALLI REPUBLIC. 232 W. Main St., Hamilton, MT 59840. Telephone: 406-363-3300. FAX: 406-363-1767. E-MAIL: editor@ravallirepublic.com. URL: http://www.ravallirepublic.com. Year Established: 1889. Pub. Frequency: d. (Mon.-Fri.) Page Size: broadsheet. Subscrip. Rate: $.50 newsstand/cover; $85.32/yr home delivery in county; $100.90/yr mailed in state; $112.40/yr mailed out of state. Circulation: 5,294 morning (paid). **Owner(s):** Lee Enterprises, Inc., 201 N. Harrison St, Ste 600, Davenport, IA 52801-1924. **Management:** Sharon Schroeder, Publisher. **Editorial:** Wayne Adair, Editor. John Andiollis, Sports.

HAVRE

HAVRE DAILY NEWS, THE. 119 Second St., Havre, MT 59501. Telephone: 406-265-6796. FAX: 406-265-6798. E-MAIL: hdn@havredailynews.com. URL: http://www.havredailynews.com. Mailing Address: PO Box 431, Havre, MT 59501. Year Established: 1915. Pub. Frequency: d. (Mon.-Fri.) Page Size: standard. Subscrip. Rate: $.50 newsstand/cover; $.75 newsstand/cover Friday; $129/yr carrier delivery; $207/yr mailed out of state. Freelance Pay: $1/column-inch. **Wire Service(s):** AP. Circulation: 4,300 evening (paid). **Owner(s):** Pioneer Newspapers, 221 First Ave., W., Ste. 405, Seattle, WA 98119. Telephone: 206-284-4424. **Management:** Val Murri, Publisher. Stacy Mantle, Advertising Manager. Craig Otterstrom, Circulation Manager. Dixie English, Classified Adv. Mgr.. **Editorial:** Alan Sorensen, Managing Editor. George Ferguson, Sports.

HELENA

INDEPENDENT RECORD. 317 Cruse Ave., Helena, MT 59601. Telephone: 406-447-4000. FAX: 406-447-4052. E-MAIL: irstaff@helenair.com. URL: http://www.helenair.com. Mailing Address: PO Box 4249, Helena, MT 59604. Pub. Frequency: d. Page Size: broadsheet. Subscrip. Rate: $.75 newsstand/cover; $1.50 Sun.; $163.50/yr carrier delivery local; $196.50/yr mailed in county; $222.75/yr mailed elsewhere. **Wire Service(s):** AP, NYT. Circulation: 14,500 morning (paid); 15,000 evening (paid). **Owner(s):** Lee Enterprises, Inc., See address and contact information above. **Management:** Pat Schlauch, Publisher. Jim Rickman, Advertising Manager. Anita Fasbender, Circulation Manager. Tonda Meyer, Classified Adv. Mgr.. **Editorial:** Dave Shors, Editor.

KALISPELL

DAILY INTER LAKE, THE. 727 E. Idaho St., Kalispell, MT 59901. Telephone: 406-755-7000. FAX: 406-752-6114. URL: http://www.dailyinterlake.com. Mailing Address: PO Box 7610, Kalispell, MT 59904. Year Established: 1888. Pub. Frequency: d. Page Size: broadsheet. Subscrip. Rate: $.50 newsstand/cover; $.75 Sat.; $1.50 Sun.; $183.25/yr carrier delivery; $189.25/yr motor route. **Wire Service(s):** AP, LAT-WAT. Circulation: 17,500 evening (paid); 19,000 Sunday (paid). **Owner(s):** Hagadone Corp., 111 S. First St., Coeur d'Alene, ID 83814-1937. Telephone: 208-667-3431. **Management:** Duane B. Hagadone, Owner. Tom Kurdy, Publisher. Lisa Fleming, Advertising Manager. Brant Horn, Circulation Manager. Dorothy Glencross, Business Manager. **Editorial:** Frank Miele, Managing Editor. Bill Spence, Business Editor. Lynnette Hintze, Church Editor. Scott Crandell, City Editor. David Lesnick, Sports.

LIVINGSTON

LIVINGSTON (MT) ENTERPRISE. 401 S. Main, Livingston, MT 59047. Telephone: 406-222-2000. FAX: 406-222-8580. E-MAIL: ads@livent.net. URL: http://www.livingstonenterprise.com. Mailing Address: PO Box 2000, Livingston, MT 59047. Year Established: 1883. Pub. Frequency: d. (Mon.-Fri.) Page Size: broadsheet. Subscrip. Rate: $.50 newsstand/cover; $111.15/yr carrier delivery local; $122.55/yr mailed in Clyde Park & Wilsall; $189.55/yr mailed elsewhere. Adv. Rate: col. inch $5.90 **Wire Service(s):** AP. Circulation: 3,500 evening (paid). **Owner(s):** Yellowstone Newspapers, See address and contact information above. **Management:** John Sullivan, Publisher. Jim Durfey, Advertising Manager. **Editorial:** John Sullivan, Editor. Stephen Matlow, Managing Editor. Lynette Zwerneman, Community Editor. Dwight Harriman, News Editor. Garrett Cheane, Photo Editor. Tom Gersack, Sports.

MILES CITY

MILES CITY STAR. ISSN 0891-8988
818 Main St., Miles City, MT 59301. Telephone: 406-234-0450. FAX: 406-234-6687. E-MAIL: mcstar@midrivers.com. URL: http://www.milescitystar.com. Mailing Address: PO Box 1216, Miles City, MT 59301. Year Established: 1910. Pub. Frequency: d. (Mon.-Fri.) Page Size: broadsheet. Subscrip. Rate: $.75 newsstand/cover; $114/yr home delivery in city; $124.40/yr motor route; $171/yr mailed in state. Adv. Rate: col. inch $6.75 **Wire Service(s):** AP. Circulation: 3,700 evening (paid). **Owner(s):** Yellowstone Newspapers, 401 S. Main, Livingston, MT 59047. Telephone: 406-222-2000. **Management:** Dan Killoy, Publisher. Giff Wood, Advertising Manager. **Editorial:** Marla Prell, Managing Editor. Jeff Virag, Circulation Editor. Denise Hartse, Community Editor. Elaine Swanson, News. Steve Allison, Photo.

MISSOULA

MISSOULIAN, THE. ISSN 0746-4495
500 S. Higgins Ave., Missoula, MT 59801. Telephone: 406-523-5200. FAX: 406-523-5221. URL: http://www.missoulian.com. Mailing Address: PO Box 8029, Missoula, MT 59807. Year Established: 1873. Pub. Frequency: d. Page Size: broadsheet. Subscrip. Rate: $.50 newsstand/cover; $1.75 newsstand/cover Sun.; $49.75 carrier delivery for 13 wks.. **Wire Service(s):** AP, LAT-WAT, MCT. Circulation: 31,680 morning (paid); 38,000 Sunday (paid). **Owner(s):** Lee Enterprises, Inc., 201 N. Harrison St, Ste 600, Davenport, IA 52801-1924. **Management:** John VanStrydonck, Publisher. Kristin Eberhart, Advertising Director. Tyler Fraiser, Circulation Manager. Jim McGowan, Classified Adv. Mgr.. **Editorial:** Mike McInally, Editor. Sherry Devlin, City Editor. Steve Woodruff, Editorial Page Editor. Bob Meseroll, Sports Editor.

NEBRASKA

ALLIANCE

ALLIANCE TIMES-HERALD. 114 E. Fourth St., Alliance, NE 69301. E-MAIL: hehnews@alliancetimes.com. URL: http://www.alliancetimes.com. Mailing Address: PO Box G, Alliance, NE 69301. Year Established: 1887. Pub. Frequency: d. (Mon.-Sat.) Page Size: broadsheet. Subscrip. Rate: $.50 newsstand/cover; $66/yr home delivery local; $86/yr mailed local; $99/yr mailed elsewhere. **Wire Service(s):** AP. Circulation: 3,030 evening (paid). **Owner(s):** Alliance Publishing Co. Inc., See address and contact information above. **Management:** Fred G. Kuhlman, Publisher. Steve Stackonwalt, Advertising. **Editorial:** John Weare, Managing Editor. Luayne Weisgerber, Lifestyle Editor. Tammy Coward, Sports.

BEATRICE

BEATRICE DAILY SUN. 200 N. Seventh St., Beatrice, NE 68310. Telephone: 402-223-5233. FAX: 402-228-3571. URL: http://www.beatricedailysun.com. Mailing Address: PO Box 847, Beatrice, NE 68310-0847. Year Established: 1902. Pub. Frequency: d. (Mon.-Sat.) Page Size: broadsheet. Subscrip. Rate: $.50 newsstand/cover; $9 home delivery/mo. local; $105.20/yr mailed in area; $112.20/yr mailed in NE & KS. **Wire Service(s):** AP. Circulation: 8,700 evening (paid). **Owner(s):** Lee Enterprises, Inc., 201 N. Harrison St, Ste 600, Davenport, IA 52801-1924. **Management:** Jim Shanks, Publisher. Shawna Hilbert, Advertising Manager. Stacy Specht, Circulation Manager. **Editorial:** Diane Vicars, Managing Editor.

COLUMBUS

COLUMBUS TELEGRAM. 1254 27th Ave., Columbus, NE 68601. Telephone: 402-564-2741. FAX: 402-563-7500. E-MAIL: col.editor@lee.net. URL: http://www.columbustelegram.com. Mailing Address: PO Box 648, Columbus, NE 68602-0648. Year Established: 1879. Pub. Frequency: d. (Sun.-Fri.) Page Size: broadsheet. Subscrip. Rate: $.75 newsstand/cover; $1.25 newsstand/cover Sun.; $107.75/yr mailed in city; $126.50/yr mailed in state. **Wire Service(s):** AP, MCT. Circulation: 11,100 evening (paid); 11,700 Sunday (paid). **Owner(s):** Lee Enterprises, Inc., 201 N. Harrison St., Davenport, IA 52801-1924. **Management:** Bob Blackman, Publisher. Ann Blunt, Advertising Director. Greg Pehrson, Circulation Director. **Editorial:** James Dean, Editor.

FREMONT

FREMONT TRIBUNE. ISSN 1049-8338
135 N. Main St., Fremont, NE 68025. Telephone: 402-721-5000. FAX: 402-721-8047. E-MAIL: tribnews@ftrib.com. URL: http://www.ftrib.com. Mailing Address: PO Box 9, Fremont, NE 68026-0009. Year Established: 1865. Pub. Frequency: d. (Mon.-Sat.) Page Size: broadsheet. Subscrip. Rate: $.50 newsstand/cover; $120.25/yr carrier delivery; $154.44/yr mailed local; $164.06/yr mailed elsewhere. **Wire Service(s):** AP, GNS. Circulation: 8,300 evening (paid). **Owner(s):** Lee Enterprises, Inc., 201 N. Harrison St., Davenport, IA 52801-1924. **Management:** Bill Vobejda, Publisher. Ken Knepper, Advertising Manager. Greg Pehrson, Circulation Manager. Rose Kuhns, Classified Adv. Mgr.. **Editorial:** Tracy Buffington, Editor. Tammy McKeighan, News Editor. Brent Wasenius, Sports Editor.

GRAND ISLAND

GRAND ISLAND INDEPENDENT. ISSN 1049-3018
422 W. First St., Grand Island, NE 68801. Telephone: 308-382-1000. FAX: 308-382-8129. E-MAIL: newsdesk@theindependent.com. URL: http://www.theindependent.com. Mailing Address: PO Box 1208, Grand Island, NE 68802-1208. Year Established: 1872. Pub. Frequency: d. Page Size: broadsheet. Subscrip. Rate: $.50 newsstand/cover; $1 Sun.; $105/yr carrier delivery; $117.50/yr mailed local; $163.75/yr elsewhere. Adv. Rate: col. inch $16.50 **Wire Service(s):** AP, SH. Circulation: 24,900 morning (paid); 26,200 Sunday (paid). **Owner(s):** Morris Multimedia, Inc., PO Box 936, Augusta, GA 30903. Telephone: 706-724-0851. **Management:** Don Smith, Publisher. Sonia Schultz, Advertising Director. Micah Young, Circulation Manager. **Editorial:** Bill Dunn, Editor. Dennis Kraus, Production Manager.

HASTINGS

HASTINGS DAILY TRIBUNE. 908-912 W. Second St., Hastings, NE 68901. Telephone: 402-462-2131. FAX: 402-461-4657. URL: http://www.hastingstribune.com. Mailing Address: PO Box 788, Hastings, NE 68902. Year Established: 1905. Pub. Frequency: d. (Mon.-Sat.) Page Size: broadsheet. Subscrip. Rate: $.50 newsstand/cover; $87/yr carrier delivery; $93/yr motor route; $126/yr mailed out of state. **Wire Service(s):** AP, SH, LAT-WAT. Circulation: 13,200 evening (paid). **Owner(s):** Seaton Publishing Co., See address and contact information above. **Management:** Donald R. Seaton, Publisher. Doug Edwards, Operations Manager. Ken Gettner, Advertising Manager. Cary Beurskens, Circulation Manager. **Editorial:** Donald R. Seaton, Editor. Darran Fowler, Managing Editor. Tami Humphreys, News Editor. Rich Houchin, Photographer. Kyle Svec, Sports Editor.

HOLDREGE

HOLDREGE DAILY CITIZEN. 418 Garfield, Holdrege, NE 68949. Telephone: 308-995-4441. FAX: 308-995-5992. Year Established: 1886. Pub. Frequency: d. (Mon.-Fri.) Page Size: broadsheet. Subscrip. Rate: $.25 newsstand/cover; $60/yr carrier delivery. **Wire Service(s):** AP. Circulation: 3,300 evening (paid). **Owner(s):** Holdrege Daily Citizen, Inc., See address and contact information above. **Management:** Robert King, President. Barbara J. Penrod, Advertising Director. Barb Green, Circulation Manager. Barbara J. Penrod, Classified Adv. Mgr.. **Editorial:** Tunney Price, Editor. Richard Headley, Sports.

KEARNEY

KEARNEY HUB. 13 E. 22nd St., Kearney, NE 68847. Telephone: 308-237-2152. FAX: 308-233-9745. E-MAIL: kearneyhub@kearney.net. URL: http://www.kearneyhub.com. Mailing Address: PO Box 1988, Kearney, NE 68848. Year Established: 1888. Pub. Frequency: d. (Mon.-Sat.) Page Size: broadsheet. Subscrip. Rate: $.50 newsstand/cover; $1.25 Sat.; $9.25 carrier delivery/mo.; $109.50/yr; $135.25/yr mailed regional. **Wire Service(s):** AP. Circulation: 13,000 evening (paid). **Owner(s):** World Newspapers, Inc., World Herald Sq., Omaha, NE 68102. Telephone: 402-444-1000. FAX: 402-345-9115. **Management:** Julie Speirs, General Manager. Steve Chatelain, President. Lori Guthard, Advertising Director. Brenda Allen, Circulation Manager. **Editorial:** Mike Konz, Managing Editor. Brad Norton, Photographer. Buck Mahoney, Sports Editor.

LINCOLN

LINCOLN JOURNAL STAR (LINCOLN). 926 P St., Lincoln, NE 68508. Telephone: 402-475-4200. FAX: 402-473-7466. E-MAIL: feedback@nebweb.com. URL: http://www.journalstar.com. Mailing Address: PO Box 81609, Lincoln, NE 68508-1609. Year Established: 1894. Pub. Frequency: d. Page Size: broadsheet. Subscrip. Rate: $.50 newsstand/cover; $1.75 newsstand/cover Sun.; $57.85 home delivery in city for 13 wks.. **Wire Service(s):** AP, UPI. Circulation: 10,700. **Owner(s):** Lee Enterprises, Inc., 201 N. Harrison St, Ste 600, Davenport, IA 52801-1924. **Management:** John Meher, Publisher. Tom Hiskey, Advertising Manager. Brady Svendgard, Circulation Manager. **Editorial:** Kathleen Rutledge, Editor. Peter Salter, City Editor. Linda Olig, Feature Editor. Jim Johnson, News Editor. John Mabry, Sports Editor. Catherine Huddle, Sunday Editor.

MCCOOK

MCCOOK DAILY GAZETTE. W. First & E. Sts., McCook, NE 69001. Telephone: 308-345-4500. FAX: 308-345-7881. Mailing Address: PO Box 1268, McCook, NE 69001. Year Established: 1911. Pub. Frequency: d. (Mon.-Sat.) Page Size: broadsheet. Subscrip. Rate: $.50 newsstand/cover; $99/yr home delivery. **Wire Service(s):** AP. Circulation: 7,200 evening (paid). **Owner(s):** Rust Communications, Inc., 301 Broadway, Cape Girardeau, MO 63701. Telephone: 573-335-6611. **Management:** Gene Morris, Publisher. Kenny Johnson, Advertising Director. Mary Beth Orsnoski, Circulation Manager. **Editorial:** Bruce Crosby, Editor.

NEBRASKA CITY

NEBRASKA CITY NEWS-PRESS. 806 Central Ave, Nebraska City, NE 68410. Telephone: 402-873-3334. FAX: 402-873-5436. URL: http://www.ncnewspress.com. Mailing Address: PO Box 757, Nebraska City, NE 68410. Year Established: 1854. Pub. Frequency: d. (Mon.-Fri.) Page Size: broadsheet. Subscrip. Rate: $.50 newsstand/cover; $50/yr in county & Fremont Cy., IA; $60/yr in state & IA; $94/yr out of area. **Wire Service(s):** AP. Circulation: 2,500 evening (paid). **Owner(s):** GateHouse Media, Inc, 350 WillowBrook Office Park, Fairport, NY 14450. Telephone: 585-598-0030. FAX: 585-248-2631. **Management:** Tim Larson, Publisher. Kathleen Kaufman, Advertising Manager. Janet Entler, Circulation Manager. **Editorial:** Tammy Pearson, Executive Editor. Kirt Manion, Sports Editor.

NORFOLK

NORFOLK DAILY NEWS. 525 Norfolk Ave., Norfolk, NE 68701-0977. Telephone: 402-371-1020. FAX: 402-371-5802. E-MAIL: ndnews@norfolkdailynews.com. URL: http://www.norfolkdailynews.com. Mailing Address: PO Box 977, Norfolk, NE 68702-0977. Year Established: 1887. Pub. Frequency: d. (Mon.-Sat.) Page Size: broadsheet. Subscrip. Rate: $.50 newsstand/cover; $111/yr carrier delivery; $123/yr motor route; $160/yr mailed in state. **Wire Service(s):** AP. Circulation: 17,500 evening (paid). **Owner(s):** Huse Publishing Co., See address and contact information above. **Management:** Les Mann, General Manager. Jerry Huse, Publisher. Larry Bartscher, Advertising Manager. Missy Bryde, Circulation Manager. Deb Warneke, Business Manager. **Editorial:** Kent Warneke, Editor. Sheryl Schmeckpepper, Lifestyle Editor. Jay Prauner, Sports Editor.

NORTH PLATTE

TELEGRAPH (NORTH PLATTE), THE. ISSN 0747-4008
621 N Chestnut, North Platte, NE 69101. Telephone: 308-532-6000. FAX: 308-532-9268. URL: http://www.nptelegraph.com. Mailing Address: PO Box 370, North Platte, NE 69103. Year Established: 1881. Pub. Frequency: d. (Tue.-Sun.) Page Size: broadsheet. Subscrip. Rate: $.50 newsstand/cover; $1 newsstand/cover Sun.; $132.50/yr mailed. **Wire Service(s):** AP. Circulation: 14,500 morning (paid); 15,050 Sunday (paid). **Owner(s):** Omaha World-Herald Co., 1314 Douglas St, Omaha, NE 68102. Telephone: 402-444-1000. FAX: 402-345-0183. **Management:** Peter Rogers, Publisher. Dee Klein, Advertising Manager. **Editorial:** Job Vigil, Managing Editor. Joe Volcek, Circulation Editor.

OMAHA

OMAHA WORLD-HERALD. ISSN 0276-4962
1314 Douglas St, Omaha, NE 68102. Telephone: 402-444-1000. FAX: 402-345-0183. E-MAIL: davidwingarder@owh.com. URL: http://www.omaha.com. Year Established: 1885. Pub. Frequency: d. Page Size: broadsheet. Subscrip. Rate: $.50 newsstand/cover; $1.75 Sun.; $2.50/wk.. **Wire Service(s):** AP, NYT, LAT-WAT. Circulation: 192,607 morning (paid); 242,964 Sunday (paid). **Owner(s):** Omaha World-Herald Co., See address and contact information above. **Bureau(s): Management:** John Gottschalk, Publisher. Dave Wiinegarder, Advertising Director. Thom Kastrup, Advertising Manager. Alex Skovgaard, Circulation Director. Larry Etienne, Classified Adv. Mgr.. **Editorial:** Larry King, Executive Editor. Don Sumerside, News Editor.

SCOTTSBLUFF

STAR-HERALD. 1405 Broadway, Scottsbluff, NE 69361. Telephone: 308-632-9000. FAX: 308-632-9001. E-MAIL: starherald@starherald.com. URL: http://www.starherald.com. Mailing Address: PO Box 1709, Scottsbluff, NE 69363-1709. Year Established: 1903. Pub. Frequency: d. (Tue.-Sun.) Page Size: broadsheet. Subscrip. Rate: $.50 newsstand/cover; $.75 newsstand/cover Sat. & Sun.; $115/yr mailed in county; $126/yr mailed out of county. **Wire Service(s):** AP, SH. Circulation: 16,000 morning (paid); 16,566 Sunday (paid). **Owner(s):** World Newspapers, Inc., Landmark Ctr., 1299 Farnam St., 15th Fl., Omaha, NE 68102-1841. Telephone: 402-444-1000. FAX: 402-345-9115. **Management:** Jim Holland, Publisher. Doug Southard, Advertising Director. **Editorial:** Steve Frederick, Editor.

SIDNEY

SIDNEY SUN-TELEGRAPH. PO Box 193, Sidney, NE 69162. Telephone: 308-254-2818. FAX: 308-254-3925. E-MAIL: admin@sidneysun.com. URL: http://www.sidneysun.com. Year Established: 1997. Pub. Frequency: d. (Tue.-Sat.) Page Size: broadsheet. Subscrip. Rate: $.50 newsstand/cover; $89/yr. Adv. Rate: col. inch $7.65 **Wire Service(s):** AP. Circulation: 3,300 morning (paid). **Owner(s):** Excellence in Publishing, Inc., See address and contact information above. **Management:** Dennis Cheatham, General Manager. Gary Stevenson, Publisher. Brenda Blanke, Circulation Manager. **Editorial:** Doug Law, Sports.

YORK

YORK NEWS-TIMES. 327 Platte Ave., York, NE 68467. Telephone: 402-362-4478. FAX: 402-362-6748. E-MAIL: rita.thomas@yorknewstimes.com. URL: http//www.yorknewstimes.com. Mailing Address: PO Box 279, York, NE 68467. Year Established: 1887. Pub. Frequency: d. (Mon.-Sat.) Page Size: broadsheet. Subscrip. Rate: $.35 newsstand/cover; $75.60/yr mailed in county; $88/yr mailed elsewhere. **Wire Service(s):** AP. Circulation: 4,500 morning (paid). **Owner(s):** Morris Multimedia, Inc., PO Box 936, Augusta, GA 30903-0936. Telephone: 706-724-0851. **Management:** Rita Thomas, Publisher. Dawn Kush, Circulation Manager. Carol Faller, Business Manager. **Editorial:** Melanie Wilkinson, Managing Editor. Carol Faller, Business Editor.

NEVADA

CARSON CITY

NEVADA APPEAL. 580 Mallory Way, Carson City, NV 89701. Telephone: 775-882-2111. FAX: 775-887-2426. E-MAIL: appeal@tahoe.com. URL: http://www.tahoe.com. Mailing Address: PO Box 2288, Carson City, NV 89702-2288. Year Established: 1865. Pub. Frequency: d. Page Size: broadsheet. Subscrip. Rate: $.50 newsstand/cover; $1.50 newsstand/cover Sun.; $87/yr; $19.50 mailed/mo.. Freelance Pay: $0.60/column-inch. **Wire Service(s):** AP. Circulation: 30,000 evening (paid). **Owner(s):** Swift Newspapers, Inc., 500 Double Eagle Ct., Reno, NV 89511. Telephone: 775-850-7676. FAX: 775-850-7677. **Management:** John Dimambro, Publisher. Keith Tanoos, Circulation Manager. Peter Kostos, Associate Publisher. Anne McLaine, Business Manager. **Editorial:** Barry Smith, Managing Editor. Rhonda Costa-Landers, Lifestyle Editor. Rick Gunn, Photographer. Charles Whisman, Sports Editor.

ELKO

ELKO DAILY FREE PRESS. 3720 Idaho St., Elko, NV 89801. Telephone: 775-738-3118. FAX: 775-738-2215. E-MAIL: swoody@elkodaily.com. URL: http://www.elkodaily.com. Year Established: 1883. Pub. Frequency: d. (Mon.-Sat.) Page Size: broadsheet. Subscrip. Rate: $.50 newsstand/cover; $1 newsstand/cover Sat.; $125/yr carrier delivery local; $153/yr mailed in county. **Wire Service(s):** AP. Circulation: 7,000 evening (paid). **Owner(s):** GateHouse Media, Inc, 3000 Dundee Rd., Ste. 203, Northbrook, IL 60062. Telephone: 847-272-2244. FAX: 847-272-6244. **Management:** Rhonda Zuroff, Publisher. Summer Ehrmann, Advertising Director. Deb Sampson, Circulation Manager. **Editorial:** Sam Brown, Sports Editor.

ELY

ELY TIMES. 297 11th St., E., Ely, NV 89301. Telephone: 775-289-4491. FAX: 775-289-4566. E-MAIL: publisher@elynews.com. URL: http://www.elynews.com. Mailing Address: PO Box 70, Las Vegas, NV 89125. Year Established: 1920. Pub. Frequency: w. (Wed.) Page Size: standard. Subscrip. Rate: $4 mailed/mo. in county; $.75 newsstand/cover. Freelance Pay: $0.35/column-inch. **Wire Service(s):** AP. Circulation: 1,800 evening (paid). **Owner(s):** Stephens Media LLC, See address and contact information above. **Bureau(s):** Contact: Steve Tetreault, Bureau Chief. **Management:** Kenneth Kliewer, Publisher. **Editorial:** Kent Harper, Editor. Shari Gilson, Production Manager.

FALLON

LAHONTAN VALLEY NEWS & FALLON EAGLE STANDARD. 562 N Maine St, Fallon, NV 89406. Telephone: 775-423-6041. FAX: 775-423-0474. E-MAIL: news@lahontanvalleynews.com. URL: http://www.lahontanvalleynews.com. Mailing Address: PO Box 1297, Fallon, NV 89407. Year Established: 1912. Pub. Frequency: d. (Mon.-Sat.) Page Size: broadsheet. Subscrip. Rate: $.50 newsstand/cover; $105/yr home delivery in county; $145/yr mailed out of county. **Wire Service(s):** AP. Circulation: 4,700 morning (paid). **Owner(s):** Swift Newspapers, Inc., 500 Double Eagle Ct., Reno, NV 89511. Telephone: 775-850-7676. FAX: 775-850-7677. **Management:** Kevin Todd, Publisher. **Editorial:** Josh Johnson, Editor.

HENDERSON

LAS VEGAS SUN. 2275 Corporate Circle, Henderson, NV 89074. Telephone: 702-385-3111. FAX: 702-383-7264. E-MAIL: letters@lasvegassun.com. URL: http://www.lasvegassun.com. Mailing Address: PO Box 98970, Las Vegas, NV 89193-8970. Year Established: 1950. Pub. Frequency: d. (Mon.-Fri.) Page Size: broadsheet. Subscrip. Rate: $.50 newsstand/cover; $3 carrier delivery/wk.. Freelance Pay: $25-$100/article. **Wire Service(s):** AP, NYT, GNS. Circulation: 120,000 evening (paid); 250,000 Sunday (paid). **Owner(s):** Barbara Greenspun, See address and contact information above. **Bureau(s):** State Capital Bldg., Carson City, NV 89710. Telephone: 775-687-5032. FAX: 775-684-5305. Contact: Cy Ryan, Bureau Chief. **Management:** Brian Greenspun, President. Barbara Greenspun, Publisher. **Editorial:** Michael J. Kelley, Managing Editor. Mike Campbell, Editorial Page Editor. Mark Whittington, Feature Editor. Drex Heikes, Metro Editor. Mark Damon, Photo Editor.

LAS VEGAS

LAS VEGAS REVIEW-JOURNAL. ISSN 1097-1645
1111 W. Bonanza Rd., Las Vegas, NV 89125-0070. Telephone: 702-383-0211. FAX: 702-383-4665. URL: http://www.lvrj.com. Mailing Address: PO Box 70, Las Vegas, NV 89125. Year Established: 1905. Pub. Frequency: d. Page Size: standard. Subscrip. Rate: $.50 newsstand/cover; $2.50 newsstand/cover Sun.; $3.50 carrier delivery/wk.; $182/yr carrier delivery. **Wire Service(s):** AP, LAT-WAT, MCT. Circulation: 190,100 morning (paid); 218,879 Sunday (paid). **Owner(s):** Stephens Media LLC, 1111 W. Bonanza Rd., Las Vegas, NV 89106. Telephone: 702-383-0211. **Bureau(s):** 666 11th St. NW, Ste. 535, Washington, DC 20001. Telephone: 202-783-1760. Contact: Steve Tetrault, Bureau Chief. **Management:** Allan Fleming, General Manager. Sherman Frederick, Publisher. Bob Brown, Advertising Director. Diane Winnemuller, Advertising Manager. Ed Parker, Circulation Director. Rebecca Bradner, Classified Adv. Mgr.. Terry Duck, Production Director. Patricia Little, Business Manager. Trudy Patterson, Promotion Manager. **Editorial:** Tom Mitchell, Editor. Charles Zobell, Managing Editor. Michael Hiesiger, Business Editor. Mary Hynes, City Editor. John Kerr, Editorial Page Editor. Frank Fertado, Entertainment Editor. Mary Greely, News Editor. Jeff Scheid, Photo Editor. Dorothy Huffy, Society Editor. Jim Fossom, Sports Editor. Melissa Sullivan, Travel Editor. Christopher Stanley, TV Editor.

RENO

RENO GAZETTE-JOURNAL. ISSN 0745-1415
955 Kuenzli St., Reno, NV 89502. Telephone: 775-788-6200. FAX: 775-788-6458. E-MAIL: newsroom@nevadanet.com. URL: http://www.rgj.com. Mailing Address: PO Box 22000, Reno, NV 89520-2000. Year Established: 1870. Pub. Frequency: d. Page Size: broadsheet. Subscrip. Rate: $16.25 carrier delivery/mo.. **Wire Service(s):** AP, NYT, DJNS, GNS. Circulation: 64,995 morning (paid); 91,232 Sunday (paid). **Owner(s):** Gannett Company, Inc., 7950 Jones Branch Dr., McLean, VA 22107-0001. Telephone: 703-854-6000. **Bureau(s):** Nevada State Capitol Bldg., Carson City, NV 89710. Telephone: 702-882-3553. **Management:** Ted Power, Publisher. Karen Ferguson, Advertising Director. Tim Dunn, Photography Director. **Editorial:** Beryl Love, Executive Editor. Peggy Santoro, Asst. Managing Ed.. Edward Shur, Business Editor. Michael Martinez, City Editor. Steve Falcone, Editorial Page Editor. Mark Lundahl, News Editor.

SPARKS

DAILY SPARKS TRIBUNE, THE. 1002 C St., Sparks, NV 89431-4929. Telephone: 775-358-8061. FAX: 775-359-3837. E-MAIL: tribunenews@sparkstribune.net. Mailing Address: PO Box 887, Sparks, NV 89432. Year Established: 1910. Pub. Frequency: d. Page Size: broadsheet. Subscrip. Rate: $.50 newsstand/cover; $.75 newsstand/cover Sun.; $9 carrier delivery/mo.. **Wire Service(s):** AP. Circulation: 7,000 evening (paid); 10,000 Sunday (paid). **Owner(s):** Butch Alford, 505 C St., Lewiston, ID 83501. Telephone: 208-743-9600. **Management:** Ed McCaffrey, Publisher. Nancy Streets, Advertising Manager. Sheryl Bein, Circulation Manager. Darlene Sharp, Classified Adv. Mgr.. **Editorial:** Jainene Kerney, Editor. Debra Reed, Photographer. Dan Eckles, Sports Editor.

NEW HAMPSHIRE

BERLIN

BERLIN DAILY SUN. 177 Main St., Berlin, NH 03570. Telephone: 603-752-5858. FAX: 603-752-4160. E-MAIL: bds@mcia.net. URL: http://www.berlindailysun.com. Mailing Address: PO Box 279, Berlin, NH 03570. Year Established: 1992. Pub. Frequency: d. (Mon.-Fri.) Page Size: tabloid. Subscrip. Rate: $5.50 mailed/wk.; $286/yr mailed. **Wire Service(s):** AP. Circulation: 8,000 morning (free). **Owner(s):** Country Club News, Inc., 64 Seavey St., North Conway, NH 03860. Telephone: 603-356-2999. **Management:** Mark Guerringue, Publisher. Catherine Rarick, Advertising Manager. Mark Guerringue, Circulation Manager. **Editorial:** Adam Hirshan, Editor. Rose Dodge, Managing Editor. Brooks Payette, Sports Editor.

CLAREMONT

EAGLE TIMES. 401 River Rd, Claremont, NH 03743. Telephone: 603-543-3100. FAX: 603-542-9705. E-MAIL: etimes@cyberportal.net. URL: http://www.eagletimes.com. Year Established: 1892. Pub. Frequency: d. (Sun.-Fri.) Page Size: broadsheet. Subscrip. Rate: $.50 newsstand/cover; $1.50 newsstand/cover Sun.; $135.20/yr home delivery local or motor rte; $210.60/yr mailed out of area. Adv. Rate: col. inch $13.50 Freelance Pay: $25/story. **Wire Service(s):** AP. Circulation: 8,700 evening (paid); 9,700 Sunday (paid). **Owner(s):** Eagle Publications, Inc., See address and contact information above. **Management:** Harvey Hill, Publisher. Randy Yanick, Circulation Manager. **Editorial:** Archire Mountain, Managing Editor. John Kelleher, Feature Editor. Patrick O'Grady, News Editor. Charlie Hentz, Sports Editor.

CONCORD

CONCORD MONITOR. One Monitor Dr, Concord, NH 03302. Telephone: 603-224-5301. FAX: 603-228-5868. E-MAIL: letters@concordmonitor.com. URL: http://www.concordmonitor.com. Mailing Address: PO Box 1177, Concord, NH 03302-1177. Year Established: 1802. Pub. Frequency: d. Page Size: broadsheet. Subscrip. Rate: $.50 newsstand/cover; $1.75 newsstand/cover Sun.; $208/yr home delivery; $283.40/yr mailed. **Wire Service(s):** AP, LAT-WAT. Circulation: 21,145 morning (paid); 22,573 Sunday (paid). **Owner(s):** Newspapers of New England, Inc., See address and contact information above. **Management:** Chuck Vincent, General Manager. Tom C. Brown, Publisher. Ann-Marie Forrester, Advertising Manager. Mark Travis, Circulation Manager. Deborah Sanborn, Classified Adv. Mgr.. **Editorial:** Mike Pride, Editor.

DOVER

FOSTER'S DAILY DEMOCRAT. ISSN 0892-6026
333 Central Ave., Dover, NH 03820. Telephone: 603-742-4455. FAX: 603-749-7079. E-MAIL: letters@fosters.com. URL: http://www.fosters.com. Year Established: 1873. Pub. Frequency: d. Page Size: broadsheet. Subscrip. Rate: $.50 newsstand/cover; $1.75 Sun.; $159.90/yr home delivery; $246/yr mailed in state; $249.20/yr mailed out of state; $143/yr Sr. Citizens. **Wire Service(s):** AP, NYT. Circulation: 26,442 evening (paid); 31,673 Sunday (paid). **Owner(s):** George J. Foster Co, Inc., See address and contact information above. **Management:** Robert H. Foster, Publisher. Gail Boysick, Advertising Director. Gerald Perkins, Circulation Manager. Joyce Norton, Classified Adv. Mgr.. **Editorial:** Therese D. Foster, Editor-in-Chief. Rod Doherty, Executive Editor. Mary Rowland, Managing Editor.

HUDSON

TELEGRAPH (HUDSON), THE. 17 Executive Dr., Hudson, NH 03051-1008. Telephone: 603-882-2741. FAX: 603-882-2681. E-MAIL: geers@telegraph-nh.com. Year Established: 1832. Pub. Frequency: d. Page Size: broadsheet. Subscrip. Rate: $.50 newsstand/cover; $1.50 Sun.; $2.25/wk.; $156/yr. **Wire Service(s):** AP, SH, LAT-WAT. Circulation: 21,000 morning (paid). **Owner(s):** Independent Publications, Inc., PO Box 1008, Nashua, NH 03061. **Management:** William McLean, President. Terrence Williams, Publisher. John Vistorino, Advertising Manager. Michael Sheehan, Circulation Manager. John Armenio, Classified Adv. Mgr..

KEENE

KEENE SENTINEL. 60 West St., Keene, NH 03431. Telephone: 603-352-1234. FAX: 603-352-0437. E-MAIL: news@keenesentinel.com. URL: http://www.keenesentinel.com. Mailing Address: PO Box 546, Keene, NH 03431. Year Established: 1799. Pub. Frequency: d. Page Size: broadsheet. Subscrip. Rate: $.50 newsstand/cover; $1.50 newsstand/cover Sun.; $147.50/yr carrier delivery local or motor rte; $185/yr mailed in county; $210/yr out of county. Adv. Rate: col. inch $11.95 **Wire Service(s):** AP, LAT-WAT. Circulation: 13,500 evening (paid); 13,517 Sunday (paid). **Owner(s):** Keene Publishing Corp., See address and contact information above. **Management:** James A. Rousmaniere Jr., President. Colin R. Lyle, Advertising Manager. Patrick J. Trubiano, Circulation Manager. Lorraine Ellis, Classified Adv. Mgr.. **Editorial:** James A. Rousmaniere Jr., Editor. Tom Kearney, Executive Editor.

LACONIA

CITIZEN (DOVER), THE. 171 Fair St., Laconia, NH 03246. Telephone: 603-524-3800. FAX: 603-524-6702. E-MAIL: news@citizen.com. URL: http://www.citizen.com. Year Established: 1925. Pub. Frequency: d. Page Size: broadsheet. Subscrip. Rate: $.50 newsstand/cover; $1.75 newsstand/cover Sun.; $150/yr home delivery. **Wire Service(s):** AP. Circulation: 20,000 evening (paid). **Owner(s):** Robert H. Foster, 333 Central Ave., Dover, NH 03820. Telephone: 603-742-4455. **Management:** John Howe, General Manager. Robert H. Foster, President. Mitch Hansen, Advertising Director. Paul Duboys, Circulation Manager. **Editorial:** John Howe, Executive Editor.

MANCHESTER

UNION LEADER/NEW HAMPSHIRE SUNDAY NEWS. ISSN 0745-5798
100 William Loeb Dr., Manchester, NH 03108. Telephone: 603-668-4321. FAX: 603-668-0382. E-MAIL: writeus@theunionleader.com. URL: http://www.theunionleader.com. Mailing Address: PO Box 9555, Manchester, NH 03108. Year Established: 1863. Pub. Frequency: d. Page Size: standard. Subscrip. Rate: $.50 newsstand/cover; $1.75 newsstand/cover Sun.; $199.16/yr; $248.56/yr mailed in state; $282.88/yr mailed out of state. **Wire Service(s):** AP. Circulation: 60,000 morning (paid); 82,000 Sunday (paid). **Owner(s):** Nackey S. Loeb School of Communications, Inc., See address and contact information above. **Management:** Joseph W. McQuaid, President. Dirk F. Ruemenapp, Executive VP. Lou Trahan, Circulation Manager. **Editorial:** Charles Perkins III, Executive Editor. John Toole, City Editor. Vin Sylvia, Sports Editor.

NORTH CONWAY

CONWAY DAILY SUN, THE. 64 Seavey St., North Conway, NH 03860. Telephone: 603-356-2999. FAX: 603-356-8774. E-MAIL: dailysun@mountwashingtonvalley.com. URL: http://www.mountwashingtonvalley.com. Year Established: 1989. Pub. Frequency: d. (Mon.-Sat.) Page Size: tabloid. Subscrip. Rate: $5.50 mailed/wk.; $286/yr mailed. **Wire Service(s):** AP. Circulation: 16,000 morning (paid and free). **Owner(s):** Country Club News, Inc., See address and contact information above. **Management:** Mark Guerringue, Publisher. Joyce Brothers, Advertising Manager. **Editorial:** Adam Hirshan, Editor. Bart Bachman, Business Editor. Lloyd Jones, Sports Editor.

PORTSMOUTH

PORTSMOUTH HERALD. ISSN 0746-6218
111 Maplewood Ave., Portsmouth, NH 03801. Telephone: 603-436-1800. FAX: 603-427-0550. E-MAIL: herald@rcnewspapers.com. URL: http://www.seacoastonline.com. Year Established: 1886. Pub. Frequency: d. Page Size: broadsheet. Subscrip. Rate: $.50 newsstand/cover; $1.75 newsstand/cover Sun.; $172.04/yr in area; $230.88/yr mailed. **Wire Service(s):** AP. Circulation: 15,109 morning (paid); 24,000 Sunday (paid). **Owner(s):** Ottaway Newspapers, Inc., PO Box 401, Campbell Hall, NY 10916. Telephone: 914-294-8181. **Management:** John Tabor, Publisher. Kymberlee Lauton, Advertising Manager. Kelvin Parker, Circulation Manager. **Editorial:** Howard Altschiller, Executive Editor. Michael Keating, Lifestyle Editor. Ed Flaherty, Sports Editor.

WEST LEBANON

VALLEY NEWS (WEST LEBANON). 24 Interchange Dr., West Lebanon, NH 03784. Telephone: 603-298-8711. FAX: 603-298-0212. E-MAIL: news@vnews.com. URL: http://www.vnews.com. Mailing Address: PO Box 877, White River Junction, VT 05001. Year Established: 1952. Pub. Frequency: d. Page Size: broadsheet. Subscrip. Rate: $.75 newsstand/cover; $2 Sun.; $195/yr home delivery; $362.96/yr mailed. **Wire Service(s):** LAT-WAT. Circulation: 17,158 morning (paid); 17,300 Sunday (paid). **Owner(s):** Newspapers of New England, Inc., PO Box 1177, Concord, NH 03302. Telephone: 603-224-5301. **Management:** Mark Travis, Publisher. Richard Wallace, Advertising Director. Jim Carey, Circulation Director. Kelly T. Vigue, Classified Adv. Mgr.. **Editorial:** Jeff Good, Editor-in-Chief. Ann Adams, Feature Editor. Don Mahler, Sports Editor.

NEW JERSEY

BRIDGETON

BRIDGETON NEWS. 100 E. Commerce St, Bridgeton, NJ 08. Telephone: 856-451-1000. FAX: 856-455-3098. URL: http://www.bridgetonews.com. Year Established: 1879. Pub. Frequency: d. (Mon.-Sat.) Page Size: broadsheet. Subscrip. Rate: $.50 newsstand/cover; $119.60/yr. **Wire Service(s):** AP. Circulation: 10,000 evening (paid). **Owner(s):** Advance Publications, Inc., See address and contact information above. **Management:** Frank Gargano, General Manager. Jim DeFillipo, Publisher. Mark Gawel, Advertising Manager. John Petracci Jr., Circulation Director. **Editorial:** Matt Gray, Managing Editor. Eric Goldstein, Sports Editor.

MILLVILLE NEWS. 100 E. Commerce St, Bridgeton, NJ 08. Telephone: 856-451-1000. FAX: 856-455-3098. Year Established: 1990. Pub. Frequency: d. (Mon.-Sat.) Page Size: broadsheet. Subscrip. Rate: $.50 newsstand/cover; $119.60/yr. **Wire Service(s):** AP. Circulation: 1,100 evening (paid). **Owner(s):** Advance Publications, Inc., See address and contact information above. **Management:** Frank Gargano, General Manager. Jim DeFillipo, Publisher. Mark Gawel, Advertising Director. John Petrazzi, Circulation Director. **Editorial:** Matt Gray, Managing Editor. Eric Goldstein, Sports Editor.

BRIDGEWATER

COURIER NEWS (BRIDGEWATER), THE. ISSN 0895-8785
1201 Rte. 22 W., Bridgewater, NJ 08807-0600. Telephone: 908-722-8800. FAX: 908-707-3252. E-MAIL: metro@c-n.com. URL: http://www.c-n.com. Mailing Address: PO Box 6600, Bridgewater, NJ 08807. Year Established: 1884. Pub. Frequency: d. Page Size: broadsheet. Subscrip. Rate: $.35 newsstand/cover; $1 newsstand/cover Sun.; $2.75 home delivery/wk.; $156/yr home delivery; $190.84/yr mailed. **Wire Service(s):** AP, LAT-WAT, GNS. Circulation: 47,484 morning (paid); 49,087 Sunday (paid). **Owner(s):** Gannett Company, Inc., 7950 Jones Branch Dr., McLean, VA 22107-0001. Telephone: 703-854-6000. **Bureau(s):** 122 Main St., Flemington, NJ 08822. Telephone: 908-782-2230. FAX: 908-782-2366. **Management:** Charles W. Nutt Jr., President. Andrea L. Thorne, Advertising Director. Linda Mast, Circulation Director. **Editorial:** James Flachsenhaar, Editor. Marilyn Dillon, Managing Editor.

CHERRY HILL

COURIER-POST, THE. ISSN 1050-432X
301 Cuthbert Blvd., Cherry Hill, NJ 08002. Telephone: 856-663-6000. FAX: 856-663-2831. E-MAIL: cphotline@aol.com. URL: http://www.courierpostonline.com. Mailing Address: PO Box 5300, Cherry Hill, NJ 08034. Year Established: 1875. Pub. Frequency: d. Page Size: broadsheet. Subscrip. Rate: $.50 newsstand/cover; $1.50 Sun.; $169/yr home delivery. **Wire Service(s):** AP, GNS. Circulation: 96,000 morning (paid); 101,000 Sunday (paid). **Owner(s):** Gannett Company, Inc., 7950 Jones Branch Dr., McLean, VA 22107-0001. Telephone: 703-854-6000. **Management:** Mark Frisby, Publisher. Tom Geonnotti, Advertising Director. Jim Gregory, Circulation Director. **Editorial:** Derek Osenenko, Executive Editor. Stuart Shinske, Managing Editor. Contact: Mark Frisby, Publisher; Joe Colagero, Circulation Manager; Tom Engleman, Editor; .

EAST BRUNSWICK

HOME NEWS TRIBUNE, THE. 35 Kennedy Blvd., East Brunswick, NJ 08816-1049. Telephone: 732-246-5500. FAX: 732-565-7208. E-MAIL: hntmetro@thnt.com. URL: http://www.thnt.com. Mailing Address: PO Box 1049, East Brunswick, NJ 08816-1049. Year Established: 1879. Pub. Frequency: d. Page Size: broadsheet. Subscrip. Rate: $.35 newsstand/cover; $.75 newsstand/cover Sun.; $13 home delivery/mo.. **Wire Service(s):** AP, GNS. Circulation: 68,000 morning (paid); 71,000 Sunday (paid). **Owner(s):** Gannett Company, Inc., 7950 Jones Branch Dr., McLean, VA 22107-0001. Telephone: 703-854-6000. **Management:** Robert Collins, Publisher. **Editorial:** Charles Paolino, Editor. Cheryl Sarfaty, Business Editor. Jack Genung, Sports Editor.

JERSEY CITY

JERSEY JOURNAL, THE. 30 Journal Sq., Jersey City, NJ 07306. Telephone: 201-653-1000. FAX: 201-963-5854. URL: http://www.thejerseyjournal.com. Year Established: 1879. Pub. Frequency: d. (Mon.-Sat.) Page Size: broadsheet. Subscrip. Rate: $.50 newsstand/cover; $3.30 home delivery/wk. local; $36 home delivery local for 13 wks.; $120/yr home delivery local. **Wire Service(s):** AP, MCT. Circulation: 150,000 morning (paid). **Owner(s):** Evening Journal Association, See address and contact information above. **Management:** Scott Ring, Publisher. Paul Lonaris, Advertising Director. Mandy Otero, Circulation Manager. William Bayer, Photography Director. **Editorial:** Judith A. Locorriere, Editor. Augie Torres, City Editor. Margaret Schmidt, Feature Editor. Ron Zeitlinger, Sports Editor.

NEPTUNE

ASBURY PARK PRESS. 3601 Hwy. 66, Neptune, NJ 07754. Telephone: 732-922-6000. FAX: 732-643-4014. E-MAIL: editors@app.com. URL: http://www.app.com. Mailing Address: PO Box 1550, Neptune, NJ 07754. Year Established: 1879. Pub. Frequency: d. Page Size: broadsheet. Subscrip. Rate: $.50 newsstand/cover; $1.50 newsstand/cover Sun.; $15.17 home delivery/mo.. **Wire Service(s):** AP, GNS. Circulation: 160,069 morning (paid); 222,347 Sunday (paid). **Owner(s):** Gannett Company, Inc., 7950 Jones Branch Dr., McLean, VA 22107-0001. Telephone: 703-854-6000. **Bureau(s):** 235 Willowbrook Rd., Freehold, NJ 07728. **Management:** Thomas Foster, Circulation Director. Sharon Cole, Classified Adv. Mgr.. **Editorial:** Skip Hidlay, Executive Editor. Gary Schoening, Managing Editor. Bob Hordt, Business Editor. Ronna Sutow, Feature Editor. Eric Girard, Sports Editor.

NEWARK

STAR-LEDGER, THE. One Star Ledger Plz., Newark, NJ 07102-1200. Telephone: 973-877-4141. FAX: 973-643-4945. URL: http://www.nj.com/starledger. Year Established: 1938. Pub. Frequency: d. Page Size: broadsheet. Subscrip. Rate: $.35 newsstand/cover; $1.25 newsstand/cover Sun.; $3.85 home delivery/wk.. **Wire Service(s):** RN, AP, LAT-WAT. Circulation: 433,300 morning (paid); 641,390 Sunday (paid). **Owner(s):** Advance Publications, Inc., One Star Ledger Plz., Newark, NJ 07101. Telephone: 973-877-4141. **Management:** Linda Dennery, Publisher. Sandra L. Lohr, Advertising Director. Dennis Carletta, Circulation Director. **Editorial:** Jim Willse, Editor. Dave Allen, Business Editor. Susan Alai, Lifestyle Editor. Pim Van Hemmen, Photo Editor. Chris D'Amico, Sports Editor. Kathleen Casey, Travel Editor.

NEWTON

NEW JERSEY HERALD. ISSN 0893-3677
2 Spring St., Newton, NJ 07860. Telephone: 973-383-1500. FAX: 973-383-8477. E-MAIL: newsroom@njhrald.com. URL: http://www.njherald.com. Mailing Address: PO Box 10, Newton, NJ 07860. Year Established: 1829. Pub. Frequency: d. (Sun.-Fri.) Page Size: broadsheet. Subscrip. Rate: $.35 newsstand/cover; $1.25 Sun.; $123.50/yr carrier delivery; $130.91/yr motor route; $164/yr mailed NJ, NY, PA; $182.50/yr mailed elsewhere. **Wire Service(s):** AP. Circulation: 16,500 morning (paid); 23,500 Sunday (paid). **Owner(s):** New Jersey Herald, See address and contact information above. **Management:** Bruce Tomlinson, General Manager. Lee Williams, Circulation Manager. **Editorial:** Chris Frear, Managing Editor. Kathy Stevens, Lifestyle Editor. Anna Murphey, Photographer. Dan Cleary, Sports Editor.

PARSIPPANY

DAILY RECORD (PARSIPPANY). 800 Jefferson Rd., Parsippany, NJ 07054-0217. Telephone: 973-428-6200. FAX: 973-428-6666. E-MAIL: newsroom@dailyrecord.com. URL: http://www.dailyrecord.com. Mailing Address: PO Box 217, Parsippany, NJ 07054-0217. Year Established: 1900. Pub. Frequency: d. Page Size: broadsheet. Subscrip. Rate: $.35 newsstand/cover; $1 newsstand/cover Sun.; $161.20/yr. Adv. Rate: col. inch $42.50 Freelance Pay: $30-$50/article. **Wire Service(s):** AP. Circulation: 51,811 morning (paid); 60,862 Sunday (paid). **Owner(s):** Gannett Company, Inc., 7950 Jones Branch Dr., McLean, VA 22107-0001. Telephone: 703-854-6000. **Management:** Walt Lafferty, Publisher. Tom Morgan, Advertising Director. Mary Luvone, Photography Director. **Editorial:** Dennis Lyons, Editor-in-Chief. Jack Bowie, Managing Editor. Kathy Shwiff, Business Editor. Fred Snowflack, Editorial Page Editor. Frank Dileo, Sports Editor.

PLEASANTVILLE

PRESS OF ATLANTIC CITY, THE. 11 Devins Ln., Pleasantville, NJ 08232-3806. E-MAIL: pmerkoski@pressofac.com. URL: http://www.pressofatlanticcity.com. Year Established: 1895. Pub. Frequency: d. Page Size: broadsheet. Subscrip. Rate: $.50 newsstand/cover; $1.50 newsstand/cover Sun.; $4.05 carrier delivery/wk.; $28 mailed for 4 weeks. **Wire Service(s):** AP, UPI, SH, LAT-WAT. Circulation: 78,228 morning (paid); 98,070 Sunday (paid). **Owner(s):** Abarta, Inc., 1000 R.I.D.C. Plz., Pittsburgh, PA 15238. Telephone: 412-963-6226. **Bureau(s):** One S. Main St., Cape May Courthouse, NJ 08210. Telephone: 609-463-0300. FAX: 609-463-6701. **Management:** Keith L. Dawn, Publisher. Vito Cicero, Circulation Director. John Celestino, Sales Manager. **Editorial:** Paul Merkoski, Executive Editor. Maryjane Briant, Managing Editor.

SALEM

TODAY'S SUNBEAM. ISSN 0890-9830
93 Fifth St., Salem, NJ 08079. Telephone: 856-935-1500. FAX: 856-845-3139. E-MAIL: tsnews@medianewsgroup.com. URL: http://www.south.nj.com. Year Established: 1972. Pub. Frequency: d. Page Size: broadsheet. Subscrip. Rate: $.35 newsstand/cover; $1 newsstand/cover Sun.; $121.70/yr. **Wire Service(s):** AP. Circulation: 12,000 morning (paid); 11,800 Sunday (paid). **Owner(s):** Advance Publications, Inc., 950 Fingerboard Rd., Staten Island, NY 10305. **Management:** Ceil Smith, General Manager. John Petracci Jr., Circulation Director. Marie Vito, Classified Adv. Mgr.. **Editorial:** Bill Gallo, Managing Editor.

TOMS RIVER

OBSERVER REPORTER. 1451 Rt 37 W, Toms River, NJ 08753. E-MAIL: observer@app.com. URL: http://www.app.com/observer. Year Established: 1850. Pub. Frequency: d. Page Size: broadsheet. Subscrip. Rate: $.50 newsstand/cover; $.75 newsstand/cover Sun.; $2.25 carrier delivery/wk.; $191.40/yr carrier delivery; $150.80/yr mailed in county; $156/yr mailed out of county. **Wire Service(s):** AP. **Owner(s):** Gannett Company, Inc., 7950 Jones Branch Dr., McLean, VA 22107-0001. Telephone: 703-854-6000. **Management:** Bonnie Russell, Advertising. Paul J. Haney, Advertising Director. **Editorial:** John Hudzinski, Executive Editor. Tom Spader, Photographer.

TRENTON

TIMES (TRENTON), THE. ISSN 8750-9083
500 Perry St., Trenton, NJ 08618. Telephone: 609-396-3232. FAX: 609-396-5644. E-MAIL: news@njtimes.com. URL: http://www.nj.com/times. Mailing Address: PO Box 847, Trenton, NJ 08605. Year Established: 1883. Pub. Frequency: d. Page Size: broadsheet. Subscrip. Rate: $.25 newsstand/cover; $1.50 newsstand/cover Sun.; $2.95 carrier delivery/wk.; $3.15 motor route/wk.. **Wire Service(s):** AP, NYT, LAT-WAT. Circulation: 77,405 morning (paid); 84,000 Sunday (paid). **Owner(s):** Advance Publications, Inc., See address and contact information above. **Management:** Richard Bilotti, Publisher. Diane Day, Advertising Director. Mark Vinciguerra, Circulation Director. **Editorial:** Brian Malone, Editor. Peter Callas, Managing Editor. Tony Hagen, Business Editor. Nora O'Dowd, Feature Editor. Anita Shaffer, Metro Editor.

TRENTONIAN, THE. 600 Perry St., Trenton, NJ 08618-3996. Telephone: 609-989-7800. FAX: 609-393-6072. E-MAIL: editor@trentonian.com. URL: http://www.trentonian.com. Mailing Address: PO Box 231, Trenton, NJ 08602-3996. Year Established: 1946. Pub. Frequency: d. Page Size: tabloid. Subscrip. Rate: $.50 newsstand/cover; $1.25 newsstand/cover Sun.; $3.40 home delivery/wk.; $177/yr. **Wire Service(s):** AP, SH. Circulation: 40,000 morning (paid); 30,000 Sunday (paid). **Owner(s):** Journal Register Co., 50 W State St, 12th Fl, Trenton, NJ 08608. Telephone: 609-396-2200. **Management:** Bill Murray, Publisher. Domenic Zanghi, Advertising Director. Jim Lindsey, Circulation Director. **Editorial:** Andrea Y Carter, Editor. Aaron Nobel, Managing Editor. Paul Mickle, City Editor.

VINELAND

DAILY JOURNAL (VINELAND), THE. 891 E. Oak Rd., Vineland, NJ 08360. Telephone: 856-691-5000. FAX: 856-563-5308. E-MAIL: djlocalnews@thedailyjournal.com. URL: http://www.thedailyjournal.com. Year Established: 1864. Pub. Frequency: d. (Mon.-Sat.) Page Size: broadsheet. Subscrip. Rate: $.50 newsstand/cover; $137.80/yr carrier delivery local. Freelance Pay: $35/article. **Wire Service(s):** AP. Circulation: 17,000 evening (paid). **Owner(s):** Gannett Company, Inc., 7950 Jones Branch Dr., McLean, VA 22107-0001. Telephone: 703-854-6000. **Management:** Nancy Monaghan, Publisher. Ray Breitwieser, Advertising Manager. Amy Winter, Circulation Director. **Editorial:** Dave Stump, Managing Editor. Jason Carris, Sports Editor.

WEST PATERSON

RECORD (WEST PATERSON), THE. One Garret Mtn. Plz, 6th Fl, West Paterson, NJ 07424. E-MAIL: editor@northjersey.com. URL: http://www.northjersey.com. Mailing Address: P.O. Box 471, West Paterson, NJ 07424. Year Established: 1895. Pub. Frequency: d. Page Size: broadsheet. Subscrip. Rate: $.50 newsstand/cover; $1.50 newsstand/cover Sun.; $105.56 for 6 mos.; $204.36/yr. **Wire Service(s):** RN, AP, UPI, LAT-WAT. Circulation: 181,166 morning (paid); 215,560 Sunday (paid). **Owner(s):** North Jersey Media Group, 150 River St, Hackensack, NJ 07061-7172. **Management:** Stephen Borg, Publisher. Charles Rowe, Advertising Director. Kerry Rubin, Classified Adv. Mgr.. Mala Lawrence, Assistant Publisher. **Editorial:** Vivian Waixel, Executive Editor. Barbara Jaeger, Feature Editor.

WILLINGBORO

BURLINGTON COUNTY TIMES. 4284 Rte. 130, Willingboro, NJ 08046. Telephone: 609-871-8000. FAX: 609-871-0490. URL: http://www.phillyburbs.com. Year Established: 1958. Pub. Frequency: d. Page Size: broadsheet. Subscrip. Rate: $.50 newsstand/cover; $1.50 newsstand/cover Sun.; $152.10/yr carrier delivery; $163.80/yr motor route; $196/yr mailed. **Wire Service(s):** AP. Circulation: 40,067 morning (paid); 44,964 Sunday (paid). **Owner(s):** Calkins Media Inc., 8400 Rte. 13, Levittown, PA 19057. Telephone: 215-949-4000. **Management:** Stanley Ellis, Publisher. Brenda F. Coumo III, Advertising Director. Steve Todd, Circulation Manager. **Editorial:** Ron Martin, Executive Editor. Gary Lindenmuth, Managing Editor. Louis Gaul, Entertainment Editor. Martha Esposito, Feature Editor. Wayne Richards, Sports Editor.

WOODBURY

GLOUCESTER COUNTY TIMES. 309 S. Broad St., Woodbury, NJ 08096. Telephone: 856-845-3300. FAX: 856-845-5480. E-MAIL: gctimes@medianewsgroup.com. URL: http://www.newjersey.com. Mailing Address: PO Box 639, Woodbury, NJ 08096. Year Established: 1897. Pub. Frequency: d. Page Size: broadsheet. Subscrip. Rate: $.35 newsstand/cover; $1 newsstand/cover Sun.. **Wire Service(s):** AP. Circulation: 29,200 evening (paid); 29,800 Sunday (paid). **Owner(s):** Advance Publications, Inc., See address and contact information above. **Management:** Frank Gargano, Publisher. Sheila Gallagar Montone, Advertising Manager. John Petracci, Circulation Manager. **Editorial:** Gary Grossman, Editor. John Barna, City Editor. Tim Hawk, Photographer. Shawn Leary, Sports.

NEW MEXICO

ALAMOGORDO

ALAMOGORDO DAILY NEWS. 518 24th St, Alamogordo, NM 88310-6104. Telephone: 505-437-7120. FAX: 505-437-7795. URL: http://www.alamogordonews.com. Year Established: 1898. Pub. Frequency: d. (Sun.-Fri.) Page Size: broadsheet. Subscrip. Rate: $.50 newsstand/cover; $1 newsstand/cover Sun.; $90/yr carrier delivery in area; $175/yr mailed in county. **Wire Service(s):** AP. Circulation: 8,710 evening (paid); 9,652 Sunday (paid). **Owner(s):** MediaNews Group, Inc., 101 W Colfax Ave, Ste 1100, Denver, CO 80202. **Management:** Richard Coltharp, Publisher. Rex Goodin, Circulation Manager. Helen Hopkins, Classified Editor. **Editorial:** Michael Becker, Editor.

ALBUQUERQUE

ALBUQUERQUE JOURNAL. 7777 Jefferson St., N.E., Albuquerque, NM 87109. Telephone: 505-823-3800. FAX: 505-823-3994. E-MAIL: journal@abqjournal.com. URL: http://www.abqjournal.com. Mailing Address: P.O. Drawer J, Albuquerque, NM 87103-1136. Year Established: 1880. Pub. Frequency: d. Page Size: broadsheet. Subscrip. Rate: $.50 newsstand/cover; $1 newsstand/cover Sun.; $11.25 carrier delivery/mo.; $240/yr mailed in state; $264/yr out of state. **Wire Service(s):** AP, LAT-WAT, MCT, CNS. Circulation: 107,947 morning (paid); 151,671 Sunday (paid). **Owner(s):** T.H. Lang, See address and contact information above. **Bureau(s):** 7777 Jefferson N E, Albuquerque, NM 87109. Telephone: 505-823-3333. **Management:** T.H. Lang, Publisher. **Editorial:** Kent Walz, Editor. Karen Moses, Managing Editor. Michael Murphy, Business Editor. Charlie Moore, City Editor. Steve Mills, Editorial Page Editor. Judy Giannettino, Feature Editor. Jaime Dispenza, Photo Editor. Sam Aselstine, Sports Editor.

ALBUQUERQUE TRIBUNE, THE. ISSN 1097-2048
7777 Jefferson, N.E., Albuquerque, NM 87109. Telephone: 505-823-7777. FAX: 505-823-3689. URL: http://www.abqtrib.com. Mailing Address: P.O. Drawer T, Albuquerque, NM 87103. Year Established: 1922. Pub. Frequency: d. (Mon.-Sat.) Page Size: broadsheet. Subscrip. Rate: $.50 newsstand/cover; $18 home delivery for 3 mos.; $46.50 mailed out of state for 3 mos.. Freelance Pay: $30-$75/article. **Wire Service(s):** AP, SH, NYT, LAT-WAT. Circulation: 28,000 evening (paid and free). **Owner(s):** E.W. Scripps Co., 312 Walnut St., 28th Fl., Cincinnati, OH 45202. Telephone: 513-977-3000. FAX: 513-977-3689. **Bureau(s):** 1090 Vermont Ave., N.W., 10thFl., Washington, DC 20006. Telephone: 202-408-2726. FAX: 202-408-5950. **Editorial:** Phill Casaus, Editor-in-Chief. Kate Nelson, Managing Editor. Rick Hindley, Bureau Editor. Bill Slakey, City Editor. Jack Ehn, Editorial Page Editor. Nancy Salem, Entertainment Editor. Michael Garcia, Sports Editor.

ARTESIA

ARTESIA DAILY PRESS. 503 W. Main, Artesia, NM 88210-2067. Telephone: 505-746-3524. FAX: 505-746-8795. E-MAIL: ads@artesianews.com. URL: http://www.artesianews.com. Mailing Address: PO Box 190, Artesia, NM 88210-0190. Year Established: 1954. Pub. Frequency: d. (Tue.-Fri. & Sun.) Page Size: broadsheet. Subscrip. Rate: $.35 newsstand/cover; $.75 newsstand/cover Sun.; $6.75 carrier delivery/mo. local; $7.25 motor route/mo.; $108/yr mailed. **Wire Service(s):** AP. Circulation: 4,000 evening (paid); 4,200 Sunday (paid). **Owner(s):** Valley Newspapers, Inc., See address and contact information above. **Management:** Gary Scott, Publisher. Barbara Boans, Office Manager. **Editorial:** Harry Readel, Managing Editor. Elizabeth Grobes, Feature Editor. Amanda Lamb, Photographer. Brienne Green, Sports.

CARLSBAD

CARLSBAD CURRENT-ARGUS. 620 S Main St, Carlsbad, NM 88220. Telephone: 505-887-5501. FAX: 505-885-1066. E-MAIL: dgiuliani@currentargus.com. URL: http://www.currentargus.com. Mailing Address: PO Box 1629, Carlsbad, NM 88221-1629. Year Established: 1889. Pub. Frequency: d. (Tue.-Sun.) Page Size: broadsheet. Subscrip. Rate: $.50 newsstand/cover; $1.50 newsstand/cover Sun.; $126/yr. **Wire Service(s):** AP. Circulation: 8,600 morning (paid); 9,000 Sunday (paid). **Owner(s):** MediaNews Group, Inc., 101 W Colfax Ave, Ste 1100, Denver, CO 80202. FAX: 303-954-6320. **Management:** Rockford Hayes, Publisher. Larry Hubner, Advertising Director. Brett Murphy, Circulation Manager. **Editorial:** Martha Mauritson, Managing Editor. Tom Schultes, News Editor.

CLOVIS

CLOVIS NEWS JOURNAL. 521 Pile St., Clovis, NM 88101. Telephone: 505-763-3431. FAX: 505-762-3879. E-MAIL: clovisnews@yahoo.com. URL: http://www.clovis-news-nm.com. Mailing Address: PO Box 1689, Clovis, NM 88102-1689. Year Established: 1929. Pub. Frequency: d. (Sun.-Fri.) Page Size: broadsheet. Subscrip. Rate: $.50 newsstand/cover; $1 newsstand/cover Sun.; $114/yr home delivery local; $129/yr mailed in county; $147/yr mailed out of county. Adv. Rate: col. inch $10.82 **Wire Service(s):** AP. Circulation: 10,000 morning (paid); 12,000 Sunday (paid). **Owner(s):** Freedom Communications, Inc., 17666 Fitch, Irvine, CA 92714. Telephone: 949-253-2300. **Management:** Ray Sullivan, Publisher. Ian Cooke, Advertising Director. Mike Grigg, Circulation Manager. **Editorial:** David Stevens, Editor. Rick White, News Editor.

DEMING

DEMING HEADLIGHT, THE. ISSN 0738-8349
219 E Maple St, Deming, NM 88031. E-MAIL: jbyers@demingheadlight.com. URL: http://www.demingheadlight.com. Mailing Address: PO Box 881, Deming, NM 88031. Year Established: 1881. Pub. Frequency: d. (Mon.-Fri.) Page Size: tabloid. Subscrip. Rate: $.50 newsstand/cover; $59.50/yr carrier delivery; $69.50/yr motor route; $87/yr mailed. Freelance Pay: $0.40/column-inch. **Wire Service(s):** AP. Circulation: 4,200 evening (paid). **Owner(s):** MediaNews Group, Inc., 101 W Colfax Ave, Ste 1100, Denver, CO 80202. **Management:** Wayne Barnard, General Manager. Monica Gutierrez, Advertising. Deborah Alstock, Circulation Director. Joann Castro, Classified Adv. Mgr.. **Editorial:** Bill Armendariz, Editor.

FARMINGTON

DAILY TIMES (FARMINGTON), THE. 201 N Allen Ave, Farmington, NM 87401. Telephone: 505-325-4545. FAX: 505-564-4630. E-MAIL: slopez@daily-times.com. URL: http://www.daily-times.com. Mailing Address: PO Box 450, Farmington, NM 87499-0450. Year Established: 1894. Pub. Frequency: d. Page Size: broadsheet. Subscrip. Rate: $.50 newsstand/cover; $1 newsstand/cover Sun.; $107.50/yr home delivery in area; $185/yr mailed. **Wire Service(s):** AP. Circulation: 18,000 morning (paid); 19,500 Sunday (paid). **Owner(s):** MediaNews Group, Inc., 101 W Colfax Ave, Ste 1100, Denver, CO 80202. FAX: 303-954-6320. **Management:** Sammy Lopez, Publisher. Connie Pruitt, Advertising Director. James Whittington, Circulation Manager. Robert Waller, Classified Adv. Mgr.. **Editorial:** Troy Turner, Editor.

GALLUP

INDEPENDENT (GALLUP). ISSN 1099-6052
500 N. Ninth St., Gallup, NM 87301. Telephone: 505-863-6811. FAX: 505-722-5750. E-MAIL: gallpind@cia-g.com. URL: http://www.gallupindependent.com/. Mailing Address: PO Box 1210, Gallup, NM 87305. Pub. Frequency: d. (Mon.-Sat.) Page Size: broadsheet. Subscrip. Rate: $.50 newsstand/cover; $.75 newsstand/cover Sat.; $10.50 home delivery/mo.. Freelance Pay: $1/column-inch. **Wire Service(s):** AP, NYT. Circulation: 16,000 morning (paid). **Owner(s):** John K. Zollinger, See address and contact information above. **Bureau(s):** Navajo Reservation, Window Rock, AZ. Telephone: 505-371-5443. Contact: Jim Maniaci, Bureau Chief. **Management:** Bob Zollinger, Publisher. Doug Veazey, Advertising Manager. Valda Brown, Circulation Manager. **Editorial:** Ken Leopold, City Editor. Gay Brown, Lifestyle Editor. Michael Peretti, Sports Editor.

HOBBS

HOBBS NEWS-SUN. 201 N. Thorp, Hobbs, NM 88240. Telephone: 505-393-2123. FAX: 505-393-5724. E-MAIL: editor@hobbsnews.com. URL: http://www.hobbsnews.com. Mailing Address: PO Box 850, Hobbs, NM 88241. Year Established: 1937. Pub. Frequency: d. (Tue.-Sun.) Page Size: broadsheet. Subscrip. Rate: $.50 newsstand/cover; $1 newsstand/cover Sun.; $99/yr home delivery local; $117/yr home delivery in county; $132/yr mailed out of county; $141.60/yr mailed out of state. **Wire Service(s):** AP. Circulation: 10,000 morning (paid); 10,000 Sunday (paid). **Owner(s):** Sun Publishing, Inc., See address and contact information above. **Management:** W. H. Shearman, President. Kathi Bearden, Publisher. **Editorial:** Daniel Russell, Editor. Richard Trout, Business Editor. James Watkins, Sports.

LAS CRUCES

LAS CRUCES SUN-NEWS. ISSN 1081-2172
256 W Las Cruces Ave, Las Cruces, NM 88004. Telephone: 505-541-5400. FAX: 505-541-5498. E-MAIL: editorlcsn@zianet.com. URL: http://www.lcsun-news.com. Mailing Address: PO Box 1749, Las Cruces, NM 88004-1749. Year Established: 1937. Pub. Frequency: d. Page Size: broadsheet. Subscrip. Rate: $.50 newsstand/cover; $1.25 newsstand/cover Sun.; $96.25/yr carrier delivery; $192/yr mailed in state. **Wire Service(s):** AP, LAT-WAT. Circulation: 25,000 morning (paid); 26,000 Sunday (paid). **Owner(s):** MediaNews Group, Inc., 101 W Colfax Ave, Ste 1100, Denver, CO 80202. FAX: 303-954-6320. **Management:** David McClain, Publisher. Bill Pitchkolan, Advertising Manager. **Editorial:** Jim Lawitz, Editor. Geoff Grammer, Sports Editor.

LAS VEGAS

LAS VEGAS DAILY OPTIC. 614 Lincoln Ave., Las Vegas, NM 87701. Telephone: 505-425-6796. FAX: 505-425-1005. E-MAIL: lvoptic@hotmail.com. URL: http://www.lasvegasoptic.com. Mailing Address: PO Box 2670, Las Vegas, NM 87701. Year Established: 1879. Pub. Frequency: d. (Mon.-Fri.) Page Size: broadsheet. Subscrip. Rate: $.50 newsstand/cover; $75/yr home delivery; $9.50 mailed/mo. in county; $10.50 mailed/mo. in state; $12.50 mailed/mo. out of state. **Wire Service(s):** AP. Circulation: 6,300 evening (paid). **Owner(s):** Landmark Community Newspapers, Inc., PO Box 549, Shelbyville, KY 40065. Telephone: 502-633-2526. **Management:** Tom McDonald, Publisher. Sherry Ann Clancy, Advertising Manager. **Editorial:** Tom McDonald, Editor. David Guiliani, Managing Editor.

LOS ALAMOS

LOS ALAMOS MONITOR. ISSN 0893-3456
256 D.P. Rd., Los Alamos, NM 87544. Telephone: 505-662-4185. FAX: 505-662-4334. E-MAIL: lamonitor@lamonitor.com. URL: http://www.lamonitor.com. Mailing Address: PO Box 1268, Los Alamos, NM 87544. Year Established: 1963. Pub. Frequency: d. (Tue.-Fri. & Sun.) Page Size: broadsheet. Subscrip. Rate: $.50 newsstand/cover; $75/yr carrier delivery; $120/yr mailed elsewhere. **Wire Service(s):** AP, NYT. Circulation: 5,400 evening (paid); 5,400 Sunday (paid). **Owner(s):** Landmark Community Newspapers, Inc., PO Box 549, Shelbyville, KY 40065. Telephone: 502-633-2526. **Management:** Kevin Todd, General Manager. Gary Dickson, Publisher. Storm Hurwin, Advertising Director. **Editorial:** Roger Snodgrass, Editor. Carol Clark, Managing Editor. Mike Maez-Cote, Sports Editor.Readers: General circulation

LOVINGTON

LOVINGTON DAILY LEADER. 14 W. Ave. B, Lovington, NM 88260. Telephone: 505-396-2844. FAX: 505-396-5775. E-MAIL: leader@leaco.net. Mailing Address: PO Drawer 1717, Lovington, NM 88260. Year Established: 1909. Pub. Frequency: d. (Tue.-Fri. & Sun.) Page Size: broadsheet. Subscrip. Rate: $.50 newsstand/cover; $90/yr home delivery; $96/yr mailed in county; $99/yr mailed out of county. Adv. Rate: col. inch $5.50 **Wire Service(s):** AP. Circulation: 2,100 evening (paid); 2,400 Sunday (paid). **Owner(s):** John Graham, See address and contact information above. **Management:** John Graham, Publisher. Joyce Clemens, Advertising Manager. Michael Hatfield, Circulation Manager. **Editorial:** John Graham, Editor. Jeanine Graham, Society Editor.

PORTALES

PORTALES NEWS-TRIBUNE. 101 E. First St., Portales, NM 88130. Telephone: 505-356-4481. FAX: 505-356-3630. E-MAIL: pnt@yucca.net. URL: http://www.portales.com. Mailing Address: PO Box 848, Portales, NM 88130. Year Established: 1957. Pub. Frequency: d. (Tue.-Fri. & Sun.) Page Size: broadsheet. Subscrip. Rate: $.50 newsstand/cover; $1 Sun.; $87/yr local; $105/yr motor route local. **Wire Service(s):** AP. Circulation: 2,900 morning (paid); 3,400 Sunday (paid). **Owner(s):** Freedom Communications, Inc., 17666 Fitch, Irvine, CA 92614. Telephone: 714-553-9292. **Management:** Ray Sullivan, Publisher. Viola Gonzales, Advertising Manager. Sestella Garcia, Circulation Manager. Rusty Galloway, Assistant Publisher. **Editorial:** Kevin Wilson, Editor.

ROSWELL

ROSWELL DAILY RECORD. 2301 N. Main St., Roswell, NM 88201-6452. Telephone: 505-622-7710. FAX: 505-625-0421. URL: http://www.roswell-record.com. Mailing Address: PO Box 1897, Roswell, NM 88202-1897. Year Established: 1891. Pub. Frequency: d. (Sun.-Fri.) Page Size: broadsheet. Subscrip. Rate: $.50 newsstand/cover; $1 Sun.; $8.25 carrier delivery/mo. local deliv. Adv. Rate: col. inch $11.88 **Wire Service(s):** AP. Circulation: 12,000 morning (paid); 13,000 Sunday (paid). **Owner(s):** Roswell Daily Record, Inc., See address and contact information above. **Management:** Robert H. Beck, President. R. Cory Beck, Publisher. Ann Burns, Advertising Manager. Josh Stephenson, Circulation Manager. Marlyn Skipper, Business Manager. **Editorial:** Mike Bush, Editor. Andrew Poertner, Managing Editor. Melissa Hilgeman, Society Editor. Shawn Millender, Sports.

SILVER CITY

SILVER CITY DAILY PRESS & INDEPENDENT. ISSN 0891-7981
300 W. Market St., Silver City, NM 88061. Telephone: 505-388-1576. E-MAIL: mail@thedailypress.com. URL: http://www.thedailypress.com. Mailing Address: P.O. Box 740, Silver City, NM 88061-0740. Year Established: 1896. Pub. Frequency: d. (Mon.-Sat.) Page Size: broadsheet. Subscrip. Rate: $.50 newsstand/cover; $2.30/wk. in town; $119.60/yr in town; $120/yr out of town; $130/yr out of state. **Wire Service(s):** AP. Circulation: 8,175 evening (paid). **Owner(s):** Silver City Daily Press & Independent Pub. Co., See address and contact information above. **Management:** Mary L. Ybarra, General Manager. Betty Jane Ely, President. Tina Ely, Publisher. Wanda Sleep, Advertising Manager. Susie Torrez, Circulation Manager. Pat Alexander, Classified Adv. Mgr.. **Editorial:** Dean Thompson, Managing Editor. Ernie Misquez, Photographer.

NEW YORK

ALBANY

TIMES UNION. News Plz. Box 15000, Albany, NY 12212. Telephone: 518-454-5694. FAX: 518-454-5869. E-MAIL: nmeyer@timesunion.com. URL: http://www.timesunion.com. Mailing Address: PO Box 15000, Albany, NY 12212. Year Established: 1856. Pub. Frequency: d. Page Size: broadsheet. Subscrip. Rate: $.50, $2 newsstand/cover; $24 carrier delivery for 10 wks.. **Wire Service(s):** AP, SH, NYT, LAT-WAT, MCT, CNS. Circulation: 101,210 morning (paid); 147,059 Sunday (paid). **Owner(s):** Hearst Corp., 959 Eighth Ave, New York, NY 10019. **Management:** David White, Publisher. Lou Saccoco, Circulation Director. John Knott, Circulation Manager. Bob Provost, Marketing Director. Mike Danieli, Development Manager. **Editorial:** Rex Smith, Editor. Howard Healy, Editorial Page Editor.

AMSTERDAM

RECORDER (AMSTERDAM), THE. ISSN 0739-2540
One Venner Rd., Amsterdam, NY 12010. Telephone: 518-843-1100. FAX: 518-843-1338. E-MAIL: news@recorder .com. URL: http://www.recordernews.com. Mailing Address: PO Box 640, Amsterdam, NY 12010. Year Established: 1878. Pub. Frequency: d. Page Size: broadsheet. Subscrip. Rate: $.50 newsstand/cover; $1.25 newsstand/cover Sun.; $2.50 home delivery/wk.. **Wire Service(s):** AP, MCT. Circulation: 9,727 evening (paid); 10,012 Sunday (paid). **Owner(s):** Wm. J. Kline & Sons, Inc., See address and contact information above. **Management:** Kevin McClary, Publisher. Michael Lawson, Circulation Manager. **Editorial:** Kevin Mattison, Executive Editor. John DeNeuville, Sports.

AUBURN

CITIZEN (AUBURN), THE. 25 Dill St, Auburn, NY 13021. Telephone: 315-253-5311. FAX: 315-253-6031. Year Established: 1816. Pub. Frequency: d. Subscrip. Rate: $.35 newsstand/cover; $1.50 newsstand/cover Sun.; $140.40/yr. **Wire Service(s):** AP. Circulation: 17,500 per issue (paid and controlled). **Owner(s):** Lee Enterprises, Inc., 201 N. Harrison St, Ste 600, Davenport, IA 52801-1924. **Management:** Rick Emanuel, Publisher. Mike Rifanburg, Advertising Manager. Matt Lang, Circulation Manager. **Editorial:** Michael LeFort, Executive Editor. Jeremy Boyer, Managing Editor.

BATAVIA

BATAVIA DAILY NEWS. 2 Apollo Dr., Batavia, NY 14020. Telephone: 585-343-8000. FAX: 585-343-2623. E-MAIL: news@batavianews.com. URL: http://www.batavianews.com. Mailing Address: PO Box 870, Batavia, NY 14021. Year Established: 1878. Pub. Frequency: d. (Mon.-Sat.) Page Size: standard. Subscrip. Rate: $.50 newsstand/cover; $37.70 home delivery for 13 weeks. Adv. Rate: col. inch $22.94 **Wire Service(s):** AP. Circulation: 17,000 evening (paid). **Owner(s):** Johnson Newspaper Corp., 260 Washington St., Watertown, NY 13601. Telephone: 315-782-1000. **Management:** Tom Turnbull, Publisher. Sheila Mitchell, Advertising Manager. Christine Smith, Circulation Manager. **Editorial:** Tom Turnbull, Editor. Mark Graczyk, Managing Editor. Ben Beagle, Feature Editor. Bill Bruton, Sports Editor.

BROOKLYN

BROOKLYN DAILY EAGLE & DAILY BULLETIN. 30 Henry St., Brooklyn, NY 11201. Telephone: 718-422-7400. FAX: 718-858-4483. E-MAIL: bdeagle@idt .net. Year Established: 1841. Pub. Frequency: d. (Mon.-Fri.) Page Size: tabloid. Subscrip. Rate: $.50 newsstand/cover; $65 for 6 mos. local; $150/yr home delivery. **Wire Service(s):** CNS. Circulation: 5,300 morning (paid). **Owner(s):** Brooklyn Eagle Publications, Inc., See address and contact information above. **Management:** Dozier Hasty, Publisher. Patricia Higgins, Advertising Manager. Katherina Ramus, Circulation Manager. **Editorial:** Sam Howe, Editor-in-Chief. Raanan Geberer, Managing Editor. Gina Klein, Lifestyle Editor. Dennis Holt, Political Editor.

BUFFALO

BUFFALO NEWS. ISSN 0745-2691
One News Plz., Buffalo, NY 14203. Telephone: 716-849-4444. FAX: 716-856-5150. URL: http://www.buffalonews.com/. Mailing Address: PO Box 100, Buffalo, NY 14240. Year Established: 1880. Pub. Frequency: d. Page Size: broadsheet. Subscrip. Rate: $.75 newsstand/cover; $2 newsstand/cover Sun.. **Wire Service(s):** RN, AP, LAT-WAT, MCT. **Owner(s):** Berkshire Hathaway, Inc., 1440 Kiewit Plz., Omaha, NE 68131. Telephone: 402-346-1400. FAX: 402-346-3375. **Bureau(s):** 1141 National Press Bldg., Washington, DC 20045. Telephone: 202-737-3188. FAX: 202-783-3224. Contact: Douglas Turner, Bureau Chief. **Management:** Stanford Lipsey, Publisher. Rich Williams, Circulation Director. John Davis, Photography Director. John Kindelan, Classified Editor. **Editorial:** Stephen Bell, Managing Editor. John Neville, Asst. Managing Ed.. Grove Potter, Business Editor. Bill Flynn, City Editor. Michael Vogel, Editorial Page Editor. Elizabeth Kahn, Feature Editor. John Davis, Graphics Editor. Henry Davis, Health Editor. David Valenzuela, Librarian. Stan Evans, News Editor. Bob McCarthy, Political Editor. Howard Smith, Sports Editor.

CANANDAIGUA

DAILY MESSENGER. 73 Buffalo St, Canandaigua, NY 14424. Telephone: 585-394-0770. FAX: 585-394-1675. E-MAIL: messengr@frontiernet.net. URL: http://www.mpnewspapers.com. Year Established: 1796. Pub. Frequency: d. (Sun.-Fri.) Page Size: broadsheet. Subscrip. Rate: $.50 newsstand/cover; $1.25 newsstand/cover Sun.; $149.90/yr in county. **Wire Service(s):** AP, SH, LAT-WAT. Circulation: 12,952 evening (paid); 14,217 Sunday (paid). **Owner(s):** GateHouse Media, Inc, 350 WillowBrook Office Park, Fairport, NY 14450. Telephone: 585-598-0030. FAX: 585-248-2631. **Management:** Carl Helbig, Publisher. Jerry Grundman, Advertising Director. **Editorial:** Robert Matson, Executive Editor. Kevin Frisch, Managing Editor. Tim Belknap, City Editor.

CATSKILL

DAILY MAIL. 414 Main St., Catskill, NY 12414. Telephone: 518-943-2100. FAX: 518-943-2063. Mailing Address: PO Box 484, Catskill, NY 12414. Year Established: 1879. Pub. Frequency: d. (Mon.-Sat.) Page Size: broadsheet. Subscrip. Rate: $.50 newsstand/cover; $1.50 newsstand/cover Sun.; $140/yr motor route in area. **Wire Service(s):** AP. Circulation: 4,700 evening (paid). **Owner(s):** Johnson Newspaper Corp., 260 Washington St., Watertown, NY 13601. Telephone: 315-782-1000. **Management:** Pamela Geskie, General Manager. Roger Coleman, Publisher. Brenda Nickles, Circulation Director. **Editorial:** Ray Pignone, Editor. Robert Ragaini, Photographer.

CORNING

LEADER (CORNING), THE. 34 W Pulteney St, Corning, NY 14830. Telephone: 607-936-4651. FAX: 607-936-9939. URL: http://www.the-leader.com. Mailing Address: PO Box 1017, Corning, NY 14830. Pub. Frequency: d. Page Size: broadsheet. Subscrip. Rate: $.50 newsstand/cover; $1.50 newsstand/cover Sun.; $3.50 carrier delivery/wk.; $3.70 motor route/wk.. **Wire Service(s):** AP. Circulation: 11,559 morning (paid); 16,000 Sunday (paid). **Owner(s):** GateHouse Media, Inc, 350 WillowBrook Office Park, Fairport, NY 14450. Telephone: 585-598-0030. FAX: 585-248-2631. **Management:** Dannis Bruen, Publisher. Lisa Van De Hey, Advertising Manager. Elmer Kuehner, Circulation Director. **Editorial:** Suzanne Dunn, Editor. Stella Dupree, City Editor.

Dailies

CORTLAND

CORTLAND STANDARD. 110 Main St., Cortland, NY 13045-5548. Telephone: 607-756-5665. FAX: 607-756-5665. E-MAIL: office@cortlandstandard.net. Mailing Address: PO Box 5548, Cortland, NY 13045-5548. Year Established: 1867. Pub. Frequency: d. (Mon.-Sat.) Page Size: broadsheet. Subscrip. Rate: $.50 newsstand/cover; $140.40/yr carrier delivery; $251.40/yr mailed. **Wire Service(s):** AP. Circulation: 10,900 evening (paid and free); 10,100 per issue (paid and free). **Owner(s):** Cortland Standard Printing Co., Inc., 110 Main St., Cortland, NY 13045. Telephone: 607-756-5665. **Management:** Wayne L. Clark, General Manager. Kevin Howe, Publisher. Mike Anderson, Advertising Director. Guy C Ussery, Circulation Director. Tom Shattuck, Classified Adv. Mgr. **Editorial:** Kevin Conlon, Managing Editor. Alan Butler, Sports Editor.

DUNKIRK

OBSERVER (DUNKIRK). 8-10 E. Second St., Dunkirk, NY 14048-0391. Telephone: 716-366-3000. FAX: 716-366-3005. E-MAIL: observer@observertoday.com. URL: http://www.observertoday.com. Mailing Address: PO Box 391, Dunkirk, NY 14048-0391. Year Established: 1882. Pub. Frequency: d. Page Size: broadsheet. Subscrip. Rate: $.50 newsstand/cover; $1.25 newsstand/cover Sun.; $132.60/yr home delivery; $167.88/yr mailed in state; $258.48/yr mailed out of state. **Wire Service(s):** AP. Circulation: 13,305 morning (paid); 13,440 Sunday (paid). **Owner(s):** Ogden Newspapers of Minnesota, Inc., 19260 San Carlos Blvd., Fort Myers Beach, FL 33931. Telephone: 239-463-4421. **Management:** Karl T. Davis, General Manager. Meredith V. Patton, Advertising Director. Jeffrey Dolley, Circulation Manager. Brenda Musacchio, Business Manager. **Editorial:** John D'Agostino, Editor.

ELMIRA

STAR-GAZETTE. 201 Baldwin St., Elmira, NY 14901. Telephone: 607-734-5151. FAX: 607-733-4408. E-MAIL: jspaulding@stargazette.com. URL: http://www.stargazette.com. Mailing Address: PO Box 285, Elmira, NY 14902-0285. Year Established: 1828. Pub. Frequency: d. Page Size: broadsheet. Subscrip. Rate: $.50 newsstand/cover; $1.50 newsstand/cover Sun.; $3.50 carrier delivery/wk.; $182/yr carrier delivery; $195/yr motor route; $243/yr mailed. **Wire Service(s):** AP, GNS. Circulation: 28,833 morning (paid); 39,778 Sunday (paid). **Owner(s):** Gannett Company, Inc., 7950 Jones Branch Dr, McLean, VA 22107. Telephone: 703-854-6000. **Management:** Monte I. Trammer, Publisher. **Editorial:** Bill Church, Executive Editor. Lois Wilson, Managing Editor. David W Kubissa, Associate Editor. Jennifer Lyon, Copy Chief. Kyle Elston, Copy Editor. Eric Banks, Graphics Editor. Peggy Ridosh, Librarian. Jeff Richards, Photographer. Contact: Daniel Aldi, Editor.

GENEVA

FINGER LAKES TIMES, THE. 218 Genesee St., Geneva, NY 14456. Telephone: 315-789-3333. FAX: 315-789-4077. E-MAIL: fltimes@fltimes.com. URL: http://www.fltimes.com. Year Established: 1872. Pub. Frequency: d. (Sun.-Fri.) Page Size: broadsheet. Subscrip. Rate: $.50 newsstand/cover; $1.25 newsstand/cover Sun.; $126.90/yr carrier delivery. **Wire Service(s):** AP, LAT-WAT. Circulation: 19,000 evening (paid); 20,400 Sunday (paid). **Owner(s):** Independent Publications, Inc., See address and contact information above. **Management:** Phillip Beckley, Publisher. Diane Lahr-Smith, Advertising Director. Audrey DaMatties, Circulation Director. **Editorial:** Anne Schuhle, Managing Editor.

GLENS FALLS

POST-STAR, THE.　ISSN 0897-0505
Lawrence & Cooper Sts., Glens Falls, NY 12801. Telephone: 518-792-3131. FAX: 518-743-1684. E-MAIL: poststar@upstatepapers.com. URL: http://www.poststar.com. Mailing Address: PO Box 2157, Glens Falls, NY 12801. Year Established: 1889. Pub. Frequency: d. Page Size: broadsheet. Subscrip. Rate: $.50 newsstand/cover; $1.75 newsstand/cover Sun.; $3.25 carrier delivery/wk.; $4.10/wk. for rural deliv; $5 mailed/wk. **Wire Service(s):** AP. Circulation: 32,600 morning (paid); 34,500 Sunday (paid). **Owner(s):** Lee Enterprises, Inc., 201 N. Harrison St., Davenport, IA 52801-1924. **Management:** James G. Marshall, Publisher. Judith Goralski, Advertising Manager. Bill Sara, Circulation Manager. Bobbi Mead, Classified Adv. Mgr. **Editorial:** Ken Tingley, Managing Editor. Monty Calvert, Photographer. Greg Brownell, Sports Editor.

GLOVERSVILLE

LEADER-HERALD, THE. 8 E. Fulton St., Gloversville, NY 12078. Telephone: 518-725-8616. FAX: 518-725-7407. E-MAIL: leader@superior.net. URL: http://www.leaderherald.com. Mailing Address: PO Box 1280, Gloversville, NY 12078. Year Established: 1887. Pub. Frequency: d. Page Size: broadsheet. Subscrip. Rate: $.50 newsstand/cover; $1.25 newsstand/cover Sun.; $2.70 home delivery/wk. local; $12.80 home delivery/wk. local rural. **Wire Service(s):** AP. Circulation: 13,000 morning (paid); 13,000 Sunday (paid). **Owner(s):** Ogden Newspapers of Minnesota, Inc., 19260 San Carlos Blvd., Fort Myers Beach, FL 33931. **Management:** Patricia Beck, Publisher. Doug Hill, Advertising Director. Tony Muscani, Circulation Manager. **Editorial:** Tim Fonda, Managing Editor.

HERKIMER

EVENING TELEGRAM, THE. 111 Green St., Herkimer, NY 13350. Telephone: 315-866-2220. FAX: 315-866-5913. URL: http://www.herkimertelegram.com. Mailing Address: PO Box 551, Herkimer, NY 13350. Year Established: 1898. Pub. Frequency: d. (Mon.-Sat.) Page Size: broadsheet. Subscrip. Rate: $.50 newsstand/cover; $143/yr carrier delivery; $141.95/yr mailed. Adv. Rate: col. inch $11.75 **Wire Service(s):** AP. Circulation: 6,500 evening (paid). **Owner(s):** GateHouse Media, Inc, 350 WillowBrook Office Park, Fairport, NY 14450. Telephone: 585-598-0030. FAX: 585-248-2631. **Management:** Beth Brewer, Publisher. Pam Grande, Advertising Manager. Beth Brewer, Circulation Manager. **Editorial:** Richard Petrillo, Managing Editor. Gary Urich, Sports Editor.

HORNELL

HORNELL EVENING TRIBUNE/SUNDAY SPECTATOR. 85 Canisteo St., Hornell, NY 14843. Telephone: 607-324-1425. FAX: 607-324-1753. E-MAIL: eveningtribune@eveningtribune.com. URL: http://www.eveningtribune.com. Year Established: 1851. Pub. Frequency: d. (Sun.-Fri.) Page Size: broadsheet. Subscrip. Rate: $.75 newsstand/cover; $13.50 carrier delivery/mo.; $13.70 motor route/mo.; $14.30 mailed/mo. in county; $25 mailed/mo. out of county. **Wire Service(s):** AP. Circulation: 8,000 morning (paid); 16,500 Sunday (paid). **Owner(s):** GateHouse Media, Inc, 350 WillowBrook Office Park, Fairport, NY 14450. Telephone: 585-598-0030. FAX: 585-248-2631. **Management:** Tom Connors, Publisher. Gary Shaver, Circulation Manager. John Frungillo, Marketing Director. **Editorial:** Andy Thompson, Managing Editor. Derrick Balinsky, Sports Editor.

HUDSON

REGISTER-STAR.　ISSN 0747-2374
364 Warren St., Hudson, NY 12534. Telephone: 518-828-1616. FAX: 518-828-9437. Mailing Address: PO Box 635, Hudson, NY 12534. Year Established: 1785. Pub. Frequency: d. (Sun.-Fri.) Page Size: broadsheet. Subscrip. Rate: $.50 newsstand/cover; $1.50 newsstand/cover Sun.; $140/yr home delivery; $228/yr mailed. **Wire Service(s):** AP. Circulation: 7,944 evening (paid); 7,900 Sunday (paid). **Owner(s):** Johnson Newspaper Corp., 260 Washington St., Watertown, NY 13601. Telephone: 315-782-1000. **Management:** Roger Coleman, Publisher. Pamela Geskie, Advertising Director. Brenda Nickles, Circulation Director. **Editorial:** Theresa Hyland, City Editor. Robert Ragaini, Photographer. C.J. Mellor, Sports Editor.

ITHACA

ITHACA JOURNAL, THE. 123-127 W. State St., Ithaca, NY 14850. Telephone: 607-272-2321. FAX: 607-272-4335. URL: http://www.theithacajournal.com. Mailing Address: PO Box 430, Ithaca, NY 14851-0430. Year Established: 1815. Pub. Frequency: d. (Mon.-Sat.) Page Size: broadsheet. Subscrip. Rate: $.35 newsstand/cover; $.50 newsstand/cover Sat.; $2.75 home delivery/wk.; $143/yr home delivery; $3 motor route/wk.; $156/yr motor route. Freelance Pay: $30/article. **Wire Service(s):** AP, GNS. Circulation: 21,000 morning (paid). **Owner(s):** Gannett Company, Inc., 7950 Jones Branch Dr., McLean, VA 22107-0001. Telephone: 703-854-6000. **Management:** Jim Fogler, Publisher. Carol Becker, Advertising Director. Anthony Rapczynski, Circulation Director. Dave Warmbrodt, Circulation Manager. Lisa Weeks, Classified Adv. Mgr. **Editorial:** Bruce Estes, Managing Editor. Dave Bohrer, Asst. Managing Ed.. Simon Wheeler, Photo Editor.

JAMESTOWN

POST-JOURNAL, THE. 15 W. Second St., Jamestown, NY 14701. Telephone: 716-487-1111. FAX: 716-664-5305. E-MAIL: post-journal@oweb.com. URL: http://www.post-journal.com. Mailing Address: PO Box 190, Jamestown, NY 14702. Year Established: 1826. Pub. Frequency: d. Page Size: broadsheet. Subscrip. Rate: $.50 newsstand/cover; $1.25 newsstand/cover Sun.; $132.60/yr home delivery; $138/yr mailed in county. Adv. Rate: col. inch $22 **Wire Service(s):** AP. Circulation: 25,000 evening (paid); 30,000 Sunday (paid). **Owner(s):** Ogden Newspapers of Minnesota, Inc., 19260 San Carlos Blvd., Fort Myers Beach, FL 33931. Telephone: 239-463-4421. **Management:** James Austin, Publisher. Debbie Brunner, Advertising Manager. Sean Spielvogel, Circulation Manager. **Editorial:** Cristie L. Herbst, Managing Editor. Rodney Stebbins, City Editor. John Whittaker, Religion Editor. Jim Riggs, Sports Editor.

KINGSTON

DAILY FREEMAN.　ISSN 0746-4932
79 Hurley Ave., Kingston, NY 12401. Telephone: 845-331-5000. FAX: 845-331-3557. E-MAIL: publisher@freemanonline.com. URL: http://www.freemanonline.com. Year Established: 1871. Pub. Frequency: d. Page Size: broadsheet. Subscrip. Rate: $.50 newsstand/cover; $1.50 newsstand/cover Sun.; $19.50 home delivery/mo.; $58.50 home delivery/quarter; $113.50 home delivery for 6 mos.; $225/yr home delivery. **Wire Service(s):** AP. Circulation: 21,662 morning (paid); 28,684 Sunday (paid). **Owner(s):** Journal Register Co., 50 W State St, 12th Fl, Trenton, NJ 08608. Telephone: 609-396-2200. **Management:** Ira Fusfeld, Publisher. Greg Appel, Advertising Director. Barbara Norton, Advertising Manager. David Fogden, Circulation Manager. Penny Ducker, Classified Adv. Mgr. **Editorial:** Sam Daleo, Managing Editor. Bill Studt, Production Manager. Jeremy Schiffres, City Editor.

LITTLE FALLS

EVENING TIMES (LITTLE FALLS), THE. 347 S. Second St., Little Falls, NY 13365-1007. Telephone: 315-823-3680. FAX: 315-823-4086. E-MAIL: editor@littlefallstimes.com. URL: http://www.littlefallstimes.com. Mailing Address: PO Box 1007, Little Falls, NY 13365-1007. Year Established: 1886. Pub. Frequency: d. (Mon.-Sat.) Page Size: broadsheet. Subscrip. Rate: $.50 newsstand/cover; $2.65 carrier delivery/wk. Adv. Rate: col. inch $8.95 **Wire Service(s):** AP. Circulation: 5,047 evening (paid). **Owner(s):** GateHouse Media, Inc, 350 WillowBrook Office Park, Fairport, NY 14450. Telephone: 585-598-0030. FAX: 585-248-2631. **Management:** Beth Brewer, Publisher. Peggy Vespi, Advertising Manager. Steve Sterusky, Circulation Manager. **Editorial:** Todd Dewan, Editor. Wayne Gallt, Production Manager.

LOCKPORT

LOCKPORT UNION-SUN & JOURNAL.　ISSN 1099-6060
170 East Ave., Lockport, NY 14094. Telephone: 716-439-9222. FAX: 716-439-9239. E-MAIL: journal@localnet.com. URL: http://www.lockportjournal.com. Mailing Address: PO Box 503, Lockport, NY 14095. Year Established: 1821. Pub. Frequency: d. Page Size: broadsheet. Subscrip. Rate: $.50 newsstand/cover; $1.25 newsstand/cover Sun.; $157.56/yr carrier delivery in area; $208/yr mailed out of area. **Wire Service(s):** AP. Circulation: 17,500 morning (paid). **Owner(s):** Community Newspaper Holdings, Inc., 3500 Colonnade Pkwy., Ste. 600, Birmingham, AL 35243. Telephone: 205-298-7100. FAX: 205-298-7101. **Management:** Steve Hall, Publisher. Diane Crowe, Advertising Manager. Sue Wadosky, Circulation Manager. **Editorial:** Tim Marren, Managing Editor. Anne Calos, Feature Editor. John D'Onofrio, Sports Editor.

MALONE

MALONE TELEGRAM. 469 E. Main St., Ste. 4, Malone, NY 12953. Telephone: 518-483-4700. FAX: 518-483-8579. E-MAIL: news@mtelegram.com. URL: http://www.mtelegram.com. Mailing Address: PO Box 69, Malone, NY 12953. Year Established: 1905. Pub. Frequency: d. (Mon.-Sat.) Page Size: broadsheet. Subscrip. Rate: $.50 newsstand/cover; $124.80/yr motor route. Adv. Rate: col. inch $9.16 **Wire Service(s):** AP. Circulation: 6,000 morning (paid). **Owner(s):** Johnson Newspaper Corp., 260 Washington St., Watertown, NY 13601. Telephone: 315-782-1000. **Management:** John B. Johnson, President. Charles W. Kelly, Publisher. James Richard, Circulation Manager. **Editorial:** Connie Jenkins, Editor.

MASSENA

DAILY COURIER OBSERVER, THE. One Harrowgate Commons, Massena, NY 13662. Telephone: 315-769-2451. FAX: 315-764-0337. Mailing Address: PO Box 300, Massena, NY 13662. Year Established: 1891. Pub. Frequency: d. (Tue.-Sat.) Page Size: standard. Subscrip. Rate: $.50 newsstand/cover; $99/yr mailed in county; $107/yr mailed out of county. Circulation: 6,000 morning (paid). **Owner(s):** Johnson Newspaper Corp., 260 Washington St., Watertown, NY 13601. Telephone: 315-782-1000. **Management:** Charles Kelly, General Manager. Jackie Mitchell, Office Manager. Sean McNamara, Advertising Manager. **Editorial:** Ryan R. Martin, Managing Editor.

MEDINA

JOURNAL-REGISTER, THE. 413 Main St., Medina, NY 14103-1416. Telephone: 585-798-1400. FAX: 585-798-0290. URL: http://www.journal-register.com. Year Established: 1903. Pub. Frequency: d. (Mon.-Fri.) Page Size: broadsheet. Subscrip. Rate: $.50 newsstand/cover; $110.24/yr motor route; $182/yr mailed. Adv. Rate: col. inch $9.43 **Wire Service(s):** AP. Circulation: 4,800 evening (paid). **Owner(s):** Community Newspaper Holdings, Inc., 3500 Colonnade Pkwy., Ste. 600, Birmingham, AL 35243. Telephone: 205-298-7100. FAX: 205-298-7101. **Management:** Steve Hall, Publisher. Matt Green, Advertising Manager. Paul Glaeser, Circulation Director. AndreeRenee Simpson, Classified Adv. Mgr.. **Editorial:** Mike Regan, Managing Editor.

MELVILLE

NEWSDAY. ISSN 0278-5587
235 Pinelawn Rd., Melville, NY 11747-4250. Telephone: 516-843-2020. FAX: 631-843-2953. URL: http://www.newsday.com. Year Established: 1940. Pub. Frequency: d. Page Size: tabloid. Subscrip. Rate: $.50 newsstand/cover; $1.50 newsstand/cover Sun.; $5 home delivery/wk. in Nassau & Suffolk cys.. **Wire Service(s):** RN, AP, LAT-WAT, DJNS. Circulation: 577,354 morning (paid); 675,619 Sunday (paid). **Owner(s):** Tribune Company, 435 N Michigan Ave, Chicago, IL 60601. Telephone: 312.222.9100. **Bureau(s):** P.O. Box 7255, Albany, NY 12224-0255. Telephone: 518-465-2311. Contact: Jordan Rau, Bureau Chief. **Management:** Timothy P. Knight, General Manager. Raymond A. Jansen, Publisher. Raymond Koupal, Finance Director. Paul Barbetta, Circulation Director. Andrea Rothchild, Classified Adv. Mgr.. Paul Fleischman, Marketing Director. **Editorial:** John Mancini, Editor. Les Payne, Assoc. Managing Ed.. James Klurfeld, Editorial Page Editor.

MIDDLETOWN

TIMES HERALD-RECORD. 40 Mulberry St., Middletown, NY 10940. Telephone: 845-341-1100. FAX: 845-343-2170. E-MAIL: comments@th-record.com. URL: http://www.recordonline.com. Mailing Address: PO Box 2046, Middletown, NY 10940. Year Established: 1956. Pub. Frequency: d. Page Size: tabloid. Subscrip. Rate: $.50 newsstand/cover; $1.75 Sun.; $15 carrier delivery/mo. in area. Freelance Pay: $35-$100/article. **Wire Service(s):** AP, SH, NYT, MCT. Circulation: 86,310 morning (paid); 102,040 Sunday (paid). **Owner(s):** Ottaway Newspapers, Inc., PO Box 401, Campbell Hall, NY 10916. Telephone: 845-294-8181. **Management:** Joe A. Vanderhoof, Publisher. Kathy Hammer, Classified Adv. Mgr.. **Editorial:** Mike Levine, Executive Editor. Meg McGuire, Managing Editor. Doug Cunningham, Business Editor. Michael Carey, City Editor.

NEW YORK

COURIER (HOUMA), THE. 620 8th Ave, New York, NY 10018. Telephone: 212-556-1234. FAX: 212-556-7614. E-MAIL: info@houmatoday.com. URL: http://www.houmatoday.com. Mailing Address: PO Box 2717, Houma, LA 70361. Year Established: 1878. Pub. Frequency: d. Page Size: broadsheet. Subscrip. Rate: $.50 newsstand/cover; $1 newsstand/cover Sun.; $144/yr home delivery local. **Wire Service(s):** AP, NYT. Circulation: 19,000 evening (paid); 21,000 Sunday (paid). **Owner(s):** New York Times Company, See address and contact information above. **Management:** Miles Forrest, Publisher. Marian Long, Advertising Manager. David Simon, Circulation Director. Robin Naquin, Classified Adv. Mgr..

DAILY COMET. 620 8th Ave, New York, NY 10018. Telephone: 212-556-1234. FAX: 212-556-7614. URL: http://www.dailycomet.com. Mailing Address: PO Box 5238, Thibodaux, LA 70302. Year Established: 1889. Pub. Frequency: d. (Mon.-Fri.) Page Size: broadsheet. Subscrip. Rate: $.50 newsstand/cover; $88/yr home delivery local. **Wire Service(s):** AP. Circulation: 12,500 evening (paid). **Owner(s):** New York Times Company, See address and contact information above. **Management:** Miles Forrest, Publisher. Emmet McKinley, Advertising Director. David Simon, Circulation Director. Robin Naquin, Classified Adv. Mgr.. **Editorial:** Jeff Zeringue, Executive Editor. Mike Gorman, City Editor. Edward Guidry, Copy Editor. Abby Tabor, Photo Editor. Brent St. Germain, Sports Editor.

DISPATCH (LEXINGTON), THE. ISSN 0163-3090
620 8th Ave, New York, NY 10018. Telephone: 212-556-1234. FAX: 212-556-7614. E-MAIL: info@the-dispatch.com. URL: http://www.the-dispatch.com. Mailing Address: PO Box 908, Lexington, NC 27293. Year Established: 1882. Pub. Frequency: d. (Tue.-Sat.) Page Size: broadsheet. Subscrip. Rate: $.50 newsstand/cover; $132/mo.. **Wire Service(s):** AP, NYT. Circulation: 10,200 evening (paid). **Owner(s):** New York Times Company, See address and contact information above. **Management:** Ned Cowan, Publisher. Jeff West, Circulation Manager. **Editorial:** Chad Killebrew, Executive Editor. Vikki Hodges, Lifestyle Editor. Graig Allen, News Editor. Mike Duprez, Sports Editor.

GADSDEN TIMES. 620 8th Ave, New York, NY 10018. Telephone: 212-556-1234. FAX: 212-556-7614. URL: http://www.gadsdentimes.com. Mailing Address: PO Box 188, Gadsden, AL 35999. Year Established: 1867. Pub. Frequency: d. Page Size: broadsheet. Subscrip. Rate: $.50 newsstand/cover; $1.25 newsstand/cover Sun.; $11 home delivery/mo.. **Wire Service(s):** AP, NYT. Circulation: 30,000 morning (paid). **Owner(s):** New York Times Company, See address and contact information above. **Management:** Roger Quinn, Publisher. Glen Porter, Advertising Director. **Editorial:** Ron Reaves, Executive Editor. Steve Howard, Automotive Editor. Donna Thornton, Business Editor. Randy Johnson, City Editor. Cyndi Nelson, Feature Editor. Steve Howard, Government Affrs. Ed.. Randy Johnson, Metro Editor. Andy Powell, Political Editor. Jimmy Smothers, Sports.

GAINESVILLE SUN, THE. ISSN 0163-4925
620 8th Ave, New York, NY 10018. Telephone: 212-556-1234. FAX: 212-556-7614. E-MAIL: srenbarger@gvillesun.com. URL: http://www.sunone.com. Mailing Address: PO Box 147147, Gainesville, FL 32614. Year Established: 1876. Pub. Frequency: d. Page Size: broadsheet. Subscrip. Rate: $.50 newsstand/cover; $1.25 newsstand/cover Sun.; $151.58/yr home delivery. **Wire Service(s):** AP, NYT. Circulation: 55,972 morning (paid); 61,389 Sunday (paid). **Owner(s):** New York Times Company, See address and contact information above. **Management:** Jim Doughton, Publisher. Susan Pinder, Advertising. **Editorial:** Jim Osteen, Executive Editor. Jacki Levine, Managing Editor.

HENDERSONVILLE TIMES-NEWS. ISSN 1042-2323
620 8th Ave, New York, NY 10018. Telephone: 212-556-1234. FAX: 212-556-7614. E-MAIL: tnletters@/blueridgenow.com. URL: http://www.blueridgenow.com. Mailing Address: PO Box 490, Hendersonville, NC 28793. Year Established: 1881. Pub. Frequency: d. Page Size: broadsheet. Subscrip. Rate: $.50 newsstand/cover; $1 newsstand/cover Sun.; $150.80/yr home delivery in state; $345/yr mailed out of state; $109.20/yr Fri, Sat, Sun; $226.20/yr mailed Fri, Sat, Sun. **Wire Service(s):** AP, NYT. Circulation: 18,500 morning (paid); 18,900 Sunday (paid). **Owner(s):** New York Times Company, See address and contact information above. **Management:** Ruth Birge, Publisher. Kevin Drake, Advertising Director. Beth Corn, Circulation Manager. Heather Staton, Classified Adv. Mgr.. **Editorial:** Bill Moss, Executive Editor. Todd Callaway, City Editor. Harrison Metzger, Editorial Page Editor. Dean Hensley, Sports Editor.

HERALD-JOURNAL. ISSN 0740-4743
620 8th Ave, New York, NY 10018. Telephone: 212-556-1234. FAX: 212-556-7614. E-MAIL: goupstate@shj.com. URL: http://www.goupstate.com. Mailing Address: PO Box 1657, Spartanburg, SC 29304-1657. Year Established: 1842. Pub. Frequency: d. Page Size: broadsheet. Subscrip. Rate: $.50 newsstand/cover; $1 newsstand/cover Sun.; $14.50 home delivery/mo.; $153.40/yr home delivery; $25 mailed/mo.; $299/yr mailed. **Wire Service(s):** AP. Circulation: 55,000 morning (paid); 65,000 Sunday (paid). **Owner(s):** New York Times Company, See address and contact information above. **Management:** David O Roberts, Publisher. Kathy Powell, Advertising Director. Ken Smith, Circulation Director. Kathy Shepherd, Classified Adv. Mgr.. **Editorial:** Carl Beck, Executive Editor. Greg Retinas, Managing Editor.

LEDGER, THE. ISSN 0163-0288
620 8th Ave, New York, NY 10018. Telephone: 212-556-1234. FAX: 212-556-7614. E-MAIL: online@theledger.com. URL: http://www.theledger.com. Mailing Address: PO Box 408, Lakeland, FL 33802. Year Established: 1924. Pub. Frequency: d. Page Size: broadsheet. Subscrip. Rate: $.50 newsstand/cover; $1 Sun.; $12/mo.; $156/yr home delivery. **Wire Service(s):** AP, NYT. Circulation: 88,500 morning (paid); 106,134 Sunday (paid). **Owner(s):** New York Times Company, See address and contact information above. **Management:** John Fitzwater, Publisher. Steve Schmidt, Advertising. **Editorial:** Louis M Perez, Executive Editor. Lenore Beecken, Managing Editor.

NEW YORK DAILY NEWS, THE. 450 W. 33rd St., New York, NY 10001. Telephone: 212-210-2100. FAX: 212-643-7831. URL: http://www.nydailynews.com. Year Established: 1919. Pub. Frequency: d. Page Size: tabloid. Subscrip. Rate: $.50 newsstand/cover; $1 newsstand/cover Sun.. **Wire Service(s):** RN, AP. Circulation: 763,975 morning (paid); 874,520 Sunday (paid). **Owner(s):** Mortimer Zuckerman, See address and contact information above. **Management:** Les Goodstein, President. Mortimer Zuckerman, Publisher. John Polizano, Advertising Director. **Editorial:** Michael Cooke, Editor-in-Chief. Martin Dunn, Editorial Director. Robert Sapio, Executive Editor. Dick Belsky, Managing Editor. Bill Boyle, Senior Managing Editor. Arthur Brown, Editorial Page Editor. Faigi Rosenthal, Librarian. Dean Chang, Metro Editor. Leon Carter, Sports Editor.

NEW YORK POST. ISSN 1090-3321
1211 Ave. of the Americas, New York, NY 10036-8790. Telephone: 212-930-8000. FAX: 212-930-8540. E-MAIL: aaquilina@nypost.com. URL: http://www.nypost.com. Year Established: 1801. Pub. Frequency: d. Page Size: tabloid. Subscrip. Rate: $.25 newsstand/cover; $3.49/wk.; $119.08/yr. **Wire Service(s):** AP, LAT-WAT, AFP. Circulation: 436,544 evening (paid). **Owner(s):** N.Y.P. Holdings Inc., 1211 Ave. of the Americas, New York, NY 10036. Telephone: 212-930-8000. **Management:** Patrick Judge, Director. Geoff Booth, General Manager. Rupert Murdoch, Owner. John Ancona, Advertising Director. Joe Gilkey, Circulation Manager. Ralph D'Onforio, Classified Adv. Mgr.. Vin Montuori, Promotion Manager. **Editorial:** Jesse Angelo, Editor. Col Allen, Editor-in-Chief. Jesse Angelo, Assignment Editor. Dan Colarusso, Business Editor. Robert McManus, Editorial Page Editor. Faye Penn, Entertainment Editor. Laura Harris, Librarian. David Boyle, Photo Editor. Mike Shain, Radio-TV Editor. Steve Cuozzo, Society Editor. Greg Gallo, Sports Editor. Pucci Meyer, Travel Editor.

NEW YORK TIMES, THE. ISSN 0362-4331
620 8th Ave, New York, NY 10018. Telephone: 212-556-1234. FAX: 212-556-7614. URL: http://www.nytimes.com. Year Established: 1851. Pub. Frequency: d. Page Size: broadsheet. Subscrip. Rate: $10.20 home delivery/wk.. Adv. Rate: B&W page $92,421, color page $101,821 **Wire Service(s):** RN, AP, NYT, DJNS, PR. Circulation: 1,118,565. **Owner(s):** New York Times Company, See address and contact information above. **Management:** Arthur Ochs Sulzberger Jr., Publisher. Daniel H Cohen, Advertising. **Editorial:** Gail Collins, Editor. Bill Keller, Executive Editor.

SANTA ROSA PRESS DEMOCRAT. ISSN 0747-220X
620 8th Ave, New York, NY 10018. Telephone: 212-556-1234. FAX: 212-556-7614. E-MAIL: bkyce@pressdemo.com. URL: http://www.pressdemo.com. Mailing Address: PO Box 569, Santa Rosa, CA 95402. Year Established: 1857. Pub. Frequency: d. Page Size: tabloid. Subscrip. Rate: $.50 newsstand/cover; $1.25 newsstand/cover Sun.; $6.45 mailed/wk.; $162/yr home delivery. Freelance Pay: $50/article. **Wire Service(s):** AP, NYT, LAT-WAT, CNS. Circulation: 94,000 morning (paid); 103,000 Sunday (paid). **Owner(s):** New York Times Company, See address and contact information above. **Management:** Michael Parman, Publisher. Joanne Davey, Advertising Director. Tim Cambra, Circulation Manager. **Editorial:** Peter Golis, Editorial Director. Catherine Barnett, Executive Editor. Robert Swofford, Managing Editor. Brad Bollinger, Business Editor. Paul Gullixson, Editorial Page Editor. Dan Taylor, Feature Editor. James Fremgen, News Editor. George Manes, Sports. Dan Taylor, Theatrical Editor.

SARASOTA HERALD-TRIBUNE. 620 8th Ave, New York, NY 10018. Telephone: 212-556-1234. FAX: 212-556-7614. URL: http://www.newscoast.com. Mailing Address: PO Box 1719, Sarasota, FL 34230. Year Established: 1925. Pub. Frequency: d. Page Size: broadsheet. Subscrip. Rate: $.50 newsstand/cover; $1.25 newsstand/cover Sun.. **Wire Service(s):** AP, SH, NYT, LAT-WAT. Circulation: 109,000 morning (paid); 160,000 Sunday (paid). **Owner(s):** New York Times Company, See address and contact information above. **Management:** Diane McFarlin, Publisher. **Editorial:** Janet Weaver, Executive Editor. Diane Tennant, Managing Editor. Mathew Sauer, Business Editor. Tom Tryon, Editorial Page Editor. Scott Peterson, Sports.

STAR BANNER. ISSN 1084-8088
620 8th Ave, New York, NY 10018. Telephone: 212-556-1234. FAX: 212-556-7614. E-MAIL: cheriebeers@starbanner.com. URL: http://www.starbanner.com. Mailing Address: PO Box 490, Ocala, FL 34478-0490. Year Established: 1866. Pub. Frequency: d. Page Size: broadsheet. Subscrip. Rate: $.50 newsstand/cover; $.75 newsstand/cover Sat.; $1.25 newsstand/cover Sun.. **Wire Service(s):** AP, NYT, LAT-WAT, MCT. Circulation: 50,000 morning (paid); 54,000 Sunday (paid). **Owner(s):** New York Times Company, See address and contact information above. **Management:** Bruce Gaultney, Publisher. Susan Pinder, Advertising Director. Jim Miller, Circulation Manager. **Editorial:** Chirie Beers, Executive Editor. Tom McNiff, Managing Editor. Kisha Dunn, Business Editor. Joe Byrnes, City Editor. Brad Rogers, Editorial Page Editor. Christopher Lloyd, Entertainment Editor. David Moore, Fashion Editor. Richard Anguiano, News Editor. Alan Youngblood, Photo Editor. Eric Barnes, Sports Editor.

TIMES DAILY. ISSN 0743-1511
620 8th Ave, New York, NY 10018. Telephone: 212-556-1234. FAX: 212-556-7614. E-MAIL: timesdly@timesdaily.com. URL: http://www.timesdaily.com. Mailing Address: PO Box 797, Florence, AL 35631. Year Established: 1869. Pub. Frequency: d. Page Size: broadsheet. Subscrip. Rate: $.50 newsstand/cover; $1.25 newsstand/cover Sun.; $11.25 home delivery for 4 wks.; $135/yr home delivery. Wire Service(s): UPI. Circulation: 34,000 morning (paid); 36,000 Sunday (paid). Owner(s): New York Times Company, See address and contact information above. Management: Robert Gruber, Publisher. Kevin Austin, Advertising. Steve Learn, Circulation Director. Editorial: David Brown, Executive Editor. Mike Goens, Managing Editor.

TUSCALOOSA NEWS, THE. 620 8th Ave, New York, NY 10018. Telephone: 212-556-1234. FAX: 212-556-7614. URL: http://www.tuscaloosanews.com. Mailing Address: PO Box 20587, Tuscaloosa, AL 35402. Year Established: 1818. Pub. Frequency: d. Page Size: broadsheet. Subscrip. Rate: $.50 newsstand/cover; $1.50 newsstand/cover Sun.; $3.75/wk.; $195/yr. Wire Service(s): AP, NYT. Circulation: 35,000 morning (paid); 35,000 Sunday (paid). Owner(s): New York Times Company, See address and contact information above. Management: Timothy M Thompson, Publisher. Paul Hass, Circulation Manager. Newell Allen, Classified Adv. Mgr.. Editorial: Douglas W Ray, Executive Editor. Robert Sutton, Photographer. Tommy Deas, Sports Editor.

WILMINGTON STAR NEWS. ISSN 0163-402X
620 8th Ave, New York, NY 10018. Telephone: 212-556-1234. FAX: 212-556-7614. E-MAIL: citydesk@wilmingtonstar.com. URL: http://www.wilmingtonstar.com. Mailing Address: PO Box 840, Wilmington, NC 28402-0840. Year Established: 1867. Pub. Frequency: d. Page Size: broadsheet. Subscrip. Rate: $.50 newsstand/cover; $1.50 Sun.; $11.92/mo.. Wire Service(s): AP, NYT, LAT-WAT, MCT. Circulation: 54,862 morning (paid); 63,098 Sunday (paid). Owner(s): New York Times Company, See address and contact information above. Management: Ken Svanum, Publisher. Diane Keenan, Advertising. Aileen Hood, Circulation Manager. Editorial: Allen Parsons, Editor. Brian Hendrickson, Sports Editor.

NIAGARA FALLS

NIAGARA GAZETTE. 310 Niagara St., Niagara Falls, NY 14303. Telephone: 716-282-2311. FAX: 716-286-3895. URL: http://www.niagara-gazette.com. Mailing Address: PO Box 549, Niagara Falls, NY 14302-0549. Year Established: 1854. Pub. Frequency: d. Page Size: broadsheet. Subscrip. Rate: $.50 newsstand/cover; $1.50 newsstand/cover Sun.; $185.64/yr home delivery in county; $286/yr mailed out of county. Freelance Pay: $25-$100/article. Wire Service(s): AP, GNS. Circulation: 22,876 morning (paid); 45,139 Sunday (paid). Owner(s): Community Newspaper Holdings, Inc., 3500 Colonnade Pkwy., Ste. 600, Birmingham, AL 35243. Telephone: 205-298-7100. FAX: 205-298-7101. Management: Matt Green, Advertising Manager. Paul Glaeser, Circulation Director. AndreeRenee Simpson, Classified Adv. Mgr.. Editorial: Tim Schmitt, Editor. Dick Lucinski, Managing Editor.

NORTH TONAWANDA

TONAWANDA NEWS. 435 River Rd., North Tonawanda, NY 14120. Telephone: 716-693-1000. FAX: 716-693-8573. URL: http://www.tonawanda-news.com. Mailing Address: PO Box 668, North Tonawanda, NY 14120-0668. Year Established: 1880. Pub. Frequency: d. Page Size: broadsheet. Subscrip. Rate: $.50 newsstand/cover; $1.25 newsstand/cover Sun.; $135.20/yr home delivery in area; $182/yr mailed out of area. Freelance Pay: $25-$100/article. Wire Service(s): AP. Circulation: 7,855 evening (paid). Owner(s): Community Newspaper Holdings, Inc., 3500 Colonnade Pkwy., Ste. 600, Birmingham, AL 35243. Telephone: 205-298-7100. FAX: 205-298-7101. Management: Steve Hall, Publisher. Matt Green, Advertising Manager. Paul Glaeser, Circulation Director. AndreeRenee Simpson, Classified Adv. Mgr.. Editorial: Carlene Peterson, Managing Editor.

NORWICH

EVENING SUN, THE. ISSN 0747-0355
29 Lackawanna Ave., Norwich, NY 13815. Telephone: 607-334-3276. FAX: 607-334-8273. E-MAIL: news@evesun.com. URL: http://www.evesun.com. Mailing Address: PO Box 151, Norwich, NY 13815-0151. Year Established: 1891. Pub. Frequency: d. (Mon.-Fri.) Page Size: broadsheet. Subscrip. Rate: $.50 newsstand/cover; $119.60/yr carrier delivery; $124.80/yr motor route; $32.50 mailed in county for 3 mos.; $39 mailed out of county for 3 mos.. Freelance Pay: $0.50/column-inch. Wire Service(s): AP. Circulation: 7,000 evening (paid). Owner(s): Snyder Communication Corp., See address and contact information above. Management: Richard Snyder, Publisher. Russ Foote, Advertising Manager. Brad Dick, Circulation Manager. Jan Rowe, Classified Adv. Mgr.. Editorial: Jeffrey Genung, Managing Editor. Patrick Newell, Sports Editor.

OGDENSBURG

THE/OGDENSBURG JOURNAL/ADVANCE NEWS. ISSN 0893-5149
308 Isabella, Ogdensburg, NY 13669. Telephone: 315-393-1000. FAX: 315-393-5108. URL: http://www.ogd.com. Mailing Address: PO Box 409, Ogdensburg, NY 13669. Year Established: 1830. Pub. Frequency: d. Page Size: broadsheet. Subscrip. Rate: $.50 newsstand/cover; $1.50 newsstand/cover Sun.. Wire Service(s): AP. Circulation: 5,200 per issue (paid); 10,700 Sunday (paid). Owner(s): Johnson Newspaper Corp., 260 Washington St., Watertown, NY 13601. Telephone: 315-782-1000. Management: Charles W. Kelly, General Manager. Sean McNamara, Advertising Manager. John Wilson, Circulation Manager. Brenda LaBrake, Business Manager. Editorial: Charles W. Kelly, Editor. James Reagen, Managing Editor. David Shea, Sports Editor.

OLEAN

TIMES HERALD (OLEAN), THE. 639 Norton Dr., Olean, NY 14760. Telephone: 716-372-3121. FAX: 716-372-0740. E-MAIL: oleanews@netsync.net. URL: http://www.oleantimesherald.com. Year Established: 1860. Pub. Frequency: d. Page Size: broadsheet. Subscrip. Rate: $.50 newsstand/cover; $1.50 newsstand/cover Sun.; $16.50 carrier delivery/mo.; $19 mailed/mo.. Wire Service(s): AP, UPI. Circulation: 18,600 morning (paid); 19,000 Sunday (paid). Owner(s): Bradford Publishing Co., 43 Main St., Bradford, PA 16701. Telephone: 814-368-3173. Management: Bill Fitzpatrick, Publisher. Larry Chiott, Advertising Director. Editorial: Bill Fitzpatrick, Editor. Jim Eckstrom, Managing Editor. George Nianiatus, Business Editor. Tom Donehue, Entertainment Editor. Darrell Gronemeier, Photo Editor. Charles Pollack, Sports Editor.

ONEIDA

ONEIDA DAILY DISPATCH. 130 Broad St., Oneida, NY 13421. Telephone: 315-363-5100. FAX: 315-363-9832. URL: http://www.oneidadispatch.com. Mailing Address: PO Box 120, Oneida, NY 13421. Year Established: 1851. Pub. Frequency: d. (Mon.-Sat.) Page Size: broadsheet. Subscrip. Rate: $.50 newsstand/cover; $156/yr carrier delivery. Wire Service(s): AP. Circulation: 18,500 morning (paid). Owner(s): Journal Register Co., 50 W State St, 12th Fl, Trenton, NJ 08608. Telephone: 609-396-2200. Management: Phil Austin, Publisher. Marc Alvord, Circulation Director. Editorial: Kurt Wanfried, Managing Editor. Perry L. Novak, Sports Editor.

ONEONTA

DAILY STAR (ONEONTA), THE. 102 Chestnut St, Oneonta, NY 13820. Telephone: 607-432-1000. FAX: 607-432-5843. URL: http://www.thedailystar.com. Year Established: 1890. Pub. Frequency: d. (Mon.-Sat.) Page Size: broadsheet. Subscrip. Rate: $.50 newsstand/cover; $1 newsstand/cover Sat.; $156/yr carrier delivery; $208/yr mailed. Wire Service(s): AP. Circulation: 19,000 morning (paid). Owner(s): Community Newspaper Holdings, Inc., 3500 Colonnade Pkwy., Ste. 600, Birmingham, AL 35242. Management: Bill Reeves, Advertising Director. Editorial: Sam Polak, Editor. Cary Brunswick, Managing Editor.

OSWEGO

PALLADIUM-TIMES, THE. 140 W. First St., Oswego, NY 13126. Telephone: 315-343-3800. FAX: 315-343-0273. E-MAIL: ptimes@bridgemicro.com. URL: www.pall-times.com. Year Established: 1845. Pub. Frequency: d. (Mon.-Sat.) Page Size: broadsheet. Subscrip. Rate: $.75 newsstand/cover; $110/yr mailed in county; $168/yr mailed out of county. Freelance Pay: $15/story. Wire Service(s): AP, SH. Circulation: 8,500 evening (paid). Owner(s): GateHouse Media, Inc, 350 WillowBrook Office Park, Fairport, NY 14450. Telephone: 585-598-0030. FAX: 585-248-2631. Management: Paul Scott, Publisher. Michael Russo, Advertising Manager. Toby Clawson, Circulation Manager. Editorial: Gary Catt, Editor. Mike LeBouef, Sports Editor.

PLATTSBURGH

PRESS-REPUBLICAN. ISSN 1041-4754
170 Margaret St, Plattsburgh, NY 12901. Telephone: 518-561-2300. FAX: 518-561-3362. E-MAIL: bparks@pressrepublican.com. URL: http://www.pressrepublican.com. Year Established: 1942. Pub. Frequency: d. Page Size: broadsheet. Subscrip. Rate: $.50 newsstand/cover; $1.75 newsstand/cover Sun.; $166.14/yr carrier delivery; $189.54/yr motor route. Freelance Pay: $30/story. Wire Service(s): AP, SH, DJNS. Circulation: 22,780 morning (paid); 25,232 Sunday (paid). Owner(s): Community Newspaper Holdings, Inc., 3500 Colonnade Pkwy., Ste. 600, Birmingham, AL 35243. Management: Robert Parks, Publisher. George Rock, Advertising Director. James Frenya, Circulation Director. Editorial: Robert Grady, Editor-in-Chief.

POTSDAM

COURIER-OBSERVER. 5 Beal St., Potsdam, NY 13676-1746. Telephone: 315-322-4416. FAX: 315-265-6001. Mailing Address: PO Box 5205, Potsdam, NY 13676. Pub. Frequency: d. (Tue.-Sat.) Page Size: broadsheet. Subscrip. Rate: $.50 newsstand/cover; $26.25 carrier delivery/quarter in county; $29.20 motor route/quarter in county. Circulation: 9,000 morning (paid). Owner(s): Johnson Newspaper Corp., 260 Washington St., Watertown, NY 13601. Telephone: 316-782-1000. Management: Charles Kelly, Publisher. Sean McNamara, Advertising Manager. Jane Moore, Circulation Manager. Editorial: Charles Kelly, Editor-in-Chief. Ryan R. Martin, Managing Editor.

POUGHKEEPSIE

POUGHKEEPSIE JOURNAL. 85 Civic Center Plz., Poughkeepsie, NY 12601. Telephone: 845-454-2000. FAX: 845-437-4921. E-MAIL: pdaugher@poughkee.gannett.com. URL: http://www.pojonews.com. Year Established: 1785. Pub. Frequency: d. Page Size: broadsheet. Subscrip. Rate: $.50 newsstand/cover; $1.50 newsstand/cover Sun.; $16 carrier delivery/mo.; $16.50 motor route/mo.. Freelance Pay: $25/article. Wire Service(s): AP, MCT, GNS. Circulation: 43,390 morning (paid); 56,514 Sunday (paid). Owner(s): Gannett Company, Inc., 7950 Jones Branch Dr., McLean, VA 22107-0001. Telephone: 703-284-6000. Management: Barry Rothfeld, Publisher. Jan Dewey, Advertising Director. Paul Felicissimo, Circulation Director. Jeff Reiss, Classified Adv. Mgr.. Editorial: Ann Gross, Editor. Margaretta Downey, Executive Editor. Richard Kleban, Managing Editor. John Ferro, City Editor. John Penney, Editorial Page Editor. Ray Fashona, Lifestyle Editor.

ROCHESTER

ROCHESTER DEMOCRAT & CHRONICLE. ISSN 1088-5153
55 Exchange Blvd., Rochester, NY 14614. Telephone: 585-232-7100. FAX: 585-258-2237. URL: http://www.democratandchronicle.com. Year Established: 1833. Pub. Frequency: d. Page Size: broadsheet. Subscrip. Rate: $.50 newsstand/cover; $1.50 newsstand/cover Sun.; $3.85 carrier delivery/wk.; $200.20/yr. Wire Service(s): RN, AP, LAT-WAT, GNS. Circulation: 363,300 morning (paid); 468,300 Sunday (paid). Owner(s): Gannett Company, Inc., 7950 Jones Branch Dr, McLean, VA 22107. Telephone: 703-854-6000. Management: David L. Hunke, Publisher. Bradley Harmon, Advertising Director. Janet Hasson, Circulation Director. Jeffrey Kapuscinski, Marketing Director. Editorial: Karen Magnuson, Editor. Jane Sutter, Managing Editor. Ellen Rosen, Business Editor. James Lawrence, Editorial Page Editor. Gini Wheeler, Librarian. Gary Fallesen, Outdoor Editor. Scott Norris, Photo Editor.

ROME

DAILY SENTINEL & SUN SENTINEL. 333 W. Dominick St., Rome, NY 13440. Telephone: 315-337-4000. FAX: 315-337-4704. URL: http://www.romesentinel.com. Year Established: 1865. Pub. Frequency: d. Page Size: tabloid. Subscrip. Rate: $.50 newsstand/cover; $143/yr carrier delivery local; $150.80/yr motor route local; $187.20/yr mailed in county. Adv. Rate: col. inch $12.50 Wire Service(s): AP. Circulation: 15,000 evening (paid and free); 25,000 Sunday (paid and free). Owner(s): Rome Sentinel Co., See address and contact information above. Management: George B Waters, President. Stephen B Waters, Publisher. Michael Brockway, Office Manager. Shirley B Waters, Vice President. Joe Entelisano, Advertising Manager. Zeb Swinney, Circulation Manager. Linda Carlson, Classified Adv. Mgr.. Ken Kakaty, Controller. Editorial: George B Waters, Editor. David C Swanson, Managing Editor. Barbara Charzuk, Editorial Page Editor. Thomas Merz, News Editor. Joseph Silkowski, Sports.

SALAMANCA

SALAMANCA PRESS. ISSN 8755-9110
36 River St., Salamanca, NY 14779. Telephone: 716-945-1644. FAX: 716-945-4285. E-MAIL: salowpress@ezet.net. URL: http://www.salamancapress.com. Mailing Address: PO Box 111, Salamanca, NY 14779. Year Established: 1868. Pub. Frequency: d. (Mon.-Fri.) Page Size: broadsheet. Subscrip. Rate: $.50 newsstand/cover; $10.25 carrier delivery/mo. in county; $13.50 motor route/mo. in county. Wire Service(s): AP. Circulation: 2,500 evening (paid). Owner(s): Bradford Publishing Co., 43 Main St., Bradford, PA 16701. Telephone: 814-368-3173. Management: Laura Howard, Publisher. Kasey Stockman, Advertising Manager. Theresa Holms, Circulation Manager. Beverly Durow, Classified Adv. Mgr.. Editorial: Laura Howard, Editor. Darren Riethmiller, Sports.

SARANAC LAKE

ADIRONDACK DAILY ENTERPRISE. 61 Broadway, Saranac Lake, NY 12983. Telephone: 518-891-2600. FAX: 518-891-2756. E-MAIL: adenews@adirondackguide.com. URL: http://www.oweb.com/enterprise. Mailing Address: PO Box 318, Saranac Lake, NY 12983-0318. Year Established: 1895. Pub. Frequency: d. (Mon.-Sat.) Page Size: broadsheet. Subscrip. Rate: $.50 newsstand/cover; $112/yr home delivery local; $130/yr mailed in county; $164/yr mailed elsewhere. **Wire Service(s):** AP. Circulation: 6,000 evening (paid). **Owner(s):** Ogden Newspapers of Minnesota, Inc., 1500 Main St., Wheeling, WV 26003. Telephone: 304-233-0100. FAX: 304-233-0327. **Management:** Catherine Moore, Publisher. Connie Amell, Advertising. Ruby Vann, Circulation Manager. **Editorial:** Steve Bradley, Editor. Sanford Sanford, Production Manager. Bill Johnson, Sports Editor.

SARATOGA SPRINGS

SARATOGIAN, THE. ISSN 1071-4448
20 Lake Ave., Saratoga Springs, NY 12866-2356. Telephone: 518-584-4242. FAX: 518-587-7750. E-MAIL: news@saratogian.com. URL: http://www.saratogian.com. Year Established: 1855. Pub. Frequency: d. Page Size: broadsheet. Subscrip. Rate: $.50 newsstand/cover; $1.75 newsstand/cover Sun.; $50.70 home delivery for 13 wks.; $202.80/yr home delivery. **Wire Service(s):** AP. Circulation: 12,000 morning (paid); 14,000 Sunday (paid). **Owner(s):** Journal Register Co., 50 W State St, 12th Fl, Trenton, NJ 08608. Telephone: 609-396-2200. FAX: 609-396-2292. **Management:** Frank McGivern, Publisher. **Editorial:** Barbara Lombardo, Managing Editor. Beverly McKim, City Editor. Jill Wing, Lifestyle Editor. Ed Burke, Photographer.

SCHENECTADY

DAILY GAZETTE. ISSN 1050-0340
2345 Maxon Rd. Ext., Schenectady, NY 12308. Telephone: 518-374-4141. FAX: 518-395-3084. E-MAIL: gazette@dailygazette.com. URL: http://www.dailygazette.com. Mailing Address: PO Box 1090, Schenectady, NY 12301-1090. Year Established: 1894. Pub. Frequency: d. Page Size: broadsheet. Subscrip. Rate: $.50 newsstand/cover; $1.75 newsstand/cover Sun.; $3.50 home delivery/wk. for 13 wks.; $182/yr home delivery; $3.65 mailed/wk. for 13 wks.. **Wire Service(s):** AP, LAT-WAT. Circulation: 68,200 morning (paid); 74,500 Sunday (paid). **Owner(s):** Daily Gazette Co., Inc., See address and contact information above. **Management:** John E.N. Hume III, President. Daniel T. Beck, Advertising Director. Scott Osswald, Advertising Manager. Christine Palmer, Classified Adv. Mgr.. Michael Lisi, Art Director. **Editorial:** Thomas Woodman, Managing Editor. Eric Anderson, Business Editor. Tim Coakley, Chief Copy Editor. George Walsh, City Editor. Lou Rappaport, Copy Chief. Dick Bennett, Entertainment Editor. Eric Anderson, Financial Editor. Dick Bennett, Lifestyle Editor. Dave Kraus, Photographer. Cecil Walker, Sports Editor.

STATEN ISLAND

STATEN ISLAND ADVANCE. 950 Fingerboard Rd., Staten Island, NY 10305. Telephone: 718-981-1234. URL: http://www.silive.com. Year Established: 1886. Pub. Frequency: d. Page Size: broadsheet. Subscrip. Rate: $.50 newsstand/cover; $1.50 newsstand/cover Sun.; $3 home delivery/wk.; $156/yr home delivery. **Wire Service(s):** AP, LAT-WAT. Circulation: 72,000 evening (paid); 93,000 Sunday (paid). **Owner(s):** Advance Publications, Inc., See address and contact information above. **Management:** Richard E. Diamond, Publisher. Gary Cognetta, Advertising Manager. Ted Wnoroski, Circulation Manager. **Editorial:** Brian J. Laline, Editor. William Huus, Managing Editor. Mark Hanley, Editorial Page Editor. Richard Ryan, Entertainment Editor. Melinda Gottlieb, Librarian. Steve Zaffarano, Photo Editor. Judy Randall, Political Editor. Todd Hill, Science Editor. Carmine Angioli, Sports Editor.

SYRACUSE

POST-STANDARD. One Clinton Sq., Syracuse, NY 13221. Telephone: 315-470-0032. FAX: 315-470-3081. URL: http://www.syracuse.com. Mailing Address: PO Box 4915, Syracuse, NY 13221. Pub. Frequency: d. Page Size: broadsheet. Subscrip. Rate: $.50 newsstand/cover; $1.75 newsstand/cover Sun.; $182/yr local. **Wire Service(s):** AP, NYT, LAT-WAT, MCT. Circulation: 89,000 morning (paid). **Owner(s):** Advance Publications, Inc., 950 Fingerboard Rd., Staten Island, NY 10305. Telephone: 718-981-1234. FAX: 718-981-1456. **Bureau(s):** 601 Lakeport Rd., P.O. Box 298, Chittenango, NY 13037. Telephone: 315-687-9139. FAX: 315-687-5176. Contact: Greg Munno, Bureau Chief. **Management:** Stephen A. Rogers, Publisher. Bill Allison, Advertising Director. Jeff Barber, Circulation Manager. Gerard Carrol, Classified Adv. Mgr.. **Editorial:** Stephen A. Rogers, Editor. Michael Connor, Executive Editor. Stan Linhorst, Senior Managing Editor. Marie Morelli, Business Editor. Gina Williams, Lifestyle Editor. Steve Carlic, Sports Editor.

TROY

RECORD (TROY), THE. ISSN 1053-8976
501 Broadway, Troy, NY 12180-3381. Telephone: 518-270-1200. FAX: 518-270-1202. E-MAIL: newsroom@troyrecord.com. URL: http://www.troyrecord.com. Year Established: 1896. Pub. Frequency: d. Page Size: broadsheet. Subscrip. Rate: $.50 newsstand/cover; $1.50 newsstand/cover Sun.; $47.45 carrier delivery for 13 wks.; $189.80/yr carrier delivery. Freelance Pay: $20-$65/article. **Wire Service(s):** AP, MCT. Circulation: 22,291 morning (paid); 23,908 Sunday (paid). **Owner(s):** Journal Register Co., 50 W State St, 12th Fl, Trenton, NJ 08608. Telephone: 609-396-2200. FAX: 609-396-2292. **Management:** Michael Sullivan, Publisher. Joan Marro-Harris, Advertising Director. Bryan Brown, Circulation Director. Lois Carson, Classified Adv. Mgr.. **Editorial:** Lisa Robert-Lewis, Editor. Nicholas Cantiello, City Editor. Mike McMahon, Photographer. Kevin . Moran, Sports Editor.

UTICA

OBSERVER-DISPATCH. ISSN 0890-0329
221 Oriskany Plz., Utica, NY 13501. Telephone: 315-792-5000. FAX: 315-792-5033. E-MAIL: nsollida@utica.gannett.com. URL: http://www.uticaod.com. Year Established: 1817. Pub. Frequency: d. Page Size: standard. Subscrip. Rate: $.50 newsstand/cover; $1.50 newsstand/cover Sun.; $189.80/yr home delivery; $384.80/yr mailed. **Wire Service(s):** AP, GNS. Circulation: 51,000 morning (paid); 63,000 Sunday (paid). **Owner(s):** Gannett Company, Inc., 7950 Jones Branch Dr., McLean, VA 22107-0001. Telephone: 703-854-6000. **Management:** Donna Donovan, President. Emilia Borelli, Advertising Manager. Rich Procida, Circulation Manager. Susan Woods, Classified Adv. Mgr.. **Editorial:** John Dye, Executive Editor. Mike Killian, Managing Editor. Fran Perritano, News Editor. Craig Muder, Sports.

VESTAL

PRESS & SUN-BULLETIN. 4421 Vestal Pkwy., E., Vestal, NY 13850. Telephone: 607-798-1234. FAX: 607-798-1113. URL: http://www.pressconnects.com. Mailing Address: PO Box 1270, Binghamton, NY 13902-1270. Year Established: 1822. Pub. Frequency: d. Page Size: broadsheet. Subscrip. Rate: $.50 newsstand/cover; $1.50 newsstand/cover Sun.; $140.40, $195/yr carrier delivery. **Wire Service(s):** AP, LAT-WAT, GNS. Circulation: 55,912 morning (paid); 70,861 evening (paid). **Owner(s):** Gannett Company, Inc., 7950 Jones Branch Dr, McLean, VA 22107. Telephone: 703-854-6000. **Management:** Bernie Griffin, Publisher. Tom Claybaugh, Advertising Director. Anthony Rapczynski, Circulation Director. Jodi Riesbeck, Classified Adv. Mgr.. Joy Peak, Marketing Director. **Editorial:** Rick Jensen, Executive Editor. Al Vieira, Asst. Managing Ed.. Jeff Platsky, Business Editor. Frank Roessner, Editorial Page Editor. Wayne Hansen, Photo Editor. Charlie Jaworski, Sports Editor. Jennifer Micale, Sunday Editor.

WATERTOWN

WATERTOWN (NY) DAILY TIMES. ISSN 0891-009X
260 Washington St, Watertown, NY 13601. Telephone: 315-782-1000. FAX: 315-661-2520. URL: http://www.watertowndailytimes.com. Year Established: 1861. Pub. Frequency: d. Page Size: broadsheet. Subscrip. Rate: $.50 newsstand/cover; $2.25 newsstand/cover Sun.; $5.25 carrier delivery/wk.; $190/yr carrier delivery; $190/yr motor route. **Wire Service(s):** AP, NYT. Circulation: 32,828 morning (paid); 36,387 Sunday (paid). **Owner(s):** John B. Johnson, Jr., See address and contact information above. **Bureau(s):** 327 State St., Albany, NY 12210. Telephone: 518-499-5506. **Management:** John B. Johnson Jr., Publisher. Barbara Peck, Classified Adv. Mgr.. **Editorial:** John B. Johnson Jr., Editor. Bert Gault, Executive Editor. Robert Gorman, Managing Editor. John McFadden, Editorial Page Editor. Norman Johnston, Photo Editor. Greg Gay, Sports Editor.

WELLSVILLE

WELLSVILLE DAILY REPORTER/SUNDAY SPECTATOR. 159 N. Main St., Wellsville, NY 14895. Telephone: 585-593-5300. FAX: 585-593-5303. E-MAIL: editor@wellsvilledaily.com. URL: http://www.wellsvilledaily.com. Year Established: 1880. Pub. Frequency: d. (Sun.-Fri.) Page Size: broadsheet. Subscrip. Rate: $.75 newsstand/cover; $1.50 newsstand/cover Sun.; $15 carrier delivery/mo.; $15.25 motor route/mo.. Freelance Pay: $0.50/column-inch. **Wire Service(s):** AP. Circulation: 5,000 evening (paid); 12,000 Sunday (paid). **Owner(s):** GateHouse Media, Inc, 350 WillowBrook Office Park, Fairport, NY 14450. Telephone: 585-598-0030. FAX: 585-248-2631. **Management:** Oak Duke, Publisher. Robert Polley, Circulation Manager. Jody Wood, Classified Adv. Mgr.. **Editorial:** John Anderson, Managing Editor. Jim Sweet, Sports.

WHITE PLAINS

JOURNAL NEWS (WHITE PLAINS), THE. One Gannett Dr., White Plains, NY 10604. Telephone: 914-694-9300. FAX: 914-694-5018. URL: http://www.thejournalnews.com. Year Established: 1889. Pub. Frequency: d. Page Size: broadsheet. Subscrip. Rate: $.50 newsstand/cover; $1.50 newsstand/cover Sun.; $4.50 carrier delivery/wk.; $234/yr carrier delivery. **Wire Service(s):** AP, GNS. Circulation: 150,000 morning (paid); 175,000 Sunday (paid). **Owner(s):** Gannett Company, Inc., 7950 Jones Branch Dr., McLean, VA 22107-0001. Telephone: 703-854-6000. **Management:** Gary Sherlock, President. Sean Kelly, Advertising Manager. Charles Farrell, Circulation Manager. **Editorial:** Tony Davenport, Managing Editor. John Humenn, Sports.

NORTH CAROLINA

ASHEBORO

COURIER-TRIBUNE, THE. 500 Sunset Ave., Asheboro, NC 27203. Telephone: 336-625-2101. FAX: 336-626-7074. E-MAIL: rcriscoe@courier-tribune.com. URL: http://www.courier-tribune.com. Mailing Address: PO Box 340, Asheboro, NC 27203. Year Established: 1876. Pub. Frequency: d. Page Size: broadsheet. Subscrip. Rate: $.50 newsstand/cover; $1 newsstand/cover Sun.; $117/yr home delivery; $200/yr mailed. **Wire Service(s):** AP. Circulation: 13,500 morning (paid); 15,000 Sunday (paid). **Owner(s):** Stephens Media LLC, PO Box 70, Las Vegas, NV 89125. Telephone: 702-383-0211. FAX: 702-383-4676. **Management:** David Renfro, Publisher. Reg Freemyer, Advertising Manager. Gary Lockhart, Circulation Manager. Wanda Lambert, Classified Adv. Mgr.. **Editorial:** Ray Criscoe, Editor. Annette Jordan, News Editor. Dennis Garcia, Sports.

ASHEVILLE

ASHEVILLE CITIZEN-TIMES. ISSN 1060-3255
14 O'Henry Ave., Asheville, NC 28801. Telephone: 828-252-5611. FAX: 828-251-2659. URL: http://www.citizen-times.com. Mailing Address: PO Box 2090, Asheville, NC 28802. Year Established: 1870. Pub. Frequency: d. Page Size: broadsheet. Subscrip. Rate: $.50 newsstand/cover; $1.50 Sun.; $15.17 home delivery/mo.. **Wire Service(s):** AP, MCT. Circulation: 59,000 morning (paid); 72,000 Sunday (paid). **Owner(s):** Gannett Company, Inc., 7950 Jones Branch Dr, McLean, VA 22107. Telephone: 703-854-6000. **Bureau(s):** 224 Montgomery St., Waynesville, NC 28786. Telephone: 828-452-1467. FAX: 828-452-1470. Contact: Sandy Wall, Bureau Chief. **Management:** Virgil L Smith, President. Kerry Johnson, Advertising Director. Richard Baker, Circulation Director. Sandra Shelton, Classified Adv. Mgr.. Jim Burns, Production Director. **Editorial:** Virgil L Smith, Editor. Robert Gabordi, Executive Editor. Kathleen Davis, Business Editor. Joy Franklin, Editorial Page Editor. Tony Kiss, Entertainment Editor. Polly McDaniel, Feature Editor. Brian Ponder, Metro Editor. Bob Berghouse, Sports Editor.

BURLINGTON

TIMES-NEWS, THE. 707 S. Main St., Burlington, NC 27215. Telephone: 336-227-0131. FAX: 336-229-2463. Mailing Address: PO Box 481, Burlington, NC 27216. Year Established: 1887. Pub. Frequency: d. Page Size: standard. Subscrip. Rate: $.50 newsstand/cover; $1 Sun.; $10 carrier delivery/mo.. **Wire Service(s):** AP. Circulation: 30,000 morning (paid); 32,000 Sunday (paid). **Owner(s):** Freedom Communications, Inc., 17666 Fitch, Irvine, CA 92714. Telephone: 714-253-9292. FAX: 714-474-7675. **Management:** Paul Mauney, General Manager. J. Stephen Buckley, Publisher. Zachary Creech, Advertising. Jim Purdon, Circulation Manager. Malissa Blaylock, Classified Adv. Mgr.. **Editorial:** Lee Barnes, Executive Editor. Jack Sink, Photographer. Bob Sutton, Sports Editor.

CHAPEL HILL

CHAPEL HILL HERALD. 106 Mallette St., Chapel Hill, NC 27516. Telephone: 919-967-6581. FAX: 919-918-1055. E-MAIL: noffen@heraldsun.com. URL: http://www.heraldsun.com. Year Established: 1988. Pub. Frequency: d. Page Size: standard. Subscrip. Rate: $.50 newsstand/cover; $1.50 newsstand/cover Sun.; $13.50 carrier delivery/mo.; $22.43 mailed/mo. in state. **Wire Service(s):** AP, NYT, LAT-WAT. Circulation: 12,250 morning (paid); 12,250 Sunday (paid). **Owner(s):** Durham Herald-Sun Co., See address and contact information above. **Management:** Bob Childress, Publisher. Ed Rose, Circulation Director. **Editorial:** Neil Offen, Editor. Bob Ashley, Editor-in-Chief. Bill Stagg, Managing Editor.

CHARLOTTE

CHARLOTTE OBSERVER. 600 S Tryon St, Charlotte, NC 28202-1880. Telephone: 704-358-5000. FAX: 704-358-5022. E-MAIL: gnielson@charlotte.infi.net. URL: http://www.charlotte.com. Mailing Address: PO Box 32188, Charlotte, NC 28232. Year Established: 1886. Pub. Frequency: d. Page Size: broadsheet. Subscrip. Rate: $.50 newsstand/cover; $1.50 Sun.. **Wire Service(s):** AP, NYT, LAT-WAT. Circulation: 235,469 morning (paid); 291,177 Sunday (paid). **Owner(s):** The/McClatchy Company, 2100 Q St, Sacramento, CA 95816. Telephone: 916-321-1936. FAX: 916-321-1869. **Management:** Ann Caulkins, Publisher. Jim Lamm, VP Circulation. Steve Cageao, Sales Manager. **Editorial:** Rick Thames, Editor.

CLINTON

SAMPSON INDEPENDENT, THE. 300 Elizabeth St, Clinton, NC 28328. Telephone: 910-592-8137. FAX: 910-592-1419. URL: http://www.clintonnc.com. Mailing Address: PO Box 89, Clinton, NC 28329. Year Established: 1929. Pub. Frequency: d. (Tue.-Sun.) Page Size: broadsheet. Subscrip. Rate: $.50 newsstand/cover; $1 newsstand/cover Sun.; $84/yr home delivery in county; $169.80/yr mailed in state; $181.80/yr mailed out of state. **Wire Service(s):** AP. Circulation: 8,811 evening (paid); 9,298 Sunday (paid). **Owner(s):** Heartland Publications, LLC, 20 Research Pkwy, Ste G, Old Saybrook, CT 06475. Telephone: 860-388-3470. FAX: 860-388-3490. **Management:** Sandy Hurley, Publisher. Becky Jones, Advertising Manager. Alissa Bradford', Circulation Manager. Brenda McCullen, Classified Adv. Mgr.. **Editorial:** Sherry Matthews, Editor.

DUNN

DAILY RECORD (DUNN), THE. 99 W. Broad St., Dunn, NC 28334. Telephone: 910-891-1234. FAX: 910-891-5253. E-MAIL: badams@mydailyrecord.com. URL: http://www.mydailyrecord.com. Mailing Address: PO Box 1448, Dunn, NC 28335. Year Established: 1950. Pub. Frequency: d. (Mon.-Fri.) Page Size: broadsheet. Subscrip. Rate: $.50 newsstand/cover; $73.50/yr carrier delivery; $143.20/yr mailed in state. Adv. Rate: col. inch $13.40 **Wire Service(s):** AP. Circulation: 10,400 evening (paid). **Owner(s):** Record Publishing Co., See address and contact information above. **Management:** Karen Wooten, General Manager. Bart Adams, Publisher. Maria House, Advertising Manager. Jeff Herman, Circulation Manager. Brenda Fryar, Classified Adv. Mgr.. **Editorial:** Lisa Farmer, Managing Editor. Laura McHale, Lifestyle Editor. Patrick Love, Sports.

DURHAM

HERALD-SUN, THE. ISSN 1055-4467 2828 Pickett Rd., Durham, NC 27705. Telephone: 919-419-6500. FAX: 919-419-6889. E-MAIL: jch@herald-sun.com. URL: http://www.herald-sun.com. Year Established: 1889. Pub. Frequency: d. Page Size: broadsheet. Subscrip. Rate: $.50 newsstand/cover; $1.50 newsstand/cover Sun.; $13.50 carrier delivery/mo.; $40.50 carrier delivery for 3 mos.; $67.30/yr mailed in state. **Wire Service(s):** RN, AP, SH, NYT, MCT. Circulation: 62,191 morning (paid); 59,017 Sunday (paid). **Owner(s):** E.T. Rollins, PO Box 2092, Durham, NC 27702. Telephone: 919-419-6500. **Management:** Robert Childress, President. Elaine Morgan, Advertising Director. Ed Rose, Circulation Director. Bob Blanchard, Classified Adv. Mgr.. Chuck Friend, Production Director. **Editorial:** Robert Ashley, Executive Editor. Ron Landfried, Editorial Page Editor.

EDEN

EDEN DAILY NEWS. ISSN 1541-3349 PO Box 398, Eden, NC 27289. Telephone: 336-623-2155. FAX: 336-623-2228. URL: http://www.edendailynews.com/. Year Established: 1980. Pub. Frequency: d. **Owner(s):** Media General, Inc., See address and contact information above. **Management:** Steven Kaylor, Publisher. **Editorial:** Angela Evans, Editor.

ELIZABETH CITY

DAILY ADVANCE. 216 S. Poindexter St., Elizabeth City, NC 27909. Telephone: 252-335-0841. FAX: 252-335-4415. URL: http://www.dailyadvance.com. Mailing Address: PO Box 588, Elizabeth City, NC 27907. Year Established: 1911. Pub. Frequency: d. Page Size: broadsheet. Subscrip. Rate: $.50 newsstand/cover; $1.25 newsstand/cover Sun.; $126/yr home delivery; $158.40/yr mailed. **Wire Service(s):** AP. Circulation: 13,000 evening (paid); 14,000 Sunday (paid). **Owner(s):** Cox Newspapers, Inc., 6205 Peachtree Dunwoody Rd., Atlanta, GA 30328. Telephone: 678-645-0000. **Management:** Tim Hobbs, General Manager. Jordan Whichard, President. Tim Hobbs, Publisher. Gene Fowler, Advertising Director. Rick Easley, Circulation Manager. **Editorial:** Michael Goodman, Editor. Juilian Eure, Managing Editor. Thom Chalfan, Sports Editor.

FAYETTEVILLE

FAYETTEVILLE OBSERVER, THE. ISSN 1052-9829 458 Whitfield St., Fayetteville, NC 28301. Telephone: 910-323-4848. FAX: 910-486-3545. E-MAIL: news@fayobserver.com. URL: http://www.fayobserver.com. Mailing Address: PO Box 849, Fayetteville, NC 28302. Year Established: 1816. Pub. Frequency: d. Page Size: broadsheet. Subscrip. Rate: $.50 newsstand/cover; $1.50 newsstand/cover Sun.; $24 home delivery for 8 wks.; $39 home delivery for 13 wks.; $146/yr home delivery. **Wire Service(s):** AP, LAT-WAT. Circulation: 61,875 morning (paid); 65,595 Sunday (paid). **Owner(s):** Fayetteville Publishing Co., See address and contact information above. **Management:** Charles W. Broadwell, Publisher. Fred Benson, Advertising Director. Jim Adkins, Circulation Director. **Editorial:** Brian Tolley, Executive Editor. Michael Arnholt, Managing Editor. Dennis Hall, Asst. Managing Ed.. Kristin Askelson, Community Editor. Johnny Horne, Photo Editor.

FOREST CITY

DAILY COURIER (FOREST CITY). 601 Oak St., Forest City, NC 28043. Telephone: 828-245-6431. FAX: 828-248-2790. E-MAIL: dailycourier@blueridge.net. Mailing Address: PO Box 1149, Forest City, NC 28043. Year Established: 1978. Pub. Frequency: d. (Tues.-Sun.) Page Size: broadsheet. Subscrip. Rate: $.50 newsstand/cover; $1.25 newsstand/cover Sun.; $8.50 home delivery/mo.; $102/yr. **Wire Service(s):** AP. Circulation: 11,200 evening (paid); 11,200 Sunday (paid). **Owner(s):** Paxton Media Group LLC, 201 S. Fourth St., Paducah, KY 42003. Telephone: 270-575-8600. FAX: 270-442-8188. **Management:** Jim Brown, Publisher. Bruce Cole, Circulation Manager. Heather Rhodes, Classified Adv. Mgr.. Joyce Fergus, Business Manager. **Editorial:** Steve Parlham, Executive Editor. Mike Gavin, Managing Editor. Alex Podlogar, Sports Editor.

GASTONIA

GASTON GAZETTE. 1893 Remount Rd., Gastonia, NC 28054. Telephone: 704-869-1700. FAX: 704-867-6988. E-MAIL: gastongazette@link.freedom.com. URL: http://www.gastongazette.com. Mailing Address: PO Box 1538, Gastonia, NC 28053. Year Established: 1880. Pub. Frequency: d. Page Size: broadsheet. Subscrip. Rate: $.50 newsstand/cover; $1.25 newsstand/cover Sun.; $123/yr home delivery; $224.76/yr mailed in state; $210/yr mailed out of state. Freelance Pay: $10/article. **Wire Service(s):** AP. Circulation: 43,000 morning (paid); 46,000 Sunday (paid). **Owner(s):** Freedom Communications, Inc., 17666 Fitch, Irvine, CA 92614. Telephone: 949-553-6000. **Management:** Duane McCallister, Publisher. Larry Grey, Circulation Director. Sandra Panther, Circulation Manager. Donna Ritter, Classified Adv. Mgr.. **Editorial:** Jon Jimision, Managing Editor. Mike Banks, Asst. Managing Ed.. Thomas Monigan, Business Editor. Kevin Ellis, City Editor. Barry Bridges, Editorial Page Editor. Will MacDonald, Lifestyle Editor. John Clark, Photographer. Derick Moss, Sports Editor.

GOLDSBORO

GOLDSBORO NEWS-ARGUS. 310 N. Berkeley Blvd., Goldsboro, NC 27534. Telephone: 919-778-2211. FAX: 919-778-9891. E-MAIL: news@newsargus.com. URL: http://www.newsargus.com. Mailing Address: PO Box 10629, Goldsboro, NC 27532. Year Established: 1885. Pub. Frequency: d. (Sun.-Fri.) Page Size: broadsheet. Subscrip. Rate: $.50 newsstand/cover; $1.25 newsstand/cover Sun.; $10.35 home delivery/mo.. Adv. Rate: col. inch $19.10 **Wire Service(s):** AP. Circulation: 22,000 evening (paid); 24,000 Sunday (paid). **Owner(s):** Wayne Printing Co., Inc., See address and contact information above. **Management:** Hal Tanner III, General Manager. Hal Tanner Jr., Publisher. Roger Stephenson, Advertising Director. Ryan Carter, Circulation Manager. Paul Worrell, Classified Adv. Mgr.. **Editorial:** Renee Corey, Editor. Jim Meachen, Business Editor. Dennis Hill, City Editor. Neil Fuller, Sports.

GREENSBORO

NEWS & RECORD, THE. ISSN 0747-1858 200 E. Market St., Greensboro, NC 27401. Telephone: 336-373-7000. FAX: 336-373-7067. URL: http://www.news-record.com. Mailing Address: PO Box 20848, Greensboro, NC 27420. Year Established: 1972. Pub. Frequency: d. Page Size: broadsheet. Subscrip. Rate: $.50 newsstand/cover; $1.25 newsstand/cover Sun.; $2.95 carrier delivery/wk.. **Wire Service(s):** AP, NYT, LAT-WAT. Circulation: 93,400 morning (paid); 120,300 Sunday (paid). **Owner(s):** Landmark Communications, Inc., 150 W. Brambleton Ave., Norfolk, VA 23510. Telephone: 804-446-2000. **Management:** Robin Saul, Publisher. Jeff LaGrange, Classified Adv. Mgr.. **Editorial:** John Robinson, Editor. Linda Austin, Managing Editor. Ed Williams, Business Editor. Mark Sutter, City Editor. Allen Johnson, Editorial Page Editor.

GREENVILLE

DAILY REFLECTOR. ISSN 1060-6130 1150 Sugg Pkwy., Greenville, NC 27834. Telephone: 252-329-9500. FAX: 252-752-9583. URL: http://www.reflector.com. Mailing Address: PO Box 1967, Greenville, NC 27835-1967. Year Established: 1882. Pub. Frequency: d. Page Size: broadsheet. Subscrip. Rate: $.50 newsstand/cover; $1.25 newsstand/cover Sun.; $131.40/yr home delivery; $186/yr mailed in state; $198/yr mailed out of state. **Wire Service(s):** AP. Circulation: 20,701 morning (paid); 23,179 Sunday (paid). **Owner(s):** Cox Newspapers, Inc., 6205 Peachtree Dunwoody Rd., Atlanta, GA 30328. Telephone: 678-645-0000. **Management:** D. Jordan Wichard, Publisher. J. Tim Holt, Advertising Manager. Keven Zepezauer, Circulation Director. Pat Wilkins, Classified Adv. Mgr.. **Editorial:** M. Allen Clark, Executive Editor. Roger Silvey, Production Manager. Bobby Burns, City Editor. Mary Schulken, Editorial Page Editor.

HENDERSON

DAILY DISPATCH (HENDERSON), THE. 304 S. Chestnut St., Henderson, NC 27536. Telephone: 252-436-2700. FAX: 252-430-0125. E-MAIL: gcraven@hendersondispatch.com. URL: http://www.hendersondispatch.com. Mailing Address: PO Box 908, Henderson, NC 27536. Year Established: 1914. Pub. Frequency: d. (Tue.-Sun.) Page Size: broadsheet. Subscrip. Rate: $.50 newsstand/cover; $1.25 Sun.; $132/yr home delivery local; $144/yr mailed in state; $168/yr mailed out of state. **Wire Service(s):** AP. Circulation: 10,500 morning (paid); 11,000 Sunday (paid). **Owner(s):** Paxton Media Group LLC, 201 S. Fourth St., Paducah, KY 42003. Telephone: 270-575-8600. FAX: 270-442-8188. **Management:** James Edwards, Publisher. Deborah Tuck, Advertising Director. A.J. Woodell, Circulation Manager. Nancy Baker, Business Manager. **Editorial:** Glen Craver, Editor. Kelly Wheeler, Local News Editor. Ashley Ayscue, Photographer. Chad Saleska, Sports.

HICKORY

HICKORY DAILY RECORD. ISSN 1061-5628 1100 Park Pl. & 11th Ave. Blvd., S.E., Hickory, NC 28602. Telephone: 828-322-4510. FAX: 828-328-9378. URL: http://www.hickoryrecord.com. Mailing Address: PO Box 968, Hickory, NC 28603. Year Established: 1915. Pub. Frequency: d. Page Size: broadsheet. Subscrip. Rate: $.50 newsstand/cover; $1 newsstand/cover Sun.; $69.16 home delivery for 26 wks.; $138.32/yr home delivery; $208/yr mailed out of state. Adv. Rate: col. inch $15.19 Freelance Pay: $0.25/column-inch. **Wire Service(s):** AP. Circulation: 20,065 morning (paid); 21,000 Sunday (paid). **Owner(s):** Media General, Inc., 333 E. Franklin St., Richmond, VA 23219. Telephone: 804-649-6000. **Management:** David King, Publisher. Cathy Fagan, Advertising Director. David Eggers, Circulation Manager. **Editorial:** Eric Millsaps, Executive Editor. Jim Lillagore, Production Manager. John Dayberry, Business Editor. Scott Ramsey, Lifestyle Editor. Michelle Bloomfield, News Editor. Chris Hobbs, Sports Editor.

HIGH POINT

HIGH POINT ENTERPRISE. ISSN 0747-1491 210 Church St, High Point, NC 27261. Telephone: 336-888-3500. FAX: 336842-5165. E-MAIL: gbm@hpe.com. URL: http://www.hpe.com. Mailing Address: PO Box 1009, High Point, NC 27261-1009. Year Established: 1885. Pub. Frequency: d. Page Size: broadsheet. Subscrip. Rate: $.50 newsstand/cover; $1 newsstand/cover Sun.; $126/yr home delivery in area. **Wire Service(s):** AP, MCT. Circulation: 31,600 morning (paid); 32,700 Sunday (paid). **Owner(s):** Paxton Media Group LLC, 201 S. Fourth St., Paducah, KY 42003. Telephone: 270-575-8600. **Management:** Rick Bean, Publisher. Rick Shelton, Advertising Director. Daniel Pittman, Circulation Director. **Editorial:** Tom Blount, Editor.

JACKSONVILLE

DAILY NEWS (JACKSONVILLE). ISSN 8750-3565 724 Bell Fork Rd., Jacksonville, NC 28546. Telephone: 910-353-1171. FAX: 910-353-7316. URL: http://www.jdnews.com. Mailing Address: P.O. Drawer 196, Jacksonville, NC 28541. Year Established: 1953. Pub. Frequency: d. Page Size: broadsheet. Subscrip. Rate: $.50 newsstand/cover; $1.25 Sun.; $115/yr; $20 mailed/mo.; $240/yr. **Wire Service(s):** AP. Circulation: 22,650 morning (paid); 24,660 Sunday (paid). **Owner(s):** Freedom Communications, Inc., 17666 Fitch St., Irvine, CA 92614. Telephone: 949-253-9292. FAX: 949-474-7675. **Management:** Elliott Potter, Publisher. Bobby Williams, Circulation Director. Richard Plucker, Classified Adv. Mgr.. Don Bryan, Photography Director. Elliott Potter, Associate Publisher. **Editorial:** Elliott Potter, Executive Editor. Madison Taylor, Managing Editor. Liz Biro, City Editor. Carolyn Alford, Education Editor. Eric Beam, Local News Editor. Robert Holland, News Editor. Paul Thompson, Sports.

KANNAPOLIS

INDEPENDENT TRIBUNE. 924 Cloverleaf Plz., Kannapolis, NC 28083. Telephone: 704-782-3155. FAX: 704-786-0645. E-MAIL: news@independenttribune.com. URL: http://www.independenttribune.com. Mailing Address: PO Box 608, Concord, NC 28026-0608. Year Established: 1900. Pub. Frequency: d. Page Size: broadsheet. Subscrip. Rate: $.50 newsstand/cover; $1 newsstand/cover Sun.; $110.93/yr home delivery; $194.77/yr mailed. **Wire Service(s):** AP. Circulation: 22,000 evening (paid); 24,000 Sunday (paid). **Owner(s):** Media General, Inc., 333 E. Franklin St., Richmond, VA 23219. Telephone: 804-649-6000. FAX: 804-775-8090. **Management:** Rick V. Martin, Publisher. Larry Norris, Advertising Manager. Frank Shipman, Circulation Manager. Suzie Perkins, Classified Adv. Mgr.. **Editorial:** Kathy Nelson, Editor. Steve Linebarrier, Production Manager. Sabian Worren, News Editor. Donnie Biggers, Sports.

KINSTON

KINSTON DAILY FREE PRESS. 2103 N. Queen St., Kinston, NC 28501. Telephone: 252-527-3191. FAX: 252-527-1813. E-MAIL: freepress@link.freedom.com. URL: http://www.kinston.com. Mailing Address: PO Box 129, Kinston, NC 28502. Year Established: 1882. Pub. Frequency: d. Page Size: standard. Subscrip. Rate: $.50 newsstand/cover; $1 newsstand/cover Sun.; $30.25 home delivery for 13 wks.; $63.25 mailed in state for 13 wks.. **Wire Service(s):** AP, SH, MCT. Circulation: 26,947 morning (paid); 35,149 Sunday (paid). **Owner(s):** Freedom Communications, Inc., 17666 Fitch, Irvine, CA 92614. Telephone: 949-553-9292. **Management:** Pat Holmes, Publisher. Billy Moore, Advertising Director. Francis Jones, Circulation Manager. Lynnell Burch, Classified Adv. Mgr.. **Editorial:** Lee Raynor, Editor. Brian Hanks, Sports Editor.

LAURINBURG

LAURINBURG EXCHANGE. 211 W. Cronly St., Laurinburg, NC 28352. Telephone: 910-276-2311. FAX: 910-276-3815. E-MAIL: laurinburgexchange@carolina.net. URL: http://www.laurinburgexchange.com. Mailing Address: PO Box 459, Laurinburg, NC 28353. Year Established: 1882. Pub. Frequency: d. (Mon.-Fri.) Page Size: broadsheet. Subscrip. Rate: $.50 newsstand/cover; $70/yr home delivery in county; $80/yr mailed out of county. Circulation: 9,400 evening (paid). **Owner(s):** Mid-South Management Co., Inc., See address and contact information above. **Management:** Kevin Milligan, Publisher. Allen Johnson, Advertising Manager. Clyde Marsh, Circulation Manager. Celeste Jackson, Classified Adv. Mgr.. **Editorial:** Ricky Allen, Editor.

LENOIR

NEWS-TOPIC. 123 Pennton Ave., Lenoir, NC 28645. Telephone: 828-758-7381. FAX: 828-754-0110. E-MAIL: ntnews@newstopic.net. URL: http://www.newstopic.net. Mailing Address: PO Box 1110, Lenoir, NC 28645. Year Established: 1875. Pub. Frequency: d. (Tue.-Sun.) Page Size: broadsheet. Subscrip. Rate: $.50 newsstand/cover; $1 newsstand/cover Sun.; $130/yr home delivery; $189/yr mailed. Adv. Rate: col. inch $16.65 **Wire Service(s):** AP, SH. Circulation: 9,810 morning (paid); 9,600 Sunday (paid). **Owner(s):** Paxton Media Group, LLC, 201 S. Fourth St., Paducah, KY 42003. Telephone: 270-575-8600. FAX: 270-442-8188. **Management:** Deborah Murray, Publisher. Mike Lambert, Circulation Director. **Editorial:** Edward Terry, Executive Editor. Merry Cable, Composing Room Manager. Laura Beach, Lifestyle Editor. Kyle Phipps, Sports Editor.

LUMBERTON

ROBESONIAN, THE. 2175 N Roberts Ave, Lumberton, NC 28359. Telephone: 910-739-4322. FAX: 910-739-6553. E-MAIL: cvilla@cnhi.com. URL: http://www.robesonian.com. Mailing Address: PO Box 1028, Lumberton, NC 28359. Year Established: 1870. Pub. Frequency: d. Page Size: broadsheet. Subscrip. Rate: $.50 newsstand/cover; $1 newsstand/cover Sun.; $119.40/yr. **Wire Service(s):** AP. Circulation: 14,769 evening (paid); 16,956 Sunday (paid). **Owner(s):** Heartland Publications, LLC, 20 Research Pkwy, Ste G, Old Saybrook, CT 06475. Telephone: 860-388-3470. FAX: 860-388-3490. **Management:** Trip Hatley, Advertising Director. Ed Knight, Circulation Manager. **Editorial:** Donnie Douglas, Editor.

MARION

MCDOWELL NEWS, THE. 46 Logan St., Marion, NC 28752-0610. Telephone: 828-652-3313. FAX: 828-652-4769. URL: http://www.mcdowellnews.com. Mailing Address: PO Box 610, Marion, NC 28752-0610. Year Established: 1929. Pub. Frequency: d. (Mon.-Fri.) Page Size: broadsheet. Subscrip. Rate: $.50 newsstand/cover; $81.90/yr carrier delivery; $117/yr mailed. **Wire Service(s):** AP. Circulation: 6,200 evening (paid). **Owner(s):** Media General, Inc., 333 E. Franklin St., Richmond, VA 23219. Telephone: 804-649-6000. FAX: 804-775-8090. **Management:** David Setzer, Publisher. Keith Austin, Advertising Manager. Kimberly Mahle, Circulation Director. Stacey Young, Classified Adv. Mgr.. **Editorial:** Scott Hollifield, Editor. Sam Hollifield, Business Editor. Ragan Robinson, Lifestyle Editor. Marty Queen, Sports Editor.

MONROE

ENQUIRER-JOURNAL, THE. 500 W. Jefferson St., Monroe, NC 28112-4647. Telephone: 704-289-1541. FAX: 704-289-2929. URL: http://www.enquirerjournal.com. Mailing Address: PO Box 5040, Monroe, NC 28111-5040. Year Established: 1873. Pub. Frequency: 6/w. (Tue.-Sun.) Page Size: broadsheet. Subscrip. Rate: $.50 newsstand/cover; $1.25 newsstand/cover Sun.; $38.75 for 13 wks.; $72.50 for 6 mos.; $138/yr. **Wire Service(s):** AP. **Owner(s):** Paxton Media Group LLC, 201 S. Fourth St., Paducah, KY 42003. Telephone: 270-575-8600. FAX: 270-442-8188. **Management:** Marvin Enderle, Publisher. Gary Grunwald, Circulation Manager. **Editorial:** Jerry Snow, Sports.Readers: Local content for Union Cty, NC.

MORGANTON

NEWS HERALD (MORGANTON), THE. ISSN 8750-3980 301 Collett St., Morganton, NC 28655. Telephone: 828-437-2161. FAX: 828-437-5372. E-MAIL: newsherald@hci.net. URL: http://www.morganton.com. Mailing Address: PO Box 280, Morganton, NC 28680-0280. Year Established: 1885. Pub. Frequency: d. (Sun.-Fri.) Page Size: broadsheet. Subscrip. Rate: $.50 newsstand/cover; $1 newsstand/cover Sun.; $124/yr home delivery. **Wire Service(s):** AP. Circulation: 12,600 evening (paid); 13,000 Sunday (paid). **Owner(s):** Media General, Inc., 333 E. Franklin St., Richmond, VA 23219. Telephone: 804-649-6000. FAX: 804-775-8090. **Management:** David Crawley, Publisher. Randy Hart, Advertising Director. Kimberly Mahle, Circulation Director. Wanda Walls, Classified Adv. Mgr.. **Editorial:** Duke Conover, Editor. Anna Wilson, Lifestyle Editor. Kevin Lumpkin, Sports Editor.

MT. AIRY

MOUNT AIRY NEWS. 319 Renfro St., Mt. Airy, NC 27030. Telephone: 336-786-4141. FAX: 336-789-2816. Mailing Address: PO Box 808, Mt. Airy, NC 27030-0808. Year Established: 1880. Pub. Frequency: d. Page Size: broadsheet. Subscrip. Rate: $.50 newsstand/cover; $1.25 newsstand/cover Sun.; $98/yr carrier delivery; $128.92/yr mailed in county; $144.21/yr mailed out of county. **Wire Service(s):** AP. Circulation: 9,500 evening (paid); 10,000 Sunday (paid). **Owner(s):** Mid-South Management Co., Inc., PO Box 1634, Spartensburg, SC 29304. Telephone: 864-583-2907. **Management:** Michael Milligan, President. Kenny Snow, Advertising Director. **Editorial:** Angela Small, Editor. Angela Leonard, Managing Editor. Eleanor Powell, Lifestyle Editor. Michael Howlett, Political Editor. Keith Barber, Sports Editor.

NEW BERN

SUN-JOURNAL. 3200 Wellons Blvd., New Bern, NC 28562. Telephone: 252-638-8101. FAX: 252-638-4664. URL: http://www.newbernsj.com. Mailing Address: PO Box 1149, New Bern, NC 28563. Year Established: 1871. Pub. Frequency: d. Page Size: standard. Subscrip. Rate: $.50 newsstand/cover; $1 newsstand/cover Sun.; $117.16/yr. **Wire Service(s):** AP. Circulation: 18,000 morning (paid); 18,000 Sunday (paid). **Owner(s):** Freedom Communications, Inc., 17666 Fitch, Irvine, CA 92614. Telephone: 949-253-2300. **Management:** Vernon Debolt, Publisher. Wanda Lingman, Advertising Director. Sheila Meadows, Circulation Manager. **Editorial:** Mark McKillop, Editor. Ken Buday, Managing Editor.

NEWTON

OBSERVER NEWS ENTERPRISE, THE. 309 N. College Ave., Newton, NC 28658. Telephone: 828-464-0221. FAX: 828-464-1267. E-MAIL: onepublisher@charter.net. URL: http://www.observernewsonline.com. Mailing Address: PO Box 48, Newton, NC 28658. Year Established: 1879. Pub. Frequency: d. (Mon.-Fri.) Page Size: broadsheet. Subscrip. Rate: $.50 newsstand/cover; $30 for 6 mos. local; $48/yr local. Freelance Pay: $0.40/column-inch. **Wire Service(s):** AP. Circulation: 4,000 evening (controlled and free). **Owner(s):** Horizon Publications, Inc., 1120 N. Carbon St., Ste.100, Marion, IL 62959. Telephone: 618-993-1693. **Management:** Michael Willard, Publisher. Cindy Tamez, Circulation Manager. Tina Cox, Classified Adv. Mgr.. **Editorial:** Chris Gilfillan, Managing Editor. John Josey, Sports Editor.

RALEIGH

NEWS & OBSERVER, THE. 215 S. McDowell St., Raleigh, NC 27601. Telephone: 919-829-4500. FAX: 919-829-4529. URL: http://www.newsobserver.com. Mailing Address: PO Box 191, Raleigh, NC 27602. Year Established: 1865. Pub. Frequency: d. Page Size: broadsheet. Subscrip. Rate: $.50 newsstand/cover; $1.50 newsstand/cover Sun.; $11.60/mo.. **Wire Service(s):** AP, SH, NYT, LAT-WAT, MCT. Circulation: 175,000 morning (paid); 212,000 Sunday (paid). **Owner(s):** The/McClatchy Company, 2100 Q St., Sacramento, CA 95816-6816. **Bureau(s): Management:** Orage Quarles III, Publisher. Jim McClure, Advertising Director. Carol Chapman, Circulation Director. Durwood Canaday, Classified Adv. Mgr.. **Editorial:** Melanie Sill, Executive Editor. Dan Barkin, Managing Editor.

REIDSVILLE

REIDSVILLE REVIEW. 1921 Vance St., Reidsville, NC 27320. Telephone: 336-349-4331. FAX: 336-342-2513. URL: http://www.reidsvillereview.com. Mailing Address: PO Box 2157, Reidsville, NC 27323. Year Established: 1888. Pub. Frequency: d. (Tue.-Fri. & Sun.) Page Size: broadsheet. Subscrip. Rate: $.50 newsstand/cover; $1 newsstand/cover Sun.; $42 home delivery for 6 mos.; $75/yr home delivery. **Wire Service(s):** UPI. Circulation: 6,600 evening (paid); 6,600 Sunday (paid). **Owner(s):** Media General, Inc., 333 E. Franklin St., Richmond, VA 23219. Telephone: 804-649-6000. FAX: 804-775-8090. **Management:** Ellen Ishmael, Publisher. Jodi Vasquez, Advertising Director. Jessica Byerly, Advertising Manager. Paul Richman, Circulation Manager. **Editorial:** John Trump, Group Editor.

ROANOKE RAPIDS

ROANOKE RAPIDS DAILY & SUNDAY HERALD. 916 Roanoke Ave., Roanoke Rapids, NC 27870. Telephone: 252-537-2505. FAX: 252-537-2314. E-MAIL: herald@costalnet.com. URL: http://www.rrdailyherald.com. Mailing Address: PO Box 520, Roanoke Rapids, NC 27870. Year Established: 1914. Pub. Frequency: d. (Sun.-Fri.) Page Size: broadsheet. Subscrip. Rate: $.50 newsstand/cover; $1.25 newsstand/cover Sun.; $109.20/yr home delivery; $118.56/yr mailed. **Wire Service(s):** UPI. Circulation: 13,500 morning (paid); 13,500 Sunday (paid). **Owner(s):** Wick Communications, Inc., 333 W. Wilcox Dr., Ste. 302, Sierra Vista, AZ 85635. **Management:** Ronnie Bell, Publisher. Patsey Ferguson, Advertising Director. Carol Moseley, Circulation Manager. Linda Foster, Classified Adv. Mgr.. **Editorial:** John Moeur, Managing Editor. Rodney Pierce, Sports Editor.

ROCKINGHAM

RICHMOND COUNTY DAILY JOURNAL. ISSN 1050-7639 105 E Washington St, Rockingham, NC 28379. Telephone: 910-997-3111. FAX: 910-997-4321. E-MAIL: ads@yourdailyjournal.com. URL: http://www.yourdailyjournal.com. Mailing Address: PO Box 1888, Rockingham, NC 28380. Year Established: 1931. Pub. Frequency: d. (Sun.-Fri.) Page Size: broadsheet. Subscrip. Rate: $.50 newsstand/cover; $1 newsstand/cover Sun.; $81/yr carrier delivery in county; $98/yr mailed in county; $120/yr mailed out of county. Adv. Rate: col. inch $10.50 **Wire Service(s):** AP. Circulation: 9,000 morning (paid). **Owner(s):** Heartland Publications, LLC, 20 Research Pkwy, Ste G, Old Saybrook, CT 06475. Telephone: 860-388-3470. FAX: 860-388-3490. **Management:** Rick Bacon, Publisher. Sharon Jimenez, Advertising Director. Randy Lohrenz, Classified Adv. Mgr.. **Editorial:** Stacy Stenberg, Editor.

ROCKY MOUNT

ROCKY MOUNT TELEGRAM. ISSN 1082-3727 800 Tiffany Blvd., Rocky Mount, NC 27804-1080. Telephone: 252-446-5161. FAX: 252-446-4057. URL: http://www.rockymounttelegram.com. Mailing Address: PO Box 1080, Rocky Mount, NC 27802-1080. Year Established: 1910. Pub. Frequency: d. Page Size: broadsheet. Subscrip. Rate: $.75 newsstand/cover; $1.25 newsstand/cover Sun.; $120.12/yr home delivery; $187.20/yr mailed. **Wire Service(s):** AP. Circulation: 15,127 morning (paid); 16,406 Sunday (paid); 1,300 per issue (paid). **Owner(s):** Cox Newspapers, Inc., 6205 Peachtree Dunwoody Rd., Atlanta, GA 30328. Telephone: 678-645-0000. **Management:** Rip Woodin, Publisher. Mike Schuttinga, Advertising Director. Norman Sinclair, Circulation Director. **Editorial:** Jeff Herrin, Editor. Gene Metrick, City Editor. Ross Chandler, Feature Editor. Ben Jones, Sports Editor.

Dailies

SALISBURY

SALISBURY POST. ISSN 0747-0738
131 W. Innes St., Salisbury, NC 28144-0105. Telephone: 704-633-8950. FAX: 704-630-0410. E-MAIL: jlesley@salisburypost.com. URL: http://www.salisburypost.com. Mailing Address: PO Box 4639, Salisbury, NC 28145-4639. Year Established: 1905. Pub. Frequency: d. Page Size: broadsheet. Subscrip. Rate: $.50 newsstand/cover; $1 newsstand/cover Sun.; $123/yr home delivery local; $168/yr mailed in state. **Wire Service(s):** AP. Circulation: 26,500 evening (paid); 28,000 Sunday (paid). **Owner(s):** Evening Post Publishing Co., 134 Columbus St., Charleston, SC 29403. **Management:** Greg Anderson, Publisher. Ron Brooks, Circulation Director. Len Clark, Classified Adv. Mgr.. **Editorial:** Elizabeth G Cook, Editor. Frank DeLoache, Managing Editor. Linda Braswell, Business Editor. Ronnie Gallagher, Sports Editor.

SANFORD

SANFORD (NC) HERALD, THE. ISSN 1067-179X
208 St. Clair Ct., Sanford, NC 27330-0100. Telephone: 919-708-9000. FAX: 919-708-9001. E-MAIL: bhorner3@interpath.com. URL: http://www.sanfordherald.com. Mailing Address: PO Box 100, Sanford, NC 27331-0100. Year Established: 1930. Pub. Frequency: d. (Tue.-Sun) Page Size: broadsheet. Subscrip. Rate: $.50 newsstand/cover; $1.25 newsstand/cover Sun.; $120/yr carrier delivery. Freelance Pay: $0.90/column-inch. **Wire Service(s):** AP. Circulation: 13,500 evening (paid). **Owner(s):** Paxton Media Group LLC, 201 S. Fourth St., Paducah, KY 42003. Telephone: 270-575-8600. FAX: 270-442-8188. **Management:** W.E. Horner III, Publisher. Doug Rowe, Advertising Director. Dawn Melvin, Advertising Manager. Jeff Ayers, Circulation Manager. **Editorial:** Jay Thwaite, Editor.

SHELBY

SHELBY STAR, THE. ISSN 1043-1950
315 E. Graham St., Shelby, NC 28150. Telephone: 704-484-7000. FAX: 704-484-0805. URL: http://www.shelbystar.com. Mailing Address: PO Box 48, Shelby, NC 28151. Year Established: 1894. Pub. Frequency: d. Page Size: standard. Subscrip. Rate: $.50 newsstand/cover; $1 newsstand/cover Sun.; $12 carrier delivery/mo.; $12.50 mailed/mo. in state. Adv. Rate: col. inch $17.95 **Wire Service(s):** AP, SH. Circulation: 15,150 evening (paid); 15,150 Sunday (paid). **Owner(s):** Freedom Communications, Inc., 17666 Fitch St., Irvine, CA 92614-6022. Telephone: 714-553-9292. FAX: 714-553-8468. **Management:** Jennie L. Lambert, Publisher. Aron Goss, Advertising Manager. Barry Croucher, Circulation Manager. **Editorial:** Skip Foster, Editor. Margarita Venegas, Managing Editor. Alan Ford, Sports Editor.

STATESVILLE

STATESVILLE RECORD & LANDMARK. ISSN 0745-7804
222 E. Broad St., Statesville, NC 28677. Telephone: 704-873-1451. FAX: 704-872-3150. URL: http://www.statesville.com. Mailing Address: PO Box 1071, Statesville, NC 28687. Year Established: 1874. Pub. Frequency: d. Page Size: broadsheet. Subscrip. Rate: $.50 newsstand/cover; $1 newsstand/cover Sun.; $2.37 carrier delivery/wk.; $61.62 carrier delivery for 6 mos.; $123.24/yr carrier delivery. **Wire Service(s):** AP. Circulation: 16,000 evening (paid); 17,400 Sunday (paid). **Owner(s):** Media General, Inc., 333 E. Franklin St., Richmond, VA 23219. Telephone: 804-649-6000. FAX: 804-775-8090. **Management:** Tim Dearman, Publisher. Jon Dunham, Advertising Manager. Bud Welch, Circulation Manager. **Editorial:** Mike Fuhrman, Managing Editor.

TARBORO

DAILY SOUTHERNER, THE. 504 W. Wilson St., Tarboro, NC 27886-4239. Telephone: 252-823-3106. FAX: 252-823-4599. E-MAIL: grfain@cnhi.com. URL: http://www.dailysoutherner.com. Mailing Address: PO Box 1199, Tarboro, NC 27886. Year Established: 1826. Pub. Frequency: d. (Mon.-Fri.) Page Size: broadsheet. Subscrip. Rate: $.50 newsstand/cover; $84/yr home delivery; $102/yr mailed. **Wire Service(s):** AP. Circulation: 3,850 evening (paid). **Owner(s):** Community Newspaper Holdings, Inc., 3500 Colonnade Pkwy., Ste. 600, Birmingham, AL 35243. Telephone: 205-298-7100. FAX: 205-298-7101. **Management:** Mike Blanton, Publisher. Denise Taylor, Advertising Manager. Allen Cale, Circulation Manager. Martha Hartley, Classified Adv. Mgr.. **Editorial:** W. Terry Smith, Editor.

TRYON

TRYON DAILY BULLETIN. 16 N. Trade St., Tryon, NC 28782. Telephone: 828-859-9151. FAX: 828-859-5575. URL: http://www.dailybulletin.com. Year Established: 1928. Pub. Frequency: d. (Mon.-Fri.) Page Size: standard. Subscrip. Rate: $.35 newsstand/cover; $50/yr. Adv. Rate: col. inch $6.75 Freelance Pay: $25/article. Circulation: 5,500 morning (paid). **Owner(s):** Jeffrey Byrd, See address and contact information above. **Management:** Jeffrey A. Byrd, President. Mike Edwards, Advertising Manager. Wanda Cash, Circulation Manager.

WASHINGTON

WASHINGTON DAILY NEWS. ISSN 1057-7068
217 N. Market St., Washington, NC 27889. Telephone: 919-946-2144. FAX: 919-946-9797. E-MAIL: news@wdnweb.com. URL: http://www.wdnweb.com. Mailing Address: PO Box 1788, Washington, NC 27889. Year Established: 1909. Pub. Frequency: d. Page Size: broadsheet. Subscrip. Rate: $.50 newsstand/cover; $1 newsstand/cover Sun.; $27 carrier delivery for 3 mos.; $33 mailed in state for 3 mos.. **Wire Service(s):** AP. Circulation: 10,000 morning (paid); 10,000 Sunday (paid). **Owner(s):** Washington News Publishing Co., See address and contact information above. **Management:** Ray McKeithan, General Manager. Ashley B. Futrell Jr., Publisher. Jerry Cox, Circulation Director. Lou Firth, Circulation Manager. Brenda Foster, Classified Adv. Mgr.. **Editorial:** Rachel Hackney, Managing Editor. Kevin Travis, Sports Editor.

WILSON

WILSON DAILY TIMES. 2001 Downing St. Ext., Wilson, NC 27893. Telephone: 252-243-5151. FAX: 252-243-2999. URL: http://www.wilsondaily.com. Mailing Address: PO Box 2447, Wilson, NC 27894. Year Established: 1902. Pub. Frequency: d. (Mon.-Sat.) Page Size: broadsheet. Subscrip. Rate: $.50 newsstand/cover; $1 newsstand/cover Sat.; $8.75 home delivery/mo. local; $11.05 mailed/mo. in state; $12.75 mailed/mo. out of state. **Wire Service(s):** AP. Circulation: 17,000 evening (paid). **Owner(s):** Morgan P. & Margaret Dickerman, See address and contact information above. **Management:** Morgan Dickerman, Publisher. Wayne Johnson, Advertising Manager. James Howell, Circulation Manager. **Editorial:** Hal Tarleton, Editor. Giles Lambertson, City Editor. Lisa Batts, Lifestyle Editor. Tom Ham, Sports Editor.

WINSTON-SALEM

WINSTON-SALEM JOURNAL. 418 N. Marshall St., Winston-Salem, NC 27101. Telephone: 336-727-7211. FAX: 336-727-7354. E-MAIL: news@journalnow.com:. URL: http://www.journalnow.com. Mailing Address: PO Box 3159, Winston-Salem, NC 27102. Year Established: 1897. Pub. Frequency: d. Page Size: broadsheet. Subscrip. Rate: $.75 newsstand/cover; $1.25 newsstand/cover Sun.; $159.63/yr carrier delivery. **Wire Service(s):** AP, NYT, LAT-WAT. Circulation: 82,175 morning (paid); 93,868 Sunday (paid); 90,792 Saturday (paid). **Owner(s):** Media General, Inc., 333 E. Franklin St., Richmond, VA 23219. Telephone: 804-649-6000. **Bureau(s): Management:** Michael Miller, President. Jon Witherspoon, Publisher. **Editorial:** Carl Crothers, Executive Editor. Ken Otterbourg, Managing Editor. Les Gura, Senior Editor. Phoebe Zerwick, Columnist. Linda Brinson, Editorial Page Editor.Readers: Northwest North Carolina

NORTH DAKOTA

BISMARCK

BISMARCK TRIBUNE. ISSN 0745-1091
707 E. Front Ave., Bismarck, ND 58504. Telephone: 701-258-6900. FAX: 701-223-0195. E-MAIL: bismarck_tribune@ndonline.com. URL: http://www.ndonline.com/. Mailing Address: PO Box 5516, Bismarck, ND 58506. Year Established: 1873. Pub. Frequency: d. Page Size: broadsheet. Subscrip. Rate: $.75 newsstand/cover; $1.75 newsstand/cover Sun.; $55.25 carrier delivery for 13 wks.; $210.40/yr carrier delivery. **Wire Service(s):** AP, LAT-WAT. Circulation: 33,000 morning (paid); 32,000 Sunday (paid). **Owner(s):** Lee Enterprises, Inc., 215 N. Main St., Davenport, IA 52801. Telephone: 563-383-2100. FAX: 563-323-9608. **Management:** Julie Bechtel, Publisher. Kristin Wilson, Advertising Manager. Laura Sweep, Circulation Manager. **Editorial:** Dave Bundy, Editor. Ken Rogers, Managing Editor. Tom Stromme, Photographer.

DEVIL'S LAKE

DEVIL'S LAKE JOURNAL. 516 Fourth St, NE, Devil's Lake, ND 58301. Telephone: 701-662-2127. FAX: 701-662-3115. URL: http://www.devilslakejournal.com. Mailing Address: PO Box 1200, Devil's Lake, ND 58301. Year Established: 1905. Pub. Frequency: d. (Mon.-Fri.) Page Size: broadsheet. Subscrip. Rate: $.75 newsstand/cover; $40 home delivery for 3 mos.; $122/yr in state. **Wire Service(s):** AP. Circulation: 4,300 evening (paid). **Owner(s):** GateHouse Media, Inc, 350 WillowBrook Office Park, Fairport, NY 14450. Telephone: 585-598-0030. FAX: 585-248-2631. **Management:** Kathy Svidal, General Manager. Paula Ramsey, Advertising Manager. Mary Jo Dimmler, Circulation Manager. **Editorial:** Mike Bellmore, Feature Editor. Sue Kraft-Fisher, Lifestyle Editor. Ray Maloney, Sports Editor.

DICKINSON

DICKINSON PRESS, THE. ISSN 1049-6718
1815 First St., W., Dickinson, ND 58601. Telephone: 701-225-8111. FAX: 701-225-6653. E-MAIL: newsroom@thedickinsonpress.com. URL: http://www.thedickinsonpress.com. Mailing Address: PO Box 1367, Dickinson, ND 58602. Year Established: 1883. Pub. Frequency: d. (Tue.-Sun.) Page Size: broadsheet. Subscrip. Rate: $.50 newsstand/cover; $1.25 newsstand/cover Sun.; $74/yr; $138/yr mailed in state. **Wire Service(s):** AP. Circulation: 7,600 morning (paid); 7,800 Sunday (paid). **Owner(s):** Jeff Meyer, PO Box 2020, Fargo, ND 58107. Telephone: 701-223-7311. **Management:** Ruth Newman, Publisher. Jerry Obrigewitsch, Advertising Manager. Deb Bahley, Circulation Manager. **Editorial:** Alan Reed, Managing Editor. Linda Sailer, Lifestyle Editor. Alan Reed, Political Editor. Brian Alexander, Sports Editor.

FARGO

DULUTH NEWS TRIBUNE. ISSN 0896-9418
101 5th St N, Fargo, ND 58102. Telephone: 701-235-7311. FAX: 701-241-5406. E-MAIL: news@duluthnews.com. URL: http://www.duluthnewstribune.com. Year Established: 1870. Pub. Frequency: d. Page Size: broadsheet. Subscrip. Rate: $.50 newsstand/cover; $1.50 newsstand/cover Sun.. **Wire Service(s):** AP, LAT-WAT, MCT. Circulation: 40,000 morning (paid); 60,000 Sunday (paid). **Owner(s):** Forum Communications Company, See address and contact information above. Knight Ridder, Inc., 424 W. First St., Duluth, MN 55802. **Management:** Steve McLister, Publisher. Aaron Becher, Advertising Director. Tim McLoughlin, Circulation Manager. **Editorial:** Rob Karwath, Executive Editor. Andrea Novel Buck, Managing Editor. Robin Washington, Editorial Page Editor. Rick Lubbers, Sports Editor.

FORUM, THE. ISSN 0895-1292
101 Fifth St., N., Fargo, ND 58102. Telephone: 701-235-7311. FAX: 701-241-5487. E-MAIL: lziegler@forumcomm.com. URL: http://www.in-forum.com. Year Established: 1878. Pub. Frequency: d. Page Size: standard. Subscrip. Rate: $.75 newsstand/cover; $1 newsstand/cover Sat.; $2 newsstand/cover Sun.; $192/yr motor route; $192/yr mailed in ND, SD, MN; $211.50/yr mailed elsewhere. **Wire Service(s):** AP, NYT. Circulation: 51,000 morning (paid); 62,000 Sunday (paid). **Owner(s):** Jeff Meyer, PO Box 2020, Fargo, ND 58107. Telephone: 701-223-7311. **Management:** William C. Marcil, Publisher. James Boberg, Advertising Director. Dan Schmidt, Advertising Manager. Jeff Nyquist, Circulation Director. Sandy Olsen, Classified Adv. Mgr.. **Editorial:** Peggy Bellows, Managing Editor. Matt VonPinnon, City Editor. Dean Rhodes, Feature Editor. Dave Jurgens, News Editor. Mike Vosburg, Photo Editor. Kevin Schnepf, Sports Editor.

GRAND FORKS

GRAND FORKS HERALD. ISSN 0745-9661
375 Second Ave N, Grand Forks, ND 58206. Telephone: 701-780-1202. FAX: 701-780-1231. E-MAIL: tdutcher@gfherald.com. URL: http://www.grandforksherald.com/. Mailing Address: PO Box 6008, Grand Forks, ND 58206-6008. Year Established: 1916. Pub. Frequency: d. Page Size: broadsheet. Subscrip. Rate: $.50 newsstand/cover; $179.40/yr carrier delivery in city; $196.56/yr carrier delivery in state. **Wire Service(s):** AP, NYT. Circulation: 40,000 morning (paid); 40,785 Sunday (paid). **Owner(s):** Jeff Meyer, 101 Fifth St., N., Fargo, ND 58207. PO Box 2020, Fargo, ND 58107. **Management:** Mike Jacobs, Publisher. Dave Austin, Advertising Director. Dawn Zimney, Circulation Director. DaLonna Bjorge, Classified Adv. Mgr.. **Editorial:** Mike Jacobs, Editor. Kevin Grinde, Managing Editor. Tom Dennis, Editorial Page Editor. Kirsten Stromsodt, News Editor. John Stennes, Photographer. Kevin Fee, Sports Editor.

JAMESTOWN

JAMESTOWN SUN, THE. 121 Third St., N.W., Jamestown, ND 58401. Telephone: 701-252-3120. FAX: 701-251-2873. E-MAIL: js@jamestownsun.com. URL: http://www.jamestownsun.com. Mailing Address: PO Box 1760, Jamestown, ND 58402. Year Established: 1925. Pub. Frequency: d. (Mon.-Sat.) Page Size: broadsheet. Subscrip. Rate: $.50 newsstand/cover; $15 carrier delivery/mo.; $145/yr in state. **Wire Service(s):** AP. Circulation: 7,300 morning (paid). **Owner(s):** Jeff Meyer, PO Box 2020, Fargo, ND 58107. Telephone: 701-201-7311. **Management:** I. Bruce Henke, Publisher. Gene Keller, Advertising Manager. Brenda Kincaide, Circulation Manager. Robyn McDonald, Classified Adv. Mgr.. **Editorial:** Kathy Steiner, Managing Editor. Scott Throlson, Sports.

MINOT

MINOT DAILY NEWS. ISSN 0885-3053
301 Fourth St., S.E., Minot, ND 58701. Telephone: 701-857-1900. FAX: 701-857-1961. URL: http://www.ndweb.com. Mailing Address: PO Box 1150, Minot, ND 58702. Year Established: 1884. Pub. Frequency: d. Page Size: standard. Subscrip. Rate: $.50 newsstand/cover; $.75 newsstand/cover Sat.; $1.75 newsstand/cover Sun.; $13.50 carrier delivery/wk. in county. **Wire Service(s):** AP. Circulation: 26,000 morning (paid); 27,000 Sunday (paid). **Owner(s):** Ogden Newspapers of Minnesota, Inc., 1500 Main St., Wheeling, WV 26003. Telephone: 304-233-0100. **Management:** Jim Eykyn, Publisher. Doug Corbit, Advertising Manager. Brian Basil, Circulation Manager. **Editorial:** Bryan Obenchain, Editor. Cindy Peterson, Sports.

VALLEY CITY

VALLEY CITY TIMES-RECORD. 146 Third St, Valley City, ND 58072. Telephone: 701-845-0463. FAX: 701-845-0175. E-MAIL: vctr@daktel.com. URL: http://www.times-online.com. Mailing Address: PO Box 697, Valley City, ND 58072. Year Established: 1879. Pub. Frequency: d. (Mon.-Fri.) Page Size: broadsheet. Subscrip. Rate: $.75 newsstand/cover; $93/yr carrier delivery in city; $96/yr motor route in city & mailed in state; $102/yr mailed out of state. Adv. Rate: col. inch $9.56 Freelance Pay: $0.50/column-inch. **Wire Service(s):** AP. Circulation: 3,000 evening (paid). **Owner(s):** Horizon Publications, Inc., 1120 N. Carbon St, Ste 100, Marion, IL 62959. **Management:** Nikki Laine Zinke, Publisher. Chrissy Komrosky, Advertising. Brenda Tompt, Circulation Manager.

WAHPETON

DAILY NEWS (WAHPETON). 601 Dakota Ave., Wahpeton, ND 58075. Telephone: 701-642-8585. FAX: 701-642-1501. E-MAIL: thedaily@rrt.net. Mailing Address: PO Box 760, Wahpeton, ND 58074. Year Established: 1880. Pub. Frequency: d. (Tue.-Fri. & Sun.) Page Size: broadsheet. Subscrip. Rate: $.50 newsstand/cover; $1.25 Sun.; $102/yr. Adv. Rate: col. inch $7.28 **Wire Service(s):** AP. Circulation: 4,100 morning (paid); 4,700 Sunday (paid). **Owner(s):** Wick Communications, Inc., 333 W. Wilcox Dr., Ste. 302, Sierra Vista, AZ 83635. Telephone: 520-458-0200. FAX: 520-458-6166. **Management:** Ken Harty, Publisher. Pam Marquardt, Advertising Manager. Sandy Kraft, Circulation Manager.

WILLISTON

WILLISTON HERALD. 14 W. Fourth St., Williston, ND 58801. Telephone: 701-572-2165. FAX: 701-572-9563. E-MAIL: news@willistonherald.com. URL: http://www.willistonherald.com. Mailing Address: PO Box 1447, Williston, ND 58802. Year Established: 1899. Pub. Frequency: d. (Sun.-Fri.) Page Size: standard. Subscrip. Rate: $.50 newsstand/cover; $1 newsstand/cover Sun.; $9 carrier delivery/mo.; $99/yr mailed in county; $108/yr mailed out of county. **Wire Service(s):** AP. Circulation: 6,600 morning (paid); 6,750 Sunday (paid). **Owner(s):** Wick Communications, Inc., 333 W. Wilcox Dr., Ste. 302, Sierra Vista, AZ 85635. Telephone: 520-458-0200. FAX: 520-458-6166. **Management:** Donald J. Mrachek, Publisher. Wanda Olaf, Advertising Manager. Dave Boeck, Circulation Manager. **Editorial:** Tim Pederson, Managing Editor. Dan Bundy, Production Manager. Tim Pederson, Editorial Page Editor. Sue Neft, Entertainment Editor. Sean Pitman, Sports Editor.

OHIO

ALLIANCE

ALLIANCE REVIEW, THE. 40 S. Linden Ave., Alliance, OH 44601-0180. Telephone: 330-821-1300. FAX: 330-821-8258. E-MAIL: reviewads@alliancelink.com. URL: http://www.the-review.com. Mailing Address: PO Box 2180, Alliance, OH 44601-0180. Year Established: 1888. Pub. Frequency: d. (Mon.-Sat.) Page Size: broadsheet. Subscrip. Rate: $.50 newsstand/cover; $96/yr carrier delivery; $97.90/yr motor route; $125/yr mailed in state. **Wire Service(s):** AP. Circulation: 12,200 evening (paid). **Owner(s):** Dix Communications Group, 212 E. Liberty St., Wooster, OH 44691. Telephone: 330-264-1125. FAX: 216-264-3756. **Management:** Robert Shaffer, General Manager. G. Charles Dix II, Publisher. Jeff Kaplan, Advertising Director. Kenneth Pagani, Circulation Manager. **Editorial:** Sarah Gold, Executive Editor. Michael Brown, Sports.

ASHLAND

ASHLAND TIMES-GAZETTE. 40 E. Second St., Ashland, OH 44805. Telephone: 419-281-0581. FAX: 419-281-5591. E-MAIL: newsroom@times-gazette.com. URL: http://www.times-gazette.com. Year Established: 1850. Pub. Frequency: d. (Mon.-Sat.) Page Size: broadsheet. Subscrip. Rate: $.50 newsstand/cover; $99.75/yr carrier delivery; $103.25/yr motor route; $163.28/yr mailed in county. **Wire Service(s):** AP. Circulation: 11,562 evening (paid). **Owner(s):** Ashland Publishing Co. LLC, See address and contact information above. **Management:** Troy Dix, Publisher. Jason Gwinnup, Advertising Manager. Deb Boreman, Circulation Manager. **Editorial:** Ted Daniels, Managing Editor. Tim Busby, News Editor. Tom Puskar, Photographer. Dusty Sloan, Sports Editor.

ASHTABULA

STAR BEACON. 4626 Park Ave., Ashtabula, OH 44004. Telephone: 440-998-2323. FAX: 440-998-7938. E-MAIL: editorial@starbeacon.com. URL: http://www.starbeacon.com. Mailing Address: PO Box 2100, Ashtabula, OH 44005-2100. Year Established: 1891. Pub. Frequency: d. Page Size: broadsheet. Subscrip. Rate: $.35 newsstand/cover; $1.25 newsstand/cover Sun.; $36.40 carrier delivery for 13 wks.; $139/yr carrier delivery; $46.23 mailed for 13 wks.. **Wire Service(s):** UPI. Circulation: 21,000 morning (paid); 22,500 Sunday (paid). **Owner(s):** Community Newspaper Holdings, Inc., 3500 Colonnade Pkwy., Ste. 600, Birmingham, AL 35243. Telephone: 205-298-7100. FAX: 205-298-7101. **Management:** Ed Looman, Publisher. Kim Rich, Advertising Manager. Mark Shorts, Circulation Manager. **Editorial:** Neil Frieder, Editor.

ATHENS

ATHENS MESSENGER, THE. ISSN 1064-2005
9300 Johnson Rd., Athens, OH 45701. Telephone: 740-592-6612. FAX: 740-592-4647. E-MAIL: info@athensmessenger.com. URL: http://www.athensmessenger.com. Mailing Address: PO Box 4210, Athens, OH 45701. Year Established: 1905. Pub. Frequency: d. Page Size: broadsheet. Subscrip. Rate: $.50, $1.25 newsstand/cover; $138.75/yr home delivery; $141.25/yr motor route; $173/yr mailed in state. Adv. Rate: col. inch $5.75 **Wire Service(s):** AP, SH. Circulation: 12,662 evening (paid); 15,594 Sunday (paid). **Owner(s):** Brown Publishing Co., 10222 Alliance Rd, Cincinnati, OH 45040. Telephone: 513-794-5040. FAX: 513-794-5480. **Management:** Gary Lamberg, Publisher. Sherrie Bossart, Advertising Manager. Joe Essman, Circulation Manager. **Editorial:** Monica Nieporte, Managing Editor. Steve Robb, News Editor. Kevin Wiseman, Sports Editor.

BELLEFONTAINE

BELLEFONTAINE EXAMINER. ISSN 0747-3273
127 E. Chillicothe Ave., Bellefontaine, OH 43311. Telephone: 937-592-3060. FAX: 937-592-4463. E-MAIL: news@examiner.org. URL: http://www.examiner.org. Mailing Address: PO Box 40, Bellefontaine, OH 43311. Year Established: 1891. Pub. Frequency: d. (Mon.-Sat.) Page Size: broadsheet. Subscrip. Rate: $.50 newsstand/cover; $2/wk.; $114/yr mailed in county; $134/yr mailed out of county. Adv. Rate: col. inch $11.10 **Wire Service(s):** AP. Circulation: 9,500 evening (paid). **Owner(s):** Hubbard Publishing Co., Inc., PO Box 40, Bellefontaine, OH 43311-0040. Telephone: 937-592-3060. FAX: 937-592-4463. **Management:** Janet Hubbard, Publisher. Barbara Campbell, Advertising Manager. John L. Sullivan, Circulation Manager. Diane Lewis, Classified Adv. Mgr.. Jon Hubbard, Business Manager. **Editorial:** Jim Mason, Editor. Doug Loehr, Photographer. Matt Hammond, Sports. Sue Pitts, Womens Interest Editor.

BELLEVUE

BELLEVUE GAZETTE, THE. 107 N. Sandusky St., Bellevue, OH 44811. Telephone: 419-483-4190. FAX: 419-483-3737. E-MAIL: gazette@cros.net. Year Established: 1867. Pub. Frequency: d. (Mon.-Sat.) Page Size: broadsheet. Subscrip. Rate: $.50 newsstand/cover; $121/yr carrier delivery; $134.50/yr motor route; $185/yr mailed in state. **Wire Service(s):** AP. Circulation: 3,200 evening (paid). **Owner(s):** Gazette Publishing Co., See address and contact information above. **Management:** Thomas R. Smith, President. Rick Miller, Advertising Manager. **Editorial:** Brian Liskai, Editor. Sally Boyd, Lifestyle Editor.

BOWLING GREEN

SENTINEL-TRIBUNE. 300 E. Poe Rd., Bowling Green, OH 43402. Telephone: 419-352-4611. FAX: 419-354-0314. E-MAIL: letters@sentinel-tribune.com. URL: http://www.sentinel-tribune.com. Mailing Address: PO Box 88, Bowling Green, OH 43402. Year Established: 1867. Pub. Frequency: d. (Mon.-Sat.) Page Size: broadsheet. Subscrip. Rate: $.50 newsstand/cover; $110/yr carrier delivery; $120/yr mailed in county; $125/yr mailed out of county; $135/yr mailed out of state. **Wire Service(s):** AP, SH. Circulation: 12,250 evening (paid). **Owner(s):** Thomas M. Haswell, See address and contact information above. **Management:** Richard Morris, General Manager. Thomas M. Haswell, Publisher. Vicky Graf, Advertising Director. Michael Morrow, Circulation Manager. **Editorial:** David C. Miller, Editor. Marie Thomas, Education Editor. Bill Ryan, Farm Editor. Karen Cota, Lifestyle Editor. J.D. Pooley, Photo Editor. David Dupont, Real Estate Editor. Jack Carle, Sports Editor. Contact: Bill Ryan, Farm Editor. Contact: Bill Ryan, Farm Editor.

BRYAN

BRYAN TIMES, THE. 127 S. Walnut St., Bryan, OH 43506. Telephone: 419-636-1111. FAX: 419-636-8937. E-MAIL: editor@bryantimes.com. URL: http://www.bryantimes.com. Mailing Address: PO Box 471, Bryan, OH 43506. Year Established: 1949. Pub. Frequency: d. (Mon.-Sat.) Page Size: broadsheet. Subscrip. Rate: $.50 newsstand/cover; $8.50 carrier delivery/wk.; $134/yr in state; $137/yr mailed out of area. Freelance Pay: $20-$30/story. **Wire Service(s):** AP. Circulation: 11,008 evening (paid). **Owner(s):** Bryan Publishing Co., The, See address and contact information above. **Management:** Tom Voigt, General Manager. Christopher Cullis, President. Mary Nickels, Advertising Manager. Mark Keller, Circulation Manager. Amy Thompson, Classified Adv. Mgr.. **Editorial:** Don Allison, Editor. Teresa Melcher, Senior Editor. Marci Hummel, Business Editor. Linda Freed, Consumer Affrs. Ed.. Shannon Hulbert, Copy Editor. Don Allison, County Editor. Christopher Cullis, Editorial Page Editor. Nancy Jackson, Education Editor. Cookie Brodbeck, Entertainment Editor. Dave Maurer, Outdoor Editor. Carla Allhouse, Photographer. John Fryman, Sports Editor.

BUCYRUS

TELEGRAPH-FORUM. 119 W. Rensselaer St., Bucyrus, OH 44820. Telephone: 419-562-3333. FAX: 419-562-9162. URL: http://www.bucyrustelegraphforum.com. Mailing Address: PO Box 471, Bucyrus, OH 44820. Year Established: 1923. Pub. Frequency: d. (Mon.-Sat.) Page Size: broadsheet. Subscrip. Rate: $.35 newsstand/cover; $.50 newsstand/cover Sat.; $111.80/yr carrier delivery. **Wire Service(s):** AP. Circulation: 7,400 evening (paid and free). **Owner(s):** Gannett Company, Inc., 7950 Jones Branch Dr., McLean, VA 22107-0001. Telephone: 703-854-6000. **Management:** Rob Jenney, General Manager. Tom Brennan, Publisher. Vicki Taylor, Advertising Director. Stacia King, Classified Adv. Mgr.. **Editorial:** Holly Fackler, Managing Editor. Lisa Miller, City Editor. Dan Clutter, Sports Editor.

CAMBRIDGE

DAILY JEFFERSONIAN, THE. 831 Wheeling Ave., Cambridge, OH 43725. Telephone: 740-439-3531. FAX: 740-432-6219. E-MAIL: jeffersonian@jadeinc.com. URL: http://www.daily-jeff.com. Mailing Address: PO Box 10, Cambridge, OH 43725. Year Established: 1824. Pub. Frequency: d. (Sun.-Fri.) Page Size: broadsheet. Subscrip. Rate: $.35 newsstand/cover; $1 newsstand/cover Sun.; $130/yr carrier delivery local; $143/yr motor route local; $145/yr mailed in state. Adv. Rate: col. inch $13.25 Freelance Pay: $0.25/column-inch. **Wire Service(s):** AP, SH. Circulation: 14,150 evening (paid); 15,000 Sunday (paid). **Owner(s):** Dix Communications Group, 212 E. Liberty St., Wooster, OH 44691. Telephone: 330-264-3511. **Management:** Peggy Murgatroyd, General Manager. Robert C. Dix, Publisher. Ed Archibald, Advertising Director. Chris Cryder, Circulation Manager. Lynn Berger, Classified Adv. Mgr.. **Editorial:** Greg Parks, Editor. Ray Booth, Executive Editor. Heath Dawson, Sports Editor.

CANTON

REPOSITORY, THE. 500 Market Ave, S, Canton, OH 44702-2193. Telephone: 330-580-8300. FAX: 330-454-5610. E-MAIL: webmaster@cantonrep.com. URL: http://www.cantonrep.com. Mailing Address: PO Box 9901, Canton, OH 44711. Year Established: 1815. Pub. Frequency: d. Page Size: broadsheet. Subscrip. Rate: $.50 newsstand/cover; $1.50 newsstand/cover Sun.; $17.02 home delivery/mo.; $204.26/yr home delivery. **Wire Service(s):** AP, NYT. Circulation: 62,500 morning (paid); 82,000 Sunday (paid). **Owner(s):** GateHouse Media, Inc, 350 WillowBrook Office Park, Fairport, NY 14450. Telephone: 585-598-0030. FAX: 585-248-2631. **Management:** Christopher T White, General Manager. Kevin Kampan, Publisher. **Editorial:** Jeff Gauger, Executive Editor.

CELINA

DAILY STANDARD, THE. 123 E. Market St., Celina, OH 45822. Telephone: 419-586-2371. FAX: 419-586-6271. E-MAIL: newsdept@dailystandard.com. URL: http://www.dailystandard.com. Mailing Address: PO Box 140, Celina, OH 45822-0140. Year Established: 1848. Pub. Frequency: d. (Mon.-Sat.) Page Size: broadsheet. Subscrip. Rate: $.50 newsstand/cover; $130/yr in county; $185/yr mailed out of county. **Wire Service(s):** AP. Circulation: 10,500 evening (paid). **Owner(s):** Standard Printing Co., See address and contact information above. **Management:** Frank Snyder, Publisher. John Lake, Advertising Manager. Diane Buening, Circulation Manager. **Editorial:** Frank Snyder, Editorial Page Editor. Ryan Hines, Sports. Betty Lawrence, Womens Interest Editor.

CHILICOTHE

CHILLICOTHE GAZETTE. 50 W Main St, Chilicothe, OH 45601. Telephone: 740-773-2111. FAX: 740-772-9501. E-MAIL: mthrone@nncogannett.com. URL: http://www.chillicothegazette.com. Year Established: 1800. Pub. Frequency: d. Page Size: broadsheet. Subscrip. Rate: $.50 newsstand/cover; $.75 newsstand/cover Sat.; $1 newsstand/cover Sun.; $160.80/yr carrier delivery local; $225/yr mailed in state. **Wire Service(s):** AP, GNS. Circulation: 17,400 Sunday (paid); 17,100 evening (paid). **Owner(s):** Gannett Company, Inc., 7950 Jones Branch Dr., McLean, VA 22107-0001. Telephone: 703-854-6000.

CINCINNATI

CINCINNATI ENQUIRER, THE. 312 Elm St., Cincinnati, OH 45202. Telephone: 513-721-2700. FAX: 513-768-8340. E-MAIL: enqedit@aol.com. URL: http://www.enquirer.com. Year Established: 1841. Pub. Frequency: d. Page Size: broadsheet. Subscrip. Rate: $.50 newsstand/cover; $1.50 newsstand/cover Sun.; $15.17 home delivery/mo.. **Wire Service(s):** AP, NYT, LAT-WAT, MCT, GNS. Circulation: 206,403 morning (paid); 310,516 Sunday (paid). **Owner(s):** Gannett Company, Inc., 7950 Jones Branch Dr, McLean, VA 22107. Telephone: 703-854-6000. **Management:** Margaret Buchanan, Publisher. Tom Smith, Advertising Director. Gary DiSanto, Circulation Director. Stephanie Zimmerman, Circulation Manager. **Editorial:** Tom Callinan, Editor. David Wells, Editorial Page Editor. Sarah Pearce, Entertainment Editor. Sara Pearce, Feature Editor. Chuck Martin, Food Editor. Julie Engebrecht, Local News Editor. Elizabeth Dufour, Photo Editor. Dan Sewell, Suburban Editor. Ann Haas, Travel Editor.

CINCINNATI POST. 125 E. Court St., Cincinnati, OH 45202. Telephone: 513-352-2000. FAX: 513-621-3962. E-MAIL: mphillips@cincypost.com. URL: http://www.cincypost.com. Year Established: 1881. Pub. Frequency: d. (Mon.-Sat.) Page Size: broadsheet. Subscrip. Rate: $.50 newsstand/cover; $8.59 home delivery/mo.; $25.77 for 3 mos.. **Wire Service(s):** AP, SH. Circulation: 69,687 evening (paid). **Owner(s):** E.W. Scripps Co., 312 Walnut St., 28th Fl., Cincinnati, OH 45202. Telephone: 513-977-3000. FAX: 513-977-3689. **Management:** Allen Horton, Publisher. Gary DiSanto, Circulation Manager. **Editorial:** Mike Philipps, Editor. Mark Neikirk, Managing Editor. David Holthaus, Business Editor. Tim Stein, Photo Editor. Keith Herrell, Sports Editor.

KENTUCKY ENQUIRER. 312 Elm St., Cincinnati, OH 45202. Telephone: 513-721-2700. FAX: 513-768-8340. URL: http://www.cincinnatienquirer.com. Pub. Frequency: d. Page Size: broadsheet. Subscrip. Rate: $.50 newsstand/cover; $1.50 Sun.; $15.17 home delivery/mo.. **Owner(s):** Gannett Company, Inc., 7950 Jones Branch Dr, McLean, VA 22107. Telephone: 703-854-6000. **Management:** Margaret Buchanan, Publisher. Tom Smith, Advertising Director. Stephanie Zimmerman, Circulation Manager. **Editorial:** Tom Callinan, Editor. Hollis Towns, Managing Editor. David Wells, Editorial Page Editor. Sarah Pearce, Entertainment Editor. Julie Engebrecht, Local News Editor. Elizabeth Dufour, Photo Editor. Michael Perry, Sports Editor. Ann Haas, Travel Editor.

LOGAN DAILY NEWS. 10222 Alliance Rd, Cincinnati, OH 45040. Telephone: 513-794-5040. FAX: 513-794-5480. URL: http://www.logandaily.com. Year Established: 1842. Pub. Frequency: d. (Mon.-Sat.) Page Size: broadsheet. Subscrip. Rate: $.75 newsstand/cover; $126/yr home delivery in city; $200/yr mailed out of city. Adv. Rate: col. inch $12.45 **Wire Service(s):** AP. Circulation: 4,500 evening (paid). **Owner(s):** American Consolidated Media, Inc., See address and contact information above. **Management:** Lucille Burcham, General Manager.

CLEVELAND

PLAIN DEALER, THE. 1801 Superior Ave., Cleveland, OH 44114. Telephone: 216-999-4360. URL: http://www.cleveland.com/. Year Established: 1842. Pub. Frequency: d. Page Size: broadsheet. Subscrip. Rate: $.35 newsstand/cover; $1 Sun.; $93.60/yr. **Wire Service(s):** AP, NYT, LAT-WAT. Circulation: 386,312 per issue (paid). **Owner(s):** Advance Publications, Inc., See address and contact information above. **Management:** Alex Machaskee, Publisher. Margaret Draper, Classified Adv. Mgr.. **Editorial:** Doug Clifton, Editor. Tom O'Hara, Managing Editor. Debbie VanTassell, Business Editor. Roy Hewitt, Sports Editor.

COLUMBUS

COLUMBUS DISPATCH. ISSN 1074-097X
34 S. Third St., Columbus, OH 43215. Telephone: 614-461-5000. FAX: 614-461-7580. E-MAIL: storyideas@dispatch.com. URL: http://www.dispatch.com. Year Established: 1871. Pub. Frequency: d. Page Size: broadsheet. Subscrip. Rate: $.50 newsstand/cover; $1.75 newsstand/cover Sun.; $3.20 home delivery/wk.; $6.50 mailed/wk.. **Wire Service(s):** AP, SH, NYT, LAT-WAT. Circulation: 250,000 morning (paid); 370,000 Sunday (paid). **Owner(s):** Dispatch Printing, Inc., See address and contact information above. **Bureau(s):** 809 National Press Bldg., Washington, DC 20045. Telephone: 202-347-3144. **Management:** John F. Wolfe, Publisher. Tim Doty, Advertising. Robert Bolone, Circulation Director. Michael Curtin, Associate Publisher. **Editorial:** Andy Murphy, Managing Editor. Ron Carter, Business Editor. Alan Miller, News Editor. Craig Holman, Photo Editor. Roy Stein, Sports Editor.

COSHOCTON

COSHOCTON TRIBUNE. 550 Main St., Coshocton, OH 43812. Telephone: 740-622-1122. FAX: 740-295-3460. E-MAIL: coshocton@nncogannett.com. URL: http://www.coshoctontribune.com. Mailing Address: PO Box 10, Coshocton, OH 43812. Year Established: 1909. Pub. Frequency: d. Page Size: standard. Subscrip. Rate: $.35 newsstand/cover; $1 newsstand/cover Sun.; $148.80/yr home delivery local; $170.40/yr mailed in state; $192/yr mailed out of state. Adv. Rate: col. inch $14 **Wire Service(s):** AP. Circulation: 7,200 evening (paid); 7,600 Sunday (paid). **Owner(s):** Gannett Company, Inc., 7950 Jones Branch Dr., McLean, VA 22107-0001. Telephone: 703-854-6000. **Management:** Dan Shaw, Publisher. Brandie Curtis, Advertising Manager. Wayne Carrier, Circulation Manager. **Editorial:** Monica Torline, City Editor. Jim Barstow, Sports.

DAYTON

DAYTON DAILY NEWS. ISSN 0897-0920
1611 S Main St, Dayton, OH 45409. URL: http://www.daytondailynews.com. Year Established: 1898. Pub. Frequency: d. Page Size: broadsheet. Subscrip. Rate: $.75 newsstand/cover; $1.85 Sun.; $129.48/yr home delivery; $306.80/yr mailed. **Wire Service(s):** AP. Circulation: 139,462 morning (paid); 194,067 Sunday (paid). **Owner(s):** Cox Newspapers, Inc., 6205 Peachtree Dunwoody Rd., Atlanta, GA 30328. Telephone: 678-645-0000. **Management:** Mike Goheen, Director. Larry Price, Photography Director. **Editorial:** Kevin Riley, Editor. David Goodwin, Managing Editor. Ellen Belcher, Editorial Page Editor. Connie Post, Feature Editor. Brian Kollars, Sports Editor.

DEFIANCE

CRESCENT-NEWS. 624 W Second St, Defiance, OH 43512. Telephone: 419-784-5441. FAX: 419-784-1492. E-MAIL: crescent@crescent-news.com. URL: http://www.crescent-news.com. Year Established: 1878. Pub. Frequency: d. (Sun.-Fri.) Page Size: broadsheet. Subscrip. Rate: $.50 newsstand/cover; $1 newsstand/cover Sun.; $102/yr carrier delivery; $106/yr motor route; $130/yr mailed in county. Adv. Rate: col. inch $15.68 **Wire Service(s):** AP. Circulation: 17,564 evening (paid); 18,842 Sunday (paid). **Owner(s):** Dix Communications Group, 212 E. Liberty St., Wooster, OH 44691. Telephone: 330-264-1125. FAX: 216-264-3756. **Management:** Steve VanDemark, General Manager. Mark Ryan, Advertising Manager. Betty Lentz, Circulation Manager. Gina Beatty, Classified Adv. Mgr.. **Editorial:** Dennis Van Scoder, Editor.

DELAWARE

DELAWARE GAZETTE. ISSN 1064-2013
PO Box 100, Delaware, OH 43015. Telephone: 740-363-1161. FAX: 740-363-6262. E-MAIL: addept@delgazette.com. URL: http://www.delgazette.com. Year Established: 1818. Pub. Frequency: d. (Mon.-Sat.) Page Size: broadsheet. Subscrip. Rate: $.50 newsstand/cover; $10.50 carrier delivery/mo.; $114/yr carrier delivery; $124/yr motor route. Adv. Rate: col. inch $12.50 **Wire Service(s):** AP. Circulation: 7,975 evening (paid). **Owner(s):** Gary Atkinson, See address and contact information above. **Management:** Gary Adkisson, Publisher. Marsha Carmetti, Advertising Manager. Paula Millisor, Circulation Director. Judy Kern, Classified Adv. Mgr.. Matt Emmons, Photography Director. **Editorial:** Larry Gibbs, Editor. Mary Motz, Managing Editor. Michael Moore, Asst. Managing Ed.. Margo Bartlett, Feature Editor. Donn Walden, Sports Editor.

DELPHOS

DELPHOS DAILY HERALD. 405 N. Main St., Delphos, OH 45833. Telephone: 419-695-0015. FAX: 419-692-7704. URL: http://www.delphosherald.com. Year Established: 1869. Pub. Frequency: d. (Mon.-Sat.) Page Size: broadsheet. Subscrip. Rate: $.50 newsstand/cover; $79/yr local; $105/yr mailed elsewhere. **Wire Service(s):** AP. Circulation: 4,200 evening (controlled). **Owner(s):** Delphos Newspapers, See address and contact information above. **Management:** Doug Nutter, Advertising. Jane Gorrgens, Circulation Manager. **Editorial:** Sue Gerker, Editor.

EAST LIVERPOOL

REVIEW (EAST LIVERPOOL), THE. 210 E. Fourth St., East Liverpool, OH 43920. Telephone: 330-385-4545. FAX: 330-385-7114. URL: http://www.reviewonline.com. Year Established: 1879. Pub. Frequency: d. (Mon.-Sun.) Page Size: broadsheet. Subscrip. Rate: $.35 newsstand/cover; $.75 newsstand/cover Sun.; $10.65/mo.. **Wire Service(s):** UPI. Circulation: 11,500 evening (paid). **Owner(s):** Ogden Newspapers of Minnesota, Inc., 1500 Main St., Wheeling, WV 26003. Telephone: 304-233-0100. FAX: 304-233-0327. **Management:** Tammie McIntosh, Publisher. Lisa Ludovici, Advertising Director. Kevin Fenton, Circulation Director. **Editorial:** Sandra Fitzgerald, Editor. Rocco Longo, Sports Editor.

ELYRIA

CHRONICLE TELEGRAM, THE. 225 East Ave., Elyria, OH 44035. Telephone: 440-329-7000. FAX: 440-329-7282. E-MAIL: ctnews@chroniclet.com. URL: http://www.chroniclet.com. Mailing Address: PO Box 4010, Elyria, OH 44036. Year Established: 1829. Pub. Frequency: d. Page Size: broadsheet. Subscrip. Rate: $.50 newsstand/cover; $1.25 newsstand/cover Sun.; $3.10 home delivery/wk.. **Wire Service(s):** AP, LAT-WAT, MCT. Circulation: 25,248 morning (paid); 24,889 Sunday (paid). **Owner(s):** Lorain County Printing & Publishing Co., See address and contact information above. **Management:** A. Cooper Hudnutt, President. Jeff Pfeiffer, Advertising Manager. Bruce Bishop, Photography Director. **Editorial:** Andrew Young, Editor-in-Chief. Patti Ewald, Managing Editor. Kyle Kondik, Editorial Page Editor. Dave Porozek, Entertainment Editor. Julie Wallace, Metro Editor. Ben Nagy, News Editor. Kevin Aprile, Sports Editor.

FINDLAY

COURIER (FINDLAY), THE. 701 W. Sandusky St., Findlay, OH 45840. Telephone: 419-422-5151. FAX: 419-422-2937. E-MAIL: webmaster@thecourier.com. URL: http://www.thecourier.com. Mailing Address: PO Box 609, Findlay, OH 45839-0609. Year Established: 1836. Pub. Frequency: d. (Mon.-Sat.) Page Size: broadsheet. Subscrip. Rate: $.50 newsstand/cover; $60.40 home delivery for 6 mos.; $118.80/yr home delivery; $114/yr mailed in adj. cys.. **Wire Service(s):** AP. Circulation: 22,284 morning (paid). **Owner(s):** Findlay Publishing Co., See address and contact information above. **Management:** Karl L. Heminger, Publisher. Kari M. Faulkner, Advertising Manager. Terry Kah, Circulation Manager. Chris Collins, Classified Adv. Mgr.. **Editorial:** Robert Hesse, Editor. Jim Harrold, Managing Editor. Kurt Leonard, City Editor. Ted Radick, News Editor. Larry Alter, Sports Editor.

FOSTORIA

REVIEW TIMES. 113 E. Center St., Fostoria, OH 44830. Telephone: 419-435-6641. FAX: 419-435-9073. URL: http://www.reviewtimes.com. Mailing Address: PO Box 947, Fostoria, OH 44830. Year Established: 1860. Pub. Frequency: d. (Mon.-Sat.) Page Size: broadsheet. Subscrip. Rate: $.50 newsstand/cover; $103/yr home delivery; $111/yr mailed in state; $133/yr mailed elsewhere. Freelance Pay: $0.30/column-inch. **Wire Service(s):** AP. Circulation: 5,000 evening (paid). **Owner(s):** Findlay Publishing Co., 701 W. Sandusky St., Findlay, OH 45840. FAX: 419-422-2937. **Management:** Mary Perkins, Publisher. Anthony Rettig, Circulation Manager. Veronica Taylor, Classified Adv. Mgr.. **Editorial:** Linda Woodland, Managing Editor. Patti Stahl, Lifestyle Editor. Scott Cottos, Sports Editor.

FREMONT

NEWS-MESSENGER (FREMONT), THE. ISSN 0746-8148
1700 Cedar St., Fremont, OH 43420. Telephone: 419-332-5511. FAX: 419-334-1037. E-MAIL: newsdesk@thenews-messenger.com. URL: http://www.thenews-messenger.com. Mailing Address: PO Box 1230, Fremont, OH 43420. Year Established: 1856. Pub. Frequency: d. (Mon.-Sat.) Page Size: broadsheet. Subscrip. Rate: $.50 newsstand/cover; $130/yr. **Wire Service(s):** AP, GNS. Circulation: 14,000 evening (paid). **Owner(s):** Gannett Company, Inc., 7950 Jones Branch Dr., McLean, VA 22107-0001. Telephone: 703-284-6000. **Management:** Lucinda Bealer-George, Publisher. Jeff Coppler, Advertising Director. Tom LaPlant, Circulation Director. **Editorial:** Dan Bowerman, Executive Editor.

GALION

GALION INQUIRER. 366 Portland Way N, Galion, OH 44833. Telephone: 419-468-1117. FAX: 419-468-7255. E-MAIL: inquirernews@core.com. URL: http://www.brownpublishing.com. Year Established: 1877. Pub. Frequency: d. (Mon.-Sat.) Page Size: broadsheet. Subscrip. Rate: $.50 newsstand/cover; $10.50/mo.; $9.45/mo. seniors. **Wire Service(s):** AP. Circulation: 3,860 evening (paid). **Owner(s):** Brown Publishing Co., 10222 Alliance Rd, Cincinnati, OH 45040. Telephone: 513-794-5040. FAX: 513-794-5480. **Management:** Vicki Taylor, Publisher. Yvonne Hawes, Circulation Manager. Angie Caldwell, Classified Adv. Mgr.. **Editorial:** Cindy Shroyer, Editor.

GALLIPOLIS

GALLIPOLIS DAILY TRIBUNE. 825 Third Ave, Gallipolis, OH 45631. Telephone: 740-446-2342. FAX: 740-446-3008. URL: http://www.mydailytribune.com. Mailing Address: PO Box 469, Gallipolis, OH 45631-0469. Year Established: 1893. Pub. Frequency: d. Page Size: broadsheet. Subscrip. Rate: $.50 newsstand/cover; $1.25 newsstand/cover Sun.; $115.84/yr carrier delivery in county; $214.21/yr mailed out of county. Adv. Rate: col. inch $9.66 **Wire Service(s):** AP. Circulation: 5,100 evening (paid); 12,000 Sunday (paid). **Owner(s):** Heartland Publications, LLC, 20 Research Pkwy, Ste G, Old Saybrook, CT 06475. Telephone: 860-388-3470. FAX: 860-388-3490. **Management:** Dan Goodrich, Publisher. Matt Rogers, Advertising Manager. Paul Barker, Circulation Manager. Rachel Saunders, Classified Adv. Mgr.. **Editorial:** Kevin Kelly, Managing Editor.

GREENVILLE

DAILY ADVOCATE. 428 S. Broadway, Greenville, OH 45331. Telephone: 937-548-3151. FAX: 937-548-3913. URL: http://www.dailyadvocate.com. Mailing Address: PO Box 220, Greenville, OH 45331. Year Established: 1883. Pub. Frequency: d. Page Size: broadsheet. Subscrip. Rate: $.50 newsstand/cover; $117/yr home delivery in county & mailed in cy.; $135/yr mailed out of county .. **Wire Service(s):** AP. Circulation: 8,000 evening (paid and free). **Owner(s):** Brown Publishing Co., 10222 Alliance Rd, Cincinnati, OH 45040. Telephone: 513-794-5040. FAX: 513-794-5480. **Management:** David Compton, Publisher. Laura Shepherd, Advertising Manager. Barb Wilson, Circulation Manager. **Editorial:** Bob Robinson, Editor. Michael Buckmaster, News Editor. George Starks, Sports.

HAMILTON

JOURNAL-NEWS. 228 Court St., Hamilton, OH 45011. Telephone: 513-863-8200. FAX: 513-896-9489. URL: http://www.journal-news.com. Mailing Address: PO Box 298, Hamilton, OH 45012. Year Established: 1879. Pub. Frequency: d. Page Size: broadsheet. Subscrip. Rate: $.35 newsstand/cover; $1.35 newsstand/cover Sun.; $87/yr home delivery; $257.40/yr mailed. **Wire Service(s):** AP, NYT. Circulation: 26,000 evening (paid); 29,000 Sunday (paid). **Owner(s):** Cox Newspapers, Inc., 6205 Peachtree Dunwoody Rd., Atlanta, GA 30328. Telephone: 678-645-0000. **Management:** Ann Hoffman, Publisher. Rob Rhor, Advertising Manager. Mike Stevens, Circulation Manager. **Editorial:** Mike Wallace, City Editor. Pete Conrad, Sports Editor.

HILLSBORO

TIMES-GAZETTE, THE. 209 S High St, Hillsboro, OH 45133. Telephone: 937-393-3456. FAX: 937-393-2059. E-MAIL: webmaster@timesgazette.com. URL: http://www.timesgazette.com. Year Established: 1818. Pub. Frequency: d. (Mon.-Sat.) Page Size: broadsheet. Subscrip. Rate: $.50 newsstand/cover; $95/yr mailed in county; $107/yr mailed out of county. Adv. Rate: col. inch $9.50 **Wire Service(s):** AP. Circulation: 5,000 evening (paid). **Owner(s):** Dix Communications Group, 212 E. Liberty St., Wooster, OH 44691. Telephone: 216-264-1125, 330-264-1125. **Management:** Rory Ryan, Publisher. Sharon Kersey, Advertising Manager. Brenda Earley, Circulation Director. **Editorial:** Steve Roush, Editor. Stephen Fosha, Sports Editor.

IRONTON

IRONTON TRIBUNE. ISSN 0279-5124
2903 S. Fifth St., Ironton, OH 45638. Telephone: 740-532-1441. FAX: 740-532-1506. E-MAIL: shawn.doyle@irontontribune.com. URL: http://www.irontontribune.com. Mailing Address: PO Box 647, Ironton, OH 45638. Year Established: 1850. Pub. Frequency: d. (Sun.-Fri.) Page Size: broadsheet. Subscrip. Rate: $.50 newsstand/cover; $1.25 newsstand/cover Sun.; $21.90 in county for 12 wks.; $126/yr in county. **Wire Service(s):** AP. Circulation: 7,500 evening (paid); 8,000 Sunday (paid). **Owner(s):** Boone Newspapers, Inc., PO Box 2370, Tuscaloosa, AL 35403. Telephone: 205-752-3381. **Management:** Michael Caldwell, Publisher. Dale Evans, Advertising Director. Richard Duvendeck, Circulation Manager. **Editorial:** Shawn Doyle, Managing Editor. Mark Shaffer, News Editor. Jessica St. James, Photographer. Jim Walker, Sports Editor.

KENTON

KENTON TIMES. 201 E. Columbus St., Kenton, OH 43326. Telephone: 419-674-4066. FAX: 419-673-1125. E-MAIL: keditor@kentontimes.com. URL: http://www.kentontimes.com. Year Established: 1953. Pub. Frequency: d. (Mon.-Sat.) Page Size: standard. Subscrip. Rate: $.50 newsstand/cover; $116.65/yr. Freelance Pay: $0.20/column-inch. **Wire Service(s):** AP. Circulation: 7,100 evening (paid). **Owner(s):** Hardin County Publishing Co., See address and contact information above. **Management:** Jeff Barnes, Publisher. Lesa Heacock, Advertising Manager. Jeff Barnes, Business Manager. **Editorial:** Tim Thomas, Editor. Jim Taylor, Production Manager. Penny Grauel, Circulation Editor. Kendrick Jesionowski, Sports Editor.

KETTERING

BEAVERCREEK NEWS-CURRENT. ISSN 1065-979X
3085 Woodman Dr., Kettering, OH 45420. Telephone: 937-294-7000. FAX: 937-294-2981. E-MAIL: wbaker@xenizgazette.com. URL: http://www.tcnewsnet.com. Year Established: 1959. Pub. Frequency: d. (Mon.-Sat.) Page Size: broadsheet. Subscrip. Rate: $.50 newsstand/cover; $98.80/yr carrier delivery; $110/yr mailed. **Wire Service(s):** AP. Circulation: 6,000 evening (paid). **Owner(s):** Brown Publishing Co., 10222 Alliance Rd, Cincinnati, OH 45040. Telephone: 513-794-5040. FAX: 513-794-5480. **Management:** Frank Beeson, Publisher. Barbara Van De Venter, Advertising Director. **Editorial:** Doug Skinner, Editor. Terry Baver, Managing Editor.

LANCASTER

LANCASTER EAGLE-GAZETTE. 138 W. Chestnut St., Lancaster, OH 43130. Telephone: 740-681-4500. FAX: 740-681-4505. E-MAIL: ataylor-thomas@nncogannett.com. URL: http://www.lancastereaglegazette.com. Mailing Address: PO Box 848, Lancaster, OH 43130-0848. Year Established: 1807. Pub. Frequency: d. Page Size: broadsheet. Subscrip. Rate: $.35 newsstand/cover; $1.25 Sun.; $150.68/yr home delivery; $186/yr mailed. Circulation: 10,000 morning (paid); 18,000 evening (paid). **Owner(s):** Gannett Company, Inc., 7950 Jones Branch Dr., McLean, VA 22107-0001. Telephone: 703-854-6000. **Management:** Greg Ptacin, Publisher. **Editorial:** Antoinette Taylor-Thomas, Editor.

LIMA

LIMA NEWS. 3515 Elida Rd., Lima, OH 45807. Telephone: 419-223-1010. FAX: 419-229-0426. URL: http://www.limanews.com. Mailing Address: P.O. Drawer 690, Lima, OH 45802. Year Established: 1884. Pub. Frequency: d. Page Size: broadsheet. Subscrip. Rate: $.50 newsstand/cover; $1.50 newsstand/cover Sun.; $39.50 home delivery for 13 wks.; $56 mailed for 13 wks.. Adv. Rate: col. inch $30.25 **Wire Service(s):** AP, MCT. Circulation: 35,482 evening (paid); 42,312 Sunday (paid). **Owner(s):** Freedom Communications, Inc., 17666 Fitch, Irvine, CA 92614. Telephone: 949-553-9292. **Management:** Stephen Johnson, Publisher. Jim Shine, Advertising Director. Natalie Buzzard, Advertising Manager. Todd Russell, Circulation Director. **Editorial:** Jim Krumel, Editor. Diane Pacetti, Managing Editor. Karen Jantzi, City Editor. Thomas Lucente, Editorial Page Editor. Adrienne Mauk, Lifestyle Editor. Tom Williams, News Editor. Craig Droiz, Photo Editor. Tim Wolfrum, Sports Editor.

LISBON

MORNING JOURNAL (LISBON). 308 Maple St., Lisbon, OH 44432. Telephone: 330-424-9541. FAX: 330-424-0048. E-MAIL: jcoolman@valunet.com. URL: http://www.morningjournalnews.com. Year Established: 1852. Pub. Frequency: d. Page Size: broadsheet. Subscrip. Rate: $.35 newsstand/cover; $1 newsstand/cover Sun.; $9.40 carrier delivery for 4 wks.; $13 mailed in county for 4 wks.. **Wire Service(s):** AP. Circulation: 13,560 morning (paid); 48,973 Sunday (paid and free). **Owner(s):** Buckeye Publishing Co., Inc., See address and contact information above. **Management:** Larry Dorschner, Publisher. Lisa Arter, Advertising Manager. John Hale, Circulation Director. **Editorial:** Dorma Tolson, Editor. Denny Spalvieri, Assistant Editor. Stephanie Ujhelyi, News Editor. Ron Firth, Sports Editor.

LONDON

MADISON PRESS, THE. 30 S Oak St, London, OH 43140. Telephone: 740-852-1616. FAX: 740-852-1620. E-MAIL: news@madison-press.com. URL: http://www.madison-press.com. Mailing Address: PO Box 390, London, OH 43140-0390. Year Established: 1845. Pub. Frequency: d. (Mon.-Fri.) Page Size: broadsheet. Subscrip. Rate: $.50 newsstand/cover; $85/yr carrier delivery. **Wire Service(s):** AP. Circulation: 6,500 evening (paid). **Owner(s):** Central Ohio Printing Corporation, See address and contact information above. **Management:** Gregg Rettig, Publisher. Kim Boyd, Advertising Manager. Tim Yost, Circulation Manager. Linda Marx, Classified Adv. Mgr.. **Editorial:** Mac Cordell, Managing Editor. Ryan Yocum, Sports Editor.

LORAIN

MORNING JOURNAL (LORAIN). 1657 Broadway Ave., Lorain, OH 44052. Telephone: 440-245-6901. FAX: 440-245-5637. E-MAIL: jcole@morningjournal.com. URL: http://www.morningjournal.com. Year Established: 1921. Pub. Frequency: d. Page Size: broadsheet. Subscrip. Rate: $.50 newsstand/cover; $1.25 newsstand/cover Sun.; $87.10 home delivery for 6 mos.; $174.20/yr home delivery. **Wire Service(s):** AP, SH. Circulation: 30,885 morning (paid); 35,562 Sunday (paid). **Owner(s):** Journal Register Co., 50 W State St, 12th Fl, Trenton, NJ 08608. Telephone: 609-396-2200. **Bureau(s):** 123 Market St., Sandusky, OH. Telephone: 419-625-4431. **Management:** Jeff Sudbrook, Publisher. Ron Beal, Advertising Director. Micah Young, Circulation Director. **Editorial:** John G. Cole, Editor. April Elliott, Managing Editor. Eric Stoessel, Sports Editor.

MANSFIELD

NEWS JOURNAL (MANSFIELD). 70 W. Fourth St., Mansfield, OH 44903. Telephone: 419-522-3311. FAX: 419-521-7415. E-MAIL: tbrennan@nncogannett.com. URL: http://www.mansfieldnewsjournal.com. Mailing Address: PO Box 25, Mansfield, OH 44901. Year Established: 1933. Pub. Frequency: d. Page Size: broadsheet. Subscrip. Rate: $.50 newsstand/cover; $1.50 newsstand/cover Sun.; $169.80/yr carrier delivery; $174.60/yr motor route; $223.80/yr mailed. **Wire Service(s):** AP, MCT. Circulation: 33,379 morning (paid); 42,650 Sunday (paid). **Owner(s):** Gannett Company, Inc., 7950 Jones Branch Dr., McLean, VA 22107-0001. Telephone: 703-854-6000. **Management:** Tom Brennan, Publisher. Bob Scott, Circulation Director. Dave Milligan, Sales Manager. **Editorial:** Tom Brennan, Editor. Carl Hunnell, Managing Editor. Calvin Jefferson, City Editor. Carl Hunnell, Editorial Page Editor. Dave Polcyn, Photo Editor. Larry Phillips, Sports Editor.

MARIETTA

MARIETTA TIMES. 700 Channel Ln., Marietta, OH 45750. Telephone: 740-373-2121. FAX: 740-376-5475. E-MAIL: jhautman@mariettatimes.com. URL: http://www.mariettatimes.com. Mailing Address: PO Box 635, Marietta, OH 45750. Year Established: 1864. Pub. Frequency: d. (Mon.-Sat.) Page Size: broadsheet. Subscrip. Rate: $.50 newsstand/cover; $1 newsstand/cover Sat.; $130/yr carrier delivery /motor rte; $208/yr mailed. **Wire Service(s):** AP, GNS. Circulation: 12,348 evening (paid). **Owner(s):** Ogden Newspapers of Minnesota, Inc., 1500 Main St., Wheeling, WV 26003. Telephone: 304-233-0100. **Management:** James Spanner, Publisher. Aaron Jones, Circulation Manager. Lisa Kehl, Classified Adv. Mgr.. **Editorial:** Jennifer Houtman, Managing Editor. Jim Bartholow, Copy Editor. Tom Hrack, News Editor. Mitch Casey, Photographer.

MARION

MARION STAR, THE. ISSN 1087-7495
150 Court St., Marion, OH 43302. Telephone: 740-387-0400. FAX: 740-375-5188. E-MAIL: tgraser@nncogannett.com. URL: http://www.marionstar.com. Year Established: 1877. Pub. Frequency: d. Page Size: broadsheet. Subscrip. Rate: $.50 newsstand/cover; $1.25 newsstand/cover Sun.; $143.52/yr carrier delivery. **Wire Service(s):** AP. Circulation: 17,695 evening (paid); 13,788 Sunday (paid). **Owner(s):** Gannett Company, Inc., 7950 Jones Branch Dr., McLean, VA 22107-0001. Telephone: 703-854-6000. **Management:** Ron Frailly, Publisher. Michael Morrow, Circulation Manager. Stacia King, Classified Adv. Mgr.. **Editorial:** Tom Graser, Editor. Michelle Leppert, Sports Editor.

MARTINS FERRY

TIMES LEADER (MARTINS FERRY). 200 S. Fourth St., Martins Ferry, OH 43935-1925. Telephone: 740-633-1131. FAX: 740-633-3496. E-MAIL: timesleader@timesleaderonline.com. URL: http://www.timesleaderonline.com. Year Established: 1891. Pub. Frequency: d. Page Size: broadsheet. Subscrip. Rate: $.50 newsstand/cover; $1.25 newsstand/cover Sun.; $7.50 carrier delivery/mo.. **Wire Service(s):** AP. Circulation: 18,241 evening (paid); 20,557 Sunday (paid). **Owner(s):** Ogden Newspapers of Minnesota, Inc., 1500 Main St., Wheeling, WV 26003. Telephone: 304-233-0100. **Management:** Alexander F. Marshall III, Publisher. Kevin Kolanski, Advertising Manager. E. J. Miller, Circulation Manager. Anita Wallace, Classified Adv. Mgr.. April Lanham, Marketing Director. **Editorial:** Christina Elliott, Editor. Betty Pokas, Librarian. Mike Harwella, Photographer. Hariett Mikilas, Society Editor. Bob Kapral, Sports Editor.

MARYSVILLE

MARYSVILLE JOURNAL-TRIBUNE. ISSN 1069-2207
207 N. Main St., Marysville, OH 43040. Telephone: 937-644-9111. FAX: 937-644-9211. E-MAIL: chad@marysvillejt.com. URL: http://www.marysvillejt.com. Mailing Address: PO Box 226, Marysville, OH 43040-0207. Year Established: 1849. Pub. Frequency: d. (Mon.-Sat.) Page Size: broadsheet. Subscrip. Rate: $.50 newsstand/cover; $99/yr mailed in state; $109/yr out of state. **Wire Service(s):** AP. Circulation: 6,300 evening (paid). **Owner(s):** Daniel E. Behrens, See address and contact information above. **Management:** Daniel E. Behrens, Publisher. Marie Woodford, Advertising Manager. Carol Craft, Circulation Manager. Brenda Maxwell, Classified Adv. Mgr.. **Editorial:** Daniel E. Behrens, Editor. Chad Williamson, Managing Editor. Tim Miller, Sports Editor.

MASSILLON

INDEPENDENT (MASSILLON), THE. 50 North Ave, NW, Massillon, OH 44647. Telephone: 330-833-2631. FAX: 330-833-2635. E-MAIL: indenews@indeonline.com. URL: http://www.indeonline.com. Mailing Address: PO Box 730, Massillon, OH 44648. Year Established: 1863. Pub. Frequency: d. Page Size: broadsheet. Subscrip. Rate: $.50 newsstand/cover; $.75 newsstand/cover Sat.; $23.13 home delivery for 13 wks.; $171.60/yr carrier delivery. **Wire Service(s):** AP, SH. Circulation: 15,000 morning (paid). **Owner(s):** GateHouse Media, Inc, 350 WillowBrook Office Park, Fairport, NY 14450. Telephone: 585-598-0030. FAX: 585-248-2631. **Management:** Ron Frailly, Publisher. Shelia Cassler, Circulation Manager. **Editorial:** Robert McCune, Editor.

MEDINA

MEDINA COUNTY GAZETTE. 885 W. Liberty St., Medina, OH 44256. Telephone: 330-725-4166. FAX: 330-725-4299. E-MAIL: manage@ohio.net. URL: http://www.medina-gazette.com. Year Established: 1832. Pub. Frequency: d. (Mon.-Sat.) Page Size: broadsheet. Subscrip. Rate: $.35 newsstand/cover; $78/yr in county; $96/yr mailed out of county. Freelance Pay: $35/story. **Wire Service(s):** AP, LAT-WAT. Circulation: 14,500 morning (paid). **Owner(s):** Medina County Publications, Inc., See address and contact information above. **Management:** George Hudnutt, Publisher. Kris High, Advertising Director. Wayne Workman, Circulation Manager. **Editorial:** Liz Sheaffer, Managing Editor. Pam Coleman, News Editor. Betty Szudlo, Sports Editor.

MIDDLETOWN

MIDDLETOWN JOURNAL, THE. 52 S. Broad St., Middletown, OH 45044. Telephone: 513-422-3611. FAX: 513-423-6940. E-MAIL: news@journalink.com. URL: http://www.middletown.com. Mailing Address: PO Box 490, Middletown, OH 45042. Year Established: 1857. Pub. Frequency: d. Page Size: broadsheet. Subscrip. Rate: $.50 newsstand/cover; $1.25 newsstand/cover Sun.; $161.20/yr carrier delivery local; $247/yr mailed. Freelance Pay: $20-$25/article. **Wire Service(s):** AP. Circulation: 18,000 evening (paid); 22,000 Sunday (paid). **Owner(s):** Cox Newspapers, Inc., 6205 Peachtree Dunwoody Rd, Atlanta, GA 30328. Telephone: 404-843-5000. **Management:** Ann Hoffman, Publisher. Joann Hyland, Advertising Manager. Mike Stevens, Circulation Manager. **Editorial:** Lisa Warren, Editor. David Goodwin, Managing Editor. Kevin Aldredge, City Editor. Michael Williams, Editorial Page Editor. Susan Carroll, News Editor. Pat Aukerman, Photographer. John Boyle, Sports.

MT. VERNON

MOUNT VERNON NEWS. 18 E. Vine St., Mt. Vernon, OH 43050. Telephone: 740-397-5333. FAX: 740-397-1321. URL: http://www.mountvernonnews.com. Year Established: 1837. Pub. Frequency: d. (Mon.-Sat.) Page Size: broadsheet. Subscrip. Rate: $.50 newsstand/cover; $73/yr carrier delivery; $104/yr motor route; $120/yr mailed in county; $124/yr mailed out of county. **Wire Service(s):** AP. Circulation: 10,000 evening (paid). **Owner(s):** Kay Culbertson, See address and contact information above. **Management:** Kay Culbertson, Publisher. Corby Wise, Advertising Manager. Mike McNichols, Circulation Manager. **Editorial:** Cheryl Splain, Editor. Virgil Shipley, Photographer. Joe Huddleston, Sports Editor.

NAPOLEON

NORTHWEST SIGNAL. 595 E. Riverview Ave., Napoleon, OH 43545. Telephone: 419-592-5055. FAX: 419-592-9778. E-MAIL: ads@northwestsignal.net. URL: http://www.northwestsignal.net. Year Established: 1966. Pub. Frequency: d. (Mon.-Sat.) Page Size: broadsheet. Subscrip. Rate: $.50 newsstand/cover; $88/yr in county; $134/yr mailed out of state. Adv. Rate: col. inch $11 **Wire Service(s):** UPI. Circulation: 4,800 evening (paid); 7,400 per issue (free). **Owner(s):** Christopher Cullis, See address and contact information above. **Management:** Tom Voight, General Manager. Christopher Cullis, Publisher. Celeste Breece, Circulation Manager. Sally Heaston, Classified Adv. Mgr.. **Editorial:** Brian Koeller, Editor. Jeff Ratliff, Sports Editor.

NEW PHILADELPHIA

TIMES-REPORTER, THE. 629 Wabash NW, New Philadelphia, OH 44663. Telephone: 330-364-5577. FAX: 330-364-8449. E-MAIL: news@timesreporter.com. URL: http://www.timesreporter.com. Mailing Address: PO Box 667, New Philadelphia, OH 44663-0667. Year Established: 1872. Pub. Frequency: d. Page Size: broadsheet. Subscrip. Rate: $.50 newsstand/cover; $1.50 newsstand/cover Sun.; $202.80/yr carrier delivery in county; $210.60/yr motor route in county; $257.40/yr mailed. Adv. Rate: col. inch $25.95 **Wire Service(s):** AP. Circulation: 23,000 morning (paid); 23,000 Sunday (paid). **Owner(s):** GateHouse Media, Inc, 350 WillowBrook Office Park, Fairport, NY 14450. Telephone: 585-598-0030. FAX: 585-248-2631. **Management:** Jac A Clay, Publisher. Marla Miskimen, Advertising Director. Mike Gorsich, Circulation Manager. **Editorial:** Richard Farrell, Editor.

NEWARK

ADVOCATE (NEWARK), THE. ISSN 0740-2120
22 N. First St., Newark, OH 43055. Telephone: 740-345-4053. FAX: 740-349-7469. E-MAIL: mshearer@nncogannett.com. URL: http://www.newarkadvocate.com. Year Established: 1821. Pub. Frequency: d. Page Size: broadsheet. Subscrip. Rate: $.35 newsstand/cover; $1 newsstand/cover Sun.; $148.20/yr carrier delivery; $137.80/yr mailed in county; $157.80/yr mailed out of county. **Wire Service(s):** AP. Circulation: 22,500 evening (paid); 22,500 Sunday (paid). **Owner(s):** Gannett Company, Inc., 7950 Jones Branch Dr., McLean, VA 22107-0001. Telephone: 703-854-6000. **Management:** Jeff Simmons, Circulation Manager.

PIQUA

PIQUA DAILY CALL. 310 Spring St., Piqua, OH 45356. Telephone: 937-773-2721. FAX: 937-773-2782. E-MAIL: editorial@dailycall.com. URL: http://www.dailycall.com. Mailing Address: PO Box 910, Piqua, OH 45356-0910. Year Established: 1883. Pub. Frequency: d. (Mon.-Sat.) Page Size: broadsheet. Subscrip. Rate: $.50 newsstand/cover; $118.50/yr home delivery; $148.80/yr mailed. **Wire Service(s):** AP. Circulation: 7,600 evening (paid). **Owner(s):** Brown Publishing Co., 10222 Alliance Rd, Cincinnati, OH 45040. Telephone: 513-794-5040. FAX: 513-794-5480. **Management:** Frank Beeson, Group Publisher. Leiann Stewart, Advertising Manager. Cheryl Hall, Circulation Manager. **Editorial:** Susan Hartley, Editor.

POMEROY

DAILY SENTINEL (POMEROY), THE. 111 Court St, Pomeroy, OH 458769. Telephone: 740-992-2156. FAX: 740-992-2157. URL: http://www.mydailysentinel.com. Mailing Address: PO Box 729, Pomeroy, OH 45769-0729. Year Established: 1948. Pub. Frequency: d. (Sun.-Fri.) Page Size: broadsheet. Subscrip. Rate: $.50 newsstand/cover; $1.25 Sun.; $115.84/yr carrier delivery in county & motor route; $214.21/yr mailed out of county. **Wire Service(s):** AP. Circulation: 5,000 evening (paid); 14,500 Sunday (paid). **Owner(s):** Heartland Publications, LLC, 20 Research Pkwy, Ste G, Old Saybrook, CT 06475. Telephone: 860-388-3470. FAX: 860-388-3490. **Management:** Charlene Hoeflich, General Manager. Dan Goodrich, Publisher. Judy Clark, Circulation Manager. Linda McTurner, Classified Adv. Mgr.. **Editorial:** Charlene Hoeflich, News Editor.

PORT CLINTON

NEWS-HERALD (PORT CLINTON). 115 W. Second St., Port Clinton, OH 43452. Telephone: 419-734-3141. FAX: 419-734-1850. E-MAIL: newsherald@cros.net. URL: http://www.portclintonnewsherald.com. Mailing Address: PO Box 550, Port Clinton, OH 43452. Year Established: 1865. Pub. Frequency: d. (Mon.-Sat.) Page Size: broadsheet. Subscrip. Rate: $.50 newsstand/cover; $117/yr in county; $130/yr motor route in county; $169.15/yr mailed. **Wire Service(s):** AP, GNS. Circulation: 6,500 evening (paid). **Owner(s):** Gannett Company, Inc., 7950 Jones Branch Dr., McLean, VA 22107-0001. Telephone: 703-854-6000. **Management:** David Barth, General Manager. Cindy George, Publisher. David Barth, Advertising Manager. Pam Sanford, Circulation Manager. **Editorial:** Dan Bowerman, Executive Editor.

PORTSMOUTH

PORTSMOUTH DAILY TIMES. ISSN 8750-6963
637 Sixth St, Portsmouth, OH 45662. Telephone: 740-3535-3101. FAX: 740-353-7280. E-MAIL: spelfrey@heartlandpubliations.com. URL: http://www.portsmouth-dailytimes.com. Mailing Address: PO Box 581, Portsmouth, OH 45662. Year Established: 1852. Pub. Frequency: d. Page Size: broadsheet. Subscrip. Rate: $.50 newsstand/cover; $1.25 newsstand/cover Sun.; $179.20/yr carrier delivery in city; $179.40/yr motor route in city; $210/yr mailed in county & adj. cys.. **Wire Service(s):** AP. Circulation: 17,101 evening (paid); 17,500 Sunday (paid). **Owner(s):** Heartland Publications, LLC, 20 Research Pkwy, Ste G, Old Saybrook, CT 06475. Telephone: 860-388-3470. FAX: 860-388-3490. **Management:** Jim Freeland, Publisher. LouAnn Blair, Circulation Manager. Wilma Coffey, Classified Adv. Mgr.. **Editorial:** Art Kuhn, Managing Editor.

RAVENNA

RECORD-COURIER. 126 N Chestnut St, Ravenna, OH 44266. Telephone: 330-296-9657. FAX: 330-296-2698. E-MAIL: editor@recordpub.com. URL: http://www.recordpub.com. Year Established: 1830. Pub. Frequency: d. Page Size: broadsheet. Subscrip. Rate: $.50 newsstand/cover; $1 newsstand/cover Sun.; $112/yr home delivery; $125/yr mailed in county; $145/yr mailed out of county. Adv. Rate: col. inch $17.08 Freelance Pay: $15/article. **Wire Service(s):** AP, SH. Circulation: 19,915 evening (paid); 19,476 Sunday (paid). **Owner(s):** Dix Communications Group, 212 E. Liberty St., Wooster, OH 44691. Telephone: 330-264-1125. FAX: 216-264-3756. **Management:** Robert C. Dix, Publisher. Charlotte Doherty, Classified Adv. Mgr.. **Editorial:** Roger Di Paolo, Editor. Heather Rainone, Managing Editor. Contact: Kasha Legela, Real Estate Editor.

SALEM

SALEM (OH) NEWS. 161 N. Lincoln Ave., Salem, OH 44460. Telephone: 330-332-4601. FAX: 330-332-1441. URL: http://www.oweb.com. Mailing Address: PO Box 268, Salem, OH 44460. Year Established: 1889. Pub. Frequency: d. (Mon.-Sat.) Page Size: broadsheet. Subscrip. Rate: $.35 newsstand/cover; $112.30/yr home delivery; $180/yr mailed. **Wire Service(s):** AP. Circulation: 8,300 morning (paid). **Owner(s):** Ogden Newspapers of Minnesota, Inc., 1500 Main St., Wheeling, WV 26003. Telephone: 304-233-0100. FAX: 304-233-0327. **Management:** Mike Bird, Publisher. Kelli Hurley, Advertising Manager. Aaron Jones, Circulation Manager. **Editorial:** J.D. Creer, Managing Editor. John Celidonio, Editorial Page Editor.

SANDUSKY

SANDUSKY REGISTER. 314 W. Market St., Sandusky, OH 44870. Telephone: 419-625-5500. FAX: 419-625-3007. URL: http://www.sanduskyregister.com. Year Established: 1822. Pub. Frequency: d. Page Size: broadsheet. Subscrip. Rate: $.50 newsstand/cover; $1.25 newsstand/cover Sun.; $2.65 carrier delivery/wk.. **Wire Service(s):** AP. Circulation: 25,000 evening (paid); 27,600 Sunday (paid). **Owner(s):** Sandusky Newspapers, Inc., See address and contact information above. **Management:** Doug Phares, Publisher. Mark Yocum, Advertising Director. William Ney, Circulation Director. James Rusincovitch, Classified Adv. Mgr.. Jason Werlong, Photography Director. **Editorial:** Annette La Cross, Managing Editor.

SHELBY

SHELBY DAILY GLOBE. 37 W. Main St., Shelby, OH 44875. Telephone: 419-342-4276. FAX: 419-342-4246. E-MAIL: globe@sdgnewsgroup.com. URL: http://www.sdgnewsgroup.com. Mailing Address: PO Box 674, Shelby, OH 44875. Year Established: 1900. Pub. Frequency: d. (Mon.-Sat.) Page Size: broadsheet. Subscrip. Rate: $.35 newsstand/cover; $1.85 home delivery/wk. local; $92/yr mailed in county & adj. cys.; $123/yr mailed out of area. **Wire Service(s):** AP. Circulation: 4,200 evening (paid). **Owner(s):** Shelby Daily Globe, Inc., See address and contact information above. **Management:** Scott Gove, Publisher. Patty Schaub, Advertising Manager. **Editorial:** Sheryl DeLong, News Editor.

SIDNEY

SIDNEY DAILY NEWS. 1451 Vandemark Rd., Sidney, OH 45365-4099. Telephone: 937-498-8088. FAX: 937-498-5991. E-MAIL: sdn@sdnccg.com. URL: http://www.sidneydailynews.com. Mailing Address: PO Box 4099, Sidney, OH 45365-4099. Year Established: 1891. Pub. Frequency: d. (Mon.-Sat.) Page Size: broadsheet. Subscrip. Rate: $.50 newsstand/cover; $138.06/yr home delivery; $199.99/yr mailed. Adv. Rate: col. inch $10.80 **Wire Service(s):** AP. Circulation: 13,000 evening (paid). **Owner(s):** Brown Publishing Co., 10222 Alliance Rd, Cincinnati, OH 45040. Telephone: 513-794-5040. FAX: 513-794-5480. **Management:** Frank Beeson, Group Publisher. Jeffrey Billiel, Publisher. Becky Smith, Advertising Manager. Ronda Schutte, Circulation Manager. Mandy Yagle, Classified Adv. Mgr.. **Editorial:** Melanie Speicher, News Editor.

SPRINGFIELD

SPRINGFIELD NEWS-SUN. ISSN 0744-6101
202 N. Limestone St., Springfield, OH 45503. Telephone: 937-328-0300. FAX: 937-328-0328. URL: http://www.springfieldnewssun.com. Year Established: 1817. Pub. Frequency: d. Page Size: broadsheet. Subscrip. Rate: $.50 newsstand/cover; $1.25 newsstand/cover Sun.; $3.76 home delivery/wk.; $195.52/yr home delivery; $286/yr mailed. Adv. Rate: col. inch $40.60 **Wire Service(s):** AP, NYT, MCT. Circulation: 28,742 morning (paid); 36,144 Sunday (paid). **Owner(s):** Cox Newspapers, Inc., 6205 Peachtree Dunwoody Rd, Atlanta, GA 30328. Telephone: 404-843-5000. **Management:** William Swaim, Publisher. Rob Mercer, Advertising Director. Sam Ronicker, Circulation Director. **Editorial:** Karla Garrett Harshaw, Editor. Jack Bianchi, Managing Editor. Ben McLaughlin, City Editor. Keith Streitenberger, Editorial Page Editor. Paul Profeta, News Editor. Marshall Gorby, Photo Editor.

ST. MARYS

EVENING LEADER, THE. ISSN 0745-5550
102 E Spring St, St. Marys, OH 45885. Telephone: 419-394-7414. FAX: 419-394-7202. E-MAIL: ads@theeveningleader.com. URL: http://www.theeveningleader.com. Year Established: 1905. Pub. Frequency: d. (Mon.-Sat.) Page Size: broadsheet. Subscrip. Rate: $.50 newsstand/cover; $2.70 carrier delivery/wk.; $11.70 carrier delivery/mo.; $35.10 carrier delivery for 3 mos.; $135/yr carrier delivery; $165/yr mailed. Adv. Rate: col. inch $10.02 **Wire Service(s):** AP. Circulation: 5,412 evening (paid). **Owner(s):** Horizon Publications, Inc., 1120 N. Carbon St, Ste 100, Marion, IL 62959. **Management:** Deb Zwez, Publisher. Quinn Gilbert, Circulation Manager. Karen Brown, Marketing Manager. **Editorial:** Tom Wehrhahn, Managing Editor.

STEUBENVILLE

HERALD-STAR & WEIRTON DAILY TIMES. 401 Herald Sq., Steubenville, OH 43952. Telephone: 740-283-4711. FAX: 740-282-4261. E-MAIL: newsroom@heraldstaronline.com. URL: http://www.heraldstaronline.com. Year Established: 1806. Pub. Frequency: d. Page Size: broadsheet. Subscrip. Rate: $.50 newsstand/cover; $1.25 newsstand/cover Sun.; $33.15 home delivery for 13 wks.. **Wire Service(s):** AP. Circulation: 20,359 evening (paid); 24,934 Sunday (paid). **Owner(s):** Ogden Newspapers of Minnesota, Inc., 1500 Main St., Wheeling, WV 26003. FAX: 304-233-0327. **Management:** Alex Marshall, General Manager. Chris Doyle, Publisher. Jason Mayberry, Advertising Director. John Hale, Circulation Manager. **Editorial:** Ross Gallabrese, Managing Editor.

SYLVANIA

BLADE (TOLEDO), THE. 6450 Monroae St, Sylvania, OH 43560. Telephone: 419-724-6035. E-MAIL: citydesk@theblade.com. URL: http://www.toledoblade.com. Year Established: 1835. Pub. Frequency: d. Page Size: broadsheet. Subscrip. Rate: $.75 newsstand/cover; $2 newsstand/cover Sun.; $3.50/wk. local. **Wire Service(s):** RN, AP, SH, NYT, LAT-WAT, MCT. Circulation: 119,000 evening (paid); 145,000 Sunday (paid). **Owner(s):** Block Communications Inc., See address and contact information above. Block Communications, 541 N. Superior St., Toledo, OH 43660. Telephone: 419-724-6000. FAX: 419-724-6439. **Bureau(s):** 955 National Press Bldg., Washington D.C.., 20045. Telephone: 202-662-7070. **Management:** John Robinson Block, Publisher. Kim Bergman, Classified Adv. Mgr.. Nate Parsons, Photography Director. **Editorial:** David Shutt, Editor. John Robinson Block, Editor-in-Chief. Ron Royhab, Executive Editor. Kurt Franck, Managing Editor. Luann Sharp, Asst. Managing Ed.. Kim Bates, City Editor. Luann Sharp, Feature Editor.

TIFFIN

ADVERTISER-TRIBUNE. 320 Nelson St., Tiffin, OH 44883. Telephone: 419-448-3200. FAX: 419-447-3274. E-MAIL: adtrib@bright.net. URL: http://www.advertiser-tribune.com. Mailing Address: PO Box 778, Tiffin, OH 44883. Year Established: 1832. Pub. Frequency: d. Page Size: broadsheet. Subscrip. Rate: $.50 newsstand/cover; $1.25 newsstand/cover Sun.; $12.50 carrier delivery/mo.; $13.50 motor route/mo.; $16.50 mailed/mo.. **Wire Service(s):** AP. Circulation: 11,500 morning (paid); 12,000 Sunday (paid). **Owner(s):** Ogden Newspapers of Minnesota, Inc., 1500 Main St., Wheeling, WV 26003. Telephone: 304-233-0100. **Management:** David Frisch, Publisher. Chris Dixon, Advertising Manager. Ron Clark, Circulation Manager. Chris Dixon, Classified Adv. Mgr.. Mary Huss, Business Manager. **Editorial:** Rob Weaver, Editor. Ryan Good, News Editor. Jim Shobe, Photographer. Dave Feltner, Sports Editor.

TROY

TROY DAILY NEWS. 224 S. Market St., Troy, OH 45373. Telephone: 937-335-5634. FAX: 937-335-3552. URL: http://www.tdn-net.com. Year Established: 1909. Pub. Frequency: d. Page Size: broadsheet. Subscrip. Rate: $.50 newsstand/cover; $1.50 newsstand/cover Sun.; $150/yr home delivery; $234/yr mailed. **Wire Service(s):** AP. Circulation: 12,000 evening (paid); 14,000 Sunday (paid). **Owner(s):** Brown Publishing Co., 10222 Alliance Rd, Cincinnati, OH 45040. Telephone: 513-794-5040. FAX: 513-794-5480. **Management:** Frank Beeson, Group Publisher. Leiann Stewart, Advertising Manager. Ken Bowen, Circulation Manager. Jodie Vagedes, Classified Adv. Mgr.. **Editorial:** David Fong, Executive Editor.

UPPER SANDUSKY

UPPER SANDUSKY DAILY CHIEF-UNION. 111 W. Wyandot, Upper Sandusky, OH 43351-0180. Telephone: 419-294-2331. FAX: 419-294-5608. URL: http://www.dailychiefunion.com. Mailing Address: PO Box 180, Upper Sandusky, OH 43351-0180. Year Established: 1936. Pub. Frequency: d. (Mon.-Sat.) Page Size: broadsheet. Subscrip. Rate: $.50 newsstand/cover; $107.90/yr in county. **Wire Service(s):** AP. Circulation: 4,500 evening (paid). **Owner(s):** Hardin County Publishing Co., 317 S. Anderson St., Elwood, IN 46036. Telephone: 317-552-3355. **Management:** Jeff Barnes, Publisher. Bonnie Carpenter, Classified Adv. Mgr.. David Barnes, Business Manager. **Editorial:** Jeff Barnes, Editor. Aaron Korte, Columnist.

URBANA

URBANA DAILY CITIZEN. 220 E. Court St., Urbana, OH 43078. Telephone: 937-652-1331. FAX: 937-652-1336. URL: http://www.urbanacitizen.com. Mailing Address: PO Box 191, Urbana, OH 43078. Year Established: 1837. Pub. Frequency: d. Page Size: broadsheet. Subscrip. Rate: $.50 newsstand/cover; $114.85/yr home delivery; $138.60/yr mailed in county; $180.90/yr mailed out of county. Adv. Rate: col. inch $11.75 **Wire Service(s):** AP. Circulation: 6,264 evening (paid). **Owner(s):** Brown Publishing Co., 10222 Alliance Rd, Cincinnati, OH 45040. Telephone: 513-794-5040. FAX: 513-794-5480. **Management:** Lane Moon, Publisher. **Editorial:** Brenda Burns, Managing Editor. Steve Stout, Sports Editor.

VAN WERT

TIMES-BULLETIN, THE. ISSN 8750-1503
700 Fox Rd., Van Wert, OH 45891. Telephone: 419-238-2285. FAX: 419-238-0447. E-MAIL: info@timesbulletin.com. URL: http://www.timesbulletin.com. Mailing Address: PO Box 271, Van Wert, OH 45891. Year Established: 1846. Pub. Frequency: d. (Mon.-Sat.) Page Size: broadsheet. Subscrip. Rate: $.50 newsstand/cover; $120/yr home delivery; $185/yr mailed. Adv. Rate: col. inch $12.70 Freelance Pay: $25/article. **Wire Service(s):** AP. Circulation: 7,000 evening (paid). **Owner(s):** Brown Publishing Co., 10222 Alliance Rd, Cincinnati, OH 45040. **Management:** Robb Krecklow, Publisher. Tracy Bishop, Advertising Manager. Christal McConnell, Circulation Manager. **Editorial:** Cindy Wood, Editor.

WAPAKONETA

WAPAKONETA DAILY NEWS. 520 Industrial Dr., Wapakoneta, OH 45895. Telephone: 419-738-2128. FAX: 419-738-5352. URL: http://www.wapakdailynews.com. Mailing Address: PO Box 389, Wapakoneta, OH 45895. Year Established: 1904. Pub. Frequency: d. (Mon.-Sat.) Page Size: broadsheet. Subscrip. Rate: $.50 newsstand/cover; $126/yr carrier delivery; $134.20/yr motor route; $156.75/yr mailed. Adv. Rate: col. inch $12.80 **Wire Service(s):** AP. Circulation: 5,300 evening (paid). **Owner(s):** Horizon Publications, Inc., 1120 N. Carbon St., Ste.100, Marion, IL 62959. Telephone: 618-993-1693. **Management:** Dianna Epperly, Publisher. Karen Brown, Advertising Director. Beverly Putman, Circulation Manager. **Editorial:** William Laney, Editor. Brian Craft, Sports Editor.

WARREN

TRIBUNE CHRONICLE. 240 Franklin, S.E., Warren, OH 44482-1431. Telephone: 330-841-1600. FAX: 330-841-1721. URL: http://www.tribune-chronicle.com. Pub. Frequency: d. Page Size: broadsheet. Subscrip. Rate: $.35 newsstand/cover; $1 newsstand/cover Sun.; $2.75 home delivery/wk.; $143/yr home delivery. **Wire Service(s):** AP. Circulation: 36,500 morning (paid); 42,000 Sunday (paid). **Owner(s):** Eastern Ohio Newspapers, Inc., 1500 Main St., Wheeling, WV 26003. Telephone: 304-233-0100. FAX: 304-233-0327. **Management:** Len Blose, General Manager. Charles Jarvis, Publisher. Chris D'Angelo, Advertising Manager. Ted Snyder, Circulation Director. Pam Bissell, Classified Adv. Mgr.. **Editorial:** Frank Robinson, Editor. Lisa Solley, Managing Editor. Brenda Linert, Metro Editor. Dave Burcham, Sports Editor.

WASHINGTON COURT HOUSE

RECORD HERALD (CINCINNATI). 138 S. Fayette St., Washington Court House, OH 43160. Telephone: 740-335-3611. FAX: 740-335-5728. URL: http://www.recordherald.com. Year Established: 1937. Pub. Frequency: d. (Mon.-Sat.) Page Size: broadsheet. Subscrip. Rate: $.50 newsstand/cover; $114.40/yr home delivery; $188.23/yr mailed. Adv. Rate: col. inch $11 **Wire Service(s):** AP. Circulation: 6,200 evening (paid). **Owner(s):** Brown Publishing Co., 10222 Alliance Rd, Cincinnati, OH 45040. Telephone: 513-794-5040. FAX: 513-794-5480. **Management:** Gary Brock, Publisher. Sherri Sattler, Advertising Manager. **Editorial:** Margaret Jones, Editor.

WILLOUGHBY

NEWS-HERALD (WILLOUGHBY). 7085 Mentor Ave., Willoughby, OH 44094-7900. Telephone: 440-951-0000. FAX: 440-975-2293. E-MAIL: lknews@ctcentral.com. URL: http://www.news-herald.com. Year Established: 1879. Pub. Frequency: d. Page Size: broadsheet. Subscrip. Rate: $.50 newsstand/cover; $1.50 newsstand/cover Sun.; $4 carrier delivery/wk.; $208/yr carrier delivery. **Wire Service(s):** AP, LAT-WAT, MCT. Circulation: 50,000 evening (paid); 59,000 Sunday (paid). **Owner(s):** Journal Register Co., 50 W. State St., 12th Fl., Trenton, NJ 08608-1298. Telephone: 609-396-2200. **Management:** Steve Roszczyk, Publisher. Mitch Perin, Classified Adv. Mgr.. **Editorial:** James Collins, Editor. Tricia Ambrose, Executive Editor. Laura Kessel, Managing Editor.

WILMINGTON

WILMINGTON NEWS-JOURNAL. ISSN 8750-4847
47 S. South St., Wilmington, OH 45177. Telephone: 937-382-2574. FAX: 937-382-4392. URL: http://www.wnewsj.com. Year Established: 1838. Pub. Frequency: d. (Mon.-Sat.) Page Size: broadsheet. Subscrip. Rate: $.50 newsstand/cover; $115/yr in county; $200/yr mailed. Adv. Rate: col. inch $15.30 **Wire Service(s):** AP. Circulation: 7,292 evening (paid). **Owner(s):** Brown Publishing Co., 10222 Alliance Rd, Cincinnati, OH 45040. Telephone: 513-794-5040. FAX: 513-794-5480. **Management:** Pamela Stricker, Publisher. Sharon Kersey, Advertising Manager. Lori Holcomb, Circulation Director. **Editorial:** Rachel Colliver, Editor. Sarah Clark, Sports Editor.

WOOSTER

DAILY RECORD (WOOSTER), THE. ISSN 0892-8215
212 E. Liberty St., Wooster, OH 44691. Telephone: 330-264-1125. FAX: 216-264-3756. E-MAIL: adv@bright.net. URL: http://www.the-daily-record.com. Year Established: 1898. Pub. Frequency: d. Page Size: broadsheet. Subscrip. Rate: $.50 newsstand/cover; $1 newsstand/cover Sun.; $136.15/yr carrier delivery local; $140.85/yr motor route local; $181.64/yr mailed out of area. **Wire Service(s):** AP, NYT. Circulation: 23,064 evening (paid); 23,399 Sunday (paid). **Owner(s):** Dix Communications Group, See address and contact information above. **Management:** William McKinney, General Manager. R. Victor Dix, Publisher. Rhonda Geer, Advertising Director. Jake Volcsko, Circulation Director. Bruce Polen, Classified Adv. Mgr.. **Editorial:** Lance White, Managing Editor.

XENIA

FAIRBORN DAILY HERALD. 30 S. Detroit St., Xenia, OH 45385. Telephone: 937-878-3993. E-MAIL: wbajer@xebuagazette,cin. URL: http://www.fairborndailyherald.com. Pub. Frequency: d. (Mon.-Sat.) Page Size: broadsheet. Subscrip. Rate: $.50 newsstand/cover; $85.20/yr home delivery; $175/yr mailed. **Wire Service(s):** UPI. Circulation: 13,300 evening (paid). **Owner(s):** Brown Publishing Co., 10222 Alliance Rd, Cincinnati, OH 45040. Telephone: 513-794-5040. FAX: 513-794-5480. **Management:** Jon Noel, Publisher. Barbara Van De Venter, Advertising Director. Gina Riefstahl, Circulation Director. Marsha Robinson, Classified Adv. Mgr.. **Editorial:** Josh Richardson, Managing Editor.

XENIA DAILY GAZETTE. ISSN 8750-4650
30 S. Detroit St., Xenia, OH 45385. E-MAIL: nblizzard@xeniagazette.com. URL: http://www.xeniagazette.com. Year Established: 1868. Pub. Frequency: d. (Mon.-Sat.) Page Size: broadsheet. Subscrip. Rate: $.50 newsstand/cover; $101.40/yr home delivery local; $175/yr mailed local. Adv. Rate: col. inch $13.88 **Wire Service(s):** AP. Circulation: 10,217 evening (paid). **Owner(s):** Brown Publishing Co., 10222 Alliance Rd, Cincinnati, OH 45040. Telephone: 513-794-5040. FAX: 513-794-5480. **Management:** Jon Noel, Publisher. Barbara Van De Venter, Advertising Director. Gina Riefstahl, Circulation Director. **Editorial:** Josh Richardson, Managing Editor. Steve Black, Sports Editor.

YOUNGSTOWN

VINDICATOR (YOUNGSTOWN), THE. ISSN 0890-9857
107 Vindicator Sq., Youngstown, OH 44503. Telephone: 330-747-1471. FAX: 330-747-6712. E-MAIL: news@vindy.com. URL: http://www.vindy.com. Mailing Address: PO Box 780, Youngstown, OH 44501-0780. Year Established: 1869. Pub. Frequency: d. Page Size: broadsheet. Subscrip. Rate: $.35 newsstand/cover; $1 newsstand/cover Sun.; $2.50 carrier delivery/wk.; $130/yr carrier delivery. Adv. Rate: col. inch $54.90 **Wire Service(s):** AP, SH, LAT-WAT, MCT. Circulation: 67,888 evening (paid); 97,476 Sunday (paid). **Owner(s):** Vindicator Printing Co., See address and contact information above. **Management:** Mark A. Brown, General Manager. Allen Bowlby, Circulation Director. Rich Hay, Classified Adv. Mgr.. **Editorial:** Michael McGowen, Editor. Paul C. Jagnow, Managing Editor. Don Shilling, Business Editor. Deb Shaulis, Entertainment Editor. Rick Logan, News Editor. Barbara Shaffer, Womens Interest Editor.

ZANESVILLE

TIMES RECORDER, THE. 34 S. Fourth St., Zanesville, OH 43701-3449. Telephone: 740-452-4561. FAX: 740-450-6759. E-MAIL: 75563.306@compuserve.com. URL: http://www.zanesvilletimesrecorder.com. Year Established: 1852. Pub. Frequency: d. Page Size: broadsheet. Subscrip. Rate: $.50 newsstand/cover; $1.50 newsstand/cover Sun.; $143/yr carrier delivery local. **Wire Service(s):** AP. Circulation: 19,945 morning (paid); 19,735 Sunday (paid). **Owner(s):** Gannett Company, Inc., 7950 Jones Branch Dr., McLean, VA 22107-0001. Telephone: 703-854-6000. **Management:** Tom Claybaugh, Publisher. Leslee Peth, Advertising Director. Wayne Carrier, Circulation Manager. **Editorial:** Jason Maddux, Managing Editor. Pam James, Lifestyle Editor. Dave Weidig, Sports Editor.

OKLAHOMA

ADA

ADA EVENING NEWS. 116 N. Broadway, Ada, OK 74820. Telephone: 580-332-4433. FAX: 580-332-8841. E-MAIL: news@adaeveningnews.com. URL: http://www.adaeveningnews.com. Mailing Address: PO Box 489, Ada, OK 74821. Year Established: 1904. Pub. Frequency: d. (Sun.-Fri.) Page Size: broadsheet. Subscrip. Rate: $.50 newsstand/cover; $1.25 newsstand/cover Sun.; $8.95 home delivery/mo.; $98.50/yr; $10.35 mailed/mo.. Adv. Rate: col. inch $.50 Freelance Pay: $0.50/column-inch. **Wire Service(s):** AP. Circulation: 10,000 evening (paid); 10,500 Sunday (paid). **Owner(s):** Community Newspaper Holdings, Inc., 3500 Colonnade Pkwy., Ste. 600, Birmingham, AL 35243. Telephone: 205-298-7100. FAX: 205-298-7101. **Management:** Lonnie Beasley, Publisher. Chris Robbins, Advertising Director. Dawn Keathley, Circulation Manager. LaDawna Fry, Classified Adv. Mgr.. **Editorial:** Brenda Tollett, Managing Editor. Jeff Cali, Sports Editor.

ALTUS

ALTUS TIMES. 218 W Commerce, Altus, OK 73521. Telephone: 580-482-1221. FAX: 580-482-5709. URL: http://www.altustimes.com. Mailing Address: PO Box 578, Altus, OK 73521-0578. Year Established: 1900. Pub. Frequency: d. Page Size: broadsheet. Subscrip. Rate: $.50 newsstand/cover; $1 Sun.; $84/yr carrier delivery local; $99/yr mailed in state; $114/yr mailed out of state. **Wire Service(s):** AP. Circulation: 5,000 evening (paid); 5,500 Sunday (paid). **Owner(s):** Heartland Publications, LLC, 20 Research Pkwy, Ste G, Old Saybrook, CT 06475. Telephone: 860-388-3470. FAX: 860-388-3490. **Management:** Bill Murphy, Publisher. Sandy Graham, Circulation Manager. **Editorial:** Michael Bush, Editor.

ALVA

ALVA REVIEW-COURIER. 620 Choctaw St., Alva, OK 73717-1600. Telephone: 580-327-2200. FAX: 580-327-2454. E-MAIL: alvareview@aol.com. URL: http://www.alvareviewcourier.com. Year Established: 1893. Pub. Frequency: d. (Sun.-Fri.) Page Size: tabloid. Subscrip. Rate: $.50 newsstand/cover; $1 newsstand/cover Sun.; $96/yr in county; $132/yr out of state. **Wire Service(s):** AP. Circulation: 2,000 morning (paid); 2,200 Sunday (paid). **Owner(s):** Martin Broadcasting Corp., 620 Choctaw, Alva, OK 73717. Telephone: 580-327-2200. FAX: 580-327-2454. **Management:** Lynn L. Martin, Publisher. Sara Bird, Advertising Manager. **Editorial:** Marione E. Martin, Editor. Helen Barrett, Assignment Editor.

ANADARKO

ANADARKO DAILY NEWS. 117-119 E. Broadway, Anadarko, OK 73005-0548. Telephone: 405-247-3331. FAX: 405-247-5571. E-MAIL: dailynews@tanet.net. Mailing Address: PO Box 548, Anadarko, OK 73005-0548. Year Established: 1901. Pub. Frequency: d. (Mon.-Sat.) Page Size: broadsheet. Subscrip. Rate: $.50 newsstand/cover; $75/yr home delivery in county; $75/yr mailed in county. **Wire Service(s):** AP. Circulation: 4,800 morning (paid). **Owner(s):** Anadarko Publishing Co., 117-119 E. Broadway, Anadarko, OK 73005. Telephone: 405-247-3331. **Management:** Carolyn N. McBride, Publisher. Carla McBride-Alexander, Advertising. Phillip F. Gomez, Circulation Manager. **Editorial:** Carolyn N. McBride, Editor. Joe W. McBride Jr., Political Editor. Earl Savage, Sports Editor.

ARDMORE

DAILY ARDMOREITE, THE. 117 W. Broadway, Ardmore, OK 73401. Telephone: 580-223-2200. FAX: 580-226-0050. E-MAIL: jbridwell@ardmorite.com. URL: http://www.ardmoreite.com. Mailing Address: PO Box 1328, Ardmore, OK 73402. Year Established: 1893. Pub. Frequency: d. (Sun.-Fri.) Page Size: broadsheet. Subscrip. Rate: $.50 newsstand/cover; $1 newsstand/cover Sun.; $8.50 home delivery/mo.; $90/yr local. **Wire Service(s):** AP. Circulation: 11,500 evening (paid); 13,980 Sunday (paid). **Owner(s):** Morris Multimedia, Inc., PO Box 936, Augusta, GA 30903. Telephone: 706-724-0851. **Management:** Bill Stauffer, Publisher. Deborah Dietz, Advertising Manager. Stan Middleton, Circulation Manager. Martha Porter, Classified Adv. Mgr.. Mary Lou Bennett, Marketing Director. Kathy Worley, Business Manager. **Editorial:** John Bridwell, Managing Editor. Mark Finley, Asst. Managing Ed.. Karen Treat, City Editor. Marsha Miller, News Editor. Steve Biehn, Photo Editor.

BARTLESVILLE

BARTLESVILLE EXAMINER-ENTERPRISE. ISSN 0883-7015
4125 S.E. Nowata Rd., Bartlesville, OK 74006. Telephone: 918-335-8200. FAX: 918-335-3111. E-MAIL: ads@examiner-enterprise.com. URL: http://www.examiner-enterprise.com. Mailing Address: PO Box 1278, Bartlesville, OK 74005. Year Established: 1895. Pub. Frequency: d. (Sun.-Fri.) Page Size: broadsheet. Subscrip. Rate: $.50 newsstand/cover; $1.25 newsstand/cover Sun.; $8.50 carrier delivery/mo.. **Wire Service(s):** AP. Circulation: 13,100 evening (paid); 15,300 Sunday (paid). **Owner(s):** Stephens Media LLC, 1111 W. Bonanza Rd., Las Vegas, NV 89106. Telephone: 702-383-0211. **Bureau(s):** National Press Club Bldg., Washington, DC. Contact: Steve Tetreault, Bureau Chief. **Management:** Jerry Quinn, Publisher. Tom Bradley, Advertising Manager. Richard Yakle, Circulation Manager. **Editorial:** Kelli Williams, Managing Editor. Mike Tupa, Sports Editor.

CHICKASHA

EXPRESS-STAR, THE. 302 N. Third St., Chickasha, OK 73018. Telephone: 405-224-2600. FAX: 405-224-7087. E-MAIL: advertising@chickashanews.com. URL: http://www.chickashanews.com. Mailing Address: P.O. Drawer E, Chickasha, OK 73023. Year Established: 1892. Pub. Frequency: d. (Sun.-Fri.) Page Size: broadsheet. Subscrip. Rate: $.50 newsstand/cover; $1 newsstand/cover Sun.; $81/yr home delivery; $114/yr mailed. **Wire Service(s):** AP. Circulation: 5,400 evening (paid); 6,200 Sunday (paid). **Owner(s):** Community Newspaper Holdings, Inc., 3500 Colonnade Pkwy., Ste. 600, Birmingham, AL 35243. Telephone: 205-298-7100. FAX: 205-298-7101. **Management:** Jerry Pittman, Publisher. Theresa Smith, Circulation Manager. **Editorial:** Kent Bush, Managing Editor. Karen Brady, Lifestyle Editor. Chuck Larson, Sports.

CLAREMORE

CLAREMORE DAILY PROGRESS. 315 W. Will Rogers Blvd., Claremore, OK 74017. Telephone: 918-341-1101. FAX: 918-341-1131. E-MAIL: editor@claremoreprogress.com. URL: http://www.claremoreprogress.com. Mailing Address: PO Box 248, Claremore, OK 74018. Year Established: 1893. Pub. Frequency: d. (Tue.-Fri. & Sun.) Page Size: broadsheet. Subscrip. Rate: $.50 newsstand/cover; $1 newsstand/cover Sun.; $6.50 carrier delivery/mo.; $8 mailed/mo. in county; $9.50 mailed/mo. out of county. **Wire Service(s):** AP. Circulation: 6,100 evening (paid); 7,100 Sunday (paid). **Owner(s):** Community Newspaper Holdings, Inc., 3500 Colonnade Pkwy., Ste. 600, Birmingham, AL 35243. Telephone: 205-298-7100. FAX: 205-298-7101. **Management:** Bailey Dabney, Publisher. Cinda Vaughan, Advertising Director. Tommy Dowdy, Circulation Director. Almetha Sizemore, Business Manager. Sheila Knight, Human Res. Mgr.. **Editorial:** Clarice Doyle, Editor.

CLINTON

CLINTON DAILY NEWS. 522 Avant Ave., Clinton, OK 73601. Telephone: 580-323-5151. FAX: 580-323-5154. E-MAIL: clintondailynews.com. URL: http://www.clintondailynews.com. Year Established: 1903. Pub. Frequency: d. (Sun.-Fri.) Page Size: standard. Subscrip. Rate: $.50 newsstand/cover; $.75 newsstand/cover Sun.; $7 home delivery/mo.. Adv. Rate: col. inch $5.95 **Wire Service(s):** AP. Circulation: 5,200 evening (paid); 5,400 Sunday (paid). **Owner(s):** Clinton Daily News Co., See address and contact information above. **Management:** Reba Donley, Advertising Manager. Cindy Gagne, Circulation Manager. Rod Serfoss, Associate Publisher. **Editorial:** Rod Serfoss, Editor. Steve Belcher, City Editor. Brittany Wagnon, Lifestyle Editor.

CUSHING

CUSHING DAILY CITIZEN. 115 S. Cleveland St., Cushing, OK 74023-1031. Telephone: 918-225-3333. FAX: 918-225-1050. E-MAIL: news@cushingdaily.com. URL: http://www.cushingdaily.com. Mailing Address: PO Box 1031, Cushing, OK 74023-1031. Year Established: 1895. Pub. Frequency: d. (Tue.-Fri. & Sun.) Page Size: broadsheet. Subscrip. Rate: $.50 newsstand/cover; $67/yr carrier delivery in city; $115/yr mailed out of city. **Wire Service(s):** AP. Circulation: 3,200 morning (paid). **Owner(s):** Community Newspaper Holdings, Inc., 3500 Colonnade Pkwy., Ste. 600, Birmingham, AL 35243-1031. Telephone: 205-298-7100. FAX: 205-298-7101. **Management:** Gina Felix, Publisher. Donna Judd, Advertising Manager. Lydia McCall, Circulation Manager. Cecilia Bias, Classified Adv. Mgr.. **Editorial:** Molly Payne, Managing Editor.

DUNCAN

DUNCAN BANNER, THE. 1001 Elm St., Duncan, OK 73533. Telephone: 580-255-5354. FAX: 580-255-8889. E-MAIL: circulation@bannernet.net. URL: http://www.duncanbanner.com. Mailing Address: PO Box 1268, Duncan, OK 73534-1268. Year Established: 1892. Pub. Frequency: d. (Sun.-Fri.) Page Size: broadsheet. Subscrip. Rate: $.50 newsstand/cover; $1 newsstand/cover Sun.; $99/yr home delivery; $39 mailed for 3 mos.. Adv. Rate: col. inch $8.40 **Wire Service(s):** AP. Circulation: 10,097 evening (paid); 10,941 Sunday (paid). **Owner(s):** Community Newspaper Holdings, Inc., 3500 Colonnade Pkwy., Ste. 600, Birmingham, AL 35243. Telephone: 205-298-7100. FAX: 205-298-7101. **Management:** Floyd Jernigan, Publisher. Dana Boyles, Advertising Manager. **Editorial:** Floyd Jernigan, Editor.

DURANT

DURANT DAILY DEMOCRAT. 200 W Beech St, Durant, OK 74701. Telephone: 580-924-4388. FAX: 580-924-0962. E-MAIL: ads@durantdemocrat.com. URL: http://www.durantdemocrat.com. Mailing Address: PO Box 250, Durant, OK 74702. Year Established: 1900. Pub. Frequency: d. (Sun.-Fri.) Page Size: broadsheet. Subscrip. Rate: $.50 newsstand/cover; $1 newsstand/cover Sun.; $84/yr home delivery; $94/yr mailed in county; $144/yr mailed in state. Adv. Rate: col. inch $8.80 **Wire Service(s):** AP. Circulation: 7,000 evening (paid); 7,600 Sunday (paid). **Owner(s):** Heartland Publications, LLC, 20 Research Pkwy, Ste G, Old Saybrook, CT 06475. Telephone: 860-388-3470. FAX: 860-388-3490. **Management:** Steve Boggs, Publisher. Paula M. Howell, Advertising Manager. Sheila Millard, Classified Adv. Mgr.. **Editorial:** Brad House, Editor.

EDMOND

EDMOND SUN, THE. ISSN 1522-5828
123 S Broadway, Edmond, OK 73034. Telephone: 405-341-2121. FAX: 405-340-7363. E-MAIL: cwhite@edmondsun.com. URL: http://www.edmondsun.com. Mailing Address: PO Box 2470, Edmond, OK 73083. Year Established: 1889. Pub. Frequency: d. (Tue.-Sat.) Page Size: broadsheet. Subscrip. Rate: $.50 newsstand/cover; $1 newsstand/cover Sun.; $97/yr mailed in county; $144/yr mailed out of county. Adv. Rate: col. inch $12.60 **Wire Service(s):** AP, LAT-WAT. Circulation: 6,907 evening (paid); 12,341 Sunday (paid). **Owner(s):** Community Newspaper Holdings, Inc., 3500 Colonnade Pkwy., Ste. 600, Birmingham, AL 35243-1031. **Management:** Steve Paterson, Publisher. Krean Ediger, Advertising Director. Richard Foster, Circulation Manager. Alice Duree, Classified Adv. Mgr.. **Editorial:** Lisa Shearer, Managing Editor.

ELK CITY

ELK CITY DAILY NEWS. 200-206 W. Broadway, Elk City, OK 73644. Telephone: 580-225-3000. FAX: 580-243-2414. E-MAIL: elkcitydailynews@itlnet.net. URL: http://www.elkcitydailynews.com. Mailing Address: PO Box 1009, Elk City, OK 73648-1009. Year Established: 1901. Pub. Frequency: d. (Sun.-Fri.) Page Size: broadsheet. Subscrip. Rate: $.50 newsstand/cover; $9 home delivery/mo.; $75/yr home delivery; $83/yr mailed in county; $110/yr mailed out of county. **Wire Service(s):** AP. Circulation: 6,176 evening (paid); 10,795 Sunday (paid). **Owner(s):** Larry R. Wade, See address and contact information above. **Management:** Mary Jane Wade, Director. Larry R. Wade, Publisher. Sharon Denny, Advertising Manager. Calvin Stone, Circulation Manager. Vonnie Kelln, Classified Adv. Mgr.. **Editorial:** Bob Fisher, Executive Editor. Cheryl Overstreet, Lifestyle Editor. John Cannon, Sports Editor.

ENID

ENID NEWS & EAGLE. 227 W. Broadway, Enid, OK 73701. Telephone: 580-233-6600. FAX: 580-233-7645. E-MAIL: info@enidnews.com. URL: http://www.enidnews.com. Mailing Address: PO Box 1192, Enid, OK 73702-1192. Year Established: 1893. Pub. Frequency: d. Page Size: broadsheet. Subscrip. Rate: $.50 newsstand/cover; $1.50 newsstand/cover Sun.; $11.95 home delivery/mo.; $131.45/yr home delivery; $130/yr mailed. Adv. Rate: col. inch $22.84 **Wire Service(s):** AP. Circulation: 18,372 morning (paid); 18,985 Sunday (paid). **Owner(s):** Community Newspaper Holdings, Inc., 3500 Colonnade Pkwy., Ste. 600, Birmingham, AL 35243. Telephone: 205-298-7100. **Management:** Jeff Funk, Publisher. Dennis Warren, Advertising Manager. Robert Robertson, Circulation Manager. Becky Allen, Classified Adv. Mgr.. **Editorial:** Cindy Allen, Managing Editor. Mark Roundtree, Sports Editor.

GROVE

GROVE SUN, THE. 27 W. Third St., Ste A, Grove, OK 74344. Telephone: 918-786-2228. FAX: 918-786-2156. E-MAIL: editor@grovesun.com. URL: http://www.grovesun.com. Mailing Address: PO Box 450969, Grove, OK 74345. Year Established: 1898. Pub. Frequency: 4/w. (Tue.-Fri.) Page Size: broadsheet. Subscrip. Rate: $1 newsstand/cover; $62/yr home delivery in county; $180/yr mailed out of state. Circulation: 6,000 morning (paid). **Owner(s):** Grove Sun Newspaper Co., See address and contact information above. **Management:** Cheryl Franklin, Publisher. Tom Gray, Advertising Manager. Billie Organ, Circulation Manager. **Editorial:** Kirsten Mustain, Editor.

GUTHRIE

GUTHRIE NEWS LEADER. ISSN 1091-9333
107 W. Harrison, PO Box 879, Guthrie, OK 73044. E-MAIL: online@guthrienewsleader.net. URL: http://www.guthrienewsleader.net/. Year Established: 1889. Pub. Frequency: 3/w. (Wed., Fri. & Sun.) Page Size: broadsheet. Subscrip. Rate: $72/yr carrier delivery local; $93/yr mailed in county; $123/yr mailed out of county. **Wire Service(s):** AP. Circulation: 3,500 evening (paid); 3,700 Sunday (paid). **Owner(s):** American Hometown Publishing, Inc., 110 Third Ave. N., Franklin, TN 37064. Telephone: 615-599-8751. FAX: 615-599-8752. **Management:** Belinda Ramsey, Publisher. Teri Large, Advertising. Sharon Beckner, Circulation Manager. **Editorial:** Belinda Ramsey, Editor. Jarrett George, Photographer.

GUYMON

GUYMON DAILY HERALD. 515 N Ellison St, Guymon, OK 73942. Telephone: 580-338-3355. FAX: 580-338-5000. E-MAIL: publisher@guymondailyherald.com. URL: http://www.guymondailyherald.com. Mailing Address: PO Box 19, Guymon, OK 73942-0019. Year Established: 1890. Pub. Frequency: d. (Mon.-Sat.) Page Size: broadsheet. Subscrip. Rate: $.50 newsstand/cover; $86/yr home delivery local; $96/yr mailed in county; $99/yr mailed out of county. Adv. Rate: col. inch $7.45 **Wire Service(s):** AP. Circulation: 2,800 evening (paid). **Owner(s):** Horizon Publications, Inc., 1120 N. Carbon St, Ste 100, Marion, IL 62959. **Management:** Alison Gipe, General Manager. Peggy Martinez, Circulation Manager. Carol Rayo, Classified Adv. Mgr.. **Editorial:** Debbie Browning, Managing Editor.

HUGO

HUGO DAILY NEWS. 128 E. Jackson St., Hugo, OK 74743. Telephone: 580-326-3311. FAX: 580-326-6397. E-MAIL: sstamper@sbcglobal.net. URL: http://www.hugonews.com. Year Established: 1907. Pub. Frequency: d. (Mon.-Fri.) Page Size: broadsheet. Subscrip. Rate: $.50 newsstand/cover; $7 carrier delivery/mo.; $72.50/yr; $8 mailed/mo. in county; $69.50/yr mailed in county; $88.50/yr mailed elsewhere. Adv. Rate: col. inch $4 **Wire Service(s):** AP. Circulation: 2,800 morning (paid). **Owner(s):** Hugo Publishing Co., Inc., See address and contact information above. **Management:** Stan Stamper, Publisher. Linda Packard, Advertising Manager. **Editorial:** Stan Stamper, Editor.

IDABEL

MCCURTAIN DAILY GAZETTE. 107 S. Central St., Idabel, OK 74745. Telephone: 580-286-3321. FAX: 580-286-2208. E-MAIL: piper@mccurtain.com. URL: http://www.mccurtain.com. Mailing Address: PO Box 179, Idabel, OK 74745. Year Established: 1906. Pub. Frequency: d. (Tue.-Fri. & Sun.) Page Size: broadsheet. Subscrip. Rate: $.50 newsstand/cover; $.75 newsstand/cover Sun.; $61/yr home delivery; $62.50/yr mailed in county; $117.50/yr mailed out of county. **Wire Service(s):** AP. Circulation: 6,400 evening (paid); 8,400 Sunday (paid). **Owner(s):** Gwen & Bruce Willingham, See address and contact information above. **Management:** Bruce Willingham, Publisher. Margie Cockerham, Advertising Manager. Donna Barber, Circulation Manager. Cecilia Wilson, Classified Adv. Mgr.. **Editorial:** Bruce Willingham, Editor. Brad Reesing, Sports Editor.

LAWTON

LAWTON CONSTITUTION. ISSN 0889-566X
102 S.W. Third St., Lawton, OK 73501. Telephone: 580-353-0620. FAX: 580-585-5140. E-MAIL: paper@sirinet.net. URL: http://www.lawton-constitution.com. Mailing Address: PO Box 2069, Lawton, OK 73502. Year Established: 1910. Pub. Frequency: d. Page Size: broadsheet. Subscrip. Rate: $.50 newsstand/cover; $1.50 newsstand/cover Sun.; $130/yr carrier delivery; $167/yr mailed. **Wire Service(s):** AP, NYT, CNS. Circulation: 23,824 morning (paid); 28,696 Sunday (paid). **Owner(s):** Lawton Publishing Co., Inc., See address and contact information above. **Management:** Donald S. Bentley, Co-Publisher. Mike Owensby, General Manager. Jim Garrett, Advertising Manager. Larry Toth, Circulation Manager. **Editorial:** David Hale, Managing Editor. Dee Ann Patterson, City Editor. Charles Clark, Lifestyle Editor. Jeff Dixon, Photographer. Joey Goodman, Sports Editor.

MCALESTER

NEWS-CAPITAL & DEMOCRAT. 500 S. Second St, McAlester, OK 74501. Telephone: 918-423-1700. FAX: 918-426-3081. E-MAIL: publisher@mcalesternews.com. URL: http://www.mcalesternews.com. Mailing Address: PO Box 987, McAlester, OK 74502. Year Established: 1898. Pub. Frequency: d. (Sun.-Fri.) Page Size: broadsheet. Subscrip. Rate: $.50 newsstand/cover; $1 newsstand/cover Sun.; $102/yr carrier delivery in county; $141/yr mailed in state. Freelance Pay: $25-$50/article. **Wire Service(s):** AP. Circulation: 10,956 evening (paid); 10,581 Sunday (paid). **Owner(s):** Community Newspaper Holdings, Inc., 3500 Colonnade Pkwy., Ste. 600, Birmingham, AL 35243. Telephone: 205-298-7100. **Management:** John Tucker, Publisher. LeeAnn Johns, Circulation Director. Carol Shackelford, Classified Adv. Mgr.. **Editorial:** James Beaty, Senior Editor. Laura Wilson, Lifestyle Editor.

MIAMI

CHANUTE TRIBUNE. 215 1st Ave NE, Miami, OK 74354. Telephone: 948-541-1934. E-MAIL: tribune@chanute.com. URL: http://www.chanute.com. Year Established: 1892. Pub. Frequency: d. (Tue.-Sat.) Page Size: broadsheet. Subscrip. Rate: $.50 newsstand/cover; $47.22 carrier delivery for 6 mos.; $89.49/yr carrier delivery. Adv. Rate: col. inch $8 **Wire Service(s):** AP. Circulation: 4,100 evening (paid). **Owner(s):** Family Media, Inc., See address and contact information above. **Management:** Kate Thompson, Publisher. Amy Jenson, Circulation Manager. Ann Smith, Classified Adv. Mgr.. Contact: James Rubow, Advertising Director.

MIAMI NEWS-RECORD. 14 First Ave., N.W., Miami, OK 74354. Telephone: 918-542-5533. FAX: 918-542-1903. E-MAIL: mnr@mmind.net. URL: http://www.miaminewsrecord.com. Mailing Address: PO Box 940, Miami, OK 74355. Year Established: 1903. Pub. Frequency: d. (Sun.-Fri.) Page Size: broadsheet. Subscrip. Rate: $.50 newsstand/cover; $1.25 newsstand/cover Sun.; $8.50 home delivery/mo. local; $10 mailed/mo. in state. Circulation: 7,000 morning (paid). **Owner(s):** American Consolidated Media, Inc., 1420 N. Mockingbird Ln, Ste 100, Dallas, TX 75247. Telephone: 214-691-4066. FAX: 214-691-4086. **Management:** Charity Armstrong, General Manager. Shannon Duhon, Publisher. Mark Rogers, Advertising Director. Bill Brisbois, Circulation Manager. Brends Martin, Classified Adv. Mgr.. **Editorial:** Krista Duhon, Managing Editor.

MUSKOGEE

MUSKOGEE DAILY PHOENIX & TIMES-DEMOCRAT. 214 Wall St, Muskogee, OK 74402. Telephone: 918-684-2828. FAX: 918-687-6270. URL: http://www.muskogeephoenix.com. Mailing Address: PO Box 1968, Muskogee, OK 74402. Year Established: 1888. Pub. Frequency: d. Page Size: broadsheet. Subscrip. Rate: $.50 newsstand/cover; $1.25 newsstand/cover Sun.; $138/yr carrier delivery in area. **Wire Service(s):** AP, UPI. Circulation: 18,883 morning (paid); 19,737 Sunday (paid). **Owner(s):** Community Newspaper Holdings, Inc., 3500 Colonnade Pkwy., Ste. 600, Birmingham, AL 35242. **Management:** Larry Corvi, Publisher. Stephen Schultheis, Circulation Manager. Tina Frost, Classified Adv. Mgr.. **Editorial:** Vicky Holland, Executive Editor.

NORMAN

NORMAN TRANSCRIPT. 215 E. Comanche St., Norman, OK 73069. Telephone: 405-321-1800. FAX: 405-366-3516. E-MAIL: news@normantranscript.com. URL: http://www.normantranscript.com. Mailing Address: P.O. Drawer 1058, Norman, OK 73070. Year Established: 1889. Pub. Frequency: d. Page Size: broadsheet. Subscrip. Rate: $.50 newsstand/cover; $1 newsstand/cover Sun.; $104/yr local; $13/mo. in adj. cys.; $18/mo. out of area. **Wire Service(s):** AP. Circulation: 15,000 evening (paid); 18,500 Sunday (paid). **Owner(s):** Community Newspaper Holdings, Inc., 3500 Colonnade Pkwy., Ste. 600, Birmingham, AL 35243. Telephone: 205-298-7100. FAX: 205-298-7101. **Management:** David Stringer, Publisher. Saundra Morris, Advertising Manager. Maurice Barcomb, Circulation Manager. Nicole Losoya, Classified Adv. Mgr.. **Editorial:** Andy Rieger, Managing Editor. Linda Henley, City Editor. Clay Horning, Sports Editor.

OKLAHOMA CITY

OKLAHOMAN, THE. 9000 N. Broadway, Oklahoma City, OK 73114. Telephone: 405-475-3311. FAX: 405-475-3183. URL: http://www.newsok.com. Mailing Address: PO Box 25125, Oklahoma City, OK 73125. Year Established: 1903. Pub. Frequency: d. Page Size: broadsheet. Subscrip. Rate: $.25 newsstand/cover; $1.50 newsstand/cover Sun.; $14 home delivery/mo.. **Wire Service(s):** RN, AP. Circulation: 207,749 morning (paid); 292,988 Sunday (paid). **Owner(s):** Oklahoma Publishing Co., See address and contact information above. **Management:** David Thompson, General Manager. Christie Everest, President. David Thompson, Publisher. Sergio Salinas, Advertising Director. Pat Dennis, Circulation Manager. Tom Hite, Classified Adv. Mgr.. **Editorial:** Susan Hale, Executive Editor. Joe Height, Managing Editor. Clytie Bunyan, Business Editor. Ed Kelly, Editorial Page Editor. Gene Triplett, Entertainment Editor. Sharon Dowell, Food Editor. Bryan Painter, Lifestyle Editor. Bill Waugh, Photographer. Penny Soldan, Radio-TV Editor. Carla Hintopn, Religion Editor.

OKMULGEE

OKMULGEE DAILY TIMES. 114 E. Seventh St., Okmulgee, OK 74447. Telephone: 918-756-3600. FAX: 918-756-8197. URL: http://www.okmulgeetimes.com. Year Established: 1903. Pub. Frequency: d. (Tue.-Sun.) Page Size: broadsheet. Subscrip. Rate: $.50 newsstand/cover; $1 newsstand/cover Sun.; $6.50 home delivery/mo. local; $23.25 mailed/mo.. **Wire Service(s):** AP. Circulation: 4,500 morning (paid); 7,500 Sunday (paid). **Owner(s):** Sumner Media Group, See address and contact information above. **Management:** Joe Gray, Publisher. Robin Brown Field, Advertising Director. Phyllis Argyle, Circulation Manager. **Editorial:** Herman Brown, Editor. Patrick Ford, Lifestyle Editor. Larry Owen, Sports Editor.

PAULS VALLEY

PAULS VALLEY DAILY DEMOCRAT. 108 S. Willow St., Pauls Valley, OK 73075. Telephone: 405-238-6464. FAX: 405-238-3042. E-MAIL: pvpub@swbellnet. URL: http://www.paulsvalleydailydemocrat.com. Mailing Address: PO Box 790, Pauls Valley, OK 73075. Year Established: 1904. Pub. Frequency: d. (Tue.-Fri. & Sun.) Page Size: broadsheet. Subscrip. Rate: $.50 newsstand/cover; $1 newsstand/cover Sun.; $84/yr carrier delivery local; $132/yr mailed out of county. Adv. Rate: col. inch $5.20 **Wire Service(s):** AP. Circulation: 3,000 evening (paid); 3,200 Sunday (paid). **Owner(s):** Community Newspaper Holdings, Inc., 3500 Colonnade Pkwy., Ste. 600, Birmingham, AL 35243. Telephone: 205-298-7100. FAX: 205-298-7101. **Management:** Shelley Ridenour, Publisher. Wendy Chick, Advertising Director. **Editorial:** Mike Arie, Sports.

PERRY

PERRY DAILY JOURNAL. ISSN 0746-7559
714 Delaware St., Perry, OK 73077. Telephone: 580-336-2222. FAX: 580-336-3222. E-MAIL: editor@perrydailyjournal.com. URL: http://www.perrydailyjournal.com. Mailing Address: PO Box 311, Perry, OK 73077-0311. Year Established: 1893. Pub. Frequency: d. (Tue.-Sat.) Page Size: broadsheet. Subscrip. Rate: $.50 newsstand/cover; $10.50 home delivery/mo. local. **Wire Service(s):** AP. Circulation: 3,250 evening (paid). **Owner(s):** Perry Daily Journal, Inc., PO Box 191, Weatherford, OK 73096. Telephone: 580-772-3301. **Management:** Phillip Reid, Publisher. Maria Lemons, Advertising. Mickey Anson, Circulation Manager. **Editorial:** Gloria Brown, Managing Editor. Matt Dvorak, Sports Editor.

PONCA CITY

PONCA CITY NEWS. 300 N. Third, Ponca City, OK 74601. Telephone: 580-765-3311. E-MAIL: news@poncacitynews.com. URL: http://www.poncacitynews.com. Mailing Address: PO Box 191, Ponca City, OK 74601. Year Established: 1893. Pub. Frequency: d. (Sun.-Fri.) Page Size: standard. Subscrip. Rate: $.35 newsstand/cover; $1 newsstand/cover Sun.; $7.25 carrier delivery/mo.. Adv. Rate: col. inch $11 **Wire Service(s):** AP. Circulation: 10,931 evening (paid); 12,470 Sunday (paid). **Owner(s):** Ponca City Publishing Co., Inc., See address and contact information above. **Management:** Tom Muchmore, Publisher. Pat Jordan, Advertising Manager. Kevin Kreger, Circulation Manager. Pat Jordan, Promotion Manager. **Editorial:** Tom Muchmore, Editor. Kristi Hayes, Managing Editor. Jerry Helems, Production Manager.

POTEAU

POTEAU DAILY NEWS. 804 N Broadway, Poteau, OK 74953. Telephone: 918-647-3188. FAX: 918-647-8198. URL: http://www.poteaudailynews.com. Mailing Address: PO Box 1237, Poteau, OK 74953. Year Established: 1895. Pub. Frequency: d. (Tue.-Sat.) Page Size: broadsheet. Subscrip. Rate: $.50 newsstand/cover; $1 newsstand/cover Sat.; $72/yr home delivery in city & mailed in cy.; $108/yr out of county. **Wire Service(s):** AP. Circulation: 5,000 morning (paid). **Owner(s):** Horizon Publications, Inc., 1120 N. Carbon St, Ste 100, Marion, IL 62959. **Management:** Samantha Hess, Publisher. Martha McClure, Circulation Manager. **Editorial:** Laura Young, Editor.

PRYOR

DAILY TIMES (PRYOR), THE. 105 South Adair, Pryor, OK 74361. Telephone: 918-825-3292. FAX: 918-825-1965. URL: http://www.pryordailytimes.com. Mailing Address: PO Box 308, Pryor, OK 74362. Pub. Frequency: d. Page Size: broadsheet. Subscrip. Rate: $.50 newsstand/cover; $1 newsstand/cover Sun.; $90 carrier delivery Sun. in county; $176 mailed Sun. in county. Circulation: 3,500 per issue (paid). **Owner(s):** Community Newspaper Holdings, Inc., 3500 Colonnade Pkwy., Ste. 600, Birmingham, AL 35243. **Management:** Amy Johns, Publisher. Vickie Willyard, Circulation Manager. **Editorial:** Kathy Parker, Managing Editor.

SAPULPA

SAPULPA DAILY HERALD, THE. 16 S. Park St, Sapulpa, OK 74067. Telephone: 918-224-5185. FAX: 918-224-5196. E-MAIL: sdheditor@sbcglobal.net. URL: http://www.sapulpaheraldonline.com. Mailing Address: PO Box 1370, Sapulpa, OK 74067-1370. Year Established: 1914. Pub. Frequency: d. (Sun.-Fri.) Page Size: broadsheet. Subscrip. Rate: $.50 newsstand/cover; $.50 newsstand/cover Sun.; $102/yr carrier delivery; $165/yr mailed. **Wire Service(s):** AP. Circulation: 5,475 evening (paid); 6,000 Sunday (paid). **Owner(s):** Sumner Newspaper Inc., See address and contact information above. **Management:** Darren Sumner, Publisher. Cindy Leslie, Advertising Manager. Diane Raper, Circulation Manager. **Editorial:** Brenda Shance, Editor. Ben Johnson, Sports.

SEMINOLE

SEMINOLE PRODUCER. 121 N. Main St., Seminole, OK 74868. Telephone: 405-382-1100. FAX: 405-382-1104. E-MAIL: producer@brightok.net. URL: http://www.seminoleproducer.com. Mailing Address: PO Box 431, Seminole, OK 74818-0431. Year Established: 1927. Pub. Frequency: d. (Tue.-Fri. & Sun.) Page Size: broadsheet. Subscrip. Rate: $.35 newsstand/cover; $.75 newsstand/cover Sun.; $6 home delivery/mo.. Circulation: 5,400 evening (paid); 5,400 Sunday (paid). **Owner(s):** Seminole Producer, Inc., See address and contact information above. **Management:** Ted Phillips, Publisher. Jim Keisman, Advertising Manager. John Lewis, Circulation Manager. Stuart Phillips, Associate Publisher. Shirlene Coffer, Business Manager. **Editorial:** Karen Anson, Managing Editor. John Lewis, Production Manager. Karen Anson, News Editor.

SHAWNEE

SHAWNEE NEWS-STAR, THE. 215 N. Bell, Shawnee, OK 74801. Telephone: 405-273-4200. FAX: 405-273-4207. URL: http://www.news-star.com. Mailing Address: PO Box 1688, Shawnee, OK 74802-1688. Year Established: 1902. Pub. Frequency: d. (Tue.-Sun.) Page Size: broadsheet. Subscrip. Rate: $.50 newsstand/cover; $1 newsstand/cover Sun.; $113/yr carrier delivery in city; $121/yr motor route; $132/yr mailed in state. Adv. Rate: col. inch $8.40 **Wire Service(s):** AP. Circulation: 9,805 morning (paid); 10,889 Sunday (paid). **Owner(s):** Morris Multimedia, Inc., PO Box 936, Augusta, GA 30903-0936. Telephone: 706-724-0851. **Management:** Peter Esser, Publisher. Sherry Lankford, Advertising Director. Don Poe, Circulation Director. Tammy Lee, Classified Adv. Mgr.. **Editorial:** Mike McCormick, Executive Editor. Karen Green, Managing Editor. April Wilkerson, Entertainment Editor. Ed Blochowiak, Photographer. Fred Fehr, Sports.

STILLWATER

STILLWATER NEWSPRESS. 211 W. Ninth St., Stillwater, OK 74074. Telephone: 405-372-5000. FAX: 405-372-3112. E-MAIL: ads@stwnewspress.com. URL: http://www.stwnewspress.com. Mailing Address: PO Box 2288, Stillwater, OK 74076. Year Established: 1940. Pub. Frequency: d. Page Size: broadsheet. Subscrip. Rate: $.50 newsstand/cover; $1 newsstand/cover Sun.; $97/yr carrier delivery in county; $111.60/yr mailed in county; $142.80/yr mailed in state. **Wire Service(s):** AP, MCT. Circulation: 9,500 evening (paid); 10,300 Sunday (paid). **Owner(s):** Community Newspaper Holdings, Inc., 3500 Colonnade Pkwy., Ste. 600, Birmingham, AL 35243. Telephone: 205-298-7100. FAX: 205-298-7101. **Management:** Mike Kellogg, Publisher. Jill Hunt, Advertising Manager. Mary Ann Driskel, Circulation Manager. Shelley Dryden, Classified Adv. Mgr.. **Editorial:** Rick Hoover, Editor. Dale Homes, Business Editor. Laura Wilson, Lifestyle Editor. Roger Moore, Sports Editor.

TAHLEQUAH

TAHLEQUAH DAILY PRESS. 106 W. Second St., Tahlequah, OK 74464. Telephone: 918-456-8833. FAX: 918-456-2019. E-MAIL: pressadvertising@intellex.com. URL: http://www.tahlequahdailypress.com. Mailing Address: PO Box 888, Tahlequah, OK 74465. Year Established: 1850. Pub. Frequency: d. (Tue.-Fri. & Sun.) Page Size: broadsheet. Subscrip. Rate: $.50 newsstand/cover; $1 newsstand/cover Sun.; $84/yr carrier delivery in area; $94.40/yr mailed in county; $150/yr mailed in state. Circulation: 7,500 evening (paid); 8,000 Sunday (paid). **Owner(s):** Community Newspaper Holdings, Inc., 3500 Colonnade Pkwy., Ste. 600, Birmingham, AL 35243. Telephone: 205-298-7100. FAX: 205-298-7101. **Management:** Pam Hutson, Publisher. Tom Dunavin, Circulation Manager. Barbara Fritts, Business Manager. **Editorial:** Kim Poindexter, Managing Editor.

TULSA

TULSA WORLD. ISSN 8750-5959
318 Main Mall, Tulsa, OK 74103. Telephone: 918-581-8400. FAX: 918-581-8353. E-MAIL: tulsaworld@tulsaworld.com. URL: http://www.tulsaworld.com. Mailing Address: PO Box 1770, Tulsa, OK 74102. Year Established: 1905. Pub. Frequency: d. Page Size: broadsheet. Subscrip. Rate: $.50 newsstand/cover; $1.50 newsstand/cover Sun.; $17 home delivery/mo.; $192.80/yr home delivery. **Wire Service(s):** AP, NYT, LAT-WAT, MCT, GNS. Circulation: 142,000 morning (paid); 203,000 Sunday (paid). **Owner(s):** World Publishing Co., See address and contact information above. **Management:** Robert E. Lorton, Publisher. Tom Morrison, Advertising Manager. Bill King, Circulation Director. Bates Frayser, Classified Adv. Mgr.. **Editorial:** Joe Worley, Executive Editor. Susan Ellerbach, Managing Editor. Wayne Greene, City Editor. Cathy Logan, Entertainment Editor. John Klein, Sports Editor. Debbie Jackson, Sunday Editor.

VINITA

VINITA DAILY JOURNAL. 138 S Wilson, Vinita, OK 74301. Telephone: 918-256-6422. FAX: 918-256-7100. E-MAIL: vdjnews@cableone.net. Mailing Address: PO Box 328, Vinita, OK 74301. Year Established: 1907. Pub. Frequency: d. (Mon.-Fri.) Page Size: broadsheet. Subscrip. Rate: $.50 newsstand/cover; $8.70/mo. in city; $36.75 in city for 3 mos.. **Wire Service(s):** UPI. Circulation: 4,475 evening (paid). **Owner(s):** Vinita Printing Co., Inc., See address and contact information above. **Management:** John Link, General Manager. Janet Link, Advertising. Freddie Montana, Circulation Manager. **Editorial:** David Burgess, Managing Editor. Brenda Haskell, Lifestyle Editor. David Johnson, Sports Editor.

WEATHERFORD

WEATHERFORD DAILY NEWS. PO Box 191, Weatherford, OK 73096. Telephone: 580-772-3301. FAX: 580-772-7329. E-MAIL: wdn@wdnonline.com. URL: http://www.wdnonline.com. Year Established: 1889. Pub. Frequency: d. (Tue.-Sat.) Page Size: broadsheet. Subscrip. Rate: $.50 newsstand/cover; $68/yr mailed in county; $70/yr mailed out of county. Freelance Pay: $0.25/column-inch. **Wire Service(s):** AP. Circulation: 5,400 evening (paid and free); 5,600 Sunday (paid and free). **Owner(s):** Weatherford News, Inc., See address and contact information above. **Management:** Philip Reid, President. Brenda Johnson, Advertising Manager. Philip Reid, Business Manager. **Editorial:** Larry Gittings, Managing Editor. James Resneder, Production Manager. Beth Roach, Circulation Editor.

WOODWARD

WOODWARD NEWS. ISSN 0883-8755
904 Oklahoma Ave., Woodward, OK 73801. Telephone: 580-256-2200. FAX: 580-254-2159. E-MAIL: adman@woodwardnews.net. URL: http://www.woodwardnews.net. Mailing Address: PO Box 928, Woodward, OK 73802. Year Established: 1983. Pub. Frequency: d. (Tue.-Sun.) Page Size: broadsheet. Subscrip. Rate: $.50 newsstand/cover; $1 newsstand/cover Sun.; $92/yr carrier delivery in area; $109/yr mailed in county; $115.50/yr mailed in state. **Wire Service(s):** AP. Circulation: 6,500 evening (paid); 6,500 Sunday (paid). **Owner(s):** Community Newspaper Holdings, Inc., 3500 Colonnade Pkwy., Ste. 600, Birmingham, AL 35243. Telephone: 205-298-7100. FAX: 205-298-7101. **Management:** Robbie Davis, Publisher. Lettie Laakman, Office Manager. Sheila Gay, Advertising Manager. Lettie Laakman, Business Manager. **Editorial:** John McMahan, Editor.

OREGON

ALBANY

ALBANY DEMOCRAT-HERALD. 600 Lyon St., S.W., Albany, OR 97321. Telephone: 541-926-2211. FAX: 541-926-5298. E-MAIL: albanydh@proqxis.com. URL: http://www.mvonline.com. Mailing Address: PO Box 130, Albany, OR 97321-0041. Year Established: 1865. Pub. Frequency: d. Page Size: broadsheet. Subscrip. Rate: $.50 newsstand/cover; $1.25 newsstand/cover Sun.; $36 carrier delivery for 13 wks.; $137/yr carrier delivery. Adv. Rate: col. inch $14.51 **Wire Service(s):** AP. Circulation: 21,745 evening (paid); 20,000 Sunday (paid). **Owner(s):** Lee Enterprises, Inc., 201 N. Harrison St., Ste. 600, Davenport, IA 52801-1924. **Management:** Martha Wells, Publisher. Judie Weissert, Advertising Manager. Cody Castellano, Circulation Manager. **Editorial:** Graham Kislingbury, Managing Editor. Hasso Hering, Book Review Editor. Bennett Hall, Business Editor. Mike Henneke, News Editor. Mark Ylen, Photo. Steve Lundeberg, Sports Editor.

ASHLAND

ASHLAND DAILY TIDINGS. 1661 Siskiyou Blvd., Ashland, OR 97520. Telephone: 541-482-3456. FAX: 541-482-3688. E-MAIL: lberteau@dailytidings.com. URL: http://www.dailytidings.com. Year Established: 1876. Pub. Frequency: d. (Mon.-Sat.) Page Size: broadsheet. Subscrip. Rate: $.50 newsstand/cover; $108/yr carrier delivery; $141.60/yr mailed in county; $195.60/yr mailed out of county. Adv. Rate: col. inch $16.03 **Wire Service(s):** AP. Circulation: 6,000 evening (paid). **Owner(s):** Ottaway Newspapers, Inc., PO Box 401, Campbell Hall, NY 10916. Telephone: 845-294-8181. **Management:** Grady Singletary, Publisher. Krystal Jordan, Advertising. John Mihalyo, Circulation Director. **Editorial:** Andrew Scot Bolsinger, Editor. Myles Murphy, City Editor.

Dailies

ASTORIA

DAILY ASTORIAN, THE. ISSN 0739-5078
949 Exchange St., Astoria, OR 97103. Telephone: 503-325-3211. FAX: 503-325-6573. E-MAIL: astorian@dailyastorian.com. URL: http://www.dailyastorian.com. Mailing Address: PO Box 210, Astoria, OR 97103. Year Established: 1873. Pub. Frequency: d. (Mon.-Fri.) Page Size: broadsheet. Subscrip. Rate: $.50 newsstand/cover; $10 carrier delivery/mo.; $99/yr carrier delivery in county; $99/yr mailed out of county. **Wire Service(s):** AP. Circulation: 9,000 evening (paid). **Owner(s):** East Oregonian Publishing Co., P.O. Box 1089, Pendleton, OR 97801. Telephone: 541-966-0800. **Management:** Debbie Schendel, General Manager. Steve Forrester, Publisher. Betty Smith, Advertising Manager. **Editorial:** Steve Forrester, Editor. Patrick Webb, Managing Editor. Samantha McLaren, Circulation Editor. Laurie Assa, Photographer. Gary Henley, Sports Editor.

BAKER CITY

BAKER CITY HERALD. 1915 First St., Baker City, OR 97814-0807. Telephone: 541-523-3673. FAX: 541-523-6426. E-MAIL: bcherald@triax.com. URL: http://www.bakercityherald.com. Mailing Address: PO Box 807, Baker City, OR 97814-0807. Year Established: 1870. Pub. Frequency: d. (Mon.-Fri.) Page Size: standard. Subscrip. Rate: $.50 newsstand/cover; $93/yr carrier delivery; $96/yr motor route domestic; $138/yr mailed. Adv. Rate: col. inch $1 Freelance Pay: $1/column-inch. **Wire Service(s):** AP. Circulation: 3,680 evening (paid). **Owner(s):** Western Communication, Inc., 1777 S.W. Chandler Ave., Bend, OR 97702. Telephone: 541-382-1811. FAX: 541-383-0372. **Management:** Kari Borgen, Publisher. Jim Sherman, Circulation Manager. **Editorial:** Mark Furman, Editor. Gerry Steele, Business Editor.

BEND

BULLETIN (BEND), THE. 1777 S.W. Chandler Ave., Bend, OR 97702. Telephone: 541-382-1811. FAX: 541-385-5804. E-MAIL: bulletin@bendbulletin.com. URL: http://www.bendbulletin.com. Mailing Address: PO Box 6020, Bend, OR 97708-6020. Year Established: 1903. Pub. Frequency: d. Page Size: standard. Subscrip. Rate: $.35 newsstand/cover; $.50 Sat.; $1.25 Sun.; $10.50 carrier delivery/mo.; $126/yr; $15.50 mailed/mo. $186/yr. Freelance Pay: $1/column-inch. **Wire Service(s):** AP, NYT, LAT-WAT, MCT. Circulation: 30,000 morning (paid). **Owner(s):** Western Communication, Inc., See address and contact information above. **Bureau(s):** Capitol Press, Rm. 43, Salem, OR 97310. Telephone: 503-566-2839. FAX: 503-566-2842. **Management:** Gordon Black, Publisher. Debbie Pattenburg, Advertising Director. Julie Story, Classified Adv. Mgr.. **Editorial:** John Costa, Editor-in-Chief. Tim Doran, Managing Editor. John Stearns, Business Editor. Richard Coe, City Editor. Erik Lukens, Editorial Page Editor. Denise Costa, Entertainment Editor. Dean Guernsey, Photo Editor. Bill Bigelow, Sports Editor.

COOS BAY

WORLD (COOS BAY), THE. ISSN 1062-8495
350 Commercial St., Coos Bay, OR 97420. Telephone: 541-269-1222. FAX: 541-267-0294. URL: http://www.theworldlink.com/. Mailing Address: P.O. Box 1840, Coos Bay, OR 97420. Year Established: 1878. Pub. Frequency: d. (Mon.-Sat.) Subscrip. Rate: $.50 newsstand/cover; $1.25 newsstand/cover Sat.; $168/yr carrier delivery local. Adv. Rate: col. inch $18.95 **Wire Service(s):** AP. Circulation: 8,000 per issue (paid). **Owner(s):** Southwestern Oregon Publishing Co., See address and contact information above. **Management:** Greg Stevens, Publisher. Bob Reitz, Advertising Director. Albert Glick, Circulation Manager. Peggy Roberson, Classified Adv. Mgr.. **Editorial:** Kathy Erickson, Editor. Elise Hamner, City Editor. John Gunther, Sports Editor.

CORVALLIS

CORVALLIS GAZETTE-TIMES. ISSN 0746-3995
600 Jefferson St., SW, Corvallis, OR 97333. Telephone: 541-753-2641. FAX: 541-758-9505. E-MAIL: gtnews@gtconnect.com. URL: http://www.gazettetimes.com. Mailing Address: PO Box 368, Corvallis, OR 97339. Year Established: 1862. Pub. Frequency: d. Page Size: broadsheet. Subscrip. Rate: $.50 newsstand/cover; $1.25 newsstand/cover Sun.; $36 home delivery for 13 wks.; $139.95/yr home delivery. Freelance Pay: $10-$50/article. **Wire Service(s):** AP, LAT-WAT, MCT. Circulation: 14,000 morning (paid); 25,000 Sunday (paid). **Owner(s):** Lee Enterprises, Inc., 201 N. Harrison St, Ste 600, Davenport, IA 52801-1924. **Management:** Brenda Speth, Publisher. Cody Castellano, Circulation Manager. Kathy Turgeon, Classified Adv. Mgr.. **Editorial:** Rob Priewe, Managing Editor. Bennett Hall, Business Editor. Theresa Novak, Editorial Page Editor. Steve Gress, Sports Editor.

EUGENE

REGISTER-GUARD, THE. ISSN 0739-8557
3500 Chad Dr., Eugene, OR 97408. Telephone: 541-485-1234. FAX: 541-984-4699. E-MAIL: altonbaker@guardnet.com. URL: http://www.registerguard.com. Mailing Address: PO Box 10188, Eugene, OR 97440-2188. Year Established: 1867. Pub. Frequency: d. Page Size: broadsheet. Subscrip. Rate: $.50 newsstand/cover; $1.25 newsstand/cover Sun.; $11.50 home delivery/mo.. **Wire Service(s):** AP, NYT, LAT-WAT. Circulation: 75,120 morning (paid); 78,510 Sunday (paid). **Owner(s):** Guard Publishing Co., See address and contact information above. **Management:** R. Fletcher Little, General Manager. Alton F. Baker III, Publisher. Michael Raz, Advertising Director. Chuck Downing, Circulation Manager. Kelly Gant, Classified Adv. Mgr.. **Editorial:** Alton F. Baker III, Editor. Dave Baker, Managing Editor. Jackman Wilson, Editorial Page Editor. Mark Johnson, Feature Editor. Chris Frisella, News Editor. Ron Bellamy, Sports Editor.

GRANTS PASS

GRANTS PASS DAILY COURIER. 409 SE Seventh St, Grants Pass, OR 97526. Telephone: 541-474-3700. FAX: 541-474-3824. E-MAIL: courier@thedailycourier.com. URL: http://www.thedailycourier.com. Mailing Address: PO Box 1468, Grants Pass, OR 97528. Year Established: 1885. Pub. Frequency: d. (Mon.-Sat.) Page Size: broadsheet. Subscrip. Rate: $.50 newsstand/cover; $12 home delivery/mo.; $15 mailed/mo. in county. Adv. Rate: col. inch $10.32 **Wire Service(s):** AP. Circulation: 18,000 morning (paid). **Owner(s):** Courier Publishing Co., See address and contact information above. **Management:** Dennis Mack, Publisher. Gene Napler, Advertising Manager. Dean Rich, Circulation Director. Debbie Thomas, Classified Adv. Mgr.. **Editorial:** Dennis Roler, Editor. Edith Decker, Feature Editor. Jim Mitchell, News Editor.

KLAMATH FALLS

HERALD & NEWS. 1301 Esplanade, Klamath Falls, OR 97601. Telephone: 541-885-4410. FAX: 541-883-4007. E-MAIL: heraldandnews@heraldandnews.com. URL: http://www.heraldandnews.com. Mailing Address: PO Box 788, Klamath Falls, OR 97601. Year Established: 1906. Pub. Frequency: d. (Sun.-Fri.) Page Size: broadsheet. Subscrip. Rate: $.50 newsstand/cover; $1 newsstand/cover Sun.; $10.50 home delivery/mo. in city; $12.25 mailed/mo. in Klamath & Lake cys; $13 mailed/mo. in Modoc & Siskiyou cys.. **Wire Service(s):** AP. Circulation: 18,337 evening (paid); 18,885 Sunday (paid). **Owner(s):** Pioneer Newspapers, Inc., 221 First Ave., W., Ste. 405, Seattle, WA 98119. Telephone: 206-284-4424. **Management:** Heidi Wright, Publisher. Lucille Wagner, Advertising. Michelle Rockwell, Circulation Manager. **Editorial:** Steve Miller, Editor. Gerald Baksys, Business Editor. Marica McGonigle, City Editor. Steve Matthies, Sports Editor.

LA GRANDE

OBSERVER (LA GRANDE), THE. 1406 Fifth St., La Grande, OR 97850. Telephone: 541-963-3161. FAX: 541-963-7804. URL: http://www.lagrandeobserver.com. Mailing Address: PO Box 3170, La Grande, OR 97850. Year Established: 1896. Pub. Frequency: d. (Mon.-Sat.) Page Size: broadsheet. Subscrip. Rate: $.50 newsstand/cover; $8.50 carrier delivery/mo.; $9.50 motor route/mo.; $15 mailed/mo.. Freelance Pay: $1.50/column-inch. **Wire Service(s):** AP. Circulation: 7,000 evening (paid). **Owner(s):** Western Communication, Inc., 1777 S.W. Chandler Ave., Bend, OR 97702. Telephone: 541-382-1811. FAX: 541-383-0372. **Management:** Mike Waltman, General Manager. Ted Kramer, Publisher. Mona Tuck, Office Manager. Mike Waltman, Advertising Director. Steve DeVore, Circulation Director. Frank Everidge, Production Director. **Editorial:** Ted Kramer, Editor.

MEDFORD

MAIL TRIBUNE. 111 N. Fir St., Medford, OR 97501-0229. Telephone: 541-776-4411. FAX: 541-776-4376. E-MAIL: news@mailtribune.com. URL: http://www.mailtribune.com. Mailing Address: PO Box 1108, Medford, OR 97501. Year Established: 1906. Pub. Frequency: d. Page Size: broadsheet. Subscrip. Rate: $.75 newsstand/cover; $1.50 newsstand/cover Sun.; $158/yr home delivery local. **Wire Service(s):** AP, LAT-WAT. Circulation: 29,000 morning (paid); 33,000 Sunday (paid). **Owner(s):** Ottaway Newspapers, Inc., PO Box 401, Campbell Hall, NY 10916. Telephone: 845-294-8181. **Management:** Grady Singletary, Publisher. Tim Tergeolou, Advertising Manager. John Mihalyo, Circulation Director. Susie Wenaus, Classified Adv. Mgr.. Dena DeRose, Sales Manager. **Editorial:** Robert Hunter, Editor. Cathy Noah, City Editor. Rob Galvin, News Editor. Tim Trower, Sports.

ONTARIO

ARGUS OBSERVER. 1160 S.W. Fourth St., Ontario, OR 97914-0130. Telephone: 541-889-5387. FAX: 541-889-3347. E-MAIL: ads@argusobserver.com. URL: http://www.argusobserver.com. Mailing Address: PO Box 130, Ontario, OR 97914-0130. Year Established: 1897. Pub. Frequency: d. (Sun.-Fri.) Page Size: broadsheet. Subscrip. Rate: $.50 newsstand/cover; $1.25 newsstand/cover Sun.; $9 home delivery/mo. local; $112/yr home delivery local; $149.76/yr mailed in county & adj. cys.. Adv. Rate: col. inch $11.40 **Wire Service(s):** AP. Circulation: 7,500 evening (paid); 8,500 Sunday (paid). **Owner(s):** Wick Communications, Inc., 333 W. Wilcox Dr., Ste. 302, Sierra Vista, AZ 85635. Telephone: 520-458-0200. **Management:** Steve Krehl, Publisher. John Dillon, Advertising Director. Andy Shimojima, Advertising Manager. Tom Hooton, Circulation Manager. **Editorial:** Pat Caldwell, Editor. Casey Keller, Lifestyle Editor. Andrew Cutler, Sports Editor.

PENDLETON

EAST OREGONIAN, THE. 211 S. E. Byers, Pendleton, OR 97801. Telephone: 541-276-2211. FAX: 541-278-2688. URL: http://www.eastoregonian.com. Mailing Address: P.O. Box 1089, Pendleton, OR 97801-1089. Year Established: 1875. Pub. Frequency: d. Page Size: standard. Subscrip. Rate: $.50 newsstand/cover; $1 newsstand/cover Sun.; $125.50/yr carrier delivery local; $138/yr out of area. **Wire Service(s):** AP. Circulation: 9,100 Sunday (paid); 9,100 evening (paid). **Owner(s):** East Oregonian Publishing Co., 1089 Pendleton, Astoria, OR 97801. Telephone: 503-276-2211. **Management:** Wendy DalPez, General Manager. Steve Forrester, President. George Murdock, Publisher. Yolanda Lennon, Advertising Manager. Deb Sampson, Circulation Manager. **Editorial:** Steve Brown, Managing Editor. Ivy Murrell, Sports Editor.

PORTLAND

OREGONIAN, THE. ISSN 8750-1317
1320 S.W. Broadway, Portland, OR 97201. Telephone: 503-221-8327. FAX: 503-294-4193. E-MAIL: letters@news.oregonian.com. URL: http://www.oregonlive.com. Year Established: 1850. Pub. Frequency: d. Page Size: broadsheet. Subscrip. Rate: $.35 newsstand/cover; $1.50 newsstand/cover Sun.; $156/yr local. **Wire Service(s):** AP, NYT, LAT-WAT, CNS. Circulation: 436,003 morning (paid); 411,759 Sunday (paid). **Owner(s):** Advance Publications, Inc., See address and contact information above. **Management:** Patrick Stickel, President. Fred A. Stickel, Publisher. John Mannix, Advertising Director. Kevin Denny, Circulation Director. Ed Merrick, Classified Adv. Mgr.. **Editorial:** Sandra Rowe, Editor. Peter Bhatia, Executive Editor. Mark Hester, Business Editor. Jack Ohman, Cartoonist. Jonathan Nicholas, Columnist. Robert J. Caldwell, Editorial Page Editor. Grant Butler, Entertainment Editor. Jolene Krawczak, Feature Editor. John Harvey, Government Affrs. Ed.. Dennis Peck, Sports Editor. Sue Hobart, Travel Editor.

ROSEBURG

NEWS-REVIEW (ROSEBURG), THE. 345 N.E. Winchester, Roseburg, OR 97470. Telephone: 541-672-3321. FAX: 541-957-4270. E-MAIL: newsdesk@nrtoday.com. URL: http://www.nrtoday.com. Mailing Address: PO Box 1248, Roseburg, OR 97470. Year Established: 1867. Pub. Frequency: d. (Sun.-Fri.) Page Size: standard. Subscrip. Rate: $.50 newsstand/cover; $1 newsstand/cover Sun.; $119.95/yr home delivery local; $156/yr mailed in county; $199/yr mailed out of county. **Wire Service(s):** AP. Circulation: 20,000 evening (paid); 22,000 Sunday (paid). **Owner(s):** Swift Newspapers, Inc., 500 Double Eagle Ct., Reno, NV 89511. Telephone: 775-850-7676. **Management:** Mark Raymond, Publisher. Pat Bridges, Advertising Director. Robert Franks, Circulation Manager. Alsy Brinkmeyer, Classified Adv. Mgr.. Sam Hollenbeck, Business Manager. **Editorial:** Vicki Menard, Editor. Mark Adams, City Editor. Craig Reed, Feature Editor. Tom Eggers, Sports Editor.

SALEM

STATESMAN JOURNAL. ISSN 0739-5507
280 Church St., N.E., Salem, OR 97301. Telephone: 503-399-6611. FAX: 503-399-6706. E-MAIL: dhughes@statesmanjournal.com. URL: http://www.statesmanjournal.com. Mailing Address: PO Box 13009, Salem, OR 97309. Year Established: 1851. Pub. Frequency: d. Page Size: broadsheet. Subscrip. Rate: $.50 newsstand/cover; $1.50 newsstand/cover Sun.; $13.95 carrier delivery/mo. local; $13.50 motor route/mo.. **Wire Service(s):** AP, LAT-WAT, GNS. Circulation: 61,000 morning (paid); 69,201 Sunday (paid). **Owner(s):** Gannett Company, Inc., 7950 Jones Branch Dr, McLean, VA 22107. Telephone: 703-854-6000. **Management:** Sonja Sorenson Craig, President. Teresa M. Keplinger, Advertising Manager. Susan Rovegno, Circulation Director. Michael Keith, Marketing Director. Diane Stevenson, Photography Director. **Editorial:** David Risser, Executive Editor. Don Currie, Business Editor. Dick Hughes, Editorial Page Editor. Barbara Curtin, Opinion Editor. James Day, Sports Editor.

THE DALLES

THE DALLES CHRONICLE. ISSN 0747-3443
414 Federal St., The Dalles, OR 97058. Telephone: 541-296-2141. FAX: 541-298-1365. URL: http://www.thedalleschronicle.com. Mailing Address: PO Box 1910, The Dalles, OR 97058. Year Established: 1890. Pub. Frequency: d. (Sun.-Fri.) Page Size: broadsheet. Subscrip. Rate: $.50 newsstand/cover; $90/yr carrier delivery in city; $101/yr motor route; $110/yr mailed. **Wire Service(s):** AP. Circulation: 5,800 evening (paid); 5,800 Sunday (paid). **Owner(s):** Eagle Newspapers, Inc., 4901 Indian School Rd, NE, Salem, OR 97309. Telephone: 503-393-1774. **Management:** Marilyn Roth, Publisher. Ray Swift, Advertising Manager. Jose Almazan, Circulation Manager. Virginia Delco, Classified Adv. Mgr.. **Editorial:** Kathy Gray, Managing Editor.

PENNSYLVANIA

ALLENTOWN

MORNING CALL, THE. ISSN 0884-5557
101 N. Sixth St., Allentown, PA 18101. Telephone: 610-820-6500. FAX: 610-820-6175. URL: http://www.mcall.com. Mailing Address: PO Box 1260, Allentown, PA 18105. Year Established: 1883. Pub. Frequency: d. Page Size: broadsheet. Subscrip. Rate: $.50 newsstand/cover; $1.75 Sun.; $4/wk.; $221/yr. **Wire Service(s):** AP, NYT, LAT-WAT, MCT. Circulation: 120,912 morning (paid); 164,723 Sunday (paid). **Owner(s):** Tribune Company, 435 N Michigan Ave, Chicago, IL 60601. Telephone: 312.222.9100. **Bureau(s):** 400 N. Hampton, Easton, PA 18042. Telephone: 610-258-5580. FAX: 610-258-1749. Contact: Robert Orenstein, Editor. **Management:** Susan Hunt, Publisher. Linda McDonald, Circulation Director. **Editorial:** David Erdman, Managing Editor. Mike Miorelli, Metro Editor. Glen Kranzley, Opinion Editor. Naomi Halperin, Photo Editor. Terry Larimer, Sports Editor.

ALTOONA

ALTOONA MIRROR. 301 Cayuga Ave., Altoona, PA 16602. Telephone: 814-946-7411. FAX: 814-946-7547. E-MAIL: altmirror@aol.com. Mailing Address: PO Box 2008, Altoona, PA 16603. Year Established: 1874. Pub. Frequency: d. Page Size: broadsheet. Subscrip. Rate: $.50 newsstand/cover; $1.50 newsstand/cover Sun.; $48.50/yr home delivery. **Wire Service(s):** AP. Circulation: 32,606 morning (paid); 39,577 Sunday (paid). **Owner(s):** Ogden Newspapers of Minnesota, Inc., 1500 Main St., Wheeling, WV 26003. Telephone: 304-233-0100. FAX: 304-233-0327. **Management:** Ray Eckenrode, General Manager. Ed Kruger, Publisher. Jamie Powers, Advertising Director. Dan Slep, Circulation Director. **Editorial:** Pete Banko, Managing Editor.

BEAVER

BEAVER COUNTY TIMES. 400 Fair Ave., Beaver, PA 15009. Telephone: 724-775-3200. FAX: 724-775-4180. E-MAIL: kbriscoe@timesonline.com. URL: http://www.timesonline.com. Mailing Address: PO Box 400, Beaver, PA 15009. Year Established: 1876. Pub. Frequency: d. Page Size: broadsheet. Subscrip. Rate: $.50 newsstand/cover; $1.50 newsstand/cover Sun.; $3.25 home delivery/wk. & motor rte. **Wire Service(s):** AP, MCT. Circulation: 43,000 morning (paid); 51,000 Sunday (paid). **Owner(s):** Calkins Media Inc., Rte. 13, Levittown, PA 19058. Telephone: 215-949-4000. **Management:** Alan Buncher, Publisher. Bob Woelfel, Advertising Director. Larry Boggs, Circulation Manager. **Editorial:** Keith Briscoe, Executive Editor. Tom Bickert, Managing Editor. Robert A. Uhriniak, Editorial Page Editor. Laura Rauch, Feature Editor.

BEDFORD

BEDFORD GAZETTE/GAZETTE SUNDAY. ISSN 0744-8457
424 W. Penn St., Bedford, PA 15522. Telephone: 814-623-1151. FAX: 814-623-5055. URL: http://www.bedfordgazette.com. Mailing Address: PO Box 671, Bedford, PA 15522-0671. Year Established: 1805. Pub. Frequency: d. Page Size: broadsheet. Subscrip. Rate: $.50 newsstand/cover; $118.50/yr home delivery. **Wire Service(s):** AP. Circulation: 10,400 morning (paid); 19,100 Sunday (paid). **Owner(s):** Bedford Gazette LLC, See address and contact information above. **Management:** Joseph Beegle, Publisher. Barbara Diehl, Circulation Manager. **Editorial:** Vicki Henry, Feature Editor. Chris Wechtenhiser, Sports Editor.

BLOOMSBURG

PRESS ENTERPRISE. ISSN 0746-0724
3185 Lackawanna Ave., Bloomsburg, PA 17815. Telephone: 570-784-2121. FAX: 570-784-9226. E-MAIL: news@pressenterprise.com. URL: http://www.pressenterpriseonline.com. Year Established: 1902. Pub. Frequency: d. Page Size: broadsheet. Subscrip. Rate: $.50 newsstand/cover; $1 newsstand/cover Sat.-Sun.; $127.95/yr carrier delivery; $189/yr mailed. **Wire Service(s):** AP, MCT. Circulation: 22,000 morning (paid); 22,000 Sunday (paid). **Owner(s):** Press Enterprise, Inc., See address and contact information above. **Management:** Paul R. Eyerly IV, President. Brandon Eyerly, Publisher. Sandy Bower, Advertising Manager. Don Whitmire, Circulation Manager. **Editorial:** Jim Sachetti, Editor. Dean Kashner, Managing Editor. Patricia Boggs, Lifestyle Editor. Dean Kashner, News Editor. Bill Hughes, Photo Editor. Mathew Traub, Sports.

BRADFORD

BRADFORD ERA, THE. 43 Main St., Bradford, PA 16701. Telephone: 814-368-3173. FAX: 814-362-6510. E-MAIL: martyw@bradfordera.com. URL: http://www.bradfordera.com. Year Established: 1877. Pub. Frequency: d. (Mon.-Sat.) Page Size: broadsheet. Subscrip. Rate: $.50 newsstand/cover; $14 carrier delivery/mo.; $159.50/yr carrier delivery; $14.50 motor route/mo.; $186/yr motor route. **Wire Service(s):** AP. Circulation: 10,400 morning (paid). **Owner(s):** Bradford Publishing Co., See address and contact information above. **Management:** John H. Satterwhite, Publisher. Richard C. Kautz, Circulation Manager. **Editorial:** John H. Satterwhite, Editor. Marty Wilder, Managing Editor. Sandra Rhodes, City Editor.

BUTLER

BUTLER EAGLE. ISSN 0744-401X
114 W. Diamond St., Butler, PA 16001. Telephone: 724-282-8000. FAX: 724-282-4180. URL: http://www.butlereagle.com. Mailing Address: PO Box 271, Butler, PA 16003. Year Established: 1869. Pub. Frequency: d. (Sun.-Fri.) Page Size: broadsheet. Subscrip. Rate: $.50 newsstand/cover; $.75 newsstand/cover Sun.; $107.80/yr local. Freelance Pay: $10-$30/article. **Wire Service(s):** AP, NYT. Circulation: 31,032 evening (paid); 32,500 Sunday (paid). **Owner(s):** Eagle Printing Co., See address and contact information above. **Management:** Vernon L. Wise Jr., Publisher. Mace Pavelek, Advertising Director. Richard Brest, Circulation Director. Jay McKain, Classified Adv. Mgr.. **Editorial:** Mark Mann, Managing Editor. John Enrietto, Sports Editor.

CARLISLE

CARLISLE SENTINEL. 457 E. North St., Carlisle, PA 17013. Telephone: 717-243-2611. FAX: 717-243-3121. E-MAIL: wpowell@cumberlink.com. URL: http://www.cumberlink.com. Mailing Address: PO Box 130, Carlisle, PA 17013. Year Established: 1861. Pub. Frequency: d. Page Size: broadsheet. Subscrip. Rate: $.50 newsstand/cover; $1 newsstand/cover Sun.; $150/yr home delivery local. **Wire Service(s):** AP. Circulation: 16,700 evening (paid); 17,000 Sunday (paid). **Owner(s):** Lee Enterprises, Inc., 201 N. Harrison St, Ste 600, Davenport, IA 52801-1924. **Management:** Mark Blum, Publisher. Ken Knepper, Advertising Manager. Tammy Shoemaker, Classified Adv. Mgr.. **Editorial:** Hope Stephan, Executive Editor. Steve Morelli, News Editor.

CHAMBERSBURG

PUBLIC OPINION, THE. 77 N Third St, Chambersburg, PA 17201. Telephone: 717-264-6161. FAX: 717-264-0377. E-MAIL: bbennett@chambers.gannett.com. URL: http://www.publicopiniononline.com. Year Established: 1869. Pub. Frequency: d. (Mon.-Sat.) Page Size: broadsheet. Subscrip. Rate: $.35 newsstand/cover; $.75 newsstand/cover Sat.; $130/yr carrier delivery; $143/yr motor route; $195/yr mailed in county; $234/yr mailed out of county. Freelance Pay: $25/article. **Wire Service(s):** AP, SH. Circulation: 21,500 evening (paid). **Owner(s):** MediaNews Group, Inc., 101 W Colfax Ave, Ste 1100, Denver, CO 80202. FAX: 303-954-6320. **Management:** Ron Clausen, Publisher. Ginny Harriger, Advertising Director. George Fuller, Circulation Director. **Editorial:** Becky Bennett, Editor. Ed Gotwals, Sports Editor.

CONNELLSVILLE

DAILY COURIER (CONNELLSVILLE). 127 W. Apple St., Connellsville, PA 15425. Telephone: 724-628-2000. FAX: 724-626-3567. E-MAIL: dailycourier@tribweb.com. URL: http://www.dailycourier.com. Mailing Address: PO Box 864, Connellsville, PA 15425-0864. Year Established: 1902. Pub. Frequency: d. (Mon.-Sat.) Page Size: broadsheet. Subscrip. Rate: $.50 newsstand/cover; $184/yr carrier delivery & motor rte.; $182.12/yr mailed in county; $198.24/yr mailed out of county. **Wire Service(s):** AP. Circulation: 10,000 evening (paid). **Owner(s):** Tribune-Review Publishing Co., 535 Keystone Dr., Warrendale, PA 15086. Telephone: 724-779-8742. **Management:** Richard Scaife, Publisher. Karen Strickland, Advertising Manager. Mark Malone, Circulation Manager. **Editorial:** Roxanne Abramowitz, Editor. Craig Smith, Executive Editor. Rose Snyder, City Editor.

CORRY

CORRY JOURNAL. 28 W. South St., Corry, PA 16407. Telephone: 814-665-8291. FAX: 814-664-2288. E-MAIL: corryjournal@tbscc.com. URL: http://www.corrypa.com/journal. Pub. Frequency: d. (Mon.-Sat.) Page Size: broadsheet. Subscrip. Rate: $.50 newsstand/cover; $11 home delivery/mo.; $132/yr home delivery. Circulation: 4,400 evening (paid). **Owner(s):** Sample News Group, See address and contact information above. **Management:** Bob Williams, General Manager. George R. Sample, Publisher. Bob Williams, Advertising Manager. Alverna Hellyer, Circulation Manager. **Editorial:** Maryann Mook, City Editor. Rob McCray, Sports.

DANVILLE

DANVILLE NEWS. 14 Mahoning St, Danville, PA 17821-2916. Telephone: 570-275-3235. FAX: 570-275-7624. URL: http://www.dailyitem.com. Year Established: 1897. Pub. Frequency: d. (Mon.-Fri.) Page Size: broadsheet. Subscrip. Rate: $.25 newsstand/cover; $65/yr in county. **Wire Service(s):** AP. Circulation: 4,200 evening (paid). **Owner(s):** Community Newspaper Holdings, Inc., 3500 Colonnade Pkwy., Ste. 600, Birmingham, AL 35242. **Management:** Janet Tippett, Publisher. Brad Bailey, Advertising Director. Fred Scheller, Circulation Manager. **Editorial:** Leondard Ingrassia, Editor. Dave Hillard, Managing Editor.

DOYLESTOWN

INTELLIGENCER (DOYLESTOWN), THE. 333 N. Broad St., Doylestown, PA 18901. Telephone: 215-345-3000. FAX: 215-345-3150. E-MAIL: lmorgnanesi@phillyburbs.com. URL: http://www.phillyburbs.com. Mailing Address: PO Box 858, Doylestown, PA 18901. Year Established: 1804. Pub. Frequency: d. Page Size: broadsheet. Subscrip. Rate: $.50 newsstand/cover; $1.50 newsstand/cover Sun.; $4.80 carrier delivery/wk. in county; $5.25 motor route/wk.; $245.70/yr carrier delivery in county. Freelance Pay: $50/article. **Wire Service(s):** AP. Circulation: 43,802 morning (paid); 51,973 Sunday (paid). **Owner(s):** Calkins Media Inc., Rte. 13, Levittown, PA 19057. Telephone: 215-949-4000. **Management:** Michael Scobey, Publisher. Kim Noble, Advertising Director. Bill Loebecker, Circulation Manager. Dale Machesoc, Classified Adv. Mgr.. **Editorial:** Lanny Morgnanesi, Executive Editor. David Gilmartin, Managing Editor. Jeff Beideman, Sports Editor. Contact: Stacy Briggs, Feature Editor.

DU BOIS

COURIER-EXPRESS/TRI-COUNTY SUNDAY. ISSN 8750-4049
500 Jeffers St., Du Bois, PA 15801-0407. Telephone: 814-371-4200. FAX: 814-371-3241. E-MAIL: cexpress@penn.com. URL: http://www.courierexpress.com. Mailing Address: PO Box 407, Du Bois, PA 15801-0407. Year Established: 1879. Pub. Frequency: d. (Sun.-Fri.) Page Size: broadsheet. Subscrip. Rate: $.50 newsstand/cover; $1 newsstand/cover Sun.; $26.50 home delivery for 3 mos.; $52 home delivery for 6 mos.; $103/yr home delivery includes Tri-County Sunday. **Wire Service(s):** AP, SH. Circulation: 10,180 evening (paid); 15,000 Sunday (paid). **Owner(s):** McLean Publishing, 945 Haverford Rd., Bryn Mawr, PA 19010. Telephone: 215-527-6330. **Management:** Joe Grecco, General Manager. Linda Smith, Advertising Manager. James Nestlerode, Circulation Manager. **Editorial:** A J Sylvis, Editor. Nick Hoffman, Managing Editor. Barbara Azzato, Lifestyle Editor. Scott Shindledecker, Sports Editor. Joy Norwood, Sunday Editor.

EASTON

EXPRESS-TIMES, THE. ISSN 1062-3620
30 N. Fourth St., Easton, PA 18042. Telephone: 610-258-7171. E-MAIL: newsf@express-times.com. URL: http://www.express-times.com. Mailing Address: PO Box 391, Easton, PA 18044. Year Established: 1855. Pub. Frequency: d. Page Size: broadsheet. Subscrip. Rate: $.35 newsstand/cover; $1 newsstand/cover Sun.; $157.15/yr home delivery; $294.40/yr mailed PA & NJ. Freelance Pay: $25-$35/article. **Wire Service(s):** AP, LAT-WAT, MCT. Circulation: 49,557 morning (paid); 49,026 Sunday (paid). **Owner(s):** Advance Publications, Inc., See address and contact information above. **Management:** Martin Till, Publisher. David Yanoshik, VP Mktg. & Sales. Robert F. Rothacker Jr., Circulation Director. Chris Smith, Circulation Manager. Denise L. Smith, Classified Adv. Mgr.. Ken Vance, Controller. **Editorial:** Joseph P Owens, Editor. Jim Deegan, Managing Editor. Scott Toole, News Editor. Edward Laubach, Sports Editor.

ELLWOOD CITY

ELLWOOD CITY LEDGER. PO Box 471, Ellwood City, PA 16117. E-MAIL: ecledger@ellwoodcityledger.com. URL: http://www.ellwoodcityledger.com. Year Established: 1920. Pub. Frequency: d. (Mon.-Sat.) Page Size: broadsheet. Subscrip. Rate: $.40 newsstand/cover; $25.20 home delivery for 3 mos.. Adv. Rate: col. inch $9.25 **Wire Service(s):** AP. Circulation: 5,400 evening (paid). **Owner(s):** Citizens Publishing & Printing Co., See address and contact information above. **Management:** Scott Kegel, General Manager. W.R. Kegel, Publisher. Dom A. Viccari, Advertising Manager. E. Crawford, Circulation Manager. Pam Hallberg, Classified Adv. Mgr.. Mary Rueckl, Business Manager. **Editorial:** Mary Ann Caputo, Editor. Randy Senior, Sports Editor.

ERIE

ERIE TIMES-NEWS. 205 W. 12th St., Erie, PA 16534. Telephone: 814-870-1612. FAX: 814-870-1615. E-MAIL: jim.dible@timesnews.com. URL: http://www.goerie.com. Year Established: 1888. Pub. Frequency: d. Page Size: broadsheet. Subscrip. Rate: $.50 newsstand/cover; $1.50 newsstand/cover Sun.; $169/yr home delivery. Adv. Rate: col. inch $83.07 **Wire Service(s):** AP. Circulation: 60,107 morning (paid); 86,713 Sunday (paid). **Owner(s):** Times Publishing Co., See address and contact information above. **Management:** Jim Dible, Publisher. Glenn Caruso, Circulation Director. Jocelyn Papesch, Classified Adv. Mgr.. **Editorial:** Rick Sayers, Executive Editor. Jeff Hileman, Feature Editor. Matt Martin, Sports Editor. Contact: Doug Rieder, Editor. Contact: Sherry Rieder, Production Editor. Contact: Jeff Hileman, Feature Editor. Contact: Jeff Hileman, Feature Editor. Contact: Jennifer Smith, Editor. Contact: Jeff Hileman, Feature Editor. Contact: Doug Oathout, Business Editor.

GETTYSBURG

GETTYSBURG TIMES. 1570 Fairfield Rd., Gettysburg, PA 17325. Telephone: 717-334-1131. FAX: 717-334-4243. E-MAIL: news@gburgtimes.com. URL: http://www.gettysburgtimes.com. Year Established: 1902. Pub. Frequency: d. (Mon.-Sat.) Page Size: broadsheet. Subscrip. Rate: $.50 newsstand/cover; $89/yr home delivery. **Wire Service(s):** AP, SH. Circulation: 10,000 morning (paid). **Owner(s):** Times & News Publishing Co., See address and contact information above. **Management:** Cynthia Ford, Publisher. Tom Bair, Circulation Manager. Tammy Signor, Classified Adv. Mgr.. **Editorial:** B.J. Small, Editor. Josh Martin, Sports Editor.

GREENSBURG

TRIBUNE-REVIEW. 622 Cabin Hill Dr., Greensburg, PA 15601-1692. Telephone: 724-834-1151. FAX: 724-838-5171. E-MAIL: letters@tribune-review.com. URL: http://www.tribune-review.com. Year Established: 1889. Pub. Frequency: d. Page Size: broadsheet. Subscrip. Rate: $.50 newsstand/cover; $1.50 newsstand/cover Sun.; $143/yr carrier delivery. **Wire Service(s):** RN, AP, LAT-WAT. Circulation: 116,346 morning (paid); 107,139 Sunday (paid). **Owner(s):** Tribune-Review Publishing Co., 535 Keystone Dr., Warrendale, PA 15086. Telephone: 724-779-8742. **Management:** Art McMullen, General Manager. Richard Scaife, Publisher. Pat Mellish, Classified Adv. Mgr.. **Editorial:** Susan McFarland, Editor. Gloria M. Ruane, City Editor. Keith Barnes, Sports.

GREENVILLE

GREENVILLE RECORD-ARGUS. 10 Penn Ave., Greenville, PA 16125. Telephone: 724-588-5000. FAX: 724-588-4691. E-MAIL: ranews@nauticom.net. Mailing Address: PO Box 711, Greenville, PA 16125. Year Established: 1848. Pub. Frequency: d. (Mon.-Sat.) Page Size: broadsheet. Subscrip. Rate: $.50 newsstand/cover; $95.40/yr carrier delivery & motor rte.; $144/yr mailed in county; $162/yr mailed elsewhere. **Wire Service(s):** AP. Circulation: 5,600 morning (paid). **Owner(s):** Greenville Newspapers, Inc., See address and contact information above. **Management:** Robert N. Bracey, Publisher. Jim Rust, Advertising Manager. Scott Bracey, Circulation Manager. **Editorial:** Natalie Kennedy, Managing Editor. Wendy Kozminski, Sports.

HANOVER

EVENING SUN. 135 Baltimore St., Hanover, PA 17331. Telephone: 717-637-3736. FAX: 717-637-7730. E-MAIL: news@eveningsun.com. URL: http://www.eveningsun.com. Mailing Address: PO Box 514, Hanover, PA 17331. Year Established: 1915. Pub. Frequency: d. Page Size: broadsheet. Subscrip. Rate: $.35 newsstand/cover; $1 newsstand/cover Sun.; $117/yr home delivery; $125/yr mailed elsewhere. **Wire Service(s):** AP. Circulation: 25,000 evening (paid); 21,200 Sunday (paid). **Owner(s):** MediaNews Group, Inc., 101 W Colfax Ave, Ste 1100, Denver, CO 80202. FAX: 303-954-6320. **Management:** Doug Cooper, Publisher. Janelle Coolaugh, Advertising Manager. Bob Trazkovich, Circulation Manager. **Editorial:** Lori Goodlin, Editor. Carl Whitehill, Managing Editor. John Pavoncello, Photographer. Phil Glatfelter, Sports.

HARRISBURG

PATRIOT-NEWS. ISSN 0887-7939
812 Market St., Harrisburg, PA 17101. Telephone: 717-255-8178. E-MAIL: jkirkpatrick@pnco.com. URL: http://www.patriot-news.com. Mailing Address: P.O. Box 2265, Harrisburg, PA 17105-2265. Year Established: 1854. Pub. Frequency: d. Page Size: broadsheet. Subscrip. Rate: $.50 newsstand/cover; $1.75 newsstand/cover Sun.; $223.60/yr home delivery; $364/yr mailed elsewhere. **Wire Service(s):** AP, NYT, LAT-WAT, MCT. Circulation: 101,421 morning (paid); 152,370 Sunday (paid). **Owner(s):** Advance Publications, Inc., See address and contact information above. **Bureau(s):** Contact: Nick Turo, Bureau Chief. **Management:** John A. Kirkpatrick, Publisher. Danny J Diego, Circulation Manager. Sue Mumma, Classified Adv. Mgr.. Anne Detter, Marketing Director. **Editorial:** John Kirkpatrick, Editor. David Newhouse, Executive Editor. Cate Barron, Managing Editor. Fred Stickel, Production Manager. Tom Barstow, Business Editor. John McGinley, Feature Editor. Monica Von Doveneck, Reporter. Nick Horvath, Sports Editor.

HAZLETON

HAZLETON STANDARD SPEAKER. 21 N. Wyoming St., Hazleton, PA 18201. Telephone: 570-455-3636. FAX: 570-455-4244. URL: http://www.standardspeaker.com. Mailing Address: PO Box 578, Hazleton, PA 18201-0578. Year Established: 1866. Pub. Frequency: d. Page Size: broadsheet. Subscrip. Rate: $.50 newsstand/cover; $1 newsstand/cover Sun.; $3.25/wk.; $35.75 home delivery/mo.. **Wire Service(s):** AP, CNS. Circulation: 24,000 morning (paid); 21,000 Sunday (paid). **Owner(s):** Hazleton Standard-Speaker, Inc., See address and contact information above. **Management:** Paul N. Walser, Publisher. Gary Yacubek, Advertising Director. Sandy Hoilko, Advertising Manager. Richard DeHaven, Circulation Manager. **Editorial:** Carl Christopher, Editor-in-Chief. Mildred Rubinate, Local News Editor. Eric Conover, Photo Editor. Babe Conroy, Sports.

HONESDALE

WAYNE INDEPENDENT, THE. 220 Eighth St., Honesdale, PA 18431. Telephone: 570-253-3055. FAX: 570-253-5387. E-MAIL: twinews@wayneindependent.com. URL: http://www.wayneindependent.com. Mailing Address: PO Box 122, Honesdale, PA 18431. Year Established: 1878. Pub. Frequency: d. (Tue.-Sat.) Page Size: broadsheet. Subscrip. Rate: $.75 newsstand/cover; $120/yr in county; $145/yr out of county. Freelance Pay: $25/article. **Wire Service(s):** AP. Circulation: 9,400 evening (paid). **Owner(s):** GateHouse Media, Inc, 350 WillowBrook Office Park, Fairport, NY 14450. Telephone: 585-598-0030. FAX: 585-248-2631. **Management:** Donald Doyle, General Manager. Michelle Hessling, Advertising Manager. Joe Hessling, Circulation Manager. Stephanie Dennis, Classified Adv. Mgr.. **Editorial:** Peter Becker, Managing Editor. Kevin Edwards, Sports Editor.

HORSHAM

INTELLIGENCER-RECORD, THE. 145 Easton Rd., Horsham, PA 19044-3194. Telephone: 215-957-8100. FAX: 215-957-8165. E-MAIL: 75703.3217@compuserve.com. URL: http://www.phillyburbs.com. Pub. Frequency: d. Page Size: broadsheet. Subscrip. Rate: $.50 newsstand/cover; $1.50 newsstand/cover Sun.; $236.34/yr carrier delivery. Circulation: 47,000 morning (paid); 53,000 Sunday (paid). **Owner(s):** Calkins Media Inc., 8400 Rte. 13, Levittown, PA 19057. Telephone: 215-949-4000. **Management:** Michael Scobey, Publisher. Kim Noble, Advertising Director. Ed Balceniuk, Circulation Manager. Dave Emann, Classified Adv. Mgr.. **Editorial:** Lanny Morgnanesi, Executive Editor. David Gilmartin, Managing Editor. Amy Gianficaro, City Editor. Stacy Briggs, Feature Editor. Jeff Beideman, Sports Editor.

HUNTINGDON

DAILY NEWS (HUNTINGDON). 325 Penn St., Huntingdon, PA 16652. Telephone: 814-643-4040. FAX: 814-643-9628. E-MAIL: dnews@getwireless.com. Mailing Address: PO Box 384, Huntingdon, PA 16652. Pub. Frequency: d. (Mon.-Sat.) Page Size: broadsheet. Subscrip. Rate: $.50 newsstand/cover; $10/mo.; $122/yr. **Wire Service(s):** UPI. Circulation: 10,200 evening (paid). **Owner(s):** George Sample, III, See address and contact information above. **Management:** George Sample III, Publisher. Carol Cutshall, Advertising Manager. Betsy Clinger, Circulation Manager. **Editorial:** Polly McMullen III, Editor. Terry Bowser, Sports.

INDIANA

INDIANA GAZETTE, THE. 899 Water St., Indiana, PA 15701. Telephone: 724-465-5555. FAX: 724-465-0402. E-MAIL: gazedit@indianagazette.net. URL: http://www.indianagazette.com. Mailing Address: PO Box 10, Indiana, PA 15701. Year Established: 1890. Pub. Frequency: d. Page Size: standard. Subscrip. Rate: $.50 newsstand/cover; $1 newsstand/cover Sun.; $146/yr carrier delivery. **Wire Service(s):** AP, NYT. Circulation: 16,000 evening (paid); 16,000 Sunday (paid). **Owner(s):** Indiana Printing & Publishing, See address and contact information above. **Management:** Joseph Geary, General Manager. Michael Donnely, Publisher. Michael J. Donnelly, Vice President. Bob Yesilonis, Advertising Manager. Ron Seckar, Circulation Manager. Beverly Daudet, Classified Adv. Mgr.. **Editorial:** Will Kennedy, Executive Editor. Mike Petersen, Managing Editor. Tony Coccagna, Sports.

JOHNSTOWN

TRIBUNE-DEMOCRAT, THE. 425 Locust St., Johnstown, PA 15907-0340. Telephone: 814-532-5050. FAX: 814-539-1409. E-MAIL: tribdem@tribune-democrat.com. URL: http://www.tribune-democrat.com. Year Established: 1853. Pub. Frequency: d. Page Size: broadsheet. Subscrip. Rate: $.50 newsstand/cover; $1.25 newsstand/cover Sun.. Freelance Pay: $20-$50/article. **Wire Service(s):** AP, MCT. Circulation: 49,646 morning (paid); 52,043 Sunday (paid). **Owner(s):** Johnstown Tribune Publishing Co., See address and contact information above. **Management:** Chris Voccio, Publisher. Marcia Miller, Advertising Director. Keith West, Circulation Director. Dawn Edmiston, Marketing Director. Stevc Sindleri, Production Director. **Editorial:** Chip Minemyer, Editor. Sean Roane, City Editor. Bruce Wissinger, Editorial Page Editor. Renee Carthew, Feature Editor. Eric Knopsnyder, Sports Editor.

KANE

KANE REPUBLICAN, THE. 200 N Fraley St, Kane, PA 16735. Telephone: 814-837-6000. FAX: 814-837-2227. E-MAIL: krnews@verizon.com. URL: http://www.kanerepublican.com. Mailing Address: PO Box 838, Kane, PA 16735-0838. Year Established: 1894. Pub. Frequency: d. (Mon.-Sat.) Page Size: broadsheet. Subscrip. Rate: $.50 newsstand/cover; $128/yr carrier delivery; $138/yr motor route; $132/yr mailed in county. **Wire Service(s):** AP. Circulation: 2,450 evening (paid). **Owner(s):** Horizon Publications, Inc., 1120 N. Carbon St, Ste 100, Marion, IL 62959. **Management:** Peg Kepler, Publisher. **Editorial:** Jerry Martin, Editor.

KITTANNING

LEADER TIMES. 11931 State Rte 85, Ste E, Kittanning, PA 16201. Telephone: 724-543-1303. FAX: 724-545-6768. E-MAIL: leadertimes@tribweb.com. URL: http://www.leadertimes.com. Mailing Address: PO Box 978, Kittanning, PA 16201. Year Established: 1898. Pub. Frequency: d. (Mon.-Sat.) Page Size: broadsheet. Subscrip. Rate: $.35 newsstand/cover; $86.50/yr home delivery; $94/yr motor route; $132/yr mailed in county; $138/yr mailed out of county. **Wire Service(s):** AP. Circulation: 11,500 evening (paid). **Owner(s):** Tribune-Review Publishing Co., 535 Keystone Dr., Warrendale, PA 15086. Telephone: 724-779-8742. **Management:** Richard Scaife, Publisher. Barbara Sheasley, Advertising Director. Larry Schuster, Circulation Manager. Donna Helit, Classified Adv. Mgr.. Larry Shuster, Marketing Director. **Editorial:** Jim Heasley, Assistant Editor.

LANCASTER

INTELLIGENCER JOURNAL. ISSN 0889-4140
8 W. King St., Lancaster, PA 17603. Telephone: 717-291-8811. FAX: 717-291-8653. E-MAIL: lnp@lnpnews.com. URL: http://www.lancasteronline.com. Mailing Address: PO Box 1328, Lancaster, PA 17608-1328. Year Established: 1794. Pub. Frequency: d. (Mon.-Sat.) Page Size: broadsheet. Subscrip. Rate: $.50 newsstand/cover; $37.05 for 3 mos.; $72.10 for 6 mos.; $143.20/yr. **Wire Service(s):** AP, NYT. Circulation: 45,636 morning (paid). **Owner(s):** Lancaster Newspapers, Inc., See address and contact information above. **Management:** John Buckwalter, Publisher. Harold Miller, Advertising Director. John Derr, Advertising Manager. Keith Kirchner, Circulation Manager. Russell Gillespie, Classified Adv. Mgr.. **Editorial:** Charles Shaw, Editor. Lynn Schmidt, Lifestyle Editor. Jon Ferguson, News Editor. Jeff Young, Sports Editor.

LANCASTER NEW ERA. 8 W. King St., Lancaster, PA 17603. FAX: 717-399-6506. E-MAIL: newera@lnpnews.com. URL: http://www.lancasteronline.com. Mailing Address: PO Box 1328, Lancaster, PA 17608-1328. Year Established: 1877. Pub. Frequency: d. (Mon.-Sat.) Page Size: broadsheet. Subscrip. Rate: $.50 newsstand/cover; $143.20/yr carrier delivery. **Wire Service(s):** AP, NYT, MCT. Circulation: 43,000 evening (paid). **Owner(s):** Lancaster Newspapers, Inc., See address and contact information above. **Management:** Harold Miller, President. John Derr, Advertising Director. Keith Kirchner, Circulation Manager. Russell Gillespie, Classified Adv. Mgr.. **Editorial:** Ernie Schreiber, Editor. Peter Mekeel, Managing Editor. Rick Hertzler, Photographer. Dennis A. Fisher, Sports Editor.

LANSDALE

REPORTER, THE. ISSN 0890-8443
307 Derstine Ave., Lansdale, PA 19446. Telephone: 215-855-8440. FAX: 215-855-3432. E-MAIL: letters@thereporteronline.com. URL: http://www.thereporteronline.com. Mailing Address: PO Box 390, Lansdale, PA 19446. Year Established: 1870. Pub. Frequency: d. Page Size: broadsheet. Subscrip. Rate: $.50 newsstand/cover; $1.50 Sun.; $195/yr home delivery; $260/yr mailed in county; $286/yr mailed out of county. **Wire Service(s):** AP, NYT. Circulation: 19,900 evening (paid). **Owner(s):** Journal Register Co., 50 W State St, 12th Fl, Trenton, NJ 08608. Telephone: 609-396-2200. FAX: 609-396-2292. **Management:** Angel Hernandez, Publisher. Thomas Brook, Advertising Director. Larry Butts, Circulation Director. **Editorial:** Nona Breaux, Executive Editor. Aixa Torregrosa Vazquez, Lifestyle Editor.

LATROBE

LATROBE BULLETIN. 1211 Ligonier St., Latrobe, PA 15650-0111. Telephone: 724-537-3351. FAX: 724-537-0489. E-MAIL: lb.news@verizon.net. Mailing Address: PO Box 111, Latrobe, PA 15650-0111. Year Established: 1902. Pub. Frequency: d. (Mon.-Sat.) Page Size: broadsheet. Subscrip. Rate: $.35 newsstand/cover; $34.50 home delivery in county for 3 mos.; $130/yr home delivery in county; $39 mailed out of county for 3 mos.; $135/yr mailed out of county. **Wire Service(s):** AP. Circulation: 8,100 evening (paid). **Owner(s):** Latrobe Printing & Publishing, See address and contact information above. **Management:** Gary Seigel, Publisher. Patty Sherback, Classified Adv. Mgr.. **Editorial:** Marie McCandless, Editor. Steve Kitty, Managing Editor. Louise F. Fritz, Society Editor. Randy Skubek, Sports.

LEBANON

LEBANON DAILY NEWS. 718 Poplar St., Lebanon, PA 17042. Telephone: 717-272-5611. FAX: 717-274-1608. E-MAIL: lebnews@leba.net. URL: http://www.ldnews.com. Mailing Address: PO Box 600, Lebanon, PA 17042. Year Established: 1872. Pub. Frequency: d. Page Size: broadsheet. Subscrip. Rate: $.50 newsstand/cover; $1.50 newsstand/cover Sun.; $39 carrier delivery for 3 mos.; $160.55/yr carrier delivery. **Wire Service(s):** UPI. Circulation: 24,088 evening (paid); 22,960 Sunday (paid). **Owner(s):** MediaNews Group, Inc., 101 W Colfax Ave, Ste 1100, Denver, CO 80202. FAX: 303-954-6320. **Management:** David Smith, Publisher. Glenn Jessee, Operations Manager. Ron Sisto, Circulation Manager. Coleen Novak, Classified Adv. Mgr.. **Editorial:** Paul Baker, Managing Editor. Mike Givler, Sports Editor.

LEHIGHTON

TIMES NEWS, THE. 594 Blakeslee Blvd. Dr., W., Lehighton, PA 18235-0239. Telephone: 610-377-2051. FAX: 610-826-9608. E-MAIL: tnonline@postoffice.ptd.net. URL: http://www.tnonline.com. Mailing Address: PO Box 239, Lehighton, PA 18235-0239. Year Established: 1883. Pub. Frequency: d. (Mon.-Sat.) Page Size: broadsheet. Subscrip. Rate: $.50 newsstand/cover; $114.80/yr carrier delivery local; $146/yr mailed. Adv. Rate: col. inch $8.95 **Wire Service(s):** AP. Circulation: 16,000 evening (paid). **Owner(s):** Pencor Inc., 613 Third St., Palmerton, PA 18071. Telephone: 610-826-2115. FAX: 610-826-7626. **Management:** Fred Masenheimer, Publisher. Donald Reese, Advertising Director. Kathy Carpenter, Circulation Manager. Linda Moyer, Classified Adv. Mgr.. **Editorial:** Robert Parfitt, Editor. Bob Urban, Managing Editor. Pattie Mihalik, Feature Editor. Marigrace Heyer, Lifestyle Editor. Emmett McCall, Sports Editor.

LEVITTOWN

BUCKS COUNTY COURIER TIMES. 8400 Rte. 13, Levittown, PA 19057. Telephone: 215-949-4000. FAX: 215-949-4177. E-MAIL: pwalker@phillyburbs.com. URL: http://www.phillyburbs.com. Year Established: 1910. Pub. Frequency: d. Page Size: broadsheet. Subscrip. Rate: $.50 newsstand/cover; $1.50 newsstand/cover Sun.; $210.60/yr carrier delivery. Freelance Pay: $25-$50/article. **Wire Service(s):** AP, SH. Circulation: 62,699 morning (paid); 67,208 Sunday (paid). **Owner(s):** Calkins Media Inc., See address and contact information above. **Management:** Dale Larson, Publisher. Tim Birch, Advertising Director. George Stevenson, Circulation Manager. **Editorial:** Patricia Meagher-Walker, Executive Editor. Guy Petroziello, Editorial Page Editor. Gary Silvers, Sports Editor.

LEWISTOWN

SENTINEL (LEWISTOWN), THE. 352 Sixth St., Lewistown, PA 17044. Telephone: 717-248-6741. FAX: 717-248-3481. E-MAIL: sentinel@pacentral.com. URL: http://www.lewistownsentinel.com. Mailing Address: PO Box 588, Lewistown, PA 17044. Year Established: 1903. Pub. Frequency: d. (Mon.-Sat.) Page Size: broadsheet. Subscrip. Rate: $.50 newsstand/cover; $.75 newsstand/cover Sat.; $9.25 carrier delivery/mo. local; $10.25 motor route/mo. local. **Wire Service(s):** AP. Circulation: 13,500 morning (paid). **Owner(s):** Ogden Newspapers of Minnesota, Inc., 1500 Main St., Wheeling, WV 26003. Telephone: 304-233-0100. **Management:** Ruth Eddy, Publisher. Bernie Oravec, Advertising Director. Holly Smith, Business Manager. **Editorial:** Heather Henline, Managing Editor. Dan Graybill, Sports Editor.

LOCK HAVEN

EXPRESS (LOCK HAVEN), THE. 9-11 W. Main St., Lock Haven, PA 17745-6791. Telephone: 570-748-6791. FAX: 570-748-1544. E-MAIL: news@lockhaven.com. URL: http://www.lockhaven.com. Mailing Address: PO Box 208, Lock Haven, PA 17745-0208. Year Established: 1882. Pub. Frequency: d. (Mon.-Sat.) Page Size: broadsheet. Subscrip. Rate: $.50 newsstand/cover; $.75 newsstand/cover Sat.; $109.20/yr carrier delivery in county; $132/yr mailed out of county; $156 mailed/mo. out of state. **Wire Service(s):** AP. Circulation: 10,000 evening (paid). **Owner(s):** Ogden Newspapers of Minnesota, Inc., 19260 San Carlos Blvd., Fort Myers Beach, FL 33931. Telephone: 239-463-4421. **Management:** Bob Rolley, Publisher. Rick Noll, Advertising Manager. Larry Rupert, Circulation Manager. Charlie Gephart, Classified Adv. Mgr.. **Editorial:** Robert Sealy, Managing Editor. Wendy Stiver, Associate Editor.

MCKEESPORT

MCKEESPORT DAILY NEWS. 409 Walnut St., McKeesport, PA 15132-2613. Telephone: 412-664-9161. FAX: 412-664-3972. E-MAIL: mcknews@bellatlantic.net. URL: http://www.dailynewsmckeesport.com. Mailing Address: PO Box 128, McKeesport, PA 15134. Year Established: 1884. Pub. Frequency: d. (Mon.-Sat.) Page Size: standard. Subscrip. Rate: $.50 newsstand/cover; $11.50 mailed/mo. local; $156/yr mailed local. Adv. Rate: col. inch $23 **Wire Service(s):** AP, LAT-WAT. Circulation: 25,000 evening (paid). **Owner(s):** Daily News Publishing Co., 409 Walnut St., McKeesport, PA 15132. Telephone: 412-664-9161. FAX: 412-664-3972. **Editorial:** Jeffery Sisk, Managing Editor. Bonniejean Adams, City Editor. Carol Frazer, Lifestyle Editor. Mark Kaboly, Sports.

MEADVILLE

MEADVILLE TRIBUNE, THE. ISSN 0747-2412
947 Federal Ct., Meadville, PA 16335. Telephone: 814-724-6370. FAX: 814-724-8755. E-MAIL: tribune@meadvilletribune.com. URL: http://www.meadvilletribune.com. Year Established: 1884. Pub. Frequency: d. Page Size: broadsheet. Subscrip. Rate: $.50 newsstand/cover; $1 newsstand/cover Sun.; $122.40/yr carrier delivery in area; $172/yr mailed out of area. **Wire Service(s):** AP, SH. Circulation: 16,335 morning (paid); 17,000 Sunday (paid). **Owner(s):** Community Newspaper Holdings, Inc., 3500 Colonnade Pkwy., Ste. 600, Birmingham, AL 35243. Telephone: 205-298-7100. FAX: 205-298-7101. **Management:** Jeanne Moore-Yount, Publisher. Lon Wilson, Advertising Director. Laura Hamilton, Circulation Director. Diane Ringer, Classified Adv. Mgr.. **Editorial:** Pat Bywater, Executive Editor. Kevin M. Hart, News Editor. Domanic DiRienzo, Sports Editor.

MILTON

STANDARD-JOURNAL. 21 N Arch St, Milton, PA 17847. Telephone: 570-742-9671. FAX: 570-742-9876. E-MAIL: newsroom@standard-journal.com. URL: http://www.standard-journal.com. Year Established: 1890. Pub. Frequency: d. (Mon.-Sat.) Page Size: broadsheet. Subscrip. Rate: $.50 newsstand/cover; $1.95 carrier delivery/wk.; $108.11/yr carrier delivery. **Wire Service(s):** AP. Circulation: 5,000 evening (paid). **Owner(s):** GateHouse Media, Inc, 350 WillowBrook Office Park, Fairport, NY 14450. Telephone: 585-598-0030. FAX: 585-248-2631. **Management:** Amy Moyer, Publisher. Jim Guinn-Bailey, Advertising Manager. Kevin Mertz, Circulation Manager. **Editorial:** Mike Redding, Managing Editor. Chris Brady, Sports.

MONESSEN

VALLEY INDEPENDENT, THE. Eastgate 19, Monessen, PA 15062. Telephone: 724-684-5200. FAX: 724-684-2602. URL: http://www.valleyindependent.com. Year Established: 1901. Pub. Frequency: d. (Mon.-Sat.) Page Size: broadsheet. Subscrip. Rate: $.50 newsstand/cover; $38.35 carrier delivery for 3 mos.; $153.40/yr carrier delivery & motor rte.. **Wire Service(s):** AP. Circulation: 16,600 evening (paid). **Owner(s):** Tribune-Review Publishing Co., 535 Keystone Dr., Warrendale, PA 15086. Telephone: 724-779-8742. **Bureau(s): Management:** Richard Scaife, Publisher. Karen Strickland, Advertising Manager. Linda Hutchinson, Circulation Manager. Michele Conte, Classified Adv. Mgr.. **Editorial:** Bob Burk, Managing Editor. Joe Abramowitz, City Editor. Carl Hill, News Editor. Jim Ference, Photographer. Brian Herman, Sports Editor.

NEW CASTLE

NEW CASTLE NEWS. 27 N. Mercer St., New Castle, PA 16101. Telephone: 724-654-6651. FAX: 724-654-9593. E-MAIL: nenclass@aol.com. URL: http://www.ncnewsonline.com. Mailing Address: PO Box 60, New Castle, PA 16103. Year Established: 1880. Pub. Frequency: d. (Mon.-Sat.) Page Size: broadsheet. Subscrip. Rate: $.50 newsstand/cover; $2.30 carrier delivery/wk.; $2.40 motor route/wk.. Adv. Rate: col. inch $29.95 **Wire Service(s):** UPI. Circulation: 19,300 evening (paid). **Owner(s):** Community Newspaper Holdings, Inc., 3500 Colonnade Pkwy., Ste. 600, Birmingham, AL 35243. Telephone: 205-298-7100. FAX: 205-298-7101. **Management:** Max Thomson, Publisher. Ed Gaydos, Advertising Manager. DuWayne Nelson, Circulation Manager. Bryan Zeigler, Classified Adv. Mgr.. **Editorial:** Mitchell Olszak, Managing Editor. Dan Irwin, Asst. Managing Ed..

NORRISTOWN

TIMES HERALD (NORRISTOWN), THE. 410 Markley St., Norristown, PA 19401. Telephone: 610-272-2500. FAX: 610-272-4003. E-MAIL: montcotime@aol.com. URL: http://www.timesherald.com. Mailing Address: PO Box 591, Norristown, PA 19404. Year Established: 1799. Pub. Frequency: d. Page Size: broadsheet. Subscrip. Rate: $.50 newsstand/cover; $1.50 newsstand/cover Sun.; $52 home delivery local for 13 wks.; $208/yr home delivery. **Wire Service(s):** AP, SH. Circulation: 23,131 morning (paid); 19,580 Sunday (paid). **Owner(s):** Journal Register Co., 50 W State St, 12th Fl, Trenton, NJ 08608. Telephone: 609-396-2200. **Management:** Dena Fritz, Publisher. Robert Ortolano, Classified Adv. Mgr.. **Editorial:** Stan Huskey, Editor. Gordon Glantz, Managing Editor. Gene Walsh, Photographer. Dave Kurtz, Sports.

OIL CITY

DERRICK, THE. 1510 W. First St., Oil City, PA 16301-0928. E-MAIL: info@thederrick.comnet. URL: http://www.thederrick.com. Mailing Address: PO Box 928, Oil City, PA 16301. Year Established: 1871. Pub. Frequency: d. (Mon.-Sat.) Page Size: broadsheet. Subscrip. Rate: $.50 newsstand/cover; $9.95 carrier delivery for 4 wks.; $250.04/yr mailed in county; $266.16/yr mailed in state; $281.08/yr mailed out of state; $129.48/yr home delivery in county. Adv. Rate: col. inch $33.31 Circulation: 19,000 morning (paid). **Owner(s):** Venango Newspapers Co., See address and contact information above. **Management:** P.C. Boyle, Publisher. Ned Cowart, Advertising Manager. Mel Basham, Circulation Manager. Carla Sheatz, Classified Adv. Mgr.. **Editorial:** Glen Mohnkern, Managing Editor.

NEWS-HERALD (OIL CITY), THE. 1510 W. First St., Oil City, PA 16301-0928. Telephone: 814-676-7444. FAX: 814-677-8347. E-MAIL: info@thederrick.com. URL: http://www.thenewsherald.com. Mailing Address: PO Box 928, Oil City, PA 16301. Year Established: 1878. Pub. Frequency: d. (Mon.-Sat.) Page Size: broadsheet. Subscrip. Rate: $.50 newsstand/cover; $9.95 home delivery for 4 wks.; $129.48/yr home delivery. **Wire Service(s):** AP. Circulation: 7,600 morning (paid). **Owner(s):** Venango Newspapers Co., See address and contact information above. **Management:** P.C. Boyle, Publisher. Ned Cowart, Advertising Manager. Mel Basham, Circulation Manager. Carla Sheatz, Classified Adv. Mgr.. **Editorial:** Glen Mohnkern, Managing Editor. Ed Brannon, Sports.

PHILADELPHIA

METRO (PHILADELPHIA). 30 S. 15th St., 9th Fl., Graham Bldg., Philadelphia, PA 19102. Telephone: 215-717-2600. FAX: 215-717-2626. E-MAIL: adphilly@metro.us. URL: http://www.metro.us. Year Established: 2000. Pub. Frequency: d. (Mon.-Fri.) Page Size: tabloid Circulation: 170,587 morning (free). **Owner(s):** TPI Metro PA, See address and contact information above. **Management:** Eric Mayberry, Publisher. Ed Abrams, Advertising Director. Brian O'Keefe, Circulation Manager. **Editorial:** Ron Varrial, Editor. Mark Moore, Editor-in-Chief.

PHILADELPHIA DAILY NEWS. 400 N. Broad St., Philadelphia, PA 19130. Telephone: 215-854-5900. FAX: 215-854-5910. E-MAIL: dailynews.opinion@phillynews.com. URL: http://www.philly.com. Mailing Address: PO Box 7788, Philadelphia, PA 19101. Year Established: 1925. Pub. Frequency: d. (Mon.-Sat.) Page Size: tabloid. Subscrip. Rate: $.60 newsstand/cover; $61.75/quarter; $247/yr. **Wire Service(s):** RN, AP, MCT. Circulation: 175,290 evening (paid). **Owner(s):** Knight Ridder, Inc., 50 W. San Fernando St., Ste. 1200, San Jose, CA 95113. Telephone: 831-938-7700. FAX: 831-938-7755. **Management:** Robert J. Hall, Publisher. Harvey Hill, Advertising Director. Roseann Oleyn, Classified Adv. Mgr.. **Editorial:** Michael Days, Editor. Frank Burgos, Editorial Page Editor. Theresa Johnson, Feature Editor. Kurt Heine, News Editor. Pat McLoone, Sports.

PHILADELPHIA INQUIRER. ISSN 0885-6613
400 N. Broad St., Philadelphia, PA 19130. Telephone: 215-854-2000. FAX: 215-854-5553. URL: http://www.philly.com. Mailing Address: PO Box 8263, Philadelphia, PA 19101. Year Established: 1829. Pub. Frequency: d. Page Size: broadsheet. Subscrip. Rate: $.50 newsstand/cover; $1.50 newsstand/cover Sun.; $38 home delivery 8 wks.; $247/yr. **Wire Service(s):** AP, LAT-WAT. Circulation: 404,860 morning (paid); 838,296 Sunday (paid). **Owner(s):** Knight Ridder, Inc., 50 W. San Fernando St., Ste. 1200, San Jose, CA 95113. Telephone: 831-938-7700. FAX: 831-938-7755. **Bureau(s):** 830 Town Center Dr., Langhorne, PA 19047. Telephone: 215-702-7800. FAX: 215-702-7820. **Management:** Clem Murray, Photography Director. **Editorial:** Acel Moore, Associate Editor. Mary Flannery, Business Editor. Virginia Smith, City Editor. Chris Satullo, Editorial Page Editor. Barbara Sadek, Food Editor. Chuck Melvin, Technical Editor. Jack Severson, Travel Editor.

PHOENIXVILLE

PHOENIX (PHOENIXVILLE), THE. 225 Bridge St., Phoenixville, PA 19460. Telephone: 610-933-8926. FAX: 610-933-1187. E-MAIL: pheonixnews@enter.net. URL: http://www.phoenixvillenews.com. Mailing Address: P O Box 689, Phoenixville, PA 19460. Year Established: 1888. Pub. Frequency: d. (Mon.-Sat.) Page Size: broadsheet. Subscrip. Rate: $.50 newsstand/cover; $3.15 home delivery/wk. local; $163/yr home delivery. Freelance Pay: $25/article. **Wire Service(s):** AP. Circulation: 5,000 evening (paid). **Owner(s):** Journal Register Co., 50 W State St, 12th Fl, Trenton, NJ 08608. Telephone: 609-396-2200. **Management:** Alexander N Gould, General Manager. Jim Kelly, Publisher. Mike Doyle, Advertising Director. Robert Dodd, Circulation Manager. **Editorial:** Patricia Matson, Editor. Jason Feather, Sports.

PITTSBURGH

PITTSBURGH POST-GAZETTE. ISSN 1068-624X
34 Blvd. of the Allies, Pittsburgh, PA 15222. Telephone: 412-263-1100. FAX: 412-391-8452. URL: http://www.post-gazette.com. Year Established: 1786. Pub. Frequency: d. Page Size: broadsheet. Subscrip. Rate: $.50 newsstand/cover; $1.50 newsstand/cover Sun.; $3 carrier delivery/wk.. **Wire Service(s):** AP, NYT. Circulation: 244,969 morning (paid); 410,879 Sunday (paid). **Owner(s):** Block Communications Inc., 6450 Monroae St, Sylvania, OH 43560. **Management:** Diana Block, Co-Publisher. David Shribman, Vice President. Randy Waugaman, Circulation Director. Tracey DeAngelo, Marketing Director. **Editorial:** David Shribman, Executive Editor. Thomas Birdsong, Asst. Managing Ed.. Bob Hoover, Book Review Editor. Tom Waseleski, Editorial Page Editor. Steven Massey, Feature Editor. Susan Smith, Science Editor. Jerry Micco, Sports Editor. Rob Owen, TV Editor.

PITTSBURGH TRIBUNE-REVIEW. 503 Martindale St., 3rd Fl., Pittsburgh, PA 15212. Telephone: 412-321-6460. FAX: 412-320-7860. URL: http://www.pittsburghlive.com. Year Established: 1992. Pub. Frequency: d. Page Size: broadsheet. Subscrip. Rate: $.50 newsstand/cover; $1.50 Sun.; $35.75 per 13 wks.. **Wire Service(s):** RN, AP, LAT-WAT. Circulation: 75,400 morning (paid). **Owner(s):** Tribune-Review Publishing Co., 535 Keystone Dr., Warrendale, PA 15086. Telephone: 724-779-8742. **Management:** Richard Scaife, Publisher. Lou Naples, Advertising Manager. Jeff Simmons, Circulation Manager. **Editorial:** Frank Craig, Editor. Robert Fryer, Managing Editor. Bill Steigerwald, Associate Editor. Jack Markowitz, Business Editor. Jolie Williamson, Feature Editor.

POTTSTOWN

MERCURY (POTTSTOWN), THE. 24 N. Hanover St., Pottstown, PA 19464. Telephone: 610-323-3000. FAX: 610-323-0682. E-MAIL: mercury@pottsmerc.com. URL: http://www.pottsmerc.com. Year Established: 1931. Pub. Frequency: d. Page Size: broadsheet. Subscrip. Rate: $.50 newsstand/cover; $1.50 newsstand/cover Sun.; $234/yr home delivery. **Wire Service(s):** AP. Circulation: 414,815 morning (paid). **Owner(s):** Journal Register Co., 50 W State St, 12th Fl, Trenton, NJ 08608. Telephone: 609-396-2200. **Management:** Tom Abbott, Publisher. Steve Batten, Advertising Director. Dan Moriarty, Circulation Director. **Editorial:** Nancy March, Managing Editor.

POTTSVILLE

POTTSVILLE REPUBLICAN - HERALD. 111 Mahantongo St., Pottsville, PA 17901. Telephone: 570-622-3456. FAX: 570-628-6092. E-MAIL: ads@republicanherald.com. URL: http://www.republicanherald.com. Mailing Address: PO Box 209, Pottsville, PA 17901-0209. Year Established: 1884. Pub. Frequency: d. (Mon.-Sat.) Page Size: broadsheet. Subscrip. Rate: $1 newsstand/cover; $2 newsstand/cover Sun.; $169.20/yr home delivery in county; $228/yr mailed. Adv. Rate: col. inch $29.25 **Wire Service(s):** AP. Circulation: 28,000 evening (paid); 40,000 Sunday (paid). **Owner(s):** Times-Shamrock Communications, 149 Penn Ave., Scranton, PA 18503. Telephone: 717-348-9101. **Management:** Henry H. Nyce Jr., Publisher. Michael A. Joyce, Advertising Director. Charlie Trapani, Advertising Manager. David Sickle, Circulation Director. Janet Joyce, Marketing Director. **Editorial:** Pete Banko, Editor. Leroy Boyer, Sports Editor.

PRIMOS

DELAWARE COUNTY DAILY/SUNDAY TIMES. 500 Mildred Ave., Primos, PA 19018. Telephone: 610-622-8800. FAX: 610-622-8829. E-MAIL: newsroom@delcotimes.com. URL: http://www.delcotimes.com. Year Established: 1876. Pub. Frequency: d. Page Size: tabloid. Subscrip. Rate: $.75 newsstand/cover; $1.75 newsstand/cover Sun.; $183.60 home delivery for 6 mos.; $367/yr home delivery. **Wire Service(s):** AP. Circulation: 40,000 morning (paid); 36,000 Sunday (paid). **Owner(s):** Journal Register Co., Lower Makefield Corporate Center, 790 Towndship Line Rd, 3rd Fl, Yardley, PA 19067. **Management:** Frank Gothie, Publisher. Leisha Shaeffer, Advertising Manager. Joe Potts, Circulation Manager. Larry Hochberger, Classified Adv. Mgr.. **Editorial:** Philip Heron, Editor. Linda DeMeglio, Managing Editor. Rob Parent, Sports Editor.

PUNXUTAWNEY

PUNXSUTAWNEY SPIRIT, THE. 510 Pine St, Punxutawney, PA 15767. Telephone: 814-938-8740. FAX: 814-938-3794. E-MAIL: publisher@punxsutawneyspirit.com. URL: http://www.punxsutawneyspirit.com. Mailing Address: PO Box 444, Punxutawney, PA 15767. Pub. Frequency: d. (Mon.-Sat.) Page Size: standard. Subscrip. Rate: $.50 newsstand/cover; $126/yr in county & adj. cys.; $17.50/mo. out of area. Circulation: 10,000 per issue (paid). **Owner(s):** Horizon Publications, Inc., 1120 N. Carbon St, Ste 100, Marion, IL 62959. **Management:** Mary Jude Troupe, Publisher. Helen Long, Circulation Manager. Annette Hetrick, Classified Adv. Mgr.. **Editorial:** Tom Chapin, Editor.

READING

READING EAGLE. 345 Penn St., Reading, PA 19601. Telephone: 610-371-5000. FAX: 610-371-5098. E-MAIL: news@readingeagle.com. URL: http://www.readingeagle.com. Mailing Address: PO Box 582, Reading, PA 19603. Year Established: 1868. Pub. Frequency: d. Page Size: broadsheet. Subscrip. Rate: $.50 newsstand/cover; $1.75 newsstand/cover Sun.; $215.80/yr home delivery; $91/yr home delivery for Sun.; $117/yr home delivery for weekend only. Adv. Rate: col. inch $33.28 **Wire Service(s):** AP, SH, MCT, CNS. Circulation: 61,907 morning (paid); 88,603 Sunday (paid). **Owner(s):** Reading Eagle Co., See address and contact information above. **Management:** William S. Flippin, Publisher. Walter Woolwine, Advertising Director. Richard D. Auman, Circulation Director. Lori Gerhart, Sales Manager. Larry R. Orkus, Associate Publisher. **Editorial:** Charles M. Gallagher, Managing Editor. Karen Miller, Business Editor. David Mowery, City Editor. Jim Homan, Editorial Page Editor. George Hatza, Entertainment Editor. George Landis, Farm Editor. Kathy Folk, Feature Editor. Christine Burger, Lifestyle Editor. James Kerr, Metro Editor. Dennis Deysher, News Editor. William Uhrich, Photo Editor. Carol Balinski, Religion Editor. Terry Bickhart, Sports Editor.

RIDGWAY

RIDGWAY RECORD. 20 Main St., Ridgway, PA 15853-1718. Telephone: 814-773-3161. FAX: 814-776-1086. E-MAIL: record@penn.com. URL: http://www.ridgwayrecord.com. Mailing Address: PO Box T, Ridgway, PA 15853-1718. Year Established: 1892. Pub. Frequency: d. (Mon.-Sat.) Page Size: broadsheet. Subscrip. Rate: $.50 newsstand/cover; $128/yr carrier delivery in county; $138/yr motor route in county; $132/yr mailed in county. **Wire Service(s):** AP. Circulation: 2,760 evening (paid). **Owner(s):** Horizon Publications, Inc., 1120 N. Carbon St., Ste.100, Marion, IL 62959. Telephone: 618-993-1693. **Management:** Darlene Coder, Publisher. **Editorial:** Michael Maneval, Editor.

SAYRE

MORNING TIMES. ISSN 1553-2283
201 N. Lehigh Ave., Sayre, PA 18840. Telephone: 570-888-9643. FAX: 570-888-6463. E-MAIL: news@morning-times.com. URL: http://www.morning-times.com. Year Established: 1891. Pub. Frequency: d. (Mon.-Sat.) Page Size: broadsheet. Subscrip. Rate: $.75 newsstand/cover; $126/yr carrier delivery; $168/yr mailed. **Wire Service(s):** AP. Circulation: 9,000 evening (paid). **Owner(s):** GateHouse Media, Inc, 350 WillowBrook Office Park, Fairport, NY 14450. Telephone: 585-598-0030. FAX: 585-248-2631. **Management:** Ted Mike Jr., Publisher. Vickee Mike, Advertising Director. **Editorial:** Warren Howler, Managing Editor. Holly Loeffler, Lifestyle Editor. Dave Post, Sports Editor.

SCRANTON

SCRANTON TIMES TRIBUNE. 149 Penn Ave., Scranton, PA 18503. URL: http://www.nepanews.com. Mailing Address: PO Box 3311, Scranton, PA 18505. Year Established: 1990. Pub. Frequency: d. Page Size: broadsheet. Subscrip. Rate: $.50 newsstand/cover; $1.50 newsstand/cover Sun.; $195/yr home delivery in area; $244.40/yr mailed in state. **Wire Service(s):** AP, NYT, MCT. Circulation: 40,500 evening (paid); 800,000 Sunday (paid). **Owner(s):** Times-Shamrock Communications, See address and contact information above. **Management:** Harold Marion, General Manager. Edward J. Lynett Jr., Publisher. Steve Sauder, Advertising Director. Michael Gaither, Circulation Manager. Susan Shotwell, Classified Adv. Mgr.. **Editorial:** Edward J. Lynett Jr., Editor. Larry Beaupre, Managing Editor. Terry Bonifanti, City Editor. Faith Golay, Feature Editor.

VIRGIN ISLANDS DAILY NEWS, THE. 149 Penn Ave,, Scranton, PA 18503. E-MAIL: dailynews@islands.vi. URL: http://www.virginislandsdailynews.com. Year Established: 1930. Pub. Frequency: 6/w. (Mon.-Sat.) Page Size: tabloid. Subscrip. Rate: $1 newsstand/cover. Adv. Rate: col. inch $36 Freelance Pay: $35-$60/article. **Wire Service(s):** AP, LAT-WAT, MCT. Circulation: 17,000 morning (paid); 17,000 Sunday (paid). **Owner(s):** Times-Shamrock Communications, See address and contact information above. **Management:** Jason Robbins, Publisher. Alfred Loiten, Circulation Director. Ken E Ryan, Production Director.Readers: Local and regional residents and tourists

SHAMOKIN

NEWS-ITEM. 707 N. Rock St., Shamokin, PA 17872. Telephone: 570-644-6397. FAX: 570-644-0892. E-MAIL: publisher@newsitem.com. URL: http://www.newsitem.com. Mailing Address: PO Box 587, Shamokin, PA 17872. Year Established: 1970. Pub. Frequency: d. (Mon.-Sat.) Page Size: broadsheet. Subscrip. Rate: $.50 newsstand/cover; $1.50 newsstand/cover Sun.; $158.60/yr carrier delivery. Adv. Rate: col. inch $13.75 **Wire Service(s):** AP. Circulation: 10,000 morning (paid). **Owner(s):** Times-Shamrock Communications, 149 Penn Ave., Scranton, PA 18503. Telephone: 717-348-9101. **Management:** Henry H Nyce, Publisher. Michael A. Joyce, Advertising Director. David Sickle, Circulation Director. **Editorial:** Andy Heintzelman, Editor. Charlie Roth, Sports.

SHARON

HERALD (SHARON), THE. 52 S Dock St, Sharon, PA 16146. Telephone: 724-981-6100. FAX: 724-981-7844. URL: http://www.sharonherald.com. Mailing Address: PO Box 51, Sharon, PA 16146-0051. Year Established: 1864. Pub. Frequency: d. Page Size: broadsheet. Subscrip. Rate: $.50 newsstand/cover; $1.25 newsstand/cover Sun.; $3.05 carrier delivery/wk.; $3.15 motor route/wk.; $14 mailed/mo. in county. Adv. Rate: col. inch $32.40 Circulation: 20,416 per issue (paid); 21,455 Sunday (paid). **Owner(s):** Community Newspaper Holdings, Inc., 3500 Colonnade Pkwy., Ste. 600, Birmingham, AL 25243. **Management:** John L. Lima, Publisher. Sharon Sorg, Advertising Director. Michael Linden, Circulation Manager.

SOMERSET

DAILY AMERICAN. ISSN 8750-247X
334 W. Main St., Somerset, PA 15501-0638. Telephone: 814-444-5900. FAX: 814-444-5966. E-MAIL: news@dailyamerican.com. URL: http://www.dailyamerican.com. Mailing Address: PO Box 638, Somerset, PA 15501-0638. Year Established: 1929. Pub. Frequency: d. (Mon.-Sat.) Page Size: broadsheet. Subscrip. Rate: $112/yr mailed in county; $180/yr mailed out of county; $60/yr online only. **Wire Service(s):** AP. Circulation: 13,971 morning (paid). **Owner(s):** Schurz Communications, Inc., 225 W. Colfax Ave., South Bend, IN 46626. Telephone: 219-287-1001. **Management:** Franklin O. Schurz Jr., President. Andrew Bruns, Publisher. Tom Koppenhofer, Advertising Manager. Samuel Foglesong, Circulation Manager. Patricia Foley, Classified Adv. Mgr.. **Editorial:** Brian Whipkey, Managing Editor. Christine Schircto, City Editor. Madolin Edwards, Community Editor. Ronald Pritts, Outdoor Editor. Mike O'Brien, Photographer. Madolin Edwards, Society Editor. Ronald Pritts, Sports Editor.

ST. MARYS

DAILY PRESS (ST. MARYS), THE. 245 Brussells St, St. Marys, PA 15857. Telephone: 814-781-1596. FAX: 814-834-7175. E-MAIL: dailypressadv@alltel.com. URL: http://www.smdailypress.com. Mailing Address: PO Box 353, St. Marys, PA 15857-0353. Year Established: 1910. Pub. Frequency: d. (Mon.-Sat.) Page Size: broadsheet. Subscrip. Rate: $.50 newsstand/cover; $128/yr carrier delivery local; $132/yr mailed in county; $138/yr mailed out of county. **Wire Service(s):** AP. Circulation: 5,700 evening (paid and free). **Owner(s):** Horizon Publications, Inc., 1120 N. Carbon St, Ste 100, Marion, IL 62959. **Management:** Darlene Coder, Publisher. Grace Catalano, Advertising Manager. Karen McKenna, Circulation Manager. Dawn Cheatle, Classified Adv. Mgr.. **Editorial:** Matt Madurski, Editor.

STATE COLLEGE

CENTRE DAILY TIMES. ISSN 0745-483X
3400 E College Ave, State College, PA 16801-7526. Telephone: 814-238-5000. FAX: 814-237-5966. E-MAIL: cfoley@centredaily.com. URL: http://www.centredaily.com. Mailing Address: PO Box 89, State College, PA 16804-0089. Year Established: 1898. Pub. Frequency: d. Page Size: broadsheet. Subscrip. Rate: $.50 newsstand/cover; $1 Sun.; $151.75/yr home delivery. **Wire Service(s):** AP, LAT-WAT. Circulation: 25,811 morning (paid); 33,733 Sunday (paid). **Owner(s):** The/McClatchy Company, 2100 Q St, Sacramento, CA 95816. Telephone: 916-321-1936. FAX: 916-321-1869. **Management:** Adrian Pratt, Publisher. Susan Leath, Advertising Director. Rod Burnham, Advertising Manager. **Editorial:** Teresa Bonner, City Editor.

STROUDSBURG

POCONO RECORD. 511 Lenox St., Stroudsburg, PA 18360. Telephone: 570-421-3000. FAX: 570-421-6284. E-MAIL: newsroom@poconorecord.com. URL: http://www.poconorecord.com. Year Established: 1894. Pub. Frequency: d. Page Size: broadsheet. Subscrip. Rate: $.50 newsstand/cover; $1.50 newsstand/cover Sun.; $53.95/yr for 13 wks.. Adv. Rate: col. inch $13.83 **Wire Service(s):** AP. Circulation: 24,000 morning (paid); 28,000 Sunday (paid). **Owner(s):** Ottaway Newspapers, Inc., PO Box 401, Campbell Hall, NY 10916. Telephone: 914-294-8181. **Management:** Peter L. Berry, Advertising Director. Barbara S. Schoebel, Advertising Manager. Lori-Ann Racki, Circulation Director. **Editorial:** Kim deBourbon, Editor. William J. Watson, Managing Editor. Susan Koomar, News Editor. Mike Kuhns, Sports Editor.

SUNBURY

DAILY ITEM (SUNBURY), THE. 200 Market St, Sunbury, PA 17801. Telephone: 800-792-2303. FAX: 870-286-2570. E-MAIL: news@dailyitem.com. URL: http://www.dailyitem.com. Year Established: 1937. Pub. Frequency: d. Page Size: broadsheet. Subscrip. Rate: $.50 newsstand/cover; $1.75 newsstand/cover Sun.; $172/yr home delivery local; $6 mailed/wk. in state. **Wire Service(s):** AP, LAT-WAT. Circulation: 28,000 evening (paid); 32,000 Sunday (paid). **Owner(s):** Community Newspaper Holdings, Inc., 3500 Colonnade Pkwy., Ste. 600, Birmingham, AL 35243-7017. **Management:** Janet Tippett, Publisher. Brad Bailey, Advertising Director. Fred Scheller, Circulation Manager. **Editorial:** Leonardd Ingrassia, Editor. Dave Hillard, Managing Editor.

TARENTUM

VALLEY NEWS DISPATCH. 210 Fourth Ave., Tarentum, PA 15084. Telephone: 724-224-4321. FAX: 724-226-7787. E-MAIL: vndnews@aol.com. URL: http://www.valleynewsdispatch.com. Mailing Address: PO Box 311, Tarentum, PA 15084. Year Established: 1891. Pub. Frequency: d. Page Size: broadsheet. Subscrip. Rate: $.50 newsstand/cover; $1 newsstand/cover Sun.; $26 carrier delivery/wk. in city for 13 wks., & motor rte.; $156/yr carrier delivery; $169/yr motor route. **Wire Service(s):** AP, GNS. Circulation: 35,000 evening (paid). **Owner(s):** Tribune-Review Publishing Co., 535 Keystone Dr., Warrendale, PA 15086. Telephone: 724-779-8742. **Management:** Richard Scaife, Publisher. Melanie Murray, Advertising Director. Randy Cook, Circulation Manager. Grace Barrett, Sales Manager. **Editorial:** Jeff Domenick, Managing Editor. Matt Provenzo, City Editor. Rebecca Killian, Lifestyle Editor. Bill Beckner, Sports Editor.

TITUSVILLE

TITUSVILLE HERALD. 209 W Spring St, Titusville, PA 16354. Telephone: 814-827-3634. FAX: 814-827-2512. E-MAIL: news@titusvilleherald.com. URL: http://www.titusvilleherald.com. Mailing Address: PO Box 328, Titusville, PA 16354. Year Established: 1865. Pub. Frequency: d. (Mon.-Sat.) Page Size: broadsheet. Subscrip. Rate: $.50 newsstand/cover; $10.30 motor route/mo. in city; $126.88/yr motor route in city. **Wire Service(s):** AP. Circulation: 5,000 morning (paid). **Owner(s):** Titusville Herald, Inc., See address and contact information above. **Management:** Michael Sample, Publisher.

TOWANDA

DAILY REVIEW/SUNDAY REVIEW. 116 Main St., Towanda, PA 18848. Telephone: 570-265-2151. FAX: 570-265-1648. E-MAIL: vharkness@epiz.net. URL: http://www.thedailyreview.com. Mailing Address: PO Box 503, Towanda, PA 18848. Year Established: 1880. Pub. Frequency: d. Page Size: broadsheet. Subscrip. Rate: $.50 newsstand/cover; $1.50 newsstand/cover Sun.; $169/yr carrier delivery; $182/yr mailed. Adv. Rate: col. inch $9 Freelance Pay: $5-$50/article. **Wire Service(s):** AP. Circulation: 9,800 morning (paid); 10,800 Sunday (paid). **Owner(s):** Towanda Printing Co., See address and contact information above. **Bureau(s):** 222 Desmond St., Sayre, PA 18840. Telephone: 570-888-9652. Contact: Ron Hosie, Editor. **Management:** James E. Towner, Publisher. Vickie Harkness, Advertising Manager. Debbie Fero, Circulation Manager. **Editorial:** C.J. Marshall, Business Editor. Kelly Andrus, Feature Editor. Ed Boardman, Photo Editor. Brian Fees, Sports.

TYRONE

DAILY HERALD (TYRONE), THE. 1018 Pennsylvania Ave., Tyrone, PA 16686. Telephone: 814-684-4000. FAX: 814-684-4238. Mailing Address: PO Box 246, Tyrone, PA 16686. Year Established: 1857. Pub. Frequency: d. (Mon.-Sat.) Page Size: broadsheet. Subscrip. Rate: $.50 newsstand/cover; $92.80/yr in town; $135/yr out of town. Adv. Rate: col. inch $3.80 **Wire Service(s):** AP. Circulation: 2,500 evening (paid). **Owner(s):** George Sample, III, 325 Penn St., Huntingdon, PA 16652. Telephone: 814-643-4040. FAX: 814-643-9628. **Management:** George Sample III, Publisher. Deb Shope, Advertising Manager. Joyce Alley, Circulation Manager. **Editorial:** Christina G Seiner, Editor. Bob Miller, Sports Editor.

UNIONTOWN

HERALD STANDARD. 8-18 E Church St, Uniontown, PA 15401. Telephone: 724-439-7500. FAX: 724-439-7528. E-MAIL: hsnews@hhs.net. URL: http://www.heraldstandard.com. Year Established: 1888. Pub. Frequency: d. Page Size: broadsheet. Subscrip. Rate: $.50 newsstand/cover; $1.25 newsstand/cover Sun.; $163.80/yr carrier delivery; $175/yr motor route. Adv. Rate: col. inch $33.80 Freelance Pay: $0.26/column-inch. **Wire Service(s):** AP. Circulation: 31,098 morning (paid); 32,986 Sunday (paid). **Owner(s):** Calkins Media Inc., 8400 Rte. 13, Levittown, PA 19057. Telephone: 215-949-4000. **Management:** Maureen Hranec, Advertising Director. Mary Ellen Friend, Classified Adv. Mgr.. **Editorial:** Mark O'Keefe, Executive Editor. Phil Brown, Managing Editor.

WARREN

TIMES OBSERVER. 205 Pennsylvania Ave., W., Warren, PA 16365. Telephone: 814-723-8200. FAX: 814-723-6922. URL: http://www.timesobserver.com. Mailing Address: PO Box 188, Warren, PA 16365. Year Established: 1966. Pub. Frequency: d. (Mon.-Sat.) Page Size: broadsheet. Subscrip. Rate: $.50 newsstand/cover; $.75 newsstand/cover Sat.; $10 carrier delivery/mo.; $10.50 motor route/mo.. **Wire Service(s):** AP. Circulation: 11,233 morning (paid). **Owner(s):** Ogden Newspapers, 19260 San Carlos Blvd, Fort Myers, FL 33931. Telephone: 239-463-4421. FAX: 304-233-0327. **Management:** Craig Bartoldson, Publisher. Gail Robillard, Advertising Manager. Kathy Hastings, Circulation Manager. Judy Miller, Business Manager. **Editorial:** Jude Dippold, Managing Editor. Eric Paddock, City Editor. John Sitler, Sports Editor.

WASHINGTON

OBSERVER-REPORTER/WASHINGTON COUNTY. ISSN 0891-0693
122 S. Main St., Washington, PA 15301. Telephone: 724-222-2200. FAX: 724-229-2754. E-MAIL: obspubco@cobweb.net. URL: http://www.observer-reporter.com. Year Established: 1808. Pub. Frequency: d. Page Size: broadsheet. Subscrip. Rate: $.50 newsstand/cover; $1 newsstand/cover Sun.; $142.50/yr carrier delivery. **Wire Service(s):** AP, NYT. Circulation: 35,426 morning (paid); 37,843 Sunday (paid). **Owner(s):** Observer Publishing Co., See address and contact information above. **Management:** Thomas P. Northrop, Publisher. Matt Chisler, Advertising Director. **Editorial:** A. Parker Burroughs, Editor. Louis Florian, Editorial Page Editor. Harry Funk, Feature Editor.

WAYNESBORO

RECORD HERALD (WAYNESBORO). 30 Walnut St., Waynesboro, PA 17268. Telephone: 717-762-2151. FAX: 717-762-3824. E-MAIL: news@therecordherald.com. URL: http://www.therecordherald.com. Mailing Address: PO Box 271, Waynesboro, PA 17268. Year Established: 1847. Pub. Frequency: d. (Mon.-Sat.) Page Size: broadsheet. Subscrip. Rate: $.75 newsstand/cover; $132.50/yr carrier delivery; $145.07/yr motor route; $180.32/yr mailed. **Wire Service(s):** AP. Circulation: 10,200 evening (paid). **Owner(s):** GateHouse Media, Inc, 350 WillowBrook Office Park, Fairport, NY 14450. Telephone: 585-598-0030. FAX: 585-248-2631. **Management:** Pat Patterson, Publisher. Dennis Shockey, Advertising Manager. Michael Straly, Circulation Manager. Shirley Gossert, Classified Adv. Mgr.. George McKee, Business Manager. **Editorial:** Sue Hadden, Managing Editor. Shawn Hardy, Lifestyle Editor. Scott Weaver, Sports Editor.

WAYNESBURG

OBSERVER-REPORTER/GREEN COUNTY. 32 Church St., Waynesburg, PA 15370. Telephone: 724-852-2602. FAX: 724-852-1497. URL: http://www.observer-reporter.com. Mailing Address: PO Box 960, Waynesburg, PA 15370. Year Established: 1808. Pub. Frequency: d. Page Size: broadsheet. Subscrip. Rate: $.50 newsstand/cover; $1 Sun.; $142.50/yr carrier delivery. **Wire Service(s):** AP, NYT. Circulation: 7,000 morning (paid); 7,532 Sunday (paid). **Owner(s):** Observer Publishing Co., 122 S. Main St., Washington, PA 15301. Telephone: 412-222-2200. **Management:** John Northrop, President. Thomas Northrop, Publisher. William B. Northrop Sr., Vice President. Matt Chisler, Advertising Director. Ed Martin, Circulation Manager. Mary Jo Spina, Classified Adv. Mgr.. **Editorial:** Louis Florian, Editorial Page Editor. Harry Funk, Feature Editor.

WESTCHESTER

DAILY LOCAL NEWS. ISSN 0163-3082
250 N. Bradford Ave., Westchester, PA 19382-2800. Telephone: 610-518-1363. FAX: 610-518-1358. E-MAIL: news@dailylocal.com. URL: http://www.dailylocal.com. Year Established: 1872. Pub. Frequency: d. Page Size: broadsheet. Subscrip. Rate: $.50 newsstand/cover; $1.50 Sun.; $4.75 home delivery/wk. local; $234.67/yr home delivery. **Wire Service(s):** AP, SH, CNS. Circulation: 33,420 morning (paid); 31,047 Sunday (paid). **Owner(s):** Journal Register Co., 50 W State St, 12th Fl, Trenton, NJ 08608. Telephone: 609-396-2200. **Management:** Shelley Meenan, Publisher. Christopher Smith, Circulation Director. **Editorial:** Andy Hachadorian, Executive Editor. Bill March, Managing Editor. Mike Rellahan, City Editor.

WILKES BARRE

CITIZEN'S VOICE, THE. ISSN 0163-4224
75 N. Washington St., Wilkes Barre, PA 18711. Telephone: 570-821-2000. FAX: 570-821-2247. URL: http://www.citizensvoice.com. Year Established: 1978. Pub. Frequency: d. Page Size: tabloid. Subscrip. Rate: $.50 newsstand/cover; $1.25 newsstand/cover Sun.; $170/yr home delivery local; $198/yr mailed in state. **Wire Service(s):** AP, SH. Circulation: 34,000 morning (paid); 30,000 Sunday (paid). **Owner(s):** Times-Shamrock Communications, 149 Penn Ave., Scranton, PA 18503. **Management:** Scott Lynette, Publisher. Lynn Ceccarelli, Advertising. Ann Marie Arnone, Advertising Director. Katey Lisk, Classified Adv. Mgr.. **Editorial:** Larry Holeva, Managing Editor. Claire Schechter, Asst. Managing Ed.. Neil Corbett, Sports Editor.

TIMES LEADER (WILKES BARRE), THE. ISSN 0896-4084
15 N. Main St., Wilkes Barre, PA 18711. Telephone: 570-829-7100. FAX: 570-829-5537. E-MAIL: allisonw@leader.net. URL: http://www.timesleader.com. Year Established: 1810. Pub. Frequency: d. Page Size: broadsheet. Subscrip. Rate: $.25 newsstand/cover; $1.50 newsstand/cover Sun.; $91 carrier delivery for 6 mos.. **Wire Service(s):** AP, MCT. Circulation: 48,000 morning (paid); 77,705 Sunday (paid). **Owner(s):** Knight Ridder, Inc., 50 W. San Fernando St., Ste. 1200, San Jose, CA 95113. Telephone: 831-938-7777. FAX: 831-938-7755. **Management:** Pat McHugh, Publisher. **Editorial:** Matt Golas, Editor. Joe Butkiewicz, Editorial Page Editor.

WILLIAMSPORT

WILLIAMSPORT SUN-GAZETTE. ISSN 1056-3083
252 W. Fourth St., Williamsport, PA 17701. Telephone: 570-326-1551. FAX: 570-323-0948. URL: http://www.sungazette.com. Mailing Address: PO Box 728, Williamsport, PA 17703-0728. Year Established: 1801. Pub. Frequency: d. Page Size: broadsheet. Subscrip. Rate: $.50 newsstand/cover; $1.25 newsstand/cover Sun.; $2.15 carrier delivery/wk.; $2.25 motor route/wk.; $117/yr. **Wire Service(s):** AP. Circulation: 33,000 evening (paid); 42,000 Sunday (paid). **Owner(s):** Ogden Newspapers of Minnesota, Inc., 1500 Main St., Wheeling, WV 26003. Telephone: 304-233-0100. **Management:** John Yahner, Publisher. John Leeser, Advertising Director. Jerry Newhouse, Circulation Manager. Linda Neupauer, Classified Adv. Mgr.. **Editorial:** Dave Troisi, Editor. Laura Janssen, News Editor.

YORK

YORK DAILY RECORD - YORK SUNDAY NEWS. 1891 Loucks Rd, York, PA 17408-9708. Telephone: 717-771-2000. FAX: 717-771-2009. E-MAIL: news@ydr.com. URL: http://www.ydr.com. Year Established: 1796. Pub. Frequency: d. (Mon.-Sun) Page Size: broadsheet. Subscrip. Rate: $.50 newsstand/cover; $14.95 carrier delivery/mo.. **Wire Service(s):** AP. Circulation: 76,000 Saturday (paid); 92,000 Sunday (paid); 45,000 morning (paid). **Owner(s):** MediaNews Group, Inc., 101 W Colfax Ave, Ste 1100, Denver, CO 80202. FAX: 303-954-6320. **Management:** Fred Uffelman, Publisher. George Sepic, VP Circulation. **Editorial:** Jim McClure, Editor. Randy Parker, Managing Editor. Cathy Hirko, Business Editor. Buffy Andrews, Feature Editor. Susan Martin, Metro Editor. Janeen Jones, News Editor. Chris Otto, Sports.

YORK DISPATCH/YORK SUNDAY NEWS. ISSN 1050-267X
205 N. George St., York, PA 17401. Telephone: 717-854-1575. E-MAIL: news@yorkdispatch.com. URL: http://www.yorkdispatch.com. Mailing Address: PO Box 2807, York, PA 17405. Year Established: 1876. Pub. Frequency: d. (Sun.-Fri.) Page Size: broadsheet. Subscrip. Rate: $.35 newsstand/cover; $1.25 newsstand/cover Sun.; $9 carrier delivery/mo.; $10 motor route/mo.. **Wire Service(s):** AP, SH, NYT, LAT-WAT. Circulation: 40,000 evening (paid); 95,000 Sunday (paid). **Owner(s):** MediaNews Group, Inc., 101 W Colfax Ave, Ste 1100, Denver, CO 80202. FAX: 303-954-6320. **Management:** William Dean Singleton, Publisher. Tamara Krebs, Classified Adv. Mgr.. **Editorial:** Deena Gross, Editor. Marc Charisse, Managing Editor. Pat Delany, City Editor. Greg Bowers, Sports Editor.

RHODE ISLAND

NEWPORT

NEWPORT DAILY NEWS, THE. ISSN 1053-2560
101 Malbone Rd., Newport, RI 02840. Telephone: 401-849-3300. FAX: 401-849-3306. URL: http://www.newportdailynews.com. Mailing Address: PO Box 420, Newport, RI 02840-0420. Year Established: 1846. Pub. Frequency: d. (Mon.-Sat.) Page Size: broadsheet. Subscrip. Rate: $.50 newsstand/cover; $.75 newsstand/cover Sat.; $132/yr home delivery; $150/yr mailed. Adv. Rate: col. inch $21 **Wire Service(s):** AP, SH. Circulation: 15,800 evening (paid). **Owner(s):** E. A. Sherman Publishing Co., See address and contact information above. **Management:** William F. Lucey III, General Manager. Albert K. Sherman Jr., Publisher. Bob Cross, Advertising Director. Robert Bidlack, Circulation Manager. **Editorial:** Sheila Mullowney, Managing Editor. Harvey Peters, News Editor. Scott Barrett, Sports Editor.

PAWTUCKET

TIMES (PAWTUCKET), THE. ISSN 1060-2747
23 Exchange St., Pawtucket, RI 02860. Telephone: 401-722-4000. FAX: 401-727-9252. E-MAIL: editort@pawtuckettimes.com. URL: http://www.pawtuckettimes.com. Year Established: 1885. Pub. Frequency: d. (Mon.-Sat.) Page Size: broadsheet. Subscrip. Rate: $.50 newsstand/cover; $3.40 home delivery/wk. local. Adv. Rate: col. inch $28.34 Freelance Pay: $25-$40/story. **Wire Service(s):** AP. Circulation: 15,649 morning (paid). **Owner(s):** Northeast Publishing Co., See address and contact information above. **Management:** Robert Jelenic, President. John Shields, Publisher. Melissa Emmott, Advertising Director. Mikel Saunby, Circulation Director. Sherri Oldfield, Classified Adv. Mgr.. **Editorial:** Bianca Pavoncello, Managing Editor. Terry Nau, Sports Editor.

PROVIDENCE

PROVIDENCE JOURNAL. 75 Fountain St., Providence, RI 02902. Telephone: 401-277-7000. FAX: 401-277-7346. URL: http://www.projo.com. Year Established: 1863. Pub. Frequency: d. Page Size: broadsheet. Subscrip. Rate: $.50 newsstand/cover; $2.05 newsstand/cover Sun.; $4.25 carrier delivery/wk.; $221/yr. **Wire Service(s):** AP, NYT, LAT-WAT, MCT. Circulation: 173,000 morning (paid); 254,000 Sunday (paid). **Owner(s):** Belo Corp., 400 S. Record St., Ste. 1300, Dallas, TX 75202. Telephone: 214-977-6606. **Management:** Howard Sutton, President. Michael Harwood, Advertising Director. Larry Ricardo, Classified Adv. Mgr.. Moira Broder, Marketing Director. **Editorial:** Joel Rawson, Executive Editor. Michael Delaney, Managing Editor. Carol Young, Associate Editor. Phil Kukielski, Feature Editor. Art Martone, Sports Editor.

WEST WARWICK

KENT COUNTY DAILY TIMES. 1353 Main St., West Warwick, RI 02893. Telephone: 401-821-7400. FAX: 401-828-0810. URL: http://www.ricentral.com. Mailing Address: P. O. Box 589, West Warwick, RI 02893-0589. Year Established: 1892. Pub. Frequency: d. (Mon.-Sat.) Page Size: broadsheet. Subscrip. Rate: $.50 newsstand/cover; $34.45 carrier delivery 13 wks; $137.80/yr carrier delivery. **Wire Service(s):** AP. Circulation: 138,030 evening (paid). **Owner(s):** Michael O'Sullivan, See address and contact information above. **Management:** David Dear, Publisher. Liz Scott, Advertising Director. Phil Rowell, Circulation Manager. Judy Hogan, Classified Adv. Mgr.. **Editorial:** Dan Trafford, Managing Editor.

WESTERLY

WESTERLY SUN, THE. ISSN 1065-1209
56 Main St., Westerly, RI 02891. Telephone: 401-348-1000. FAX: 401-348-5080. E-MAIL: rroy@thewesterlysun.com. URL: http://www.thewesterlysun.com. Mailing Address: PO Box 520, Westerly, RI 02891. Year Established: 1893. Pub. Frequency: d. Page Size: broadsheet. Subscrip. Rate: $.50 newsstand/cover; $1.50 newsstand/cover Sun.; $4.25 home delivery/wk.; $110.50 home delivery for 6 mos.; $221/yr home delivery. **Wire Service(s):** AP. Circulation: 10,100 morning (paid); 10,400 Sunday (paid). **Owner(s):** Record-Journal Publishing Co., See address and contact information above. **Management:** Raymond Roy, General Manager. Tim Ryan, Publisher. John Layton, Advertising Director. Michael Smith, Circulation Director. Karen Davis, Classified Adv. Mgr.. Bob Cardosa, Marketing Director. **Editorial:** David Tranchida, Editor. Angela Algier, City Editor.Readers: Southeast CT/Southwest RI

WOONSOCKET

CALL, THE. 75 Main St., Woonsocket, RI 02895. Telephone: 401-762-3000. FAX: 401-765-2834. E-MAIL: news@woonsocketcall.com. URL: http://www.woonsocketcall.com. Mailing Address: PO Box A, Woonsocket, RI 02895. Year Established: 1892. Pub. Frequency: d. Page Size: broadsheet. Subscrip. Rate: $.50 newsstand/cover; $1.50 newsstand/cover Sun.; $46.80 home delivery for 13 wks.; $187.20/yr home delivery. **Wire Service(s):** AP. Circulation: 26,600 morning (paid); 26,600 Sunday (paid). **Owner(s):** Journal Register Co., 50 W State St, 12th Fl, Trenton, NJ 08608. Telephone: 609-396-2200. **Management:** Mike Moses, Publisher. Marylynn St. Louis, Advertising Director. **Editorial:** Dan Trafford, Managing Editor. Kathie Raleigh, Lifestyle Editor. Mark Pickering, News Editor. Arlen Schweiger, Sports Editor.

SOUTH CAROLINA

AIKEN

AIKEN STANDARD. ISSN 0893-2557
326 Rutland Dr., Aiken, SC 29801. Telephone: 803-648-2311. FAX: 803-648-6052. E-MAIL: editorial@scescape-net. URL: http://www.aikenstandard.com. Mailing Address: PO Box 456, Aiken, SC 29802. Year Established: 1867. Pub. Frequency: d. Page Size: broadsheet. Subscrip. Rate: $.50 newsstand/cover; $1 newsstand/cover Sun.; $114/yr home delivery local. **Wire Service(s):** AP, MCT. Circulation: 16,000 evening (paid); 16,000 Sunday (paid). **Owner(s):** Evening Post Publishing Co., 134 Columbus St., Charleston, SC 29403. Telephone: 843-577-7111. FAX: 843-937-5545. **Management:** Scott B Hunter, Publisher. Arthur Zappa, Advertising Director. Scot Newcome, Circulation Manager. **Editorial:** Mike Gibbons, City Editor. Kenton Makin, Sports.

ANDERSON

ANDERSON INDEPENDENT-MAIL. ISSN 1093-9318
1000 Williamston Rd., Anderson, SC 29621. Telephone: 864-224-4321. FAX: 864-260-1276. URL: http://www.andersonindependentmail.com. Mailing Address: PO Box 2507, Anderson, SC 29622. Year Established: 1899. Pub. Frequency: d. Page Size: broadsheet. Subscrip. Rate: $.50 newsstand/cover; $1.50 newsstand/cover Sun.; $179/yr home delivery. **Wire Service(s):** AP, NYT. Circulation: 40,197 morning (paid); 46,302 Sunday (paid). **Owner(s):** E.W. Scripps Co., 312 Walnut St., 28th Fl., Cincinnati, OH 45202. Telephone: 513-977-3000. **Bureau(s):** P.O. Box 762, Lavonia, GA 30553. Telephone: 706-356-4308. **Management:** Fred L. Foster, President. Tony G. Marroni, Advertising. Jim C. Lasley, Circulation Manager. **Editorial:** T. Wayne Mitchell, Editor. Don Kausler Jr., Managing Editor. Tony Rogers, Automotive Editor. Leah Daniels, Beauty Editor. Wendy Weinhold, Business Editor. Leah Daniels, Church Editor. Bonnie C. Williams, Columnist. Leah Daniels, Entertainment Editor. John Brasier, Sports Editor.

BEAUFORT

BEAUFORT GAZETTE. ISSN 1090-8285
1556 Salem Rd., Beaufort, SC 29902. Telephone: 843-524-3183. FAX: 843-524-8728. E-MAIL: gazette@beaufortgazette.com. URL: http://www.beaufortgazette.com. Mailing Address: PO Box 399, Beaufort, SC 29901-0399. Year Established: 1897. Pub. Frequency: d. Page Size: broadsheet. Subscrip. Rate: $.25 newsstand/cover; $1 newsstand/cover Sun.; $120/yr home delivery in county; $136/yr mailed in state. **Wire Service(s):** AP. Circulation: 11,500 morning (paid); 11,500 Sunday (paid). **Owner(s):** The/McClatchy Company, 2100 Q St, Sacramento, CA 95816. Telephone: 916-321-1936. FAX: 916-321-1869. **Management:** Sara Borton, Publisher. Fitz McAden, Vice President. Sandy Gillis, VP Advertising.

BLUFFTON

BLUFFTON TODAY. 52 Persimmon St., Bluffton, SC 29910-6525. Telephone: 843-815-0800. FAX: 843-815-0898. URL: http://www.blufftontoday.com. Mailing Address: PO Box 486, Bluffton, SC 29910. Year Established: 2005.Pub. Frequency: d. Page Size: tabloid Circulation: 15,000 morning (free). **Owner(s):** Morris Multimedia, Inc., PO Box 936, Augusta, GA. Telephone: 706-724-0851. **Management:** Tim Anderson, Publisher. Marc Jenkins, Advertising Manager. Lee Blue, Circulation Manager. **Editorial:** Kyle Poplin, Executive Editor. Robert C Holquist, Managing Editor. Tim Wood, Sports Editor.

ISLAND PACKET. ISSN 0746-4886
10 Buck Island Rd., Bluffton, SC 29910. Telephone: 843-706-8100. FAX: 843-706-3070. E-MAIL: publisher@islandpacket.com. URL: http://www.islandpacket.com. Mailing Address: PO Box 5727, Hilton Head, SC 29938. Year Established: 1970. Pub. Frequency: d. Page Size: broadsheet. Subscrip. Rate: $.25 newsstand/cover; $1 newsstand/cover Sun.; $114/yr home delivery. **Wire Service(s):** AP, NYT. Circulation: 18,000 morning (paid); 19,500 Sunday (paid). **Owner(s):** The/McClatchy Company, 2100 Q St, Sacramento, CA 95816. Telephone: 916-321-1936. FAX: 916-321-1869. **Bureau(s): Management:** Sara Borton, Publisher. Sandy Gillis, Advertising Director. Robert Jones, Circulation Director. Susan Green, Classified Adv. Mgr.. **Editorial:** Fitz McAden, Executive Editor. Sally Mahan, Managing Editor. Jeff Kidd, Sports Editor.

CHARLESTON

POST AND COURIER, THE. ISSN 1061-5105
134 Columbus St., Charleston, SC 29403. Telephone: 843-577-7111. FAX: 843-937-5545. E-MAIL: ltarleton@postandcourier.com. URL: http://www.charleston.net. Year Established: 1803. Pub. Frequency: d. Page Size: broadsheet. Subscrip. Rate: $.50 newsstand/cover; $1.50 newsstand/cover Sun.; $13.50 home delivery/mo.; $40.50 home delivery for 3 mos.; $150/yr home delivery. **Wire Service(s):** AP, LAT-WAT, MCT. Circulation: 101,288 morning (paid); 113,999 Sunday (paid). **Owner(s):** Evening Post Publishing Co., See address and contact information above. **Management:** Mickey Bella, General Manager. Larry Tarleton, Publisher. Bill Cranford, Advertising Director. Steve Wagenlander, Circulation Director. Joel Cardwell, Classified Adv. Mgr.. **Editorial:** Barbara Williams, Editor. William Hawkins, Executive Editor. John McDermott, Business Editor. Rick Nelson, City Editor. Ron Menchaca, Environmental Editor. Steve Mullins, Lifestyle Editor. Malcolm DeWitt, Sports Editor.

Dailies

COLUMBIA

STATE (COLUMBIA), THE. 1401 Shop Rd, Columbia, SC 29201. Telephone: 803-771-6161. FAX: 803-771-8363. URL: http://www.thestate.com. Mailing Address: PO Box 1333, Columbia, SC 29202. Year Established: 1891. Pub. Frequency: d. Page Size: broadsheet. Subscrip. Rate: $.50 newsstand/cover; $1.50 newsstand/cover Sun.; $45.50/yr. **Wire Service(s):** AP, UPI, NYT. Circulation: 107,153 morning (paid); 139,521 Sunday (paid). **Owner(s):** The/McClatchy Company, 2100 Q St, Sacramento, CA 95816. Telephone: 916-321-1936. FAX: 916-321-1869. **Management:** Henry Haitz III, Publisher. Parks Rogers, VP Advertising. Pat McFarland, VP Circulation. **Editorial:** Mark Lett, Executive Editor. Tonnya Kennedy Kohn, Managing Editor.

FLORENCE

MORNING NEWS (FLORENCE). 310 S. Dargan St., Florence, SC 29501. Telephone: 843-317-6397. FAX: 843-317-7292. URL: http://www.morningnewsonline.com. Mailing Address: PO Box 100528, Florence, SC 29501. Year Established: 1922. Pub. Frequency: d. Page Size: broadsheet. Subscrip. Rate: $.50 newsstand/cover; $1.25 newsstand/cover Sun.; $11.50/mo.; $138/yr. Freelance Pay: $20/article. **Wire Service(s):** AP, SH. Circulation: 36,600 morning (paid); 38,500 Sunday (paid). **Owner(s):** Media General, Inc., 333 E. Franklin St., Richmond, VA 23219. Telephone: 804-649-6000. FAX: 804-649-6898. **Management:** Michael Miller, Publisher. Mark Miller, Advertising Director. John Barlow, Advertising Manager. Mark Campbell, Circulation Director. Fay Morris, Classified Adv. Mgr.. **Editorial:** Harry Logan, Editor. Daniel Perry, Entertainment Editor. Anna Bowman, Librarian. Andy Cole, Metro Editor. Chris Clark, Outdoor Editor. David Ackerman, Photographer. Traci Bridges, Political Editor. Sam Bundy, Sports Editor.

GREENVILLE

GREENVILLE NEWS. 305 S. Main St., Greenville, SC 29601. Telephone: 864-298-4259. FAX: 864-298-4395. E-MAIL: adinfo@greenville.infi.net. URL: http://www.greenvilleonline.com. Mailing Address: PO Box 1688, Greenville, SC 29602. Year Established: 1875. Pub. Frequency: d. Page Size: broadsheet. Subscrip. Rate: $.50 newsstand/cover; $1.50 newsstand/cover Sun.; $3.92 carrier delivery/wk.; $196.64/yr carrier delivery. **Wire Service(s):** AP, NYT, LAT-WAT. Circulation: 95,468 morning (paid); 127,494 Sunday (paid). **Owner(s):** Gannett Company, Inc., 7950 Jones Branch Dr, McLean, VA 22107. Telephone: 703-854-6000. **Management:** Steve Brandt, Publisher. Steve Lundblade, Advertising Director. Mike McKillip, Circulation Director. George Gardner, Photography Director. **Editorial:** John S Pittman, Executive Editor. Chris Weston, Managing Editor. Woody White, Business Editor. Beth Padgett, Editorial Page Editor. Jan Phillips, Feature Editor. Ralph Jeffery, News Editor. Bart Wright, Sports Editor. Marion Elliott, Suburban Editor.

GREENWOOD

INDEX-JOURNAL. 610 Phoenix St., Greenwood, SC 29646. Telephone: 864-223-1411. FAX: 864-223-7331. URL: http://www.indexjournal.com. Mailing Address: PO Box 1018, Greenwood, SC 29648-1018. Year Established: 1919. Pub. Frequency: d. Page Size: standard. Subscrip. Rate: $.50 newsstand/cover; $1.50 newsstand/cover Sun.; $156.60/yr home delivery; $304.80/yr mailed. **Wire Service(s):** AP. Circulation: 17,000 evening (paid); 18,800 Sunday (paid). **Owner(s):** Judith M. Burns, See address and contact information above. **Management:** Judith M. Burns, Publisher. Pam Still, Advertising Director. Albert Ashley, Circulation Manager. Ashley Henry, Classified Adv. Mgr.. **Editorial:** Richard Whiting, Executive Editor. Shawn Lewis, Managing Editor. William A. Collins, Editorial Page Editor.

MYRTLE BEACH

SUN NEWS, THE. 914 Frontage Rd, E, Myrtle Beach, SC 29577-6700. Telephone: 843-626-8555. FAX: 843-626-0208. URL: http://www.myrtlebeachonline.com. Mailing Address: PO Box 406, Myrtle Beach, SC 29578-0406. Year Established: 1935. Pub. Frequency: d. Page Size: broadsheet. Subscrip. Rate: $.50 newsstand/cover; $1.50 newsstand/cover Sun.; $43 home delivery for 13 wks.; $156/yr home delivery. **Wire Service(s):** AP, NYT. Circulation: 48,003 morning (paid); 58,544 Sunday (paid). **Owner(s):** The/McClatchy Company, 2100 Q St, Sacramento, CA 95816. Telephone: 916-321-1936. FAX: 916-321-1869. **Management:** Gary Wortel, Publisher. Bill Galer, Advertising Director. **Editorial:** Trisha O'Connor, Editor. Cassidy Strader, News Editor.

ORANGEBURG

TIMES & DEMOCRAT, THE. 1010 Broughton St., Orangeburg, SC 29115. Telephone: 803-533-5500. FAX: 803-533-5526. E-MAIL: ttad@oburg.net. URL: http://www.thetandd.com. Mailing Address: P.O. Drawer 1766, Orangeburg, SC 29116. Year Established: 1881. Pub. Frequency: d. Page Size: broadsheet. Subscrip. Rate: $.35 newsstand/cover; $1 newsstand/cover Sun.; $75.25 carrier delivery for 6 mos.; $112.40 mailed for 6 mos.. **Wire Service(s):** AP. Circulation: 18,000 morning (paid); 18,000 Sunday (paid). **Owner(s):** Lee Enterprises, Inc., 201 N. Harrison St., Davenport, IA 52801-1924. **Management:** Cathy C Hughes, Publisher. Barbara West-Ravenell, Circulation Manager. **Editorial:** Lee Harter, Managing Editor. Nancy Wooten, Lifestyle Editor. Van Hope, Photographer.

ROCK HILL

HERALD (ROCK HILL), THE. 132 W Main, Rock Hill, SC 29730. Telephone: 803-329-4000. FAX: 803-329-4021. URL: http://www.heraldonline.com. Mailing Address: PO Box 11707, Rock Hill, SC 29731. Year Established: 1872. Pub. Frequency: d. Page Size: broadsheet. Subscrip. Rate: $.35 newsstand/cover; $1 newsstand/cover Sun.; $78/yr. Adv. Rate: col. inch $5.80 Freelance Pay: $25/article. **Wire Service(s):** AP, SH, LAT-WAT. Circulation: 31,614 morning (paid); 33,020 Sunday (paid). **Owner(s):** The/McClatchy Company, 2100 Q St, Sacramento, CA 95816. Telephone: 916-321-1936. FAX: 916-321-1869. **Management:** Valerie Canepa, Publisher. Andy Bass, Advertising Director. Michelle Reid, Circulation Manager. **Editorial:** Paul Osmundson, Editor.

SENECA

DAILY JOURNAL (SENECA), THE. 210 W N. First St, Seneca, SC 29678. Telephone: 864-882-2375. FAX: 864-882-2381. URL: http://www.dailyjm.com. Mailing Address: PO Box 547, Seneca, SC 29679-0547. Pub. Frequency: d. (Tue.-Sat.) Subscrip. Rate: $.50 newsstand/cover; $89/yr home delivery Circulation: 8,050 (paid). **Owner(s):** Edwards Group Inc, 125 Eagles Nest, Seneca, SC 29678. Telephone: 864-882-3272. **Management:** Joni Weerheim, Publisher. Jay Brooks, Advertising Director. Scott Nickles, Circulation Director. Diane Winstead, Classified Adv. Mgr.. **Editorial:** Brett McLaughlin, Editor.

DAILY MESSENGER, THE. 210 W N. First St, Seneca, SC 29678. Telephone: 864-882-2375. FAX: 864-882-2381. URL: http://www.upstatetoday.com. Mailing Address: PO Box 547, Seneca, SC 29679. Year Established: 1954. Pub. Frequency: d. (Tue.-Sat.) Page Size: standard. Subscrip. Rate: $.50 newsstand/cover; $89/yr local. Circulation: 15,000 per issue (paid). **Owner(s):** Edwards Group Inc, 125 Eagles Nest, Seneca, SC 29678. Telephone: 864-882-3272. **Management:** Joni Weerheim, Publisher. Jay Brooks, Advertising Director. Scott Nickles, Circulation Director. Diane Winstead, Classified Adv. Mgr.. **Editorial:** Brett McLaughlin, Editor.

SUMTER

ITEM (SUMTER), THE. 20 N. Magnolia St., Sumter, SC 29150. Telephone: 803-774-1200. FAX: 803-774-1288. E-MAIL: jack@theitem.com. URL: http://www.theitem.com. Year Established: 1894. Pub. Frequency: d. Page Size: broadsheet. Subscrip. Rate: $.50 newsstand/cover; $1.25 newsstand/cover Sun.; $113.40/yr home delivery; $198/yr mailed. Adv. Rate: col. inch $22.35 **Wire Service(s):** AP. Circulation: 20,500 morning (paid); 21,250 Sunday (paid). **Owner(s):** Osteen Publishing Co., PO Box 1677, Sumter, SC 29151. Telephone: 803-774-1200. **Management:** Kyle Osteen, General Manager. Jack Osteen, Publisher. Bob Neimon, Advertising Director. Earle Woodward, Circulation Director. Bobby Touchberry, Classified Adv. Mgr.. Barry Lewis, Controller. **Editorial:** Hubert D. Osteen Jr., Editor. Robbie Evens, Managing Editor. Keith Gedemke, Photo Editor. Dennis Brunson, Sports Editor.

UNION

UNION DAILY TIMES. 100 Times Blvd., Union, SC 29379. Telephone: 864-427-1234. FAX: 864-427-1237. E-MAIL: gwilliams@uniondailytimes.com. URL: http://www.uniondailytimes.com. Mailing Address: P.O. Box 749, Union, SC 29379-0749. Year Established: 1850. Pub. Frequency: d. (Mon.-Sat.) Page Size: broadsheet. Subscrip. Rate: $.50 newsstand/cover; $96/yr home delivery; $142.80/yr mailed. **Wire Service(s):** AP. Circulation: 7,000 evening (paid). **Owner(s):** Mid-South Management Co., Inc., See address and contact information above. **Management:** Anthony Summerlin, Publisher. Don Cody, Circulation Manager. Brenda Gallo, Classified Adv. Mgr.. **Editorial:** Graham Williams, Managing Editor. Mark Brasington, Photographer. Brian Whitmore, Sports.

SOUTH DAKOTA

ABERDEEN

AMERICAN NEWS. 124 S Second St, Aberdeen, SD 57401-4010. Telephone: 605-225-4100. FAX: 800-925-4100. E-MAIL: americannews@aberdeennews. URL: http://www.aberdeennews.com. Year Established: 1885. Pub. Frequency: d. Page Size: standard. Subscrip. Rate: $43.99 carrier delivery for 13 wks.; $167.44/yr carrier delivery; $171.60/yr mailed in SD & ND. **Wire Service(s):** AP, MCT. Circulation: 16,259 morning (paid); 18,000 Sunday (paid). **Owner(s):** Schurz Communications, Inc., See address and contact information above. **Management:** David Leone, Publisher. Christy Orwig, Advertising Director. David Nelson, Circulation Manager. **Editorial:** Cindy Eikamp, Executive Editor. Terry Salfrank, Production Manager. Anita Meyer, City Editor. Todd Anderson, Copy Editor. Dawn Dietrich-Sahli, Photographer. Angela Mettler, Reporter.

BROOKINGS

BROOKINGS REGISTER. 312 Fifth St., Brookings, SD 57006-0177. Telephone: 605-692-6271. FAX: 605-692-2979. E-MAIL: registernews@brookingsregister.com. URL: http://www.brookingsregister.com. Mailing Address: PO Box 177, Brookings, SD 57006-0177. Year Established: 1879. Pub. Frequency: d. (Mon.-Sat.) Page Size: broadsheet. Subscrip. Rate: $.50 newsstand/cover; $106.36/yr home delivery local; $162.05/yr mailed out of area. **Wire Service(s):** AP. Circulation: 5,200 evening (paid). **Owner(s):** News Media Corp., PO Box 46, Rochelle, IL 61068. Telephone: 815-562-2061. FAX: 815-562-2060. **Management:** John C. Tompkins, President. Will McMacken, Publisher. Jessica Johnson, Circulation Manager. Hillary Bullis, Production Director. Christina Nelson, Business Manager. **Editorial:** Jerrod Niedermyer, Managing Editor. Tigh Lessman, Sports Editor.

HURON

PLAINSMAN, THE. 49 Third St., S.E., Huron, SD 57350. Telephone: 605-352-6401. FAX: 605-352-7754. URL: http://www.plainsman.com. Mailing Address: PO Box 1278, Huron, SD 57350. Year Established: 1886. Pub. Frequency: d. (Tue.-Sun.) Page Size: broadsheet. Subscrip. Rate: $.50 newsstand/cover; $1 newsstand/cover Sun.; $10.11 carrier delivery/mo.. Adv. Rate: col. inch $12.70 **Wire Service(s):** AP. Circulation: 8,000 morning (paid); 9,000 Sunday (paid). **Owner(s):** News Media Corp., PO Box 46, Rochelle, IL 61068. Telephone: 815-562-2061. FAX: 815-562-2060. **Management:** Mark Davis, Publisher. **Editorial:** George Thompson, Executive Editor. Allen Creecy, Production Manager. Mike Carroll, Sports.

MADISON

MADISON DAILY LEADER. 214 S Eagan Ave, Madison, SD 57042. Telephone: 605-256-4555. FAX: 605-256-6190. E-MAIL: jon@madisondailyleader.com. URL: http://www.madisonet.com. Mailing Address: PO Box 348, Madison, SD 57042. Year Established: 1890. Pub. Frequency: d. (Mon.-Fri.) Page Size: broadsheet. Subscrip. Rate: $.50 newsstand/cover; $98/yr carrier delivery in town; $90.80/yr mailed in county & adj. cys.; $99.80/yr mailed in state. **Wire Service(s):** AP. Circulation: 8,000 evening (paid and free). **Owner(s):** Hunter Publishing, Inc., See address and contact information above. **Management:** Jon M. Hunter, Publisher. Autumn Rasmussen, Advertising Manager. Laurie Walker, Classified Adv. Mgr.. **Editorial:** Marcia Schoeberl, Editor. Elisa Sand, Photographer. Dan Holsworth, Sports Editor.

MITCHELL

DAILY REPUBLIC (MITCHELL). 120 S. Lawler St., Mitchell, SD 57301. Telephone: 605-996-5514. FAX: 605-996-7793. URL: http://www.mitchellrepublic.com. Mailing Address: PO Box 1288, Mitchell, SD 57301. Year Established: 1882. Pub. Frequency: d. (Mon.-Sat.) Page Size: broadsheet. Subscrip. Rate: $.50 newsstand/cover; $122/yr mailed in state; $177/yr mailed out of state. **Wire Service(s):** AP. Circulation: 12,000 evening (paid). **Owner(s):** Jeff Meyer, 101 Fifth St., N., Fargo, ND 58207. Telephone: 701-223-7311. **Management:** Noel Hamiel, Publisher. Kevin Flemmer, Advertising Manager. Jon Louder, Circulation Manager. **Editorial:** Kim Galliano, Managing Editor. Korrie Wenzel, Sports Editor.

PIERRE

CAPITAL JOURNAL. 333 W Dakota, Pierre, SD 575601. E-MAIL: news@capjournal.com. URL: http://www.capjournal.com. Mailing Address: PO Box 878, Pierre, SD 57501-0878. Pub. Frequency: d. (Mon.-Fri.) Page Size: broadsheet. Subscrip. Rate: $.75 newsstand/cover; $95/yr carrier delivery; $122/yr mailed. Adv. Rate: col. inch $7.14 Circulation: 10,000 morning (paid). **Owner(s):** Wick Communications, Inc., 333 W. Wilcox, Ste. 302, Sierra Vista, AZ 85632. **Management:** Russell Cannon, Publisher. Lois Ries, Advertising Manager. Amanda Peck, Classified Adv. Mgr.. **Editorial:** Andrew Cutler, Editor. Mike Smith, Sports Editor.

RAPID CITY

RAPID CITY JOURNAL. 507 Main St., Rapid City, SD 57701. Telephone: 605-394-8300. FAX: 605-394-8462. E-MAIL: journal@rapidnet.com. URL: http://www.rapidcityjournal.com. Mailing Address: PO Box 450, Rapid City, SD 57709. Year Established: 1878. Pub. Frequency: d. Page Size: broadsheet. Subscrip. Rate: $.60 newsstand/cover; $1.75 newsstand/cover Sun.; $170/yr home delivery; $190/yr mailed. **Wire Service(s):** AP, NYT. Circulation: 32,000 morning (paid); 36,500 Sunday (paid). **Owner(s):** Lee Enterprises, Inc., 201 N. Harrison St, Ste 600, Davenport, IA 52801-1924. **Management:** Bill Masterson Jr., Publisher. Brad Slater, Advertising Director. Troy Kilpatrick, Circulation Manager. Jim Wilber, Classified Adv. Mgr.. **Editorial:** Peggy Sagen, Editor. Ron Bender, Local News Editor.

SIOUX FALLS

ARGUS LEADER. 200 S. Minnesota Ave., Sioux Falls, SD 57104. Telephone: 605-331-2200. FAX: 605-331-2260. URL: http://www.argusleader.com. Mailing Address: PO Box 5034, Sioux Falls, SD 57117-5034. Year Established: 1881. Pub. Frequency: d. Page Size: broadsheet. Subscrip. Rate: $.50 newsstand/cover; $1.50 newsstand/cover Sun.; $16.26 carrier delivery/mo.; $195/yr carrier delivery; $17.33 motor route/mo.; $208/yr mailed $2102/mo sd ia mn ne. **Wire Service(s):** AP, LAT-WAT, MCT, GNS. Circulation: 54,000 morning (paid); 77,000 Sunday (paid). **Owner(s):** Gannett Company, Inc., 7950 Jones Branch Dr., McLean, VA 22107-0001. Telephone: 703-854-6000. **Management:** Arnold Garson, Publisher. Coreen Fisher, Advertising Director. Jay Winkler, Circulation Director. **Editorial:** Randell Beck, Executive Editor. Maricarrol Kueter, Managing Editor. Jacqueline Palfy, Lifestyle Editor. Laura Buseman, News Editor.

SPEARFISH

BLACK HILLS PIONEER. ISSN 1061-6179
315 Seaton Cir., Spearfish, SD 57783. Telephone: 605-642-2761. E-MAIL: news@bhpioneer.com. URL: http://www.bhpioneer.com. Mailing Address: PO Box 7, Spearfish, SD 57783. Year Established: 1876. Pub. Frequency: d. (Mon.-Sat.) Page Size: tabloid. Subscrip. Rate: $.50 newsstand/cover; $9 carrier delivery/mo. & motor rte. Adv. Rate: col. inch $9.95 **Wire Service(s):** AP. Circulation: 25,000 evening (paid). **Owner(s):** Seaton Publishing Co., See address and contact information above. **Management:** Letti Lister, General Manager. Stewart Huntington, Publisher. Letti Lister, Advertising Manager. Dale Audis, Circulation Manager. Ardy Richards, Classified Adv. Mgr.. **Editorial:** Heather Murschel, Managing Editor.

WATERTOWN

WATERTOWN PUBLIC OPINION. 120 Third Ave., N.W., Watertown, SD 57201. Telephone: 605-886-6901. FAX: 605-886-4280. E-MAIL: advertise@thepublicopinion.com. URL: http://www.thepublicopinion.com. Mailing Address: PO Box 10, Watertown, SD 57201. Year Established: 1887. Pub. Frequency: d. (Mon.-Sat.) Page Size: broadsheet. Subscrip. Rate: $.50 newsstand/cover; $107.38/yr home delivery local. Adv. Rate: col. inch $14.75 **Wire Service(s):** AP. Circulation: 13,000 evening (controlled and free). **Owner(s):** Watertown Public Opinion Company, See address and contact information above. **Management:** Mark Roby, Publisher. Paul Reinschmidt, Circulation Manager. **Editorial:** Jerry Steinley, Editor. Bob Mooney, City Editor.

YANKTON

YANKTON DAILY PRESS & DAKOTAN. 319 Walnut St., Yankton, SD 57078. Telephone: 605-665-7811. FAX: 605-665-1721. E-MAIL: newsroom@yankton.net; classified@yankton.net. URL: http://www.yankton.net. Mailing Address: PO Box 56, Yankton, SD 57078. Year Established: 1861. Pub. Frequency: d. (Mon.-Sat.) Page Size: standard. Subscrip. Rate: $.50 newsstand/cover; $.75 newsstand/cover Sat.; $25.86 mailed for 3 mos.; $39.89 mailed out of area for 3 mos.. Circulation: 8,200 evening (paid). **Owner(s):** Morris Multimedia, Inc., PO Box 936, Augusta, GA 30903-0936. Telephone: 706-724-0851. **Management:** Gary Wood, Publisher. David Jeffcoat, Circulation Manager. Heather Heimes, Classified Adv. Mgr.. Tonya Schild, Business Manager. **Editorial:** Kelly Hertz, Managing Editor. James Cimburek, Sports.

TENNESSEE

ATHENS

DAILY POST-ATHENIAN. 320 S Jackson St, Athens, TN 37371. Telephone: 423-745-5664. FAX: 423-745-8295. URL: http://www.dpa.xtn.net. Mailing Address: PO Box 340, Athens, TN 37371-0340. Year Established: 1848. Pub. Frequency: d. (Mon.-Fri.) Page Size: broadsheet. Subscrip. Rate: $.50 newsstand/cover; $1.25 newsstand/cover for Fri.; $93/yr home delivery. Adv. Rate: col. inch $15.10 **Wire Service(s):** AP. Circulation: 20,000 evening (paid and free). **Owner(s):** Jones Media Group, 121 W Summer St, Greenville, TN 37745. Telephone: 423-581-0088. FAX: 423-235-7012. **Management:** Ralph Baldwin, Publisher. Rhonda Elkins, Advertising Manager. **Editorial:** Doug Headrick, Editor.

CHATTANOOGA

CHATTANOOGA TIMES FREE PRESS. 400 E 11th St, Chattanooga, TN 37403. Telephone: 423-756-6900. FAX: 423-756-3683. URL: http://www.timesfreepress.com. Year Established: 1936. Pub. Frequency: d. Page Size: broadsheet. Subscrip. Rate: $.50 newsstand/cover; $1.50 newsstand/cover Sun.; $135.60/yr home delivery. Circulation: 80,000 morning (paid); 110,000 Sunday (paid). **Owner(s):** Wehco Media, Inc., PO Box 2221, Little Rock, AR 72203. FAX: 501-378-3527. **Management:** Tom Griscom, Publisher. Mike Baskin, Advertising Director. Pamela Austin, Advertising Manager. David Enoch, Circulation Director. Mike Machaskee, Classified Adv. Mgr.. **Editorial:** Tom Griscom, Executive Editor. John Vass, Business Editor. Rick Moore, News Editor. Jay Greeson, Sports Editor.

CLARKSVILLE

LEAF-CHRONICLE, THE. ISSN 0745-7367
200 Commerce St., Clarksville, TN 37040. Telephone: 931-552-1808. FAX: 931-648-8001. E-MAIL: genewasher@theleafchronicle.com. URL: http://www.theleafchronicle.com. Mailing Address: PO Box 31029, Clarksville, TN 37040-0018. Year Established: 1808. Pub. Frequency: d. Page Size: broadsheet. Subscrip. Rate: $.50 newsstand/cover; $1.50 newsstand/cover Sun.; $148.20/yr home delivery. **Wire Service(s):** AP. Circulation: 22,500 morning (paid); 26,000 Sunday (paid). **Owner(s):** Gannett Company, Inc., 7950 Jones Branch Dr., McLean, VA 22107-0001. Telephone: 703-854-6000. **Management:** F. Gene Washer, President. Tim Koewler, Circulation Manager. **Editorial:** Richard Stevens, Executive Editor. Thomya Hogan, City Editor. Chris Smith, News Editor. Jimmy Trodglen, Sports Editor.

CLEVELAND

CLEVELAND DAILY BANNER. 1505 25th St., N.W., Cleveland, TN 37311. Telephone: 423-472-5041. FAX: 423-476-1046, 423-614-6529. E-MAIL: advertising@clevelandbanner.com. URL: http://www.clevelandbanner.com. Mailing Address: PO Box 3600, Cleveland, TN 37320-3600. Year Established: 1854. Pub. Frequency: d. (Sun.-Fri.) Page Size: broadsheet. Subscrip. Rate: $.50 newsstand/cover; $1 newsstand/cover Sun.; $38 home delivery for 6 mos.; $75/yr home delivery. **Wire Service(s):** AP. Circulation: 16,000 evening (paid); 17,500 Sunday (paid). **Owner(s):** Cleveland Newspapers, Inc., See address and contact information above. **Management:** Jim Bryant, General Manager. C. Lee Walls, President. Stephen Crass, Publisher. Jack Bennett, Advertising Manager. Herb Lacy, Circulation Manager. **Editorial:** Gwenn Swiger, Executive Editor. David Davis, Managing Editor. Samantha Serum, Beauty Editor. Bettie Marlowe, Fashion Editor. Richard Melvin, Sports Editor.

COLUMBIA

DAILY HERALD (COLUMBIA). 1115 S. Main St., Columbia, TN 38401. Telephone: 931-388-6464. FAX: 931-388-1003. URL: http://www.columbiadailyherald.com. Mailing Address: PO Box 1425, Columbia, TN 38402. Year Established: 1848. Pub. Frequency: d. (Sun.-Fri.) Page Size: broadsheet. Subscrip. Rate: $.50 newsstand/cover; $1 newsstand/cover Sun.; $22.95 home delivery for 3 mos.; $91.80/yr home delivery prepaid. **Wire Service(s):** AP. Circulation: 11,567 morning (paid); 13,344 Sunday (paid). **Owner(s):** Donrey Media Group, 1111 W. Bonanza Rd., Las Vegas, NV 89106. Telephone: 702-382-5020. **Management:** Mark Palmer, Publisher. Shirley Brady, Advertising Manager. Fred Chappell, Circulation Manager. **Editorial:** Betty Stewart, Business Editor. Chris Fletcher, City Editor. Marvine Sugg, Fashion Editor. Susan Thurman, Photo Editor. Marion Wilhoite, Sports.

COOKEVILLE

HERALD-CITIZEN. ISSN 8750-5541
1300 Neal St., Cookeville, TN 38501-2729. E-MAIL: editor@herald-citizencom. URL: http://www.herald-citizen.com. Mailing Address: PO Box 2729, Cookeville, TN 38502-2729. Year Established: 1903. Pub. Frequency: d. (Sun.-Fri.) Page Size: broadsheet. Subscrip. Rate: $.50 newsstand/cover; $1 newsstand/cover Sun.; $75/yr home delivery. **Wire Service(s):** AP. Circulation: 13,000 evening (paid); 15,000 Sunday (paid). **Owner(s):** Cookeville Newspapers, Inc., See address and contact information above. **Management:** Bill Shuster, Publisher. Albert Thompson, Advertising Manager. Keith McCormick, Circulation Manager. **Editorial:** Charles Denning, Managing Editor. Margaret Schuster, Family Editor. Buddy Pearson, Sports.

DYERSBURG

STATE GAZETTE. 294 Hwy. 51 Bypass N., Dyersburg, TN 38024. Telephone: 731-285-4091. FAX: 731-285-9747. Mailing Address: PO Box 808, Dyersburg, TN 38025. Year Established: 1865. Pub. Frequency: d. (Tue.-Sun.) Page Size: broadsheet. Subscrip. Rate: $.50 newsstand/cover; $1 newsstand/cover Sun.; $133.20/yr mailed. **Wire Service(s):** AP. Circulation: 7,822 morning (paid); 7,293 Sunday (paid). **Owner(s):** Rust Communications, Inc., 301 Broadway, Cape Girardeau, MO 63701. Telephone: 573-335-6611. **Management:** Shelia Rouse Kelly, Publisher. Todd Hayes, Advertising Director. Terry Brock, Circulation Director. **Editorial:** Chris Rimel, Executive Editor. Tara Temple, Feature Editor. Michael Kenny, Sports Editor.

ELIZABETHTON

ELIZABETHTON STAR. 300 Sycamore St., Elizabethton, TN 37643. Telephone: 423-542-4151. FAX: 423-542-2004. E-MAIL: frobinson@starhq.com. URL: http://www.starhq.com. Mailing Address: PO Box 1960, Elizabethton, TN 37644-1960. Pub. Frequency: d. (Sun.-Fri.) Page Size: broadsheet. Subscrip. Rate: $.50 newsstand/cover; $1.50 newsstand/cover Sun.; $96/yr home delivery; $135/yr mailed; $92/yr home delivery to senior citizens. **Wire Service(s):** AP. Circulation: 9,166 evening (paid); 10,081 Sunday (paid). **Owner(s):** Elizabethton Newspaper, Inc., See address and contact information above. **Management:** Frank Robinson, Owner. Nathan C Goode, Publisher. Kathy Scalf, Circulation Manager. Harvey Prichard, Associate Publisher. **Editorial:** Rozella Hardin, Editor. Bryan Stevens, Lifestyle Editor. Wes Holtsclaw, Sports Editor.

FRANKLIN

REVIEW APPEAL. 121 Second Ave., N., Franklin, TN 37064. URL: http://www.reviewappeal.com. Mailing Address: PO Box 681988, Franklin, TN 37068-1988. Pub. Frequency: d. (Wed., Fri.-Sun.) Page Size: broadsheet. Subscrip. Rate: $.50 newsstand/cover; $.75 newsstand/cover Sun.; $64/yr home delivery in county; $74/yr mailed out of county. Circulation: 10,000 morning (paid and free); 10,000 Sunday (paid and free). **Owner(s):** Morris Multimedia, Inc., 725 Broad St, Augusta, GA 30901. Telephone: 706-724-0851. FAX: 706-722-7125. **Management:** Mike Giangreco, General Manager. Jolene McKenzie, Advertising Manager. **Editorial:** Doug Dyer, Sports Editor.

JACKSON

JACKSON SUN, THE. ISSN 0890-9938
245 W. Lafayette, Jackson, TN 38301. Telephone: 731-427-3333. FAX: 731-425-9639. URL: http://www.jacksonsun.com. Mailing Address: PO Box 1059, Jackson, TN 38302. Year Established: 1848. Pub. Frequency: d. Page Size: broadsheet. Subscrip. Rate: $.50 newsstand/cover; $1.50 newsstand/cover Sun.; $13.65 carrier delivery/mo. in county; $27.30 carrier delivery in county for 2 mos.. **Wire Service(s):** AP, GNS. Circulation: 41,500 morning (paid); 45,500 Sunday (paid). **Owner(s):** Gannett Company, Inc., 7950 Jones Branch Dr., McLean, VA 22107-0001. Telephone: 703-854-6000. **Bureau(s):** 204 College St., Trenton, TN 38382. Telephone: 901-427-3610. **Management:** Edward Graves, President. Ed Graves, Publisher. Cheryle Platt, Circulation Director. Phillip Gallemore, Classified Adv. Mgr.. **Editorial:** Dick Schneider, Executive Editor. Africa Price, Managing Editor.

JOHNSON CITY

JOHNSON CITY PRESS. 204 W. Main St., Johnson City, TN 37604. Telephone: 423-929-3111. FAX: 423-929-1674. Year Established: 1934. Pub. Frequency: d. Page Size: broadsheet. Subscrip. Rate: $.50 newsstand/cover; $1.50 newsstand/cover Sun.; $12 carrier delivery/mo.; $144/yr carrier delivery; $105 mailed for 6 mos. within 100 mi radius; $188/yr mailed. **Wire Service(s):** AP, NYT. Circulation: 30,847 morning (paid); 34,671 Sunday (paid). **Owner(s):** Sandusky Newspapers, Inc., See address and contact information above. **Bureau(s):** 904 Broad St., Elizabethton, TN 37643. Telephone: 423-543-2841. Contact: Robert Houk, Bureau Chief. **Management:** Arthur S Powers, Publisher. Phil Hensley, Circulation Manager. **Editorial:** John Molley, Managing Editor. Jeff Keeling, Business Editor. Brad Jolly, City Editor. Lee Talbert, Photo Editor. Kelly Hodge, Sports Editor.

KINGSPORT

DAILY NEWS OF KINGSPORT. 310 E. Sullivan, Kingsport, TN 37660. Telephone: 423-246-4800. FAX: 423-247-2502. E-MAIL: dr22charterten.net. URL: http://www.kingsportdailynews.com. Year Established: 1963. Pub. Frequency: d. (Tue.-Fri.) Page Size: tabloid. Subscrip. Rate: $.25 newsstand/cover; $90/yr local; $120/yr out of area. Freelance Pay: $0.20/column-inch. **Wire Service(s):** RN. Circulation: 7,600 morning (paid). **Owner(s):** Daily News of Kingsport, Inc., See address and contact information above. **Management:** Pete Dykes, President. Steve Dykes, Publisher. Dot Dykes, Circulation Manager. **Editorial:** Pete Dykes, Editor. Jean Fletcher, Associate Editor. Robin Harris, Lifestyle Editor. Jean Fletcher, News Editor.

KINGSPORT TIMES-NEWS. 701 Lynn Garden Dr., Kingsport, TN 37662. Telephone: 423-929-2197. FAX: 423-392-1392. Mailing Address: PO Box 479, Kingsport, TN 37662. Year Established: 1918. Pub. Frequency: d. Page Size: broadsheet. Subscrip. Rate: $.50 newsstand/cover; $1.25 newsstand/cover Sun.; $132/yr; $240/yr mailed. **Wire Service(s):** AP. Circulation: 43,677 morning (paid and free); 47,206 Sunday (paid and free). **Owner(s):** Sandusky Newspapers, Inc., 314 W. Market St., Sandusky, OH 44870. Telephone: 419-625-5500. **Management:** Keith Wilson, Publisher. Pat Donaldson, Advertising Manager. Glen Tabor, Circulation Manager. **Editorial:** Ted Como, Managing Editor. Stephanie McDlellan, City Editor. Becky Whitlock, Feature Editor. David Grace, Photographer. Ron Bliss, Sports.

KNOXVILLE

NEWS SENTINEL. 2332 News Sentinel Dr., Knoxville, TN 37950. Telephone: 865-523-3131. FAX: 865-342-6400. E-MAIL: kns@knoxnews.com. URL: http://www.knoxnews.com/. Mailing Address: PO Box 59038, Knoxville, TN 37950. Year Established: 1886. Pub. Frequency: d. Page Size: oversize. Subscrip. Rate: $.50 newsstand/cover; $2 newsstand/cover Sun.; $17.50 home delivery/mo.. **Wire Service(s):** AP, SH, NYT. Circulation: 167,000 morning (paid); 168,078 Sunday (paid). **Owner(s):** E.W. Scripps Co., 312 Walnut St., 28th Fl., Cincinnati, OH 45202. Telephone: 513-977-3000. **Management:** Bruce Hartmann, Publisher. Diana Condon, Advertising Director. Jim Boyd, Circulation Director. **Editorial:** Jack McElroy, Editor. Lara Edge, Managing Editor. Dave Keim, Business Editor. Steve Ahillen, Sports.

LEBANON

LEBANON DEMOCRAT, THE. 402 N. Cumberland St., Lebanon, TN 37087. Telephone: 615-444-3952. FAX: 615-444-1358. E-MAIL: production@lebanondemocrat.com. URL: http://www.lebanondemocrat.com. Mailing Address: PO Box 430, Lebanon, TN 37088. Year Established: 1888. Pub. Frequency: d. (Mon.-Sat.) Page Size: broadsheet. Subscrip. Rate: $.50 newsstand/cover; $27 mailed in county for 3 mos.; $44/yr mailed out of county for 3 mos.. **Wire Service(s):** AP. Circulation; 9,500 morning (paid). **Owner(s):** Sandusky Newspapers, Inc., 314 W. Market St., Sandusky, OH 44870. Telephone: 419-625-5500. **Management:** Joseph H Adams, Publisher. Roger Wells, Advertising Director. **Editorial:** Amelia Hipps, Managing Editor. Dallus Whitfield, Photographer. Andy Reed, Sports Editor.

MARYVILLE

DAILY TIMES (MARYVILLE). 307 E. Harper Ave., Maryville, TN 37801-9740. Telephone: 865-981-1100. FAX: 865-981-1175. E-MAIL: evelyn.sandlin@thedailytimes.com. URL: http://www.thedailytimes.com. Mailing Address: PO Box 9740, Maryville, TN 37802-9740. Year Established: 1883. Pub. Frequency: d. Page Size: broadsheet. Subscrip. Rate: $.35 newsstand/cover; $1 newsstand/cover Sun.; $114/yr motor route; $218.40/yr mailed. **Wire Service(s):** AP. Circulation: 24,000 morning (paid). **Owner(s):** Horvitz Newspapers, Inc., 500 180th Ave N E, #1750, Bellevue, WA 98004. Telephone: 425-274-4780. FAX: 425-274-4781. **Management:** Peter Horvitz, President. F. Max Crotser, Publisher. Evelyn Sandlin, Advertising Director. Doug Hurst, Classified Adv. Mgr.. **Editorial:** Dean Stone, Editor. Larry Aldridge, Executive Editor. Fred Tipton, Production Manager. Rick Laney, Business Editor. Melanie Tucker, Lifestyle Editor. Anna C. Irwin, Photographer. Melanie Tucker, Radio-TV Editor. John Brice, Sports Editor.

MEMPHIS

COMMERCIAL APPEAL, THE. ISSN 0745-4856
495 Union Ave., Memphis, TN 38103. Telephone: 901-529-2211. FAX: 901-529-2245. URL: http://www.commercialappeal.com. Mailing Address: PO Box 364, Memphis, TN 38101. Year Established: 1894. Pub. Frequency: d. Page Size: broadsheet. Subscrip. Rate: $.50 newsstand/cover; $2 newsstand/cover Sun.; $18.69 home delivery/mo.. **Wire Service(s):** RN, AP, SH, NYT, LAT-WAT. Circulation: 344,766 morning (paid); 233,639 Sunday (paid). **Owner(s):** E.W. Scripps Co., 312 Walnut St., 28th Fl., Cincinnati, OH 45202. Telephone: 513-977-3000. **Bureau(s):** Scripps Howard News Service, Washington, DC 20005. Telephone: 202-408-2710. Contact: Woody Brosnan, Editor. **Management:** John Wilcox, Publisher. Brad Lackey, Advertising Director. Darrell Jones, Circulation Director. Dennis Copeland, Photography Director. **Editorial:** Chris Peck, Editor. Otis Sanford, Managing Editor. Lianne Kleinman, Asst. Managing Ed.. Sonny Albardo, Business Editor. Peggy Burch, Entertainment Editor. Peggy McKenzie, Feature Editor. Charles Bernsen, Metro Editor. Kevin McDaniel, National Editor. John Stamm, News Editor. Gary Robinson, Sports Editor. Rick Kelley, Weekend Editor.

MORRISTOWN

CITIZEN TRIBUNE. 1609 W First N St., Morristown, TN 37814. Telephone: 423-581-5630. FAX: 423-581-3061. URL: http://www.citizentribune.com. Mailing Address: PO Box 625, Morristown, TN 37815. Year Established: 1966. Pub. Frequency: d. (Sun.-Fri.) Page Size: broadsheet. Subscrip. Rate: $.50 newsstand/cover; $1.25 newsstand/cover Sun.; $111/yr carrier delivery. **Wire Service(s):** AP. Circulation: 21,322 evening (paid); 25,750 Sunday (paid). **Owner(s):** Lakeway Publishers, Inc., See address and contact information above. **Management:** R. Jack Fishman, President. Mike Walker, Advertising Manager. Jeff Seals, Circulation Manager. Mike Fishman, Assistant Publisher. **Editorial:** R. Jack Fishman, Editor-in-Chief. John Ross, Managing Editor. Dianne Barnes, Lifestyle Editor. Gary Smith, Photo Editor. Brian Trent, Sports. Stan Johnson, State Editor.

MURFREESBORO

DAILY NEWS JOURNAL, THE. 224 N. Walnut St., Murfreesboro, TN 37133. Telephone: 615-893-5860. FAX: 615-896-8702. E-MAIL: pirtle@dnj.com. URL: http://dnj.midsouthnews.com/. Mailing Address: PO Box 68, Murfreesboro, TN 37133. Year Established: 1849. Pub. Frequency: d. Page Size: standard. Subscrip. Rate: $.50 newsstand/cover; $1.25 newsstand/cover Sun.; $11/mo. local; $144/yr mailed in state. **Wire Service(s):** AP. Circulation: 167,000 morning (paid). **Owner(s):** Morris Multimedia, Inc., 725 Broad St, Augusta, GA 30901. Telephone: 706-724-0851. FAX: 706-722-7125. **Management:** Judy Teuzotis, Publisher. Jolene McKenzie, Advertising Director. **Editorial:** Jimmy Hart, Executive Editor. Gary Frazier, News Editor. Monte Hale, Sports Editor.

NASHVILLE

TENNESSEAN, THE. ISSN 1053-6590
1100 Broadway, Nashville, TN 37203. Telephone: 615-259-8000. FAX: 615-259-8093. E-MAIL: newstips@tennessean.com. URL: http://www.tennessean.com. Year Established: 1812. Pub. Frequency: d. Page Size: broadsheet. Subscrip. Rate: $.50 newsstand/cover; $1 newsstand/cover Sun.; $15.20 carrier delivery/mo.. **Wire Service(s):** AP, UPI, NYT. Circulation: 292,175 morning (paid); 294,510 Sunday (paid). **Owner(s):** Gannett Company, Inc., 7950 Jones Branch Dr, McLean, VA 22107. Telephone: 703-854-6000. **Management:** Leslie Giallombardo, Publisher. Dave Gould, VP Advertising. Patricia Yates, Classified Adv. Mgr.. **Editorial:** Frank Sutherland, Editor. David Green, Managing Editor. Alan Bostick, Book Review Editor. Bill Choyke, Business Editor. Tom Goldsmith, City Editor. Sandra Roberts, Opinion Editor. Mike Sherman, Religion Editor.

NEWPORT

NEWPORT PLAIN TALK, THE. 145 E Broadway, Newport, TN 37821. Telephone: 423-623-6171. FAX: 423-625-1995. E-MAIL: doopie@xtn.net. URL: http://www.cocke.xtn.net. Mailing Address: PO Box 279, Newport, TN 37822. Year Established: 1900. Pub. Frequency: d. (Tue-Fri. & Sun.) Page Size: broadsheet. Subscrip. Rate: $.50 newsstand/cover; $1 newsstand/cover Sun.; $86/yr carrier delivery in county; $88/yr mailed in county; $99.75/yr mailed out of county. Adv. Rate: col. inch $16.27 Circulation: 13,476 Sunday (paid); 7,250 evening (paid). **Owner(s):** Jones Media Group, 121 W Summer St, Greenville, TN 37745. Telephone: 423-581-0088. FAX: 423-235-7012. **Management:** David Popiel, Co-Publisher. John M Jones, Publisher. Betty McMillan, Advertising Director. Patrick Helms, Circulation Manager. Brenda Crum, Classified Adv. Mgr.. **Editorial:** David Popiel, Editor.

OAK RIDGE

OAK RIDGER, THE. ISSN 0890-6009
785 Oak Ridge Tpke., Oak Ridge, TN 37831. Telephone: 865-482-1021. FAX: 865-482-7834. E-MAIL: oakridge@oakridger.com. URL: http://www.oakridger.com. Mailing Address: PO Box 3446, Oak Ridge, TN 37831. Year Established: 1949. Pub. Frequency: d. (Mon.-Fri.) Page Size: broadsheet. Subscrip. Rate: $.50 newsstand/cover; $1 newsstand/cover Fri.; $113/yr carrier delivery; $148/yr mailed. **Wire Service(s):** AP. Circulation: 11,000 evening (paid). **Owner(s):** Morris Multimedia, Inc., PO Box 936, Augusta, GA 30903. Telephone: 706-724-0851. **Management:** John Miller, Publisher. Janet Wood, Advertising Director. Don Jarnagin, Circulation Manager. Janet Wood, Classified Adv. Mgr.. Carol Skyberg, Business Manager. **Editorial:** Donna Smith, News Editor.

PARIS

PARIS POST-INTELLIGENCER. ISSN 0893-3669
208 E Wood St, Paris, TN 38242-0310. Telephone: 731-642-1162. FAX: 731-642-1165. E-MAIL: parispi@parispi.net. URL: http://www.parispi.net. Mailing Address: PO Box 310, Paris, TN 38424-0310. Year Established: 1866. Pub. Frequency: d. (Mon.-Fri.) Page Size: broadsheet. Subscrip. Rate: $96/yr; $.50 newsstand/cover. Adv. Rate: B&W page $1,005.28 **Wire Service(s):** AP. Circulation: 8,050 (paid). **Owner(s):** Paris Publishing Co. Inc., See address and contact information above. **Management:** Michael Williams, Publisher. Laura Daugherty, Advertising Manager. Tim Forrest, Circulation Manager. Evonne Williams, Business Manager. **Editorial:** Michael Williams, Editor. Jimmy Williams, Production Manager. Ken Walker, News Editor. Steve McCadams, Outdoor Editor. Tom Priddy, Sports Editor.

SHELBYVILLE

SHELBYVILLE TIMES-GAZETTE. 323 E. Depot St., Shelbyville, TN 37160. E-MAIL: news@t-g.com. URL: http://www.t-g.com. Mailing Address: PO Box 380, Shelbyville, TN 37162-0380. Year Established: 1874. Pub. Frequency: d. (Mon.-Fri.) Page Size: broadsheet. Subscrip. Rate: $.50 newsstand/cover; $65/yr carrier delivery in county; $50/yr mailed out of area. **Wire Service(s):** AP. Circulation: 8,200 evening (paid). **Owner(s):** Shelbyville Publishing Co., Inc., See address and contact information above. **Management:** Hugh Jones, Publisher. Sandra Smith, Advertising Manager. Angel Gresham, Circulation Manager. Rita Holliman, Classified Adv. Mgr.. Wilene Sanders, Associate Publisher. **Editorial:** Kay Rose, Editor.

UNION CITY

UNION CITY DAILY MESSENGER. ISSN 0745-5534
613 E Jackson St, Union City, TN 38281. Telephone: 731-885-0744. FAX: 731-885-0782. E-MAIL: ucdm@ucmessenger.com. URL: http://www.ucmessenger.com. Mailing Address: PO Box 430, Union City, TN 38281. Year Established: 1926. Pub. Frequency: d. (Mon.-Fri.) Page Size: broadsheet. Subscrip. Rate: $.50 newsstand/cover; $88/yr carrier delivery in area; $108/yr out of area. Adv. Rate: col. inch $8.50 **Wire Service(s):** AP. Circulation: 8,700 evening (paid). **Owner(s):** Critchlow/David Sr., David, Jr. & Scott, See address and contact information above. **Management:** David Critchlow, Sr., Publisher. Gloria Chesteen, Advertising Manager. Glenda Langford, Classified Adv. Mgr.. **Editorial:** David Critchlow, Jr., Managing Editor.

TEXAS

ABILENE

ABILENE REPORTER-NEWS. ISSN 0199-3267
101 Cypress St., Abilene, TX 79601. Telephone: 325-673-4271. FAX: 325-673-1901. E-MAIL: reagan@texnews.com. URL: http://www.texnews.com. Mailing Address: PO Box 30, Abilene, TX 79604. Year Established: 1881. Pub. Frequency: d. Page Size: broadsheet. Subscrip. Rate: $.50 newsstand/cover; $1.50 newsstand/cover Sun.; $16.25 carrier delivery/mo.; $17.33 mailed/mo.. **Wire Service(s):** AP, SH, MCT. Circulation: 40,000 morning (paid); 50,000 Sunday (paid). **Owner(s):** E.W. Scripps Co., 312 Walnut St., 28th Fl., Cincinnati, OH 45202. Telephone: 513-977-3000. **Management:** George Cogswell, Publisher. Jim Grahn, Advertising Director. Lauren Brownell, Advertising Manager. **Editorial:** Terri Burke, Editor. Barton Cromeens, Managing Editor. Loretta Fulton, City Editor. Jeff Wolf, Editorial Page Editor.

ALICE

ALICE ECHO-NEWS JOURNAL. 405 E. Main, Alice, TX 78332. Telephone: 361-664-6588. FAX: 361-668-1030. URL: http://www.aliceechonews.com. Mailing Address: PO Box 1610, Alice, TX 78333. Year Established: 1896. Pub. Frequency: d. (Sun.-Fri.) Page Size: broadsheet. Subscrip. Rate: $.50 newsstand/cover; $1.50 newsstand/cover Sun.; $27 carrier delivery local for 3 mos.; $108/yr carrier delivery local. **Wire Service(s):** AP. Circulation: 20,000 evening (paid); 6,000 Sunday (paid). **Owner(s):** American Consolidated Media, Inc., 1420 N. Mockingbird Ln, Ste 100, Dallas, TX 75247. Telephone: 214-691-4066. FAX: 214-691-4086. **Management:** Tony Morris, Publisher. Javier Ramos, Advertising. Prissy Asuna, Circulation Director. **Editorial:** Nichole Prepez, Editor.

AMARILLO

AMARILLO GLOBE-NEWS. 900 S. Harrison St., Amarillo, TX 79101. Telephone: 806-376-4488. FAX: 806-373-0810. E-MAIL: dwilmarth@amarillonet.com. URL: http://amarillonet.com. Mailing Address: PO Box 2091, Amarillo, TX 79166-2091. Year Established: 1909. Pub. Frequency: d. Page Size: broadsheet. Subscrip. Rate: $.50 newsstand/cover; $1.50 newsstand/cover Sun.; $19.75 carrier delivery/mo.; $29.55 carrier delivery for 3 months. **Wire Service(s):** AP, LAT-WAT, MCT. Circulation: 43,801 morning (paid); 74,791 Sunday (paid). **Owner(s):** Morris Multimedia, Inc., PO Box 936, Augusta, GA 30903-2091. Telephone: 706-724-0851. **Management:** Joanne Gosselin, General Manager. Les Simpson, Publisher. Rob Leivo, Advertising Director. James Adkins, Circulation Director. **Editorial:** Dawn Dressler, Executive Editor. Michael Schumacher, Photo Editor. Lance Lehnert, Sports Editor.

ARLINGTON

ARLINGTON STAR-TELEGRAM. 1111 W. Abram St., Arlington, TX 76013. Telephone: 817-548-5400. FAX: 817-261-1193. E-MAIL: newsroom@star-telegram.com. URL: http://www.arlingtonnow.com. Mailing Address: PO Box 915006, Fort Worth, TX 76115. Year Established: 1883. Pub. Frequency: d. Page Size: broadsheet. Subscrip. Rate: $.50 newsstand/cover; $1.50 newsstand/cover Sun.; $14 carrier delivery/mo.; $159/yr. **Wire Service(s):** RN, AP, NYT. Circulation: 245,000 morning (paid); 540,000 Sunday (paid). **Owner(s):** Knight Ridder, Inc., 50 W. San Fernando St., Ste. 1200, San Jose, CA 95113. Telephone: 831-938-7700. FAX: 831-938-7755. **Management:** Gary Hardee, Publisher. Bill Vincent, Advertising Director. Bob Paul, Advertising Manager. Mike Fillner, Circulation Manager. Leslie Collier, Classified Adv. Mgr.. Gregg Elman, Photography Director. **Editorial:** Jeanmarie Brown, Editor. Tara Ranson, Business Editor. Kristi Payne, City Editor. Angie Summers, Society Editor. Kevin Lyons, Sports Editor.

ATHENS

ATHENS DAILY REVIEW. ISSN 1040-6522
201 S. Prairieville St., Athens, TX 75751. Telephone: 903-675-5626. FAX: 903-675-9450. E-MAIL: dyoungman@athensreview.com. URL: http://www.athensreview.com. Mailing Address: PO Box 32, Athens, TX 75751. Year Established: 1885. Pub. Frequency: d. (Sun.-Fri.) Page Size: broadsheet. Subscrip. Rate: $.50 newsstand/cover; $1 newsstand/cover Sun.; $96/yr carrier delivery in area; $116.65/yr mailed out of city. Adv. Rate: col. inch $9.72 **Wire Service(s):** AP. Circulation: 5,665 evening (paid); 6,215 Sunday (paid). **Owner(s):** Community Newspaper Holdings, Inc., 3500 Colonnade Pkwy., Ste. 600, Birmingham, AL 35243. Telephone: 205-298-7100. **Management:** David Sullens, Publisher. Andi Green, Advertising Director. Sandra Frazier, Circulation Manager. **Editorial:** Jayson Larson, Editor. Cristin Ross, News Editor. Benny Rogers, Sports Editor.

AUSTIN

AUSTIN AMERICAN-STATESMAN. ISSN 0199-8560
305 S. Congress Ave., Austin, TX 78704. Telephone: 512-445-3500. FAX: 512-445-3557. E-MAIL: news@statesman.com. URL: http://www.statesman.com. Mailing Address: PO Box 670, Austin, TX 78767. Year Established: 1885. Pub. Frequency: d. Page Size: broadsheet. Subscrip. Rate: $.50 newsstand/cover; $1.50 newsstand/cover Sun.; $16 carrier delivery/mo.. **Wire Service(s):** AP, NYT, LAT-WAT, MCT. Circulation: 183,300 morning (paid); 241,970 Sunday (paid). **Owner(s):** Cox Newspapers, Inc., 6205 Peachtree Dunwoody Rd., Atlanta, GA 30328. Telephone: 678-645-0000. **Management:** Mike Laosa, Publisher. George Gutierrez, Advertising. Harry Davis, Circulation Manager. Zack Ryall, Photography Director. **Editorial:** Rich Oppel, Editor. Kathy Warbelow, Business Editor. Arnold Garcia, Editorial Page Editor. Vasin Omar Douglas, Graphics Editor. Tim Lott, News Editor. John Bridges, Sports Editor.

BAY CITY

BAY CITY TRIBUNE. 2901 Carey Smith Blvd., Bay City, TX 77414. Telephone: 979-245-5555. FAX: 979-244-5908. URL: http://www.baycitytribune.com. Mailing Address: PO Box 2450, Bay City, TX 77404-2450. Year Established: 1845. Pub. Frequency: d. (Tue.-Fri. & Sun.) Page Size: broadsheet. Subscrip. Rate: $.50 newsstand/cover; $50/yr carrier delivery in county. **Wire Service(s):** AP. Circulation: 5,000 evening (paid); 5,200 Sunday (paid). **Owner(s):** Southern Newspapers, Inc., 5701 Woodway Dr., Ste. 131, Houston, TX 77057-1589. **Management:** Mike Reddell, Publisher. Sharon Vacek, Advertising Director. Resendez Rosario, Classified Adv. Mgr.. Jessica Wright, Business Manager. **Editorial:** Shelly Gormey, Managing Editor. Justin Daily, Sports Editor.

BAYTOWN

BAYTOWN SUN. 1301 Memorial Dr., Baytown, TX 77520. Telephone: 281-422-8302. FAX: 281-427-6283. E-MAIL: baytownsun@aol.com. URL: http://www.baytownsun.com. Mailing Address: PO Box 90, Baytown, TX 77522. Year Established: 1931. Pub. Frequency: d. (Mon.-Sun.) Page Size: broadsheet. Subscrip. Rate: $.50 newsstand/cover; $1 newsstand/cover Sun.; $13.20 mailed/mo.; $119.40/yr home delivery; $157.60/yr mailed. **Wire Service(s):** AP, UPI. Circulation: 16,000 evening (paid). **Owner(s):** Southern Newspapers, Inc., 5701 Woodway Dr., Ste. 131, Houston, TX 77057-1589. **Management:** Cliff Clements, Publisher. Janie Halter, Advertising Manager. Angie Pagel, Classified Adv. Mgr.. Sandy Denson, Business Manager. **Editorial:** Cliff Clements, Editor. David Bloom, Managing Editor.

BEAUMONT

BEAUMONT ENTERPRISE. ISSN 0744-1207
380 Main St., Beaumont, TX 77701. Telephone: 409-833-3311. FAX: 409-880-0757. E-MAIL: jnewhouse@hearstnp.com. URL: http://www.beaumontenterprise.com. Mailing Address: PO Box 3071, Beaumont, TX 77704. Year Established: 1880. Pub. Frequency: d. Page Size: broadsheet. Subscrip. Rate: $.50 newsstand/cover; $1.50 newsstand/cover Sun.; $12 home delivery/mo.; $17 mailed/mo.. **Wire Service(s):** AP, NYT. Circulation: 50,000 morning (paid); 55,000 Sunday (paid). **Owner(s):** Hearst Corp., 250 W. 55th St., New York, NY 10019-5288. **Management:** John E Newhouse, Publisher. Jeff Noble, Advertising Manager. Rolland Ramos, Classified Adv. Mgr.. **Editorial:** Brian Pearson, Managing Editor. Chris Clausen, Business Editor. Michael Peters, Sports Editor.

BIG SPRING

BIG SPRING HERALD. ISSN 0746-6811
710 Scurry, Big Spring, TX 79721. Telephone: 432-263-7331. FAX: 432-264-7205. E-MAIL: publisher@bigspringherald.com. URL: http://www.bigspringherald.com. Mailing Address: PO Box 1431, Big Spring, TX 79721. Year Established: 1904. Pub. Frequency: d. (Sun.-Fri.) Page Size: broadsheet. Subscrip. Rate: $.50 newsstand/cover; $1.25 newsstand/cover Sun.; $93.42/yr home delivery. Freelance Pay: $15/story. **Wire Service(s):** AP. Circulation: 5,000 evening (paid); 5,700 Sunday (paid). **Owner(s):** Horizon Publications, Inc., 1120 N. Carbon St, Ste 100, Marion, IL 62959. **Management:** Ron Midkiff, Publisher. Rick Nunez, Advertising Manager. Duane McCollum, Circulation Manager. Ellen Talbot, Classified Adv. Mgr.. **Editorial:** John Mosley, Editor.

BORGER

BORGER NEWS-HERALD. 207 N Main St, Borger, TX 79007. Telephone: 806-273-5611. FAX: 806-273-2552. E-MAIL: publisher@borgernewsherald.com. URL: http://www.borgernewsherald.com. Mailing Address: PO Box 5130, Borger, TX 79008. Year Established: 1926. Pub. Frequency: d. (Mon.-Sat.) Page Size: broadsheet. Subscrip. Rate: $.50 newsstand/cover; $1 newsstand/cover Sun.; $90/yr home delivery in county; $150/yr mailed out of county. Adv. Rate: col. inch $9.23 **Wire Service(s):** AP. Circulation: 5,000 evening (paid); 5,500 Sunday (paid). **Owner(s):** Horizon Publications, Inc., 1120 N. Carbon St, Ste 100, Marion, IL 62959. **Management:** L.W. McCall, Publisher. Pat Landrum, Circulation Manager. Amanda Smith, Classified Adv. Mgr.. **Editorial:** Kim Duso, Editor.

BRENHAM

BANNER-PRESS (BRENHAM), THE. ISSN 8750-5800
2430 Stringer St., Brenham, TX 77833. Telephone: 979-836-7956. FAX: 979-830-8577. E-MAIL: download@banner-press.com. URL: http://www.banner-press.com. Mailing Address: PO Box 585, Brenham, TX 77834-0585. Year Established: 1866. Pub. Frequency: d. (Mon.-Sat.) Page Size: broadsheet. Subscrip. Rate: $.50 newsstand/cover; $1 newsstand/cover Sat.; $90/yr home delivery in city; $102/yr mailed out of city; $108/yr mailed out of state. **Wire Service(s):** AP. Circulation: 6,500 per issue (paid). **Owner(s):** Hartman Newspapers, Inc., PO Box 1390, Rosenberg, TX 77471. Telephone: 281-342-7304. FAX: 281-342-6968. **Management:** Charles Moser, Publisher. Helen Nowicki, Advertising Manager. Carol Kruger, Classified Adv. Mgr.. **Editorial:** Charles Moser, Editor. Arthur Hahn, Managing Editor.

BROWNSVILLE

BROWNSVILLE HERALD, THE. ISSN 0894-2064
1135 E. Van Buren St., Brownsville, TX 78520. Telephone: 956-542-4301. FAX: 956-542-0840. E-MAIL: tbhletters@link.freedom.com. URL: http://www.brownsvilleherald.com. Mailing Address: PO Box 351, Brownsville, TX 78520-0351. Year Established: 1892. Pub. Frequency: d. Page Size: standard. Subscrip. Rate: $.50 newsstand/cover; $1.25 newsstand/cover Sun.; $8 carrier delivery/mo.; $99/yr carrier delivery. **Wire Service(s):** AP. Circulation: 19,285 morning (paid); 20,800 Sunday (paid). **Owner(s):** Freedom Communications, Inc., 17666 Fitch, Irvine, CA 92614. Telephone: 714-553-9292. FAX: 714-474-7675. **Management:** R. Daniel Cavazos, Publisher. Rusty Hall, Circulation Manager. **Editorial:** Rachel Benavidez, Editor. Carlos Rodriguez, Managing Editor. Melissa Zamora, City Editor.

BROWNWOOD

BROWNWOOD BULLETIN, THE. 700 Carnegie, Brownwood, TX 76801. Telephone: 325-646-2541. FAX: 325-646-6835. E-MAIL: news@brownwoodbulletin.com. URL: http://www.brownwoodbulletin.com. Mailing Address: PO Box 1189, Brownwood, TX 76804. Year Established: 1900. Pub. Frequency: d. Page Size: broadsheet. Subscrip. Rate: $.50 newsstand/cover; $1.50 newsstand/cover Sun.; $11.95 home delivery/mo. local; $15 mailed/mo. in state; $17 mailed/mo. out of state. **Wire Service(s):** AP. Circulation: 6,500 evening (paid); 8,000 Sunday (paid). **Owner(s):** American Consolidated Media, Inc., 1420 N. Mockingbird Ln, Ste 100, Dallas, TX 75247. Telephone: 214-691-4066. FAX: 214-691-4086. **Management:** Robert W. Brincefield, Publisher. Juliet Lemond, Advertising Manager. John Kliebenstein, Circulation Manager. Bill Crist, Associate Publisher. **Editorial:** Gene Deason, Managing Editor. Derrick Stuckley, Sports.

BRYAN

BRYAN-COLLEGE STATION EAGLE. ISSN 0739-8727
1729 Briarcrest Dr, Bryan, TX 77802. Telephone: 979-776-4444. E-MAIL: news@theeagle.com. URL: http://www.theeagle.com. Mailing Address: PO Box 3000, Bryan, TX 77805. Year Established: 1876. Pub. Frequency: d. Page Size: broadsheet. Subscrip. Rate: $.50 newsstand/cover; $1.25 newsstand/cover Sun.; $122.76/yr home delivery local; $156/yr mailed in state; $216/yr mailed out of state. **Wire Service(s):** AP. Circulation: 24,500 morning (paid); 31,000 Sunday (paid). **Owner(s):** Evening Post Publishing Co., 134 Columbus St., Charleston, SC 29403. Telephone: 843-577-7111. **Management:** Jim Wilson, Publisher. Lee Neely, Circulation Director. Leslie Lueckemeyer, Classified Adv. Mgr.. **Editorial:** Donnis Baggett, Editor. Kelly Brown, Managing Editor. Darren Benson, City Editor. Robert Premeaux, Sports Editor.

CLEBURNE

CLEBURNE TIMES-REVIEW. 108 S. Anglin St., Cleburne, TX 76031. Telephone: 817-645-2441. FAX: 817-645-4020. E-MAIL: editor@trcle.com. URL: http://www.cleburnetimesreview.com. Mailing Address: PO Box 1569, Cleburne, TX 76033-1569. Year Established: 1904. Pub. Frequency: d. (Sun.-Fri.) Page Size: broadsheet. Subscrip. Rate: $.50 newsstand/cover; $1 newsstand/cover Sun.; $87/yr carrier delivery; $96/yr mailed in state; $100/yr mailed out of state. **Wire Service(s):** AP. Circulation: 7,500 evening (paid); 8,500 Sunday (paid). **Owner(s):** Community Newspaper Holdings, Inc., 3500 Colonnade Pkwy., Ste. 600, Birmingham, AL 35243. Telephone: 205-298-7100. FAX: 205-298-7101. **Management:** Kay Helms, Publisher. Nancy Laws, Circulation Manager. Lynn Coplin, Classified Adv. Mgr.. **Editorial:** Dale Gosser, Managing Editor.

CLUTE

FACTS (CLUTE), THE. 720 S. Main St., Clute, TX 77531. Telephone: 979-265-7411. FAX: 979-265-9052. E-MAIL: yuonnemintz@thefacts.com. URL: http://www.thefacts.com. Mailing Address: PO Box 549, Clute, TX 77531. Year Established: 1913. Pub. Frequency: d. Page Size: broadsheet. Subscrip. Rate: $.50 newsstand/cover; $1.25 newsstand/cover Sun.; $129/yr home delivery; $10 home delivery/mo. to senior citizens; $12 mailed/mo. in state to senior citizens. **Wire Service(s):** AP. Circulation: 19,958 evening (paid); 21,530 Sunday (paid). **Owner(s):** Southern Newspapers, Inc., 5701 Woodway Dr., Ste. 131, Houston, TX 77057-1589. **Management:** Judy Starnes, General Manager. Bill Cornwell, Publisher. Deana Lesco, Advertising Manager. Glenn Blount, Circulation Manager. Dena Matthews, Classified Adv. Mgr.. **Editorial:** Yuonne Mintz, Managing Editor.

CONROE

COURIER (CONROE), THE. 100 Ave. A, Conroe, TX 77301. Telephone: 936-756-6671. FAX: 936-756-6676. E-MAIL: courier@lcc.net. URL: http://www.thecourier-online.com. Mailing Address: PO Box 609, Conroe, TX 77305-0609. Year Established: 1892. Pub. Frequency: d. Page Size: broadsheet. Subscrip. Rate: $.50 newsstand/cover; $1 newsstand/cover Sun.; $117/yr carrier delivery; $156/yr mailed in county; $180/yr mailed out of county. **Wire Service(s):** AP. Circulation: 12,000 morning (paid); 16,200 Sunday (paid). **Owner(s):** ASP Westward LP, 523-N Sam Houston Pkwy, Ste 600, Houston, TX 77060. Telephone: 281-668-1100. **Management:** Robb Reeves, Publisher. Karen Mauermann, Advertising Manager. Linda Mickelson, Classified Adv. Mgr.. Ann Toppel, Business Manager. **Editorial:** Jim Fredricks, Editor. Bubba Hand, Lifestyle Editor. Jana-Lynn Hill, Photographer. Mike Jones, Sports Editor.

CORPUS CHRISTI

CORPUS CHRISTI CALLER-TIMES. ISSN 0894-5365
820 Lower N. Broadway, Corpus Christi, TX 78401. Telephone: 361-884-2011. FAX: 361-886-3780. URL: http://www.caller.com. Mailing Address: PO Box 9136, Corpus Christi, TX 78469-9136. Year Established: 1883. Pub. Frequency: d. Page Size: broadsheet. Subscrip. Rate: $.50 newsstand/cover; $1.50 newsstand/cover Sun.; $195/yr home delivery; $260/yr mailed in county; $338/yr mailed out of county. **Wire Service(s):** AP, SH, NYT, MCT. Circulation: 62,093 morning (paid); 81,099 Sunday (paid). **Owner(s):** E.W. Scripps Co., 312 Walnut St., 28th Fl., Cincinnati, OH 45202. Telephone: 513-977-3820. **Management:** Patrick Birmingham, Publisher. Steve McConnell, Advertising Director. **Editorial:** Libby Averyt, Editor. Shane Fitzgerald, Managing Editor. Nick Jimenez, Editorial Page Editor. Cynthia Williams, Feature Editor. Tom Whitehurst, Metro Editor. John Allen, Sports Editor.

CORSICANA

CORSICANA DAILY SUN. ISSN 8750-2518
405 E. Collin St., Corsicana, TX 75110. Telephone: 903-872-3931. FAX: 903-872-6878. E-MAIL: rlinex@corsicanadailysun.com. URL: http://www.corsicanadailysun.com. Mailing Address: PO Box 622, Corsicana, TX 75151. Year Established: 1894. Pub. Frequency: d. Page Size: broadsheet. Subscrip. Rate: $.50 newsstand/cover; $1 newsstand/cover Sun.; $117/yr carrier delivery; $135/yr mailed. **Wire Service(s):** AP. Circulation: 7,100 evening (paid); 8,100 Sunday (paid). **Owner(s):** Community Newspaper Holdings, Inc., 3500 Colonnade Pkwy., Ste. 600, Birmingham, AL 35243. Telephone: 205-298-7100. FAX: 205-289-7101. **Management:** Bob Dennis, Publisher. Linda Dozier, Advertising Director. David Smith, Circulation Manager. Karen Davis, Classified Adv. Mgr.. **Editorial:** Raymond Linex, Editor.

DALLAS

CIRCLEVILLE HERALD. 1420 N. Mockingbird Ln, Ste 100, Dallas, TX 75247. E-MAIL: news@circlevilleherald.com. URL: http://www.circlevilleherald.com. Year Established: 1883. Pub. Frequency: d. (Mon.-Sat.) Page Size: broadsheet. Subscrip. Rate: $.50 newsstand/cover; $120/yr carrier delivery; $120/yr motor route in county; $185/yr mailed in county. **Wire Service(s):** AP. Circulation: 6,500 evening (paid). **Owner(s):** American Consolidated Media, Inc., See address and contact information above. Brown Publishing Co., 120 Watt St, Circleville, OH 43113. 10222 Alliance Rd, Cincinnati, OH 45040. **Management:** Steve Davies, Publisher. Jerry Shasteen, Advertising Manager. Dick Lamb, Circulation Manager. **Editorial:** David Amey, Editor.Readers: County residents

DALLAS MORNING NEWS, THE. 508 Young St., Dallas, TX 75202. Telephone: 214-977-8222. FAX: 214-977-7586. E-MAIL: nbarry@dallasnews.com. URL: http://www.dallasnews.com. Year Established: 1885. Pub. Frequency: d. Page Size: broadsheet. Subscrip. Rate: $.50 newsstand/cover; $1.50 newsstand/cover Sun.; $149.40/yr home delivery in county. **Wire Service(s):** AP, NYT, AFP. Circulation: 496,182 morning (paid); 783,944 Sunday (paid). **Owner(s):** Belo Corp., P.O. Box 655237, Dallas, TX 75265-5237. **Bureau(s):** 314 E. Commerce St., Ste. 401, San Antonio, TX 78205. Telephone: 210-226-9083. FAX: 210-226-0633. Contact: David McLemore, Bureau Chief. **Management:** Bob Mong, President. Jim Moroney, Publisher. Paul Webb, Production Director. **Editorial:** John Cranfill, Editor. Stuart Wilk, Managing Editor. Jerome Weeks, Book Review Editor. Ed. Dufner, Business Editor. Chris Kelley, City Editor. Rena Pederson, Editorial Page Editor. Rick Holter, Entertainment Editor. Tracy A. Hayes, Fashion Editor. Sue Smith, Lifestyle Editor. Raul Reyes, National Editor. Bob Moos, Opinion Editor. Ray Sasser, Outdoor Editor. Steve Brown, Real Estate Editor. Tom Siegfried, Science Editor. Bob Yates, Sports Editor. Rodger Jones, State Editor. Leona Allen, Suburban Editor. Vernon Smith, Sunday Editor. Ed Bark, TV Critic.

DEL RIO

DEL RIO NEWS-HERALD. 2205 Bedell Ave., Del Rio, TX 78842. Telephone: 830-775-1551. FAX: 830-774-2610. E-MAIL: newsroom@delrionewsherald.com. URL: http://www.delrionewsherald.com. Mailing Address: P.O.Box 420397, Del Rio, TX 78841. Year Established: 1929. Pub. Frequency: d. Page Size: broadsheet. Subscrip. Rate: $.50 newsstand/cover; $1.25 newsstand/cover Sun.; $8 carrier delivery/mo.; $96/yr carrier delivery; $20 mailed/mo.; $240/yr mailed. Freelance Pay: $0.50/column-inch. **Wire Service(s):** AP. Circulation: 5,400 evening (paid); 5,750 Sunday (paid). **Owner(s):** Southern Newspapers, Inc., 5701 Woodway Dr., Ste. 131, Houston, TX 77057-1589. **Management:** Joe San Miguel, Publisher. Guy Aguirre, Advertising Manager. Pedro Salazar, Circulation Manager. **Editorial:** Jennifer Robles, Managing Editor. Joe San Miguel, Military Editor. Brian Arqabright, Sports Editor.

DENTON

DENTON RECORD-CHRONICLE. 314 E. Hickory St., Denton, TX 76201. Telephone: 940-566-6800. FAX: 940-566-6888. E-MAIL: drc@dentonrc.com. URL: http://www.dentonrc.com. Mailing Address: PO Box 369, Denton, TX 76202. Year Established: 1903. Pub. Frequency: d. Page Size: broadsheet. Subscrip. Rate: $.50 newsstand/cover; $1 newsstand/cover Sun.; $11.25 carrier delivery/mo.; $135/yr carrier delivery. **Wire Service(s):** AP. Circulation: 17,140 evening (paid); 20,058 Sunday (paid). **Owner(s):** Belo Corp., 400 S. Record St., Ste. 1300, Dallas, TX 75202. Telephone: 214-977-6606. **Management:** Bill Patterson, Publisher. Sandra Hammond, Advertising Director. Dan Hammond, Circulation Director. **Editorial:** Dawn Cobb, Managing Editor. Matt Zabel, City Editor. Lucinda Breeding, Feature Editor. Barron Ludlum, Photo Editor.

EL PASO

EL PASO TIMES. ISSN 0746-3588
300 N Campbell St, El Paso, TX 79901. Telephone: 915-546-6100. FAX: 915-546-6284. URL: http://www.elpasotimes.com. Mailing Address: PO Box 20, El Paso, TX 79999. Year Established: 1881. Pub. Frequency: d. Page Size: broadsheet. Subscrip. Rate: $.50 newsstand/cover; $1.50 newsstand/cover Sun.; $12.75 carrier delivery/mo.. **Wire Service(s):** AP, GNS. Circulation: 87,500 morning (paid); 103,000 Sunday (paid). **Owner(s):** MediaNews Group, Inc., 101 W Colfax Ave, Ste 1100, Denver, CO 80202. FAX: 303-954-6320. **Management:** Ray Stafford, Publisher. **Editorial:** Don Flores, Editor. Laurie Muller, News Editor.

ENNIS

ENNIS DAILY NEWS. ISSN 8755-9056
213 N. Dallas, Ennis, TX 75119. Telephone: 972-875-3801. FAX: 972-875-9747. E-MAIL: ennisnews@vetec.com. URL: http://www.ennisdailynews.com. Mailing Address: P.O. Drawer 100, Ennis, TX 75120-0100. Year Established: 1891. Pub. Frequency: d. (Sun.-Fri.) Page Size: broadsheet. Subscrip. Rate: $.50 newsstand/cover; $84/yr home delivery in county; $114/yr home delivery out of county. Adv. Rate: col. inch $6.25 **Wire Service(s):** AP. Circulation: 3,845 evening (paid); 4,000 Sunday (paid). **Owner(s):** Ellis County Newspapers, Inc., P.O. Drawer 100, Ennis, TX 75120. Telephone: 972-875-3801. **Management:** Lange Svehlak, Advertising Manager. **Editorial:** Sandy Manning, Managing Editor.

FRISCO

LITTLE ELM JOURNAL. 8820 W Main St, Ste 2000, Frisco, TX 75034. Telephone: 469-633-7777. FAX: 469-633-7779. URL: http://www.scntx.com. Pub. Frequency: w. (Thu.) Page Size: broadsheet. Subscrip. Rate: $.50 newsstand/cover; $25/yr home delivery local; $39.95/yr mailed in county; $59.95/yr mailed out of county. Circulation: 2,500 per issue (free). **Owner(s):** Star Community Newspapers, 14875 Landmark Blvd, Ste 110, Addison, TX 75254. Telephone: 972-628-4061. **Management:** Bill Weaver, Publisher. Donna Zarnbiosi, Advertising Manager.

GAINESVILLE

GAINESVILLE DAILY REGISTER. 306 E. California, Gainesville, TX 76240. Telephone: 940-665-5511. FAX: 940-665-0920. E-MAIL: dailyregister@ntin.net. URL: http://www.gainesvilleregister.com. Mailing Address: PO Box 309, Gainesville, TX 76241. Year Established: 1890. Pub. Frequency: d. (Sun.-Fri.) Page Size: broadsheet. Subscrip. Rate: $.50 newsstand/cover; $1 newsstand/cover Sun.; $96/yr home delivery in county; $108/yr mailed out of county. **Wire Service(s):** AP. Circulation: 8,000 evening (paid); 8,000 Sunday (paid). **Owner(s):** Community Newspaper Holdings, Inc., 3500 Colonnade Pkwy., Ste. 600, Birmingham, AL 35243. Telephone: 205-298-7100. FAX: 205-298-7101. **Management:** David Scott, Publisher. David Mann, Advertising Manager. Juanietta Kiser, Circulation Manager. Sharon Pharr, Classified Adv. Mgr.. **Editorial:** J. Osborne, Managing Editor.

GALVESTON

GALVESTON COUNTY DAILY NEWS, THE. ISSN 0738-8047
8522 Teichman Rd., Galveston, TX 77554. Telephone: 409-683-5200. FAX: 409-740-3421. E-MAIL: newsroom@galvnews.com. URL: http://www.galvnews.com. Mailing Address: PO Box 628, Galveston, TX 77553-0628. Year Established: 1842. Pub. Frequency: d. Page Size: broadsheet. Subscrip. Rate: $.50 newsstand/cover; $1.50 newsstand/cover Sun.; $39 carrier delivery for 3 mos.. **Wire Service(s):** AP. Circulation: 25,000 morning (paid); 25,000 Sunday (paid). **Owner(s):** Galveston Newspapers, Inc., See address and contact information above. **Management:** Dolph Tillotson, Publisher. Scott Moon, Advertising Manager. Yvonne Mascorro, Circulation Manager. Angela Taylor, Community Affrs. Dir.. **Editorial:** Heber Taylor, Editor. Michael Smith, Associate Editor. Jennifer Reynolds, Photo Editor.

GREENVILLE

HERALD BANNER. ISSN 1042-3710
2305 King St., Greenville, TX 75401-3299. Telephone: 903-455-4220. FAX: 903-455-6281. URL: http://www.heraldbanner.com. Mailing Address: PO Box 6000, Greenville, TX 75403-6000. Year Established: 1869. Pub. Frequency: d. Page Size: broadsheet. Subscrip. Rate: $.50 newsstand/cover; $1 newsstand/cover Sun.; $57 carrier delivery for 6 mos.; $111/yr carrier delivery. **Wire Service(s):** AP. Circulation: 9,019 morning (paid); 10,444 Sunday (paid). **Owner(s):** Community Newspaper Holdings, Inc., 3500 Colonnade Pkwy., Ste. 600, Birmingham, AL 35243. Telephone: 205-298-7100. FAX: 205-298-7101. **Management:** Lisa Chappell, Publisher. Deb Gentry, Advertising Director. Robert Spillers, Circulation Director. Shelley Morgan, Classified Adv. Mgr.. **Editorial:** Derek Price, Editor. Warren Morrison, Managing Editor. David Claybourn, Sports Editor.

HARLINGEN

VALLEY MORNING STAR. 1310 S. Commerce, Harlingen, TX 78551. Telephone: 956-430-6200. FAX: 956-430-6204. URL: http://www.valleystar.com. Mailing Address: PO Box 511, Harlingen, TX 78551. Year Established: 1911. Pub. Frequency: d. Page Size: broadsheet. Subscrip. Rate: $.50 newsstand/cover; $1.25 newsstand/cover Sun.; $10 home delivery/mo.. **Wire Service(s):** AP. Circulation: 34,000 morning (paid); 35,004 Sunday (paid). **Owner(s):** Freedom Communications, Inc., 17666 Fitch, Irvine, CA 92714. **Bureau(s):** State Capitol Bldg., P.O. Box 2910, Austin, TX 78769. **Management:** Tyler Patton, Publisher. Richard Guerrero, Advertising Director. Rusty Hall, Circulation Manager. **Editorial:** Paul Binz, Editor. Lucio Castillo, Managing Editor. Contact: Tyler Patton, Publisher.

HENDERSON

HENDERSON DAILY NEWS. 1711 Hwy. 79 S., Henderson, TX 75654. Telephone: 903-657-2501. FAX: 903-657-2452. E-MAIL: randallg@hendersondailynews.com. URL: http://www.hendersondailynews.com. Mailing Address: PO Box 30, Henderson, TX 75653-0030. Year Established: 1930. Pub. Frequency: d. (Sun.-Fri.) Page Size: broadsheet. Subscrip. Rate: $.50 newsstand/cover; $1 newsstand/cover Sun.; $92/yr carrier delivery in county & mailed in cy.; $156/yr mailed out of county. Adv. Rate: col. inch $7.25 **Wire Service(s):** AP. Circulation: 6,215 evening (paid). **Owner(s):** Henderson Newspapers, Inc., PO Box 1390, Rosenberg, TX 77471-1390. Telephone: 281-342-8691. **Management:** Noble Welch, Publisher. Randall Gill, Advertising Director. **Editorial:** Tony Floyd, Managing Editor.

HEREFORD

HEREFORD BRAND. 313 N. Lee St., Hereford, TX 79045. Telephone: 806-364-2030. FAX: 806-364-8364. URL: http://www.herefordbrand.com. Mailing Address: PO Box 673, Hereford, TX 79045. Year Established: 1901. Pub. Frequency: d. (Tue.-Sat.) Page Size: broadsheet. Subscrip. Rate: $.75 newsstand/cover; $1 newsstand/cover Sat.; $75.20/yr in county; $82.70/yr mailed out of county. **Wire Service(s):** AP. Circulation: 3,200 evening (paid); 4,300 Sunday (paid). **Owner(s):** Roberts Publishing Co., 210 E. Broadway, Andrews, TX 79714. **Management:** Brian Brisendine, General Manager. Freddie Flores, Advertising Director. Julius Bodner, Advertising Manager. Jay Guerero, Circulation Manager. Becky Bridges, Classified Adv. Mgr.. **Editorial:** Donald M. Cooper, Editor. Becky Thorn, Lifestyle Editor.

HOUSTON

HOUSTON CHRONICLE. ISSN 1074-7109
801 Texas Ave., Houston, TX 77002. Telephone: 713-220-7171. FAX: 713-220-6806. E-MAIL: hci@chron.com. URL: http://www.chron.com. Mailing Address: PO Box 4260, Houston, TX 77210. Year Established: 1901. Pub. Frequency: d. Page Size: broadsheet. Subscrip. Rate: $.50 newsstand/cover; $1.75 newsstand/cover Sun.; $51 home delivery for 6 mos.; $102/yr home delivery in county. **Wire Service(s):** AP, SH, NYT, AFP, MCT. Circulation: 553,462 morning (paid); 747,803 Sunday (paid). **Owner(s):** Hearst Corp., 959 Eighth Ave, New York, NY 10019. **Bureau(s):** 400 South Record, Ste. 850, Dallas, TX 75202. Telephone: 214-747-5995. Contact: Jim Henderson, Bureau Chief. **Management:** Jack Sweeney, Publisher. Lynn Cook, Advertising Director. Bill Offill, Classified Adv. Mgr.. Dave Insel, Photography Director. Jack Loftis, Associate Publisher. **Editorial:** Jeff Cohen, Editor. Dan Cunningham, Asst. Managing Ed.. Melissa Aguilar, Entertainment Editor. Susan Bishoff, Feature Editor.

HUNTSVILLE

HUNTSVILLE ITEM, THE. ISSN 0888-4145
1409 Tenth St., Huntsville, TX 77320. Telephone: 936-295-5407. FAX: 936-435-0135. E-MAIL: item@icc.net. URL: http://www.itemonline.com. Mailing Address: PO Box 539, Huntsville, TX 77342-0539. Year Established: 1850. Pub. Frequency: d. Page Size: broadsheet. Subscrip. Rate: $.50 newsstand/cover; $1.50 newsstand/cover Sun.; $11.45 carrier delivery/mo. in city; $11.75 carrier delivery/mo. out of city; $174/yr mailed in county; $198/yr mailed out of county. Adv. Rate: col. inch $14 **Wire Service(s):** AP. Circulation: 7,000 evening (paid); 8,000 Sunday (paid). **Owner(s):** Community Newspaper Holdings, Inc., 3500 Colonnade Pkwy., Ste. 600, Birmingham, AL 35243. Telephone: 205-298-7100. FAX: 205-298-7101. **Management:** Rex Maynor, Publisher. Dennis Garrison, Advertising Director. Charles Blakeley, Circulation Director. Sheila Youngbird, Classified Adv. Mgr.. **Editorial:** Jay Ermis, Managing Editor. Robbie Byrd, News Editor.

JACKSONVILLE

JACKSONVILLE DAILY PROGRESS. 525 E. Commerce St., Jacksonville, TX 75766-0071. Telephone: 903-586-2236. FAX: 903-586-0987. E-MAIL: publisher@jacksonvilleprogress.com. URL: http://www.jacksonvilleprogress.com. Mailing Address: PO Box 711, Jacksonville, TX 75766-0711. Year Established: 1910. Pub. Frequency: d. (Sun.-Fri.) Page Size: broadsheet. Subscrip. Rate: $.50 newsstand/cover; $1 newsstand/cover Sun.; $87/yr carrier delivery in county; $102/yr mailed out of county; $114/yr mailed out of state. Adv. Rate: col. inch $9.20 **Wire Service(s):** AP. Circulation: 4,186 evening (paid); 4,800 Sunday (paid). **Owner(s):** Community Newspaper Holdings, Inc., 3500 Colonnade Pkwy., Ste. 600, Birmingham, AL 35243. Telephone: 205-298-7100. **Management:** Amy Miller, Publisher. Tammy Minton, Office Manager. Heather Metzig, Advertising Director. Josh Hart, Circulation Manager. **Editorial:** Jim Goodson, Editor.

KERRVILLE

KERRVILLE DAILY TIMES. 429 Jefferson St., Kerrville, TX 78028-1428. Telephone: 830-896-7000. FAX: 830-896-1150. E-MAIL: kdt@ktc.com. URL: http://www.dailytimes.com. Mailing Address: PO Box 291428, Kerrville, TX 78029. Year Established: 1908. Pub. Frequency: d. (Sun.-Fri.) Page Size: broadsheet. Subscrip. Rate: $.50 newsstand/cover; $1 newsstand/cover Sun.; $9.95 mailed/mo. in county; $107.40/yr mailed in county; $11.10 mailed/mo. out of county; $125/yr mailed out of county. Adv. Rate: col. inch $9 **Wire Service(s):** AP. Circulation: 9,283 evening (paid and free); 11,000 Sunday (paid and free). **Owner(s):** Southern Newspapers, Inc., 5701 Woodway Dr., Ste. 131, Houston, TX 77057-1589. **Management:** Greg Shrader, Publisher. Marie Schwartzkopf, Advertising Manager. Judy Rodgers, Circulation Manager. **Editorial:** Greg Shrader, Editor. Rayanne Schmid, Managing Editor. John Schmid, Photographer. Doug Mitchell, Sports Editor.

KILGORE

KILGORE NEWS HERALD. 610 E. Main St., Kilgore, TX 75662. Telephone: 903-984-2593. FAX: 903-984-7462. URL: http://www.kilgorenewsherald.com. Mailing Address: PO Box 1210, Kilgore, TX 75663. Year Established: 1931. Pub. Frequency: d. (Sun.-Fri.) Page Size: broadsheet. Subscrip. Rate: $.25 newsstand/cover; $.75 newsstand/cover Sun. (effective 2005); $72/yr carrier delivery; $90/yr mailed. **Wire Service(s):** AP. Circulation: 3,500 evening (paid); 4,200 Sunday (paid). **Owner(s):** Bluebonnet Publishing, See address and contact information above. **Management:** Bill Woodall, Publisher. Valerie Larsen, Advertising. Candy Cole, Circulation Manager. **Editorial:** Bill Woodall, Editor. Mitch Lucas, Sports.

KILLEEN

KILLEEN DAILY HERALD. 1809 Florence Rd., Killeen, TX 76541. Telephone: 254-634-2125. FAX: 254-634-8204. E-MAIL: kdh@vvm.com. URL: http://www.kdhnews.com. Mailing Address: PO Box 1300, Killeen, TX 76540. Year Established: 1890. Pub. Frequency: d. Page Size: broadsheet. Subscrip. Rate: $.50 newsstand/cover; $1 newsstand/cover Sun.; $110/yr home delivery local; $130.80/yr mailed in county; $157.20/yr mailed out of county. Adv. Rate: col. inch $17.50 **Wire Service(s):** AP, SH. Circulation: 21,000 morning (paid); 26,000 Sunday (paid). **Owner(s):** F. Mayborn Enterprises, Inc., PO Box 614, Temple, TX 76503. Telephone: 254-778-4444. **Management:** Terry Gandy, General Manager. Sue Mayborn, Publisher. Sam Clark, Circulation Director. **Editorial:** Lee Trigg, Managing Editor. Dave Miller, Asst. Managing Ed.. Mark Miller, Sports.

LONGVIEW

LONGVIEW NEWS-JOURNAL. 320 E. Methvin St., Longview, TX 75601. Telephone: 903-757-3311. FAX: 903-757-3742. E-MAIL: newsjournal@coxnews.com. URL: http://www.news-journal.com. Mailing Address: PO Box 1792, Longview, TX 75606. Year Established: 1871. Pub. Frequency: d. Page Size: broadsheet. Subscrip. Rate: $.50 newsstand/cover; $1.50 newsstand/cover Sun.; $12.50 carrier delivery/mo.; $150/yr carrier delivery; $225/yr mailed. **Wire Service(s):** AP, SH, NYT, CNS. Circulation: 35,977 morning (paid); 42,034 Sunday (paid). **Owner(s):** Cox Newspapers, Inc., 6205 Peachtree Dunwoody Rd, Atlanta, GA 30328. Telephone: 404-843-5000. **Management:** Glen McCutchen, Publisher. Alan Todd, Advertising Director. Erik Buck, Circulation Director. **Editorial:** Ana Walker, Editor. Juan Elizondo, Managing Editor. Pete Litterski, Senior Editor. Kevin Green, Photographer. Gabriel Brooks, Sports Editor.

LUBBOCK

LUBBOCK AVALANCHE-JOURNAL. 710 Ave. J, Lubbock, TX 79401. Telephone: 806-762-8844. FAX: 806-744-9603. URL: http://www.lubbockonline.com. Mailing Address: PO Box 491, Lubbock, TX 79408. Year Established: 1904. Pub. Frequency: d. Page Size: broadsheet. Subscrip. Rate: $.50 newsstand/cover; $1.50 newsstand/cover Sun.; $13.95 carrier delivery/mo.; $167.40/yr carrier delivery. **Wire Service(s):** AP, SH, LAT-WAT, MCT. Circulation: 65,000 morning (paid); 76,000 Sunday (paid). **Owner(s):** Morris Multimedia, Inc., PO Box 936, Augusta, GA 30903. Telephone: 706-724-0851. **Management:** Mark Nusbaum, Publisher. Carol McWhorter, Advertising Director. **Editorial:** Randy Sanders, Editor. Mel Tittle, Managing Editor.

LUFKIN

LUFKIN DAILY NEWS, THE. 300 Ellis at Herndon, Lufkin, TX 75901-1089. Telephone: 936-632-6631. FAX: 936-632-6655. E-MAIL: lufnews@coxnews.com. URL: http://www.lufkindailynews.com. Mailing Address: PO Box 1089, Lufkin, TX 75902. Year Established: 1906. Pub. Frequency: d. Page Size: broadsheet. Subscrip. Rate: $.50 newsstand/cover; $1.50 newsstand/cover Sun.; $144/yr home delivery; $264/yr mailed. **Wire Service(s):** AP. Circulation: 14,550 morning (paid and free); 16,514 Sunday (paid and free). **Owner(s):** Cox Newspapers, Inc., 6205 Peachtree Dunwoody Rd., Atlanta, GA 30328. Telephone: 678-645-0000. **Management:** Gary Borders, Publisher. Jeannie Cook, Advertising Director. Jennifer Ferrell, Circulation Director. **Editorial:** Andy Adams, Editor. Ashley Cook, City Editor. Beverly Johnson, Lifestyle Editor. Joel Andrews, Photographer. Josh Harvard, Sports Editor.

MARSHALL

MARSHALL NEWS MESSENGER, THE. 309 E. Austin St., Marshall, TX 75670. Telephone: 903-935-7914. FAX: 903-935-6242. E-MAIL: newsmessenger@coxmnm.com. URL: http://www.marshallnewsmessenger.com. Mailing Address: PO Box 730, Marshall, TX 75671. Pub. Frequency: d. Page Size: standard. Subscrip. Rate: $.50 newsstand/cover; $120.60/yr home delivery; $141/yr mailed. **Wire Service(s):** AP. Circulation: 7,000 morning (paid); 8,000 Sunday (paid). **Owner(s):** Cox Newspapers, Inc., 6205 Peachtree Dunwoody Rd., Atlanta, GA 30328. Telephone: 678-645-0000. **Management:** Phil Latham, Publisher. Nan Friend, Advertising Manager. Erik Buck, Circulation Director. **Editorial:** Phil Latham, Editor. DD Turner, Managing Editor. Robin Y Richardson, Feature Editor. Jon Dustin Brooks, Sports Editor.

MCALLEN

MONITOR, THE. 1400 E. Nolona, McAllen, TX 78504. Telephone: 956-686-4343. FAX: 956-683-4401. E-MAIL: comments@themonitor.com. URL: http://www.themonitor.com. Mailing Address: PO Box 3267, McAllen, TX 78502-3267. Year Established: 1911. Pub. Frequency: d. Page Size: broadsheet. Subscrip. Rate: $.50 newsstand/cover; $1.25 newsstand/cover Sun.; $9.75 carrier delivery/mo.; $117/yr carrier delivery in county; $210/yr mailed out of county. **Wire Service(s):** AP, MCT. Circulation: 42,068 morning (paid); 50,281 Sunday (paid). **Owner(s):** Freedom Communications, Inc., 17666 Fitch, Irvine, CA 92614. Telephone: 949-253-2300. **Management:** Benita Mendell, General Manager. Olaf Frandsen, Publisher. Brian Sales, Advertising Director. Robert Levier, Circulation Director. Tammy Risica, Marketing Director. **Editorial:** Stephen Fagan, Editor. Mack Harrison, Editorial Page Editor. Marcia Caltibiano, Metro Editor. Oscar Gonzales, Sports.

MCKINNEY

MCKINNEY COURIER GAZETTE. 1650 W Virginia, Ste 202, McKinney, TX 75069. Telephone: 972-542-2631. FAX: 972-529-1684. URL: http://www.courier-gazette.com. Year Established: 1847. Pub. Frequency: d. (Sun.-Fri.) Page Size: broadsheet. Subscrip. Rate: $.50 newsstand/cover; $1 newsstand/cover Sun.; $75/yr home delivery in county & mailed in cy.; $112.50/yr mailed out of county. Circulation: 55,000 morning (paid). **Owner(s):** Star Community Newspapers, 14875 Landmark Blvd, Ste 110, Addison, TX 75254. Telephone: 972-628-4061. FAX: 971-436-7432. **Management:** Bill Weaver, Publisher. Joani Dittrich, Advertising Manager. Joni Craghead, Classified Adv. Mgr.. **Editorial:** Dave Sorter, Managing Editor.

MEXIA

MEXIA DAILY NEWS. 214 N. Railroad St., Mexia, TX 76667. Telephone: 254-562-2868. FAX: 254-562-3121. URL: http://www.mexiadailynews.com. Mailing Address: PO Box 431, Mexia, TX 76667. Year Established: 1872. Pub. Frequency: d. (Tue.-Sat.) Page Size: broadsheet. Subscrip. Rate: $.50 newsstand/cover; $34.50 carrier delivery for 6 mos. in county; $43.55 mailed/mo. in county 6 mos.; $46.15 mailed/mo. out of county 6 mos.. **Wire Service(s):** AP. Circulation: 2,800 evening (paid). **Owner(s):** Community Newspaper Holdings, Inc., 3500 Colonnade Pkwy., Ste. 600, Birmingham, AL 35243. Telephone: 205-298-7100. FAX: 205-298-7101. **Management:** Lynette Copley, Publisher. Vicky Thomas, Circulation Manager. Doris Miller, Classified Adv. Mgr.. **Editorial:** Robert E. Wright, Editor.

MIDLAND

MIDLAND REPORTER-TELEGRAM. ISSN 0890-5932
201 E. Illinois Ave., Midland, TX 79701. Telephone: 432-682-5311. FAX: 432-570-7650. E-MAIL: gott@hearstnp.com. URL: http://www.mywesttexas.com. Mailing Address: PO Box 1650, Midland, TX 79702. Year Established: 1929. Pub. Frequency: d. Page Size: broadsheet. Subscrip. Rate: $.50 newsstand/cover; $1.50 newsstand/cover Sun.; $12 home delivery/mo.; $132/yr home delivery. Adv. Rate: col. inch $26.10 **Wire Service(s):** AP, LAT-WAT. Circulation: 19,894 morning (paid); 23,428 Sunday (paid). **Owner(s):** Hearst Corp., 959 Eighth Ave, New York, NY 10019. **Management:** Charles Spence, Publisher. Chuck Evers, Advertising Manager. Gary Wamsley, Circulation Director. Dick Hardin, Classified Adv. Mgr.. **Editorial:** Gary Ott, Editor. Stewart Doreen, Managing Editor. Mella McEwen, Business Editor. Georgia Temple, Entertainment Editor. Tim Fisher, Photographer. Len Hayward, Sports Editor.

MINERAL WELLS

MINERAL WELLS INDEX. 300 S.E. First St., Mineral Wells, TX 76067. Telephone: 940-325-4465. FAX: 940-325-2020. E-MAIL: editor@mineralindex.com. URL: http://www.mineralwellsindex.com. Mailing Address: PO Box 370, Mineral Wells, TX 76068. Year Established: 1900. Pub. Frequency: d. (Tue.-Fri. & Sun.) Page Size: broadsheet. Subscrip. Rate: $.50 newsstand/cover; $1 newsstand/cover Sun.; $84/yr home delivery; $108/yr mailed out of area. **Wire Service(s):** AP, MCT. Circulation: 4,000 evening (paid); 4,750 Sunday (paid). **Owner(s):** Community Newspaper Holdings, Inc., 3500 Colonnade Pkwy., Ste. 600, Birmingham, AL 35243. Telephone: 205-298-7100. FAX: 205-298-7101. **Management:** Mel Rhodes, Publisher. Stacy Choate, Circulation Director. Glenna Barham, Classified Adv. Mgr.. **Editorial:** David May, Editor. Craig Holamon, Sports.

MT. PLEASANT

MOUNT PLEASANT DAILY TRIBUNE. 1705 Industrial St., Mt. Pleasant, TX 75455. Telephone: 903-572-1700. FAX: 903-572-6026. E-MAIL: newsroom@bluebonnet.net. URL: http://www.etxmp.com. Mailing Address: PO Box 1177, Mt. Pleasant, TX 75456. Year Established: 1874. Pub. Frequency: d. (Sun.-Fri.) Page Size: broadsheet. Subscrip. Rate: $.50 newsstand/cover; $1.25 newsstand/cover Sun.; $30 mailed in county for 3 mos.; $88/yr mailed in county; $99/yr mailed out of county. **Wire Service(s):** AP. Circulation: 5,500 evening (paid); 6,000 Sunday (paid). **Owner(s):** Palmer Media, Inc., See address and contact information above. **Management:** Robert L. Palmer, Publisher. Amy Hinton, Advertising Manager. Larry Belcher, Circulation Manager. Michelle Rains, Classified Adv. Mgr.. **Editorial:** Robert L. Palmer, Editor. John Whitten, Asst. Managing Ed.. Linda Harton, Lifestyle Editor. Brian Gegere, Sports Editor.

NACOGDOCHES

DAILY SENTINEL (NACOGDOCHES), THE. 4920 Colonial Dr., Nacogdoches, TX 75961. Telephone: 936-564-8361. FAX: 936-560-4267. E-MAIL: sentinel@lcc.net. URL: http://www.dailysentinel.com. Mailing Address: PO Box 630068, Nacogdoches, TX 75963. Year Established: 1972. Pub. Frequency: d. Page Size: broadsheet. Subscrip. Rate: $.50 newsstand/cover; $1.50 newsstand/cover Sun.; $144/yr home delivery; $264/yr mailed. **Wire Service(s):** AP. Circulation: 9,000 morning (paid); 11,000 Sunday (paid). **Owner(s):** Cox Newspapers, Inc., 6205 Peachtree Dunwoody Rd., Atlanta, GA 30328. Telephone: 678-645-0000. **Management:** Ferris H. Fain, General Manager. Carla DeLuca, Publisher. David Lawrence, Advertising Manager. Rayford Williams, Circulation Manager. **Editorial:** Carla DeLuca, Editor. Robbie Goodrich, Managing Editor. Debra Ryan, News Editor. Kevin Gore, Sports Editor.

NEW BRAUNFELS

HERALD-ZEITUNG. 707 Landa St., New Braunfels, TX 78130. Telephone: 830-625-9144. FAX: 830-625-1224. URL: http://www.herald-zeitung.com. Mailing Address: PO Box 311328, New Braunfels, TX 78131-1328. Year Established: 1852. Pub. Frequency: d. (Tue.- Sun.) Page Size: broadsheet. Subscrip. Rate: $.50 newsstand/cover; $1 newsstand/cover Sun.; $25 carrier delivery/quarter; $79/yr carrier delivery. **Wire Service(s):** AP. Circulation: 8,500 evening (paid); 11,000 Sunday (paid). **Owner(s):** Southern Newspapers, Inc., 5701 Woodway Dr., Ste. 131, Houston, TX 77057-1589. **Management:** Douglas Toney, Publisher. Chuck Evers, Advertising Manager. Jeff Fowler, Circulation Manager. Valerie Shields, Business Manager. **Editorial:** Jeremy Pafford, Managing Editor. Henry Coello, Production Manager. David Ingram, Photo Editor. Will Wright, Sports Editor.

ODESSA

ODESSA AMERICAN. 222 E. Fourth St., Odessa, TX 79761. Telephone: 800-375-9661. FAX: 432-333-7700. E-MAIL: oaoa@link.freedom.com. URL: http://www.oaoa.com. Mailing Address: PO Box 2952, Odessa, TX 79760. Year Established: 1940. Pub. Frequency: d. Page Size: broadsheet. Subscrip. Rate: $.50 newsstand/cover; $1.50 newsstand/cover Sun.; $12.50 carrier delivery/mo.; $18.50 mailed/mo.. **Wire Service(s):** AP. Circulation: 24,139 morning (paid); 26,896 Sunday (paid). **Owner(s):** Freedom Communications, Inc., 17666 Fitch St., Irvine, CA 92614. **Management:** Pat Canty, Publisher. Stacey Rean, Advertising Director. Brandi Hill, Advertising Manager. Linda Fury, Circulation Manager. Angie Fuentes, Classified Adv. Mgr.. **Editorial:** John Kerr, Executive Editor. Ken Brodnax, Editorial Page Editor.

ORANGE

ORANGE LEADER. ISSN 0885-8047
200 Front Ave., Orange, TX 77630. Telephone: 409-883-3571. FAX: 409-883-6342. E-MAIL: orangeleader@yahoo.com. URL: www.orangeleader.com. Mailing Address: PO Box 1028, Orange, TX 77631. Year Established: 1875. Pub. Frequency: d. Page Size: broadsheet. Subscrip. Rate: $.50 newsstand/cover; $1 newsstand/cover Sun.; $117/yr home delivery; $15 mailed/mo.. Adv. Rate: col. inch $16.54 Freelance Pay: $15/article. **Wire Service(s):** AP. Circulation: 8,800 morning (paid); 9,800 Sunday (paid). **Owner(s):** Community Newspaper Holdings, Inc., 3500 Colonnade Pkwy., Ste. 600, Birmingham, AL 35243. Telephone: 205-298-7100. FAX: 205-298-7101. **Management:** Eric Bauer, Publisher. Becky Hatfield, Advertising Manager. Glenda Bland, Circulation Manager. **Editorial:** Richard Nelson, Editor. Van Wade, Sports Editor.

PALESTINE

PALESTINE HERALD-PRESS. ISSN 1053-5748
519 N. Elm St., Palestine, TX 75802. Telephone: 903-729-0281. FAX: 903-729-0284. E-MAIL: pheraldp@flash.net. URL: http://www.palestineherald.com. Mailing Address: PO Box 379, Palestine, TX 75802. Year Established: 1898. Pub. Frequency: d. Page Size: broadsheet. Subscrip. Rate: $.50 newsstand/cover; $1.25 newsstand/cover Sun.; $105/yr home delivery local; $138/yr mailed out of county. **Wire Service(s):** AP. Circulation: 9,368 evening (paid); 9,613 Sunday (paid). **Owner(s):** Community Newspaper Holdings, Inc., 3500 Colonnade Pkwy., Ste. 600, Birmingham, AL 35243. Telephone: 205-298-7100. FAX: 205-298-7101. **Management:** Gary Connor, Publisher. Mandy Meazell, Advertising Manager. Maria Beazley, Classified Adv. Mgr.. **Editorial:** Angie Tawater, Managing Editor. Cheryl Vernon, Lifestyle Editor. Scott Tyler, Sports.

PAMPA

PAMPA NEWS. 403 W. Atchison, Pampa, TX 79065. Telephone: 806-669-2525. FAX: 806-669-2520. E-MAIL: editor@thepampenews.com. URL: http://www.thepampanews.com. Mailing Address: P.O. Drawer 2198, Pampa, TX 79066. Year Established: 1927. Pub. Frequency: d. (Sun.-Fri.) Page Size: broadsheet. Subscrip. Rate: $.50 newsstand/cover; $1 newsstand/cover Sun.; $84/yr home delivery in area; $102/yr mailed in state; $114/yr mailed out of state. **Wire Service(s):** AP. Circulation: 5,000 evening (paid); 6,200 Sunday (paid). **Owner(s):** PTS Inc., 221A 35th St., N.E., Fort Payne, AL 35967. Telephone: 205-845-4590. **Management:** Sean Smith, Publisher. ReDonn Woods, Advertising Director. Leon Watson, Circulation Manager. Beverly Taylor, Classified Adv. Mgr.. **Editorial:** Dennis Spies, Editor. Michael Stevens, Sports Editor.

PARIS

PARIS NEWS, THE. ISSN 8756-2081
5050 S.E. Loop 286, Paris, TX 75461-5050. Telephone: 903-785-8744. FAX: 903-785-1263. E-MAIL: editor@theparisnews.com. URL: http://theparisnews.com. Mailing Address: PO Box 1078, Paris, TX 75461. Year Established: 1869. Pub. Frequency: d. (Sun.-Fri.) Page Size: broadsheet. Subscrip. Rate: $.50 newsstand/cover; $1.25 newsstand/cover Sun.; $9.75 carrier delivery/mo.. **Wire Service(s):** AP. Circulation: 11,700 evening (paid); 13,000 Sunday (paid). **Owner(s):** Southern Newspapers, Inc., 5701 Woodway Dr., Ste. 131, Houston, TX 77057-1589. **Management:** Michael Graxiola, President. Toni Barron, Advertising Manager. Dean Foster, Circulation Manager. Dorothy Crawford, Classified Adv. Mgr.. Fred Downs, Production Director. Relan Walker, Business Manager. **Editorial:** Phillip Hamilton, Editor. Contact: Sally Boswell, Editor. Contact: Phillip Hamilton, Managing Editor.

PASADENA

PASADENA CITIZEN. ISSN 0896-3320
102 S. Shaver St., Pasadena, TX 77506. Telephone: 713-477-0221. FAX: 713-477-9090. E-MAIL: ggallatin@hcnonline.com. URL: http://www.hcnonline.com. Mailing Address: PO Box 6192, Pasadena, TX 77506. Year Established: 1947. Pub. Frequency: d. (Tue.-Fri. & Sun.) Page Size: broadsheet. Subscrip. Rate: $.50 newsstand/cover; $5.95 carrier delivery/mo.; $17.85 for 3 months. Adv. Rate: col. inch $20.84 **Wire Service(s):** AP. Circulation: 8,100 morning (paid); 13,900 Sunday (paid). **Owner(s):** ASP Westward LP, 523-N Sam Houston Pkwy, Ste 600, Houston, TX 77060. Telephone: 281-668-1100. **Management:** Kevin Barry, Chief Executive Ofc. . Gordon Gallatin, Publisher. Jim Wadzinski, Advertising Director. **Editorial:** David Taylor, Editor. Robert Avery, Sports Editor.

PLAINVIEW

PLAINVIEW DAILY HERALD. 820 Broadway, Plainview, TX 79072. Telephone: 806-296-1300. FAX: 806-296-1315. URL: http://www.myplainview.com. Mailing Address: PO Box 1240, Plainview, TX 79073-1240. Year Established: 1889. Pub. Frequency: d. (Sun.-Fri.) Page Size: standard. Subscrip. Rate: $.50 newsstand/cover; $1.25 newsstand/cover Sun.; $105/yr home delivery; $138/yr mailed. **Wire Service(s):** AP. Circulation: 7,500 evening (paid); 9,000 Sunday (paid). **Owner(s):** Hearst Corp., 959 Eighth Ave, New York, NY 10019. **Management:** Rollie D. Hyde, Publisher. Vernah Ramsower, Advertising Manager. Charles Lawson, Circulation Director. Jason Johnson, Classified Adv. Mgr.. **Editorial:** Danny Andrews, Editor. Bill Rushing, Production Manager. Nicki Logan, Lifestyle Editor. Doug McDonough, News Editor. Richard Porter, Photographer. Mark Turner, Sports Editor.

PLANO

PLANO STAR COURIER. ISSN 0895-4305
624 Krona Dr, Ste 170, Plano, TX 75074. Telephone: 972-398-4200. FAX: 972-398-4470. URL: http://www.planostar.com. Year Established: 1888. Pub. Frequency: d. (Wed.-Sun.) Page Size: broadsheet. Subscrip. Rate: $.50 newsstand/cover; $1 newsstand/cover Sun.; $85/yr home delivery in county .; $114.95/yr mailed out of county .; $154.95/yr mailed out of state .. Circulation: 3,040 morning (paid); 3,040 Sunday (paid). **Owner(s):** Star Community Newspapers, 14875 Landmark Blvd, Ste 110, Addison, TX 75254. Telephone: 972-628-4061. FAX: 971-436-7432. **Management:** Bill Weaver, Publisher. Ken McEwen, Circulation Manager. **Editorial:** Rick Mann, Managing Editor.

PORT ARTHUR

PORT ARTHUR NEWS. ISSN 0889-6755
3501 Turtle Creek Dr., Port Arthur, TX 77642. Telephone: 409-721-2431. FAX: 409-724-6854. E-MAIL: panews@panews.com. URL: http://www.panews.com. Mailing Address: PO Box 789, Port Arthur, TX 77641. Year Established: 1897. Pub. Frequency: d. Page Size: broadsheet. Subscrip. Rate: $.50 newsstand/cover; $1 newsstand/cover Sun.; $9 carrier delivery/mo. local; $98/yr carrier delivery local; $14 mailed/mo. out of area. **Wire Service(s):** AP, NYT, LAT-WAT. Circulation: 19,196 morning (paid); 19,605 Sunday (paid). **Owner(s):** Community Newspaper Holdings, Inc., 3500 Colonnade Pkwy., Ste. 600, Birmingham, AL 35243. Telephone: 205-298-7100. FAX: 205-298-7101. **Management:** Glenn Stifflemire, Publisher. Renae Alexander, Advertising Manager. Don Richter, Circulation Manager. Tara Ford, Classified Adv. Mgr.. **Editorial:** Roger Cowles, Editor. Bob West, Sports Editor.

ROSENBERG

HERALD COASTER, THE. 1902 Fourth St., Rosenberg, TX 77471-5142. Telephone: 281-342-4474. FAX: 281-342-3219. E-MAIL: newsroom@herald-coaster.com. URL: http://www.herald-coaster.com. Mailing Address: PO Box 1088, Rosenberg, TX 77471-1088. Year Established: 1892. Pub. Frequency: d. (Sun.-Fri.) Page Size: broadsheet. Subscrip. Rate: $.50 newsstand/cover; $1 newsstand/cover Sun.; $75/yr carrier delivery; $133/yr mailed out of state. **Wire Service(s):** AP. Circulation: 9,200 evening (paid); 9,200 Sunday (paid). **Owner(s):** Hartman Newspapers, Inc., PO Box 1390, Rosenberg, TX 77471. Telephone: 281-342-4474. FAX: 281-342-3219. **Management:** David Lyons Jr., Publisher. Lee Hartman, Advertising Manager. Steve Fristoe, Circulation Manager. **Editorial:** Bob Haenel, Managing Editor. Gary Martin, Sports Editor.

SAN ANGELO

SAN ANGELO STANDARD-TIMES. 34 W. Harris Ave., San Angelo, TX 76903. Telephone: 325-653-1221. FAX: 325-659-8171. E-MAIL: comments@texaswest.com. URL: http://www.sastandardtimes.com. Mailing Address: PO Box 5111, San Angelo, TX 76902. Year Established: 1884. Pub. Frequency: d. Page Size: broadsheet. Subscrip. Rate: $.50 newsstand/cover; $1.50 newsstand/cover Sun.; $14.95 home delivery/mo.; $179.40/yr home delivery. Adv. Rate: col. inch $38.29 **Wire Service(s):** AP, SH. Circulation: 27,000 morning (paid); 31,866 Sunday (paid). **Owner(s):** E.W. Scripps Co., 312 Walnut St., 28th Fl., Cincinnati, OH 45202. Telephone: 513-977-3000. **Management:** Robert Aguilar, Publisher. Rich Barnes, Advertising Manager. Joe Solley, Circulation Manager. **Editorial:** Tim Archuletta, Editor. Jack Cowan, Editorial Page Editor. Jason Hunter, Sports Editor.

SAN ANTONIO

SAN ANTONIO EXPRESS-NEWS. ISSN 1065-7908
301 Ave E, San Antonio, TX 78205-2171. Telephone: 210-250-3000. FAX: 210-250-3105. E-MAIL: cthomason@express-news.net. URL: http://www.mysanantonio.com/expressnews. Mailing Address: PO Box 2171, San Antonio, TX 78297-2171. Year Established: 1984. Pub. Frequency: d. Page Size: broadsheet. Subscrip. Rate: $.50 newsstand/cover; $9.99 home delivery/mo. in county; $16 home delivery/mo. out of county. **Wire Service(s):** AP, SH, NYT, LAT-WAT. Circulation: 356,377 per issue. **Owner(s):** Hearst Corp., 959 Eighth Ave, New York, NY 10019. **Management:** Thomas Stevenson, General Manager. W. Lawrence Walker Jr., Publisher. **Editorial:** Robert Rivard, Editor. Brett Thacker, Managing Editor. Kathy Foley, Asst. Managing Ed.. Vicky Vaugh, Business Editor. Lynnell Burkett, Editorial Page Editor. Steve Quintana, Sports Editor.

SAN MARCOS

SAN MARCOS DAILY RECORD. 1910 IH-35 S., San Marcos, TX 78666. Telephone: 512-392-2458. FAX: 512-392-1514. URL: http://www.sanmarcosrecord.com. Mailing Address: PO Box 1109, San Marcos, TX 78667. Year Established: 1912. Pub. Frequency: d. Page Size: broadsheet. Subscrip. Rate: $.50 newsstand/cover; $1 newsstand/cover Sun.; $72/yr carrier delivery local; $108/yr mailed in county. **Wire Service(s):** AP. Circulation: 7,500 evening (paid); 8,500 Sunday (paid). **Owner(s):** Community Newspaper Holdings, Inc., 3500 Colonnade Pkwy., Ste. 600, Birmingham, AL 35243. Telephone: 205-298-7100. FAX: 205-298-7101. **Management:** Cathy Fagan, Publisher. Cheryl Sosa, Advertising Director. **Editorial:** Rowe Ray, Managing Editor. Jeff Walker, Community Editor. Anita Miller, News Editor. Randy Stevens, Sports Editor.

SEGUIN

GAZETTE-ENTERPRISE. 1012 Schriewer Rd., Seguin, TX 78155. Telephone: 830-379-5441. FAX: 830-379-8328. URL: http://www.seguingazette.com. Mailing Address: PO Box 1200, Seguin, TX 78156-1200. Year Established: 1979. Pub. Frequency: d. (Tue.-Fri. & Sun.) Page Size: broadsheet. Subscrip. Rate: $.50 newsstand/cover; $1 newsstand/cover Sun.; $72/yr carrier delivery. **Wire Service(s):** AP. Circulation: 6,500 evening (paid); 8,500 Sunday (paid). **Owner(s):** Southern Newspapers, Inc., 5701 Woodway Dr., Ste. 131, Houston, TX 77057-1589. **Management:** Neice Bell, Publisher. Gaylyn Olsovsky, Advertising Manager. Jessie Fausto, Circulation Manager. Gaylyn Olsovsky, Classified Adv. Mgr.. Maggie Clarkson, Business Manager. **Editorial:** Christopher Lykins, Editor. Jamie Mobley, Feature Editor. Chris Chase, Sports Editor.

SHERMAN

HERALD DEMOCRAT. 603 S. Sam Rayburn Fwy., Sherman, TX 75090-7258. Telephone: 903-893-8181. FAX: 903-868-1930. URL: http://www.herald-democrat.com. Mailing Address: PO Box 1128, Sherman, TX 75091. Year Established: 1879. Pub. Frequency: d. (Sun.-Fri.) Page Size: standard. Subscrip. Rate: $.50 newsstand/cover; $1 newsstand/cover Sun.; $126/yr carrier delivery; $78/yr carrier delivery Sun only. **Wire Service(s):** AP, SH. Circulation: 26,700 morning (paid); 29,600 Sunday (paid). **Owner(s):** Stephens Media LLC, 1111 W. Bonanza Rd., Las Vegas, NV 89106. Telephone: 501-785-7810. **Management:** John Wright, Publisher. Wes King, Advertising Director. Mike Brezina, Circulation Manager. Ken Lanford, Classified Adv. Mgr.. **Editorial:** Don Eldredge, Editor. Kathy Williams, Assistant Editor. Gary Carter, City Editor. Lynette George, Lifestyle Editor. Alec Richards, Photographer. Todd Hutchinson, Sports Editor.

SNYDER

SNYDER DAILY NEWS. ISSN 1934-7014
3600 College Ave., Snyder, TX 79549. Telephone: 325-573-5486. FAX: 325-573-0044. E-MAIL: publisher@snyderdailynews.com. URL: http://www.snyderdailynews.com. Mailing Address: PO Box 949, Snyder, TX 79550. Year Established: 1950. Pub. Frequency: d. (Sun.-Fri.) Page Size: broadsheet. Subscrip. Rate: $.50 newsstand/cover; $1 newsstand/cover Sun.; $93.20/yr home delivery in county; $119.50/yr mailed out of county. **Wire Service(s):** AP. Circulation: 5,500 evening (paid); 6,000 Sunday (paid). **Owner(s):** Roberts Publishing Co., 210 E. Broadway, Andrews, TX 79714. **Management:** Roy McQueen, Publisher. Wayne Burney, Advertising Director. Donna Browning, Classified Adv. Mgr.. **Editorial:** Bobby Allen, Managing Editor. JoAnn Nunley, Feature Editor. Carry McCarty, Sports Editor.

STEPHENVILLE

STEPHENVILLE EMPIRE-TRIBUNE. 590 S. Loop, Stephenville, TX 76401. Telephone: 254-965-3124. FAX: 254-965-4269. E-MAIL: gene.deason@empiretribune.com. URL: www.empiretribune.com. Mailing Address: PO Box 958, Stephenville, TX 76401. Year Established: 1870. Pub. Frequency: d. (Sun.-Fri.) Page Size: broadsheet. Subscrip. Rate: $.50 newsstand/cover; $1.50 newsstand/cover Sun.; $9.90 carrier delivery/mo.. Adv. Rate: col. inch $12.50 Freelance Pay: $25/story. **Wire Service(s):** AP. Circulation: 4,400 evening (paid); 4,700 Sunday (paid). **Owner(s):** American Consolidated Media, Inc., 1420 N. Mockingbird Ln, Ste 100, Dallas, TX 75247. Telephone: 214-691-4066. FAX: 214-691-4086. **Management:** Mike P Coggins, Publisher. Mike Coggins, Advertising Director. **Editorial:** Jimmy Galvan, Managing Editor. Bud Jones, Sports Editor.

SULPHUR SPRINGS

SULPHUR SPRINGS NEWS-TELEGRAM. ISSN 0745-6425
401 Church St., Sulphur Springs, TX 75482. Telephone: 903-885-8663. E-MAIL: news@ssecho.com. URL: http://www.ssecho.com/nt.html. Mailing Address: PO Box 598, Sulphur Springs, TX 75483. Year Established: 1881. Pub. Frequency: d. (Sun.-Fri.) Page Size: broadsheet. Subscrip. Rate: $.50 newsstand/cover; $1.25 newsstand/cover Fri. & Sun.; $97/yr home delivery in city; $103/yr home delivery out of city; $107/yr mailed out of city. **Wire Service(s):** AP. Circulation: 6,800 evening (paid); 7,400 Sunday (paid). **Owner(s):** Echo Publishing Co., See address and contact information above. **Management:** Dan Smith, General Manager. Scott Keys, President. Jim Butler, Vice President. **Editorial:** Bruce Alsobrook, Managing Editor. Angela Pitts, Photographer. Butch Burney, Sports.

SWEETWATER

SWEETWATER REPORTER. 112 W Third St, Sweetwater, TX 79556. Telephone: 325-236-6677. FAX: 325-235-4967. E-MAIL: publisher@sweetwaterreporter.com. URL: http://www.sweetwaterreporter.com. Mailing Address: PO Box 750, Sweetwater, TX 79556-0750. Year Established: 1881. Pub. Frequency: d. (Sun.-Fri.) Page Size: broadsheet. Subscrip. Rate: $.50 newsstand/cover; $1 newsstand/cover Sun.; $87/yr home delivery in county; $75/yr mailed in county. Adv. Rate: col. inch $8 **Wire Service(s):** AP. Circulation: 3,400 evening (paid); 4,000 Sunday (paid). **Owner(s):** Horizon Publications, Inc., 1120 N. Carbon St, Ste 100, Marion, IL 62959. **Management:** Janice Boil, Advertising Manager. Terri Garza, Circulation Manager. **Editorial:** Ben Barkley, Editor.

TAYLOR

TAYLOR DAILY PRESS. ISSN 1054-3171
211 W. Third St., Taylor, TX 76574. Telephone: 512-352-8535. FAX: 512-352-2227. E-MAIL: news@taylordailypress.net. URL: http://www.tailordailypress.net. Mailing Address: P.O. Box 1040, Taylor, TX 76574. Year Established: 1912. Pub. Frequency: d. (Mon.-Fri.) Page Size: broadsheet. Subscrip. Rate: $.50 newsstand/cover; $84/yr in county; $122/yr out of county. Adv. Rate: col. inch $10 **Wire Service(s):** AP. Circulation: 5,300 evening (paid). **Owner(s):** Jim Chiosini, See address and contact information above. **Management:** Don Wilson, Advertising Manager. Albert Tovar, Circulation Manager. Charlotte Bengston, Classified Adv. Mgr.. **Editorial:** David King, Executive Editor. Heather Allee, Lifestyle Editor.

TEMPLE

TEMPLE DAILY TELEGRAM. 10 S. Third St., Temple, TX 76501. Telephone: 254-778-4444. FAX: 254-778-4444. E-MAIL: tdt@vvm.com or tdt@temple-telegram.com. URL: http://www.temple-telegram.com. Mailing Address: PO Box 6114, Temple, TX 76503-6114. Year Established: 1907. Pub. Frequency: d. Page Size: broadsheet. Subscrip. Rate: $.50 newsstand/cover; $1 newsstand/cover Sun.; $110/yr home delivery; $121/yr mailed in county & part of adj. cys.; $138/yr mailed elsewhere. **Wire Service(s):** CNS. Circulation: 21,926 morning (paid); 24,738 Sunday (paid). **Owner(s):** Frank Mayborn Enterprises, Inc., See address and contact information above. **Management:** Sue Mayborn, Publisher. Gary Garner, Advertising Manager. Pat Graham, Circulation Manager. Stan Thomas, Classified Adv. Mgr.. **Editorial:** Sue Mayborn, Editor. Steve Walters, Managing Editor. Janice Gibbs, City Editor. Randy Ray, Entertainment Editor. David Stevens, News Editor. Todd Glasscock, Society Editor.

TERRELL

TERRELL TRIBUNE, THE. 150 Ninth St., Terrell, TX 75160. Telephone: 972-563-6476. FAX: 972-563-0340. E-MAIL: ttrib@swbell.net. URL: http://www.terrelltribune.com. Mailing Address: PO Box 669, Terrell, TX 75160. Year Established: 1916. Pub. Frequency: d. (Sun.-Fri.) Page Size: broadsheet. Subscrip. Rate: $.50 newsstand/cover; $19.50 home delivery in city for 3 mos.; $30 mailed in county for 3 mos; $45 mailed elsewhere for 3 mos.. **Wire Service(s):** AP. Circulation: 6,200 evening (paid); 6,500 Sunday (paid). **Owner(s):** Hartman Newspapers, Inc., PO Box 1390, Rosenberg, TX 77471. Telephone: 713-342-4474. FAX: 713-342-3219. **Management:** Bill Jordan, Publisher. Rhonda McCormick, Classified Adv. Mgr.. **Editorial:** Kent Miller, Managing Editor. Cliff Gibson, Sports.

TEXARKANA

TEXARKANA GAZETTE. 315 Pine St, Texarkana, TX 75501. Telephone: 903-794-3311. FAX: 903-792-7183. URL: http://www.texarkangazette.com. Mailing Address: PO Box 621, Texarkana, TX 75504-0621. Year Established: 1875. Pub. Frequency: d. Page Size: broadsheet. Subscrip. Rate: $.50 newsstand/cover; $1.25 newsstand/cover Sun.; $138/yr carrier delivery; $153/yr mailed. Circulation: 31,000 morning (paid); 33,000 Sunday (paid). **Owner(s):** Wehco Media, Inc., PO Box 2221, Little Rock, AR 72203. Telephone: 501-378-3400. **Management:** Walter E. Hussman Jr., Publisher. Rick Meredith, Advertising Manager. Bobby Perry, Circulation Manager. **Editorial:** Les Minor, Managing Editor. Russell McDermott, News Editor. Johnny Green, Sports Editor.

TEXAS CITY

TEXAS CITY SUN. 7800 Emmett Lowry Expy., Texas City, TX 77591. Telephone: 409-945-3441. FAX: 409-935-0428. E-MAIL: tjaulds@texascitysun.com. URL: http://www.texascitysun.com. Mailing Address: PO Box 2249, Texas City, TX 77592. Year Established: 1912. Pub. Frequency: d. Page Size: broadsheet. Subscrip. Rate: $.50 newsstand/cover; $1 newsstand/cover Sun.; $9.95 carrier delivery/mo.; $14 mailed/mo.; $168/yr mailed. **Wire Service(s):** AP. Circulation: 8,800 morning (paid); 10,500 Sunday (paid). **Owner(s):** Walls Investment Co., 10 Willcrest Dr., Houston, TX 77042. Telephone: 713-266-5481. **Management:** Les Daughtery Jr., Publisher. Patti Shelton, Advertising Manager. Kay Whitley, Circulation Manager. Jan Hines, Business Manager. **Editorial:** Les Daughtery Jr., Editor. T J Avids, Managing Editor. Floyd Sims, Production Manager. Jim Levesque, Sports Editor.

TYLER

TYLER MORNING TELEGRAPH. 410 W. Erwin St., Tyler, TX 75702. Telephone: 903-597-8111. FAX: 903-595-0335. Mailing Address: PO Box 2030, Tyler, TX 75710. Year Established: 1877. Pub. Frequency: d. Page Size: broadsheet. Subscrip. Rate: $.50 newsstand/cover; $1.25 newsstand/cover Sun.; $9.75 carrier delivery/mo.. Adv. Rate: col. inch $22.93 **Wire Service(s):** AP. Circulation: 43,954 morning (paid); 50,188 Sunday (paid). **Owner(s):** T.B. Butler Publishing Co., Inc., See address and contact information above. **Management:** J.D. Osborn, General Manager. Nelson Clyde III, Publisher. Art McClelland, Advertising Director. Jerry Rives, Circulation Manager. Lauren Ballard, Classified Adv. Mgr.. **Editorial:** Everett Taylor, Editor-in-Chief. Jim Giametta, Executive Editor. Dave Berry, Managing Editor. Richard Loomis, City Editor. Joyce Turner, Feature Editor. David Branch, Photo Editor. Phil Hicks, Sports.

VERNON

VERNON DAILY RECORD. ISSN 1046-1426
3214 Wilbarger St., Vernon, TX 76384. Telephone: 940-552-5454. FAX: 940-553-4823. E-MAIL: editor@vernonrecord.com. URL: http://www.vernonrecord.com. Year Established: 1923. Pub. Frequency: d. (Sun.-Fri.) Page Size: broadsheet. Subscrip. Rate: $.50 newsstand/cover; $1 newsstand/cover Sun.; $51.50 home delivery for 6 mos.; $92.50/yr home delivery. **Wire Service(s):** AP. Circulation: 4,350 evening (paid); 5,150 Sunday (paid). **Owner(s):** Larry L. Crabtree, See address and contact information above. **Management:** Larry L. Crabtree, General Manager. Jim Surber, Advertising Manager. Beverly Cannady, Circulation Manager. Virginia Perez, Classified Adv. Mgr.. **Editorial:** Jimmy Carr, Managing Editor. Joyce Ashley, Society Editor. Kathy McClellan, Sports.

VICTORIA

VICTORIA ADVOCATE. 311 E. Constitution, Victoria, TX 77901. Telephone: 361-575-1451. FAX: 361-574-1225. E-MAIL: feedback@vicad.com. URL: http://www.victoriaadvocate.com. Mailing Address: PO Box 1518, Victoria, TX 77902. Year Established: 1846. Pub. Frequency: d. Page Size: broadsheet. Subscrip. Rate: $.50 newsstand/cover; $1.25 newsstand/cover Sun.; $144/yr home delivery in area; $156/yr motor route in county; $174/yr mailed in county. **Wire Service(s):** AP, LAT-WAT. Circulation: 40,000 morning (paid); 42,000 Sunday (paid). **Owner(s):** Victoria Advocate Publishing Co., See address and contact information above. **Management:** John M. Roberts, Publisher. Ed Gambardella, Advertising Director. Hamp Rogers, Circulation Director. **Editorial:** Chris Cobler, Editor. Thomas Martinez, Asst. Managing Ed.. Coy Slavik, Sports.

Dailies

WACO

WACO TRIBUNE HERALD. 900 Franklin Ave., Waco, TX 76701. Telephone: 254-757-5757. FAX: 254-757-0302. E-MAIL: letters@mail.iamerica.net. URL: http://www.wacotrib.com. Mailing Address: PO Box 2588, Waco, TX 76702-2588. Year Established: 1909. Pub. Frequency: d. Page Size: broadsheet. Subscrip. Rate: $.50 newsstand/cover; $1.50 newsstand/cover Sun.; $14.50 carrier delivery/mo.; $160.08/yr carrier delivery; $219/yr mailed. **Wire Service(s):** AP, NYT. Circulation: 46,331 morning (paid); 58,382 Sunday (paid). **Owner(s):** Cox Newspapers, Inc., 6205 Peachtree Dunwoody Rd, Atlanta, GA 30328. **Management:** Dan C Savage, President. Carlos Sanchez, Advertising Manager. Rick Deaver, Circulation Director. **Editorial:** Becky Gregory, Managing Editor. Mike Copeland, Business Editor. John Young, Editorial Page Editor. Paula Blesener, News Editor.

WAXAHACHIE

WAXAHACHIE DAILY LIGHT. ISSN 0896-0291 200 W. Marvin Ave., Waxahachie, TX 75168. Telephone: 972-937-3310. FAX: 972-937-1139. E-MAIL: thelight@azmail.net. URL: http://www.thedailylight.com. Mailing Address: PO Box 877, Waxahachie, TX 75165. Year Established: 1867. Pub. Frequency: d. (Sun.-Fri.) Page Size: broadsheet. Subscrip. Rate: $.50 newsstand/cover; $1.50 newsstand/cover Sun.; $28.50 carrier delivery in county for 3 mos.; $35.50 mailed in state for 3 mos.; $42 mailed out of state for 3 mos.. **Wire Service(s):** UPI. Circulation: 7,000 evening (paid); 7,000 Sunday (paid). **Owner(s):** American Consolidated Media, Inc., 841 Preston Rd., Dallas, TX 75225. Telephone: 214-691-4066. **Management:** Floyd Ingram, Publisher. Jennifer Kesterson, Advertising Manager. Brian Jones, Circulation Manager. **Editorial:** Neal White, Editor. Joann Livingston, Managing Editor. Patrick Walker, News Editor.

WEATHERFORD

WEATHERFORD DEMOCRAT. 512 Palo Pinto St., Weatherford, TX 76086. Telephone: 817-594-7447. FAX: 817-594-9734. E-MAIL: wfdd.editor@airmail.net. URL: http://www.weatherforddemocrat.com. Year Established: 1895. Pub. Frequency: d. (Sun.-Fri.) Page Size: broadsheet. Subscrip. Rate: $.50 newsstand/cover; $1 newsstand/cover Sun.; $87.95/yr carrier delivery in county; $108/yr mailed out of county. **Wire Service(s):** AP. Circulation: 7,000 morning (paid); 9,000 Sunday (paid). **Owner(s):** Community Newspaper Holdings, Inc., 3500 Colonnade Pkwy., Ste. 600, Birmingham, AL 35243. Telephone: 205-298-7100. FAX: 205-298-7101. **Management:** David Thornberry, Publisher. Paula Sears, Advertising Manager. Misty Harvey, Circulation Manager. **Editorial:** Phil Riddle, Editor. Matt DeWalt, Sports Editor.

WICHITA FALLS

TIMES RECORD NEWS. ISSN 0895-6138 1301 Lamar St., Wichita Falls, TX 76301. Telephone: 940-767-8341. FAX: 940-767-5201. E-MAIL: schutzb@wtr.com. URL: http://www.trnonline.com. Mailing Address: PO Box 120, Wichita Falls, TX 76307. Year Established: 1907. Pub. Frequency: d. Page Size: standard. Subscrip. Rate: $.50 newsstand/cover; $1.50 newsstand/cover Sun.; $13.45 home delivery/mo.. Freelance Pay: $15/article. **Wire Service(s):** AP, MCT. Circulation: 40,000 morning (paid); 50,000 Sunday (paid). **Owner(s):** E.W. Scripps Co., 312 Walnut St., 28th Fl., Cincinnati, OH 45202. Telephone: 513-977-3000. **Management:** Darrell Coleman, Publisher. Duane Bivona, Circulation Manager. **Editorial:** Carroll Wilson, Editor. Deanna Watson, Editorial Page Editor. Bridget Knight, Feature Editor. Judy McGinnis, Food Editor. Julie Gaynor, Graphics Editor. Bruce Smith, News Editor. Gary Lawson, Photo Editor. Nick Gholson, Sports Editor.

UTAH

LOGAN

HERALD JOURNAL (LOGAN), THE. 75 W. 300 N., Logan, UT 84321. Telephone: 435-752-2121. FAX: 435-753-6642. E-MAIL: hjnews@hjnews.com. URL: http://www.hjnews.com. Mailing Address: PO Box 487, Logan, UT 84323-0487. Year Established: 1931. Pub. Frequency: d. Page Size: broadsheet. Subscrip. Rate: $.50 newsstand/cover; $1.25 newsstand/cover Sun.; $117/yr in county; $18.50 mailed/mo. out of county. Adv. Rate: col. inch $13.50 **Wire Service(s):** AP, SH. Circulation: 15,000 evening (paid); 15,500 Sunday (paid). **Owner(s):** Pioneer Newspapers, Inc., 221 First Ave., W., Ste. 405, Seattle, WA 98119. **Management:** Bruce K. Smith, Publisher. Shawn Brady, Advertising Director. Russ Davis, Circulation Manager. Vicki Perry, Classified Adv. Mgr.. **Editorial:** Charles McCollum, Managing Editor. David Nelson, City Editor. Jasmine Michaelson, Feature Editor. Christian Hansen, News Editor. Mitch Mascaro, Photo Editor. Shawn Harrison, Sports.

OGDEN

STANDARD-EXAMINER. 332 Standard Way, Ogden, UT 84404. Telephone: 801-625-4200. FAX: 801-625-4508. E-MAIL: broghaar@standard.net. URL: http://www.standard.net. Mailing Address: PO Box 12790, Ogden, UT 84412-2790. Year Established: 1888. Pub. Frequency: d. Page Size: broadsheet. Subscrip. Rate: $.50 newsstand/cover; $1.50 Sun.; $162.37/yr home delivery; $252.37/yr mailed. Adv. Rate: col. inch $55.116 **Wire Service(s):** AP. Circulation: 60,768 morning (paid); 64,347 Sunday (paid). **Owner(s):** Ogden Publishing Corp., See address and contact information above. **Bureau(s):** 67 S Main St, Layton, UT 84041. Telephone: 801-629-5238. Contact: Julie Williamson, Editor. **Management:** Mark Shenefelt, Director. Lee Carter, Publisher. Brad Roghaar, Advertising Director. Ron Thornburg, Circulation Director. Bart Wade, Production Director. Vaughn Jacobsen, Business Manager. **Editorial:** Andy Howell, Managing Editor. Don Porter, Editorial Page Editor. Vanessa Zimmer, Feature Editor. Chris Miller, Sports Editor.Readers: General market

PROVO

DAILY HERALD (PROVO), THE. ISSN 0891-2777 1555 N. Freedom Blvd., Provo, UT 84604-0717. Telephone: 801-373-5050. FAX: 801-373-5489. E-MAIL: dhads@heraldextra.com. URL: http://www.heraldextra.com. Mailing Address: PO Box 717, Provo, UT 84603-0717. Year Established: 1873. Pub. Frequency: d. Page Size: broadsheet. Subscrip. Rate: $.50 newsstand/cover; $1.50 newsstand/cover Sun.; $13.20 carrier delivery/wk.; $24.60 carrier delivery/mo.. Freelance Pay: $0.75-$1.25/column-inch. **Wire Service(s):** AP, MCT, CNS. Circulation: 29,985 morning (paid); 35,600 Sunday (paid). **Owner(s):** Lee Enterprises, Inc., 201 N. Harrison St., Ste 600, Davenport, IA 52801-1924. **Management:** Al Manzi, Publisher. Cindy Richards, Advertising Manager. Karl Wurzbach, Circulation Director. **Editorial:** Randy Wright, Executive Editor. Elyssa Andrus, Lifestyle Editor. Joe Pyrah, Metro Editor.

SALT LAKE CITY

DESERET MORNING NEWS. ISSN 1545-5939 30 E. 100 South, Salt Lake City, UT 84111. URL: http://www.desnews.com. Mailing Address: PO Box 1257, Salt Lake City, UT 84110. Pub. Frequency: d. Page Size: broadsheet. Subscrip. Rate: $.50 newsstand/cover; $1.50 newsstand/cover Sun.; $3.40 carrier delivery/wk.; $327.60/yr mailed in ID, NV, WY, UT; $410.80/yr mailed elsewhere. **Wire Service(s):** RN, AP, UPI, SH, NYT, LAT-WAT. Circulation: 71,741 per issue (paid); 71,126 Sunday (paid). **Owner(s):** Deseret News Publishing Co., See address and contact information above. **Management:** Jim M. Wall, Publisher. Ravell Call, Photography Director. **Editorial:** Joseph A Cannon, Editor. Richard Hall, Managing Editor. Greg Kratz, Business Editor. Gerry Avant, Church Editor. Wendy Ogata, City Editor. Jay Evensen, Editorial Page Editor. John Robinson, National Editor. David Schneider, Sports Editor.

SALT LAKE CTY

SALT LAKE TRIBUNE, THE. ISSN 0746-3502 90 S 400 W Ste 700, Salt Lake Cty, UT 84101-1431. E-MAIL: tkm@sltrib.com. URL: http://www.sltrib.com. Year Established: 1871. Pub. Frequency: d. Page Size: broadsheet. Subscrip. Rate: $.50 newsstand/cover; $1.75 newsstand/cover Sun.; $107/yr carrier delivery. **Wire Service(s):** RN, AP, LAT-WAT, GNS. Circulation: 138,038 morning (paid); 175,000 Sunday (paid). **Owner(s):** MediaNews Group, Inc., 101 W Colfax Ave, Ste 1100, Denver, CO 80202. FAX: 303-954-6320. **Management:** Dean Singleton, Publisher. Diane Butcher, Advertising Manager. **Editorial:** Perry Orme, Editor. Lori Post, Photo Editor. Kurt Kragthorpe, Sports.

ST. GEORGE

SPECTRUM (ST. GEORGE), THE. ISSN 0745-6611 275 E. St. George Blvd., St. George, UT 84770. Telephone: 435-674-6200. FAX: 435-674-6264. E-MAIL: llindus@thespectrum.com. URL: http://www.thespectrum.com. Year Established: 1963. Pub. Frequency: d. Page Size: broadsheet. Subscrip. Rate: $.50 newsstand/cover; $1.50 newsstand/cover Sun.; $8.50 home delivery/mo.. Freelance Pay: $0.75/column-inch. **Wire Service(s):** AP. Circulation: 23,000 morning (paid). **Owner(s):** Gannett Company, Inc., 7950 Jones Branch Dr, McLean, VA 22107. Telephone: 703-854-6000. **Management:** Brent Lowe, Publisher. James English, Advertising Director. **Editorial:** Todd Seifert, Editor. Scott Porter, Production Manager.

VERMONT

BARRE

TIMES ARGUS. 540 N. Main St., Barre, VT 05641. Telephone: 802-479-0191. FAX: 802-479-4032. E-MAIL: info@timesargus.com. URL: http://www.timesargus.com. Mailing Address: PO Box 707, Barre, VT 05641. Year Established: 1897. Pub. Frequency: d. Page Size: broadsheet. Subscrip. Rate: $.75 newsstand/cover; $1.75 newsstand/cover Sun.; $3.45 home delivery/wk. town; $51.35 motor route 3 Mos. **Wire Service(s):** AP, NYT, MCT. Circulation: 8,749 evening (paid); 9,664 Sunday (paid). **Owner(s):** Herald Association, Inc., 27 Wales St., Rutland, VT 05701. Telephone: 802-476-0912. **Management:** Anita Ancel, General Manager. R. John Mitchell, Publisher. Beth Wechsler, Advertising Manager. Robert Arrowsmith, Circulation Director. **Editorial:** Sue Allen, Managing Editor. Jim Lowe, Entertainment Editor. Dirk VanSusteren, Sunday Editor.

BENNINGTON

BENNINGTON BANNER. 425 Main St., Bennington, VT 05201. Telephone: 802-447-7567. FAX: 802-442-3413. E-MAIL: news@benningtonbanner.com. URL: http://www.benningtonbanner.com. Mailing Address: PO Box 5027, Bennington, VT 05201. Year Established: 1841. Pub. Frequency: d. (Mon.-Sat.) Page Size: broadsheet. Subscrip. Rate: $.50 newsstand/cover; $.75 newsstand/cover Sat.; $105/yr home delivery; $132/yr mailed in county. **Wire Service(s):** AP. Circulation: 8,800 morning (paid). **Owner(s):** MediaNews Group, Inc., 101 W Colfax Ave, Ste 1100, Denver, CO 80202. FAX: 303-954-6320. **Management:** Edward L Wood, Publisher. Doug Woodward, Advertising Manager. Marianne Sawyer, Classified Adv. Mgr. **Editorial:** James Therrien, Editor.

BRATTLEBORO

BRATTLEBORO REFORMER. 62 Black Mountain Rd., Brattleboro, VT 05302-0802. Telephone: 802-254-2311. FAX: 802-257-1305. URL: http://www.reformer.com. Mailing Address: PO Box 802, Brattleboro, VT 05302-0802. Year Established: 1913. Pub. Frequency: d. (Mon.-Sat.) Page Size: broadsheet. Subscrip. Rate: $.50 newsstand/cover; $.75 newsstand/cover Sat.; $118/yr carrier delivery; $137/yr mailed in county. **Wire Service(s):** AP. Circulation: 11,235 morning (paid). **Owner(s):** MediaNews Group, Inc., 101 W Colfax Ave, Ste 1100, Denver, CO 80202. FAX: 303-954-6320. **Management:** Jim Wells, Publisher. Anton Kaufer, Advertising Manager. Tim Gorts, Circulation Manager. Melissa Wetherby, Classified Adv. Mgr.. **Editorial:** Kevin Moran, Managing Editor. Daniel Watson, Sports Editor.

BURLINGTON

BURLINGTON FREE PRESS. ISSN 0894-8844 191 College St., Burlington, VT 05402. Telephone: 802-863-3441. FAX: 802-660-1802. E-MAIL: bfreepress@aol.com. URL: http://www.burlingtonfreepress.com. Mailing Address: PO Box 10, Burlington, VT 05402. Year Established: 1827. Pub. Frequency: d. Page Size: broadsheet. Subscrip. Rate: $.50 newsstand/cover; $1.75 newsstand/cover Sun.; $45.50 carrier delivery for 13 wks.; $29.90 carrier delivery 13 wks. daily only. Freelance Pay: $60/article. **Wire Service(s):** AP, LAT-WAT, GNS. Circulation: 51,467 morning (paid); 61,245 Sunday (paid). **Owner(s):** Gannett Company, Inc., 7950 Jones Branch Dr, McLean, VA 22107. Telephone: 703-854-6000. **Management:** James Carey, President. Pam Swartz, Advertising Manager. **Editorial:** Mike Townsend, Executive Editor.

NEWPORT

NEWPORT DAILY EXPRESS. 178 Hill St, Newport, VT 05855. Telephone: 802-334-6568. FAX: 802-334-6891. E-MAIL: ctemple@newportdailyadv.com. Mailing Address: PO Box 347, Newport, VT 05855-0347. Year Established: 1936. Pub. Frequency: d. Page Size: standard. Subscrip. Rate: $.50 newsstand/cover; $112.99/yr. Freelance Pay: $35/story. **Wire Service(s):** AP. Circulation: 4,581 morning (paid). **Owner(s):** Horizon Publications, Inc., 1120 N. Carbon St, Ste 100, Marion, IL 62959. **Management:** Kenneth Wells, Publisher. Jana Graves, Advertising Manager. Sadie Keement, Circulation Manager. **Editorial:** Stephen Blake, Managing Editor.

RUTLAND

RUTLAND HERALD. 27 Wales St., Rutland, VT 05701. Telephone: 802-747-6121. FAX: 802-775-2423. E-MAIL: info@rutlandherald.com. URL: www.rutlandherald.com. Mailing Address: PO Box 668, Rutland, VT 05702-0668. Year Established: 1794. Pub. Frequency: d. Page Size: broadsheet. Subscrip. Rate: $.75 newsstand/cover; $1.75 newsstand/cover Sun.; $3.50 carrier delivery/wk.; $3.90 motor route/wk.. **Wire Service(s):** AP, NYT, MCT. Circulation: 21,770 morning (paid); 21,741 Sunday (paid). **Owner(s):** Herald Association, Inc., See address and contact information above. **Bureau(s):** 112 Main Street, Montpelier, VT 05602. Telephone: 802-223-3931. FAX: 802-229-9894. **Management:** Robert G. Miller, General Manager. R. John Mitchell, President. Glenda Hawley, Advertising Director. Robert Arrowsmith, Circulation Director. **Editorial:** John Dolan, Managing Editor. David Moats, Editorial Page Editor. Bob Fredette, Sports Editor.

ST. JOHNSBURY

CALEDONIAN-RECORD, THE. PO Box 8, St. Johnsbury, VT 05819. Telephone: 802-748-8121. FAX: 802-748-1613. E-MAIL: news@caledonian-record.com. URL: http://www.caledonian-record.com. Year Established: 1837. Pub. Frequency: d. (Mon.-Sat.) Page Size: broadsheet. Subscrip. Rate: $.50 newsstand/cover; $150/yr mailed in VT.& NH; $175/yr mailed elsewhere. Adv. Rate: col. inch $7.20 Freelance Pay: $30-$60/article. **Wire Service(s):** AP. Circulation: 10,600 evening (paid). **Owner(s):** Caledonian-Record Publishing Co., Inc., See address and contact information above. **Management:** Dana Gray, General Manager. Barbara Smith, President. Mark Smith, Publisher. Michael Gonyaw, Advertising Director. Ken White, Advertising Manager. Judy Burke, Circulation Manager. Susan Donna, Business Manager. **Editorial:** Lyn Bixby, Executive Editor. Jan Newpher, City Editor. Craig Beck, Sports.

VIRGIN ISLANDS

ST. CROIX

ST. CROIX AVIS. 36 ANB La Grande Princesse, St. Croix, VI 00820. Telephone: 340-773-2300. E-MAIL: stxavis@viaaccess.net. Mailing Address: PO Box 750, Christiansted, VI 00821. Year Established: 1844. Pub. Frequency: d. (Tue.-Sun.) Page Size: tabloid. Subscrip. Rate: $.50 newsstand/cover; $.60 newsstand/cover Sun.; $95/yr mailed local; $172/yr mailed out of area. **Wire Service(s):** AP. Circulation: 14,500 morning (paid); 14,500 Sunday (paid). **Owner(s):** St. Croix Avis, See address and contact information above. **Management:** Rena Broadhust, Publisher. Maria Morales, Circulation Director. Linda Clark, Production Director. **Editorial:** Michael Cisco, Managing Editor.

VIRGINIA

BRISTOL

BRISTOL HERALD COURIER. ISSN 1552-2458
320 Morrison Blvd., Bristol, VA 24201. Telephone: 276-669-2181. FAX: 276-669-3696. URL: http://www.tricities.com. Mailing Address: PO Box 609, Bristol, VA 24203. Year Established: 1985. Pub. Frequency: d. Page Size: broadsheet. Subscrip. Rate: $.75 newsstand/cover; $1.50 newsstand/cover Sun.; $14.69 carrier delivery/mo.; $291.20/yr mailed. **Wire Service(s):** AP, SH, LAT-WAT. Circulation: 32,164 Saturday (paid); 33,033 morning (paid); 35,877 Sunday (paid). **Owner(s):** Media General, Inc., 333 E. Franklin St., Richmond, VA 23219. Telephone: 804-649-6000. FAX: 804-649-6898. **Management:** Carl Esposito, Publisher. Michael Schuttinga, Advertising Director. **Editorial:** J Todd Foster, Managing Editor. Susan Cameron, City Editor. David Crigger, Photographer.

CHARLOTTESVILLE

DAILY PROGRESS. ISSN 0746-0430
685 W. Rio Rd., Charlottesville, VA 22901. Telephone: 434-978-7210. FAX: 434-978-7214. E-MAIL: dpnews@dailyprogress.com. URL: http://www.dailyprogress.com. Mailing Address: PO Box 9030, Charlottesville, VA 22902. Year Established: 1892. Pub. Frequency: d. Page Size: broadsheet. Subscrip. Rate: $.50 newsstand/cover; $1.50 newsstand/cover Sun.; $2.99 motor route/wk.. **Wire Service(s):** AP, NYT, LAT-WAT. Circulation: 35,000 morning (paid); 37,000 Sunday (paid). **Owner(s):** Media General, Inc., 333 E. Franklin St., Richmond, VA 23219. Telephone: 804-649-6000. FAX: 804-775-8090. **Management:** Lawrence McConnell, Publisher. Tina Hancock, Advertising. Wanda Birckhead, Advertising Director. Alan West, Circulation Manager. Mark Berry, Classified Adv. Mgr.. Paul Davis, Business Manager.

COVINGTON

VIRGINIAN REVIEW. 128 N. Maple Ave., Covington, VA 24426-0271. Telephone: 540-962-2121. FAX: 540-962-5072. E-MAIL: virginianreview@aol.com. URL: http://www.alleghanyhighlands.com. Mailing Address: PO Box 271, Covington, VA 24426-0271. Year Established: 1914. Pub. Frequency: d. (Mon.-Sat.) Page Size: broadsheet. Subscrip. Rate: $.50 newsstand/cover; $92.40/yr carrier delivery; $138.60/yr mailed. Freelance Pay: $0.21/column-inch. **Wire Service(s):** AP. Circulation: 8,000 evening (paid). **Owner(s):** Covington Virginian Inc., See address and contact information above. **Management:** Horton P. Beirne, Publisher. Ewell S. Beirne, Vice President. Maryanne Beirne, Advertising Manager. David Crosier, Circulation Manager. Donna Via, Classified Adv. Mgr.. **Editorial:** Horton P. Beirne, Editor-in-Chief. Gavin Dressler, Photographer. Adam Crawfor, Sports.

CULPEPER

CULPEPER STAR EXPONENT. ISSN 0899-4803
122 W. Spencer St., Culpeper, VA 22701. Telephone: 540-825-0771. FAX: 540-825-0778. E-MAIL: rhumphreys@starexponent.com. URL: http://www.starexponent.com. Mailing Address: PO Box 111, Culpeper, VA 22701. Year Established: 1882. Pub. Frequency: d. Page Size: broadsheet. Subscrip. Rate: $.50 newsstand/cover; $1 newsstand/cover Sun.; $59.80/yr home delivery in county. **Wire Service(s):** AP. Circulation: 7,897 morning (paid). **Owner(s):** Media General, Inc., 333 E. Franklin St., Richmond, VA 23219. Telephone: 804-649-6000. FAX: 804-775-8090. **Management:** C. Kirk Read, Publisher. Gloria Williams, Advertising Director. Patricia Graham, Circulation Manager. **Editorial:** Rob Humphreys, Managing Editor. George Lanun, News Editor. Jeff Say, Sports Editor.

DANVILLE

DANVILLE REGISTER & BEE. ISSN 1527-5620
700 Monument St., Danville, VA 24541. Telephone: 434-793-2311. FAX: 434-797-2299. E-MAIL: rbnews@gamewood.net. URL: http://www.registerbee.com. Mailing Address: PO Box 331, Danville, VA 24543. Year Established: 1848. Pub. Frequency: d. Page Size: broadsheet. Subscrip. Rate: $.50 newsstand/cover; $1.25 newsstand/cover Sun.; $119.80/yr home delivery; $140.40/yr mailed. Adv. Rate: col. inch $22 **Wire Service(s):** AP. Circulation: 22,032 morning (paid); 25,981 Sunday (paid). **Owner(s):** Media General, Inc., 333 E. Franklin St., Richmond, VA 23219. Telephone: 804-649-6000. FAX: 804-649-6898. **Management:** Bob McPherson, Publisher. Jodi Vasquez, Advertising Director. Linda Willis, Business Manager. Valerie Tilley, Classified Editor. **Editorial:** Arnold Hendrix, Managing Editor. Alta LeCompte, News Editor.

FREDERICKSBURG

FREE LANCE-STAR, THE. 616 Amelia St., Fredericksburg, VA 22401-3887. Telephone: 540-374-5000. FAX: 540-374-5449. E-MAIL: information@freelancestar.com. URL: http://www.fredericksburg.com. Year Established: 1885. Pub. Frequency: d. Page Size: broadsheet. Subscrip. Rate: $.50 newsstand/cover; $1.25 newsstand/cover Sun.; $156/yr carrier delivery; $318/yr mailed. **Wire Service(s):** AP, MCT. Circulation: 44,367 morning (paid); 47,323 Sunday (paid). **Owner(s):** Free Lance-Star Publishing Co., See address and contact information above. **Management:** Josiah P Rowe III, Publisher. Bill Smith, Advertising Director. Thomas Bibs, Circulation Manager. **Editorial:** Edward W Jones, Editor. Nancy Moore, Managing Editor. Howard Owen, Business Editor. Annette Jones, Community Editor. Phil Jenkins, Metro Editor. Clint Schemmer, News Editor. Steve DeShazo, Sports Editor.

HARRISONBURG

DAILY NEWS-RECORD. 231 S. Liberty St., Harrisonburg, VA 22801. Telephone: 540-574-6200. FAX: 540-574-6299. URL: http://www.dnronline.com. Mailing Address: PO Box 193, Harrisonburg, VA 22803-0193. Year Established: 1913. Pub. Frequency: d. (Mon.-Sat.) Page Size: broadsheet. Subscrip. Rate: $.35 newsstand/cover; $80/yr in state; $93/yr out of state. **Wire Service(s):** AP. Circulation: 33,300 morning (paid). **Owner(s):** Page-Shenandoah News Corp., See address and contact information above. **Management:** Peter Yates, General Manager. Tom Byrd, President. Thomas H. Bridges, Circulation Director. Linda Swecker, Classified Adv. Mgr.. Pete Marovich, Photography Director. David Shiplett Jr., Production Director. Betty L. Hinkle, Business Manager. **Editorial:** Peter Yates, Editor. Cort Kirkwood, Managing Editor. Brad Jenkins, City Editor. Kathryn Huff, Feature Editor. Lewis Sword, News Editor. Tom Mitchell, Religion Editor. Chris Simmons, Sports Editor.

HOPEWELL

HOPEWELL NEWS. 516 E. Randolph Rd., Hopewell, VA 23860. Telephone: 804-458-8511. FAX: 804-458-7556. E-MAIL: newsroom@hopewellnews.com. URL: http://www.hopewellnews.com. Mailing Address: P.O. Box 481, Hopewell, VA 23860-0481. Year Established: 1926. Pub. Frequency: d. (Mon.-Fri.) Page Size: broadsheet. Subscrip. Rate: $.50 newsstand/cover; $6.50 carrier delivery/mo.; $78/yr carrier delivery; $9 mailed/mo.; $108/yr mailed. **Wire Service(s):** UPI. Circulation: 6,000 evening (paid). **Owner(s):** Hopewell Publishing Co., Inc., See address and contact information above. **Management:** James Lancaster, President. Rod Collins, Publisher. **Editorial:** Dan Ehrlich, Editor. Kenny Holley, Photographer. Hank Bilyeu, Sports Editor.

LYNCHBURG

NEWS & ADVANCE. 101 Wyndale Dr., Lynchburg, VA 24501. Telephone: 434-385-5400. FAX: 434-385-5538. E-MAIL: newsroom@newsadvance.com. URL: http://www.newsadvance.com. Mailing Address: PO Box 10129, Lynchburg, VA 24506-0129. Year Established: 1866. Pub. Frequency: d. Page Size: broadsheet. Subscrip. Rate: $.50 newsstand/cover; $1.25 newsstand/cover Sun.; $169/yr home delivery. **Wire Service(s):** AP, NYT. Circulation: 38,000 morning (paid); 44,000 Sunday (paid). **Owner(s):** Media General, Inc., 333 E. Franklin St., Richmond, VA 23219. Telephone: 434-649-6000. **Management:** Terry Jamerson, Publisher. Tony Stophel, Circulation Manager. Dinaoy Inbiani, Classified Adv. Mgr.. **Editorial:** Bob Morgan, Editor. Joe Stinnett, Managing Editor. Logan Anderson, Business Editor. Robert C. Wimer, Editorial Page Editor. Jessie Martin Thompson, Lifestyle Editor. Mark Thompson, Photo Editor.

Dailies

MANASSAS

MANASSAS JOURNAL MESSENGER. ISSN 0745-6859
9009 Church St., Manassas, VA 20110. Telephone: 703-368-3101. FAX: 703-368-9017. E-MAIL: opinion@potomacnews.com. URL: http://www.manassasjm.com. Mailing Address: P.O. Drawer 431, Manassas, VA 20108. Year Established: 1869. Pub. Frequency: d. Page Size: broadsheet. Subscrip. Rate: $.35 newsstand/cover; $.75 newsstand/cover Sun.; $124/yr home delivery; $291/yr mailed. Freelance Pay: $25-$30/article. **Wire Service(s):** AP. Circulation: 6,500 evening (paid); 5,000 Sunday (paid). **Owner(s):** Media General, Inc., 333 E. Franklin St., Richmond, VA 23219. Telephone: 804-649-6000. FAX: 804-775-8090. **Management:** Mark Laskowski, Publisher. Paula Downey, Advertising Director. Bob Spessard, Circulation Director. **Editorial:** Susan Svihlik, Executive Editor. Caryn Gobel, Managing Editor. Bennie Scarton, Business Editor. Helen Steinberg, Feature Editor.

MARTINSVILLE

MARTINSVILLE BULLETIN. 204 Broad St., Martinsville, VA 24112. Telephone: 276-638-8801. FAX: 276-638-7409. E-MAIL: info@martinsvillebulletin.com. URL: http://www.martinsvillebulletin.com. Mailing Address: PO Box 3711, Martinsville, VA 24115. Year Established: 1889. Pub. Frequency: d. (Sun.-Fri.) Page Size: broadsheet. Subscrip. Rate: $.35 newsstand/cover; $1 newsstand/cover Sun.; $95/yr carrier delivery (effective 2005); $144/yr mailed. **Wire Service(s):** AP, UPI. Circulation: 20,000 evening (paid); 22,000 Sunday (paid). **Owner(s):** Robert Haskell, See address and contact information above. **Management:** George H. Harris, General Manager. Robert Haskell, President. Robert Cox, Advertising Manager. Matt Dishman, Circulation Manager. **Editorial:** Virginia Wray, Editor. Michael Wray, Photographer.

MCLEAN

▼**SOUTH OAKLAND ECCENTRIC.** 7950 Jones Branch Dr, McLean, VA 22107. Telephone: 703-854-5000. Year Established: 2009. Pub. Frequency: w. (Sun.) **Owner(s):** Observer, Eccentric & Mirror Newspapers, Inc., See address and contact information above.VA see NATIONAL NEWSPAPERS

NORFOLK

VIRGINIAN-PILOT, THE. ISSN 0889-6127
150 W. Brambleton Ave., Norfolk, VA 23510. Telephone: 757-446-2000. URL: http://www.pilotonline.com. Mailing Address: PO Box 449, Norfolk, VA 23501. Year Established: 1865. Pub. Frequency: d. Page Size: broadsheet. Subscrip. Rate: $.50 newsstand/cover; $1.25 newsstand/cover Sun.; $34.99 home delivery for 13 weeks; $124.99/yr home delivery; $290/yr mailed. Adv. Rate: col. inch $67.41 **Wire Service(s):** AP, NYT, LAT-WAT, MCT. Circulation: 201,163 morning (paid); 234,706 Sunday (paid). **Owner(s):** Landmark Communications, Inc., See address and contact information above. **Management:** D.R. Carpenter III, Publisher. Alan Levenstein, Advertising Manager. Pam Smith-Rodden, Circulation Director. Barbara Elliott, Classified Adv. Mgr.. Alex Burrows, Photography Director. **Editorial:** Denis Finley, Managing Editor. Margaret E. Edds, Associate Editor. Bill Choyke, Business Editor. Dennis Hartig, Editorial Page Editor. Lorraine M. Eaton, Education Editor. Melinda Forbes, Lifestyle Editor.

PETERSBURG

PROGRESS-INDEX. 15 Franklin St., Petersburg, VA 23803. Telephone: 804-732-3456. FAX: 804-732-8417. Mailing Address: PO Box 71, Petersburg, VA 23804. Year Established: 1865. Pub. Frequency: d. Page Size: broadsheet. Subscrip. Rate: $.50 newsstand/cover; $1.25 newsstand/cover Sun.; $12 carrier delivery/mo.; $19 mailed/mo. in state; $26 mailed/mo. out of state. Adv. Rate: col. inch $21 **Wire Service(s):** AP, SH. Circulation: 15,000 evening (paid); 16,500 Sunday (paid). **Owner(s):** Scranton Times, 149 Penn Ave., Scranton, PA 18503. Telephone: 717-348-9101. **Management:** Catherine Oakley, Advertising Director. Bob Seals, Circulation Director. Peggy Simon, Business Manager. **Editorial:** Brian Couturier, Managing Editor.

PULASKI

SOUTHWEST TIMES, THE. 34 Fifth St., N.E., Pulaski, VA 24301. Telephone: 540-980-5220. FAX: 540-980-3618. E-MAIL: editor@southwest.com. URL: http://www.southwesttimes.com. Year Established: 1906. Pub. Frequency: d. (Sun.-Fri.) Page Size: broadsheet. Subscrip. Rate: $.50 newsstand/cover; $1 newsstand/cover Sun.; $95/yr carrier delivery; $195/yr mailed. Adv. Rate: col. inch $10.30 Freelance Pay: $15/article. **Wire Service(s):** AP. Circulation: 7,497 evening (paid); 8,600 Sunday (paid). **Owner(s):** Southwest Publishers LLC, See address and contact information above. **Management:** Mike Williams, Publisher. Vanessa Young, Advertising Director. Jake Walters, Circulation Manager. Courtney Dunavant, Classified Adv. Mgr.. **Editorial:** Dave Bisset, Sports Editor.

RICHMOND

RICHMOND TIMES-DISPATCH. 333 E. Franklin St., Richmond, VA 23219. Telephone: 804-649-6000. FAX: 804-649-6898. URL: http://www.timesdispatch.com/. Mailing Address: PO Box 85333, Richmond, VA 23293. Year Established: 1850. Pub. Frequency: d. Page Size: broadsheet. Subscrip. Rate: $.50 newsstand/cover; $.75 newsstand/cover Sat.; $1.75 newsstand/cover Sun.; $182/yr carrier delivery. **Wire Service(s):** AP, SH, NYT, LAT-WAT. Circulation: 195,000 morning (paid); 230,000 Sunday (paid). **Owner(s):** Media General, Inc., See address and contact information above. **Bureau(s):** Contact: Marsha Mercer, Bureau Chief. **Management:** Albert T. August, General Manager. J. Stewart Bryan III, Publisher. Charles Ritscher, Advertising Manager. Raymond G. Bruett, Circulation Director. Scott Christino, Classified Adv. Mgr.. Scott Leath, Business Manager. **Editorial:** William H. Millsaps Jr., Executive Editor. Louise Seals, Managing Editor. Robert Powell, Associate Editor. Pam Feibish, Business Editor. Lewis Brissman, Chief Copy Editor. Ross McKenzie, Editorial Page Editor. Andy Taylor, Metro Editor. Harry Meem, News Editor. Jack Berninger, Sports Editor. Tom Kapsidelis, State Editor.

ROANOKE

ROANOKE TIMES, THE. 201 W. Campbell Ave., Roanoke, VA 24011. Telephone: 800-346-1234. FAX: 276-981-3318. URL: http://www.roanoke.com. Mailing Address: PO Box 2491, Roanoke, VA 24010-2491. Year Established: 1886. Pub. Frequency: d. Page Size: broadsheet. Subscrip. Rate: $.50 newsstand/cover; $1.50 newsstand/cover Sun.; $29.95 home delivery for 13 wks.. **Wire Service(s):** AP, NYT, LAT-WAT, MCT. Circulation: 100,249 morning (paid); 115,848 Sunday (paid). **Owner(s):** Landmark Communications, Inc., 150 W. Brambleton Ave., Norfolk, VA 23510. Telephone: 804-446-2000. **Bureau(s):** 110 Peppers Ferry Rd., P.O. Box 540, Christianburg, VA 24073. Telephone: 540-382-4905. **Management:** Wendy Zomparelli, President. Dan Wheeler, Circulation Director. Tracy Murray, Classified Adv. Mgr.. Robyn Porterfield, Sales Manager. **Editorial:** Rich Martin, Managing Editor. Mike Reiley, News Editor.

STAUNTON

NEWS LEADER (STAUNTON), THE. ISSN 0747-2501
11 N. Central Ave., Staunton, VA 24402. Telephone: 540-885-7281. FAX: 540-885-1904. E-MAIL: news@newsleader.com. URL: http://www.newsleader.com. Mailing Address: PO Box 59, Staunton, VA 24402. Year Established: 1904. Pub. Frequency: d. Page Size: broadsheet. Subscrip. Rate: $.50 newsstand/cover; $1.25 Sun.; $119.60/yr home delivery local; $171.60/yr mailed in state. **Wire Service(s):** AP. Circulation: 18,500 morning (paid); 22,000 Sunday (paid). **Owner(s):** Gannett Company, Inc., 7950 Jones Branch Dr., McLean, VA 22107-0001. Telephone: 703-854-6000. **Management:** Gary Stout, President. Jim Clark, Advertising Director. Danny Allen, Circulation Director. Dirk Poe, Classified Adv. Mgr.. **Editorial:** David Fritz, Managing Editor. Vince Lerz, Photographer. Hubert Grimm III, Sports Editor.

STRASBURG

NORTHERN VIRGINIA DAILY. 152 N. Holliday St., Strasburg, VA 22657. Telephone: 540-465-5137. FAX: 540-465-6169. E-MAIL: nvd@shentel.net. URL: http://www.nvdaily.com. Mailing Address: PO Box 69, Strasburg, VA 22657-0069. Year Established: 1932. Pub. Frequency: d. (Mon.-Sat.) Page Size: broadsheet. Subscrip. Rate: $.35 newsstand/cover; $69/yr carrier delivery; $73/yr mailed. **Wire Service(s):** AP, SH. Circulation: 17,300 morning (paid). **Owner(s):** Shenandoah Publishing House, Inc., See address and contact information above. **Bureau(s):** 133 S. Main St., P.O. Box 254, Woodstock, VA 22664. Telephone: 540-459-3729. FAX: 540-459-5991. Contact: Mary Beiler, Bureau Chief. **Management:** Elizabeth Smoot, General Manager. James Gainey, Advertising Manager. Randy Taylor, Circulation Manager. **Editorial:** John F. Horan Jr., Editor. Bob Wooten, Managing Editor. John F. Horan Jr., Editorial Page Editor. Natalie Austin, Feature Editor.

SUFFOLK

SUFFOLK NEWS-HERALD. ISSN 8750-9598
130 S. Saratoga St., Suffolk, VA 23434. Telephone: 757-539-3437. FAX: 757-539-8804. E-MAIL: dgrant@mediageneral.com. URL: http://www.hamptonroadsmedia.com. Mailing Address: PO Box 1220, Suffolk, VA 23439. Year Established: 1873. Pub. Frequency: d. (Tue.-Sun.) Page Size: broadsheet. Subscrip. Rate: $.50 newsstand/cover; $1 newsstand/cover Sun.; $119.60/yr carrier delivery; $112/yr mailed in state. Circulation: 6,000 morning (paid); 6,000 Sunday (paid). **Owner(s):** Boone Newspapers, Inc., 15222 Freemen's Bend Rd., Northport, AL 35475. Telephone: 205-330-4100. **Management:** Jesse Lindsey, Publisher. Earl Jones, Advertising Manager. Connie Knapp, Circulation Director. **Editorial:** Douglas Grant, Managing Editor. Harvey White, Photographer.

WAYNESBORO

NEWS VIRGINIAN, THE. ISSN 8750-7862
544 W. Main St., Waynesboro, VA 22980. Telephone: 540-949-8213. FAX: 540-942-4542. E-MAIL: nvnews@mgads.com. URL: http://www.newsvirginian.com. Mailing Address: PO Box 1027, Waynesboro, VA 22980. Year Established: 1892. Pub. Frequency: d. Page Size: broadsheet. Subscrip. Rate: $.50 newsstand/cover; $1 newsstand/cover Sun.; $51.12 home delivery for 6 mos.; $96.85/yr home delivery. **Wire Service(s):** AP. Circulation: 8,070 morning (paid); 8,037 Sunday (paid). **Owner(s):** Media General, Inc., 333 E. Franklin St., Richmond, VA 23219. Telephone: 804-649-6000. **Management:** Bruce Potter, Publisher. Tina Hancock, Advertising Manager. Randy Terwilliger, Circulation Director. Tina Hancock, Classified Adv. Mgr.. **Editorial:** J Todd Foster, Managing Editor. Courtney Huckabay, Lifestyle Editor. Jim Sacco, News Editor.

WINCHESTER

WINCHESTER STAR, THE. ISSN 1064-0665
2 N. Kent St., Winchester, VA 22601. Telephone: 540-667-3200. FAX: 540-667-0012. E-MAIL: news@winchesterstar.com. URL: http://www.winchesterstar.com. Pub. Frequency: d. (Mon.-Sat.) Page Size: broadsheet. Subscrip. Rate: $.50 newsstand/cover; $80/yr home delivery local; $99/yr mailed out of area. **Wire Service(s):** AP, NYT. Circulation: 22,000 evening (paid). **Owner(s):** Winchester Star, Inc., See address and contact information above. **Management:** Thomas T. Byrd, Publisher. John Parkinson, Advertising Manager. Bill Green, Circulation Director. Ann Whitacre, Classified Adv. Mgr.. **Editorial:** Robert Ford, Managing Editor. Adrian O'Connor, Asst. Managing Ed.. Brian Brehm, City Editor. Robyn Fontes Taylor, Feature Editor. Frances Lowe, Lifestyle Editor. Ben Brooks, Sports Editor.

WOODBRIDGE

POTOMAC NEWS. 14010 Smoketown Rd., Woodbridge, VA 22193. Telephone: 703-878-8000. FAX: 703-878-8099. E-MAIL: emitchell@potomacnews.com. URL: http://www.potomacnews.com. Mailing Address: PO Box 2470, Woodbridge, VA 22195-2470. Year Established: 1959. Pub. Frequency: d. Page Size: broadsheet. Subscrip. Rate: $.35 newsstand/cover; $1 newsstand/cover Sun.; $124/yr carrier delivery; $291/yr mailed. **Wire Service(s):** AP, NYT, GNS. Circulation: 23,110 evening (paid); 26,500 Sunday (paid). **Owner(s):** Media General, Inc., 333 E. Franklin St., Richmond, VA 23219. Telephone: 804-649-6000. **Management:** Mark Laskowski, Publisher. Paula Downey, Advertising Manager. Robert Spessard, Circulation Manager. Paula Downey, Classified Adv. Mgr.. **Editorial:** Alfred Biddlecomb, Editorial Page Editor. Diane Freda, Education Editor. Susan Neer, Feature Editor. Tammy Minnick, Lifestyle Editor. Lynn Hrivnak, Local News Editor. Ellen Mitchell, News Editor. Dave Ellis, Photographer. David Faucett, Sports Editor.

WASHINGTON

ABERDEEN

DAILY WORLD (ABERDEEN), THE. ISSN 0740-3135
315 S. Michigan St., Aberdeen, WA 98520. Telephone: 360-532-4000. FAX: 360-533-1328. E-MAIL: www.thedailyworld.com. Mailing Address: PO Box 269, Aberdeen, WA 98520. Year Established: 1890. Pub. Frequency: d. Page Size: broadsheet. Subscrip. Rate: $.50 newsstand/cover; $1 Sun.; $120/yr carrier delivery local. Adv. Rate: col. inch $17.50 **Wire Service(s):** AP. Circulation: 17,000 evening (paid); 17,000 Sunday (paid). **Owner(s):** Stephens Media LLC, 1111 W. Bonanza Rd., Las Vegas, NV 89106. Telephone: 702-382-5020. **Management:** John Hughes, Publisher. Bridget Pannell, Advertising Manager. Gerald Atkinson, Circulation Manager. **Editorial:** Doug Barker, Managing Editor. Tommi Gatlin, Lifestyle Editor. Kathy Quigg, Photographer. Rick Anderson, Sports Editor.

BELLINGHAM

BELLINGHAM HERALD. 1155 N State St, Bellingham, WA 98225. Telephone: 360-676-2600. FAX: 360-756-2826. URL: http://www.bellinghamherald.com. Mailing Address: PO Box 1277, Bellingham, WA 98227. Year Established: 1890. Pub. Frequency: d. Page Size: broadsheet. Subscrip. Rate: $.50 newsstand/cover; $1.50 newsstand/cover Sun.; $14 home delivery/mo. in city; $19.25 mailed/mo. in county. **Wire Service(s):** AP. Circulation: 23,372 morning (paid); 29,950 Sunday (paid). **Owner(s):** The/McClatchy Company, 2100 Q St, Sacramento, CA 95816. Telephone: 916-321-1936. FAX: 916-321-1869. **Management:** Glen Nardi, Publisher. Sam Aldrich, Advertising Manager. Amber Aldrich, Classified Adv. Mgr.. **Editorial:** Julie Shirley, Executive Editor. Debbie Townsend, Managing Editor.

BREMERTON

KITSAP SUN. 545 Fifth St., Bremerton, WA 98337-0053. Telephone: 360-377-3711. FAX: 360-479-7681. E-MAIL: sunnews @kitsapsun.com. URL: http://www.kitsapsun.com. Mailing Address: PO Box 259, Bremerton, WA 98337-0053. Year Established: 1935. Pub. Frequency: d. Page Size: broadsheet. Subscrip. Rate: $.50 newsstand/cover; $1.50 newsstand/cover Sun.; $11.50 home delivery for 4 wks.; $130/yr. **Wire Service(s):** AP, SH, LAT-WAT. Circulation: 34,000 morning (paid); 36,000 Sunday (paid). **Owner(s):** E.W. Scripps Co., 312 Walnut St., 28th Fl., Cincinnati, OH 45202. Telephone: 513-977-3000. **Management:** Mike Levi, Publisher. Tom Larsen, Operations Manager. John Carr, Advertising Director. Sandy Atkins, Circulation Director. Gussie Schaeffer, Marketing Director. **Editorial:** Scott Ware, Editor. Jeff Brody, Managing Editor. Darcy Himes, Entertainment Editor. Carolyn Yaschur, Photographer. Jeff Rosen, Sports Editor.

CENTRALIA

CHRONICLE (CENTRALIA), THE. 321 N. Pearl St., Centralia, WA 98531. Telephone: 360-736-3311. FAX: 360-736-4796. URL: http://www. chronline.com. Mailing Address: PO Box 580, Centralia, WA 98531-0580. Year Established: 1889. Pub. Frequency: d. (Mon.-Sat.) Page Size: broadsheet. Subscrip. Rate: $.50 newsstand/cover; $10.95 carrier delivery/mo. town; $29.75/quarter; $96.75/yr. **Wire Service(s):** AP. Circulation: 15,000 evening (paid). **Owner(s):** Lafromboise Newspapers, Inc., See address and contact information above. **Management:** J.R. Lafromboise, President. Dennis R. Waller, Publisher. Randy Morrison, Circulation Manager. **Editorial:** Gordon MacCracken, Editor. Pat Jones, Lifestyle Editor. Sam Bakotich, Sports Editor.

ELLENSBURG

DAILY RECORD. 401 N. Main St., Ellensburg, WA 98926-0248. Telephone: 509-925-1414. FAX: 509-925-5696. E-MAIL: dailyrecord@kvnews.com. URL: http://www.kvnews.com. Year Established: 1909. Pub. Frequency: d. (Mon.-Sat.) Page Size: broadsheet. Subscrip. Rate: $.50 newsstand/cover; $9.75 home delivery/mo. in county; $17.50 mailed/mo. out of county; $112/yr mailed. **Wire Service(s):** AP. Circulation: 6,000 evening (paid). **Owner(s):** Pioneer Newspapers, Inc., 221 First Ave., W., Ste. 405, Seattle, WA 98119-4224. Telephone: 206-284-4424. FAX: 206-282-2143. **Management:** Matt Davison, Publisher. Pam Shuart, Advertising. Cory Young, Circulation Manager. Matt Beyer, Classified Adv. Mgr.. **Editorial:** Jeff Robinson, Managing Editor. Michael Gallaher, Assistant Editor. Andrea Paris, Feature Editor. Kate Fagan, Sports.

EVERETT

HERALD (EVERETTE), THE. 1213 California St, Everett, WA 98201. Telephone: 425-339-3000. FAX: 425-339-3049. E-MAIL: frank@heraldnet.com. URL: http://www.heraldnet.com. Mailing Address: PO Box 930, Everett, WA 98206. Year Established: 1891. Pub. Frequency: d. Subscrip. Rate: $.35 newsstand/cover; $1.50 newsstand/cover Sun.; $35.85 home delivery in county for 3 mos.; $131.40/yr home delivery in county. **Owner(s):** Washington Post Co., 1150 15th St., N.W., Washington, DC 20071-0001. Telephone: 202-334-7100. **Management:** Allen Funk, Publisher. Steve Hwes, Advertising Director. Robin Prendergast, Advertising Manager. Kelly Hulin, Marketing Director. **Editorial:** Stan Strick, Executive Editor. Mike Benbow, Business Editor. Robert Frank, City Editor. Melanie Munk, Feature Editor. Robert Frank, News Editor. Justin Best, Photo Editor. Kevin Brown, Sports Editor.

KENNEWICK

TRI-CITY HERALD. 107 N. Cascade St., Kennewick, WA 99336. Telephone: 509-582-1500. FAX: 509-582-1453. URL: http://www.tri-cityherald.com. Mailing Address: PO Box 2608, Tri-Cities, WA 99302-2608. Year Established: 1947. Pub. Frequency: d. Page Size: broadsheet. Subscrip. Rate: $.50 newsstand/cover; $1.25 newsstand/cover Sun.; $135/yr home delivery; $141/yr motor route. **Wire Service(s):** AP, NYT. Circulation: 41,152 morning (paid); 44,591 Sunday (paid). **Owner(s):** The/McClatchy Company, 2100 Q St, Sacramento, CA 95816. Telephone: 916-321-1936. FAX: 916-321-1869. **Management:** Rufus Friday, Publisher. Dave Gillcrest, Advertising Manager. Vivian Terrell, Circulation Director. **Editorial:** Ken Robertson, Executive Editor. Rick Larson, Managing Editor. Laurie Williams, Asst. Managing Ed.. Jeff Morrow, Sports Editor.

LONGVIEW

DAILY NEWS (LONG VIEW), THE. ISSN 0889-0005
770 11th Ave., Longview, WA 98632. Telephone: 360-577-2500. FAX: 360-577-2538. E-MAIL: pyork@tdn.com. URL: http://www.tdn.com. Mailing Address: PO Box 189, Longview, WA 98632. Year Established: 1923. Pub. Frequency: d. Page Size: broadsheet. Subscrip. Rate: $.50 newsstand/cover; $1.25 newsstand/cover Sun.; $12.85/mo.. **Wire Service(s):** AP. Circulation: 23,000 morning (paid); 23,000 Sunday (paid). **Owner(s):** Lee Enterprises, Inc., 201 N. Harrison St, Ste 600, Davenport, IA 52801-1924. **Management:** Peter M. York, Publisher. Steve Quaife, Advertising Manager. **Editorial:** Jim Bross, Editorial Page Editor. Bill Wagner, Photographer. Rick Alvord, Sports Editor.

LYNNWOOD

SHORELINE/LAKE FOREST PARK ENTERPRISE. 4303 198th St, SW, Lynnwood, WA 98036. Telephone: 425-673-6500. FAX: 425-774-8622. E-MAIL: shoreline@heraldnet.com. URL: http://www.enterprisenewspapers.com. Year Established: 1958. Pub. Frequency: w. (Wed.) Page Size: tabloid.Subscrip. Rate: $30/yr mailed Circulation: 23,000 evening (free); 104,747 Sunday (paid). **Owner(s):** Washington Post Co., 1150 15th St., N.W., Washington, DC 20071-0001. **Management:** John Souza, Advertising Director. Monica Moyer, Circulation Manager. **Editorial:** Amy Daybert, Editor. Sarah Koenig, Education Editor. Andrea Miller, Feature Editor. David Pan, Sports Editor.

MOSES LAKE

COLUMBIA BASIN HERALD. ISSN 1041-1658
813 W. Third Ave., Moses Lake, WA 98837. Telephone: 509-765-4561. FAX: 509-765-8659. E-MAIL: hbeagley@columbiabasinherald.com. URL: http://www.columbiabasinherald.com. Mailing Address: PO Box 910, Moses Lake, WA 98837. Year Established: 1942. Pub. Frequency: d. (Mon.-Fri.) Page Size: broadsheet. Subscrip. Rate: $.50 newsstand/cover; $9.25 mailed/mo. in county; $12.42 mailed/mo. out of county. Adv. Rate: col. inch $13.30 **Wire Service(s):** AP. Circulation: 8,300 evening (paid). **Owner(s):** Hagadone Corp., 111 S. First St., Coeur d'Alene, ID 83814-1937. **Management:** Harlan Beagley, Publisher. Samantha Houston, Advertising Director. Tom Hinde, Circulation Manager. **Editorial:** Bill Stevenson, Managing Editor. Neil Pierson, Sports.

MT. VERNON

SKAGIT VALLEY HERALD. ISSN 1071-197X
1000 E. College Way, Mt. Vernon, WA 98273-0578. Telephone: 360-424-3251. FAX: 360-424-5300. E-MAIL: webmaster@skagitvalleyherald.com. URL: http://www.skagitvalleyherald.com. Mailing Address: PO Box 578, Mt. Vernon, WA 98273-0578. Year Established: 1884. Pub. Frequency: d. Page Size: broadsheet. Subscrip. Rate: $.50 newsstand/cover; $1.25 Sun.; $11.25 carrier delivery/mo.; $33.75/quarter; $120/yr. Adv. Rate: col. inch $20.30 **Wire Service(s):** AP. Circulation: 17,389 evening (paid); 18,556 Sunday (paid). **Owner(s):** Skagit Valley Publishing Co., PO Box 578, Mt. Vernon, WA 98273. Telephone: 360-424-3251. FAX: 360-424-5300. **Management:** Leighton P. Wood, President. L. Stedem Wood, Publisher. Ron Thayer, Advertising Manager. Brian Naplachowski, Circulation Manager. Kelly Bachman, Business Manager. **Editorial:** Don Nelson, Managing Editor. Dan Abshier, News Editor. Scott Terrell, Photo Editor. Dan Ruthemeyer, Sports Editor.

OLYMPIA

OLYMPIAN, THE. ISSN 0746-7575
111 Bethel St, NE, Olympia, WA 98506. Telephone: 360-754-5400. FAX: 360-357-0740. E-MAIL: rritter@theolympian.com. URL: http://www.theolympian.com. Mailing Address: PO Box 407, Olympia, WA 98507. Year Established: 1889. Pub. Frequency: d. Page Size: broadsheet. Subscrip. Rate: $.50 newsstand/cover; $1.50 Sun.; $13.75 in county for 4 wks.; $14.25 out of county for 4 wks.. **Wire Service(s):** AP. Circulation: 38,155 morning (paid); 44,786 Sunday (paid). **Owner(s):** The/McClatchy Company, 2100 Q St, Sacramento, CA 95816. Telephone: 916-321-1936. FAX: 916-321-1869. **Management:** John Miller, Publisher. Frank Bauer, Advertising Director. Christian Lee, Circulation Manager. Cindy Broome, Classified Adv. Mgr.. **Editorial:** Vickie Kilgore, Executive Editor. Jerry Wakefield, Managing Editor. Ron Newberry, Sports Editor.

POINT PLEASANT

POINT PLEASANT REGISTER. 200 Main St, Point Pleasant, WA 25550. Telephone: 304-675-1333. FAX: 304-675-5234. URL: http://www.mydailyregister.com. Pub. Frequency: d. Page Size: standard. Subscrip. Rate: $.50 newsstand/cover; $25.48 home delivery for 13 wks.; $97.56/yr home delivery; $29.25 mailed for 13 wks.; $109.72/yr mailed. **Wire Service(s):** AP. Circulation: 6,000 evening (paid). **Owner(s):** Heartland Publications, LLC, 20 Research Pkwy, Ste G, Old Saybrook, CT 06475. Telephone: 860-388-3470. FAX: 860-388-3490. **Management:** Dan Goodrich, Publisher. Pam Caldwell, Advertising Manager. David Hill, Circulation Manager. **Editorial:** Nicole Fields, News Editor.

PORT ANGELES

PENINSULA DAILY NEWS. ISSN 1050-7000
305 W. First St., Port Angeles, WA 98362-0246. Telephone: 360-452-2345. FAX: 360-417-3521. E-MAIL: news@peninsuladailynews.com. URL: http://www.peninsuladailynews.com. Mailing Address: PO Box 1330, Port Angeles, WA 98362. Year Established: 1916. Pub. Frequency: d. (Sun.-Fri. AM) Page Size: broadsheet. Subscrip. Rate: $.50 newsstand/cover; $1.25 newsstand/cover Sun.; $135/yr carrier delivery. Adv. Rate: col. inch $17.50 Freelance Pay: $10-$50/article. **Wire Service(s):** AP. Circulation: 17,200 morning (paid); 18,500 Sunday (paid). **Owner(s):** Horvitz Newspapers, Inc., 500 180th Ave N E, #1750, Bellevue, WA 98004. Telephone: 425-274-4780. FAX: 425-274-4781. **Bureau(s):** 1939 E Sims Way, Port Townsend, WA 98368. Telephone: 360-385-7421. FAX: 360-385-3917. **Management:** John Brewer, Publisher. Suzanne Williams, Advertising Director. Sue Stoneman, Advertising Manager. Jason McNeely, Circulation Manager. Ann Ashley, Human Res. Mgr.. **Editorial:** John Brewer, Editor. Rex Wilson, Executive Editor. Leah Leach, Managing Editor. Dean Mangiantini, Production Manager. Marcie Miller, Feature Editor. Brad LaBrie, Sports Editor. Contact: Laura Rosser, Feature Editor. Contact: Laura Rosser, Feature Editor.

POULSBO

AKRON BEACON JOURNAL. 19351 8th Ave. NE, Ste. 106, Poulsbo, WA 98370. Telephone: 360-394-5800. FAX: 360-394-5829. E-MAIL: scageao@thebeaconjournal.com. URL: http://www.ohio.com. Year Established: 1839. Pub. Frequency: d. Page Size: broadsheet. Subscrip. Rate: $.50 newsstand/cover; $1.50 Sun.; $175.50/yr; $446.68/yr mailed out of state. **Wire Service(s):** AP, NYT, MCT. Circulation: 122,373 morning (paid); 157,713 Sunday (paid). **Owner(s):** Sound Publishing, Inc., See address and contact information above. **Management:** Steve Cageao, Director. Alton Brown, General Manager. Andrea C Mathewson, Publisher. Alton Brown, Executive VP. Jim DeLuca, VP Circulation. Christine Sabo, Marketing Director. Dawn Bonfiglio, Information Director. Aaron Burr, Human Res. Mgr.. **Editorial:** Bruce Winges, Editor. Doug Oplinger, Managing Editor. Michael Douglas, Editorial Page Editor.

SEATTLE

IDAHO STATE JOURNAL. 221 First Ave, W, Ste 405, Seattle, WA 98119. E-MAIL: drounkles@journalnet.com. URL: http://www.idahostatejournal.com. Mailing Address: PO Box 431, Pocatello, ID 83202. Year Established: 1893. Pub. Frequency: d. Page Size: broadsheet. Subscrip. Rate: $.50 newsstand/cover; $1.50 newsstand/cover Sun.; $12.25/mo. in city. Adv. Rate: col. inch $24.95 **Wire Service(s):** AP. Circulation: 18,553 evening (paid); 19,425 Sunday (paid). **Owner(s):** Idaho State Publishing, Inc., See address and contact information above. **Management:** Bill Kunerth, Publisher. Dale Rounkles, Advertising Director. Nathan Slater, Circulation Director. Susie Tubbs, Classified Adv. Mgr.. **Editorial:** Ian Fennell, Managing Editor. John O'Connell, City Editor. Tim Flagstad, Sports Editor.

SEATTLE POST-INTELLIGENCER (ONLINE). 101 Elliott Ave., W., Seattle, WA 98119-4220. Telephone: 206-448-8000. FAX: 206-448-8166. URL: http://www.seattlepi.com/. Mailing Address: PO Box 1909, Seattle, WA 98111-1909. Pub. Frequency: d. **Owner(s):** Hearst Corp., See address and contact information above.

SPOKANE

SPOKESMAN-REVIEW, THE. 999 W Riverside Ave, Spokane, WA 99201-1010. Telephone: 509-459-5000. FAX: 509-459-5258. E-MAIL: shaunh@spokesman.com. URL: http://www.spokane.net. Mailing Address: PO Box 2160, Spokane, WA 99210-1615. Year Established: 1883. Pub. Frequency: d. Page Size: broadsheet. Subscrip. Rate: $.50 newsstand/cover; $1.50 newsstand/cover Sun.; $13 home delivery/mo.. **Wire Service(s):** AP, NYT, MCT. Circulation: 105,000 morning (paid); 134,000 Sunday (paid). **Owner(s):** Cowles Publishing Co., See address and contact information above. **Management:** Shaun Higgins, Marketing Director. **Editorial:** Steve Smith, Editor. Rick Bonino, Entertainment Editor. Jamie Neeley, Feature Editor. Vince Grippi, Graphics Editor. Kevin Graman, News Editor. Richard Landers, Outdoor Editor. Joe Palmcuist, Sports Editor.

SUNNYSIDE

DAILY SUN NEWS. ISSN 1046-1612
600 S. Sixth St., Sunnyside, WA 98944-0878. Telephone: 509-837-4500. FAX: 509-837-6397. E-MAIL: dailysunnews@eaglenewspapers.com. URL: http://www.dailysunnews.com. Mailing Address: PO Box 878, Sunnyside, WA 98944-0878. Year Established: 1901. Pub. Frequency: d. (Mon.-Fri.) Page Size: tabloid. Subscrip. Rate: $.50 newsstand/cover; $4.75 carrier delivery/mo. in area; $57/yr mailed in county; $60/yr mailed out of county. Adv. Rate: col. inch $8 Circulation: 4,000 evening (paid and free). **Owner(s):** Eagle Newspapers, Inc., 4901 Indian School Rd., N.E., Salem, OR 97305. Telephone: 503-393-1774. FAX: 503-463-9898. **Management:** Tim Graff, Publisher. Bob Dedolph, Advertising Manager. Debbie Marez, Circulation Manager. **Editorial:** Bob Story, News Editor.

TACOMA

NEWS TRIBUNE, THE. ISSN 1073-5860
1950 S State St, Tacoma, WA 98405. Telephone: 253-597-8742. FAX: 253-597-8274. URL: http://www.tribnet.com. Mailing Address: PO Box 11000, Tacoma, WA 98411. Year Established: 1883. Pub. Frequency: d. Page Size: broadsheet. Subscrip. Rate: $.35 newsstand/cover; $1.50 Sun.; $34.50 carrier delivery/quarter; $69 for 6 mos.; $138/yr. **Wire Service(s):** AP, SH, NYT. Circulation: 130,000 morning (paid); 150,000 Sunday (paid). **Owner(s):** The/McClatchy Company, 2100 Q St, Sacramento, CA 95816. Telephone: 916-321-1936. **Management:** Cheryl E. Dell, Publisher. Suzanne Pepper, Advertising Director. Mike Burlingame, Circulation Director. **Editorial:** David Zeek, Executive Editor.

WALLA WALLA

WALLA WALLA UNION-BULLETIN. 112 S. First St., Walla Walla, WA 99362. Telephone: 509-525-3300. FAX: 509-525-1232. E-MAIL: mcibart@ubnet.com. URL: http://www.union-bulletin.com. Mailing Address: PO Box 1358, Walla Walla, WA 99362. Year Established: 1869. Pub. Frequency: d. (Sun.-Fri.) Page Size: broadsheet. Subscrip. Rate: $.50 newsstand/cover; $1 newsstand/cover Sun.; $10/mo.. **Wire Service(s):** AP, LAT-WAT. Circulation: 14,200 evening (paid); 15,200 Sunday (paid). **Owner(s):** Seattle Times Co., PO Box 70, Seattle, WA 98111. Telephone: 509-525-3300. **Management:** Rob Blethen, Publisher. Jay Brodt, Advertising Manager. Michael Cibart, Circulation Manager. **Editorial:** Rick Doyle, Editor. Vicki Hillhouse, Business Editor. Rick Eskil, Editorial Page Editor. Alasdair Stewart, News Editor. Greg Lehman, Photographer. Jim Buchan, Sports.

WENATCHEE

WENATCHEE WORLD. 14 N. Mission St., Wenatchee, WA 98801. Telephone: 509-663-5161. FAX: 509-665-1183. E-MAIL: newsroom@wenworld.com. URL: http://www.wenatcheeworld.com. Mailing Address: PO Box 1511, Wenatchee, WA 98807-1511. Year Established: 1905. Pub. Frequency: d. Page Size: broadsheet. Subscrip. Rate: $.50 newsstand/cover; $1.50 newsstand/cover Sun.; $11.25 carrier delivery/mo. in city; $11.75 motor route/mo. in city. Freelance Pay: $20/article. **Wire Service(s):** AP. Circulation: 24,900 evening (paid); 27,100 Sunday (paid). **Owner(s):** World Publishing Co., See address and contact information above. **Management:** Steve Robinson, General Manager. Rufus Woods, Publisher. Jackie Swant, Advertising Director. Ed Navarro, Circulation Manager. Matt Kearny, Classified Adv. Mgr.. **Editorial:** Rufus Woods, Editor. Christine Pratt, Business Editor. Andrew Wahl, Feature Editor. Steve Maher, Sports Editor.

YAKIMA

YAKIMA HERALD-REPUBLIC. 114 N. Fourth St., Yakima, WA 98901. Telephone: 509-248-1251. FAX: 509-577-7766. E-MAIL: news@yakima-herald.com. URL: http://www.yakima-herald.com. Mailing Address: PO Box 9668, Yakima, WA 98909. Year Established: 1903. Pub. Frequency: d. Page Size: standard. Subscrip. Rate: $.50 newsstand/cover; $1.25 newsstand/cover Sun.; $11.75 carrier delivery/mo.. **Wire Service(s):** AP, UPI, MCT. Circulation: 41,500 morning (paid); 42,000 Sunday (paid). **Owner(s):** Seattle Times Co., PO Box 70, Seattle, WA 98111. **Management:** James Stickel, Advertising Director. Michelle Smith, Marketing Manager. Brian Fitzgerald, Photography Director. **Editorial:** Sara Jenkins, Editor. Bob Crider, Managing Editor. Bill Lee, Editorial Page Editor. John Taylor, Feature Editor. Donean Brown, Librarian. Kathy Harestad, News Editor.

WEST VIRGINIA

BECKLEY

REGISTER-HERALD (BECKLEY), THE.   ISSN 0746-6854
801 N. Kanawha St., Beckley, WV 25801. Telephone: 304-255-4400. FAX: 304-255-4427. E-MAIL: news@register-herald.com. URL: http://www.register-herald.com. Mailing Address: PO Box 2398, Beckley, WV 25802. Year Established: 1880. Pub. Frequency: d. Page Size: broadsheet. Subscrip. Rate: $.50 newsstand/cover; $1.50 newsstand/cover Sun.; $167.40/yr carrier delivery in county & adj. cys; $204/yr mailed out of area & adj. cys. **Wire Service(s):** AP. Circulation: 29,854 morning (paid); 31,356 Sunday (paid). **Owner(s):** Community Newspaper Holdings, Inc., 3500 Colonnade Pkwy., Ste. 600, Birmingham, AL 35243. Telephone: 205-298-7100. FAX: 205-298-7101. **Management:** Frank Wood, Publisher. Chuck Jessup, Advertising Director. Mark Campbell, Circulation Director. Diana Slone, Classified Adv. Mgr.. **Editorial:** Butch Antolini, Executive Editor. Beverly Davis, Lifestyle Editor. Dawn Dayton, News Editor.

BLUEFIELD

BLUEFIELD DAILY TELEGRAPH. 928 Bluefield Ave., Bluefield, WV 24701. Telephone: 304-327-2800. FAX: 304-327-6179. E-MAIL: editor@bdtonline.com. URL: http://www.bdtonline.com. Mailing Address: PO Box 1599, Bluefield, WV 24701. Year Established: 1893. Pub. Frequency: d. Page Size: broadsheet. Subscrip. Rate: $.50 newsstand/cover; $1.50 newsstand/cover Sun.; $151.20/yr home delivery; $210/yr mailed. **Wire Service(s):** AP. Circulation: 25,500 morning (paid); 27,000 Sunday (paid). **Owner(s):** Community Newspaper Holdings, Inc., 3500 Colonnade Pkwy., Ste. 600, Birmingham, AL 35243. Telephone: 205-298-7100. FAX: 205-298-7101. **Management:** Randy Deason, Publisher. Terri Hale, Advertising Manager. Chris Dorton, Circulation Manager. Joyce Anderson, Classified Adv. Mgr.. **Editorial:** Tom Colley, Editor.

CHARLESTON

CHARLESTON DAILY MAIL. 1001 Virginia St., E., Charleston, WV 25301. Telephone: 304-348-5140. FAX: 304-348-4847. E-MAIL: cstadelman@dailymail.com. URL: http://www.dailymail.com. Mailing Address: PO Box 2993, Charleston, WV 25330. Year Established: 1920. Pub. Frequency: d. (Mon.-Sat.) Page Size: broadsheet. Subscrip. Rate: $.50 newsstand/cover; $1.50 newsstand/cover Sun.; $147/yr home delivery local. Freelance Pay: $25-$100/article. **Wire Service(s):** AP, LAT-WAT. Circulation: 40,000 evening (paid); 98,000 Sunday (paid). **Owner(s):** MediaNews Group, Inc., 101 W Colfax Ave, Ste 1100, Denver, CO 80202. FAX: 303-954-6320. **Management:** Larry Levak, Advertising Director. **Editorial:** Nanya Friend, Editor.

CHARLESTON GAZETTE, THE. 1001 Virginia St., E., Charleston, WV 25301. Telephone: 304-348-5140. FAX: 304-348-1233. E-MAIL: gazette@wvgazette.com. URL: http://www.wvgazette.com. Mailing Address: PO Box 2993, Charleston, WV 25330. Year Established: 1872. Pub. Frequency: d. Page Size: broadsheet. Subscrip. Rate: $.50 newsstand/cover; $1.25 newsstand/cover Sun.; $26 home delivery for 2 mos.. **Wire Service(s):** AP, NYT. Circulation: 50,737 morning (paid); 91,511 Sunday (paid). **Owner(s):** Betty Chilton, See address and contact information above. **Management:** Betty Chilton, Publisher. Larry Levak, Advertising Manager. Jerry Briggs, Circulation Manager. Melissa Dickerson, Marketing Director. **Editorial:** James Haught, Editor-in-Chief. Patty Vandergrift Tompkins, Managing Editor. Robert Byers, City Editor. Rosalie Earle, Lifestyle Editor. Vic Burkhammer, News Editor. Mitch Vingle, Sports Editor. James Haught, Sunday Editor.

CLARKSBURG

CLARKSBURG EXPONENT TELEGRAM. 324 Hewes Ave, Clarksburg, WV 26301. Telephone: 304-624-1400. FAX: 304-622-3629. E-MAIL: advertising@exponent-telegram.com. URL: http://www.cpubco.com. Mailing Address: PO Box 2000, Clarksburg, WV 26302. Year Established: 1906. Pub. Frequency: d. Page Size: broadsheet. Subscrip. Rate: $.50 newsstand/cover; $1.25 newsstand/cover Sun.; $161.20/yr home delivery; $204.88/yr mailed. Adv. Rate: col. inch $16.60 Circulation: 19,000 morning (paid); 22,000 Sunday (paid). **Owner(s):** Clarksburg Publishing Co., See address and contact information above. **Management:** J. Cecil Jarvis, Publisher. Deborah Veltri, Advertising Manager. Sara Shingleton, Classified Adv. Mgr.. **Editorial:** Robert F. Stealey, Editor. John G. Miller, Managing Editor. Matt Harvey, City Editor. Julie Perrine, Lifestyle Editor. Danny Carpenter, Sports Editor.

ELKINS

INTER-MOUNTAIN, THE. 520 Railroad Ave., Elkins, WV 26241. Telephone: 304-636-2121. FAX: 304-636-8252. Mailing Address: PO Box 1339, Elkins, WV 26241. Year Established: 1893. Pub. Frequency: d. (Mon.-Sat.) Page Size: broadsheet. Subscrip. Rate: $.50 newsstand/cover; $.75 newsstand/cover Sat.; $92.80 carrier delivery $9280yr. **Wire Service(s):** AP. Circulation: 12,700 evening (paid). **Owner(s):** Ogden Newspapers of Minnesota, Inc., 1500 Main St., Wheeling, WV 26003. Telephone: 304-233-0100. **Management:** Don Smith, Publisher. Samantha Storch, Advertising Director. Jerry Ferguson, Circulation Manager. **Editorial:** Don Smith, Editor. Tracy Marsh, Photographer. Edgar Kelley, Sports Editor.

FAIRMONT

TIMES WEST VIRGINIAN. Quincy & Ogden Sts., Fairmont, WV 26554. Telephone: 304-367-2500. FAX: 304-367-2569. E-MAIL: timeswv@timeswv.com. URL: http://www.timeswv.com. Mailing Address: PO Box 2530, Fairmont, WV 26555-2530. Year Established: 1845. Pub. Frequency: d. Page Size: broadsheet. Subscrip. Rate: $.50 newsstand/cover; $1.25 newsstand/cover Sun.; $16.90 carrier delivery/mo. in area; $173.75/yr carrier delivery; $24 mailed/mo. out of area. **Wire Service(s):** AP. Circulation: 13,000 morning (paid). **Owner(s):** Community Newspaper Holdings, Inc., 3500 Colonnade Pkwy., Ste. 600, Birmingham, AL 35243. Telephone: 205-298-7100. **Management:** Andy Kniceley, Publisher. Craig Richards, Advertising Manager. Jim Smith, Circulation Director. Toni Ricer, Classified Adv. Mgr.. **Editorial:** Misty Poe, City Editor. John Veasey, Community Editor. Jennifer Roush, Lifestyle Editor. Mike Bowen, Sports Editor.

HUNTINGTON

HERALD-DISPATCH, THE. 946 Fifth Ave., Huntington, WV 25701. Telephone: 304-526-4000. FAX: 304-526-2857. URL: http://www.hdonline.com. Mailing Address: PO Box 2017, Huntington, WV 25720. Year Established: 1889. Pub. Frequency: d. Page Size: broadsheet. Subscrip. Rate: $.50 newsstand/cover; $1.50 newsstand/cover Sun.; $15.50 home delivery/mo.. **Wire Service(s):** AP, GNS. Circulation: 34,966 morning (paid); 40,983 Sunday (paid). **Owner(s):** Gannett Company, Inc., 7950 Jones Branch Dr, McLean, VA 22107. Telephone: 703-854-6000. **Management:** Pat Thompson Frantz, Publisher. Cheryl Lindus, Advertising Director. Lisa Marcum, Advertising Manager. Scott Daily, Circulation Director. Gail Patton, Classified Adv. Mgr.. **Editorial:** Edward Dawson Jr., Executive Editor. Jill Nevels-Haus, Managing Editor. Jim Ross, Editorial Page Editor. Rick McCann, Sports Editor.

KEYSER

MINERAL DAILY NEWS-TRIBUNE. 24 Armstrong St., Keyser, WV 26726. Telephone: 304-788-3333. FAX: 304-788-3398. E-MAIL: newstribune@mindspring.com. URL: http://www.newstribune.com. Mailing Address: PO Box 879, Keyser, WV 26726. Pub. Frequency: d. (Mon.-Sat.) Page Size: broadsheet. Subscrip. Rate: $.50 newsstand/cover; $131/yr carrier delivery in county; $131/yr mailed in county. **Wire Service(s):** AP. Circulation: 4,800 morning (paid). **Owner(s):** GateHouse Media, Inc, 350 WillowBrook Office Park, Fairport, NY 14450. Telephone: 585-598-0030. FAX: 585-248-2631. **Management:** Randy Lewis, Publisher. Christy Jamison, Circulation Manager. Kathy Murphy, Classified Adv. Mgr.. **Editorial:** Tony Cimaglia, Managing Editor. Andrew Arthur, News Editor.

LEWISBURG

WEST VIRGINIA DAILY NEWS. 200 S. Court St., Lewisburg, WV 24901-0471. Telephone: 304-645-1206. FAX: 304-645-7104. E-MAIL: dailynewsad@charter.net. Mailing Address: PO Box 471, Lewisburg, WV 24901-0471. Year Established: 1967. Pub. Frequency: d. (Mon.-Fri.) Page Size: broadsheet. Subscrip. Rate: $.30 newsstand/cover; $59.40/yr carrier delivery; $97.52/yr mailed in state; $92/yr mailed out of state. Adv. Rate: col. inch $6.75 Circulation: 4,000 evening (paid). **Owner(s):** Moffitt Newspapers, Inc., PO Box 8565, Roanoke, VA 24014. Telephone: 703-344-2489. **Management:** Frank Spicer, Publisher. Judy K. Steele, Advertising Manager. Crystal McNeely, Circulation Manager. **Editorial:** Tina Alvey, Editor.

LOGAN

LOGAN BANNER.   ISSN 0746-0570
437-447 Stratton St, Logan, WV 25601. Telephone: 304-752-6950. FAX: 304-752-1239. URL: http://www.loganbanner.com. Mailing Address: PO Box 720, Logan, WV 25601-0720. Year Established: 1888. Pub. Frequency: d. (Sun.-Fri.) Page Size: broadsheet. Subscrip. Rate: $.50 newsstand/cover; $1 newsstand/cover Sun.; $54 carrier delivery for 6 mos.; $143/yr carrier delivery. Adv. Rate: col. inch $6.15 **Wire Service(s):** AP. Circulation: 9,500 morning (paid); 11,000 Sunday (paid). **Owner(s):** Heartland Publications, LLC, 20 Research Pkwy, Ste G, Old Saybrook, CT 06475. Telephone: 860-388-3470. FAX: 860-388-3490. **Management:** Richard Osborne, Publisher. Kathy Chafin, Advertising Manager. Dottie Hatfield, Classified Adv. Mgr.. **Editorial:** Richard Browning, Managing Editor. Martha Sparks, Society Editor.

MARTINSBURG

JOURNAL (MARTAINSBURG), THE. 207 W. King St., Martinsburg, WV 25401. Telephone: 304-263-8931. FAX: 304-263-8058. URL: http://www.journal-news.net. Mailing Address: PO Box 807, Martinsburg, WV 25402. Year Established: 1927. Pub. Frequency: d. Page Size: broadsheet. Subscrip. Rate: $.50 newsstand/cover; $1.25 newsstand/cover Sun.; $109.20/yr home delivery; $150/yr mailed in state. **Wire Service(s):** UPI. Circulation: 19,344 morning (paid); 19,988 Sunday (paid). **Owner(s):** Ogden Newspapers of Minnesota, Inc., 1500 Main St., Wheeling, WV 26003. Telephone: 304-233-0100. **Management:** L. Craig Bohrer, Publisher. Jeff Weshmyer, Advertising Director. John Swint, Circulation Director. David Smith, Business Manager. **Editorial:** Maria Lorensen, Editor. Ron Agnir, Photographer. Matt Tabeek, Sports Editor.

MORGANTOWN

DOMINION POST, THE. 1251 Earl Core Rd., Morgantown, WV 26505-6298. Telephone: 304-292-6301. FAX: 304-291-2326. E-MAIL: newsroom@dominionpost.com. URL: http://www.dominionpost.com. Year Established: 1873. Pub. Frequency: d. Page Size: broadsheet. Subscrip. Rate: $.50 newsstand/cover; $1.50 newsstand/cover Sun.; $45.50 home delivery local for 13 wks.; $60.45 home delivery out of area for 13 wks.. **Wire Service(s):** AP. Circulation: 25,000 morning (paid); 30,000 Sunday (paid). **Owner(s):** David A. Raese, See address and contact information above. **Bureau(s):** 150 Morgan St., Kingwood, WV 26537-1481. Telephone: 304-329-1406. FAX: 304-329-3001. **Management:** David A. Raese, Publisher. James F. Matuga, Advertising Director. Rod Phillips, Circulation Director. **Editorial:** Geri Ferrara, Editor. David Beard, Managing Editor.

MOUNDSVILLE

MOUNDSVILLE DAILY ECHO. 713 Lafayette Ave., Moundsville, WV 26041-0369. Telephone: 304-845-2660. FAX: 304-845-2661. Mailing Address: PO Box 369, Moundsville, WV 26041-0369. Year Established: 1891. Pub. Frequency: d. (Mon.-Sat.) Page Size: broadsheet. Subscrip. Rate: $.20 newsstand/cover; $1 home delivery/wk.; $47.70/yr mailed. **Wire Service(s):** AP. Circulation: 4,000 evening (paid). **Owner(s):** Charles L. Walton, See address and contact information above. **Management:** Charles Walton, General Manager. Marian Walton, Publisher. Linda Massie, Classified Adv. Mgr.. **Editorial:** Hugh Anderson, City Editor. Charles Walton, Sports Editor.

PARKERSBURG

▼PARKERSBURG NEWS AND SENTINEL. 519 Juliana St., Parkersburg, WV 26101. Telephone: 304-485-1891. FAX: 304-485-5122. URL: http://newsandsentinel.com/. Mailing Address: PO Box 1787, Parkersburg, WV 26102. Year Established: 2009. Pub. Frequency: d. Subscrip. Rate: $160/yr (Mon.-Sun.); $82/yr (Sun.); $78/yr (Mon.-Sat.). Owner(s): Ogden Newspapers of Minnesota, Inc., 1500 Main St., Wheeling, WV 26003. Telephone: 304-233-0100. FAX: 304-233-0327.

WAYNE

WAYNE COUNTY (WV) NEWS. 310 Central Ave., Wayne, WV 25570. Telephone: 304-272-3433. FAX: 304-272-6516. E-MAIL: advertising@waynecountynews.com. URL: http://www.waynecountynews.com. Year Established: 1874. Pub. Frequency: d. (Mon.-Sat.) Page Size: broadsheet. Subscrip. Rate: $.50 newsstand/cover; $104/yr in county; $128/yr out of area. Circulation: 5,000 per issue (paid). Owner(s): Thomas J. George, See address and contact information above. Management: Thomas J. George, Publisher. Ruth Adkins, Advertising Manager. Editorial: Thomas J. George, Editor. Randy Payton, Sports.

WEIRTON

WEIRTON DAILY TIMES. 114 Lee Ave., Weirton, WV 26062. Telephone: 304-748-0606. FAX: 304-748-2202. URL: http://www.weir.net/dailytimes. Year Established: 1928. Pub. Frequency: d. Page Size: broadsheet. Subscrip. Rate: $.50 newsstand/cover; $1.25 newsstand/cover Sun.; $111.80/yr carrier delivery; $117/yr motor route. Wire Service(s): AP, SH. Circulation: 6,000 evening (paid); 6,000 Sunday (paid). Owner(s): Ogden Newspapers of Minnesota, Inc., 19260 San Carlos Blvd., Fort Myers Beach, FL 33931. Telephone: 239-463-4421. Management: Richard Crofton, Publisher. Thomas Peck, Circulation Manager. Editorial: Richard Crofton, Editor. Linda Harris, Managing Editor.

WELCH

WELCH DAILY NEWS. 125 Wyoming St., Welch, WV 24801. Telephone: 304-436-3144. FAX: 304-294-4144. Mailing Address: PO Box 569, Welch, WV 24801. Year Established: 1923. Pub. Frequency: d. (Mon.-Fri.) Page Size: broadsheet. Subscrip. Rate: $.40 newsstand/cover; $75/yr home delivery. Freelance Pay: $0.15/column-inch. Wire Service(s): UPI. Circulation: 6,000 evening (paid). Owner(s): Jack Moffitt, See address and contact information above. Management: Jack Moffitt, President. Greg Spinella, Publisher. Pamela Riggs, Advertising Manager. Tom Molin, Circulation Manager. Editorial: Shanelle Rucker, Editor.

WHEELING

FORT WAYNE NEWS-SENTINEL. 1500 Main St, Wheeling, WV 26003. Telephone: 304-233-0100. E-MAIL: nsmetro@news-sentinel.com. URL: http://www.news-sentinel.com. Year Established: 1918. Pub. Frequency: d. (Mon.-Sat.) Page Size: broadsheet. Subscrip. Rate: $.50 newsstand/cover; $32.50 for 13 wks.. Wire Service(s): AP, MCT. Circulation: 30,000 evening (paid). Owner(s): Ogden Newspapers Inc., See address and contact information above. Management: Michael Christman, Publisher. Brian Tombaugh, Photography Director. Editorial: Kerry Hubartt, Executive Editor. Mary Lou Brink, Managing Editor. Lisa Esquivel Long, Business Editor. Kevin Kilbane, Feature Editor. Rob Joesbury, Metro Editor. Elbert Starks, Sports Editor.

INTELLIGENCER, THE. 1500 Main St., Wheeling, WV 26003. Telephone: 304-233-0100. E-MAIL: myer@news-register.net. URL: http://www.theintelligencer.com. Year Established: 1852. Pub. Frequency: d. (Mon.-Sat.) Page Size: broadsheet. Subscrip. Rate: $.50 newsstand/cover; $1.25 newsstand/cover Sat.; $10.85 home delivery/mo.; $124.80/yr home delivery. Wire Service(s): AP. Circulation: 22,000 morning (paid); 42,000 Saturday (paid). Owner(s): Ogden Newspapers of Minnesota, Inc., See address and contact information above. Management: Perry Nardo, General Manager. Lori Figurski, Advertising Manager. Greg Pohl, Circulation Manager. Brian Clutter, Classified Adv. Mgr.. Editorial: J. Michael Myer, Executive Editor. Nick Bedway, Sports Editor.

WHEELING NEWS-REGISTER. 1500 Main St., Wheeling, WV 26003. Telephone: 304-233-0100. E-MAIL: myer@news-register.net. URL: http://www.news-register.net. Year Established: 1890. Pub. Frequency: d. (Sun.-Fri.) Page Size: broadsheet. Subscrip. Rate: $.50 newsstand/cover; $1.25 newsstand/cover Sun.; $10 carrier delivery/mo.; $249/yr mailed. Wire Service(s): AP. Circulation: 16,679 evening (paid); 40,838 Sunday (paid). Owner(s): Ogden Newspapers of Minnesota, Inc., See address and contact information above. Bureau(s): Court Ave., Moundsville, WV 06041. Telephone: 304-845-3603. Management: Perry Nardo, General Manager. Lori Figurski, Advertising Director. Greg Pohl, Circulation Manager. Editorial: J. Michael Meyer, Executive Editor. John McCabe, City Editor. Nick Bedway, Sports Editor.

WILLIAMSON

WILLIAMSON DAILY NEWS.   ISSN 0883-1602
100 Block E Third Ave, Williamson, WV 25661. Telephone: 304-235-4242. FAX: 304-235-0730. URL: http://www.williamsondailynews.com. Mailing Address: PO Box 1660, Williamson, WV 25661. Year Established: 1904. Pub. Frequency: d. Page Size: broadsheet. Subscrip. Rate: $.50 newsstand/cover; $1 newsstand/cover Sun.; $111.60/yr carrier delivery; $160.28/yr mailed in county; $180/yr mailed out of county. Wire Service(s): AP. Circulation: 11,000 evening (paid); 11,000 Sunday (paid). Owner(s): Heartland Publications, LLC, 20 Research Pkwy, Ste G, Old Saybrook, CT 06475. Telephone: 860-388-3470. FAX: 860-388-3490. Management: D. Gaither Perry, Publisher. Renee Kessler, Advertising Manager. Chad Whitt, Circulation Manager. Kasey Baldwin, Classified Adv. Mgr.. Editorial: Teddy Paynter, Editor.

WISCONSIN

ANTIGO

ANTIGO DAILY JOURNAL. 612 Superior St., Antigo, WI 54409. Telephone: 715-623-4191. FAX: 715-623-4193. URL: http://www.antigodailyjournal.com. Year Established: 1905. Pub. Frequency: d. (Mon.-Sat.) Page Size: broadsheet. Subscrip. Rate: $.50 newsstand/cover; $81.95/yr carrier delivery; $118.60/yr motor route; $87/yr mailed in county. Wire Service(s): AP. Circulation: 6,500 evening (paid). Owner(s): Berner Bros. Publishing Co., Inc., See address and contact information above. Management: Marie F. Berner, Publisher. Jon Croce, Advertising Director. Editorial: Fred A. Berner, Editor. Lisa Haefs, Society Editor. Larry Ebitz, Sports Editor.

APPLETON

POST-CRESCENT, THE. 306 W. Washington St., Appleton, WI 54911. Telephone: 920-733-4411. FAX: 920-733-1945. E-MAIL: email@postcsescent.com. URL: http://www.postcrescent.com. Mailing Address: PO Box 59, Appleton, WI 54912. Year Established: 1853. Pub. Frequency: d. Page Size: broadsheet. Subscrip. Rate: $.50 newsstand/cover; $1.75 newsstand/cover Sun.; $200.20/yr carrier delivery & motor rte; $312/yr mailed in state; $364/yr mailed out of state. Wire Service(s): AP, SH. Circulation: 67,643 evening (paid); 74,930 Sunday (paid). Owner(s): Gannett Company, Inc., 7950 Jones Branch Dr., McLean, VA 22107-0001. Telephone: 703-854-6000. Bureau(s): 216 W. Wisconsin Ave., Neenah, WI 54956. Telephone: 414-722-4243. Management: Ellen Leifeld, Publisher. Paul Gaier, Advertising Director. Joe Braunschwieg, Circulation Manager. Editorial: Andrew Oppmann, Executive Editor. Dan Flannery, Managing Editor. Larry Gallup, Editorial Page Editor. Bob Vitale, News Editor. Brad Zimanek, Sports Editor.

ASHLAND

DAILY PRESS (ASHLAND), THE.   ISSN 1050-4095
122 W. Third St., Ashland, WI 54806. Telephone: 715-682-2313. FAX: 715-682-4699. E-MAIL: ashpress@cheqnet.net. URL: http://www.ashlandwi.com. Mailing Address: PO Box 313, Ashland, WI 54806. Year Established: 1888. Pub. Frequency: d. (Mon.-Sat.) Page Size: broadsheet. Subscrip. Rate: $.75 newsstand/cover; $120/yr carrier delivery local; $145/yr mailed out of area; $145/yr mailed elsewhere. Adv. Rate: col. inch $11.63 Wire Service(s): AP. Circulation: 6,739 morning (paid). Owner(s): Superior Publishing Corp., 1105 Tower Ave., Superior, WI 54880-1502. Management: Gary Pennington, General Manager. Karen Petros, Circulation Manager. Editorial: Claire Duquette, Editor. Cindi Shrider, Society Editor. Larry Servinsky, Sports.

BARABOO

BARABOO NEWS REPUBLIC. 714 Matt's Ferry Rd., Baraboo, WI 53913. Telephone: 608-356-4808. FAX: 608-356-0344. E-MAIL: bnreditor@scwn.com. URL: http://www.bnr.wiscnews.com. Mailing Address: PO Box 9, Baraboo, WI 53913-0009. Year Established: 1855. Pub. Frequency: d. (Mon.-Sat.) Page Size: broadsheet. Subscrip. Rate: $.50 newsstand/cover; $.75 newsstand/cover Sat.; $119/yr carrier delivery; $125/yr mailed in state; $145.70/yr mailed out of state. Adv. Rate: col. inch $49.68 Wire Service(s): AP. Circulation: 4,200 morning (paid). Owner(s): Capital Newspapers, Inc., 1901 Fish Hatchery Rd., Madison, WI 53713. Management: George Althoff, Publisher. Julie Brown, Advertising Manager. Teresa Klinger, Circulation Manager. Editorial: Brendan Leonard, Editor. Jennifer McBride, Assistant Editor. Ben Bromley, Feature Editor. Andy Davis, Sports Editor.

BEAVER DAM

DAILY CITIZEN.   ISSN 0749-1379
805 Park Ave., Beaver Dam, WI 53916. Telephone: 920-887-0321. FAX: 920-887-8790. URL: http://www.wiscnews.com/bdc. Mailing Address: PO Box 558, Beaver Dam, WI 53916. Year Established: 1856. Pub. Frequency: d. (Mon.-Sat.) Page Size: broadsheet. Subscrip. Rate: $.50 newsstand/cover; $1 newsstand/cover Sat.; $35.75/yr home delivery for 13 wks.; $143/yr home delivery. Wire Service(s): AP, NYT. Circulation: 10,500 evening (paid). Owner(s): Capital Newspapers, Inc., 1901 Fish Hatchery Rd., Madison, WI 53713. Telephone: 608-252-6200. Management: Jim Kelsh, Publisher. Scott Zeinemann, Advertising Manager. Teresa Klinger, Circulation Manager. Editorial: Aaron Holbrook, Editor. Tom Kahl, Sports Editor.

BELOIT

BELOIT DAILY NEWS. 149 State St., Beloit, WI 53511. Telephone: 608-365-8811. FAX: 608-365-1420. E-MAIL: keymann@beloitdailynews.com. URL: http://www.beloitdailynews.com. Year Established: 1892. Pub. Frequency: d. (Mon.-Sat.) Page Size: broadsheet. Subscrip. Rate: $.50 newsstand/cover; $1 newsstand/cover Sat.; $11.50 home delivery for 4 wks.; $149.50/yr home delivery. Wire Service(s): AP. Circulation: 13,936 evening (paid). Owner(s): Greater Beloit Publishing Co., See address and contact information above. Management: Kent Eymann, Publisher. Jim Rees, Circulation Director. Steve Elkins, Marketing Director. Angie Meals, Business Manager. Editorial: William Barth, Editor. Don Behling, Production Manager. Hillary Wundrow, Business Editor. Deb Jenson Dehart, Feature Editor. Clint Wolf, Health Editor. Jim Franz, Sports.

CHIPPEWA FALLS

CHIPPEWA HERALD,THE.   ISSN 8756-2960
321 Frenette Dr., Chippewa Falls, WI 54729-0069. Telephone: 715-723-5515. FAX: 715-723-9644. E-MAIL: publisher@chippewa.com. URL: http://www.chippewa.com. Mailing Address: PO Box 69, Chippewa Falls, WI 54729-0069. Year Established: 1879. Pub. Frequency: d. (Sat.-Thu.) Page Size: broadsheet. Subscrip. Rate: $.50 newsstand/cover; $1 newsstand/cover Sun.; $132/yr home delivery local. Wire Service(s): AP. Circulation: 7,150 evening (paid and free); 7,150 Sunday (paid and free). Owner(s): Lee Enterprises, Inc., 201 N. Harrison St, Ste 600, Davenport, IA 52801-1924. Management: Mark Baker, Publisher. Steve Jahn, Advertising Director. Patrick Milliren, Advertising Manager. Mike McClure, Circulation Manager. Editorial: Ross Evavold, Managing Editor. Jeff Jackson, Sports.

EAU CLAIRE

LEADER-TELEGRAM.   ISSN 0891-0227
701 S. Farwell St., Eau Claire, WI 54701. Telephone: 715-833-9200. FAX: 715-833-9244. E-MAIL: leadertelegram@cvol.net. URL: http://www.leadertelegram.com. Mailing Address: PO Box 570, Eau Claire, WI 54702-0570. Year Established: 1881. Pub. Frequency: d. Page Size: broadsheet. Subscrip. Rate: $.50 newsstand/cover; $3.30/wk.; $161.20/yr Freelance Pay: $0.40/column-inch. Wire Service(s): AP, SH, MCT. Circulation: 32,779 Saturday (paid); 38,785 Sunday (paid); 27,028 evening (paid). Owner(s): Eau Claire Press Co., See address and contact information above. Management: Pieter Graaskamp, General Manager. Dan Graaskamp, Advertising Manager. Steve Svihovec, Circulation Manager. Lisa Behlke, Classified Adv. Mgr.. Editorial: Don Huebscher, Editor. Gary Johnson, City Editor. Dan Pherson, Sports Editor.

FOND DU LAC

REPORTER (FOND DU LAC), THE. 33 W. Second St., Fond Du Lac, WI 54935-0630. Telephone: 920-922-4600. FAX: 920-922-5388. E-MAIL: treporter@smgopo.gannett.com. URL: http://www.fdlreporter.com. Mailing Address: PO Box 630, Fond Du Lac, WI 54936-0630. Year Established: 1870. Pub. Frequency: d. (Sun-Fri.) Page Size: broadsheet. Subscrip. Rate: $.50 newsstand/cover; $1.25 newsstand/cover Sun.; $169/yr home delivery. Wire Service(s): AP, SH, GNS. Circulation: 20,000 evening (paid); 21,500 Sunday (paid). Owner(s): Gannett Company, Inc., 7950 Jones Branch Dr., McLean, VA 22107-0001. Telephone: 703-854-6000. Management: Lani Dorlack, Publisher. Jennifer Sorenson, Advertising Director. Editorial: Steve Fountain, Editor. Michael Mentzer, City Editor.

FORT ATKINSON

DAILY JEFFERSON COUNTY UNION. 28 W. Milwaukee Ave., Fort Atkinson, WI 53538-2018. Telephone: 920-563-5553. FAX: 920-563-2329. E-MAIL: dniemeyer@dailyunion.com. URL: http://www.dailyunion.com. Year Established: 1870. Pub. Frequency: d. (Mon.-Fri.) Page Size: broadsheet. Subscrip. Rate: $.50 newsstand/cover; $85/yr home delivery; $90/yr mailed. Adv. Rate: col. inch $10.75 **Wire Service(s):** AP. Circulation: 8,600 evening (paid). **Owner(s):** W.D. Hoard & Sons Co., See address and contact information above. **Management:** Brian Knox, Publisher. Diane Niemeyer, Advertising Director. Judy Schnell, Circulation Manager. Paulette Cook, Classified Adv. Mgr.. Diane Niemeyer, Marketing Director. **Editorial:** Christine Spangler, Managing Editor. Randall Dullum, News Editor. Jeff Seisser, Sports Editor.

GREEN BAY

GREEN BAY PRESS-GAZETTE. 435 E. Walnut St., Green Bay, WI 54305-3430. Telephone: 920-435-4411. FAX: 920-431-8379. URL: http://www.greenbaypressgazette.com. Mailing Address: PO Box 23430, Green Bay, WI 54305-3430. Year Established: 1915. Pub. Frequency: d. Page Size: broadsheet. Subscrip. Rate: $.50 newsstand/cover; $1.75 newsstand/cover Sun.; $16.31 carrier delivery/mo.; $195/yr carrier delivery. **Wire Service(s):** AP, MCT, GNS. Circulation: 61,000 evening (paid); 86,000 Sunday (paid). **Owner(s):** Gannett Company, Inc., 7950 Jones Branch Dr, McLean, VA 22107. Telephone: 703-854-6000. **Management:** William T. Nusbaum, Publisher. Scott Johnson, Advertising Director. Bill Johnson, Circulation Director. **Editorial:** John Dye, Executive Editor. Barbara Janesh, Managing Editor. Kim McAuliffe, Lifestyle Editor.

JANESVILLE

JANESVILLE GAZETTE. One S. Parker Dr., Janesville, WI 53545. Telephone: 608-754-3311. FAX: 608-754-8003. URL: http://www.gazetteextra.com. Mailing Address: PO Box 5001, Janesville, WI 53547. Year Established: 1845. Pub. Frequency: d. Page Size: broadsheet. Subscrip. Rate: $.50 newsstand/cover; $1.75 newsstand/cover Sun.; $49.40 carrier delivery for 13 wks.; $176.80/yr carrier delivery. **Wire Service(s):** AP. Circulation: 26,990 evening (paid); 27,876 Sunday (paid). **Owner(s):** Bliss Communications, Inc., See address and contact information above. **Management:** David A;. Johnson, General Manager. Sidney H. Bliss, Publisher. Dan White, Advertising Director. Rudy Frank, Circulation Manager. **Editorial:** Scott Angus, Editor. Barbara Uebelacker, Managing Editor. Shelly Birkelo, Lifestyle Editor. Bill Olmsted, Photo Editor. David Wedeward, Sports Editor.

KENOSHA

KENOSHA NEWS. ISSN 0749-713X
5800 Seventh Ave., Kenosha, WI 53140. Telephone: 262-657-1000. FAX: 262-657-1617. E-MAIL: hjb@kenoshanews.com. URL: http://www.kenoshanews.com. Year Established: 1894. Pub. Frequency: d. Page Size: broadsheet. Subscrip. Rate: $.50 newsstand/cover; $1.75 newsstand/cover Sun.; $4/wk.. Adv. Rate: col. inch $22.05 **Wire Service(s):** AP, SH, LAT-WAT. Circulation: 26,572 morning (paid); 29,191 Sunday (paid). **Owner(s):** United Communications Corp., See address and contact information above. **Management:** Ron J. Montemurro, General Manager. Kenneth L. Dowdell, Publisher. Kenneth McElroy, Advertising Manager. James DeMarco, Circulation Manager. Jared Thorson, Marketing Director. **Editorial:** Steve Lund, Editorial Page Editor. Dave Marren, Sports Editor.

LA CROSSE

LA CROSSE TRIBUNE. ISSN 0745-9793
401 N. Third St., La Crosse, WI 54601-3281. Telephone: 608-782-9710. FAX: 608-782-9723. E-MAIL: news@lacrossetribune.com. URL: http://www.lacrossetribune.com. Year Established: 1904. Pub. Frequency: d. Page Size: broadsheet. Subscrip. Rate: $.75 newsstand/cover; $1.75 newsstand/cover Sun.; $234/yr carrier delivery local; $247/yr motor route local. **Wire Service(s):** AP, SH, MCT. Circulation: 32,743 morning (paid); 40,894 Sunday (paid). **Owner(s):** Lee Enterprises, Inc., 201 N. Harrison St, Ste 600, Davenport, IA 52801-1924. **Management:** Rusty Cunningham, Publisher. Becky Bjork, Advertising Manager. Nick Nicks, Circulation Manager. **Editorial:** John Smalley, Editor. Richard Mial, Editorial Page Editor. Jeff Brown, Sports Editor.

MADISON

CAPITAL TIMES, THE. ISSN 0749-4068
1901 Fish Hatchery Rd, Madison WI 53713. Telephone: 608-252-6200. FAX: 608-250-4155. E-MAIL: tctvoice@captimes.madison.com. URL: http://www.madison.com/tct/. Mailing Address: PO Box 8056, Madison, WI 53708. Year Established: 1917. Pub. Frequency: d. (Mon.-Sat.) Page Size: broadsheet. Subscrip. Rate: $.50 newsstand/cover; $135.85/yr carrier delivery; $177.85/yr mailed in state. Freelance Pay: $15-$100/article. **Wire Service(s):** AP, SH, LAT-WAT. Circulation: 19,892 evening (paid). **Owner(s):** Capital Newspapers, Inc., See address and contact information above. **Management:** Clayton Frink, Publisher. Jeff Schroeter, Advertising Director. Phil Stoddard, Circulation Director. **Editorial:** Dave Zweifel, Editor. Phil Haslanger, Managing Editor. Linda Brazzil, Feature Editor. Adam Mertz, Sports Editor.

WISCONSIN STATE JOURNAL. ISSN 0749-405X
1901 Fish Hatchery Rd., Madison, WI 53713. Telephone: 608-252-6100. FAX: 608-252-6119. URL: http://www.madison.com/wsj. Mailing Address: PO Box 8058, Madison, WI 53708. Year Established: 1901. Pub. Frequency: d. Page Size: broadsheet. Subscrip. Rate: $.50 newsstand/cover; $1.75 newsstand/cover Sun.; $4.15 carrier delivery/wk.; $185.25/yr carrier delivery. **Wire Service(s):** AP, NYT, MCT. Circulation: 89,084 morning (paid); 152,899 Sunday (paid). **Owner(s):** Lee Enterprises, Inc., 201 N. Harrison St, Ste 600, Davenport, IA 52801-1924. **Management:** James Hopson, Publisher. Mary DeNiro, Advertising Manager. Marci Rosen, Classified Adv. Mgr.. **Editorial:** Ellen Foley, Editor. Tim Kelley, Managing Editor. Cliff Behnke, Senior Managing Editor. Teryl Franklin, Business Editor. Phil Glende, City Editor. Scott Milfred, Editorial Page Editor. Chris Juzwik, Feature Editor. Greg Sprout, Sports Editor.

MANITOWOC

HERALD TIMES REPORTER. 902 Franklin St., Manitowoc, WI 54220-0790. Telephone: 920-684-4433. FAX: 920-684-4416. E-MAIL: htrnews@smgpo.gannett.com. URL: http://www.htrnews.com. Mailing Address: PO Box 790, Manitowoc, WI 54221-0790. Year Established: 1875. Pub. Frequency: d. Page Size: broadsheet. Subscrip. Rate: $.50 newsstand/cover; $1.25 newsstand/cover Sun.; $156.95/yr carrier delivery in city; $162.95/yr motor route in city; $195.52/yr mailed. **Wire Service(s):** AP. Circulation: 17,500 evening (paid); 18,500 Sunday (paid). **Owner(s):** Gannett Company, Inc., 7950 Jones Branch Dr, McLean, VA 22107. Telephone: 703-854-6000. **Management:** Bill Hackney, General Manager. Bill Nusbaum, Publisher. Lowell Johnson, Advertising Director. Bill Hackney, Circulation Director. **Editorial:** Barbara Janesh, Editor. Amy Holschbach, Lifestyle Editor. Tim Swoboda, Photographer. Steve Clark, Sports Editor.

MARINETTE

EAGLE-HERALD. 1809 Dunlap Ave., Marinette, WI 54143. Telephone: 715-735-6611. FAX: 715-735-7580. E-MAIL: news@eagleherald.com. URL: http://www.eagleherald.com. Mailing Address: P.O. Box 77, Marinette, WI 54143. Year Established: 1871. Pub. Frequency: d. (Mon.-Sat.) Page Size: broadsheet. Subscrip. Rate: $.50 newsstand/cover; $.75 newsstand/cover Sat.; $135.40/yr carrier delivery; $148.33/yr motor route; $169.43/yr mailed in county; $183.42/yr mailed out of county. Circulation: 11,500 evening (paid). **Owner(s):** Eagle-Herald Publishing LLC, See address and contact information above. **Management:** Dennis Colling, General Manager. Jim Hofer, Advertising Manager. Wayne Jessel, Circulation Manager. **Editorial:** Terri Lescelius, Editor. Jody Korch, Sports Editor.

MARSHFIELD

MARSHFIELD NEWS-HERALD. 111 W. Third St., Marshfield, WI 54449. Telephone: 715-384-3131. FAX: 715-387-4175. URL: http://www.wisinfo.com. Mailing Address: PO Box 70, Marshfield, WI 54449. Year Established: 1927. Pub. Frequency: d. Page Size: broadsheet. Subscrip. Rate: $.50 newsstand/cover; $1.25 newsstand/cover Sun.; $96/yr carrier delivery. Freelance Pay: $1/column-inch. **Wire Service(s):** AP, GNS. Circulation: 14,803 evening (paid); 18,800 Sunday (paid). **Owner(s):** Gannett Company, Inc., 7950 Jones Branch Dr., McLean, VA 22107-0001. Telephone: 703-854-6000. **Management:** Helen Jungwirth, Publisher. **Editorial:** Tom Berger, Editor.

MILWAUKEE

MILWAUKEE JOURNAL SENTINEL. ISSN 1082-8850
333 W State St, PO Box 661, Milwaukee, WI 53203. Telephone: 414-224-2000. E-MAIL: mkaiser@journalsentinel.com. URL: http://www.jsonline.com. Mailing Address: PO Box 371, Milwaukee, WI 53201-0371. Year Established: 1995. Pub. Frequency: d. Page Size: broadsheet. Subscrip. Rate: $.50 newsstand/cover; $1.75 newsstand/cover Sun.; $3.65 carrier delivery/wk.. **Wire Service(s):** AP, NYT, LAT-WAT. Circulation: 244,288 morning (paid); 437,578 Sunday (paid). **Owner(s):** Journal Communications, Inc., See address and contact information above. **Bureau(s):** 24 National Press Bldg., Washington, DC 20045. Telephone: 202-488-7755. Contact: Craig Gilbert, Bureau Chief. **Management:** Keith Spore, President. Steven Smith, Chairman of the Board. Richard Dobson, Advertising Director. Hugh McNamel, Circulation Director. **Editorial:** Martin Kaiser, Editor. George Stanley, Managing Editor. Gary Miller, Bus. & Fin. Editor. Michael Ruby, Editorial Page Editor. Diane Bacha, Feature Editor. Dave Vogel, News Editor.

MONROE

MONROE TIMES, THE. ISSN 1068-5820
1065 Fourth Ave., W, Monroe, WI 53566. Telephone: 608-328-4202. FAX: 608-328-4217. URL: http://www.themonroetimes.com. Mailing Address: PO Box 230, Monroe, WI 53566. Year Established: 1898. Pub. Frequency: d. (Mon.-Sat.) Page Size: broadsheet. Subscrip. Rate: $.75 newsstand/cover; $117/yr home delivery. Adv. Rate: col. inch $14.65 **Wire Service(s):** AP. Circulation: 6,300 evening (paid). **Owner(s):** Monroe Publishing LLC, One S Parker Dr., Janesville, WI 53547. Telephone: 608-754-3311. **Management:** Carl Hearing, General Manager. Sidney "Skip" Bliss, President. Laura Hughes, Advertising Manager. Cindy Rotblat, Circulation Manager. Laura Hughes, Classified Adv. Mgr.. **Editorial:** Jeff Rogers, Editor. Jim Winter, News Editor.

OSHKOSH

OSHKOSH NORTHWESTERN. 224 State St., Oshkosh, WI 54902. Telephone: 920-235-7700. FAX: 920-426-6600. E-MAIL: sriechman@oshkosh.gannett.com. URL: http://www.thenorthwestern.com. Mailing Address: PO Box 2926, Oshkosh, WI 54903. Year Established: 1868. Pub. Frequency: d. Page Size: broadsheet. Subscrip. Rate: $.50 newsstand/cover; $1.50 newsstand/cover Sun.; $182/yr carrier delivery; $195/yr motor route; $212.68/yr mailed in state; $249.08/yr mailed out of state. **Wire Service(s):** AP. Circulation: 26,500 morning (paid); 28,500 Sunday (paid). **Owner(s):** Gannett Company, Inc., 7950 Jones Branch Dr, McLean, VA 22107. Telephone: 703-854-6000. **Management:** Kevin Doyle, Publisher. Marilyn Duquaine, Advertising Manager. Amy Reitzke, Circulation Manager. **Editorial:** Stewart Riechman, Editor. Amanda Schultz, Feature Editor. Joe Sienkiewicz, Photographer.

PORTAGE

PORTAGE DAILY REGISTER, THE. ISSN 0747-2927
1640 LaDawn Dr., Portage, WI 53901-0470. Telephone: 608-745-3500. FAX: 608-355-8328. URL: http://www.wiscnews.com. Mailing Address: PO Box 470, Portage, WI 53901-0470. Year Established: 1886. Pub. Frequency: d. (Mon.-Sat.) Page Size: broadsheet. Subscrip. Rate: $.50 newsstand/cover; $.75 newsstand/cover Sat.; $113.60/yr mailed in county; $145.70/yr mailed out of state. **Wire Service(s):** AP. Circulation: 5,500 morning (paid); 5,500 Sunday (paid). **Owner(s):** Capital Newspapers, Inc., 1901 Fish Hatchery Rd., Madison, WI 53713. **Management:** George Althoff, Publisher. Julie Brown, Advertising Manager. Teresa Klinger, Circulation Manager. **Editorial:** Jason Maddux, Editor. Nate Frandsen, Sports Editor.

RACINE

JOURNAL TIMES. ISSN 0746-2867
212 Fourth St., Racine, WI 53403. Telephone: 262-634-3322. FAX: 262-631-1702. E-MAIL: news@journaltimes.com. URL: http://www.journaltimes.com. Year Established: 1857. Pub. Frequency: d. Page Size: standard. Subscrip. Rate: $.50 newsstand/cover; $1.75 newsstand/cover Sun.; $16 carrier delivery/mo.. **Wire Service(s):** AP, MCT. Circulation: 36,385 morning (paid); 40,000 Sunday (paid). **Owner(s):** Lee Enterprises, Inc., 201 N. Harrison St., Ste. 600, Davenport, IA 52801-1924. **Management:** Richard Johnston, Publisher. Michael Rehberg, Circulation Manager. Donna Melby, Classified Adv. Mgr.. **Editorial:** Randy Brandt, Editor. Michael Burke, Business Editor. Sirena Mankins, Feature Editor. Mark Hertzberg, Photo Editor. Sue Shemanske, Sports Editor.

RHINELANDER

DAILY NEWS (RHINELANDER), THE. ISSN 0746-5866
314 Courtney St., Rhinelander, WI 54501. Telephone: 715-365-6397. FAX: 715-365-6367. E-MAIL: malbright@pulitzer.net. URL: http://www.rhinelanderdailynews.com. Mailing Address: PO Box 778, Rhinelander, WI 54501. Year Established: 1882. Pub. Frequency: d. (Sun.-Fri.) Page Size: broadsheet. Subscrip. Rate: $.50 newsstand/cover; $1.25 Sun.; $114/yr carrier delivery; $120/yr in county; $144/yr out of county; $168/yr elsewhere. **Wire Service(s):** AP. Circulation: 5,500 evening (paid); 6,000 Sunday (paid). **Owner(s):** Lee Enterprises, Inc., 900 N. Tucker Blvd., St. Louis, MO 63101. Telephone: 314-340-8000. **Management:** Jay Anderle, Publisher. Jan Juedes, Advertising Manager. Cindy Kennedy, Circulation Manager. Evan Lesch, Business Manager. **Editorial:** Meredith Albright, Managing Editor. Brian Sharp, Sports.

SHAWANO

SHAWANO LEADER. ISSN 0749-7148
1464 E. Green Bay St., Shawano, WI 54166. Telephone: 715-526-2121. FAX: 715-524-3941. E-MAIL: editor@shawanoleader.com. URL: http://www.shawanoleader.com. Mailing Address: PO Box 416, Shawano, WI 54166. Year Established: 1881. Pub. Frequency: d. (Mon.-Fri. & Sat.) Page Size: broadsheet. Subscrip. Rate: $.50 newsstand/cover; $1 newsstand/cover Sun.; $104/yr carrier delivery in city; $127/yr mailed in state; $149/yr mailed out of state. **Wire Service(s):** AP. Circulation: 20,250 evening (paid and free); 6,800 Sunday (paid and free). **Owner(s):** Capital Newspapers, Inc., 1901 Fish Hatchery Rd., Madison, WI 53713. Telephone: 608-252-6200. **Management:** Paul Seveska, Publisher. Chris Kennedy, Advertising Director. Marie Reed, Circulation Director. Patti Peterson, Marketing Director. **Editorial:** Kent Tempus, Editor. Donna Hobscheid, Asst. Managing Ed..

SHEBOYGAN

SHEBOYGAN PRESS, THE. ISSN 0749-7121
632 Center Ave., Sheboygan, WI 53081-0358. Telephone: 920-457-7711. FAX: 920-457-0178. URL: http://www.sheboygan-press.com. Mailing Address: PO Box 358, Sheboygan, WI 53082-0358. Year Established: 1907. Pub. Frequency: d. Page Size: broadsheet. Subscrip. Rate: $.50 newsstand/cover; $1.50 Sun.; $168/yr carrier delivery; $182/yr motor route; $254.15/yr mailed elsewhere. **Wire Service(s):** AP, NYT. Circulation: 27,500 evening (paid); 28,500 Sunday (paid). **Owner(s):** Gannett Company, Inc., 7950 Jones Branch Dr., McLean, VA 22107-0001. Telephone: 703-854-6000. **Management:** Richard Roesgen, Publisher. Scott Harlan, Advertising Director. Manny Nevarez, Circulation Director. **Editorial:** Mike Knuth, Editor. Mike McQuade, Managing Editor. Bob Farina, Feature Editor. Pete Barth, Sports Editor.

STEVENS POINT

STEVENS POINT JOURNAL, THE. ISSN 0748-6332
1200 Third Ct., Stevens Point, WI 54481. Telephone: 715-344-6100. FAX: 715-344-7229. E-MAIL: news@stevenspointjournal.com. URL: http://www.stevenspointjournal.com. Year Established: 1873. Pub. Frequency: d. Page Size: broadsheet. Subscrip. Rate: $.50 newsstand/cover; $1.25 newsstand/cover Sun.; $2.50 carrier delivery/wk.; $65 carrier delivery 26 wks.; $130/yr mailed. **Wire Service(s):** AP, NYT. Circulation: 12,868 evening (paid); 17,632 Sunday (paid). **Owner(s):** Gannett Company, Inc., 7950 Jones Branch Dr., McLean, VA 22107-0001. Telephone: 703-854-6000. **Editorial:** Lisa Nelleson-Lara, Managing Editor. Doug Wojak, Photo.

SUPERIOR

DAILY TELEGRAM (SUPERIOR). 1226 Ogden Ave., Superior, WI 54880. Telephone: 715-394-4411. FAX: 715-394-9404. E-MAIL: telegram@superiorwi.com. URL: http://www.superiorwi.com. Year Established: 1890. Pub. Frequency: d. (Mon.-Sat.) Page Size: broadsheet. Subscrip. Rate: $.50 newsstand/cover; $1 newsstand/cover Sat.; $56.98 home delivery for 6 mos. local; $56.98 motor route for 6 mos. local; $74.88 mailed for 6 mos. in county (effective 2006); $85.80 for 6 mos. out of county. **Wire Service(s):** AP. Circulation: 10,750 evening (paid). **Owner(s):** Superior Publishing Corp., 1105 Tower Ave., Superior, WI 54880-1502. **Management:** Todd Keute, General Manager. Nate Hunt, Circulation Manager. Aaron Becher, Classified Adv. Mgr.. **Editorial:** Rick Lubbers, Managing Editor. Jim Biros, Entertainment Editor. Linda McGonegal, Lifestyle Editor. Ken Olson, Sports.

WATERTOWN

WATERTOWN (WI) DAILY TIMES. ISSN 0885-680X
113-115 W. Main St., Watertown, WI 53094. Telephone: 920-261-5161. FAX: 920-261-5102. E-MAIL: news@wdtimes.com. URL: http://www.wdtimes.com. Mailing Address: PO Box 140, Watertown, WI 53094-0410. Year Established: 1895. Pub. Frequency: d. (Mon.-Sat.) Page Size: broadsheet. Subscrip. Rate: $.50 newsstand/cover; $130/yr carrier delivery; $140/yr motor route; $132/yr mailed in state & out of state. **Wire Service(s):** AP. Circulation: 9,100 evening (paid). **Owner(s):** Times Publishing Co., See address and contact information above. **Management:** Kevin C. Clifford, General Manager. James M. Clifford, Publisher. Judy A. Kluetzman, Advertising Manager. Mark D. Kuehl, Circulation Manager. Mark Shingler, Classified Adv. Mgr.. Ralph H. Krueger, Business Manager. **Editorial:** Thomas Schultz, Managing Editor. Kevin Wilson, Sports Editor.

WAUKESHA

WAUKESHA FREEMAN. ISSN 1062-9041
801 N. Barstow St., Waukesha, WI 53187-0007. Telephone: 262-542-2501. FAX: 262-542-2015. URL: http://www.gmtoday.com. Mailing Address: PO Box 7, Waukesha, WI 53187-0007. Year Established: 1859. Pub. Frequency: d. (Mon.-Sat.) Page Size: broadsheet. Subscrip. Rate: $.50 newsstand/cover; $.75 newsstand/cover Sat.; $112.32/yr carrier delivery; $121.68/yr motor route. Adv. Rate: col. inch $19.35 **Wire Service(s):** AP, MCT. Circulation: 17,000 evening (paid). **Owner(s):** Conley Publishing Group, Ltd., 119 Monroe St., Beaver Dam, WI 53916. Telephone: 920-885-7800. **Management:** Phil Paige, Publisher. Jim Baumgart, Advertising Manager. Art Montgomery, Circulation Director. Tina Wolf, Classified Adv. Mgr.. **Editorial:** Bill Yorth, Editor. Lee Fensin, Sports Editor.

WAUSAU

WAUSAU DAILY HERALD. ISSN 0887-4271
800 Scott St., Wausau, WI 54401. Telephone: 715-842-2101. FAX: 715-848-9360. URL: http://www.wausaudailyherald.com. Mailing Address: PO Box 1286, Wausau, WI 54403-1286. Year Established: 1907. Pub. Frequency: d. Page Size: broadsheet. Subscrip. Rate: $.50 newsstand/cover; $1.50 newsstand/cover Sun.; $38.35 home delivery for 3 months; $40.95 motor route for 3 months. Adv. Rate: col. inch $31.21 **Wire Service(s):** AP, GNS. Circulation: 30,000 evening (paid); 33,000 Sunday (paid). **Owner(s):** Gannett Company, Inc., 7950 Jones Branch Dr., McLean, VA 22107-0001. Telephone: 703-854-6000. **Management:** Genia Lovett, Publisher. Sandy Falk, Advertising Director. Scott Hehir, Advertising Manager. Bobby Novak, Circulation Manager. **Editorial:** Mark Baldwin, Executive Editor. Jamie Orcutt, Feature Editor. Pete Wasson, Opinion Editor. Rob Orcutt, Photographer. Mark Multer, Sports Editor.

WEST BEND

DAILY NEWS (WEST BEND). ISSN 0899-2444
100 S. Sixth Ave., West Bend, WI 53095. Telephone: 262-306-5000. FAX: 262-338-1984. E-MAIL: dailynews@conleynet.com. URL: http://daily.fnpinteractive.com/. Mailing Address: PO Box 478, West Bend, WI 53095. Year Established: 1855. Pub. Frequency: d. (Mon.-Sat.) Page Size: broadsheet. Subscrip. Rate: $.50 newsstand/cover; $119.50/yr motor route. Adv. Rate: col. inch $12.92 **Wire Service(s):** AP. Circulation: 11,500 evening (paid). **Owner(s):** Conley Publishing Group, Ltd., 119 Monroe St., Beaver Dam, WI 53916. Telephone: 920-885-7800. **Management:** Steve Ciccantelli, Publisher. Lois Evans, Advertising Manager. Kristi Wolf, Classified Adv. Mgr.. **Editorial:** Jill Badzinski, Managing Editor.

WISCONSIN RAPIDS

DAILY TRIBUNE. 220 First Ave., S., Wisconsin Rapids, WI 54495-8090. Telephone: 715-423-7200. FAX: 715-421-1545. E-MAIL: tribune@wctc.net. URL: http://www.wisconsinrapidstribune.com. Mailing Address: P.O. Box 8090, Wisconsin Rapids, WI 54495-8090. Year Established: 1914. Pub. Frequency: d. (Mon.-Sat.) Page Size: broadsheet. Subscrip. Rate: $.50 newsstand/cover; $1.25 newsstand/cover Sun.; $12/mo. local; $188/yr mailed; $198/yr mailed out of area. **Wire Service(s):** AP. Circulation: 14,132 evening (paid). **Owner(s):** Gannett Company, Inc., 7950 Jones Branch Dr, McLean, VA 22107. Telephone: 703-854-6000. **Management:** Helen Jungworth, Publisher. Steve Bandy, Sales Manager. **Editorial:** Allen Hicks, Managing Editor. Jamie Jung-Rokus, Lifestyle Editor.

WYOMING

CASPER

CASPER STAR TRIBUNE. 170 Star Ln., Casper, WY 82604. Telephone: 307-266-0500. FAX: 307-266-0501. URL: http://www.casperstartribune.net. Mailing Address: PO Box 80, Casper, WY 82602. Year Established: 1891. Pub. Frequency: d. Page Size: broadsheet. Subscrip. Rate: $.50 newsstand/cover; $.56 newsstand/cover Sun.; $192/yr home delivery local. **Wire Service(s):** AP, NYT. Circulation: 30,502 morning (paid); 32,255 Sunday (paid). **Owner(s):** Lee Enterprises, Inc., 201 N. Harrison St., Davenport, IA 52801-1924. **Management:** Nathan Bekke, Publisher. Ryan Moffat, Advertising Director. Maurice Elhart, Circulation Director. Ron Kay, Business Manager. **Editorial:** Clark Walworth, Executive Editor.

CHEYENNE

WYOMING TRIBUNE-EAGLE. ISSN 1075-783X
702 W. Lincolnway, Cheyenne, WY 82001. Telephone: 307-634-3361. FAX: 307-633-3189. URL: http://www.wyomingnews.com. Year Established: 1867. Pub. Frequency: d. Page Size: broadsheet. Subscrip. Rate: $.50 newsstand/cover; $.75 newsstand/cover for Wed.; $1.25 newsstand/cover Sun.; $137.50/yr carrier delivery; $148.50/yr motor route; $240/yr mailed out of county. **Wire Service(s):** AP. Circulation: 16,425 morning (paid); 18,176 Sunday (paid). **Owner(s):** Cheyenne Newspapers, Inc., See address and contact information above. **Management:** L. Michael McCracken, Publisher. Scott Walker, Advertising Director. LaShay Hernandez, Classified Adv. Mgr.. Larry Catalano, Business Manager. **Editorial:** D. Reed Eckhardt, Executive Editor. Brian K. Martin, Managing Editor. Scott Smith, Editorial Page Editor. Michael Smith, Photo Editor. Robert Gagliard, Sports Editor.

LARAMIE

LARAMIE BOOMERANG. 320 E. Grand Ave., Laramie, WY 82070-3712. Telephone: 307-742-2176. FAX: 307-742-2046. URL: http://www.laramieboomerang.com. Year Established: 1881. Pub. Frequency: d. (Tue.-Sun.) Page Size: broadsheet. Subscrip. Rate: $.50 newsstand/cover; $1.50 Sun.; $103/yr home delivery; $125/yr mailed in state; $182/yr mailed elsewhere. Adv. Rate: col. inch $11.20 **Wire Service(s):** AP. Circulation: 6,179 morning (paid); 6,487 Sunday (paid). **Owner(s):** Laramie Newspapers, Inc., See address and contact information above. **Management:** Don Black, Publisher. Matt Petrie, Advertising Director. Steve Warner, Circulation Manager. Dianne Gallatin, Classified Adv. Mgr.. **Editorial:** Deb Thomsen, Managing Editor. Bob Hammond, Sports.

RAWLINS

RAWLINS DAILY TIMES, THE. 522 W Buffalo, Rawlins, WY 82301. Telephone: 307-324-3411. FAX: 307-324-2797. E-MAIL: dtimes@tribcsp.com. Mailing Address: PO Box 370, Rawlins, WY 82301-0370. Year Established: 1890. Pub. Frequency: d. (Tue.-Sat.) Page Size: tabloid. Subscrip. Rate: $.50 newsstand/cover; $65/yr carrier delivery; $75/yr mailed. Adv. Rate: col. inch $7 **Wire Service(s):** AP. Circulation: 3,870 morning (paid). **Owner(s):** Rawlins Newspapers, Inc., See address and contact information above. **Management:** Shelley Ridenaur, Publisher. Shelley Ridenour, Advertising Manager. Linda Brantner, Circulation Manager. **Editorial:** Kyle Dudo, Sports Writer.

RIVERTON

RANGER, THE. 421 E. Main St., Riverton, WY 82501. Telephone: 307-856-2244. FAX: 307-856-0189. E-MAIL: ranger@wyoming.com. URL: http://www.dailyranger.com. Mailing Address: P.O. Box 993, Riverton, WY 82501-0993. Year Established: 1953. Pub. Frequency: d. (Sun.-Fri.) Page Size: broadsheet. Subscrip. Rate: $.50 newsstand/cover; $60/yr home delivery. **Wire Service(s):** AP. Circulation: 7,280 evening (paid). **Owner(s):** Robert & Steve Peck, See address and contact information above. **Management:** Robert A Peck, President. Heidi Coulson, Advertising Manager. Carl Manning, Circulation Manager. Steve Peck, Associate Publisher. **Editorial:** Steve Peck, Editor. Robert A Peck, Editorial Page Editor. Steve Peck, Education Editor. Bruce Tippets, Sports Editor.

Dailies

ROCK SPRINGS

DAILY ROCKET-MINER.   ISSN 0893-3650
215 D St, Rock Springs, WY 82901. Telephone: 307-362-3736.
E-MAIL: publisher@rocketminer.com. URL:
http://www.rocketminer.com. Mailing Address: P.O. Box 98, Rock
Springs, WY 82902-0098. Year Established: 1880. Pub.
Frequency: d. (Tue.-Sat.) Page Size: broadsheet. Subscrip. Rate:
$.50 newsstand/cover; $80/yr carrier delivery; $100/yr mailed in
county; $110/yr mailed in state. Freelance Pay: $0.20/column-inch.
Wire Service(s): AP. Circulation: 8,361 morning (paid). **Owner(s):**
Rock Springs Newspapers, Inc., See address and contact
information above. **Management:** Holly Dabb, Publisher. Rick Lee,
Advertising Manager. Pam Haynes, Circulation Manager. Stacey.
Turcate, Business Manager. **Editorial:** Michele Depue, Editor.
Carlos Harryman, Photographer.

SHERIDAN

SHERIDAN PRESS.   ISSN 1074-682X
144 Grinnell St., Sheridan, WY 82801. Telephone: 307-672-2431.
FAX: 307-672-7950. URL: http://www.thesheridanpress.com.
Mailing Address: P.O. Box 2006, Sheridan, WY 82801. Year
Established: 1886. Pub. Frequency: d. (Mon.-Sat.) Page Size:
broadsheet. Subscrip. Rate: $.50 newsstand/cover; $93/yr carrier
delivery; $105/yr mailed. **Wire Service(s):** AP. Circulation: 12,500
evening (paid). **Owner(s):** Sheridan Newspapers, See address
and contact information above. **Management:** Carl Sanders,
Publisher. Rick Schmidt, Operations Manager. Aimee Fabre,
Circulation Manager. **Editorial:** Patrick Murphy, Managing Editor.
Pat Blair, Society Editor. Ken Hamrick, Sports Editor.

WORLAND

NORTHERN WYOMING DAILY NEWS, 201 N. Eighth, Worland, WY
82401. Telephone: 307-347-3241. FAX: 307-347-4267. E-MAIL:
nwdn@trib.com. Year Established: 1905. Pub. Frequency: d.
(Tue.-Sat.) Page Size: broadsheet. Subscrip. Rate: $.50
newsstand/cover; $30.25 mailed for 6 mos. in county; $77.50/yr
mailed in county. **Wire Service(s):** AP. Circulation: 5,000 morning
(paid). **Owner(s):** Big Horn Basin Newspapers, Inc., See address
and contact information above. **Management:** Lee Lockhart,
President. Dustin Fuller, Advertising. Dennis Koch, Circulation
Manager. **Editorial:** Lee Lockhart, Editor-in-Chief. Bobby
Matthews, Managing Editor. Judy Lockhart, Sports Editor.

Weekly Newspaper

ALABAMA

ABBEVILLE

ABBEVILLE HERALD. PO Box 609, Abbeville, AL 36310. Telephone: 334-585-2331. FAX: 334-585-6875. E-MAIL: herald@ala.net. Year Established: 1941. Pub. Frequency: w. (Thu.) Page Size: tabloid. Subscrip. Rate: $.50 newsstand/cover; $19.98/yr mailed in county; $26.46/yr mailed out of county; $28.25/yr mailed out of state. Circulation: 2,350 per issue (paid). **Owner(s):** J. Edward Dodd, III, See address and contact information above. **Management:** J. Edward Dodd III, Publisher. **Editorial:** J. Edward Dodd III, Editor.

ALBERTVILLE

SAND MOUNTAIN REPORTER, THE. 1603 Progress Dr., Albertville, AL 35950. Telephone: 256-840-3000. FAX: 256-840-2987. E-MAIL: news@sandmountainreporter.com. URL: http://www.sandmountainreporter.com. Mailing Address: PO Box 1729, Albertville, AL 35950. Year Established: 1955. Pub. Frequency: 3/w. (Tue., Thu., Sat.) Page Size: broadsheet. Subscrip. Rate: $.50 newsstand/cover; $35.50/yr in county; $57/yr out of county. **Wire Service(s):** AP. Circulation: 10,241 per issue (controlled and free). **Owner(s):** Southern Newspapers of Alabama, Inc., 5701 Woodway Dr., Ste. 131, Houston, TX 77057-1589. **Management:** Martha Walls, President. Ben Shurett, Publisher. Teresa Lien, Advertising Manager. Linda Allen, Classified Adv. Mgr.. **Editorial:** Ben Shurett, Editor. David Clemons, Managing Editor.

ALEXANDER CITY

DADEVILLE RECORD. 548 Cherokee Rd, Alexander City, AL 35010. Telephone: 256-234-4281. FAX: 256-234-6550. E-MAIL: acoutlook@webshoppe.net. URL: http://www.thedadevillerecord.com. Mailing Address: P.O. Box 999, Alexander City, AL 35011. Year Established: 1896. Pub. Frequency: w. (Thu.) Page Size: standard. Subscrip. Rate: $.50 newsstand/cover; $25/yr mailed in county. Circulation: 1,700 per issue (paid). **Owner(s):** Boone Newspapers, Inc., 15222 Freemen's Bend Rd., Northport, AL 35475. Telephone: 205-330-4100. **Management:** Tim Reeves, Publisher. Drew Heederick, Circulation Manager. **Editorial:** Laura McAlister, Managing Editor. Brandon Shields, Sports Editor.

ARAB

ARAB TRIBUNE. 619 S. Brindlee Mountain Pkwy., Arab, AL 35016-1502. Telephone: 256-586-3188. FAX: 256-586-3190. E-MAIL: tribnews@otelco.net. Year Established: 1958. Pub. Frequency: s-w. (Wed. & Sat.) Page Size: broadsheet. Subscrip. Rate: $.50 newsstand/cover; $19/yr local; $30/yr elsewhere. Circulation: 6,400 per issue (paid). **Owner(s):** Edwin H. Reed, See address and contact information above. **Management:** Edwin H. Reed, Publisher. Phil Baker, Advertising Manager. **Editorial:** David Moore, Editor.

ATMORE

ATMORE ADVANCE. ISSN 0746-1968
301 S Main St, Atmore, AL 36504. Telephone: 251-368-2123. E-MAIL: prcarter@frontiernet.net. Year Established: 1927. Pub. Frequency: s-w. (Wed. & Sun.) Page Size: broadsheet. Subscrip. Rate: $.75 newsstand/cover; $50/yr carrier delivery domestic area; $60/yr in state; $65/yr out of state. Freelance Pay: $0.05/column-inch. Circulation: 10,000 per issue (paid). **Owner(s):** Boone Newspapers, Inc., P O Box 28, Atmore, AL 36504. PO Box 2370, Tuscaloosa, AL 35403. Telephone: 205-752-3381. FAX: 205-752-3392. **Management:** Chuck Bodiford, Publisher. Lauri Hall, Advertising. Blaire Nassar, Circulation Manager. **Editorial:** Arthur McLean, Managing Editor.

AUBURN

CORNER NEWS, THE. 117 N. College St., Auburn, AL 36831-3240. Telephone: 334-821-7150. FAX: 334-887-0037. E-MAIL: virginiafarmer@thecornernews.com. URL: http://www.thecornernews.com. Mailing Address: PO Box 3240, Auburn, AL 36831-3240. Year Established: 1937. Pub. Frequency: w. (Wed.) Page Size: broadsheet Circulation: 10,000 per issue (paid). **Owner(s):** Media General, Inc., 333 E. Franklin St., Richmond, VA 23219. Telephone: 804-649-6000. **Management:** James Rainey, Publisher. **Editorial:** Virginia Farmer, Editor.

BAY MINETTE

BALDWIN TIMES. 329 Courthouse Sq., Bay Minette, AL 36507. Telephone: 251-937-2511. FAX: 251-937-1637. E-MAIL: timenews@gulftel.com. Mailing Address: PO Box 519, Bay Minette, AL 36507. Year Established: 1890. Pub. Frequency: w. (Thu.) Page Size: broadsheet. Subscrip. Rate: $.50 newsstand/cover; $26.75/yr home delivery local; $39/yr mailed out of state. Circulation: 4,000 per issue (paid). **Owner(s):** Crescent Media Group, See address and contact information above. **Management:** James G. Walther, Group Publisher. Dave Williams, Advertising Director. Jeannette Chandler, Classified Adv. Mgr.. **Editorial:** Dan Rutledge, Editor.

BESSEMER

WESTERN STAR. 1709 Third Ave N., Bessemer, AL 35020. Telephone: 205-424-7827. FAX: 205-424-8118. E-MAIL: editor@thewesternstarnews.com. Mailing Address: PO Box 1900, Bessemer, AL 35021. Year Established: 1984. Pub. Frequency: w. (Wed.) Page Size: broadsheet. Subscrip. Rate: $.50 newsstand/cover; $24.80/yr local; $29/yr out of area; $33/yr out of state. Adv. Rate: col. inch $7.90 Circulation: 9,000 per issue (paid). **Owner(s):** Tribble Publications, Inc., PO Box 648, Manchester, GA 31816. Telephone: 706-846-4336. **Management:** Robert Tribble, President. Dan Delonge, Publisher. Julie Bradley, Office Manager. **Editorial:** Dan Delonge, Editor.

BIRMINGHAM

ALABAMA MESSENGER. 205 N. 20th St., Ste. 706, Birmingham, AL 35203. Telephone: 205-252-3672. FAX: 205-252-3679. Year Established: 1959. Pub. Frequency: w. (Sat.) Page Size: broadsheet. Subscrip. Rate: $.25 newsstand/cover; $10/yr mailed. Circulation: 2,500 per issue (paid). **Owner(s):** Alabama Messenger, 205 N. 20th St., Ste. 706, Birmingham, AL 35103. Telephone: 205-252-3672. **Management:** Traci A. Smeraglia, Advertising Manager. **Editorial:** Karen Abercrombie, Editor.

BIRMINGHAM WEEKLY. 2014 6th Ave N, Birmingham, AL 35203-2702. Telephone: 205-939-4030. FAX: 205-212-1005. E-MAIL: editor@bhamweekly.com. URL: http://www.birminghamweekly.com/. Year Established: 1997. Pub. Frequency: w. (Thu.) Page Size: tabloid Circulation: 30,000 per issue (free). **Owner(s):** Birmingham Weekly Publishing Co. Inc., See address and contact information above. **Editorial:** Glenny Brock, Managing Editor.

OVER THE MOUNTAIN JOURNAL. 2016 Columbiana Rd., Birmingham, AL 35216. Telephone: 205-823-9646. FAX: 205-824-1246. URL: http://www.bham.net. Mailing Address: PO Box 660502, Birmingham, AL 35216. Year Established: 1980. Pub. Frequency: bi-m. Page Size: tabloid. Subscrip. Rate: $24/yr mailed. Circulation: 44,000 per issue (paid and free). **Owner(s):** Maurice G. Wald, III, See address and contact information above. **Management:** Maurice G. Wald III, Publisher. Butch Glass, Circulation Manager. **Editorial:** Cara Morrison, Editor-in-Chief.

THOMASTON TIMES, THE. 3500 Collonade Pkwy., Ste 600, Birmingham, AL 35243. URL: www.thomastontimes.com. Mailing Address: PO Box 430, Thomaston, GA 30286. Year Established: 1868. Pub. Frequency: 3/w. (Mon., Wed., Fri.) Page Size: broadsheet. Subscrip. Rate: $.75 newsstand/cover; $45/yr home delivery local; $55/yr mailed in state; $65/yr mailed elsewhere. Circulation: 6,500 per issue (paid and free); 5,000 per issue (paid and controlled). **Owner(s):** Thomaston Publishing Co., Inc., See address and contact information above. **Management:** Debbie Black, Publisher. Don Powers, Advertising Manager. Willie Green, Circulation Manager. Linda Knight, Classified Adv. Mgr.. **Editorial:** Kelly Stephenson, Editor. Billy Vaughn, News.

BREWTON

BREWTON STANDARD, THE. 407 St. Nicholas Ave., Brewton, AL 36426. Telephone: 251-867-4876. FAX: 251-867-4877. E-MAIL: newsroon@brewtonstandard.com. URL: http://www.brewtonstandard.com. Mailing Address: PO Box 887, Brewton, AL 36427. Year Established: 1906. Pub. Frequency: s-w. (Wed. & Sun.) Page Size: broadsheet. Subscrip. Rate: $.75 newsstand/cover; $50/yr mailed in county; $62.32/yr mailed out of county; $70.20/yr mailed out of state. Circulation: 4,200 per issue (paid). **Owner(s):** Boone Newspapers, PO Box 2370, Tuscaloosa, AL 35403. Telephone: 205-752-3381. **Management:** Kerry Whipple Bean, Publisher. Marilyn Raines, Advertising Director. Rodica Angel, Circulation Manager. Charity Welcher, Classified Adv. Mgr.. **Editorial:** Mary-Allison Lancaster, Managing Editor. Bruce Hixon, Sports Editor.

BUTLER

CHOCTAW ADVOCATE. 210 N. Mulberry St., Butler, AL 36904. Telephone: 205-459-2858. FAX: 205-459-3000. E-MAIL: choctawadvocate@tds.net. Mailing Address: PO Box 475, Butler, AL 36904. Year Established: 1890. Pub. Frequency: w. (Thu.) Page Size: standard. Subscrip. Rate: $.75 newsstand/cover; $20.52/yr mailed in county; $28.08/yr mailed out of county; $29/yr mailed out of state. **Wire Service(s):** AP. Circulation: 4,600 per issue (paid). **Owner(s):** Choctaw Advocate, Inc., See address and contact information above. **Management:** Elaine Shields, Advertising Manager. Sharon Shepard, Circulation Manager. **Editorial:** Jenna Doggett Robbins, Managing Editor.

CAMDEN

WILCOX PROGRESSIVE ERA. P.O. Box 100, Camden, AL 36726-0100. Telephone: 334-682-4422. FAX: 334-682-5163. E-MAIL: progressiveera@mchsi.com. Year Established: 1860. Pub. Frequency: w. (Wed.) Page Size: standard. Subscrip. Rate: $.50 newsstand/cover; $30/yr in county; $37/yr out of county. Adv. Rate: col. inch $5.90 Circulation: 3,060 per issue (paid). **Owner(s):** M. Hollis Curl, PO Box 100, Camden, AL 36726. Telephone: 334-682-4422. **Management:** M. Hollis Curl, President. LeAnn Stallings, Advertising Manager. **Editorial:** M. Hollis Curl, Editor.

CARROLLTON

PICKENS COUNTY HERALD. 215 Reform St., Carrollton, AL 35447-0390. Telephone: 205-367-2217. FAX: 205-367-2217. E-MAIL: theherald@pickens.net. URL: http://www.theherald-pickens.net. Mailing Address: PO Box 390, Carrollton, AL 35447-0390. Year Established: 1848. Pub. Frequency: w. (Wed.) Page Size: standard. Subscrip. Rate: $.50 newsstand/cover; $25/yr mailed in county; $36/yr mailed in adj. counties. Adv. Rate: col. inch $7.35 Circulation: 5,500 per issue (paid). **Owner(s):** Hershel Lake, PO Box 390, Carrollton, AL 35447. Telephone: 205-367-2217. **Management:** Hershel Lake, President. Doug Sanders, Publisher. **Editorial:** Doug Sanders, Editor.

CENTRE

CHEROKEE COUNTY HERALD. 107 1st Ave W, Centre, AL 35960-1901. Telephone: 256-927-5037. FAX: 256-927-4853. E-MAIL: kroe@cherokeeherald.com. URL: http://www.cherokeeherald.com. Year Established: 1938. Pub. Frequency: w. (Wed.) Page Size: broadsheet. Subscrip. Rate: $.50 newsstand/cover; $27/yr mailed in county; $41.40/yr mailed out of county; $40/yr mailed out of state. Adv. Rate: col. inch $7.57 Freelance Pay: $0.60/column-inch. Circulation: 3,611 per issue (paid). **Owner(s):** News Publishing Co., PO Box 1633, Rome, GA 30162. **Management:** Kathy Roe, Publisher. Vickie Evans Robinson, Advertising Manager. **Editorial:** Kathy Roe, Editor.

CENTREVILLE

CENTREVILLE PRESS. 32 Court Sq., W., Centreville, AL 35042. Telephone: 205-926-9769. FAX: 205-926-9760. E-MAIL: cpress@dbtech.net. Mailing Address: PO Box 127, Centreville, AL 35042-0127. Year Established: 1879. Pub. Frequency: w. (Wed.) Page Size: broadsheet. Subscrip. Rate: $.50 newsstand/cover; $21.60/yr mailed in county; $35/yr mailed out of state. Circulation: 4,200 per issue (paid). **Owner(s):** Trib Publications, Inc., PO Box 648, Manchester, GA 31816. Telephone: 706-846-4336. **Management:** Lorrie Rinehart, General Manager. **Editorial:** Lorrie Rinehart, Editor.

CHATOM

WASHINGTON COUNTY NEWS (CHATOM). PO Box 510, Chatom, AL 36518. Telephone: 251-847-2599. FAX: 251-847-3847. E-MAIL: wcnews@millry.net. Year Established: 1892. Pub. Frequency: w. (Wed.) Page Size: standard. Subscrip. Rate: $.50 newsstand/cover; $23.76/yr in county; $28.08/yr out of county. Circulation: 4,000 per issue (paid). **Owner(s):** Shirley Specht, See address and contact information above. **Management:** Cathy Beach, General Manager. Shirley Specht, Publisher. **Editorial:** Shirley Specht, Editor. Jillian Pope, Sports.

CITRONELLE

CALL NEWS, THE. 7870 State St., Citronelle, AL 36522. Telephone: 251-866-5998. FAX: 251-866-5981. E-MAIL: callnews@bellsouth.net. URL: http://www.thecallnews.com. Year Established: 1897. Pub. Frequency: w. (Wed.) Page Size: broadsheet. Subscrip. Rate: $.50 newsstand/cover; $19.50/yr home delivery; $28/yr mailed out of state. Adv. Rate: col. inch $6 Circulation: 12,500 per issue (paid). **Owner(s):** Willa Gray, See address and contact information above. **Management:** Willie Gray, Owner. Rhonda Gray, Publisher. **Editorial:** Nikki Whitner, Editor.

CLAYTON

CLAYTON RECORD. PO Box 69, Clayton, AL 36016. Telephone: 334-775-3254. FAX: 334-775-8554. E-MAIL: clayrecord@earthlink.net. Pub. Frequency: w. (Thu.) Page Size: broadsheet. Subscrip. Rate: $.50 newsstand/cover; $20/yr mailed in state; $22/yr mailed out of state. Adv. Rate: col. inch $5.25 Circulation: 2,500 per issue (paid). **Owner(s):** Rebecca P. Beasley, See address and contact information above. **Management:** Rebecca Beasley, Publisher. **Editorial:** Rebecca Beasley, Managing Editor.

COLUMBIANA

SHELBY COUNTY REPORTER. ISSN 1063-9489
115 Main St., Columbiana, AL 35051. Telephone: 205-669-3131. FAX: 205-669-4217. E-MAIL: shelbynews@shelbycountyreporter.com. URL: http://www.shelbycountyreporter.com. Mailing Address: PO Box 947, Columbiana, AL 35051. Year Established: 1843. Pub. Frequency: w. (Wed.) Page Size: broadsheet. Subscrip. Rate: $.50 newsstand/cover; $29.15/yr carrier delivery; $20.52/yr carrier delivery to senior citizens; $53.60/yr mailed out of state. Circulation: 11,235 per issue (paid). **Owner(s):** Boone Newspapers, Inc., PO Box 2370, Tuscaloosa, AL 35403. Telephone: 205-752-3381. **Management:** Tim Prince, Publisher. Allen Matthew, Advertising Manager. **Editorial:** Tim Prince, Editor. Asley Vanfant, Managing Editor. Justin Averette, News Editor.

CULLMAN

CULLMAN TRIBUNE. ISSN 0739-523X
219 Second Ave., S.E., Cullman, AL 35055-3513. Telephone: 256-739-1351. FAX: 256-739-4422. E-MAIL: culltrib@bellsouth.net. Year Established: 1874. Pub. Frequency: w. (Thu.) Page Size: broadsheet. Subscrip. Rate: $.50 newsstand/cover; $30/yr home delivery in county; $40/yr mailed out of county. Freelance Pay: $8/column-inch. Circulation: 16,000 per issue (paid). **Owner(s):** Delton Blalock, See address and contact information above. **Management:** Robin Vest, General Manager. Delton Blalock, Publisher. Shirley Ludlow, Advertising Manager. Robin Vest, Circulation Manager. **Editorial:** Delton Blalock, Editor.

DAPHNE

DAPHNE BULLETIN. 1805 Main St., Daphne, AL 36526. Telephone: 251-626-9300. FAX: 251-626-0144. Mailing Address: PO Box 1560, Daphne, AL 36526. Pub. Frequency: s-w. (Wed. & Sat.) Page Size: standard. Subscrip. Rate: $.50 newsstand/cover; $35.50/yr in county; $37.50/yr out of county. Circulation: 2,850 per issue (paid). **Owner(s):** Crescent Media Group, PO Box 1634, Spartanburg, SC 29304. Telephone: 864-583-2907. **Management:** James G. Walther, Group Publisher. Sharell Duddy, Advertising. **Editorial:** Wendy Ladnier, Editor.

DEMOPOLIS

BLACKBELT GAZETTE. 115 E Washington St, Demopolis, AL 36732. Telephone: 334-289-2013. FAX: 334-289-2014. E-MAIL: news@blackbeltgazette.com. URL: http://www.blackbeltgazette.com. Year Established: 2003. Pub. Frequency: w. (Wed.) Page Size: tabloid. Subscrip. Rate: $20/yr. Adv. Rate: col. inch $9 Circulation: 10,913 per issue (paid). **Owner(s):** Boone Newspapers, Inc., 15222 Freemen's Bend Rd., Northport, AL 35475. Telephone: 205-330-4100. **Management:** Lee Parker, Publisher. Charlie Partridge, Advertising. Janet Marlowe, Advertising Manager. **Editorial:** Leewanna Parker, Editor. Kathy Odom, Production Manager. Charlie Partridge, Photographer.

CLARKE COUNTY SHOPPERS GUIDE. 315 E. Jefferson St., Demopolis, AL 36732. Telephone: 334-289-4017. FAX: 334-289-4019. E-MAIL: demtimes@westal.net. URL: Http://www.demopolistimes.com. Mailing Address: PO Box 860, Demopolis, AL 36732.Pub. Frequency: w. Circulation: 12,000 per issue (free). **Owner(s):** Boone Newspapers, Inc., 15222 Freemen's Bend Rd., Northport, AL 35475. Telephone: 205-330-4100. **Management:** Sam R Hall, Publisher. Brandy Philips, Advertising Manager. **Editorial:** Gennie Phillips, Managing Editor.

GREEN/HALE SHOPPERS GUIDE. 315 E. Jefferson St., Demopolis, AL 36732. Telephone: 334-289-4017. FAX: 334-289-4019. E-MAIL: demtimes@westal.net. URL: http://www.demopolistimes.com. Mailing Address: PO Box 860, Demopolis, AL 36732.Pub. Frequency: w. Circulation: 12,400 per issue (free). **Owner(s):** Boone Newspapers, Inc., 15222 Freemen's Bend Rd., Northport, AL 35475. Telephone: 205-330-4100. **Management:** Sam R Hall, Publisher. Brandy Philips, Advertising Manager. **Editorial:** Gennie Phillips, Managing Editor.

MARENGO COUNTY SHOPPERS GUIDE. 315 E. Jefferson St., Demopolis, AL 36732. Telephone: 334-289-4017. FAX: 334-289-4019. E-MAIL: demtimes@westal.net. URL: http://www.demopolistimes.com. Mailing Address: PO Box 860, Demopolis, AL 36732.Pub. Frequency: w. Circulation: 9,200 per issue (free). **Owner(s):** Boone Newspapers, Inc., 15222 Freemen's Bend Rd., Northport, AL 35475. Telephone: 205-330-4100. **Management:** Sam R Hall, Publisher. Brandy Philips, Advertising Manager. Heather Miller, Circulation Manager. Brandy Maddox, Classified Adv. Mgr.. **Editorial:** Sam R Hall, Editor. Gennie Phillips, Managing Editor.

WILCOX COUNTY SHOPPERS GUIDE. 315 E. Jefferson St., Demopolis, AL 36732. Telephone: 334-289-4017. FAX: 334-289-4019. E-MAIL: demtimes@westal.net. URL: http://www.demopolistimes.com. Mailing Address: PO Box 860, Demopolis, AL 36732.Pub. Frequency: w. Circulation: 5,200 per issue (free). **Owner(s):** Boone Newspapers, Inc., 15222 Freemen's Bend Rd., Northport, AL 35475. Telephone: 205-330-4100. **Management:** Sam R Hall, Publisher. Brandy Philips, Advertising Manager. **Editorial:** Gennie Phillips, Managing Editor.

DOTHAN

ASHFORD POWER. 227 N. Oats St., Dothan, AL 36303. Telephone: 334-792-3141. FAX: 334-712-7975. E-MAIL: ebrackin@dothanprogress.com. Mailing Address: PO Box 1968, Dothan, AL 36302. Pub. Frequency: w. (Thu.) Page Size: broadsheet. Subscrip. Rate: $.50 newsstand/cover; $15/yr in county; $18/yr out of county. Circulation: 1,100 per issue (paid). **Owner(s):** Media General, Inc., 333 E. Franklin St., Richmond, VA 23219. Telephone: 804-649-6000. **Management:** Alan Davis, Publisher. Jerry Morgan, Advertising Manager. Marshall Andrews, Circulation Manager. **Editorial:** Elaine Brackin, Editor.

DOTHAN PROGRESS. 227 N. Oats St., Dothan, AL 36303. Telephone: 334-792-3141. FAX: 334-712-7975. E-MAIL: ebrackin@dothanprogress.com. Mailing Address: PO Box 1968, Dothan, AL 36302-1968. Pub. Frequency: w. (Thu.) Page Size: broadsheet. Subscrip. Rate: $.50 newsstand/cover; $15/yr mailed in county; $18/yr mailed out of county. Circulation: 7,500 per issue (paid). **Owner(s):** Media General, Inc., 333 E. Franklin St., Richmond, VA 23219. Telephone: 804-649-6000. **Management:** Alan Davis, Publisher. Jerry Morgan, Advertising Manager. Marshall Andrews, Circulation Manager. **Editorial:** Elaine Brackin, Editor.

HEADLAND OBSERVER. 227 N. Oates St., Dothan, AL 36303. E-MAIL: ebrackin@dothanprogress.com. Mailing Address: PO Box 1968, Dothan, AL 36302-1968. Year Established: 1965. Pub. Frequency: w. (Thu.) Page Size: broadsheet. Subscrip. Rate: $.50 newsstand/cover; $15/yr in county; $18/yr out of county; $21/yr mailed out of state. Circulation: 2,000 per issue (paid). **Owner(s):** Media General, Inc., 333 E. Franklin St., Richmond, VA 23219. Telephone: 804-649-6000. **Management:** Alan Davis, Publisher. Jerry Morgan, Advertising Manager. Marshall Andrews, Circulation Manager. **Editorial:** Elaine Brackin, Editor.

ELBA

ELBA CLIPPER, THE. 417 W. Buford St., Elba, AL 36323. Telephone: 334-897-2823. FAX: 334-897-7434. E-MAIL: clipper@2laweb.com. Mailing Address: PO Box 677, Elba, AL 36323-0677. Year Established: 1897. Pub. Frequency: w. (Thu.) Page Size: broadsheet. Subscrip. Rate: $.50 newsstand/cover; $19/yr in county; $21/yr mailed out of county; $24/yr mailed out of state. Adv. Rate: col. inch $4.50 Circulation: 3,200 per issue (paid). **Owner(s):** John Ferrin Cox, See address and contact information above. **Management:** John Ferrin Cox, Publisher. Heddy J. Cox, Business Manager. **Editorial:** Linda Hodge, Editor. Ricky Mularz, Sports Editor.

EUFAULA

EUFAULA TRIBUNE. 514 E. Barbour St., Eufaula, AL 36027. Telephone: 334-687-3506. FAX: 334-687-3229. E-MAIL: editor@eufaulatribune.com. URL: http://www.eufaulatribune.com. Mailing Address: PO Box 628, Eufaula, AL 36072-0628. Year Established: 1929. Pub. Frequency: s-w. (Wed. & Sun.) Page Size: broadsheet. Subscrip. Rate: $.50 newsstand/cover; $39.50/yr carrier delivery in Eufaula & Barbour cys.; $52/yr mailed in state; $69.95/yr mailed out of state. Circulation: 5,500 per issue (paid). **Owner(s):** Tribune Publishing Company, Inc., See address and contact information above. **Management:** Joel P. Smith, President. Dennis Shelley, Advertising Manager. Cynrhia Pastre, Circulation Manager. **Editorial:** Patrick Johnston, Managing Editor.

EUTAW

GREENE COUNTY INDEPENDENT. 106 Main St., Eutaw, AL 35462-1104. Telephone: 205-372-2232. FAX: 205-372-2232. E-MAIL: greenecoind@aol.com. Year Established: 1985. Pub. Frequency: w. (Wed.) Page Size: standard. Subscrip. Rate: $.50 newsstand/cover; $18/yr in county; $25/yr out of county. Circulation: 1,500 per issue (paid). **Owner(s):** Greene County Independent Newspapers, Inc., 106 Main St., Eutaw, AL 35462. Telephone: 205-372-2232. **Management:** Sharon S. Trammell, General Manager. Betty C. Banks, Publisher. **Editorial:** Leewanna Parker, Editor.

EVERGREEN

EVERGREEN COURANT, THE. 204 Rural St., Evergreen, AL 36401. Telephone: 251-578-1492. FAX: 251-578-1496. E-MAIL: evergreencourant@earthlink.net. Mailing Address: PO Box 440, Evergreen, AL 36401-0440. Year Established: 1895. Pub. Frequency: w. (Thu.) Page Size: standard. Subscrip. Rate: $.50 newsstand/cover; $23/yr in county; $35/yr mailed out of county. Circulation: 3,800 per issue (paid). **Owner(s):** R.G. Bozeman, III, See address and contact information above. **Management:** R.G. Bozeman III, Publisher. **Editorial:** R.G. Bozeman III, Editor.

FAIRHOPE

FAIRHOPE COURIER, THE. 325 Fairhope Ave, Fairhope, AL 36533. Telephone: 251-928-2321. FAX: 251-928-9963. E-MAIL: courier@gulfcoastnewspapers.com. Mailing Address: PO Box 549, Fairhope, AL 36533. Year Established: 1894. Pub. Frequency: s-w. (Wed. & Sat.) Page Size: broadsheet. Subscrip. Rate: $.50 newsstand/cover; $37/yr mailed in county; $78/yr mailed out of county. Freelance Pay: $10-$50/article. Circulation: 3,200 per issue (paid). **Owner(s):** Crescent Media Group, PO Box 1634, Spartanburg, SC 29304. **Management:** James G. Walther, Publisher. David Williams, Advertising Manager. **Editorial:** Sheila Propp, Editor.

FAYETTE

TIMES RECORD (FAYETTE), THE. 106 First St., S.E., Fayette, AL 35555. Telephone: 205-932-6271. FAX: 205-932-6998. E-MAIL: trnews@fayette.net. Mailing Address: P.O. Drawer 159, Fayette, AL 35555. Year Established: 1977. Pub. Frequency: w. (Wed.) Page Size: standard. Subscrip. Rate: $.50 newsstand/cover; $25/yr in county; $28/yr adjoining cys; $36/yr mailed elsewhere. Adv. Rate: col. inch $9.10 Circulation: 5,000 per issue (paid). **Owner(s):** Mid-South Publishing Co., N.W. Alabamian, P.O. Box 430, Haleyville, AL 35565. **Management:** Horace Moore, Publisher. Gina Lynn, Advertising Manager. Jerrie Elliott, Business Manager. **Editorial:** Teresa Sanders, Editor.

FLOMATON

TRI-CITY LEDGER. 20766 Hwy. 31, Flomaton, AL 36441. E-MAIL: newsroom@tricityledger.com. Mailing Address: PO Box 1916, Flomaton, AL 36441. Year Established: 1971. Pub. Frequency: w. (Thu.) Page Size: broadsheet. Subscrip. Rate: $.75 newsstand/cover; $25/yr local; $30/yr out of county; $35/yr mailed out of state. Circulation: 5,300 per issue (paid). **Owner(s):** Tri-City Newspapers, Inc., See address and contact information above. **Management:** Bo Bolton, President. Joe Thomas, Publisher. Gary Murph, Advertising Manager. Cheryl Hicks, Circulation Manager. **Editorial:** Joe Thomas, Editor. Anne S. Anderson, Lifestyle Editor.

FLORALA

FLORALA NEWS, THE. 1155 Fifth St., Florala, AL 36442. Telephone: 334-858-3342. FAX: 334-858-3786. E-MAIL: floralanews@fairpoint.net. Year Established: 1900. Pub. Frequency: w. (Thu.) Page Size: broadsheet. Subscrip. Rate: $.50 newsstand/cover; $27/yr in state; $25/yr mailed out of state. Adv. Rate: col. inch $4.50 Circulation: 2,100 per issue (paid). **Owner(s):** Larry & Merle Woodham, See address and contact information above. **Management:** Larry Woodham, President. Gary Woodham, Publisher. Lisa Windham, Business Manager. **Editorial:** Lisa Windham, Editor.

FLORENCE

COURIER JOURNAL (FLORENCE). 1828 Darby Dr., Florence, AL 35630. Telephone: 256-764-4268. FAX: 256-760-9618. E-MAIL: editor@courierjournal.net. URL: http://www.courierjournal.net. Year Established: 1884. Pub. Frequency: w. (Wed.) Page Size: tabloid. Subscrip. Rate: $39/yr mailed out of area. Adv. Rate: col. inch $10.75 Circulation: 66,042 per issue (controlled). **Owner(s):** L&L Services, Inc., See address and contact information above. **Management:** Thomas V. Magazzu, Publisher. **Editorial:** Thomas V. Magazzu, Editor.

FOLEY

ONLOOKER, THE. 217 N. McKenzie St., Foley, AL 36535. Telephone: 251-943-2151. FAX: 334-934-3441. Mailing Address: PO Box 1687, Foley, AL 36536. Year Established: 1907. Pub. Frequency: s-w. (Wed. & Sat.) Page Size: broadsheet. Subscrip. Rate: $.50 newsstand/cover; $35.25/yr in county; $78/yr out of county. Circulation: 4,250 per issue (paid). **Owner(s):** Crescent Media Group, PO Box 1634, Spartanburg, SC 29304. Telephone: 864-583-2907. **Management:** James G. Walther, Group Publisher. David Williams, Advertising Manager.

FT PAYNE

MOUNTAIN ECHO, THE. PO Box 680027, Ft Payne, AL 35967. Telephone: 256-845-5512. FAX: 256-845-5509. E-MAIL: jschaaf@socket.net. Mailing Address: PO Box 25, Ironton, MO 63650. Year Established: 1937. Pub. Frequency: w. (Wed.) Page Size: broadsheet. Subscrip. Rate: $.50 newsstand/cover; $24/yr local; $37/yr out of area; $37/yr out of state. Circulation: 63,000 per issue (paid and free). **Owner(s):** Smith Newspapers, Inc., 110 N. Main St., Ironton, MO 63650-0025. Telephone: 573-546-3917. FAX: 573-546-3919. **Management:** Judy Schaaf-Wheeler, Publisher. Cherrie Reinagel, Advertising Manager. **Editorial:** Kevin Jenkins, Editor.

GARDENDALE

NORTH JEFFERSON NEWS. 118 Main St., Gardendale, AL 35071. Telephone: 205-631-8716. FAX: 205-631-9902. E-MAIL: newsroom@njeffersonnews.com. Mailing Address: PO Box 849, Gardendale, AL 35071. Pub. Frequency: s-w. (Wed. & Sat.) Page Size: broadsheet. Subscrip. Rate: $.75 newsstand/cover; $35/yr in county; $50/yr out of county. Adv. Rate: col. inch $7.25 **Wire Service(s):** AP. Circulation: 5,000 per issue (paid). **Owner(s):** Community Newspaper Holdings, Inc., 3500 Colonnade Pkwy., Ste. 600, Birmingham, AL 35243. Telephone: 205-298-7100. FAX: 205-298-7101. **Management:** Bill Morgan, Publisher. Becky Johnson, Advertising Manager. **Editorial:** Adam Smith, Editor.

GENEVA

GENEVA COUNTY REAPER. 803 E. Town Ave., Geneva, AL 36340. Telephone: 334-684-2280. FAX: 334-684-3099. E-MAIL: genevanewspapers@centurytel.net. Mailing Address: PO Box 160, Geneva, AL 36340-3099. Year Established: 1899. Pub. Frequency: w. (Wed.) Page Size: broadsheet. Subscrip. Rate: $.50 newsstand/cover; $24/yr in county; $30/yr out of county; $35/yr mailed out of state. Adv. Rate: col. inch $6.40 Circulation: 2,500 per issue (paid). **Owner(s):** Geneva County Publishing, See address and contact information above. **Management:** Randy Pebworth, Publisher. Rich Williams, Advertising Manager. Judi Vaughn, Circulation Manager. **Editorial:** Stephen Crews, Editor.

GENEVA COUNTY SHOPPER. 803 E. Town Ave., Geneva, AL 36340. Telephone: 334-684-2280. FAX: 334-684-3099. E-MAIL: genevanewspapers@centurytel.net. Mailing Address: PO Box 160, Geneva, AL 36340-3099. Year Established: 1990. Pub. Frequency: w. (Tue.) Page Size: broadsheet.Adv. Rate: col. inch $7.10 Circulation: 8,714 per issue (paid). **Owner(s):** Geneva County Publishing, See address and contact information above. **Management:** Randy Pebworth, Publisher. Rich Williams, Advertising Manager. Judi Vaughn, Circulation Manager. **Editorial:** Stephen Crews, Editor.

HARTFORD NEWS-HERALD. 803 E. Town Ave., Geneva, AL 36340. Telephone: 334-684-2280. FAX: 334-684-3099. E-MAIL: genevanewspapers@centurytel.net. Mailing Address: PO Box 160, Geneva, AL 36340-3099. Pub. Frequency: w. (Wed.) Page Size: broadsheet. Subscrip. Rate: $.50 newsstand/cover; $22/yr in county; $27/yr out of county. Adv. Rate: col. inch $6.40 Circulation: 1,000 per issue (paid). **Owner(s):** Geneva County Publishing, See address and contact information above. **Management:** Randy Pebworth, Publisher. Rich Williams, Advertising Manager. Judi Vaughn, Circulation Manager. **Editorial:** Stephen Crews, Editor.

SAMSON LEDGER. 803 E. Town Ave., Geneva, AL 36340. Telephone: 334-684-2280. FAX: 334-684-3099. E-MAIL: genevanewspapers@centurytel.net. Mailing Address: PO Box 160, Geneva, AL 36340-0160. Year Established: 1933. Pub. Frequency: w. (Wed.) Page Size: broadsheet. Subscrip. Rate: $.50 newsstand/cover; $24/yr in county; $30/yr out of county; $35/yr mailed out of state. Adv. Rate: col. inch $6.40 Circulation: 800 per issue (paid). **Owner(s):** Geneva Newspapers, Inc., See address and contact information above. **Management:** Randy Pebworth, Publisher. Rich Williams, Advertising Manager. Judi Vaughn, Circulation Manager. **Editorial:** Stephen Crews, Editor.

GREENSBORO

GREENSBORO WATCHMAN, THE. P.O. Drawer 550, Greensboro, AL 36744-0550. E-MAIL: gwatchman@bellsouth.net. Mailing Address: P.O. Drawer 550, Greensboro, AL 36744-0550. Year Established: 1876. Pub. Frequency: w. (Thu.) Page Size: broadsheet. Subscrip. Rate: $.50 newsstand/cover; $20.50/yr in state; $26.50/yr out of state; $18.50/yr in county. Adv. Rate: col. inch $6.30 Circulation: 3,100 per issue (paid). **Owner(s):** Willie Jean Arrington, 1005 Market St, Greensboro, AL 34744. Telephone: 334-624-8323. FAX: 334-624-8327. **Management:** Willie Jean Arrington, Publisher. **Editorial:** Willie Jean Arrington, Editor.

GREENVILLE

BUTLER COUNTY NEWS. 103 Hickory St, Greenville, AL 36037. Telephone: 334-382-3111. FAX: 334-382-7104. E-MAIL: editor@greenvilleadvocate.com. URL: http://www.greenvilleadvocate.com. Year Established: 1911. Pub. Frequency: w. (Thu.) Page Size: broadsheet. Subscrip. Rate: $.50 newsstand/cover; $21.60/yr mailed in county; $32.40/yr mailed out of county. Adv. Rate: col. inch $5.25 Circulation: 900 per issue (paid). **Owner(s):** Boone Newspapers, Inc., P.O. Box 507, Greenville, AL 36037. 15222 Freewmen's Bend Rd., Northport, AL 35475. **Management:** Ed Darling, President. Cheryl Gates, Office Manager. **Editorial:** Kevin Pearcey, Managing Editor. Austin Phillips, Sports Editor.

BUTLER EXPRESS, THE. 103 Hickory St, Greenville, AL 36037. Telephone: 334-382-3111. FAX: 334-382-7104. E-MAIL: editor@greenvilleadvoccate.com. URL: http://www.greenvilleadvocate.com.Pub. Frequency: w. (Fri.) Circulation: 10,400 per issue (free). **Owner(s):** Boone Newspapers, Inc., P.O. Box 507, Greenville, AL 36037. 15222 Freemen's Bend Rd., Northport, AL 35475. Telephone: 205-330-4100. **Management:** Ed Darling, President. Cheryl Gates, Office Manager. Tracy Salter, Advertising Manager. **Editorial:** Kevin Pearcey, Managing Editor. Austin Phillips, Sports Editor.

GREENVILLE (AL) ADVOCATE, THE. 103 Hickory St, Greenville, AL 36037. Telephone: 334-382-3111. FAX: 334-382-7104. E-MAIL: editor@greenvilleadvocate.com. URL: http://www.greenvilleadvocate.com. Year Established: 1865. Pub. Frequency: s-w. (Wed. & Sat.) Page Size: broadsheet. Subscrip. Rate: $.75 newsstand/cover; $49.05/yr mailed in county; $59.95/yr mailed out of county. Adv. Rate: col. inch $10.45 Circulation: 3,000 per issue (paid). **Owner(s):** Boone Newspapers, Inc., P.O. Box 507, Greenville, AL 36037. 15222 Freemen's Bend Rd., Northport, AL 35475. Telephone: 205-330-4100. **Management:** Ed Darling, President. Cheryl Gates, Office Manager. Tracy Salter, Advertising Manager. **Editorial:** Kevin Pearcey, Managing Editor. Austin Phillips, Sports Editor.

LOWNDES SIGNAL, THE. 103 Hickory St, Greenville, AL 36037. Telephone: 334-382-3111. FAX: 334-382-7104. E-MAIL: editor@lowndessignal.com. URL: http://www.greenvilleadvocate.com. Pub. Frequency: w. (Thu.) Page Size: broadsheet. Subscrip. Rate: $.25 newsstand/cover; $22/yr mailed in county; $33/yr mailed out of county. Adv. Rate: col. inch $5 Circulation: 1,300 per issue (paid). **Owner(s):** Boone Newspapers, Inc., P.O. Box 507, Greenville, AL 36037. 15222 Freemen's Bend Rd., Northport, AL 35475. Telephone: 205-330-4100. **Management:** Ed Darling, President. Cheryl Gates, Office Manager. Tracy Salter, Advertising Manager. **Editorial:** Kevin Pearcey, Managing Editor. Austin Phillips, Sports Editor.

LUVERNE JOURNAL, THE. 103 Hickory St, Greenville, AL 36037. Telephone: 334-382-3111. FAX: 334-382-7104. E-MAIL: editor@luvernejournal.com. URL: http://www.luvernejournal.com. Mailing Address: PO Box 146, Gatesville, NC 27938. Year Established: 1888. Pub. Frequency: w. (Thu.) Page Size: broadsheet. Subscrip. Rate: $.50 newsstand/cover; $28.34/yr mailed in county; $39.24/yr mailed out of county. Adv. Rate: col. inch $7,050 Circulation: 3,000 per issue (paid). **Owner(s):** Boone Newspapers, Inc., 15222 Freemen's Bend Rd., Northport, AL 35475. Telephone: 205-330-4100. **Management:** Ed Darling, President. Cheryl Gates, Office Manager. Tracy Salter, Advertising Manager. **Editorial:** Kevin Pearcey, Managing Editor. Austin Phillips, Sports Editor.

GROVE HILL

CLARKE COUNTY DEMOCRAT, THE. 261 N. Jackson, Grove Hill, AL 36451. Telephone: 251-275-3375. FAX: 251-275-3060. E-MAIL: cedemo@mygalaxyexpress.com. URL: http://www.clarkecountydemocrat.com. Mailing Address: PO Box 39, Grove Hill, AL 36451-0039. Year Established: 1856. Pub. Frequency: w. (Thu.) Page Size: broadsheet. Subscrip. Rate: $.50 newsstand/cover; $21.80/yr in county; $30/yr mailed elsewhere. Circulation: 5,300 per issue (paid). **Owner(s):** James A. Cox, See address and contact information above. **Management:** Mike Williamson, General Manager. James A. Cox, Publisher. **Editorial:** James A. Cox, Editor. Ross Wood, Sports Editor.

GULF SHORES

ISLANDER (GULF SHORES), THE. ISSN 1041-2662
128 Cove Ave., Gulf Shores, AL 36542. Telephone: 251-968-6414. FAX: 251-968-5233. E-MAIL: islander@gulfcoastnewspapers.com. URL: http://www.gulfcoastnewspapers.com. Mailing Address: PO Box 1128, Gulf Shores, AL 36547. Year Established: 1977. Pub. Frequency: s-w. (Wed. & Sat.) Page Size: broadsheet. Subscrip. Rate: $.50 newsstand/cover; $37.25/yr in county; $78/yr mailed elsewhere; $31.25/yr mailed in county to senior citizens. Circulation: 5,000 per issue (paid). **Owner(s):** Crescent Publishing Co., The, See address and contact information above. **Management:** Harry Clarke, Advertising. Carolyn W Dugger, Classified Adv. Mgr.. Angela King, Business Manager. **Editorial:** Mary-Allison Bauer, Editor.

Weeklies

GUNTERSVILLE

ADVERTISER-GLEAM. 2218 Taylor St, Guntersville, AL 35976. Telephone: 256-582-3232. FAX: 256-582-3231. E-MAIL: ads@advertisergleam.com. URL: http://www.advertisergleam.com. Mailing Address: PO Box 190, Guntersville, AL 35976-0190. Year Established: 1880. Pub. Frequency: 2/w. (Wed. & Sat.) Page Size: broadsheet. Subscrip. Rate: $.50 newsstand/cover; $26/yr in county; $45/yr elsewhere. Adv. Rate: col. inch $8.95 Circulation: 11,307 per issue (paid). **Owner(s):** Advertiser Gleam Inc., See address and contact information above. **Management:** John Harvey, General Manager. Taunya Buchanan, Advertising Manager. **Editorial:** Sam Harvey, Editor.

HALEYVILLE

NORTHWEST ALABAMIAN. 1530 21st St., Haleyville, AL 35565. Telephone: 205-486-9461. FAX: 205-486-4847. E-MAIL: nwanews@sonet.net. Mailing Address: PO Box 430, Haleyville, AL 35565. Year Established: 1906. Pub. Frequency: s-w. (Wed. & Sat.) Page Size: broadsheet. Subscrip. Rate: $.50 newsstand/cover; $30/yr mailed in county; $34/yr mailed adj. counties; $27/yr mailed in county senior citizens. Freelance Pay: $0.15/column-inch. Circulation: 8,600 per issue (paid). **Owner(s):** Hershel Lake, See address and contact information above. **Management:** Horace Moore, Publisher. Roger Carden, Advertising Manager. Phillip Brooks, Production Director. **Editorial:** Melica Allen, News Editor.

HAMILTON

JOURNAL RECORD (HAMILTON). 401 State Hwy. 17, Hamilton, AL 35570. Telephone: 205-921-3104. FAX: 205-921-3105. E-MAIL: tjr@sonet.net. Mailing Address: PO Drawer 1477, Hamilton, AL 35570. Year Established: 1970. Pub. Frequency: s-w. (Wed. & Sat.) Page Size: broadsheet. Subscrip. Rate: $.50 newsstand/cover; $30.95/yr in county; $34/yr adjacent cys; $46/yr mailed elsewhere. Circulation: 8,500 per issue (paid). **Owner(s):** Mid-South Publishing Co., N.W. Alabamian, P.O. Box 430, Haleyville, AL 35565. Telephone: 205-486-9461. FAX: 205-486-4849. **Bureau(s):** P.O. Drawer 458, Winfield, AL 35594. Telephone: 205-487-3278. Contact: Tracy Estes, Bureau Chief. **Management:** Horace Moore, Publisher. Krisit White, Advertising Manager. **Editorial:** Les Walters, Managing Editor. Tracy Estes, News Editor.

HANCEVILLE

HANCEVILLE HERALD. 107 Bangor Ave., Hanceville, AL 35077. Telephone: 256-352-4775. FAX: 256-352-0224. E-MAIL: hherald@hiwaay.net. URL: http://www.hancevilleherald.com. Mailing Address: PO Box 880, Hanceville, AL 35077. Year Established: 1977. Pub. Frequency: w. (Wed.) Page Size: broadsheet. Subscrip. Rate: $.50 newsstand/cover; $19.99/yr Culman & Blount cys.; $39.99/yr mailed elsewhere. Circulation: 2,700 per issue (paid). **Owner(s):** Ginger Grantham, See address and contact information above. **Editorial:** Ed Flaig, Editor.

HARTSELLE

HARTSELLE ENQUIRER. 407 W. Chestnut St., Hartselle, AL 35640. Telephone: 256-773-6566. FAX: 256-773-1953. E-MAIL: leada.gore@hartselleenquirer.com. URL: http://www.hartselleenquirer.com. Mailing Address: PO Box 929, Hartselle, AL 35640. Year Established: 1874. Pub. Frequency: w. (Thu.) Page Size: broadsheet. Subscrip. Rate: $.50 newsstand/cover; $25/yr mailed in county; $30/yr mailed out of county; $35/yr mailed out of state. Circulation: 7,800 per issue (paid). **Owner(s):** Boone Newspapers, Inc., PO Box 2370, Tuscaloosa, AL 35403. Telephone: 205-330-4100. **Management:** Leada Gore, Publisher. Tabbetha Williams, Office Manager. Randy Garrison, Advertising Manager. Sherman Kirby, Circulation Director. Barbara Davis, Classified Adv. Mgr. **Editorial:** Leada Gore, Editor. Justin Schuver, Sports Editor.

HEFLIN

CLEBURNE NEWS, THE. 926 Ross St., Heflin, AL 36264. Telephone: 256-463-2872. FAX: 256-463-7127. E-MAIL: news@cleburnenews.com. URL: http://www.cleburnenews.com. Mailing Address: PO Box 67, Heflin, AL 36264. Year Established: 1906. Pub. Frequency: w. (Thu.) Page Size: broadsheet. Subscrip. Rate: $.50 newsstand/cover; $10 for 6 mos. in county; $18/yr in county; $14 for 6 mos. out of county; $24/yr out of county. Circulation: 3,200 per issue (paid). **Owner(s):** Consolidated Publishing Co., 4305 McClellan Blvd., Anniston, AL 36201. Telephone: 256-236-1551. FAX: 256-231-0027. **Management:** Mickey Cook, General Manager. Stacy Camp, Advertising. **Editorial:** Wayne Ruple, Editor. Misty Pointer, Production Manager.

JACKSON

SOUTH ALABAMIAN. 1064 Cotterville Rd., Jackson, AL 36545. Telephone: 251-246-4494. FAX: 251-246-7486. E-MAIL: ad@southalabamian.com. URL: http://www.southalabamian.com.. Mailing Address: PO Box 68, Jackson, AL 36545. Year Established: 1887. Pub. Frequency: w. (Thu.) Page Size: broadsheet. Subscrip. Rate: $.50 newsstand/cover; $20/yr local; $26/yr out of area. Circulation: 4,800 per issue (paid). **Owner(s):** Jim Cox, See address and contact information above. **Management:** Jim Cox, Publisher. Bill Williams, Advertising Manager. Shelly Menz, Circulation Manager. **Editorial:** Evan Carden, Editor.

JACKSONVILLE

JACKSONVILLE NEWS, THE. 203 S. Pelham Rd., Jacksonville, AL 36265. Telephone: 256-435-5021. FAX: 256-435-1028. E-MAIL: news@jaxnews.com. URL: http://www.jaxnews.com. Year Established: 1936. Pub. Frequency: w. (Wed.) Page Size: broadsheet. Subscrip. Rate: $.50 newsstand/cover; $24/yr in county (effective 2005); $35/yr mailed out of county. Circulation: 3,500 per issue (paid). **Owner(s):** Consolidated Publishing Co., 4305 McClellan Blvd., Anniston, AL 36201. Telephone: 256-235-9200. **Management:** Julia Brock, General Manager. Phillip A. Sanguinetti, Publisher. Jim Haynes, Advertising Manager. Pat O'Malley, Circulation Manager. **Editorial:** Julia Brock, Editor. Anita Kilgore, Photo.

LEEDS

LEEDS NEWS. 8024 Parkway Dr., Leeds, AL 35094. Telephone: 205-699-2214. FAX: 205-699-3157. Year Established: 1939. Pub. Frequency: w. (Thu.) Page Size: broadsheet. Subscrip. Rate: $.50 newsstand/cover; $20/yr. Adv. Rate: col. inch $5.90 Freelance Pay: $20/article. Circulation: 4,300 per issue (paid). **Owner(s):** Community Newspaper Holdings, Inc., 3500 Colonnade Pkwy., Ste. 600, Birmingham, AL 35243. Telephone: 205-298-7100. FAX: 205-298-7101. **Management:** Bill Mogan, Publisher. Angela Knight, Advertising Manager. **Editorial:** Robert Blankenship, Editor.

LINDEN

DEMOCRAT-REPORTER, THE, 108 Coats, Linden, AL 36748. Telephone: 334-295-5224. FAX: 334-295-5563. Mailing Address: PO Box 480040, Linden, AL 36748. Year Established: 1879. Pub. Frequency: w. (Thu.) Page Size: broadsheet. Subscrip. Rate: $1 newsstand/cover; $35/yr in county; $50/yr mailed out of county; $60/yr mailed out of state. Adv. Rate: col. inch $7.50 Circulation: 10,000 per issue (paid). **Owner(s):** Goodloe Sutton, See address and contact information above. **Management:** Goodloe Sutton, Publisher. **Editorial:** Goodloe Sutton, Editor.

LINEVILLE

CLAY TIMES JOURNAL.   ISSN 1053-9123
60132 Hwy. 49, Lineville, AL 36266-0097. Telephone: 256-396-5760. FAX: 256-396-5760. E-MAIL: timesjournal@centurytel.net. Mailing Address: PO Box 97, Lineville, AL 36266-0097. Year Established: 1903. Pub. Frequency: w. (Wed.) Page Size: standard. Subscrip. Rate: $.50 newsstand/cover; $22/yr mailed in county; $27/yr mailed out of county. Circulation: 3,800 per issue (paid). **Owner(s):** Connie & David Proctor, PO Box 97, Lineville, AL 36266. Telephone: 205-396-5760. **Management:** David Proctor, Publisher. Linda McDonald, Advertising Manager. **Editorial:** David Proctor, Editor.

LIVINGSTON

SUMTER COUNTY RECORD-JOURNAL, THE. P.O. Drawer B, Livingston, AL 35470. Telephone: 205-652-6100. FAX: 205-652-4466. E-MAIL: news@recordjournal.net. URL: http://www.recordjournal.net. Year Established: 1968. Pub. Frequency: w. (Thu.) Page Size: broadsheet. Subscrip. Rate: $.75 newsstand/cover; $22/yr mailed in county; $25/yr mailed out of county; $30/yr mailed out of state. Circulation: 5,000 per issue (paid). **Owner(s):** Tommy McGraw, See address and contact information above. **Management:** Sherry Doggett, General Manager. Tommy McGraw, Publisher. **Editorial:** Tommy McGraw, Editor. Herman Ward, Sports Editor.

MADISON

MADISON COUNTY (AL) RECORD.   ISSN 0889-4205
151-C Hughes Rd, Madison, AL 35758. Telephone: 256-772-6677. FAX: 256-772-6655. E-MAIL: leada.gore@madisoncountyrecord.com. URL: http://www.madisoncountyrecord.com. Year Established: 1967. Pub. Frequency: w. (Fri.) Page Size: broadsheet. Subscrip. Rate: $.50 newsstand/cover; $21/yr in county; $30/yr out of county; $35/yr mailed out of state. Circulation: 4,000 per issue (paid). **Owner(s):** Boone Newspapers, Inc., 15222 Freemen's Bend Rd., Northport, AL 35475. Telephone: 205-330-4100. **Management:** Leada Gore, Publisher. Randy Garrison, Advertising Manager. **Editorial:** Leada Gore, Editor. Emily Howard, Managing Editor. Justin Schuver, Sports Editor.

MARION

MARION TIMES-STANDARD. 414 Washington St., Marion, AL 36756. Telephone: 334-683-6318. FAX: 334-683-4616. Mailing Address: PO Box 418, Marion, AL 36756. Year Established: 1839. Pub. Frequency: w. (Wed.) Page Size: standard. Subscrip. Rate: $.50 newsstand/cover; $19.62/yr in county; $27.25/yr out of county; $35/yr out of state. Circulation: 2,100 per issue (paid). **Owner(s):** Trib Publications, Inc., PO Box 648, Manchester, GA 31816. Telephone: 706-846-4336. **Management:** Lorrie Rinehart, General Manager. Robert Tribble, President. Lorrie Rinehart, Circulation Manager. **Editorial:** B. Parrish, Editor.

MILLPORT

WEST ALABAMA GAZETTE. PO Box 249, Millport, AL 35576-0249. Telephone: 205-662-4296. FAX: 205-662-4740. E-MAIL: gazettenews@frontiernet.net. URL: http://www.gazettefrontiernet.net. Year Established: 1976. Pub. Frequency: w. (Wed.) Page Size: broadsheet. Subscrip. Rate: $.50 newsstand/cover; $20/yr in county; $25/yr in state; $30/yr mailed out of state. Circulation: 4,200 per issue (paid). **Owner(s):** Peyton & Barbara Bobo, See address and contact information above. **Management:** Peyton Bobo, Publisher. Janis Hollis, Advertising Manager. **Editorial:** Barbara Bobo, Editor.

MONROEVILLE

MONROE JOURNAL.   ISSN 0884-8750
49 Hines St., Monroeville, AL 36460. Telephone: 251-575-3282. FAX: 251-575-3284. E-MAIL: news@monroejournal.com. URL: http://www.monroejournal.com. Mailing Address: PO Box 826, Monroeville, AL 36461-0826. Year Established: 1866. Pub. Frequency: w. (Thu.) Page Size: broadsheet. Subscrip. Rate: $.50 newsstand/cover; $26/yr in county; $32/yr mailed in state; $37/yr mailed out of state. Circulation: 7,600 per issue (paid). **Owner(s):** Bolton Newspapers, Inc., See address and contact information above. **Management:** Kermit Bolton, President. Bo Bolton, Publisher. **Editorial:** Mike Qualls, Managing Editor. Beth Norris, Lifestyle Editor.

MONTGOMERY

MONTGOMERY INDEPENDENT. 141 Market Pl, Montgomery, AL 36117-4900. Telephone: 334-265-7323. FAX: 334-265-7320. E-MAIL: ads@montgomeryindependent.com. URL: http://www.al.com/independent/. Mailing Address: PO Box 231297, Montgomery, AL 36123-1297. Year Established: 1964. Pub. Frequency: w. (Thu.) Page Size: tabloid. Subscrip. Rate: $.75 newsstand/cover; $28/yr mailed; $34/yr out of county. Adv. Rate: col. inch $8.73 Circulation: 8,000 per issue (paid). **Owner(s):** Robert Martin, See address and contact information above. **Management:** Robert Martin, Publisher. James Martin, Circulation Manager. **Editorial:** Robert Martin, Editor. John Woolf, Production Manager.

MOULTON

MOULTON ADVERTISER, THE. 659 Main St., Moulton, AL 35650. Telephone: 256-974-1114. FAX: 256-974-3097. E-MAIL: luke@moultonadvertiser.com. URL: http://www.moultonadvertiser.com. Mailing Address: PO Box 517, Moulton, AL 35650. Year Established: 1828. Pub. Frequency: w. (Wed.) Page Size: standard. Subscrip. Rate: $.75 newsstand/cover; $25/yr in county; $34/yr out of county. Adv. Rate: col. inch $9.35 Circulation: 14,000 per issue (paid). **Owner(s):** Slaton Newspapers, Inc., See address and contact information above. **Management:** Luke Slaton, Publisher. Teresa Woodruff, Advertising Manager. Rice Towry, Circulation Manager. **Editorial:** Luke Slaton, Editor.

MOUNDVILLE

MOUNDVILLE TIMES. 298 Market St., Moundville, AL 35474-4018. Telephone: 205-371-2488. FAX: 205-371-2788. E-MAIL: times@mound.net. Mailing Address: PO Box 683, Moundville, AL 35474-0683. Year Established: 1988. Pub. Frequency: w. (Wed.) Page Size: broadsheet. Subscrip. Rate: $.50 newsstand/cover; $16/yr in county; $18/yr in state; $20/yr out of state. Adv. Rate: col. inch $6 Circulation: 2,500 per issue (paid). **Owner(s):** Larry Taylor, See address and contact information above. **Management:** Larry Taylor, Publisher. Cindy Bolling, Circulation Manager. **Editorial:** Cindy Bolling, Editor.

NORTHPORT

NORTHPORT GAZETTE, THE. 401 20th Ave, Ste 5, Northport, AL 35476. Telephone: 205-759-3891. FAX: 205-759-5449. Pub. Frequency: w. (Wed.) Subscrip. Rate: $.50 newsstand/cover; $25/yr in county; $35/yr out of county. **Owner(s):** Peyton & Barbara Bobo, PO Box 749, Northport, AL 35476.

ONEONTA

BLOUNT COUNTIAN, THE. 217 Third St., S., Oneonta, AL 35121. Telephone: 205-625-3231. E-MAIL: countian@otelco.net. Mailing Address: PO Box 310, Oneonta, AL 35121-0310. Year Established: 1894. Pub. Frequency: w. (Wed.) Page Size: broadsheet. Subscrip. Rate: $.50 newsstand/cover; $17/yr in county; $28/yr out of county; $35/yr out of state; $13/yr in county seniors citizens. Circulation: 6,700 per issue (paid). **Owner(s):** Southern Democrat, Inc., See address and contact information above. **Management:** Molly Howard Ryan, President. Barbara Davis, Circulation Manager. **Editorial:** Lisa Ryan, Editor.

OPP

OPP NEWS. 200 W. Covington Ave., Opp, AL 36467. Telephone: 334-493-3595. FAX: 334-493-4901. E-MAIL: oppnews@oppcatu.com. Mailing Address: PO Box 870, Opp, AL 36467. Year Established: 1901. Pub. Frequency: w. (Thu.) Page Size: broadsheet. Subscrip. Rate: $.50 newsstand/cover; $24/yr in county; $30/yr out of county; $35/yr out of state. Circulation: 5,300 per issue (paid). **Owner(s):** Covington Publishing Corp., See address and contact information above. **Management:** Rupert Phillips, President. Randy Pebworth, Publisher. Wanda Sasser, Advertising Manager. Amzie Lawson, Business Manager. **Editorial:** Doris Wisner, Editor.

OZARK

SOUTHERN STAR. 373 Ed Lisenby Dr., Ozark, AL 36360. Telephone: 334-774-2715. FAX: 334-774-9619. E-MAIL: southstar@centurytel.net. Year Established: 1867. Pub. Frequency: w. (Wed.) Page Size: broadsheet. Subscrip. Rate: $.50 newsstand/cover; $23.22/yr mailed in county; $25.38/yr mailed out of county; $29/yr mailed out of state. Circulation: 5,000 morning (paid); 5,200 per issue (paid). **Owner(s):** Joseph H. Adams, PO Box 1729, Ozark, AL 36361. Telephone: 205-774-2715. **Management:** Joseph H. Adams, Publisher. Charles Dawkins, Advertising Manager. **Editorial:** Joseph H. Adams, Editor.

PELHAM

AMERICAN CLASSIFIEDS. 250 Yeager Parkway, Pelham, AL 35124-1800. Telephone: 205-942-2555. FAX: 205-942-5770. E-MAIL: Birmongham, Al. URL: http://www.americanclassifieds.com. Year Established: 1982. Pub. Frequency: w. (Thu.) Page Size: tabloid Circulation: 40,000 per issue (free). **Owner(s):** Brian Merrill, See address and contact information above. **Management:** Brian Merrill, Publisher.

PELL CITY

ST. CLAIR NEWS-AEGIS. ISSN 1044-1964
1820 Second Ave, N, Pell City, AL 35125. Telephone: 205-884-2310. FAX: 205-884-2312. E-MAIL: scna@newsaegis.com. Mailing Address: PO Box 750, Pell City, AL 35125-0750. Year Established: 1873. Pub. Frequency: w. (Thu.) Page Size: standard. Subscrip. Rate: $.50 newsstand/cover; $20/yr in county; $28/yr out of county. **Wire Service(s):** UPI. Circulation: 7,000 per issue (paid). **Owner(s):** Community Newspaper Holdings, Inc., 3500 Colonnade Pkwy., Ste. 600, Birmingham, AL 35242. **Management:** Bill Morgan, Publisher. Melissa Blankenship, Advertising Manager. Dale McCurry, Circulation Manager. **Editorial:** Kyle Shilton, Editor.

ST. CLAIR TIMES. 1911 Martin St. S, Pell City, AL 35128. Telephone: 205-884-3400. FAX: 205-814-9194. E-MAIL: klong@dailyhome.com. URL: http://www.dailyhome.com. Year Established: 2000. Pub. Frequency: w. (Thu.) Page Size: broadsheet.Adv. Rate: col. inch $6.75 Circulation: 20,500 per issue (free). **Owner(s):** Consolidated Publishing Co., 4305 McClennen Blvd., Anniston, AL 36206. Telephone: 256-236-1551. **Management:** Carol Pappas, Publisher. **Editorial:** Kellie Long, Editor.

PRATTVILLE

PRATTVILLE PROGRESS. ISSN 1044-0380
152 W. Third St., Prattville, AL 36068. Telephone: 334-365-6739. FAX: 334-365-1400. Year Established: 1886. Pub. Frequency: s-w. (Wed. & Sat.) Page Size: broadsheet. Subscrip. Rate: $.50 newsstand/cover; $17/yr carrier delivery. Circulation: 9,000 per issue (paid). **Owner(s):** Gannett Company, Inc., 7950 Jones Branch Dr, McLean, VA 22107. Telephone: 703-854-6000. **Editorial:** Sarah Stephens, Editor.

RAINSVILLE

WEEKLY POST, THE. 690 McCurdy Ave. N., Rainsville, AL 35986-0849. Telephone: 256-638-4027. FAX: 256-638-2329. E-MAIL: teri@theweeklypost.com. URL: http://www.theweeklypost.com. Mailing Address: PO Box 849, Rainsville, AL 35986-0849. Year Established: 1987. Pub. Frequency: w. (Thu.) Page Size: broadsheet. Subscrip. Rate: $.50 newsstand/cover; $20/yr out of county; $30/yr mailed out of county; $15/yr in county to senior citizens. Circulation: 4,000 per issue (paid). **Owner(s):** Southern Newspapers, Inc., 5701 Woodway Dr., Ste. 131, Houston, TX 77057-1589. **Management:** Fay McBride, Publisher. Lori Stone, Advertising Director. **Editorial:** Terry Baker, Editor. Dwayne Patterson, Managing Editor.

RED BAY

RED BAY NEWS. 120 Fourth Ave., S.E., Red Bay, AL 35582. Telephone: 256-356-2148. FAX: 256-356-2787. E-MAIL: rbnews@hiwaay.net. Mailing Address: PO Box 1339, Red Bay, AL 35582. Year Established: 1963. Pub. Frequency: w. (Wed.) Page Size: broadsheet. Subscrip. Rate: $.50 newsstand/cover; $22/yr local; $27/yr mailed elsewhere. **Wire Service(s):** CNS. Circulation: 4,020 per issue (paid). **Owner(s):** Harden Publishers, Inc., See address and contact information above. **Management:** LaVale Mills, Publisher. Lennetta Jackson, Classified Adv. Mgr.. **Editorial:** Keith Ledbetter, Editor.

ROANOKE

RANDOLPH LEADER. 524 Main St., Roanoke, AL 36274. Telephone: 334-863-2819. FAX: 334-863-4006. E-MAIL: john@therandolphleader.com. URL: http://www.therandolphleader.com. Mailing Address: PO Box 1267, Roanoke, AL 36274-1267. Year Established: 1892. Pub. Frequency: w. (Wed.) Page Size: standard. Subscrip. Rate: $.50 newsstand/cover; $22/yr local; $28/yr mailed elsewhere. Adv. Rate: col. inch $5.70 Circulation: 6,800 per issue (paid). **Owner(s):** Randolph Publishers, See address and contact information above. **Management:** John Wo. Stevenson, Publisher. Peggy Seabolt, Advertising Manager. **Editorial:** John Wo. Stevenson, Editor. Vanessa Sorrell Burnside, News Editor.

ROBERTSDALE

INDEPENDENT (ROBERTSDALE), THE. 21764 Media Dr., Robertsdale, AL 36567. Telephone: 251-947-7318. FAX: 251-947-7652. Mailing Address: PO Box 509, Robertsdale, AL 36567. Year Established: 1975. Pub. Frequency: w. (Thu.) Page Size: broadsheet. Subscrip. Rate: $.50 newsstand/cover; $26.75/yr mailed in state; $39/yr mailed out of state. Circulation: 3,000 per issue (paid). **Owner(s):** Crescent Media Group, PO Box 1634, Spartanburg, SC 29304. Telephone: 864-583-2907. **Management:** James G. Walther, Publisher. Amber Kimbler, Circulation Manager. **Editorial:** John Underwood, Editor.

ROGERSVILLE

EAST LAUDERDALE NEWS. E. Lee St., Rogersville, AL 35652. Telephone: 256-247-5565. FAX: 256-247-1902. Year Established: 1965. Pub. Frequency: w. (Thu.) Page Size: broadsheet. Subscrip. Rate: $.50 newsstand/cover; $25/yr in state; $25/yr domestic; $25/yr elsewhere. Adv. Rate: col. inch $8.57 Circulation: 4,500 per issue (paid). **Owner(s):** James B. & Phyllis D. Cox, PO Box 479, Rogersville, AL 35652-0479. Telephone: 256-247-5565. FAX: 256-247-1902. **Management:** James B. Cox, Publisher. **Editorial:** James B. Cox, Editor.

RUSSELLVILLE

FRANKLIN COUNTY PLUS. 14131 Hwy. 43, Russellville, AL 35653. Telephone: 256-332-1881. FAX: 256-332-1883. Mailing Address: PO Box 1088, Russellville, AL 35653. Pub. Frequency: w. (Wed.) Page Size: broadsheet Circulation: 8,125 per issue (free). **Owner(s):** Boone Newspapers, Inc., 15222 Freemen's Bend Rd., Northport, AL 35475. Telephone: 205-330-4100. **Management:** Jason Cannon, Publisher. Charles Pounders, Circulation Manager. **Editorial:** Jason Cannon, Editor. Mike Self, Managing Editor.

FRANKLIN COUNTY TIMES. 14131 Hwy. 43, Russellville, AL 35653. Telephone: 256-332-1881. FAX: 256-332-1883. URL: http://www.franklincountytimes.com. Mailing Address: PO Box 1088, Russellville, AL 35653. Year Established: 1879. Pub. Frequency: 3/w. (Wed., Fri., Sun.) Page Size: broadsheet. Subscrip. Rate: $.75 newsstand/cover; $58.34/yr in county; $73.44/yr mailed out of county; $80.99/yr mailed out of state; $54/yr in county. Circulation: 2,500 (paid). **Owner(s):** Boone Newspapers, Inc., PO Box 2370, Tuscaloosa, AL 35403. Telephone: 205-330-4100. **Management:** Jason Cannon, Publisher. Charles Pounders, Circulation Manager. Nicole Pell, Classified Adv. Mgr.. **Editorial:** Jason Cannon, Editor. Mike Self, Managing Editor.

SCOTTSBORO

VALLEY SUN, THE. 701 Veterans Dr., Scottsboro, AL 35768. Telephone: 256-259-1020. FAX: 256-259-2707. E-MAIL: dsnews@dailysentinel.com. Pub. Frequency: w. (Wed.) Page Size: broadsheet. **Wire Service(s):** AP. Circulation: 10,500 per issue (free). **Owner(s):** Scottsboro Newspapers, Inc., See address and contact information above. **Management:** Mike DeLapp, Publisher. Laurie Chapman, Advertising Director. Rebecca Long, Business Manager. **Editorial:** Mike DeLapp, Editor. Mazie Aldrich, Managing Editor.

SULLIGENT

LAMAR LEADER. 55071 Hwy. 17, Sulligent, AL 35586. Telephone: 205-698-8148. FAX: 205-698-8146. E-MAIL: leader@bamacomm.com. Year Established: 1973. Pub. Frequency: w. (Wed.) Page Size: broadsheet. Subscrip. Rate: $.50 newsstand/cover; $14/yr in county; $16/yr domestic adjacent cys; $17/yr in state; $20/yr out of state. Adv. Rate: col. inch $5 Circulation: 3,400 per issue (paid). **Owner(s):** Orman & Camille Wilson, See address and contact information above. **Management:** Orman Wilson, Publisher. Stephanie Wilson, Office Manager. Keith Bryson, Advertising. **Editorial:** Orman Wilson, Editor.

TALLASSEE

TALLASSEE TRIBUNE. 301 Gilmer Ave., Tallassee, AL 36078. Telephone: 334-283-6568. FAX: 334-283-6569. URL: http://www.tallasseetribune.com. Mailing Address: P.O. Drawer 780730, Tallassee, AL 36078-0730. Year Established: 1899. Pub. Frequency: w. (Thu.) Page Size: broadsheet. Subscrip. Rate: $.50 newsstand/cover; $26/yr in county; $28/yr out of county; $35/yr mailed out of state. Circulation: 4,200 per issue (paid). **Owner(s):** Josephine M Venable, See address and contact information above. **Management:** Josephine M Venable, Publisher. Barbara Morrow, Advertising Manager. Jane Parker, Circulation Manager. **Editorial:** Josephine M Venable, Editor. Jane Parker, Womens Interest Editor.

TROY

TROY MESSENGER, THE. 98 S Brundidge St, Troy, AL 36081. Telephone: 334-566-4270. FAX: 334-566-4281. E-MAIL: stacy.graning@troymessenger.com. URL: http://www.troymessenger.com. Year Established: 1866. Pub. Frequency: d. Subscrip. Rate: $108/yr home delivery in county; $125/yr out of county. Circulation: 3,000 per issue (paid). **Owner(s):** Boone Newspapers, Inc., P.O. Box 727, Troy, AL 36081. 15222 Freemen's Bend Rd., Northport, AL 35475. Telephone: 205-330-4100. **Management:** Stacy Graning, Publisher. Deedie Carter, Advertising Manager. Tim Davenport, Circulation Manager. **Editorial:** Jenny Humphryers, Editor.

TUSCUMBIA

COLBERT COUNTY REPORTER. 106 W. Fifth St., Tuscumbia, AL 35674. Telephone: 256-383-8471. FAX: 256-383-8476. E-MAIL: colbertcountyreporter@earthlink.net. Mailing Address: PO Box 969, Tuscumbia, AL 35674-0969. Year Established: 1911. Pub. Frequency: w. (Fri.) Page Size: broadsheet. Subscrip. Rate: $.50 newsstand/cover; $18/yr mailed in state; $21/yr mailed out of state; $16/yr in state to senior citizens. Circulation: 4,500 per issue (paid). **Owner(s):** Jim Crawford, Jr., See address and contact information above. **Management:** Jim Crawford Jr., Publisher. Estelle C. Whitehead, Office Manager. Charles Crawford, Advertising. **Editorial:** Jim Crawford Jr., Editor.

STANDARD & TIMES. 106 W. Fifth St., Tuscumbia, AL 35674. Telephone: 256-383-8471. FAX: 256-383-8476. E-MAIL: colbertcountyreporter@earthlink.net. Mailing Address: PO Box 969, Tuscumbia, AL 35674-0969. Year Established: 1829. Pub. Frequency: w. (Sat.) Page Size: broadsheet. Subscrip. Rate: $.50 newsstand/cover; $14/yr in county. Circulation: 1,500 per issue (paid). **Owner(s):** Jim Crawford, Jr., See address and contact information above. **Management:** Jim Crawford Jr., Publisher. Estelle C. Whitehead, Office Manager. Charles Crawford, Advertising. **Editorial:** Jim Crawford Jr., Editor.

TUSKEGEE

TUSKEGEE NEWS. 103 S. Main St., Tuskegee, AL 36083. Telephone: 334-727-3020. FAX: 334-727-7700. E-MAIL: pauldavis@bellsouth.net. Year Established: 1865. Pub. Frequency: w. (Thu.) Page Size: broadsheet. Subscrip. Rate: $.75 newsstand/cover; $27.50/yr in county; $34/yr mailed in state; $39/yr mailed out of state. Circulation: 4,800 per issue (paid). **Owner(s):** Paul Davis, See address and contact information above. **Management:** Jacquelyn Carlisle, General Manager. Paul Davis, Publisher. **Editorial:** Jacquelyn Carlisle, News Editor.

UNION SPRINGS

UNION SPRINGS HERALD. 104 E. Conecuh Ave., Union Springs, AL 36089. Telephone: 334-738-2360. FAX: 334-738-2342. Year Established: 1866. Pub. Frequency: w. (Wed.) Page Size: broadsheet. Subscrip. Rate: $.50 newsstand/cover; $20/yr mailed in state; $25/yr mailed out of state. Circulation: 3,000 per issue (paid). **Owner(s):** U S Newspapers, Inc., See address and contact information above. **Management:** Jared Falkins, Publisher. Tim Piorior, Office Manager.

VERNON

LAMAR DEMOCRAT (VERNON). 125 First Ave., N.E., Vernon, AL 35592-0587. Telephone: 205-695-7029. FAX: 205-695-9501. E-MAIL: democrat@fayette.net. Mailing Address: PO Box 587, Vernon, AL 35592-0587. Year Established: 1896. Pub. Frequency: w. (Wed.) Page Size: broadsheet. Subscrip. Rate: $.75 newsstand/cover; $25/yr mailed in county; $35/yr mailed out of county; $40/yr mailed out of state. Adv. Rate: col. inch $6 Circulation: 3,400 per issue (paid). **Owner(s):** Howard Reeves, See address and contact information above. **Management:** Howard Reeves, President. Tammy Bardon, Publisher. **Editorial:** Howard Reeves, Editor.

WETUMPKA

ECLECTIC OBSERVER, THE. 300 Green St., Wetumpka, AL 36092. Telephone: 334-567-7811. FAX: 334-567-3284. Mailing Address: PO Box 99, Wetumpka, AL 36092-0099. Pub. Frequency: w. (Thu.) Page Size: tabloid. Subscrip. Rate: $.50 newsstand/cover; $20/yr in county; $25/yr out of county. Circulation: 2,000 per issue (paid). **Owner(s):** Price Publications, Inc., See address and contact information above. **Management:** Kim N. Price, Publisher. Cheryll Focthmann, Advertising. Jay Goodwin, Circulation Manager. Shannon Elliott, Classified Editor. **Editorial:** Donna Sparks, Managing Editor.

WETUMPKA HERALD, THE. 300 Green St., Wetumpka, AL 36092. Telephone: 334-567-7811. FAX: 334-567-3284. E-MAIL: wetumpkaherald@elmore.rr.com. Mailing Address: PO Box 99, Wetumpka, AL 36092-0099. Year Established: 1898. Pub. Frequency: s-w. (Wed. & Sat.) Page Size: standard. Subscrip. Rate: $.50 newsstand/cover; $34/yr mailed in county; $38/yr mailed in state. Adv. Rate: col. inch $5.55 Circulation: 5,000 per issue (paid and free). **Owner(s):** Price Publications, Inc., See address and contact information above. **Management:** Kim N. Price, Publisher. Cheryll Focthmann, Advertising. Jay Goodwin, Circulation Manager. Shannon Elliott, Classified Editor. **Editorial:** Peggy Blackburn, Managing Editor.

ALASKA

ANCHORAGE

GREAT LANDER BUSH MAILER. 3110 Spenard Rd., Anchorage, AK 99503. Telephone: 907-274-0611. FAX: 907-272-2105. E-MAIL: marketingak@greatlander.com. URL: http://www.greatlander.com. Year Established: 1984. Pub. Frequency: m. Page Size: tabloid.Adv. Rate: B&W page $975 Circulation: 129,000 per issue (free). **Owner(s):** Anchorage Printing, Inc., See address and contact information above. **Management:** Charles Rhodes, President. Dennis Ford, Advertising Manager. **Editorial:** Charles Rhodes, Editor.

TUNDRA DRUMS, THE. ISSN 1937-2183
301 Calista Ct., Ste. B, Anchorage, AK 99518. Telephone: 907-349-6220. FAX: 907-543-3312. E-MAIL: drums@unicom-alaska.com. URL: http://www.alaskanewspapers.com. Mailing Address: PO Box 868, Bethel, AK 99559. Year Established: 1974. Pub. Frequency: w. (Thu.) Page Size: tabloid. Subscrip. Rate: $1 newsstand/cover; $75/yr mailed 2nd class; $100/yr mailed 1st class. **Wire Service(s):** AP. Circulation: 6,300 per issue (paid). **Owner(s):** Alaska Newspapers, Inc., See address and contact information above. **Management:** Linda Fernau, General Manager. **Editorial:** R A Dillon, Managing Editor. Ron Irwin, Reporter.

BARROW

ARCTIC SOUNDER, THE. 980 Stevenson St., Apt. B, Barrow, AK 99723. Telephone: 907-852-2531. FAX: 907-852-2255. URL: http://www.alaskanewspapers.com. Mailing Address: PO Box 942, Barrow, AK 99723. Pub. Frequency: w. (Thu.) Page Size: broadsheet. Subscrip. Rate: $1 newsstand/cover; $75/yr 2nd class; $100/yr 1st class. Circulation: 3,000 per issue (paid). **Owner(s):** Alaska Newspapers, Inc., 301 Calista Ct., Ste. B, Anchorage, AK 99518. Telephone: 907-543-3550. FAX: 907-543-3312. **Bureau(s):** P.O. Box 290, Kotzebue, AK 99752. Telephone: 907-442-2716. **Editorial:** Alex De Marban, Editor-in-Chief. Randall Howell, Managing Editor. Heather Reeze, Assistant Editor.

CORDOVA

CORDOVA TIMES. 528 Second St., Cordova, AK 99574-0200. Telephone: 907-424-7181. FAX: 907-424-5799. E-MAIL: cdvtimes@ptialaska.net. URL: http://alaskanewspapers.com. Mailing Address: PO Box 200, Cordova, AK 99574-0200. Year Established: 1914. Pub. Frequency: w. (Thu.) Page Size: standard. Subscrip. Rate: $1 newsstand/cover; $39/yr carrier delivery; $75/yr mailed 2nd class. Freelance Pay: $0.75-$1.25/column-inch. **Wire Service(s):** AP. Circulation: 1,200 per issue (paid). **Owner(s):** Alaska Newspapers, Inc., 301 Calista Ct., Ste. B, Anchorage, AK 99518. Telephone: 907-349-6220. FAX: 907-543-3312. **Management:** Christopher Casati, Publisher. Joy Landaluce, Advertising Manager. **Editorial:** James MacPherson, Editor-in-Chief. Alberto Cagliano, Managing Editor. Melissa Campbell, Assistant Editor.

DELTA JUNCTION

DELTA WIND, THE. 2887 Alaska Hwy., Delta Junction, AK 99737-0986. Telephone: 907-895-5115. FAX: 907-895-5116. E-MAIL: deltawind@wildak.net. URL: http://www.deltawindonline.com. Mailing Address: PO Box 986, Delta Junction, AK 99737-0986. Year Established: 1976. Pub. Frequency: w. (Thu.) Page Size: tabloid. Subscrip. Rate: $.50 newsstand/cover; $26/yr mailed. Adv. Rate: col. inch $10 **Wire Service(s):** AP. Circulation: 1,300 per issue (paid and free). **Owner(s):** TriDelta, Inc., PO Box 986, Delta Junction, AK 99737. Telephone: 907-895-4200. **Editorial:** Michael Paschall, Managing Editor.

DILLINGHAM

BRISTOL BAY TIMES, THE. ISSN 1937-2167
P.O. Box 1770, Dillingham, AK 99576. Telephone: 907-842-5572. FAX: 907-842-5562. E-MAIL: bbtimes@nushtel.com. URL: http://www.alaskanewspapers.com/bristolbay.asp. Year Established: 1980. Pub. Frequency: w. (Thu.) Page Size: tabloid. Subscrip. Rate: $1 newsstand/cover; $75/yr mailed 2nd class; $100/yr mailed 1st class. Circulation: 2,000 per issue (paid). **Owner(s):** Alaska Newspapers, Inc., 301 Calista Ct., Ste. B, Anchorage, AK 99518. Telephone: 907-349-6220. FAX: 907-543-3312. **Management:** Heidi Bohi, Publisher. John Linnehan, Advertising Manager. **Editorial:** Alex De Marban, Editor-in-Chief. Jed Ediah, Managing Editor.

DUTCH HARBOR

DUTCH HARBOR FISHERMAN, THE. ISSN 1937-2175
P.O. Box 920472, Dutch Harbor, AK 99692. Telephone: 907-581-2092. FAX: 907-581-2090. E-MAIL: fisherman@artic.net. URL: http://www.alaskanewspapers.com. Year Established: 1992. Pub. Frequency: w. (Thu.) Page Size: tabloid. Subscrip. Rate: $1 newsstand/cover; $75/yr mailed 2nd class; $100/yr mailed 1st class. Circulation: 1,000 per issue (paid). **Owner(s):** Alaska Newspapers, Inc., 301 Calista Ct., Ste. B, Anchorage, AK 99518. Telephone: 907-349-6220. FAX: 907-543-3312. **Management:** Heidi Bohi, Publisher. Carmen Zimbrick, Advertising. Brandy Johnson, Advertising Director. **Editorial:** Alex DeMarban, Editor-in-Chief. Jeff Richardson, Managing Editor.

EAGLE RIVER

ALASKA STAR. 16941 N. Eagle River Loop Rd., Eagle River, AK 99577-7499. Telephone: 907-694-2727. FAX: 907-694-1545. E-MAIL: akstar@micronet.net. URL: http://www.alaskastar.com. Year Established: 1971. Pub. Frequency: w. (Thu.) Page Size: tabloid. Subscrip. Rate: $.50 newsstand/cover; $32/yr home delivery in state or mailed; $34/yr mailed out of state. Adv. Rate: col. inch $17.80 Circulation: 6,200 per issue (paid). **Owner(s):** Morris Multimedia, Inc., PO Box 936, Augusta, GA 30903-0936. Telephone: 706-724-0851. FAX: 706-722-7125. **Management:** Jeff Jones, Publisher. Joyce Little, Advertising Manager. John Narsavich, Circulation Manager. **Editorial:** Tony Bickert, Editor.

HAINES

CHILKAT VALLEY NEWS. 229 Main St., Haines, AK 99827-0630. Telephone: 907-766-2688. FAX: 907-766-2689. E-MAIL: cvn@chilkatvalleynews.com. URL: http://www.chilkatvalleynews.com. Mailing Address: PO Box 630, Haines, AK 99827-0630. Year Established: 1966. Pub. Frequency: w. (Thu.) Page Size: tabloid. Subscrip. Rate: $1 newsstand/cover; $42/yr local; $48/yr mailed in state 2nd class; $54/yr mailed out of state 2nd class. Adv. Rate: col. inch $10 Circulation: 1,100 per issue (paid). **Owner(s):** Bonnie Hedrick, See address and contact information above. **Management:** Bonnie Hedrick, Publisher. **Editorial:** Bonnie Hedrick, Editor.

HOMER

HOMER NEWS. 3482 Landings St., Homer, AK 99603. Telephone: 907-235-7767. FAX: 907-275-4199. E-MAIL: news@homernews.com. URL: http://www.homernews.com. Year Established: 1964. Pub. Frequency: w. (Thu.) Page Size: tabloid. Subscrip. Rate: $.75 newsstand/cover; $38/yr local; $48/yr mailed in state; $59/yr mailed out of state; $105/yr mailed out of state 1st class. Adv. Rate: col. inch $10.85 Circulation: 4,000 per issue (paid). **Owner(s):** Homer News, Inc., See address and contact information above. **Management:** Lori Evans, Publisher. Gary Thomas, Advertising Director. **Editorial:** Lori Evans, Editor. Contact: Celeste Novak, Editor.

JUNEAU

CAPITAL CITY WEEKLY. 1910 Alex Holden Way, Juneau, AK 99801. Telephone: 907-789-4144. FAX: 907-789-0987. URL: http://www.capweek.com. Year Established: 1980. Pub. Frequency: w. (Wed.) Page Size: tabloid. Subscrip. Rate: $69.50/yr mailed. Circulation: 20,000 per issue (paid and free). **Owner(s):** Morris Multimedia, Inc., 725 Broad St, Augusta, GA 30901. **Management:** Karen Wright, General Manager. **Editorial:** Amanda Gragert, Editor.

NOME

NOME NUGGET. ISSN 0745-9106
PO Box 610, Nome, AK 99762. Telephone: 907-443-5235. FAX: 907-443-5112. E-MAIL: nugget@nomenugget.com. URL: http://www.nomenugget.com. Year Established: 1900. Pub. Frequency: w. (Thu.) Page Size: tabloid. Subscrip. Rate: $.50 newsstand/cover; $60/yr mailed in state; $65/yr mailed out of state. **Wire Service(s):** AP. Circulation: 6,000 per issue (paid). **Owner(s):** Nancy McGuire, See address and contact information above. **Management:** Nancy McGuire, Publisher. Jay Peterson, Advertising Manager. **Editorial:** Nancy McGuire, Editor.

PETERSBURG

PETERSBURG PILOT. 207 N Nordic Dr, Petersburg, AK 99833. Telephone: 907-772-9393. FAX: 907-772-4871. E-MAIL: psgpub@gci.net. URL: http://www.petersburgpilot.com. Mailing Address: PO Box 930, Petersburg, AK 99833. Year Established: 1974. Pub. Frequency: w. (Thu.) Page Size: tabloid. Subscrip. Rate: $1 newsstand/cover; $42/yr local; $54/yr in state; $64/yr out of state; $98/yr mailed 1st class. Adv. Rate: col. inch $10 **Wire Service(s):** AP. Circulation: 1,900 per issue (paid). **Owner(s):** Pilot Publishing, Inc., See address and contact information above. **Management:** Anne Loesch, Publisher. **Editorial:** Ronald J Loesch, Editor.

SEWARD

SEWARD PHOENIX LOG, THE. ISSN 1937-2191
302 Railway Ave., Seward, AK 99664. Telephone: 907-224-8070. FAX: 907-224-3157. E-MAIL: log@gci.net. URL: http://www.alaskanewspapers.com. Mailing Address: PO Box 89, Seward, AK 99664. Year Established: 1966. Pub. Frequency: w. (Thu.) Page Size: tabloid. Subscrip. Rate: $1 newsstand/cover; $75/yr mailed 2nd class; $100/yr mailed 1st class. **Wire Service(s):** AP. Circulation: 2,000 per issue (paid). **Owner(s):** Alaska Newspapers, Inc., 301 Calista Ct., Ste. B, Anchorage, AK 99518. Telephone: 907-349-6220. FAX: 907-543-3312. **Management:** Heidi Bohi, Publisher. Bruce Swanson, Advertising Manager. **Editorial:** Alex Demarloan, Editor-in-Chief. Nancy Erickson, Managing Editor. Colleen Kelly, Reporter.

VALDEZ

VALDEZ VANGUARD. 224 Galena, Valdez, AK 99686. Telephone: 907-835-2211. FAX: 907-835-5101. E-MAIL: vangrd@alaska.net. URL: http://www.alaskanewspapers.com. Mailing Address: PO Box 98, Valdez, AK 99686. Year Established: 1975. Pub. Frequency: w. (Wed.) Page Size: tabloid. Subscrip. Rate: $1 newsstand/cover; $75/yr. **Wire Service(s):** AP. Circulation: 1,650 per issue (paid). **Owner(s):** Alaska Newspapers, Inc., 301 Calista Ct., Ste. B, Anchorage, AK 99518. Telephone: 907-349-6220. FAX: 907-543-3312. **Management:** Christopher Casati, Publisher. Michelle Camarena, Business Manager. **Editorial:** Tony Bickert, Managing Editor. Terry Wilson, Photographer. Ruth Case, Reporter.

WASILLA

MAT - SU VALLEY FRONTIERSMAN, THE. 5751 E. Mayflower Ct., Wasilla, AK 99654-7880. Telephone: 907-352-2250. FAX: 907-352-2277. E-MAIL: contact@frontiersman.com. URL: http://www.frontiersman.com. Year Established: 1947. Pub. Frequency: 3/w. (Tue., Fri., Sun.) Page Size: broadsheet. Subscrip. Rate: $.50 newsstand/cover; $62/yr carrier delivery in city; $87/yr mailed out of city; $120/yr mailed out of state. Adv. Rate: col. inch $18.50 Freelance Pay: $25/story. **Wire Service(s):** AP. Circulation: 5,500 per issue (paid). **Owner(s):** Wick Communications, Inc., 333 W. Wilcox Dr., Ste. 302, Sierra Vista, AZ 85635. Telephone: 520-458-0200. FAX: 520-458-6166. **Management:** Kari Sleight, Publisher. Jerry Starcevic, Advertising Director. Lynn Pursley, Classified Adv. Mgr.. Jacque Sielaff, Marketing. Tracy Ressler, Business Manager. **Editorial:** Frank Ameduri, Managing Editor. Jimmy McDowell, Production Manager. Jerimiah Bartz, Sports Editor.Readers: Matanuska-Susitna Valley residents

VALLEY SUN. 5751 E. Mayflower Ct., Wasilla, AK 99654-7880. Telephone: 907-352-2250. FAX: 907-352-2277. E-MAIL: contact@frontiersman.com. Pub. Frequency: w. (Wed.) Page Size: broadsheet Circulation: 9,500 per issue (free). **Owner(s):** Wick Communications, Inc., 333 W. Wilcox Dr., Ste. 302, Sierra Vista, AZ 85635. Telephone: 520-458-0200. FAX: 520-458-6166. **Management:** Kari Sleight, Publisher. Jerry Starcevic, Advertising Director. **Editorial:** Greg Johnson, Managing Editor.

WRANGELL

WRANGELL SENTINEL. 250 Front St., Wrangell, AK 99929. Telephone: 907-874-2301. FAX: 907-874-2303. E-MAIL: wrgsent@gci.net. Mailing Address: PO Box 798, Wrangell, AK 99929-0798. Year Established: 1902. Pub. Frequency: w. (Thu.) Page Size: tabloid. Subscrip. Rate: $1 newsstand/cover; $38/yr local; $54/yr mailed in county 2nd class; $64/yr mailed out of county 1st class. Circulation: 1,500 per issue (paid). **Owner(s):** Pibot Publishing, Inc., See address and contact information above. **Management:** Ron Loesch, Publisher. **Editorial:** Ron Loesch, Editor.

AMERICAN SAMOA

PAGO PAGO

SAMOA NEWS (PAGO PAGO). PO Box 516, Pago Pago, AS 96799. Telephone: 684-633-5599. FAX: 684-633-4684. E-MAIL: editor@samoanews.com. URL: http://www.samoanews.com.Year Established: 198? Pub. Frequency: 6/w. Circulation: 8,000 per issue (paid). **Owner(s):** Osini Faleatasi, Inc., See address and contact information above. Samoa Journal & Advertiser, PO Box 909, Pago Pago, AS 96799. **Management:** Robin Annesley Dalton, General Manager.Readers: Samoan communities

ARIZONA

AJO

AJO COPPER NEWS. ISSN 1546-2846
PO Box 39, Ajo, AZ 85321. Telephone: 520-387-7688. FAX: 520-387-7688. E-MAIL: editor@cunews.info. URL: http://www.cunews.info. Year Established: 1916. Pub. Frequency: w. (Wed.) Page Size: tabloid. Subscrip. Rate: $.35 newsstand/cover; $30/yr mailed. Adv. Rate: col. inch $3.75 Circulation: 2,100 per issue (paid). **Owner(s):** Gabrielle David & Hollister J. David, See address and contact information above. **Management:** Hollister J. David, Publisher. Michelle Pacheco, Advertising Manager. **Editorial:** Gabrielle David, Editor-in-Chief. Kate Garmise, Writer.

APACHE JUNCTION

APACHE JUNCTION - GOLD CANYON INDEPENDENT. 850 S. Ironwood Dr., Ste. 112, Apache Junction, AZ 85220. Telephone: 480-982-7799. FAX: 480-671-0016. E-MAIL: ajeditor@newszap.com. URL: http://www.newszap.com. Year Established: 1959. Pub. Frequency: w. (Tue.) Page Size: broadsheet.Adv. Rate: col. inch $22.60 Circulation: 20,000 per issue (controlled and free). **Owner(s):** Independent Newspapers, Inc., PO Box 737, Dover, DE 19903. Telephone: 302-674-3600. FAX: 302-674-9510. **Management:** Lisa Grassie, Advertising Manager. Nancy Tudor, Circulation Manager. Angie Mendez, Classified Adv. Mgr.. **Editorial:** Terrance Thorton, Editor.

MESA INDEPENDENT. 850 S. Ironwood Dr., Ste. 112, Apache Junction, AZ 85220. Telephone: 480-982-7799. FAX: 480-671-0016. E-MAIL: emesanews@newszap.com. URL: http://www.newszap.com. Year Established: 1963. Pub. Frequency: w. (Tue.) Page Size: broadsheet.Adv. Rate: col. inch $24.96 Circulation: 25,000 per issue (free). **Owner(s):** Independent Newspapers, Inc., PO Box 737, Dover, DE 19903. Telephone: 302-674-3600. FAX: 302-674-9510. **Management:** Lisa Grassie, Advertising Manager. Nancy Tudor, Circulation Manager. Angie Mendez, Classified Adv. Mgr.. **Editorial:** Todd Hoover, Editor.

QUEEN CREEK INDEPENDENT. 850 S. Ironwood Dr., Ste. 112, Apache Junction, AZ 85220. Telephone: 480-982-7799. FAX: 480-671-0016. E-MAIL: qcnews@newszap.com. URL: http://www.newszap.com. Year Established: 2004. Pub. Frequency: w. (Wed.) Page Size: broadsheet. Subscrip. Rate: $.50 newsstand/cover. Adv. Rate: col. inch $20.20 Circulation: 16,000 per issue (paid and free). **Owner(s):** Independent Newspapers, Inc., PO Box 737, Dover, DE 19903. Telephone: 302-674-3600. FAX: 302-674-9510. **Management:** Lisa Grassie, Advertising Manager. Nancy Tudor, Circulation Manager. Angie Mendez, Classified Adv. Mgr.. Dan Sepulveda, Marketing. **Editorial:** Angela DeWelles, Editor.

ARIZONA CITY

ARIZONA CITY INDEPENDENT EDITION. 13350 S. Sunland Gin Rd., Ste. 1-C, Arizona City, AZ 85223-2014. Telephone: 520-466-6277. FAX: 520-466-6676. E-MAIL: editor@arizonacityindependent.com. URL: http://www.trivalleycentral.com. Mailing Address: PO Box 2014, Arizona City, AZ 85223-2014. Pub. Frequency: w. (Wed.) Page Size: tabloid. Subscrip. Rate: $.50 newsstand/cover; $25/yr mailed in county; $56/yr mailed out of county. Adv. Rate: col. inch $5.18 Circulation: 1,000 per issue (paid). **Owner(s):** Casa Grande Valley Newspapers, Inc., 200 W Second St, Casa Grande, AZ 85222. Telephone: 520-836-7461. FAX: 520-836-0343. **Management:** Donovan Kramer, Sr. Sr., Publisher. Mary Klukas, Advertising. Kara Cooper, Advertising Director. Richard Rosales, Circulation Director. **Editorial:** Kayne Crison, Editor.

AVONDALE

WEST VALLEY VIEW. 1050 E Riley Dr, Avondale, AZ 85323. E-MAIL: advertising@westvalleyview.com. URL: http://www.westvalleyview.com. Year Established: 1985. Pub. Frequency: s-w. (Tue. & Fri.) Page Size: tabloid. Subscrip. Rate: $150/yr. Adv. Rate: col. inch $39.22 Circulation: 80,458 per issue (paid and free). **Owner(s):** Freireich, See address and contact information above. **Management:** Elliott Freireich, Publisher. Stephanie Hillebrand, Advertising Director. Chris Yee, Circulation Manager. Art Schneider, Production Director. **Editorial:** Jim Painter, Editor.

BENSON

SAN PEDRO VALLEY NEWS-SUN. 200 S. Ocotillo Ave., Benson, AZ 85602. Telephone: 520-586-3382. FAX: 520-586-2382. URL: http://www.bensonnews-sun.com. Mailing Address: P.O. Drawer 1000, Benson, AZ 85602. Year Established: 1900. Pub. Frequency: w. (Wed.) Page Size: broadsheet. Subscrip. Rate: $.50 newsstand/cover; $28/yr in county; $32/yr in state; $35/yr out of state. Circulation: 3,200 per issue (paid). **Owner(s):** Wick Communications, Inc., 333 W. Wilcox Dr., Ste. 302, Sierra Vista, AZ 85635. Telephone: 520-458-0200. FAX: 520-458-6166. **Management:** Brendan Fitzsimons, Publisher. Donna Fenn, Circulation Manager. **Editorial:** Chris Dabovich, Editor.

BISBEE

BISBEE OBSERVER, THE. ISSN 0895-2450
7 Bisbee Rd., Ste. L, Bisbee, AZ 85603. Telephone: 520-432-7254. FAX: 520-432-4192. E-MAIL: bisbeeobserver@cableone.net. URL: http://www.thebisbeeobserver.com. Year Established: 1985. Pub. Frequency: w. (Thu.) Page Size: tabloid. Subscrip. Rate: $.50 newsstand/cover; $33/yr in county; $40/yr in state; $44/yr out of state. Adv. Rate: col. inch $6 Circulation: 2,300 per issue (paid). **Owner(s):** Laura Swan, See address and contact information above. **Management:** Laura Swan, Publisher.

BUCKEYE

BUCKEYE SUN, THE. 208 N Fourth St, Buckeye, AZ 85326-2440. Telephone: 623-474-6000. FAX: 623-386-7019. E-MAIL: information@buckeyesun.com. Year Established: 1993. Pub. Frequency: w. (Thu.) Page Size: tabloid.Adv. Rate: col. inch $17.40 Circulation: 25,000 per issue (free). **Owner(s):** West Valley Media One, 1416 Litchfield Rd., Ste. 240, Goodyear, AZ 85338. **Management:** Phyllis Duran, Publisher. **Editorial:** Cynthia Mae Howard, Editor.

BUCKEYE VALLEY NEWS. 122 S. Fourth St., Buckeye, AZ 85326. Telephone: 623-386-4426. FAX: 623-386-4426. E-MAIL: bvalnews@aol.com. Mailing Address: PO Box 217, Buckeye, AZ 85326-0217. Year Established: 1912. Pub. Frequency: w. (Tue.) Page Size: tabloid. Subscrip. Rate: $.40 newsstand/cover; $15.95/yr in county; $17.95/yr out of county. Circulation: 2,000 per issue (paid). **Owner(s):** Mark Shepard, See address and contact information above. **Management:** Sharon Butler, Publisher. **Editorial:** Sharon Butler, Editor.

BULLHEAD CITY

BULLHEAD CITY BEE. ISSN 1049-0884
1905 Lakeside Dr., Bullhead City, AZ 86442-5726. Telephone: 928-763-9339. FAX: 928-763-1510. E-MAIL: buzzybee@bullcity-bee.com. URL: http://www.bullheadcity-bee.com. Pub. Frequency: w. (Fri.) Page Size: broadsheet. Subscrip. Rate: $.25 newsstand/cover; $14.95/yr in county; $39/yr mailed out of county. Circulation: 6,000 per issue (paid). **Owner(s):** Thom McGraham, See address and contact information above. **Management:** Thom McGraham, Publisher. Belinda Canning, Advertising Manager. **Editorial:** Shirin McGraham, Editor. Contact: Thom McGraham, Publisher.

CLIPPIN' THE RIVER. 1610 Riverview Dr, Ste 4, Bullhead City, AZ 86442. Telephone: 928-704-6245. FAX: 928-704-6284. URL: http://www.clippintheriver.com. Pub. Frequency: w. (Wed.) Page Size: tabloid Circulation: 20,000 per issue (free). **Owner(s):** Brehm Communications, Inc., 16644 W. Bernardo Dr., Ste. 300, San Diego, CA 92127. Telephone: 619-451-6200. **Management:** Wells Andrews, General Manager. Chuck Rathbun, Publisher. Larry Imoe, Circulation Manager. Kathy Jones, Classified Adv. Mgr.. Sue Anderson, Business Manager.

THE/BOOSTER (BULLHEAD CITY). 2435 Miracle Mile, Bullhead City, AZ 86442. Telephone: 928-763-2505. FAX: 928-763-7820. URL: http://www.mohavedailynews.com. Mailing Address: PO Box 21209, Bullhead City, AZ 86439. Year Established: 1969. Pub. Frequency: s-w. (Wed. & Sun.) Page Size: tabloid.Adv. Rate: col. inch $6.85 Circulation: 15,200 per issue (free); 10,325 Sunday (free). **Owner(s):** Brehm Communications, Inc., 16644 W. Bernardo Dr., Ste. 300, San Diego, CA 92127. Telephone: 619-451-6200. **Management:** Paul Stubler, General Manager. Chuck Rathbun, Publisher. Maria Pynakker, Advertising Manager. Ed Clary, Circulation Manager. Kathy Jones, Classified Adv. Mgr..

CAMP VERDE

CAMP VERDE JOURNAL, THE. 406 S. First St., Camp Verde, AZ 86322. Telephone: 928-567-3341. FAX: 928-567-2373. E-MAIL: cveditor@larsonnwewspapers.com. Mailing Address: PO Box 2048, Camp Verde, AZ 86322-2048. Year Established: 1980. Pub. Frequency: w. (Wed.) Page Size: standard. Subscrip. Rate: $.50 newsstand/cover; $16/yr local; $22/yr elsewhere. Adv. Rate: col. inch $8.50 Circulation: 2,400 per issue (paid and free). **Owner(s):** Camp Verde Journal LLC, The, See address and contact information above. **Management:** Robert B. Larson, Publisher. Eric Mageary, Circulation Manager. **Editorial:** Doug McDaniel, Editor.

CASA GRANDE

PINAL COUNTY STAR WATCH. 200 W Second St, Casa Grande, AZ 85222. Telephone: 520-836-7461. FAX: 520-836-0343. E-MAIL: ad@trivalleycentral.com. URL: http://www.trivalleycentral.com. Mailing Address: PO Box 15002, Casa Grande, AZ 85222-5002. Pub. Frequency: w. (Sat.) Page Size: tabloid.Adv. Rate: col. inch $9.76 Circulation: 23,000 per issue (free). **Owner(s):** Casa Grande Valley Newspapers, Inc., See address and contact information above. **Management:** Donovan Kramer, Jr., Publisher. Kara Cooper, Advertising Director. Richard Rosales, Circulation Director. Kim Sumpter, Classified Adv. Mgr..

WAMPUM SAVER (CASA GRANDE). 200 W Second St, Casa Grande, AZ 85222. Telephone: 520-836-7461. FAX: 520-836-0343. Mailing Address: PO Box 15002, Casa Grande, AZ 85222-5002. Pub. Frequency: w. (Tue.) Page Size: tabloid Circulation: 23,000 per issue (free). **Owner(s):** Casa Grande Valley Newspapers, Inc., See address and contact information above. **Management:** Kara Cooper, Advertising Director. Richard Rosales, Circulation Director. Kim Sumpter, Classified Adv. Mgr..

CAVE CREEK

SONORAN NEWS. 6812 E. Cave Creek Rd., Cave Creek, AZ 85331. Telephone: 480-488-2021. FAX: 480-488-6216. URL: http://www.sonorannews.com. Pub. Frequency: w. (Wed.) Page Size: broadsheet. Subscrip. Rate: $20.20 mailed for 13 wks.; $78.55/yr mailed. Adv. Rate: col. inch $28 Circulation: 43,000 per issue (free). **Owner(s):** Conestoga Merchants, Inc., See address and contact information above. **Management:** Don Sorchych, Publisher. Charles Anthony, Advertising. Sandy Hapkowskij, Classified Adv. Mgr.. **Editorial:** Don Sorchych, Editor.Readers: North Maricopa County

CHANDLER

SANTAN SUN NEWS. PO Box 23, Chandler, AZ 85244-0023. Telephone: 480-732-0250. FAX: 480-883-8714. E-MAIL: info@santansun.com. URL: http://www.santansunnews.com. Year Established: 1995. Pub. Frequency: s-m. (1st. & 3rd. Sat.) Page Size: tabloid. Subscrip. Rate: $40/yr. Circulation: 35,000 per issue (paid and free). Owner(s): Fagen-Hancock, LLC, See address and contact information above. Management: Laurie Fagen, Publisher. Geoff Hancock, Advertising Director. Editorial: Linda Exley, Editor. Susan Henderson, Managing Editor. Shawn Patrick, Graphics Editor.Readers: Middle to upper class families with children; seniors

CHINO VALLEY

CHINO VALLEY REVIEW. 401 W. Palomino Rd., Chino Valley, AZ 86323. Telephone: 928-636-2653. FAX: 928-636-1334. URL: http://www.prescottaz.com. Mailing Address: PO Box 428, Chino Valley, AZ 86323. Pub. Frequency: w. (Wed.) Page Size: broadsheet. Subscrip. Rate: $.50 newsstand/cover; $104/yr mailed 1st class. Freelance Pay: $1/column-inch. Circulation: 8,000 per issue (paid and free). Owner(s): Western News & Info., Inc., 201 S. First St., Ste 4, Yuma, AZ 85364. Telephone: 928-783-3311. Management: Kit Atwell, Publisher. Sarah Vaughn, Advertising. John Harrell, Circulation Director. Diane DeHamer, Classified Adv. Mgr.. Editorial: Ben Hansen, Editor. Andy Draper, Managing Editor.

COOLIDGE

COOLIDGE EXAMINER. 353 W. Central Ave., Coolidge, AZ 85228. Telephone: 520-723-5441. FAX: 520-723-7899. URL: http://www.trivalleycentral.com. Mailing Address: PO Box 129, Coolidge, AZ 85228. Pub. Frequency: w. (Wed.) Page Size: broadsheet. Subscrip. Rate: $.50 newsstand/cover; $29/yr mailed in county; $45/yr mailed out of county; $56/yr mailed out of state. Adv. Rate: col. inch $7.84 Circulation: 2,288 per issue (paid). Owner(s): Casa Grande Valley Newspapers, Inc., 200 W Second St, Casa Grande, AZ 85222. Telephone: 520-836-7461. FAX: 520-836-0343. Management: Donovan Kramer, Jr., Publisher. Kara Cooper, Advertising Director. Bob Tuley, Advertising Manager. Kim Sumpter, Classified Adv. Mgr.. Editorial: Brian Ahnmark, Editor. Edward Petruska, Sports Editor.

COTTONWOOD

COTTONWOOD JOURNAL EXTRA. 830 S. Main., Ste. 1-E, Cottonwood, AZ 86326. E-MAIL: editor@larsonnewspapers.com. URL: http://www.journalaz.com. Year Established: 1988. Pub. Frequency: w. (Wed.) Page Size: broadsheet. Subscrip. Rate: $.50 newsstand/cover; $16/yr in county; $22/yr out of county. Circulation: 7,250 per issue (paid). Owner(s): Larson Newspapers, PO Box 619, Sedona, AZ 86336. Management: Robert Larson Jr., Publisher. Eric McGuerey, Circulation Manager. Editorial: Ryan Van Benthuyfen, Managing Editor. Lu Stitt, News Editor.

VERDE INDEPENDENT. 116 S. Main St., Cottonwood, AZ 86326. Telephone: 928-634-2241. FAX: 928-634-2312. E-MAIL: pmiller@verdevalleynews.com. URL: http://www.verdenews.com. Mailing Address: PO Box 429, Cottonwood, AZ 86326. Year Established: 1948. Pub. Frequency: 3/w. (Wed., Fri., Sun.) Page Size: broadsheet. Subscrip. Rate: $.50 newsstand/cover; $59/yr carrier delivery. Freelance Pay: $1/column-inch. Circulation: 4,800 per issue (paid). Owner(s): Western News & Info., Inc., 1748 S. Arizona Ave., Yuma, AZ 85364-5727. Management: Pam Miller, Publisher. Shelley VanderKraats, Advertising Manager. Pam Miller, Circulation Manager. Editorial: Dan Engler, Editor. Raquel Hendrickson, Associate Editor.Readers: Local community

DE WITT

DE WITT ERA ENTERPRISE. 326 Court Sq., PO Box 431, De Witt, AZ 72042. Telephone: 870-946-3241. FAX: 870-946-1888. E-MAIL: dewitt@cpomail.net. URL: http://www.dewitt-ee.com. Year Established: 1882. Pub. Frequency: w. (Wed.) Page Size: broadsheet. Subscrip. Rate: $.50 newsstand/cover; $17/yr in county; $21/yr in state; $24/yr elsewhere. Adv. Rate: col. inch $5 Circulation: 3,100 per issue (paid). Owner(s): Frank Scott and Christina Verderosa, See address and contact information above. Management: C.F. Scott, Publisher. Christina Verderosa, Advertising Manager. Editorial: C.F. Scott, Editor. Ann Cox, Production Manager.

DOUGLAS

VALLEY VISTA. 530 11th St., Douglas, AZ 85607. Telephone: 520-364-3424. FAX: 520-364-6750. Mailing Address: PO Box H, Douglas, AZ 85608. Pub. Frequency: w. (Fri.) Owner(s): Wick Communications, Inc., 333 W. Wilcox Dr., Ste. 302, Sierra Vista, AZ 83635. Telephone: 520-458-0200. FAX: 520-458-6166. Management: Larry Blaskey, Publisher. Ana Maria Santana, Advertising Manager. Karl Sproule, Circulation Manager. Marta Gallegos, Business Manager. Editorial: Larry Blaskey, Editor. April Martin, Managing Editor.

VIVA. 530 11th St., Douglas, AZ 85607. Telephone: 520-364-3424. FAX: 520-364-6750. Mailing Address: PO Box H, Douglas, AZ 85608.Pub. Frequency: w. (Tue.) Circulation: 20,500 per issue (free). Owner(s): Wick Communications, Inc., 333 W. Wilcox Dr., Ste. 302, Sierra Vista, AZ 83635. Telephone: 520-458-0200. FAX: 520-458-6166. Management: Larry Blaskey, Publisher. Ana Maria Santana, Advertising Manager. Karl Sproule, Circulation Manager. Marta Gallegos, Business Manager. Editorial: April Martin, Managing Editor.

ELOY

ELOY ENTERPRISE. 710 N. Main St., Eloy, AZ 85231. Telephone: 520-466-7333. FAX: 520-466-7334. E-MAIL: enterprise@theriver.com. URL: http://www.trivalleycentral.com. Mailing Address: PO Box 15002, Casa Grande, AZ 85222-5002. Year Established: 1947. Pub. Frequency: w. (Thu.) Page Size: broadsheet. Subscrip. Rate: $.50 newsstand/cover; $29/yr local; $45/yr mailed out of county; $56/yr mailed out of state. Adv. Rate: col. inch $6.15 Circulation: 1,200 per issue (paid). Owner(s): Casa Grande Valley Newspapers, Inc., 200 W Second St, Casa Grande, AZ 85222. Telephone: 520-836-7461. FAX: 520-836-0343. Management: Donovan Kramer, Jr., Publisher. Kara Cooper, Advertising Director. Kim Sumpter, Classified Adv. Mgr.. Editorial: Jose Garcia, Editor. Edward Petruska, Sports Editor.

FLORENCE

FLORENCE REMINDER & BLADE-TRIBUNE. 190 N. Main St., Florence, AZ 85232. Telephone: 520-868-5897. FAX: 520-868-5898. URL: http://www.trivalleycentral.com. Mailing Address: PO Box 15002, Casa Grande, AZ 85222-5002. Year Established: 1882. Pub. Frequency: w. (Thu.) Page Size: broadsheet. Subscrip. Rate: $.50 newsstand/cover; $29/yr mailed in county; $45/yr mailed out of county; $56/yr mailed out of state. Wire Service(s): AP. Circulation: 1,800 per issue (paid). Owner(s): Casa Grande Valley Newspapers, Inc., 200 W Second St, Casa Grande, AZ 85222. Telephone: 520-836-7461. Management: Donovan Kramer, Sr. Sr., Publisher. Kara Cooper, Advertising Director. Bob Tuley, Advertising Manager. Richard Rosales, Circulation Director. Kim Sumpter, Classified Adv. Mgr.. Editorial: Mark Cowling, Editor.

FOUNTAIN HILLS

FOUNTAIN HILLS TIMES, THE. 16929 E. Enterprise Dr., Fountain Hills, AZ 85269. Telephone: 480-837-1925. FAX: 480-837-1951. E-MAIL: alan@fhtimes.goodnet.com. URL: http://www.fhtimes.com. Pub. Frequency: w. (Wed.) Page Size: broadsheet. Subscrip. Rate: $.75 newsstand/cover; $32/yr. Adv. Rate: col. inch $6.83 Circulation: 6,200 per issue (paid). Owner(s): L. Alan Cruikshank, See address and contact information above. Management: L. Alan Cruikshank, Publisher. Dani Cordaro, Circulation Manager. Editorial: Michael Scharnow, Editor.

GLENDALE

GLENDALE STAR, THE.   ISSN 1053-7600
7122 N. 59th Ave., Glendale, AZ 85301. Telephone: 623-842-6000. FAX: 623-842-6017. E-MAIL: wtoops@star-times.com. URL: http://www.glendalestar.com. Year Established: 1979. Pub. Frequency: w. (Thu.) Page Size: tabloid. Subscrip. Rate: $.50 newsstand/cover; $25/yr in county; $30/yr out of county. Adv. Rate: col. inch $8.65 Circulation: 9,975 per issue (paid); 2,025 per issue (free). Owner(s): Pueblo Publishers, Inc., See address and contact information above. Management: William V. Toops, President. William E. Toops, Publisher. Connie Williams, Advertising Manager. Noel G. Lucht, Circulation Manager. Brenda Fenimore, Classified Adv. Mgr.. Editorial: Carolyn Dryer, Editor-in-Chief.

PEORIA TIMES. 7122 N. 59th Ave., Glendale, AZ 85301. Telephone: 623-842-6000. FAX: 623-842-6017. E-MAIL: wtoops@star-times.com. URL: http://www.peoriatimes.com. Year Established: 1952. Pub. Frequency: w. (Fri.) Page Size: tabloid. Subscrip. Rate: $.50 newsstand/cover; $25/yr in county; $30/yr out of county. Adv. Rate: col. inch $7.20 Circulation: 6,450 per issue (paid); 1,550 per issue (free). Owner(s): Pueblo Publishers, Inc., See address and contact information above. Management: William V. Toops, President. William E. Toops, Publisher. Connie Williams, Advertising Manager. Noel G. Lucht, Circulation Manager. Brenda Fenimore, Classified Adv. Mgr.. Editorial: Carolyn Dryer, Editor.

GLOBE

ARIZONA SILVER BELT. 298 N. Pine St., Globe, AZ 85501. Telephone: 928-425-7121. FAX: 928-425-7001. URL: http://www.silverbelt.com. Mailing Address: PO Box 31, Globe, AZ 85502. Year Established: 1878. Pub. Frequency: w. (Wed.) Page Size: broadsheet. Subscrip. Rate: $.75 newsstand/cover; $28/yr mailed in county; $33/yr mailed out of county. Circulation: 5,200 per issue (paid). Owner(s): GateHouse Media, Inc, 350 WillowBrook Office Park, Fairport, NY 14450. Telephone: 585-598-0030. FAX: 585-248-2631. Management: John Bennett, Publisher. Andrea Marcenti, Circulation Manager. Megan Clark, Classified Adv. Mgr.. Editorial: John Bennett, Editor.

COPPER COUNTRY NEWS. 1776 E. Ash St, Globe, AZ 85501. Telephone: 928-425-0355. FAX: 928-425-6535. E-MAIL: globeccn@yahoo.com. Year Established: 1984. Pub. Frequency: w. (Wed.) Page Size: tabloid. Subscrip. Rate: $50/yr mailed local. Adv. Rate: col. inch $8.25 Circulation: 16,000 per issue (paid). Owner(s): Rita & Glen Hassard, See address and contact information above. Management: Rita Hassard, Publisher. MaryLou Hussaker, Advertising Manager. Editorial: Rita Hassard, Editor.

GILA COUNTY ADVANTAGE. 298 N. Pine St., Globe, AZ 85501. Telephone: 928-425-7121. FAX: 928-425-7001. Mailing Address: PO Box 31, Globe, AZ 85502. Pub. Frequency: w. (Tue.) Page Size: standard Circulation: 4,600 per issue (free). Owner(s): GateHouse Media, Inc, 350 WillowBrook Office Park, Fairport, NY 14450. Telephone: 585-598-0030. Management: John Bennett, Publisher. Andrea Marcenti, Circulation Manager. Megan Clark, Classified Adv. Mgr..

SAN CARLOS APACHE MOCCASIN. 298 N. Pine St., Globe, AZ 85501. Telephone: 928-425-7121. FAX: 928-425-7001. URL: http://www.silverbelt.com. Mailing Address: PO Box 31, Globe, AZ 85502. Pub. Frequency: w. (Wed.) Page Size: broadsheet. Subscrip. Rate: $.75 newsstand/cover; $28/yr in county; $33/yr out of county. Circulation: 2,100 per issue (paid). Owner(s): GateHouse Media, Inc, 350 WillowBrook Office Park, Fairport, NY 14450. Telephone: 585-598-0030. FAX: 585-248-2631. Management: John Bennett, Publisher. Andrea Marcenti, Circulation Manager. Megan Clark, Classified Adv. Mgr.. Editorial: John Bennett, Editor.

GREEN VALLEY

GREEN VALLEY NEWS & SUN. 101-42 S. LaCanada, Green Valley, AZ 85614. Telephone: 520-625-5511. FAX: 520-625-8046. E-MAIL: editorial@gvnews.com. URL: http://www.gvnews.com. Mailing Address: PO Box 567, Green Valley, AZ 85622. Year Established: 1964. Pub. Frequency: 3/w. (Wed., Fri., Sun.) Page Size: standard. Subscrip. Rate: $.75 newsstand/cover; $55/yr carrier delivery; $75/yr mailed; $70/yr mailed for snowbirds. Adv. Rate: col. inch $13.25 Circulation: 11,500 per issue (paid). Owner(s): Wick Communications, Inc., 333 Wilcox Dr., Ste. 302, Sierra Vista, AZ 85635-1756. Telephone: 520-458-0200. Management: Pamela K. Mox, Publisher. Kelly Walter, Advertising Manager. Donna West, Circulation Director. Peggy Dorio, Classified Adv. Mgr.. Editorial: Pamela K. Mox, Editor. Kathy Engle, Managing Editor. Jim Lamb, Asst. Managing Ed..

HOLBROOK

HOLBROOK TRIBUNE NEWS. 200 E. Hopi Dr., Holbrook, AZ 86025. Telephone: 928-524-6205. FAX: 928-524-3541. E-MAIL: francie@azjournal.com. URL: http://www.azjournal.com. Mailing Address: PO Box 670, Holbrook, AZ 86025-0670. Year Established: 1909. Pub. Frequency: s-w. (Wed. & Fri.) Page Size: broadsheet. Subscrip. Rate: $.50 newsstand/cover; $33/yr mailed in county; $39/yr mailed in state; $47/yr mailed out of state. Circulation: 3,600 per issue (paid). Owner(s): Navajo County Publishers, Inc., See address and contact information above. Management: Matthew Barger, Co-Publisher. Bill Wiegand, Advertising. Matthew Barger, Advertising Director. Editorial: Francie Payne, Editor.

KEARNY

COPPER BASIN NEWS. 366 Alden Rd., Kearny, AZ 85237-9900. Telephone: 520-363-5554. FAX: 520-363-9663. URL: http://www.copperarea.com. Mailing Address: PO Box 579, Kearny, AZ 85237-0579. Year Established: 1958. Pub. Frequency: w. (Wed.) Page Size: broadsheet. Subscrip. Rate: $.50 newsstand/cover; $30.50/yr in county; $35.50/yr out of county. Adv. Rate: col. inch $5.60 Freelance Pay: $1/column-inch. Circulation: 2,500 per issue (paid). Owner(s): James Carnes, See address and contact information above. Management: James Carnes, Publisher. Editorial: Gayle Carnes, Managing Editor.

LAKE HAVASU CITY

LAKE HAVASU CITY WHITE SHEET. 2099 W. Acoma Blvd., Ste. A, Lake Havasu City, AZ 86403. Telephone: 928-855-7871. FAX: 928-855-8183. E-MAIL: whitesheet@online.net. Year Established: 1955. Pub. Frequency: w. (Tue.) Page Size: tabloid Circulation: 12,500 per issue (free). Owner(s): Schurz Communications, Inc., 225 W. Colfax Ave., South Bend, IN 46626. Telephone: 574-287-1001. FAX: 574-287-2257. Management: Hal Paradis, Publisher. John Schneider, Sales Manager. Esperanza Barrett, Controller.

PARKER-BLYTHE WHITE SHEET. 2099 W. Acoma Blvd., Ste. A, Lake Havasu City, AZ 86403. Telephone: 928-855-7871. FAX: 928-855-8183. E-MAIL: whitesheet@online.net. Year Established: 1955. Pub. Frequency: w. (Tue.) Page Size: tabloid Circulation: 15,000 per issue (free). Owner(s): Schurz Communications, Inc., 225 W. Colfax Ave., South Bend, IN 46626. Telephone: 574-287-1001. FAX: 574-287-2257. Management: Hal Paradis, Publisher. John Schneider, Sales Manager.

TRI STATE WHITE SHEET. 2099 W. Acoma Blvd., Ste. A, Lake Havasu City, AZ 86403. Telephone: 928-855-7871. FAX: 928-855-8183. E-MAIL: whitesheet@online.net. Year Established: 1955. Pub. Frequency: w. (Tue.) Page Size: tabloid Circulation: 11,000 per issue (free). **Owner(s):** Schurz Communications, Inc., 225 W. Colfax Ave., South Bend, IN 46626. Telephone: 574-287-1001. FAX: 574-287-2257. **Management:** Hal Paradis, Publisher. John Schneider, Sales Manager.

MARICOPA

MARICOPA MONITOR. 19756 N John Wayne Pkwy, Ste 106, Maricopa, AZ 852239. Telephone: 520-568-4198. FAX: 520-568-4729. E-MAIL: monitor@theriver.com. URL: http://www.trivalleycentral.com. Mailing Address: PO Box 15002, Casa Grande, AZ 85222-5002. Pub. Frequency: w. (Fri.) Page Size: broadsheet. Subscrip. Rate: $.50 newsstand/cover; $25/yr mailed in county; $45/yr mailed out of county; $56/yr mailed out of state. Adv. Rate: col. inch $6.34 Circulation: 3,000 per issue (paid). **Owner(s):** Casa Grande Valley Newspapers, Inc., 200 W Second St, Casa Grande, AZ 85222. Telephone: 520-836-7461. **Management:** Donovan Kramer, Jr., Publisher. Kara Cooper, Advertising Director. Richard Rosales, Circulation Director. Kim Sumpter, Classified Adv. Mgr.. **Editorial:** Kathy Hall, Editor. Edward Petruska, Sports Editor.

NOGALES

NOGALES INTERNATIONAL. 268 W. View Point Dr., Nogales, AZ 85621-4114. Telephone: 520-281-9706. FAX: 520-761-3115. URL: http://www.nogalesinternational.com. Mailing Address: PO Box 579, Nogales, AZ 85628-0579. Year Established: 1925. Pub. Frequency: s-w. (Tue. & Fri.) Page Size: standard. Subscrip. Rate: $.75 newsstand/cover; $49/yr in county; $59/yr out of county. Adv. Rate: col. inch $7.50 Circulation: 5,000 per issue (paid). **Owner(s):** Wick Communications, Inc., 333 W. Wilcox Dr., Ste. 302, Sierra Vista, AZ 85635. Telephone: 520-458-0200. FAX: 520-458-6166. **Management:** Robert Kimball, Publisher. Guetvo Lopez, Advertising. Sandra Morales, Business Manager. **Editorial:** Robert Kimball, Editor. Kathleen Vandervoet, Managing Editor.

PAGE

LAKE POWELL CHRONICLE. 3 Elm St Mall, PO Box 1716, Page, AZ 86040. Telephone: 928-645-8888. FAX: 928-645-2209. E-MAIL: christopher@lakepowellchronicle.com. URL: http://www.lakepowellchronicle.com. Year Established: 1965. Pub. Frequency: w. (Wed.) Page Size: broadsheet. Subscrip. Rate: $.75 newsstand/cover; $38/yr in county; $52/yr mailed in state; $66/yr mailed out of state. Circulation: 3,400 per issue (paid). **Owner(s):** News Media Corp., 211 Hwy. 38 E., Rochelle, IL 61608. Telephone: 815-562-2061. FAX: 815-562-5060. **Management:** Sue Shenniman, Publisher. Ed Pease, Advertising Director. Sharon Douglas, Circulation Manager. **Editorial:** Christopher Sheid, Editor.

PARKER

PARKER PIONEER. 1001 W. 12th St., Parker, AZ 85344. Telephone: 928-669-2275. FAX: 928-669-9624. Mailing Address: PO Box 3365, Parker, AZ 85344. Year Established: 1954. Pub. Frequency: w. (Wed.) Page Size: broadsheet. Subscrip. Rate: $.50 newsstand/cover; $23.10/yr mailed in county; $27.72/yr mailed in state; $40.32/yr mailed out of state. Circulation: 5,000 per issue (paid). **Owner(s):** River City Newspapers LLC, 2225 W. Acoma Blvd., Lake Havasu City, AZ 86403-1756. Telephone: 928-453-4237. **Management:** Mike Quinn, Publisher. Steve Stevens, Advertising Director. Jim Abdon, Circulation Manager. **Editorial:** Joan M. Travis, Editor.

PAYSON

PAYSON ROUNDUP. 708 N. Beeline Hwy., Payson, AZ 85547. Telephone: 928-474-5251. FAX: 928-474-1893. E-MAIL: rounduppro@aol.com. URL: http://www.paysonroundup.com. Mailing Address: PO Box 2520, Payson, AZ 85547. Year Established: 1937. Pub. Frequency: s-w. (Tue. & Fri.) Page Size: standard. Subscrip. Rate: $.50 newsstand/cover; $39.50/yr in county; $65.50/yr out of county. **Wire Service(s):** AP. Circulation: 7,200 per issue (paid). **Owner(s):** WorldWest LLC, 609 New Hampshire, P.O. Box 688, Lawrence, KS 66044. Telephone: 785-843-1000. **Management:** Richard Haddad, Publisher. Julie Haught, Advertising Director. **Editorial:** Jerry Thebado, Editor.

PHOENIX

NEW TIMES (PHOENIX). ISSN 0279-3962
1201 E Jefferson St, Phoenix, AZ 85034. Telephone: 415-541-0700. FAX: 415-541-9096. E-MAIL: editor@newtimes.com. URL: http://www.phoenixnewtimes.com. Mailing Address: PO Box 2510, Phoenix, AZ 85002. Year Established: 1970.Pub. Frequency: w. Page Size: tabloid Circulation: 140,000 (free). **Owner(s):** Village Voice Media, Inc., See address and contact information above. **Management:** Kurtis Barton, Publisher. Jennifer Rockstad, Advertising Director. Jack Erickson, Circulation Director. Ellis Alvarez, Classified Adv. Mgr.. **Editorial:** Rick Barrs, Editor. Amy Silverman, Associate Editor. Niki D'Andrea, Music Editor.

PHOENIX PRESS WEEKLY. 623 E Euclid Ave, Phoenix, AZ 85066. Telephone: 602-243-1857. Mailing Address: PO Box 8753, Phoenix, AZ 85066-8753.Pub. Frequency: w. Page Size: standard Circulation: 8,200 per issue (free). **Owner(s):** Ellison Publications Inc., See address and contact information above. **Management:** Deborah Ellison, Publisher. **Editorial:** Lee Norman, Editor.

PRESCOTT VALLEY

PRESCOTT VALLEY TRIBUNE, THE. 8303 State Rte. 69 E., Prescott Valley, AZ 86314. Telephone: 928-775-4440. FAX: 928-772-3393. E-MAIL: editorial@prescottaz.com. URL: http://www.prescottvalleytribune.com. Pub. Frequency: s-w. (Wed. & Fri.) Page Size: broadsheet. Subscrip. Rate: $.50 newsstand/cover; $260/yr mailed. Circulation: 15,367 per issue (paid and controlled). **Owner(s):** Western News & Info., Inc., 201 S. First St., Ste 4, Yuma, AZ 85364. Telephone: 928-783-3311. **Management:** Kit Atwell, Publisher. JohnPam Gremaldi, Advertising Director. John Harrell, Circulation Director. **Editorial:** Ben Hansen, Editor. Jerry Herrmann, Managing Editor.

SAFFORD

COPPER ERA, THE. 301 E.U.S. Hwy 70 #A, Safford, AZ 85546-2043. Telephone: 928-865-3162. FAX: 928-428-3110. E-MAIL: eacourier@aepnet.com. URL: http://www.eacourier.com. Year Established: 1899. Pub. Frequency: w. (Wed.) Page Size: broadsheet. Subscrip. Rate: $.75 newsstand/cover; $24/yr home delivery in county; $34/yr mailed in state; $39/yr mailed out of state. Freelance Pay: $0.50/column-inch. Circulation: 2,500 per issue (paid). **Owner(s):** Wick Communications, Inc., 333 W. Wilcox Dr., Ste. 302, Sierra Vista, AZ 85635-1357. Telephone: 520-458-0200. FAX: 520-458-6166. **Management:** Rick Schneider, President. Chad Christenson, Advertising Manager. **Editorial:** Walter Mares, News Editor.

EASTERN ARIZONA COURIER. 301 Hwy. 70 E., Ste. A, Safford, AZ 85546. Telephone: 928-428-2560. FAX: 928-428-4901. E-MAIL: publisher@eacourier.com. URL: http://www.eacourier.com. Year Established: 1967. Pub. Frequency: w. (Wed.) Page Size: broadsheet. Subscrip. Rate: $.75 newsstand/cover; $29/yr mailed in cy. & adj. cys.; $39/yr mailed in state. Freelance Pay: $25/article. Circulation: 9,700 per issue (paid and free). **Owner(s):** Wick Communications, Inc., 333 W. Wilcox Dr., Ste. 302, Sierra Vista, AZ 85635. Telephone: 928-458-0200. FAX: 928-458-6166. **Management:** Rick Schneider, Publisher. Chad Christenson, Advertising Manager. Jerry Robinson, Classified Adv. Mgr.. **Editorial:** Aimee Staten, Managing Editor. John Kamin, Assistant Editor. Daniel McKillop, Sports Editor.

SAN MANUEL

SAN MANUEL MINER, THE. 139 W 8th Ave., San Manuel, AZ 85631-1161. Telephone: 520-385-2266. FAX: 520-385-4666. Pub. Frequency: w. (Wed.) Page Size: broadsheet. Subscrip. Rate: $.50 newsstand/cover; $35.50/yr in county; $40.50/yr elsewhere. Adv. Rate: col. inch $5.50 Circulation: 3,100 evening (paid). **Owner(s):** Central Pinal Publishing Co., PO Box 60, San Manuel, AZ 85631-0060. **Management:** James Carnes, Publisher. **Editorial:** Gayle Carnes, Editor.

SCOTTSDALE

NORTH SCOTTSDALE INDEPENDENT. 11000 N Scottsdale Rd, Ste 210, Scottsdale, AZ 85254. Telephone: 480-483-0977. FAX: 480-946-0496. URL: http://www.newszap.com. Year Established: 1985. Pub. Frequency: w. Page Size: broadsheet.Subscrip. Rate: $.50 newsstand/cover Circulation: 13,000 per issue (free). **Owner(s):** Independent Newspapers, Inc., PO Box 737, Dover, DE 19903. Telephone: 302-629-5505. FAX: 302-674-9510. **Management:** Ed Dulin, President. Mark Lindsey, Advertising. Angie Mendez, Classified Adv. Mgr.. **Editorial:** Jennifer Amsler, Editor.

TOWN OF PARADISE VALLEY INDEPENDENT. 11000 N Scottsdale Rd, Ste 210, Scottsdale, AZ 85254. Telephone: 480-483-0977. FAX: 480-946-0496. E-MAIL: pvalleynews@newszap.com. URL: http://www.newszap.com. Year Established: 1982. Pub. Frequency: w. (Wed.) Page Size: broadsheet. Subscrip. Rate: $.50 newsstand/cover; $44/yr mailed 3rd class. Adv. Rate: col. inch $15.28 Circulation: 6,500 per issue (paid and controlled). **Owner(s):** Independent Newspapers, Inc., PO Box 737, Dover, DE 19903. Telephone: 302-674-3600. FAX: 302-674-9510. **Management:** Ed Dulin, President. Mark Lindsey, Advertising. Angie Mendez, Classified Adv. Mgr.. **Editorial:** Jennifer Amsler, Editor.

SEDONA

SEDONA RED ROCK NEWS. 298 Van Deren Rd., Sedona, AZ 86336. Telephone: 928-282-7795. FAX: 928-282-6011. E-MAIL: editor@larsonnewspapers.com. URL: http://www.redrocknews.com. Mailing Address: PO Box 619, Sedona, AZ 86339. Year Established: 1963. Pub. Frequency: s-w. (Wed. & Fri.) Page Size: broadsheet. Subscrip. Rate: $.50 newsstand/cover; $43/yr carrier delivery local; $64/yr mailed out of area. Freelance Pay: $1.25/column-inch. Circulation: 7,500 per issue (paid). **Owner(s):** Larson Publishing, See address and contact information above. **Management:** Robert S. Larson, President. Robert B. Larson, Publisher. Rebecca Tarnow, Advertising Director. **Editorial:** Ryan Van Benthuysen, Editor-in-Chief.

SHOW LOW

WAMPUM SAVER. 3191 S. White Mountain Rd., Show Low, AZ 85902-1570. Telephone: 928-537-5721. FAX: 928-537-1780. E-MAIL: gtock@wmicentral.com. URL: http//www.wmicentral.com. Mailing Address: PO Box 1570, Show Low, AZ 85902-1570. Year Established: 1975. Pub. Frequency: s-w. (Wed. & Sat.) Page Size: tabloid Circulation: 17,829 per issue (free). **Owner(s):** White Mountain Publishing Co., See address and contact information above. **Management:** Greg Tock, Publisher.

WHITE MOUNTAIN INDEPENDENT. 3191 S. White Mountain Rd., Show Low, AZ 85902-1570. Telephone: 928-537-5721. FAX: 928-537-1780. E-MAIL: gtock@wmicentral.com. URL: http://www.wmicentral.com. Mailing Address: PO Box 1570, Show Low, AZ 85902-1570. Year Established: 1909. Pub. Frequency: s-w. (Tue. & Fri.) Page Size: broadsheet. Subscrip. Rate: $.50 newsstand/cover; $38/yr navajo & apache cys; $74 for 2 yrs. navajo & apache cys. Adv. Rate: col. inch $15.93 Circulation: 9,143 per issue (paid). **Owner(s):** White Mountain Publishing Co., See address and contact information above. **Management:** Donovan M. Kramer Sr., Owner. Greg Tock, Publisher.

SNOWFLAKE

SILVER CREEK HERALD. PO Box 924, Snowflake, AZ 86047. Telephone: 928-536-3994. FAX: 928-524-3541. URL: http://www.azjournal.com. Mailing Address: PO Box 670, Holbrook, AZ 86025-0670. Pub. Frequency: w. (Wed.) Page Size: broadsheet. **Owner(s):** Navajo County Publishers, Inc., 200 E. Hopi Dr., Holbrook, AZ 86025. Telephone: 928-524-6205. FAX: 928-524-3541. **Management:** Matthew Barger, Co-Publisher. Francie Payne, General Manager. Bill Wiegand, Advertising. Matthew Barger, Advertising Director.

SUN CITY

NORTHWEST VALLEY NEWS. 10102 Santa Fe Dr., Sun City, AZ 85351. Telephone: 623-977-8351. FAX: 623-876-3698. URL: http://www.dailynews-sun.com. Mailing Address: PO Box 1779, Sun City, AZ 85372-1180. Pub. Frequency: w. (Fri.) Page Size: broadsheet Circulation: 34,500 per issue (free). **Owner(s):** Freedom Communications, Inc., 17666 Fitch St., Irvine, CA 92614-6022. Telephone: 949-253-2300. FAX: 949-474-7675. **Management:** Hal Dekeyser, Publisher. Cathy Carlson, Circulation Manager. **Editorial:** Patrick O'Grady, Editor. Dan McCarthy, Executive Editor.

PEORIA INDEPENDENT. 17220 N Boswell Blvd, Ste L101, Sun City, AZ 85373. Telephone: 623-972-6101. FAX: 623-974-6004. URL: http://www.newszap.com. Pub. Frequency: w. (Wed.) Page Size: broadsheet. Subscrip. Rate: $.50 newsstand/cover; $30 mailed for 3 mos.. Circulation: 10,000 per issue (free). **Owner(s):** Independent Newspapers, Inc., PO Box 737, Dover, DE 19903. Telephone: 302-674-3600. FAX: 302-674-9510. **Management:** Charlene Bisson, Publisher. **Editorial:** Rusty Bradshaw, Editor.

TOMBSTONE

NATIONAL TOMBSTONE EPITAPH, THE. 9 S. Fifth St., Tombstone, AZ 85638. Telephone: 520-457-2211. Mailing Address: PO Box 1880, Tombstone, AZ 85638. Year Established: 1880. Pub. Frequency: m. Page Size: tabloid.Subscrip. Rate: $20/yr; $25/yr mailed Circulation: 8,500 per issue (paid). **Owner(s):** Sara E. Love, See address and contact information above. **Management:** Sara E. Love, President. E. Dean Prichard, Advertising Manager. Carol Winkelmann, Circulation Manager. **Editorial:** E. Dean Prichard, Editor.

Weeklies

TUCSON

EXPLORER NEWSPAPER (TUCSON), THE. 7235 N. Paseo Del Norte, Tucson, AZ 85704. Telephone: 520-797-4384. FAX: 520-575-8891. E-MAIL: editor@explorernews.com. URL: http://www.explorernews.com. Year Established: 1993. Pub. Frequency: w. (Wed.) Page Size: tabloid. Subscrip. Rate: $47.50/yr mailed in state; $49.50/yr mailed out of state. Adv. Rate: page $2,690 Freelance Pay: $50-$100/story. Circulation: 47,750 per issue (paid and free). **Owner(s):** Thirteenth Street Media Inc., See address and contact information above. **Management:** Randy Miller, Owner. Dave Perry, Publisher. Jim Humphrey, Advertising Director. Jaime Hood, Business Manager. **Editorial:** Dave Perry, Editor. Ty Bowers, Managing Editor. Grace Heike, Production Manager.

TUCSON WEEKLY. 3280 E. Hemisphere Loop, Ste 180, Tucson, AZ 85706-5027. Telephone: 520-792-3630. FAX: 520-792-2096. E-MAIL: info@tucsonweekly.com. URL: http://www.tucsonweekly.com. Mailing Address: PO Box 27087, Tucson, AZ 85726-7087. Pub. Frequency: w. (Thu.) Page Size: standard. Circulation: 40,000 per issue (controlled and free). **Owner(s):** Tucson Weekly Inc., See address and contact information above. **Management:** Joann Hardy Carranza, General Manager. Thomas P Lee, Publisher. Jill A'Hearn, Advertising Director. Josie Lindstrom, Circulation Manager. Sean B. Ardry, Classified Adv. Mgr.. **Editorial:** Jimmy Boegle, Editor.

WICKENBURG

WICKENBURG SUN, THE. 180 N. Washington St., Wickenburg, AZ 85390. Telephone: 928-684-5454. FAX: 928-684-3185. E-MAIL: wicksun@futureone.com. URL: http://www.wickenburgsun.com. Year Established: 1933. Pub. Frequency: w. (Wed.) Page Size: broadsheet. Subscrip. Rate: $.75 newsstand/cover; $28/yr mailed in county; $36/yr mailed out of county; $40/yr mailed out of state. Freelance Pay: $0.50/column-inch. Circulation: 5,200 per issue (paid). **Owner(s):** Brehm Communications, Inc., 16644 W. Bernardo Dr., Ste. 300, San Diego, CA 92127. Telephone: 858-451-6200. **Management:** Kevin Cloe, Publisher. Vic Porto, Advertising Director. Robert Pinchawsky, Circulation Manager. Sherri Heizer, Classified Adv. Mgr.. **Editorial:** Tamara Thomas, Editor.

WILLIAMS

WILLIAMS GRAND CANYON NEWS. 118 S. Third St., Williams, AZ 86046. Telephone: 928-635-4426. FAX: 928-635-4887. E-MAIL: editorial@williamsnews.com. URL: http//www.williamsnews.com. Mailing Address: PO Box 667, Williams, AZ 86046. Year Established: 1889. Pub. Frequency: w. (Wed.) Page Size: broadsheet. Subscrip. Rate: $.50 newsstand/cover; $24.50/yr in county; $34.50/yr in state; $36.50/yr out of state. Circulation: 5,000 per issue (paid). **Owner(s):** Western News & Info., Inc., 1748 S. Arizona Ave., Yuma, AZ 85364-5727. **Management:** Doug Wells, Publisher. Jason Miller, Advertising. Connie Hiemenz, Advertising Manager. Kyle Johnson, Circulation Manager. Carol DeLander, Business Manager. **Editorial:** Lynda Duffy, Editor. Tracey Cerami, Graphics Editor.

WINSLOW

WINSLOW MAIL. ISSN 8750-5711
208 W. First St., Winslow, AZ 86047. Telephone: 928-289-2467. FAX: 928-289-4151. URL: http://www.winslowaznews.com. Year Established: 1894. Pub. Frequency: w. (Wed.) Page Size: broadsheet. Subscrip. Rate: $.50 newsstand/cover; $24/yr in county; $31.50/yr out of county; $39.90/yr out of state. Adv. Rate: col. inch $7.68 Circulation: 4,200 per issue (paid and free). **Owner(s):** Western News & Info., Inc., 1748 S. Arizona Ave., Yuma, AZ 85364. **Management:** Joe Soldwedel, President. Douglas Wells, Publisher. Katie Stewart, Advertising Manager. **Editorial:** Jeff Pope, Editor.

YUMA

SUPER SHOPPER. 1203 W. 16th St., Yuma, AZ 85364-4447. Telephone: 928-783-1201. FAX: 928-343-4763. E-MAIL: superads@yumasupershopper.com. URL: http://www.yumasupershopper.com.Pub. Frequency: w. (Sun.) Page Size: standard Circulation: 58,000 Winter (free); 38,000 Summer (free). **Owner(s):** Freedom Newspapers of S.W. Arizona Inc., See address and contact information above. **Management:** John Courtis, Managing Director. Julie Mareno, Advertising.

YUMA WHITE SHEET. 1355 W. 16th St., Ste. 10, Yuma, AZ 85364. Telephone: 928-782-3663. FAX: 928-782-3403. E-MAIL: katurner@desertshoppers.net. URL: http://www.greenandwhitesheet.com. Pub. Frequency: w. (Tue.) Page Size: standard Circulation: 32,000 per issue (free). **Owner(s):** Associated Desert Shoppers, Inc., 73-400 Hwy. 111, Palm Desert, CA 92260. Telephone: 760-346-1729. **Management:** Hal Paradis, Publisher. Kim Turner, Sales Manager. Esperanza Barrett, Controller. **Editorial:** Hal Paradis, Editor.

ARKANSAS

ARKADELPHIA

ARKADELPHIA EXTRA. 205 S 26th St, Arkadelphia, AR 71923. Telephone: 870-246-5525. FAX: 870-246-6556. URL: http://www.siftingsherald.com. Mailing Address: PO Box 10, Arkadelphia, AR 71923. Pub. Frequency: w. (Wed.) Page Size: standard Circulation: 11,180 per issue (free). **Owner(s):** GateHouse Media, Inc, 350 WillowBrook Office Park, Fairport, NY 14450. Telephone: 585-598-0030. FAX: 585-248-2631. **Management:** George Jinks, Publisher. Sherry Kizziar, Advertising Manager. Donnie Hollis, Circulation Manager.

ASHDOWN

LITTLE RIVER NEWS. 45 E. Commerce, Ashdown, AR 71822. Telephone: 870-898-3462. FAX: 870-898-6213. E-MAIL: littlerivernews@sbcglobal.net. Year Established: 1898. Pub. Frequency: w. (Thu.) Page Size: broadsheet. Subscrip. Rate: $.50 newsstand/cover; $20/yr in county; $25/yr in state; $35/yr out of state. Adv. Rate: col. inch $6.50 Circulation: 3,000 per issue (paid). **Owner(s):** Little River News, See address and contact information above. **Editorial:** Carolyn Myers, Editor.

ATKINS

ATKINS CHRONICLE, THE. PO Box 188, Atkins, AR 72823. Telephone: 479-641-2688. FAX: 479-641-1604. E-MAIL: news@atkinschronicle.com. URL: http://www.atkinschronicle.com. Year Established: 1894. Pub. Frequency: w. (Wed.) Page Size: broadsheet. Subscrip. Rate: $.50 newsstand/cover; $25/yr mailed in county & adj. cys.; $30/yr mailed in state; $35/yr mailed out of state. Adv. Rate: col. inch $5.25 Circulation: 2,400 per issue (paid). **Owner(s):** Ginnie & Van Allen Tyson, See address and contact information above. **Management:** Ginnie Tyson, Publisher. Mitzi Henderson, Advertising. Beverly Davis, Circulation Manager. **Editorial:** Van Allen Tyson, Editor. Rebecca Tyson, Managing Editor.Readers: Residents of Central Arkansas

DOVER TIMES, THE. PO Box 188, Atkins, AR 72823. Telephone: 479-641-2688. FAX: 479-641-1604. E-MAIL: news@atkinschronicle.com. URL: http://www.atkinschronicle.com. Pub. Frequency: w. (Wed.) Page Size: broadsheet. Subscrip. Rate: $.25 newsstand/cover; $18/yr mailed in county & adj. cys.; $27/yr mailed in state; $32/yr mailed out of state. Adv. Rate: col. inch $4.25 Circulation: 1,400 per issue (paid). **Owner(s):** Ginnie & Van Allen Tyson, See address and contact information above. **Management:** Ginnie Tyson, Publisher. Mitzi Henderson, Advertising. Beverly Davis, Circulation Manager. **Editorial:** Van Allen Tyson, Editor.Readers: Central Arkansas

BALD KNOB

BALD KNOB BANNER. 3203 Hwy 367 N, Bald Knob, AR 72010-1480. Telephone: 501-724-0398. FAX: 501-724-6362. E-MAIL: wcrecord@ipa.net. Mailing Address: P.O. Box 1480, Bold Knob, AR 72010-1480. Year Established: 1905. Pub. Frequency: w. (Thu.) Page Size: standard. Subscrip. Rate: $.50 newsstand/cover; $25/yr in county; $20/yr in county to senior citizens. Adv. Rate: col. inch $7 Freelance Pay: $20/article. Circulation: 650 per issue (paid). **Owner(s):** Wagon Wheel Publishing, Inc., See address and contact information above. **Management:** Barth Grayson, Publisher. **Editorial:** Terry Gabrion, Managing Editor.

WHITE COUNTY RECORD. 3203 Hwy 367 N, Bald Knob, AR 72010-1480. Telephone: 501-724-0398. FAX: 501-724-6362. E-MAIL: wcrecord@ipa.net. Year Established: 1866. Pub. Frequency: w. (Wed.) Page Size: standard. Subscrip. Rate: $.50 newsstand/cover; $25/yr local; $20/yr to senior citizens. Adv. Rate: col. inch $7 Freelance Pay: $20/article. Circulation: 771 per issue (paid). **Owner(s):** Wagon Wheel Publishing, Inc., See address and contact information above. **Management:** Barth Grayson, Publisher. **Editorial:** Terry Gabrion, Managing Editor.

BEEBE

BEEBE NEWS. 107 E. Center, Beebe, AR 72012. Telephone: 501-882-5414. FAX: 501-882-3576. E-MAIL: tbn@beebenews.com. URL: http://www.beebenews.com. Mailing Address: PO Box 910, Beebe, AR 72012. Year Established: 1934. Pub. Frequency: w. (Thu.) Page Size: broadsheet. Subscrip. Rate: $.75 newsstand/cover; $30/yr mailed in county; $35/yr mailed in state; $45/yr mailed out of state. Circulation: 2,500 per issue (paid). **Owner(s):** Lee K. McLane, See address and contact information above. **Management:** Lee K. McLane, Publisher. Christian McLane, Circulation Manager. **Editorial:** Lee K. McLane, Editor.

BELLA VISTA

WEEKLY VISTA, THE. 313 Town Center W, Bella Vista, AR 72714. Telephone: 479-855-3724. FAX: 479-855-6992. E-MAIL: weeklyvista@nwanews.com. URL: http://nwanews.com/weeklyvista. Pub. Frequency: w. (Wed.) Page Size: broadsheet. Subscrip. Rate: $.50 newsstand/cover; $27/yr in county; $30/yr out of county. Adv. Rate: col. inch $10.56 Circulation: 4,598 per issue (paid). **Owner(s):** Wehco Media, Inc., PO Box 2221, Little Rock, AR 72203. Telephone: 501-378-3400. **Management:** Jeff Jeffus, Publisher. John Mobbs, Advertising Director. Hector Cueva, Circulation Director. **Editorial:** Linda Caldwell, Editor.

BERRYVILLE

OZARK MOUNTAIN TRADER, THE. 602 Hwy. 62 Spur, Berryville, AR 72616. Telephone: 870-423-6636. FAX: 870-423-6640. E-MAIL: ccnews@aol.com. Mailing Address: PO Box 232, Berryville, AR 72616. Pub. Frequency: w. (Tue.) Page Size: broadsheet Circulation: 18,000 per issue (free). **Owner(s):** Rust Communications, Inc., 301 Broadway, Cape Girardeau, MO 63701. Telephone: 573-335-6611. **Management:** Bob Moore, Publisher.

STAR-TRIBUNE (BERRYVILLE). 602 Hwy. 62 Spur, Berryville, AR 72616. Telephone: 870-423-6636. FAX: 870-423-6640. E-MAIL: bmoore@mynewroads.com. URL: http://www.ccnstartribune.com/. Mailing Address: PO Box 232, Berryville, AR 72616. Year Established: 1889. Pub. Frequency: w. (Tue) Page Size: broadsheet. Subscrip. Rate: $.75 newsstand/cover; $32.50/yr mailed local; $46/yr mailed in state. Adv. Rate: col. inch $7.40 Circulation: 3,600 per issue (paid). **Owner(s):** Rust Communications, Inc., 301 Broadway, Cape Girardeau, MO 63701. Telephone: 573-335-6611. **Management:** Bob Moore, Publisher. **Editorial:** Jerry Dupy, Managing Editor. Ken O'Toole, News Editor.

BOONEVILLE

BOONEVILLE DEMOCRAT. 72 W. Second St., Booneville, AR 72927. Telephone: 479-675-4455. FAX: 479-675-5457. URL: http://www.boonevilledemocrat.com. Mailing Address: PO Box 208, Booneville, AR 72927-0208. Pub. Frequency: w. (Wed.) Page Size: broadsheet. Subscrip. Rate: $.50 newsstand/cover; $20.75/yr in county; $30.50/yr in state; $34.50/yr out of state. Circulation: 2,800 per issue (paid). **Owner(s):** Stephens Group, Inc., 1111 W. Bonanza Rd., Las Vegas, NV 89106. Telephone: 702-383-0211. **Management:** Vickey Wiggins, Publisher. Christina Coffee, Circulation Manager. **Editorial:** Glenn Parrish, Editor.

BRINKLEY

BRINKLEY ARGUS. 308 W. Cedar St., Brinkley, AR 72021. Telephone: 870-734-1056. FAX: 870-734-1474. E-MAIL: argus@tigernet.tv; brinkleyargus@sbcglobal.net. Mailing Address: PO Box 711, Brinkley, AR 72021-0711. Year Established: 1875. Pub. Frequency: s-w. (Wed. & Fri.) Page Size: broadsheet. Subscrip. Rate: $.50 newsstand/cover; $35/yr mailed in state; $60/yr mailed out of state. Circulation: 3,800 per issue (paid). **Owner(s):** Franklin & Flora Jane Elledge, See address and contact information above. **Management:** Katie Jacques, General Manager. **Editorial:** Thomas Jacques, Editor.

CABOT

CABOT STAR-HERALD. 903 South Pine St, Cabot, AR 72023. Telephone: 501-843-3534. FAX: 501-843-6447. E-MAIL: editor@cabotstarherald.com. URL: http://www.cabotstarherald.com. Mailing Address: PO Box 1058, Cabot, AR 72023. Pub. Frequency: w. (Wed.) Page Size: broadsheet. Subscrip. Rate: $.50 newsstand/cover; $19/yr in county; $25/yr out of county; $35/yr out of state. Circulation: 8,100 per issue (paid). **Owner(s):** Stephens Media LLC, See address and contact information above. **Management:** Dennis Byrd, Publisher. Kenneth Jones, Advertising Director. Gary Ford, Circulation Manager. Claudine Mitchell, Business Manager. **Editorial:** Jesse Gonzalez, Production Manager. Tyler Tucker, News Editor.

CABOT STAR HERALD/WEEKEND. 903 South Pine St, Cabot, AR 72023. Telephone: 501-843-3534. FAX: 501-843-6447. E-MAIL: editor@cabotstarherald.com. Mailing Address: PO Box 1058, Cabot, AR 72023. Pub. Frequency: w. (Sat) Page Size: broadsheet Circulation: 20,900 per issue (free). **Owner(s):** Stephens Media LLC, See address and contact information above. **Management:** Dennis Byrd, Publisher. Kenneth Jones, Advertising Director. Gary Ford, Circulation Manager. Claudine Mitchell, Business Manager. **Editorial:** Jesse Gonzalez, Production Manager. Tyler Tucker, News Editor.

JACKSONVILLE PATRIOT. ISSN 1064-7260
903 South Pine St, Cabot, AR 72023. Telephone: 501-982-6506. FAX: 501-843-6447. URL: http://www.jacksonvillepatriot.com/. Mailing Address: PO Box 5329, Jacksonville, AR 72078. Year Established: 1957. Pub. Frequency: s-w. (Mon. & Fri.) Page Size: broadsheet. Subscrip. Rate: $14/yr in county; $42/yr mailed in state; $53/yr mailed out of state. Circulation: 3,000 per issue (paid). **Owner(s):** Stephens Media LLC, See address and contact information above. **Management:** Dennis Byrd, Publisher. Kenneth Jones, Advertising Director. Gary Ford, Circulation Manager. Claudine Mitchell, Business Manager. **Editorial:** Peggy Kenyon, Editor. Jesse Gonzalez, Production Manager. Tyler Tucker, News Editor. Chad Matchett, Sports Editor.

CALICO ROCK

WHITE RIVER CURRENT. PO Box 570, Calico Rock, AR 72519. Telephone: 870-297-3010. FAX: 870-297-3070. E-MAIL: wrcnews@centraltel.net. Year Established: 1972. Pub. Frequency: w. (Thu.) Page Size: broadsheet. Subscrip. Rate: $.50 newsstand/cover; $18/yr in county; $25/yr out of county. Adv. Rate: col. inch $4.50 Circulation: 1,700 per issue (paid). **Owner(s):** Jeannie Day, See address and contact information above. **Management:** Debbie Dutton, Publisher. **Editorial:** Debbie Dutton, Editor-in-Chief. Cindy Stewart, Managing Editor.

CARLISLE

CARLISLE INDEPENDENT. 220 W Main St, Carlisle, AR 72024. Telephone: 870-552-3111. FAX: 870-552-3111. E-MAIL: editor@carlisleindependent.com. URL: http://www.carlisleindependent.com. Mailing Address: PO Box 47, Carlisle, AR 72024. Year Established: 1904. Pub. Frequency: w. (Wed.) Page Size: broadsheet. Subscrip. Rate: $.50 newsstand/cover; $14/yr in county; $17/yr out of county; $28/yr out of state. Circulation: 1,700 per issue (paid). **Owner(s):** Stephens Media LLC, See address and contact information above. **Management:** Dennis Byrd, Publisher. Kenneth Jones, Advertising Director. Gary Ford, Circulation Manager. Claudine Mitchell, Business Manager. **Editorial:** Jesse Gonzalez, Production Manager. Tyler Tucker, News Editor.

CHARLESTON

CHARLESTON EXPRESS. 511 Main St., Charleston, AR 72933. Telephone: 479-965-7368. FAX: 479-965-7206. Mailing Address: P.O. Box 39, Charleston, AR 72933. Pub. Frequency: w. (Wed.) Page Size: tabloid. Subscrip. Rate: $.50 newsstand/cover; $20/yr mailed in county & adj. counties; $24/yr mailed out of area. Circulation: 22,050 per issue (paid). **Owner(s):** Stephens Media LLC, 1111 W. Bonanza Rd., Las Vegas, NV 89106. Telephone: 702-383-0211. **Management:** Kristyn Sims, General Manager. **Editorial:** Paul Gramich, Editor.

CLARENDON

MONROE COUNTY SUN, THE. 237 Madison St., Clarendon, AR 72029. Telephone: 870-747-3373. FAX: 870-734-1494. Pub. Frequency: w. (Thu.) Page Size: broadsheet. Subscrip. Rate: $.50 newsstand/cover; $25/yr in state; $40/yr out of state. Circulation: 1,500 per issue (paid). **Owner(s):** River Publishing Co., PO Box 315, Clarendon, AR 72029-0315. Telephone: 870-747-3373. FAX: 870-734-1494. **Management:** Katie Jacques, Publisher. **Editorial:** Tricia Rogers, Editor.

CLARKSVILLE

JOHNSON COUNTY GRAPHIC. 203 E. Cherry, Clarksville, AR 72830-3101. Telephone: 479-754-2005. FAX: 479-754-2098. E-MAIL: graphic@thegraphic.org. URL: http://www.thegraphic.org. Mailing Address: PO Box 289, Clarksville, AR 72830-0289. Year Established: 1877. Pub. Frequency: w. (Wed.) Page Size: standard.Subscrip. Rate: $.50 newsstand/cover; $35/yr Circulation: 8,200 per issue (paid). **Owner(s):** Johnson County Graphic, Inc., See address and contact information above. **Management:** Ron Wylie, General Manager. Debra Grey, Advertising Manager. **Editorial:** Margaret Wylie, Editor.

CLINTON

VAN BUREN COUNTY DEMOCRAT. 319 S. Court St., Clinton, AR 72031-0119. Telephone: 501-745-5175. FAX: 501-745-8865. E-MAIL: ads@clintoncable.net. Mailing Address: PO Box 119, Clinton, AR 72031-0119. Year Established: 1909. Pub. Frequency: w. (Wed.) Page Size: standard. Subscrip. Rate: $.50 newsstand/cover; $20/yr home delivery in county; $23/yr mailed in state; $29/yr mailed out of state. Adv. Rate: col. inch $6.60 Circulation: 4,000 per issue (paid). **Owner(s):** Stephens Media LLC, PO Box 70, Las Vegas, NV 89125-0070. Telephone: 702-477-3846. FAX: 702-251-0736. **Management:** Roger Smith, Publisher. **Editorial:** Roger Smith, Editor.

CORNING

CLAY COUNTY COURIER. 810 N. Missouri, Corning, AR 72422-2709. Telephone: 870-857-3531. FAX: 870-857-5204. URL: http://www.corningpublishing.com. Mailing Address: PO Box 85, Corning, AR 72422-0128. Pub. Frequency: w. (Thu.) Page Size: broadsheet. Subscrip. Rate: $.50 newsstand/cover; $20/yr in county. Circulation: 3,500 per issue (paid). **Owner(s):** Corning & J.V. Rockwell Publishing Inc., See address and contact information above. **Management:** J.V. Rockwell, Publisher. Fred Martin, Advertising Manager. **Editorial:** J.V. Rockwell, Editor.

NORTHEAST ARKANSAS MERCHANDISER. 810 N. Missouri, Corning, AR 72422-2709. Telephone: 870-857-3531. FAX: 870-857-5204. E-MAIL: fredmartin@jvrhomes.com. URL: http://www.corningpublishing.com. Mailing Address: PO Box 85, Corning, AR 72422-0128. Pub. Frequency: w. (Wed.) Page Size: broadsheet Circulation: 7,000 per issue (free). **Owner(s):** Corning & J.V. Rockwell Publishing Inc., 810 N. Missouri Ave., Corning, AR 72422. Telephone: 870-857-3531. FAX: 870-857-5204. **Management:** J.V. Rockwell, Publisher. Fred Martin, Advertising Manager. **Editorial:** J.V. Rockwell, Editor.

CROSSETT

ASHLEY COUNTY SHOPPERS GUIDE. 106 E. Second Ave., Crossett, AR 71635. Telephone: 870-364-5186. FAX: 870-364-2116. URL: http://www.ashleynewsobserver.com. Pub. Frequency: w. (Mon.) Page Size: broadsheet Circulation: 10,653 per issue (free). **Owner(s):** Ashley County Publishing Co., See address and contact information above. **Management:** Barney W. White, Publisher. Kelli Caldwell, Advertising Manager.

ASHLEY NEWS OBSERVER, THE. 106 E. Second Ave., Crossett, AR 71635. Telephone: 870-364-5186. FAX: 870-364-2116. E-MAIL: news@ashleynewsobserver.com. URL: http://www.ashleynewsobserver.com. Mailing Address: PO Box 798, Crossett, AR 71635. Year Established: 1907. Pub. Frequency: w. (Wed.) Page Size: broadsheet. Subscrip. Rate: $.75 newsstand/cover; $29/yr mailed in county; $37/yr mailed in adj. cys.; $45/yr mailed out of county. Circulation: 4,300 per issue (paid). **Owner(s):** Ashley County Publishing Co., See address and contact information above. **Management:** Barney White, Publisher. Kelli Caldwell, Advertising Manager. **Editorial:** Heath Waldrop, Editor.

DANVILLE

YELL COUNTY RECORD. 602 Main St., Danville, AR 72833. Telephone: 479-495-2354. FAX: 479-495-3501. Mailing Address: PO Box 188, Danville, AR 72833-0188. Pub. Frequency: w. (Wed.) Page Size: broadsheet.Subscrip. Rate: $.50 newsstand/cover; $18/yr Circulation: 4,700 per issue (paid). **Owner(s):** David Fisher, See address and contact information above. **Management:** David Fisher, Publisher. **Editorial:** David Fisher, Editor.

DEQUEEN

DEQUEEN BEE. 404 DeQueen Ave., DeQueen, AR 71832. Telephone: 870-642-2111. FAX: 870-642-3138. E-MAIL: dqbee@ipa.net. URL: http://www.dequeen.com. Year Established: 1897. Pub. Frequency: w. (Thu.) Page Size: broadsheet. Subscrip. Rate: $.50 newsstand/cover; $15/yr local; $30/yr mailed out of area. Circulation: 1,500 per issue (paid). **Owner(s):** Anita Kimball Marshall, See address and contact information above. **Management:** Anita Marshall, Publisher. Leoda Matthews, Advertising Manager. Melissa Blankenship, Circulation Manager. **Editorial:** Scott Smith, Editor.

DES ARC

WHITE RIVER JOURNAL. 424 Main St, Des Arc, AR 72040. Telephone: 870-256-4254. E-MAIL: wrjnews@ipa.net. Mailing Address: PO Box 1051, Des Arc, AR 72040-1051. Year Established: 1907. Pub. Frequency: w. (Wed.) Page Size: broadsheet. Subscrip. Rate: $.50 newsstand/cover; $15/yr in county; $20/yr out of county; $25/yr out of state. Adv. Rate: col. inch $5 Circulation: 2,400 per issue (paid). **Owner(s):** White River Journal Corp., See address and contact information above.

DUMAS

DUMAS CLARION. 136 E. Waterman St., Dumas, AR 71639-0220. Telephone: 870-382-4925. FAX: 870-382-6421. E-MAIL: thawkins@centurytel.net. Mailing Address: PO Box 220, Dumas, AR 71639-0220. Year Established: 1899. Pub. Frequency: w. (Wed.) Page Size: broadsheet. Subscrip. Rate: $.50 newsstand/cover; $24/yr local; $27/yr out of county; $34/yr out of state. Freelance Pay: $20/article. Circulation: 3,200 per issue (paid). **Owner(s):** Emmerich Newspapers, Inc., See address and contact information above. **Management:** Terry Hawkins, Publisher. Dorothy Patterson, Office Manager. **Editorial:** Terry Hawkins, Editor.

ENGLAND

ENGLAND DEMOCRAT. 121 E. Haywood, England, AR 72046. Telephone: 501-842-3111. FAX: 501-842-3081. E-MAIL: englanddemo@centurytel.net. Mailing Address: PO Drawer 250, England, AZ 72046. Pub. Frequency: w. (Wed.) Page Size: standard. Subscrip. Rate: $.50 newsstand/cover; $15/yr in county; $18/yr mailed out of county; $24/yr mailed out of state. Circulation: 1,800 per issue (paid). **Owner(s):** Jerry Jackson, See address and contact information above. **Management:** Jerry Jackson, Publisher. **Editorial:** Jerry Jackson, Editor.

EUREKA SPRINGS

EUREKA SPRINGS TIMES-ECHO. ISSN 8750-6467
5 Forest Park Ave., Ste. B, Eureka Springs, AR 72631. Telephone: 479-253-9719. FAX: 479-253-5960. E-MAIL: bmoore@cox-internet.com. URL: http://www.eurekaspringstimesecho.com. Mailing Address: PO Box 232, Berryville, AR 72616. Year Established: 1879. Pub. Frequency: w. (Tue.) Page Size: broadsheet. Subscrip. Rate: $.75 newsstand/cover; $36/yr in county; $49/yr in state; $52/yr out of state. Adv. Rate: col. inch $7.40 Freelance Pay: $75/article. **Wire Service(s):** AP. Circulation: 2,526 per issue (paid). **Owner(s):** Rust Communications, Inc., 301 Broadway, Cape Girardeau, MO 63701. Telephone: 573-335-6611. **Management:** Bob Moore, Publisher. **Editorial:** Jerry Dupy, Managing Editor. Ken O'Toole, News Editor.

FAYETTEVILLE

WHITE RIVER VALLEY NEWS. 2684 Hollybrooke Dr, Fayetteville, AR 72701. Telephone: 479-443-9786. FAX: 479-443-9788. URL: http://www.nwanews.com. Mailing Address: PO Box 766, Elkins, AR 72727. Pub. Frequency: w. (Thu.) Page Size: broadsheet. Subscrip. Rate: $.50 newsstand/cover; $20/yr in county. Adv. Rate: col. inch $3.81 Circulation: 1,270 per issue (paid). **Owner(s):** Wehco Media, Inc., PO Box 2221, Little Rock, AR 72203. Telephone: 501-378-3400. **Management:** Pat Harris, General Manager. Hector Cueva, Circulation Director. Ted Rancifer, Admin. Assistant. **Editorial:** Pat Harris, Editor.

FLIPPIN

MOUNTAINEER ECHO, THE. 210 Main Ste 3, Flippin, AR 72634. Telephone: 870-453-3731. FAX: 870-453-3071. E-MAIL: staff@themountaineer.com. Mailing Address: PO Box 1199, Flippin, AR 72634. Year Established: 1886. Pub. Frequency: w. (Thu.) Page Size: broadsheet. Subscrip. Rate: $.50 newsstand/cover; $21.50/yr in county; $28.50/yr out of county; $34/yr mailed out of state. Circulation: 2,500 per issue (paid). **Owner(s):** Dale Estes & Jane Estes, See address and contact information above. **Management:** Dale Estes, Publisher. **Editorial:** Jane Estes, Editor.

FORDYCE

FORDYCE NEWS-ADVOCATE. 509 Spring St., Fordyce, AR 71742-3318. Telephone: 870-352-3144. FAX: 870-352-8091. E-MAIL: newsadvo@ipa.net. Mailing Address: PO Box 559, Fordyce, AR 71742-0559. Pub. Frequency: w. (Wed.) Page Size: broadsheet. Subscrip. Rate: $.50 newsstand/cover; $22/yr in county; $24/yr out of county; $30/yr out of state. Circulation: 3,400 per issue (paid). **Owner(s):** Bill Whitehead, Jr., See address and contact information above. **Management:** Bill Whitehead Jr., Publisher. Ann Mathews, Advertising Manager. **Editorial:** Bill Whitehead Jr., Editor.

GENTRY

DECATUR HERALD. 103 N Collins, Gentry, AR 72734. Telephone: 479-787-5300. FAX: 479-524-5144. URL: http://www.nwanews.com. Mailing Address: PO Box 677, Gentry, AR 72734-0677. Pub. Frequency: w. (Wed.) Page Size: broadsheet. Subscrip. Rate: $.50 newsstand/cover; $25/yr in county; $31/yr out of county. Adv. Rate: col. inch $7.55 Circulation: 1,000 per issue (paid). **Owner(s):** Wehco Media, Inc., PO Box 2221, Little Rock, AR 72203. Telephone: 501-378-3400. **Management:** Shelly Moran, Publisher. Sherry DuBois, Advertising.

GENTRY COURIER-JOURNAL. ISSN 1048-8278
103 N Collins, Gentry, AR 72734. Telephone: 479-787-5300. FAX: 479-524-5144. URL: http://www.nwanews.com/leader. Mailing Address: PO Box 677, Gentry, AR 72734-0677. Pub. Frequency: w. (Wed.) Page Size: broadsheet. Subscrip. Rate: $.50 newsstand/cover; $25/yr in county; $31/yr out of county. Adv. Rate: col. inch $7.55 Circulation: 1,050 per issue (paid). **Owner(s):** Wehco Media, Inc., PO Box 2221, Little Rock, AR 72203. Telephone: 501-378-3400. **Management:** Shelly Moran, Publisher. Sherry DuBois, Advertising. Hector Cueva, Circulation Director. **Editorial:** Treena Harp, Managing Editor.

Weeklies

GLENWOOD

GLENWOOD HERALD. 209 E. Broadway, Glenwood, AR 71943. Telephone: 870-356-2111. FAX: 870-356-4400. E-MAIL: gwherald@ipa.net. Mailing Address: PO Box 1130, Glenwood, AR 71943. Year Established: 1926. Pub. Frequency: w. (Thu.) Page Size: broadsheet. Subscrip. Rate: $.75 newsstand/cover; $16.50/yr local; $31.50/yr mailed in state; $36.50/yr mailed out of state. Circulation: 2,700 per issue (paid). **Owner(s):** Graves Publishing Co., Inc., 418 N. Main St., Nashville, AR 71852. Telephone: 807-845-2010. **Management:** Lawrence Graves, Publisher. Theresa Ross Parrish, Advertising Manager. Lois Welch, Circulation Manager. **Editorial:** Mike McCoy, Editor.

GRAVETTE

GRAVETTE NEWS HERALD. 123 E Main St, Gravette, AR 72736. Telephone: 479-787-5300. FAX: 479-787-5332. URL: http://www.nwanews.com. Mailing Address: PO Box 640, Gravette, AR 72736. Year Established: 1894. Pub. Frequency: w. (Wed.) Page Size: broadsheet. Subscrip. Rate: $.50 newsstand/cover; $21/yr local; $27/yr mailed elsewhere. Adv. Rate: col. inch $5.86 Circulation: 1,950 per issue (paid). **Owner(s):** Wehco Media, Inc., PO Box 2221, Little Rock, AR 72203. Telephone: 501-378-3400. **Management:** Shelly Moran, Publisher. Hector Cueva, Circulation Director. **Editorial:** Robert Evans, Editor.

GREENWOOD

GREENWOOD DEMOCRAT. 38 Towne Sq., Greenwood, AR 72936-0398. Telephone: 479-996-4494. FAX: 479-996-4122. E-MAIL: mcole@greenwooddemocrat.com. URL: http://www.greenwooddemocrat.com. Mailing Address: PO Box 398, Greenwood, AR 72936-0398. Year Established: 1882. Pub. Frequency: w. (Wed.) Page Size: broadsheet. Subscrip. Rate: $.50 newsstand/cover; $22/yr in county; $29/yr in state; $32.50/yr out of state. Circulation: 2,500 per issue (paid). **Owner(s):** Stephens Media LLC, PO Box 70, Las Vegas, NV 89125. Telephone: 702-383-0211. FAX: 702-383-4676. **Management:** Robert Hager, Publisher. Amy Lowdermilk, Business Manager. **Editorial:** Martha Cole, Editor.

GURDON

GURDON TIMES, THE. 107 N Second St, Gurdon, AR 71743. Telephone: 870-353-4482. FAX: 870-887-2949. E-MAIL: brags@iocc.com. URL: http://www.picayune-times.com. Mailing Address: PO Box 250, Gurdon, AR 71743-0250. Pub. Frequency: w. (Wed.) Page Size: standard. Subscrip. Rate: $.50 newsstand/cover; $15.50/yr local; $19.50/yr in state; $27/yr out of state. Circulation: 1,400 per issue (paid). **Owner(s):** GateHouse Media, Inc, 350 WillowBrook Office Park, Fairport, NY 14450. Telephone: 585-598-0030. FAX: 585-248-2631. **Management:** George Jinks, Publisher. **Editorial:** Wendy Ledbetter, Editor.

HAMBURG

ASHLEY COUNTY LEDGER. PO Box 471, Hamburg, AR 71646-0471. Telephone: 870-853-2424. FAX: 870-853-8203. E-MAIL: theledger@seark.net. URL: http://www.ashleycountyledger.com. Pub. Frequency: w. (Wed.) Page Size: broadsheet. Subscrip. Rate: $.50 newsstand/cover; $25/yr local; $30/yr out of county. Adv. Rate: col. inch $5 Circulation: 3,000 per issue (paid). **Owner(s):** Ashley Publishing, Inc., See address and contact information above. **Management:** David Moyers, Publisher. Jan Roberts, Advertising Manager. **Editorial:** David Moyers, Editor.

HAMPTON

SOUTH ARKANSAS SUN. ISSN 1072-3323
305 E. Main St., Hampton, AR 71744-1069. Telephone: 870-798-3786. E-MAIL: brenda@southarkansassunc.om. URL: http://www.southarkansassun.com. Pub. Frequency: w. (Thu.) Page Size: broadsheet. Subscrip. Rate: $.50 newsstand/cover; $23/yr in county; $26/yr mailed out of county; $29/yr mailed out of state. Circulation: 1,300 per issue (paid). **Owner(s):** Brenda Clark, See address and contact information above. **Management:** Brenda G. Clark, Publisher. Pat Stringfellow, Advertising Manager. Brenda G. Clark, Circulation Manager. **Editorial:** Brenda G. Clark, Editor.

HARRISBURG

MODERN NEWS. 206 Main St, PO Box 400, Harrisburg, AR 72432. Telephone: 870-578-2121. FAX: 870-578-9415. E-MAIL: modernn@pcsii.com. Year Established: 1888. Pub. Frequency: w. (Wed.) Page Size: broadsheet. Subscrip. Rate: $.75 newsstand/cover; $22/yr in county; $27/yr mailed in state; $32/yr mailed out of state. Adv. Rate: col. inch $5.25 Circulation: 2,000 per issue (paid). **Owner(s):** Charles & Elaine Nix, See address and contact information above. **Management:** Charles D. Nix, Publisher. **Editorial:** Charles D. Nix, Managing Editor.

HAZEN

DE VALLS BLUFF TIMES. 77 Hwy 70 E, Hazen, AR 72064-0370. Telephone: 870-255-4538. FAX: 870-255-4539. E-MAIL: editor@herald-publishing.com. URL: http://www.herald-publishing.com. Pub. Frequency: w. (Wed.) Subscrip. Rate: $.50 newsstand/cover; $15/yr in county; $20/yr out of county; $25/yr out of state. Circulation: 650 per issue (paid). **Owner(s):** Herald Publising Co., Inc., P O Drawer B, Court-Sq Sta, Dublin, GA 31040. Telephone: 478-272-5522. **Management:** Roxanne W. Bradow, Publisher. Chris Bradow, Advertising. Martha Shinley, Circulation Manager. **Editorial:** Mathaniel Bradow, Editor.

GRAND PRAIRIE HERALD. 77 Hwy 70 E, Hazen, AR 72064-0370. Telephone: 870-255-4538. FAX: 870-255-4539. E-MAIL: editor@herald-publishing.com. URL: http://www.herald-publishing.com. Pub. Frequency: w. (Wed.) Page Size: standard. Subscrip. Rate: $.50 newsstand/cover; $15/yr in county; $20/yr out of county; $25/yr out of state. Circulation: 1,750 per issue (paid). **Owner(s):** Herald Publising Co., Inc., P O Drawer B, Court-Sq Sta, Dublin, GA 31040. Telephone: 478-272-5522. **Management:** Roxanne W. Bradow, Publisher. Chris Bradow, Advertising. Martha Shinley, Circulation Manager. Roxanne W. Bradow, Business Manager. **Editorial:** Mathaniel Bradow, Editor.

HEBER SPRINGS

SUN-TIMES, THE. ISSN 1050-5105
107 N. Fourth St., Heber Springs, AR 72543-0669. Telephone: 501-362-2425. FAX: 501-362-5877. URL: http://www.thesuntimes.com. Mailing Address: PO Box 669, Heber Springs, AR 72543-0669. Year Established: 1888. Pub. Frequency: s-w. (Wed. & Fri.) Page Size: broadsheet. Subscrip. Rate: $.75 newsstand/cover; $44.99, $54.99/yr out of county. Adv. Rate: col. inch $8.20 Circulation: 5,797 per issue (paid). **Owner(s):** GateHouse Media, Inc, 350 WillowBrook Office Park, Fairport, NY 14450. Telephone: 585-598-0030. FAX: 585-248-2631. **Management:** David J. Lee, Publisher. Ashley Gualtney, Circulation Manager. Donetta Sterling, Classified Adv. Mgr.. **Editorial:** Lorie Thompson, Editor. Will Gilbert, Sports Editor.

HELENA

DAILY WORLD T M C. 417 York St., Helena, AR 72342. Telephone: 870-338-9181. FAX: 870-338-9184. URL: http://www.helena-arkansas.com. Mailing Address: PO Box 340, Helena, AR 72342-0340. Pub. Frequency: w. (Thu.) Page Size: broadsheet Circulation: 7,700 per issue (free). **Owner(s):** GateHouse Media, Inc, 350 WillowBrook Office Park, Fairport, NY 14450. Telephone: 585-598-0030. FAX: 585-248-2631. **Management:** Clark Smith, Publisher. Ann Puckett, Advertising Manager. Donna Ginn, Circulation Manager. Kerri Dunlap-Davis, Classified Adv. Mgr..

HOPE

STAR EXTRA. 522 W Third St, Hope, AR 71801. Telephone: 870-777-8841. FAX: 870-777-3311. Mailing Address: PO Box 648, Hope, AR 71802-0648. Pub. Frequency: w. (Tue.) Page Size: broadsheet Circulation: 15,517 per issue (free). **Owner(s):** GateHouse Media, Inc, 350 WillowBrook Office Park, Fairport, NY 14450. Telephone: 585-598-0030. FAX: 585-248-2631. **Management:** George Jinks, Publisher. Richard Haycox, Advertising Manager. Donnie Hollis, Circulation Manager.

HUNTSVILLE

MADISON COUNTY (AR) RECORD. 201 Church St., Huntsville, AR 72740. Telephone: 479-738-2141. FAX: 479-738-1550. Year Established: 1879. Pub. Frequency: w. (Thu.) Page Size: broadsheet. Subscrip. Rate: $.50 newsstand/cover; $22/yr in county; $24/yr out of county; $26/yr out of state. Circulation: 5,500 per issue (paid). **Owner(s):** Fara Faubus & Ellen Kreth, See address and contact information above. **Management:** Ellen Kreth, Publisher. **Editorial:** Kyle Mooty, Editor.

IMBODEN

OZARK JOURNAL, THE. PO Box 598, Imboden, AR 72434-0598. Telephone: 870-869-2220. Year Established: 1915. Pub. Frequency: w. (Thu.) Page Size: standard. Subscrip. Rate: $.25 newsstand/cover; $12/yr mailed in state; $16/yr mailed out of state. Adv. Rate: col. inch $4.67 Circulation: 1,483 per issue (paid). **Owner(s):** Ozark Journal, Inc., See address and contact information above. **Editorial:** Karen Glass, Editor.

JASPER

NEWTON COUNTY TIMES, THE. 201 Locust St., Jasper, AR 72641-0453. Telephone: 870-446-2645. FAX: 870-446-6286. E-MAIL: nctimes@jasper.yournet.com. URL: http://www.newtoncountytimes.com. Mailing Address: PO Box 453, Jasper, AR 72641-0453. Pub. Frequency: w. (Thu.) Page Size: standard. Subscrip. Rate: $.50 newsstand/cover; $20/yr in county; $22/yr out of county; $25/yr out of state. Circulation: 2,875 per issue (paid). **Owner(s):** Community Publishers, Inc., PO Box 1049, Bentonville, AR 72172. Telephone: 501-271-3700. FAX: 501-271-3744. **Management:** Jane Christenson, Publisher. **Editorial:** Jeff Dezort, Editor.

LAKE VILLAGE

CHICOT COUNTY SPECTATOR. 105 N. Court, Lake Village, AR 71653-1917. Telephone: 870-265-2071. FAX: 870-265-2807. E-MAIL: arccs@sbcglobal.net. Year Established: 1906. Pub. Frequency: w. (Wed.) Page Size: broadsheet. Subscrip. Rate: $.50 newsstand/cover; $21/yr in county; $32/yr out of county. Circulation: 1,500 per issue (paid). **Owner(s):** Chicot County Newspapers LLC, See address and contact information above. **Management:** Barney White, Publisher. Rick Thompson, Advertising Manager. **Editorial:** John Corbitt, Editor.

EUDORA ENTERPRISE. 105 N. Court, Lake Village, AR 71653-1917. Telephone: 870-265-2071. FAX: 870-265-2807. E-MAIL: arccs@sbcglobal.net. Pub. Frequency: w. (Wed.) Page Size: broadsheet. Subscrip. Rate: $.50 newsstand/cover; $21/yr in county; $32/yr out of county. Adv. Rate: col. inch $5.50 Circulation: 1,500 per issue (paid). **Owner(s):** Chicot County Newspapers LLC, See address and contact information above. **Management:** John Corbitt, General Manager. Rick Thompson, Advertising Manager. **Editorial:** John Corbitt, Editor.

LEWISVILLE

LAFAYETTE COUNTY DEMOCRAT. 107 Spruce St., Lewisville, AR 71845. Telephone: 870-921-5711. Mailing Address: PO Box 507, Lewisville, AR 71845-0507. Pub. Frequency: w. (Thu.) Page Size: standard. Subscrip. Rate: $.50 newsstand/cover; $19/yr; $38 for 2 yrs.. Circulation: 1,000 per issue (paid). **Owner(s):** Graves Publishing Company, See address and contact information above. **Editorial:** Jeremy Langley, Editor.

LINCOLN

LINCOLN LEADER, THE. P.O. Box 520, Lincoln, AR 72744-0520. Telephone: 479-824-3263. FAX: 479-824-5540. E-MAIL: washconews@nwaonline.net. Pub. Frequency: w. (Wed.) Page Size: broadsheet. Subscrip. Rate: $.50 newsstand/cover; $18/yr in county; $25/yr out of county. Adv. Rate: col. inch $4.03 Circulation: 1,800 per issue (paid). **Owner(s):** Stephens Media LLC, 1111 W. Bonanza Rd., Las Vegas, NV 89106. Telephone: 702-383-0211. FAX: 702-383-0402. **Management:** Johnna Kidd, General Manager. Rosemary Johnson, Circulation Manager. **Editorial:** Martha Brock, Editor.

LITTLE ROCK

ARKANSAS TIMES. ISSN 0164-6273
201 E. Markham, Ste. 200, Little Rock, AR 72201-1627. Telephone: 501-375-2985. FAX: 501-375-3623. E-MAIL: arktimes@arktimes.com. URL: http://www.arktimes.com. Mailing Address: PO Box 34010, Little Rock, AR 72203-4010. Pub. Frequency: w. (Fri.) Page Size: tabloid. Subscrip. Rate: $32/yr mailed in state; $39/yr mailed out of state; $168/yr mailed foreign. Circulation: 43,000 per issue (paid and free). **Owner(s):** Arkansas Times LP, See address and contact information above. **Management:** Alan Leveritt, Publisher. Phyllis Britton, Advertising Director. Robert Curfman, Circulation Director. **Editorial:** Max Brantley, Editor. Michael Spain, Advertising Editor. Leslie Peacock, Feature Editor.

LITTLE ROCK FREE PRESS. 1300 S. Main St., Little Rock, AR 72202. Telephone: 501-372-4719. FAX: 501-372-4739. E-MAIL: freep@aristotle.net/freep. URL: http://www.aristotle.net/freep. Mailing Address: PO Box 165117, Little Rock, AR 72216. Year Established: 1993. Pub. Frequency: s-m. (Wed.) Page Size: tabloid Circulation: 20,000 per issue (free). **Owner(s):** Aristotle. net Inc., See address and contact information above. **Management:** Dotty Oliver, Publisher. **Editorial:** Dotty Oliver, Editor.

LONOKE

LONOKE DEMOCRAT. 402 N Center St, Lonoke, AR 72086. Telephone: 501-676-2463. FAX: 501-676-2463. E-MAIL: advertising@lonokedemocrat.com. URL: http://www.lonokedemocrat.com. Mailing Address: PO Box 747, Lonoke, AR 72086. Year Established: 1872. Pub. Frequency: w. (Wed.) Page Size: broadsheet. Subscrip. Rate: $.25 newsstand/cover; $14/yr in county; $17/yr in state; $28/yr out of state. Circulation: 2,700 per issue (paid). **Owner(s):** Stephens Media LLC, See address and contact information above. **Management:** Dennis Byrd, Publisher. Kenneth Jones, Advertising Director. Gary Ford, Circulation Manager. Claudine Mitchell, Business Manager. **Editorial:** Jesse Gonzalez, Production Manager.

MARIANNA

MARIANNA COURIER INDEX. 31 S. Poplar St., Marianna, AR 72360. Telephone: 870-295-2521. FAX: 870-295-9662. Mailing Address: PO Box 569, Marianna, AR 72360. Year Established: 1874. Pub. Frequency: w. (Thu.) Page Size: broadsheet. Subscrip. Rate: $.50 newsstand/cover; $24/yr mailed in county; $38/yr mailed in state; $50/yr mailed out of state. Circulation: 2,500 per issue (paid). **Owner(s):** Times-Herald Publishing Co., Inc., PO Box 1699, Forrest City, AR 72335. Telephone: 870-633-3130. **Management:** Melinda Huff, General Manager. Weston M. Lewey, Publisher. **Editorial:** Amanda Vondarn, Editor.

MARKED TREE

TRI-CITY TRIBUNE. 15 Elm St., Marked Tree, AR 72365. Telephone: 870-358-2993. FAX: 870-358-4538. E-MAIL: tctnews@eritter.net. URL: http://www.tri-citytribune.com. Mailing Address: PO Box 490, Marked Tree, AR 72365. Year Established: 1905. Pub. Frequency: w. (Thu.) Page Size: broadsheet. Subscrip. Rate: $.50 newsstand/cover; $23/yr local. Circulation: 1,700 per issue (paid). **Owner(s):** Rust Communications, Inc., 301 Broadway, Cape Girardeau, MO 63701. Telephone: 573-335-6611. **Management:** Ronald Kemp, Publisher. Samantha Martin, Advertising. **Editorial:** Samantha Martin, Editor.

MARSHALL

MARSHALL MOUNTAIN WAVE. PO Box 220, Marshall, AR 72650. E-MAIL: mmw@windstream.net. Year Established: 1890. Pub. Frequency: w. (Wed.) Page Size: broadsheet. Subscrip. Rate: $.50 newsstand/cover; $21/yr in county; $25/yr out of county; $28/yr out of state. Circulation: 4,500 per issue (paid). **Owner(s):** Marshall Mountain Wave Pub. Co., Inc., 215 Hwy.27 S, Marshall, AR 72650. Telephone: 870-448-3321. FAX: 870-448-5659. **Management:** Al Tilley, Publisher. **Editorial:** Debbie Horton, Managing Editor. Helen Horton, Circulation Editor.

MAUMELLE

MAUMELLE MONITOR. 1501 Club Manor Dr, Ste 2, Maumelle, AR 72113. Telephone: 501-851-6220. URL: http://www.maumellemonitor.com. Year Established: 1985. Pub. Frequency: w. (Wed.) Page Size: broadsheet. Subscrip. Rate: $22/yr in county; $26/yr in state; $34/yr out of state. Adv. Rate: col. inch $9.60 Circulation: 3,000 per issue (paid). **Owner(s):** Stephens Media LLC, See address and contact information above. **Management:** Dennis Byrd, Publisher. Kenneth Jones, Advertising Director. Gary Ford, Circulation Manager. Claudine Mitchell, Business Manager. **Editorial:** Jesse Gonzalez, Production Manager.

MCCRORY

WOODRUFF COUNTY MONITOR LEADER ADVOCATE. 301 N Edmonds Ave, McCrory, AR 72101. Telephone: 870-731-2263. FAX: 870-731-5899. Year Established: 1990. Pub. Frequency: w. (Wed.) Page Size: broadsheet. Subscrip. Rate: $.50 newsstand/cover; $23/yr in county; $29/yr out of county; $34/yr out of state. Freelance Pay: $10/article. Circulation: 2,200 per issue (paid). **Owner(s):** Gladys Price Press, See address and contact information above. **Management:** Paula Barnett, General Manager.

MCGEHEE

MCGEHEE-DERMOTT TIMES NEWS. 9211 N. Second St., McGehee, AR 71654-0290. Telephone: 870-222-3922. FAX: 870-222-3726. E-MAIL: timeseditor@allegiance.tv. Pub. Frequency: w. (Wed.) Page Size: broadsheet. Subscrip. Rate: $.50 newsstand/cover; $25/yr home delivery local; $35/yr mailed out of area. Circulation: 34,000 per issue (paid). **Owner(s):** James P. & Arlene White, See address and contact information above. **Management:** James P. White Jr., Publisher. Arlene White, Advertising Manager. **Editorial:** Rachel Freeze, Editor.

MELBOURNE

MELBOURNE TIMES, THE. 408 Court St., Melbourne, AR 72556. Telephone: 870-368-4421. FAX: 870-368-4721. Mailing Address: PO Box 308, Melbourne, AR 72556-0308. Pub. Frequency: w. (Wed.) Page Size: broadsheet. Subscrip. Rate: $.50 newsstand/cover; $20/yr in county; $30/yr out of county. Circulation: 3,500 per issue (paid). **Owner(s):** Dutton Printing Inc., See address and contact information above. **Management:** Debbie Dutton, Publisher. **Editorial:** Debbie Dutton, Managing Editor.

MENA

MENA STAR. ISSN 0747-1513
501 Mena St., Mena, AR 71953. Telephone: 479-394-1900. FAX: 479-394-1524. E-MAIL: jay@menastar.com. URL: http://www.menastar.com. Mailing Address: PO Box 1307, Mena, AR 71953. Year Established: 1896. Pub. Frequency: w. (Thu.) Page Size: broadsheet. Subscrip. Rate: $.50 newsstand/cover; $27/yr local; $37/yr mailed elsewhere. **Wire Service(s):** AP. Circulation: 4,500 per issue (paid). **Owner(s):** Lancaster Management, Inc., PO Box 609, Gadsden, AL 35902. **Management:** Joe Ben Oller, Publisher. Debbie Frost, Advertising Director. Rhonda Lambert, Circulation Manager. **Editorial:** Joe Ben Oller, Editor. Jay Strasner, Managing Editor.

MONTICELLO

ADVANCE MONTICELLONIAN. 314 N. Main St., Monticello, AR 71655. Telephone: 870-367-5325. FAX: 870-367-6612. E-MAIL: editor@monticellonews.net. Mailing Address: PO Box 486, Monticello, AR 71657. Year Established: 1870. Pub. Frequency: w. (Wed.) Page Size: broadsheet. Subscrip. Rate: $.75 newsstand/cover; $34/yr local area; $45/yr mailed elsewhere. Adv. Rate: col. inch $6.75 Circulation: 4,200 per issue (paid). **Owner(s):** DLS Inc., PO Box 27, Fort Payne, AL 35967. **Management:** Tom White, Publisher. Wendy Tassin, Advertising. **Editorial:** Beverly Burks, Editor.

MORRILTON

CONWAY COUNTY PETIT JEAN COUNTRY HEADLIGHT. 908 W Broadway, Morrilton, AR 72110. Telephone: 501-354-2451. FAX: 501-354-4225. E-MAIL: pjch@ipa.net. URL: http://www.headlightnews.com. Mailing Address: PO Box 540, Morrilton, AR 72110. Year Established: 1874. Pub. Frequency: w. (Wed.) Page Size: broadsheet. Subscrip. Rate: $.75 newsstand/cover; $35/yr mailed in county; $43/yr mailed in state; $45/yr mailed out of state. Circulation: 6,700 per issue (paid). **Owner(s):** Fisher Publications, See address and contact information above. **Management:** David Fisher, President. Sharon Judkins, Advertising Manager. Donna Ferren, Circulation Manager. Eddy Hodge, Business Manager. **Editorial:** Charlotte Hodge, Editor.

PERRY COUNTY PETIT JEAN COUNTRY HEADLIGHT. 908 W Broadway, Morrilton, AR 72110. Telephone: 501-354-2451. FAX: 501-354-4225. URL: http://www.headlightnews.com. Mailing Address: PO Box 540, Morrilton, AR 72110. Pub. Frequency: w. (Wed.) Page Size: broadsheet. Subscrip. Rate: $.75 newsstand/cover; $32/yr in county; $45/yr in state. Circulation: 8,200 per issue (paid). **Owner(s):** Fisher Publications, See address and contact information above. **Management:** David Fisher, Publisher. Sharon Judkins, Advertising Manager. Donna Ferren, Circulation Manager. Eddy Hodge, Business Manager. **Editorial:** Charlotte Hodge, Editor.

MOUNTAIN VIEW

STONE COUNTY CITIZEN. PO Box 6, Mountain View, AR 72560. Telephone: 870-269-8626. FAX: 870-269-8634. E-MAIL: stonecountycitizen@yahoo.com. Year Established: 1986. Pub. Frequency: w. (Wed.) Page Size: standard. Subscrip. Rate: $.35 newsstand/cover; $16/yr in county; $26/yr mailed out of county. Circulation: 4,000 per issue (paid and free). **Owner(s):** Dennis Brannon, See address and contact information above. **Management:** Dennis Brannon, Publisher. Ellen Brannon, Advertising Manager. **Editorial:** Dennis Brannon, Editor.

STONE COUNTY LEADER. 104 W. Main, Mountain View, AR 72560. Telephone: 870-269-3841. FAX: 870-269-2171. E-MAIL: leader@mvtel.net. URL: http://www.stonecountyleader.com. Mailing Address: PO Box 509, Mountain View, AR 72560. Year Established: 1952. Pub. Frequency: w. (Wed.) Page Size: broadsheet. Subscrip. Rate: $.50 newsstand/cover; $20/yr in county & adj. cys.; $31/yr mailed out of area. Adv. Rate: col. inch $5.25 Circulation: 5,000 per issue (paid). **Owner(s):** Stone County Publishing Co., Inc., See address and contact information above. **Management:** James R;. Fraser, Publisher. Linda Kroon Van Diest, Advertising. **Editorial:** Lori Freeze, News Editor.

MT. IDA

MONTGOMERY COUNTY NEWS. 154 S. George St., Mt. Ida, AR 71957. Telephone: 870-867-2010. FAX: 870-356-4400. Mailing Address: PO Box 187, Mt. Ida, AR 71957-0187. Pub. Frequency: w. (Thu.) Page Size: broadsheet. Subscrip. Rate: $.75 newsstand/cover; $22/yr in county; $37/yr out of county; $42/yr out of state. Circulation: 1,800 per issue (paid). **Owner(s):** Graves Publishing Co., Inc., 418 N. Main St., Nashville, AR 71852. Telephone: 870-845-2010. FAX: 870-845-5091. **Management:** Lawrence Graves, Publisher. **Editorial:** Mike Wallace, Managing Editor.

MURFREESBORO

MURFREESBORO DIAMOND. 201 S Washington Ave, Ste C, Murfreesboro, AR 71958. Telephone: 870-285-2723. FAX: 870-285-3820. Mailing Address: PO Box 550, Murfreesboro, AR 71958. Year Established: 1975. Pub. Frequency: w. (Wed.) Page Size: broadsheet. Subscrip. Rate: $.75 newsstand/cover; $33/yr local; $50/yr elsewhere. Adv. Rate: col. inch $6 Circulation: 1,800 per issue (paid). **Owner(s):** Graves Publishing Co., Inc., 418 N. Main St., Nashville, AR 71852. Telephone: 870-845-2010. **Management:** Lawrence Graves, Publisher. Alicia Berry, Advertising Manager. **Editorial:** John L. Balch, Editor. Linda Twilley, Assistant Editor. Jane Graves, News Editor.

NASHVILLE

NASHVILLE NEWS. 418 N. Main St., Nashville, AR 71852. Telephone: 870-845-2010. FAX: 870-845-5091. E-MAIL: nashnews@cswnet.com. URL: http://www.nashvillenews.org. Year Established: 1878. Pub. Frequency: s-w. (Mon. & Thu.) Page Size: broadsheet. Subscrip. Rate: $.75 newsstand/cover; $27/yr mailed local trade area; $50/yr mailed elsewhere. **Wire Service(s):** AP. Circulation: 5,000 per issue (paid). **Owner(s):** Graves Publishing Co., Inc., See address and contact information above. **Management:** Lawrence Graves, Publisher. Sarah Rodgers, Advertising Manager. Ellen Ward, Circulation Manager. Mike Graves, Business Manager. **Editorial:** Jay Strasner, Editor. Jane Graves, News Editor.

Weeklies

NEWPORT

NEWPORT INDEPENDENT. 2408 Hwy 367 N., Newport, AR 72112-1750. Telephone: 870-523-5855. FAX: 870-523-6540. URL: http://www.newportindependent.com. Mailing Address: PO Box 1750, Newport, AR 72112-1750. Year Established: 1901. Pub. Frequency: s-w. (Wed. & Fri.) Page Size: broadsheet. Subscrip. Rate: $.50 newsstand/cover; $43/yr mailed in state; $50/yr mailed out of state. **Wire Service(s):** AP. Circulation: 2,500 per issue (paid). **Owner(s):** GateHouse Media, Inc, 350 WillowBrook Office Park, Fairport, NY 14450. Telephone: 585-598-0030. FAX: 585-248-2631. **Management:** Gina Slagley, Publisher. Pat Breckenridge, Circulation Manager. **Editorial:** Melissa Lore, Reporter. Ken Duvall, Sports.

NORTH LITTLE ROCK

TIMES (NORTH LITTLE ROCK), THE. 5301 McClanahan Dr, Ste D7, North Little Rock, AR 72116. Telephone: 501-353-1830. FAX: 501-370-8391. URL: http://www.nlrtimes.com/. Mailing Address: 119 Main St., PO Box 428, Little Rock, AR 72201. Year Established: 1922. Pub. Frequency: w. Subscrip. Rate: $22/yr in county; $26/yr in state; $34/yr out of state. **Owner(s):** Stephens Media LLC, See address and contact information above. **Management:** Dennis Byrd, Publisher. Kenneth Jones, Advertising Director. Gary Ford, Circulation Manager. Claudine Mitchell, Business Manager. **Editorial:** Jesse Gonzalez, Production Manager.

OSCEOLA

OSCEOLA TIMES, THE. 112 N. Poplar St., Osceola, AR 72370. Telephone: 870-563-2615. FAX: 870-563-2616. URL: http://www.osceolatimes.com. Mailing Address: PO Box 408, Osceola, AR 72370. Year Established: 1870. Pub. Frequency: w. (Thu.) Page Size: broadsheet. Subscrip. Rate: $.75 newsstand/cover; $24/yr mailed in county; $48/yr mailed out of county. Adv. Rate: col. inch $5.75 **Wire Service(s):** AP. Circulation: 9,000 per issue (paid). **Owner(s):** Tennyson Publishing, 900 N. Broadway, Blytheville, AR 72316. Telephone: 870-763-4461. FAX: 870-763-6874. **Management:** David Tennyson, Publisher. Steve Knox, Advertising Manager. David Pierce, Circulation Manager. **Editorial:** Sandra Brand, Editor.

OZARK

SPECTATOR (OZARK), THE. 207 W. Main St., Ozark, AR 72949-3231. Telephone: 501-667-2136. FAX: 501-667-4365. E-MAIL: spectator@ar-digit.net. URL: http://www.ozarkspectator.com. Pub. Frequency: w. (Wed.) Page Size: broadsheet. Subscrip. Rate: $.25 newsstand/cover; $18/yr in county & adj. cys.; $22/yr elsewhere in state; $24/yr out of state. Adv. Rate: col. inch $5 Circulation: 5,800 per issue (paid). **Owner(s):** Bob Bevil, See address and contact information above. **Management:** Bob Bevil, Advertising Manager. **Editorial:** Jo Eveld, Editor.

PARIS

PARIS EXPRESS. ISSN 1071-9709
22 S. Express St., Paris, AR 72855. Telephone: 479-963-2901. FAX: 479-963-3062. URL: http://www.paris-express.com. Mailing Address: PO Box 551, Paris, AR 72855. Year Established: 1880. Pub. Frequency: w. (Wed.) Page Size: broadsheet. Subscrip. Rate: $.50 newsstand/cover; $26/yr local. Circulation: 3,600 per issue (paid). **Owner(s):** Stephens Media LLC, 1111 W. Bonanza Rd., Las Vegas, NV 89106. Telephone: 702-383-0211. FAX: 702-383-4676. **Management:** Vickey Wiggins, Publisher. Mary Harrison, Advertising Manager. **Editorial:** Pat McHughes, Editor.

PEA RIDGE

TIMES OF NORTHEAST BENTON COUNTY. 186A Lee Town Rd, Pea Ridge, AR 72751. Telephone: 479-451-1196. FAX: 479-451-9456. E-MAIL: annetteb@nwannews.com. URL: http://www.nwarktimes.com. Mailing Address: PO Box 25, Pea Ridge, AR 72751-0025. Year Established: 1966. Pub. Frequency: w. (Wed.) Page Size: broadsheet. Subscrip. Rate: $.50 newsstand/cover; $20/yr in county; $26/yr mailed out of county. Adv. Rate: col. inch $4.68 Circulation: 1,425 per issue (paid). **Owner(s):** Wehco Media, Inc., PO Box 2221, Little Rock, AR 72203. Telephone: 501-378-3400. **Management:** Annette Beard, General Manager. Jeff Jeffus, Publisher. Hector Cueva, Circulation Director.

PIGGOTT

PIGGOTT TIMES, THE. 209 W. Main St., Piggott, AR 72454. Telephone: 870-598-2201. FAX: 870-598-5189. E-MAIL: rkemp@scwnet.com. Mailing Address: PO Box 59, Piggott, AR 72454. Year Established: 1967. Pub. Frequency: w. (Wed.) Page Size: standard. Subscrip. Rate: $.75 newsstand/cover; $23/yr mailed in county; $28/yr mailed out of county; $33/yr mailed out of state. Circulation: 3,200 per issue (paid). **Owner(s):** Rust Communications, Inc., 301 Broadway, Cape Girardeau, MO 63701. Telephone: 573-335-6611. **Management:** Ronald Kemp, Publisher. Alex Routszong, Advertising Manager. **Editorial:** Ronald Kemp, Editor. Robbie Wells, News Director. Carla Wagster, Production Manager.

POCAHONTAS

POCAHONTAS STAR HERALD. 109 N. Van Bibber St., Pocahontas, AR 72455. Telephone: 870-892-4451. FAX: 870-892-4453. E-MAIL: starherald@jvrhomes.com. Mailing Address: PO Box 608, Pocahontas, AR 72455. Year Established: 1880. Pub. Frequency: w. (Thu.) Page Size: broadsheet. Subscrip. Rate: $.50 newsstand/cover; $20/yr mailed in cy. & adj. cys.; $30/yr mailed out of area. Freelance Pay: $0.60/column-inch. Circulation: 5,000 per issue (paid and free). **Owner(s):** J.V. Rockwell Publishing Co., PO Box 128, Corning, AR 72422. Telephone: 501-857-3531. **Management:** J.V. Rockwell, President. Susan Thielemier, Advertising Manager. Pam Russell, Circulation Manager. **Editorial:** Anita Murphy, Editor.

PRESCOTT

NEVADA COUNTY PICAYUNE. 100 E Elm St, Prescott, AR 71857. Telephone: 870-887-2002. FAX: 870-887-2949. URL: http://www.picayune-times.com. Mailing Address: PO Box 60, Prescott, AR 71857-0060. Year Established: 1878. Pub. Frequency: w. (Wed.) Page Size: broadsheet. Subscrip. Rate: $.75 newsstand/cover; $22/yr in county; $24/yr out of county; $39/yr out of state. Circulation: 2,500 per issue (paid). **Owner(s):** GateHouse Media, Inc, 350 WillowBrook Office Park, Fairport, NY 14450. Telephone: 585-598-0030. FAX: 585-248-2631. **Management:** George Jinks, Publisher. Richard Hycox, Advertising Manager. Lisa Martin, Classified Adv. Mgr.. **Editorial:** Wendy Ledbetter, Editor.

RECTOR

CLAY COUNTY DEMOCRAT. 306 Main St., Rector, AR 72461. Telephone: 870-595-3549. FAX: 870-595-3611. E-MAIL: ccd@centurytel.net. URL: http://www.claycountydemocrat.com. Mailing Address: PO Box 366, Rector, AR 72461. Pub. Frequency: w. (Wed.) Page Size: broadsheet. Subscrip. Rate: $.75 newsstand/cover; $20/yr in clay & adjoining cys; $25/yr in state; $30/yr out of state. Circulation: 2,400 per issue (paid). **Owner(s):** Rust Communications, Inc., 301 Broadway, Cape Girardeau, MO 63701. **Management:** Nancy Kemp, Publisher.

RISON

CLEVELAND COUNTY HERALD. 215 Main St., Rison, AR 71665. Telephone: 870-325-6412. FAX: 870-325-6127. E-MAIL: ccherald@tds.net. URL: http://www.clevelandcountyherald.com. Mailing Address: PO Box 657, Rison, AR 71665-0657. Year Established: 1888. Pub. Frequency: w. (Wed.) Page Size: broadsheet. Subscrip. Rate: $.50 newsstand/cover; $20/yr in county; $25/yr in state; $27/yr out of state. Adv. Rate: col. inch $5.50 Circulation: 2,700 per issue (paid). **Owner(s):** Talent Publishing LLC, See address and contact information above. **Management:** Britt Talent, Publisher. Shannon Ingram, Circulation Manager. **Editorial:** Britt Talent, Editor.

ROGERS

ROGERS HOMETOWN NEWS. 1400 W Walnut St, Ste 123, Rogers, AR 72757. Telephone: 479-621-6397. FAX: 479-621-6399. E-MAIL: ads@nwanews.com. URL: http://nwanews.com. Mailing Address: PO Box 1320, Rogers, AR 72757. Pub. Frequency: w. (Wed.) Page Size: standard. Subscrip. Rate: $.50 newsstand/cover; $20/yr in county. Adv. Rate: col. inch $8.02 Freelance Pay: $25/story. Circulation: 2,380 per issue (paid). **Owner(s):** Wehco Media, Inc., PO Box 2221, Little Rock, AR 72203. Telephone: 501-378-3400. **Management:** Jeff Jeffus, General Manager. Linda Gilmore, Advertising. Hector Cueva, Circulation Director. **Editorial:** Michael Roark, Editor.

RUSSELLVILLE

POST-DISPATCH. 201 E Second St, PO Box 887, Russellville, AR 72811-0887. Telephone: 479-229-2250. FAX: 479-229-1159. E-MAIL: postdispatch@centurytel.net. Mailing Address: PO Box 270, Dardanelle, AR 72834. Year Established: 1854. Pub. Frequency: w. (Wed.) Page Size: broadsheet. Subscrip. Rate: $.50 newsstand/cover; $16/yr in county; $27/yr out of state. Circulation: 2,300 per issue (paid). **Owner(s):** Paxton Media Group Llc, 201 S. Fourth St., Paducah, KY 42003. Telephone: 270-575-8600. FAX: 270-442-8188. **Management:** Neal Ronquist, Publisher. Michelle Harris, Advertising Manager. Mike Geiss, Circulation Manager. **Editorial:** Todd Brooks, Editor.

TRI-COUNTY RECORD (RUSSELLVILLE). 201 E. Second St., Russellville, AR 72801-5102. Telephone: 479-968-5252. FAX: 479-968-4037. E-MAIL: editor@couriernews.com. URL: http://www.couriernews.com. Mailing Address: PO Box 887, Russellville, AR 72811. Pub. Frequency: w. (Wed.) Page Size: broadsheet.Adv. Rate: col. inch $10.25 Circulation: 19,670 per issue (free). **Owner(s):** Paxton Media Group LLC, 201 S. Fourth St., Paducah, KY 42003. Telephone: 270-575-8600. FAX: 270-442-8188. **Management:** Marvin Enderle, Publisher. Michelle Harris, Advertising Manager. **Editorial:** Scott Perkins, Editor.

TRI-PEAKS TRADER. 104 Modesto, Russellville, AR 72801-2322. Telephone: 479-968-2720. FAX: 479-890-6098. Year Established: 1991. Pub. Frequency: w. (Wed.) Page Size: tabloid.Adv. Rate: color page $500 Circulation: 14,000 per issue (free). **Owner(s):** Ruby Jenkins, See address and contact information above. **Management:** Ruby Jenkins, Publisher. **Editorial:** Ruby Jenkins, Editor.

SALEM

IZARD-FULTON RECORD. 388 Hwy. 62-412, Salem, AR 72576. Telephone: 870-895-3207. FAX: 870-895-4277. E-MAIL: news@areawidenews.com. Mailing Address: PO Box 248, Salem, AR 72576-0248. Pub. Frequency: w. (Wed.) Page Size: broadsheet.Adv. Rate: col. inch $6.75 Circulation: 6,100 per issue (free). **Owner(s):** Rust Communications, Inc., 301 Broadway, Cape Girardeau, MO 63701. Telephone: 573-335-6611. **Management:** Erma Harris, General Manager. Kathy Kleinman, Advertising Manager. **Editorial:** Erma Harris, Editor.

NEWS (SALEM), THE. 388 Hwy. 62-412, Salem, AR 72576. Telephone: 870-895-3207. FAX: 870-895-4277. E-MAIL: news@areawidenews.com. URL: http://www.areawidenews.com. Mailing Address: PO Box 248, Salem, AR 72576-0248. Pub. Frequency: w. (Thu.) Page Size: broadsheet. Subscrip. Rate: $.75 newsstand/cover; $33/yr in county; $40/yr out of county. Adv. Rate: col. inch $13 Freelance Pay: $0.50/column-inch. Circulation: 3,362 per issue (paid). **Owner(s):** Rust Communications, Inc., 301 Broadway, Cape Girardeau, MO 63701. Telephone: 573-335-6611. FAX: 573-335-5018. **Management:** Erma Harris, General Manager. Kathy Kleinman, Advertising Manager. Debra Perryman, Circulation Manager. **Editorial:** Erma Harris, Editor.

OREGON COUNTY RECORD. 388 Hwy. 62-412, Salem, AR 72576. Telephone: 870-895-3207. FAX: 870-895-4277. E-MAIL: news@areawidenews.com. URL: http://www.areawidenews.com. Mailing Address: PO Box 248, Salem, AR 72576-0248. Pub. Frequency: w. (Wed.) Page Size: broadsheet.Adv. Rate: col. inch $13.80 Circulation: 5,625 per issue (free). **Owner(s):** Rust Communications, Inc., 301 Broadway, Cape Girardeau, MO 63701. Telephone: 573-335-6611. FAX: 573-335-5018. **Management:** Erma Harris, General Manager. Kathy Kleinman, Advertising Manager. Debra Perryman, Circulation Manager. **Editorial:** Erma Harris, Editor.

SHARP COUNTY RECORD. 388 Hwy. 62/412 E., Salem, AR 72576. Telephone: 870-895-3207. FAX: 870-895-4277. E-MAIL: areawidemedia@centurytel.net. Mailing Address: PO Box 248, Salem, AR 72575-0248. Pub. Frequency: w. (Wed.) Page Size: broadsheet.Adv. Rate: col. inch $6.75 Circulation: 8,000 per issue (free). **Owner(s):** Rust Communications, 301 Broadway, Cape Girardeau, MO 63701. Telephone: 800-879-1210. **Management:** Janie Flynn, General Manager. Kathy Kleinman, Advertising Manager. **Editorial:** Erma Harris, Editor.

VILLAGER JOURNAL, THE. 388 Hwy. 62-412 E, Salem, AR 72576. Telephone: 870-895-3207. FAX: 870-895-4277. E-MAIL: news@areawidenews.com. URL: villageronline.com. Mailing Address: PO Box 248, Salem, AR 72576-0248. Pub. Frequency: w. (Wed.) Page Size: broadsheet. Subscrip. Rate: $.75 newsstand/cover; $33/yr in county; $40/yr out of county. Circulation: 3,400 per issue (paid). **Owner(s):** Roundhouse Publishing, See address and contact information above. **Management:** Janie Flynn, Publisher. Debra Perryman, Circulation Manager. **Editorial:** Erma Harris, Managing Editor.

SEARCY

COMMUNITY SHOPPER (SEARCY). 3000 E. Race Ave., Searcy, AR 72143. Telephone: 501-268-0702. FAX: 501-268-3868. E-MAIL: shopper@dailycitizen.com. URL: http://www.advertisingdailycitizen.com. Year Established: 1999. Pub. Frequency: w. (Wed.) Page Size: broadsheet Circulation: 29,538 per issue (free). **Owner(s):** Paxton Media Group LLC, 201 S. Fourth St., Paducah, KY 42003. Telephone: 270-575-8600. FAX: 270-442-8188. **Management:** Billy Roberts, Manager.

SHERIDAN

SHERIDAN HEADLIGHT, THE. 211 W High St, Sheridan, AR 72150. Telephone: 870-942-2142. FAX: 870-942-8823. E-MAIL: sheadlite1@aol.com. URL: http://www.thesheridanheadlight.com. Mailing Address: PO Box 539, Sheridan, AR 72150. Year Established: 1881. Pub. Frequency: w. (Wed.) Page Size: broadsheet. Subscrip. Rate: $.50 newsstand/cover; $20/yr in county; $26/yr mailed out of county; $33/yr mailed elsewhere. Adv. Rate: col. inch $5 Circulation: 4,050 per issue (paid). **Owner(s):** Katherine Webb, See address and contact information above. **Management:** Melody A. Morehouse, Publisher. Sheila Phillips, Advertising. **Editorial:** Rob Patrick, Sports Editor.

SHERWOOD

SHERWOOD VOICE. PO Box 6166, Sherwood, AR 72124. E-MAIL: news@sherwoodvoice.com. URL: http://www.sherwoodvoice.com. Year Established: 1964. Pub. Frequency: w. (Thu.) Page Size: broadsheet. Subscrip. Rate: $17/yr in county; $19/yr in state; $30/yr out of state. Adv. Rate: col. inch $7.15 Circulation: 3,000 per issue (paid). **Owner(s):** Stephens Media LLC, 5301 McClanahan Dr, Ste D7, North Little Rock, AR 72116. Telephone: 501-353-1830. FAX: 501-353-1832. **Management:** Dennis Byrd, Publisher. Kenneth Jones, Advertising Director. Gary Ford, Circulation Manager. Claudine Mitchell, Business Manager. **Editorial:** Jesse Gonzalez, Production Manager. Tyler Tucker, News Editor.

SILOAM SPRINGS

HERALD-LEADER, THE. 101 N Mt. Olive, Siloam Springs, AR 72761. Telephone: 479-524-5144. FAX: 479-524-5159. E-MAIL: compub95@aol.com. URL: http://nwanews.com/leader. Year Established: 1892. Pub. Frequency: s-w. (Wed. & Sun.) Page Size: broadsheet. Subscrip. Rate: $.50 newsstand/cover for Wed.; $1.25 newsstand/cover Sun.; $22/yr home delivery local; $35/yr out of area. Adv. Rate: col. inch $6.80 Circulation: 10,000 per issue (paid). **Owner(s):** Wehco Media, Inc., PO Box 2221, Little Rock, AR 72203. Telephone: 501-378-3400. **Management:** Shelly Moran, Publisher. Hector Cueva, Circulation Director. **Editorial:** Sara Gatling, Managing Editor. Gary Trembly, Sports Editor.

SMACKOVER

SMACKOVER JOURNAL. 618 N. Broadway, Smackover, AR 71762-1821. Telephone: 870-725-3131. FAX: 870-725-3131. Mailing Address: PO Box 147, Smackover, AR 71762. Year Established: 1922. Pub. Frequency: w. (Thu.) Page Size: broadsheet. Subscrip. Rate: $.35 newsstand/cover; $16.50/yr in county; $20/yr out of county. Circulation: 1,121 per issue (paid and free). **Owner(s):** Wehco Media, Inc., PO Box 2221, Little Rock, AR 72203. Telephone: 501-378-3400. FAX: 501-378-3527. **Management:** Donna Faulkner, General Manager. Tammy Holloway, Advertising. **Editorial:** Donna Faulkner, Editor.

STAR CITY

LINCOLN LEDGER. Town Sq., Star City, AR 71667. Telephone: 870-628-4161. FAX: 870-628-3802. Year Established: 1876. Pub. Frequency: w. (Wed.) Page Size: standard. Subscrip. Rate: $.25 newsstand/cover; $9/yr in county; $12/yr out of county; $15/yr mailed out of state. Circulation: 2,550 per issue (paid). **Owner(s):** Lincoln County Publishing Co., Inc., See address and contact information above. **Management:** Joe V. Mason, Publisher. Peggy Mason, Advertising Manager. **Editorial:** Joe V. Mason, Editor.

STUTTGART

EXTRA (STUTTGART), THE. 111 W. Sixth St., Stuttgart, AR 72160-0531. Telephone: 870-673-8533. FAX: 870-673-3671. URL: http://www.stuttgartdailyleader.com. Year Established: 1928. Pub. Frequency: w. (Tue.) Page Size: broadsheet Circulation: 5,707 per issue (free). **Owner(s):** GateHouse Media, Inc, 350 WillowBrook Office Park, Fairport, NY 14450. Telephone: 585-598-0030. **Management:** Clark Smith, Publisher. Tony Cooper, Advertising Manager. Willene Boehn, Circulation Manager. Dannie Jo Bueker, Classified Adv. Mgr..

TRUMANN

TRUMANN DEMOCRAT. 405 Hwy. 463 N., Trumann, AR 72472. Telephone: 870-483-6317. FAX: 870-483-6031. E-MAIL: tdemocrat@centurytel.net. URL: http://www.trumanndemocrat.com. Mailing Address: PO Box 5, Trumann, AR 72472-0005. Year Established: 1922. Pub. Frequency: w. (Wed.) Page Size: broadsheet. Subscrip. Rate: $.50 newsstand/cover; $23/yr in county; $28/yr mailed out of county; $33/yr mailed out of state. Adv. Rate: col. inch $6 Circulation: 1,275 per issue (paid). **Owner(s):** Ron Kemp, See address and contact information above. **Management:** Nancy Kemp, Co-Publisher. Joyce Minor, Advertising Director. **Editorial:** Samantha Martin, Editor. Dan Brawner, Sports.

VAN BUREN

PRESS ARGUS-COURIER. ISSN 0885-9086
100 N. 11th St., Van Buren, AR 72956. Telephone: 479-474-5215. FAX: 479-471-5607. E-MAIL: bhager@pressargus.com. URL: http://www.pressargus.com. Mailing Address: PO Box 369, Van Buren, AR 72956. Year Established: 1859. Pub. Frequency: s-w. (Wed. & Sat.) Page Size: broadsheet. Subscrip. Rate: $.50 newsstand/cover; $36/yr area; $41/yr out of area; $46/yr mailed out of state. Circulation: 7,000 per issue (paid). **Owner(s):** Stephens Media LLC, 1111 W. Bonanza Rd., Las Vegas, NV 89106. Telephone: 702-383-0211. FAX: 702-383-0402. **Management:** Bill Hager, Publisher. Judy Weese, Advertising Manager. **Editorial:** Kenneth Fry, Editor. George Mitchell IV, Sports.

RIVER VALLEY ADVERTISER, THE. 100 N. 11th St., Van Buren, AR 72957. Telephone: 479-474-5215. FAX: 479-471-5607. Mailing Address: PO Box 369, Van Buren, AR 72957. Pub. Frequency: w. (Wed.) Page Size: broadsheet Circulation: 13,000 per issue (free). **Owner(s):** Stephens Media LLC, 1111 W. Bonanza Rd., Las Vegas, NV 89106. Telephone: 702-383-0211. FAX: 702-383-4676. **Management:** Bill Hager, Publisher. Judy Weese, Advertising Manager. **Editorial:** Kenneth Fry, Editor.

WALDRON

CITIZEN (MANSFIELD), THE. 200 S. Main St., Waldron, AR 72958-1816. Telephone: 479-637-4161. FAX: 479-637-4162. Mailing Address: PO Box 36, Mansfield, AR 72944-0036. Year Established: 1967. Pub. Frequency: w. (Wed.) Page Size: broadsheet. Subscrip. Rate: $.50 newsstand/cover; $16/yr local; $22/yr in state; $26/yr out of state. Circulation: 3,000 per issue (paid and free). **Owner(s):** Waldron Newspapers, Inc., PO Box 745, Waldron, AR 72958-0347. **Management:** Joe Ben Oller, Publisher. Don Jones, Advertising Manager. **Editorial:** Joe Ben Oller, Editor.

SCOTT COUNTY ADVERTISER. 200 S. Main St., Waldron, AR 72958-1816. Telephone: 479-637-4161. FAX: 479-637-4162. Year Established: 1987. Pub. Frequency: w. (Wed.) Page Size: broadsheet Circulation: 4,600 per issue (free). **Owner(s):** Waldron Newspapers, Inc., PO Box 745, Waldron, AR 72958-0347. **Management:** Joe Ben Oller, Publisher. Don Jones, Advertising Manager. **Editorial:** Joe Ben Oller, Editor.

WALDRON NEWS. 200 S. Main St., Waldron, AR 72958-1816. E-MAIL: carla@waldronnews.com. URL: http://www.waldronnews.com. Pub. Frequency: w. (Wed.) Page Size: tabloid. Subscrip. Rate: $.50 newsstand/cover; $21/yr local; $26/yr mailed out of area; $33/yr mailed out of state. Circulation: 2,125 per issue (paid). **Owner(s):** Waldron Newspapers, Inc., PO Box 745, Waldron, AR 72958. Telephone: 479-637-4161. FAX: 479-637-4162. **Management:** Joe Ben Oller, Publisher. Don Jones, Advertising Manager. **Editorial:** Joe Ben Oller, Editor.

WALNUT RIDGE

TIMES DISPATCH. 225 W. Main St., Walnut Ridge, AR 72476. Telephone: 870-886-2464. FAX: 870-886-9369. E-MAIL: thetd@bscn.com. URL: http://www.thetd.com. Mailing Address: PO Box 389, Walnut Ridge, AR 72476-0389. Year Established: 1910. Pub. Frequency: w. (Wed.) Page Size: broadsheet. Subscrip. Rate: $.50 newsstand/cover; $26/yr in county & adj. cys.; $32/yr in state; $34/yr out of state. Circulation: 5,700 per issue (paid). **Owner(s):** Times Dispatch, Inc., See address and contact information above. **Management:** Janice Hibbard, Advertising Manager. **Editorial:** Gretchen Hunt, Editor. Debbie Richey, Sports. Virginia Bland, Writer.

WARREN

WARREN EAGLE-DEMOCRAT. 200 W. Cypress St., Warren, AR 71671-2743. Telephone: 870-226-5831. FAX: 870-226-6601. E-MAIL: eaglepub@sbcglobal.net. Year Established: 1885. Pub. Frequency: w. (Wed.) Page Size: broadsheet. Subscrip. Rate: $.50 newsstand/cover; $30/yr mailed in state; $38/yr mailed out of state. Adv. Rate: col. inch $6.75 Circulation: 3,900 evening (paid). **Owner(s):** Danny Cook, See address and contact information above. **Management:** Danny Cook, Publisher. **Editorial:** Zack Plair, Editor.

WHITE HALL

WHITE HALL JOURNAL. ISSN 0747-1572
7400 Dollarway Rd., Ste. E, White Hall, AR 71602. Telephone: 870-247-4700. FAX: 870-247-4755. E-MAIL: whjnews@cablelynx.com. Mailing Address: PO Box 20755, White Hall, AR 71612. Year Established: 1983. Pub. Frequency: w. (Wed.) Page Size: broadsheet. Subscrip. Rate: $.50 newsstand/cover; $22/yr in county; $28/yr mailed out of county; $33/yr mailed out of state. Circulation: 2,390 per issue (paid). **Owner(s):** Forest Communicators, Inc., See address and contact information above. **Management:** Frank Lightfoot, President. Vicki Kelly, Advertising Manager. **Editorial:** Frank Lightfoot, Editor-in-Chief.

WYNNE

EAST ARKANSAS NEWS LEADER, THE. 702 N. Falls Blvd., Wynne, AR 72396-2209. Telephone: 870-238-2375. FAX: 870-238-4655. Mailing Address: PO Box 308, Wynne, AR 72396-0308. Year Established: 1971. Pub. Frequency: w. (Wed.) Page Size: broadsheet.Adv. Rate: col. inch $10 Circulation: 21,500 per issue (free). **Owner(s):** David & Sandra Boger, See address and contact information above. **Management:** David M. Boger, Publisher. Brandon Boger, Advertising Manager. Melissa Watson, Classified Adv. Mgr.. **Editorial:** Joe Halm, Managing Editor.

WYNNE PROGRESS. 702 N. Falls Blvd., Wynne, AR 72396-2209. Telephone: 870-238-2375. FAX: 870-238-4655. E-MAIL: wynnenews@cablelynx.com. Mailing Address: PO Box 308, Wynne, AR 72396-0308. Year Established: 1898. Pub. Frequency: w. (Fri.) Page Size: broadsheet. Subscrip. Rate: $.75 newsstand/cover; $33/yr in county; $40/yr mailed out of county; $44/yr mailed out of state. Adv. Rate: col. inch $8.50 Circulation: 3,000 per issue (paid and free). **Owner(s):** David & Sandra Boger, See address and contact information above. **Management:** David M. Boger, Publisher. Brandon Boger, Advertising Manager. Melissa Watson, Classified Adv. Mgr.. **Editorial:** Joe Halm, Managing Editor.

CALIFORNIA

AGOURA HILLS

ACORN, THE. 30423 Canwood St., Ste. 108, Agoura Hills, CA 91301-4316. Telephone: 818-706-0266. FAX: 818-706-8733. E-MAIL: info@theacorn.com. URL: http://www.theacorn.com. Year Established: 1974. Pub. Frequency: w. (Thu.) Page Size: standard. Subscrip. Rate: $.25 newsstand/cover; $120/yr mailed. Freelance Pay: $30/article. Circulation: 60,000 per issue (paid and free). **Owner(s):** J. Bee NP Publishing Ltd., See address and contact information above. **Management:** Jim Rule, Owner. Mona Uttal, Classified Adv. Mgr.. **Editorial:** Steve Holt, Managing Editor. Jann Hendry, Photo Editor.

THOUSAND OAKS ACORN. 30423 Canwood St., Ste. 108, Agoura Hills, CA 91301-4316. E-MAIL: moreinfo@theacorn.com. URL: http://www.toacorn.com. Year Established: 1998. Pub. Frequency: w. (Thu.) Page Size: tabloid. Subscrip. Rate: $120/yr mailed. Adv. Rate: col. inch $12.55 Circulation: 40,466 per issue (free). **Owner(s):** J. Bee NP Publishing Ltd., See address and contact information above. **Management:** Jim Rule, Owner. Jennifer Corlo-Valdez, Classified Adv. Mgr.. **Editorial:** Steve Holt, Managing Editor. Jann Hendry, Photo Editor.

ALAMEDA

MONTCLARION. 1516 Oak St, Alameda, CA 94501. Telephone: 510-748-1683. FAX: 510-748-1680. E-MAIL: ccnmontclarion@bayareanewsgroup.com. URL: http://www.contracostatimes.com. Year Established: 1943. Pub. Frequency: s-w. (Tue. & Fri.) Page Size: broadsheet. Subscrip. Rate: $.50 newsstand/cover; $30/yr mailed in county. Freelance Pay: $1.50/column-inch. **Wire Service(s):** CNS. Circulation: 63,000 per issue (controlled). **Owner(s):** MediaNews Group, Inc., 101 W Colfax Ave, Ste 1100, Denver, CO 80202. FAX: 303-954-6320. **Management:** John Armstrong, Publisher. Patricia Vetner, Advertising Manager. **Editorial:** Jon Kawamoto, Editor.

PIEDMONTER, THE. 1516 Oak St, Alameda, CA 94501. Telephone: 510-748-1683. FAX: 510-748-1680. E-MAIL: piedmont@bayareanewsgroup.com. URL: http://www.contracostatimes.com. Year Established: 1916. Pub. Frequency: w. (Fri.) Page Size: standard. Subscrip. Rate: $.50 newsstand/cover; $30/yr local area. Circulation: 7,000 per issue (paid). **Owner(s):** MediaNews Group, Inc., 101 W Colfax Ave, Ste 1100, Denver, CO 80202. FAX: 303-954-6320. **Management:** John Armstrong, Publisher. Patricia Vetner, Advertising Manager. **Editorial:** Jon Kawamoto, Editor.

ALPINE

ALPINE SUN. ISSN 8750-8257
2144 Alpine Blvd., Alpine, CA 91901. Telephone: 619-445-3288. FAX: 619-445-6776. E-MAIL: editor@alpinesun.com. URL: http://www.alpinesun.com. Mailing Address: PO Box 1089, Alpine, CA 91903. Year Established: 1952. Pub. Frequency: w. (Thu.) Page Size: tabloid. Subscrip. Rate: $20/yr in county; $26/yr out of county. Circulation: 2,300 per issue (free). **Owner(s):** San Diego Neighborhood Newspapers, Inc., 119 N. Magnolia Ave., El Cajon, CA 92020. Telephone: 619-441-0400. **Management:** Linda Marie Peterson, Advertising Manager. Vonnie Sanchez, Associate Publisher. **Editorial:** Christy Scott, Editor. Greg Eichelberger, Sports Editor.

ALTURAS

MODOC COUNTY RECORD. 201 W. Carlos St., Alturas, CA 96101. Telephone: 530-233-2632. FAX: 530-233-5113. E-MAIL: record1@modocrecord.com. URL: http://www.modocrecord.com. Mailing Address: PO Box 531, Alturas, CA 96101. Year Established: 1892. Pub. Frequency: w. (Thu.) Page Size: broadsheet. Subscrip. Rate: $.50 newsstand/cover; $25/yr local; $30/yr mailed elsewhere. Adv. Rate: col. inch $4 Circulation: 4,500 per issue (paid). **Owner(s):** Rick & Jane Holloway, See address and contact information above. **Management:** Jane Holloway, Publisher. **Editorial:** Rick Holloway, Editor.

ANAHEIM

ANAHEIM BULLETIN. 1771 S. Lewis St., Anaheim, CA 92805. Telephone: 714-634-1567. FAX: 714-796-3681. E-MAIL: anaheimbulletin@ocregister.com. URL: http://www.ocregister.com/anaheim. Year Established: 1923. Pub. Frequency: w. (Thu.) Page Size: tabloid. **Owner(s):** Freedom Communications, Inc., 17666 Fitch, Irvine, CA 92714. Telephone: 714-553-9292. **Management:** Chris Anderson, Publisher. Judy Silvers, Advertising Manager. Susan Perratano, Classified Adv. Mgr.. **Editorial:** John Swanson, Managing Editor.

ANAHEIM HILLS NEWS. 1771 S. Lewis St., Anaheim, CA 92805. Telephone: 714-634-1567. FAX: 714-796-3681. E-MAIL: jswanson@ocregister.com. URL: http://www.ocregister.com. Year Established: 1969. Pub. Frequency: w. (Thu.) Page Size: tabloid. Subscrip. Rate: $78/yr mailed. Circulation: 14,000 per issue (paid and controlled). **Owner(s):** Freedom Communications, Inc., 17666 Fitch, Irvine, CA 92714. **Management:** Chris Anderson, Publisher. **Editorial:** Bill Diepenbrock, Editor.

BREA PROGRESS. 1771 S. Lewis St., Anaheim, CA 92805. Telephone: 714-634-1567. FAX: 714-796-3681. E-MAIL: hmccluskey@ocregister.com. URL: http://www.ocregister.com. Year Established: 1922. Pub. Frequency: w. (Thu.) Page Size: tabloid. Subscrip. Rate: $78/yr mailed. Circulation: 10,000 per issue (controlled and free). **Owner(s):** Freedom Communications, Inc., 17666 Fitch, Irvine, CA 92714. Telephone: 714-253-9292. **Management:** Chris Anderson, Publisher. **Editorial:** Jeff Light, Editor.

PLACENTIA NEWS-TIMES. 1771 S. Lewis St., Anaheim, CA 92805. Telephone: 714-634-1567. FAX: 714-796-3681. Year Established: 1924. Pub. Frequency: w. (Thu) Page Size: broadsheet. Subscrip. Rate: $.25 newsstand/cover. Circulation: 12,000 per issue (controlled). **Owner(s):** Freedom Communications, Inc., 17666 Fitch, Irvine, CA 92614. Telephone: 714-553-9292. **Management:** Chris Anderson, Publisher. **Editorial:** Donna Johnson, City Editor. Stan Bird, Photographer. Lowell Bennink, Sports.

STAR PROGRESS. 1771 S. Lewis St., Anaheim, CA 92805. Telephone: 714-634-1567. FAX: 714-796-3681. URL: http://www.ocregister.com. Year Established: 1916. Pub. Frequency: w. (Thu.) Page Size: broadsheet. **Wire Service(s):** AP. Circulation: 15,203 per issue (paid and controlled). **Owner(s):** Freedom Communications, Inc., 17666 Fitch, Irvine, CA 92614. Telephone: 714-553-9292. **Management:** Frank Michodiet, General Manager. Chris Anderson, Publisher. Michael Hayes, Advertising Manager. **Editorial:** Heather McCluskey, Editor.

APPLE VALLEY

APPLE VALLEY NEWS. 17993 Hwy. 18, Ste. 104, Apple Valley, CA 92307. Telephone: 760-242-1930. FAX: 760-244-6609. Year Established: 1965. Pub. Frequency: w. (Fri.) Page Size: broadsheet. Subscrip. Rate: $15/yr mailed local; $25/yr mailed out of area. Circulation: 5,000 per issue (paid and free). **Owner(s):** Raymond Pryke, See address and contact information above. **Management:** Raymond Pryke, Publisher. Renee Carlson, Advertising. **Editorial:** Sandy Martinez, Managing Editor.

ARCATA

NORTH COAST JOURNAL OF POLITICS, PEOPLE & ART, THE. ISSN 1099-7571
145 G St., Ste. A, Arcata, CA 95521. Telephone: 707-826-2000. FAX: 707-826-2060. E-MAIL: ncjournal@northcoastjournal.com. URL: http://www.northcoastjournal.com. Year Established: 1990. Pub. Frequency: w. Page Size: tabloid. Subscrip. Rate: $25/yr mailed. Adv. Rate: B&W page $910, color page $1,160 Circulation: 20,000 per issue (paid and free). **Owner(s):** North Coast Journal, Inc., See address and contact information above. **Management:** Judy Hodgson, Publisher. Colleen Dickens, Advertising. **Editorial:** Hank Sims, Editor.

ARROYO GRANDE

FIVE CITIES TIMES PRESS-RECORDER. 260 Station Way, Ste. F, Arroyo Grande, CA 93420. Telephone: 805-489-4206. FAX: 805-473-0571. E-MAIL: vahrendes@pulitzer.net. URL: http://www.timespressrecorder.com. Mailing Address: PO Box 460, Arroyo Grande, CA 93421-0460. Year Established: 1887. Pub. Frequency: s-w. (Wed. & Fri.) Page Size: broadsheet. Subscrip. Rate: $.50 newsstand/cover; $24/yr in county; $46/yr mailed in state. Adv. Rate: col. inch $14.25 Circulation: 7,500 per issue (paid). **Owner(s):** Pulitzer Publishing Co., 900 N. Tucker Blvd., St. Louis, MO 63101. Telephone: 314-340-8000. **Management:** Vern Ahrendes, General Manager. Cynthia Schur, Publisher. Kathy Knobbe, Circulation Manager. **Editorial:** Michael R. Hodgson, Editor.

ATASCADERO

NORTH COUNTY SHOPPING NEWS. 5660 El Camino Real, Atascadero, CA 93422. Telephone: 805-466-2585. FAX: 805-466-2714. E-MAIL: graphis@astascaderonews.com. URL: http://www.astascaderonews.com. Mailing Address: PO Box 6068, Atascadero, CA 93423. Pub. Frequency: w. (Thu.) Page Size: standard Circulation: 5,600 per issue (free). **Owner(s):** News Media Corp., 211 Hwy. 38 E., Rochelle, IL 61608. Telephone: 815-562-2961. **Management:** Jack Porter, Publisher. Gary Porter, Advertising. Venessa Williams, Circulation Manager. **Editorial:** Ben Banuchi, Editor.

AUBERRY

MOUNTAIN PRESS. 33171 Auberry Rd., Auberry, CA 93602. Mailing Address: PO Box 97, Prather, CA 93651-0097. Year Established: 1973. Pub. Frequency: w. (Wed.) Page Size: tabloid. Subscrip. Rate: $.25 newsstand/cover; $10.50/yr local; $28/yr out of county. Adv. Rate: col. inch $6 Freelance Pay: $3/column-inch. Circulation: 2,200 per issue (paid). **Owner(s):** Marceline Scott, See address and contact information above. **Editorial:** Alyson Nelson, Editor.

AUBURN

AUBURN TRADER. 11899 Edgewood, Ste. C, Auburn, CA 95603. Telephone: 530-888-7653. FAX: 530-268-3326. E-MAIL: bonniep@goldcountrymedia.com. URL: http://www.auburntrader.com. Year Established: 1981. Pub. Frequency: w. (Thu.) Page Size: tabloid. Subscrip. Rate: $32/yr. Circulation: 25,000 per issue (paid and free). **Owner(s):** Brehm Communications, Inc., 16644 W. Bernardo Dr., Ste. 300, San Diego, CA 92127. Telephone: 858-451-6200. **Management:** Bonnie Pebley, General Manager.

GRASS VALLEY TRADER. 11899 Edgewood, Ste. C, Auburn, CA 95603. Telephone: 530-888-7653. FAX: 530-268-3326. URL: http://www.grassvalleytrader.com. Year Established: 1982. Pub. Frequency: w. (Wed.) Page Size: tabloid. Subscrip. Rate: $32/yr out of area. Circulation: 26,000 per issue (paid and free). **Owner(s):** Brehm Communications, Inc., 16644 W. Bernardo Dr., Ste. 300, San Diego, CA 92127. Telephone: 858-451-6200. FAX: 858-451-3814. **Management:** Bonnie Pebley, General Manager.

PLACER SENTINEL (AUBURN). 1226 High St, Auburn, CA 95603. Telephone: 530-823-2463. FAX: 530-823-1309. E-MAIL: editor@placersentinel.com. URL: http://www.placersentinel.com. Mailing Address: P.O. Box 9148, Auburn, CA 95604. Year Established: 1987. Pub. Frequency: w. (Fri.) Page Size: broadsheet. Circulation: 10,000 per issue (controlled and free). **Owner(s):** Janice Forbes & Robert Evans, See address and contact information above. **Management:** Robert Evans, Chief Executive Ofc. . Janice Forbes, Publisher. **Editorial:** Donna Lach, Managing Editor.

AVALON

AVALON BAY NEWS, THE. 117 Whittley, Avalon, CA 90704-1809. Telephone: 310-510-1500. FAX: 310-510-1371. E-MAIL: abn@catalinas.net. Mailing Address: PO Box 1809, Avalon, CA 90704-1809. Year Established: 1990. Pub. Frequency: w. (Thu) Page Size: tabloid. Subscrip. Rate: $.60 newsstand/cover; $32/yr. Circulation: 2,000 per issue (paid and free). **Owner(s):** Barbara L. Crow, 117 Whittley, Avalon, CA 90704. Telephone: 310-510-1500. FAX: 310-510-1371. **Management:** Barbara L. Crow, Publisher. **Editorial:** Barbara L. Crow, Editor-in-Chief. Iris Duchesneau, Managing Editor.

CATALINA ISLANDER, THE. 101 Marila Ave, Avalon, CA 90704. Telephone: 310-510-0500. FAX: 310-510-2882. E-MAIL: catislander@catalinaisp.com. Mailing Address: PO Box 428, Avalon, CA 90704-0428. Year Established: 1914. Pub. Frequency: w. (Fri.) Page Size: tabloid. Subscrip. Rate: $.50 newsstand/cover; $52/yr. Circulation: 5,000 per issue (paid and free). **Owner(s):** Community Media Corp., See address and contact information above. **Management:** Danny Verdugo, Publisher. **Editorial:** Dan Tecknesoff, Editor.

AVENAL

AVENAL PROGRESS. 524 E. Merced St., Avenal, CA 93204. Telephone: 559-386-9385. FAX: 559-386-4661. E-MAIL: progress@tcsn.net. URL: http://www.newzcentral.com. Mailing Address: PO Box 607, Avenal, CA 93204-0607. Year Established: 1986. Pub. Frequency: w. (Wed.) Page Size: broadsheet. Subscrip. Rate: $.50 newsstand/cover; $25/yr mailed in county; $35/yr mailed out of county. Circulation: 1,300 per issue (paid). **Owner(s):** Lee Enterprises, Inc., 201 N. Harrison St, Ste 600, Davenport, IA 52801-1924. 900 N. Tucker Blvd., St. Louis, MO 63101. **Management:** Randy Rickman, Publisher. Joy Redding, Advertising Manager. Greg Barkley, Circulation Director. Kevin Crawford, Classified Adv. Mgr.. **Editorial:** Arlene Santino, Editor. Denis Bohannan, Editor-in-Chief. Jon Matsune, Sports Editor.

BANNING

RECORD GAZETTE. ISSN 0747-1521
218 N. Murray St., Banning, CA 92220-0727. Telephone: 951-849-4586. FAX: 951-849-2437. E-MAIL: editor@recordgazette.net. URL: http://www.recordgazette.net. Mailing Address: PO Box 727, Banning, CA 92220-0727. Year Established: 1908. Pub. Frequency: w. (Fri.) Page Size: broadsheet. Subscrip. Rate: $.50 newsstand/cover; $22/yr area; $17/yr to senior citizens; $31/yr out of county to senior citizens; $35/yr mailed out of state to senior citizens. Circulation: 19,000 per issue (paid and free). **Owner(s):** Century Publishing Co., Inc., 218 N. Murray St., Banning, CA 92220. Telephone: 951-849-4586. **Management:** Gerald A. Bean, President. Toebe Bush, Publisher. Richard Klein, Circulation Manager. Amber Diekow, Classified Adv. Mgr.. **Editorial:** Charlie Ferrell, Editor.

BEVERLY HILLS

BEVERLY HILLS COURIER. ISSN 0892-645X
8840 W. Olympic Blvd., Beverly Hills, CA 90211. Telephone: 310-278-1322. FAX: 310-271-5118. URL: http://www.bhcourier.com. Year Established: 1965. Pub. Frequency: s-w. (Wed. & Fri.) Page Size: tabloid. Subscrip. Rate: $75/yr in county. **Wire Service(s):** AP. Circulation: 43,000 per issue (paid and free). **Owner(s):** Clifton Smith, See address and contact information above. **Management:** Clifton Smith, Publisher. M W Hobbs, Associate Publisher. **Editorial:** Chris Sieroty, Managing Editor. John Seitz, Senior Editor.Readers: Affluent West Los Angeles

BEVERLY HILLS WEEKLY. ISSN 1528-851X
140 S. Beverly Dr., Ste. 201, Beverly Hills, CA 90212-3050. Telephone: 310-887-0788. FAX: 310-887-0789. E-MAIL: editor@bhweekly.com. URL: http://www.bhweekly.com. Year Established: 1999. Pub. Frequency: w. (Thu.) Page Size: tabloid. Subscrip. Rate: $75/yr mailed. Circulation: 17,000 per issue (paid and free). **Owner(s):** Josh Gross, See address and contact information above. **Management:** Josh Gross, Publisher. Patricia Massachi, Advertising Manager. **Editorial:** Jacquelyn Ryan, Editor.

BIG BEAR LAKE

BIG BEAR GRIZZLY. ISSN 1073-6867
42007 Fox Farm Rd., Ste. 3B, Big Bear Lake, CA 92315-1789. Telephone: 909-866-3456. FAX: 909-866-2302. URL: http://www.bigbeargrizzly.net. Mailing Address: PO Box 1789, Big Bear Lake, CA 92315-1789. Year Established: 1941. Pub. Frequency: w. (Wed.) Page Size: broadsheet. Subscrip. Rate: $.50 newsstand/cover; $30/yr in county; $41/yr out of county; $52/yr out of state. Adv. Rate: col. inch $15.90 Circulation: 10,000 per issue (paid). **Owner(s):** Brehm Communications, Inc., 16644 W. Bernardo Dr., Ste. 300, San Diego, CA 92127. Telephone: 858-451-6200. FAX: 858-451-3814. **Management:** Jerry Wright, Publisher. Sally Cornett, Circulation Manager. Karen Osuna, Classified Adv. Mgr.. **Editorial:** Judi Bowers, Editor.

BIG BEAR SHOPPER. 42007 Fox Farm Rd., Ste. 3B, Big Bear Lake, CA 92315-1789. Telephone: 909-866-3456. FAX: 909-866-2302. Mailing Address: PO Box 1789, Big Bear Lake, CA 92315-1789. Year Established: 1983. Pub. Frequency: w. (Thu.) Page Size: standard.Adv. Rate: col. inch $15.30 Circulation: 10,000 per issue (free). **Owner(s):** Brehm Communications, Inc., 16644 W. Bernardo Dr., Ste. 300, San Diego, CA 92127. Telephone: 858-451-6200. **Management:** Jerry Wright, Publisher. Sally Cornett, Circulation Manager. Karen Osuna, Classified Adv. Mgr.. **Editorial:** Kathy Portie, Sports.

GRIZZLY WEEKENDER. 42007 Fox Farm Rd., Ste. 3B, Big Bear Lake, CA 92315-1789. Telephone: 909-866-3456. FAX: 909-866-2302. URL: http://www.bigbeargrizzly.net. Mailing Address: PO Box 1789, Big Bear Lake, CA 92315-1789. Year Established: 1958. Pub. Frequency: w. (Sat.) Page Size: tabloid.Adv. Rate: col. inch $15.30 Circulation: 10,000 per issue (free). **Owner(s):** Brehm Communications, Inc., 16644 W. Bernardo Dr., Ste. 300, San Diego, CA 92127. **Management:** Jerry Wright, Publisher. Sally Cornett, Circulation Manager. Karen Osuna, Classified Adv. Mgr.. **Editorial:** Judi Bowers, Editor. Kathy Portie, Sports.

BLYTHE

PALO VERDE VALLEY TIMES. 231 N. Spring.St., Blythe, CA 92225. Telephone: 760-922-3181. FAX: 760-922-3184. Mailing Address: PO Box 1159, Blythe, CA 92226. Year Established: 1924. Pub. Frequency: s-w. (Wed. & Fri.) Page Size: broadsheet. Subscrip. Rate: $.50 newsstand/cover; $38/yr in county; $43/yr mailed out of county; $58/yr mailed out of area. Freelance Pay: $0.50/column-inch. Circulation: 4,500 per issue (paid). **Owner(s):** Western News & Info., Inc., PO Box 1271, Yuma, AZ 85366. Telephone: 602-783-3311. **Management:** Debbie Hoel, Publisher. Jill Madsen, Advertising. Robin Echard, Circulation Manager. Tye Castor, Classified Adv. Mgr.. **Editorial:** Marty Backman, Managing Editor.

BODEGA BAY

BODEGA BAY NAVIGATOR. PO Box 969, Bodega Bay, CA 94923. Telephone: 707-875-3574. FAX: 707-875-3875. E-MAIL: editor@bodegabaynavigator.com. URL: http://www.bodegabaynavigator.com. Year Established: 1987. Pub. Frequency: w. (Thu.) Page Size: tabloid. Subscrip. Rate: $.50 newsstand/cover; $20/yr local area; $34/yr elsewhere. Adv. Rate: col. inch $7.50 Circulation: 1,600 per issue (paid and free). **Owner(s):** Joel Hack, See address and contact information above. **Management:** Joel Hack, Publisher.

BOLINAS

COASTAL POST. ISSN 0739-2028
41 Wharf Rd., Bolinas, CA 94924. Telephone: 415-868-1600. FAX: 415-868-0502. E-MAIL: editor@coastalpost.com. URL: http://www.coastalpost.com. Mailing Address: PO Box 31, Bolinas, CA 94924-0031. Year Established: 1975. Pub. Frequency: m. Page Size: tabloid. Subscrip. Rate: $24/yr mailed. Circulation: 13,500 per issue (paid and free). **Owner(s):** Don Deane, See address and contact information above. **Management:** Don Deane, Publisher. **Editorial:** Don Deane, Editor.

BREA

PENNYSAVER (BREA). 2830 Orbiter St., Brea, CA 92821. Telephone: 714-996-8900. FAX: 714-577-4294. URL: http://www.pennysaverusa.com. Year Established: 1962. Pub. Frequency: w. (Wed.) Page Size: standard Circulation: 870,000 per issue (free). **Owner(s):** Harte-Hanks, Inc., PO Box 269, San Antonio, TX 78291. Telephone: 210-829-9000. **Management:** Pete Gorman, President.

BURLINGAME

BOUTIQUE & VILLAGER. 1828 El Camino Real, Ste 508, Burlingame, CA 94010. Telephone: 650-692-9406. FAX: 650-692-7565. URL: http://www.smindependent.com. Year Established: 1965. Pub. Frequency: s-w. (Tue. & Sat.) Page Size: broadsheet Circulation: 17,000 per issue (paid). **Owner(s):** S F Newspaper Co., See address and contact information above. **Management:** Scott McKibben, Publisher. Mark Hutt, Advertising. Jose Diaz, Circulation Manager. **Editorial:** Lambert Clay, Editor. Barbara Backer, Managing Editor. Jamie Casini, City Editor.

ENQUIRER-BULLETIN. 1828 El Camino Real, Ste 508, Burlingame, CA 94010. Telephone: 650-692-9406. FAX: 650-692-7565. E-MAIL: smiedit@aol.com. Year Established: 1924. Pub. Frequency: s-w. (Tue.. & Sat.) Page Size: broadsheet Circulation: 22,600 per issue (paid). **Owner(s):** S F Newspaper Co., See address and contact information above. **Management:** Scott McKibben, Publisher. Mark Hutt, Advertising. Jose Diaz, Circulation Manager. **Editorial:** Lambert Clay, Editor. Barbara Backer, Managing Editor. Jamie Casini, City Editor.

FOSTER CITY PROGRESS. 1828 El Camino Real, Ste 508, Burlingame, CA 94010. Telephone: 650-692-9406. FAX: 650-692-7565. Year Established: 1966. Pub. Frequency: s-w. (Wed. & Sat.) Page Size: broadsheet Circulation: 10,700 per issue (paid). **Owner(s):** S F Newspaper Co., See address and contact information above. **Management:** Scott McKibben, Publisher. Mark Hutt, Advertising. Jose Diaz, Circulation Manager. **Editorial:** Lambert Clay, Editor. Barbara Backer, Managing Editor. Jamie Casini, City Editor.

PENINSULA INDEPENDENT. 1828 El Camino Real, Ste 508, Burlingame, CA 94010. Telephone: 650-692-9406. FAX: 650-692-7565. E-MAIL: smi-edit@aol.com. Year Established: 1994. Pub. Frequency: s-w. (Tue. & Sat.) Page Size: broadsheet Circulation: 43,600 per issue (free). **Owner(s):** S F Newspaper Co., See address and contact information above. **Management:** Scott McKibben, Publisher. Mark Hutt, Advertising. Jose Diaz, Circulation Manager. **Editorial:** Lambert Clay, Editor. Barbara Backer, Managing Editor. Jamie Casini, City Editor.

REDWOOD CITY TRIBUNE. 1828 El Camino Real, Ste 508, Burlingame, CA 94010. Telephone: 650-692-9406. FAX: 650-692-7565. E-MAIL: rwcedit@aol.com. Year Established: 1994. Pub. Frequency: s-w. (Tue. & Sat.) Page Size: broadsheet Circulation: 28,905 per issue (free). **Owner(s):** S F Newspaper Co., See address and contact information above. **Management:** Scott McKibben, Publisher. Mark Hutt, Advertising. Jose Diaz, Circulation Manager. **Editorial:** Lambert Clay, Editor. Barbara Backer, Managing Editor. Jamie Casini, City Editor.

SAN MATEO WEEKLY. 1828 El Camino Real, Ste 508, Burlingame, CA 94010. Telephone: 650-692-9406. FAX: 650-692-7565. E-MAIL: smjedit@aol.com. Pub. Frequency: s-w. (Tue. & Sat.) Page Size: broadsheet Circulation: 28,800 per issue (free). **Owner(s):** S F Newspaper Co., See address and contact information above. **Management:** Scott McKibben, Publisher. Mark Hutt, Advertising. Jose Diaz, Circulation Manager. **Editorial:** Lambert Clay, Editor. Barbara Backer, Managing Editor. Jamie Casini, City Editor.

BURNEY

INTERMOUNTAIN NEWS, THE. 37095 Main St Ste C, Burney, CA 96013-4216. E-MAIL: intermountain-news@mac.com. URL: http://www.im-news.com. Mailing Address: PO Box 1030, Burney, CA 96013-1030. Year Established: 1958. Pub. Frequency: w. (Wed.) Page Size: broadsheet. Subscrip. Rate: $.75 newsstand/cover; $32/yr mailed in county & adj. cys.; $40/yr mailed out of area. Adv. Rate: page $693 Circulation: 3,335 per issue (paid). **Owner(s):** Craig Harrington, See address and contact information above. **Management:** Craig Harrington, Publisher.

CALIFORNIA CITY

MOJAVE DESERT NEWS, THE. ISSN 1065-1152
8046 California City Blvd., California City, CA 93505. Telephone: 760-373-4812. E-MAIL: advertise@desertnews.com. URL: http://www.desertnews.com. Mailing Address: PO Box 2698, California City, CA 93505. Year Established: 1938. Pub. Frequency: w. (Thu.) Page Size: standard. Subscrip. Rate: $.50 newsstand/cover; $15/yr in county; $30/yr out of county; $35/yr mailed out of state. Circulation: 5,500 per issue (paid). **Owner(s):** MOCAL News Corp., See address and contact information above. **Management:** Joe Schultheiss, General Manager. Bill Deaver, Publisher. Joe Schultheiss, Circulation Manager. Michelle Williamson, Classified Adv. Mgr.. Barbara Schultheiss, Business Manager. **Editorial:** Christina Scott, Editor.

CARMICHAEL

CARMICHAEL TIMES. 5921 Stanley Ave, Ste. C, Carmichael, CA 95609. Telephone: 916-773-1111. FAX: 916-773-2999. E-MAIL: publisher@carmichaeltimes.com. URL: http://www.carmichaeltimes.com. Mailing Address: PO Box 14, Carmichael, CA 95609. Year Established: 1981. Pub. Frequency: w. (Tue.) Page Size: tabloid. Subscrip. Rate: $39/yr mailed. **Wire Service(s):** CaNS, PR. Circulation: 10,000 per issue (paid and free). **Owner(s):** Paul V Scholl, See address and contact information above. **Management:** Paul V Scholl, Publisher. Shirley Turner, Advertising Manager. **Editorial:** Paul V Scholl, Editor.Readers: 25 and older living within the community

CARPINTERIA

COASTAL VIEW NEWS. 4856 Carpinteria Ave., Carpinteria, CA 93013. Telephone: 805-684-4428. FAX: 805-684-4650. E-MAIL: news@coastalview.com. URL: http://www.coastalview.com. Year Established: 1994. Pub. Frequency: w. (Thu.) Page Size: tabloid. Subscrip. Rate: $57/yr mailed. Circulation: 7,000 evening (paid and free). **Owner(s):** RMG Ventures, 4856 Carpinteria Ave., Carpenteria, CA 93103. Telephone: 805-684-4428. FAX: 805-684-4650. **Management:** Michael VanStry, Publisher. Betty Lloyd, Sales Manager. **Editorial:** Amy Orozco, Editor. Ryan Hawk, Photo Editor. Andres Nuno, Sports Editor.

CATHEDRAL CITY

DESERT POST WEEKLY. 68625 Perez Rd., Ste. 6, Cathedral City, CA 92234. Telephone: 760-202-3200. FAX: 760-324-2751. E-MAIL: brianmedricka@desertpostweekly.com. URL: http://www.desertpostweekly.com. Year Established: 1941. Pub. Frequency: w. (Thu.) Page Size: tabloid. Subscrip. Rate: $9 for 6 wks.. Adv. Rate: col. inch $24 Circulation: 23,000 per issue (paid and free). **Owner(s):** Gannett Company, Inc., 7950 Jones Branch Dr, McLean, VA 22107. Telephone: 703-854-6000. **Management:** Steve Gaines, Circulation Manager. Kurt Jaeger, Sales Manager. Kevin Necessary, Art Director. **Editorial:** Brian Medricka, Editor. Judith Salkin, Entertainment Editor.

CERES

CERES COURIER. 2940 Fourth St, PO Box 7, Ceres, CA 95307. Telephone: 290-537-5032. FAX: 290-537-0543. URL: http://www.cerescourier.com. Year Established: 1910. Pub. Frequency: w. (Wed.) Page Size: broadsheet. Subscrip. Rate: $.50 newsstand/cover; $42/yr in county. Circulation: 19,500 per issue (paid). **Owner(s):** Morris Newspaper Corporation, 27 Abercorn St., Savannah, GA 31401. Telephone: 912-233-1281. FAX: 912-232-4639. **Management:** Jeffrey Benziger, Publisher. Bill Sanborn, Advertising Manager. Brad Barnes, Circulation Manager. **Editorial:** Jeffrey Benziger, Editor.

CHICO

CHICO NEWS & REVIEW. 353 E. Second St., Chico, CA 95928. Telephone: 530-894-2300. FAX: 530-894-0143. E-MAIL: tomg@newsreview.com. URL: http://www.newsreview.com. Mailing Address: PO Box 7847, Chico, CA 95927. Year Established: 1977. Pub. Frequency: w. (Thu.) Page Size: tabloid.Subscrip. Rate: $39/yr mailed Circulation: 47,000 per issue (free). **Owner(s):** Chico Community Publishing, Inc., See address and contact information above. **Management:** Jeff von Kaenel, President. Lee Craft, Publisher. **Editorial:** Evan Tuchinsky, Editor.

CHULA VISTA

STAR NEWS (CHULA VISTA), THE. 321 E. St., Chula Vista, CA 91910. Telephone: 619-427-3000. FAX: 619-426-6346. E-MAIL: editor@thestarnews.com. URL: http://www.thestarnews.com. Year Established: 1882. Pub. Frequency: w. (Fri.) Page Size: tabloid.Subscrip. Rate: $25/yr mailed Circulation: 32,000 per issue (free). **Owner(s):** Pacific Sierra Publishing, Inc., See address and contact information above. **Management:** Linda R. Townson, Publisher. Adrian Ortiz, Advertising. Linda Rosas, Advertising Manager. Jutta Vanderheyden, Circulation Manager. **Editorial:** Carlos Davalos, Editor. Philip Brents, Sports.

CLAREMONT

CLAREMONT COURIER. 1420 N Claremont Blvd., Ste.205B, Claremont, CA 91711-5051. Telephone: 909-621-4761. FAX: 909-621-4072. E-MAIL: editor@claremont-courier.com. URL: http://www.claremont-courier.com. Year Established: 1908. Pub. Frequency: 2/w. Page Size: tabloid. Subscrip. Rate: $.75 newsstand/cover; $52/yr; $47/yr seniors. Adv. Rate: col. inch $11 Circulation: 6,250 per issue (paid). **Owner(s):** Peter Weinberger, See address and contact information above. **Management:** Peter Weinberger, Publisher. Mary Rose, Advertising Manager. **Editorial:** Judy Rodriguez, Circulation Editor. Tony Kricki, City Editor.

CLEARLAKE

CLEAR LAKE OBSERVER-AMERICAN. 14913 Lakeshore Dr. Ste B, Clearlake, CA 95422. Telephone: 707-994-6444. FAX: 707-994-5335. E-MAIL: news@clearlakeobserver.com. URL: http://www.clearlakeobserveramerican.com. Year Established: 1936. Pub. Frequency: s-w. (Wed. & Sat.) Page Size: broadsheet. Subscrip. Rate: $.35 newsstand/cover; $30/yr in county; $60/yr out of county. Circulation: 1,615 per issue (paid). **Owner(s):** MediaNews Group, Inc., 101 W Colfax Ave, Ste 1100, Denver, CO 80202. FAX: 303-954-6320. **Management:** Gregg McConnell, Publisher. Shawn Garrison, Advertising. **Editorial:** Rick Kennedy, Managing Editor. Jim Davis, Circulation Editor.

CLOVERDALE

CLOVERDALE REVEILLE. 207 N Cloverdale Blvd, Cloverdale, CA 95425. Telephone: 707-894-3339. FAX: 707-894-3343. E-MAIL: reveille@cloverdalereveille.com. Mailing Address: PO Box 157, Cloverdale, CA 95425. Year Established: 1879. Pub. Frequency: w. (Wed.) Page Size: broadsheet. Subscrip. Rate: $.50 newsstand/cover; $28.50/yr in county. Circulation: 2,500 per issue (paid). **Owner(s):** Hanchett Publishing, Inc., See address and contact information above. **Management:** Bonny J. Hanchett, Publisher. **Editorial:** Bonny J. Hanchett, Editor.

CLOVIS

CLOVIS INDEPENDENT. ISSN 1068-5944
420 Bullard, Ste. 105, Clovis, CA 93612. Telephone: 559-298-8081. FAX: 559-298-0459. E-MAIL: plippert@clovisindependent.com. URL: http://www.clovisindependent.com. Year Established: 1905. Pub. Frequency: w. (Fri.) Page Size: broadsheet. Subscrip. Rate: $.50 newsstand/cover; $24/yr; $36/yr mailed. Circulation: 5,000 per issue (paid). **Owner(s):** The/McClatchy Company, 2100 Q St, Sacramento, CA 95816. Telephone: 916-321-1936. FAX: 916-321-1869. **Management:** Valerie Bender, Publisher. Bill Gutierrez, Advertising Manager. **Editorial:** Patti Lippert, Editor. Pete Boele, Sports Editor.

COALINGA

COALINGA RECORD. 152 E. Elm Ave., Ste. 103, Coalinga, CA 93210. Telephone: 559-935-2906. FAX: 559-935-5257. E-MAIL: record@cvcca.com. URL: http://www.newzcentral.com. Mailing Address: PO Box 496, Coalinga, CA 93210. Year Established: 1904. Pub. Frequency: w. (Wed.) Page Size: standard. Subscrip. Rate: $.50 newsstand/cover; $25/yr in county; $30/yr out of county. Circulation: 9,000 per issue (paid). **Owner(s):** Lee Enterprises, Inc., 900 N. Tucker Blvd., St. Louis, MO 63101. Telephone: 314-340-8000. **Management:** Mark Daniel, Publisher. Joy Redding, Advertising Manager. Robert Van Wagoner, Circulation Manager. **Editorial:** Pamela Pond, Editor.

Weeklies

COLFAX

COLFAX RECORD. 25 W. Church St, Colfax, CA 95713. Telephone: 530-346-2232. FAX: 530-346-2700. URL: http://www.colfaxrecord.com. Mailing Address: PO Box 755, Colfax, CA 95713. Year Established: 1908. Pub. Frequency: w. (Thu.) Page Size: standard. Subscrip. Rate: $.50 newsstand/cover; $26/yr home delivery local. Circulation: 1,700 per issue (paid). **Owner(s):** Brehm Communications, Inc., 16644 W. Bernardo Dr., Ste. 300, San Diego, CA 92127. Telephone: 858-451-6200. **Management:** Tony Hazarian, Publisher. Steve Jameson, Classified Adv. Mgr.. **Editorial:** Carol Feiniman, Editor. Michael Kirby, Photographer.

COLUSA

COLUSA COUNTY SUN-HERALD. ISSN 0897-8743
131 5th St, Colusa, CA 95932. Telephone: 530-458-2121. FAX: 530-458-5711. E-MAIL: sunherald@frontiernet.net. Year Established: 1862. Pub. Frequency: s-w. (Wed. & Fri.) Page Size: broadsheet. Subscrip. Rate: $.75 newsstand/cover; $50/yr home delivery in county; $62/yr mailed out of county. Circulation: 6,500 per issue (paid). **Owner(s):** Morris Newspaper Corporation, 27 Abercorn St., Savannah, GA 31401. Telephone: 912-233-1281. FAX: 912-232-4639. **Management:** Christine Hammers, Advertising Manager. **Editorial:** Bill Rozak, Managing Editor.

COMPTON

CARSON BULLETIN. 800 E Compton Blvd, Compton, CA 90221. Telephone: 310-635-6776. FAX: 310-635-4045. E-MAIL: news@thecomptonbulletin.com. URL: http://www.thecomptonbulletin.com. Mailing Address: PO Box 4248, Compton, CA 90224. Year Established: 1980. Pub. Frequency: w. (Wed.) Page Size: broadsheet. Subscrip. Rate: $.35 newsstand/cover; $25/yr local deliv; $50/yr mailed out of area. Circulation: 18,000 per issue (paid). **Owner(s):** American Print Media, Inc., See address and contact information above. **Management:** Lucille Daniels, General Manager. Lisa Grace-Kellogg, Publisher. Clay McDonald, Advertising. **Editorial:** Lisa Grace-Kellogg, Editor.

COMPTON BULLETIN. 800 E Compton Blvd, Compton, CA 90221. Telephone: 310-635-6776. FAX: 310-635-4045. E-MAIL: newa@thecomptonbulletin.com. URL: http://www.thecomptonbulletin.com. Mailing Address: PO Box 4248, Compton, CA 90224. Year Established: 1980. Pub. Frequency: w. (Wed.) Page Size: broadsheet.Subscrip. Rate: $.35 newsstand/cover; $50/yr Circulation: 22,000 per issue (paid). **Owner(s):** American Print Media, Inc., See address and contact information above. **Management:** Lucille Daniels, General Manager. Lisa Grace-Kellogg, Publisher. Clay McDonald, Advertising. **Editorial:** Lisa Grace-Kellogg, Editor.

INGLEWOOD TRIBUNE. 800 E Compton Blvd, Compton, CA 90221. Telephone: 310-635-6776. FAX: 310-635-4045. E-MAIL: news@thecomptonbulletin.com. URL: http://www.thecomptonbulletin.com. Mailing Address: PO Box 4248, Compton, CA 90224. Pub. Frequency: w. (Wed.) Page Size: broadsheet.Subscrip. Rate: $.35 newsstand/cover; $50/yr Circulation: 10,000 per issue (paid). **Owner(s):** American Print Media, Inc., See address and contact information above. **Management:** Lucille Daniels, General Manager. Lisa Grace-Kellogg, Publisher. Clay McDonald, Advertising. **Editorial:** Lisa Grace-Kellogg, Editor.

LYNWOOD JOURNAL. 800 E Comton Blvd, Compton, CA 90221. E-MAIL: news@thecomptonbulletin.com. URL: http://www.thecomptonbulletin.com. Year Established: 1980. Pub. Frequency: w. (Wed.) Page Size: broadsheet. Subscrip. Rate: $.35 newsstand/cover; $50/yr mailed. Circulation: 15,000 per issue (paid). **Owner(s):** American Press, See address and contact information above. **Management:** Lisa Grace-Kellogg, Publisher. **Editorial:** Lisa Grace-Kellogg, Editor.

WILMINGTON BEACON. 800 E Compton Blvd, Compton, CA 90221. Telephone: 310-635-6776. E-MAIL: news@thecomptonbulletin.com. URL: http://www.thecomptonbulletin.com. Mailing Address: PO Box 4248, Compton, CA 90224. Year Established: 1980. Pub. Frequency: w. (Wed.) Page Size: broadsheet. Subscrip. Rate: $.35 newsstand/cover; $25/yr local deliv; $50/yr mailed. Circulation: 10,000 per issue (paid). **Owner(s):** American Print Media, Inc., See address and contact information above. **Management:** Lucille Daniels, General Manager. Lisa Grace-Kellogg, Publisher. Clay McDonald, Advertising. **Editorial:** Lisa Grace-Kellogg, Editor.

COPPEROPOLIS

COPPEROPOLIS HERALD. P.O. Box 220, Copperopolis, CA 95228. Telephone: 209-887-3112. FAX: 209-887-3111. Year Established: 1998. Pub. Frequency: m. Page Size: broadsheet. Subscrip. Rate: $.50 newsstand/cover; $35/yr. Adv. Rate: col. inch $9.50 Freelance Pay: $0.50/column-inch. Circulation: 1,500 per issue (paid). **Owner(s):** Brian Reilly, 18974 E. Main St., Linden, CA 95236. **Management:** Kelly Wright, Publisher. **Editorial:** Brian Reilly, Editor.

CORNING

CORNING OBSERVER. 1208 Solano St, Corning, CA 96021. Telephone: 530-824-5464. FAX: 530-824-4804. E-MAIL: editor@tcnpress.com. URL: www.tcnpress.com. Year Established: 1887. Pub. Frequency: s-w. (Wed. & Fri.) Page Size: broadsheet. Subscrip. Rate: $.75 newsstand/cover; $50/yr home delivery; $62/yr mailed. Circulation: 7,000 per issue (paid). **Owner(s):** Morris Newspaper Corporation, 27 Abercorn St., Savannah, GA 31401. Telephone: 912-233-1281. FAX: 912-232-4639. **Management:** Dale Bean, General Manager. Dan Hammers, Advertising Manager. Mike Compton, Circulation Manager. **Editorial:** Bill Rozak, Executive Editor.

CORONADO

CORONADO EAGLE & JOURNAL. 1116 Tenth St., Coronado, CA 92118. Telephone: 619-437-8800. FAX: 619-437-8635. E-MAIL: journaledit@eaglenewsca.com. URL: http://www.coronadonewsca.com. Year Established: 1912. Pub. Frequency: w. (Wed.) Page Size: tabloid. Subscrip. Rate: $36/yr mailed. Circulation: 12,500 per issue (paid and free). **Owner(s):** Eagle Newspapers LLC, See address and contact information above. **Management:** Dean Eckenroth Jr., General Manager. Dean Eckenroth, Publisher. Pamela Thornton Willis, Advertising Manager. Janice Wright, Classified Adv. Mgr. **Editorial:** Jared Cohen, News Editor.

COSTA MESA

HUNTINGTON BEACH/FOUNTAIN VALLEY INDEPENDENT. ISSN 0194-6021
1375 Sunflower Ave, Costa Mesa, CA 92626. Telephone: 714-966-4600. FAX: 714-966-4611. Year Established: 1966. Pub. Frequency: w. (Thu.) Page Size: tabloid Circulation: 40,000 per issue (free). **Owner(s):** Los Angeles Times Communications LLC, 202 W First St, Los Angeles, CA 90012. Telephone: 213-237-5000. **Management:** Tom Johnson, Publisher. **Editorial:** Tony Dodero, Editor. S J Cahn, Managing Editor. Carol Chambers, City Editor.

DELANO

DELANO RECORD, THE. 1231 Jefferson St., Delano, CA 93215. Telephone: 661-725-0600. FAX: 661-725-4373. Year Established: 1908. Pub. Frequency: w. (Thu.) Page Size: broadsheet. Subscrip. Rate: $.35 newsstand/cover; $19/yr mailed in county; $21/yr mailed out of county; $24/yr mailed out of state. Adv. Rate: col. inch $7.50 Circulation: 4,500 per issue (paid). **Owner(s):** Reed Print, Inc., 5409 Aldrin Ct., Bakersfield, CA 93313. Telephone: 805-834-0496. **Management:** Donald Reed, Publisher. Jason Reed, Advertising Manager. Helen Oros, Circulation Manager. Angel Sapien, Classified Adv. Mgr..

MARKET SHOPPER, THE. 1231 Jefferson St., Delano, CA 93215. Telephone: 661-725-0600. FAX: 661-725-4373. Year Established: 1914. Pub. Frequency: w. (Wed.) Page Size: broadsheet.Adv. Rate: col. inch $9.24 Circulation: 11,500 per issue (free). **Owner(s):** Reed Print, Inc., 5409 Aldrin Ct., Bakersfield, CA 93313. Telephone: 805-834-0496. **Management:** Donald Reed, Publisher. Jason Reed, Advertising Manager. Helen Oros, Circulation Manager. Angel Sapien, Classified Adv. Mgr..

DIXON

DIXON TRIBUNE. 145 E. A St, Dixon, CA 95620. Telephone: 707-678-5594. FAX: 707-678-5404. Pub. Frequency: 3/w. (Wed., Fri., Sun.) Page Size: broadsheet. Subscrip. Rate: $.50 newsstand/cover; $37/yr local. Circulation: 5,000 per issue (paid). **Owner(s):** Gibson Publications, Inc., 544 Curtola Pkwy, Vallejo, CA 94590. Telephone: 707-643-2552. **Management:** David L. Payne, Publisher. Sarah Villec, Advertising. **Editorial:** Brianna Boyd, Editor.

DOWNEY

DOWNEY PATRIOT. 11525 Downey Ave, Ste A, Downey, CA 90241-5808. Telephone: 562-803-0902. FAX: 562-803-0942. E-MAIL: downeypatriot@yahoo.com. URL: http://www.downeypatriot.com. Year Established: 2002. Pub. Frequency: w. (Fri.) Page Size: broadsheet.Adv. Rate: col. inch $18 Circulation: 25,000 per issue (paid and free). **Owner(s):** John Adams, See address and contact information above. **Management:** John Adams, Publisher. Jerry Brady, Advertising Director. **Editorial:** John Adams, Editor.

DOWNIEVILLE

MOUNTAIN MESSENGER. ISSN 0278-4394
313 Main St, Downieville, CA 95936. Telephone: 530-289-3262. FAX: 530-289-3262. E-MAIL: mtnmess@cwo.com. Mailing Address: P.O. Drawer A, Downieville, CA 95936. Year Established: 1853. Pub. Frequency: w. (Thu.) Page Size: broadsheet. Subscrip. Rate: $.50 newsstand/cover; $20/yr in county; $25/yr mailed out of county. Adv. Rate: col. inch $5.50 Circulation: 2,680 per issue (paid). **Owner(s):** Donald S. Russell, Inc., See address and contact information above. James Roos, **Management:** Donald S Russell, Publisher. **Editorial:** Donald S Russell, Executive Editor.

EL CAJON

EAST COUNTY CALIFORNIAN. 119 N. Magnolia Ave., El Cajon, CA 92020. Telephone: 619-441-0400. E-MAIL: editor@eccalifornian.com. Year Established: 1892. Pub. Frequency: w. (Thu.) Page Size: tabloid.Subscrip. Rate: $30, $40/yr out of county Circulation: 32,500 per issue (free). **Owner(s):** San Diego Neighborhood Newspapers, Inc., See address and contact information above. **Management:** Linda Townson, Group Publisher. David Kelso, Sales Manager. **Editorial:** Chris Coburn, Editor.

EL MONTE

MID VALLEY NEWS. 11401 E. Valley Blvd., Ste. 100, El Monte, CA 91731. Telephone: 626-443-1753. FAX: 626-443-2245. E-MAIL: connie@midvalleynews.com. URL: http://www.midvalleynews.com. Year Established: 1966. Pub. Frequency: w. (Wed.) Page Size: tabloid. Subscrip. Rate: $49/yr mailed in county. Freelance Pay: $1/column-inch. Circulation: 15,000 per issue (paid and free). **Owner(s):** Connie Keenan & Virginia Moseley, See address and contact information above. **Management:** Connie Keenan, Advertising Manager. Zulema Sandoval, Classified Adv. Mgr.. **Editorial:** Connie Keenan, Editor-in-Chief. Joe Torosian, Sports Editor.

EL SEGUNDO

EL SEGUNDO HERALD. 312 E. Imperial Ave., El Segundo, CA 90245. Telephone: 310-322-1830. E-MAIL: sales@heraldpublications.com. Mailing Address: PO Box 188, El Segundo, CA 90245-0188. Year Established: 1911. Pub. Frequency: w. (Thu.) Page Size: tabloid. Subscrip. Rate: $60/yr mailed in county. Circulation: 16,000 per issue (paid and free). **Owner(s):** Herald Publications, See address and contact information above. **Management:** Richard Van Vraken, Publisher. **Editorial:** Heidi Maerker, Editor.

ELK GROVE

ELK GROVE CITIZEN. 8970 Elk Grove Blvd., Elk Grove, CA 95624. Telephone: 916-685-5533. FAX: 916-686-6675. E-MAIL: advertising@herburger.net. URL: http://www.egcitizen.com. Mailing Address: PO Box 1777, Elk Grove, CA 95759. Year Established: 1903. Pub. Frequency: s-w. (Wed. & Fri.) Page Size: broadsheet. Subscrip. Rate: $.35 newsstand/cover; $35/yr in county. Circulation: 27,941 per issue (paid). **Owner(s):** Herburger Publications, Inc., 604 N. Lincoln, Galt, CA 95632. Telephone: 209-745-1551. **Management:** Roy Herburger, President. David Herburger, Publisher. Jim O'Donald, Advertising Manager. Adell Wycoff, Classified Adv. Mgr.. **Editorial:** Jeff Forward, Editor. Jon Gudel, Sports Editor.

EMERYVILLE

EAST BAY EXPRESS. 1335 Stanford Ave., Ste. 100, Emeryville, CA 94608. Telephone: 510-879-3700. FAX: 510-601-0217. E-MAIL: info@eastbayexpress.com. URL: http://www.eastbayexpress.com. Year Established: 1978. Pub. Frequency: w. (Wed.) Page Size: tabloid.Subscrip. Rate: $100/yr mailed in county Circulation: 85,000 per issue (free). **Owner(s):** Village Voice Media, Inc., 1201 E Jefferson St, Phoenix, AZ 85034. Telephone: 415-541-0700. FAX: 415-541-9096. **Management:** Josh Fromson, Publisher. Troy Larkin, Advertising Director. Wesley Chung, Circulation Director. Kent Winkler, Classified Adv. Mgr.. **Editorial:** Steven Buel, Executive Editor. Michael Mechanic, Managing Editor. David Downs, Music Editor.

ESCALON

ESCALON TIMES, THE. PO Box 98, Escalon, CA 95320. Telephone: 209-838-7043. FAX: 209-847-9750. E-MAIL: marge@escalontimes.net. URL: http://www.escalontimes.com. Pub. Frequency: w. (Fri.) Page Size: broadsheet. Subscrip. Rate: $.75 newsstand/cover; $31/yr mailed in county; $38/yr mailed out of county; $26/yr mailed in county to senior citizens. Circulation: 8,000 per issue (paid). **Owner(s):** Morris Newspaper Corporation, See address and contact information above. **Management:** Bill Camp, General Manager. Randy McCants, Publisher. Carol Williams, Office Manager. Melinda Owen, Advertising Manager. **Editorial:** Marg Jackson, Editor. Mitchell Naylor, Managing Editor.

EXETER

EXETER SUN, THE. ISSN 1072-1584
120 N. E St., Exeter, CA 93221. URL: http://www.theexetersun.com. Mailing Address: PO Box 7, Exeter, CA 93221-0007. Year Established: 1903. Pub. Frequency: w. (Wed.) Page Size: broadsheet. Subscrip. Rate: $.50 newsstand/cover; $25/yr local; $30/yr mailed out of county; $35/yr mailed out of state. Circulation: 25,000 per issue (paid). **Owner(s):** Mineral King Publishing Co., See address and contact information above. **Management:** Bill Brown, Publisher. JoAnn Wright, Advertising. Pam Bradsteen, Circulation Manager. Terri Garcia, Classified Adv. Mgr.. **Editorial:** Reggie Ellis, Editor.

LINDSAY GAZETTE. ISSN 1072-1800
120 N. E St., Exeter, CA 93221. Telephone: 559-592-3171. FAX: 559-592-4308. E-MAIL: editor@theexetersun.com. URL: http://www.lindsaygazette.com. Mailing Address: PO Box 7, Exeter, CA 93221-0007. Year Established: 1901. Pub. Frequency: w. (Wed.) Page Size: broadsheet. Subscrip. Rate: $.50 newsstand/cover; $25/yr in county; $30/yr mailed out of county. Circulation: 17,300 per issue (paid). **Owner(s):** Mineral King Publishing Co., See address and contact information above. **Management:** Katherine Byrne, General Manager. Bill Brown, Publisher. JoAnn Wright, Advertising. Terri Garcia, Classified Adv. Mgr.. **Editorial:** Reggie Ellis, Editor.

FILLMORE

FILLMORE HERALD. 505 Santa Clara St, Fillmore, CA 93016-0727. Telephone: 805-524-0153. FAX: 805-524-0154. E-MAIL: info@fillmorehearld.com. URL: http://www.fillmoreherald.com. Mailing Address: P.O. Box 727, Fillmore, CA 93016-0727. Year Established: 1907. Pub. Frequency: w. (Thu.) Page Size: broadsheet. Subscrip. Rate: $.50 newsstand/cover; $30/yr local; $33/yr out of county; $40/yr out of state. Adv. Rate: col. inch $4.65, page $5 Circulation: 3,000 per issue (controlled and free). **Owner(s):** San Canetano Investment, Inc., See address and contact information above. **Editorial:** Terry Timmons, Editor-in-Chief. Linda Roberts, Managing Editor. Charles Mozley, Senior Editor. Jill Lapple, Photographer.

FOLSOM

EL DORADO HILLS TELEGRAPH. 49 Natoma St., Ste. D, Folsom, CA 95630. Telephone: 916-985-2581. FAX: 916-985-0720. E-MAIL: gloriab@goldcountrymedia.com. URL: http://www.edhtelegraph.com. Year Established: 2001. Pub. Frequency: w. (Wed.) Page Size: broadsheet. Subscrip. Rate: $.50 newsstand/cover; $26/yr home delivery local. Adv. Rate: col. inch $9.50 Freelance Pay: $35/article. Circulation: 8,650 per issue (free). **Owner(s):** Brehm Communications, Inc., 16644 W. Bernardo Dr., Ste. 300, San Diego, CA 92128. Telephone: 858-451-6200. FAX: 858-451-3814. **Management:** Allison Perkes, General Manager. Debbie Elmore, Circulation Manager. **Editorial:** Gloria Beverage, Editor. Matt Long, Sports Editor.

FOLSOM TELEGRAPH. 49 Natoma St., Ste. D, Folsom, CA 95630. Telephone: 916-985-2581. FAX: 916-985-0720. E-MAIL: gloriab@goldcountrymedia.com. URL: http://www.folsomtelegraph.com. Year Established: 1856. Pub. Frequency: w. (Wed.) Page Size: broadsheet. Subscrip. Rate: $.50 newsstand/cover; $26/yr home delivery. Adv. Rate: col. inch $13 Freelance Pay: $35/article. Circulation: 18,650 per issue (controlled and free). **Owner(s):** Brehm Communications, Inc., 16644 W. Bernardo Dr., Ste. 300, San Diego, CA 92127. Telephone: 858-451-6200. **Management:** Allison Perkes, General Manager. Debbie Elmore, Circulation Director. **Editorial:** Gloria Beverage, Editor. Matt Long, Sports Editor.

FONTANA

FONTANA HERALD NEWS. 16981 Foothill Blvd., Ste. N., Fontana, CA 92335. Telephone: 909-822-2231. FAX: 909-355-9358. E-MAIL: adsales@fontanaheraldnews.com. URL: http://www.fontanaheraldnews.com. Mailing Address: PO Box 549, Fontana, CA 92334. Year Established: 1923. Pub. Frequency: w. (Fri.) Page Size: tabloid. Subscrip. Rate: $19.95/yr mailed. Adv. Rate: col. inch $15.40 Freelance Pay: $1/column-inch. Circulation: 11,000 per issue (paid). **Owner(s):** Century Group, The, 35154 Yucaipa Blvd., Yucaipa, CA 92399. Telephone: 909-797-9101. FAX: 909-797-0502. **Management:** Grace Barnett, Publisher. Christina Rocha, Office Manager. Janice Chilcote, Circulation Manager. **Editorial:** Russell Ingold, Editor. Ruell Asuncion, Production Manager.Readers: Local community, families

FONTUNA

HUMBOLDT BEACON, THE. 936 Main St, Fontuna, CA 95540. Telephone: 707-725-6166. FAX: 707-725-6837. E-MAIL: beacon@humboldt1.com. URL: http://www.humboldtbeacon.com. Year Established: 1902. Pub. Frequency: w. (Thu.) Page Size: standard. Subscrip. Rate: $.50 newsstand/cover; $10 for 6 mos. in county; $17.50/yr in county; $25/yr in state; $30/yr out of state. Freelance Pay: $1.35/column-inch. Circulation: 4,000 per issue (paid). **Owner(s):** MediaNews Group, Inc., 101 W Colfax Ave, Ste 1100, Denver, CO 80202. FAX: 303-954-6320. **Management:** Patrick O'Dell, President. **Editorial:** Christine Sackey, Editor.

FT. BRAGG

FORT BRAGG ADVOCATE-NEWS. ISSN 0886-8840
450 N. Franklin St., Ft. Bragg, CA 95437. Telephone: 707-964-5642. FAX: 707-964-0424. E-MAIL: advocatenews@mcn.org. URL: http://www.advocate-news.com. Mailing Address: PO Box 1188, Ft. Bragg, CA 95437. Year Established: 1889. Pub. Frequency: w. (Thu.) Page Size: standard. Subscrip. Rate: $37/yr in county; $50/yr out of county. Adv. Rate: col. inch $9.85 Circulation: 5,400 per issue (paid). **Owner(s):** MediaNews Group, Inc., 101 W Colfax Ave, Ste 1100, Denver, CO 80202. FAX: 303-954-6320. **Management:** Sharon DiMauro, Publisher. Antonio Garcia, Circulation Manager. **Editorial:** Katherine Lee, Managing Editor.

MENDOCINO BEACON, THE. 450 N. Franklin St., Ft. Bragg, CA 95437. Telephone: 707-964-5642. FAX: 707-964-0424. E-MAIL: beacon@mcn.com. URL: http://www.mendocinobeacon.com. Mailing Address: PO Box 1188, Ft. Bragg, CA 95437. Year Established: 1877. Pub. Frequency: w. (Thu.) Page Size: standard. Subscrip. Rate: $.50 newsstand/cover; $16.50 for 6 mos. in county; $30/yr in county; $43/yr out of county. Adv. Rate: col. inch $7.45 Circulation: 2,400 per issue (paid). **Owner(s):** MediaNews Group, Inc., 101 W Colfax Ave, Ste 1100, Denver, CO 80202. FAX: 303-954-6320. **Management:** Sharon Brewer, Publisher. Antonio Garcia, Circulation Manager. **Editorial:** Katherine Lee, Managing Editor.

GALT

GALT HERALD, THE. 604 N. Lincoln, Galt, CA 95632. Telephone: 209-745-1551. FAX: 209-745-4492. E-MAIL: galtnews@herburger.net. URL: http://www.galtherald.com. Mailing Address: PO Box 307, Galt, CA 95632-0307. Year Established: 1903. Pub. Frequency: w. (Wed.) Page Size: broadsheet. Subscrip. Rate: $.35 newsstand/cover; $18/yr in county. Adv. Rate: col. inch $9 Circulation: 10,500 per issue (paid). **Owner(s):** Herburger Publications, Inc., See address and contact information above. **Management:** Roy Herburger, President. David Herburger, Publisher. Jim O'Donald, Advertising Manager. **Editorial:** Rachel Roberts, News Editor. Mike Bush, Sports.

GARBERVILLE

REDWOOD TIMES. 442 Maple Lane, Garberville, CA 95542. Telephone: 707-923—1396. FAX: 707-923-7735. E-MAIL: sgardner@redwoodtimes.com. URL: http://www.redwoodtimes.com. Mailing Address: PO Box 897, Garberville, CA 95542. Year Established: 2004. Pub. Frequency: w. Subscrip. Rate: $32.50/yr Circulation: 4,500 per issue (paid). **Owner(s):** MediaNews Group, Inc., 101 W Colfax Ave, Ste 1100, Denver, CO 80202. FAX: 303-954-6320. **Management:** Susan Gardner, General Manager. Dru Cherubini, Advertising Director. **Editorial:** Susan Gardner, Editor. Mary Anderson, Writer.

GARDEN GROVE

ORANGE COUNTY NEWS. 7441 Garden Grove Blvd. Ste. G, Garden Grove, CA 92841-4209. Telephone: 714-894-2575. FAX: 714-894-0809. E-MAIL: ocn@localnewspapers.org. Year Established: 1909. Pub. Frequency: s-w. (Wed. & Fri.) Page Size: tabloid. Subscrip. Rate: $55/yr mailed in county. Circulation: 21,700 per issue (paid and free). **Owner(s):** Community Media Corporation, See address and contact information above. **Management:** Eddie Verdugo, Publisher. Daniel Verdugo, Vice President. **Editorial:** John Seymour, Editor.

GARDENA

GARDENA VALLEY NEWS. ISSN 1930-9252
16417 S. Western Ave., Gardena, CA 90247. Telephone: 310-329-6351. FAX: 310-329-7501. E-MAIL: gvneditorial@covad.net. Mailing Address: PO Box 219, Gardena, CA 90248. Year Established: 1904. Pub. Frequency: w. (Thu.) Page Size: broadsheet. Subscrip. Rate: $.25 newsstand/cover; $12/yr home delivery; $55/yr mailed. Freelance Pay: $15-$40/story. Circulation: 7,000 per issue (paid). **Owner(s):** Don Algie, See address and contact information above. **Management:** Don Algie, President. Dan Gagajena, Advertising Manager. Donald Oyama, Assistant Publisher. Ruriko Yatabe, Business Manager. **Editorial:** Gary Kohatsu, Editor-in-Chief. James Fujita, Sports.

GILROY

RAMONA SENTINEL. 6400 Monterey Rd, Gilroy, CA 95020. Telephone: 408-842-6400. FAX: 408-842-4302. E-MAIL: news@ramonasentinel.com. URL: http://www.ramonasentinel.com. Mailing Address: PO Box 367, Ramona, CA 92065-0367. Year Established: 1886. Pub. Frequency: w. (Thu.) Page Size: broadsheet. Subscrip. Rate: $.50 newsstand/cover; $25/yr in county; $30/yr mailed out of county; $30/yr mailed out of state. Circulation: 5,600 per issue (paid). **Owner(s):** Main Street Media Group, 425-A 10th St, Ramona, CA 92065. **Management:** Jeff Mitchell, Publisher.

GREENFIELD

GREENFIELD NEWS. 845 Oak Ave., Greenfield, CA 93927. Telephone: 831-385-4880. FAX: 831-385-4799. E-MAIL: sceditor@redshift.com. URL: http://www.greenfieldnews.com. Mailing Address: PO Box 710, King City, CA 93930. Pub. Frequency: w. (Wed.) Page Size: broadsheet. Subscrip. Rate: $.75 newsstand/cover; $32.50/yr in county; $37.50/yr out of county. Circulation: 1,700 per issue (paid). **Owner(s):** News Media Corp., PO Box 46, Rochelle, IL 61068. **Management:** Scott Brennan, Publisher. **Editorial:** Richard Sitts, Editor.

GRIDLEY

GRIDLEY HERALD, THE. 630 Washington St., Gridley, CA 95948. Telephone: 530-846-3661. FAX: 530-846-4519. E-MAIL: news@gridleyherald.com. URL: http://www.gridleyherald.com. Mailing Address: PO Box 68, Gridley, CA 95948. Year Established: 1880. Pub. Frequency: s-w. (Wed. & Fri.) Page Size: broadsheet. Subscrip. Rate: $.50 newsstand/cover; $43/yr in county; $49/yr out of county. Adv. Rate: col. inch $8.40 Circulation: 2,500 per issue (paid). **Owner(s):** GateHouse Media, Inc, 350 WillowBrook Office Park, Fairport, NY 14450. Telephone: 585-598-0030. **Management:** Lisa Van De Hey, Publisher. Lynne Farris, Advertising. Judy Quist, Circulation Director. Alice Johnson, Classified Adv. Mgr.. **Editorial:** Lisa Van De Hey, Editor.

GRIDLEY SHOPPING NEWS, THE. 630 Washington St., Gridley, CA 95948. Telephone: 530-846-3661. FAX: 530-846-4519. Mailing Address: PO Box 68, Gridley, CA 95948. Pub. Frequency: w. (Wed.) Page Size: standard Circulation: 5,500 per issue (free). **Owner(s):** GateHouse Media, Inc, 350 WillowBrook Office Park, Fairport, NY 14450. Telephone: 585-598-0030. **Management:** Lisa Van De Hey, Publisher. Lynne Farris, Advertising. Judy Quist, Circulation Director. Alice Johnson, Classified Adv. Mgr..

HALF MOON BAY

HALF MOON BAY REVIEW. 714 Kelly Ave., Half Moon Bay, CA 94019. Telephone: 650-726-4424. FAX: 650-726-7054. E-MAIL: hmbreview@hmbreview.com. URL: http://www.hmbreview.com. Mailing Address: PO Box 68, Half Moon Bay, CA 94019. Year Established: 1898. Pub. Frequency: w. (Wed.) Page Size: broadsheet. Subscrip. Rate: $.75 newsstand/cover; $34/yr home delivery; $34/yr in county; $48/yr out of county. Adv. Rate: col. inch $2 Circulation: 7,200 per issue (paid). **Owner(s):** Wick Communications, Inc., 333 W. Wilcox Dr., Ste. 302, Sierra Vista, AZ 85635. Telephone: 602-458-0200. **Management:** Debra Godshall, Publisher. Martha Ransom, Circulation Manager.

HEALDSBURG

HEALDSBURG TRIBUNE. 5 Mitchell Ln., Healdsburg, CA 95448. Telephone: 707-433-4451. FAX: 707-431-2623. E-MAIL: capfitch@pacbell.net. URL: http://www.hbgtrib.com. Mailing Address: P.O Box 518, Healdsburg, CA 95448. Year Established: 1856. Pub. Frequency: w. (Wed.) Page Size: broadsheet. Subscrip. Rate: $.50 newsstand/cover; $30/yr in county; $40/yr out of county; $20/yr in county to senior citizens. Adv. Rate: col. inch $21.95 Circulation: 5,000 per issue (paid). **Owner(s):** Sonoma West Publishers, Inc., See address and contact information above. **Management:** Rollie Atkinson, Publisher. Cherie Kelsay, Advertising Manager. Grace Garner, Circulation Manager. Jeanne Ellis, Classified Adv. Mgr.. **Editorial:** Barry Dugan, Managing Editor. Kerrie Russell, Senior Editor. Greg Clementi, Sports Editor.

HERMOSA BEACH

EASY READER. 83 Hermosa Ave., Hermosa Beach, CA 90254. Telephone: 310-372-4611. FAX: 310-318-6292. E-MAIL: easyreader@easyreader.info. URL: http://www.easyreader.info. Mailing Address: PO Box 427, Hermosa Beach, CA 90254. Year Established: 1970. Pub. Frequency: w. (Thu.) Page Size: tabloid. Subscrip. Rate: $50/yr in county. Circulation: 65,000 per issue (paid and free). **Owner(s):** Kevin Cody, See address and contact information above. **Management:** Joseph Nicosia, General Manager. Kevin Cody, Publisher.

HESPERIA

HESPERIA RESORTER. 16925 Main St., Hesperia, CA 92345. Telephone: 760-244-0021. FAX: 760-244-6609. E-MAIL: valleywide@compu-ad.net. Mailing Address: PO Box 400937, Hesperia, CA 92340-0937. Year Established: 1959. Pub. Frequency: w. (Thu.) Page Size: broadsheet. Subscrip. Rate: $15/yr mailed local; $21/yr mailed elsewhere. Circulation: 5,000 per issue (paid and free). **Owner(s):** Raymond Pryke, See address and contact information above. **Management:** Raymond Pryke, President. Jenny Jones, Publisher. Renee Carlson, Classified Adv. Mgr.. **Editorial:** Rhonda Lee, Managing Editor.

HESPERIA STAR. ISSN 1530-3519
17045 Main St., Hesperia, CA 92345. Telephone: 760-956-7827. FAX: 760-956-6803. URL: http://www.hesperiastar.com. Year Established: 2000. Pub. Frequency: w. (Tue.) Page Size: tabloid.Subscrip. Rate: $6/yr mailed Circulation: 19,500 per issue (free). **Owner(s):** Freedom Communications, Inc., 17666 Fitch, Irvine, CA 92614. Telephone: 949-253-2300. **Management:** Stephen Wingert, Publisher. David Griffith, Advertising Manager. **Editorial:** Peter Day, Editor.

HOLLISTER

PINNACLE, THE. 380 San Benito St, Hollister, CA 95203. Telephone: 831-637-6300. FAX: 831-637-8174. Mailing Address: PO Box 22365, Gilroy, CA 95021-2365. Year Established: 1986. Pub. Frequency: w. (Fri.) Page Size: tabloid. Subscrip. Rate: $45/yr mailed out of county. Circulation: 54,500 per issue (paid and free). **Owner(s):** Main Street Media Group, 6400 Monterey St, Gilroy, CA 95020. Telephone: 408-842-6400. FAX: 408-802-7105. **Management:** Mark Paxton, Publisher. Linda Moore, Advertising Director. **Editorial:** Melissa Flores, News Editor.

HOLTVILLE

HOLTVILLE TRIBUNE. 570 Holt Ave., Holtville, CA 92250. Telephone: 760-356-2995. FAX: 760-756-4715. URL: http://www.imperialvalleynews.com. Year Established: 1906. Pub. Frequency: w. (Thu.) Page Size: tabloid. Subscrip. Rate: $.50 newsstand/cover; $22/yr in county; $26.50/yr mailed in state. Adv. Rate: col. inch $7.20 Circulation: 3,000 per issue (paid). **Owner(s):** Steve Larson, See address and contact information above. **Management:** Steve Larson, Publisher. Brenda Torres, Business Manager. **Editorial:** Steve Larson, Editor.

IDYLLWILD

IDYLLWILD TOWN CRIER. 54295 Village Center Dr., Idyllwild, CA 92549-0157. Telephone: 951-659-2145. FAX: 951-659-2071. E-MAIL: itc@towncrier.com. URL: http://www.towncrier.com. Mailing Address: PO Box 157, Idyllwild, CA 92549-0157. Year Established: 1946. Pub. Frequency: w. (Thu.) Page Size: tabloid. Subscrip. Rate: $.75 newsstand/cover; $29/yr home delivery in county; $33/yr home delivery out of county; $34/yr combined subscription in county print & online eds.; $38/yr combined subscription out of county print & online eds.. Adv. Rate: col. inch $9.50 Freelance Pay: $0.10/word. Circulation: 3,700 per issue (paid); 262 per issue (free). **Owner(s):** Idyllwild Publications, Inc., 54295 Village Center Dr., Idyllwild, CA 92549. Telephone: 909-659-2145. **Management:** Becky Clark, Publisher. Grace Reed, Advertising Manager. **Editorial:** Becky Clark, Editor. J P Crumrine, News Editor.Readers: Community news aimed at Idyllwild residents, part-timers, and visitors

Weeklies

IMPERIAL BEACH

IMPERIAL BEACH EAGLE & TIMESN. 1223 Palm Ave, Imperial Beach, CA 91922. Telephone: 619-429-5555. FAX: 619-429-5556. Pub. Frequency: w. (Fri.) Page Size: tabloid.Subscrip. Rate: $25/yr mailed Circulation: 10,000 per issue (free). **Owner(s):** Eagle Newspapers LLC, 1116 Tenth St., Coronado, CA 92118. Telephone: 619-437-8800. FAX: 619-437-8635. **Management:** Dean Eckenroth Jr., General Manager. Dean Eckenroth, Publisher. Dean Eckenroth Jr., Advertising Manager. Janice Wright, Classified Adv. Mgr.. **Editorial:** Jared Cohen, News Editor.

IRVINE

IRVINE WORLD NEWS, THE. ISSN 0195-4822 2006 Mcgaw Ave., Irvine, CA 92614. Telephone: 949-553-2900. FAX: 949-553-2925. E-MAIL: iwpadv@aol.com. URL: http://www.irvineworldnews.com. Year Established: 1970. Pub. Frequency: s-w. (Thu. & Sun.) Page Size: tabloid. Circulation: 43,000 per issue (controlled). **Owner(s):** Orange County Register, 625 N. Grand Ave., Santa Ana, CA 92701. Telephone: 877-469-7344. **Management:** Paul Davison, General Manager. Chris Anderson, Publisher. **Editorial:** Don Dennis, Editor. Peggy Blizzard, Entertainment Editor. Tim Burt, Sports.

LOG, THE. 17782 Cowan, Ste A, Irvine, CA 92614. Telephone: 949-660-6150. FAX: 949-660-6172. E-MAIL: log1edit@aol.com. URL: http://www.thelog.com. Year Established: 1971. Pub. Frequency: bi-w. (Fri.) Page Size: tabloid. Subscrip. Rate: $29.95/yr mailed 3rd class; $53.95/yr mailed 1st class. Circulation: 18,000 per issue (free). **Owner(s):** Pacific Sierra Publishing, Inc., See address and contact information above. **Management:** Teresa Ybarra McIntosh, Co-Publisher. Duncan McIntosh, Publisher. Janette Hood, Advertising Director. Richard Nelson, Circulation Manager. Jon Sorenson, Classified Adv. Mgr.. **Editorial:** Jane Hascher, Editor. Jeffrey Fleming, Associate Editor.

LOG: SAN DIEGO EDITION, THE. 17782 Cowan, Ste A, Irvine, CA 92614. Telephone: 949-660-6150. FAX: 949-660-6172. URL: http://www.thelog.com. Pub. Frequency: bi-w. (Fri) Page Size: standard. Subscrip. Rate: $29.95/yr mailed 3rd class; $53.95/yr 1st class. Circulation: 15,000 per issue (free). **Owner(s):** Pacific Sierra Publishing, Inc., See address and contact information above. **Management:** Teresa Ybarra McIntosh, Co-Publisher. Duncan McIntosh, Publisher. Janette Hood, Advertising Director. Richard Nelson, Circulation Manager. Jon Sorenson, Classified Adv. Mgr.. **Editorial:** Jane Hascher, Editor. Jeffrey Fleming, Associate Editor.

LOG: SOUTHERN CALIFORNIA EDITION, THE. 17782 Cowan, Ste A, Irvine, CA 92614. Telephone: 949-660-6150. FAX: 949-660-6172. URL: http://www.thelog.com. Pub. Frequency: bi-w. (Fri.) Page Size: standard. Subscrip. Rate: $29.95/yr mailed 3rd class; $53.95/yr mailed 1st class. Circulation: 19,000 per issue (free). **Owner(s):** Pacific Sierra Publishing, Inc., See address and contact information above. **Management:** Teresa Ybarra McIntosh, Co-Publisher. Duncan McIntosh, Publisher. Janette Hood, Advertising Director. Richard Nelson, Circulation Manager. Jon Sorenson, Classified Adv. Mgr.. **Editorial:** Jane Hascher, Editor. Jeffrey Fleming, Associate Editor.

TUSTIN NEWS, THE. 2006 McGaw Ave, Irvine, CA 92614. Telephone: 949-553-2918. FAX: 947-353-2925. E-MAIL: tunews@link-freedom.com. URL: http://www.ocregister.com/community/tustin_news/. Year Established: 1922. Pub. Frequency: w. (Thu.) Page Size: broadsheet Circulation: 35,000 per issue (free). **Owner(s):** Freedom Communications, Inc., 17666 Fitch St., Irvine, CA 92614. **Management:** Chris Anderson, Publisher. Bobbi Ayers, Advertising. **Editorial:** Jill Leach, City Editor. Keenon Singleton, Sports Editor.

JACKSON

AMADOR LEDGER-DISPATCH. ISSN 1045-8336 10776 Argonaut Ln, Jackson, CA 95642. Telephone: 209-223-1767. FAX: 209-223-4245. URL: http://www.ledger-dispatch.com. Mailing Address: PO Box 22365, Gilroy, CA 95021-2365. Year Established: 1855. Pub. Frequency: s-w. (Wed. & Fri.) Page Size: broadsheet. Subscrip. Rate: $.75 newsstand/cover; $55/yr home delivery in county; $77/yr mailed in county; $99/yr mailed out of county. Freelance Pay: $1.50/column-inch. Circulation: 7,500 per issue (controlled and free). **Owner(s):** Main Street Media Group, 6400 Monterey St, Gilroy, CA 95020. Telephone: 408-842-6400. FAX: 408-802-7105. **Management:** Jack Mitchell, Publisher. David Marin, VP Advertising. Diana Stewart, Classified Adv. Mgr.. **Editorial:** Jim Reece, Sports Editor.

KERMAN

FIREBAUGH/MENDOTA JOURNAL. 14689 W. Whitesbridge, Kerman, CA 93630. Telephone: 559-846-6689. FAX: 559-846-8045. E-MAIL: kerwest@msn.com. Mailing Address: PO Box 336, Kerman, CA 93630-0336. Pub. Frequency: w. (Wed.) Page Size: broadsheet. Subscrip. Rate: $.55 newsstand/cover; $30/yr mailed. Circulation: 7,700 per issue (paid). **Owner(s):** KerWest, Inc., See address and contact information above. **Management:** Merlyn Wilcox, General Manager. **Editorial:** Mark Kilen, Editor.

KERMAN NEWS. 14689 W. Whitesbridge, Kerman, CA 93630. Telephone: 559-846-6689. FAX: 559-846-8045. E-MAIL: kerwest@msn.com. Mailing Address: PO Box 336, Kerman, CA 93630-0336. Year Established: 1905. Pub. Frequency: w. (Wed.) Page Size: broadsheet. Subscrip. Rate: $.55 newsstand/cover; $30/yr mailed in county. Circulation: 2,000 per issue (paid). **Owner(s):** KerWest, Inc., See address and contact information above. **Management:** Mark Kilen, General Manager. Merlyn Wilcox, Advertising Manager. **Editorial:** Mark Kilen, Editor.

WEST SIDE ADVANCE. 14689 W. Whitesbridge, Kerman, CA 93630. Telephone: 559-846-6689. FAX: 559-846-8045. E-MAIL: kerwest@msn.com. Mailing Address: PO Box 336, Kerman, CA 93630-0336. Year Established: 1905. Pub. Frequency: w. (Wed.) Page Size: broadsheet. Subscrip. Rate: $.55 newsstand/cover; $30/yr mailed in county. Circulation: 2,700 per issue (paid and free). **Owner(s):** KerWest, Inc., See address and contact information above. **Management:** Merlyn Wilcox, General Manager. **Editorial:** Mark Kilen, Editor.

KING CITY

KING CITY RUSTLER. 522A Broadway, King City, CA 93930. Telephone: 831-385-4880. FAX: 831-385-4799. E-MAIL: kcrustler@redshift.com. URL: http://www.kingcityrustler.com. Mailing Address: PO Box 710, King City, CA 93930. Year Established: 1901. Pub. Frequency: w. (Wed.) Page Size: broadsheet. Subscrip. Rate: $.50 newsstand/cover; $32.50/yr in county; $37.50/yr mailed out of county. Circulation: 4,486 per issue (paid). **Owner(s):** News Media Corp., PO Box 46, Rochelle, IL 61068. **Management:** Scott Brennan, Publisher. Sheryl Bailey, Advertising. **Editorial:** Scott Brennan, Editor. Kellie Hicks, Graphics Editor.

VISTAS. 522-A Broadway, King City, CA 93930. Telephone: 831-385-4880. FAX: 831-385-4799. Mailing Address: PO Box 710, King City, CA 93930. Pub. Frequency: w. (Wed.) Page Size: broadsheet Circulation: 5,400 per issue (free). **Owner(s):** News Media Corp., PO Box 46, Rochelle, IL 61068. **Management:** Scott Brennan, Publisher. Bess Brennan, Advertising. **Editorial:** Scott Brennan, Editor. Joseph Soqui, Sports.

KINGSBURG

KINGSBURG RECORDER. 1467 Marion St., Kingsburg, CA 93631. Telephone: 559-897-2993. FAX: 559-897-4868. URL: http://www.kingsburgrecorder.com. Mailing Address: PO Box 128, Kingsburg, CA 93631. Pub. Frequency: w. (Wed.) Page Size: broadsheet. Subscrip. Rate: $.50 newsstand/cover; $25/yr in county; $28/yr out of county; $30/yr mailed elsewhere. Circulation: 3,100 per issue (paid). **Owner(s):** Lee Enterprises, Inc., 900 N. Tucker Blvd., St. Louis, MO 63101. Telephone: 314-340-8000. **Management:** Mark Daniel, Publisher. Joe Sciotis, Advertising Manager. Greg Barkley, Circulation Manager. **Editorial:** Michael Miyamoto, Editor.

LA CANADA

LA CANADA VALLEY SUN. 1061 Valley Sun Ln., La Canada, CA 91011. Telephone: 818-790-8774. FAX: 818-790-5690. E-MAIL: lcnews@valleysun.net. URL: http://www.lacanadaonline.com. Mailing Address: PO Box 38, La Canada, CA 91012. Year Established: 1946. Pub. Frequency: w. (Thu.) Page Size: tabloid. Subscrip. Rate: $.50 newsstand/cover; $25/yr in county; $32/yr out of county. Adv. Rate: col. inch $9.95 Circulation: 10,000 per issue (paid and free). **Owner(s):** Gerald A. Bean, See address and contact information above. **Management:** Carol Cormaci, Publisher. April Sperling, Classified Adv. Mgr.. Katrina Ten, Production Director. **Editorial:** Carol Cormaci, Managing Editor. Katrina Ten, Photographer. Ralph Saenz, Sports Editor.

LA JOLLA

LA JOLLA LIGHT. 565 Pearl St., Ste. 300, La Jolla, CA 92037. Telephone: 858-459-4201. FAX: 858-459-5507. E-MAIL: karas@lajollanews.com. URL: http://www.lajollalight.com. Mailing Address: PO Box 1417, Hollister, CA 95024. Year Established: 1913. Pub. Frequency: w. (Thu.) Page Size: broadsheet. Subscrip. Rate: $75/yr mailed out of area. Freelance Pay: $15-$75/article. Circulation: 30,000 per issue (paid and free). **Owner(s):** Main Street Media Group, 350 Sixth St, Hollister, CA 95023. **Management:** Brendan Ruff, Publisher. Ryan Ruff, Classified Adv. Mgr.. Dann Sorensen, Business Manager. **Editorial:** Kara Snow, Executive Editor. David Schwab, Business Editor.

LAGUNA WOODS

LEISURE WORLD NEWS. 24351 El Toro Rd., Laguna Woods, CA 92653. Telephone: 949-837-5200. FAX: 949-837-0106. E-MAIL: mneben@ocregister.com. Mailing Address: PO Box 2068, Laguna Hills, CA 92654. Year Established: 1965. Pub. Frequency: w. (Thu.) Page Size: tabloid. Subscrip. Rate: $.50 newsstand/cover; $13/yr home delivery. Circulation: 11,567 per issue (paid). **Owner(s):** Freedom Communications, Inc., 17666 Fitch, Irvine, CA 92614. Telephone: 849-553-9292. **Management:** Pat Bicoy, Advertising. **Editorial:** Myra Neben, City Editor. Cheryl Walker, Reporter.

LAKE ARROWHEAD

CRESTLINE COURIER-NEWS. 28200 Hwy. 189, Ste. 200, Lake Arrowhead, CA 92352. Telephone: 909-338-1893. FAX: 909-337-5275. URL: www.crestlinecourier-news.com. Mailing Address: PO Box 2410, Lake Arrowhead, CA 92352. Year Established: 1924. Pub. Frequency: w. (Thu.) Page Size: broadsheet. Subscrip. Rate: $.50 newsstand/cover; $21/yr in county. Adv. Rate: col. inch $6.50 Circulation: 2,300 per issue (paid). **Owner(s):** Brehm Communications, Inc., 16644 W. Bernardo Dr., Ste. 300, San Diego, CA 92127. Telephone: 858-451-6200. **Management:** Harry Bradley, Publisher. Allison Hathaway, Business Manager. **Editorial:** Mary Justine Lanyon, Editor.

MOUNTAIN NEWS, THE. 28200 Hwy. 189, Ste. 200, Lake Arrowhead, CA 92352. Telephone: 909-336-3555. FAX: 909-337-5275. E-MAIL: production@mountain-news.com. URL: http://www.mountain-news.com. Mailing Address: PO Box 2410, Lake Arrowhead, CA 92352. Year Established: 1920. Pub. Frequency: w. (Thu.) Page Size: broadsheet. Subscrip. Rate: $.50 newsstand/cover; $26/yr in county; $38/yr out of county. Circulation: 5,700 per issue (paid). **Owner(s):** Brehm Communications, Inc., 16644 W. Bernardo Dr., Ste. 300, San Diego, CA 92127. Telephone: 858-451-6200. **Management:** Harry Bradley, Publisher. Allison Hathaway, Business Manager. **Editorial:** Mary Justine Lanyon, Editor.

MOUNTAIN SHOPPER. 28200 Hwy. 189, Ste. 200, Lake Arrowhead, CA 92352. Telephone: 909-336-3555. FAX: 909-337-5275. URL: http://www.moutain-news.com. Mailing Address: PO Box 2410, Lake Arrowhead, CA 92352. Pub. Frequency: w. (Tue.) Page Size: tabloid Circulation: 16,000 per issue (free). **Owner(s):** Brehm Communications, Inc., 16644 W. Bernardo Dr., Ste. 300, San Diego, CA 92127. Telephone: 858-451-6200. **Management:** Harry Bradley, Publisher. Allison Hathaway, Business Manager. **Editorial:** Mary Justine Lanyon, Editor.

LAKE FOREST

ALISO VIEJO NEWS. 22481 Aspan St., Lake Forest, CA 92630. Telephone: 949-454-7355. FAX: 949-454-7354. E-MAIL: alisoviego@ocregister.com. URL: http://www.ocregister/alisoviego.com. Pub. Frequency: w. (Thu.) Page Size: tabloid Circulation: 7,247 per issue (free). **Owner(s):** Freedom Communications, Inc., 17666 Fitch, Irvine, CA 92614. Telephone: 949-553-9292. **Management:** Chris Anderson, Publisher. Susan Sewell, Advertising. **Editorial:** Cindy O'Dell, City Editor. Larry Shield, Sports.

CAPISTRANO VALLEY NEWS. 22481 Aspan St., Lake Forest, CA 92630. Telephone: 949-454-7355. FAX: 949-454-7354. E-MAIL: capistranovalleynews@ocregister.com. Year Established: 1972. Pub. Frequency: w. (Thu.) Page Size: tabloid Circulation: 15,000 per issue (free). **Owner(s):** Freedom Communications, Inc., 17666 Fitch, Irvine, CA 92614. Telephone: 714-553-9292. **Management:** Tom Gordon, Manager. **Editorial:** Ryan Hammill, Editor. Nellene Teubner, City Editor.

DANA POINT NEWS. 22481 Aspan St., Lake Forest, CA 92630. Telephone: 949-454-7355. FAX: 949-454-7354. E-MAIL: danapoint@ocregister. URL: Http://www.ocregister..com/danapoint. Pub. Frequency: w. (Thu.) Page Size: tabloid Circulation: 10,340 per issue (free). **Owner(s):** Freedom Communications, Inc., 17666 Fitch, Irvine, CA 92614. Telephone: 714-553-9292. **Management:** Chris Anderson, Publisher. Nicole Lindstrom, Advertising Manager. **Editorial:** Magda Liszewska, Editor.

LAGUAN NIGUEL NEWS. 22481 Aspan St., Lake Forest, CA 92630-1630. FAX: 949-454-7354. E-MAIL: saddleback@link.freedom.com. URL: http://www.ocregister.com/lagunaniguel. Year Established: 1972. Pub. Frequency: w. (Thu.) Page Size: tabloid Circulation: 28,701 per issue (free). **Owner(s):** Freedom Communications, Inc., 17666 Fitch, Irvine, CA 92614. Telephone: 949-553-9292. **Management:** Chris Anderson, Publisher. Susan Sewell, Advertising. **Editorial:** Cindy O'Dell, City Editor. Larry Shield, Sports Editor.

LAGUNA NEWS POST. 22481 Aspan St., Lake Forest, CA 92630. Telephone: 949-454-7355. E-MAIL: saddleback@link.freedom.com. URL: http://www.ocregister.com. Year Established: 1915. Pub. Frequency: w. (Thu.) Page Size: tabloid Circulation: 12,000 per issue (free). **Owner(s):** Freedom Communications, Inc., 17666 Fitch, Irvine, CA 92714. Telephone: 714-553-9292. FAX: 714-474-7675. **Management:** Chris Anderson, Publisher. David McDomara, Advertising Manager. **Editorial:** Cathy Lawhon, City Editor. Larry Shield, Sports Editor.

RANCHO SANTA MARGARITA NEWS. 22481 Aspan St., Lake Forest, CA 92630. Telephone: 949-454-7355. FAX: 949-454-7354. E-MAIL: saddleback@link.freedom.com. Pub. Frequency: w. (Fri.) Page Size: tabloid Circulation: 10,000 per issue (free). **Owner(s):** Freedom Communications, Inc., 17666 Fitch, Irvine, CA 92614. Telephone: 714-553-9292. **Management:** Chris Anderson, Publisher. Terry Ludin, Advertising Manager. **Editorial:** Lynn Montagna, Editor.

SADDLEBACK VALLEY NEWS. 22481 Aspan St., Lake Forest, CA 92630. Telephone: 949-454-7355. FAX: 949-454-7354. Pub. Frequency: w. (Fri.) Page Size: tabloid Circulation: 60,528 per issue (free). **Owner(s):** Freedom Communications, Inc., 17666 Fitch, Irvine, CA 92614. Telephone: 714-553-9292. **Management:** Chris Anderson, Publisher. **Editorial:** Warren Esterline, City Editor. Eric LaPack, Sports.

LAKE ISABELLA

KERN VALLEY SUN. 6404 Lake Isabella Blvd., Lake Isabella, CA 93240. Telephone: 760-379-3667. FAX: 760-379-4343. URL: http://www.kvsun.com. Mailing Address: PO Box 3074, Lake Isabella, CA 93240. Year Established: 1957. Pub. Frequency: w. (Wed.) Page Size: broadsheet. Subscrip. Rate: $.50 newsstand/cover; $28/yr home delivery; $34.50/yr mailed in county; $43.60/yr mailed out of county. Circulation: 6,300 per issue (paid). **Owner(s):** Wick Communications, Inc., 333 W. Wilcox Dr., Ste. 302, Sierra Vista, AZ 85635. Telephone: 520-458-0200. FAX: 520-458-6166. **Management:** Marsha Smith, Publisher. Michele Lyn, Advertising. Steve Wheeler, Circulation Manager. **Editorial:** Mike Devich, Managing Editor. Ray Conner, Sports Editor.

LAKE LOS ANGELES

LAKE LOS ANGELES NEWS. 4030 N. 170th St. E., Lake Los Angeles, CA 93591-0109. Telephone: 661-264-0578. FAX: 661-269-2139. E-MAIL: joycemed@pacbell.net. Mailing Address: PO Box 500109, Lake Los Angeles, CA 93591-0109. Pub. Frequency: w. (Fri) Page Size: tabloid. Subscrip. Rate: $.25 newsstand/cover; $49/yr. **Wire Service(s):** UPI. Circulation: 3,100 per issue (paid). **Owner(s):** Joyce Media, Inc., 3413 Soledad Canyon Rd., Acton, CA 93510-0057. Telephone: 661-269-1169. FAX: 661-269-2139. **Management:** Gayle Joyce, President. John Joyce, Publisher. Lynne Sickler, Advertising. John Joyce, Sales Manager. **Editorial:** Gayle Joyce, News Editor.

LAMONT

LAMONT REPORTER. 9717 Main St., Lamont, CA 93241. Telephone: 661-845-3704. FAX: 661-832-0841. Mailing Address: PO Box 548, Lamont, CA 93241. Pub. Frequency: w. (Wed.) Page Size: broadsheet. Subscrip. Rate: $19/yr mailed in county; $21/yr out of county; $24/yr elsewhere. Circulation: 8,100 per issue (paid and free). **Owner(s):** Reed Print, Inc., 5409 Aldrin Ct., Bakersfield, CA 93313. Telephone: 661-834-0496. **Management:** Donald Reed, Publisher. Jason Reed, Advertising. **Editorial:** Jesse Atondo, Editor. Donald L. Reed, Editor-in-Chief.

LINCOLN

LINCOLN NEWS MESSENGER. 553 F St, Lincoln, CA 95648. Telephone: 916-645-7733. FAX: 916-645-2776. E-MAIL: messenger@goldcountrymedia.com. URL: http://www.lincolnnewsmessenger.com. Pub. Frequency: w. (Thu.) Page Size: broadsheet.Subscrip. Rate: $20/yr Circulation: 5,000 per issue (paid). **Owner(s):** Brehm Communications, Inc., 16644 W. Bernardo Dr., Ste. 300, San Diego, CA 92127. Telephone: 858-451-6200. **Management:** Jean Lund, General Manager. Steve Jameson, Classified Adv. Mgr.. **Editorial:** Wendy Lautner, Editor.

LINDEN

LINDEN HERALD. 18974 E. Main St., Linden, CA 95236. Telephone: 209-887-3112. FAX: 209-887-3111. Mailing Address: PO Box 929, Linden, CA 95236. Year Established: 1959. Pub. Frequency: w. (Thu.) Page Size: broadsheet. Subscrip. Rate: $.50 newsstand/cover; $35/yr. Adv. Rate: col. inch $9.50 Freelance Pay: $0.50/column-inch. Circulation: 1,200 per issue (paid). **Owner(s):** Brian Reilly, See address and contact information above. **Management:** Brian Reilly, Publisher. **Editorial:** Brian Reilly, Editor-in-Chief.

LIVERMORE

INDEPENDENT (LIVERMORE), THE. 2250 First St., Livermore, CA 94550. Telephone: 925-447-8700. FAX: 925-447-0212. E-MAIL: editmail@compuserve.com. URL: http://www.independentnews.com. Year Established: 1963. Pub. Frequency: w. (Thu.) Page Size: broadsheet. Subscrip. Rate: $18/yr mailed local; $60/yr mailed out of area. Adv. Rate: col. inch $26.95 Circulation: 49,000 per issue (controlled and free). **Owner(s):** Inland Valley Publishing, See address and contact information above. **Management:** Joan Seppala, Publisher. Tina Rose, Classified Adv. Mgr., David Powell, Associate Publisher. **Editorial:** Janet Armantrout, Editor.

LOCKEFORD

LOCKEFORD CLEMENTS NEWS. 19000 N. Hwy. 88, Ste. B, Lockeford, CA 95237. Telephone: 209-727-5776. FAX: 209-727-3931. E-MAIL: lcnews@inreach.com. Mailing Address: PO Box 76, Lockeford, CA 95237-0076. Year Established: 1948. Pub. Frequency: w. (Wed.) Page Size: tabloid. Subscrip. Rate: $18/yr. Adv. Rate: col. inch $7.27 Freelance Pay: $25/article. Circulation: 4,800 per issue (paid and free). **Owner(s):** Lockeford Clements News, See address and contact information above. **Management:** Mike Henry, Publisher. Robin Sharp, Classified Adv. Mgr.. **Editorial:** Mike Henry, Editor.

LONG BEACH

BEACHCOMBER (LONG BEACH). 5199 E. Pacific Coast Hwy., Ste. 608, Long Beach, CA 90804-3364. E-MAIL: info@longbeachcomber.com. URL: http://www.longbeachcomber.com. Mailing Address: PO Box 15679, Long Beach, CA 90815-0679. Year Established: 1992. Pub. Frequency: bi-w. Page Size: tabloid. Subscrip. Rate: $30/yr. Adv. Rate: B&W page $1,639, color page $2,295 Freelance Pay: $0.12/word. Circulation: 42,000 per issue (paid and controlled). **Owner(s):** Beeler & Associates, See address and contact information above. **Management:** Jay Beeler, Publisher. John Tosdal, Advertising. **Editorial:** Jeff Beeler, Editor.Readers: Homeowners

DOWNTOWN GAZETTE. 5225 E Second St, Long Beach, CA 90803. Telephone: 562-433-2000. FAX: 562-434-8826. E-MAIL: editor@gazettes.com. URL: http://www.gazettes.com. Year Established: 1978. Pub. Frequency: w. (Mon.) Page Size: tabloid.Adv. Rate: col. inch $14 Freelance Pay: $25/article. Circulation: 29,500 per issue (free). **Owner(s):** MediaNews Group, Inc., 101 W Colfax Ave, Ste 1100, Denver, CO 80202. FAX: 303-954-6320. **Management:** Simon Grieve, Publisher. Jonathan Chandler, Advertising Manager. **Editorial:** Harry Saltzgaver, Executive Editor. Kelly Garrison, Feature Editor.

GRUNION GAZETTE. 5225 E Second St, Long Beach, CA 90803. Telephone: 562-433-2000. FAX: 562-434-8826. E-MAIL: editor@gazette.com. URL: http://www.gazettes.com. Year Established: 1978. Pub. Frequency: w. (Thu.) Page Size: tabloid. Subscrip. Rate: $40/yr mailed. Adv. Rate: col. inch $17 Freelance Pay: $25/article. Circulation: 44,000 per issue (free). **Owner(s):** MediaNews Group, Inc., 101 W Colfax Ave, Ste 1100, Denver, CO 80202. FAX: 303-954-6320. **Management:** Simon Grieve, Publisher. Jonathan Chandler, Advertising Manager. **Editorial:** Harry Saltzgaver, Executive Editor.

LOOMIS

LOOMIS NEWS, THE. 3550 Taylor Rd, Loomis, CA 95650. Telephone: 916-652-7939. FAX: 916-652-7879. URL: http://www.theloomisnews.com. Year Established: 1940. Pub. Frequency: w. (Thu.) Page Size: broadsheet. Subscrip. Rate: $.50 newsstand/cover; $26/yr mailed local. Circulation: 5,000 per issue (paid). **Owner(s):** Brehm Communications, Inc., 16644 W. Bernardo Dr., Ste. 300, San Diego, CA 92127. Telephone: 619-451-6200. **Management:** Bill Wallace, Publisher. Martha Garcia, Office Manager. **Editorial:** Martha Garcia, Editor.

LOS ALAMITOS

NEWS ENTERPRISE, THE. ISSN 1095-0850
11110 Los Alamitos Blvd., Ste. 101, Los Alamitos, CA 90720. Telephone: 562-431-1397. FAX: 562-493-2310. E-MAIL: patc@newsenterprise.net. Year Established: 1923. Pub. Frequency: w. (Wed.) Page Size: tabloid. Subscrip. Rate: $40/yr mailed in county; $45/yr mailed out of state. Adv. Rate: page $16 Circulation: 30,000 per issue (paid and free). **Owner(s):** Community Media Inc, 9559 Valley View St., Cyress, CA 90630. Telephone: 714-220-0292. **Management:** Edward Verdugo, Publisher. Gwen Parker, Advertising Manager. **Editorial:** Sean Emory, Editor.

LOS ALTOS

LOS ALTOS TOWN CRIER. ISSN 8750-4588
138 Main St., Los Altos, CA 94022. Telephone: 650-948-9000. FAX: 650-948-6647. E-MAIL: bruceb@latc.com. URL: http://www.latc.com. Year Established: 1947. Pub. Frequency: w. (Wed.) Page Size: tabloid. Subscrip. Rate: $.50 newsstand/cover; $20/yr in county; $40/yr out of county; $15/yr to senior citizens. Freelance Pay: $30-$50/article. Circulation: 16,500 per issue (controlled). **Owner(s):** Los Altos Town Crier Co., Inc., The, See address and contact information above. **Management:** Paul Nyberg, Publisher. Tom Zahiralis, Advertising Manager. Howard Bischoff, Circulation Manager. **Editorial:** Bruce Barton, Editor. Pete Borello, Sports Editor.

LOS ANGELES

ARGONAUT, THE. 5355 McConnell Ave., Los Angeles, CA 90066. Telephone: 310-822-1629. E-MAIL: argienews@aol.com. URL: http://www.argonautnewspaper.com. Mailing Address: PO Box 11209, Marina del Rey, CA 90295-7209. Year Established: 1971. Pub. Frequency: w. (Thu.) Page Size: tabloid. Subscrip. Rate: $4 mailed per issue; $120/yr mailed local 1st class. Adv. Rate: col. inch $36.25 Circulation: 42,000 per issue (paid and free). **Owner(s):** Argonaut, Inc., See address and contact information above. **Management:** David Asper Johnson, Publisher. Rikki Barker, Advertising Director. Carole Keenan, Business Manager. **Editorial:** David Asper Johnson, Editor. Cindy Frazier, News Editor.

EASTWAVE. 4201 Wilshire Blvd., Ste. 600, Los Angeles, CA 90011. Telephone: 323-556-5720. FAX: 323-291-0219. URL: http://www.wavenewspapers.com. Year Established: 1923. Pub. Frequency: w. (Thu.) Page Size: broadsheet. Subscrip. Rate: $25/yr mailed; $35/yr mailed out of area. Adv. Rate: col. inch $65 **Wire Service(s):** CiNS. Circulation: 15,133 per issue (paid and free). **Owner(s):** Wave Community Newspapers, Inc., See address and contact information above. **Management:** Robert Bush, General Manager. Pluria Marshall Jr., Publisher. Andrew Jackson, Circulation Manager. **Editorial:** Don Wanlass, Managing Editor.

ESCONDIDO NEWS-REPORTER. 210 S. Spring St., Los Angeles, CA 90012-3710. Telephone: 213-628-4384. FAX: 213-687-3886. E-MAIL: info@mnc.net. URL: http://www.mnc.net. Mailing Address: PO Box 60859, Los Angeles, CA 90080-0859. Year Established: 1983. Pub. Frequency: w. (Fri.) Page Size: standard. Subscrip. Rate: $.25 newsstand/cover; $48/yr mailed local. **Wire Service(s):** AP. Circulation: 5,000 per issue (paid). **Owner(s):** Metropolitan News Co., See address and contact information above. **Management:** Vahn Babigian, General Manager. Jo-Ann Grace, Publisher. **Editorial:** Roger M. Grace, Editor.

HERALD AMERICAN. 4201 Wilshire Blvd., Ste. 600, Los Angeles, CA 90010. Telephone: 323-556-5720. FAX: 323-556-5704. URL: http://www.wavenewspapers.com. Year Established: 1905. Pub. Frequency: w. (Thu.) Page Size: broadsheet. Subscrip. Rate: $90/yr mailed out of area. Adv. Rate: col. inch $65 **Wire Service(s):** CiNS. Circulation: 15,250 per issue (free). **Owner(s):** Wave Community Newspapers, Inc., See address and contact information above. **Management:** Pluria Marshall Jr., Publisher. Danielle Jake, Sales Manager. **Editorial:** Don Wanlass, Managing Editor.

HOLLYWOOD INDEPENDENT. 4201 Wilshire Blvd., Ste. 600, Los Angeles, CA 90011. Telephone: 323-556-5720. FAX: 323-556-5704. E-MAIL: laingroup@aol.com. URL: http://www.laindependent.com. Year Established: 1935. Pub. Frequency: w. (Wed.) Page Size: broadsheet. Subscrip. Rate: $.25 newsstand/cover; $40 mailed for 6 mos. local; $80/yr mailed out of area. Adv. Rate: col. inch $83.10 **Wire Service(s):** CiNS. Circulation: 159,400 per issue (controlled). **Owner(s):** Wave Newspapers, Inc., See address and contact information above. **Management:** Pluria Marshall Jr., Publisher. Andrew Jackson, Circulation Manager. Danielle Jake, Sales Manager. **Editorial:** Tony Castro, Managing Editor.

L A WEEKLY. ISSN 0192-1940
6715 Sunset Blvd., Los Angeles, CA 90028. Telephone: 323-465-9909. FAX: 323-465-3220. URL: http://www.laweekly.com/. Year Established: 1978. Pub. Frequency: w. **Owner(s):** Village Voice Media, Inc., See address and contact information above. **Management:** Beth Sestanovich, Publisher. **Editorial:** Laurie Ochoa, Editor-in-Chief.

LYNWOOD PRESS EDITION. 4201 Wilshire Blvd., Ste. 600, Los Angeles, CA 90010. Telephone: 323-556-5720. FAX: 323-556-5704. URL: http://www.wavenewspapers.com. Year Established: 1922. Pub. Frequency: s-w. (Wed. & Sat.) Page Size: broadsheet. Subscrip. Rate: $90/yr mailed out of area. Adv. Rate: col. inch $65 **Wire Service(s):** CiNS. Circulation: 24,006 per issue (controlled). **Owner(s):** Wave Community Newspapers, Inc., See address and contact information above. **Management:** Pluria Marshall Jr., Publisher. Andrew Jackson, Circulation Manager. Danielle Jake, Sales Manager. **Editorial:** Don Wanlass, Managing Editor.

NORTHEAST EDITION. 4201 Wilshire Blvd., Ste. 600, Los Angeles, CA 90010. Telephone: 323-556-5720. FAX: 323-556-5704. E-MAIL: djake@wavepublications.com. URL: http://www.wavenewspapers.com. Pub. Frequency: w. (Wed.) Page Size: standard. Subscrip. Rate: $.25 newsstand/cover; $90/yr in state. Adv. Rate: col. inch $65 **Wire Service(s):** CiNS. Circulation: 19,059 per issue (paid). **Owner(s):** Wave Community Newspapers, Inc., See address and contact information above. **Management:** Pluria Marshall Jr., Publisher. Danielle Jake, Sales Manager. **Editorial:** Tony Castro, Executive Editor. Don Wanlass, Managing Editor.

PARK LABREA NEWS/BEVERLY PRESS. 6720 Melrose Ave., Los Angeles, CA 90038. Telephone: 323-933-5518. FAX: 323-933-5812. Mailing Address: PO Box 36036, Los Angeles, CA 90036. Year Established: 1947. Pub. Frequency: w. (Thu.) Page Size: tabloid. Subscrip. Rate: $120/yr mailed. Circulation: 11,000 per issue (controlled). **Owner(s):** Michael & Karen Villalpando, See address and contact information above. **Management:** Karen Villalpando, Publisher. **Editorial:** Ed Folven, Editor.

PRESS (LOS ANGELES), THE. 4201 Wilshire Blvd., Ste. 600, Los Angeles, CA 90010. Telephone: 323-556-5720. FAX: 323-556-5704. URL: http://www.wavenewspapers.com. Year Established: 1943. Pub. Frequency: w. (Thu.) Page Size: broadsheet. Subscrip. Rate: $90/yr mailed. Adv. Rate: col. inch $65 **Wire Service(s):** CiNS. Circulation: 150,000 per issue (free). **Owner(s):** Wave Community Newspapers, Inc., See address and contact information above. **Management:** Pluria Marshall Jr., Publisher. Danielle Jake, Sales Manager. **Editorial:** Don Wanlass, Managing Editor.

RIVERSIDE BULLETIN, THE. 210 S. Spring St., Los Angeles, CA 90012-3710. Telephone: 213-628-4384. FAX: 213-687-3886. E-MAIL: info@mnc.net. URL: http://www.mnc.net. Mailing Address: PO Box 60859, Los Angeles, CA 90060. Pub. Frequency: w. (Fri.) Page Size: standard. Subscrip. Rate: $.25 newsstand/cover; $10/yr in county. **Wire Service(s):** AP. Circulation: 500 per issue (paid). **Owner(s):** Metropolitan News Co., See address and contact information above. **Management:** Jo-Ann W. Grace, Publisher. **Editorial:** Roger M. Grace, Editor.

SAN BERNARDINO BULLETIN, THE. 210 S. Spring St., Los Angeles, CA 90012-3710. Telephone: 213-628-4384. FAX: 213-687-3886. E-MAIL: info@mnc.net. URL: http://www.mnc.net. Mailing Address: PO Box 60859, Los Angeles, CA 90060. Pub. Frequency: w. (Thu.) Page Size: standard. Subscrip. Rate: $.50 newsstand/cover; $69/yr. **Wire Service(s):** AP. Circulation: 300 per issue (paid). **Owner(s):** Metropolitan News Co., See address and contact information above. **Management:** Jo-Ann W. Grace, Publisher. Veronica Lopez, Advertising. Vahn C. Babigian, Asst. General Mgr.. **Editorial:** Roger M. Grace, Editor-in-Chief.

SOULVINE. 4201 Wilshire Blvd., Ste. 600, Los Angeles, CA 90010. Telephone: 323-556-5720. FAX: 323-556-5704. URL: http://www.wavenewspapers.com. Year Established: 1923. Pub. Frequency: w. (Thu.) Page Size: broadsheet. Subscrip. Rate: $90/yr mailed. Adv. Rate: col. inch $65 **Wire Service(s):** CiNS. Circulation: 30,731 per issue (free). **Owner(s):** Wave Community Newspapers, Inc., See address and contact information above. **Management:** Danielle Jake, Sales Manager. Pluria Marshall Jr., Associate Publisher. **Editorial:** Don Wanlass, Executive Editor.

WAVE, THE. 4201 Wilshire Blvd., Ste. 600, Los Angeles, CA 90010. Telephone: 323-556-5720. FAX: 323-556-5704. URL: http://www.wavenewspapers.com. Year Established: 1918. Pub. Frequency: w. (Thu.) Page Size: broadsheet. Subscrip. Rate: $90/yr mailed. Adv. Rate: col. inch $65 **Wire Service(s):** CiNS. Circulation: 150,000 per issue (free). **Owner(s):** Wave Community Newspapers, Inc., See address and contact information above. **Management:** Pluria Marshall Jr., Publisher. Danielle Jake, Sales Manager.

WEST EDITION. 4201 Wilshire Blvd., Ste. 600, Los Angeles, CA 90010. Telephone: 323-556-5720. FAX: 323-556-5704. E-MAIL: djake@wavepublications.com. URL: http://www.wavenewspapers.com. Year Established: 1923. Pub. Frequency: w. (Thu.) Page Size: broadsheet. Subscrip. Rate: $90/yr mailed out of area. Adv. Rate: col. inch $65 **Wire Service(s):** CiNS. Circulation: 31,609 per issue (free). **Owner(s):** Wave Community Newspapers, Inc., See address and contact information above. **Management:** Pluria Marshall Jr., Publisher. Andrew Jackson, Circulation Manager. Danielle Jake, Sales Manager. **Editorial:** Tony Castro, Executive Editor. Don Wanlass, Managing Editor.

LOS BANOS

LOS BANOS ENTERPRISE. 1253 W I St, Los Banos, CA 93635. Telephone: 209-826-3831. FAX: 209-826-2005. E-MAIL: publisher@losbanosenterprise.com. URL: http://www.losbanosenterprise.com. Year Established: 1891. Pub. Frequency: s-w. (Tue. & Fri.) Page Size: broadsheet. Subscrip. Rate: $.50 newsstand/cover; $3.69/mo. in county; $50/yr mailed in county. Circulation: 4,400 per issue (paid); 10,700 per issue (free). **Owner(s):** The/McClatchy Company, 2100 Q St, Sacramento, CA 95816. Telephone: 916-321-1936. FAX: 916-321-1869. **Management:** Gene Lieb, Publisher. Doris McGary, Advertising Manager. Theresa Wood, Circulation Director. **Editorial:** Gene Lieb, Editor. Kim Yancey, Managing Editor.

LOS GATOS

LOS GATOS WEEKLY-TIMES. ISSN 0748-4704
245 Almendra Ave., Los Gatos, CA 95030. Telephone: 408-354-3110. FAX: 408-354-3917. E-MAIL: lgwt@svcn.com. URL: http://www.lgwt.com. Year Established: 1881. Pub. Frequency: w. (Tue.) Page Size: tabloid.Subscrip. Rate: $36/yr mailed in city Circulation: 20,300 per issue (paid). **Owner(s):** Silicon Valley Community Newspapers, 1095 The Alemeda, San Jose, CA 95126. Telephone: 408-200-1000. **Management:** David Cohen, Publisher. Nancy Weigel, Advertising Manager. Kate Fitzgerald, Classified Adv. Mgr.. **Editorial:** Dick Sparrer, Editor. Dale Bryant, Executive Editor. George Sakkestad, Photographer.

SARATOGA NEWS. ISSN 0745-6255
245 Almendra Ave., Los Gatos, CA 95030. Telephone: 408-354-3110. FAX: 408-354-3917. E-MAIL: sn@svcn.com. URL: http://www.svcn.com. Mailing Address: PO Box 65, Los Gatos, CA 95030. Year Established: 1955. Pub. Frequency: w. (Wed.) Page Size: tabloid. Subscrip. Rate: $.50 newsstand/cover; $26/yr local; $52/yr out of area. Circulation: 9,200 per issue (paid). **Owner(s):** Silicon Valley Community Newspapers, 1095 The Alameda, San Jose, CA 95126. Telephone: 408-200-1000. **Management:** David Cohen, Publisher. Jeannette Close, Advertising Manager. **Editorial:** Dale Bryant, Editor. Dick Sparrer, Sports.

MALIBU

MALIBU SURFSIDE NEWS. ISSN 0191-7307
28990 Pacific Coast Hwy., Malibu, CA 90265. Telephone: 310-457-2112. FAX: 310-457-9908. E-MAIL: editor@malibusurfsidenews.com. URL: http://www.malibusurfsidenews.com. Mailing Address: P.O. Box 903, Malibu, CA 90265. Year Established: 1972. Pub. Frequency: w. (Thu.) Page Size: tabloid. Subscrip. Rate: $.25 newsstand/cover; $50/yr home delivery local; $95/yr mailed out of city; $150/yr mailed elsewhere. Adv. Rate: col. inch $20 Circulation: 13,500 per issue (controlled). **Owner(s):** Malibu News Enterprises, Inc., See address and contact information above. **Management:** Anne C. Soble, Publisher. Kaori Ueda Ibrahim, Production Director. **Editorial:** Anne C. Soble, Editor. Peggy Hall Kaplan, Feature Editor.

MALIBU TIMES. ISSN 1050-4931
PO Box 1127, Malibu, CA 90265. Telephone: 310-456-5507. FAX: 310-456-8786. E-MAIL: agyork@malibutimes.com. URL: http://www.malibutimes.com. Year Established: 1946. Pub. Frequency: w. (Thu.) Page Size: broadsheet. Subscrip. Rate: $.50 newsstand/cover; $50 mailed for 6 mos.; $70/yr mailed. Circulation: 12,000 per issue (paid and free). **Owner(s):** Arnold G. & Karen P. York, See address and contact information above. **Management:** Arnold G. York, Publisher. **Editorial:** Laura Tate, Editor. Arnold G. York, Managing Editor.

MAMMOTH LAKES

MAMMOTH TIMES. 452 Old Mamouth Rd, Mammoth Lakes, CA 93546. Telephone: 760-934-3929. FAX: 760-934-3951. E-MAIL: news@mammothtimes.com. URL: http://mammothtimes.com/. Year Established: 1987. Pub. Frequency: w. (Thu.) Page Size: tabloid. Subscrip. Rate: $.50 newsstand/cover; $36/yr local; $56/yr mailed out of area. Circulation: 8,500 per issue (paid and free). **Owner(s):** Horizon Publications, Inc., 1120 N. Carbon St., Ste.100, Marion, IL 62959. Telephone: 618-993-1693. **Management:** Patti Cole, General Manager. Sharon Dare, Publisher. Dave Michalski, Advertising. **Editorial:** Diane Eagle, Editor.

MANHATTAN BEACH

BEACH REPORTER, THE. 400 S Sepulvedo Blvd, Ste 247, Manhattan Beach, CA 90266. Telephone: 310-372-0388. FAX: 310-372-6113. URL: http://www.tbrnews.com. Year Established: 1977. Pub. Frequency: w. (Thu.) Page Size: tabloid. Subscrip. Rate: $80 mailed for 6 mos. in county; $160/yr mailed. Circulation: 55,500 per issue (free). **Owner(s):** MediaNews Group, Inc., PO Box 65210, Colorado Springs, CO 80962. **Management:** Paul Silva, Publisher. Jim Curnutt, Advertising Manager. **Editorial:** Paul Silva, Editor. Dawnya Pring, Managing Editor.

MANTECA

LATHROP BULLETIN. 531 E Yosemite Ave, Manteca, CA 95336. Telephone: 209-249-3500. FAX: 209-549-3559. Pub. Frequency: w. (Fri) **Owner(s):** Morris Newspaper Corporation, 27 Abercorn St., Savannah, GA 31401. Telephone: 912-233-1281. FAX: 912-232-4639.

RIPON BULLETIN. 531 E Yosemite Ave, Manteca, CA 95336. Telephone: 209-249-3500. FAX: 209-549-3559. Pub. Frequency: w. (Wed) **Owner(s):** Morris Newspaper Corporation, 27 Abercorn St., Savannah, GA 31401. Telephone: 912-233-1281. FAX: 912-232-4639.

MARIPOSA

MARIPOSA GAZETTE. PO Box 38, Mariposa, CA 95338. Telephone: 209-966-2500. FAX: 209-966-3384. E-MAIL: jballinger@sti.net. Year Established: 1854. Pub. Frequency: w. (Wed.) Page Size: broadsheet. Subscrip. Rate: $.50 newsstand/cover; $29/yr mailed in county; $38/yr mailed out of county. Circulation: 5,300 per issue (paid). **Owner(s):** Dan Tucker, See address and contact information above. **Management:** Dan Tucker, Publisher. **Editorial:** Jill Ballinger, Managing Editor.

MARTINEZ

MARTINEZ NEWS GAZETTE. 615 Estudillo St., Martinez, CA 94553. Telephone: 925-228-6400. FAX: 925-228-1536. E-MAIL: mtzgaz@dnai.com. Mailing Address: PO Box 151, Martinez, CA 94553. Year Established: 1858. Pub. Frequency: 3/w. (Tue., Thu., Sat.) Page Size: broadsheet. Subscrip. Rate: $.50 newsstand/cover; $50/yr home delivery. Circulation: 15,000 per issue (paid). **Owner(s):** Gibson Publications, Inc., 544 Curtola Pkwy, Vallejo, CA 94590. Telephone: 707-643-2552. **Management:** David Payne, Publisher. Sam LiRon, Circulation Manager. **Editorial:** Richie Parks, Editor.

MENLO PARK

ALMANAC (MENLO PARK), THE. ISSN 0192-0111
3525 Alameda De Las Pulgas, Menlo Park, CA 94025-4455. Telephone: 650-854-2626. FAX: 650-854-0677. E-MAIL: editor@calmanac.com. URL: http://www.almanacnews.com. Mailing Address: PO Box 1610, Palo Alto, CA 94302. Year Established: 1965. Pub. Frequency: w. (Wed.) Page Size: tabloid. Subscrip. Rate: $.50 newsstand/cover; $50/yr mailed elsewhere. Adv. Rate: col. inch $22.05 Circulation: 17,500 per issue (paid and free). **Owner(s):** Embarcadero Media, 703 High St, Palo Alto, CA 94302. Telephone: 650-326-8210. FAX: 650-326-3928. **Management:** Tom Gibboney, Publisher. Neal Fine, Advertising Director. Bill Rayburn, Classified Adv. Mgr.. **Editorial:** Tom Gibboney, Editor. Richard Hine, Managing Editor. Renee Batti, News Editor.

MERCED

ATWATER SIGNAL, THE. 3033 N. G St., Merced, CA 95340. Telephone: 209-722-1511. FAX: 209-385-2460. E-MAIL: creitor@mercedsunstar.com. URL: http://www.mercedsunstar.com. Mailing Address: PO Box 739, Merced, CA 95341. Year Established: 1911. Pub. Frequency: w. (Fri.) Page Size: broadsheet. Circulation: 11,500 per issue (controlled and free). **Owner(s):** The/McClatchy Company, 2100 Q St, Sacramento, CA 95816. Telephone: 916-321-1936. **Management:** Hank VanderVeen, Publisher. Larry Dovichi, Advertising Director. **Editorial:** Joe Kieta, Editor. Mike Fitzgerald, City Editor.

ATWATER TIMES. 2221 K St., Merced, CA 95340. E-MAIL: midvalleypub@aol.com. Mailing Address: PO Box 772, Merced, CA 95341. Pub. Frequency: w. (Thu.) Page Size: tabloid. Subscrip. Rate: $.50 newsstand/cover; $27/yr mailed in county; $27/yr mailed out of county. Adv. Rate: col. inch $11.95 Circulation: 2,800 per issue (paid). **Owner(s):** Mid-Valley Publications, Inc., 6950 Gerard St., Winton, CA 95388. Telephone: 209-358-5311. FAX: 209-358-7108. **Management:** John Derby, Publisher. Fran Sodini, Circulation Manager. Kim McGowen, Classified Adv. Mgr.. **Editorial:** Sarah Sanders, Editor. John Derby, Managing Editor.

DENAIR DISPATCH. 2221 K St., Merced, CA 95340. E-MAIL: midvalleypub@aol.com. Mailing Address: PO Box 772, Merced, CA 95341. Pub. Frequency: w. (Wed.) Page Size: broadsheet. Subscrip. Rate: $.50 newsstand/cover; $27/yr mailed in county; $30/yr mailed out of county. Adv. Rate: col. inch $11.95 Circulation: 2,500 per issue (paid). **Owner(s):** Mid-Valley Publications, Inc., 6950 Gerard St., Winton, CA 95388. Telephone: 209-358-5311. FAX: 209-358-7108. **Management:** John Derby, Publisher. Fran Sodini, Circulation Manager. Kim McGowen, Classified Adv. Mgr.. **Editorial:** Cindy Citti, Editor. John Derby, Managing Editor.

HILMAR TIMES. 2221 K St., Merced, CA 95340. E-MAIL: midvalleypub@aol.com. Mailing Address: PO Box 772, Merced, CA 95341. Pub. Frequency: w. (Thu.) Page Size: broadsheet. Subscrip. Rate: $.50 newsstand/cover; $27/yr mailed in county; $30/yr mailed out of county. Adv. Rate: col. inch $11.95 Circulation: 700 per issue (paid). **Owner(s):** Mid-Valley Publications, Inc., 6950 Gerard St., Winton, CA 95388. Telephone: 209-358-5311. FAX: 209-358-7108. **Management:** John Derby, Publisher. Fran Sodini, Circulation Manager. Kim McGowen, Classified Adv. Mgr.. **Editorial:** Michelle Harvey, Editor.

HUGHSON CHRONICLE. 2221 K St., Merced, CA 95340. E-MAIL: midvalleypub@aol.com. Mailing Address: PO Box 772, Merced, CA 95341. Pub. Frequency: w. (Tue.) Page Size: broadsheet. Subscrip. Rate: $.50 newsstand/cover; $27/yr mailed in county; $30/yr mailed out of county. Adv. Rate: col. inch $11.95 Circulation: 4,200 per issue (paid). **Owner(s):** Mid-Valley Publications, Inc., 6950 Gerard St., Winton, CA 95388. Telephone: 209-358-5311. FAX: 209-358-7108. **Management:** John Derby, Publisher. Fran Sodini, Circulation Manager. Kim McGowen, Classified Adv. Mgr.. **Editorial:** Caprice Epp, Editor. John Derby, Managing Editor.

LIVINGSTON CHRONICLE, THE. 3033 N. G St., Merced, CA 95340. Telephone: 209-722-1511. FAX: 209-385-2460. URL: http://www.mercedsun-star.com. Mailing Address: PO Box 739, Merced, CA 95341. Pub. Frequency: w. (Wed.) Page Size: broadsheet. Circulation: 8,500 per issue (controlled and free). **Owner(s):** The/McClatchy Company, 2100 Q St, Sacramento, CA 95816. Telephone: 916-321-1936. FAX: 916-321-1869. **Management:** Hank VanderVeen, Publisher. Larry Dovichi, Advertising Director. Victor Quiralte, Circulation Director.

MERCED COUNTY TIMES. 2221 K St., Merced, CA 95340. E-MAIL: midvalleypub@aol.com. Mailing Address: PO Box 772, Merced, CA 95341. Pub. Frequency: w. (Thu.) Page Size: tabloid. Subscrip. Rate: $.50 newsstand/cover; $27/yr mailed in county; $30/yr mailed out of county. Circulation: 2,200 per issue (paid). **Owner(s):** Mid-Valley Publications, Inc., 6950 Gerard St., Winton, CA 95388. Telephone: 209-358-5311. FAX: 209-358-7108. **Management:** John Derby, Publisher. Fran Sodini, Circulation Manager. Kim McGowen, Classified Adv. Mgr.. **Editorial:** Sarah Sanders, Editor. John Derby, Managing Editor.

WATERFORD NEWS. 2221 K St., Merced, CA 95340. E-MAIL: midvalleypub@aol.com. Mailing Address: PO Box 772, Merced, CA 95341. Pub. Frequency: w. (Tue.) Page Size: broadsheet. Subscrip. Rate: $.50 newsstand/cover; $27/yr mailed in county; $30/yr mailed out of county. Adv. Rate: col. inch $11.95 Circulation: 6,000 per issue (paid). **Owner(s):** Mid-Valley Publications, Inc., 6950 Gerard St., Winton, CA 95388. Telephone: 209-358-5311. FAX: 209-358-7108. **Management:** John Derby, Publisher. Fran Sodini, Circulation Manager. Kim McGowen, Classified Adv. Mgr.. **Editorial:** Paul Kelly, Editor. John Derby, Managing Editor.

WINTON TIMES. 2221 K St., Merced, CA 95340. Telephone: 209-383-0433. FAX: 209-383-0344. Mailing Address: PO Box 772, Merced, CA 95341. Pub. Frequency: w. (Thu.) Page Size: broadsheet. Subscrip. Rate: $.50 newsstand/cover; $27/yr mailed in county; $29/yr mailed out of county. Adv. Rate: col. inch $11.95 Circulation: 1,600 per issue (paid). **Owner(s):** Mid-Valley Publications, Inc., 6950 Gerard St., Winton, CA 95388. Telephone: 209-358-5311. **Management:** John Derby, Publisher. Kim McGowen, Classified Adv. Mgr.. **Editorial:** Kelly Thomas, Editor. John Derby, Managing Editor.

MILIPITAS

BERRYESSA SUN. 59 Marylinn Dr, Milipitas, CA 95035. Telephone: 408-262-2454. FAX: 408-263-9710. E-MAIL: news@themilpitaspost.com. URL: http://www.themilpitaspost.com. Year Established: 1992. Pub. Frequency: m. Page Size: tabloid.Subscrip. Rate: $.50 newsstand/cover; $13/yr Circulation: 15,900 per issue (paid). **Owner(s):** MediaNews Group, Inc., 101 W Colfax Ave, Ste 1100, Denver, CO 80202. FAX: 303-954-6320. **Management:** Rob Devincenzi, Publisher. **Editorial:** Rob Devincenzi, Editor.

FREMONT BULLETIN. 59 Marylinn Dr, Milipitas, CA 95035. Telephone: 408-262-2454. FAX: 408-263-9710. E-MAIL: thepost@cwo.com. URL: http://www.themilpitaspost.com. Pub. Frequency: w. (Sat.) Page Size: broadsheet. Subscrip. Rate: $.50 newsstand/cover; $30/yr local town; $35/yr mailed. Circulation: 30,000 per issue (paid). **Owner(s):** MediaNews Group, Inc., 101 W Colfax Ave, Ste 1100, Denver, CO 80202. FAX: 303-954-6320. **Management:** Rob Devincenzi, Publisher. **Editorial:** Rob Devincenzi, Editor.

MILPITAS POST. ISSN 0745-6212
59 Marylinn Dr, Milipitas, CA 95035. Telephone: 408-262-2454. FAX: 408-263-9710. E-MAIL: thepost@themilpitaspost.com. URL: http://www.themilpitaspost.com. Year Established: 1955. Pub. Frequency: w. (Thu.) Page Size: tabloid. Subscrip. Rate: $.50 newsstand/cover; $25/yr carrier delivery town; $35/yr mailed out of county. Freelance Pay: $15-$20/article. Circulation: 23,000 per issue (paid). **Owner(s):** MediaNews Group, Inc., 101 W Colfax Ave, Ste 1100, Denver, CO 80202. FAX: 303-954-6320. **Management:** Rob Devincenzi, Publisher. **Editorial:** Rob Devincenzi, Editor.

MORGAN HILL

MORGAN HILL TIMES. 30 E Third St, Morgan Hill, CA 95038. Telephone: 408-842-6400. FAX: 408-779-3886. E-MAIL: waltglines@morganhilltimes.com. URL: http://www.morganhilltimes.com. Mailing Address: PO Box 757, Morgan Hill, CA 95038. Year Established: 1894. Pub. Frequency: s-w. (Tue. & Fri.) Page Size: broadsheet. Subscrip. Rate: $.50 newsstand/cover; $30/yr carrier delivery; $54.38/yr mailed; $93.75/yr out of town. Freelance Pay: $20/article. Circulation: 4,200 per issue (controlled). **Owner(s):** Main Street Media Group, 6400 Monterey St, Gilroy, CA 95020. Telephone: 408-842-6400. FAX: 408-802-7105. **Management:** Steve Staloch, Publisher. David Marin, VP Advertising. Walt Glines, Circulation Manager. Carrie Gault, Classified Adv. Mgr..

MORRO BAY

CENTRAL COAST SUN BULLETIN. 1149 Market Ave., Morro Bay, CA 93442. Telephone: 805-772-7346. FAX: 805-772-7044. Mailing Address: PO Box 112, San Luis Obispo, CA 93406. Year Established: 1931. Pub. Frequency: w. (Wed.) Page Size: tabloid. Subscrip. Rate: $.50 newsstand/cover; $26/yr home delivery; $45/yr mailed. Adv. Rate: col. inch $9.25 Circulation: 3,400 per issue (paid); 1,000 per issue (free). **Owner(s):** Knight Ridder, Inc., 50 W. San Fernando St., Ste. 1200, San Jose, CA 95113. Telephone: 831-938-7777. FAX: 831-938-7755. **Management:** Frank Virnig, Advertising Manager. Mark Smith, Circulation Manager. **Editorial:** Antonio A. Prado, Editor. Lindsay Christians, Reporter.

MOUNTAIN VIEW

MOUNTAIN VIEW VOICE. 655 W. Evelyn Ave., Mountain View, CA 94041. Telephone: 650-964-6300. FAX: 650-964-0294. URL: http://www.mv-voice.com. Mailing Address: PO Box 1610, Palo Alto, CA 94302. Pub. Frequency: w. (Fri.) Page Size: tabloid. Subscrip. Rate: $50/yr out of area. Adv. Rate: col. inch $18.40 Circulation: 18,000 per issue (paid). **Owner(s):** Embarcadero Media, 703 High St, Palo Alto, CA 94302. Telephone: 650-326-8210. FAX: 650-326-3928. **Management:** Tom Gibboney, Publisher. Britt Calloway, Advertising Manager. **Editorial:** Don Frances, Managing Editor.

MT. SHASTA

DUNSMUIR NEWS. 924B N. Mt. Shasta Blvd., Mt. Shasta, CA 96067-0127. Telephone: 530-926-5214. FAX: 530-926-4166. E-MAIL: news@mtshastanews.com. URL: http://www.mtshastanews.com. Mailing Address: PO Box 127, Mt. Shasta, CA 96067-0127. Year Established: 1890. Pub. Frequency: w. (Wed.) Page Size: standard. Subscrip. Rate: $.75 newsstand/cover; $28.50/yr in county; $31.50/yr mailed out of county (effective 2007); $33.50/yr mailed out of state. Circulation: 12,000 per issue (paid). **Owner(s):** GateHouse Media, Inc, 350 WillowBrook Office Park, Fairport, NY 14450. Telephone: 585-598-0030. **Management:** Genny Axtman, Publisher. Julie Anderson, Advertising. Dave Reynolds, Circulation Manager. Angie Case, Classified Adv. Mgr.. **Editorial:** Steve Gerace, Editor.

LINK (MT. SHASTA), THE. 924B N. Mt. Shasta Blvd., Mt. Shasta, CA 96067-0127. Telephone: 530-926-6166. FAX: 530-926-4166. Mailing Address: PO Box 360, Mt. Shasta, CA 96067. Pub. Frequency: w. (Wed.) Page Size: standard Circulation: 16,000 per issue (free). **Owner(s):** GateHouse Media, Inc, 350 WillowBrook Office Park, Fairport, NY 14450. Telephone: 585-598-0030. FAX: 585-248-2631. **Management:** Genny Axtman, Publisher. Charlies Poulis, Advertising. Dave Reynolds, Circulation Manager. Miki Simonson, Classified Adv. Mgr..

MOUNT SHASTA HERALD. 924B N. Mt. Shasta Blvd., Mt. Shasta, CA 96067-0127. Telephone: 530-926-5214. FAX: 530-926-4166. E-MAIL: news@mtshastanews.com. URL: http://www.mtshastanews.com. Mailing Address: PO Box 127, Mt. Shasta, CA 96067-0127. Year Established: 1887. Pub. Frequency: w. (Wed.) Page Size: broadsheet. Subscrip. Rate: $.75 newsstand/cover; $28.50/yr carrier delivery in county; $31.50/yr mailed in county; $33.50/yr mailed out of county. Adv. Rate: col. inch $9.75 Circulation: 3,500 per issue (paid). **Owner(s):** GateHouse Media, Inc, 350 WillowBrook Office Park, Fairport, NY 14450. Telephone: 585-598-0030. **Management:** Genny Axtman, Publisher. Julie Anderson, Advertising. Dave Reynolds, Circulation Manager. Angie Case, Classified Adv. Mgr.. **Editorial:** Steve Gerace, Editor. Rob McCallum, Sports.

VOICE OF THE MOUNTAIN. 924B N. Mt. Shasta Blvd., Mt. Shasta, CA 96067-0127. Telephone: 530-926-6166, 530-926-5214. Mailing Address: PO Box 127, Mt. Shasta, CA 96067-0127. Pub. Frequency: w. (Wed.) Page Size: standard Circulation: 4,050 per issue (free). **Owner(s):** GateHouse Media, Inc, See address and contact information above. **Management:** Genny Axtman, Publisher. Julie Anderson, Advertising. Dave Reynolds, Circulation Manager. Angie Case, Classified Adv. Mgr..

WEED PRESS. 924B N. Mt. Shasta Blvd., Mt. Shasta, CA 96067-0127. Telephone: 530-926-5214. FAX: 530-926-4166. E-MAIL: news@mtshastanews.com. URL: http://www.mtshastanews.com. Mailing Address: PO Box 127, Mt. Shasta, CA 96067-0127. Year Established: 1925. Pub. Frequency: w. (Wed.) Page Size: broadsheet. Subscrip. Rate: $.75 newsstand/cover; $28.50/yr in county; $33.50/yr out of county. Adv. Rate: col. inch $9.75 Circulation: 1,700 per issue (paid). **Owner(s):** GateHouse Media, Inc, 350 WillowBrook Office Park, Fairport, NY 14450. Telephone: 585-598-0030. **Management:** Genny Axtman, Publisher. Julie Anderson, Advertising. Dave Reynolds, Circulation Manager. Angie Case, Classified Adv. Mgr.. **Editorial:** Steve Gerace, Editor.

NEEDLES

NEEDLES DESERT STAR. 911 Third St., Needles, CA 92363. Telephone: 760-326-2222. FAX: 760-326-3480. E-MAIL: needlesdesertstar@sitlink.net. URL: http://www.thedesertstar.com. Year Established: 1888. Pub. Frequency: w. (Wed.) Page Size: standard. Subscrip. Rate: $.50 newsstand/cover; $13.95/yr local; $36.30/yr in county; $40.70/yr elsewhere. Circulation: 24,000 per issue (paid). **Owner(s):** Brehm Communications, Inc., 16644 W. Bernardo Dr., Ste. 300, San Diego, CA 92127. Telephone: 858-451-6200. **Management:** Steve Seager, General Manager. Chuck Rathbun, Publisher. Wells Andrews, Advertising Manager. Larry Imoe, Circulation Manager. Kathy Jones, Classified Adv. Mgr.. **Editorial:** Robin Richards, Editor.

NOVATO

NORTH MARIN NEWS. 1068 Machin Ave., Novato, CA 94945. Telephone: 415-892-1516. FAX: 415-897-0940. E-MAIL: publisher@novatoadvance.com. URL: http://www.novatoadvance.com. Mailing Address: PO Box 8, Novato, CA 94948. Pub. Frequency: w. (Wed.) Page Size: broadsheet. Subscrip. Rate: $41/yr. Adv. Rate: col. inch $26.50 Circulation: 7,500 per issue (free). **Owner(s):** Scripps Enterprises, PO Box 1109, Herndon, VA 22070. **Management:** Paul D Hutchesen, Publisher. Dick Blaustein, Advertising Manager. Linda Mallin, Circulation Manager. **Editorial:** Mary Connell, Editor. Dan Stebbins, Executive Editor.

NOVATO ADVANCE. 1068 Machin Ave., Novato, CA 94945. Telephone: 415-892-1516. FAX: 415-897-0940. E-MAIL: publisher@ novatoadvance.com. URL: http://www.novatoadvance.com. Mailing Address: PO Box 8, Novato, CA 94948. Year Established: 1922. Pub. Frequency: w. (Wed.) Page Size: standard. Subscrip. Rate: $.50 newsstand/cover; $41/yr home delivery. Adv. Rate: col. inch $23.70 Circulation: 8,000 per issue (paid). **Owner(s):** Scripps Enterprises, PO Box 1109, Herndon, VA 22070. **Management:** Paul D Hutchesen, Publisher. Dick Blaustein, Advertising Director. Susan Coddington, Circulation Manager. **Editorial:** Mary Connell, Editor. Patricia Goodin, Reporter.

OAKDALE

OAKDALE LEADER. PO Box 278, Oakdale, CA 95361. Telephone: 209-847-3021. FAX: 209-847-9750. E-MAIL: mitch@oakdaleleader.net. Year Established: 1882. Pub. Frequency: w. (Wed.) Page Size: broadsheet. Subscrip. Rate: $.50 newsstand/cover; $31/yr mailed in county; $38/yr mailed out of county; $26/yr mailed in county to senior citizens. Circulation: 10,000 per issue (paid and free). **Owner(s):** Morris Newspaper Corporation, 27 Abercorn St., Savannah, GA 31401. Telephone: 912-233-1281. FAX: 912-232-4639. **Management:** Bill Camp, Publisher. Melinda Owen, Advertising Manager. Peggy Ragle, Circulation Manager. **Editorial:** Mitchell Naylor, Managing Editor. Marg Jackson, Assistant Editor.

OAKHURST

SIERRA STAR, THE. 49165 Crane Valley Rd, Oakhurst, CA 93644. Telephone: 559-683-4464. FAX: 559-683-8102. URL: http://www.sierrastar.com. Mailing Address: PO Box 305, Oakhurst, CA 93644-0305. Year Established: 1958. Pub. Frequency: s-w. (Wed. & Fri.) Page Size: standard. Subscrip. Rate: $.50 newsstand/cover; $50.64/yr home delivery in county; $72/yr mailed out of county. Circulation: 15,700 per issue (paid and free). **Owner(s):** The/McClatchy Company, 2100 Q St, Sacramento, CA 95816. Telephone: 916-321-1936. FAX: 916-321-1869. **Management:** Betty E Linn, Publisher. Greg Wilde, Advertising Manager. **Editorial:** David Richards, Editor.

OJAI

OJAI VALLEY NEWS. 408-A Bryant Cir, Ojai, CA 93023. Telephone: 805-646-1476. FAX: 805-646-4281. URL: http://www.ojaivalleynews.com. Mailing Address: PO Box 277, Ojai, CA 93024. Year Established: 1891. Pub. Frequency: s-w. (Wed. & Fri.) Page Size: broadsheet. Subscrip. Rate: $.50 newsstand/cover; $30 home delivery for 6 mos. local; $48/yr home delivery; $50 mailed for 6 mos.; $75/yr mailed. Circulation: 11,100 per issue (paid and free). **Owner(s):** Ojai Newspapers LLC, See address and contact information above. **Management:** Bill Buchanan, Owner. Bret Bradigan, Publisher. Jeanne Miller, Classified Adv. Mgr.. Jodie Miller, Business Manager. **Editorial:** Lenny Roberts, Managing Editor. Chris Contle, Photographer. Misty Volaski, Sports Editor.

ORLAND

ORLAND PRESS-REGISTER. 401 Walker St, Orland, CA 95988. Telephone: 530-865-4433. FAX: 530-865-3110. E-MAIL: editor@tcnpress.com. Year Established: 1868. Pub. Frequency: s-w. (Wed. & Fri.) Page Size: broadsheet. Subscrip. Rate: $.75 newsstand/cover; $65/yr mailed out of county. Circulation: 5,000 per issue (paid and free). **Owner(s):** Morris Newspaper Corporation, 27 Abercorn St., Savannah, GA 31401. Telephone: 912-233-1281. FAX: 912-232-4639. **Management:** Dale Bean, General Manager. Christine Hammers, Advertising Manager. Deanna McGarr, Circulation Manager. **Editorial:** Bill Rozak, Managing Editor.

OROVILLE

DIGGER SHOPPER & NEWS, THE. 2057 Mitchell Ave., Oroville, CA 95966. Telephone: 530-533-2170. FAX: 530-533-2181. E-MAIL: suzanne@diggernews.com. URL: http://www.diggernews.com/. Mailing Address: PO Box 5006, Oroville, CA 95966-5006. Year Established: 1977. Pub. Frequency: w. (Tue.) Page Size: tabloid Subscrip. Rate: $52/yr Circulation: 19,000 per issue (free). **Owner(s):** David Miller, See address and contact information above. **Management:** David Miller, Publisher. Tammy DeLuccia, Classified Adv. Mgr.. Suzanne Legg, Business Manager. **Editorial:** Patti Day-Miller, Editor. Lee Elmore, Production Manager.

PACIFIC GROVE

CARMEL PINE CONE. 734 Lighthouse, Pacific Grove, CA 93950. Telephone: 831-274-8603. FAX: 831-375-5018. E-MAIL: mail@carmelpinecone.com. URL: http://www.carmelpinecone.com. Mailing Address: P.O. Box G-1, Carmel, CA 93950. Year Established: 1915. Pub. Frequency: w. (Fri.) Page Size: tabloid. Subscrip. Rate: $143 mailed for 6 mos. 1st class mail; $78 mailed for 6 mos. 3 rd.class mail. Circulation: 23,000 per issue (paid and free). **Owner(s):** Carmel Communications, Inc., See address and contact information above. **Management:** Paul Miller, Publisher. Tim Cadigan, Advertising Manager.Readers: Affluent residents - Pebble Beach, Carmel.

PACIFIC PALISADES

PALISADIAN-POST. 839 Via De La Paz, Pacific Palisades, CA 90272. Telephone: 310-454-1321. FAX: 310-454-1078. E-MAIL: palipost@aol.com. URL: http://www.palisadespost.com. Mailing Address: PO Box 725, Pacific Palisades, CA 90272. Year Established: 1928. Pub. Frequency: w. (Thu.) Page Size: broadsheet. Subscrip. Rate: $.50 newsstand/cover; $45/yr mailed in county; $65/yr mailed out of county. Circulation: 6,000 per issue (paid). **Owner(s):** Small Newspaper Group, 8 Dearborn Sq., Kankakee, IL 60901. **Bureau(s):** 1063 National Press Building, Washington, DC 20045. Telephone: 202-393-0418. **Management:** Roberta Donahue, Publisher. Eve DeVeir, Advertising Manager. Sharon Reynolds, Circulation Manager. **Editorial:** Bill Bruns, Managing Editor. Libby Motika, Senior Editor. Laura Witsenhausen, Associate Editor. Steve Galluzzo, Sports Editor.

POST SHOPPER. 839 Via de la Paz, Pacific Palisades, CA 90272-0725. Telephone: 310-454-1321. FAX: 310-454-1078. E-MAIL: palipost@aol.com. URL: http://www.palisadespost.com. Mailing Address: PO Box 725, Pacific Palisades, CA 90272. Year Established: 1928. Pub. Frequency: w. (Thu.) Page Size: broadsheet Circulation: 11,600 per issue (free). **Owner(s):** Small Newspaper Group, 8 Dearborn Sq., Kankakee, IL 60901. **Management:** Tom Small, President. Roberta Donohue, Publisher. Eve DeVeir, Advertising Manager. Sharon Reynolds, Circulation Manager. Cheryel Kanan, Business Manager. **Editorial:** Bill Bruns, Managing Editor. Libby Motika, Senior Editor. Laura Witsenhausen, Feature Editor. Linda Renaud, News Editor. Steve Galluzzo, Sports Editor.

PACIFICA

PACIFICA TRIBUNE. 59 Aura Vista, Pacifica, CA 94044. Telephone: 650-359-6666. FAX: 650-359-3821. E-MAIL: pactrib@hax.com. URL: http://www.pacificatribune.com. Mailing Address: P O Box 1189, Pacifica, CA 94044. Year Established: 1947. Pub. Frequency: w. (Wed.) Page Size: broadsheet. Subscrip. Rate: $.50 newsstand/cover; $30/yr carrier delivery; $35/yr mailed in county; $36/yr out of county. Circulation: 7,451 per issue (paid). **Owner(s):** MediaNews Group, Inc., 101 W Colfax Ave, Ste 1100, Denver, CO 80202. FAX: 303-954-6320. **Management:** Elaine Larsen, Publisher. Gregory Brand, Circulation Manager. Lavern Meeks, Classified Adv. Mgr.. **Editorial:** Elaine Larsen, Editor.

PALM DESERT

COACHELLA VALLEY WHITE SHEET. 73-400 Hwy. 111, Palm Desert, CA 92260. Telephone: 760-346-0601. FAX: 760-779-1354. E-MAIL: katurner@desertshoppers.net. URL: http://www.greenandwhitesheet.com.Pub. Frequency: w. (Thu.) Circulation: 38,000 per issue (free). **Owner(s):** Schurz Communications, Inc., 225 W. Colfax Ave., South Bend, IN 46626. Telephone: 574-287-1001. FAX: 574-287-2257. **Management:** Hal Paradis, Publisher. Robert Witt, Circulation Manager. Kim Turner, Sales Manager.

DESERT MOBILE HOME NEWS. 74-361 Hwy 111, Ste 12, Palm Desert, CA 92260. Telephone: 790-568-6633. FAX: 790-776-5733n. E-MAIL: ads@desertmobilehomenews.com. Mailing Address: PO Box 3386, Palm Desert, CA 92260-3386. Year Established: 1954. Pub. Frequency: w. (Fri. (Oct.-May)) Page Size: tabloid Circulation: 14,000 per issue (free). **Owner(s):** Brehm Communications, Inc., 16644 W. Bernardo Dr., Ste. 300, San Diego, CA 92128. **Management:** John McGucken, General Manager. Ken Larson, Advertising Director.

PALO ALTO

PACIFIC SUN. ISSN 0048-2641
703 High St, Palo Alto, CA 94302. Telephone: 650-326-8210. FAX: 650-326-3928. URL: http://www.pacificsun.com. Year Established: 1963. Pub. Frequency: w. (Fri.) Page Size: tabloid. Subscrip. Rate: $60/yr mailed. Circulation: 31,000. **Owner(s):** Embarcadero Media, See address and contact information above. **Management:** Linda Black, Advertising Director. Beth Allen, Production Director.Readers: All of Marin County

PALO ALTO WEEKLY. ISSN 0199-1159
450 Cambridge Ave, Palo Alto, CA 94306. E-MAIL: editor@paweekly.com. URL: http://www.paloaltoonline.com. Mailing Address: PO Box 1610, Palo Alto, CA 94302. Year Established: 1979. Pub. Frequency: s-w. (Wed. & Fri.) Page Size: tabloid. Subscrip. Rate: $.50 newsstand/cover; $25/yr local; $50/yr out of area. Adv. Rate: col. inch $37.10 Circulation: 49,500 per issue (controlled and free). **Owner(s):** Embarcadero Media, See address and contact information above. **Management:** William Johnson, Publisher. Walter Kupiec, Advertising Director. Bob Lampkin, Circulation Manager. **Editorial:** Jay Thorwaldson, Editor-in-Chief. Jocelyn Dong, Associate Editor.

PARADISE

PARADISE POST. 5399 Clark Rd., Paradise, CA 95969. Telephone: 530-877-4413. FAX: 530-877-1326. E-MAIL: advertising@ppp1.com. URL: http://www.paradisepost.com. Mailing Address: PO Drawer 70, Paradise, CA 95967. Year Established: 1945. Pub. Frequency: 3/w. (Tue., Thu., Sat.) Page Size: broadsheet. Subscrip. Rate: $.50 newsstand/cover; $49.35/yr home delivery in county; $89.50/yr home delivery out of county. Circulation: 9,000 per issue (paid). **Owner(s):** MediaNews Group, Inc., 101 W Colfax Ave, Ste 1100, Denver, CO 80202. FAX: 303-954-6320. **Management:** Randy Goldberg, General Manager. Jerry Urban, Advertising Director. Gene Ghimenti, Circulation Manager.

PASADENA

PASADENA WEEKLY. 50 S De Lacey Ave, Rm 200, Pasadena, CA 91105-1904. Telephone: 626-584-1500. FAX: 626-795-0149. E-MAIL: weekly@pasadenaweekly.com. URL: http://www.pasadenaweekly.com. Year Established: 1984. Pub. Frequency: w. (Thu.) Page Size: tabloid. Subscrip. Rate: $99/yr mailed. Circulation: 40,000 per issue (controlled and free). **Owner(s):** Southland Publishing, Inc., 700 E. Main St., Ventura, CA 93001. Telephone: 805-648-2244. **Management:** Marc Brancaccio, Publisher. Fred Bankston, Advertising Manager. Patrick Lund, Circulation Manager. **Editorial:** Kevin Uhrich, Managing Editor. Andre Coleman, Entertainment Editor. Judy Seckler, Reporter.

V C REPORTER. 50 S Delacey Ave, 200, Pasadena, CA 91105. Telephone: 805-658-2244. FAX: 805-658-2245. URL: http://www.vcreporter.com. Pub. Frequency: w. (Thu.) **Owner(s):** Ventura Newspaper, Inc., See address and contact information above. **Management:** David Comden, Group Publisher.

PASO ROBLES

PASO ROBLES PRESS, THE. 502 First St, Ste C, Paso Robles, CA 98446. Telephone: 805-237-6060. FAX: 805-237-6066. E-MAIL: news@pasoroblespress.com. URL: http://www.pasoroblespress.com. Mailing Address: PO Box 427, Paso Robles, CA 93447-0427. Year Established: 1886. Pub. Frequency: s-w. (Tues & Fri) Page Size: broadsheet. Subscrip. Rate: $.50 newsstand/cover; $39/yr in county; $60/yr out of county. Adv. Rate: col. inch $13.25 **Wire Service(s):** CNS. Circulation: 10,000 per issue (paid). **Owner(s):** News Media Corp., See address and contact information above. **Management:** Jason Cross, Publisher. Rachel Fox, Circulation Manager.

PLEASANTON

PLEASANTON WEEKLY. 5506 Sunol Blvd, Ste 100, Pleasanton, CA 94566. Telephone: 925-600-0840. FAX: 925-600-9559. URL: http://www.pleasantonweekly.com. Mailing Address: PO Box 1610, Palo Alto, CA 94302. Year Established: 2000. Pub. Frequency: w. (Fri.) Page Size: tabloid. Subscrip. Rate: $40/yr in city; $60/yr out of city. Adv. Rate: col. inch $17.10 Circulation: 25,000 per issue (paid). **Owner(s):** Embarcadero Media, 703 High St, Palo Alto, CA 94302. Telephone: 650-326-8210. FAX: 650-326-3928. **Management:** Jeb Bing, Publisher. Esmeralda Escovedo-Flores, Advertising Manager. Bob Lampkin, Circulation Manager. Susan Thomas, Classified Adv. Mgr.. **Editorial:** Jeb Bing, Editor. Janet Pelletier, Assistant Editor.

POINT REYES STATION

POINT REYES LIGHT. 11431 Hwy. 1, Point Reyes Station, CA 94956-0210. Telephone: 415-663-8404. FAX: 415-663-8458. E-MAIL: editor@ptreyeslight.com. URL: http://www.editor@ptreyeslight.com. Mailing Address: PO Box 210, Point Reyes Station, CA 94956-0210. Year Established: 1948. Pub. Frequency: w. (Thu.) Page Size: tabloid. Subscrip. Rate: $1 newsstand/cover; $46/yr in county; $52/yr out of county. Circulation: 4,500 per issue (paid). **Owner(s):** Robert Plotkin, See address and contact information above. **Management:** Robert Plotkin, Publisher. Renee Shannon, Advertising Manager. Missy Patterson, Circulation Manager. Donna Blum, Business Manager. **Editorial:** Robert Plotkin, Editor. Tess Elliott, Managing Editor.

POWAY

CORRIDOR NEWS. 13247 Poway Rd., Poway, CA 92064. Telephone: 858-748-2311. FAX: 858-748-7695. E-MAIL: editor@cts.com. URL: http://www.pomeradonews.com. Mailing Address: PO Box 685, Poway, CA 92064-0685. Year Established: 1971. Pub. Frequency: w. (Thu.) Page Size: broadsheet. Subscrip. Rate: $.50 newsstand/cover; $24/yr home delivery in county; $135/yr mailed 1st class. Circulation: 4,750 per issue (paid). **Owner(s):** Calvert Communications Inc., See address and contact information above. **Management:** David Calvert, Publisher. Trudy Armstrong, Advertising Director. Shannon Brandau, Circulation Manager. **Editorial:** Steve Dreyer, Executive Editor. David Garrick, Managing Editor. Kevin Gemmell, Sports Editor.

POWAY NEWS CHIEFTAIN. 13247 Poway Rd., Poway, CA 92064. Telephone: 858-748-2311. FAX: 858-748-7695. E-MAIL: editor@pomeradonews.com. URL: http://www.pomeradonews.com. Mailing Address: PO Box 685, Poway, CA 92074-0685. Year Established: 1955. Pub. Frequency: w. (Thu.) Page Size: broadsheet. Subscrip. Rate: $.50 newsstand/cover; $24/yr home delivery in county; $42/yr mailed in county. Circulation: 17,000 per issue (paid and free). **Owner(s):** Calvert Communications Inc., See address and contact information above. **Management:** David Calvert, Publisher. Trudy Armstrong, Advertising Director. Shannon Brandau, Circulation Manager. **Editorial:** Steve Dreyer, Executive Editor. David Garrick, Managing Editor. Erin Allin, Community Editor. Kevin Gemmell, Sports Editor.

RANCHO BERNARDO NEWS JOURNAL. 13247 Poway Rd., Poway, CA 92064. Telephone: 858-487-5757. FAX: 858-748-7695. E-MAIL: editor@pomeradonews.commpan@adnc.com. URL: http://www.pomeradonews.com. Mailing Address: PO Box 685, Poway, CA 92064-4613. Year Established: 1970. Pub. Frequency: w. (Thu.) Page Size: broadsheet. Subscrip. Rate: $.50 newsstand/cover; $24/yr home delivery in county. Circulation: 45,000 per issue (controlled and free). **Owner(s):** Calvert Communications Inc., See address and contact information above. **Management:** David Calvert, Publisher. Trudy Armstrong, Advertising Manager. **Editorial:** Pat Kumpan, Editor. Steve Dreyer, Executive Editor. David Garrick, Managing Editor.

RANCHO PALOS VERDES

PALOS VERDES PENINSULA NEWS. 500 Silver Spur Rd, Ste 300, Rancho Palos Verdes, CA 90275. Telephone: 310-377-6877. FAX: 310-377-4520. E-MAIL: editorial@pvnews.com. URL: http://www.pvnews.com. Year Established: 1937. Pub. Frequency: s-w. (Thu. & Sat.) Page Size: broadsheet. Subscrip. Rate: $.50 newsstand/cover; $41.41/yr home delivery. Freelance Pay: $0.20/column-inch. **Wire Service(s):** CiNS. Circulation: 13,600 per issue (paid and free); 5,000 Saturday (paid and free). **Owner(s):** MediaNews Group, Inc., 101 W Colfax Ave, Ste 1100, Denver, CO 80202. FAX: 303-954-6320. **Management:** Julia Parton, Publisher. **Editorial:** Chris Boyd, Managing Editor.

REDLANDS

REDLANDS GREEN SHEET. 611 W. Redlands Blvd., Redlands, CA 92373. Telephone: 909-793-3768. FAX: 909-793-3699. E-MAIL: greensheet@desertshopper.net. URL: http://www.greeandwhitesheet.com. Year Established: 1955. Pub. Frequency: w. (Thu.) Page Size: tabloid Circulation: 100,000 per issue (free). **Owner(s):** Schurz Communications, Inc., 225 W. Colfax Ave., South Bend, IN 46626. Telephone: 219-287-1001. FAX: 219-287-2257. **Management:** Hal Paradis, Publisher. Charles Holcombe, Sales Manager.

RIVERSIDE GREEN SHEET. 611 W. Redlands Blvd., Redlands, CA 92373. Telephone: 909-793-3768. FAX: 909-793-3699. E-MAIL: greensheet@desertshopper.net. URL: http://www.greenandwhitesheet.com. Year Established: 1955. Pub. Frequency: w. (Thu.) Page Size: tabloid Circulation: 100,000 per issue (free). **Owner(s):** Schurz Communications, Inc., 225 W. Colfax Ave., South Bend, IN 46626. Telephone: 219-287-1001. FAX: 219-287-2257. **Management:** Hal Paradis, Publisher. Charles Holcombe, Sales Manager. Esperanza Barrett, Controller.

SAN BERNARDINO GREEN SHEET. 611 W. Redlands Blvd., Redlands, CA 92373. Telephone: 909-793-3768. FAX: 909-793-3699. E-MAIL: greensheet@desertshopper.net. URL: http://www.greenandwhitesheet.com. Year Established: 1955. Pub. Frequency: w. (Wed.) Page Size: standard Circulation: 10,000 per issue (free). **Owner(s):** Schurz Communications, Inc., 225 W. Colfax Ave., South Bend, IN 46626. Telephone: 219-287-1001. FAX: 219-287-2257. **Management:** Hal Paradis, Publisher. Charles Holcombe, Sales Manager. Esperanza Barrett, Controller.

WEST SAN BERNARDINO GREEN SHEET. 611 W. Redlands Blvd., Redlands, CA 92373. Telephone: 909-793-3768. FAX: 909-793-3699. E-MAIL: greensheet@desertshopper.net. URL: http://www.greenandwhitesheet.com. Year Established: 1955. Pub. Frequency: w. (Thu.) Page Size: tabloid Circulation: 20,000 per issue (free). **Owner(s):** Schurz Communications, Inc., 225 W. Colfax Ave., South Bend, IN 46626. Telephone: 219-287-1001. **Management:** Hal Paradis, Publisher. Charles Holcombe, Sales Manager. Esperanza Barrett, Controller.

REEDLEY

ORANGE COVE MOUNTAIN TIMES. 1130 G St., Reedley, CA 93654. Telephone: 559-638-2244. FAX: 559-638-5021. Mailing Address: PO Box 432, Reedley, CA 93654. Year Established: 1984. Pub. Frequency: w. (Wed.) Page Size: standard.Subscrip. Rate: $.30 newsstand/cover Circulation: 3,785 per issue (paid). **Owner(s):** Mid-Valley Publications, Inc., See address and contact information above. **Management:** Fred Hall, Publisher. Janie Lucio, Advertising. **Editorial:** Mark Kistler, Editor.

PARLIER POST. 1130 G St., Reedley, CA 93654. Telephone: 559-638-2244. FAX: 559-638-5021. E-MAIL: markk@mid-valleypublishing.com. Mailing Address: PO Box 432, Reedley, CA 93654. Year Established: 1984. Pub. Frequency: w. (Wed.) Page Size: standard. Subscrip. Rate: $.30 newsstand/cover; $24.50/yr mailed in county; $26.50/yr mailed out of county. Circulation: 6,000 per issue (paid and free). **Owner(s):** Mid-Valley Publications, Inc., See address and contact information above. **Management:** Fred Hall, Publisher. Janie Lucio, Advertising. **Editorial:** Mark Kistler, Editor.

REEDLEY EXPONENT. 1130 G St., Reedley, CA 93654. Telephone: 559-638-2244. FAX: 559-638-5021. E-MAIL: buddb@reedleyexponent.com. URL: http://www.reedleyexponent.com. Mailing Address: PO Box 432, Reedley, CA 93654. Year Established: 1891. Pub. Frequency: w. (Thu.) Page Size: broadsheet. Subscrip. Rate: $.50 newsstand/cover; $20/yr in county. Circulation: 3,845 per issue (paid). **Owner(s):** Mid-Valley Publications, Inc., See address and contact information above. **Management:** Fred Hall, Publisher. Janie Lucio, Advertising. **Editorial:** Budd Budd Brockett, Editor.

RIDGECREST

NEWS REVIEW. 109 N. Sanders, Ridgecrest, CA 93555. Telephone: 760-371-4301. FAX: 760-371-4304. E-MAIL: newsreview@iwvisp.com. URL: http://www.news-ridgecrest.com. Year Established: 1976. Pub. Frequency: w. (Wed.) Page Size: broadsheet. Subscrip. Rate: $.50 newsstand/cover; $25/yr carrier delivery local; $30/yr mailed out of county. Freelance Pay: $1.25/column-inch. Circulation: 7,500 per issue (paid and free). **Owner(s):** Patricia Farris, See address and contact information above. **Management:** Patricia Farris, Publisher. **Editorial:** Patti Cosner, Editor.

PENNY PINCHER (RIDGECREST). 224 E. Ridgecrest Blvd., Ridgecrest, CA 93555. Telephone: 760-375-4481. FAX: 760-375-4880. Mailing Address: PO Box 7, Ridgecrest, CA 93556. Pub. Frequency: w. (Wed.) Page Size: standard Circulation: 5,200 per issue (free). **Owner(s):** GateHouse Media, Inc, 350 WillowBrook Office Park, Fairport, NY 14450. Telephone: 585-598-0030. FAX: 585-248-2631. **Management:** John Watkins, Publisher. Karen Sanders, Advertising Director. Chris Bradley, Circulation Manager.

SWAP SHEET. 619 W. Ridgecrest Blvd., Ste. D, Ridgecrest, CA 93555. Telephone: 760-375-5400. FAX: 760-375-1901. E-MAIL: wap@iwvisp.com. URL: http://www.swapsheet.org. Pub. Frequency: w. (Thu.) Page Size: tabloid.Adv. Rate: B&W page $243.43 Circulation: 9,000 per issue (free). **Owner(s):** Patty Sutton & Peggy Breeden, See address and contact information above. **Management:** Patty Sutton, Publisher. **Editorial:** Peggy Breeden, Editor.

RIVERBANK

RIVERBANK NEWS, THE. PO Box 887, Riverbank, CA 95367. URL: http://www.theriverbanknews.com. Pub. Frequency: w. (Wed.) Page Size: broadsheet. Subscrip. Rate: $.75 newsstand/cover; $31/yr mailed in county; $38/yr mailed out of county; $28/yr mailed in county to senior citizens. Circulation: 6,000 per issue (paid). **Owner(s):** Morris Newspaper Corporation, 27 Abercorn St., Savannah, GA 31401. **Management:** Bill Camp, General Manager. Melinda Owen, Advertising Manager. Peggy Ragle, Circulation Manager. **Editorial:** Marg Jackson, News Editor.

RIVERDALE

TWIN CITY TIMES/RIVERDALE FREE PRESS. 3356 W. Mt. Whitney, Riverdale, CA 93656. Telephone: 559-867-3671. FAX: 559-867-4154. E-MAIL: twintimes@tcfn.net. URL: http://www.twincitytimes.townnews.com. Mailing Address: PO Box 757, Riverdale, CA 93656. Pub. Frequency: w. (Wed.) Page Size: standard. Subscrip. Rate: $.50 newsstand/cover; $26/yr mailed in county; $29/yr mailed out of county; $31/yr mailed out of state. Circulation: 6,000 per issue (paid). **Owner(s):** Lee Enterprises, Inc., 900 N. Tucker Blvd., St. Louis, MO 63101. Telephone: 314-340-8000. FAX: 314-340-3125. **Management:** Mark Daniel, Publisher. Lance Cardoza, Advertising Director. Greg Barkley, Circulation Director. Kevin Crawford, Classified Adv. Mgr.. Julie Pendley, Assistant Publisher. **Editorial:** Linda Renn, Editor. Denis Bohannan, Editor-in-Chief. Jon Matsune, Sports Editor.

RIVERSIDE

CORONA-NORCO INDEPENDENT. ISSN 0745-3930 3450 14th St., Riverside, CA 92501. Telephone: 951-368-9761. FAX: 951-368-9021. E-MAIL: sbarry@pe.com. URL: http://www.pe.com. Year Established: 1887. Pub. Frequency: w. (Fri.) Page Size: tabloid Subscrip. Rate: $10/yr Circulation: 1,272 per issue (paid). **Owner(s):** Belo Corp., 400 S. Record St., Ste. 1300, Dallas, TX 75202. Telephone: 214-977-6606. **Management:** Sue Barry, VP Advertising. Shelly Yepez, Circulation Director. **Editorial:** Eric Velchis, Editor. Robert Kirkemo, Sports Editor.

LAKE ELSINORE VALLEY SUN-TRIBUNE. 3450 14th St., Riverside, CA 92501. Telephone: 951-368-9761. FAX: 951-368-9021. E-MAIL: syepez@pe.com. URL: http://www.pe.com. Year Established: 1885. Pub. Frequency: w. (Fri.) Page Size: tabloid Subscrip. Rate: $10/yr Circulation: 927 per issue (paid). **Owner(s):** Belo Corp., 400 S. Record St., Ste. 1300, Dallas, TX 75202. Telephone: 214-977-6606. **Management:** Sue Barry, VP Advertising. Shelly Yepez, Circulation Director. **Editorial:** Eric Velchis, Editor. Robert Kirkemo, Sports Editor.

RANCHO NEWS. 3450 14th St., Riverside, CA 92501. Telephone: 951-368-9761. FAX: 951-368-9021. E-MAIL: syepez@pe.com. URL: http://www.pe.com. Year Established: 1965. Pub. Frequency: w. (Fri.) Page Size: tabloid Subscrip. Rate: $10/yr Circulation: 1,127 per issue (paid). **Owner(s):** Belo Corp., 400 S. Record St., Ste. 1300, Dallas, TX 75202. Telephone: 214-977-6606. **Management:** Sue Barry, VP Advertising. Shelly Yepez, Circulation Director. **Editorial:** Eric Velchis, Editor. Robert Kirkemo, Sports Editor.

SUN CITY NEWS. 3450 14th St., Riverside, CA 92501. Telephone: 951-368-9761. FAX: 951-368-9021. E-MAIL: syepez@pe.com. URL: http://www.pe.com. Year Established: 1962. Pub. Frequency: w. (Fri.) Page Size: tabloid Subscrip. Rate: $10/yr Circulation: 1,664 per issue (paid). **Owner(s):** Belo Corp., 400 S. Record St., Ste. 1300, Dallas, TX 75202. Telephone: 214-977-6606. **Management:** Sue Barry, VP Advertising. Shelly Yepez, Circulation Director. **Editorial:** Eric Velchis, Editor. Robert Kirkemo, Sports Editor.

VALLEY TIMES (RIVERSIDE), THE. 3450 14th St., Riverside, CA 92501. Telephone: 951-368-9761. FAX: 951-368-9021. E-MAIL: sbarry@pe.com. URL: http://www.pe.com. Year Established: 1954. Pub. Frequency: w. (Fri.) Page Size: tabloid Subscrip. Rate: $10/yr Circulation: 947 per issue (paid). **Owner(s):** Belo Corp., 400 S. Record St., Ste. 1300, Dallas, TX 75202. Telephone: 214-977-6606. **Management:** Sue Barry, VP Advertising. Shelly Yepez, Circulation Director. **Editorial:** Eric Velchis, Editor. Robert Kirkemo, Sports Editor.

ROCKLIN

PLACER HERALD, THE. 4253 Rocklin Rd., Rocklin, CA 95677. Telephone: 916-624-9713. FAX: 916-624-7469. E-MAIL: pherald@tsyber.com. URL: http://www.placerherald.com. Year Established: 1852. Pub. Frequency: w. (Wed.) Page Size: broadsheet.Subscrip. Rate: $.50 newsstand/cover; $55/yr Circulation: 13,000 per issue (paid). **Owner(s):** Brehm Communications, Inc., 16644 W. Bernardo Dr., Ste. 300, San Diego, CA 92127. Telephone: 858-451-6200. **Management:** Bill Wallace, Publisher. Mike Maniscal, Advertising Manager. **Editorial:** Toby Lewis, Editor. Karina Williams, Photographer. Russ Edmondsun, Sports.

ROSAMOND

ROSAMOND WEEKLY NEWS. 2654 Diamond St., Rosamond, CA 93560-0848. Telephone: 661-269-1169. FAX: 661-269-2139. E-MAIL: joycemed@pacbell.net. Year Established: 1988. Pub. Frequency: w. (Fri.) Page Size: tabloid. Subscrip. Rate: $.25 newsstand/cover; $49/yr. **Wire Service(s):** UPI. Circulation: 3,100 per issue (paid). **Owner(s):** Joyce Media, Inc., See address and contact information above. **Management:** Gayle Joyce, President. John Joyce, Publisher. Lynne Sickler, Advertising Manager. Gayle Joyce, Circulation Manager. **Editorial:** Gayle Joyce, News Editor.

ROSEVILLE

PRESS-TRIBUNE, THE. 188 Cirby Way, Roseville, CA 95678. Telephone: 916-786-8746. FAX: 916-786-6501. URL: http://www.thepresstribune.com. Year Established: 1906. Pub. Frequency: s-w. (Wed. & Sat.) Page Size: broadsheet. Subscrip. Rate: $.50 newsstand/cover; $39/yr home delivery. Adv. Rate: col. inch $25 **Wire Service(s):** CNS. Circulation: 10,000 per issue (paid). **Owner(s):** Brehm Communications, Inc., 16644 W. Bernardo Dr., Ste. 300, San Diego, CA 92127. Telephone: 858-451-6200. **Management:** Jim Easterly, General Manager. Kelly Leibold, Circulation Director. Suzanne Steveson, Classified Adv. Mgr.. Erin Mezzetti, Business Manager. **Editorial:** Susan Belknap, Editor. Kurt Johnson, Sports Editor.

SACRAMENTO

SACRAMENTO BULLETIN, THE. 530 Bercut Dr., Ste. E, Sacramento, CA 95814. Telephone: 916-445-6336. FAX: 916-443-5871. E-MAIL: info@mnc.net. URL: http://www.mnc.net. Pub. Frequency: w. (Thu.) Page Size: standard. Subscrip. Rate: $.50 newsstand/cover; $10/yr. **Wire Service(s):** AP. **Owner(s):** Metropolitan News Co., 210 S. Spring St., Los Angeles, CA 90012-3710. Telephone: 213-628-4384. FAX: 213-687-3886. **Management:** Vahn Babigian, General Manager. Jo-Ann W. Grace, Publisher.

SACRAMENTO NEWS & REVIEW. 1015 20th St., Sacramento, CA 95814. Telephone: 916-498-1234. FAX: 916-498-7910. URL: http://www.newsreview.com. Pub. Frequency: w. (Thu.) Page Size: tabloid.Subscrip. Rate: $39/yr mailed Circulation: 93,000 per issue (free). **Owner(s):** Chico Community Publishing, Inc., 353 E. Second St., Chico, CA 95928. Telephone: 530-894-2300. **Management:** Jeff von Kaenel, President. Deborah Redmond, Operations Manager. Rosemarie Messina, Advertising Manager. **Editorial:** Melinda Welsh, Editor. Anne Lesemann, Production Manager. Becca Costello, Art Editor.

SAN BERNARDINO

COLTON COURIER, THE. 1809 S.Commerce Ctr., W., San Bernardino, CA 92408. Telephone: 909-381-9898. FAX: 909-384-0406. E-MAIL: lecn1@mac.com. Mailing Address: PO Box 789, San Marcos, CA 92079. Pub. Frequency: w. (Thu.) Page Size: tabloid Subscrip. Rate: $100/yr Circulation: 4,500 per issue (free). **Owner(s):** CCRR Publishing Co., Inc., See address and contact information above. **Management:** William D. Harrison, Publisher. Kathy Boswell, Advertising Manager. **Editorial:** MaryJoy Duncan, Editor. William D. Harrison, Managing Editor.

RIALTO RECORD. 1809 S.Commerce Ctr., W., San Bernardino, CA 92408. Telephone: 909-381-9898. FAX: 909-384-0406. E-MAIL: iecn@gte.net. Mailing Address: PO Box 789, San Marcos, CA 92079. Year Established: 1879. Pub. Frequency: w. (Thu.) Page Size: broadsheet. Subscrip. Rate: $103/yr mailed 1st class. Freelance Pay: $0.65/column-inch. **Wire Service(s):** AP. Circulation: 16,000 per issue (paid and free). **Owner(s):** CCRR Publishing Co., Inc., See address and contact information above. **Management:** William D. Harrison, Publisher. Kathy Boswell, Advertising Manager. **Editorial:** MaryJoy Duncan, Editor.

SUN NEWSPAPERS (SAN DIEGO). 1809 S.Commerce Ctr., W., San Bernardino, CA 92408. Telephone: 909-381-9898. FAX: 909-384-0406. URL: http://www.sunpapers.com. Mailing Address: PO Box 789, San Marcos, CA 92079. Year Established: 1925. Pub. Frequency: w. (Thu.) Page Size: tabloid. Subscrip. Rate: $80/yr. Circulation: 6,000 per issue (controlled and free). **Owner(s):** CCRR Publishing Co., Inc., See address and contact information above. **Management:** William D. Harrison, Publisher. Kathy Boswell, Advertising Manager. **Editorial:** MaryJoy Duncan, Editor.

SAN CLEMENTE

SUN POST NEWS, THE. 95 Avenida Del Mar, San Clemente, CA 92672. Telephone: 949-492-5121. FAX: 949-492-0401. E-MAIL: sunpostnews@ocregister.com. Year Established: 1937. Pub. Frequency: 3/w. (Tue., Thu., Fri.) Page Size: broadsheet Circulation: 11,038 per issue (paid). **Owner(s):** Freedom Communications, Inc., 17666 Fitch, Irvine, CA 92614. Telephone: 949-553-9292. **Management:** Larry Garner, Advertising Manager. **Editorial:** Paul Bersebach, Photographer. Mark Garcia, Sports Editor.

SAN DIEGO

BEACH & BAY PRESS. 4645 Cass St, 2nd Fl, San Diego, CA 92109. Telephone: 858-270-3103. FAX: 858-713-0095. E-MAIL: mail@sdnews.com. URL: http://www.sdnews.com/vnews/display.v/ Year Established: 1988. Pub. Frequency: w. (Thu.) Page Size: tabloid. Subscrip. Rate: $62/yr mailed. Adv. Rate: B&W page $1,480, color page $1,780 Circulation: 19,000 per issue (paid and free). **Owner(s):** San Diego Community Newspaper Group, See address and contact information above. **Management:** David Mannis, Publisher. Julie Mannis-Hoisington, Advertising Manager. **Editorial:** Larry Harmon, Editor.

GOLDEN TRIANGLE NEWS. 4645 Cass St, 2nd Fl, San Diego, CA 92109. Telephone: 858-270-3103. FAX: 858-713-0095. E-MAIL: mail@sdnews.com. Year Established: 1988. Pub. Frequency: w. (Thu.) Page Size: tabloid. Subscrip. Rate: $38.35/yr. Adv. Rate: col. inch $1,278 Circulation: 3,500 per issue (paid and free). **Owner(s):** San Diego Community Newspaper Group, See address and contact information above. **Management:** David Mannis, President. Julie Mannis-Hoisington, Advertising Manager. **Editorial:** Anne Terhune, Editor-in-Chief. John Gregory, Managing Editor.

LA JOLLA VILLAGE NEWS. 4645 Cass St, 2nd Fl, San Diego, CA 92109. Telephone: 858-270-3103. FAX: 858-713-0095. E-MAIL: mail@sdnews.com. URL: http://www.sdnews.com/vnews/display.v/ Pub. Frequency: w. (Thu.) Page Size: tabloid.Adv. Rate: B&W page $1,410, color page $1,710 Circulation: 20,000 per issue (free). **Owner(s):** San Diego Community Newspaper Group, See address and contact information above. **Management:** David Mannis, President. Julie Mannis-Hoisington, Publisher. **Editorial:** Anne Terhune, Editor-in-Chief. John Gregory, Managing Editor.

PENINSULA BEACON, THE. 4645 Cass St, 2nd Fl, San Diego, CA 92109. Telephone: 858-270-3103. FAX: 858-713-0095. E-MAIL: sales@sdnews.com. URL: http://www.sdnews.com/vnews/display.v/ Year Established: 1981. Pub. Frequency: w. (Thu.) Page Size: tabloid.Adv. Rate: B&W page $1,410, color page $1,310 Freelance Pay: $15-$20/article. Circulation: 16,000 per issue (free). **Owner(s):** San Diego Community Newspaper Group, See address and contact information above. **Management:** David Mannis, Publisher. **Editorial:** Eric Yates, Editor. Anne Terhune, Editor-in-Chief. John Gregory, Managing Editor.

RANCHO BERNARDO SUN. 12712 Caminito Cancion, #121, San Diego, CA 92128. Telephone: 858-385-5195. FAX: 858-385-5197. E-MAIL: rbsun@sbcglobal.net. URL: http://www.ranchobernardosun.com. Year Established: 1985. Pub. Frequency: m. Page Size: tabloid. Subscrip. Rate: $45/yr. Adv. Rate: col. inch $17,364 Circulation: 23,000 per issue (free). **Owner(s):** M B A Communications, See address and contact information above. **Management:** Mark Brenner, Publisher. Samantha Brenner, Business Manager. **Editorial:** Mark Brenner, Editor.Readers: Age 50+

SAN DIEGO DOWNTOWN NEWS. 4645 Cass St, 2nd Fl, San Diego, CA 92109. Telephone: 858-270-3103. FAX: 858-713-0095. E-MAIL: sales@sdnews.com. URL: http://www.sdnews.com/vnews/display.v/ Pub. Frequency: w. (Thu.) Page Size: tabloid. Subscrip. Rate: $62/yr; $32 for 6 mos.. Adv. Rate: page $1,480; 10.5 x 15.375 Circulation: 20,000 per issue (free). **Owner(s):** San Diego Community Newspaper Group, See address and contact information above. **Management:** David Mannis, Publisher. Heather Synder, Advertising. **Editorial:** Lori Martinez, Editor. Anne Terhune, Editor-in-Chief. Marty Westlin, Managing Editor.

SAN DIEGO READER. 1703 India St., San Diego, CA 92101-0583. Telephone: 619-235-3000. FAX: 619-231-0489. URL: http://www.sandiegoreader.com. Year Established: 1972. Pub. Frequency: w. (Thu.) Page Size: tabloid.Subscrip. Rate: $175 mailed for 6 mos. Circulation: 176,000 per issue (free). **Owner(s):** James E. Holman, PO Box 85803, San Diego, CA 92186. Telephone: 619-235-3000. FAX: 619-231-0489. **Management:** James E. Holman, Publisher. Linda Flounders, Advertising Manager. Gene Rochamdeau, Classified Adv. Mgr.. **Editorial:** James E. Holman, Editor.

SAN FERNANDO

SAN FERNANDO VALLEY SUN. 601 S. Brand Blvd., Ste. 202, San Fernando, CA 91340. Telephone: 818-365-3111. FAX: 818-898-7135. URL: http://www.sanfernandosun.com. Year Established: 1904. Pub. Frequency: w. (Thu.) Page Size: tabloid. Subscrip. Rate: $85/yr mailed in state. **Wire Service(s):** AP, CiNS. Circulation: 10,000 per issue (paid and free). **Owner(s):** Sev Aszkenazy, See address and contact information above. **Management:** Martha Aszkenazy, Co-Publisher. **Editorial:** Diana Martinez, Editor.

VALLEY VIEW (SAN FERNANDO). 601 S. Brand Blvd., Ste. 202, San Fernando, CA 91340. Telephone: 818-365-3111. Pub. Frequency: w. (Thu.) Page Size: broadsheet. Subscrip. Rate: $85/yr mailed. Circulation: 12,000 per issue (controlled and free). **Owner(s):** Sev Aszkenazy, See address and contact information above. **Management:** Sev Aszkenazy, Co-Publisher. Andres Chavez, Sales Manager. **Editorial:** Diana Martinez, Editor.

SAN FRANCISCO

S F WEEKLY. ISSN 1060-2526
185 Berry, Lobby 4, Ste 3800, San Francisco, CA 94107-1729. Telephone: 415-536-8100. FAX: 415-541-9096. URL: http://www.sfweekly.com. Year Established: 1981. Pub. Frequency: w. Page Size: broadsheet. Subscrip. Rate: $80/yr mailed. Circulation: 100,000 (controlled). **Owner(s):** Village Voice Media, See address and contact information above. **Editorial:** Tom Walsh, Editor.

SAN FRANCISCO INDEPENDENT. 450 Mission St., San Francisco, CA 94105. Telephone: 415-359-2600. FAX: 415-826-2766. Year Established: 1958. Pub. Frequency: s-w. (Tue. & Sat.) Page Size: broadsheet Circulation: 537,000 per issue (free). **Owner(s):** S F Newspaper Co., 1213 Evans St., San Francisco, CA 94124. Telephone: 415-862-5371. **Management:** James Fang, President. Scott McKibben, Publisher. Dan Payomo, Advertising Director. Jason Phillips, Advertising Manager. Jose Diaz, Circulation Manager. **Editorial:** Jim Pimentel, Managing Editor.

SAN FRANCISCO METRO REPORTER. 270 Francisco St., San Francisco, CA 94133-2012. Telephone: 415-391-2030. FAX: 415-391-2525. Pub. Frequency: w. (Wed.) Page Size: tabloid. Circulation: 125,000 per issue (paid and controlled). **Owner(s):** Garry M. Goodlett, 1366 Turk St., San Francisco, CA 94115. Telephone: 415-576-1149. **Management:** Dr. Gary M. Goodlett, Publisher. **Editorial:** Charles E. Belle, Editor.

SAN FRANCISCO OBSERVER. PO Box 15102, San Francisco, CA 94115-0102. Telephone: 415-863-6397. FAX: 415-431-2021. E-MAIL: advertising@sfobserver.com. URL: http://www.sfobserver.com. Year Established: 1997. Pub. Frequency: s-m. Page Size: tabloid. Subscrip. Rate: $15/yr out of county. Freelance Pay: $0.15/word. Circulation: 40,000 per issue (free). **Owner(s):** San Francisco Observer Newspaper Group, See address and contact information above. **Management:** Sandy Staggs, Publisher. **Editorial:** Sandy Staggs, Editor. Alex Selim, Book Review Editor.

SUN REPORTER. 270 Francisco, San Francisco, CA 94133-2012. Telephone: 415-391-2030. FAX: 415-391-2527. Year Established: 1944. Pub. Frequency: w. (Wed.) Page Size: tabloid. Subscrip. Rate: $.50 newsstand/cover; $15/yr. Circulation: 160,000 per issue (paid and free). **Owner(s):** Garry M. Goodlett, 1366 Turk St., San Francisco, CA 94115. Telephone: 415-931-5778. **Management:** Dr. Gary M. Goodlett, Publisher. Jessica Castle, Advertising Manager. **Editorial:** Charles E. Belle, Editor. Amelia Ashley-Ward, Managing Editor.

SAN JOSE

CAMPBELL REPORTER, THE. 1095 The Alameda, San Jose, CA 95126. Telephone: 408-200-1000. E-MAIL: campbellreporter@svcn.com. URL: http://www.svcn.com. Pub. Frequency: w. (Tue.) Page Size: tabloid. Subscrip. Rate: $36/yr. Circulation: 18,800 per issue (paid and free). **Owner(s):** Silicon Valley Community Newspapers, See address and contact information above. **Management:** David Cohen, Publisher. Jeannette Close, Advertising Manager. Joe Lauletta, Circulation Manager. **Editorial:** Sandy Sims, Editor. Dale Bryant, Executive Editor. Jacquelin Ramseyer, Photographer. Dick Sparrer, Sports Editor.

CUPERTINO COURIER. 1095 The Alameda, San Jose, CA 95126. Telephone: 408-200-1000. E-MAIL: cc@svcn.com. URL: http://www.svcn.com. Year Established: 1947. Pub. Frequency: w. (Wed.) Page Size: tabloid. Subscrip. Rate: $.50 newsstand/cover; $36/yr out of county. Circulation: 19,000 per issue (paid and free). **Owner(s):** Silicon Valley Community Newspapers, See address and contact information above. **Management:** David Cohen, Owner. Jeannette Close, Advertising Manager. Joe Lauletta, Circulation Manager. **Editorial:** Carol Bogart, Editor. Dick Sparrer, Sports Editor.

METRO SILICON VALLEY. 550 S. First St., San Jose, CA 95113. Telephone: 408-298-8000. FAX: 408-298-6992. E-MAIL: dpulcrano@metro.com. URL: http://www.metroactive.com/metro/. Year Established: 1985. Pub. Frequency: w. (Wed.) Page Size: tabloid. Subscrip. Rate: $76/yr mailed. Adv. Rate: col. inch $18 Circulation: 83,000 (free). **Owner(s):** Metro Publishing, Inc., See address and contact information above. **Management:** Dan Pulcrano, President. Alisa Cromer, Advertising Manager. Holly Carthew, Classified Adv. Mgr.. **Editorial:** Dan Pulcrano, Editor.

SUNNYVALE SUN. 1095 The Alameda, San Jose, CA 95126. Telephone: 408-200-1000. FAX: 408-200-1013. E-MAIL: sun@svcn.com. URL: http://www.sunnyvalesun.com. Year Established: 1994. Pub. Frequency: w. (Wed.) Page Size: tabloid. Subscrip. Rate: $36/yr in county; $62/yr out of county. Circulation: 36,600 per issue (paid and free). **Owner(s):** Silicon Valley Community Newspapers, See address and contact information above. **Management:** David Cohen, Publisher. Joe Lauletta, Circulation Manager. Kate Fitzgerald, Classified Adv. Mgr.. Jeannette Close, Associate Publisher. **Editorial:** Carol Bogart, Editor. Dale Bryant, Executive Editor. Jacqueline Ramseyer, Photographer. Dick Sparrer, Sports Editor.

WILLOW GLEN RESIDENT. 1095 The Alameda, San Jose, CA 95126-3142. Telephone: 408-200-1000. FAX: 408-200-1013. E-MAIL: wgr@svcn.com. URL: http://www.wgresident.com. Pub. Frequency: w. (Tue.) Page Size: tabloid Subscrip. Rate: $26/yr Circulation: 20,800 per issue (paid and free). **Owner(s):** Silicon Valley Community Newspapers, 550 W. First St., San Jose, CA 95113. Telephone: 408-200-1000. **Management:** David Cohen, Publisher. Jeannette Close, Advertising Manager. Joe Lauletta, Circulation Manager. **Editorial:** Carol Bogart, Editor. Dale Bryant, Executive Editor. Dick Sparrer, Sports Editor.

SAN LUIS OBISPO

NEW TIMES. 1010 Marsh St, San Luis Obispo, CA 93401. Telephone: 805-546-8208. FAX: 805-546-8641. E-MAIL: mail@newtimesslo.com. URL: http://www.newtimesslo.com. Year Established: 1986. Pub. Frequency: w. (Thu.) Page Size: tabloid. Subscrip. Rate: $52 for 6 mos.; $104/yr. Adv. Rate: page $1,395 Circulation: 40,000 per issue (paid and controlled). **Owner(s):** New Times Publishing, See address and contact information above. **Management:** Bob Rucker, General Manager. Fred Bohnhoff, Circulation Manager. Alex Zuniga, Art Director. **Editorial:** King Harris, Managing Editor.

SAN MARINO

SAN MARINO TRIBUNE. 1441 San Marino Ave., San Marino, CA 91108. Telephone: 626-792-6397. FAX: 626-792-4915. E-MAIL: smtribune@earthlink.net. URL: http://www.sanmarinotribune.com. Year Established: 1929. Pub. Frequency: w. (Thu.) Page Size: broadsheet. Subscrip. Rate: $1.75 per issue; $89/yr mailed in state; $109/yr mailed out of state. Circulation: 20,000 per issue (paid). **Owner(s):** Clifton Smith, See address and contact information above. **Management:** Clifton Smith, President. Ann Luke, Advertising Manager. Kate Boyce, Circulation Manager. Richard Jones, Marketing. **Editorial:** Winston Chua, Editor. Mitch Lehman, City Editor. Liz Hezlep, Society Editor. Steve Simmons, Travel Editor.

SAN PEDRO

RANDOM LENGTHS NEWS. 1300 S. Pacific Ave., San Pedro, CA 90731-1442. Telephone: 310-519-1442. FAX: 310-832-1000. E-MAIL: adv@randomlengthsnews.com. URL: http://www.randomlengthsnews.com. Mailing Address: PO Box 731, San Pedro, CA 90733-0731. Year Established: 1979. Pub. Frequency: bi-w. (Thu.) Page Size: tabloid. Subscrip. Rate: $26/yr mailed; $40/yr mailed 1st class. Adv. Rate: B&W page $1,180 Freelance Pay: $0.05/word. Circulation: 25,000 per issue (paid and free). **Owner(s):** Random Lengths News, Inc., See address and contact information above. **Management:** James P. Allen, Publisher. Rodney Golden, Advertising Manager. Suzanne Matsumiya, Associate Publisher. **Editorial:** Terrelle Jerricks, Managing Editor. Paul Rosenberg, Senior Editor.

SAN RAFAEL

CLASSIFIED GAZETTE. 716 Fourth St., San Rafael, CA 94901. Telephone: 415-457-4151. FAX: 415-457-5731. E-MAIL: jpowers@classifiedgazette.com. URL: http://www.classifiedgazette.com. Year Established: 1968. Pub. Frequency: s-w. (Wed. & Fri.) Page Size: tabloid Circulation: 56,000 per issue (free). **Owner(s):** News Media Corp., 211 Hwy. 38 E., Rochelle, IL 61608. Telephone: 815-562-2060. **Management:** Joann Powers, General Manager.

SANGER

FOWLER ENSIGN. 740 N St., Sanger, CA 93657. Telephone: 559-875-2511. FAX: 559-875-2521. Pub. Frequency: w. (Thu.) Page Size: broadsheet. Subscrip. Rate: $.27 newsstand/cover; $20/yr in county; $24.50/yr out of county; $26.50/yr mailed out of state. Circulation: 700 per issue (paid). **Owner(s):** Mid-Valley Publications, Inc., PO Box 432, Reedley, CA 93654. Telephone: 559-638-2244. FAX: 559-638-5021. **Management:** Fred Hall, Publisher. Madlyn Esquer, Advertising. **Editorial:** Cathy Willingham, Editor.

SANGER HERALD. 740 N St., Sanger, CA 93657. Telephone: 559-875-2511. FAX: 559-875-2521. Year Established: 1888. Pub. Frequency: w. (Thu.) Page Size: standard. Subscrip. Rate: $.50 newsstand/cover; $20/yr in county; $24.50/yr out of county; $26.50/yr out of state. Adv. Rate: col. inch $110.45 Freelance Pay: $1/column-inch. Circulation: 2,900 per issue (paid). **Owner(s):** Mid-Valley Publications, Inc., PO Box 432, Reedley, CA 93654. Telephone: 209-638-2244. FAX: 209-638-5021. **Management:** Fred Hall, Publisher. Madlyn Esquer, Advertising. **Editorial:** Dawn Pearson, Editor.

SANTA ANA

O C WEEKLY. 1666 N. Main St., Ste. 500, Santa Ana, CA 92701. Telephone: 714-550-5950. FAX: 714-550-5908. E-MAIL: letters@ocweekly.com. URL: http://www.ocweekly.com. Year Established: 1995. Pub. Frequency: w. (Thu.) Page Size: tabloid Circulation: 70,000 per issue (free). **Owner(s):** Village Voice Media, Inc., 36 Cooper Square, New York, NY 10003-1205. Telephone: 516-877-7373. **Editorial:** Will Swaim, Editor. Matt Coker, Managing Editor. Steve Lowery, Feature Editor.NDEX-CITY-STATESanta Ana, CA see SPECIAL INTEREST NEWSPAPERS: Legal

SANTA BARBARA

SANTA BARBARA INDEPENDENT. 122 W. Figueroa St., Santa Barbara, CA 93101. Telephone: 805-965-5205. FAX: 805-965-5518. E-MAIL: admin@independent.com. URL: http://www.independent.com. Year Established: 1986. Pub. Frequency: w. (Thu.) Page Size: tabloid. Subscrip. Rate: $88/yr mailed. Freelance Pay: $1-$2.25/column-inch. Circulation: 40,000 per issue (paid and free). **Owner(s):** Santa Barbara Independent Inc., The, See address and contact information above. **Management:** George Thurlow, Publisher. Scott Kaufman, Circulation Manager. Penelope Huston, Classified Adv. Mgr.. Tom Morey, Sales Manager. **Editorial:** Marianne Partridge, Editor-in-Chief. Audrey Berman, Editorial Director. Nick Welsh, Executive Editor. Duncan Wright, Art Editor. Cathy Murillo, News Editor. Paul Wellman, Photo Editor.

SANTA CRUZ

GOOD TIMES. ISSN 0164-4033
1205 Pacific Ave, Ste 301, Santa Cruz, CA 95060. Telephone: 831-458-1100. FAX: 831-458-1296. E-MAIL: rslack@gtweekly.com. URL: http://www.gtweekly.com. Year Established: 1975. Pub. Frequency: w. (Thu.) Page Size: tabloid. Subscrip. Rate: $100/yr mailed. Adv. Rate: B&W page $1,828 Freelance Pay: $0.15/word. Circulation: 45,000 per issue (controlled). **Owner(s):** Main Street Media Group, See address and contact information above. **Management:** Ron Slack, Publisher. Penelope Brown, Advertising Director. **Editorial:** Greg Archer, Editor. Christa Martin, Feature Editor. Linda Koffman, Music Editor. Elizabeth Limbach, News Editor.Readers: Ages 25-66

METRO SANTA CRUZ. 115 Cooper St., Santa Cruz, CA 95060. Telephone: 831-457-9000. FAX: 831-457-5828. E-MAIL: editorial2metrosantacruz.com. URL: http://www.metroactive.com. Pub. Frequency: w. (Wed.) Page Size: tabloid. Subscrip. Rate: $40 mailed for 6 mos.; $76/yr. **Owner(s):** Metro Newspapers, 550 S. First St., San Jose, CA 95113. Telephone: 408-298-8000. **Management:** Debra Wkezin, General Manager. Elisa Cromer, Publisher. Neil Smyth, Circulation Manager. **Editorial:** Bill Forman, Editor. Dan Pulcrano, Executive Editor. Bill Forman, Feature Editor. Sara Phelan, News Editor.

SANTA PAULA

SANTA PAULA TIMES. 944 E. Main St., Santa Paula, CA 93060. Telephone: 805-525-1890. FAX: 805-525-7375. E-MAIL: santapaulatimes@skypipeline.com. URL: Http://www.santapaulatimes.com. Mailing Address: PO Box 431, Santa Paula, CA 93061. Year Established: 1993. Pub. Frequency: s-w. (Wed. & Fri.) Page Size: broadsheet. Subscrip. Rate: $.50 newsstand/cover; $36/yr home delivery; $53 mailed for 6 mos.; $106/yr mailed. Circulation: 9,000 per issue (paid and free). **Owner(s):** Donald & Deborah Johnson, See address and contact information above. **Management:** Donald Johnson, Publisher. Deborah Johnson, Advertising Manager. **Editorial:** Donald Johnson, Editor. Brian Wilson, Sports.

SANTA ROSA

NORTH BAY BOHEMIAN. 216 E St., Santa Rosa, CA 95404. Telephone: 707-527-1200. FAX: 707-527-1288. E-MAIL: editorial@metronews.com. URL: http://www.metronews.com. Pub. Frequency: w. (Thu.) Page Size: tabloid. Subscrip. Rate: $65/yr in county; $80/yr out of county. Circulation: 33,191 per issue (controlled). **Owner(s):** Metro Newspapers, 550 S. First St., San Jose, CA 95113. Telephone: 408-298-8000. **Management:** Alisa Cromer, Group Publisher. Rosemary Olson, Publisher. Lisa Santos, Advertising Director. Clara Evans, Classified Adv. Mgr.. **Editorial:** Gretchen Giles, Editor.

SAUSALITO

MARIN SCOPE. 1050 Bridgeway, Ste. 290, Sausalito, CA 94966. Telephone: 415-339-8510. FAX: 415-331-1882. E-MAIL: mscope@marinscope.com. URL: http://www.marinscope.com. Year Established: 1971. Pub. Frequency: w. (Tue.) Page Size: standard. Subscrip. Rate: $.50 newsstand/cover; $24/yr mailed. Circulation: 15,000 per issue (paid). **Owner(s):** Marin Scope Community Newspapers, PO Box 1689, Sausalito, CA 94966-1689. Telephone: 415-289-4040. FAX: 415-332-8714. **Management:** Dijay Mallya, Publisher. Mel Copeland, Advertising Director. **Editorial:** Damien English, Editor. Chris Rooney, Managing Editor.

MILL VALLEY HERALD. 1050 Bridgeway, Ste. 290, Sausalito, CA 94966. Telephone: 415-339-8510. FAX: 415-331-1882. E-MAIL: mscope@marinscope.com. URL: http://www.marinscope.com. Mailing Address: PO Box 1016, Mill Valley, CA 94941. Pub. Frequency: w. (Mon.) Page Size: standard. Subscrip. Rate: $.50 newsstand/cover; $24/yr mailed. Circulation: 11,500 per issue (paid). **Owner(s):** Marin Scope Community Newspapers, PO Box 1689, Sausalito, CA 94966. Telephone: 415-339-8510. FAX: 415-331-1882. **Editorial:** Joshua Sabatini, Editor. Chris Rooney, Managing Editor.

ROSS VALLEY REPORTER. 1050 Bridgeway, Ste. 290, Sausalito, CA 94966. FAX: 415-331-1897. E-MAIL: mscope@marinscope.com. URL: http://www.marinscope.com. Mailing Address: PO Box 1689, Sausalito, CA 94966. Year Established: 1964. Pub. Frequency: w. (Tue.) Page Size: broadsheet. Subscrip. Rate: $.50 newsstand/cover; $24/yr home delivery. Freelance Pay: $10-$35/article. Circulation: 11,050 per issue (paid and free). **Owner(s):** Marin Scope Community Newspapers, See address and contact information above. **Management:** Pual Anderson, Publisher. **Editorial:** Olga Czar, Editor. Chris Rooney, Managing Editor.

SAN RAFAEL NEWS POINTER. PO Box 1689, Sausalito, CA 94966-1689. Telephone: 415-339-8510. FAX: 415-331-1882. E-MAIL: newspointer@yahoo.com. URL: http://www.marinscope.com. Mailing Address: PO Box T, San Rafael, CA 94966. Pub. Frequency: w. (Tue.) Page Size: standard. Subscrip. Rate: $.50 newsstand/cover; $25/yr mailed. Circulation: 9,500 per issue (free). **Owner(s):** Marin Scope Community Newspapers, See address and contact information above. **Editorial:** Chris Rooney, Editor.

TWIN CITIES TIMES. 1050 Bridgeway, Ste. 290, Sausalito, CA 94966. Telephone: 415-339-8510. FAX: 415-331-1882. E-MAIL: mscope@marinscope.com. URL: http://www.marinscope.com. Year Established: 1975. Pub. Frequency: w. (Wed.) Page Size: standard. Subscrip. Rate: $.50 newsstand/cover; $24/yr mailed. Circulation: 9,200 per issue (controlled and free). **Owner(s):** Marin Scope Community Newspapers, PO Box 1689, Sausalito, CA 94966-1689. Telephone: 415-289-4040. **Management:** Dijay Mallya, Publisher. Harlan Cross, Sales Manager. **Editorial:** Trevor Noren, Editor. Chris Rooney, Managing Editor.

SEAL BEACH

SUN NEWSPAPER, THE. 216 Main St., Seal Beach, CA 90740. Telephone: 562-430-7555. FAX: 562-430-3469. E-MAIL: editor@sunnews.org. Year Established: 1967. Pub. Frequency: w. (Thu.) Page Size: tabloid. Subscrip. Rate: $75/yr mailed 1st class. Freelance Pay: $1.50/column-inch. Circulation: 32,000 per issue (paid and free). **Owner(s):** Community Media, See address and contact information above. **Management:** Beth Gates, Publisher. **Editorial:** Dennis Kais, Editor. Kate Korp, Assistant Editor.

SEASIDE

MONTEREY COUNTY WEEKLY. 668 Williams Ave, Seaside, CA 93955. Telephone: 831-394-5656. FAX: 831-394-0409. E-MAIL: mcweekly.com. URL: http://www.montereycountyweekly.com. Year Established: 1988. Pub. Frequency: w. (Thu.) Subscrip. Rate: $52/yr mailed. Circulation: 40,000 morning. **Owner(s):** Milestone Communications, Inc., See address and contact information above. **Management:** Erik Cushman, Publisher. George Kassal, Advertising Director. Kevin Smith, Classified Adv. Mgr.. **Editorial:** Eric Johnson, Editor. Bradley Zeve, Executive Editor.

SEBASTOPOL

SONOMA WEST/TIMES & NEWS. 130 S. Main St., Ste. 114, Sebastopol, CA 95472. Telephone: 707-823-7845. FAX: 707-823-7508. E-MAIL: news@sonomawest.com. URL: http://www.sonomawest.com. Mailing Address: PO Box 521, Sebastopol, CA 95473. Year Established: 1889. Pub. Frequency: w. (Thu.) Page Size: standard. Subscrip. Rate: $.50 newsstand/cover; $30/yr home delivery in county; $50/yr home delivery out of county; $20/yr home delivery to senior citizens. Circulation: 6,000 per issue (paid and controlled). **Owner(s):** Sonoma West Publishers, Inc., See address and contact information above. **Management:** Rollie Atkinson, Publisher. Sara Bradbury, Advertising Director. Grace Garner, Circulation Manager. **Editorial:** Barry Dugan, Managing Editor. Greg Clementi, Sports Editor.

SELMA

SELMA ENTERPRISE. 2045 Grant St., Selma, CA 93662. Telephone: 559-896-1976. FAX: 559-896-9160. URL: http://www.selmaenterprise.com. Mailing Address: PO Box 100, Selma, CA 93662-0100. Year Established: 1886. Pub. Frequency: w. (Wed.) Page Size: broadsheet. Subscrip. Rate: $.50 newsstand/cover; $26/yr in county; $36/yr out of county; $36/yr mailed out of state. Adv. Rate: col. inch $10 Circulation: 4,000 per issue (paid). **Owner(s):** Lee Enterprises, Inc., 1555 N. Freedom Blvd., Provo, UT 84604. Telephone: 810-344-2935. FAX: 810-373-5489. **Management:** Randy Rickman, Advertising Director. Joe Schiotis, Advertising Manager. Cliff Donaldson, Circulation Manager. **Editorial:** Michael Miyamoto, Editor.

SHAFTER

SHAFTER PRESS. 107 E. Lerdo Hwy., Shafter, CA 93263. Telephone: 661-746-4942. FAX: 661-746-5571. Mailing Address: PO Box 1600, Shafter, CA 93263. Pub. Frequency: w. (Wed.) Page Size: broadsheet. Subscrip. Rate: $.35 newsstand/cover; $19/yr in county; $21/yr out of county; $24/yr out of state. Circulation: 6,300 per issue (paid and free). **Owner(s):** Reed Print, Inc., 5409 Aldrin Ct., Bakersfield, CA 93313. Telephone: 805-834-0496. **Management:** Donald Reed, Publisher. Diane Givens, Office Manager. Jason Reed, Advertising Manager. **Editorial:** Margaret Baker, Editor. Frank W Reed, Editor-in-Chief.

SOLEDAD

GONZALES TRIBUNE. 635 Front St., Soledad, CA 93960. Telephone: 831-385-4880. FAX: 831-385-4799. E-MAIL: kcrustler@redshift.com. Mailing Address: PO Box 710, King City, CA 93930. Pub. Frequency: w. (Wed.) Page Size: broadsheet. Subscrip. Rate: $.50 newsstand/cover; $32.50/yr in county; $37.50/yr mailed out of county. Circulation: 13,000 per issue (paid). **Owner(s):** News Media Corp., PO Box 46, Rochelle, IL 61068. **Management:** Scott Brennan, Publisher. Bess Brennan, Advertising. **Editorial:** Scott Brennan, Editor.

SOLEDAD BEE. 635 Front St., Soledad, CA 93960. Telephone: 831-678-2660. FAX: 831-678-3676. Mailing Address: PO Box 710, King City, CA 93930. Pub. Frequency: w. (Wed.) Page Size: broadsheet. Subscrip. Rate: $.50 newsstand/cover; $29.50/yr in county; $34.50/yr out of county. Circulation: 1,262 per issue (paid). **Owner(s):** News Media Corp., PO Box 46, Rochelle, IL 61068. Telephone: 815-562-2061. FAX: 815-562-2060. **Management:** Scott Brennan, Publisher. Bess Brennan, Advertising. **Editorial:** Scott Brennan, Editor.

SOLVANG

SANTA YNEZ VALLEY EXTRA EDITION. 423 Second St., Solvang, CA 93463. Telephone: 805-688-5522. FAX: 805-688-7685. Pub. Frequency: w. (Tue.) Page Size: broadsheet Circulation: 13,500 per issue (free). **Owner(s):** Lee Enterprises, Inc., 201 N. Harrison St., Davenport, IA 52801. **Management:** Ronn Iverson, General Manager. Cynthia L Schur, Publisher. **Editorial:** John Lankfork, Editor.

SANTA YNEZ VALLEY NEWS. 423 Second St., Solvang, CA 93463. Telephone: 805-688-5522. FAX: 805-688-7685. Year Established: 1925. Pub. Frequency: s-w. (Tue. & Thu.) Page Size: broadsheet. Subscrip. Rate: $.35 newsstand/cover; $20/yr home delivery. Circulation: 13,900 per issue (paid). **Owner(s):** Lee Enterprises, Inc., 201 N. Harrison St., Davenport, IA 52801. **Management:** Ronn Iverson, General Manager. Cynthia L Schur, Publisher. **Editorial:** John Lankfork, Editor.

SOUTH PASADENA

SOUTH PASADENA REVIEW. ISSN 1094-9801
1020-C Mission St., South Pasadena, CA 91030. Telephone: 626-799-1161. FAX: 626-799-2892. E-MAIL: reviewsp@aol.com. Mailing Address: PO Box 310, South Pasadena, CA 91031-2092. Year Established: 1888. Pub. Frequency: w. (Wed.) Page Size: standard. Subscrip. Rate: $.25 newsstand/cover; $35/yr in county; $35/yr mailed in state 2nd class. Circulation: 4,000 per issue (paid). **Owner(s):** South Pasadena Publishing Co., See address and contact information above. **Management:** William Ericson, President. Laurie Woiflick, Advertising Manager. Loretta Brantley, Circulation Manager. **Editorial:** Bill Glazier, Editor.

ST. HELENA

ST. HELENA STAR. 1200 Main St, St. Helena, CA 94574. Telephone: 707-963-2731. FAX: 707-963-8957. E-MAIL: starnews@sthelenastar.com. URL: http://www.sthelenastar.com. Mailing Address: PO Box 346, St. Helena, CA 94574. Year Established: 1874. Pub. Frequency: w. (Thu.) Page Size: broadsheet. Subscrip. Rate: $.50 newsstand/cover; $25/yr home delivery in county; $28.50/yr mailed out of county. Circulation: 6,000 per issue (paid). **Owner(s):** Lee Enterprises, Inc., 201 N Harrison St, Davenport, IA 52801-1939. Telephone: 563-383-2100. **Management:** Doug Ernst, Publisher. Robyn Higginbotham, Advertising Director. **Editorial:** Doug Ernst, Editor. Vince D'Adamo, Sports.

TAFT

BARGAIN HUNTER (TAFT). 800 Center St., Taft, CA 93268. Telephone: 661-763-3171. FAX: 661-763-5638. Mailing Address: PO Box 958, Taft, CA 93268. Pub. Frequency: w. (Tue.) Page Size: standard Circulation: 3,000 per issue (free). **Owner(s):** GateHouse Media, Inc, 350 WillowBrook Office Park, Fairport, NY 14450. Telephone: 585-598-0030. **Management:** Deana Long, General Manager. Melissa Robertson, Circulation Manager. Teri Walgren, Classified Adv. Mgr..

MIDWAY DRILLER. 800 Center St., Taft, CA 93268. Telephone: 661-763-3171. FAX: 661-763-5638. E-MAIL: editor@bak.rr.com. URL: http://www.taftmidwaydriller.com. Mailing Address: PO Box 958, Taft, CA 93268. Year Established: 1910. Pub. Frequency: s-w. (Tue. & Fri.) Page Size: broadsheet. Subscrip. Rate: $.50 newsstand/cover; $83.66/yr. **Wire Service(s):** AP. Circulation: 4,500 evening (paid). **Owner(s):** GateHouse Media, Inc, See address and contact information above. **Management:** John Watkins, Publisher. Melissa Robertson, Circulation Manager. Teri Walgren, Classified Adv. Mgr.. **Editorial:** Doug Keeler, Editor. Jason Blasco, Sports Editor.

TAHOE CITY

TAHOE WORLD. 395 N. Lake Blvd., Tahoe City, CA 96145. Telephone: 530-583-3487. FAX: 530-583-7109. E-MAIL: editor@tahoe-world.com. URL: http://www.tahoe.com. Mailing Address: PO Box 138, Tahoe City, CA 96145-0138. Year Established: 1963. Pub. Frequency: w. (Thu.) Page Size: broadsheet. Subscrip. Rate: $.50 newsstand/cover; $31.95/yr home delivery local; $52/yr mailed out of area. Freelance Pay: $0.50/column-inch. Circulation: 6,250 per issue (paid). **Owner(s):** Swift Newspapers, Inc., See address and contact information above. **Management:** Lee Denmark, Publisher. Charles Carey, Office Manager. **Editorial:** Keith Sheffield, Editor. Peter Staren, Group Editor.

TEHACHAPI

TEHACHAPI NEWS. 411 N. Mill St., Tehachapi, CA 93561. Telephone: 661-822-6828. FAX: 661-822-4053. E-MAIL: acrisalli@tehachapinews.com. URL: http://www.tehachapinews.com/. Mailing Address: PO Box 1840, Tehachapi, CA 93561. Year Established: 1900. Pub. Frequency: w. (Wed.) Page Size: broadsheet. Subscrip. Rate: $.50 newsstand/cover; $26/yr in county; $30/yr mailed in state. Circulation: 9,000 per issue (paid). **Owner(s):** Valley Direct, Inc., See address and contact information above. **Management:** Vicky Thrasher, General Manager. Lisa Baldridge, Publisher. Stefani Parks, Advertising Manager. Ron Fishgold, Classified Adv. Mgr.. **Editorial:** Carol Holmes, Editor. Michael Duffy, Sports.

TIBURON

ARK (TIBURON), THE. 1550 Tiburon Blvd., Tiburon, CA 94920. Telephone: 415-435-2652. FAX: 415-435-0849. E-MAIL: editor@thearknewspaper.com. URL: http://www.thearknewspaper.com. Year Established: 1972. Pub. Frequency: w. (Wed.) Page Size: tabloid. Subscrip. Rate: $1 newsstand/cover; $40/yr domestic 94920 & 94941area; $50/yr out of area. Adv. Rate: page $765 Circulation: 3,500 per issue (paid). **Owner(s):** Barbara Gnoss & Marilyn Kessler, See address and contact information above. **Management:** Barbara Gnoss, Publisher. Azi Najafi, Advertising Manager. **Editorial:** Barbara Gnoss, Editor.

ARK (TIBURON), THE. 1550 Tiburon Blvd, Tiburon, CA 94920. Telephone: 415-435-2652. FAX: 415-435-0849. URL: http://www.thearknewspaper.com. Year Established: 1973. Pub. Frequency: w. (Wed.) Subscrip. Rate: $1 newsstand/cover; $50/yr 94920 & 94941 zip code areas (effective 2008); $65/yr elsewhere. Circulation: 4,300. **Owner(s):** Ark Publishing Co., See address and contact information above. **Management:** Marilyn Kessler, Publisher. Henriette Corn, Advertising. **Editorial:** Marilyn Kessler, Editor.

TRUCKEE

SIERRA SUN. 12315 Deerfield Dr, Truckee, CA 96160. E-MAIL: editor@sierrasun.com. URL: http://www.sierrasun.com. Year Established: 1869. Pub. Frequency: w. (Thu.) Page Size: broadsheet. Subscrip. Rate: $.50 newsstand/cover; $150/yr local area; $175/yr out of area. Adv. Rate: col. inch $14.20 Freelance Pay: $0.50/column-inch. Circulation: 6,300 per issue (paid). **Owner(s):** Swift Newspapers, Inc., 500 Double Eagle Ct., Reno, NV 89511. Telephone: 775-850-7676. FAX: 775-850-7677.

TURLOCK

TURLOCK JOURNAL. 138 S Center St, Turlock, CA 95380. Telephone: 209-634-9141. FAX: 209-632-8813. URL: http://www.turlockjournal.com. Year Established: 1904. Pub. Frequency: s-w. (Wed. & Sat.) Page Size: broadsheet. Subscrip. Rate: $.75 newsstand/cover; $39/yr home delivery. **Wire Service(s):** AP. Circulation: 7,461 evening (paid). **Owner(s):** Morris Newspaper Corporation, 27 Abercorn St., Savannah, GA 31401. Telephone: 912-233-1281. FAX: 912-232-4639. **Management:** Doug Miller, Publisher. Dave Shabaz, Advertising Manager. Amy Hitchcock, Circulation Manager. **Editorial:** Kristina Hacker, Sports.

TWENTYNINE PALMS

DESERT TRAIL. 6396 Adobe Rd., Twentynine Palms, CA 92277. Telephone: 760-367-3577. FAX: 760-367-1798. E-MAIL: kurts@deserttrail.com. URL: http://www.deserttrail.com. Year Established: 1935. Pub. Frequency: w. (Thu.) Page Size: standard. Subscrip. Rate: $.50 newsstand/cover; $22/yr in county; $37/yr out of county; $52/yr out of state. Circulation: 3,500 per issue (paid). **Owner(s):** Brehm Communications, Inc., 16644 W. Bernardo Dr., Ste. 300, San Diego, CA 92127. Telephone: 858-451-6200. **Management:** Cindy Melland, General Manager. Eldon McKinnis, Publisher. Vivian McKinnis, Advertising Manager. Linda McNeeley, Classified Adv. Mgr.. **Editorial:** Kurt Schauppner, Editor.

VALLEY CENTER

VALLEY ROADRUNNER. 29277 Valley Center Rd., Valley Center, CA 92082. Telephone: 760-749-1112. FAX: 760-749-1688. E-MAIL: advertising@valleycenter.com. URL: http://www.valleycenter.com. Mailing Address: PO Box 1529, Valley Center, CA 92082. Year Established: 1974. Pub. Frequency: w. (Wed.) Page Size: broadsheet.Subscrip. Rate: $.50 newsstand/cover; $24/yr Circulation: 3,400 per issue (paid). **Owner(s):** Dale & Shirley Good, See address and contact information above. **Management:** Dale Good, President. Shirley Good, Publisher. Theresa Trogdon, Advertising Manager. Valerie Jonas, Art Director. **Editorial:** David Ross, Editor.

VENTURA

VENTURA COUNTY REPORTER. 700 E. Main St., Ventura, CA 93001. Telephone: 805-648-2244. FAX: 805-648-7801. E-MAIL: david@vcreporter.com. URL: http://www.vcreporter.com. Year Established: 1978. Pub. Frequency: w. (Thu.) Page Size: tabloid. Subscrip. Rate: $99/yr mailed. Freelance Pay: $75-$250/article. Circulation: 35,000 per issue (paid and free). **Owner(s):** Southland Publishing, Inc., See address and contact information above. **Management:** David Comden, Publisher. Teresa Wann-Davis, Office Manager. Kelly-Marie Tracy, Advertising. Teresa Wann-Davis, Circulation Manager. **Editorial:** Michael Sullivan, Editor.

WALNUT CREEK

CONTRA COSTA SUN. 2640 Shadelands Dr, Walnut Creek, CA 94598. Telephone: 925-935-2525. FAX: 925-977-8457. E-MAIL: ccsun@cctimes.com. URL: http://www.contracostatimes.com. Year Established: 1938. Pub. Frequency: w. (Fri.) Page Size: broadsheet Circulation: 13,500 per issue (paid). **Owner(s):** MediaNews Group, Inc., 101 W Colfax Ave, Ste 1100, Denver, CO 80202. FAX: 303-954-6320. **Management:** George E Armstrong, Publisher.

WASCO

WASCO TRIBUNE. 440 E St., Ste. C, Wasco, CA 93280. Telephone: 661-758-3063. FAX: 661-758-3064. Mailing Address: PO Box Y, Wasco, CA 93280. Pub. Frequency: w. (Wed.) Page Size: broadsheet. Subscrip. Rate: $.35 newsstand/cover. Circulation: 5,600 per issue (paid and free). **Owner(s):** Reed Print, Inc., 5409 Aldrin Ct., Bakersfield, CA 93313. Telephone: 661-834-0496. **Management:** Donald Reed, Publisher. Diane Givens, Office Manager. Jason Reed, Advertising Manager. **Editorial:** Roy Patrick, Editor. Frank W Reed, Editor-in-Chief.

WEAVERVILLE

TRINITY JOURNAL, THE. 500 Main St, Weaverville, CA 96093. Telephone: 530-623-2055. FAX: 530-623-5382. E-MAIL: trinityjournal@dcacable.net. URL: http:www.trinityjournal.com. Mailing Address: PO Box 340, Weaverville, CA 96093-0340. Year Established: 1856. Pub. Frequency: w. (Wed.) Page Size: standard. Subscrip. Rate: $.50 newsstand/cover; $29/yr in county; $46/yr out of county; $35/yr combined subscription in county print & online eds; $52/yr combined subscription out of county print & online eds.. Adv. Rate: col. inch $8.25 Freelance Pay: $1.25/column-inch. Circulation: 4,500 per issue (paid). **Owner(s):** W R A Enterprises, Inc., See address and contact information above. **Management:** Wayne Agner, Publisher. **Editorial:** Wayne Agner, Editor.

WEST COVINA

AZUSA HERALD. 1210 N. Azusa Canyon Rd., West Covina, CA 91790-1003. Telephone: 626-854-8700. FAX: 626-854-8719. E-MAIL: weeklies@yahoo.com. Year Established: 1887.Pub. Frequency: w. (Thu.) Page Size: tabloid Circulation: 483 per issue (free). **Owner(s):** MediaNews Group, Inc., 101 W Colfax Ave, Ste 1100, Denver, CO 80202. FAX: 303-954-6320. **Management:** Ron Wood, Publisher. Stacy DeHenau, Advertising Manager. Tim Guesman, Classified Adv. Mgr.. **Editorial:** Scott Swanson, Editor.

GLENDORA PRESS HIGHLANDER. 1210 N. Azusa Canyon Rd., West Covina, CA 91790-1003. URL: http://www.sgvn.com. Year Established: 1890. Pub. Frequency: w. (Thu.) Page Size: tabloid. Freelance Pay: $0.75/column-inch. Circulation: 17,460 per issue (free). **Owner(s):** MediaNews Group, Inc., 101 W Colfax Ave, Ste 1100, Denver, CO 80202. FAX: 303-954-6320. **Management:** Randy Heltsley, Advertising Director. Bryan Muldoon, Circulation Director. Jesse Dillon, Classified Adv. Mgr..

HIGHLANDER, THE. 1210 N. Azusa Canyon Rd., West Covina, CA 91790-1003. Telephone: 626-962-8811. Year Established: 1962. Pub. Frequency: w. (Thu.) Page Size: tabloid. Freelance Pay: $20/article. Circulation: 1,312 per issue (free). **Owner(s):** MediaNews Group, Inc., 101 W Colfax Ave, Ste 1100, Denver, CO 80202. FAX: 303-954-6320. **Management:** Ron Wood, Publisher. Ed Loescher, Advertising Manager. **Editorial:** Scott Swanson, Editor. Doug Spoon, Sports Editor.

WEST SACRAMENTO

NEWS-LEDGER, THE. PO Box 463, West Sacramento, CA 95691. Telephone: 916-371-8030. FAX: 916-371-8055. Year Established: 1964. Pub. Frequency: w. (Wed.) Page Size: broadsheet. Subscrip. Rate: $.35 newsstand/cover; $20/yr in county; $25/yr mailed elsewhere. Adv. Rate: col. inch $5.75 Circulation: 2,300 per issue (paid). **Owner(s):** Michael P. Garten, See address and contact information above. **Management:** Michael P. Garten, Publisher. **Editorial:** Steven K. Marschke, Editor.

WILLITS

THE/WILLITS NEWS. 77 W Commercial St, Willits, CA 95490. Telephone: 707-459-4643. FAX: 707-459-7664. E-MAIL: dclark@willitsnews.com. URL: http://www.willitsnews.com. Year Established: 1903. Pub. Frequency: s-w. (Wed. & Fri.) Page Size: broadsheet. Subscrip. Rate: $51.25/yr mailed in county; $63.52/yr mailed out of county; $45.10/yr mailed in county to senior citizens. **Owner(s):** MediaNews Group, Inc., 101 W Colfax Ave, Ste 1100, Denver, CO 80202. FAX: 303-954-6320. **Management:** Debbie Clark, Publisher. Christa Banzhaf, Advertising Director. Scott DeMuth, Classified Editor. **Editorial:** Dan McKee, Editor.

WILLOWS

WILLOWS JOURNAL. 101 Airport Rd, Willows, CA 95988. Telephone: 530-934-6800. FAX: 530-934-6815. E-MAIL: editor@tcnpress.com. Year Established: 1877. Pub. Frequency: s-w. (Wed. & Fri.) Page Size: broadsheet. Subscrip. Rate: $.75 newsstand/cover; $50/yr in county; $65/yr mailed out of county. Freelance Pay: $0.35/column-inch. Circulation: 5,486 per issue (paid and free). **Owner(s):** Morris Newspaper Corporation, 27 Abercorn St., Savannah, GA 31401. Telephone: 912-233-1281. FAX: 912-232-4639. **Management:** Dale Bean, General Manager. Christine Hammers, Advertising Manager. **Editorial:** Bill Rozak, Managing Editor.

WINDSOR

WINDSOR TIMES, THE. P O Box 799, Windsor, CA 95492. Telephone: 707-838-9211. FAX: 707-431-2623. URL: http://www.sonomawest.com/windsor/front/. Pub. Frequency: w. (Wed.) Subscrip. Rate: $.50 newsstand/cover per issue; $30/yr in city; $40/yr out of city; $20/yr in city to senior citizens. Circulation: 2,950 per issue (controlled). **Owner(s):** Sonoma West Publishers, Inc., 5 Mitchell Ln., Healdsburg, CA 95448. Telephone: 707-433-4451. **Management:** Rollie Atkinson, Publisher. Cherie Kelsay, Advertising Director. Grace Garner, Circulation Manager. **Editorial:** Matthew Hall, Managing Editor. Greg Clementi, Sports Editor.

WINTON

DELHI EXPRESS. 6950 Gerard St., Winton, CA 95388. Telephone: 209-358-5311. E-MAIL: mustardseedpub@hotmail.com. Pub. Frequency: w. (Thu.) Page Size: broadsheet.Subscrip. Rate: $27/yr mailed Circulation: 3,300 per issue (free). **Owner(s):** Mid-Valley Publications, Inc., See address and contact information above.

WOODLAND HILLS

LAS VIRGENES ENTERPRISE. ISSN 0193-9904
23009 Ventura Blvd., Woodland Hills, CA 91364-1107. Telephone: 818-223-9545. FAX: 818-223-9552. E-MAIL: wnrcnew@instanet.com. Year Established: 1980. Pub. Frequency: w. (Fri.) Page Size: tabloid. Subscrip. Rate: $30/yr mailed. Adv. Rate: col. inch $7 Circulation: 7,000 per issue (free). **Owner(s):** Valley News Group, See address and contact information above. **Management:** Kathleen Sterling, President. Rodger Sterling, Publisher. Kathleen Sterling, Advertising Manager. **Editorial:** Rodger Sterling, Editor-in-Chief.

VALLEY VANTAGE. 23009 Ventura Blvd., Woodland Hills, CA 91364-1107. Telephone: 818-223-9545. FAX: 818-223-9552. E-MAIL: wnrcnews@instanet.com. Year Established: 1949. Pub. Frequency: w. (Thu.) Page Size: tabloid. Subscrip. Rate: $45/yr mailed. Adv. Rate: col. inch $15 Circulation: 20,000 per issue (paid and free). **Owner(s):** Valley News Group, See address and contact information above. **Management:** Kathleen Sterling, President. Robert Skolnick, Advertising Manager. **Editorial:** Rodger Sterling, Editor.

WARNER CENTER NEWS. 23009 Ventura Blvd., Woodland Hills, CA 91364-1107. E-MAIL: wnrc@instanet.com. Year Established: 1980. Pub. Frequency: w. (Fri.) Page Size: tabloid. Subscrip. Rate: $40/yr mailed. Adv. Rate: col. inch $15 Circulation: 10,000 per issue (paid). **Owner(s):** Valley News Group, See address and contact information above. **Management:** Kathleen Sterling, President. Rodger Sterling, Publisher. Robert Skolnick, Advertising Manager. **Editorial:** Rodger Sterling, Editor-in-Chief.

YUCAIPA

YUCAIPA & CALIMESA NEWS MIRROR. 35154 Yucaipa Blvd., Yucaipa, CA 92399. Telephone: 909-797-9101. FAX: 909-797-0502. E-MAIL: news@newmirror.net. Year Established: 1915. Pub. Frequency: w. (Thu.) Page Size: tabloid. Subscrip. Rate: $.50 newsstand/cover; $22/yr. Adv. Rate: col. inch $17.70 Circulation: 19,265 per issue (paid). **Owner(s):** Century Group, The, See address and contact information above. **Management:** Gerald Bean, President. Toebe Bush, Publisher. Julie O'Connor, Advertising Director. Kathy Shepard, Circulation Manager. Pamela Eldridge, Human Res. Mgr.. **Editorial:** Claire Marie Teeters, Editor.

YUCCA VALLEY

H-DESERT SHOPPER. 56445 29 Palms Hwy., Yucca Valley, CA 92284. Telephone: 760-365-3315. FAX: 760-365-2650. Mailing Address: PO Box 880, Yucca Valley, CA 92286. Year Established: 1970. Pub. Frequency: w. (Thu.) Page Size: standard Circulation: 6,500 per issue (free). **Owner(s):** Brehm Communications, Inc., 16644 W. Bernardo Dr., Ste. 300, San Diego, CA 92128. **Management:** Cindy Melland, General Manager. Eldon McKinnis, Publisher. Vivian McKinnis, Advertising Manager. Kimberly Herrera, Circulation Manager. Roberta Huff, Classified Adv. Mgr..

HI-DESERT STAR. ISSN 0746-2301
56445 29 Palms Hwy., Yucca Valley, CA 92284. Telephone: 760-365-3315. FAX: 760-365-2650. E-MAIL: news@hidesertstar. URL: http://www.hidesertstar.com. Mailing Address: PO Box 880, Yucca Valley, CA 92286. Year Established: 1957. Pub. Frequency: s-w. (Wed. & Sat.) Page Size: standard. Subscrip. Rate: $.50 newsstand/cover; $33/yr home delivery in county; $63.36/yr mailed out of county; $74.70/yr mailed out of state. **Wire Service(s):** AP. Circulation: 7,752 per issue (paid). **Owner(s):** Brehm Communications, Inc., 16644 W. Bernardo Dr., Ste. 300, San Diego, CA 92127. Telephone: 858-451-6200. **Management:** Cindy Melland, General Manager. Eldon McKinnis, Publisher. Vivian McKinnis, Advertising Manager. Kimberly Herrera, Circulation Manager. Roberta Huff, Classified Adv. Mgr.. **Editorial:** Stacy Moore, Editor.

COLORADO

AKRON

AKRON NEWS REPORTER. 69 Main Ave, Akron, CO 80720-1439. Telephone: 970-345-2296. FAX: 970-345-6638. E-MAIL: akronews@plains.net. Year Established: 1910. Pub. Frequency: w. (Thu.) Page Size: broadsheet. Subscrip. Rate: $.50 newsstand/cover; $23/yr in state; $27/yr out of state. Circulation: 2,300 per issue (paid). **Owner(s):** MediaNews Group, Inc., 101 W Colfax Ave, Ste 1100, Denver, CO 80202. FAX: 303-954-6320. **Management:** Timi McCormick, Publisher. **Editorial:** JoAnne Busing, Editor.

ARVADA

ARVADA SENTINEL. ISSN 1524-5241
5777 Old Wadsworth Blvd, Ste R-900, Arvada, CO 80002. Telephone: 303-425-8755. FAX: 303-239-9808. E-MAIL: circulation@jeffconews.com. URL: http://www.jeffconews.com. Year Established: 1967. Pub. Frequency: w. (Thu.) Page Size: tabloid. Subscrip. Rate: $.50 newsstand/cover; $30/yr home delivery in county; $35/yr mailed out of county. Adv. Rate: col. inch $42 Circulation: 10,000 per issue (paid). **Owner(s):** Jeffco Publishing Co., 1000 Tenth St., Golden, CO 80401. Telephone: 303-279-5541. **Management:** David Lewis, President. Dee Schofer, Advertising. **Editorial:** Thomas Martinez, Editor. Steve Graham, Assistant Editor.

AURORA

AURORA SENTINEL. 10730 E. Bethany Dr., Ste. 304, Aurora, CO 80012. Telephone: 303-750-7555. FAX: 303-750-7699. E-MAIL: editor@aurorasentinel.com. URL: http://www.aurorasentinel.com. Year Established: 1910. Pub. Frequency: w. (Thu.) Page Size: tabloid. Subscrip. Rate: $.50 newsstand/cover; $20/yr mailed. Circulation: 22,950 per issue (paid and free). **Owner(s):** Aurora Publishing, See address and contact information above. **Management:** Harrison Cochran, Publisher. Bob Guerrero, Circulation Manager. **Editorial:** Dave Perry, Editor. Jake Hawkins, Feature Editor. Courtney Oakes, Sports Editor.

AVON

VAIL TRAIL. ISSN 1061-1770
40780 US Hwy. 6 & 24, Avon, CO 81620. Telephone: 970-748-0049. FAX: 970-748-6427. URL: http://www.vailtrail.com. Year Established: 1965. Pub. Frequency: w. (Thu.) Page Size: tabloid. Circulation: 14,000 per issue (controlled and free). **Owner(s):** Swift Newspapers, Inc., 500 Double Eagle Ct., Reno, NV 89511. **Editorial:** Tamara Miller, Editor.

BAILEY

FLUME, THE. 5138 County Rd. 64, Bailey, CO 80421-0460. Telephone: 303-838-4423. FAX: 303-838-8414. E-MAIL: info@theflume.com. URL: http://www.theflume.com. Mailing Address: PO Box 460, Bailey, CO 80421-0460. Year Established: 1879. Pub. Frequency: w. (Fri.) Page Size: tabloid. Subscrip. Rate: $.75 newsstand/cover; $24/yr in county; $29/yr in state; $33/yr out of state. Circulation: 3,200 per issue (paid). **Owner(s):** Arkansas Valley Publishing, 125 E. Second St., Salida, CO 81201. Telephone: 719-539-6691. FAX: 719-539-6630. **Management:** Lori Crawford, General Manager. Merle Baranczyk, Publisher. Lyndsay Gunter, Advertising Manager. **Editorial:** Tom Locke, Editor.

BAYFIELD

PINE RIVER TIMES. 110 Mill St., Bayfield, CO 81122-0830. Telephone: 970-884-2331. FAX: 970-884-4385. E-MAIL: prt@pinerivertimes.com. Mailing Address: PO Box 830, Bayfield, CO 81122-0830. Year Established: 1985. Pub. Frequency: w. (Fri.) Page Size: broadsheet. Subscrip. Rate: $.50 newsstand/cover; $27/yr in county; $33/yr out of county. Adv. Rate: col. inch $8 Circulation: 1,800 per issue (paid). **Owner(s):** Robert & Melanie Mazur, See address and contact information above. **Management:** Melanie Mazur, Publisher. Robert Mazur, Advertising Manager.

BOULDER

NORWOOD POST. PO Box 20788, Boulder, CO 80308. Telephone: 970-728-9788. FAX: 970-728-8061. E-MAIL: norwoodpost@yahoo.com. URL: http://www.norwoodpost.com. Pub. Frequency: w. (Thu.) Page Size: broadsheet.Subscrip. Rate: $.50 newsstand/cover; $36/yr Circulation: 1,100 per issue (paid). **Owner(s):** Telluride Newspapers, Inc., See address and contact information above. **Management:** Andrew Mirrington, Publisher. Jen Roach, Advertising. **Editorial:** Ellen Marie Mettrick, Editor.

BRIGHTON

BRIGHTON STANDARD BLADE. 139 N. Main St., Brighton, CO 80601. Telephone: 303-659-2522. FAX: 303-659-2901. E-MAIL: news@metrowestnewspapers.com. URL: http://www.metrowestfyi.com. Mailing Address: PO Box 646, Brighton, CO 80601. Year Established: 1903. Pub. Frequency: w. (Wed.) Page Size: broadsheet. Subscrip. Rate: $.50 newsstand/cover; $30/yr carrier delivery in state; $47/yr out of state. Adv. Rate: col. inch $21.78 Circulation: 10,200 per issue (paid). **Owner(s):** Landmark Community Newspapers, Inc., PO Box 549, Shelbyville, KY 40065. Telephone: 502-633-2526. **Management:** Karen Lambert, Publisher. Rick Fox, Advertising Manager. Frank Frazier, Circulation Manager. **Editorial:** Ken Eysaman, Editor.

FARMER & MINER. 139 N. Main St., Brighton, CO 80061. Telephone: 303-659-2522. FAX: 303-659-2901. E-MAIL: news@metrowestnewspapers.com. URL: http://www.metrowestfyi.com. Mailing Address: PO Box 400, Frederick, CO 80530. Year Established: 1930. Pub. Frequency: w. (Wed.) Page Size: tabloid. Subscrip. Rate: $.50 newsstand/cover per issue; $24/yr in state; $31/yr out of state. Adv. Rate: col. inch $13.95 Circulation: 1,100 per issue (paid). **Owner(s):** Landmark Community Newspapers, Inc., PO Box 549, Shelbyville, KY 40065. Telephone: 502-633-2526. **Management:** Karen Lambert, Publisher. Rick Fox, Advertising Manager. Frank Frazier, Circulation Manager. **Editorial:** Ken Eysaman, Editor.

FORT LUPTON PRESS. ISSN 1056-2419
139 N. Main St., Brighton, CO 80601. Telephone: 303-659-1141. FAX: 303-857-6801. URL: http://www.metrowest.com. Mailing Address: PO Box 646, Brighton, CO 80601. Year Established: 1906. Pub. Frequency: s-w. (Wed. & Sat.) Page Size: tabloid. Subscrip. Rate: $.50 newsstand/cover; $30/yr carrier delivery in state; $47/yr carrier delivery out of state. Circulation: 5,300 per issue (paid). **Owner(s):** Landmark Community Newspapers, Inc., PO Box 549, Shelbyville, KY 40065. Telephone: 502-633-4344. **Management:** Terry Gogerty, Publisher. Rick Fox, Advertising Manager. Frank Frazier, Circulation Manager. **Editorial:** Annette Reisel, Editor.

BROOMFIELD

BROOMFIELD ENTERPRISE. 1006 Depot Hill Rd., Ste. G, Broomfield, CO 80020. Telephone: 303-466-3636. FAX: 303-466-8168. URL: http://www.broomfieldenterprise.com. Year Established: 1975. Pub. Frequency: s-w. (Wed. & Sat.) Page Size: tabloid. Subscrip. Rate: $.50 newsstand/cover; $52/yr mailed. Circulation: 18,500 per issue (controlled and free). **Owner(s):** Boulder Publishing, Inc., 1048 Pearl St., Boulder, CO 80302. **Management:** Shera Warde, Advertising Manager. Bill Essex, Circulation Manager. **Editorial:** Kristin Hamm, Editor.

BRUSH

BRUSH NEWS-TRIBUNE. 109 Clayton St., Brush, CO 80723-0008. Telephone: 970-842-5516. FAX: 970-842-5519. E-MAIL: horner@brushnewstribune.com. URL: http://www.brushnewstribune.com. Mailing Address: PO Box 8, Brush, CO 80723-0008. Year Established: 1896. Pub. Frequency: w. (Wed.) Page Size: broadsheet. Subscrip. Rate: $.50 newsstand/cover; $26/yr mailed in county; $35/yr mailed elsewhere. Adv. Rate: col. inch $6.55 Circulation: 2,000 per issue (paid). **Owner(s):** MediaNews Group, Inc., 101 W Colfax Ave, Ste 1100, Denver, CO 80202. FAX: 303-954-6320. **Management:** Iva Kay Horner, Publisher. Rene Henry, Advertising. **Editorial:** Iva Kay Horner, Editor. Katie Collins, Reporter.

BUENA VISTA

CHAFFEE COUNTY TIMES, THE. 209 E. Main St., Buena Vista, CO 81211. Telephone: 719-395-8621. FAX: 719-395-8623. E-MAIL: allnews@chaffeecountytimes.com. URL: http://www.chaffeecountytimes.com. Mailing Address: PO Box 2048, Buena Vista, CO 81211. Year Established: 1880. Pub. Frequency: w. (Thu.) Page Size: tabloid. Subscrip. Rate: $28/yr in county; $35/yr out of county. Circulation: 3,000 per issue (paid). **Owner(s):** Arkansas Valley Publishing, 125 E. Second St., Salida, CO 81201. Telephone: 719-539-6691. FAX: 719-539-6630. **Management:** Merle Baranczyk, Publisher. Joy Duprey, Advertising Manager. Judie Moorhead, Classified Adv. Mgr.. **Editorial:** Mike Bulock, Editor. Theresa Williamson, Copy Editor.

CARBONDALE

VALLEY JOURNAL. 467 Main St., Carbondale, CO 81623. Telephone: 970-963-3211. FAX: 970-963-3259. Mailing Address: PO Box 1150, Carbondale, CO 81623-1150. Year Established: 1974. Pub. Frequency: s-w. (Thu. & Sun.) Page Size: tabloid. Subscrip. Rate: $30/yr local area; $35/yr out of area. Freelance Pay: $1.50/column-inch. Circulation: 5,700 per issue (paid and free). **Owner(s):** Swift Newspapers, Inc., 500 Double Eagle Ct., Reno, NV 89511. Telephone: 775-850-7676. FAX: 775-850-7677. **Management:** Karl Terry, Publisher. **Editorial:** John Colson, Editor. John Stroud, Managing Editor.

CASTLE ROCK

CASTLE ROCK NEWS-PRESS. 125 Stephanie Pl, Castle Rock, CO 81090. Telephone: 303-688-3128. FAX: 303-660-0240. E-MAIL: dceditor@ccnewspapers.com. URL: http://www.ccnewspapers.com. Mailing Address: PO Box 1270, Castle Rock, CO 80104. Pub. Frequency: w. (Thu.) Page Size: broadsheet. Subscrip. Rate: $.50 newsstand/cover per issue; $24.95/yr. **Owner(s):** ASP Westward LP, 523 N Sam Houston Pkwy Ste, 600, Houston, TX 77060-4011. **Management:** Asa Cole, Publisher. Stacy Vogel, Advertising Manager. Effie Ward, Circulation Director. **Editorial:** Jeremy Bangs, Editor.

DOUGLAS COUNTY NEWS PRESS. 125 Stephanie Pl, Castle Rock, CO 81090. Telephone: 303-688-3128. FAX: 303-660-0240. URL: http://www.ccnewspapers.com. Mailing Address: PO Box 1270, Castle Rock, CO 80104. Year Established: 1892. Pub. Frequency: w. (Thu.) Page Size: broadsheet.Subscrip. Rate: $.50 newsstand/cover; $24.95/yr Circulation: 38,000 per issue (paid). **Owner(s):** ASP Westward LP, 523 N Sam Houston Pkwy Ste, 600, Houston, TX 77060-4011. **Management:** Steve Lencke, Publisher. Cindy Paytask, Advertising Manager. Vivian McKinnis, Circulation Manager. **Editorial:** Heide Harden, Managing Editor. Sean Hadden, Sports Editor.

ELBERT COUNTY NEWS. 125 Stephanie Pl, Castle Rock, CO 81090. Telephone: 303-688-3128. FAX: 303-660-0240. URL: http://www.ccnewspapers.com. Mailing Address: PO Box 1270, Castle Rock, CO 80104. Pub. Frequency: w. (Thu.) Page Size: broadsheet.Subscrip. Rate: $.50 newsstand/cover; $24.95/yr Circulation: 3,000 per issue (paid). **Owner(s):** ASP Westward LP, 523 N Sam Houston Pkwy Ste, 600, Houston, TX 77060-4011. **Management:** Steven Lencke, Publisher. Bill Gibson, Advertising Manager. **Editorial:** Karen Kendig, Editor. Greg Johnson, Managing Editor.

LONE TREE VOICE. 125 Stephanie Pl, Castle Rock, CO 81090. Telephone: 303-688-3128. FAX: 303-660-0240. E-MAIL: jbangs@ccnewspapers.com. URL: http://www.ccnewspapers.com. Pub. Frequency: w. (Thu) Page Size: broadsheet. Subscrip. Rate: $52/yr mailed out of area. **Owner(s):** ASP Westward LP, 523 N Sam Houston Pkwy Ste, 600, Houston, TX 77060-4011. **Management:** Asa Cole, Publisher. Stacy Vogel, Advertising Manager. Effie Ward, Circulation Director. **Editorial:** Jeremy Bangs, Editor.

PARKER CHRONICLE. 125 Stephanie Pl, Castle Rock, CO 81090. Telephone: 303-841-5497. FAX: 303-660-0240. E-MAIL: dceditor@ccnewspapers.com. URL: http://ccnewspapers.com. Mailing Address: PO Box 1270, Castle Rock, CO 80104. Year Established: 2001. Pub. Frequency: w. (Thu.) Page Size: broadsheet Circulation: 21,700 per issue (free). **Owner(s):** ASP Westward LP, 523 N Sam Houston Pkwy Ste, 600, Houston, TX 77060-4011. **Management:** Asa Cole, Publisher. Stacy Vogel, Advertising Manager. Effie Ward, Circulation Director. **Editorial:** Jeremy Bangs, Editor.

COLORADO SPRINGS

BLACK FOREST NEWS & PALMER DIVIDE PIONEER. ISSN 0745-533X
11425 Black Forest Rd., Colorado Springs, CO 80908. Telephone: 719-495-8750. FAX: 719-495-8758. E-MAIL: blackforestnews@earthlink.net. URL: http://blackforestnews-co.com. Year Established: 1960. Pub. Frequency: w. (Thu.) Page Size: tabloid. Subscrip. Rate: $.35 newsstand/cover; $15/yr home delivery in county; $17/yr mailed out of state. Adv. Rate: col. inch $5.25 Circulation: 1,300 per issue (paid). **Owner(s):** Judy vonAhlefeldt, See address and contact information above. **Management:** Judy vonAhlefeldt, Publisher. **Editorial:** Judy vonAhlefeldt, Editor.

CORTEZ

CORTEZ JOURNAL, THE. 123 Roger Smith Ave., Cortez, CO 81321. Telephone: 970-565-8527. FAX: 970-565-8532. E-MAIL: news@cortezjournal.com. URL: http://www.cortezjournal.com. Mailing Address: PO Box J, Cortez, CO 81321. Year Established: 1936. Pub. Frequency: 3/w. (Tue., Thu., Sat.) Page Size: standard. Subscrip. Rate: $.35 newsstand/cover; $43/yr home delivery in county; $68/yr mailed out of county. Circulation: 7,150 per issue (paid). **Owner(s):** Animas Publishing, See address and contact information above. **Management:** Suzy Meyer, Publisher. Tammy Wright, Advertising. Joyce Nidiffer, Circulation Manager. Cathy McCully, Classified Adv. Mgr.. **Editorial:** Paula Pennell, Managing Editor. Mike Larson, Sports Editor.

MANCOS TIMES, THE. 123 Roger Smith Ave., Cortez, CO 81321. Telephone: 970-565-8527. FAX: 970-565-8532. URL: http://www.cortezjournal.com. Mailing Address: PO Box J, Cortez, CO 81321. Year Established: 1892. Pub. Frequency: w. (Wed.) Page Size: tabloid. Subscrip. Rate: $.35 newsstand/cover; $18/yr home delivery in area; $26/yr mailed out of area. Circulation: 850 evening (paid). **Owner(s):** Animas Publishing, See address and contact information above. **Management:** Suzy Meyer, General Manager. Tammy Wright, Advertising. Joyce Nidiffer, Circulation Manager. Cathy McCully, Classified Adv. Mgr.. Sue Patterson, Business Manager. **Editorial:** Tom Vaughan, Managing Editor. Mike Larson, Sports Editor.

CRAIG

SATURDAY MORNING PRESS. 466 Yampa Ave., Craig, CO 81625. Telephone: 970-824-7031. FAX: 970-824-6810. URL: http://www.craigdailypress.com. Mailing Address: PO Box 5, Craig, CO 81626. Pub. Frequency: w. (Sat.) Page Size: standard Circulation: 9,600 per issue (free). **Owner(s):** WorldWest LLC, 609 New Hampshire, P.O. Box 688, Lawrence, KS 66044. Telephone: 785-843-1000. **Management:** Bryce Jacobson, Publisher. Renee Campbell, Advertising Manager. Amy Fontenot, Circulation Manager. **Editorial:** Jennifer Grubbs, Managing Editor.

DELTA

DELTA COUNTY INDEPENDENT. ISSN 0891-9704
401 Meeker St., Delta, CO 81416. Telephone: 970-874-4421. FAX: 970-874-4424. E-MAIL: editor@daltacountyindependent.com. URL: http://www.deltacountyindependent.com. Mailing Address: PO Box 809, Delta, CO 81416-0809. Year Established: 1883. Pub. Frequency: w. (Wed.) Page Size: broadsheet. Subscrip. Rate: $.40 newsstand/cover; $17/yr home delivery in county; $20/yr mailed in state. Circulation: 7,320 per issue (paid). **Owner(s):** Leader Publishing Co., Inc., See address and contact information above. **Management:** Randy Sunderland, General Manager. Norman Sunderland, Publisher. Roxanne McCormick, Advertising Manager. **Editorial:** Pat Sunderland, Managing Editor. Gary Burke, Sports Editor.

DENVER

DENVER HERALD-DISPATCH. ISSN 0898-1701
2200 S Federal Blvd #6, Denver, CO 80219. E-MAIL: nancy@hdnewspaper.com. Year Established: 1926. Pub. Frequency: w. (Thu.) Page Size: tabloid. Subscrip. Rate: $.50 newsstand/cover; $30/yr home delivery in county; $42/yr home delivery out of county. Adv. Rate: col. inch $15 **Wire Service(s):** AP. Circulation: 3,600 per issue (paid). **Owner(s):** Robert Sweeney, See address and contact information above. **Management:** Nancy Russell, General Manager. Robert Sweeney, Publisher. **Editorial:** Elizabeth Denton, Editor.

ESTES PARK TRAIL-GAZETTE. 101 W Colfax Ave, Ste 1100, Denver, CO 80202. FAX: 303-954-6320. E-MAIL: geditor@eptrail.com. URL: http://www.eptrail.com. Mailing Address: P O Box 1707, Estes Park, CO 80517. Year Established: 1915. Pub. Frequency: s-w. (Wed. & Fri.) Page Size: broadsheet. Subscrip. Rate: $.75 newsstand/cover; $36/yr home delivery in county; $47/yr mailed in state; $55/yr mailed out of state. Circulation: 5,800 per issue (paid). **Owner(s):** MediaNews Group, Inc., See address and contact information above. **Management:** Bill Ferguson, Publisher. Cat Harvilla, Advertising Director. Annette Ackerland, Circulation Manager. **Editorial:** John Cordsen, Managing Editor.

PARK RECORD, THE. ISSN 0745-9483
101 W Colfax Ave, Ste 1100, Denver, CO 80202. FAX: 303-954-6320. URL: http://www.parkrecord.com. Mailing Address: PO Box 3688, Park City, UT 84060. Year Established: 1880. Pub. Frequency: bi-w. (Wed. & Sat.) Page Size: broadsheet. Subscrip. Rate: $.50 newsstand/cover; $37/yr in county; $70/yr elsewhere. Circulation: 8,500 per issue (controlled and free). **Owner(s):** MediaNews Group, Inc., See address and contact information above. **Management:** Andy Bernhard, Publisher. Valerie Deming, Advertising Director. Cristin Hicks, Classified Adv. Mgr.. **Editorial:** Nan Chalat-Noaker, Editor.

WESTWORD. 969 Broadway, Denver, CO 80203. Telephone: 303-296-7744. FAX: 303-296-5416. E-MAIL: denver-editorial@westword.com. URL: http://www.westword.com. Mailing Address: PO Box 5970, Denver, CO 80217. Year Established: 1977. Pub. Frequency: w. (Thu) Page Size: tabloid.Subscrip. Rate: $50/yr mailed Circulation: 108,000 per issue (free). **Owner(s):** Village Voice Media, Inc., 1201 E Jefferson St, Phoenix, AZ 85034. Telephone: 415-541-0700. FAX: 415-541-9096. **Management:** Scott Tobias, Publisher. Mandy Mortimer, Advertising Director. Taylor Wheeler, Classified Adv. Mgr.. **Editorial:** Patricia Calhoun, Editor. Amy Haimerl, Associate Editor.

DOLORES

DOLORES STAR, THE. 211 Railroad Ave., Dolores, CO 81323. Telephone: 970-882-4486. FAX: 970-882-4476. E-MAIL: judy@doloresstar.com. Mailing Address: PO Box 660, Dolores, CO 81323-0211. Year Established: 1897. Pub. Frequency: w. (Fri.) Page Size: tabloid. Subscrip. Rate: $.50 newsstand/cover; $14/yr local; $21/yr out of area. Circulation: 1,200 per issue (paid). **Owner(s):** Montezuma Valley Publishing, PO Box J, Cortez, CO 81321. Telephone: 970-565-8527. **Management:** Suzy Meyer, Publisher. Sue Patterson, Business Manager. **Editorial:** Judy Englehart, Editor.

DOVE CREEK

DOVE CREEK PRESS. 321 N. Main, Dove Creek, CO 81324. Telephone: 970-677-2214. FAX: 970-677-3002g. E-MAIL: dcpress@centurytel.net. Mailing Address: PO Box 598, Dove Creek, CO 81324-0598. Year Established: 1940. Pub. Frequency: w. (Thu.) Page Size: tabloid. Subscrip. Rate: $.35 newsstand/cover; $15/yr in county; $22/yr mailed out of county. Circulation: 1,245 per issue (paid). **Owner(s):** Doug & Linda Funk, See address and contact information above. **Management:** Linda Funk, Publisher. Tina Coker, Circulation Manager. **Editorial:** Doug Funk, Editor.

EADS

KIOWA COUNTY PRESS. 1208 Maine St., Eads, CO 81036. Telephone: 719-438-5800. E-MAIL: release@kiowacountypress.com. URL: http://www.kiowacountypress.com. Mailing Address: PO Box 248, Eads, CO 81036-0248. Year Established: 1887. Pub. Frequency: w. (Fri.) Page Size: standard. Subscrip. Rate: $.50 newsstand/cover; $19/yr in county; $21/yr in state; $24/yr out of state. Adv. Rate: col. inch $5.80 Circulation: 725 per issue (paid). **Owner(s):** Christopher Sorensen, See address and contact information above. **Management:** Chris Sorensen, Publisher. Connie McPherson, Circulation Manager. **Editorial:** Connie McPherson, Editor.

EVERGREEN

CANYON COURIER. ISSN 0192-0197
27902 Meadow Dr., Ste. 200, Evergreen, CO 80439-2106. Telephone: 303-674-5534. FAX: 303-674-4104. E-MAIL: news@evergreenco.com. URL: http://www.canyoncourier.com. Year Established: 1954. Pub. Frequency: w. (Wed.) Page Size: tabloid. Subscrip. Rate: $.50 newsstand/cover; $25/yr home delivery in county; $31/yr mailed out of county. Freelance Pay: $20/story. Circulation: 8,350 per issue (paid). **Owner(s):** Landmark Community Newspapers, Inc., PO Box 549, Shelbyville, KY 40065. Telephone: 502-633-2526. FAX: 502-633-2618. **Management:** Brad W. Bradberry, Publisher. Russell Puls, Advertising Manager. **Editorial:** Dan Johnson, Editor.

HIGH TIMBER TIMES. 27902 Meadow Rd., Ste. 200, Evergreen, CO 80439. Telephone: 303-838-5830. FAX: 303-838-6007. E-MAIL: news@evergreenco.com. URL: http://www.hightimbertimes.com. Year Established: 1977. Pub. Frequency: w. (Thu.) Page Size: tabloid. Subscrip. Rate: $.50 newsstand/cover; $22/yr local; $30/yr elsewhere. Freelance Pay: $20/story. Circulation: 2,500 per issue (paid). **Owner(s):** Landmark Community Newspapers, Inc., PO Box 549, Shelbyville, KY 40065. Telephone: 502-633-2526. FAX: 502-633-2618. **Management:** Brad Bradberry, Publisher. Russell Puls, Advertising Manager. **Editorial:** Steve Jackson, Editor.

FLORENCE

FLORENCE CITIZEN. 200 S. Pikes Peak Ave., Florence, CO 81226. Telephone: 719-784-6383. FAX: 719-784-6384. Pub. Frequency: w. (Thu.) Page Size: tabloid. Subscrip. Rate: $.50 newsstand/cover; $20/yr local; $22/yr out of area. Circulation: 1,200 per issue (paid). **Owner(s):** Robert & Sue Wood, See address and contact information above. **Management:** Robert M. Wood, Publisher. **Editorial:** Robert M. Wood, Editor.

FOUNTAIN

FOUNTAIN VALLEY NEWS / EL PASO COUNTY NEWS. PO Box 400, Fountain, CO 80817. Telephone: 719-382-5611. FAX: 719-382-5614. E-MAIL: ftvalley@earthlink.net. Year Established: 1958. Pub. Frequency: w. (Wed.) Page Size: tabloid. Subscrip. Rate: $.75 newsstand/cover; $18/yr home delivery in county; $17/yr mailed in county; $20/yr mailed out of county. Circulation: 5,000 per issue (paid and free). **Owner(s):** Shopper Press, Inc., See address and contact information above. **Management:** Kathryn A. Wiese, Publisher. **Editorial:** Patricia St. Louis, Managing Editor.

FOWLER

FOWLER TRIBUNE, THE. 112 E Cranston, Fowler, CO 81039. Telephone: 719-263-5311. FAX: 719-263-5549. URL: http://www.fowlertribune.com. Year Established: 1898. Pub. Frequency: w. (Thu.) Page Size: broadsheet. Subscrip. Rate: $.50 newsstand/cover; $22/yr in county; $28/yr out of county; $32/yr out of state. Circulation: 1,600 per issue (paid). **Owner(s):** GateHouse Media, Inc, 350 WillowBrook Office Park, Fairport, NY 14450. Telephone: 585-598-0030. **Management:** Pat Ptolemy, Publisher. **Editorial:** Candi Miell, Editor.

FRISCO

SUMMIT COUNTY JOURNAL. 40 W. Main St., Frisco, CO 80443. Telephone: 970-668-0750. FAX: 970-668-3859. URL: http://www.summitcounty.com. Mailing Address: PO Box 709, Frisco, CO 80443. Year Established: 1880. Pub. Frequency: w. (Fri.) Page Size: tabloid. Subscrip. Rate: $30 mailed for 6 mos. in state; $40/yr mailed in state. Circulation: 11,000 per issue (paid and free). **Owner(s):** Swift Newspapers, Inc., 500 Double Eagle Ct., Reno, NV 89511. **Management:** James Morgan, Publisher. David Mercier, Advertising Director. Ed Pankevicius, Circulation Manager. **Editorial:** Jim Pokrandt, Editor.

FRUITA

FRUITA TIMES. 217 E. Aspen Ave., Fruita, CO 81521-2238. Telephone: 970-858-3924. FAX: 970-858-7658. Year Established: 1892. Pub. Frequency: w. (Thu.) Page Size: tabloid. Subscrip. Rate: $.50 newsstand/cover; $20/yr in county; $30/yr out of county. Adv. Rate: col. inch $7.06 Freelance Pay: $0.75/column-inch. Circulation: 1,500 per issue (paid). **Owner(s):** Robert Sweeney & Robert Dougherty, See address and contact information above. **Management:** Robert Dougherty, Publisher. **Editorial:** Robert Dougherty, Editor.

GOLDEN

GOLDEN TRANSCRIPT. ISSN 0746-6382
1000 Tenth St., Golden, CO 80401. Telephone: 303-279-5541. FAX: 303-279-7157. E-MAIL: circulation@jeffconews.com. URL: http://www.jeffconews.com. Year Established: 1866. Pub. Frequency: w. (Wed.) Page Size: tabloid. Subscrip. Rate: $.50 newsstand/cover; $30/yr in county; $35/yr out of county. Adv. Rate: col. inch $19 Circulation: 4,200 per issue (paid and controlled). **Owner(s):** Jeffco Publishing Co., See address and contact information above. **Management:** David Lewis, President. **Editorial:** Thomas Martinez, Editor. Steve Graham, Assistant Editor.

WHEAT RIDGE TRANSCRIPT. ISSN 1089-9197
1000 Tenth St., Golden, CO 80401. Telephone: 303-279-5541. FAX: 303-279-7157. E-MAIL: circulation@milehighnews.com. URL: http://www.milehighnews.com. Pub. Frequency: w. (Wed.) Page Size: tabloid. Subscrip. Rate: $.50 newsstand/cover; $30/yr in county; $35/yr out of county. Adv. Rate: col. inch $18 Circulation: 3,000 per issue (controlled and free). **Owner(s):** Jeffco Publishing Co., See address and contact information above. **Management:** David Lewis, Publisher. **Editorial:** Thomas Martinez, Editor. Steve Graham, Assistant Editor.

GUNNISON

GUNNISON COUNTRY TIMES. ISSN 0892-1113
218 N. Wisconsin St., Gunnison, CO 81230. Telephone: 970-641-1414. FAX: 970-641-6515. E-MAIL: publisher@gunnisontimes.com. URL: http://www.gunnisontimes.com. Year Established: 1880. Pub. Frequency: w. (Thu.) Page Size: tabloid. Subscrip. Rate: $.50 newsstand/cover; $36/yr home delivery in county; $44/yr mailed out of county. Adv. Rate: col. inch $10.50 Circulation: 4,000 per issue (paid). **Owner(s):** Gunnison Country Publications LLC, See address and contact information above. **Management:** Chris Dickey, Owner. Stephen J. Pierotti, Publisher. Drew Nelson, Advertising Manager. Larry Jenson, Classified Adv. Mgr.. **Editorial:** Chris Dickey, Managing Editor.Readers: Gunnison County

GYPSUM

EAGLE VALLEY ENTERPRISE. 0200 Lindberg Dr, Gypsum, CO 81637. Telephone: 970-328-6656. FAX: 970-328-6393. E-MAIL: getnews@vail.net. URL: http://www.searchcolorado.com. Mailing Address: PO Box 450, Eagle, CO 81631. Year Established: 1898. Pub. Frequency: w. (Thu.) Page Size: tabloid. Subscrip. Rate: $.25 newsstand/cover; $20/yr in state; $30/yr out of state. Circulation: 3,200 per issue (paid and free). **Owner(s):** Swift Newspapers, Inc., 500 Double Eagle Ct., Reno, NV 89511. Telephone: 775-850-7676. FAX: 775-850-7677. **Management:** Andrea Palm-Porter, Publisher. **Editorial:** Kathy Heicher, Editor.

HAXTUN

HAXTUN-FLEMING HERALD, THE. PO Box 128, Haxtun, CO 80731. Telephone: 970-774-6118. FAX: 970-774-7690. E-MAIL: news@hfherald.com. URL: http://www.hfherald.com. Year Established: 1975. Pub. Frequency: w. (Wed.) Page Size: tabloid.Subscrip. Rate: $26/yr local; $28/yr out of area Circulation: 1,300 per issue (paid). **Owner(s):** Fletcher Street, Inc., See address and contact information above. **Management:** Jean Gray, Publisher. Candie Salyards, Advertising. **Editorial:** Jean Gray, Editor.

HUGO

EASTERN COLORADO PLAINSMAN. PO Box 98, Hugo, CO 80821-0098. Telephone: 719-743-2371. E-MAIL: ecp@rebeltec.net. Year Established: 1912. Pub. Frequency: w. (Thu.) Page Size: tabloid. Subscrip. Rate: $.50 newsstand/cover; $20/yr in county; $25/yr out of county. Adv. Rate: col. inch $5.75 Circulation: 1,300 per issue (paid). **Owner(s):** Becky Osterwald, See address and contact information above. **Management:** Becky Osterwald, Advertising Manager. **Editorial:** Becky Osterwald, Editor.

JULESBURG

JULESBURG ADVOCATE. 108 Cedar St., Julesburg, CO 80737-1520. Telephone: 970-474-3388. FAX: 970-474-3389. E-MAIL: julesadv@ria.net. Year Established: 1899. Pub. Frequency: w. (Thu.) Page Size: broadsheet. Subscrip. Rate: $.50 newsstand/cover; $24/yr in county; $26/yr out of county. Circulation: 2,000 per issue (paid). **Owner(s):** MediaNews Group, Inc., 101 W Colfax Ave, Ste 1100, Denver, CO 80202. FAX: 303-954-6320. **Management:** Kay Johnson, General Manager. Jan Howett, Office Manager. Lona McCollister, Advertising.

LAKEWOOD

LAKEWOOD SENTINEL. ISSN 1060-5215
1224 Wadsworth Blvd., Lakewood, CO 80215. Telephone: 303-239-9890. FAX: 303-239-9808. E-MAIL: circulation@jeffconews.com. URL: http://www.jeffconews.com. Year Established: 1924. Pub. Frequency: w. (Thu.) Page Size: tabloid. Subscrip. Rate: $.50 newsstand/cover; $30/yr in county; $35/yr out of county; $35/yr out of county to alumni. Circulation: 10,000 per issue (controlled and free). **Owner(s):** Jeffco Publishing Co., 1000 Tenth St., Golden, CO 80401. Telephone: 303-279-5541. FAX: 303-279-7157. **Management:** David Lewis, President. **Editorial:** Steve Graham, Assistant Editor.

LAS ANIMAS

BENT COUNTY DEMOCRAT. 516 Carson Ave, Las Animas, CO 81054. Telephone: 719-456-1333. FAX: 719-456-1420. URL: http://www.bentcountydemocrat.com. Mailing Address: PO Box 467, Las Animas, CO 81054-0467. Year Established: 1883. Pub. Frequency: w. (Thu.) Page Size: broadsheet. Subscrip. Rate: $.50 newsstand/cover; $23/yr local. **Owner(s):** GateHouse Media, Inc, 350 WillowBrook Office Park, Fairport, NY 14450. Telephone: 585-598-0030. FAX: 585-248-2631. **Management:** Pat Ptolemy, Publisher. **Editorial:** Dan Cunningham, Editor.

LEADVILLE

HERALD-DEMOCRAT (LEADVILLE). 717 Harrison Ave., Leadville, CO 80461. Telephone: 719-486-0641. FAX: 719-486-0611. E-MAIL: allnews@leadvilleherald.com. URL: http://www.leadvilleherald.com. Mailing Address: PO Box 980, Leadville, CO 80461. Year Established: 1879. Pub. Frequency: w. (Thu.) Page Size: tabloid. Subscrip. Rate: $.75 newsstand/cover; $19/yr in county; $27/yr out of county. Adv. Rate: col. inch $6.25 Circulation: 2,500 per issue (paid). **Owner(s):** Arkansas Valley Publishing, PO Box 189, Salida, CO 81201. Telephone: 719-539-6691. FAX: 719-539-6630. **Management:** Merle Baranczyk, Publisher. Dave Lindley, Advertising Manager. Carol MacKelvie, Circulation Manager. Mary Franz, Classified Adv. Mgr.. **Editorial:** Marcia Martinek, Editor. Carol Werckman, News Editor.

LEADVILLE CHRONICLE, THE. 613 Harrison Ave, Leadville, CO 80461. Telephone: 719-486-3666. FAX: 719-486-3444. URL: http://www.leadvillechronicle.com. Year Established: 1998. Pub. Frequency: w. (Thu.) Page Size: tabloid.Adv. Rate: col. inch $7.50 Circulation: 4,500 per issue (free). **Owner(s):** Swift Newspapers, Inc., 500 Double Eagle Ct., Reno, NV 89511. Telephone: 775-850-7676. FAX: 775-850-7677. **Editorial:** Christine Ina Casillas, Editor.

LITTLETON

ENGLEWOOD HERALD. ISSN 1058-9899
2329 W. Main St., Littleton, CO 80120. Telephone: 303-794-7877. FAX: 303-794-1909. E-MAIL: craig@ccnewspapers.com. URL: http://www.ccnewspapers.com. Year Established: 1911. Pub. Frequency: w. (Fri.) Page Size: tabloid. Subscrip. Rate: $.75 newsstand/cover; $24.95/yr in county; $30/yr out of county; $40/yr mailed out of state. Circulation: 2,100 per issue (paid). **Owner(s):** ASP Westward LP, 523 N Sam Houston Pkwy, Ste 600, Houston, TX 77060. **Management:** Tim Craig, Publisher. Vivian MxKinnis, Circulation Manager. **Editorial:** Jeremy Bangs, Editor.

HIGHLANDS RANCH HERALD. 2329 W. Main St., Littleton, CO 80120. Telephone: 303-794-7877. FAX: 303-794-1909. E-MAIL: tspargur@ccnewspapers.com. URL: http://www.ccnewspapers.com. Pub. Frequency: w. (Thu.) Page Size: broadsheet. Subscrip. Rate: $.75 newsstand/cover; $52/yr. Adv. Rate: col. inch $22.50 Circulation: 11,000 per issue (paid). **Owner(s):** ASP Westward LP, 523 N Sam Houston Pkwy Ste, 600, Houston, TX 77060-4011. Telephone: 281-668-1100. **Management:** Tim Craig, Publisher. Vivian MxKinnis, Circulation Manager. **Editorial:** Jeremy Bangs, Editor.

LITTLETON INDEPENDENT (LITTLETON). 2329 W. Main St., Littleton, CO 80120. Telephone: 303-794-7877. FAX: 303-794-1909. E-MAIL: tcraig@ccnewspapers.com. URL: http://www.dcnewspress.com. Year Established: 1888. Pub. Frequency: w. (Thu.) Page Size: tabloid. Subscrip. Rate: $.75 newsstand/cover; $24.95/yr in county; $30/yr mailed out of county. Adv. Rate: col. inch $17.95 Circulation: 6,100 per issue (paid). **Owner(s):** ASP Westward LP, 523 N Sam Houston Pkwy Ste, 600, Houston, TX 77060-4011. Telephone: 281-668-1100. **Management:** Tim Craig, Publisher. Vivian McKinnis, Circulation Manager. **Editorial:** Jeremy Bangs, Editor.

LYONS

LYONS RECORDER, THE. 304 Main St #C, Lyons, CO 80540. E-MAIL: lreditor@lyonsrecorder.com. URL: http://www.lyonsrecorder.com. Year Established: 1910. Pub. Frequency: w. (Thu.) Page Size: tabloid. Subscrip. Rate: $22/yr mailed; $.50 newsstand/cover. Adv. Rate: col. inch $8 Freelance Pay: $0.75/column-inch. Circulation: 900 per issue (paid and free). **Owner(s):** Berthoud News, Inc., 1501 S County Rd 23E, Berthoud, CO 80513. Telephone: 970-532-3898. **Management:** Gary Wamsley, Owner. **Editorial:** Sharlynn Wamsley, Editor.

MEEKER

RIO BLANCO HERALD TIMES. 592 Main St, Ste 6, Meeker, CO 81641. E-MAIL: editor@theheraldtimes.com. Year Established: 1885. Pub. Frequency: w. (Thu.) Page Size: broadsheet. Subscrip. Rate: $.50 newsstand/cover; $15 for 6 mos. in county; $25/yr in county; $25 for 6 mos. out of county; $40/yr out of county. Adv. Rate: col. inch $6.50 Circulation: 2,700 per issue (paid). **Owner(s):** Mitch & Meg Bettis, PO Box 720, Meeker, CO 81641-0720. Telephone: 970-878-4017. FAX: 970-878-4016. **Management:** Mitch Bettis, Publisher. Deb Pettijohn, Advertising. **Editorial:** Jeff Burkhead, Editor. Tonya Morris, Production Editor.Mar. - Spring edition)

MONTE VISTA

CENTER POST DISPATCH. 229 Adams St., Monte Vista, CO 81144. Telephone: 719-852-3531. FAX: 719-852-3387. Mailing Address: PO Box 607, Monte Vista, CO 81144. Pub. Frequency: w. (Wed.) Page Size: tabloid. Subscrip. Rate: $.50 newsstand/cover; $27.75/yr in county; $33.75/yr mailed out of county; $38.75/yr mailed out of state. Circulation: 830 per issue (paid). **Owner(s):** News Media Corp., PO Box 46, Rochelle, IL 61068. **Management:** Jennifer Alonzo, Publisher. **Editorial:** James Shea, Editor.

Weeklies

CONEJOS COUNTY CITIZEN, THE. 229 Adams St., Monte Vista, CO 81144. Telephone: 719-852-3531. FAX: 719-852-3387. Year Established: 1892. Pub. Frequency: w. (Wed.) Page Size: tabloid. Subscrip. Rate: $.50 newsstand/cover; $22.75/yr in county; $33.75/yr out of county; $38.75/yr out of state. Circulation: 1,000 per issue (paid). **Owner(s):** News Media Corp., 228 Main St., Lingle, WY 82223. Telephone: 307-532-2184. FAX: 307-532-2283. **Management:** Jennifer Alonzo, Publisher. Shasta Hunter, Circulation Manager. **Editorial:** James Shea, Editor.

DEL NORTE PROSPECTOR. 229 Adams St., Monte Vista, CO 81144. Telephone: 719-852-3531. FAX: 719-852-3387. Mailing Address: PO Box 607, Monte Vista, CO 81144. Pub. Frequency: w. (Thu.) Page Size: tabloid. Subscrip. Rate: $.50 newsstand/cover; $27.75/yr in county; $33.75/yr out of county; $38.75/yr mailed out of state. Circulation: 800 per issue (paid). **Owner(s):** News Media Corp., PO Box 46, Rochelle, IL 61068. **Management:** Jennifer Alonzo, Publisher. Yvonne Steiehl, Circulation Manager. **Editorial:** James Shea, Editor.

MINERAL COUNTY MINER. 229 Adams St., Monte Vista, CO 81144. Telephone: 719-852-3531. FAX: 719-852-3387. Mailing Address: PO Box 607, Monte Vista, CO 81144. Pub. Frequency: w. (Thu.) Page Size: tabloid. Subscrip. Rate: $.50 newsstand/cover; $27.75/yr in county; $33.75/yr out of county; $38.75/yr out of state. Circulation: 776 per issue (paid). **Owner(s):** News Media Corp., PO Box 46, Rochelle, IL 61068. **Management:** Marsha Triplett, Publisher. Shasta Hunter, Circulation Manager. **Editorial:** Marsha Triplett, Editor.

MONTE VISTA JOURNAL. 229 Adams St., Monte Vista, CO 81144. Telephone: 719-852-3531. FAX: 719-852-3387. URL: http://www.montevistajournal.com. Mailing Address: PO Box 607, Monte Vista, CO 81144. Year Established: 1888. Pub. Frequency: w. (Wed.) Page Size: tabloid. Subscrip. Rate: $.50 newsstand/cover; $27.75/yr mailed in county; $33.75/yr mailed out of county; $38.75/yr mailed out of state. Freelance Pay: $0.50/column-inch. Circulation: 2,500 per issue (paid). **Owner(s):** News Media Corp., PO Box 46, Rochelle, IL 61068. Telephone: 815-562-2061. **Management:** Jennifer Alonzo, Publisher. Marsha Triplett, Advertising Manager. Shasta Hunter, Circulation Manager. **Editorial:** Marsha Tripplet, Editor.

SATURDAY ADVANTAGE, THE. 229 Adams St., Monte Vista, CO 81144. Telephone: 719-852-3531. FAX: 719-852-3387. Pub. Frequency: w. (Sat.) Page Size: tabloid Circulation: 15,000 per issue (free). **Owner(s):** News Media Corp., PO Box 46, Rochelle, IL 61068. **Management:** Marsha Triplett, Publisher. Shasta Hunter, Circulation Manager. **Editorial:** Marsha Triplett, Editor.

SOUTH FORK TIMES, THE. 229 Adams St., Monte Vista, CO 81144. Telephone: 719-852-3531. FAX: 719-852-3387. URL: http://www.southforktines.com. Mailing Address: PO Box 607, Monte Vista, CO 81144. Pub. Frequency: w. (Wed.) Page Size: tabloid. Subscrip. Rate: $.50 newsstand/cover; $27.75/yr in county; $33.75/yr mailed out of county; $38.75/yr mailed out of state. Circulation: 2,500 per issue (paid). **Owner(s):** News Media Corp., See address and contact information above. **Management:** Jennifer Alonzo, Publisher. **Editorial:** Thomas Phillips, Editor.

MONUMENT

TRI-LAKES TRIBUNE. 1850 Woodmoor Dr., Ste. 102, Monument, CO 80132. Telephone: 719-481-3423. FAX: 719-481-9005. E-MAIL: tribunenews@aol.com. URL: http://www.ccnewspapers.com. Mailing Address: PO Box 488, Monument, CO 80132-0488. Year Established: 1965. Pub. Frequency: w. (Thu.) Page Size: broadsheet. Subscrip. Rate: $.50 newsstand/cover; $19.50/yr out of county; $26.50/yr out of state. Adv. Rate: col. inch $7.85 Circulation: 4,700 per issue (paid). **Owner(s):** ASP Westward LP, 523 N Sam Houston Pkwy Ste, 600, Houston, TX 77060-4011. Telephone: 281-446-5929. **Management:** Rob Carrigan, Publisher. **Editorial:** Bryan Grossman, Editor.

OURAY

OURAY COUNTY PLAINDEALER. 302 Sixth Ave., Ouray, CO 81427-0607. Telephone: 970-325-4412. FAX: 970-325-4413. E-MAIL: plaindealer@ouraynews.com. Mailing Address: PO Box 607, Ouray, CO 81427-0607. Year Established: 1877. Pub. Frequency: w. (Fri.) Page Size: tabloid. Subscrip. Rate: $.50 newsstand/cover; $30/yr in county; $36/yr out of county. Circulation: 1,900 per issue (paid). **Owner(s):** David Mullings, See address and contact information above. **Management:** David Mullings, Publisher. Tonya Chelf, Office Manager. **Editorial:** David Mullings, Editor.

PAGOSA SPRINGS

PAGOSA SPRINGS SUN. 466 Pagosa St, Pagosa Springs, CO 81147. Telephone: 970-264-2100. FAX: 970-264-2103. E-MAIL: pagosaspringssun@pagosasprings.net. URL: http://www.pagosaspringssun.com. Mailing Address: PO Box 9, Pagosa Springs, CM 81147. Year Established: 1909. Pub. Frequency: w. (Thu.) Page Size: tabloid. Subscrip. Rate: $2 newsstand/cover; $20/yr in county; $30/yr out of county. Circulation: 30,000 per issue (paid). **Owner(s):** Pagosa Springs Sun, Inc., See address and contact information above. **Management:** Terri House, Publisher. Shari Pierce, Advertising Manager. **Editorial:** Karl Isberg, Managing Editor.

PALISADE

PALISADE TRIBUNE. 124 W Third St., Palisade, CO 81526. Telephone: 970-464-5614. E-MAIL: bobd@palisadetribune.com. URL: http://www.palisadetribune.com. Mailing Address: PO Box 8, Palisade, CO 81526. Year Established: 1903. Pub. Frequency: w. (Thu.) Page Size: tabloid. Subscrip. Rate: $.50 newsstand/cover; $24/yr in county; $29/yr out of county; $34/yr out of state. Adv. Rate: col. inch $11.50 Circulation: 4,100 per issue (paid and free). **Owner(s):** Robert Sweeney & Robert Dougherty, See address and contact information above. **Management:** Robert C Dougherty, Co-Publisher.

RIDGWAY

RIDGWAY SUN. 565 Sherman Ste. 6, Ridgway, CO 81432-0529. Telephone: 970-626-5100. FAX: 970-325-4413. E-MAIL: ridgwaysun@ouraynews.com. Mailing Address: PO Box 529, Ridgway, CO 81432-0529. Year Established: 1918. Pub. Frequency: w. (Wed.) Page Size: tabloid. Subscrip. Rate: $.50 newsstand/cover; $30/yr in county; $36/yr out of county. Adv. Rate: col. inch $7 Freelance Pay: $1.50/column-inch. Circulation: 1,020 per issue (paid). **Owner(s):** David Mullings, PO Box 607, Ouray, CO 81427. Telephone: 970-325-4412. FAX: 970-325-4413. **Management:** David Mullings, Publisher. **Editorial:** David Mullings, Editor.

RIFLE

CITIZEN TELEGRAM, THE. 132 E. Third St., Rifle, CO 81650. Telephone: 970-625-3245. FAX: 970-625-3628. E-MAIL: editor@citizentelegram.com. URL: http://www.searchcolorado.com. Mailing Address: PO Box 111, Rifle, CO 81650. Year Established: 1903. Pub. Frequency: w. (Thu.) Page Size: tabloid. Subscrip. Rate: $.50 newsstand/cover; $.75 newsstand/cover Sun.; $20/yr home delivery. Freelance Pay: $15-$25/article. Circulation: 3,500 per issue (controlled and free). **Owner(s):** Swift Newspapers, Inc., 500 Double Eagle Ct., Reno, NV 89511. Telephone: 775-850-7676. FAX: 775-850-7677. **Management:** Michael Bennett, Publisher. Sally Dahl, Advertising. **Editorial:** Dale Shrull, Editor. Melanie Handl, Production Manager.

SILVERTON

SILVERTON STANDARD & THE MINER. 1315 Snowden St, Silverton, CO 81433. Telephone: 970-387-5477. FAX: 970-387-5291. E-MAIL: editor@silvertonstandard.com. URL: http://www.silvertonstandard.com. Mailing Address: PO Box 8, Silverton, CO 81433-0008. Year Established: 1875. Pub. Frequency: w. (Thu.) Page Size: tabloid. Subscrip. Rate: $.50 newsstand/cover; $24/yr local; $40/yr elsewhere. Circulation: 1,200 per issue (paid). **Owner(s):** GateHouse Media, Inc, 350 WillowBrook Office Park, Fairport, NY 14450. Telephone: 585-598-0030. FAX: 585-248-2631. **Management:** Gary Dickson, Publisher. Kristi Smith, Advertising. **Editorial:** Deb Dion, Editor.

SNOWMASS VILLAGE

SNOWMASS VILLAGE SUN. P.O. Box 5770, Snowmass Village, CO 81615. Telephone: 970-923-5829. FAX: 970-923-2571. URL: http://www.searchcolorado.com. Mailing Address: PO Box 5770, Snowmass Village, CO 81615-5770. Pub. Frequency: w. (Fri.) Page Size: standard. Subscrip. Rate: $.25 newsstand/cover; $30/yr. Adv. Rate: col. inch $6.50 Circulation: 3,500 per issue (paid). **Owner(s):** Swift Newspapers, Inc., 500 Double Eagle Ct., Reno, NV 89511. Telephone: 775-850-7676. FAX: 775-850-7677. **Management:** Carolyn Sackarason, Publisher. Michele Wurtsmith, Circulation Manager. Bryan Gonzales, Sales Manager. **Editorial:** Madeleine Osberger, Editor.

STEAMBOAT SPRINGS

HIDDEN VALLEY PRESS. 1901 Curve Plz., Steamboat Springs, CO 80477-4872. Telephone: 970-879-1502. FAX: 970-879-2888. E-MAIL: editor@steamboatpilot.com. URL: http://www.steamboatpilot.com. Mailing Address: PO Box 4827, Steamboat Springs, CO 80477-4872. Pub. Frequency: w. (Wed.) Page Size: standard. Subscrip. Rate: $1 newsstand/cover; $24/yr in county; $32/yr elsewhere. **Wire Service(s):** AP. Circulation: 6,500 per issue (paid). **Owner(s):** WorldWest LLC, 609 New Hampshire, P.O. Box 688, Lawrence, KS 66044. Telephone: 785-843-1000. FAX: 785-832-7213. **Management:** Suzanne Schlicht, General Manager. Bryna Larsen, Publisher. Samantha Johnston, Advertising Director. Laura Soard, Classified Adv. Mgr.. **Editorial:** Scott Stanford, Managing Editor.

STEAMBOAT PILOT. 1901 Curve Plz., Steamboat Springs, CO 80477-4872. Telephone: 970-879-1502. FAX: 970-879-2888. E-MAIL: editor@steamboatpilot.com. URL: http://www.steamboatpilot.com. Mailing Address: PO Box 4827, Steamboat Springs, CO 80477-4872. Year Established: 1989. Pub. Frequency: w. (Sun) Page Size: broadsheet. Subscrip. Rate: $1 newsstand/cover Sun.; $29/yr mailed in county; $37/yr mailed out of county. **Wire Service(s):** AP. Circulation: 6,500 per issue (paid and free). **Owner(s):** WorldWest LLC, 609 New Hampshire, P.O. Box 688, Lawrence, KS 66044. Telephone: 785-843-1000. FAX: 785-832-7213. **Management:** Suzanne Schlicht, General Manager. Bryna Larsen, Publisher. Samantha Johnston, Advertising Director. Laura Soard, Classified Adv. Mgr.. **Editorial:** Scott Stanford, Managing Editor.

THORNTON

NORTHGLENN-THORNTON SENTINEL. ISSN 1044-4254 8710 Grant St., Thornton, CO 80229. E-MAIL: scottperriman@metronorthnews.com. Year Established: 1968. Pub. Frequency: w. (Thu.) Page Size: tabloid. Subscrip. Rate: $.50 newsstand/cover; $24/yr in county. Adv. Rate: col. inch $11.77 Circulation: 5,850 per issue (paid). **Owner(s):** Scott D. Perriman, PO Box 350070, Westminster, CO 80035. Telephone: 303-426-6000. FAX: 303-426-4209. **Management:** Scott D. Perriman, Publisher. **Editorial:** Mikkel Kelly, Managing Editor.

WESTMINSTER WINDOW. 8710 Grant St., Thornton, CO 80229. Telephone: 303-426-6000. FAX: 303-426-4209. E-MAIL: scottperriman@metronorthnews.com. Year Established: 1947. Pub. Frequency: w. (Thu.) Page Size: tabloid. Subscrip. Rate: $.50 newsstand/cover; $24/yr mailed in county. Adv. Rate: col. inch $140,019 Circulation: 5,850 per issue (paid). **Owner(s):** Scott D. Perriman, PO Box 350070, Westminster, CO 80035-0070. Telephone: 303-426-6000. FAX: 303-426-4209. **Management:** Scott D. Perriman, Publisher. **Editorial:** Mikkel Kelly, Managing Editor.

WESTSIDER. 8710 Grant St., Thornton, CO 80229. Telephone: 303-426-6000. FAX: 303-426-4209. E-MAIL: scottperriman@metronorthnews.com. URL: http://www.metronorthnews.com. Year Established: 1999. Pub. Frequency: w. (Fri.) Page Size: broadsheet.Adv. Rate: col. inch $22 Circulation: 15,000 per issue (free). **Owner(s):** Scott D. Perriman, PO Box 350070, Westminster, CO 80035-0070. Telephone: 303-426-6000. FAX: 303-426-4209. **Management:** Scott D. Perriman, Publisher. **Editorial:** Mikkel Kelly, Managing Editor.

WALDEN

JACKSON COUNTY STAR. 417 Fifth St., Walden, CO 80480-0397. Telephone: 970-723-4404. FAX: 970-723-4474. Mailing Address: PO Box 397, Walden, CO 80480-0397. Year Established: 1913. Pub. Frequency: w. (Thu.) Page Size: tabloid. Subscrip. Rate: $.50 newsstand/cover; $20/yr in county; $26/yr out of county. Adv. Rate: page $20 Circulation: 1,400 per issue (paid). **Owner(s):** Dustin Publishing Inc., See address and contact information above. **Management:** Jim Dustin, Publisher. Debbie Wilson, Advertising Manager. **Editorial:** Jim Dustin, Editor-in-Chief.

WESTCLIFFE

WET MOUNTAIN TRIBUNE. 404 Main St., Westcliffe, CO 81252-0300. Telephone: 719-783-2361. FAX: 719-783-3725. E-MAIL: wmtrib@ris.net. URL: www.wetmountaintribune.com. Mailing Address: PO Box 300, Westcliffe, CO 81252-0300. Year Established: 1883. Pub. Frequency: w. (Thu.) Page Size: tabloid. Subscrip. Rate: $.50 newsstand/cover; $33/yr. Adv. Rate: col. inch $9 Freelance Pay: $0.05/word. Circulation: 3,043 per issue (paid). **Owner(s):** Jim Little, 404 Main St., Westcliffe, CO 81252. Telephone: 719-783-2361. FAX: 719-783-3725. **Management:** Jim Little, President. Jean Paxton, Advertising Manager. Art Solomon, Circulation Manager. **Editorial:** Jim Little, Editor-in-Chief. Constance Little, Managing Editor.

WINDSOR

WINDSOR BEACON. 425 Main St, Windsor, CO 80550. Telephone: 970-686-9646. FAX: 970-686-9647. E-MAIL: sales@adv.com. URL: http://www.windsorbeacon.com. Year Established: 1896. Pub. Frequency: w. (Thu.) Page Size: standard Circulation: 3,200 per issue (paid). **Owner(s):** Gannett Company, Inc., 7950 Jones Branch Dr., McLean, VA 22107-0001. Telephone: 703-854-6000.

WINTER PARK

WINTER PARK MANIFEST. 78622 Winter Park Dr., Winter Park, CO 80482. Telephone: 970-726-5721. FAX: 970-726-8789. Mailing Address: PO Box 409, Winter Park, CO 80482. Year Established: 1977. Pub. Frequency: w. (Wed.) Page Size: tabloid. Subscrip. Rate: $.50 newsstand/cover; $16/yr mailed in county; $22/yr mailed out of county. Circulation: 4,300 per issue (paid). **Owner(s):** William Potter Johnson, 445 W. Rapa Pl., Tucson, AZ 85737. Telephone: 520-726-5721. **Management:** Patrick Brower, Publisher. **Editorial:** Stephanie Buss, Editor.

WOODLAND PARK

PIKES PEAK COURIER VIEW. 1200 Hwy 24, Woodland Park, CO 80866. Telephone: 719-687-3006. E-MAIL: rcarrigan@aol.com. URL: http://www.ccnewspapers.com. Mailing Address: PO Box 340, Woodland Park, CO 80866. Pub. Frequency: w. (Wed.) Page Size: standard. Subscrip. Rate: $.75 newsstand/cover; $22/yr in county; $28/yr out of county; $34/yr elsewhere. Circulation: 5,200 per issue (paid). **Owner(s):** ASP Westward LP, 523 N Sam Houston Pkwy Ste, 600, Houston, TX 77060-4011. **Management:** Rob Carrigan, Publisher. Myra Krider, Advertising Manager. **Editorial:** Joel Quevillon, Editor.

WRAY

WRAY GAZETTE. 411 Main St., Wray, CO 80758. Telephone: 970-332-4846. E-MAIL: wraygaztte@plains.net. URL: http://wraygazette.com. Year Established: 1903. Pub. Frequency: w. (Wed.) Page Size: broadsheet. Subscrip. Rate: $.50 newsstand/cover; $27/yr home delivery local; $30/yr mailed out of area. Circulation: 3,300 per issue (paid). **Owner(s):** Ron Rieb, See address and contact information above. **Management:** Ron Rieb, Publisher. Janette Rieb, Advertising Manager. **Editorial:** Rose Kent, Editor.

YUMA

YUMA PIONEER. 207 S. Main St., Yuma, CO 80759. Telephone: 970-848-2174. FAX: 970-848-2895. E-MAIL: yumapioneer@centurytel.net. Mailing Address: P.O.Box 326, Yuma, CO 80759. Year Established: 1886. Pub. Frequency: w. (Thu.) Page Size: standard. Subscrip. Rate: $.75 newsstand/cover; $28/yr home delivery in state; $32/yr home delivery out of state. Adv. Rate: col. inch $4.90 Circulation: 2,850 per issue (paid). **Owner(s):** Yuma Pioneer Corp., See address and contact information above. **Management:** Ida Mathies, Advertising. **Editorial:** Anthony Rayl, Editor.

CONNECTICUT

BRIDGETPORT

FAIRFIELD COUNTY WEEKLY, THE. 350 Fairfield Ave., Ste. 605, Bridgetport, CT 06640. Telephone: 203-382-9666. FAX: 203-382-9657. E-MAIL: editor@fairfieldweekly.com. URL: http://www.fairfieldweekly.com. Year Established: 1979. Pub. Frequency: w. (Wed.) Page Size: tabloid. Subscrip. Rate: $160/yr mailed. Adv. Rate: B&W page $2,000 Freelance Pay: $20-$300/article. Circulation: 70,000 per issue (paid and free). **Owner(s):** New Mass Media, Inc., See address and contact information above. **Management:** Joshua Mamis, Publisher.

BRISTOL

BLOOMFIELD JOURNAL. ISSN 0746-9632
188 Main St., Bristol, CT 06010. Telephone: 860-236-3571. FAX: 860-233-2080. E-MAIL: bloomfieldjournal@ctcentral.com. URL: http://www.bloomfieldjournal.com. Year Established: 1976. Pub. Frequency: w. (Fri.) Page Size: tabloid. Subscrip. Rate: $31/yr mailed in state; $52/yr mailed out of state. Circulation: 1,750 per issue (paid). **Owner(s):** Journal Register Co., 50 W State St, 12th Fl, Trenton, NJ 08608. Telephone: 609-396-2200. **Management:** William Sheedy, Publisher. Gary Curran, Advertising Manager. **Editorial:** Barbara Thomas, Editor.

FARMINGTON VALLEY POST, THE. 188 Main St., Bristol, CT 06010. Telephone: 860-674-9660. FAX: 860-674-9680. E-MAIL: inprintnews@ctcentral.com. URL: http://www.farmingtonvalleypost.com. Year Established: 1990. Pub. Frequency: s-m. Page Size: tabloid. Subscrip. Rate: $29/yr mailed. Freelance Pay: $1/column-inch. Circulation: 37,900 per issue (free). **Owner(s):** Journal Register Co., 50 W State St, 12th Fl, Trenton, NJ 08608. Telephone: 609-396-2200. FAX: 609-396-2292. **Management:** William Sheedy, Publisher. **Editorial:** Barbara Thomas, Editor.

NEWINGTON TOWN CRIER. ISSN 0745-0796
188 Main St., Bristol, CT 06010. Telephone: 860-236-3571. FAX: 860-233-2080. E-MAIL: newingtontowncrier@ctcentral.com. URL: http://www.newingtontowncrier.com. Year Established: 1959. Pub. Frequency: w. (Fri.) Page Size: tabloid. Subscrip. Rate: $.75 newsstand/cover; $31/yr mailed; $22/yr mailed to senior citizens; $52/yr mailed out of state. Circulation: 2,800 per issue (paid). **Owner(s):** Journal Register Co., 50 W State St, 12th Fl, Trenton, NJ 08608. Telephone: 609-396-2200. **Management:** Bill Sheedy, Publisher. Leslie Friedlander, Advertising. Beverly Forestiere, Classified Adv. Mgr.. **Editorial:** Barbara Thomas, Managing Editor. Christopher Wendrychowicz, Sports.

ROCKY HILL POST. 99 Main St., Bristol, CT 06010-6528. FAX: 860-584-2192. E-MAIL: rockyhillpost@centralctcommunications.com. URL: http://www.rockyhillpost.com. Year Established: 1978. Pub. Frequency: w. (Fri.) Page Size: tabloid. Subscrip. Rate: $1 newsstand/cover; $31/yr mailed; $22/yr mailed in state to senior citizens; $52/yr mailed out of state. Circulation: 900 per issue (paid). **Owner(s):** Journal Register Co., 50 W State St, 12th Fl, Trenton, NJ 08608. Telephone: 609-396-2200. FAX: 609-396-2292. **Management:** Michael Schroeder, Publisher. Angels Prestridge, Operations Manager. Brenda Vumback, Advertising. **Editorial:** John Fits, Editor.

WEST HARTFORD NEWS. 188 Main St., Bristol, CT 06010. Telephone: 860-236-3571. FAX: 860-233-2080. E-MAIL: westhartfordnews@ctcentral.com. URL: http://www.westhartfordnews.com. Mailing Address: 1224 Farmington Ave., West Hartford, CT 06107. Year Established: 1931. Pub. Frequency: w. (Thu.) Page Size: tabloid. Subscrip. Rate: $.75 newsstand/cover; $34/yr home delivery; $27.50/yr home delivery to senior citizens; $55.50/yr mailed out of state. Circulation: 11,000 per issue (paid). **Owner(s):** Journal Register Co., 50 W State St, 12th Fl, Trenton, NJ 08608. Telephone: 609-396-2200. **Management:** Lisa Basile, Advertising Manager. Beverly Forestiere, Classified Adv. Mgr.. **Editorial:** Barbara Thomas, Managing Editor. Robert Mayer, Sports Editor.

WETHERSFIELD POST. 188 Main St., Bristol, CT 06010. Telephone: 860-236-3571. FAX: 860-236-0490. E-MAIL: wethersfieldpost@ctcentral.com. URL: http://www.wethersfieldpost.com. Year Established: 1959. Pub. Frequency: w. (Fri.) Page Size: tabloid. Subscrip. Rate: $.75 newsstand/cover; $31/yr home delivery; $22/yr home delivery to senior citizens; $52/yr mailed out of state. Circulation: 3,700 per issue (paid). **Owner(s):** Journal Register Co., 50 W State St, 12th Fl, Trenton, NJ 08608. Telephone: 609-396-2200. **Management:** William Sheedy, Publisher. Gary Curran, Advertising Manager. Brenda Kelley, Circulation Director. **Editorial:** Barbara Thomas, Managing Editor.

WINDSOR JOURNAL. 188 Main St., Bristol, CT 06010. Telephone: 860-236-3571. FAX: 860-233-2080. E-MAIL: windsorjournal@ctcentral.com. URL: http://www.windsorjournal.com. Year Established: 1973. Pub. Frequency: w. (Fri.) Page Size: tabloid. Subscrip. Rate: $.75 newsstand/cover; $31/yr home delivery; $22/yr home delivery to senior citizens; $52/yr mailed out of state. Circulation: 2,263 per issue (paid). **Owner(s):** Journal Register Co., 50 W State St, 12th Fl, Trenton, NJ 08608. Telephone: 609-396-2200. **Management:** William Sheedy, Publisher. Gary Curran, Advertising Manager. Brenda Kelley, Circulation Director. **Editorial:** Nancy Johnson, Editor. Barbara Thomas, Managing Editor.

WINDSOR LOCKS JOURNAL. 188 Main St., Bristol, CT 06010. Telephone: 860-236-3571. FAX: 860-233-2080. URL: http://www.windsorlocksjournal.com. Year Established: 1880. Pub. Frequency: w. (Fri.) Page Size: tabloid. Subscrip. Rate: $.75 newsstand/cover; $31/yr home delivery; $22/yr home delivery to senior citizens; $52/yr mailed out of state. Circulation: 1,052 per issue (paid). **Owner(s):** Journal Register Co., 50 W State St, 12th Fl, Trenton, NJ 08608. Telephone: 609-396-2200. FAX: 609-396-2292. **Management:** William Sheedy, Publisher. Lisa Basile, Advertising Manager. Sam Tibbols, Circulation Manager. Beverly Forestiere, Classified Adv. Mgr.. **Editorial:** Barbara Thomas, Managing Editor. Bob Mayer, Sports Editor.

CHESHIRE

CHESHIRE HERALD. ISSN 1090-5049
1079 S. Main St., Cheshire, CT 06410-3414. Telephone: 203-272-5316. FAX: 203-250-7145. E-MAIL: news@cheshireherald.com. URL: http://www.cheshireherald.com. Mailing Address: PO Box 247, Cheshire, CT 06410. Year Established: 1953. Pub. Frequency: w. (Thu.) Page Size: tabloid. Subscrip. Rate: $.70 newsstand/cover; $24/yr home delivery in county; $33/yr home delivery out of county; $33/yr mailed out of state. Adv. Rate: col. inch $9.70 Circulation: 7,400 per issue (paid). **Owner(s):** Joseph & Maureen Jakubisyn, See address and contact information above. **Management:** Joseph Jakubisyn, Publisher. Maureen Jakubisyn, Vice President. Susan Keany, Advertising Manager. **Editorial:** Shannon Becker, Managing Editor.

CLINTON

TRIBUNE (ELKIN), THE. 1 W Main St, Clinton, CT 06413. Telephone: 860-664-1075. FAX: 860-664-1085. URL: http://www.elkintribune.com. Year Established: 1911. Pub. Frequency: 3/w. (Mon.-Wed.-Fri.) Subscrip. Rate: $.50 newsstand/cover; $52/yr mailed tri-cy. area. Adv. Rate: col. inch $7.95 Circulation: 5,300 per issue. **Owner(s):** Heartland Publications, LLC, See address and contact information above. **Management:** Wanda Walls, General Manager. Chris Lane, Circulation Manager. Holly Lamm, Classified Adv. Mgr.. **Editorial:** Steve Steiner, Editor.

Weeklies

DARIEN

DARIEN NEWS-REVIEW. ISSN 0744-3862
24 Old Kings Hwy S, Darien, CT 06820-4537. Telephone: 203-655-7476. FAX: 203-655-1442. URL: http://www.dariennews-review.com. Year Established: 1973. Pub. Frequency: w. (Thu.) Page Size: tabloid. Subscrip. Rate: $.55 newsstand/cover; $16.50/yr home delivery in county. Circulation: 7,947 per issue (paid). **Owner(s):** MediaNews Group, Inc., 101 W Colfax Ave, Ste 1100, Denver, CO 80202. FAX: 303-954-6320. **Management:** Kevin Lally, Publisher. Ed Majersky, Advertising Director. **Editorial:** Chuck Dianis, Editor. Linda Goodman, Managing Editor.

DARIEN TIMES, THE. 4 Corbin Dr., Darien, CT 06820-5401. Telephone: 203-656-4230. FAX: 203-656-4240. E-MAIL: editor@darientimes.com. URL: http://www.acorn-online.com. Pub. Frequency: w. (Thu.) Page Size: broadsheet. Subscrip. Rate: $.50 newsstand/cover; $30/yr out of city; $42/yr out of area. Adv. Rate: col. inch $11 Circulation: 7,200 per issue (controlled and free). **Owner(s):** Hersam Acorn Newspapers LLC, 16 Bailey Ave., Ridgefield, CT 06877. Telephone: 203-438-6544. **Management:** Thomas Nash, Publisher. Bruce McDougall, Circulation Manager. Rose Sayers, Classified Adv. Mgr.. **Editorial:** Joshua Fisher, Editor. Jack Sanders, Executive Editor. Steve Buono, Sports.

DERBY

VALLEY TIMES (DERBY), THE. 7 Francis St., Derby, CT 06418-1505. Telephone: 203-735-6696. FAX: 203-735-0334. E-MAIL: mail@thevalleytimes.com. URL: http://www.thevalleytimes.com. Year Established: 1993. Pub. Frequency: w. (Fri.) Page Size: broadsheet. Subscrip. Rate: $.50 newsstand/cover; $19/yr in county; $22/yr mailed out of county; $25/yr mailed out of state. Adv. Rate: col. inch $9.75 Circulation: 21,000 per issue (paid). **Owner(s):** Valley Publishing Co., Inc., See address and contact information above. **Management:** Irene Platt, General Manager. Blaze Garbatini, Publisher. Bill Blaze, Advertising Manager. Angela Burke, Classified Adv. Mgr.. **Editorial:** Sandy Mendyk, Editor. Bill Pucci, Sports.

EAST HARTFORD

EAST HARTFORD GAZETTE, THE. ISSN 8750-9156
1406 Main St., East Hartford, CT 06108. Telephone: 860-289-6468. FAX: 860-289-6469. E-MAIL: ehgazette@ctcentral.com. URL: http://www.easthartfordgazette.com. Year Established: 1885. Pub. Frequency: w. (Thu.) Page Size: tabloid. Subscrip. Rate: $45.20/yr mailed 1st class. Adv. Rate: col. inch $22.25 Circulation: 19,100 per issue (paid and free). **Owner(s):** Journal Register Co., Lower Makefield Corporate Center, 790 Township Line Rd, 3rd. flr, Yardley, PA 19067. Telephone: 215-504-4200. **Management:** Ed Gunderson, Publisher. Nancy Phaneuf, Advertising Manager. Leona Regalis, Circulation Manager. **Editorial:** William A. Doak, Editor.

ENFIELD

ENFIELD PRESS. 399 Enfield St., Enfield, CT 06083. Telephone: 860-745-3348. FAX: 413-562-4185. E-MAIL: kevin.johnson@wenpub.com. Mailing Address: PO Box 1141, Enfield, CT 06083. Year Established: 1880. Pub. Frequency: w. (Thu.) Page Size: tabloid. Subscrip. Rate: $.50 newsstand/cover; $20/yr mailed in state; $28/yr mailed out of state. Freelance Pay: $15-$20/article. Circulation: 2,300 per issue (paid). **Owner(s):** Westfield News Publishing, Inc., 62-64 School St., Westfield, MA 01086. Telephone: 413-562-4181. **Management:** Carol Mazza, Publisher. Marty Baillaigeron, Advertising Manager. **Editorial:** Kevin Johnson, Editor. James Corwin, Feature Editor.

ESSEX

MAIN STREET NEWS. 242 Essex Plz., Essex, CT 06426-1477. E-MAIL: mainstreetnews@ctcentral.com. URL: http://www.ctmainstreetnews.com. Mailing Address: PO Box 349, Guilford, CT 06437. Year Established: 1993. Pub. Frequency: w. (Thu.) Page Size: tabloid. Subscrip. Rate: $.50 newsstand/cover; $23/yr home delivery local; $33/yr mailed out of area. Adv. Rate: col. inch $9.85 Circulation: 5,300 per issue (paid). **Owner(s):** Journal Register Co., 66 High St, Guilford, CT 06437. 50 W State St, 12th Fl, Trenton, NJ 08608. Telephone: 845-677-8241. FAX: 609-396-2292. **Management:** John Slater, General Manager. Laura Carpenter, Advertising. **Editorial:** Erik Hesselberg, Executive Editor. Laura Robida, News Editor. Jimmy Zanor, Sports Editor.

FAIRFIELD

FAIRFIELD CITIZEN NEWS, THE. ISSN 0191-5134
220 Carter Henry Dr., Fairfield, CT 06824. Telephone: 203-255-4561. E-MAIL: phines@bcnnews.com. URL: http://www.fairfieldcitizen-news.com. Year Established: 1973. Pub. Frequency: s-w. (Wed. & Fri.) Page Size: tabloid. Subscrip. Rate: $.55 newsstand/cover; $27.50/yr home delivery in county; $36.50/yr mailed out of county; $36.50/yr mailed out of state. Circulation: 12,325 per issue (paid). **Owner(s):** MediaNews Group, Inc., 101 W Colfax Ave, Ste 1100, Denver, CO 80202. FAX: 303-954-6320. **Editorial:** Patricia Hines, Editor. Rachel Sadlowski, Managing Editor. Erin Lynch, Reporter.

GEORGETOWN

REDDING PILOT, THE. 3 Main St., Georgetown, CT 06829. Telephone: 203-544-9519. E-MAIL: pilot@acorn-online.com. URL: http://www.acorn-online.com. Mailing Address: PO Box 389, Georgetown, CT 06829. Year Established: 1966. Pub. Frequency: w. (Thu.) Page Size: broadsheet. Subscrip. Rate: $.75 newsstand/cover; $39/yr in county; $45/yr mailed out of county. Freelance Pay: $40-$60/article. **Wire Service(s):** AP. Circulation: 2,340 per issue (paid and free). **Owner(s):** Hersam Acorn Newspapers LLC, 16 Bailey Ave., Ridgefield, CT 06877. Telephone: 203-438-6544. **Management:** Thomas Nash, Publisher. Shelagh Barrett, Advertising Director. Bruce McDougall, Circulation Manager. Rose Sayers, Classified Adv. Mgr.. **Editorial:** Susan Wolf, Editor. Jack Sanders, Executive Editor. Tim Murphy, Sports.

WESTON FORUM, THE. 3 Main St., Georgetown, CT 06883. Telephone: 203-544-9990. FAX: 203-544-9382. E-MAIL: acorn@compuserve.com. URL: http://www.acornonline.com. Mailing Address: PO Box 1185, Weston, CT 06883. Year Established: 1970. Pub. Frequency: w. (Thu.) Page Size: broadsheet. Subscrip. Rate: $.50 newsstand/cover; $39/yr in county out of town; $45/yr out of county out of town. **Wire Service(s):** AP. Circulation: 3,500 per issue (controlled and free). **Owner(s):** Hersam Acorn Newspapers LLC, 16 Bailey Ave., Ridgefield, CT 06877. Telephone: 203-438-6544. **Management:** Thomas Nash, Publisher. Shelagh Barrett, Advertising Director. Bruce McDougall, Circulation Manager. Rose Sayers, Classified Adv. Mgr.. **Editorial:** Kim Donnelly, Editor. Jack Sanders, Executive Editor.

GLASTONBURY

GLASTONBURY CITIZEN. 1510 Main St., Glastonbury, CT 06033. Telephone: 860-633-4691. FAX: 860-657-3258. E-MAIL: citizen@snet.net. URL: http://www.glastonburycitizen.com. Year Established: 1950. Pub. Frequency: w. (Thu.) Page Size: tabloid. Subscrip. Rate: $1 newsstand/cover; $25/yr mailed in state; $28/yr mailed out of state. Adv. Rate: page $11 Circulation: 2,700 per issue (paid). **Owner(s):** Hallas Family, See address and contact information above. **Management:** John Ultee, General Manager. James Hallas, Publisher. Carole Saucier, Advertising Manager. Janki Buch, Circulation Manager. **Editorial:** Kathleen Stack, Editor.

RIVER EAST NEWS BULLETIN. 1510 Main St., Glastonbury, CT 06033. Telephone: 860-633-4691. FAX: 860-657-3258. E-MAIL: rivereast@snet.net. URL: http://www.rivereastnews.com. Year Established: 1984. Pub. Frequency: w. (Fri.) Page Size: tabloid. Subscrip. Rate: $75/yr mailed. Adv. Rate: col. inch $9 Circulation: 26,000 per issue (free). **Owner(s):** Hallas Family, See address and contact information above. **Management:** John Ultee, General Manager. James Hallas, Publisher. Carole Saucier, Advertising Manager. **Editorial:** James Hallas, Editor.

GREENWICH

GREENWICH CITIZEN. 41 W Putman Ave, Greenwich, CT 06830. Telephone: 203-422-5230. FAX: 203-422-5242. E-MAIL: dharrison@bcnnew.com. URL: http://www.greenwichcitizen.com. Pub. Frequency: w. (Fri.) Page Size: tabloid Circulation: 15,000 per issue (free). **Owner(s):** MediaNews Group, Inc., 101 W Colfax Ave, Ste 1100, Denver, CO 80202. FAX: 303-954-6320. **Management:** Kevin Lally, Publisher. Ed Majersky, Advertising Director. **Editorial:** Don Harrison, Editor.

NORWALK CITIZEN-NEWS. 41 W Putman Ave, Greenwich, CT 06830. Telephone: 203-422-5230. FAX: 203-422-5242. E-MAIL: lnailen@bcnnews.com. URL: http://www.norwalkcitizen-news.com. Pub. Frequency: w. (Fri.) Page Size: tabloid Circulation: 18,500 per issue (free). **Owner(s):** MediaNews Group, Inc., 101 W Colfax Ave, Ste 1100, Denver, CO 80202. FAX: 303-954-6320. **Management:** Kevin Lally, Publisher. Ed Majersky, Advertising Director. **Editorial:** Laura Nailen, Editor. Jeanne Goodman, Managing Editor.

GUILFORD

BRANFORD REVIEW, THE. 66 High St, Guilford, CT 06437. Telephone: 203-488-2535. FAX: 203-481-4125. E-MAIL: branfordreview@ctcentral.com. URL: http://www.branfordreview.com. Mailing Address: PO Box 349, Guilford, CT 06437. Pub. Frequency: w. (Wed.) Page Size: tabloid. Subscrip. Rate: $.50 newsstand/cover; $34/yr mailed in county; $57/yr mailed out of county; $57/yr mailed out of state. Circulation: 2,000 per issue (paid). **Owner(s):** Journal Register Co., 50 W State St, 12th Fl, Trenton, NJ 08608. Telephone: 609-396-2200. FAX: 609-396-2292. **Management:** David W Compton, Publisher. William Keim, Advertising. Donna Smiley, Circulation Manager. **Editorial:** Sally Bahner, Editor. Susan Braden, Entertainment Editor. Hal Levy, Sports Editor.

CLINTON RECORDER. ISSN 0886-6112
66 High St, Guilford, CT 06437. E-MAIL: clintonrecorder@ctcentral.com. URL: http://www.clintonrecorder.com. Mailing Address: PO Box 349, Guilford, CT 06437-0349. Year Established: 1900. Pub. Frequency: w. (Tue.) Page Size: tabloid. Subscrip. Rate: $.50 newsstand/cover; $32/yr home delivery in county; $57/yr mailed out of county; $57/yr mailed out of state. Freelance Pay: $15-$30/article. Circulation: 3,600 per issue (paid). **Owner(s):** Journal Register Co., 50 W State St, 12th Fl, Trenton, NJ 08608. Telephone: 609-396-2200. **Management:** John Slater, General Manager. **Editorial:** Erik Hesselberg, Executive Editor. Hal Levy, Sports Editor.

EAST HAVEN ADVERTISER. 66 High St., Guilford, CT 06437. Telephone: 203-488-2535. FAX: 203-481-4125. E-MAIL: chadvertiser@ctcentral.com. URL: http://www.easthavenadvertiser.com. Mailing Address: PO Box 349, Guilford, CT 06437. Pub. Frequency: w. (Sat.) Page Size: tabloid. Subscrip. Rate: $.50 newsstand/cover; $20/yr mailed in county; $57/yr mailed out of county; $57/yr mailed out of state. Circulation: 1,745 per issue (paid and free). **Owner(s):** Journal Register Co., 50 W State St, 12th Fl, Trenton, NJ 08608. Telephone: 609-396-2200. **Management:** Dave Phillips, Publisher. Bill Klem, Advertising Manager. Donna Smiley, Circulation Manager. **Editorial:** Sally Bahner, Editor. Erik Hesselberg, Executive Editor. Hal Levy, Sports Editor.

PICTORIAL GAZETTE. 66 High St, Guilford, CT 06437. E-MAIL: pictorialgazette@ctcentral.com. URL: http://www.pictorialgazette.com. Mailing Address: PO Box 349, Guilford, CT 06437. Pub. Frequency: s-w. (Tue. & Sat.) Page Size: broadsheet. Subscrip. Rate: $.50 newsstand/cover; $34/yr mailed in county; $57/yr mailed out of county; $57/yr mailed out of state. Circulation: 10,000 per issue (paid). **Owner(s):** Journal Register Co., 50 W State St, 12th Fl, Trenton, NJ 08608. Telephone: 609-396-2200. **Management:** John Slater, General Manager. **Editorial:** Erik Hesselberg, Executive Editor. Laura Robida, News Editor. Jimmy Zanor, Sports Editor.

SHORE LINE TIMES. ISSN 0887-7912
66 High St., Guilford, CT 06437. Telephone: 203-453-2711. FAX: 203-453-4152. E-MAIL: shorelinetimes@ctcentral.com. URL: http://www.shorelinetimes.com. Mailing Address: PO Box 349, Guilford, CT 06437-0349. Pub. Frequency: s-w. (Wed. & Sat.) Page Size: broadsheet. Subscrip. Rate: $.50 newsstand/cover; $39/yr in county; $57/yr out of county; $57/yr mailed out of state. Circulation: 9,000 per issue (paid). **Owner(s):** Journal Register Co., 50 W State St, 12th Fl, Trenton, NJ 08608. Telephone: 609-396-2200. FAX: 609-396-2292. **Management:** John Slater, General Manager. Tony Santamaria, Advertising. Sam Tibbals, Circulation Director. **Editorial:** Barbara Douglas, Editor. Erik Hesselberg, Executive Editor. Hal Levy, Sports Editor.

HARTFORD

HARTFORD NEWS. 99-A Hammer St., Hartford, CT 06114-1373. Telephone: 860-296-6128. FAX: 860-296-3350. E-MAIL: hartfordnews@aol.com. URL: http://www.hartfordnews.com. Year Established: 1977. Pub. Frequency: w. (Wed.) Page Size: tabloid. Freelance Pay: $1/column-inch. Circulation: 30,000 per issue (free). **Owner(s):** JBH Communications, Inc., See address and contact information above. **Management:** Andy Hart, General Manager. Jon B. Harden, Publisher. **Editorial:** Jon B. Harden, Editor.

NORTH END AGENTS. 680 Blue Hills Ave., Hartford, CT 06112. Telephone: 860-522-1888. FAX: 860-286-0316. Mailing Address: PO Box 2308, Hartford, CT 06143-2308. Pub. Frequency: w. (Wed) Page Size: tabloid Circulation: 40,000 per issue (free). **Owner(s):** John Allen, PO Box 2308, Hartford, CT 06146-2308. Telephone: 860-522-1888. FAX: 860-286-0316. **Management:** John Allen, Publisher. **Editorial:** John Allen, Editor.

LAKEVILLE

LAKEVILLE JOURNAL, THE. PO Box 1688, Lakeville, CT 06039-1688. E-MAIL: publisher@lakevillejournal.com. URL: http://www.lakevillejournal. com. Year Established: 1897. Pub. Frequency: w. (Thu.) Page Size: broadsheet.Subscrip. Rate: $1.25 newsstand/cover Circulation: 10,000 per issue (paid). **Owner(s):** Lakeville Journal LLC, See address and contact information above. **Management:** A. Whitney Ellsworth, General Manager. Janet Manko, Publisher. Anna Mae Kupferer, Advertising Manager. **Editorial:** Cynthia Hochwender, Editor.

MADISON

EAST HAVEN COURIER. 724 Boston Post Rd., Ste. 202, Madison, CT 06443. Telephone: 203-245-1877. FAX: 203-245-9773. E-MAIL: news@shorepublishing.com. URL: http://www.shorepublishing.com. Mailing Address: P.O. Box 1010, Madison, CT 06443. Year Established: 2002. Pub. Frequency: w. (Thu.) Page Size: broadsheet.Adv. Rate: col. inch $11.80 Circulation: 13,952 per issue (free). **Owner(s):** Shore Publishing LLC, See address and contact information above. **Management:** James A. Warner, Publisher. Lisa Miksis, Advertising Manager. David A. Ellis, Classified Adv. Mgr.. **Editorial:** Brian Boyd, Editor. Amy J. Barry, Feature Editor. David Phillips, Sports Editor.

GUILFORD COURIER, THE. 724 Boston Post Rd., Ste. 202, Madison, CT 06443. Telephone: 203-245-1877. FAX: 203-245-9773. E-MAIL: news@shorepublishing.com. URL: http://www.shorepublishing.com. Mailing Address: P.O. Box 1010, Madison, CT 06443. Year Established: 1998. Pub. Frequency: w. (Thu.) Page Size: broadsheet.Adv. Rate: col. inch $11.80 Circulation: 9,176 per issue (free). **Owner(s):** Shore Publishing LLC, See address and contact information above. **Management:** James Warner, Publisher. Lisa Miksis, Advertising Manager. David A. Ellis, Classified Adv. Mgr.. **Editorial:** Brian Boyd, Editor. Alan Ellis, Production Manager. Amy J. Barry, Feature Editor. David Phillips, Sports Editor.

HARBOR NEWS, THE. 724 Boston Post Rd., Ste. 202, Madison, CT 06443. Telephone: 203-245-1877. FAX: 203-245-9773. E-MAIL: news@shorepublishing.com. URL: http://www.shorepublishing.com. Mailing Address: P.O. Box 1010, Madison, CT 06443. Pub. Frequency: w. (Thu.) Page Size: broadsheet.Adv. Rate: col. inch $9.80 Circulation: 18,000 per issue (free). **Owner(s):** Shore Publishing LLC, See address and contact information above. **Management:** James Warner, Publisher. Michelle DiPietro, Advertising Director. David A. Ellis, Classified Adv. Mgr.. **Editorial:** Brian Boyd, Editor. Alan Ellis, Production Manager. Amy J. Barry, Feature Editor. Jim Duffy, Sports Editor.

NORTH HAVEN COURIER. 724 Boston Post Rd., Ste. 202, Madison, CT 06443. Telephone: 203-245-1877. FAX: 203-245-9773. E-MAIL: news@shorepublishing.com. URL: http://www.shorepublishing.com. Mailing Address: P.O. Box 1010, Madison, CT 06443. Year Established: 2000. Pub. Frequency: w. (Thu.) Page Size: broadsheet.Adv. Rate: col. inch $9.80 Circulation: 10,261 per issue (free). **Owner(s):** Shore Publishing LLC, See address and contact information above. **Management:** James Warner, Publisher. Michelle DiPietro, Advertising Manager. David A. Ellis, Classified Adv. Mgr.. **Editorial:** Brian Boyd, Editor. Alan Ellis, Production Manager. Amy J. Barry, Feature Editor. Jim Duffy, Sports Editor.

SOUND, THE. 724 Boston Post Rd., Ste. 202, Madison, CT 06443. Telephone: 203-245-1877. FAX: 203-245-9773. E-MAIL: news@shorepublishing.com. URL: http://www.shorepublishing.com. Mailing Address: P.O. Box 1010, Madison, CT 06443. Year Established: 1997. Pub. Frequency: w. (Thu.) Page Size: broadsheet.Adv. Rate: col. inch $11.80 Circulation: 19,082 per issue (free). **Owner(s):** Shore Publishing LLC, See address and contact information above. **Management:** James Warner, Publisher. Lisa Miksis, Advertising Manager. David A. Ellis, Classified Adv. Mgr.. **Editorial:** Brian Boyd, Editor. Alan Ellis, Production Manager. Amy J. Barry, Feature Editor. David Phillips, Sports Editor.

SOURCE (MADISON), THE. 724 Boston Post Rd., Ste. 202, Madison, CT 06443. Telephone: 203-245-1877. FAX: 203-245-9773. E-MAIL: news@shorepublishing.com. URL: http://www.shorepublishing.com. Mailing Address: P.O. Box 1010, Madison, CT 06443. Pub. Frequency: w. (Thu.) Page Size: broadsheet.Adv. Rate: col. inch $9.80 Circulation: 8,500 per issue (free). **Owner(s):** Shore Publishing LLC, See address and contact information above. **Management:** James Warner, Publisher. Michelle DiPietro, Advertising Director. David A. Ellis, Classified Adv. Mgr.. **Editorial:** Brian Boyd, Editor. Alan Ellis, Production Manager. Amy Barry, Feature Editor. Jim Duffy, Sports Editor.

VALLEY COURIER (MADISON). 724 Boston Post Rd., Ste. 202, Madison, CT 06443. Telephone: 203-245-1877. FAX: 203-245-9773. E-MAIL: news@shorepublishing.com. URL: http://www.shorepublishing.com. Mailing Address: P.O. Box 1010, Madison, CT 06443. Year Established: 2001. Pub. Frequency: w. (Thu.) Page Size: broadsheet.Adv. Rate: col. inch $11.80 Circulation: 6,222 per issue (free). **Owner(s):** Shore Publishing LLC, See address and contact information above. **Management:** James Warner, Publisher. Lisa Miksis, Advertising Manager. **Editorial:** Brian Boyd, Editor. Alan C. Ellis, Production Manager. Amy J. Barry, Feature Editor. David Phillips, Sports Editor.

MIDDLEFIELD

TOWN TIMES (MIDDLEFIELD). 488 Main St., Middlefield, CT 06455. Telephone: 860-349-8000. FAX: 860-349-8027. E-MAIL: news@towntimes.com. URL: http://www.towntimes.com. Mailing Address: PO Box 265, Middlesex, CT 06455-0265. Year Established: 1994. Pub. Frequency: w. (Fri.) Page Size: tabloid Circulation: 6,500 per issue (free). **Owner(s):** Meriden Record-Journal Publishing Co., 75 S. Colony St., Meriden, CT 06450. Telephone: 203-317-2420. FAX: 203-235-3482. **Management:** Dave Lucy, Publisher. Dick LaValle, Advertising Director. **Editorial:** Sue VanDerzee, Editor. Betsy White Booz, Production Manager.

MIDDLETOWN

REGIONAL STANDARD. 2 Main St., Middletown, CT 06457. Telephone: 860-347-3331. FAX: 860-347-3380. E-MAIL: regionalstandard@ctcentral.com. URL: http://www.regionalstandard.com. Pub. Frequency: w. (Fri.) Page Size: tabloid.Subscrip. Rate: $.50 newsstand/cover; $16.96/yr Circulation: 5,000 per issue (paid). **Owner(s):** Journal Register Co., 50 W State St, 12th Fl, Trenton, NJ 08608. Telephone: 609-396-2200. FAX: 609-396-2292. **Management:** John Slater, General Manager. Lee Warren, Advertising Manager. Patricia Russell, Classified Adv. Mgr.. **Editorial:** Eric Montgomery, Editor. Erik Hesselberg, Executive Editor. Deby Bishop, Sports Editor.

MILFORD

BULLETIN (MILFORD), THE. 349 New Haven Ave., Milford, CT 06460. Telephone: 203-876-6800. FAX: 203-877-4772. E-MAIL: elmcity@ctcentral.com. URL: http://www.orangebulletin.com. Mailing Address: PO Box 5339, Milford, CT 06460. Pub. Frequency: w. (Thu.) Page Size: tabloid Circulation: 9,730 per issue (free). **Owner(s):** Journal Register Co., 50 W State St, 12th Fl, Trenton, NJ 08608. Telephone: 609-396-2200. **Management:** David W Compton, Publisher. Keith Buth, Advertising Director. Sam Tibbals, Circulation Manager. **Editorial:** Bridget Albert, Editor. Erik Hesselberg, Executive Editor.

HAMDEN CHRONICLE, THE. 349 New Haven Ave., Milford, CT 06460. Telephone: 203-876-6800. FAX: 203-877-4772. E-MAIL: hamdenchronicle@ctcentral.com. URL: http://www.hamdenchronicle.com. Mailing Address: PO Box 5339, Milford, CT 06460. Pub. Frequency: w. (Thu.) Page Size: broadsheet. Circulation: 20,000 per issue (paid and free). **Owner(s):** Journal Register Co., 50 W State St, 12th Fl, Trenton, NJ 08608. Telephone: 609-396-2200. **Management:** David W Compton, Publisher. Keith Buth, Advertising Director. Sam Tibbals, Circulation Manager. Edith Williams Pryne, Classified Adv. Mgr.. **Editorial:** Chad Odefey, Editor. Erik Hesselberg, Executive Editor. Vinnie Salzo, Sports Editor.

MILFORD WEEKLY. 349 New Haven Ave., Milford, CT 06460. Telephone: 203-876-6800. FAX: 203-877-4772. E-MAIL: http://www.milfordweekly.com. URL: http://www.milfordweekly.com. Mailing Address: PO Box 5339, Milford, CT 06460. Pub. Frequency: w. (Fri.) Page Size: broadsheet Circulation: 10,000 per issue (free). **Owner(s):** Journal Register Co., 50 W State St, 12th Fl, Trenton, NJ 08608. Telephone: 609-396-2200. FAX: 609-396-2292. **Management:** David Compton, Publisher. Keith Buth, Advertising Director. Sam Tibbals, Circulation Manager. **Editorial:** Chad Odefey, Editor. Erik Hesselberg, Executive Editor.

NORTH HAVEN POST, THE. 349 New Haven Ave, Milford, CT 06460. Telephone: 203-876-6800. FAX: 203-877-4772. E-MAIL: nhavenpost@ctcentral.com. URL: http://www.northhavenpost.com. Mailing Address: PO Box 5339, Milford, CT 06460. Pub. Frequency: w. (Fri.) Page Size: broadsheet. Subscrip. Rate: $16/yr. Circulation: 2,893 per issue (paid and free). **Owner(s):** Journal Register Co., 50 W State St, 12th Fl, Trenton, NJ 08608. Telephone: 609-396-2200. **Management:** David Compton, Publisher. Keith Buth, Advertising Director. Sam Tibbals, Circulation Manager. **Editorial:** Fred Nevin, Editor. Gail Celentano, Editorial Assistant.

STRATFORD BARD. ISSN 1077-0844 349 New Haven Ave., Milford, CT 06460. Telephone: 203-876-6800. FAX: 203-877-4772. E-MAIL: stratfordbard@ctcentral.com. URL: http://www.stratfordbard.com. Mailing Address: PO Box 5339, Milford, CT 06460. Year Established: 1970. Pub. Frequency: w. (Fri.) Page Size: tabloid. Subscrip. Rate: $18/yr home delivery in county. Freelance Pay: $1/column-inch. Circulation: 4,300 per issue (free). **Owner(s):** Journal Register Co., 50 W State St, 12th Fl, Trenton, NJ 08608. Telephone: 609-396-2200. **Management:** David W Compton, Publisher. Magda M. Ballaro, Advertising Manager. Sam Tibbals, Circulation Manager. Shannon White, Classified Adv. Mgr.. **Editorial:** Tristram DeRoma, Editor. Ann Freely, Editorial Assistant.

WEST HAVEN NEWS. 349 New Haven Ave., Milford, CT 06460. Telephone: 203-876-6800. FAX: 203-877-4772. E-MAIL: westhavennews@ctcentral.com. URL: http://www.westhavennews.com. Mailing Address: PO Box 5339, Milford, CT 06460. Year Established: 1931. Pub. Frequency: w. (Fri.) Page Size: tabloid Circulation: 9,000 per issue (free). **Owner(s):** Journal Register Co., 50 W State St, 12th Fl, Trenton, NJ 08608. Telephone: 609-396-2200. **Management:** David W Compton, Publisher. Magda M. Ballaro, Advertising Manager. Sam Tibbals, Circulation Director. Shannon White, Classified Adv. Mgr.. **Editorial:** Chad Odefey, Editor. Ann Freely, Editorial Assistant. Vinnie Salzo, Sports Editor.

MYSTIC

MYSTIC RIVER PRESS. 10 Water St., Mystic, CT 06355. Telephone: 860-536-9577. FAX: 860-536-1276. E-MAIL: utter02891@aol.com. Year Established: 1992. Pub. Frequency: w. (Thu.) Page Size: tabloid. Subscrip. Rate: $30 mailed for 6 mos. 1st class; $56/yr mailed. Circulation: 10,000 per issue (paid and free). **Owner(s):** Record -Journal Publishing Co., 11 Crown St., Meriden, CT 06450-5788. Telephone: 203-235-1661. **Management:** Dave Lucey, Publisher. Bob Cardosa, Advertising Director. Peter Griggs, Advertising Manager. Ann Capalbo, Admin. Assistant. **Editorial:** Greg Benoit, Editor.

NAUGATUCK

CITIZEN'S NEWS. 71 Weid Dr., Naugatuck, CT 06770. Telephone: 203-729-2228. FAX: 203-729-9099. Year Established: 1885. Pub. Frequency: w. (Fri.) Page Size: broadsheet. Subscrip. Rate: $50 newsstand/cover; $41.60/yr mailed. Adv. Rate: col. inch $7.30 Circulation: 5,250 per issue (paid). **Owner(s):** Maitland Publishing LLC, See address and contact information above. **Editorial:** Kendra Bobowick, Managing Editor.

NEW CANAAN

NEW CANAAN ADVERTISER. 42 Vitti St., New Canaan, CT 06840. Telephone: 203-966-9541. FAX: 203-966-8006. E-MAIL: editor@ncadvertiser.com. URL: http://www.acorn-online.com. Mailing Address: PO Box 605, New Canaan, CT 06840. Year Established: 1908. Pub. Frequency: w. (Thu.) Page Size: standard. Subscrip. Rate: $.75 newsstand/cover; $39/yr in state. Adv. Rate: col. inch $11 Circulation: 7,500 per issue (paid). **Owner(s):** Hersam Acorn Newspapers LLC, 16 Bailey Ave., Ridgefield, CT 06877. Telephone: 203-438-6544. **Management:** Thomas Nash, Publisher. Shelagh Barrett, Advertising Director. Bruce McDougall, Circulation Manager. Rose Sayers, Classified Adv. Mgr.. **Editorial:** John Kovach, Editor. Jack Sanders, Executive Editor.

NEW CANAAN NEWS-REVIEW. 161 Cherry St., New Canaan, CT 16840. Telephone: 203-972-4400. FAX: 203-972-4404. E-MAIL: ncnr@bcnnnew.com. URL: http://www.newcanaannews-review.com. Pub. Frequency: w. (Fri.) Page Size: tabloid Circulation: 8,000 per issue (free). **Owner(s):** MediaNews Group, Inc., 101 W Colfax Ave, Ste 1100, Denver, CO 80202. FAX: 303-954-6320. **Management:** Kevin Lally, Publisher. Ed Majersky, Advertising Director. **Editorial:** Phil Soto-Oritz, Editor.

NEW FAIRFIELD

NEW FAIRFIELD CITIZEN NEWS. 79 Rte 39, New Fairfield, CT 06812. Telephone: 203-746-4669. FAX: 203-746-5606. E-MAIL: citiznnews@aol.com. Mailing Address: PO Box 8048, New Fairfield, CT 06812-8048. Year Established: 1972. Pub. Frequency: w. (Wed.) Page Size: tabloid. Subscrip. Rate: $.35 newsstand/cover; $40/yr mailed. Adv. Rate: col. inch $7 Circulation: 7,600 per issue (paid). **Owner(s):** Ellen Burnett, See address and contact information above. **Management:** Ellen Burnett, Publisher. **Editorial:** Ellen Burnett, Editor. William Merritt, Sports Editor.

NEW HAVEN

INNER CITY. 50 Fitch St., New Haven, CT 06515-1319. Telephone: 203-387-0354. FAX: 203-387-2684. E-MAIL: tomficklin@aol.com. Pub. Frequency: w. (Fri.) Page Size: broadsheet. Subscrip. Rate: $30/yr mailed. Circulation: 35,000 per issue (paid and free). **Owner(s):** Pennfield Communications, Inc., See address and contact information above. **Management:** John Thomas, President. Diane Payton, Advertising Manager. **Editorial:** Diane Payton, Editor.

NEW HAVEN ADVOCATE. ISSN 0192-8511 900 Chapel St., Ste. 1100, New Haven, CT 06510-5991. Telephone: 203-789-0010. FAX: 203-787-1418. E-MAIL: editor@newhavenadvocate.com. URL: http://www.newhavenadvocate.com. Year Established: 1975. Pub. Frequency: w. Page Size: tabloid. Subscrip. Rate: $160/yr mailed. Adv. Rate: page $1,875 Freelance Pay: $75-$300/article. Circulation: 55,000 per issue (paid and free). **Owner(s):** New Mass Media, Inc., See address and contact information above. **Management:** Joshua Mamis, Publisher. Susan Leighton, Advertising Director. Jose Luyando, Circulation Manager. **Editorial:** Mark Oppenheimer, Editor. Tom Gogola, Managing Editor.

NEW MILFORD

BETHEL BEACON. 65 Bank St., New Milford, CT 06776. FAX: 860-354-8706. E-MAIL: betheleditor@ctcentral.com. URL: http://www.bethelbeacon.com. Year Established: 1996. Pub. Frequency: w. (Fri.) Page Size: broadsheet. Subscrip. Rate: $1 newsstand/cover; $37.95/yr home delivery in county; $47.95/yr mailed out of county. Adv. Rate: col. inch $11.03 Circulation: 1,382 per issue (paid). **Owner(s):** Journal Register Co., Lower Makefield Corporate Center, 790 Township Line Rd, 3rd Fl, Yardley, PA 19067. **Management:** Paula Walsh, Publisher. Ray Filbert, Advertising Manager. **Editorial:** Douglas Clement, Editor.

BROOKFIELD JOURNAL. 65 Bank St., New Milford, CT 06776. Telephone: 860-354-2261. FAX: 860-210-2609. E-MAIL: brookfieldeditor@ctcentral.com. URL: http://www.brookfieldjournal.com. Year Established: 1957. Pub. Frequency: w. (Fri.) Page Size: broadsheet. Subscrip. Rate: $1 newsstand/cover; $32.95/yr home delivery in county; $42.95/yr mailed out of county. Adv. Rate: col. inch $14.54 Circulation: 1,855 per issue (paid). **Owner(s):** Journal Register Co., Lower Makefield Corporate Center, 790 Township Line Rd, 3rd Fl, Yardley, PA 19067. **Management:** Paula Walsh, Publisher. Ray Filbert, Advertising Manager. **Editorial:** Doug Clement, Executive Editor. Alice Tessier, Managing Editor.

HOUSATONIC LIVING. 65 Bank St., New Milford, CT 06776. Telephone: 860-354-2261. FAX: 860-210-2609. E-MAIL: goodlivingeditor@ctcentral.com. URL: http://www.newmilfordtimes.com. Year Established: 1948. Pub. Frequency: w. (Fri.) Page Size: broadsheet.Adv. Rate: col. inch $19.64 Circulation: 39,000 per issue (free). **Owner(s):** Journal Register Co., Lower Makefield Corporate Center, 790 Township Line Rd, 3rd Fl, Yardley, PA 19067. **Management:** Paula Walsh, Publisher. Ray Filbert, Advertising Manager. Heidi Haug, Classified Adv. Mgr.. **Editorial:** Douglas Clement, Executive Editor. Jaime Ferris, Associate Editor.

LITCHFIELD COUNTY TIMES, THE. 65 Bank St., New Milford, CT 06776. E-MAIL: news@countytimes.com. URL: http://www.countytimes.com. Year Established: 1981. Pub. Frequency: w. (Fri.) Page Size: broadsheet. Subscrip. Rate: $1.25 newsstand/cover; $40/yr in county; $37/yr to senior citizens; $50/yr out of county. Adv. Rate: col. inch $24.10 Circulation: 13,502 per issue (paid). **Owner(s):** Journal Register Co., Lower Makefield Corporate Center, 790 Township Line Rd, 3rd Fl, Yardley, PA 19067. **Management:** Paula Walsh, Publisher. Ray Filbert, Advertising Manager. Heidi Haug, Classified Adv. Mgr.. Laurie Gaboardi, Photography Director. **Editorial:** Douglas Clement, Executive Editor.

LITCHFIELD ENQUIRER. 65 Bank St., New Milford, CT 06776. Telephone: 860-354-2261. FAX: 860-210-2609. E-MAIL: litchfieldeditor@ctcentral.com. URL: http://www.litchfieldenquirer.com. Year Established: 1825. Pub. Frequency: w. (Fri.) Page Size: broadsheet. Subscrip. Rate: $1 newsstand/cover; $32.95/yr home delivery in county; $42.95/yr mailed out of county; $27.95/yr home delivery in county to senior citizens. Adv. Rate: col. inch $11.03 Circulation: 1,478 per issue (paid and free). **Owner(s):** Journal Register Co., Lower Makefield Corporate Center, 790 Township Line Rd, 3rd. flr, Yardley, PA 19067. Telephone: 215-504-4200. FAX: 215-504-4201. **Management:** Paula Walsh, Publisher. Ray Filbert, Advertising Manager. **Editorial:** Douglas Clement, Executive Editor. Alice Tessier, Managing Editor.

NEW MILFORD TIMES. 65 Bank St., New Milford, CT 06776. Telephone: 860-354-2261. FAX: 860-210-2150. E-MAIL: litchfieldeditor@ctcentral.com. URL: http://www.newmilfordtimes.com. Pub. Frequency: w. (Fri.) Subscrip. Rate: $1 newsstand/cover; $36.95/yr in county; $31.95/yr in county to senior citizens; $46.95/yr out of county. Adv. Rate: col. inch $17.54 Circulation: 2,940 per issue. **Owner(s):** Journal Register Co., Lower Makefield Corporate Center, 790 Township Line Rd, 3rd. flr, Yardley, PA 19067. **Management:** Paula Walsh, Publisher. Ray Filbert, Advertising Manager. Heidi Haug, Classified Adv. Mgr.. **Editorial:** Doug Clement, Executive Editor. Emily Olson, Managing Editor.

NEWTOWN

NEWTOWN BEE, THE. 5 Church Hill Rd., Newtown, CT 06470-5503. Telephone: 203-426-3141. FAX: 203-426-5169. E-MAIL: info@thebee.com. URL: http://www.thenewtownbee.com. Mailing Address: PO Box 5503, Newtown, CT 06470-5503. Year Established: 1877. Pub. Frequency: w. (Fri.) Page Size: broadsheet. Subscrip. Rate: $.65 newsstand/cover; $30/yr home delivery; $53 home delivery for 2 yrs.. Adv. Rate: col. inch $9.99 Circulation: 9,000 per issue (paid). **Owner(s):** The Bee Publishing Co., 5 Church Hill Rd., Newtown, CT 06470. Telephone: 203-426-3141. FAX: 203-426-1394. **Management:** R. Scudder Smith, Publisher. Scott Baggett, Advertising Manager. **Editorial:** R. Scudder Smith, Editor. Curtis Clark, Managing Editor.

NORTH HAVEN

ADVISOR (NORTH HAVEN), THE. 83 State St., North Haven, CT 06473-2208. Telephone: 203-239-5404. FAX: 203-239-7097. URL: http://www.advisor-newspaper.com. Year Established: 1965. Pub. Frequency: w. (Tue.) Page Size: tabloid.Subscrip. Rate: $21/yr mailed Circulation: 33,000 per issue (free). **Owner(s):** Patricia Flagg, PO Box 460, North Haven, CT 06473-0460. Telephone: 203-239-5404. **Management:** Patricia Flagg, Publisher. Donna Kelly, Advertising. Joyce Scott, Circulation Manager. **Editorial:** Danielle Flagg, Editor.

NORWALK

STAMFORD LIFESTYLES. 542 Westport Ave., Norwalk, CT 06851. Telephone: 203-849-1600. FAX: 203-840-4844. URL: http://www.brooksnewspapers.com.Pub. Frequency: m. Page Size: tabloid Circulation: 10,000 per issue (free). **Owner(s):** MediaNews Group, Inc., 101 W Colfax Ave, Ste 1100, Denver, CO 80202. FAX: 303-954-6320. **Management:** Kevin Lally, Publisher. Ed Majersky, Advertising Director. **Editorial:** Don Harrison, Editor.

WILTON LIFESTYLES. 542 Westport Ave., Norwalk, CT 06851. Telephone: 203-849-1600. FAX: 203-840-4844. URL: http://www.brooksnewspapers.com.Pub. Frequency: m. Page Size: tabloid Circulation: 4,500 per issue (free). **Owner(s):** MediaNews Group, Inc., 101 W Colfax Ave, Ste 1100, Denver, CO 80202. FAX: 303-954-6320. **Management:** Kevin Lally, Publisher. Ed Majersky, Advertising Director. **Editorial:** Don Harrison, Editor.

OLD SAYBROOK

NEW LONDON COUNTY PENNYSAVER. 210 Main St., Old Saybrook, CT 06475. Telephone: 860-388-3441. FAX: 860-388-5613. Mailing Address: PO Box 813, Old Saybrook, CT 06475. Pub. Frequency: w. (Thu.) Page Size: tabloid Circulation: 6,000 per issue (free). **Owner(s):** Journal Register Co., 50 W State St, 12th Fl, Trenton, NJ 08608. Telephone: 609-396-2200. FAX: 609-396-2292. **Management:** Tammy West, Publisher. **Editorial:** Bill Keim, Editor.

PAWCATUCK

RESIDENT (STONINGTON), THE. ISSN 1085-7591
252 S. Broad St., Pawcatuck, CT 06379. Telephone: 860-599-1221. FAX: 860-599-1400. E-MAIL: alexis@theresident.com. URL: http://www.theresident.com. Mailing Address: PO Box 269, Stonington, CT 06378-0269. Year Established: 1990. Pub. Frequency: bi-w. (Wed.) Page Size: tabloid. Subscrip. Rate: $28/yr. Adv. Rate: col. inch $26 Freelance Pay: $55/story. Circulation: 45,000 per issue (free). **Owner(s):** Alexis Ann, 427 Noank Rd, Mystic, CT 06355. Telephone: 860-572-2054. FAX: 860-572-2038. **Management:** Alexis Ann, Publisher.

RIDGEFIELD

GREENWICH POST. ISSN 1554-2025
16 Bailey Ave, Ridgefield, CT 06877. Telephone: 203-438-6544. FAX: 203-861-0027. E-MAIL: editor@greenwichpost.com. URL: http://www.acorn-online.com. Mailing Address: PO Box 1019, Ridgefield, CT 06877. Year Established: 1996. Pub. Frequency: w. (Thu.) Page Size: tabloid. Subscrip. Rate: $.50 newsstand/cover; $42/yr mailed out of area. Adv. Rate: col. inch $15.50 Circulation: 24,000 per issue (free). **Owner(s):** Hersom Acorn Newspapers, LLC, See address and contact information above. **Management:** Thomas B. Nash, Publisher. Shelagh Barrett, Advertising Director. Bruce McDougall, Circulation Manager. Rose Sayers, Classified Adv. Mgr.. **Editorial:** Jack Sanders, Executive Editor.

LEWISBORO LEDGER, THE. 16 Bailey Ave., Ridgefield, CT 06877. Telephone: 203-438-6544. FAX: 203-861-0023. E-MAIL: ledger@acorn-online.com. URL: http://www.acorn-online.com. Mailing Address: PO Box 188, Cross River, NY 10518. Year Established: 1976. Pub. Frequency: w. (Thu.) Page Size: broadsheet. Subscrip. Rate: $.75 newsstand/cover; $39/yr mailed in county; $45/yr mailed out of county. **Wire Service(s):** AP. Circulation: 1,800 per issue (paid). **Owner(s):** Hersam Acorn Newspapers LLC, See address and contact information above. **Management:** Thomas Nash, Publisher. Shelagh Barrett, Advertising Director. Bruce McDougall, Circulation Manager. Rose Sayers, Classified Adv. Mgr.. **Editorial:** Ken Mastro, Editor. Jack Sanders, Executive Editor.

RIDGEFIELD PRESS, THE. 16 Bailey Ave., Ridgefield, CT 06877. Telephone: 203-438-6544. FAX: 203-861-0023. E-MAIL: newsroom@acorn-online.com. URL: http://www.acorn-online.com. Mailing Address: PO Box 1019, Ridgefield, CT 06877-1019. Year Established: 1875. Pub. Frequency: w. (Thu.) Page Size: broadsheet. Subscrip. Rate: $.75 newsstand/cover; $39/yr in county; $45/yr out of county. **Wire Service(s):** AP. Circulation: 7,010 per issue (paid). **Owner(s):** Hersam Acorn Newspapers LLC, See address and contact information above. **Management:** Thomas Nash, Publisher. Shelagh Barrett, Advertising Director. Bruce McDougall, Circulation Manager. Rose Sayers, Classified Adv. Mgr.. **Editorial:** Macklin Reid, Editor. Jack Sanders, Executive Editor. Tim Murphy, Sports.

TRI-STATE PENNYSAVER PRESS. 16 Bailey Ave, Ridgefield, CT 06877. Telephone: 203-894-3310. FAX: 203-861-0027. E-MAIL: ads@hersamacornvt.com. URL: http://www.vtliving.com/newspapers/tristatepennysaver/index.shtml. Year Established: 1958. Pub. Frequency: w. (Wed.) Page Size: tabloid Circulation: 37,000 per issue (free). **Owner(s):** Hersom Acorn Newspapers, LLC, See address and contact information above. **Management:** Renee Tassore, General Manager. Linda Devlin, Circulation Manager.

VERMONT NEWS GUIDE. 16 Bailey Ave., Ridgefield, CT 06877. URL: http://www.hersamacorn.com. Mailing Address: 99 Bonnet St, Manchester Center, VT 05255-1265. Year Established: 1960. Pub. Frequency: w. (Wed.) Page Size: tabloid. Subscrip. Rate: $35/yr mailed out of state. Circulation: 16,000 per issue (paid and free). **Owner(s):** Hersam Acorn Newspapers LLC, See address and contact information above. **Management:** Renee Tassone, General Manager.

ROCKY HILL

RARE REMINDER. 222 Dividend Rd., Rocky Hill, CT 06067. Telephone: 860-563-9386. FAX: 860-257-4688. URL: http://www.rarereminder.com. Mailing Address: PO Box 289, Rocky Hill, CT 06067-0289. Year Established: 1953. Pub. Frequency: w. (Tue.) Page Size: tabloid Circulation: 58,000 per issue (free). **Owner(s):** Rare Reminder, Inc., See address and contact information above. **Management:** Kevin Rarey, Publisher. Carol Flagg, Advertising Manager. Brian Klatt, Circulation Manager.

SHELTON

AMITY OBSERVER. 1000 Bridgeport Ave, Shelton, CT 06484. Telephone: 203-926-2080. FAX: 203-926-2091. E-MAIL: amityobserver@icpgroup.com. URL: http://www.amityobserver.com. Mailing Address: PO Box 1019, Ridgefield, CT 06877-1019. Pub. Frequency: w. (Thu.) Page Size: broadsheet. Subscrip. Rate: $18/yr in county; $26.50/yr out of county. Circulation: 9,750 per issue (paid and free). **Owner(s):** Hersam Acorn Newspapers LLC, 16 Bailey Ave., Ridgefield, CT 06877-1019. **Management:** Regina Burkhart, Publisher. John Schneider, Advertising Director. **Editorial:** Terri Miles, Editor. Lorraine Bukowski, News Editor. Ellen Beveridge, Society Editor. Bill Bloxsom, Sports Editor.

BRIDGEPORT NEWS (SHELTON), THE. 1000 Bridgeport Ave, Shelton, CT 06484. Telephone: 203-926-2080. FAX: 203-926-2091. E-MAIL: HomePubl@aol.com. Pub. Frequency: w. (Thu.) Page Size: broadsheet.Subscrip. Rate: $37.50/yr mailed out of county Circulation: 4,940 per issue (paid). **Owner(s):** Hersam Acorn Newspapers LLC, 16 Bailey Ave., Ridgefield, CT 06877. Telephone: 203-438-6544. FAX: 203-861-0023. **Management:** Regina Burkhart, Publisher. John Schneider, Advertising Director. Sharon Sako, Circulation Director. **Editorial:** Lorraine Bukowski, News Editor. Ellen Beveridge, Society Editor. Bill Bloxsom, Sports Editor.

EASTON COURIER. 1000 Bridgeport Ave, Shelton, CT 06484. Telephone: 203-926-2080. FAX: 203-926-2091. E-MAIL: eastoncourier@add-inc.com. Pub. Frequency: w. (Thu) Page Size: broadsheet. Subscrip. Rate: $1.06 newsstand/cover; $16/yr local town; $37.50/yr out of area out of town. Circulation: 1,688 per issue (paid). **Owner(s):** Hersam Acorn Newspapers LLC, 16 Bailey Ave., Ridgefield, CT 06877. Telephone: 203-438-6544. FAX: 203-861-0023. **Management:** Regina Burkhart, Publisher. John Schneider, Advertising Director. Sharon Sako, Circulation Director. **Editorial:** Larissa Lytwyn, Editor. Ellen Beveridge, Society Editor.

HUNTINGTON HERALD, THE. 1000 Bridgeport Ave, Shelton, CT 06484. Telephone: 203-926-2080. FAX: 203-926-2091. URL: http://www.huntingtonherald.com. Pub. Frequency: w. (Wed.) Page Size: broadsheet. Subscrip. Rate: $1.06 newsstand/cover; $16/yr local; $37.50/yr out of area. Circulation: 8,110 per issue (paid). **Owner(s):** Hersam Acorn Newspapers LLC, 16 Bailey Ave., Ridgefield, CT 06877. Telephone: 203-438-6544. FAX: 203-861-0023. **Management:** Regina Burkhart, Publisher. Sharon Sako, Circulation Director. **Editorial:** Christian Meagher, Editor. Bill Bloxsom, Sports Editor.

MILFORD MIRROR. ISSN 1527-6759
1000 Bridgeport Ave, Shelton, CT 06484. Telephone: 203-926-2080. FAX: 203-926-2091. E-MAIL: HomePubl@aol.com. URL: http://www.milfordmirror.com. Year Established: 1986. Pub. Frequency: w. (Thu.) Page Size: broadsheet. Subscrip. Rate: $37.50/yr. Circulation: 16,800 per issue (paid and free). **Owner(s):** Hersam Acorn Newspapers LLC, 16 Bailey Ave., Ridgefield, CT 06877. Telephone: 203-438-6544. FAX: 203-861-0023. **Management:** Regina Burkhart, Publisher. John Schneider, Advertising Director. Sharon Sako, Circulation Director. **Editorial:** Lorraine Bukowski, News Editor. Ellen Beveridge, Society Editor. Bill Bloxsom, Sports Editor.

MONROE COURIER. 1000 Bridgeport Ave, Shelton, CT 06484. Telephone: 203-926-2080. FAX: 203-926-2091. E-MAIL: monroecourier@add-inc.com. URL: http://www.monroecourier.com. Year Established: 1965. Pub. Frequency: w. (Thu.) Page Size: broadsheet. Subscrip. Rate: $1.06 newsstand/cover; $16/yr home delivery in county; $37.50/yr mailed out of county. **Wire Service(s):** AP. Circulation: 4,364 per issue (paid). **Owner(s):** Hersam Acorn Newspapers LLC, 16 Bailey Ave., Ridgefield, CT 06877. Telephone: 203-438-6544. FAX: 203-861-0023. **Management:** Regina Burkhart, Publisher. John Schneider, Advertising Director. Sharon Sako, Circulation Director. **Editorial:** Lorraine Bukowski, News Editor. Ellen Beveridge, Society Editor. Bill Bloxsom, Sports Editor.

STRATFORD STAR (SHELTON). 1000 Bridgeport Ave, Shelton, CT 06484. Telephone: 203-926-2080. FAX: 203-926-2091. E-MAIL: HomePubl@aol.com. URL: http://www.stratfordstar.com. Pub. Frequency: w. (Thu.) Page Size: broadsheet. Subscrip. Rate: $37.50/yr mailed out of county. Circulation: 18,120 per issue (paid and free). **Owner(s):** Hersam Acorn Newspapers LLC, 16 Bailey Ave., Ridgefield, CT 06877. Telephone: 203-438-6544. FAX: 203-861-0023. **Management:** Regina Burkhart, Publisher. Hank Misiak, Advertising Director. Sharon Sako, Circulation Director. **Editorial:** Fred Musante, Editor. Lorraine Bukowski, News Editor. Ellen Beveridge, Society Editor. Bill Bloxsom, Sports Editor.

TRUMBULL TIMES. 1000 Bridgeport Ave, Shelton, CT 06484. Telephone: 203-926-2080. FAX: 203-926-2091. E-MAIL: HomePubl@aol.com. URL: http://www.trumbulltimes.com. Year Established: 1958. Pub. Frequency: w. (Thu.) Page Size: broadsheet. Subscrip. Rate: $1.06 newsstand/cover; $16/yr home delivery in county town; $37.50/yr mailed out of county out of town. Freelance Pay: $0.75/column-inch. Circulation: 7,480 per issue (paid). **Owner(s):** Hersam Acorn Newspapers LLC, 16 Bailey Ave., Ridgefield, CT 06877. Telephone: 203-438-6544. FAX: 203-861-0023. **Management:** Regina Burkhart, Publisher. John Schneider, Advertising Director. **Editorial:** Donald Eng, Editor. Lorraine Bukowski, News Editor.

VALLEY GAZETTE. 1000 Bridgeport Ave, Shelton, CT 06484. Telephone: 203-926-2080. FAX: 203-926-2091. E-MAIL: homepubl@aol.com. Year Established: 1992. Pub. Frequency: w. (Wed.) Page Size: broadsheet. Subscrip. Rate: $37.50/yr out of town. Freelance Pay: $1-$2/column-inch. Circulation: 15,690 per issue (paid and free). **Owner(s):** Hersam Acorn Newspapers LLC, 16 Bailey Ave., Ridgefield, CT 06877. Telephone: 203-438-6544. FAX: 203-861-0023. **Management:** Regina Burkhart, Publisher. John Schneider, Advertising Director. **Editorial:** Lorraine Bukowski, News Editor. Ellen Beveridge, Society Editor.

SOUTHBURY

HERITAGE VILLAGER. 519 Heritage Rd., Ste. 3B, Southbury, CT 06488. Telephone: 203-264-0123. FAX: 203-264-9467. E-MAIL: hvillager@aol.com. Pub. Frequency: s-m. (Fri.) Page Size: tabloid.Subscrip. Rate: $1 newsstand/cover; $18/yr Circulation: 2,500 per issue (paid). **Owner(s):** Maitland Publishing LLC, PO Box 269, Southbury, CT 06488-0269. Telephone: 203-264-0123. FAX: 203-264-9467. **Management:** Marcey Tweedie, Sales Manager. **Editorial:** Frances Chamberlain, Editor.

THOMASTON

THOMASTON EXPRESS, THE. 44 Union St., Thomaston, CT 06787. Telephone: 860-283-4355. FAX: 860-283-4356. E-MAIL: thomaston@ctcentral.com. URL: http://www.thomastonexpress.com. Mailing Address: PO Box 250, Thomaston, CT 06787-0250. Year Established: 1874. Pub. Frequency: w. (Thu.) Page Size: tabloid. Subscrip. Rate: $.35 newsstand/cover; $21/yr local; $27/yr in state; $33/yr out of state. Circulation: 1,900 per issue (paid). **Owner(s):** Journal Register Co., 50 W State St, 12th Fl, Trenton, NJ 08608. Telephone: 609-396-2200. FAX: 609-396-2292. **Management:** William Sheedy, Publisher. Melanie Koles, Advertising Manager. **Editorial:** Samantha Friedrich, Editor. Rick Wilson, Sports.

TORRINGTON

FOOTHILLS TRADER. 190 Water St., Torrington, CT 06790-0058. URL: http:www.foothillstrader.com. Mailing Address: PO Box 58, Torrington, CT 06790. Year Established: 1964. Pub. Frequency: w. (Mon.) Page Size: standard.Adv. Rate: col. inch $16 Circulation: 50,000 per issue (free). **Owner(s):** Journal Register Co., 50 W State St, 12th Fl, Trenton, NJ 08608. Telephone: 609-396-2200. FAX: 609-396-2292. **Management:** Marc Romanow, Publisher.

TRUMBULL

BARGAIN NEWS. 30 Nutmeg Dr., Trumbull, CT 06611. Telephone: 203-377-3000. FAX: 203-377-2632. E-MAIL: drindos@bargainnews.com. URL: http://www.bargainnews.com. Pub. Frequency: w. (Thu.) Page Size: tabloid.Subscrip. Rate: $1.75 newsstand/cover; $255/yr Circulation: 100,000 per issue (paid). **Owner(s):** Bargain News LLC, See address and contact information above. **Management:** John F. Roy, Publisher. David Reno, Advertising Manager. Gary Ferris, Circulation Director. **Editorial:** Carol Leach, Editor. William Caple, Production Manager.

WATERBURY

SOUTHINGTON OBSERVER. 213 Spring St., Waterbury, CT 06489. Telephone: 203-628-9645. FAX: 203-621-1841. E-MAIL: obsnews@megahits.com. Year Established: 1975. Pub. Frequency: w. (Thu.) Page Size: broadsheet. Subscrip. Rate: $.50 newsstand/cover; $22/yr local. Adv. Rate: col. inch $7.50 Circulation: 6,000 per issue (paid). **Owner(s):** Maitland Corp., See address and contact information above. **Editorial:** Harry Kyle, Editor.

WATERTOWN

TOWN TIMES (WATERTOWN). 469 Main St., Watertown, CT 06795-2628. Telephone: 860-274-8851. FAX: 860-945-3116. Mailing Address: PO Box 1, Watertown, CT 06795-0001. Pub. Frequency: w. (Thu.) Page Size: broadsheet Circulation: 10,000 per issue (free). **Owner(s):** Prime Publishers, Inc., See address and contact information above. **Management:** Rudolph Mazurosky, Publisher. **Editorial:** Susan Pfeifer, Editor.

WESTPORT

WESTPORT MINUTEMAN, THE. 1175 Post Rd., E., Westport, CT 06880. Telephone: 203-226-8877. FAX: 203-221-7540. E-MAIL: editor@westportminuteman.com. URL: http://www.westportminuteman.com. Year Established: 1993. Pub. Frequency: w. (Thu.) Page Size: tabloid.Adv. Rate: page $1,588 Circulation: 38,000 per issue (free). **Owner(s):** Journal Register Co., 50 W State St, 12th Fl, Trenton, NJ 08608. Telephone: 609-396-2200. FAX: 609-396-2292. **Management:** Linette Ginnon, Publisher. Gary Kealey, Advertising Director. **Editorial:** Tom Henry, Editor.

WESTPORT NEWS. 15 Myrtle Ave, Ste 1-A, Westport, CT 06880. Telephone: 203-226-6311. FAX: 203-454-2765. E-MAIL: wrowlands@bcnew.com. URL: http://www.westport-news.com. Year Established: 1964. Pub. Frequency: s-w. (Wed. & Fri.) Page Size: tabloid. Subscrip. Rate: $.52 newsstand/cover; $33.92/yr in county; $43.20/yr out of county; $43/yr mailed out of state. Circulation: 12,134 per issue (paid). **Owner(s):** MediaNews Group, Inc., 101 W Colfax Ave, Ste 1100, Denver, CO 80202. FAX: 303-954-6320. **Management:** Kevin Lally, Publisher. Ed Majersky, Advertising Director. **Editorial:** Frances Moore, Editor.

WILLIMANTIC

HOMETOWN SHOPPER. PO Box 148, Willimantic, CT 06226-1932. Telephone: 860-423-8466. FAX: 860-423-7641. E-MAIL: sales@thechronicle.com. URL: http://www.thechronicle.com.Pub. Frequency: w. (Wed.) Circulation: 44,873 per issue (free). **Owner(s):** Chronicle Printing Co., Inc., See address and contact information above. **Management:** Lucy Crosbie, President. Kevin Crosbie, Publisher. Jean Beckley, Advertising Manager. **Editorial:** Ron Robillard, Editor.

WILTON

WILTON BULLETIN. 47 Old Ridgefield Rd., Wilton, CT 06897. Telephone: 203-762-3456. FAX: 203-762-3120. E-MAIL: gbartlett@wiltonbulletin.com. URL: http://www.acorn-online.com. Mailing Address: PO Box 367, Wilton, CT 06897. Year Established: 1937. Pub. Frequency: w. (Thu.) Page Size: broadsheet. Subscrip. Rate: $.75 newsstand/cover; $30/yr in county; $42/yr mailed out of county. Adv. Rate: col. inch $10.50 **Wire Service(s):** AP. Circulation: 4,600 per issue (paid). **Owner(s):** Hersam Acorn Newspapers LLC, 16 Bailey Ave., Ridgefield, CT 06877. Telephone: 203-438-6544. **Management:** Thomas Nash, Publisher. Shelagh Barrett, Advertising Director. Bruce McDougall, Circulation Manager. Rose Sayers, Classified Adv. Mgr.. **Editorial:** Jeff Yates, Editor. Jack Sanders, Executive Editor. Tim Murphy, Sports Editor.

WINSTED

WINSTED JOURNAL, THE. 396 Main St., Winsted, CT 06098. Telephone: 860-738-4418. FAX: 860-738-3709. E-MAIL: winstedjournal@sbcglobal.net. URL: http://www.winstedjournal.com. Mailing Address: PO Box 835, Winsted, CT 06098. Year Established: 1995. Pub. Frequency: w. (Fri.) Page Size: broadsheet. Subscrip. Rate: $1.25 newsstand/cover; $28 for 6 mos. in county; $53/yr. Circulation: 1,690 per issue (paid). **Owner(s):** Lakeville Journal LLC, PO Box 1688, Lakeville, CT 06039-1688. **Editorial:** Michael Marciano, Editor.

WOODBURY

VOICES. ISSN 0193-1474
90 Middle Quarter Mall, Woodbury, CT 06798. Telephone: 203-263-2116. FAX: 203-266-0199. E-MAIL: sleo@ctvoices.com. URL: http://www.voicesnews.com. Year Established: 1970. Pub. Frequency: w. (Wed.) Page Size: tabloid. Subscrip. Rate: $1 newsstand/cover; $15 carrier delivery/mo.; $55/yr mailed. Adv. Rate: col. inch $18.48 Circulation: 32,000 per issue (paid). **Owner(s):** Prime Publishers, Inc., PO Box 383, Southbury, CT 06488. Telephone: 203-263-2116. **Management:** Rudy Mazurosky, General Manager. **Editorial:** Pattie Wesley, Editor.

DELAWARE

BETHANY BEACH

DELAWARE WAVE. Rte. 1, Lem Hickman Plz., Bethany Beach, DE 19930. Telephone: 302-537-1881. FAX: 302-537-9705. E-MAIL: wave@gannett.com. URL: http://www.delawarewave.com. Mailing Address: PO Box 1420, Bethany Beach, DE 19930. Year Established: 1936. Pub. Frequency: w. (Wed.) Page Size: tabloid. **Wire Service(s):** AP. Circulation: 22,000 evening (free). **Owner(s):** Gannett Company, Inc., 7950 Jones Branch Dr., McLean, VA 22107-0001. Telephone: 703-854-6000. **Management:** Joni Silverstein, Publisher. Janet Powell, Circulation Manager. **Editorial:** Dennis Friedel, Editor.

DOVER

DOVER POST, THE. 609 E. Division St., Dover, DE 19901. Telephone: 302-678-3616. FAX: 302-678-8291. E-MAIL: don.flood@doverpost.com. URL: http://www.doverpost.com. Mailing Address: PO Box 664, Dover, MD 19903. Year Established: 1975. Pub. Frequency: w. (Wed.) Page Size: broadsheet. Subscrip. Rate: $.50 newsstand/cover; $39/yr mailed in area. Circulation: 29,400 per issue (paid). **Owner(s):** Dover Post Co., See address and contact information above. **Management:** James A Flood Jr., General Manager. James A. Flood Sr., Publisher. Fred Kaltreider, Advertising Manager. Mary Wessel, Circulation Manager. **Editorial:** Don G. Flood, Editor.

EXPRESS-SOUTHERN EDITION, THE. 609 E. Division St., Dover, DE 19901. Telephone: 302-678-3616. FAX: 302-678-8291. E-MAIL: don.flood@doverpost.com. URL: http://www.doverpost.com. Mailing Address: PO Box 664, Dover, MD 19903. Pub. Frequency: w. (Thu.) Page Size: broadsheet Circulation: 26,000 per issue (free). **Owner(s):** Dover Post Co., See address and contact information above. **Management:** James A. Flood Sr., Publisher. Fred Kaltreider, Advertising Manager. Mary Wessel, Circulation Manager. **Editorial:** Don Flood, Editor.

SUN CITIES INDEPENDENT. PO Box 737, Dover, DE 19903. Telephone: 302-674-3600. FAX: 302-674-9510. E-MAIL: suncitynews@newszap.com. Mailing Address: Bell Plaza Professional Bldg. South, 17220 N Boswell Blvd, Ste L101, Sun City, AZ 85353. Year Established: 1960. Pub. Frequency: w. (Wed.) Page Size: broadsheet. Subscrip. Rate: $.50 newsstand/cover; $30 mailed for 3 mos.; $120/yr mailed. Circulation: 39,500 per issue (paid and free). **Owner(s):** Independent Newspapers, Inc., See address and contact information above. **Management:** Chris Purcell, Advertising. Diane Runion, Circulation Manager. Angie Mendez, Classified Adv. Mgr.. **Editorial:** Matt Loeschman, Editor. Charlene Bisson, Managing Editor.

SUN CITY WEST INDEPENDENT. PO Box 737, Dover, DE 19903. Telephone: 302-674-3600. FAX: 302-674-9510. E-MAIL: suncitynews@newszap.com. Mailing Address: Bell Plaza Professional Bldg. South, 17220 N Boswell Blvd, Ste L101, Sun City, AZ 85353. Year Established: 1978. Pub. Frequency: w. (Wed.) Page Size: broadsheet. Subscrip. Rate: $.50 newsstand/cover; $30 mailed for 3 mos.. Adv. Rate: col. inch $13.72 Circulation: 15,000 per issue (free). **Owner(s):** Independent Newspapers, Inc., See address and contact information above. **Management:** Chris Purcell, Advertising. Angie Mendez, Classified Adv. Mgr.. **Editorial:** Rusty Bradshaw, Editor. Charlene Bisson, Managing Editor.

SURPRISE INDEPENDENT. PO Box 737, Dover, DE 19903. Telephone: 302-674-3600. FAX: 302-674-9510. E-MAIL: surprisenews@newszap.com. URL: http://www.newszap.com. Mailing Address: Bell Plaza Professional Bldg. South, 17220 N Boswell Blvd, Ste L101, Sun City, AZ 85353. Year Established: 1998. Pub. Frequency: w. (Wed) Page Size: broadsheet. Subscrip. Rate: $.50 newsstand/cover; $40 mailed for 6 mos.. Circulation: 19,000 per issue (free). **Owner(s):** Independent Newspapers, Inc., See address and contact information above. **Management:** Laura Riffle, Advertising. Angie Mendez, Classified Adv. Mgr.. **Editorial:** Matt Loeschman, Editor. Charlene Bisson, Managing Editor.

GEORGETOWN

SUSSEX COUNTIAN. 13 S Front St, Georgetown, DE 19947. Telephone: 302-856-0026. FAX: 302-556-0925. Year Established: 1886. Pub. Frequency: w. (Wed.) Page Size: tabloid. Subscrip. Rate: $.50 newsstand/cover; $18/yr mailed in state; $22/yr mailed out of state. Adv. Rate: col. inch $9.60 Circulation: 5,000 per issue (paid). **Owner(s):** Flood Family, See address and contact information above. **Management:** Jim Flood, Publisher. **Editorial:** Valerie Lemoi Jr., Editor. John Trumpower, Managing Editor.

HARRINGTON

HARRINGTON JOURNAL, THE. ISSN 0747-0975
110 Center St., Harrington, DE 19952. Telephone: 302-398-3206. FAX: 302-741-8261. URL: http://www.newszap.com. Mailing Address: PO Box 239, Harrington, DE 19952. Year Established: 1913. Pub. Frequency: w. (Wed.) Page Size: broadsheet. Subscrip. Rate: $.50 newsstand/cover; $15/yr in state; $17/yr out of state. Circulation: 3,000 per issue (paid). **Owner(s):** Independent Newspapers, Inc., PO Box 737, Dover, DE 19903. Telephone: 302-674-3600. FAX: 302-674-9510. **Management:** Pat Lee, Advertising. **Editorial:** Andy West, Managing Editor. Tom Eldred, News Editor.

HOCKESSIN

GREENVILLE COMMUNITY NEWS. 6300 Limestone Rd., Hockessin, DE 19707. Telephone: 302-239-4644. FAX: 302-239-7033. E-MAIL: editor@communitypub.com. URL: http://www.communitypub.com. Mailing Address: PO Box 549, Hockessin, DE 19707. Pub. Frequency: w. (Tue.) Page Size: tabloid. Subscrip. Rate: $30/yr mailed in state; $35/yr mailed out of state. Circulation: 10,418 per issue (free). **Owner(s):** Community Publications, Inc., See address and contact information above. **Management:** Joseph Amon, Publisher. John Wisniewski, Circulation Manager. Richard Gaw, Marketing Manager. **Editorial:** Jason Brimmer, Editor. William Chanin, Executive Editor.

HOCKESSIN COMMUNITY NEWS. 6300 Limestone Rd., Hockessin, DE 19707. Telephone: 302-239-4644. FAX: 302-239-7033. E-MAIL: editor@communitypub.com. URL: http://www.communitypub.com. Mailing Address: PO Box 549, Hockessin, DE 19707. Pub. Frequency: w. (Thu.) Page Size: tabloid. Subscrip. Rate: $30/yr mailed in state; $35/yr mailed out of state. Circulation: 16,061 per issue (paid and free). **Owner(s):** Community Publications, Inc., See address and contact information above. **Management:** Joseph Amon, Publisher. John Wisniewski, Circulation Manager. Richard Gaw, Marketing Manager. **Editorial:** Jason Brimmer, Editor. William Chanin, Executive Editor.

MILL CREEK COMMUNITY NEWS. 6300 Limestone Rd., Hockessin, DE 19707. Telephone: 302-239-4644. FAX: 302-239-7033. E-MAIL: editor@commjnithypub.com. URL: http://www.communitypub.com. Mailing Address: PO Box 549, Hockessin, DE 19707. Pub. Frequency: w. (Wed.) Page Size: tabloid. Subscrip. Rate: $30/yr mailed in state; $35/yr mailed out of state. Adv. Rate: col. inch $10.70 Circulation: 11,000 per issue (paid and free). **Owner(s):** Community Publications, Inc., See address and contact information above. **Management:** Joseph Amon, President. **Editorial:** Jason Brimmer, Editor. William Chanin, Editor-in-Chief.

LEWES

CAPE GAZETTE. 17585 Nassau Commons Blvd., Lewes, DE 19958. Telephone: 302-645-7700. FAX: 302-645-1664. E-MAIL: dnf@capegazette.com. URL: http://www.capegazette.com. Mailing Address: PO Box 213, Lewes, DE 19958-0213. Year Established: 1993. Pub. Frequency: s-w. (Tue & Fri) Page Size: tabloid. Subscrip. Rate: $.50 newsstand/cover; $30/yr in county; $50/yr out of county. Adv. Rate: col. inch $10.75 Circulation: 12,500 per issue (paid). **Owner(s):** Dennis Forney & Patricia Vernon, See address and contact information above. **Management:** Dennis Forney, Publisher. Kathy Emery, Office Manager. Joni Weber, Circulation Director. Sandy Barr, Classified Adv. Mgr.. **Editorial:** Trish Vernon, News Editor. Dave Frederick, Sports Editor.

MIDDLETOWN

MIDDLETOWN TRANSCRIPT. 24 W. Main St., Middletown, DE 19709-1039. Telephone: 302-378-9531. FAX: 302-378-0647. E-MAIL: Kristenkrenzer@doverpost.com. URL: http://www.middletowntranscript.com. Year Established: 1868. Pub. Frequency: w. (Thu.) Page Size: tabloid. Subscrip. Rate: $.50 newsstand/cover; $18.95/yr mailed. Circulation: 6,100 per issue (paid). **Owner(s):** Dover Post Co., 609 E. Division St., Dover, DE 19901. Telephone: 302-678-3616. **Management:** Don G. Flood, General Manager. James A. Flood Sr., Publisher. Debra Kalinowksi, Advertising Manager. **Editorial:** Kristen Krenzer, Managing Editor.

MILFORD

MILFORD CHRONICLE. 37A N. Walnut St., Milford, DE 19963. Telephone: 302-422-1200. FAX: 302-422-1208. E-MAIL: mc@newszap.com. URL: http://www.newszap.com. Mailing Address: PO Box 297, Milford, DE 19963-0297. Year Established: 1848. Pub. Frequency: w. (Thu.) Page Size: broadsheet.Subscrip. Rate: $.50 newsstand/cover; $18/yr Circulation: 8,500 per issue (paid). **Owner(s):** Independent Newspapers, Inc., PO Box 737, Dover, DE 19903. Telephone: 302-674-3600. FAX: 302-674-9510. **Management:** Laura Owens, Advertising. **Editorial:** Gwen Guerke, Editor.

NEW CASTLE

NEW CASTLE WEEKLY, THE. 203 Delaware St., New Castle, DE 19720-4815. Telephone: 302-328-6005. Year Established: 1991. Pub. Frequency: w. (Wed.) Page Size: broadsheet. Subscrip. Rate: $.25 newsstand/cover; $18/yr mailed. Circulation: 1,200 per issue (paid). **Owner(s):** Mimi Carpenter, 203 Delaware St., New Castle, DE 19720. Telephone: 302-328-6005. **Management:** Mimi Carpenter, Publisher. **Editorial:** Mimi Carpenter, Editor.

NEWARK

NEWARK POST, THE. ISSN 1056-7658 168 Elkton Rd., Ste. 206, Newark, DE 19711. Telephone: 302-737-0724. FAX: 302-737-9019. E-MAIL: postnews@chespub.com. URL: http://www.newarkpostonline.com. Year Established: 1910. Pub. Frequency: w. (Fri.) Page Size: tabloid. Subscrip. Rate: $.50 newsstand/cover; $87.95/yr home delivery. Freelance Pay: $35/article. Circulation: 18,000 per issue (paid). **Owner(s):** Chesapeake Publishing Corp., 29088 Airpark Dr., Easton, MD 21601. Telephone: 410-810-6505. FAX: 410-770-4019. **Management:** Marty Valania Jr., Publisher. Ed Hoffman, Advertising Director. **Editorial:** Christine W. Neff, News Editor. Joe Becker, Sports Editor.

ROUTE 40 FLIER, THE. 168 Elkton Rd., Ste. 206, Newark, DE 19711. Telephone: 302-737-0724. FAX: 302-737-9019. E-MAIL: postnews@chespub.com. URL: http://www.newarkpostonline.com.Pub. Frequency: m. Page Size: broadsheet Circulation: 24,000 per issue (free). **Owner(s):** Chesapeake Publishing Corp., 29088 Airpark Dr., Easton, MD 21601. Telephone: 410-810-6505. FAX: 410-770-4012. **Management:** Marty Valania Jr., Publisher. Ed Hoffman, Advertising Director.

REHOBOTH BEACH

DELAWARE BEACHCOMBER. 3712 Hwy. 1, Rehoboth Beach, DE 19971. Telephone: 302-227-9466. FAX: 302-227-9469. E-MAIL: dcp@smgpo.gannett.com. URL: http://www.delmarvanow.com. Mailing Address: PO Box 309, Rehoboth Beach, DE 19971. Year Established: 1968. Pub. Frequency: w. (Fri.) Page Size: tabloid. Freelance Pay: $25/story. Circulation: 15,000 per issue (free). **Owner(s):** Gannett Company, Inc., 7950 Jones Branch Dr., McLean, VA 22107-0001. Telephone: 703-854-6000. **Management:** Joni Silverstein, Publisher. **Editorial:** Ashley Dawson, Editor. Jane Meleady, Managing Editor. Marc Clery, Photographer.

DELAWARE COAST PRESS. ISSN 0740-2023 3712 Hwy. 1, Rehoboth Beach, DE 19971. Telephone: 302-227-9466. FAX: 302-227-9469. E-MAIL: dcp@smgpo.gannett.com. URL: http://www.delmarvanow.com. Mailing Address: PO Box 309, Rehoboth Beach, DE 19971. Year Established: 1899. Pub. Frequency: w. (Wed.) Page Size: tabloid. Subscrip. Rate: $45/yr. Freelance Pay: $25/story. Circulation: 15,000 per issue (paid and controlled). **Owner(s):** Gannett Company, Inc., 7950 Jones Branch Dr., McLean, VA 22107-0001. Telephone: 703-854-6000. **Management:** Jane Meleady, General Manager. Joni Silverstein, Publisher. **Editorial:** Ashley Dawson, Editor. Marc Clery, Photographer.

SEAFORD

LEADER-STATE REGISTER, THE. 302 W Stein Hwy, Seaford, DE 19973. Telephone: 302-629-5505. FAX: 302-629-6700. URL: http://www.newszap.com. Mailing Address: PO Box 1130, Seaford, DE 19973. Year Established: 1890. Pub. Frequency: w. (Thu.) Page Size: broadsheet. Subscrip. Rate: $.50 newsstand/cover; $23.50/yr elsewhere. Adv. Rate: col. inch $15.88 Circulation: 9,645 per issue (paid and free). **Owner(s):** Independent Newspapers, Inc., PO Box 737, Dover, DE 19903. Telephone: 302-674-3600. FAX: 302-674-9510. **Management:** Joyce Ramsey, Advertising. Don Clendaniel, Circulation Manager. **Editorial:** Glenn Rolfe, Editor.

SUSSEX POST, THE. 302 W Stein Hwy, Seaford, DE 19973. Telephone: 302-629-5505. FAX: 302-629-6700. E-MAIL: sussexpost@newszap.com. URL: http://www.newszap.com. Mailing Address: PO Box 1130, Seaford, DE 19973. Year Established: 1972. Pub. Frequency: w. (Thu.) Page Size: broadsheet. Subscrip. Rate: $.50 newsstand/cover; $13/yr home delivery in county; $16/yr mailed elsewhere. Circulation: 20,000 per issue (paid and free). **Owner(s):** Independent Newspapers, Inc., PO Box 737, Dover, DE 19903. Telephone: 302-674-3600. FAX: 302-674-9510. **Management:** Joyce Ramsey, Advertising. Don Clendaniel, Circulation Manager. **Editorial:** Michael Short, Editor. Michael Pelrine, Executive Editor. Andy West, Managing Editor.

SMYRNA

SMYRNA/CLAYTON SUN-TIMES. 25 W. Commerce St., Smyrna, DE 19977. Telephone: 302-653-2083. FAX: 302-653-8821. URL: http://www.scsuntimes.com. Mailing Address: PO Box 327, Smyrna, DE 19977-0327. Year Established: 1854. Pub. Frequency: w. (Wed.) Page Size: tabloid. Subscrip. Rate: $.50 newsstand/cover; $21/yr mailed. Circulation: 3,600 per issue (paid). **Owner(s):** Dover Post Co., 609 E. Division St., Dover, DE 19901. Telephone: 302-678-3616. FAX: 302-678-8291. **Management:** Don G. Flood, General Manager. James A. Flood Sr., Publisher. Brigitte McKinney, Advertising Manager. **Editorial:** Ben Mace, Editor.

YORKLYN

BRANDYWINE COMMUNITY NEWS. 1157 Yorklyn Rd, Yorklyn, DE 19736. Telephone: 302-239-4644. FAX: 302-239-7033. Mailing Address: PO Box 549, Hockessin, DE 19707. Pub. Frequency: w. (Fri.) Page Size: tabloid. Subscrip. Rate: $30/yr in state; $35/yr out of state. Adv. Rate: col. inch $10.70 Circulation: 14,000 per issue (paid and free). **Owner(s):** Community Publications, Inc., 6300 Limestone Rd., Hockessin, DE 19707. **Management:** Joseph Amon, President. John Wisniewski, Circulation Manager. **Editorial:** Jason Brimmer, Editor. William Chanin, Executive Editor.

DISTRICT OF COLUMBIA

WASHINGTON

DOWNTOWNER, THE. 1054 Potomac St., N.W., Washington, DC 20007. Telephone: 202-338-4833. FAX: 202-342-0751. URL: http://www.downtowner.org. Year Established: 2003. Pub. Frequency: bi-w. (Thu.) Page Size: tabloid Circulation: 30,000 per issue (free). **Owner(s):** Sonya Bernhardt, See address and contact information above. **Management:** Sonya Bernhardt, Publisher. **Editorial:** Dave Roffman, Editor. Gary Tischler, Feature Editor.

GEORGETOWN CURRENT, THE. 5185 McArthur Blvd., N.W., Ste. 102, Washington, DC 20016. Telephone: 202-244-7223. E-MAIL: newsdesk@currentnewspapers.com. URL: http://www.currentnewspapers.com. Mailing Address: PO Box 40400, Washington, DC 20016-0400. Year Established: 1967. Pub. Frequency: w. (Wed.) Page Size: tabloid. Subscrip. Rate: $52/yr. Adv. Rate: col. inch $37 Circulation: 8,855 per issue (paid and free). **Owner(s):** Current Newspapers, Inc., See address and contact information above. **Management:** Davis Kennedy, Publisher. Gary Socha, Advertising Director. Davis Kennedy, Circulation Manager. **Editorial:** Chris Kain, Managing Editor.AJOR_METROX see NATIONAL NEWSPAPERS

INTOWNER, THE. 1730-B Corcoran St., N.W., Washington, DC 20009-2406. Telephone: 202-234-1717. E-MAIL: intowner@intowner.com. URL: http://www.intowner.com. Year Established: 1968. Pub. Frequency: m. (2nd Fri. of mo.) Page Size: tabloid.Adv. Rate: B&W page $1,050 Circulation: 30,000 per issue (free). **Owner(s):** InTowner Publishing Corp., See address and contact information above. **Management:** P.L. Wolff, Publisher. **Editorial:** P.L. Wolff, Editor.

NORTHWEST CURRENT, THE. 5185 Mc Arthur Blvd., N.W., Ste. 102, Washington, DC 20016-0400. Telephone: 202-244-7223. FAX: 202-244-5924. E-MAIL: newsdesk@currentnewspapers.com. URL: http://www.currentnewspapers.com. Year Established: 1967. Pub. Frequency: w. (Wed.) Page Size: tabloid. Subscrip. Rate: $52/yr. Adv. Rate: col. inch $37 Circulation: 31,215 per issue (paid and free). **Owner(s):** Current Newspapers, Inc., See address and contact information above. **Management:** Davis Kennedy, Publisher. Gary Socha, Advertising Director. Apryl Wines, Circulation Manager. **Editorial:** Chris Kain, Managing Editor.

SPRING VALLEY TRIBUNE. 1 Massachusetts Ave, NW, Ste 610, Washington, DC 20001. Telephone: 202-842-2002. E-MAIL: tribune@clear.lakes.com. URL: http://www.hometown-pages.com. Year Established: 1880. Pub. Frequency: w. (Wed.) Page Size: broadsheet. Subscrip. Rate: $.60 newsstand/cover; $20/yr local. Circulation: 1,729 per issue (paid). **Owner(s):** Phillips International, Inc., See address and contact information above.

WASHINGTON CITY PAPER. 2390 Champlain St. N.W., Washington, DC 20009. Telephone: 202-332-2100. FAX: 202-332-8500. E-MAIL: mail@washcp.com. URL: http://www.washingtoncitypaper.com. Year Established: 1981. Pub. Frequency: w. (Thu.) Page Size: tabloid. Subscrip. Rate: $90/yr. Circulation: 98,000 per issue (paid and free). **Owner(s):** Tom Yoder, Robert Roth, Robert McCamant & Amy Austin, See address and contact information above. **Management:** Amy Austin, Publisher. Mike McClanahan, Advertising Manager. Kris Koth, Circulation Manager. **Editorial:** Erik Wemple, Editor.n, DC 20071-0001 see NATIONAL NEWSPAPERS

WASHINGTON'S HILL RAG. 224 Seventh St., S.E., Ste 300, Washington, DC 20003. E-MAIL: hillraginc@aol.com. URL: http://www.capitalnews.com. Year Established: 1976. Pub. Frequency: 24/yr. Adv. Rate: page $1,175; trim 12 x 10 Circulation: 20,000 (controlled). **Owner(s):** Fagon Publishing Group, See address and contact information above. **Management:** Jean Fagon, Publisher. **Editorial:** Melissa Ashabranner, Executive Editor.

FLORIDA

APALACHICOLA

APALACHICOLA TIMES, THE. 82 Market St., Apalachicola, FL 32320-1430. Telephone: 850-653-8868. E-MAIL: newspaper@apalachtimes.com. URL: http://www.apalachtimes.com. Pub. Frequency: w. (Thu.) Page Size: broadsheet. Subscrip. Rate: $.50 newsstand/cover; $20/yr in county; $24/yr elsewhere. Circulation: 5,100 per issue (paid). **Owner(s):** The Star Publishing Co of Port St. Joe Inc., P.O. Drawer 820, Apalachicola, FL 32320. Telephone: 850-653-8868. FAX: 850-653-8036. **Management:** William H Ramsey, Publisher. **Editorial:** William H Ramsey, Managing Editor.

CARRABELLE TIMES, THE. 82 Market St., Apalachicola, FL 32320-1430. Telephone: 850-653-8868. FAX: 850-653-8036. E-MAIL: news@apalachtimes.com. URL: http://www.apalachtimes.com. Mailing Address: P.O. Drawer 820, Apalachicola, FL 32320. Pub. Frequency: w. (Thu.) Page Size: broadsheet. Subscrip. Rate: $.50 newsstand/cover; $20/yr local; $24/yr elsewhere. Circulation: 1,600 per issue (paid). **Owner(s):** The Star Publishing Co of Port St. Joe Inc., P.O. Drawer 820, Apalachicola, FL 32320. Telephone: 850-653-8868. **Management:** William H Ramsey, Publisher. **Editorial:** William H Ramsey, Editor.

APOPKA

APOPKA CHIEF, THE. 439 W. Main St., Apopka, FL 32712. Telephone: 407-886-2777. FAX: 407-889-4121. E-MAIL: apopkachief@earthlink.net. URL: http://www.theapopkachief.com. Year Established: 1923. Pub. Frequency: w. (Fri.) Page Size: broadsheet. Subscrip. Rate: $.50 newsstand/cover; $18/yr in county; $23/yr elsewhere. Adv. Rate: col. inch $10 Circulation: 4,600 per issue (paid). **Owner(s):** Foliage Enterprises, Inc., See address and contact information above. **Management:** Neoma DeGard Knox, General Manager. John E. Ricketson, Publisher. **Editorial:** John Peery, Editor.

PLANTER, THE. 439 W. Main St., Apopka, FL 32712. Telephone: 407-886-2777. FAX: 407-889-4121. E-MAIL: theapopkachief@earthlink.net. Pub. Frequency: s-w. (Thu., Fri.) Page Size: broadsheet Circulation: 10,000 per issue (free). **Owner(s):** Foliage Enterprises, Inc., See address and contact information above. **Management:** Neoma DeGard Knox, General Manager. John E. Ricketson, Publisher. **Editorial:** John Peery, Editor.

BELLEVIEW

VOICE OF SOUTH MARION. 5516 SE 113th St, Belleview, FL 34420. Telephone: 352-245-3161. FAX: 352-347-7444. E-MAIL: vosm@aol.com. Mailing Address: PO Box 700, Belleview, FL 34421-0700. Year Established: 1969. Pub. Frequency: w. (Thu.) Page Size: tabloid. Subscrip. Rate: $.25 newsstand/cover; $15/yr in county; $20/yr out of county. Circulation: 2,500 per issue (paid). **Owner(s):** Sandy Waldron, PO Box 700, Belleview, FL 34421. Telephone: 352-245-3161. FAX: 352-347-7444. **Management:** Sandy Waldron, Publisher. **Editorial:** Sandy Waldron, Editor.

BEVERLY HILL

VISITOR (BEVERLY HILL), THE. PO Box 640850, Beverly Hill, FL 32665. Telephone: 352-746-4292. FAX: 352-746-5401. E-MAIL: info@visitornews.com. Mailing Address: PO Box 640850, Beverly Hill, FL 34464. Pub. Frequency: w. (Sat.) Page Size: broadsheet Circulation: 11,000 per issue (free). **Owner(s):** Citrus Publishing, Inc., See address and contact information above. **Management:** Gerald Mulligan, Publisher. Christine Ordway, Operations Manager. **Editorial:** Sandra Koonce, Editor.

BOCA GRANDE

BOCA BEACON. P.O. Box 313, Boca Grande, FL 33921-0313. Telephone: 941-964-2995. FAX: 941-964-0372. E-MAIL: kathi@bocabeacon.com. URL: http://bocabeacon.com. Pub. Frequency: w. (Fri.) Page Size: tabloid. Subscrip. Rate: $.50 newsstand/cover; $42/yr in state; $39.50/yr out of state. Circulation: 7,000 per issue (paid). **Owner(s):** Hopkins & Daughter, Inc., 431 Park Ave., Boca Grande, FL 33921. **Management:** Dusty Hopkins, Publisher. Sue Dutery, Circulation Manager. Kathi Strapp, Classified Adv. Mgr.. **Editorial:** Gary Dutery, Editor.

GASPARILLA GAZETTE. 5800 Gasparilla Rd, Ste F, Boca Grande, FL 33921. Telephone: 941-964-2728. FAX: 941-964-2850. URL: http://www.gasparillagazette.com. Mailing Address: PO Box 929, Boca Grande, FL 33921. Pub. Frequency: w. (Thu.) Page Size: tabloid. Subscrip. Rate: $.25 newsstand/cover; $22/yr in county; $30/yr in state. Circulation: 5,000 per issue (paid). **Owner(s):** Breeze Corp., 2510 Del Prado Blvd, Cape Coral, FL 33904. Telephone: 941-574-1110. **Management:** Ed Kellam, Group Publisher. Deb Oliviera, Advertising. **Editorial:** Marcy Shortuse, Editor. Chris Stine, Managing Editor.

BOCA RATON TY(Palm Beach) see NATIONAL NEWSPAPERS

BONIFAY

HOLMES COUNTY TIMES-ADVERTISER. 112 E Virginia Ave, Bonifay, FL 32425. Telephone: 850-547-9414. FAX: 850-638-4601. E-MAIL: cni@digitalexp.com. URL: http://www.bonifaynow.com. Mailing Address: PO Box 67, Bonifay, FL 32425-0067. Pub. Frequency: w. (Wed.) Page Size: broadsheet. Subscrip. Rate: $.50 newsstand/cover; $22/yr mailed in county; $30/yr mailed out of county. Circulation: 3,000 per issue (paid). **Owner(s):** Chipley Newspapers, Inc., 112 E Virginia Ave, Bonifay, FL 32425-2326. Telephone: 850-547-9414. FAX: 850-638-4601. **Management:** Maurice Pujol, Publisher. Zola Anderson, Classified Adv. Mgr.. Brenda Pujol, Associate Publisher. **Editorial:** Maurice Pujol, Editor. Jay Felsberg, Managing Editor.

HOLMES COUNTY TIMES ADVERTISER. 112 E. Virginia Ave., Bonifay, FL 32425-0067. Telephone: 850-638-0212. FAX: 850-638-4601. E-MAIL: mail@wfp-webpress.com. URL: http://www.bonifaynow.com. Mailing Address: P.O. Box 67, Bonifay, FL 32428-0067. Year Established: 1892. Pub. Frequency: w. (Wed.) Page Size: broadsheet. Subscrip. Rate: $.50 newsstand/cover; $25.68/yr in county; $35/yr out of county. Freelance Pay: $1/column-inch. Circulation: 4,000 per issue (paid and free). **Owner(s):** Larry & Gary Woodham, See address and contact information above. **Management:** Maurice Pujol, Publisher. Lynn Chapman, Business Manager. **Editorial:** Jay Felsberg, Managing Editor. Jermy Raines, Sports Editor.

BONITA SPRINGS

BONITA BANNER. ISSN 0191-5479
9102 Bonita Beach Rd., Bonita Springs, FL 34135. Telephone: 239-213-6000. FAX: 239-213-6099. E-MAIL: banner@naplesnews.com. URL: http://www.bonitabanner.com. Mailing Address: PO Box 40, Bonita Springs, FL 34133. Year Established: 1959. Pub. Frequency: s-w. (Wed. & Sat.) Page Size: broadsheet. Subscrip. Rate: $26 for 6 mos.; $41.60/yr. **Wire Service(s):** SH. Circulation: 35,000 per issue (paid and free). **Owner(s):** E.W. Scripps Co., 312 Walnut St., 28th Fl., Cincinnati, OH 45202. Telephone: 513-977-3000. **Management:** Steve Akers, Publisher. **Editorial:** Todd Pratt, Editor. Cathy Cottrill, Managing Editor. Karie Partington, Bureau Chief. Kristen Smith, Feature Editor. Dana Oppedisano, Sports Editor.

BRANDON

BRANDON NEWS & SHOPPER, THE. 505 W. Robertson St., Brandon, FL 33511-2800. Telephone: 813-657-4500. FAX: 813-689-9545. Year Established: 1958. Pub. Frequency: w. (Wed.) Page Size: tabloid. Subscrip. Rate: $20/yr out of county. Circulation: 45,500 per issue (paid and free). **Owner(s):** Media General, Inc., 333 E. Franklin St., Richmond, VA 23219. Telephone: 804-649-6000. FAX: 804-649-6898. **Management:** Carla Floyd, Publisher. Tami Donaldson, Advertising Manager. Kevin Brady, Circulation Manager. **Editorial:** D'Ann White, Editor. Russ Holecek, Managing Editor.

BRANFORD

BRANFORD NEWS. 705 NW Suwannee Ave, Branford, FL 32008. Telephone: 386-938-1427. FAX: 386-935-3043. E-MAIL: branfordnews@alltel.net. URL: http://www.suwanneedemocrat.com. Mailing Address: PO Box 148, Branford, FL 32008-0148. Year Established: 1967. Pub. Frequency: w. (Thu.) Page Size: broadsheet. Subscrip. Rate: $.50 newsstand/cover; $16/yr in county; $23/yr out of county. Adv. Rate: col. inch $4.33 Circulation: 2,000 per issue (paid). **Owner(s):** Community Newspaper Holdings, Inc., 3500 Colonnade Pkwy., Ste. 600, Birmingham, AL 25243. **Management:** Shirley Hatch, Publisher. **Editorial:** Shirley Hatch, Managing Editor.

MAYO FREE PRESS. 705 NW Suwannee Ave, Branford, FL 32008. E-MAIL: mayofreepress@alltel.net. URL: http://www.suwanneedemocrate.com. Mailing Address: PO Box 248, Mayo, FL 32066. Pub. Frequency: w. (Thu.) Page Size: broadsheet. Subscrip. Rate: $.50 newsstand/cover; $16/yr in county; $23/yr out of county. Circulation: 2,000 per issue (paid). **Owner(s):** Community Newspaper Holdings, Inc., 3500 Colonnade Pkwy., Ste. 600, Birmingham, AL 25243. **Management:** Linda Smith, Publisher. **Editorial:** Linda Smith, Editor.

BRISTOL

CALHOUN-LIBERTY JOURNAL, THE. 11493 Summers Rd., N.W., Bristol, FL 32321. Telephone: 850-643-3333. FAX: 850-643-3334. E-MAIL: thejournal@nettally.com. Pub. Frequency: w. (Wed.) Page Size: broadsheet. Subscrip. Rate: $.50 newsstand/cover; $18/yr in area. Circulation: 4,900 per issue (paid). **Owner(s):** Liberty Journal, Inc., PO Box 536, Bristol, FL 32321-0536. Telephone: 850-643-3333. FAX: 850-643-3334. **Management:** John Eubanks, Owner. Teresa Eubanks, Advertising Manager. **Editorial:** Teresa Eubanks, Editor.

BRONSON

LEVY COUNTY JOURNAL. 440 S. Court St., Bronson, FL 32621. Telephone: 352-486-2312. FAX: 352-486-5042. E-MAIL: editor@levyjournal.com. URL: http://www.levyjournal.com. Mailing Address: PO Box 159, Bronson, FL 32621-0159. Year Established: 1923. Pub. Frequency: w. (Thu.) Page Size: standard. Subscrip. Rate: $.50 newsstand/cover; $17/yr in county & Gilchrist & Dixie cys.; $22/yr mailed in state; $27/yr mailed out of state. Adv. Rate: col. inch $4.85 Circulation: 1,200 evening (paid). **Owner(s):** Andy Andrews, See address and contact information above. **Management:** Andy Andrews, Publisher. **Editorial:** Carolyn Risner, Managing Editor.

BUSHNELL

SUMTER COUNTY TIMES. 204 E. McCollum Ave., Bushnell, FL 33513. Telephone: 352-793-2161. FAX: 352-793-1486. E-MAIL: news@sctnews.com. URL: http://www.sumtercountytimes.com. Year Established: 1881. Pub. Frequency: w. (Thu.) Page Size: broadsheet. Subscrip. Rate: $.50 newsstand/cover; $21/yr in county. Adv. Rate: col. inch $9.54 Circulation: 5,600 per issue (paid). **Owner(s):** Landmark Community Newspapers, Inc., PO Box 549, Shelbyville, KY 40065. Telephone: 502-633-2526. FAX: 502-633-2618. **Management:** Gerard Mulligan, Publisher. Alan Place, Sales Manager. **Editorial:** Bob Reichman, Editor.

CALLAHAN

NASSAU COUNTY RECORD. 617317 Brandies Ave, Callahan, FL 32011. Telephone: 904-879-2727. FAX: 904-879-5155. E-MAIL: fmaloy@nassaucountyrecord.com. URL: http://www.nassaucountyrecord.com. Mailing Address: P O Box 609, Callahan, FL 32011. Pub. Frequency: w. (Thu.) Page Size: standard. Subscrip. Rate: $.50 newsstand/cover; $20/yr carrier delivery in county; $33/yr mailed out of county. Circulation: 5,000 per issue (paid). **Owner(s):** Community Newspapers (Athens), Inc., PO Box 792, Athens, GA 30603. **Management:** Foy Maloy, Publisher. Mike Hankins, Advertising Director. Bob Timpe, Circulation Director. **Editorial:** Amanda Bishop, Managing Editor.

CEDAR KEY

CEDAR KEY BEACON. 1018 Whiddon Ave., Cedar Key, FL 32625-0998. Telephone: 352-543-5701. FAX: 352-543-5928. E-MAIL: connie@cedarkeybeacon.com. URL: http://www.cedarkeybeacon.com. Mailing Address: PO Box 532, Cedar Key, FL 32625. Year Established: 1984. Pub. Frequency: w. (Thu.) Page Size: tabloid. Subscrip. Rate: $.50 newsstand/cover; $30/yr in state (effective 2005); $30/yr out of state. Adv. Rate: page $292 Circulation: 1,500 per issue (paid). **Owner(s):** Advertising Design, Inc., See address and contact information above. **Management:** Connie Raftis, President. Michael J. Raftis, Sales Manager. **Editorial:** Michael J. Raftis, Editor. Mark Stockhus, Writer.

CHARLOTTE HARBOR

POLK COUNTY DEMOCRAT, THE. ISSN 1522-0354
23170 Harbor View Rd., Charlotte Harbor, FL 33980. Telephone: 941-206-1003. FAX: 941-206-1007. E-MAIL: news@polkcountydemocrat.com. URL: http://www.polkcountydemocrat.com. Year Established: 1931. Pub. Frequency: s-w. (Wed. & Sat.) Page Size: broadsheet. Subscrip. Rate: $.50 newsstand/cover; $37.50/yr in county; $62/yr out of county; $68.50/yr out of state. Adv. Rate: col. inch $10.15 Circulation: 4,030 per issue (paid and free). **Owner(s):** Sun Coast Media Group, Inc., See address and contact information above. Frisbie Publishing Co., Inc., 190 S. Florida Ave., Bartow, FL 33830-4701. PO Box 120, Bartow, FL 33831-0120. **Management:** S.L. Frisbie IV, Publisher. Melodie Willis, Advertising Manager. **Editorial:** S.L. Frisbie IV, Editor. Peggy Kehoe, Managing Editor.Readers: General audience

CHATTAHOOCHEE

TWIN CITY NEWS (CHATTAHOOCHIE), THE. ISSN 0889-2245
314 W Washington, Chattahoochee, FL 32324. Telephone: 850-663-2255. E-MAIL: tcnews@gtcom.net. Year Established: 1964. Pub. Frequency: w. (Thu.) Page Size: broadsheet. Subscrip. Rate: $.50 newsstand/cover; $20/yr in county; $25/yr mailed elsewhere. Adv. Rate: col. inch $5 Circulation: 2,000 per issue (paid). **Owner(s):** John N. Bert, See address and contact information above. **Management:** John N. Bert, Publisher. **Editorial:** Kathy Johnson, Managing Editor.

CHIEFLAND

CHIEFLAND CITIZEN. 624 W. Park Ave., Chiefland, FL 32626-0430. Telephone: 352-493-4796. FAX: 352-493-9336. E-MAIL: citizen@svic.net. URL: http://www.chieflandcitizen.com. Mailing Address: P.O. Drawer 980, Chiefland, FL 32644. Pub. Frequency: w. (Thu.) Page Size: broadsheet. Subscrip. Rate: $.50 newsstand/cover; $22/yr in county; $29/yr out of county; $32/yr out of state. Circulation: 3,600 per issue (paid). **Owner(s):** Landmark Community Newspapers, Inc., PO Box 549, Shelbyville, KY 40065. Telephone: 502-633-2526. **Management:** Dale Bowen, General Manager. Deah King, Circulation Manager. **Editorial:** Jim Clark, Editor.

CHIPLEY

WASHINGTON COUNTY NEWS (CHIPLEY). ISSN 0279-795X
1364 Railroad Ave., Chipley, FL 32428. Telephone: 850-638-0212. FAX: 850-638-4601. URL: http://www.chipleypaper.com. Mailing Address: PO Box 627, Chipley, FL 32428-0627. Year Established: 1924. Pub. Frequency: s-w. (Wed. & Sat.) Page Size: broadsheet. Subscrip. Rate: $.50 newsstand/cover; $34/yr local; $42/yr out of area. Circulation: 7,800 per issue (paid). **Owner(s):** Chipley Newspapers, Inc., See address and contact information above. **Management:** Maurice Pujol, Publisher. Zola Anderson, Classified Adv. Mgr.. Brenda Pujol, Associate Publisher. **Editorial:** Maurice Pujol, Editor. Jay Felsberg, Managing Editor.

CLEARWATER

CLEARWATER GAZETTE & BEACH VIEWS. 25 Causeway Blvd., Ste. 32, Clearwater, FL 33767. Telephone: 727-446-6723. FAX: 727-461-5659. E-MAIL: cni@digital.exp.com. Pub. Frequency: w. (Thu.) Page Size: broadsheet Circulation: 17,000 per issue (free). **Owner(s):** Clearwater Gazette & Beach Views, Inc., See address and contact information above. **Management:** Charles Pollick, Publisher. Sandy Pollick, Advertising. **Editorial:** Charles Pollick, Editor.

Weeklies

CLERMONT

NEWS LEADER (CLERMONT), THE. 628 Eighth St., Clermont, FL 34711-2160. Telephone: 352-242-9818. FAX: 352-242-9820. Pub. Frequency: w. (Wed.) Page Size: broadsheet Circulation: 25,800 per issue (free). **Owner(s):** News Leader, The, PO Box 187T., Tampa, FL 33526-2160. **Management:** Donna Covert, Publisher. **Editorial:** Donna Covert, Editor.

SOUTH LAKE PRESS. 732 W. Montrose St., Clermont, FL 34711. Telephone: 352-394-2183. FAX: 352-394-8001. E-MAIL: southlakepress@earthlink.net. URL: http://www.southlakepress.com. Year Established: 1913. Pub. Frequency: w. (Fri.) Page Size: broadsheet. Subscrip. Rate: $.50 newsstand/cover; $16.95/yr in county; $29.95/yr out of county. Freelance Pay: $25/article. Circulation: 3,500 per issue (paid). **Owner(s):** HarborPoint Media, LLC, 125 Basin St., Ste. 200, Daytona Beach, FL 32114. **Management:** Ron Wallace, Publisher. **Editorial:** Dan Fields, Managing Editor. Adam Minichino, Sports Editor.

CLEWISTON

CLEWISTON NEWS. 820 W Sugarland Hwy., Clewiston, FL 33440. E-MAIL: clewnews@gate.net. URL: http://www.newszap.com. Mailing Address: PO Box 1236, Clewiston, FL 33440. Year Established: 1928. Pub. Frequency: w. (Thu.) Page Size: broadsheet.Subscrip. Rate: $.50 newsstand/cover; $24.61/yr Circulation: 3,100 per issue (paid). **Owner(s):** Independent Newspapers, Inc., PO Box 737, Dover, DE 19903. Telephone: 302-674-3600. FAX: 302-674-9510. **Management:** Brenda Jaramillo, Advertising Manager. **Editorial:** Jose Zaragoza, Editor.

GLADES COUNTY DEMOCRAT. 820 W Sugarland Hwy., Clewiston, FL 33440. Telephone: 863-983-9148. FAX: 863-983-7537. URL: http://www.newszap.com. Mailing Address: PO Box 1236, Clewiston, FL 33440. Year Established: 1923. Pub. Frequency: w. (Thu.) Page Size: tabloid.Subscrip. Rate: $.50 newsstand/cover; $24.61/yr Circulation: 1,100 per issue (paid). **Owner(s):** Independent Newspapers, Inc., PO Box 737, Dover, DE 19903. Telephone: 302-674-3600. FAX: 302-674-9510. **Management:** Brenda Jaramillo, Advertising Manager. **Editorial:** Jose Zaragoza, Editor.

SUN (CLEWISTON), THE. 820 W Sugarland Hwy., Clewiston, FL 33440. Telephone: 863-983-9148. FAX: 863-983-7537. URL: http://www.newszap.com. Mailing Address: PO Box 1236, Clewiston, FL 33440. Pub. Frequency: w. (Thu.) Page Size: broadsheet. Subscrip. Rate: $.50 newsstand/cover; $24.61/yr in area. Circulation: 2,400 per issue (paid). **Owner(s):** Independent Newspapers, Inc., PO Box 737, Dover, DE 19903. Telephone: 302-674-3600. FAX: 302-674-9510. **Management:** Brenda Jaramillo, Advertising Manager. **Editorial:** Jose Zaragoza, Editor.

COCONUT CREEK

CORAL SPRINGS FORUM. 4611 Johnson Rd., Ste. 4, Coconut Creek, FL 33073. Telephone: 954-420-0955. FAX: 954-420-0415. E-MAIL: ldellarocca@tribune.com. Year Established: 1980. Pub. Frequency: w. (Thu.) Page Size: tabloid. Freelance Pay: $35/article. **Wire Service(s):** CNS. Circulation: 30,690 per issue (free). **Owner(s):** Tribune Company, 435 N Michigan Ave, Chicago, IL 60601. Telephone: 312.222.9100. **Management:** Joann Zollo, Advertising Manager. Ed Wilder, Circulation Manager. **Editorial:** Lenny Dellarocca, Editor. Rick Menning, Sports Editor.

MARGATE FORUM. 4611 Johnson Rd., Ste. 4, Coconut Creek, FL 33073. Telephone: 954-420-0955. FAX: 954-420-0415. E-MAIL: ldellarocca@tribune.com. Pub. Frequency: w. (Thu.) Page Size: tabloid. **Wire Service(s):** CNS. Circulation: 21,810 per issue (free). **Owner(s):** Tribune Company, 435 N Michigan Ave, Chicago, IL 60601. Telephone: 312.222.9100. **Management:** Joann Zollo, Advertising Manager. Ed Wilder, Circulation Manager. **Editorial:** Lenny Dellarocca, Editor.

SUNRISE FORUM. 4611 Johnson Rd., Ste. 4, Coconut Creek, FL 33073. Telephone: 954-420-0955. FAX: 954-420-0415. E-MAIL: ldellarocca@tribune.com. Pub. Frequency: w. (Fri.) Page Size: tabloid Circulation: 18,785 per issue (free). **Owner(s):** Tribune Company, 435 N Michigan Ave, Chicago, IL 60601. Telephone: 312.222.9100. **Management:** Joann Zollo, Advertising Manager. Ed Wilder, Circulation Manager. **Editorial:** Lenny Dellarocca, Editor.

TAMARAC FORUM. 4611 Johnson Rd., Ste. 4, Coconut Creek, FL 33073. Telephone: 954-420-0955. FAX: 954-420-0415. E-MAIL: ldellarocca@tribune.com. Pub. Frequency: w. (Fri.) Page Size: tabloid Circulation: 15,900 per issue (free). **Owner(s):** Tribune Company, 435 N Michigan Ave, Chicago, IL 60601. Telephone: 312.222.9100. **Management:** Joann Zollo, Advertising. Mickie Caruso, Advertising Manager. Ed Wilder, Circulation Manager. **Editorial:** Lenny Dellarocca, Editor.

CORAL SPRINGS

OUR TOWN NEWS. 11874 Wiles Rd., Coral Springs, FL 33076. Telephone: 954-977-7770. FAX: 954-977-7779. E-MAIL: brdsnrnews@aol.com. URL: http://www.flabrowardseniornews.com. Year Established: 1977. Pub. Frequency: w. (Thu.) Page Size: tabloid.Adv. Rate: col. inch $11 Circulation: 60,000 per issue (free). **Owner(s):** Harvey Lustig, Pub., 11874 Wiles Rd., Coral Springs, FL 33076. Telephone: 954-977-7770. FAX: 954-977-7779. **Management:** Harvey Lustig, President.

PARKLAND GAZETTE. 9660 W. Sample Rd., Coral Springs, FL 33065. Telephone: 954-752-7474. FAX: 954-752-7855.Pub. Frequency: m. Page Size: tabloid Circulation: 21,000 per issue (free). **Owner(s):** Tribune Company, 435 N Michigan Ave, Chicago, IL 60601. Telephone: 312.222.9100. **Management:** Joann Zollo, Advertising. Ed Wilder, Circulation Manager. **Editorial:** Lenny Dellarocca, Editor.

CRAWFORDVILLE

WAKULLA NEWS. 3119 Crawfordville Hwy., Crawfordville, FL 32327. Telephone: 850-926-7102. FAX: 850-926-3815. Mailing Address: PO Box 307, Crawfordville, FL 32326. Year Established: 1895. Pub. Frequency: w. (Thu.) Page Size: broadsheet. Subscrip. Rate: $.50 newsstand/cover; $25/yr in county; $30/yr out of county; $35/yr out of state. Circulation: 5,700 per issue (paid). **Owner(s):** Wakulla Publishing Co., See address and contact information above. **Management:** Lynda Kinsey, Advertising Manager. **Editorial:** Stacie M. Phillips, Editor. Shannon Joiner, Managing Editor.

CRESCENT CITY

COURIER JOURNAL (CRESCENT CITY), THE. 330 N. Summit St., Crescent City, FL 32112-2334. Telephone: 386-698-1644. FAX: 386-698-1994. E-MAIL: news@cjnewspaper.com. Year Established: 1898. Pub. Frequency: w. (Wed.) Page Size: broadsheet. Subscrip. Rate: $.50 newsstand/cover; $24/yr in county; $28/yr mailed out of county. Circulation: 3,000 per issue (paid). **Owner(s):** Lake Street Publishing Co., See address and contact information above. **Management:** William "BJ" Laurie, Publisher. **Editorial:** William "BJ" Laurie, Editor.

CRESTVIEW

BULLETIN (CRESTVIEW), THE. 295 W. James Lee Blvd., Crestview, FL 32536-3313. E-MAIL: cnleader@aol.com. Year Established: 1975. Pub. Frequency: w. (Wed.) Page Size: broadsheet. Subscrip. Rate: $32.50/yr mailed. Circulation: 14,500 per issue (paid and free). **Owner(s):** Okaloosa Publishing Co., See address and contact information above. **Management:** James J Knudsen Jr., Publisher. Reid Walker, Circulation Director. Gail Zabriskie, Classified Adv. Mgr.. **Editorial:** David Hein, Editor. Greg Langley, Sports.

CRESTVIEW NEWS BULLETIN. 295 W. James Lee Blvd., Crestview, FL 32536-3313. E-MAIL: okpublishing@earthlink.net. Mailing Address: PO Box 447, Crestview, FL 32536-0447. Year Established: 1992. Pub. Frequency: w. (Wed.) Page Size: broadsheet. Subscrip. Rate: $.50 newsstand/cover; $22.50/yr in county; $32.50/yr mailed out of county. Freelance Pay: $25/column-inch. Circulation: 4,000 per issue (free). **Owner(s):** Okaloosa Publishing Co., See address and contact information above. **Management:** James J Knudsen Jr., Publisher. Jennifer Knudsen, Advertising Manager. Reid Walker, Circulation Director. **Editorial:** Steve Andrews, Managing Editor.

OKALOOSA NEWS EXTRA. 295 W. James Lee Blvd., Crestview, FL 32536-3313. Mailing Address: PO Box 447, Crestview, FL 32536-0447. Pub. Frequency: w. (Wed.) Page Size: broadsheet.Subscrip. Rate: $52/yr mailed Circulation: 13,500 per issue (free). **Owner(s):** Okaloosa Publishing Co., 295 W. James Lee Blvd., Crestview, FL 32536-3313. **Management:** James J. Knudsen. Jr., Publisher. Jennifer Knudsen, Advertising Manager. Reid Walker, Circulation Director. **Editorial:** Steve Andrews, Managing Editor.

DAVIE

PLANTATION FORUM. 4801 S. University Dr., Ste. 101, Davie, FL 33328. Telephone: 954-680-4460. FAX: 954-680-6695, 954-429-1207. Pub. Frequency: w. (Wed.) Page Size: tabloid Circulation: 19,000 per issue (free). **Owner(s):** Tribune Company, 435 N Michigan Ave, Chicago, IL 60601. Telephone: 312.222.9100. **Management:** Gregg Behar, Advertising Manager. Ed Wilder, Circulation Director. **Editorial:** Lenny Dellarocca, Editor.

WESTON GAZETTE. 4801 S. University Dr., Ste. 101, Davie, FL 33328. Telephone: 954-680-4460. FAX: 954-680-6695.Pub. Frequency: m. Page Size: tabloid Circulation: 8,000 per issue (free). **Owner(s):** Tribune Company, 435 N Michigan Ave, Chicago, IL 60601. Telephone: 312.222.9100. **Management:** William Groves, Advertising Manager. **Editorial:** Rubin Cueto, Editor.

DE LAND

DE LAND-DELTONA BEACON, THE. 110 W. New York Ave, De Land, FL 32721-2397. Telephone: 386-734-4622. FAX: 386-734-4641. E-MAIL: info@delandbeacon.com. URL: http://www.delandbeacon.com. Mailing Address: P.O. Box 2397, Deland, FL 32721-2397. Year Established: 1992. Pub. Frequency: s-w. (Mon. & Thu.) Page Size: broadsheet. Subscrip. Rate: $.50 newsstand/cover; $29/yr online; $32/yr print; $52/yr combined subscription print & online. Adv. Rate: col. inch $11.50 Freelance Pay: $15/article. Circulation: 5,200 evening (paid); 11,543 per issue (free). **Owner(s):** Barbara Shepherd, See address and contact information above. Joann Kramer, Eileen Everett, **Management:** Barbara Shepherd, Publisher. Sammie Wiggins, Advertising Manager.

WEST VOLUSIA PENNYSAVER. 245 S. Woodland Blvd., De Land, FL 32720. Telephone: 386-736-2880. FAX: 386-736-3587. E-MAIL: readwvps@psavers.com. URL: http://www.floridapennysavers.com. Year Established: 1971. Pub. Frequency: s-w. (Wed. & Sat.) Page Size: tabloid Circulation: 50,000 per issue (free). **Owner(s):** News-Journal Corp., 245 S. Woodland Blvd., De Land, FL 32723-3536. Telephone: 386-736-2880. FAX: 386-736-3587. **Management:** Stephen Blais, Publisher. Chris Padilla, Advertising Director. Kathleen Mason, Advertising Manager. Bill Johnson, Circulation Director. **Editorial:** Stephen Blais, Editor.

DEERFIELD BEACH

DEERFIELD BEACH OBSERVER. 43 N.E. Second St., Deerfield Beach, FL 33441. Telephone: 954-428-9045. FAX: 954-428-9096. E-MAIL: observer@gate.net. Year Established: 1972. Pub. Frequency: w. (Thu.) Page Size: tabloid. Subscrip. Rate: $60/yr. Circulation: 30,000 per issue (paid and free). **Owner(s):** Deerfield Publishing, Inc., See address and contact information above. **Management:** Judith V. Wilson, President. David Eller, Publisher. **Editorial:** Joan Durbin, Editor. Judith V. Wilson, Managing Editor.

DEFUNIAK SPRINGS

DEFUNIAK SPRINGS HERALD-BREEZE. 676 Baldwin Ave, DeFuniak Springs, FL 32433. Telephone: 850-892-3232. FAX: 850-892-2270. E-MAIL: herald@dfsi.net. URL: http://www.defuniakherald.com. Mailing Address: PO Box 1546, DeFuniak Springs, FL 32435-1546. Year Established: 1888. Pub. Frequency: w. (Thu.) Page Size: broadsheet. Subscrip. Rate: $.50 newsstand/cover; $25/yr in state; $30/yr out of state. Circulation: 6,300 per issue (paid). **Owner(s):** Larry & Merle Woodham, See address and contact information above. **Management:** Gary Woodham, Publisher. **Editorial:** Ron Kelley, Editor. Chuck Hinson, Sports.

DESTIN

DESTIN LOG. 1225 Airport Rd., Destin, FL 32541. Telephone: 850-837-2828. FAX: 850-654-5982. E-MAIL: thelog@emeraldcoast.com. URL: http://www.destin.com. Mailing Address: PO Box 957, Destin, FL 32540. Year Established: 1974. Pub. Frequency: s-w. (Wed. & Sat.) Page Size: broadsheet. Subscrip. Rate: $.50 newsstand/cover; $38.50/yr in county; $44.45/yr in state; $51.84/yr out of state. Circulation: 13,500 per issue (paid). **Owner(s):** Freedom Communications, Inc., 17666 Fitch, Irvine, CA 92614. Telephone: 949-253-2300. **Management:** Rick Thomason, Publisher. Tom Stephens, Advertising Director. Mark Hurt, Circulation Manager. **Editorial:** Jim Wagner, Editor. Tina Harbuck, Sports.

DUNNELLON

RIVERLAND NEWS. 20441 E. Pennsylvania Ave., Dunnellon, FL 34432. Telephone: 352-489-2731. FAX: 352-489-6593. URL: http://www.riverlandnews.com. Mailing Address: PO Box 807, Dunnellon, FL 34430-0807. Pub. Frequency: w. (Thu.) Page Size: broadsheet. Subscrip. Rate: $.50 newsstand/cover; $20/yr in county; $26/yr out of county. Circulation: 7,100 per issue (paid). **Owner(s):** Landmark Community Newspapers, Inc., 601 Taylorsville Rd, Shelbyville, KY 40065-0549. Telephone: 502-633-4334. PO Box 549, Shelbyville, KY 40065. **Management:** Jim Hunter, General Manager. Gerry Mulligan, Publisher. **Editorial:** Michel Northsea, Editor.

ENGLEWOOD

ENGLEWOOD REVIEW, THE. 370 W. Dearborn St., Ste. B, Englewood, FL 34223-3146. Telephone: 941-474-4351. FAX: 941-474-8317. E-MAIL: pat@thereview.ws. Year Established: 1988. Pub. Frequency: bi-m. (Thu.) Page Size: tabloid.Subscrip. Rate: $50/yr mailed Circulation: 5,000 per issue (free). **Owner(s):** Newton Studios, Inc., See address and contact information above. **Management:** Pat Newton, Publisher. **Editorial:** Pat Newton, Editor.

FERNANDINA BEACH

NEWS-LEADER (FERNANDINA BEACH). 511 Ash St, Fernandina Beach, FL 32034. Telephone: 904-261-3696. FAX: 904-261-3698. E-MAIL: editor@fbnewsleader.com. URL: http://www.fbnewsleader.com. Mailing Address: P O Box 766, Fernandina Beach, FL 32035. Year Established: 1858. Pub. Frequency: s-w. (Wed. & Fri.) Page Size: broadsheet. Subscrip. Rate: $.50 newsstand/cover; $36/yr in county; $63/yr mailed out of county. Freelance Pay: $20-$50/story. Circulation: 11,600 per issue (paid). **Owner(s):** Community Newspapers (Athens), Inc., PO Box 792, Athens, GA 30603. Telephone: 706-548-0010. **Management:** Foy Maloy, Publisher. Mike Hankins, Advertising Director. Bob Timpe, Circulation Director. April Butler, Classified Adv. Mgr.. **Editorial:** Michael Parnell, Editor.

NEWS LEADER (FERNANDINA). 511 Ash St, Fernandina Beach, FL 32034. Telephone: 904-261-3696. FAX: 904-261-3698. E-MAIL: fmaloy@fbnewsleader.com. URL: http://www.fbnewsleader.com. Mailing Address: P O Box 766, Fernandina Beach, FL 32035. Pub. Frequency: w. (Wed.) Subscrip. Rate: $36/yr in county; $63/yr out of county. **Owner(s):** Community Newspapers (Athens), Inc., PO Box 792, Athens, GA 30603. **Management:** Foy Maloy, Publisher. Mike Hankins, Advertising Director. Bob Timpe, Circulation Director. April Butler, Classified Adv. Mgr.. Angeline Mudd, Business Manager. **Editorial:** Michael Parnell, Editor.

FORT LAUDERDALE

BROWARD TIMES. ISSN 1065-1462
3301 NW 55th St, Fort Lauderdale, FL 33309. Telephone: 954-497-3190. FAX: 954-497-3193. Year Established: 1990. Pub. Frequency: w. (Fri.) Page Size: broadsheet. Subscrip. Rate: $.50 newsstand/cover per issue; $52/yr home delivery. Freelance Pay: $45/article. **Wire Service(s):** AP. Circulation: 25,000 (controlled). **Owner(s):** Broward Times, Inc., PO Box 670038, Coral Springs, FL 33067-0001. **Management:** Keith A Clayborne, Publisher. Bernadette P Clayborne, Advertising. **Editorial:** Mara Kiffin, Editor.

PROMENADE (FORT LAUDERDALE). PO Box 030397, Fort Lauderdale, FL 33303-0397. Telephone: 954-467-0020. FAX: 954-463-2674. E-MAIL: voicehab@gate.net. Year Established: 1992. Pub. Frequency: m. Page Size: tabloid. Subscrip. Rate: $25/yr. Adv. Rate: B&W page $760 Circulation: 15,000 per issue (controlled). **Owner(s):** Ray Brasted, See address and contact information above. **Editorial:** Ray Brasted, Editor.

FORT MEADE

FORT MEADE LEADER, THE. 25 W. Broadway, Fort Meade, FL 33841-0893. Telephone: 863-285-8625. FAX: 863-285-7634. E-MAIL: fpcslfiv@aol.com. URL: http://www.polkcountydemocrat.com. Mailing Address: PO Box 893, Fort Meade, FL 33841-0893. Year Established: 1971. Pub. Frequency: s-w. (Tue. & Fri.) Page Size: broadsheet. Subscrip. Rate: $.25 newsstand/cover; $21/yr in county; $31.50/yr out of county; $36.75/yr mailed out of state. Adv. Rate: col. inch $6.95 Circulation: 1,394 per issue (paid and free). **Owner(s):** Frisbie Publishing Co., Inc., PO Box 120, Bartow, FL 33831-0120. Telephone: 863-533-4183. FAX: 863-533-0402. **Management:** S.L. Frisbie IV, Publisher. **Editorial:** S.L. Frisbie IV, Editor. Peggy Kehoe, Managing Editor.

FORT MYERS

FORT MYERS BEACH BULLETIN. 19260 San Carlos Blvd, Fort Myers, FL 33931. Telephone: 239-463-4421. FAX: 239-463-1402. E-MAIL: bchbulletin@breezenewspapers.com. URL: http://www.breezenewspapers.com. Year Established: 1951. Pub. Frequency: w. (Fri.) Page Size: tabloid. Subscrip. Rate: $30/yr mailed out of county. Circulation: 14,000 per issue (paid and free). **Owner(s):** Ogden Newspapers, See address and contact information above. **Management:** Robin Calabrese, General Manager. **Editorial:** Sue Starkweather, Editor.

PINE ISLAND EAGLE. 19260 San Carlos Blvd, Fort Myers, FL 33931. Telephone: 239-463-4421. FAX: 239-463-1402. E-MAIL: swfnews1@aol.com. Year Established: 1976. Pub. Frequency: w. (Wed.) Page Size: tabloid. Subscrip. Rate: $30/yr mailed in county 3rd class. Circulation: 8,500 per issue (paid and free). **Owner(s):** Ogden Newspapers, See address and contact information above. **Management:** Jack Glarrow, Publisher. Charlene Russ, Advertising. Judy Housewright, Circulation Manager. **Editorial:** Marianne Paton, Editor.

FORT MYERS BEACH

FORT MYERS BEACH OBSERVER. 19260 San Carlos Blvd., Fort Myers Beach, FL 33931. Telephone: 239-765-0400. FAX: 239-765-0846. E-MAIL: observer@breezenewspapers.com. URL: http://www.breezenewspapers.com. Year Established: 1985. Pub. Frequency: w. (Wed.) Page Size: tabloid. Subscrip. Rate: $30/yr mailed in county 3rd class. Circulation: 14,000 per issue (paid). **Owner(s):** Ogden Newspapers of Minnesota, Inc., 1500 Main St., Wheeling, WV 26003. Telephone: 304-233-0100. **Management:** Steve Dubose, General Manager. Jack Garrow, Publisher. Steve Dubose, Advertising Manager. **Editorial:** Joe Taylor, Editor.

FROSTPROOF

FROSTPROOF NEWS, THE. 19 S. Scenic Hwy., Frostproof, FL 33843. Telephone: 863-635-2171. FAX: 863-635-0032. E-MAIL: frostnews@newszap.com. URL: http://www.newszap.com. Mailing Address: PO Box 67, Frostproof, FL 33843. Year Established: 1914. Pub. Frequency: w. (Thu.) Page Size: broadsheet. Subscrip. Rate: $.50 newsstand/cover; $24.61/yr in county. Adv. Rate: col. inch $6.18 Circulation: 1,100 per issue (paid). **Owner(s):** Independent Newspapers, Inc., PO Box 737, Dover, DE 19903. Telephone: 302-674-3600. FAX: 302-674-9510. **Editorial:** Cindy Monk, Editor.

FRUITLAND PARK

LAKE NEWS (FRUITLAND PARK). 2891 Hwy. 441-27, Fruitland Park, FL 34731-2438. Telephone: 352-787-6277. FAX: 352-787-8479. E-MAIL: mspln@aol.com. Pub. Frequency: w. (Wed.) Page Size: tabloid Circulation: 16,700 per issue (free). **Owner(s):** Mid-Florida Sun Publications, 4645 Hwy. 19-A, Mt. Dora, FL 32757. **Management:** Cheryl Crisp, Publisher. Bob Horne, Circulation Manager. **Editorial:** Dixie Glessner, Editor.

SUMTER SHOPPER. 2891 Hwy. 27-441, Fruitland Park, FL 34731-4483. Telephone: 352-787-6277. FAX: 352-787-8479. Pub. Frequency: w. (Wed.) Page Size: tabloid Circulation: 20,000 per issue (free). **Owner(s):** Mid-Florida Sun Publications, 4645 Hwy. 19-A, Mt. Dora, FL 32757. **Management:** Cheryl Crisp, Publisher. Jim Callop, Advertising Manager. Cheryl Crisp, Circulation Manager. Paula Heines, Classified Adv. Mgr.. **Editorial:** Cheryl Crisp, Editor.

GAINESVILLE

GAINESVILLE BUYERS GUIDE. 2251 N.W. 41st St., Ste. B, Gainesville, FL 32606. Telephone: 352-372-5468. FAX: 352-373-9178. E-MAIL: charley@towerpublications.com. Pub. Frequency: w. (Thu.) Page Size: broadsheet Circulation: 28,500 per issue (free). **Owner(s):** Carlos Delatorre, See address and contact information above. **Management:** Carlos Delatorre, Publisher. **Editorial:** Carlos Delatorre, Editor.

GAINSVILLE

RECORD (GAINSVILLE), THE. 620 N. Main St., Gainsville, FL 32602. Telephone: 352-377-2444. FAX: 352-338-1986. E-MAIL: record620@aol.com. Mailing Address: PO Box 806, Gainsville, FL 32602. Year Established: 1965. Pub. Frequency: w. (Thu.) Subscrip. Rate: $.50/yr newsstand/cover; $20/yr in state; $25/yr mailed elsewhere. Circulation: 6,800 (paid). **Owner(s):** Santa Fe Publishing Co., Inc., See address and contact information above. **Management:** Constance D Rowe, Publisher. **Editorial:** Marcy Yozgat, Editor.

HIGH SPRINGS

HIGH SPRINGS HERALD, THE. ISSN 0746-1046
5 N.W. First St., High Springs, FL 32643. Telephone: 386-454-1297. FAX: 386-454-4559. E-MAIL: news@highspringsherald.com. URL: http://www.highspringsherald.com. Mailing Address: PO Box 745, High Springs, FL 32655. Year Established: 1952. Pub. Frequency: w. (Thu.) Page Size: standard. Subscrip. Rate: $.25 newsstand/cover; $12/yr in county; $15/yr mailed; $17/yr out of state. **Wire Service(s):** AP. Circulation: 4,500 per issue (paid and free). **Owner(s):** Campus Communications, Inc., PO Box 14257, Gainesville, FL 32604-3275. Telephone: 352-376-4446. FAX: 352-376-4556. **Management:** Ed Barber, President. Darcy Lanton, Advertising Manager. Jamie Walker, Art Director. **Editorial:** Ronald Dupont Jr., Managing Editor.

HOMESTEAD

SOUTH DADE NEWS LEADER. 15 N.E. First Rd., Homestead, FL 33030. Telephone: 305-245-2311. FAX: 305-248-0596. Mailing Address: PO Box 900340, Homestead, FL 33090. Year Established: 1912. Pub. Frequency: 3/w. (Mon., Wed., Fri.) Page Size: broadsheet. Subscrip. Rate: $.50 newsstand/cover; $18 mailed in county. **Wire Service(s):** UPI. Circulation: 12,514 per issue (paid). **Owner(s):** Homestead Newspapers, Inc., See address and contact information above. **Management:** Glen Martin, General Manager. Tracy Lovitt, Advertising. Bobby Williams, Circulation Manager. Larry Wiggins, Controller. **Editorial:** Yolanda Ulrich, Editor. John Baxter, Sports Editor.

JACKSONVILLE BEACH

BEACHES LEADER, THE. ISSN 1059-647X
1114 Beach Blvd, Jacksonville Beach, FL 32250. Telephone: 904-249-9033. FAX: 904-249-1501. E-MAIL: editor@beachesleader.com. URL: http://www.beachesleader.com. Year Established: 1963. Pub. Frequency: s-w. (Wed. & Fri.) Page Size: broadsheet. Subscrip. Rate: $.50 newsstand/cover; $30/yr mailed in county; $48/yr mailed out of county. Circulation: 23,000 per issue (paid). **Owner(s):** T H Wood, See address and contact information above. **Management:** Thomas H Wood, Publisher. Joanne Jund, Advertising Director. Marie Adams, Circulation Manager. **Editorial:** Kathleen Feindt Bailey, Editor.

SUN TIMES WEEKLY. 1114 Beach Blvd., Jacksonville Beach, FL 32250. E-MAIL: ldrgrp@aol.com. Pub. Frequency: w. (Fri.) Page Size: standard Circulation: 11,000 evening (paid). **Owner(s):** Community Newspapers (Athens), Inc., PO Box 792, Athens, GA 30603. **Management:** Thomas Wood, Publisher. **Editorial:** Kathleen Bailey, Editor.

JASPER

JASPER NEWS. 105 N.E. Second Ave., Jasper, FL 32052. Telephone: 386-792-2487. FAX: 386-792-3009. E-MAIL: jaspernews1@alltel.net. Year Established: 1870. Pub. Frequency: w. (Thu.) Page Size: broadsheet. Subscrip. Rate: $.50 newsstand/cover; $16/yr in county; $23/yr mailed out of county. Circulation: 2,300 per issue (paid). **Owner(s):** Community Newspaper Holdings, Inc., 3500 Colonnade Pkwy., Ste. 600, Birmingham, AL 35243. Telephone: 205-298-7100. FAX: 205-298-7101. **Management:** Myra Regan, Publisher. John Tucker, Advertising Manager. Melody Lee, Manager.

JUPITER

JUPITER COURIER. ISSN 0896-0283
800 W. Indiantown Rd., Jupiter, FL 33458. Telephone: 561-746-5111. FAX: 561-743-0673. URL: http://www.tcpalm.com. Mailing Address: PO Box 1486, Jupiter, FL 33468. Year Established: 1958. Pub. Frequency: s-w. (Wed. & Sun.) Page Size: broadsheet. Subscrip. Rate: $.50 newsstand/cover; $57.24/yr home delivery; $82.68/yr mailed. Circulation: 17,000 per issue (paid). **Owner(s):** E.W. Scripps Co., 312 Walnut St., 28th Fl., Cincinnati, OH 45202. Telephone: 513-977-3000. **Management:** Jerry Rupar, General Manager. John Maletzke, Circulation Manager. **Editorial:** Sy O'Neill, Managing Editor. Randall Murray, Community Editor. Sy O'Neill, Editorial Page Editor.

KEY BISCAYNE

ISLANDER NEWS, THE. 104 Crandon Blvd., Ste. 301, Key Biscayne, FL 33149-1526. Telephone: 305-361-3333. FAX: 305-361-5051. E-MAIL: islnews@aksi.net. URL: http://www.islandernews.com. Pub. Frequency: w. (Thu) Page Size: standard. Subscrip. Rate: $1.25 newsstand/cover; $48.15/yr mailed in county; $83.46/yr mailed out of county; $78/yr mailed out of state. Adv. Rate: B&W page $865 Circulation: 3,600 per issue (paid). **Owner(s):** Crescent Media Goup, PO Box 1634, Spartanburg, SC 29304. Telephone: 864-583-2907. **Management:** Nancy Ray, Publisher. James Owen, Advertising Director. Karen Chamarro, Circulation Director. **Editorial:** Nancy Ray, Editor.

KEY LARGO

OCEAN REEF PRESS. 3 Barracuda Ln, Key Largo, FL 33037. Telephone: 305-367-4911. FAX: 305-367-2191. URL: http://www.keysnews.com. Mailing Address: PO Box 1800, Key West, FL 33041. Pub. Frequency: w. (Fri.) Page Size: broadsheet Circulation: 4,000 per issue (free). **Owner(s):** Cooke Communications LLC, 3420 Northside Dr., Key West, FL 33040. Telephone: 305-292-7777. **Management:** John Kent Cook Jr., Publisher. Todd Milligan, Advertising. Bob Timmerman, Circulation Manager. Connie Fitzgerald, Sales Manager. **Editorial:** Tom Tuell, Managing Editor.

KEY WEST

KEY WEST KEYNOTER, THE. 2720-A N Roosevelt Blvd., Key West, FL 33040. Telephone: 305-296-6989. FAX: 305-296-1924. URL: http://wwwkeynoter.com. Pub. Frequency: s-w. (Sat. & Wed.) Page Size: tabloid. Subscrip. Rate: $.25 newsstand/cover; $37.63/yr home delivery in county; $47.74/yr mailed in state. Circulation: 5,000 per issue (paid). **Owner(s):** The/McClatchy Company, 2100 Q St, Sacramento, CA 95816. Telephone: 916-321-1936. FAX: 916-321-1869. **Management:** Wayne Markham, Publisher. Juliana Waldrop, Advertising. Craig Skinner, Circulation Manager. Melanie Elder, Marketing Director. **Editorial:** Larry Kahn, Editor.

SOLARES HILL. 3420 Northside Dr., Key West, FL 33040. Telephone: 305-294-6641. FAX: 305-294-0768. E-MAIL: solareshill@keysnews.com. URL: http://www.keysnews.com. Pub. Frequency: w. (Fri.) Page Size: tabloid Circulation: 18,000 per issue (free). **Owner(s):** Cooke Communications LLC, See address and contact information above. **Management:** John Kent Cooke Jr., Publisher. Kim Works, Advertising Manager. Bob Timmerman, Circulation Manager. **Editorial:** Nancy Klingener, Editor. Nadja Hansen, Assistant Editor.

Weeklies

ULRICH'S PERIODICALS DIRECTORY 2010

KEYSTONE HEIGHTS

LAKE REGION MONITOR. 7082 State Rd., 21, Keystone Heights, FL 32656-9381. Telephone: 352-473-2210. FAX: 352-473-2210. Pub. Frequency: w. (Thu.) Page Size: standard. Subscrip. Rate: $19.26/yr mailed. Adv. Rate: col. inch $4 Circulation: 4,000 per issue (paid). **Owner(s):** Bradford County Telegraph, See address and contact information above. **Management:** John Miller, Publisher. Kevin Miller, Advertising Manager. **Editorial:** James Williams, Editor.

KISSIMMEE

OSCEOLA NEWS-GAZETTE. ISSN 1060-1244
108 Church St., Kissimmee, FL 34741. Telephone: 407-846-7600. FAX: 407-933-6856. E-MAIL: borben@osceolanewsgazette.com. URL: http://www.oscnewsgazette.com. Mailing Address: PO Box 422068, Kissimmee, FL 34742-2068. Year Established: 1895. Pub. Frequency: s-w. (Thu. & Sat.) Page Size: broadsheet. Subscrip. Rate: $.50 newsstand/cover; $52/yr in state & other states. Circulation: 29,500 per issue (controlled and free). **Owner(s):** Florida Sun Publication, PO Box 811, Bradenton, FL 34206. Telephone: 800-282-3953. **Management:** Paula Stark, General Manager. John Lowe, Advertising Manager. Kathy Beckham, Circulation Manager. Cheryl Christian, Classified Adv. Mgr.. **Editorial:** Bill Orben, Editor. Marvin Cortner, Assistant Editor. Peter Covino, Entertainment Editor. Rick Pedone, Sports Editor.

LA BELLE

CALOOSA BELLE. 22 Fort Thompson Ave., La Belle, FL 33935. Telephone: 239-657-6000. FAX: 239-675-1449. URL: http://www.newszap.com. Mailing Address: PO Box 518, La Belle, FL 33975. Year Established: 1922. Pub. Frequency: w. (Thu.) Page Size: broadsheet. Subscrip. Rate: $25 mailed for 6 mos. 1st class; $54/yr mailed. Circulation: 7,500 per issue (paid). **Owner(s):** Independent Newspapers, Inc., PO Box 737, Dover, DE 19903. Telephone: 302-674-3600. FAX: 302-674-9510. **Management:** Dale Conyers, Advertising Manager. Janet Madrey, Circulation Manager. **Editorial:** Patty Brant, Editor.

IMMOKALEE BULLETIN. 22 Fort Thompson Ave., La Belle, FL 33935. Telephone: 239-657-6000. FAX: 239-657-1449. E-MAIL: cb-editor@lha.net. URL: http://www.newszap.com. Mailing Address: PO Box 518, La Belle, FL 33975. Pub. Frequency: w. (Thu.) Page Size: broadsheet.Subscrip. Rate: $20 mailed for 6 mos.; $40/yr Circulation: 3,500 per issue (paid). **Owner(s):** Independent Newspapers, Inc., PO Box 737, Dover, DE 19903. Telephone: 302-674-3600. FAX: 302-674-9510. **Management:** Dale Conyers, Advertising Manager. Janet Madrey, Circulation Manager. **Editorial:** Patty Brant, Editor.

LAKE BUTLER

UNION COUNTY TIMES (LAKE BUTLER). 150 W. Main St., Lake Butler, FL 32054-1640. Telephone: 386-496-2261. FAX: 386-964-8628. URL: http://www.uctimesonline.com. Pub. Frequency: w. (Thu.) Page Size: standard. Subscrip. Rate: $.50 newsstand/cover; $26/yr in area. Adv. Rate: col. inch $4.60 Circulation: 2,500 per issue (paid). **Owner(s):** Bradford County Telegraph Inc., See address and contact information above. **Management:** John Miller, Publisher. Kevin Miller, Sales Manager. **Editorial:** Gail D. Livingston, Editor. Evelyn Crawford, Circulation Editor.

LAKE PARK

WEEKDAY. 826 Park Ave., Lake Park, FL 33403-2402. Telephone: 561-844-2408. FAX: 561-844-5917. Pub. Frequency: w. (Fri.) Page Size: standard.Adv. Rate: col. inch $8 Circulation: 16,500 per issue (free). **Owner(s):** American Press Association, See address and contact information above. **Management:** John Carroll, Publisher. **Editorial:** John Carroll, Editor.

LAKE PLACID

LAKE PLACID JOURNAL. 232 N. Main St., Lake Placid, FL 33852. Telephone: 863-465-2521. FAX: 863-699-0331. E-MAIL: lpjournal@htn.net. Year Established: 1957. Pub. Frequency: w. (Thu.) Page Size: broadsheet. Subscrip. Rate: $.50 newsstand/cover; $24.61/yr in state; $28.89/yr mailed out of state. Circulation: 6,000 per issue (paid). **Owner(s):** Constance Delaney, PO Box 785, Lake Placid, FL 33862. Telephone: 863-465-4122. FAX: 863-699-0331. **Management:** Constance Delaney, Co-Publisher. Tom Staik, General Manager. Matt Delaney, Publisher. Michael Ridgeway, Advertising Manager. Kaye Ridgeway, Circulation Manager. **Editorial:** Matt Delaney, Assignment Editor. Tom Staik, Religion Editor. David Rinald, Sports.

LAKE WALES

LAKE WALES NEWS. 140 E. Stuart Ave., Lake Wales, FL 33853-4198. Telephone: 863-676-3467. FAX: 863-676-3468. URL: http://www.lakewalesnews.com. Year Established: 1926. Pub. Frequency: w. (Thu.) Page Size: broadsheet. Subscrip. Rate: $.50 newsstand/cover; $16.50/yr in county; $20/yr out of county. Adv. Rate: col. inch $4.75 Circulation: 3,500 per issue (paid). **Owner(s):** Frisbie Publishing Co., Inc., PO Box 120, Bartow, FL 33831-0120. Telephone: 863-533-4183. FAX: 863-533-0402. **Management:** S.L. Frisbee IV, Publisher. Dale Bresett, Advertising. **Editorial:** S.L. Frisbie IV, Editor.

LAKE WORTH

COASTAL OBSERVER (LAKE WORTH). 130 S. H St., Lake Worth, FL 33460. Telephone: 561-585-9387. FAX: 561-585-5434. Mailing Address: PO Box 191, Lake Worth, FL 33460-0191. Year Established: 1970. Pub. Frequency: w. (Thu.) Page Size: tabloid.Adv. Rate: col. inch $11.50 Circulation: 20,000 per issue (free). **Owner(s):** Mark & Sarajo Easton, See address and contact information above. **Management:** Mark J. Easton, Publisher. **Editorial:** H. Patrick Parrish, Editor.

GREENACRES OBSERVER. 130 S. H St., Lake Worth, FL 33460. Telephone: 561-585-9387. FAX: 561-585-5434. Mailing Address: PO Box 191, Lake Worth, FL 33460-0191. Pub. Frequency: w. (Thu.) Page Size: tabloid.Adv. Rate: col. inch $11.50 Circulation: 15,000 per issue (free). **Owner(s):** Mark & Sarajo Easton, See address and contact information above. **Management:** Mark J. Easton, Publisher. **Editorial:** H. Patrick Parrish, Editor.

LAKE WORTH HERALD. 130 S. H St., Lake Worth, FL 33460. Telephone: 561-585-9387. FAX: 561-585-5434. Mailing Address: PO Box 191, Lake Worth, FL 33460-0191. Year Established: 1912. Pub. Frequency: w. (Thu.) Page Size: tabloid. Subscrip. Rate: $.50 newsstand/cover; $15 for 6 mos.; $25/yr. Circulation: 38,000 per issue (paid). **Owner(s):** Mark & Sarajo Easton, See address and contact information above. **Management:** Mark J. Easton, Publisher. **Editorial:** H. Patrick Parrish, Editor.

LEHIGH ACRES

LEHIGH ACRES NEWS STAR. 1280 Lee Blvd., Lehigh Acres, FL 33936-0908. Telephone: 239-369-2191. FAX: 239-369-1396. E-MAIL: news@lehighnewsstar.com. URL: http://www.lehighnewsstar.com. Mailing Address: PO Box 908, Lehigh Acres, FL 33970-0908. Year Established: 1962. Pub. Frequency: s-w. (Wed. & Sat.) Page Size: broadsheet. Subscrip. Rate: $28.50/yr in county; $56.50/yr out of county; $62/yr mailed out of state. Freelance Pay: $25/article. Circulation: 15,000 per issue (paid and controlled). **Owner(s):** Gannett Company, Inc., 7950 Jones Branch Dr, McLean, VA 22107. Telephone: 703-854-6000. **Management:** Jim Wyatt, General Manager. Carol Hudler, Publisher. **Editorial:** Michelle Hudson, Editor.

LIVE OAK

SUWANNEE DEMOCRAT. 211 Howard St, E, Live Oak, FL 32064. Telephone: 386-362-1734. FAX: 386-364-5578. URL: http://www.suwanneedemocrat.com. Pub. Frequency: s-w. (Wed. & Fri.) Page Size: broadsheet. Subscrip. Rate: $.50 newsstand/cover; $32/yr carrier delivery in county; $45/yr mailed out of county. Circulation: 4,500 per issue (paid). **Owner(s):** Community Newspaper Holdings, Inc., 3500 Colonnade Pkwy., Ste. 600, Birmingham, AL 35243. **Management:** Myra Regan, Publisher. Monja Robinson, Advertising. Angie Sparks, Circulation Manager. Tami Stevenson, Classified Adv. Mgr.. **Editorial:** Robert Bridges, Editor.

LUTZ

LAKER (LUTZ), THE. 1930 Lando-Lakes Blvd, Lutz, FL 33549. Telephone: 813-909-2800. FAX: 813-909-2802. E-MAIL: cnews@ij.net. Pub. Frequency: w. (Wed.) Page Size: tabloid Subscrip. Rate: $90/yr Circulation: 34,000 per issue (paid). **Owner(s):** Community News, PO Box 271880, Lutz, FL 33688-1880. Telephone: 813-909-2800. FAX: 813-909-2802. **Management:** Mark Mathes, Publisher. **Editorial:** Mark Mathes, Editor.

LUTZ COMMUNITY NEWS. 1930 Lando-Lakes Blvd, Lutz, FL 33549. Telephone: 813-909-2800. FAX: 813-909-2802. E-MAIL: cnews@ij.net. Year Established: 1961. Pub. Frequency: w. (Wed.) Page Size: tabloid. Subscrip. Rate: $5.95/yr in state; $12/yr mailed out of state. Circulation: 11,000 per issue (controlled and free). **Owner(s):** Community News, PO Box 271880, Lutz, FL 33688-1880. Telephone: 813-964-1919. FAX: 813-963-5876. **Management:** Mark Mathes, Publisher. Diane Mathes, Advertising Manager. **Editorial:** Mark Mathes, Editor.

TEMPLE TERRACE BEACON. 1930 Lando-Lakes Blvd, Lutz, FL 33549. Telephone: 813-909-2800. FAX: 813-909-2802. E-MAIL: cnews@ij.net. Pub. Frequency: w. (Wed.) Page Size: tabloid. Subscrip. Rate: $60/yr in state; $60/yr mailed out of state. Circulation: 10,000 per issue (paid). **Owner(s):** Community News, PO Box 271880, Lutz, FL 33688-1880. Telephone: 813-909-2800. FAX: 813-909-2802. **Management:** Mark Mathes, Publisher. Diane Mathes, Advertising Manager. **Editorial:** Mark Mathes, Editor.

MACCLENNY

BAKER COUNTY PRESS, THE. 104 S. Fifth St., MacClenny, FL 32063. Telephone: 904-259-2400. FAX: 904-259-6502. E-MAIL: bcpress@nefcon.net. Year Established: 1929. Pub. Frequency: w. (Wed.) Page Size: broadsheet. Subscrip. Rate: $.50 newsstand/cover; $20/yr in county; $25/yr out of county. Adv. Rate: col. inch $6.15 Circulation: 5,400 per issue (paid). **Owner(s):** Baker County Press, Inc., See address and contact information above. **Management:** James C. McGauley, Publisher. Jessica Prevatt, Advertising. Barbara Blackshear, Classified Adv. Mgr.. **Editorial:** James C. McGauley, Editor.

MADISON

MADISON COUNTY CARRIER. P.O. Drawer 772, Madison, FL 32340. Telephone: 850-973-4141. FAX: 850-973-4122. URL: http://www.greenepublishing.com. Mailing Address: P.O. Drawer 772, Madison, FL 32341. Year Established: 1964. Pub. Frequency: w. (Wed.) Page Size: broadsheet. Subscrip. Rate: $.50 newsstand/cover; $26/yr mailed in county; $31/yr mailed out of county. Circulation: 4,500 per issue (paid). **Owner(s):** Emerald Kinsley, See address and contact information above. **Management:** Emerald Kinsley, General Manager. Mary Ellen Greene, Advertising Manager. **Editorial:** Lisa Greene, Editor.

MADISON ENTERPRISE-RECORDER, THE. P.O. Drawer 772, Madison, FL 32341. Telephone: 850-973-4141. FAX: 850-973-4121. URL: http://www.greenepublishing.com. Mailing Address: P.O. Drawer 772, Madison, FL 32341. Year Established: 1864. Pub. Frequency: w. (Fri.) Page Size: broadsheet. Subscrip. Rate: $.50 newsstand/cover; $26/yr mailed in county; $31/yr mailed out of county. Circulation: 4,000 per issue (paid). **Owner(s):** Emerald Kinsley, See address and contact information above. **Management:** Emerald Kinsley, General Manager. Mary Ellen Greene, Advertising Manager.

MARATHON

FLORIDA KEYS KEYNOTER. ISSN 8756-6427
3015 Overseas Hwy, Marathon, FL 33050. Telephone: 305-743-5551. FAX: 305-743-9586. E-MAIL: keynoter@keynoter.com. URL: http://www.keynoter.com. Mailing Address: PO Box 500158, Marathon, FL 33050. Year Established: 1953. Pub. Frequency: s-w. (Wed. & Sat.) Page Size: tabloid. Subscrip. Rate: $.25 newsstand/cover; $35/yr in county; $45/yr mailed elsewhere. **Wire Service(s):** AP. Circulation: 19,000 per issue (paid). **Owner(s):** The/McClatchy Company, 2100 Q St, Sacramento, CA 95816. Telephone: 916-321-1936. FAX: 916-321-1869. **Management:** Wayne Markham, Publisher. Craig Skinner, Circulation Manager. Melanie Elder, Marketing Director. **Editorial:** Larry Kahn, Editor.

MARATHON/BIG PINE/LOWER KEYS FREE PRESS. 6363 Overseas Hwy., Marathon, FL 33050. Telephone: 305-743-8766. FAX: 305-743-9977. E-MAIL: marathon@keysnews.com. URL: http://www.keysnews.com. Year Established: 1989. Pub. Frequency: w. (Wed.) Page Size: broadsheet.Adv. Rate: col. inch $13.10 Circulation: 11,000 per issue (free). **Owner(s):** Cooke Communications LLC, 3420 Northside Dr., Key West, FL 33040. Telephone: 305-292-7777. FAX: 305-294-0768. **Management:** John Kent Cook Jr., Publisher. Adrian Jones, Advertising Manager. Bob Timmerman, Circulation Manager. **Editorial:** Marc Phelps, Managing Editor.

MARCO ISLAND

MARCO ISLAND EAGLE. 579 Elkcam Cir., Marco Island, FL 34146. Telephone: 239-213-5300. FAX: 239-213-5390. E-MAIL: marcoeagle@aol.com. URL: http://www.marcoeagle.com. Mailing Address: PO Box 579, Marco Island, FL 34146. Year Established: 1968. Pub. Frequency: w. (Wed.) Page Size: tabloid. Subscrip. Rate: $.50 newsstand/cover; $25/yr mailed in state. Adv. Rate: col. inch $14.35 Circulation: 9,095 per issue (paid). **Owner(s):** E.W. Scripps Co., 312 Walnut St., 28th Fl., Cincinnati, OH 45202. Telephone: 513-977-3000. **Management:** Cheryl Ferrara, Publisher. Mary Quinton, Advertising Manager. Donald Eggeman, Circulation Manager. **Editorial:** Jamie Kuser, Editor. Nadine Ouillette, Assistant Editor.

MELBOURNE

BAY BULLETIN, THE. One Gannett Plz., Melbourne, FL 32940-9000. Telephone: 321-242-3801. FAX: 321-242-0760. URL: http://www.floridatoday.com. Mailing Address: PO Box 419000, Melbourne, FL 32941-9000. Pub. Frequency: w. (Wed.) Page Size: broadsheet Circulation: 32,825 per issue (free). **Owner(s):** Gannett Company, Inc., 7950 Jones Branch Dr., McLean, VA 22107-0001. Telephone: 703-854-6000. **Management:** Michael Coleman, Publisher. Nancy Solliday, Advertising Director. Cedric Johnson, Circulation Manager. **Editorial:** Susan Smiley-Hieght, Editor. Tom Palermo, Managing Editor.

PRESS TRIBUNE, THE. One Gannett Plz., Melbourne, FL 32940-9000. Telephone: 321-242-3500. FAX: 321-242-6620. URL: http://www.presstribune.com. Mailing Address: PO Box 419000, Melbourne, FL 32941-9000. Year Established: 1917. Pub. Frequency: w. (Wed.) Page Size: broadsheet.Subscrip. Rate: $17.24 mailed/mo. Circulation: 40,651 per issue (free). **Owner(s):** Gannett Company, Inc., 7950 Jones Branch Dr., McLean, VA 22107-0001. Telephone: 703-854-6000. **Management:** Michael J Coleman, Publisher. Nancy Solliday, Advertising Director. Cedric Johnson, Circulation Manager. Barry Barlow, Classified Adv. Mgr.. **Editorial:** Bob Stover, Managing Editor.

REPORTER (MELBOURNE), THE. One Gannett Plz., Melbourne, FL 32940. Mailing Address: PO Box 419000, Melbourne, FL 32941-9000. Year Established: 1981. Pub. Frequency: w. (Thu.) Subscrip. Rate: $26/yr mailed in area. **Owner(s):** Gannett Company, Inc., 7950 Jones Branch Dr., McLean, VA 22107-0001. Telephone: 703-854-6000. **Management:** Michael J Coleman, Publisher.

STAR-ADVOCATE, THE. One Gannett Plz., Melbourne, FL 32940. Telephone: 321-242-3801. FAX: 321-242-0760. E-MAIL: weeklies@flatoday.net. URL: http://www.floridatoday.com. Mailing Address: PO Box 419000, Melbourne, FL 32941-9000. Year Established: 1880. Pub. Frequency: w. (Wed.) Page Size: broadsheet Circulation: 24,000 per issue (free). **Owner(s):** Gannett Company, Inc., 7950 Jones Branch Dr., McLean, VA 22107-0001. Telephone: 703-854-6000. **Management:** Michael Coleman, Publisher. Nancy Solliday, Advertising Director. Cedric Johnson, Circulation Manager. **Editorial:** Susan Smiley-Hieght, Editor. Tom Palermo, Managing Editor. Debbie Roberts, Reporter.

TIMES (MELBOURNE), THE. One Gannett Plz., Melbourne, FL 32940-9000. Telephone: 321-242-3801. FAX: 321-242-6620. Mailing Address: PO Box 419000, Melbourne, FL 32941-9000. Year Established: 1894. Pub. Frequency: w. (Wed.) Page Size: broadsheet Circulation: 56,160 per issue (free). **Owner(s):** Gannett Company, Inc., 7950 Jones Branch Dr., McLean, VA 22107-0001. Telephone: 703-854-6000. **Management:** Michael J Coleman, Publisher. Nancy Solliday, Advertising Director. Cedric Johnson, Circulation Manager. **Editorial:** Tom Palermo, Managing Editor. Susan Smiley, Asst. Managing Ed..

MIAMI

MIAMI NEW TIMES. 2800 Biscayne Blvd., Miami, FL 33137. Telephone: 305-576-8000. FAX: 305-571-7677. URL: http://www.miaminewtimes.com. Mailing Address: PO Box 011591, Miami, FL 33101-1591. Year Established: 1987. Pub. Frequency: w. (Thu.) Page Size: tabloid Circulation: 105,000 per issue (free). **Owner(s):** Village Voice Media, Inc., 1201 E Jefferson St, Phoenix, AZ 85034. Telephone: 415-541-0700. FAX: 415-541-9096. **Management:** Derek Warriner, Advertising Manager. Julian Suardi, Circulation Director. Ladyane Lopez, Classified Adv. Mgr.. Michael Shavalies, Art Director. Ewald Fuchs, Associate Publisher. **Editorial:** Frank Houston, Associate Editor. Mosi Reeves, Music Editor.

MIAMI BEACH

SUN POST, THE. 1688 Meridian Ave., Ste. 200, Miami Beach, FL 33139. Telephone: 305-538-9700. FAX: 305-538-6077. Mailing Address: PO Box 19-1870, Miami Beach, FL 33119. Pub. Frequency: w. (Thu.) Page Size: tabloid. Subscrip. Rate: $150/yr mailed 1st class. Circulation: 35,000 per issue (controlled). **Owner(s):** Caxton Publishing Co., See address and contact information above. **Management:** Jeannette Stark, President. Andrew Stark, Publisher. Andrew Stock, Advertising Manager. **Editorial:** Erik Bojnansky, Editor.

MIAMI LAKES

MIAMI LAKER. 6843 Main St., Miami Lakes, FL 33014. Telephone: 305-821-1130. FAX: 305-817-4199. E-MAIL: miamilaker1@aol.com. Year Established: 1975. Pub. Frequency: s-m. (1st. & 3rd. Fri.) Page Size: tabloid. Circulation: 26,500 per issue (controlled). **Owner(s):** Graham Companies, The, See address and contact information above. **Management:** Gil Mendez, Sales Manager. **Editorial:** Roger Reece, Editor.

MILTON

SANTA ROSA FREE PRESS. ISSN 0273-5857
6629 Elva St., Milton, FL 32572. Telephone: 850-623-3616. FAX: 850-623-2007. Year Established: 1907. Pub. Frequency: s-w. (Wed. & Sat.) Page Size: broadsheet Circulation: 7,500 per issue (paid). **Owner(s):** Santa Rosa Press Gazette, See address and contact information above. **Management:** Michael Coulter, Publisher. Jim Martin, Advertising Manager. Tracie Smelstoys, Circulation Manager. Carol Barnes, Business Manager. **Editorial:** Jim Fletcher, Editor.

MONTICELLO

MONTICELLO NEWS. ISSN 0746-5297
180 W Washington St, Monticello, FL 32344. E-MAIL: monticellonews@embarqmail.com. Mailing Address: PO Box 428, Monticello, FL 32344. Year Established: 1869. Pub. Frequency: s-w. (Wed. & Fri.) Page Size: broadsheet. Subscrip. Rate: $.50 newsstand/cover; $45/yr in state; $52/yr out of state. Circulation: 3,000 per issue (paid). **Owner(s):** E C B Publishing Co., Inc., See address and contact information above. **Management:** Ron Cichon, President. Cliff Miller, Advertising. **Editorial:** Ray Cichon, Editor-in-Chief.

MT. DORA

EUSTIS LAKE REGION NEWS. 4645 Hwy. 19 A, Mt. Dora, FL 32757-2039. Telephone: 352-589-8811. FAX: 352-357-3202. Pub. Frequency: w. (Thu.) Page Size: broadsheet. Subscrip. Rate: $.25 newsstand/cover; $10.30/yr in county; $12.20/yr out of county. Circulation: 700 per issue (paid). **Owner(s):** Mid-Florida Sun Publications, See address and contact information above. **Management:** Cheryl Crisp, Publisher. Cindy Thibodeau, Advertising Manager. **Editorial:** Dixie Glessner, Editor.

PASCO NEWS. 4645 Hwy. 19 A, Mt. Dora, FL 32757-2039. Telephone: 352-589-8811. FAX: 352-357-3202. E-MAIL: owens@pasconews.com. URL: http://www.pasconews.com. Year Established: 1904. Pub. Frequency: w. (Thu.) Page Size: broadsheet. Subscrip. Rate: $.50 newsstand/cover; $18/yr in county; $23/yr out of county. Circulation: 6,000 per issue (paid). **Owner(s):** Mid-Florida Sun Publications, See address and contact information above. **Management:** J W Owens, Publisher. Joanna Hinson, Advertising Manager. John Hinson, Circulation Manager. **Editorial:** Joe Potter, Editor.

TAVARES CITIZEN. 4645 Hwy. 19-A, Mt. Dora, FL 32757. FAX: 352-357-3202. Year Established: 1882. Pub. Frequency: w. (Thu.) Page Size: broadsheet. Subscrip. Rate: $.25 newsstand/cover; $10.30/yr in county; $12.20/yr out of county. Freelance Pay: $20/story. Circulation: 2,000 per issue (controlled and free). **Owner(s):** Mid-Florida Sun Publications, See address and contact information above. **Management:** Cheryl Crisp, Publisher. **Editorial:** Dixie Glessner, Editor.

MULBERRY

POLK COUNTY PRESS. 1020 N. Church Ave., Hwy. 37-N., Mulberry, FL 33860. Telephone: 863-425-3411. E-MAIL: mulberrypress@juno.com. Year Established: 1909. Pub. Frequency: w. (Wed.) Page Size: broadsheet. Subscrip. Rate: $.50 newsstand/cover; $25/yr in county. Adv. Rate: col. inch $9 Circulation: 6,000 per issue (paid). **Owner(s):** Histed Media Group, See address and contact information above. **Management:** William M Histed, President. **Editorial:** William M Histed, Editor.

NEW PORT RICHEY

SUN COAST NEWS. 6214 US Hwy. 19, New Port Richey, FL 34652. Telephone: 727-815-1000. FAX: 727-847-2902. E-MAIL: neckard@suncoastnews.com. Mailing Address: PO Box 785, New Port Richey, FL 34652. Pub. Frequency: s-w. (Wed. & Sat.) Page Size: tabloid. Subscrip. Rate: $5.30 mailed/mo.; $53.60/yr mailed Wed & Sat. Circulation: 136,675 per issue (paid and free). **Owner(s):** Media General, Inc., 333 E. Franklin St., Richmond, VA 23219. Telephone: 804-649-6000. FAX: 804-649-6898. **Management:** Rosemary Curtiss, General Manager. Nancy Eckard, Advertising Manager. Tom Manzak, Circulation Manager. Tim Smolarick, Classified Adv. Mgr.. **Editorial:** John Tischner, Managing Editor.

NEW SMYRNA BEACH

EDGE, THE (NEW SMYRNA BEACH). 823 S. Dixie Fwy., New Smyrna Beach, FL 32168. Telephone: 386-427-1000. FAX: 386-424-9858. URL: http://www.nsb-observer.com. Mailing Address: PO Box 10, New Smyrna Beach, FL 32170. Pub. Frequency: w. (Thu.) Page Size: broadsheet Circulation: 8,700 per issue (free). **Owner(s):** Horizon Publications, Inc., 1120 N. Carbon St, Ste 100, Marion, IL 62959. **Management:** Philip Jackson, Publisher. John Haglof, Circulation Manager.

SMYRNA BREEZE, THE. 823 S. Dixie Fwy., New Smyrna Beach, FL 32168. Telephone: 386-427-1000. FAX: 386-424-9858. URL: http://www.nsb-observer.com. Mailing Address: PO Box 10, New Smyrna Beach, FL 32170. Pub. Frequency: w. (Tue.) Page Size: broadsheet.Adv. Rate: col. inch $7.15 Circulation: 10,000 per issue (free). **Owner(s):** Horizon Publications, Inc., 1120 N. Carbon St, Ste 100, Marion, IL 62959. **Management:** Philip Jackson, Publisher. John Haglof, Circulation Manager.

NICEVILLE

BAY BEACON, THE. 1181 E. John Sims Pkwy., Niceville, FL 32578-2752. Telephone: 850-678-1080. FAX: 850-729-3225. E-MAIL: info@baybeacon.com. URL: tp://www.baybeacon.com. Year Established: 1992. Pub. Frequency: w. (Wed.) Page Size: broadsheet. Subscrip. Rate: $.50 newsstand/cover per issue; $104/yr mailed. Adv. Rate: col. inch $11.75 Freelance Pay: $25/article. Circulation: 15,500 per issue (paid and free). **Owner(s):** Stephen W. Kent, See address and contact information above. **Management:** Stephen W. Kent, Publisher. Sara Kent, Advertising Manager. **Editorial:** Stephen W. Kent, Editor-in-Chief.

ORANGE PARK

CLAY TODAY. 1564 Kingsley Ave., Orange Park, FL 32073. Telephone: 904-264-3200. FAX: 904-269-6958. E-MAIL: jlclay@jax-inter.net. Year Established: 1950. Pub. Frequency: w. (Thu.) Page Size: tabloid. Subscrip. Rate: $.50 newsstand/cover; $24/yr; $45 for 2 yrs.. Circulation: 25,000 per issue (paid). **Owner(s):** Journal Community Publishing Group, 600 Industrial Dr., PO Box 609, Waupaca, WI 54981. Telephone: 715-258-8450. **Management:** Vincent Grassia, General Manager. Jon Cantrell, Publisher. Leah Davis, Circulation Manager. Jaime Jadwin, Classified Editor. **Editorial:** Bob Henderson, Managing Editor. Bette Jadwin, Production Manager. Bill Austin, News Editor.

ORLANDO

ORLANDO WEEKLY, THE. 111 W. Livingston, Orlando, FL 32801. Telephone: 407-377-0400. FAX: 407-377-0420. URL: http://www.orlandoweekly.com. Year Established: 1990. Pub. Frequency: w. (Thu.) Page Size: tabloid. Subscrip. Rate: $65/yr. Circulation: 50,000 per issue (paid and controlled). **Owner(s):** Times-Shamrock Communications, 149 Penn Ave,, Scranton, PA 18503. Telephone: 570-348-7287. **Management:** Rick Schreiber, Publisher. Graham Jarrett, Advertising Director. John Prinzo, Circulation Manager. Brian Martin, Classified Editor. **Editorial:** Bob Whitby, Editor. Lindy Shepherd, Managing Editor. Jason Ferguson, Music Editor.

WORLD (BARRE), THE. 460 N Orlando Ave, Ste 200, Orlando, FL 32789. Telephone: 407-628-4802. FAX: 407-628-7061. E-MAIL: sales@vt-world.com. URL: http://www.vt-world.com. Year Established: 1972. Pub. Frequency: w. (Wed.) Page Size: tabloid Circulation: 28,000 per issue (free). **Owner(s):** Bonnier Corp., See address and contact information above.

ORMOND BEACH

DAYTONA PENNYSAVER. 454 S. Yonge St., Ormond Beach, FL 32174. Telephone: 386-677-4262. FAX: 386-672-7453. URL: http://www.floridapennysavers.com. Mailing Address: PO Box 67, Ormond Beach, FL 32175. Year Established: 1976. Pub. Frequency: w. (Wed.) Page Size: tabloid Circulation: 75,000 per issue (free). **Owner(s):** News-Journal Corp., 901 Sixth St., Daytona Beach, FL 32117-8099. Telephone: 904-252-1511. **Management:** Leonard Marsh, General Manager. Toni Maddux, Advertising Director. Jeff Hull, Circulation Director. Kelli Hull, Business Manager.

OVIEDO

OVIEDO VOICE, THE. 1401 W. Broadway, Oviedo, FL 32765. Telephone: 407-366-9181. FAX: 407-366-7580. E-MAIL: editor@theoviedovoice.com. URL: http://www.theoviedovoice.com. Year Established: 1992. Pub. Frequency: w. (Thu.) Page Size: broadsheet. Subscrip. Rate: $.35 newsstand/cover; $24.80/yr mailed. Adv. Rate: col. inch $7 Freelance Pay: $1-$1.75/column-inch. Circulation: 4,000 per issue (paid). **Owner(s):** Investment Holdings LLC, See address and contact information above. **Management:** Zachary Warrner, Publisher. **Editorial:** Zachary Warrner, Executive Editor.

WINTER SPRING VOICE. 1401 W. Broadway, Oviedo, FL 32765. Telephone: 407-366-9181. FAX: 407-366-7580. E-MAIL: oviedovoice@mpinet.net. URL: http://www.theoviedovoice.com. Year Established: 1998. Pub. Frequency: w. (Thu.) Page Size: broadsheet. Subscrip. Rate: $24.80/yr mailed. Adv. Rate: col. inch $7 Freelance Pay: $1.50/column-inch. Circulation: 4,000 per issue (free). **Owner(s):** Investment Holdings LLC, See address and contact information above. **Management:** Zachary Warrner, Publisher. **Editorial:** Zachary Warrner, Executive Editor.

Weeklies

PALM COAST

FLAGLER/PALM COAST NEWS TRIBUNE, THE. 2 McCormick Dr., Palm Coast, FL 32164. Telephone: 386-437-2491. FAX: 386-437-0139. Year Established: 1981. Pub. Frequency: s-w. (Wed. & Sat.) Page Size: broadsheet. Subscrip. Rate: $.35 newsstand/cover; $16.70/yr carrier delivery; $36.40/yr mailed. Circulation: 10,000 per issue (paid). **Owner(s):** News-Journal Corp., 901 Sixth St., Daytona Beach, FL 32117. Telephone: 386-252-1511. FAX: 386-258-8465. **Management:** Georgia Kaney, Publisher. Lisa Gardner, Advertising. Doug Davis, Circulation Director. Guy Beasley, Classified Adv. Mgr.. **Editorial:** Ron Hurtibise, Editor. Donald Lindley, Executive Editor.

PENSACOLA

ESCAMBIA SUN PRESS. PO Box 4625, Pensacola, FL 32507. Telephone: 850-456-3121. FAX: 850-456-0103. Year Established: 1948. Pub. Frequency: w. (Thu.) Page Size: broadsheet. Subscrip. Rate: $.25 newsstand/cover; $17.20/yr in county; $22.57/yr out of county (effective 2005); $27.95/yr out of state. Circulation: 3,500 per issue (paid). **Owner(s):** Michael Driver, See address and contact information above. **Management:** Michael Driver, Publisher. Denise Turner, Office Manager. **Editorial:** Michael Driver, Editor.

MULLET WRAPPER. PO Box 34403, Pensacola, FL 32507. Telephone: 850-492-5221. FAX: 251-975-6397. Year Established: 1985. Pub. Frequency: bi-w. (Wed.) Page Size: tabloid Circulation: 10,000 per issue (free). **Owner(s):** Gulf Breeze Publishing Co., See address and contact information above. **Management:** Fran Thompson, Publisher. **Editorial:** Fran Thompson, Editor.

PELICAN, THE. 101 E. Romana St., Pensacola, FL 32502. Telephone: 850-232-3127. FAX: 850-469-8216. E-MAIL: news@thepelicanonline.com. URL: http://www.thepelicanonline.com. Mailing Address: PO Box 2470, Orange Beach, AL 36561. Pub. Frequency: w. (Fri.) Page Size: tabloid Circulation: 15,400 per issue (free). **Owner(s):** Gannett Company, Inc., 7950 Jones Branch Dr., McLean, VA 22107-0001. Telephone: 703-854-6000. **Management:** Nigel Allen, General Manager. Mo Osborn, Publisher. Kim Roegner, Advertising Manager.

PENSACOLA VOICE. 213 E. Yonge St., Pensacola, FL 32503. Telephone: 850-434-6963. FAX: 850-469-8745. E-MAIL: info@pensacolavoic.com. URL: http://www.pensacolavoice.com. Year Established: 1965. Pub. Frequency: w. (Thu.) Page Size: broadsheet. Subscrip. Rate: $.50 newsstand/cover; $20/yr carrier delivery. Adv. Rate: col. inch $19.20 Circulation: 10,000 per issue (paid). **Owner(s):** Jacqueline Miles Williams, See address and contact information above. **Management:** Jacqueline Miles Williams, Publisher. Jacqueline Miles, Advertising Manager. **Editorial:** LaDonna Williams, Editor. Marni Woodson, Associate Editor. LaDonna Spivey, Consulting Editor.

SHOPPER (PENSACOLA), THE. 3041 E. Olive Rd., Pensacola, FL 32514. Telephone: 850-478-3813. FAX: 850-478-2222. Year Established: 1975. Pub. Frequency: s-w. (Tue. & Fri.) Page Size: tabloid.Subscrip. Rate: $.75 newsstand/cover Circulation: 65,000 per issue (paid). **Owner(s):** Susan Thibodeaux, See address and contact information above. **Editorial:** Susan Thibodeaux, Editor.

PERRY

PERRY NEWS-HERALD. ISSN 0747-0967
123 N. Jefferson, Perry, FL 32347. Telephone: 850-584-5513. FAX: 850-838-1566. E-MAIL: perrynews@perry.gulfnet.com. Mailing Address: PO Box 888, Perry, FL 32348. Year Established: 1887. Pub. Frequency: w. (Fri.) Page Size: broadsheet. Subscrip. Rate: $.50 newsstand/cover; $35/yr mailed in county; $49/yr mailed out of county. Circulation: 5,100 per issue (paid). **Owner(s):** Perry Newspapers, Inc., See address and contact information above. **Management:** Don Lincoln, Publisher. Beth Mann, Advertising Manager. Richard Fletcher, Circulation Manager. **Editorial:** Susan Lincoln, Managing Editor.

PERRY TACO TIMES. ISSN 0747-2358
123 N. Jefferson, Perry, FL 32347. Telephone: 850-584-5513. FAX: 850-838-1566. E-MAIL: perrynews@perry.gulfnet.com. Mailing Address: PO Box 888, Perry, FL 32348. Year Established: 1962. Pub. Frequency: w. (Wed.) Page Size: standard. Subscrip. Rate: $.50 newsstand/cover; $35/yr mailed in county; $49/yr mailed out of county. Circulation: 5,100 per issue (paid). **Owner(s):** Perry Newspapers, Inc., See address and contact information above. **Management:** Don Lincoln, Publisher. Beth Mann, Advertising Manager. Richard Fletcher, Circulation Manager. **Editorial:** Susan Lincoln, Managing Editor.

PLANT CITY

COURIER (PLANT CITY), THE. 101 N. Wheeler St., Plant City, FL 33563-5455. Telephone: 813-752-3113. FAX: 813-865-4449. E-MAIL: kbrady@mediageneral.com. Year Established: 1884. Pub. Frequency: w. (Thu.) Page Size: tabloid. Subscrip. Rate: $25/yr mailed. Circulation: 11,300 per issue (paid and free). **Owner(s):** Media General, Inc., 333 E. Franklin St., Richmond, VA 23219. Telephone: 804-649-6000. **Management:** Carla Floyd, General Manager. Josephine Frisco, Circulation Manager. **Editorial:** Kevin Brady, Editor.

PLANT CITY SHOPPER. 101 N. Wheeler St., Plant City, FL 33563-5455. Telephone: 813-752-3113. FAX: 813-865-4449. E-MAIL: tmarrero@mediageneral.com. Year Established: 1946. Pub. Frequency: w. (Wed.) Page Size: tabloid Circulation: 26,800 per issue (free). **Owner(s):** Media General, Inc., 333 E. Franklin St., Richmond, VA 23219-2800. Telephone: 804-649-6000. FAX: 804-649-6898. **Management:** Carla Floyd, Publisher. Melissa Poage, Advertising Manager. **Editorial:** Tony Marrero, Editor.

POMPANO BEACH

BOCA TIMES, THE. 1701 Green Rd., Ste. B, Pompano Beach, FL 33064. Telephone: 954-698-6397. FAX: 954-429-1207. Mailing Address: P.O. Box 1189, Deerfield Beach, FL 33432. Pub. Frequency: w. (Wed.) Page Size: tabloid Circulation: 41,600 per issue (free). **Owner(s):** Tribune Company, 435 N Michigan Ave, Chicago, IL 60601. Telephone: 312.222.9100. **Management:** Mickie Caruso, Advertising Manager. Ed Wilder, Circulation Director. Lori York, Classified Adv. Mgr.. **Editorial:** Lisa Freed, Editor. Pamela Doto, Executive Editor.

BOYNTON TIMES, THE. 1701 Green Rd., Ste. B, Pompano Beach, FL 33064. Telephone: 954-698-6397. FAX: 954-429-1207. Mailing Address: P.O. Box 1189, Deerfield Beach, FL 33432. Pub. Frequency: w. (Wed.) Page Size: tabloid Circulation: 36,150 per issue (free). **Owner(s):** Tribune Company, 435 N Michigan Ave, Chicago, IL 60601. Telephone: 312.222.9100. **Management:** Keri Lurtz, Advertising Manager. Olga Lorimer, Classified Adv. Mgr.. **Editorial:** Tracy Kolody, Editor. Pamela Doto, Executive Editor. Rick Menning, Sports.

DEERFIELD TIMES, THE. 1701 Green Rd., Ste. B, Pompano Beach, FL 33064. Telephone: 954-698-6397. FAX: 954-429-1207. Mailing Address: P.O. Box 1189, Deerfield Beach, FL 33432. Pub. Frequency: w. (Thu.) Page Size: tabloid.Adv. Rate: col. inch $26.35 Circulation: 18,500 per issue (paid and controlled). **Owner(s):** Tribune Company, 435 N Michigan Ave, Chicago, IL 60601. Telephone: 312.222.9100. **Management:** Suzanne Gallagher, Advertising Manager. Ed Wilder, Circulation Manager. Tony Digregoiro, Classified Adv. Mgr.. **Editorial:** David Rush, Editor. Pamela Doto, Executive Editor.

DELRAY TIMES, THE. 1701 Green Rd., Ste. B, Pompano Beach, FL 33064. Telephone: 954-698-6397. FAX: 954-429-1207. Mailing Address: P.O. Box 1189, Deerfield Beach, FL 33432. Year Established: 2002. Pub. Frequency: w. (Wed.) Page Size: tabloid Circulation: 29,425 per issue (free). **Owner(s):** Tribune Company, 435 N Michigan Ave, Chicago, IL 60601. Telephone: 312.222.9100. **Management:** Barey Shrier, Advertising Manager. Ed Wilder, Circulation Director. Olga Lorimer, Classified Adv. Mgr.. **Editorial:** Tracy Kolody, Editor. Pamela Doto, Executive Editor. Rick Menning, Sports.

EASTSIDER. 1701 Green Rd., Ste. B, Pompano Beach, FL 33064. Telephone: 954-698-6397. FAX: 954-429-1207. Mailing Address: P.O. Box 1189, Deerfield Beach, FL 33432. Pub. Frequency: w. (Thu.) Page Size: tabloid Circulation: 29,900 per issue (free). **Owner(s):** Tribune Company, 435 N Michigan Ave, Chicago, IL 60601. Telephone: 312.222.9100. **Management:** Barey Shrier, Advertising Manager. Ed Wilder, Circulation Director. **Editorial:** Colleen Webb, Editor. Pamela Doto, Executive Editor.

FT. LAUDERDALE EASTSIDER, THE. 1701 Green Rd., Ste. B, Pompano Beach, FL 33064. Telephone: 954-698-6397. FAX: 954-480-8426. Pub. Frequency: w. (Thu.) Page Size: tabloid Circulation: 30,875 per issue (free). **Owner(s):** Forum Publishing Group, See address and contact information above. **Management:** Suzanne Gallagher, Publisher. Ed Wilder, Circulation Director. Mickie Carusos, Classified Adv. Mgr..

HI-RISER. ISSN 0191-7153
1701 Green Rd., Ste. B, Pompano Beach, FL 33064. Telephone: 954-698-6397. FAX: 954-429-1207. Year Established: 1967. Pub. Frequency: w. (Thu.) Page Size: tabloid. Freelance Pay: $35/story. Circulation: 17,800 per issue (free). **Owner(s):** Tribune Company, 435 N Michigan Ave, Chicago, IL 60601. Telephone: 312.222.9100. **Management:** Barey Shrier, Advertising Manager. Ed Wilder, Circulation Manager. **Editorial:** Robin Shear, Editor. Pamelo Doto, Executive Editor.

POMPANO TIMES, THE. 1701 Green Rd., Ste. B, Pompano Beach, FL 33064. Telephone: 954-698-6397. FAX: 954-429-1207. Pub. Frequency: w. (Thu.) Page Size: tabloid Circulation: 20,000 per issue (free). **Owner(s):** Tribune Company, 435 N Michigan Ave, Chicago, IL 60601. Telephone: 312.222.9100. **Management:** Barey Shrier, Advertising Manager. Ed Wilder, Circulation Director. **Editorial:** Tom Turner, Editor. Pamela Doto, Executive Editor. Rick Menning, Sports.

SENTRY, THE. 2500 S.E. Fifth Ct., Pompano Beach, FL 33062-6106. Telephone: 954-532-2000. E-MAIL: editor@flsentry.com. URL: http://www.flsentry.com. Year Established: 1980. Pub. Frequency: w. (Thu.) Page Size: broadsheet. Subscrip. Rate: $.25 newsstand/cover; $13.78/yr mailed. Adv. Rate: col. inch $12.95 **Wire Service(s):** AP. Circulation: 55,000 per issue (paid and free). **Owner(s):** Benita V. Rosin, See address and contact information above. **Management:** Karen M. Foley, Publisher. **Editorial:** Ross Shaulmister, Managing Editor.

WEST BOCA TIMES, THE. 1701 Green Rd., Ste. B, Pompano Beach, FL 33064. Telephone: 954-698-6397. FAX: 954-429-1207. Pub. Frequency: w. (Wed.) Page Size: tabloid Circulation: 33,625 per issue (free). **Owner(s):** Tribune Company, 435 N Michigan Ave, Chicago, IL 60601. Telephone: 312.222.9100. **Management:** Barey Shrier, Advertising Manager. Ed Wilder, Circulation Director. **Editorial:** Lisa Freed, Editor. Pamela Doto, Executive Editor. Rick Menning, Sports.

QUINCY

GADSDEN COUNTY TIMES. 15 S. Madison St., Quincy, FL 32351. Telephone: 850-627-7649. FAX: 850-627-7191. E-MAIL: editor@gadcotimes.com. URL: http://www.gadcotimes.com. Year Established: 1901. Pub. Frequency: w. (Thu.) Page Size: broadsheet. Subscrip. Rate: $.50 newsstand/cover; $26/yr mailed in county; $30/yr mailed out of county. Adv. Rate: col. inch $8 Circulation: 5,200 per issue (paid and free). **Owner(s):** Gemini Newspapers Inc, 260 Willow St., Port St. Joe, FL 32456. **Management:** Ronald Isbell, Publisher. **Editorial:** Alice Dupont, Editor. Byron Spires, Writer.Readers: 60% African-American, 12% Latino, 28% White Deadline: Ads-Thu., 5:00 pm. - Display ads for proof, legals, classified, community news, obits. Fri. 5:00 pm - Display ads camera ready or non-proof.; Features-Mon., 5:00 pm; News-Mon., 5:00 pm; Photo-Mon., 5:00 pm

ROYAL PALM BEACH

OBSERVER (ROYAL PALM BEACH), THE. 240 Royal Palm Beach Blvd., Royal Palm Beach, FL 33411. Telephone: 561-791-9687. FAX: 561-791-9690. E-MAIL: news@observer-news.com. Year Established: 1992. Pub. Frequency: w. (Fri.) Page Size: tabloid Circulation: 20,000 per issue (free). **Owner(s):** Bruce H. & Mark J. Easton, See address and contact information above. **Management:** Bruce H. Easton, Publisher. **Editorial:** Lynda Dematteo, Assistant Editor.

RUSKIN

OBSERVER NEWS, THE. 210 Woodland Estates Ave., Ruskin, FL 33570. Telephone: 813-645-4048. FAX: 813-645-1792. E-MAIL: news@observernews.net. URL: http://www.observernews.net. Year Established: 1958. Pub. Frequency: w. (Thu.) Page Size: tabloid. Subscrip. Rate: $36/yr mailed. Adv. Rate: col. inch $22.25 Circulation: 39,000 per issue (paid and free). **Owner(s):** M & M Printing Co., Inc., See address and contact information above. **Management:** Stephen Mixon, President. Brenda Knowles, Publisher. **Editorial:** Brenda Knowles, Editor.

SOUTH SHORE NEWS. 3036 College Ave., Ruskin, FL 33570. E-MAIL: southshorenews@mediageneral.com. Year Established: 1981. Pub. Frequency: w. (Wed.) Page Size: tabloid Circulation: 16,000 per issue (free). **Owner(s):** Media General, Inc., 333 E. Franklin St., Richmond, VA 23219. Telephone: 804-649-6000. FAX: 804-649-6898. **Management:** Tami Donaldson, Advertising Manager.

SUN (RUSKIN), THE. 3036 College Ave., Ruskin, FL 33570. E-MAIL: southshorenews@mediageneral.com. Year Established: 1973. Pub. Frequency: w. (Wed.) Page Size: tabloid Circulation: 15,000 per issue (free). **Owner(s):** Media General, Inc., 333 E. Franklin St., Richmond, VA 23219. Telephone: 804-649-6000. FAX: 804-649-6898. **Management:** Carla Floyd, Publisher. Tami Donaldson, Advertising Manager. **Editorial:** Penny Fletcher, Editor.

SANFORD

SANFORD (FL) HERALD, THE. 300 N. French Ave., Sanford, FL 32771. Telephone: 407-322-2611. FAX: 407-323-9408. E-MAIL: dping@seminoleherald.com. URL: http://www.seminoleherald.com. Mailing Address: PO Box 1667, Sanford, FL 32772. Year Established: 1908. Pub. Frequency: s-w. (Wed. & Sun.) Page Size: standard. Subscrip. Rate: $.50 newsstand/cover; $36/yr in county; $42/yr out of county; $52/yr out of state. Adv. Rate: page $900 **Wire Service(s):** AP. Circulation: 6,000 Sunday (paid); 6,000 per issue (paid). **Owner(s):** Republic Newspapers Inc., 11863 Kingston Pike, Knoxville, TN 37922. Telephone: 423-675-6397. FAX: 423-675-0675. **Management:** Dan Ping, Publisher. Rozxie Lavendar, Advertising Director. Ed Kramarcik, Circulation Manager. **Editorial:** Dan Ping, Editor. Steve Paradis, Managing Editor. Tom Vincent, Photographer. Dean Smith, Sports Editor.

SANIBEL

CAPTIVA CURRENT. 2340 Periwinkle Way, Sanibel, FL 33957. FAX: 239-472-8398. E-MAIL: sancapnews@figuide.com. URL: http://www.flguide.com. Mailing Address: PO Box 809, Sanibel, FL 33957. Year Established: 1989. Pub. Frequency: w. (Fri.) Page Size: tabloid. Subscrip. Rate: $.50 newsstand/cover; $19.25/yr mailed in county; $25/yr mailed out of county. Circulation: 2,000 per issue (paid). **Owner(s):** Ogden Newspapers of Minnesota, Inc., 1500 Main St., Wheeling, WV 26003. Telephone: 304-233-0100. FAX: 304-233-0327. **Management:** Robin Calabrese, Publisher. **Editorial:** Renny Severance, Executive Editor.

ISLAND REPORTER. 2340 Periwinkle Way, Sanibel, FL 33957. Telephone: 239-472-1587. FAX: 239-472-8398. E-MAIL: sarcapnews@flguide.com. Mailing Address: PO Box 809, Sanibel, FL 33957. Year Established: 1973. Pub. Frequency: w. (Thu.) Page Size: tabloid. Subscrip. Rate: $.75 newsstand/cover; $25/yr in county; $31/yr mailed out of county. Circulation: 6,000 per issue (paid). **Owner(s):** Ogden Newspapers of Minnesota, Inc., 1500 Main St., Wheeling, WV 26003. Telephone: 304-233-0100. FAX: 304-233-0327. **Management:** Robin Calabrese, Group Publisher. Jack Glarrow, Publisher. Rich Martin, Advertising Manager. **Editorial:** Renny Severance, Editor.

SANIBEL-CAPTIVA ISLANDER. 695 Tarpon Bay Rd., Sanibel, FL 33957. Telephone: 239-472-5185. FAX: 239-472-1372. E-MAIL: islandnews@flguide.com. URL: http://www.breezenewspapers.com. Mailing Address: PO Box 56, Sanibel, FL 33957. Year Established: 1961. Pub. Frequency: w. (Fri.) Page Size: tabloid.Subscrip. Rate: $28/yr mailed Circulation: 12,000 per issue (paid). **Owner(s):** Ogden Newspapers of Minnesota, Inc., 1500 Main St., Wheeling, WV 26003. Telephone: 304-233-0100. **Management:** Terri Blackmore, General Manager. Robin Calabrese, Publisher. **Editorial:** Renny Severance, Editor.

SARASOTA

PELICAN PRESS. 5011 Ocean Blvd, Sarasota, FL 34242. Telephone: 941-349-4949. FAX: 941-346-7118. Year Established: 1971. Pub. Frequency: w. (Thu.) Page Size: tabloid. Freelance Pay: $30-$40/article. Circulation: 25,000 per issue (paid and free). **Owner(s):** Journal Community Publishing Group, 600 Industrial Dr., PO Box 609, Waupaca, WI 54981. Telephone: 715-258-8450. FAX: 715-258-4896. **Management:** Jay Kemp, General Manager. Karen Koblenz, Publisher. **Editorial:** Rachel Hackney, Editor. Anne Johnson, News Editor.

SEBASTIAN

SEBASTIAN SUN. 717 Coolidge St., Sebastian, FL 32958. Telephone: 772-978-2371. FAX: 772-978-2366. URL: http://www.sebastiansun.com. Mailing Address: PO Box 1268, Vero Beach, FL 32961. Year Established: 1980. Pub. Frequency: w. (Fri.) Page Size: tabloid Circulation: 14,500 per issue (free). **Owner(s):** E.W. Scripps Co., 312 Walnut St., 28th Fl., Cincinnati, OH 45202. Telephone: 513-977-3000. **Editorial:** Kathrine Bauman, Editor. Larry Reisman, Executive Editor.

SEBRING

NEWS SUN. ISSN 0163-3988
2227 US 27 S, Sebring, FL 33870. Telephone: 863-465-0426. FAX: 863-385-1954. E-MAIL: editor@newssun.com. URL: http://www.newssun.com. Year Established: 1927. Pub. Frequency: 3/w. (Wed., Fri., Sun.) Page Size: broadsheet. Subscrip. Rate: $.50 per issue Wed. & Fri.; $.75 newsstand/cover Sun.; $50.83/yr carrier delivery in area; $78/yr mailed in state; $78/yr mailed out of state. **Wire Service(s):** NYT. Circulation: 18,000 Sunday (paid); 17,000 per issue (paid). **Owner(s):** HarborPoint Media, LLC, 125 Basin St., Ste. 200, Daytona Beach, FL 32114. Telephone: 386-252-9921. FAX: 386-252-9925. **Management:** "Chip" Wigginton, Publisher. Vickie Jones, Advertising. Craig Sutter, Production Director. **Editorial:** Romona Washington, Editor.

SEMINOLE

BELLAIR BEE. 9911 Seminole Blvd., Seminole, FL 33772. Telephone: 727-397-5563. FAX: 727-397-5900. E-MAIL: dautrey@tbnweekly.com. URL: http://www.tbnweekly.com. Year Established: 1976. Pub. Frequency: w. (Thu.) Page Size: tabloid.Adv. Rate: col. inch $12.85 Circulation: 14,000 per issue (free). **Owner(s):** Times Publishing Co., 490 First Ave., S., St. Petersburg, FL 33701-1121. Telephone: 727-893-8111. FAX: 727-892-2328. **Management:** Dan Autrey, Publisher. Jay Rey, Advertising Manager. Shelly Fournier, Classified Adv. Mgr.. **Editorial:** Chary Southmayd, Editor. Tom Germond, Executive Editor.Readers: Adults

CLEARWATER CITIZEN. 9911 Seminole Blvd., Seminole, FL 33772. Telephone: 727-397-5563. FAX: 727-397-5900. E-MAIL: dautrey@tbnweekly.com. URL: http://www.tbnweekly.com. Pub. Frequency: w. (Fri.) Page Size: tabloid. Subscrip. Rate: $100/yr mailed 1st class. Adv. Rate: col. inch $12.85 Circulation: 25,000 per issue (free). **Owner(s):** Times Publishing Co., 490 First Ave., S., St. Petersburg, FL 33701-1121. Telephone: 727-893-8111. FAX: 727-892-2328. **Management:** Dan Autrey, Publisher. Jay Rey, Advertising Manager. Shelly Fournier, Classified Adv. Mgr.. **Editorial:** Tom Germond, Executive Editor.Readers: Adults

LARGO LEADER. 9911 Seminole Blvd., Seminole, FL 33772. Telephone: 727-397-5563. FAX: 727-397-5900. E-MAIL: dautrey@tbnweekly.com. URL: http:www.tbnweekly.com. Year Established: 1977. Pub. Frequency: w. (Thu.) Page Size: tabloid.Adv. Rate: col. inch $12.85 Circulation: 25,000 per issue (free). **Owner(s):** Times Publishing Co., 490 First Ave., S., St. Petersburg, FL 33701-1121. Telephone: 727-893-8111. FAX: 727-892-2328. **Management:** Dan Autrey, Publisher. Jay Rey, Advertising Manager. Shelly Fournier, Classified Adv. Mgr.. **Editorial:** Jim Harrington, Editor. Tom Germond, Executive Editor.Readers: Adults

SEMINOLE BEACON. 9911 Seminole Blvd., Seminole, FL 33772. Telephone: 727-397-5563. FAX: 727-397-5900. E-MAIL: tbnpub@hotmail.com. URL: http://www.tbnweekly.com. Year Established: 1978. Pub. Frequency: w. (Thu.) Page Size: tabloid.Adv. Rate: col. inch $12.85 Circulation: 40,000 per issue (free). **Owner(s):** Times Publishing Co., 490 First Ave., S., St. Petersburg, FL 33701-1121. Telephone: 727-893-8111. **Management:** Dan Autrey, Publisher. Jay Rey, Advertising Manager. Shelly Fournier, Classified Adv. Mgr.. **Editorial:** Tom Germond, Executive Editor.Readers: Adults

SOUTH MIAMI

AVENTURA NEWS. 6796 S.W. 62 Ave, South Miami, FL 33143. Telephone: 305-669-7355. FAX: 305-661-0954. E-MAIL: cnews@gate.net. URL: http://www.communitynewspapers.com. Pub. Frequency: w. (Wed.) Page Size: tabloid. **Wire Service(s):** AP. Circulation: 15,000 per issue (free). **Owner(s):** Miami's Community Newspapers, See address and contact information above. **Management:** Grant Miller, Publisher. Georgia Tate, Advertising Manager. **Editorial:** Ron Beasley, Editor. Michael Miller, Executive Editor.

BISCAYNE BAY TRIBUNE. 6796 S.W. 62 Ave, South Miami, FL 33143. Telephone: 305-669-7355. FAX: 305-661-0954. E-MAIL: cnews@gate.net. URL: http://www.communitynewspapers.com. Pub. Frequency: w. (Tue.) Page Size: tabloid Circulation: 10,000 per issue (free). **Owner(s):** Miami's Community Newspapers, See address and contact information above. **Management:** Grant Miller, Publisher. Georgia Tate, Advertising Manager. **Editorial:** Ron Beasley, Editor. Michael Miller, Executive Editor.

COMMUNITY NEWSPAPER, THE. 6796 S.W. 62 Ave, South Miami, FL 33143. Telephone: 305-669-7355. FAX: 305-661-0954. E-MAIL: cnews@gate.net. URL: http://www.communitynewspapers.com. Year Established: 1958. Pub. Frequency: w. (Mon.) Page Size: tabloid. **Wire Service(s):** UPI. Circulation: 15,000 per issue (free). **Owner(s):** Miami's Community Newspapers, See address and contact information above. **Management:** Grant Miller, Publisher. Georgia Tate, Advertising Manager. **Editorial:** Ron Beasley, Editor. Michael Miller, Executive Editor.

CORAL GABLES NEWS. 6796 S.W. 62 Ave, South Miami, FL 33143. Telephone: 305-669-7355. FAX: 305-661-0954. E-MAIL: cnews@gate.net. URL: http://www.communitynewspapers.com. Year Established: 1958. Pub. Frequency: w. (Thu.) Page Size: tabloid. **Wire Service(s):** UPI. Circulation: 7,000 per issue (controlled and free). **Owner(s):** Miami's Community Newspapers, See address and contact information above. **Management:** Grant Miller, Publisher. Georgia Tate, Advertising Manager. **Editorial:** Ron Beasley, Editor. Michael Miller, Executive Editor.

DORAL TRIBUNE, THE. 6796 S.W. 62 Ave, South Miami, FL 33143. Telephone: 305-669-7355. FAX: 305-661-0954. E-MAIL: cnews@gate.net. URL: http://www.communitynewspapers.com. Year Established: 1965. Pub. Frequency: m. Page Size: tabloid. **Wire Service(s):** UPI. Circulation: 10,000 per issue (free). **Owner(s):** Miami's Community Newspapers, See address and contact information above. **Management:** Grant Miller, Publisher. Georgia Tate, Advertising Manager. **Editorial:** Ron Beasley, Editor. Michael Miller, Executive Editor.

DOWNTOWN NEWS. 6796 S.W. 62 Ave, South Miami, FL 33143. Telephone: 305-669-7355. FAX: 305-661-0954. E-MAIL: cnews@gate.net. URL: http://www.communitynewspapers.com. Year Established: 1958. Pub. Frequency: w. (Mon.) Page Size: tabloid. **Wire Service(s):** AP. Circulation: 4,500 per issue (free). **Owner(s):** Miami's Community Newspapers, See address and contact information above. **Management:** Grant Miller, Publisher. Georgia Tate, Advertising Manager. **Editorial:** Ron Beasley, Editor. Michael Miller, Executive Editor.

HOMESTEAD NEWS. 6796 S.W. 62 Ave, South Miami, FL 33143. Telephone: 305-669-7355. FAX: 305-661-0954. E-MAIL: mmiller@community news.com. URL: http://www.communitynewspapers.com. Year Established: 1958. Pub. Frequency: w. (Wed.) Page Size: tabloid. Subscrip. Rate: $27.50/yr in county. **Wire Service(s):** AP. Circulation: 15,000 per issue (free). **Owner(s):** Miami's Community Newspapers, See address and contact information above. **Management:** Grant Miller, Publisher. Georgia Tate, Advertising Manager. **Editorial:** Ron Beasley, Editor. Michael Miller, Executive Editor.

KENDALL GAZETTE. 6796 S.W. 62 Ave, South Miami, FL 33143. Telephone: 305-669-7355. FAX: 305-661-0954. E-MAIL: cnews@gate.net. URL: http://www.communitynewspapers.com. Year Established: 1958. Pub. Frequency: w. (Tue.) Page Size: tabloid. **Wire Service(s):** UPI. Circulation: 15,000 per issue (free). **Owner(s):** Miami's Community Newspapers, See address and contact information above. **Management:** Grant Miller, Publisher. Georgia Tate, Advertising Manager. **Editorial:** Ron Beasley, Editor. Michael Miller, Executive Editor.

SUNNY ISLES BEACH SUN. 6796 S.W. 62 Ave, South Miami, FL 33143. Telephone: 305-669-7355. FAX: 305-661-0954. E-MAIL: cnews@gate.net. URL: http://www.communitynewspapers.com. Pub. Frequency: bi-w. (Mon.) Page Size: tabloid Circulation: 8,000 per issue (free). **Owner(s):** Miami's Community Newspapers, See address and contact information above. **Management:** Grant Miller, Publisher. Georgia Tate, Advertising Manager. **Editorial:** Ron Beasley, Editor. Michael Miller, Executive Editor.

ST. PETERSBURG

WEEKLY CHALLENGER. 2500 Martin Luther King S., St. Petersburg, FL 33705. Telephone: 727-896-2922. FAX: 727-823-2568. E-MAIL: tchallen@tampabay.rr.com. Year Established: 1967. Pub. Frequency: w. (Thu.) Page Size: broadsheet. Subscrip. Rate: $.25 newsstand/cover; $30/yr in state. Circulation: 45,000 per issue (paid). **Owner(s):** Ethel Johnson, See address and contact information above. **Management:** Lootha Cleveland, General Manager. Ethel Johnson, President.

STARKE

BRADFORD COUNTY TELEGRAPH. P.O. Drawer A, Starke, FL 32091. Telephone: 904-964-6305. FAX: 904-964-8628. E-MAIL: editor@bctelegraph.com. URL: http://www.bctelegraph.com. Year Established: 1879. Pub. Frequency: w. (Thu.) Page Size: broadsheet. Subscrip. Rate: $.50 newsstand/cover; $30/yr in county; $30/yr out of county. Circulation: 10,400 per issue (paid). **Owner(s):** John M. Miller, See address and contact information above. **Management:** John M. Miller, Publisher. Melanie Ellington, Classified Adv. Mgr.. John M. Miller, Sales Manager. **Editorial:** Marcia Miller, Editor.

TAMPA

CARROLLWOOD NEWS. Thompson Ctr., 5501 W. Waters Ave., Ste. 404, Tampa, FL 33634-2800. Telephone: 813-865-1515. FAX: 813-689-9545. Year Established: 1980. Pub. Frequency: w. (Wed.) Page Size: tabloid Circulation: 44,700 per issue (free). **Owner(s):** Media General, Inc., 333 E. Franklin St., Richmond, VA 23219. Telephone: 804-649-6000. FAX: 804-649-6898. **Management:** Carla Floyd, Publisher. Ann Drake, Advertising Manager. Josephine Frisco, Circulation Manager. **Editorial:** Sherri Lonon, Editor.

FREE PRESS (TAMPA), THE. 1010 W. Cass St, Tampa, FL 33606. Telephone: 813-254-5888. FAX: 813-251-0511. Mailing Address: PO Box 1333, Tampa, FL 33681. Year Established: 1911. Pub. Frequency: w. (Sat.) Page Size: standard.Subscrip. Rate: $.25 newsstand/cover; $15/yr Circulation: 1,100 per issue (paid). **Owner(s):** Free Press Publishing Co., See address and contact information above. **Management:** John N. Harrison IV, Owner.

SOUTH TAMPA NEWS. 3251 Bay to Bay Blvd., Tampa, FL 33629. Telephone: 813-835-2113. FAX: 813-831-4686. E-MAIL: hvalentine@mediageneral.com. Year Established: 1994. Pub. Frequency: w. (Wed.) Page Size: tabloid Circulation: 32,000 per issue (free). **Owner(s):** Media General, Inc., 333 E. Franklin St., Richmond, VA 23219. Telephone: 804-649-6000. FAX: 804-649-6898. **Management:** Carla Floyd, Publisher. **Editorial:** J Pilarczyk, Editor.

Weeklies

TEMPLE TERRACE NEWS. 15310 Amberly Dr., Ste. 102, Tampa, FL 33647. Telephone: 813-977-2854. FAX: 813-977-2854. E-MAIL: jmckenzie@mediageneral.com. Year Established: 1988. Pub. Frequency: w. (Wed.) Page Size: tabloid Circulation: 24,000 per issue (free). **Owner(s):** Media General, Inc., 333 E. Franklin St., Richmond, VA 23219. Telephone: 804-649-6000. FAX: 804-649-6898. **Management:** Tami Donaldson, Advertising Manager. **Editorial:** Joyce McKenzie, Editor. Russel Holecek, Managing Editor.

TOWN 'N COUNTRY NEWS. 5625 W. Waters Ave., Tampa, FL 33634. FAX: 813-865-1500. Year Established: 1988. Pub. Frequency: w. (Wed.) Page Size: tabloid Circulation: 23,700 per issue (free). **Owner(s):** Media General, Inc., 5501 W. Waters Ave., Tampa, FL 33634. 333 E. Franklin St., Richmond, VA 23219. Telephone: 804-648-6000. FAX: 804-649-6898. **Management:** Carla Floyd, Publisher. Beth Ann Drake, Advertising Manager. Josephine Frisco, Circulation Manager.

TAVERNIER

ISLAMORADA FREE PRESS. 91731 Overseas Hwy, Tavernier, FL 33070. Telephone: 305-853-7277. FAX: 305-853-0556. E-MAIL: freepress@keysnews.com. URL: http://www.keysnews.com. Pub. Frequency: w. (Wed.) Page Size: tabloid Circulation: 10,000 per issue (free). **Owner(s):** Cooke Communications LLC, 3420 Northside Dr., Key West, FL 33040. Telephone: 305-292-7777. FAX: 305-294-0768. **Management:** John Kent Cooke Jr., Publisher. Heather Warren, Advertising. Bob Timmerman, Circulation Manager. Isis Bargallo, Classified Adv. Mgr.. Connie Fitzgerald, Sales Manager. **Editorial:** Dan Campbell, Managing Editor.

KEY LARGO FREE PRESS. 91731 Overseas Hwy, Tavernier, FL 33070. Telephone: 305-853-7277. FAX: 305-853-0556. E-MAIL: freepress@keysnews.com. URL: http://www.keysnews.com. Pub. Frequency: w. (Wed.) Page Size: tabloid.Subscrip. Rate: $52/yr mailed Circulation: 14,000 per issue (free). **Owner(s):** Cooke Communications LLC, 3420 Northside Dr., Key West, FL 33040. Telephone: 305-292-7777. FAX: 305-294-0768. **Management:** John Kent Cooke Jr., Publisher. Heather Warren, Advertising. Bob Timmerman, Circulation Manager. Isis Bargallo, Classified Adv. Mgr.. Connie Fitzgerald, Sales Manager. **Editorial:** Dan Campbell, Managing Editor.

REPORTER (TAVERNIER), THE. 91655 Overseas Hwy, Tavernier, FL 33037. Telephone: 305-852-3216. FAX: 305-852-0199. URL: http://www.upperkeysreporter.com. Mailing Address: PO Box 1197, Tavernier, FL 33070-1197. Pub. Frequency: w. (Fri.) Page Size: tabloid. Subscrip. Rate: $.25 newsstand/cover; $24.04/yr home delivery local & in cy.; $37.49/yr mailed in state. Circulation: 4,500 per issue (paid). **Owner(s):** The/McClatchy Company, 2100 Q St, Sacramento, CA 95816. Telephone: 916-321-1936. FAX: 916-321-1869. **Management:** Wayne Markham, Publisher. Peter Hirsch, Advertising. Carol Drumheller, Circulation Manager. **Editorial:** David Goodhue, Editor. David Hawkins, Assistant Editor.

VENICE

VENICE GONDOLIER SUN. ISSN 1536-1063
200 E. Venice Ave., Venice, FL 34285. Telephone: 941-207-1000. FAX: 941-485-3036. E-MAIL: ravedder@sunline.net. URL: http://www.venicegondolier.com. Year Established: 1946. Pub. Frequency: 3/w. (Wed., Fri., Sun.) Page Size: broadsheet. Subscrip. Rate: $.50 newsstand/cover; $40.08/yr home delivery local; $66.83/yr mailed in state; $62.45/yr mailed out of state. Circulation: 31,000 per issue (paid and free). **Owner(s):** Sun Coast Media Group, Inc., 23170 Harbor View Rd., Charlotte Harbor, FL 33980. Telephone: 941-206-1000. FAX: 941-629-2085. **Management:** Derek Dunn-Rankin, Owner. Bob Vedder, Publisher. Donna Denson, Advertising Manager. Karen Gardner, Circulation Manager. **Editorial:** Bob Mudge, Editor. Jeff Tavares, Photographer.

WELLINGTON

LAKE WORTH FORUM. 11576 Pierson Rd., Ste. K-5, Wellington, FL 33414. Telephone: 561-791-7790. FAX: 561-791-7593. E-MAIL: m.martin@tribune.com. Pub. Frequency: w. (Tue.) Page Size: tabloid Circulation: 42,000 per issue (free). **Owner(s):** Tribune Company, 435 N Michigan Ave, Chicago, IL 60601. Telephone: 312.222.9100. **Management:** Keri Lurtz, Advertising Manager. Ed Wilder, Circulation Manager. **Editorial:** Mara Martin, Editor.

TOWN - CRIER. 12794 W. Forest Hill Blvd., Ste. 31, Wellington, FL 33414. Telephone: 561-793-7606. FAX: 561-793-1470, 561-793-7606. E-MAIL: towncrierads@aol.com. URL: http://www.gotowncrier.com. Year Established: 1980. Pub. Frequency: w. (Fri.) Page Size: tabloid.Adv. Rate: col. inch $11 Circulation: 30,000 per issue (free). **Owner(s):** Barry Manning, See address and contact information above. **Management:** Dawn Rivera, General Manager. Barry Manning, Publisher. Wanda Glockson, Classified Adv. Mgr.. Jody Gorran, Associate Publisher. **Editorial:** Josh Manning, Editorial Director.

WELLINGTON FORUM. 11576 Pierson Rd., Ste. K-5, Wellington, FL 33414-8765. Telephone: 561-791-7790. FAX: 561-791-7593. E-MAIL: rbuckley@tribune.com. Pub. Frequency: w. (Wed.) Page Size: tabloid Circulation: 25,000 per issue (free). **Owner(s):** Tribune Company, 435 N Michigan Ave, Chicago, IL 60601. Telephone: 312.222.9100. **Management:** Keri Lurtz, Advertising Manager. Ed Wilder, Circulation Manager. **Editorial:** Mara Martin, Editor.

WINTER GARDEN

WEST ORANGE TIMES. 720 S. Dillard, Winter Garden, FL 34787. Telephone: 407-656-2121. FAX: 404-656-3908. E-MAIL: wotimes@aol.com. URL: http://www.wotimes.com. Year Established: 1911. Pub. Frequency: w. (Thu.) Page Size: standard. Subscrip. Rate: $.50 newsstand/cover; $21.50/yr in county; $35/yr out of county. Circulation: 9,000 per issue (paid). **Owner(s):** George Bailey, See address and contact information above. **Management:** Andrew Bailey, Publisher. Jackie Browder, Office Manager. Jana Krouch, Advertising. **Editorial:** Mary Anne Swickerath, Editor.

WINTER HAVEN

POLK SHOPPER. 650 Sixth St., S.W., Winter Haven, FL 33880. Telephone: 863-294-7731. FAX: 863-294-2008. URL: http://www.polkonline.com. Pub. Frequency: w. (Wed.) Page Size: tabloid Circulation: 53,000 per issue (free). **Owner(s):** Morris Multimedia, Inc., PO Box 936, Augusta, GA 30903. Telephone: 706-724-0851. FAX: 706-722-7125. **Management:** Susan Holley, Advertising Director. Linda Mooney, Circulation Manager. Bill Megivern, Classified Adv. Mgr.. **Editorial:** Christie Gilpin, Editor.

WINTER PARK

WINTER PARK-MAITLAND OBSERVER. ISSN 1064-3613
P.O. Box 2426, Winter Park, FL 32790. E-MAIL: editor@observernewspapers.com. URL: www.observernewspapers.net. Year Established: 1989. Pub. Frequency: w. Page Size: tabloid. Subscrip. Rate: $.35 newsstand/cover; $24/yr; $30/yr mailed. Adv. Rate: col. inch $14 Circulation: 10,000 per issue (paid). **Owner(s):** Community Press Corp., 609 Executive Dr., Winter Park, FL 32789. Telephone: 407-628-8500 ext 303. FAX: 407-628-4053. **Management:** Kyle Taylor, President. Carole Arthurs, Sales Manager. **Editorial:** Kyle Taylor, Editor-in-Chief.

ZEPHYRHILLS

ZEPHYRHILLS NEWS. 38333 Fifth Ave., Zephyrhills, FL 33542. Telephone: 813-782-1558. FAX: 813-788-7987. E-MAIL: readznews@aol.com. URL: http://www.zephyrhillsnews.com. Mailing Address: PO Box 638, Zephyrhills, FL 33539. Year Established: 1911. Pub. Frequency: w. (Thu.) Page Size: broadsheet. Subscrip. Rate: $.50 newsstand/cover; $17/yr local. Circulation: 5,000 per issue (paid). **Owner(s):** E.W. Scripps Co., 312 Walnut St., 28th Fl., Cincinnati, OH 45202. Telephone: 513-977-3000. FAX: 513-977-3689. **Management:** Chris Drews, Publisher. Linda Wood, Business Manager. **Editorial:** Gary Hatrick, Editor. Darlene Sanders, Graphics Editor.

GEORGIA

ADAIRSVILLE

NORTH BARTOW NEWS. 321-B N Main St, Adairsville, GA 30103. Telephone: 770-773-3754. FAX: 770-773-3757. Mailing Address: PO Box 374, Adairsville, GA 30103. Pub. Frequency: w. (Tue.) Page Size: broadsheet. Subscrip. Rate: $.50 newsstand/cover; $35/yr mailed. Circulation: 36,458 per issue (controlled and free). **Owner(s):** Walls Newspapers, Inc., 525 Office Park Dr., Birmingham, AL 35223. Telephone: 205-870-1684. **Management:** Charles Hurley, Publisher. Sherry Ray, Office Manager. Eric Pass, Advertising Manager. **Editorial:** Johnette Dawson, Editor.

ADEL

ADEL NEWS TRIBUNE. 131 S. Hutchinson Ave., Adel, GA 31620. Telephone: 229-896-2233. E-MAIL: 1ant@surfsouth.com. Year Established: 1888. Pub. Frequency: w. (Wed.) Page Size: broadsheet. Subscrip. Rate: $.50 newsstand/cover; $21.40/yr in county; $19.08/yr in county to senior citizens. Circulation: 4,200 per issue (paid). **Owner(s):** Cook Publishing Co., Inc., See address and contact information above. **Management:** Ann Knight, General Manager. Lucille Seelye, Office Manager. Pat Ashcroft, Advertising Manager. Lance Williford, Circulation Manager. **Editorial:** Ann Knight, Editor.

ALBANY

ALBANY AREA ADVERTISER. 126 N Washington St, Albany, GA 31701. Telephone: 229-888-9300. FAX: 229-888-9357. URL: http://www.albanyherald.com. Mailing Address: PO Box 48, Albany, GA 31702. Pub. Frequency: w. (Tue.) Page Size: standard Circulation: 20,000 per issue (free). **Owner(s):** Triple Crown Media, Inc., 546 E Main St, Lexington, KY 40508. Telephone: 859-226-4678. FAX: 859-226-4308. **Management:** Michael Gebhart, Publisher. Tami Abbott, Advertising Director. J. Michael Hill, Circulation Director. John Bush, Classified Adv. Mgr..

ALBANY JOURNAL. 118 Roosevelt Ave., Albany, GA 31701-1628. Telephone: 229-435-6222. FAX: 229-435-0557. E-MAIL: ajournal@thealbanyjournal.com. URL: http://www.thealbanyjournal.com. Mailing Address: PO Box 1628, Albany, GA 31702-1628. Year Established: 1939. Pub. Frequency: w. (Thu.) Page Size: standard.Subscrip. Rate: $.50 newsstand/cover; $36/yr Circulation: 3,000 per issue (paid). **Owner(s):** Sam Farkas, See address and contact information above. **Management:** Sam Farkas, Publisher. Tara Elizondo, Advertising. Wilbur Rainey, Circulation Manager. **Editorial:** Sam Farkas, Editor.

ALPHARETTA

FORSYTH HERALD. 319 N Main St, Alpharetta, GA 30201. Telephone: 770-442-3278. E-MAIL: advertising@northfulton.com. URL: http://www.northfulton.com. Pub. Frequency: w. (Wed.) Page Size: tabloid. Subscrip. Rate: $.50 newsstand/cover; $75/yr. Adv. Rate: page $1,025 Circulation: 16,500 per issue (paid). **Owner(s):** Appen Newspapers, Inc., See address and contact information above. **Management:** Ray Appen, President. Trey Hayes, Marketing Director. **Editorial:** Jennifer Howard, Editor.

JOHNS CREEK HERALD. 319 N. Main St., Alpharetta, GA 30004. Telephone: 770-442-3278. FAX: 770-475-1216. E-MAIL: advertising@northfulton.com. URL: http://www.northfulton.com. Year Established: 1997. Pub. Frequency: w. (Wed.) Page Size: tabloid. Subscrip. Rate: $.50 newsstand/cover; $75/yr. Adv. Rate: page $1,025 Circulation: 14,500 per issue (paid). **Owner(s):** Appen Newspapers, Inc., 319 N Main St, Alpharetta, GA 30201. Telephone: 770-442-3278. **Management:** Ray Appen, President. Trey Hayes, Marketing Director. **Editorial:** Hatcher Hurd, Editor.

REVUE & NEWS. 319 N Main St, Alpharetta, GA 30201. Telephone: 770-442-3278. E-MAIL: advertising@northfulton.com. URL: http://www.northfulton.com. Pub. Frequency: w. (Thu.) Page Size: tabloid. Subscrip. Rate: $.50 newsstand/cover; $75/yr. Adv. Rate: page $1,325 Circulation: 24,500 per issue (paid). **Owner(s):** Appen Newspapers, Inc., See address and contact information above. **Management:** Ray Appen, President. Trey Hayes, Marketing Director. **Editorial:** Hatcher Hurd, Editor.

ASHBURN

WIREGRASS FARMER, THE. 109 N. Gordon St., Ashburn, GA 31714-5208. Telephone: 229-567-3655. FAX: 229-567-4402. E-MAIL: wiregrassfarmer@yahoo.com. Mailing Address: PO Box 309, Ashburn, GA 31714. Pub. Frequency: w. (Wed.) Page Size: standard. Subscrip. Rate: $.50 newsstand/cover; $21.40/yr in county; $26.75/yr mailed out of county; $35/yr mailed out of state. Circulation: 3,500 per issue (paid). **Owner(s):** Cook Publishing, Inc., PO Box 1500-A, Adel, GA 31620. Telephone: 229-896-2233. **Management:** Ann Knight, Publisher. Linda Sellars, Advertising Manager. **Editorial:** Ben Baker, Editor.

ATLANTA

ATLANTA DAILY WORLD. 145 Auburn Ave., N.E., Atlanta, GA 30303-1201. Telephone: 404-659-1110. FAX: 404-659-4988. E-MAIL: publisher@atlantadailyworld.com. URL: http://www.atlantadailyworld.com. Year Established: 1928. Pub. Frequency: w. (Thu) Page Size: broadsheet. Subscrip. Rate: $.50 newsstand/cover; $49/yr mailed; $75 mailed for 2 yrs.. **Wire Service(s):** UPI. Circulation: 10,000 per issue (paid). **Owner(s):** Atlanta Daily World, Inc., 145 Auburn Ave., N.E., Atlanta, GA 30303. Telephone: 404-659-1110. **Management:** M. Alexis Scott, Publisher. Charles Hamm, Advertising Manager. Dyra Parker, Circulation Manager. James McFarland, Assistant Publisher. **Editorial:** Hal Lamar, Sports Editor.

DUNWOODY CRIER. 16 Perimeter Park Dr., Ste. 10 1, Atlanta, GA 30341. Telephone: 770-451-4147. FAX: 770-451-4223. E-MAIL: thecrier@mindspring.com. Mailing Address: PO Box 888044, Atlanta, GA 30356. Year Established: 1975. Pub. Frequency: w. (Wed.) Page Size: tabloid. Subscrip. Rate: $60/yr mailed. Circulation: 23,500 per issue (paid and controlled). **Owner(s):** Crier Newspapers LLC, See address and contact information above. **Management:** James Hart, Advertising Director. **Editorial:** Dick Williams, Editor.

NORTHSIDE NEIGHBOR, THE. 5290 Roswell Rd., N.W., Ste. M, Atlanta, GA 30342. Telephone: 404-256-3100. FAX: 404-256-3292. E-MAIL: inside@neighbornewspapers.com. URL: http://www.neighbornewspapers.com. Year Established: 1968. Pub. Frequency: w. (Wed.) Page Size: broadsheet.Adv. Rate: col. inch $30.60 **Wire Service(s):** AP. Circulation: 2,400 per issue (paid and controlled). **Owner(s):** Marietta Daily Journal & Neighbor Newspapers, 580 Fairground St., Marietta, GA 30060. Telephone: 770-428-9411. FAX: 770-422-9533. **Management:** Otis A Brumby Jr., Publisher. Stephanie Dejarnette, Advertising. **Editorial:** Thornton Kennedy, Editor.

SANDY SPRINGS NEIGHBOR, THE. 5290 Roswell Rd., N.W., Ste. M, Atlanta, GA 30342. Telephone: 404-256-3100. FAX: 404-256-3292. Pub. Frequency: w. (Wed.) Page Size: broadsheet Circulation: 36,000 per issue (free). **Owner(s):** Marietta Daily Journal & Neighbor Newspapers, 580 Fairground St., Marietta, GA 30060. Telephone: 770-428-9411. FAX: 770-422-9533. **Management:** Otis A Brumby Jr., Publisher. **Editorial:** Thorton Kennedy, Editor.

AUGUSTA

GIRARD PRESS. 725 Broad St, Augusta, GA 30901. Telephone: 706-724-0851. FAX: 706-722-7125. E-MAIL: thepress@seqw.com. Year Established: 1869. Pub. Frequency: w. (Wed.) Page Size: broadsheet. Subscrip. Rate: $.50 newsstand/cover; $19.25/yr in county; $24.95/yr out of county. Adv. Rate: col. inch $3.50 Circulation: 2,600 per issue (paid and free). **Owner(s):** Morris Multimedia, Inc., See address and contact information above. **Management:** Stephen Wade, Publisher. Cindy Clingon, Advertising Director. **Editorial:** Mark Schremmer, Managing Editor. Kevin Abbatt, Sports Editor.

BAINBRIDGE

BAINBRIDGE POST-SEARCHLIGHT. 301 N. Crawford St., Bainbridge, GA 39818. Telephone: 229-246-2827. FAX: 229-246-7665. E-MAIL: postsearch@e-postprint.com. URL: www.thepostsearchlight.com. Mailing Address: PO Box 277, Bainbridge, GA 39818. Year Established: 1907. Pub. Frequency: s-w. (Wed. & Sat.) Page Size: broadsheet. Subscrip. Rate: $.50 newsstand/cover; $34/yr local; $50/yr mailed out of area. Circulation: 6,600 per issue (paid). **Owner(s):** Samuel M. Griffin, Jr., PO Box 277, Bainbridge, GA 31717. Telephone: 229-246-2827. **Management:** Samuel M. Griffin Jr., Publisher. Samuel M. Griffin III, Advertising Manager. Ike Manuel, Circulation Manager. **Editorial:** Carol P. Heard, Managing Editor. Joe Crine, Sports Editor.

BARNESVILLE

HERALD GAZETTE (BARNESVILLE), THE. 509 Greenwood St., Barnesville, GA 30204. Telephone: 770-358-0754. FAX: 770-358-0756. E-MAIL: news@barnesville.com. URL: http://www.barnesville.com. Mailing Address: P.O. Box 220, Barnesville, GA 30204. Pub. Frequency: w. (Tue.) Page Size: broadsheet. Subscrip. Rate: $.50 newsstand/cover; $18.50/yr local; $28.75/yr out of county; $33.80/yr out of state. Adv. Rate: col. inch $5.50 Circulation: 6,500 per issue (paid). **Owner(s):** Hometown Press, Inc., See address and contact information above. **Management:** Walter B Geiger Sr., Publisher. Laura Geiger, Advertising Manager. Missy Ware, Circulation Manager. **Editorial:** Walter B Geiger Sr., Editor. Laura Geiger, Managing Editor.

BAXLEY

BAXLEY NEWS-BANNER, THE. 241 E. Parker, Baxley, GA 31513. Telephone: 912-367-2468. FAX: 912-367-0277. E-MAIL: mail@baxleynewsbanner.com. URL: http://www.baxleynewsbanner.com. Mailing Address: PO Box 410, Baxley, GA 31515. Year Established: 1884. Pub. Frequency: w. (Wed.) Page Size: broadsheet. Subscrip. Rate: $.50 newsstand/cover; $26.22/yr in county; $34.24/yr mailed out of county; $37/yr mailed out of state. Adv. Rate: col. inch $5.45 Circulation: 5,000 per issue (paid). **Owner(s):** Baxley News-Banner, Inc., See address and contact information above. **Management:** Helen Gardner, Co-Publisher. Jamie Gardner, Advertising Manager. **Editorial:** Helen Gardner, Editor.

BLACKSHEAR

ALMA TIMES, THE. 113 S. Central Ave., Blackshear, GA 31516-1208. E-MAIL: mail@thealmatimes.com. URL: http://www.thealmatimes.com. Mailing Address: PO Box 428, Alma, GA 31510. Year Established: 1906. Pub. Frequency: w. (Thu.) Page Size: broadsheet. Subscrip. Rate: $.50 newsstand/cover; $25/yr in county; $30/yr out of county; $35/yr out of state. Adv. Rate: col. inch $6.50 Circulation: 3,100 per issue (paid). **Owner(s):** SouthFire Newspapers, See address and contact information above. **Management:** Cheryl Williams, President. Robert Williams, Publisher. Courson Sherrie, Advertising. Jenny Pritchett, Secretary. **Editorial:** John DuPont, Editor.

BLACKSHEAR TIMES, THE. 113 S. Central Ave., Blackshear, GA 31516-1208. Telephone: 912-449-6693. FAX: 912-449-1719. E-MAIL: mail@theblackSheartimes.com. URL: http://www.theblacksheartimes.com. Mailing Address: PO Box 410, Blackshear, GA 31516. Pub. Frequency: w. (Wed.) Page Size: broadsheet. Subscrip. Rate: $.75 newsstand/cover; $22/yr in county & adj. cys.; $30/yr elsewhere. Circulation: 3,200 per issue (paid). **Owner(s):** SouthFire Newspapers, See address and contact information above. **Management:** Robert M. Williams Jr., Publisher. LaVerne Boatright, Advertising Manager. Cheryl S. Williams, Associate Publisher. **Editorial:** Robert M. Williams Jr., Editor. DeAnn Komanecky, Managing Editor.

BLAIRSVILLE

NORTH GEORGIA NEWS. PO Box 2029, Blairsville, GA 30514. Telephone: 706-745-6343. FAX: 706-745-1830. E-MAIL: northgeorgianews@hotmail.com. URL: http://www.nganews.com. Year Established: 1912. Pub. Frequency: w. (Wed.) Page Size: broadsheet. Subscrip. Rate: $.50 newsstand/cover; $35/yr mailed. Circulation: 9,700 per issue (paid). **Owner(s):** Kenneth West, See address and contact information above. **Management:** Kenneth West, General Manager. **Editorial:** Norman Cooper, Editor.

BLAKELY

EARLY COUNTY NEWS. 115 College St., Blakely, GA 39823. Telephone: 229-723-4376. FAX: 229-723-6097. E-MAIL: ecnews@alltol.net. Mailing Address: PO Box 748, Blakely, GA 39823. Pub. Frequency: w. (Wed.) Page Size: broadsheet. Subscrip. Rate: $.50 newsstand/cover; $21.40/yr in county; $36.92/yr mailed out of county. Circulation: 4,000 per issue (paid). **Owner(s):** Billy Fleming, See address and contact information above. **Management:** Billy Fleming, Publisher. Judy Fleming, Advertising Manager. **Editorial:** Billy Fleming, Editor.

BLUE RIDGE

NEWS OBSERVER, THE. 5748 Appalachian Hwy., Blue Ridge, GA 30513. Telephone: 706-632-2019. FAX: 706-632-2577. E-MAIL: news@thenewsobserver.com. URL: http://www.thenewsobserver.com. Mailing Address: PO Box 989, Blue Ridge, GA 30513-0989. Pub. Frequency: s-w. (Tue. & Fri.) Page Size: broadsheet. Subscrip. Rate: $.50 newsstand/cover; $22.47/yr in county; $40.66/yr out of county. Circulation: 9,000 per issue (paid). **Owner(s):** Community Newspapers (Athens), Inc., PO Box 792, Athens, GA 30603. Telephone: 706-548-0010. FAX: 706-548-0808. **Management:** Glenn Harbison, Publisher. Stacy Chastain, Associate Publisher. **Editorial:** Brian Finnicum, Editor.

BREMEN

HARALSON GATEWAY-BEACON, THE. 222 Tallapoosa St., Bremen, GA 30110. Telephone: 770-537-2434. FAX: 770-537-0826. E-MAIL: hgbtj@times-georgian.com. Mailing Address: PO Box 685, Bremen, GA 30110. Year Established: 1895. Pub. Frequency: w. (Thu.) Page Size: broadsheet. Subscrip. Rate: $.50 newsstand/cover; $25/yr home delivery in county area; $31/yr mailed out of county; $35/yr mailed out of state. Circulation: 5,000 per issue (paid). **Owner(s):** Paxton Media Group LLC, 201 S. Fourth St., Paducah, KY 42003. Telephone: 270-575-8600. FAX: 270-442-8188. **Management:** Tom Overton, Publisher. Judy Westmoreland, Office Manager. Heather Gilley, Advertising Manager. **Editorial:** Stephine Rebman, Editor. Jamie Cohran, News.

BRUNSWICK

GLYNCO OBSERVER, THE. 3395 Cypress Mill Rd., Ste. E, Brunswick, GA 31520-2871. Telephone: 912-267-7878. FAX: 912-264-3357. E-MAIL: glynnpress@bellsouth.net. Year Established: 1984. Pub. Frequency: bi-w. (Thu.) Page Size: tabloid.Adv. Rate: col. inch $7.50 Circulation: 2,600 per issue (free). **Owner(s):** Glynn Press, Inc., 3395 Cypress Mill Rd., Ste. E, Brunswick, GA 31525-2871. **Management:** Troy Fore, Publisher. Noel Watson, Advertising. **Editorial:** Troy Fore, Editor.

HARBOR SOUND. 1326 Newcastle St., Brunswick, GA 31520. Telephone: 912-265-2130. E-MAIL: harborsoundads@yahoo.com. Mailing Address: PO Box 606, Brunswick, GA 31521-0606. Year Established: 1984. Pub. Frequency: w. (Tue.) Page Size: tabloid.Subscrip. Rate: $30/yr out of area Circulation: 30,000 per issue (free). **Owner(s):** Jim Dryden, See address and contact information above. **Editorial:** Jim Dryden, Editor.

ISLANDER (BRUNSWICK), THE. 3596 Darien Hwy., Ste. 6, Brunswick, GA 31525. Telephone: 912-265-9654. FAX: 912-265-3699. E-MAIL: ssislander@bellsouth.net. URL: http://www.theislanderonline.com. Year Established: 1972. Pub. Frequency: w. (Mon.) Page Size: tabloid. Subscrip. Rate: $.50 newsstand/cover; $17/yr in county; $19/yr mailed out of county. Circulation: 4,000 per issue (paid). **Owner(s):** Permar Publications, Inc., PO Box 20539, St. Simons Island, GA 31522. Telephone: 912-265-9654. FAX: 912-265-3699. **Management:** Matthew J. Permar, Publisher. Pam Shierling, Advertising Manager. **Editorial:** Pam Shierling, Editor.

JEKYLL'S GOLDEN ISLANDER. 3395 Cypress Mill Rd., Ste. E, Brunswick, GA 31520-2871. Telephone: 912-267-7878. FAX: 912-264-3357. E-MAIL: glynnpres@bellsouth.net. Year Established: 1972. Pub. Frequency: bi-w. (Thu.) Page Size: tabloid. Subscrip. Rate: $23/yr mailed 3rd class; $37/yr mailed 1st class. Adv. Rate: col. inch $7.50 Circulation: 6,000 per issue (free). **Owner(s):** Glynn Press, Inc., See address and contact information above. **Management:** Troy Fore, Publisher. Noel Watson, Advertising Manager. **Editorial:** Troy Fore, Editor.

BUTLER

TAYLOR COUNTY NEWS. 302 Meadowdale St., Butler, GA 31006. Telephone: 478-862-5101. FAX: 478-862-9668. E-MAIL: tcnnews@gnat.net. Year Established: 1886. Pub. Frequency: w. (Thu.) Page Size: broadsheet. Subscrip. Rate: $.50 newsstand/cover; $18/yr local; $26/yr out of county. Circulation: 2,500 per issue (paid). **Owner(s):** Valori Moore, See address and contact information above. **Management:** Valori Moore, Publisher. **Editorial:** Valori Moore, Editor.

CAIRO

CAIRO MESSENGER. 31-35 First Ave., N.E., Cairo, GA 39828. Telephone: 229-377-2032. E-MAIL: rwind@cairomessenger.com. URL: http://www.cairomessenger.com. Mailing Address: P.O. Box 30, Cairo, GA 39828. Year Established: 1904. Pub. Frequency: w. (Wed.) Page Size: broadsheet. Subscrip. Rate: $.50 newsstand/cover; $16.94/yr home delivery local; $24.35/yr home delivery; $15.25/yr home delivery in state seniors; $21.91/yr mailed out of state. Circulation: 13,000 per issue (paid). **Owner(s):** Messenger Publishing Co., Inc., See address and contact information above. **Management:** Herbert W. Wind, President. Randolph H. Wind, Publisher. **Editorial:** Randolph H. Wind, Editor. Herbert S. Wind, Production Manager. Randolph H. Wind, Advertising Editor.

CALHOUN

CALHOUN (GA) TIMES. 215 W. Line St., Calhoun, GA 30701. Telephone: 706-629-2231. FAX: 706-625-0899. E-MAIL: mtalley@calhountimes.com. URL: calhountimes.com. Mailing Address: PO Box 8, Calhoun, GA 30703. Year Established: 1870. Pub. Frequency: s-w. (Wed. & Sat.) Page Size: broadsheet. Subscrip. Rate: $.50 newsstand/cover; $35.31/yr home delivery in county; $48.88/yr home delivery out of county. Circulation: 8,000 per issue (paid). **Owner(s):** News Publishing Co., PO Box 1633, Rome, GA 30162. Telephone: 706-291-6297. **Management:** Burgett Mooney, Publisher. Billy Steele, Advertising Manager. Robert Ronco, Circulation Manager. **Editorial:** Mitch Talley, Managing Editor. Rob Broadway, Production Manager. Nathan Smith, Sports Editor.

CAMILLA

CAMILLA ENTERPRISE. 13 S. Scott St., Camilla, GA 31730. Telephone: 229-336-5265. FAX: 229-336-8476. E-MAIL: camillaenterprise@camillaga.net. Mailing Address: PO Box 365, Camilla, GA 31730. Year Established: 1903. Pub. Frequency: w. (Wed.) Page Size: broadsheet. Subscrip. Rate: $.50 newsstand/cover; $29/yr in county; $43/yr out of county. Adv. Rate: col. inch $6 Circulation: 3,600 per issue (paid). **Owner(s):** Robert Tribble, PO Box 426, Manchester, GA. **Management:** Kim McKeown, Advertising. Sandra Williams, Circulation Manager.

CARROLLTON

BOWDON BULLETIN. 901 Hays Mill Rd., Carrollton, GA 30117-5005. Telephone: 770-834-6631. FAX: 770-830-9425. E-MAIL: center@time.georgian.com. Mailing Address: PO Box 460, Carrollton, GA 30117-5005. Pub. Frequency: w. (Wed.) Page Size: broadsheet. Subscrip. Rate: $.50 newsstand/cover; $26/yr; $32/yr mailed in state; $34/yr mailed out of state. Circulation: 1,100 per issue (paid). **Owner(s):** Paxton Media Group Llc, 201 S. Fourth St., Paducah, KY 42003. Telephone: 270-575-8600. FAX: 270-442-8188. **Management:** Tom Overton, Publisher. **Editorial:** Bruce Browning, Managing Editor. Stephaine Rebman, News Editor.

CARROLTON

VILLA RICAN, THE. ISSN 0895-7312
901 Hay's Mill Rd., Carrolton, GA 30117. Telephone: 770-834-6631. FAX: 770-834-9991, 770-830-9425. E-MAIL: center@time.georgian.com. Mailing Address: PO Box 460, Carrolton, GA 30112. Year Established: 1935. Pub. Frequency: w. (Thu.) Page Size: broadsheet. Subscrip. Rate: $.50 newsstand/cover; $25/yr in county; $31/yr out of county; $34/yr mailed out of state. Circulation: 1,200 per issue (paid). **Owner(s):** Paxton Media Group Llc, 201 S. Fourth St., Paducah, KY 42003. Telephone: 270-575-8600. FAX: 270-442-8188. **Management:** Tom Overton, Publisher. Valerie Copeland, Advertising. **Editorial:** Spencer Crawford, News Editor.

Weeklies

CARTERSVILLE

BARTOW NEIGHBOR, THE. 10 Wall St., Cartersville, GA 30120. Telephone: 770-386-0872. FAX: 770-386-0879. Pub. Frequency: w. (Wed.) Page Size: broadsheet Circulation: 15,000 per issue (free). Owner(s): Marietta Daily Journal & Neighbor Newspapers, 580 Fairground St., Marietta, GA 30060. Telephone: 770-428-9411. FAX: 770-422-9533. **Management:** Otis Brumby Jr., Publisher. Katherine Strawn, Advertising Manager. **Editorial:** Amy McGee, Editor.

HERALD-TRIBUNE, THE. 251 S. Tennessee St., Cartersville, GA 30120. Telephone: 770-382-4545. FAX: 770-382-2711. E-MAIL: news@daily-tribune.com. URL: http://www.daily-tribune.com. Mailing Address: PO Box 70, Cartersville, GA 30120-0070. Year Established: 1926. Pub. Frequency: w. (Tue) Page Size: broadsheet. Circulation: 22,100 per issue (controlled). Owner(s): Cleveland Newspapers, Inc., 1505 25th St., N.W., Cleveland, TN 37311. Telephone: 423-472-5041. **Management:** Johnette Dawson, Publisher. Jennifer Moates, Advertising Director. Tony Henderson, Circulation Manager. Mandy Soloman, Classified Adv. Mgr. **Editorial:** Johnette Dawson, Editor. Joe Hiett, Managing Editor. Ryan Rees, Sports Editor.

CEDARTOWN

CEDARTOWN STANDARD. 213 Main St., Cedartown, GA 30125. Telephone: 770-748-1520. FAX: 770-748-1524. URL: http://www.cedartownstd.com. Mailing Address: PO Box 308, Cedartown, GA 30125. Year Established: 1869. Pub. Frequency: s-w. (Tue. & Thu.) Page Size: broadsheet. Subscrip. Rate: $.50 newsstand/cover; $39.59/yr home delivery in county; $53.04/yr mailed out of county; $51/yr mailed out of state. Circulation: 3,600 per issue (paid). Owner(s): News Publishing Co., 305 E. Sixth Ave., Rome, GA 30161. **Management:** James M Penney, Publisher. Clarissa Aiken, Advertising. Ann Wood, Advertising Manager. **Editorial:** James M Penney, Editor. Brad Easterwood, Sports.

CHAMBLEE

DEKALB NEIGHBOR, THE. 3060 Mercer University Dr, Ste 210, Chamblee, GA 30341. Telephone: 770-454-9388. FAX: 770-454-9131. E-MAIL: dekalbAneighbornewspapers.com. URL: http://www.neighbornewspapers.com. Year Established: 1969. Pub. Frequency: w. (Wed.) Page Size: broadsheet. Circulation: 5,325 per issue (controlled). Owner(s): Marietta Daily Journal & Neighbor Newspapers, 580 Fairground St., Marietta, GA 30060. Telephone: 770-428-9411. FAX: 770-422-9533. **Management:** Otis A Brumby Jr., Publisher. Mike Gilmer, Advertising Manager. **Editorial:** Brian Clark, Editor.

ROCKDALE NEIGHBOR, THE. 3060 Mercer University Dr, Ste 210, Chamblee, GA 30341. Telephone: 770-454-9388. FAX: 770-454-9131. E-MAIL: rockdale@neighbornewspapers.com. Year Established: 1980. Pub. Frequency: w. (Thu.) Page Size: broadsheet Circulation: 16,550 per issue (free). Owner(s): Marietta Daily Journal & Neighbor Newspapers, 580 Fairground St., Marietta, GA 30060. Telephone: 770-428-9411. FAX: 770-422-9533. **Management:** Otis Brumby, Publisher. Nat Long, Advertising Manager. **Editorial:** Tom Spigolon, Editor.

CHATSWORTH

CHATSWORTH TIMES, THE. 224 N. Third Ave., Chatsworth, GA 30705. Telephone: 706-695-4646. FAX: 706-695-7181. E-MAIL: chatsworthtimes@alltel.net. Mailing Address: PO Box 130, Chatsworth, GA 30705. Year Established: 1885. Pub. Frequency: w. (Wed.) Page Size: standard. Subscrip. Rate: $.50 newsstand/cover; $21.95/yr home delivery in county; $35/yr mailed in state. Circulation: 6,000 per issue (paid). Owner(s): Walls Newspapers, Inc., 525 Office Park Dr., Birmingham, AL 35223. Telephone: 205-870-1684. **Management:** Trannon Goble, General Manager. Johnette Dawson, Publisher. Cari Sluder, Advertising. Ronnie Bridges, Circulation Manager. **Editorial:** Vivian Dixon, Managing Editor. Chicke Nwakamma, Sports.

CLAXTON

CLAXTON ENTERPRISE. 24 S Newton St, PO Box 218, Claxton, GA 30417-2044. Telephone: 912-739-2132. FAX: 912-739-2140. URL: http://www.claxtonenterprise.com. Mailing Address: PO Box 218, Claxton, GA 30417. Pub. Frequency: w. (Thu.) Page Size: broadsheet. Subscrip. Rate: $.50 newsstand/cover; $25/yr in county; $27/yr out of state. Circulation: 4,894 per issue (paid). Owner(s): Mitchell Peace, See address and contact information above. **Management:** Mitchell Peace, Publisher. Paula McNeely, Vice President. **Editorial:** Al Hackle, Editor. Angye Morrison, Associate Editor.

CLAYTON

CLAYTON TRIBUNE, THE. 120 N Main St, Clayton, GA 30525. Telephone: 706-782-3312. FAX: 706-782-4230. E-MAIL: thetribune@theclaytontribune.com. URL: http://www.theclaytontribune.com. Mailing Address: PO Box 425, Clayton, GA 30525. Year Established: 1897. Pub. Frequency: w. (Thu.) Page Size: broadsheet. Subscrip. Rate: $.50 newsstand/cover; $24/yr in county; $30/yr out of county. Circulation: 8,000 per issue (controlled and free). Owner(s): Community Newspapers (Athens), Inc., PO Box 792, Athens, GA 30603. Telephone: 800-226-0692. FAX: 706-548-0808. **Management:** Steve Meadows, Publisher. Cyndy Brogdon, Advertising Manager. **Editorial:** Blake Spurney, Editor.

CLEVELAND

WHITE COUNTY NEWS-TELEGRAPH. 13 E. Jarrard St., Cleveland, GA 30528-1228. Telephone: 706-865-4718. FAX: 706-865-3048. E-MAIL: wnewstelegraph@alltel.net. URL: http://www.whitecountynewstelegraph.com. Pub. Frequency: w. (Thu.) Page Size: broadsheet. Subscrip. Rate: $.50 newsstand/cover; $22/yr in county; $33/yr out of county; $40/yr out of state. Circulation: 7,000 per issue (paid). Owner(s): Community Newspapers (Athens), Inc., PO Box 792, Athens, GA 30603. Telephone: 706-548-0010. FAX: 706-548-0808. **Management:** Will Davis, Publisher. Melanie Peck, Advertising. **Editorial:** Will Davis, Editor. Anne Cole, Circulation Editor.

COCHRAN

COCHRAN JOURNAL. 125 Second St., Cochran, GA 31014. Telephone: 478-934-6303. FAX: 478-934-6800. E-MAIL: cochranjournal@yahou.com. Mailing Address: P.O. Box 856, Cochran, GA 31014. Year Established: 1908. Pub. Frequency: w. (Tue.) Page Size: broadsheet. Subscrip. Rate: $.50 newsstand/cover; $23.90/yr in county; $31.91/yr out of county; $38.45/yr out of state; $21.33/yr to senior citizens. Adv. Rate: col. inch $5 Circulation: 4,500 per issue (paid). Owner(s): Courier Publishing Co., 115 S. Jefferson St., Dublin, GA 31040. Telephone: 478-272-5522. **Management:** DuBose Porter, Publisher. Cheryl Burton-Trawick, Office Manager. **Editorial:** Brandy Perry, Editor. Leah Stanley, Managing Editor.

COLQUITT

MILLER COUNTY LIBERAL. 157 E. Main St., Colquitt, GA 39837-0037. Telephone: 229-758-5549. FAX: 229-758-5540. E-MAIL: terrytoole@bellsouth.net. URL: http://www.millercountyliberal.com. Mailing Address: PO Box 37, Colquitt, GA 39837. Year Established: 1897. Pub. Frequency: w. (Wed.) Page Size: broadsheet. Subscrip. Rate: $.50 newsstand/cover; $21.40/yr local; $36.92/yr mailed elsewhere. Adv. Rate: col. inch $5 Wire Service(s): AP. Circulation: 3,000 per issue (controlled and free). Owner(s): Terry Toole, See address and contact information above. **Management:** Terry Toole, Publisher. **Editorial:** Terry Toole, Managing Editor.

COMER

COMER NEWS, THE. 1976 Main St., Comer, GA 30629-0007. Telephone: 706-783-2553. FAX: 706-783-2278. Mailing Address: PO Box 7, Comer, GA 30629-0007. Pub. Frequency: w. (Thu.) Page Size: broadsheet. Subscrip. Rate: $.25 newsstand/cover; $10.70/yr in county; $32.10/yr out of county; $42.80/yr out of state. Adv. Rate: col. inch $3.08 Circulation: 1,700 per issue (paid). Owner(s): Madison County Newspapers, Inc., See address and contact information above. **Management:** Jere Ayers, Publisher. **Editorial:** Jennifer Fogal, Editor.

DANIELSVILLE MONITOR, THE. 422 Main St., Comer, GA 30629. Telephone: 706-783-2553. FAX: 706-783-2278. E-MAIL: mcnews@nejia.net. Pub. Frequency: w. (Fri.) Page Size: broadsheet. Subscrip. Rate: $.25 newsstand/cover; $16.05/yr in county. Circulation: 1,850 per issue (paid). Owner(s): Madison County Newspapers, Inc., 7Comer, GA 30629-0007. **Management:** Jere Ayers, Publisher. **Editorial:** Jere Ayers, Editor.

COMMERCE

COMMERCE NEWS. 1672 S. Broad St., Commerce, GA 30529. Telephone: 706-335-2927. FAX: 706-335-4531. E-MAIL: news@mainstreetnews.com. URL: http://www.mainstreetnews.com. Mailing Address: PO Box 459, Commerce, GA 30529. Year Established: 1875. Pub. Frequency: w. (Wed.) Page Size: broadsheet. Subscrip. Rate: $.50 newsstand/cover; $19.75/yr home delivery in county; $38.85/yr mailed out of county; $17.75/yr home delivery in county to senior citizens; $44.50/yr mailed out of state. Circulation: 3,000 per issue (paid). Owner(s): MainStreet Newspapers, Inc., 33 Lee St, Jefferson, GA 30549. Telephone: 706-367-5233. **Management:** Herman Buffington, Owner. Connie Owensby, Advertising. Scott Buffington, Advertising Director. Debbie Castellaw, Circulation Manager. **Editorial:** Mark Beardsley, Editor. Ben Munroe, Sports.

CORDELE

SUNBELT SHOPPER. 306 13th. Ave., W., Cordele, GA 31015. Telephone: 229-273-2277. FAX: 229-273-7239. URL: http://www.cordeledispatch.com. Mailing Address: PO Box 1058, Cordele, GA 31010. Pub. Frequency: w. (Tue.) Page Size: standard. Circulation: 15,000 per issue (free). Owner(s): Community Newspaper Holdings, Inc., See address and contact information above. **Management:** Peggy King, Publisher. Ashli Garrick, Circulation Manager. **Editorial:** Peggy King, Editor.

CORNELIA

NORTHEAST GEORGIAN, THE. 2440 Old Athens Hwy., Cornelia, GA 30531. Telephone: 706-778-4215. FAX: 706-776-9510. E-MAIL: news@thenortheastgeorgian.com. URL: http://www.thenortheastgeorgian.com. Mailing Address: PO Box 1555, Cornelia, GA 30531. Year Established: 1892. Pub. Frequency: s-w. (Tue. & Fri.) Page Size: broadsheet. Subscrip. Rate: $.50 newsstand/cover; $30/yr in county; $40, $50/yr out of county. Circulation: 9,500 per issue (paid). Owner(s): Community Newspapers (Athens), Inc., PO Box 792, Athens, GA 30603. Telephone: 800-226-0692. FAX: 706-548-0808. **Management:** John D. Solesbee, Publisher. **Editorial:** John D. Solesbee, Editor. Chuck Bodiford, Circulation Editor. Rob Moore, News Editor.

COVINGTON

COVINGTON NEWS. 1166 Usher St NW, Covington, GA 30014. Telephone: 770-787-6397. FAX: 770-786-6451. E-MAIL: rhorne@covnews.com. URL: http://www.covnews.com. Year Established: 1865. Pub. Frequency: 3/w. (Tue., Thu., Sat.) Page Size: broadsheet. Subscrip. Rate: $.50 newsstand/cover; $44.95/yr mailed in state; $46.64/yr mailed out of state. Circulation: 7,500 per issue (controlled and free). Owner(s): Morris Newspaper Corporation, 27 Abercorn St., Savannah, GA 31401. Telephone: 912-233-1281. FAX: 912-232-4639. **Management:** David Riges, General Manager. **Editorial:** Robert Horne, Editor. Brian Knapp, Sports.

CRAWFORDVILLE

ADVOCATE DEMOCRAT, THE. 184 Davidson St., S.E., Crawfordville, GA 30631-3800. Telephone: 706-453-7988. Pub. Frequency: w. (Fri.) Page Size: standard. Subscrip. Rate: $.25 newsstand/cover; $8.56/yr local; $9.53/yr in state; $10.70/yr out of state. Circulation: 550 per issue (paid). Owner(s): Carey Williams Jr., 107 Main St, Greensboro, GA 30642. Telephone: 706-453-7988. **Management:** Carey Williams Jr., Publisher. **Editorial:** Dr. Kathie Allen, Editor. Carey Williams Jr., Managing Editor.

CUMMING

BARROW COUNTY NEWS, THE. PO Box 210, Cumming, GA 30028. E-MAIL: news@barrowcountynews.com. URL: http://www.barrowcountynews.com. Year Established: 1893. Pub. Frequency: s-w. (Wed. & Sun.) Page Size: broadsheet. Subscrip. Rate: $.50 newsstand/cover; $40/yr in county; $54/yr mailed out of county. Circulation: 8,000 per issue (paid). Owner(s): Swartz Morris Media, See address and contact information above. **Management:** Debby Burgamy, Publisher. Joann Craven, Circulation Manager. **Editorial:** Leanne Akin, Editor.

FORSYTH COUNTY NEWS. 302 Veterans Memorial Blvd., Cumming, GA 30040. Telephone: 770-887-3126. FAX: 770-844-9779. E-MAIL: editor@forsythnews.com. URL: http://www.forsythnews.com. Mailing Address: PO Box 210, Cumming, GA 30028-0210. Year Established: 1908. Pub. Frequency: w. (Sun., Wed., Thu., Fri.) Page Size: broadsheet. Subscrip. Rate: $.50 newsstand/cover per issue; $1 newsstand/cover Sun.; $52/yr home delivery. Circulation: 15,500 per issue (paid). Owner(s): Morris Multimedia, Inc., PO Box 210, Cumming, GA 30028. Telephone: 770-887-3126. **Management:** Norman Boggs, General Manager. Dennis Stockton, Publisher. Gary Tensley, Circulation Manager. **Editorial:** Tom Spigolon, Editor.

DAHLONEGA

DAHLONEGA NUGGET, THE. 1074 Morrison Moore Pkwy., Dahlonega, GA 30533. Telephone: 706-864-3613. FAX: 706-864-4360. E-MAIL: thenug@stc.net. URL: http://www.thedahloneganugget.com. Mailing Address: PO Box 36, Dahlonega, GA 30533-0036. Year Established: 1890. Pub. Frequency: w. (Wed.) Page Size: broadsheet. Subscrip. Rate: $.50 newsstand/cover; $22/yr in county; $33/yr out of area; $40/yr mailed out of state. Circulation: 6,500 per issue (paid). Owner(s): Community Newspapers (Athens), Inc., PO Box 792, Athens, GA 30603. Telephone: 706-548-0010. FAX: 706-548-0808. **Management:** Terrie Ellerbee, Publisher. Lynn Clarke, Advertising. **Editorial:** Terrie Ellerbee, Editor.

DALLAS

DALLAS NEW ERA. 121 W. Spring St., Dallas, GA 30132. Telephone: 770-495-3379. FAX: 770-495-3379. E-MAIL: newerapr@bellsouth.net. Year Established: 1882. Pub. Frequency: w. (Thu.) Page Size: broadsheet. Subscrip. Rate: $.25 newsstand/cover; $15/yr home delivery; $25 home delivery for 2 yrs.. Circulation: 8,000 per issue (paid). **Owner(s):** William T & Joseph S Parker, See address and contact information above. **Management:** Joseph S Parker, Owner. Jolee Kitchen, Advertising Manager. Joseph S Parker, Circulation Director. **Editorial:** Joseph S Parker, Editor.

PAULDING NEIGHBOR, THE. 31 Courthouse Sq., Dallas, GA 30132. Telephone: 770-445-9401. FAX: 770-445-0565. E-MAIL: paidling@neighbornewspapers.com. Pub. Frequency: w. (Thu.) Page Size: broadsheet. Subscrip. Rate: $112/yr mailed. **Wire Service(s):** AP. Circulation: 24,000 per issue (paid and free). **Owner(s):** Marietta Daily Journal & Neighbor Newspapers, 580 Fairground St., Marietta, GA 30060. Telephone: 770-428-9411. FAX: 770-422-9533. **Management:** Otis A Brumby Jr., Publisher. Wade Stephens, Advertising Director. **Editorial:** John Barker, Editor.

DANIELSVILLE

MADISON COUNTY JOURNAL. PO Box 658, Danielsville, GA 30633. Telephone: 706-367-5233. FAX: 706-367-8056. E-MAIL: news@mainstreetnews.com. URL: http://www.mainstreetnews.com. Pub. Frequency: w. (Wed.) Page Size: broadsheet. Subscrip. Rate: $.50 newsstand/cover; $14.98/yr in county; $38.85/yr out of county; $44.50/yr out of state. Circulation: 3,500 per issue (paid). **Owner(s):** Main Street Newspapers, Inc., PO Box 908, Jefferson, GA 30549. Telephone: 706-367-5233. FAX: 706-367-8056. **Management:** Mike Buffington, General Manager. Herman Buffington, Publisher. Scott Buffington, Advertising Manager. **Editorial:** Angela Gary, Editor.

DARIEN

DARIEN NEWS. PO Box 496, Darien, GA 31305-0498. Telephone: 912-437-4251. FAX: 912-437-2299. Year Established: 1951. Pub. Frequency: w. (Thu.) Page Size: broadsheet. Subscrip. Rate: $.50 newsstand/cover; $26.75/yr in county; $30/yr out of county; $30/yr out of state. Circulation: 3,600 per issue (paid). **Owner(s):** Charles M. Williamson, Jr., See address and contact information above. **Management:** Charles M. Williamson Jr., Publisher. **Editorial:** Kathleen W. Russell, Editor.

DAWSON

DAWSON NEWS, INC., THE. 139 W. Lee St., Dawson, GA 39842. Telephone: 229-995-2175. FAX: 229-995-2176. E-MAIL: dnews@windstream.net. Mailing Address: PO Box 350, Dawson, GA 39842-0350. Year Established: 1866. Pub. Frequency: w. (Thu.) Page Size: standard. Subscrip. Rate: $.50 newsstand/cover; $20/yr local; $24/yr in state; $30/yr out of state. Adv. Rate: col. inch $6.25 Circulation: 8,300 per issue (paid and free). **Owner(s):** Tommy Rountree, See address and contact information above. **Management:** Tommy Rountree, Publisher. **Editorial:** Tommy Rountree, Editor.

DAWSONVILLE

DAWSON COMMUNITY NEWS. 514 Academy Ave., Dawsonville, GA 30534. Telephone: 706-265-3384. FAX: 706-265-3276. E-MAIL: editor@dawsonnews.com. URL: http://www.dawsonnews.com. Pub. Frequency: w. (Wed.) Page Size: tabloid. Subscrip. Rate: $.50 newsstand/cover; $12/yr in county; $25/yr out of county. **Owner(s):** Swartz-Morris Media, Inc., 302 Veterans Memorial Blvd., Cumming, GA 30040. Telephone: 912-233-1281. **Management:** John Hall, Publisher. Jennifer Lyness, Advertising Director. **Editorial:** Tammy Cox, Editor.

DAWSON NEWS & ADVERTISER. 40 Hwy. 9 N., Dawsonville, GA 30534-3500. Telephone: 706-265-2345. FAX: 706-265-7842. E-MAIL: news@dcadvert.com. URL: http://www.dawsonadvertiser.com. Mailing Address: PO Box 225, Dawsonville, GA 30534-3500. Year Established: 1887. Pub. Frequency: w. (Wed.) Page Size: broadsheet. Subscrip. Rate: $.50 newsstand/cover; $15/yr in county; $25/yr out of county; $32/yr out of state. Circulation: 5,500 per issue (paid). **Owner(s):** Community Newspapers (Athens), Inc., PO Box 792, Athens, GA 30603. **Management:** Linda Carder, Publisher. Carrie Smith, Office Manager. Crystal Austin, Advertising. Carrie Smith, Circulation Manager. **Editorial:** Linda Carder, Editor. Lori Sexton, Sports Editor.

DONALSONVILLE

DONALSONVILLE NEWS. 120 W. 2nd St., Donalsonville, GA 39845-0338. Telephone: 229-524-2343. FAX: 229-524-2343. E-MAIL: bo@donalsonvillenews.com. Mailing Address: PO Box 338, Donalsonville, GA 39845-0338. Year Established: 1916. Pub. Frequency: w. (Wed.) Page Size: broadsheet. Subscrip. Rate: $.50 newsstand/cover; $16.05/yr local; $21.40/yr mailed elsewhere. Circulation: 3,600 per issue (paid). **Owner(s):** Donalsonville News, Inc., PO Box 338, Donalsonville, GA 39845. Telephone: 229-524-2343. **Management:** Bo McLeod, Publisher. **Editorial:** Bo McLeod, Editor.

DOUGLAS

DOUGLAS ENTERPRISE. 1823 S. Peterson Ave., Douglas, GA 31533. Telephone: 912-384-2323. FAX: 912-383-0218. E-MAIL: dougent@surfsouth.com. Mailing Address: PO Box 750, Douglas, GA 31534. Year Established: 1888. Pub. Frequency: s-w. (Wed. & Sun.) Page Size: standard. Subscrip. Rate: $.50 newsstand/cover; $24.50/yr home delivery in county; $55/yr mailed elsewhere. Circulation: 8,100 per issue (paid). **Owner(s):** Lovan B. & Patricia W. Thomas, See address and contact information above. **Management:** Tracy Mayo, Publisher. Darlene Guise, Circulation Manager. **Editorial:** Kathy Hudson, Editor.

DOUGLAS SHOPPER. 213 N. Peterson Ave., Douglas, GA 31533-3251. Telephone: 912-384-9112. FAX: 912-384-4220. Pub. Frequency: w. (Thu.) Page Size: standard Circulation: 19,252 per issue (free). **Owner(s):** Community Newspaper Holdings, Inc., See address and contact information above. **Management:** Gwen Torminey, General Manager. Wendy McNalley, Advertising.

DOUGLASVILLE

DOUGLAS NEIGHBOR, THE. 8434 Price Ave., Douglasville, GA 30135. Telephone: 770-942-1611. FAX: 770-942-4348. URL: http://www.neighbornewspapers.com. Year Established: 1978. Pub. Frequency: w. (Wed.) Page Size: broadsheet Circulation: 23,000 per issue (free). **Owner(s):** Marietta Daily Journal & Neighbor Newspapers, 580 Fairground St., Marietta, GA 30060. Telephone: 770-428-9411. FAX: 770-422-9533. **Management:** Otis A Brumby Jr., Publisher. Lisa Whitfield, Advertising Manager. **Editorial:** Mike Rieman, Editor.

PAULDING COUNTY SENTINEL. 8501 Bowden St., Douglasville, GA 30134. Telephone: 770-942-6571. FAX: 770-949-7556. Mailing Address: PO Box 1586, Douglasville, GA 30133. Pub. Frequency: w. (Wed.) Page Size: broadsheet.Subscrip. Rate: $.25 newsstand/cover; $109/yr Circulation: 10,800 per issue (paid). **Owner(s):** Paxton Media Group Llc, 201 S. Fourth St., Paducah, KY 42003. Telephone: 270-575-8600. FAX: 270-442-8188. **Management:** Mitchell Lynch, Publisher. Harriet Vincent, Advertising Director. Phil Jones, Circulation Director. **Editorial:** Chris Barker, Editor.

EASTMAN

DODGE COUNTY NEWS, THE. 226 Main St., Eastman, GA 31023-1650. Telephone: 478-374-6397. FAX: 478-374-0361. E-MAIL: dcn@dodgecountynews.com. URL: http://www.dodgecountynews.com. Mailing Address: PO Box 69, Eastman, GA 31023-0069. Year Established: 1989. Pub. Frequency: w. (Wed.) Page Size: broadsheet. Subscrip. Rate: $.50 newsstand/cover; $21/yr in county; $27/yr out of county; $32/yr out of state. Adv. Rate: col. inch $5.25 Circulation: 5,515 per issue (paid and free). **Owner(s):** Chuck & Cindy Eckles, See address and contact information above. **Management:** Chuck Eckles, Publisher. Cindy Eckles, Advertising Manager. **Editorial:** Cindy Eckles, Managing Editor.

EATONTON

EATONTON MESSENGER, THE. 100 N. Jefferson Ave., Eatonton, GA 31024. Telephone: 706-485-3501. FAX: 706-485-4166. E-MAIL: amsmith@msgr.com. URL: http://www.msgr.com. Mailing Address: PO Box 4027, Eatonton, GA 31024. Year Established: 1861. Pub. Frequency: 2/w. (Thu. & Sat.) Page Size: broadsheet. Subscrip. Rate: $.50 newsstand/cover; $20/yr in county; $25/yr out of county; $30/yr out of state. Circulation: 13,324 per issue (paid). **Owner(s):** Smith Communications Inc., PO Box 4027, Eatonton, GA. Telephone: 706-485-3501. **Management:** Micky Smith, Publisher. **Editorial:** Don Richenson, News Editor.

ELBERTON

ELBERTON STAR & EXAMINER, THE. 25 N. Public Sq., Elberton, GA 30635-2416. Telephone: 706-283-8500. FAX: 706-283-9700. E-MAIL: starexaminer@elberton.com. URL: http://www.elberton.com. Mailing Address: PO Box 280, Elberton, GA 30635. Pub. Frequency: w. (Wed.) Page Size: broadsheet. Subscrip. Rate: $.50 newsstand/cover; $18/yr in county; $18/yr in county to senior citizens; $22/yr out of county; $30/yr out of state. Circulation: 6,000 per issue (paid). **Owner(s):** Community Newspapers (Athens), Inc., PO Box 792, Athens, GA 30603. Telephone: 706-548-0010. **Management:** Gary Jones, General Manager. Melinda Turner, Advertising Manager. Earl Saxon, Circulation Director. Kerri Pruitt, Classified Adv. Mgr.. Barbara Slay, Production Director. **Editorial:** Shane Scoggins, Managing Editor.

ELLLJAY

TIMES-COURIER (ELLIJAY). 47 River St., Ellljay, GA 30540. Telephone: 706-635-4313. FAX: 706-635-7006. E-MAIL: shanaparks@timescourier.com. URL: http://www.timescourier.com. Mailing Address: PO Box 1076, Ellijay, GA 30540. Year Established: 1875. Pub. Frequency: w. (Wed.) Page Size: broadsheet. Subscrip. Rate: $.50 newsstand/cover; $24/yr in county; $28/yr out of county. Circulation: 7,550 per issue (paid). **Owner(s):** George N. Bunch, See address and contact information above. **Management:** George N. Bunch III III, Publisher. Shana Parks, Advertising Manager. **Editorial:** George N. Bunch III III, Editor. Annetta B. Bunch, Associate Editor.

EVANS

COLUMBIA COUNTY NEWS TIMES, THE. 4272 Washington Rd, Ste 3B, Evans, GA 30809. Telephone: 706-863-6165. E-MAIL: cnt@newstimesonline.com. URL: http://www.newstimesonline.com. Year Established: 1881. Pub. Frequency: s-w. (Wed. & Sun.) Page Size: broadsheet. Subscrip. Rate: $.50 newsstand/cover per issue; $38/yr mailed. Adv. Rate: col. inch $18 Circulation: 25,500 per issue (paid). **Owner(s):** Southeastern Newspapers Corp., See address and contact information above. **Management:** Barry Paschal, Publisher. Ryan Hewett, Advertising. **Editorial:** Barry Paschal, Editor. Donnie Fetter, News Editor. Stephen Fastenau, Sports Writer.Readers: Columbia County only

FAYETTEVILLE

CITIZEN (FAYETTEVILLE), THE. 310-B N. Glynn St., Fayetteville, GA 30214. Telephone: 770-719-1880. FAX: 770-719-1976. E-MAIL: editor@thecitizenn.com. URL: http://www.thecitizen.com. Year Established: 1993. Pub. Frequency: w. (Wed.) Page Size: broadsheet. Subscrip. Rate: $.50 newsstand/cover; $26/yr. Adv. Rate: col. inch $14.50 Circulation: 28,000 per issue (paid and free). **Owner(s):** Fayette Publishing, Inc., See address and contact information above. **Management:** Cal Beverly, Publisher. Joyce Beverly, Advertising Manager. Karen Ratcliffe, Classified Adv. Mgr.. **Editorial:** Cal Beverly, Editor. Emily Baldwin, Lifestyle Editor.

COWETA CITIZEN REVIEW, THE. 310-B N. Glynn St., Fayetteville, GA 30214. Telephone: 770-719-1880. FAX: 770-719-1976. E-MAIL: editor@thecitizen.com. URL: http://www.thecitizen.com. Mailing Address: Drawer 1719, Fayetteville, GA 30214. Year Established: 1996. Pub. Frequency: w. (Fri.) Page Size: broadsheet. Subscrip. Rate: $.50 newsstand/cover; $26/yr. Adv. Rate: col. inch $10.50 Circulation: 8,694 per issue (paid and free). **Owner(s):** Fayette Publishing, Inc., See address and contact information above. **Management:** Cal Beverly, Publisher. Joyce Beverly, Advertising Manager. Karen Ratcliffe, Classified Adv. Mgr.. **Editorial:** John Thompson, Editor. Emily Baldwin, Lifestyle Editor.

PEACHTREE CITIZEN REVIEW, THE. 310-B N. Glynn St., Fayetteville, GA 30214. Telephone: 770-719-1880. FAX: 770-719-1976. E-MAIL: editor@thecitizennews.com. URL: http://www.thecitizen.com. Year Established: 1995. Pub. Frequency: w. (Fri.) Page Size: broadsheet. Subscrip. Rate: $.50 newsstand/cover; $26/yr in state. Adv. Rate: col. inch $10.50 **Owner(s):** Fayette Publishing, Inc., See address and contact information above. **Management:** Cal Beverly, Publisher. Joyce Beverly, Advertising Manager. Karen Ratcliffe, Classified Adv. Mgr.. **Editorial:** Cal Beverly, Editor. Emily Baldwin, Lifestyle Editor.

SOUTH FULTON CITIZEN. 310-B N. Glynn St., Fayetteville, GA 30214. Telephone: 770-719-1880. FAX: 770-719-1976. E-MAIL: editor@thecitizennews.com. URL: http://www.thecitizennews.com. Year Established: 2000. Pub. Frequency: w. (Fri.) Page Size: broadsheet. Subscrip. Rate: $.50 newsstand/cover; $26/yr. Adv. Rate: col. inch $9 Circulation: 6,000 per issue (paid). **Owner(s):** Fayette Publishing, Inc., See address and contact information above. **Management:** Cal Beverly, Publisher. Joyce Beverly, Advertising Manager. Karen Ratcliffe, Classified Adv. Mgr.. **Editorial:** Ben Nelms, Editor. Emily Baldwin, Lifestyle Editor.

TYRONE CITIZEN, THE. 310-B N. Glynn St., Fayetteville, GA 30214. Telephone: 770-719-1880. FAX: 770-719-1976. E-MAIL: editor@thecitizen.com. URL: http://www.thecitizen.com. Mailing Address: Drawer 1719, Fayetteville, GA 30214. Year Established: 1998. Pub. Frequency: w. (Sun.) Page Size: broadsheet. Subscrip. Rate: $.50 newsstand/cover; $26/yr. Adv. Rate: col. inch $9 Circulation: 6,000 Sunday (paid and free). **Owner(s):** Fayette Publishing, Inc., See address and contact information above. **Management:** Cal Beverly, Publisher. Joyce Beverly, Advertising Manager. Karen Ratcliffe, Classified Adv. Mgr.. **Editorial:** Ben Nelms, Editor. Emily Baldwin, Lifestyle Editor.

FITZGERALD

HERALD-LEADER (FITZGERALD), THE. 202-204 E. Central Ave., Fitzgerald, GA 31750. Telephone: 229-423-9331. FAX: 229-423-6533. E-MAIL: mail@herald-leader.net. URL: http://www.herald-leader.net. Mailing Address: PO Box 40, Fitzgerald, GA 31750. Year Established: 1895. Pub. Frequency: w. (Wed.) Page Size: standard. Subscrip. Rate: $.50 newsstand/cover; $18.73/yr in county & adj. cys.; $30.50/yr in state. Circulation: 5,400 per issue (paid). **Owner(s):** Pryor Publications, Inc., See address and contact information above. **Management:** Tim Anderson, Publisher. Becky Anderson, Advertising Manager. Anne Taylor, Circulation Manager. **Editorial:** Tim Anderson, Editor.

FOLKSTON

CHARLTON COUNTY HERALD. 204 S. First St., Folkston, GA 31537-9998. Telephone: 912-496-3585. FAX: 912-496-4585. E-MAIL: cherald@planttel.net. Mailing Address: PO Box 398, Folkston, GA 31537-0398. Year Established: 1898. Pub. Frequency: w. (Wed.) Page Size: broadsheet. Subscrip. Rate: $.50 newsstand/cover; $17.26/yr mailed in county; $20.47/yr mailed out of county. Circulation: 3,000 per issue (paid). **Owner(s):** David Thompson, See address and contact information above. **Management:** David Thompson, Publisher. **Editorial:** David Thompson, Editor.

FOREST PARK

CLAYTON NEIGHBOR. 5300 Frontage Rd., Ste. B, Forest Park, GA 30297. Telephone: 404-363-8484. FAX: 404-363-0212. Year Established: 1976. Pub. Frequency: w. (Wed.) Page Size: broadsheet. Circulation: 42,000 per issue (controlled). **Owner(s):** Marietta Daily Journal & Neighbor Newspapers, 580 Fairground St., Marietta, GA 30060. Telephone: 770-428-9411. FAX: 770-422-9533. **Management:** Otis A Brumby Jr., Publisher. Nat Long, Advertising. **Editorial:** Towanda Freeman, Editor.

SOUTH FULTON NEIGHBOR, THE. ISSN 0192-0693
5300 Frontage Rd., Ste. B, Forest Park, GA 30297. Telephone: 404-363-8484. FAX: 404-363-0212. Year Established: 1968. Pub. Frequency: w. (Wed.) Page Size: broadsheet Circulation: 26,500 per issue (free). **Owner(s):** Marietta Daily Journal & Neighbor Newspapers, 580 Fairground St., Marietta, GA 30060. Telephone: 770-428-9411. FAX: 770-422-9533. **Management:** Otis A Brumby Jr., Publisher. Nat Long, Advertising Manager. **Editorial:** Bill Baldowski, Managing Editor.

FORSYTH

MONROE COUNTY REPORTER, THE. 30 E. Johnston St., Forsyth, GA 31029-2230. Telephone: 478-994-2358. FAX: 478-994-2359. E-MAIL: michaelstone@gellsouth.net. Mailing Address: PO Box 795, Forsyth, GA 31029-0795. Pub. Frequency: w. (Wed.) Page Size: standard. Subscrip. Rate: $.50 newsstand/cover; $21/yr local; $36/yr out of area. Circulation: 4,200 per issue (paid). **Owner(s):** Crescent Media, 314 S. Pine St., Spartanburg, SC 29304. Telephone: 205-298-7100. FAX: 205-298-7101. **Management:** Wanda Fountain, General Manager. Carolyn Martel, Advertising Manager. **Editorial:** Michael Stone, Editor.

FORT OGLETHORPE

SIGNAL MOUNTAIN POST. 2712 LaFayette Rd., Fort Oglethorpe, GA 30742. Telephone: 706-866-1020. FAX: 706-866-1128. E-MAIL: signalmountainpost@comcast.net. URL: http://www.signalmountainpost.com. Mailing Address: P.O. Box 2070, Fort Oglethorpe, GA 30742. Pub. Frequency: bi-w. (Thu.) Page Size: tabloid Circulation: 7,500 per issue (free). **Owner(s):** Community Newspaper Holdings, Inc., 3500 Colonnade Pkwy., Ste. 600, Birmingham, AL 35243. Telephone: 205-298-7100. FAX: 205-298-7101. **Management:** Debbie Buck, Advertising. Joanne Cox, Classified Adv. Mgr.. **Editorial:** Daryl Cole, Editor.

FORT VALLEY

LEADER-TRIBUNE, THE. 109 Anderson Ave., Fort Valley, GA 31030. Telephone: 478-825-2432. FAX: 478-825-4130. E-MAIL: leadertribune@georgiaspeed.net. Year Established: 1888. Pub. Frequency: w. (Wed.) Page Size: broadsheet. Subscrip. Rate: $.50 newsstand/cover; $21.60/yr home delivery in county; $29.15/yr mailed in state; $37/yr mailed out of state. Adv. Rate: col. inch $7.10 Freelance Pay: $20/article. Circulation: 14,110 per issue (paid and free). **Owner(s):** Peach Publishing Co., Inc., See address and contact information above. **Management:** Vicky Davis, General Manager. Aven Simmans, Advertising. **Editorial:** Vicky Davis, Editor.

GLENNVILLE

GLENNVILLE SENTINEL, THE. 105 W. Barnard St., Glennville, GA 30427. Telephone: 912-654-2515. FAX: 912-654-2527. E-MAIL: gsasstededitor@alltel.net. Mailing Address: PO Box 218, Glennville, GA 30427. Year Established: 1925. Pub. Frequency: w. (Thu.) Page Size: broadsheet. Subscrip. Rate: $.50 newsstand/cover; $21.44/yr in state; $25.68/yr mailed elsewhere. Adv. Rate: col. inch $5 Circulation: 4,900 per issue (paid and free). **Owner(s):** Pam & Russell Terry Waters, See address and contact information above. **Management:** Pam Waters, Publisher. Gwenda Murphy, Advertising. **Editorial:** Pam Waters, Editor-in-Chief.

GRAY

JONES COUNTY NEWS. 103 Atlanta Rd, Gray, GA 31032. Telephone: 478-986-3929. FAX: 478-986-1935. E-MAIL: info@jcnews.com. URL: http://www.jcnews.com. Mailing Address: PO Box 1538, Gray, GA 31032-1538. Year Established: 1895. Pub. Frequency: w. (Thu.) Page Size: broadsheet. Subscrip. Rate: $.50 newsstand/cover; $21.40/yr in county; $23.54/yr out of county; $25.68/yr out of state. Adv. Rate: col. inch $5 Circulation: 4,300 per issue (paid). **Owner(s):** Community Voice Media, See address and contact information above. **Management:** Josh Lurie, Publisher. Karen Hunsinger, Advertising. **Editorial:** Debbie Lurie-Smith, Editor.

GREENSBORO

HERALD JOURNAL, THE. 107 N. Main St., Greensboro, GA 30642-1143. Telephone: 706-453-7988. FAX: 706-453-2311. Pub. Frequency: w. (Thu.) Subscrip. Rate: $.50 newsstand/cover; $20.33/yr in county; $23.54/yr out of county; $26.75/yr out of state. Circulation: 4,500 per issue (paid). **Owner(s):** Carey J. Williams, Jr., See address and contact information above. **Management:** Carey J. Williams Jr., Publisher. Jill Foster, Advertising Manager. **Editorial:** Carey J. Williams Jr., Editor.

HARTWELL

HARTWELL SUN, THE. 8 Benson St., Hartwell, GA 30643. Telephone: 706-376-8025. FAX: 706-376-3016. E-MAIL: hartwellsun@hartcom.net. URL: http://www.thehartwellsun.com. Mailing Address: PO Box 700, Hartwell, GA 30643-0700. Year Established: 1877. Pub. Frequency: w. (Thu.) Page Size: broadsheet. Subscrip. Rate: $.50 newsstand/cover; $22/yr in county; $24/yr in state; $32/yr out of state. Adv. Rate: col. inch $10.59 Circulation: 8,000 per issue (paid and free). **Owner(s):** Commmunity Newspapers, Inc., PO Box 792, Athens, GA 30603. Telephone: 706-548-0010. **Management:** Peggy Vickery, General Manager. Robert Rider, Publisher. **Editorial:** Judith Salter, Editor.

HAWKINSVILLE

HAWKINSVILLE DISPATCH & NEWS. 329 Commerce St., Hawkinsville, GA 31036-1344. Telephone: 478-783-1291. FAX: 478-783-1293. Mailing Address: PO Box 30, Hawkinsville, GA 31036-0339. Pub. Frequency: w. (Wed.) Page Size: broadsheet. Subscrip. Rate: $.50 newsstand/cover; $21.40/yr in county; $28.99/yr out of county; $35/yr out of state. Circulation: 3,100 per issue (paid). **Owner(s):** Hawkinsville Publishing Co., See address and contact information above. **Management:** Chuck Southerland, Owner. Monika Robert, Circulation Manager.

HAZLEHURST

JEFF DAVIS LEDGER. 12 Latimer St., Hazlehurst, GA 31539. Telephone: 912-375-4225. FAX: 912-375-3704. E-MAIL: news@jdledger.com. URL: http://www.jdledger.com. Mailing Address: PO Box 460, Hazlehurst, GA 31539. Year Established: 1940. Pub. Frequency: w. (Wed.) Page Size: broadsheet. Subscrip. Rate: $.50 newsstand/cover; $18.19/yr home delivery local; $21.40/yr mailed out of county; $28.89/yr mailed out of state. Circulation: 3,900 per issue (paid). **Owner(s):** Hazlehurst Publishing Co. Inc., See address and contact information above. **Management:** Kay Purser, Advertising. Carolyn Thompson, Business Manager. **Editorial:** Thomas H. Purser, Editor.

HIAWASSEE

TOWNS COUNTY HERALD. PO Box 365, Hiawassee, GA 30546-0365. Telephone: 706-896-4454. FAX: 706-896-1745. Pub. Frequency: w. (Thu.) Page Size: broadsheet. Subscrip. Rate: $.50 newsstand/cover; $20/yr in county; $25/yr out of county. Circulation: 3,500 per issue (paid). **Owner(s):** Wanda West, See address and contact information above. **Management:** Kenneth West, General Manager. Wanda West, Publisher. **Editorial:** Carl Vanzura, Editor.

HINESVILLE

COASTAL COURIER. ISSN 1047-6636
125 S Main St, PO Box 498, Hinesville, GA 31310. Telephone: 912-876-0156. FAX: 912-368-6329. E-MAIL: editor@coastalcourier.com. URL: http://www.coastalcourier.com. Year Established: 1871. Pub. Frequency: 3/w. (Wed., Fri., Sun.) Page Size: standard. Subscrip. Rate: $45/yr in county; $62.50/yr out of county; $75/yr mailed out of state. Circulation: 5,600 per issue (paid). **Owner(s):** Morris Newspaper Corporation, 27 Abercorn St., Savannah, GA 31401. Telephone: 912-233-1281. FAX: 912-232-4639. **Management:** Mark Griffin, Publisher. MaryAnn Wilson, Advertising. **Editorial:** Patrick Donahue, Editor.

HOMER

BANKS COUNTY NEWS. Main St., Homer, GA 30547. Telephone: 706-677-3491. FAX: 706-677-3263. E-MAIL: news@mainstreetnews.com. URL: http://www.mainstreetnews.com. Mailing Address: PO Box 920, Homer, GA 30547-0920. Year Established: 1968. Pub. Frequency: w. (Wed.) Page Size: broadsheet. Subscrip. Rate: $.50 newsstand/cover; $19.75/yr in county; $38.85/yr out of county; $44.50/yr out of state. Circulation: 3,000 per issue (paid). **Owner(s):** Main Street Newspapers, Inc., PO Box 908, Jefferson, GA 30549. Telephone: 706-367-5233. FAX: 706-367-8056. **Management:** Mike Buffington, General Manager. Herman Buffington, Publisher. Scott Buffington, Advertising Manager. **Editorial:** Angela Gary, Editor. Adam Fouche, Sports.

HOMERVILLE

CLINCH COUNTY NEWS, THE. 210 E. Dame Ave., Homerville, GA 31634. Telephone: 912-487-5337. FAX: 912-487-3227. E-MAIL: clinnews@alltel.net. URL: http://www.theclinchcountynews.com. Mailing Address: PO Box 377, Homerville, GA 31634-0377. Year Established: 1894. Pub. Frequency: w. (Wed.) Page Size: broadsheet. Subscrip. Rate: $.75 newsstand/cover; $20/yr in county; $28/yr out of county. Adv. Rate: color page $4.75 Circulation: 2,200 per issue (paid and free). **Owner(s):** Len Robbins, See address and contact information above. **Management:** Len Robbins, Publisher. Bonnie Whitley, Classified Adv. Mgr.. Jenny Robins, Sales Manager. **Editorial:** Len Robbins, Editor.

IRWINTON

WILKINSON COUNTY NEWS. 100 High Hill St., Irwinton, GA 31042-9789. Telephone: 478-946-2218. FAX: 478-946-7226. Mailing Address: PO Box 205, Irwinton, GA 31042. Pub. Frequency: w. (Thu.) Page Size: broadsheet. Subscrip. Rate: $.50 newsstand/cover; $18.73/yr in county area; $26.75/yr out of county; $35/yr out of state. Circulation: 3,000 per issue (paid). **Owner(s):** Trib Publications, Inc., PO Box 648, Manchester, GA 31816. Telephone: 706-846-4336. **Management:** Heidi Daniel, Publisher. Teresa Wells, Advertising. **Editorial:** Heidi Daniel, Editor.

JACKSON

JACKSON PROGRESS-ARGUS. 129 Mulberry St, Jackson, GA 30233. Telephone: 770-775-3107. FAX: 770-775-3855. E-MAIL: joethehobo@hotmail.com. Year Established: 1873. Pub. Frequency: w. (Wed.) Page Size: broadsheet. Subscrip. Rate: $.50 newsstand/cover; $24/yr home delivery local; $46/yr mailed out of county; $47.73/yr mailed out of state. Circulation: 4,400 per issue (paid). **Owner(s):** Triple Crown Media, Inc., 546 E Main St, Lexington, KY 40508. Telephone: 859-226-4678. FAX: 859-226-4308. **Management:** Marshall Avett, Publisher. Brenda Hardman, Advertising. **Editorial:** Marshall Avett, Managing Editor.

JASPER

PICKENS COUNTY PROGRESS. 94 N. Main St., Jasper, GA 30143-1504. Telephone: 706-253-2457. FAX: 706-253-9738. E-MAIL: progress@ellijay.com. URL: http://www.pickensprogress.com. Mailing Address: PO Box 67, Jasper, GA 30143. Pub. Frequency: w. (Thu.) Page Size: broadsheet. Subscrip. Rate: $.50 newsstand/cover; $21.40/yr in county & adj. cys.; $28.89/yr mailed in state; $34.24/yr mailed out of state. Circulation: 7,500 per issue (paid). **Owner(s):** Pickens County Progress, Inc., See address and contact information above. **Management:** John R. Pool, Publisher. Martha F. Pool, Advertising Manager. Sheri Crowe, Circulation Manager. **Editorial:** William E. Pool, Managing Editor. Dan Pool, News Editor.

JEFFERSON

JACKSON HERALD (JEFFERSON). 33 Lee St, Jefferson, GA 30549. Telephone: 706-367-5233. E-MAIL: news@mainstreetnews.com. URL: http://www.mainstreetnews.com. Mailing Address: P.O. Box 908, Jefferson, GA 30549. Year Established: 1875. Pub. Frequency: w. (Wed.) Page Size: broadsheet. Subscrip. Rate: $.50 newsstand/cover; $19.75/yr home delivery in county; $38.85/yr mailed out of county; $17.75/yr home delivery in county to senior citizens; $44.50/yr mailed out of state. Circulation: 10,000 per issue (paid). **Owner(s):** MainStreet Newspapers, Inc., See address and contact information above. **Management:** Mike Buffington, General Manager. Herman Buffington, Publisher. Scott Buffington, Advertising Manager. **Editorial:** Mike Buffington, Editor.

JESUP

PINELAND PENNYSAVER, THE. 155 E. Cherry St., Jesup, GA 31545. Telephone: 912-427-8912. FAX: 912-427-0055. Mailing Address: PO Box 606, Jesup, GA 31545. Pub. Frequency: w. (Tue.) Page Size: tabloid. Circulation: 13,000 per issue (controlled). **Owner(s):** Morris Multimedia, Inc., PO Box 210, Cumming, GA 30028. Telephone: 770-887-3126. **Management:** Mark Griffin, Publisher. Goldie Myers, Advertising. **Editorial:** Patrick Watkins, Editor.

PRESS-SENTINEL, THE. 252 W Walnut St, Jesup, GA 31535. Telephone: 912-427-3757. FAX: 912-427—4092. E-MAIL: staff@thepress-sentinel.com. URL: http://www.thepress-sentinel.com. Mailing Address: P.O. Box 607, Jesup, GA 31598-0607. Year Established: 1977. Pub. Frequency: s-w. (Wed. & Sun.) Page Size: broadsheet. Subscrip. Rate: $.50 newsstand/cover; $34/yr mailed in county; $42/yr mailed in state. Adv. Rate: col. inch $9.50 Freelance Pay: $1/column-inch. Circulation: 6,900 per issue (paid). **Owner(s):** Community Newspapers (Athens), Inc., PO Box 792, Athens, GA 30603. **Management:** Eric Denty, Publisher. Melissa Millard, Advertising Director. **Editorial:** Drew Davis, Editor.

LA FAYETTE

WALKER COUNTY MESSENGER. 120 E. Patton St., La Fayette, GA 30728. Telephone: 706-638-1859. FAX: 706-638-7045. URL: http://www.walkermessenger.com. Mailing Address: PO Box 766, La Fayette, GA 30728-0766. Year Established: 1877. Pub. Frequency: s-w. (Wed. & Fri.) Page Size: broadsheet. Subscrip. Rate: $.50 newsstand/cover; $35.31/yr home delivery in county; $48.88/yr mailed out of county; $47/yr mailed out of state. Circulation: 4,050 per issue (paid). **Owner(s):** News Publishing Co., PO Box 1633, Rome, GA 30162. Telephone: 706-291-6397. **Management:** Don Stilwell, Publisher. Pammy Hamilton, Advertising Manager. Angie Dearing, Classified Adv. Mgr.. **Editorial:** Andy Diffendorfer, Editor. Cathy Edgemon, News Editor. Scott Herpst, Sports Editor.

LAKELAND

LANIER COUNTY NEWS. 114 W. Church St., Lakeland, GA 31635-1110. Telephone: 229-896-2233. FAX: 229-896-6353. Mailing Address: PO Box 216, Lakeland, GA 31635-1110. Pub. Frequency: w. (Wed.) Page Size: broadsheet. Subscrip. Rate: $.50 newsstand/cover; $18.75/yr in county; $23.85/yr out of county; $35/yr out of state. Circulation: 1,100 per issue (paid). **Owner(s):** Trib Publications, Inc., PO Box 648, Manchester, GA 31816. Telephone: 706-846-4336. **Management:** Ann Knight, General Manager. Lorrie Rinehart, Publisher.

LAVONIA

FRANKLIN COUNTY CITIZEN. 12150 Augusta Rd., Lavonia, GA 30553. Telephone: 706-356-8557. FAX: 706-356-2008. E-MAIL: fccitizen@alltel.net. URL: http://www.franklincountycitizen.com. Mailing Address: PO Box 580, Lavonia, GA 30553. Year Established: 1971. Pub. Frequency: w. (Thu.) Page Size: broadsheet. Subscrip. Rate: $.50 newsstand/cover; $21/yr in county; $28/yr out of county; $34/yr out of state. Adv. Rate: col. inch $9.95 Circulation: 6,200 per issue (paid). **Owner(s):** Community Newspapers (Athens), Inc., PO Box 792, Athens, GA 30603. Telephone: 800-226-0692. **Management:** Tom Ten Broeck, Publisher. Jennifer Greenway, Office Manager. Lola Breeden, Circulation Manager. **Editorial:** Denise Matthews, Editor.

LEESBURG

LEE COUNTY LEDGER. 124 Fourth St., Leesburg, GA 31763-3131. Telephone: 229-759-2413. FAX: 229-759-6599. E-MAIL: dquinn@leecountyledger.com. URL: http://www.leecountyledger.com. Mailing Address: PO Box 715, Leesburg, GA 31763-0715. Pub. Frequency: w. (Wed.) Page Size: broadsheet. Subscrip. Rate: $.50 newsstand/cover; $17/yr in county; $22/yr out of county. Adv. Rate: col. inch $2.90 Circulation: 3,300 per issue (paid). **Owner(s):** Lee County Ledger Corp., See address and contact information above. **Management:** Derryl Quinn, Publisher. Tina Maples, Advertising Manager. **Editorial:** Jim Quinn, Editor.

LEXINGTON

OGLETHORPE ECHO, THE. 121 Main St., Lexington, GA 30648-0268. Telephone: 706-743-3111. FAX: 706-743-5510. Mailing Address: PO Box 268, Lexington, GA 30648-0268. Pub. Frequency: w. (Thu.) Page Size: broadsheet. Subscrip. Rate: $.35 newsstand/cover; $19.26/yr in county; $25.68/yr mailed out of county; $30/yr mailed out of state. Circulation: 3,400 per issue (paid). **Owner(s):** Ralph B. Maxwell, Sr., PO Box 268, Lexington, GA 30648. Telephone: 706-743-3111. **Management:** Ralph B. Maxwell Jr., Publisher. **Editorial:** Ralph B. Maxwell Jr., Editor.

LOUISVILLE

NEWS & FARMER/JEFFERSON REPORTER. 615 Mulberry St., Louisville, GA 30434. Telephone: 478-625-7722. FAX: 478-625-8816. E-MAIL: editor@thenewsandfarmer.com. URL: http://www.thenewsandfarmer.com. Mailing Address: P.O Box 487, Louisville, GA 30434. Pub. Frequency: w. (Thu.) Page Size: broadsheet. Subscrip. Rate: $.75 newsstand/cover; $22/yr in county; $30/yr out of county; $35/yr out of state. Circulation: 5,100 per issue (paid). **Owner(s):** Morris Publishing Group, See address and contact information above. **Management:** Sam Eason, General Manager. Becky Irwin, Circulation Manager. David Irwin, Sales Manager. **Editorial:** Parish Howard, Editor.

MADISON

LAKE OCONEE BREEZE. 131 E. Jefferson St., Madison, GA 30650-0191. Telephone: 478-453-1454. FAX: 478-453-1429. Mailing Address: PO Box 520, Milledgeville, GA 31061. Year Established: 1985. Pub. Frequency: w. (Wed.) Page Size: broadsheet Circulation: 4,000 per issue (free). **Owner(s):** Community Newspaper Holdings, Inc., 3500 Colonnade Pkwy., Ste. 600, Birmingham, AL 35243. Telephone: 205-298-7100. FAX: 205-298-7101. **Management:** Keith Barlow, Publisher. Billy Sutton, Advertising. **Editorial:** Judy Bailey, Executive Editor.

MANCHESTER

HARRIS COUNTY JOURNAL. 3051 Roosevelt Hwy, Manchester, GA 31816. Telephone: 706-846-3188. FAX: 706-846-2206. Mailing Address: PO Box 426, Manchester, GA 31816-0426. Pub. Frequency: w. (Thu.) Page Size: broadsheet. Subscrip. Rate: $.50 newsstand/cover; $20/yr in county; $26/yr out of county. Circulation: 2,200 per issue (paid). **Owner(s):** Grimes Publications, See address and contact information above. **Management:** Millard Grimes, Owner. Johnny Kuykendall, Publisher. **Editorial:** Johnny Kuykendall, Editor.

HOGANSVILLE HERALD. 3051 Roosevelt Hwy, Manchester, GA 31816. Telephone: 706-846-3188. FAX: 706-846-2206. Mailing Address: PO Box 426, Manchester, GA 31816-0426. Pub. Frequency: w. (Thu.) Page Size: broadsheet. Subscrip. Rate: $.50 newsstand/cover; $20/yr in county; $26/yr out of county. Circulation: 1,150 per issue (paid). **Owner(s):** Grimes Publications, See address and contact information above. **Management:** Millard Grimes, Owner. Johnny Kuykendall, Publisher.

MANCHESTER STAR-MERCURY. 3051 Roosevelt Hwy, Manchester, GA 31816. Telephone: 706-846-3188. FAX: 706-846-2206. E-MAIL: starmercury2@earthlink.net. Mailing Address: PO Box 426, Manchester, GA 31816-0426. Year Established: 1911. Pub. Frequency: w. (Wed.) Page Size: broadsheet. Subscrip. Rate: $.50 newsstand/cover; $20/yr in county; $26/yr mailed out of county. Circulation: 3,650 per issue (paid). **Owner(s):** Grimes Publications, See address and contact information above. **Management:** Millard Grimes, Owner. Johnny Kuykendall, Publisher. **Editorial:** Rob Richardson, Editor.

MERIWETHER VINDICATOR. 3051 Roosevelt Hwy, Manchester, GA 31816. Telephone: 706-846-3188. FAX: 706-846-2206. E-MAIL: starmercury2@earthlink.net. Mailing Address: PO Box 426, Manchester, GA 31816-0426. Year Established: 1876. Pub. Frequency: w. (Fri.) Page Size: broadsheet. Subscrip. Rate: $.50 newsstand/cover; $20/yr mailed in county; $26/yr mailed out of county. Circulation: 1,700 per issue (paid). **Owner(s):** Grimes Publications, See address and contact information above. **Management:** Millard Grimes, Owner. Johnny Kuykendall, Publisher. **Editorial:** Rob Richardson, Editor.

TALBOTTON NEW ERA. 3051 Roosevelt Hwy, Manchester, GA 31816. Telephone: 706-846-3188. FAX: 706-846-2206. E-MAIL: starmercury2@earthlink.net. Mailing Address: PO Box 426, Manchester, GA 31816-0426. Pub. Frequency: w. (Thu.) Page Size: broadsheet. Subscrip. Rate: $.50 newsstand/cover; $20/yr in county; $26/yr out of county. Circulation: 1,000 per issue (paid). **Owner(s):** Grimes Publications, See address and contact information above. **Management:** Millard Grimes, Owner. Johnny Kuykendall, Publisher. **Editorial:** Billy Bryant, Editor.

MARIETTA

ACWORTH NEIGHBOR. ISSN 0191-7269
580 Fairground St., Marietta, GA 30060. Telephone: 770-428-9411. FAX: 770-422-9533. Mailing Address: PO Box 449, Marietta, GA 30061. Year Established: 1815. Pub. Frequency: w. (Thu.) Page Size: broadsheet.Subscrip. Rate: $28; $56 for 6 mos.; $112 Circulation: 20,850 per issue (free). **Owner(s):** Marietta Daily Journal & Neighbor Newspapers, Inc., See address and contact information above. **Management:** Otis A. Brumby Jr., Publisher. Wade Stephens, Advertising Manager. Rusty Powell, Circulation Manager. **Editorial:** Robert Nesmith, Editor.

AUSTELL NEIGHBOR. ISSN 0191-7382
580 Fairground St., Marietta, GA 30060. Telephone: 770-428-9411. FAX: 770-422-9533. Mailing Address: PO Box 449, Marietta, GA 30061. Pub. Frequency: w. (Thu.) Page Size: broadsheet. Subscrip. Rate: $112 mailed local deliv. Circulation: 6,500 per issue (paid and free). **Owner(s):** Marietta Daily Journal & Neighbor Newspapers, Inc., See address and contact information above. **Management:** Otis A. Brumby Jr., Publisher. Wade Stephens, Advertising Manager. Rusty Powell, Circulation Manager.

EAST COBBER. PO Box 672121, Marietta, GA 30006-0036. Pub. Frequency: m. Subscrip. Rate: $12/yr. Adv. Rate: page $800 Circulation: 40,000. **Owner(s):** Community Communications, See address and contact information above. **Management:** Cynthia M Rozzo, Publisher. **Editorial:** Cynthia M Rozzo, Editor.

KENNESAW NEIGHBOR, THE. ISSN 0191-7072
580 Fairground St., Marietta, GA 30060. Telephone: 770-428-9411. FAX: 770-422-9533. Mailing Address: PO Box 449, Marietta, GA 30061. Pub. Frequency: w. (Wed.) Page Size: broadsheet. Subscrip. Rate: $50 newsstand/cover; $28 mailed; $56 for 6 mos.; $112/yr. **Owner(s):** Marietta Daily Journal & Neighbor Newspapers, Inc., See address and contact information above. **Management:** Otis A. Brumby Jr., Publisher. Wade Stephens, Advertising Manager. Rusty Powell, Circulation Manager. **Editorial:** Mark Maguire, Editor.

MABLETON NEIGHBOR, THE. ISSN 0192-2483
580 Fairground St., Marietta, GA 30060. Telephone: 770-428-9411. FAX: 770-422-9533. Mailing Address: PO Box 449, Marietta, GA 30061. Year Established: 1973. Pub. Frequency: w. (Wed.) Page Size: broadsheet Circulation: 6,375 per issue (free). **Owner(s):** Marietta Daily Journal & Neighbor Newspapers, Inc., See address and contact information above. **Management:** Otis A. Brumby Jr., Publisher. Wade Stephens, Advertising Manager. Terry Toth, Classified Adv. Mgr.. **Editorial:** Mark Maguire, Editor.

POWDER SPRINGS NEIGHBOR, THE. ISSN 0191-5525
580 Fairground St., Marietta, GA 30060. Telephone: 770-428-9411. FAX: 770-422-9533. Mailing Address: PO Box 449, Marietta, GA 30061. Pub. Frequency: w. (Thu.) Page Size: broadsheet. Subscrip. Rate: $.50 newsstand/cover; $28 for 3 mos.; $112/yr mailed. Circulation: 7,864 per issue (free). **Owner(s):** Marietta Daily Journal & Neighbor Newspapers, Inc., See address and contact information above. **Management:** Otis A. Brumby Jr., Publisher. Wade Stephens, Advertising Manager. Rusty Powell, Circulation Manager. Terry Toth, Classified Adv. Mgr.. **Editorial:** Joe Kirby, Editor.

MCRAE

TELFAIR ENTERPRISE, THE. 237 W Oak St, McRae, GA 31055. Telephone: 229-868-6015. FAX: 229-868-5486. E-MAIL: telfairenterprise@alltel.net. URL: http://www.thetelfairenterprise.com. Mailing Address: P.O. Boc 269, McRae, GA 31055. Year Established: 1887. Pub. Frequency: w. (Wed.) Page Size: standard. Subscrip. Rate: $.75 newsstand/cover; $25/yr in county; $32/yr out of county; $34/yr out of state. Circulation: 3,200 per issue (paid). **Owner(s):** Community Newspapers (Athens), Inc., PO Box 792, Athens, GA 30603. **Management:** Donna Bell, General Manager. Eric Denty, Publisher. Jennifer Swain, Advertising Manager. **Editorial:** Kelly Arnold, Editor.

METTER

METTER ADVERTISER, THE. PO Box 8, Metter, GA 30439. Telephone: 912-685-6566. FAX: 912-685-4901. E-MAIL: news@metteradvertiser.com. URL: http://www.metteradvertiser.com. Year Established: 1912. Pub. Frequency: w. (Wed.) Page Size: broadsheet. Subscrip. Rate: $.50 newsstand/cover; $21.40/yr in county; $26.75/yr in state; $32.10/yr out of state. Circulation: 3,000 per issue (paid). **Owner(s):** Snell Publications, Inc., See address and contact information above. **Management:** Carvy Snell III, Publisher. Michelle Booth, Advertising Manager. Mandi Carroll, Circulation Manager. **Editorial:** Carvy Snell III, Editor.

MILLEN

MILLEN NEWS, THE. 856 Cotton Ave, Millen, GA 30442. Telephone: 478-982-5460. FAX: 478-982-1785. Mailing Address: PO Box 909, Millen, GA 30442-0909. Year Established: 1903. Pub. Frequency: w. (Wed.) Page Size: broadsheet. Subscrip. Rate: $.50 newsstand/cover; $20/yr in county. Adv. Rate: col. inch $6 Circulation: 2,200 per issue (paid). **Owner(s):** Chalker Publishing Co., 547 E. Sixth St., Waynesboro, GA 30830. Telephone: 706-554-7888. FAX: 706-554-2437. **Management:** Roy F. Chalker, Publisher. **Editorial:** Roy F. Chalker, Editor.

MONROE

WALTON TRIBUNE, THE. ISSN 0893-410X
124 N. Broad St., Monroe, GA 30655. E-MAIL: tribstaff@waltontribune.com. URL: http://www.waltontribune.com. Mailing Address: PO Box 808, Monroe, GA 30655. Year Established: 1900. Pub. Frequency: s-w. (Wed. & Sun.) Page Size: broadsheet. Subscrip. Rate: $.75 newsstand/cover; $52/yr home delivery. Adv. Rate: col. inch $8.95 Circulation: 5,500 per issue (paid). **Owner(s):** Southern Newspapers, Inc., 5701 Woodway Dr., Ste. 131, Houston, TX 77057-1589. **Management:** David Clemons, Publisher. Peggy Wheldon, Advertising Manager. Lisa Owens, Business Manager. **Editorial:** David Clemons, Editor. Brian Arrington, Managing Editor. Robbie Schwartz, News Editor. Danny Daniels, Sports Editor.

MONTEZUMA

CITIZEN & GEORGIAN. 305 S. Dooley St., Montezuma, GA 31063. Telephone: 478-472-7755. FAX: 478-472-5753. Pub. Frequency: w. (Wed.) Page Size: broadsheet. Subscrip. Rate: $.50 newsstand/cover; $18.65/yr in county; $25.80/yr out of county. Circulation: 3,000 per issue (paid). **Owner(s):** Danny Evans Newspapers, PO Box 220, Montezuma, GA 31063-0220. Telephone: 912-472-7755. **Management:** Danny Evans, Publisher. **Editorial:** Judy Robinson, Editor. Sherri Martin, Associate Editor.

MONTICELLO

MONTICELLO NEWS, THE. 237 W. Washington St., Monticello, GA 31064-1241. Telephone: 706-468-6511. FAX: 706-468-6576. E-MAIL: editor@themonticellonews.com. Year Established: 1881. Pub. Frequency: w. (Thu.) Page Size: broadsheet. Subscrip. Rate: $.50 newsstand/cover; $21/yr in county; $26/yr out of county. Adv. Rate: col. inch $4.50 **Wire Service(s):** AP. Circulation: 3,100 per issue (paid). **Owner(s):** Kathy Mudd, PO Box 30, Monticello, GA 31064-0030. Telephone: 706-468-6511. **Management:** Jenny Phillips, Advertising Manager. **Editorial:** Kathy Mudd, Editor.

NAHUNTA

BRANTLEY ENTERPRISE, THE. 108A N Main St., Nahunta, GA 31553. Telephone: 912-462-6776. FAX: 912-462-8047. E-MAIL: news@brantleyenterprise.com. URL: http://www.brantleyenterprise.com. Mailing Address: PO Box 454, Nahunta, GA 31553-0454. Year Established: 1920. Pub. Frequency: w. (Thu.) Page Size: broadsheet. Subscrip. Rate: $.50 newsstand/cover; $20/yr in county; $25/yr out of county. Circulation: 3,000 per issue (paid). **Owner(s):** Ken Buchanan, See address and contact information above. **Management:** Ken Buchanan, Publisher. **Editorial:** Ken Buchanan, Editor.

NASHVILLE

BERRIEN PRESS. 200 E. McPherson Ave., Nashville, GA 31639. Telephone: 229-686-3523. FAX: 229-686-7771. E-MAIL: theberrienpress@alltel.net. Year Established: 1959. Pub. Frequency: w. (Wed.) Page Size: broadsheet. Subscrip. Rate: $.50 newsstand/cover; $21.50/yr in county; $32/yr mailed out of county; $43.50/yr mailed out of state. Circulation: 4,800 per issue (paid). **Owner(s):** Barbara H. Boyd, See address and contact information above. **Management:** Jonna Exum, General Manager. **Editorial:** Donald Boyd, Editor. Debbie Cole, Assistant Editor.

PEARSON

ATKINSON COUNTY CITIZEN. 302 Austin Ave., Pearson, GA 31642. Telephone: 912-422-3824. FAX: 912-422-6050. Mailing Address: PO Box 398, Pearson, GA 31642-0398. Year Established: 1914. Pub. Frequency: w. (Thu.) Page Size: broadsheet. Subscrip. Rate: $.50 newsstand/cover; $19.26/yr in county; $28.89/yr out of county. Adv. Rate: col. inch $4 Circulation: 1,400 per issue (paid). **Owner(s):** Blalock Lovett & Assoc., Inc., 1802 Lee Ave., Ste. 332, Tifton, GA 31794. Telephone: 229-388-9580. FAX: 229-382-1022. **Management:** Blalock Lovett, Publisher. **Editorial:** Joan Vickers, Editor.

PELHAM

PELHAM JOURNAL. 310 W. Railroad St., Pelham, GA 31779. Telephone: 229-294-3661. FAX: 229-336-8426. Year Established: 1902. Pub. Frequency: w. (Wed.) Page Size: standard. Subscrip. Rate: $.50 newsstand/cover; $21.50/yr home delivery in county; $30/yr mailed in state; $35/yr mailed out of state. Circulation: 1,950 per issue (paid). **Owner(s):** Trib Publications, Inc., PO Box 648, Manchester, GA 31816. Telephone: 706-846-4336. **Management:** Roger Anne Davis, Publisher. Susan Sowell, Advertising Manager. **Editorial:** Roger Anne Davis, Editor.

POOLER

POOLER NEWS. 504 W Hwy 80, Unit 4, Pooler, GA 31322. Telephone: 912-748-3446. FAX: 912-450-6397. E-MAIL: dcamma@poolernews.com. URL: http://www.poolernews.com. Pub. Frequency: w. (Thu.) Page Size: broadsheet Circulation: 6,500 per issue (free). **Owner(s):** Morris Newspaper Corporation, 27 Abercorn St., Savannah, GA 31401. Telephone: 912-233-1281. FAX: 912-232-4639. **Management:** David Camma, Advertising. **Editorial:** William Saunders, Editor. Lynnette Spratley, Writer.

QUITMAN

QUITMAN FREE PRESS. 112 N. Lee St., Quitman, GA 31643-2124. Telephone: 229-263-4615. FAX: 229-263-5282. Mailing Address: PO Box 72, Quitman, GA 31643. Year Established: 1876. Pub. Frequency: w. (Wed.) Page Size: broadsheet. Subscrip. Rate: $.50 newsstand/cover; $21.40/yr in county; $26.75/yr mailed out of county; $35/yr mailed out of state. Circulation: 3,600 per issue (paid). **Owner(s):** Trib Publications, Inc., PO Box 648, Manchester, GA 31816. Telephone: 706-846-4336. **Management:** Ann Knight, General Manager. **Editorial:** Bonnell Holmes, Editor.

REIDSVILLE

TATTNALL JOURNAL. 114B N. Main St., Reidsville, GA 30453. Telephone: 912-557-6761. FAX: 912-557-4132. E-MAIL: mail@tatnalljournal.com. URL: http://www.tattnalljournal.com. Mailing Address: PO Box 278, Reidsville, GA 30453. Year Established: 1879. Pub. Frequency: w. (Thu.) Page Size: broadsheet. Subscrip. Rate: $.50 newsstand/cover; $22/yr in county; $26/yr out of county. Circulation: 4,406 per issue (paid). **Owner(s):** Russell J. Rhoden, See address and contact information above. **Management:** Lillian Durrence, Advertising Manager. **Editorial:** Allison Cobb, Editor.

RICHLAND

STEWART-WEBSTER-JOURNAL-PATRIOT. 106 E. Broad St., Richland, GA 31825-0250. Telephone: 229-887-3674. FAX: 229-887-2800. E-MAIL: swjcp@bellsouth.net. Mailing Address: P.O. Box 250, Richland, GA 31825-0250. Pub. Frequency: w. (Thu.) Page Size: broadsheet. Subscrip. Rate: $.50 newsstand/cover; $19.95/yr in county; $27/yr out of county; $36/yr mailed out of state. Circulation: 1,800 per issue (paid). **Owner(s):** Rolin Publishing Co., See address and contact information above. **Management:** Ron Provencher, Publisher. **Editorial:** Linda Provencher, Editor.

RICHMOND HILL

BRYAN COUNTY NEWS. PO Box 1239, Richmond Hill, GA 31324. Telephone: 912-756-2668. FAX: 912-756-5907. E-MAIL: bcnewseditor@bryancountynews.net. URL: www.bryancountynews.net. Pub. Frequency: w. (Thu.) Page Size: broadsheet. Subscrip. Rate: $.50 newsstand/cover; $24/yr in county; $27/yr out of county; $34/yr out of state. Circulation: 2,100 per issue (paid). **Owner(s):** Morris Newspaper Corporation, 27 Abercorn St., Savannah, GA 31401. **Management:** Jamie Lawson, General Manager. Marla Busbee, Office Manager. Tina Lamson, Advertising. **Editorial:** Sonya Campbell, Editor.

RINCON

EFFINGHAM HERALD, THE. 586 South Columbia Ave #13, Rincon, GA 31326. Telephone: 912-826-5012. FAX: 912-826-0381. E-MAIL: efulford@effinghamherald.net. URL: http://www.effinghamherald.net. Year Established: 1908. Pub. Frequency: s-w. (Tue & Fri..) Page Size: broadsheet. Subscrip. Rate: $.50 newsstand/cover; $35/yr in county; $40/yr out of county. Adv. Rate: col. inch $7.50 Circulation: 4,100 per issue (paid). **Owner(s):** Morris Newspaper Corporation, 27 Abercorn St., Savannah, GA 31401. Telephone: 912-233-1281. FAX: 912-232-4639. **Management:** Karen Tanksley, Publisher. Julie Hales, Advertising Manager. Melissa Mincey, Classified Adv. Mgr.. **Editorial:** Edward Fulford, Managing Editor.

RINGGOLD

CATOOSA COUNTY NEWS, THE. 7513 Nashville St., Ringgold, GA 30736. Telephone: 706-935-2621. FAX: 706-965-5934. E-MAIL: rball@catoosanews.com. URL: http://www.catoosanews.com. Mailing Address: PO Box 40, Ringgold, GA 30736. Year Established: 1949. Pub. Frequency: w. (Wed.) Page Size: broadsheet. Subscrip. Rate: $.50 newsstand/cover; $22.47/yr in county; $37.45/yr out of county; $35/yr out of state. Circulation: 3,500 per issue (paid). **Owner(s):** News Publishing Co., PO Box 1633, Rome, GA 30162. Telephone: 706-290-5290. **Management:** B H Mooney III, Owner. Don Stilwell, Publisher. Cindy Block, Classified Editor. **Editorial:** Stan Guess, Editor. Chris Zelk, News Editor. Misty Chastin-Martin, Sports Editor.

ROBERTA

GEORGIA POST, THE. 58 S. Dugger Ave., Roberta, GA 31078. Telephone: 479-836-3195. FAX: 478-836-9634. Mailing Address: PO Box 860, Roberta, GA 31078. Year Established: 1921. Pub. Frequency: w. (Thu.) Page Size: broadsheet. Subscrip. Rate: $.50 newsstand/cover; $15/yr in county; $20/yr out of county. Adv. Rate: col. inch $4 Circulation: 1,900 per issue (paid). **Owner(s):** Crawford Publishing LLC, See address and contact information above. **Management:** Floyd M. Buford Jr., Publisher. **Editorial:** Glisa Buford, Editor. Celia Martin, Managing Editor.

ROCKMART

ROCKMART JOURNAL. 238 S. Piedmont Ave., Rockmart, GA 30153. Telephone: 770-684-7811. FAX: 770-684-8468. E-MAIL: lvickers@rockmartjrl.com. URL: http://www.rockmartjournal.com. Mailing Address: PO Box 609, Rockmart, GA 30153. Year Established: 1873. Pub. Frequency: w. (Wed.) Page Size: broadsheet. Subscrip. Rate: $.50 newsstand/cover; $26.75/yr in county; $41/yr out of county. Circulation: 11,000 per issue (paid and free). **Owner(s):** B.H. Mooney, III, PO Box 1633, Rome, GA 30162. Telephone: 706-291-6397. **Management:** Lowell Vickers, Publisher. Rick Stone, Advertising Manager. **Editorial:** Lowell Vickers, Editor. Agnes Hagin, News Editor. Jerome Stewart, Sports Editor.

ROME

CHATTOOGA PRESS. 305 E. Sixth Ave., Rome, GA 30161. Telephone: 706-857-5433. FAX: 706-234-6478. Mailing Address: PO Box 485, Summerville, GA 30747. Year Established: 1982. Pub. Frequency: w. (Wed.) Page Size: broadsheet Circulation: 11,500 per issue (free). **Owner(s):** News Publishing Co., PO Box 1633, Rome, GA 30162. Telephone: 706-290-5330. **Management:** Trip Hatley, Advertising Manager. **Editorial:** Pamella Purcell, Editor.

ROSWELL

ROSWELL-ALPHARETTA NEIGHBOR. ISSN 0192-2637
10930 Crabapple Rd., Ste. 210, Roswell, GA 30075. Telephone: 770-993-7400. FAX: 770-518-6062. Year Established: 1980. Pub. Frequency: w. (Wed.) Page Size: broadsheet. Subscrip. Rate: $.50 newsstand/cover. Circulation: 48,000 per issue (controlled and free). **Owner(s):** Marietta Daily Journal & Neighbor Newspapers, 580 Fairground St., Marietta, GA 30060. Telephone: 770-428-9411. FAX: 770-422-9533. **Management:** Otis A Brumby Jr., Publisher. Terri Toth, Classified Adv. Mgr.. **Editorial:** Everett Catts, Editor. Mark McGuire, Managing Editor. Charles Strong, Sports Editor.

ROYSTON

ROYSTON NEWS LEADER. 70 Lee St., Royston, GA 30662. Telephone: 706-245-7351. FAX: 706-245-5991. URL: http://www.roystonnewsleader.com. Mailing Address: PO Box 26, Royston, GA 30662. Year Established: 1978. Pub. Frequency: w. (Thu.) Page Size: broadsheet. Subscrip. Rate: $.50 newsstand/cover; $21/yr in county; $28/yr out of county; $34/yr out of state. Circulation: 4,000 per issue (paid). **Owner(s):** Community Newspapers (Athens), Inc., PO Box 792, Athens, GA 30603. Telephone: 706-548-0808. **Management:** Tom Ten Broeck, Publisher. Bonnie Partain, Office Manager. Brandy Harris, Advertising. **Editorial:** Denise Matthews, Editor.

SANDERSVILLE

SANDERSVILLE PROGRESS. 118 E. Haynes St., Sandersville, GA 31082. Telephone: 478-552-3161. FAX: 478-552-5177. E-MAIL: heidie@sandersvilleprogress.net. URL: http://www.sandersvilleprogress.com. Mailing Address: P.O. Box 431, Sandersville, GA 31082. Year Established: 1887. Pub. Frequency: w. (Wed.) Page Size: broadsheet. Subscrip. Rate: $.50 newsstand/cover; $21.40/yr home delivery in county; $29.96/yr mailed out of county plus tax; $35/yr mailed out of state. Circulation: 5,300 per issue (paid). **Owner(s):** Robert Tribble, See address and contact information above. **Management:** Robert Tribble, President. Theresa Wheels, Advertising Manager. Heidie Daniels, Circulation Manager.

SAVANNAH

CONNECT SAVANNAH. 1800 E. Victory Dr., Savannah, GA 31404. Telephone: 912-231-0250. FAX: 912-231-9932. E-MAIL: jim@connectsavannah.com. URL: www.connectsavannah.com. Pub. Frequency: w. (Wed.) Page Size: broadsheet. Subscrip. Rate: $39 mailed for 6 mos.; $78/yr. Circulation: 21,000 per issue (paid and free). **Owner(s):** Morris Multimedia, Inc., 725 Broad St, Augusta, GA 30901. Telephone: 706-724-0851. FAX: 706-722-7125. **Editorial:** Jim Morekis, Editor.

SOPERTON

MONTGOMERY MONITOR. P.O. Box 527, Soperton, GA 30457. Telephone: 912-529-6624. FAX: 912-529-5399. E-MAIL: monitor@nlamerica.com. Pub. Frequency: w. (Wed.) Page Size: broadsheet. Subscrip. Rate: $.50 newsstand/cover; $20/yr in county; $31/yr out of county. Circulation: 1,950 per issue (paid). **Owner(s):** Herald Publishing Co., P.O. Drawer B, Court-Square Sta., Dublin, GA 31040. Telephone: 478-272-5522. **Management:** Griffin Lovett, Publisher. Marsha Green, Advertising Manager. **Editorial:** Dubose Porter, Editor.

SOPERTON NEWS, THE. P.O. Box 527, Soperton, GA 30457. Telephone: 912-529-6624. FAX: 912-529-5399. E-MAIL: sopertonnews@nlamerica.com. Year Established: 1914. Pub. Frequency: w. (Wed.) Page Size: broadsheet. Subscrip. Rate: $.50 newsstand/cover; $20/yr in county; $31/yr out of county. Adv. Rate: col. inch $5 Circulation: 2,050 per issue (paid). **Owner(s):** Herald Publishing Co., P.O. Drawer B, Court-Square Sta., Dublin, GA 31040. Telephone: 478-272-5522. **Management:** Griffin Lovett, Publisher. Marsha Green, Advertising Manager. **Editorial:** Jonathan Findley, Editor. Dubose Porter, Executive Editor. Griffin Lovett, Managing Editor.

WHEELER COUNTY EAGLE. P.O. Box 527, Soperton, GA 30457. Telephone: 912-529-6624. E-MAIL: eagle@nlamerica.com. Mailing Address: PO Box 409, Alamo, GA 30411. Pub. Frequency: w. (Wed.) Page Size: broadsheet. Subscrip. Rate: $.50 newsstand/cover; $19.32/yr in county; $30.77/yr out of county. Adv. Rate: col. inch $5 Circulation: 1,081 per issue (paid). **Owner(s):** Herald Publishing Co., P.O. Drawer B, Court-Square Sta., Dublin, GA 31040. Telephone: 478-272-5522. **Management:** Griffin Lovett, Publisher. Marsha Green, Advertising Manager. **Editorial:** Dubose Porter, Editor.

ST. MARYS

TRIBUNE & GEORGIAN. ISSN 1551-8353
206 Osborne St, St. Marys, GA 31558. Telephone: 912-882-4927. FAX: 912-882-6519. E-MAIL: editor1@tds.net. URL: http://www.tribune-georgian.com. Mailing Address: PO Box 470, St. Marys, GA 31558. Year Established: 1996. Pub. Frequency: s-w. (Wed. & Fri.) Page Size: broadsheet. Subscrip. Rate: $.50 newsstand/cover; $24/yr in county; $50/yr mailed out of county; $50/yr mailed out of state. Freelance Pay: $12/article. Circulation: 7,800 per issue (paid). **Owner(s):** Community Newspapers (Athens), Inc., PO Box 792, Athens, GA 30603. Telephone: 800-226-0692. FAX: 706-548-0808. **Management:** Alan NeSmith, Publisher. Tom Latos, Advertising Director. Terri Teston, Circulation Manager. **Editorial:** Jill Helton, Editor. Chris Fernsler, Sports Editor.

SUMMERVILLE

SUMMERVILLE NEWS, THE. 20 Wildlife Lake Rd., Summerville, GA 30747-0310. Telephone: 706-857-2494. FAX: 706-857-2393. Mailing Address: PO Box 310, Summerville, GA 30747-0310. Year Established: 1886. Pub. Frequency: w. (Thu.) Page Size: broadsheet. Subscrip. Rate: $.50 newsstand/cover; $19.26/yr in county. Circulation: 7,800 per issue (paid). **Owner(s):** David, Winston E., Greg, Tracy Espy, See address and contact information above. **Management:** David Espy, General Manager. Winston E. Espy, Publisher. **Editorial:** Winston E. Espy, Editor. Greg Espy, Production Manager.

SWAINSBORO

FOREST-BLADE, THE. 416 W. Moring St., Swainsboro, GA 30401. Telephone: 478-237-9971. FAX: 478-237-9451. E-MAIL: news@forest-blade.com. URL: http://www.forest-blade.com. Mailing Address: PO Box 938, Swainsboro, GA 30401. Year Established: 1859. Pub. Frequency: w. (Wed.) Page Size: broadsheet. Subscrip. Rate: $.50 newsstand/cover; $35/yr in state; $46/yr out of state. Circulation: 16,000 per issue (paid and free). **Owner(s):** Smith Newspapers Inc., PO Box 27, Fort Payne, AL 35968. Telephone: 256-845-5510. FAX: 256-845-5509. **Management:** Wally Gallian, Publisher. Gail Douglas, Advertising. **Editorial:** Wally Gillian, Managing Editor. Jacquie Brasher, Feature Editor. Martha Lewis, Society Editor. Mac Kanady, Sports Editor.

SYLVANIA

SYLVANIA TELEPHONE, THE. 208 N. Main St., Sylvania, GA 30467-0010. Telephone: 912-564-2045. FAX: 912-564-7055. E-MAIL: sylte2@planters.net. URL: http://www.sylvaniatelephone.com. Mailing Address: PO Box 10, Sylvania, GA 30467-0010. Year Established: 1879. Pub. Frequency: w. (Thu.) Page Size: broadsheet. Subscrip. Rate: $.50 newsstand/cover; $20/yr in county; $25/yr out of county; $30/yr out of state. Freelance Pay: $50/story. Circulation: 5,000 per issue (paid). **Owner(s):** Community Newspapers (Athens), Inc., PO Box 792, Athens, GA 30603. Telephone: 706-548-0010. FAX: 706-548-0808. **Management:** Enoch Autry, Publisher. Kim Mitchell, Advertising. Betsy Carver, Circulation Manager. **Editorial:** Enoch Autry, Editor.

SYLVESTER

SYLVESTER LOCAL NEWS. PO Box 387, Sylvester, GA 31791. Telephone: 229-776-7713. Year Established: 1884. Pub. Frequency: w. (Wed.) Page Size: standard. Subscrip. Rate: $.50 newsstand/cover; $18/yr in county; $22/yr out of county; $30/yr elsewhere. Circulation: 3,800 per issue (paid). **Owner(s):** Leigh H. Ford, See address and contact information above. **Management:** Leigh H. Ford, Publisher. Marilyn Powell, Advertising Manager. **Editorial:** Leigh H. Ford, Editor.

THOMSON

MCDUFFIE PROGRESS, THE. 101 Church St., S.W., Thomson, GA 30824-1090. Telephone: 706-595-1601. FAX: 706-597-8974. E-MAIL: kfoutz@jeffersonenergy.com. URL: http://www.mcduffieprogress.com. Mailing Address: PO Box 1090, Thomson, GA 30824-1090. Year Established: 1899. Pub. Frequency: s-w. (Wed. & Sun.) Page Size: broadsheet. Subscrip. Rate: $.50 newsstand/cover; $25 mailed for 6 mos. in county; $40/yr in county; $65/yr mailed out of county. Circulation: 4,500 per issue (paid). **Owner(s):** McDuffie County Newspapers, Inc., PO Box 1090, Thomson, GA 30824. Telephone: 706-595-1601. **Management:** Matt Reynolds, Publisher. Dan Dyches, Advertising Manager. Debbie Reese, Circulation Manager. Michele Hagerman, Classified Editor. **Editorial:** Tom Turner, Managing Editor.

TIFTON

TIFTAREA SHOPPER. 147 Love Ave., Tifton, GA 31794-4832. Telephone: 229-386-0472. FAX: 229-386-0478. E-MAIL: tiftareashoper@friendlycity.net. Mailing Address: PO Box 1549, Tifton, GA 31794. Year Established: 1973. Pub. Frequency: w. (Tue.) Page Size: broadsheet Circulation: 19,500 per issue (free). **Owner(s):** Tracy Mayo, See address and contact information above. **Management:** Tracy Mayo, Publisher. Boyd Sumler, Manager. **Editorial:** Tracy Mayo, Editor.

TOCCOA

TOCCOA RECORD. 151 W. Doyle St., Toccoa, GA 30577. Telephone: 706-886-9476. FAX: 706-886-2161. E-MAIL: chieftain@alltel.net. URL: http://www.thetaccoarecord.com. Mailing Address: P.O. Drawer 1069, Toccoa, GA 30577. Pub. Frequency: s-w. (Tue. & Fri.) Page Size: standard. Subscrip. Rate: $.50 newsstand/cover; $25/yr in county; $34/yr out of county; $40/yr mailed out of state. Circulation: 7,300 per issue (paid). **Owner(s):** Community Newspapers (Athens), Inc., PO Box 792, Athens, GA 30603. Telephone: 706-548-0010. FAX: 706-548-0808. **Management:** Tom Law, Publisher. Joel Jenkins, Advertising Director. **Editorial:** Ralph Willis, Editor. Tom Law, Managing Editor. Gloria Robinson, Circulation Editor.

VIDALIA

ADVANCE PROGRESS, THE. ISSN 1059-3608
205 E. First St., Vidalia, GA 30474. Telephone: 912-537-3131. FAX: 912-537-4899. E-MAIL: wfladvance@bellsouth.net. Mailing Address: PO Box 669, Vidalia, GA 30475-0669. Pub. Frequency: w. (Wed.) Page Size: broadsheet. Subscrip. Rate: $.50 newsstand/cover; $30/yr local; $45/yr out of area. Circulation: 7,000 per issue (paid). **Owner(s):** Advance Publications, Inc., See address and contact information above. **Management:** William F. Ledford Jr., Publisher. Daniel Ford, Advertising Manager. Gail Cauley, Circulation Director. **Editorial:** William F. Ledford Jr., Editor. Melissa Holdren, Production Manager.

ADVANTAGE (VIDALIA), THE. 205 E. First St., Vidalia, GA 30474. Telephone: 912-537-3131. FAX: 912-537-4899. E-MAIL: advance@cybersouth.com. Mailing Address: PO Box 669, Vidalia, GA 30475-0669. Year Established: 1978. Pub. Frequency: w. (Mon.) Page Size: tabloid Circulation: 23,000 per issue (free). **Owner(s):** Advance Publications, Inc., See address and contact information above. **Management:** William F Ledford Jr., Publisher. Daniel Ford, Advertising Manager. Gail Cauley, Classified Adv. Mgr.. **Editorial:** William F Ledford Jr., Editor. William F. Ledford Jr., Managing Editor. Melissa Holdren, Production Manager.

WASHINGTON

NEWS-REPORTER, THE. 116 W. Robert Toombs Ave., Washington, GA 30673-1664. Telephone: 706-678-2636. FAX: 706-678-3857. E-MAIL: editor@news-reporter.com. URL: http://www.news-reporter.com. Mailing Address: PO Box 340, Washington, GA 30673-0340. Year Established: 1896. Pub. Frequency: w. (Thu.) Page Size: broadsheet. Subscrip. Rate: $.50 per issue; $21/yr local; $28/yr out of county. Circulation: 4,200 per issue (paid). **Owner(s):** Parks S. & Mary J. Newsome, See address and contact information above. **Management:** Parks S. Newsome Jr., Publisher. Cathy Lannae, Advertising. Teri Eno, Circulation Manager. **Editorial:** Parks S. Newsome Jr., Editor. Mary J. Newsome, Managing Editor. Kip Burke, News Editor.

WASHINGTON NEWS-REPORTER. 116 W. Robert Toombs Ave., Washington, GA 30673. Telephone: 706-678-2636. FAX: 706-678-3857. E-MAIL: ncc1701@g-net.net. Year Established: 1919. Pub. Frequency: w. (Thu.) Page Size: standard. Subscrip. Rate: $.50 newsstand/cover; $21/yr in county; $28/yr out of county. Circulation: 5,000 per issue (paid). **Owner(s):** Wilkes Publishing Co., See address and contact information above. **Management:** Sparky Newsome, Publisher. **Editorial:** Sparky Newsome, Editor.

WATKINSVILLE

OCONEE ENTERPRISE, THE. 26 Barnett Shoals Rd., Watkinsville, GA 30677-2500. Telephone: 706-769-5175. FAX: 706-769-8532. E-MAIL: oconeeenterprise@mindspring.com. URL: http://www.oconeeenterprise.com. Mailing Address: PO Box 535, Watkinsville, GA 30677-0535. Pub. Frequency: w. (Thu.) Page Size: broadsheet. Subscrip. Rate: $.50 newsstand/cover; $16/yr in county; $18/yr out of county; $20/yr out of state. Circulation: 4,006 per issue (paid). **Owner(s):** Vinnie Williams, See address and contact information above. **Management:** Maridee Williams, General Manager. Vinnie Williams, Publisher. Maridee Williams, Advertising Manager. **Editorial:** Billy Vaughn, Editor. Sarah Thuerk, Assistant Editor. Jeff Cochran, Sports.

WAYNESBORO

TRUE CITIZEN, THE. 547 E. Sixth St., Waynesboro, GA 30830. Telephone: 706-554-7888. FAX: 706-554-2437. E-MAIL: bonniet@thetruecitizen.com. URL: http://www.thetruecitizen.com. Mailing Address: PO Box 948, Waynesboro, GA 30830-0948. Year Established: 1882. Pub. Frequency: w. (Wed.) Page Size: broadsheet. Subscrip. Rate: $1 newsstand/cover; $28.10/yr in county; $35/yr in state; $44.30/yr out of state. Adv. Rate: col. inch $7.35 Circulation: 5,200 per issue (paid). **Owner(s):** Chalker Publishing Co., See address and contact information above. **Management:** Bonnie K. Taylor, General Manager. Roy F. Chalker, Publisher. **Editorial:** Roy F. Chalker, Editor. Elizabeth Billips, Associate Editor.

WOODSTOCK

CHEROKEE LEDGER-NEWS. 103 E. Main St., Woodstock, GA 30188. Telephone: 770-928-0706. FAX: 770-928-3152. E-MAIL: editor@legernews.com. URL: http://www.ledgernews.com. Mailing Address: PO Box 2369, Woodstock, GA 30188. Year Established: 1995. Pub. Frequency: w. (Wed.) Page Size: tabloid. Subscrip. Rate: $24.95/yr out of county. Adv. Rate: col. inch UGX18.95 Circulation: 40,000 per issue (paid and free). **Owner(s):** David & Sherry Caughman, See address and contact information above. **Management:** Dave Caughman, Publisher. Susan Dumpis, Circulation Manager. Melissa Davies, Classified Adv. Mgr.. **Editorial:** Gerry Yandel, Managing Editor. Brian Purcell, Production Manager. Brandon Michea, Sports Editor.Readers: Cherokee County, GA

WRIGHTSVILLE

WRIGHTSVILLE HEADLIGHT, THE. ISSN 0747-3737
102 W. Elm St., Wrightsville, GA 31096. Telephone: 478-864-3528. FAX: 478-864-2166. E-MAIL: headlight@washemc.net. Mailing Address: P.O. Box 290, Wrightsville, GA 31096. Year Established: 1880. Pub. Frequency: w. (Thu.) Page Size: broadsheet. Subscrip. Rate: $.50 newsstand/cover; $18/yr local; $26.50/yr out of county; $35/yr out of state. Circulation: 1,500 per issue (paid and free). **Owner(s):** Trib Publications, Inc., PO Box 648, Manchester, GA 31816. Telephone: 706-846-4336. **Management:** Robert Tribble, President. Heidi Daniel, Publisher. **Editorial:** Heidi Daniel, Editor.

ZEBULON

PIKE COUNTY JOURNAL & REPORTER. P.O. Box 789, Zebulon, GA 30295. Telephone: 770-567-3446. FAX: 770-567-8814. E-MAIL: walterg@barnesville.com. URL: http://www.pikecountygeorgia.com. Pub. Frequency: w. (Wed.) Page Size: broadsheet. Subscrip. Rate: $.50 newsstand/cover; $16/yr local; $20/yr out of county; $25/yr out of state. Circulation: 3,000 per issue (paid). **Owner(s):** Hometown Press, Inc., 509 Greenwood St., Barnesville, GA 30204. Telephone: 770-358-0754. **Management:** Walter B Geiger Sr., Publisher. Brenda Sanchez, Advertising Manager. **Editorial:** Laura Geiger, Editor.

Weeklies

HAWAII

KANEOHE

MIDWEEK (KANEOHE). 45-525 Luluku Rd., Kaneohe, HI 96744. Telephone: 808-235-5881. FAX: 808-247-7246. URL: http://www.midweek.com. Pub. Frequency: w. (Wed.) Page Size: broadsheet Circulation: 270,000 per issue (free). **Owner(s):** Ron Nagasawa, See address and contact information above. **Management:** Sharene Chun, Circulation Manager. **Editorial:** Don Chapman, Editor-in-Chief. Terri Hefner, Managing Editor.

LAHAINA

MAUI TIME WEEKLY. 658 Front St, Ste 7278, Lahaina, HI 96761. Telephone: 808-661-3786. FAX: 808-661-0446. E-MAIL: jen@mauitime.com. URL: http://www.mauitime.com. Year Established: 1997. Pub. Frequency: w. (Thu.) Page Size: tabloid Circulation: 11,000 per issue (free). **Owner(s):** Maui Time Weekly, See address and contact information above. **Management:** Jennifer Russo, General Manager. Tommy Russo, Publisher. Brad Chambers, Classified Adv. Mgr.. Rudi King, Art Director. **Editorial:** Anthony Pignataro, Editor. Samantha Campos, Associate Editor. Kristen Guenther, Photographer.

LIHUE

KAUAI TIMES. 3137 Kuhio Hwy., Lihue, HI 96766. Telephone: 808-245-3681. FAX: 808-245-5286. E-MAIL: ginews@aloha.net. Mailing Address: PO Box 231, Lihue, HI 96766. Year Established: 1902. Pub. Frequency: w. (Sat.) Page Size: standard Circulation: 22,000 per issue (free). **Owner(s):** Lee Enterprises, Inc., 900 N. Tucker Blvd., St. Louis, MO 63101. Telephone: 314-340-8000. **Management:** Cynthia Schur, Publisher. June Tada, Advertising Manager. **Editorial:** Sue Dixon-Strong, Editor.

IDAHO

ABERDEEN

ABERDEEN TIMES. 31 S Main, Aberdeen, ID 83210. Telephone: 208-397-4440. FAX: 208-397-4440. URL: http://www.press-times.com. Mailing Address: PO Box 856, Aberdeen, ID 83210. Year Established: 1911. Pub. Frequency: w. (Wed.) Page Size: broadsheet. Subscrip. Rate: $.75 newsstand/cover; $25.95/yr in state; $30.95/yr out of state. Adv. Rate: col. inch $7.20 Circulation: 1,350 per issue (paid). **Owner(s):** Brett Crompton, 174 Idaho St., American Falls, ID 83211-1923. Telephone: 208-226-5294. FAX: 208-226-5295. **Management:** Brett Crompton, Publisher. Debbie Crompton, Advertising. **Editorial:** Vicki Gamble, Editor.

AMERICAN FALLS

POWER COUNTY PRESS, THE. 174 Idaho St., American Falls, ID 83211-1923. Telephone: 208-226-5294. FAX: 208-226-5295. E-MAIL: press1@dcdi.net. URL: http://www.press-times.com. Mailing Address: PO Box 547, American Falls, ID 83211-0547. Year Established: 1898. Pub. Frequency: w. (Wed.) Page Size: broadsheet. Subscrip. Rate: $.75 newsstand/cover; $27/yr motor route local. Adv. Rate: col. inch $7.05 Circulation: 2,000 per issue (paid). **Owner(s):** Brett Crompton, See address and contact information above. **Management:** Debbie Crompton, Advertising. **Editorial:** Brett Crompton, Editor.Readers: For local and rural readers.

ARCO

ARCO ADVERTISER. ISSN 0890-1511
146 S. Front St., Arco, ID 83213. E-MAIL: arcoadv@aol.com. URL: http://www.arcoadvertiser.com. Mailing Address: PO Box 803, Arco, ID 83213-0803. Year Established: 1909. Pub. Frequency: w. (Thu.) Page Size: broadsheet. Subscrip. Rate: $.60 newsstand/cover; $23/yr mailed local; $26/yr mailed out of area. Adv. Rate: col. inch $4.50 Circulation: 2,185 per issue (paid). **Owner(s):** Arco Advertiser, Inc., The, See address and contact information above. **Management:** Don Cammack, Publisher. **Editorial:** Charles L. Cammack, Editor.

BLACKFOOT

SHOPPERS EXTRA. 34 N. Ash St., Blackfoot, ID 83221-2101. Telephone: 208-785-1100. FAX: 208-785-4239. E-MAIL: editor@am-news.com. URL: http://www.am-news.com. Mailing Address: PO Box 70, Blackfoot, ID 83221. Pub. Frequency: w. (Wed) Page Size: broadsheet Circulation: 5,500 evening (free). **Owner(s):** Horizon Publications, Inc., 1120 N. Carbon St., Ste.100, Marion, IL 62959. Telephone: 618-993-1693. **Management:** Leonard Martin, Publisher. Wayne Ingram, Advertising Manager. Phil Ward, Circulation Manager. Jackie Graham, Classified Adv. Mgr.. **Editorial:** Chris O'Nan, Managing Editor.

BOISE

BOISE WEEKLY. ISSN 1944-6314
523 Broad St, Boise, ID 83702. Telephone: 208-344-2055. FAX: 208-342-4733. E-MAIL: sally@boiseweekly.com. URL: http://www.boiseweekly.com. Year Established: 1992. Pub. Frequency: w. (Wed.) Page Size: tabloid. Circulation: 30,000 per issue (paid and free). **Owner(s):** Sally Freeman, PO Box 1657, Boise, ID 83701-1657. Telephone: 208-344-2055. FAX: 208-342-4733. **Management:** Sally Freeman, Publisher. Leila Ramella Rader, Art Director. **Editorial:** Rachel Daigle, Editor.

BONNERS FERRY

BONNERS FERRY HERALD. 7183 Main St, Bonners Ferry, ID 83805. Telephone: 208-267-5521. FAX: 208-267-5523. E-MAIL: keyes@bdmi.net. URL: http://www.bonnersferryherald.com. Mailing Address: P O Box 539, Bonners Ferry, ID 83805-0539. Year Established: 1891. Pub. Frequency: w. (Thu.) Page Size: broadsheet. Subscrip. Rate: $1 newsstand/cover; $29.50/yr mailed in state; $33.50/yr mailed out of state. Circulation: 3,000 per issue (paid). **Owner(s):** Hagadone Corp., 111 S. First St., Coeur d'Alene, ID 83814-1937. **Management:** Myrtle McLean, General Manager. David Keyes, Publisher. **Editorial:** Kathy Nussberger, Editor. Elaine Sandman, Reporter.

BUHL

BUHL HERALD. PO Box 312, Buhl, ID 83316. Telephone: 208-543-4335. Mailing Address: PO Box 312, Buhl, ID 83316-0312. Year Established: 1909. Pub. Frequency: w. (Wed.) Page Size: broadsheet. Subscrip. Rate: $.40 newsstand/cover; $22/yr mailed in county; $25/yr mailed out of county; $27/yr mailed out of state. Circulation: 2,900 per issue (paid). **Owner(s):** Sandra Wisekaver, See address and contact information above. **Management:** Sandra Wisekaver, Publisher. **Editorial:** Sandra Wisekaver, Editor.

CAMBRIDGE

UPPER COUNTRY NEWS-REPORTER. PO Box 9, Cambridge, ID 83610. Telephone: 208-257-3515. FAX: 208-257-3540. E-MAIL: reporter@cpcweb.net. Year Established: 1889. Pub. Frequency: w. (Thu.) Page Size: broadsheet. Subscrip. Rate: $.75 newsstand/cover; $25/yr mailed in state; $25/yr mailed out of state. Circulation: 900 per issue (paid). **Owner(s):** Norman Dopf, See address and contact information above. **Management:** Norman Dopf, Publisher. **Editorial:** Norman Dopf, Editor.

CASCADE

LONG VALLEY ADVOCATE, THE. P O Box 1079, Cascade, ID 83611. Telephone: 208-382-3233. FAX: 208-382-6728. Year Established: 1985. Pub. Frequency: w. (Wed.) Page Size: tabloid. Subscrip. Rate: $.50 newsstand/cover; $19/yr local; $24/yr mailed elsewhere. Circulation: 3,400 per issue (paid and free). **Owner(s):** Michael Stewart, See address and contact information above. **Management:** Michael Stewart, Publisher. **Editorial:** Michael Stewart, Editor.

CHALLIS

CHALLIS MESSENGER. 310 N. Main St., Challis, ID 83226-0405. Telephone: 208-879-4445. FAX: 208-879-5276. E-MAIL: info@challismessenger.com. URL: http://challismessenger.com. Mailing Address: PO Box 405, Challis, ID 83226-0405. Year Established: 1881. Pub. Frequency: w. (Thu.) Page Size: tabloid. Subscrip. Rate: $.60 newsstand/cover; $23.25/yr mailed in county; $31.60/yr mailed out of county. Adv. Rate: col. inch $5.25 Circulation: 1,850 per issue (paid and free). **Owner(s):** Custer Publishing, Inc., PO Box 405, Challis, ID 83226. Telephone: 208-879-4445. **Management:** Margaret Wimborne, Publisher. **Editorial:** Margaret Wimborne, Editor.

COEUR D'ALENE

EXPRESSIONS. 201 Second St, Coeur d'Alene, ID 83814. Telephone: 208-664-8176-. FAX: 208-664-0212. E-MAIL: pburke@cdapress. Mailing Address: PO Box 700, Coeur d'Alene, ID 83816. Pub. Frequency: w. (Wed) Page Size: broadsheet Circulation: 29,500 per issue (free). **Owner(s):** Hagadone Corp., 111 S. First St., Coeur d'Alene, ID 83814-1937. Telephone: 208-667-3431. **Management:** Jeannie Peugh, Office Manager. **Editorial:** Mike Tatrick, Editor.

COTTONWOOD

COTTONWOOD CHRONICLE. PO Box 157, Cottonwood, ID 83522-0157. Telephone: 208-962-3851. FAX: 208-962-7131. E-MAIL: cotchron@camasnet.com. Year Established: 1892. Pub. Frequency: w. (Thu.) Page Size: tabloid. Subscrip. Rate: $24/yr in state; $28/yr out of state. Circulation: 1,000 per issue (paid). **Owner(s):** Wherry Publishing, Inc., See address and contact information above. **Management:** Patricia Wherry, Publisher. **Editorial:** Greg Wherry, Editor.

COUNCIL

ADAMS COUNTY RECORD, THE. 100 Illinois Ave, Council, ID 83612. E-MAIL: record@ctcweb.net. URL: http://www.theadamscountyrecord.com. Year Established: 1977. Pub. Frequency: w. (Thu.) Page Size: broadsheet. Subscrip. Rate: $.75 newsstand/cover; $30/yr mailed in state; $35/yr mailed out of state. Adv. Rate: col. inch $5.48 Circulation: 1,300 per issue (paid). **Owner(s):** Adams County Record Publishing Co, LLC, PO Box R, Council, ID 83612. Telephone: 208-253-6961. FAX: 208-253-6801. **Management:** Lyle Sall, Publisher. Jennifer DeHaas, Office Manager. **Editorial:** Cody Cahill, Managing Editor.

DRIGGS

TETON VALLEY NEWS. 75 N. Main, Driggs, ID 83422. Telephone: 208-354-8101. FAX: 208-354-8621. E-MAIL: tvnews@tetontel.com. Year Established: 1909. Pub. Frequency: w. (Thu.) Page Size: tabloid. Subscrip. Rate: $.75 newsstand/cover; $35/yr mailed in county; $39/yr mailed out of county. Circulation: 2,600 per issue (paid). **Owner(s):** Grand Teton News LLC, See address and contact information above. **Management:** Susan Carr, Associate Publisher. **Editorial:** Jeannette Blosel, Editor. Contact: Jeannette Blosel, Editor.

EMMETT

MESSENGER INDEX. 120 N. Washington Ave., Emmett, ID 83617. Telephone: 208-365-6066. FAX: 208-365-6068. E-MAIL: ksteed@messenger.index.com. Mailing Address: PO Box 577, Emmett, ID 83617. Year Established: 1896. Pub. Frequency: w. (Wed.) Page Size: broadsheet. Subscrip. Rate: $.50 newsstand/cover; $29/yr in county; $48/yr out of county. Circulation: 7,000 per issue (paid and free). **Owner(s):** Idaho Press-Tribune, 1618 N. Midland, Nampa, ID 83652. Telephone: 208-465-8127. **Management:** Stephanie Pressly Jr., Publisher. Ron Tincher, Advertising Manager. Tonja Hydor, Circulation Manager. Nicki Lee, Classified Adv. Mgr.. **Editorial:** Joe Sova, Managing Editor.

GOODING

GOODING COUNTY LEADER. 438 Idaho St., Gooding, ID 83330. Telephone: 208-934-4449. FAX: 208-934-8815. Year Established: 1908. Pub. Frequency: w. (Thu.) Page Size: tabloid. Subscrip. Rate: $.75 newsstand/cover; $24/yr in county; $29/yr out of county; $19/yr in county to senior citizens. Adv. Rate: col. inch $6 Freelance Pay: $0.40/column-inch. Circulation: 1,200 per issue (paid). **Owner(s):** Lee Enterprises, Inc., See address and contact information above. **Management:** Norma DeVoe, General Manager. **Editorial:** Kelly Kasp, Editor.

NORTH SIDE NEWS. 438 Idaho St., Gooding, ID 83330. Telephone: 208-934-4449. FAX: 208-934-8815. E-MAIL: mvtrio@safelink. Year Established: 1907. Pub. Frequency: w. (Thu.) Page Size: tabloid. Subscrip. Rate: $.75 newsstand/cover; $24/yr in county; $29/yr out of state; $19/yr to senior citizens. Adv. Rate: col. inch $6.25 Freelance Pay: $0.80/column-inch. Circulation: 1,800 per issue (paid). **Owner(s):** Lee Enterprises, Inc., See address and contact information above. **Management:** Norma DeVoe, General Manager. Todd Sears, Advertising. Valinda Roehl, Circulation Manager. **Editorial:** Elizabeth Devena, Editor.

GRANGEVILLE

IDAHO COUNTY FREE PRESS. 900 W. Main St., Grangeville, ID 83530. Telephone: 208-983-1200. FAX: 208-983-1336. E-MAIL: freepressnews@eaglenewspapers.com. URL: http://www.idahocountyfreepress.com. Mailing Address: PO Box 690, Grangeville, ID 83530. Year Established: 1886. Pub. Frequency: w. (Wed.) Page Size: broadsheet. Subscrip. Rate: $.50 newsstand/cover; $29/yr in county; $39/yr out of county. Circulation: 3,766 per issue (paid). **Owner(s):** Eagle Newspapers, Inc., 4901 Indian School Rd, NE, Salem, OR 97309. Telephone: 503-393-1774. **Management:** Andy McNab, Publisher. Linda Mort, Classified Adv. Mgr.. **Editorial:** David Rauzi, Editor.

HOMEDALE

OWYHEE AVALANCHE. PO Box 97, Homedale, ID 83628. Telephone: 208-337-4681. FAX: 208-337-4867. E-MAIL: cableone@net. Year Established: 1865. Pub. Frequency: w. (Wed.) Page Size: tabloid. Subscrip. Rate: $.75 newsstand/cover; $31.50/yr mailed in county; $36.75/yr mailed out of county; $40/yr mailed elsewhere. Circulation: 1,500 per issue (paid). **Owner(s):** Joe Aman, See address and contact information above. **Management:** Joe Aman, Publisher. Rob Aman, Advertising Manager. **Editorial:** Jon Brown, Editor.

KAMIAH

CLEARWATER PROGRESS, THE. 417 Main St, Kamiah, ID 83536. E-MAIL: progress@cybrquest.com. URL: http://www.clearwaterprogress.com. Mailing Address: PO Box 428, Kamiah, ID 83536-0428. Year Established: 1905. Pub. Frequency: w. (Thu.) Page Size: tabloid. Subscrip. Rate: $.50 newsstand/cover; $29.50/yr in state; $34.25/yr out of state. Adv. Rate: col. inch $7.25 Circulation: 4,200 per issue (paid). **Owner(s):** Clearwater Progress, Inc., See address and contact information above. **Management:** John Bennet, Publisher. Sunnie Renshaw, Advertising. **Editorial:** Ben Jorgensen, Editor.

KETCHUM

IDAHO MOUNTAIN EXPRESS.   ISSN 0279-8964
591 First Ave., N., Ketchum, ID 83340-1013. Telephone: 208-726-8060. FAX: 208-726-2329. E-MAIL: news@mtexpress.com. URL: http://www.mtexpress.com. Mailing Address: PO Box 1013, Ketchum, ID 83340-1013. Year Established: 1974. Pub. Frequency: s-w. (Wed. & Fri.) Page Size: tabloid. Subscrip. Rate: $42/yr home delivery; $38/yr mailed in county; $57/yr mailed out of county. Adv. Rate: col. inch $14.85 Wire Service(s): AP. Circulation: 13,700 per issue (paid and free). **Owner(s):** Express Publishing Co., Inc., See address and contact information above. **Management:** Pam Morris, Publisher. David Thouvenel, Advertising Manager. Connie Johnson, Business Manager. **Editorial:** Gregory Foley, Editor. Jennifer Tuohy, Entertainment Editor. Jeff Cordes, Sports Editor.

MALAD CITY

IDAHO ENTERPRISE. 100 E. 90 S., Malad City, ID 83252. E-MAIL: idahoenterprise@atcnet.net. Year Established: 1887. Pub. Frequency: w. (Thu.) Page Size: broadsheet. Subscrip. Rate: $.65 newsstand/cover; $22/yr mailed in county; $27/yr mailed out of county. Adv. Rate: col. inch $6.82 Circulation: 1,500 per issue (paid). **Owner(s):** Kris Smith, PO Box 205, Malad City, ID 83252. Telephone: 208-766-4773. FAX: 208-766-4774. **Management:** Kris Smith, Publisher. **Editorial:** Kris Smith, Editor.

MCCALL

STAR-NEWS, THE.   ISSN 0747-248X
100 First St., McCall, ID 83638. Telephone: 208-634-2123. FAX: 208-634-4950. E-MAIL: strnews@aol.com. Year Established: 1966. Pub. Frequency: w. (Thu.) Page Size: broadsheet. Subscrip. Rate: $.75 newsstand/cover; $30/yr area. Adv. Rate: col. inch $8.75 Freelance Pay: $2/column-inch. Circulation: 4,000 per issue (paid). **Owner(s):** Central Idaho Publishing, Inc., See address and contact information above. **Management:** A.L. "Butch" Alford Jr., Publisher.

MIDDLETON

MIDDLETON GAZETTE. 501 N Dewey, Middleton, ID 83644-5616. Telephone: 208-585-3472. FAX: 208-585-2582. Mailing Address: PO Box 1099, Middleton, ID 83644-1099. Pub. Frequency: m. Page Size: tabloid. Subscrip. Rate: $10/yr. Circulation: 5,580 per issue (paid and free). **Owner(s):** Becky O'Meara, See address and contact information above. **Management:** Becky O'Meara, Publisher. **Editorial:** Becky O'Meara, Editor.

MONTPELIER

NEWS-EXAMINER (MONTPELIER). 847 Washington, Montpelier, ID 83254. Telephone: 208-847-0552. FAX: 208-847-0553. E-MAIL: Editor@news-examiner.net. URL: http://www.news-examiner.net. Mailing Address: PO Box 278, Montpelier, ID 83254-0278. Year Established: 1895. Pub. Frequency: w. (Wed.) Page Size: standard. Subscrip. Rate: $.75 newsstand/cover; $26/yr local; $35/yr out of area. Adv. Rate: col. inch $5.90 Freelance Pay: $0.45/column-inch. Circulation: 2,500 per issue (paid). **Owner(s):** Bob Marshall & Kris Passey, 77 S. State St., Preston, ID 83263-1242. Telephone: 208-852-0155. FAX: 208-852-0158. **Management:** Bob Marshall, Co-Publisher. **Editorial:** Rosa Moosman, Editor.

PRESTON CITIZEN. 847 Washington, Montpelier, ID 83254. Mailing Address: PO Box 278, Montpelier, ID 83254-0278. Year Established: 1890. Pub. Frequency: w. (Wed.) Page Size: broadsheet. Subscrip. Rate: $.75 newsstand/cover; $26/yr in area; $35/yr out of area. Adv. Rate: col. inch $8.65 Freelance Pay: $15/article. Circulation: 3,000 per issue (paid and free). **Owner(s):** Bob Marshall & Kris Passey, 77 S. State St., Preston, ID 83263-1242. Telephone: 208-852-0155. FAX: 208-852-0158. **Management:** Kelly Mickelsen, Publisher. Nancy Cale, Advertising Manager. **Editorial:** Rod Boam, Editor.

MOSCOW

PALOUSE LIVING. 409 S. Jackson St., Moscow, ID 83843-2251. Telephone: 208-882-5561. FAX: 208-882-8205. E-MAIL: briefs@dnews.com. URL: http://www.dnews.com. Mailing Address: PO Box 8187, Moscow, ID 83843-8187. Pub. Frequency: w. (Tue.) Page Size: broadsheet.Adv. Rate: col. inch $10 Circulation: 14,500 evening (free). **Owner(s):** TCI Holdings, PO Box 957, Lewiston, ID 87501. **Management:** Nathan Alford, Publisher. Doug Weber, Advertising Manager. Jim Crowl, Circulation Manager. Heather Frazier, Classified Adv. Mgr.. **Editorial:** Steve McClure, Managing Editor.

MOUNTAIN HOME

MOUNTAIN HOME NEWS. 195 S. Third E., Mountain Home, ID 83647. Telephone: 208-587-3331. FAX: 208-587-9205. URL: http://www.mountainhomenews.com. Mailing Address: PO Box 1330, Mountain Home, ID 83647. Year Established: 1888. Pub. Frequency: w. (Wed.) Page Size: broadsheet. Subscrip. Rate: $.75 newsstand/cover; $33/yr home delivery in county; $38/yr mailed in state; $43/yr out of state. Circulation: 4,000 per issue (paid). **Owner(s):** Rust Communications, Inc., 301 Broadway, Cape Girardeau, MO 63701. Telephone: 573-335-6611. **Management:** Coleen W Swenson, Publisher. Brenda Fincher, Business Manager. **Editorial:** Kelly Everitt, Editor.

NEZPERCE

LEWIS COUNTY HERALD (NEZPERCE). 517 Oak St., Nezperce, ID 83543-0159. Telephone: 208-937-2671. FAX: 208-962-7131. Mailing Address: PO Box 159, Nezperce, ID 83543-0159. Year Established: 1897. Pub. Frequency: w. (Thu.) Page Size: tabloid. Subscrip. Rate: $.50 newsstand/cover; $24/yr mailed in state; $28/yr mailed out of state. Circulation: 1,100 per issue (paid). **Owner(s):** Wherry Publishing, Inc., 517 Oak St., Nezperce, ID 83543. Telephone: 208-937-2671. **Management:** Patricia Wherry, Publisher. **Editorial:** Steve Wherry, Editor.

OROFINO

CLEARWATER TRIBUNE. PO Box 71, Orofino, ID 83544. Telephone: 208-476-4571. FAX: 208-476-0765. E-MAIL: cleartrib@clearwater.net. URL: http://www.clearwatertribune.com. Year Established: 1912. Pub. Frequency: w. (Thu.) Page Size: broadsheet. Subscrip. Rate: $.50 newsstand/cover; $27/yr in county; $35/yr out of county. Adv. Rate: col. inch $4.90 Circulation: 3,250 per issue (paid). **Owner(s):** Clearwater Publishing Co., Inc., See address and contact information above. **Management:** Cloann Wilkins-McNall, Publisher.

PAYETTE

INDEPENDENT ENTERPRISE. 124 S. Main St., Payette, ID 83661-0520. Telephone: 208-642-3357. FAX: 208-642-3560. E-MAIL: iepub@fmtc.com. Year Established: 1891. Pub. Frequency: w. (Wed.) Page Size: standard. Subscrip. Rate: $.50 newsstand/cover; $26/yr local; $33/yr mailed out of area. Adv. Rate: col. inch $7.15 Circulation: 2,400 per issue (paid). **Owner(s):** Wick Communications, Inc., 333 W. Wilcox Dr., Ste. 302, Sierra Vista, AZ 85635. **Management:** Larry Hurrle, Publisher. Lisa Allison, Office Manager. **Editorial:** Larry Hurrle, Editor.

POST FALLS

POST FALLS TRIBUNE, THE. 318 Spokane St., Post Falls, ID 83854. Telephone: 208-773-7501. FAX: 208-773-7002. URL: http://www.cdapress.com. Mailing Address: PO Box 700, Coeur d'Alene, ID 83816. Year Established: 1896. Pub. Frequency: w. (Wed.) Page Size: broadsheet Circulation: 6,010 per issue (free). **Owner(s):** Hagadone Corp., 111 S. First St., Coeur d'Alene, ID 83814. Telephone: 208-667-3431. **Management:** Jim Thompson, Publisher. Paul Burke, Advertising Manager. Walt Haskett, Circulation Manager. Robert Stevens, Classified Adv. Mgr.. **Editorial:** Mike Patrick, Managing Editor.

PRIEST RIVER

PRIEST RIVER TIMES.   ISSN 0740-3348
910 Albeni Hwy., Ste C, Priest River, ID 83856. Telephone: 208-448-2431. FAX: 208-448-2938. E-MAIL: prtimes@cdapress.com. URL: http://www.priestrivertimes.com. Mailing Address: PO Box 10, Priest River, ID 83856. Year Established: 1914. Pub. Frequency: w. (Wed.) Page Size: broadsheet. Subscrip. Rate: $.75 newsstand/cover; $21.50/yr home delivery area; $27/yr mailed out of area; $31/yr mailed out of state. Circulation: 11,200 per issue (paid and free). **Owner(s):** Hagadone Corp., 111 S. First St., Coeur d'Alene, ID 83814-1937. Telephone: 208-667-3431. **Management:** David Keyes, Publisher. Shannon Foote, Office Manager. Angela Vaage, Advertising Manager. Heather Cunningham, Circulation Manager. **Editorial:** Terri Ivie, Managing Editor.

RIGBY

JEFFERSON STAR, THE. 134 W. Main St., Rigby, ID 83442. Telephone: 208-745-8701. FAX: 208-745-8703. E-MAIL: piopub@onewest.net. Mailing Address: PO Box 37, Rigby, ID 83442. Year Established: 1903. Pub. Frequency: w. (Wed.) Page Size: tabloid. Subscrip. Rate: $.50 newsstand/cover; $23.75/yr in county. Adv. Rate: col. inch $7.25 Circulation: 1,750 per issue (paid). **Owner(s):** Pioneer Publications, Inc., PO Box P, Shelley, ID 83274. Telephone: 208-745-8701. FAX: 208-745-8703. **Management:** Earlene Poole, General Manager. Terry Carr, Publisher. Crystal Foster, Circulation Manager. **Editorial:** Terry Carr, Editor.

SALMON

RECORDER-HERALD. PO Box 310, Salmon, ID 83467. Telephone: 208-756-2221. FAX: 208-756-2222. Year Established: 1886. Pub. Frequency: w. (Thu.) Page Size: broadsheet. Subscrip. Rate: $.62 newsstand/cover; $23.50/yr local; $26.50/yr in state; $30.50/yr out of state. Adv. Rate: col. inch $6.90 Circulation: 3,400 per issue (paid). **Owner(s):** Ricky G. Hodges, See address and contact information above. **Management:** Ricky G. Hodges, Publisher. Sheila Hodges, Advertising Manager. Ricky G. Hodges, Sales Manager. **Editorial:** Ricky G. Hodges, Editor. Christy Hewitt, Reporter.

SHELLEY

SHELLEY PIONEER. 154 E.Center, Shelley, ID 83274. Telephone: 208-357-7661. FAX: 208-357-3435. Year Established: 1905. Pub. Frequency: w. (Thu.) Page Size: tabloid. Subscrip. Rate: $.50 newsstand/cover; $19.50/yr in county; $24/yr mailed out of county; $28.50/yr mailed out of state. Circulation: 1,500 per issue (paid). **Owner(s):** Terry Carr, See address and contact information above. **Management:** Crystal Foster, General Manager. Terry Carr, Publisher. **Editorial:** Terry Carr, Editor.

SODA SPRINGS

CARIBOU COUNTY SUN. PO Box 815, Soda Springs, ID 83276. Telephone: 208-547-3260. FAX: 208-547-4422. Year Established: 1930. Pub. Frequency: w. (Thu.) Page Size: tabloid. Subscrip. Rate: $.67 newsstand/cover; $20/yr in county; $25/yr out of county. Adv. Rate: col. inch $6.60 Circulation: 3,100 per issue (paid). **Owner(s):** Mark Steele, See address and contact information above. **Management:** Mark Steele, Publisher. **Editorial:** Mark Steele, Editor.

ST. ANTHONY

STANDARD JOURNAL, THE. 44 N. Bridge St., St. Anthony, ID 83445. Telephone: 208-624-4455. FAX: 208-624-4456. E-MAIL: jedlefsen@rexburgstandardjournal.com. URL: http://www.rexburgstandardjournal.com. Mailing Address: PO Box 568, St. Anthony, ID 83445. Year Established: 1891. Pub. Frequency: 3/w. (Mon., Wed., Fri.) Page Size: broadsheet. Subscrip. Rate: $.50 newsstand/cover; $59.95/yr home delivery; $69.95/yr mailed in state; $98/yr mailed out of state. Wire Service(s): AP. Circulation: 19,800 per issue (paid). **Owner(s):** Pioneer Publications, PO Box P, Shelley, ID 83274. Telephone: 208-745-8701. FAX: 208-745-8703. **Management:** Rich Ballou, Publisher. Kristy Geisler, Advertising Director. Jeremy Cooley, Circulation Manager. **Editorial:** Joyce Edlefsen, Managing Editor.

ST. MARIES

ST. MARIES GAZETTE RECORD. 610 Main Ave., St. Maries, ID 83861. Telephone: 208-245-4538. FAX: 208-245-4011. E-MAIL: dano@stmariesidaho.com. URL: http://www.smgazette.com. Year Established: 1906. Pub. Frequency: w. (Wed.) Page Size: broadsheet. Subscrip. Rate: $1 newsstand/cover; $34.50/yr in county & adj. cys.; $37.75/yr out of area incl. WA, MT, OR; $48.50/yr mailed elsewhere. Circulation: 3,600 per issue (paid). **Owner(s):** St. Maries Gazette Record Corp., See address and contact information above. **Management:** Daniel Hammes, Publisher. Shenelle Craack, Advertising Manager. **Editorial:** Daniel Hammes, Editor.

WEISER

WEISER SIGNAL AMERICAN.   ISSN 1087-514X
PO Box 709, Weiser, ID 83672-0709. Telephone: 208-549-1717. FAX: 208-549-1718. E-MAIL: newsroom@ruralnetwork.net. Year Established: 1882. Pub. Frequency: s-w. (Mon. & Wed.) Page Size: broadsheet. Subscrip. Rate: $.50 newsstand/cover; $27/yr mailed in state; $39/yr out of state. Adv. Rate: col. inch $8.95 Circulation: 2,200 per issue (paid); 950 per issue (free). **Owner(s):** Signal-American Printers, Inc., See address and contact information above. **Management:** James R. Simpson, Publisher. Eydie Fenton, Advertising Manager. Sarah Boles, Circulation Manager. **Editorial:** Rob Ruth, Editor.

Weeklies

ILLINOIS

ABINGDON

ABINGDON ARGUS. 507 N. Monroe St., Ste. 3, Abingdon, IL 61410. Telephone: 309-462-3189. FAX: 309-462-3221. E-MAIL: argus@abingdon.net. Year Established: 1957. Pub. Frequency: w. (Thu.) Page Size: tabloid. Subscrip. Rate: $.50 newsstand/cover; $25/yr mailed in county; $30/yr mailed out of county; $35/yr mailed out of state. Adv. Rate: col. inch $4.50 Circulation: 1,500 per issue (paid and free). **Owner(s):** Eagle Publications, 210 S. Randolph, Macomb, IL 61455. Telephone: 309-837-4428. **Management:** Tom Hutson, Publisher. Kathy Hahn, Advertising Manager. **Editorial:** Deb Folks, Editor.

AVON SENTINEL. 507 N. Monroe St., Ste. 3, Abingdon, IL 61410. Telephone: 309-462-3189. FAX: 309-462-3221. E-MAIL: argus@abingdon.net. Year Established: 1879. Pub. Frequency: w. (Thu..) Page Size: tabloid. Subscrip. Rate: $.50 newsstand/cover; $25/yr mailed in county; $30/yr mailed in state; $35/yr mailed out of state. Circulation: 600 per issue (paid and free). **Owner(s):** Eagle Publications, 210 S. Randolph, Macomb, IL 61455. Telephone: 309-837-4428. **Management:** Tom Hutson, Publisher. Kathy Hahn, Advertising Manager. **Editorial:** Deb Folks, Editor.

ALEDO

TIMES RECORD. 219 S. College Ave., Aledo, IL 61231. Telephone: 309-582-5112. FAX: 309-582-5319. URL: http://www.aledotimesrecord.com. Mailing Address: PO Box 309, Aledo, IL 61231. Year Established: 1856. Pub. Frequency: w. (Wed.) Page Size: broadsheet. Subscrip. Rate: $1 newsstand/cover; $40/yr local; $55/yr mailed elsewhere. Circulation: 10,700 per issue (paid and free). **Owner(s):** GateHouse Media, Inc, 350 WillowBrook Office Park, Fairport, NY 14450. Telephone: 585-598-0030. FAX: 585-248-2631. **Management:** Tony Scott, Publisher. Davina Logsdon, Advertising. Peggy Schaechter, Circulation Manager. **Editorial:** Cathy Decker, Editor. Robert Blackford, Sports Editor.

TOWN CRIER ADVERTISER. 219 S. College Ave., Aledo, IL 61231. Telephone: 309-582-5112. FAX: 309-582-5319. Mailing Address: PO Box 309, Aledo, IL 61231. Pub. Frequency: w. (Tue.) Page Size: tabloid Circulation: 7,100 per issue (free). **Owner(s):** GateHouse Media, Inc, 350 WillowBrook Office Park, Fairport, NY 14450. Telephone: 585-598-0030. FAX: 585-248-2631. **Management:** Tony Scott, Publisher. Davina Logsdon, Advertising. Peggy Schaechter, Circulation Manager.

ALGONQUIN

ALGONQUIN COUNTRYSIDE. ISSN 0744-527X 1485 Merchant Dr., Algonquin, IL 60102. Telephone: 847-458-5300. FAX: 847-458-5325. E-MAIL: display@pioneerlocal.com. URL: http://www.pioneerlocal.com/algonquincountryside/. Year Established: 1972. Pub. Frequency: w. (Thu.) Page Size: tabloid. Subscrip. Rate: $1 newsstand/cover; $21.95/yr in county; $51.95/yr out of county. Adv. Rate: col. inch $17.86 Circulation: 2,377 per issue (paid). **Owner(s):** Pioneer Press, Inc., 3701 W. Lake Ave., Glenview, IL 60025. Telephone: 847-486-9200. **Management:** Ed Rooney, Advertising Director. **Editorial:** Mike Martinez, Editor. Andrea Brown, Managing Editor.

BARRINGTON COURIER-REVIEW. ISSN 1086-8216 1485 Merchant Dr., Algonquin, IL 60102. Telephone: 847-458-5300. FAX: 847-458-5325. E-MAIL: display@pioneerlocal.com. URL: http://www.pioneerlocal.com. Year Established: 1890. Pub. Frequency: w. (Thu.) Page Size: tabloid. Subscrip. Rate: $1 newsstand/cover; $21.95/yr in county; $51.95/yr out of county. Adv. Rate: col. inch $25.14 Circulation: 7,426 per issue (paid). **Owner(s):** Pioneer Press, Inc., 3701 W. Lake Ave., Glenview, IL 60025. Telephone: 847-486-9200. **Management:** Ed Rooney, Advertising Director. **Editorial:** Mike Martinez, Editor. Andrea Brown, Managing Editor.

CARY-GROVE COUNTRYSIDE. 1485 Merchant Dr., Algonquin, IL 60102. Telephone: 847-458-5300. FAX: 847-458-5325. E-MAIL: display@pioneerlocal.com. URL: http://www.pioneerlocal.com. Year Established: 1972. Pub. Frequency: w. (Thu.) Page Size: tabloid. Subscrip. Rate: $1 newsstand/cover; $21.95/yr in county; $51.95/yr out of county. Adv. Rate: col. inch $17.86 Circulation: 2,535 per issue (paid). **Owner(s):** Pioneer Press, Inc., 3701 W. Lake Ave., Glenview, IL 60025. Telephone: 847-486-9200. **Management:** Ed Rooney, Advertising Director. **Editorial:** Mike Martinez, Editor.

LAKE ZURICH COURIER. 1485 Merchant Dr., Algonquin, IL 60102. Telephone: 847-458-5300. FAX: 847-458-5325. E-MAIL: display@pioneerlocal.com. URL: http://www.pioneerlocal.com. Year Established: 1981. Pub. Frequency: w. (Thu.) Page Size: tabloid. Subscrip. Rate: $1 newsstand/cover; $21.95/yr in county; $51.95/yr out of county. Adv. Rate: col. inch $17.86 Circulation: 3,328 per issue (paid). **Owner(s):** Pioneer Press, Inc., 3701 W. Lake Ave., Glenview, IL 60025. Telephone: 847-486-9200. **Management:** Ed Rooney, Advertising Director. David Perham, Circulation Manager. **Editorial:** Mike Martinez, Editor.

WAUCONDA COURIER. 1485 Merchant Dr., Algonquin, IL 60102. Telephone: 847-458-5300. FAX: 847-458-5325. Year Established: 2004. Pub. Frequency: w. (Thu.) Subscrip. Rate: $1 newsstand/cover; $21.95/yr in county; $51.95/yr out of county. Adv. Rate: col. inch $17.86 Circulation: 1,500 per issue. **Owner(s):** Pioneer Press, Inc., 3701 W. Lake Ave., Glenview, IL 60025. Telephone: 847-486-9200. FAX: 847-496-7454. **Management:** Ed Rooney, Advertising Director. **Editorial:** Mike Martinez, Editor.

ALTAMONT

ALTAMONT NEWS, THE. 111 N. Main, Altamont, IL 62411. Telephone: 618-483-6176. FAX: 618-483-5177. E-MAIL: altnewsban@frontiernet.net. Year Established: 1881. Pub. Frequency: w. (Tue.) Page Size: standard. Subscrip. Rate: $.75 newsstand/cover; $27/yr mailed in county; $31/yr mailed out of county. Circulation: 1,600 per issue (paid). **Owner(s):** Greg Hoskins, See address and contact information above. **Management:** Barbara Barr, Publisher. **Editorial:** Clyde Barr, Editor.

AMBOY

AMBOY NEWS, THE. 219 E. Main St., Amboy, IL 61310-0162. Telephone: 815-857-2311. FAX: 815-857-2517. E-MAIL: phil@amboynews.com. URL: http:www.amboynews.com. Mailing Address: PO Box 162, Amboy, IL 61310-0162. Year Established: 1854. Pub. Frequency: w. (Wed.) Page Size: tabloid. Subscrip. Rate: $.50 newsstand/cover per issue; $23/yr local; $28/yr mailed elsewhere. Adv. Rate: col. inch $4.75 Circulation: 2,500 per issue (paid). **Owner(s):** News Media Corp., PO Box 46, Rochelle, IL 61068. Telephone: 815-562-2061. FAX: 815-562-2060. **Management:** Kip Cheek, President. Mark Elston, Circulation Manager. **Editorial:** Jessie Johnson, Editor.

ANNA

GAZETTE-DEMOCRAT. 12 Lafayette St., Anna, IL 62906. Telephone: 618-833-2158. FAX: 618-833-5813. E-MAIL: reppert@midwest.net. Mailing Address: P.O. Box 529, Anna, IL 62906. Year Established: 1849. Pub. Frequency: w. (Thu.) Page Size: broadsheet. Subscrip. Rate: $.50 newsstand/cover; $25/yr. Adv. Rate: col. inch $9.75 Circulation: 6,500 per issue (paid). **Owner(s):** Jerry L. Reppert, See address and contact information above. **Management:** Jerry L. Reppert, President. Russell Mertz, Advertising Manager. Diane Reppert, Circulation Manager. **Editorial:** Geof Skinner, Editor.

ARCOLA

ARCOLA RECORD HERALD. 118 E. Main St., Arcola, IL 61910. Telephone: 217-268-4950. FAX: 217-268-4938. E-MAIL: slackpub@arcola-il.com. Year Established: 1866. Pub. Frequency: w. (Thu.) Page Size: broadsheet. Subscrip. Rate: $.50 newsstand/cover; $26/yr mailed in state; $29/yr mailed out of state. Adv. Rate: col. inch $4 Circulation: 2,500 per issue (paid). **Owner(s):** Chris Slack, See address and contact information above. **Management:** Chris Slack, Publisher. **Editorial:** Chris Slack, Editor.

ARLINGTON HEIGHTS

ARLINGTON HEIGHTS POST. 291 N. Dunton Ave., Arlington Heights, IL 60004. Telephone: 847-797-5100. FAX: 847-797-5151. E-MAIL: display@pioneerlocal.com. URL: http://www.pioneerlocal.com/arlingtonheights. Year Established: 1996. Pub. Frequency: w. (Thu.) Page Size: tabloid. Subscrip. Rate: $1 newsstand/cover; $21.95/yr in county; $51.95/yr out of county. Adv. Rate: col. inch $17.86 Circulation: 5,904 per issue (paid). **Owner(s):** Pioneer Press, Inc., 3701 W. Lake Ave., Glenview, IL 60025. Telephone: 847-486-9200. **Management:** Ed Rooney, Advertising Director. **Editorial:** John Korinek, Managing Editor. Jennifer Thomas, Entertainment Editor. Jennifer Clark, Group Editor.

BUFFALO GROVE COUNTRYSIDE. 291 N. Dunton Ave., Arlington Heights, IL 60004. Telephone: 847-797-5100. FAX: 847-797-5151. E-MAIL: display@pioneerlocal.com. URL: http://www.pioneerlocal.com. Year Established: 1981. Pub. Frequency: w. (Thu.) Page Size: tabloid. Subscrip. Rate: $1 newsstand/cover; $21.95/yr in county; $51.95/yr out of county. Adv. Rate: col. inch $21.29 Circulation: 5,862 per issue (paid). **Owner(s):** Pioneer Press, Inc., 3701 W. Lake Ave., Glenview, IL 60025. Telephone: 847-486-9200. **Management:** Ed Rooney, Advertising Director. **Editorial:** Jeff Finley, Managing Editor. Jennifer Thomas, Entertainment Editor. Jennifer Clark, Group Editor.

ELK GROVE VILLAGE TIMES. 291 N. Dunton Ave., Arlington Heights, IL 60004. Telephone: 847-797-5100. FAX: 847-797-5151. E-MAIL: display@pioneerlocal.com. URL: http://www.pioneerlocal.com. Pub. Frequency: w. (Thu.) Page Size: tabloid. Subscrip. Rate: $1 newsstand/cover; $21.95/yr in county; $51.95/yr out of county. Adv. Rate: col. inch $21.29 Circulation: 1,989 per issue (paid). **Owner(s):** Pioneer Press, Inc., 3701 W. Lake Ave., Glenview, IL 60025. Telephone: 847-486-9200. **Management:** Ed Rooney, Advertising Director. **Editorial:** Jennifer Clark, Managing Editor. Jennifer Thomas, Entertainment Editor. Jennifer Clark, Group Editor.

HOFFMAN ESTATES REVIEW. 291 N. Dunton Ave., Arlington Heights, IL 60004. Telephone: 847-797-5100. FAX: 847-797-5151. E-MAIL: display@pioneerlocal.com. URL: http://www.pioneerlocal.com. Year Established: 1989. Pub. Frequency: w. (Thu.) Page Size: tabloid. Subscrip. Rate: $1 newsstand/cover; $21.95/yr in county; $51.95/yr out of county. Adv. Rate: col. inch $21.29 Circulation: 1,923 per issue (paid). **Owner(s):** Pioneer Press, Inc., 3701 W. Lake Ave., Glenview, IL 60025. Telephone: 847-486-9200. **Management:** Ed Rooney, Advertising Director. **Editorial:** Jennifer Clark, Managing Editor. Jennifer Thomas, Entertainment Editor. Jennifer Clark, Group Editor.

PALATINE COUNTRYSIDE. 291 N. Dunton Ave., Arlington Heights, IL 60004. Telephone: 847-797-5100. FAX: 847-797-5151. E-MAIL: display@pioneerlocal.com. URL: http://www.pioneerlocal.com. Year Established: 1972. Pub. Frequency: w. (Thu.) Page Size: tabloid. Subscrip. Rate: $1 newsstand/cover; $21.95/yr in county; $51.95/yr out of county. Adv. Rate: col. inch $21.29 Circulation: 5,835 per issue (paid). **Owner(s):** Pioneer Press, Inc., 3701 W. Lake Ave., Glenview, IL 60025. Telephone: 847-486-9200. **Management:** Ed Rooney, Advertising Director. **Editorial:** Jeff Finley, Managing Editor. Jennifer Thomas, Entertainment Editor. Jennifer Clark, Group Editor.

ROLLING MEADOWS REVIEW. 291 N. Dunton Ave., Arlington Heights, IL 60004. Telephone: 847-797-5100. FAX: 847-797-5151. E-MAIL: display@pioneerlocal.com. URL: http://www.pioneerlocal.com. Year Established: 1989. Pub. Frequency: w. (Thu.) Page Size: tabloid. Subscrip. Rate: $1 newsstand/cover; $21.95/yr in county; $51.95/yr out of county. Adv. Rate: col. inch $17.86 Circulation: 1,278 per issue (paid). **Owner(s):** Pioneer Press, Inc., 3701 W. Lake Ave., Glenview, IL 60025. Telephone: 847-486-9200. **Management:** Ed Rooney, Advertising Director. **Editorial:** John Korinek, Managing Editor. Jennifer Thomas, Entertainment Editor. Jennifer Clark, Group Editor.

SCHAUMBURG REVIEW. 291 N. Dunton Ave., Arlington Heights, IL 60004. Telephone: 847-797-5100. FAX: 847-797-5151. E-MAIL: display@pioneerlocal.com. URL: http://www.pioneerlocal.com. Year Established: 1989. Pub. Frequency: w. (Thu.) Page Size: tabloid. Subscrip. Rate: $1 newsstand/cover; $21.95/yr in county; $51.95/yr out of county. Adv. Rate: col. inch $21.29 Circulation: 5,309 per issue (paid). **Owner(s):** Pioneer Press, Inc., 3701 W. Lake Ave., Glenview, IL 60025. Telephone: 847-486-9200. **Management:** Ed Rooney, Advertising Director. **Editorial:** Jennifer Clark, Managing Editor. Jennifer Thomas, Entertainment Editor. Jennifer Clark, Group Editor.

WHEELING COUNTRYSIDE. 291 N. Dunton Ave., Arlington Heights, IL 60004. Telephone: 847-797-5100. FAX: 847-797-5151. E-MAIL: display@pioneerlocal.com. URL: http://www.pioneerlocal.com. Year Established: 1981. Pub. Frequency: w. (Thu.) Page Size: tabloid. Subscrip. Rate: $1 newsstand/cover; $21.95/yr in county; $51.95/yr out of county. Adv. Rate: col. inch $21.29 Circulation: 1,683 per issue (paid). **Owner(s):** Pioneer Press, Inc., 3701 W. Lake Ave., Glenview, IL 60025. Telephone: 847-486-9200. **Management:** Ed Rooney, Advertising Director. **Editorial:** Jeff Finley, Managing Editor. Jennifer Thomas, Entertainment Editor. Jennifer Clark, Group Editor.

ARTHUR

ARTHUR GRAPHIC CLARION. 113 E. Illinois St., Arthur, IL 61911. Telephone: 217-543-2151. FAX: 217-543-2152. Year Established: 1887. Pub. Frequency: w. (Thu.) Page Size: broadsheet. Subscrip. Rate: $.50 newsstand/cover; $19/yr mailed in county; $22/yr mailed out of county. Circulation: 3,000 per issue (paid). **Owner(s):** Arthur Graphic Clarion, Inc., See address and contact information above. **Management:** Greg Hoskins, Owner. Stephanie Weirman, Advertising Manager. **Editorial:** Roger Bonham, Managing Editor.

ASHTON

ASHTON GAZETTE. 813 Main St., Ashton, IL 61006-0287. Telephone: 815-453-2551. FAX: 815-453-2422. Mailing Address: PO Box 287, Ashton, IL 61006-0287. Year Established: 1895. Pub. Frequency: w. (Wed.) Page Size: tabloid. Subscrip. Rate: $.50 newsstand/cover; $23/yr in county; $28/yr out of county. Circulation: 1,000 per issue (paid). **Owner(s):** News Media Corp., PO Box 46, Rochelle, IL 61068. Telephone: 815-562-2061. FAX: 815-562-2060. **Management:** John Shank, General Manager. **Editorial:** Monetla Young, Managing Editor.

ASSUMPTION

GOLDEN PRAIRIE NEWS. 301 S. Chestnut St., Assumption, IL 62510. Telephone: 217-226-3721. FAX: 217-226-3579. Year Established: 1880. Pub. Frequency: w. (Thu.) Page Size: standard.Subscrip. Rate: $.40 newsstand/cover; $20/yr area Circulation: 2,200 per issue (paid). **Owner(s):** Willard Raymond, See address and contact information above. **Management:** Willard Raymond, Publisher. **Editorial:** Willard Raymond, Editor.

ASTORIA

ASTORIA SOUTH FULTON ARGUS. PO Box 590, Astoria, IL 61501-0590. Telephone: 309-329-2151. FAX: 309-329-2344. E-MAIL: argus@kkspc.com/argus. URL: http://www.kkspc.com/argus. Year Established: 1959. Pub. Frequency: w. (Wed.) Page Size: tabloid. Subscrip. Rate: $22.95/yr in county; $27.95/yr out of county. Adv. Rate: col. inch $3 Circulation: 2,050 per issue (paid and free). **Owner(s):** K.K. Stevens Publishing Co., 100 N Pearl St, Astoria, IL 61501. **Management:** Thomas B Stevens, President. Bill Hand, Advertising. Jodie Ragle, Circulation Manager. **Editorial:** Judy Beaird, Editor. Ellen Stevens, Advertising Editor. Laura Hickle, Art.

AUBURN

AUBURN CITIZEN. PO Box 50, Auburn, IL 62615. Year Established: 1874. Pub. Frequency: w. (Thu.) Page Size: tabloid. Subscrip. Rate: $.75 newsstand/cover; $30/yr in county. Adv. Rate: col. inch $5.50 Circulation: 1,700 per issue (paid). **Owner(s):** South County Publications Ltd, 110 N Fifth St., Auburn, IL 62615. Telephone: 217-438-6155. FAX: 217-438-6156. **Management:** Joe Michelich, Publisher. Connie Michelich, Advertising Manager. **Editorial:** Joe M Michelich, Editor.

CHATHAM CLARION. 110 N Fifth St., Auburn, IL 62615. Telephone: 217-438-6155. FAX: 217-438-6156. Year Established: 1962. Pub. Frequency: w. (Thu.) Page Size: tabloid. Subscrip. Rate: $.75 newsstand/cover; $29/yr home delivery in county. Adv. Rate: col. inch $5.50 Circulation: 1,900 per issue (paid). **Owner(s):** South County Publications Ltd, See address and contact information above. **Management:** Joe Michelich, Publisher. Connie Michelich, Advertising Manager. **Editorial:** Joe Pritchett, Editor.

DIVERNON NEWS. 110 N Fifth St., Auburn, IL 62615. Telephone: 217-438-6155. FAX: 217-438-6156. Year Established: 1897. Pub. Frequency: w. (Thu.) Page Size: tabloid. Subscrip. Rate: $.75 newsstand/cover; $29/yr in county. Adv. Rate: col. inch $5.50 Circulation: 400 per issue (paid). **Owner(s):** South County Publications Ltd, See address and contact information above. **Management:** Joe Michelich, Publisher. Connie Michelich, Advertising Manager. **Editorial:** Joe M Michelich, Editor.

NEW BERLIN BEE. PO Box 50, Auburn, IL 62615. Pub. Frequency: w. (Fri.) Page Size: tabloid. Subscrip. Rate: $.50 newsstand/cover; $22/yr in county. Adv. Rate: col. inch $5.50 Circulation: 1,000 per issue (paid). **Owner(s):** South County Publications Ltd, 110 N Fifth St., Auburn, IL 62615. Telephone: 217-438-6155. FAX: 217-438-6156. **Management:** Connie Michelich, Advertising Manager. **Editorial:** Joe M Michelich, Editor.

PAWNEE POST. PO Box 50, Auburn, IL 62615. Year Established: 1965. Pub. Frequency: w. (Thu.) Page Size: tabloid. Subscrip. Rate: $.75 newsstand/cover; $30/yr home delivery in county. Adv. Rate: col. inch $5.50 Circulation: 675 per issue (paid). **Owner(s):** South County Publications Ltd, 110 N Fifth St., Auburn, IL 62615. Telephone: 217-438-6155. FAX: 217-438-6156. **Management:** Joe Michelich, Publisher. Connie Michelich, Advertising Manager. **Editorial:** Joe M Michelich, Editor.

PLEASANT PLAINS PRESS. PO Box 50, Auburn, IL 62615. Pub. Frequency: w. (Fri.) Page Size: tabloid. Subscrip. Rate: $.50 newsstand/cover; $22/yr in county. Adv. Rate: col. inch $5.50 Circulation: 600 per issue (paid). **Owner(s):** South County Publications Ltd, 110 N Fifth St., Auburn, IL 62615. Telephone: 217-438-6155. FAX: 217-438-6156. **Management:** Joe Michelich, Publisher. Connie Michelich, Advertising Manager. **Editorial:** Joe M Michelich, Editor.

ROCHESTER TIMES (AUBURN). PO Box 50, Auburn, IL 62615. Pub. Frequency: w. (Thu.) Page Size: tabloid. Subscrip. Rate: $30/yr mailed in county; $.75 newsstand/cover. Adv. Rate: col. inch $3.75 Circulation: 1,000 per issue (paid). **Owner(s):** South County Publications Ltd, 110 N Fifth St., Auburn, IL 62615. Telephone: 217-438-6155. FAX: 217-438-6156. **Management:** Joe Michelich, Publisher. Connie Michelich, Advertising Manager. **Editorial:** Joe M Michelich, Editor.

TRI - CITY REGISTER. PO Box 50, Auburn, IL 62615. Year Established: 1986. Pub. Frequency: w. (Sat.) Page Size: tabloid. Subscrip. Rate: $.50 newsstand/cover per issue; $20/yr. Adv. Rate: col. inch $3 Circulation: 2,300 per issue (free). **Owner(s):** South County Publications Ltd, 110 N Fifth St., Auburn, IL 62615. Telephone: 217-438-6155. FAX: 217-438-6156. **Management:** Joe Michelich, Publisher. Connie Michelich, Advertising Manager. **Editorial:** Byron Painter, Editor.

AURORA

BATAVIA SUN. 101 S. River St., Aurora, IL 60506. Telephone: 630-844-5844. FAX: 630-844-5818. Pub. Frequency: w. (Wed.) Page Size: broadsheet Circulation: 3,000 per issue (free). **Owner(s):** Sun-Times Media Group, 350 N Orleans St, Ste 10-S, Chicago, IL 60654. Telephone: 312-321-2299. **Management:** Rick Nagel, Publisher. Mike Bertok, Advertising Manager. **Editorial:** Kim Williams, Managing Editor.

GENEVA SUN. 101 S. River St., Aurora, IL 60506. Telephone: 630-844-5844. FAX: 630-844-5818. Pub. Frequency: w. (Wed.) Page Size: broadsheet Circulation: 2,500 per issue (free). **Owner(s):** Sun-Times Media Group, 350 N Orleans St, Ste 10-S, Chicago, IL 60654. Telephone: 312-321-2299. **Management:** Rick Nagel, Publisher. Mike Bertok, Advertising Manager. **Editorial:** Kim Williams, Managing Editor. John Russell, Associate Editor.

ST. CHARLES SUN. 101 S. River St., Aurora, IL 60506. Telephone: 630-844-5844. FAX: 630-844-5818. Pub. Frequency: w. (Wed.) Page Size: broadsheet Circulation: 2,500 per issue (free). **Owner(s):** Sun-Times Media Group, 350 N Orleans St, Ste 10-S, Chicago, IL 60654. Telephone: 312-321-2299. **Management:** Rick Nagel, Publisher. Mike Bertok, Advertising Manager. **Editorial:** Kim Williams, Managing Editor. John Russell, Associate Editor.

BARRY

PAPER (BARRY), THE. 725 Bainbridge St., Barry, IL 62312. Telephone: 217-335-2112. FAX: 217-335-2112. E-MAIL: rnews1@adams.net. Year Established: 1962. Pub. Frequency: w. (Wed.) Page Size: tabloid. Subscrip. Rate: $.35 newsstand/cover; $20/yr in county; $26/yr out of county. Circulation: 2,200 per issue (paid). **Owner(s):** Debbie Harshman, See address and contact information above. **Management:** Debbie Harshman, President.

BARTONVILLE

LIMESTONE INDEPENDENT NEWS. 114 Roosevelt, Bartonville, IL 61607. Telephone: 309-697-1859. FAX: 309-697-1851. E-MAIL: limestonenews@yahoo.com. Year Established: 1967. Pub. Frequency: w. (Wed.) Page Size: tabloid.Subscrip. Rate: $.50 newsstand/cover; $22/yr Circulation: 2,500 per issue (paid). **Owner(s):** Barbara Widener, See address and contact information above. **Management:** Barbara Widener, Publisher. Joy Haun, Advertising Manager. Rhonda Welk, Circulation Manager. **Editorial:** Barbara Widener, Editor.

BEARDSTOWN

CASS COUNTY STAR-GAZETTE. 1210 Wall St, Beardstown, IL 62610. Telephone: 217-323-1010. FAX: 217-323-5402. E-MAIL: stargazette@casscomm.com. URL: http://www.beardstownnewspapers.com. Mailing Address: PO Box 79, Beardstown, IL 62610. Year Established: 1840. Pub. Frequency: w. (Thu.) Page Size: broadsheet. Subscrip. Rate: $.75 newsstand/cover; $31/yr mailed in county & adj. cys.; $39/yr mailed in state; $44/yr mailed out of state. Circulation: 3,300 per issue (paid). **Owner(s):** Delphos Newspapers, 405 N. Main St., Delphos, OH 45833. Telephone: 419-695-0015. FAX: 419-692-7704. **Management:** Pat Wellenkamp, Publisher. **Editorial:** Bill Beard, Editor.

STAR-GAZETTE EXTRA. 1210 Wall St, Beardstown, IL 62610. Telephone: 217-323-1010. FAX: 217-323-5402. URL: http://www.beardstownnewspapers.com. Mailing Address: PO Box 79, Beardstown, IL 62610. Pub. Frequency: w. (Mon.) Page Size: standard Circulation: 9,700 per issue (free). **Owner(s):** Delphos Newspapers, 405 N. Main St., Delphos, OH 45833. Telephone: 419-695-0015. FAX: 419-692-7704. **Management:** Pat Wellenkamp, Publisher. **Editorial:** Bill Beard, Editor.

STAR TRADER. 1210 Wall St, Beardstown, IL 62610. Telephone: 217-323-1010. FAX: 217-323-5402. Mailing Address: PO Box 79, Beardstown, IL 62610. Pub. Frequency: w. (Tue.) Page Size: standard Circulation: 4,500 per issue (free). **Owner(s):** Delphos Newspapers, 405 N. Main St., Delphos, OH 45833. Telephone: 419-695-0015. FAX: 419-692-7704. **Management:** Pat Wellenkamp, Publisher. **Editorial:** Bill Beard, Editor.

TRI-COUNTY TIMES. 1210 Wall St, Beardstown, IL 62610. Telephone: 217-323-1010. FAX: 217-323-5402. Mailing Address: PO Box 79, Beardstown, IL 62610. Pub. Frequency: w. (Wed.) Page Size: standard. Subscrip. Rate: $.50 newsstand/cover; $21/yr in county. Circulation: 500 per issue (paid). **Owner(s):** Delphos Newspapers, 405 N. Main St., Delphos, OH 45833. Telephone: 419-695-0015. **Management:** Pat Wellenkamp, Publisher. **Editorial:** Bill Beard, Editor. Contact: Debbie Milton, Publisher; Kim Holcombe, Advertising Manager; Patricia Buster, Classified Adv. Mgr.; Tom Burkdine, Editor; Steve Williams, Sports Editor.

BEECHER CITY

BEECHER CITY JOURNAL. ISSN 1066-7970
104 S. Charles St., Beecher City, IL 62414. Telephone: 618-487-5634. FAX: 618-487-5180. E-MAIL: bcj@xel.net. Mailing Address: P.O. Box 38, Beecher City, IL 62414. Year Established: 1915. Pub. Frequency: w. (Mon.) Page Size: tabloid. Subscrip. Rate: $.50 newsstand/cover; $22/yr home delivery in county; $25/yr home delivery out of county; $27/yr mailed elsewhere. Adv. Rate: col. inch $4 Circulation: 1,500 per issue (paid). **Owner(s):** P.J. Ryan & Cherie Ryan, See address and contact information above. **Management:** P.J. Ryan, President. **Editorial:** P.J. Ryan, Editor. Cherie Ryan, Associate Editor.

BELVIDERE

BELVIDERE REPUBLICAN. 130 S. State St., Ste. 203, Belvidere, IL 61008. Telephone: 815-547-0084. FAX: 815-547-0045. URL: http://www.rockvalleypublishing.com. Year Established: 1894. Pub. Frequency: 3/w. (Tue., Wed., Fri.) Page Size: tabloid. Subscrip. Rate: $.50 newsstand/cover; $19 for 13 wks.; $35 for 26 wks.; $65/yr. **Wire Service(s):** AP. Circulation: 5,488 per issue (paid). **Owner(s):** Rock Valley Publishing LLC, 11512 N. Second St., Machesney Park, IL 61115. Telephone: 815-877-4044. FAX: 815-654-4857. **Management:** Jack Cruger, President. Randy Johnson, Advertising Director. Lindy Sweet, Circulation Manager. **Editorial:** Meline Brady, Managing Editor.

BLUE MOUND

BLUE MOUND LEADER. 205 W. Niles, Blue Mound, IL 62513-0318. Telephone: 217-692-2323. FAX: 217-692-2323. E-MAIL: bmleader1@yahoo.com. Year Established: 1886. Pub. Frequency: w. (Wed.) Page Size: tabloid. Subscrip. Rate: $.50 newsstand/cover; $22/yr in county; $22/yr mailed out of county. Adv. Rate: col. inch $4.50 Circulation: 850 per issue (paid and free). **Owner(s):** Cindy Ervin, PO Box 318, Blue Mound, IL 62513. Telephone: 217-692-2323. FAX: 217-692-2323. **Management:** Cindy Ervin, President.

Weeklies

BOLINBROOK

BUGLE, THE. 340-B Quadrangle Dr, Bolinbrook, IL 60440. Telephone: 630-759-4709. FAX: 630-759-6423. E-MAIL: publisher@buglenewspapers.com. Year Established: 1957. Pub. Frequency: w. (Thu.) Page Size: tabloid. Subscrip. Rate: $75/yr carrier delivery local. Freelance Pay: $25/article. **Wire Service(s):** AP. Circulation: 15,000 per issue (controlled and free). **Owner(s):** Bugle Newspapers, Inc., See address and contact information above. **Management:** Richard Masterson, Publisher.

BOURBONNAIS

HERALD/COUNTRY MARKET, THE. 500 Brown Blvd., Bourbonnais, IL 60914-2328. Telephone: 815-933-1131. FAX: 815-933-3785. E-MAIL: news@bbherald.com. URL: http://www.bbherald.com. Year Established: 1975. Pub. Frequency: w. (Tue.) Page Size: tabloid. Subscrip. Rate: $.60 newsstand/cover; $25/yr mailed in state. Circulation: 35,000 per issue (paid and free). **Owner(s):** B & B Publishing, Inc., See address and contact information above. **Management:** Toby Olszewski, Publisher. Teresa Hensley, Classified Adv. Mgr.. **Editorial:** Mary Kay Blankestyn, Copy Editor.

BREESE

BREESE JOURNAL. 8060 Old Hwy. 50, Breese, IL 62230. Telephone: 618-526-7211. FAX: 618-526-2590. Year Established: 1921. Pub. Frequency: w. (Wed.) Page Size: broadsheet. Subscrip. Rate: $.50 newsstand/cover; $18.50/yr home delivery in county; $22/yr home delivery out of county. Adv. Rate: col. inch $6.44 Circulation: 6,226 per issue (paid and free). **Owner(s):** Breese Publishing Co., See address and contact information above. **Management:** Steven Mahlandt, President. Dave Mahlandt, Publisher. Mandy Jankowski, Advertising Manager. **Editorial:** Vicky Albers, Editor.

BRIDGEPORT

BRIDGEPORT LEADER. 131 E. Olive St., Bridgeport, IL 62417-1935. Telephone: 618-945-2111. FAX: 618-945-7405. E-MAIL: editor@bridgeportleader.com. Mailing Address: PO Box 317, Bridgeport, IL 62417-0317. Year Established: 1907. Pub. Frequency: w. (Thu.) Page Size: broadsheet. Subscrip. Rate: $.50 newsstand/cover; $25/yr local; $35/yr out of state. Adv. Rate: col. inch $5 Circulation: 2,950 per issue (paid). **Owner(s):** James Herring, See address and contact information above. **Management:** James Herring, Owner. Lindy Stivers, Advertising Manager. **Editorial:** Barbara Allender, Editor.

BRIGHTON

SOUTHWESTERN JOURNAL NEWS. 117 N. Main St., Brighton, IL 62012. Telephone: 618-372-8451. FAX: 618-372-4925. E-MAIL: swjnews@sbcglobal.net. Mailing Address: PO Box 606, Brighton, IL 62012. Year Established: 1972. Pub. Frequency: w. (Thu.) Page Size: tabloid. Subscrip. Rate: $.35 newsstand/cover; $21/yr in county; $28/yr mailed out of county. Adv. Rate: col. inch $3.30 Circulation: 1,550 per issue (paid). **Owner(s):** Galer Publishing Co., PO Box 100, Hillsboro, IL 62046. Telephone: 217-532-3933. **Management:** John M, Galer, Publisher. Courtney Wood, Advertising Manager. **Editorial:** Tera Wiseman, Managing Editor.

BUNKER HILL

ADVERTISER (BUNKER HILL), THE. 150 N. Washington, Bunker Hill, IL 62014. Telephone: 618-585-4411. FAX: 618-585-3354. Year Established: 1970. Pub. Frequency: w. (Mon.) Page Size: broadsheet.Adv. Rate: col. inch $3.30 **Owner(s):** Bunker Hill Publishing Co., See address and contact information above. **Management:** John M. Galer, President. **Editorial:** Courtney Wood, Editor.

BUSHNELL

MCDONOUGH DEMOCRAT. 358 E. Main St., Bushnell, IL 61422. Telephone: 309-772-2129. FAX: 309-772-3994. E-MAIL: lorton1@bushnell.net. Year Established: 1884. Pub. Frequency: w. (Mon.) Page Size: standard. Subscrip. Rate: $.50 newsstand/cover; $18/yr mailed in state; $22/yr mailed out of state. Circulation: 2,250 per issue (paid). **Owner(s):** David Norton, See address and contact information above. **Management:** David Norton, Publisher. Darlene Norton, Advertising Manager. **Editorial:** David Norton, Editor.

BYRON

TEMPO, THE. 418 W. Blackhawk St., Byron, IL 61010. Telephone: 815-234-4821. FAX: 815-234-4809. E-MAIL: rvcpress@aol.com. URL: http://www.rockvalleypublishing.com. Pub. Frequency: w. (Thu.) Page Size: tabloid. Subscrip. Rate: $.60 newsstand/cover; $25.95/yr in county; $28.95/yr out of county; $44.65/yr mailed out of state. Circulation: 6,000 per issue (paid and free). **Owner(s):** Rock Valley Publishing LLC, 11512 N. Second St., Machesney Park, IL 61115. Telephone: 815-877-4044. FAX: 815-654-4857. **Management:** Randy Johnston, General Manager. Peter Cruger, President. Jack Cruger, Publisher. Kelly Perris, Advertising. **Editorial:** Amy Kennedy, Editor.

CAHOKIA

HERALD (CAHOKIA), THE. 713 Range Ln., Cahokia, IL 62206. Telephone: 618-337-7300. FAX: 618-939-3815. Pub. Frequency: w. (Wed.) Page Size: broadsheet. Subscrip. Rate: $.50 newsstand/cover; $22/yr. Circulation: 3,000 per issue (paid and free). **Owner(s):** Breese Publishing Co., 8060 Old Hwy. 50, Breese, IL 62230. Telephone: 618-526-7211. FAX: 618-526-2590. **Editorial:** Monte Miller, Editor.

CAIRO

CAIRO CITIZEN. 711 Washington Ave., Cairo, IL 62914. Telephone: 618-734-4242. FAX: 618-734-4244. E-MAIL: editor@cairocitizen.com. URL: http://www.cairocitizen.com. Mailing Address: PO Box 33, Cairo, IL 62914-0033. Year Established: 1887. Pub. Frequency: w. (Thu.) Page Size: broadsheet. Subscrip. Rate: $.50 newsstand/cover; $27/yr mailed local. Circulation: 3,500 per issue (paid). **Owner(s):** North Scott Publishing, Inc., PO Box 529, Anna, IL 62906. Telephone: 618-833-2158. **Management:** James West Jr., Publisher. Lara Sullivan, Advertising Manager. **Editorial:** Barbara Wilson, Managing Editor.

CANTON

FULTON COUNTY SHOPPER. 53 W. Elm St., Canton, IL 61520. Telephone: 309-647-5100. FAX: 309-647-4665. URL: http://www.gatehousemedia.com. Mailing Address: PO Box 540, Canton, IL 61520. Pub. Frequency: w. (Tue.) Page Size: tabloid Circulation: 16,250 per issue (free). **Owner(s):** GateHouse Media, Inc, 350 WillowBrook Office Park, Fairport, NY 14450. Telephone: 585-598-0030. **Management:** Scott Koon, Publisher. Jackie Caulkins, Advertising Manager. Rick Baybee, Circulation Manager.

CARLINVILLE

MACOUPIN COUNTY ENQUIRER-DEMOCRAT. 125 E. Main St., Carlinville, IL 62626-0200. Telephone: 217-854-2534. FAX: 217-854-2535. E-MAIL: enquirer@dtnspeed.net. Year Established: 1852. Pub. Frequency: w. (Thu.) Page Size: broadsheet. Subscrip. Rate: $.50 newsstand/cover; $20/yr in county; $27/yr mailed out of county. Circulation: 5,500 per issue (paid). **Owner(s):** Chris Schmitt, See address and contact information above. **Management:** Chris Schmitt, Publisher. Beverly Neighbors, Advertising. **Editorial:** Chris Schmitt, Editor.

CARLYLE

CARLYLE UNION BANNER. 671 Tenth St., Carlyle, IL 62231. Telephone: 618-594-3131. FAX: 618-594-3115. E-MAIL: dempsey@unionbanner.com. Year Established: 1863. Pub. Frequency: w. (Wed.) Page Size: broadsheet. Subscrip. Rate: $.35 newsstand/cover; $17.50/yr in county; $27.50/yr out of county. Circulation: 6,200 per issue (paid). **Owner(s):** Dempsey Publishing Co., See address and contact information above. **Management:** Warren Dempsey, Publisher. Mike Langham, Advertising Manager. **Editorial:** Warren Dempsey, Editor.

CARMI

WHITE COUNTY SHOPPER NEWS. 323 E. Main St., Carmi, IL 62821. Telephone: 618-382-4176. FAX: 618-384-2163. Mailing Address: PO Box 190, Carmi, IL 62821. Pub. Frequency: w. (Mon.) Page Size: standard Circulation: 8,500 per issue (free). **Owner(s):** GateHouse Media, Inc, 350 WillowBrook Office Park, Fairport, NY 14450. Telephone: 585-598-0030. **Management:** Barry C. Cleveland, Publisher. Linda Devoy, Advertising Manager. Brenda Pennington, Circulation Manager.

CARROLLTON

CARROLLTON GAZETTE PATRIOT. 428 N. Main St., Carrollton, IL 62016-0231. Telephone: 217-942-3626. FAX: 217-942-3699. E-MAIL: gazette@midwest.net. Mailing Address: PO Box 231, Carrollton, IL 62016-0231. Year Established: 1846. Pub. Frequency: w. (Thu.) Page Size: broadsheet. Subscrip. Rate: $.55 newsstand/cover; $25/yr home delivery in county; $30/yr mailed out of county. Adv. Rate: col. inch $4 Circulation: 1,568 per issue (paid). **Owner(s):** Albert W. Scott, III, 428 N. Main St., Carrollton, IL 62016. Telephone: 217-942-3626. FAX: 217-942-3699. **Management:** Albert W. Scott III, Publisher. Sheryl Cook, Circulation Manager. **Editorial:** Albert W. Scott III, Editor.

CARTHAGE

HANCOCK COUNTY JOURNAL-PILOT. 31 N. Washington, Carthage, IL 62321. Telephone: 217-357-2149. FAX: 217-357-2177. E-MAIL: editor@journalpilot.com. URL: http://www.journalpilot.com. Mailing Address: PO Box 478, Carthage, IL 62321. Year Established: 1887. Pub. Frequency: w. (Wed.) Page Size: broadsheet. Subscrip. Rate: $.75 newsstand/cover; $25/yr carrier delivery in county motor rte. & mailed; $38/yr mailed out of county. Adv. Rate: col. inch $5.85 Circulation: 4,500 per issue (paid and free). **Owner(s):** Brehm Communications, Inc., 16644 W. Bernardo Dr., Ste. 300, San Diego, CA 92127. Telephone: 858-451-6200. **Management:** Mark Smidt, Publisher. Hollis Dear, Advertising Manager. Carrie Thompson, Circulation Manager. Leta Shumaker, Classified Adv. Mgr.. **Editorial:** Joy Swearingen, Managing Editor. Doug Endres, Sports Editor.

CASEY

CASEY REPORTER, THE. 216 S Central, Casey, IL 62420. Telephone: 217-826-2102. FAX: 217-923-9214. Mailing Address: PO Box 158, Casey, IL 62420. Year Established: 1938. Pub. Frequency: w. (Mon.) Page Size: broadsheet. Subscrip. Rate: $.75 newsstand/cover; $24/yr in county; $30/yr out of county. Circulation: 3,500 per issue (paid). **Owner(s):** Community Media Group, Inc, PO Box 10, West Frankfort, IL 62896. Telephone: 618-937-6412. **Management:** Charlotte Roach, Publisher. **Editorial:** Debbie Sowers, Editor.

MARSHALL INDEPENDENT CHOICE, THE. 216 S Central, Casey, IL 62420. Telephone: 217-826-2102. FAX: 217-923-9214. Mailing Address: PO Box 158, Casey, IL 62420. Pub. Frequency: w. (Mon.) Page Size: standard. Subscrip. Rate: $.75 newsstand/cover; $28/yr in county. Circulation: 1,500 per issue (paid). **Owner(s):** Community Media Group, Inc, PO Box 10, West Frankfort, IL 62896. Telephone: 618-937-6412. **Management:** Charlotte Roach, Publisher. **Editorial:** Debbie Sowers, Editor.

NEOGA NEWS. 216 S Central, Casey, IL 62420. Telephone: 217-826-2102. FAX: 217-923-9214. Mailing Address: PO Box 158, Casey, IL 62420. Pub. Frequency: w. (Mon.) Page Size: standard. Subscrip. Rate: $.75 newsstand/cover; $22/yr in county. Circulation: 600 per issue (paid). **Owner(s):** Community Media Group, Inc, PO Box 10, West Frankfort, IL 62896. Telephone: 618-937-6412. **Management:** Charlotte Roach, Publisher. **Editorial:** Nancy Larson, Editor.

CERRO GORDO

NEWS-RECORD, THE. 221 E. South St., Cerro Gordo, IL 61818-0049. FAX: 217-864-4711. Mailing Address: PO Box 49, Cerro Gordo, IL 61818-0049. Year Established: 1889. Pub. Frequency: w. (Wed.) Page Size: broadsheet. Subscrip. Rate: $.50 newsstand/cover; $18/yr mailed. Adv. Rate: col. inch $3.75 Circulation: 1,250 per issue (paid). **Owner(s):** Mt. Zion Publications, Inc., P O Box 79, Mt. Zion, IL 62549-0079. Telephone: 217-864-4212. **Management:** Cleon Birkemeyer, President. Mike Brothers, Publisher. Michael Vargo, Advertising Manager. Mike Brothers, Circulation Manager.

CHAMPAIGN

AMERICAM CLASSIFIEDS. 61 E. University Ave., Champaign, IL 61820-4109. Telephone: 217-356-4804. FAX: 217-356-4970. URL: http://www.americanclassifieds.com. Year Established: 1985. Pub. Frequency: w. (Thu.) Page Size: tabloid.Adv. Rate: col. inch $9.60 Circulation: 50,000 per issue (free). **Owner(s):** Gabrielle Cooper, 306 W Springfield, Champaign, IL 61820. **Management:** Gabrielle Cooper, General Manager. Bob Craft, Circulation Manager.

PIATT COUNTY JOURNAL-REPUBLICAN. 15 Main St., Champaign, IL 61820. Telephone: 217-351-5266, 217-762-2511. FAX: 217-762-8591. E-MAIL: journal@journal-republicam.com. Year Established: 1856. Pub. Frequency: w. (Wed.) Page Size: broadsheet. Subscrip. Rate: $.75 newsstand/cover; $30/yr mailed in county; $35/yr mailed out of county; $18/yr mailed to students. Adv. Rate: col. inch $9.45 Circulation: 3,900 per issue (paid). **Owner(s):** News Gazette, 118 W Washington St, Monticelli, IL 61856. 15 Main St, Champaign, IL 61820. **Management:** John Foreman, Publisher. Laurel Cripe, Office Manager. Stephanie Davenport, Advertising Manager. **Editorial:** Ken Hartman, Editor.

CHESTER

RANDOLPH COUNTY HERALD TRIBUNE. 1205 Swanwick St, Chester, IL 62233. Telephone: 618-826-2385. FAX: 618-826-5181. E-MAIL: tribuneeditor@verizon.net. URL: http://www.randolphcountyheraldtribune.com. Mailing Address: PO Box 269, Chester, IL 62233. Year Established: 1926. Pub. Frequency: w. (Thu.) Page Size: broadsheet. Subscrip. Rate: $.50 newsstand/cover; $22.30/yr in county; $26.45/yr elsewhere. Freelance Pay: $5/article. Circulation: 3,400 per issue (paid). **Owner(s):** GateHouse Media, Inc, 350 WillowBrook Office Park, Fairport, NY 14450. Telephone: 585-598-0030. **Management:** Brent Easton, Publisher. Linda Lang, Classified Adv. Mgr.. **Editorial:** Carrie Gonzales, Editor.

CHICAGO

BEVERLY REVIEW, THE. ISSN 0006-0410
10546 S Western Ave, Chicago, IL 60643. Telephone: 776-238-3366. FAX: 776-238-1492. Year Established: 1905. Pub. Frequency: w. Page Size: tabloid. Subscrip. Rate: $.75 newsstand/cover; $23/yr in area. Adv. Rate: col. inch $9.40 Circulation: 6,300 (paid). **Owner(s):** T R Communications, See address and contact information above. **Management:** Robert Olszewski, Advertising. **Editorial:** Robert M Olszewski Jr., Editor.

BRIDGEPORT NEWS (CHICAGO). 3252 S. Halsted, Chicago, IL 60608. Telephone: 312-842-5883. FAX: 312-842-5097. URL: http://www.bridgeportnews.net. Year Established: 1943. Pub. Frequency: w. (Wed.) Page Size: broadsheet.Subscrip. Rate: $.20 newsstand/cover Circulation: 25,300 per issue (paid). **Owner(s):** Chicago Bridgeport News, Inc., See address and contact information above. **Management:** Joseph S. Feldman, Publisher. Janice Racinowski, Advertising Manager. David Witkowski, Circulation Manager. **Editorial:** Janice Racinowski, Editor.

BRIGHTON PARK LIFE. ISSN 0007-0149
2949 W 43rd St, Chicago, IL 60632. Year Established: 1933. Pub. Frequency: w. Page Size: standard. Subscrip. Rate: $60/yr. Circulation: 30,000. **Owner(s):** Brighton Publishing Co., See address and contact information above. **Management:** Albert H Silinski, Publisher. **Editorial:** Albert H Silinski, Editor.

CHICAGO GAZETTE. 1335 W. Harrison St., Chicago, IL 60607-3318. Telephone: 312-243-4288. FAX: 312-243-4270. E-MAIL: nearwestgazette@comcast.net. URL: www.nearwestgazette.com. Year Established: 1983. Pub. Frequency: w. (Fri.) Page Size: tabloid. Subscrip. Rate: $25/yr. Freelance Pay: $75/article. Circulation: 17,000 per issue (paid and controlled). **Owner(s):** Mark J. Valentino, 1335 W. Harrison, Chicago, IL 60607. Telephone: 312-243-4288. FAX: 312-243-4270. **Management:** Mark J. Valentino, President. Carmen Valentino, Advertising Manager. **Editorial:** Mark J. Valentino, Editor-in-Chief. William S. Bike, Managing Editor. Anne M. Nordhaus-Bike, Feature Editor.

CLEAR-RIDGE REPORTER. 6225 S. Kedzie Ave., Chicago, IL 60629. Telephone: 773-476-4800. FAX: 773-476-7811. E-MAIL: vonpub@aol.com. URL: http://www.swnewsherald.com. Year Established: 1961. Pub. Frequency: w. (Wed.) Page Size: tabloid Circulation: 24,000 per issue (free). **Owner(s):** Southwest Community Newspapers, See address and contact information above. **Management:** James C Vondrak, Publisher. Robert W Gusanders, Vice President. Jose Reyes, Classified Adv. Mgr.. **Editorial:** Joseph Boyle, Editor.

HYDE PARK HERALD. 5240 S. Harper Ave., Chicago, IL 60615. Telephone: 773-643-8533. FAX: 773-667-0938. E-MAIL: hpherald@aol.com. URL: http://www.hpherald.com. Year Established: 1881. Pub. Frequency: w. (Wed.) Page Size: tabloid.Subscrip. Rate: $.50 newsstand/cover; $15/yr Circulation: 28,000 per issue (paid). **Owner(s):** Hyde Park Herald Newspapers, Inc., See address and contact information above. **Management:** Susan J. Walker, General Manager. Bruce Sagan, Publisher. Carol Cichocki, Advertising Manager. **Editorial:** Brian Wellner, Editor.

INSIDE PUBLICATION. 4159 N Western Ave,, 2nd fl., Chicago, IL 60618-2813. Telephone: 773-313-2000. FAX: 773-313-2006. E-MAIL: inside@britsys.net. Year Established: 1968. Pub. Frequency: w. (Wed.) Page Size: tabloid. Subscrip. Rate: $100/yr. Adv. Rate: col. inch $26 Freelance Pay: $25/article. Circulation: 49,500 per issue (free). **Owner(s):** Ronald Roenigk, See address and contact information above. **Management:** Ronald Roenigk, Advertising Manager. Karen Sonnefeldt, Circulation Manager. **Editorial:** Jeff Borgardt, Editor.

JOURNAL NEWS. 1751 W 47th St., 2nd Fl Chicago, IL 60609. Telephone: 773-927-7204. FAX: 773-927-7940. E-MAIL: journalnews@bync.org. Year Established: 1932. Pub. Frequency: w. (Wed.) Page Size: tabloid. Subscrip. Rate: $30/yr. Adv. Rate: col. inch $22 Circulation: 44,000 per issue (paid and free). **Owner(s):** Back of the Yards Journal, See address and contact information above. **Management:** Patrick J. Salmon, Publisher. **Editorial:** Sonja Schneider, Editor.

LINCOLN PARK PRESS. 1708 W. Belmont Ave., Chicago, IL 60657. Telephone: 773-472-6904. FAX: 773-472-7806. Year Established: 1930. Pub. Frequency: w. Page Size: tabloid. Subscrip. Rate: $35/yr. Circulation: 24,700 (controlled). **Owner(s):** Rick Goss, See address and contact information above. **Management:** Arthur Diaz, President. Rick Goss, Publisher. Ann Thomas, Advertising Manager. Sabina Jankowski, Business Manager.

NEW CITY. 770 N. Halsted, Ste. 306, Chicago, IL 60622. Telephone: 312-243-8786. FAX: 312-243-8802. E-MAIL: advertising@newcitynet.com. URL: http://www.newcitychicago.com. Year Established: 1986. Pub. Frequency: w. (Thu.) Page Size: tabloid. Subscrip. Rate: $75/yr. Circulation: 70,000 per issue (paid and controlled). **Owner(s):** New City Communications, Inc., See address and contact information above. **Management:** Jan Hieggelke, Publisher. Michael Hartnett, Advertising Manager. **Editorial:** Brian Hieggelke, Editor.

NORTHWEST SIDE PRESS. 4937 N. Milwaukee Ave., Chicago, IL 60630-2191. Telephone: 773-286-6100. FAX: 773-286-8151. Year Established: 1940. Pub. Frequency: w. (Wed.) Page Size: broadsheet. Subscrip. Rate: $.50 newsstand/cover; $115/yr mailed. Adv. Rate: col. inch $37 Circulation: 34,000 per issue (paid and controlled). **Owner(s):** Nadig Newspapers, Inc., See address and contact information above. **Management:** Glenn H. Nadig, President. Brian Nadig, Publisher. **Editorial:** Randy Erickson, Editor.

REPORTER (CHICAGO), THE. 4937 N. Milwaukee Ave., Chicago, IL 60630-2191. Telephone: 773-286-6100. FAX: 773-286-8151. Year Established: 1964. Pub. Frequency: w. (Sat.) Page Size: tabloid. Subscrip. Rate: $.50 newsstand/cover; $115/yr mailed. Adv. Rate: col. inch $18.50 Circulation: 10,000 per issue (paid and free). **Owner(s):** Nadig Newspapers, Inc., See address and contact information above. **Management:** Glenn H. Nadig, President. Brian Nadig, Publisher. **Editorial:** Randy Erickson, Editor.

SOUTHWEST HERALD/ZONE B. 6225 S. Kedzie Ave., Chicago, IL 60629. Telephone: 773-476-4800. FAX: 773-476-7811. E-MAIL: vonpub@aol.com. URL: swnewsherald.com. Year Established: 1982. Pub. Frequency: w. (Thu.) Page Size: tabloid. Subscrip. Rate: $.50 newsstand/cover; $20.10/yr mailed. Circulation: 25,685 per issue (paid and free). **Owner(s):** Southwest Community Newspapers, See address and contact information above. **Management:** James C Vondrak, Publisher. Robert W Gusanders, Vice President. John Briggs, Circulation Manager. Jose Reyes, Classified Adv. Mgr. **Editorial:** Joe Boyle, Editor.

SOUTHWEST NEWS-HERALD. ISSN 0038-4704 6225 S. Kedzie Ave., Chicago, IL 60629. Telephone: 773-476-4800. FAX: 773-476-7811. E-MAIL: vonpub@aol.com. URL: http://www.swnewsherald.com. Year Established: 1924. Pub. Frequency: w. Page Size: broadsheet. Subscrip. Rate: $15/yr. Circulation: 27,604. **Owner(s):** Southwest Community Newspapers, See address and contact information above. **Management:** James C Vondrak, Publisher. Robert W Gusanders, Vice President. John Briggs, Circulation Manager. Jose Reyes, Classified Adv. Mgr.. **Editorial:** Joe Boyle, Editor.

SOUTHWEST NEWS HERALD/ZONE A. 6225 S. Kedzie Ave., Chicago, IL 60629. Telephone: 773-476-4800. FAX: 773-476-7811. E-MAIL: vonpub@aol.com. URL: http://www. swnewsherald.com. Year Established: 1986. Pub. Frequency: w. (Thu.) Page Size: tabloid. Subscrip. Rate: $.50 newsstand/cover. Circulation: 11,500 per issue (paid and free). **Owner(s):** Southwest Community Newspapers, See address and contact information above. **Management:** James C Vondrak, Publisher. Robert W Gusanders, Vice President. Joyce Erickson, Circulation Manager. Jose Reyes, Classified Adv. Mgr. Jim Vondrak Jr., Sales Manager. **Editorial:** Joe Boyle, Editor.

SOUTHWEST SHOPPER. 6225 S. Kedzie Ave., Chicago, IL 60629. Telephone: 773-476-4800. FAX: 773-476-7811. E-MAIL: vonpub@aol.com. URL: http://www.swnewsherald.com. Year Established: 1960. Pub. Frequency: w. (Tue.) Page Size: broadsheet. Subscrip. Rate: $.15 newsstand/cover. Circulation: 30,000 per issue (paid and free). **Owner(s):** Southwest Community Newspapers, See address and contact information above. **Management:** James C Vondrak, Publisher. Robert W Gusanders, Vice President. John Briggs, Circulation Manager. Jose Reyes, Classified Adv. Mgr. **Editorial:** Joe Boyle, Editor.

CHRISMAN

CHRISMAN LEADER, THE. 107 N. Indiana St., Chrisman, IL 61924. Telephone: 217-269-2811. FAX: 217-269-3611. E-MAIL: xman@tigerpaw.com. Year Established: 1972. Pub. Frequency: w. (Thu.) Page Size: tabloid. Subscrip. Rate: $.35 newsstand/cover; $25/yr home delivery local; $30/yr mailed elsewhere. Circulation: 2,000 per issue (paid). **Owner(s):** Hometown Publications, See address and contact information above. **Management:** Louis Valbert, President. **Editorial:** Phyllis Mullenax, Editor.

CICERO

CHICAGO LAWNDALE NEWS. 5416 W. 25th St., Cicero, IL 60804. Telephone: 708-656-6400. FAX: 708-656-2433. E-MAIL: jn@chicagonet.net. URL: http://www.lawndalenews.com. Year Established: 1937. Pub. Frequency: w. (Thu.) Page Size: tabloid. Subscrip. Rate: $50/yr mailed. Adv. Rate: col. inch $55 Circulation: 198,000 per issue (paid and free). **Owner(s):** Linda Nardini, See address and contact information above. **Management:** Robert Nardini, President. Linda Nardini, Publisher. Jim Nardini, Vice President. **Editorial:** Daniel Nardini, Editor. Pilar Dazzo, Editor-in-Chief.

CHICAGO WEST SIDE TIMES. 5416 W. 25th St., Cicero, IL 60804. Telephone: 708-656-6400. FAX: 708-656-2433. E-MAIL: sales@lawndalenews.com. URL: http://www.lawndalenews.com. Year Established: 1940. Pub. Frequency: w. (Thu. & Sun.) Page Size: tabloid. Subscrip. Rate: $50/yr mailed. Circulation: 50,000 Sunday (paid and free); 150,000 per issue (paid and free). **Owner(s):** Linda Nardini, See address and contact information above. **Management:** Pilar Dazzo, General Manager. Robert Nardini, President. Linda Nardini, Publisher. Jim Nardini, Vice President.

CISSNA PARK

CISSNA PARK NEWS. 119 W. Garfield, PO Box 8, Cissna Park, IL 60924-0008. Telephone: 815-457-2245. FAX: 815-457-3245. Year Established: 1941. Pub. Frequency: w. (Thu.) Page Size: tabloid. Subscrip. Rate: $.50 newsstand/cover per issue; $26/yr home delivery in county; $28/yr home delivery out of city. Adv. Rate: col. inch $5 Circulation: 12,000. **Owner(s):** Baier Publishing Co., See address and contact information above. **Management:** Rick A. Baier, Publisher. **Editorial:** Rick A. Baier, Editor.

RANKIN INDEPENDENT. 119 W. Garfield, PO Box 8, Cissna Park, IL 60924-0008. Telephone: 815-457-2245. FAX: 815-457-3245. Year Established: 1897. Pub. Frequency: w. (Thu.) Page Size: tabloid. Subscrip. Rate: $.50 newsstand/cover; $26/yr in county; $28/yr out of county. Adv. Rate: col. inch $5 Circulation: 1,900 per issue (paid). **Owner(s):** Baier Publishing Co., See address and contact information above. **Management:** Rick A. Baier, Publisher. **Editorial:** Mary Ann Scott, Editor.

CLIFTON

ADVOCATE (CLIFTON), THE. 330 N. Fourth St., Clifton, IL 60927-0548. Telephone: 815-694-2122. FAX: 815-694-2649. Year Established: 1883. Pub. Frequency: w. (Thu.) Page Size: tabloid. Subscrip. Rate: $.50 newsstand/cover; $18.95/yr in state; $19.95/yr out of state. Adv. Rate: col. inch $3.75 Circulation: 2,100 per issue (controlled and free). **Owner(s):** Therese Simoneau, See address and contact information above. **Management:** Therese Simoneau, Publisher. **Editorial:** Therese Simoneau, Editor.

COLLINSVILLE

COLLINSVILLE HERALD JOURNAL. 2 Executive Dr., Collinsville, IL 62234. Telephone: 618-344-0264. FAX: 618-344-3831. E-MAIL: cfredeking@yourjournal.com. URL: http://www.yourjournal.com. Year Established: 1974. Pub. Frequency: s-w. (Wed. & Sun.) Page Size: broadsheet. Circulation: 13,441 per issue (paid and free). **Owner(s):** Suburban Journals, 1714 Deer Tracks Trail, St. Louis, MO 63101. Telephone: 314-831-1110. **Management:** Rick Jarvis, Publisher. Carol Fredeking, Advertising Manager. John Mackelden, Circulation Manager. **Editorial:** Harry Weiner, Managing Editor. Joey Cavato, Sports Editor.

EDWARDSVILLE JOURNAL. 2 Executive Dr., Collinsville, IL 62234. Telephone: 618-656-8000. FAX: 618-344-3831. E-MAIL: cfredeking@yourjournal.com. URL: http://www.yourjournal.com. Year Established: 1965. Pub. Frequency: w. (Wed.) Page Size: broadsheet. Subscrip. Rate: $.50 newsstand/cover Circulation: 13,441 per issue (free). **Owner(s):** Suburban Journals, 1714 Deer Tracks Trail, St. Louis, MO 63101. Telephone: 314-821-1110. **Management:** Rick Jarvis, Publisher. Carol Fredeking, Advertising Manager. John Mackelden, Circulation Manager. **Editorial:** Harry Weiner, Managing Editor. Joey Cabato, Sports Editor.

GRANITE CITY PRESS RECORD JOURNAL. 2 Executive Dr., Collinsville, IL 62234. Telephone: 618-344-0264. FAX: 618-344-3831. E-MAIL: cfredeking@yourjournal.com. URL: http://www.yourjournal.com. Year Established: 2000. Pub. Frequency: s-w. (Wed. & Sun.) Page Size: broadsheet. Circulation: 2,757 per issue (controlled and free). **Owner(s):** Suburban Journals, 1714 Deer Tracks Trail, St. Louis, MO 63101. Telephone: 314-821-1110. **Management:** Rick Jarvis, Publisher. Carol Fredeking, Advertising Manager. John Mackelden, Circulation Manager. **Editorial:** Harry Weiner, Managing Editor. Joey Cabato, Sports Editor.

COLUMBIA

CLARION JOURNAL, THE. 212 W. Locust, Columbia, IL 62236. Telephone: 618-281-7691. FAX: 618-281-7693. E-MAIL: dbarger@yourjournal.com. URL: http://www.yourjournal.com. Pub. Frequency: s-w. (Wed. & Sun.) Page Size: broadsheet. Subscrip. Rate: $.50 newsstand/cover. Circulation: 1,500 per issue (controlled and free). **Owner(s):** Suburban Journals, 1714 Deer Tracks Trail, St. Louis, MO 63131. Telephone: 314-821-1110. **Management:** Tina Kapocky, Publisher. Sam Clines, Circulation Manager. **Editorial:** Garen Vartanian, Managing Editor.

ENTERPRISE JOURNAL. 212 W. Locust, Columbia, IL 62236. Telephone: 618-281-7691. FAX: 618-281-7693. E-MAIL: dbarger@yourjournal.com. URL: http://www.yourjournal.com. Pub. Frequency: w. (Wed.) Page Size: broadsheet. Subscrip. Rate: $.50 newsstand/cover; $58/yr mailed in county. Circulation: 4,000 per issue (paid and free). **Owner(s):** Suburban Journals, 1714 Deer Tracks Trail, St. Louis, MO 63131. Telephone: 314-821-1110. **Management:** Tina Kapocky, Publisher. Sam Clines, Circulation Manager. **Editorial:** Garen Vartanian, Managing Editor.

DECATUR

DECATUR TRIBUNE. 240 N. Park St., Decatur, IL 62523. Telephone: 217-422-9702. E-MAIL: decaturtrb@aol.com. URL: http://www.decaturtribune.com. Mailing Address: PO Box 1490, Decatur, IL 62525-1490. Year Established: 1969. Pub. Frequency: w. (Wed.) Page Size: tabloid. Subscrip. Rate: $.60 newsstand/cover; $30/yr mailed in area; $50 mailed for 2 yrs. in area. Adv. Rate: col. inch $6 Circulation: 8,000 per issue (paid). **Owner(s):** Paul V. Osborne, See address and contact information above. **Management:** Paul V. Osborne, Publisher. **Editorial:** Paul V. Osborne, Editor.

DEKALB

MIDWEEK, THE. 650 Peace Rd., DeKalb, IL 60115. Telephone: 815-758-0696. FAX: 815-758-1418. E-MAIL: readit@midweeknews.com. URL: http://www.midweeknews.com. Mailing Address: PO Box 546, DeKalb, IL 60115. Year Established: 1967. Pub. Frequency: w. (Wed.) Page Size: tabloid. Subscrip. Rate: $91/yr out of area. Circulation: 30,000 per issue (paid and free). **Owner(s):** Lee Enterprises, Inc., 900 N. Tucker Blvd., St. Louis, MO 63101. Telephone: 314-340-8000. **Management:** Ken Doubler, General Manager. Stacey Miller, Circulation Manager. **Editorial:** Josh Albrecht, Managing Editor. Hank Brockett, News Editor.

DELAVAN

DELAVAN TIMES, THE. 314 Locust, Delavan, IL 61734-0199. Telephone: 309-244-7111. E-MAIL: delavantimes@sbcglobal.net. Mailing Address: PO Box 199, Delavan, IL 61734-0199. Year Established: 1874. Pub. Frequency: w. (Wed.) Page Size: tabloid. Subscrip. Rate: $.50 newsstand/cover; $20/yr in state; $22/yr out of state. Circulation: 1,550 per issue (paid). **Owner(s):** Sandra Larimore Denman, PO Box 199, Delavan, IL 61734. Telephone: 309-244-7111. **Management:** Sandra Larimore Denman, Publisher. **Editorial:** Sandra Larimore Denman, Editor.

DES PLAINES

ARLINGTON HEIGHTS JOURNAL & TOPICS. 622 Graceland Ave., Des Plaines, IL 60016-4556. Telephone: 847-299-5511. E-MAIL: journalnews@mail.com. URL: http://www.journal-topics.com. Pub. Frequency: w. (Thu.) Page Size: tabloid. Subscrip. Rate: $1 newsstand/cover; $28/yr in county; $33/yr out of county; $23/yr in county to senior citizens. Circulation: 3,923 per issue (paid). **Owner(s):** Journal & Topics Newspapers, The, See address and contact information above. **Management:** Richard C. Wessell Sr., Publisher. Robert H Wessell, Advertising Director. Richard C. Wessell Jr., Advertising Manager. Jack Carbery, Classified Adv. Mgr.. **Editorial:** Todd Wessell, Editor. Dwight Esau, Sports.

Weeklies

BUFFALO GROVE JOURNAL & TOPICS. 622 Graceland Ave., Des Plaines, IL 60016-4556. Telephone: 847-299-5511. FAX: 847-298-8549. E-MAIL: journalnews@mail.com. URL: http://www.journal-topics.com. Pub. Frequency: w. (Thu.) Page Size: tabloid. Subscrip. Rate: $1 newsstand/cover; $28/yr in county; $33/yr out of county; $23/yr in county to senior citizens. Circulation: 3,217 per issue (paid). **Owner(s):** Journal & Topics Newspapers, The, See address and contact information above. **Management:** Richard C. Wessell Sr., Publisher. Robert H Wessell, Advertising Director. Jack Carbery, Classified Adv. Mgr.. **Editorial:** Todd Wessell, Editor. Dwight Esau, Sports.

DES PLAINES JOURNAL. 622 Graceland Ave., Des Plaines, IL 60016-4556. Telephone: 847-299-5511. FAX: 847-298-8549. E-MAIL: journalnews@mail.com. URL: http://www.journal-topics.com. Year Established: 1933. Pub. Frequency: s-w. (Wed. & Fri.) Page Size: standard. Subscrip. Rate: $1 newsstand/cover; $28/yr in county; $33/yr out of county; $23/yr to senior citizens. Circulation: 10,022 per issue (paid). **Owner(s):** Journal & Topics Newspapers, The, See address and contact information above. **Management:** Todd Wessell, Publisher. Richard C. Wessell Jr., Advertising Manager. Jack Carbery, Classified Adv. Mgr.. **Editorial:** Dwight Esau, Sports.

ELK GROVE JOURNAL. 622 Graceland Ave., Des Plaines, IL 60016-4556. Telephone: 847-299-5511. FAX: 847-298-8549. E-MAIL: jounralnews@mail.com. URL: http://www.journal-topics.com. Year Established: 1982. Pub. Frequency: w. (Thu.) Page Size: tabloid. Subscrip. Rate: $1 newsstand/cover; $28/yr in county; $33/yr out of county; $23/yr in county to senior citizens. Circulation: 4,128 per issue (paid). **Owner(s):** Journal & Topics Newspapers, The, See address and contact information above. **Management:** Todd Wessell, Publisher. Robert H Wessell, Advertising Director. Richard C. Wessell Jr., Advertising Manager. **Editorial:** Todd Wessell, Editor. Dwight Esau, Sports.

GOLF MILL JOURNAL. 622 Graceland Ave., Des Plaines, IL 60016-4556. Telephone: 847-299-5511. FAX: 847-298-8549. E-MAIL: journalnews@mail.com. URL: http://www.journal-topics.com. Pub. Frequency: s-w. (Wed. & Fri.) Page Size: tabloid. Subscrip. Rate: $1 newsstand/cover; $28/yr in county; $33/yr out of county; $23/yr in county to senior citizens. Circulation: 1,224 per issue (paid). **Owner(s):** Journal & Topics Newspapers, The, See address and contact information above. **Management:** Todd Wessell, Publisher. Robert H Wessell, Advertising Director. Richard C. Wessell Jr., Advertising Manager. Jack Carbery, Classified Adv. Mgr.. **Editorial:** Todd Wessell, Editor. Dwight Esau, Sports.

MOUNT PROSPECT JOURNAL. 622 Graceland Ave., Des Plaines, IL 60016-4556. Telephone: 847-299-5511. FAX: 847-298-8549. E-MAIL: journalnews@mail.com. URL: http://www.journal-topics.com. Pub. Frequency: s-w. (Wed. & Fri.) Page Size: tabloid. Subscrip. Rate: $1 newsstand/cover; $28/yr in county; $33/yr out of county; $23/yr to senior citizens. Circulation: 5,818 per issue (paid). **Owner(s):** Journal & Topics Newspapers, The, See address and contact information above. **Management:** Todd Wessell, Publisher. Robert H Wessell, Advertising Director. Richard C. Wessell Jr., Advertising Manager. Jack Carbery, Classified Adv. Mgr.. **Editorial:** Todd Wessell, Editor. Dwight Esau, Sports.

NILES JOURNAL. 622 Graceland Ave., Des Plaines, IL 60016-4556. Telephone: 847-299-5511. E-MAIL: journalnews@mail.com. URL: http://www.journal-topics.com. Pub. Frequency: w. (Wed.) Page Size: tabloid. Subscrip. Rate: $1 newsstand/cover; $28/yr in county; $33/yr out of county; $23/yr in county to senior citizens. Circulation: 4,301 per issue (paid). **Owner(s):** Journal & Topics Newspapers, The, See address and contact information above. **Management:** Todd Wessell, Publisher. Robert H Wessell, Advertising Director. Richard C. Wessell Jr., Advertising Manager. Jack Carbery, Classified Adv. Mgr.. **Editorial:** Todd Wessell, Editor. Dwight Esau, Sports.

NORTHWEST JOURNAL. 622 Graceland Ave., Des Plaines, IL 60016-4556. Telephone: 847-299-5511. FAX: 847-298-8549. E-MAIL: journalnews@mail.com. URL: http://www.journal-topics.com. Pub. Frequency: w. (Mon.) Page Size: tabloid. Subscrip. Rate: $1 newsstand/cover; $28/yr home delivery in county; $23/yr mailed in county to senior citizens; $33/yr mailed out of county. Circulation: 4,317 per issue (paid). **Owner(s):** Journal & Topics Newspapers, The, See address and contact information above. **Management:** Todd Wessell, Publisher. Richard C. Wessell Jr., Advertising Manager. Jack Carbery, Classified Adv. Mgr.. **Editorial:** Todd Wessell, Editor. Dwight Esau, Sports.

PALATINE JOURNAL/TOPICS. 622 Graceland Ave., Des Plaines, IL 60016-4556. Telephone: 847-299-5511. FAX: 847-298-8549. E-MAIL: journalnews@mail.com. URL: http://www.journal-topics.com. Pub. Frequency: w. (Thu.) Page Size: tabloid. Subscrip. Rate: $1 newsstand/cover; $28/yr in county; $33/yr out of county; $23/yr in county to senior citizens. Circulation: 3,016 per issue (paid). **Owner(s):** Journal & Topics Newspapers, The, See address and contact information above. **Management:** Todd Wessell, Publisher. Richard C. Wessell Jr., Advertising Director. Jack Carbery, Classified Adv. Mgr.. **Editorial:** Todd Wessell, Editor. Dwight Esau, Sports. Mary Jane Wessell, Travel Editor.

PARK RIDGE JOURNAL. 622 Graceland Ave., Des Plaines, IL 60016-4556. Telephone: 847-299-5511. FAX: 847-298-8549. E-MAIL: journalnews@mail.com. URL: http://www.journal-topics.com. Pub. Frequency: w. (Wed.) Page Size: tabloid. Subscrip. Rate: $1 newsstand/cover; $28/yr in county; $23/yr in county to senior citizens; $33/yr out of county. Circulation: 3,724 per issue (paid). **Owner(s):** Journal & Topics Newspapers, The, See address and contact information above. **Management:** Todd Wessell, Publisher. Robert H Wessell, Advertising Director. Richard C. Wessell Jr., Advertising Manager. **Editorial:** Todd Wessell, Editor. Dwight Esau, Sports.

PROSPECT HEIGHTS JOURNAL. 622 Graceland Ave., Des Plaines, IL 60016. Telephone: 847-299-5511. FAX: 847-298-8549. E-MAIL: journalnews@mail.com. URL: http://www.journal-topics.com. Pub. Frequency: s-w. (Wed. & Fri.) Page Size: tabloid. Subscrip. Rate: $1 newsstand/cover; $28/yr in county; $33/yr out of county; $23/yr in county to senior citizens. Circulation: 1,679 per issue (paid). **Owner(s):** Des Plaines Journal, Inc., See address and contact information above. **Management:** Todd Wessell, Publisher. Robert H Wessell, Advertising Director. Richard C. Wessell Jr., Advertising Manager. Jack Carbery, Classified Adv. Mgr.. **Editorial:** Todd Wessell, Editor. Dwight Esau, Sports.

ROLLING MEADOWS JOURNAL/TOPICS. 622 Graceland Ave., Des Plaines, IL 60016-4556. Telephone: 847-299-5511. FAX: 847-298-8549. E-MAIL: journalnews@mail.com. URL: http://www.journal-topics.com. Year Established: 1967. Pub. Frequency: w. (Thu.) Page Size: tabloid. Subscrip. Rate: $1 newsstand/cover; $28/yr in county; $23/yr in county to senior citizens; $33/yr out of county. Circulation: 3,171 per issue (paid). **Owner(s):** Journal & Topics Newspapers, The, See address and contact information above. **Management:** Todd Wessell, Publisher. Robert H Wessell, Advertising Director. Richard C. Wessell Jr., Advertising Manager. Jack Carbery, Classified Adv. Mgr.. **Editorial:** Todd Wessell, Editor. Dwight Esau, Sports.

ROSEMONT JOURNAL. 622 Graceland Ave., Des Plaines, IL 60016-4556. Telephone: 847-299-5511. FAX: 847-298-8549. E-MAIL: journalnews@mail.com. URL: http://www.journal-topics.com. Pub. Frequency: w. (Wed.) Page Size: tabloid. Subscrip. Rate: $1 newsstand/cover; $28/yr in county; $33/yr out of county; $23/yr local to senior citizens. Circulation: 604 per issue (paid). **Owner(s):** Journal & Topics Newspapers, The, See address and contact information above. **Management:** Todd Wessell, Publisher. Robert H Wessell, Advertising Director. Richard C. Wessell Jr., Advertising Manager. **Editorial:** Todd Wessell, Editor. Dwight Esau, Sports.

SUBURBAN JOURNAL. 622 Graceland Ave., Des Plaines, IL 60016-4556. Telephone: 847-299-5511. E-MAIL: journalnews@mail.com. URL: http://www.journal-topics.com. Pub. Frequency: w. (Sat.) Page Size: tabloid. Subscrip. Rate: $1 newsstand/cover; $28/yr in county; $33/yr out of county; $23/yr to senior citizens. Circulation: 4,422 per issue (paid). **Owner(s):** Journal & Topics Newspapers, The, See address and contact information above. **Management:** Todd Wessell, Publisher. Richard C. Wessell Jr., Advertising Director. Jack Carbery, Classified Adv. Mgr.. **Editorial:** Todd Wessell, Editor. Dwight Esau, Sports Editor.

WHEELING JOURNAL/TOPICS. 622 Graceland Ave., Des Plaines, IL 60016-4556. Telephone: 847-299-5511. FAX: 847-298-8549. E-MAIL: journalnews@mail.com. URL: http://www.journal-topics.com. Pub. Frequency: w. (Thu.) Page Size: tabloid. Subscrip. Rate: $1 newsstand/cover; $28/yr in county; $33/yr out of county; $23/yr in county to senior citizens. Circulation: 1,112 per issue (paid). **Owner(s):** Journal & Topics Newspapers, The, See address and contact information above. **Management:** Todd Wessell, Publisher. Robert H Wessell, Advertising Director. Richard C. Wessell Jr., Advertising Manager. **Editorial:** Todd Wessell, Editor. Dwight Esau, Sports.

DOWNERS GROVE

BARTLETT/HANOVER PARK/STREAM WOOD PRESS. 1101 W 31st St, Ste 100, Downers Grove, IL 60515-5581. Telephone: 630-368-1100. FAX: 630-368-1333. URL: http://www.gatehousemedia.com. Pub. Frequency: w. (Thu.) Page Size: tabloid. Subscrip. Rate: $.75 newsstand/cover; $30/yr in county area. Adv. Rate: col. inch $9.95 Circulation: 1,500 per issue (paid). **Owner(s):** GateHouse Media, Inc, 350 WillowBrook Office Park, Fairport, NY 14450. Telephone: 585-598-0030. **Management:** Caroll Stacklin, Publisher. Bill Casey, VP Advertising. John Novosel, Circulation Director. Rita Feigl, Classified Adv. Mgr..

BOLINGBROOK/WOODRIDGE/LISLE REPORTER. 1101 W 31st St, Ste 100, Downers Grove, IL 60515-5581. Telephone: 630-368-1100. FAX: 630-368-1333. URL: http://www.chicagosuburbannews.com. Year Established: 1969. Pub. Frequency: w. (Wed.) Page Size: tabloid. Subscrip. Rate: $1 newsstand/cover; $38/yr. Adv. Rate: col. inch $23.30 Circulation: 10,400 per issue (paid and free). **Owner(s):** GateHouse Media, Inc, 350 WillowBrook Office Park, Fairport, NY 14450. Telephone: 585-598-0030. FAX: 585-248-2631. **Management:** Caroll Stacklin, Publisher. Bill Casey, VP Advertising. John Novosel, Circulation Director. Rita Feigl, Classified Adv. Mgr..

CLARENDON HILLS/DARIEN SUBURBAN LIFE. 1101 W 31st St, Ste 100, Downers Grove, IL 60515-5581. Telephone: 630-368-1100. FAX: 630-368-1333. E-MAIL: localnews@libertysuburban.com. URL: http://www.chicagosuburbannews.com/. Year Established: 1959. Pub. Frequency: s-w. (Wed. & Sat.) Page Size: tabloid. Subscrip. Rate: $1 newsstand/cover; $30/yr in county. Adv. Rate: col. inch $17.65 Circulation: 6,750 per issue (paid and free). **Owner(s):** GateHouse Media, Inc, 350 WillowBrook Office Park, Fairport, NY 14450. Telephone: 585-598-0030. FAX: 585-248-2631. **Management:** Caroll Stacklin, Publisher. Bill Casey, VP Advertising. John Novosel, Circulation Director. **Editorial:** Jon Schuler, City Editor.

COUNTRYSIDE SUBURBAN LIFE. 1101 W 31st St, Ste 100, Downers Grove, IL 60515-5581. Telephone: 630-368-1100. FAX: 630-368-1333. E-MAIL: localnews@libertysuburban.com. URL: http://www.chicagosuburbannews.com. Year Established: 1926. Pub. Frequency: w. (Fri.) Page Size: broadsheet. Subscrip. Rate: $.75 newsstand/cover; $25/yr. Adv. Rate: col. inch $23.55 Circulation: 5,000 per issue (paid). **Owner(s):** GateHouse Media, Inc, 350 WillowBrook Office Park, Fairport, NY 14450. Telephone: 585-598-0030. FAX: 585-248-2631. **Management:** Caroll Stacklin, Publisher. Bill Casey, VP Advertising. John Novosel, Circulation Director. Rita Feigl, Classified Adv. Mgr.. **Editorial:** Jon Schuler, City Editor.

HINSDALE/OAKBROOK/WILLOWBROOK SUBURBAN LIFE. 1101 W 31st St, Ste 100, Downers Grove, IL 60515-5581. Telephone: 630-368-1100. FAX: 630-368-1333. E-MAIL: jjd@libertysuburban.com. URL: http://www.chicagosuburbannews.com. Year Established: 1895. Pub. Frequency: s-w. (Wed. & Sat.) Page Size: broadsheet. Subscrip. Rate: $1 newsstand/cover; $30/yr in city; $38/yr out of city. Adv. Rate: col. inch $10.25 Circulation: 500 per issue (paid). **Owner(s):** GateHouse Media, Inc, 350 WillowBrook Office Park, Fairport, NY 14450. Telephone: 585-598-0030. FAX: 585-248-2631. **Management:** Caroll Stacklin, Publisher. Bill Casey, VP Advertising. John Novosel, Circulation Director. Rita Feigl, Classified Adv. Mgr.. **Editorial:** Jon Schuler, City Editor.

LEMONT REPORTER. 1101 W 31st St, Ste 100, Downers Grove, IL 60515-5581. Telephone: 630-368-1100. FAX: 630-368-1333. URL: http://www.chicagosuburbannews.com. Year Established: 1990. Pub. Frequency: w. (Fri.) Page Size: tabloid. Subscrip. Rate: $.75 newsstand/cover; $25/yr. Adv. Rate: col. inch $13.55 Circulation: 9,000 per issue (paid and free). **Owner(s):** GateHouse Media, Inc, 350 WillowBrook Office Park, Fairport, NY 14450. Telephone: 585-598-0030. FAX: 585-248-2631. **Management:** Caroll Stacklin, Publisher. Bill Casey, VP Advertising. John Novosel, Circulation Director. Rita Feigl, Classified Adv. Mgr.. Michael Kolpas, Associate Publisher.

REPORTER (DOWNERS GROVE). 1101 W 31st St, Ste 100, Downers Grove, IL 60515-5581. Telephone: 630-368-1100. FAX: 630-368-1333. E-MAIL: yournews@libertysuburban.com. URL: http://www.chicagosuburbannews.com. Year Established: 1883. Pub. Frequency: s-w. (Wed. & Fri.) Page Size: tabloid. Subscrip. Rate: $1 newsstand/cover; $25/yr. Adv. Rate: col. inch $23.30 Circulation: 10,400 per issue (paid and free). **Owner(s):** GateHouse Media, Inc, 350 WillowBrook Office Park, Fairport, NY 14450. Telephone: 585-598-0030. **Management:** Caroll Stacklin, Publisher. Bill Casey, VP Advertising. John Novosel, Circulation Director. Rita Feigl, Classified Adv. Mgr.. Michael Kolpas, Associate Publisher.

WESTMONT PROGRESS. 1101 W 31st St, Ste 100, Downers Grove, IL 60515-5581. Telephone: 630-368-1100. FAX: 630-368-1333. URL: http://www.chicagosuburbannews.com. Year Established: 1959. Pub. Frequency: s-w. (Wed. & Sat.) Page Size: tabloid. Subscrip. Rate: $1 newsstand/cover; $38/yr. Adv. Rate: col. inch $23.30 Circulation: 10,400 per issue (paid and free). **Owner(s):** GateHouse Media, Inc, 350 WillowBrook Office Park, Fairport, NY 14450. Telephone: 585-598-0030. FAX: 585-248-2631. **Management:** Caroll Stacklin, Publisher. Bill Casey, VP Advertising. John Novosel, Circulation Director. Rita Feigl, Classified Adv. Mgr.. Michael Kolpas, Associate Publisher.

DU QUOIN

ASHLEY NEWS. 9 N. Division St., Du Quoin, IL 62832. Telephone: 618-542-2133. FAX: 618-542-2726. Mailing Address: PO Box 184, Du Quoin, IL 62832. Pub. Frequency: w. (Tue.) Page Size: standard.Subscrip. Rate: $18/yr mailed Circulation: 100 per issue (paid). **Owner(s):** GateHouse Media, Inc, 350 WillowBrook Office Park, Fairport, NY 14450. Telephone: 585-598-0030. FAX: 585-248-2631. **Management:** John Croessman, Publisher. Terri Fisher, Advertising Manager. Patty Malinee, Circulation Manager.

DU QUOIN NEWS, THE. 9 N. Division St., Du Quoin, IL 62832. Telephone: 618-542-2133. FAX: 618-542-2726. Mailing Address: PO Box 184, Du Quoin, IL 62832. Pub. Frequency: w. (Fri.) Page Size: standard.Subscrip. Rate: $27/yr mailed Circulation: 200 per issue (paid). **Owner(s):** GateHouse Media, Inc, 350 WillowBrook Office Park, Fairport, NY 14450. Telephone: 585-598-0030. FAX: 585-248-2631. **Management:** John Croessman, Publisher. Terri Fisher, Advertising Manager. Patty Malinee, Circulation Manager.

DURAND

VOLUNTEER, THE. 109 E. Oak St., Durand, IL 61024. Telephone: 815-248-4407. FAX: 815-248-9176. E-MAIL: volunteer@stateline-isp.com. Year Established: 1990. Pub. Frequency: w. (Thu.) Page Size: tabloid. Subscrip. Rate: $.75 newsstand/cover; $28/yr in county; $42/yr elsewhere. Freelance Pay: $25/article. Circulation: 5,000 per issue (paid). **Owner(s):** The Volunteer, Inc., See address and contact information above. **Management:** Gary Haughton, President. Curt Stalheim, Publisher. C.J. Gregg, Advertising Manager. Cheryl Bradt, Circulation Manager. **Editorial:** Curt Stalheim, Editor.

EAST ST. LOUIS

EAST ST. LOUIS MONITOR. 1501 State St., East St. Louis, IL 62205. Telephone: 618-271-0468. E-MAIL: media@estlmonitor.com. Mailing Address: P.O. Box 2137, East St. Louis, IL 62202-2137. Year Established: 1963. Pub. Frequency: w. (Thu.) Page Size: broadsheet. Subscrip. Rate: $.50 newsstand/cover; $125/yr mailed. Adv. Rate: col. inch $14.60 Freelance Pay: $25-$35/article. Circulation: 12,500 per issue (paid). **Owner(s):** Anne E. Jordan, See address and contact information above. **Management:** Anne E. Jordan, Publisher. George Laktzian, Advertising Director. **Editorial:** Frazier Garner, Editor.

EDINBURG

HERALD-STAR, THE. 103 S. Eaton, Edinburg, IL 62531. Telephone: 217-623-5523. FAX: 217-623-5523. E-MAIL: heraldstar@consolidated.net. Mailing Address: PO Box 50, Edinburg, IL 62531-0050. Year Established: 1882. Pub. Frequency: w. (Thu.) Page Size: broadsheet. Subscrip. Rate: $.35 newsstand/cover; $19/yr in county; $22/yr mailed out of county. Adv. Rate: col. inch $3 Circulation: 650 per issue (paid). **Owner(s):** Glenn W. Luttrell, See address and contact information above. **Editorial:** Elizabeth Luttrell, Editor.

EL PASO

EL PASO JOURNAL. 51 W Front St, El Paso, IL 61738. Telephone: 309-527-8595. FAX: 309-527-8850. E-MAIL: journal@elpaso.net. URL: http://www.elpaso.net/~journal/. Year Established: 1991. Pub. Frequency: w. (Wed.) Page Size: broadsheet. Subscrip. Rate: $.75 newsstand/cover; $26/yr mailed in county; $29/yr mailed in McLean cy.; $39/yr mailed out of county. Freelance Pay: $25/article. Circulation: 1,100 per issue (paid). **Owner(s):** El Paso Journal Inc., See address and contact information above. **Management:** Jim Glassman, Publisher. Elizabeth Kearney, Advertising. **Editorial:** Kim Kearney, Editor.

ELBURN

ELBURN HERALD. 123 N. Main St., Elburn, IL 60119. Telephone: 630-365-6446. FAX: 630-365-2251. E-MAIL: info@elburnherald.com. URL: http://www.elburnherald.com. Year Established: 1908. Pub. Frequency: w. (Thu.) Page Size: tabloid. Subscrip. Rate: $.75 newsstand/cover; $22/yr in county; $28/yr out of county; $35/yr out of state. Adv. Rate: col. inch $11.77 Circulation: 4,425 per issue (paid). **Owner(s):** Kaneland Publications, Inc., 123 N. Main St., Elburn, IL 60119-9166. Telephone: 630-365-6446. FAX: 630-365-2251. **Management:** Richard L. Cooper, Publisher. Luanne Hume, Business Manager. **Editorial:** Ryan Wells, Editor. Andy Tavegia, Assistant Editor.

ELIZABETHTOWN

HARDIN COUNTY (IL) INDEPENDENT. 25-27 W First St, Elizabethtown, IL 62931-0328. E-MAIL: etownnews@yahoo.com. Mailing Address: PO Box 328, Elizabethtown, IL 62931-0328. Year Established: 1871. Pub. Frequency: w. (Thu.) Page Size: broadsheet. Subscrip. Rate: $.75 newsstand/cover; $25/yr out of county. Adv. Rate: col. inch $3.80 Circulation: 2,700 per issue (paid). **Owner(s):** Noel E. Hurford, See address and contact information above. **Management:** Julie Rash, Publisher. **Editorial:** Julie Rash, Editor.

ELMHURST

GLEN ELLYN PRESS. 112 S. York St., Elmhurst, IL 60126-3432. Telephone: 630-469-0100. FAX: 630-545-1142. E-MAIL: news@libertysuburban.com. URL: http://www.chicagosuburbannews.com. Pub. Frequency: w. (Thu.) Page Size: tabloid. Subscrip. Rate: $.75 newsstand/cover; $30/yr local; $36/yr mailed out of state. Adv. Rate: col. inch $9.55 Circulation: 10,003 per issue (paid). **Owner(s):** Liberty Suburban Chicago Newspapers, 709 Enterprise Dr., Oak Brook, IL 60523. Telephone: 630-368-1100. **Management:** Gerry Smith, Publisher. Jeff Serota, Advertising Director. **Editorial:** Jim Harris, Editor.

ELMWOOD

TRI-COUNTY NEWS (ELMWOOD). 116 S. Magnolia, Elmwood, IL 61529. Telephone: 309-742-2521. FAX: 309-742-2511. E-MAIL: homeshopper@mchsi.com. Mailing Address: PO Box 289, Elmwood, IL 615529. Year Established: 1875. Pub. Frequency: w. (Thu.) Page Size: tabloid. Subscrip. Rate: $.50 newsstand/cover; $22/yr mailed in state; $25/yr mailed out of state. Adv. Rate: col. inch $3.20 Circulation: 600 per issue (paid). **Owner(s):** Tri-County News, See address and contact information above. **Management:** DeEllda Swindler, Owner. Sue Swindler, Advertising Manager. **Editorial:** Sue Swindler, Editor.

ERIE

REVIEW (ERIE), THE. 910 Albany St., Erie, IL 61250-0357. Telephone: 309-659-2761. FAX: 309-659-7751. E-MAIL: review@whitesidesentinel.com. Mailing Address: PO Box 357, Erie, IL 61250-0357. Year Established: 1857. Pub. Frequency: w. (Wed.) Page Size: broadsheet. Subscrip. Rate: $.75 newsstand/cover; $30/yr in county; $36/yr out of county; $47/yr out of state. Adv. Rate: col. inch $9 Circulation: 2,300 per issue (paid). **Owner(s):** W.N.S. Publications, 100 E. Main St., P.O. Box 31, Morrison, IL 61270. Telephone: 800-245-4927. FAX: 815-772-4105. **Management:** Tony Komlanc, President. Beth Armstrong, Advertising Manager. **Editorial:** Judy James, Editor.

EUREKA

WOODFORD COUNTY JOURNAL. 1926 S. Main St., Eureka, IL 61530. Telephone: 309-467-3314. FAX: 309-467-4563. E-MAIL: woodcojo@mtco.com. Mailing Address: PO Box 36, Eureka, IL 61530. Year Established: 1913. Pub. Frequency: w. (Thu.) Page Size: broadsheet. Subscrip. Rate: $.75 newsstand/cover; $33/yr local; $35/yr out of county; $40/yr out of state. Adv. Rate: col. inch $7.88 Circulation: 3,251 per issue (paid). **Owner(s):** Lee Enterprises, Inc., 201 N. Harrison St, Ste 600, Davenport, IA 52801-1924. **Management:** Mark Barra, General Manager. **Editorial:** Jason Shults, Editor.

FAIRBURY

BLADE (FAIRBURY), THE. 125 W Locust St, Fairbury, IL 61739. Telephone: 815-692-2366. FAX: 815-692-3782. URL: http://www.gatehousemedia.com. Pub. Frequency: w. (Wed.) Page Size: standard. Subscrip. Rate: $1 newsstand/cover; $30/yr in county. Circulation: 1,720 per issue (paid). **Owner(s):** GateHouse Media, Inc, 350 WillowBrook Office Park, Fairport, NY 14450. Telephone: 585-598-0030. FAX: 585-248-2631. **Management:** Scharon Shifflet, Publisher. Brenda Travis, Advertising.

FAIRFIELD

WAYNE COUNTY PRESS. 213 E. Main St., Fairfield, IL 62837-2028. Telephone: 618-842-2662. FAX: 618-842-7912. Year Established: 1866. Pub. Frequency: s-w. (Mon. & Thu.) Page Size: broadsheet. Subscrip. Rate: $.75 newsstand/cover; $49/yr in county. Adv. Rate: col. inch $11.20 Circulation: 7,250 per issue (paid). **Owner(s):** Wayne County Press, Inc., See address and contact information above. **Management:** Preston Mathews, President. Tom Mathews Jr., Publisher. Carol Tannahill, Advertising Manager. Sherry Auvil, Circulation Manager. **Editorial:** Tom Mathews Jr., Editor. Brian Turner, Sports.

FARINA

FARINA NEWS, THE. 109 N. Walnut, Farina, IL 62838. Telephone: 618-245-6216. FAX: 618—245-6216. Year Established: 1882. Pub. Frequency: w. (Thu.) Page Size: standard. Subscrip. Rate: $.45 newsstand/cover; $18/yr mailed in county; $22/yr mailed out of county; $26/yr mailed out of state. Circulation: 1,250 per issue (paid). **Owner(s):** Shirley Ann Quick, See address and contact information above. **Management:** Shirley Ann Quick, Publisher. **Editorial:** Shirley Ann Quick, Editor.

FARMER CITY

FARMER CITY JOURNAL. PO Box 80, Farmer City, IL 61842-0080. Telephone: 309-928-2193. FAX: 309-928-2194. E-MAIL: fcjournal@mchsi.com. Year Established: 1872. Pub. Frequency: w. (Wed.) Page Size: broadsheet. Subscrip. Rate: $30/yr in county; $33/yr mailed out of county. Circulation: 3,100 per issue (paid). **Owner(s):** Illinois Valley Press, See address and contact information above. **Management:** Steve Hoffman, General Manager.

FISHER

FISHER REPORTER, THE. 114 S. Third St., Fisher, IL 61843. Telephone: 217-897-1525. FAX: 217-897-1525. E-MAIL: fisherreporter@prairieinet.net. Mailing Address: PO Box 400, Fisher, IL 61843-0400. Year Established: 1880. Pub. Frequency: w. (Wed.) Page Size: broadsheet. Subscrip. Rate: $.50 newsstand/cover; $20/yr. Adv. Rate: col. inch $4 Circulation: 1,100 per issue (paid). **Owner(s):** Karen Henson, See address and contact information above. **Management:** Karen Henson, Publisher. **Editorial:** Karen Henson, Editor.

FREEPORT

FREEPORT SHOPPING NEWS. 1342 S Harlem Ave, Freeport, IL 61032. Telephone: 815-235-4106. FAX: 815-235-7077. E-MAIL: freeportshopnews@themonroetimes.com. Mailing Address: PO Box 230, Monroe, WI 53566. Year Established: 1970. Pub. Frequency: w. (Wed.) Page Size: tabloid. Subscrip. Rate: $25/yr mailed 3rd class. Adv. Rate: col. inch $12.90 Circulation: 23,000 per issue (free). **Owner(s):** Monroe Publishing LLC, See address and contact information above. **Management:** Carl Hearing, General Manager. Laura Hughes, Advertising Manager.

SCENE (FREEPORT), THE. 27 S State Ave, Freeport, IL 61032. Telephone: 815-232-1171. FAX: 815-232-3601. URL: http://www.gatehousemedia.com. Mailing Address: PO Box 330, Freeport, IL 61032-0330. Pub. Frequency: w. (Wed.) Page Size: standard Circulation: 14,600 per issue (free). **Owner(s):** GateHouse Media, Inc, 350 WillowBrook Office Park, Fairport, NY 14450. Telephone: 585-598-0030. **Management:** Steve Trosley, Publisher. Ann Young, Advertising Manager. Lisa Ray, Circulation Manager.

FULTON

FULTON JOURNAL. 408 Tenth Ave., Fulton, IL 61252. Telephone: 815-589-2424. FAX: 815-589-2568. Year Established: 1854. Pub. Frequency: w. (Wed.) Page Size: tabloid. Subscrip. Rate: $.50 newsstand/cover; $20/yr in county; $30/yr out of county; $34/yr mailed out of state. Circulation: 2,200 per issue (paid). **Owner(s):** Fulton Press, Inc., See address and contact information above. **Management:** Doris Kramer, Publisher. **Editorial:** Henry Kramer, Editor. Doris Kramer, Managing Editor.

WHITESIDE SHOPPER. 408 Tenth Ave., Fulton, IL 61252. Telephone: 815-589-2424. FAX: 815-589-2568. Year Established: 1940. Pub. Frequency: w. (Tue.) Page Size: tabloid Circulation: 3,300 per issue (free). **Owner(s):** Fulton Press, Inc., See address and contact information above. **Management:** Doris Kramer, Publisher. **Editorial:** Henry Kramer, Editor. Doris Kramer, Managing Editor.

GALATIA

MONEY STRETCHER. PO Box 99, Galatia, IL 62935. Telephone: 618-268-6291. FAX: 618-268-4325. URL: http://www.galatiamoneystretcher.com. Pub. Frequency: w. (Tue.) Page Size: standard Circulation: 27,011 per issue (free). **Owner(s):** GateHouse Media, Inc, 350 WillowBrook Office Park, Fairport, NY 14450. Telephone: 585-598-0030. FAX: 585-248-2631. **Management:** John Pfeifer, Publisher.

GALENA

GALENA GAZETTE. 716 S. Bench St., Galena, IL 61036-0319. Telephone: 815-777-0019. FAX: 815-777-3809. E-MAIL: cnewton999@aol.com. URL: http://www.galenagazette.com. Mailing Address: PO Box 319, Galena, IL 61036-0319. Year Established: 1834. Pub. Frequency: w. (Wed.) Page Size: tabloid. Subscrip. Rate: $1 newsstand/cover; $29/yr mailed local; $35/yr mailed tri-state; $48/yr mailed elsewhere. Circulation: 5,300 per issue (paid). **Owner(s):** P. Carter & Sarah Newton, See address and contact information above. **Management:** P. Carter Newton, President. Sarah Newton, Classified Adv. Mgr.. **Editorial:** Jay Dickerson, Editor.

GALESBURG

PAPER (GALESBURG), THE. 1445 Monmouth Blvd., Galesburg, IL 61401. Telephone: 309-344-3800. FAX: 309-344-3341. URL: http://www.gatehousemedia.com. Pub. Frequency: w. (Wed.) Page Size: standard Circulation: 21,600 per issue (free). **Owner(s):** GateHouse Media, Inc, 350 WillowBrook Office Park, Fairport, NY 14450. Telephone: 585-598-0030. FAX: 585-248-2631. **Management:** Tony Scott, Publisher. Tommy Todd, Advertising Manager. **Editorial:** Terry Haywood, Editor.

GALVA

GALVA NEWS. 348 Front St, Galva, IL 61434. Telephone: 309-932-2103. FAX: 309-932-3282. E-MAIL: galvanews@mchsi.com. URL: http://www.galvanews.com. Year Established: 1879. Pub. Frequency: w. (Wed.) Page Size: broadsheet. Subscrip. Rate: $.60 newsstand/cover; $29/yr mailed in state; $35/yr mailed out of state. Circulation: 2,400 per issue (paid). **Owner(s):** GateHouse Media, Inc, 350 WillowBrook Office Park, Fairport, NY 14450. Telephone: 585-598-0030. FAX: 585-248-2631. **Management:** Don Cooper, Publisher. Kelly Duke, Advertising Manager. Amber Weber, Circulation Manager. **Editorial:** Doug Boock, Editor.

GENESEO

CAMBRIDGE CHRONICLE (GENESEO). 108 W. First St., Geneseo, IL 61254-0209. Telephone: 309-944-2119. FAX: 309-944-5615. E-MAIL: editor@geneseorepublic.com. URL: http://www.geneseorepublic.com. Mailing Address: PO Box 132, Cambridge, IL 61238. Year Established: 1853. Pub. Frequency: w. (Thu.) Page Size: broadsheet. Subscrip. Rate: $1 newsstand/cover; $39/yr in state; $45/yr out of state. Circulation: 1,200 per issue (paid). **Owner(s):** GateHouse Media, Inc, 350 WillowBrook Office Park, Fairport, NY 14450. Telephone: 585-598-0030. FAX: 585-248-2631. **Management:** Dee Evans, General Manager. Deb Anderson, Advertising Manager. Marnie Eggen, Circulation Manager. Carol Clementz, Classified Adv. Mgr.. **Editorial:** Mindy Carls, Editor.

GENESEO REPUBLIC. 108 W. First St., Geneseo, IL 61254-0209. Telephone: 309-944-2119. FAX: 309-944-5615. E-MAIL: editor@geneseorepublic.com. URL: http://www.geneseorepublic.com. Mailing Address: PO Box 209, Geneseo, IL 61254. Year Established: 1856. Pub. Frequency: w. (Fri.) Page Size: broadsheet. Subscrip. Rate: $1 newsstand/cover; $39/yr mailed in state; $45/yr mailed out of state. Circulation: 3,150 per issue (paid and free). **Owner(s):** GateHouse Media, Inc, 350 WillowBrook Office Park, Fairport, NY 14450. Telephone: 585-598-0030. FAX: 585-248-2631. **Management:** Dee Evans, General Manager. Deb Anderson, Advertising Manager. Marnie Eggen, Circulation Manager. Carol Clementz, Classified Adv. Mgr.. **Editorial:** Lisa Depies, Editor. Amy Boldt, Sports Editor.

HENRY COUNTY ADVERTIZER-SHOPPER. 108 W. First St., Geneseo, IL 61254-0209. Telephone: 309-944-2119. FAX: 309-944-5615. E-MAIL: publisher@genescorepublic.com. URL: http://www.geneseorepublic.com. Mailing Address: PO Box 209, Geneseo, IL 61254. Year Established: 1856. Pub. Frequency: w. (Wed.) Page Size: broadsheet. Subscrip. Rate: $1 newsstand/cover; $39/yr mailed in state; $45/yr mailed out of state. Circulation: 18,000 per issue (paid and free). **Owner(s):** GateHouse Media, Inc, 350 WillowBrook Office Park, Fairport, NY 14450. Telephone: 585-598-0030. FAX: 585-248-2631. **Management:** Dee Evans, General Manager. Marnie Eggen, Circulation Manager. Carol Clementz, Classified Adv. Mgr..

ORION GAZETTE. 108 W. First St., Geneseo, IL 61254-0209. Telephone: 309-944-2119. FAX: 309-944-5615. E-MAIL: editor@netexpress.net. URL: http://www.geneseorepublic.com. Mailing Address: PO Box 400, Orion, IL 61273. Year Established: 1992. Pub. Frequency: w. (Thu.) Page Size: broadsheet. Subscrip. Rate: $1 newsstand/cover; $39/yr in state; $45/yr out of state. Circulation: 1,671 per issue (paid). **Owner(s):** GateHouse Media, Inc, 350 WillowBrook Office Park, Fairport, NY 14450. Telephone: 585-598-0030. FAX: 585-248-2631. **Management:** Dee Evans, General Manager. Deb Anderson, Advertising Manager. Marnie Eggen, Circulation Manager. Carol Clementz, Classified Adv. Mgr.. **Editorial:** Mindy Carls, Editor.

GEORGETOWN

INDEPENDENT NEWS. 302 Mill St., Georgetown, IL 61846. Telephone: 217-662-2556. FAX: 217-662-2484. E-MAIL: indnews@charter.net. Year Established: 1976. Pub. Frequency: w. (Wed.) Page Size: tabloid. Subscrip. Rate: $25/yr mailed out of area. Circulation: 17,000 per issue (paid and free). **Owner(s):** Doyne & Marcia Lenhart, See address and contact information above. **Management:** Vicki Delhaye, General Manager. Doyne Lenhart, Publisher. **Editorial:** Katie Marrow, Editor.

GIBSON CITY

GIBSON CITY COURIER. 310 N. Sangamon Ave., Gibson City, IL 60936. Telephone: 217-784-4244. FAX: 217-784-4246. E-MAIL: dbenter_gc@sbcglobal.net. Mailing Address: PO Box 549, Gibson City, IL 60936-0549. Year Established: 1873. Pub. Frequency: w. (Wed.) Page Size: broadsheet. Subscrip. Rate: $.50 newsstand/cover; $26/yr in county; $28/yr out of county. Adv. Rate: col. inch $7.86 Circulation: 2,013 per issue (paid). **Owner(s):** Lee Enterprises, Inc., 201 N. Harrison St, Ste 600, Davenport, IA 52801-1924. **Management:** Linda Lindus, Publisher. **Editorial:** Doris Benter, Editor.

GILLESPIE

GILLESPIE AREA NEWS. 112 W. Chestnut St., Gillespie, IL 62033. Telephone: 217-839-2130. FAX: 217-839-2139. E-MAIL: intouch@ctnet.net. Mailing Address: PO Box 209, Gillespie, IL 62033-0209. Year Established: 1905. Pub. Frequency: w. (Thu.) Page Size: broadsheet. Subscrip. Rate: $.50 newsstand/cover; $22/yr in county; $25/yr out of county. Adv. Rate: col. inch $4.20 Circulation: 3,000 per issue (paid). **Owner(s):** David & Patty Ambrose, See address and contact information above. **Management:** Patty Ambrose, General Manager. David Ambrose, Publisher. Patty Ambrose, Advertising. Jan Allan, Circulation Manager. **Editorial:** David Ambrose, Editor.

GILMAN

GILMAN STAR. 203 N. Central St., Gilman, IL 60938. Telephone: 815-265-7332. FAX: 815-265-7880. Mailing Address: PO Box 7, Gilman, IL 60938. Year Established: 1869. Pub. Frequency: w. (Thu.) Page Size: broadsheet. Subscrip. Rate: $.60 newsstand/cover; $27/yr mailed in county; $30/yr mailed out of county. Adv. Rate: col. inch $3.25 Circulation: 2,900 per issue (paid). **Owner(s):** John T. Elliot, See address and contact information above. **Management:** John T Elliot, Publisher. **Editorial:** John T Elliot, Editor.

GLASFORD

GLASFORD GAZETTE, THE. 309 Main St., Glasford, IL 61533-0260. Telephone: 309-389-2811. FAX: 309-384-4949. Year Established: 1899. Pub. Frequency: w. (Thu.) Page Size: tabloid. Subscrip. Rate: $.50 newsstand/cover; $21/yr in state; $23.50/yr out of state. Circulation: 1,200 per issue (paid). **Owner(s):** Gazette Printing Co., See address and contact information above. **Management:** William Watkins, Publisher. **Editorial:** William Watkins, Editor.

GLEN ELLYN

CAROL STREAM PRESS. 800 Roosevelt Rd, Bldg D, Ste 107, Glen Ellyn, IL 60137. Telephone: 630-469-0100. FAX: 630-469-4472. URL: http://www.chicagosuburbannews.com. Year Established: 1900. Pub. Frequency: w. (Thu.) Page Size: tabloid. Subscrip. Rate: $1 newsstand/cover; $25/yr. Adv. Rate: col. inch $17.65 Circulation: 11,200 per issue (paid and free). **Owner(s):** GateHouse Media, Inc, 350 WillowBrook Office Park, Fairport, NY 14450. Telephone: 585-598-0030. FAX: 585-248-2631. **Management:** John Novosel, Circulation Director. Rita Feigl, Classified Adv. Mgr.. **Editorial:** Jerry Moore, Editor.

ELMHURST PRESS. ISSN 1043-3236
800 Roosevelt Rd, Bldg D, Ste 107, Glen Ellyn, IL 60137. Telephone: 630-469-0100. FAX: 630-469-4472. E-MAIL: news@libertysuburban.com. URL: http://www.chicagosuburbannews.com. Year Established: 1889. Pub. Frequency: w. (Wed.) Page Size: broadsheet. Subscrip. Rate: $1 newsstand/cover; $25/yr. Adv. Rate: col. inch $25.90 Freelance Pay: $25-$50/article. Circulation: 9,000 per issue (paid and free). **Owner(s):** GateHouse Media, Inc, 350 WillowBrook Office Park, Fairport, NY 14450. Telephone: 585-598-0030. **Management:** Caroll Stacklin, Publisher. Bill Casey, VP Advertising. John Novosel, Circulation Director. Rita Feigl, Classified Adv. Mgr.. **Editorial:** Jerry Moore, Editor.

GENEVA REPUBLICAN, THE. 800 Roosevelt Rd, Bldg D, Ste 107, Glen Ellyn, IL 60137. Telephone: 630-469-0100. FAX: 630-469-4472. E-MAIL: editorial@libertysuburban.com. URL: http://www.chicagosuburbannews.com. Year Established: 1847. Pub. Frequency: w. (Thu.) Page Size: tabloid. Subscrip. Rate: $1 newsstand/cover; $38/yr mailed. Adv. Rate: col. inch $31.30 Circulation: 17,300 per issue (paid and free). **Owner(s):** GateHouse Media, Inc, 350 WillowBrook Office Park, Fairport, NY 14450. Telephone: 585-598-0030. FAX: 585-248-2631. **Management:** Caroll Stacklin, Publisher. Bill Casey, VP Advertising. John Novosel, Circulation Director. Rita Feigl, Classified Adv. Mgr.. **Editorial:** Jerry Moore, Editor.

GLEN ELLYN NEWS. ISSN 1059-8146
800 Roosevelt Rd, Bldg D, Ste 107, Glen Ellyn, IL 60137. Telephone: 630-469-0100. FAX: 630-469-4472. URL: http://www.chicagosuburbannews.com. Year Established: 1922. Pub. Frequency: w. (Thu.) Page Size: tabloid. Subscrip. Rate: $1 newsstand/cover; $30/yr mailed. Adv. Rate: col. inch $15 Circulation: 12,500 per issue (paid and free). **Owner(s):** GateHouse Media, Inc, 350 WillowBrook Office Park, Fairport, NY 14450. Telephone: 585-598-0030. FAX: 585-248-2631. **Management:** Caroll Stacklin, Publisher. Bill Casey, VP Advertising. John Novosel, Circulation Director. Rita Feigl, Classified Adv. Mgr.. **Editorial:** Jerry Moore, Editor.

LOMBARD SPECTATOR. 800 Roosevelt Rd, Bldg D, Ste 107, Glen Ellyn, IL 60137. Telephone: 630-469-0100. FAX: 630-469-4472. E-MAIL: news@libertysuburban.com. URL: http://www.chicagosuburbannews.com. Pub. Frequency: s-w. (Wed. & Fri.) Page Size: broadsheet. Subscrip. Rate: $1 newsstand/cover; $30/yr. Adv. Rate: col. inch $25.90 Circulation: 9,000 per issue (paid and free). **Owner(s):** GateHouse Media, Inc, 350 WillowBrook Office Park, Fairport, NY 14450. Telephone: 585-598-0030. FAX: 585-248-2631. **Management:** Caroll Stacklin, Publisher. Bill Casey, VP Advertising. John Novosel, Circulation Director. Rita Feigl, Classified Adv. Mgr.. **Editorial:** Jerry Moore, Editor.

VILLA PARK ARGUS. 800 Roosevelt Rd, Bldg D, Ste 107, Glen Ellyn, IL 60137. Telephone: 630-469-0100. FAX: 630-469-4472. E-MAIL: news@libertysuburban.com. URL: http://www.chicagosuburbannews.com. Pub. Frequency: s-w. (Wed. & Fri.) Page Size: broadsheet. Subscrip. Rate: $1 newsstand/cover; $36/yr. Adv. Rate: col. inch $25.90 Freelance Pay: $35-$100/article. Circulation: 15,000 per issue (paid and free). **Owner(s):** GateHouse Media, Inc, 350 WillowBrook Office Park, Fairport, NY 14450. Telephone: 585-598-0030. **Management:** Caroll Stacklin, Publisher. Bill Casey, VP Advertising. John Novosel, Circulation Director. Rita Feigl, Classified Adv. Mgr.. **Editorial:** Jerry Moore, Editor.

WHEATON LEADER. 800 Roosevelt Rd, Bldg D, Ste 107, Glen Ellyn, IL 60137. Telephone: 630-469-0100. FAX: 630-469-4472. URL: http://www.chicagosuburbannews.com. Year Established: 1954. Pub. Frequency: w. (Thu.) Page Size: tabloid. Subscrip. Rate: $1 newsstand/cover; $30/yr. Adv. Rate: col. inch $15 Circulation: 11,250 per issue (paid and free). **Owner(s):** GateHouse Media, Inc, 350 WillowBrook Office Park, Fairport, NY 14450. Telephone: 585-598-0030. FAX: 585-248-2631. **Management:** Caroll Stacklin, Publisher. Bill Casey, VP Advertising. John Novosel, Circulation Director. Rita Feigl, Classified Adv. Mgr.. **Editorial:** Jerry Moore, Editor.

GLENVIEW

EVANSTON REVIEW. ISSN 1044-7733
3701 W. Lake Ave., Glenview, IL 60025. Telephone: 847-486-7300. FAX: 847-486-7453. E-MAIL: display@pioneerlocal.com. URL: http://www.evanston-review.com. Year Established: 1925. Pub. Frequency: w. (Thu.) Page Size: tabloid. Subscrip. Rate: $1 newsstand/cover; $29.95/yr in county; $51.95/yr out of county. Adv. Rate: col. inch $30.29 Circulation: 10,447 per issue (paid). **Owner(s):** Pioneer Press, Inc., See address and contact information above. **Management:** Peggy Cunniff, Advertising Director. **Editorial:** Jeff Wisser, Editor-in-Chief. Gary Taylor, Managing Editor. Michael Bonesteel, Entertainment Editor. Gary Taylor, Group Editor.

GLENCOE NEWS. ISSN 0841-1646
3701 W. Lake Ave., Glenview, IL 60025. Telephone: 847-486-9200, 847-486-7300. FAX: 847-486-7453. E-MAIL: display@pioneerlocal.com. URL: http://www.pioneerlocal.com. Year Established: 1916. Pub. Frequency: w. (Thu.) Page Size: tabloid. Subscrip. Rate: $1 newsstand/cover; $39.95/yr in county; $51.95/yr out of county. Adv. Rate: col. inch $17.86 Circulation: 2,271 per issue (paid). **Owner(s):** Pioneer Press, Inc., See address and contact information above. **Management:** Peggy Cunniff, Advertising Director. **Editorial:** Jeff Wisser, Editor-in-Chief. Sheila Richard, Managing Editor. Michael Bonesteel, Entertainment Editor. Gary Taylor, Group Editor.

GLENVIEW ANNOUNCEMENTS. ISSN 1087-5409
3701 W. Lake Ave., Glenview, IL 60025. Telephone: 847-486-9200, 847-486-7300. FAX: 847-486-7453. E-MAIL: display@pioneerlocal.com. URL: http://www.pioneerlocal.com. Year Established: 1940. Pub. Frequency: w. (Thu.) Page Size: tabloid. Subscrip. Rate: $1 newsstand/cover; $39.95/yr in county; $51.95/yr out of county. Adv. Rate: col. inch $22.71 Circulation: 9,546 per issue (paid). **Owner(s):** Pioneer Press, Inc., See address and contact information above. **Management:** Peggy Cunniff, Advertising Director. **Editorial:** Jeff Wisser, Editor-in-Chief. Cathy Backer, Managing Editor. Michael Bonesteel, Entertainment Editor. Gary Taylor, Group Editor.

NORTHBROOK STAR. ISSN 0744-9550
3701 W. Lake Ave., Glenview, IL 60025. Telephone: 847-486-7300. FAX: 847-486-7453. E-MAIL: display@pioneerlocal.com. URL: http://www.pioneerlocal.com. Year Established: 1954. Pub. Frequency: w. (Thu.) Page Size: tabloid. Subscrip. Rate: $1 newsstand/cover; $39.95/yr in county; $51.95/yr out of county. Adv. Rate: col. inch $22.71 Circulation: 8,167 per issue (paid). **Owner(s):** Pioneer Press, Inc., See address and contact information above. **Management:** Peggy Cunniff, Advertising Director. **Editorial:** Jeff Wisser, Editor-in-Chief. Cathy Backer, Managing Editor. Michael Bonesteel, Entertainment Editor. Gary Taylor, Group Editor.

WILMETTE LIFE. ISSN 0745-0044
3701 W. Lake Ave., Glenview, IL 60025. Telephone: 847-486-9200. FAX: 847-496-7454. E-MAIL: display@pioneerlocal.com. URL: http://www.pioneerlocal.com. Year Established: 1916. Pub. Frequency: w. (Thu.) Page Size: tabloid. Subscrip. Rate: $1 newsstand/cover; $39.95/yr in county; $51.95/yr out of county. Adv. Rate: col. inch $22.71 Circulation: 6,852 per issue (paid). **Owner(s):** Pioneer Press, Inc., See address and contact information above. **Management:** Peggy Cunniff, Advertising Director. **Editorial:** Jeff Wisser, Editor-in-Chief. Gary Taylor, Managing Editor. Michael Bonesteel, Entertainment Editor. Gary Taylor, Group Editor.

WINNETKA TALK. 3701 W. Lake Ave., Glenview, IL 60025. Telephone: 847-486-7300. FAX: 847-486-7453. E-MAIL: display@pioneerlocal.com. URL: http://www.pioneerlocal.com. Year Established: 1914. Pub. Frequency: w. (Thu.) Page Size: tabloid. Subscrip. Rate: $1 newsstand/cover; $39.95/yr in county; $51.95/yr out of county. Adv. Rate: col. inch $22.71 Circulation: 5,218 per issue (paid). **Owner(s):** Pioneer Press, Inc., See address and contact information above. **Management:** Peggy Cunniff, Advertising Director. **Editorial:** Jeff Wisser, Editor-in-Chief. Sheila Richard, Managing Editor. Michael Bonesteel, Entertainment Editor. Gary Taylor, Group Editor.

GOLCONDA

HERALD-ENTERPRISE. 211 Main St., Golconda, IL 62938-0400. Telephone: 618-683-3531. FAX: 618-683-3831. E-MAIL: sandee@shawneelink.net. Mailing Address: PO Box 400, Golconda, IL 62938. Year Established: 1858. Pub. Frequency: w. (Wed.) Page Size: broadsheet. Subscrip. Rate: $.55 newsstand/cover; $25/yr mailed in county & adjoining area; $28/yr mailed out of area. Adv. Rate: col. inch $5 Circulation: 2,100 per issue (paid). **Owner(s):** Sandra Cowsert, See address and contact information above. **Management:** Sandra Cowsert, President. **Editorial:** Pamela Joiner, Production Manager.

GRANVILLE

PUTNAM COUNTY RECORD. 325 S. McCoy St., Granville, IL 61326. Telephone: 815-339-2321. FAX: 815-339-6727. E-MAIL: pcrtnews@aol.com. URL: http://www.pcrtnews.com. Mailing Address: PO Box 48, Granville, IL 61326-0048. Year Established: 1868. Pub. Frequency: w. (Wed.) Page Size: tabloid. Subscrip. Rate: $.50 newsstand/cover; $20/yr mailed in county; $40/yr mailed out of county. Adv. Rate: col. inch $4.75 Circulation: 3,431 per issue (controlled and free). **Owner(s):** Elin Arnold, See address and contact information above. **Management:** Elin Arnold, President. **Editorial:** Elin Arnold, Editor.

GRAYSLAKE

ANTIOCH NEWS. 30 S. Whitney St., Grayslake, IL 60030. Telephone: 847-223-8161. FAX: 847-223-8810. E-MAIL: newseditor@weeklyjournals.com. URL: http://www.weeklyjournals.com. Year Established: 1886. Pub. Frequency: w. (Thu.) Page Size: tabloid. Subscrip. Rate: $.75 newsstand/cover; $24.50/yr mailed. Circulation: 4,132 per issue (paid). **Owner(s):** Northwest News Group, See address and contact information above. **Management:** Robert J. Schroeder, General Manager. William Schroeder, Publisher. Jo Ann Chase, Circulation Manager. **Editorial:** Larry Lough, Executive Editor.

FOX LAKE PRESS. 30 S. Whitney St., Grayslake, IL 60030. Telephone: 847-223-8161. FAX: 847-223-8810. E-MAIL: newseditor@weeklyjournals.com. URL: http://www.weeklyjournals.com. Year Established: 1934. Pub. Frequency: w. (Thu.) Page Size: tabloid. Subscrip. Rate: $.75 newsstand/cover; $24.50/yr mailed. Freelance Pay: $50/story. Circulation: 5,000 per issue (paid). **Owner(s):** Northwest News Group, See address and contact information above. **Management:** Robert Schroeder, General Manager. William Schroeder, Publisher. Robert J. Schroeder, Advertising Manager. Jo Ann Chase, Circulation Manager. **Editorial:** Larry Lough, Executive Editor. Rob Backus, Sports.

GRAYSLAKE TIMES. 30 S. Whitney St., Grayslake, IL 60030. Telephone: 847-223-8161. FAX: 847-223-8810. E-MAIL: ednewseditor@weeklyjournals.com. URL: http://www.weeklyjournals.com. Year Established: 1900. Pub. Frequency: w. (Thu.) Page Size: tabloid. Subscrip. Rate: $.75 newsstand/cover; $24.50/yr mailed. Circulation: 4,700 per issue (paid). **Owner(s):** Northwest News Group, See address and contact information above. **Management:** Robert J. Schroeder, General Manager. William Schroeder, Publisher. Dave Sherman, Advertising Manager. Jo Ann Chase, Circulation Manager. **Editorial:** Larry Lough, Executive Editor.

GURNEE JOURNAL. ISSN 1931-9444
30 S. Whitney St., Grayslake, IL 60030. Telephone: 847-223-8161. FAX: 847-223-8810. E-MAIL: newseditor@weeklyjournals.com. URL: http://www.weeklyjournals.com. Year Established: 1973. Pub. Frequency: w. (Thu.) Page Size: tabloid. Subscrip. Rate: $.75 newsstand/cover; $24.50/yr mailed. Circulation: 4,842 per issue (paid). **Owner(s):** Northwest News Group, See address and contact information above. **Management:** Robert Schroeder, General Manager. William Schroeder, Publisher. Dave Sherman, Advertising Manager. Jo Ann Chase, Circulation Manager. **Editorial:** Larry Lough, Executive Editor.

LAKE VILLA RECORD. 30 S. Whitney St., Grayslake, IL 60030. Telephone: 847-223-8161. FAX: 847-223-8810. E-MAIL: newseditor@weeklyjournals.com. URL: http://www.weeklyjournals.com. Year Established: 1955. Pub. Frequency: w. (Thu.) Page Size: tabloid. Subscrip. Rate: $.75 newsstand/cover; $24.50/yr mailed. Circulation: 2,500 per issue (paid). **Owner(s):** Northwest News Group, See address and contact information above. **Management:** Robert J. Schroeder, General Manager. William Schroeder, Publisher. Robert J. Schroeder, Advertising Manager. Jo Ann Chase, Circulation Manager. **Editorial:** Larry Lough, Executive Editor. Rob Backus, Sports.

LIBERTYVILLE NEWS. 30 S. Whitney St., Grayslake, IL 60030. Telephone: 847-223-8161. FAX: 847-223-8810. E-MAIL: newseditor@weeklyjournals.com. URL: http://www.weeklyjournals.com. Year Established: 1989. Pub. Frequency: w. (Thu.) Page Size: tabloid. Subscrip. Rate: $.75 newsstand/cover; $24.50/yr; $23.50/yr to senior citizens. Circulation: 2,700 per issue (paid). **Owner(s):** Northwest News Group, See address and contact information above. **Management:** Robert Schroeder, General Manager. William Schroeder, Publisher. Robert J. Schroeder, Advertising Manager. Jo Ann Chase, Circulation Manager. **Editorial:** Larry Lough, Executive Editor. Rob Backus, Sports.

LINDENHURST NEWS. 30 S. Whitney St., Grayslake, IL 60030. Telephone: 847-223-8161. FAX: 847-223-8810. E-MAIL: newseditor@weeklyjournals.com. URL: http://www.weeklyjournals.com. Year Established: 1988. Pub. Frequency: w. (Thu.) Page Size: tabloid. Subscrip. Rate: $.75 newsstand/cover; $24.50/yr mailed in county; $22.50/yr to senior citizens. Circulation: 2,300 per issue (paid). **Owner(s):** Northwest News Group, See address and contact information above. **Management:** Robert J. Schroeder, General Manager. William Schroeder, Publisher. Dave Sherman, Advertising Manager. Jo Ann Chase, Circulation Manager. Crystal Reed, Classified Adv. Mgr.. **Editorial:** Larry Lough, Executive Editor. Brendan O'Neill, Sports Editor.

MUNDELEIN JOURNAL. ISSN 1931-9452
30 S. Whitney St., Grayslake, IL 60030. Telephone: 847-223-8161. FAX: 847-223-8810. E-MAIL: ednewseditor@weeklyjournals.com. URL: http://www.weeklyjournals.com. Year Established: 1942. Pub. Frequency: w. (Thu.) Page Size: tabloid. Subscrip. Rate: $.75 newsstand/cover; $24.50/yr mailed. Circulation: 3,000 per issue (paid). **Owner(s):** Northwest News Group, See address and contact information above. **Management:** Robert Schroeder, General Manager. William Schroeder, Publisher. Robert J. Schroeder, Advertising Manager. Jo Ann Chase, Circulation Manager. **Editorial:** Larry Lough, Executive Editor. Rob Backus, Sports.

ROUND LAKE NEWS. 30 S. Whitney St., Grayslake, IL 60030. Telephone: 847-223-8161. FAX: 847-223-8810. E-MAIL: newseditor@weeklyjournals.com. URL: http://www.weeklyjournals.com. Year Established: 1938. Pub. Frequency: w. (Thu.) Page Size: tabloid. Subscrip. Rate: $.75 newsstand/cover; $24.50/yr mailed. Circulation: 4,500 per issue (paid). **Owner(s):** Northwest News Group, See address and contact information above. **Management:** Robert Schroeder, General Manager. William Schroeder, Publisher. Robert J. Schroeder, Advertising Manager. Jo Ann Chase, Circulation Manager. **Editorial:** Larry Lough, Executive Editor. Marc Jenkins, Managing Editor. Rob Backus, Sports.

WADSWORTH JOURNAL. ISSN 1931-9460
30 S. Whitney St., Grayslake, IL 60030. Telephone: 847-223-8161. FAX: 847-223-8810. E-MAIL: newseditor@weeklyjournals.com. URL: http://www.weeklyjournals.com. Year Established: 1960. Pub. Frequency: w. (Thu.) Page Size: tabloid. Subscrip. Rate: $.75 newsstand/cover; $14.95/yr mailed in county. Circulation: 1,900 per issue (paid). **Owner(s):** Northwest News Group, See address and contact information above. **Management:** Robert Schroeder, General Manager. William Schroeder, Publisher. Robert J. Schroeder, Advertising Manager. Jo Ann Chase, Circulation Manager. **Editorial:** Larry Lough, Executive Editor.

WAUCONDA LEADER. 30 S. Whitney St., Grayslake, IL 60030. Telephone: 847-223-8161. FAX: 847-223-8810. E-MAIL: newseditor@weeklyjournals.com. URL: http://www.weeklyjournals.com. Year Established: 1888. Pub. Frequency: w. (Thu.) Page Size: tabloid. Subscrip. Rate: $.75 newsstand/cover; $14.95/yr mailed. Circulation: 3,700 per issue (paid). **Owner(s):** Northwest News Group, See address and contact information above. **Management:** Robert Schroeder, General Manager. William Schroeder, Publisher. Robert J. Schroeder, Advertising Manager. **Editorial:** Larry Lough, Executive Editor. Rob Backus, Sports.

GREENUP

GREENUP PRESS. 104 E. Cumberland St., Greenup, IL 62428. Telephone: 217-923-3704. FAX: 217-923-3704. Year Established: 1889. Pub. Frequency: w. (Thu.) Page Size: standard. Subscrip. Rate: $.50 newsstand/cover; $25/yr mailed in state; $30/yr mailed out of state. Adv. Rate: col. inch $6 Circulation: 1,850 per issue (paid). **Owner(s):** William D. McMorris, PO Box 127, Greenup, IL 62428-0127. Telephone: 217-923-3704. FAX: 217-923-3704. **Management:** William D McMorris, Publisher. Tony McMorris, Advertising Manager. William D McMorris, Circulation Manager.

GREENVILLE

GREENVILLE (IL) ADVOCATE, THE. 305 S Second St, Greenville, IL 62246. E-MAIL: advocateil@sbcglobal.net. URL: http://www.thegreenvilleadvocate.com. Year Established: 1858. Pub. Frequency: s-w. (Tue. & Thu.) Page Size: broadsheet. Subscrip. Rate: $.50 newsstand/cover; $25/yr mailed in city; $40/yr mailed out of area. Circulation: 5,100 per issue (paid). **Owner(s):** Richard D. & Rhonda K. Reeves, P O Box 9, Greenville, IL 62246. Telephone: 618-664-3144. **Management:** Richard D Reeves, General Manager. Duane L Reeves, President. Richard D Reeves, Advertising Manager. Nancy Nowlin, Classified Adv. Mgr.. **Editorial:** Jeffry Leidel, News Editor.

HARDIN

CALHOUN NEWS-HERALD. 310 S. County Rd., Hardin, IL 62047. Telephone: 618-576-2244. FAX: 618-576-2245. E-MAIL: newsherald@ezl.com. Year Established: 1915. Pub. Frequency: w. (Wed.) Page Size: standard. Subscrip. Rate: $.75 newsstand/cover; $28/yr local; $38/yr out of area. Circulation: 4,000 per issue (paid). **Owner(s):** Bruce Campbell, See address and contact information above. **Management:** Bruce Campbell, President. Vicki Moore, Advertising Manager. Karen Ballan, Circulation Manager. **Editorial:** Julie Boren, Editor.

HAVANA

MASON COUNTY DEMOCRAT. ISSN 1060-2437
219 W. Market St., Havana, IL 62644. Telephone: 309-543-3311. E-MAIL: mcdemo@havanaprint.com. URL: http://www.masoncountydemocrat.com. Mailing Address: PO Box 380, Havana, IL 62644. Year Established: 1849. Pub. Frequency: w. (Wed.) Page Size: broadsheet. Subscrip. Rate: $1 newsstand/cover; $37/yr; $52/yr out of county. Adv. Rate: col. inch $13 Freelance Pay: $0.05/word. Circulation: 6,300 per issue (paid and free). **Owner(s):** Martin Publishing Co., Inc., See address and contact information above. **Management:** Robert Martin, Publisher. **Editorial:** Wendy Jo Martin, Editor.Readers: Residents of Mason County

HENRY

HENRY NEWS REPUBLICAN. 709 Third St., Henry, IL 61537. Telephone: 309-364-3250. FAX: 309-364-3858. E-MAIL: henrynews@verizon.net. Year Established: 1852. Pub. Frequency: w. (Wed.) Page Size: broadsheet. Subscrip. Rate: $.50 newsstand/cover; $24/yr mailed Marshall & Putnam cys.; $30/yr mailed out of area. Adv. Rate: col. inch $4.25 Circulation: 2,850 per issue (paid). **Owner(s):** Douglas Ziegler, PO Box 190, Henry, IL 61537-0190. Telephone: 309-364-3250. FAX: 309-364-3858. **Management:** Douglas Ziegler, Publisher. Amy Ziegler, Advertising Manager. **Editorial:** Douglas Ziegler, Editor.

WENONA INDEX. PO Box 190, Henry, IL 61537-0190. Telephone: 309-364-3250. FAX: 309-364-3858. Pub. Frequency: w. (Thur.) Page Size: standard. Subscrip. Rate: $.30 newsstand/cover; $14/yr mailed in state; $16/yr mailed out of state. Circulation: 900 per issue (paid). **Owner(s):** Douglas Ziegler, See address and contact information above. **Management:** Douglas Ziegler, Publisher. Amy Ziegler, Advertising Manager.

HERRIN

FREETIME. 216 N. Park Ave., Herrin, IL 62948. Telephone: 618-942-5000. FAX: 618-942-4630. URL: http://www.gatehousemedia.com. Mailing Address: PO Box 128, Herrin, IL 62948. Year Established: 1995. Pub. Frequency: w. (Sun.) Page Size: tabloid.Adv. Rate: col. inch $15.25 Circulation: 7,825 per issue (free). **Owner(s):** GateHouse Media, Inc, 350 WillowBrook Office Park, Fairport, NY 14450. Telephone: 585-598-0030. **Management:** Tim Petrowich, Publisher. **Editorial:** Bill Swinford, Editor.

HERRIN SPOKESMAN. 216 N. Park Ave., Herrin, IL 62948. Telephone: 618-942-5000. FAX: 618-942-4630. E-MAIL: herrin@intrnet.net. URL: http://www.gatehousemedia.com. Mailing Address: PO Box 128, Herrin, IL 62948. Year Established: 1942. Pub. Frequency: w. (Mon.) Page Size: broadsheet. Subscrip. Rate: $1 newsstand/cover; $29.95/yr mailed in county; $37.95/yr mailed out of county. Freelance Pay: $0.50/column-inch. Circulation: 1,043 per issue (paid). **Owner(s):** GateHouse Media, Inc, 350 WillowBrook Office Park, Fairport, NY 14450. Telephone: 585-598-0030. FAX: 585-248-2631. **Management:** Tim Petrowich, Publisher. **Editorial:** Bill Swinford, Editor.

HERSCHER

HERSCHER PILOT. PO Box 709, Herscher, IL 60941. Telephone: 815-426-2132. Year Established: 1976. Pub. Frequency: w. (Thu.) Page Size: tabloid. Subscrip. Rate: $.30 newsstand/cover; $20/yr mailed in state; $25/yr mailed out of state. Circulation: 2,500 per issue (paid). **Owner(s):** Robert A. Mau, See address and contact information above. **Management:** Robert A. Mau, Publisher. **Editorial:** Robert A. Mau, Editor.

HIGHLAND

HIGHLAND NEWS LEADER. ISSN 8750-0957
One Woodcrest Professional Pk, Highland, IL 62249. Telephone: 618-654-2366. FAX: 618-654-1181. Mailing Address: PO Box 250, Highland, IL 62249. Year Established: 1861. Pub. Frequency: s-w. (Mon. & Thu.) Page Size: broadsheet. Subscrip. Rate: $.50 newsstand/cover; $29/yr local. Circulation: 15,800 per issue (paid and free). **Owner(s):** The/McClatchy Company, 2100 Q St, Sacramento, CA 95816. Telephone: 916-321-1936. FAX: 916-321-1869. **Management:** Jane Dotson, General Manager. Gay Bentlage, Advertising. **Editorial:** Dave Trinka, Editor.

HILLSBORO

BUNKER HILL GAZETTE NEWS. PO Box 100, Hillsboro, IL 62014. Telephone: 217-532-3933. Year Established: 1866. Pub. Frequency: w. (Thu.) Page Size: tabloid. Subscrip. Rate: $.30 newsstand/cover; $13/yr in county; $15/yr out of county; $17/yr out of state. Adv. Rate: col. inch $3.30 Circulation: 1,500 per issue (paid). **Owner(s):** Galer Publishing Co., See address and contact information above. **Management:** Courtney Wood, General Manager. John M, Galer, President. Courtney Wood, Advertising Manager.

HILLSBORO JOURNAL. 431 S. Main St., Hillsboro, IL 62049. Telephone: 217-532-3933. FAX: 217-532-3632. E-MAIL: thejournal-news@consolidated.net. URL: http://www.thejournal-news.net. Year Established: 1853. Pub. Frequency: s-w. (Mon. & Thu.) Page Size: broadsheet. Subscrip. Rate: $.50 newsstand/cover; $26/yr mailed in county; $39/yr mailed out of county; $45/yr mailed out of state. Adv. Rate: col. inch $6 Circulation: 7,000 per issue (paid). **Owner(s):** Hillsboro Journal, See address and contact information above. **Management:** John Galer, Publisher. Connie Carney, Circulation Manager. **Editorial:** Nancy Galer, Editor.

M & M JOURNAL. 431 S. Main St., Hillsboro, IL 62049. Telephone: 217-532-3933. FAX: 217-532-3632. Year Established: 1968. Pub. Frequency: w. (Mon.) Page Size: broadsheet Circulation: 21,945 per issue (free). **Owner(s):** Hillsboro Journal, See address and contact information above. **Management:** John Galer, General Manager. Phillip C. Galer, Publisher. Connie Carney, Circulation Manager.

MACOUPIN COUNTY SHOPPER. 431 S. Main St., Hillsboro, IL 62049. Telephone: 217-532-3933. FAX: 217-532-3632. Year Established: 1968. Pub. Frequency: w. (Mon.) Page Size: broadsheet Circulation: 13,500 per issue (free). **Owner(s):** Hillsboro Journal, See address and contact information above. **Management:** John Galer, General Manager. Connie Carney, Circulation Manager. **Editorial:** John. Galer, Editor.

MONTGOMERY COUNTY NEWS, THE. 431 S Main, Hillsboro, IL 62049. Telephone: 217-532-3933. E-MAIL: thenews@consolidated.net. URL: http://www.themontgomerynews.com. Year Established: 1869. Pub. Frequency: 3/w. (Tue., Thu., Sat.) Page Size: broadsheet. Subscrip. Rate: $.35 newsstand/cover; $28/yr in county; $40/yr out of county; $48/yr mailed out of state. Circulation: 4,000 per issue (paid). **Owner(s):** Hillsboro & Montgomery County News, Inc., See address and contact information above. **Management:** Phillip C. Galer, Publisher. Connie Carney, Circulation Manager. **Editorial:** John Galer, Editor.

SORENTO NEWS. 431 S. Main St., Hillsboro, IL 62049. Telephone: 217-532-3933. FAX: 217-532-3632. E-MAIL: journal@consolidated.net. URL: htt//:www.thejournal-news@consolidated.net. Year Established: 1927. Pub. Frequency: w. (Thu.) Page Size: broadsheet. Subscrip. Rate: $.30 newsstand/cover; $8/yr in county; $14/yr out of county. Circulation: 320 per issue (paid). **Owner(s):** Journal Publications, See address and contact information above. **Management:** John Galer, General Manager. Phillip C. Galer, Publisher. John Galer, Advertising Manager. Connie Carney, Circulation Manager. **Editorial:** Phillip C. Galer, Editor.

HINSDALE

CLARENDON HILLS DOINGS, THE. 440 E. Ogden, Hinsdale, IL 60521. Telephone: 630-887-0600. FAX: 630-887-9646. URL: http://www.pioneerlocal.com. Year Established: 1895. Pub. Frequency: w. (Thu.) Page Size: tabloid. Subscrip. Rate: $1 newsstand/cover; $41.95/yr in county; $51.95/yr out of county. Adv. Rate: col. inch $17.14 Circulation: 1,408 per issue (paid). **Owner(s):** Pioneer Press, Inc., 3701 W. Lake Ave., Glenview, IL 60025. Telephone: 847-486-9200. FAX: 847-496-7454. **Editorial:** Dawn Rafferty, Managing Editor.

ELMHURST DOINGS, THE. 440 E. Ogden, Hinsdale, IL 60521. Telephone: 630-887-0600. FAX: 630-887-9646. URL: http://www.pioneerlocal.com. Year Established: 2001. Pub. Frequency: w. (Thu.) Page Size: tabloid. Subscrip. Rate: $1 newsstand/cover; $21.95/yr in county; $51.95/yr out of county. Adv. Rate: col. inch $17.14 Circulation: 3,566 per issue (paid). **Owner(s):** Pioneer Press, Inc., 3701 W. Lake Ave., Glenview, IL 60025. Telephone: 847-486-9200. FAX: 847-496-7454. **Management:** Jim Golden, Advertising. **Editorial:** Karen Chadra, Managing Editor. Dawn Rafferty, Group Editor.

HINSDALE DOINGS, THE. 440 E. Ogden, Hinsdale, IL 60521. Telephone: 630-887-0600. FAX: 630-887-9646. URL: http://www.pioneerlocal.com. Year Established: 1895. Pub. Frequency: w. (Thu.) Page Size: tabloid. Subscrip. Rate: $1 newsstand/cover; $39.95/yr in county; $51.95/yr out of county. Adv. Rate: page $17.14 Circulation: 4,865 per issue (paid). **Owner(s):** Pioneer Press, Inc., 3701 W. Lake Ave., Glenview, IL 60025. Telephone: 847-486-9200. FAX: 847-496-7454. **Management:** Brenda Wible, Advertising. **Editorial:** Dawn Rafferty, Managing Editor.

LA GRANGE DOINGS, THE. 440 E. Ogden, Hinsdale, IL 60521. Telephone: 630-887-0600. FAX: 630-887-9646. URL: http://www.pioneerlocal.com. Year Established: 2000. Pub. Frequency: w. (Thu.) Page Size: tabloid. Subscrip. Rate: $1 newsstand/cover; $21.95/yr in county; $51.95/yr out of county. Adv. Rate: col. inch $13.57 Circulation: 3,343 per issue (paid). **Owner(s):** Pioneer Press, Inc., 3701 W. Lake Ave., Glenview, IL 60025. Telephone: 847-486-9200. FAX: 847-496-7454. **Management:** Colette Kaufman, Advertising. **Editorial:** Brett Johnson, Managing Editor. Dawn Rafferty, Group Editor.

OAK BROOK DOINGS, THE. 440 E. Ogden, Hinsdale, IL 60521. Telephone: 630-887-0600. FAX: 630-887-9646. URL: http://www.pioneerlocal.com. Year Established: 1999. Pub. Frequency: w. (Thu.) Page Size: tabloid. Subscrip. Rate: $1 newsstand/cover; $29.95/yr in county; $51.95/yr out of county. Adv. Rate: col. inch $17.14 Circulation: 1,179 per issue (paid). **Owner(s):** Pioneer Press, Inc., 3701 W. Lake Ave., Glenview, IL 60025. Telephone: 847-486-9200. FAX: 847-496-7454. **Management:** Kelly Colby, Advertising. **Editorial:** Karen Chadra, Managing Editor. Dawn Rafferty, Group Editor.

WEEKLY DOINGS, THE. 440 E. Ogden, Hinsdale, IL 60521. Telephone: 630-887-0600. FAX: 630-887-9646. URL: http://www.pioneerlocal.com. Year Established: 1999. Pub. Frequency: w. (Thu.) Page Size: tabloid. Subscrip. Rate: $1 newsstand/cover; $21.95/yr in county; $51.95/yr out of county. Adv. Rate: col. inch $13.57 Circulation: 3,737 per issue (paid). **Owner(s):** Pioneer Press, Inc., 3701 W. Lake Ave., Glenview, IL 60025. Telephone: 847-486-9200. FAX: 847-496-7454. **Management:** Colette Kaufman, Advertising. **Editorial:** Karen Chadra, Managing Editor. Dawn Rafferty, Group Editor.

WESTERN SPRINGS DOINGS. 440 E. Ogden, Hinsdale, IL 60521. Telephone: 630-887-0600. FAX: 630-887-9646. Year Established: 1999. Pub. Frequency: w. (Thu.) Page Size: tabloid. Subscrip. Rate: $1 newsstand/cover; $29.95/yr in county; $51.95/yr out of county. Adv. Rate: col. inch $13.57 Circulation: 2,141 per issue (paid). **Owner(s):** Pioneer Press, Inc., 3701 W. Lake Ave., Glenview, IL 60025. Telephone: 847-486-9200. FAX: 847-496-7454. **Management:** Tony Ralenkotter, Advertising. **Editorial:** Brett Johnson, Managing Editor. Dawn Rafferty, Group Editor.

HOOPESTON

CHRONICLE (HOOPESTON), THE. 308 E. Main St., Hoopeston, IL 60942. Telephone: 217-283-5111. FAX: 217-283-5846. E-MAIL: chronicle@dtnspeed.net. URL: http://www.thehoopestonchronicle.com. Pub. Frequency: w. (Wed.) Page Size: standard. Subscrip. Rate: $1 newsstand/cover; $36/yr in county; $52/yr out of county. Circulation: 2,300 per issue (paid). **Owner(s):** Community Media Group, Inc, PO Box 10, West Frankfort, IL 62896. Telephone: 618-937-6412. **Management:** Bertha Parsons, General Manager. Don Hurd, Publisher. Bertha Parsons, Advertising Manager. Mary Jo Petersen, Circulation Manager. **Editorial:** Charles Ordoqui, Managing Editor.

ILLIOPOLIS

ILLIOPOLIS SENTINEL. PO Box 300, Illiopolis, IL 62539. Telephone: 217-486-6496. FAX: 217-486-6496. Year Established: 1924. Pub. Frequency: w. (Thu.) Page Size: tabloid. Subscrip. Rate: $.50 newsstand/cover; $20/yr in county; $22.50/yr out of county. Circulation: 700 per issue (paid). **Owner(s):** Wilson Publications, See address and contact information above. **Management:** Cindy Wilson, Publisher. Maurice Wilson, Advertising Manager. **Editorial:** Cindy Wilson, Editor.

JERSEYVILLE

TELEGRAPH (QUAD COUNTY EDITION), THE. 201 N. State St., Jerseyville, IL 62052. Telephone: 618-498-5551. FAX: 618-498-3964. URL: http://www.thetelegraph.com. Mailing Address: PO Box 389, Jerseyville, IL 62052-0389. Year Established: 1989. Pub. Frequency: w. (Wed.) Page Size: standard. Subscrip. Rate: $22.68 home delivery for 6 wks.; $176.90/yr home delivery; $.50 newsstand/cover. Circulation: 10,000 per issue (paid). **Owner(s):** Freedom Communications, Inc., 17666 Fitch St., Irvine, CA 92614. Telephone: 949-253-9292. FAX: 949-474-7675. **Management:** James E Shrader, Publisher. John Aguire, Advertising Manager. **Editorial:** Dan Brannan, Managing Editor. Tom Wrausmann, Writer.

JOLIET

FARMER'S WEEKLY REVIEW. 100 Manhattan Rd., Joliet, IL 60433. Telephone: 815-727-4811. FAX: 815-727-5570. E-MAIL: farmersweekly@sbcglobal.net. Year Established: 1921. Pub. Frequency: w. (Thu.) Page Size: tabloid Subscrip. Rate: $15/yr Circulation: 11,500 per issue (paid). **Owner(s):** Will COunty Publications, Inc., See address and contact information above. **Management:** Michael Cleary, Publisher. Debbie Werner, Advertising Manager. **Editorial:** Michael Cleary, Editor.

LINCOLN-WAY SUN. 300 Caterpillar Dr., Joliet, IL 60436-1097. Telephone: 815-729-6161. FAX: 815-729-6059. Pub. Frequency: w. (Wed.) Page Size: standard Circulation: 3,100 per issue (free). **Owner(s):** Sun-Times Media Group, 350 N Orleans St, Ste 10-S, Chicago, IL 60654. Telephone: 312-321-2299. **Management:** Larry Randa, Publisher. Brian Garrigan, Advertising Manager. **Editorial:** Nick Reiher, Editor. Dave Monaghan, Managing Editor.

KEWANEE

TRI-COUNTY ADVERTISER (KEWANEE). 105 E. Central Blvd., Kewanee, IL 61443. Telephone: 309-852-2181. FAX: 309-852-0010. Mailing Address: PO Box A, Kewanee, IL 61443. Pub. Frequency: w. (Tue.) Page Size: tabloid Circulation: 4,800 per issue (free). **Owner(s):** GateHouse Media, Inc, 350 WillowBrook Office Park, Fairport, NY 14450. Telephone: 585-598-0030. FAX: 585-248-2631. **Management:** Susan Griffith, Publisher. Jolene Clark, Classified Adv. Mgr..

KINMUNDY

KINMUNDY EXPRESS. 210 S. Madison, Kinmundy, IL 62854. Telephone: 618-547-3111. Year Established: 1883. Pub. Frequency: w. (Thu.) Page Size: broadsheet. Subscrip. Rate: $.30 newsstand/cover; $15/yr mailed in county; $17/yr mailed in state; $20/yr mailed elsewhere. Circulation: 925 per issue (paid). **Owner(s):** Rudolph Slane, See address and contact information above. **Management:** Rudolph Slane, Publisher. **Editorial:** Rudolph Slane, Editor.

LA FAYETTE

PRAIRIE SHOPPER, THE. 101 Jefferson St., La Fayette, IL 61449. Telephone: 309-995-3877. FAX: 309-995-3975. Year Established: 1981. Pub. Frequency: w. (Wed.) Page Size: tabloid Circulation: 6,315 per issue (free). **Owner(s):** Lowell McKirgan, See address and contact information above. **Management:** Lowell McKirgan, President. Ruth Hollis, Advertising Manager.

LACON

LACON HOME JOURNAL. 204 S. Washington St., Lacon, IL 61540. Telephone: 309-246-2865. FAX: 309-246-3214. Year Established: 1837. Pub. Frequency: w. (Thu.) Page Size: tabloid. Subscrip. Rate: $50 newsstand/cover; $24/yr in county; $26/yr mailed out of county. Circulation: 2,400 per issue (paid). **Owner(s):** Marshall County Publishing Co., See address and contact information above. **Management:** William H. Sondag, Publisher. **Editorial:** William H. Sondag, Editor.

LAGRANGE PARK

LAGRANGE/LAGRANGE PARK/WESTERN SPRINGS SUBURBAN LIFE. 1128 N Maple Ave, LaGrange Park, IL 60525. Telephone: 708-469-3900. FAX: 708-482-7726. E-MAIL: localnews@libertysuburban.com. URL: http://www.chicagosuburbannews.com. Pub. Frequency: s-w. (Wed. & Sat.) Page Size: tabloid. Subscrip. Rate: $1 newsstand/cover; $38/yr. Adv. Rate: col. inch $26.75 Freelance Pay: $20-$75/article. Circulation: 20,850 per issue (paid). **Owner(s):** GateHouse Media, Inc, 350 WillowBrook Office Park, Fairport, NY 14450. Telephone: 585-598-0030. FAX: 585-248-2631. **Management:** Caroll Stacklin, Publisher. Bill Casey, VP Advertising. Carrie Banas, Advertising Manager. John Novosel, Circulation Director. Rita Feigl, Classified Adv. Mgr..

LAWRENCEVILLE

LAWRENCE COUNTY NEWS. 1209 State St., Lawrenceville, IL 62439. Telephone: 618-943-2331. E-MAIL: drecord@midwest.net. Year Established: 1842. Pub. Frequency: w. (Wed.) Page Size: standard.Subscrip. Rate: $28/yr mailed Circulation: 300 per issue (paid). **Owner(s):** Larry H. Lewis, See address and contact information above. **Management:** Larry H. Lewis, President. **Editorial:** Larry H. Lewis, Editor.

LENA

SCOOP TODAY, THE. 213 S. Center St., Lena, IL 61048. Telephone: 815-369-4112. FAX: 815-369-9093. URL: http://www.rockvalleypublishing.com. Pub. Frequency: w. (Wed.) Page Size: tabloid. Subscrip. Rate: $15/yr mailed area; $35/yr mailed out of area. Circulation: 5,100 per issue (free). **Owner(s):** Rock Valley Publishing LLC, 11512 N. Second St., Machesney Park, IL 61115. Telephone: 815-877-4044. FAX: 815-654-4857. **Management:** Jack Cruger, Publisher. Brandy Brown, Advertising. **Editorial:** Cynthia Carton, Editor.

SHOPPERS GUIDE, THE. 213 S. Center St., Lena, IL 61048. Telephone: 815-369-4112. FAX: 815-369-9093. Pub. Frequency: w. (Thu) Page Size: tabloid. Subscrip. Rate: $15/yr mailed in county; $35/yr mailed out of county. Circulation: 5,162 per issue (free). **Owner(s):** Rock Valley Publishing LLC, 11512 N. Second St., Machesney Park, IL 61115. Telephone: 815-877-4044. FAX: 815-654-4857. **Management:** Jack Cruger, Publisher.

LEWISTOWN

FULTON DEMOCRAT. ISSN 1058-9619
165 W. Lincoln, Lewistown, IL 61542. Telephone: 309-547-3055. FAX: 309-543-6844. E-MAIL: mcdemo@havanprint.com. URL: http://fultondemocrat.com. Mailing Address: PO Box 191, Lewistown, IL 61542. Year Established: 1855. Pub. Frequency: w. (Wed.) Page Size: broadsheet. Subscrip. Rate: $.75 newsstand/cover; $34/yr in county; $47/yr out of county. Freelance Pay: $0.05/word. Circulation: 3,200 per issue (paid). **Owner(s):** Martin Publishing Co., Inc., 219 W. Market St., Havana, IL 62644. Telephone: 309-543-3311. **Management:** Robert Martin, General Manager. **Editorial:** Wendy Martin, Editor.Readers: Residents of Fulton County

LOMBARD

LOMBARDIAN, THE. 116 S. Main St., Lombard, IL 60148. Telephone: 630-627-7010. FAX: 630-627-7027. E-MAIL: lombardian@sbcglobal.net. Year Established: 1957. Pub. Frequency: w. (Wed.) Page Size: tabloid. Subscrip. Rate: $.50 newsstand/cover; $40/yr in county; $45/yr out of county. Circulation: 21,500 per issue (paid). **Owner(s):** E.A. MacKay Enterprises, See address and contact information above. **Management:** Bonnie Lee MacKay, Publisher. Marguerite Micken, Advertising. Scott MacKay, Advertising Manager. **Editorial:** Lawrence Synett, Editor. Bonnie Lee MacKay, Managing Editor. Jane Charmelo, Community Editor. Steve Spoden, Photographer. Chris Fox, Sports Editor.

VILLA PARK REVIEW. 116 S. Main St., Lombard, IL 60148. Telephone: 630-627-7010. FAX: 630-627-7027. E-MAIL: lombardian@sbcglobal.net. Year Established: 1958. Pub. Frequency: w. (Wed.) Page Size: tabloid. Subscrip. Rate: $.50 newsstand/cover; $40/yr in county; $45/yr out of county. Circulation: 21,000 per issue (paid). **Owner(s):** E.A. MacKay Enterprises, See address and contact information above. **Management:** Bonnie Lee MacKay, Publisher. Marguerite Micken, Advertising. Scott MacKay, Advertising Manager. **Editorial:** Lawrence Synett, Editor. Bonnie Lee MacKay, Managing Editor. Jane Charmelo, Community Editor. Steve Spoden, Photographer. Chris Fox, Sports Editor.

MACHESNEY PARK

POST JOURNAL, THE. 11512 N. Second St., Machesney Park, IL 61115. Telephone: 815-877-4044. FAX: 815-654-4857. Pub. Frequency: w. (Thu.) Page Size: standard. Subscrip. Rate: $.60 newsstand/cover; $25.95/yr in county; $28.95/yr out of county. Circulation: 11,189 per issue (paid). **Owner(s):** Rock Valley Publishing LLC, See address and contact information above. **Management:** Randy Johnson, General Manager. Peter Cruger, President. Jack Cruger, Publisher. Maxine Bayer, Advertising. Lindy Sweet, Circulation Manager. **Editorial:** Dan Moeller, Editor.

ROCKFORD JOURNAL, THE. 11512 N. Second St., Machesney Park, IL 61115. Telephone: 815-877-4044. FAX: 815-654-4857. Pub. Frequency: w. (Thu.) Page Size: standard. Subscrip. Rate: $.60 newsstand/cover; $25.95/yr in county; $28.95/yr out of county. Circulation: 14,189 per issue (paid). **Owner(s):** Rock Valley Publishing LLC, See address and contact information above. **Management:** Randy Johnson, General Manager. Peter Cruger, President. Jack Cruger, Publisher. Maxine Bayer, Advertising. Lindy Sweet, Circulation Manager. **Editorial:** Dan Moeller, Editor. Jim Swans, Sports.

MACOMB

MACOMB EAGLE. ISSN 1526-7881
210 S. Randolph, Macomb, IL 61455. Telephone: 309-837-4428. FAX: 309-837-7188. E-MAIL: eaglenews@eaglepublications.com. URL: http://www.eaglepublications.com. Year Established: 1999. Pub. Frequency: 3/w. (Mon., Wed., Fri.) Page Size: tabloid. Subscrip. Rate: $40/yr in county; $70/yr out of county; $85/yr out of state. Freelance Pay: $25/article. Circulation: 2,600 per issue (paid). **Owner(s):** Eagle Publications of Western Illinois, Inc., See address and contact information above. **Management:** Tom Hutson, Publisher. Lynne Campbell, Advertising Manager. **Editorial:** Tom Hutson, Editor-in-Chief.

ROSEVILLE INDEPENDENT. 210 S. Randolph, Macomb, IL 61455. Telephone: 309-837-4428. FAX: 309-837-7188. E-MAIL: argus@abingdon.net. URL: http://www.eaglepublications.com. Pub. Frequency: w. (Wed.) Page Size: tabloid. Subscrip. Rate: $.50 newsstand/cover; $25/yr mailed in county; $30/yr mailed out of county; $35/yr mailed out of state. Circulation: 775 per issue (paid). **Owner(s):** Eagle Publications of Western Illinois, Inc., See address and contact information above. **Management:** Tom Hutson, Publisher. Kathy Hahn, Advertising Manager. **Editorial:** Phil Gerding, Editor.

MARION

INYO REGISTER. 1120 N. Carbon St, Ste 100, Marion, IL 62959. E-MAIL: pub@inyoregister.com. URL: http://www.inyoregister.com. Year Established: 1870. Pub. Frequency: 3/w. (Tue., Thu., Sat.) Page Size: broadsheet. Subscrip. Rate: $.50 newsstand/cover; $64.20/yr home delivery local; $81.39/yr mailed in Inyo & Mono cys.; $89.45/yr mailed elsewhere. **Wire Service(s):** SH. Circulation: 6,300 per issue (paid). **Owner(s):** Horizon Publications, Inc., See address and contact information above. **Management:** Bob Reitz, Publisher. Sonja Spry, Advertising. Teresa Brooks, Circulation Manager. **Editorial:** Darcy Ellis, Editor.

MARION DAILY EXTRA. 502 W. Jackson St., Marion, IL 62959. Telephone: 618-993-2626. FAX: 618-993-8326. URL: http://www.gatehousemedia.com. Mailing Address: PO Box 490, Marion, IL 62959. Year Established: 1973. Pub. Frequency: w. (Sun.) Page Size: tabloid.Adv. Rate: col. inch $15.25 Circulation: 9,000 per issue (free). **Owner(s):** GateHouse Media, Inc, 350 WillowBrook Office Park, Fairport, NY 14450. Telephone: 585-598-0030. **Management:** Tim Petrowich, Publisher. Dave Broy, Advertising Director. Jim Nobles, Circulation Manager. Betty Caraker, Classified Adv. Mgr..

WEEKLY REVIEW, THE. 1120 N. Carbon St., Ste.100, Marion, IL 62959. Telephone: 618-997-2222. FAX: 618-997-4018. E-MAIL: review@ilwllc.net. Year Established: 1990. Pub. Frequency: w. (Sat.) Page Size: tabloid.Adv. Rate: col. inch $5 Circulation: 7,500 per issue (free). **Owner(s):** Horizon Publications, Inc., See address and contact information above. **Management:** Roland McBride, Publisher. Judy Moore, Advertising Manager. Steve Sheldon, Circulation Manager.

MASCOUTAH

CLINTON COUNTY NEWS (MASCOUTAH). P O Box C, Mascoutah, IL 62258. Telephone: 618-566-8282. FAX: 618-566-8283. Year Established: 1937. Pub. Frequency: w. (Thu.) Page Size: broadsheet. Subscrip. Rate: $1 newsstand/cover; $27/yr in county; $32/yr out of county; $24.50/yr in county to senior citizens; $22/yr in county to students. Circulation: 1,200 per issue (paid). **Owner(s):** Herald Publications, See address and contact information above. **Management:** Greg Hoskins, Publisher. Debbie Mense, Business Manager. **Editorial:** Tom Palmer, Editor.

FAIRVIEW HEIGHTS TRIBUNE. P O Box C, Mascoutah, IL 62258. Telephone: 618-566-8282. FAX: 618-566-8283. E-MAIL: heraldpubs@cbnstl.com. Year Established: 1972. Pub. Frequency: w. (Thu.) Page Size: broadsheet. Subscrip. Rate: $1 newsstand/cover; $27/yr in county; $30/yr out of county. Circulation: 1,250 per issue (paid). **Owner(s):** Herald Publications, See address and contact information above. **Management:** Greg Hoskins, Publisher. Debbie Mensee, Office Manager. **Editorial:** Tom Palmer, Editor.

MASCOUTAH HERALD. P O Box C, Mascoutah, IL 62258. Telephone: 618-566-8282. FAX: 618-566-8283. E-MAIL: herald@accessus.net. URL: http://www.better-newspapers.com. Year Established: 1885. Pub. Frequency: w. (Thu.) Page Size: broadsheet. Subscrip. Rate: $.50 newsstand/cover; $25/yr in county; $30/yr out of county. Circulation: 2,400 per issue (paid). **Owner(s):** Herald Publications, See address and contact information above. **Management:** Greg Hoskins, Publisher. Debbie Mense, Office Manager.

MCLEANSBORO

MCLEANSBORO TIMES-LEADER. 123 S. Jackson, McLeansboro, IL 62859. Telephone: 618-643-2387. FAX: 618-643-3426. Mailing Address: PO Box 489, Mount Vernon, IL 62864. Year Established: 1855. Pub. Frequency: w. (Thu.) Page Size: broadsheet. Subscrip. Rate: $.50 newsstand/cover; $26/yr in county. Circulation: 3,600 per issue (paid). **Owner(s):** Community Newspaper Holdings, Inc., 3500 Colonnade Pkwy., Ste. 600, Birmingham, AL 35243. Telephone: 205-298-7101. **Management:** Bart McDowell, Advertising Manager. **Editorial:** Paul Lorenz, Editor.

MELVIN

FORD COUNTY PRESS. 115 W. Main St., Melvin, IL 60952. Telephone: 217-388-7721. FAX: 217-388-2864. E-MAIL: fcpress@illicom.net. Year Established: 1918. Pub. Frequency: w. (Thu.) Page Size: standard. Subscrip. Rate: $.35 newsstand/cover; $17/yr in county; $18/yr out of county. Adv. Rate: col. inch $2.50 Circulation: 875 per issue (controlled and free). **Owner(s):** Alan Thackeray, See address and contact information above. **Management:** Alan Thackeray, Publisher. **Editorial:** Alan Thackery, Editor.

MENDOTA

MENDOTA REPORTER, THE. 703 ILL. Ave, PO Box 300, Mendota, IL 61342. Telephone: 815-539-9396. FAX: 815-539-7862. E-MAIL: editor@mendotareporter.com. URL: http://www.mendotareporter.com. Year Established: 1878. Pub. Frequency: w. (Wed.) Page Size: broadsheet. Subscrip. Rate: $.75 newsstand/cover; $29.50/yr mailed in state; $42.75/yr mailed out of state. Adv. Rate: col. inch $9.50 Circulation: 4,400 per issue (paid). **Owner(s):** Mendota Publishing Corp., See address and contact information above. **Management:** Mark Elston, General Manager. Kip Cheek, Publisher. Mark Elston, Advertising Manager. Ann Caylor, Circulation Manager. **Editorial:** Jessie Johnson, Editor. Pete Wilson, Sports Editor.

METROPOLIS

METROPOLIS PLANET. 111 E. Fifth St., Metropolis, IL 62960-0820. Telephone: 618-524-2141. FAX: 618-524-4727. E-MAIL: news@metropolisplanet.com; ads@metropolisplanet.com. URL: http://www.metropolisplanet.com. Mailing Address: PO Box 820, Metropolis, IL 62960-0820. Year Established: 1865. Pub. Frequency: w. (Wed.) Page Size: broadsheet. Subscrip. Rate: $.85 newsstand/cover; $31.50/yr mailed local; $43/yr mailed elsewhere. Adv. Rate: col. inch $8.29 Circulation: 4,200 per issue (paid). **Owner(s):** Paxton Media Group LLC, 201 S. Fourth St., Paducah, KY 42003. Telephone: 270-575-8600. FAX: 270-575-8780. **Management:** Matt Jones, General Manager. Clyde Wills, Publisher. Lisa Davis, Advertising Manager. **Editorial:** Linda Kennedy, News Editor.

SOUTHERN SCENE, THE. 111 E. Fifth St., Metropolis, IL 62960-0820. Telephone: 618-524-2141. FAX: 618-524-4727. E-MAIL: news@metropolisplanet.com. URL: http://www.metropolisplanet.com. Mailing Address: PO Box 820, Metropolis, IL 62960-0820. Pub. Frequency: w. (Mon.) Page Size: broadsheet Circulation: 13,300 per issue (free). **Owner(s):** Paxton Media Group LLC, 201 S. Fourth St., Paducah, KY 42003. Telephone: 270-575-8600. FAX: 270-442-8188. **Management:** Matt Jones, General Manager. Lisa Davis, Advertising Manager. Betsy Fellows, Circulation Manager. **Editorial:** Linda Kennedy, News Editor.

MIDLOTHIAN

ALSIP EXPRESS. 3840 W. 147th St., Midlothian, IL 60445. Telephone: 708-388-2425. FAX: 708-385-7811. E-MAIL: spressnews@aol.com. Year Established: 1945. Pub. Frequency: w. (Thu.) Page Size: tabloid. Subscrip. Rate: $.50 newsstand/cover; $18/yr in county; $21/yr out of county; $27/yr mailed out of state. Circulation: 4,970 per issue (paid). **Owner(s):** Southwest Messenger Press, Inc., See address and contact information above. **Management:** Margaret D. Lysen, Publisher. Thomas Gavin, Executive VP. **Editorial:** Lucinda Lysen, Editor.

BEVERLY NEWS. 3840 W. 147th St., Midlothian, IL 60445. Telephone: 708-388-2425. E-MAIL: spressnews@aol.com. Year Established: 1948. Pub. Frequency: w. (Thu.) Page Size: tabloid. Subscrip. Rate: $.50 newsstand/cover; $45/yr Circulation: 4,080 per issue (paid). **Owner(s):** Southwest Messenger Press, Inc., See address and contact information above. **Management:** Margaret D. Lysen, Publisher. Thomas Gavin, Executive VP. Lucinda Lysen, Advertising Director. **Editorial:** Lori Taylor, Editor.

BRIDGEVIEW INDEPENDENT. 3840 W. 147th St., Midlothian, IL 60445. Telephone: 708-388-2425. FAX: 708-385-7811. E-MAIL: spressnews@aol.com. Year Established: 1962. Pub. Frequency: w. (Wed.) Page Size: tabloid. Subscrip. Rate: $.50 newsstand/cover; $45/yr Circulation: 2,740 per issue (paid). **Owner(s):** Southwest Messenger Press, Inc., See address and contact information above. **Management:** Margaret D. Lysen, Publisher. Thomas Gavin, Executive VP. **Editorial:** Lucinda Lysen, Editor.

BURBANK-STICKNEY INDEPENDENT. 3840 W. 147th St., Midlothian, IL 60445. Telephone: 708-388-2425. FAX: 708-385-7811. E-MAIL: spressnews@aol.com. Year Established: 1962. Pub. Frequency: w. (Thu.) Page Size: tabloid. Subscrip. Rate: $.50 newsstand/cover; $18/yr in county; $21/yr out of county; $27/yr mailed out of state. Circulation: 6,110 per issue (paid). **Owner(s):** Southwest Messenger Press, Inc., See address and contact information above. **Management:** Margaret D. Lysen, Publisher. Thomas Gavin, Executive VP. **Editorial:** Lucinda Lysen, Editor.

CHICAGO RIDGE CITIZEN. 3840 W. 147th St., Midlothian, IL 60445. Telephone: 708-388-2425. FAX: 708-385-7811. E-MAIL: spressnews@aol.com. Year Established: 1962. Pub. Frequency: w. (Thu.) Page Size: tabloid. Subscrip. Rate: $.50 newsstand/cover; $18/yr in county; $21/yr out of county; $27/yr out of state. Circulation: 2,915 per issue (paid). **Owner(s):** Southwest Messenger Press, Inc., See address and contact information above. **Management:** Margaret D. Lysen, Publisher. Thomas Gavin, Executive VP. **Editorial:** Lucinda Lysen, Editor.

EVERGREEN PARK COURIER. 3840 W. 147th St., Midlothian, IL 60445. Telephone: 708-388-2425. FAX: 708-385-7811. E-MAIL: spressnews@aol.com. Year Established: 1930. Pub. Frequency: w. (Thu.) Page Size: tabloid. Subscrip. Rate: $.50 newsstand/cover; $18/yr in county; $21/yr out of county; $27/yr out of state. Circulation: 4,410 per issue (paid). **Owner(s):** Southwest Messenger Press, Inc., See address and contact information above. **Management:** Lucinda Lysen, President. Margaret D. Lysen, Publisher. Thomas Gavin, Executive VP. **Editorial:** Lucinda Lysen, Editor.

HICKORY HILLS CITIZEN. 3840 W. 147th St., Midlothian, IL 60445. Telephone: 708-388-2425. FAX: 708-385-7811. E-MAIL: spressnews@aol.com. Year Established: 1958. Pub. Frequency: w. (Thu.) Page Size: tabloid. Subscrip. Rate: $.50 newsstand/cover; $18/yr in county; $21/yr out of county; $27/yr out of state. Circulation: 3,530 per issue (paid). **Owner(s):** Southwest Messenger Press, Inc., See address and contact information above. **Management:** Margaret D. Lysen, Publisher. **Editorial:** Lucinda Lysen, Editor.

MIDLOTHIAN-BREMEN MESSENGER. 3840 W. 147th St., Midlothian, IL 60445. Telephone: 708-388-2425. FAX: 708-385-7811. E-MAIL: spressnews@aol.com. Year Established: 1930. Pub. Frequency: w. (Thu.) Page Size: tabloid. Subscrip. Rate: $.50 newsstand/cover; $18/yr in county; $21/yr out of county; $27/yr out of state. Circulation: 10,200 per issue (paid). **Owner(s):** Southwest Messenger Press, Inc., See address and contact information above. **Management:** Margaret D. Lysen, Publisher. Thomas Gavin, Executive VP. **Editorial:** Lucinda Lysen, Editor.

MOUNT GREENWOOD EXPRESS. 3840 W. 147th St., Midlothian, IL 60445. Telephone: 708-388-2425. FAX: 708-385-7811. E-MAIL: spressnews@aol.com. Year Established: 1945. Pub. Frequency: w. (Thu.) Page Size: tabloid. Subscrip. Rate: $.50 newsstand/cover; $18/yr in county; $21/yr out of county; $27/yr out of state. Circulation: 7,471 per issue (paid). **Owner(s):** Southwest Messenger Press, Inc., See address and contact information above. **Management:** Margaret D. Lysen, Publisher. Thomas Gavin, Executive VP. **Editorial:** Lucinda Lysen, Editor.

OAK LAWN INDEPENDENT. 3840 W. 147th St., Midlothian, IL 60445. Telephone: 708-388-2425. FAX: 708-385-7811. E-MAIL: spressnews@aol.com. Year Established: 1930. Pub. Frequency: w. (Thu.) Page Size: tabloid. Subscrip. Rate: $.50 newsstand/cover; $18/yr in county; $21/yr out of county; $27/yr out of state. Circulation: 10,880 per issue (paid). **Owner(s):** Southwest Messenger Press, Inc., See address and contact information above. **Management:** Margaret D. Lysen, Publisher. Thomas Gavin, Executive VP. **Editorial:** Lucinda Lysen, Editor.

ORLAND TOWNSHIP MESSENGER. 3840 W. 147th St., Midlothian, IL 60445. Telephone: 708-388-2425. FAX: 708-385-7811. E-MAIL: spressnews@aol.com. Year Established: 1980. Pub. Frequency: w. (Thu.) Page Size: tabloid. Subscrip. Rate: $.50 newsstand/cover; $45/yr Circulation: 3,788 per issue (paid). **Owner(s):** Southwest Messenger Press, Inc., See address and contact information above. **Management:** Margaret D. Lysen, Publisher. Thomas Gavin, Executive VP. **Editorial:** Lucinda Lysen, Editor.

PALOS CITIZEN. 3840 W. 147th St., Midlothian, IL 60445. Telephone: 708-388-2425. FAX: 708-385-7811. E-MAIL: spressnews@aol.com. Mailing Address: PO Box 548, Midlothian, IL 60445. Year Established: 1958. Pub. Frequency: w. (Thu.) Page Size: tabloid. Subscrip. Rate: $.50 newsstand/cover; $18/yr in county; $21/yr out of county; $27/yr out of state. Circulation: 4,610 per issue (paid). **Owner(s):** Southwest Messenger Press, Inc., 3840 W. 147th St., Midlothian, IL 06045. Telephone: 708-388-2425. FAX: 708-385-7811. **Management:** Margaret D. Lysen, Publisher. **Editorial:** Lucinda Lysen, Editor.

SCOTTSDALE-ASHBURN INDEPENDENT. 3840 W. 147th St., Midlothian, IL 60445. Telephone: 708-388-2425. FAX: 708-385-7811. E-MAIL: spressnews@aol.com. Year Established: 1962. Pub. Frequency: w. (Thu.) Page Size: tabloid. Subscrip. Rate: $.50 newsstand/cover; $45/yr Circulation: 5,975 per issue (paid). **Owner(s):** Southwest Messenger Press, Inc., See address and contact information above. **Management:** Margaret D. Lysen, Publisher. Thomas Gavin, Executive VP. **Editorial:** Lucinda Lysen, Editor.

WORTH CITIZEN. 3840 W. 147th St., Midlothian, IL 60445. Telephone: 708-388-2425. FAX: 708-385-7811. E-MAIL: spressnews@aol.com. Year Established: 1930. Pub. Frequency: w. (Thu.) Page Size: tabloid. Subscrip. Rate: $.50 newsstand/cover; $18/yr in county; $21/yr out of county; $27/yr out of state. Circulation: 2,660 per issue (paid). **Owner(s):** Southwest Messenger Press, Inc., See address and contact information above. **Management:** Margaret D. Lysen, Publisher. Thomas Gavin, Executive VP. **Editorial:** Lucinda Lysen, Editor.

MINIER

OLYMPIA REVIEW. 102 S. Main St., Minier, IL 61759. Telephone: 309-392-2414. FAX: 309-392-2169. Mailing Address: PO Box 710, Minier, IL 61759. Year Established: 1967. Pub. Frequency: w. (Tue.) Page Size: broadsheet. Subscrip. Rate: $.50 newsstand/cover; $30/yr mailed. Circulation: 6,950 per issue (paid). **Owner(s):** Rickard Publishing Co., PO Box 71, Mason City, IL 62664. **Management:** Lois Rickard, Publisher. **Editorial:** Lois Rickard, Editor.

MINONK

MINONK NEWS DISPATCH EDITION. 224 E. Fifth, Minonk, IL 61760. Telephone: 309-432-2505. FAX: 309-467-4563. Mailing Address: PO Box 68, Minonk, IL 61760. Pub. Frequency: w. (Thu.) Page Size: broadsheet. Subscrip. Rate: $.75 newsstand/cover; $30/yr local; $33/yr mailed out of county; $37/yr mailed out of state. Circulation: 672 per issue (paid and free). **Owner(s):** Illinois Valley Press, 301 W. Washington, Normal, IL 61761. Telephone: 309-829-9411. **Management:** Mark Barra, General Manager. **Editorial:** Julia Voss, Editor.

MONMOUTH

PENNYSAVER (MONMOUTH). 400 S. Main St., Monmouth, IL 61462. Telephone: 309-734-3176. FAX: 309-734-7649. Mailing Address: PO Box 650, Monmouth, IL 61462. Pub. Frequency: w. (Wed.) Page Size: standard Circulation: 14,278 per issue (free). **Owner(s):** GateHouse Media, Inc, 350 WillowBrook Office Park, Fairport, NY 14450. Telephone: 585-598-0030. FAX: 585-248-2631. **Management:** Tony Scott, Publisher. Wendy Todd, Advertising Manager. Brian Elliott, Circulation Manager.

MORRISONVILLE

MORRISONVILLE TIMES. 511 Carlin St., Morrisonville, IL 62546. Telephone: 217-526-3323. FAX: 217-526-3323. E-MAIL: pananews@consolidated.net. Mailing Address: PO Box 16, Morrisonville, IL 62546. Pub. Frequency: w. (Wed.) Page Size: broadsheet. Subscrip. Rate: $.50 newsstand/cover; $28/yr in county; $33/yr in state. Adv. Rate: col. inch $2.45 Circulation: 600 per issue (paid). **Owner(s):** Pana News, Inc., 205 S. Locust St., Pana, IL 62557. Telephone: 217-562-2111. **Management:** Thomas J. Phillips Jr., Publisher. Cindy Latonis, Circulation Manager. **Editorial:** Tom Latonis, Editor.

MORTON

MORTON COURIER. 780 W Jefferson, Morton, IL 61550. Telephone: 309-263-7414. FAX: 309-266-9905. E-MAIL: haglnews1@mtco.com. Mailing Address: PO Box 349, Washington, IL 61571. Pub. Frequency: w. (Wed) Page Size: tabloid. Subscrip. Rate: $.50 newsstand/cover; $34/yr Adv. Rate: col. inch $11.98 Circulation: 7,000 per issue (paid). **Owner(s):** Hagel Publications, Inc., 100 Ford Ln., Washington, IL 61571. Telephone: 309-444-3139. FAX: 309-444-8505. **Management:** Roger Hagel, Publisher. **Editorial:** Joi DeArmond, Editor.

MT ZION

ATWOOD HERALD. P O Box 79, Mt Zion, IL 62549. Telephone: 217-864-4212. Year Established: 1892. Pub. Frequency: w. (Wed.) Page Size: broadsheet. Subscrip. Rate: $.50 newsstand/cover; $18/yr Circulation: 1,000 per issue (paid). **Owner(s):** Mt. Zion Publications, Inc., See address and contact information above. **Management:** Mike Brothers, Publisher. Stephanie Wierman, Advertising Manager. **Editorial:** Mike Brothers, Editor.

MT. OLIVE

MT. OLIVE HERALD, THE. 102 E. Main St., Mt. Olive, IL 62069. Telephone: 217-999-3941. FAX: 217-999-5105. E-MAIL: moherald1880@yahoo.com. Mailing Address: PO Box 300, Mt. Olive, IL 62069. Year Established: 1880. Pub. Frequency: w. (Thu.) Page Size: tabloid. Subscrip. Rate: $.50 newsstand/cover; $18/yr local; $22/yr out of state. Adv. Rate: col. inch $3.30 Circulation: 1,650 per issue (paid). **Owner(s):** John M. Galer, See address and contact information above. **Management:** John M. Galer, President. **Editorial:** Linda Hasquin, Editor.

MT. STERLING

DEMOCRAT-MESSAGE. 123 W. Main St., Mt. Sterling, IL 62353. Telephone: 217-773-3371. FAX: 217-773-3369. Year Established: 1848. Pub. Frequency: w. (Wed.) Page Size: tabloid. Subscrip. Rate: $.50 newsstand/cover; $22/yr mailed in county; $32/yr mailed elsewhere. Circulation: 2,700 per issue (paid). **Owner(s):** Coulson Publications, See address and contact information above. **Management:** Warren Coulson, Publisher. **Editorial:** Warren Coulson, Editor.

MT. ZION

MT. ZION REGION NEWS. 433 Hwy. 121, Mt. Zion, IL 62549. Telephone: 217-864-4212. FAX: 217-864-4711. Mailing Address: PO Box 79, Mt. Zion, IL 62549. Year Established: 1959. Pub. Frequency: w. (Wed.) Page Size: broadsheet. Subscrip. Rate: $.75 newsstand/cover; $26/yr; $24/yr to senior citizens. Adv. Rate: col. inch $6.25 Circulation: 1,350 per issue (paid). **Owner(s):** Mt. Zion Publications, Inc., P O Box 79, Mt Zion, IL 62549. Telephone: 217-864-4212. **Management:** Mike Brothers, Publisher. Bonnie Burcham, Office Manager. Stephanie Wierman, Advertising Manager. **Editorial:** Bonnie Burcham, Reporter.

MURPHYSBORO

AMERICAN MONDAY. 1400 Walnut St, Murphysboro, IL 62966. Telephone: 618-684-5833. FAX: 618-684-5080. URL: http://www.gatehousemedia.com. Year Established: 1946. Pub. Frequency: w. (Mon.) Page Size: broadsheet. Adv. Rate: col. inch $19.99 Circulation: 8,300 per issue (free). **Owner(s):** GateHouse Media, Inc, 350 WillowBrook Office Park, Fairport, NY 14450. Telephone: 585-598-0030. FAX: 585-248-2631. **Management:** Tom Tiernan, Publisher.

MURPHYSBORO AMERICAN. 1400 Walnut St, Murphysboro, IL 62966. Telephone: 618-684-5833. FAX: 618-684-5080. URL: http://www.murphysboroamerican.com. Pub. Frequency: s-w. (Mon. & Thu.) Page Size: standard. Subscrip. Rate: $.50 newsstand/cover; $39.95/yr in area; $48.25/yr out of area. Circulation: 1,200 per issue (paid). **Owner(s):** GateHouse Media, Inc, 350 WillowBrook Office Park, Fairport, NY 14450. Telephone: 585-598-0030. FAX: 585-248-2631. **Management:** Tom Tiernan, Publisher. **Editorial:** John Gojkovich, Executive Editor.

NAPERVILLE

DOWNERS GROVE SUN. 1500 W. Ogden Ave., Naperville, IL 60540. Telephone: 630-355-8014. FAX: 630-416-5163. URL: http://www.suburbanchicagonews.com. Mailing Address: PO Box 269, Naperville, IL 60566. Pub. Frequency: w. (Fri.) Page Size: standard. Circulation: 3,000 per issue (paid and free). **Owner(s):** Sun-Times Media Group, 350 N Orleans St, Ste 10-S, Chicago, IL 60654. Telephone: 312-321-2299. **Management:** Jim Lynch, Publisher. Lois Mayer, Advertising Manager. **Editorial:** Lisa Yee, Editor. Ted Slowik, Managing Editor.

FOX VALLEY VILLAGES SUN. 1500 W. Ogden Ave., Naperville, IL 60540. Telephone: 630-355-8014. FAX: 630-416-5163. URL: http://www.suburbanchicagonews.com. Mailing Address: PO Box 269, Naperville, IL 60566. Year Established: 1984. Pub. Frequency: w. (Thu.) Page Size: tabloid. Subscrip. Rate: $.50 newsstand/cover. Circulation: 12,700 per issue (paid and controlled). **Owner(s):** Sun-Times Media Group, 350 N Orleans St, Ste 10-S, Chicago, IL 60654. Telephone: 312-321-2299. **Management:** Jim Lynch, Publisher. Lois Mayer, Advertising Manager. **Editorial:** Lisa Yee, Editor.

GLEN ELLYN SUN. 1500 W. Ogden Ave., Naperville, IL 60540. Telephone: 630-355-8014. FAX: 630-416-5163. URL: http://www.glenellynsun.com. Mailing Address: PO Box 269, Naperville, IL 60566. Pub. Frequency: w. (Fri.) Page Size: standard Circulation: 4,500 per issue (free). **Owner(s):** Sun-Times Media Group, 350 N Orleans St, Ste 10-S, Chicago, IL 60654. Telephone: 312-321-2299. **Management:** Jim Lynch, Publisher. Lois Mayer, Advertising Manager. **Editorial:** Lisa Yee, Editor. Ted Slowik, Managing Editor.

LISLE SUN, THE. 1500 W. Ogden Ave., Naperville, IL 60540. Telephone: 630-355-8014. FAX: 630-416-5163. E-MAIL: thesun@copleypress.com. URL: http://www.thelislesun.com. Year Established: 1938. Pub. Frequency: w. (Fri.) Page Size: tabloid. Subscrip. Rate: $.50 newsstand/cover. Adv. Rate: col. inch $14 **Wire Service(s):** AP. Circulation: 4,300 per issue (free). **Owner(s):** Sun-Times Media Group, 350 N Orleans St, Ste 10-S, Chicago, IL 60654. Telephone: 312-321-2299. **Management:** Jim Lynch, Publisher. Lois Mayer, Advertising Manager. **Editorial:** Lisa Yee, Editor. Ted Slowik, Managing Editor.

WHEATON SUN. 1500 W. Ogden Ave., Naperville, IL 60540. Telephone: 630-355-8014. FAX: 630-416-5163. URL: http://www.suburbanchicagonews.com/wheatonsun/. Mailing Address: PO Box 269, Naperville, IL 60566. Year Established: 1910. Pub. Frequency: w. (Fri.) Page Size: tabloid. Subscrip. Rate: $.50 newsstand/cover. Adv. Rate: col. inch $20 **Wire Service(s):** AP. Circulation: 23,000 per issue (free). **Owner(s):** Sun-Times Media Group, 350 N Orleans St, Ste 10-S, Chicago, IL 60654. Telephone: 312-321-2299. **Management:** Jim Lynch, Publisher. Lois Mayer, Advertising Manager. Mary Alltop, Circulation Manager. **Editorial:** Lisa Yee, Editor.

NASHVILLE

NASHVILLE NEWS, THE. 211 W. St. Louis St., Nashville, IL 62263-0047. Telephone: 618-327-3411. FAX: 618-327-3299. Year Established: 1934. Pub. Frequency: w. (Wed.) Page Size: broadsheet. Subscrip. Rate: $.50 newsstand/cover; $24/yr mailed in cy. & adj. cys.; $28/yr mailed elsewhere. Adv. Rate: col. inch $6.10 Circulation: 5,500 per issue (paid). **Owner(s):** Richard & Constance Tomaszewski, See address and contact information above. **Management:** Richard Tomaszewski, Publisher. **Editorial:** David Volz, Editor.

NEWTON

NEWTON PRESS-MENTOR. ISSN 0745-788X
700 W. Washington St., Newton, IL 62448-9998. Telephone: 618-783-2324. FAX: 618-783-2325. E-MAIL: newtonpressmentor@psbnewton.com. Mailing Address: PO Box 151, Newton, IL 62448-9998. Year Established: 1862. Pub. Frequency: w. (Thu.) Page Size: broadsheet. Subscrip. Rate: $.50 newsstand/cover; $29.50/yr in county & adj. cys.; $40/yr in state; $45/yr out of state. Circulation: 3,000 per issue (paid). **Owner(s):** GateHouse Media, Inc, 350 WillowBrook Office Park, Fairport, NY 14450. Telephone: 585-598-0030. FAX: 585-248-2631. **Management:** Ray McGrew, Publisher. Kathy Slounker, Advertising. **Editorial:** Vanette King, Editor.

NOKOMIS

NOKOMIS FREE PRESS-PROGRESS. 112 W. State St., Nokomis, IL 62075. Telephone: 217-563-2115. FAX: 217-563-7464. E-MAIL: pananews@consolidated.net. Mailing Address: PO Box 130, Nokomis, IL 62075-0130. Year Established: 1877. Pub. Frequency: w. (Wed.) Page Size: broadsheet. Subscrip. Rate: $.50 newsstand/cover; $28/yr in county; $33/yr out of county; $38/yr out of state. Circulation: 2,700 per issue (paid). **Owner(s):** Pana News, Inc., 205 S. Locust St., Pana, IL 62557. Telephone: 217-562-2111. **Management:** Thomas J. Phillips Jr., President. Cindy Latonis, Circulation Manager. **Editorial:** Brenda Compton, Editor.

NORRIS CITY

NORRIS CITY BANNER. 112 S Division St, Norris City, IL 62869. URL: http//www.gatehousemedia.com. Pub. Frequency: w. (Wed.) Page Size: broadsheet. Subscrip. Rate: $.75 newsstand/cover; $29/yr in county. Circulation: 1,215 per issue (paid). **Owner(s):** GateHouse Media, Inc, 350 WillowBrook Office Park, Fairport, NY 14450. Telephone: 585-598-0030. FAX: 585-248-2631. **Management:** Karrie Scott, Publisher. **Editorial:** Karrie Scott, Editor.

NORTH RIVERSIDE

BERWYN/CICERO LIFE. 7222 W Cermak Rd, Ste 505, North Riverside, IL 60546. Telephone: 708-447-9810. FAX: 708-447-9871. E-MAIL: localnews@libertysuburban.com. URL: http://www.chicagosuburbannews.com. Pub. Frequency: s-w. (Wed. & Fri.) Page Size: broadsheet. Subscrip. Rate: $1 newsstand/cover; $38/yr. Adv. Rate: col. inch $23.55 Circulation: 11,500 per issue (paid). **Owner(s):** GateHouse Media, Inc, 350 WillowBrook Office Park, Fairport, NY 14450. Telephone: 585-598-0030. **Management:** Bill Casey, VP Advertising. John Novosel, Circulation Director. Rita Feigl, Classified Adv. Mgr.. **Editorial:** Jon Schuler, City Editor.

BROOKFIELD SUBURBAN LIFE. 7222 W Cermak Rd, Ste 505, North Riverside, IL 60546. Telephone: 708-447-9810. FAX: 708-447-9871. E-MAIL: news@libertysuburban.com. URL: http://www.chicagosuburbannews.com. Year Established: 1949. Pub. Frequency: s-w. (Wed. & Sat.) Page Size: broadsheet. Subscrip. Rate: $1 newsstand/cover; $38/yr carrier delivery. Circulation: 29,295 per issue (paid). **Owner(s):** GateHouse Media, Inc, 350 WillowBrook Office Park, Fairport, NY 14450. Telephone: 585-598-0030. FAX: 585-248-2631. **Management:** Caroll Stacklin, Publisher. Bill Casey, VP Advertising. John Novosel, Circulation Director. Rita Feigl, Classified Adv. Mgr.. **Editorial:** Jon Schuler, City Editor.

RIVERSIDE SUBURBAN LIFE. 7222 W Cermak Rd, Ste 505, North Riverside, IL 60546. Telephone: 708-447-9810. FAX: 708-447-9871. URL: http://www.chicagosuburbannews.com. Year Established: 1949. Pub. Frequency: s-w. (Wed. & Sat.) Page Size: tabloid. Subscrip. Rate: $1 newsstand/cover; $38/yr. Adv. Rate: col. inch $26.75 Freelance Pay: $20-$75/article. Circulation: 20,850 per issue (paid). **Owner(s):** GateHouse Media, Inc, 350 WillowBrook Office Park, Fairport, NY 14450. Telephone: 585-598-0030. FAX: 585-248-2631. **Management:** Caroll Stacklin, Publisher. Bill Casey, VP Advertising. John Novosel, Circulation Director. Rita Feigl, Classified Adv. Mgr.. **Editorial:** Jon Schuler, City Editor.

WESTCHESTER/BROADVIEW/HILLSIDE SUBURBAN LIFE. 7222 W Cermak Rd, Ste 505, North Riverside, IL 60546. Telephone: 708-447-9810. FAX: 708-447-9871. E-MAIL: localnews@libertysuburban.com. URL: http://www.chicagosuburbannews.com. Year Established: 1949. Pub. Frequency: s-w. (Wed. & Sat.) Page Size: tabloid. Subscrip. Rate: $1 newsstand/cover; $38/yr. Adv. Rate: col. inch $26.75 Freelance Pay: $20-$75/article. Circulation: 20,850 per issue (paid). **Owner(s):** GateHouse Media, Inc, 350 WillowBrook Office Park, Fairport, NY 14450. Telephone: 585-598-0030. FAX: 585-248-2631. **Management:** Caroll Stacklin, Publisher. Bill Casey, VP Advertising. John Novosel, Circulation Director. Rita Feigl, Classified Adv. Mgr.. **Editorial:** Jon Schuler, City Editor.

O'FALLON

METRO EAST WEEKENDER, THE. 1480 Green Mount Rd, Ste 200, O'Fallon, IL 62269. Telephone: 619-632-3643. FAX: 619-632-6438. Mailing Address: PO Box 970, O'Fallon, IL 62269-0970. Pub. Frequency: w. (Fri.) Page Size: standard Circulation: 1,500 per issue (free). **Owner(s):** The/McClatchy Company, 2100 Q St, Sacramento, CA 95816. Telephone: 916-321-1936. FAX: 916-321-1869. **Management:** Todd Eschman, General Manager. Judy Weatherly, Advertising. **Editorial:** Todd Eschman, Editor.

O'FALLON PROGRESS. 1480 Green Mount Rd, Ste 200, O'Fallon, IL 62269. Telephone: 619-632-3643. FAX: 619-632-6438. E-MAIL: ofprogress@bnd.com. Mailing Address: PO Box 970, O'Fallon, IL 62269-0970. Year Established: 1895. Pub. Frequency: w. (Thu.) Page Size: broadsheet. Subscrip. Rate: $.50 newsstand/cover; $23/yr in county. Adv. Rate: col. inch $11.55 Circulation: 4,000 per issue (paid and free). **Owner(s):** The/McClatchy Company, 2100 Q St, Sacramento, CA 95816. Telephone: 916-321-1936. FAX: 916-321-1869. **Management:** Todd Eschman, General Manager. Judy Weatherly, Advertising. **Editorial:** Todd Eschman, Editor.

OAK BROOK

BENSENVILLE/WOOD DALE PRESS. 709 Enterprise Dr., Oak Brook, IL 60523-8814. Telephone: 630-368-1100. FAX: 630-368-1199. E-MAIL: news@libertysuburban.com. URL: http://www.chicagosuburbannews.com. Year Established: 1988. Pub. Frequency: w. (Thu.) Page Size: broadsheet. Subscrip. Rate: $1 newsstand/cover; $25/yr. Adv. Rate: col. inch $16.90 Circulation: 6,000 per issue (paid and free). **Owner(s):** Liberty Suburban Chicago Newspapers, See address and contact information above. **Management:** Gerry Smith, President. Susan Smith, Advertising Director. John Novosel, Circulation Manager. **Editorial:** Tim Bryers, Managing Editor.

BROOKFIELD/LYONS/MCCOOK SUBURBAN LIFE. 709 Enterprise Dr., Oak Brook, IL 60523-8814. Telephone: 630-368-1100. FAX: 630-368-1199. E-MAIL: localnews@libertysuburban.com. URL: http://www.chicagosuburbannews.com. Year Established: 1949. Pub. Frequency: s-w. (Wed. & Sat.) Page Size: tabloid. Subscrip. Rate: $1 newsstand/cover; $38/yr. Adv. Rate: col. inch $26.75 Freelance Pay: $20-$75/article. Circulation: 20,850 per issue (paid). **Owner(s):** Liberty Suburban Chicago Newspapers, See address and contact information above. **Management:** Gerry Smith, Publisher. Michael James, Advertising Manager. **Editorial:** Joe DeRosier, Managing Editor.

BURR RIDGE/DARIEN/WILLOWBROOK SUBURBAN LIFE. 709 Enterprise Dr., Oak Brook, IL 60523-8814. Telephone: 630-368-1100. FAX: 630-638-1199. E-MAIL: localnews@libertysuburban.com. URL: http://www.chicagosuburbannews.com. Year Established: 1974. Pub. Frequency: s-w. (Wed. & Sat.) Page Size: tabloid. Subscrip. Rate: $1 newsstand/cover; $38/yr. Adv. Rate: col. inch $17.65 Circulation: 6,750 per issue (paid and free). **Owner(s):** Liberty Suburban Chicago Newspapers, See address and contact information above. **Management:** Gerry Smith, Publisher. Neil Shannon, Advertising Manager. John Novosel, Circulation Manager. Rita Fiego, Classified Adv. Mgr.. Sue Smith, Associate Publisher. **Editorial:** Joe DeRosier, Managing Editor.

COUNTRYSIDE/INDIAN HEAD PK/HODGKINS/WILLOW SPR./PLEASANTDALE SUBURBAN LIFE. 709 Enterprise Dr., Oak Brook, IL 60523-8814. Telephone: 630-368-1100. FAX: 630-368-1199. E-MAIL: localnews@libertysuburban.com. URL: http://www.chicagosuburbannews.com. Year Established: 1949. Pub. Frequency: s-w. (Wed. & Sat.) Page Size: tabloid. Subscrip. Rate: $1 newsstand/cover; $38/yr. Adv. Rate: col. inch $26.75 Freelance Pay: $20-$75/article. Circulation: 20,850 per issue (paid). **Owner(s):** Liberty Suburban Chicago Newspapers, See address and contact information above. **Management:** Gerry Smith, Publisher. Jeff Serota, Advertising Manager. Rita Hendren Feigl, Circulation Manager. Dorothy Bratko, Classified Adv. Mgr.. **Editorial:** Joseph DeRosier, Executive Editor. Peggi Mannion, Managing Editor.

SUBURBAN LIFE (OAK BROOK). 709 Enterprise Dr., Oak Brook, IL 60523-8814. Telephone: 630-368-1100. FAX: 630-368-1199. E-MAIL: news@libertysuburban.com. URL: http://www.chicagosuburbannews.com. Year Established: 1949. Pub. Frequency: s-w. (Wed. & Sun.) Page Size: broadsheet. Subscrip. Rate: $1 newsstand/cover; $30/yr carrier delivery. Circulation: 34,000 per issue (paid). **Owner(s):** Liberty Suburban Chicago Newspapers, See address and contact information above. **Management:** Gerry Smith, President. Michael James, Advertising Director. John Novosel, Circulation Manager. **Editorial:** Jim Pokin, Executive Editor.

WHEATON PRESS. 709 Enterprise Dr., Oak Brook, IL 60523-8814. Telephone: 630-368-1100. FAX: 630-368-1199. E-MAIL: news@libertysuburban.com. URL: http://www.chicagosuburbannews.com. Year Established: 1922. Pub. Frequency: w. (Thu.) Page Size: tabloid. Subscrip. Rate: $.50 newsstand/cover; $25/yr. Adv. Rate: col. inch $9.55 Freelance Pay: $35/article. Circulation: 28,000 per issue (paid). **Owner(s):** Liberty Suburban Chicago Newspapers, See address and contact information above. **Management:** Gerry Smith, President. Michael James, Advertising Director. John Novosel, Circulation Manager. **Editorial:** Jim Pokin, Executive Editor.

OAK PARK

AUSTIN WEEKLY NEWS. 141 S. Oak Park Ave., Oak Park, IL 60302. Telephone: 708-524-8300. FAX: 708-524-0447. E-MAIL: tdean@wjinc.com. URL: http://www.austinweeklynews.com. Year Established: 1987. Pub. Frequency: w. (Thu.) Page Size: tabloid Circulation: 10,000 per issue (free). **Owner(s):** Wednesday Journal, Inc., See address and contact information above. **Management:** Dan Haley, President. Andrew Johnston, Operations Manager. Marc Stopeck, Advertising Manager. Kathy Hanson, Circulation Manager. **Editorial:** Terry Dean, Editor.

BOOSTER LAKE VIEW EDITION. 1140 Lake St., Oak Park, IL 60301. Telephone: 708-383-3200. FAX: 708-383-3678. URL: http://www.pioneerlocal.com. Year Established: 1902. Pub. Frequency: w. (Wed.) Page Size: tabloid. Subscrip. Rate: $1 newsstand/cover; $21.95/yr in county; $51.95/yr out of county. Adv. Rate: col. inch $17.29 Circulation: 4,000 per issue (paid and free). **Owner(s):** Pioneer Press, Inc., 3701 W. Lake Ave., Glenview, IL 60025. Telephone: 847-486-9200. FAX: 847-496-7454. **Management:** Chuck Agresti, Advertising Manager. **Editorial:** Beth Burmahl, Managing Editor. Holly Anderson, Asst. Managing Ed.. Michael Bonesteel, Entertainment Editor. Rick Hibbert, Group Editor.

BOOSTER WICKER EDITION. 1140 Lake St., Oak Park, IL 60301. Telephone: 708-383-3200. FAX: 708-383-3678. URL: http://www.pioneerlocal.com. Pub. Frequency: w. (Wed.) Page Size: tabloid. Subscrip. Rate: $1 newsstand/cover; $21.95/yr in county; $51.95/yr out of county. Adv. Rate: col. inch $17.29 Circulation: 1,600 per issue (paid and free). **Owner(s):** Pioneer Press, Inc., 3701 W. Lake Ave., Glenview, IL 60025. Telephone: 847-486-9200. FAX: 847-496-7454. **Management:** Chuck Agresti, Advertising Manager. **Editorial:** Beth Burmahl, Managing Editor. Holly Anderson, Asst. Managing Ed.. Michael Bonesteel, Entertainment Editor. Rick Hibbert, Group Editor.

CHICAGO JOURNAL. 141 S. Oak Park Ave., Oak Park, IL 60302. Telephone: 708-524-8300. FAX: 708-524-0447. E-MAIL: mmaidenberg@chicagojournal.com. URL: http://www.chicagojournal.com. Year Established: 2000. Pub. Frequency: w. (Thu.) Page Size: tabloid Circulation: 16,000 per issue (free). **Owner(s):** Wednesday Journal, Inc., See address and contact information above. **Management:** Dan Haley, President. Andrew Johnston, Operations Manager. Marc Stopeck, Advertising Manager. Kathy Hanson, Circulation Manager. **Editorial:** Micah Maidenberg, Editor.Readers: Urban residents

ELM LEAVES. 1140 Lake St., Oak Park, IL 60301. Telephone: 708-383-3200. FAX: 708-383-3678. E-MAIL: display@pioneerlocal.com. URL: http://www.pioneerlocal.com. Year Established: 1970. Pub. Frequency: w. (Wed.) Page Size: tabloid. Subscrip. Rate: $1 newsstand/cover; $21.95/yr in county; $51.95/yr out of county. Adv. Rate: col. inch $17.86 Circulation: 3,462 per issue (paid). **Owner(s):** Pioneer Press, Inc., 3701 W. Lake Ave., Glenview, IL 60025. Telephone: 847-486-9200. **Management:** Chuck Agresti, Advertising Manager. **Editorial:** Cristel Mohrman, Managing Editor. Holly Anderson, Asst. Managing Ed.. Jennifer Thomas, Entertainment Editor. Rick Hibbert, Group Editor.

FOREST LEAVES. 1140 Lake St., Oak Park, IL 60301. Telephone: 708-383-3200. FAX: 708-383-3678. E-MAIL: display@pioneerlocal.com. URL: http://www.pioneerlocal.com. Year Established: 1906. Pub. Frequency: w. (Wed.) Page Size: tabloid. Subscrip. Rate: $1 newsstand/cover; $21.95/yr in county; $51.95/yr out of county. Adv. Rate: col. inch $28 Circulation: 2,284 per issue (paid). **Owner(s):** Pioneer Press, Inc., 3701 W. Lake Ave., Glenview, IL 60025. Telephone: 847-486-9200. **Management:** Chuck Agresti, Advertising Manager. **Editorial:** Cheri Bentrup, Managing Editor. Holly Anderson, Asst. Managing Ed.. Jennifer Thomas, Entertainment Editor. Rick Hibbert, Group Editor.

FOREST PARK REVIEW. 141 S. Oak Park Ave., Oak Park, IL 60302. Telephone: 708-524-8300. E-MAIL: jadams@wjinc.com. URL: http://www.forestparkreview.com. Year Established: 1915. Pub. Frequency: w. (Wed.) Page Size: tabloid. Subscrip. Rate: $1 newsstand/cover; $18/yr mailed. Circulation: 2,200 per issue (paid and free). **Owner(s):** Wednesday Journal, Inc., See address and contact information above. **Management:** Dan Haley, President. Andrew Johnston, Operations Manager. Marc Stopeck, Advertising Manager. Kathy Hanson, Circulation Manager. **Editorial:** Josh Adams, Editor.

FRANKLIN PARK HERALD-JOURNAL, THE. ISSN 1044-906X 1140 Lake St., Oak Park, IL 60301. Telephone: 708-383-3200. FAX: 708-383-3678. E-MAIL: display@pioneerlocal.com. URL: http://www.pioneerlocal.com. Year Established: 1970. Pub. Frequency: w. (Wed.) Page Size: tabloid. Subscrip. Rate: $1 newsstand/cover; $21.95/yr in county; $51.95/yr out of county. Adv. Rate: col. inch $17.86 Circulation: 2,522 per issue (paid). **Owner(s):** Pioneer Press, Inc., 3701 W. Lake Ave., Glenview, IL 60025. Telephone: 847-486-9200. **Management:** Chuck Agresti, Advertising Manager. **Editorial:** Cristel Mohrman, Managing Editor. Holly Anderson, Asst. Managing Ed.. Jennifer Thomas, Entertainment Editor. Rick Hibbert, Group Editor.

LANDMARK, THE. 141 S. Oak Park Ave., Oak Park, IL 60302. Telephone: 708-524-8300. URL: http://www.rblandmark.com. Year Established: 1985. Pub. Frequency: w. (Wed.) Page Size: tabloid. Subscrip. Rate: $.50 newsstand/cover; $20/yr in county; $30/yr out of county. Circulation: 7,500 per issue (paid and free). **Owner(s):** Wednesday Journal, Inc., See address and contact information above. **Management:** Dan Haley, President. Andrew Johnston, Operations Manager. Marc Stopeck, Advertising Manager. Kathy Hanson, Circulation Manager. **Editorial:** Bob Uphues, Managing Editor.

MELROSE PARK HERALD. 1140 Lake St., Oak Park, IL 60301. Telephone: 708-524-4460. FAX: 708-383-3678. E-MAIL: display@pioneerlocal.com. URL: http://www.pioneerlocal.com. Year Established: 1970. Pub. Frequency: w. (Wed.) Page Size: tabloid. Subscrip. Rate: $1 newsstand/cover; $19.95/yr in county; $51.95/yr out of county. Adv. Rate: col. inch $20.57 Circulation: 2,128 per issue (paid). **Owner(s):** Pioneer Press, Inc., 3701 W. Lake Ave., Glenview, IL 60025. Telephone: 847-486-9200. **Management:** Larry Green, President. Mike Sperling, Advertising Manager. Dave Perham, Circulation Manager. Kyle Leonard, Promotion Manager. **Editorial:** Dan Obermaier, Editor. Paul Sassone, Bureau Chief.

NEWS-STAR. 1140 Lake St., Oak Park, IL 60301. Telephone: 708-383-3200. FAX: 708-383-3678. E-MAIL: lerner@enteract.com. URL: http://www.pioneerlocal.com. Year Established: 1902. Pub. Frequency: w. (Wed.) Page Size: tabloid. Subscrip. Rate: $.50 newsstand/cover; $21.95/yr in county; $51.95/yr out of county. Adv. Rate: col. inch $17.29 Circulation: 5,510 per issue (paid and free). **Owner(s):** Pioneer Press, Inc., 3701 W. Lake Ave., Glenview, IL 60025. Telephone: 847-486-9200. FAX: 847-496-7454. **Management:** Chuck Agresti, Advertising Manager. **Editorial:** Beth Burmahl, Managing Editor. Holly Anderson, Asst. Managing Ed.. Michael Bonesteel, Entertainment Editor. Rick Hibbert, Group Editor.

OAK LEAVES, THE. 1140 Lake St., Oak Park, IL 60301. Telephone: 708-383-3200. FAX: 708-383-3678. E-MAIL: display@pioneerlocal.com. URL: http://www.pioneerlocal.com. Year Established: 1902. Pub. Frequency: w. (Wed.) Page Size: tabloid. Subscrip. Rate: $1 newsstand/cover; $21.95/yr in county; $51.95/yr out of county. Adv. Rate: col. inch $28 Circulation: 9,690 per issue (paid). **Owner(s):** Pioneer Press, Inc., 3701 W. Lake Ave., Glenview, IL 60025. Telephone: 847-486-9200. **Management:** Chuck Agresti, Advertising Manager. **Editorial:** Cheri Bentrup, Managing Editor. Holly Anderson, Asst. Managing Ed.. Jennifer Thomas, Entertainment Editor. Rick Hibbert, Group Editor.

PROVISO HERALD. 1140 Lake St., Oak Park, IL 60301. Telephone: 708-383-3200. FAX: 708-383-3678. E-MAIL: display@pioneerlocal.com. URL: http://www.pioneerlocal.com. Year Established: 1970. Pub. Frequency: w. (Wed.) Page Size: tabloid. Subscrip. Rate: $1 newsstand/cover; $21.95/yr in county; $51.95/yr out of county. Adv. Rate: col. inch $20.57 Circulation: 2,916 per issue (paid). **Owner(s):** Pioneer Press, Inc., 3701 W. Lake Ave., Glenview, IL 60025. Telephone: 847-486-9200. **Management:** Chuck Agresti, Advertising Manager. **Editorial:** Cristel Mohrman, Managing Editor. Holly Anderson, Asst. Managing Ed.. Jennifer Thomas, Entertainment Editor. Rick Hibbert, Group Editor.

RIVER GROVE MESSENGER. 1140 Lake St., Oak Park, IL 60301. Telephone: 708-383-3200. FAX: 708-383-3678. E-MAIL: display@pioneerlocal.com. URL: http://www.pioneerlocal.com. Year Established: 1951. Pub. Frequency: w. (Wed.) Page Size: tabloid. Subscrip. Rate: $1 newsstand/cover; $21.95/yr in county; $51.95/yr out of county. Adv. Rate: col. inch $17.86 Circulation: 1,165 per issue (paid). **Owner(s):** Pioneer Press, Inc., 3701 W. Lake Ave., Glenview, IL 60025. Telephone: 847-486-9200. **Management:** Chuck Agresti, Advertising Manager. **Editorial:** Cristel Mohrman, Managing Editor. Holly Anderson, Asst. Managing Ed.. Jennifer Thomas, Entertainment Editor. Rick Hibbert, Group Editor.

SKYLINE. 1140 Lake St., Oak Park, IL 60301. Telephone: 708-383-3200. FAX: 708-383-3678. E-MAIL: skyline@lernernews.com. URL: http://www. Pub. Frequency: w. (Thu.) Page Size: tabloid.Adv. Rate: col. inch $21.57 Circulation: 15,258 per issue (paid and free). **Owner(s):** Pioneer Press, Inc., 3701 W. Lake Ave., Glenview, IL 60025. Telephone: 847-486-9200. FAX: 847-496-7454. **Management:** Chuck Agresti, Advertising Manager. **Editorial:** Beth Burmahl, Managing Editor. Holly Anderson, Asst. Managing Ed.. Michael Bonesteel, Entertainment Editor. Rick Hibbert, Group Editor.

WEDNESDAY JOURNAL OF OAK PARK & RIVER FOREST. 141 S. Oak Park Ave., Oak Park, IL 60302. Telephone: 708-524-8300. FAX: 708-524-0447. E-MAIL: ajohnston@wjinc.com. URL: http://www.wednesdayjournalonline.com. Year Established: 1980. Pub. Frequency: w. (Wed.) Page Size: tabloid. Subscrip. Rate: $1 newsstand/cover; $18/yr mailed. Circulation: 10,000 per issue (controlled and free). **Owner(s):** Wednesday Journal, Inc., See address and contact information above. **Management:** Dan Haley, Publisher. Andrew Johnston, Operations Manager. Marc Stopeck, Advertising Manager. Kathy Hanson, Circulation Manager. **Editorial:** Helen Karakoudas, Managing Editor.Readers: Local residents

WEST PROVISO HERALD. 1140 Lake St., Oak Park, IL 60301. Telephone: 708-524-4460. FAX: 708-383-3678. E-MAIL: display@pioneerlocal.com. URL: http://www.pioneerlocal.com. Year Established: 1970. Pub. Frequency: w. (Wed.) Page Size: tabloid. Subscrip. Rate: $1 newsstand/cover; $19.95/yr in county; $51.95/yr out of county. Adv. Rate: col. inch $20.57 Circulation: 2,883 per issue (paid). **Owner(s):** Pioneer Press, Inc., 3701 W. Lake Ave., Glenview, IL 60025. Telephone: 847-486-9200. **Management:** Larry Green, President. Susan Karol, VP Advertising. Mike Sperling, Advertising Manager. Dave Perham, Circulation Manager. Mike Kolpas, Classified Adv. Mgr.. Marty Kroschel, Production Director. Kyle Leonard, Promotion Manager. **Editorial:** Kevin Beese, Editor. John Korinek, Managing Editor. Paul Sassone, Bureau Chief. Dan Long, Sports Editor.

OLNEY

ADVANTAGE (OLNEY). 206 Whittle Ave., Olney, IL 62450-0340. Telephone: 618-393-2931. FAX: 618-392-2953. URL: http://www.olneydailymail.com. Mailing Address: PO Box 340, Olney, IL 62450-0340. Pub. Frequency: w. (Mon.) Page Size: tabloid Circulation: 3,300 per issue (free). **Owner(s):** GateHouse Media, Inc, 350 WillowBrook Office Park, Fairport, NY 14450. Telephone: 585-598-0030. **Management:** Ray McGrew, Publisher. Joe Gardner, Circulation Manager.

JASPER COUNTY NEW EAGLE. 206 Whittle Ave., Olney, IL 62450-0340. Telephone: 618-393-2931. FAX: 618-392-2953. URL: http://www.olneydailymail.com. Mailing Address: PO Box 340, Olney, IL 62450-0340. Pub. Frequency: w. (Mon.) Page Size: tabloid Circulation: 3,300 per issue (free). **Owner(s):** GateHouse Media, Inc, 350 WillowBrook Office Park, Fairport, NY 14450. Telephone: 585-598-0030. **Management:** Ray McGrew, Publisher. Joe Gardner, Circulation Manager.

WEEKLY MAIL, THE. 206 Whittle Ave., Olney, IL 62450-0340. Telephone: 618-393-2931. FAX: 618-392-2953. Mailing Address: PO Box 340, Olney, IL 62450-0340. Pub. Frequency: w. (Thu.) Page Size: standard.Subscrip. Rate: $34/yr mailed Circulation: 190 per issue (paid). **Owner(s):** GateHouse Media, Inc, 350 WillowBrook Office Park, Fairport, NY 14450. Telephone: 585-598-0030. FAX: 585-248-2631. **Management:** Ray McGrew, Publisher. **Editorial:** Mark Allen, Editor.

OQUAWKA

OQUAWKA CURRENT. 206 Schuyler St, Oquawka, IL 61469. Telephone: 309-867-2515. FAX: 309-867-6215. URL: http://www.gatehousemedia.com. Pub. Frequency: w. (Wed.) Page Size: standard. Subscrip. Rate: $.60 newsstand/cover; $24/yr in county. Circulation: 900 per issue (paid). **Owner(s):** GateHouse Media, Inc, 350 WillowBrook Office Park, Fairport, NY 14450. Telephone: 585-598-0030. FAX: 585-248-2631. **Management:** Scott Champion, Publisher.

OREGON

FORRESTON JOURNAL. 121-A Fourth St, Oregon, IL 61061. Telephone: 815-732-6166. FAX: 815-732-4238. E-MAIL: vwells@shawnewspapers.com. URL: http://www.shawnewspapers.com. Mailing Address: PO Box 8, Oregon, IL 61061. Year Established: 1865. Pub. Frequency: w. (Thu.) Page Size: broadsheet. Subscrip. Rate: $1 newsstand/cover; $39/yr mailed in county; $52/yr mailed out of county. Circulation: 1,000 per issue (paid). **Owner(s):** Shaw Newspapers, 444 Pine Hill Dr., Dixon, IL 61021. Telephone: 815-284-2222. **Management:** Earleen Hinton, General Manager. Trevis Mayfield, Publisher. **Editorial:** Vinde Wells, Editor.

OGLE COUNTY LIFE. 200 N. Third St., Ste. 2, Oregon, IL 61061. Telephone: 815-732-2156. FAX: 815-732-6154. E-MAIL: tonja@oglecountylife.com. URL: http://www.oglecountylife.com. Mailing Address: PO Box 378, Oregon, IL 61061. Year Established: 1968. Pub. Frequency: w. (Mon.) Page Size: tabloid.Subscrip. Rate: $35/yr out of area Circulation: 12,800 per issue (free). **Owner(s):** News Media Corp, PO Box 46, Rochelle, IL 61068. Telephone: 815-562-2061. **Management:** John Shank, General Manager. C. Thomas Cross, Publisher. Lesley Divers, Advertising. **Editorial:** Tanya Greenfield, Editor.

OTTAWA

THRIF-T-NIKEL COMMUNITY SHOPPING GUIDE. 801 Canal St., Ottawa, IL 61350. Telephone: 815-433-5595. Year Established: 1973. Pub. Frequency: w. (Wed.) Page Size: tabloid. Subscrip. Rate: $52/yr mailed elsewhere. Circulation: 18,990 per issue (controlled and free). **Owner(s):** Steven F.W. Gray & Associates Ltd., See address and contact information above. **Management:** Steven F Gray, President. **Editorial:** Jody Gray, Editor.

TOWN & COUNTRY WEEKLY. 801 Canal St., Ottawa, IL 61350. Telephone: 815-433-5595. Year Established: 1979. Pub. Frequency: w. (Wed.) Page Size: tabloid. Subscrip. Rate: $13/yr local; $76/yr mailed elsewhere. Circulation: 19,000 per issue (controlled and free). **Owner(s):** Steven F.W. Gray & Associates Ltd., See address and contact information above. **Management:** Steven F Gray, President. Jody Gray, Circulation Manager. **Editorial:** Jody Gray, Editor.

PALOS HEIGHTS

REGIONAL NEWS. 12243 S. Harlem Ave., Palos Heights, IL 60463-0932. Telephone: 708-448-4000. FAX: 708-448-4012. E-MAIL: regional@comcast.net. Year Established: 1941. Pub. Frequency: w. (Thu.) Page Size: broadsheet. Subscrip. Rate: $.75 newsstand/cover; $39/yr mailed in county; $49/yr mailed out of county. Adv. Rate: col. inch $17.22 Freelance Pay: $40/article. Circulation: 18,297 per issue (paid). **Owner(s):** Regional Publishing Corp., See address and contact information above. **Management:** Amy Richards, Publisher. **Editorial:** Jack Murray, Managing Editor.

REPORTER (PALOS HEIGHTS), THE. 12243 S Harlem Ave, Palos Heights, IL 60463. E-MAIL: thereporter@comcast.net. URL: http://www.thereporteronline.net. Year Established: 1960.Pub. Frequency: w. (Thu.) Subscrip. Rate: $33/yr Circulation: 18,800 (paid). **Owner(s):** Regional Publishing Corp., See address and contact information above. **Management:** Amy Richards, Publisher. **Editorial:** Jason Maholy, Editor.

REPORTER NEWSPAPER, THE. 12247 S. Harlem Ave., Palos Heights, IL 60463-1431. Telephone: 708-448-6161. FAX: 708-448-4012. E-MAIL: reporter@comcast.net. Year Established: 1960. Pub. Frequency: w. (Thu.) Page Size: broadsheet. Subscrip. Rate: $.75 newsstand/cover; $33/yr in county; $43/yr out of county. Freelance Pay: $30/story. Circulation: 18,486 per issue (paid). **Owner(s):** Regional Publishing Corp., See address and contact information above. **Management:** Amy Richards, Publisher. **Editorial:** Jason Maholy, Editor. Ken Karrson, Sports.

PANA

PANA NEWS-PALLADIUM. 205 S. Locust St., Pana, IL 62557. Telephone: 217-562-2113. FAX: 217-562-3729. E-MAIL: pananews@consolidated.net. Year Established: 1869. Pub. Frequency: s-w. (Mon. & Thu.) Page Size: broadsheet. Subscrip. Rate: $.75 newsstand/cover; $49/yr mailed in county; $57/yr mailed in state; $63/yr mailed out of state. Circulation: 4,300 per issue (paid). **Owner(s):** Pana News, Inc., See address and contact information above. **Management:** Thomas J. Phillips Jr., Publisher. Holly Satterlee, Advertising Manager. Cindy Latonis, Circulation Manager. **Editorial:** Tom Latonis, Editor.

PARK RIDGE

DES PLAINES TIMES. ISSN 0745-8681
130 S. Prospect Ave., Park Ridge, IL 60068. FAX: 847-696-3229. E-MAIL: display@pioneerlocal.com. URL: http://www.pioneerlocal.com. Year Established: 1887. Pub. Frequency: w. (Thu.) Page Size: tabloid. Subscrip. Rate: $1 newsstand/cover; $21.95/yr in county; $51.95/yr out of county. Adv. Rate: col. inch $16.29 Circulation: 3,017 per issue (paid). **Owner(s):** Pioneer Press, Inc., 3701 W. Lake Ave., Glenview, IL 60025. Telephone: 847-486-9200. **Management:** Peggy Cunniff, Advertising Director. **Editorial:** Anne Lunde, Managing Editor. Marc Alberts, Group Editor.

EDGEBROOK-SAUGANASH TIMES REVIEW. ISSN 0895-0105
130 S. Prospect Ave., Park Ridge, IL 60068. FAX: 847-696-3229. E-MAIL: display@pioneerlocal.com. URL: http://www.pioneerlocal.com. Year Established: 1985. Pub. Frequency: w. (Thu.) Page Size: tabloid. Subscrip. Rate: $1 newsstand/cover; $21.95/yr in county; $51.95/yr out of county. Adv. Rate: col. inch $16.29 Circulation: 1,426 per issue (paid). **Owner(s):** Pioneer Press, Inc., 3701 W. Lake Ave., Glenview, IL 60025. Telephone: 847-486-9200. **Editorial:** Anne Lunde, Managing Editor. Marc Alberts, Group Editor.

EDISON-NORWOOD TIMES REVIEW. 130 S. Prospect Ave., Park Ridge, IL 60068. FAX: 847-696-3229. E-MAIL: display@pioneerlocal.com. URL: http://www.pioneerlocal.com. Year Established: 1937. Pub. Frequency: w. (Thu.) Page Size: broadsheet. Subscrip. Rate: $1 newsstand/cover; $21.95/yr in county; $51.95/yr out of county. Adv. Rate: col. inch $16.29 Circulation: 4,607 per issue (paid). **Owner(s):** Pioneer Press, Inc., 3701 W. Lake Ave., Glenview, IL 60025. Telephone: 847-486-9200. **Management:** Peggy Cunniff, Advertising Director. **Editorial:** Anne Lunde, Editor. Marc Alberts, Group Editor.

HARLEM IRVING TIMES. 130 S. Prospect Ave., Park Ridge, IL 60068. FAX: 847-696-3229. E-MAIL: lerner@enteract.com. Year Established: 1946. Pub. Frequency: w. (Thu.) Page Size: broadsheet. Subscrip. Rate: $1 newsstand/cover; $19.95/yr in county; $59.95/yr out of county. Adv. Rate: col. inch $16.29 Circulation: 2,447 per issue (paid and free). **Owner(s):** Pioneer Press, Inc., 3701 W. Lake Ave., Glenview, IL 60025. Telephone: 847-486-9200. FAX: 847-496-7454. **Management:** Peggy Cunniff, Advertising Director. **Editorial:** Nicole Wagner, Managing Editor. Marc Alberts, Group Editor.

JEFFERSON PARK/PORTAGE PARK/BELMONT CRAGIN TIMES.
130 S. Prospect Ave., Park Ridge, IL 60068. FAX: 847-696-3229. E-MAIL: lerner@enteract.com. Year Established: 1946. Pub. Frequency: w. (Thu.) Page Size: broadsheet. Subscrip. Rate: $1 newsstand/cover; $21.95/yr in county; $51.95/yr mailed out of county. Adv. Rate: col. inch $16.29 Circulation: 2,771 per issue (paid and free). **Owner(s):** Pioneer Press, Inc., 3701 W. Lake Ave., Glenview, IL 60025. Telephone: 847-486-9200. FAX: 847-496-7454. **Management:** Peggy Cunniff, Advertising Director. **Editorial:** Anne Lunde, Managing Editor. Marc Alberts, Group Editor.

LINCOLNWOOD REVIEW. 130 S. Prospect Ave., Park Ridge, IL 60068-4074. E-MAIL: display@pioneerlocal.com. URL: http://www.pioneerlocal.com. Pub. Frequency: w. (Thu.) Page Size: tabloid. Subscrip. Rate: $1 newsstand/cover; $21.95/yr in county; $51.95/yr mailed out of state. Adv. Rate: col. inch $17.86 Circulation: 1,680 per issue (paid). **Owner(s):** Pioneer Press, Inc., 3701 W. Lake Ave., Glenview, IL 60025. Telephone: 847-486-9200. **Management:** Peggy Cunniff, Advertising Director. **Editorial:** Marc Alberts, Managing Editor.

MORTON GROVE CHAMPION. ISSN 0193-7251
130 S. Prospect Ave., Park Ridge, IL 60068. FAX: 847-696-3229. E-MAIL: display@pioneerlocal.com. URL: http://www.pioneerlocal.com. Year Established: 1957. Pub. Frequency: w. (Thu.) Page Size: tabloid. Subscrip. Rate: $1 newsstand/cover; $21.95/yr in county; $51.95/yr out of county. Adv. Rate: col. inch $16.29 Circulation: 3,148 per issue (paid). **Owner(s):** Pioneer Press, Inc., 3701 W. Lake Ave., Glenview, IL 60025. Telephone: 847-486-9200. **Management:** Peggy Cunniff, Advertising Director. **Editorial:** Marc Alberts, Managing Editor.

MOUNT PROSPECT TIMES. ISSN 0747-2595
130 S. Prospect Ave., Park Ridge, IL 60068. FAX: 847-696-3229. E-MAIL: display@pioneerlocal.com. URL: http://www.pioneerlocal.com. Year Established: 1987. Pub. Frequency: w. (Thu.) Page Size: tabloid. Subscrip. Rate: $1 newsstand/cover; $21.95/yr in county; $51.95/yr out of county. Adv. Rate: col. inch $16.29 Circulation: 2,195 per issue (paid). **Owner(s):** Pioneer Press, Inc., 3701 W. Lake Ave., Glenview, IL 60025. Telephone: 847-486-9200. **Management:** Peggy Cunniff, Advertising Director. **Editorial:** Marc Alberts, Managing Editor.

NILES HERALD-SPECTATOR. ISSN 0895-0121
130 S. Prospect Ave., Park Ridge, IL 60068. E-MAIL: display@pioneerlocal.com. URL: http://www.pioneerlocal.com. Year Established: 1950. Pub. Frequency: w. (Wed.) Page Size: tabloid. Subscrip. Rate: $1 newsstand/cover; $21.95/yr in county; $51.95/yr out of state. Adv. Rate: col. inch $15.71 Circulation: 7,948 per issue (paid). **Owner(s):** Pioneer Press, Inc., 3701 W. Lake Ave., Glenview, IL 60025. Telephone: 847-486-9200. **Management:** Peggy Cunniff, Advertising Director. **Editorial:** Anne Lunde, Editor. Marc Alberts, Group Editor.

NORRIDGE/HARWOOD HEIGHTS NEWS. ISSN 0885-7814
130 S. Prospect Ave., Park Ridge, IL 60068. Telephone: 847-486-7317. E-MAIL: display@pioneerlocal.com. URL: http://www.pioneerlocal.com. Year Established: 1984. Pub. Frequency: w. (Thu.) Page Size: tabloid. Subscrip. Rate: $1 newsstand/cover; $21.95/yr in county; $51.95/yr mailed out of state. Adv. Rate: col. inch $16.29 Circulation: 3,604 per issue (paid). **Owner(s):** Pioneer Press, Inc., 3701 W. Lake Ave., Glenview, IL 60025. **Management:** Peggy Cunniff, Advertising Director. **Editorial:** Anne Lunde, Managing Editor. Marc Alberts, Group Editor.

NORRIDGE-HARWOOD HEIGHTS NEWS. 130 S. Prospect Ave., Park Ridge, IL 60068. URL: http://www.pioneerlife.com. Pub. Frequency: w. (Wed.) Page Size: broadsheet. Subscrip. Rate: $1 newsstand/cover; $21.95/yr in county (effective 2007); $51.95/yr out of county. Circulation: 3,200 per issue (paid). **Owner(s):** Pioneer Press, Inc., 3701 W. Lake Ave., Glenview, IL 60025. Telephone: 847-486-9200. **Management:** Peggy Cunniff, Advertising Director. **Editorial:** Anne Lunde, Managing Editor.

PARK RIDGE HERALD-ADVOCATE. ISSN 0744-5385
130 S. Prospect Ave., Park Ridge, IL 60068. FAX: 847-696-3229. E-MAIL: display@pioneerlocal.com. URL: http://www.parkridge-heraldadvocate.com. Year Established: 1993. Pub. Frequency: w. (Thu.) Page Size: tabloid. Subscrip. Rate: $1 newsstand/cover; $21.95/yr in county; $51.95/yr out of county. Adv. Rate: col. inch $17.86 Circulation: 7,806 per issue (paid). **Owner(s):** Pioneer Press, Inc., 3701 W. Lake Ave., Glenview, IL 60025. Telephone: 847-486-9200. **Management:** Peggy Cunniff, Advertising Director. **Editorial:** Anne Lunde, Editor. Marc Alberts, Group Editor.

SKOKIE REVIEW. ISSN 0192-2742
130 S. Prospect Ave., Park Ridge, IL 60068-4074. E-MAIL: display@pioneerlocal.com. URL: http://www.pioneerlocal.com. Year Established: 1946. Pub. Frequency: w. (Thu.) Page Size: tabloid. Subscrip. Rate: $1 newsstand/cover; $19.95/yr in county; $51.95/yr out of county. Adv. Rate: col. inch $17.86 Circulation: 7,339 per issue (paid). **Owner(s):** Pioneer Press, Inc., 3701 W. Lake Ave., Glenview, IL 60025. Telephone: 847-486-9200. **Management:** Peggy Cunniff, Advertising Director. **Editorial:** Marc Alberts, Managing Editor.

PAXTON

LODA TIMES. 218 N. Market St., Paxton, IL 60957. Telephone: 217-379-2356. E-MAIL: advpaxtonrecord@illiwm.net. Year Established: 1888. Pub. Frequency: w. (Wed.) Page Size: broadsheet. Subscrip. Rate: $.50 newsstand/cover; $30/yr in county; $35/yr out of county. Adv. Rate: col. inch $8.65 Circulation: 3,600 per issue (paid). **Owner(s):** Paxton Printing Co., See address and contact information above. **Management:** Joyce Sage, Circulation Manager. Cathy Younker, Classified Adv. Mgr.. **Editorial:** David Hinton, Editor. Will Brumleve, Sports.

RECORD (PAXTON), THE. 218 N. Market St., Paxton, IL 60957. Telephone: 217-379-2356. FAX: 217-379-3104. E-MAIL: advpaxtonrecord@ilicom.net. Mailing Address: PO Box 73, Paxton, IL 60957. Year Established: 1865. Pub. Frequency: w. (Wed.) Page Size: broadsheet. Subscrip. Rate: $.50 newsstand/cover; $30/yr in county; $35/yr out of county. Adv. Rate: col. inch $8.65 Circulation: 2,100 per issue (paid). **Owner(s):** Paxton Printing Co., See address and contact information above. **Management:** Joyce Sage, Circulation Manager. Cathy Younker, Classified Adv. Mgr.. **Editorial:** Bob Maney, Editor.

PECATONICA

GAZETTE (PECATONICA), THE. 111 W Fourth St., Pecatonica, IL 61063. Telephone: 815-239-1028. FAX: 815-239-9198. E-MAIL: llceditors@aol.com. URL: http://www.rockvalleypublishing.com. Year Established: 1953. Pub. Frequency: w. (Thu.) Page Size: tabloid. Subscrip. Rate: $.75 newsstand/cover; $25.95/yr in county; $28.95/yr out of county. Circulation: 5,672 per issue (paid). **Owner(s):** Rock Valley Publishing LLC, 11512 N. Second St., Machesney Park, IL 61115. Telephone: 815-877-4044. FAX: 815-654-4857. **Management:** Randy Johnson, General Manager. Peter Cruger, President. Jack Cruger, Publisher. **Editorial:** Amy Kennedy, Editor.

PEKIN

TAZEWELL COUNTY SHOPPER. 20 S. Fourth St., Pekin, IL 61554. Telephone: 309-346-1111. FAX: 309-346-9815. URL: http://www.gatehousemedia.com. Mailing Address: PO Box 430, Pekin, IL 61555. Pub. Frequency: w. (Wed.) Page Size: standard Circulation: 11,000 per issue (free). **Owner(s):** GateHouse Media, Inc, 350 WillowBrook Office Park, Fairport, NY 14450. Telephone: 585-598-0030. FAX: 585-248-2631. **Management:** Greg Ratliff, Publisher. Michele Long, Advertising Director. Anthony Moreno, Circulation Manager.

PEORIA

CHILLICOTHE TIMES-BULLETIN. 1616 W. Pioneer Pkwy., Peoria, IL 61615. Telephone: 309-692-6600. FAX: 309-690-3399. E-MAIL: mgillespie@timestoday.com. URL: http://www.chillicothetimesbulletin.com. Mailing Address: PO Box 9426, Peoria, IL 61612-9426. Year Established: 1883. Pub. Frequency: w. (Wed.) Page Size: broadsheet. Subscrip. Rate: $.75 newsstand/cover; $26/yr in county; $39/yr out of county. Adv. Rate: col. inch $18.50 Circulation: 1,871 per issue (paid). **Owner(s):** Community Service Newspapers, See address and contact information above. **Management:** Beth Gehrt, General Manager. Jim Glassman, President. Henry Balfanz, Publisher. Julie Howell, Circulation Manager. **Editorial:** Marianne Gillespie, Editor.

EAST PEORIA TIMES-COURIER. 1616 W. Pioneer Pkwy., Peoria, IL 61615. Telephone: 309-692-6600. FAX: 309-691-7857. Mailing Address: PO Box 9426, Peoria, IL 61612-9426. Year Established: 1922. Pub. Frequency: w. (Wed.) Page Size: broadsheet. Subscrip. Rate: $.75 newsstand/cover; $26/yr in county; $39/yr out of county. Adv. Rate: col. inch $16 Circulation: 2,026 per issue (paid). **Owner(s):** Community Service Newspapers, See address and contact information above. **Management:** Beth Gehrt, General Manager. Jim Glassman, President. Henry Balfanz, Publisher. Julie Howell, Circulation Manager. **Editorial:** Jeanette Kendall, Editor.

MORTON TIMES-NEWS. 1616 W. Pioneer Pkwy., Peoria, IL 61615. Telephone: 309-692-6600. FAX: 309-690-3399. Mailing Address: PO Box 9426, Peoria, IL 61612-9426. Year Established: 1888. Pub. Frequency: w. (Wed.) Page Size: broadsheet. Subscrip. Rate: $1 newsstand/cover; $26/yr in county; $39/yr out of county. Adv. Rate: col. inch $22 Circulation: 2,416 per issue (paid). **Owner(s):** Community Service Newspapers, See address and contact information above. **Management:** Beth Gehrt, General Manager. Jim Glassman, President. Henry Balfanz, Publisher. Julie Howell, Circulation Manager. **Editorial:** Nathan Domenighini, Editor.

PEORIA TIMES OBSERVER. 1616 W. Pioneer Pkwy., Peoria, IL 61615. Telephone: 309-692-6600. FAX: 309-690-3399. URL: http://www.peoriatimesobserver.com. Mailing Address: PO Box 9426, Peoria, IL 61612-9426. Year Established: 1962. Pub. Frequency: w. (Wed.) Page Size: broadsheet. Subscrip. Rate: $1 newsstand/cover; $26/yr mailed in county; $39/yr mailed out of county. Adv. Rate: col. inch $32 Circulation: 15,277 per issue (paid). **Owner(s):** Community Service Newspapers, See address and contact information above. **Management:** Beth Gehrt, General Manager. Jim Glassman, President. Henry Balfanz, Publisher. Julie Howell, Circulation Manager. **Editorial:** Tom Batter, Editor.

WASHINGTON TIMES REPORTER, THE. 1616 W. Pioneer Pkwy., Peoria, IL 61615. Telephone: 309-692-6600. FAX: 309-690-3399. URL: http://www.washingtontimesreporter.com. Mailing Address: PO Box 9426, Peoria, IL 61612-9426. Year Established: 1840. Pub. Frequency: w. (Wed.) Page Size: broadsheet. Subscrip. Rate: $1 newsstand/cover; $31/yr mailed in county; $39/yr mailed out of county. Adv. Rate: col. inch $13.40 **Wire Service(s):** CNS. Circulation: 9,248 per issue. **Owner(s):** Community Service Newspapers, See address and contact information above. **Management:** Beth Gehrt, General Manager. Jim Glassman, President. Henry Balfanz, Publisher. Julie Howell, Circulation Manager. **Editorial:** Donelle Whiting, Editor.

PERCY

COUNTY JOURNAL (PERCY). 1101 E. Pine, Percy, IL 62272. Telephone: 618-497-8272. FAX: 618-497-2607. E-MAIL: cjournal@egyptian.net. Mailing Address: PO Box 369, Percy, IL 62272. Year Established: 1980. Pub. Frequency: w. (Thu.) Page Size: broadsheet. Subscrip. Rate: $.50 newsstand/cover; $21/yr in county; $23/yr out of county. Adv. Rate: col. inch $6.50 Circulation: 7,300 per issue (paid). **Owner(s):** Gerald & Larry Willis, See address and contact information above. **Management:** Gerald Willis, President. Larry Willis, Publisher. John Falkenhein, Advertising Manager. Delma Rubach, Circulation Manager. **Editorial:** Greg Myers, Editor.

PETERSBURG

MENARD COUNTY REVIEW. 235 E Sangamon, Petersburg, IL 62675. E-MAIL: observer@gcctb.com. Mailing Address: PO Box 350, Petersburg, IL 62675. Year Established: 1883. Pub. Frequency: w. (Thu.) Page Size: tabloid. Subscrip. Rate: $.50 newsstand/cover; $18/yr mailed in state; $21/yr mailed out of state. Circulation: 1,450 per issue (paid). **Owner(s):** Petersburg Observer Co., See address and contact information above. **Management:** Jane Cutright, Publisher. Keri Vogt, Advertising Manager.

PETERSBURG OBSERVER. PO Box 350, Petersburg, IL 62675. Telephone: 217-632-2236. E-MAIL: observer@gcctv.com. Year Established: 1874. Pub. Frequency: w. (Thu.) Page Size: broadsheet. Subscrip. Rate: $.60 newsstand/cover; $24/yr mailed in state. Adv. Rate: col. inch $4.40 Circulation: 3,100 per issue (paid). **Owner(s):** Petersburg Observer Co., 235 E. Sangamon St., Petersburg, IL 62675-0350. **Management:** Keri Vogt, Advertising Manager. Jane Cutright, Secretary. **Editorial:** Jane Cutright, Editor.

PITTSFIELD

PIKE COUNTY EXPRESS. P.O. Box 537, Pittsfield, IL 62363. Telephone: 217-285-5415. FAX: 217-285-9564. Pub. Frequency: w. (Wed.) Page Size: standard. Subscrip. Rate: $.50 newsstand/cover; $22/yr mailed in county; $32/yr mailed elsewhere. Adv. Rate: col. inch $5.50 Circulation: 4,200 per issue (paid). **Owner(s):** Coulson Publications, 123 W. Main St., Mt. Sterling, IL 62312. Telephone: 217-335-2348. FAX: 217-335-2342. **Management:** Joan Coulson, Publisher. Jackie Taylor, Advertising. **Editorial:** Tom Coulson, Editor.

PLAINFIELD

BOLINGBROOK SUN, THE. ISSN 0885-6389 3101 N. US Hwy. 30, Plainfield, IL 60544. Telephone: 815-439-5300. FAX: 815-439-4362. URL: http://www.thebolingbrooksun.com. Year Established: 1963. Pub. Frequency: w. (Fri.) Page Size: tabloid. Subscrip. Rate: $.50 newsstand/cover; $22/yr; $51.95/yr out of county. Adv. Rate: col. inch $18 **Wire Service(s):** CNS. Circulation: 7,300 per issue (paid). **Owner(s):** Sun-Times Media Group, 350 N Orleans St, Ste 10-S, Chicago, IL 60654. Telephone: 312-321-2299. **Management:** Jim Lynch, Publisher. Lois Mayer, Advertising Manager. Mary Alltop, Circulation Manager. **Editorial:** Dan Cassidy, Editor.

HOMER SUN. 3101 N. US Hwy. 30, Plainfield, IL 60544. Telephone: 815-439-5300. FAX: 815-439-4362. URL: http://www.homersun.com. Pub. Frequency: w. (Fri.) Page Size: broadsheet. Subscrip. Rate: $1 newsstand/cover; $21.95/yr in county; $51.95/yr out of city. Circulation: 4,300 per issue (paid). **Owner(s):** Sun-Times Media Group, 350 N Orleans St, Ste 10-S, Chicago, IL 60654. Telephone: 312-321-2299. **Management:** Jim Lynch, Publisher. Lois Mayer, Advertising Manager. Mary Alltop, Circulation Manager. **Editorial:** Dan Cassidy, Editor.

PLAINFIELD SUN. 3101 N. US Hwy. 30, Plainfield, IL 60544. Telephone: 815-439-5300. FAX: 815-439-4362. URL: http://www.suburbanchicagonews.com. Year Established: 1997. Pub. Frequency: w. (Wed.) Page Size: tabloid Circulation: 13,000 per issue (free). **Owner(s):** Sun-Times Media Group, 350 N Orleans St, Ste 10-S, Chicago, IL 60654. Telephone: 312-321-2299. **Management:** Jim Lynch, Publisher. Lois Mayer, Advertising Manager. **Editorial:** Dan Cassidy, Editor.

PONTIAC

FLANAGAN HOME TIMES. 318 N. Main St., Pontiac, IL 61764. Telephone: 815-842-1153. FAX: 815-842-4388. Mailing Address: PO Box 170, Pontiac, IL 61764. Year Established: 1885. Pub. Frequency: w. (Wed.) Page Size: standard. Subscrip. Rate: $.50 newsstand/cover; $25/yr in state; $27.50/yr mailed out of state. Circulation: 250 per issue (paid). **Owner(s):** GateHouse Media, Inc, 3000 Dundee Rd., Ste. 203, Northbrook, IL 60062. Telephone: 847-272-2244. FAX: 847-272-6244. **Management:** Thomas E Hutson, Publisher. Gary DeVault, Advertising Manager. Roger Swearingen, Circulation Manager. **Editorial:** John Holloway, Editor.

LIVINGSTON SHOPPING NEWS. 318 N. Main St., Pontiac, IL 61764. Telephone: 815-842-1153. FAX: 815-842-4388. Mailing Address: PO Box 170, Pontiac, IL 61764. Pub. Frequency: w. (Wed.) Page Size: standard Circulation: 19,570 per issue (free). **Owner(s):** GateHouse Media, Inc, 350 WillowBrook Office Park, Fairport, NY 14450. Telephone: 585-598-0030. FAX: 585-248-2631. **Management:** Thomas E Hutson, Publisher. Gary DeVault, Advertising Manager. Roger Swearingen, Circulation Manager. **Editorial:** John Holloway, News Editor.

PRINCETON

BUREAU COUNTY REPUBLICAN. ISSN 0894-1181 316 S. Main St., Princeton, IL 61356. Telephone: 815-875-4461. FAX: 815-875-1235. E-MAIL: bcrnews@theramp.net. URL: http://www.bcrnews.com. Mailing Address: PO Box 340, Princeton, IL 61356-0340. Year Established: 1847. Pub. Frequency: 3/w. (Tue., Thu., Sat.) Page Size: broadsheet. Subscrip. Rate: $.75 newsstand/cover; $85/yr carrier delivery in county; $94/yr mailed out of county. Circulation: 7,271 per issue (paid). **Owner(s):** Shaw Newspaper Co., 444 Pine Hill Dr., Dixon, IL 61021. Telephone: 815-284-4000. **Management:** Sam Fisher, Publisher. Sandy Pistole, Advertising Manager. Geoff Vanderlin, Circulation Manager. **Editorial:** Terri Simon, Managing Editor.

RANTOUL

RANTOUL PRESS. 1332 E. Harmon Dr., PO Box 5110, Rantoul, IL 61866-5110. Telephone: 217-892-9615. FAX: 217-892-9451. E-MAIL: news@rantoulpress.com. Year Established: 1874. Pub. Frequency: w. (Wed.) Page Size: tabloid. Subscrip. Rate: $.50 newsstand/cover; $34/yr. Adv. Rate: col. inch $15.40 Circulation: 9,625 per issue (paid and free). **Owner(s):** News Gazette, PO Box 677, Champaign, IL 61824-0677. Telephone: 217-351-5252. **Management:** Ronald Wilcox, General Manager. Melinda Carpenter, Circulation Manager.

RED BUD

NORTH COUNTY NEWS (RED BUD). 124 S. Main St., Red Bud, IL 62278. Telephone: 618-282-3803. FAX: 618-282-6134. E-MAIL: ncnews@hotmail.com. URL: http://www.blossomcity.com. Mailing Address: PO Box 68, Red Bud, IL 62278-0068. Year Established: 1959. Pub. Frequency: w. (Thu.) Page Size: broadsheet. Subscrip. Rate: $.50 newsstand/cover; $19/yr 3 cys.; $22/yr out of area. Adv. Rate: col. inch $5.75 Circulation: 4,000 per issue (paid). **Owner(s):** Victor L. Mohr, See address and contact information above. **Management:** Victor L. Mohr, Publisher. Kathy Bauer, Advertising Manager. **Editorial:** Mary Koester, Managing Editor.

RIVERTON

RIVERTON REGISTER & TRI CITY REGISTER. 100 N. Sixth St., Riverton, IL 62561-0200. Telephone: 217-629-9247. Year Established: 1948. Pub. Frequency: w. (Wed.) Page Size: tabloid. Subscrip. Rate: $.35 newsstand/cover; $16/yr mailed in county; $20/yr mailed out of county. Adv. Rate: col. inch $4.50 Circulation: 2,000 per issue (paid). **Owner(s):** Rhodes Publications, See address and contact information above. **Management:** Barbara Rhodes, Publisher. **Editorial:** Barbara Rhodes, Editor.

TRI-CITY REGISTER. 100 N. Sixth St., Riverton, IL 62561-0200. Telephone: 217-629-9247. Year Established: 1948. Pub. Frequency: w. (Wed.) Page Size: tabloid. Subscrip. Rate: $.30 newsstand/cover; $16/yr mailed in county; $20/yr mailed out of county. Circulation: 1,000 per issue (paid). **Owner(s):** Rhodes Publications, See address and contact information above. **Management:** Barbara Rhodes, Publisher. **Editorial:** Barbara Rhodes, Editor.

WILLIAMSVILLE SUN. 100 N. Sixth St., Riverton, IL 62561-0200. Telephone: 217-629-9247. Year Established: 1948. Pub. Frequency: w. (Wed.) Page Size: tabloid. Subscrip. Rate: $.35 newsstand/cover; $16/yr mailed in county; $20/yr mailed out of county. Circulation: 1,000 per issue (paid). **Owner(s):** Rhodes Publications, See address and contact information above. **Management:** Barbara Rhodes, Publisher. **Editorial:** Barbara Rhodes, Editor.

ROANOKE

WOODFORD COUNTY JOURNAL/ROANOKE BENSON EDITION. P.O. Box 200, Roanoke, IL 61561. Telephone: 309-923-5841. FAX: 309-467-4583. E-MAIL: woodcojo@mtco.com. Year Established: 1867. Pub. Frequency: w. (Thu.) Page Size: broadsheet. Subscrip. Rate: $.75 newsstand/cover; $33/yr mailed in county; $36/yr mailed out of county; $40/yr mailed out of state. Circulation: 934 per issue (paid and free). **Owner(s):** Lee Enterprises, Inc., 201 N. Harrison St, Ste 600, Davenport, IA 52801-1924. **Management:** Mark Barra, General Manager. **Editorial:** Cheryl Wolfe, Editor.

ROCHELLE

ATASCADERO NEWS. PO Box 46, Rochelle, IL 61068. E-MAIL: atascaderonews@charter.net. Year Established: 1916. Pub. Frequency: s-w. (Wed. & Fri.) Page Size: broadsheet. Subscrip. Rate: $.50 newsstand/cover; $31/yr in county; $36.25/yr out of county; $40/yr mailed out of state. Adv. Rate: col. inch $9.50 Circulation: 26,000 per issue (paid and free). **Owner(s):** News Media Corp., 228 Main St., Lingle, WY 82223. Telephone: 307-532-2184. FAX: 307-532-2283. **Management:** J J Tompkins, General Manager. John Porter, Publisher. Venessa Williams, Circulation Manager. **Editorial:** Ben Banuchi, Editor. Chris Cauly, Sports Editor.

ROCHELLE NEWS LEADER. 211 Hwy. 38 E., Rochelle, IL 61608. E-MAIL: rchnwsldr1@aol.com. URL: http://www.rochellenews-leader.com. Mailing Address: PO Box 46, Rochelle, IL 61608. Year Established: 1921. Pub. Frequency: 3/w. (Tue., Thu., Sun.) Page Size: broadsheet. Subscrip. Rate: $.50 newsstand/cover; $42.25 for 6 mos.; $81/yr; $72.90/yr to senior citizens. Circulation: 5,000 per issue (paid). **Owner(s):** News Media Corp., See address and contact information above. **Management:** Tom Cross, Publisher. Patrick Duffy, Advertising Director. Wanda Brimhall, Circulation Manager. **Editorial:** John Shank, Managing Editor. Shannon Kruse, City Editor. Larry Hanson, Sports Editor.

ROCKTON

HERALD (ROCKTON), THE. 555 W. Blackhawk Blvd., Rockton, IL 61072-2003. Telephone: 815-624-6211. FAX: 815-624-8018. Year Established: 1865. Pub. Frequency: w. (Thu.) Page Size: tabloid. Subscrip. Rate: $.60 newsstand/cover; $27.95/yr in county; $28.95/yr out of county. Circulation: 7,500 per issue (paid and free). **Owner(s):** Rock Valley Publishing LLC, 11512 N. Second St., Machesney Park, IL 61115. Telephone: 815-877-4044. FAX: 815-654-4857. **Management:** Randy Johnson, General Manager. Peter Cruger, President. Jack Cruger, Publisher. Maxine Bayer, Advertising Manager. Lindi Sweet, Circulation Manager. **Editorial:** Mike Ruggles, Editor. Linda Lano, Production Manager. Dan Moeller, Sports.

RUSHVILLE

RUSHVILLE TIMES, THE. PO Box 226, Rushville, IL 62681. Telephone: 217-322-3321. FAX: 217-322-2770. Year Established: 1848. Pub. Frequency: w. (Wed.) Page Size: broadsheet. Subscrip. Rate: $.50 newsstand/cover; $18/yr mailed in cy. & adj.cys.; $24/yr mailed in county; $30/yr out of state. Circulation: 3,400 per issue (paid). **Owner(s):** Wayne Perry, See address and contact information above. **Management:** Wayne Perry, Publisher. Teresa Haines, Advertising Manager. **Editorial:** Alan Icenogle, Editor.

SAINT CHARLES

WARRENVILLE POST, THE. 3755 E. Main St., Ste. 170, Saint Charles, IL 60174-2463. E-MAIL: news@press-repub.com. URL: http://www.chicagosuburbannews.com. Year Established: 1986. Pub. Frequency: w. (Thu.) Page Size: tabloid. Subscrip. Rate: $.75 newsstand/cover; $33/yr. Adv. Rate: col. inch $15.25 Circulation: 7,800 per issue (paid and free). **Owner(s):** Liberty Suburban Chicago Newspapers, 709 Enterprise Dr., Oak Brook, IL 60523-8814. Telephone: 630-368-1100. FAX: 630-368-1188. **Management:** Gerry Smith, Publisher. Terri Pereira, Advertising Manager. John Novosel, Circulation Manager. Rita Fietel, Classified Adv. Mgr.. **Editorial:** Kris Kochanek, Managing Editor. Jason Bromwelo, News Editor. Mark Busch, Photo Editor. Craig Brueski, Sports Editor.

SALEM

SALEM TIMES-COMMONER. 120 S. Broadway, Salem, IL 62881-0548. Telephone: 618-548-3330. FAX: 618-548-3593. E-MAIL: stc@accessus.net. URL: http://www.salem-tc.com. Year Established: 1860. Pub. Frequency: 3/w. (Mon., Wed., Fri.) Page Size: broadsheet. Subscrip. Rate: $.50 newsstand/cover; $38.92/yr mailed in county; $41.16/yr mailed in state; $51.25/yr mailed out of state. Adv. Rate: col. inch $5.92 Circulation: 4,500 per issue (paid). **Owner(s):** William Perrine, See address and contact information above. **Management:** Dan Nichols, General Manager. William Perrine, President. Debra Spencer, Advertising Manager. Kimberly Lowery, Circulation Manager. **Editorial:** Kim Keller, Editor. Dennis Rosenberger, Assistant Editor.

SAVANNA

NORTHWESTERN ILLINOIS DISPATCH. 121 Main St., Savanna, IL 61074. Telephone: 815-273-2277. FAX: 815-273-2715. Year Established: 1960. Pub. Frequency: w. (Thu.) Page Size: tabloid Circulation: 9,700 per issue (free). **Owner(s):** Robert W. Watson, See address and contact information above. **Management:** Robert W. Watson, Publisher. Kristin Bortano, Advertising Manager. Pam Villalobos, Circulation Manager. **Editorial:** Robert W. Watson, Editor. Janice Smith, Production Manager.

SAVANNA TIMES JOURNAL. 121 Main St., Savanna, IL 61074. Telephone: 815-273-2277. FAX: 815-273-2715. Year Established: 1875. Pub. Frequency: w. (Thu.) Page Size: tabloid. Subscrip. Rate: $.75 newsstand/cover; $24/yr mailed in county; $29/yr mailed out of county; $35/yr mailed out of state. Circulation: 2,250 per issue (paid). **Owner(s):** Robert W. Watson, See address and contact information above. **Management:** Robert W. Watson, Publisher. Kristin Bortano, Advertising Manager. Pam Villalobos, Circulation Manager. **Editorial:** Robert W. Watson, Editor. Janice Smith, Production Manager.

SHAWNEETOWN

GALLATIN DEMOCRAT. 288 N Lincoln Blvd. E, Shawneetown, IL 62984. URL: http://www.gatehousemedia.com. Pub. Frequency: w. (Thu.) Page Size: broadsheet. Subscrip. Rate: $.50 newsstand/cover; $30/yr in county; $33/yr out of county. Circulation: 800 per issue (paid). **Owner(s):** GateHouse Media, Inc, 350 WillowBrook Office Park, Fairport, NY 14450. Telephone: 585-598-0030. FAX: 585-248-2631. **Management:** George Wilson, Publisher. **Editorial:** George Wilson, Editor.

RIDGEWAY NEWS. 288 N Lincoln Blvd. E, Shawneetown, IL 62984. URL: http://www.gatehousemedia.com. Pub. Frequency: w. (Thu.) Page Size: broadsheet. Subscrip. Rate: $.50 newsstand/cover; $30/yr in county; $33/yr out of county. Circulation: 700 per issue (paid). **Owner(s):** GateHouse Media, Inc, 350 WillowBrook Office Park, Fairport, NY 14450. Telephone: 585-598-0030. FAX: 585-248-2631. **Management:** George Wilson, Publisher. **Editorial:** George Wilson, Editor.

SOUTH HOLLAND

SHOPPER (SOUTH HOLLAND), THE. 924 E. 162nd St., South Holland, IL 60473. Telephone: 708-333-5901. FAX: 708-333-9630. Year Established: 1957. Pub. Frequency: w. (Wed.) Page Size: tabloid Circulation: 64,000 per issue (free). **Owner(s):** Arlo Kallemeyn, See address and contact information above. **Management:** Arlo Kallemeyn, Publisher.

SPARTA

JOURNAL-MESSENGER, THE. 116 W Main, Sparta, IL 62286. Telephone: 618-443-2145. FAX: 618-443-2780. Mailing Address: PO Box 217, Sparta, IL 62286. Pub. Frequency: w. (Wed.) Page Size: broadsheet. Subscrip. Rate: $.50 newsstand/cover; $21/yr in county. Circulation: 2,475 per issue (paid). **Owner(s):** The/McClatchy Company, 2100 Q St, Sacramento, CA 95816. Telephone: 916-321-1936. FAX: 916-321-1869. **Management:** Carol Mulholland, General Manager. Darleen Conner, Advertising Manager. Linda Bird, Circulation Manager. **Editorial:** Mike Springton, Editor.

SPARTA NEWS-PLAINDEALER. 116 W Main, Sparta, IL 62286. Telephone: 618-443-2145. FAX: 618-443-2780. E-MAIL: kc@bnd.com. Mailing Address: PO Box 217, Sparta, IL 62286. Year Established: 1863. Pub. Frequency: w. (Tue.) Page Size: broadsheet. Subscrip. Rate: $.50 newsstand/cover; $21/yr mailed in county; $26/yr mailed out of county; $31/yr mailed out of state. Circulation: 9,225 per issue (paid). **Owner(s):** The/McClatchy Company, 2100 Q St, Sacramento, CA 95816. Telephone: 916-321-1936. FAX: 916-321-1869. **Management:** Carol Mulholland, General Manager. Jill Povolish, Advertising Manager. Linda Bird, Circulation Manager. **Editorial:** Mike Springton, Editor.

SPRINGFIELD

ILLINOIS TIMES. 1320 S. State St., Springfield, IL 62704. Telephone: 217-753-2226. FAX: 217-753-2281. E-MAIL: editor@illinoistimes.com. URL: http://www.illinoistimes.com. Year Established: 1975. Pub. Frequency: w. (Thu.) Page Size: tabloid. Subscrip. Rate: $75/yr mailed. Circulation: 30,000 per issue (paid and free). **Owner(s):** Yesse Communications, See address and contact information above. **Management:** Sharon Whalen, Publisher. Tauna King, Classified Adv. Mgr.. Beth Parkes-Irwin, Sales Manager. Sharon Whalen, Promotion Manager. **Editorial:** Fletcher Farrar, Editor.Readers: For adults 25-54

SPRINGFIELD SHOPPER. 2001 W. Monroe St., Springfield, IL 62704. Telephone: 217-546-3295. FAX: 217-546-3133. E-MAIL: classified@springfield-shopper.net. URL: http://www.springfield-shopper.net. Year Established: 1975. Pub. Frequency: w. (Thu.) Page Size: tabloid. Subscrip. Rate: $25/yr mailed. Adv. Rate: col. inch $12.50 Circulation: 32,300 per issue (paid and free). **Owner(s):** GateHouse Media, Inc, 3000 Dundee Rd., Ste. 203, Northbrook, IL 60062. Telephone: 847-272-2244. FAX: 847-272-6244. **Management:** Teri Hill, Advertising Manager. **Editorial:** Teri Hill, Editor.

ST. CHARLES

ADDISON/BENSENVILLE PRESS. 3755 E Main St, Ste 170, St. Charles, IL 60174-4712. Telephone: 630-513-5050. FAX: 630-513-6660. E-MAIL: rnovak@gatehousemedia.com. URL: http://www.mysuburbanlife.com. Year Established: 1953. Pub. Frequency: w. (Thu.) Page Size: tabloid. Subscrip. Rate: $1 newsstand/cover; $25/yr. Adv. Rate: col. inch $23 Circulation: 1,550 per issue (paid and free). **Owner(s):** GateHouse Media, Inc, 350 WillowBrook Office Park, Fairport, NY 14450. Telephone: 585-598-0030. FAX: 585-248-2631. **Management:** Caroll Stacklin, Publisher. Bill Casey, VP Advertising. Carrie Banas, Advertising Manager. John Novosel, Circulation Director. Loryn Hawkins, Classified Adv. Mgr..Readers: Local population

BATAVIA REPUBLICAN, THE. 3755 E Main St, Ste 170, St. Charles, IL 60174-4712. Telephone: 630-513-5050. FAX: 630-513-6660. E-MAIL: rnovak@gatehousemedia.com. URL: http://www.mysuburbanlife.com. Pub. Frequency: w. (Thu.) Page Size: tabloid. Subscrip. Rate: $1 newsstand/cover; $38/yr. Adv. Rate: col. inch $48 Circulation: 31,200 per issue (paid and free). **Owner(s):** GateHouse Media, Inc, 350 WillowBrook Office Park, Fairport, NY 14450. Telephone: 585-598-0030. FAX: 585-248-2631. **Management:** Caroll Stacklin, Publisher. Bill Casey, VP Advertising. Jim Ringness, Advertising Manager. John Novosel, Circulation Director. Loryn Hawkins, Classified Adv. Mgr..

FARMSIDE OF HUNTLEY/MARENGO/UNION, THE. 3755 E Main St, Ste 170, St. Charles, IL 60174-4712. Telephone: 630-513-5050. FAX: 630-513-6660. E-MAIL: rnovak@gatehousemedia.com. URL: http://www.mysuburbanlife.com. Year Established: 1961. Pub. Frequency: w. (Thu.) Page Size: tabloid.Subscrip. Rate: $1 newsstand/cover; $33/yr Circulation: 1,083 per issue (paid). **Owner(s):** GateHouse Media, Inc, 350 WillowBrook Office Park, Fairport, NY 14450. Telephone: 585-598-0030. FAX: 585-248-2631. **Management:** Caroll Stacklin, Publisher. Bill Casey, VP Advertising. Jim Ringness, Advertising Manager. John Novosel, Circulation Director. Loryn Hawkins, Classified Adv. Mgr..

GLENDALE HEIGHTS/BLOOMINGDALE PRESS. 3755 E Main St, Ste 170, St. Charles, IL 60174-4712. Telephone: 630-513-5050. FAX: 630-513-6660. E-MAIL: rnovak@gatehousemedia.com. URL: http://www.mysuburbanlife.com. Year Established: 1922. Pub. Frequency: w. (Fri.) Page Size: tabloid. Subscrip. Rate: $1 newsstand/cover; $38/yr. Adv. Rate: col. inch $23 Freelance Pay: $35-$100/article. Circulation: 10,000 per issue (paid and free). **Owner(s):** GateHouse Media, Inc, 350 WillowBrook Office Park, Fairport, NY 14450. Telephone: 585-598-0030. FAX: 585-248-2631. **Management:** Caroll Stacklin, Publisher. Bill Casey, VP Advertising. Jim Ringness, Advertising Manager. John Novosel, Circulation Director. Loryn Hawkins, Classified Adv. Mgr..

ROSELLE/ITASCA PRESS. 3755 E Main St, Ste 170, St. Charles, IL 60174-4712. Telephone: 630-513-5050. FAX: 630-513-6660. E-MAIL: rnovak@gatehousemedia.com. URL: http://www.mysuburbanlife.com. Pub. Frequency: w. (Fri.) Page Size: tabloid. Subscrip. Rate: $.75 newsstand/cover; $25/yr. Adv. Rate: col. inch $23 Circulation: 10,000 per issue (paid and free). **Owner(s):** GateHouse Media, Inc, 350 WillowBrook Office Park, Fairport, NY 14450. Telephone: 585-598-0030. FAX: 585-248-2631. **Management:** Caroll Stacklin, Publisher. Bill Casey, VP Advertising. Jim Ringness, Advertising Manager. John Novosel, Circulation Director. Loryn Hawkins, Classified Adv. Mgr..

ST. CHARLES REPUBLICAN, THE. 3755 E Main St, Ste 170, St. Charles, IL 60174-4712. Telephone: 630-513-5050. FAX: 630-513-6660. E-MAIL: rnovak@gatehousemedia.com. URL: http://www.mysuburbanlife.com. Pub. Frequency: w. (Thu.) Page Size: tabloid. Subscrip. Rate: $1 newsstand/cover; $38/yr local. Adv. Rate: col. inch $48 Circulation: 31,200 per issue (paid and free). **Owner(s):** GateHouse Media, Inc, 350 WillowBrook Office Park, Fairport, NY 14450. Telephone: 585-598-0030. FAX: 585-248-2631. **Management:** Caroll Stacklin, Publisher. Bill Casey, VP Advertising. Jim Ringness, Advertising Manager. John Novosel, Circulation Director. Loryn Hawkins, Classified Adv. Mgr..

WEST CHICAGO/WINFIELD/WARRENVILLE PRESS, THE. 3755 E Main St, Ste 170, St. Charles, IL 60174-4712. Telephone: 630-513-5050. FAX: 630-513-6660. URL: http://www.mysuburbanlife.com. Year Established: 1907. Pub. Frequency: w. (Thu.) Page Size: tabloid. Subscrip. Rate: $.75 newsstand/cover; $30/yr home delivery. Adv. Rate: col. inch $24 Circulation: 5,500 per issue (paid and free). **Owner(s):** GateHouse Media, Inc, 350 WillowBrook Office Park, Fairport, NY 14450. Telephone: 585-598-0030. FAX: 585-248-2631. **Management:** Caroll Stacklin, Publisher. Bill Casey, VP Advertising. Jim Ringness, Advertising Manager. John Novosel, Circulation Director. Loryn Hawkins, Classified Adv. Mgr..

ST. ELMO

SAINT ELMO BANNER. PO Box 10, St. Elmo, IL 62458. Telephone: 618-829-3246. Pub. Frequency: w. (Tue.) Page Size: tabloid. Subscrip. Rate: $.50 newsstand/cover; $18.75/yr in county; $21.75/yr elsewhere. Freelance Pay: $0.30/column-inch. Circulation: 900 per issue (paid). **Owner(s):** Greg Hoskins, See address and contact information above. **Management:** Barbara Barr, General Manager. **Editorial:** Clyde Barr, Editor.

STAUNTON

STAUNTON STAR TIMES. 108 W. Main St., Staunton, IL 62088. Telephone: 618-635-2000. FAX: 618-635-5281. E-MAIL: startime@madisontelco.com. URL: http://www.stauntonstartimes.com. Mailing Address: PO Box 180, Staunton, IL 62088-0180. Year Established: 1878. Pub. Frequency: w. (Wed.) Page Size: broadsheet. Subscrip. Rate: $.50 newsstand/cover; $19/yr mailed in county; $24/yr mailed out of county. Adv. Rate: col. inch $7.50 Circulation: 3,900 per issue (paid). **Owner(s):** Star Times Publishing Co., Inc., See address and contact information above. **Management:** Carol Haase, Publisher. Liz Sigafoos, Advertising Manager. **Editorial:** Carol Haase, Editor.

STEELEVILLE

STEELVILLE LEDGER. 108 N Sparta St, Steeleville, IL 62288. Telephone: 618-965-3417. FAX: 618-965-3548. Pub. Frequency: w. (Wed.) Page Size: broadsheet. Subscrip. Rate: $.35 newsstand/cover; $18/yr in county. Circulation: 603 per issue (paid). **Owner(s):** GateHouse Media, Inc, 350 WillowBrook Office Park, Fairport, NY 14450. Telephone: 585-598-0030. FAX: 585-248-2631. **Management:** Brent Easton, Publisher. **Editorial:** Dennis Cole, Editor.

STRONGHURST

HANCOCK COUNTY QUILL. 102 N. Broadway, Stronghurst, IL 61480. Telephone: 309-924-1871. FAX: 309-924-1212. Mailing Address: PO Box 149, Stronghurst, IL 61480-0149. Year Established: 1926. Pub. Frequency: w. (Wed.) Page Size: tabloid. Subscrip. Rate: $.60 newsstand/cover; $22/yr mailed in state; $23/yr mailed out of state. Circulation: 1,200 per issue (paid). **Owner(s):** Dessa Rodeffer, See address and contact information above. **Management:** Dessa Rodeffer, Publisher. Shirley Linder, Advertising Manager. Gloria Snyder, Marketing. **Editorial:** Dessa Rodeffer, Editor.

HENDERSON COUNTY QUILL. 102 N. Broadway, Stronghurst, IL 61480. Telephone: 309-924-1871. FAX: 309-924-1212. E-MAIL: quill@hcil.net. URL: http://www.quillnewspaper.com. Mailing Address: PO Box 149, Stronghurst, IL 61480-0149. Year Established: 1926. Pub. Frequency: w. (Wed.) Page Size: tabloid. Subscrip. Rate: $.60 newsstand/cover; $24/yr mailed in state; $25/yr mailed out of state. Circulation: 1,700 per issue (paid). **Owner(s):** Dessa Rodeffer, See address and contact information above. **Management:** Dessa Rodeffer, Publisher. Shirley Linder, Advertising Manager. **Editorial:** Dessa Rodeffer, Editor.

SULLIVAN

NEWS-PROGRESS. ISSN 0744-141X
100 W. Monroe St., Sullivan, IL 61951. Telephone: 217-728-7381. FAX: 217-728-2020. E-MAIL: newspro@advancenet.net. Year Established: 1961. Pub. Frequency: w. (Wed.) Page Size: broadsheet. Subscrip. Rate: $.60 newsstand/cover; $24.50/yr in county; $29.50/yr out of county. **Wire Service(s):** AP. Circulation: 4,000 per issue (paid). **Owner(s):** Marion E. Best, See address and contact information above. **Management:** R. R. Best, General Manager. Marion E. Best, President. Barry Morgan, Advertising Director. Carolyn Collier, Circulation Manager. **Editorial:** Krista Laiven, Managing Editor.

Weeklies

SUMNER

SUMNER PRESS. PO Box 126, Sumner, IL 62466. Telephone: 618-936-2212. FAX: 618-936-2858. E-MAIL: sumner.press@juno.com. URL: http://www.sumnerpress.com. Year Established: 1876. Pub. Frequency: w. (Thu.) Page Size: standard. Subscrip. Rate: $.35 newsstand/cover; $20/yr out of county; $17.50/yr in county. Circulation: 2,150 per issue (paid and free). **Owner(s):** J.C., Roscoe, Mary Ellen Cunningham, Inc., See address and contact information above. **Management:** J.C. Cunningham, Publisher. **Editorial:** Jo Ann Dowty, Editor.

SWANSEE

BELLEVILLE JOURNAL. 5050 Old Collinsville Rd, Swansee, IL 62226-2009. Telephone: 618-277-7000. FAX: 877-277-7018. URL: http://www.yourjournal.com. Pub. Frequency: s-w. (Wed. & Sun.) Page Size: broadsheet. Subscrip. Rate: $35/yr mailed. Circulation: 35,000 per issue (paid and free). **Owner(s):** Suburban Journals, 1714 Deer Tracks Trail, St. Louis, MO 63101. Telephone: 314-821-1110. **Management:** Steve Holt, Publisher. Theresa Willmann, Advertising Manager. John Ver Straten, Circulation Manager. **Editorial:** Tat Warner, Managing Editor. Scott Marion, Sports.

CAHOKIA-DUPO JOURNAL. 5050 Old Collinsville Rd, Swansee, IL 62226-2009. Telephone: 877-622-5050. FAX: 877-277-7018. URL: http://www.yourjournal.com. Year Established: 1969. Pub. Frequency: s-w. (Wed. & Sun.) Page Size: broadsheet. Subscrip. Rate: $38/yr mailed. Circulation: 13,000 per issue (paid and free). **Owner(s):** Suburban Journals, 1714 Deer Tracks Trail, St. Louis, MO 63101. Telephone: 314-821-1110. **Management:** Steve Holt, Publisher. Theresa Willmann, Advertising Manager. John Ver Straten, Circulation Manager. **Editorial:** Tat Warner, Managing Editor.

EAST ST. LOUIS JOURNAL. 5050 Old Collinsville Rd, Swansee, IL 62226-2009. Telephone: 877-622-5050. FAX: 877-277-7018. E-MAIL: twillmann@yourjournal.com. URL: http://www.yourjournal.com. Year Established: 1954. Pub. Frequency: w. (Wed.) Page Size: broadsheet. Circulation: 20,100 per issue (paid and free). **Owner(s):** Suburban Journals, 1714 Deer Tracks Trail, St. Louis, MO 63101. Telephone: 314-821-1110. **Management:** Steve Holt, Publisher. Theresa Willmann, Advertising Manager. John Ver Straten, Circulation Manager. **Editorial:** Tat Warner, Managing Editor.

FAIRVIEW HEIGHTS JOURNAL. 5050 Old Collinsville Rd, Swansee, IL 62226-2009. Telephone: 877-622-5050. FAX: 618-622-5057. URL: http://www.yourjournal.com. Pub. Frequency: s-w. (Wed. & Sun.) Page Size: broadsheet. Subscrip. Rate: $35/yr mailed. Circulation: 1,500 per issue (paid and controlled). **Owner(s):** Suburban Journals, 1714 Deer Tracks Trail, St. Louis, MO 63131. Telephone: 314-821-1110. FAX: 314-821-0745. **Management:** Steve Holt, Publisher. Theresa Willmann, Advertising Manager. John Ver Straten, Circulation Manager. **Editorial:** Tat Warner, Managing Editor. Scott Marion, Sports Editor.

SYCAMORE

GENOA JOURNAL. ISSN 1557-4806. 513 N State St, Sycamore, IL 60178. Telephone: 815-899-6397. FAX: 815-899-4329. E-MAIL: syc@shawnews.com. Year Established: 2005. Pub. Frequency: w. (Thu.) Subscrip. Rate: $.50 newsstand/cover; $33/yr mailed in county; $33/yr mailed out of county. **Owner(s):** Shaw Newspapers, 444 Pine Hill Dr., Dixon, IL 61021. Telephone: 815-284-2222. FAX: 815-254-9290. **Management:** John Rung, Publisher. Peter Shaw, Advertising Manager. **Editorial:** Clyde Hutchby, Editor. Paul Rock, Managing Editor.

HAMPSHIRE JOURNAL. 513 N State St, Sycamore, IL 60178. Telephone: 815-899-6397. FAX: 815-899-4329. E-MAIL: syc@shawnews.com. Year Established: 1894. Pub. Frequency: w. (Thu.) Page Size: broadsheet. Subscrip. Rate: $.50 newsstand/cover; $33/yr mailed in county; $45/yr mailed out of county. Freelance Pay: $15/article. Circulation: 4,000 per issue (paid). **Owner(s):** Shaw Newspapers, 444 Pine Hill Dr., Dixon, IL 61021. Telephone: 815-284-2222. **Management:** John Rung, Publisher. Peter Shaw, Advertising Manager. **Editorial:** Clyde Hutchby, Editor. Paul Rock, Managing Editor.

TEUTOPOLIS

TEUTOPOLIS PRESS. 107 E Main St, Teutopolis, IL 62467. Telephone: 217-857-3116. FAX: 217-857-3623. URL: http://www.gatehousemedia.com. Pub. Frequency: w. (Wed.) Page Size: broadsheet. Subscrip. Rate: $.50 newsstand/cover; $28/yr in county & adj. cys. Circulation: 1,006 per issue (paid). **Owner(s):** GateHouse Media, Inc, 350 WillowBrook Office Park, Fairport, NY 14450. Telephone: 585-598-0030. FAX: 585-248-2631. **Management:** Ray McGrew, Publisher. **Editorial:** Nancy Bence, Editor.

THOMSON

CARROLL COUNTY REVIEW. 809 Main St., Thomson, IL 61285-0369. Telephone: 815-259-2131. FAX: 815-259-3226. E-MAIL: ccreview@grics.net. Mailing Address: PO Box 369, Thomson, IL 61285-0369. Year Established: 1863. Pub. Frequency: w. (Wed.) Page Size: tabloid. Subscrip. Rate: $.75 newsstand/cover; $28/yr home delivery in county. Adv. Rate: col. inch $7.50 Circulation: 1,983 per issue (paid). **Owner(s):** Jonathan K. Whitney, PO Box 369, Thomson, IL 61285. Telephone: 815-259-2131. **Management:** Jonathan K. Whitney, Publisher. Nancy G. Whitney, Advertising Manager. **Editorial:** Bill Gengenbach, Editor.

TINLEY PARK

ALSIP-BLUE ISLAND STAR. 6901 W 159th St, Tinley Park, IL 60477. Telephone: 708-802-8800. FAX: 708-633-4859. Pub. Frequency: s-w. (Thu. & Sun.) Page Size: tabloid. Subscrip. Rate: $.50 newsstand/cover; $1 newsstand/cover Sun.; $41.08/yr home delivery; $81.64/yr mailed. **Owner(s):** Sun-Times Media Group, 350 N Orleans St, Ste 10-S, Chicago, IL 60654. Telephone: 312-321-2299. **Management:** Franklin Schuftan, Publisher. Rita Feigel, Advertising Manager. **Editorial:** Margaret Seltzer, Managing Editor. Alan Macey, Sports Editor.

COUNTRY CLUB HILLS-HAZEL CREST STAR. 6901 W 159th St, Tinley Park, IL 60477. Telephone: 708-802-8800. FAX: 708-633-4859. URL: http://www.countryclubhills.com. Pub. Frequency: s-w. (Thu. & Sun.) Page Size: tabloid. Subscrip. Rate: $.50 newsstand/cover; $1 newsstand/cover Sun.; $41.08/yr home delivery; $81.64/yr mailed. **Owner(s):** Sun-Times Media Group, 350 N Orleans St, Ste 10-S, Chicago, IL 60654. Telephone: 312-321-2299. **Management:** Franklin Schuftan, Publisher. Rita Feigel, Advertising Manager. **Editorial:** Margaret Seltzer, Managing Editor. Alan Macey, Sports Editor.

CRETE-UNIVERSITY PARK-BEECHER STAR. 6901 W 159th St, Tinley Park, IL 60477. Telephone: 708-802-8800. FAX: 708-633-4859. URL: http://www.starnewspapers.com. Pub. Frequency: s-w. (Thu. & Sun.) Page Size: tabloid. Subscrip. Rate: $.05 newsstand/cover; $1 newsstand/cover Sun.; $41.08/yr home delivery; $81.64/yr mailed. **Owner(s):** Sun-Times Media Group, 350 N Orleans St, Ste 10-S, Chicago, IL 60654. Telephone: 312-321-2299. **Management:** Franklin Schuftan, Publisher. Rita Feigel, Advertising Manager. **Editorial:** Margaret Seltzer, Managing Editor. Alan Macey, Sports Editor.

FRANKFORT-MOKENA STAR. 6901 W 159th St, Tinley Park, IL 60477. Telephone: 708-802-8800. FAX: 708-633-4859. Pub. Frequency: s-w. (Thu. & Sun.) Page Size: broadsheet. Subscrip. Rate: $.50 newsstand/cover; $1 newsstand/cover Sun.; $41.08/yr home delivery; $81.64/yr mailed in state. Circulation: 4,000 per issue (paid). **Owner(s):** Sun-Times Media Group, 350 N Orleans St, Ste 10-S, Chicago, IL 60654. Telephone: 312-321-2299. **Management:** Franklin Schuftan, Publisher. Rita Feigel, Advertising Manager. **Editorial:** Margaret Seltzer, Managing Editor. Alan Macey, Sports Editor.

HOMER GLEN-LOCKPORT-LEMON STAR. 6901 W 159th St, Tinley Park, IL 60477. Telephone: 708-802-8800. FAX: 708-633-4859. URL: http://www.suburbanchicagonews.com. Pub. Frequency: s-w. (Thu. & Sun.) Page Size: tabloid. Subscrip. Rate: $.50 newsstand/cover; $1 newsstand/cover Sun.; $41.08/yr home delivery; $81.64/yr mailed. **Owner(s):** Sun-Times Media Group, 350 N Orleans St, Ste 10-S, Chicago, IL 60654. Telephone: 312-321-2299. **Management:** Franklin Schuftan, Publisher. Rita Feigel, Advertising Manager. **Editorial:** Margaret Seltzer, Managing Editor. Alan Macey, Sports Editor.

HOMEWOOD-FLOSSMOORE-GLENWOOD-OLYMPIA FIELDS STAR. 6901 W 159th St, Tinley Park, IL 60477. Telephone: 708-802-8800. FAX: 708-633-4859. URL: http://www.starnewspapers.com. Pub. Frequency: s-w. (Thu. & Sun.) Page Size: tabloid. Subscrip. Rate: $.50 newsstand/cover; $1 newsstand/cover Sun.; $41.08/yr home delivery; $81.64/yr mailed. **Owner(s):** Sun-Times Media Group, 350 N Orleans St, Ste 10-S, Chicago, IL 60654. Telephone: 312-321-2299. **Management:** Franklin Schuftan, Publisher. Rita Feigel, Advertising Manager. **Editorial:** Margaret Seltzer, Managing Editor. Alan Macey, Sports Editor.

OAK FOREST-CRESTWOOD-MIDLOTHIAN STAR. 6901 W 159th St, Tinley Park, IL 60477. Telephone: 708-802-8800. FAX: 708-633-4859. URL: http://www.starnewspapers.com/oakforest/indexhtml. Pub. Frequency: s-w. (Thu. & Sun.) Page Size: tabloid. Subscrip. Rate: $.50 newsstand/cover; $1 newsstand/cover Sun.; $41.08/yr home delivery; $81.64/yr mailed. **Owner(s):** Sun-Times Media Group, 350 N Orleans St, Ste 10-S, Chicago, IL 60654. Telephone: 312-321-2299. **Management:** Franklin Schuftan, Publisher. Rita Feigel, Advertising Manager. **Editorial:** Margaret Seltzer, Managing Editor. Alan Macey, Sports Editor.

OAK LAWN-PALOS-WORTH TOWNSHIPS. 6901 W 159th St, Tinley Park, IL 60477. Telephone: 708-802-8800. FAX: 708-633-4859. URL: http://www.starnewspapers.com/oaklawn/indexhtml. Pub. Frequency: s-w. (Thu. & Sun.) Page Size: tabloid. Subscrip. Rate: $.50 newsstand/cover; $1 newsstand/cover Sun.; $41.08/yr home delivery; $81.64/yr mailed. **Owner(s):** Sun-Times Media Group, 350 N Orleans St, Ste 10-S, Chicago, IL 60654. Telephone: 312-321-2299. **Management:** Franklin Schuftan, Publisher. Rita Feigel, Advertising Manager. **Editorial:** Margaret Seltzer, Managing Editor. Alan Macey, Sports Editor.

ORLAND PARK-ORLAND HILLS. 6901 W 159th St, Tinley Park, IL 60477. Telephone: 708-802-8800. FAX: 708-633-4859. URL: http://www.starnewspapers.com. Year Established: 1989. Pub. Frequency: s-w. (Thu. & Sun.) Page Size: tabloid. Subscrip. Rate: $1, $.50 newsstand/cover; $41.08/yr home delivery in county; $81.64/yr mailed out of county. Adv. Rate: col. inch $17.86 Circulation: 1,374 per issue (paid). **Owner(s):** Sun-Times Media Group, 350 N Orleans St, Ste 10-S, Chicago, IL 60654. Telephone: 312-321-2299. **Management:** Franklin Schuftan, Publisher. Rita Feigel, Advertising Manager. **Editorial:** Margaret Seltzer, Managing Editor.

PARK FOREST-MATTESON-RICHTON PARK STAR. 6901 W 159th St, Tinley Park, IL 60477. Telephone: 708-802-8800. FAX: 708-633-4859. Pub. Frequency: s-w. (Thu. & Sun.) Page Size: tabloid. Subscrip. Rate: $.50 newsstand/cover; $1 newsstand/cover Sun.; $41.08/yr home delivery; $81.64/yr mailed. **Owner(s):** Sun-Times Media Group, 350 N Orleans St, Ste 10-S, Chicago, IL 60654. Telephone: 312-321-2299. **Management:** Franklin Schuftan, Publisher. Rita Feigel, Advertising Manager. **Editorial:** Margaret Seltzer, Managing Editor. Alan Macey, Sports Editor.

PENNY SAVER (TINLEY PARK), THE. 6901 W. 159th St., Tinley Park, IL 60477. Year Established: 1965. Pub. Frequency: w. (Tue.) Page Size: tabloid Circulation: 300,000 per issue (free). **Owner(s):** Midwest Suburban Publishing, Inc., See address and contact information above. **Management:** Boni Fine, President. John Doolin, Advertising Manager. Terry Kandle, Circulation Manager.

SOUTH HOLLAND-THORTON TOWNSHIP STAR. 6901 W 159th St, Tinley Park, IL 60477. Telephone: 708-802-8800. FAX: 708-633-4859. URL: http://www.starnewspapers.com. Pub. Frequency: s-w. (Thu. & Sun.) Page Size: tabloid. Subscrip. Rate: $.50 newsstand/cover; $1 newsstand/cover Sun.; $41.05/yr home delivery; $81.64/yr mailed. **Owner(s):** Sun-Times Media Group, 350 N Orleans St, Ste 10-S, Chicago, IL 60654. Telephone: 312-321-2299. **Management:** Franklin Schuftan, Publisher. Rita Feigel, Advertising Manager. **Editorial:** Margaret Seltzer, Managing Editor. Alan Macey, Sports Editor.

TINLEY PARK STAR. 6901 W 159th St, Tinley Park, IL 60477. Telephone: 708-802-8800. FAX: 708-633-4859. URL: http://www.thesuntimesnewsgroup.com. Pub. Frequency: s-w. (Thu. & Sun.) Page Size: standard. Subscrip. Rate: $.50 newsstand/cover; $1 newsstand/cover Sun.; $41.08/yr home delivery; $81.64/yr mailed. Circulation: 38,870 per issue (paid); 39,626 Sunday (paid). **Owner(s):** Sun-Times Media Group, 350 N Orleans St, Ste 10-S, Chicago, IL 60654. Telephone: 312-321-2299. **Management:** Franklin Schuftan, Publisher. Rita Feigel, Advertising Manager. **Editorial:** Margaret Seltzer, Managing Editor. Alan Macey, Sports Editor.

TRENTON

TRENTON SUN. 15 W. Broadway, Trenton, IL 62293-1303. Telephone: 618-224-9422. FAX: 618-224-2646. E-MAIL: sybil@trentonsun.net. URL: http://www.trentonsun.net. Mailing Address: PO Box 118, Trenton, IL 62293-0118. Year Established: 1880. Pub. Frequency: w. (Wed.) Page Size: broadsheet. Subscrip. Rate: $.50 newsstand/cover; $21/yr in county; $35/yr out of county. Adv. Rate: col. inch $3.80 Circulation: 1,750 per issue (paid). **Owner(s):** Sybil & Michael Conley, See address and contact information above. **Management:** Michael L. Conley, Publisher. Sybil Conley, Advertising. **Editorial:** Michael L. Conley, Editor.

TUSCOLA

TUSCOLA REVIEW. 115 W. Sale St., Tuscola, IL 61953. Telephone: 217-253-2358. FAX: 217-253-3265. E-MAIL: rhastings@tuscolanews.net. Mailing Address: PO Box 350, Tuscola, IL 61953-0350. Year Established: 1875. Pub. Frequency: w. (Tue.) Page Size: broadsheet. Subscrip. Rate: $.50 newsstand/cover; $25/yr mailed in county; $30/yr mailed out of county. Adv. Rate: col. inch $4 Circulation: 3,600 per issue (paid). **Owner(s):** Downstate News Group, See address and contact information above. **Management:** Brian Timpone, Publisher. Randy H. Hastings, Advertising Manager.

VANDALIA

LEADER-UNION, THE. 229 S. Fifth St., Vandalia, IL 62471. Telephone: 618-283-3374. FAX: 618-283-0977. E-MAIL: leader@fginet.com. URL: http://www.leaderunion.com. Mailing Address: PO Box 315, Vandalia, IL 62471. Year Established: 1865. Pub. Frequency: s-w. (Wed. & Fri.) Page Size: broadsheet. Subscrip. Rate: $.50 newsstand/cover; $34/yr mailed in county; $49.95/yr mailed in state; $61/yr mailed out of state. Adv. Rate: col. inch $7.30 Circulation: 5,300 per issue (paid). **Owner(s):** Landmark Community Newspapers, Inc., PO Box 549, Shelbyville, KY 40065. Telephone: 502-633-2526. **Management:** David R. Bell, Publisher. Linda Poninski, Advertising Manager. LaTisha Paslay, Circulation Manager. **Editorial:** Rich Bauer, Managing Editor. Katie Thaman, Feature Editor. Chris Stalter, Sports Editor.

VIENNA

VIENNA TIMES, THE. 305 W. Main, Vienna, IL 62995. Telephone: 618-658-4321. FAX: 618-658-4322. Year Established: 1882. Pub. Frequency: w. (Thu.) Page Size: broadsheet. Subscrip. Rate: $.50 newsstand/cover; $26/yr in county. Adv. Rate: col. inch $5.06 Circulation: 2,800 per issue (paid). **Owner(s):** Donald L. Sanders, See address and contact information above. **Management:** Donald L. Sanders, Publisher. **Editorial:** Donald L. Sanders, Editor.

WASHBURN

HERALD (WASHBURN), THE. 614 N. E. Jefferson St., Washburn, IL 61570. Telephone: 309-367-2335. FAX: 309-367-2616. E-MAIL: herald@mtco.com. Mailing Address: P.O. Box 490, Washburn, IL 61570. Pub. Frequency: w. (Thu.) Page Size: broadsheet. Subscrip. Rate: $.75 newsstand/cover; $25/yr in county; $27/yr out of county. Circulation: 2,500 per issue (paid). **Owner(s):** Scott Hubbel, See address and contact information above. **Management:** Scott Hubbel, Publisher. **Editorial:** Scott Hubell, Editor. Scott Hubbel, Sports Editor.

WASHBURN LEADER. 614 N. E. Jefferson St., Washburn, IL 61570. Telephone: 309-367-2335. FAX: 309-367-2616. E-MAIL: herald@mtco. Mailing Address: P.O. Box 490, Washburn, IL 61570. Year Established: 1892. Pub. Frequency: w. (Thu.) Page Size: broadsheet. Subscrip. Rate: $.75 newsstand/cover; $25/yr in county; $27/yr out of county. Circulation: 925 per issue (paid). **Owner(s):** Scott Hubbel, See address and contact information above. **Management:** Scott Hubbel, Publisher. **Editorial:** Scott Hubell, Editor. Scott Hubbel, Production Manager.

WASHINGTON

WASHINGTON COURIER. 100 Ford Ln., Washington, IL 61571. Telephone: 309-444-3139. FAX: 309-444-8505. E-MAIL: haglnews1@mteo.com. Mailing Address: PO Box 349, Washington, IL 61571. Year Established: 1958. Pub. Frequency: w. (Wed.) Page Size: tabloid. Subscrip. Rate: $34/yr home delivery local. Adv. Rate: col. inch $11.98 Circulation: 8,500 per issue (paid and free). **Owner(s):** Hagel Publications, Inc., See address and contact information above. **Management:** Roger Hagel, Publisher. **Editorial:** Joi DeArmond, Editor.

WOODFORD COURIER. 100 Ford Ln., Washington, IL 61571. Telephone: 309-444-3139. FAX: 309-444-8505. E-MAIL: haglnews@mtco.com. Mailing Address: PO Box 349, Washington, IL 61571. Pub. Frequency: w. (Wed.) Page Size: tabloid. Subscrip. Rate: $.50 newsstand/cover; $34.50/yr. Adv. Rate: col. inch $8.55 Circulation: 3,400 per issue (paid). **Owner(s):** Hagel Publications, Inc., See address and contact information above. **Management:** Roger Hagel, Publisher. **Editorial:** Joi DeArmond, Editor.

WATERLOO

REPUBLIC-TIMES. 114 Main St., Waterloo, IL 62298. Telephone: 618-939-3814. FAX: 618-939-3815. E-MAIL: rtsales2@htc.net. URL: http://www.republic-times.com. Mailing Address: P.O. Box 147, Waterloo, IL 62298. Year Established: 1844. Pub. Frequency: w. (Wed.) Page Size: broadsheet. Subscrip. Rate: $.50 newsstand/cover; $22/yr in county; $27/yr out of county; $35/yr out of state. Adv. Rate: col. inch $8.50 Circulation: 4,500 per issue (paid). **Owner(s):** Breese Publishing Co., 8060 Old Hwy. 50, Breese, IL 62230. Telephone: 618-526-7211. FAX: 618-526-2590. **Management:** Lynn Venhaus, Publisher. **Editorial:** Lynn Venhaus, Editor.

WAUKEGAN

ANTIOCH REVIEW. 2383 N. Delany Rd., Waukegan, IL 60087. Telephone: 847-599-6900. FAX: 847-599-6902. E-MAIL: display@pioneerlocal.com. URL: http://www.pioneerlocal.com. Year Established: 1998. Pub. Frequency: w. (Thu.) Page Size: tabloid. Subscrip. Rate: $1 newsstand/cover; $21.95/yr in county; $51.95/yr out of county. Adv. Rate: col. inch $19.57 Circulation: 1,920 per issue (paid). **Owner(s):** Pioneer Press, Inc., 3701 W. Lake Ave., Glenview, IL 60025. Telephone: 847-486-9200. **Management:** Peggy Cunniff, Advertising Director. **Editorial:** Michael Bivona, Managing Editor. Dorothy Andries, Entertainment Editor. David Sweet, Group Editor.

DEERFIELD REVIEW. ISSN 1084-7952
2383 N. Delany Rd., Waukegan, IL 60087. Telephone: 847-599-6900. FAX: 847-599-6902. URL: http://www.pioneerlocal.com. Year Established: 1924. Pub. Frequency: w. (Thu.) Page Size: tabloid. Subscrip. Rate: $1 newsstand/cover; $39.95/yr in county; $51.95/yr out of county. Adv. Rate: col. inch $22.71 Circulation: 4,852 per issue (paid). **Owner(s):** Pioneer Press, Inc., 3701 W. Lake Ave., Glenview, IL 60025. Telephone: 847-486-9200. FAX: 847-496-7454. **Management:** Peggy Cunniff, Advertising Director. **Editorial:** Arnold Grahl, Managing Editor. David Sweet, Group Editor.

GRAYSLAKE REVIEW. 2383 N. Delany Rd., Waukegan, IL 60087. Telephone: 847-599-6900. FAX: 847-599-6902. E-MAIL: lake@pioneerlocal.com. URL: http://www.pioneerlocal.com. Year Established: 1989. Pub. Frequency: w. (Thu.) Page Size: tabloid. Subscrip. Rate: $1 newsstand/cover; $21.95/yr in county; $51.95/yr out of county. Adv. Rate: col. inch $19.57 Circulation: 3,081 per issue (paid). **Owner(s):** Pioneer Press, Inc., 3701 W. Lake Ave., Glenview, IL 60025. Telephone: 847-486-9200. **Management:** Peggy Cunniff, Advertising Director. **Editorial:** Michael Bivona, Managing Editor. Dorothy Andries, Entertainment Editor. David Sweet, Group Editor.

GURNEE REVIEW. 2383 N. Delany Rd., Waukegan, IL 60087. Telephone: 847-599-6900. FAX: 847-599-6902. E-MAIL: display@pioneerlocal.com. URL: http://www.pioneerlocal.com. Year Established: 1989. Pub. Frequency: w. (Thu.) Page Size: tabloid. Subscrip. Rate: $1 newsstand/cover; $21.95/yr in county; $51.95/yr out of county. Adv. Rate: col. inch $19.57 Circulation: 3,844 per issue (paid). **Owner(s):** Pioneer Press, Inc., 3701 W. Lake Ave., Glenview, IL 60025. Telephone: 847-486-9200. **Management:** Peggy Cunniff, Advertising Director. **Editorial:** Michael Bivona, Managing Editor. Dorothy Andries, Entertainment Editor. David Sweet, Group Editor.

HIGHLAND PARK NEWS. 2383 N. Delany Rd., Waukegan, IL 60087. Telephone: 847-599-6900. FAX: 847-599-6902. E-MAIL: lake@pioneerlocal.com. URL: http://www.pioneerlocal.com. Year Established: 1924. Pub. Frequency: w. (Thu.) Page Size: tabloid. Subscrip. Rate: $1 newsstand/cover; $39.95/yr in county; $51.95/yr out of county. Adv. Rate: col. inch $22.71 Circulation: 7,541 per issue (paid). **Owner(s):** Pioneer Press, Inc., 3701 W. Lake Ave., Glenview, IL 60025. Telephone: 847-486-9200. **Management:** Peggy Cunniff, Advertising Director. **Editorial:** David Sweet, Managing Editor.

LAKE FORESTER. ISSN 0744-7973
2383 N. Delany Rd., Waukegan, IL 60087. Telephone: 847-599-6900. FAX: 847-599-6902. E-MAIL: display@pioneerlocal.com. URL: http://www.pioneerlocal.com. Year Established: 1895. Pub. Frequency: w. (Thu.) Page Size: tabloid. Subscrip. Rate: $1 newsstand/cover; $39.95/yr in county; $51.95/yr out of county. Adv. Rate: col. inch $22.71 Circulation: 6,718 per issue (paid). **Owner(s):** Pioneer Press, Inc., 3701 W. Lake Ave., Glenview, IL 60025. Telephone: 847-486-9200. **Management:** Peggy Cunniff, Advertising Director. **Editorial:** David Sweet, Managing Editor.

LAKE VILLA/LINDENHURST REVIEW. 2383 N. Delany Rd., Waukegan, IL 60087. Telephone: 847-599-6900. FAX: 847-599-6902. E-MAIL: display@pioneerlocal.com. URL: http://www.pioneerlocal.com. Year Established: 1989. Pub. Frequency: w. (Thu.) Page Size: tabloid. Subscrip. Rate: $1 newsstand/cover; $21.95/yr in county; $51.95/yr out of county. Adv. Rate: col. inch $19.57 Circulation: 2,121 per issue (paid). **Owner(s):** Pioneer Press, Inc., 3701 W. Lake Ave., Glenview, IL 60025. Telephone: 847-486-9200. **Management:** Peggy Cunniff, Advertising Director. **Editorial:** Michael Bivona, Managing Editor. Dorothy Andries, Entertainment Editor. David Sweet, Group Editor.

LIBERTYVILLE REVIEW. ISSN 0744-852X
2383 N. Delany Rd., Waukegan, IL 60087. Telephone: 847-599-6900. FAX: 847-599-6902. E-MAIL: display@pioneerlocal.com. URL: http://www.pioneerlocal.com. Year Established: 1895. Pub. Frequency: w. (Thu.) Page Size: tabloid. Subscrip. Rate: $1 newsstand/cover; $39.95/yr in county; $51.95/yr out of county. Adv. Rate: col. inch $22.71 Circulation: 6,718 per issue (paid). **Owner(s):** Pioneer Press, Inc., 3701 W. Lake Ave., Glenview, IL 60025. Telephone: 847-486-9200. **Management:** Peggy Cunniff, Advertising Director. **Editorial:** Jim Powers, Managing Editor. Dorothy Andries, Entertainment Editor. David Sweet, Group Editor.

LINCOLNSHIRE REVIEW. 2383 N. Delany Rd., Waukegan, IL 60087. Telephone: 847-599-6900. FAX: 847-599-6902. E-MAIL: display@pioneerlocal.com. URL: http://www.pioneerlocal.com. Year Established: 2000. Pub. Frequency: w. (Thu.) Page Size: tabloid. Subscrip. Rate: $1 newsstand/cover; $39.95/yr in county; $51.95/yr out of county. Adv. Rate: col. inch $22.71 Circulation: 1,254 per issue (paid). **Owner(s):** Pioneer Press, Inc., 3701 W. Lake Ave., Glenview, IL 60025. Telephone: 847-486-9200. **Management:** Peggy Cunniff, Advertising Director. **Editorial:** Arnold Grahl, Managing Editor. David Sweet, Group Editor.

MUNDELEIN REVIEW. 2383 N. Delany Rd., Waukegan, IL 60087. Telephone: 847-599-6900. FAX: 847-599-6902. E-MAIL: display@pioneerlocal.com. URL: http://www.pioneerlocal.com. Year Established: 1981. Pub. Frequency: w. (Thu.) Page Size: tabloid. Subscrip. Rate: $1 newsstand/cover; $21.95/yr in county; $51.95/yr out of county. Adv. Rate: col. inch $17.86 Circulation: 2,283 per issue (paid). **Owner(s):** Pioneer Press, Inc., 3701 W. Lake Ave., Glenview, IL 60025. Telephone: 847-486-9200. **Management:** Peggy Cunniff, Advertising Director. **Editorial:** Jim Powers, Managing Editor. Dorothy Andries, Entertainment Editor. David Sweet, Group Editor.

VERNON HILLS REVIEW. 2383 N. Delany Rd., Waukegan, IL 60087. Telephone: 847-599-6900. FAX: 847-599-6902. E-MAIL: display@pioneerlocal.com. URL: http://www.pioneerlocal.com. Year Established: 1972. Pub. Frequency: w. (Thu.) Page Size: tabloid. Subscrip. Rate: $1 newsstand/cover; $21.95/yr in county; $51.95/yr out of county. Adv. Rate: col. inch $17.86 Circulation: 2,180 per issue (paid). **Owner(s):** Pioneer Press, Inc., 3701 W. Lake Ave., Glenview, IL 60025. Telephone: 847-486-9200. **Management:** Peggy Cunniff, Advertising Director. **Editorial:** Jim Powers, Managing Editor. Dorothy Andries, Entertainment Editor. David Sweet, Group Editor.

WAVERLY

WAVERLY JOURNAL. 130 S. Pearl St., Waverly, IL 62692. Telephone: 217-435-9221. FAX: 217-435-4511. Year Established: 1872. Pub. Frequency: w. (Fri.) Page Size: tabloid. Subscrip. Rate: $.50 newsstand/cover; $24/yr mailed in state (effective 2005); $28/yr mailed out of state. Adv. Rate: col. inch $3 Circulation: 1,577 per issue (paid). **Owner(s):** Nancy Copelin, See address and contact information above. **Management:** Nancy Copelin, Publisher. Julie A. Springer, Advertising Manager. **Editorial:** Julie A. Springer, Editor.

WEST FRANKFORT

FRANKLIN PRESS (WEST FRANKFORT). 111 S. Emma St., West Frankfort, IL 62896. Telephone: 618-932-2146. FAX: 618-937-6006. URL: http://www.gatehousemedia.com. Mailing Address: PO Box 617, West Frankfort, IL 62896. Pub. Frequency: w. (Sat.) Page Size: tabloid Circulation: 5,650 per issue (free). **Owner(s):** GateHouse Media, Inc, 350 WillowBrook Office Park, Fairport, NY 14450. Telephone: 585-598-0030. **Management:** Lynn Kidd, Publisher. Diann Walthes, Advertising Manager. Pat Hampton, Circulation Manager.

S I TRADER. 111 S. Emma St., West Frankfort, IL 62896. Telephone: 800-642-3564. FAX: 618-937-2958. Mailing Address: PO Box 617, West Frankfort, IL 62896. Pub. Frequency: w. (Fri.) Page Size: tabloid. Subscrip. Rate: $1.50 newsstand/cover; $62.40 mailed 3rd class; $273 mailed 1st class. Circulation: 25,169 per issue (paid). **Owner(s):** GateHouse Media, Inc, 350 WillowBrook Office Park, Fairport, NY 14450. Telephone: 585-598-0030. FAX: 585-248-2631. **Management:** Lynn Kidd, Publisher. Sherry Claycame, Advertising. Kathy Stubblefield, Classified Adv. Mgr..

WILMINGTON

BRAIDWOOD JOURNAL, THE. 111 S. Water St., Wilmington, IL 60481. Telephone: 815-476-7966. FAX: 815-476-7002. E-MAIL: fpnnews@cabcast.com. URL: http://www.freepressnewspapers.com. Year Established: 1958. Pub. Frequency: w. (Wed.) Page Size: broadsheet. Subscrip. Rate: $.75 newsstand/cover; $34/yr in county; $40/yr out of county; $45/yr out of state. Adv. Rate: col. inch $8 Circulation: 1,310 per issue (paid). **Owner(s):** G.W. Communications, Inc., See address and contact information above. **Management:** Eric Fisher, Publisher. **Editorial:** Pam Monson, Editor. Eric Fisher, Managing Editor.

COAL CITY COURANT. 111 S. Water St., Wilmington, IL 60481. Telephone: 815-476-7966. FAX: 815-476-7002. E-MAIL: fpnnews@cabcast.com. URL: http://www.freepressnewspapers.com. Year Established: 1903. Pub. Frequency: w. (Wed.) Page Size: broadsheet. Subscrip. Rate: $.75 newsstand/cover; $34/yr in county grundy & will cys; $40/yr in state; $45/yr out of state. Adv. Rate: col. inch $8 Circulation: 2,360 per issue (paid). **Owner(s):** G.W. Communications, Inc., See address and contact information above. **Management:** Eric Fisher, Publisher. **Editorial:** Janet Fisher, Managing Editor.

FREE PRESS ADVOCATE. 111 S. Water St., Wilmington, IL 60481. Telephone: 815-476-7966. FAX: 815-476-7002. E-MAIL: fpnnews@cabcast.com. URL: http://www.freepressnewspapers.com. Year Established: 1870. Pub. Frequency: w. (Wed.) Page Size: broadsheet. Subscrip. Rate: $.75 newsstand/cover; $34/yr in county; $40/yr out of county; $45/yr mailed out of state. Adv. Rate: col. inch $8 Circulation: 2,425 per issue (paid). **Owner(s):** G.W. Communications, Inc., See address and contact information above. **Management:** Eric Fisher, Publisher. **Editorial:** Eric Fisher, Managing Editor.

PRAIRIE SHOPPER (WILMINGTON), THE. 111 S. Water St., Wilmington, IL 60481. Telephone: 815-476-7966. FAX: 815-476-7002. E-MAIL: Fpnnews@cabcast.com. URL: http://www.freepressnewspapers.com. Year Established: 1982. Pub. Frequency: w. (Mon.) Page Size: broadsheet.Adv. Rate: col. inch $12 Circulation: 17,912 per issue (free). Owner(s): G.W. Communications, Inc., See address and contact information above. Management: Eric Fisher, Publisher. Editorial: Eric Fisher, Managing Editor.

WOODSTOCK

WOODSTOCK INDEPENDENT, THE. 671 E. Calhoun St., Woodstock, IL 60098. Telephone: 815-338-8040. FAX: 815-338-8177. E-MAIL: pressrelease@inde-news.com. URL: http://www.inde-news.com. Year Established: 1987. Pub. Frequency: w. (Wed.) Page Size: tabloid. Subscrip. Rate: $1 newsstand/cover; $33/yr local. Freelance Pay: $50/article. Circulation: 3,300 per issue (paid). Owner(s): Cheryl B. Wormley & Paul Wormley, See address and contact information above. Management: Paul Wormley, President. Cheryl B. Wormley, Publisher. Marjorie Moore, Advertising Manager.

WORDEN

MADISON COUNTY CHRONICLE. 125 E. Wall St., Worden, IL 62097-0490. Telephone: 618-459-3655. FAX: 618-459-3655. Mailing Address: PO Box 490, Worden, IL 62097-0490. Year Established: 1978. Pub. Frequency: w. (Thu.) Page Size: tabloid. Subscrip. Rate: $.30 newsstand/cover; $16/yr in county; $17/yr out of county; $20/yr out of state. Adv. Rate: col. inch $3.30 Circulation: 1,200 per issue (paid). Owner(s): Bunker Hill Publishing Co., 150 N. Washington, Bunker Hill, IL 62014. Telephone: 618-585-4411. Management: John M. Galer, President. Courtney Wood, Advertising Manager. Editorial: Vera Eckhardt, Managing Editor.

YORKVILLE

FOX VALLEY SHOPPING NEWS, THE. 110 Countryside Pkwy., Ste. C, Yorkville, IL 60560. Telephone: 630-553-7431. FAX: 630-553-0310. E-MAIL: lmelhouse@scn1.com. Mailing Address: PO Box 609, Yorkville, IL 60560. Year Established: 1873. Pub. Frequency: w. (Wed.) Page Size: tabloid.Subscrip. Rate: $48/yr mailed elsewhere Circulation: 35,000 per issue (paid). Owner(s): Suburban Chicago Newspapers, 3101 N. Rte. 30, Plainfield, IL 60544. Telephone: 815-439-5300. Management: Dick Whitfield, General Manager. Bill Hardecopf, Advertising Manager. Editorial: Dick Whitfield, Editor.

KENDALL COUNTY RECORD. 222 S. Bridge St., Yorkville, IL 60560. Telephone: 630-553-7034. FAX: 630-553-7085. E-MAIL: jfarren290@aol.com. Year Established: 1864. Pub. Frequency: w. (Thu.) Page Size: tabloid. Subscrip. Rate: $.50 newsstand/cover; $24/yr mailed in county; $31/yr mailed out of county. Circulation: 4,650 per issue (paid). Owner(s): Jeff & Kathy Farren, See address and contact information above. Management: Jeff Farren, Publisher. Kristin Hawkins, Advertising Manager. Jeff Farren, Circulation Manager. Editorial: Kathy Farren, Editor.

ZION

BARGAINEER. 2711 Sheridan Rd, Unit 202, Zion, IL 60099. Telephone: 847-746-9000. FAX: 847-746-9150. Pub. Frequency: w. (Tue.) Page Size: broadsheet. Freelance Pay: $1.15/column-inch. Circulation: 39,000 per issue (paid). Owner(s): United Communications Corp., 5800 Seventh Ave., Kenosha, WI 53140. Telephone: 262-657-1000. FAX: 262-656-1255. Management: Frank Misareli, Publisher. B T Adams, Advertising. Anthony Decesaro, Circulation Manager. Editorial: Mona Shannon, Editor.

ZION-BENTON NEWS. 2711 Sheridan Rd, Unit 202, Zion, IL 60099. Telephone: 847-746-9000. FAX: 847-746-9150. E-MAIL: zion@kenoshanews.com. Mailing Address: PO Box 111, Zion, IL 60099. Year Established: 1929. Pub. Frequency: w. (Thu.) Page Size: tabloid. Subscrip. Rate: $.75 newsstand/cover; $32.95/yr mailed in county; $34.95/yr mailed out of county. Circulation: 3,000 per issue (paid). Owner(s): United Communications Corp., 5800 Seventh Ave., Kenosha, WI 53141. Telephone: 262-657-1000. Management: Frank Misareli, Publisher. B T Adams, Advertising. Anthony Decesaro, Circulation Manager. Editorial: Mona Shannon, Editor.

INDIANA
ATTICA

MESSENGER (ATTICA), THE. 113 S. Perry St., Attica, IN 47918. Telephone: 765-762-2411. FAX: 765-762-2163. Pub. Frequency: w. (Tue.) Page Size: broadsheet.Adv. Rate: col. inch $10.65 Circulation: 11,621 per issue (free). Owner(s): Community Media Group, Inc, PO Box 10, West Frankfort, IL 62896. Telephone: 618-937-6412. Management: Nancy Mickle, Office Manager. Greg Willhite, Advertising Manager. Editorial: Jared Jernagan, Managing Editor.

NEIGHBOR, THE.   ISSN 1556-9144
113 S. Perry St., Attica, IN 47918. Telephone: 765-762-2411. FAX: 765-762-2163. E-MAIL: editor@k-inc.com. URL: http://www.fountaincountyneighbor.com. Year Established: 1851. Pub. Frequency: w. (Wed.) Page Size: broadsheet. Subscrip. Rate: $1 newsstand/cover; $42/yr in county; $54/yr out of county. Adv. Rate: col. inch $6 Circulation: 2,158 per issue (paid and free). Owner(s): Community Media Group, Inc, PO Box 10, West Frankfort, IL 62896. Telephone: 618-937-6412. Management: Nancy Mickle, Office Manager. Greg Willhite, Advertising Manager. Editorial: Jared Jernagan, Managing Editor.

REVIEW-REPUBLICAN, THE. 113 S. Perry St., Attica, IN 47918. E-MAIL: revrep@sbcglobal.net. URL: http://newsbug.info/williamsport_review_republican. Mailing Address: PO Box 216, Williamsport, IN 47993. Year Established: 1914. Pub. Frequency: w. (; Thu.) Page Size: standard. Subscrip. Rate: $1.25 newsstand/cover; $42/yr in county; $54/yr out of county. Adv. Rate: col. inch $8.95 Circulation: 2,400 per issue (paid). Owner(s): Community Media Group, Inc, PO Box 10, West Frankfort, IL 62896. Telephone: 618-937-6412. Management: Don Hurd, Publisher. Greg Wilhite, Classified Adv. Mgr.. Editorial: Jane Jernagan, Editor.Readers: General population

AURORA

JOURNAL-PRESS. 414 Third St., Aurora, IN 47001. Telephone: 812-926-0063. FAX: 812-537-5576. E-MAIL: regpub@seieata.com. Mailing Address: PO Box 59, Aurora, IN 47001. Year Established: 1858. Pub. Frequency: w. (Tue.) Page Size: broadsheet. Subscrip. Rate: $.75 newsstand/cover; $26/yr in county; $37/yr mailed in OH & KY; $64/yr mailed elsewhere. Adv. Rate: col. inch $9.20 Circulation: 6,183 per issue (paid). Owner(s): Delphos Newspapers, 405 N. Main St., Delphos, OH 45833. Telephone: 419-695-0015. Management: Joe Awad, Publisher. Janet Essert, Advertising Manager. Editorial: Erika Schmidt Russell, Editor. Jim Buchberger, Sports Editor.

AVON

HENDRICKS COUNTY FLYER.   ISSN 0193-4910
8109 Kingston St., Ste. 500, Avon, IN 46123. Telephone: 317-272-5800. FAX: 317-272-5887. E-MAIL: flyer@flyergroup.com. URL: http://www.flyergroup.com. Year Established: 1965. Pub. Frequency: d. (Tue.-Sat.) Page Size: broadsheet. Subscrip. Rate: $.50 newsstand/cover; $52/yr carrier delivery in county; $225/yr mailed in state. Circulation: 43,000 per issue (paid and free). Owner(s): Community Newspaper Holdings, Inc., 3500 Colonnade Pkwy., Ste. 600, Birmingham, AL 35243. Telephone: 205-298-7100. FAX: 205-298-7101. Management: Harold Allen, Publisher. Bill Jarchow, Advertising Director. Dawn Carman, Circulation Manager. Editorial: Kathy Linton, Managing Editor. Brent Glasgow, Sports.

WESTSIDE FLYER. 8109 Kingston St., Ste. 500, Avon, IN 46123. Telephone: 317-272-5800. FAX: 317-272-5887. E-MAIL: flyer@flyergroup.com. URL: http://www.flyergroup.com. Year Established: 1993. Pub. Frequency: w. (Mon.) Page Size: broadsheet. Subscrip. Rate: $.50 newsstand/cover; $25/yr carrier delivery in county. Circulation: 43,000 per issue (paid and free). Owner(s): Community Newspaper Holdings, Inc., 3500 Colonnade Pkwy., Ste. 600, Birmingham, AL 35243. Telephone: 205-298-7100. Management: Harold Allen, Publisher. Bill Jarchow, Advertising Director. Dawn Carman, Circulation Manager. Annette Burcharts, Classified Adv. Mgr.. Editorial: Kathy Linton, Editor. Brent Glasgow, Sports.

BATESVILLE

HERALD-TRIBUNE.   ISSN 0746-2042
701 Tekulve Rd., Batesville, IN 47006. Telephone: 812-934-4343. FAX: 812-934-6406. E-MAIL: herald@seidata.com. URL: http://www.batesvilleheraldtribune.com. Mailing Address: PO Box 89, Batesville, IN 47006. Year Established: 1890. Pub. Frequency: s-w. (Tue. & Fri.) Page Size: broadsheet. Subscrip. Rate: $.75 newsstand/cover; $48/yr carrier delivery local; $52/yr mailed in county. Circulation: 4,000 per issue (paid). Owner(s): Community Newspaper Holdings, Inc., 3500 Colonnade Pkwy., Ste. 600, Birmingham, AL 35243. Telephone: 205-298-7100. FAX: 205-298-7101. Management: Peter Van Baalen, Publisher. Bonnie Motz, Advertising. Laura Welborn, Advertising Director. Sue Gillespie, Circulation Manager. Editorial: Bryan Helvie, Managing Editor. Debbie Blank, Assistant Editor.

BEECH GROVE

SOUTHSIDE TIMES. 301 Main St., Beech Grove, IN 46107. Telephone: 317-787-3291. FAX: 317-787-3325. E-MAIL: news@ss-times.com. URL: http://www.ss-times.com. Year Established: 1928. Pub. Frequency: w. (Thu.) Page Size: broadsheet Circulation: 21,500 per issue (free). Owner(s): Times Leader Publications LLC, See address and contact information above. Management: Roger Huntzinger, Publisher. Eric Moore, Advertising. Editorial: Sara Gentry, Editor.

BERNE

BERNE TRI-WEEKLY NEWS. 153 S. Jefferson St., Berne, IN 46711. Telephone: 219-589-2101. FAX: 260-589-8614. E-MAIL: canderson@adamswells.com. URL: http://www.bernetriweekly.com. Year Established: 1896. Pub. Frequency: 3/w. (Mon., Wed., Fri.) Page Size: standard. Subscrip. Rate: $.50 newsstand/cover; $49.95/yr. Adv. Rate: col. inch $5 Circulation: 3,000 per issue (paid). Owner(s): EP Graphics, See address and contact information above. Management: Clint Anderson, General Manager. John Muselman, President. Carl H. Muselman, Publisher. Kay Bower, Office Manager. Jessica Smith, Advertising Manager. Editorial: Kim Permor, News Editor.

BOONVILLE

BOONVILLE STANDARD, THE. 204 W. Locust St., Boonville, IN 47601. Telephone: 812-897-2330. FAX: 812-897-3703. E-MAIL: newsroom@warricknews.com. URL: http://www.tristate-media.com. Mailing Address: PO Box 266, Boonville, IN 47601. Year Established: 1875. Pub. Frequency: w. (Wed.) Page Size: broadsheet. Subscrip. Rate: $.75 newsstand/cover; $30/yr in county; $40/yr mailed in state; $50/yr mailed out of state. Freelance Pay: $0.40/column-inch. Circulation: 4,000 per issue (paid). Owner(s): Brehm Communications, Inc., 16644 W. Bernardo Dr., Ste. 300, San Diego, CA 92127. Telephone: 858-451-6200. Management: Gary Neal, Publisher. Byran Marshall, Advertising Director. Karen Monks, Circulation Manager. Debbie Whitaker, Classified Adv. Mgr.. Editorial: Nathan Blackford, Editor.

WARRICK EAST. 204 W. Locust St., Boonville, IN 47601. Telephone: 812-897-2330. FAX: 812-897-3703. Mailing Address: PO Box 266, Boonville, IN 47601. Pub. Frequency: d. (w. We) Page Size: broadsheet Circulation: 4,000 per issue (free). Owner(s): Brehm Communications, inc, 16644 W. Bernardo Dr., Ste. 300, San Diego, CA 92127. Telephone: 619-451-6200. FAX: 858-451-3814. Management: Gary Neal, Publisher. Byran Marshall, Advertising Director. Karen Monks, Circulation Manager. Debbie Whitaker, Classified Adv. Mgr.. Editorial: Nathan Blackford, Editor.

BOURBON

BOURBON NEWS-MIRROR. 208 N Main St, Bourbon, IN 46504. Telephone: 574-342-5143. FAX: 574-342-3002. E-MAIL: bnmnews@kconline.com. URL: http://www.thepilotnews.com. Pub. Frequency: w. (Wed.) Page Size: standard. Subscrip. Rate: $.50 newsstand/cover; $21/yr mailed in state; $26/yr mailed out of state. Circulation: 1,600 per issue (paid). Owner(s): Horizon Publications, Inc., 1120 N. Carbon St, Ste 100, Marion, IL 62959. Management: Rick A. Kreps, Publisher. Cindy Stockton, Advertising Manager. James Radican, Circulation Manager. Editorial: Angela Perkins, Editor.

BREMEN

BREMEN ENQUIRER, THE. 126 E Plymouth St, Bremen, IN 46506. Telephone: 574-546-2941. FAX: 574-546-5170. E-MAIL: enquirer@fourway.net. URL: http://www.thepilotnews.com. Pub. Frequency: w. (Wed.) Page Size: standard. Subscrip. Rate: $.50 newsstand/cover; $21/yr mailed in state; $26/yr mailed out of state. Circulation: 1,500 per issue (paid). Owner(s): Horizon Publications, Inc., 1120 N. Carbon St, Ste 100, Marion, IL 62959. Management: Rick A. Kreps, Publisher. Cindy Stockton, Advertising Manager. James Radican, Circulation Manager. Editorial: Holly Heller, Editor. Maggie Nixon, Managing Editor.

BROOKVILLE

BROOKVILLE AMERICAN. PO Box 38, Brookville, IN 47012. Telephone: 765-647-4221. FAX: 765-647-4811. E-MAIL: ww-pub@cnz.com. Year Established: 1832. Pub. Frequency: w. (Wed.) Page Size: broadsheet. Subscrip. Rate: $.50 newsstand/cover; $18/yr mailed. Circulation: 6,250 per issue (paid). Owner(s): Whitewater Publications, See address and contact information above. Management: Gary Wolf, President. Becky Trammell, Advertising Manager. Donna Minton, Classified Adv. Mgr.. Editorial: John Estridge, Managing Editor. Andy Sallee, Sports.

BROOKVILLE DEMOCRAT. PO Box 38, Brookville, IN 47012. Telephone: 765-647-4221. FAX: 765-647-4811. E-MAIL: ww-pub@cnz.com. Pub. Frequency: w. (Wed.) Page Size: broadsheet.Subscrip. Rate: $.50 newsstand/cover; $18/yr Circulation: 4,500 per issue (paid). **Owner(s):** Whitewater Publications, See address and contact information above. **Management:** Gary Wolf, President. Becky Trammell, Advertising Manager. Donna Minton, Classified Adv. Mgr..

BROWNSTOWN

JACKSON COUNTY BANNER, THE.   ISSN 1055-775X
116 E. Cross St., Brownstown, IN 47220. Telephone: 812-358-2111. FAX: 812-358-5606. E-MAIL: banner@hsonline.net. URL: http://www.thebanner.com. Mailing Address: PO Box G, Brownstown, IN 47220. Year Established: 1869. Pub. Frequency: s-w. (Mon. & Thu.) Page Size: broadsheet. Subscrip. Rate: $.50 newsstand/cover; $47/yr mailed in county & adj. cys.; $52/yr mailed in state; $58/yr mailed out of state. Adv. Rate: col. inch $8.45 **Wire Service(s):** AP. Circulation: 2,600 per issue (paid). **Owner(s):** Community Media Group, Inc, PO Box 10, West Frankfort, IL 62896. Telephone: 618-937-6412. **Management:** Patricia Robertson, General Manager. Helen Nolting, Advertising Manager. **Editorial:** Larry Morris, Editor. Steven Crawford, Sports.

CAMBRIDGE CITY

WESTERN WAYNE NEWS. 120 W. Main St., Cambridge City, IN 47327. Telephone: 765-478-5448. FAX: 317-478-5155. E-MAIL: wwnews@firstbankconnect.com. Year Established: 1991. Pub. Frequency: w. (Wed.) Page Size: tabloid. Subscrip. Rate: $.50 newsstand/cover; $16/yr in county; $20/yr out of county; $24/yr out of state. Adv. Rate: col. inch $4 Circulation: 2,600 per issue (paid). **Owner(s):** Janis Buhl, See address and contact information above. **Management:** Janis Buhl, Publisher.

CHARLESTOWN

LEADER (CHARLESTOWN), THE. PO Box 382, Charlestown, IN 47111. Telephone: 812-967-3176. FAX: 812-256-3377. URL: http://www.gbpnews.com. Year Established: 1919. Pub. Frequency: w. (Wed.) Page Size: tabloid.Subscrip. Rate: $18.50/yr Circulation: 13,150 per issue (free). **Owner(s):** Green Banner Publications, See address and contact information above. **Management:** Joe Green, General Manager. John Roberts, Advertising Manager. Heather Marlman, Art Director. **Editorial:** Mark Grigsby, Managing Editor. Janna Ross, Associate Editor.

CLAY CITY

CLAY CITY, THE. 717 Main St, PO Box 38, Clay City, IN 47841. Telephone: 812-939-2163. FAX: 812-939-2286. Year Established: 1912. Pub. Frequency: w. (Wed.) Subscrip. Rate: $.35 newsstand/cover; $16/yr **Owner(s):** The Clay City, See address and contact information above. **Management:** John A Gillaspy, General Manager. Kim Howell, Advertising. **Editorial:** John A Gillaspy, Editor.

CORYDON

CLARION NEWS (CORYDON). 301 N. Capitol Ave., Corydon, IN 47112. Telephone: 812-738-4552. FAX: 812-738-1909. E-MAIL: clarionnews@seidata.com. Year Established: 1930. Pub. Frequency: w. (Wed.) Page Size: standard. Subscrip. Rate: $.50 newsstand/cover; $24/yr mailed elsewhere. Circulation: 15,000 per issue (free). **Owner(s):** O'Bannon Publishing Co., Inc., See address and contact information above. **Management:** Jon O'Bannon, Publisher. Jan Crosby, Advertising Manager. Betty Andriot, Circulation Manager. **Editorial:** Chris Adam, Managing Editor.

CORYDON DEMOCRAT. 301 N. Capitol Ave., Corydon, IN 47112. Telephone: 812-738-2211. FAX: 812-738-1909. E-MAIL: democrat@seidata.com. URL: http://www.corydondemocrat.com. Year Established: 1856. Pub. Frequency: w. (Wed.) Page Size: broadsheet. Subscrip. Rate: $1 newsstand/cover; $30/yr mailed in cy. & adj. cys.; $25/yr mailed to senior citizens; $36/yr mailed in IN & KY; $46/yr mailed elsewhere in IN & KY. Circulation: 8,100 per issue (paid). **Owner(s):** O'Bannon Publishing Co., Inc., See address and contact information above. **Management:** Jon O'Bannon, Publisher. Mark Young, Advertising. Betty Andriot, Circulation Manager. **Editorial:** Randy West, Editor.

CROTHERSVILLE

CROTHERSVILLE TIMES. 570 Moore St., Crothersville, IN 47229. Telephone: 812-793-2188. FAX: 812-793-2188. E-MAIL: ctimes@hsonline.net. URL: http://www.crothersville.net/times. Mailing Address: PO Box 141, Crothersville, IN 47229-0141. Year Established: 1980. Pub. Frequency: w. (Wed.) Page Size: tabloid. Subscrip. Rate: $.40 newsstand/cover; $18/yr mailed in county; $30/yr mailed out of area. Circulation: 1,200 per issue (paid). **Owner(s):** Curt & Mary A. Kovener, See address and contact information above. **Management:** Mary A. Kovener, President. Curt Kovener, Publisher. **Editorial:** Curt Kovener, Editor-in-Chief.

CROWN POINT

CROWN POINT STAR. 112 W. Clark St., Crown Point, IN 46307. Telephone: 219-663-4212. FAX: 219-663-0137. E-MAIL: star shopperl@post-trib.com. Mailing Address: PO Box 419, Crown Point, IN 46308. Year Established: 1857. Pub. Frequency: w. (Thu.) Page Size: broadsheet. Subscrip. Rate: $.50 newsstand/cover; $26/yr mailed in state; $32/yr mailed out of state. Freelance Pay: $0.75/column-inch. Circulation: 4,000 per issue (paid and free). **Owner(s):** Sun-Times Media Group, 350 N Orleans St, Ste 10-S, Chicago, IL 60654. Telephone: 312-321-2299. **Management:** Murdoch L. Davis, Publisher. Shirley Knanga, Circulation Manager. **Editorial:** Andy Steele, Managing Editor. Kitty Conley, Feature Editor.

CULVER

CULVER CITIZEN. 110 N Main St, Culver, IN, 46511. E-MAIL: citizen@culcom.net. URL: http://www.thepilotnews.com. Year Established: 1894. Pub. Frequency: w. (Wed.) Page Size: broadsheet. Subscrip. Rate: $.50 newsstand/cover; $21/yr in state; $26/yr out of state. Circulation: 1,600 per issue (paid). **Owner(s):** Horizon Publications, Inc., 1120 N. Carbon St, Ste 100, Marion, IL 62959. **Management:** Rick A. Kreps, Publisher. Cindy Stockton, Advertising Manager. James Radican, Circulation Manager. **Editorial:** Dee Grenert, Editor.

DALE

SPENCER COUNTY LEADER. 218 East Medcalf St, Dale, IN 47523-9040. Mailing Address: PO Box 38, Ferdinand, IN 47532. Year Established: 1960. Pub. Frequency: w. (Thu.) Page Size: broadsheet. Subscrip. Rate: $.50 newsstand/cover; $25/yr local; $37.50/yr in state; $48/yr mailed out of state. Circulation: 2,050 per issue (paid). **Owner(s):** Dubois-Spencer County Publishing, Inc., See address and contact information above. **Management:** Miriam Ash, Advertising Manager. Paul Ash, Circulation Manager. **Editorial:** Kathy Tretter, Editor.

DANVILLE

REPUBLICAN (HENDRICKS), THE. 6 E. Main St., Danville, IN 46122. Telephone: 317-745-2777. FAX: 317-745-2777. E-MAIL: therepublican@sbcglobal.net. Mailing Address: PO Box 149, Danville, IN 46122-0149. Year Established: 1847. Pub. Frequency: w. (Thu.) Page Size: standard. Subscrip. Rate: $.50 newsstand/cover; $20/yr mailed in county. Adv. Rate: col. inch $5 Circulation: 1,600 per issue (paid). **Owner(s):** Betty J. Weesner, See address and contact information above. **Management:** Betty J. Weesner, Publisher. **Editorial:** Betty J. Weesner, Editor.

DEMOTTE

KANKAKEE VALLEY POST-NEWS. 827 S Halleck St, Demotte, IN 46310. Telephone: 219-987-5111. FAX: 219-987-5119. Mailing Address: PO Box 110, Demotte, IN 46310-0110. Pub. Frequency: w. (Thu.) Page Size: broadsheet. Subscrip. Rate: $1 newsstand/cover; $47/yr in county; $52/yr out of county. Circulation: 2,200 per issue (paid). **Owner(s):** Community Media Group, Inc, PO Box 10, West Frankfort, IL 62896. Telephone: 618-937-6412. **Management:** Don Hurd, Publisher. **Editorial:** Cindy Ward, Editor.

ELLETTSVILLE

JOURNAL (ELLETTSVILLE), THE. 211 N. Sale St., Ellettsville, IN 47429. Telephone: 812-876-2254. FAX: 812-876-2853. Year Established: 1939. Pub. Frequency: w. (Wed.) Page Size: standard. Subscrip. Rate: $16/yr; $.30 newsstand/cover. Freelance Pay: $0.50-$1/column-inch. Circulation: 2,000 per issue (paid). **Owner(s):** John T. Gillaspy, See address and contact information above. **Management:** John T Gillaspy, Publisher. Ranee Brown-Mounce, Advertising Manager. **Editorial:** Tom Douglas, Editor. Steve Sturgeon, Sports.

FAIRMOUNT

NEWS-SUN. 122 S. Main St., Fairmount, IN 46928-1923. Telephone: 765-948-4165. Year Established: 1872. Pub. Frequency: w. (Wed.) Page Size: tabloid. Subscrip. Rate: $.25 newsstand/cover; $54/yr mailed 3rd class. Adv. Rate: col. inch $6 Circulation: 4,400 per issue (paid and free). **Owner(s):** Allen Terhune & Associates, See address and contact information above. **Management:** Jim Terhune, Publisher. **Editorial:** Jim Terhune, Editor.

FERDINAND

FERDINAND NEWS, THE. 113 West 6th St, Ferdinand, IN 47532-9517. E-MAIL: ferdnews@psci.net. Mailing Address: PO Box 38, Ferdinand, IN 47532. Year Established: 1906. Pub. Frequency: w. (Wed.) Page Size: broadsheet. Subscrip. Rate: $.50 newsstand/cover; $27/yr local; $37.50/yr in state; $48/yr mailed out of state. Circulation: 3,100 per issue (paid). **Owner(s):** Dubois-Spencer County Publishing, Inc., See address and contact information above. **Editorial:** Kathy Tretter, Editor.

FISHERS

DAILY LEDGER (FISHERS). 13095 Publishers Dr., Fishers, IN 46038. Telephone: 317-773-1210. FAX: 317-773-3872. E-MAIL: Letters@topics.com. Mailing Address: PO Box 1478, Noblesville, IN 46061. Year Established: 1888. Pub. Frequency: s-w. (Tue. & Fri.) Page Size: broadsheet. Subscrip. Rate: $.50 newsstand/cover; $1 carrier delivery/wk.; $13. **Wire Service(s):** AP. Circulation: 12,000 evening (paid). **Owner(s):** Gannett Company, Inc., 7950 Jones Branch Dr., McLean, VA 22107-0001. Telephone: 703-854-6000. **Management:** Tom Jekel, Publisher. Jack Stoner, Sales Manager. **Editorial:** Leslie Collins, Managing Editor. Ted Schultz, Sports Editor.

GEIST TOPICS/NORTHEAST EDITION. 13095 Publishers Dr., Fishers, IN 46038. Telephone: 317-444-5500. FAX: 317-444-5530. URL: http://www.topics.com. Mailing Address: PO Box 1478, Noblesville, IN 46060-7478. Year Established: 1961. Pub. Frequency: w. (Wed.) Page Size: broadsheet. Circulation: 2,000 per issue (paid and free). **Owner(s):** Gannett Company, Inc., 7950 Jones Branch Dr., McLean, VA 22107-0001. Telephone: 703-854-6000. **Management:** Tom Jekel, General Manager. David Lewis, Publisher. Jack Stoner, Advertising Manager. Mick Siemers, Circulation Manager. Felicia Hence, Classified Adv. Mgr..

NOBLESVILLE LEDGER, THE. 13095 Publishers Dr., Fishers, IN 46038. Telephone: 317-773-1210. FAX: 317-773-3872. E-MAIL: topic@1net.direct.net. URL: http://www.thenobelsvilleledger.com. Mailing Address: PO Box 1478, Noblesville, IN 46061-7478. Year Established: 1978. Pub. Frequency: s-w. (Tue & Fri.) Page Size: broadsheet. Subscrip. Rate: $20/yr mailed. **Wire Service(s):** AP. Circulation: 4,338 per issue (paid and free). **Owner(s):** Gannett Company, Inc., 7950 Jones Branch Dr., McLean, VA 22107-0001. Telephone: 703-854-6000. **Management:** Tom Jekel, Publisher. Jay Fredrickson, Advertising Manager. Mick Siemers, Circulation Manager.

NORTH SIDE TOPICS. 13095 Publishers Dr., Fishers, IN 46038. Telephone: 317-444-5500. FAX: 317-444-5530. E-MAIL: topic@1net.direct.net. Mailing Address: PO Box 1478, Noblesville, IN 46060-7478. Year Established: 1922. Pub. Frequency: w. (Wed.) Page Size: broadsheet. Subscrip. Rate: $20/yr mailed. **Wire Service(s):** UPI. Circulation: 18,891 per issue (paid and free). **Owner(s):** Gannett Company, Inc., 7950 Jones Branch Dr., McLean, VA 22107-0001. Telephone: 703-854-6000. **Management:** David Lewis, Publisher. Jay Fredrickson, Advertising Director. Mick Siemers, Circulation Manager. **Editorial:** Tom Jekel, Editor-in-Chief.

NORTHWEST TOPICS. 13095 Publishers Dr., Fishers, IN 46038. Telephone: 317-444-5500. FAX: 317-444-5530. E-MAIL: letters@topics.com. URL: http://www.topics.com. Year Established: 1969. Pub. Frequency: w. (Thu.) Page Size: broadsheet. Subscrip. Rate: $20/yr mailed. Circulation: 17,750 per issue (paid and free). **Owner(s):** Gannett Company, Inc., 7950 Jones Branch Dr., McLean, VA 22107-0001. Telephone: 703-854-6000. **Management:** Tom Jekel, General Manager. **Editorial:** Ted Schultz, Sports Editor.

FLORA

CARROLL COUNTY COMET. 14 E. Main St., Flora, IN 46929-0026. Telephone: 574-967-4135. FAX: 574-967-3384. E-MAIL: editor@carrollcountycomet.com. URL: http://www.carrollcountycomet.com. Mailing Address: PO Box 26, Flora, IN 46929. Year Established: 1974. Pub. Frequency: w. (Wed.) Page Size: broadsheet. Subscrip. Rate: $1 newsstand/cover; $30/yr local. Adv. Rate: col. inch $9.70 Circulation: 4,800 per issue (paid). **Owner(s):** Carroll Papers, Inc., See address and contact information above. **Management:** Joseph L. Moss, Publisher. **Editorial:** Susan Scholl, Editor.

FOWLER

BENTON REVIEW, THE. 102 E. Fifth St., Fowler, IN 47944-0527. Telephone: 765-884-1902. FAX: 765-884-8110. E-MAIL: bentonreview@sbcglobel.net. Year Established: 1875. Pub. Frequency: w. (Wed.) Page Size: broadsheet. Subscrip. Rate: $.50 newsstand/cover; $21/yr in county; $24/yr out of county. Adv. Rate: col. inch $2.50 Circulation: 3,450 per issue (paid). **Owner(s):** Benton Review Newspaper, See address and contact information above. **Management:** Don Moyars, General Manager. Karen Moyars, Publisher. Sheila Cain, Office Manager. **Editorial:** Karen Moyars, Editor. Don Moyars, Outdoor Editor.

FRENCH LICK

SPRINGS VALLEY HERALD. PO Box 311, French Lick, IN 47432. Telephone: 812-936-9630. FAX: 812-936-9559. E-MAIL: svh@bluemarble.net. Year Established: 1903. Pub. Frequency: w. (Wed.) Page Size: broadsheet. Subscrip. Rate: $.50 newsstand/cover; $22.95/yr home delivery out of county; $29.95/yr out of county. Adv. Rate: col. inch $3.50 Circulation: 3,000 per issue (paid and free). **Owner(s):** Art Hampton, See address and contact information above. **Management:** Art Hampton, President. Malissa Wiseman, Advertising. **Editorial:** Dennis Ellis, Editor.

GARY

GARY CRUSADER. ISSN 1930-7012
1549 Broadway, Gary, IN 46407. Telephone: 219-885-4357. FAX: 219-883-3317. E-MAIL: crusaderil@aol.com. Pub. Frequency: w. (Thu.) Page Size: tabloid. Subscrip. Rate: $.25 newsstand/cover; $20/yr; $36 for 2 yrs.. Circulation: 36,373 per issue (paid). **Owner(s):** Dorothy R. Leavell, See address and contact information above. **Management:** Dorothy R. Leavell, Publisher. John Smith, Advertising Manager. **Editorial:** Dorothy R. Leavell, Editor. David Denson, Managing Editor.

INFO (GARY). 4800 W. Fifth Ave., Gary, IN 46401. Telephone: 219-977-9710. FAX: 219-977-8120. Mailing Address: PO Box 64587, Gary, IN 46401. Year Established: 1963. Pub. Frequency: w. (Thu.) Page Size: tabloid. Subscrip. Rate: $.35 newsstand/cover; $16/yr local; $30/yr out of county. Adv. Rate: col. inch $14.91 Circulation: 27,000 per issue (paid). **Owner(s):** Info Printing & Publishing, Inc., See address and contact information above. **Management:** Imogene Harris, Publisher. Huston Pugh, Advertising Manager. **Editorial:** Imogene Harris, Editor.

GOSHEN

PAPER (ELKHART COUNTY EDITION), THE. 134 S. Main St., Goshen, IN 46526. Telephone: 574-534-2591. FAX: 219-533-4820. Year Established: 1973. Pub. Frequency: w. (Tue.) Page Size: tabloid.Adv. Rate: col. inch $9.15 Circulation: 33,550 per issue (free). **Owner(s):** The Papers, Inc., 206 S. Main St, Milford, IN 46542. Telephone: 574-658-4111. FAX: 574-658-4701. **Management:** Ronald Baumgartner, Publisher. Kip Schumm, Advertising Manager. Suzanne Robinson, Circulation Manager. **Editorial:** Jeri Seely, Editor.

GREENFIELD

IMAGE (GREENFIELD). 119 W. North St., Greenfield, IN 46140-0602. Telephone: 317-462-7368. FAX: 317-462-7779. E-MAIL: indysuburbanimage@cnhiindiana.com. URL: www.imagenews.com. Mailing Address: PO Box 602, Greenfield, IN 46140-0602. Year Established: 1999. Pub. Frequency: w. (Thu.) Page Size: tabloid Circulation: 25,000 per issue (free). **Owner(s):** Community Newspaper Holdings, Inc., 3500 Colonnade Pkwy., Ste. 600, Birmingham, AL 35243. Telephone: 205-298-7100. **Management:** Debbie Yozipovich, Publisher. Jeanie Cole, Advertising Manager. Dawn Harmon, Circulation Manager. **Editorial:** Debbie Yozipovich, Editor. David Marlowe, Production Manager.

GREENWOOD

FRANKLIN CHALLENGER. ISSN 8750-7390
400 E Main St, Greenwood, IN 46143. E-MAIL: news@indychallenger.com. Year Established: 1984. Pub. Frequency: w. (Thu.) Page Size: tabloid. Subscrip. Rate: $.50 newsstand/cover; $25/yr mailed. Adv. Rate: col. inch $12 Circulation: 3,150 per issue (paid). **Owner(s):** Greenwood Newspapers, Inc., PO Box 708, Greenwood, IN 46143. Telephone: 317-888-3376. FAX: 317-888-3377. **Management:** Kelly R. Chambers, President. Doug L. Chambers, Publisher. **Editorial:** Doug L. Chambers, Editor-in-Chief.

GREENWOOD & SOUTHSIDE CHALLENGER. ISSN 1068-6673
400 E Main St, Greenwood, IN 46143. E-MAIL: news@indychallenger.com. URL: http://www.challengernewspapers.com. Year Established: 1972. Pub. Frequency: w. (Wed.) Page Size: tabloid. Subscrip. Rate: $.50 newsstand/cover; $25/yr; $35/yr out of state. Adv. Rate: col. inch $12 Circulation: 4,275 per issue (paid). **Owner(s):** Greenwood Newspapers, Inc., PO Box 708, Greenwood, IN 46143. Telephone: 317-888-3376. FAX: 317-888-3377. **Management:** Kelly R. Chambers, President. Doug L. Chambers, Publisher. **Editorial:** Doug L. Chambers, Editor-in-Chief.

HAGERSTOWN

HAGERSTOWN EXPONENT, THE. 35 W. Main St., Hagerstown, IN 47346-1214. Telephone: 765-489-4035. FAX: 765-489-5323. E-MAIL: hagersexpo@verizon.com. Year Established: 1875. Pub. Frequency: w. (Wed.) Page Size: broadsheet. Subscrip. Rate: $.60 newsstand/cover; $24.50/yr. Adv. Rate: col. inch $4.75 Circulation: 6,550 per issue (paid and free). **Owner(s):** Hagerstown Newspapers, Inc., See address and contact information above. **Management:** David Quinn, Publisher. Katherine Hopper, Office Manager.

HAMMOND

CALUMET PRESS, THE. ISSN 1075-6981
6405 Olcott, Hammond, IN 46320. Telephone: 219-844-1230. FAX: 219-989-8516. E-MAIL: philip@calumetpress.com. Year Established: 1957. Pub. Frequency: w. (Wed.) Page Size: tabloid.Subscrip. Rate: $54/yr mailed Circulation: 42,000 per issue (free). **Owner(s):** Jim Dedlow, See address and contact information above. **Management:** Jim Dedlow, Publisher. **Editorial:** Jim Dedlow, Editor.

HOPE

HOPE STAR-JOURNAL. PO Box 65, Hope, IN 47246. E-MAIL: news@hopestarjournal.com. URL: http://www.hopestarjournal.com. Year Established: 1912. Pub. Frequency: w. (Thu.) Page Size: broadsheet. Subscrip. Rate: $.50 newsstand/cover; $25/yr in county; $30/yr out of county. Adv. Rate: col. inch $6.50 Circulation: 1,000 per issue (paid). **Owner(s):** Larry Simpson, Tony Davich, 308 Jackson St, Hope, IN 47246. **Management:** Larry Simpson, Publisher. **Editorial:** Larry Simpson, Editor.Readers: Area residents of all ages

INDIANAPOLIS

EAST SIDE HERALD. 4309 E. Michigan St., Indianapolis, IN 46201. Telephone: 317-356-2487. FAX: 317-356-5871. URL: http://www.essnnews.com. Year Established: 1968. Pub. Frequency: w. (Fri.) Page Size: broadsheet.Adv. Rate: col. inch $22.75 Circulation: 20,000 per issue (free). **Owner(s):** Phoenix Publishing, Inc., See address and contact information above. **Management:** Connie Hammond, Publisher. **Editorial:** Connie Hammond, Editor.

EAST SIDE HERALD, THE. 4309 E Michigan St, Box 11042, Indianapolis, IN 46201. E-MAIL: ethelwinslow@essn.com. URL: http://www.essnnews.com.Year Established: 1935 Pub. Frequency: w. Circulation: 32,500 (free). **Owner(s):** East Side Communication Corp., See address and contact information above. **Editorial:** Tom Jekel, Editor.

ESSN'S INOY HERALD WEEKLY. 4309 E. Michigan St., Indianapolis, IN 46201. Telephone: 317-356-2487. FAX: 317-356-5871. E-MAIL: essnnews@aol.com. URL: http://www.essnnews.com. Year Established: 1935. Pub. Frequency: w. (Fri.) Page Size: broadsheet.Adv. Rate: col. inch $22.75 Circulation: 32,500 per issue (free). **Owner(s):** Phoenix Publications, Inc., See address and contact information above. **Management:** Connie Hammond, Publisher. **Editorial:** Ethel Winslow, Editor.

INDIANAPOLIS RECORDER. 2901 N. Tacoma Ave., Indianapolis, IN 46218. Telephone: 317-924-5143. FAX: 317-921-6653. E-MAIL: newsroom@indyrecorder.com. URL: http://www.indianapolisrecorder.com. Year Established: 1895. Pub. Frequency: w. (Fri.) Page Size: broadsheet. Subscrip. Rate: $.75 newsstand/cover; $39/yr. Adv. Rate: col. inch $30 **Wire Service(s):** AP. Circulation: 13,300 per issue (paid and free). **Owner(s):** William Mays, See address and contact information above. **Management:** Carolene Mays, President. Leroy Lewis, Advertising Manager. Angie Kuhn, Circulation Manager. **Editorial:** Shannon Williams, Editor.

NORTHEAST HERALD, THE. 4309 E. Michigan St., Indianapolis, IN 46201. Telephone: 317-356-2487. FAX: 317-356-5871. URL: http://www.essnnews.com. Year Established: 1966. Pub. Frequency: w. (Fri.) Page Size: broadsheet.Adv. Rate: col. inch $22.75 Circulation: 5,000 per issue (free). **Owner(s):** Phoenix Publications, Inc., See address and contact information above. **Management:** Connie Hammond, Publisher. **Editorial:** Connie Hammond, Editor.

NUVO. 3951 N. Meridian St., Ste. 200, Indianapolis, IN 46208. Telephone: 317-254-2400. FAX: 317-254-2405. E-MAIL: nuvo@nuvo.net. URL: http://www.nuvo.net. Year Established: 1990. Pub. Frequency: w. (Wed.) Page Size: tabloid. Subscrip. Rate: $52/yr mailed. Freelance Pay: $0.10/word. Circulation: 48,000 per issue (paid and free). **Owner(s):** Kevin McKinney, See address and contact information above. **Management:** Kevin K. McKinney, Publisher. Dave Wicting, Circulation Manager. **Editorial:** Kevin K. McKinney, Editor-in-Chief. Jim Poyser, Managing Editor. David Hoppe, Art Editor. Terry Kirts, Food Editor. Leslie Benson, Music Editor. Laura McPhee, News Editor.

SPOTLIGHT (INDIANAPOLIS), THE. 4217 S. Meridian St, Indianapolis, IN 46217. Telephone: 317-444-4554. FAX: 317-788-4570. E-MAIL: spotlight@indyweb.net. URL: http://www.indyspotlight.com. Year Established: 1939. Pub. Frequency: w. (Wed.) Page Size: broadsheet. Subscrip. Rate: $50/yr mailed 1st class. Adv. Rate: col. inch $10 Circulation: 25,000 per issue (paid and free). **Owner(s):** Gannett Company, Inc., 7950 Jones Branch Dr., McLean, VA 22102. **Management:** Tom Jekel, General Manager. **Editorial:** Rosalyn Dumarel, Editor.

KENTLAND

BROOK REPORTER, THE. 305 E Graham St, Kentland, IN 47951. Telephone: 219-474-5532. FAX: 219-474-5354. Mailing Address: PO Box 107, Kentland, IN 47951-0107. Pub. Frequency: w. (Wed.) Page Size: broadsheet. Subscrip. Rate: $1 newsstand/cover; $38/yr mailed in county; $46/yr mailed out of county. Circulation: 200 per issue (paid). **Owner(s):** Community Media Group, Inc, PO Box 10, West Frankfort, IL 62896. Telephone: 618-937-6412. **Management:** Don Hurd, Publisher. Randy Pruden, Advertising Manager. **Editorial:** Cheri Glancy, Managing Editor.

ENTERPRISE (KENTLAND), THE. 305 E Graham St, Kentland, IN 47951. Telephone: 219-474-5532. FAX: 219-474-5354. URL: http://www.newtoncountyenterprise.com. Mailing Address: PO Box 107, Kentland, IN 47951-0107. Year Established: 1865. Pub. Frequency: w. (Wed.) Page Size: broadsheet. Subscrip. Rate: $.75 newsstand/cover; $39/yr in county; $50/yr elsewhere. Circulation: 1,650 per issue (paid). **Owner(s):** Community Media Group, Inc, PO Box 10, West Frankfort, IL 62896. Telephone: 618-937-6412. **Management:** Don Hurd, Publisher. Randy Pruden, Advertising Manager. **Editorial:** Cheri Glancy, Managing Editor.

MOROCCO COURIER, THE. 305 E Graham St, Kentland, IN 47951. Telephone: 219-474-5532. FAX: 219-474-5354. Mailing Address: PO Box 107, Kentland, IN 47951-0107. Pub. Frequency: w. (Wed.) Page Size: broadsheet. Subscrip. Rate: $1 newsstand/cover; $38/yr in county; $46/yr out of county. Circulation: 370 per issue (paid). **Owner(s):** Community Media Group, Inc, PO Box 10, West Frankfort, IL 62896. Telephone: 618-937-6412. **Management:** Don Hurd, Publisher. Randy Pruden, Advertising Manager. **Editorial:** Cheri Glancy, Managing Editor.

KNOX

LEADER OF STARKE COUNTY, THE. 15 N Main St, Knox, IN 46554. Telephone: 574-772-2101. FAX: 574-772-7041. E-MAIL: theleader@nitline.net. URL: http://www.thepilotnews.com. Pub. Frequency: w. (Wed.) Page Size: broadsheet. Subscrip. Rate: $.50 newsstand/cover; $21/yr mailed in state; $26/yr mailed out of state. Circulation: 1,500 per issue (free). **Owner(s):** Horizon Publications, Inc., 1120 N. Carbon St., Ste.100, Marion, IL 62959. Telephone: 618-993-1693. **Management:** Rick A. Kreps, Publisher. Cindy Stockton, Advertising Manager. James Radican, Circulation Manager. **Editorial:** John Reed, Editor.

LA GRANGE

LA GRANGE STANDARD NEWS. PO Box 148, La Grange, IN 46761. Telephone: 260-463-2167. FAX: 260-463-2734. E-MAIL: lagpubco@kountrynet.com. Year Established: 1856. Pub. Frequency: s-w. (Tue. & Fri..) Page Size: broadsheet. Subscrip. Rate: $.50 newsstand/cover; $30/yr local. Circulation: 7,200 per issue (paid). **Owner(s):** La Grange Publishing Co., Inc., See address and contact information above. **Management:** William Connelly, Publisher. Kim Hicks, Circulation Manager. Marcia Kitchen, Classified Adv. Mgr.. **Editorial:** William Connelly, Editor.

LA PORTE

REGIONAL NEWS, THE. 9852 W. State Rd. 2, La Porte, IN 46350. Telephone: 219-785-2234. FAX: 219-785-2442. Mailing Address: PO Box 828, Westville, IN 46350. Year Established: 1915. Pub. Frequency: w. (Thu.) Page Size: broadsheet. Subscrip. Rate: $.45 newsstand/cover; $22/yr mailed in county; $26/yr mailed out of county; $39/yr mailed out of state. Circulation: 650 per issue (paid). **Owner(s):** Galen L. Armstrong, PO Box 828, Westville, IN 46391. Telephone: 219-785-2234. **Management:** Galen L. Armstrong, Publisher. Nancy Armstrong, Circulation Manager. **Editorial:** Galen L. Armstrong, Editor.

LAFAYETTE

LAFAYETTE LEADER. 2218 Main St, Ste C-1, Lafayette, IN 47902. Telephone: 765-449-8123. FAX: 765-742-5156. E-MAIL: lafleader@aol.com. URL: http://www.communitymediagroup.com/publications. Mailing Address: PO Box 908, Lafayette, IN 47902. Year Established: 1883. Pub. Frequency: w. (Thu.) Page Size: tabloid. Subscrip. Rate: $1 newsstand/cover; $48/yr. Freelance Pay: $0.07/word. Circulation: 5,000 per issue (paid). **Owner(s):** Community Media Group, Inc, PO Box 10, West Frankfort, IL 62896. Telephone: 618-937-6412. **Management:** Don Hurd, Publisher. Julie Korkos, Advertising. **Editorial:** Don Hurd, Editor.

LAWRENCE

LAWRENCE TOWNSHIP JOURNAL. 7968 Pendleton Pike, Lawrence, IN 46226. Telephone: 317-542-1137. FAX: 317-542-1137. E-MAIL: ltjnews@aol.com. Year Established: 1944. Pub. Frequency: w. (Wed.) Page Size: broadsheet. Subscrip. Rate: $.50 newsstand/cover; $26/yr. Adv. Rate: col. inch $9.50 Circulation: 16,275 per issue (paid). **Owner(s):** M.A. Zainey Enterprises, Inc., See address and contact information above. **Management:** Shelly Zainey, Publisher. **Editorial:** Sandy Zainey, Editor.

LAWRENCEBURG

DEARBORN COUNTY REGISTER. 126 W. High St., Lawrenceburg, IN 47025. Telephone: 812-537-0063. FAX: 812-537-5576. URL: http://www.dearborncountyregister.com. Mailing Address: PO Box 4128, Lawrenceburg, IN 47025. Year Established: 1825. Pub. Frequency: w. (Thu.) Page Size: broadsheet. Subscrip. Rate: $.75 newsstand/cover; $26/yr in county; $37/yr in OH & KY; $54/yr elsewhere. Adv. Rate: col. inch $10.55 Circulation: 7,561 per issue (paid). **Owner(s):** Delphos Newspapers, 405 N. Main St., Delphos, OH 45833. Telephone: 419-695-0015. **Management:** Joe Awad, Publisher. Janet Essert, Advertising Manager. **Editorial:** Joe Awad, Editor. Jim Buchberger, Sports.

LIGONIER

LIGONIER ADVANCE-LEADER. 121 S. Cavin St., Ligonier, IN 46767. Telephone: 260-894-3102. FAX: 260-894-3104. E-MAIL: bobreprt@ligtel.com. URL: http://www.kpcnews.com. Mailing Address: PO Box 30, Ligonier, IN 46767. Year Established: 1880. Pub. Frequency: w. (Thu.) Page Size: broadsheet. Subscrip. Rate: $.75 newsstand/cover; $17 for 26 wks.; $34/yr in state; $37/yr out of state. Adv. Rate: col. inch $7.08 Circulation: 1,500 per issue (paid). **Owner(s):** Kendallville Publishing Co., 112 N. Main St., Kendallville, IN 46755. Telephone: 219-347-0400. **Management:** Bob Buttgen, Sales Manager. **Editorial:** Bob Buttgen, Editor.

SMART SHOPPER (LIGONIER), THE. 121 S. Cavin St., Ligonier, IN 46767. Telephone: 260-894-3102. FAX: 260-894-3104. E-MAIL: bobreprt@ligtel.com. URL: http://www.kpcnews.com. Mailing Address: PO Box 30, Ligonier, IN 46767. Pub. Frequency: w. (Tue.) Page Size: standard Circulation: 44,000 per issue (free). **Owner(s):** Kendallville Publishing Co., 112 N. Main St., Kendallville, IN 46755. Telephone: 219-347-0400. **Management:** Terry Housholder, Publisher. Rich Fisher, Advertising Manager. Sam Ashe, Circulation Manager. **Editorial:** Bob Buttgen, Editor.

LOGAN

LOGAN HERALD OBSERVER. 107 N Fourth Ave, Ste 3, Logan, IN 51546. Telephone: 712-644-2705. FAX: 712-644-2788. Mailing Address: PO Box 148, Logan, IA 51546-0148. Year Established: 1886. Pub. Frequency: w. (Wed.) Page Size: broadsheet. Subscrip. Rate: $.75 newsstand/cover; $32/yr in county & adj. cys.; $34.50/yr mailed in state & NE; $38.50/yr mailed elsewhere. Circulation: 2,100 per issue (paid). **Owner(s):** Omaha World-Herald Co., 1314 Douglas St, Omaha, NE 68102. Telephone: 402-444-1000. FAX: 402-345-0183. **Management:** John Beaudoin, Publisher. Mary Darling, Circulation Manager.

LOWELL

CEDAR LAKE JOURNAL. 116 Clark St., Lowell, IN 46356. Telephone: 219-698-7711. FAX: 219-696-7713. E-MAIL: pilcher@xvi.net. Mailing Address: PO Box 248, Lowell, IN 46356-0248. Year Established: 1968. Pub. Frequency: w. (Tue.) Page Size: broadsheet. Subscrip. Rate: $.50 newsstand/cover; $24/yr in county; $30/yr out of county. Adv. Rate: col. inch $7 Circulation: 1,550 per issue (paid and free). **Owner(s):** Pilcher Publishing Co., Inc., See address and contact information above. **Management:** Mary Jeanette Pilcher, Publisher. Gary Pilcher, Advertising Manager. **Editorial:** Craig Pilcher, Editor.

LOWELL TRIBUNE. 116 Clark St., Lowell, IN 46356. Telephone: 219-696-7711. FAX: 219-696-7713. E-MAIL: pilcher@xvi.net. Mailing Address: PO Box 248, Lowell, IN 46356-0248. Year Established: 1885. Pub. Frequency: w. (Tue.) Page Size: broadsheet. Subscrip. Rate: $.50 newsstand/cover; $24/yr in county; $30/yr out of county. Adv. Rate: col. inch $7 Circulation: 5,000 per issue (paid). **Owner(s):** Pilcher Publishing Co., Inc., See address and contact information above. **Management:** Mary Jeanette Pilcher, Publisher. Gary Pilcher, Advertising Manager. **Editorial:** Craig Pilcher, Editor.

SOUTH LAKE ADVERTISER. 116 Clark St., Lowell, IN 46356. Telephone: 219-698-7711. FAX: 219-696-7713. E-MAIL: pilcher@xvi.net. Mailing Address: PO Box 248, Lowell, IN 46356-0248. Year Established: 1962. Pub. Frequency: w. (Tue.) Page Size: broadsheet.Adv. Rate: col. inch $7 Circulation: 2,650 per issue (free). **Owner(s):** Pilcher Publishing Co., Inc., See address and contact information above. **Management:** Mary Jeanette Pilcher, Publisher. Gary Pilcher, Advertising Manager. **Editorial:** Craig Pilcher, Editor.

MIDDLETOWN

MIDDLETOWN NEWS, THE. 106 N. Fifth St., Middletown, IN 47356-0096. Telephone: 765-354-2221. FAX: 765-354-2221. E-MAIL: drew@themiddletownnews.com. URL: http://www.themiddletownnews.com. Year Established: 1885. Pub. Frequency: w. (Thu.) Page Size: broadsheet. Subscrip. Rate: $.50 newsstand/cover; $20.75/yr in county; $24.50/yr out of county; $39/yr out of state. Adv. Rate: col. inch $4.40 Circulation: 2,000 per issue (paid). **Owner(s):** Drew Cooper, See address and contact information above. **Management:** Drew Cooper, Co-Publisher. Joey Cooper, Advertising Manager. **Editorial:** Drew Cooper, Managing Editor.

MILFORD

MAIL-JOURNAL, THE. 206 S. Main St, Milford, IN 46542. Telephone: 574-658-4111. FAX: 574-658-4701. E-MAIL: adcomp@the-papers.com; jseely@the-papers.com. Mailing Address: PO Box 188, Milford, IN 46542. Year Established: 1888. Pub. Frequency: w. (Wed.) Page Size: broadsheet. Subscrip. Rate: $.75 newsstand/cover; $30/yr in county; $35/yr in state; $38/yr out of state. Circulation: 3,800 per issue (paid). **Owner(s):** The Papers, Inc., See address and contact information above. **Management:** Ron Baumgartner, Publisher. Kip Schumn, Advertising Manager. Elaine Pearson, Circulation Manager. Lisa Schiefelbein, Classified Adv. Mgr.. **Editorial:** Jeri Seely, Editor.

MISHAWAKA

MISHAWAKA ENTERPRISE. 419 W. 7th St., Mishawaka, IN 46544. Telephone: 574-255-4789. FAX: 574-255-4789. E-MAIL: mishawakanews@aol.com. Year Established: 1855. Pub. Frequency: w. (Thu.) Page Size: tabloid. Subscrip. Rate: $.40 newsstand/cover; $15/yr in county; $23/yr out of county; $13/yr in county to senior citizens. Circulation: 2,000 per issue (paid). **Owner(s):** Ecom Publishing, PO Box 584, Mishawaka, IN 46546-0584. Telephone: 574-255-4789. FAX: 574-255-4789. **Management:** Bruce Behling, Sales Manager. **Editorial:** William Nich, Editor.

MOORESVILLE

MOORESVILLE DECATUR TIMES, THE. 23 E. Main St., Mooresville, IN 46158-0308. Telephone: 317-831-0280. FAX: 317-831-7068. E-MAIL: edit@md-times.com. URL: http://www.md-times.com. Mailing Address: PO Box 308, Mooresville, IN 46158. Year Established: 1871. Pub. Frequency: s-w. (Wed. & Sat.) Page Size: broadsheet. Subscrip. Rate: $.50 newsstand/cover; $43/yr. Adv. Rate: col. inch $12 Circulation: 5,100 per issue (paid). **Owner(s):** Schurz Communications, Inc., 225 W. Colfax Ave., South Bend, IN 46626. Telephone: 219-287-1001. **Management:** James Krodner, General Manager. E. Mayer Maloney, Publisher. Shawn Everett, Advertising Manager. **Editorial:** Michele Suter, Production Manager. Steve Page, Sports Editor.

MT. VERNON

MOUNT VERNON DEMOCRAT. 231A Main St., Mt. Vernon, IN 47620. Telephone: 812-838-4811. FAX: 812-838-3696. E-MAIL: mvdemocrat-editor @insightbb.com. Mailing Address: PO Box 767, Mt. Vernon, IN 47620. Year Established: 1867. Pub. Frequency: w. (Wed.) Page Size: broadsheet. Subscrip. Rate: $.75 newsstand/cover; $28/yr home delivery in county; $35/yr mailed in state; $45/yr mailed out of state. Adv. Rate: col. inch $9.50 Circulation: 3,200 per issue (paid). **Owner(s):** Landmark Community Newspapers, Inc., PO Box 549, Shelbyville, KY 40065. Telephone: 502-633-2526. **Management:** Beth Foster, General Manager. Brenda Higgins, Advertising Manager. **Editorial:** Beth Foster, Editor.

MUNSTER

TIMES (MUNSTER), THE. 601 W. 45th Ave., Munster, IN 46321-2875. E-MAIL: thetimes@mwt.net. Year Established: 1906. Pub. Frequency: w. (Thu.) Page Size: broadsheet. Subscrip. Rate: $.50 newsstand/cover; $29.25 local 13 wks.; $34.50 in state 13 wks.. Circulation: 1,800 per issue (paid). **Owner(s):** Lee Enterprises, Inc., See address and contact information above. **Management:** Kevin Mulberry, Publisher. Karen Bloom, Advertising Manager. **Editorial:** William Nangle, Executive Editor. Theresa Badovich, Managing Editor. Joe Puchek, City Editor.

NAPPANEE

ADVANCE NEWS OF ELKHART COUNTY. 158 W Market St, Nappanee, IN 46550. Telephone: 574-773-3127. FAX: 574-773-3512. E-MAIL: advance@npcc.net. URL: http://www.thepilotnews.com. Mailing Address: PO Box 230, Nappanee, IN 46550. Pub. Frequency: w. (Wed.) Page Size: broadsheet. Subscrip. Rate: $.50 newsstand/cover; $21/yr mailed in state; $26/yr mailed out of state. **Owner(s):** Horizon Publications, Inc., 1120 N. Carbon St., Ste.100, Marion, IL 62959. Telephone: 618-993-1693. **Management:** Rick A. Kreps, Publisher. Cindy Stockton, Advertising Manager. James Radican, Circulation Manager. **Editorial:** Mandy McFarland, Editor.

NASHVILLE

BROWN COUNTY DEMOCRAT. 147 E. Main, Nashville, IN 47448-0277. Telephone: 812-988-2221. FAX: 812-988-6502. E-MAIL: newsroom@bcdemocrat.com. URL: http://www.browncountyindiana.com. Mailing Address: PO Box 277, Nashville, IN 47448. Year Established: 1870. Pub. Frequency: w. (Wed.) Page Size: broadsheet. Subscrip. Rate: $.75 newsstand/cover; $31/yr mailed in county; $41/yr mailed out of county. Circulation: 4,700 per issue (paid). **Owner(s):** Home News Enterprises, See address and contact information above. **Management:** Steve Marshall, General Manager. Keith Fleener, Advertising Manager. **Editorial:** Linda Margison, Managing Editor.

NEW HAVEN

ALLEN COUNTY TIMES. 512 Broadway, Ste. 103, New Haven, IN 46774-1404. Telephone: 260-493-2464. E-MAIL: rkoassociates@yahoo.com. Mailing Address: P.O.Box 1, New Haven, IN 46774-0001. Year Established: 1991. Pub. Frequency: m. Page Size: tabloid.Adv. Rate: col. inch $6 Circulation: 15,000 per issue (controlled). **Owner(s):** Ronald Oetting, See address and contact information above. **Management:** Ronald Oetting, Publisher. **Editorial:** Lois Eminhiser, City Editor.

NEWBURGH

NEWBURGH-CHANDLER REGISTER. 501 State St., Newburgh, IN 47629. Telephone: 812-853-3366. FAX: 812-853-8685. E-MAIL: newsroom@warricknews.com. URL: http://www.tristate-media.com. Mailing Address: PO Box 535, Newburgh, IN 47629. Year Established: 1886. Pub. Frequency: w. (Wed.) Page Size: standard. Subscrip. Rate: $.75 newsstand/cover; $30/yr home delivery in county; $95/yr mailed 1st class. Circulation: 10,000 per issue (paid). **Owner(s):** Brehm Communications, Inc., 16644 W. Bernardo Dr., Ste. 300, San Diego, CA 92127. Telephone: 619-451-6200. FAX: 858-451-3814. **Management:** Byran Marshall, Advertising Manager. Karen Monks, Circulation Manager. Debbie Whitaker, Classified Adv. Mgr.. **Editorial:** Nathan Blackford, Editor.

NORTH MANCHESTER

NEWS-JOURNAL (NORTH MANCHESTER), THE. 1306 State Rd. 114 W, North Manchester, IN 46962. E-MAIL: news@nmpaper.com. Mailing Address: PO Box 368, North Manchester, IN 46962-0368. Year Established: 1873. Pub. Frequency: w. (Wed.) Page Size: tabloid. Subscrip. Rate: $.50 newsstand/cover; $30/yr mailed in county; $35/yr mailed out of county. Circulation: 1,800 per issue (paid). **Owner(s):** Mike Rees, 1306 State Rd. 114 W, North Mancheste r, IN 46962. Telephone: 260-982-6383. FAX: 260-982-8233. **Management:** Mike Rees, Publisher. **Editorial:** Eric Christiansen, Editor.

NORTH VERNON

NORTH VERNON PLAIN DEALER. PO Box 988, North Vernon, IN 47265. Telephone: 812-346-3973. FAX: 812-346-8368. E-MAIL: pds@northvernon.com. URL: http://www.northvernon.com. Year Established: 1862. Pub. Frequency: w. (Thu.) Page Size: standard. Subscrip. Rate: $.50 newsstand/cover; $32/yr local; $40/yr mailed elsewhere. Circulation: 6,800 per issue (paid). **Owner(s):** Barbara, Madelon, Susan King, See address and contact information above. **Management:** Barbara King, Publisher. Josh Taylor, Advertising Manager. **Editorial:** Bryce Mayer, Editor.

NORTH VERNON SUN. PO Box 988, North Vernon, IN 47265. Telephone: 812-346-3973. FAX: 812-346-8368. E-MAIL: pds@northvernon.com. URL: http://www.northvernon.com. Year Established: 1876. Pub. Frequency: w. (Tue.) Page Size: standard. Subscrip. Rate: $.50 newsstand/cover; $32/yr local; $40/yr in state & surrounding states; $45/yr elsewhere. Circulation: 6,200 per issue (paid). **Owner(s):** Barbara, Madelon & Susan King, See address and contact information above. **Management:** Patrick Morley, General Manager. Barbara King, Publisher. Josh Taylor, Advertising Manager. **Editorial:** Bryce Mayer, Editor.

OSSIAN

OSSIAN JOURNAL. 1002 Dehner Dr., Ossian, IN 46777. Telephone: 260-622-4108. FAX: 260-622-6439. E-MAIL: ossianj@adamswells.com. Mailing Address: PO Box 365, Ossian, IN 46777. Year Established: 1912. Pub. Frequency: w. (Thu.) Page Size: broadsheet. Subscrip. Rate: $.50 newsstand/cover; $19/yr in county. **Wire Service(s):** AP. Circulation: 504 per issue (paid). **Owner(s):** News-Banner Publications, Inc., 125 N. Johnson, Bluffton, IN 46714. Telephone: 260-824-0224. FAX: 260-824-0700. **Management:** Mark Miller, Publisher. Penny Meadows, Advertising. Rhonda Hesher, Circulation Manager. **Editorial:** James C. Barbieri, Managing Editor.

SUNRISER NEWS. 1002 Dehner Dr., Ossian, IN 46777. Telephone: 260-622-4108. FAX: 260-622-6439. E-MAIL: ossianj@adamswells.com. Mailing Address: PO Box 365, Ossian, IN 46777. Year Established: 1978. Pub. Frequency: w. (Tue.) Page Size: tabloid Circulation: 9,060 per issue (free). **Owner(s):** News-Banner Publications, Inc., 125 N. Johnson, Bluffton, IN 46714. Telephone: 260-824-0224. **Management:** Mark Miller, Publisher. Eric McEvoy, Advertising. **Editorial:** James C. Barbieri, Managing Editor. Rhonda Hesher, Circulation Editor.

PAOLI

ORANGE COUNTIAN. PO Box 190, Paoli, IN 47454. Telephone: 812-723-2572. FAX: 812-723-2592. Year Established: 1984. Pub. Frequency: w. (Wed.) Page Size: broadsheet.Adv. Rate: col. inch $5.50 Circulation: 11,848 per issue (free). **Owner(s):** Orange County Publishing Co., Inc., See address and contact information above. **Management:** Arthur Hampton, Publisher. Malissa Wiseman, Advertising Manager. **Editorial:** Arthur Hampton, Managing Editor.

PAOLI NEWS. PO Box 190, Paoli, IN 47454. Telephone: 812-723-2572. FAX: 812-723-2592. E-MAIL: ocpinc@ocpnews.com. URL: http://www.paolinews.com. Year Established: 1872. Pub. Frequency: w. (Thu.) Page Size: broadsheet. Subscrip. Rate: $.50/yr newsstand/cover; $33.95/yr mailed in county & adj cys; $42.95/yr mailed elsewhere. Adv. Rate: col. inch $4 Circulation: 3,050 per issue (paid). **Owner(s):** Orange County Publishing Co., Inc., See address and contact information above. **Management:** Arthur Hampton, President. Malissa Wiseman, Advertising Manager. **Editorial:** Dennis Ellis, Editor.

PAOLI REPUBLICAN. PO Box 190, Paoli, IN 47454. Telephone: 812-723-2572. FAX: 812-723-2592. E-MAIL: ocpinc@ocpnews.com. Year Established: 1872. Pub. Frequency: w. (Tue.) Page Size: broadsheet. Subscrip. Rate: $.50 newsstand/cover; $31.95/yr mailed local; $33.95/yr mailed in county & adj cys; $42.95/yr mailed elsewhere. Adv. Rate: col. inch $4 Circulation: 3,150 per issue (paid). **Owner(s):** Orange County Publishing Co., Inc., See address and contact information above. **Management:** Arthur Hampton, Publisher. Malissa Wiseman, Advertising Manager. **Editorial:** Dennis Ellis, Editor.

PEKIN

AUCTIONER, THE. ISSN 1053-2218
PO Box 38, Pekin, IN 47165. Telephone: 812-967-3176. FAX: 812-752-6486. E-MAIL: paperman@gbpnews.com. URL: http://www.gbpnews.com. Year Established: 1989. Pub. Frequency: w. (Wed.) Page Size: tabloid.Subscrip. Rate: $25/yr mailed local Circulation: 500 per issue (paid). **Owner(s):** Green Banner Publications, See address and contact information above. **Management:** Joe Green, General Manager. John Roberts, Advertising Manager. **Editorial:** Mark Grigsby, Managing Editor.

BANNER-GAZETTE. ISSN 0194-3545
PO Box 38, Pekin, IN 47165. Telephone: 812-967-3176. FAX: 812-752-6486. URL: http://www.gbpnews.com. Year Established: 1919. Pub. Frequency: w. (Wed.) Page Size: tabloid.Subscrip. Rate: $.25 newsstand/cover; $18.50/yr Circulation: 17,237 per issue (free). **Owner(s):** Green Banner Publications, See address and contact information above. **Management:** Joe Green, Owner. John Roberts, Advertising Manager. Heather Marlman, Art Director. **Editorial:** Mark Grigsby, Editor. Jason Nelson, Associate Editor. Mark Grigsby, Sports.

SCOTT COUNTY JOURNAL. PO Box 38, Pekin, IN 47165. Telephone: 812-967-3176. FAX: 812-752-6486. E-MAIL: paperman@gbpnews.com. URL: http://www.gbpnews.com. Pub. Frequency: w. (Sat.) Page Size: broadsheet. Subscrip. Rate: $.25 newsstand/cover; $9.95/yr in county & adj cys; $16.50/yr out of area. Circulation: 4,784 per issue (paid). **Owner(s):** Green Banner Publications, See address and contact information above. **Management:** Joe Green, Publisher. John Roberts, Advertising Manager. **Editorial:** Marcus Amos, Managing Editor.

PETERSBURG

PRESS-DISPATCH, THE. 820 Poplar St., Petersburg, IN 47567. Telephone: 812-354-8500. FAX: 812-354-2014. E-MAIL: editor@pressdispatch.net. URL: http://www.pressdispatch.net. Mailing Address: P.O. Box 68, Petersburg, IN 47567-0068. Year Established: 1885. Pub. Frequency: w. (Wed.) Page Size: broadsheet. Subscrip. Rate: $.75 newsstand/cover; $22/yr mailed. Adv. Rate: col. inch $5.50 Circulation: 5,800 per issue (paid). **Owner(s):** Pike Publishing, See address and contact information above. **Management:** Frank Heuring, Publisher. John Heuring, Advertising Manager. **Editorial:** Andy Heuring, Editor. Mike Johansen, Sports Editor.Readers: Rural, farming & mining community

PRINCETON

GIBSON COUNTY TODAY. 100 N. Gibson St., Princeton, IN 47670. Telephone: 812-385-2525. FAX: 812-386-6199. Mailing Address: PO Box 30, Princeton, IN 47670. Pub. Frequency: w. (Monl) Page Size: broadsheet Circulation: 8,100 per issue (free). **Owner(s):** Brehm Communications, Inc., 16644 W. Bernardo Dr., Ste. 300, San Diego, CA 92127. Telephone: 619-451-6200. FAX: 858-451-3814. **Management:** Gary Blackburn, President. Debra Walker, Advertising Manager. Jim Hansen, Circulation Director. Maggie Armstrong, Classified Adv. Mgr..

OAKLAND CITY JOURNAL. 100 N. Gibson St., Princeton, IN 47670. Telephone: 812-385-2525. FAX: 812-386-6199. Mailing Address: PO Box 30, Princeton, IN 47670. Year Established: 1892. Pub. Frequency: w. (Wed.) Page Size: broadsheet Circulation: 9,000 per issue (free). **Owner(s):** Brehm Communications, Inc., 16644 W. Bernardo Dr., Ste. 300, San Diego, CA 92127. Telephone: 619-451-6200. FAX: 858-451-3814. **Management:** Gary Blackburn, Publisher. Debra Walker, Advertising Manager. Jim Hansen, Circulation Director. Maggie Armstrong, Classified Adv. Mgr..

RENSSELAER

COURIER (RENSSELAER), THE. ISSN 1060-5231
117 N. Van Rensselaer St., Rensselaer, IN 47978. Telephone: 219-866-5111. FAX: 219-866-3775. Pub. Frequency: w. (Wed.) Page Size: standard. Subscrip. Rate: $.50 newsstand/cover; $25/yr in county; $27/yr out of county; $32/yr out of state. Circulation: 1,000 per issue (paid). **Owner(s):** Kankakee Valley Publishing Co., See address and contact information above. **Management:** Sally Snow, Publisher. **Editorial:** Harley Tomlinson, Editor.

HOOPESTON CHRONICLE. ISSN 1076-4186
117 N. Van Rensselaer St., Rensselaer, IN 47978. Telephone: 219-866-5111. FAX: 219-866-3775. E-MAIL: cchristy@intranix.com. Year Established: 1872. Pub. Frequency: w. (Wed.) Page Size: tabloid. Subscrip. Rate: $.75 newsstand/cover; $30/yr in county; $45/yr elsewhere. Circulation: 1,963 per issue (paid). **Owner(s):** Kankakee Valley Publishing Co., See address and contact information above. **Management:** Berthaa Parsons, General Manager. Mary Jo Petersen, Circulation Manager.

REMINGTON PRESS. 117 N. Van Rensselaer St., Rensselaer, IN 47978. Telephone: 219-866-5111. FAX: 219-866-3775. Year Established: 1873. Pub. Frequency: w. (Wed.) Page Size: standard. Subscrip. Rate: $.50 newsstand/cover; $31/yr in county; $34/yr in state; $38/yr out of state. Circulation: 1,000 per issue (paid). **Owner(s):** Kankakee Valley Publishing Co., See address and contact information above. **Management:** Sally Snow, Publisher. JoAnn Lloyd, Circulation Manager. Sally Snow, Sales Manager. **Editorial:** Harlen Tomlinson, Editor.

RISING SUN

OHIO COUNTY NEWS. 235 Main St., PO Box 4128, Rising Sun, IN 47040. Telephone: 812-438-2011. FAX: 812-537-5576. Year Established: 1833. Pub. Frequency: w. (Thu.) Page Size: broadsheet. Subscrip. Rate: $.60 newsstand/cover; $20/yr mailed in county; $31/yr mailed out of county. Adv. Rate: col. inch $4.90 Circulation: 579 per issue (paid and free). **Owner(s):** Register Publications, 126 W. High St., Lawrenceburg, IN 47025. Telephone: 812-537-0063. **Management:** Joe Awad, Publisher. Janet Essert, Advertising Manager. **Editorial:** Tim Hillman, Managing Editor.

RISING SUN RECORDER. 235 Main St., PO Box 4128, Rising Sun, IN 47040. Telephone: 812-438-2011. FAX: 812-537-5576. Year Established: 1834. Pub. Frequency: w. (Thu.) Page Size: broadsheet. Subscrip. Rate: $.60 newsstand/cover; $20/yr mailed in county. Adv. Rate: col. inch $5.90 Circulation: 2,009 per issue (paid). **Owner(s):** Register Publications, 126 W. High St., Lawrenceburg, IN 47025. Telephone: 812-537-0063. **Management:** Joe Awad, Publisher. Janet Essert, Advertising Manager. **Editorial:** Tim Hillman, Editor.

ROCKPORT

SPENCER COUNTY JOURNAL DEMOCRAT. 541 Main St., Rockport, IN 47635. Telephone: 812-649-4440. FAX: 812-649-9197. E-MAIL: journal@psci.net. Mailing Address: PO Box 6, Rockport, IN 47635. Year Established: 1853. Pub. Frequency: w. (Thu.) Page Size: broadsheet. Subscrip. Rate: $.75 newsstand/cover; $26/yr in county; $40/yr out of state. Circulation: 4,500 per issue (paid). **Owner(s):** Landmark Community Newspapers, Inc., PO Box 549, Shelbyville, KY 40065. Telephone: 502-633-2526. **Management:** Teresa Rice, Publisher. **Editorial:** Melissa Miller, Editor. Kyann Bays, Production Manager.

ROCKVILLE

PARKE COUNTY SENTINEL. ISSN 1044-7822
PO Box 187, Rockville, IN 47872. Telephone: 765-569-2033. FAX: 765-569-1424. E-MAIL: sentinel@ticz.com. Year Established: 1833. Pub. Frequency: w. (Wed.) Page Size: broadsheet. Subscrip. Rate: $.50 newsstand/cover; $32/yr mailed in state; $37/yr mailed out of state. Circulation: 4,400 per issue (paid). **Owner(s):** Torch Newspapers, Inc., 125 W High St, Rockville, IN 47872. **Management:** Jessica M. Harney-Lynk, President. Jane Kelp, Advertising Manager. Jamie Brehmer, Circulation Manager. **Editorial:** Larry Bemis, Editor.

SALEM

SALEM DEMOCRAT, THE. PO Box 506, Salem, IN 47167. Telephone: 812-883-3282. FAX: 812-883-4446. E-MAIL: sales@salemleader.com. Year Established: 1827. Pub. Frequency: w. (Thu.) Page Size: broadsheet. Subscrip. Rate: $.50 newsstand/cover; $31/yr mailed in county; $40.50/yr mailed in state; $47.50/yr mailed out of state. Circulation: 6,500 per issue (paid). **Owner(s):** Leader Publishing Co., Inc., See address and contact information above. **Management:** Nancy Grossman, General Manager. Debbi Hayes, Advertising Manager. Rhonda Smith, Classified Adv. Mgr.. **Editorial:** Stephanie Taylor, Editor. George Browning, Sports.

SALEM LEADER, THE. PO Box 506, Salem, IN 47167. Telephone: 812-883-3281. FAX: 812-883-4446. E-MAIL: sales@salemleader.com. Year Established: 1878. Pub. Frequency: w. (Tue.) Page Size: broadsheet. Subscrip. Rate: $.50 newsstand/cover; $31/yr mailed in county; $40.50/yr mailed in state; $47.50/yr mailed out of state. Circulation: 6,000 per issue (paid). **Owner(s):** Leader Publishing Co., Inc., See address and contact information above. **Management:** Nancy Grossman, Publisher. Debbi Hayes, Advertising Manager. Rhonda Smith, Classified Adv. Mgr.. **Editorial:** Stephanie Taylor, Editor.

WASHINGTON COUNTY EDITION. 105 E. Walnut St., Salem, IN 47167. Telephone: 812-883-5555. FAX: 812-883-3688. E-MAIL: newsroom@gbpnews.com. URL: http://www.gbpnews.com. Year Established: 1982. Pub. Frequency: w. (Wed.) Page Size: tabloid. Subscrip. Rate: $15/yr mailed. Adv. Rate: col. inch $4.50 Circulation: 11,242 per issue (paid and free). **Owner(s):** Green Banner Publications, PO Box 38, Pekin, IN 47165. Telephone: 812-967-3176. **Management:** Joe Green, General Manager. John Roberts, Advertising Manager. **Editorial:** Mark Grigsby, Editor.

SCOTTSBURG

GIVEAWAY, THE. 183 E. McClain St., Scottsburg, IN 47170. Telephone: 812-752-3171. FAX: 812-752-6468. E-MAIL: paperman@gbpnews.com. URL: http://www.gbpnews.com. Year Established: 1937. Pub. Frequency: w. (Wed.) Page Size: tabloid. Subscrip. Rate: $18.50/yr mailed out of state. Circulation: 18,560 per issue (paid and free). **Owner(s):** Green Banner Publications, PO Box 38, Pekin, IN 47165. Telephone: 812-967-3176. **Management:** Joe Green, General Manager. Wanda Green, Executive VP. John Roberts, Advertising Manager. **Editorial:** Mark Grigsby, Editor.

JOURNAL & AUSTIN CHRONICLE. 183 E. McClain St., Scottsburg, IN 47170. Telephone: 812-752-3171. FAX: 812-752-6468. E-MAIL: newsroom@gbpnews.com. URL: http://www.gbpnews.com. Year Established: 1882. Pub. Frequency: w. (Sat.) Page Size: broadsheet. Subscrip. Rate: $.25 newsstand/cover; $9.95/yr mailed local. Circulation: 5,000 per issue (paid). **Owner(s):** Green Banner Publications, PO Box 38, Pekin, IN 47165. Telephone: 812-967-3176. **Management:** Joe Green, General Manager. Wanda Green, Executive VP. John Roberts, Advertising Manager. **Editorial:** Mark Grigsby, Editor. Marcus Amos, Managing Editor.

SOUTH BEND

TRI-COUNTY NEWS (SOUTH BEND). 2517 Edison Rd., South Bend, IN 46615. Telephone: 574-287-0285. FAX: 574-282-1716. URL: http://www.tricountynewsinc.com. Mailing Address: P.O. Box 6666, South Bend, IN 46660-6666. Year Established: 1923. Pub. Frequency: w. (Fri.) Page Size: tabloid. Subscrip. Rate: $12/yr mailed in county; $20 mailed for 2 yrs. in county; $17/yr mailed out of county. Adv. Rate: col. inch $4 Circulation: 1,000 per issue (paid). **Owner(s):** Cherie Jolly, See address and contact information above. **Management:** Cherie Jolly, Publisher. **Editorial:** Cherie Jolly, Managing Editor.

SPEEDWAY

SPEEDWAY TOWN PRESS. 1564 Main St., Speedway, IN 46224. Telephone: 317-241-4345. FAX: 317-241-4386. E-MAIL: thepress@in-motion.net. Year Established: 1956. Pub. Frequency: w. (Wed.) Page Size: tabloid.Adv. Rate: col. inch $10 Circulation: 6,000 per issue (free). **Owner(s):** Speedway Northwest Press, Inc., See address and contact information above. **Management:** Elizabeth Sullivan, Publisher. Shirley Nelson, Advertising Manager. **Editorial:** Elizabeth Sullivan, Editor.

WESTSIDE MESSENGER. 1564 Main St., Speedway, IN 46224. Telephone: 317-241-4345. FAX: 317-241-4386. E-MAIL: thepress@in-motion.net. Year Established: 1915. Pub. Frequency: w. (Wed.) Page Size: tabloid.Adv. Rate: col. inch $10 Circulation: 6,000 per issue (free). **Owner(s):** Speedway Northwest Press, Inc., See address and contact information above. **Management:** Elizabeth Sullivan, Publisher. Shirley Nelson, Advertising Manager. **Editorial:** Elizabeth Sullivan, Editor.

TELL CITY

PERRY COUNTY NEWS, THE. 537 Main St., Tell City, IN 47586. Telephone: 812-547-3424. FAX: 812-547-2847. E-MAIL: pcnews@psci.com. URL: http://www.perrycountynews.com. Mailing Address: PO Box 309, Tell City, IN 47586. Year Established: 1891. Pub. Frequency: s-w. (Mon. & Thu.) Page Size: broadsheet. Subscrip. Rate: $.50 newsstand/cover; $40/yr mailed in county; $53/yr mailed out of county; $67/yr mailed out of state. Circulation: 7,450 per issue (paid). **Owner(s):** Landmark Community Newspapers, Inc., PO Box 549, Shelbyville, KY 40065. Telephone: 502-633-2526. **Management:** Teresa Rice, Publisher. Cindy Dauby, Advertising Manager. Corliss Krueger, Classified Adv. Mgr.. **Editorial:** Vince Luecke, Editor. Kevin Koelling, Managing Editor. Larry Goffinet, Sports Editor.

VALPARAISO

HOBART CHRONICLE. 10 N. Washington St., Valparaiso, IN 46383. Telephone: 219-462-1488. FAX: 219-462-3897. Year Established: 1887. Pub. Frequency: w. (Wed.) Page Size: tabloid Circulation: 7,000 per issue (paid). **Owner(s):** Great Lakes Publishing, Inc., See address and contact information above. **Management:** Brenda Kleihege, Publisher. **Editorial:** Erin Ciszczon, Editor.

PORTAGE CHRONICLE. 10 N. Washington St., Valparaiso, IN 46383. Telephone: 219-462-1488. FAX: 219-462-3897. E-MAIL: glpubs@aol.com. Pub. Frequency: w. (Wed.) Page Size: tabloid Circulation: 10,000 per issue (free). **Owner(s):** Great Lakes Publishing, Inc., See address and contact information above. **Management:** Brenda Kleihege, Publisher. **Editorial:** Erin Ciszczon, Editor.

VALPARAISO NEWS. 10 N. Washington St., Valparaiso, IN 46383. Telephone: 219-462-1488. FAX: 219-462-3897. E-MAIL: glpubs@aol.com. Pub. Frequency: w. (Wed.) Page Size: tabloid Circulation: 9,200 per issue (free). **Owner(s):** Great Lakes Publishing, Inc., See address and contact information above. **Management:** Brenda Kleihege, Publisher. **Editorial:** Julia Versau, Managing Editor.

VERSAILLES

OSGOOD JOURNAL. 115 S. Washington St., Versailles, IN 47042. Telephone: 812-689-6364. FAX: 812-689-6508. E-MAIL: ripleynews@seidata.com. URL: http://www.ripleynews.com. Mailing Address: PO Box 158, Versailles, IN 47042. Year Established: 1865. Pub. Frequency: w. (Tue.) Page Size: broadsheet. Subscrip. Rate: $.75 newsstand/cover; $43/yr in county; $45/yr out of county; $50/yr out of state. Circulation: 5,200 per issue (paid). **Owner(s):** Gene Demaree, 6709 Mad River Rd., Centerville, OH 45459. Telephone: 812-689-6364. FAX: 812-689-6508. **Management:** Gene Demaree, President. Linda Chandler, Publisher. **Editorial:** Wanda Burnett, Editor.

VERSAILLES REPUBLICAN. 115 S. Washington St., Versailles, IN 47042. Telephone: 812-689-6364. FAX: 812-689-6508. E-MAIL: ripleynews@seidata.com. URL: http://www.ripleynews.com. Mailing Address: PO Box 158, Versailles, IN 47042. Year Established: 1856. Pub. Frequency: w. (Thu.) Page Size: broadsheet. Subscrip. Rate: $.50 newsstand/cover; $38/yr in county; $41/yr out of county; $45/yr mailed out of state. Circulation: 5,200 per issue (paid). **Owner(s):** Gene Demaree, 6709 Mad River Rd., Centerville, OH 45459. Telephone: 812-689-6364. FAX: 812-689-6508. **Management:** Linda Chandler, Publisher. **Editorial:** Wanda Burnett, Editor.

VEVAY

SWITZERLAND DEMOCRAT. 111 W. Market St., Vevay, IN 47043. Telephone: 812-427-2311. FAX: 812-427-2793. E-MAIL: vevnews@seidata.com. Mailing Address: PO Box 157, Vevay, IN 47043. Year Established: 1868. Pub. Frequency: w. (Thu.) Page Size: broadsheet. Subscrip. Rate: $.50 newsstand/cover; $25/yr in county & surrounding cys; $30/yr IN, OH, KY.; $35/yr elsewhere. Circulation: 600 per issue (paid). **Owner(s):** Vevay Newspapers, Inc., See address and contact information above. **Management:** Don R. Wallis Jr., Publisher. Julie Sharp, Advertising. Ginny Leap, Circulation Manager. **Editorial:** Patrick Lanman, Managing Editor.

VEVAY REVEILLE-ENTERPRISE. 111 W. Market St., Vevay, IN 47043. Telephone: 812-427-2311. FAX: 812-427-2793. Mailing Address: PO Box 157, Vevay, IN 47043. Year Established: 1816. Pub. Frequency: w. (Thu.) Page Size: broadsheet. Subscrip. Rate: $.50 newsstand/cover; $25/yr home delivery in county; $30/yr mailed in IN, OH, KY; $35/yr mailed elsewhere. Circulation: 3,600 per issue (paid). **Owner(s):** Vevay Newspapers, Inc., See address and contact information above. **Management:** Patrick Lanman, General Manager. Don R. Wallis Jr., Publisher. Julie Sharp, Advertising Manager. Ginny Leap, Circulation Manager. **Editorial:** Patrick Lanman, Editor.

WABASH

PAPER OF WABASH COUNTY, THE. PO Box 603, Wabash, IN 46992. Telephone: 260-563-8326. FAX: 260-563-2863. E-MAIL: thepaper@ctlnet.com. URL: http://www.thepaperofwabash.com. Year Established: 1977. Pub. Frequency: w. (Tue.) Page Size: tabloid. Subscrip. Rate: $35/yr mailed. Circulation: 16,225 per issue (paid and controlled). **Owner(s):** Wayne & Michael Rees, Julie Frieden, See address and contact information above. **Management:** Mike Rees, General Manager. Wayne Rees, Publisher. Julie Frieden, Advertising Manager. Teressa Guy, Circulation Manager.

WARSAW

PAPER (KOSCIUSKO COUNTY EDITION), THE. 114 W. Market, Warsaw, IN 46580. Telephone: 574-269-2932. FAX: 219-269-5850. E-MAIL: jseely@the-papers.com. Year Established: 1971. Pub. Frequency: w. (Wed.) Page Size: tabloid.Adv. Rate: col. inch $8.90 Circulation: 22,425 per issue (free). **Owner(s):** The Papers, Inc., 206 S. Main St, Milford, IN 46542. Telephone: 574-658-4111. **Management:** Ronald Baumgartner, Publisher. Kip Schumm, Advertising Manager. Suzanne Robinson, Circulation Manager. **Editorial:** Jeri Seely, Editor.

WESTVILLE

WESTVILLE INDICATOR. PO Box 828, Westville, IN 46391. Telephone: 219-785-2234. FAX: 219-785-2442. Year Established: 1882. Pub. Frequency: w. (Thu.) Page Size: broadsheet. Subscrip. Rate: $.45 newsstand/cover; $22/yr mailed in county; $26/yr mailed out of county. Circulation: 5,200 per issue (paid). **Owner(s):** Gaylen L. Armstrong, See address and contact information above. **Management:** Gaylen L. Armstrong, Publisher. Nancy Armstrong, Circulation Manager. **Editorial:** Gaylen L. Armstrong, Editor.

WINAMAC

INDEPENDENT (WINAMAC), THE. PO Box 19, Winamac, IN 46996. Telephone: 574-946-6629. FAX: 574-946-7471. E-MAIL: ads@pulaskijournal.com. URL: http://www.pulaskijournal.com. Year Established: 1962. Pub. Frequency: w. (Mon.) Page Size: tabloid.Adv. Rate: col. inch $4.70 Circulation: 10,003 per issue (free). **Owner(s):** Winamac Publishing, Inc., See address and contact information above. **Management:** John Plowman, General Manager. John Haley, Publisher. **Editorial:** John Plowman, Editor.

PULASKI COUNTY JOURNAL. ISSN 1940-9710 PO Box 19, Winamac, IN 46996. Telephone: 574-946-6628. FAX: 574-946-7471. E-MAIL: results@pulaskijournal.com. URL: http://www.pulaskijournal.com. Year Established: 1872. Pub. Frequency: w. (Wed.) Page Size: tabloid. Subscrip. Rate: $1 newsstand/cover; $32/yr mailed in county; $40/yr mailed in state; $48/yr mailed out of state. Adv. Rate: col. inch $4.40 Circulation: 3,800 per issue (paid). **Owner(s):** Winamac Publishing, Inc., See address and contact information above. **Management:** John Plowman, General Manager. John Haley, Publisher. Venell Risner, Advertising Manager. **Editorial:** John Plowman, Editor.

WOLCOTT

WOLCOTT ENTERPRISE. 125 W. Market St., Wolcott, IN 47995-0078. Telephone: 219-279-2167. FAX: 219-279-2167. E-MAIL: wolcott@sugardog.com. Mailing Address: P.O.Box 78, Wolcott, IN 47995-0078. Pub. Frequency: w. (Thu.) Page Size: standard. Subscrip. Rate: $.60 newsstand/cover; $27/yr local; $30/yr out of area. Circulation: 950 per issue (paid). **Owner(s):** Barbara Lawson, See address and contact information above. **Management:** Barbara Lawson, Publisher. **Editorial:** Barbara Lawson, Editor.

ZIONSVILLE

ZIONSVILLE TIMES SENTINEL. ISSN 0886-4330 250 S. Elm St., Zionsville, IN 46077-6397. Telephone: 317-873-6397. FAX: 317-873-6259. E-MAIL: news@timessentinel.com. URL: http://www.timessentinel.com. Year Established: 1860. Pub. Frequency: w. (Wed.) Page Size: broadsheet. Subscrip. Rate: $.75 newsstand/cover; $30/yr in county; $38/yr out of county; $50/yr out of state. Circulation: 4,300 per issue (paid). **Owner(s):** Community Newspaper Holdings, Inc., 3500 Colonnade Pkwy., Ste. 600, Birmingham, AL 35243. Telephone: 205-298-7100. FAX: 205-298-7101. **Management:** Harold Allen, Publisher. Bill Jarchow, Advertising Director. **Editorial:** Harold Allen, Editor. Greta Sanderson, Executive Editor. Jennifer Dawson, Managing Editor. Will Willems, Sports.

IOWA

ADAIR

ADAIR NEWS, THE. 403 Audubon St., Adair, IA 50002. Telephone: 641-742-3241. FAX: 641-742-3489. Pub. Frequency: w. (Thu.) Page Size: standard.Subscrip. Rate: $.75 newsstand/cover; $20/yr Circulation: 1,443 per issue (paid). **Owner(s):** W. E. Littller, III, See address and contact information above. **Management:** W. E. Littler III, Publisher. **Editorial:** W. E. Littler III, Editor.

AFTON

AFTON STAR-ENTERPRISE. 274 N Douglas St, Afton, IA 50830. Telephone: 641-347-8721. FAX: 641-347-8721. Mailing Address: PO Box 128, Afton, IA 50830. Year Established: 1880. Pub. Frequency: w. (Thu.) Page Size: tabloid. Subscrip. Rate: $.50 newsstand/cover; $19/yr mailed in state; $24/yr mailed out of state. Adv. Rate: col. inch $3 Circulation: 1,220 per issue (paid). **Owner(s):** Afton Star-Enterprise, See address and contact information above. **Management:** David A. Pugh, President.

AKRON

AKRON HOMETOWNER. 110 Reed St, Akron, IA 51001. Telephone: 712-568-2208. FAX: 712-568-2271. Mailing Address: PO Box 797, Akron, IA 51001. Pub. Frequency: w. (Wed.) Page Size: broadsheet. Subscrip. Rate: $.75 newsstand/cover; $26/yr in county. Circulation: 1,800 per issue (paid). **Owner(s):** Doris Hook, See address and contact information above. **Management:** Doris Hook, Publisher. **Editorial:** Doris Hook, Editor.

ALBIA

ALBIA UNION-REPUBLICAN. 109 Benton Ave., E., Albia, IA 52531. Telephone: 641-932-7121. FAX: 641-932-2822. E-MAIL: theresa@albianews.com. URL: www.albianews.com. Mailing Address: PO Box 338, Albia, IA 52531. Year Established: 1862. Pub. Frequency: s-w. (Tue. & Thu.) Page Size: broadsheet. Subscrip. Rate: $.50 newsstand/cover; $36/yr mailed in state; $47/yr mailed out of state. Circulation: 3,500 per issue (paid). **Owner(s):** Lancaster Management, Inc., PO Box 609, Gadsden, AL 35902. Telephone: 256-543-3417. **Management:** David A. Paxton, Publisher. Carol Ann Faber, Advertising. Theresa Christofferson, Circulation Manager. **Editorial:** David A. Paxton, Editor.

MONROE NEWS. 109-111 Benton Ave., E., Albia, IA 52531. Telephone: 641-932-7121. FAX: 641-932-2822. E-MAIL: dave@albianews.com. URL: http://www.albianews.com. Mailing Address: PO Box 338, Albia, IA 52531. Year Established: 1890. Pub. Frequency: w. (Tue.) Page Size: broadsheet. Subscrip. Rate: $.50 newsstand/cover; $36/yr mailed in state; $47/yr mailed out of state. Circulation: 3,400 per issue (paid). **Owner(s):** Lancaster Management, Inc., PO Box 609, Gadsden, AL 35902. Telephone: 205-543-3417. **Management:** David A. Paxton, Publisher. Carol Ann Faber, Advertising. Theresa Christofferson, Circulation Manager. **Editorial:** David A. Paxton, Editor. Dien Judge, Sports.

ALGONA

ALGONA UPPER DES MOINES. 14 E. Nebraska St., Algona, IA 50511. Telephone: 515-295-3535. FAX: 515-295-7217. URL: http:www.algona.com. Mailing Address: PO Box 400, Algona, IA 50511. Year Established: 1866. Pub. Frequency: w. (Thu.) Page Size: broadsheet. Subscrip. Rate: $1.25 newsstand/cover; $49/yr local. Circulation: 5,100 per issue (paid). **Owner(s):** World Newspapers, Inc., World Herald Sq., Omaha, NE 68102. Telephone: 402-444-1000. **Management:** Joe Warren, Publisher. Nancy Steburg, Advertising Director. Cookie Bilyeu, Circulation Manager. **Editorial:** Jeff Robinson, Editor. Shari Hegland, Managing Editor. Scott Shannon, Sports.

ALLISON

BUTLER COUNTY TRIBUNE JOURNAL. 308 N Main St, Allison, IA 50602. URL: http://www.butlercountytribune.com. Mailing Address: PO Box 8, Allison, IA 50602. Pub. Frequency: w. (Thu.) Page Size: broadsheet. Subscrip. Rate: $.75 newsstand/cover; $32/yr in county; $37/yr out of county. Circulation: 1,800 per issue (paid). **Owner(s):** Mid-America Publishing Corp., PO Box 29, Hampton, IA 50441. Telephone: 641-456-2585. FAX: 641-456-2587.

ALTOONA

ALTOONA HERALD, THE. 100 Eighth St., S. E., Ste. H, Altoona, IA 50009. Telephone: 515-699-7000. FAX: 515-699-7098. URL: http://www.altoonaherald.com. Mailing Address: PO Box 427, Altoona, IA 50009. Year Established: 1888. Pub. Frequency: w. (Wed.) Page Size: broadsheet. Subscrip. Rate: $.75 newsstand/cover; $25/yr carrier delivery in county; $30/yr mailed. Circulation: 5,900 per issue (controlled and free). **Owner(s):** Gannett Company, Inc., 7950 Jones Branch Dr., McLean, VA 22107-0001. Telephone: 703-854-6000. **Management:** Amy Duncan, Publisher. **Editorial:** Adam Wilson, Editor.

AMES

TRI-COUNTY TIMES, THE. ISSN 0749-7040 317 Fifth St., Ames, IA 50010. Telephone: 515-232-2160. FAX: 515-232-2364. URL: http://www.tricountytimes.com. Year Established: 1890. Pub. Frequency: w. (Thu.) Page Size: broadsheet. Subscrip. Rate: $.75 newsstand/cover; $29.95/yr in county; $40/yr mailed out of county; $40/yr mailed out of state. Adv. Rate: col. inch $3.85 Circulation: 2,300 per issue (paid). **Owner(s):** World Newspapers, Inc., World Herald Sq., Omaha, NE 68102. Telephone: 402-444-1000. **Management:** Marlys Barker, General Manager.

ANAMOSA

ANAMOSA JOURNAL-EUREKA. 208 W. Main St., Anamosa, IA 52205-0108. Telephone: 319-462-3511. FAX: 319-462-4540. Mailing Address: PO Box 108, Anamosa, IA 52205-0108. Year Established: 1854. Pub. Frequency: w. (Thu.) Page Size: tabloid. Subscrip. Rate: $.75 newsstand/cover; $25/yr local; $32/yr out of area. Circulation: 2,500 per issue (paid). **Owner(s):** News Publishing Co., PO Box 286, Black Earth, WI 53515-0108. Telephone: 608-767-3655. **Management:** Larry K Woellert, Publisher. Becky Dirks, Circulation Manager. Cindy Wollum, Sales Manager. **Editorial:** Michelle Phillips, Editor.

JONES COUNTY TOWN CRIER. 208 W. Main St., Anamosa, IA 52205. Telephone: 319-462-3511. FAX: 319-462-4540. Mailing Address: PO Box 108, Anamosa, IA 52205-0108. Year Established: 1966. Pub. Frequency: w. (Tue.) Page Size: tabloid Circulation: 8,058 per issue (free). **Owner(s):** News Publishing Co., PO Box 286, Black Earth, WI 53515. Telephone: 608-767-3655. **Management:** Brian Cook, Publisher. Lori Menke, Advertising Manager. Becky Dirks, Circulation Manager.

Weeklies

ANKENY

ANKENY PRESS CITIZEN. 106 E. First St., Ankeny, IA 50021-1703. Telephone: 515-964-0639. FAX: 515-964-7019. E-MAIL: ssanderson@presscitizen-shopper.com. URL: http://www.presscitizen-shopper.com. Year Established: 1955. Pub. Frequency: w. (Tue.) Page Size: tabloid.Adv. Rate: col. inch $6.75 Circulation: 20,155 per issue (free). **Owner(s):** Ogden Newspapers of Minnesota, Inc., 1500 Main St., Wheeling, WV 26003. Telephone: 304-233-0100. FAX: 304-233-0327. **Management:** Brad Robertson, General Manager. Linda Vanderlinden, Office Manager. Jennifer Vanderpool, Advertising Director. Tom Landes, Circulation Director. Suzanne Cruz, Classified Editor. **Editorial:** Sandy Sanderson, Editor. Dan Holm, Sports Editor.

ATLANTIC

SOUTHWEST IOWA SHOPPER, THE. 410 Walnut St., Atlantic, IA 50022. Telephone: 712-243-2624. FAX: 712-243-4988. Mailing Address: PO Box 230, Atlantic, IA 50022. Pub. Frequency: w. (Tue.) Page Size: standard Circulation: 17,000 per issue (free). **Owner(s):** Community Media Group, Inc, PO Box 10, West Frankfort, IL 62896. Telephone: 618-937-6412. **Management:** Ron Sohl, Publisher. Connie Collins, Advertising Manager. Deb Baker, Circulation Manager.

AUBURN

TRI-COUNTY SPECIAL. P.O. Box E, Auburn, IA 51433. Telephone: 712-688-2216. FAX: 712-688-2216. Pub. Frequency: w. (Wed.) Page Size: tabloid.Subscrip. Rate: $30/yr mailed Circulation: 7,000 per issue (free). **Owner(s):** Dudley Publishing, See address and contact information above. **Management:** Gary D. Dudley, Publisher. **Editorial:** Tesa Cates, Editor.

AUDUBON

AUDUBON COUNTY ADVOCATE JOURNAL. 301 Broadway, Audubon, IA 50025-1101. E-MAIL: acenews@iowatelecom.net. URL: http://www.auduboncountynews.com. Pub. Frequency: w. (Fri.) Page Size: broadsheet. Subscrip. Rate: $1 newsstand/cover; $27.50/yr in county; $37.50/yr out of county. Circulation: 2,550 per issue (paid). **Owner(s):** Audubon Media Corp., See address and contact information above. **Management:** Keith McGlade, Publisher. Jeanne Meike, Advertising. **Editorial:** Judy Lauridesen, Editor. Joyce Bergmann, Managing Editor.

NISHNA VALLEY TRIBUNE. 301 Broadway, Audubon, IA 50025. Telephone: 712-563-2661. FAX: 712-563-3118. E-MAIL: acnnews@iowatelecom.net. URL: http://www.auduboncountynews.com. Mailing Address: PO Box 247, Audubon, IA 50025-0247. Pub. Frequency: w. (Tue.) Page Size: broadsheet.Subscrip. Rate: $32.50/yr mailed out of area Circulation: 6,504 per issue (free). **Owner(s):** Audubon Media Corp., See address and contact information above. **Management:** Keith McGlade, Publisher. Jeanne Meike, Advertising. **Editorial:** Judy Lauridsen, Editor. Joyce Bergmann, Managing Editor.

AVOCA

JOURNAL-HERALD (AVOCA), THE. 124 S. Elm St., Avoca, IA 51521. Telephone: 712-343-2154. FAX: 712-343-2262. Mailing Address: PO Box 308, Avoca, IA 51521-0308. Pub. Frequency: w. (Thu.) Page Size: broadsheet. Subscrip. Rate: $.50 newsstand/cover; $18/yr in county; $30/yr out of state. Circulation: 1,700 per issue (paid). **Owner(s):** Donald L. Nielson, See address and contact information above. **Management:** Donald L. Nielson, Publisher. **Editorial:** Rich Price, Editor.

OAKLAND HERALD, THE. 124 S. Elm St., Avoca, IA 51521. Telephone: 712-343-2154. FAX: 712-343-2262. Pub. Frequency: w. (Wed.) Page Size: tabloid.Subscrip. Rate: $.50 newsstand/cover; $18/yr Circulation: 1,400 per issue (paid). **Owner(s):** Donald L. Nielson, See address and contact information above. **Management:** Donald L. Nielson, Publisher. **Editorial:** Rich Price, Editor.

BANCROFT

BANCROFT REGISTER, THE. PO Box 175, Bancroft, IA 50517-0220. Telephone: 515-885-2531. FAX: 515-885-2771. Pub. Frequency: w. (Wed.) Page Size: standard. Subscrip. Rate: $.75 newsstand/cover; $18/yr in county; $23.50/yr out of county. Circulation: 1,100 per issue (paid). **Owner(s):** Jerry D. Wiseman, See address and contact information above. **Management:** Jerry D. Wiseman, Publisher.

BAYARD

NEWS GAZETTE, THE. 409 Main St., Bayard, IA 50029-0130. Telephone: 712-651-2321. FAX: 712-651-2599. E-MAIL: ciapub@netins.net. Mailing Address: PO Box 130, Bayard, IA 50029. Pub. Frequency: w. (Thu.) Page Size: standard. Subscrip. Rate: $.75 newsstand/cover; $23/yr in county; $28/yr out of county; $33/yr out of state. Adv. Rate: col. inch $4.50 Circulation: 2,200 per issue (paid). **Owner(s):** Central Iowa Publishing, See address and contact information above. **Editorial:** Lu-Ann Waldo, Editor.

BEDFORD

BEDFORD TIMES-PRESS, THE. 310 Main St., Bedford, IA 50833-1319. Telephone: 712-523-2525. Pub. Frequency: w. (Wed.) Page Size: standard. Subscrip. Rate: $.75 newsstand/cover; $21/yr in county; $26/yr out of county. Circulation: 2,100 per issue (paid). **Owner(s):** Colleen & Randall Larimer, See address and contact information above. **Management:** Randall Larimer, Publisher. **Editorial:** Colleen Larimer, Editor.

BELLE PLAINE

BELLE PLAINS UNION. PO Box 208, Belle Plaine, IA 52208-0208. Telephone: 319-444-2520. FAX: 319-444-2522. E-MAIL: bpunion@netins.net. URL: http://wwwshowcase.netins.net/web/bpunion/.. Mailing Address: PO Box 208, Belle Plaine, IA 52208-0208. Pub. Frequency: w. (Tue.) Page Size: broadsheet.Subscrip. Rate: $1 newsstand/cover; $26/yr Circulation: 1,753 per issue (paid). **Owner(s):** Gannett Company, Inc., 7950 Jones Branch Dr, McLean, VA 22107. Telephone: 703-854-6000.

SOUTH BENTON STAR-PRESS. 502 Seventh Ave., Belle Plaine, IA 52208-1757. Telephone: 319-444-2520. FAX: 319-444-2522. URL: http://www.showcase.netins.net/web/bpunion. Mailing Address: PO Box 208, Belle Plaine, IA 52208-0208. Pub. Frequency: w. (Wed.) Page Size: broadsheet.Subscrip. Rate: $1 newsstand/cover; $28/yr Circulation: 1,488 per issue (paid). **Owner(s):** Gannett Company, Inc., 7950 Jones Branch Dr, McLean, VA 22107. Telephone: 703-854-6000. **Editorial:** Jim Magdefrau, Editor.

BELLEVUE

BELLEVUE HERALD-LEADER. 118 S. Second St., Bellevue, IA 52031-1381. Telephone: 563-872-4159. FAX: 563-872-4298. Pub. Frequency: w. (Thu.) Page Size: broadsheet. Subscrip. Rate: $.75 newsstand/cover; $34/yr in county; $38/yr out of county; $44/yr elsewhere. Circulation: 2,900 per issue (paid). **Owner(s):** Maquoketa Newspapers, Inc., 108 W. Quarry St., Maquoketa, IA 52060. FAX: 563-652-6094. **Management:** Douglas Melvold, Publisher. Lynn Hager, Advertising Manager. **Editorial:** Lowell Carlson, Editor. Willy Frieburger, Sports Editor.

BELMOND

BELMOND INDEPENDENT. 215 E. Main St., Belmond, IA 50421. Telephone: 641-444-3333. URL: http://www.belmondnews.com. Mailing Address: PO Box 126, Belmond, IA 50421-0126. Year Established: 1876. Pub. Frequency: w. (Wed.) Page Size: broadsheet. Subscrip. Rate: $1 newsstand/cover; $30/yr in county; $34/yr out of county; $38/yr elsewhere. Circulation: 2,000 per issue (paid). **Owner(s):** Dirk & Lee Van Der Linden, See address and contact information above. **Management:** Dirk Van Der Linden, Publisher. Lee Van Der Linden, Advertising Manager. Connie Mattison, Circulation Manager. **Editorial:** Lee Van Der Linden, Editor.

BETTENDORF

BETTENDORF NEWS. P.O. Box 460, Bettendorf, IA 52722. FAX: 563-383-2370. E-MAIL: bettnews@qctimes.com. URL: http://www.thebettendorfnews.com. Year Established: 1927. Pub. Frequency: w. (Thu.) Page Size: tabloid. Subscrip. Rate: $.75 newsstand/cover; $25/yr in county. Adv. Rate: col. inch $16.60 Circulation: 10,000 per issue (paid). **Owner(s):** Lee Enterprises, Inc., 215 N. Main St., Davenport, IA 52801. Telephone: 563-383-2100. **Management:** Brenda Minkalis, Advertising. Ann Boyd, Advertising Manager. **Editorial:** Janet Hill, Editor.

BLOOMFIELD

BLOOMFIELD DEMOCRAT, THE. 207 S Madison, Bloomfield, IA 52537. Telephone: 641-664-2334. FAX: 641-664-2316. E-MAIL: bdemo@netins.net. URL: http://www.bdemo.com. Mailing Address: PO Box 19, Bloomfield, IA 52537. Pub. Frequency: w. (Wed.) Page Size: broadsheet. Subscrip. Rate: $1 newsstand/cover; $40/yr in county; $52/yr out of county. Circulation: 3,000 per issue (paid). **Owner(s):** C. Gary Spurgeon, See address and contact information above. **Management:** C. Gary Spurgeon, Publisher. Phil Norton, Advertising Manager. **Editorial:** Scott Spurgeon, Editor.

BOONE

BOONE COUNTY SHOPPING NEWS. 2136 E Mamie Eisenhower, Boone, IA 50036. Telephone: 515-432-6694. FAX: 515-432-7811. E-MAIL: results@boonetoday.com. URL: http://www.boonetoday.com. Mailing Address: PO Box 100, Boone, IA 50036-0100. Pub. Frequency: w. (Tue.) Page Size: tabloid Circulation: 12,000 per issue (free). **Owner(s):** Iowa Newspapers, Inc., 317 Fifth St., Ames, IA 50010. Telephone: 515-232-2160. FAX: 515-323-2364. **Management:** Claudia Lovin, Publisher. Sandi Hilsabeck, Circulation Manager. **Editorial:** Susan Hildreth, Editor.

BREDA

BREDA NEWS. PO Box 183, Breda, IA 51436-0183. Telephone: 712-673-2318. FAX: 712-673-4246. E-MAIL: bredanews@win-4-u.net. Pub. Frequency: w. (Wed.) Page Size: standard.Subscrip. Rate: $.35 newsstand/cover; $15/yr Circulation: 700 per issue (paid). **Owner(s):** R. D. & D., See address and contact information above. **Editorial:** Diane Lucas, Managing Editor.

BRITT

BRITT NEWS-TRIBUNE. 42 W. Center St., Britt, IA 50423. Telephone: 641-843-3851. FAX: 641-843-3307. URL: http://www.forestcitysummit.com/britt. Mailing Address: PO Box 38, Britt, IA 50423. Year Established: 1881. Pub. Frequency: w. (Wed.) Page Size: broadsheet. Subscrip. Rate: $.75 newsstand/cover; $29/yr mailed in county; $36/yr mailed out of county; $41/yr mailed out of state. Circulation: 2,000 per issue (paid). **Owner(s):** Lee Enterprises, Inc., 201 N. Harrison St., Davenport, IA 52801-1924. **Management:** Joe McDermott, Publisher. Kristi Kirchbaum, Advertising. **Editorial:** Angie Johannsen, Editor. Jill McNeese, Composing Room Manager. Christy Johnson, Sports.

BROOKLYN

BROOKLYN CHRONICLE. 132 Jackson St., Brooklyn, IA 52211. Telephone: 641-522-7155. FAX: 641-522-7909. Mailing Address: PO Box 533, Brooklyn, IA 52211-0533. Pub. Frequency: w. (Wed.) Page Size: standard. Subscrip. Rate: $1 newsstand/cover; $26/yr local; $28/yr in state; $34/yr elsewhere. Circulation: 1,400 per issue (paid). **Owner(s):** Brooklyn Publishing Co., See address and contact information above. **Management:** Dan Deibettignies, Publisher. Vicki Watts, Advertising. **Editorial:** Amber Williams, Editor. Dan Deibettignies, Managing Editor.

BUFFALO CENTER

BUFFALO CENTER TRIBUNE. 124 N. Main, Buffalo Center, IA 50424-0367. Telephone: 641-562-2606. FAX: 641-562-2636. E-MAIL: bctrib@wctatel.net. URL: http://www.buffalocentertribune.com. Mailing Address: PO Box 367, Buffalo Center, IA 50424. Year Established: 1892. Pub. Frequency: w. (Thu.) Page Size: standard. Subscrip. Rate: $.75 newsstand/cover; $31/yr local; $35/yr elsewhere. Circulation: 1,700 per issue (paid). **Owner(s):** Merlyn R. Elman, See address and contact information above. **Editorial:** Lanita Kardoes, Managing Editor.

BURLINGTON

SHOPPER SPREE. 3208 Division St., Burlington, IA 52601. Telephone: 319-752-4555. FAX: 319-752-6410. E-MAIL: shoppers@interl.net. URL: http://www.interl.net/~shoppers. Pub. Frequency: w. (Wed.) Page Size: tabloid Circulation: 21,000 per issue (paid). **Owner(s):** Brehm Communications, Inc., 16644 W. Bernardo Dr., Ste. 300, San Diego, CA 92127. Telephone: 858-451-6200. **Management:** Ron Storey, General Manager. Sue Stratton, Circulation Manager.

CALMAR

CALMAR COURIER. 109 N. Maryville, Calmar, IA 52132. Telephone: 563-562-3488. FAX: 563-562-3940. E-MAIL: driscoll@calmar.polaristel.net. Pub. Frequency: w. (Tue.) Page Size: tabloid. Subscrip. Rate: $.50 newsstand/cover; $20/yr local; $25/yr in county; $30/yr elsewhere. Circulation: 3,500 per issue (paid). **Owner(s):** Tina Hagenan, See address and contact information above. **Management:** Tina Hagenan, Publisher. Becca Berger, Advertising Manager. **Editorial:** Tina Hagenan, Editor.

CARLISLE

CARLISLE CITIZEN, THE. 210 S. First St., Carlisle, IA 50047-7720. Telephone: 515-989-3251. Pub. Frequency: w. (Thu.) Page Size: standard.Subscrip. Rate: $.50 newsstand/cover Circulation: 1,650 per issue (paid). **Owner(s):** Klein Publications, See address and contact information above. **Management:** Steve Klein, Publisher. Kim Hartshorn, Advertising Manager. **Editorial:** Kim Hartshorn, Editor.

CENTERVILLE

AD EXPRESS. 105 N Main St, Centerville, IA 52544. Telephone: 641-856-6336. FAX: 641-856-8118. Mailing Address: PO Box 610, Centerville, IA 52544-0610. Pub. Frequency: w. (Wed.) Page Size: standard Circulation: 14,000 per issue (free). **Owner(s):** Community Newspaper Holdings, Inc., 3500 Colonnade Pkwy., Ste. 600, Birmingham, AL 35243-1031. **Management:** Becky Maxwell, Publisher. Jean Clark, Circulation Manager. Sheila Selix, Classified Adv. Mgr.. **Editorial:** Dan Ehl, Managing Editor.

CHARITON

CHARITON HERALD-PATRIOT. 815 Braden Ave., Chariton, IA 50049. Telephone: 641-774-2137. FAX: 641-774-2139. URL: http://www.charitonleader.com. Mailing Address: PO Box 651, Chariton, IA 50049. Year Established: 1857. Pub. Frequency: w. (Thu.) Page Size: broadsheet. Subscrip. Rate: $.50 newsstand/cover; $37/yr mailed in county. Adv. Rate: col. inch $6.95 Circulation: 3,317 per issue (paid and free). **Owner(s):** Lancaster Management, Inc., PO Box 609, Gadsden, AL 35902. **Management:** Dave Paxton, Publisher. Susan Smith, Advertising Manager. **Editorial:** Bill Howes, Associate Editor. Dave Paxton, News Editor.

CHARITON LEADER, THE. 815 Braden Ave., Chariton, IA 50049. Mailing Address: PO Box 651, Chariton, IA 50049. Year Established: 1867. Pub. Frequency: w. (Tue.) Page Size: broadsheet. Subscrip. Rate: $.50 newsstand/cover; $34/yr in county. Adv. Rate: col. inch $5.40 Circulation: 3,317 per issue (paid and free). **Owner(s):** Lancaster Management, Inc., PO Box 609, Gadsden, AL 35902. **Management:** Dave Paxton, Publisher. Ellie Barnes, Advertising Manager. **Editorial:** Eleaine McCullough, Editor. Bill Hower, Associate Editor.

CHARLES CITY

LOOK & SHOP-SHOPPER. 801 Riverside Dr., Charles City, IA 50616. Telephone: 641-228-3211. FAX: 641-228-2641. URL: http://www.gatehousemedia.com. Mailing Address: PO Box 397, Charles City, IA 50616. Pub. Frequency: w. (Fri.) Page Size: tabloid.Adv. Rate: col. inch $15.25 Circulation: 17,175 per issue (free). **Owner(s):** GateHouse Media, Inc, 350 WillowBrook Office Park, Fairport, NY 14450. Telephone: 585-598-0030. **Management:** Gene A. Hall, Publisher. **Editorial:** Mark Wicks, Managing Editor.

CLARINDA

CLARINDA HERALD JOURNAL. 205 E Main St, Clarinda, IA 51632. Telephone: 712-542-2181. FAX: 712-542-5424. E-MAIL: hjournal@clarinda.heartland.net. Mailing Address: PO Box 278, Clarinda, IA 51632-0278. Year Established: 1858. Pub. Frequency: w. (Wed.) Page Size: broadsheet. Subscrip. Rate: $.75 newsstand/cover; $30/yr mailed in state; $50/yr mailed out of state. Circulation: 24,000 per issue (paid). **Owner(s):** Omaha World-Herald Co., 1314 Douglas St, Omaha, NE 68102. Telephone: 402-444-1000. FAX: 402-345-0183. **Management:** Kevin Brown, Publisher. Marilyn Jones, Classified Adv. Mgr.. **Editorial:** Kent Dinnebier, News Editor. Contact: Barry C. Cleveland, Publisher; .

CLIVE

MID-IOWA ENTERPRISE. 10963 Lincoln Ave, Clive, IA 50325. Telephone: 641-751-3965. E-MAIL: jstrawn@iowatelecom.net. URL: http://www.midiowaenterprise.com. Mailing Address: P.O. Box 634, State Center, IA 50247-0634. Year Established: 1871. Pub. Frequency: w. (Thu.) Page Size: broadsheet. Subscrip. Rate: $1 newsstand/cover; $30/yr local; $35/yr elsewhere. Adv. Rate: col. inch $4.50 Circulation: 1,500 per issue (paid). **Owner(s):** John & Diane Strawn, 408 2nd St., S.W., State Center, IA 50247-0634. Telephone: 641-483-2120. FAX: 641-483-2938. **Management:** John C. Strawn II, Publisher. **Editorial:** Joel Lively, Editor-in-Chief.

COLFAX

COLFAX JASPER CO. TRIBUNE. 1 W Howard St, Colfax, IA 50054-1011. Telephone: 515-674-3591. FAX: 515-674-3591. E-MAIL: jctribune@qwest.net. Mailing Address: P O Box 7, Colfax, IA 50054-0007. Pub. Frequency: w. (Thu.) Subscrip. Rate: $.60 newsstand/cover; $20/yr mailed in county; $23/yr mailed out of county. Circulation: 1,715 per issue (paid). **Owner(s):** Shaw Newspapers, 444 Pine Hill Dr., Dixon, IL 61021. **Management:** Allyn Arthur, Publisher. **Editorial:** Allyn Arthur, Editor.

CORYDON

TIMES-REPUBLICAN (CORYDON). 205 W. Jackson, Corydon, IA 50060. Telephone: 641-872-1234. FAX: 641-872-1985. Mailing Address: PO Box 258, Corydon, IA 50060-0258. Pub. Frequency: w. (Tue.) Page Size: broadsheet. Subscrip. Rate: $.50 newsstand/cover; $26/yr mailed in county; $29/yr mailed in state; $33/yr mailed out of state. Circulation: 3,000 per issue (paid). **Owner(s):** Lancaster Management, Inc., PO Box 609, Gadsden, AL 35902. **Management:** Rhonda Bennett, Publisher. **Editorial:** Tammy C. Helm, Editor.

CRESCO

TIMES-PLAIN DEALER. ISSN 1089-8271
214 N. Elm St., Cresco, IA 52136. Telephone: 563-547-3601. FAX: 563-547-4602. E-MAIL: info@crescotimes.com. URL: http://www.crescotimes.com. Mailing Address: PO Box 350, Cresco, IA 52136-0350. Year Established: 1866. Pub. Frequency: w. (Wed.) Page Size: broadsheet. Subscrip. Rate: $1 newsstand/cover; $31.95/yr in area; $55/yr mailed out of area. Freelance Pay: $0.50/column-inch. Circulation: 3,000 per issue (paid). **Owner(s):** GateHouse Media, Inc, 350 WillowBrook Office Park, Fairport, NY 14450. Telephone: 585-598-0030. FAX: 585-248-2631. **Management:** Zach Jensen, General Manager. Matthew Bryant, Publisher. Lacey Mader, Advertising. Barb Moore, Circulation Manager. **Editorial:** Zach Jensen, News Editor.

DAVENPORT

CHADRON RECORD, THE. 201 N. Harrison St., Davenport, IA 52801. E-MAIL: cdrrecord@bbc.net. URL: http://www.thechadronnews.com. Year Established: 1887. Pub. Frequency: w. (Wed.) Page Size: broadsheet. Subscrip. Rate: $1 newsstand/cover per issue; $36/yr home delivery in county; $52.50/yr mailed out of county; $59.25/yr mailed out of state. Adv. Rate: col. inch $7.55 Circulation: 7,100 per issue (paid and free). **Owner(s):** Lee Enterprises, Inc., See address and contact information above.

LEADER (DAVENPORT), THE. 3719 Bridge Ave, Ste 4, Davenport, IA 52807. Telephone: 563-386-3670. FAX: 563-386-3731. Year Established: 1986. Pub. Frequency: w. (Fri.) Subscrip. Rate: $26/yr out of area. Adv. Rate: col. inch $1.25 Circulation: 50,000 per issue (paid and controlled). **Owner(s):** Small Newspaper Group, 8 Dearborn Sq., Kankakee, IL 60901. Telephone: 815-937-3300. **Management:** Gerald J Taylor, Publisher. Nick Norman, Advertising Director. Ron Manning, Circulation Manager. **Editorial:** Michael Romkey, Editor.

MINIDOKA COUNTY NEWS. 201 N. Harrison St., Davenport, IA 52801. E-MAIL: mcn@safelink.net. Year Established: 1906. Pub. Frequency: w. (Wed.) Page Size: broadsheet. Subscrip. Rate: $.50 newsstand/cover; $28/yr in city; $25/yr local to senior citizens; $41/yr mailed. Circulation: 1,414 per issue (paid). **Owner(s):** Lee Enterprises, Inc., See address and contact information above. **Management:** Steve Baker, Publisher. Annie Holmes, Office Manager. Rose Bryan, Advertising. **Editorial:** Judy Albertson, Editor.

THRIFTY NICKEL WANT ADS. 500 E. Third St., Davenport, IA 52802. Telephone: 563-333-2601. FAX: 563-333-2666. E-MAIL: qcnickel@qcthriftynickel.com. URL: http://www.qcthriftynickel.com. Mailing Address: P.O. Box 3828, Davenport, IA 52808. Year Established: 1982. Pub. Frequency: w. (Thu.) Page Size: tabloid Circulation: 55,000 per issue (free). **Owner(s):** Lee Enterprises, Inc., 201 N. Harrison St, Ste 600, Davenport, IA 52801-1924. **Management:** Peggy Dykes, General Manager.

DECORAH

DECORAH PUBLIC OPINION & DECORAH JOURNAL. 107 E Water St, Decorah, IA 52101. Telephone: 563-382-4221. FAX: 563-382-5949. E-MAIL: news@decorahnewspapers.com. URL: http://www.decorahnewspaper.com. Mailing Address: PO Box 350, Decorah, IA 52101. Year Established: 1864. Pub. Frequency: s-w. (Tue. Public Opinion; Thu. Journal) Page Size: broadsheet. Subscrip. Rate: $.75 newsstand/cover; $35/yr in county & adj. cys.; $40/yr out of area; $45/yr out of state. Adv. Rate: col. inch $6 Circulation: 6,400 per issue (paid). **Owner(s):** Decorah News Co., See address and contact information above. **Management:** John Anundsen, Publisher. Julie Ude, Advertising Manager. **Editorial:** Richard Fromm, Editor. Roz Weis, Lifestyle Editor. Sarah Strandberg, News Editor. Nate Troy, Sports.

DENISON

DENISON BULLETIN & REVIEW. 1410 Broadway, Denison, IA 51442. Telephone: 712-263-2121. FAX: 712-263-8484. E-MAIL: gwehle@bulletinreview.com. URL: http://www.bulletinreview.com. Mailing Address: PO Box 550, Denison, IA 51442. Year Established: 1873. Pub. Frequency: s-w. (Tue. & Sat.) Page Size: broadsheet. Subscrip. Rate: $.75 newsstand/cover; $55/yr local; $62/yr elsewhere. Adv. Rate: col. inch $8.75 Freelance Pay: $0.10/column-inch. Circulation: 4,000 per issue (paid). **Owner(s):** Omaha World-Herald Co., 1314 Douglas St, Omaha, NE 68102. Telephone: 402-444-1000. FAX: 402-345-0183. **Management:** Greg Wahle, Publisher. Jackie Gallagher, Circulation Manager. Eileen Mullin, Classified Adv. Mgr.. **Editorial:** Gordon Wolf, News Editor.

DES MOINES

ALTOONA/PLEASANT HILL PRESS CITIZEN. 525 S.W. Fifth St., Des Moines, IA 50309. Telephone: 515-262-1190. FAX: 515-286-2555. E-MAIL: news@presscitizen-shopper.com. URL: http://www.presscitizen-shopper.com. Mailing Address: PO Box 957, Des Moines, IA 50304. Pub. Frequency: w. (Wed.) Page Size: tabloid.Adv. Rate: col. inch $9.50 Circulation: 10,940 per issue (free). **Owner(s):** Gannett Company, Inc., 7950 Jones Branch Dr., McLean, VA 22107-0001. Telephone: 703-854-6000. **Management:** Brett Mathis, Publisher. Jalene Siemsglusz, Advertising.

CLIVE/WINDSOR HEIGHTS PRESS CITIZEN. 2221 E. Ovid St., Des Moines, IA 50313. Telephone: 515-262-1724. FAX: 515-262-2267. E-MAIL: rstrenge@presscitizen-shopper.com. URL: http://www.presscitizen-shopper.com. Mailing Address: PO Box 4826, Des Moines, IA 50306. Pub. Frequency: w. (Wed.) Page Size: tabloid.Adv. Rate: col. inch $10 Circulation: 11,111 per issue (free). **Owner(s):** Ogden Newspapers of Minnesota, Inc., 19260 San Carlos Blvd., Fort Myers Beach, FL 33931. Telephone: 239-463-4421. **Management:** Brad Robertson, Publisher. Jennifer Vanderpool, Advertising Director. Tom Landes, Circulation Director. Jolene Siemsglusz, Classified Adv. Mgr.. **Editorial:** Rose Strenge, Editor. Jeff Hage, News Editor. Dan Holm, Sports Editor.

DES MOINES PRESS CITIZEN. 525 S.W. Fifth St., Des Moines, IA 50309. Telephone: 515-262-1190. FAX: 515-286-2555. E-MAIL: news@presscitizen-shopper.com. URL: http://www.presscitizen-shopper.com. Mailing Address: PO Box 957, Des Moines, IA 50304. Pub. Frequency: w. (Wed.) Page Size: tabloid.Adv. Rate: col. inch $7 Circulation: 38,929 per issue (free). **Owner(s):** Gannett Company, Inc., 7950 Jones Branch Dr., McLean, VA 22107-0001. Telephone: 703-854-6000. **Management:** Jalene Siemsglusz, Advertising.

EAST DES MOINES PRESS CITIZEN. 2221 E. Ovid St., Des Moines, IA 50313. Telephone: 515-262-1724. FAX: 515-262-2267. E-MAIL: jhage@presscitizen-shopper.com. URL: http://www.presscitizen-shopper.com. Mailing Address: PO Box 4826, Des Moines, IA 50306. Year Established: 1958. Pub. Frequency: w. (Wed.) Page Size: tabloid.Adv. Rate: col. inch $6.75 Circulation: 15,362 per issue (free). **Owner(s):** Ogden Newspapers of Minnesota, Inc., 19260 San Carlos Blvd., Fort Myers Beach, FL 33931. Telephone: 239-463-4421. **Management:** Brad Robertson, General Manager. Jennifer Vanderpool, Advertising Director. Tom Landes, Circulation Director. Jolene Siemsglusz, Classified Adv. Mgr.. **Editorial:** Dan Holm, Sports Editor.

JOHNSTON PRESS CITIZEN. 2221 E. Ovid St., Des Moines, IA 50313. Telephone: 515-262-1190. FAX: 515-564-0577. E-MAIL: cflesher@presscitizen-shopper.com. URL: http://www.presscitizen-shopper.com. Mailing Address: PO Box 4826, Des Moines, IA 50306. Pub. Frequency: w. (Wed.) Page Size: tabloid.Adv. Rate: col. inch $7.50 Circulation: 11,452 per issue (free). **Owner(s):** Ogden Newspapers of Minnesota, Inc., 19260 San Carlos Blvd., Fort Myers Beach, FL 33931. Telephone: 239-463-4421. **Management:** Brad Robertson, Publisher. Jennifer Vanderpool, Advertising Director. Tom Landes, Circulation Director. Jolene Siemsglusz, Classified Adv. Mgr.. **Editorial:** Charles Flesher, Managing Editor. Jeff Hage, News Editor. Dan Holm, Sports Editor.

POLK COUNTY PRESS CITIZEN. 525 S.W. Fifth St., Des Moines, IA 50309. Telephone: 515-262-1190. FAX: 515-286-2555. E-MAIL: cflesher@presscitizen-shopper.com. URL: http://www.presscitizen-shopper.com. Mailing Address: PO Box 957, Des Moines, IA 50304. Pub. Frequency: w. (Fri.) Page Size: tabloid. Subscrip. Rate: $.50 newsstand/cover; $30/yr mailed. Adv. Rate: col. inch $9.50, page $5 Circulation: 1,429 per issue (paid). **Owner(s):** Gannett Company, Inc., 7950 Jones Branch Dr., McLean, VA 22107-0001. Telephone: 703-854-6000. **Management:** Brett Mathis, Publisher. Jalene Siemsglusz, Advertising.

SOUTH DES MOINES PRESS CITIZEN. 525 S.W. Fifth St., Des Moines, IA 50309. Telephone: 515-262-1190. FAX: 515-286-2555. E-MAIL: jhage@presscitizen-shopper.com. URL: http://www.presscitizen-shopper.com. Mailing Address: PO Box 957, Des Moines, IA 50304. Pub. Frequency: w. (Wed.) Page Size: tabloid.Adv. Rate: col. inch $8 Circulation: 24,995 per issue (free). **Owner(s):** Gannett Company, Inc., 7950 Jones Branch Dr., McLean, VA 22107-0001. Telephone: 703-854-6000. **Management:** Jalene Siemsglusz, Advertising.

URBANDALE PRESS CITIZEN. 2221 E. Ovid St., Des Moines, IA 50313. Telephone: 515-262-1190. FAX: 515-564-0577. E-MAIL: rstrenge@presscitizen-shopper.com. URL: http://www.presscitizen-shopper.com. Mailing Address: PO Box 4826, Des Moines, IA 50306. Pub. Frequency: w. (Wed.) Page Size: broadsheet.Adv. Rate: col. inch $7.50 Circulation: 15,661 per issue (free). **Owner(s):** Ogden Newspapers of Minnesota, Inc., 19260 San Carlos Blvd., Fort Myers Beach, FL 33931. **Management:** Brad Robertson, Publisher. Jennifer Vanderpool, Advertising Director. Tom Landes, Circulation Director. Jolene Siemsglusz, Classified Adv. Mgr.. **Editorial:** Rose Strenge, Managing Editor. Dan Holm, Sports Editor.

WEST DES MOINES PRESS CITIZEN. 525 S.W. Fifth St., Des Moines, IA 50309. Telephone: 515-262-1190. FAX: 515-286-2555. E-MAIL: khurley@presscitizen-shopper.com. URL: http://www.presscitizen-shopper.com. Mailing Address: PO Box 957, Des Moines, IA 50304. Pub. Frequency: w. (Wed.) Page Size: tabloid.Adv. Rate: col. inch $9.50 Circulation: 17,844 per issue (free). **Owner(s):** Gannett Company, Inc., See address and contact information above. **Management:** Jalene Siemsglusz, Advertising.

DEWITT

OBSERVER (DEWITT), THE. ISSN 0886-8808
512 Seventh St., DeWitt, IA 52742-0049. Telephone: 563-659-3121. FAX: 563-659-3778. E-MAIL: observer@iowatelecom.net. URL: http://www.dewittobserver.com. Mailing Address: PO Box 49, DeWitt, IA 52742-0049. Year Established: 1864. Pub. Frequency: s-w. (Wed. & Sat.) Page Size: tabloid. Subscrip. Rate: $.75 newsstand/cover; $35/yr local. Adv. Rate: col. inch $10 Circulation: 7,003 per issue (paid and free). **Owner(s):** DeWitt Observer Publishing Inc, See address and contact information above. **Management:** Jean Bormann, Advertising Director. **Editorial:** Mary Rueter, Editor. Steve Thiltgen, Sports.

DOON

DOON PRESS. 104 First Ave., Doon, IA 51235. Telephone: 712-726-3313. Mailing Address: PO Box 100, Doon, IA 51235. Year Established: 1872. Pub. Frequency: w. (Thu.) Page Size: tabloid. Subscrip. Rate: $.50 newsstand/cover; $17.25/yr in area; $18.50/yr within 50 mi. radius; $19.50/yr in county; $23.50/yr mailed elsewhere. Circulation: 2,800 per issue (paid). **Owner(s):** Bridget Vander Tuin, See address and contact information above. **Management:** Bridget Vander Tuin, President. **Editorial:** Harold Aardema, Editor.

DYERSVILLE

DYERSVILLE COMMERCIAL. 223 First Ave., E., Dyersville, IA 52040-0350. Telephone: 563-875-7131. FAX: 563-875-2279. E-MAIL: dceditor@wcinet.com. Mailing Address: PO Box 350, Dyersville, IA 52040-0350. Year Established: 1873. Pub. Frequency: w. (Wed.) Page Size: broadsheet. Subscrip. Rate: $1 newsstand/cover; $30/yr local; $44/yr in state; $47/yr out of state. Adv. Rate: col. inch $7.70 Freelance Pay: $0.04/word. Circulation: 4,000 per issue (paid). **Owner(s):** Woodward Communications Inc., PO Box 688, Dubuque, IA 52004. Telephone: 563-588-5687. FAX: 563-588-5739. **Management:** Mary Ungs-Sogaard, General Manager. Shannon Funke, Circulation Manager. **Editorial:** Josh Jorgeson, Editor.

EAGLE GROVE

EAGLE GROVE EAGLE. 314 W. Broadway, Eagle Grove, IA 50533. Telephone: 515-448-4745. FAX: 515-448-3182. E-MAIL: egeagle@netins.net. Mailing Address: PO Box 6, Eagle Grove, IA 50533-0006. Year Established: 1896. Pub. Frequency: w. (Wed.) Page Size: broadsheet. Subscrip. Rate: $1 newsstand/cover; $41/yr local; $44/yr mailed in state; $47/yr mailed out of state. Adv. Rate: col. inch $5.90 Circulation: 2,500 per issue (paid). **Owner(s):** Mid-America Publishing Corp., See address and contact information above. **Management:** Ryan Harvey, Publisher. Leigh Banwell, Advertising Manager. Regina Lesher, Circulation Manager. **Editorial:** Kim Demory, Editor.

EDGEWOOD

EDGEWOOD REMINDER. 108 E. Union St., Edgewood, IA 52042. Telephone: 563-928-6876. FAX: 563-928-6876. E-MAIL: reminder@mwc.net. Pub. Frequency: w. (Tue.) Page Size: tabloid. Subscrip. Rate: $.80 newsstand/cover; $22/yr in state; $26/yr out of state. Circulation: 1,500 per issue (paid and free). **Owner(s):** John & Julie Miller, See address and contact information above. **Management:** John Miller, President. Julie Miller, Publisher. **Editorial:** Julie Miller, News Editor.

ELDORA

ELDORA HERALD-LEDGER. 1513 W. Edgington Ave., Eldora, IA 50627. Telephone: 641-939-5051. FAX: 641-939-5541. URL: http://www.eldoraheraldledger.com. Year Established: 1880. Pub. Frequency: w. (Tue.) Page Size: broadsheet. Subscrip. Rate: $.75 newsstand/cover; $36/yr. Adv. Rate: col. inch $7.10 Circulation: 2,850 per issue (paid). **Owner(s):** GateHouse Media, Inc, 350 WillowBrook Office Park, Fairport, NY 14450. Telephone: 585-598-0030. FAX: 585-248-2631. **Management:** Scott Bierle, General Manager. Susan Woodman, Advertising. **Editorial:** Rick Patrie, Editor. Scott Bierle, Sports.

HARDIN COUNTY INDEX. 1513 W. Edgington Ave., Eldora, IA 50627. Telephone: 641-939-5051. FAX: 641-939-5541. Year Established: 1940. Pub. Frequency: w. (Fri.) Page Size: broadsheet.Subscrip. Rate: $.75 newsstand/cover; $36/yr Circulation: 2,850 per issue (paid). **Owner(s):** GateHouse Media, Inc, 350 WillowBrook Office Park, Fairport, NY 14450. Telephone: 585-598-0030. FAX: 585-248-2631. **Management:** Scott Bierle, General Manager. **Editorial:** Rick Patrie, Editor. Scott Bierle, Sports.

ELDRIDGE

NORTH SCOTT PRESS, THE. 214 N. Second St., Eldridge, IA 52748. Telephone: 563-285-8111. FAX: 563-285-8114. E-MAIL: btubbs@northscottpress.com. URL: http://www.northscottpress.com. Mailing Address: PO Box 200, Eldridge, IA 52748-0200. Year Established: 1968. Pub. Frequency: w. (Wed.) Page Size: tabloid. Subscrip. Rate: $1 newsstand/cover; $33/yr in county. Adv. Rate: col. inch $12 Circulation: 5,600 per issue (paid). **Owner(s):** North Scott Press, Inc., See address and contact information above. **Management:** William F. Tubbs, Publisher. **Editorial:** Charles Scott Campbell, Editor.

ELKADER

CLAYTON COUNTY REGISTER, THE. 106 Cedar, N.W., Elkader, IA 52043-0130. Telephone: 563-245-1311. FAX: 563-245-1312. E-MAIL: ccrnews@pinecom.net. Mailing Address: PO Box 130, Elkader, IA 52043-0130. Year Established: 1878. Pub. Frequency: w. (Wed.) Page Size: broadsheet. Subscrip. Rate: $1 newsstand/cover; $29/yr local; $38/yr out of state. Adv. Rate: col. inch $7.18 Circulation: 3,000 per issue (paid). **Owner(s):** News Publishing Co., PO Box 286, Black Earth, WI 53515. Telephone: 608-767-3655. FAX: 608-767-2222. **Management:** Tom Johnson, Publisher. Curtis Ruhser, Advertising Manager. Joanne Gray, Circulation Manager. **Editorial:** Robert Andersen, Editor.

EMMETSBURG

EMMETSBURG DEMOCRAT. 1901 Main St., Emmetsburg, IA 50536. Telephone: 712-852-2323. FAX: 712-852-3184. Mailing Address: PO Box 73, Emmetsburg, IA 50536. Year Established: 1877. Pub. Frequency: w. (Thu.) Page Size: broadsheet. Subscrip. Rate: $.50 newsstand/cover; $29.50/yr mailed in county. Circulation: 2,268 per issue (paid). **Owner(s):** Ogden Newspapers of Minnesota, Inc., 1500 Main St., Wheeling, WV 26003. **Management:** John Schmidt, General Manager. Dan McCain, Advertising Manager. **Editorial:** Jane Whitmore, Editor.

EMMETSBURG REPORTER. 1901 Main St., Emmetsburg, IA 50536. Telephone: 712-852-2323. FAX: 712-852-3184. Mailing Address: PO Box 73, Emmetsburg, IA 50536. Year Established: 1877. Pub. Frequency: w. (Tue.) Page Size: broadsheet. Subscrip. Rate: $.50 newsstand/cover; $29.50/yr in county; $33/yr out of county. Circulation: 2,500 per issue (paid). **Owner(s):** Ogden Newspapers of Minnesota, Inc., 1500 Main St., Wheeling, WV 26003. **Management:** John Schmidt, Publisher. Dan McCain, Advertising Manager. **Editorial:** Jane Whitmore, Editor. Dan Voigt, Sports.

FOREST CITY

FOREST CITY SUMMIT. 105 S. Clark St., Forest City, IA 50436. Telephone: 641-585-2112. FAX: 641-585-4442. URL: http://www.forestcitysummit.com. Mailing Address: PO Box 350, Forest City, IA 50436. Year Established: 1867. Pub. Frequency: w. (Tue.) Page Size: broadsheet. Subscrip. Rate: $.75 newsstand/cover; $29/yr in county & adj cys; $36/yr IA & MN; $41/yr mailed elsewhere. Circulation: 10,500 per issue (paid). **Owner(s):** Lee Enterprises, Inc., 201 N. Harrison St., Davenport, IA 52801-1924. **Management:** Joyce Paul, Advertising. **Editorial:** Bob Fenske, Editor. Matt Foy, Sports.

WINNEBAGO HANCOCK SHOPPER. 105 S. Clark St., Forest City, IA 50436. Telephone: 641-585-2112. FAX: 641-585-4442. E-MAIL: fcsummit@wctatel.net. URL: http://www.forestcitysummit.com. Mailing Address: PO Box 350, Forest City, IA 50346-0350. Pub. Frequency: w. (Tue.) Page Size: broadsheet Circulation: 13,000 per issue (free). **Owner(s):** Lee Enterprises, Inc., 215 N. Main St., Davenport, IA 52801. Telephone: 563-383-2100. FAX: 563-323-9608. **Management:** Joe McDermott, Publisher. Joyce Paul, Advertising. **Editorial:** Angie Johannsen, Managing Editor.

FREMONT

VILLAGE VINE. Main St, Fremont, IA 52561. Telephone: 641-634-2092. FAX: 641-933-4471. Year Established: 2004. Pub. Frequency: w. (Wed.) Page Size: broadsheet. Subscrip. Rate: $.50 newsstand/cover; $25/yr in state; $30/yr out of state. Circulation: 501 per issue (paid). **Owner(s):** Mid-America Publishing, Inc., PO Box 29, Hampton, IA 50441. Telephone: 641-456-2585. FAX: 641-456-2587. **Management:** Chad Hicks, Publisher.

GLENWOOD

GLENWOOD OPINION-TRIBUNE. ISSN 0746-4398
116 S. Walnut St., Glenwood, IA 51534-0191. Telephone: 712-527-3191. FAX: 712-527-3193. E-MAIL: editorjoe@stratomail.com. URL: http://www.glenwoodopiniontribune.com. Mailing Address: PO Box 191, Glenwood, IA 51534-0191. Year Established: 1864. Pub. Frequency: w. (Wed.) Page Size: broadsheet. Subscrip. Rate: $.75 newsstand/cover; $28/yr in county; $47/yr out of county. Circulation: 3,800 per issue (paid). **Owner(s):** Landmark Community Newspapers, Inc., PO Box 549, Shelbyville, KY 40065. Telephone: 502-633-2526. **Management:** Tim Craig, General Manager. Erica Childers, Circulation Manager. **Editorial:** Joe Foreman, Editor. Chad Inman, Sports Editor.

GREENE

GREENE RECORDER, THE. P.O. Box 370, Greene, IA 50636-0370. Telephone: 641-816-4525. E-MAIL: news2greenrecorder.com. URL: http://www.greenrecorder.com. Year Established: 1883. Pub. Frequency: w. (Wed.) Page Size: broadsheet. Subscrip. Rate: $.50 newsstand/cover; $24/yr local; $26/yr in state; $28/yr out of state. Circulation: 1,218 per issue (paid and free). **Owner(s):** Ross & Sarah Hawker, 219 Second St., N, Greene, IA 50636. Telephone: 641-816-4525. FAX: 641-816-4525. **Management:** Fred J. Hawker, Publisher. **Editorial:** Syliva J. Hawker, Editor-in-Chief.

GREENFIELD

ADAIR COUNTY FREE PRESS. ISSN 1072-7523
108 E. Iowa St., Greenfield, IA 50849. Telephone: 641-743-6121. FAX: 641-743-6378. E-MAIL: FREEPRS@mddc.com. Year Established: 1889. Pub. Frequency: w. (Wed.) Page Size: broadsheet. Subscrip. Rate: $.75 newsstand/cover; $22/yr. Adv. Rate: col. inch $5 Circulation: 3,000 per issue (paid). **Owner(s):** Ed J. Sidey, See address and contact information above. **Management:** Ed J. Sidey, Publisher. Linda Sidey, Advertising. Denna Mitchell, Circulation Manager. **Editorial:** Terri Queck-Matzie, Editor.

GRINNELL

GRINNELL HERALD-REGISTER. 813 Fifth Ave., Grinnell, IA 50112-0360. Telephone: 641-236-3113. FAX: 641-236-5135. Mailing Address: PO Box 360, Grinnell, IA 50112-0360. Year Established: 1868. Pub. Frequency: s-w. (Mon. & Thu.) Page Size: broadsheet. Subscrip. Rate: $.75 newsstand/cover; $41.50/yr local; $47.50/yr out of area. Adv. Rate: col. inch $8.40 Circulation: 3,550 per issue (paid and free). **Owner(s):** Mr. & Mrs. A.J. Pinder, 813 Fifth Ave., Grinnell, IA 50112. Telephone: 641-236-3113. FAX: 641-236-5135. **Management:** A.J. Pinder, Publisher. Larry Pinder, Operations Manager. **Editorial:** Martha Pinder, Managing Editor. Dorothy Pinder, Lifestyle Editor. Larry Pinder, Sports Editor.

GRUNDY CENTER

GRUNDY REGISTER. 601 G Ave., Grundy Center, IA 50638. Telephone: 319-824-6958. FAX: 319-824-6288. Mailing Address: PO Box 245, Grundy Center, IA 50638-0245. Year Established: 1868. Pub. Frequency: w. (Wed.) Page Size: broadsheet. Subscrip. Rate: $1 newsstand/cover; $32/yr in county; $41/yr out of county. Adv. Rate: col. inch $5 Circulation: 3,000 per issue (paid). **Owner(s):** Mid-America Publishing Corp., PO Box 29, Hampton, IA 50441. Telephone: 641-456-2585. **Management:** Steve Tilkes, Publisher. **Editorial:** Steve Tilkes, Editor.

GUTHRIE CENTER

GUTHRIE CENTER TIMES. 205 State St., Guthrie Center, IA 50115. Telephone: 641-332-2380. FAX: 641-332-2382. E-MAIL: gctimes@netins.net. URL: http://www.guthrian.com. Year Established: 1856. Pub. Frequency: w. (Wed.) Page Size: broadsheet. Subscrip. Rate: $.50 newsstand/cover; $20/yr in county; $25/yr mailed elsewhere. Circulation: 2,360 per issue (paid). **Owner(s):** Scott Gonzales, See address and contact information above. **Management:** Scott Gonzales, Publisher. Beth Rogers, Advertising Manager. **Editorial:** Scott Gonzales, Editor. Betty Thompson, Society Editor.

GUTTENBERG

GUTTENBERG PRESS, THE. 10 Schiller St., Guttenberg, IA 52052. Telephone: 563-252-2421. FAX: 563-252-1275. E-MAIL: gbpress@alpinecom.net. URL: http://www.guttenbergpress.com. Mailing Address: PO Box 937, Guttenberg, IA 52052. Year Established: 1897. Pub. Frequency: w. (Wed.) Page Size: tabloid. Subscrip. Rate: $.75 newsstand/cover; $26/yr local; $34/yr out of county. Circulation: 2,600 per issue (paid and free). **Owner(s):** Howe Printing Co., PO Box 149, Prairie du Chien, WI 53821. **Management:** Jane Thein, Advertising Manager.

HAMBURG

HAMBURG REPORTER, THE. 1009 Main, Hamburg, IA 51640. Telephone: 712-382-1234. FAX: 712-382-1222. URL: http://www.hamburgreporter.com. Mailing Address: PO Box 99, Hamburg, IA 51640-0099. Pub. Frequency: w. (Thu.) Page Size: standard. Subscrip. Rate: $.50 newsstand/cover; $25/yr in county; $35/yr out of county. Circulation: 1,100 per issue (paid). **Owner(s):** GateHouse Media, Inc, 350 WillowBrook Office Park, Fairport, NY 14450. Telephone: 585-598-0030. **Management:** Tim Larson, Publisher. Kathleen Kaufman, Advertising Manager. Janet Entler, Circulation Manager. **Editorial:** Tammy Pearson, Executive Editor.

HAMPTON

HAMPTON CHRONICLE. 9 Second St., N.W., Hampton, IA 50441. URL: http://www.hamptonchronicle.com. Mailing Address: PO Box 29, Hampton, IA 50441. Year Established: 1876. Pub. Frequency: w. (Wed.) Page Size: broadsheet. Subscrip. Rate: $1 newsstand/cover; $38/yr in county; $43/yr out of county; $48/yr out of state. Circulation: 72,000 per issue (paid and free). **Owner(s):** Hampton Publishing Co., PO Box 29, Hampton, IA. Telephone: 641-456-2585. **Management:** Joseph P. Roth, President. Brad Hicks, Publisher. Deb Cheney, Circulation Manager.

SIGOURNEY NEWS-REVIEW. 9 2nd St NW, Hampton, IA 50441. E-MAIL: signred@lisco.com. URL: http://www.sigourneynewsreview.com. Year Established: 1870. Pub. Frequency: w. (Wed.) Page Size: broadsheet. Subscrip. Rate: $1 newsstand/cover; $40/yr in state; $43/yr out of state. Adv. Rate: col. inch $7.10 Freelance Pay: $20/article. Circulation: 2,649 per issue (paid). **Owner(s):** Mid-America Publishing Corp., See address and contact information above.

HARLAN

HARLAN NEWS-ADVERTISER. Press Bldg., 1114 Seventh St, Harlan, IA 51537-0721. Telephone: 712-755-3111. FAX: 712-755-3324. E-MAIL: news2@harlanonline.com. URL: http://www.harlanonline.com. Mailing Address: PO Box 721, Harlan, IA 51537-0721. Year Established: 1870. Pub. Frequency: w. (Fri.) Page Size: broadsheet. Subscrip. Rate: $1 newsstand/cover; $44/yr includes "tribune". Adv. Rate: col. inch $7.25 Circulation: 4,725 per issue (paid). **Owner(s):** Alan & Steve Mores, See address and contact information above. **Management:** Alan Mores, Publisher. Mike Kolbe, Advertising Manager. **Editorial:** Bob Bjoin, Editor-in-Chief. Mike Oeffner, Sports.

HARLAN TRIBUNE. Press Bldg., 1114 Seventh St, Harlan, IA 51537-0721. Telephone: 712-755-3111. FAX: 712-755-3324. E-MAIL: news@harlanonline.com. URL: http://www.harlanonline.com. Mailing Address: PO Box 721, Harlan, IA 51537-0721. Year Established: 1879. Pub. Frequency: w. (Tue.) Page Size: broadsheet. Subscrip. Rate: $1 newsstand/cover; $44/yr for 2 papers incl. Adv.. Adv. Rate: col. inch $7.25 Circulation: 4,725 per issue (paid). **Owner(s):** Alan & Steve Mores, See address and contact information above. **Management:** Alan Mores, Publisher. Mike Kolbe, Advertising Manager. **Editorial:** Bob Bjoin, Editor.

HUDSON

HUDSON HERALD, THE. 411 Jefferson St., Hudson, IA 50643-0210. Telephone: 319-988-3855. FAX: 319-988-3855. E-MAIL: hudherald@forbin.net. Year Established: 1911. Pub. Frequency: w. (Thu.) Page Size: broadsheet. Subscrip. Rate: $.50 newsstand/cover; $28/yr. Adv. Rate: col. inch $4 Circulation: 1,500 per issue (paid). **Owner(s):** Hudson Printing Co., See address and contact information above. **Management:** Clifford Murray, Owner. **Editorial:** Clifford Murray, Editor-in-Chief.

HUMBOLDT

HUMBOLDT INDEPENDENT. 512 Sumner Ave., Humboldt, IA 50548. Telephone: 515-332-2514. FAX: 515-332-1505. E-MAIL: independent@humboldtnews.com. URL: http://www.humboldtnews.com. Year Established: 1889. Pub. Frequency: w. (Thu.) Page Size: broadsheet. Subscrip. Rate: $1 newsstand/cover; $34/yr in state; $44/yr out of state. Circulation: 4,200 per issue (paid). **Owner(s):** Gargano Communications, Inc., See address and contact information above. **Management:** James Gargano, Publisher. **Editorial:** Jeffrey Gargano, Editor.

INDEPENDENCE

INDEPENDENCE BULLETIN-JOURNAL. 116 Fifth Ave, NE, Independence, IA 50644. Telephone: 319-334-2557. FAX: 319-334-6752. URL: http://www.bulletinjournal.com. Mailing Address: PO Box 290, Independence, IA 50644. Year Established: 1860. Pub. Frequency: s-w. (Wed. & Sat.) Page Size: broadsheet. Subscrip. Rate: $1 newsstand/cover; $47/yr mailed in area; $55/yr out of area. Circulation: 4,000 per issue (paid). **Owner(s):** Community Media Group, Inc, PO Box 10, West Frankfort, IL 62896. Telephone: 618-937-6412. **Management:** John Perratto, Publisher. Cindy Klendworth, Advertising. Susan Hosto, Circulation Manager. Lori Smith, Classified Adv. Mgr.. **Editorial:** Jessica Birthisel, Editor. Jacki Ellenwood, News Editor. John Jensen, Sports Editor.

INDIANOLA

RECORD-HERALD & INDIANOLA TRIBUNE. ISSN 0895-3287 1801 W. Second Ave., Ste. 2, Indianola, IA 50125. Telephone: 515-961-2511. FAX: 515-961-4833. E-MAIL: tevans@dmreg.com. Mailing Address: PO Box 259, Indianola, IA 50125. Year Established: 1857. Pub. Frequency: w. (Wed.) Page Size: broadsheet. Subscrip. Rate: $.75 newsstand/cover; $29/yr in county; $38/yr mailed elsewhere. Adv. Rate: col. inch $8.12 Circulation: 5,250 per issue (controlled and free). **Owner(s):** Des Moines Register & Tribune, PO Box 957, Des Moines, IA 50304. Telephone: 515-284-8000. **Management:** Amy Duncan, Publisher. Becky Vanderberg, Advertising Manager. Susie Kling, Circulation Manager. **Editorial:** Amy Duncan, Editor. Mike Rolands, Managing Editor. Bill Hendricks, Sports.

IOWA FALLS

TIMES CITIZEN. PO Box 640, Iowa Falls, IA 50126. Telephone: 641-648-2521. FAX: 641-648-4605. URL: http://www.timescitizen.com. Year Established: 1881. Pub. Frequency: s-w. (Wed. & Sat.) Page Size: broadsheet. Subscrip. Rate: $.75 newsstand/cover; $34/yr local. Circulation: 3,700 per issue (paid). **Owner(s):** Times Citizen Communications, See address and contact information above. **Management:** Jo E. Martin, General Manager. Mark Hamilton, Publisher. Susan Duncan, Circulation Manager. **Editorial:** Kent Thomson, Editor.

JEFFERSON

JEFFERSON BEE. 214 N. Wilson Ave., Jefferson, IA 50129. Telephone: 515-386-4161. FAX: 515-386-4162. Year Established: 1866. Pub. Frequency: w. (Tue.) Page Size: broadsheet. Subscrip. Rate: $26/yr mailed in state; $34.50/yr mailed out of state. Adv. Rate: col. inch $6.10 Circulation: 7,300 per issue (free). **Owner(s):** Bee Herald Publishing Co., See address and contact information above. **Management:** Frederick G. Morain, Publisher. Deb Geisler, Advertising. **Editorial:** Frederick G. Morain, Editor. Doug Rieder, Sports. Tori Chargo, Writer.

JEFFERSON HERALD, THE. 214 N. Wilson Ave., Jefferson, IA 50129. Telephone: 515-386-4161. FAX: 515-386-4162. Year Established: 1891. Pub. Frequency: w. (Fri.) Page Size: broadsheet. Subscrip. Rate: $.75 newsstand/cover; $26/yr mailed in state; $35.50/yr mailed out of state. Adv. Rate: col. inch $4.60 Circulation: 3,300 per issue (paid). **Owner(s):** Bee Herald Publishing Co., See address and contact information above. **Management:** Frederick G. Morain, Publisher. Deb Geisler, Advertising. **Editorial:** Frederick G. Morain, Editor. Doug Rieder, Sports. Tori Chargo, Writer.

KALONA

KALONA NEWS, THE. PO Box 430, Kalona, IA 52247-0430. Telephone: 319-656-2104. FAX: 319-656-2299. E-MAIL: knews@kctc.net. URL: http://www.kctc.net/knews. Year Established: 1891. Pub. Frequency: w. (Thu.) Page Size: broadsheet. Subscrip. Rate: $1 newsstand/cover; $33/yr in county; $35/yr in state; $40/yr mailed out of state. Circulation: 2,800 per issue (paid). **Owner(s):** Sleckta Communications, See address and contact information above. **Management:** Ronald C. Slechta, Publisher. Helen M. Slechta, Circulation Manager. **Editorial:** Ronald C. Slechta, Editor-in-Chief.

KEOKUK

GATE CITY FREE PRESS. 1016 Main St., Keokuk, IA 52632-0430. Telephone: 319-524-8300. FAX: 319-524-4363. URL: http://www.gatecity. Mailing Address: PO Box 430, Keokuk, IA 52632-0430. Pub. Frequency: w. (Wed.) Page Size: tabloid Circulation: 6,000 per issue (free). **Owner(s):** Brehm Communications, Inc., 16644 W. Bernardo Dr., Ste. 300, San Diego, CA 92128. **Management:** Mark Smidt, Publisher. Doug Shipman, Advertising Manager. Diane Bolton, Circulation Manager.

KNOXVILLE

KNOXVILLE JOURNAL EXPRESS, THE. 122 E. Robinson, Knoxville, IA 50138. Telephone: 641-842-2155. FAX: 641-842-2929. URL: http://www.journalexpress.net. Mailing Address: PO Box 458, Knoxville, IA 50138. Year Established: 1855. Pub. Frequency: w. (Fri.) Page Size: broadsheet. Subscrip. Rate: $.75 newsstand/cover; $32/yr in county; $37/yr elsewhere. Adv. Rate: col. inch $7.57 Freelance Pay: $5-$50/article. Circulation: 2,500 per issue (paid). **Owner(s):** Community Newspaper Holdings, Inc., 3500 Colonnade Pkwy., Ste. 600, Birmingham, AL 35243. Telephone: 205-298-7100. FAX: 205-298-7101. **Management:** Sandy Selvy, Publisher. Reggie Dodd, Circulation Manager. **Editorial:** Steve Woodhouse, Editor.

MARION COUNTY REMINDER. 122 E. Robinson, Knoxville, IA 50138. Telephone: 641-842-2155. FAX: 641-842-2929. URL: http://www.journalexpress.net. Mailing Address: PO Box 458, Knoxville, IA 50138. Year Established: 1969. Pub. Frequency: w. (Tue.) Page Size: tabloid.Adv. Rate: col. inch $8.65 Circulation: 21,500 per issue (free). **Owner(s):** Community Newspaper Holdings, Inc., 3500 Colonnade Pkwy., Ste. 600, Birmingham, AL 35243-1031. **Management:** Sandy Selvy, Publisher. Carrie Short, Circulation Manager. **Editorial:** Clint Brown, Editor.

LEON

LEON JOURNAL-REPORTER. 110 N. Main St., Leon, IA 50144. Telephone: 641-446-4151. FAX: 641-446-7645. Mailing Address: PO Box 580, Leon, IA 50144-0580. Year Established: 1861. Pub. Frequency: w. (Wed.) Page Size: standard. Subscrip. Rate: $.50 newsstand/cover; $22/yr in county; $32/yr out of county. Circulation: 2,144 per issue (paid). **Owner(s):** Gary D. Lindsey & Corey R. Lindsey, See address and contact information above. **Management:** Gary D. Lindsey, Chairman of the Board. Corey R. Lindsey, Advertising Manager.

LIME SPRINGS

LIME SPRINGS HERALD. PO Box 187, Lime Springs, IA 52155. Telephone: 563-566-2687. FAX: 507-324-5267. E-MAIL: evanssppc@smig.net. Year Established: 1888. Pub. Frequency: w. (Thu.) Page Size: broadsheet. Subscrip. Rate: $.75 newsstand/cover; $27/yr area; $30/yr out of area. Circulation: 750 per issue (paid). **Owner(s):** Dan & Joyce Evans, See address and contact information above. **Management:** Dan Evans, Publisher. **Editorial:** Dan Evans, Editor.

LONE TREE

LONE TREE REPORTER, THE. 117 LaVoe, Lone Tree, IA 52755-0235. Telephone: 319-629-5207. FAX: 319-629-4203. E-MAIL: itnews@iowatelecom.net. URL: http://www.lonetreereporter.com. Mailing Address: PO Box 235, Lone Tree, IA 52755. Year Established: 1893. Pub. Frequency: w. (Thu.) Page Size: tabloid. Subscrip. Rate: $.75 newsstand/cover; $25/yr mailed in state; $30/yr mailed out of state. Freelance Pay: $10/article. Circulation: 6,350 per issue (paid). **Owner(s):** Slechta Communications, Inc., PO Box 430, Kalena, IA 52247. Telephone: 319-656-2273. FAX: 319-656-2299. **Management:** Ronald C. Slechta, Publisher. **Editorial:** Jonathan E Green, Editor-in-Chief.

MALVERN

FREMONT MILLS BEACON ENTERPRISE. PO Box 129, Malvern, IA 51551. Telephone: 712-624-8512. FAX: 712-624-9250. Pub. Frequency: w. (Thu.) Page Size: broadsheet. Subscrip. Rate: $.50 newsstand/cover; $20/yr in county; $26/yr out of county; $28/yr out of state. Circulation: 600 per issue (paid). **Owner(s):** Mark A. & Karol Siekman, See address and contact information above. **Management:** Karol Siekman, Publisher. Margaret Waugh, Advertising. **Editorial:** Karol Siekman, Editor.

MALVERN LEADER, THE. PO Box 129, Malvern, IA 51551. Telephone: 712-624-8512. FAX: 712-624-9250. E-MAIL: msiekman@radiks.net. Year Established: 1874. Pub. Frequency: w. (Thu.) Page Size: broadsheet. Subscrip. Rate: $.50 newsstand/cover; $20/yr in county; $26/yr out of county; $28/yr out of state; $19/yr to senior citizens. Circulation: 700 per issue (paid). **Owner(s):** Mark A. & Karol Siekman, See address and contact information above. **Management:** Karol Siekman, Publisher. Margaret Waugh, Advertising Manager. **Editorial:** Karol Siekman, Editor.

MANCHESTER

MANCHESTER PRESS. 109 E. Delaware St., Manchester, IA 52057. Telephone: 563-927-2020. FAX: 563-927-4945. Mailing Address: PO Box C, Manchester, IA 52057. Year Established: 1871. Pub. Frequency: w. (Tue.) Page Size: broadsheet.Subscrip. Rate: $1 newsstand/cover; $41/yr Circulation: 5,000 per issue (paid). **Owner(s):** News Publishing Co., PO Box 286, Black Earth, WI 53515. Telephone: 608-767-3655. **Management:** Brian Cook, Publisher. Barbara Passeho, Advertising Manager.

Weeklies

MAQUOKETA

MAQUOKETA SENTINEL-PRESS. 108 W. Quarry St., Maquoketa, IA 52060. Telephone: 563-652-2441. FAX: 563-652-6094. E-MAIL: mspress@mspress.net. URL: http://www.mspress.jimdo.com. Year Established: 1854. Pub. Frequency: s-w. (Wed. & Sat.) Page Size: broadsheet. Subscrip. Rate: $1 newsstand/cover; $50/yr in county; $65/yr out of county; $72/yr mailed elsewhere. Circulation: 5,000 per issue (paid). **Owner(s):** Maquoketa Newspapers, Inc., See address and contact information above. **Management:** Douglas Melvold, Publisher. Nan Tracy, Advertising. Rosie Morehead, Advertising Manager. Dianne Barker, Circulation Manager. Nancy Rockwell, Classified Adv. Mgr.. **Editorial:** Douglas Melvold, Editor. Beth Melvold, Production Manager. Vickie Earles, Family Editor. Mike Earles, Sports Editor.

MARENGO

PIONEER REPUBLICAN, THE. ISSN 1087-1179
100 W. Main St., Marengo, IA 52301. Telephone: 319-642-5506. FAX: 319-642-5509. E-MAIL: publish@netins.net. Mailing Address: PO Box 208, Marengo, IA 52301. Year Established: 1853. Pub. Frequency: w. (Thu.) Page Size: broadsheet. Subscrip. Rate: $1 newsstand/cover (effective 2005); $28/yr in state (effective 2004); $37/yr out of state. Adv. Rate: col. inch $6.75 Circulation: 2,100 per issue (paid). **Owner(s):** Gannett Company, Inc., 7950 Jones Branch Dr., McLean, VA 22107-0001. Telephone: 703-854-6000. **Management:** Martin Bunge, Publisher. John Rotter, Advertising Manager. Audrey Yardley, Circulation Manager. **Editorial:** Dan Adix, Editor.

MISSOURI VALLEY

MISSOURI VALLEY TIMES-NEWS. 501 E. Erie St., Missouri Valley, IA 51555. E-MAIL: news@missourivalleytimes.com. URL: http://www.missourivalleytimes.com. Mailing Address: PO Box 159, Missouri Valley, IA 51555-0159. Year Established: 1868. Pub. Frequency: s-w. (Wed. & Fri.) Page Size: broadsheet. Subscrip. Rate: $.75 newsstand/cover; $42/yr in area; $55/yr mailed out of area; $64/yr mailed out of state. Adv. Rate: col. inch $8 Circulation: 2,100 per issue (paid). **Owner(s):** Mark Rhoades, 138 N. 16th, Blair, NE 68008. Telephone: 402-426-2121. FAX: 402-426-2227. **Management:** Mark Rhoades, President. Brad Swensen, Publisher. Kris Gash, Office Manager. **Editorial:** Pete Graham, Editor. Matt Gengler, Sports Editor.

MONROE

MONROE LEGACY. 213 W Mills, Monroe, IA 50170-0340. Telephone: 641-259-2708. Mailing Address: P O Box 340, Monroe, IA 50170-0340. Pub. Frequency: w. (Thu.) Subscrip. Rate: $.45 newsstand/cover; $20/yr mailed in county; $21/yr mailed out of county. Circulation: 936 per issue (paid). **Owner(s):** Shaw Newspapers, See address and contact information above. **Management:** Kathleen Darrach, Publisher. **Editorial:** Kathleen Darrach, Editor.

MONTEZUMA

MONTEZUMA REPUBLICAN, THE. 406 E. Main St., Montezuma, IA 50171. Telephone: 641-623-5116. FAX: 641-623-5580. Mailing Address: PO Box 100, Montezuma, IA 50171. Year Established: 1856. Pub. Frequency: w. (Wed.) Page Size: broadsheet. Subscrip. Rate: $26/yr in county; $28/yr mailed in state. Circulation: 1,900 per issue (paid). **Owner(s):** Gannett Company, Inc., 7950 Jones Branch Dr., McLean, VA 22107-0001. Telephone: 703-854-6000. **Management:** Dan DeBettignies, Publisher. **Editorial:** J. O. Parker, Editor.

MONTICELLO

MONTICELLO EXPRESS. 111 E. Grand, Monticello, IA 52310. Telephone: 319-465-3555. FAX: 319-465-4611. E-MAIL: mexpress@n-connect.net. URL: http://www.monticelloexpress.com. Mailing Address: PO Box 191, Monticello, ID 52310. Year Established: 1865. Pub. Frequency: w. (Wed.) Page Size: tabloid. Subscrip. Rate: $1 newsstand/cover; $28/yr in county. Circulation: 3,400 per issue (paid). **Owner(s):** Monticello Express, Inc., See address and contact information above. **Management:** Dan Goodyear, Co-Publisher. Mark Spensley, Advertising Manager. **Editorial:** Angela Owen, Editor-in-Chief. Pete Temple, Sports.

MOUNT AYR

MOUNT AYR RECORD-NEWS. PO Box 346, Mount Ayr, IA 50854-0346. Telephone: 641-464-2440. FAX: 641-464-2229. E-MAIL: recnews@iowatelecom.net. URL: http://www.mountayrnews.com. Year Established: 1864. Pub. Frequency: w. (Thu.) Page Size: broadsheet. Subscrip. Rate: $.75 newsstand/cover; $27.50/yr in county. Adv. Rate: col. inch $3.85 Circulation: 2,493 per issue (paid). **Owner(s):** H. Alan Smith, 122 W Madison St, Mount Ayr, IA 59854. **Management:** H. Alan Smith, Publisher. Veva Haley, Advertising Manager. Sandy Main, Circulation Manager. **Editorial:** H. Alan Smith, Editor.

MT. VERNON

SUN (MT. VERNON), THE. Main St., Mt. Vernon, IA 52314. E-MAIL: news@mtvernonlisbonsun.com. URL: http://www.mtvernonlisbonsun.com. Year Established: 1869. Pub. Frequency: w. (Thu.) Page Size: broadsheet. Subscrip. Rate: $1 newsstand/cover; $29/yr in county; $39/yr out of county; $43/yr out of state. Circulation: 3,200 per issue (paid and free). **Owner(s):** West Branch Communications, PO Box 129, Mt. Vernon, IA 52314. Telephone: 319-895-6216. FAX: 319-895-6217. **Management:** Jake Krob, Publisher. Stephanie Hasselmann, Advertising Manager. **Editorial:** Margaret Stevens, Managing Editor.

NASHUA

NASHUA REPORTER. 216 Main St., Nashua, IA 50658. Telephone: 641-435-4151. Mailing Address: PO Box 67, Nashua, IA 50658-0067. Year Established: 1878. Pub. Frequency: w. (Wed.) Page Size: broadsheet. Subscrip. Rate: $.50 newsstand/cover; $20/yr in county; $23/yr in state. Adv. Rate: col. inch $4 Circulation: 1,000 per issue (paid). **Owner(s):** Carmen Conklin & Wanda Orric, See address and contact information above. **Management:** Carmen Conklin, Publisher. **Editorial:** Conklin Orric, Editor-in-Chief. Wanda Orric, Managing Editor.

NEVADA

NEVADA JOURNAL (OMAHA). ISSN 0747-430X
922 Lincoln Hwy, Nevada, IA 50201. Telephone: 515-382-2161. FAX: 515-382-4299. E-MAIL: results@nevadaiowajournal.com. URL: http://www.nevadaiowajournal.com. Mailing Address: PO Box 89, Nevada, IA 50201. Year Established: 1895. Pub. Frequency: w. (Thu.) Page Size: standard. Subscrip. Rate: $1 newsstand/cover; $35/yr in county; $49/yr out of county. **Wire Service(s):** AP. Circulation: 3,300 per issue (paid). **Owner(s):** World Newspapers, Inc., World Herald Sq., Omaha, NE 68102. Telephone: 402-444-1000. **Management:** Marlys Barker, General Manager. Wynne Landgraf, Office Manager. Mary Husske, Advertising. Steve Huntrods, Circulation Manager. **Editorial:** Joe Randleman, Sports.

NEW HAMPTON

NEW HAMPTON TRIBUNE. 10 N. Chestnut Ave., New Hampton, IA 50659-0380. Telephone: 641-394-2111. FAX: 641-394-2113. E-MAIL: nhtribune@mchsi.com. URL: http://www.newhamptontribune.com. Mailing Address: PO Box 380, New Hampton, IA 50659-0380. Year Established: 1874. Pub. Frequency: s-w. (Tue. & Fri.) Page Size: broadsheet. Subscrip. Rate: $.75 newsstand/cover; $46/yr in area; $55/yr out of area. Adv. Rate: col. inch $9.26 Circulation: 10,000 per issue (paid and free). **Owner(s):** GateHouse Media, Inc, 350 WillowBrook Office Park, Fairport, NY 14450. Telephone: 585-598-0030. FAX: 585-248-2631. **Management:** Matthew Bryant, Publisher. Misti Shawver, Advertising. **Editorial:** Elaine Denner, Feature Editor. Dorothy Huber, Sports.

NORTHEAST IOWA SHOPPER, THE. 10 N. Chestnut Ave., New Hampton, IA 50659-0380. Telephone: 641-394-2111. FAX: 641-394-2113. URL: http://www.gatehousemedia.com. Mailing Address: PO Box 380, New Hampton, IA 50659-0380. Pub. Frequency: w. (Tue.) Page Size: standard Circulation: 7,440 per issue (free). **Owner(s):** GateHouse Media, Inc, 350 WillowBrook Office Park, Fairport, NY 14450. Telephone: 585-598-0030. **Management:** Matthew Bryant, Publisher. Misti Shawver, Advertising.

ONAWA

ONAWA DEMOCRAT. ISSN 0899-6520
720 Iowa Ave., Onawa, IA 51040-0418. Telephone: 712-423-2411. FAX: 712-423-2411. E-MAIL: democrat@longlines.com. Mailing Address: PO Box 418, Onawa, IA 51040-0418. Year Established: 1890. Pub. Frequency: w. (Wed.) Page Size: standard. Subscrip. Rate: $.50 newsstand/cover; $22/yr local; $28/yr mailed elsewhere. Adv. Rate: col. inch $5 Circulation: 2,870 per issue (paid). **Owner(s):** Wonder & Son Publishing, 720 Iowa Ave., Onawa, IA 51040. Telephone: 712-423-2134. FAX: 712-423-2411. **Management:** Freddie. Wonder, Owner. William Wonder, Publisher.

ONAWA SENTINEL. 1014 Ninth St., Onawa, IA 51040. Telephone: 712-423-2021. FAX: 712-423-3038. Year Established: 1885. Pub. Frequency: w. (Thu.) Page Size: broadsheet. Subscrip. Rate: $.50 newsstand/cover; $14/yr local; $18/yr mailed in state; $24/yr mailed out of state. Adv. Rate: col. inch $3.50 Circulation: 1,800 per issue (paid). **Owner(s):** Verlee Sawyer, See address and contact information above. **Management:** Verlee Sawyer, Publisher. **Editorial:** Verlee Sawyer, Editor.

OSAGE

MITCHELL COUNTY PRESS-NEWS. 112 N. Sixth St., Osage, IA 50461. Telephone: 641-732-3721. FAX: 641-732-5689. E-MAIL: mcpress@osage.net. URL: http://www.mcpress.com. Mailing Address: PO Box 60, Osage, IA 50461. Year Established: 1865. Pub. Frequency: w. (Wed.) Page Size: broadsheet. Subscrip. Rate: $1 newsstand/cover; $32/yr in county; $42/yr out of county. Freelance Pay: $0.12/column-inch. Circulation: 7,000 per issue (paid). **Owner(s):** Lee Enterprises, Inc., 201 N. Harrison St., Davenport, IA 52801-1924. **Management:** Dave Stanley, Publisher. Shari Pohren, Advertising. **Editorial:** Larry Kershner, Editor. Mary Loden, Reporter.

OSCEOLA

OSCEOLA SENTINEL-TRIBUNE. ISSN 0745-6247
115 E. Washington St., Osceola, IA 50213-1244. Telephone: 641-342-2131. FAX: 6641-342-2060. E-MAIL: sentrib@pionet.net. URL: http://www.osceolaiowa.com. Year Established: 1859. Pub. Frequency: w. (Thu.) Page Size: broadsheet. Subscrip. Rate: $.75 newsstand/cover; $22/yr adj cys; $27/yr in state; $32/yr mailed out of state. Adv. Rate: col. inch $4.18 Circulation: 4,200 per issue (paid). **Owner(s):** Sally & Frank Morlan, See address and contact information above. **Editorial:** Frank E. Morlan, Editor.

OSSIAN

OSSIAN BEE, THE. 107 W. Main St., Ossian, IA 52161-0096. Telephone: 563-532-9113. FAX: 563-532-9081. E-MAIL: thebee@acegroup.cc. Mailing Address: PO Box 96, Ossian, IA 52161-0096. Year Established: 1889. Pub. Frequency: w. (Wed.) Page Size: broadsheet. Subscrip. Rate: $.50 newsstand/cover; $15/yr in county; $18/yr out of county. Adv. Rate: col. inch $4.50 Circulation: 1,143 per issue (paid). **Owner(s):** Janell Bradley, 107 W. Main St., Ossian, IA 52161. Telephone: 563-532-9113. FAX: 563-532-9081. **Management:** Janell Bradley, Publisher.

PAULLINA

PAULLINA TIMES. 144 E. Broadway, Paullina, IA 51046-0677. Telephone: 712-949-3622. Mailing Address: PO Box 637, Paullina, IA 51046-0637. Year Established: 1883. Pub. Frequency: w. (Thu.) Page Size: broadsheet. Subscrip. Rate: $.50 newsstand/cover; $20/yr in county; $24/yr out of county. Circulation: 1,400 per issue (paid and free). **Owner(s):** Richard Rodke Enterprises, Inc., See address and contact information above. **Management:** Richard Radke, Publisher.

PELLA

PELLA CHRONICLE. 812 Main St., Pella, IA 50219. Telephone: 641-628-3882. FAX: 641-628-3905. E-MAIL: thechronicle@iowatelecom.net. URL: http://www.pellachronicle.com. Mailing Address: PO Box 126, Pella, IA 50219. Year Established: 1865. Pub. Frequency: w. (Thu.) Page Size: broadsheet. Subscrip. Rate: $.75 newsstand/cover; $27/yr in county; $32/yr mailed out of county. Adv. Rate: col. inch $7.57 Circulation: 2,600 per issue (paid). **Owner(s):** Community Newspaper Holdings, Inc., 3500 Colonnade Pkwy., Ste. 600, Birmingham, AL 35243. Telephone: 205-298-7100. FAX: 205-298-7101. **Management:** Maureen Miller, Publisher. Connie Davis, Circulation Manager. **Editorial:** Clint Brown, Editor.

PERRY

PERRY CHIEF. ISSN 0746-7222
PO Box 98, Perry, IA 50220. Telephone: 515-465-4666. FAX: 515-465-3087. URL: http://www.perrychief.com. Year Established: 1874. Pub. Frequency: w. (Thu.) Page Size: broadsheet. Subscrip. Rate: $.65 newsstand/cover; $17.50 for 6 mos.; $30/yr. Adv. Rate: col. inch $5.81 Circulation: 3,300 per issue (paid). **Owner(s):** Stephen R. Whitehead, See address and contact information above. **Management:** Linda Schumacher, Advertising Manager. **Editorial:** Howard Balaban, Editor.

POCAHONTAS

POCAHONTAS RECORD-DEMOCRAT. 218 N. Main St., Pocahontas, IA 50574. Telephone: 712-335-3553. FAX: 712-335-3856. E-MAIL: rd@evertek.net. Year Established: 1884. Pub. Frequency: w. (Wed.) Page Size: broadsheet. Subscrip. Rate: $.75 newsstand/cover; $23/yr in county; $25.50/yr in adj cys; $27.50/yr in state; $29.50/yr out of state. Circulation: 5,000 per issue (paid). **Owner(s):** Brooks Taylor & Jerry Wiseman, See address and contact information above. **Management:** Brooks Taylor, Publisher. **Editorial:** Brooks Taylor, Editor.

PRAIRIE CITY

PRAIRIE CITY NEWS. P.O.Box 249, Prairie City, IA 50228-0249. Telephone: 515-994-2349. FAX: 515-994-3169. E-MAIL: prairiecitynews@aol.com. Mailing Address: 13533 S. 60th Ave W., Mitchellville, IA 50169-8552. Year Established: 1874. Pub. Frequency: w. (Thu.) Page Size: tabloid. Subscrip. Rate: $.45 newsstand/cover; $19/yr in state; $22/yr out of state. Adv. Rate: col. inch $3.90 Circulation: 1,014 per issue (paid). **Owner(s):** Orian Woods, 108 E. Jefferson, Prairie City, IA 50228. Telephone: 515-994-2349. FAX: 515-994-3169. **Management:** Peter Scarnati, Publisher. **Editorial:** Peter Scarnati, Editor.

RED OAK

RED OAK EXPRESS. ISSN 0747-3281
2012 Commerce Dr., Red Oak, IA 51566. Telephone: 712-623-2566. FAX: 712-623-2568. Mailing Address: PO Box 377, Red Oak, IA 51566. Year Established: 1868. Pub. Frequency: w. (Tue.) Page Size: broadsheet. Subscrip. Rate: $.75 newsstand/cover; $30/yr mailed in county; $51/yr mailed out of state. Adv. Rate: col. inch $6.70 Circulation: 4,800 per issue (paid). **Owner(s):** Landmark Community Newspapers, Inc., PO Box 549, Shelbyville, KY 40065. Telephone: 502-633-2526. FAX: 502-633-2618. **Management:** Jan Castle Renander, General Manager. Laura Schraeder, Circulation Manager. **Editorial:** Jan Castle Renander, Editor.

ROCK RAPIDS

LYON-SIOUX PRESS. 310 First Ave., Rock Rapids, IA 51246. Telephone: 712-472-2525. FAX: 712-472-3414. Year Established: 1888. Pub. Frequency: w. (Wed.) Page Size: broadsheet. Subscrip. Rate: $.75 newsstand/cover; $26/yr in county & adj cys; $40/yr mailed elsewhere. Circulation: 2,900 per issue (paid). **Owner(s):** New Century Press, Inc., See address and contact information above. **Management:** Jim Houck, Publisher. **Editorial:** Jodie Hoogendoorn, Editor.

WESTBROOK SENTINEL/TRIBUNE. 310 First Ave., Rock Rapids, IA 51246. Telephone: 712-472-2525. FAX: 712-472-3414. E-MAIL: sentrib@ncppub.com. URL: http://www.ncppub.com/sentinel.html. Pub. Frequency: w. (Wed..) Page Size: broadsheet. Subscrip. Rate: $1 newsstand/cover; $38/yr mailed in county; $42/yr mailed out of county. Adv. Rate: col. inch $.15 Circulation: 1,320 per issue (paid). **Owner(s):** New Century Press, Inc., See address and contact information above.Readers: General public

SCHALLER

SCHALLER HERALD. PO Box 129, Schaller, IA 51053. Telephone: 712-275-4229. Year Established: 1881. Pub. Frequency: w. (Wed.) Page Size: broadsheet. Subscrip. Rate: $.50 newsstand/cover; $20/yr in county; $23/yr out of county; $25/yr out of state. Circulation: 900 per issue (paid). **Owner(s):** Betty Bailey, See address and contact information above. **Management:** Betty Bailey, Publisher. **Editorial:** Betty Bailey, Editor.

SHELDON

N'WEST IOWA REVIEW. 227 Ninth St., Sheldon, IA 51201-1419. Telephone: 712-324-2514. FAX: 712-324-2345. E-MAIL: pww@iowainformation.com. Mailing Address: PO Box 160, Sheldon, IA 51201-0160. Year Established: 1972. Pub. Frequency: w. (Sat.) Page Size: broadsheet. Subscrip. Rate: $1.25 newsstand/cover; $37.95/yr mailed in county; $52.50/yr mailed out of county. Adv. Rate: col. inch $6.93 Freelance Pay: $50-$250/article. Circulation: 5,500 per issue (paid). **Owner(s):** Iowa Information, Inc., See address and contact information above. **Management:** Jeff Wagner, General Manager. Peter W Wagner, Publisher. Denise Rust, Advertising Manager. **Editorial:** Jeff Grant, Editor.

SHELDON MAIL-SUN. 227 Ninth St., Sheldon, IA 51201-1419. Telephone: 712-324-2514. FAX: 712-324-2345. Mailing Address: PO Box 160, Sheldon, IA 51201-0160. Year Established: 1873. Pub. Frequency: w. (Wed.) Page Size: broadsheet. Subscrip. Rate: $.85 newsstand/cover; $29.95/yr in county; $39.95/yr out of county. Adv. Rate: col. inch $6.93 Freelance Pay: $1/column-inch. Circulation: 3,000 per issue (paid). **Owner(s):** Iowa Information, Inc., See address and contact information above. **Management:** Jeff Wagner, General Manager. Peter W Wagner, Publisher. Denise Rust, Advertising Manager. **Editorial:** Jeff Grant, Editor.

SHENANDOAH

ESSEX INDEPENDENT, THE. P.O. Box 369, Shenandoah, IA 51601. Telephone: 712-246-3097. FAX: 712-246-3099. Year Established: 1894. Pub. Frequency: w. (Thu.) Page Size: broadsheet. Subscrip. Rate: $.50 newsstand/cover; $20/yr in county; $26/yr out of county. Adv. Rate: col. inch $5.50 Circulation: 450 per issue (paid and free). **Owner(s):** Omaha World-Herald Co, 117 Pearl St., Council Bluffs, IA 51503-0864. Telephone: 712-246-3097. FAX: 712-246-3099. **Management:** Alan Cross, Publisher. **Editorial:** Alan Cross, Editor.

SIBLEY

OSCEOLA COUNTY GAZETTE-TRIBUNE. 201 Ninth St., Sibley, IA 51249. Telephone: 712-754-2551. FAX: 712-754-2552. Year Established: 1872. Pub. Frequency: w. (Wed.) Page Size: broadsheet. Subscrip. Rate: $.75 newsstand/cover; $21.50/yr in county; $26.50/yr out of county. Circulation: 1,700 per issue (paid). **Owner(s):** Sibley Printing & Publishing, See address and contact information above. **Management:** Jerry Wiseman, Publisher. **Editorial:** Zach Jensen, Editor.

SOLON

NORTH LIBERTY LEADER, THE. PO Box 249, Solon, IA 52333. Telephone: 319-644-2233. FAX: 319-624-1356. E-MAIL: hybrid@southslope.net. Year Established: 1950. Pub. Frequency: w. (Wed.) Page Size: tabloid. Subscrip. Rate: $.75 newsstand/cover; $25/yr in county. Circulation: 775 per issue (paid). **Owner(s):** Hybrid Publications, See address and contact information above. **Management:** Doug Lindner, Owner. Rena Nevada, Advertising. **Editorial:** Doug Lindner, Editor.

SPENCER

NORTHWEST IOWA SHOPPER. 310 E. Milwaukee, Spencer, IA 51301. Telephone: 712-262-6610. FAX: 712-262-3044. E-MAIL: news@spencerdailyreporter.com. URL: http://www.spencerdailyreporter.com. Mailing Address: PO Box 197, Spencer, IA 51301. Pub. Frequency: s-w. (Wed. & Sat.) Page Size: standard. Subscrip. Rate: $80/yr mailed in area. Circulation: 25,000 per issue (paid and controlled). **Owner(s):** Rust Communications, Inc., 301 Broadway, Cape Girardeau, MO 63701. Telephone: 573-335-6611. **Management:** Paula Buenger, Publisher. Janelle Madison, Advertising Director. **Editorial:** Randy Cauthron, Managing Editor.

SPIRIT LAKE

DICKINSON COUNTY NEWS, THE. 1706 Ithaca St., Spirit Lake, IA 51360. Telephone: 712-336-1211. FAX: 712-336-1219. E-MAIL: dcn@ncn.net. Mailing Address: PO Box AE, Spirit Lake, IA 51360. Year Established: 1870. Pub. Frequency: s-w. (Wed. & Sat.) Page Size: broadsheet. Subscrip. Rate: $.75 newsstand/cover; $33/yr in county; $44/yr out of county. Circulation: 4,000 per issue (paid). **Owner(s):** Rust Communications Inc., 301 Broadway, Cape Girardeau, MO 63701. Telephone: 573-335-6611. **Management:** Paula Buenger, Publisher. Lisa Johnson, Advertising Manager. **Editorial:** Anitra Wolf, Editor. Kelli Lins, Sports.

STORM LAKE

STORM LAKE PILOT TRIBUNE. ISSN 0893-8555
527 Cayuga, Storm Lake, IA 50588. Telephone: 712-732-3130. FAX: 712-732-3152. E-MAIL: sled@iowaone.net. URL: http://www.stormlakepilottribune.com. Mailing Address: PO Box 1187, Storm Lake, IA 50588. Year Established: 1870. Pub. Frequency: 3/w. (Tue., Thu., Sat.) Page Size: broadsheet. Subscrip. Rate: $.50 newsstand/cover; $50/yr. **Wire Service(s):** AP. Circulation: 3,000 morning (paid). **Owner(s):** Rust Communications, Inc., 301 Broadway, Cape Girardeau, MO 63701. Telephone: 573-335-6611. **Management:** Robert L. Madsen, General Manager. **Editorial:** Dana Larsen, Editor.

STORM LAKE TIMES, THE. 220 W. Railroad St., Storm Lake, IA 50588. Telephone: 712-732-4991. FAX: 712-732-4331. E-MAIL: times@stormlake.com. URL: http://www.stormlake.com. Mailing Address: PO Box 487, Storm Lake, IA 50588-0487. Year Established: 1990. Pub. Frequency: s-w. (Wed. & Sat.) Page Size: broadsheet. Subscrip. Rate: $.75 newsstand/cover; $54.95/yr home delivery in county; $66.95/yr mailed out of county; $71.95/yr mailed elsewhere. Adv. Rate: col. inch $6.20 Circulation: 3,200 per issue (paid). **Owner(s):** Storm Lake Times Co., See address and contact information above. **Management:** John Cullen, Publisher. R. Michael Diercks, Advertising Manager. **Editorial:** Art Cullen, Editor.Readers: Geneeral public

STORY CITY

STORY CITY HERALD. 511 Broad St., Story City, IA 50248. Telephone: 515-733-4318. FAX: 515-733-4319. E-MAIL: scherald@storycity.com. Year Established: 1881. Pub. Frequency: w. (Wed.) Page Size: broadsheet. Subscrip. Rate: $.75 newsstand/cover; $30/yr in state; $37/yr out of state. Adv. Rate: col. inch $6 Circulation: 2,000 per issue (paid and free). **Owner(s):** Todd Thorson, 846 Lafayette Ave., Story City, IA 50248. Telephone: 515-733-4551. FAX: 515-733-4319. **Management:** Todd Thorson, Publisher. **Editorial:** Erin Feaker, Editor.Readers: Story City, Roland, IA and surrounding area residents

SULLY

DIAMOND TRAIL NEWS. 301 Seventh Ave., Ste. 101, Sully, IA 50251. E-MAIL: dtnews@netesn.net. Year Established: 1975. Pub. Frequency: w. (Wed.) Page Size: tabloid. Subscrip. Rate: $.75 newsstand/cover; $28/yr in state; $35/yr out of state. Adv. Rate: col. inch $6.50 Circulation: 1,900 per issue (paid). **Owner(s):** Diamond Trail News, P O Box 267, Sully, IA 50251-0267. **Management:** Amber Vander Linden, Publisher. **Editorial:** Amber Vander Linden, Editor.

SUMNER

SUMNER GAZETTE. 106 E. First St., Sumner, IA 50674. Telephone: 563-578-3351. FAX: 563-578-5784. Year Established: 1800. Pub. Frequency: w. (Thu.) Page Size: broadsheet. Subscrip. Rate: $.75 newsstand/cover; $24/yr carrier delivery; $26/yr motor route in county; $28.50/yr mailed out of county. Circulation: 3,000 per issue (paid). **Owner(s):** Angi & Doug Daniels, See address and contact information above. **Management:** Angi Daniels, Publisher. **Editorial:** Angi Daniels, Editor.

TAMA

TAMA NEWS-HERALD, THE. 220 W. Third St., Tama, IA 52339. Telephone: 641-484-2841. FAX: 641-484-5705. E-MAIL: editor@tamatoledonews.com. Mailing Address: PO Box 118, Tama, IA 52339. Year Established: 1915. Pub. Frequency: w. (Thu.) Page Size: broadsheet. Subscrip. Rate: $.75 newsstand/cover; $42/yr in county. Circulation: 3,100 per issue (paid). **Owner(s):** Ogden Newspapers of Minnesota, Inc., 19260 San Carlos Blvd., Fort Myers Beach, FL 33931. Telephone: 239-463-4421. **Management:** Nancy Sund, General Manager. Mike Schlesinger, Publisher. Nancy Sund, Advertising. **Editorial:** John Speer, Editor.

TOLEDO CHRONICLE. 220 W. Third St., Tama, IA 52339. Telephone: 641-484-2841. FAX: 641-484-5705. E-MAIL: editor@tamatoledonews.com. URL: http://www.tamatoledonews.com. Mailing Address: PO Box 118, Tama, IA 52339. Year Established: 1856. Pub. Frequency: w. (Tue.) Page Size: broadsheet. Subscrip. Rate: $.75 newsstand/cover; $47.20/yr in county. Circulation: 3,100 per issue (paid). **Owner(s):** Ogden Newspapers of Minnesota, Inc., 19260 San Carlos Blvd., Fort Myers Beach, FL 33931. Telephone: 239-463-4421. **Management:** Nancy Sund, General Manager. Mike Schlesinger, Publisher. Nancy Sund, Advertising. **Editorial:** John Speer, Sports.

THOMPSON

THOMPSON COURIER & RAKE REGISTER. 150 Jackson St., Thompson, IA 50478-5006. Telephone: 641-584-2770. FAX: 641-584-2802. E-MAIL: editor@trnews.com. URL: http://www.trnews.com. Mailing Address: PO Box 318, Thompson, IA 50473-0318. Pub. Frequency: w. (Thu.) Page Size: tabloid. Subscrip. Rate: $.50 newsstand/cover; $23/yr in county; $28/yr out of county. Adv. Rate: col. inch $3 Circulation: 1,000 per issue (paid and free). **Owner(s):** Gretchen Daniels, See address and contact information above. **Management:** Gretchen Daniels, Publisher. **Editorial:** Gretchen Daniels, Editor.

THORNTON

SOUTHERN COUNTY NEWS. 300 Main St., Thornton, IA 50479-0096. E-MAIL: soconews@frontiernet.net. Mailing Address: PO Box 96, Thornton, IA 50479. Pub. Frequency: w. (Thu.) Page Size: broadsheet. Subscrip. Rate: $.75 newsstand/cover; $25/yr in state; $30/yr mailed out of state. Circulation: 1,300 per issue (paid and free). **Owner(s):** Southern County News, See address and contact information above. **Management:** William Schrader, Publisher. Jennifer Roberts, Office Manager. **Editorial:** Ana Diaz, Editor.

TIPTON

TIPTON CONSERVATIVE & ADVERTISER. PO Box 271, Tipton, IA 52772. Telephone: 563-886-2131. FAX: 563-886-6466. E-MAIL: stuartc108@aol.com. Year Established: 1846. Pub. Frequency: w. (Wed.) Page Size: broadsheet. Subscrip. Rate: $.75 newsstand/cover; $32/yr home delivery. Adv. Rate: col. inch $6.49 Circulation: 4,400 per issue (paid). **Owner(s):** Stuart and Sharon Clark, See address and contact information above. **Management:** Stuart Clark, Publisher. Becky Young, Office Manager. Annie Schroeder, Advertising. Pat Kroemer, Advertising Manager. Darla Walling, Circulation Manager. **Editorial:** Kris Clark, Editor. Ryan Stonebraker III, Sports Editor.

TRAER

TRAER STAR-CLIPPER. 625 Second St., Traer, IA 50675. Telephone: 319-478-2323. FAX: 319-478-2818. E-MAIL: editor@traerstarclipper.com. Mailing Address: PO Box 156, Traer, IA 50675. Year Established: 1873. Pub. Frequency: w. (Thu.) Page Size: broadsheet. Subscrip. Rate: $.75 newsstand/cover; $39/yr in state. Circulation: 2,000 per issue (paid). **Owner(s):** Marshalltown Newspapers, Inc., 135 W. Main, Marshalltown, IA 50158. Telephone: 800-542-7893. **Editorial:** Jody Stover, Managing Editor.

WAUKON

WAUKON STANDARD. 15 First St., N.W., Waukon, IA 52172. Telephone: 563-568-3431. FAX: 563-568-4242. E-MAIL: wstd@salamander.com. URL: http://www.waukonstandard.com. Mailing Address: PO Box 286, Waukon, IA 52172. Year Established: 1870. Pub. Frequency: w. (Wed.) Page Size: broadsheet. Subscrip. Rate: $1 newsstand/cover; $29/yr local; $45/yr mailed out of area; $54/yr mailed out of state. Circulation: 3,700 per issue (paid). **Owner(s):** News Publishing Co., PO Box 286, Black Earth, WI 53515. Telephone: 563-568-3431. **Management:** Jeremy Troendle, Publisher. Barbara Neverman, Advertising Manager. **Editorial:** Jeremy Troendle, Editor.

WAVERLY

BREMER COUNTY INDEPENDENT. ISSN 0899-8698 311 W. Bremer, Waverly, IA 50677-0858. Telephone: 319-352-3334. FAX: 319-352-5135. E-MAIL: wavnews@mcleodusa.net. URL: http://www.waverlynewspapers.com. Mailing Address: PO Box 858, Waverly, IA 50677-0858. Year Established: 1856. Pub. Frequency: w. (Tue.) Page Size: broadsheet. Subscrip. Rate: $1 newsstand/cover; $52/yr in county with Waverly Democrat (Thu); $78/yr out of county. Adv. Rate: col. inch $8.65 Circulation: 6,000 per issue (paid). **Owner(s):** Community Media Group, Inc, PO Box 10, West Frankfort, IL 62896. Telephone: 618-937-6412. **Management:** John Perratto, Publisher. Michael Izer, Advertising Manager. **Editorial:** Anelia Dimitrova, Editor. Stephanie Able, Lifestyle Editor. Dick Fridley, Sports.

WAVERLY DEMOCRAT. 311 W. Bremer Ave., Waverly, IA 50677. Telephone: 319-352-3335. FAX: 319-352-5135. E-MAIL: ad@waverlynewspapers.com. URL: http://www.waverlynewspapers.com. Mailing Address: PO Box 858, Waverly, IA 50677. Year Established: 1876. Pub. Frequency: s-w. (Tue. & Thu.) Page Size: broadsheet. Subscrip. Rate: $1 newsstand/cover; $52/yr mailed in county; $78/yr mailed out of county. Adv. Rate: col. inch $8.45 Circulation: 6,300 per issue (paid). **Owner(s):** Community Media Group, Inc, PO Box 10, West Frankfort, IL 62896. Telephone: 618-937-6412. **Management:** Andy Kukutschka, General Manager. John Perratto, Publisher. Michael Izer, Advertising Manager. Susan Hosto, Circulation Manager. **Editorial:** Anelia Dimitrova, Editor. Dick Fridley, Sports.

WEST BURLINGTON

DES MOINES COUNTY NEWS, THE. 204 Broadway St., West Burlington, IA 52655-0177. Telephone: 319-752-8328. FAX: 319-752-8328. E-MAIL: lpc@louisacomm.net. Mailing Address: PO Box 177, West Burlington, IA 51655-0177. Year Established: 1956. Pub. Frequency: w. (Thu.) Page Size: tabloid. Subscrip. Rate: $.50 newsstand/cover; $24/yr mailed in county; $29/yr mailed in state; $33/yr mailed out of state. Adv. Rate: col. inch $4.90 Circulation: 1,900 per issue (paid). **Owner(s):** Louisa Publishing LLC, PO Box 306, Wapello, IA 52653. Telephone: 319-523-4631. FAX: 319-523-8167. **Management:** Mike Hodges, Publisher. Reginia Brown, Advertising. **Editorial:** Sherry Kaestner, Reporter.

WEST LIBERTY

WEST LIBERTY INDEX. 201 E. Third St., West Liberty, IA 52776. Telephone: 319-627-2814. FAX: 319-627-2110. E-MAIL: index@lcom.net. URL: http://www.westlibertyindex.com. Year Established: 1868. Pub. Frequency: w. (Thu.) Page Size: tabloid. Subscrip. Rate: $.75 newsstand/cover; $29/yr in county; $31/yr in state; $33/yr elsewhere. Adv. Rate: col. inch $5 Circulation: 2,000 per issue (paid). **Owner(s):** Jake Krob & Stuart Clark, PO Box 96, West Liberty, IA 52776-0096. Telephone: 319-627-2814. FAX: 319-627-2110. **Management:** Jake Krob, Publisher. Mary Sue Kruse, Advertising Manager. **Editorial:** Sara Sedlacek, Managing Editor.

WEST POINT

BONNY BUYER. 403 Ave. D, West Point, IA 52656. Telephone: 319-837-6232. FAX: 319-837-6913. URL: http://www.bonnybuyer.net. Mailing Address: PO Box 6, West Point, IA 52656. Year Established: 1972. Pub. Frequency: w. (Wed.) Page Size: tabloid.Adv. Rate: col. inch $8.75 Circulation: 23,000 per issue (free). **Owner(s):** Brehm Communications, Inc., 16644 W. Bernardo Dr., Ste. 300, San Diego, CA 92127. Telephone: 858-451-6200. **Management:** Wendy Vonderhaar, General Manager. Diana Spickenmeier, Advertising. Sandy Martin, Classified Adv. Mgr..

DONNELSON STAR. 403 Ave. D, West Point, IA 52656. Telephone: 319-837-6232. FAX: 319-837-6913. Mailing Address: PO Box 6, West Point, IA 52656. Pub. Frequency: w. (Thu.) Page Size: tabloid. Subscrip. Rate: $.50 newsstand/cover; $24/yr local. Circulation: 3,500 per issue (paid). **Owner(s):** Brehm Communications, Inc., 188 Cirby Way, Roseville, CA 95678. **Management:** Wendy Vonderhaar, General Manager. Diana Spickenmeier, Advertising. Sandy Martin, Classified Adv. Mgr..

WEST POINT BEE, THE. 403 Ave. D, West Point, IA 52656. Telephone: 319-837-6232. FAX: 319-837-6913. URL: http://www.brehmcommunications.com. Year Established: 1878. Pub. Frequency: w. (Thu) Page Size: tabloid.Subscrip. Rate: $.50 newsstand/cover; $24/yr Circulation: 3,500 per issue (paid). **Owner(s):** Brehm Communications, Inc., 16644 W. Bernardo Dr., Ste. 300, San Diego, CA 92127. Telephone: 858-451-6200. **Management:** Wendy Vonderhaar, General Manager. Diana Spickenmeier, Advertising. Sandy Martin, Classified Adv. Mgr.. **Editorial:** Lucinda Ward, Editor.

WEST UNION

FAYETTE COUNTY UNION. 119 S. Vine, West Union, IA 52175. Telephone: 563-422-3888. FAX: 563-422-3488. E-MAIL: theunion@alpinecom.net. URL: http://www.westunionfayettecountyunion.com. Mailing Address: PO Box 153, West Union, IA 52175-0153. Year Established: 1866. Pub. Frequency: w. (Wed.) Page Size: broadsheet. Subscrip. Rate: $1 newsstand/cover; $38/yr in county; $48/yr mailed out of area. Circulation: 7,200 per issue (paid and free). **Owner(s):** Fayette County Union, Inc., See address and contact information above. **Management:** Leann Larson, Co-Publisher. Gerald H. Blue, Publisher. Leann Larson, Advertising Director. **Editorial:** Gerald H. Blue, Editor-in-Chief. Rich Holm, Sports.

WHAT CHEER

WHAT CHEER PAPER. 102 N. Barnes St., What Cheer, IA 50268. Telephone: 641-634-2092. E-MAIL: whatcheerpaper@iowatelecom.net. Mailing Address: PO Box 414, What Cheer, IA 50268-0414. Year Established: 1880. Pub. Frequency: w. (Thu.) Page Size: broadsheet. Subscrip. Rate: $.50 newsstand/cover; $20/yr in county; $25/yr out of county; $30/yr out of state. Adv. Rate: col. inch $3.50 Circulation: 1,588 per issue (paid). **Owner(s):** Mid-America Publishing, Inc., PO Box 29, Hampton, IA 50441. Telephone: 641-456-2585. FAX: 641-456-2587. **Management:** Chad Hicks, Publisher.

WILLIAMSBURG

JOURNAL TRIBUNE. 208 W. State St., Williamsburg, IA 52361. Telephone: 319-668-1240. FAX: 319-668-9112. Mailing Address: PO Box 690, Williamsburg, IA 52361. Year Established: 1900. Pub. Frequency: w. (Thu.) Page Size: broadsheet. Subscrip. Rate: $1 newsstand/cover; $28/yr in county; $30/yr out of county; $37/yr out of state. Circulation: 2,000 per issue (paid). **Owner(s):** Gannett Company, Inc., 7950 Jones Branch Dr., McLean, VA 22107-0001. Telephone: 703-854-6000. **Management:** Martin Bunge, Publisher. John Rotter, Advertising Manager. **Editorial:** Callie Wetjen, Editor. Dan Adix, Editor-in-Chief.

WINTERSET

WINTERSET MADISONIAN. 112 W. Court Ave., Winterset, IA 50273-0350. Telephone: 515-462-2101. FAX: 515-462-2102. E-MAIL: editor@i-rule.net. URL: http://www.wintersetmadisonian.com. Mailing Address: P.O. Box 350, Winterset, IA 50273. Year Established: 1856. Pub. Frequency: w. (Wed.) Page Size: broadsheet. Subscrip. Rate: $.75 newsstand/cover; $29.50/yr in county; $34.50/yr elsewhere. Freelance Pay: $1.50/column-inch. Circulation: 3,500 per issue (paid). **Owner(s):** Ted Gorman, See address and contact information above. **Bureau(s):** 319 E. Fifth St., Des Moines, IA 50309. Telephone: 515-244-2145. **Management:** Ted Gorman, Publisher. **Editorial:** Dave Braga, Editor.

WOODBINE

WOODBINE TWINER. 509 Walker St, Woodbine, IA 51579. Telephone: 712-647-2821. FAX: 712-647-3081. Pub. Frequency: w. (Wed.) Subscrip. Rate: $.50 newsstand/cover; $32/yr in county & adj. cys.; $34.50/yr in state & NE; $38.50/yr elsewhere. **Owner(s):** Omaha World-Herald Co., 1314 Douglas St, Omaha, NE 68102. Telephone: 402-444-1000. FAX: 402-345-0183. **Management:** John Beaudoin, Publisher. Melissa Stillman, Advertising. Nikki Davis, Classified Adv. Mgr..

KANSAS

ANTHONY

ANTHONY REPUBLICAN, THE. 121 E. Main St., Anthony, KS 67003. Telephone: 620-842-5129. E-MAIL: republican@cyberlodge.com. Year Established: 1879. Pub. Frequency: w. (Wed.) Page Size: broadsheet. Subscrip. Rate: $.74 newsstand/cover; $25/yr mailed in county & adj. counties; $30/yr mailed in state. Adv. Rate: col. inch $4 Circulation: 2,600 per issue (paid). **Owner(s):** Larry J. & Bonnie L. Dunn, See address and contact information above. **Management:** Larry J. Dunn, Publisher. **Editorial:** Larry J. Dunn, News Editor.

BELLE PLAINE

BELLE PLAINE NEWS, THE. 431 N. Merchant, Belle Plaine, KS 67013. Telephone: 620-488-2234. FAX: 620-488-3241. E-MAIL: bpnews@oldwiz.net. Mailing Address: PO Box 128, Belle Plaine, KS 67013-0128. Year Established: 1879. Pub. Frequency: w. (Thu.) Page Size: tabloid. Subscrip. Rate: $.50 newsstand/cover; $36/yr in zone area; $49/yr in state; $57/yr out of state. Freelance Pay: $0.25/column-inch. Circulation: 1,000 per issue (paid and free). **Owner(s):** Shayleen Casteel, See address and contact information above. **Management:** Shayleen Casteel, Publisher. **Editorial:** Joshua Delaugh, Editor.

OXFORD REGISTER, THE. 431 N. Merchant, Belle Plaine, KS 67013. Telephone: 620-488-2234. FAX: 620-488-3241. E-MAIL: bpnews@oldwiz.net. Mailing Address: PO Box 128, Belle Plaine, KS 67013-0128. Year Established: 1879. Pub. Frequency: w. (Thu.) Page Size: tabloid. Subscrip. Rate: $.50 newsstand/cover; $27/yr in county; $43/yr out of state. Freelance Pay: $0.25/column-inch. Circulation: 1,000 per issue (paid and free). **Owner(s):** Shayleen Casteel, See address and contact information above. **Management:** Shayleen Casteel, Publisher. **Editorial:** Joshua Delaugh, Editor.

BELLEVILLE

BELLEVILLE TELESCOPE. ISSN 0740-0985 PO Box 349, Belleville, KS 66935-0349. Telephone: 785-527-2244. FAX: 785-527-2225. E-MAIL: telescope@nckcn.com. Year Established: 1870. Pub. Frequency: w. (Thu.) Page Size: broadsheet. Subscrip. Rate: $.75 newsstand/cover; $29/yr in county. Circulation: 4,900 per issue (paid). **Owner(s):** Telescope, Inc., See address and contact information above. **Management:** Mark Miller, Publisher. Paul Hasse, Business Manager. **Editorial:** Mark L. Miller, Editor-in-Chief.

BELOIT

BELOIT CALL. ISSN 1557-4121 119 Main St., Beloit, KS 67420. Telephone: 785-738-3537. FAX: 785-738-6442. E-MAIL: beloitcall@nckcen.com. Mailing Address: PO Box 366, Beloit, KS 67420. Year Established: 1901. Pub. Frequency: 3/w. (Mon, Wed., Fri.) Page Size: broadsheet. Subscrip. Rate: $.50 newsstand/cover; $52.33/yr in area. Circulation: 1,700 evening (paid). **Owner(s):** Blade-Empire Publishing Co., Inc., 510 Washington St., Concordia, KS 66901. Telephone: 785-243-2424. **Management:** Barbara Axtell, General Manager. **Editorial:** Barbara Axtell, Editor.

BIRD CITY

BIRD CITY TIMES. 312 Bird Ave, Bird City, KS 67731-0167. Telephone: 785-734-2621. FAX: 785-734-2659. E-MAIL: bctimes@nwkansas.com. URL: http://www.nwkansas.com. Mailing Address: PO Box 220, Bird City, KS 67731-0167. Pub. Frequency: w. (Thu.) Page Size: broadsheet. Subscrip. Rate: $.65 newsstand/cover; $25/yr in county & adj cys; $28/yr elsewhere. Adv. Rate: col. inch $3.89 Circulation: 550 per issue (paid and free). **Owner(s):** NorWest Newspapers, Inc., 170 S Penn Ave, Oberlin, KS 67749. Telephone: 785-475-2206. FAX: 785-475-2800. **Management:** Karen Krien, Publisher. Casey McCormick, Advertising. Jennifer Boyles, Advertising Manager. **Editorial:** Casey McCormick, Editor. Steve Haynes, Editor-in-Chief.

BONNER SPRINGS

BONNER SPRINGS-EDWARDSVILLE CHIEFTAIN, THE. 128 Oak St, Bonner Springs, KS 66012. Telephone: 913-422-4048. FAX: 913-422-4233. E-MAIL: editor@bonnersprings.com. URL: http://www.bonnersprings.com. Mailing Address: PO Box 256, Bonner Springs, KS 66012. Year Established: 1896. Pub. Frequency: w. (Thu.) Page Size: broadsheet. Subscrip. Rate: $.75 newsstand/cover; $30/yr in county & adj cys; $45/yr out of area; $50/yr mailed out of state. Circulation: 1,500 per issue (paid). **Owner(s):** World Co., 609 New Hampshire St., Lawrence, KS 66044. Telephone: 785-843-1000. **Management:** Maria Preston, Advertising Manager. Adreanna Jacobs, Classified Adv. Mgr.. **Editorial:** John Beal, Editor. Matt Tait, Sports.

BURLINGAME

OSAGE COUNTY CHRONICLE. ISSN 1040-6077
107 E. Santa Fe, Burlingame, KS 66413. Telephone: 785-654-3621. FAX: 785-654-3438. E-MAIL: durt@aol.com. Mailing Address: PO Box 65, Burlingame, KS 66413-0065. Year Established: 1863. Pub. Frequency: w. (Thu.) Page Size: broadsheet. Subscrip. Rate: $.75 newsstand/cover; $28/yr in county; $32/yr mailed out of county. Circulation: 5,200 per issue (paid). **Owner(s):** Incunabula, Inc., See address and contact information above. **Management:** Kathleen Kessinger, Publisher. **Editorial:** Kathleen Kessinger, Editor.

BURLINGTON

COFFEY COUNTY REPUBLICAN, THE. 324 Hudson St., Burlington, KS 66839. Telephone: 620-364-5325. FAX: 620-364-2607. E-MAIL: ccrepub@kans.com. URL: http://www.coffeycountyonline.com. Mailing Address: PO Drawer A, Burlington, KS 66839-0218. Year Established: 1856. Pub. Frequency: s-w. (Tue. & Fri.) Page Size: broadsheet. Subscrip. Rate: $.75 newsstand/cover; $46/yr carrier delivery local; $48/yr mailed in state; $56/yr out of state. Adv. Rate: col. inch $6.56 Circulation: 2,800 per issue (paid). **Owner(s):** Faimon Publications, Inc., See address and contact information above. **Management:** Catherine Faimon, Co-Publisher. **Editorial:** Mark Petterson, Managing Editor. Becky Reeves, News Editor.

COTTONWOOD FALLS

CHASE COUNTY LEADER-NEWS. ISSN 1079-8188
306 Broadway, Cottonwood Falls, KS 66845-0046. Telephone: 620-273-6391. FAX: 620-273-8674. Mailing Address: PO Box K, Cottonwood Falls, KS 66845-0436. Year Established: 1871. Pub. Frequency: w. (Thu.) Page Size: standard. Subscrip. Rate: $.75 newsstand/cover; $30/yr in county; $36/yr out of county. Adv. Rate: col. inch $3.75 Circulation: 1,700 per issue (paid). **Owner(s):** Chase County Publishing Co., Inc., See address and contact information above. **Management:** Jerry Schwilling, Publisher. **Editorial:** Jerry Schwilling, Editor.

COURTLAND

COURTLAND JOURNAL-EMPIRE. ISSN 0746-5750
420 Main St., Courtland, KS 66939-0318. Telephone: 785-374-4428. FAX: 785-374-4209. E-MAIL: cjournal@courtland.net. Mailing Address: PO Box 318, Courtland, KS 66939-0318. Year Established: 1891. Pub. Frequency: w. (Thu.) Page Size: standard. Subscrip. Rate: $.35 newsstand/cover; $17.17/yr in state. Circulation: 700 per issue (paid). **Owner(s):** Robert & Colleen Mainquist, See address and contact information above. **Management:** Robert Mainquist, Publisher. **Editorial:** Colleen Mainquist, Editor.

DERBY

SHOPPER GUIDE (DERBY). 201 S. Baltimore St., Derby, KS 67037. Telephone: 316-788-2835. FAX: 316-788-0854. Mailing Address: PO Box 190, Derby, KS 67037. Pub. Frequency: w. (Thu.) Page Size: tabloid Circulation: 11,000 per issue (free). **Owner(s):** GateHouse Media, Inc, 350 WillowBrook Office Park, Fairport, NY 14450. FAX: 585-248-2631. **Management:** Jim Clements, Publisher. Fred Bonner, Advertising. Lori Rubendall, Circulation Manager.

DODGE CITY

SHOPPER'S WEEKLY, THE. 705 Second Ave., Dodge City, KS 67801. Telephone: 620-225-4151. FAX: 620-225-4154. Mailing Address: PO Box 820, Dodge City, KS 67801-0820. Pub. Frequency: w. (Wed.) Page Size: broadsheet Circulation: 21,000 per issue (free). **Owner(s):** Morris Multimedia, Inc., PO Box 936, Augusta, GA 30903. Telephone: 706-724-0851. FAX: 706-722-7125. **Management:** Terry Cochran, Publisher. Linda Berry, Office Manager. Frank Solis, Circulation Manager. **Editorial:** Rick Druse, Editor.

ELLSWORTH

ELLSWORTH COUNTY INDEPENDENT REPORTER, THE. 220 N Douglas, Ellsworth, KS 67439. Telephone: 785-472-5085. FAX: 785-472-5087. E-MAIL: reporter@infomatics.net. URL: http://www.ellsworthinderep.com. Year Established: 1871. Pub. Frequency: w. (Wed.) Page Size: broadsheet. Subscrip. Rate: $1 newsstand/cover; $32.95/yr in county; $38.50/yr in state. Adv. Rate: col. inch $3.99 Circulation: 3,000 per issue (paid). **Owner(s):** Morris Newspaper Corporation, 27 Abercorn St., Savannah, GA 31401. Telephone: 912-233-1281. FAX: 912-232-4639. **Management:** Linda Mowery-Denning, Publisher. David Rains, Advertising Director. **Editorial:** Linda Mowery-Denning, Editor-in-Chief. Amy Eck, Managing Editor.

EUREKA

EUREKA HERALD. PO Box 590, Eureka, KS 67045. Telephone: 620-583-5721. FAX: 620-583-5922. E-MAIL: dclasen@eurekaherald.com. URL: http://www.eurekaherald.com. Year Established: 1868. Pub. Frequency: w. (Thu.) Page Size: broadsheet. Subscrip. Rate: $1 newsstand/cover; $35/yr area; $42/yr out of area. Circulation: 3,300 per issue (paid). **Owner(s):** Greenwood County Publishing, Inc., See address and contact information above. **Management:** Richard W. Clasen, Publisher. **Editorial:** Richard W. Clasen, Editor.

FREDONIA

WILSON COUNTY CITIZEN. 406 N. Seventh St., Fredonia, KS 66736-1315. Telephone: 620-378-4415. FAX: 620-378-4688. E-MAIL: wccitizen@earthlink.net. Year Established: 1870. Pub. Frequency: s-w. (Mon. & Thu.) Page Size: broadsheet. Subscrip. Rate: $.50 newsstand/cover; $32.25/yr in state; $35/yr out of state. Circulation: 3,995 per issue (paid). **Owner(s):** Joe & Rita Relph, See address and contact information above. **Management:** Joe Relph, Co-Publisher. Meredith Wilson, Advertising Manager. **Editorial:** Mina DeBerry, Managing Editor.

GODDARD

TIMES-SENTINEL, THE. P O Box 697, Goddard, KS 67052. FAX: 316-794-2455. E-MAIL: tsnews@fn.net. URL: http://www.tsnews.com. Year Established: 1894. Pub. Frequency: w. (Thu.) Page Size: tabloid. Subscrip. Rate: $.75 newsstand/cover; $30/yr. Freelance Pay: $15-$20/article. Circulation: 3,550 per issue (paid). **Owner(s):** Paul Rhodes & Amy Crouch, 211 N. Garfield St., Cheney, KS 67025. Telephone: 316-794-2445. **Management:** Amy Crouch, Co-Publisher. Paul Rhodes, Advertising Manager. **Editorial:** Paul Rhodes, Editor-in-Chief. Travis Mounts, Production Manager.

GOODLAND

GOODLAND STAR NEWS, THE. ISSN 0893-0562
1205 Main St., Goodland, KS 67735-0500. Telephone: 785-899-2338. FAX: 785-899-6186. E-MAIL: starnews@nwkansas.com. URL: http://www.nwkansas.com. Year Established: 1932. Pub. Frequency: s-w. (Tue & Fri.) Page Size: standard. Subscrip. Rate: $.75 newsstand/cover; $76/yr local; $84/yr in state; $119/yr out of state. Wire Service(s): AP. Circulation: 2,000 evening (paid). **Owner(s):** Norwest Newspapers Inc., 170 S. Penn Ave., Oberlin, KS 67749. Telephone: 785-475-2206. **Management:** Jim Bowker, General Manager. Steve Haynes, Publisher. Doug Jackson, Advertising. Sheila Smith, Circulation Manager. **Editorial:** Tom Betz, Editor. Sharon Corcoran, Society Editor.

GREENBURG

KIOWA COUNTY SIGNAL. 320 S Main St, Greenburg, KS 67054. Telephone: 620-672-5511. FAX: 620-723-1031. URL: http://www.kiowacountysignal.com. Mailing Address: PO Box 368, Greenburg, KS 67054-0368. Pub. Frequency: w. (Wed.) Page Size: standard. Subscrip. Rate: $.75 newsstand/cover; $41.46/yr in county. Circulation: 1,012 per issue (paid). **Owner(s):** GateHouse Media, Inc, 350 WillowBrook Office Park, Fairport, NY 14450. Telephone: 585-598-0030. FAX: 585-248-2631. **Management:** Keith Lippoldt, Publisher. Laurie Anderson, Advertising Manager. Stan Navarrette, Classified Adv. Mgr.. **Editorial:** Mark Anderson, Editor.

HERINGTON

HERINGTON TIMES. PO Box 310, Herington, KS 67449. Telephone: 785-258-2211. FAX: 785-258-2400. E-MAIL: thtinc@tctelco.net. Year Established: 1889. Pub. Frequency: w. (Thu.) Page Size: broadsheet. Subscrip. Rate: $1 newsstand/cover; $45.07/yr local. Circulation: 2,200 per issue (paid). **Owner(s):** Larry L. Byers, See address and contact information above. **Management:** Larry L. Byers, Publisher. **Editorial:** Larry L. Byers, Editor.

HIAWATHA

HIAWATHA WORLD. 607 Utah St., Hiawatha, KS 66434-2319. Telephone: 785-742-2111. FAX: 785-742-2276. E-MAIL: world@npgco.com. Year Established: 1908. Pub. Frequency: s-w. (Tue. & Fri.) Page Size: broadsheet. Subscrip. Rate: $.75 newsstand/cover; $52.58/yr in county; $64.23/yr out of county; $77/yr out of state. Circulation: 2,300 per issue (paid). **Owner(s):** N P G Newspapers, Inc., 825 Edmond St., St. Joseph, MO 64501. **Management:** Dan Glynn, General Manager. Mary Adcock, Office Manager. Bobbi Dozier, Advertising. **Editorial:** Deb Rosenberger, Editor-in-Chief.

HILLSBORO

HILLSBORO STAR-JOURNAL. 105 E Grand Ave, Hillsboro, KS 67063. Telephone: 620-947-3975. FAX: 620-947-3883. URL: http://www.starj.com. Mailing Address: PO Box 10, Hillsboro, KS 67063. Year Established: 1903. Pub. Frequency: w. (Thu.) Page Size: broadsheet. Subscrip. Rate: $.75 newsstand/cover; $39/yr local; $44/yr in state; $49/yr out of state. Circulation: 2,000 per issue (paid and free). **Owner(s):** Hoch Publishing Co., Inc., 117 S.Third St., Marion, KS 66861. Telephone: 620-382-2165. **Management:** Donna Bernhardt, Publisher. Melissa Parmley, Advertising Manager. Jean Stuchlik, Circulation Manager. **Editorial:** Grant Overstake, Editor.

HOISINGTON

HOISINGTON DISPATCH. PO Box 330, Hoisington, KS 67544. Telephone: 620-653-4154. FAX: 620-653-4720. Year Established: 1889. Pub. Frequency: w. (Thu.) Page Size: broadsheet. Subscrip. Rate: $.50 newsstand/cover; $22.38/yr local. Circulation: 2,200 per issue (paid). **Owner(s):** Brown Family Publishing, Inc., See address and contact information above. **Management:** Luke Brown, Publisher. Debbie Reif, Office Manager. **Editorial:** Luke Brown, Editor. Megan Brown, Photographer. Nathan Brown, Sports Editor.

HOLTON

HOLTON RECORDER. 109 W. 4th St, Holton, KS 66436-1701. Telephone: 785-364-3141. FAX: 785-364-3422. E-MAIL: holtonrecorder@earthlink.net. URL: http://www.holtonrecorder.com. Year Established: 1867. Pub. Frequency: s-w. (Mon. & Wed.) Page Size: broadsheet. Subscrip. Rate: $.75 newsstand/cover; $31/yr in county; $36/yr out of county; $46/yr out of state. Circulation: 4,800 per issue (paid). **Owner(s):** David Powls, See address and contact information above. **Management:** David Powls, Publisher. **Editorial:** David Powls, Editor.

INDEPENDENCE

INDEPENDENCE NEWS, THE. ISSN 1067-5906
210 W. Main St., Independence, KS 67301. Telephone: 620-331-4711. FAX: 620-251-1905. Year Established: 1948. Pub. Frequency: w. (Thu.) Page Size: broadsheet. Subscrip. Rate: $45/yr home delivery. Adv. Rate: col. inch $6 Circulation: 1,085 per issue (paid and free). **Owner(s):** John F. Vermillion, See address and contact information above. **Management:** John F. Vermillion, President. **Editorial:** John F. Vermillion, Editor-in-Chief.

JETMORE

JETMORE REPUBLICAN. 415 Main St., Jetmore, KS 67854-0337. Telephone: 620-357-8316. FAX: 620-357-8464. E-MAIL: jetreoub@pld.com. Mailing Address: PO Box 337, Jetmore, KS 67854-0337. Year Established: 1887. Pub. Frequency: w. (Wed.) Page Size: broadsheet. Subscrip. Rate: $.65 newsstand/cover; $24.98/yr in state; $26/yr mailed out of state. Circulation: 8,960 per issue (paid). **Owner(s):** Jerry Anderson, PO Box 536, Cimarron, KS 67835. Telephone: 620-855-3902. **Management:** Jerry Anderson, Publisher. **Editorial:** Michael Thornburg, Editor.

JOHNSON

JOHNSON PIONEER. PO Box 10, Johnson, KS 67855-0010. Telephone: 620-492-6244. FAX: 620-492-6245. Year Established: 1890. Pub. Frequency: w. (Thu.) Page Size: broadsheet. Subscrip. Rate: $.65 newsstand/cover; $18.60/yr in county; $20.73/yr out of county. Circulation: 1,100 per issue (paid). **Owner(s):** Ronda Ford, See address and contact information above. **Management:** Ronda Ford, President.

KANSAS CITY

RECORD, THE. 3414 Strong Ave, Kansas City, KS 66106. Telephone: 913-362-1988. FAX: 913-362-8406. Year Established: 1887. Pub. Frequency: w. Subscrip. Rate: $13.75/yr. Circulation: 4,000 per issue (paid and controlled). **Owner(s):** Jon A. Males, See address and contact information above. **Management:** Jon A. Males, Publisher. **Editorial:** Jon A. Males, Editor.

KINGMAN

KINGMAN LEADER-COURIER, THE. PO Box 353, Kingman, KS 67068. Telephone: 316-532-3151, 620-532-3152. E-MAIL: leadercourier@websurf.net. Year Established: 1885. Pub. Frequency: s-w. (Tue. & Fri.) Page Size: broadsheet. Subscrip. Rate: $.75 newsstand/cover; $34/yr local; $37/yr out of state. Circulation: 3,400 per issue (paid). **Owner(s):** Robert McQuin, See address and contact information above. **Management:** Robert McQuin, Publisher. Sarah Solomon, Advertising Director. **Editorial:** Robert McQuin, Editor.

LA CROSSE

RUSH COUNTY NEWS. 112 W. Eighth St., La Crosse, KS 67548-0060. Telephone: 785-222-2555. FAX: 785-222-2557. Year Established: 1940. Pub. Frequency: w. (Thu.) Page Size: broadsheet. Subscrip. Rate: $.50 newsstand/cover; $23.50/yr in county; $27.50/yr in state; $29.50/yr out of state. Adv. Rate: col. inch $3.95 Circulation: 2,000 per issue (paid). **Owner(s):** Rush County News, 112 W. Eighth St., La Crosse, KS 67548. Telephone: 785-222-2555. FAX: 785-222-2557. **Management:** Mary Engel, Publisher. Tim Engel, Advertising Manager. **Editorial:** Tim Engel, Managing Editor.

LEAVENWORTH

CHRONICLE SHOPPER. 422 Seneca St., Leavenworth, KS 66048. Telephone: 913-682-0305. FAX: 913-682-1114. URL: http://www.leavenworthshopper.com. Mailing Address: PO Box 144, Leavenworth, KS 66048. Pub. Frequency: w. (Wed.) Page Size: broadsheet.Adv. Rate: col. inch $23.98 Circulation: 20,500 per issue (free). **Owner(s):** GateHouse Media, Inc, 350 WillowBrook Office Park, Fairport, NY 14450. Telephone: 585-598-0030. FAX: 585-248-2631. **Management:** David Thompson, General Manager. Meredith Timmons, Advertising Manager. James Castle, Circulation Manager.

LANSING THIS WEEK WEEKLY. 422 Seneca St., Leavenworth, KS 66048. Telephone: 913-682-0305. FAX: 913-682-1114. URL: http://www.lansingchronicletimes.com. Mailing Address: PO Box 144, Leavenworth, KS 66048. Pub. Frequency: w. (Sun.) Page Size: standard Circulation: 6,000 per issue (free). **Owner(s):** GateHouse Media, Inc, 350 WillowBrook Office Park, Fairport, NY 14450. Telephone: 585-598-0030. FAX: 585-248-2631. **Management:** David Thompson, Publisher. Meredith Timmons, Advertising Manager. James Castle, Circulation Manager. Tanya Wilder, Classified Adv. Mgr.. **Editorial:** Scott Lowder, Managing Editor. Neil Fuller, Sports Editor.

MADISON

MADISON NEWS, THE. 242 Rd. H, Madison, KS 66860. Telephone: 620-475-3453. FAX: 620-437-2433. E-MAIL: madnews@madtel.net. Year Established: 1879. Pub. Frequency: w. (Thu.) Page Size: standard. Subscrip. Rate: $.50 newsstand/cover; $25.88/yr local; $27/yr out of state. Circulation: 850 per issue (paid and free). **Owner(s):** Earl, Patsy, Calvin & Chris Murphy, See address and contact information above. **Management:** Patsy Murphy, Office Manager. Chris Murphy, Advertising Manager. **Editorial:** Jola Casey, Editor.

MANKATO

JEWELL COUNTY RECORD. 111 E Main, Mankato, KS 66956. Telephone: 785-378-3705. FAX: 785-378-3782. E-MAIL: jc.record@windstream.net. Mailing Address: PO Box 305, Mankato, KS 66956. Year Established: 1890. Pub. Frequency: w. (Thu.) Page Size: broadsheet. Subscrip. Rate: $.50 newsstand/cover; $22/yr in state; $34/yr elsewhere. Circulation: 1,500 per issue (paid). **Owner(s):** Superior Publishing Co., 148 E. Third St., Superior, NE 68978. Telephone: 402-879-3291. FAX: 402-879-3463. **Management:** Bill Blauvelt, Publisher. Rita Blauvelt, Advertising Manager. **Editorial:** Gloria Schlaefli, Feature Editor.

MARION

MARION COUNTY RECORD. 117 S.Third St., Marion, KS 66861. E-MAIL: editor@marionrecord.com. URL: http://www.marionrecord.com. Mailing Address: PO Box 278, Marion, KS 66861-0278. Year Established: 1869. Pub. Frequency: w. (Wed.) Page Size: broadsheet. Subscrip. Rate: $39/yr mailed local; $44/yr mailed in state; $49/yr mailed out of state. Circulation: 3,023 per issue (paid). **Owner(s):** Hoch Publishing Co., Inc., See address and contact information above. **Management:** Donna Bernhardt, Publisher. Melissa Parmley, Advertising Manager. Jean Stuchlik, Circulation Manager. **Editorial:** Donna Bernhardt, Editor.

MARQUETTE

MARQUETTE TRIBUNE (MARQUETTE). PO Box 308, Marquette, KS 67464. Telephone: 785-546-2266. FAX: 785-546-2266. Pub. Frequency: w. (Wed.) Subscrip. Rate: $27.95/yr in state; $31/yr out of state. **Owner(s):** Morris Newspaper Corporation, 27 Abercorn St., Savannah, GA 31401. Telephone: 912-233-1281. FAX: 912-232-4639. **Editorial:** Liz Ponting, Editor.

MARYSVILLE

MARYSVILLE ADVOCATE, THE. 107 S. Ninth St., Marysville, KS 66508-0271. Telephone: 785-562-2317. FAX: 785-562-5589. E-MAIL: skess@mvleadvocate.com. URL: http://www.mvleadvocate.com. Mailing Address: PO Box 271, Marysville, KS 66508-0271. Year Established: 1885. Pub. Frequency: w. (Thu.) Page Size: broadsheet. Subscrip. Rate: $1 newsstand/cover; $38/yr in area; $45/yr mailed in state; $46/yr mailed out of state. Freelance Pay: $0.50/column-inch. Circulation: 5,534 per issue (paid). **Owner(s):** Howard & Sharon Kessinger, 107 S. Ninth St., Marysville, KS 66508. Telephone: 913-562-2317. FAX: 913-562-5589. **Management:** Howard D. Kessinger, Co-Publisher. Janet Harms, Advertising. Jan Smith, Circulation Manager. **Editorial:** Howard D. Kessinger, Editor. Julie Perry, Sports Editor.

MCPHERSON

SOUTH CENTRAL SHOPPER. 301 S. Main, McPherson, KS 67460. Telephone: 620-241-2422. FAX: 620-241-2425. E-MAIL: macsentinelpub@sbcglobal.net. URL: http://www.gatehousemedia.com. Mailing Address: PO Box 926, McPherson, KS 67460. Pub. Frequency: w. (Wed.) Page Size: tabloid.Adv. Rate: col. inch $10 Circulation: 6,000 per issue (free). **Owner(s):** GateHouse Media, Inc, 350 WillowBrook Office Park, Fairport, NY 14450. Telephone: 585-598-0030. **Management:** Gary Mehl, Publisher. Joni Regnier, Advertising Manager. Linda Born, Classified Adv. Mgr..

MEDICINE LODGE

BARBER COUNTY INDEX. 103 E Kansas Ave., Medicine Lodge, KS 67104. Telephone: 620-886-5617. FAX: 620-886-3547. URL: http://www.gatehousemedia.com. Mailing Address: PO Box 349, Medicine Lodge, KS 67104-0349. Pub. Frequency: w. (Wed.) Page Size: broadsheet. Subscrip. Rate: $.50 newsstand/cover; $41.75/yr in county. Circulation: 1,200 per issue (paid). **Owner(s):** GateHouse Media, Inc, 350 WillowBrook Office Park, Fairport, NY 14450. Telephone: 585-598-0030. FAX: 585-248-2631. **Management:** Steve Lippoldt, Publisher. Deana Horn, Advertising. **Editorial:** Conrad Easterday, Managing Editor.

MILTONVALE

MILTONVALE RECORD. 12 Spruce St., Miltonvale, KS 67466-0414. Telephone: 785-427-2680. FAX: 785-427-2680. Year Established: 1899. Pub. Frequency: w. (Thu.) Page Size: broadsheet. Subscrip. Rate: $.40 newsstand/cover; $20/yr home delivery in county; $21.50/yr mailed out of county; $22.50/yr mailed out of state. Adv. Rate: col. inch $2.50 Circulation: 650 per issue (paid). **Owner(s):** Richard & Deanna Phelps, 412 Ash, Miltonvale, KS 67466. Telephone: 785-427-3203. **Management:** Richard Phelps, President. Barbara Mikels, Advertising Manager. **Editorial:** Richard Phelps, Editor-in-Chief.

MOUNDRIDGE

LEDGER (MOUNDRIDGE), THE. 135 S. Christian, Moundridge, KS 67107. Telephone: 620-345-6353. FAX: 620-345-2170. E-MAIL: theledger@wwwebservice.net. Year Established: 1887. Pub. Frequency: w. (Thu.) Page Size: tabloid. Subscrip. Rate: $.75 newsstand/cover; $25.75/yr in state; $32.75/yr out of state. Circulation: 1,500 per issue (paid). **Owner(s):** Davies Communications, Inc., See address and contact information above. **Management:** Jerry Davies, Publisher. **Editorial:** Brian Williams, Managing Editor.

NEODESHA

NEODESHA DERRICK, THE. 502 Main, Neodesha, KS 66757. Telephone: 620-325-3000. E-MAIL: thederrick@cableone.net. Year Established: 1883. Pub. Frequency: w. (Thu.) Page Size: broadsheet. Subscrip. Rate: $.75 newsstand/cover; $35/yr in state; $40/yr mailed out of state. Adv. Rate: col. inch $4 Circulation: 1,900 per issue (paid). **Owner(s):** JoAnne Hartley Harper, See address and contact information above. **Management:** JoAnne Hartley Harper, Publisher. Deeanne Tigner, Advertising Manager.

NESS CITY

NESS COUNTY NEWS, THE. 110 S. Kansas, Ness City, KS 67560. Telephone: 785-798-2213. FAX: 785-798-2214. E-MAIL: nessnews@ruraltel.net. Year Established: 1884. Pub. Frequency: w. (Thu.) Page Size: standard. Subscrip. Rate: $.65 newsstand/cover; $23.39/yr local; $25.50/yr out of state. Circulation: 2,425 per issue (paid). **Owner(s):** Jerry Clarke, See address and contact information above. **Management:** Jerry Clarke, Publisher. **Editorial:** Jerry Clarke, Editor.

NORTON

NORTON TELEGRAM, THE. 215 S Kansas, Norton, KS 67654. Telephone: 785-877-3361. FAX: 785-877-3732. E-MAIL: chaynes-nwkansas.com. URL: http://www.nwkansas.com/NCTwebpages/ntmain.html. Year Established: 1906. Pub. Frequency: 3/w. (Mon., Tue., Fri.) Page Size: broadsheet. Subscrip. Rate: $.75 newsstand/cover per issue; $60/yr carrier delivery in county; $67/yr mailed out of county. **Wire Service(s):** AP. Circulation: 2,000 evening (paid). **Owner(s):** NorWest Newspapers, Inc., 170 S Penn Ave, Oberlin, KS 67749. Telephone: 785-475-2206. **Management:** Cynthia Haynes, Publisher. Sherry Hickman, Classified Adv. Mgr.. **Editorial:** Cynthia Haynes, Editor. Erica Bradley, Writer.

OAKLEY

OAKLEY GRAPHIC. 118 N. Center Ave., Oakley, KS 67748. Telephone: 785-672-3228. FAX: 785-672-3229. E-MAIL: bglover@carrollsweb.com. Year Established: 1887. Pub. Frequency: w. (Wed.) Page Size: broadsheet. Subscrip. Rate: $.65 newsstand/cover; $25.18/yr local; $26.18/yr out of area. Circulation: 1,250 per issue (paid and controlled). **Owner(s):** Mark Anderson, PO Box 528, Cimarron, KS 67835. Telephone: 316-855-3902. **Management:** Mark Anderson, Publisher. Gloria Pabst, Advertising Manager. **Editorial:** Barbara Glover, Editor.

OBERLIN

OBERLIN HERALD, THE. 170 S Penn Ave, Oberlin, KS 67749-2243. Telephone: 785-475-2206. FAX: 785-475-2800. E-MAIL: shaynes@nwkansas.com. URL: http://www.nwkansas.com. Year Established: 1879. Pub. Frequency: w. (Wed.) Page Size: broadsheet. Subscrip. Rate: $.75 newsstand/cover; $30/yr in county; $34/yr in state; $37/yr out of state. Adv. Rate: col. inch $4.65 Freelance Pay: $0.50/column-inch. Circulation: 2,777 per issue (paid). **Owner(s):** NorWest Newspapers, Inc., 170 S Penn Ave, Oberlin, KS 67745-2243. Telephone: 785-475-2206. FAX: 785-475-2800. **Management:** Steve Haynes, President. Dave Bergling, Advertising. Pat Cozad, Circulation Manager. **Editorial:** Kimberly Brandt, Editor. Steve Haynes, Editor-in-Chief.

OSAWATOMIE

OSAWATOMIE GRAPHIC. 635 Main St, Osawatomie, KS 66064. Telephone: 913-755-4151. FAX: 913-755-6544. E-MAIL: graphic@graphic-online.com. URL: http:\\www.graphic-online.com. Year Established: 1887. Pub. Frequency: w. (Wed.) Page Size: standard. Subscrip. Rate: $.75 newsstand/cover; $41/yr in county; $51/yr in state; $60/yr mailed out of state. Circulation: 4,500 per issue (paid). **Owner(s):** News-Press & Gazette Co., PO Box 29, St. Joseph, MO 64502. Telephone: 816-271-8500. **Management:** Paul L Branson, Advertising Manager. Larry Dwyer, Circulation Director. Jennifer Husted, Classified Adv. Mgr.. **Editorial:** Larry Chiott, Editor. Jennifer McDaniel, News Editor. Jeff Gulley, Sports.

OSKALOOSA

OSKALOOSA INDEPENDENT. 607 Delaware St., Oskaloosa, KS 66066. Telephone: 785-863-2520. FAX: 785-863-2730. E-MAIL: independent@grasshoppernet.com. URL: http://oskaloosaindependent.com. Mailing Address: PO Box 187, Valley Falls, KS 66088. Year Established: 1869. Pub. Frequency: w. (Thu.) Page Size: broadsheet. Subscrip. Rate: $.75 newsstand/cover; $22.50/yr in county; $24/yr in state; $30/yr out of state. Adv. Rate: col. inch $5.05 Circulation: 2,331 per issue (paid). **Owner(s):** Davis Publications, Inc., 416 Broadway, Valley Falls, KS 66088-0187. Telephone: 785-945-3257. **Management:** Corey Davis, General Manager. Clarke Davis, Publisher. Corey Davis, Advertising. Carol Meneley, Circulation Manager. **Editorial:** Ken Lassiter, Editor.

OTTAWA

OTTAWA TIMES SHOPPER, THE. 104 S. Cedar, Ottawa, KS 66067. Telephone: 785-242-4700. FAX: 785-242-9420. E-MAIL: ads@ottawaherald.com. Year Established: 1974. Pub. Frequency: w. (Tue.) Page Size: tabloid.Adv. Rate: col. inch $6.70 Circulation: 14,585 per issue (free). **Owner(s):** Kansas Newspapers LLC, One N Main St, Hutchinson, KS 67501-5229. Telephone: 620-694-5830. **Management:** Jeanny J. Sharp, Publisher. Linda Brown, Classified Adv. Mgr.. **Editorial:** Jeanny J. Sharp, Editor.

OVERLAND PARK

JOHNSON COUNTY SUN. 4370 W 109th St, Overland Park, KS 66212. Telephone: 913-381-1010. FAX: 913-381-9889. E-MAIL: kmoore@sunpublications.com. URL: http://www.sunpublications.com. Year Established: 1950. Pub. Frequency: w. (Thu.) Page Size: broadsheet. Subscrip. Rate: $.50 newsstand/cover; $78.46/yr mailed in county; $85.40/yr mailed elsewhere. Circulation: 11,000 per issue (paid and free). **Owner(s):** News-Press & Gazette Co., PO Box 29, St. Joseph, MO 64502. Telephone: 816-271-8500. **Management:** Roy Biondi, Publisher. Peter Cook, Advertising Director. David Pine, Circulation Manager. Brooke Wilkens, Classified Adv. Mgr.. **Editorial:** Jack Miles, Editor.

LEAWOOD SUN/BLUE VALLEY. 4370 W 109th St, Overland Park, KS 66212. Telephone: 913-381-1010. FAX: 913-381-9889. E-MAIL: jmiles@sunpublications.com. URL: http://www.sunpublications.com. Year Established: 1928. Pub. Frequency: s-w. (Wed. & Fri.) Page Size: broadsheet. Subscrip. Rate: $.50 newsstand/cover; $78.46/yr mailed in county; $85.40/yr mailed elsewhere. Circulation: 26,130 per issue (paid and free). **Owner(s):** News-Press & Gazette Co., PO Box 29, St. Joseph, MO 64502. Telephone: 816-271-8500. **Management:** Roy Biondi, Publisher. Peter Cook, Advertising Director. David Pine, Circulation Manager. Brooke Wilkens, Classified Adv. Mgr.. **Editorial:** Jack Miles, Editor.

LENEXA SUN. 4370 W 109th St, Overland Park, KS 66212. Telephone: 913-381-1010. FAX: 913-381-9889. E-MAIL: jmiles@sunpublications.com. URL: http://www.sunpublications.com. Year Established: 1921. Pub. Frequency: s-w. (Wed. & Fri.) Page Size: broadsheet. Subscrip. Rate: $.50 newsstand/cover; $78.46/yr mailed in county; $85.40/yr mailed elsewhere. Circulation: 19,900 per issue (paid and free). **Owner(s):** News-Press & Gazette Co., PO Box 29, St. Joseph, MO 64502. Telephone: 816-271-8500. **Management:** Roy Biondi, Publisher. Peter Cook, Advertising Director. David Pine, Circulation Manager. Brooke Wilkens, Classified Adv. Mgr.. **Editorial:** Jack Miles, Editor.

NORTHEAST JOHNSON COUNTY SUN. 4370 W 109th St, Overland Park, KS 66212. Telephone: 913-381-1010. FAX: 913-381-9889. E-MAIL: jmiles@sunpublications.com. URL: http://www.sunpublications.com. Year Established: 1950. Pub. Frequency: w. (Thu.) Page Size: broadsheet. Subscrip. Rate: $.50 newsstand/cover; $84/yr mailed. Circulation: 19,633 per issue (paid and free). **Owner(s):** News-Press & Gazette Co., PO Box 29, St. Joseph, MO 64502. Telephone: 816-271-8500. **Management:** Roy Biondi, Publisher. Peter Cook, Advertising Director. David Pine, Circulation Manager. Brooke Wilkens, Classified Adv. Mgr.. **Editorial:** Jack Miles, Editor.

OLATHE SUN. 4370 W 109th St, Overland Park, KS 66212. Telephone: 913-381-1010. FAX: 913-381-9889. E-MAIL: jmiles@sunpublications.com. URL: http://www.sunpublications.com. Year Established: 1950. Pub. Frequency: w. (Thu.) Page Size: broadsheet. Subscrip. Rate: $.50 newsstand/cover; $78.46/yr mailed in county; $85.40/yr mailed out of county. Circulation: 14,500 per issue (paid and free). **Owner(s):** News-Press & Gazette Co., PO Box 29, St. Joseph, MO 64502. Telephone: 816-271-8500. **Management:** Roy Biondi, Publisher. Peter Cook, Advertising Director. David Pine, Circulation Manager. Brooke Wilkens, Classified Adv. Mgr.. **Editorial:** Jack Miles, Editor.

OVERLAND PARK SUN. 4370 W 109th St, Overland Park, KS 66212. Telephone: 913-381-1010. FAX: 913-381-9889. E-MAIL: jmiles@sunpublications.com. URL: http://www.sunpublications.com. Pub. Frequency: w. (Thu.) Page Size: broadsheet. Subscrip. Rate: $.50 newsstand/cover; $78.46/yr mailed in county; $85.40/yr mailed elsewhere. Circulation: 23,195 per issue (paid and free). **Owner(s):** News-Press & Gazette Co., PO Box 29, St. Joseph, MO 64502. Telephone: 816-271-8500. **Management:** Roy Biondi, Publisher. Peter Cook, Advertising Director. David Pine, Circulation Manager. Brooke Wilkens, Classified Adv. Mgr.. **Editorial:** Jack Miles, Editor.

PRAIRIE VILLAGE SUN. 4370 W 109th St, Overland Park, KS 66212. Telephone: 913-381-1010. FAX: 913-381-9889. E-MAIL: kmoore@sunpublications.com. URL: http://www.sunpublications.com. Year Established: 1950. Pub. Frequency: s-w. (Wed. & Fri.) Page Size: broadsheet. Subscrip. Rate: $.50 newsstand/cover; $78.46/yr mailed in county; $85.40/yr mailed elsewhere. Circulation: 7,700 per issue (paid and free). **Owner(s):** News-Press & Gazette Co., PO Box 29, St. Joseph, MO 64502. Telephone: 816-271-8500. **Management:** Roy Biondi, Publisher. Peter Cook, Advertising Director. David Pine, Circulation Manager. Brooke Wilkens, Classified Adv. Mgr.. **Editorial:** Jack Miles, Editor.

SHAWNEE/MERRIAM SUN. 4370 W 109th St, Overland Park, KS 66212. Telephone: 913-381-1010. FAX: 913-381-9889. E-MAIL: jmiles@sunpublications.com. URL: http://www.sunpublications.com. Year Established: 1911. Pub. Frequency: s-w. (Wed. & Fri.) Page Size: broadsheet. Subscrip. Rate: $.50 newsstand/cover; $78.46/yr mailed in county; $85.40/yr mailed elsewhere. Circulation: 13,100 per issue (paid and free). **Owner(s):** News-Press & Gazette Co., PO Box 29, St. Joseph, MO 64502. Telephone: 816-271-8500. **Management:** Roy Biondi, Publisher. Peter Cook, Advertising Director. David Pine, Circulation Manager. Brooke Wilkens, Classified Adv. Mgr.. **Editorial:** Jack Miles, Editor.

WEDNESDAY MAGAZINE. 4370 W 109th St, Overland Park, KS 66211-1361. Telephone: 913-381-1010. URL: http://www.kccommunitynews.com. Year Established: 1937. Pub. Frequency: w. (Wed.) Page Size: tabloid.Subscrip. Rate: $20/yr in county Circulation: 23,111 per issue (paid). **Owner(s):** N P G Newspapers, Inc., See address and contact information above. **Management:** David Small, General Manager. David Thompson, Advertising Manager. **Editorial:** Chris Rodgers, Associate Editor.

PAOLA

MIAMI COUNTY REPUBLIC. 121 S Pearl St, Paola, KS 66071. Telephone: 913-294-2311. FAX: 913-294-5318. E-MAIL: republic@republic-online.com. URL: http://www.republic-online.com. Year Established: 1866. Pub. Frequency: s-w. (Wed. & Fri.) Page Size: broadsheet. Subscrip. Rate: $.75 newsstand/cover; $50/yr in county; $72/yr out of county. Circulation: 5,000 per issue (paid). **Owner(s):** News-Press & Gazette Co., PO Box 29, St. Joseph, MO 64502. Telephone: 816-271-8500. **Management:** Sandy Nelson, Publisher. Teresa Morrow, Advertising Manager. **Editorial:** Brian McCauley, Editor. Gene Morris, Sports.

PEABODY

PEABODY GAZETTE BULLETIN. 113 N Walnut St, Peabody, KS 66866. Telephone: 620-983-2185. FAX: 620-983-2185. Pub. Frequency: w. (Wed.) Page Size: broadsheet. Subscrip. Rate: $.75 newsstand/cover; $39/yr local; $44/yr in state; $49/yr out of state. Circulation: 1,800 per issue (free). **Owner(s):** Hoch Publishing Co., Inc., 117 S.Third St., Marion, KS 66861. Telephone: 620-382-2165. FAX: 620-382-2265. **Management:** Donna Bernhardt, Publisher. Melissa Parmley, Advertising Manager. Jean Stuchlik, Circulation Manager. **Editorial:** Susan Marshall, News Editor.

PHILLIPSBURG

PHILLIPS COUNTY REVIEW. 257 F St., Phillipsburg, KS 67661. Telephone: 785-543-5242. FAX: 785-543-5243. E-MAIL: pcreview@ruraltel.net. URL: http://www.phillipscountyreview.com. Mailing Address: PO Box 446, Phillipsburg, KS 67661. Year Established: 1905. Pub. Frequency: w. (Wed.) Page Size: broadsheet. Subscrip. Rate: $.50 newsstand/cover; $23.65/yr in state; $29/yr mailed out of state. Circulation: 2,000 per issue (paid). **Owner(s):** Main Street Media, See address and contact information above. **Management:** Irene Allen, Advertising. **Editorial:** Randy Moll, Editor. Contact: Tracey Altman, Publisher;; Jeff Dunetz, Marketing Director; Charlie Cox, Executive Editor; Stuart Englert, Senior Editor.

PRATT

SUNFLOWER SHOPPER. 320 S. Main St., Pratt, KS 67124. URL: http://www.gatehousemedia.com. Mailing Address: PO Box 909, Pratt, KS 67124. Pub. Frequency: w. (Wed.) Page Size: tabloid Circulation: 8,000 per issue (free). **Owner(s):** GateHouse Media, Inc, 350 WillowBrook Office Park, Fairport, NY 14450. **Management:** Keith Lippoldt, Publisher. Laurie Anderson, Advertising Manager. Leslie Barnes, Circulation Manager.

RUSSELL

LEBANON TIMES, THE. PO Box 513, Russell, KS 67665. Telephone: 785-483-2116. FAX: 785-483-4012. Year Established: 1887. Pub. Frequency: w. (Wed.) Page Size: standard. Subscrip. Rate: $.50 newsstand/cover; $15.41/yr in county; $16.76/yr in state; $16.50/yr out of state. Circulation: 600 per issue (paid and free). **Owner(s):** Jack & Kathy Krier, See address and contact information above.

RUSSELL COUNTY NEWS. PO Box 513, Russell, KS 67665. Telephone: 785-483-2116. FAX: 785-483-4012. E-MAIL: russellnews@eaglecom.net. Year Established: 1947. Pub. Frequency: s-w. (Wed. & Fri.) Page Size: tabloid.Subscrip. Rate: $.75 newsstand/cover; $43.05/yr Circulation: 2,400 evening (paid). **Owner(s):** Jack & Kathy Krier, See address and contact information above. **Management:** Ruth Newman, General Manager. Jack Krier, Owner. Pam Soetaert, Advertising Manager. Myra Thompson, Circulation Manager. Cindy Reed, Business Manager. **Editorial:** Pam Soetaert, Editor. David Thompson, Sports.

SHAWNEE

JOURNAL HERALD, THE. 11004 Johnson Dr., Shawnee, KS 66203. Telephone: 913-631-2550. FAX: 913-631-6552. E-MAIL: editor@shawneejournalherald.com. URL: http://www.shawneejournalherald.com. Mailing Address: PO Box 3886, Shawnee, KS 66203. Year Established: 1924. Pub. Frequency: w. (Thu.) Page Size: standard. Subscrip. Rate: $.50 newsstand/cover; $27.50/yr in county; $32.50/yr out of county; $37.50/yr mailed out of state. Circulation: 10,000 per issue (paid and free). **Owner(s):** GateHouse Media, Inc, 350 WillowBrook Office Park, Fairport, NY 14450. Telephone: 585-598-0030. FAX: 585-248-2631. **Management:** Pat Morrison, Publisher. Kathy Rowe, Office Manager. Pat Morrison, Advertising. John Harris, Circulation Manager. **Editorial:** Angie Davis, Graphics Editor. Tammy Worth, News Editor.

SMITH CENTER

SMITH COUNTY PIONEER. 201 S. Main St., Smith Center, KS 66967. Telephone: 785-282-3371. FAX: 785-282-6383. E-MAIL: pioneer@ruraltel.net. URL: http://www.smithcountypioneer.com. Year Established: 1871. Pub. Frequency: w. (Thu.) Page Size: standard. Subscrip. Rate: $.75 newsstand/cover; $23.28/yr in county; $24.23/yr out of county; $26/yr mailed out of state. Circulation: 3,198 per issue (paid). **Owner(s):** Jack & Kathy Krier, PO Box 513, Russell, KS 67665. Telephone: 785-483-2116. FAX: 785-483-4012. **Management:** Linda Baetz, General Manager. Jack Krier, Publisher. **Editorial:** Darrel Miller, Editor. Jack Krier, Managing Editor.

ST. FRANCIS

SAINT FRANCIS HERALD, THE. 310 Washington, St. Francis, KS 67756. Telephone: 785-332-3162. FAX: 785-332-3001. E-MAIL: sfherald@nwkansas.com. URL: http://www.nwkansas.com. Mailing Address: PO Box 1050, St. Francis, KS 67756-1050. Year Established: 1885. Pub. Frequency: w. (Thu.) Page Size: broadsheet. Subscrip. Rate: $.75 newsstand/cover; $30/yr local; $34/yr in state; $37/yr out of state. Adv. Rate: col. inch $4.05 Circulation: 1,681 per issue (paid and free). **Owner(s):** NorWest Newspapers, Inc., 170 S Penn Ave, Oberlin, KS 67749. Telephone: 785-475-2206. FAX: 785-475-2800. **Management:** Steve Haynes, President. Karen Krien, Publisher. Casey McCormick, Advertising. Leslie Hilt, Circulation Manager. **Editorial:** Karen Krien, Managing Editor.

ST. JOHN

ST. JOHN NEWS. 318 N. Main St., St. John, KS 67576. Telephone: 620-549-3201. FAX: 620-549-3829. E-MAIL: sjnews@stjohnks.net. Mailing Address: PO Box 488, St. John, KS 67576. Year Established: 1880. Pub. Frequency: w. (Wed.) Page Size: tabloid. Subscrip. Rate: $.75 newsstand/cover; $44/yr mailed in county; $55/yr mailed out of county. Adv. Rate: col. inch $4.28 Circulation: 1,500 per issue (paid). **Owner(s):** GateHouse Media, Inc, 350 WillowBrook Office Park, Fairport, NY 14450. Telephone: 585-598-0030. **Management:** Keith Lippoldt, Publisher. **Editorial:** Terry Spradley, Editor.

Weeklies

ST. MARYS

ST. MARYS STAR. 517 W. Bertrand, St. Marys, KS 66536-1618. Telephone: 785-437-2935. FAX: 785-437-2095. E-MAIL: star@oct.net. Year Established: 1884. Pub. Frequency: w. (Tue.) Page Size: tabloid. Subscrip. Rate: $.75 newsstand/cover; $31.89/yr in county; $32/yr in state; $36/yr out of state. Adv. Rate: col. inch $3.50 Circulation: 1,800 per issue (paid and free). **Owner(s):** Anita H. Janssen, PO Box 190, St. Marys, KS 66536-0190. Telephone: 785-437-2935. FAX: 785-437-2095. **Management:** Anita H. Janssen, Publisher. **Editorial:** Anita H. Janssen, Managing Editor. Rhonda Slagle, Assistant Editor.

ULYSSES

ULYSSES NEWS. PO Box 706, Ulysses, KS 67880. Telephone: 620-356-1201. FAX: 620-356-4610. E-MAIL: ulynews@pld.com. Year Established: 1892. Pub. Frequency: w. (Thu.) Page Size: broadsheet. Subscrip. Rate: $.75 newsstand/cover; $25/yr in county; $28.50/yr out of county. Circulation: 2,600 per issue (paid). **Owner(s):** Karla Wood, See address and contact information above. **Management:** Karla Wood, Publisher. **Editorial:** Karla Wood, Editor. Kellie Euliss, Managing Editor.

VALLEY FALLS

VALLEY FALLS VINDICATOR. 416 Broadway, Valley Falls, KS 66088-0187. Telephone: 785-945-3257. FAX: 785-945-3444. E-MAIL: vindicator@grasshoppernet.com. URL: http://www.valleyfallsvindicator.com. Mailing Address: P.O. Box 187, Valley Falls, KS 66088-0187. Year Established: 1864. Pub. Frequency: w. (Thu.) Page Size: broadsheet. Subscrip. Rate: $.75 newsstand/cover; $22.50/yr home delivery in county; $24/yr mailed in state; $30/yr mailed elsewhere. Adv. Rate: col. inch $5.05 Circulation: 2,536 per issue (paid). **Owner(s):** Davis Publications, Inc., See address and contact information above. **Management:** Corey Davis, General Manager. Clarke Davis, Advertising Manager. Carol Meneley, Circulation Manager. **Editorial:** Clarke Davis, Editor. Ken Lassiter, Reporter. Marveta Davis, Society Editor.

WASHINGTON

WASHINGTON COUNTY (KS) NEWS. 303 C St., Washington, KS 66968-0316. E-MAIL: newseditor@sbcglobal.net. Year Established: 1869. Pub. Frequency: w. (Thu.) Page Size: broadsheet. Subscrip. Rate: $.75 newsstand/cover; $28.50/yr mailed in county; $33/yr mailed out of county; $36/yr mailed out of state. Adv. Rate: col. inch $5 Circulation: 3,000 per issue (paid). **Owner(s):** Dan Thalmann, PO Box 316, Washington, KS 66968. Telephone: 785-325-2219. FAX: 785-325-3255. **Management:** Dan Thalmann, Publisher. Marcia Hubbard, Advertising. **Editorial:** Dan Thalmann, Editor.

KENTUCKY

ALBANY

CLINTON COUNTY NEWS (ALBANY). 116 Washington St., Albany, KY 42602. Telephone: 606-387-5144. FAX: 606-387-7949. E-MAIL: gp@clintonnews.net. URL: http:www.clintonnews.net. Year Established: 1949. Pub. Frequency: w. (Thu.) Page Size: standard. Subscrip. Rate: $.50 newsstand/cover; $14/yr local; $17/yr mailed in state; $21/yr mailed out of state. Circulation: 3,750 per issue (paid). **Owner(s):** Gibson Printing Co., Inc., See address and contact information above. **Management:** Alan B. Gibson, Publisher. Janie U. Gibson, Advertising Manager. **Editorial:** Alan B. Gibson, Editor.

BARBOURVILLE

BARBOURVILLE MOUNTAIN ADVOCATE. 214 Knox St., Barbourville, KY 40906. Telephone: 606-546-9225. FAX: 606-546-2830. E-MAIL: advocate@barbourville.com. URL: http://www.barbourvilleadvocate.com. Mailing Address: PO Box 140, Barbourville, KY 40906. Year Established: 1904. Pub. Frequency: w. (Thu.) Page Size: broadsheet. Subscrip. Rate: $.50 newsstand/cover; $23/yr mailed in county; $32/yr mailed out of county; $38/yr mailed out of state. Adv. Rate: col. inch $8.76 Circulation: 6,700 per issue (paid). **Owner(s):** Robert K. Wilson, See address and contact information above. **Management:** J.T. H. Hurst, Publisher. Wanda Blevins, Advertising Manager. **Editorial:** Marilynn Brittain, Editor. Eddie Arnold, City Editor. Steve Foley, Sports Editor.

BARDSTOWN

KENTUCKY STANDARD. ISSN 8750-0760
110 W. Stephen Foster Ave., Bardstown, KY 40004. Telephone: 502-348-9003. FAX: 502-348-1971. E-MAIL: standard@bardstown.com. URL: http://www.kystandard.com. Mailing Address: PO Box 639, Bardstown, KY 40004. Year Established: 1900. Pub. Frequency: 3/w. (Sun., Wed., Fri.) Page Size: broadsheet. Subscrip. Rate: $.50 newsstand/cover; $54/yr in county; $75.26/yr in state; $97/yr out of state. **Wire Service(s):** AP. Circulation: 9,350 per issue (paid). **Owner(s):** Landmark Community Newspapers, Inc., PO Box 549, Shelbyville, KY 40065. **Management:** Ron Filkins, Publisher. Robin Phelan, Advertising Manager. Rita Durbin, Circulation Manager. Carol Mudd, Classified Adv. Mgr.. **Editorial:** Lisa Tolliver, Editor. Peter Zubaty, Sports Editor.

SHOPPER'S GUIDE. 110 W. Stephen Foster Ave., Bardstown, KY 40004. Telephone: 502-348-9003. FAX: 502-348-1971. Mailing Address: PO Box 639, Bardstown, KY 40004. Pub. Frequency: w. (Wed.) Page Size: broadsheet Circulation: 12,286 per issue (free). **Owner(s):** Landmark Community Newspapers, Inc., PO Box 549, Shelbyville, KY 40065. **Management:** Ron Filkins, Publisher. Robin Phelan, Advertising Manager. Rita Durbin, Circulation Manager. Carol Mudd, Classified Adv. Mgr.. **Editorial:** Lisa Tolliter, Editor.

BARDWELL

CARLISLE COUNTY NEWS, THE. PO Box 309, Bardwell, KY 42023. Telephone: 270-628-5490. FAX: 270-628-3167. E-MAIL: ccn@galaxycable.net. Pub. Frequency: w. (Wed.) Page Size: standard. Subscrip. Rate: $.75 newsstand/cover; $29/yr in county; $39/yr mailed out of county. Circulation: 1,500 per issue (paid). **Owner(s):** Kentucky Publishing, Inc., See address and contact information above. **Management:** Greg LeNeave, Publisher. Clint Dennis, Advertising Manager. **Editorial:** Lilly Morefield, Editor.

BEATTYVILLE

BEATTYVILLE ENTERPRISE. 147 Main St., Beattyville, KY 41311-9249. Telephone: 606-464-2444. FAX: 606-464-8858. E-MAIL: beattyill@bellsouth.net. Mailing Address: PO Box 126, Beattyville, KY 41311-0126. Pub. Frequency: w. (Wed.) Page Size: standard. Subscrip. Rate: $.50 newsstand/cover; $15/yr in county; $23/yr out of county. Circulation: 2,300 per issue (paid). **Owner(s):** Intermountain Publishing, See address and contact information above. **Management:** James Nolan, Publisher. Cheryle Walton, Advertising Manager. **Editorial:** Edmund Shelby, Editor.

BEDFORD

TRIMBLE BANNER. 322 Hwy. 42E, Bedford, KY 40006-0289. Telephone: 502-255-3205. FAX: 502-255-7797. URL: http://www.trimblebanner.com. Mailing Address: PO Box 289, Bedford, KY 40006-0289. Pub. Frequency: w. (Wed.) Page Size: standard. Subscrip. Rate: $.50 newsstand/cover; $23.32/yr in county; $31.80/yr mailed out of county; $38/yr mailed out of state. Circulation: 1,800 per issue (paid). **Owner(s):** Landmark Community Newspapers, Inc., PO Box 549, Shelbyville, KY 40065. Telephone: 502-633-2526. FAX: 502-633-2618. **Management:** Jeff Moore, Publisher. Carla Kidwell, Advertising Manager. **Editorial:** Darren Pike, Editor.

BENTON

TRIBUNE-COURIER (PADUCAH). 100 W. 11th St., Benton, KY 42025. Telephone: 270-527-3162. FAX: 270-527-4567. E-MAIL: editor@tribunecourier.com. URL: http://www.tribunecourier.com. Mailing Address: PO Box 410, Benton, KY 42025. Year Established: 1888. Pub. Frequency: w. (Wed.) Page Size: broadsheet. Subscrip. Rate: $.75 newsstand/cover; $30/yr in county; $36/yr out of county; $38/yr out of state. Circulation: 5,000 per issue (paid). **Owner(s):** Paxton Media Group Llc, 201 S. Fourth St., Paducah, KY 42003. Telephone: 270-575-8600. FAX: 270-442-8188. **Management:** Jim Ward, Publisher. Burt Dunn, Circulation Manager. **Editorial:** Tabitha Armstrong, Editor. Chris Jung, Sports Editor.

BEREA

BEREA CITIZEN, THE. 711 Chestnut St., Berea, KY 40403. Telephone: 859-986-0959. FAX: 859-986-0960. Year Established: 1899. Pub. Frequency: w. (Thu.) Page Size: broadsheet. Subscrip. Rate: $.50 newsstand/cover; $19/yr in county; $26/yr out of county. Circulation: 4,000 per issue (paid). **Owner(s):** Berea Publishing Inc., PO Box 207, Berea, KY 40403-0207. Telephone: 859-986-0959. **Management:** Teresa Senters, Publisher. Kristi Johnson, Advertising Manager. **Editorial:** Scott Powell, Editor.

BOWLING GREEN

COUNTRY PEDDLER. 326 E 8th Ave, Bowling Green, KY 42101-2270. Telephone: 270-842-3314. FAX: 270-842-4220. Mailing Address: PO Box 492, Bowling Green, KY 42101-0492. Year Established: 1971. Pub. Frequency: w. (Thu.) Page Size: tabloid Circulation: 33,700 per issue (free). **Owner(s):** News Publishing Co., Inc., PO Box 492, Bowling Green, KY 42102-0492. Telephone: 270-842-3314. **Management:** Belinda Saltzman, Publisher. **Editorial:** Kyda H West, Editor.

BRANDENBURG

COUNTY MESSENGER, THE. 138 Broadway, Brandenburg, KY 40108. Telephone: 270-422-2155. FAX: 270-422-2110. E-MAIL: messenger@bbtel.com. Mailing Address: PO Box 678, Brandenburg, KY 40108. Year Established: 1892. Pub. Frequency: w. (Wed.) Page Size: broadsheet. Subscrip. Rate: $.60 newsstand/cover; $22/yr home delivery in county; $29/yr mailed elsewhere. Circulation: 6,000 per issue (paid). **Owner(s):** Mead County Messenger Corp., See address and contact information above. **Management:** Roxanne Curts, General Manager. Rena Singleton, Publisher. Linda Riddell, Advertising Manager.

BROOKSVILLE

BRACKEN COUNTY NEWS, THE. 216 Frankfort St., Brooksville, KY 41001. Telephone: 606-735-2198. FAX: 606-735-2199. E-MAIL: bcnews@alltel.net. Mailing Address: PO Box 68, Brooksville, KY 41004. Year Established: 1927. Pub. Frequency: w. (Thu.) Page Size: standard. Subscrip. Rate: $.50 newsstand/cover; $20/yr local; $25/yr out of county; $30/yr out of state. Circulation: 3,000 per issue (paid). **Owner(s):** Kathy Bay, See address and contact information above. **Management:** Kathy Bay, Publisher. **Editorial:** Lynn Darnell, Editor.

BROWNSVILLE

EDMONSON NEWS. PO Box 69, Brownsville, KY 42210. Telephone: 270-597-3115. FAX: 270-597-3115. Pub. Frequency: w. (Thu.) Page Size: standard. Subscrip. Rate: $.50 newsstand/cover; $12/yr in county; $18/yr in state; $21/yr out of state. Circulation: 4,000 per issue (paid). **Owner(s):** William & Cathy Canty, See address and contact information above. **Management:** William Canty, Publisher. **Editorial:** Cathy Canty, Editor.

BURKESVILLE

CUMBERLAND COUNTY NEWS. 412 Courthouse Sq., Burkesville, KY 42717. Telephone: 270-864-3891. FAX: 270-864-3497. E-MAIL: ccn@burkesville.com. URL: http://www.burkesville.com/ccn. Mailing Address: PO Box 307, Burkesville, KY 42717. Year Established: 1920. Pub. Frequency: w. (Wed.) Page Size: broadsheet. Subscrip. Rate: $.35 newsstand/cover; $15/yr in county & adj cys; $21/yr in state; $24/yr out of state. Circulation: 3,000 per issue (paid). **Owner(s):** Patsy Judd, See address and contact information above. **Management:** Patsy Judd, Publisher. Chris Garland, Advertising Manager. **Editorial:** Cyndi Pritchett, Editor. Danny Stilts, Sports.

CADIZ

CADIZ RECORD, THE. 58 Nunn Blvd., Cadiz, KY 42211. Telephone: 270-522-6605. FAX: 270-522-3001. E-MAIL: news@cadizrecord.com. URL: http://www.cadizrecord.com. Mailing Address: PO Box 1670, Cadiz, KY 42211. Year Established: 1881. Pub. Frequency: w. (Wed.) Page Size: broadsheet. Subscrip. Rate: $.75 newsstand/cover; $32/yr mailed in county; $38/yr mailed out of county; $45/yr mailed out of state. Adv. Rate: col. inch $6.20 Circulation: 5,000 per issue (paid). **Owner(s):** Paxton Media Group Llc, 201 S. Fourth St., Paducah, KY 42003. Telephone: 270-575-8600. FAX: 270-442-8188. **Management:** Mary B Carlock, General Manager. **Editorial:** Justin McGill, Executive Editor.

CALHOUN

MCLEAN COUNTY NEWS. 166 E. Second St., Calhoun, KY 42327. Telephone: 270-273-3287. FAX: 270-273-3544. Mailing Address: PO Box 266, Calhoun, KY 42327. Year Established: 1884. Pub. Frequency: w. (Thu.) Page Size: broadsheet. Subscrip. Rate: $.75 newsstand/cover; $26.50/yr in state; $35/yr mailed out of state. Circulation: 3,000 per issue (paid). **Owner(s):** Paxton Media Group Llc, 201 S. Fourth St., Paducah, KY 42003. Telephone: 270-575-8600. **Management:** Bob Morris, Publisher. **Editorial:** Jessica Bratcher, Editor.

CALVERT CITY

LAKE NEWS (CALVERT CITY), THE. 153 E. Fifth Ave.., Calvert City, KY 42029. Telephone: 270-395-5858. FAX: 270-395-5858. E-MAIL: news@thelakenews.net. URL: http://www.thelakenews.net. Mailing Address: PO Box 498, Calvert City, KY 42029. Year Established: 1984. Pub. Frequency: w. (Wed.) Page Size: standard. Subscrip. Rate: $.75 newsstand/cover; $20/yr in county; $30/yr out of county & state. Adv. Rate: col. inch $5.93 Circulation: 2,700 per issue (paid). **Owner(s):** Loyd Ford, See address and contact information above. **Management:** Loyd Ford, Publisher. **Editorial:** Loyd Ford, Editor.

CAMPBELLSVILLE

CENTRAL KENTUCKY NEWS-JOURNAL. 428 Woodlawn Ave., Campbellsville, KY 42718. Telephone: 270-465-8111. FAX: 270-465-2500. E-MAIL: cknj@cknj.com. URL: http://www.cknj.com. Mailing Address: PO Box 1138, Campbellsville, KY 42719. Year Established: 1910. Pub. Frequency: s-w. (Mon. & Thu.) Page Size: broadsheet. Subscrip. Rate: $.50 newsstand/cover; $45/yr mailed in county; $63.60/yr mailed in state; $77/yr mailed out of state. Adv. Rate: col. inch $11.46 Circulation: 7,000 per issue (paid). **Owner(s):** Landmark Community Newspapers, Inc., PO Box 549, Shelbyville, KY 40065. Telephone: 502-633-2526. FAX: 502-633-2618. **Management:** Patrick M Keefe, Publisher. Kristi Campbell, Advertising. Patrick M Keefe, Advertising Manager. Rose Rainwater, Circulation Manager. **Editorial:** Rebecca Cassell, Editor. Bobby Brockman, Sports Editor.

CAMPTON

WOLFE COUNTY NEWS, THE. 270 Main St., Campton, KY 41301-0129. Telephone: 606-668-3595. FAX: 606-668-6001. Mailing Address: PO Box 129, Campton, KY 41301-0129. Pub. Frequency: w. (Fri.) Page Size: broadsheet. Subscrip. Rate: $.50 newsstand/cover; $21/yr mailed in state; $24/yr mailed out of state. Circulation: 2,800 per issue (paid). **Owner(s):** Courier Publishing Co. Inc., See address and contact information above. **Management:** Earl W. Kinner, Publisher. JB Stamper, Advertising Manager. **Editorial:** Earl W. Kinner, Editor.

CARLISLE

NICHOLAS COUNTIAN AND THE CARLISLE MERCURY, THE. 218 N. Locust St., Carlisle, KY 40311. Telephone: 859-289-6424. FAX: 859-289-6947. E-MAIL: nich_co@bellsouth.net. URL: http://www.nicholascountian.com. Year Established: 1867. Pub. Frequency: w. (Thu.) Page Size: broadsheet. Subscrip. Rate: $.50 newsstand/cover; $25/yr mailed in state; $30/yr mailed out of state. Circulation: 3,600 per issue (paid). **Owner(s):** William D. Crawford, See address and contact information above. **Management:** William D. Crawford, Publisher. Brandy Evans, Advertising Manager. **Editorial:** William D. Crawford, Editor.

CARROLLTON

NEWS-DEMOCRAT, THE. 122 Sixth St., Carrollton, KY 41008. Telephone: 502-732-4261. FAX: 502-732-0453. Mailing Address: PO Box 60, Carrollton, KY 41008. Year Established: 1867. Pub. Frequency: w. (Wed.) Page Size: broadsheet. Subscrip. Rate: $.75 newsstand/cover; $31.80/yr home delivery in county; $40.28/yr mailed out of county; $48/yr mailed out of state. Adv. Rate: col. inch $7.80 Circulation: 3,400 per issue (paid). **Owner(s):** Landmark Community Newspapers, Inc., PO Box 549, Shelbyville, KY 40065. **Management:** Jeff Moore, Publisher. Carla Kidwell, Circulation Manager.

CAVE CITY

PROGRESS (CAVE CITY), THE. P O Box 546, Cave City, KY 42127. Telephone: 270-786-2679. FAX: 270-786-4470. Year Established: 1935. Pub. Frequency: w. (Thu.) Page Size: broadsheet. Subscrip. Rate: $.50 newsstand/cover; $25/yr in county; $40/yr in state; $55/yr out of state. Adv. Rate: col. inch $5.35 Circulation: 8,500 per issue (paid). **Owner(s):** Jobe Publishing Inc., P O Box 340, Horse Cave, KY 42149. **Management:** Judy Wright, Publisher. Teresia Sexton, Advertising Manager. **Editorial:** Josh Hampton, Editor.

CENTRAL CITY

LEADER-NEWS (GREENVILLE). 1730 W. Everly Bros. Blvd., Central City, KY 42330. Telephone: 270-754-3000. FAX: 270-754-9484. URL: http://www.ky-leadernews.com. Mailing Address: PO Box 138, Greenville, KY 42345-0138. Year Established: 1912. Pub. Frequency: w. (Wed.) Page Size: broadsheet. Subscrip. Rate: $.50 newsstand/cover; $13 mailed for 6 mos. in county; $14 mailed for 6 mos. out of county; $16 mailed for 6 mos. out of state. Circulation: 8,600 per issue (paid). **Owner(s):** Vickie Anderson, PO Box 138, Greenville, KY 42345. Telephone: 502-754-3000. FAX: 502-754-9484. **Management:** Jowanna Bandy, General Manager. Vickie Anderson, Publisher. Angela Wilson, Advertising. **Editorial:** Rita Dukes, Editor.

TIMES-ARGUS. 202 W. Broad St., Central City, KY 42330. Telephone: 270-754-2331. FAX: 270-754-1805. E-MAIL: thetimesargus@bellsouth.net. URL: http://www.times-argus.net. Mailing Address: PO Box 31, Central City, KY 42330. Year Established: 1906. Pub. Frequency: w. (Wed.) Page Size: broadsheet. Subscrip. Rate: $.50 newsstand/cover; $18.80/yr in state; $23/yr out of state. Circulation: 3,000 per issue (paid). **Owner(s):** Central City Publishing Corp., See address and contact information above. **Management:** Mark Stone, Publisher. Debbie Harris, Advertising. **Editorial:** Mark Stone, Editor. Richard Deavers, Managing Editor. Charlotte Ball, Graphics Editor.

CLINTON

HICKMAN COUNTY GAZETTE. 308 S. Washington Ave., Clinton, KY 42031. Telephone: 270-653-3381. FAX: 270-653-3322. E-MAIL: gazette@purchasearea.net. Year Established: 1901. Pub. Frequency: w. (Wed.) Page Size: standard. Subscrip. Rate: $.50 newsstand/cover; $22.90/yr in county; $25.90/yr out of county. Adv. Rate: col. inch $4.75 Circulation: 2,000 per issue (paid). **Owner(s):** Lewis Publishing Co.Inc., PO Box 200, Clinton, KY 42031-0200. **Management:** Larry Lewis, Publisher. Nancy Evans, Advertising Manager. **Editorial:** Gaye Bencini, Editor.

COLUMBIA

ADAIR PROGRESS, THE. 98 Grant Ln, Columbia, KY 42728. Telephone: 270-384-6471. FAX: 270-384-6474. E-MAIL: adairpro1@alltel.net. URL: http://www.adairprogress.com. Mailing Address: P.O. Box 595, Columbia, KY 42728-0595. Year Established: 1988. Pub. Frequency: s-w. (Tue. & Thu.) Page Size: broadsheet. Subscrip. Rate: $.50 newsstand/cover; $19/yr in county & adj. cys.; $31/yr out of area. Adv. Rate: col. inch $5.41 Circulation: 5,900 per issue (paid). **Owner(s):** The Adair Progress, Inc., See address and contact information above. **Management:** Donna Hancock, Publisher. Lee Babbitt, Advertising Manager. **Editorial:** Tiffany Hadley, Managing Editor.

ADAIR RUSSELL SHOPPER, THE. 98 Grant Ln, Columbia, KY 42728. Telephone: 270-384-6471. FAX: 270-384-6474. E-MAIL: adairpco1@alltel.net. URL: http://www.adairprogress.com. Year Established: 1988. Pub. Frequency: w. (Mon.) Page Size: tabloid.Adv. Rate: col. inch $7.13 Circulation: 16,000 per issue (free). **Owner(s):** The Adair Progress, Inc., See address and contact information above. **Management:** Donna Hancock, Publisher. Lee Babbitt, Advertising Manager. **Editorial:** Tiffany Hadley, Managing Editor.

CASEY COUNTY SHOPPER, THE. 98 Grant Ln, Columbia, KY 42728. Telephone: 270-384-6471. FAX: 270-384-6474. E-MAIL: adairpro1@alltel.net. Year Established: 1988. Pub. Frequency: w. (Mon.) Page Size: tabloid.Adv. Rate: col. inch $5.95 Circulation: 7,000 per issue (paid and controlled). **Owner(s):** The Adair Progress, Inc., See address and contact information above. **Management:** Donna Hancock, Publisher. Lee Babbitt, Advertising Manager. **Editorial:** Tiffany Hadley, Managing Editor.

CROMONA

LETCHER COUNTY COMMUNITY NEWS-PRESS.   ISSN 0899-1820 PO Box 156, Cromona, KY 41810. Telephone: 606-855-4541. FAX: 606-855-9290. Year Established: 1959. Pub. Frequency: w. (Wed.) Page Size: broadsheet. Subscrip. Rate: $.75 newsstand/cover; $20/yr in county; $32/yr elsewhere. Adv. Rate: col. inch $5 Circulation: 2,000 per issue (controlled and free). **Owner(s):** Superior Printing & Publishing Co., Inc., See address and contact information above. **Management:** Charles Whitaker, Publisher. **Editorial:** Tina Whitaker, Editor. Mike Whitaker, Managing Editor.

CUMBERLAND

TRI-CITY NEWS. 850 E. Main St., Cumberland, KY 40823. Telephone: 606-589-2588. FAX: 606-589-2589. E-MAIL: tricitynews@yahoo.com. Year Established: 1929. Pub. Frequency: w. (Wed.) Page Size: broadsheet. Subscrip. Rate: $.50 newsstand/cover; $18/yr local; $20/yr mailed in state; $24/yr mailed out of state. Adv. Rate: col. inch $7 Circulation: 2,500 per issue (paid). **Owner(s):** Jeff Wilder, See address and contact information above. **Management:** Tammy Deal, Assistant Manager. **Editorial:** Jeff Wilder, Editor. Rachel Ison, Production Editor.

CYNTHIANA

CYNTHIANA DEMOCRAT, THE. 302 Webster Ave., Cynthiana, KY 41031. Telephone: 859-234-1035. FAX: 859-234-8096. E-MAIL: cyndem@kih.net. URL: http://www.cynthianademocrat.com. Mailing Address: PO Box 160, Cynthiana, KY 41031. Year Established: 1868. Pub. Frequency: w. (Thu.) Page Size: broadsheet. Subscrip. Rate: $.50 newsstand/cover; $30.74/yr in county & adj. counties; $40.28/yr mailed in state; $50/yr mailed out of state. Circulation: 5,800 per issue (paid). **Owner(s):** Landmark Community Newspapers, Inc., PO Box 549, Shelbyville, KY 40065. Telephone: 502-633-2526. **Management:** Jeff Moore, Publisher. Patricia Jenkins, Advertising Manager. Linda Wright, Circulation Manager. Wanda Gaunce, Classified Adv. Mgr.. **Editorial:** Becky Barnes, Editor. Donal Richie, Writer.

DAWSON SPRINGS

DAWSON SPRINGS PROGRESS. 131 S. Main St., Dawson Springs, KY 42408. Telephone: 270-797-3271. FAX: 270-797—3271. Year Established: 1919. Pub. Frequency: w. (Thu.) Page Size: standard. Subscrip. Rate: $.50 newsstand/cover; $19/yr mailed in county; $25/yr mailed out of county; $30/yr mailed out of state. Adv. Rate: col. inch $4.50 Circulation: 2,200 per issue (paid). **Owner(s):** Progress Publishing Co., Inc., See address and contact information above. **Management:** Jed Dillingham, Co-Publisher. Scott Dillingham, Advertising Manager. **Editorial:** Jed Dillingham, Editor.

DRY RIDGE

GRANT COUNTY NEWS (WILLIAMSTOWN). 129 S Main St, Dry Ridge, KY 41035. E-MAIL: grantnews@fuse.net. URL: http://www.grantky.com. Mailing Address: PO Box 247, Williamstown, KY 41097-0247. Year Established: 1906. Pub. Frequency: w. (Thu.) Page Size: broadsheet. Subscrip. Rate: $.50 newsstand/cover; $28.62/yr in area; $42.40/yr in state; $54/yr out of state. Adv. Rate: col. inch $10.62 Circulation: 5,958 per issue (paid). **Owner(s):** Landmark Community Newspapers, Inc., PO Box 549, Shelbyville, KY 40065. Telephone: 502-633-2526. FAX: 502-633-2618. **Management:** Ken Stone, Publisher. **Editorial:** Jamie Baker-Nantz, Editor.Readers: Local county and area

EDDYVILLE

HERALD LEDGER. 143 Main St, Eddyville, KY 42038. Telephone: 270-388-2269. FAX: 270-388-5540. E-MAIL: jstovall@heraldledger.com. URL: http://www.heraldledger.com. Mailing Address: PO Box 747, Eddyville, KY 42038. Year Established: 1905. Pub. Frequency: w. (Wed.) Page Size: broadsheet. Subscrip. Rate: $.75 newsstand/cover; $27/yr mailed in county; $32/yr mailed out of county; $34/yr mailed out of state. Circulation: 2,600 per issue (paid). **Owner(s):** Paxton Media Group, LLC., 201 S. Fourth St., Paducah, KY 42003. Telephone: 270-575-8600. FAX: 270-442-8188. **Management:** Jim Ward, General Manager. Selena Ward, Advertising Manager. **Editorial:** Jayne Stoval, Editor. Jody Norwood, Sports Editor.

EDMONTON

EDMONTON HERALD-NEWS. 116 S Main St, Edmonton, KY 42129. Mailing Address: PO Box 67, Edmonton, KY 42129. Pub. Frequency: s-w. (Wed. & Sat.) Page Size: standard. Subscrip. Rate: $.50 newsstand/cover; $21.95/yr in county; $36/yr out of county. Circulation: 3,100 per issue (paid). **Owner(s):** Jobe Publishing Inc., 514 S Green St, Glasgow, KY 42141. **Management:** Jeffrey S. Jobe, Publisher. Kathy Riddle, Advertising. **Editorial:** Shirley Mayrand, Editor.

METCALFE COUNTY LIGHT. P O Box 87, Edmonton, KY 42129. Telephone: 270-786-2679. FAX: 270-786-4470. URL: http://www.jobepublishinginc.com. Pub. Frequency: w. (Sun) Subscrip. Rate: $.50 newsstand/cover; $25/yr home delivery in county; $40/yr mailed out of county; $55/yr mailed out of state. Circulation: 1,956 per issue (paid). **Owner(s):** Jobe Publishing Inc., P O Box 340, Horse Cave, KY 42149. **Management:** Jeffrey S. Jobe, Publisher. Kathy Riddle, Advertising.

ELIZABETHTOWN

HARDIN COUNTY (KY) INDEPENDENT. 318 N. Mulberry St., Elizabethtown, KY 42701-1033. Telephone: 270-737-5585. FAX: 270-737-6634. E-MAIL: glush@hardincountyindependent.com. URL: http://www.hardincountyindependent.com. Mailing Address: PO Box 1117, Elizabethtown, KY 42702. Pub. Frequency: w. (Thu.) Page Size: standard. Subscrip. Rate: $.50 newsstand/cover; $20/yr in county; $26/yr out of county; $35/yr out of state. Circulation: 5,000 per issue (paid). **Owner(s):** Gerald Lush, See address and contact information above. **Management:** Gerald Lush, Publisher. **Editorial:** Gerald Lush, Editor.

ELKTON

TODD COUNTY STANDARD, THE. PO Box 308, Elkton, KY 42220. Telephone: 270-265-2439. E-MAIL: tcstandard@kypress.com. Year Established: 1892. Pub. Frequency: w. (Wed.) Page Size: broadsheet. Subscrip. Rate: $.50 newsstand/cover; $18.50/yr mailed in county; $24/yr mailed out of county. Circulation: 2,300 per issue (paid). **Owner(s):** Mike Finch, See address and contact information above. **Management:** Mike Finch, Publisher. Jo Tribble, Advertising. **Editorial:** Michael Finch II, Editor.

EMINENCE

HENRY COUNTY LOCAL. 1378 Eminence Rd., Eminence, KY 40019. Telephone: 502-845-2858. FAX: 502-845-2921. E-MAIL: hclocal@kih.net. URL: http:www.hclocal.com. Mailing Address: PO Box 209, New Castle, KY 40050. Year Established: 1876. Pub. Frequency: w. (Wed.) Page Size: broadsheet. Subscrip. Rate: $.50 newsstand/cover; $28.62/yr in county; $37.10/yr in state $3710; $46/yr out of state. Circulation: 4,100 per issue (paid). **Owner(s):** Landmark Community Newspapers, Inc., PO Box 549, Shelbyville, KY 40065. Telephone: 502-633-4334. **Management:** Melissa Blankenship, General Manager. Tiffany Clark, Advertising Manager. Angela Courtney, Circulation Manager. **Editorial:** Melissa Blankenship, Editor. Mike Smith, Sports Editor.

FALMOUTH

FALMOUTH OUTLOOK, THE.   ISSN 0891-8694 210 Main St., Falmouth, KY 41040-0111. Telephone: 859-654-3332. FAX: 859-654-4365. E-MAIL: falout@fuse.net. URL: http://www.falmouthoutlook.com. Mailing Address: PO Box 111, Falmouth, KY 41040-0111. Year Established: 1907. Pub. Frequency: w. (Tue.) Page Size: broadsheet. Subscrip. Rate: $.75 newsstand/cover; $26.50/yr in county; $35.50/yr out of county; $43/yr out of state. Circulation: 4,950 per issue (paid). **Owner(s):** Delphos Newspapers, 405 N. Main St., Delphos, OH 45833. Telephone: 419-695-0015. **Management:** Deborrah Dennie, Publisher. Valerie Cookendorfer, Advertising. **Editorial:** Deborrah Dennie, Editor.

FLEMINGSBURG

FLEMINGSBURG GAZETTE. 151 E Water St, Flemingsburg, KY 41041-1218. Telephone: 606-845-9211. FAX: 606-845-3299. E-MAIL: gazette@fleminggazette.com. URL: http://www.fleminggazette.com. Mailing Address: PO Box 32, Flemingsburg, KY 41041. Year Established: 1880. Pub. Frequency: w. (Wed.) Page Size: standard. Subscrip. Rate: $.50 newsstand/cover; $17/yr in county; $30/yr out of county; $40/yr out of state. Circulation: 4,100 per issue (paid). **Owner(s):** Barker Publications LLC, See address and contact information above. **Management:** Gary Barker, Publisher. **Editorial:** Danetta Barker, Editor.

FLORENCE

DIXIE NEWS. 6603 Dixie Hwy., Florence, KY 41042. Telephone: 859-371-6177. Year Established: 1962. Pub. Frequency: w. (Thu.) Page Size: broadsheet. Subscrip. Rate: $25 newsstand/cover. Circulation: 24,200 per issue (controlled and free). **Owner(s):** Lee Thomas, See address and contact information above. **Management:** Lee Thomas, Publisher. **Editorial:** Lee Thomas, Editor.

FORT MITCHELL

BOONE COUNTY RECORDER. 228 Grandview Dr, Fort Mitchell, KY 41017. Telephone: 859-283-0404. FAX: 859-283-7285. E-MAIL: mhornback@nky.com. URL: http://www.communitypress.com. Year Established: 1875. Pub. Frequency: w. (Thu.) Page Size: broadsheet. Subscrip. Rate: $.50 newsstand/cover; $18.02/yr mailed in county; $23.32/yr mailed in state; $27.56/yr mailed out of state. Adv. Rate: col. inch $13.50 Freelance Pay: $20/article. Circulation: 2,938 per issue (paid). **Owner(s):** Community Recorder Newspapers, 7950 Jones Branch Dr, McLean, VA 22107. Telephone: 703-854-6000. **Management:** Susan McHugh, General Manager. Mike Hornback, Advertising Manager. Sharon Schachleiter, Circulation Manager. **Editorial:** Susan McHugh, Editor. Nancy Daly, Senior Editor. James Weber, Sports.

CAMPBELL COMMUNITY RECORDER. 228 Grandview Dr, Fort Mitchell, KY 41017. Telephone: 859-283-0404. FAX: 859-283-7285. E-MAIL: mhornback@nky.com. URL: http://www.communitypress.com. Pub. Frequency: w. (Thu.) Page Size: broadsheet. Subscrip. Rate: $.50 newsstand/cover; $18.02/yr in county. Circulation: 10,015 per issue (paid). **Owner(s):** Community Recorder Newspapers, 7950 Jones Branch Dr, McLean, VA 22107. Telephone: 703-854-6000. **Management:** Susan McHugh, General Manager. Mike Hornback, Advertising Manager. Sharon Schachleiter, Circulation Manager. **Editorial:** Susan McHugh, Editor. Nancy Daly, Senior Editor. James Weber, Sports.

CAMPBELL COUNTY RECORDER. 228 Grandview Dr, Fort Mitchell, KY 41017. Telephone: 859-283-0404. FAX: 859-283-7285. E-MAIL: mhornback@inky.com. URL: http://www.communitypress.com. Year Established: 1978. Pub. Frequency: w. (Thu.) Page Size: broadsheet. Subscrip. Rate: $.50 newsstand/cover; $18.02/yr in county; $23.32/yr out of county; $27.56/yr out of state. Circulation: 1,617 per issue (paid). **Owner(s):** Community Recorder Newspapers, 7950 Jones Branch Dr, McLean, VA 22107. Telephone: 703-854-6000. **Management:** Susan McHugh, General Manager. Mike Hornback, Advertising Manager. Sharon Schachleiter, Circulation Manager. **Editorial:** Jordan Kellogg, Editor. Nancy Daly, Senior Editor. James Weber, Sports.

COMMUNITY RECORDER OF NORTHERN KENTUCKY. 228 Grandview Dr, Fort Mitchell, KY 41017. Telephone: 859-283-0404. FAX: 859-283-7285. E-MAIL: mhornback@nky.com. URL: http://www.communitypress.com. Pub. Frequency: w. (Thu.) Page Size: broadsheet. Subscrip. Rate: $18/yr in county; $20/yr out of county. Circulation: 13,860 per issue (free). **Owner(s):** Community Recorder Newspapers, 7950 Jones Branch Dr, McLean, VA 22107. Telephone: 703-854-6000. **Management:** Susan McHugh, General Manager. Mike Hornback, Advertising Manager. Sharon Schachleiter, Circulation Manager. **Editorial:** Susan McHugh, Editor. Nancy Daly, Senior Editor. James Weber, Sports.

ERLANGER RECORDER. 228 Grandview Dr, Fort Mitchell, KY 41017. Telephone: 859-283-0404. FAX: 859-283-7285. E-MAIL: mhornback@nky.com. URL: http://www.communitypress.com. Pub. Frequency: w. (Thu.) Page Size: standard. Subscrip. Rate: $.50 newsstand/cover; $18/yr in county; $20/yr out of county. Circulation: 8,036 per issue (free). **Owner(s):** Community Recorder Newspapers, 7950 Jones Branch Dr, McLean, VA 22107. Telephone: 703-854-6000. **Management:** Susan McHugh, General Manager. Mike Hornback, Advertising Manager. Sharon Schachleiter, Circulation Manager. **Editorial:** Susan McHugh, Editor. Nancy Daly, Senior Editor. James Weber, Sports.

FLORENCE RECORDER. 228 Grandview Dr, Fort Mitchell, KY 41017. Telephone: 859-283-0404. FAX: 859-283-7285. E-MAIL: mhornback@nky.com. URL: http://www.communitypress.com. Pub. Frequency: w. (Thu.) Page Size: broadsheet. Subscrip. Rate: $.50 newsstand/cover voluntary pay; $18/yr in county; $20/yr out of county. Circulation: 14,656 per issue (paid and free). **Owner(s):** Community Recorder Newspapers, 7950 Jones Branch Dr, McLean, VA 22107. Telephone: 703-854-6000. **Management:** Susan McHugh, General Manager. Mike Hornback, Advertising Manager. Sharon Schachleiter, Circulation Manager. **Editorial:** Brian Mains, Editor. Nancy Daly, Senior Editor. James Weber, Sports.

FORT THOMAS RECORDER. 228 Grandview Dr, Fort Mitchell, KY 41017. Telephone: 859-283-0404. FAX: 859-283-7285. E-MAIL: mhornback@nky.com. URL: http://www.communitypress.com. Pub. Frequency: w. (Thu.) Page Size: broadsheet. Subscrip. Rate: $.50 newsstand/cover; $18/yr in county; $20/yr out of county. Circulation: 5,674 per issue (free). **Owner(s):** Community Recorder Newspapers, 7950 Jones Branch Dr, McLean, VA 22107. Telephone: 703-854-6000. **Management:** Susan McHugh, General Manager. Mike Hornback, Advertising Manager. Sharon Schachleiter, Circulation Manager. **Editorial:** Susan McHugh, Editor. Nancy Daly, Senior Editor. James Weber, Sports.

KENTON COMMUNITY RECORDER. 228 Grandview Dr, Fort Mitchell, KY 41017. Telephone: 859-283-0404. FAX: 859-283-7285. E-MAIL: mhornback@nky.com. URL: http://www.communitynews.com. Year Established: 1978. Pub. Frequency: w. (Thu.) Page Size: broadsheet. Subscrip. Rate: $.50 newsstand/cover; $18/yr mailed in county; $20/yr mailed out of county. Freelance Pay: $20/article. Circulation: 11,910 per issue (free). **Owner(s):** Community Recorder Newspapers, 7950 Jones Branch Dr, McLean, VA 22107. Telephone: 703-854-6000. **Management:** Susan McHugh, General Manager. Mike Hornback, Advertising Manager. **Editorial:** Susan McHugh, Editor. Nancy Daly, Senior Editor. James Weber, Sports.

FRANKFORT

KENTUCKY GAZETTE, THE. 311 W. Main St., Frankfort, KY 40602. Telephone: 502-875-8325. FAX: 502-875-8330. URL: http://www.kentuckyrollcall.com. Pub. Frequency: s-m. (Tue.) Page Size: tabloid Subscrip. Rate: $179/yr Circulation: 1,200 per issue (paid). **Owner(s):** Lowell Reese, PO Box 778, Frankfort, KY 40602-0778. Telephone: 502-875-8325. **Management:** Lowell Reese, Publisher. **Editorial:** Lowell Reese, Editor.

FRANKLIN

FRANKLIN FAVORITE. 103 N. High St., Franklin, KY 42134. Telephone: 270-586-4481. FAX: 270-586-6031. E-MAIL: cportmann@franklinfavorite.com. URL: http://www.franklinfavorite.com. Mailing Address: PO Box 309, Franklin, KY 42135-0309. Year Established: 1857. Pub. Frequency: w. (Thu.) Page Size: broadsheet. Subscrip. Rate: $.75 newsstand/cover; $26/yr mailed in Franklin & Simpson counties; $31/yr mailed in adj. counties; $34.50/yr mailed in state. Circulation: 6,300 per issue (controlled and free). **Owner(s):** Paxton Media Group Llc, 201 S. Fourth St., Paducah, KY 42003. Telephone: 270-575-8600. FAX: 270-442-8188. **Management:** Ben Sheroan, Publisher. Betty Gentry, Advertising Manager. Paulette Thomas, Circulation Manager. Deb Shelton, Classified Adv. Mgr. Jeff Richardson, Business Manager. **Editorial:** Charles Portmann, Editor. Amy Ellis, Photographer. Charles Portmann, Sports.

FULTON

FULTON LEADER. 304 E. State Line St., Fulton, KY 42041-1200. Telephone: 270-472-1121. FAX: 270-472-1129. Mailing Address: PO Box 1200, Fulton, KY 42041-1200. Year Established: 1898. Pub. Frequency: w. (Wed.) Page Size: broadsheet. Subscrip. Rate: $.75 newsstand/cover; $25/yr local. Circulation: 2,600 per issue (paid). **Owner(s):** Magic Valley Publishing, 144 W. Main St., Camden, TN 38320. Telephone: 731-584-7200. FAX: 731-584-4943. **Management:** Dennis Richardson, Publisher. Benita Gammon, Advertising. Sabrina Bondurant, Circulation Manager. **Editorial:** John Jones, Editor. Joe Dacus, Sports Editor.

FULTON SHOPPER. 304 E. State Line St., Fulton, KY 42041. Telephone: 270-472-1121. FAX: 270-472-1129. E-MAIL: fulpub@apex.net. Mailing Address: PO Box 1200, Fulton, KY 42041. Pub. Frequency: w. (Wed.) Page Size: standard Circulation: 15,064 per issue (free). **Owner(s):** Magic Valley Publishing, 144 W. Main St., Camden, TN 38320. Telephone: 731-584-7200. FAX: 731-584-4943. **Management:** Dennis Richardson, Publisher. Benita Gammon, Advertising. Sabrina Bondurant, Circulation Manager. **Editorial:** John Jones, Editor. Joe Dacus, Sports Editor.

GEORGETOWN

GEORGETOWN NEWS-GRAPHIC. ISSN 1072-9305 1481 Cherry Blossom Way, Georgetown, KY 40324. Telephone: 502-863-1111. FAX: 502-863-6296. E-MAIL: news@news-graphic.com. URL: http://www.news-graphic.com. Year Established: 1867. Pub. Frequency: 3/w. (Wed., Fri., Sun.) Page Size: broadsheet. Subscrip. Rate: $.50 newsstand/cover; $90/yr home delivery. **Wire Service(s):** AP. Circulation: 5,300 per issue (paid). **Owner(s):** Lancaster Management, Inc., PO Box 609, Gadsden, AL 35902. **Management:** Mike Scogin, Publisher. Sabra Oller, Advertising Director. Ralph Tackett, Circulation Manager. Sabrina Hounshell, Classified Adv. Mgr. Andrea Giusti, Marketing Director. **Editorial:** Mike Scogin, Editor. Ty Johnston, Managing Editor.

GRAYSON

GRAYSON JOURNAL-ENQUIRER. 211 S Carol Malone Blvd., Grayson, KY 41143. URL: http://www.journal-times.com. Year Established: 1968. Pub. Frequency: w. (Wed.) Page Size: broadsheet. Subscrip. Rate: $.50 newsstand/cover; $22/yr mailed in county; $38/yr mailed out of county; $42/yr mailed out of state. Circulation: 3,000 per issue (paid). **Owner(s):** Community Newspaper Holdings, Inc., 3500 Colonnade Pkwy., Ste. 600, Birmingham, AL 35243. Telephone: 205-298-7100. FAX: 205-298-7101. **Management:** Rob McCullough, Publisher. Bonnie Pence, Advertising. Mara Harlow, Circulation Manager. **Editorial:** Denver Brown, Editor.

GREENSBURG

GREENSBURG RECORD-HERALD. PO Box 130, Greensburg, KY 42743. Telephone: 270-932-4381. FAX: 270-932-4441. E-MAIL: news@record-herald.com. Pub. Frequency: w. (Wed.) Page Size: standard. Subscrip. Rate: $.50 newsstand/cover; $19/yr in county; $24/yr out of county; $29/yr out of state. Circulation: 7,000 per issue (paid). **Owner(s):** Walt C. Gorin, See address and contact information above. **Management:** Walt C. Gorin, Publisher. **Editorial:** Tom Mills, Editor.

GREENUP

GREENUP COUNTY NEWS-TIMES. 203 Harrison St., Greenup, KY 41144. Telephone: 606-473-9851. FAX: 606-473-7591. Mailing Address: PO Box 724, Greenup, KY 41144-0724. Year Established: 1867. Pub. Frequency: w. (Thu.) Page Size: broadsheet. Subscrip. Rate: $.50 newsstand/cover; $22/yr mailed in county; $28/yr mailed out of county; $34/yr mailed out of state. Circulation: 3,700 per issue (paid). **Owner(s):** Community Newspaper Holdings, Inc., 3500 Colonnade Pkwy., Ste. 600, Birmingham, AL 35243. Telephone: 205-298-7100. FAX: 205-298-7101. **Management:** Eddie Blakley, Publisher. Nikki Clay, Advertising Manager. Stefanie Scott, Classified Adv. Mgr.. **Editorial:** Kathie Shaffer, Executive Editor. Mason Branham, Managing Editor.

HARDINSBURG

BRECKINRIDGE HERALD-NEWS. 120 US Hwy. 60 E., Hardinsburg, KY 40143-0006. Telephone: 270-756-2109. FAX: 270-756-1003. E-MAIL: editorialthn@bbtel.com. Mailing Address: PO Box 6, Hardinsburg, KY 40143-0006. Year Established: 1876. Pub. Frequency: w. (Wed.) Page Size: broadsheet. Subscrip. Rate: $.75 newsstand/cover; $32.50/yr in county; $36.50/yr in state; $39.50/yr out of state. Adv. Rate: col. inch $6.25 Circulation: 5,750 per issue (paid). **Owner(s):** Breckinridge Herald-News, Inc., See address and contact information above. **Management:** Chris McGehee, General Manager. Nadean Croan, Advertising. **Editorial:** David Hayes, Editor.

HARLAN

BARGAIN BANNER, THE. 102 S. Main St., Harlan, KY 40831. Telephone: 606-573-5609. FAX: 606-573-5380. URL: http://www.thebargainbanner.com. Year Established: 1989. Pub. Frequency: w. (Thu.) Page Size: tabloid.Adv. Rate: col. inch $4.25 Circulation: 15,000 per issue (free). **Owner(s):** Bargain Banner, The, PO Box 104, Harlan, KY 40831-0104. Telephone: 606-573-5609. **Management:** Lavondi Browning, Publisher. **Editorial:** Lavondi Browning, Editor.

HARRODSBURG

HARRODSBURG HERALD, THE. 101 W Broadway, Harrodsburg, KY 40330. Telephone: 859-734-2726. FAX: 859-734-0737. E-MAIL: hherald@searnet.com. Mailing Address: P O Box 68, Harrodsburg, KY 40330. Year Established: 1884. Pub. Frequency: w. (Thu.) Page Size: broadsheet. Subscrip. Rate: $.50 newsstand/cover; $27/yr in county; $36/yr out of county; $44/yr out of state. Circulation: 6,000 per issue (paid). **Owner(s):** Hutton Pyles Trust, See address and contact information above. **Management:** Chris Freeman, Publisher. Cathy Caton, Advertising. April Ellis, Circulation Manager. **Editorial:** Rosalind Turner, News Editor.

HARTFORD

OHIO COUNTY TIMES NEWS. PO Box 226, Hartford, KY 42347. Telephone: 270-298-7100. FAX: 270-298-9572. URL: http://www.octimes.com. Year Established: 1965. Pub. Frequency: w. (Thu.) Page Size: broadsheet. Subscrip. Rate: $.50 newsstand/cover; $22.40/yr mailed in county; $26/yr mailed in adj. counties; $28/yr mailed in state; $32/yr mailed out of state. Adv. Rate: col. inch $3.25 Circulation: 6,500 per issue (paid). **Owner(s):** Andy Anderson Corp., See address and contact information above. **Management:** Victoria Anderson, Publisher. Sue Vincent, Advertising Manager. Linda Whitten, Circulation Manager. Doris Hicks, Business Manager. **Editorial:** Don Wilkins, Editor. Neil Grant, Sports.

HAWESVILLE

HANCOCK CLARION. 230 Main, Hawesville, KY 42348. Telephone: 270-927-6945. FAX: 270-927-6947. E-MAIL: clarion@tds.com. Mailing Address: PO Box 39, Hawesville, KY 42348-0039. Year Established: 1893. Pub. Frequency: w. (Thu.) Page Size: broadsheet. Subscrip. Rate: $.50 newsstand/cover; $20/yr in county; $24/yr out of county. Circulation: 4,300 per issue (paid). **Owner(s):** Donn K. Wimmer, See address and contact information above. **Management:** Donn K. Wimmer, Publisher. Paul Young, Advertising Manager. **Editorial:** Steve Wimmer, Editor.

HAZARD

HAZARD HERALD. 439 High St, Hazard, KY 41701. Telephone: 606-436-5771. FAX: 606-436-3140. E-MAIL: hazardherold@setel.com. URL: http://www.hazard-herald.com. Mailing Address: PO Box 869, Hazard, KY 41702. Year Established: 1911. Pub. Frequency: w. (Wed.) Page Size: broadsheet. Subscrip. Rate: $.50 newsstand/cover; $25/yr mailed in county; $30/yr mailed in state; $35/yr mailed out of state. Adv. Rate: col. inch $9.25 Circulation: 5,500 per issue (paid). **Owner(s):** Heartland Publications, LLC, 20 Research Pkwy, Ste G, Old Saybrook, CT 06475. Telephone: 860-388-3470. FAX: 860-388-3490. **Management:** Luke Keith Jr., Publisher. Barbara Marshall, Advertising Manager. Jenny Jones, Circulation Manager. **Editorial:** Cris Ritchie, Editor.

HICKMAN

HICKMAN COURIER. 1232 Moscow Ave., Hickman, KY 42050-1467. Telephone: 270-236-2726. FAX: 270-236-2726. E-MAIL: hickcourier@apea.net. Mailing Address: P.O. Box 70, Hickman, KY 42050-1467. Pub. Frequency: w. (Thu.) Page Size: standard. Subscrip. Rate: $.50 newsstand/cover; $22/yr in county; $25/yr in state. Circulation: 2,000 per issue (paid). **Owner(s):** Mary Jo & Larry Lewis, See address and contact information above. **Management:** Larry Lewis, Publisher. Barbara Atwill, Advertising Manager. **Editorial:** Cherry Pyron, Managing Editor.

HINDMAN

TROUBLESOME CREEK TIMES. E. Main St., Hindman, KY 41822. Telephone: 606-785-5134. FAX: 606-785-0105. Pub. Frequency: w. (Wed.) Page Size: standard. Subscrip. Rate: $.50 newsstand/cover; $16/yr local; $20/yr in state; $24/yr out of state. Circulation: 4,100 per issue (paid). **Owner(s):** Sharon Hall & Karen Jones, E. Main St., Hindman, KY 41822-0700. Telephone: 606-785-5134. FAX: 606-785-0105. **Management:** Sharon Hall, Publisher. **Editorial:** Karen Jones, Editor.

HODGENVILLE

LARUE COUNTY HERALD-NEWS. 40 Shawnee Dr., Hodgenville, KY 42748. Telephone: 270-358-3118. FAX: 270-358-4852. E-MAIL: heraldnews@kynet.org. Year Established: 1885. Pub. Frequency: w. (Wed.) Page Size: broadsheet. Subscrip. Rate: $.50 newsstand/cover; $28.62/yr in area; $34.98/yr in state. Adv. Rate: col. inch $6.94 Circulation: 4,667 per issue (paid). **Owner(s):** Landmark Community Newspapers, Inc., PO Box 549, Shelbyville, KY 40065. Telephone: 502-633-2526. **Management:** Melissa Nalley, General Manager. Mona Coffey, Circulation Manager. **Editorial:** Linda Ireland, Editor.

HORSE CAVE

GREEN RIVER REPUBLICAN. P O Box 340, Horse Cave, KY 42149. URL: http://www.jobepublishinginc.com. Mailing Address: PO Box 219, Morgantown, KY 42261-0219. Pub. Frequency: w. (Sun) Subscrip. Rate: $.50 newsstand/cover; $40/yr in county; $50/yr out of county. Circulation: 4,606 per issue (paid and free). **Owner(s):** Jobe Publishing Inc., See address and contact information above. **Management:** Judy Jobe, Publisher. **Editorial:** John Embry, Editor.

HART COUNTY NEWS-HERALD, THE. 570 S Dixie St, Horse Cave, KY 42749-1253. Telephone: 270-786-2676. FAX: 270-786-4470. Mailing Address: P O Box 340, Horse Cave, KY 42749-0340. Year Established: 1878. Pub. Frequency: w. (Thu.) Page Size: standard. Subscrip. Rate: $.50 newsstand/cover; $25/yr in county; $40/yr mailed in state; $55/yr mailed out of state. Adv. Rate: col. inch $8.40 Circulation: 8,500 per issue (paid). **Owner(s):** Jobe Publishing Inc., See address and contact information above. **Management:** Judy Wright, Publisher. Teresia Sexton, Advertising Manager. **Editorial:** Josh Hampton, Editor.

HYDEN

LESLIE COUNTY NEWS. PO Box 967, Hyden, KY 41749-0967. Telephone: 606-672-2841. FAX: 606-672-7409. Year Established: 1968. Pub. Frequency: w. (Thu.) Page Size: broadsheet. Subscrip. Rate: $.50 newsstand/cover; $28/yr mailed in county; $33/yr mailed out of county. Freelance Pay: $2/column-inch. Circulation: 5,000 per issue (paid). **Owner(s):** Reba & Vernon Baker, See address and contact information above. **Management:** Reba Baker, Publisher. Bernetta York, Advertising. **Editorial:** Reba Baker, Editor. Vernon Baker, Managing Editor.

THOUSANDSTICKS NEWS. 22009 Main St., Hyden, KY 41749. Telephone: 606-672-2841. FAX: 606-672-7409. Mailing Address: PO Box 917, Hyden, KY 41749-0967. Pub. Frequency: w. (Tue.) Page Size: standard. Subscrip. Rate: $.50 newsstand/cover; $26/yr in county; $33/yr out of county. Circulation: 4,100 per issue (paid). **Owner(s):** Vernon & Reba Baker, See address and contact information above. **Management:** Reba Baker, Publisher. Ron Williams, Advertising.

INEZ

MOUNTAIN CITIZEN, THE. PO Box 1029, Inez, KY 41224. Telephone: 606-298-7570. FAX: 606-298-3711. E-MAIL: mtncit@eastky.net. Year Established: 1975. Pub. Frequency: w. (Wed.) Page Size: broadsheet. Subscrip. Rate: $.50 newsstand/cover; $18/yr in county; $25/yr out of county. Circulation: 6,000 per issue (paid). **Owner(s):** Lisa Stayton, See address and contact information above. **Management:** Lisa Stayton, President. Roger Smith, Publisher. Diane Smith, Advertising. Becky Smith, Circulation Manager. **Editorial:** Gary Ball, Editor.

IRVINE

CITIZEN VOICE & TIMES. P O Box 660, Irvine, KY 40336. E-MAIL: cvt@irvineonline.net. URL: Http://www.hatfieldnewspapers.com. Year Established: 1973. Pub. Frequency: w. (Thu.) Page Size: broadsheet. Subscrip. Rate: $.50 newsstand/cover; $15.95/yr mailed in county; $23.95/yr mailed out of county; $32/yr mailed out of state. **Wire Service(s):** AP. Circulation: 4,200 per issue (paid). **Owner(s):** Hatfield Newspapers, Inc., 108 Court St, Irvine, KY 40336-1093. **Management:** Teresa Hatfield, Publisher. Arvin Cheryl, Circulation Manager.

ESTILL COUNTY TRIBUNE, THE. 6135 Winchester Rd., Irvine, KY 40336-9706. Telephone: 606-723-5012. FAX: 606-723-5012. E-MAIL: tribune@urbanonline.net. Year Established: 1982. Pub. Frequency: w. (Wed.) Page Size: standard. Subscrip. Rate: $.25 newsstand/cover; $11.50/yr in county; $21/yr out of county; $24/yr out of state. Adv. Rate: col. inch $2 Circulation: 2,257 per issue (paid). **Owner(s):** Tracy R. Patrick, 7665 Winchester Rd., Irvine, KY 40336. Telephone: 606-723-7155. **Management:** Tracy R. Patrick, Publisher. **Editorial:** Delores L. Rowland, Editor.

JACKSON

JACKSON TIMES. PO Box 999, Jackson, KY 41339. Telephone: 606-666-2451. FAX: 606-666-5757. E-MAIL: jacksontimes@yahoo.com. Pub. Frequency: w. (Thu.) Page Size: broadsheet. Subscrip. Rate: $.50 newsstand/cover; $18/yr in county; $25/yr out of county. Circulation: 4,500 per issue (paid). **Owner(s):** Intermountain Publishing, See address and contact information above. **Management:** Edmund Shelby, General Manager. Glen Gray, Publisher. Tracy Gillum, Advertising Manager. **Editorial:** Edmund Shelby, Editor.

JAMESTOWN

RUSSELL REGISTER. 300 Monument Sq., Jamestown, KY 42629. Telephone: 270-343-6397. FAX: 270-343-6363. E-MAIL: staff@russellregister.com. URL: http://www.russellregister.com. Pub. Frequency: w. (Thu.) Page Size: standard. Subscrip. Rate: $.50 newsstand/cover; $15/yr in county; $20/yr out of county; $25/yr out of state. Circulation: 5,800 per issue (paid). **Owner(s):** Russell Media Inc., PO Box 5, Jamestown, KY 42629-0005. Telephone: 270-343-6397. **Management:** Wade Daffron, Publisher. Ashlea Fugate, Advertising Manager. **Editorial:** Wade Daffron, Editor.

LA GRANGE

OLDHAM ERA, THE. 204 S. First St., La Grange, KY 40031-0005. Telephone: 502-222-7183. FAX: 502-222-7194. E-MAIL: oldhamera@kth.net. URL: http://www.oldhamera.com. Mailing Address: PO Box 5, La Grange, KY 40031. Year Established: 1876. Pub. Frequency: w. (Thu.) Page Size: broadsheet. Subscrip. Rate: $.50 newsstand/cover; $29.68/yr in county & adj. counties; $52/yr out of county. Circulation: 7,100 per issue (paid). **Owner(s):** Landmark Community Newspapers, Inc., PO Box 549, Shelbyville, KY 40065. Telephone: 502-633-2526. **Management:** Jim Patrick, Publisher. Jo Kerr, Advertising Manager. Mary Johnson, Circulation Manager. **Editorial:** Julie Satterly, Editor.

LANCASTER

GARRARD CENTRAL RECORD, THE. PO Box 800, Lancaster, KY 40444. Telephone: 859-792-2831. FAX: 859-792-3448. E-MAIL: centralrecord@windstream.net. Year Established: 1889. Pub. Frequency: w. (Thu.) Page Size: broadsheet. Subscrip. Rate: $.50 newsstand/cover; $25.44/yr home delivery in county; $34.66/yr home delivery out of county; $40/yr mailed out of state. Circulation: 4,800 per issue (paid). **Owner(s):** Jim Walker Cox, See address and contact information above. **Management:** Jim Walker Cox, Publisher. **Editorial:** Pattie Cox, Editor.Readers: Garrard County, KY

LAWRENCEBURG

ANDERSON NEWS, THE. 133 S. Main St., Lawrenceburg, KY 40342. Telephone: 502-839-6906. FAX: 502-839-3118. E-MAIL: news@theandersonnews.com. URL: http://www.theandersonnews.com. Mailing Address: PO Box 410, Lawrenceburg, KY 40342. Year Established: 1903. Pub. Frequency: w. (Wed.) Page Size: broadsheet. Subscrip. Rate: $.75 newsstand/cover; $30.74/yr in county; $40.28/yr out of county; $52/yr out of state. Circulation: 6,000 per issue (paid). **Owner(s):** Landmark Community Newspapers, Inc., PO Box 549, Shelbyville, KY 40065. Telephone: 502-633-2526. **Management:** Don White, Publisher. Bud Garrison, Advertising Manager. Mattie Spaulding, Circulation Manager. **Editorial:** Don White, Editor.

LEBANON

LEBANON ENTERPRISE, THE. 119 S. Proctor Knott Ave., Lebanon, KY 40033-1259. Telephone: 270-692-6026. FAX: 270-692-2119. E-MAIL: heine@kyol.net. URL: http://www.lebanonenterprise.com. Year Established: 1885. Pub. Frequency: w. (Wed.) Page Size: broadsheet. Subscrip. Rate: $.75 newsstand/cover; $30.74/yr mailed in county; $38.16/yr mailed out of county. Circulation: 6,400 per issue (paid). **Owner(s):** Landmark Community Newspapers, Inc., PO Box 549, Shelbyville, KY 40065. Telephone: 270-633-4334. **Management:** Chris Hamilton, Publisher. Mary Anne Blair, Advertising Manager. Jane Ballard, Circulation Manager. **Editorial:** Chris Hamilton, Editor. Stevie Lowery, News Editor.

LEITCHFIELD

GRAYSON COUNTY NEWS-GAZETTE. 307 W Market St, Leitchfield, KY 42754. Telephone: 270-259-9622. FAX: 270-259-5537. E-MAIL: newsgazette@alltel.net. URL: http://www.gcnewsgazette.com. Mailing Address: PO Box 305, Leitchfield, KY 42755. Year Established: 1881. Pub. Frequency: s-w. (Mon. & Thu.) Page Size: broadsheet. Subscrip. Rate: $.75 newsstand/cover; $26/yr mailed in county; $36/yr mailed in state; $42/yr mailed out of state. Circulation: 6,000 per issue (paid). **Owner(s):** Heartland Publications, LLC, 20 Research Pkwy, Ste G, Old Saybrook, CT 06475. Telephone: 860-388-3470. FAX: 860-388-3490. **Management:** Tim Kiger, Publisher. Kristy Willis, Advertising. Beverly White, Circulation Manager. Vanessa VanNatta, Classified Adv. Mgr.. **Editorial:** Tim Kiger, Editor.

RECORD (LEITCHFIELD), THE. 209-C W. White Oak St, Leitchfield, KY 42754. Telephone: 270-259-6061. FAX: 270-230-8405. Year Established: 1980. Pub. Frequency: w. (Thu.) Page Size: broadsheet. Subscrip. Rate: $.25 newsstand/cover; $15/yr in county; $20/yr out of county; $30/yr out of state. Circulation: 6,333 per issue (paid). **Owner(s):** Landmark Community Newspapers, Inc., 601 Taylorsville Rd, Shelbyville, KY 40065-0549. Telephone: 502-633-4334. PO Box 549, Shelbyville, KY 40065. **Management:** Stephanie Hornback, General Manager. **Editorial:** Stephanie Hornback, Editor.

LIBERTY

CASEY COUNTY NEWS. 720 Campbellsville St., Liberty, KY 42539. Telephone: 606-787-7171. FAX: 606-787-8306. E-MAIL: dcarman@caseynews.net. URL: http://www.caseynews.net. Mailing Address: PO Box 40, Liberty, KY 42539. Year Established: 1904. Pub. Frequency: w. (Wed.) Page Size: broadsheet. Subscrip. Rate: $.75 newsstand/cover; $31.80/yr in county; $43.46/yr out of county. Circulation: 6,400 per issue (paid). **Owner(s):** Landmark Community Newspapers, Inc., PO Box 549, Shelbyville, KY 40065. Telephone: 502-633-2526. **Management:** Donna Carman, General Manager. Brittany Emerson, Advertising. Randall Vaught, Advertising Director. Karla Raney, Circulation Manager. **Editorial:** Donna Carman, Editor.

LONDON

SENTINEL-ECHO, THE. 123 W Fifth St, London, KY 40741. Telephone: 606-878-7400. FAX: 606-878-7404. E-MAIL: sentinel1@sunspot.com. URL: http://www.sentinel-echo.com. Mailing Address: PO Box 830, London, KY 40743. Year Established: 1873. Pub. Frequency: 3/w. (Mon., Wed., Fri.) Page Size: broadsheet. Subscrip. Rate: $.50 newsstand/cover; $50/yr mailed in county. Circulation: 8,000 per issue (controlled and free). **Owner(s):** Community Newspaper Holdings, Inc., 3500 Colonnade Pkwy., Ste. 600, Birmingham, AL 35243-7017. **Management:** Willie Sawyers, Publisher. Kathy Jones, Advertising Manager. Earlette Sparkman, Circulation Manager. Erin Sizemore, Classified Adv. Mgr.. **Editorial:** Sue Minton, Lifestyle Editor. Allison Altizer, News Editor.

LOUISA

ADVERTISER (LOUISA), THE. 101 Ricky Skaggs Blvd., Louisa, KY 41230. Telephone: 606-638-4581. FAX: 606-638-9949. E-MAIL: erma@bigsandynews.com. URL: http://www.bigsandynews.com. Mailing Address: PO Box 766, Louisa, KY 41230. Year Established: 1982. Pub. Frequency: w. (Sun.) Page Size: tabloid.Adv. Rate: col. inch $4.50 Circulation: 26,000 per issue (free). **Owner(s):** Sandy Valley Press, Inc., See address and contact information above. **Management:** Marjie Hale, President. **Editorial:** Marjie Hale, Editor-in-Chief.

BIG SANDY NEWS, THE. 101 Ricky Skaggs Blvd., Louisa, KY 41230. Telephone: 606-638-4581. FAX: 606-638-9949. E-MAIL: bsnews@footheels.com. URL: http://www.bigsandynews.com/. Mailing Address: PO Box 766, Louisa, KY 41230. Year Established: 1885. Pub. Frequency: s-w. (Wed. & Fri.) Page Size: standard. Subscrip. Rate: $.50 newsstand/cover; $25/yr mailed in county & adj cys; $35/yr mailed out of area. Circulation: 12,000 per issue (paid). **Owner(s):** Sandy Valley Press, Inc., See address and contact information above. **Management:** Marjie Hale, Publisher. **Editorial:** Marjie Hale, Editor-in-Chief.

LOUISVILLE

VOICE-TRIBUNE, THE. ISSN 1076-7398
130 St Matthews Ave, Ste 300, Louisville, KY 40207. Telephone: 502-897-8900. FAX: 502-897-8915. URL: http://www.voice-tribune.com. Year Established: 1949. Pub. Frequency: w. (Wed.) Page Size: broadsheet. Subscrip. Rate: $.50 newsstand/cover; $25.95/yr in county; $30.95/yr out of county. Adv. Rate: col. inch $28.18 Freelance Pay: $0.75/column-inch. **Wire Service(s):** AP. Circulation: 13,860 per issue (paid). **Owner(s):** Blue Equity LLC, See address and contact information above. **Management:** Jonathan S Blue, Managing Director. Julie Klotter, Advertising. **Editorial:** Jacob Glassner, Editor. Earl Cox, Sports Writer. Ashley Medley, Writer. Harry Clegg Jr., .Readers: Louisville and surrounding areas.

MANCHESTER

MANCHESTER (KY) ENTERPRISE, THE. 103 Third St., Manchester, KY 40962. Telephone: 606-598-6174. FAX: 606-598-2330. Mailing Address: PO Box 449, Manchester, KY 40962. Year Established: 1890. Pub. Frequency: w. (Thu.) Page Size: broadsheet. Subscrip. Rate: $.75 newsstand/cover; $26/yr mailed in county; $30/yr mailed out of county. Adv. Rate: col. inch $6 Freelance Pay: $5/story. Circulation: 6,500 per issue (paid). **Owner(s):** James F. Nolan, Jr., See address and contact information above. **Management:** Mark Hoskins, General Manager. Glenn Gray, Vice President. Dean Howard, Advertising Manager. **Editorial:** John Dobson, Editor. Joe Burchell, Sports.

MARION

CRITTENDEN PRESS, THE. 125 E. Bellville St., Marion, KY 42064. Telephone: 270-965-3191. FAX: 270-965-2516. URL: http://www.the-press.com. Mailing Address: P.O. Box 191, Marion, KY 42064-0191. Year Established: 1879. Pub. Frequency: w. (Thu.) Page Size: broadsheet. Subscrip. Rate: $.50 newsstand/cover; $23/yr in county; $28/yr in state; $30/yr out of state. **Wire Service(s):** AP. Circulation: 4,500 per issue (paid). **Owner(s):** Chris & Allison Evans, See address and contact information above. **Management:** Chris Evans, Publisher. Marty Kares, Advertising Manager. **Editorial:** Chris Evans, Editor. Allison Mick-Evans, Assistant Editor.

MAYSVILLE

ADVERTISER (MAYSVILLE). 120 Limestone St., Maysville, KY 41056-1101. Telephone: 606-564-9091. FAX: 606-564-6893. Mailing Address: PO Box 518, Maysville, KY 41056-0518. Pub. Frequency: w. (Mon.) Page Size: standard Circulation: 21,000 per issue (free). **Owner(s):** Lee Enterprises, Inc., 215 N. Main St., Davenport, IA 52801. Telephone: 563-383-2100. **Management:** Bob Hendrickson, Publisher. Patty Moore, Advertising Manager. **Editorial:** Mary Ann Kerns, Editor.

MCKEE

JACKSON COUNTY SUN, THE. Main St., McKee, KY 40447. Telephone: 606-287-7197. FAX: 606-287-7196. URL: http://www.jacksoncountysun.com. Pub. Frequency: w. (Thu.) Page Size: standard. Subscrip. Rate: $.50 newsstand/cover; $12/yr in county; $13/yr in state; $15/yr out of state. Circulation: 4,650 per issue (paid). **Owner(s):** Jackson County Sun, Inc., See address and contact information above. **Management:** Tammy Spurlock, General Manager. Marti Roberts, Advertising. **Editorial:** George Farrell, Editor. Connie Esh, Associate Editor.

MIDDLESBORO

CUMBERLAND TRADING POST, THE. 120 N. 11th St., Middlesboro, KY 40965. Telephone: 606-248-1010. FAX: 606-248-7614. URL: http://www.middlesborodailynews.com. Year Established: 1978. Pub. Frequency: w. (Thu.) Page Size: tabloid. Subscrip. Rate: $60/yr mailed. Adv. Rate: col. inch $6.12, page $477.36 Circulation: 20,000 per issue (free). **Owner(s):** Heartland Publications, LLC, 20 Research Pkwy, Ste G, Old Saybrook, CT 06475. Telephone: 860-388-3470. FAX: 860-388-3490. **Management:** Tom Spargur, Publisher. Patricia Cheek, Advertising Director. Lisa Gray, Circulation Manager. Mary Gordon, Classified Adv. Mgr..

MONTICELLO

WAYNE COUNTY OUTLOOK. 109 E. Columbia Ave., Monticello, KY 42633. Telephone: 606-348-3338. FAX: 606-348-8848. E-MAIL: mjones@kih.net. URL: http://www.waynecountyoutlook.com. Mailing Address: PO Box 432, Monticello, KY 42633. Year Established: 1904. Pub. Frequency: w. (Wed.) Page Size: broadsheet. Subscrip. Rate: $.50 newsstand/cover; $26/yr mailed in county & adj. cys.; $36/yr mailed elsewhere. Adv. Rate: col. inch $5.50 Circulation: 6,000 per issue (paid). **Owner(s):** Community Newspaper Holdings, Inc., 3500 Colonnade Pkwy., Ste. 600, Birmingham, AL 35243. Telephone: 205-298-7100. **Management:** Melinda Jones, Publisher. Lisa Lowe, Advertising. Nikki Dishman, Classified Adv. Mgr.. **Editorial:** Melodie Phelps, Editor. Sylvia McGinnis, Reporter.

MOREHEAD

MOREHEAD NEWS, THE. 722 W. First St., Morehead, KY 40351. Telephone: 606-784-4116. FAX: 606-784-7337. Year Established: 1883. Pub. Frequency: s-w. (Tue. & Fri.) Page Size: broadsheet. Subscrip. Rate: $.50 newsstand/cover; $35/yr in county & adj cys; $47/yr in state; $50/yr out of state. Adv. Rate: col. inch $6.10 Circulation: 5,800 per issue (paid). **Owner(s):** Community Newspaper Holdings, Inc., 3500 Colonnade Pkwy., Ste. 600, Birmingham, AL 35243. Telephone: 205-298-7100. **Management:** Rob McCullough, Publisher. Dan Duncan, Advertising Manager. Chimila Hargett, Circulation Manager. Amy Nickell, Classified Adv. Mgr.. **Editorial:** Stephanie Ockerman, Managing Editor.

OLIVE HILL TIMES. 722 W. First St., Morehead, KY 40351. Telephone: 606-784-4116. FAX: 606-784-7337. Mailing Address: PO Box 484, Olive Hill, KY 41164. Pub. Frequency: w. (Wed.) Page Size: broadsheet. Subscrip. Rate: $.50 newsstand/cover; $22/yr mailed in county; $38/yr mailed out of county; $42/yr mailed out of state. Circulation: 2,350 per issue (paid). **Owner(s):** Community Newspaper Holdings, Inc., 3500 Colonnade Pkwy., Ste. 600, Birmingham, AL 35243. Telephone: 205-298-7100. FAX: 205-298-7101. **Management:** Rob McCullough, Publisher. Dan Duncan, Advertising Manager. Chimila Hargett, Circulation Manager. Amy Nickell, Classified Adv. Mgr.. **Editorial:** Stephanie Ockerman, Managing Editor.

MORGANFIELD

UNION COUNTY ADVOCATE, THE. 214 W. Main St., Morganfield, KY 42437. Telephone: 270-389-1833. FAX: 270-389-3926. E-MAIL: news@ucadvocate.com. URL: http://www.ucadvocate.com. Mailing Address: PO Box 370, Morganfield, KY 42437. Year Established: 1924. Pub. Frequency: w. (Wed.) Page Size: broadsheet. Subscrip. Rate: $.50 newsstand/cover; $23.50/yr in county; $32/yr out of county; $37/yr out of state. Circulation: 5,000 per issue (paid). **Owner(s):** E.W. Scripps Co., 312 Walnut St., 28th Fl., Cincinnati, OH 45202. Telephone: 513-977-3000. FAX: 513-977-3689. **Management:** Paula Smith, General Manager. Steve Austin, Publisher. Lisa Turner, Advertising. Stephanie Hite, Classified Adv. Mgr.. **Editorial:** LeighAnn Tipto, Editor.

MORGANTOWN

BUTLER COUNTY BANNER, THE. ISSN 0745-7006
120 E. Ohio St, Morgantown, KY 42261. Telephone: 270-526-4151. FAX: 270-526-3111. E-MAIL: bcbanner@logantele.com. URL: http://www.jobepublishinginc.com. Mailing Address: PO Box 219, Morgantown, KY 42261-0219. Year Established: 1982. Pub. Frequency: s-w. (Wed. & Sun.) Page Size: broadsheet. Subscrip. Rate: $.50 newsstand/cover Sun.; $40/yr mailed out of county; $50/yr mailed out of state. Circulation: 5,885 per issue (paid). **Owner(s):** Jobe Publishing Inc., P O Box 340, Horse Cave, KY 42149. **Management:** Jeffrey S. Jobe, Publisher. **Editorial:** Susan Lorenz Jobe, Editor.

MT. STERLING

ADVERTISER (MT. STERLING), THE. 219 Midland Dr, Mt. Sterling, KY 40353. Telephone: 859-498-2222. FAX: 859-498-2228. Year Established: 1978. Pub. Frequency: w. (Mon.) Page Size: broadsheet Circulation: 19,779 per issue (free). **Owner(s):** Hasco Newspapers, See address and contact information above. **Management:** Matt Hall, Publisher. JoAnne Halsey, Advertising. **Editorial:** Steven Wilson, Editor. Martha Greer, Circulation Editor.

MOUNT STERLING ADVOCATE. 219 Midland Dr, Mt. Sterling, KY 40353. Telephone: 859-498-2222. Pub. Frequency: w. (Thu.) Page Size: broadsheet. Subscrip. Rate: $.50 newsstand/cover; $19.61/yr in county. Circulation: 7,145 per issue (paid). **Owner(s):** Hasco Newspapers, See address and contact information above. **Management:** Matt Hall, Publisher. **Editorial:** Steven Wilson, Editor.

NICHOLASVILLE

JESSAMINE JOURNAL, THE. 507 N. Main St., Nicholasville, KY 40356. Telephone: 859-885-5381. FAX: 859-887-2966. E-MAIL: sschurz@jessaminejournal.com. URL: http:www.jessaminejournal.com. Mailing Address: PO Box 8, Nicholasville, KY 40340. Year Established: 1873. Pub. Frequency: w. (Thu.) Page Size: broadsheet. Subscrip. Rate: $.75 newsstand/cover; $30/yr in county; $36/yr out of county; $45/yr out of state. Circulation: 7,329 per issue (paid). **Owner(s):** Advocate Communications, Inc., See address and contact information above. **Management:** Scott Schurz, Publisher. Brad Toy, Advertising Manager. **Editorial:** Mike Moore, Editor. Casey Castle, Sports.

OWINGSVILLE

BATH COUNTY NEWS-OUTLOOK. PO Box 577, Owingsville, KY 40360. Telephone: 606-674-2181. Year Established: 1878. Pub. Frequency: w. (Thu.) Page Size: broadsheet. Subscrip. Rate: $.75 newsstand/cover; $18/yr in county; $22/yr mailed in state; $27/yr out of state. Circulation: 2,900 per issue (paid). **Owner(s):** Margaret C., Ken E., Gloria Metz, See address and contact information above. **Management:** Ken E. Metz, Publisher. **Editorial:** Ken E. Metz, Executive Editor.

PADUCAH

ADVANCE-YEOMAN. ISSN 1088-5684
701 Jefferson St., Paducah, KY 42002-1135. Telephone: 270-442-7389. FAX: 270-442-5220. E-MAIL: kyyeoman@brtc.net. URL: http://www.ky-news.com. Mailing Address: P.O. Box 1135, Paducah, KY 42002-1135. Year Established: 1882. Pub. Frequency: w. (Wed.) Page Size: standard. Subscrip. Rate: $.75 newsstand/cover; $29/yr mailed in county; $43/yr mailed out of county. Circulation: 1,700 per issue (paid). **Owner(s):** Kentucky Publishing, Inc., See address and contact information above. **Management:** Greg LeNeave, General Manager. Larrah Workman, Advertising Manager. **Editorial:** Monica Glisson, Editor. Michael Powell, Managing Editor.

WEST KENTUCKY NEWS. 701 Jefferson St., Paducah, KY 42002-1135. Telephone: 270-442-7389. FAX: 270-442-5220. E-MAIL: kip123@comcast.net. URL: http//www.ky-news.com. Mailing Address: P.O. Box 1135, Paducah, KY 42002-1135. Year Established: 1967. Pub. Frequency: w. (Thu.) Page Size: broadsheet. Subscrip. Rate: $29/yr mailed in county; $39/yr mailed out of state; $.75 newsstand/cover per issue. Circulation: 20,000 per issue (paid). **Owner(s):** Kentucky Publishing, Inc., See address and contact information above. **Management:** Greg LeNeave, Owner. Larrah Workman, Advertising Manager. **Editorial:** Michael Powell, Managing Editor. Gregory Vaught, Production Manager.

PAINTSVILLE

EASTERN KENTUCKY SHOPPER. 209 Main St., Paintsville, KY 41240. Telephone: 606-789-5315. FAX: 606-789-9717. URL: http://www.paintsvilleherald.com. Mailing Address: PO Box 1547, Paintsville, KY 41240. Year Established: 1990. Pub. Frequency: w. (Mon.) Page Size: broadsheet Circulation: 16,500 per issue (free). **Owner(s):** Lancaster Publications, 645 Walnut St., Gadsden, AL 35901. Telephone: 256-543-3417. FAX: 256-543-3548. **Management:** Paula Holm, Publisher. John McKenzie, Advertising. Nancy Daniel, Classified Adv. Mgr.. **Editorial:** Loretta Blackburn, Editor.

PAINTSVILLE HERALD, THE. 209 Main St., Paintsville, KY 41240. Telephone: 606-789-5315. FAX: 606-789-9717. URL: http://www.paintsvilleherald.com. Mailing Address: PO Box 1547, Paintsville, KY 41240. Year Established: 1901. Pub. Frequency: s-w. (Wed. & Fri.) Page Size: broadsheet. Subscrip. Rate: $.50 newsstand/cover; $26/yr mailed in county; $50/yr mailed in state; $55/yr mailed out of state. Circulation: 5,300 per issue (paid). **Owner(s):** Lancaster Publications, 645 Walnut St., Gadsden, AL 35901. Telephone: 256-543-3417. FAX: 256-543-3548. **Management:** Paula Holm, Publisher. John McKenzie, Advertising. **Editorial:** Loretta Blackburn, Editor. Melinda Robinson, Sports.

PARIS

ADVERTISER (PARIS), THE. 123 W. Eighth St., Paris, KY 40361. Telephone: 859-987-1870. FAX: 859-987-3729. Mailing Address: PO Box 158, Paris, KY 40362. Year Established: 1807. Pub. Frequency: w. (Mon.) Page Size: standard.Subscrip. Rate: $30/yr mailed Circulation: 11,700 per issue (free). **Owner(s):** Brannon Family, See address and contact information above. **Management:** Genevieve Brannon, Publisher. Rebecca Brannon, Advertising Manager. Beverly Brannon, Sales Manager. **Editorial:** Jim Brannon, Editor.

BOURBON COUNTY CITIZEN. 123 W. Eighth St., Paris, KY 40361. Telephone: 859-987-1870. FAX: 859-987-3729. Mailing Address: PO Box 158, Paris, KY 40362. Pub. Frequency: w. (Wed.) Page Size: standard. Subscrip. Rate: $.50 newsstand/cover; $14/yr local; $18/yr mailed out of state. Circulation: 2,600 per issue (paid). **Owner(s):** Brannon Family, See address and contact information above. **Management:** Genevieve Brannon, Publisher. Rebecca Brannon, Advertising Manager. Beverly Brannon, Sales Manager. **Editorial:** Jim Brannon, Editor. Rebecca Lawyer, Assistant Editor.

PIKEVILLE

APPALACHIAN NEWS-EXPRESS. 129 Caroline Ave., Pikeville, KY 41501. Telephone: 606-437-4054. FAX: 606-437-4246. E-MAIL: dpotter@news-expressky.com. URL: http://www.news-expressky.com. Year Established: 1913. Pub. Frequency: 3/w. (Wed., Fri., Sun.) Page Size: broadsheet. Subscrip. Rate: $.75 newsstand/cover; $75/yr home delivery in county; $90/yr mailed out of county; $110/yr mailed out of state. Freelance Pay: $0.60/column-inch. **Wire Service(s):** AP. Circulation: 11,000 per issue (paid). **Owner(s):** Appalachian Newspapers, Inc., PO Box 802, Pikeville, KY 41502. Telephone: 606-437-4054. **Management:** Jeff Vanderbeck, General Manager. Danny Coleman, Advertising Director. John D. Spears, Circulation Manager. **Editorial:** Mike Moore, Editor. Rachel Stanley, Managing Editor.

PINEVILLE

PINEVILLE SUN-CUMBERLAND COURIER. 210 Virginia Ave., Pineville, KY 40977-1616. Telephone: 606-337-2333. Mailing Address: PO Box 250, Pineville, KY 40977-0250. Year Established: 1907. Pub. Frequency: w. (Thu.) Page Size: broadsheet. Subscrip. Rate: $.50 newsstand/cover; $25/yr in county; $35/yr elsewhere. Circulation: 3,500 per issue (paid). **Owner(s):** Pineville Sun-Cumberland Courier, See address and contact information above. **Management:** Gary Ferguson, General Manager. James Nolan, President. Gary Ferguson, Advertising Manager. **Editorial:** Kellie Grubb, Editor.

PRESTONSBURG

FLOYD COUNTY TIMES, THE. 263 S Central Ave, Prestonsburg, KY 41653. Telephone: 606-886-8506. FAX: 606-886-3603. URL: http://www.floydcountytimes.com. Mailing Address: PO Box 390, Prestonsburg, KY 41653. Year Established: 1928. Pub. Frequency: 3/w. (Wed., Fri., Sun.) Page Size: broadsheet. Subscrip. Rate: $.75 newsstand/cover; $59/yr carrier delivery in county; $76/yr elsewhere. Circulation: 8,200 per issue (paid). **Owner(s):** Heartland Publications, LLC, 20 Research Pkwy, Ste G, Old Saybrook, CT 06475. Telephone: 860-388-3470. FAX: 860-388-3490. **Management:** Joshua Byers, Publisher. Kim Frasure, Advertising Manager. Jenny Ousley, Circulation Manager. LeeAnn Williams, Classified Adv. Mgr.. **Editorial:** Ralph Davis, Editor.

PRINCETON

TIMES LEADER (PRINCETON), THE. 607 W. Washington St., Princeton, KY 42445. Telephone: 270-365-5588. FAX: 270-365-7299. E-MAIL: chiphutcheson@timesleader.net. URL: http://www.timesleader.net. Mailing Address: PO Box 439, Princeton, KY 42445. Year Established: 1871. Pub. Frequency: s-w. (Wed. & Sat.) Page Size: broadsheet. Subscrip. Rate: $.50 newsstand/cover; $39/yr in county; $44/yr in state; $54/yr out of state. Adv. Rate: col. inch $6 **Wire Service(s):** AP. Circulation: 5,740 per issue (paid). **Owner(s):** Times Leader, See address and contact information above. **Management:** John Hutcheson III, Publisher. Kathy Boyd, Advertising Manager. LeAnn Felker, Circulation Manager. **Editorial:** Anita Baker, Editor.

PROVIDENCE

JOURNAL-ENTERPRISE, THE. 100 Walnut St., Providence, KY 42450. Telephone: 270-667-2068. FAX: 270-667-9160. E-MAIL: staff@journalenterprise.com. URL: http://www.journalenterprise.com. Mailing Address: PO Box 190, Providence, KY 42450. Year Established: 1899. Pub. Frequency: w. (Wed.) Page Size: broadsheet. Subscrip. Rate: $.50 newsstand/cover; $21/yr in county; $23/yr in state; $25/yr out of state. Circulation: 5,400 per issue (paid). **Owner(s):** The Journal-Enterprise, Inc., See address and contact information above. **Management:** Charles Hust, Owner. Maggie Utley, Circulation Manager. Kristie Dunbar, Classified Editor. **Editorial:** Dennis Beard, Editor.

RADCLIFF

SENTINEL (RADCLIFF), THE. 1558 Hill St., Radcliff, KY 40160. Telephone: 270-351-4407. FAX: 270-351-4407. Year Established: 1961. Pub. Frequency: w. (Thu.) Page Size: broadsheet. Subscrip. Rate: $.35 newsstand/cover; $9.75/yr in county. Adv. Rate: col. inch $5.52 Circulation: 3,400 per issue (paid). **Owner(s):** Royalty Printing Co., See address and contact information above. **Management:** O.J. Royalty, Publisher. **Editorial:** O.J. Royalty, Editor. Marlene Lawson, News Editor.

RUSSELL SPRINGS

RUSSELL COUNTY NEWS, THE. ISSN 8750-1651
120 Wilson St., Russell Springs, KY 42642-0190. Telephone: 270-866-3191. FAX: 270-866-3198. URL: http://www.russellcounty.net. Year Established: 1913. Pub. Frequency: w. (Sat.) Page Size: broadsheet. Circulation: 9,000 Sunday (paid and free). **Owner(s):** Russell County Newspapers, Inc., PO Box 190, Russell Springs, KY 42642. Telephone: 270-866-3191. FAX: 270-866-3198. **Management:** David Davenport, Publisher. Stephanie George, Advertising Manager. Karla Suchland, Circulation Manager. **Editorial:** David Davenport, Managing Editor.

TIMES JOURNAL, THE. 120 Wilson St., Russell Springs, KY 42642-0190. Telephone: 270-866-3191. FAX: 270-866-3198. E-MAIL: tjnews@duo-county.com. URL: http://www.russellcounty.net. Mailing Address: PO Box 190, Russell Springs, KY 42642-0190. Year Established: 1949. Pub. Frequency: w. (Thu.) Page Size: broadsheet. Subscrip. Rate: $.50 newsstand/cover; $17.57/yr in county; $27.11/yr out of county; $26/yr out of state; $80/yr elsewhere. Circulation: 4,200 per issue (paid). **Owner(s):** Russell County Newspapers, Inc., PO Box 190, Russell Springs, KY 42642. Telephone: 270-866-3191. FAX: 270-866-3198. **Management:** David Davenport, Publisher. Stephanie George, Advertising Manager. Kim Haydon, Circulation Manager. **Editorial:** David Davenport, Managing Editor.

RUSSELLVILLE

NEWS-DEMOCRAT & LEADER. 120 Public Sq., Russellville, KY 42276. Telephone: 270-726-8394. FAX: 270-726-8398. E-MAIL: newsdem@net. URL: http://www.newsdemocratleader.com. Mailing Address: PO Box 270, Russellville, KY 42276. Year Established: 1806. Pub. Frequency: s-w. (Tue. & Fri.) Page Size: standard. Subscrip. Rate: $.75 newsstand/cover; $33/yr in county; $45/yr elsewhere. Circulation: 6,600 per issue (paid and free). **Owner(s):** Heartland Publications, LLC, 20 Research Pkwy, Ste G, Old Saybrook, CT 06475. Telephone: 860-388-3470. FAX: 860-388-3490. **Management:** Randall Fuqua, Publisher. Tonya Anding, Advertising. Rita Osborne, Circulation Manager. **Editorial:** Jim Turner, Editor.

SALYERSVILLE

SALYERSVILLE INDEPENDENT, THE. 7 W. Maple St., Salyersville, KY 41465. Telephone: 606-349-2915. FAX: 606-349-8609. Mailing Address: PO Box 29, Salyersville, KY 41465. Year Established: 1921. Pub. Frequency: w. (Thu.) Page Size: standard. Subscrip. Rate: $.50 newsstand/cover; $22/yr in county; $26/yr out of state. Adv. Rate: col. inch $3.40 Circulation: 5,500 per issue (paid). **Owner(s):** M. David Prater, PO Box 29, Salyersville, KY 44165. Telephone: 606-349-2915. **Management:** David Prater, Publisher. Rita Hall, Circulation Manager. **Editorial:** Jeremy Stewart, Editor.

SCOTTSVILLE

SCOTTSVILLE CITIZEN-TIMES. PO Box 310, Scottsville, KY 42164-0310. Telephone: 270-237-3441. FAX: 270-237-4943. E-MAIL: ctimes@nctc.com. Year Established: 1890. Pub. Frequency: w. (Thu.) Page Size: standard. Subscrip. Rate: $.50 newsstand/cover; $17/yr in county; $20/yr out of county. Adv. Rate: col. inch $6.75 Circulation: 5,633 per issue (paid). **Owner(s):** Robert B. Pitchford, III, See address and contact information above. **Management:** Robert B. Pitchford III, Publisher. **Editorial:** Matt Pedigo, Editor.

SHELBYVILLE

CLEAR CREEK COURANT. ISSN 1084-3493
601 Taylorsville Rd, Shelbyville, KY 40065-0549. E-MAIL: cccourant@bwn.net. Mailing Address: PO Box 549, Shelbyville, KY 40065-0399. Year Established: 1973. Pub. Frequency: w. (Wed.) Page Size: tabloid. Subscrip. Rate: $.75 newsstand/cover; $28/yr in county; $36/yr out of county; $22/yr to senior citizens. Circulation: 2,200 per issue (paid). **Owner(s):** Landmark Community Newspapers, Inc., See address and contact information above. **Management:** Brad Bradberry, Publisher. Jan Paradise, Advertising. **Editorial:** Meghan Murphy, Editor.

SHELBYVILLE SENTINEL-NEWS. PO Box 549, Shelbyville, KY 40065. FAX: 502-633-2618. E-MAIL: jmulcahy@sentinelnews.com. URL: www.sentinelnews.com. Year Established: 1840. Pub. Frequency: s-w. (Wed. & Fri.) Page Size: broadsheet. Subscrip. Rate: $.50 newsstand/cover; $40/yr in area; $58/yr out of area; $69/yr out of state. Circulation: 8,500 per issue (paid). **Owner(s):** Landmark Community Newspapers, Inc., See address and contact information above. **Management:** James L. Edelen, Publisher. Jim Irish, Advertising Manager. Tonya Stormes, Circulation Manager. Becky Block, Classified Editor. **Editorial:** James Mulcahy, Editor. Todd Martin, Sports.

SHOPPER/PLUS. PO Box 549, Shelbyville, KY 40065. Telephone: 502-633-4334. E-MAIL: sentinelnews@ka.net. URL: http://www.shelbyconnect.com. Year Established: 1983. Pub. Frequency: w. (Mon.) Page Size: broadsheet Circulation: 18,100 per issue (free). **Owner(s):** Landmark Community Newspapers, Inc., See address and contact information above. **Management:** James L. Edelen, Publisher. Jim Irish, Advertising Manager. Tonya Stormes, Circulation Manager. **Editorial:** James Mulcahy, Editor.

SHEPHERDSVILLE

PIONEER NEWS. 455 N. Buckman St., Shepherdsville, KY 40165. Telephone: 502-543-2288. FAX: 502-955-9704. URL: http://www.pioneernews.net. Mailing Address: PO Box 98, Shepherdsville, KY 40165. Year Established: 1882. Pub. Frequency: s-w. (Mon. & Wed.) Page Size: broadsheet. Subscrip. Rate: $.50 newsstand/cover; $32.99/yr in area; $56.25/yr elsewhere. Freelance Pay: $0.17/column-inch. Circulation: 22,500 per issue (paid and free). **Owner(s):** Landmark Community Newspapers, Inc., PO Box 549, Shelbyville, KY 40065. Telephone: 502-633-2526. **Management:** Thomas Barr, Publisher. Sue Myers, Circulation Manager. **Editorial:** Thomas Barr, Editor. Mike Farner, Sports.

SPRINGFIELD

SPRINGFIELD (KY) SUN. 108 Progress Ave., Springfield, KY 40069. Telephone: 859-336-3716. FAX: 859-336-7718. E-MAIL: editor@thespringfieldsun.com. URL: http://www.thespringfieldsun.com. Mailing Address: PO Box 31, Springfield, KY 40069. Year Established: 1904. Pub. Frequency: w. (Wed.) Page Size: broadsheet. Subscrip. Rate: $.75 newsstand/cover; $30.74/yr in county; $38.16/yr out of county; $49/yr out of state. Circulation: 4,400 per issue (paid). **Owner(s):** Landmark Community Newspapers, Inc., PO Box 549, Shelbyville, KY 40065. Telephone: 502-633-2526. FAX: 502-633-2618. **Management:** Shorty Lassiter, General Manager. Pamela Barr, Office Manager. Shorty Lassiter, Advertising. Renee Webb, Circulation Manager. **Editorial:** Chris O'Nan, Editor. Tom Bystrek, Sports.

STANFORD

INTERIOR JOURNAL, THE. ISSN 8750-7609
111 E. Main St., Stanford, KY 40484-1252. Telephone: 606-365-2104. FAX: 606-365-2105. E-MAIL: news@theinteriorjournal.com. Year Established: 1860. Pub. Frequency: w. (Thu.) Page Size: broadsheet. Subscrip. Rate: $.50 newsstand/cover; $17.50/yr mailed in state; $35/yr mailed out of state. Adv. Rate: col. inch $4.25 Circulation: 4,339 per issue (paid). **Owner(s):** Schurz Communications, Inc., 225 W. Colfax Ave., South Bend, IN 46626. Telephone: 574-287-1001. FAX: 574-287-2257. **Management:** Karen Rolff, Advertising. **Editorial:** George Lewis, Editor.

STANTON

CLAY CITY TIMES, THE. ISSN 1940-9699
208 N Main St, Stanton, KY 40380. Telephone: 606-663-5540. FAX: 606-663-6397. URL: http://www.hatfieldnewspapers.com. Mailing Address: P O Box 547, Stanton, KY 40380. Year Established: 1896. Pub. Frequency: w. (Thu.) Page Size: broadsheet. Subscrip. Rate: $.50 newsstand/cover; $15.95/yr local; $23.95/yr mailed in state. Circulation: 4,050 per issue (paid). **Owner(s):** Hatfield Newspapers, Inc., See address and contact information above. **Management:** Teresa Hatfield, Publisher. **Editorial:** James Cook, Editor.

STURGIS

STURGIS NEWS. 617 N. Adams St., Sturgis, KY 42459-0218. Telephone: 270-333-5545. FAX: 270-333-9943. E-MAIL: sebroebanner@bellsouth.net. Mailing Address: PO Box 218, Sturgis, KY 42459-0218. Year Established: 1885. Pub. Frequency: w. (Wed.) Page Size: standard. Subscrip. Rate: $.35 newsstand/cover; $11.66/yr mailed in county; $15.90/yr mailed out of county; $18/yr mailed out of state. Circulation: 3,200 per issue (paid). **Owner(s):** Catlett Publishing Co., Inc., PO Box 36, Sebree, KY 42455. Telephone: 270-835-7521. FAX: 270-835-9521. **Management:** Betty P. Catlett, Publisher. **Editorial:** Tony Catlett, Editor.

TAYLORSVILLE

SPENCER MAGNET. 51 W. Main St., Taylorsville, KY 40071. Telephone: 502-477-2239. FAX: 502-477-2110. URL: http://www.spencermagnet.com. Mailing Address: PO Box 219, Taylorsville, KY 40071. Pub. Frequency: w. (Wed.) Page Size: broadsheet. Subscrip. Rate: $.50 newsstand/cover; $29.68/yr area; $42.40/yr mailed in state; $52/yr mailed out of state. Circulation: 3,500 per issue (paid). **Owner(s):** Landmark Community Newspapers, Inc., PO Box 549, Shelbyville, KY 40065. Telephone: 502-633-4334. **Management:** Lynette Mason, General Manager. Wesley Martin, Advertising Manager. Susan Collins, Circulation Manager. **Editorial:** Robin Bass, Editor.

TOMPKINSVILLE

MONROE COUNTY CITIZEN. 301 N Main St, Ste B, Tompkinsville, KY 42167. Telephone: 270-786-2679. FAX: 270-786-4470. URL: http://www.jobepublishinginc.com. Pub. Frequency: w. (Wed.) Subscrip. Rate: $.50 newsstand/cover; $20/yr in county; $40/yr mailed out of county; $55/yr mailed out of state. Circulation: 810 per issue (paid). **Owner(s):** Jobe Publishing Inc., P O Box 340, Horse Cave, KY 42149. **Management:** Jeffrey S. Jobe, Publisher. Kathy Riddle, Advertising. **Editorial:** Candace Geralds, Editor.

TOMPKINSVILLE NEWS. 105 N. Main St., Tompkinsville, KY 42167. Telephone: 270-487-5576. FAX: 270-487-8839. E-MAIL: tvillenews@alltel.net. URL: http://www.tompkinsvillenews.com. Year Established: 1903. Pub. Frequency: w. (Thu.) Page Size: broadsheet. Subscrip. Rate: $.50 newsstand/cover; $18/yr in county; $22/yr out of county; $27/yr out of state. Adv. Rate: col. inch $5 Circulation: 4,500 per issue (paid). **Owner(s):** Monroe County Press, Inc., See address and contact information above. **Management:** Blanche Trimble, Publisher. Teresa Gerughty, Advertising. Carol Depta, Circulation Manager. **Editorial:** Blanche Trimble, Editor.

VERSAILLES

WOODFORD SUN. 184 S. Main St., Versailles, KY 40383. Telephone: 859-873-4131. FAX: 859-873-0300. E-MAIL: information@woodfordsun.co. URL: http://www.woodfordsun.com. Mailing Address: PO Box 29, Versailles, KY 40383. Year Established: 1869. Pub. Frequency: w. (Thu.) Page Size: broadsheet. Subscrip. Rate: $.75 newsstand/cover; $21/yr in county; $27/yr mailed out of county; $34/yr mailed out of state. Adv. Rate: col. inch $7 Circulation: 6,000 per issue (paid). **Owner(s):** Woodford Sun Co., Inc., See address and contact information above. **Management:** A. Ben Chandler Jr., Publisher. Morjorie Holbrook, Advertising. **Editorial:** Steve Peterson, Managing Editor. Forrest Rutherford, Sports.

WEST LIBERTY

LICKING VALLEY COURIER, THE. PO Box 187, West Liberty, KY 41472. Telephone: 606-743-3551. FAX: 606-743-3565. Year Established: 1910. Pub. Frequency: w. (Thu.) Page Size: broadsheet. Subscrip. Rate: $.50 newsstand/cover; $19.50/yr in county; $22/yr out of county; $24/yr out of state. Circulation: 4,200 per issue (paid). **Owner(s):** Courier Publishing Co., Inc., See address and contact information above. **Management:** Earl W. Kinner, Publisher. Greg Kinner, Circulation Manager. **Editorial:** Earl W. Kinner, Editor.

WHITESBURG

MOUNTAIN EAGLE, THE. PO Box 808, Whitesburg, KY 41858. Telephone: 606-633-2252. FAX: 606-633-2843. E-MAIL: mteagle@tgtel.com. Year Established: 1907. Pub. Frequency: w. (Wed.) Page Size: broadsheet. Subscrip. Rate: $.75 newsstand/cover; $24.50/yr in county; $31.50/yr out of county. Circulation: 7,800 per issue (paid). **Owner(s):** Tom Gish, See address and contact information above. **Management:** Tom Gish, Publisher. Freddy Oakes, Advertising Manager. Pam Walker, Circulation Manager. **Editorial:** Ben Gish, Editor.

WHITLEY CITY

MCCREARY COUNTY RECORD. 48 N Main St, Whitley City, KY 42653. E-MAIL: mcrec@highland.net. URL: http://www.mccrearyrecord.com. Mailing Address: PO Box 9, Whitley City, KY 42653-0009. Year Established: 1919. Pub. Frequency: w. (Tue.) Page Size: broadsheet. Subscrip. Rate: $.50 newsstand/cover; $19.50/yr in county; $28/yr in state; $30/yr out of state. Circulation: 4,717 per issue (paid). **Owner(s):** Community Newspaper Holdings, Inc., 3500 Colonnade Pkwy., Ste. 600, Birmingham, AL 35243-2304. **Management:** Ken Shmidheiser, Publisher. Janie West, Advertising Manager. Carolyn Anderson, Circulation Manager. **Editorial:** Ken Shmidheiser, Editor.

WILLIAMSBURG

CORBIN WHITLEY NEWS JOURNAL. 105 S. Second St., Williamsburg, KY 40769. Telephone: 606-549-0643. FAX: 606-549-0644. E-MAIL: destep@corbinnewsjournal.com. URL: http://www.corbinnewsjournal.com. Mailing Address: PO Box 1524, Corbin, KY 40702. Year Established: 1908. Pub. Frequency: w. (Wed.) Page Size: broadsheet. Subscrip. Rate: $.50 newsstand/cover; $26/yr mailed in county; $38/yr mailed out of county; $46/yr mailed out of state. Adv. Rate: col. inch $9.10 Circulation: 9,000 per issue (paid). **Owner(s):** Terry Forcht & Don Estep, See address and contact information above. **Management:** Don Estep, Publisher. Debra Wright, Advertising. **Editorial:** Mark White, Editor. Trent Knuckles, News Editor. Jim McAlister, Sports.

LOUISIANA

ALEXANDRIA

ALEXANDRIA NEWS WEEKLY. 1746 Mason St., Alexandria, LA 71301. Telephone: 318-443-7664. Year Established: 1963. Pub. Frequency: w. (Thu.) Page Size: broadsheet. Subscrip. Rate: $.50 newsstand/cover; $59/yr in state. Circulation: 10,000 per issue (paid). **Owner(s):** Leon Coleman, Sr. & Alice G. Coleman, PO Box 608, Alexandria, LA 71309. Telephone: 318-443-7664. **Management:** Alice G. Coleman, Publisher. Leon Coleman Sr., Advertising Manager. **Editorial:** Alice G. Coleman, Editor.

AMITE

AMITE TANGI DIGEST. 120 N.E. Central Ave., Amite, LA 70422. Telephone: 985-748-6343. FAX: 985-748-7104. E-MAIL: atdnews@i-55.com. URL: http://www.amitetangidigest.com. Mailing Address: PO Box 698, Amite, LA 70422. Year Established: 1928. Pub. Frequency: w. (Wed.) Page Size: broadsheet. Subscrip. Rate: $.75 newsstand/cover; $24/yr in parish; $38/yr out of parish; $48/yr out of state. Circulation: 4,100 per issue (paid). **Owner(s):** Louisiana State Newspapers, 600 Jefferson St., Lafayette, LA 70501. Telephone: 337-266-2154. **Management:** Carol Brooke, Publisher. Ruth White, Circulation Manager. Jerri Robertson, Business Manager. **Editorial:** Carol Brooke, Editor.

ARABI

ST. BERNARD VOICE, THE. 234 Mehle Ave., Arabi, LA 70032-0088. Telephone: 504-279-7488. FAX: 504-277-2231. E-MAIL: roy@lastbv.nocoxmail.com. URL: http://www.stbernardvoice.com. Mailing Address: PO Box 88, Arabi, LA 70032-0088. Year Established: 1890. Pub. Frequency: w. (Fri.) Page Size: broadsheet. Subscrip. Rate: $.30 newsstand/cover; $12/yr in state; $14/yr out of state. Circulation: 3,200 per issue (paid). **Owner(s):** St. Bernard Voice, Inc., The, 234 Mehle Ave., Arabi, LA 70032. Telephone: 504-279-7488. FAX: 504-277-2231. **Management:** Edwin M. Roy Jr., Publisher. Mazie Roy Doody, Business Manager. **Editorial:** Edwin M. Roy Jr., Editor.

ARCADIA

BIENVILLE DEMOCRAT & RINGGOLD RECORD. 1952 Railroad St., Arcadia, LA 71001. Telephone: 318-263-2922. FAX: 318-263-8897. Mailing Address: PO Box 29, Arcadia, LA 71001. Year Established: 1909. Pub. Frequency: w. (Thu.) Page Size: broadsheet. Subscrip. Rate: $.50 newsstand/cover; $25/yr mailed in parish; $35/yr mailed in state; $45/yr mailed out of state. Adv. Rate: col. inch $5.85 Circulation: 3,500 per issue (paid). **Owner(s):** Natchitoches Times, Inc., PO Box 448, Natchitoches, LA 71458. Telephone: 318-375-3294. **Management:** Wayne E. Dring, Publisher. Priscilla Smith, Advertising. **Editorial:** Wayne E. Dring, Editor.

BAKER

BAKER OBSERVER. 5240 Groom Rd., Baker, LA 70714-3126. Telephone: 225-775-2315. FAX: 225-774-9212. E-MAIL: news@kso.brcoxmail.com. Year Established: 1957. Pub. Frequency: w. (Thu.) Page Size: broadsheet. Subscrip. Rate: $.75 newsstand/cover; $24/yr in parish; $50/yr mailed out of state. Circulation: 750 per issue (paid and free). **Owner(s):** Louisiana Suburban Press, See address and contact information above. **Management:** William Holliday, Publisher. Terri Whittington, Advertising Manager. **Editorial:** Jackie Alford, Editor.

BATON ROUGE

BATON ROUGE SHOPPER. 8252 W. El Cajon Dr., Baton Rouge, LA 70815. Telephone: 225-926-8882. Pub. Frequency: w. (Wed.) Page Size: tabloid.Subscrip. Rate: $1.75 newsstand/cover Circulation: 35,000 per issue (paid). **Owner(s):** H.M. Mike Cannon, See address and contact information above. **Management:** H.M. Mike Cannon, General Manager. **Editorial:** Veronica Spegell, Editor.

CONSUMERS' EDGE. 8252 W. El Cajon Dr., Baton Rouge, LA 70815. Telephone: 225-926-8882. Pub. Frequency: w. (Wed.) Page Size: tabloid Circulation: 30,000 per issue (free). **Owner(s):** H.M. Mike Cannon, See address and contact information above. **Management:** H.M. Mike Cannon, General Manager. **Editorial:** Veronica Spegell, Editor.

WEEKLY PRESS. 1283 Rosenwald Rd., Ste. 1, Baton Rouge, LA 70807-4173. Telephone: 225-775-2002. FAX: 225-775-4216. E-MAIL: theweeklypress@yahoo.com. URL: http://www.weeklypress.com. Year Established: 1981. Pub. Frequency: w. (Thu.) Page Size: broadsheet. Subscrip. Rate: $.50 newsstand/cover; $38/yr local; $40/yr out of state. Circulation: 7,500 per issue (paid). **Owner(s):** Ivory Payne, See address and contact information above. **Management:** Ivory Payne, Publisher.

BELLE CHASSE

PLAQUEMINES GAZETTE. ISSN 0740-266X
7952 Hwy. 23, Belle Chasse, LA 70037. Telephone: 504-392-1619. FAX: 504-393-9327. Year Established: 1926. Pub. Frequency: w. (Fri.) Page Size: broadsheet. Subscrip. Rate: $.35 newsstand/cover; $25/yr in parish. Circulation: 3,000 per issue (paid). **Owner(s):** Plaquemines Newspaper Publishing, Inc., See address and contact information above. **Management:** Dale Benoit, President. Norris J. Babin Jr., Advertising Manager. Dale Benoit, Business Manager. **Editorial:** Dale Benoit, Editor-in-Chief.

PLAQUEMINES WATCHMAN. 7952 Hwy. 23, Belle Chasse, LA 70037. Telephone: 504-392-1619. FAX: 504-393-9327. Year Established: 1981. Pub. Frequency: w. (Tue.) Page Size: broadsheet. Subscrip. Rate: $.35 newsstand/cover; $25/yr in parish; $30/yr out of parish; $35/yr out of state. Circulation: 2,950 per issue (paid). **Owner(s):** Plaquemines Newspaper Publishing, Inc., See address and contact information above. **Management:** Theresa Furgesson, Advertising. Dale Benoit, Business Manager. **Editorial:** Dale Benoit, Editor.

BOSSIER CITY

BOSSIER BANNER-PROGRESS. PO Box 6267, Bossier City, LA 71171. Telephone: 318-747-7900. FAX: 318-747-5298. E-MAIL: bpress@ciai.net. Year Established: 1859. Pub. Frequency: w. (Wed.) Page Size: broadsheet. Subscrip. Rate: $.50 newsstand/cover; $17.50 for 6 mos. in parish; $35/yr out of parish. Circulation: 1,500 per issue (paid). **Owner(s):** Specht Newspapers Co., See address and contact information above. **Management:** David Specht Jr., Publisher. Randy Brown, Advertising Manager. Kenny Clark, Circulation Manager. **Editorial:** Rachel Hayes, Managing Editor.

BOSSIER PRESS-TRIBUNE. ISSN 0747-4733
4250 Viking Dr., Bossier City, LA 71111. Telephone: 318-747-7900. FAX: 318-747-5298. E-MAIL: dspecht@bossierpress.com. URL: http://www.bossierpress.com. Year Established: 1928. Pub. Frequency: s-w. (Mon. & Thu.) Page Size: broadsheet. Subscrip. Rate: $.50 newsstand/cover; $13.50 for 6 mos. in parish; $35/yr in parish; $43/yr out of parish. Circulation: 7,000 per issue (paid). **Owner(s):** Specht Newspapers Co., See address and contact information above. **Management:** David Specht Jr., Publisher. Randall Brown, Advertising Manager. Barbara Prudhome, Circulation Manager. **Editorial:** David Specht Jr., Editor. Jerry Byrd, Sports Editor.

CHURCH POINT

CHURCH POINT NEWS. 315 N. Main St., Church Point, LA 70525. Telephone: 337-684-5711. FAX: 337-684-5793. E-MAIL: cpnews@centurytel.net. Mailing Address: P.O. Drawer 319, Church Point, LA 70525. Year Established: 1933. Pub. Frequency: w. (Wed.) Page Size: broadsheet. Subscrip. Rate: $1 newsstand/cover; $30/yr in parish; $38/yr in state; $48/yr mailed out of state. Circulation: 1,400 per issue (paid). **Owner(s):** Louisiana State Newspapers, 600 Jefferson St., Lafayette, LA 70501. Telephone: 337-266-2154. **Management:** Darrell Guillory, Publisher. Liz Horecky, Advertising Manager. **Editorial:** Diane Daigle, Editor.

CLINTON

WATCHMAN, THE. 11317B Church St., Clinton, LA 70722. Telephone: 225-683-5195. FAX: 225-683-4276. Mailing Address: PO Box 368, Clinton, LA 70722. Year Established: 1878. Pub. Frequency: w. (Thu.) Page Size: standard. Subscrip. Rate: $.75 newsstand/cover; $24/yr in parish; $35/yr mailed out of parish; $50/yr mailed out of state. Adv. Rate: col. inch $6.70 Circulation: 1,700 per issue (paid). **Owner(s):** Louisiana State Newspapers, See address and contact information above. **Management:** Bill Holliday, Publisher.

COUSHATTA

COUSHATTA CITIZEN. 1904 Ringgold Ave., Coushatta, LA 71019-1365. Telephone: 318-932-4201. FAX: 318-932-4285. Year Established: 1871. Pub. Frequency: w. (Thu.) Page Size: broadsheet. Subscrip. Rate: $.50 newsstand/cover; $21/yr. Circulation: 6,200 per issue (paid and free). **Owner(s):** Lovan Thomas, See address and contact information above. **Management:** Lovan Thomas, President. Jennifer Canan, Advertising Manager. Barbara Richey, Circulation Manager. **Editorial:** Emerson Sherra, News Editor.

COVINGTON

NEWS-BANNER, THE. 19290 19th Ave., Covington, LA 70433. Telephone: 985-892-7980. FAX: 985-867-8572. E-MAIL: editor@newsbanner.com. URL: http://www.newsbanner.com. Mailing Address: P.O. Drawer 90, Covington, LA 70434. Year Established: 1963. Pub. Frequency: 3/w. (Wed., Fri., Sun.) Page Size: broadsheet. Subscrip. Rate: $.75 newsstand/cover; $51/yr home delivery; $72/yr mailed in parish. Circulation: 26,500 per issue (paid). **Owner(s):** Wick Communications, Inc., 333 W. Wilcox, Ste. 302, Sierra Vista, AZ 85632. Telephone: 928-458-0200. FAX: 928-458-6166. **Management:** J. Kennon, Publisher. Barbara Eckert, Advertising Director. Richie Calamia, Circulation Manager. Rae Aguero, Marketing Director. Genia Baughman, Business Manager. **Editorial:** Sandy Cunningham, Managing Editor.

ST. TAMMANY FARMER. 321 N. New Hampshire St., Covington, LA 70433. Telephone: 985-892-2323. FAX: 985-892-2325. Year Established: 1874. Pub. Frequency: w. (Thu.) Page Size: broadsheet.Subscrip. Rate: $.50 newsstand/cover; $17.50/yr Circulation: 4,000 per issue (paid). **Owner(s):** St. Tammany Farmer, Inc., PO Box 269, Covington, LA 70434-0269. Telephone: 985-892-2323. FAX: 985-892-2232. **Management:** Karen Courtney, Publisher. Brenda Willis, Advertising. **Editorial:** Danny Nowlin, Editor. Paul Salvant, Sports Editor.

DENHAM SPRINGS

NEWS (DENHAM SPRINGS), THE. 688 Hatchell Ln., Denham Springs, LA 70726. Telephone: 225-665-5176. FAX: 225-667-0167. URL: http://www.livingstonparishnews.com. Year Established: 1898. Pub. Frequency: s-w. (Thu. & Sun.) Page Size: broadsheet. Subscrip. Rate: $40.56/yr in parish; $50.96/yr adjacent parishes; $74.88/yr elsewhere; $.50 newsstand/cover. Circulation: 11,327 per issue (paid). **Owner(s):** Denham Springs Publishing Co., PO Box 1529, Denham Springs, LA 70727. Telephone: 504-665-5342. **Management:** Jeff M David, President. Lauren Katz, Advertising Director. Dianne Patterson, Circulation Manager. Amy Ferguson, Classified Adv. Mgr.. **Editorial:** Mike Dowty, Editor. David Normand, Photographer. Sam Muffoletto, Sports.

DEQUINCY

DE QUINCY NEWS. 203 E Harrison, DeQuincy, LA 70633-3545. Telephone: 318-786-8004. FAX: 318-786-8131. E-MAIL: dequincynews@century.tel.net. URL: http://www.dequincynews.com. Year Established: 1923. Pub. Frequency: w. (Wed.) Page Size: broadsheet. Subscrip. Rate: $.50 newsstand/cover; $18/yr in county & adj. cys.; $19.40/yr elsewhere in LA & TX. Adv. Rate: col. inch $7.50 Circulation: 3,800 per issue (paid). **Owner(s):** Wise Newspapers, Inc., See address and contact information above. **Management:** Jerry Wise, Publisher. Jeffra DeViney, Advertising. **Editorial:** Jerry Wise, Editor.

DONALDSONVILLE

DONALDSONVILLE CHIEF. 120 Railroad Ave., Donaldsonville, LA 70346. Telephone: 225-473-3101. FAX: 225-473-4060. Mailing Address: PO Box 309, Donaldsonville, LA 70346. Year Established: 1871. Pub. Frequency: w. (Thu.) Page Size: standard. Subscrip. Rate: $.50 newsstand/cover; $29/yr in parish; $38.34/yr out of parish. Freelance Pay: $10-$25/story. Circulation: 2,700 per issue (paid). **Owner(s):** GateHouse Media, Inc, 350 WillowBrook Office Park, Fairport, NY 14450. Telephone: 585-598-0030. **Management:** Bob Prejean, Advertising Manager. **Editorial:** Allison B Hudson, Editor.

EUNICE

EUNICE NEWS. 465 Aymond St., Eunice, LA 70535. Telephone: 337-457-3061. FAX: 337-457-3122. E-MAIL: eunice@lsnweb.com. Mailing Address: PO Box 989, Eunice, LA 70535. Year Established: 1904. Pub. Frequency: s-w. (Thu. & Sun.) Page Size: broadsheet. Subscrip. Rate: $1 newsstand/cover; $36/yr in parish; $50/yr out of parish; $60/yr mailed elsewhere. Circulation: 3,500 per issue (paid). **Owner(s):** Louisiana State Newspapers, 600 Jefferson St., Lafayette, LA 70501. Telephone: 337-266-2154. **Management:** Darrell Guillory, Publisher. Chad Fontenot, Advertising Manager. James Street, Circulation Manager. **Editorial:** Bobby Gerard, Editor. Myra Miller, Lifestyle Editor.

FERRIDAY

CONCORDIA SENTINEL. 1308 1st St, Ferriday, LA 71334. Telephone: 318-757-3646. FAX: 318-757-3001. E-MAIL: consentinel@cricket.net. URL: http://www.concordiasentinel.com. Mailing Address: PO Box 1485, Ferriday, LA 71334. Year Established: 1876. Pub. Frequency: w. (Wed.) Page Size: broadsheet. Subscrip. Rate: $.50 newsstand/cover; $25/yr in parish; $30/yr in state; $35/yr mailed out of state. Circulation: 5,500 per issue (paid). **Owner(s):** Hanna Publishing Co., See address and contact information above. **Management:** Leslie Capdepon, General Manager. Mary Sue Hanna, Publisher. Barbara Jackson, Advertising Manager. **Editorial:** Leslie Capdepon, Editor.

GONZALES

COMMUNITY MIRROR. 205 W. Worthey Rd., Gonzales, LA 70737. Telephone: 225-647-4569. FAX: 225-644-8238. E-MAIL: gonzwkly@eatel.net. URL: http://www.gonzalesweekly.com. Mailing Address: PO Box 38, Gonzales, LA 70707-0038. Pub. Frequency: w. (Tue.) Page Size: broadsheet.Adv. Rate: col. inch $8.70 Circulation: 32,000 per issue (free). **Owner(s):** Gonzales Weekly, Inc., See address and contact information above. **Management:** Alana Bishop, Publisher. Tony Tortoreo, Advertising Manager. **Editorial:** Wade McIntyre, Editor. Dean Bourque, Sports Editor.

GONZALES WEEKLY CITIZEN. 231 W Cornerview, Gonzales, LA 70737. Telephone: 225-644-6397. FAX: 225-644-2069. E-MAIL: gonzwkly@eatel.net. URL: http://www.gonzalesweekly.com. Mailing Address: PO Box 430, Gonzales, LA 70707. Year Established: 1920. Pub. Frequency: w. (Fri.) Page Size: broadsheet. Subscrip. Rate: $.50 newsstand/cover; $39/yr mailed in state. Adv. Rate: col. inch $8.70 **Wire Service(s):** AP. Circulation: 10,000 per issue (paid). **Owner(s):** GateHouse Media, Inc, 350 WillowBrook Office Park, Fairport, NY 14450. Telephone: 585-598-0030. FAX: 585-248-2631. **Management:** Tony Cooper, Publisher. Brenda Gautreau, Classified Adv. Mgr.. **Editorial:** Mike Kiral, Sports Editor.

MARKETEER (GONZALES), THE. 231 W Cornerview, Gonzales, LA 70737. Telephone: 225-644-6397. FAX: 225-644-2069. URL: http://www.ascensioncitizen.com. Mailing Address: PO Box 430, Gonzales, LA 70707. Pub. Frequency: w. (Mon.) Page Size: standard Circulation: 26,000 per issue (free). **Owner(s):** GateHouse Media, Inc, 350 WillowBrook Office Park, Fairport, NY 14450. Telephone: 585-598-0030. **Management:** Tony Cooper, Publisher. Brenda Gautreau, Classified Adv. Mgr..

JEANERETTE

JEANERETTE ENTERPRISE. 808 E. Main St., Jeanerette, LA 70544. Telephone: 337-276-5171. FAX: 337-367-9640. Mailing Address: PO Box 327, Jeanerette, LA 70544. Year Established: 1942. Pub. Frequency: w. (Wed.) Page Size: broadsheet.Subscrip. Rate: $.25 newsstand/cover; $30/yr Circulation: 4,500 per issue (paid). **Owner(s):** Wick Communications, Inc., 333 W. Wilcox Dr., Ste. 302, Sierra Vista, AZ 85635. Telephone: 928-728-4488. FAX: 928-728-6090. **Management:** Will Chapman, Publisher. Alan Rini, Advertising Manager. **Editorial:** Karma Champaigne, Editor.

JENA

JENA TIMES OLLA-TULLOS-URANIA SIGNAL. PO Box 3050, Jena, LA 71342. Telephone: 318-992-4121. FAX: 318-992-2287. E-MAIL: editor@thejenatimes.net. URL: http://www.thejenatimes.net. Year Established: 1905. Pub. Frequency: w. (Wed.) Page Size: broadsheet. Subscrip. Rate: $.75 newsstand/cover; $45/yr. Adv. Rate: col. inch $6 Circulation: 4,600 per issue (paid). **Owner(s):** Sammy J. Franklin, See address and contact information above. **Management:** Sammy J Franklin, Publisher. Chris Lee, Advertising Manager. Ashley Keene, Circulation Manager. Kristie Taylor, Classified Adv. Mgr.. **Editorial:** Sammy J Franklin, Editor.

JONESBORO

JACKSON INDEPENDENT, THE. 624 Hudson Ave., Jonesboro, LA 71251. Telephone: 318-259-2551. FAX: 318-259-8537. E-MAIL: jackson@pineynet.com. URL: http://www.jackson-ind.com. Year Established: 1892. Pub. Frequency: w. (Thu.) Page Size: broadsheet. Subscrip. Rate: $.50 newsstand/cover; $22.95/yr in parish; $36/yr out of parish. Adv. Rate: col. inch $4.68 Circulation: 12,500 per issue (paid and free). **Owner(s):** Chris Smith, See address and contact information above. **Management:** Chris Smith, President. **Editorial:** Chris Smith, Managing Editor.

KENTWOOD

KENTWOOD LEDGER. 202 Ave. F, Kentwood, LA 70444. Telephone: 985-229-8607. FAX: 985-229-8698. Year Established: 1965. Pub. Frequency: w. (Wed.) Page Size: broadsheet. Subscrip. Rate: $1 newsstand/cover; $26/yr in parish; $34/yr out of parish; $44/yr mailed out of state. Circulation: 14,646 per issue (paid). **Owner(s):** Louisiana State Newspapers, 600 Jefferson St., Ste. 1500, Lafayette, LA 70451. Telephone: 337-266-2154. **Management:** Carol Brooke, Publisher. Diane Faust, Advertising Manager. **Editorial:** Cathy Chapman, Editor.

LA PLACE

OBSERVATEUR, L'. 116 Newspaper Dr., La Place, LA 70068. Telephone: 985-652-9545. FAX: 985-652-3885. URL: http://www.lobservateur.com. Mailing Address: PO Box 1010, La Place, LA 70069. Year Established: 1913. Pub. Frequency: s-w. (Wed. & Sat.) Page Size: broadsheet. Subscrip. Rate: $.50 newsstand/cover; $30/yr home delivery; $40/yr mailed. Circulation: 3,800 per issue (paid). **Owner(s):** Wick Communications, Inc., 333 W. Wilcox Dr., Ste. 302, Sierra Vista, AZ 85635. Telephone: 520-728-4488. FAX: 520-728-6090. **Management:** Ellen Ishmael, Publisher. Laura Anthony, Advertising Manager. Thomas Williams, Circulation Manager. **Editorial:** Leonard Gray, Managing Editor.

LAFAYETTE

LAFAYETTE SUN, THE. 116 Lafayette St, Lafayette, LA 36862. Telephone: 334-864-8885. FAX: 334-864-8310. E-MAIL: thelafayettesun@emailnc.com. Mailing Address: PO Box 378, Lafayette, AL 36862. Year Established: 1880. Pub. Frequency: w. (Wed.) Page Size: broadsheet. Subscrip. Rate: $.25 newsstand/cover; $14.75/yr in county; $16/yr mailed out of county. Adv. Rate: col. inch $5,015 Circulation: 3,000 per issue (paid). **Owner(s):** Michael Hand, See address and contact information above. **Management:** Michael Hand, Publisher. Sherry Bishop, Advertising Manager. **Editorial:** Michael Hand, Editor.

TIMES OF ACADIANA, THE. 221 Jefferson St., Lafayette, LA 70501. Telephone: 337-289-6300. FAX: 337-289-6496. E-MAIL: timesedit@thomnews.com. URL: http://www.timesofacadiana.com. Year Established: 1980. Pub. Frequency: w. (Wed.) Page Size: tabloid. Subscrip. Rate: $28.50/yr mailed in county. Adv. Rate: color page $1,748, B&W page $1,368 Circulation: 33,500 per issue (controlled). **Owner(s):** Gannett Company, Inc., 7950 Jones Branch Dr., McLean, VA 22107-0001. Telephone: 703-854-6000. **Management:** Ted Power, Publisher. William Bronson, Advertising Manager. **Editorial:** Doug Gruse, Managing Editor. Eileen Fontenot, Associate Editor. Peter Piacsa, Photo Editor. Don Allen, Sports.

LUTCHER

NEWS EXAMINER, THE. 2290 Texas St., Lutcher, LA 70071. Telephone: 225-869-5784. FAX: 225-869-4386. E-MAIL: ruhrvalley@earthlink.com. Mailing Address: P.O. Box 460, Lutcher, LA 70071. Pub. Frequency: w. (Thu.) Page Size: broadsheet. Subscrip. Rate: $.50 newsstand/cover; $15.60/yr mailed in county. Circulation: 3,900 per issue (paid). **Owner(s):** Ruhr Valley Publishing, See address and contact information above. **Management:** Wilbur Raynaud, Publisher. Kathleen Becnel, Advertising Manager. Connie Frederic, Classified Adv. Mgr.. **Editorial:** David Raynaud Jr., Editor.

MANSFIELD

MANSFIELD ENTERPRISE. 202 Adams St., Mansfield, LA 71052. Telephone: 318-872-4120. FAX: 318-872-6038. E-MAIL: enterprise@wnonline.net. URL: http://www.mansfieldenterprise.com. Mailing Address: PO Box 840, Mansfield, LA 71052. Year Established: 1904. Pub. Frequency: w. (Thu.) Page Size: broadsheet. Subscrip. Rate: $.50 newsstand/cover; $25/yr in parish; $40/yr mailed out of parish; $50/yr mailed out of state. Circulation: 4,200 per issue (paid). **Owner(s):** Natchitoches Times, Inc., PO Box 448, Natchitoches, LA 71458. FAX: 318-375-4578. **Management:** Bennie Hall, General Manager. **Editorial:** Tammy Overton, Editor.

MANY

SABINE BANNER. 850 San Antonio Ave., Many, LA 71449. E-MAIL: ads@sabineindex.net. Mailing Address: P.O. Box 850, Many, LA 71449-0850. Year Established: 1879. Pub. Frequency: w. (Tue.) Page Size: standard Circulation: 13,000 per issue (free). **Owner(s):** Robert Gentry, See address and contact information above. **Management:** Robert Gentry, Publisher. Shannon Greer, Advertising Manager.

SABINE INDEX. 850 San Antonio Ave., Many, LA 71449. E-MAIL: ads@sbineindex.net. Mailing Address: P.O. Box 850, Many, LA 71449-0850. Year Established: 1879. Pub. Frequency: w. (Wed.) Page Size: standard. Subscrip. Rate: $.75 newsstand/cover; $34/yr in parish; $48/yr out of parish. Circulation: 6,000 per issue (controlled and free). **Owner(s):** Robert Gentry, See address and contact information above. **Management:** Robert Gentry, Publisher. Shannon Greer, Advertising Manager. **Editorial:** Robert Gentry, Editor.

MARKSVILLE

AVOYELLES JOURNAL. PO Box 523, Marksville, LA 71351. Telephone: 318-253-9247. FAX: 318-253-7223. Year Established: 1978. Pub. Frequency: s-w. (Sun. & Wed.) Page Size: broadsheet Circulation: 17,119 per issue (free). **Owner(s):** Avoyelles Publishing Co., See address and contact information above. **Management:** Randy DeCuir, Publisher. Kathy Lipe, Advertising Manager. **Editorial:** Randy DeCuir, Editor. Garland Foreman, Sports Editor.

WEEKLY NEWS. PO Box 523, Marksville, LA 71351. Telephone: 318-253-9247. FAX: 318-253-7223. Pub. Frequency: w. (Thu.) Page Size: broadsheet. Subscrip. Rate: $.50 newsstand/cover; $15/yr in parish; $27/yr mailed out of parish; $31/yr mailed out of state. Circulation: 2,850 per issue (paid). **Owner(s):** Avoyelles Publishing Co., See address and contact information above. **Management:** Randy DeCuir, Publisher. Kathy Lipe, Advertising Manager. **Editorial:** Randy DeCuir, Editor. Garland Foreman, Sports Editor.

MORGAN CITY

ST. MARY JOURNAL. 1014 Front St., Morgan City, LA 70380. Telephone: 985-384-1350. FAX: 985-384-4255. E-MAIL: news@daily-review.com. URL: http://www.daily-review.com. Mailing Address: P.O. Box 948, Morgan City, LA 70381. Year Established: 1960. Pub. Frequency: s-w. (Sun. & Wed.) Page Size: broadsheet Circulation: 10,500 per issue (free). **Owner(s):** Morgan City Newspapers, Inc., See address and contact information above. **Management:** Andy Shirley, General Manager. Steve Shirley, Publisher. Charles LeJeune, Advertising Manager. Andy Shirley, Circulation Manager. **Editorial:** Steve Shirley, Editor-in-Chief.

NATCHITOCHES

WINN PARISH ENTERPRISE. PO Box 448, Natchitoches, LA 71458. Mailing Address: PO Box 750, Winnfield, LA 71483. Year Established: 1925. Pub. Frequency: w. (Wed.) Page Size: broadsheet. Subscrip. Rate: $.50 newsstand/cover; $20/yr local. Circulation: 4,300 per issue (paid). **Owner(s):** Lovan B. & Patricia W. Thomas, See address and contact information above. **Management:** Bob Holeman, Publisher. Minnie Young, Advertising Manager. Bob Holeman, Circulation Manager. Verlene Henderson, Classified Adv. Mgr.. **Editorial:** Sherri Taylor, News Editor.

NEW ROADS

POINTE COUPEE BANNER. 123 St. Mary St., New Roads, LA 70760. Telephone: 225-638-7155. FAX: 225-638-8442. E-MAIL: thpcbanner@aol.com. Mailing Address: P.O. Box 400, New Roads, LA 70760. Year Established: 1880. Pub. Frequency: w. (Thu.) Page Size: broadsheet. Subscrip. Rate: $.60 newsstand/cover; $31.20/yr in state; $35/yr out of state; $60/yr mailed elsewhere. Circulation: 5,000 per issue (paid). **Owner(s):** Pointe Coupee Printing & Publishing, Inc., See address and contact information above. **Management:** Brent Roy, Co-Publisher. E.M. White, Publisher. Mary Denny, Advertising. **Editorial:** Tommy Comeaux, Editor.

OAK GROVE

WEST CARROLL GAZETTE. 512 S. Constitution Ave., Oak Grove, LA 71263-1007. Telephone: 318-428-3207. FAX: 318-428-2747. E-MAIL: lsnoak@aol.com. Mailing Address: PO Box 1007, Oak Grove, LA 71263-1007. Year Established: 1910. Pub. Frequency: w. (Wed.) Page Size: standard. Subscrip. Rate: $.75 newsstand/cover; $31/yr mailed in parish; $37/yr mailed out of parish; $43/yr mailed out of state. Circulation: 2,000 per issue (paid). **Owner(s):** Moody Co., PO Box 4033C, Lafayette, LA 70502. **Management:** Mary Terry, Publisher. Melba West, Office Manager. Renee Graham, Advertising Manager. Melba West, Circulation Manager. **Editorial:** Johney Turner, Editor. Jessica Townsend, Feature Editor.

OAKDALE

OAKDALE JOURNAL. ISSN 0746-5920
231 E. Sixth Ave., Oakdale, LA 71463. Telephone: 318-335-0635. FAX: 318-335-0431. E-MAIL: barbara@wnonline.net. Mailing Address: PO Box 668, Oakdale, LA 71463. Year Established: 1913. Pub. Frequency: w. (Thu.) Page Size: broadsheet. Subscrip. Rate: $1 newsstand/cover; $24/yr in parish; $30/yr out of parish; $44/yr out of state. Adv. Rate: col. inch $7.75 Circulation: 1,700 per issue (paid). **Owner(s):** Louisiana State Newspapers, 600 Jefferson St., Lafayette, LA 70501. Telephone: 318-266-2154. **Management:** David Ortego, General Manager. **Editorial:** Barbara Doyle, Editor.

PIERRE PART

CAJUN GAZETTE, THE. 2939 Hwy 70, Pierre Part, LA 70339. Telephone: 985-252-6435. FAX: 985-252-3836. Mailing Address: PO Box 160, Pierre Part, LA 70339-0160. Pub. Frequency: w. (Wed.) Page Size: broadsheet. Subscrip. Rate: $.50 newsstand/cover; $27/yr local. Circulation: 2,500 per issue (paid). **Owner(s):** GateHouse Media, Inc, 350 WillowBrook Office Park, Fairport, NY 14450. Telephone: 585-598-0030. FAX: 585-248-2631. **Editorial:** Zelma Landry, Editor.

PLAQUEMINE

POST/SOUTH. ISSN 1053-5691
58650 Belleview Rd., Plaquemine, LA 70764. Telephone: 225-687-3288. FAX: 225-687-1814. E-MAIL: news@postsouth. URL: http://www.postsouth.com. Mailing Address: PO Box 589, Plaquemine, LA 70765-0589. Year Established: 1957. Pub. Frequency: w. (Thu.) Page Size: broadsheet. Subscrip. Rate: $.75 newsstand/cover; $31.50/yr local; $39.30/yr in state; $43/yr out of state. Adv. Rate: col. inch $6.76 Freelance Pay: $50-$75/article. Circulation: 4,000 per issue (paid). **Owner(s):** GateHouse Media, Inc, 350 WillowBrook Office Park, Fairport, NY 14450. Telephone: 585-598-0030. **Management:** Alan Curran, General Manager. Liz Troxclair, Office Manager. Brandy Brewer, Advertising. Jim Ringness, Advertising Manager. Loryn Hawkins, Classified Adv. Mgr.. **Editorial:** Steve Colwell, Editor. Keith Byars, Production Manager. Jean Paul Keller, Graphics Editor. Candace Edwards, Lifestyle Editor.

WEST BANK SHOPPER. 58650 Belleview Rd., Plaquemine, LA 70764. Telephone: 225-687-3288. FAX: 225-687-1814. URL: http://www.postsouth.com. Mailing Address: PO Box 589, Plaquemine, LA 70765-0589. Pub. Frequency: w. (Mon.) Page Size: broadsheet.Adv. Rate: col. inch $13.15 Circulation: 13,000 per issue (free). **Owner(s):** GateHouse Media, Inc, 350 WillowBrook Office Park, Fairport, NY 14450. Telephone: 585-598-0030. **Management:** Alan Curran, General Manager. Liz Troxclair, Office Manager. **Editorial:** Tryne Bracken, Editor.

PONCHATOULA

ENTERPRISE (PONCHATOULA), THE. ISSN 0889-0684
PO Box 218, Ponchatoula, LA 70454. Telephone: 985-386-6537. Year Established: 1921. Pub. Frequency: w. (Wed.) Page Size: broadsheet.Subscrip. Rate: $.25 newsstand/cover; $12/yr Circulation: 2,500 per issue (paid). **Owner(s):** Don Ellzey, See address and contact information above. **Management:** Carol Robertson, Publisher. Jan Heider, Office Manager.

PONCHATOULA TIMES, THE. 145 W. Pine St., Ste. A, Ponchatoula, LA 70454-3347. Telephone: 985-386-2877. FAX: 985-386-0458. E-MAIL: editor@ponchatoula.com. URL: http://www.ponchatoula.com/ptimes/. Year Established: 1981. Pub. Frequency: w. (Thu.) Page Size: broadsheet. Subscrip. Rate: $.50 newsstand/cover; $20/yr mailed. Adv. Rate: col. inch $5.49 Circulation: 7,025 per issue (controlled and free). **Owner(s):** Bryan T. McMahon, See address and contact information above. **Management:** Bryan T. McMahon, Co-Publisher. **Editorial:** Brendan B'Iarde McMahon, Editor.

PORT ALLEN

WEST SIDE JOURNAL. 668 N. Jefferson Ave, Port Allen, LA 70767. Telephone: 225-343-2540. FAX: 225-344-0923. E-MAIL: westside@westsidejournal.com. URL: http://www.westsidejournal.com. Year Established: 1937. Pub. Frequency: w. (Thu.) Page Size: broadsheet. Subscrip. Rate: $.75 newsstand/cover; $24/yr in parish; $42/yr out of parish. Circulation: 3,000 per issue (paid). **Owner(s):** Venture Capital Publishers LLC, See address and contact information above. **Management:** Joyce Jenne, Publisher. Darryl Guilbeau, Advertising Manager. Angela Robertson, Circulation Manager. **Editorial:** Courtney Lacy, Editor.

RAYNE

RAYNE ACADIAN-TRIBUNE, THE. ISSN 1069-2398
108 N. Adams St, Rayne, LA 70578. Telephone: 337-334-3186. FAX: 337-334-8474. E-MAIL: raynenews@aol.com. URL: http://www.acadian-tribune.com. Mailing Address: PO Box 260, Rayne, LA 70578. Year Established: 1893. Pub. Frequency: w. (Thu.) Page Size: broadsheet. Subscrip. Rate: $.75 newsstand/cover; $20/yr in state; $22/yr mailed out of state. Circulation: 2,700 per issue (paid and free). **Owner(s):** Louisiana State Newspapers, 600 Jefferson St., Lafayette, LA 70501. Telephone: 337-266-2154. **Management:** Carol Stutes, General Manager. **Editorial:** Paul Kedinger, Managing Editor.

RAYNE INDEPENDENT. 201 E.S. First St., Rayne, LA 70578. Telephone: 337-334-2128. FAX: 337-334-2120. E-MAIL: rayneind@bellsouth.net. Mailing Address: P.O. Box 428, Rayne, LA 70578-0428. Year Established: 1967. Pub. Frequency: w. (Thu.) Page Size: broadsheet. Subscrip. Rate: $.50 newsstand/cover; $17/yr in state; $20/yr out of state. Adv. Rate: col. inch $5.90 Circulation: 3,200 per issue (paid); 450 per issue (free). **Owner(s):** Independent Publishing Corp., See address and contact information above. **Management:** Walter T. Cart, Publisher. Walter T. Cart, Advertising Manager. **Editorial:** Jo Cart, Editor.

RAYVILLE

RICHLAND BEACON-NEWS. 603 N. Louisa St., Rayville, LA 71269. Telephone: 318-728-2250. FAX: 318-728-5991. E-MAIL: maryterry@bellsouth.net. URL: http://www.lsnbeacon.com. Mailing Address: PO Box 209, Rayville, LA 71269. Year Established: 1846. Pub. Frequency: w. (Thu.) Page Size: broadsheet. Subscrip. Rate: $.75 newsstand/cover; $28/yr in parish; $34/yr out of state. Freelance Pay: $25/article. Circulation: 10,918 per issue (paid). **Owner(s):** Louisiana State Newspapers, 600 Jefferson St., Lafayette, LA 70501. Telephone: 337-266-2154. **Management:** Mary Terry, Publisher. **Editorial:** Darryl Riser, Editor.

SPRINGHILL

SPRINGHILL PRESS. 127 Main St., Springhill, LA 71075. Telephone: 318-539-3511. Mailing Address: PO Box 668, Springhill, LA 71075. Pub. Frequency: w. (Thu.) Page Size: broadsheet. Subscrip. Rate: $.50 newsstand/cover; $25/yr local; $40/yr out of parish; $50/yr mailed out of state. Circulation: 4,000 per issue (paid). **Owner(s):** Lovan B. & Patricia W. Thomas, See address and contact information above. **Management:** Vicky Darst, Publisher. **Editorial:** Vicky Darst, Editor.

ST. MARTINVILLE

ST. MARTINVILLE TECHE NEWS. 214 N. Main St., P.O. Box 69, St. Martinville, LA 70582. Telephone: 337-394-6232. FAX: 337-394-7511. E-MAIL: news@bellsouth.net. Year Established: 1886. Pub. Frequency: w. (Wed.) Page Size: broadsheet. Subscrip. Rate: $1 newsstand/cover; $35.36/yr in parish; $41.60/yr out of parish; $50/yr out of state. Adv. Rate: col. inch $6.50 Circulation: 5,800 per issue (paid). **Owner(s):** Louisiana Suburban Press, See address and contact information above. **Management:** Ken Grissom, Publisher. Kristy Bourque, Advertising Manager. **Editorial:** Ken Grissom, Editor.

SULPHUR

VINTON NEWS. 716 E. Napoleon St., Sulphur, LA 70663. Telephone: 337-527-7075. FAX: 337-528-3044. Mailing Address: PO Box 1999, Sulphur, LA 70664-1999. Pub. Frequency: w. (Thu.) Page Size: broadsheet. Subscrip. Rate: $.50 newsstand/cover; $16.80/yr local. Circulation: 2,500 per issue (paid). **Owner(s):** GateHouse Media, Inc, 350 WillowBrook Office Park, Fairport, NY 14450. Telephone: 585-598-0030. **Management:** Lewis Cain, Publisher. **Editorial:** Carla Bastos, Editor.

TALLULAH

MADISON JOURNAL. 300 S. Chestnut St., Tallulah, LA 71282. Telephone: 318-574-1404. FAX: 318-574-4219. E-MAIL: madison@louisiana-internet.com. Year Established: 1869. Pub. Frequency: w. (Wed.) Page Size: broadsheet. Subscrip. Rate: $.50 newsstand/cover; $18/yr in parish; $22/yr out of parish. Circulation: 3,400 per issue (paid and free). **Owner(s):** Emmrich Newspaper Group, See address and contact information above. **Management:** Bert Bryant, Publisher. Carla Lopez, Circulation Manager.

VILLE PLATTE

MAMOU ACADIAN PRESS. 145 Court St., Ville Platte, LA 70586. Telephone: 337-363-3939. FAX: 337-363-2841. E-MAIL: vpgaz@asbank.com. Mailing Address: P o Box 240, Ville Platte, LA 70486. Year Established: 1956. Pub. Frequency: w. (Tue.) Page Size: broadsheet.Subscrip. Rate: $18/yr mailed Circulation: 4,000 per issue (free). **Owner(s):** Louisiana State Newspapers, 600 Jefferson St., Lafayette, LA 70501. Telephone: 337-266-2151. **Management:** David Ortego, Publisher. **Editorial:** Carissa Hebert, Editor.

VILLE PLATTE GAZETTE. 145 Court St., Ville Platte, LA 70586. Telephone: 337-363-3939. FAX: 337-363-2841. E-MAIL: vpgaz@asbank.com. Mailing Address: PO Box 220, Ville Platte, LA 70586. Year Established: 1914. Pub. Frequency: s-w. (Thu. & Sun.) Page Size: broadsheet. Subscrip. Rate: $1 newsstand/cover; $34/yr local; $39/yr out of area. Circulation: 4,000 per issue (paid). **Owner(s):** Louisiana State Newspapers, 600 Jefferson St., Lafayette, LA 70501. Telephone: 337-266-2154. **Management:** David Ortego, General Manager. Bob Hadding, Sales Manager. **Editorial:** Kathy Longino, Editor. Carissa Hebert, News Editor. Heather Bogard, Society Editor. Lance Reed, Sports Editor.

VIVIAN

CADDO CITIZEN. 203 S Spruce, Vivian, LA 71082. Telephone: 318-375-3294. FAX: 318-375-4578. E-MAIL: caddocitizen@centurytell.net. Year Established: 1912. Pub. Frequency: w. (Thu.) Page Size: broadsheet. Subscrip. Rate: $.50 newsstand/cover; $24/yr in parish; $29/yr mailed in state; $33/yr mailed out of state. Adv. Rate: col. inch $6.85 Freelance Pay: $0.35/column-inch. Circulation: 1,200 per issue (paid). **Owner(s):** Natchitoches Times, Inc., PO Box 448, Natchitoches, LA 71458. Telephone: 318-375-3294. **Management:** Mary Haddox, Publisher. **Editorial:** Mary Haddox, Editor.

WINNSBORO

FRANKLIN SUN, THE. 514 Prairie St., Winnsboro, LA 71295-0550. Telephone: 318-435-4521. FAX: 318-435-9220. Year Established: 1856. Pub. Frequency: w. (Wed.) Page Size: broadsheet. Subscrip. Rate: $.50 newsstand/cover; $25/yr in parish; $33/yr mailed out of parish; $38/yr mailed out of state. Circulation: 6,200 per issue (paid). **Owner(s):** Hanna Publishing Co., 1308 1st St, Ferriday, LA 71334. Telephone: 318-757-3646. **Management:** Mary Sue Hanna, Publisher. Sharon Ferrington, Office Manager. Monica Huff, Advertising Manager. **Editorial:** Leslie Young, Editor.

ZACHARY

ZACHARY PLAINSMAN-NEWS. 5145 Main St., Ste. C, Zachary, LA 70791. Telephone: 225-654-6841. FAX: 225-654-8271. Year Established: 1953. Pub. Frequency: w. (Thu.) Page Size: broadsheet. Subscrip. Rate: $.75 newsstand/cover; $24/yr in state; $35/yr out of parish; $50/yr mailed out of state. Circulation: 2,000 per issue (paid). **Owner(s):** Louisiana State Newspapers, 600 Jefferson St., Lafayette, LA 70501. Telephone: 337-266-2154. **Management:** William Holliday, Publisher. **Editorial:** Mindy Miller-Head, Editor.

MAINE

AUGUSTA

CAPITAL WEEKLY. ISSN 1087-3856
1 Mulliken Ct., Augusta, ME 04330. Telephone: 207-621-6000. FAX: 207-621-6006. E-MAIL: cwmail@courierpub.com. URL: http://www.mainecoastnow.com. Mailing Address: PO Box 2788, Augusta, ME 04338. Year Established: 1995. Pub. Frequency: w. (Thu.) Page Size: broadsheet. Subscrip. Rate: $1 newsstand/cover; $37/yr in state; $60/yr out of state. Adv. Rate: col. inch $8.25 Circulation: 5,500 per issue (paid). **Owner(s):** Courier Publications, 301 Park St., Rockland, ME 04841. **Management:** Diane Norton, Group Publisher. Peter Lynch, Advertising Director. Donna Culbertson, Circulation Director. **Editorial:** Joyce Grondin, Editor.

BANGOR

WEEKLY, THE. 491 Main St., Bangor, ME 04401. Telephone: 207-990-8000. FAX: 207-947-7508. E-MAIL: theweekly@bangordailynews.net. Mailing Address: PO Box 1329, Bangor, ME 04402-2237. Pub. Frequency: w. (Fri.) Page Size: tabloid.Subscrip. Rate: $1.25/wk. Circulation: 38,470 per issue (free). **Owner(s):** Bangor Publishing Co., See address and contact information above. **Management:** Lorie Ireland, Classified Adv. Mgr.. **Editorial:** Roxanne Saucier, Editor.

BAR HARBOR

BAR HARBOR TIMES. 74 Cottage St., Bar Harbor, ME 04609. Telephone: 207-288-3311. FAX: 207-288-5813. E-MAIL: cgmail@courierpub.com. URL: http://www.mainecoastnow.com/#bht. Year Established: 1914. Pub. Frequency: w. (Thu.) Page Size: broadsheet. Subscrip. Rate: $1 newsstand/cover; $37/yr in state; $60/yr mailed out of state. Adv. Rate: col. inch $12.25 Circulation: 8,266 per issue (paid). **Owner(s):** Courier Publications, 301 Park St., Rockland, ME 04841. Telephone: 207-594-4401. FAX: 207-596-6981. **Management:** Diane Norton, Group Publisher. Cathy McDonald, Advertising Manager. Donna Culbertson, Circulation Director. **Editorial:** Greg Fish, Editor.

BATH

COASTAL JOURNAL. ISSN 0192-4524
832 Washington St., Bath, ME 04530. Telephone: 207-443-6241. FAX: 207-443-5605. E-MAIL: editor@coastaljournal.com. URL: http://www.coastaljournal.com. Mailing Address: PO Box 705, Bath, ME 04530-0705. Year Established: 1966. Pub. Frequency: w. (Thu.) Page Size: tabloid. Subscrip. Rate: $65 mailed for 6 mos.; $120/yr mailed. Adv. Rate: col. inch $16.50 Circulation: 18,200 per issue (free). **Owner(s):** Seattle Times Co., PO Box 70, Seattle, WA 98111. Telephone: 509-525-3300. **Management:** Ralph Stetson, General Manager. Dave Kaufman, Publisher. Bruce Hardina, Advertising. **Editorial:** Fred Kahrl, Editor.

BELFAST

REPUBLICAN JOURNAL (BELFAST). ISSN 0034-5075
71 High St., Belfast, ME 04915. Telephone: 207-594-4401. FAX: 207-596-6981. E-MAIL: trgmail@courierpub.com. URL: http://www.courierpub.com. Mailing Address: PO Box 327, Belfast, ME 04915. Year Established: 1829. Pub. Frequency: w. Page Size: broadsheet. Subscrip. Rate: $.75/yr newsstand/cover; $37/yr in state; $60/yr out of state. Freelance Pay: $10-$25/story. Circulation: 7,820. **Owner(s):** Courier Publications, 301 Park St., Rockland, ME 04841. Telephone: 207-594-4401. FAX: 207-596-6981. **Management:** Diane Norton, Group Publisher. Chum Berry, Advertising Director. Donna Culbertson, Circulation Director. **Editorial:** Daniel Dunkle, Editor.

WALDO INDEPENDENT, THE. 71 High St., Belfast, ME 04915. Telephone: 207-594-4401. FAX: 207-596-6981. E-MAIL: waldoindependent@courierpub.com. URL: http://www.mainecoastnow.com. Mailing Address: PO Box 327, Belfast, ME 04915. Year Established: 1993. Pub. Frequency: w. (Thu.) Page Size: broadsheet. Subscrip. Rate: $.75 newsstand/cover; $37 for 6 mos. in state; $60/yr mailed out of state. Circulation: 7,500 per issue (paid). **Owner(s):** Courier Publications, 301 Park St., Rockland, ME 04841. Telephone: 207-594-4401. FAX: 207-596-6981. **Management:** Diane Norton, Group Publisher. Chum Berry, Advertising Director. Donna Culbertson, Circulation Director. Connie Vaccaro, Classified Adv. Mgr.. **Editorial:** Daniel Dunkle, Editor.

BETHEL

BETHEL CITIZEN, THE. 19 Main St., Bethel, ME 04217. Telephone: 207-824-2444. FAX: 207-824-2426. E-MAIL: news@bethelcitizen.com. URL: http://www.bethelcitizen.com. Mailing Address: PO Box 109, Bethel, ME 04217. Year Established: 1895. Pub. Frequency: w. (Thu.) Page Size: broadsheet. Subscrip. Rate: $.50 newsstand/cover; $24/yr in county; $29/yr out of county; $39/yr out of state. Adv. Rate: col. inch $5.45 Circulation: 3,600 per issue (paid). **Owner(s):** C's Publishing, 104 Park St., Lewiston, ME. **Management:** Edward M. Snook, Publisher. **Editorial:** Michael Daniels, Editor.

BIDDEFORD

BIDDEFORD-SACO-OLD ORCHARD BEACH COURIER. 180 Main St., Biddeford, ME 04005. Telephone: 207-282-4337. FAX: 207-282-4339. Mailing Address: PO Box 1894, Biddeford, ME 04005-1894. Year Established: 1989. Pub. Frequency: w. (Thu.) Page Size: tabloid. Subscrip. Rate: $100/yr mailed out of city. **Wire Service(s):** AP. Circulation: 22,000 per issue (paid and controlled). **Owner(s):** Mainely Newspapers, See address and contact information above. **Management:** Carolyn Flood, Publisher. David Clark, Advertising Manager. Mike Gagne, Circulation Manager. **Editorial:** Randy Seaver, Editor.

SCARBOROUGH LEADER. 180 Main St., Biddeford, ME 04005. Telephone: 207-282-4337. FAX: 207-282-4339. E-MAIL: news@scarboroughleader.com. URL: http://www.scarboroughleader.com. Mailing Address: PO Box 907, Scarborough, ME 04070-0907. Pub. Frequency: w. (Fri.) Page Size: tabloid. Subscrip. Rate: $100/yr out of town. Circulation: 8,000 per issue (paid and free). **Owner(s):** Mainely Newspapers, See address and contact information above. **Management:** Carolyn Flood, Publisher. David Clark, Advertising Manager. Mike Gagne, Circulation Manager. **Editorial:** Elizabeth Elder, Editor.

SOUTH PORTLAND SENTRY. 180 Main St., Biddeford, ME 04005. Telephone: 207-282-4337. FAX: 207-282-4339. Mailing Address: PO Box 2399, South Portland, ME 04116. Pub. Frequency: w. (Fri.) Page Size: tabloid.Subscrip. Rate: $100/yr out of town Circulation: 12,000 per issue (paid). **Owner(s):** Mainely Newspapers, See address and contact information above. **Management:** Carolyn Flood, Publisher. David Clark, Advertising Manager. Mike Gagne, Circulation Manager. **Editorial:** Elizabeth Elder, Editor.

SUMMER BEACON. 180 Main St., Biddeford, ME 04005. Telephone: 207-282-4337. FAX: 207-282-4339. URL: http://www.mainlynewspapers.com. Mailing Address: PO Box 1894, Biddeford, ME 04005-1894. Pub. Frequency: w. (Fri. (May-Sep.)) Page Size: tabloid.Subscrip. Rate: $100/yr out of county Circulation: 10,000 per issue (free). **Owner(s):** Mainely Newspapers, See address and contact information above. **Management:** Carolyn Flood, Publisher. **Editorial:** Chris Flood, Editor.

BLUE HILL

WEEKLY PACKET. Main St., Blue Hill, ME 04614. Telephone: 207-374-2341. FAX: 207-374-2343. E-MAIL: wp@penobscotbaypress.com. URL: http://www.penobscotbaypress.com. Mailing Address: PO Box 646, Blue Hill, ME 04614. Year Established: 1961. Pub. Frequency: w. (Thu.) Page Size: tabloid. Subscrip. Rate: $.70 newsstand/cover; $27.95/yr in state; $39.95/yr mailed out of state; $69.96/yr mailed elsewhere. Adv. Rate: col. inch $9.75 Freelance Pay: $1.50/column-inch. Circulation: 2,600 per issue (paid). **Owner(s):** Penobscot Bay Press, PO Box 36, Stonington, ME 04681. Telephone: 207-367-2200. FAX: 207-367-6397. **Management:** R. Nathaniel W. Barrows, Publisher. Darcy Grindal, Classified Adv. Mgr.. **Editorial:** R. Nathaniel W. Barrows, Editor.

BOOTHBAY HARBOR

BOOTHBAY REGISTER. 97 Townsend Ave., Boothbay Harbor, ME 04538. Telephone: 207-633-4620. FAX: 207-633-7123. E-MAIL: editcopy@boothbayregister.com. URL: http://www.boothbayregister.maine.com. Mailing Address: PO Box 357, Boothbay Harbor, ME 04538-0357. Year Established: 1876. Pub. Frequency: w. (Thu.) Page Size: broadsheet. Subscrip. Rate: $.50 newsstand/cover; $25/yr in county; $35/yr out of county. Adv. Rate: col. inch $9.06 Circulation: 5,563 per issue (paid). **Owner(s):** Maine-OK Enterprises, Inc., See address and contact information above. **Management:** Marylouise Cowan, Publisher. Kathy Frizzell, Advertising. Patricia Schmid, Business Manager. **Editorial:** Kevin Burnham, Editor. Mary Brewer, Managing Editor. Contact: Kathy Frizzell, Advertising Manager.

BRIDGTON

BRIDGTON NEWS, THE. 118 Main St., Bridgton, ME 04009. Telephone: 207-647-2851. FAX: 207-647-5001. E-MAIL: bnews@roadrunner.com. Mailing Address: PO Box 244, Bridgton, ME 04009. Year Established: 1870. Pub. Frequency: w. (Thu.) Page Size: broadsheet. Subscrip. Rate: $.60 newsstand/cover; $26/yr in state; $28/yr mailed out of state. Circulation: 6,800 per issue (paid and free). **Owner(s):** Bridgton News Corp., PO Box 244, Bridgton, ME. Telephone: 207-647-2851. **Management:** Stephen E. Shorey, President. Henry A. Shorey, Publisher. Gail Stretton, Advertising Manager. **Editorial:** Wayne E. Rivet, Editor.

BUCKSPORT

BUCKSPORT ENTERPRISE, THE. 105 Main St., Bucksport, ME 04416-0829. Telephone: 207-469-6722. FAX: 207-469-2114. E-MAIL: theenterpr@aol.com. Mailing Address: PO Box 829, Bucksport, ME 04416. Year Established: 1992. Pub. Frequency: w. (Thu.) Page Size: tabloid. Subscrip. Rate: $.60 newsstand/cover; $30/yr in state; $35/yr mailed out of state; $45/yr mailed foreign. Adv. Rate: col. inch $6 Freelance Pay: $25/story. Circulation: 2,200 per issue (paid). **Owner(s):** Donald M. Houghton, See address and contact information above. **Management:** Donald Houghton, Publisher. Sandra Holmes, Advertising Manager. **Editorial:** Donald Houghton, Editor.

CALAIS

CALAIS ADVERTISER. PO Box 660, Calais, ME 04619. Telephone: 207-454-3561. FAX: 207-454-3458. E-MAIL: calaisadvertiser@myfairpoint.net. URL: http://www.the-calais-advertiser.com. Year Established: 1836. Pub. Frequency: w. (Wed.) Page Size: tabloid. Subscrip. Rate: $1.25 newsstand/cover; $47/yr in state; $52/yr mailed out of state. Circulation: 4,250 per issue (paid). **Owner(s):** Calais Advertiser, The, See address and contact information above. **Management:** Brenda Dempsey, Office Manager. Beverley Mains, Advertising Manager. **Editorial:** Ferguson Calder, Editor. Cheryl Stabinski, Production Manager. Mike Boise, Sports.

CALOUS

MACHIAS VALLEY NEWS OBSERVER. Willow St, Calous, ME 04619. Telephone: 207-454-3758. E-MAIL: news@machiasnews.com. Year Established: 1853. Pub. Frequency: w. (Wed.) Page Size: tabloid. Subscrip. Rate: $1 newsstand/cover; $35/yr in county; $40/yr out of county. Adv. Rate: col. inch $4.75 Circulation: 3,400 per issue (paid). **Owner(s):** Gener & Patricia Townsend, See address and contact information above. Jay & Karen Hinson, 31 Broadway, Machias, ME 04654. Telephone: 207-255-6561. FAX: 207-255-4058. **Management:** Gene Townsend, Owner. Mary Bury, Business Manager. **Editorial:** Karen Hinson, Editor-in-Chief.

CAMDEN

CAMDEN HERALD, THE. 56 Elm St., Camden, ME 04843. Telephone: 207-236-8511. FAX: 207-523-6424. URL: http://www.camdenherald.com. Year Established: 1869. Pub. Frequency: w. (Thu.) Page Size: broadsheet. Subscrip. Rate: $1 newsstand/cover; $37/yr in state; $60/yr mailed out of state. Circulation: 5,200 per issue (paid). **Owner(s):** Courier Publications, 301 Park St., Rockland, ME 04841. Telephone: 207-594-4401. FAX: 207-596-6981. **Management:** Diane Norton, Group Publisher. Peter Lynch, Advertising Director. Donna Culbertson, Circulation Director. **Editorial:** David Grima, Editor. Steve Rzasa, Assistant Editor.

CAPE ELIZABETH

CAPE COURIER, THE. 320 Ocean House Rd., Cape Elizabeth, ME 04107-6242. Telephone: 207-767-5023. E-MAIL: courier@gwi.net. URL: http://www.capecourier.com. Mailing Address: PO Box 6242, Cape Elizabeth, ME 04107-0042. Year Established: 1988. Pub. Frequency: bi-w. (1st & 3rd Sat.) Page Size: tabloid. Subscrip. Rate: $18/yr in state; $20/yr mailed out of state. Adv. Rate: col. inch $7.50 Circulation: 3,600 per issue (paid and free). **Owner(s):** Cape Courier, The, See address and contact information above. **Management:** Pat Adler, Publisher. Carolyn Young, Advertising Manager. **Editorial:** Tina Harnden, Editor.

CARIBOU

AROOSTOOK REPUBLICAN & NEWS. 159 Bennett Dr., Caribou, ME 04736. Telephone: 207-496-3251. FAX: 207-492-4351. E-MAIL: aroosrep@bangornews.infi.net. Mailing Address: PO Box 608, Caribou, ME 04736. Year Established: 1880. Pub. Frequency: w. (Wed.) Page Size: broadsheet. Subscrip. Rate: $.75 newsstand/cover; $39/yr in county; $48.40/yr out of county; $50.60/yr mailed out of state; $77/yr mailed foreign. Adv. Rate: col. inch $13.45 Circulation: 5,075 per issue (paid). **Owner(s):** Northeast Publishing Co., PO Box 510, Presque Isle, ME 04769. Telephone: 207-768-4471. **Management:** Gayle Smith, Advertising Manager. **Editorial:** Mark Putnam, Editor.

CASTINE

CASTINE PATRIOT. Water St., Castine, ME 04421. Telephone: 207-326-9300. FAX: 207-326-4383. E-MAIL: cp@penobscottbaypress.com. URL: http://www.penobscotbaypress.com. Mailing Address: PO Box 205, Castine, ME 04421. Pub. Frequency: w. (Thu.) Page Size: broadsheet. Subscrip. Rate: $.70 newsstand/cover; $27.95/yr in state area. Adv. Rate: col. inch $9.75 Circulation: 1,200 per issue (paid). **Owner(s):** Penobscot Bay Press Inc., PO Box 205, Castine, ME 04421-0205. Telephone: 207-326-4383. FAX: 207-326-4383. **Management:** R. Nathaniel Barrows, Publisher. Sandy Bush, Circulation Manager. **Editorial:** R. Nathaniel Barrows, Editor.

CUTLER

DOWNEAST COASTAL PRESS, THE. 2413 Cutler Rd., Cutler, ME 04626-9601. Telephone: 207-259-7751. FAX: 207-259-2026. E-MAIL: downeastcoastal@earthlink.net. Pub. Frequency: w. (Tue.) Page Size: tabloid. Subscrip. Rate: $.75 newsstand/cover; $30/yr in county; $35/yr out of county. Adv. Rate: col. inch $5 Circulation: 3,535 per issue (paid). **Owner(s):** Nancy L. & Frederick G. Hastings, See address and contact information above. **Management:** Frederick G. Hastings, Publisher. **Editorial:** Frederick G. Hastings, Editor.

DEXTER

EASTERN GAZETTE, THE. 21 Main St., Dexter, ME 04930-0306. Telephone: 207-924-7402. FAX: 207-924-6215. E-MAIL: gazette@kynd.net. Mailing Address: PO Box 306, Dexter, ME 04930-0306. Year Established: 1853. Pub. Frequency: w. (Sat.) Page Size: tabloid. Subscrip. Rate: $45/yr mailed. Adv. Rate: col. inch $10 Circulation: 17,000 per issue (paid and free). **Owner(s):** Robert & Janice Shank, PO Box 306, Dexter, ME 04930. Telephone: 207-924-7402. FAX: 207-924-6215. **Management:** Janice Shank, President. Robert Shank, Publisher. **Editorial:** Robert Shank, Editor.

DOVER-FOXCROFT

PISCATAQUIS OBSERVER, THE. 12 E. Main St., Dover-Foxcroft, ME 04426. Telephone: 207-564-8355. FAX: 207-564-7056. E-MAIL: observer@nepublish.com. Mailing Address: PO Box 30, Dover-Foxcroft, ME 04426. Year Established: 1838. Pub. Frequency: w. (Wed.) Page Size: standard. Subscrip. Rate: $.60 newsstand/cover; $42.10/yr in state; $44.20/yr out of state; $66/yr foreign. Adv. Rate: col. inch $12.50 Circulation: 5,000 per issue (paid). **Owner(s):** Northeast Publishing Co., PO Box 510, Presque Isle, ME 04769. FAX: 207-764-7585. **Management:** Richard Warren, Publisher. Jeannette Hughes, Office Manager. Keri Foster, Advertising. **Editorial:** Mark Putnam, Executive Editor.

ELLSWORTH

ELLSWORTH AMERICAN, THE. ISSN 1541-6720
PO Box 509, Ellsworth, ME 04605-0509. E-MAIL: info@ellsworthamerican.com. URL: http://www.ellsworthamerican.com. Year Established: 1851. Pub. Frequency: w. (Thu.) Page Size: broadsheet. Subscrip. Rate: $1 newsstand/cover; $39/yr local; $44/yr out of area; $55/yr out of state. Adv. Rate: col. inch $15.85 Circulation: 10,702 per issue (paid). **Owner(s):** Ellsworth American, Inc, 30 Water St, Ellsworth, ME 04605-0509. Telephone: 207-667-2576. FAX: 207-667-7656. **Management:** Terry L. Carlisle, General Manager. Alan Baker, President. Brian Hewitt, Advertising Manager. **Editorial:** Stephen Fay, Managing Editor.

FARMINGDALE

COMMUNITY ADVERTISER. 20 Peter Path, Farmingdale, ME 04344. Telephone: 207-582-8486. FAX: 207-582-4530. Year Established: 1936. Pub. Frequency: w. (Mon.) Page Size: tabloid. Freelance Pay: $0.65/column-inch. Circulation: 12,000 per issue (paid and free). **Owner(s):** Keith Peters, See address and contact information above. **Management:** Keith Peters, Publisher. **Editorial:** Keith Peters, Editor.

FARMINGTON

FRANKLIN JOURNAL. 187 Wilton Rd., Farmington, ME 04938-0750. Telephone: 207-778-2075. FAX: 207-778-6970. E-MAIL: editon@megalink.net. Mailing Address: PO Box 750, Farmington, ME 04938-0750. Year Established: 1840. Pub. Frequency: s-w. (Tue. & Fri.) Page Size: broadsheet. Subscrip. Rate: $.50 newsstand/cover Tue.; $.75 newsstand/cover Fri.; $33/yr in state; $44/yr mailed out of state. Adv. Rate: col. inch $8.91 Circulation: 10,000 per issue (paid). **Owner(s):** Kirkland Newspapers, PO Box 750, Farmington, ME 04938. Telephone: 207-778-2075. FAX: 207-778-6970. **Management:** Bob Wallack, Publisher. Leslie Bull, Advertising. Patty Storer, Circulation Manager. **Editorial:** Bobby Hanstein, Editor.

GREENVILLE

MOOSEHEAD MESSENGER. 16 Moosehead Lake Rd, Greenville, ME 04441. Telephone: 207-695-3077. FAX: 207-695-3780. E-MAIL: kopentonllc@verizon.net. URL: http://www.moosemessenger.com. Mailing Address: PO Box 400, Greenville, ME 04441. Year Established: 1952. Pub. Frequency: w. (Fri.) Page Size: broadsheet. Subscrip. Rate: $.75 newsstand/cover; $48/yr. Adv. Rate: col. inch $8 Circulation: 4,000 per issue (paid). **Owner(s):** Kopenton LLC, See address and contact information above. **Management:** Rachel Clawson, Advertising Manager. Heidi St. Jean, Production Director. **Editorial:** Fran Emmons, Editor.

HOULTON

HOULTON PIONEER TIMES. 23 Court St., Houlton, ME 04730. Telephone: 207-532-2281. FAX: 207-532-2403. E-MAIL: pioneertimes@nepublish.com. Mailing Address: PO Box 456, Houlton, ME 04730. Year Established: 1857. Pub. Frequency: w. (Wed.) Page Size: broadsheet. Subscrip. Rate: $.75 newsstand/cover; $39/yr in county; $48.40/yr out of county; $50.60/yr out of state. Adv. Rate: col. inch $11.70 Circulation: 5,575 per issue (paid). **Owner(s):** Northeast Publishing Co., PO Box 510, Presque Isle, ME 04769. FAX: 207-764-7585. **Management:** Roger Tremblay, General Manager. Dave Russell, Advertising. Wanda MacIlroy, Circulation Manager. **Editorial:** Mark Putnam, Managing Editor. Sarah Berthiaume, Reporter. Gloria Austin, Sports.

ISLESBORO

ISLESBORO ISLAND NEWS. ISSN 1071-1473
103 W. Shore Dr., Islesboro, ME 04848. Telephone: 207-754-6921. FAX: 207-734-6519. E-MAIL: iinew@mint.net. Mailing Address: PO Box 104, Islesboro, ME 04048-0104. Year Established: 1985. Pub. Frequency: bi-m. Page Size: tabloid. Subscrip. Rate: $24/yr mailed. Circulation: 600 per issue (paid and free). **Owner(s):** Brenda Craig, See address and contact information above. **Management:** Brenda Craig, Publisher. **Editorial:** Brenda Craig, Editor.

KENNEBUNK

YORK COUNTY COAST STAR. 39 Main St, Kennebunk, ME 04043. Telephone: 207-985-2961. FAX: 207-985-9050. E-MAIL: dking@seacoastonline.com. URL: http://www.seacoastonline.com. Mailing Address: PO Box 979, Kennebunk, ME 04043-0979. Year Established: 1878. Pub. Frequency: w. (Thu.) Page Size: broadsheet. Subscrip. Rate: $1 newsstand/cover; $36.75/yr mailed in county; $45.75/yr mailed in state; $60.50/yr mailed out of state. Circulation: 9,724 per issue (paid). **Owner(s):** Ottaway Newspapers, Inc., PO Box 401, Campbell Hall, NY 10916. Telephone: 914-294-8181. **Management:** John Tabor, Publisher. Pat Lee, Advertising Director. **Editorial:** Howard Altscheller, Editor.

LINCOLN

LINCOLN NEWS. PO Box 35, Lincoln, ME 04457. Telephone: 207-794-6532. FAX: 207-794-2004. E-MAIL: lincnews@midmaine.com. Year Established: 1959. Pub. Frequency: w. (Thu.) Page Size: tabloid. Subscrip. Rate: $.60 newsstand/cover; $32/yr in state; $36/yr mailed out of state. Freelance Pay: $10/article. Circulation: 5,696 per issue (paid). **Owner(s):** M. Sheila Tenggren, See address and contact information above. **Management:** M. Sheila Tenggren, Publisher. Laverne Carll, Office Manager. M. Sheila Tenggren, Advertising. David Whalen, Production Director. **Editorial:** M. Sheila Tenggren, Editor. Kevin Tenggren, Photographer.

LIVERMORE FALLS

LIVERMORE FALLS ADVERTISER. 59 Main St., Livermore Falls, ME 04254-0701. Telephone: 207-788-2075. FAX: 207-788-6970. E-MAIL: lfa@megalink. Year Established: 1892. Pub. Frequency: w. (Thu.) Page Size: broadsheet. Subscrip. Rate: $.50 newsstand/cover; $19/yr in state; $26/yr mailed out of state. Adv. Rate: col. inch $5.94 Circulation: 8,000 per issue (paid). **Owner(s):** Kirkland Newspapers, See address and contact information above. **Management:** Bob Wallack, Publisher. Leslie Bull, Advertising. **Editorial:** Abbie Nixon, Editor.

LUBEC

LUBEC LIGHT, THE. 43 S. Lubec Rd., Lubec, ME 04652. Telephone: 207-733-2939. FAX: 207-733-2847. E-MAIL: lubeclight@rmcl.org. Year Established: 1991. Pub. Frequency: m. (Thu.) Page Size: tabloid. Subscrip. Rate: $1 newsstand/cover; $20/yr in county; $25/yr out of county; $28/yr mailed out of state. Adv. Rate: col. inch $5 Circulation: 1,000 per issue (paid). **Owner(s):** Regional Medical Center at Lubec, See address and contact information above. **Management:** Jill Belt, General Manager. John MacCarthy, Advertising Manager. **Editorial:** Robin Gautier, Editor.

MACHIAS

COUNTY WIDE. 26 Main St, Machias, ME 04654-0497. Telephone: 207-753-0919. E-MAIL: countywidenews@hotmail.com. URL: http://www.mainemagazine.com. Mailing Address: PO Box 497, Machias, ME 04654-0497. Year Established: 1977. Pub. Frequency: w. (Mon.) Page Size: tabloid. Subscrip. Rate: $28/yr. Circulation: 4,400 per issue (paid and free). **Owner(s):** County Wide Communications, Inc., See address and contact information above. **Management:** Bob Berta, Publisher. Joan Casey, Advertising. **Editorial:** Lester J Reynolds, Editor.

MADAWASKA

ST. JOHN VALLEY TIMES. 160 Main St., Madawaska, ME 04756. Telephone: 207-728-3336. FAX: 207-728-3825. E-MAIL: publisher@sjvalley-times.com. Mailing Address: PO Box 419, Madawaska, ME 04756. Year Established: 1957. Pub. Frequency: w. (Wed.) Page Size: tabloid. Subscrip. Rate: $.90 newsstand/cover; $48/yr. Circulation: 6,550 per issue (controlled and free). **Owner(s):** Walls Newspapers, Inc., 525 Office Park Dr., Birmingham, AL 35223. Telephone: 205-870-1684. **Management:** Don Levesque, Publisher. Denise Cote, Advertising Manager. Myra A. Tardie, Circulation Manager. **Editorial:** Don Levesque, Managing Editor. Don Arnold, Sports.

MILLINOCKET

KATAHDIN TIMES. ISSN 1064-0657
202 Penobscot Ave., Millinocket, ME 04462. Telephone: 207-723-8118. FAX: 207-723-4434. E-MAIL: editor@kattimes.com. Year Established: 1976. Pub. Frequency: w. (Tue.) Page Size: broadsheet. Subscrip. Rate: $.70 newsstand/cover; $34/yr in county; $41/yr in state; $48/yr out of state. Circulation: 3,600 per issue (paid and free). **Owner(s):** David S. & Marlene Henley, PO Box 304, Houlton, ME 04730. Telephone: 506-328-8863. **Management:** David S. Henley, Publisher. Christine Parker, Advertising Manager. **Editorial:** Benjamin D Hutchins, Editor-in-Chief.

NEW GLOUCESTER

NEW GLOUCESTER NEWS. 379 Intervale Rd., New Gloucester, ME 04260-0102. Telephone: 207-926-4036. FAX: 207-926-4034. E-MAIL: ngnews@aol.com. URL: http://www.newgloucesternews.com. Mailing Address: P.O. Box 102, New Gloucester, ME 04260-0102. Year Established: 1972. Pub. Frequency: w. (Sat.) Page Size: standard. Subscrip. Rate: $35/yr out of state. Circulation: 3,500 per issue (paid and free). **Owner(s):** New Gloucester News Inc., See address and contact information above. **Management:** Jackie Rybeck, Advertising Manager. **Editorial:** Amy Green, Editor.

NEWCASTLE

LINCOLN COUNTY NEWS. Mills Rd., Newcastle, ME 04553-0520. Telephone: 207-563-3171. FAX: 207-563-3127. E-MAIL: lcn@lincoln.midcoast.com. URL: http://www.mainelincolncountynews.com. Year Established: 1875. Pub. Frequency: w. (Thu.) Page Size: broadsheet. Subscrip. Rate: $.40 newsstand/cover; $18.50/yr in county; $24.50/yr out of county. Adv. Rate: col. inch $6.25 Circulation: 8,000 per issue (paid). **Owner(s):** Lincoln County Publishing Co., Inc., PO Box 36, Damariscotta, ME 04543. Telephone: 207-563-3171. FAX: 207-563-3127. **Management:** Christopher A. Roberts, Publisher. **Editorial:** Judi Finn, Editor.

NORWAY

ADVERTISER-DEMOCRAT. 1 Pikes Hill, Norway, ME 04268. Telephone: 207-743-7011. FAX: 207-743-2256. E-MAIL: arena@advertiserdemocrat.com. URL: http://www.advertiserdemocrat.com. Mailing Address: P.O. Box 269, Norway, ME 04268. Year Established: 1824. Pub. Frequency: w. (Thu.) Page Size: standard. Subscrip. Rate: $.50 newsstand/cover; $17.50 for 6 mos. in county. Adv. Rate: col. inch $5.80 Freelance Pay: $25/story. Circulation: 7,100 per issue (paid). **Owner(s):** James Newspapers, Inc., See address and contact information above. **Editorial:** Susan Arena, Editor.

OLD TOWN

PENOBSCOT TIMES. 266 Main St., Old Town, ME 04468. Telephone: 207-827-4451. FAX: 207-827-2280. E-MAIL: penobtimes@midmaine.com. Year Established: 1891. Pub. Frequency: w. (Thu.) Page Size: tabloid. Subscrip. Rate: $.75 newsstand/cover; $24/yr in county; $39/yr out of county. Freelance Pay: $15/story. Circulation: 4,000 per issue (paid). **Owner(s):** Penobscot Times, Inc., See address and contact information above. **Editorial:** Rick Redmond, Editor. Lynn Higgins, Managing Editor.

PRESQUE ISLE

STAR-HERALD (PRESQUE ISLE), THE. PO Box 510, Presque Isle, ME 04769. Telephone: 207-768-4471. FAX: 207-764-7585. E-MAIL: starherald@nepublish.com. Year Established: 1871. Pub. Frequency: w. (Wed.) Page Size: broadsheet. Subscrip. Rate: $.75 newsstand/cover; $39/yr in county; $48.80/yr in state; $50.60/yr mailed out of state. Circulation: 7,000 per issue (paid). **Owner(s):** Northeast Publishing Co., See address and contact information above. **Management:** John Bishop, Publisher. Jim Berry, Advertising Manager. **Editorial:** Mark Putnam, Executive Editor. Kevin Sjoberg, Sports Editor.

RANGELEY

RANGELEY HIGHLANDER. PO Box 542, Rangeley, ME 04970. Telephone: 207-864-3756. FAX: 207-864-2447. E-MAIL: info@therangeleyhighlander.com. Year Established: 1953. Pub. Frequency: s-m. (Fri.) Page Size: broadsheet. Subscrip. Rate: $.95 newsstand/cover; $24/yr. Adv. Rate: col. inch $9.75 Circulation: 1,350 per issue (paid). **Owner(s):** Kevin and Amy Bree, See address and contact information above. **Management:** Amy Bree, Publisher. **Editorial:** James Bree, Editor. Amy Bree, Managing Editor.

ROCKLAND

COURIER GAZETTE. 301 Park St., Rockland, ME 04841. Telephone: 207-594-4401. FAX: 207-596-6981. URL: http://www.mainecoastnow.com/#cg. Year Established: 1846. Pub. Frequency: w. (Fri.) Page Size: broadsheet. Subscrip. Rate: $.75 newsstand/cover for Tue.; $1 newsstand/cover for Thu. & Sat.; $13.50/mo. in state; $98/yr in state; $110/yr out of state. Circulation: 4,000 per issue (paid). **Owner(s):** Courier Publications, See address and contact information above. **Management:** Diane Norton, Group Publisher. Peter Lynch, Advertising Director. Donna Culbertson, Circulation Director. **Editorial:** Steve Betts, News Editor.

COURIER-GAZETTE, THE. 301 Park St., Rockland, ME 04841. Telephone: 207-594-4401. FAX: 207-596-6981. E-MAIL: cgmail@courierpub.com. URL: http://www.courierpub.com. Year Established: 1846. Pub. Frequency: 3/w. (Tue., Thu., Sat.) Page Size: broadsheet. Subscrip. Rate: $.75 newsstand/cover; $12.50/mo. in state; $94.25/yr; $14 mailed/mo. out of state; $117.95/yr mailed. Circulation: 9,145 per issue (paid). **Owner(s):** Courier Publications, See address and contact information above. **Management:** Diane Norton, Group Publisher. Peter Lynch, Advertising Director. Cathy McDonald, Advertising Manager. Donna Culbertson, Circulation Director. **Editorial:** Steve Betts, News Editor.

FREE PRESS (ROCKLAND), THE. 6 Leland St., Rockland, ME 04841-3016. Telephone: 207-596-0055. FAX: 207-596-6698. E-MAIL: freepress@freepressonline.com. URL: http://www.freepressonline.com/. Year Established: 1985. Pub. Frequency: w. (Thu) Page Size: tabloid. Subscrip. Rate: $52/yr. Adv. Rate: col. inch $9.95 Circulation: 11,000 per issue (free). **Owner(s):** Reade F. Brower, See address and contact information above. **Management:** Alice McFadden, Publisher. Steve Davis, Advertising Manager. **Editorial:** Patricia Poe, Editor. Contact: Steve Davis, Advertising Manager. Contact: Steve Davis, Advertising Manager.

RUMFORD

RUMFORD FALLS TIMES. 81 Canal St., Rumford, ME 04276. Telephone: 207-364-7893. FAX: 207-369-0170. E-MAIL: rfttimes@gwi.net. URL: http://www.rumfordfallstimes.com. Mailing Address: PO Box 490, Rumford, ME 04276. Pub. Frequency: w. (Wed.) Page Size: broadsheet. Subscrip. Rate: $.50 newsstand/cover; $30/yr in county; $36/yr northern New England; $44/yr western New England. Adv. Rate: col. inch $5.80 Circulation: 5,000 per issue (paid). **Owner(s):** James Newspapers, Bridge St., Norway, ME 04268. Telephone: 207-743-8996. FAX: 207-743-2256. **Management:** Bruce Farrin Jr., General Manager. **Editorial:** Bruce Farrin Jr., Editor.

SANFORD

SANFORD NEWS. ISSN 1090-8293
835 Main St., Sanford, ME 04073. Telephone: 207-324-5986. FAX: 207-490-1431. E-MAIL: news@sanfordnews.com. Mailing Address: PO Box D, Sanford, ME 04073. Year Established: 1980. Pub. Frequency: w. (Thu.) Page Size: broadsheet. Subscrip. Rate: $.50 newsstand/cover; $18.20/yr home delivery. Adv. Rate: col. inch $11.88 Circulation: 6,500 per issue (paid). **Owner(s):** George J. Foster Co., See address and contact information above. **Management:** Kristan Robinson, Advertising Manager. **Editorial:** Ann Fisher, Editor.

SOUTH WATERFORD

BEAR FACTS OF MAINE, INC., THE. Sweden Hill Rd., South Waterford, ME 04081. Telephone: 207-583-2851. FAX: 207-583-4637. E-MAIL: editor@bearfactsme.com. URL: http://www.bearfactsme.com. Mailing Address: PO Box 718, Norway, ME 04268-0718. Year Established: 1986. Pub. Frequency: s-m. (1st and 3rd Mon.) Page Size: tabloid. Subscrip. Rate: $2.50 newsstand/cover; $27/yr. Freelance Pay: $0.30/column-inch. Circulation: 40,000 per issue (free). **Owner(s):** Stanley & Diana Wright, PO Box 718, Norway, ME 04268. Telephone: 207-583-2851. FAX: 207-583-4637. **Management:** John Wright, General Manager. Diana D. Taylor-Wright, Publisher. Lee Wright, Circulation Director. Stan Wright, Classified Adv. Mgr.. **Editorial:** Ken Wright, Editor.

STONINGTON

ISLAND AD-VANTAGES. 69 Main St., Stonington, ME 04681-0036. Telephone: 207-367-2200. FAX: 207-367-6397. E-MAIL: ia@penobscotbaypress.com. URL: http://www.penobscotbaypress.com. Mailing Address: PO Box 36, Stonington, ME 04681-0036. Year Established: 1934. Pub. Frequency: w. (Thu.) Page Size: tabloid. Subscrip. Rate: $.70 newsstand/cover; $27.95/yr in state; $39.95/yr out of state. Adv. Rate: col. inch $9.50 Freelance Pay: $1.50/column-inch. Circulation: 2,600 per issue (paid). **Owner(s):** Penobscot Bay Press, PO Box 36, Stonington, ME 04681. Telephone: 207-367-2200. FAX: 207-367-6397. **Management:** R. Nathaniel W. Barrows, Publisher. **Editorial:** R. Nathaniel W. Barrows, Editor.

WESTBROOK

AMERICAN JOURNAL (WESTBROOK). 910Main St, Westbrook, ME 04092. Telephone: 207-854-2577. FAX: 207-854-0018. URL: http://www.keepmecurrent.com. Year Established: 1950. Pub. Frequency: w. (Wed.) Page Size: tabloid. Subscrip. Rate: $.50 newsstand/cover; $25/yr; $44 for 2 yrs.. Adv. Rate: col. inch $13.50 Circulation: 6,600 per issue (paid and free). **Owner(s):** Lee Hews Cassler., See address and contact information above. **Management:** Lee Hews Cassler, Publisher. **Editorial:** Brendan Moran, Editor.

WISE GUIDE, THE. 538 Main St., Westbrook, ME 04092. Telephone: 207-856-5655. FAX: 207-856-5688. Pub. Frequency: w. (Mon.) Page Size: broadsheet.Adv. Rate: col. inch $10 Circulation: 30,000 per issue (free). **Owner(s):** Paula Theriault, See address and contact information above. **Management:** Dee Batista, Owner. **Editorial:** Dee Batista, Editor.

WISCASSET

WISCASSET NEWSPAPER. 47 Gardiner Rd., Wiscasset, ME 04578. Telephone: 207-882-6355. FAX: 207-882-4280. E-MAIL: wiscassetnewspaper@verizon.net. URL: http://wiscassetnewspaper.maine.com. Mailing Address: PO Box 429, Wiscasset, ME 04578-0429. Year Established: 1969. Pub. Frequency: w. (Thu.) Page Size: broadsheet. Subscrip. Rate: $.50 newsstand/cover; $25/yr in county; $35/yr out of county. Adv. Rate: col. inch $9.06 Circulation: 1,300 per issue (paid). **Owner(s):** Maine-OK Enterprises, Inc., PO Box 357, Boothbay Harbor, ME 04538-0357. Telephone: 207-633-4620. FAX: 207-633-7123. **Management:** Marylouise Cowan, Publisher. Kathy Frizzell, Advertising. Patricia Schmid, Business Manager. **Editorial:** Paula Gibbs, Editor. Mary Brewer, Managing Editor.

YARMOUTH

NOTES, THE. 33 Yarmouth Crossing Dr., Yarmouth, ME 04096. Telephone: 207-846-4112. URL: http://www.thenotes.org. Mailing Address: PO Box 905, Yarmouth, ME 04906. Year Established: 1952. Pub. Frequency: w. (Tue.) Page Size: tabloid.Adv. Rate: col. inch $7.50 Circulation: 1,600 per issue (free). **Owner(s):** Andrew & Mark LaBrie, 33 Yarmouth Crossing Dr., Yarmouth, ME 04096-1307. Telephone: 207-846-3321. **Management:** Andrew LaBrie, Publisher. Mark LaBrie, Advertising. Cathi Landry, Classified Adv. Mgr.. **Editorial:** Alyssa Barker, News Editor.

MARYLAND

ABERDEEN

BARGAINEER, THE. 214 W. Bel Air Ave., Aberdeen, MD 21001. Telephone: 410-272-3131. FAX: 410-272-4208. URL: http://www.chespub.com. Mailing Address: PO Box 190, Aberdeen, MD 21001. Year Established: 1975. Pub. Frequency: w. (Mon.) Page Size: broadsheet Circulation: 45,000 per issue (free). **Owner(s):** Chesapeake Publishing Corp., 29088 Airpark Dr., Easton, MD 21601. FAX: 410-770-4019, 410-770-4012. **Management:** Claudia Nimmo, General Manager.

ANNAPOLIS

NEW BAY WEEKLY. 1629 Forest Dr, Annapolis, MD 21403. Telephone: 410-626-9999. FAX: 410-626-0008. E-MAIL: lisa@bayweekly.com. URL: http://www.bayweekly.com. Year Established: 1993. Pub. Frequency: w. (Thu.) Page Size: tabloid. Subscrip. Rate: $75/yr mailed 1st class. Adv. Rate: col. inch $30 Circulation: 20,000 per issue (free). **Owner(s):** New Bay Enterprises, Inc., See address and contact information above. **Management:** Alex Knoll, Chief Executive Ofc. . Bill Lambrecht, Publisher. Lisa Knoll, Marketing. **Editorial:** Sandra O. Martin, Editor.Readers: Chesapeake Bay region

SOUTH COUNTY GAZETTE. 2000 Capital Dr., Annapolis, MD 21401. Telephone: 410-268-5000. FAX: 410-280-5953. Pub. Frequency: w. (Thu.) Page Size: standard Circulation: 10,000 per issue (free). **Owner(s):** Capital Gazette Newspapers, Inc., See address and contact information above. **Management:** James B. Brown, Publisher. Bernie Hoff, Advertising Director. John R. Bieberich, Circulation Director. Kim Welty, Classified Adv. Mgr.. **Editorial:** Roxanne Powell, Editor.

WEST COUNTY GAZETTE. 2000 Capital Dr., Annapolis, MD 21401. URL: http://www.hometownannapolis.com. Pub. Frequency: w. (Thu.) Page Size: standard Circulation: 15,000 per issue (free). **Owner(s):** Capital Gazette Newspapers, Inc., See address and contact information above. **Management:** James B. Brown, Publisher. Bernie Hoff, Advertising Director. John R. Bieberich, Circulation Director. Kim Welty, Classified Adv. Mgr.. **Editorial:** Roxanne Powell, Editor.

APG

A P G NEWS. APG Public Affairs Office, Bldg 2201 AMSSB-GIM-P, APG, MD 21005-5001. Telephone: 410-278-1150. FAX: 410-278-2570. E-MAIL: editor@usag.apg.army.mil. URL: http://www.apgnews.apg.army.mil. Year Established: 1856. Pub. Frequency: w. (Thu.) Page Size: broadsheet Circulation: 8,900 per issue (free). **Owner(s):** Homestead Publishing Co., 10 Hays St., Bel Air, MD 21014-0189. Telephone: 410-838-4400. FAX: 410-838-7867. **Editorial:** Debi Horne, Editor.

BALTIMORE

ARBUTUS TIMES. ISSN 0748-5271
757 Frederick Rd., Ste. 103, Baltimore, MD 21228. Telephone: 410-788-4500. FAX: 410-788-4103. URL: http://www.arbutustimes.com. Year Established: 1961. Pub. Frequency: w. (Wed.) Page Size: tabloid.Subscrip. Rate: $.50 newsstand/cover; $20.95/yr Circulation: 4,820 per issue (paid). **Owner(s):** Patuxent Publishing Co., 10750 Little Patuxent Pkwy., Columbia, MD 21044. Telephone: 410-730-3620. FAX: 410-715-9631. **Management:** Jim Quimby, Publisher. Heather Deitrich, Advertising Manager. Pat Harrington, Circulation Manager. Dotty Daub, Marketing Director. **Editorial:** Keith Meisel, Editor. Kenneth Weiss, Managing Editor. Craig Clary, Sports.

AVENUE NEWS, THE. 442 Eastern Ave., Baltimore, MD 21221. Telephone: 410-687-7775. FAX: 410-687-7881. E-MAIL: aveeditorial@chespub.com. URL: http://www.chespub.com. Mailing Address: PO Box 7889, Baltimore, MD 21221. Year Established: 1974. Pub. Frequency: w. (Thu.) Page Size: tabloid Circulation: 65,000 per issue (free). **Owner(s):** Chesapeake Publishing Corp., 29088 Airpark Dr., Easton, MD 21601. FAX: 410-770-4012. **Management:** Jeffrey Mezzatesta, Publisher. Terry Crawford, Advertising Director. **Editorial:** Jean Flanaghan, Editor. Patrick Wagner, Entertainment Editor.

BALTIMORE CITY PAPER. 812 Park Ave., Baltimore, MD 21201. Telephone: 410-523-2300. FAX: 410-523-2222. E-MAIL: amarkowitz@citypaper.com. URL: http://www.citypaper.com. Year Established: 1977. Pub. Frequency: w. (Wed.) Page Size: tabloid.Subscrip. Rate: $75/yr mailed Circulation: 90,000 per issue (free). **Owner(s):** Times-Shamrock Communications, 149 Penn Ave,, Scranton, PA 18503. **Management:** Don Farley, Publisher. Jennifer Marsh, Advertising Director. Christine Grabowski, Circulation Manager. **Editorial:** Lee Gardner, Editor. Jess Harvell, Music Editor. Erin Sullivan, News Editor.

BALTIMORE GUIDE, THE. 526 S. Conkling St., Baltimore, MD 21224. Telephone: 410-732-6600. FAX: 410-732-6336. E-MAIL: rbpublisher@ebguide.com. URL: http://www.baltimoreguide.com. Year Established: 1927. Pub. Frequency: w. (Wed.) Page Size: tabloid. Subscrip. Rate: $.25 newsstand/cover; $20/yr southeast edition only. **Wire Service(s):** AP. Circulation: 42,000 per issue (controlled and free). **Owner(s):** R & B Publishing Co., See address and contact information above. **Management:** Richard W. Sandza, President. Claudia Picarello, Office Manager. Fran Schuyler, Advertising. **Editorial:** Jacqueline Watts, Editor.

BALTIMORE TIMES. 2513 N. Charles St., Baltimore, MD 21218. Telephone: 410-366-3900. FAX: 410-243-1627. E-MAIL: btimes@btimes.com. URL: http://www.baltimoretimes-online.com. Year Established: 1986. Pub. Frequency: w. (Fri.) Page Size: tabloid Circulation: 32,000 per issue (free). **Owner(s):** Joy Bramble, See address and contact information above. **Management:** Joy Bramble, Publisher. Donnie Manuel, Advertising Director. **Editorial:** Joy Bramble, Managing Editor.

CATONSVILLE TIMES. ISSN 0748-5263
757 Frederick Rd., Ste. 103, Baltimore, MD 21228. Telephone: 410-788-4500. FAX: 410-788-4103. URL: http://www.catonsvilletimes.com. Year Established: 1881. Pub. Frequency: w. (Wed.) Page Size: tabloid. Subscrip. Rate: $.50 newsstand/cover; $20.95/yr in state; $25/yr out of state. Circulation: 8,630 per issue (paid and free). **Owner(s):** Patuxent Publishing Co., 10750 Little Patuxent Pkwy., Columbia, MD 21044. Telephone: 410-730-3990. FAX: 410-730-7053. **Management:** Jim Quimby, Publisher. Heather Deitrich, Advertising Manager. Phil Baldyga, Circulation Manager. Shirlanda Braxton, Classified Adv. Mgr.. Dotty Daub, Marketing Director. **Editorial:** Keith Meisel, Editor. Kenneth Weiss, Managing Editor. Craig Clary, Sports.

DUNDALK EAGLE, THE. 4 N. Center Pl., Baltimore, MD 21222. Telephone: 410-288-6060. FAX: 410-288-2712. E-MAIL: info@dundalkeagle.com. URL: http://www.dundalkeagle.net. Mailing Address: P.O. Box 8936, Dundalk, MD 21222. Year Established: 1969. Pub. Frequency: w. (Thu.) Page Size: tabloid. Subscrip. Rate: $.25 newsstand/cover; $14.84/yr local; $25/yr out of city. Circulation: 21,000 per issue (paid). **Owner(s):** Dundalk Eagle, The, See address and contact information above. **Management:** Mary G. Oelke, Publisher. Kim Boone, Advertising Manager. Deborah Cornely, Associate Publisher. **Editorial:** Wayne Laufert, Managing Editor.

OWINGS MILLS TIMES. 409 Washington Ave., Baltimore, MD 21204. Telephone: 410-337-2400. FAX: 410-337-2490. URL: http://www.owingsmillstimes.com. Year Established: 1986. Pub. Frequency: w. (Thu.) Page Size: tabloid. Subscrip. Rate: $.50 newsstand/cover. Circulation: 35,925 per issue (paid and free). **Owner(s):** Patuxent Publishing Co./ The Tribune Co., 10750 Little Patuxent Pkwy., Columbia, MD 21044. Telephone: 410-730-3620. **Management:** Jim Quimby, Publisher. **Editorial:** Janice Jewell, Editor. Ken Weiss, Managing Editor. Nelson Coffin, Sports Editor.

SOUTH BALTIMORE GUIDE. 526 S. Conkling St., Baltimore, MD 21224. Telephone: 410-732-6600. FAX: 410-732-6336. E-MAIL: rbpublisher@ebguide.com. URL: http://www.ebguide.com. Year Established: 1998. Pub. Frequency: w. (Wed.) Page Size: tabloid. Subscrip. Rate: $20/yr. **Wire Service(s):** AP. Circulation: 25,000 per issue (controlled and free). **Owner(s):** R & B Publishing Co., See address and contact information above. **Management:** Richard W. Sandza, President. Claudia Picarello, Office Manager. Fran Schuyler, Advertising. **Editorial:** Jacqueline Watts, Editor.

BEL AIR

AEGIS, THE. 10 Hays St., Bel Air, MD 21014. Telephone: 410-838-4400. FAX: 410-638-0357. E-MAIL: news@theaegis.com. URL: http://www.theaegis.com. Mailing Address: PO Box 189, Bel Air, MD 21014. Year Established: 1856. Pub. Frequency: w. (Wed. & Fri.) Page Size: broadsheet. Subscrip. Rate: $.75 newsstand/cover; $40/yr in county. Circulation: 60,000 per issue (paid). **Owner(s):** Tribune Company, 435 N Michigan Ave, Chicago, IL 60601. Telephone: 312.222.9100. **Management:** Jim Quimby, President. John D. Worthington, Publisher. Marianne Pfeffer, Advertising Manager. **Editorial:** Ted Hendricks, Executive Editor. Allan Vought, Managing Editor. Jim Kennedy, Copy Editor. Kathleen Gran, Feature Editor. Erika Compton, News Editor. Randy McRoberts, Sports.

TERRAPIN TIMES, THE. PO Box 993, Bel Air, MD 21014-0993. Telephone: 301-656-8257. FAX: 301-530-7704. URL: http://www.terrapintimes.com. Pub. Frequency: bi-w. Subscrip. Rate: $9.95/mo.; $99.95 per academic year. Circulation: 20,000 per issue (paid). **Owner(s):** Cavanaugh Publishing Inc., See address and contact information above.

WEEKENDER (BEL AIR), THE. 10 Hays St., Bel Air, MD 21014-0189. Telephone: 410-838-4400. FAX: 410-638-0357. URL: http://www.theaegis.com/weekender.htm. Mailing Address: P.O. Box 189, Bel Air, MD 21014. Year Established: 1985. Pub. Frequency: w. (Fri.) Page Size: tabloid Circulation: 91,650 per issue (free). **Owner(s):** Homestead Publishing Co., See address and contact information above. **Management:** Jim Quimby, President. John Worthington IV, Publisher. Marianne Pfeffer, Advertising Director. Frank Schwind, Circulation Manager. **Editorial:** Kathleen Gran, Editor. Ted Hendricks, Executive Editor.

BOWIE

BOWIE BLADE-NEWS. 6000 Laurel-Bowie Rd., Ste. 101, Bowie, MD 20715. Telephone: 301-262-3700. FAX: 301-262-7314. E-MAIL: letters@bladenews.com. URL: http://www.bowieblade.com. Mailing Address: PO Box 770, Bowie, MD 20718. Year Established: 1958. Pub. Frequency: w. (Thu.) Page Size: standard. Subscrip. Rate: $52/yr mailed. **Wire Service(s):** AP. Circulation: 25,000 per issue (free). **Owner(s):** Capital Gazette Newspapers, Inc., 2000 Capital Dr., Annapolis, MD 21401. Telephone: 301-261-2200. **Management:** John Rouse, General Manager. Toni Adams, Advertising Manager. Carla Wetzel, Circulation Manager. **Editorial:** John Rouse, Editor. Jacob Linger, Sports Editor.

CROFTON NEWS-CRIER. 6000 Laurel-Bowie Rd., Ste. 101, Bowie, MD 20715. Telephone: 301-262-3700. FAX: 301-262-3714. E-MAIL: rpowell@croftoncrier.com. URL: http://www.capitalonline.com. Mailing Address: PO Box 770, Bowie, MD 20718. Year Established: 1972. Pub. Frequency: w. (Thu.) Page Size: standard Circulation: 10,200 per issue (free). **Owner(s):** Capital Gazette Newspapers, Inc., 2000 Capital Dr., Annapolis, MD 21401. Telephone: 301-261-2200. FAX: 410-268-4543. **Management:** James B. Brown, Publisher. Bernie Hoff, Advertising Director. Kim Welty, Classified Adv. Mgr.. **Editorial:** Roxanne Powell, Editor.

BRUNSWICK

BRUNSWICK CITIZEN. 101 W. Potomac St., Brunswick, MD 21716. Telephone: 301-834-7722. Year Established: 1974. Pub. Frequency: w. (Thu.) Page Size: tabloid. Subscrip. Rate: $.35 newsstand/cover; $13.50/yr in county. Circulation: 3,500 per issue (paid). **Owner(s):** Citizen Communications, Inc., See address and contact information above. **Management:** Peter Maynard, Publisher. **Editorial:** Julia Maynard, Editor.

MIDDLETOWN VALLEY CITIZEN. ISSN 1056-7674
101 W. Potomac St., Brunswick, MD 21716. Telephone: 301-834-7722. E-MAIL: citizen@mit.net. Year Established: 1990. Pub. Frequency: w. (Thu.) Page Size: tabloid.Subscrip. Rate: $.35 newsstand/cover; $13.50/yr Circulation: 1,400 per issue (paid). **Owner(s):** Citizen Communications, Inc., See address and contact information above. **Management:** Julia Maynard, Publisher. **Editorial:** Julia Maynard, Editor.

CALIFORNIA

ENTERPRISE (LEXINGTON PARK), THE. 23125 Camden Way, California, MD 20619. Telephone: 301-862-2111. FAX: 301-737-1665. E-MAIL: dmorgan@somdnews.com. URL: http://www.somdnews.com. Mailing Address: PO Box 700, Lexington Park, MD 20653. Year Established: 1883. Pub. Frequency: s-w. (Wed. & Fri.) Page Size: broadsheet. Subscrip. Rate: $.75 newsstand/cover; $39.90/yr. Circulation: 19,000 per issue (paid and free). **Owner(s):** Washington Post Co., 1150 15th St., N.W., Washington, DC 20071-0001. Telephone: 202-334-6000. **Management:** Karen Acton, Publisher. Ron Notter, Circulation Manager. Pauline Cardello, Classified Adv. Mgr.. Al Dailey, Associate Publisher. **Editorial:** Rick Boyd, Editor. Donnie Morgan, Managing Editor. Susan Craton, Community Editor. Kayvon Pourmand, Sports Editor.Readers: St. Mary's County; Southern Maryland

ST. MARY'S TODAY. PO Box 689, California, MD 20619-0689. Telephone: 301-535-8624. E-MAIL: staff@stmarystoday.com. URL: http://www.stmarystoday.com. Year Established: 1989. Pub. Frequency: w. (Sun.) Page Size: tabloid. Subscrip. Rate: $43.16/yr. Adv. Rate: col. inch $10 Circulation: 6,000 per issue (paid). **Owner(s):** Kenneth Rossignol, See address and contact information above. **Management:** Kenneth Rossignol, Publisher. Pat Martone, Advertising Manager. **Editorial:** Kenneth Rossignol, Editor.

CAMBRIDGE

DORCHESTER STAR. 535 Poplar St, Cambridge, MD 21613. Telephone: 410-228-0222. FAX: 410-228-0685. URL: http://www.dorchesterstar.com. Mailing Address: PO Box 176, Cambridge, MD 21613. Year Established: 1867. Pub. Frequency: w. (Fri.) Page Size: broadsheet Circulation: 12,500 per issue (free). **Owner(s):** Chesapeake Publishing Corp., 29088 Airpark Dr., Easton, MD 21601. FAX: 410-770-4019, 410-770-4012. **Management:** Larry Effingham, Publisher. Paul Myers, Advertising Manager. Louis Walls, Circulation Director. **Editorial:** Gail Dean, Editor.

CENTREVILLE

RECORD-OBSERVER. 114 Broadway, Centreville, MD 21617. Telephone: 410-758-1400. FAX: 410-758-1701. URL: http://www.chespub.com. Year Established: 1864. Pub. Frequency: w. (Fri.) Page Size: broadsheet. Subscrip. Rate: $.50 newsstand/cover; $27.95/yr home delivery in county; $45/yr mailed in county. Circulation: 3,500 per issue (paid). **Owner(s):** Chesapeake Publishing Corp., 29088 Airpark Dr., Easton, MD 21601. FAX: 410-770-4019, 410-770-4012. **Management:** Larry Effingham, Publisher. Louis Walls, Circulation Director. David Fike, Marketing Director. **Editorial:** Janice Colvin, Editor.

CHESTERTOWN

KENT COUNTY NEWS. 217 High St., Chestertown, MD 21620. Telephone: 410-778-2011. FAX: 410-778-6522. E-MAIL: jvotel@cpc.chespub.com. URL: http://www.thekentcountynews.com. Mailing Address: PO Box 30, Chestertown, MD 21620-0030. Year Established: 1793. Pub. Frequency: w. (Thu.) Page Size: broadsheet. Subscrip. Rate: $.50 newsstand/cover; $27.95/yr in county; $47.95/yr out of county. Circulation: 8,500 per issue (paid). **Owner(s):** Chesapeake Publishing Corp., 29088 Airpark Dr., Easton, MD 21601. FAX: 410-770-4019, 410-770-4012. **Management:** Mary Burton, General Manager. Liz Meekins, Advertising Director. Katherine McLaughlin, Circulation Manager. **Editorial:** Kevin Hemstock, Editor.

TIDEWATER TRADER. 300 S. Cross St., Chestertown, MD 21620. Telephone: 410-778-1262. FAX: 410-778-0381. E-MAIL: traderbird@friend.ly.net. URL: http://www.tidewatertrader.com. Year Established: 1981. Pub. Frequency: w. (Wed.) Page Size: tabloid Circulation: 15,000 per issue (free). **Owner(s):** Tidewater Trader, Inc., See address and contact information above. **Management:** Carla Johnson, Publisher. Mary Helen Bowers, Advertising. George Kennedy Sr., Circulation Manager. Doris Plummer, Classified Adv. Mgr.. **Editorial:** Carla Johnson, Editor. Karen Trout Reed, Creative Director.

COLUMBIA

COLUMBIA FLIER. ISSN 0192-7841
10750 Little Patuxent Pkwy., Columbia, MD 21044. Telephone: 410-730-3990. URL: http://www.columbiaflier.com. Year Established: 1969. Pub. Frequency: w. (Thu.) Page Size: tabloid.Subscrip. Rate: $.50 newsstand/cover Circulation: 39,204 per issue (free). **Owner(s):** Patuxent Publishing Co., See address and contact information above. **Management:** Jim Quimby, Publisher. Heather Deitrich, Advertising Manager. Pat Harrington, Circulation Manager. Shirlanda Braxton, Classified Adv. Mgr.. Dotty Daub, Marketing Manager. **Editorial:** Steve Kelly, Editor. Paul Milton, Executive Editor.

HOWARD COUNTY TIMES. ISSN 0748-5298
10750 Little Patuxent Pkwy., Columbia, MD 21044. Telephone: 410-730-3620, 410-730-3990. FAX: 410-730-7053, 410-715-9631. E-MAIL: circulation@patuxent.com. URL: http://www.howardcountytimes.com. Year Established: 1979. Pub. Frequency: w. (Thu.) Page Size: tabloid. Subscrip. Rate: $.50 newsstand/cover; $24.95/yr mailed in county. Circulation: 20,528 per issue (paid). **Owner(s):** Patuxent Publishing Co., See address and contact information above. **Management:** Jim Quimby, Publisher. Phil Baldyga, Circulation Manager. Shirlanda Braxton, Classified Adv. Mgr.. Dotty Daub, Marketing Director. **Editorial:** Steve Kelly, Editor.

CRISFIELD

CRISFIELD TIMES, THE. 914 W. Main St., Crisfield, MD 21817-1016. Telephone: 410-968-1188. FAX: 410-968-1197. E-MAIL: crisfieldnews@newszap.com. URL: http://www.newszap.com. Mailing Address: PO Box 230, Crisfield, MD 21817-0230. Year Established: 1889. Pub. Frequency: w. (Wed.) Page Size: broadsheet. Subscrip. Rate: $.35 newsstand/cover; $16.80/yr. Adv. Rate: col. inch $9.75 Circulation: 3,000 per issue (paid). **Owner(s):** Independent Newspapers, Inc., PO Box 737, Dover, DE 19903. Telephone: 302-674-3600. FAX: 302-674-9510. **Management:** Tamra Brittingham, Publisher. Linda Mister, Advertising. **Editorial:** Michael Pelrine, Executive Editor. Richard Crumeacker, News Editor.

DENTON

TIMES-RECORD (DENTON), THE. ISSN 0746-1658
219 Market St., Denton, MD 21629. Telephone: 410-479-1800. FAX: 410-479-3174. E-MAIL: timesrecord@chespub.com. URL: http://www.chespub.com. Mailing Address: PO Box 160, Denton, MD 21629. Year Established: 1929. Pub. Frequency: w. (Wed.) Page Size: broadsheet. Subscrip. Rate: $.50 newsstand/cover; $27.95/yr home delivery in county; $32/yr out of county; $35/yr out of state. Circulation: 3,500 per issue (paid). **Owner(s):** Chesapeake Publishing Corp., 29088 Airpark Dr., Easton, MD 21601. FAX: 410-770-4019, 410-770-4012. **Management:** Tom Bradlee, President. Larry Effingham, Publisher. Julia Millionie, Advertising Manager. **Editorial:** John Evans, Editor. Shean Venables, Sports Editor.

FREDERICK

COUNTY GLOBE, THE. 247 W. Patrick St., Frederick, MD 21701-6946. Telephone: 301-696-8301. FAX: 301-696-8302.Pub. Frequency: bi-w. Page Size: tabloid Circulation: 50,000 per issue (free). **Owner(s):** GED, Inc., See address and contact information above. **Management:** George Dredden, Publisher. Toni Bowie, Advertising Manager. **Editorial:** Earlene Thornton, Editor.

FREDERICK CITY GAZETTE. 2A N. Market St., 4th Fl., Frederick, MD 21701. Telephone: 301-846-2100. FAX: 301-846-2124. E-MAIL: jallanach@gazette.net. URL: http://www.gazette.net. Pub. Frequency: w. (Thu.) Page Size: tabloid.Adv. Rate: col. inch $20.69 Circulation: 29,505 per issue (free). **Owner(s):** Washington Post Co., 1150 15th St, N W, Washington, DC 20071. Telephone: 202-334-7100. **Management:** Jim Mannarino, Group Publisher. **Editorial:** Jeff Allanach, Managing Editor.

MIDDLETOWN/BRUNSWICK GAZETTE. 2A N. Market St., 4th Fl., Frederick, MD 21701. Telephone: 301-846-2100. FAX: 301-846-2124. E-MAIL: jallanach@gazette.net. URL: http://www.gazette.net. Pub. Frequency: w. (Thu.) Page Size: tabloid.Adv. Rate: col. inch $11.77 Circulation: 10,907 per issue (free). **Owner(s):** Washington Post Co., 1150 15th St, N W, Washington, DC 20071. Telephone: 202-334-7100. **Management:** Jim Mannarino, Group Publisher. Chuck Lyons, President. **Editorial:** Jeff Allanach, Managing Editor.

NEW MARKET/URBANA GAZETTE. 2A N. Market St., 4th Fl., Frederick, MD 21701. Telephone: 301-846-2100. FAX: 301-846-2124. E-MAIL: jallanach@gazette.net. URL: http://www.gazette.net. Pub. Frequency: w. (Thu.) Page Size: tabloid Circulation: 10,732 per issue (free). **Owner(s):** Washington Post Co., 1150 15th St, N W, Washington, DC 20071. Telephone: 202-334-6000. **Management:** Jim Mannarino, Group Publisher. Chuck Lyons, President. **Editorial:** Jeff Allanach, Managing Editor.

WALKERSVILLE/THURMONT GAZETTE. 2A N. Market St., 4th Fl., Frederick, MD 21701. Telephone: 301-846-2100. FAX: 301-846-2124. E-MAIL: jallanach@gazette.net. URL: http://www.gazette.net. Pub. Frequency: w. (Thu.) Page Size: tabloid.Adv. Rate: col. inch $11.91 Circulation: 8,001 per issue (free). **Owner(s):** Washington Post Co., 1150 15th St, N W, Washington, DC 20071. Telephone: 202-334-7100. **Management:** Jim Mannarino, Group Publisher. Chuck Lyons, President. **Editorial:** Jeff Allanach, Managing Editor.

GAITHERSBURG

ASPEN HILL GAZETTE. 1200 Quince Orchard Blvd., Gaithersburg, MD 20878. Telephone: 301-670-2073. FAX: 301-670-7183. E-MAIL: jhruz@gazette.net. URL: http://www.gazette.net. Pub. Frequency: w. (Wed..) Page Size: tabloid.Adv. Rate: col. inch $11.41 Circulation: 9,211 per issue (free). **Owner(s):** Washington Post Co., 1150 15th St, N W, Washington, DC 20071. Telephone: 202-334-6000. **Management:** Chuck Lyons, President. **Editorial:** Judy Hruz, Managing Editor.

BETHESDA GAZETTE. 1200 Quince Orchard Blvd., Gaithersburg, MD 20878. Telephone: 301-280-3120. FAX: 301-670-7183. E-MAIL: class@gazette.net. URL: http://www.gazette.net. Pub. Frequency: w. (Wed.) Page Size: tabloid.Adv. Rate: col. inch $25.40 Circulation: 6,700 per issue (free). **Owner(s):** Washington Post Co., 1150 15th St, N W, Washington, DC 20071. Telephone: 202-334-6000. **Management:** Jim Mannarino, Group Publisher. Chuck Lyons, President. **Editorial:** Joann Grbach, Managing Editor.

CHEVY CHASE GAZETTE. 1200 Quince Orchard Blvd., Gaithersburg, MD 20878. Telephone: 301-280-3120. FAX: 301-670-7183. E-MAIL: jgrbach@gazette.net. URL: http://www.gazette.net. Pub. Frequency: w. (Wed.) Page Size: tabloid.Adv. Rate: col. inch $14.89 Circulation: 5,605 per issue (free). **Owner(s):** Washington Post Co., 1150 15th St, N W, Washington, DC 20071. Telephone: 202-334-6000. **Management:** Jim Mannarino, Group Publisher. Chuck Lyons, President. **Editorial:** Joann Grbach, Managing Editor.

DAMASCUS GAZETTE. 1200 Quince Orchard Blvd., Gaithersburg, MD 20878. Telephone: 301-670-7155. FAX: 301-670-7183. E-MAIL: tmurphy@gazette.net. URL: http://www.gazette.net. Year Established: 1964. Pub. Frequency: w. (Wed.) Page Size: tabloid.Adv. Rate: col. inch $9.31 Circulation: 7,923 per issue (free). **Owner(s):** Washington Post Co., 1150 15th St, N W, Washington, DC 20071. Telephone: 202-334-6000. **Management:** Chuck Lyons, President. **Editorial:** Tammy Murphy, Editor. Brian Gnatt, Managing Editor.

FORT WASHINGTON GAZETTE. 1200 Quince Orchard Blvd., Gaithersburg, MD 20878. Telephone: 301-948-3120. FAX: 301-670-7170. E-MAIL: aslee@gazette.net. URL: http://www.gazette.net. Year Established: 1943. Pub. Frequency: w. (Thu.) Page Size: tabloid.Adv. Rate: col. inch $17.46 Circulation: 32,516 per issue (free). **Owner(s):** Washington Post Co., 1150 15th St, N W, Washington, DC 20071. Telephone: 202-334-6000. **Management:** Jim Mannarino, Group Publisher. Chuck Lyons, President. Cliff Chiet, Advertising Director. Jean Casey, Circulation Director. **Editorial:** Angela Swinson Lee, Editor.

GAITHERSBURG GAZETTE. 1200 Quince Orchard Blvd., Gaithersburg, MD 20878. Telephone: 301-670-2066. FAX: 301-670-7183. E-MAIL: lbatzler@gazette.net. URL: http://www.gazette.net. Year Established: 1959. Pub. Frequency: w. (Wed.) Page Size: tabloid.Adv. Rate: col. inch $23.96 Circulation: 42,672 per issue (free). **Owner(s):** Washington Post Co., 1150 15th St, N W, Washington, DC 20071. Telephone: 202-334-6000. **Management:** Chuck Lyons, President. **Editorial:** Lloyd Batzler, Editor.

GAZETTE (GAITHERSBURG), THE. 1200 Quince Orchard Blvd., Gaithersburg, MD 20878. Telephone: 301-948-3120. FAX: 301-670-7183. E-MAIL: lbatzler@gazette.net. URL: http://www.gazette.net. Pub. Frequency: w. (Fri.) Page Size: broadsheet. Subscrip. Rate: $.50 newsstand/cover; $26/yr in county; $32/yr out of county. Adv. Rate: col. inch $6.30 Circulation: 23,000 per issue (paid). **Owner(s):** Washington Post Co., 1150 15th St, N W, Washington, DC 20071. Telephone: 202-334-6000. **Management:** Jim Mannarino, Group Publisher. Chuck Lyons, President. Art Dwight, Advertising Director. Jean Casey, Circulation Director. **Editorial:** Lloyd Batzler, Editor. Jack Murphy, Executive Editor. Michelle LeComte, Managing Editor.

GERMANTOWN GAZETTE. 1200 Quince Orchard Blvd., Gaithersburg, MD 20878. Telephone: 301-670-7155. FAX: 301-670-7183. E-MAIL: tmurphy@gazette.net. URL: http://www.gazette.net. Pub. Frequency: w. (Wed.) Page Size: tabloid.Adv. Rate: col. inch $14.27 Circulation: 29,193 per issue (free). **Owner(s):** Washington Post Co., 1150 15th St, N W, Washington, DC 20071. Telephone: 202-334-6000. **Management:** Chuck Lyons, President. **Editorial:** Tammy Murphy, Editor. Brian Gnatt, Managing Editor.

KENSINGTON GAZETTE. 1200 Quince Orchard Blvd., Gaithersburg, MD 20878. Telephone: 301-280-3120. FAX: 301-670-7183. E-MAIL: jgrbach@gazette.net. URL: http://www.gazette.net. Pub. Frequency: w. (Wed.) Page Size: tabloid.Adv. Rate: col. inch $14.89 Circulation: 10,000 per issue (free). **Owner(s):** Washington Post Co., 1150 15th St, N W, Washington, DC 20071. Telephone: 202-334-6000. **Management:** Jim Mannarino, Group Publisher. Chuck Lyons, President. **Editorial:** Joann Grbach, Managing Editor.

MONTGOMERY VILLAGE GAZETTE. 1200 Quince Orchard Blvd., Gaithersburg, MD 20878. Telephone: 301-670-2066. FAX: 301-670-7183. E-MAIL: lbatzler@gazette.net. URL: http://www.gazette.net. Pub. Frequency: w. (Wed.) Page Size: tabloid.Adv. Rate: col. inch $23.96 Circulation: 42,000 per issue (free). **Owner(s):** Washington Post Co., 1150 15th St, N W, Washington, DC 20071. Telephone: 202-334-6000. **Management:** Jim Mannarino, Group Publisher. Chuck Lyons, President. **Editorial:** Lloyd Batzler, Editor.

NORTH POTOMAC GAZETTE. 1200 Quince Orchard Blvd., Gaithersburg, MD 20878. Telephone: 301-280-3120. FAX: 301-670-7183. E-MAIL: jgrbach@gazette.net. URL: http://www.gazette.net. Pub. Frequency: w. (Wed.) Page Size: tabloid.Adv. Rate: col. inch $15.66 Circulation: 22,661 per issue (free). **Owner(s):** Washington Post Co., 1150 15th St, N W, Washington, DC 20071. Telephone: 202-334-6000. **Management:** Jim Mannarino, Group Publisher. Chuck Lyons, President. **Editorial:** Joann Grbach, Managing Editor.

OLNEY GAZETTE. 1200 Quince Orchard Blvd., Gaithersburg, MD 20878. Telephone: 301-670-2073. FAX: 301-670-7183. E-MAIL: jhruz@gazette.net. URL: http://www.gazette.net. Pub. Frequency: w. (Wed.) Page Size: tabloid.Adv. Rate: col. inch $12.84 Circulation: 15,675 per issue (paid). **Owner(s):** Washington Post Co., 1150 15th St, N W, Washington, DC 20071. Telephone: 202-334-7100. **Management:** Chuck Lyons, President. **Editorial:** Judith Hruz, Managing Editor.

POOLESVILLE GAZETTE. 1200 Quince Orchard Blvd., Gaithersburg, MD 20878. Telephone: 301-670-7155. FAX: 301-670-7183. E-MAIL: tmurphy@gazette.net. URL: http://www.gazette.net. Pub. Frequency: w. (Wed.) Page Size: tabloid.Adv. Rate: col. inch $8.83 Circulation: 3,167 per issue (free). **Owner(s):** Washington Post Co., 1150 15th St, N W, Washington, DC 20071. Telephone: 202-334-6000. **Management:** Chuck Lyons, President. **Editorial:** Tammy Murphy, Editor. Brian Gnatt, Managing Editor.

POTOMAC GAZETTE. 1200 Quince Orchard Blvd., Gaithersburg, MD 20878. Telephone: 301-280-3120. FAX: 301-670-7183. E-MAIL: jgrbach@gazette.net. URL: http://www.gazette.net. Pub. Frequency: w. (Wed.) Page Size: tabloid.Adv. Rate: col. inch $15.66 Circulation: 22,661 per issue (free). **Owner(s):** Washington Post Co., 1150 15th St, N W, Washington, DC 20071. Telephone: 202-334-6000. **Management:** Jim Mannarino, Group Publisher. Chuck Lyons, President. **Editorial:** Joann Grbach, Managing Editor.

ROCKVILLE GAZETTE. 1200 Quince Orchard Blvd., Gaithersburg, MD 20878. Telephone: 301-670-2073. FAX: 301-670-0718. E-MAIL: jhruz@gazette.net. URL: http://www.gazette.net. Pub. Frequency: w. (Wed.) Page Size: tabloid.Adv. Rate: col. inch $21.43 Circulation: 23,390 per issue (free). **Owner(s):** Washington Post Co., 1150 15th St, N W, Washington, DC 20071. Telephone: 202-334-6000. **Management:** Chuck Lyons, President. **Editorial:** Judy Hruz, Editor.

GLEN BURNIE

MARYLAND GAZETTE. 306 Crain Hwy., S.W., Glen Burnie, MD 21061. Telephone: 410-766-3700. FAX: 410-768-5189. E-MAIL: gazstaff@annap.infi.net. URL: http://www.hometownannapolis.com. Year Established: 1727. Pub. Frequency: s-w. (Wed. & Sat.) Page Size: standard. Subscrip. Rate: $.50 newsstand/cover; $52/yr home delivery. Circulation: 34,000 per issue (paid). **Owner(s):** Capital Gazette Newspapers, Inc., 2000 Capital Dr., Annapolis, MD 21401. Telephone: 301-268-5000. **Management:** James B. Brown, Publisher. Tom Bazzell, Advertising Manager. Don Wright, Circulation Manager. **Editorial:** Rick Hutzell, Editor. Sean Burns, Sports Editor.

GREENBELT

GREENBELT NEWS REVIEW. 15 Crescent Rd., Ste. 100, Greenbelt, MD 20770-1887. Telephone: 301-474-4131. FAX: 301-474-5880. E-MAIL: newsreview@greenbelt.com. Year Established: 1937. Pub. Frequency: w. (Thu.) Page Size: tabloid. Subscrip. Rate: $35/yr mailed. Adv. Rate: col. inch $10 Circulation: 11,000 per issue (paid and free). **Owner(s):** Greenbelt Cooperative Publishing Association, Inc., See address and contact information above. **Management:** James Farnham, President. **Editorial:** Mary Lou Williamson, Editor. Elaine Skolnik, News Editor.

HANCOCK

HANCOCK NEWS. 263 Pennsylvania Ave., Hancock, MD 21750. Telephone: 301-678-6255. FAX: 301-678-5520. E-MAIL: news@hancocknews.us. Year Established: 1914. Pub. Frequency: w. (Wed.) Page Size: broadsheet. Subscrip. Rate: $.74 newsstand/cover; $21/yr in state; $23/yr out of state. Adv. Rate: col. inch $4 Circulation: 2,600 per issue (paid). **Owner(s):** Berkeley Springs Morgan Messenger, Mercer St., Berkeley Springs, WV 25411. Telephone: 304-258-1800. FAX: 304-258-8441. **Management:** Sandra Howard, Office Manager. Sandy Buzzerd, Advertising Manager. **Editorial:** J. Warren Buzzerd, Editor.

LANDOVER

BOWIE STAR. 8201 Corporate Dr., Ste.1200, Landover, MD 20785. Telephone: 301-731-2101. FAX: 301-731-2141. E-MAIL: dharrison@gazette.net. URL: http://www.gazette.net. Pub. Frequency: w. (Thu.) Page Size: tabloid.Adv. Rate: col. inch $18.81 Circulation: 23,043 per issue (free). **Owner(s):** Washington Post Co., 1150 15th St, N W, Washington, DC 20071. Telephone: 202-334-6000. **Management:** Frank Abbott, Group Publisher. Chuck Lyons, President. **Editorial:** Darren Harrison, Managing Editor.

COLLEGE PARK GAZETTE. 8201 Corporate Dr., Ste.1200, Landover, MD 20785. Telephone: 301-731-2110. FAX: 301-731-2141. E-MAIL: lgreve@gazette.net. URL: http://www.gazette.net. Pub. Frequency: w. (Thu.) Page Size: tabloid.Adv. Rate: col. inch $18.81 Circulation: 26,117 per issue (free). **Owner(s):** Washington Post Co., 1150 15th St, N W, Washington, DC 20071. Telephone: 202-334-6000. **Management:** Jim Mannarino, Group Publisher. Chuck Lyons, President. **Editorial:** Ulric Hetsberger, Managing Editor. Lee Greve, Asst. Managing Ed..

GREENBELT GAZETTE. 8201 Corporate Dr., Ste.1200, Landover, MD 20785. Telephone: 301-731-2110. FAX: 301-731-2141. E-MAIL: lgreves@gazette.net. URL: http://www.gazette.net. Pub. Frequency: w. (Thu.) Page Size: tabloid.Adv. Rate: col. inch $18.81 Circulation: 8,100 per issue (free). **Owner(s):** Washington Post Co., 1150 15th St, N W, Washington, DC 20071. Telephone: 202-334-6000. **Management:** Jim Mannarino, Group Publisher. Chuck Lyons, President. **Editorial:** Lee Greve, Asst. Managing Ed..

HYATTSVILLE/RIVERDALE GAZETTE. 8201 Corporate Dr., Ste.1200, Landover, MD 20785. Telephone: 301-731-2110. FAX: 301-731-2141. E-MAIL: wgivens@gazette.net. URL: http://www.gazette.net. Pub. Frequency: w. (Thu.) Page Size: tabloid.Adv. Rate: col. inch $18.81 Circulation: 24,296 per issue (free). **Owner(s):** Washington Post Co., 1150 15th St, N W, Washington, DC 20071. Telephone: 202-334-6000. **Management:** Jim Mannarino, Group Publisher. Chuck Lyons, President. **Editorial:** Willie Givens, Editor.

LANDOVER GAZETTE. 8201 Corporate Dr., Ste.1200, Landover, MD 20785. Telephone: 301-731-2101. FAX: 301-731-2141. E-MAIL: wgivens@gazette.net. URL: http://www.gazette.net. Pub. Frequency: w. (Thu.) Page Size: tabloid.Adv. Rate: col. inch $18.81 Circulation: 18,000 per issue (free). **Owner(s):** Washington Post Co., 1150 15th St, N W, Washington, DC 20071. Telephone: 202-334-6000. **Management:** Jim Mannarino, Group Publisher. Chuck Lyons, President. **Editorial:** Willie Givens, Editor.

LANHAM GAZETTE. 8201 Corporate Dr., Ste.1200, Landover, MD 20785. Telephone: 301-731-2101. FAX: 301-731-2141. E-MAIL: dharrison@gazette.net. URL: http://www.gazette.net. Pub. Frequency: w. (Thu.) Page Size: tabloid.Adv. Rate: col. inch $18.81 Circulation: 28,520 per issue (free). **Owner(s):** Washington Post Co., 1150 15th St, N W, Washington, DC 20071. Telephone: 202-334-6000. **Management:** Frank Abbott, Group Publisher. Chuck Lyons, President. **Editorial:** Darren Harrison, Managing Editor.

LARGO GAZETTE. 8201 Corporate Dr., Ste.1200, Landover, MD 20785. Telephone: 301-731-2101. FAX: 301-731-2141. E-MAIL: dharrison@gazette.net. URL: http://www.gazette.net. Pub. Frequency: w. (Thu.) Page Size: tabloid.Adv. Rate: col. inch $18.81 Circulation: 18,800 per issue (free). **Owner(s):** Washington Post Co., 1150 15th St, N W, Washington, DC 20071. Telephone: 202-334-6000. **Management:** Jim Mannarino, Group Publisher. Chuck Lyons, President. **Editorial:** Darren Harrison, Managing Editor.

LAUREL GAZETTE. 8201 Corporate Dr., Ste.1200, Landover, MD 20785. Telephone: 301-731-2110. FAX: 301-731-2141. E-MAIL: lgreve@gazette.net. URL: http://www.gazette.net. Pub. Frequency: w. (Thu.) Page Size: tabloid.Adv. Rate: col. inch $18.81 Circulation: 26,345 per issue (free). **Owner(s):** Washington Post Co., 1150 15th St, N W, Washington, DC 20071. Telephone: 202-334-6000. **Management:** Frank Abbott, Group Publisher. Chuck Lyons, President. **Editorial:** Ulric Hetsberger, Managing Editor. Lee Greve, Asst. Managing Ed..

NEW CARROLLTON GAZETTE. 8201 Corporate Dr., Ste.1200, Landover, MD 20785. Telephone: 301-731-2101. FAX: 301-731-2141. E-MAIL: wgivens@gazette.net. URL: http://www.gazette.net. Pub. Frequency: w. (Thu.) Page Size: tabloid.Adv. Rate: col. inch $18.81 Circulation: 26,312 per issue (free). **Owner(s):** Washington Post Co., 1150 15th St, N W, Washington, DC 20071. Telephone: 202-334-6000. **Management:** Frank Abbott, Group Publisher. Chuck Lyons, President. **Editorial:** Willie Givens, Editor.

PORT TOWNS GAZETTE. 8201 Corporate Dr., Ste.1200, Landover, MD 20785. Telephone: 301-731-2110. FAX: 301-731-2141. E-MAIL: wgivens@gazette.net. URL: http://www.gazette.net. Pub. Frequency: w. (Thu.) Page Size: tabloid.Adv. Rate: col. inch $18.81 Circulation: 10,100 per issue (free). **Owner(s):** Washington Post Co., 1150 15th St, N W, Washington, DC 20071. Telephone: 202-334-6000. **Management:** Jim Mannarino, Group Publisher. Chuck Lyons, President. **Editorial:** Willie Givens, Editor.

UPPER MARLBORO STAR. 8201 Corporate Dr., Ste.1200, Landover, MD 20785. Telephone: 301-731-2101. FAX: 301-731-2141. E-MAIL: aslee@gazette.net. URL: http://www.gazette.com. Pub. Frequency: w. (Thu.) Page Size: tabloid.Adv. Rate: col. inch $13.80 Circulation: 14,445 per issue (free). **Owner(s):** Washington Post Co., 1150 15th St, N W, Washington, DC 20071. Telephone: 202-334-6000. **Management:** Jim Mannarino, Group Publisher. Chuck Lyon, President. **Editorial:** Angela Swinson Lee, Editor. Ulric Hetsberger, Managing Editor.

LAUREL

LAUREL LEADER. ISSN 0748-528X
615 Main St., Laurel, MD 20707. Telephone: 301-725-2000. FAX: 301-317-8736. URL: http://www.laurelleader.com. Year Established: 1897. Pub. Frequency: w. (Thu.) Page Size: tabloid. Subscrip. Rate: $.50 newsstand/cover. Freelance Pay: $35/article. Circulation: 31,240 per issue (free). **Owner(s):** Patuxent Publishing Co., 10750 Little Patuxent Pkwy., Columbia, MD 21044. Telephone: 410-730-3990. FAX: 410-715-9631. **Management:** Jim Quimby, Publisher. Susan Econ, Advertising Manager. Phil Baldyga, Circulation Manager. Shirlanda Braxton, Classified Adv. Mgr.. Dotty Daub, Marketing Director. **Editorial:** Joe Murchison, Editor. Pete Pichaske, Assistant Editor. Melanie Dzwonchyk, Feature Editor.

MONTGOMERY VILLAGE

MONTGOMERY VILLAGE NEWS. 10120 Apple Ridge Rd., Montgomery Village, MD 20886-1000. Telephone: 301-948-0110. FAX: 301-869-0489. E-MAIL: mvinfo@mvf.org. URL: http://www.mvf.org. Year Established: 1968. Pub. Frequency: bi-w. (Fri.) Page Size: tabloid. Subscrip. Rate: $25/yr out of county. Circulation: 12,000 per issue (paid and free). **Owner(s):** Montgomery Village Foundation Inc., See address and contact information above. **Management:** john Zakian, Executive VP. **Editorial:** Sharon Goldberg, Executive Editor. Sharon O'Donnell, Managing Editor.

MT. AIRY

MOUNT AIRY GAZETTE. 218 S. Main St., Mt. Airy, MD 21771. Telephone: 301-831-0047. FAX: 301-829-9101. E-MAIL: dmorgan@gazette.net. URL: http://www.gazette.net. Pub. Frequency: w. (Thu.) Page Size: tabloid.Adv. Rate: col. inch $13.86 Circulation: 21,150 per issue (paid and free). **Owner(s):** Washington Post Co., 1150 15th St, N W, Washington, DC 20071. Telephone: 202-334-6000. **Management:** Jim Mannarino, Group Publisher. Chuck Lyons, President. **Editorial:** Diana Morgan, Managing Editor. Carolyne Fitzpatrick, Reporter.

SYKESVILLE/ELDERSBURG GAZETTE. 218 S. Main St., Mt. Airy, MD 21771. Telephone: 301-831-0047. FAX: 301-829-9101. E-MAIL: cblackburn@gazette.net. URL: http://www.gazette.net. Pub. Frequency: w. (Thu.) Page Size: tabloid.Adv. Rate: col. inch $12.84 Circulation: 15,000 per issue (free). **Owner(s):** Washington Post Co., 1150 15th St, N W, Washington, DC 20071. Telephone: 202-334-6000. **Management:** Jim Mannarino, Group Publisher. Chuck Lyons, President. **Editorial:** Carol Blackburn, Managing Editor. Katie Champion, Reporter.

NOTTINGHAM

TIMES-HERALD (NOTTINGHAM). 8846 Belair Rd., Nottingham, MD 21236-2401. Year Established: 1963. Pub. Frequency: bi-w. (Thu.) Page Size: tabloid. Freelance Pay: $1.50/column-inch. Circulation: 20,000 per issue (free). **Owner(s):** JRM Inc., 526 S. Conkling St., Baltimore, MD 21224. **Management:** Richard Sandza, Publisher. Jeff Harris, Advertising Manager. **Editorial:** Don Dohler, Editor.

OAKLAND

REPUBLICAN, THE. 108 S. Second St., Oakland, MD 21550. Telephone: 301-334-3963. FAX: 301-334-5904. E-MAIL: newsroom@therepublicannews.com. URL: http://www.therepublicannews.com. Mailing Address: PO Box 326, Oakland, MD 21550. Year Established: 1877. Pub. Frequency: w. (Thu.) Page Size: broadsheet. Subscrip. Rate: $.61 newsstand/cover; $23.10/yr in state; $24.50/yr out of state. Circulation: 11,500 per issue (controlled and free). **Owner(s):** Sincell Publishing Co., See address and contact information above. **Management:** Donald W. Sincell, Publisher. Lisa Rook, Advertising Manager. **Editorial:** Donald W. Sincell, Editor.

OCEAN CITY

MARYLAND BEACHCOMBER, THE. 12417 Ocean City Gateway, Ste 7, Ocean City, MD 21842. Telephone: 410-213-9442. FAX: 410-213-9458. E-MAIL: mbc@shore-source.com. Mailing Address: PO Box 479, Ocean City, MD 21843. Pub. Frequency: w. (Fri.) Page Size: tabloid.Subscrip. Rate: $150/yr mailed Circulation: 30,000 per issue (free). **Owner(s):** Gannett Company, Inc., 7950 Jones Branch Dr., McLean, VA 22107-0001. Telephone: 703-854-6000. **Management:** Connie T. Cooper, General Manager. **Editorial:** Kathi Book, Editor.

MARYLAND TIMES PRESS. 12417 Ocean City Gateway, Ste 7, Ocean City, MD 21842. Telephone: 410-213-9442. FAX: 410-213-9458. E-MAIL: mtp@shore-source.com. URL: http://www.delmarvaheadlines.com. Mailing Address: PO Box 479, Ocean City, MD 21843. Year Established: 1923. Pub. Frequency: w. (Thu.) Page Size: tabloid. Subscrip. Rate: $.25 newsstand/cover; $20/yr in county; $18.90/yr out of county. Circulation: 4,000 per issue (paid). **Owner(s):** Gannett Company, Inc., 7950 Jones Branch Dr., McLean, VA 22107-0001. Telephone: 703-854-6000. **Management:** Connie T. Cooper, General Manager. Lawrence Jock, Publisher.

OCEAN PINES INDEPENDENT. 214 16th St., Ocean City, MD 21842. Telephone: 410-289-6534. FAX: 410-289-6838. E-MAIL: scanfora@smgpo.gannett.com. Mailing Address: PO Box 479, Ocean City, MD 21843. Pub. Frequency: w. (Wed.) Page Size: tabloid Circulation: 5,200 per issue (free). **Owner(s):** Gannett Company, Inc., 7950 Jones Branch Dr, McLean, VA 22107. Telephone: 703-854-6000. **Management:** Jane Meleady, Publisher.

POCOMOKE CITY

WORCESTER COUNTY MESSENGER. 129 Market St., Pocomoke City, MD 21851. Telephone: 410-957-1700. FAX: 410-957-4314. E-MAIL: wcm@shore.intercom.net. Year Established: 1869. Pub. Frequency: w. (Wed.) Page Size: broadsheet.Subscrip. Rate: $54.60/yr mailed Circulation: 2,500 per issue (paid). **Owner(s):** Gannett Company, Inc., 7950 Jones Branch Dr., McLean, VA 22107-0001. Telephone: 703-854-6000. **Management:** Joni Silverstein, Publisher. Lindsay Ayres, Advertising Manager. **Editorial:** Bill Kerbin, Editor.

POOLESVILLE

WESTERN MONTGOMERY BULLETIN. PO Box 195, Poolesville, MD 20837-0195. Telephone: 301-972-8100. Pub. Frequency: w. (Sat.) Page Size: tabloid Circulation: 10,000 per issue (free). **Owner(s):** Stanley Janet, See address and contact information above. **Management:** Stanley Janet, Publisher. Sophie Janet, Advertising Manager. **Editorial:** Stanley Janet, Editor.

PRINCE FREDERICK

CALVERT INDEPENDENT. 424 Soloman's Island Rd., Prince Frederick, MD 20678. Telephone: 410-535-1575. FAX: 410-535-3426. Mailing Address: PO Box 910, Prince Frederick, MD 20678. Year Established: 1940. Pub. Frequency: w. (Wed.) Page Size: broadsheet. Subscrip. Rate: $.50 newsstand/cover; $19.69/yr in county; $27/yr out of county. Freelance Pay: $30/article. Circulation: 10,000 per issue (paid). **Owner(s):** News World Communications, Inc., 3600 New York Ave., N.E., Washington, DC 20002-1947. Telephone: 202-636-4841. **Management:** Charles Mister, General Manager. Sandy Worsham, Advertising Manager. Debbie Bowen, Circulation Manager.

RECORDER (PRINCE FREDERICK), THE. 134 Main St., Prince Frederick, MD 20678. Telephone: 410-535-1214. FAX: 410-535-5883. E-MAIL: jdavis@somdnews.com. URL: http://www.washingtonpost.com. Mailing Address: PO Box 485, Prince Frederick, MD 20678. Year Established: 1971. Pub. Frequency: s-w. (Wed. & Fri.) Page Size: broadsheet. Subscrip. Rate: $.50 newsstand/cover; $24.26/yr in county. Circulation: 10,000 per issue (paid). **Owner(s):** Washington Post Co., 1150 15th St., N.W., Washington, DC 20071-0001. Telephone: 202-334-6000. **Management:** Jeannie Green, General Manager. Karen Acton, Publisher. Rick Wohlfarth, Circulation Manager. Pauline Cardello, Classified Adv. Mgr.. **Editorial:** Joel Davis, Editor. Rob Perry, Managing Editor. Kevin Conron, Business Editor. Michael Reid, Sports Editor.

PRINCESS ANNE

SOMERSET HERALD. ISSN 8756-6397
11763 Somerset Ave., Princess Anne, MD 21853. Telephone: 410-651-1600. FAX: 410-651-3785. E-MAIL: herald@intercom.net. Mailing Address: PO Box 310, Princess Anne, MD 21853-0310. Year Established: 1826. Pub. Frequency: w. (Wed.) Page Size: broadsheet. Subscrip. Rate: $.50 newsstand/cover; $18.90/yr local; $31.50/yr out of area '. Circulation: 3,000 per issue (paid). **Owner(s):** Gannett Company, Inc., 7950 Jones Branch Dr., McLean, VA 22107-0001. Telephone: 703-854-6000. **Management:** Joni Silverstein, Publisher. Mickey Justice, Advertising Manager. **Editorial:** Liz Holland, Editor.

ROCKVILLE

MONTGOMERY COUNTY SENTINEL. P O Box 1272, Rockville, MD 20849. FAX: 301-838-3458. E-MAIL: editor-mc@thesentinel.com. URL: http://www.thesentinel.com. Year Established: 1855. Pub. Frequency: w. (Thu.) Page Size: tabloid.Subscrip. Rate: $.25 newsstand/cover; $21/yr Circulation: 8,700 per issue (paid). **Owner(s):** Montgomery County Sentinel, 30 Courthouse Sq., Ste 405, Rockville, MD 29759. Telephone: 301-838-0788. **Management:** Lynn G Kapiloff, President. Bernard Kapiloff, Publisher. Sherry Sanderson, Advertising Manager. **Editorial:** Paul Grevier, Managing Editor.

SEABROOK

PRINCE GEORGE'S SENTINEL. ISSN 1041-262X
9458 Lanham-Severn Rd., Ste. 203, Seabrook, MD 20706. Telephone: 301-306-9500. FAX: 301-306-9596. E-MAIL: ads@thesentinel.com. URL: http://www.thesentinel.com. Mailing Address: PO Box 1229, Seabrook, MD 20703. Year Established: 1932. Pub. Frequency: w. (Wed.) Page Size: tabloid. Subscrip. Rate: $.25 newsstand/cover; $15.75/yr. Freelance Pay: $35/story. Circulation: 40,000 per issue (paid and free). **Owner(s):** Berlyn, Inc., PO Box 1229, Seabrook, MD 20703. Telephone: 301-306-9500. FAX: 301-306-0134. **Management:** Bernard Kapiloff, Publisher. Joe Ortega, Circulation Manager. Deborah Collins, Admin. Assistant. **Editorial:** Vincent Swanson, Editor. Marketa Ebert, Photographer.

SILVER SPRING

BURTONSVILLE GAZETTE. 8650 Georgia Ave., Silver Spring, MD 20910. Telephone: 301-562-3260. FAX: 301-562-3262. E-MAIL: jbrocker@gazette.net. URL: http://www.gazette.net. Pub. Frequency: w. (Wed.) Page Size: tabloid.Adv. Rate: col. inch $17.70 Circulation: 25,453 per issue (free). **Owner(s):** Washington Post Co., 1150 15th St, N W, Washington, DC 20071. Telephone: 202-334-6000. **Management:** Jim Mannarino, Group Publisher. Chuck Lyons, President. **Editorial:** Jim Brocker, Managing Editor.

SILVER SPRING GAZETTE. 8650 Georgia Ave., Silver Spring, MD 20910. Telephone: 301-562-3260. FAX: 301-562-3262. E-MAIL: jbroker@gazette.net. URL: http://www.gazette.net. Pub. Frequency: w. (Wed.) Page Size: tabloid.Adv. Rate: col. inch $20.33 Circulation: 25,361 per issue (free). **Owner(s):** Washington Post Co., 1150 15th St, N W, Washington, DC 20071. Telephone: 202-334-6000. **Management:** Jim Mannarino, Group Publisher. Chuck Lyons, President. Cliff Chiet, Advertising Director. Jean Casey, Circulation Director. **Editorial:** Jim Brocker, Managing Editor. Jack Murphy, Editorial Page Editor.

TAKOMA PARK GAZETTE. 8650 Georgia Ave., Silver Spring, MD 20910. Telephone: 301-562-3260. FAX: 301-562-3262. E-MAIL: jbrocker@gazette.net. URL: http://www.gazette.net. Pub. Frequency: w. (Wed.) Page Size: tabloid.Adv. Rate: col. inch $20.33 Circulation: 25,361 per issue (free). **Owner(s):** Washington Post Co., 1150 15th St, N W, Washington, DC 20071. Telephone: 202-334-6000. **Management:** Jim Mannarino, Group Publisher. Chuck Lyons, President. **Editorial:** Jim Brocker, Managing Editor.

WHEATON GAZETTE (SILVER SPRING). 8650 Georgia Ave., Silver Spring, MD 20910. Telephone: 301-562-3260. FAX: 301-562-3262. E-MAIL: jbrocker@gazette.net. URL: http://www.gazette.net. Pub. Frequency: w. (Wed.) Page Size: tabloid.Adv. Rate: col. inch $21.53 Circulation: 26,067 per issue (free). **Owner(s):** Washington Post Co., 1150 15th St, N W, Washington, DC 20071. Telephone: 202-334-6000. **Management:** Jim Mannarino, Group Publisher. Chuck Lyons, President. **Editorial:** Jim Brocker, Managing Editor.

STEVENSVILLE

BAY TIMES. 1101 Butterworth Ct., Ste. 100, Stevensville, MD 21666-4002. Telephone: 410-643-7770. FAX: 410-643-8374. E-MAIL: baytimes@cpc.chespub.com. URL: http://www.chespub.com. Year Established: 1963. Pub. Frequency: w. (Wed.) Page Size: tabloid. Subscrip. Rate: $.50 newsstand/cover; $21.95/yr in county; $25.15/yr out of county; $29.95/yr out of state. Freelance Pay: $10-$20/article. Circulation: 6,000 per issue (paid). **Owner(s):** Chesapeake Publishing Corp., 29088 Airpark Dr., Easton, MD 21601. FAX: 410-770-4019, 410-770-4012. **Management:** Larry Effingham, Publisher. **Editorial:** Angela Price, Editor.

TOWSON

BALTIMORE MESSENGER. ISSN 1041-0872
409 Washington Ave., Towson, MD 21204. Telephone: 410-337-2400. FAX: 410-337-2490. URL: http://www.baltimoremessenger.com. Pub. Frequency: w. (Thu.) Page Size: tabloid. Subscrip. Rate: $.50 newsstand/cover; $24.95/yr mailed in county. Circulation: 4,809 per issue (paid and free). **Owner(s):** Patuxent Publishing Co., 10750 Little Patuxent Pkwy., Columbia, MD 21044. Telephone: 410-730-3990. FAX: 410-730-7053. **Management:** Jim Quimby, President. Pat Sweeney, Advertising. Chuck Linn, Circulation Manager. Dotty Daub, Marketing Director. **Editorial:** Larry Perl, Editor. Kenneth Weiss, Managing Editor. Nelson Coffin, Sports Editor.

JEFFERSONIAN (TOWSON), THE. 409 Washington Ave., Towson, MD 21204. Telephone: 410-337-2400. FAX: 410-337-2490. URL: http://www.thejeffersonian.com. Year Established: 1911. Pub. Frequency: s-w. (Tue. & Thu.) Page Size: broadsheet. Subscrip. Rate: $.50 newsstand/cover; $29.95/yr in state; $35/yr out of state. Circulation: 3,542 per issue (paid). **Owner(s):** Patuxent Publishing Co., 10750 Little Patuxent Pkwy., Columbia, MD 21044. Telephone: 410-730-3990. **Management:** Jim Quimby, Publisher. Susan Econ, Advertising Manager. Dotty Daub, Marketing Manager. **Editorial:** Michael Cody, Editor. Kenneth Weiss, Managing Editor. Judi Laser, Editorial Assistant.

NORTH COUNTY NEWS (TOWSON). 409 Washington Ave., Towson, MD 21204. Telephone: 410-337-2400. FAX: 410-337-2490. URL: http://www.northconews.com. Pub. Frequency: w. (Wed.) Page Size: tabloid. Circulation: 18,233 per issue (controlled). **Owner(s):** Patuxent Publishing, Co., 10750 Little Patuxent Pkwy., Columbia, MD 21044. Telephone: 410-730-3990. **Management:** Jim Quimby, Publisher. Phil Baldyga, Circulation Manager. **Editorial:** Angela Bornemann, Editor. Kenneth Weiss, Managing Editor. Nelson Coffin, Sports Editor.

NORTHEAST BOOSTER. 409 Washington Ave., Towson, MD 21204-4920. Telephone: 410-337-2400. FAX: 410-337-2490. URL: http://www.northeastbooster.com. Pub. Frequency: w. (Wed.) Page Size: tabloid Circulation: 21,665 per issue (free). **Owner(s):** Patuxent Publishing Co., 10750 Little Patuxent Pkwy., Columbia, MD 21044. Telephone: 410-730-3990. FAX: 410-715-9631. **Management:** Jim Quimby, Publisher. Susan Econ, Advertising Manager. Phil Baldyga, Circulation Manager. Dotty Daub, Marketing Director. **Editorial:** Dave Sturm, Editor. Kenneth Weiss, Managing Editor. Nelson Coffin, Sports Editor.

NORTHEAST REPORTER. 409 Washington Ave., Towson, MD 21204. Telephone: 410-337-2400. FAX: 410-337-2490. URL: http://www.northeastreporter.com. Year Established: 1954. Pub. Frequency: w. (Wed.) Page Size: tabloid Circulation: 17,000 per issue (free). **Owner(s):** Patuxent Publishing Co., 10750 Little Patuxent Pkwy., Columbia, MD 21044. Telephone: 410-730-3990. FAX: 410-715-9631. **Management:** Jim Quimby, Publisher. Phil Baldyga, Circulation Manager. Dotty Daub, Marketing Director. **Editorial:** Dave Sturm, Editor. Nelson Coffin, Sports Editor.

TOWSON TIMES. ISSN 1041-0899
409 Washington Ave., Towson, MD 21204. Telephone: 410-337-2400. FAX: 410-337-2490. URL: http://www.towsontimes.com. Year Established: 1968. Pub. Frequency: w. (Wed.) Page Size: tabloid. Subscrip. Rate: $.50 newsstand/cover. Circulation: 38,175 per issue (paid and free). **Owner(s):** Patuxent Publishing Co., 10750 Little Patuxent Pkwy., Columbia, MD 21044. Telephone: 410-730-3990. **Management:** Jim Quimby, President. Chuck Linn, Circulation Manager. **Editorial:** Angie Bornemann, Editor. Kenneth Weiss, Managing Editor. Loni Ingraham, Local News Editor. Nelson Coffin, Sports Editor.

UPPER MARLBORO

ENQUIRER-GAZETTE. 14801 Pratt St., Upper Marlboro, MD 20772. Telephone: 301-627-2833. FAX: 301-627-2835. E-MAIL: gazette3@erols.com. URL: http://www.gazette.net. Mailing Address: PO Box 30, Upper Marlboro, MD 20773. Pub. Frequency: w. (Thu.) Page Size: broadsheet. Subscrip. Rate: $.25 newsstand/cover; $13.65/yr in county (effective 2006); $24.15/yr out of county. Circulation: 6,000 per issue (paid). **Owner(s):** Washington Post Co., 1150 15th St., N.W., Washington, DC 20071-0001. Telephone: 202-334-6000. **Management:** Dale Foster, General Manager. Karen Acton, Publisher. Kim Minopoli, Advertising Manager. Rich Wohlfarth, Circulation Manager. **Editorial:** Vanessa Harrington, Editor.

PRINCE GEORGES POST. ISSN 1053-2226
15207 Marlboro Pike, Upper Marlboro, MD 20772-3131. Telephone: 301-627-0900. FAX: 301-627-8147. E-MAIL: editor@pgpost.com. URL: http://www.pgpost.com. Mailing Address: PO Box 1001, Upper Marlboro, MD 20773. Pub. Frequency: w. (Thu.) Page Size: broadsheet.Subscrip. Rate: $.25 newsstand/cover; $15/yr Circulation: 10,000 per issue (paid). **Owner(s):** Prince Georges Post, See address and contact information above. **Management:** Legusta Floyd, Publisher. Brenda Boice, Advertising Manager. **Editorial:** David Zirin, Editor.

WALDORF

MARYLAND INDEPENDENT. 7 Industrial Park Dr., Waldorf, MD 20602. Telephone: 301-645-9480. FAX: 301-645-2175. E-MAIL: abreck@somdnews.com. URL: http://www.gazette.net. Year Established: 1872. Pub. Frequency: s-w. (Wed. & Fri.) Page Size: broadsheet. Subscrip. Rate: $.75 newsstand/cover; $39.90/yr local; $44.10/yr elsewhere. Circulation: 21,500 per issue (paid). **Owner(s):** Washington Post Co., 1150 15th St., N.W., Washington, DC 20071-0001. Telephone: 202-334-7973. **Management:** Karen Acton, Publisher. Kim Minopoli, Advertising Director. Richard Wohlfarth, Circulation Director. **Editorial:** Angela Breck, Editor.

WESTMINSTER

COMMUNITY TIMES. 201 Railroad Ave., Westminster, MD 21157. Telephone: 410-875-5449. FAX: 410-875-5401. E-MAIL: ctimes@lcniofmd.com. URL: http://www.communitytimes.com. Mailing Address: PO Box 203, Westminster, MD 21158-0203. Year Established: 1928. Pub. Frequency: w. (Wed.) Page Size: broadsheet. Subscrip. Rate: $.50 newsstand/cover; $25/yr. Circulation: 13,000 per issue (paid and free). **Owner(s):** Landmark Community Newspapers, Inc., PO Box 549, Shelbyville, KY 40065. **Management:** Charlie Baker, General Manager. Robin Saul, Publisher. Ron Thomas, Advertising Manager. **Editorial:** Baxter Smith, Editor.

WESTMINSTER EAGLE. 121 E Main St., Westminster, MD 21157. Telephone: 410-386-0334. FAX: 410-386-0340. URL: http://www.westminstereagle.com. Pub. Frequency: w. (Wed.) Page Size: tabloid.Adv. Rate: col. inch $67.50 Circulation: 25,393 per issue (free). **Owner(s):** Patuxnet Publishing, Co., 10750 Little Patuxnet Pkwy., Columbia, MD 21004. Telephone: 410-730-3990. **Management:** Jim Quimby, President. Tracey Lambert, Advertising. **Editorial:** Jim Joyner, Editor. Heidi Schroeder, Editorial Assistant.

MASSACHUSETTS

AMHERST

AMHERST BULLETIN. 55 University Dr., Amherst, MA 01002-2217. Telephone: 413-549-2000. FAX: 413-549-8181. E-MAIL: amherst@gazettenet.com. Pub. Frequency: w. (Fri.) Page Size: broadsheet Circulation: 14,000 per issue (free). **Owner(s):** H.S. Gere & Sons, Inc., 115 Conz St., Northampton, MA 01060. Telephone: 413-584-5000. **Management:** Peter DeRose, Publisher. Mark Elliot, Advertising Director. David Sikop, Classified Adv. Mgr.. **Editorial:** Nicole Cusano, Editor.

ANDOVER

ANDOVER TOWNSMAN. 33 Chestnut St, Andover, MA 01810. Telephone: 978-475-7000. FAX: 978-475-5731. E-MAIL: adsales@andovertownsman.com. URL: http://www.andovertownsman.com. Mailing Address: PO Box 1986, Andover, MA 01810-1986. Year Established: 1887. Pub. Frequency: w. (Thu.) Page Size: broadsheet. Subscrip. Rate: $.75 newsstand/cover; $40/yr in area; $45/yr mailed out of area. Adv. Rate: col. inch $22.45 Circulation: 6,935 per issue (paid). **Owner(s):** Community Newspaper Holdings, Inc., 3500 Colonnade Pkwy., Ste. 600, Birmingham, AL 35243-2304. Telephone: 205-298-7100. FAX: 205-298-7108. **Management:** Al Getler, General Manager. Ellen Zappala, Publisher. Mark Miller, Advertising Director. **Editorial:** Nell Fater, Editor.

ATTLEBORO

ADVISOR (ATTLEBORO). 34 S. Main St., Attleboro, MA 02703. Telephone: 508-222-7000. FAX: 508-236-0462. Mailing Address: PO Box 600, Attleboro, MA 02703-0600. Pub. Frequency: w. (Sat.) Page Size: broadsheet Circulation: 28,495 per issue (free). **Owner(s):** United Communications Corp., 5800 Seventh Ave., Kenosha, WI 53140. Telephone: 262-657-1000. FAX: 262-657-1617. **Management:** Roy Belcher, General Manager. Oreste D'Arconte, Publisher. Paul Morrissey, Advertising Manager. Arleen McGlone, Circulation Director. **Editorial:** Michael Kirby, Editor.

BARRE

BARRE GAZETTE, THE. 5 Exchange St., Barre, MA 01005. Telephone: 978-355-4000. FAX: 978-355-6274. E-MAIL: edowner@turley.com. URL: http://www.turley.com. Mailing Address: PO Box 448, Barre, MA 01005-0448. Year Established: 1834. Pub. Frequency: w. (Thu.) Page Size: broadsheet. Subscrip. Rate: $.75 newsstand/cover; $29/yr in state; $33/yr out of state. Adv. Rate: col. inch $9.85 Circulation: 2,900 per issue (paid). **Owner(s):** Turley Publications, Inc., 24 Water St, Palmer, MA 01069. Telephone: 413-283-8393. FAX: 413-289-1977. **Management:** Patrick H Turley, Publisher. Timothy J. Mara, Advertising Manager. Kerry McGarrett, Classified Adv. Mgr.. **Editorial:** Ellie Downer, Editor. Lou Zoldy, Sports Editor.

Weeklies

BELCHERTOWN

SENTINEL (BELCHERTOWN), THE. 10 S. Main St., Belchertown, MA 01007. Telephone: 413-323-5999. FAX: 413-323-9424. Mailing Address: PO Box 601, Belchertown, MA 01007. Year Established: 1915. Pub. Frequency: w. (Thu.) Page Size: tabloid.Adv. Rate: col. inch $11.50 Circulation: 10,521 per issue (free). **Owner(s):** Turley Publications, Inc., 24 Water St, Palmer, MA 01069. Telephone: 413-283-8393. FAX: 413-289-1977. **Management:** Patrick H Turley, Publisher. Debra Dodge, Office Manager. Dave Anderson, Advertising Manager. **Editorial:** Debbie Strauss, Editor. Lou Zoldy, Sports Editor.

BEVERLY

AMESBURY NEWS. 72 Cherry Hill Dr, Beverly, MA 01915. Telephone: 978-739-1300. FAX: 978-739-8501. E-MAIL: amesbury@cnc.com. URL: http://www.townonline.com. Year Established: 1888. Pub. Frequency: w. (Fri.) Page Size: broadsheet. Subscrip. Rate: $.75 newsstand/cover; $34/yr local. Adv. Rate: col. inch $12.15 Circulation: 1,972 per issue (paid). **Owner(s):** GateHouse Media, Inc, 350 WillowBrook Office Park, Fairport, NY 14450. Telephone: 585-598-0030. FAX: 585-248-2631. **Management:** Kirk Davis, Publisher. **Editorial:** Kevin Doyle, Editor. Marlene Switzer, Editor-in-Chief.

BEVERLY CITIZEN. 72 Cherry Hill Dr, Beverly, MA 01915. Telephone: 978-739-1300. FAX: 978-739-8501. E-MAIL: beverly@cnc.com. URL: http://www.townonline com. Pub. Frequency: w. (Thu.) Page Size: broadsheet. Subscrip. Rate: $.75 newsstand/cover; $30/yr local. Adv. Rate: col. inch $18.40 Circulation: 4,892 per issue (paid). **Owner(s):** GateHouse Media, Inc, 350 WillowBrook Office Park, Fairport, NY 14450. Telephone: 585-598-0030. FAX: 585-248-2631. **Management:** Kirk Davis, Publisher. **Editorial:** Dan Macapine, Editor. Marlene Switzer, Editor-in-Chief.

DANVERS HERALD. 72 Cherry Hill Dr, Beverly, MA 01915. Telephone: 978-739-1300. FAX: 978-739-8501. E-MAIL: danversherald@cnc.com. URL: http://www.townonline.com. Year Established: 1863. Pub. Frequency: w. (Thu.) Page Size: broadsheet. Subscrip. Rate: $.75 newsstand/cover; $34/yr in area. Adv. Rate: col. inch $15.25 Circulation: 6,652 per issue (paid). **Owner(s):** GateHouse Media, Inc, 350 WillowBrook Office Park, Fairport, NY 14450. Telephone: 585-598-0030. FAX: 585-248-2631. **Management:** Kirk Davis, Publisher. **Editorial:** Cathrine O'Hara, Editor. Marlene Switzer, Editor-in-Chief.

GEORGETOWN RECORD. 72 Cherry Hill Dr, Beverly, MA 01915. Telephone: 978-739-1300. FAX: 978-739-8501. E-MAIL: georgetown@cnc.com. URL: http://www.townonline.com. Year Established: 1982. Pub. Frequency: w. (Thu.) Page Size: broadsheet. Subscrip. Rate: $1 newsstand/cover; $42/yr local. Adv. Rate: col. inch $12 Circulation: 1,913 per issue (paid). **Owner(s):** GateHouse Media, Inc, 350 WillowBrook Office Park, Fairport, NY 14450. Telephone: 585-598-0030. FAX: 585-248-2631. **Management:** Kirk Davis, Publisher. **Editorial:** Renee Seamore, Editor. Marlene Switzer, Editor-in-Chief.

HAMILTON/WENHAM CHRONICLE. 72 Cherry Hill Dr, Beverly, MA 01915. Telephone: 978-739-1300. FAX: 978-739-8501. E-MAIL: hamilton-wenham@cnc.com. URL: http://www.townonline.com. Year Established: 1948. Pub. Frequency: w. (Thu.) Page Size: broadsheet. Subscrip. Rate: $1 newsstand/cover; $39/yr in county. Adv. Rate: col. inch $12.65 Circulation: 2,540 per issue (paid). **Owner(s):** GateHouse Media, Inc, 350 WillowBrook Office Park, Fairport, NY 14450. Telephone: 585-598-0030. FAX: 585-248-2631. **Management:** Kirk Davis, Publisher. **Editorial:** Wendell Waters, Editor. Marlene Switzer, Editor-in-Chief.

NORTH ANDOVER CITIZEN. 72 Cherry Hill Dr, Beverly, MA 01915. Telephone: 978-739-1300. FAX: 978-739-8501. E-MAIL: northandover@cnc.com. URL: http://www.townonline.com/northandover. Pub. Frequency: w. (Fri.) Page Size: broadsheet. Subscrip. Rate: $.75 newsstand/cover; $42/yr. Adv. Rate: col. inch $14.15 Circulation: 3,500 per issue (paid and free). **Owner(s):** GateHouse Media, Inc, 350 WillowBrook Office Park, Fairport, NY 14450. Telephone: 585-598-0030. FAX: 585-248-2631. **Management:** Kirk Davis, Publisher. **Editorial:** Sarah Wolf, Editor. Marlene Switzer, Editor-in-Chief.

NORTH SHORE SUNDAY. 72 Cherry Hill Dr, Beverly, MA 01915. Telephone: 978-739-1300. FAX: 978-739-8501. E-MAIL: northshore@cnc.com. URL: http://www.townonline.com. Year Established: 1977. Pub. Frequency: w. (Fri..) Page Size: broadsheet. Subscrip. Rate: $35/yr out of area. Adv. Rate: col. inch $31.75 **Wire Service(s):** AP. Circulation: 53,383 per issue (free). **Owner(s):** GateHouse Media, Inc, 350 WillowBrook Office Park, Fairport, NY 14450. Telephone: 585-598-0030. FAX: 585-248-2631. **Management:** Kirk Davis, Publisher. **Editorial:** Barbara Taormina, Editor. Marlene Switzer, Editor-in-Chief.

SAUGUS ADVERTISER. 72 Cherry Hill Dr, Beverly, MA 01915. Telephone: 978-739-1300. FAX: 978-739-8501. E-MAIL: saugus@cnc.com. URL: http://www.townonlinecom. Year Established: 1881. Pub. Frequency: w. (Thu.) Page Size: broadsheet. Subscrip. Rate: $.75 newsstand/cover; $33/yr local. Adv. Rate: col. inch $14.65 Circulation: 4,180 per issue (paid). **Owner(s):** GateHouse Media, Inc, 350 WillowBrook Office Park, Fairport, NY 14450. Telephone: 585-598-0030. FAX: 585-248-2631. **Management:** Kirk Davis, Publisher. **Editorial:** Kathleen O'Brien, Editor. Marlene Switzer, Editor-in-Chief.

STONEHAM SUN. 72 Cherry Hill Dr, Beverly, MA 01915. Telephone: 978-739-1300. FAX: 978-739-8501. E-MAIL: info@cnc.com. URL: http://www.townonline.com. Pub. Frequency: w. (Wed.) Page Size: broadsheet.Adv. Rate: col. inch $12.90 Circulation: 4,800 per issue (paid and free). **Owner(s):** GateHouse Media, Inc, 350 WillowBrook Office Park, Fairport, NY 14450. Telephone: 585-598-0030. FAX: 585-248-2631. **Management:** Kirk Davis, Publisher. **Editorial:** Jesse Kowa, Editor. Marlene Switzer, Editor-in-Chief.

TRI-TOWN TRANSCRIPT. 72 Cherry Hill Dr, Beverly, MA 01915. Telephone: 978-739-1300. FAX: 978-739-8501. E-MAIL: tri-town@cnc.com. URL: http://www.townonline.com. Year Established: 1959. Pub. Frequency: w. (Fri.) Page Size: broadsheet. Subscrip. Rate: $.75 newsstand/cover; $37/yr in area. Adv. Rate: col. inch $14.30 Circulation: 5,192 per issue (paid). **Owner(s):** GateHouse Media, Inc, 350 WillowBrook Office Park, Fairport, NY 14450. Telephone: 585-598-0030. FAX: 585-248-2631. **Management:** Patrick J. Purcell, Publisher. Chuck Goodrich, Vice President. **Editorial:** David Roger, Editor. Marlene Switzer, Editor-in-Chief.

WAKEFIELD OBSERVER. 72 Cherry Hill Dr, Beverly, MA 01915. Telephone: 978-739-1300. FAX: 978-739-8501. E-MAIL: wakefield@cnc.com. URL: http://www.townonline.com. Pub. Frequency: w. (Thu.) Page Size: broadsheet. Subscrip. Rate: $.75 newsstand/cover; $28/yr in area. Adv. Rate: col. inch $12.85 Circulation: 3,817 per issue (paid). **Owner(s):** GateHouse Media, Inc, 350 WillowBrook Office Park, Fairport, NY 14450. Telephone: 585-598-0030. FAX: 585-248-2631. **Management:** Patrick J. Purcell, Publisher. Chuck Goodrich, Vice President. **Editorial:** Lisa Guerriero, Editor. Marlene Switzer, Editor-in-Chief.

BOSTON

FENWAY NEWS, THE. 10 Gainsborough St, Boston, MA 02115. Telephone: 617-266-8790. E-MAIL: fenway.news@verizon.net. Year Established: 1974. Pub. Frequency: m. (Fri.) Page Size: broadsheet Circulation: 10,000 per issue (free). **Owner(s):** Fenway News Association, Inc., Astor Station, PO Box 230307, Boston, MA 02123-0307. Telephone: 617-266-8790. **Editorial:** Robert Hanson, Editor.

PORTLAND PHOENIX. 126 Brookline Ave., Boston, MA 02215. Telephone: 617-536-5390. FAX: 617-536-1463. E-MAIL: submit@phx.com. URL: http://www.thephoenix.com. Year Established: 1999. Pub. Frequency: w. (Thu.) Page Size: tabloid. Subscrip. Rate: $80/yr mailed 3rd class; $200/yr mailed 1st class. Adv. Rate: B&W page $11,550 Circulation: 40,000 per issue (free). **Owner(s):** Phoenix Media Communications Group, See address and contact information above. **Management:** Stephen M. Mindich, Publisher. A. William Risteen, Advertising Director. Maureen Roberts, Circulation Director. Terry Ryan, Classified Adv. Mgr.. Marc Shepard, Associate Publisher. **Editorial:** Peter Kadzis, Editor. Jeff Inglis, Managing Editor.

SOUTH BOSTON TRIBUNE. PO Box 6, Boston, MA 02127. Telephone: 617-268-3440. FAX: 617-268-6420. E-MAIL: adinfo@southbostoninfo.com. URL: http://www.southbostoninfo.com. Year Established: 1938. Pub. Frequency: w. (Thu.) Page Size: broadsheet. Subscrip. Rate: $.50 newsstand/cover; $25/yr. **Wire Service(s):** AP. Circulation: 8,500 per issue (paid). **Owner(s):** Daniel J. Horgan, See address and contact information above. **Management:** Daniel J. Horgan, Publisher. Jim Horgan, Advertising Manager. **Editorial:** Alice O'Leary, Editor.

SOUTH END NEWS. 631 Tremont St., Boston, MA 02118. Telephone: 617-266-6670. FAX: 617-266-5973. E-MAIL: sbaird@southendnews.com. Pub. Frequency: w. (Thu.) Page Size: broadsheet. Subscrip. Rate: $25/yr. Freelance Pay: $50/article. Circulation: 17,000 per issue (free). **Owner(s):** Sue O'Connell & Jeff Coakley, See address and contact information above. **Management:** Jeff Coakley, Publisher. **Editorial:** Susan Kyan Volmar, Editor-in-Chief. Loren King, Art Editor.

CANTON

CANTON CITIZEN. 866 Washington St, Canton, MA 02021-2923. Telephone: 781-821-4418. FAX: 781-821-4419. E-MAIL: cancitizen@aol.com. Year Established: 1987. Pub. Frequency: w. (Thu.) Page Size: broadsheet. Subscrip. Rate: $.50 newsstand/cover; $32/yr in county; $27/yr in county to senior citizens; $38/yr out of county. Adv. Rate: col. inch $8.50 Circulation: 3,500 per issue (paid). **Owner(s):** Beth Erickson, See address and contact information above. **Management:** Rosemary Eleuteri, Advertising Manager. Claire Joyce, Circulation Director. **Editorial:** Beth Erickson, Editor.

CARLISLE

CARLISLE MOSQUITO. 872 Westford St., Carlisle, MA 01741. Telephone: 978-369-8313. FAX: 978-369-3569. URL: http://www.carlislemosquito.org. Mailing Address: PO Box 616, Carlisle, MA 01741-0616. Pub. Frequency: w. (Fri.) Page Size: broadsheet. Subscrip. Rate: $.50 newsstand/cover; $20/yr out of area. Circulation: 2,100 per issue (paid). **Owner(s):** Carlisle Communications Inc., See address and contact information above. **Management:** Susan Emmons, General Manager. Marcy Guttadauro, Advertising Manager. Bill Koener, Circulation Manager. Janet Churchill, Classified Adv. Mgr.. **Editorial:** Marilyn Harte, Feature Editor. Maya Litepio, News Editor.

CHARLESTOWN

CHARLESTOWN PATRIOT & SOMERVILLE CHRONICLE. One Thompson Sq., Charlestown, MA 02129-3328. Telephone: 617-241-9511. Mailing Address: PO Box 290054, Charlestown, MA 02129-0054. Year Established: 1958. Pub. Frequency: w. (Thu.) Page Size: tabloid. Subscrip. Rate: $.25 newsstand/cover; $55/yr. Adv. Rate: col. inch $5.20 Circulation: 4,500 per issue (paid). **Owner(s):** Charlestown Patriot Publications, Inc., See address and contact information above. **Management:** Gloria S. Conway, Publisher. **Editorial:** Gloria S. Conway, Editor.

CHATHAM

CAPE COD CHRONICLE. 60C Munson Meeting Way, Chatham, MA 02633. Telephone: 508-945-2220. FAX: 508-945-2579. E-MAIL: twood@capecodchronicle.com. URL: http://www.capecodchronicle.com. Year Established: 1965. Pub. Frequency: w. (Thu.) Page Size: standard. Subscrip. Rate: $.75 newsstand/cover; $21/yr on cape; $25/yr elsewhere; $75/yr mailed 1st class. Circulation: 10,000 per issue (paid). **Owner(s):** Hyora Publications, Inc., See address and contact information above. **Management:** Henry C. Hyora, Publisher. Deb DeCosta, Advertising Manager. Karyn A. Hyora, Circulation Director. Peter Schall, Classified Adv. Mgr.. **Editorial:** Tim Wood, Editor. Bill Galvin, Managing Editor.

CHICOPEE

CHICOPEE REGISTER, THE. 333 Front St., Chicopee, MA 01013. Telephone: 413-592-3599. FAX: 413-592-3568. E-MAIL: tlandon@turley.com. URL: http://www.turley.com. Pub. Frequency: w. (Thu.) Page Size: tabloid.Adv. Rate: col. inch $10.75 Circulation: 17,070 per issue (free). **Owner(s):** Turley Publications, Inc., 24 Water St, Palmer, MA 01069. Telephone: 413-283-8393. FAX: 413-289-1977. **Management:** Jack R. Mead, General Manager. Patrick H Turley, Publisher. Beth Baker, Advertising Director. **Editorial:** Tammy Landon, Editor. Lou Zoldy, Sports Editor.

HOLYOKE SUN, THE. 333 Front St., Chicopee, MA 01013. Telephone: 413-592-3599. FAX: 413-592-3568. Pub. Frequency: w. (Fri.) Page Size: broadsheet.Adv. Rate: col. inch $9.75 Circulation: 7,000 per issue (free). **Owner(s):** Turley Publications, Inc., 24 Water St, Palmer, MA 01069. Telephone: 413-283-8393. **Management:** Patrick A Turley, Publisher. Beth Baker, Advertising Manager. **Editorial:** Hope Tremblay, Editor. Lou Zoldy, Sports Editor.

CLINTON

BANNER (WEST BOYLSTON & BOYLSTON), THE. ISSN 0895-7665 156 Church St, Clinton, MA 01510. Telephone: 508-835-4865. E-MAIL: editor@weeklybanner.com. URL: http://www.telegram.com/apps/pbcs.dll/section?Category=coulter03. Year Established: 1978. Pub. Frequency: w. Subscrip. Rate: $29/yr in state; $39/yr out of state. **Owner(s):** Coulter Press, See address and contact information above. **Management:** Gary Hutner, Publisher. Jeff Goldfarb, Advertising. Henry Bowden, Circulation Director. **Editorial:** Michael Kane, Editor.

LANCASTER TIMES & CLINTON COURIER. 18 High St, Clinton, MA 01510. Telephone: 978-368-3393. FAX: 978-368-1696. E-MAIL: lancaster@cnc.com. URL: http://www.townonline.com/clinton. Pub. Frequency: w. (Thu.) Page Size: tabloid. Subscrip. Rate: $.75 newsstand/cover; $29/yr local; $25/yr seniors. Circulation: 2,000 per issue (paid). **Owner(s):** GateHouse Media, Inc, 350 WillowBrook Office Park, Fairport, NY 14450. Telephone: 585-598-0030. FAX: 585-248-2631. **Management:** Kirk Davis, Publisher. **Editorial:** Noah Bombard, Editor.

CONCORD

BEACON (CONCORD), THE. ISSN 0744-7930 150 Bakers Ave., Ext., Concord, MA 01742. Telephone: 978-371-5751. E-MAIL: beacon@cnc.com. URL: http://www.townonline.com. Year Established: 1950. Pub. Frequency: w. (Thu.) Page Size: broadsheet. Subscrip. Rate: $.75 newsstand/cover; $44/yr in county. Adv. Rate: col. inch $18 Circulation: 5,940 per issue (paid). **Owner(s):** GateHouse Media, Inc, 350 WillowBrook Office Park, Fairport, NY 14450. Telephone: 585-598-0030. FAX: 585-248-2631. **Management:** Kirk Davis, Publisher. Gareth Charter, Advertising Director. Tina Hermistone, Circulation Manager. **Editorial:** Jesse Floyd, Editor. Kathy Cordeiro, Editor-in-Chief.

BEACON-VILLAGER, THE. 150 Bakers Ave., Ext., Concord, MA 01742. Telephone: 978-371-5751. FAX: 978-371-5220. E-MAIL: beaconvillager@cnc.com. URL: http://www.townonline.com. Year Established: 1976. Pub. Frequency: w. (Thu.) Page Size: broadsheet. Subscrip. Rate: $38/yr in county; $60/yr mailed out of state. Adv. Rate: col. inch $13.75 Circulation: 3,320 per issue (free). **Owner(s):** GateHouse Media, Inc, 350 WillowBrook Office Park, Fairport, NY 14450. Telephone: 585-598-0030. FAX: 585-248-2631. **Management:** Kirk Davis, Publisher. Ann Marie Magerman, Advertising Director. **Editorial:** Jesse Floyd, Editor. Kathy Cordeiro, Editor-in-Chief.

BEDFORD MINUTEMAN. 150 Bakers Ave., Ext., Concord, MA 01742. Telephone: 978-371-5754. FAX: 978-371-5220. E-MAIL: bedford@cnc.com. URL: http://www.townonline.com. Year Established: 1958. Pub. Frequency: w. (Thu.) Page Size: broadsheet. Subscrip. Rate: $1 newsstand/cover; $44/yr in area. Adv. Rate: col. inch $16.60 Circulation: 3,395 per issue (paid). **Owner(s):** GateHouse Media, Inc, 350 WillowBrook Office Park, Fairport, NY 14450. Telephone: 585-598-0030. FAX: 585-248-2631. **Management:** Kirk Davis, Publisher. Gareth Charter, Advertising Director. **Editorial:** Peter Costa, Editor. Kathy Cordeiro, Editor-in-Chief.

BILLERICA MINUTEMAN. 150 Bakers Ave., Ext., Concord, MA 01742. Telephone: 978-371-5726. FAX: 978-371-5212. E-MAIL: billerica@cnc.com. URL: http://www.townonline.com. Year Established: 1971. Pub. Frequency: w. (Thu.) Page Size: broadsheet. Subscrip. Rate: $1 newsstand/cover; $40/yr in area. Adv. Rate: col. inch $14.50 Circulation: 5,000 per issue (paid). **Owner(s):** GateHouse Media, Inc, 350 WillowBrook Office Park, Fairport, NY 14450. Telephone: 585-598-0030. FAX: 585-248-2631. **Management:** Gareth Charter, Advertising Director. Kristen Gongas, Classified Adv. Mgr.. **Editorial:** Margaret Smith, Editor. Kathy Cordeiro, Editor-in-Chief.

BURLINGTON UNION. 150 Baker Ave Ext Ste 105, Concord, MA 01742. Telephone: 781-229-0918. E-MAIL: burlington@cnc.com. URL: http://www.townonline.com. Year Established: 1956. Pub. Frequency: w. (Thu.) Page Size: broadsheet. Subscrip. Rate: $.75 newsstand/cover; $39/yr. Adv. Rate: col. inch $14.20 Circulation: 3,369 per issue (paid). **Owner(s):** GateHouse Media, Inc, 350 WillowBrook Office Park, Fairport, NY 14450. Telephone: 585-598-0030. FAX: 585-248-2631. **Management:** Kirk Davis, Publisher. Ann Marie Magerman, Advertising Director. **Editorial:** David Smith, Editor.

CHELMSFORD INDEPENDENT. 150 Bakers Ave., Ext., Concord, MA 01742. Telephone: 978-371-5724. FAX: 978-371-5212. E-MAIL: chelmsford@cnc.com. URL: http://www.townonline.com. Year Established: 1952. Pub. Frequency: w. (Thu.) Page Size: broadsheet. Subscrip. Rate: $.75 newsstand/cover; $40/yr in area. Adv. Rate: col. inch $14.20 Circulation: 4,500 per issue (paid). **Owner(s):** GateHouse Media, Inc, 350 WillowBrook Office Park, Fairport, NY 14450. Telephone: 585-598-0030. FAX: 585-248-2631. **Management:** Kirk Davis, Publisher. Gareth Charter, Advertising Director. **Editorial:** Kevin Zimmerman, Editor. Kathy Cordeiro, Editor-in-Chief.

CONCORD JOURNAL, THE. 150 Bakers Ave., Ext., Concord, MA 01742. Telephone: 978-371-5720. FAX: 978-371-5220. E-MAIL: concord@cnc.com. URL: http://www.townonline.com. Pub. Frequency: w. (Thu.) Page Size: broadsheet. Subscrip. Rate: $1 newsstand/cover; $48/yr in county. Adv. Rate: col. inch $21.50 Circulation: 6,200 per issue (paid). **Owner(s):** GateHouse Media, Inc, 350 WillowBrook Office Park, Fairport, NY 14450. Telephone: 585-598-0030. FAX: 585-248-2631. **Management:** Gareth Charter, Advertising Director. **Editorial:** Maureen O'Connell, Editor. Kathy Cordeiro, Editor-in-Chief.

LINCOLN JOURNAL (CONCORD). 150 Bakers Ave., Ext., Concord, MA 01742. Telephone: 978-371-5720. FAX: 978-371-5220. E-MAIL: lincoln@cnc.com. URL: http://www.townonline.com. Year Established: 1985. Pub. Frequency: w. (Thu.) Page Size: broadsheet. Subscrip. Rate: $1 newsstand/cover per issue; $40/yr in area. Adv. Rate: col. inch $14.95 Circulation: 1,600 per issue (paid). **Owner(s):** GateHouse Media, Inc, 350 WillowBrook Office Park, Fairport, NY 14450. Telephone: 585-598-0030. FAX: 585-248-2631. **Management:** Kirk Davis, Publisher. Gareth Charter, Advertising Director. **Editorial:** Cheryl Lecesse, Editor. Kathy Cordeiro, Editor-in-Chief.

LITTLETON INDEPENDENT. 150 Bakers Ave., Ext., Concord, MA 01742. Telephone: 978-371-5709. FAX: 978-371-5220. E-MAIL: littleton@cnc.com. URL: http://www.townonline.com. Year Established: 1950. Pub. Frequency: w. (Thu.) Page Size: broadsheet. Subscrip. Rate: $.75 newsstand/cover; $42/yr in area. Adv. Rate: col. inch $12.90 Freelance Pay: $25-$35/article. Circulation: 2,000 per issue (paid). **Owner(s):** GateHouse Media, Inc, 350 WillowBrook Office Park, Fairport, NY 14450. Telephone: 585-598-0030. FAX: 585-248-2631. **Management:** Gareth Charter, Advertising Director. **Editorial:** Betsy Levinson, Editor. Kathy Cordeiro, Editor-in-Chief.

READING ADVOCATE, THE. 150 Bakers Ave., Ext., Concord, MA 01742. Telephone: 978-371-5732. FAX: 978-371-5216. E-MAIL: reading@cnc.com. URL: http://www.townonline.com. Year Established: 1998. Pub. Frequency: w. (Thu.) Page Size: broadsheet. Subscrip. Rate: $.75 newsstand/cover; $24/yr in area. Adv. Rate: col. inch $14.50 Circulation: 3,480 per issue (paid). **Owner(s):** GateHouse Media, Inc, 350 WillowBrook Office Park, Fairport, NY 14450. FAX: 585-248-2631. **Management:** Kirk Davis, Publisher. Gareth Charter, Advertising Director. **Editorial:** Jason McEntyre, Editor. Kathy Cordeiro, Editor-in-Chief.

TEWKSBURY ADVOCATE. 150 Bakers Ave., Ext., Concord, MA 01742. Telephone: 978-371-5709. FAX: 978-371-5216. E-MAIL: tewksbury@cnc.com. URL: http://www.townonline.com. Pub. Frequency: w. (Thu.) Page Size: broadsheet. Subscrip. Rate: $.75 newsstand/cover; $24/yr in area. Adv. Rate: col. inch $16.95 Circulation: 3,062 per issue (paid). **Owner(s):** GateHouse Media, Inc, 350 WillowBrook Office Park, Fairport, NY 14450. Telephone: 585-598-0030. FAX: 585-248-2631. **Management:** Gareth Charter, Advertising Director. **Editorial:** Franklin Tucker, Editor. Kathy Cordeiro, Editor-in-Chief.

WESTFORD EAGLE. 150 Bakers Ave., Ext., Concord, MA 01742. Telephone: 978-371-5724. FAX: 978-371-5212. E-MAIL: westford@cnc.com. URL: http://www.townonline.com. Year Established: 1970. Pub. Frequency: w. (Thu.) Page Size: broadsheet. Subscrip. Rate: $.75 newsstand/cover; $44/yr in area. Adv. Rate: col. inch $16 Circulation: 4,700 per issue (paid). **Owner(s):** GateHouse Media, Inc, 350 WillowBrook Office Park, Fairport, NY 14450. FAX: 585-248-2631. **Management:** Kirk Davis, Publisher. Gareth Charter, Advertising Director. **Editorial:** Peter Costa, Editor. Kathy Cordeiro, Editor-in-Chief.

WILMINGTON ADVOCATE. 150 Bakers Ave., Ext., Concord, MA 01742. Telephone: 978-371-5709. FAX: 978-371-5216. E-MAIL: wilmington@cnc.com. URL: http://www.townonline.com. Pub. Frequency: w. (Thu.) Page Size: broadsheet.Adv. Rate: col. inch $16.95 Circulation: 3,800 per issue (free). **Owner(s):** GateHouse Media, Inc, 350 WillowBrook Office Park, Fairport, NY 14450. Telephone: 585-598-0030. FAX: 585-248-2631. **Management:** Kirk Davis, Publisher. **Editorial:** Franklin Tucker, Editor. Kathy Cordeiro, Editor-in-Chief.

WOBURN ADVOCATE. ISSN 1071-9806
150 Bakers Ave., Ext., Concord, MA 01742. Telephone: 978-371-5775. FAX: 978-371-5216. E-MAIL: woburn@cnc.com. URL: http://www.townonline.com. Year Established: 1991. Pub. Frequency: w. (Thu.) Page Size: broadsheet.Adv. Rate: col. inch $16 Circulation: 7,200 per issue (free). **Owner(s):** GateHouse Media, Inc, 350 WillowBrook Office Park, Fairport, NY 14450. Telephone: 585-598-0030. FAX: 585-248-2631. **Management:** Kirk Davis, Publisher. Ann Marie Magerman, Advertising Director. **Editorial:** Mike Marotta, Editor. Kathy Cordeiro, Editor-in-Chief.

COTUIT

OTIS NOTICE, THE. Rte. 28, Cotuit, MA 02635. Telephone: 508-428-8900. FAX: 508-428-8524. E-MAIL: otis@lujeanprinting.com. Mailing Address: PO Box 571, Osterville, MA 02655. Pub. Frequency: m. (1st. Thu.) Page Size: tabloid.Adv. Rate: col. inch $8 Circulation: 5,000 per issue (free). **Owner(s):** Lujean Printing Co., See address and contact information above. **Management:** Michael Lally, Publisher. Norm Hoppensteadt, Advertising Manager. **Editorial:** Norm Hoppensteadt, Editor.

DANVERS

MELROSE FREE PRESS. 152 Sylvan St., Danvers, MA 01923. Telephone: 781-665-4000. FAX: 978-739-8501. E-MAIL: melrose@cnc.com. URL: http://www.townonline.com. Year Established: 1901. Pub. Frequency: w. (Thu.) Page Size: broadsheet. Subscrip. Rate: $.75 newsstand/cover; $39/yr. Adv. Rate: col. inch $16.15 Circulation: 6,305 per issue (paid). **Owner(s):** GateHouse Media, Inc, 350 WillowBrook Office Park, Fairport, NY 14450. Telephone: 585-598-0030. FAX: 585-248-2631. **Management:** Patrick J. Purcell, Publisher. Chuck Goodrich, VP Advertising. **Editorial:** Daniel MacAlpine, Editor. Marlene Switzer, Editor-in-Chief.

MERRIMACK RIVER CURRENT. 152 Sylvan St., Danvers, MA 01923. Telephone: 978-739-1347. FAX: 978-739-8501. E-MAIL: merrimackvalley@cnc.com. URL: http://www.townonline.com. Pub. Frequency: w. (Fri.) Page Size: broadsheet.Adv. Rate: col. inch $15.75 Circulation: 5,312 per issue (paid). **Owner(s):** GateHouse Media, Inc, 350 WillowBrook Office Park, Fairport, NY 14450. Telephone: 585-598-0030. FAX: 585-248-2631. **Management:** Kirk Davis, Publisher. Chuck Goodrich, Vice President. **Editorial:** Peter Chianca, Editor. Marlene Switzer, Editor-in-Chief.

DEDHAM

DEDHAM TIMES. 395 Washington St., Dedham, MA 02026-4456. Telephone: 781-329-5553. FAX: 781-329-8291. E-MAIL: dtimes@rcn.com. Year Established: 1992. Pub. Frequency: w. (Fri.) Page Size: broadsheet. Subscrip. Rate: $.75 newsstand/cover; $34/yr town; $40/yr out of town; $10/yr to military out of town. Adv. Rate: col. inch $10 Circulation: 3,000 per issue (paid). **Owner(s):** Hana Heald, See address and contact information above. **Management:** Jimmy Heald, Publisher. **Editorial:** Hana Heald, Editor.

DEVENS

AYER PUBLIC SPIRIT, THE. 78 Barnum Rd., Devens, MA 01432. Telephone: 978-772-0777. FAX: 978-772-4012. E-MAIL: editor@nashobapub.com. URL: http://www.nashobapublishing.com/ayer. Mailing Address: PO Box 362, Ayer, MA 01432. Year Established: 1952. Pub. Frequency: s-w. (Wed. & Fri.) Page Size: broadsheet. Subscrip. Rate: $.75 newsstand/cover; $55.54/yr mailed in state; $88.90 mailed for 2 yrs. in state. Adv. Rate: col. inch $14 Circulation: 3,111 per issue (paid). **Owner(s):** MediaNews Group, Inc., 101 W Colfax Ave, Ste 1100, Denver, CO 80202. FAX: 303-954-6320. **Management:** Mark Iacuessa, General Manager. **Editorial:** Kate Walsh, Editor. Ken Blanchette, Sports Editor.

GROTON LANDMARK. 78 Barnum Rd., Devens, MA 01432. Telephone: 978-772-0777. FAX: 978-772-4012. E-MAIL: editor@nashobapub.com. URL: http://www.nashobapub.com. Mailing Address: PO Box 362, Ayer, MA 01432. Pub. Frequency: s-w. (Wed. & Fri.) Page Size: broadsheet. Subscrip. Rate: $.75 newsstand/cover; $50/yr in state; $65/yr out of state. Adv. Rate: col. inch $14 Circulation: 2,763 per issue (paid). **Owner(s):** MediaNews Group, Inc., 101 W Colfax Ave, Ste 1100, Denver, CO 80202. FAX: 303-954-6320. **Management:** Mark Iacuessa, General Manager. **Editorial:** Kate Walsh, Editor.

HARVARD HILLSIDE. 78 Barnum Rd., Devens, MA 01432. Telephone: 978-772-0777. FAX: 978-772-4012. E-MAIL: editor@nashobapub.com. URL: http://www.nashobapub.com. Mailing Address: PO Box 362, Ayer, MA 01432. Pub. Frequency: s-w. (Wed. & Fri.) Page Size: broadsheet. Subscrip. Rate: $.75 newsstand/cover; $50/yr in state; $65/yr out of state. Adv. Rate: col. inch $14 Circulation: 1,123 per issue (paid). **Owner(s):** MediaNews Group, Inc., 101 W Colfax Ave, Ste 1100, Denver, CO 80202. FAX: 303-954-6320. **Management:** Linda Leland, Advertising Manager. **Editorial:** Kate Walsh, Editor. John Love, Photographer. Ken Blanchette, Sports Editor.

PEPPERELL FREE PRESS. 78 Barnun Rd., Devens, MA 01432-1003. Telephone: 978-772-0777. FAX: 978-772-4012. E-MAIL: editor@nashobapub.com. URL: http://www.pepperellfreepress.com. Mailing Address: PO Box 362, Ayer, MA 01432. Pub. Frequency: s-w. (Wed. & Fri.) Page Size: broadsheet. Subscrip. Rate: $.75 newsstand/cover; $34.54/yr in state. Adv. Rate: col. inch $14 Circulation: 1,420 per issue (paid). **Owner(s):** MediaNews Group, Inc., 101 W Colfax Ave, Ste 1100, Denver, CO 80202. FAX: 303-954-6320. **Management:** Mark Iacuessa, General Manager. **Editorial:** Kate Walsh, Editor. John Love, Photographer. Ken Blanchette, Sports Editor.

SHIRLEY ORACLE. ISSN 1526-7318
78 Barnum Rd., Devens, MA 01432. Telephone: 978-772-0777. FAX: 978-772-4012. E-MAIL: editor@nashobapub.com. URL: http://www.shirleyoracle.com. Mailing Address: PO Box 362, Ayer, MA 01432. Pub. Frequency: s-w. (Wed. & Fri.) Page Size: broadsheet. Subscrip. Rate: $.75 newsstand/cover; $50/yr mailed in state; $65/yr mailed out of state. Adv. Rate: col. inch $14 Circulation: 1,863 per issue (paid). **Owner(s):** MediaNews Group, Inc., 101 W Colfax Ave, Ste 1100, Denver, CO 80202. FAX: 303-954-6320. **Management:** Asa Cole, Publisher. Linda Leland, Advertising Manager. **Editorial:** Kate Walsh, Editor. John Love, Photographer. Ken Blanchette, Sports Editor.

TOWNSEND TIMES. 78 Barnum Rd., Devens, MA 01432. Telephone: 978-772-0777. FAX: 978-772-4012. E-MAIL: editor@nashobapub.com. URL: http://www.townsendtimes.com. Mailing Address: PO Box 362, Ayer, MA 01432. Year Established: 1869. Pub. Frequency: w. (Wed. & Fri.) Page Size: broadsheet. Subscrip. Rate: $.75 newsstand/cover; $50/yr mailed in state; $65/yr mailed out of state. Adv. Rate: col. inch $14 Freelance Pay: $0.35/column-inch. Circulation: 2,420 per issue (paid). **Owner(s):** MediaNews Group, Inc., 101 W Colfax Ave, Ste 1100, Denver, CO 80202. **Management:** Linda Leland, Advertising Manager. **Editorial:** Kate Walsh, Editor. John Love, Photographer. Ken Blanchette, Sports Editor.

EAST LONGMEADOW

CHICOPEE HERALD, THE. 280 N Main St, East Longmeadow, MA 01028. Telephone: 413-525-6661. FAX: 413-525-5882. E-MAIL: heraldnews@thereminder.com. URL: http://www.reminderpublications.com. Year Established: 1927. Pub. Frequency: w. (Mon.) Page Size: tabloid. Subscrip. Rate: $25/yr mailed local area. Adv. Rate: col. inch $34 Circulation: 11,000 per issue (free). **Owner(s):** Reminder Publications, Inc., See address and contact information above. **Management:** Christopher Buendo, Co-Publisher. Winnifred Lee, Circulation Manager. Barbara Perry, Sales Manager. **Editorial:** G Michael Dobbs, Managing Editor.

REMINDER (EAST LONGMEADOW), THE. 280 N Main St, East Longmeadow, MA 01028. Telephone: 413-525-6661. FAX: 413-525-5882. E-MAIL: news@thereminder.com. URL: http://www.reminderpublications.com. Year Established: 1962. Pub. Frequency: w. (Mon.) Page Size: tabloid. Subscrip. Rate: $25/yr mailed domestic area. Adv. Rate: col. inch $32 Circulation: 26,000 per issue (free). **Owner(s):** Reminder Publications, Inc., See address and contact information above. **Management:** Christopher Buendo, Co-Publisher. Winnifred Lee, Circulation Manager. Barbara Perry, Sales Manager. **Editorial:** Christopher Buendo, Editor-in-Chief. G Michael Dobbs, Managing Editor.

REMINDER/METRO WEST, THE. 280 North Main St, East Longmeadow, MA 01028. Telephone: 413-525-6661. FAX: 413-525-5882. E-MAIL: news@thereminder.com. URL: http://www.reminderpublications.com. Year Established: 1962. Pub. Frequency: w. (Wed.) Page Size: tabloid. Subscrip. Rate: $25/yr mailed in area. Adv. Rate: col. inch $34 Circulation: 12,400 per issue (free). **Owner(s):** Reminder Publications, See address and contact information above. **Management:** Christopher Buendo, Co-Publisher. Barbara Perry, Sales Manager. **Editorial:** G. Michael Dobbs, Managing Editor.

EASTHAMPTON

VALLEY ADVOCATE. ISSN 0192-852X
116 Pleasant St., 3rd Fl., Easthampton, MA 01027-2741. FAX: 413-529-2844. E-MAIL: feedback@newmassmedia.com. URL: http://www.valleyadvocate.com. Pub. Frequency: w. Page Size: tabloid. Subscrip. Rate: $150/yr mailed. Adv. Rate: page $2,215 Circulation: 65,000 per issue (paid and controlled). **Owner(s):** New Mass Media, Inc., 121 Wawarme Ave., 1st Fl., Hartford, CT 06114-1507. Telephone: 860-548-9300. **Management:** Janet Reynolds, Publisher. S. Do-Han Allen, Advertising Director. Jeffrey Owczarski, Circulation Manager. **Editorial:** Tom Vannah, Editor.

EDGARTOWN

VINEYARD GAZETTE. PO Box 66, Edgartown, MA 02539-0066. Telephone: 508-627-4311. FAX: 508-627-7444. E-MAIL: manager@mvgazette.com. URL: http://www.mvgazette.com. Year Established: 1846. Pub. Frequency: w. (w Fri.; s-w.: Tues. & Fri. summer) Page Size: broadsheet. Subscrip. Rate: $.75 newsstand/cover; $41/yr residents; $53/yr non-residents. Circulation: 15,000 per issue (paid). **Owner(s):** Vineyard Gazette Inc., See address and contact information above. **Management:** Joe Pitt, General Manager. Richard Reston, Publisher. **Editorial:** Julia Wells, Editor.

EVERETT

EVERETT LEADER-HERALD & NEWS GAZETTE. 28 Church St., Everett, MA 02149-2719. Telephone: 617-387-4570. FAX: 617-387-0409. E-MAIL: everettleader@comcast.net. Year Established: 1885. Pub. Frequency: w. (Thu.) Page Size: standard. Subscrip. Rate: $100/yr. Adv. Rate: col. inch $10 Circulation: 15,000 per issue (free). **Owner(s):** Joseph Cumane, Jr., See address and contact information above. **Management:** Joseph Curnane Jr., Advertising Manager. **Editorial:** Jen Di Donato, Editor.

FAIRHAVEN

ADVOCATE (FAIRHAVEN), THE. 130 Main St., Fairhaven, MA 02719. Telephone: 508-961-2243. FAX: 508-961-2245. E-MAIL: theadvocatenewspaper@yahoo.com. Year Established: 1976. Pub. Frequency: w. (Thu.) Page Size: standard. Subscrip. Rate: $.50 newsstand/cover; $26.25/yr in county; $44.25/yr out of county. Adv. Rate: col. inch $7.95 Freelance Pay: $25/story. Circulation: 3,000 per issue (paid). **Owner(s):** Hathaway Publishing Corp., See address and contact information above. **Management:** Mary Harrington, General Manager. Kerry Silvia, Classified Adv. Mgr.. **Editorial:** Michael Medeiros, Editor.

FALMOUTH

BOURNE ENTERPRISE. 50 Depot Ave., Falmouth, MA 02540. Telephone: 508-548-4700. FAX: 508-540-8407. E-MAIL: news@capenews.net. URL: www.capenews.net. Pub. Frequency: w. (Fri.) Page Size: broadsheet. Subscrip. Rate: $.75 newsstand/cover; $15.60/yr in county; $17/yr out of county. Adv. Rate: col. inch $10.45 Circulation: 4,000 per issue (paid). **Owner(s):** Bill Hough, See address and contact information above. **Management:** Bill Hough, President. Chris Avis, Advertising Director. Tracy Moniz, Circulation Director. Esther Buchanan, Classified Adv. Mgr.. **Editorial:** Janice Walford, Managing Editor.

FALMOUTH ENTERPRISE, THE. ISSN 0744-2114
50 Depot Ave., Falmouth, MA 02540. Telephone: 508-548-4700. FAX: 508-540-8407. E-MAIL: enterprise@cape.com. Year Established: 1895. Pub. Frequency: s-w. (Tue. & Fri.) Page Size: broadsheet. Subscrip. Rate: $.75 newsstand/cover; $52/yr mailed in county; $56.50/yr mailed out of county. Adv. Rate: col. inch $17 Circulation: 14,000 per issue (paid). **Owner(s):** Bill Hough, See address and contact information above. **Management:** Bill Hough, President. Chris Avis, Advertising Director. Tracy Moniz, Circulation Director. Esther Buchanan, Classified Adv. Mgr.. **Editorial:** Janice Walford, Managing Editor.

MASHPEE ENTERPRISE. 50 Depot Ave., Falmouth, MA 02540. Telephone: 508-548-4700. FAX: 508-540-8407. E-MAIL: enterprise@cape.com. Pub. Frequency: w. (Fri.) Page Size: broadsheet. Subscrip. Rate: $.75 per issue; $26/yr in county; $28.15/yr elsewhere. Adv. Rate: col. inch $9.40 Circulation: 3,000 per issue (paid). **Owner(s):** Bill Hough, See address and contact information above. **Management:** Bill Hough, President. Chris Avis, Advertising Director. Tracy Moniz, Circulation Director. Esther Buchanan, Classified Adv. Mgr.. **Editorial:** Janice Walford, Managing Editor.

SANDWICH ENTERPRISE. 50 Depot Ave., Falmouth, MA 02540. Telephone: 508-548-4700. FAX: 508-540-8407. E-MAIL: enterprise@cape.com. Pub. Frequency: w. (Fri.) Page Size: broadsheet. Subscrip. Rate: $.75 newsstand/cover; $26/yr in county; $28.15/yr out of county. Adv. Rate: col. inch $10.75 Circulation: 3,400 per issue (paid). **Owner(s):** Bill Hough, See address and contact information above. **Management:** Bill Hough, President. Chris Avis, Advertising Director. Tracy Moniz, Circulation Director. **Editorial:** Janice Walford, Managing Editor.

FEEDING HILLS

AGAWAM ADVERTISER NEWS. 23 Southwick St, Feeding Hills, MA 01030. Telephone: 413-786-7747. FAX: 413-786-8457. Pub. Frequency: w. (Thu.) Page Size: broadsheet. Subscrip. Rate: $.75 newsstand/cover; $30/yr in state; $34/yr out of state. Adv. Rate: col. inch $9.40 **Owner(s):** Turley Publications, Inc., 24 Water St, Palmer, MA 01069. Telephone: 413-283-8393. FAX: 413-667-3011. **Management:** Rick Sardella, General Manager. Patrick H Turley, Publisher.

SOUTHWICK SUFFIELD NEWS. 23 Southwick St, Feeding Hills, MA 01030. Telephone: 413-786-7747. FAX: 413-786-8457. Pub. Frequency: w. (Fri.) Page Size: broadsheet.Adv. Rate: col. inch $9.20 Circulation: 6,000 per issue (free). **Owner(s):** Turley Publications, Inc., 24 Water St, Palmer, MA 01069. Telephone: 413-283-8393. **Management:** Patrick H Turley, Publisher. **Editorial:** Sarah Leete Tsitso, Editor.

FOXBORO

FOXBORO REPORTER, THE. 36 Mechanic St., Foxboro, MA 02035. Telephone: 508-543-4851. FAX: 508-543-4888. E-MAIL: foxborofile@yahoo.com. URL: http://www.foxbororeporter.com. Mailing Address: PO Box 289, Foxboro, MA 02035. Year Established: 1884. Pub. Frequency: w. (Thu.) Page Size: broadsheet. Subscrip. Rate: $.50 newsstand/cover; $26/yr in county; $32/yr out of county. Adv. Rate: col. inch $8.70 Freelance Pay: $25-$100/article. Circulation: 5,000 per issue (paid). **Owner(s):** United Communications Corp., 5800 Seventh Ave., Kenosha, WI 53140. Telephone: 262-656-1001. FAX: 262-656-1255. **Management:** Oreste P. D'Arconte, Publisher. Susan Patton, Advertising Manager. Annette Fisher, Circulation Manager. **Editorial:** Jeffrey Peterson, Managing Editor.

FRAMINGHAM

ASHLAND TAB. 33 New York Ave., Framingham, MA 01701. Telephone: 508-626-3800. FAX: 508-626-4400. E-MAIL: ashland@cnc.com. URL: http://www.townonline.com. Pub. Frequency: w. (Tue.) Page Size: broadsheet. Subscrip. Rate: $.50 newsstand/cover; $31/yr. Adv. Rate: col. inch $13.65 Circulation: 3,200 per issue (paid). **Owner(s):** GateHouse Media, Inc, 350 WillowBrook Office Park, Fairport, NY 14450. Telephone: 585-598-0030. FAX: 585-248-2631. **Management:** Kirk Davis, Publisher. Mark Olivieri, Advertising Director. **Editorial:** Jim Kleninkauf, Editor. Richard Lodge, Editor-in-Chief.

FRAMINGHAM TAB. 33 New York Ave., Framingham, MA 01701. Telephone: 508-626-3800. FAX: 508-626-4400. E-MAIL: framingham@cnc.com. URL: http://www.townonline.com. Year Established: 1979. Pub. Frequency: w. (Fri.) Page Size: broadsheet.Adv. Rate: col. inch $24.05 **Wire Service(s):** AP. Circulation: 10,187 per issue (free). **Owner(s):** GateHouse Media, Inc, 350 WillowBrook Office Park, Fairport, NY 14450. Telephone: 585-598-0030. FAX: 585-248-2631. **Management:** Kirk Davis, Publisher. Mark Olivieri, Advertising Director. **Editorial:** Jeff Adair, Editor. Richard Lodge, Editor-in-Chief.

HOLLISTON TAB. 33 New York Ave., Framingham, MA 01701. Telephone: 508-626-3800. FAX: 508-626-4400. E-MAIL: holliston@cnc.com. URL: http://www.townonline.com. Pub. Frequency: w. (Tue.) Page Size: broadsheet. Subscrip. Rate: $.50 newsstand/cover; $36/yr. Adv. Rate: col. inch $14.20 Circulation: 4,000 per issue (paid). **Owner(s):** GateHouse Media, Inc, 350 WillowBrook Office Park, Fairport, NY 14450. Telephone: 585-598-0030. FAX: 585-248-2631. **Management:** Kirk Davis, Publisher. Mark Olivieri, Advertising Director. **Editorial:** Jim Kleninkauf, Editor. Richard Lodge, Editor-in-Chief.

HOPKINTON CRIER. ISSN 1061-3250
33 New York Ave., Framingham, MA 01701. Telephone: 508-626-3800. FAX: 508-626-4400. E-MAIL: rborkows@cnc.com. URL: http://www.townonline.com. Year Established: 1987. Pub. Frequency: w. (Fri.) Page Size: broadsheet. Subscrip. Rate: $.75 newsstand/cover; $29/yr. Adv. Rate: col. inch $12 **Wire Service(s):** AP. Circulation: 2,010 per issue (paid). **Owner(s):** GateHouse Media, Inc, 350 WillowBrook Office Park, Fairport, NY 14450. Telephone: 585-598-0030. FAX: 585-248-2631. **Management:** Kirk Davis, Publisher. Mark Olivieri, Advertising Director. **Editorial:** Rob Borkowski, Editor. Richard Lodge, Editor-in-Chief.

NATICK BULLETIN & TAB. 33 New York Ave., Framingham, MA 01701. Telephone: 508-626-3800. FAX: 508-626-4400. E-MAIL: natick@cnc.com. URL: http://www.townonline.com. Pub. Frequency: w. (Fri.) Page Size: broadsheet. Subscrip. Rate: $36/yr. Adv. Rate: col. inch $15.55 Circulation: 8,164 per issue (paid and free). **Owner(s):** GateHouse Media, Inc, 350 WillowBrook Office Park, Fairport, NY 14450. Telephone: 585-598-0030. FAX: 585-248-2631. **Management:** Kirk Davis, Publisher. Mark Olivieri, Advertising Director. **Editorial:** Phil Maddocks, Editor. Richard Lodge, Editor-in-Chief.

SUDBURY TOWN CRIER, THE. 33 New York Ave., Framingham, MA 01701. Telephone: 508-626-3800. FAX: 508-626-4400. E-MAIL: sudbury@cnc.com. URL: http://www.townonline.com. Year Established: 1951. Pub. Frequency: w. (Thu.) Page Size: broadsheet. Subscrip. Rate: $.75 newsstand/cover (effective 2007); $36/yr. Adv. Rate: col. inch $12.45 Circulation: 3,838 per issue (paid). **Owner(s):** GateHouse Media, Inc, 350 WillowBrook Office Park, Fairport, NY 14450. Telephone: 585-598-0030. FAX: 585-248-2631. **Management:** Kirk Davis, Publisher. Mark Olivieri, Advertising Director. **Editorial:** Richard Lodge, Editor-in-Chief. Mike Wyner, Assistant Editor. Rick Smith, Sports Editor.

WAYLAND TOWN CRIER. 33 New York Ave., Framingham, MA 01701. Telephone: 508-626-3800. FAX: 508-626-4400. E-MAIL: wayland@cnc.com. URL: http://www.townonline.com. Year Established: 1945. Pub. Frequency: w. (Thu.) Page Size: broadsheet. Subscrip. Rate: $36/yr. Adv. Rate: col. inch $14 **Wire Service(s):** AP. Circulation: 5,300 per issue (paid and free). **Owner(s):** GateHouse Media, Inc, 350 WillowBrook Office Park, Fairport, NY 14450. Telephone: 585-598-0030. FAX: 585-248-2631. **Management:** Kirk Davis, Publisher. Mark Olivieri, Advertising Director. **Editorial:** Mike Wyner, Editor. Richard Lodge, Editor-in-Chief.

WESTON TOWN CRIER. 33 New York Ave., Framingham, MA 01701. Telephone: 508-626-3800. FAX: 508-626-4400. E-MAIL: weston@cnc.com. URL: http://www.townonline.com. Year Established: 1951. Pub. Frequency: w. (Thu.) Page Size: broadsheet. Subscrip. Rate: $.75 newsstand/cover; $39/yr. Adv. Rate: col. inch $15.66 **Wire Service(s):** AP. Circulation: 2,391 per issue (paid). **Owner(s):** GateHouse Media, Inc, 350 WillowBrook Office Park, Fairport, NY 14450. Telephone: 585-598-0030. FAX: 585-248-2631. **Management:** Kirk Davis, Publisher. Mark Olivieri, Advertising Director. **Editorial:** Michael Wyner, Editor. Richard Lodge, Editor-in-Chief.

GREAT BARRINGTON

BERKSHIRE RECORD. 21 Elm St., Great Barrington, MA 01230. Telephone: 413-528-5380. FAX: 413-528-9449. E-MAIL: berkrec@bcn.net. Year Established: 1989. Pub. Frequency: w. (Thu.) Page Size: broadsheet. Subscrip. Rate: $.50 newsstand/cover; $25/yr in county; $30/yr out of county. Circulation: 5,000 per issue (paid). **Owner(s):** Anthony & Donna Prisendorf, See address and contact information above. **Management:** Ed Shepardson, General Manager. Anthony Prisendorf, President. **Editorial:** Donna Prisendorf, Editor.

GREENFIELD

GREENFIELD ATHOL-ORANGE TOWN CRIER. 393 Main St, Greenfield, MA 01302. Telephone: 413-774-7226. FAX: 413-774-6809. E-MAIL: gtesales@reformer.com. Mailing Address: PO Box 1435, Greenfield, MA 01302-1435. Year Established: 1961. Pub. Frequency: w. (Fri.) Page Size: tabloid.Adv. Rate: col. inch $19.50 Circulation: 31,500 per issue (free). **Owner(s):** MediaNews Group, Inc., 101 W Colfax Ave, Ste 1100, Denver, CO 80202. FAX: 303-954-6320. **Management:** Bob Larson, General Manager. Martin Langeveld, Advertising Manager. **Editorial:** Cicely Eastman, Managing Editor.

GROTON

GROTON HERALD, THE. 161 Main St., Groton, MA 01450-1237. Telephone: 978-448-6061. FAX: 978-448-6031. E-MAIL: newseditor@grotonherald.com. Mailing Address: PO Box 610, Groton, MA 01450-0610. Year Established: 1979. Pub. Frequency: w. (Fri.) Page Size: tabloid. Subscrip. Rate: $.65 newsstand/cover; $28/yr in area. Adv. Rate: col. inch $8 Circulation: 2,000 per issue (paid). **Owner(s):** Groton Herald Inc., See address and contact information above. **Management:** Deborah E. Johnson, Publisher. Jane Bouvier, Advertising Manager. **Editorial:** Robert W. Stewart, Editor. Robert Mingolelli, Sports Editor.

HARVARD

BOLTON COMMON, THE. 249 Ayer Rd Ste 305, Harvard, MA 01451. Telephone: 978-456-3342. FAX: 978-456-3341. E-MAIL: bolton@cac.com. URL: http://www.townonline.com. Year Established: 1988. Pub. Frequency: w. (Fri.) Page Size: tabloid. Subscrip. Rate: $.75 newsstand/cover; $28/yr in county. Circulation: 1,446 per issue (paid). **Owner(s):** GateHouse Media, Inc, 350 WillowBrook Office Park, Fairport, NY 14450. Telephone: 585-598-0030. FAX: 585-248-2631. **Management:** Kirk Davis, Publisher. Chris Murphy, Advertising. **Editorial:** Corinne Green, Editor.

HARVARD POST, THE. 249 Ayer Rd Ste 305, Harvard, MA 01451. Telephone: 978-456-3342. FAX: 978-456-3341. E-MAIL: harvard@cnc.com. URL: http://www.townonline.com/harvard. Year Established: 1973. Pub. Frequency: w. (Fri.) Page Size: tabloid. Subscrip. Rate: $.75 newsstand/cover; $22/yr mailed. Adv. Rate: col. inch $8.50 Circulation: 3,200 per issue (paid). **Owner(s):** GateHouse Media, Inc, 350 WillowBrook Office Park, Fairport, NY 14450. Telephone: 585-598-0030. FAX: 585-248-2631. **Management:** Kirk Davis, Publisher. Chris Murphy, Advertising. **Editorial:** Linda King, Editor.

HAVERHILL

HAVERHILL GAZETTE, THE. ISSN 1082-2348
181 Merrimack St, Haverhill, MA 01830. Telephone: 978-373-1000. FAX: 978-521-6790. E-MAIL: info@hgazette.com. URL: http://www.hgazette.com. Mailing Address: PO Box 991, Haverhill, MA 01831. Year Established: 1821. Pub. Frequency: w. (Thu.) Page Size: broadsheet. Subscrip. Rate: $.75 newsstand/cover; $25/yr in county; $35/yr out of county. Adv. Rate: col. inch $12.47 Circulation: 6,350 per issue (paid). **Owner(s):** Community Newspaper Holdings, Inc., 3500 Colonnade Pkwy., Ste. 600, Birmingham, AL 35243-1031. **Management:** Ellen Zappala, Publisher. Mark Miller, Advertising Director. **Editorial:** Jean MacDougall-Tattan, Editor.

HINGHAM

COHASSET MARINER. 73 South St., Hingham, MA 02043. Telephone: 781-741-2933. FAX: 781-741-2931. E-MAIL: cohasset@cnc.. URL: http://www.townonline.com. Year Established: 1978. Pub. Frequency: w. (Thu.) Page Size: broadsheet. Subscrip. Rate: $1 newsstand/cover; $40/yr in area. Adv. Rate: col. inch $11.95 Circulation: 2,172 per issue (controlled and free). **Owner(s):** GateHouse Media, Inc, 350 WillowBrook Office Park, Fairport, NY 14450. Telephone: 585-598-0030. FAX: 585-248-2631. **Management:** Kirk Davis, Publisher. Mark Olivieri, Advertising Director. **Editorial:** Mary Ford, Editor. Mark Skala, Editor-in-Chief.

HINGHAM JOURNAL, THE. ISSN 0745-6301
73 South St., Hingham, MA 02043. Telephone: 781-741-2933. FAX: 781-741-2931. URL: http://www.townonline.com. Year Established: 1867. Pub. Frequency: w. (Thu.) Page Size: broadsheet. Subscrip. Rate: $1 newsstand/cover; $41/yr in area. Adv. Rate: col. inch $11.95 Circulation: 4,968 per issue (controlled and free). **Owner(s):** GateHouse Media, Inc, 350 WillowBrook Office Park, Fairport, NY 14450. Telephone: 585-598-0030. FAX: 585-248-2631. **Management:** Patrick J. Purcell, Publisher. Mark Olivieri, Advertising Director. **Editorial:** Mary Ford, Editor. Mark Skala, Editor-in-Chief.

HULL

HULL TIMES, THE. 41 Highland Ave, Hull, MA 02045-1133. Telephone: 781-925-9266. FAX: 781-925-0336. E-MAIL: hulltimes@aol.com. URL: http://www.hulltimes.com. Year Established: 1930. Pub. Frequency: w. (Thu.) Page Size: tabloid. Subscrip. Rate: $.75 newsstand/cover; $30/yr in city; $30/yr out of city; $30/yr in city to senior citizens. Adv. Rate: col. inch $10 Circulation: 3,000 per issue (paid). **Owner(s):** Susan Ovans, See address and contact information above. **Management:** Susan Ovans, Publisher. Roger Jackson, Advertising Director. **Editorial:** Chris Haraden, Editor.

HUNTINGTON

COUNTRY JOURNAL. 5 Main St, Huntington, MA 01050. Telephone: 413-667-3211. FAX: 413-667-3011. Mailing Address: PO Box 429, Huntington, MA 01050-0429. Year Established: 1979. Pub. Frequency: w. (Thu.) Page Size: tabloid. Subscrip. Rate: $.50 newsstand/cover; $27/yr in state; $32/yr out of state. Adv. Rate: col. inch $7 Circulation: 3,300 per issue (paid). **Owner(s):** Turley Publications, Inc., 24 Water St, Palmer, MA 01069. Telephone: 413-283-8393. FAX: 413-667-3011. **Management:** Patrick Turley, Publisher. **Editorial:** Cindy Duby, Editor.

HYANNIS

BARNSTABLE PATRIOT, THE. ISSN 0744-7221
396 Main St., Hyannis, MA 02601. Telephone: 508-771-1427. FAX: 508-790-3997. E-MAIL: news@barnstablepatriot.com. URL: http://www.barnstablepatriot.com. Mailing Address: PO Box 1208, Barnstable, MA 02601. Year Established: 1830. Pub. Frequency: w. (Fri.) Page Size: broadsheet. Subscrip. Rate: $.75 newsstand/cover; $29/yr. Adv. Rate: col. inch $12.75 Freelance Pay: $50/article. Circulation: 4,318 per issue (paid). **Owner(s):** Robert F. & Anne G. Sennott, See address and contact information above. **Management:** Anne G Sennott, Co-Publisher. Rob Sennott, Advertising Manager. **Editorial:** David Still II, Editor.

HYDE PARK

DORCHESTER ARGUS-CITIZEN. 1261 Hyde Park Ave., Hyde Park, MA 02136. Telephone: 617-361-6500. FAX: 617-268-6420. Mailing Address: PO Box 366367, Hyde Park, MA 02136. Pub. Frequency: w. Page Size: tabloid. Subscrip. Rate: $.50 newsstand/cover; $15/yr in county; $18/yr out of county. Circulation: 4,000 per issue (paid). **Owner(s):** Daniel J. Horgan, PO Box 6, Boston, MA 02127. Telephone: 617-268-3440. **Management:** Daniel J. Horgan Jr., Publisher. **Editorial:** Alice O'Leary, Editor.

HYDE PARK/MATTAPAN TRIBUNE. 1261 Hyde Park Ave., Hyde Park, MA 02136-2802. Telephone: 617-361-6500. FAX: 617-361-6503. Pub. Frequency: w. (Thu.) Page Size: tabloid. Subscrip. Rate: $.50 newsstand/cover; $15/yr in county; $18/yr out of county. Circulation: 59,000 per issue (paid). **Owner(s):** Sharp Publication Corp., See address and contact information above. **Management:** Daniel J. Horgan Jr., Publisher. Ann Diorio, Advertising Manager. **Editorial:** Alice O'Leary, Editor.

JAMAICA PLAIN CITIZEN. 1261 Hyde Park Ave., Hyde Park, MA 02136-2802. Telephone: 617-361-6500. FAX: 617-361-6503. E-MAIL: adinfo@southbostoninfo.com. Pub. Frequency: w. (Thu.) Page Size: tabloid. Subscrip. Rate: $.50 newsstand/cover; $15/yr in county; $18/yr out of county; $13/yr to senior citizens. Circulation: 5,000 per issue (paid). **Owner(s):** Sharp Publication Corp., See address and contact information above. **Management:** Daniel J. Horgan Jr., Publisher. Ann Diorio, Advertising Manager. **Editorial:** Alice O'Leary, Editor.

IPSWICH

IPSWICH CHRONICLE. 55 Market St., Ipswich, MA 01938. Telephone: 978-412-1803. FAX: 978-412-1801. E-MAIL: ipswich@cnc.com. URL: http://www.townonline. Year Established: 1872. Pub. Frequency: w. (Thu.) Page Size: broadsheet. Subscrip. Rate: $1 newsstand/cover; $40/yr in area. Adv. Rate: col. inch $15.15 Circulation: 3,900 per issue (paid). **Owner(s):** GateHouse Media, Inc, 350 WillowBrook Office Park, Fairport, NY 14450. Telephone: 585-598-0030. FAX: 585-248-2631. **Management:** Kirk Davis, Publisher. Chuck Goodrich, Vice President. **Editorial:** Jane Enos, Editor. Marlene Switzer, Editor-in-Chief.

LEE

BERKSHIRE PENNY SAVER. 14 Park Pl, Lee, MA 1238. Telephone: 413-243-2341. FAX: 413-243-4662. Mailing Address: P O Box 300, Lee, MA 1238-0300. Year Established: 1963. Pub. Frequency: w. (Tue.) Page Size: tabloid.Adv. Rate: col. inch $7.75 Circulation: 14,500 per issue (paid and controlled). **Owner(s):** Hersam Acorn Newspapers LLC, 16 Bailey Ave., Ridgefield, CT 06877. Telephone: 203-438-6544. FAX: 203-861-0023. **Management:** Scott McElhaney, President. Dani J Holmes, Publisher.

LEXINGTON

ARLINGTON ADVOCATE. 9 Meriam St., Lexington, MA 02420. Telephone: 781-674-7726. FAX: 781-674-7735. E-MAIL: arlington@cnc.com. URL: http://www.townonline.com. Year Established: 1872. Pub. Frequency: w. (Thu.) Page Size: broadsheet. Subscrip. Rate: $1 newsstand/cover; $43/yr mailed in area. Adv. Rate: col. inch $20.25 Freelance Pay: $20-$50/article. Circulation: 8,547 per issue (paid). **Owner(s):** GateHouse Media, Inc, 350 WillowBrook Office Park, Fairport, NY 14450. Telephone: 585-598-0030. FAX: 585-248-2631. **Management:** Kirk Davis, Publisher. Ann Marie Magerman, Advertising Director. **Editorial:** Les Masterson, Editor. Kathy Cordeiro, Editor-in-Chief.

BELMONT CITIZEN-HERALD. 9 Meriam St., Lexington, MA 02420. Telephone: 781-674-7723. FAX: 781-674-7735. E-MAIL: belmont@cnc.com. URL: http://www.townonline.com. Year Established: 1919. Pub. Frequency: w. (Thu.) Page Size: broadsheet. Subscrip. Rate: $1 newsstand/cover; $43/yr mailed in area. Adv. Rate: col. inch $18.25 Circulation: 5,120 per issue (paid). **Owner(s):** GateHouse Media, Inc, 350 WillowBrook Office Park, Fairport, NY 14450. Telephone: 585-598-0030. FAX: 585-248-2631. **Management:** Kirk Davis, Publisher. Ann Marie Magerman, Advertising Director. **Editorial:** Linda Pinkow, Editor. Kathy Cordeiro, Editor-in-Chief.

LEXINGTON MINUTEMAN. ISSN 1081-8146
9 Meriam St., Lexington, MA 02420. Telephone: 781-674-7725. FAX: 781-674-7735. E-MAIL: lexington@cnc.com. URL: http://www.townonline.com. Year Established: 1871. Pub. Frequency: w. (Thu.) Page Size: broadsheet. Subscrip. Rate: $1 newsstand/cover; $46/yr mailed in area. Adv. Rate: col. inch $21.20 Circulation: 7,573 per issue (paid). **Owner(s):** GateHouse Media, Inc, 350 WillowBrook Office Park, Fairport, NY 14450. Telephone: 585-598-0030. FAX: 585-248-2631. **Management:** Kirk Davis, Publisher. Ann Marie Magerman, Advertising Director. **Editorial:** Susan Bushey, Editor. Kathy Cordeiro, Editor-in-Chief.

WINCHESTER STAR. 9 Meriam St., Lexington, MA 02420. Telephone: 781-674-7733. FAX: 781-674-7735. E-MAIL: winchester@cnc.com. URL: http://www.townonline.com. Year Established: 1880. Pub. Frequency: w. (Thu.) Page Size: broadsheet. Subscrip. Rate: $1 newsstand/cover; $43/yr mailed in area. Adv. Rate: col. inch $17.50 Freelance Pay: $20-$50/article. Circulation: 4,495 per issue (paid). **Owner(s):** GateHouse Media, Inc, 350 WillowBrook Office Park, Fairport, NY 14450. Telephone: 585-598-0030. FAX: 585-248-2631. **Management:** Kirk Davis, Publisher. Ann Marie Magerman, Advertising Director. **Editorial:** David Smith, Editor. Kathy Cordeiro, Editor-in-Chief.

LOWELL

VALLEY DISPATCH, THE. 491 Dutton St, Lowell, MA 01852. Telephone: 978-458-7100. FAX: 978-970-4600. E-MAIL: circulation@lowellsun.com. URL: http://www.thevalleydispatch.com. Year Established: 1973. Pub. Frequency: w. (Fri.) Page Size: tabloid. Subscrip. Rate: $19.95/yr mailed. Adv. Rate: col. inch $17.24 Circulation: 21,000 per issue (paid and free). **Owner(s):** MediaNews Group, Inc., 101 W Colfax Ave, Ste 1100, Denver, CO 80202. FAX: 303-954-6320. **Management:** Mark O'Neil, Publisher. Mike Sheehan, Circulation Director. **Editorial:** James Campanini, Editor. Dennis Whitton, Sports Editor.

1590 BROADCASTER. ISSN 0192-8597
255 Main St, Lowell, MA 01853. Telephone: 603-886-6075. FAX: 603-866-8180. E-MAIL: BroadcasterNews@aol.com. URL: http://www.1590.com. Mailing Address: PO Box 548, Nashua, NH 03061-0548. Year Established: 1964. Pub. Frequency: w. Page Size: tabloid. Circulation: 63,500 (controlled). **Owner(s):** 1590 Broadcasting Corp., See address and contact information above. **Management:** Kendall Wallace, Publisher. Paul Schwabe, Advertising Director. Mark Iacuessa, Advertising Manager. Steven Darling, Circulation Manager. Margaret Titus, Classified Adv. Mgr.. **Editorial:** Bill Flaucher, Editor-in-Chief. John Collins, News Editor.

LYNNFIELD

LYNNFIELD VILLAGER. ISSN 1077-2308
55 Salem St., Lynnfield, MA 01940-2645. Telephone: 781-334-6319. Mailing Address: PO Box 186, Lynnfield, MA 01940-0186. Year Established: 1973. Pub. Frequency: w. (Wed.) Page Size: tabloid. Subscrip. Rate: $.50 newsstand/cover; $17/yr in county; $20/yr out of area out of town. Adv. Rate: col. inch $7.05 Circulation: 1,800 per issue (paid). **Owner(s):** Great Oak Publications, Inc., 7 Bow St., North Reading, MA 01864-2534. Telephone: 978-664-4761. FAX: 978-664-4954. **Management:** Albert E. Sylvia, Publisher. Albert E. Sylvia Jr., Advertising Manager. Eileen Eaton, Circulation Manager. **Editorial:** Albert E. Sylvia Jr., Editor. Kathleen Correale, Associate Editor. Albert E. Sylvia Jr., News Editor.

MANCHESTER

MANCHESTER CRICKET, THE. 50 Summer St., Manchester, MA 01944-1518. Telephone: 978-526-7131. FAX: 978-526-8193. E-MAIL: news@cricketpress.com. Year Established: 1888. Pub. Frequency: w. (Fri.) Page Size: standard. Subscrip. Rate: $.60 newsstand/cover; $25/yr in county. Adv. Rate: col. inch $10 Circulation: 2,515 per issue (paid). **Owner(s):** The Cricket Press, Inc., 50 Summer St., Manchester, MA 01944. Telephone: 978-526-7131. FAX: 978-526-8193. **Management:** Harry E. Slade Jr., Publisher. **Editorial:** Patricia Slade, Managing Editor.

MARBLEHEAD

MARBLEHEAD REPORTER. 122 Washington St, Marblehead, MA 01945. Telephone: 781-631-7700. FAX: 781-639-4801. E-MAIL: marblehead@cnc.com. URL: http://www.townonline.com. Year Established: 1964. Pub. Frequency: w. (Thu.) Page Size: broadsheet. Subscrip. Rate: $1 newsstand/cover; $41/yr mailed in area. Adv. Rate: col. inch $22.95 Circulation: 6,400 per issue (paid and free). **Owner(s):** GateHouse Media, Inc, 350 WillowBrook Office Park, Fairport, NY 14450. Telephone: 585-598-0030. FAX: 585-248-2631. **Management:** Kirk Davis, Publisher. Nan Weissenberger, Advertising. **Editorial:** Lou Sumner, Editor. Marlene Switzer, Editor-in-Chief.

SWAMPSCOTT REPORTER. 122 Washington St, Marblehead, MA 01945. Telephone: 781-631-7700. FAX: 781-639-4801. E-MAIL: swampscott@cnc.com. URL: http://www.townonline.com. Year Established: 1865. Pub. Frequency: w. (Thu.) Page Size: broadsheet. Subscrip. Rate: $1 newsstand/cover; $39/yr mailed in area. Adv. Rate: col. inch $22.95 Freelance Pay: $25/story. Circulation: 3,252 per issue (paid). **Owner(s):** GateHouse Media, Inc, 350 WillowBrook Office Park, Fairport, NY 14450. Telephone: 585-598-0030. FAX: 585-248-2631. **Management:** Kirk Davis, Publisher. Nan Weissenberger, Advertising. **Editorial:** Marlene Switzer, Editor-in-Chief.

MARLBOROUGH

HUDSON SUN. 40 Mechanic St Ste 220, Marlborough, MA 01752-3252. Telephone: 508-490-7455. FAX: 508-490-7471. E-MAIL: hudson@cnc.com. URL: http://www.townonline.com. Year Established: 1903. Pub. Frequency: w. (Thu.) Page Size: broadsheet. Subscrip. Rate: $.50 newsstand/cover; $36/yr mailed. Adv. Rate: col. inch $17.30 Freelance Pay: $45/article. Circulation: 3,500 per issue (paid and free). **Owner(s):** GateHouse Media, Inc, 350 WillowBrook Office Park, Fairport, NY 14450. Telephone: 585-598-0030. FAX: 585-248-2631. **Management:** Kirk Davis, Publisher. Mark Olivieri, Advertising Director. **Editorial:** Marilyn Spencer, Editor. Richard Lodge, Editor-in-Chief.

Weeklies

MARLBOROUGH ENTERPRISE. 40 Mechanic St Ste 220, Marlborough, MA 01752-3252. Telephone: 508-490-7455. FAX: 508-490-7471. E-MAIL: enterprisesun@cnc.com. URL: http://www.townonline.com. Pub. Frequency: w. (Thu.) Page Size: broadsheet. Subscrip. Rate: $1 newsstand/cover; $36/yr. Adv. Rate: col. inch $18 Freelance Pay: $40/story. Circulation: 7,254 per issue (paid). **Owner(s):** GateHouse Media, Inc, 350 WillowBrook Office Park, Fairport, NY 14450. Telephone: 585-598-0030. FAX: 585-248-2631. **Management:** Kirk Davis, Publisher. Mark Olivieri, Advertising Director. **Editorial:** Cathrine Buday, Editor. Richard Lodge, Editor-in-Chief.

NORTHBOROUGH-SOUTHBOROUGH VILLAGER, THE. 40 Mechanic St Ste 220, Marlborough, MA 01752-3252. Telephone: 508-490-7455. FAX: 508-490-7471. URL: http://www.townonline.com. Pub. Frequency: w. (Fri.) Subscrip. Rate: $.75 newsstand/cover; $35/yr. **Owner(s):** GateHouse Media, Inc, 350 WillowBrook Office Park, Fairport, NY 14450. Telephone: 585-598-0030. FAX: 585-248-2631. **Management:** Kirk Davis, Publisher. Mark Olivieri, Advertising Director. **Editorial:** Glenda Hazard, Editor. Richard Lodge, Editor-in-Chief.

SHREWSBURY CHRONICLE. ISSN 1541-7255
40 Mechanic St Ste 220, Marlborough, MA 01752-3252. Telephone: 508-490-7455. FAX: 508-490-7471. E-MAIL: shrewsbury@cnc.com. URL: http://www.townonline.com. Pub. Frequency: w. (Thu.) Page Size: broadsheet. Subscrip. Rate: $.50 newsstand/cover; $22/yr. Adv. Rate: col. inch $13.60 Circulation: 4,500 per issue (paid and free). **Owner(s):** GateHouse Media, Inc, 350 WillowBrook Office Park, Fairport, NY 14450. Telephone: 585-598-0030. FAX: 585-248-2631. **Management:** Kirk Davis, Publisher. Mark Olivieri, Advertising Director. **Editorial:** Glenda Hazard, Editor. Richard Lodge, Editor-in-Chief.

MARSHFIELD

ABINGTON MARINER. 165 Enterprise Dr, Marshfield, MA 02050. Telephone: 781-837-4555. FAX: 781-837-4547. E-MAIL: abington@cnc.com. URL: http://www.townonline.com. Pub. Frequency: w. (Fri.) Page Size: broadsheet. Subscrip. Rate: $.75 newsstand/cover; $29/yr local. Adv. Rate: col. inch $12.80 Circulation: 2,809 per issue (paid). **Owner(s):** GateHouse Media, Inc, 350 WillowBrook Office Park, Fairport, NY 14450. Telephone: 585-598-0030. FAX: 585-248-2631. **Management:** Kirk Davis, Publisher. Mark Olivieri, Advertising Director. **Editorial:** Matthew Gill, Editor.

CARVER REPORTER. 165 Enterprise Dr, Marshfield, MA 02050. Telephone: 781-837-4555. FAX: 781-837-4547. E-MAIL: carver@cnc.com. URL: http://www.wickedlocal.com. Year Established: 1988. Pub. Frequency: w. (Thu.) Page Size: tabloid. Subscrip. Rate: $.75 newsstand/cover; $28/yr in county; $37/yr out of county. Adv. Rate: col. inch $7.60 Circulation: 2,443 per issue (paid). **Owner(s):** GateHouse Media, Inc, 350 WillowBrook Office Park, Fairport, NY 14450. Telephone: 585-598-0030. FAX: 585-248-2631. **Management:** Sean Burke, Publisher. Tom Booth, Advertising Director. Lynn Pelletier, Circulation Director. Jeanette Dowd, Classified Adv. Mgr.. **Editorial:** Scott Smith, Managing Editor.

DUXBURY REPORTER. ISSN 0899-6229
165 Enterprise Dr, Marshfield, MA 02050. Telephone: 781-837-4555. FAX: 781-837-4547. E-MAIL: duxbury@cnc.com. URL: http://www.wickedlocal. Year Established: 1987. Pub. Frequency: w. (Fri.) Page Size: tabloid. Subscrip. Rate: $28/yr in county; $38/yr out of county. Adv. Rate: col. inch $7.45 Circulation: 3,373 per issue (free). **Owner(s):** GateHouse Media, Inc, 350 WillowBrook Office Park, Fairport, NY 14450. Telephone: 585-598-0030. **Management:** Sean Burke, Publisher. Tom Booth, Advertising Director. Lynn Pelletier, Circulation Director. **Editorial:** Matthew Nadler, Editor. Sarah Corbitt, Editor-in-Chief.

HALIFAX/PLYMPTON REPORTER. ISSN 8750-0485
165 Enterprise Dr, Marshfield, MA 02050. Telephone: 781-837-4555. FAX: 781-837-4547. E-MAIL: halifaxplympton@cnc.com. URL: http://www.townonline.com. Year Established: 1984. Pub. Frequency: w. (Thu.) Page Size: tabloid. Subscrip. Rate: $.75 newsstand/cover; $28/yr in county. Adv. Rate: col. inch $7.60 Circulation: 1,418 per issue (paid). **Owner(s):** GateHouse Media, Inc, 350 WillowBrook Office Park, Fairport, NY 14450. Telephone: 585-598-0030. FAX: 585-248-2631. **Management:** Sean Burke, Publisher. Tom Booth, Advertising Director. Lynn Pelletier, Circulation Director. Jeanette Dowd, Classified Adv. Mgr.. **Editorial:** Matthew Nadler, Editor. Sarah Corbitt, Editor-in-Chief.

HANOVER MARINER. ISSN 0745-7960
165 Enterprise Dr, Marshfield, MA 02050. Telephone: 781-837-4555. FAX: 781-837-4547. E-MAIL: hanover@cnc.com. URL: http://www.townonline.com. Year Established: 1981. Pub. Frequency: w. (Wed.) Page Size: broadsheet. Subscrip. Rate: $1 newsstand/cover; $37.50/yr in county. Adv. Rate: col. inch $10.95 Circulation: 2,595 per issue (paid). **Owner(s):** GateHouse Media, Inc, 350 WillowBrook Office Park, Fairport, NY 14450. Telephone: 585-598-0030. FAX: 585-248-2631. **Management:** Kirk Davis, Publisher. Mark Olivieri, Advertising Director. **Editorial:** Matthew Gill, Editor.

KINGSTON MARINER. 165 Enterprise Dr, Marshfield, MA 02050. Telephone: 781-837-4555. FAX: 781-837-4547. E-MAIL: kingston@cnc.com. URL: http://www.townonline.com/kingston. Pub. Frequency: w. (Fri.) Page Size: broadsheet. Subscrip. Rate: $.75 newsstand/cover; $30/yr mailed in area. Adv. Rate: col. inch $10.40 Circulation: 2,600 per issue (paid). **Owner(s):** GateHouse Media, Inc, 350 WillowBrook Office Park, Fairport, NY 14450. Telephone: 585-598-0030. FAX: 585-248-2631. **Management:** Kirk Davis, Publisher. Mark Olivieri, Advertising Director. **Editorial:** Paula Woodhull, Editor. Mark Skala, Editor-in-Chief.

MARSHFIELD MARINER. 165 Enterprise Dr, Marshfield, MA 02050. Telephone: 781-837-4555. FAX: 781-837-4547. E-MAIL: marshfield@cnc.com. URL: http://www.townonline.com. Year Established: 1972. Pub. Frequency: w. (Wed.) Page Size: broadsheet. Subscrip. Rate: $.75 newsstand/cover; $40/yr mailed in area. Adv. Rate: col. inch $11.95 Circulation: 4,344 per issue (controlled and free). **Owner(s):** GateHouse Media, Inc, 350 WillowBrook Office Park, Fairport, NY 14450. Telephone: 585-598-0030. FAX: 585-248-2631. **Management:** Kirk Davis, Publisher. Mark Olivieri, Advertising Director. **Editorial:** Matthew Gill, Editor. Mark Skala, Editor-in-Chief.

MARSHFIELD REPORTER. 165 Enterprise Dr, Marshfield, MA 02050. Telephone: 781-837-4555. FAX: 781-837-4547. E-MAIL: marshfield@cnc.com. URL: http://www.wickedlocal.com. Year Established: 1987. Pub. Frequency: w. (Fri.) Page Size: tabloid. Subscrip. Rate: $39/yr in county; $63/yr out of county. Adv. Rate: col. inch $7.60 Circulation: 4,341 per issue (free). **Owner(s):** GateHouse Media, Inc, 350 WillowBrook Office Park, Fairport, NY 14450. Telephone: 585-598-0030. FAX: 585-248-2631. **Management:** Kirk Davis, Publisher. Mark Olivieri, Advertising Director. **Editorial:** Bill Fonda, Editor.

NORWELL MARINER. 165 Enterprise Dr, Marshfield, MA 02050. Telephone: 781-837-4555. FAX: 781-837-4547. E-MAIL: norwell@cnc.com. URL: http://www.townonline.com. Year Established: 1974. Pub. Frequency: w. (Thu.) Page Size: broadsheet. Subscrip. Rate: $1 newsstand/cover; $44/yr mailed in area. Adv. Rate: col. inch $11.95 Circulation: 2,114 per issue (paid). **Owner(s):** GateHouse Media, Inc, 350 WillowBrook Office Park, Fairport, NY 14450. Telephone: 585-598-0030. FAX: 585-248-2631. **Management:** Kirk Davis, Publisher. Mark Olivieri, Advertising Director. **Editorial:** Matthew Gill, Editor. Mark Skala, Editor-in-Chief.

PEMBROKE MARINER. 165 Enterprise Dr, Marshfield, MA 02050. Telephone: 781-837-4555. FAX: 781-837-4547. E-MAIL: pwoodhull@cnc.com. URL: http://www.townonline.com. Year Established: 1983. Pub. Frequency: w. (Wed.) Page Size: broadsheet. Subscrip. Rate: $.75 newsstand/cover; $35/yr local. Adv. Rate: col. inch $10.40 Circulation: 1,840 per issue (paid). **Owner(s):** GateHouse Media, Inc, 350 WillowBrook Office Park, Fairport, NY 14450. Telephone: 585-598-0030. FAX: 585-248-2631. **Management:** Patrick J. Purcell, Publisher. Mark Olivieri, Advertising Director. Ryan Farrell, Circulation Manager. **Editorial:** Paula Woodhull, Editor. Mark Skala, Editor-in-Chief.

PEMBROKE MARINER/REPORTER. 165 Enterprise Dr, Marshfield, MA 02050. Telephone: 781-837-4555. FAX: 781-837-4547. E-MAIL: pembroke@cnc.com. URL: http://www.wickedlocal.com. Year Established: 1983. Pub. Frequency: w. (Thu.) Page Size: tabloid. Subscrip. Rate: $.75 newsstand/cover; $34.50/yr in county; $63/yr out of county. Adv. Rate: col. inch $7.60 Circulation: 1,407 per issue (paid). **Owner(s):** GateHouse Media, Inc, 350 WillowBrook Office Park, Fairport, NY 14450. Telephone: 585-598-0030. **Management:** Kirk Davis, Publisher. Lynn Pelletier, Circulation Director. Jeanette Dowd, Classified Adv. Mgr.. **Editorial:** Bill Fonda, Editor.

ROCKLAND MARINER. 165 Enterprise Dr, Marshfield, MA 02050. Telephone: 781-837-4555. FAX: 781-837-4547. E-MAIL: rockland@cnc.com. URL: http://www.townonline.com. Pub. Frequency: w. (Fri.) Subscrip. Rate: $.75 newsstand/cover; $29/yr local. **Owner(s):** GateHouse Media, Inc, 350 WillowBrook Office Park, Fairport, NY 14450. Telephone: 585-598-0030. FAX: 585-248-2631. **Management:** Kirk Davis, Publisher. Mark Olivieri, Advertising Director. **Editorial:** Matthew Gill, Editor.

SCITUATE MARINER. 165 Enterprise Dr, Marshfield, MA 02050. Telephone: 781-837-4555. FAX: 781-837-4547. E-MAIL: scituate@cnc.com. URL: http://www.townonline.com. Year Established: 1867. Pub. Frequency: w. (Thu.) Page Size: broadsheet. Subscrip. Rate: $.75 newsstand/cover; $42/yr in area (effective 2007); $63/yr in area. Adv. Rate: col. inch $11.95 Circulation: 4,253 per issue (paid). **Owner(s):** GateHouse Media, Inc, 350 WillowBrook Office Park, Fairport, NY 14450. Telephone: 585-598-0030. FAX: 585-248-2631. **Management:** Kirk Davis, Publisher. Mark Olivieri, Advertising Director. **Editorial:** Bill Fonda, Editor.

SENTINEL (MARSHFIELD), THE. 165 Enterprise Dr, Marshfield, MA 02050. Telephone: 781-837-4555. FAX: 781-837-4547. E-MAIL: thesentinel@cnc.com. URL: http://www.wickedlocal.com. Year Established: 1963. Pub. Frequency: w. (Thu.) Subscrip. Rate: $28/yr in county; $38/yr out of county. **Owner(s):** GateHouse Media, Inc, 350 WillowBrook Office Park, Fairport, NY 14450. Telephone: 585-598-0030. FAX: 585-248-2631. **Management:** Kirk Davis, Publisher. Tom Booth, Advertising Director. Jeanette Dowd, Classified Adv. Mgr.. **Editorial:** Matthew Nadler, Editor. Sarah Corbitt, Editor-in-Chief.

WAREHAM COURIER. 165 Enterprise Dr, Marshfield, MA 02050. Telephone: 781-837-4555. FAX: 781-837-4547. E-MAIL: wareham@cnc.com. URL: http://www.wickedlocal.com. Year Established: 1894. Pub. Frequency: w. (Thu.) Page Size: tabloid. Subscrip. Rate: $.75 newsstand/cover; $28/yr in county; $38/yr mailed out of county. Adv. Rate: col. inch $10.95 Circulation: 4,822 per issue (paid). **Owner(s):** GateHouse Media, Inc, 350 WillowBrook Office Park, Fairport, NY 14450. Telephone: 585-598-0030. FAX: 585-248-2631. **Management:** Sean Burke, Publisher. Tom Booth, Advertising Director. Lynn Pelletier, Circulation Director. Jeanette Dowd, Classified Adv. Mgr.. **Editorial:** Charles Matthewson, Editor. Sarah Corbitt, Editor-in-Chief.

WAREHAM PENNYSAVER. 165 Enterprise Dr, Marshfield, MA 02050. Telephone: 781-837-4555. FAX: 781-837-4547. URL: http://www.townonline.com. Pub. Frequency: w. (Thu.) Page Size: broadsheet.Adv. Rate: col. inch $11.95 Circulation: 8,000 per issue (free). **Owner(s):** GateHouse Media, Inc, 350 WillowBrook Office Park, Fairport, NY 14450. Telephone: 585-598-0030. FAX: 585-248-2631. **Management:** Kirk Davis, Publisher. Mark Olivieri, Advertising Director. **Editorial:** Mark Skala, Editor-in-Chief.

MATTAPOISETT

WANDERER, THE. ISSN 1559-1212
55 County Rd., Mattapoisett, MA 02739-1640. Telephone: 508-758-9055. FAX: 508-758-4845. E-MAIL: office@wanderer.com. URL: http://www.wanderer.com. Mailing Address: PO Box 102, Mattapoisett, MA 02739-0102. Year Established: 1992. Pub. Frequency: w. (Thu.) Page Size: tabloid.Subscrip. Rate: $23 for 6 mos.; $40/yr Circulation: 5,000 per issue (free). **Owner(s):** Paul Lopes, See address and contact information above. **Management:** Paul Lopes, Publisher. **Editorial:** Kenneth J. Souza, News Editor.

MEDFORD

MALDEN OBSERVER. ISSN 1093-0507
57 High St., Medford, MA 02155. Telephone: 781-393-1827. FAX: 781-739-8501. E-MAIL: malden@cnc.com. URL: http://www.wickedlocal.com/malden/. Pub. Frequency: w. (Fri.) Page Size: broadsheet. Subscrip. Rate: $.75/yr newsstand/cover local; $31/yr local. Adv. Rate: col. inch $16.65 Circulation: 8,100 per issue (paid and free). **Owner(s):** GateHouse Media, Inc, 350 WillowBrook Office Park, Fairport, NY 14450. FAX: 585-248-2631. **Management:** Kirk Davis, Publisher. **Editorial:** Timothy Lavallue, Editor. Marlene Switzer, Editor-in-Chief.

MEDFORD TRANSCRIPT, THE. ISSN 1066-8861
57 High St., Medford, MA 02155. Telephone: 781-393-1827. FAX: 781-739-8501. E-MAIL: medford@cnc.com. URL: http://www.townonline.com. Year Established: 1990. Pub. Frequency: w. (Thu.) Page Size: broadsheet. Subscrip. Rate: $.75 newsstand/cover; $28/yr mailed in area. Adv. Rate: col. inch $16.95 Circulation: 2,610 per issue (paid). **Owner(s):** GateHouse Media, Inc, 350 WillowBrook Office Park, Fairport, NY 14450. Telephone: 585-598-0030. FAX: 585-248-2631. **Management:** Kirk Davis, Publisher. **Editorial:** Neil Escobar Coakley, Editor. Marlene Switzer, Editor-in-Chief.

MIDDLEBORO

MIDDLEBORO GAZETTE. 148 W. Grove St., Middleboro, MA 02346. Telephone: 508-947-1760. FAX: 508-947-9426. E-MAIL: mgazette@gis.net. Mailing Address: PO Box 551, Middleboro, MA 02346. Year Established: 1852. Pub. Frequency: w. (Thu.) Page Size: broadsheet. Subscrip. Rate: $.50 newsstand/cover; $29.75/yr in county; $49.75/yr mailed out of county. Freelance Pay: $30/story. Circulation: 6,500 per issue (paid). **Owner(s):** Ottaway Newspapers, Inc., 1500 Main St., Wheeling, WV 26003. Telephone: 304-233-0100. FAX: 304-233-0327. **Management:** Mary Harrington, General Manager. **Editorial:** Jane Lopes, Editor.

MILFORD

COUNTRY GAZETTE, THE. 159 S. Main St., Milford, MA 01757. Telephone: 508-634-7563. FAX: 508-634-7514. E-MAIL: gazette@cnc.com. Pub. Frequency: w. (Wed.) Page Size: standard. Subscrip. Rate: $26/yr mailed. Adv. Rate: col. inch $33.40 Circulation: 29,830 per issue (free). **Owner(s):** GateHouse Media, Inc, 350 WillowBrook Office Park, Fairport, NY 14450. Telephone: 585-598-0030. FAX: 585-248-2631. **Management:** Kirk Davis, Publisher. Tom Sawyer, Advertising Director. **Editorial:** Tracey Lewis, Editor.

EASTON JOURNAL. 159 S. Main St., Milford, MA 01757. Telephone: 508-634-7563. FAX: 508-634-7514. E-MAIL: easton@cnc.com. URL: http://www.townonline.com. Pub. Frequency: w. (Fri.) Page Size: broadsheet. Subscrip. Rate: $.50 newsstand/cover; $24/yr in county. Adv. Rate: col. inch $12.85 Circulation: 5,598 per issue (paid). **Owner(s):** GateHouse Media, Inc, 350 WillowBrook Office Park, Fairport, NY 14450. Telephone: 585-598-0030. FAX: 585-248-2631. **Management:** Kirk Davis, Publisher. Mark Olivieri, Advertising Director. Tom Marquis, Circulation Director. **Editorial:** Donna Whitehead, Editor. Richard Lodge, Editor-in-Chief. Mike Hardman, Sports.

MANSFIELD NEWS, THE. 159 S. Main St., Milford, MA 01757. Telephone: 508-634-7563. FAX: 508-634-7514. E-MAIL: mansfield@cnc.com. URL: http://www.townonline.com. Year Established: 1873. Pub. Frequency: w. (Fri.) Page Size: broadsheet. Subscrip. Rate: $.50 newsstand/cover; $33/yr local area. Adv. Rate: col. inch $10.90 Circulation: 4,189 per issue (paid). **Owner(s):** GateHouse Media, Inc, 350 WillowBrook Office Park, Fairport, NY 14450. Telephone: 585-598-0030. FAX: 585-248-2631. **Management:** Kirk Davis, Publisher. Mark Olivieri, Advertising Director. **Editorial:** Donna Whitehead, Editor. Richard Lodge, Editor-in-Chief. Mike Hardman, Sports.

NORTON MIRROR. 159 S. Main St., Milford, MA 01757. Telephone: 508-634-7563. FAX: 508-634-7514. E-MAIL: norton@cnc.com. URL: http://www.townonline.com. Pub. Frequency: w. (Fri.) Page Size: broadsheet. Subscrip. Rate: $.35 newsstand/cover; $29/yr. Adv. Rate: col. inch $10.65 Circulation: 2,472 per issue (paid). **Owner(s):** GateHouse Media, Inc, 350 WillowBrook Office Park, Fairport, NY 14450. Telephone: 585-598-0030. FAX: 585-248-2631. **Management:** Kirk Davis, Publisher. Mark Olivieri, Advertising Director. **Editorial:** Donna Whitehead, Editor. Richard Lodge, Editor-in-Chief. Mike Hardman, Sports.

MILLBURY

MILLBURY-SUTTON CHRONICLE. 117 Elm St., Millbury, MA 01527. Telephone: 508-865-1645. Year Established: 1986. Pub. Frequency: w. (Thu.) Page Size: tabloid.Subscrip. Rate: $.35 newsstand/cover; $13/yr Circulation: 2,500 per issue (paid). **Owner(s):** Andree Belisle, See address and contact information above. **Management:** A.G. Belisle, Publisher. A.A. Belisle, Advertising Manager. **Editorial:** Andree Belisle, Editor-in-Chief.

MILTON VILLAGE

MILTON RECORD TRANSCRIPT. 26 High St., Milton Village, MA 02186. Telephone: 617-698-6563. FAX: 617-698-7827. Mailing Address: PO Box 126, Milton Village, MA 02187. Year Established: 1900. Pub. Frequency: w. (Fri.) Page Size: broadsheet. Subscrip. Rate: $.50 newsstand/cover (effective 2005); $20/yr in county; $22/yr out of county. Freelance Pay: $35-$50/story. Circulation: 5,900 per issue (paid). **Owner(s):** Tribune Publishing Company, Inc., 1261 Hyde Park Ave., Hyde Park, MA 02136. Telephone: 617-361-6500. **Management:** Daniel Horgan, Publisher. **Editorial:** Alice O'Leary, Editor.

NANTUCKET

INQUIRER & MIRROR, THE. One Old South Rd., Nantucket, MA 02554. Telephone: 508-228-0001. FAX: 508-325-5089. E-MAIL: newsroom@inkym.com. URL: http://www.ack.net. Mailing Address: PO Box 1198, Nantucket, MA 02554. Year Established: 1821. Pub. Frequency: w. (Thu.) Page Size: broadsheet. Subscrip. Rate: $1 newsstand/cover; $50/yr on island; $58/yr out of area. Freelance Pay: $50/story. Circulation: 15,000 per issue (paid). **Owner(s):** Ottaway Newspapers, Inc., PO Box 401, Campbell Hall, NY 10916. Telephone: 845-294-8181. **Management:** Marianne Stanton, Publisher. Lora Kebbati, Advertising. Nicole Wynne, Circulation Manager. Joshua Gray, Classified Adv. Mgr.. **Editorial:** Marianne Stanton, Editor. Joshua Balling, Managing Editor. Carrie Leland, Assistant Editor. Nicole Harnishfeger, Photographer. Dean Geddes, Sports.

NEEDHAM

ALLSTON/BRIGHTON TAB. 254 Second Ave., Needham, MA 02494. Telephone: 781-433-8200. FAX: 781-433-8202. E-MAIL: allston-brighton@cnc.com. URL: http://www.townonline.com. Pub. Frequency: w. (Fri.) Page Size: broadsheet. Subscrip. Rate: $.75 newsstand/cover; $32/yr in area. Adv. Rate: col. inch $14.05 Circulation: 5,054 per issue (paid). **Owner(s):** GateHouse Media, Inc, 350 WillowBrook Office Park, Fairport, NY 14450. Telephone: 585-598-0030. FAX: 585-248-2631. **Management:** Kirk Davis, Publisher. Christine Warren, Advertising Director. **Editorial:** Richard Lodge, Editor-in-Chief.

BROOKLINE TAB. ISSN 0745-2071
254 Second Ave., Needham, MA 02494. Telephone: 781-433-8200. FAX: 781-433-8202. E-MAIL: info@cnc.com. URL: http://www.townonline.com. Year Established: 1979. Pub. Frequency: w. (Thu.) Page Size: broadsheet. Subscrip. Rate: $30/yr mailed. Adv. Rate: col. inch $27.70 Circulation: 14,830 per issue (paid and free). **Owner(s):** GateHouse Media, Inc, 350 WillowBrook Office Park, Fairport, NY 14450. Telephone: 585-598-0030. FAX: 585-248-2631. **Management:** Kirk Davis, Publisher. Christine Warren, Advertising Director. **Editorial:** Leslie Mahoney, Editor. Richard Lodge, Editor-in-Chief.

CAMBRIDGE TAB. 254 Second Ave., Needham, MA 02494. Telephone: 781-433-8200. FAX: 781-433-8202. E-MAIL: info@cnc.com. URL: http://www.townonline.com. Pub. Frequency: w. (Fri.) Page Size: broadsheet.Adv. Rate: col. inch $22.85 Circulation: 5,854 per issue (paid and free). **Owner(s):** GateHouse Media, Inc, 350 WillowBrook Office Park, Fairport, NY 14450. Telephone: 585-598-0030. FAX: 585-248-2631. **Management:** Kirk Davis, Publisher. Christine Warren, Advertising Director. **Editorial:** Valentine Zig, Editor.

DOVER-SHERBORN PRESS, THE. 254 Second Ave., Needham, MA 02494. Telephone: 781-433-8200. FAX: 781-433-8202. E-MAIL: dover-sherborn@cnc.com. URL: http://www.townonline.com. Pub. Frequency: w. (Thu.) Page Size: broadsheet. Subscrip. Rate: $.75 newsstand/cover; $37/yr; $44/yr mailed out of state. Adv. Rate: col. inch $13 Circulation: 1,796 per issue (paid and free). **Owner(s):** GateHouse Media, Inc, 350 WillowBrook Office Park, Fairport, NY 14450. Telephone: 585-598-0030. FAX: 585-248-2631. **Management:** Kirk Davis, Publisher. Christine Warren, Advertising Director. **Editorial:** Nick Katz, Editor.

MEDFIELD PRESS. 254 Second Ave., Needham, MA 02494. Telephone: 781-433-8200. FAX: 781-433-8202. E-MAIL: medfieldpress@cnc.com. URL: http://www.townonline.com. Year Established: 1932. Pub. Frequency: w. (Thu.) Page Size: broadsheet. Subscrip. Rate: $.75 newsstand/cover; $37/yr in area. Adv. Rate: col. inch $11.40 Circulation: 2,700 per issue (paid). **Owner(s):** GateHouse Media, Inc, 350 WillowBrook Office Park, Fairport, NY 14450. Telephone: 585-598-0030. FAX: 585-248-2631. **Management:** Kirk Davis, Publisher. **Editorial:** Richard Lodge, Editor-in-Chief.

NEEDHAM TIMES. 254 Second Ave., Needham, MA 02494. Telephone: 781-433-8200. FAX: 781-433-8202. E-MAIL: info@cnc.com. URL: http://www.townonline.com. Pub. Frequency: w. (Thu.) Page Size: broadsheet.Adv. Rate: col. inch $15.90 Circulation: 12,050 per issue (paid and free). **Owner(s):** GateHouse Media, Inc, 350 WillowBrook Office Park, Fairport, NY 14450. Telephone: 585-598-0030. FAX: 585-248-2631. **Management:** Kirk Davis, Publisher. Christine Warren, Advertising Director. **Editorial:** Richard Lodge, Editor-in-Chief.

NEWTON TAB. ISSN 0739-3849
254 Second Ave., Needham, MA 02494. Telephone: 781-433-8200. FAX: 781-433-8202. E-MAIL: newton@cnc.com. URL: http://www.townonline.com. Year Established: 1872. Pub. Frequency: w. (Wed.) Page Size: broadsheet.Adv. Rate: col. inch $31.70 Freelance Pay: $25/story. Circulation: 32,310 per issue (paid and free). **Owner(s):** GateHouse Media, Inc, 350 WillowBrook Office Park, Fairport, NY 14450. Telephone: 585-598-0030. FAX: 585-248-2631. **Management:** Kirk Davis, Publisher. Christine Warren, Advertising Director. **Editorial:** Richard Lodge, Editor-in-Chief.

ROSLINDALE TRANSCRIPT. 254 Second Ave., Needham, MA 02494. Telephone: 781-433-8200. FAX: 781-433-8202. E-MAIL: transcript@cnc.com. URL: http://www.townonline.com. Year Established: 1929. Pub. Frequency: w. (Thu.) Page Size: broadsheet. Subscrip. Rate: $1 newsstand/cover; $40/yr. Adv. Rate: col. inch $16.15 Circulation: 7,780 per issue (paid). **Owner(s):** GateHouse Media, Inc, 350 WillowBrook Office Park, Fairport, NY 14450. Telephone: 585-598-0030. FAX: 585-248-2631. **Management:** Kirk Davis, Publisher. Christine Warren, Advertising Director. **Editorial:** Nick Katz, Editor. Richard Lodge, Editor-in-Chief.

STOUGHTON JOURNAL. 254 Second Ave., Needham, MA 02494. Telephone: 781-433-8200. FAX: 781-433-8202. E-MAIL: stoughton@cnc.com. URL: http://www.townonline.com. Pub. Frequency: w. (Fri.) Page Size: broadsheet. Subscrip. Rate: $30/yr in county. Adv. Rate: col. inch $11.20 Circulation: 3,132 per issue (paid). **Owner(s):** GateHouse Media, Inc, 350 WillowBrook Office Park, Fairport, NY 14450. Telephone: 585-598-0030. FAX: 585-248-2631. **Management:** Kirk Davis, Publisher. Mark Olivieri, Advertising Director. **Editorial:** Seth Jacobson, Editor. Richard Lodge, Editor-in-Chief. Tom Fargo, Sports.

WATERTOWN TAB & PRESS. 254 Second Ave., Needham, MA 02494. Telephone: 781-433-8200. FAX: 781-433-8202. E-MAIL: watertown@cnc.com. URL: http://www.townonline.com. Year Established: 1955. Pub. Frequency: w. (Thu.) Page Size: broadsheet. Subscrip. Rate: $.75 newsstand/cover; $35/yr in area. Adv. Rate: col. inch $14.55 Circulation: 3,921 per issue (paid). **Owner(s):** GateHouse Media, Inc, 350 WillowBrook Office Park, Fairport, NY 14450. Telephone: 585-598-0030. FAX: 585-248-2631. **Management:** Kirk Davis, Publisher. Christine Warren, Advertising Director. **Editorial:** Chris Helms, Editor. Greg Reibman, Editor-in-Chief.

WEST ROXBURY TRANSCRIPT. 254 Second Ave., Needham, MA 02494. Telephone: 781-433-8200. FAX: 781-433-8202. E-MAIL: wroxbury@cnc.com. URL: http://www.townonline.com. Year Established: 1941. Pub. Frequency: w. (Wed.) Page Size: broadsheet. Subscrip. Rate: $.75 newsstand/cover; $43/yr. Adv. Rate: col. inch $16.15 Circulation: 9,000 per issue (paid). **Owner(s):** GateHouse Media, Inc, 350 WillowBrook Office Park, Fairport, NY 14450. Telephone: 585-598-0030. FAX: 585-248-2631. **Management:** Kirk Davis, Publisher. Christine Warren, Advertising Director. **Editorial:** Wayne Braverman, Editor. Richard Lodge, Editor-in-Chief.

NORTH ADAMS

ADVOCATE (NORTH ADAMS), THE. 124 American Legion Dr, North Adams, MA 01247. Telephone: 413-663-3741. FAX: 413-662-2792. E-MAIL: news@advocateweekly.com. URL: http://www.advocateweekly.com. Mailing Address: P O Box 1840, North Adams, MA 01247-1840. Year Established: 1982. Pub. Frequency: w. (Thu.) Page Size: tabloid. Subscrip. Rate: $112/yr mailed. Adv. Rate: col. inch $6.50 Circulation: 22,000 per issue (paid and free). **Owner(s):** MediaNews Group, Inc., 101 W Colfax Ave, Ste 1100, Denver, CO 80202. FAX: 303-954-6320. **Management:** Robert Chapman, Publisher. Amanda Sweet, Advertising Manager. **Editorial:** Rebecca Dravis, Editor.

NORTH ANDOVER

TOWN CROSSINGS. 100 Turnpike St, North Andover, MA 01845-5096. Telephone: 978-946-2000. FAX: 978-685-1588. URL: http://www.towncrossings.com. Pub. Frequency: w. (Thu.) Page Size: broadsheet.Adv. Rate: col. inch $15.28 Circulation: 19,699 per issue (free). **Owner(s):** Community Newspaper Holdings, Inc., 3500 Colonnade Pkwy., Ste. 600, Birmingham, AL 35243. **Management:** Al Getler, Publisher. Mark Miller, Advertising Director. Steven Malone, Circulation Director. **Editorial:** Nell Fater, Editor.

NORTH ATTLEBORO

FREE PRESS (NORTH ATTLEBORO), THE. 31 N. Washington, North Attleboro, MA 02760-1605. Telephone: 508-699-6755. FAX: 508-699-8545. E-MAIL: ads@nafreepress.com. Mailing Address: PO Box 1047, North Attleborough, MA 02761-1047. Year Established: 1987. Pub. Frequency: w. (Wed.) Page Size: tabloid Circulation: 15,000 per issue (free). **Owner(s):** Douglas Reed, See address and contact information above. **Management:** Douglas Reed, Publisher. **Editorial:** Douglas Reed, Editor.

NORTH DARTMOUTH

CHRONICLE (NORTH DARTMOUTH), THE. 45 Slocum Rd., North Dartmouth, MA 02747-0268. Telephone: 508-992-1522. FAX: 508-992-1689. E-MAIL: chronnews@aol.com. Mailing Address: PO Box 80268, South Dartmouth, MA 02748-0268. Year Established: 1969. Pub. Frequency: w. (Wed.) Page Size: broadsheet. Subscrip. Rate: $.50 newsstand/cover; $29.25/yr in county; $49.25/yr mailed out of county. Circulation: 6,500 per issue (paid). **Owner(s):** Ottaway Newspapers, Inc., PO Box 401, Campbell Hall, NY 10916. Telephone: 845-294-8181. **Management:** Mary Harrington, General Manager. Angie Ferro, Advertising Manager. **Editorial:** Robert Barboza, Editor.

NORTH GRAFTON

GRAFTON NEWS, THE. PO Box 457, North Grafton, MA 01536. Telephone: 508-839-2259. FAX: 508-839-5235. Pub. Frequency: w. (Wed.) Page Size: tabloid.Subscrip. Rate: $.50 newsstand/cover; $12/yr Circulation: 4,200 per issue (paid). **Owner(s):** Charles N. Bolack, See address and contact information above. **Management:** Charles N. Bolack, Publisher. Marianne Rososky, Advertising Manager. **Editorial:** Donald Clark, Editor.

Weeklies

NORTH READING

NORTH READING TRANSCRIPT. ISSN 1077-2286
7 Bow St., North Reading, MA 01864-2534. Telephone: 978-664-4761. FAX: 978-664-4954. Mailing Address: PO Box 7, North Reading, MA 01864-0007. Year Established: 1956. Pub. Frequency: w. (Thu.) Page Size: tabloid. Subscrip. Rate: $.75 newsstand/cover; $24/yr local. Adv. Rate: col. inch $8.25 Circulation: 4,483 per issue (paid). **Owner(s):** Great Oak Publications, Inc., See address and contact information above. **Management:** Albert E. Sylvia Sr., Publisher. Albert E. Sylvia Jr., Advertising Manager. **Editorial:** Robert Turosz, Editor. Albert E. Sylvia Jr., Managing Editor.

NORWOOD

NORWOOD BULLETIN. 1091 Washington St, Norwood, MA 02062. Telephone: 781-326-5355. FAX: 781-433-8375. E-MAIL: norwood@cnc.com. URL: http://www.norwoodbulletin.com. Year Established: 1992. Pub. Frequency: w. (Thu.) Page Size: tabloid. Subscrip. Rate: $.75 newsstand/cover; $30/yr in county; $33/yr in state; $35/yr out of state. Circulation: 4,000 per issue (paid). **Owner(s):** GateHouse Media, Inc, 350 WillowBrook Office Park, Fairport, NY 14450. Telephone: 585-598-0030. FAX: 585-248-2631. **Management:** Kirk Davis, Publisher. Art Geisinger, Advertising Director. **Editorial:** Matt Cook, Editor.

SHARON ADVOCATE. 1091 Washington St, Norwood, MA 02062. Telephone: 781-784-1487. FAX: 781-433-8375. E-MAIL: sharon@cnc.com. URL: http://www.townonline.com. Year Established: 1873. Pub. Frequency: w. (Fri.) Page Size: broadsheet. Subscrip. Rate: $.35 newsstand/cover; $31/yr area. Adv. Rate: col. inch $12.35 Circulation: 4,765 per issue (paid). **Owner(s):** GateHouse Media, Inc, 350 WillowBrook Office Park, Fairport, NY 14450. Telephone: 585-598-0030. FAX: 585-248-2631. **Management:** Kirk Davis, Publisher. Mark Olivieri, Advertising Director. **Editorial:** Amy Guerrero, Editor. Richard Lodge, Editor-in-Chief. Mike Hardman, Sports.

WESTWOOD PRESS. 1091 Washington St, Norwood, MA 02062. Telephone: 781-326-5355. FAX: 781-433-8375. E-MAIL: westwood@cnc.com. URL: http://www.townonline.com. Pub. Frequency: w. (Thu.) Page Size: broadsheet. Subscrip. Rate: $.75 newsstand/cover; $40/yr mailed in town; $47/yr mailed out of county. Adv. Rate: col. inch $10.95 Circulation: 2,400 per issue (paid). **Owner(s):** GateHouse Media, Inc, 350 WillowBrook Office Park, Fairport, NY 14450. Telephone: 585-598-0030. FAX: 585-248-2631. **Management:** Kirk Davis, Publisher. AnnMarie Magman, Advertising Director. **Editorial:** Rob Borkowski, Editor. Greg Reibman, Editor-in-Chief.

ORLEANS

CAPE CODDER, THE. 5 Namskaket Rd., Orleans, MA 02653. Telephone: 508-247-3255. FAX: 508-247-3255. E-MAIL: codder@cnc.com. URL: http://www.townonline.com. Mailing Address: PO Box 39, Orleans, MA 02653. Year Established: 1946. Pub. Frequency: w. (Fri.) Page Size: tabloid. Subscrip. Rate: $.75 newsstand/cover; $37/yr on Cape. Adv. Rate: col. inch $24.30 Circulation: 12,845 per issue (paid). **Owner(s):** GateHouse Media, Inc, 350 WillowBrook Office Park, Fairport, NY 14450. Telephone: 585-598-0030. FAX: 585-248-2631. **Management:** Kirk Davis, Publisher. Janet Pooler, Advertising Director. Tom Marquis, Circulation Director. **Editorial:** Paul O'Neil, Editor. Mark Skala, Editor-in-Chief.

HARWICH ORACLE. 5 Namskaket Rd., Orleans, MA 02653. Telephone: 508-247-3255. FAX: 508-247-3255. E-MAIL: harwich@cnc.com. URL: http://www.townonline.com. Mailing Address: PO Box 39, Orleans, MA 02653. Year Established: 1986. Pub. Frequency: w. (Wed.) Page Size: broadsheet. Subscrip. Rate: $.50 newsstand/cover; $17.95/yr on Cape. Adv. Rate: col. inch $12.60 Circulation: 3,112 per issue (controlled and free). **Owner(s):** GateHouse Media, Inc, 350 WillowBrook Office Park, Fairport, NY 14450. Telephone: 585-598-0030. FAX: 585-248-2631. **Management:** Kirk Davis, Publisher. Janet Pooler, Advertising Director. **Editorial:** Scott Dalton, Editor. Mark Skala, Editor-in-Chief.

PALMER

JOURNAL REGISTER, THE. 24 Water St, Palmer, MA 01069. Telephone: 413-283-8393. FAX: 413-289-1977. E-MAIL: jhoboth@turley.com. URL: http://www.turley.com. Year Established: 1850. Pub. Frequency: w. (Thu.) Page Size: broadsheet. Subscrip. Rate: $.75 newsstand/cover; $32/yr in state; $36/yr mailed out of state. Adv. Rate: col. inch $10.20 Circulation: 5,200 per issue (paid). **Owner(s):** Turley Publications, Inc., See address and contact information above. **Management:** Jack R. Mead, General Manager. Patrick H Turley, Publisher. Beth Baker, Advertising Director. Kerry McGarrett, Classified Adv. Mgr.. **Editorial:** Jennifer Hoboth, Editor. Lou Zoldy, Sports Editor.

REGISTER (PALMER), THE. 24 Water St, Palmer, MA 01069. Telephone: 413-283-8393. FAX: 413-289-1977. E-MAIL: pkillough@turley.com. URL: http://www.turley.com. Year Established: 1946. Pub. Frequency: w. (Wed.) Page Size: tabloid. Subscrip. Rate: $27/yr in state; $31/yr mailed out of state. Adv. Rate: col. inch $11.50 Circulation: 12,600 per issue (free). **Owner(s):** Turley Publications, Inc., See address and contact information above. **Management:** Jack R. Mead, General Manager. Patrick H Turley, Publisher. Beth Baker, Advertising Director. Kerry McGarrett, Classified Adv. Mgr.. **Editorial:** Paula Killough, Editor. Lou Zoldy, Sports Editor.

SHOPPING GUIDE. 24 Water St, Palmer, MA 01069. Telephone: 413-283-8393. FAX: 413-289-1977. URL: http://www.turley.com. Pub. Frequency: w. (Wed.) Page Size: tabloid.Adv. Rate: col. inch $11.50 Circulation: 19,660 per issue (free). **Owner(s):** Turley Publications, Inc., See address and contact information above. **Management:** Jack R. Mead, General Manager. Patrick H Turley, Publisher. Beth Baker, Advertising Director. Dave Anderson, Advertising Manager.

PEABODY

PEABODY-LYNNFIELD WEEKLY NEWS. 10 First Ave., Peabody, MA 01960. Telephone: 978-532-5880. FAX: 978-532-4250. E-MAIL: info@suburbanpublishing.com. URL: http://www.weeklynews.net. Year Established: 1957. Pub. Frequency: w. (Thu.) Page Size: tabloid. Subscrip. Rate: $25/yr mailed. Adv. Rate: col. inch $19.99 Circulation: 21,000 per issue (free). **Owner(s):** Suburban Publishing Corp., See address and contact information above. **Management:** Richard H. Ayer, Publisher. Philip Broderick, Advertising Director. Steve McCarthy, Circulation Manager. Mark Moore, Classified Adv. Mgr.. **Editorial:** Robert Curtin, Editor. Amy Wyeth, Associate Editor. Gary Trask, Sports Editor.

PITTSFIELD

PITTSFIELD GAZETTE, THE. 38 West St., Pittsfield, MA 01201. Telephone: 413-443-2010. FAX: 413-443-2445. Mailing Address: PO Box 2236, Pittsfield, MA 01202-2236. Year Established: 1991. Pub. Frequency: w. (Thu.) Page Size: tabloid. Subscrip. Rate: $.50 newsstand/cover; $20/yr in county; $30/yr out of county. Adv. Rate: col. inch $7 Circulation: 2,800 per issue (paid and free). **Owner(s):** Pittsfield Gazette, Inc., See address and contact information above. **Management:** Jonathan Levine, Publisher. **Editorial:** Jonathan Levine, Editor.

PLYMOUTH

KINGSTON REPORTER. ISSN 0747-2692
182 Standish Ave, Plymouth, MA 02360. Telephone: 508-591-6600. FAX: 508-591-6601. E-MAIL: kingston@cnc.com. URL: http://www.wickedlocal.com. Year Established: 1984. Pub. Frequency: w. (Thu.) Page Size: tabloid. Subscrip. Rate: $.75 newsstand/cover; $22/yr in county. Adv. Rate: col. inch $7.60 Circulation: 3,959 per issue (paid and free). **Owner(s):** GateHouse Media, Inc, 350 WillowBrook Office Park, Fairport, NY 14450. Telephone: 585-598-0030. **Management:** Sean Burke, Publisher. Tom Booth, Advertising Director. Lynn Pelletier, Circulation Director. **Editorial:** Tamson Burgess, Editor. Sarah Corbitt, Editor-in-Chief.

OLD COLONY MEMORIAL. 182 Standish Ave, Plymouth, MA 02360. Telephone: 508-591-6600. E-MAIL: oldcolony@cnc.com. URL: http://www.wickedlocal.com. Year Established: 1822. Pub. Frequency: s-w. (Wed & Sat.) Page Size: broadsheet. Subscrip. Rate: $1 newsstand/cover; $47/yr in county; $55/yr out of county. Adv. Rate: col. inch $18.60 Freelance Pay: $10-$25/article. Circulation: 12,170 per issue (paid). **Owner(s):** GateHouse Media, Inc, 350 WillowBrook Office Park, Fairport, NY 14450. Telephone: 585-598-0030. **Management:** Sean Burke, Publisher. Tom Booth, Advertising Director. Kim Callahan, Classified Adv. Mgr.. **Editorial:** Matthew Nadler, Editor. Sarah Corbitt, Editor-in-Chief.

WHITMAN TIMES. 182 Standish Ave, Plymouth, MA 02360. Telephone: 508-591-6600. FAX: 508-591-6601. E-MAIL: whitman@cnc.com. URL: http://www.townonline.com. Year Established: 1873. Pub. Frequency: w. (Wed.) Page Size: tabloid. Freelance Pay: $0.75/column-inch. Circulation: 552 per issue (paid). **Owner(s):** GateHouse Media, Inc, 350 WillowBrook Office Park, Fairport, NY 14450. Telephone: 585-598-0030. FAX: 585-248-2631. **Management:** Kirk Davis, Publisher. **Editorial:** Stuart Green, Editor.

PROVINCETOWN

PROVINCETOWN BANNER. 167 Commercial St., Provincetown, MA 02657. Telephone: 508-487-7400. FAX: 508-487-7144. E-MAIL: general@provincetownbanner.com. URL: provincetownbanner.com/articles. Mailing Address: PO Box 977, Provincetown, MA 02657-0977. Year Established: 1995. Pub. Frequency: w. (Thu.) Page Size: tabloid. Subscrip. Rate: $1 newsstand/cover; $26/yr; $19/yr to senior citizens. Circulation: 10,000 per issue (paid). **Owner(s):** Alix Ritchie, See address and contact information above. **Management:** Joan Lenane, General Manager. Alix Ritchie, Publisher. **Editorial:** John Harley, Editor.

QUINCY

QUINCY SUN. 1372 Hancock St., Quincy, MA 02169. Telephone: 617-471-3100. FAX: 617-472-3963. Year Established: 1968. Pub. Frequency: w. (Thu.) Page Size: tabloid. Subscrip. Rate: $.40 newsstand/cover; $22/yr in town; $27/yr out of area; $35/yr mailed out of state. Adv. Rate: col. inch $10 Circulation: 7,000 per issue (paid). **Owner(s):** Henry W. Bosworth, See address and contact information above. **Management:** Henry W. Bosworth, Publisher. Donna Gray, Circulation Manager. **Editorial:** Robert Bosworth, Editor.

RANDOLPH

MONEYSAVER. 41 Highland Ave., Ste. 1, Randolph, MA 02368-4509. Telephone: 781-963-8267. Pub. Frequency: w. (Wed.) Page Size: broadsheet Circulation: 18,100 per issue (free). **Owner(s):** Randolph Printing Co., Inc., 41 Highland Ave., Ste. 1, Randolph, MA 02368. Telephone: 781-963-8267. FAX: 781-963-0028. **Management:** Roberta Harback, Publisher.

RAYHAM

AVON MESSENGER. 370 Paramount Dr, Unit 3, Rayham, MA 02767. Telephone: 508-967-3500. FAX: 508-967-3501. E-MAIL: avon@cnc.com. URL: http://www.townonline.com. Pub. Frequency: w. (Wed) Page Size: broadsheet. **Owner(s):** GateHouse Media, Inc, 350 WillowBrook Office Park, Fairport, NY 14450. Telephone: 585-598-0030. FAX: 585-248-2631. **Management:** Kirk Davis, Publisher. **Editorial:** Stuart Green, Editor.

BRIDGEWATER INDEPENDENT. 370 Paramount Dr, Unit 3, Rayham, MA 02767. Telephone: 508-967-3500. FAX: 508-967-3501. E-MAIL: bridgewater.com. URL: http://www.townonline.com. Pub. Frequency: w. (Wed) Page Size: broadsheet. **Owner(s):** GateHouse Media, Inc, 350 WillowBrook Office Park, Fairport, NY 14450. Telephone: 585-598-0030. FAX: 585-248-2631. **Management:** Kirk Davis, Publisher. **Editorial:** Stuart Green, Editor.

CANTON JOURNAL. 370 Paramount Dr, Unit 3, Rayham, MA 02767. Telephone: 508-967-3500. FAX: 508-967-3501. E-MAIL: canton@cnc.com. URL: http://www.townonline.com. Year Established: 1876. Pub. Frequency: w. (Fri.) Page Size: broadsheet. Subscrip. Rate: $.75 newsstand/cover; $48/yr mailed in county; $60/yr mailed out of state. Adv. Rate: col. inch $12.60 Circulation: 3,000 per issue (paid). **Owner(s):** GateHouse Media, Inc, 350 WillowBrook Office Park, Fairport, NY 14450. Telephone: 585-598-0030. FAX: 585-248-2631. **Management:** Kirk Davis, Publisher. **Editorial:** Seth Jacobson, Editor. Richard Lodge, Editor-in-Chief.

EAST BRIDGEWATER STAR. 370 Paramount Dr, Unit 3, Rayham, MA 02767. Telephone: 508-967-3500. FAX: 508-967-3501. E-MAIL: bridgewater@cnc.com. URL: http://www.townonline.com. Pub. Frequency: w. (Wed) Page Size: broadsheet. **Owner(s):** GateHouse Media, Inc, 350 WillowBrook Office Park, Fairport, NY 14450. Telephone: 585-598-0030. FAX: 585-248-2631. **Management:** Kirk Davis, Publisher. **Editorial:** Stuart Green, Editor.

HANSON TOWN CRIER. 370 Paramount Dr, Unit 3, Rayham, MA 02767. Telephone: 508-967-3500. FAX: 508-967-3501. E-MAIL: hanson@cnc.com. URL: http://www.townonline.com. Pub. Frequency: w. (Wed) Page Size: broadsheet. **Owner(s):** GateHouse Media, Inc, 350 WillowBrook Office Park, Fairport, NY 14450. Telephone: 585-598-0030. FAX: 585-248-2631. **Management:** Kirk Davis, Publisher. **Editorial:** Stuart Green, Editor. Mark Skala, Managing Editor.

LAKEVILLE CALL. 370 Paramount Dr, Unit 3, Rayham, MA 02767. Telephone: 508-967-3500. FAX: 508-967-3501. E-MAIL: lakeville@cnc.com. URL: Http://www.townonline.com. Pub. Frequency: w. (Wed) Page Size: broadsheet. **Owner(s):** GateHouse Media, Inc, 350 WillowBrook Office Park, Fairport, NY 14450. Telephone: 585-598-0030. FAX: 585-248-2631. **Management:** Kirk Davis, Publisher. **Editorial:** Stuart Green, Editor. Mark Skala, Managing Editor.

RANDOLPH HERALD. 370 Paramount Dr, Unit 3, Rayham, MA 02767. Telephone: 508-967-3500. FAX: 508-967-3501. E-MAIL: randolph@cnc.com. URL: http://www.townonline.com. Pub. Frequency: w. (Wed) Page Size: broadsheet. **Owner(s):** GateHouse Media, Inc, 350 WillowBrook Office Park, Fairport, NY 14450. Telephone: 585-598-0030. FAX: 585-248-2631. **Management:** Kirk Davis, Publisher. **Editorial:** Stuart Green, Editor. Mark Skala, Managing Editor.

RAYNHAM CALL. 370 Paramount Dr, Unit 3, Rayham, MA 02767. Telephone: 508-967-3500. FAX: 508-967-3501. E-MAIL: raynham@cnc.com. URL: http://www.townontown.com. Pub. Frequency: w. (Wed) Page Size: broadsheet. **Owner(s):** GateHouse Media, Inc, 350 WillowBrook Office Park, Fairport, NY 14450. Telephone: 585-598-0030. FAX: 585-248-2631. **Management:** Kirk Davis, Publisher. **Editorial:** Stuart Green, Editor. Mark Skala, Managing Editor.

TAUNTON CALL. 370 Paramount Dr, Unit 3, Rayham, MA 02767. Telephone: 508-967-3500. FAX: 508-967-3501. E-MAIL: taunton@cnc.com. URL: http://www.townonline. Pub. Frequency: w. (Wed) Page Size: broadsheet. **Owner(s):** GateHouse Media, Inc, 350 WillowBrook Office Park, Fairport, NY 14450. Telephone: 585-598-0030. FAX: 585-248-2631. **Management:** Kirk Davis, Publisher. **Editorial:** Stuart Green, Editor. Mark Skala, Managing Editor.

REVERE

CHELSEA RECORD. ISSN 1054-6529
385 Broadway, Ste. 105, Revere, MA 02151. Telephone: 781-284-2400. FAX: 781-289-5352. URL: http://www.chelsearecord.com. Mailing Address: PO Box 9103, Revere, MA 02151-9103. Year Established: 1890. Pub. Frequency: w. (Thu.) Page Size: broadsheet. Subscrip. Rate: $.35 newsstand/cover; $22/yr town; $36/yr out of town. Adv. Rate: col. inch $9.45 Circulation: 3,500 per issue (paid). **Owner(s):** Independent Newspaper Group, Inc., See address and contact information above. **Management:** Stephen Quigley, President. Sandy Davis, Advertising. Debra DiGregorio, Advertising Manager. **Editorial:** Carey Shuman, Editor.

EAST BOSTON SUN TRANSCRIPT. 385 Broadway, Ste. 105, Revere, MA 02151. Telephone: 781-284-2400. FAX: 781-289-5352. E-MAIL: ed@revereindependent.com. URL: http://www.eastbostontranscript.com. Pub. Frequency: w. (Fri.) Page Size: tabloid Circulation: 10,300 per issue (free). **Owner(s):** Independent Newspaper Group, Inc., See address and contact information above. **Management:** Stephen Quigley, President. Sandy Davis, Advertising. Deborah DeGregorio, Advertising Manager. **Editorial:** John Lynds, Editor.

EVERETT INDEPENDENT. 385 Broadway, Ste. 105, Revere, MA 02151. Telephone: 781-284-2400. FAX: 781-289-5352. URL: http://www.everettindependent.com. Mailing Address: PO Box 9103, Revere, MA 02151-9103. Pub. Frequency: w. (Wed.) Page Size: tabloid.Subscrip. Rate: $70/yr home delivery Circulation: 10,000 per issue (free). **Owner(s):** Independent Newspaper Group, Inc., See address and contact information above. **Management:** Stephen Quigley, President. Sandy Davis, Advertising. Debbie DeGregorio, Advertising Manager. **Editorial:** Joshua Resnek, Editor. Contact: Jerry Pittman, Publisher; Saundra Morris, Advertising Manager; Vonnie Clark, Circulation Manager; Kent Bush, Managing Editor.

LYNN JOURNAL. 385 Broadway, Ste. 105, Revere, MA 02151. Telephone: 781-284-2400. FAX: 781-289-5352. E-MAIL: editor@lynnjournal.com. URL: http://www.lynnjournal.com. Mailing Address: PO Box 9103, Revere, MA 02151-9103. Pub. Frequency: w. (Wed.) Page Size: tabloid.Subscrip. Rate: $70/yr home delivery in county Circulation: 21,000 per issue (free). **Owner(s):** Independent Newspaper Group, Inc., See address and contact information above. **Management:** Stephen Quigley, President. Sandy Davis, Advertising. Debbie DeGregorio, Advertising Manager. **Editorial:** Joshua Resnek, Editor.

REVERE JOURNAL, THE. 385 Broadway, Ste. 105, Revere, MA 02151. Telephone: 781-284-2400. FAX: 781-289-5352. E-MAIL: editor@reverejournal.com. URL: http://www.reverejournal.com. Year Established: 1881. Pub. Frequency: w. (Wed.) Page Size: broadsheet. Subscrip. Rate: $.50 newsstand/cover; $22/yr local; $36/yr elsewhere. Freelance Pay: $20-$50/article. Circulation: 7,500 per issue (paid). **Owner(s):** Independent Newspaper Group, Inc., See address and contact information above. **Management:** Stephen Quigley, President. Sandy Davis, Advertising. Debbie DeGregorio, Advertising Manager. **Editorial:** David O'Connor, Editor.

WINTHROP SUN TRANSCRIPT. 385 Broadway, Ste. 105, Revere, MA 02151. Telephone: 781-284-2400. FAX: 781-289-5352. E-MAIL: editor@reveretranscript.com. URL: http://www.winthroptranscript.com. Mailing Address: PO Box 9103, Revere, MA 02151-9103. Pub. Frequency: w. (Thu.) Page Size: broadsheet. Subscrip. Rate: $.50 newsstand/cover; $22/yr in county; $36/yr out of county. Adv. Rate: col. inch $6.35 Circulation: 4,300 per issue (paid). **Owner(s):** Independent Newspaper Group, Inc., See address and contact information above. **Management:** Stephen Quigley, President. Sandy Davis, Advertising. Debbie DeGregorio, Advertising Manager. **Editorial:** Joe Domelowicz, Editor.

ROCKLAND

EASTON BULLETIN. PO Box 309, Rockland, MA 02370. Telephone: 781-341-1111. FAX: 781-878-3333. E-MAIL: aweekkies@aol.com. Mailing Address: PO Box 441, Stoughton, MA 02072-0441. Year Established: 1929. Pub. Frequency: w. (Thu.) Page Size: tabloid. Subscrip. Rate: $.50 newsstand/cover; $19.50/yr; $35.50 for 2 yrs.. Freelance Pay: $40-$120/story. Circulation: 1,916 per issue (paid). **Owner(s):** Associated Newspapers, See address and contact information above. **Management:** Jesse A. Anderson, Publisher. Jay MacNevin, Circulation Manager. **Editorial:** Michael Lenney, Editor-in-Chief. Deborah Anderson, Book Review Editor. Larry Jones, Entertainment Editor. Lou Molinari, Sports Editor.

HOLBROOK TIMES. PO Box 309, Rockland, MA 02370. Telephone: 781-878-1111. FAX: 781-878-3333. E-MAIL: AWeeklies@aol.com. Year Established: 1929. Pub. Frequency: w. (Wed.) Page Size: tabloid.Subscrip. Rate: $.25 newsstand/cover; $19.50/yr Circulation: 700 per issue (paid). **Owner(s):** Associated Newspapers, PO Box 309, Rockland, MA 02370-0309. Telephone: 781-878-1111. FAX: 781-878-3333. **Management:** Jesse A. Anderson, Publisher. John Anderson, Advertising Manager. C. MacDonald, Circulation Manager. **Editorial:** Michael Lenny, Editor-in-Chief.

NORTON COURIER. PO Box 309, Rockland, MA 02370. Telephone: 781-878-1111. FAX: 781-878-3333. E-MAIL: aweeklies@aol.com. Year Established: 1986. Pub. Frequency: w. (Wed.) Page Size: tabloid. Subscrip. Rate: $.50 newsstand/cover; $19.50/yr in area. Circulation: 1,270 per issue (paid). **Owner(s):** Associated Newspapers, See address and contact information above. **Management:** Jesse A. Anderson, Publisher. Donald E. Ferguson, Advertising Manager. C. MacDonald, Circulation Manager. **Editorial:** Michael Lenney, Editor-in-Chief.

RAYNHAM JOURNAL. PO Box 309, Rockland, MA 02370. Telephone: 781-878-1111. FAX: 781-878-3333. E-MAIL: aweeklies@aol.com. Mailing Address: PO Box 441, Stoughton, MA 02072. Year Established: 1982. Pub. Frequency: w. (Thu.) Page Size: tabloid. Subscrip. Rate: $.50 newsstand/cover; $19.50/yr; $35.50 for 2 yrs.. Circulation: 1,845 per issue (paid). **Owner(s):** Associated Newspapers, See address and contact information above. **Management:** Jesse A. Anderson, Publisher. John A. Anderson III, Advertising. Jay MacNevin, Circulation Manager. **Editorial:** Michael Lenney, Managing Editor. Larry Jones, Entertainment Editor. Lou Molinari, Sports Editor.

SOUTH SHORE NEWS (ROCKLAND). PO Box 309, Rockland, MA 02370. Telephone: 781-878-1111. E-MAIL: aweeklies@aol.com. Year Established: 1853. Pub. Frequency: w. (Thu.) Page Size: tabloid. Subscrip. Rate: $.50 newsstand/cover; $28/yr in county; $50/yr out of county. Freelance Pay: $80/article. Circulation: 70,729 per issue (controlled and free). **Owner(s):** Associated Newspapers, See address and contact information above. **Management:** Jesse A. Anderson, Publisher. **Editorial:** Michael Lenny, Managing Editor.

STOUGHTON CHRONICLE. PO Box 309, Rockland, MA 02370. Telephone: 781-341-1111. FAX: 781-878-3333. E-MAIL: aweeklies@aol.com. Mailing Address: PO Box 441, Stoughton, MA 02072-0441. Year Established: 1861. Pub. Frequency: w. (Wed.) Page Size: tabloid.Subscrip. Rate: $.25 newsstand/cover; $19.50/yr Circulation: 4,469 per issue (paid). **Owner(s):** Associated Newspapers, See address and contact information above. **Management:** John A. Anderson, Publisher. Jesse A. Anderson, Advertising Manager. C. MacDonald, Circulation Manager. **Editorial:** Michael Lenney, Editor. Larry Jones, Entertainment Editor. Lou Molinari, Sports Editor.

SHELBURNE FALLS

WEST COUNTY NEWS (SHELBURNE FALLS). 87 Bridge St, Shelburne Falls, MA 01370. Telephone: 413-625-4660. FAX: 413-625-4661. E-MAIL: wcnews@comcast.net. URL: http://www.turley.com. Mailing Address: PO Box 218, Shelburne Falls, MA 01370-0218. Pub. Frequency: w. (Thu.) Page Size: broadsheet. Subscrip. Rate: $.75 newsstand/cover; $37/yr mailed in state; $42/yr mailed out of state. Adv. Rate: col. inch $7.35 Circulation: 2,221 per issue (paid). **Owner(s):** Turley Publications, Inc., 24 Water St, Palmer, MA 01069. **Management:** Patrick Turley, Publisher. **Editorial:** Patrick O'Connor, Editor.

SOMERSET

SPECTATOR (SOMERSET), THE. 780 County St., Somerset, MA 02726. Telephone: 508-674-4656. FAX: 508-677-1210. Year Established: 1932. Pub. Frequency: w. (Wed.) Page Size: broadsheet. Subscrip. Rate: $.50 newsstand/cover; $27.75/yr in county; $43.75/yr out of county. Freelance Pay: $25/story. Circulation: 8,000 per issue (paid and free). **Owner(s):** Hathaway Publishing, See address and contact information above. **Management:** Mary Harrington, General Manager. **Editorial:** George Austin, Editor.

SOMERVILLE

CAMBRIDGE CHRONICLE. 20-40 Holland St Ste 404, Somerville, MA 02144. Telephone: 617-577-7149. FAX: 617-629-3381. E-MAIL: cambridge@cnc.com. URL: http://www.townonline.com/cambridge/. Year Established: 1846. Pub. Frequency: w. (Wed.) Page Size: broadsheet. Subscrip. Rate: $.75 newsstand/cover; $36/yr. Adv. Rate: col. inch $21.50 Circulation: 8,746 per issue (paid). **Owner(s):** GateHouse Media, Inc, 350 WillowBrook Office Park, Fairport, NY 14450. Telephone: 585-598-0030. FAX: 585-248-2631. **Management:** Kirk Davis, Publisher. Christine Warren, Advertising Director. **Editorial:** David Harris, Editor.

SOMERVILLE JOURNAL. 20-40 Holland St Ste 404, Somerville, MA 02144. Telephone: 617-625-6300. FAX: 617-629-3381. E-MAIL: somerville@cnc.com. URL: http://www.townonline.com. Year Established: 1870. Pub. Frequency: w. (Thu.) Page Size: broadsheet. Subscrip. Rate: $.75 newsstand/cover; $40/yr mailed in area. Adv. Rate: col. inch $21.50 Freelance Pay: $20-$50/article. Circulation: 9,272 per issue (paid). **Owner(s):** GateHouse Media, Inc, 350 WillowBrook Office Park, Fairport, NY 14450. Telephone: 585-598-0030. FAX: 585-248-2631. **Management:** Kirk Davis, Publisher. Christine Warren, Advertising Director. **Editorial:** Kat Powers, Editor. Greg Reibman, Editor-in-Chief.

SOMERVILLE NEWS, THE. 7 Davis Sq., Somerville, MA 02144-2917. E-MAIL: somervillenews@aol.com. Pub. Frequency: m. (Thu.) Page Size: standard.Adv. Rate: col. inch $15.75 Circulation: 12,000 evening (free). **Owner(s):** Bob Publicover, See address and contact information above. **Management:** Neil McCabe, Publisher. **Editorial:** Neil McCabe, Editor.

SOUTH HADLEY

TOWN REMINDER. 136 College St, Ste 2, South Hadley, MA 01075. Telephone: 413-536-5333. FAX: 413-536-5334. E-MAIL: town-reminder@town-reminder.com. URL: http://www.town-reminder.com. Mailing Address: PO Box 61, South Hadley, MA 01075-0061. Pub. Frequency: w. (Mon.) Page Size: broadsheet Adv. Rate: col. inch $11.50 Circulation: 11,800 (free). **Owner(s):** Turley Publications, Inc., 24 Water St, Palmer, MA 01069. **Management:** Patrick H. Turley, Publisher. Beth Baker, Advertising Director. **Editorial:** Tammy Landon, Editor.

SPENCER

SPENCER NEW LEADER. ISSN 1945-6603
369 Main St., Spencer, MA 01562. Telephone: 508-885-5041. FAX: 508-885-4213. E-MAIL: sjarvis@stonebridgepress.com. URL: http://www.spencernewleader.com. Mailing Address: PO Box 911, Spencer, MA 01562. Year Established: 1977. Pub. Frequency: w. (Wed.) Page Size: tabloid. Subscrip. Rate: $.75 newsstand/cover; $39/yr in county; $49/yr mailed out of county; $35/yr in county to senior citizens. Adv. Rate: col. inch $10.80 Freelance Pay: $15/article. Circulation: 5,500 per issue (paid). **Owner(s):** Stonebridge Press, Inc., 25 Elm St., Southbridge, MA 01501. Telephone: 617-832-5876. **Management:** Frank Chilinski, Publisher. Jean Ashton, Advertising Director. Georgia Leaming, Circulation Manager. **Editorial:** Stephanie Jarvis, Editor. David Forbes, Sports Editor.

WICK-QUA-BOAG WEEKLY. 369 Main St., Spencer, MA 01562. Telephone: 508-885-9402. FAX: 508-885-4213. E-MAIL: sjarvis@stonebridcepress.com. URL: http://www.stonebridgepress.com. Year Established: 1955. Pub. Frequency: w. (Fri.) Page Size: tabloid Circulation: 15,800 per issue (free). **Owner(s):** Stonebridge Press, Inc., 25 Elm St., Southbridge, MA 01550. Telephone: 508-764-4325. **Management:** Frank Chilinski, President. Jean Ashton, Advertising Director. John Loveland, Advertising Manager. Georgia Leaming, Circulation Manager. Sarah Hynds, Classified Adv. Mgr.. **Editorial:** Stephanie Jarvis, Editor.

STONEHAM

STONEHAM INDEPENDENT, THE. 377 Main St., Stoneham, MA 02801-3514. Telephone: 781-438-1660. FAX: 781-438-6762. E-MAIL: news@stonehamonline.com. URL: http://www.stonehamonline.com. Year Established: 1870. Pub. Frequency: w. (Wed.) Page Size: broadsheet. Subscrip. Rate: $.75 newsstand/cover; $25/yr local; $27/yr mailed out of area; $29/yr mailed out of state. Adv. Rate: col. inch $9.30 **Wire Service(s):** AP. Circulation: 4,650 per issue (paid). **Owner(s):** Woburn Daily Times, Inc., One Arrow Dr., Woburn, MA 01801. Telephone: 781-933-3700. FAX: 781-932-3321. **Management:** Peter Haggerty, Publisher. Joe McCarthy, Advertising Manager. **Editorial:** Joseph Haggerty, Editor.

WALPOLE

WALPOLE TIMES, THE. 257 Elm St., Walpole, MA 02081. Telephone: 508-668-0243. E-MAIL: walptimes@aol.com. URL: http:www.walpoletimes.com. Year Established: 1915. Pub. Frequency: w. (Thu.) Page Size: broadsheet. Subscrip. Rate: $.75 newsstand/cover; $35/yr mailed in county; $40/yr out of county. Freelance Pay: $15-$35/article. Circulation: 6,400 per issue (paid). **Owner(s):** Harris D. Lang, See address and contact information above. **Management:** Harris D. Lang, Publisher. Albie Nudel, Advertising Manager. Gail Van Hoesen, Circulation Manager. Kay MacDonald, Business Manager. **Editorial:** Tom Glynn, Editor.

WARE

BUY LINE, THE. 92 Main St., Ware, MA 01082. Telephone: 413-967-3505. FAX: 413-967-6009. URL: http://www.turley.com. Pub. Frequency: w. (Sat.) Page Size: tabloid.Adv. Rate: col. inch $12 Circulation: 20,700 per issue (free). **Owner(s):** Turley Publications, Inc., 24 Water St, Palmer, MA 01069. Telephone: 413-283-8393. FAX: 413-289-1977. **Management:** Patrick H Turley, Publisher. Jacky Perrot, Advertising. **Editorial:** Tim Kane, Editor.

WARE RIVER NEWS, THE. 92 Main St., Ware, MA 01082. Telephone: 413-967-3505. FAX: 413-967-6009. E-MAIL: warerivernews@turley.com. URL: http://www.turley.com. Year Established: 1887. Pub. Frequency: w. (Thu.) Page Size: broadsheet. Subscrip. Rate: $.75 newsstand/cover; $27/yr in state; $31/yr out of state. Adv. Rate: col. inch $10.20 Circulation: 4,429 per issue (paid). **Owner(s):** Turley Publications, Inc., 24 Water St, Palmer, MA 01069. Telephone: 413-283-8393. FAX: 413-289-1977. **Management:** Patrick H Turley, Publisher. Jacky Perrot, Advertising. **Editorial:** Tim Kane, Editor.

WEBSTER

AUBURN NEWS. 43 E Main St, Webster, MA 01570. Telephone: 508-832—2222. FAX: 508-832-2431. E-MAIL: bmoffa@stonebridgepress.com. URL: http://www.stonebridgepress.com. Year Established: 1949. Pub. Frequency: w. (Wed.) Page Size: tabloid. Subscrip. Rate: $.75 newsstand/cover; $42/yr in county; $53/yr mailed out of county; $37.50/yr in county to senior citizens. Adv. Rate: col. inch $10.10 Circulation: 4,500 per issue (paid). **Owner(s):** Stonebridge Press, Inc., 25 Elm St., Southbridge, MA 01550. Telephone: 508-764-4325. **Management:** Frank Chilinski, President. Jean Ashton, Advertising Director. Georgia Leaming, Circulation Manager. Sarah Hynds, Classified Adv. Mgr.. **Editorial:** Blaine Moffa, Editor. Tim Kane, Executive Editor. David Forbes, Sports Editor.

PATRIOT (WEBSTER), THE. 15 Sutton Rd, Webster, MA 01570-3136. Telephone: 508-943-8784. FAX: 508-943-8129. E-MAIL: patriot15@charter.net. URL: http://www.patriotnewspaper.com. Mailing Address: PO Box 310, Webster, MA 01570-0310. Pub. Frequency: w. (Wed.) Page Size: standard. Subscrip. Rate: $.75 newsstand/cover; $38/yr in state; $48/yr out of state. Adv. Rate: col. inch $8 Circulation: 3,500 per issue (paid). **Owner(s):** Paul O'Donnell, See address and contact information above. **Management:** Paul O'Donnell, Publisher. **Editorial:** Paul O'Donnell, Editor-in-Chief.

SOUTH COUNTY WEEKENDER. 43 E Main St, Webster, MA 01570. Telephone: 508-832—2222. FAX: 508-832-2431. E-MAIL: websterads@stonebridgepress.com. URL: http://www.stonebridgepress.com. Year Established: 1962. Pub. Frequency: w. (Mon.) Page Size: tabloid Circulation: 17,000 per issue (free). **Owner(s):** Stonebridge Press, Inc., 25 Elm St., Southbridge, MA 01550. Telephone: 508-764-4325. **Management:** Frank Chilinski, Publisher. Diane Cameron, Advertising Manager. Georgia Leaming, Circulation Manager. Jean Ashton, Marketing Director.

WEBSTER TIMES, THE. ISSN 1945-6611
43 E Main St, Webster, MA 01570. Telephone: 508-832—2222. FAX: 508-832-2431. E-MAIL: bmoffa@stonebridgepress.com. URL: http://www.webstertimes.net. Year Established: 1849. Pub. Frequency: w. (Wed.) Page Size: broadsheet. Subscrip. Rate: $.75 newsstand/cover; $42/yr in county; $53/yr out of county; $37.50/yr in county to senior citizens. Adv. Rate: col. inch $12.77 Circulation: 3,000 per issue (paid). **Owner(s):** Stonebridge Press, Inc., 25 Elm St, Southbridge, MA 01550. Telephone: 508-764-4325. **Management:** Frank Chilinski, Publisher. Diane Cameron, Advertising Manager. Georgia Leaming, Circulation Manager. **Editorial:** Blaine Moffa, Editor. David Forbes, Sports Editor.

YANKEE SHOPPER. 15 Sutton Rd, Webster, MA 01570-3136. Telephone: 508-943-8784. FAX: 508-943-8129. Mailing Address: PO Box 310, Webster, MA 01570-0310. Pub. Frequency: w. (Thu.) Page Size: tabloid.Adv. Rate: col. inch $6.50 Circulation: 16,000 per issue (free). **Owner(s):** Paul O'Donnell, See address and contact information above. **Management:** Paul O'Donnell, Publisher.

WELLESLEY HILLS

WELLESLEY TOWNSMAN. 310 Washington St., Wellesley Hills, MA 02481. Telephone: 781-431-2000. FAX: 781-431-2001. E-MAIL: ccain@cnc.com. URL: http://www.townonline.com/wellesley. Year Established: 1906. Pub. Frequency: w. (Thu.) Page Size: broadsheet. Subscrip. Rate: $1 newsstand/cover; $52/yr in area. Adv. Rate: col. inch $16.85 Circulation: 6,817 per issue (paid). **Owner(s):** GateHouse Media, Inc, 350 WillowBrook Office Park, Fairport, NY 14450. Telephone: 585-598-0030. FAX: 585-248-2631. **Management:** Kirk Davis, Publisher. AnnMarie Magman, Advertising Director. **Editorial:** Chad Cain, Editor.

WEST SPRINGFIELD

WEST SPRINGFIELD RECORD. 516 Main St., West Springfield, MA 01089. Telephone: 413-736-1587. FAX: 413-739-2477. Mailing Address: PO Box 357, West Springfield, MA 01090. Year Established: 1953. Pub. Frequency: w. (Thu.) Page Size: tabloid. Subscrip. Rate: $.35 newsstand/cover; $15/yr in county; $28/yr out of county. Circulation: 5,600 per issue (paid). **Owner(s):** Marie Coburn-Gill, See address and contact information above. **Management:** Thomas Coburn, Publisher. Marie Coburn-Gill, Advertising. **Editorial:** Thomas Coburn, Managing Editor. Phillip T. Dassatti, Associate Editor.

WESTBOROUGH

COMMUNITY ADVOCATE, THE. 32 South St., 2nd Fl., Westborough, MA 01581-1431. Telephone: 508-366-5500. FAX: 508-366-2812. E-MAIL: commad@communityadvocate.com. URL: http://www.communityadvocate.com. Year Established: 1974. Pub. Frequency: w. (Fri.) Page Size: broadsheet.Subscrip. Rate: $14.95/yr mailed Circulation: 24,850 per issue (free). **Owner(s):** David Bagdon, See address and contact information above. **Management:** David Bagdon, Publisher. **Editorial:** David Bagdon, Editor.

WESTBOROUGH NEWS, THE. ISSN 0893-3782
10 E. Main St., Westborough, MA 01581. Telephone: 508-366-1511. FAX: 508-366-5265. E-MAIL: westboro@cnc.com. URL: http://www.townonline.com. Year Established: 1974. Pub. Frequency: w. (Fri.) Page Size: broadsheet. Subscrip. Rate: $.50 newsstand/cover; $9/yr local; $22/yr out of area. Adv. Rate: col. inch $12.25 Freelance Pay: $25/article. Circulation: 8,000 per issue (paid). **Owner(s):** GateHouse Media, Inc, 350 WillowBrook Office Park, Fairport, NY 14450. Telephone: 585-598-0030. FAX: 585-248-2631. **Management:** Kirk Davis, Publisher. AnnMarie Magman, Advertising Director. **Editorial:** Chad Cain, Editor.

WESTFIELD

LONGMEADOW NEWS. 62-64 School St., Westfield, MA 01086. Telephone: 413-562-4181. FAX: 413-562-4185. Mailing Address: PO Box 930, Westfield, MA 01086. Pub. Frequency: w. (Thu.) Page Size: standard. Subscrip. Rate: $.40 newsstand/cover; $20/yr home delivery. Circulation: 2,400 per issue (paid). **Owner(s):** Westfield News Publishing, Inc., 64 School St., Westfield, MA 01085. **Management:** Carol Mazza, Publisher. Martha Baillargeon, Advertising. **Editorial:** David Canton, Editor. Dale Oleksak, Production Manager. James Corwin, Feature Editor.

WEYMOUTH

BRAINTREE FORUM. 91 Washington St, Weymouth, MA 02188. Telephone: 781-682-4850. FAX: 781-682-4851. E-MAIL: braintree@cnc.com. URL: http://www.townonline.com. Year Established: 1877. Pub. Frequency: w. (Wed.) Page Size: broadsheet. Subscrip. Rate: $1 newsstand/cover; $37/yr mailed in area. Adv. Rate: col. inch $10.95 Circulation: 4,482 per issue (paid). **Owner(s):** GateHouse Media, Inc, 350 WillowBrook Office Park, Fairport, NY 14450. Telephone: 585-598-0030. FAX: 585-248-2631. **Management:** Kirk Davis, Publisher. AnnMarie Magman, Advertising Director. **Editorial:** Chad Cain, Editor.

HOLBROOK SUN. 91 Washington St, Weymouth, MA 02188. Telephone: 781-682-4850. FAX: 781-682-4851. E-MAIL: holbrook@cnc.com. URL: http://www.townonline.com. Year Established: 1958. Pub. Frequency: w. (Fri.) Page Size: tabloid. Subscrip. Rate: $1 newsstand/cover; $35/yr in county. Adv. Rate: col. inch $10.40 Circulation: 2,033 per issue (paid). **Owner(s):** GateHouse Media, Inc, 350 WillowBrook Office Park, Fairport, NY 14450. Telephone: 585-598-0030. FAX: 585-248-2631. **Management:** Kirk Davis, Publisher. AnnMarie Magman, Advertising Director. **Editorial:** Chad Cain, Editor.

WEYMOUTH NEWS. 91 Washington St, Weymouth, MA 02188. Telephone: 781-682-4850. FAX: 781-682-4851. E-MAIL: weymouth@cnc.com. URL: http://www.townonline.com. Year Established: 1867. Pub. Frequency: w. (Wed.) Page Size: broadsheet. Subscrip. Rate: $.75 newsstand/cover; $34/yr mailed in area. Adv. Rate: col. inch $15.80 Circulation: 11,501 per issue (paid). **Owner(s):** GateHouse Media, Inc, 350 WillowBrook Office Park, Fairport, NY 14450. Telephone: 585-598-0030. FAX: 585-248-2631. **Management:** Kirk Davis, Publisher. AnnMarie Magman, Advertising Director.

WHITINSVILLE

BLACKSTONE VALLEY TRIBUNE. ISSN 0745-8673
110 Church St., Whitinsville, MA 01588. Telephone: 508-234-2107. FAX: 508-234-7506. URL: http://www.stonebridgepress.com. Year Established: 1949. Pub. Frequency: w. (Wed.) Page Size: tabloid. Subscrip. Rate: $.75 newsstand/cover; $39/yr mailed in county; $49/yr mailed out of county; $35/yr mailed in county to senior citizens. Adv. Rate: col. inch $9.70 Freelance Pay: $15/story. Circulation: 4,500 per issue (paid and free). **Owner(s):** Stonebridge Press, Inc., 25 Elm St., Southbridge, MA 01550. Telephone: 508-764-4325. **Management:** Frank Chilinski, Publisher. Jean Ashton, Advertising Director. Georgia Leaming, Circulation Manager. Sarah Hynds, Classified Adv. Mgr.. **Editorial:** Andy Levin, Editor. David Forbes, Sports Editor.

WILBRAHAM

WILBRAHAM-HAMPDEN TIMES, THE. 2341 Boston Rd, Wilbraham, MA 01095. Telephone: 413-682-0007. FAX: 413-682-0013. E-MAIL: cbennett@turley.com. URL: http://www.wilbrahamtimes.com. Year Established: 2002. Pub. Frequency: w. (Thu.) Page Size: tabloid.Adv. Rate: col. inch $11.50 Circulation: 9,338 per issue (free). **Owner(s):** Turley Publications, Inc., 24 Water St, Palmer, MA 01069. Telephone: 413-283-8393. FAX: 413-667-3011. **Management:** Pat Turley, Publisher. Jocelyn Walker, Advertising. **Editorial:** Charles Bennett, Editor. Dave Forbes, Sports Editor.Readers: Families

WILMINGTON

TEWKSBURY TOWN CRIER. 104 Lowell St., Wilmington, MA 01887. Telephone: 978-658-2346. FAX: 978-658-2266. E-MAIL: office@yourtowncrier.com. URL: http://www.yourtowncrier.com. Pub. Frequency: w. (Wed.) Page Size: broadsheet. Subscrip. Rate: $.75 newsstand/cover; $25/yr mailed in area; $30/yr mailed out of area. Adv. Rate: col. inch $10.50 Circulation: 2,515 per issue (paid). **Owner(s):** Haggerty Family, One Arrow Dr., Woburn, MA 01801. Telephone: 781-933-3700. FAX: 781-932-3321. **Management:** Peter Haggerty, Publisher. John O'Neil, Advertising Manager. Mary Earley, Circulation Manager. **Editorial:** Stephen Bjork, Editor. Stu Neilson, Managing Editor. Jamie Pote, Sports Editor.

WILMINGTON TOWN CRIER. 104 Lowell St., Wilmington, MA 01887. Telephone: 978-658-2346. FAX: 978-658-2266. E-MAIL: office@yourtowncrier.com. URL: http://www.yourtowncrier.com. Pub. Frequency: w. (Wed.) Page Size: broadsheet. Subscrip. Rate: $.75 newsstand/cover; $25/yr mailed in area; $30/yr mailed out of area. Adv. Rate: col. inch $10.50 Circulation: 4,300 per issue (paid). **Owner(s):** Haggerty Family, One Arrow Dr., Woburn, MA 01801. Telephone: 781-933-3700. FAX: 781-932-3321. **Management:** Peter Haggerty, Publisher. John O'Neil, Advertising Manager. Mary Early, Circulation Manager. **Editorial:** Shawn Sullivan, Editor. Stu Neilson, Managing Editor. Jamie Pote, Sports Editor.

WINCHENDON

WINCHENDON COURIER. 91 Central St., Winchendon, MA 01475-1749. Telephone: 978-297-0050. FAX: 978-297-2177. URL: http://www.stonepress.com. Year Established: 1878. Pub. Frequency: w. (Thu.) Page Size: broadsheet. Subscrip. Rate: $.75 newsstand/cover; $39/yr in county; $49/yr out of county. Circulation: 2,500 per issue (paid). **Owner(s):** Stonebridge Press, Inc., 25 Elm St., Southbridge, MA 01550. Telephone: 508-764-4325. **Management:** Frank Chilinski, Publisher. Jeff Dickens, Advertising. **Editorial:** Ruth Deamicis, Managing Editor.

YARMOUTHPORT

MASHPEE/COTUIT PENNYSAVER. Sunflower Mkt., 023G Rte. 6A, Yarmouthport, MA 02675-2159. Telephone: 508-375-4945. FAX: 508-375-4901. E-MAIL: yarmouth@cnc.com. URL: http://www.townonline.com. Year Established: 1985. Pub. Frequency: w. (Wed.) Page Size: tabloid.Adv. Rate: col. inch $12.55 Circulation: 13,781 per issue (free). **Owner(s):** GateHouse Media, Inc, 350 WillowBrook Office Park, Fairport, NY 14450. Telephone: 585-598-0030. FAX: 585-248-2631. **Management:** Kirk Davis, Publisher. Janet Pooler, Advertising Director. Mark Olivieri, Advertising Manager. **Editorial:** John Basile, Editor.

REGISTER (YARMOUTHPORT), THE. Sunflower Mkt., 023G Rte. 6A, Yarmouthport, MA 02675-2159. Telephone: 508-375-4945. FAX: 508-375-4901. E-MAIL: jbasile@cnc.com. URL: http://www.townonline.com. Year Established: 1836. Pub. Frequency: w. (Thu.) Page Size: broadsheet. Subscrip. Rate: $.50 newsstand/cover; $26.95/yr; $57/yr mailed out of state. Adv. Rate: col. inch $17.40 Freelance Pay: $40-$100/article. Circulation: 8,570 per issue (paid). **Owner(s):** GateHouse Media, Inc, 350 WillowBrook Office Park, Fairport, NY 14450. Telephone: 585-598-0030. FAX: 585-248-2631. **Management:** Kirk Davis, Publisher. Janet Pooler, Advertising Director. **Editorial:** John Basile, Editor. Glen Ritt, Editor-in-Chief.

SANDWICH/SAGAMORE PENNYSAVER. Sunflower Mkt., 023G Rte. 6A, Yarmouthport, MA 02675-2159. Telephone: 508-375-4945. FAX: 508-375-4901. Mailing Address: PO Box 39, Orleans, MA 02653. Year Established: 1974. Pub. Frequency: w. (Thu.) Page Size: tabloid.Adv. Rate: col. inch $9.40 Circulation: 9,172 per issue (free). **Owner(s):** GateHouse Media, Inc, 350 WillowBrook Office Park, Fairport, NY 14450. Telephone: 585-598-0030. FAX: 585-248-2631. **Management:** Gary G. Higgins, Publisher. Mark Olivieri, Advertising Manager. **Editorial:** John Basile, Editor. Mark Skala, Editor-in-Chief.

UPPER CAPE CODDER, THE. ISSN 1525-4801
Sunflower Mkt., 023G Rte. 6A, Yarmouthport, MA 02675-2159. Telephone: 508-375-4945. FAX: 508-375-4901. E-MAIL: jbasile@cnc.com. URL: http://www.townonline.com. Year Established: 1999. Pub. Frequency: w. (Thu.) Page Size: broadsheet. Subscrip. Rate: $.50 newsstand/cover; $32/yr mailed area. Adv. Rate: col. inch $16.95 Freelance Pay: $40-$100/story. Circulation: 14,545 per issue (paid). **Owner(s):** GateHouse Media, Inc, 350 WillowBrook Office Park, Fairport, NY 14450. Telephone: 585-598-0030. FAX: 585-248-2631. **Management:** Kirk Davis, Publisher. Janet Pooler, Advertising Director. **Editorial:** John Basile, Editor. Mark Skala, Editor-in-Chief.

MICHIGAN

ADRIAN

ADRIAN ACCESS SHOPPER. 133 N. Winter St., Adrian, MI 49221. Telephone: 517-265-5111. FAX: 517-263-4152. Mailing Address: PO Box 647, Adrian, MI 49221-0647. Pub. Frequency: w. (Mon.) Page Size: standard Circulation: 39,230 per issue (free). **Owner(s):** GateHouse Media, Inc, 350 WillowBrook Office Park, Fairport, NY 14450. Telephone: 585-598-0030. FAX: 585-248-2631. **Management:** Paul Heidbreder, Publisher. Deb Werner, Advertising Director. Jeff Stahl, Circulation Director.

ADRIAN MEDLEY. 133 N. Winter St., Adrian, MI 49221. Telephone: 517-265-5111. FAX: 517-263-4152. URL: http://www.gatehousemedia.com. Mailing Address: PO Box 647, Adrian, MI 49221-0647. Pub. Frequency: w. (Mon.) Page Size: tabloid Circulation: 8,200 per issue (free). **Owner(s):** GateHouse Media, Inc, 350 WillowBrook Office Park, Fairport, NY 14450. Telephone: 585-598-0030. FAX: 585-248-2631. **Management:** Paul Heidbreder, Publisher. Deb Werner, Advertising Director. Jeff Stahl, Circulation Director.

ALBION

ALBION RECORDER. ISSN 8750-9008
125 E Cass St, Albion, MI 49224-1755. Telephone: 517-629-0041. FAX: 517-629-5210. Year Established: 1908. Pub. Frequency: w. (Thu.) Page Size: broadsheet. Subscrip. Rate: $1 newsstand/cover; $24 home delivery for 6 mos. area; $48/yr home delivery. **Wire Service(s):** AP. Circulation: 1,500 morning (paid). **Owner(s):** Betty Watson, See address and contact information above.

ALLEGAN

ALLEGAN COUNTY NEWS. 231 Trowbridge St., Ste 17, Allegan, MI 49010. E-MAIL: editor@allegannews.com. URL: http://www.allegannews.com. Mailing Address: PO Box 189, Allegan, MI 49010-0189. Year Established: 1882. Pub. Frequency: w. (Thu.) Page Size: broadsheet. Subscrip. Rate: $.75 newsstand/cover; $26/yr in county; $34/yr out of county; $40/yr out of state. Adv. Rate: col. inch $9.22 Circulation: 5,017 per issue (paid). **Owner(s):** Kaechele Publications, Inc., See address and contact information above. **Management:** Cheryl Kaechele, Publisher. Robin Clark, Advertising. Judy T Smith, Circulation Manager. **Editorial:** Ryan Lewis, Editor.

FLASHES SHOPPING GUIDE. 595 Jenner Dr., Allegan, MI 49010. Telephone: 269-673-2141. FAX: 269-673-4761. Year Established: 1934. Pub. Frequency: w. (Mon.) Page Size: tabloid. Freelance Pay: $15/page. Circulation: 148,000 per issue (free). **Owner(s):** Morris Multimedia, Inc., PO Box 936, Augusta, GA 30903-0936. Telephone: 706-724-0851. FAX: 706-722-7125. **Editorial:** Mike Hingle, Editor.

UNION ENTERPRISE. 231 Trowbridge St., Ste 17, Allegan, MI 49010. FAX: 269-673-5535. E-MAIL: editorial@allegannews.com. URL: http://www.allegannews.com. Mailing Address: PO Box 417, Plainwell, MI 49080-0417. Year Established: 1869. Pub. Frequency: w. (Thu.) Page Size: tabloid. Subscrip. Rate: $.50 newsstand/cover; $22/yr in county; $27/yr out of county; $34/yr out of state. Adv. Rate: col. inch $5.60 Circulation: 582 per issue (paid and free). **Owner(s):** Kaechele Publications, Inc., See address and contact information above. **Management:** Cheryl Kaechele, Publisher. Robin Clark, Advertising.

ALPENA

PRESQUE ISLE STAR. 431 Ripley Blvd., Alpena, MI 49707. Telephone: 989-356-2121. FAX: 989-354-8275. E-MAIL: star@star-ads.com. URL: http://www.star-ads.com. Year Established: 1975. Pub. Frequency: w. (Sun.) Page Size: tabloid.Adv. Rate: col. inch $5.84 Circulation: 5,900 Sunday (free). **Owner(s):** Morning Star Publishing, 711 W. Pickard, Mt. Pleasant, MI 48858. Telephone: 989-779-6000. **Management:** Ethan Clarke, General Manager.

ARMADA

ARMADA TIMES. 23061 E Main St, Armada, MI 48005. Telephone: 586-784-5551. FAX: 586-784-8710. Mailing Address: P O Box 915, Armada, MI 48005. Pub. Frequency: w. (Wed.) Page Size: broadsheet. Subscrip. Rate: $.50 newsstand/cover; $21/yr in county; $31/yr out of county. Circulation: 1,800 per issue (paid). **Owner(s):** Journal Register Co., 50 W State St, 12th Fl, Trenton, NJ 08608. **Management:** Donna Remer, General Manager. Ronald Wood, Publisher. Debbie Loggins, Advertising Director. **Editorial:** Donna Remer, Executive Editor. Lisa Harden, Managing Editor.

BAD AXE

HURON COUNTY PRESS. 110 E Huron Ave, Bad Axe, MI 48413. Telephone: 989-269-2893. FAX: 989-269-2917. E-MAIL: copress@avci.net. URL: http://www.huroncountypress.com. Year Established: 2002. Pub. Frequency: w. (Wed.) Page Size: broadsheet. Subscrip. Rate: $.50 newsstand/cover; $21/yr mailed in county; $31/yr mailed out of county. Circulation: 2,500 per issue (paid). **Owner(s):** Journal Register Co., 50 W State St, 12th Fl, Trenton, NJ 08608. **Management:** Jack Guza, Publisher. Shelley Adair, Advertising Director. Nadine Klee, Circulation Director. Tammy Philp, Classified Editor. **Editorial:** Molly Dando, Editor.

THUMB BLANKET. 55 Westland Dr, Bad Axe, MI 48413. Telephone: 989-269-9918. E-MAIL: tphilp@lapeergroup.com. URL: http://www.huroncountypress.com. Year Established: 1980.Pub. Frequency: w. (Sun.) Circulation: 18,000 per issue (free). **Owner(s):** Journal Register Co., 50 W. State St, 12th Fl., Trenton, NJ 08608. **Management:** Jack Guza, Publisher. Shelley Adair, Advertising Director. Nadine Klee, Circulation Director. Tammy Philp, Classified Editor. **Editorial:** Molly Dando, Editor.

BALDWIN

LAKE COUNTY STAR. 851 Michigan Ave., Baldwin, MI 49304. Telephone: 231-745-4635. FAX: 231-745-7733. E-MAIL: lcstar@pioneergroup.net. URL: http://www.pioneergroup.com. Mailing Address: PO Box 399, Baldwin, MI 49304. Year Established: 1873. Pub. Frequency: w. (Thu.) Page Size: tabloid. Subscrip. Rate: $.75 newsstand/cover; $27.40/yr mailed in county; $43.85/yr mailed out of county; $59.20/yr mailed out of state. Circulation: 3,100 per issue (paid). **Owner(s):** The Pioneer Group, 502 N. State St., Big Rapids, MI 49307. FAX: 231-796-1152. **Management:** John Norton, Publisher. Sharon Frederick, Advertising Manager. Sue Vellanti, Circulation Manager. **Editorial:** Jim Bruskotter, Managing Editor.

BATTLE CREEK

BATTLE CREEK SHOPPER NEWS. 1361 E. Columbia Ave., Battle Creek, MI 49014. Telephone: 269-965-3955. FAX: 269-968-8586. E-MAIL: j-adgraphics.com. URL: http://www.battlecreekshopper.com. Mailing Address: P O Box 163, Battle Creek, MI 49014. Year Established: 1967. Pub. Frequency: w. (Thu.) Page Size: tabloid. Subscrip. Rate: $38/yr home delivery in area. Adv. Rate: col. inch $8.40 Circulation: 49,000 per issue (controlled and free). **Owner(s):** J-AD Graphics, Inc., 1351 N. M43 Hwy, Hastings, MI 49058. Telephone: 269-945-9554. **Management:** John Jacobs, President. Fred Jacobs, Publisher. Donna Hazel, Sales Manager. **Editorial:** Shelly Sulser, Editor.

BELLAIRE

ANTRIM COUNTY NEWS. 206 N Bridge St, Bellaire, MI 49615. Telephone: 231-533-8523. FAX: 231-587-8471. URL: http://www.antrimcountynews.com. Mailing Address: P O Box 337, Bellaire, MI 49615-0337. Year Established: 1947. Pub. Frequency: w. (Wed.) Subscrip. Rate: $.75 newsstand/cover; $30/yr in county; $35/yr out of county. Circulation: 6,050 per issue (paid). **Owner(s):** Journal Register Co., 50 W State St, 12th Fl, Trenton, NJ 08608. **Management:** Larry See, General Manager. Hugh Conklin, Publisher. Jackie White, Advertising. Jackie Burley, Circulation Director. **Editorial:** Larry See, Managing Editor. Aimee Gibbert, Production Manager.

BELLEVILLE

VIEW, THE. 159 Main St, Belleville, MI 48111. Telephone: 734-697-8255. FAX: 734-697-4610. E-MAIL: editor@bellevilleview.com. URL: http://www.bellevilleview.com. Year Established: 1983. Pub. Frequency: w. (Thu.) Page Size: broadsheet. Subscrip. Rate: $.50 newsstand/cover; $12 mailed for 6 mos.; $22/yr mailed. Freelance Pay: $25-$30/story. Circulation: 1,300 per issue (paid). **Owner(s):** Journal Register Co., 50 W State St, 12th Fl, Trenton, NJ 08608. Telephone: 609-396-2200. FAX: 609-396-2292. **Management:** James Williams, Publisher. Justin Wilcox, Advertising Director. **Editorial:** Renee Collins, Editor.

YPSILANTI COURIER. 159 Main St, Belleville, MI 48111. Telephone: 734-697-8255. FAX: 734-697-4610. E-MAIL: edito@ypsilanticourier.com. URL: http://www.ypsilanticourier.com. Year Established: 1918. Pub. Frequency: w. (Thu.) Page Size: broadsheet. Subscrip. Rate: $.75 newsstand/cover; $15 home delivery for 6 mos. local; $27/yr home delivery local; $78/yr mailed in county. Adv. Rate: col. inch $9.36 Circulation: 7,000 per issue (paid). **Owner(s):** Journal Register Co., 50 W State St, 12th Fl, Trenton, NJ 08608. Telephone: 609-396-2200. FAX: 609-396-2292. **Management:** James Williams, Publisher. Justin Wilcox, Advertising Director. **Editorial:** Renee Collins, Editor.

BIRMINGHAM

REDFORD OBSERVER. 805 E Maple, Birmingham, MI 48009. Telephone: 248-644-1100. FAX: 248-644-1314. URL: http://www.hometownlife.com. Year Established: 1952. Pub. Frequency: s-w. (Sun. & Thu.) Page Size: broadsheet. Subscrip. Rate: $.75 newsstand/cover; $59.95/yr home delivery local; $83.95/yr mailed in county; $108.95/yr mailed out of county. Circulation: 7,201 Sunday (paid and free); 7,032 per issue (paid and free). **Owner(s):** Observer, Eccentric & Mirror Newspapers, Inc., 7950 Jones Branch Dr, McLean, VA 22107. Telephone: 703-854-5000. **Management:** Peter Neill, Publisher. Marty Carry, Advertising Director. Jeannie Parent, Advertising Manager. Frank Cibor, Classified Adv. Mgr. **Editorial:** Susan Rosiek, Executive Editor. Hugh Gallagher, Managing Editor. Tim Smith, Sports Editor.

BLISSFIELD

ADVANCE, THE. 121 Newspaper St., Blissfield, MI 49228. Telephone: 517-486-2400. FAX: 517-486-4675. Year Established: 1874. Pub. Frequency: w. (Wed.) Page Size: tabloid. Subscrip. Rate: $.50 newsstand/cover; $25/yr local; $35/yr out of area. Adv. Rate: col. inch $6.25 Circulation: 2,800 per issue (paid). **Owner(s):** Marcia Loader, See address and contact information above. **Management:** Marcia Loader, President. **Editorial:** Doug Goodnough, Editor.

BOYNE CITY

CITIZEN-JOURNAL, THE. 112 S Park, Boyne City, MI 49712. Telephone: 231-536-0044. FAX: 231-582+6762. E-MAIL: citizen@voyager.net. URL: http://www.citizenandjournal.com. Year Established: 1879. Pub. Frequency: w. (Wed.) Page Size: broadsheet. Subscrip. Rate: $.75 newsstand/cover; $30/yr in county; $37.50/yr out of county. Freelance Pay: $0.75/column-inch. Circulation: 5,800 per issue (paid and free). **Owner(s):** Journal Register Co., 50 W State St, 12th Fl Trenton, NJ 08608. **Management:** Albert Frattura, Publisher. Jeannine Stez, Office Manager. Windy Bittis, Advertising.

BROOKLYN

EXPONENT (BROOKLYN), THE. 160 S. Main, Brooklyn, MI 49230. Telephone: 517-592-2122. FAX: 517-592-3241. E-MAIL: exponews@frontiernet.net. URL: http://www.theexponent.com. Year Established: 1881. Pub. Frequency: w. (Tue.) Page Size: tabloid. Subscrip. Rate: $.50 newsstand/cover; $25/yr in county. Adv. Rate: col. inch $6.20 Freelance Pay: $20/article. Circulation: 5,800 per issue (paid). **Owner(s):** Schepeler Corp., See address and contact information above. **Management:** Matt Schepeler, Publisher. Dorothy Booth, Advertising Manager. **Editorial:** Jeff Steers, Editor.

BUCHANAN

BERRIEN COUNTY RECORD. 206 Main St., Buchanan, MI 49107-1612. Telephone: 269-695-3878. FAX: 269-695-3880. Mailing Address: PO Box 191, Buchanan, MI 49107-0191. Year Established: 1867. Pub. Frequency: w. (Thu) Page Size: broadsheet. Subscrip. Rate: $.75 newsstand/cover; $30/yr mailed in county; $35/yr mailed out of county. Circulation: 2,600 per issue (paid and free). **Owner(s):** Dean H. Henricksen, See address and contact information above. **Management:** Dean Henricksen, Publisher. Daleen Granger, Office Manager. **Editorial:** Dean Henricksen, Editor.

Weeklies

CADILLAC

NORTHERN MICHIGAN NEWS. ISSN 0194-3014
130 N. Mitchell, Cadillac, MI 49601-0640. Telephone: 231-775-6565. FAX: 231-775-8790. URL: http://www.cadillacnews.com. Mailing Address: PO Box 640, Cadillac, MI 49601-0640. Year Established: 1972. Pub. Frequency: w. (Mon.) Page Size: broadsheet Circulation: 17,690 per issue (free). **Owner(s):** Thomas C. Huckle, See address and contact information above. **Management:** Chris Huckle, Publisher. Charity England, Advertising Manager. Tom Alderich, Circulation Manager. **Editorial:** Matt Seward, Editor.

CARO

TUSCOLA COUNTY ADVERTISER. 344 N. State St., Caro, MI 48723. Telephone: 989-673-3181. FAX: 989-673-5662. E-MAIL: ads@tcadvertiser.com. Mailing Address: PO Box 106, Caro, MI 48723. Year Established: 1868. Pub. Frequency: s-w. (Wed. & Sat.) Page Size: broadsheet. Subscrip. Rate: $.75 newsstand/cover; $32/yr. Freelance Pay: $1/column-inch. Circulation: 8,500 per issue (paid). **Owner(s):** Edwards Group Inc, 125 Eagles Nest, Seneca, SC 29679. **Management:** Tim Murphy, Publisher. Ven Stark, Circulation Manager. Stacy Burkey, Classified Adv. Mgr.. **Editorial:** Amy Joles, Editor.

CASS CITY

CASS CITY CHRONICLE. PO Box 115, Cass City, MI 48726. Telephone: 989-872-2010. FAX: 989-872-3810. Year Established: 1917. Pub. Frequency: w. (Wed.) Page Size: broadsheet. Subscrip. Rate: $.50 newsstand/cover; $19/yr local; $23/yr in state; $25/yr elsewhere. Adv. Rate: col. inch $5.57 Circulation: 3,600 per issue (paid). **Owner(s):** Clarke Haire, See address and contact information above. **Management:** Clarke Haire, Publisher. **Editorial:** Tom Montgomery, Editor.

CHARLEVOIX

CHARLEVOIX COURIER. 112 Mason St., Charlevoix, MI 49720-1314. Telephone: 231-547-6558. FAX: 231-547-4992. E-MAIL: ad@charlevoixcourier.com. Mailing Address: PO Box 117, Charlevoix, MI 49720-0117. Year Established: 1883. Pub. Frequency: w. (Wed.) Page Size: tabloid. Subscrip. Rate: $.50 newsstand/cover; $63/yr. Adv. Rate: col. inch $10.70 Circulation: 3,200 per issue (paid). **Owner(s):** Northern Michigan Review, Inc., PO Box 528, Petoskey, MI 49770. Telephone: 231-347-2544. FAX: 231-347-6833. **Management:** Ken Winter, General Manager. Kim Taylor, Advertising Manager.

NORTH WOODS CALL. 00165 Turkey Run, Charlevoix, MI 49720-9801. Telephone: 231-547-9797. FAX: 231-547-0367. Year Established: 1953. Pub. Frequency: bi-w. (Wed.) Page Size: tabloid. Subscrip. Rate: $1.25 newsstand/cover; $20 mailed for 6 mos.; $30/yr; $54 for 2 yrs.. Circulation: 10,000 per issue (paid). **Owner(s):** North Woods Call, Inc., See address and contact information above. **Management:** Mary Sheppard, Sales Manager. **Editorial:** Glen Sheppard, Editor.

CHARLOTTE

CHARLOTTE SHOPPING GUIDE. 239 S Cochran, Charlotte, MI 48813. Telephone: 517-543-9913. FAX: 517-543-3677. E-MAIL: rgreco@gannett.com. URL: http://www.hometownlife.com. Year Established: 1948. Pub. Frequency: w. (Sun.) Page Size: tabloid. Subscrip. Rate: $.50 newsstand/cover; $104/yr mailed 1st class. Circulation: 15,681 Sunday (paid and free). **Owner(s):** Lansing Community Newspapers, 7950 Jones Branch Dr, McLean, VA 22107. Telephone: 703-854-6000. **Management:** Liza Sayre, Advertising. Ellen Kent, Advertising Manager. Betty Henry, Circulation Manager. Ann Lyon, Classified Adv. Mgr.. **Editorial:** Rachel Greco, Editor. Al Wilson, Group Editor.

EATON RAPIDS COMMUNITY NEWS. 239 S Cochran, Charlotte, MI 48813. Telephone: 517-543-9913. FAX: 517-543-3677. E-MAIL: cbumstead@gannett.com. URL: http://www.hometownlife.com. Year Established: 1854. Pub. Frequency: w. (Sun.) Page Size: tabloid. Subscrip. Rate: $.50 newsstand/cover; $104/yr mailed. Circulation: 8,541 Sunday (paid and free). **Owner(s):** Lansing Community Newspapers, 7950 Jones Branch Dr, McLean, VA 22107. Telephone: 703-854-6000. **Management:** Rich Ramhoff, Publisher. Isaac Stohrs, Advertising. Ellen Kent, Advertising Manager. Betty Henry, Circulation Manager. Ann Lyon, Classified Adv. Mgr.. **Editorial:** Carla Bumstead, Editor.

CHEBOYGAN

MACKINAW JOURNAL. 308 N. Main St., Cheboygan, MI 49721. Telephone: 231-627-7144. FAX: 231-627-5331. E-MAIL: nancykidder@cheboygantribune.com. URL: http://www.cheboygannews.com. Mailing Address: PO Box 290, Cheboygan, MI 49721. Pub. Frequency: w. (Tue.) Page Size: broadsheet. Subscrip. Rate: $.75 newsstand/cover; $20/yr in county. Circulation: 3,200 per issue (paid). **Owner(s):** GateHouse Media, Inc, 350 WillowBrook Office Park, Fairport, NY 14450. Telephone: 585-598-0030. FAX: 585-248-2631. **Management:** Nancy Kidder, General Manager. **Editorial:** Shawna Jankoviak, Editor.

CHELSEA

CHELSEA STANDARD, THE. 20750 Old US 12, Chelsea, MI 48118. Telephone: 734-475-1371. FAX: 734-475-1413. E-MAIL: editor@chelseastandard.com. URL: http://www.chelseastandard.com. Year Established: 1871. Pub. Frequency: w. (Thu.) Page Size: broadsheet. Subscrip. Rate: $.75 newsstand/cover; $19.50 mailed for 6 mos.; $33/yr mailed. Adv. Rate: col. inch $6.50 Circulation: 4,400 per issue (paid). **Owner(s):** Journal Register Co., 50 W State St, 12th Fl, Trenton, NJ 08608. Telephone: 609-396-2292, 609-396-2200. **Management:** James Williams, Publisher. Teresa Riddle, Advertising Manager. **Editorial:** Terry Jacoby, Editor.

DEXTER LEADER, THE. 20750 Old US 12, Chelsea, MI 48118. Telephone: 734-475-1371. FAX: 734-475-1413. E-MAIL: editor@dexterleader.com. URL: http://www.dexterleader.com. Year Established: 1867. Pub. Frequency: w. (Thu.) Page Size: broadsheet. Subscrip. Rate: $.75 newsstand/cover; $19.50 mailed for 6 mos.; $33/yr mailed. Adv. Rate: col. inch $5.46 Circulation: 3,500 per issue (paid). **Owner(s):** Journal Register Co., 50 W State St, 12th Fl, Trenton, NJ 08608. Telephone: 609-396-2292, 609-396-2200. **Management:** James Williams, Publisher. Teresa Riddle, Advertising Manager. **Editorial:** Terry Jacoby, Editor.

CHESANING

TRI-COUNTY CITIZEN. 9998 E. M-57, Chesaning, MI 48616. Telephone: 989-845-7403. FAX: 989-845-4397. E-MAIL: citizen@centurytel.net. Year Established: 1983. Pub. Frequency: w. (Sun.) Page Size: tabloid.Subscrip. Rate: $7 mailed/mo.; $78/yr mailed Circulation: 19,200 per issue (free). **Owner(s):** County Press, See address and contact information above. **Management:** Daniel Lea, Publisher. Melissa Lea, Advertising Director. **Editorial:** Daniel Lea, Editor.

CLARE

CLARE SENTINEL. 112 W. Fourth St., Clare, MI 48617. Telephone: 989-386-9937. FAX: 989-386-9311. Year Established: 1897. Pub. Frequency: w. (Tue.) Page Size: broadsheet.Subscrip. Rate: $.50 newsstand/cover; $20.50/yr Circulation: 3,500 per issue (paid). **Owner(s):** Alfred R. Bransdorfer, See address and contact information above. **Editorial:** Judy Kushmaul, Editor.

CLARKSTON

CLARKSTON NEWS. 5 S. Main St., Clarkston, MI 48346. Telephone: 248-625-3370. FAX: 248-625-0706. E-MAIL: clarkstonnews@gmail.com. URL: http://www.clarkstonnews.com. Year Established: 1929. Pub. Frequency: w. (Wed.) Page Size: tabloid. Subscrip. Rate: $.50 newsstand/cover; $30/yr mailed in county; $33/yr mailed out of county; $38/yr mailed out of state. Circulation: 4,500 per issue (paid and free). **Owner(s):** Sherman Publications, Inc., 666 S. Lapeer, Oxford, MI 48371. Telephone: 248-628-4801. FAX: 248-628-9750. **Management:** James A. Sherman Jr., Publisher. Cindy Burroughs, Advertising Manager. **Editorial:** Phil Custodio, Editor.

COLDWATER

BRONSON JOURNAL, THE. 15 W. Pearl St., Coldwater, MI 49036. Telephone: 517-278-2318. FAX: 517-278-6041. URL: http://www.thebronsonjournal.com. Pub. Frequency: w. (Wed.) Page Size: broadsheet. Subscrip. Rate: $.75 newsstand/cover; $32/yr in county; $38/yr out of county; $44/yr out of state. Circulation: 900 per issue (paid). **Owner(s):** GateHouse Media, Inc, 350 WillowBrook Office Park, Fairport, NY 14450. Telephone: 585-598-0030. FAX: 585-248-2631. **Management:** David Ferro, Publisher. Craig Sowers, Circulation Manager. **Editorial:** Heather Jeffrey, Executive Editor.

COLDWATER SHOPPER GUIDE. 57 S Monroe St, Coldwater, MI 49036. Telephone: 517-279-9764. FAX: 517-278-8597. Pub. Frequency: w. (Wed.) Page Size: tabloid Circulation: 22,950 per issue (free). **Owner(s):** GateHouse Media, Inc, 350 WillowBrook Office Park, Fairport, NY 14450. Telephone: 585-598-0030. **Management:** Pat Jolley, Office Manager.

JONESVILLE INDEPENDENT. 15 W. Pearl St., Coldwater, MI 49036. Telephone: 517-278-2318. FAX: 517-278-6041. URL: http://www.gatehousemedia.com. Pub. Frequency: w. (Fri.) Page Size: broadsheet. Subscrip. Rate: $.50 newsstand/cover; $20/yr in county; $24/yr out of county; $26/yr out of state. Circulation: 800 per issue (paid). **Owner(s):** GateHouse Media, Inc, 350 WillowBrook Office Park, Fairport, NY 14450. Telephone: 585-598-0030. FAX: 585-248-2631. **Management:** David Ferro, Publisher. Craig Sowers, Circulation Manager. **Editorial:** Heather Jeffrey, Executive Editor.

REPORTER EXTRA, THE. 15 W. Pearl St., Coldwater, MI 49036. Telephone: 517-278-2318. FAX: 517-278-6041. Pub. Frequency: w. (Mon.) Page Size: tabloid Circulation: 8,100 per issue (free). **Owner(s):** GateHouse Media, Inc, 57 S Monroe St, Coldwater, MI 49036. 350 WillowBrook Office Park, Fairport, NY 14450. Telephone: 585-598-0030. FAX: 585-248-2631. **Management:** David Ferro, Publisher. Craig Sowers, Circulation Manager.

UNION CITY REGISTER TRIBUNE. 15 W. Pearl St., Coldwater, MI 49036. Telephone: 517-278-2318. FAX: 517-278-6041. Pub. Frequency: w. (Tue.) Page Size: broadsheet. Subscrip. Rate: $.75 newsstand/cover; $32/yr in county; $38/yr out of county; $44/yr out of state. **Owner(s):** GateHouse Media, Inc, 350 WillowBrook Office Park, Fairport, NY 14450. Telephone: 585-598-0030. FAX: 585-248-2631. **Management:** David Ferro, Publisher. Craig Sowers, Circulation Manager. **Editorial:** Heather Jeffrey, Executive Editor.

CROSWELL

JEFFERSONIAN, THE. 14 Wells St., Croswell, MI 48422. Telephone: 810-679-4500. FAX: 810-679-4504. Year Established: 1858. Pub. Frequency: w. (Sun.) Page Size: tabloid. Circulation: 16,200 per issue (controlled and free). **Owner(s):** Journal Register Co., 50 W State St, 12th Fl, Trenton, NJ 08608. Telephone: 609-396-2200. **Editorial:** Carol Seifferlein, Editor.

DAVISON

DAVISON INDEX, THE. 220 N. Main St., Davison, MI 48423-1432. Telephone: 810-653-3511. FAX: 810-653-3077. Mailing Address: PO Box, Davison, MI 48423-0100. Year Established: 1889. Pub. Frequency: w. (Wed.) Page Size: tabloid. Subscrip. Rate: $.75 newsstand/cover; $22/yr local; $25/yr mailed out of area; $30/yr mailed out of state. Adv. Rate: col. inch $8 Circulation: 11,500 per issue (paid and free). **Owner(s):** Jim Sherman, See address and contact information above. **Management:** Jim Sherman, Publisher. **Editorial:** Jonathan Kane, Editor.

DEARBORN

DEARBORN TIMES-HERALD. ISSN 0193-0230
13730 Michigan Ave., Dearborn, MI 48126-3520. Telephone: 313-584-4000. FAX: 313-584-1357. E-MAIL: dbntherald@aol.com. Year Established: 1963. Pub. Frequency: w. (Wed.) Page Size: broadsheet. Subscrip. Rate: $.75 newsstand/cover; $32.95/yr. Circulation: 42,000 per issue (paid and free). **Owner(s):** Laurie & Scott Bewick, See address and contact information above. **Management:** Michael Bewick, Publisher. Gloria Fox, Advertising Manager. Laura Bewick, Assistant Publisher. **Editorial:** Scott Bewick, Editor.

PRESS & GUIDE. 22450 Park St, Dearborn, MI 48124. Telephone: 313-359-7820. FAX: 313-359-7833. E-MAIL: editor@pressandguide.com. URL: http://www.pressandguide.com. Year Established: 1918. Pub. Frequency: s-w. (Wed. & Sun.) Page Size: broadsheet. Subscrip. Rate: $.75 newsstand/cover; $54/yr home delivery local; $108/yr mailed. Circulation: 20,000 Sunday (paid); 25,000 weekly (paid). **Owner(s):** Journal Register Co., 50 W State St, 12th Fl, Trenton, NJ 08608. Telephone: 609-396-2200. FAX: 609-396-2292. **Management:** Denise McDonald, Publisher. Deborah Silvers, Circulation Manager. **Editorial:** Tim Powers, Editor.

SUNDAY TIMES, THE. 13730 Michigan Ave., Dearborn, MI 48126-3520. Telephone: 313-584-4000. FAX: 313-584-1357. E-MAIL: dbntherald@aol.com. Mailing Address: PO Box 706, Dearborn, MI 48126. Year Established: 1963. Pub. Frequency: w. (Sun.) Page Size: broadsheet. Subscrip. Rate: $.75 newsstand/cover; $32.95/yr. Circulation: 42,000 per issue (paid and free). **Owner(s):** Laurie & Scott Bewick, See address and contact information above. **Management:** Michael Bewick, Publisher. Louise Parker, Advertising Manager. John Walton, Circulation Manager. Gloria Fox, Classified Adv. Mgr.. **Editorial:** Scott Bewick, Editor.

DETROIT

METRO TIMES. 733 St. Antoine St., Detroit, MI 48226. Telephone: 313-961-4060. FAX: 313-961-6598. URL: http://www.metrotimes.com. Pub. Frequency: w. (Wed.) Page Size: tabloid. Subscrip. Rate: $35 mailed for 6 mos. 3rd class; $70 mailed for 6 mos. 1st class. Circulation: 105,000 per issue (paid and free). **Owner(s):** Times-Shamrock Communications, 149 Penn Ave., Scranton, PA 18503. Telephone: 570-348-9100. **Management:** Lisa Rudy, Publisher. Jim Cohen, Advertising Director. Erica Grabski, Circulation Manager. Jill Berry, Classified Adv. Mgr.. **Editorial:** W. Kim Heron, Editor. Brian Smith, Feature Editor. Curt Guyette, News Editor.

EAST TAWAS

IOSCO COUNTY NEWS-HERALD. 110 W State St, East Tawas, MI 48730. Telephone: 989-362-3456. FAX: 989-362-6601. E-MAIL: editor@iosconews.com. URL: http://www.iosconews.com. Mailing Address: PO Box 72, East Tawas, MI 48730-0072. Pub. Frequency: w. (Wed.) Page Size: tabloid. Subscrip. Rate: $1 newsstand/cover; $45/yr mailed local; $50/yr mailed in state; $55/yr mailed out of state. Adv. Rate: col. inch $8.85 Circulation: 7,500 per issue (paid). **Owner(s):** Community Media Group, Inc, PO Box 10, West Frankfort, IL 62896. Telephone: 618-937-6412. **Management:** Jim Dunn, Publisher. **Editorial:** John Morris, Editor.

FLINT

BURTON NEWS, THE. 200 E. First St., Flint, MI 48502. Telephone: 810-766-6100. URL: http://www.theburtonnews.com. Year Established: 1973. Pub. Frequency: w. (Sun.) Page Size: broadsheet. Subscrip. Rate: $.25 newsstand/cover; $72/yr mailed. Adv. Rate: col. inch $10.20 Circulation: 13,804 per issue (paid and free). **Owner(s):** Advance Publications, Inc., See address and contact information above. **Management:** Tom Eason, Advertising Director. **Editorial:** Brooke Rausch, Managing Editor. Katie Bach, Community Editor. John Foren, Local News Editor. Howard Thomas, Sports Editor.

CLIO MESSENGER, THE. ISSN 1523-6552
200 E. First St., Flint, MI 48502. E-MAIL: feedback@thecliomessenger.com. URL: http://www.thecliomessenger.com. Year Established: 1907. Pub. Frequency: w. (Sun.) Page Size: broadsheet. Subscrip. Rate: $.25 newsstand/cover; $72/yr mailed. Adv. Rate: col. inch $8.40 Circulation: 8,889 per issue (paid and free). **Owner(s):** Advance Publications, Inc., See address and contact information above. **Management:** Tom Eason, Advertising Manager. Jerry Carlson, Circulation Manager. **Editorial:** Barb Modrack, Editor. Brooke Rausch, Managing Editor. John Foren, Local News Editor. Dave Poniers, Sports Editor.

DAVISON FLAGSTAFF. ISSN 1523-6544
200 E. First St., Flint, MI 48502. Telephone: 810-766-6100. URL: http://www.heritagenews.com. Pub. Frequency: w. (Sun.) Page Size: broadsheet. Subscrip. Rate: $.50 newsstand/cover; $72/yr mailed. Adv. Rate: col. inch $8.40 Circulation: 8,808 per issue (paid and free). **Owner(s):** Advance Publications, Inc., See address and contact information above. **Management:** Tom Eason, Advertising Manager. Sam Harris, Circulation Manager. **Editorial:** Barb Modrack, Editor. Brooke Rausch, Managing Editor. John Foren, Local News Editor. Howard Thomas, Sports Editor.

FENTON PRESS, THE. 200 E. First St., Flint, MI 48502. Telephone: 810-766-6100. E-MAIL: tcn@thecommunitynewspapers.com. URL: http://www.fentonpress.com. Year Established: 2002. Pub. Frequency: w. (Sun.) Page Size: broadsheet. Subscrip. Rate: $.50 newsstand/cover; $72/yr mailed. Adv. Rate: col. inch $10.75 Circulation: 14,000 per issue (free). **Owner(s):** Advance Publications, Inc., See address and contact information above. **Management:** Tom Eason, Advertising Manager. Jerry Carlson, Circulation Manager. **Editorial:** Paul Keep, Editor. Brooke Rausch, Managing Editor. John Foren, Local News Editor. Howard Thomas, Sports Editor.

FLINT TOWNSHIP NEWS, THE. 200 E. First St., Flint, MI 48507. E-MAIL: editor@theflinttownshipnews.com. URL: http://www.theflinttownshipnews.com. Pub. Frequency: w. (Sun.) Page Size: broadsheet.Adv. Rate: col. inch $8.40 Circulation: 17,123 per issue (free). **Owner(s):** Advance Publications, Inc., 200 E. First St., Flint, MI 48502. **Management:** Tom Eason, Advertising Manager. Jerry Carlson, Circulation Manager. **Editorial:** Katie Bach, Editor. Brooke Rausch, Managing Editor. John Foren, Local News Editor. Howard Thomas, Sports Editor.

FLUSHING OBSERVER, THE. ISSN 0747-1718
200 E. First St., Flint, MI 48502. E-MAIL: feedback@theflushingobserver.com. URL: http://www.theflushingobserver.com. Year Established: 1882. Pub. Frequency: w. (Sun.) Page Size: broadsheet. Subscrip. Rate: $.25 newsstand/cover; $26/yr carrier delivery; $72/yr mailed. Adv. Rate: col. inch $8.40 Circulation: 9,318 per issue (paid and free). **Owner(s):** Advance Publications, Inc., See address and contact information above. **Editorial:** Barb Modrack, Editor. Brooke Rausch, Managing Editor. John Foren, Local News Editor. Howard Thomas, Sports Editor.

GRAND BLANC NEWS, THE. ISSN 0747-1742
200 E. First St., Flint, MI 48507. E-MAIL: editor@thegrandblancnews.com. URL: http://www.grandblancnews.com. Year Established: 1906. Pub. Frequency: w. (Sun.) Page Size: broadsheet.Adv. Rate: col. inch $10.75 Circulation: 20,790 per issue (free). **Owner(s):** Advance Publications, Inc., See address and contact information above. **Management:** Tom Eason, Advertising Director. Jerry Carlson, Circulation Manager. **Editorial:** Jim Larkin, Editor. Brooke Rausch, Managing Editor. Katie Bach, Community Editor. John Foren, Local News Editor. Howard Thomas, Sports Editor.

SWARTZ CREEK NEWS. 200 E. First St., Flint, MI 48502. URL: http://www.flintjournal.com. Year Established: 1939. Pub. Frequency: w. (Sun.) Page Size: broadsheet. Subscrip. Rate: $.50 newsstand/cover. Adv. Rate: col. inch $8.40 Circulation: 10,779 per issue (paid and free). **Owner(s):** Advance Publications, Inc., See address and contact information above. **Management:** Tom Eason, Advertising. **Editorial:** Barb Modrack, Editor. Brooke Rausch, Managing Editor. John Foren, Local News Editor. Howard Thomas, Sports Editor.

FRANKENMUTH

FRANKENMUTH NEWS. 527 N Franklin St., Frankenmuth, MI 48734. Telephone: 989-652-3246. FAX: 989-652-2417. E-MAIL: frankenmuthnews@airadv.net. URL: http://www.frankenmuthnews.com. Mailing Address: PO Box 252, Frankenmuth, MI 48734. Year Established: 1906. Pub. Frequency: w. (Wed.) Page Size: broadsheet. Subscrip. Rate: $.75 newsstand/cover; $32/yr in county; $34/yr mailed out of county; $37/yr mailed out of state. Circulation: 5,200 per issue (paid). **Owner(s):** Steven J. Grainger, 410 E. Tuscola, Frankenmuth, MI 48734. **Management:** Steven J. Grainger, Publisher. Vicky Hayden, Advertising Manager. Vanessa Sanders, Business Manager. **Editorial:** Scott A. Wenzel, Editor.

FRANKFORT

BENZIE COUNTY RECORD PATRIOT. 417 Main St., Frankfort, MI 49635. Telephone: 231-352-9659. FAX: 231-352-9874. URL: http://www.thepioneergroup.net. Mailing Address: PO Box 673, Frankfort, MI 49635-0673. Pub. Frequency: w. (Wed.) Page Size: broadsheet. Subscrip. Rate: $.75 newsstand/cover; $26/yr mailed in county & adj. counties; $33/yr mailed out of area; $44/yr mailed out of state. Circulation: 4,200 per issue (paid). **Owner(s):** The Pioneer Group, 851 Michigan Ave., Baldwin, MI 49304. **Management:** John A. Batdorff II, General Manager. John A. Batdorff, President. Marilyn Barker, Publisher. Amy Barron, Advertising Manager. Kim Hanchofky, Classified Adv. Mgr.. **Editorial:** Roland Halliday, Editor.

FREMONT

TIMES-INDICATOR. 44 W. Main St., Fremont, MI 49412. Telephone: 231-924-4400. FAX: 231-924-4066. E-MAIL: news@ncats.net. URL: http://www.timesindicator.com. Mailing Address: PO Box 7, Fremont, MI 49412. Year Established: 1878. Pub. Frequency: w. (Wed.) Page Size: broadsheet. Subscrip. Rate: $.60 newsstand/cover; $27/yr mailed in county & adj. cys.; $36/yr mailed western Michigan area; $47/yr mailed out of area. Circulation: 10,000 per issue (paid). **Owner(s):** T.I. Publications, PO Box 387, Morrison, IL 61270. Telephone: 815-772-4123. **Management:** Richard Wheater Sr., Publisher. Debbie Reinhold, Advertising Manager. Jenna Flanery, Circulation Manager. **Editorial:** Richard Wheater Sr., Editor.

GAYLORD

GAYLORD HERALD TIMES. 2058 S. Otsego Ave., Gaylord, MI 49735-0598. Telephone: 989-732-1111. FAX: 989-732-3490. E-MAIL: jim@gaylordheraldtimes.com. URL: http://www.gaylordheraldtimes.com. Mailing Address: PO Box 598, Gaylord, MI 49734-0598. Year Established: 1875. Pub. Frequency: s-w. (Wed. & Sat.) Page Size: broadsheet. Subscrip. Rate: $.75 newsstand/cover(s); $53/yr mailed local; $72/yr mailed out of area. **Wire Service(s):** AP. Circulation: 21,000 Saturday (paid and free); 7,000 (paid). **Owner(s):** Otsego County Herald Times, Inc., See address and contact information above. **Management:** James L. Grisso, Publisher. Kim Ballard, Advertising Manager. **Editorial:** Chris Grosser, Editor. Peter Comings, News Editor.

MARKETPLACE (GAYLORD). 2058 S. Otsego Ave., Gaylord, MI 49735-0598. Telephone: 989-732-1111. FAX: 989-732-3490. Mailing Address: PO Box 598, Gaylord, MI 49734-0598. Pub. Frequency: w. (Sat.) Page Size: standard Circulation: 5,000 per issue (free). **Owner(s):** Otsego County Herald Times, Inc., See address and contact information above. **Management:** James L. Grisso, Publisher. Kim Ballard, Advertising Manager. **Editorial:** Chris Grosser, Editor. Jeremy Speer, Sports Editor.

NORTHERN STAR. 1966 S. Otsego Ave., Gaylord, MI 49735. Telephone: 989-732-5125. FAX: 989-732-9323. URL: http://www.star-ads.com. Mailing Address: PO Box 620, Gaylord, MI 49734. Year Established: 1960. Pub. Frequency: w. (Sun.) Page Size: tabloid.Adv. Rate: col. inch $8.14 Circulation: 19,800 Sunday (free). **Owner(s):** Morning Star Publishing, 711 W. Pickard, Mt. Pleasant, MI 48858. Telephone: 989-779-6000. **Management:** Dan McDonald, General Manager. Paige O'Neal, Sales Manager.

OGEMAW/OSCODA COUNTY STAR. PO Box 620, Gaylord, MI 49734. Telephone: 989-732-5125. FAX: 989-732-9323. URL: http://www.star-ads.com. Pub. Frequency: w. (Sun.) Page Size: tabloid.Adv. Rate: col. inch $8.20 Circulation: 16,400 Sunday (free). **Owner(s):** Morning Star Publishing, 711 W. Pickard, Mt. Pleasant, MI 48858. Telephone: 989-779-6000. **Management:** Susan Kelly-Jacobs, General Manager. Bill McHugh, President. Mike Ithnatenko, VP Circulation. Susan Kelly-Jacobs, Advertising Manager. **Editorial:** Ethan Clarke, Editor.

PETROSKEY STAR. 1966 S. Otsego Ave., Gaylord, MI 49735. Telephone: 989-732-5125. FAX: 989-732-9323. URL: http://www.star-ads.com. Pub. Frequency: w. (Sun.) Page Size: tabloid.Adv. Rate: col. inch $9.95 Circulation: 23,000 Sunday (free). **Owner(s):** Morning Star Publishing, 711 W. Pickard, Mt. Pleasant, MI 48858. Telephone: 989-779-6000. **Management:** Ray Pike, President. Susan Kelly-Jacobs, Advertising Manager. **Editorial:** Ethan Clarke, Editor.

ROSCOMMON COUNTY STAR. 1966 S Otsego Ave, Gaylord, MI 49735. URL: http://www.star-ads.com. Pub. Frequency: w. (Sun) Page Size: tabloid.Adv. Rate: col. inch $4.75 Circulation: 14,448 Sunday (free). **Owner(s):** Journal Register Co., 50 W. State St., 12th Fl., Trenton, NJ 08608. **Management:** Mary Babb, General Manager. Ray Pike, President. Susan Kelly-Jacobs, Advertising Manager. **Editorial:** Ethan Clark, Editor.

TOWN MEETING, THE. 1966 S. Otsego Ave., Gaylord, MI 49735. Telephone: 989-732-5125. FAX: 989-732-9323. URL: http://www.star-ads.com. Pub. Frequency: w. (Sun.) Page Size: tabloid.Adv. Rate: col. inch $9.95 Circulation: 20,300 Sunday (free). **Owner(s):** Morning Star Publishing, 711 W. Pickard, Mt. Pleasant, MI 48858. Telephone: 989-779-6000. **Management:** Kathleen Weitschat, Advertising Director. Susan Kelly-Jacobs, Advertising Manager. **Editorial:** Dave Lein, Editor.

GLADWIN

GLADWIN COUNTY RECORD & BEAVERTON CLARION. 700 E. Cedar Ave., Gladwin, MI 48624-0425. Telephone: 989-426-9411. FAX: 989-426-2023. E-MAIL: edit@gladcorec.com. URL: http://www.gladcorec.com. Mailing Address: PO Box 425, Gladwin, MI 48624-0425. Year Established: 1877. Pub. Frequency: w. (Wed.) Page Size: broadsheet. Subscrip. Rate: $.50 newsstand/cover; $24.95/yr mailed in county & adj. counties; $28.95/yr mailed out of area. Circulation: 8,000 per issue (paid and free). **Owner(s):** Superior Publishing Corp., 1105 Tower Ave, Superior, WI 54880. Telephone: 715-395-5725. FAX: 715-395-5729. **Management:** Michael Drey, General Manager. **Editorial:** Marie Hopsensperger, News Editor.

GOBLES

VAN BUREN COUNTY ADVERTISER. PO Box 340, Gobles, MI 49055. Telephone: 269-628-5122. FAX: 269-628-5198. Year Established: 1946. Pub. Frequency: w. (Mon.) Page Size: tabloid Circulation: 7,800 per issue (free). **Owner(s):** Michigan Printing Co., See address and contact information above. **Management:** Pam Harris, Owner. Peggy Rose, Office Manager. **Editorial:** Pam Harris, Editor.

GRAND LEDGE

CLINTON COUNTY NEWS (GRAND LEDGE). 11936 W Andre Dr, Grand Ledge, MI 48837. Telephone: 517-627-6085. FAX: 517-627-4863. E-MAIL: sounds@gannett.com. URL: http://www.hometownlife.com. Year Established: 1930. Pub. Frequency: w. (Sun.) Page Size: tabloid. Subscrip. Rate: $.50 newsstand/cover; $104/yr mailed 1st class. Circulation: 13,994 Sunday (paid and free). **Owner(s):** Lansing Community Newspapers, 7950 Jones Branch Dr, McLean, VA 22107. Telephone: 703-854-6000. **Management:** Preston Odette, Publisher. Joel Pretzer, Advertising. Ellen Kent, Advertising Manager. Betty Henry, Circulation Manager. Ann Lyon, Classified Adv. Mgr.. **Editorial:** Sue Lounds, Editor. Al Wilson, Group Editor.

DELTA/WAVERLY COMMUNITY NEWS. 11936 W Andre Dr, Grand Ledge, MI 48837. E-MAIL: kumadden@gannett.com. URL: http://www.hometownlife.com. Year Established: 1984. Pub. Frequency: w. (Sun.) Page Size: tabloid. Subscrip. Rate: $50 newsstand/cover; $104/yr mailed 1st class. Circulation: 8,924 per issue (paid and free). **Owner(s):** Lansing Community Newspapers, 7950 Jones Branch Dr, McLean, VA 22107. **Management:** Preston Odette, Publisher. Joana Rohrs, Advertising. Ellen Kent, Advertising Manager. Betty Henry, Circulation Manager. **Editorial:** Kurt Madden, Editor. Al Wilson, Group Editor.

GRAND LEDGE INDEPENDENT, THE. 11936 W Andre Dr, Grand Ledge, MI 48837. Telephone: 517-627-6085. FAX: 517-627-4863. E-MAIL: kumadden@gannett.com. URL: http:/www.hometownlife.com. Year Established: 1869. Pub. Frequency: w. (Sun.) Page Size: broadsheet. Subscrip. Rate: $.50 newsstand/cover; $104/yr mailed 1st class. Circulation: 14,244 Sunday (paid and free). **Owner(s):** Lansing Community Newspapers, 7950 Jones Branch Dr, McLean, VA 22107. Telephone: 703-854-6000. **Management:** Preston Odette, Publisher. Joana Rohrs, Advertising. Ellen Kent, Advertising Manager. Betty Henry, Circulation Manager. Ann Lyon, Classified Adv. Mgr.. **Editorial:** Kurt Madden, Editor.

HOLT COMMUNITY NEWS. 11936 W Andre Dr, Grand Ledge, MI 48837. Telephone: 517-627-6085. FAX: 517-627-4863. E-MAIL: wkangas@gannett.com. URL: http://www.homelife.com. Year Established: 1995. Pub. Frequency: w. (Sun.) Page Size: tabloid. Subscrip. Rate: $50 newsstand/cover; $104/yr. Adv. Rate: col. inch $8 Circulation: 10,183 Sunday (paid and free). **Owner(s):** Lansing Community Newspapers, 7950 Jones Branch Dr, McLean, VA 22107. Telephone: 703-854-6000. **Management:** Joel Pretzer, Advertising. Ellen Kent, Advertising Manager. Betty Henry, Circulation Manager. Ann Lyon, Classified Adv. Mgr.. **Editorial:** Al Wilson, Group Editor. Will Kangas, Writer.

Weeklies

INGHAM COUNTY COMMUNITY NEWS. 11936 W Andre Dr, Grand Ledge, MI 48837. Telephone: 517-627-6085. FAX: 517-627-4863. E-MAIL: rgreco@gannett.com. URL: http://www.hometownlife.com. Year Established: 1858. Pub. Frequency: w. (Sun.) Page Size: tabloid. Subscrip. Rate: $.50 newsstand/cover; $20/yr. Circulation: 10,346 Sunday (paid and free). **Owner(s):** Lansing Community Newspapers, 7950 Jones Branch Dr, McLean, VA 22107. Telephone: 703-854-6000. **Management:** Mel Burke, Advertising. Ellen Kent, Advertising Manager. Betty Henry, Circulation Manager. Ann Lyon, Classified Adv. Mgr.. **Editorial:** Rachel Greco, Editor. Al Wilson, Group Editor.

PORTLAND REVIEW & OBSERVER. 11936 W Andre Dr, Grand Ledge, MI 48837. Telephone: 517-627-6085. FAX: 517-627-4863. E-MAIL: tthelan@gannett.com. URL: http://www.hometownlife.com. Year Established: 1867. Pub. Frequency: w. (Sun.) Page Size: tabloid. Subscrip. Rate: $.50 newsstand/cover; $62.60/yr mailed in county; $74/yr mailed out of county; $104/yr mailed out of state. Circulation: 7,462 Sunday (paid and free). **Owner(s):** Lansing Community Newspapers, 7950 Jones Branch Dr, McLean, VA 22107. Telephone: 703-854-6000. **Management:** Preston Odette, Publisher. Tammy Beson, Advertising. Ellen Kent, Advertising Manager. Betty Henry, Circulation Manager. Ann Lyon, Classified Adv. Mgr.. **Editorial:** Tom Thelan, Editor. Al Wilson, Group Editor.

TOWNE COURIER, THE. 11936 W Andre Dr, Grand Ledge, MI 48837. Telephone: 517-627-6085. FAX: 517-627-4863. E-MAIL: wwhelton@gannett.com. URL: http://www.hometownlife.com. Year Established: 1972. Pub. Frequency: w. (Sun.) Page Size: tabloid. Subscrip. Rate: $.50 newsstand/cover; $26 for 3 mos.; $104/yr. Circulation: 23,920 Sunday (paid and free). **Owner(s):** Lansing Community Newspapers, 7950 Jones Branch Dr, McLean, VA 22107. Telephone: 703-854-6000. **Management:** Mel Burke, Advertising. Ellen Kent, Advertising Manager. Betty Henry, Circulation Manager. Ann Lyon, Classified Adv. Mgr.. **Editorial:** Will Whelton, Editor. Al Wilson, Group Editor.

WILLIAMSTON ENTERPRISE, THE. 11936 W Andre Dr, Grand Ledge, MI 48837. Telephone: 517-627-6085. FAX: 517-627-4863. E-MAIL: wwhelton@gannett.com. URL: http://www.hometownlife.com. Pub. Frequency: w. (Sun.) Page Size: tabloid. Subscrip. Rate: $.50 newsstand/cover per issue; $104/yr mailed. Circulation: 6,063 Sunday (paid and free). **Owner(s):** Lansing Community Newspapers, 7950 Jones Branch Dr, McLean, VA 22107. Telephone: 703-854-6000. **Management:** Barb Brevick, Advertising. Ellen Kent, Advertising Manager. Betty Henry, Circulation Manager. Ann Lyon, Classified Adv. Mgr.. **Editorial:** Will Whelton, Editor. Al Wilson, Group Editor.

GRAND MARAIS

GREAT LAKES MARINERS. PO Box 339, Grand Marais, MI 49839. FAX: 906-494-2527. E-MAIL: rickcaps@jamadots.com. URL: http://www.greatlakespilotpreview.com. Year Established: 1971. Pub. Frequency: m. (15th of mo.) Page Size: tabloid.Subscrip. Rate: $1 newsstand/cover; $18/yr Circulation: 50,000 per issue (free). **Owner(s):** Great Lakes Pilot Preview Publishing Co., See address and contact information above. **Management:** Rick Capogrossa, Publisher. Mary Capogrossa, Advertising. **Editorial:** Rick Capogrossa, Editor.

GROSSE IIE

ILE CAMERA, THE. 8545 Macomb St, Grosse Ile, MI 48138. Telephone: 734-676-0515. FAX: 734-676-0638. E-MAIL: editor@ilecamera.com. URL: http://www.ilecamera.com. Year Established: 1945. Pub. Frequency: w. (Fri.) Page Size: tabloid. Subscrip. Rate: $.50 newsstand/cover; $18.50 mailed for 6 mos.; $33/yr mailed. Adv. Rate: col. inch $5.46 Circulation: 3,500 per issue (controlled and free). **Owner(s):** Journal Register Co., 50 W State St, 12th Fl, Trenton, NJ 08608. Telephone: 609-542-0200. FAX: 609-396-2292.

GROSSE POINTE FARMS

GROSSE POINTE NEWS. 96 Kercheval Rd., Grosse Pointe Farms, MI 48236. Telephone: 313-882-6900. FAX: 313-882-1585. E-MAIL: jminnis@grossepointenews.com. URL: http://www.grossepointenews.com. Year Established: 1940. Pub. Frequency: w. (Thu.) Page Size: broadsheet. Subscrip. Rate: $1 newsstand/cover; $37/yr in state; $65/yr out of state. Freelance Pay: $35/article. Circulation: 14,000 per issue (paid). **Owner(s):** Anteebo Publishers, See address and contact information above. **Management:** John Minnis, General Manager. Robert G. Edgar, Publisher. Barbara Vethacke, Classified Adv. Mgr.. **Editorial:** John Minnis, Editor.

HAMTRAMCK

CITIZEN (HAMTRAMCK), THE. ISSN 1042-6906 3020 Caniff St., Hamtramck, MI 48212-3019. Telephone: 313-365-9500. FAX: 313-365-8660. E-MAIL: hamtramckcitizen@comcast.net. Year Established: 1934. Pub. Frequency: w. (Wed.) Page Size: broadsheet. Subscrip. Rate: $.50 newsstand/cover; $27/yr mailed in county; $27/yr mailed out of county. Circulation: 9,765 per issue (paid). **Owner(s):** Meadow & Mayberry News Corp., See address and contact information above. **Editorial:** Charles Sercombe, News Editor.

HARBOR BEACH

HARBOR BEACH TIMES. 146 S Huron Ave, Harbor Beach, MI 48441. Telephone: 989-479-9620-. FAX: 989-269-2917. E-MAIL: hbtimes@hbch.com. URL: http://www.huroncountypress.com. Year Established: 1880. Pub. Frequency: w. (Wed) Page Size: tabloid. Subscrip. Rate: $.50 newsstand/cover; $18/yr mailed in county; $25/yr mailed out of county. Circulation: 5,000 per issue (paid). **Owner(s):** Journal Register Co., 50 W State St, 12th Fl, Trenton, NJ 08608. **Management:** Jack Guza, Publisher. Shelley Adair, Advertising Director. Nadine Klee, Circulation Director. **Editorial:** Molly Dando, Editor.

HART

OCEANA'S HERALD-JOURNAL. 123 S State St., Hart, MI 49420. Telephone: 231-873-5602. FAX: 231-873-4775. E-MAIL: ohj@voyager.net. URL: http://www.oceanaheraldjournal.com. Year Established: 1981. Pub. Frequency: w. (Thu.) Page Size: broadsheet. Subscrip. Rate: $.75 newsstand/cover; $31.50/yr in county; $35/yr out of county; $42/yr out of state. Adv. Rate: col. inch $7.45 Freelance Pay: $1.25/column-inch. Circulation: 7,400 per issue (paid). **Owner(s):** Shoreline Media, Inc., 202 N. Rath Ave., Ludington, MI 49431-4011. Telephone: 231-845-5181. FAX: 231-843-4011. **Management:** James O. Young, Publisher. Julie Payment, Circulation Manager. **Editorial:** Mary Sanford, Editor.

HASTINGS

HASTINGS BANNER. 1351 N. M43 Hwy, Hastings, MI 49058. Telephone: 269-945-9554. FAX: 269-945-5192. E-MAIL: news@j-adgraphics.com. URL: http://www.hastingsbanner.com. Mailing Address: PO Box 188, Hastings, MI 49058. Year Established: 1856. Pub. Frequency: w. (Thu.) Page Size: broadsheet. Subscrip. Rate: $.75 newsstand/cover; $35/yr mailed in county; $45/yr mailed out of county. **Wire Service(s):** AP. Circulation: 7,000 per issue (paid). **Owner(s):** J-AD Graphics, Inc., See address and contact information above. **Management:** Fred Jacobs, Publisher.Readers: General community

HASTINGS REMINDER. 1351 N. M43 Hwy, Hastings, MI 49058. Telephone: 269-945-9554. URL: http://www.hastingsreminder.com. Mailing Address: PO Box 188, Hastings, MI 49058. Year Established: 1940. Pub. Frequency: w. (Tue.) Page Size: tabloid. Subscrip. Rate: $40/yr mailed. Adv. Rate: col. inch $5.85 Circulation: 33,500 per issue (free). **Owner(s):** J-AD Graphics, Inc., See address and contact information above. **Management:** Fred Jacobs, Publisher. Dennis Rasey, Circulation Manager. **Editorial:** Fred Jacobs, Editor.Readers: General

MAPLE VALLEY NEWS. 1351 N. M43 Hwy, Hastings, MI 49058. Telephone: 269-945-9554. E-MAIL: news@j-adgraphics.com. URL: http://www.hastingsreminder.com. Mailing Address: PO Box 188, Hastings, MI 49058. Year Established: 1975. Pub. Frequency: w. (Tue.) Page Size: tabloid. Subscrip. Rate: $30/yr mailed. Circulation: 4,675 per issue (paid and free). **Owner(s):** J-AD Graphics, Inc., See address and contact information above. **Management:** Fred Jacobs, Publisher. Tracey Harris, Office Manager. Fred Jacobs, Advertising Manager. Dennis Rasey, Circulation Manager. **Editorial:** Fred Jacobs, Editor.Readers: Local population

SUN & NEWS, THE. 1351 N. M43 Hwy, Hastings, MI 49058. Telephone: 269-945-9554. URL: http://www.hastingsreminder.com. Mailing Address: PO Box 188, Hastings, MI 49058. Year Established: 1871. Pub. Frequency: w. (Tue.) Page Size: tabloid Subscrip. Rate: $30/yr Circulation: 11,700 per issue (free). **Owner(s):** J-AD Graphics, Inc., See address and contact information above. **Management:** John Jacobs, President. Fred Jacobs, Publisher. Chris Silverman, Advertising. Dennis Rasey, Circulation Manager. **Editorial:** Fred Jacobs, Managing Editor.Readers: General

HONOR

AD-VISOR. 10575 Main St, Honor, MI 49640. Telephone: 231-325-8600. FAX: 231-325-8602. E-MAIL: advisor@michigannewspapers.com. Year Established: 1966. Pub. Frequency: w. (Sun.) Page Size: tabloid Circulation: 9,000 per issue (free). **Owner(s):** Journal Register Co., 50 W State St, 12th Fl, Trenton, NJ 08608. **Management:** Kim Forsher, General Manager. Cathy Sanders, Advertising Manager. Cindy Kochis, Sales Manager.

HOUGHTON LAKE

HOUGHTON LAKE RESORTER. 4049 W. Houghton Lake Dr., Houghton Lake, MI 48629. E-MAIL: resorter@voyager.net. URL: http://www.houghtonlakeresorter.com. Year Established: 1939. Pub. Frequency: w. (Thu.) Page Size: broadsheet. Subscrip. Rate: $.50 newsstand/cover; $20/yr in county; $24/yr out of county. Adv. Rate: col. inch $7.70 **Wire Service(s):** AP. Circulation: 8,000 per issue (paid). **Owner(s):** Thomas W. Hamp, See address and contact information above. **Management:** Thomas W. Hamp, General Manager. Patty Tribelhorn, Advertising. Pat Durfee, Circulation Manager. **Editorial:** Thomas W. Hamp, Editor.

IMLAY CITY

TRI-CITY TIMES. PO Box 278, Imlay City, MI 48444. Year Established: 1977. Pub. Frequency: w. (Wed.) Page Size: broadsheet. Subscrip. Rate: $.50 newsstand/cover; $18/yr mailed in county; $20/yr mailed out of county; $29/yr mailed out of state. Circulation: 8,760 per issue (paid). **Owner(s):** Delores Heim, See address and contact information above. **Management:** Randy Jorgensen, General Manager. Delores Heim, Owner. Kim Jorgensen, Advertising Manager. **Editorial:** Catherine Minolli, Editor.

IRON MOUNTAIN

ADVERTISER (IRON MOUNTAIN), THE. 421 S. Stephenson Ave., Iron Mountain, MI 49801. Telephone: 906-774-3708. FAX: 906-774-1088. E-MAIL: Advert@upgroup.com. Mailing Address: PO Box 786, Iron Mountain, MI 49801. Year Established: 1975. Pub. Frequency: w. (Tue.) Page Size: tabloid Circulation: 20,600 per issue (free). **Owner(s):** Ogden Newspapers of Minnesota, Inc., 1500 Main St., Wheeling, WV 26003. Telephone: 304-233-0100. FAX: 304-233-0327. **Management:** James Walker, General Manager. **Editorial:** J. Delbeck, Editor.

IRON RIVER

IRON COUNTY REPORTER. PO Box 311, Iron River, MI 49935. Telephone: 906-265-9927. FAX: 906-265-5755. E-MAIL: reporter@up.net. URL: http://www.ironcountyreporter.com. Year Established: 1885. Pub. Frequency: w. (Wed.) Page Size: broadsheet. Subscrip. Rate: $.75 newsstand/cover; $34/yr in county; $45/yr out of county; $32/yr in county senior citizen; $35/yr out of county senior citizen. Circulation: 6,000 per issue (paid). **Owner(s):** Northland Publishers, Inc., See address and contact information above. **Management:** Dennis Christensen, General Manager. Eugene Halker, Publisher. Jennifer Couch, Advertising. Joyce Myefski, Business Manager. **Editorial:** Marian Nelson, Editor. Peter Nocerini, Sports Editor.

IRONWOOD

NORTH COUNTRY SUN. 216 E. Aurora St., Ironwood, MI 49938. Telephone: 906-932-3530. FAX: 906-932-3074. Mailing Address: PO Box 425, Ironwood, MI 49938. Year Established: 1977. Pub. Frequency: w. (Mon.) Page Size: tabloid. Subscrip. Rate: $25/yr mailed. Adv. Rate: col. inch $7.35 Circulation: 16,638 per issue (paid and free). **Owner(s):** La Pean Publications, 417 Ninth Ave., W., Ashland, WI 54806. Telephone: 715-682-8131. FAX: 715-682-6400. **Management:** Richard Barringer, General Manager. Gary La Pean, Publisher. **Editorial:** Gary La Pean, Editor.

ITHACA

GRATIOT COUNTY HERALD. 123 N. Main St., Ithaca, MI 48847. Telephone: 989-875-4151. FAX: 989-875-3159. E-MAIL: gcherald@cmsenter.net. URL: http://www.gcherald.com. Year Established: 1887. Pub. Frequency: w. (Thu.) Page Size: tabloid. Subscrip. Rate: $.75 newsstand/cover; $30/yr mailed in county & adj. counties; $32/yr mailed in state; $40/yr mailed out of state. Adv. Rate: col. inch $7.99 Circulation: 7,200 per issue (paid). **Owner(s):** Patricia R. & Thomas P. MacDonald, See address and contact information above. **Management:** Thomas P. MacDonald, Publisher. Marta Lake, Advertising. **Editorial:** Greg Nelson, Managing Editor. Seth Stapleton, Sports.

JENISON

EAST GRAND RAPIDS CADENCE. 2141 Port Sheldon St., Jenison, MI 49428. E-MAIL: retailsales@advancenewspapers.com. URL: http://www.advancenewspapers.com. Mailing Address: PO Box 9, Jenison, MI 49429-0009. Pub. Frequency: w. (Wed.) Page Size: tabloid.Adv. Rate: col. inch $10.90 Circulation: 5,125 per issue (free). **Owner(s):** Valley Media, Inc., See address and contact information above. **Management:** Joel Holland, Publisher. Terry Alvesteffer, Circulation Manager. Jeanne Anderson, Classified Adv. Mgr.. **Editorial:** Jill Read, News Editor. Larry Hirt, Sports Editor.

FOREST HILLS ADVANCE. 2141 Port Sheldon St., Jenison, MI 49428. E-MAIL: retailsales@advancenewspapers.com. URL: http://www.advancenewspapers.com. Mailing Address: PO Box 9, Jenison, MI 49429-0009. Pub. Frequency: w. (Wed.) Page Size: tabloid.Adv. Rate: col. inch $9.65 Circulation: 15,450 per issue (free). **Owner(s):** Valley Media, Inc., See address and contact information above. **Management:** Joel Holland, Publisher. Terry Alvesteffer, Circulation Manager. Jeanne Anderson, Classified Adv. Mgr.. **Editorial:** Mike Wyngarden, News Editor. Karen Waite, Photo Editor. Larry Hirt, Sports Editor.

GRAND VALLEY EAST ADVANCE. 2141 Port Sheldon St., Jenison, MI 49428. E-MAIL: retailsales@advancenewspapers.com. URL: http://www.advancenewspapers.com. Mailing Address: PO Box 9, Jenison, MI 49429-0009. Year Established: 1966. Pub. Frequency: w. (Tue.) Page Size: tabloid.Adv. Rate: col. inch $9.80 Circulation: 18,810 per issue (free). **Owner(s):** Valley Media, Inc., See address and contact information above. **Management:** Joel Holland, Publisher. Terry Alvesteffer, Circulation Manager. Jeanne Anderson, Classified Adv. Mgr.. **Editorial:** Mike Wyngarden, Managing Editor. Karen Waite, Photo Editor. Larry Hirt, Sports Editor.

GRAND VALLEY WEST ADVANCE. 2141 Port Sheldon St., Jenison, MI 49428. E-MAIL: retailsales@advancenewspapers.com. URL: http://www.advancenewspapers.com. Mailing Address: PO Box 9, Jenison, MI 49429-0009. Pub. Frequency: w. (Tue.) Page Size: tabloid.Adv. Rate: col. inch $11.40 Circulation: 18,460 per issue (free). **Owner(s):** Valley Media, Inc., See address and contact information above. **Management:** Joel Holland, Publisher. Terry Alvesteffer, Circulation Manager. Jeanne Anderson, Classified Adv. Mgr.. **Editorial:** Mike Wyngarden, Managing Editor. Larry Hirt, Sports Editor.

KENTWOOD ADVANCE. 2141 Port Sheldon St., Jenison, MI 49428. E-MAIL: retailsales@advancenewspapers.com. URL: http://www.advancenewspapers.com. Mailing Address: PO Box 9, Jenison, MI 49429-0009. Year Established: 1982. Pub. Frequency: w. (Tue.) Page Size: tabloid.Adv. Rate: col. inch $12.45 Circulation: 16,865 per issue (free). **Owner(s):** Valley Media, Inc., See address and contact information above. **Management:** Joel Holland, Publisher. Terry Alvesteffer, Circulation Manager. Jeanne Anderson, Classified Adv. Mgr.. **Editorial:** Mike Wyngarden, Managing Editor. Jill Read, News Editor. Karen Waite, Photo Editor. Larry Hirt, Sports Editor.

NORTHFIELD ADVANCE. 2141 Port Sheldon St., Jenison, MI 49428. E-MAIL: retailsales@advancenewspapers.com. URL: http://www.advancenewspapers.com. Mailing Address: PO Box 9, Jenison, MI 49429-0009. Year Established: 1982. Pub. Frequency: w. (Wed.) Page Size: tabloid.Adv. Rate: col. inch $11.30 Circulation: 19,775 per issue (free). **Owner(s):** Valley Media, Inc., See address and contact information above. **Management:** Joel Holland, Publisher. Terry Alvesteffer, Circulation Manager. Jeanne Anderson, Classified Adv. Mgr.. **Editorial:** Lindsey Ackerman, News Editor. Larry Hirt, Sports Editor.

OTTAWA ADVANCE. 2141 Port Sheldon St., Jenison, MI 49428. E-MAIL: retailsales@advancenewspapers.com. URL: http://www.advancenewspapers.com. Mailing Address: PO Box 9, Jenison, MI 49429-0009. Year Established: 1968. Pub. Frequency: w. (Tue.) Page Size: tabloid.Adv. Rate: col. inch $10.50 Circulation: 11,275 per issue (free). **Owner(s):** Valley Media, Inc., See address and contact information above. **Management:** Joel Holland, Publisher. Terry Alvesteffer, Circulation Manager. Jeanne Anderson, Classified Adv. Mgr.. **Editorial:** Mike Wyngarden, Managing Editor. Karen Waite, Photo Editor.

ROCKFORD/CEDAR SPRINGS ADVANCE. 2141 Port Sheldon St., Jenison, MI 49428. E-MAIL: retailsales@advancenewspapers.com. URL: http://www.advancenewspapers.com. Mailing Address: PO Box 9, Jenison, MI 49429-0009. Year Established: 1989. Pub. Frequency: w. (Tue.) Page Size: tabloid.Adv. Rate: col. inch $8.75 Circulation: 18,285 per issue (free). **Owner(s):** Valley Media, Inc., See address and contact information above. **Management:** Joel Holland, Publisher. Terry Alvesteffer, Circulation Manager. Jeanne Anderson, Classified Adv. Mgr.. **Editorial:** Karen Waite, Photo Editor. Larry Hirt, Sports Editor.

SOUTH ADVANCE. 2141 Port Sheldon St., Jenison, MI 49428. E-MAIL: retailsales@advancenewspapers.com. URL: http://www.advancenewspapers.com. Mailing Address: PO Box 9, Jenison, MI 49429-0009. Pub. Frequency: w. (Tue.) Page Size: tabloid.Adv. Rate: col. inch $11 Circulation: 15,735 per issue (free). **Owner(s):** Valley Media, Inc., See address and contact information above. **Management:** Joel Holland, Publisher. Terry Alvesteffer, Circulation Manager. Jeanne Anderson, Classified Adv. Mgr.. **Editorial:** Matt Russell, News Editor. Larry Hirt, Sports Editor.

SPARTA/KENT CITY ADVANCE. 2141 Port Sheldon St., Jenison, MI 49428. E-MAIL: retailsales@advancenewspapers.com. URL: http://www.advancenewspapers.com. Mailing Address: PO Box 9, Jenison, MI 49429-0009. Year Established: 1989. Pub. Frequency: w. (Tue.) Page Size: tabloid.Adv. Rate: col. inch $7.35 Circulation: 12,575 per issue (free). **Owner(s):** Valley Media, Inc., See address and contact information above. **Management:** Joel Holland, Publisher. Terry Alvesteffer, Circulation Manager. Jeanne Anderson, Classified Adv. Mgr.. **Editorial:** Jill Read, News Editor. Karen Waite, Photo Editor. Larry Hirt, Sports Editor.

WALKER/WESTSIDE ADVANCE. 2141 Port Sheldon St., Jenison, MI 49428. E-MAIL: retailsales@advancenewspapers.com. URL: http://www.advancenewspapers.com. Mailing Address: PO Box 9, Jenison, MI 49429-0009. Year Established: 1968. Pub. Frequency: w. (Tue.) Page Size: tabloid.Adv. Rate: col. inch $14.90 Circulation: 23,260 per issue (free). **Owner(s):** Valley Media, Inc., See address and contact information above. **Management:** Joel Holland, Publisher. Terry Alvesteffer, Circulation Manager. Jeanne Anderson, Classified Adv. Mgr.. **Editorial:** Jill Read, News Editor. Karen Waite, Photo Editor. Larry Hirt, Sports Editor.

WYOMING ADVANCE. 2141 Port Sheldon St., Jenison, MI 49428. E-MAIL: retailsales@advancenewspaper.com. URL: http://www.advancenewspapers.com. Mailing Address: PO Box 9, Jenison, MI 49429-0009. Year Established: 1982. Pub. Frequency: w. (Tue.) Page Size: tabloid.Adv. Rate: col. inch $14.60 Circulation: 21,615 per issue (free). **Owner(s):** Valley Media, Inc., See address and contact information above. **Management:** Joel Holland, Publisher. Terry Alvesteffer, Circulation Manager. Jeanne Anderson, Classified Adv. Mgr.. **Editorial:** Mike Wyngarden, Managing Editor. Lindsey Ackerman, News Editor. Karen Waite, Photo Editor. Larry Hirt, Sports Editor.

KALKASKA

LEADER & THE KALKASKIAN, THE. 318 N Cedar St, Kalkaska, MI 49646. Telephone: 231-258-4600. FAX: 231-258-4603. URL: http://leaderandkalkaskian.com. Year Established: 1870. Pub. Frequency: w. (Wed.) Page Size: broadsheet. Subscrip. Rate: $.75 newsstand/cover; $34.50/yr in county; $42/yr out of county; $28/yr in county to senior citizens. Circulation: 3,600 per issue (paid). **Owner(s):** Journal Register Co., 50 W State St, 12th Fl, Trenton, NJ 08608. **Management:** Albert Frattura, Publisher. Lee Hill, Office Manager. Sherry Kilbourn, Advertising. Janet Sieting, Advertising Manager. Michelle L Reichenbacher, Classified Adv. Mgr.. **Editorial:** Josh Perttunen, Editor. Chris Tredway, Sports Editor. Chris Fusciardi, Writer.

L'ANSE

L'ANSE SENTINEL. 636 Broad St., L'Anse, MI 49946. Telephone: 906-524-6194. FAX: 906-524-6197. E-MAIL: sentinel@up.net. Year Established: 1880. Pub. Frequency: w. (Wed.) Page Size: broadsheet. Subscrip. Rate: $33/yr local; $36/yr in state; $39/yr out of state. Adv. Rate: col. inch $8.20 Circulation: 3,800 per issue (paid). **Owner(s):** L D J Publishers, Inc., See address and contact information above. **Management:** Gale Eilola, General Manager. Ed Danner, Publisher. Joe Schutte, Advertising Manager. **Editorial:** Barry Drue, Editor.

LAKE LEELANAU

LEELANAU ENTERPRISE. 7200 E. Duck Lake Rd., Lake Leelanau, MI 49653-0527. Telephone: 231-256-9827. FAX: 231-256-7705. E-MAIL: info@leelanaunews.com. URL: http://www.leelanaunews.com. Year Established: 1877. Pub. Frequency: w. (Thu.) Page Size: tabloid. Subscrip. Rate: $.50 newsstand/cover; $20/yr in county; $38/yr mailed out of county. Adv. Rate: col. inch $7 Circulation: 9,000 per issue (paid). **Owner(s):** Alan Campbell, See address and contact information above. **Management:** Alan Campbell, Publisher. Debra Campbell, Advertising Manager. **Editorial:** Alan Campbell, Editor. Amy Hubbell, News Editor.

LAPEER

COUNTY PRESS (LAPEER), THE. ISSN 8750-4561 1521 Imlay City Rd., Lapeer, MI 48446. Telephone: 810-664-0811. FAX: 810-667-6309. E-MAIL: editor@countypress.com. URL: http://www.countypress.com. Year Established: 1838. Pub. Frequency: 3/w. (Wed. Fri. & Sun.) Page Size: broadsheet. Subscrip. Rate: $.75 newsstand/cover; $1 Sun.; $49.50/yr in county; $65/yr out of county. Circulation: 43,000 per issue (paid). **Owner(s):** Journal Register Co., 50 W State St, 12th Fl, Trenton, NJ 08608. **Management:** Bill Southern, President. Steve Paterson, Publisher. Evelyn Grogan, Circulation Manager. **Editorial:** Jeff Payne, Managing Editor.

LESLIE

LESLIE LOCAL INDEPENDENT. 109 Carney, Leslie, MI 49251-0617. Telephone: 517-589-8228. FAX: 517-589-8526. Mailing Address: PO Box 617, Leslie, MI 49251-0617. Year Established: 1869. Pub. Frequency: w. (Thu.) Page Size: tabloid. Subscrip. Rate: $.35 newsstand/cover; $12/yr in state; $14/yr out of state. Circulation: 7,415 per issue (paid and free). **Owner(s):** S.G. Publications, 140 E. Ash St., Mason, MI 48854-0159. Telephone: 517-676-5100. FAX: 517-676-6753. **Management:** George Raymond, Publisher. Joan Hill, Office Manager. Cindy Malcho, Advertising Manager. **Editorial:** Chris Cook, Editor.

LIVONIA

CANTON OBSERVER. 36251 Schoolcraft Rd, Livonia, MI 48150. Telephone: 734-591-2300. FAX: 734-591-7279. URL: http://www.hometownlife.com. Year Established: 1975. Pub. Frequency: s-w. (Sun. & Thu.) Page Size: broadsheet. Subscrip. Rate: $.75 newsstand/cover; $59.95/yr home delivery local; $83.95/yr mailed in county; $108.95/yr mailed out of county. Circulation: 10,359 Sunday (paid and free); 10,383 per issue (paid). **Owner(s):** Observer, Eccentric & Mirror Newspapers, Inc., 7950 Jones Branch Dr, McLean, VA 22107. Telephone: 703-854-5000. **Management:** Peter Neill, Publisher. Marty Carry, Advertising Director. Jeannie Parent, Advertising Manager. Frank Cibor, Classified Adv. Mgr.. **Editorial:** Susan Rosiek, Executive Editor. Hugh Gallagher, Managing Editor. Ed Wright, Sports Editor.

FARMINGTON OBSERVER. 36251 Schoolcraft Rd, Livonia, MI 48150. URL: http://www.hometownlife.com. Pub. Frequency: s-w. (Sun. & Thu.) Page Size: broadsheet. Subscrip. Rate: $.75 newsstand/cover; $49.95/yr in county; $72.95/yr mailed out of county; $108/yr out of state. Circulation: 11,793 Sunday (paid and free); 12,094 morning (paid and free). **Owner(s):** Observer, Eccentric & Mirror Newspapers, Inc., 7950 Jones Branch Dr, McLean, VA 22107. **Management:** Marty Carry, Advertising Director. Jeannie Parent, Advertising Manager. Frank Cibor, Classified Adv. Mgr.. **Editorial:** Susan Rosiek, Executive Editor. Hugh Gallagher, Managing Editor. Stacey Jenkins, News Editor.

GARDEN CITY OBSERVER. 36251 Schoolcraft Rd, Livonia, MI 48150. Telephone: 734-591-2300. FAX: 734-591-7279. E-MAIL: cmccloud@oe.homecomm.net. URL: http://www.hometownlife.com. Pub. Frequency: s-w. (Sun. & Thu.) Page Size: broadsheet. Subscrip. Rate: $.75 newsstand/cover; $51/yr in county; $72.95/yr mailed out of county; $108.95/yr mailed out of state. Circulation: 4,688 Sunday (paid and free); 4,157 per issue (paid and free). **Owner(s):** Observer, Eccentric & Mirror Newspapers, Inc., 7950 Jones Branch Dr, McLean, VA 22107. Telephone: 703-854-5000. **Management:** Marty Carry, Advertising Director. Jeannie Parent, Advertising Manager. Frank Cibor, Classified Adv. Mgr.. **Editorial:** Susan Rosiek, Executive Editor. Hugh Gallagher, Managing Editor. Sue Mason, News Editor.

LIVONIA OBSERVER. 36251 Schoolcraft Rd, Livonia, MI 48150. Telephone: 734-591-2300. FAX: 734-591-7279. URL: http://www.hometownlife.com. Year Established: 1939. Pub. Frequency: s-w. (Sun. & Thu.) Page Size: broadsheet. Subscrip. Rate: $.75 newsstand/cover; $59.95/yr in county; $83.95/yr mailed out of county; $108.95/yr mailed out of state. Circulation: 20,598 Sunday (paid and free); 20,684 per issue (paid and free). **Owner(s):** Observer, Eccentric & Mirror Newspapers, Inc., 7950 Jones Branch Dr, McLean, VA 22107. Telephone: 703-854-5000. **Management:** Marty Carry, Advertising Director. Jeannie Parent, Advertising Manager. Frank Cibor, Classified Adv. Mgr.. **Editorial:** Susan Rosiek, Executive Editor. Hugh Gallagher, Managing Editor. Dave Varga, News Editor. Brad Emons, Sports Editor.

OXFORD ECCENTRIC, THE. 36251 Schoolcraft Rd, Livonia, MI 48150. Telephone: 734-591-2300. FAX: 734-591-7279. URL: http://www.hometownlife.com. Pub. Frequency: w. (Thu.) Page Size: broadsheet. Subscrip. Rate: $.50 newsstand/cover; $30/yr home delivery in county; $36.48/yr mailed in county; $54.48/yr mailed out of county. Circulation: 3,438 per issue (paid and free). **Owner(s):** Observer, Eccentric & Mirror Newspapers, Inc., 7950 Jones Branch Dr, McLean, VA 22107. Telephone: 703-854-5000. **Management:** Marty Carry, Advertising Director. Frank Cibor, Classified Adv. Mgr.. **Editorial:** Susan Rosiek, Executive Editor. Joe Bauman, Managing Editor.

PLYMOUTH OBSERVER. 36251 Schoolcraft Rd, Livonia, MI 48150. E-MAIL: t. URL: http://www.hometownlife.com. Year Established: 1967. Pub. Frequency: s-w. (Sun. & Thu.) Page Size: broadsheet. Subscrip. Rate: $.75 newsstand/cover; $51/yr home delivery in county; $72.95/yr mailed in county; $108.95/yr mailed out of county. Circulation: 6,128 Sunday (paid and free); 5,844 per issue (paid and free). **Owner(s):** Observer, Eccentric & Mirror Newspapers, Inc., 7950 Jones Branch Dr, McLean, VA 22107. **Management:** Marty Carry, Advertising Director. Jeannie Parent, Advertising Manager. Frank Cibor, Classified Adv. Mgr.. **Editorial:** Susan Rosiek, Executive Editor. Hugh Gallagher, Managing Editor. Brad Kadrich, News Editor. Ed Wright, Sports Editor.

Weeklies

WEST BLOOMFIELD-LAKES ECCENTRIC. 36251 Schoolcraft Rd, Livonia, MI 48150. Telephone: 734-591-2300. FAX: 734-591-7279. URL: http://www.hometownlife.com. Year Established: 1972. Pub. Frequency: s-w. (Sun. & Thu.) Page Size: broadsheet. Subscrip. Rate: $.75 newsstand/cover; $51/yr home delivery local; $72.95/yr mailed in county; $108.95/yr mailed out of county. Circulation: 10,769 Sunday (paid); 10,889 per issue (paid). **Owner(s):** Observer, Eccentric & Mirror Newspapers, Inc., 7950 Jones Branch Dr, McLean, VA 22107. Telephone: 703-854-5000. **Management:** Marty Carry, Advertising Director. Frank Cibor, Classified Adv. Mgr.. **Editorial:** Susan Rosiek, Executive Editor. Joe Bauman, Managing Editor. Larry Ruehlen, News Editor. Mike Rosenbaum, Sports Editor.

WESTLAND OBSERVER. 36251 Schoolcraft Rd, Livonia, MI 48150. Telephone: 734-591-2300. FAX: 734-591-7279. URL: http://www.hometownlife.com. Year Established: 1965. Pub. Frequency: s-w. (Sun. & Thu.) Page Size: broadsheet. Subscrip. Rate: $.75 newsstand/cover; $51/yr home delivery local; $72.95/yr mailed in county; $108.95/yr mailed out of county. Circulation: 6,739 Sunday (paid); 6,042 per issue (paid). **Owner(s):** Observer, Eccentric & Mirror Newspapers, Inc., 7950 Jones Branch Dr, McLean, VA 22107. Telephone: 703-854-5000. **Management:** Marty Carry, Advertising Director. Frank Cibor, Classified Adv. Mgr.. **Editorial:** Susan Rosiek, Executive Editor. Hugh Gallagher, Managing Editor. Sue Mason, News Editor.

LOWELL

LOWELL LEDGER. 105 N. Broadway, Lowell, MI 49331. Telephone: 616-897-9261. FAX: 616-897-4809. E-MAIL: ledger@lowellbuyersguide.com. Year Established: 1893. Pub. Frequency: w. (Wed.) Page Size: broadsheet. Subscrip. Rate: $.35 newsstand/cover; $15/yr mailed. Circulation: 3,000 per issue (paid). **Owner(s):** Roger K. Brown, See address and contact information above. **Management:** Roger K. Brown, Publisher. **Editorial:** Jeanne Boss, Editor.

MANCELONA

STAR-PENNY STRETCHER. 112 E. State St., Mancelona, MI 49659. Telephone: 231-587-8471. FAX: 231-587-9617. Mailing Address: PO Box 1061, Kalkaska, MI 49646. Year Established: 1970. Pub. Frequency: w. (Sun.) Page Size: tabloid.Adv. Rate: col. inch $8.35 Circulation: 12,406 Sunday (free). **Owner(s):** Morning Star Publishing, 711 W. Pickard, Mt. Pleasant, MI 48858. Telephone: 989-779-6000. FAX: 989-779-6101. **Management:** Jan Anderson, General Manager. Janet Sieting, Advertising. Paige O'Neal, Sales Manager.

MANCHESTER

MANCHESTER (MI) ENTERPRISE, THE. 109 E Main St, Manchester, MI 48158. Telephone: 734-428-8173. FAX: 734-428-9044. URL: http://www.manchesterenterprise.com. Year Established: 1867. Pub. Frequency: w. (Thu.) Page Size: broadsheet. Subscrip. Rate: $.50 newsstand/cover; $15 mailed for 6 mos.; $27/yr mailed. Adv. Rate: col. inch $5.46 Circulation: 2,100 per issue (paid and free). **Owner(s):** Journal Register Co., 50 W State St, 12th Fl, Trenton, NJ 08608. Telephone: 609-396-2200. FAX: 609-396-2292. **Management:** James Williams, Publisher. Justin Wilcox, Advertising Director. **Editorial:** Daniel Lei, Editor.

MANISTEE

WEST SHORE SHOPPER GUIDE. 75 Maple St., Manistee, MI 49660. Telephone: 231-723-3593. FAX: 231-723-4733. Mailing Address: PO Box 317, Manistee, MI 49660-0317.Pub. Frequency: w. (Sun.) Page Size: tabloid Circulation: 15,000 Sunday (free). **Owner(s):** The Pioneer Group, 851 Michigan Ave., Baldwin, MI 49304. **Management:** Marilyn Barker, Publisher. Cheryl Soranno, Advertising Manager. Dawn Day, Circulation Manager. **Editorial:** David Barber, Editor.

MANISTIQUE

MANISTIQUE PIONEER-TRIBUNE. 212 Walnut St., Manistique, MI 49854. Telephone: 906-341-5200. FAX: 906-341-5914. Year Established: 1876. Pub. Frequency: w. (Thu.) Page Size: broadsheet. Subscrip. Rate: $.75 newsstand/cover; $29/yr in county; $38/yr out of county. Circulation: 3,350 per issue (paid). **Owner(s):** Four Seasons Publishing, Inc., See address and contact information above. **Management:** Lisa A. Demers, Publisher. **Editorial:** Paul Olson, Editor.

MARSHALL

MARSHALL CHRONICLE. 514 S. Kalmazoo, Marshall, MI 49068. Telephone: 269-781-5444. FAX: 269-781-7766. Year Established: 1879. Pub. Frequency: w. (Mon) Page Size: broadsheet. Subscrip. Rate: $.50 newsstand/cover; $25/yr mailed in county; $48/yr mailed out of county. **Wire Service(s):** UPI. Circulation: 1,900 evening (paid). **Owner(s):** J-AD Graphics, Inc., See address and contact information above. **Management:** John Jacobs, President. Fred Jacobs, Publisher. Scott Ommen, Advertising Manager. Dennis Rasey, Circulation Manager. **Editorial:** David T Young, Editor.

MARSHALL COMMUNITY AD-VISOR. 514 S. Kalmazoo, Marshall, MI 49068. Telephone: 269-781-5444. FAX: 269-781-7766. Mailing Address: PO Box 111, Marshall, MI 49068-0111. Pub. Frequency: w. (Wed.) Page Size: tabloid. Subscrip. Rate: $26/yr mailed. Adv. Rate: col. inch $5.57 Circulation: 18,000 per issue (free). **Owner(s):** J-AD Graphics, Inc., 1351 N. M43 Hwy, Hastings, MI 49058. Telephone: 269-945-9554. **Management:** John Jacobs, Publisher. **Editorial:** Mary Tinsley-Young, Editor.

MAYVILLE

MAYVILLE MONITOR. 6071 Fulton St., Mayville, MI 48744-0299. Telephone: 989-843-6441. FAX: 989-843-0054. E-MAIL: mayvillemonitor@hotmail.com. Mailing Address: PO Box 299, Mayville, MI 48744-0299. Year Established: 1884. Pub. Frequency: w. (Thu.) Page Size: tabloid. Subscrip. Rate: $.50 newsstand/cover; $13/yr in county; $15/yr out of county; $18/yr out of state. Circulation: 1,200 per issue (paid). **Owner(s):** Gale & Debra Langford, 6071 Fulton St., Mayville, MI 08744-0299. Telephone: 989-843-6441. **Management:** Debra Langford, Publisher. **Editorial:** Gale Langford, Editor-in-Chief. Debra Langford, Managing Editor.

MONROE

GUARDIAN, THE. 15649 S Telegraph Rd, Monroe, MI 48161. Telephone: 734-243-2100. FAX: 734-243-5196. E-MAIL: editor@monroeguardian.com. URL: http://www.monroeguardian.com. Year Established: 1939. Pub. Frequency: w. (Thu.) Page Size: broadsheet.Adv. Rate: col. inch $6.76 Circulation: 11,000 per issue (paid). **Owner(s):** Journal Register Co., 50 W State St, 12th Fl, Trenton, NJ 08608. Telephone: 609-396-2200. FAX: 609-396-2292. **Management:** James Williams, Publisher. Justin Wilcox, Advertising Director. **Editorial:** Dennis Oblander, Writer.

MORENCI

MORENCI OBSERVER. 120 North St., Morenci, MI 49256. Telephone: 517-458-6811. FAX: 517-458-6811. E-MAIL: dgreen@tc3net.com. Year Established: 1872. Pub. Frequency: w. (Wed.) Page Size: tabloid. Subscrip. Rate: $.50 newsstand/cover; $22/yr local; $25/yr out of area. Adv. Rate: col. inch $4.55 Circulation: 2,475 per issue (paid). **Owner(s):** David Green, See address and contact information above. **Management:** David Green, Publisher. **Editorial:** David Green, Editor.

MT. PLEASANT

ALPENA STAR. 711 W. Pickard, Mt. Pleasant, MI 48848. Telephone: 989-779-6000. URL: http://www.star-ads.com. Mailing Address: PO Box 464, Alpena, MI 49707. Year Established: 1972. Pub. Frequency: w. (Sun.) Page Size: tabloid.Adv. Rate: col. inch $8.14 Circulation: 19,600 Sunday (free). **Owner(s):** Morning Star Publishing, See address and contact information above. **Management:** Ethan Clarke, General Manager. Paige O'Neal, Sales Manager.

MUNISING

MUNISING NEWS. ISSN 1074-0201
132 E Superior St., Munising, MI 49862. Telephone: 906-387-3282. FAX: 906-387-4054. Year Established: 1896. Pub. Frequency: w. (Wed.) Page Size: broadsheet. Subscrip. Rate: $40/yr home delivery in county; $45/yr mailed out of county. Adv. Rate: col. inch $6 Circulation: 3,075 per issue (paid). **Owner(s):** Willie J. Peterson, See address and contact information above. **Management:** Willie J. Peterson, Publisher. **Editorial:** Dan Wilson, Editor.

MUSKEGON

NORTON-LAKESHORE EXAMINER. 950 W. Norton, Ste. 402, Muskegon, MI 49441. Telephone: 231-739-6397. FAX: 231-737-1520. E-MAIL: exnews@netonecom.net. Mailing Address: PO Box 0357, Muskegon, MI 49443. Year Established: 1968. Pub. Frequency: w. (Wed.) Page Size: tabloid. Subscrip. Rate: $.50 newsstand/cover; $24/yr in area. Freelance Pay: $0.50/column-inch. **Wire Service(s):** AP. Circulation: 3,000 per issue (paid and free). **Owner(s):** East Light Publishing Co., See address and contact information above. **Management:** David Seyferth, Publisher. **Editorial:** David Seyferth, Editor.

NEW BALTIMORE

BAY VOICE. ISSN 8750-7188
51180 Bedford St, New Baltimore, MI 48047. Telephone: 586-716-8100. FAX: 586-716-8918. E-MAIL: thevoice@voicenews.com. URL: http://www.voicenews.com. Mailing Address: P O Box 760, New Baltimore, MI 48047. Year Established: 1983. Pub. Frequency: w. (Wed.) Page Size: tabloid. Subscrip. Rate: $.50 newsstand/cover; $28/yr. Freelance Pay: $25-$40/article. Circulation: 22,000 per issue (paid and free). **Owner(s):** Journal Register Co., 50 W State St, 12th Fl, Trenton, NJ 08608. **Management:** Debbie Loggins, General Manager. Wayne Oehmke, Publisher. Anna Eerola, Advertising. **Editorial:** Donna Remer, Executive Editor.

BLUE WATER VOICE, THE. 51180 Bedford St, New Baltimore, MI 48047. Telephone: 586-716-8100. FAX: 586-716-8918. E-MAIL: thevoice@voicenews.com. URL: http://www.voicenews.com. Mailing Address: P O Box 760, New Baltimore, MI 48047. Year Established: 1990. Pub. Frequency: w. (Wed.) Page Size: tabloid. Subscrip. Rate: $.50 newsstand/cover; $28/yr mailed. Freelance Pay: $20-$40/article. Circulation: 11,000 per issue (paid and free). **Owner(s):** Journal Register Co., 50 W State St, 12th Fl, Trenton, NJ 08608. **Management:** Debbie Loggins, General Manager. Anna Eerola, Advertising. Carol Warehall, Advertising Manager. **Editorial:** Donna Remer, Executive Editor.

DOWNRIVER VOICE. 51180 Bedford St, New Baltimore, MI 48047. Telephone: 586-716-8100. FAX: 586-716-8918. URL: http://www.voicenews.com. Mailing Address: P O Box 760, New Baltimore, MI 48047. Year Established: 1985. Pub. Frequency: w. (Wed.) Page Size: tabloid. Subscrip. Rate: $.50 newsstand/cover; $28/yr mailed out of area. Freelance Pay: $20-$40/article. Circulation: 11,000 per issue (paid and free). **Owner(s):** Journal Register Co., 50 W State St, 12th Fl, Trenton, NJ 08608. **Management:** Debbie Loggins, General Manager. Anna Eerola, Advertising. Carol Warehall, Advertising Manager. **Editorial:** Donna Remer, Executive Editor.

MACOMB TOWNSHIP VOICE, THE. 51180 Bedford St, New Baltimore, MI 48047. Telephone: 586-716-8100. FAX: 586-716-8918. E-MAIL: donna.remer@voicenews.com. URL: http://www.voicenews.com. Mailing Address: P O Box 760, New Baltimore, MI 48047. Year Established: 1990. Pub. Frequency: w. (Wed.) Page Size: tabloid. Subscrip. Rate: $.50 newsstand/cover; $28/yr. Circulation: 58,000 per issue (paid and free). **Owner(s):** Journal Register Co., 50 State St 12 fl, Trenton, NJ 08608-1298. Telephone: 609-396-2000. FAX: 609-396-2292. **Management:** Debbie Loggins, General Manager. Kevin Haezebroeck, President. **Editorial:** Donna Remer, Executive Editor.

NORTH MACOMB VOICE. 51180 Bedford St, New Baltimore, MI 48047. Telephone: 586-716-8100. FAX: 586-716-8918. URL: http://www.voicenews.com. Mailing Address: P O Box 760, New Baltimore, MI 48047. Year Established: 1985. Pub. Frequency: w. (Wed.) Page Size: tabloid. Subscrip. Rate: $28/yr mailed out of area. Freelance Pay: $20-$40/article. Circulation: 9,000 per issue (paid and free). **Owner(s):** Journal Register Co., 50 W State St, 12th Fl, Trenton, NJ 08608. **Management:** Debbie Loggins, General Manager. Anna Eerola, Advertising. Carol Warehall, Advertising Manager. **Editorial:** Donna Remer, Executive Editor.

VOICE (NEW BALTIMORE), THE. 51180 Bedford St, New Baltimore, MI 48047. Telephone: 586-716-8100. FAX: 586-716-8918. URL: http://www.voicenews.com. Mailing Address: P O Box 760, New Baltimore, MI 48047. Pub. Frequency: w. (Wed.) Page Size: tabloid. Subscrip. Rate: $.50 newsstand/cover; $28/yr; $48 for 2 yrs.. Circulation: 73,000 per issue (paid and free). **Owner(s):** Journal Register Co., 50 W State St, 12th Fl, Trenton, NJ 08608. **Management:** Debbie Loggins, General Manager. Anna Eerola, Advertising. Carol Warehall, Advertising Manager. **Editorial:** Donna Remer, Executive Editor.

VOICE WEEKEND. 51180 Bedford St, New Baltimore, MI 48047. Telephone: 586-716-8100. FAX: 586-716-8918. E-MAIL: donna.remer@voicenews.com. URL: http://www.voicenews.com. Mailing Address: P O Box 760, New Baltimore, MI 48047. Pub. Frequency: w. (Sat.) Page Size: tabloid. Subscrip. Rate: $.50 newsstand/cover; $28/yr mailed out of area. Circulation: 10,000 morning (paid and free). **Owner(s):** Journal Register Co., 50 W State St, 12th Fl, Trenton, NJ 08608. **Management:** Debbie Loggins, General Manager. Anna Eerola, Advertising. Carol Warehall, Advertising Manager. **Editorial:** Donna Remer, Executive Editor.

NEW BUFFALO

NEW BUFFALO TIMES. 140 N Whittaker, New Buffalo, MI 49117-0369. Telephone: 269-469-1100. Mailing Address: PO Box 369, New Buffalo, MI 49117-0369. Year Established: 1942. Pub. Frequency: w. (Wed.) Page Size: tabloid. Subscrip. Rate: $.50 newsstand/cover; $36/yr. Freelance Pay: $20/story. Circulation: 5,000 per issue (paid). **Owner(s):** M.B. Moriarty, See address and contact information above. **Management:** M B Moriarty, Publisher. **Editorial:** M B Moriarty, Editor.

NILES

CASSOPOLIS VIGILANT. 217 N. Fourth St., Niles, MI 49120. Telephone: 269-683-2101. FAX: 269-683-2175. E-MAIL: vigilant@leaderpub.com. URL: http://www.leaderpub.com. Mailing Address: PO Box 128, Cassopolis, MI 49031. Pub. Frequency: w. (Thu.) Page Size: broadsheet. Subscrip. Rate: $.75 newsstand/cover; $25/yr mailed. Adv. Rate: col. inch $5.55 Circulation: 1,040 per issue (paid). **Owner(s):** Boone Newspapers, Inc., 15222 Freemen's Bend Rd., Northport, AL 35475. Telephone: 205-330-4100. **Management:** Jan Griffey, Publisher. Mary Cooper, Advertising Director. Julie Korkos, Classified Adv. Mgr.. Hal Shue, Marketing Manager. **Editorial:** Jan Griffey, Editor. Marcia Steffens, Managing Editor. Bob Bell, Production Manager. Scott Novak, Sports Editor.

EDWARDSBURG ARGUS. 217 N. Fourth St., Niles, MI 49120. Telephone: 269-683-2101. FAX: 269-683-2175. E-MAIL: argus@leaderpub.com. URL: http://www.edwardsburgargus.com. Pub. Frequency: w. (Thu.) Page Size: broadsheet. Subscrip. Rate: $.75 newsstand/cover; $25/yr mailed. Adv. Rate: col. inch $5.55 Circulation: 1,020 per issue (paid). **Owner(s):** Boone Newspapers, Inc., 15222 Freemen's Bend Rd., Northport, AL 35475. Telephone: 205-330-4100. **Management:** Jan Griffey, Publisher. Diana Kingsley, Advertising Director. Hal Shue, Marketing Manager. **Editorial:** Jan Griffey, Editor. Marcia Steffens, Managing Editor. Bob Bell, Production Manager.

LEADER (NILES), THE. 217 N. Fourth St., Niles, MI 49120. Telephone: 269-683-2101. FAX: 269-683-2175. URL: http://www.leaderpub.com. Pub. Frequency: w. (Mon.) Page Size: broadsheet Circulation: 37,650 per issue (free). **Owner(s):** Boone Newspapers, Inc., 15222 Freemen's Bend Rd., Northport, AL 35475. Telephone: 205-330-4100. **Management:** Jan Griffey, Publisher. Mary Cooper, Advertising Director. **Editorial:** Bob Bell, Production Manager.

NORTHVILLE

NORTHVILLE RECORD. ISSN 1050-2467 104 W Main St, Ste 101, Northville, MI 48167. Telephone: 248-349-1700. FAX: 248-349-9832. URL: http://www.hometownlife.com. Year Established: 1869. Pub. Frequency: w. (Thu.) Page Size: broadsheet. Subscrip. Rate: $.50 newsstand/cover; $26/yr in county. Circulation: 5,781 per issue (paid). **Owner(s):** Gannett Company, Inc., 7950 Jones Branch Dr., McLean, VA 22107-0001. **Management:** Rich Perlberg, General Manager. Grace Perry, Advertising Director. **Editorial:** Cal Stone, Editor. Rich Perlberg, Executive Editor.

NOVI NEWS. 104 W Main St, Ste 101, Northville, MI 48167. Telephone: 248-349-1700. FAX: 248-349-9832. URL: http://www.hometownlife.com. Year Established: 1953. Pub. Frequency: w. (Thu.) Page Size: broadsheet. Subscrip. Rate: $.50 newsstand/cover; $26/yr in county. Circulation: 5,780 per issue (paid). **Owner(s):** Gannett Company, Inc., 7950 Jones Branch Dr, McLean, VA 22107. **Management:** Rich Perlberg, General Manager. Grace Perry, Advertising Director. **Editorial:** Marilyn Mitchell, Managing Editor.

ONAWAY

ONAWAY OUTLOOK. PO Box 176, Onaway, MI 49765. Telephone: 989-733-6543. Year Established: 1974. Pub. Frequency: w. (Fri.) Page Size: tabloid. Subscrip. Rate: $.50 newsstand/cover; $23/yr mailed local. Circulation: 2,000 per issue (paid). **Owner(s):** Richard Lamb, See address and contact information above. **Management:** Richard Lamb, Publisher. Deborah Sheil, Advertising. **Editorial:** Richard Lamb, Editor.

ONTONAGON

ONTONAGON HERALD, THE. 326 River St., Ontonagon, MI 49953-0098. Telephone: 906-884-2826. FAX: 906-884-2939. E-MAIL: maureen@ontongonherald.com. Year Established: 1881. Pub. Frequency: w. (Wed.) Page Size: broadsheet. Subscrip. Rate: $1 newsstand/cover; $39.50/yr in county; $49.50/yr out of county. Circulation: 3,700 per issue (paid). **Owner(s):** Maureen Guzek, See address and contact information above. **Management:** Maureen Guzek, Publisher. **Editorial:** Maureen Guzek, Editor.

ORTONVILLE

COUNTY LINE REMINDER. 48 South St, Ortonville, MI 48462. Telephone: 248-627-2843. FAX: 248-627-3473. E-MAIL: reminder@lapeergroup.com. Mailing Address: P O Box 560, Ortonville, MI 48462-0560. Year Established: 1953. Pub. Frequency: w. (Sat.) Page Size: broadsheet Circulation: 8,200 Saturday (free). **Owner(s):** Journal Register Co., 50 W State St, 12th Fl, Trenton, NJ 08608. **Management:** Steve Paterson, Publisher. Jim Misener, Advertising Manager. **Editorial:** Phil Foley, Editor.

OSCODA

OSCODA PRESS. 311 S State St, Oscoda, MI 48750. Telephone: 989-739-2054. FAX: 989-739-3201. E-MAIL: oscodapress@voyager.net. URL: http://www.oscodapress.com. Mailing Address: PO Box 663, Oscoda, MI 48750. Year Established: 1800. Pub. Frequency: w. (Wed.) Page Size: tabloid. Subscrip. Rate: $.75 newsstand/cover; $40/yr mailed in county; $45/yr mailed out of county; $50/yr mailed out of state. Circulation: 5,750 per issue (paid). **Owner(s):** Community Media Group, Inc, PO Box 10, West Frankfort, IL 62896. Telephone: 618-937-6412. **Management:** Jim Dunn, Publisher. **Editorial:** Holly Nelson, Editor. Jeff Thomas, Sports Editor.

OWOSSO

SUNDAY INDEPENDENT, THE. 1907 W. M-21, Owosso, MI 48867-9317. Telephone: 989-723-1118. FAX: 989-725-1834. E-MAIL: indysales@chartermi.net. Year Established: 1968. Pub. Frequency: w. (Wed.) Page Size: tabloid. Subscrip. Rate: $18 for 6 mos.; $30/yr. Adv. Rate: col. inch $25 Circulation: 40,577 per issue (free). **Owner(s):** Michael Flores, 1907 W. M-21, Owosso, MI 48867. Telephone: 517-723-1118. FAX: 517-725-1834. **Management:** Michael Flores, President. Jean Yanna, Advertising Manager. Teresa Cooper, Classified Adv. Mgr.. **Editorial:** Bill Constine, Editor-in-Chief.

PARMA

COUNTY PRESS (PARMA). 123 W. Main St., Parma, MI 49269-0279. Telephone: 517-531-4542. FAX: 517-531-3576. E-MAIL: countypress@aol.com. Mailing Address: PO Box 279, Parma, MI 49269-0279. Year Established: 1868. Pub. Frequency: w. (Wed.) Page Size: tabloid. Subscrip. Rate: $.75 newsstand/cover; $24/yr. Adv. Rate: col. inch $10.47 Circulation: 1,500 per issue (paid). **Owner(s):** Carole & Ralph Rice, 123 W. Main St., Parma, MI 49269. Telephone: 517-531-4542. FAX: 517-531-3576. **Management:** Jill Carr, Advertising.

PAW PAW

PAW PAW COURIER-LEADER, THE. PO Box 129, Paw Paw, MI 49079-0129. Telephone: 269-657-3072. FAX: 269-657-5723. Year Established: 1844. Pub. Frequency: w. (Fri.) Page Size: broadsheet. Subscrip. Rate: $.75 newsstand/cover; $20/yr. Adv. Rate: col. inch $5.50 Circulation: 3,500 per issue (paid). **Owner(s):** Vineyard Press, Inc., See address and contact information above. **Management:** Steven A. Racette, General Manager. **Editorial:** Felix A. Racette, Editor. Robin Racette Griffin, Associate Editor.

PETOSKEY

PETOSKEY/CHARLEVOIX STAR. 1327 Spring St, Petoskey, MI 49770. Telephone: 231-347-8186. FAX: 231-347-5744. URL: http://www.morningstarpublishing.com. Mailing Address: PO Box 826, Petoskey, MI 49770. Year Established: 1956.Pub. Frequency: w. (Sun.) Page Size: tabloid Circulation: 19,070 Sunday (free). **Owner(s):** Morning Star Publishing, 711 W. Pickard, Mt. Pleasant, MI 48858. Telephone: 989-779-6000. **Management:** Jan Anderson, General Manager. Paige O'Neal, Sales Manager.

REED CITY

OSCEOLA PIONEER. ISSN 0192-8678 101 W. Slosson Ave., Reed City, MI 49677. Telephone: 231-832-5566. FAX: 231-832-5558. E-MAIL: l foster@pioneergroup.net. URL: http://www.pioneergroup.com Year Established: 1862. Pub. Frequency: w. (Wed.) Page Size: broadsheet. Subscrip. Rate: $.50 newsstand/cover; $27.40/yr mailed in county; $43.80/yr mailed out of county; $57.20/yr out of state. **Wire Service(s):** AP. Circulation: 2,875 per issue (paid). **Owner(s):** The Pioneer Group, 502 N. State St., Big Rapids, MI 49307. Telephone: 231-796-4831. FAX: 231-796-1152. **Management:** John A. Batdorff Sr., President. John Norton, Publisher. Sharon Frederick, Advertising Manager. **Editorial:** James Crees, Editor.

PIONEER/OSCEOLA EDITION, THE. 101 W. Slosson Ave., Reed City, MI 49677. Telephone: 231-832-5566. FAX: 231-832-5558. E-MAIL: crherald@pioneergroup.net. URL: http://www.pioneergroup.com. Pub. Frequency: w. (Wed.) Page Size: broadsheet. Subscrip. Rate: $.50 newsstand/cover; $27.40/yr mailed in county; $43.85/yr mailed out of county; $59.26/yr mailed out of state. Circulation: 2,300 per issue (paid). **Owner(s):** The Pioneer Group, 851 Michigan Ave., Baldwin, MI 49304. **Management:** John A. Batdorff, Publisher. Sharon Frederick, Advertising Manager. Sue Vellanti, Circulation Manager. **Editorial:** Jim Crees, Editor.

RICHMOND

WEEKEND VOICE. 68085 S Main St, Richmond, MI 48062. Telephone: 586-727-3745. FAX: 586-727-4413. URL: http://www.voicenews.com. Year Established: 1876.Pub. Frequency: w. (Sun) Page Size: tabloid Circulation: 12,000 Sunday (free). **Owner(s):** Journal Register Co., 50 W State St, 12th Fl, Trenton, NJ 08608. **Management:** Debbie Loggins, General Manager. Helga Wissell, Circulation Manager. **Editorial:** Chris Axon, Production Manager.

ROCHESTER

CLARKSTON ECCENTRIC. 400 Water St, Ste 203, Rochester, MI 48307. Telephone: 248-651-7575. FAX: 248-651-9080. URL: http://www.hometownlife.com. Year Established: 1995. Pub. Frequency: s-w. (Sun. & Thu.) Page Size: broadsheet. Subscrip. Rate: $.50 newsstand/cover; $59.95/yr home delivery local; $83.95/yr mailed in county; $108.95/yr mailed out of county. Circulation: 6,440 per issue (paid and free). **Owner(s):** Observer, Eccentric & Mirror Newspapers, Inc., 7950 Jones Branch Dr, McLean, VA 22107. Telephone: 703-854-5000. **Management:** Marty Carry, Advertising Director. Frank Cibor, Classified Adv. Mgr.. **Editorial:** Susan Rosiek, Executive Editor. Joe Bauman, Managing Editor.

LAKE ORION ECCENTRIC. 400 Water St, Ste 203, Rochester, MI 48307. Telephone: 248-651-7575. FAX: 248-651-9080. URL: http://www.hometownlife.com. Pub. Frequency: w. (Thu.) Page Size: broadsheet. Subscrip. Rate: $.50 newsstand/cover; $29.95/yr local; $54.48/yr mailed out of state. Circulation: 4,414 per issue (paid and free). **Owner(s):** Observer, Eccentric & Mirror Newspapers, Inc., 7950 Jones Branch Dr, McLean, VA 22107. Telephone: 703-854-5000. **Management:** Marty Carry, Advertising Director. Frank Cibor, Classified Adv. Mgr.. **Editorial:** Susan Rosiek, Executive Editor. Joe Bauman, Managing Editor.

ROCKFORD

ROCKFORD SQUIRE, THE. 51 1/2 E. Bridge St., Rockford, MI 49341. Telephone: 616-866-4465. FAX: 616-866-3810. E-MAIL: squiremail@aol.com. URL: http://www.rockfordsquire.com. Mailing Address: PO Box 498, Rockford, MI 49341-0498. Year Established: 1983. Pub. Frequency: w. (Thu.) Page Size: tabloid. Subscrip. Rate: $15/yr mailed in city; $23/yr mailed out of county; $26/yr mailed out of state. Adv. Rate: col. inch $8.50 Circulation: 8,500 per issue (paid and free). **Owner(s):** Rockford Publishing Co., 51 1/2 E. Bridge St., Rockford, MI 48341. Telephone: 616-866-4465. FAX: 616-866-3810. **Management:** Roger Allen, Publisher. Beth Alpena, Business Manager. **Editorial:** Beth Alpena, Managing Editor.

ROGERS CITY

PRESQUE ISLE ADVANCE. 104 S. Third St., Rogers City, MI 49779. Telephone: 989-734-2105. URL: http://www.piadvance.com. Year Established: 1878. Pub. Frequency: w. (Thu.) Page Size: broadsheet. Subscrip. Rate: $.75 newsstand/cover; $27/yr in county; $29/yr in state; $31/yr out of state. Circulation: 3,800 per issue (paid). **Owner(s):** Presque Isle Newspapers, Inc., See address and contact information above. **Management:** Richard Lamb, Publisher. Cella Bade, Advertising. Richard Lamb, Manager. **Editorial:** Richard Lamb, Editor. Peter Jakey, Managing Editor. Beth Kowalski, Composing Room Manager.

ROMEO

ROMEO OBSERVER, THE. 124 W. St. Clair, Romeo, MI 48065-0096. Telephone: 586-752-3524. FAX: 586-752-0548. E-MAIL: news@romeoobserver.com. URL: http://www.romeoobserver.com. Mailing Address: P.O. Box 96, Romeo, MI 48065-0096. Year Established: 1866. Pub. Frequency: w. (Wed.) Page Size: broadsheet. Subscrip. Rate: $.50 newsstand/cover; $18/yr mailed in state; $25/yr mailed out of state. Adv. Rate: col. inch $12.15 **Wire Service(s):** AP. Circulation: 12,778 per issue (paid and free). **Owner(s):** Romeo Observer Inc., See address and contact information above. **Management:** Melvin E. Bleich, Publisher. Robert Bleich, Circulation Director. **Editorial:** Melvin E. Bleich, Editor. Dennis A. Setter, Managing Editor. Michelle Tanquay, News. Karen Hamilton, Photographer.

ROSCOMMON

ROSCOMMON COUNTY HERALD-NEWS. 905 Lake St., Roscommon, MI 48653. Telephone: 989-275-5100. FAX: 989-275-5449. E-MAIL: heraldnews@voyager.net. Mailing Address: PO Box 8, Roscommon, MI 48653. Year Established: 1875. Pub. Frequency: w. (Sun.) Page Size: broadsheet. Subscrip. Rate: $.50 newsstand/cover; $25/yr mailed in state; $30/yr mailed out of state. Circulation: 15,000 Sunday (paid). **Owner(s):** Robert Perlberg, PO Box 247, West Branch, MI 48661. **Management:** Robert Perlberg, Publisher.

ROYAL OAK

WEEKLY TRIBUNE PLUS, THE. 210 E Third St, Royal Oak, MI 48067. Telephone: 248-541-3000. FAX: 248-541-7903. Pub. Frequency: w. (Sun.) Page Size: tabloid Circulation: 75,815 per issue (free). **Owner(s):** Journal Register Co., 50 W State St, 12th Fl, Trenton, NJ 08608. **Management:** Kevin Haezebroeck, President. Wayne Oehmke, Publisher. Jennifer Gorczany, Advertising Director. Betsy Karmeisool, Circulation Director. Deb Harper, Classified Adv. Mgr.. **Editorial:** Mike Beeson, Editor.

SAGINAW

SAGINAW PRESS, THE. 410 Hancock St., Saginaw, MI 48602. Telephone: 989-793-8070. Year Established: 1912. Pub. Frequency: w. (Fri.) Page Size: standard. Subscrip. Rate: $.50 newsstand/cover; $25/yr in state. Adv. Rate: col. inch $5.88 Circulation: 425 per issue (paid). **Owner(s):** Saginaw Publishing Co., See address and contact information above. **Management:** George W Baxter, President. **Editorial:** George W Baxter, Managing Editor.

TOWNSHIP TIMES. 2089 Wieneke Rd., Saginaw, MI 48603-3338. Telephone: 989-799-3200. FAX: 989-799-7085. Year Established: 1964. Pub. Frequency: w. (Wed.) Page Size: tabloid. Subscrip. Rate: $.50 newsstand/cover; $25/yr in county; $35/yr out of county; $22.50/yr in county to senior citizens. Adv. Rate: col. inch $10.25 Circulation: 5,000 per issue (paid). **Owner(s):** Saginaw Community Newspapers Co., 2089 Wieneke Rd., Saginaw, MI 48603. Telephone: 989-799-3200. **Management:** Mike Thompson, General Manager. Edward Belles, Publisher. Bob Grnak, Advertising Manager. **Editorial:** Bob Grnak, Editor.

SALINE

MILAN NEWS-LEADER, THE. 106 W Michigan Ave, Saline, MI 48176. Telephone: 734-429-7380. FAX: 734-429-3621. E-MAIL: editor@milannews.com.. URL: http://www.milannews.com. Year Established: 1881. Pub. Frequency: w. (Thu.) Page Size: tabloid. Subscrip. Rate: $.50 newsstand/cover; $16.50 mailed for 6 mos. in county; $30/yr mailed in county. Circulation: 3,000 per issue (paid). **Owner(s):** Journal Register Co., 50 W. State St., 12th Fl., Trenton, NJ 08608-1298. **Management:** James Williams, Publisher. Justin Wilcox, Advertising Director. **Editorial:** Michelle Rogers, Editor.

SALINE REPORTER, THE. 106 W Michigan Ave, Saline, MI 48176. Telephone: 734-429-7380. FAX: 734-429-3621. E-MAIL: editor@salinereporter.com. URL: http://www.salinereporter.com. Year Established: 1948. Pub. Frequency: w. (Thu.) Page Size: broadsheet. Subscrip. Rate: $.75 newsstand/cover; $16.50 mailed for 6 mos.; $30/yr mailed. Circulation: 4,700 per issue (paid). **Owner(s):** Journal Register Co., 50 W State St, 12th Fl, Trenton, NJ 08608. Telephone: 609-396-2200. FAX: 609-396-2292. **Management:** James Williams, Publisher. Justin Wilcox, Advertising Director. **Editorial:** Michelle Rogers, Editor.

SANDUSKY

SANILAC COUNTY NEWS. 356 E Sanilac Rd, Sandusky, MI 48471. Telephone: 810-648-4000. E-MAIL: sannews@avci.net. URL: http://www.sanilaccountynews.com. Year Established: 1971. Pub. Frequency: w. (Wed.) Page Size: tabloid. Subscrip. Rate: $.75 newsstand/cover; $21/yr mailed in county; $42.50/yr mailed out of county; $49/yr mailed out of state. Circulation: 900 per issue (paid). **Owner(s):** Journal Register Co., 50 W. State St., 12th Fl., Trenton, NJ 06808. **Management:** Jane Vanderpool, Publisher. Jody Woltman, Advertising Manager. **Editorial:** Eric Levine, Editor. Dale Ball, Sports.

SAUGATUCK

COMMERCIAL RECORD (ALLEGAN). 3217 Blue Star Hwy, Saugatuck, MI 49453. Telephone: 269-857-2570. FAX: 269-857-4637. Mailing Address: PO Box 189, Allegan, MI 49010-0189. Pub. Frequency: w. (Thu.) Page Size: tabloid. Subscrip. Rate: $.75 newsstand/cover; $20/yr in county; $23/yr mailed out of county; $27/yr mailed out of state. Circulation: 1,599 per issue (paid). **Owner(s):** Kaechele Publications, Inc., 231 Trowbridge St., Ste 17, Allegan, MI 49010. Telephone: 269-673-5534. FAX: 269-673-5535. **Management:** Cheryl Kaechele, Publisher. Kristine Gorno, Sales Manager.

SAULT STE. MARIE

TRI COUNTY BUYERS GUIDE. 109 Arlington St., Sault Ste. Marie, MI 49783. Telephone: 906-632-2235. FAX: 906-632-1222. Pub. Frequency: w. (Sun.) Page Size: tabloid Circulation: 18,300 per issue (free). **Owner(s):** GateHouse Media, Inc, 350 WillowBrook Office Park, Fairport, NY 14450. Telephone: 585-598-0030. FAX: 585-248-2631. **Management:** Howard Kaiser, Publisher. Penny Joss, Advertising Manager. Mike Ferraro, Circulation Manager. Kathy Kaiser, Classified Adv. Mgr..

SEBEWAING

NEWSWEEKLY, THE. 236 N Center St, Sebewaing, MI 48759. Telephone: 989-453-3100. FAX: 989-883-9211. E-MAIL: newswkly@avci.net. URL: http://www.huroncountypress.com. Year Established: 1890. Pub. Frequency: w. (Tue.) Page Size: tabloid. Subscrip. Rate: $.50 newsstand/cover; $21/yr mailed locally; $31/yr mailed elsewhere. Circulation: 4,500 per issue (paid). **Owner(s):** Journal Register Co., 50 W State St, 12th Fl, Trenton, NJ 08608. **Management:** Bill Southern, President. Jack Guza, Publisher. Shelley Adair, Advertising Director. Nadine Klee, Circulation Director. Tammy Philp, Classified Editor. **Editorial:** Molly Dando, Editor.

SHEBOYGAN

STRAITS AREA STAR. 222 N. Main St., Sheboygan, MI 49721. Telephone: 231-627-3151. FAX: 231-627-6244. E-MAIL: sheboygan@michigannewspapers.com. Year Established: 1986. Pub. Frequency: w. (Sun.) Page Size: tabloid Adv. Rate: col. inch $8 Circulation: 12,721 Sunday (free). **Owner(s):** Morning Star Publishing, 711 W. Pickard, Mt. Pleasant, MI 48885. Telephone: 989-779-6000. **Management:** Carol Northcott, General Manager.

SHELBY TOWNSHIP

ADVISOR & SOURCE, THE. 48075 Van Dyke Ave, Shelby Township, MI 48317. Telephone: 586-731-1000. FAX: 586-731-8172. URL: http://www.sourcenewspapers.com. Year Established: 1972. Pub. Frequency: w. (Sun.) Page Size: broadsheet.Adv. Rate: col. inch $58.30 Circulation: 121,749 per issue (free). **Owner(s):** Journal Register Co., 50 W State St, 12th Fl, Trenton, NJ 08608. **Management:** Chris Troszak, General Manager. Kevin Haezebroeck, President. Jared Waterstone, Circulation Manager. **Editorial:** Jody McVeigh, Editor.

SOUTH HAVEN

SOUTH HAVEN TRIBUNE. 255 Center St., South Haven, MI 49090. Telephone: 269-637-1104. FAX: 269-637-8415. E-MAIL: shtribune@comcast.net. URL: http://www.southhaventribune.com. Year Established: 1899. Pub. Frequency: w. (Sun.) Page Size: broadsheet. Subscrip. Rate: $.50 newsstand/cover; $70/yr mailed in county. Circulation: 14,500 per issue (free). **Owner(s):** Paxton Media Group LLC, 201 S. Fourth St., Paducah, KY 42003. Telephone: 270-575-8600. FAX: 270-442-8188. **Management:** Geoffrey Moser, Publisher. Sherri Pratt, Circulation Manager. Sue Spencer, Classified Adv. Mgr.. **Editorial:** Becky Burkert, Managing Editor.

SOUTH LYON

MILFORD TIMES. 101 N Lafayette St, South Lyon, MI 48178-2070. Telephone: 248-437-2011. FAX: 248-437-3386. URL: http://www.hometownlife.com. Year Established: 1871. Pub. Frequency: w. (Thu.) Page Size: broadsheet. Subscrip. Rate: $.50 newsstand/cover; $26/yr in county; $40/yr mailed out of county; $50/yr mailed out of state. Circulation: 7,500 per issue (paid). **Owner(s):** Gannett Company, Inc., 7950 Jones Branch Dr., McLean, VA 22107-0001. **Management:** Grace Perry, Advertising Director. Lisa Dranginis, Advertising Manager. **Editorial:** Philip Allmen, Editor.

SOUTH LYON HERALD. 101 N Lafayette St, South Lyon, MI 48178-2070. Telephone: 248-437-2011. FAX: 248-437-3386. E-MAIL: jamitchell@gannett.com. URL: http://www.hometownlife.com. Year Established: 1880. Pub. Frequency: w. (Thu.) Page Size: broadsheet. Subscrip. Rate: $.50 newsstand/cover; $26/yr mailed in county; $40/yr mailed out of county; $50/yr mailed out of state. Circulation: 7,800 per issue (paid). **Owner(s):** Gannett Company, Inc., 7950 Jones Branch Dr., McLean, VA 22107-0001. **Management:** Rich Perlberg, General Manager. Grace Perry, Advertising Director. Lisa Dranginis, Advertising Manager. **Editorial:** James Mitchell, Editor.

SOUTHGATE

NEWS-HERALD (SOUTHGATE), THE. One Heritage Drive Ste 100, Southgate, MI 48195. Telephone: 734-246-0800. E-MAIL: editor@thenewsherald.com. URL: http://www.heritage.com. Year Established: 1879. Pub. Frequency: 3/w. (Wed., Fri., Sun.) Page Size: broadsheet. Subscrip. Rate: $.75 newsstand/cover; $75/yr mailed in county; $99/yr mailed out of county. Adv. Rate: col. inch $63.57 Circulation: 65,150 Sunday (controlled and free); 74,000 per issue (controlled and free). **Owner(s):** Journal Register Co., 50 W State St, 12th Fl, Trenton, NJ 08608. Telephone: 609-396-2200. FAX: 609-396-2292. **Management:** James Williams, Publisher. Justin Wilcox, Advertising Director. **Editorial:** Karl Ziomek, Editor.

ST JOHNS

ST JOHNS REMINDER. 109 W Higham St, St Johns, MI 48879. Telephone: 989-224-8356. FAX: 989-224-9458. Year Established: 1949. Pub. Frequency: w. (Sun.) Page Size: tabloid Circulation: 17,600 per issue (free). **Owner(s):** Journal Register Co., 50 W State St, 12th Fl, Trenton, NJ 08608. **Management:** Bonny Fybie, General Manager.

ST. IGNACE

ST. IGNACE NEWS, THE. 359 Reagon St., St. Ignace, MI 49781-0277. Telephone: 906-643-9150. FAX: 906-643-9122. E-MAIL: news@stignacenews.com. Year Established: 1878. Pub. Frequency: w. (Thu.) Page Size: broadsheet. Subscrip. Rate: $.75 newsstand/cover (effective 2005); $31/yr in county (effective 2004); $39/yr out of county. Circulation: 6,700 per issue (paid). **Owner(s):** St. Ignace News, See address and contact information above. **Management:** Wesley H. Maurer Jr., Publisher. Dawn Huskey, Advertising Manager. Wendy Colegrove, Circulation Manager. **Editorial:** Wesley H. Maurer Jr., Editor.

ST. JOHNS

DEWITT-BATH REVIEW. 320 N. Clinton Ave., St. Johns, MI 48879. Telephone: 989-224-2361. FAX: 989-224-4452. URL: http://www.htnews.com. Year Established: 1979. Pub. Frequency: w. (Sun.) Page Size: tabloid. Subscrip. Rate: $50 newsstand/cover. Adv. Rate: col. inch $10.53 Circulation: 8,455 Sunday (paid and free). **Owner(s):** HomeTown Communications Network, 36251 Schoolcraft Rd., Livonia, MI 48150. Telephone: 734-953-2215. FAX: 734-591-9424. **Management:** Preston O'Dette, Publisher. Todd Pride, Advertising Director. **Editorial:** Jeremy Nagel, Editor. Sue Lounds, Sports Editor.

STANDISH

ARENAC COUNTY INDEPENDENT. 203 E. Cedar St., Standish, MI 48658. E-MAIL: arecoind@ch-net.com. Year Established: 1883. Pub. Frequency: w. (Wed.) Page Size: broadsheet. Subscrip. Rate: $.50 newsstand/cover; $22/yr mailed in county; $32/yr mailed out of county; $40/yr mailed out of state. Circulation: 6,000 per issue (paid). **Owner(s):** Robert Perlberg, PO Box 247, West Branch, MI 48661. PO Box 699, Standish, MI 48658. Telephone: 989-846-4531. **Management:** Robert Perlberg, Publisher. Grange Bell, Advertising Manager. **Editorial:** Stephanie Buffman, Managing Editor.

STOCKBRIDGE

TOWN CRIER. PO Box 548, Stockbridge, MI 49285. Telephone: 517-851-7833. FAX: 517-851-4641. Mailing Address: PO Box 548, Stockbridge, MI 49285-0548. Year Established: 1967. Pub. Frequency: w. (Tue.) Page Size: tabloid. Subscrip. Rate: $.50 newsstand/cover; $23/yr. Adv. Rate: col. inch $9.25 Circulation: 10,175 per issue (paid and free). **Owner(s):** Ruth Camp Wellman, See address and contact information above. **Management:** Ruth Camp Wellman, Publisher. Toni Jarvis, Advertising Manager. **Editorial:** Ruth Camp Wellman, Editor. Sandra Kay, News Editor. Michael Williamson, Sports.

STURGIS

GATEWAY SHOPPER. 201 Clay St, Sturgis, MI 49091. Telephone: 269-651-2944. FAX: 269-651-8855. Pub. Frequency: w. (Tue.) Page Size: tabloid Circulation: 25,300 per issue (free). **Owner(s):** GateHouse Media, Inc, 350 WillowBrook Office Park, Fairport, NY 14450. Telephone: 585-598-0030. FAX: 585-248-2631. **Management:** Kim Haller, Advertising Manager. Pat Burlew, Classified Adv. Mgr..

TECUMSEH

TECUMSEH HERALD. 110 E. Logan St., Tecumseh, MI 49286. Telephone: 517-423-2174. FAX: 517-423-6258. E-MAIL: herald@lni.net. URL: http://www.tecumsehherald.com. Year Established: 1850. Pub. Frequency: w. (Thu.) Page Size: broadsheet. Subscrip. Rate: $.50 newsstand/cover; $25/yr mailed in county; $27/yr mailed out of county. Adv. Rate: col. inch $8.90 Circulation: 5,600 per issue (paid). **Owner(s):** James C.Lincoln, See address and contact information above. **Management:** James C. Lincoln, Publisher. Jean Oatman, Advertising. **Editorial:** James L. Lincoln, Editor. Cristina Tropani, Feature Editor. Mickey Alvarado, Sports Editor.

THREE RIVERS

PENNY SAVER (THREE RIVERS). 124 N. Main St., Three Rivers, MI 49093. Telephone: 269-279-7488. FAX: 269-279-6007. Year Established: 1985. Pub. Frequency: w. (Sun.) Page Size: tabloid Circulation: 16,400 per issue (free). **Owner(s):** Dirk Milliman, See address and contact information above. **Management:** Dirk Milliman, President. Sharon Summers, Circulation Manager.

TRAVERSE CITY

GRAND TRAVERSE HERALD. 120 W Front St, Traverse City, MI 49684. Telephone: 231-946-2000. FAX: 231-946-8632. URL: http://www.gherald.com. Mailing Address: PO Box 632, Traverse City, MI 49685. Pub. Frequency: w. (Wed.) Page Size: standard. Subscrip. Rate: $.75 newsstand/cover. Adv. Rate: col. inch $9.53 Circulation: 13,900 per issue (paid and free). **Owner(s):** Community Newspaper Holdings, Inc., 3500 Colonnade Pkwy., Ste. 600, Birmingham, AL 35243-2304. **Management:** Ann Reed, Publisher. Jacki Krolczyk, Advertising Director. Steve Knape, Circulation Manager. Jeana Daenzer, Classified Adv. Mgr.. **Editorial:** Garrett Leiva, Editor.

PREVIEW COMMUNITY WEEKLY. 410 S. Union St., Traverse City, MI 49684. E-MAIL: star@star-ads.com. URL: http://www.star-ads.com. Mailing Address: PO Box 5847, Traverse City, MI 49696. Year Established: 1972. Pub. Frequency: w. (Sun.) Page Size: tabloid.Adv. Rate: col. inch $8.75 Circulation: 33,000 Sunday (free). **Owner(s):** Morning Star Publishing, 711 W. Pickard, Mt. Pleasant, MI 48848. **Management:** Kim Forshee, General Manager.

TROY

TROY-SOMERSET GAZETTE. 1903 E. Wattles, Troy, MI 48085. Telephone: 248-524-4868. FAX: 248-524-9140. E-MAIL: editor@troy-somersetgazette.com. URL: http://troy-somersetgazette.com. Mailing Address: PO Box 482, Troy, MI 48099. Year Established: 1980. Pub. Frequency: w. (Mon.) Page Size: tabloid.Adv. Rate: col. inch $15.60 Freelance Pay: $1.50/column-inch. **Wire Service(s):** PR. Circulation: 25,000 per issue (free). **Owner(s):** Claire M. Weber, 6506 Tanglewood, Troy, MI 48098. Telephone: 248-828-8523. **Management:** Claire M. Weber, Publisher. Todd Kmett, Circulation Manager. **Editorial:** Cynthia Kmett, Editor.

VASSAR

VASSAR PIONEER TIMES. ISSN 0193-0249
113 S. Main St., Vassar, MI 48768. Telephone: 989-823-8579. FAX: 989-823-8778. E-MAIL: vptimes@midmich.net. URL: http://www.pioneertimes.com. Mailing Address: PO Box 69, Vassar, MI 48768. Year Established: 1857. Pub. Frequency: w. (Wed.) Page Size: tabloid. Subscrip. Rate: $.50 newsstand/cover; $15.16/yr mailed. Adv. Rate: col. inch $6 Freelance Pay: $0.33/column-inch. Circulation: 1,813 per issue (paid). **Owner(s):** Hearst Corp., 959 Eighth Ave, New York, NY 10019. **Management:** Shawn Jenkins, General Manager. **Editorial:** Shawn Jenkins, Managing Editor.

VICKSBURG

COMMERCIAL-EXPRESS. 109 S. Main St., Vicksburg, MI 49097. Telephone: 269-649-2333. E-MAIL: commercialexpress@earthlink.net. Mailing Address: PO Box 154, Vicksburg, MI 49097. Year Established: 1879. Pub. Frequency: w. (Sat.) Page Size: tabloid. Subscrip. Rate: $.75 newsstand/cover; $25/yr in county; $34/yr out of county. Adv. Rate: col. inch $3.75 Freelance Pay: $0.50/column-inch. Circulation: 2,200 per issue (paid). **Owner(s):** GateHouse Media, Inc, 350 WillowBrook Office Park, Fairport, NY 14450. Telephone: 585-598-0030. FAX: 585-248-2631. **Management:** Dan Tollefson, Publisher. Debbie Hargreave, Advertising Manager. **Editorial:** Kathleen Allworth, Editor.

WATERFORD

SPINAL COLUMN NEWSWEEKLY. 7196 Cooley Lake Rd, Waterford, MI 48327-4113. Telephone: 248-360-7355. FAX: 313-360-1220. URL: http://www.spinalcolumnonline.com. Mailing Address: PO Box 14, Union Lake, MI 48387-0014. Year Established: 1960. Pub. Frequency: w. (Wed.) Page Size: tabloid. Subscrip. Rate: $.75 newsstand/cover; $35/yr mailed. Circulation: 50,000 per issue (paid and free). **Owner(s):** S C N Communications Group, See address and contact information above. **Management:** James W Fancy, Publisher. Dennis Boggs, Circulation Manager. Lori Snyder, Classified Adv. Mgr.. David Hohendorf, Associate Publisher. **Editorial:** Tim Dmoch, News Editor.

WATERVLIET

TRI-CITY RECORD, THE. 138 N. Main St., Watervliet, MI 49098. Year Established: 1882. Pub. Frequency: w. (Wed.) Page Size: broadsheet. Subscrip. Rate: $.75 newsstand/cover; $33/yr in county; $44/yr out of county; $49/yr out of state. Circulation: 2,700 per issue (paid). **Owner(s):** Anne & Karl Bayer, See address and contact information above. **Management:** Anne Bayer, Publisher. Amy Loshbough, Business Manager. **Editorial:** Bonnie Bannen, Copy Chief.

WAYLAND

PENASEE GLOBE. 133 E. Superior, Wayland, MI 49348. Telephone: 269-792-2271. FAX: 269-792-2030. E-MAIL: retailsales@advancenewspapers.com. URL: http://www.advancenewspapers.com. Mailing Address: PO Box 9, Jenison, MI 49429-0009. Pub. Frequency: w. (Mon.) Page Size: tabloid.Adv. Rate: col. inch $8.90 Circulation: 16,575 per issue (free). **Owner(s):** Valley Media, Inc., 2141 Port Sheldon St., Jenison, MI 49428. **Management:** Joel Holland, Publisher. Terry Alvesteffer, Circulation Manager. Jeanne Anderson, Classified Adv. Mgr.. **Editorial:** Matt Russell, News Editor. Karen Waite, Photo Editor. Larry Hirt, Sports Editor.

WAYNE

BELLEVILLE ENTERPRISE. 35128 W Michigan Ave, Wayne, MI 48184. Telephone: 734-467-1900. FAX: 734-729-1840. Mailing Address: PO Box 339, Wayne, MI 48184. Year Established: 1886. Pub. Frequency: w. (Thu.) Page Size: broadsheet. Subscrip. Rate: $.50 newsstand/cover; $26 mailed for 6 mos. in county & out of county; $48/yr mailed in county & out of county. Freelance Pay: $10/article. Circulation: 4,500 per issue (paid). **Owner(s):** Associated Newspapers, See address and contact information above. **Management:** Sean Rhaesa, General Manager. Susan Willett, Publisher.

CANTON EAGLE. 35540 W. Michigan Ave., Wayne, MI 48184. Telephone: 734-729-4000. FAX: 734-729-1840. Year Established: 1945. Pub. Frequency: w. (Thu.) Page Size: broadsheet. Subscrip. Rate: $.75 newsstand/cover; $48/yr mailed in county & out of county. Freelance Pay: $10/article. Circulation: 4,000 per issue (paid). **Owner(s):** Journal Newspapers, See address and contact information above. **Management:** David Willett, Owner. Susan Willett, Publisher. Doug Willett, Circulation Manager. **Editorial:** Scott Spielman, Managing Editor.

INKSTER LEDGER-STAR. 35540 W. Michigan Ave., Wayne, MI 48184. Telephone: 734-729-4000. FAX: 734-729-1840. Mailing Address: PO Box 578, Wayne, MI 48184. Pub. Frequency: w. (Thu.) Page Size: broadsheet. Subscrip. Rate: $.75 newsstand/cover; $48/yr mailed in county; $48/yr mailed out of county. Freelance Pay: $10/article. Circulation: 3,500 per issue (paid). **Owner(s):** Journal Newspapers, See address and contact information above. **Management:** David Willett, Owner. Susan Willett, Publisher. Doug Willett, Circulation Manager. **Editorial:** Scott Spielman, Managing Editor.

ROMULUS ROMAN. 35540 W. Michigan Ave., Wayne, MI 48184. Telephone: 734-729-4000. FAX: 734-729-1840. Year Established: 1885. Pub. Frequency: w. (Thu.) Page Size: broadsheet. Subscrip. Rate: $.75 newsstand/cover; $48/yr mailed in county & out of county. Freelance Pay: $10/article. Circulation: 6,500 per issue (paid). **Owner(s):** Journal Newspapers, See address and contact information above. **Management:** David Willett, Owner. Susan Willett, Publisher. Doug Willett, Circulation Manager. **Editorial:** Scott Spielman, Managing Editor.

WAYNE EAGLE. PO Box 339, Wayne, MI 48184. Telephone: 734-467-1900. FAX: 734-729-1840. Year Established: 1945. Pub. Frequency: w. (Thu.) Page Size: broadsheet. Subscrip. Rate: $.75 newsstand/cover; $45/yr mailed in county & out of county. Freelance Pay: $10/article. Circulation: 6,000 per issue (paid). **Owner(s):** Susan Willett, See address and contact information above. **Management:** Sean Rhaesa, General Manager. Susan Willett, Publisher. **Editorial:** Scott Spielman, Managing Editor.

WESTLAND EAGLE. 35128 W Michigan Ave, Wayne, MI 48184. Telephone: 734-467-1900. FAX: 734-729-1840. Mailing Address: PO Box 339, Wayne, MI 48184. Year Established: 1945. Pub. Frequency: w. (Thu.) Page Size: broadsheet. Subscrip. Rate: $.75 newsstand/cover; $48/yr in county & out of county. Freelance Pay: $10/article. Circulation: 5,000 per issue (paid). **Owner(s):** Associated Newspapers, See address and contact information above. **Management:** Sean Rhaesa, General Manager. Susan Willett, Publisher.

WEST BRANCH

OGEMAW COUNTY HERALD. PO Box 247, West Branch, MI 48661. Telephone: 989-345-0044. Year Established: 1880. Pub. Frequency: w. (Thu.) Page Size: broadsheet. Subscrip. Rate: $.75 newsstand/cover; $25/yr in county; $32/yr out of county; $40/yr out of state. Circulation: 10,000 per issue (paid). **Owner(s):** Robert Perlberg, PO Box 699, Standish, MI 48658. **Management:** Mike Dray, General Manager. Kathy Collins, Advertising Manager. **Editorial:** Kay Reeser, Editor.

WHITEHALL

WHITE LAKE BEACON. 432 Spring St, Whitehall, MI 49461. Telephone: 231-894-5356. FAX: 231-894-2174. E-MAIL: editor@whitelakebeacon.com. URL: http://www.whitelakebeacon.com. Mailing Address: PO Box 98, Whitehall, MI 49461-0098. Year Established: 1983. Pub. Frequency: w. (Sun.) Page Size: tabloid. Subscrip. Rate: $1 newsstand/cover; $30/yr mailed in county; $33/yr mailed out of county; $40/yr mailed out of state. Circulation: 11,900 per issue (free). **Owner(s):** Shoreline Media, Inc., 202 N. Rath Ave., Ludington, MI 49431-4011. Telephone: 231-845-5181. FAX: 231-843-4011. **Management:** James O. Young, Publisher. Julie Payment, Circulation Manager.

ZEELAND

ZEELAND RECORD. ISSN 1072-1304
16 S Elm St, Zeeland, MI 49464-1751 . Telephone: 616-772-2131. FAX: 616-772-9771. Year Established: 1890. Pub. Frequency: w. Subscrip. Rate: $18/yr. **Owner(s):** Zeeland Record Co., See address and contact information above.

MIDDLE PACIFIC

SAIPAN

PALAU HORIZON. PO Box 231, Saipan, MP 96950. Telephone: 670-234-6341. FAX: 680-488-4565. E-MAIL: younis@vzpacifica.net/hprinting@palaunet.com. Year Established: 1998. Pub. Frequency: w. Page Size: tabloid. Subscrip. Rate: $.50 newsstand/cover. **Wire Service(s):** RN, AP. Circulation: 3,000 per issue (paid and free). **Owner(s):** Younis Art Studio, Inc., See address and contact information above. **Management:** Abed Younis, President. Paz Younis, Vice President. Abed Younis, Manager.

MINNESOTA

ADA

NORMAN COUNTY INDEX. 307 W. Main St., Ada, MN 56510-0148. Telephone: 218-784-2541. FAX: 218-784-2551. E-MAIL: nci@losetel.net. Mailing Address: PO Box 148, Ada, MN 56510-0148. Year Established: 1880. Pub. Frequency: w. (Tue.) Page Size: broadsheet. Subscrip. Rate: $.75 newsstand/cover; $26/yr mailed in county; $30/yr mailed in state; $38/yr mailed out of state. Adv. Rate: col. inch $5 Circulation: 1,990 per issue (paid and free). **Owner(s):** Index Printing, Inc., 307 W. Main St., Ada, MN 56510. Telephone: 218-784-2541. FAX: 218-784-2551. **Management:** Ross D. Pfund, Publisher. **Editorial:** Tim Halle, Editor.

Weeklies

ADAMS

MONITOR REVIEW, THE. 318 W. Main St., Adams, MN 55909-0283. Telephone: 507-582-3542. FAX: 507-582-3542. E-MAIL: monitor@omnitelcom.com. Mailing Address: PO Box 283, Adams, MN 55909-0283. Pub. Frequency: w. (Thu.) Page Size: standard. Subscrip. Rate: $.75 newsstand/cover. **Owner(s):** Bob Adams, 318 W. Main St., Adams, MN. Telephone: 507-582-3542. **Management:** Bob Adams, Publisher. **Editorial:** Bob Adams, Editor.

ADRIAN

NOBLES COUNTY REVIEW. 108 Maine Ave., Adrian, MN 56110-0160. Telephone: 507-483-2219. FAX: 507-483-2219. E-MAIL: ncreview@prairie.lakes.com. URL: http://www.noblescountyreview.net. Pub. Frequency: w. (Wed) Page Size: standard. Subscrip. Rate: $100 newsstand/cover; $25/yr in county; $31/yr mailed elsewhere. Circulation: 1,500 per issue (paid). **Owner(s):** Jerry Johnson, See address and contact information above. **Management:** Jerry Johnson, Publisher. **Editorial:** Kathy Burzliss, Editor.

AITKIN

AITKIN INDEPENDENT AGE. 213 Minnesota Ave., N., Aitkin, MN 56431-0259. Telephone: 218-927-3761. FAX: 218-927-3763. E-MAIL: age@aitkinage.com. URL: http://www.aitkinage.com. Mailing Address: PO Box 259, Aitkin, MN 56431-0259. Year Established: 1883. Pub. Frequency: w. (Wed.) Page Size: broadsheet. Subscrip. Rate: $30/yr local; $35/yr out of county; $41/yr out of state. Adv. Rate: col. inch $10.15 Circulation: 5,241 per issue (paid). **Owner(s):** Dick Norlander, PO Box 259, Aitkin, MN 56431. Telephone: 218-927-3761. **Management:** Dick Norlander, Publisher. Roxanne Bovley, Advertising Manager. Sharon Dotzler, Circulation Manager. Bonnie Williams, Classified Adv. Mgr.. **Editorial:** Dick Norlander, Editor.

ALBANY

STEARNS-MORRISON ENTERPRISE. 561 Railroad Ave, Albany, MN 56307-0310. Telephone: 320-845-2700. FAX: 320-845-4805. E-MAIL: aenterprise@means.net. URL: http://www.albanyenterprise.com. Mailing Address: PO Box 310, Albany, MN 56307-0310. Pub. Frequency: w. (Tue.) Page Size: broadsheet. Subscrip. Rate: $.60 newsstand/cover; $25/yr in state; $35/yr out of state. **Owner(s):** American Community Newspapers LLC, See address and contact information above. **Management:** Richard Raeker, General Manager. Don Larson, Publisher. Richard Raeker, Advertising Manager. **Editorial:** Mike Kosik, Editor.

ALBERT LEA

FREEBORN COUNTY SHOPPER. 1100 Pearl, Albert Lea, MN 56007. Telephone: 507-373-1310.FAX: 507-373-4253 Pub. Frequency: w. Circulation: 17,900 per issue (free). **Owner(s):** Boone Newspapers, Inc., P.O. Box 1108, Albert Lea, MN 56007. 15222 Freemen's Bend Rd., Northport, AL 35475. Telephone: 205-330-4100. **Management:** Dennis Raiche, General Manager.

ALDEN

ALDEN ADVANCE. ISSN 0898-526X
150 E. Main St., Alden, MN 56009. Telephone: 507-874-3440. FAX: 507-874-3440. E-MAIL: aldenadv@lakes.com. Pub. Frequency: w. (Thu.) Page Size: broadsheet. Subscrip. Rate: $.50 newsstand/cover. Adv. Rate: col. inch $3.30 Circulation: 800 per issue (paid). **Owner(s):** David Gehrke, PO Box 485, Alden, MN 56009-0485. Telephone: 507-874-3440. **Management:** David Gehrke, Publisher. **Editorial:** Tami Oldfather, Writer.

ALEXANDRIA

ECHO PRESS, THE. 225 Seventh Ave., E., Alexandria, MN 56308-0549. Telephone: 320-763-3133. FAX: 320-763-3258. E-MAIL: echo@echopress.com. URL: http://www.echopress.com. Mailing Address: PO Box 549, Alexandria, MN 56308-0549. Year Established: 1875. Pub. Frequency: s-w. (Wed. & Fri.) Page Size: broadsheet. Subscrip. Rate: $.75 newsstand/cover; $50/yr local; $57/yr mailed out of area; $63/yr mailed out of state. Adv. Rate: col. inch $10 Circulation: 10,600 per issue (paid). **Owner(s):** Jeff Meyer, 101 Fifth St., N., Fargo, ND 58102. Telephone: 701-235-7311. **Management:** Jody Hanson, Publisher. Lynn Moundson, Circulation Manager. Diann Drew, Business Manager. **Editorial:** Al Edenloff, Editor. Tara Bitzan, Lifestyle Editor. Larry Holverson, Sports Editor.

LAKELAND SHOPPING GUIDE. 225 Seventh Ave., E., Alexandria, MN 56308-0549. Telephone: 320-763-3133. FAX: 320-763-3258. URL: http://www.echopress.com. Mailing Address: PO Box 549, Alexandria, MN 56308-0549. Pub. Frequency: w. (Sun.) Page Size: tabloid. Subscrip. Rate: $53/yr mailed in state. Circulation: 28,000 per issue (controlled). **Owner(s):** Jeff Meyer, 101 Fifth St., N., Fargo, ND 58102. Telephone: 701-235-7311. **Management:** Jody Hanson, Publisher. **Editorial:** Al Edenloff, Editor. Larry Holverson, Sports Editor.

ANNANDALE

ANNANDALE ADVOCATE. 73 Oak Ave., S., Annandale, MN 55302-1205. Telephone: 320-274-3052. FAX: 320-274-2301. E-MAIL: advocate@llakedale.net. URL: http://www.annandalearea.com. Year Established: 1888. Pub. Frequency: w. (Wed.) Page Size: tabloid.Subscrip. Rate: $30/yr in state; $36/yr elsewhere Circulation: 2,750 per issue (paid). **Owner(s):** Annandale Advocate, 73 Oak Ave. S.., Annandale, MN 55302. Telephone: 329-274-3052. **Management:** Sharon Schumacher, Publisher. Marlene Young, Advertising Manager. **Editorial:** Chuck Sterling, Editor.

APPLETON

APPLETON PRESS. 241 W. Snelling Ave., Appleton, MN 56208-1367. Telephone: 320-289-1323. FAX: 320-289-2702. E-MAIL: apress@maxminn.com. Pub. Frequency: w. (Wed.) Page Size: standard. Subscrip. Rate: $.75 newsstand/cover; $25/yr local; $27/yr in state; $29/yr out of state. **Owner(s):** Appleton Press, See address and contact information above. **Management:** Loren Johnson, Publisher. **Editorial:** Leslie Ehrenberg, Editor.

ARLINGTON

ARLINGTON ENTERPRISE. 402 W. Alden St., Arlington, MN 55307. Telephone: 507-964-5547. FAX: 507-964-5547. E-MAIL: agiesenpublisher@frontier.net. Pub. Frequency: w. (Thu.) Page Size: broadsheet. Subscrip. Rate: $.75 newsstand/cover; $30/yr in county. Circulation: 1,700 per issue (paid). **Owner(s):** Alan Giesen, 83, Arlington, MN 55307-0083. **Management:** Alan Giesen, Publisher. **Editorial:** Kurt Menk, Editor.

SIBLEY SHOPPER. 405 W. Main St., Arlington, MN 55307. Telephone: 507-964-2423. Pub. Frequency: w. (Sun.) Page Size: tabloid. Circulation: 7,200 per issue (controlled and free). **Owner(s):** McLeod Publishing, Inc., See address and contact information above. **Management:** William Ramige, Publisher. Sue Colden, Advertising. **Editorial:** Rich Glennie, Editor.

ASKOV

ASKOV AMERICAN. PO Box 275, Askov, MN 55704. Telephone: 320-838-3151. FAX: 320-838-3152. E-MAIL: askovam1@ecenet.com. Year Established: 1914. Pub. Frequency: w. (Thu.) Page Size: broadsheet. Subscrip. Rate: $.75 newsstand/cover; $28/yr in county; $32/yr out of county. Adv. Rate: col. inch $5.25 Circulation: 2,000 per issue (paid). **Owner(s):** Marlana Benzie-Lourey, See address and contact information above. **Management:** Marlana Benzie-Lourey, Publisher. **Editorial:** Marlana Benzie-Lourey, Editor.

AUSTIN

MOWER COUNTY SHOPPER. 3405 W. Oakland, Austin, MN 55912. Telephone: 507-437-7731. FAX: 507-437-7733. Mailing Address: PO Box 522, Austin, MN 55912-0522. Pub. Frequency: w. (Tue.) Page Size: standard Circulation: 20,000 per issue (free). **Owner(s):** Boone Newspapers, Inc., 15222 Freemen's Bend Rd., Northport, AL 35475. Telephone: 205-330-4100. **Management:** Julia Thompson, General Manager.

MOWER COUNTY SHOPPING NEWS. 310 N E Second St., Austin, MN 55912. Telephone: 507-433-8851. FAX: 507-437-8644. E-MAIL: newsroom@austindailyherald.comra. URL: http://www.austindailyherald.com. Mailing Address: PO Box 578, Austin, MN 55912.Pub. Frequency: w. (Fri.) Circulation: 10,000 per issue (free). **Owner(s):** Boone Newspapers, Inc., 15222 Freemen's Bend Rd., Northport, AL 35475. Telephone: 205-330-4100. **Management:** Kevin True, Publisher. **Editorial:** Bryan Clapper, Managing Editor. Matt Steichen, Sports Editor.

BALATON

BALATON PRESS-TRIBUNE. PO Box 310, Balaton, MN 56115. Telephone: 507-734-5421. FAX: 507-734-5457. E-MAIL: balatonpublishing@yahoo.com. Pub. Frequency: w. (Wed.) Page Size: broadsheet. Subscrip. Rate: $.50 newsstand/cover; $28/yr in county; $35/yr out of county; $40/yr out of state. Circulation: 1,000 per issue (paid). **Owner(s):** Seth Schmidt, See address and contact information above. **Management:** Seth Schmidt, Publisher. **Editorial:** Beth Stubbe, Editor.

BARNESVILLE

BARNESVILLE RECORD REVIEW. 424 Front St. S, Barnesville, MN 56514-3607. Telephone: 218-354-2606. FAX: 218-354-2246. E-MAIL: newsrecordreview@buillemn.net. Mailing Address: PO Box 70, Barnesville, MN 56514-0070. Pub. Frequency: w. (Mon.) Page Size: standard. Subscrip. Rate: $1 newsstand/cover; $25/yr in county; $28/yr out of county; $30/yr out of state. Adv. Rate: col. inch $7.50 Circulation: 2,000 per issue (paid). **Owner(s):** Papermakers Inc., See address and contact information above. **Management:** Eugene A. Prim, Publisher. **Editorial:** Eugene A. Prim, Editor.

BATTLE LAKE

BATTLE LAKE REVIEW. 114 Lake Ave. N., Battle Lake, MN 56515. Telephone: 218-864-5952. FAX: 218-864-5212. E-MAIL: blreview@arvig.net. Mailing Address: PO Box 99, Battle Lake, MN 56515-0099. Pub. Frequency: w. (Wed.) Page Size: broadsheet. Subscrip. Rate: $.75 newsstand/cover; $25/yr mailed in county; $29/yr mailed out of county; $34/yr mailed out of state. Circulation: 2,300 per issue (paid). **Owner(s):** Jon A. Tamke, PO Box 99, Battle Lake, MN 56515-0099. Telephone: 218-864-5952. **Management:** Jon A. Tamke, Publisher. **Editorial:** Jon A. Tamke, Editor.

BAUDETTE

BAUDETTE REGION, THE. 107 Main Ave., N., Baudette, MN 56623-0240. Telephone: 218-634-1722. FAX: 218-634-1224. E-MAIL: baudetteregion@wiktel.com. Mailing Address: Drawer C, Baudette, MN 56623-0240. Year Established: 1902. Pub. Frequency: w. (Tue.) Page Size: broadsheet. Subscrip. Rate: $.50 newsstand/cover; $24.25/yr local; $30.25/yr mailed out of area. Adv. Rate: col. inch $5.25 Circulation: 2,350 per issue (paid). **Owner(s):** North Star Publishing Co., 1602 Hwy 71, International Falls, MN 56649. Telephone: 218-285-7411. FAX: 218-285-7206. **Management:** Penny Mio, Publisher. **Editorial:** Penny Mio, Editor.

NORTHERN LIGHT, THE. 997 Main W., Baudette, MN 56623. Telephone: 218-634-2700. FAX: 218-634-2777. E-MAIL: norlight@wiktel.com. URL: http://www.rrv.net/page1pub. Mailing Address: PO Box 1134, Baudette, MN 56623. Year Established: 1902. Pub. Frequency: w. (Wed.) Page Size: broadsheet. Subscrip. Rate: $.50 newsstand/cover; $25/yr in county; $32/yr out of county. Circulation: 1,400 per issue (paid). **Owner(s):** Page 1 Publications, See address and contact information above. **Management:** Julie Nordine, Publisher. Delane Walker, Advertising Manager. **Editorial:** Teri Thompson, Managing Editor.

BECKER

SHERBURNE COUNTY CITIZEN, THE. 14054 Bank Street, Becker, MN 55308-0217. Telephone: 763-261-5880. FAX: 763-261-5884. E-MAIL: citizennewspaper@sherbtel.net. URL: http://www.citizennewspaper.com. Mailing Address: PO Box 217, Becker, MN 55306-0217. Pub. Frequency: w. (Sat.) Page Size: tabloid. Subscrip. Rate: $78/yr mailed. **Owner(s):** Citizen Inc., The, See address and contact information above. **Management:** Gary W. Meyer, General Manager. Mary Erikson, Advertising. Idonna Hunter, Sales Manager.

BELGRADE

OBSERVER (BELGRADE), THE. 303 Washburn Ave., Belgrade, MN 56312. Telephone: 320-254-8250. FAX: 320-254-3215. E-MAIL: observer@belgradearea.com. URL: http://www.belgradearea.com. Mailing Address: PO Box 279, Belgrade, MN 56312. Year Established: 1969. Pub. Frequency: w. (Wed.) Page Size: tabloid. Subscrip. Rate: $.50 newsstand/cover; $16/yr in county. Circulation: 1,133 per issue (controlled and free). **Owner(s):** Jim Lemmer, See address and contact information above. **Management:** Jim Lemmer, Publisher. Grace Strodtman, Advertising Manager. **Editorial:** Jim Lemmer, Editor.

BELLE PLAINE

BELLE PLAINE HERALD. 113 E. Main St., Belle Plaine, MN 56011-0007. Telephone: 952-873-2261. FAX: 952-873-2262. E-MAIL: bpherald@frontiernet.net. Year Established: 1882. Pub. Frequency: w. (Wed.) Page Size: broadsheet. Subscrip. Rate: $.75 newsstand/cover; $26/yr local; $30/yr elsewhere. Adv. Rate: col. inch $7.50 Circulation: 3,800 per issue (paid). **Owner(s):** C. Edward Townsend, See address and contact information above. **Management:** C. Edward Townsend, Publisher. **Editorial:** C. Edward Townsend, Editor.

BENSON

SWIFT COUNTY MONITOR-NEWS. 101 12th St., S., Benson, MN 56215. Telephone: 320-843-4111. FAX: 320-843-3246. URL: http://www.swiftcountymonitor.com. Year Established: 1887. Pub. Frequency: w. (Wed.) Page Size: broadsheet. Subscrip. Rate: $1 newsstand/cover; $30/yr local; $35/yr mailed in state. Circulation: 3,500 per issue (paid). **Owner(s):** Reed Anfinson, See address and contact information above. **Management:** Reed Anfinson, Publisher. Nancy Ridler, Advertising. **Editorial:** Reed Anfinson, Editor.

BIG LAKE

WEST SHERBURNE TRIBUNE. 29 Lake St., S., Big Lake, MN 55309-0276. Telephone: 763-263-3602. FAX: 763-263-8458. E-MAIL: westrib@sherbtel.net. URL: http://www.westsherburnetribune.com. Pub. Frequency: w. (Sat.) Page Size: tabloid. **Owner(s):** West Sherburne Tribune, See address and contact information above. **Management:** Gary W. Meyer, Publisher. **Editorial:** Gary W. Meyer, Editor.

BIRD ISLAND

BIRD ISLAND UNION. 750 Ash Ave., Bird Island, MN 55310. Telephone: 320-365-3266. FAX: 320-365-4506. E-MAIL: union@willmar.com. Mailing Address: PO Box 160, Bird Island, MN 55310. Year Established: 1881. Pub. Frequency: w. (Wed.) Page Size: broadsheet. Subscrip. Rate: $.75 newsstand/cover; $28/yr mailed in county; $32/yr mailed out of county; $37/yr mailed out of state. Circulation: 1,000 per issue (paid). **Owner(s):** Hubin Publishing, 201 Main St., Hector, MN. Telephone: 320-848-2248. FAX: 320-848-2249. **Management:** John Hubin, Publisher. Aaron Hubin, Advertising Manager. **Editorial:** Jake Dornseif, Editor.

BIWABIK

RANGE TIMES. 211 N. Main St., Biwabik, MN 55708-0169. Telephone: 218-865-6265. FAX: 218-865-7007. Year Established: 1901. Pub. Frequency: w. (Thu.) Page Size: standard. Subscrip. Rate: $.75 newsstand/cover; $24/yr in county; $27/yr elsewhere. Adv. Rate: col. inch $4.20 Circulation: 1,402 per issue (paid). **Owner(s):** GDA Publications Inc., See address and contact information above. **Management:** Gary Albertson, Publisher. Karen Larson, Advertising Manager.

BLACKDUCK

AMERICAN (FARGO), THE. ISSN 0747-0363
25 Main St., N.W., Blackduck, MN 56630. Telephone: 218-835-4211. FAX: 218-635-6992. Mailing Address: PO Box 100, Blackduck, MN 56630. Year Established: 19??. Pub. Frequency: w. (Sun.) Page Size: standard. Subscrip. Rate: $.50 newsstand/cover (effective 2005); $24/yr local (effective 2004); $26/yr mailed in state. Circulation: 1,100 per issue (paid). **Owner(s):** Jeff Meyer, 101 Fifth St., N., Fargo, ND 58102. Telephone: 701-235-7311. **Management:** Dennis Doeden, Publisher. Paula Bauman, Office Manager. **Editorial:** Karen Walker, Editor.

BLACKDUCK SHOPPER, THE. 25 Main St., N.W., Blackduck, MN 56630. Telephone: 218-835-4211. FAX: 218-635-6992. Mailing Address: PO Box 100, Blackduck, MN 56630.Pub. Frequency: w. (Sun.) Page Size: standard Circulation: 3,000 Sunday (free). **Owner(s):** Jeff Meyer, 101 Fifth St., N., Fargo, ND 58207. **Management:** Dennis Doeden, Publisher. Paula Bauman, Advertising Manager. **Editorial:** Karen Walker, Editor.

BLAINE

BLAINE BANNER. 12570 Raddison Rd., N.E., Blaine, MN 55449. E-MAIL: littlepaper@comcast.net. Year Established: 1985. Pub. Frequency: m. (1st Wed.) Page Size: tabloid. Subscrip. Rate: $24/yr. Circulation: 10,000 per issue (paid and free). **Owner(s):** Blaine Banner, See address and contact information above. **Management:** Marilyn Hamm, Publisher. **Editorial:** Marilyn Hamm, Editor.

BLUE EARTH

FARIBAULT COUNTY REGISTER. 125 N. Main St., Blue Earth, MN 56013. Telephone: 507-526-7324. FAX: 507-526-4080. E-MAIL: fcnews@bevcomm.net. URL: http://www.faribaultcountyregister.com. Mailing Address: PO Box 98, Blue Earth, MN 56013. Year Established: 1869. Pub. Frequency: w. (Mon.) Page Size: broadsheet. Subscrip. Rate: $1 newsstand/cover; $36/yr in county; $44/yr out of county. Circulation: 3,500 per issue (paid). **Owner(s):** Ogden Newspapers of Minnesota, Inc., 1500 Main St., Wheeling, WV 26003. Telephone: 304-233-0100. FAX: 304-233-0327. **Management:** Lori Nauman, Publisher. Amanda Wiltze, Circulation Manager. **Editorial:** Charles Hunt, Editor.

BOVEY

SCENIC RANGE NEWS. 314 Second St., Bovey, MN 55709. Telephone: 218-245-1422. Pub. Frequency: w. (Wed.) Page Size: tabloid. Subscrip. Rate: $.50 newsstand/cover; $20/yr in county; $30/yr out of county. Circulation: 1,800 per issue (paid). **Owner(s):** Ethel I. Deal, 3Bovey, MN 55709-0003. **Management:** L.L. Johnson, Publisher. **Editorial:** L.L. Johnson, Editor.

BROOTEN

BONANZA VALLEY VOICE. PO Box 280, Brooten, MN 56316. Telephone: 320-346-2400. FAX: 320-346-2400. E-MAIL: bonanzavalvoice@tds.net. Pub. Frequency: w. (Thu.) Page Size: broadsheet. Subscrip. Rate: $.50 newsstand/cover; $12/yr in county; $14/yr out of county. Circulation: 1,000 per issue (paid). **Owner(s):** Howard J. Johnson, See address and contact information above. **Management:** Howard J. Johnson, Publisher. **Editorial:** Howard J. Johnson, Editor. Jennifer Murphey, Assistant Editor.

BROWERVILLE

TODD COUNTY COUNTRY COURIER. 609 N Main St, Browerville, MN 56434. Telephone: 320-594-2911. FAX: 320-594-6111. E-MAIL: staff@bladepublishing.net. URL: http://www.tccourier.com. Mailing Address: PO Box 245, Browerville, MN 56438-0245.Pub. Frequency: m. Circulation: 1,750 per issue (free). **Owner(s):** Blade Publishing, See address and contact information above. **Management:** Aaron Quirt, General Manager. Peter Quirt, Owner. Karleen Peterson, Advertising. **Editorial:** Theresa Quirt, Editor.

BUFFALO

DRUMMER, THE. 108 Central Ave., Buffalo, MN 55313. Telephone: 763-682-1221. E-MAIL: business@thedrummer.com. URL: http://www.thedrummer.com. Year Established: 1971. Pub. Frequency: w. (Sun.) Page Size: broadsheet.Subscrip. Rate: $29/yr out of area Circulation: 50,000 per issue (free). **Owner(s):** James P. McDonnell, Jr., See address and contact information above. **Management:** James McDonnell Jr. Jr., Publisher. James McDonnell III III, Advertising. **Editorial:** James McDonnell Jr. Jr., Editor. Ed DuBois, News Editor.

WRIGHT COUNTY JOURNAL-PRESS. 108 Central Ave., Buffalo, MN 55313-0159. Telephone: 763-682-1221. FAX: 763-682-5458. E-MAIL: business@thedrummer.com. URL: http://www.thedrummer.com. Mailing Address: PO Box 159, Buffalo, MN 55313-0159. Year Established: 1887. Pub. Frequency: w. (Thu.) Page Size: broadsheet. Subscrip. Rate: $1 newsstand/cover; $31/yr mailed in state; $39/yr mailed out of state. Circulation: 5,850 per issue (paid). **Owner(s):** James P. McDonnell, Jr., 108 Central Ave., Buffalo, MN 55313. Telephone: 763-682-1221. **Management:** James McDonnell Jr. Jr., Publisher. James McDonnell III III, Advertising. **Editorial:** James McDonnell Jr. Jr., Editor. Ed DuBois, News Editor. Tim Kolehmainen, Sports.

BURNSVILLE

APPLE VALLEY THISWEEK. 12190 County Rd. 11, Burnsville, MN 55337. Telephone: 952-894-1111. FAX: 952-846-2010. URL: http://www.thisweek-online.com. Pub. Frequency: w. (Sat.) Page Size: tabloid Circulation: 15,000 per issue (free). **Owner(s):** ECM Publishers, Inc., 4095 Coon Rapids Blvd., Coon Rapids, MN 55433. Telephone: 763-712-2400. **Management:** Eric Olson, General Manager. Diane Henningen, Classified Adv. Mgr.. Cindy Clay, Sales Manager. **Editorial:** Tad Johnson, Managing Editor. Brett Anderson, News Editor.

BURNSVILLE THISWEEK. 12190 County Rd. 11, Burnsville, MN 55337. Telephone: 952-894-1111. E-MAIL: editor.thisweek@ecm-inc.com. URL: http://www.thisweek-online.com. Pub. Frequency: w. (Sat.) Page Size: tabloid. Circulation: 16,000 per issue (paid and free). **Owner(s):** ECM Publishers, Inc., 4095 Coon Rapids Blvd., Coon Rapids, MN 55433. Telephone: 763-712-2400. **Management:** Eric Olson, General Manager. Cindy Clay, Sales Manager. **Editorial:** John Gessner, Editor. Tad Johnson, Managing Editor.

DAKOTA COUNTY TRIBUNE. ISSN 8750-2895
12190 County Rd. 11, Burnsville, MN 55337. Telephone: 952-894-1111. E-MAIL: ads.thisweek@ecm.-inc.com. URL: http://www.thisweek-online.com. Year Established: 1884. Pub. Frequency: w. (Thu.) Page Size: tabloid.Subscrip. Rate: $.50 newsstand/cover; $24/yr Circulation: 1,097 per issue (paid). **Owner(s):** ECM Publishers, Inc., 4095 Coon Rapids Blvd., Coon Rapids, MN 55433. Telephone: 763-712-2400. **Management:** Eric Olson, General Manager. Craig Anderson, Circulation Manager. Cindy Clay, Sales Manager. **Editorial:** Tad Johnson, Managing Editor.

EAGAN THISWEEK. 12190 County Rd. 11, Burnsville, MN 55337. Telephone: 952-894-1111. E-MAIL: editor.thisweek@ecm-inc.com. URL: http://www.thisweek-online.com. Pub. Frequency: w. (Sat.) Page Size: tabloid. Circulation: 13,000 per issue (paid and free). **Owner(s):** ECM Publishers, Inc., 4095 Coon Rapids Blvd., Coon Rapids, MN 55433. Telephone: 763-712-2400. **Management:** Eric Olson, General Manager. Cindy Clay, Sales Manager. **Editorial:** Erin Johnson, Editor. Tad Johnson, Managing Editor. Todd Abeln, Sports Editor.

FARMINGTON THISWEEK. 12190 County Rd. 11, Burnsville, MN 55337. Telephone: 952-894-1111. E-MAIL: editor.thisweek@ecm-inc.com. URL: http://www.thisweek-online.com. Pub. Frequency: w. (Sat.) Page Size: tabloid. Circulation: 26,000 per issue (paid and free). **Owner(s):** ECM Publishers, Inc., 4095 Coon Rapids Blvd., Coon Rapids, MN 55433. Telephone: 763-712-2400. **Management:** Eric Olson, General Manager. Cindy Clay, Sales Manager. **Editorial:** Aaron Tinklenberg, Editor. Tad Johnson, Managing Editor. Todd Abeln, Sports Editor.

LAKEVILLE THISWEEK. 12190 County Rd. 11, Burnsville, MN 55337. Telephone: 952-894-1111. FAX: 952-846-2010. E-MAIL: editor.thisweek@ecm-inc.com. URL: http://www.thisweek-online.com. Year Established: 1979. Pub. Frequency: w. (Sat.) Page Size: tabloid.Adv. Rate: col. inch $15.50 Circulation: 26,000 per issue (paid and free). **Owner(s):** ECM Publishers, Inc., 4095 Coon Rapids Blvd., Coon Rapids, MN 55433. Telephone: 763-421-2400. **Management:** Eric Olson, General Manager. Craig Anderson, Circulation Manager. Cindy Clay, Sales Manager. **Editorial:** John Sucansky, Editor. Tad Johnson, Managing Editor. Todd Abeln, Sports Editor.

ROSEMOUNT THISWEEK. 12190 County Rd. 11, Burnsville, MN 55337. Telephone: 952-894-1111. E-MAIL: editor.thisweek@ecm-inc.com. URL: http://www.thisweek-online.com. Pub. Frequency: w. (Sat.) Page Size: tabloid. Circulation: 16,000 per issue (paid and free). **Owner(s):** ECM Publishers, Inc., 4095 Coon Rapids Blvd., Coon Rapids, MN 55433. Telephone: 763-712-2400. **Management:** Eric Olson, General Manager. Cindy Clay, Sales Manager. **Editorial:** John Sucansky, Editor. Tad Johnson, Managing Editor.

BYRON

BYRON REVIEW. 505 E. Frontage Rd., Byron, MN 55920. Telephone: 507-775-6180. FAX: 507-374-9327. E-MAIL: byronreview@frontiernet.com. Pub. Frequency: w. (Tues.) Page Size: broadsheet. Subscrip. Rate: $.75 newsstand/cover; $36/yr in county; $39/yr mailed out of county. Circulation: 2,000 per issue (paid). **Owner(s):** Larry & Melanie Dobson, See address and contact information above. **Management:** Larry Dobson, Publisher. **Editorial:** Melanie Dobson, Editor.

CALEDONIA

CALEDONIA ARGUS, THE. 314 W Lincoln St, Caledonia, MN 55921. E-MAIL: editor.argus@ecm-inc.com. URL: http://www.hometownargus.com. Mailing Address: PO Box 227, Caledonia, MN 55921-0227. Pub. Frequency: w. (Wed.) Page Size: standard. Subscrip. Rate: $1 newsstand/cover; $39/yr local; $41/yr elsewhere. Adv. Rate: col. inch $6.98 Circulation: 2,150 per issue. **Owner(s):** ECM Publishers, Inc., 4095 Coon Rapids Blvd., Coon Rapids, MN 55433. Telephone: 763-712-2400.

CAMBRIDGE

ISANTI COUNTY NEWS. 234 S. Main St., Cambridge, MN 55008-0352. Telephone: 763-689-1981. FAX: 763-689-4372. E-MAIL: editor.countynews@ecm-inc.com. URL: http://www.isanticountynews.com. Mailing Address: 234 Main St S., Cambridge, MN 55008-1643. Year Established: 1900. Pub. Frequency: w. (Wed.) Page Size: broadsheet. Subscrip. Rate: $.75 newsstand/cover; $45/yr; $40/yr to senior citizens. Adv. Rate: col. inch $10.10 Circulation: 12,500 per issue. **Owner(s):** ECM Publishers, Inc., 4095 Coon Rapids Blvd., Coon Rapids, MN 55433. Telephone: 763-712-2400. **Management:** Marge Winkelman, General Manager. Julian Andersen, Publisher. Tonya Orbeck, Classified Editor. **Editorial:** Jon Tatting, Editor. Greg Hunt, Sports.

SCOTSMAN, THE. 234 Main St. S., Cambridge, MN 55008. Telephone: 763-689-1981. FAX: 763-689-4372. E-MAIL: class.cambridge@ecm-inc.com. Mailing Address: 234 Main St S., Cambridge, MN 55008-1643. Pub. Frequency: w. (Sun.) Page Size: tabloid.Adv. Rate: col. inch $20.80 Circulation: 56,000 per issue. **Owner(s):** ECM Publishers, Inc., 4095 Coon Rapids Blvd., Coon Rapids, MN 55433. Telephone: 763-712-2400. **Management:** Marge Winkelman, General Manager.

SCOTSMAN (RUM RIVER AREA). 234 S. Main St., Cambridge, MN 55008. Telephone: 763-689-1981. FAX: 763-689-4372. E-MAIL: editor@ecm-inc.com. Mailing Address: 234 Main St S., Cambridge, MN 55008-1643. Pub. Frequency: w. (Sun.) Page Size: broadsheet. Subscrip. Rate: $50/yr mailed out of county 3rd class; $150/yr mailed out of county 1st class. Circulation: 55,000 per issue (paid and free). **Owner(s):** ECM Publishers, Inc., 4095 Coon Rapids Blvd., Coon Rapids, MN 55433. Telephone: 763-712-2400. **Management:** Elmer L. Anderson, Publisher. **Editorial:** Marge Winkelman, Editor.

CANBY

CANBY NEWS. PO Box 129, Canby, MN 56220. Telephone: 507-223-5303. Year Established: 1878. Pub. Frequency: w. (Wed.) Page Size: broadsheet. Subscrip. Rate: $.75 newsstand/cover; $26/yr mailed in county; $30/yr mailed out of county. Circulation: 3,900 per issue (paid). **Owner(s):** Don & Ellie Beman, See address and contact information above. **Management:** Don Beman, Co-Publisher. **Editorial:** Don Beman, Editor.

CANNON FALLS

CANNON FALLS BEACON. 120 S. Fourth St., Cannon Falls, MN 55009. Telephone: 507-263-3991. FAX: 507-263-2300. E-MAIL: beacon@cannonfalls.com. URL: http://www.cannonfalls.com. Year Established: 1876. Pub. Frequency: w. (Thu.) Page Size: broadsheet. Subscrip. Rate: $1 newsstand/cover; $29/yr in county area; $33/yr mailed in state; $36/yr mailed out of state. Adv. Rate: col. inch $6.95 Circulation: 4,100 per issue (paid). **Owner(s):** Dick Dalton, See address and contact information above. **Management:** Dick Dalton, Publisher. Dave Templin, Advertising Manager. Jenny Rutter, Classified Adv. Mgr.. **Editorial:** Dick Dalton, Editor. Mike Dalton, News Editor.

CHANHASSEN

CHANHASSEN VILLAGER. 80 W. 78th St., Ste. 170, Chanhassen, MN 55317. Telephone: 952-934-5045. FAX: 952-934-7960. E-MAIL: editor@chanvillager.com. URL: http://www.chanvillager.com. Mailing Address: PO Box 99, Chanhassen, MN 55317-0099. Year Established: 1987. Pub. Frequency: w. (Thu.) Page Size: broadsheet. Subscrip. Rate: $25/yr domestic area; $28/yr in county; $41/yr in state; $25 for 6 mos. out of state. Adv. Rate: B&W page $828 Circulation: 5,000 per issue (paid and free). **Owner(s):** Southwest Suburban Publishing Co., PO Box 8, Shakopee, MN 55379. **Management:** Mark A. Weber, Publisher. Craig Theif, Advertising Manager. Laurie Hartmann, Classified Adv. Mgr.. **Editorial:** Richard Crawford, Editor. Tom Hoen, Sports Editor.

EDEN PRAIRIE NEWS. 80 W. 78th St., Ste. 170, Chanhassen, MN 55317. Telephone: 952-934-5045. FAX: 952-934-7960. E-MAIL: weber@swpub.com. URL: http://www.edenprairienews.com. Mailing Address: PO Box 44220, Eden Prairie, MN 55317. Pub. Frequency: w. (Thu.) Page Size: standard. Subscrip. Rate: $1 newsstand/cover; $25/yr local; $41/yr in state; $45/yr out of state. Circulation: 12,552 per issue (paid). **Owner(s):** Southwest Suburban Publishing Co., PO Box 8, Shakopee, MN 55379. **Management:** Mark A. Weber, Publisher. Craig Theif, Advertising Manager. Laurie Hartmann, Classified Adv. Mgr.. **Editorial:** Stuart Sudak, Editor. Kathy Nelson, News Editor. Daniel Huss, Sports Editor.

CHASKA

CHASKA HERALD. 123 W. Second St., Chaska, MN 55318. Telephone: 952-448-2650. FAX: 952-448-3146. E-MAIL: editor@chaskaherald.com. URL: http://www.chaskaherald.com. Mailing Address: PO Box 113, Chaska, MN 55318. Year Established: 1863. Pub. Frequency: w. (Thu.) Page Size: broadsheet. Subscrip. Rate: $1 newsstand/cover; $28/yr mailed in county; $41/yr mailed out of county; $45/yr mailed out of state. Adv. Rate: col. inch $6.95 Circulation: 4,700 per issue (paid). **Owner(s):** Southwest Suburban Publishing Co., PO Box 8, Shakopee, MN 55379. **Management:** Stan Rolfsrud, Publisher. Craig Theif, Advertising Manager. **Editorial:** Robert Siegel, Editor.

CHATFIELD

CHATFIELD NEWS. 13 S.E. Third St., Ste. 4, Chatfield, MN 55923-1372. Telephone: 507-867-3870. FAX: 507-867-3870. E-MAIL: news@thechatfieldnews.com. Year Established: 1856. Pub. Frequency: w. (Tue.) Page Size: standard. Subscrip. Rate: $.50 newsstand/cover; $26/yr local; $29/yr snowbirds; $32/yr elsewhere. Adv. Rate: col. inch $5,075 Circulation: 2,500 per issue (paid). **Owner(s):** David Phillips, See address and contact information above. **Management:** David Phillips, Publisher. **Editorial:** David Phillips, Editor.

CHISHOLM

CHISHOLM TRIBUNE PRESS, THE. 327 W. Lake St., Chisholm, MN 55719. Telephone: 218-254-4432. FAX: 218-254-7141. E-MAIL: tribune@mx3.com. Year Established: 1947. Pub. Frequency: w. (Wed.) Page Size: broadsheet. Subscrip. Rate: $.50 newsstand/cover; $24/yr in county; $28/yr mailed out of county; $30/yr mailed out of state. Adv. Rate: col. inch $4.85 Freelance Pay: $10/article. Circulation: 2,300 per issue (paid). **Owner(s):** Superior Publishing Corp., 1105 Tower Ave., Superior, WI 54880-1502. **Management:** Wanda Moeller, Publisher. **Editorial:** Brian K. Anderson, Editor.

CLARA CITY

CLARA CITY HERALD. 34 E. Center Ave., Clara City, MN 56222-0458. Telephone: 320-847-3130. E-MAIL: ccherald@hcinet.net. Year Established: 1896. Pub. Frequency: w. (Wed.) Page Size: standard. Subscrip. Rate: $.75 newsstand/cover; $26/yr home delivery local; $28/yr mailed in state; $33/yr mailed elsewhere. **Owner(s):** T. J. Almen, See address and contact information above. **Management:** T. J. Almen, Publisher. **Editorial:** John White, Editor.

CLARISSA

INDEPENDENT NEWS HERALD. ISSN 1065-0628
310 W. Main St., Clarissa, MN 56440-0188. Telephone: 218-756-2131. FAX: 218-756-2126. E-MAIL: jeremy@inhnews.com. URL: http://www.inhnews.com. Mailing Address: PO Box 188, Clarissa, MN 56440-0188. Year Established: 1891. Pub. Frequency: w. (Tue.) Page Size: broadsheet. Subscrip. Rate: $.75 newsstand/cover; $25/yr local; $32/yr mailed in state; $38/yr mailed out of state. Adv. Rate: col. inch $5 Circulation: 2,600 per issue (paid). **Owner(s):** Ray Benning, 310 W. Main St., Clarissa, MN 56440. Telephone: 218-756-2131. FAX: 218-756-2126. **Management:** Marlo Benning, Publisher. **Editorial:** Ray Benning, Editor.

CLINTON

NORTHERN STAR, THE. 128 Main St., Clinton, MN 56225-0368. Telephone: 320-325-5152. FAX: 320-325-5280. E-MAIL: northernstar@mchsi.com. Mailing Address: PO Box 368, Clinton, MN 56225-0368. Year Established: 1965. Pub. Frequency: w. (Thu.) Page Size: broadsheet. Subscrip. Rate: $.75 newsstand/cover; $30/yr in county; $35/yr in state; $40/yr out of state. Adv. Rate: col. inch $4.50 Circulation: 1,950 per issue (paid). **Owner(s):** Kaercher Publications, Inc., See address and contact information above. **Management:** James D. Kaercher, Publisher. Denese Gustafson, Advertising Manager. **Editorial:** Lois Torgerson, Managing Editor.

CLOQUET

PINE JOURNAL. 813 Cloquet Ave., Cloquet, MN 55720. Telephone: 218-879-1950. FAX: 218-879-6696. E-MAIL: journalt@cloquetmn.com. URL: http://www.cloquetmn.com. Year Established: 1884. Pub. Frequency: s-w. (Wed. & Sat.) Page Size: broadsheet. Subscrip. Rate: $.75 newsstand/cover; $29/yr mailed in county; $35/yr mailed in state; $42.31/yr mailed out of state. Circulation: 3,500 per issue (paid). **Owner(s):** Superior Publishing Corp., 1105 Tower Ave, Superior, WI 54880. Telephone: 715-395-5725. FAX: 715-395-5729. **Management:** Wendy Johnson, Publisher. **Editorial:** Mike Sylvester, Editor. Kathy Clampitt, Circulation Editor.

COKATO

ENTERPRISE DISPATCH. 185 Third St. S. W., Cokato, MN 55321. Telephone: 320-286-2118. FAX: 320-286-2119. E-MAIL: news@dasselcokato.com. URL: http://www.dasselcokato.com. Mailing Address: PO Box 969, Cokato, MN 55321-0969. Year Established: 1884. Pub. Frequency: w. (Mon) Page Size: broadsheet. Subscrip. Rate: $1 newsstand/cover; $32/yr in county; $37/yr in state; $42/yr out of state. Adv. Rate: col. inch $7.45 Circulation: 3,100 per issue (paid). **Owner(s):** JEB Co. LLC, See address and contact information above. **Management:** Tom Hauer, Publisher. Sheila Rieke, Advertising Manager. **Editorial:** Dori Moudry, Editor. Bob Bradford, Sports Editor.

COLD SPRING

COLD SPRING RECORD. 403 West Wind Ct., Cold Spring, MN 56320-0456. Telephone: 320-685-8621. FAX: 320-685-8885. E-MAIL: csrecord@mcleodusa.net. Mailing Address: PO Box 456, Cold Spring, MN 56320. Pub. Frequency: w. (Tue.) Page Size: standard. Subscrip. Rate: $.65 newsstand/cover; $19/yr local; $21/yr elsewhere. **Owner(s):** Mike Austreng, See address and contact information above. **Management:** Mike Austreng, Publisher. **Editorial:** Mike Austreng, Editor.

COLUMBIA HEIGHTS

ARDEN HILLS/FALCON HEIGHTS/ROSEVILLE FOCUS NEWS. 3989 Central Ave NE #200, Columbia Heights, MN 55421. Telephone: 763-706-0890. FAX: 763-706-0891. E-MAIL: info@mnsunpub.com. URL: http://www.mnnews.com. Year Established: 1985. Pub. Frequency: w. (Thu.) Page Size: tabloid. Subscrip. Rate: $85/yr mailed. Adv. Rate: B&W page $775 Circulation: 16,442 per issue (free). **Owner(s):** Focus Newspapers, See address and contact information above. **Management:** Gene Carr, Publisher. Heather Junkert, Advertising. Anita Bednarek, Advertising Manager. Herb Hesse, Circulation Manager. **Editorial:** Yvonne Klinnert, Executive Editor. Paul Rignell, Managing Editor. Pete Agren, Sports.

COLUMBIA HEIGHTS/FRIDLEY FOCUS NEWS. 3989 Central Ave NE #200, Columbia Heights, MN 55421. Telephone: 763-706-0890. FAX: 763-706-0891. E-MAIL: info@mnsunpub.com. URL: http://www.mnnews.com. Pub. Frequency: w. (Thu.) Page Size: tabloid. Subscrip. Rate: $85/yr mailed. Adv. Rate: B&W page $1,140 Circulation: 19,253 per issue (free). **Owner(s):** Focus Newspapers, See address and contact information above. **Management:** Gene Carr, Publisher. Joanna Ambrose, Office Manager. Anita Bednarek, Advertising Manager. Todd Aldridge, Circulation Manager. **Editorial:** Paul Rignell, Managing Editor.

SUN FOCUS, THE. 3989 Central Ave., NE, Columbia Heights, MN 55421. Telephone: 763-706-0890. FAX: 763-706-0891. E-MAIL: info@mnsunpub.com. URL: http://www.mnnews.com. Year Established: 1985. Pub. Frequency: w. (Thu.) Page Size: tabloid.Adv. Rate: B&W page $1,020 Circulation: 54,583 per issue (free). **Owner(s):** Sun Newspapers, See address and contact information above. **Management:** Gene Carr, Publisher. Joanna Ambrose, Office Manager. Anita Bednarek, Advertising. Todd Aldridge, Circulation Manager. Pamela Bolander, Art Director. **Editorial:** Paul Rignell, Managing Editor. Pete Agren, Sports.

SUN FOCUS NEWS. 3989 Central Ave NE #200, Columbia Heights, MN 55421. Telephone: 763-706-0890. FAX: 763-706-0891. E-MAIL: info@mnsunpub.com. URL: http://www.mnnews.com. Pub. Frequency: w. (Thu.) Page Size: tabloid. Subscrip. Rate: $85/yr mailed. Adv. Rate: B&W page $1,130 Circulation: 16,593 per issue (paid). **Owner(s):** Focus Newspapers, See address and contact information above. **Management:** Gene Carr, Publisher. Linda McIntyre, Office Manager. Anita Bednarek, Advertising. Howard Collins, Circulation Manager. Pamela Bolander, Art Director. **Editorial:** Tyra Novic Wahman, Editor. Paul Rignell, Reporter. Pete Agren, Sports.

COON RAPIDS

ANOKA COUNTY SHOPPER. 4095 Coon Rapids Blvd., Coon Rapids, MN 55433. Telephone: 763-712-2400. URL: http://www.abcnewspapers.com. Pub. Frequency: w. (Wed.) Page Size: standard. **Owner(s):** ECM Publishers, Inc., See address and contact information above. **Management:** Eric Olson, General Manager. Mike Johnson, Advertising Manager.

ANOKA COUNTY UNION. ISSN 1059-9525
4101 Coon Rapids Blvd., Coon Rapids, MN 55433. Telephone: 763-421-4444. FAX: 763-421-4315. E-MAIL: editor.anokaunion@ecm-inc.com. URL: http://www.abcnewspapers.com/. Mailing Address: PO Box 99, Anoka, MN 55303. Year Established: 1865. Pub. Frequency: w. (Fri.) Page Size: broadsheet. Subscrip. Rate: $.75 newsstand/cover; $30/yr mailed in state; $33/yr mailed out of state. Circulation: 5,800 per issue (paid). **Owner(s):** ECM Publishers, Inc., 4095 Coon Rapids Blvd., Coon Rapids, MN 55433. Telephone: 763-421-4444. FAX: 763-421-4315. **Management:** Eric Olson, General Manager. Julian Andersen, Publisher. Mike Johnson, Advertising Manager. **Editorial:** Larry A. Jones, Editor.

BLAINE-SPRING LAKE PARK LIFE. ISSN 1059-9533
4101 Coon Rapids Blvd., Coon Rapids, MN 55433. Telephone: 763-421-4444. FAX: 763-421-4315. URL: http://www.abcnewspapers.com. Mailing Address: PO Box 99, Anoka, MN 55303. Year Established: 1961. Pub. Frequency: w. (Fri.) Page Size: broadsheet. Subscrip. Rate: $.75 newsstand/cover; $30/yr mailed in state; $36/yr mailed out of state. Circulation: 2,100 per issue (paid). **Owner(s):** ECM Publishers, Inc., 4095 Coon Rapids Blvd., Coon Rapids, MN 55433. Telephone: 763-421-4444. FAX: 763-421-4315. **Management:** Eric Olson, General Manager. Julian Andersen, Publisher. Mike Johnson, Advertising Manager. **Editorial:** Sue Austreng, Editor.

COON RAPIDS HERALD. ISSN 1059-9541
4095 Coon Rapids Blvd., Coon Rapids, MN 55433. Telephone: 763-421-4444. FAX: 763-421-4315. E-MAIL: peterbodley@ecm-inc.com. URL: http://www.coonrapidsherald.com. Mailing Address: PO Box 99, Anoka, MN 55303. Year Established: 1875. Pub. Frequency: w. (Fri.) Page Size: broadsheet. Subscrip. Rate: $.75 newsstand/cover; $30/yr mailed in state; $36/yr mailed out of state. Circulation: 4,000 per issue (paid). **Owner(s):** ECM Publishers, Inc., See address and contact information above. **Management:** Eric Olson, General Manager. Julian Andersen, Publisher. Mike Johnson, Advertising Manager. **Editorial:** Peter G. Bodley, Managing Editor. Tom Yelle, Asst. Managing Ed..

COTTAGE GROVE

SOUTH WASHINGTON COUNTY BULLETIN. 7584 80th St. S., Cottage Grove, MN 55016-0099. Telephone: 651-459-3434. FAX: 651-459-9491. E-MAIL: editor@swcbulletin.com. URL: http://www.swcbulletin.com. Mailing Address: PO Box 99, Cottage Grove, MN 55016-0099. Year Established: 1958. Pub. Frequency: w. (Wed.) Page Size: standard. Subscrip. Rate: $30/yr out of county. Circulation: 119,800 per issue (paid and free). **Owner(s):** Jeff Meyer, 101 Fifth St., N., Fargo, ND 58102-0099. Telephone: 701-235-7311. **Management:** Jeff Patterson, General Manager. Steve Messick, Publisher. **Editorial:** Chad Hyelting, Editor.

COTTONWOOD

TRI-COUNTY NEWS (COTTONWOOD). 74 W Main, Cottonwood, MN 56229. Telephone: 507-423-6239. FAX: 507-423-6230. URL: http://www.gatehousemedia.com. Mailing Address: PO Box 76, Cottonwood, MN 56229-0076. Pub. Frequency: w. (Wed.) Page Size: broadsheet. Subscrip. Rate: $1 newsstand/cover; $30/yr in county. Circulation: 2,000 per issue (paid). **Owner(s):** GateHouse Media, Inc, 350 WillowBrook Office Park, Fairport, NY 14450. Telephone: 585-598-0030. **Editorial:** Jody Isaackson, Editor.

CROOKSTON

CROOKSTON VALLEY SHOPPER. 124 S. Broadway, Crookston, MN 56716. Telephone: 218-281-2730. FAX: 218-281-7234. URL: http://www.crookstontimes.com. Mailing Address: PO Box 615, Crookston, MN 56716. Pub. Frequency: w. (Thu.) Page Size: standard Circulation: 9,670 per issue (free). **Owner(s):** GateHouse Media, Inc, 350 WillowBrook Office Park, Fairport, NY 14450. Telephone: 585-598-0030. FAX: 585-248-2631. **Management:** Randal Hultgren, Publisher. Calvin Anderson, Advertising Manager. Carl Melbye, Circulation Manager. Janelle Brekken, Classified Adv. Mgr..

CROSBY

CROSBY-IRONTON COURIER. P.O. Box 67, Crosby, MN 56441-0067. E-MAIL: courier@emily.com. Year Established: 1911. Pub. Frequency: w. (wed.) Page Size: broadsheet. Subscrip. Rate: $.75 newsstand/cover; $30/yr local; $36/yr elsewhere. Adv. Rate: col. inch $10.40 Circulation: 4,150 per issue (paid). **Owner(s):** Thomas M. Swensen, 12 E. Main St., Crosby, MN 56441-0067. Telephone: 218-546-5029. FAX: 218-546-8352. **Management:** Lori J. LaBorde, Co-Publisher. Thomas M. Swensen, Publisher. **Editorial:** Dina McDonough, Managing Editor. Bill Swensen, Sports Editor.

DELANO

DELANO EAGLE. 265 N. River St., Ste. 109, Delano, MN 55328. Telephone: 763-972-6171. FAX: 763-972-6172. E-MAIL: news@pressnews.com. URL: http://www.pressnews.com. Mailing Address: PO Box 280, Osseo, MN 55369. Year Established: 1878. Pub. Frequency: w. (Mon.) Page Size: broadsheet. Subscrip. Rate: $1 newsstand/cover; $34/yr; $49 for 2 yrs.. Adv. Rate: col. inch $7.94 Circulation: 1,439 per issue (paid); 3,420 per issue (free). **Owner(s):** American Community Newspapers LLC, 10917 Valley View Rd., Eden Prairie, MN 55344. **Management:** Jeff Coolman, President. Bruce Treichler, Publisher. Bruce Pierce, Circulation Manager. **Editorial:** Jeff Borowicz, Managing Editor.

DETROIT LAKES

BECKER COUNTY RECORD. 511 Washington Ave., Detroit Lakes, MN 56501. Telephone: 218-847-3151. FAX: 218-847-9409. URL: http://www.dl-online.com. Mailing Address: PO Box 826, Detroit Lakes, MN 56502. Year Established: 1871. Pub. Frequency: w. (Wed.) Page Size: broadsheet. Subscrip. Rate: $1 newsstand/cover. Adv. Rate: col. inch $14 Circulation: 13,500 per issue (paid and free). **Owner(s):** Jeff Meyer, 101 Fifth St., N., Fargo, ND 58102. Telephone: 701-235-7311. **Management:** Dennis Winskowski, Publisher. Mary Brenk, Advertising Manager. Viola Anderson, Circulation Manager. **Editorial:** Nathan Bowe, Editor. Brian Wierima, Sports Editor.

DETROIT LAKES TRIBUNE. 511 Washington Ave., Detroit Lakes, MN 56501. Telephone: 218-847-3151. FAX: 218-847-9409. E-MAIL: dlpaper@dlprinting.com. URL: http://www.dl-online.com. Mailing Address: PO Box 826, Detroit Lakes, MN 56502. Year Established: 1907. Pub. Frequency: w. (Sun.) Page Size: broadsheet. Subscrip. Rate: $1 newsstand/cover; $32.50/yr mailed in county; $38/yr mailed out of county; $48/yr mailed in state. Adv. Rate: col. inch $14 Circulation: 7,000 per issue (paid). **Owner(s):** Jeff Meyer, 101 Fifth St., N., Fargo, ND 58102. Telephone: 701-235-7311. **Management:** Dennis Winskowski, Publisher. Mary Brenk, Advertising Manager. Viola Anderson, Circulation Manager. **Editorial:** Nathan Bowe, Editor. Brian Basham, Photo Editor. Brian Wierima, Sports Editor.

EAST GRAND FORKS

EXPONENT (EAST GRAND FORKS), THE. 910 Central Ave., N.E., East Grand Forks, MN 56721. Telephone: 218-773-2808. FAX: 218-773-9212. E-MAIL: tribune@grandforks.polaristel.net. URL: http://www.itv.net/page1pub. Mailing Address: PO Box 285, East Grand Forks, MN 56721. Year Established: 1902. Pub. Frequency: w. (Wed.) Page Size: broadsheet. Subscrip. Rate: $.75 newsstand/cover; $30/yr in county; $37/yr out of county. Circulation: 2,100 per issue (paid). **Owner(s):** Page 1 Publications, PO Box 1134, Baudette, MN 56623. Telephone: 218-634-2700. FAX: 218-634-2777. **Management:** Julie Nordine, Publisher. Gail Schrage, Advertising Manager. **Editorial:** Steve Gust, Editor.

EDEN PRAIRIE

APPLE VALLEY/ROSEMOUNT/EAGAN SUN-CURRENT. 10917 Valley View Rd., Eden Prairie, MN 55344-3730. E-MAIL: suncurrentsouth@mnsun.com. URL: http://www.mnsun.com. Year Established: 1975. Pub. Frequency: w. (Thu.) Page Size: tabloid. Subscrip. Rate: $.75 newsstand/cover; $84/yr mailed. Adv. Rate: B&W page $1,735 Circulation: 32,102 per issue (paid and free). **Owner(s):** American Community Newspapers LLC, See address and contact information above. **Management:** Jeff Coolman, Publisher. Herb Hesse, Circulation Manager. Krista Jech, Classified Adv. Mgr..

BLOOMINGTON SUN-CURRENT. 10917 Valley View Rd., Eden Prairie, MN 55344. Telephone: 952-392-6800. FAX: 952-392-6868. E-MAIL: suncurrentcentral@mnsun.com. URL: http://www.mnsun.com. Year Established: 1954. Pub. Frequency: w. (Thu.) Page Size: tabloid. Subscrip. Rate: $.75 newsstand/cover; $84/yr mailed 1st class. Adv. Rate: B&W page $1,915 Circulation: 29,510 per issue (paid and free). **Owner(s):** American Community Newspapers LLC, See address and contact information above. **Management:** Jeff Coolman, Publisher. Herb Hesse, Circulation Manager. **Editorial:** Harvey Rockwood, Editor. Peggy Bakken, Executive Editor. Greg Kleven, Sports Editor.

BROOKLYN CENTER/BROOKLYN PARK SUN POST. 10917 Valley View Rd., Eden Prairie, MN 55344. Telephone: 952-392-6800. FAX: 952-392-6868. E-MAIL: suninfo@mnsun.com. URL: http://www.mnsun.com. Year Established: 1956. Pub. Frequency: w. (Thu.) Page Size: tabloid. Subscrip. Rate: $.75 newsstand/cover; $84/yr mailed 1st class. Adv. Rate: B&W page $1,685 Circulation: 26,410 per issue (paid and free). **Owner(s):** American Community Newspapers LLC, See address and contact information above. **Management:** Jeff Coolman, Publisher. Herb Hesse, Circulation Manager. **Editorial:** Peggy Bakken, Executive Editor. Bill Jones, Photographer. Dave Pedersen, Sports.

BROOKLYN PARK SUN POST. 10917 Valley View Rd., Eden Prairie, MN 55344. Telephone: 952-392-6800. FAX: 952-392-6868. E-MAIL: suninfo@mnsun.com. URL: http://www.mnsun.com. Year Established: 1965. Pub. Frequency: w. (Thu.) Page Size: tabloid. Subscrip. Rate: $.75 newsstand/cover; $84/yr mailed. Adv. Rate: B&W page $1,770 Circulation: 16,357 per issue (paid and free). **Owner(s):** American Community Newspapers LLC, See address and contact information above. **Management:** Jeffrey Coolman, General Manager. Jeff Coolman, Publisher. Todd Aldrich, Circulation Manager. Krista Jech, Classified Adv. Mgr.. **Editorial:** Yvonne Klinnert, Executive Editor. Bill Jones, Photographer. Dave Pedersen, Sports.

BURNSVILLE/SAVAGE/LAKEVILLE SUN-CURRENT. 10917 Valley View Rd., Eden Prairie, MN 55344. Telephone: 952-392-6800. E-MAIL: suncurrentcentral@mnsun.com. URL: http://www.mnsun.com/. Year Established: 1976. Pub. Frequency: w. (Thu.) Page Size: tabloid. Subscrip. Rate: $.75 newsstand/cover; $84/yr mailed 1st class. Adv. Rate: B&W page $1,735 Circulation: 29,254 per issue (paid and free). **Owner(s):** American Community Newspapers LLC, See address and contact information above. **Management:** Jeff Coolman, Publisher. Pam Miller, Advertising Manager. Herb Hesse, Circulation Manager. **Editorial:** Lonny Goldsmith, Editor. Peggy Bakken, Executive Editor. Mike Shaughnessy, Sports.

EAGAN SUN-CURRENT. 10917 Valley View Rd., Eden Prairie, MN 55344. Telephone: 952-392-6800. E-MAIL: suncurrentcentral@mnsun.com. URL: http://www.mnsun.com. Pub. Frequency: w. (Thu.) Page Size: tabloid. Subscrip. Rate: $.75 newsstand/cover; $84/yr mailed 1st class. Adv. Rate: B&W page $1,820 Circulation: 17,000 per issue (paid and free). **Owner(s):** American Community Newspapers LLC, See address and contact information above. **Management:** Jeff Coolman, Publisher. **Editorial:** Joshua Nichols, Editor. Peggy Bakken, Executive Editor. Andy Blenkush, Photographer. Greg Kleven, Sports Editor.

EDEN PRAIRIE SUN-CURRENT. 10917 Valley View Rd., Eden Prairie, MN 55344. Telephone: 952-392-6800. FAX: 952-392-6868. E-MAIL: suncurrentcentral@mnsun.com. URL: http://www.mnsun.com. Year Established: 1932. Pub. Frequency: w. (Thu.) Page Size: tabloid. Subscrip. Rate: $.75 newsstand/cover; $84/yr mailed. Adv. Rate: B&W page $980 Circulation: 12,840 per issue (paid and free). **Owner(s):** American Community Newspapers LLC, See address and contact information above. **Management:** Jeff Coolman, Publisher. Herb Hesse, Circulation Manager. **Editorial:** Lynn Jerde, Editor. Peggy Bakken, Executive Editor. Greg Kleven, Sports Editor.

EDINA SUN-CURRENT. 10917 Valley View Rd., Eden Prairie, MN 55344. Telephone: 952-392-6800. FAX: 952-392-6868. E-MAIL: suncurrentcentral@mnsun.com. URL: http://www.mnsun.com/. Year Established: 1932. Pub. Frequency: w. (Thu.) Page Size: tabloid. Subscrip. Rate: $.75 newsstand/cover; $84/yr mailed 1st class. Adv. Rate: B&W page $1,410 Circulation: 16,800 per issue (paid and free). **Owner(s):** American Community Newspapers LLC, 624 Krona Dr., Ste. 107, Plano, TX 75074. Telephone: 972-398-4499. FAX: 972-398-4470. **Management:** Jeff Coolman, Publisher. Herb Hesse, Circulation Manager. **Editorial:** James Zwilling, Editor. Peggy Bakken, Executive Editor. John Sherman, Sports.

EXCELSIOR/SHOREWOOD/CHANHASSEN SUN-SAILOR. 10917 Valley View Rd., Eden Prairie, MN 55344. Telephone: 952-392-6800. FAX: 952-392-6868. E-MAIL: suncurrentcentral@mnsun.com. URL: http://www.mnsun.com/. Pub. Frequency: w. (Thu.) Page Size: tabloid. Subscrip. Rate: $.75 newsstand/cover; $84/yr mailed 1st class. Adv. Rate: B&W page $835 Circulation: 6,050 per issue (paid and free). **Owner(s):** American Community Newspapers LLC, See address and contact information above. **Management:** Jeff Coolman, Publisher. Herb Hesse, Circulation Manager. Scott Carr, Classified Adv. Mgr.. **Editorial:** Mike Hanks, Editor. Peggy Bakken, Executive Editor. Mike Erickson, Production Manager. Craig Lassig, Photographer. Greg Kleven, Sports Editor.

HOPKINS/EAST MINNETONKA SUN-SAILOR. 10917 Valley View Rd., Eden Prairie, MN 55344. Telephone: 952-392-6800. FAX: 952-392-6868. E-MAIL: suncurrentcoastal@mnsun.com. URL: http://www.mnsun.com/. Pub. Frequency: w. (Thu.) Page Size: tabloid. Subscrip. Rate: $.75 newsstand/cover; $84/yr mailed 1st class. Adv. Rate: B&W page $1,015 Circulation: 14,500 per issue (paid and free). **Owner(s):** American Community Newspapers LLC, See address and contact information above. **Management:** Jeff Coolman, Publisher. Herb Hesse, Circulation Manager. **Editorial:** Marc Ingber, Editor. Peggy Bakken, Executive Editor. Mike Erickson, Production Manager. Craig Lassig, Photographer. Nick Clark, Sports.

LAKEVILLE SUN-CURRENT. 10917 Valley View Rd., Eden Prairie, MN 55344. Telephone: 952-392-6800. FAX: 952-392-6868. E-MAIL: suncurrentcentral@mnsun.com. URL: http://www.mnsun.com. Year Established: 1975. Pub. Frequency: w. (Thu.) Page Size: tabloid. Subscrip. Rate: $.75 newsstand/cover; $84/yr mailed 1st class. Adv. Rate: B&W page $1,530 Circulation: 10,000 per issue (paid and free). **Owner(s):** American Community Newspapers LLC, See address and contact information above. **Management:** Jeff Coolman, President. Herb Hesse, Circulation Manager. **Editorial:** Mike Westholder, Managing Editor. Greg Kleven, Sports Editor.

MONTICELLO TIMES. 10917 Valley View Rd., Eden Prairie, MN 55344-3730. E-MAIL: monticellotimes@monticellotimes.com. URL: http://www.monticellotimes.com. Year Established: 1857. Pub. Frequency: w. (Thu.) Page Size: broadsheet. Subscrip. Rate: $39/yr. Adv. Rate: col. inch $10.30 Circulation: 2,319 per issue (paid). **Owner(s):** American Community Newspapers LLC, See address and contact information above. **Management:** Bruce Treichler, Publisher. **Editorial:** Mike Shoemer, News Editor.Readers: Local community

PLYMOUTH SUN-SAILOR. 10917 Valley View Rd., Eden Prairie, MN 55344. Telephone: 952-392-6800. E-MAIL: suninfo@acnpapers.com. URL: http://www.mnsun.com. Pub. Frequency: w. (Thu.) Page Size: tabloid. Subscrip. Rate: $.75 newsstand/cover; $84/yr mailed 1st class. Circulation: 17,500 per issue (free). **Owner(s):** American Community Newspapers LLC, See address and contact information above. **Management:** Jeff Coolman, Publisher. **Editorial:** Sally Thompson, Editor. Peggy Bakken, Executive Editor.

RICHFIELD SUN-CURRENT. 10917 Valley View Rd., Eden Prairie, MN 55344. Telephone: 952-392-6800. FAX: 952-392-6868. E-MAIL: suninfo@acnpapers.com. URL: http://www.mnsun.com. Pub. Frequency: w. (Wed.) Page Size: tabloid. Subscrip. Rate: $.75 newsstand/cover; $24.95/yr mailed. Adv. Rate: B&W page $1,080 Circulation: 9,826 per issue (paid and free). **Owner(s):** American Community Newspapers LLC, See address and contact information above. **Management:** Jeff Coolman, Publisher. Todd Aldrich, Circulation Manager. **Editorial:** John Klun, Editor. Yvonne Klinnert, Executive Editor. David Eyestone, Photographer. John Sherman, Sports.

SOUTH ST. PAUL/INVER GROVE HEIGHTS SUN-CURRENT. 10917 Valley View Rd., Eden Prairie, MN 55344. Telephone: 952-392-6800. FAX: 952-392-6802. E-MAIL: suninfo@acnpapers.com. URL: http://www.mnsun.com. Year Established: 1950. Pub. Frequency: w. (Wed.) Page Size: tabloid. Subscrip. Rate: $.75 newsstand/cover; $24.95/yr mailed. Adv. Rate: B&W page $1,565 Circulation: 14,500 per issue (paid and free). **Owner(s):** American Community Newspapers LLC, See address and contact information above. **Management:** Gene Carr, Publisher. Jeff Coolman, Advertising Director. Krista Jech, Advertising Manager. Todd Aldrich, Circulation Manager. **Editorial:** Yvonne Klinnert, Executive Editor. Andy Blenkusch, Photographer.

ST. LOUIS PARK SUN-SAILOR. 10917 Valley View Rd., Eden Prairie, MN 05344-9730. Telephone: 952-829-0797. FAX: 952—829-6868. E-MAIL: suninfo@acnpapaers.com. URL: http://www.mnsun.com. Year Established: 1984. Pub. Frequency: w. (Thu.) Page Size: tabloid. Subscrip. Rate: $.75 newsstand/cover; $40/yr mailed. Adv. Rate: B&W page $1,265 Circulation: 12,830 per issue (free). **Owner(s):** American Community Newspapers LLC, See address and contact information above. **Management:** Jeff Coolman, President. Herb Hesse, Circulation Manager. **Editorial:** Teri Kelsh, Editor. Peggy Bakken, Executive Editor. Mike Erickson, Production Manager. Mike Shaughnessy, Sports Editor.

WAYZATA/ORONO/LONG LAKE SUN-SAILOR. 10917 Valley View Rd., Eden Prairie, MN 55344. Telephone: 952-392-6800. FAX: 952-392-6868. E-MAIL: suninfo@acnpapers.com. URL: http://www.mnsun.com. Pub. Frequency: w. (Thu.) Page Size: tabloid. Subscrip. Rate: $.75 newsstand/cover; $84/yr mailed 1st class. Adv. Rate: B&W page $1,665 Circulation: 22,900 evening (free). **Owner(s):** American Community Newspapers LLC, See address and contact information above. **Management:** Jeff Coolman, President. Herb Hesse, Circulation Manager. **Editorial:** Troy Pieper, Editor. Peggy Bakken, Executive Editor. Nick Clark, Sports.

WEST ST. PAUL/MENDOTA HEIGHTS SUN-CURRENT. 10917 Valley View Rd., Eden Prairie, MN 55344. Telephone: 952-392-6800. FAX: 952-392-6868. E-MAIL: suninfo@acnpapers.com. URL: http://www.mnsun.com/. Pub. Frequency: w. (Wed.) Page Size: tabloid. Subscrip. Rate: $.75 newsstand/cover; $84/yr mailed. Adv. Rate: B&W page $1,315 Circulation: 10,200 per issue (paid and free). **Owner(s):** American Community Newspapers LLC, See address and contact information above. **Management:** Jeff Coolman, Publisher. Herb Hesse, Circulation Manager. **Editorial:** Heather Carlson, Editor. Yvonne Klinnert, Managing Editor. Andy Blenkush, Photographer. Mike Shaughnessy, Sports.

EDGERTON

EDGERTON ENTERPRISE, THE. 831 Main St., Edgerton, MN 56128-0397. Telephone: 507-442-6161. FAX: 507-631-0061. E-MAIL: edgent@dtgnet.com. URL: http://www.edgertonminnesota.com. Year Established: 1883. Pub. Frequency: w. (Wed.) Page Size: broadsheet. Subscrip. Rate: $.75 newsstand/cover; $29/yr local; $36/yr mailed elsewhere. Adv. Rate: col. inch $4.40 Circulation: 1,800 per issue (paid). **Owner(s):** Jill Fenneman & Irene Gunnink, See address and contact information above. **Management:** Jill Fenneman, Publisher. Rose Van Nieuwenhuyzen, Circulation Manager. **Editorial:** Jill Fenneman, Editor.

ELK RIVER

STAR NEWS. 506 Freeport Ave. NW Ste. A, Elk River, MN 55330. Telephone: 763-441-3500. FAX: 763-441-6401. E-MAIL: print.elkriver@ecm-inc.com. URL: http://www.erstarnews.com. Year Established: 1872. Pub. Frequency: w. (Wed.) Page Size: broadsheet. Subscrip. Rate: $.75 newsstand/cover; $35/yr mailed. Adv. Rate: col. inch $14.30 Circulation: 23,000 per issue (controlled). **Owner(s):** ECM Publishers, Inc., 4095 Coon Rapids Blvd., Coon Rapids, MN 55433. Telephone: 763-421-2400. **Management:** Liz Harris, General Manager. Julian Andersen, Publisher. Liz Harris, Advertising Manager. Sharon Newton, Classified Adv. Mgr.. **Editorial:** Jim Boyle, Editor.

STAR SHOPPER. 506 Freeport Ave. NW Ste. A, Elk River, MN 55330. Telephone: 763-441-3500. FAX: 763-441-6401. E-MAIL: print.elkriver@ecm-inc.com. URL: http://www.erstarnews.com. Year Established: 1987. Pub. Frequency: w. (Sat.) Page Size: tabloid.Adv. Rate: col. inch $10.75 Circulation: 26,000 per issue (controlled). Owner(s): ECM Publishers, Inc., 4095 Coon Rapids Blvd., Coon Rapids, MN 55433. Telephone: 763-421-4444. FAX: 763-427-4315. **Management:** Liz Harris, General Manager.

ELY

ELY ECHO. ISSN 0746-7087
15 E. Chapman St., Ely, MN 55731-1257. Telephone: 218-365-3141. FAX: 218-365-3142. E-MAIL: elyecho@aol.com. URL: http://www.elyecho.com. Year Established: 1972. Pub. Frequency: w. (Mon.) Page Size: broadsheet. Subscrip. Rate: $1 newsstand/cover; $25/yr in county; $35/yr mailed out of county; $45/yr mailed out of state. Adv. Rate: col. inch $9.71 Circulation: 5,336 per issue (paid). Owner(s): Milestones, Inc., 15 E. Chapman St., Ely, MN 55731. Telephone: 218-365-3141. FAX: 218-365-3142. **Management:** Anne Swenson, Publisher. Nick Wognum, Office Manager. Anne Swenson, Advertising Manager. **Editorial:** Tom Coombe, Managing Editor.

FARMINGTON

FARMINGTON INDEPENDENT. 320 Third St., Farmington, MN 55024. Telephone: 651-460-6606. FAX: 651-463-7730. URL: http://www.farmingtonindependent.com. Mailing Address: PO Box 192, Farmington, MN 55024. Pub. Frequency: w. (Thu.) Page Size: standard. Subscrip. Rate: $.75 newsstand/cover; $30/yr carrier delivery; $40/yr mailed. Circulation: 2,275 per issue (paid). Owner(s): Jeff Meyer, PO Box 2020, Fargo, ND 58107. Telephone: 701-235-7311. **Management:** Steve Messick, Publisher. Aaron Rather, Advertising Manager. Maureen Northrup, Classified Adv. Mgr.. **Editorial:** Jeff Mores, Managing Editor. Nathan Hansen, News Editor.

FOREST LAKE

FOREST LAKE TIMES. 218, Forest Lake, MN 55025-0218. E-MAIL: editor.forestlaketimes@ecm-inc.com. URL: http://www.forestlaketimes.com. Year Established: 1903. Pub. Frequency: w. (Thu.) Page Size: broadsheet. Subscrip. Rate: $1 newsstand/cover; $40/yr mailed. Adv. Rate: col. inch $12.25 Circulation: 12,500 per issue (paid and free). Owner(s): ECM Publishers, Inc., 4095 Coon Rapids Blvd., Coon Rapids, MN 55433. Telephone: 763-712-2400. FAX: 763-712-2480. **Management:** Jeff Andres, General Manager. Carol Lehner, Advertising. **Editorial:** Clifford Buchan, Editor. Joe Drennan, Sports Editor.

ST. CROIX VALLEY PEACH. 218, Forest Lake, MN 55025-0218. E-MAIL: print.forestlake@ecm-inc.com. URL: http://www.hometownsource.com. Year Established: 1954. Pub. Frequency: w. (Sun.) Page Size: tabloid. Subscrip. Rate: $1 newsstand/cover out of area; $97/yr out of area. Adv. Rate: col. inch $12.20 Circulation: 32,500 per issue (paid and free). Owner(s): ECM Publishers, Inc., 4095 Coon Rapids Blvd., Coon Rapids, MN 55433. Telephone: 763-712-2400. FAX: 763-712-2480. **Management:** Jeff Andres, General Manager.

FOSSTON

FOSSTON THIRTEEN TOWNS. 118 Johnson Ave., N., Fosston, MN 56542. Telephone: 218-435-1313. FAX: 218-435-1309. E-MAIL: 13towns@gvtel.com. Mailing Address: PO Box 505, Fosston, MN 56542-0505. Year Established: 1884. Pub. Frequency: w. (Tue.) Page Size: broadsheet. Subscrip. Rate: $.75 newsstand/cover; $22/yr in county; $27/yr out of county. Adv. Rate: col. inch $5 Circulation: 3,000 per issue (paid). Owner(s): Dean Vikan & Dick Richards, See address and contact information above. **Management:** Dick Richards, Publisher. Amy Ribland, Advertising.

GAYLORD

GAYLORD HUB, THE. 234 4th St., Gaylord, MN 55334. Telephone: 507-237-2476. E-MAIL: hubpub@mnic.net. Mailing Address: PO Box 208, Gaylord, MN 55334-0208. Pub. Frequency: w. (Thu.) Page Size: broadsheet. Subscrip. Rate: $.85 newsstand/cover; $30/yr in county; $35/yr in state; $40/yr out of state. Circulation: 1,867 per issue (paid). Owner(s): Gaylord Hub, See address and contact information above. **Management:** Joe Deis, Publisher. **Editorial:** Joe Deis, Editor.

GLENCOE

GLENCOE ENTERPRISE. PO Box 97, Glencoe, MN 55336. Telephone: 320-864-4715. E-MAIL: enterp@hutchtel.net. Year Established: 1873. Pub. Frequency: w. (Thu.) Page Size: standard. Subscrip. Rate: $22/yr in county; $25/yr out of county. Circulation: 4,200 per issue (paid). Owner(s): Annamarie Tudhope, See address and contact information above. **Management:** Annamarie Tudhope, Publisher. **Editorial:** Annamarie Tudhope, Editor.

MCLEOD COUNTY CHRONICLE, THE. 716 E. Tenth St., Glencoe, MN 55336. Telephone: 320-864-5518. FAX: 320-864-5510. E-MAIL: chronicle@glencoenews.com. URL: http://www.glencoenews.com. Mailing Address: PO Box 188, Glencoe, MN 55336. Pub. Frequency: w. (Wed.) Page Size: broadsheet. Subscrip. Rate: $30/yr local; $36/yr in state; $42/yr elsewhere. Adv. Rate: col. inch $6.54 Circulation: 3,300 per issue (paid). Owner(s): McLeod County Chronicle, The, See address and contact information above. **Management:** Bill Ramige, Publisher. Susan Colden, Advertising Manager. **Editorial:** Rich Glennie, Editor. Lee Ostrom, Sports Editor.

GLENWOOD

POPE COUNTY TRIBUNE. 14 First Ave. S.E., Glenwood, MN 56334. Telephone: 320-634-4571. FAX: 320-634-5522. E-MAIL: news@pctribune.com. URL: http://www.pctribune.com. Year Established: 1920. Pub. Frequency: w. (Mon.) Page Size: broadsheet. Subscrip. Rate: $1 newsstand/cover; $31/yr home delivery in county; $36/yr mailed out of county. Circulation: 4,000 per issue (paid). Owner(s): John R. Stone, See address and contact information above. **Management:** Tim Douglas, Publisher. Mike Scott, Advertising. **Editorial:** Chad Koenan, Sports.

GONVICK

GRYGLA EAGLE. Second & Main, PO Box 159, Gonvick, MN 56644. Telephone: 218-487-5225. E-MAIL: gyrlgaeagle@gvtel.com. Mailing Address: PO Box 17, Grygla, MN 56727. Year Established: 1973. Pub. Frequency: w. (Thu.) Page Size: tabloid. Subscrip. Rate: $1 newsstand/cover; $25/yr local; $30/yr out of area. Circulation: 5,000 per issue (paid). Owner(s): Richards Publishing Co., Inc., See address and contact information above. **Management:** Dick Richards, Publisher. **Editorial:** Karla Byklum, Editor.

LEADER-RECORD. Second & Main, PO Box 159, Gonvick, MN 56644. Telephone: 218-487-5225. FAX: 218-487-5251. E-MAIL: richards@gvtel.com. Pub. Frequency: w. (Wed.) Page Size: tabloid. Subscrip. Rate: $.75 newsstand/cover; $20/yr in county; $25/yr mailed out of county. Circulation: 2,252 per issue (paid). Owner(s): Richards Publishing Co., Inc., See address and contact information above. **Management:** Corrine Richards, Publisher. **Editorial:** Corrine Richards, Editor.

GRAND MARAIS

COOK COUNTY NEWS-HERALD. 111/2 Broadway, Grand Marais, MN 55604. Telephone: 218-387-1025. FAX: 218-387-2539. E-MAIL: newsherald@grandmarais-mn.com. URL: http://www.grandmarais-mn.com. Mailing Address: PO Box 757, Grand Marais, MN 55604. Year Established: 1890. Pub. Frequency: w. (Mon.) Page Size: broadsheet. Subscrip. Rate: $.75 newsstand/cover; $28/yr mailed in county; $35/yr mailed out of county; $38/yr mailed out of state. Adv. Rate: col. inch $5.45 Circulation: 4,100 per issue (paid). Owner(s): Superior Publishing Corp., 1105 Tower Ave., Superior, WI 54880-1502. **Management:** Vicki Biggs-Anderson, Publisher. **Editorial:** Vicki Biggs-Anderson, Editor.

GRAND RAPIDS

GRAND RAPIDS/HERALD-REVIEW. 301 First Ave., N.W., Grand Rapids, MN 55744. Telephone: 218-326-6623. FAX: 218-326-6627. E-MAIL: news@grandrapidsmn.com. URL: http://www.grandrapidsmn.com. Mailing Address: PO Box 220, Grand Rapids, MN 55744. Year Established: 1894. Pub. Frequency: s-w. (Wed. & Sat.) Page Size: tabloid. Subscrip. Rate: $1 newsstand/cover; $48/yr carrier delivery; $51/yr motor route; $52/yr mailed. Circulation: 19,000 per issue (paid and free). Owner(s): Superior Publishing Corp., 1105 Tower Ave., Superior, WI 54880. Telephone: 715-395-5725. FAX: 715-395-5729. **Management:** Ronald Oleheiser, General Manager. Steve Lynch, Advertising Manager. **Editorial:** Mary Beth Biley, Editor. Britta Arendt, Reporter. Ted Anderson, Sports.

GRANITE FALLS

ADVOCATE-TRIBUNE. 713 Prentice St., Granite Falls, MN 56241. Telephone: 320-564-2126. FAX: 320-564-4293. E-MAIL: editor@mail.kilowatt.net. URL: http://www.granitefallsnews.com. Mailing Address: PO Box 99, Granite Falls, MN 56241. Year Established: 1883. Pub. Frequency: w. (Thu.) Page Size: broadsheet.Subscrip. Rate: $1 newsstand/cover; $41/yr Circulation: 3,400 per issue (paid). Owner(s): GateHouse Media, Inc, 350 WillowBrook Office Park, Fairport, NY 14450. Telephone: 585-598-0030. FAX: 585-248-2631. **Management:** Dave Smiglewski, Publisher. Teresa Ihnen, Advertising. **Editorial:** Dave Smiglewski, Editor. Dan McGonigle, News Editor. Dick Jepson, Sports.

GREENBUSH

NEW RIVER RECORD. ISSN 0747-4407
PO Box F, Greenbush, MN 56726. Telephone: 218-782-2275. FAX: 218-782-2277. E-MAIL: tribune@means.net. URL: http://www.rrv.net/page1pub. Year Established: 1902. Pub. Frequency: w. (Wed.) Page Size: broadsheet. Subscrip. Rate: $.75 newsstand/cover; $22/yr in county; $29/yr mailed out of county. Circulation: 500 per issue (paid). Owner(s): Page 1 Publications, See address and contact information above. **Management:** Julie Nordine, Publisher.

HALSTAD

SHOPPER (HALSTAD), THE. 301 Third Ave, W, Halstad, MN 56548. Telephone: 218-456-2133. FAX: 218-456-2567. Mailing Address: PO Box 267, Halstad, MN 56548. Pub. Frequency: w. (Mon.) Page Size: standard Circulation: 27,000 per issue (free). Owner(s): GateHouse Media, Inc, 350 WillowBrook Office Park, Fairport, NY 14450. Telephone: 585-598-0030. FAX: 585-248-2631. **Management:** Don Forney, Publisher.

VALLEY JOURNAL (HALSTAD), THE. 301 Third Ave, W, Halstad, MN 56548. Telephone: 218-456-2133. FAX: 218-456-2567. Mailing Address: PO Box 267, Halstad, MN 56548. Pub. Frequency: w. (Mon.) Page Size: standard. Subscrip. Rate: $1 newsstand/cover; $52/yr in county. Circulation: 3,600 per issue (paid). Owner(s): GateHouse Media, Inc, 350 WillowBrook Office Park, Fairport, NY 14450. Telephone: 585-598-0030. FAX: 585-248-2631. **Management:** Don Forney, Publisher.

HASTINGS

HASTINGS STAR GAZETTE. 741 Spiral Dr., Hastings, MN 55033. Telephone: 651-437-6153. FAX: 651-437-5911. E-MAIL: editor@hastingsstargazette.com. URL: http://www.hastingsstargazette.com. Mailing Address: PO Box 277, Hastings, MN 55033. Year Established: 1857. Pub. Frequency: w. (Thu.) Page Size: broadsheet. Subscrip. Rate: $1.25 newsstand/cover; $43/yr local area; $60/yr mailed out of area. Circulation: 6,400 per issue (paid). Owner(s): Jeff Meyer, 101 Fifth St., N., Fargo, ND 58102. Telephone: 701-235-7311. **Management:** Ross Ulrich, General Manager. Steve Messick, Publisher. Maureen Northrup, Classified Adv. Mgr.. **Editorial:** Ben Ganje, Editor.

HAWLEY

HAWLEY HERALD. PO Box 709, Hawley, MN 56549. Telephone: 218-483-3306. Year Established: 1890. Pub. Frequency: w. (Mon.) Page Size: broadsheet. Subscrip. Rate: $.75 newsstand/cover; $24/yr in county; $27/yr mailed out of county; $30/yr mailed out of state. Adv. Rate: col. inch $6.30 Circulation: 2,025 per issue (paid). Owner(s): Eugene Prim, See address and contact information above. **Management:** Eugene Prim, Publisher. **Editorial:** Marc C. Ness, Managing Editor.

HUTCHINSON

HUTCHINSON LEADER. 36 Washington Ave W, Hutchinson, MN 55350-2240. Telephone: 320-587-5000. FAX: 320-587-6104. URL: http://www.hutchinsonleader.com. Year Established: 1880. Pub. Frequency: 3/w. (Tue., Thu., Sun.) Page Size: broadsheet. Subscrip. Rate: $.75 newsstand/cover; $49.50/yr local. Circulation: 5,552 per issue (paid); 22,024 per issue (free). Owner(s): Red Wing Publishing, PO Box 2010, Red Wing, MN 55066. Telephone: 651-388-5000. FAX: 651-388-7973. **Management:** Matt McMillan, Publisher. Tina Berglund, Advertising Director. **Editorial:** Doug Hanneman, Editor.

JACKSON

JACKSON COUNTY LIVEWIRE. 310 Second St, Jackson, MN 56143-0208. Telephone: 507-847-3771. FAX: 507-847-5822. E-MAIL: info@livewireprinting.com. URL: http://www.livewireprinting.com/publications/livewire. Mailing Address: PO Box 208, Jackson, MN 56143-0208. Year Established: 1929. Pub. Frequency: w. (Mon.) Page Size: tabloid. Subscrip. Rate: $16/yr out of area. Adv. Rate: col. inch $7.20 Circulation: 10,000 per issue (free). Owner(s): Livewire Printing Co., See address and contact information above. **Management:** Jim Keul, Owner. Connie Reinert, Publisher. **Editorial:** Ed Gallagher, Editor.

JACKSON COUNTY PILOT. 310 Second St, Jackson, MN 56143-0208. Telephone: 507-847-3771. FAX: 507-847-5822. E-MAIL: info@livewireprinting.com. URL: http://www.jacksoncountypilot.com. Mailing Address: PO Box 208, Jackson, MN 56143-0208. Year Established: 1890. Pub. Frequency: w. (Thu.) Subscrip. Rate: $1 newsstand/cover; $37/yr local; $48/yr out of area. Adv. Rate: col. inch $7.30 Owner(s): Livewire Printing Co., See address and contact information above. **Management:** Jim Keul, Owner. Connie Reinert, Publisher. **Editorial:** Ed Gallagher, Editor.

LAKEFIELD STANDARD. 310 Second St, Jackson, MN 56143-0208. Telephone: 507-847-3771. FAX: 507-847-5822. URL: http://www.livewireprinting.com. Mailing Address: PO Box 208, Jackson, MN 56143-0208. Year Established: 1884. Pub. Frequency: w. (Thu.) Page Size: broadsheet. Subscrip. Rate: $1 newsstand/cover; $31/yr in county; $36.50/yr out of county. Adv. Rate: col. inch $4.90 Circulation: 1,200 per issue (paid). **Owner(s):** Livewire Printing Co., See address and contact information above. **Management:** Connie Reinert, Publisher. **Editorial:** Ed Gallagher, Editor.

JASPER

JASPER JOURNAL. ISSN 0744-3110
106 W. Wall St., Jasper, MN 56144-0188. Telephone: 507-348-4176. FAX: 507-825-2168. E-MAIL: pipepub@pipestonestar.com. URL: http://www.pipestonestar.com. Mailing Address: PO Box 188, Jasper, MN 56144. Year Established: 1888. Pub. Frequency: w. (Mon.) Page Size: tabloid. Subscrip. Rate: $.75 newsstand/cover; $25/yr local; $33/yr mailed elsewhere. Adv. Rate: col. inch $4.50 Circulation: 885 per issue (paid). **Owner(s):** Pipestone Publishing Co., 101 Second St. NE, Pipestone, MN 56164. Telephone: 507-825-3333. **Management:** John Draper, Publisher. Deloris Quissell, Advertising. **Editorial:** Steven Swenson, Editor.

KARLSTAD

NORTH STAR NEWS. 204 S. Main St., Karlstad, MN 56732-0158. Telephone: 218-436-2157. FAX: 218-436-3271. E-MAIL: norstar@wiktel.com. Mailing Address: PO Box 158, Karlstad, MN 56732. Year Established: 1902. Pub. Frequency: w. (Thu.) Page Size: broadsheet. Subscrip. Rate: $.75 newsstand/cover; $27/yr in county; $34/yr out of county. Circulation: 2,300 per issue (paid). **Owner(s):** Page 1 Publications, PO Box F, Greenbush, MN 56726. Telephone: 218-782-2275. FAX: 218-782-2277. **Management:** Julie Nordine, Publisher. Heidi Spilde, Advertising. **Editorial:** Lori Bothum, Managing Editor.

KENYON

KENYON LEADER. 638 Second St., Kenyon, MN 55946. Telephone: 507-789-6161. FAX: 507-789-5040. E-MAIL: kleader@clear.lakes.com. Year Established: 1885. Pub. Frequency: w. (Wed.) Page Size: broadsheet. Subscrip. Rate: $.75 newsstand/cover; $25/yr in county; $27/yr mailed in state; $31/yr mailed out of state. Adv. Rate: col. inch $4.25 Circulation: 1,994 per issue (paid). **Owner(s):** Noah Publishing, Inc., See address and contact information above. **Management:** Douglas A. Noah, President. **Editorial:** Bryn Schuenke, Editor-in-Chief.

LAMBERTON

LAMBERTON NEWS. 218 Main St., Lamberton, MN 56152-1377. Telephone: 507-752-7181. FAX: 507-752-7181. E-MAIL: lambnews@rrcnet.org. Mailing Address: P.O. Box 308, Lamberton, MN 56152-1377. Year Established: 1923. Pub. Frequency: w. (Wed.) Page Size: standard. Subscrip. Rate: $.75 newsstand/cover; $25/yr local; $27.50/yr mailed in state; $30/yr mailed out of state. Adv. Rate: col. inch $4.75 Circulation: 1,700 per issue (paid). **Owner(s):** Joseph G. Dietl, See address and contact information above. **Management:** Joseph G. Dietl, Publisher.

LE CENTER

LE CENTER LEADER. 62 E. Minnesota St., Le Center, MN 56057. Telephone: 507-357-2233. FAX: 507-357-6656. Year Established: 1895. Pub. Frequency: w. (Wed.) Page Size: broadsheet. Subscrip. Rate: $1 newsstand/cover; $34/yr in state; $47/yr out of state. Adv. Rate: col. inch $9.05 Circulation: 1,500 per issue (paid). **Owner(s):** James Huckle, See address and contact information above. **Management:** Terri McMillen, Publisher. **Editorial:** Terri McMillen, Editor.

LEROY

INDEPENDENT (LEROY), THE. PO Box 89, Leroy, MN 55951. Telephone: 507-324-5325. FAX: 507-324-5267. Pub. Frequency: w. (Thu.) Page Size: broadsheet. Subscrip. Rate: $.75 newsstand/cover; $27/yr in county & adj cys; $30/yr elsewhere. Circulation: 1,300 per issue (paid). **Owner(s):** Dan & Joyce Evans, See address and contact information above. **Management:** Dan Evans, Publisher. **Editorial:** Dan Evans, Editor.

LINDSTROM

CHISAGO COUNTY PRESS. ISSN 1526-9701
12631 Lake Blvd., Lindstrom, MN 55045-0748. Telephone: 651-257-5115. FAX: 651-257-5500. E-MAIL: chisago@citlink.net. URL: http://www.chisagocountypress.com. Year Established: 1898. Pub. Frequency: w. (Thu.) Page Size: broadsheet. Subscrip. Rate: $1 newsstand/cover; $45/yr in county; $47.50/yr out of county. Circulation: 4,333 per issue (paid). **Owner(s):** John A. Silver, See address and contact information above. **Management:** Matt Silver, Publisher. Ellen Glenna, Advertising Manager. **Editorial:** Denise Martin, Managing Editor.

LITCHFIELD

LITCHFIELD INDEPENDENT REVIEW. 217 N. Sibley Ave., Litchfield, MN 55355. Telephone: 320-693-3266. FAX: 320-693-9177. E-MAIL: inews@independentreview.net. URL: http://independentreview.net. Mailing Address: PO Box 921, Litchfield, MN 55355-0921. Year Established: 1876. Pub. Frequency: w. (Thu.) Page Size: broadsheet. Subscrip. Rate: $1 newsstand/cover; $30/yr mailed in county; $40/yr mailed out of county; $42/yr mailed out of state. Circulation: 4,000 per issue (paid). **Owner(s):** Red Wing Publishing, 2760 N. Service Dr., Redwing, MN 55066. Telephone: 651-388-2914. **Management:** Matt McMillan, Publisher. **Editorial:** Brent Schacherer, Editor.

LITTLE FALLS

MORRISON COUNTY RECORD. 216 SE First St, Little Falls, MN 56345. Telephone: 320-632-2348. E-MAIL: mcr@mcrecord.com. URL: http://www.mcrecord.com. Year Established: 1972. Pub. Frequency: w. (Sun) Page Size: broadsheet Circulation: 18,000 per issue (free). **Owner(s):** E M C Publishers, Inc., See address and contact information above. **Management:** Tom West, General Manager. Julian Andersen, Publisher. Kim Hansen, Advertising. Karen Grittner, Circulation Manager.

LONG PRAIRIE

LONG PRAIRIE LEADER. PO Box 479, Long Prairie, MN 56347. Telephone: 320-732-2151. E-MAIL: lpleader@rea-alp.com. URL: http://www.lpleader.com. Year Established: 1887. Pub. Frequency: w. (Wed.) Page Size: broadsheet. Subscrip. Rate: $.75 newsstand/cover; $25/yr mailed in county; $30/yr mailed out of county; $35/yr out of state. Adv. Rate: col. inch $5.80 Circulation: 3,500 per issue (paid). **Owner(s):** Gary & Sharon Brown, See address and contact information above. **Management:** Gary Brown, Publisher.

LUVERNE

ROCK COUNTY STAR HERALD. PO Box 837, Luverne, MN 56156. Telephone: 507-283-2333. E-MAIL: editor@star-herald.com. URL: http://www.star-herald.com. Year Established: 1873. Pub. Frequency: w. (Thu.) Page Size: broadsheet. Subscrip. Rate: $1 newsstand/cover; $38/yr mailed in county; $48/yr mailed out of county. Circulation: 3,000 per issue (paid). **Owner(s):** Tollefson Publishing, See address and contact information above. **Management:** Roger S. Tollefson, Publisher. **Editorial:** Lorie Ehde, Editor. Sara Quam, Assistant Editor. John Rittenhouse, Sports.

MABEL

NEWS-RECORD (MABEL). 102 W. Fillmore St., Mabel, MN 55954-0307. Telephone: 507-493-5204. FAX: 507-493-5204. E-MAIL: Melissa@means.net. URL: http://www.hometown-pages.com. Mailing Address: PO Box 307, Mabel, MN 55954-0307. Pub. Frequency: s-w. (Wed. & Thu.) Page Size: standard.Subscrip. Rate: $.60 newsstand/cover; $20/yr Circulation: 1,514 per issue (paid). **Owner(s):** Phillips Publishing, PO Box 112, Spring Valley, MN 55975. **Management:** David Phillips, Publisher. Jerry Rollie, Advertising Manager. Debby Groth, Circulation Manager. **Editorial:** Melissa Vander Plas, Editor.

MADELIA

MADELIA TIMES-MESSENGER. 112 W. Main St., Madelia, MN 56062-1440. Telephone: 507-642-3636. FAX: 507-642-3535. E-MAIL: remark@chriscomco.net. Pub. Frequency: w. (Thu) Page Size: standard. Subscrip. Rate: $1 newsstand/cover; $35/yr in county; $42/yr mailed elsewhere. Circulation: 1,233 per issue (paid). **Owner(s):** Michael Koob, See address and contact information above. **Management:** Michael Koob, Publisher. Shari Kilmer, Advertising Manager. Karla Grev, Circulation Manager. **Editorial:** Michael Koob, Editor.

MADISON LAKE

LAKE REGION TIMES. 513 Main St., Madison Lake, MN 56063-0128. Telephone: 507-243-3031. FAX: 507-243-3122. E-MAIL: lrtimes@hickorytch.net. Mailing Address: P.O. Box 128, Madison Lake, MN 56063-0128. Year Established: 1908. Pub. Frequency: w. (Wed.) Page Size: standard. Subscrip. Rate: $25/yr local; $30/yr in state; $35/yr elsewhere. Adv. Rate: col. inch $4.50 Circulation: 924 per issue (paid). **Owner(s):** Jerry Groebner, See address and contact information above. **Management:** Jerry Groebner, Publisher. **Editorial:** Jerry Groebner, Editor.

MAHNOMEN

MAHNOMEN PIONEER, THE. PO Box 219, Mahnomen, MN 56557-0219. Telephone: 218-935-5296. FAX: 218-935-2555. E-MAIL: mahpioneer@arvig.net. Year Established: 1905. Pub. Frequency: w. (Thu.) Page Size: broadsheet. Subscrip. Rate: $.50 newsstand/cover; $23/yr in county; $29/yr in state; $33/yr out of state. Adv. Rate: col. inch $4.75 Circulation: 2,775 per issue (paid). **Owner(s):** Patrick D. Kelly, See address and contact information above. **Management:** Patrick Kelly, Advertising Manager. Jeanne Kelly, Circulation Manager. **Editorial:** Sue Kraft, Editor.

MAPLE LAKE

MAPLE LAKE MESSENGER. 218 Division St. W., Maple Lake, MN 55358-0817. Telephone: 320-963-3813. FAX: 320-963-6114. E-MAIL: mlmess@lakedalelink.net. URL: http://www.maplelakemessenger.com. Mailing Address: PO Box 817, Maple Lake, MN 55358-0817. Year Established: 1895. Pub. Frequency: w. (Wed.) Page Size: standard. Subscrip. Rate: $22/yr in county; $19.80/yr in county to senior citizens; $25/yr elsewhere. Circulation: 1,300 per issue (paid). **Owner(s):** Theresa Andrus, See address and contact information above. **Management:** Theresa Andrus, Publisher. Kayla Erickson, Advertising. **Editorial:** Theresa Andrus, Editor. Angela Stegman, Photo.

Weeklies

MAPLETON

MAPLE RIVER MESSENGER. 309 Main St. N.E., Mapleton, MN 56065-0425. Telephone: 507-524-3212. FAX: 507-524-4249. E-MAIL: enterpub@gotocrystal.net. Pub. Frequency: w. (Wed.) Page Size: standard. Subscrip. Rate: $.75 newsstand/cover; $28/yr mailed in state; $30/yr out of state. Circulation: 1,700 per issue (paid). **Owner(s):** Ed and Carolyn Dorsey, See address and contact information above. **Management:** Carolyn Dorsey, Publisher. **Editorial:** Ed Dorsey, Editor.

MCGREGOR

VOYAGEUR PRESS OF MCGREGOR, THE. P O Box 59, McGregor, MN 55760. E-MAIL: vpofmg@frontiernet.net. URL: http://www.thevoyageurpress.com. Year Established: 2000. Pub. Frequency: w. (Tue.) Page Size: tabloid. Subscrip. Rate: $1 newsstand/cover; $28/yr local; $36/yr mailed in state; $39/yr mailed out of state. Circulation: 1,300 per issue (paid). **Owner(s):** John Grones, 15 Country House Ln., McGregor, MN 55760-0059. Telephone: 218-768-3405. FAX: 218-768-7046. **Management:** John Grones, Publisher. Patty Raveil, Circulation Manager. **Editorial:** Mike Heaser, Editor. Amber Lehman, Graphics Editor.

MCINTOSH

MCINTOSH TIMES. 115 Broadway, N.W., McIntosh, MN 56556. Telephone: 218-563-3585. FAX: 218-487-5251. E-MAIL: richards@gvtel.net. Mailing Address: PO Box 9, McIntosh, MN 56556. Year Established: 1888. Pub. Frequency: w. (Wed.) Page Size: tabloid. Subscrip. Rate: $.75 newsstand/cover; $20/yr mailed in county; $25/yr mailed out of county. Circulation: 1,350 per issue (paid). **Owner(s):** Richards Publishing Co., Inc., Second & Main, PO Box 159, Gonvick, MN 56644. Telephone: 218-487-5225. **Management:** Richard Richards, Publisher. **Editorial:** Mary Horacek, Editor.

MELROSE

MELROSE BEACON. PO Box 186, Melrose, MN 56352. Telephone: 320-256-3240. E-MAIL: news@acnpapers.com. URL: http://www.melrosebeacon.com. Year Established: 1890. Pub. Frequency: w. (Sat.) Page Size: broadsheet. Subscrip. Rate: $.75 newsstand/cover; $31/yr mailed in county area; $37/yr mailed in state; $41/yr mailed out of state. Freelance Pay: $5-$25/article. Circulation: 4,500 per issue (paid). **Owner(s):** Stearns County Publishing, Inc., See address and contact information above. **Management:** Richard Raeker, General Manager. **Editorial:** Roberta Olson, Editor. Herman Lansing, Assistant Editor.

MILACA

MILLE LACS COUNTY TIMES. 225 Second St., S.W., Milaca, MN 56353. Telephone: 320-983-6111. FAX: 320-983-6112. E-MAIL: editor.millelacscotimes@ecm-inc.com. URL: http://www.millelacscountytimes.com. Mailing Address: PO Box 9, Milaca, MN 56353. Year Established: 1892. Pub. Frequency: w. (Thu.) Page Size: broadsheet. Subscrip. Rate: $.75 newsstand/cover; $25/yr mailed in county & adj. cys.; $34/yr mailed out of state. Adv. Rate: col. inch $6.75 Circulation: 3,100 per issue (paid). **Owner(s):** ECM Publishers, Inc., 4095 Coon Rapids Blvd., Coon Rapids, MN 55433. Telephone: 763-712-2400. **Management:** Lois Ploeger, General Manager. Elmer L. Anderson, Publisher. **Editorial:** Gary Larson, Editor.

TOWN & COUNTRY SHOPPER. 225 Second St., Milaca, MN 56353. Telephone: 320-983-6111. FAX: 320-983-6112. URL: http://www.ecm-inc.com. Pub. Frequency: w. (Mon.) Page Size: tabloid.Adv. Rate: col. inch $8.60 Circulation: 16,800 per issue. **Owner(s):** ECM Publishers, Inc., 4095 Coon Rapids Blvd., Coon Rapids, MN 55433. Telephone: 763-421-4444. FAX: 763-421-4315. **Management:** Dawn Slade, General Manager. Julian Andersen, Publisher.

MINNEAPOLIS

CITY PAGES. 401 N. Third St., Ste. 550, Minneapolis, MN 55401. Telephone: 612-375-1015. FAX: 612-372-3737. E-MAIL: adinfo@citypages.com. URL: http://www.citypages.com. Mailing Address: PO Box 59183, Minneapolis, MN 55459. Year Established: 1981. Pub. Frequency: w. (Wed.) Page Size: tabloid. Subscrip. Rate: $65/yr mailed. Circulation: 125,000 per issue (paid and free). **Owner(s):** Village Voice Media, Inc., 36 Cooper Sq., New York, NY 10003. Telephone: 212-475-3300. **Management:** Mark Bartel, Publisher. Stephanie Hansen, Advertising Manager. Tom Imbertson, Circulation Manager. **Editorial:** Steve Perry, Editor.

NORTHEASTER. 1620 Central Ave. NE #101, Minneapolis, MN 55413. E-MAIL: mkashmore@aol.com. Pub. Frequency: s-m. Page Size: tabloid.Subscrip. Rate: $20/yr; $34/yr mailed 1st class Circulation: 33,000 per issue (paid). **Owner(s):** Kerry Ashmore, See address and contact information above. **Management:** Kerry Ashmore, Publisher. **Editorial:** Kerry Ashmore, Editor.

NORTHNEWS. 1620 Central Ave. NE #101, Minneapolis, MN 55413. E-MAIL: mkashmore@aol.com. Pub. Frequency: m. Page Size: tabloid.Subscrip. Rate: $14/yr; $22/yr mailed 1st class Circulation: 30,000 per issue (paid). **Owner(s):** Kerry Ashmore, See address and contact information above. **Management:** Kerry Ashmore, Publisher. Joy Judge, Circulation Manager. **Editorial:** Kerry Ashmore, Editor.

SKYWAY NEWS. 1115 Hennepin Ave, S., Minneapolis, MN 55403-3636. Telephone: 612-825-9205. FAX: 612-825-0929. E-MAIL: skywaynews@skywaynew.net. URL: http://www.skywaynews.net. Pub. Frequency: w. (Mon.) Page Size: standard. Subscrip. Rate: $64/yr mailed. Circulation: 30,000 per issue (paid and free). **Owner(s):** Terry Gahan, See address and contact information above. **Management:** Terry Gahan, Co-Publisher. Jen Guarino, General Manager. Janis Hall, Publisher. Melissa Ungerman, Advertising. Jen Guarino, Advertising Manager. **Editorial:** Sarah McKenzie, Editor. Robb Long, Photo Editor.

SOUTHWEST JOURNAL, THE. 1115 Hennepin Ave, S., Minneapolis, MN 55403-3636. Telephone: 612-825-9205. FAX: 612-825-0929. E-MAIL: swjournal@uswest.net. URL: http://www.swjournal.com. Pub. Frequency: bi-m. (Mon,) Page Size: standard.Subscrip. Rate: $32/yr mailed Circulation: 35,000 per issue (free). **Owner(s):** Terry Gahan, See address and contact information above. **Management:** Terry Gahan, Co-Publisher. Jen Guarino, General Manager. Janis Hall, Publisher. Melissa Ungerman, Advertising. Jen Guarino, Advertising Manager. **Editorial:** Sarah McKenzie, Editor. Robb Long, Photo Editor.

MINNEOTA

MINNEOTA MASCOT. 201 N. Jefferson St., Minneota, MN 56264-0008. Telephone: 507-872-6492. FAX: 507-872-6840. E-MAIL: mascot@centurytel.net. URL: www.minneotamascot.com. Year Established: 1891. Pub. Frequency: w. (Wed.) Page Size: standard.Subscrip. Rate: $.75 newsstand/cover; $27.50/yr Circulation: 1,395 per issue (paid). **Owner(s):** Jon Guttormsson, See address and contact information above. **Management:** Jon Guttormsson, Publisher. **Editorial:** Gail Van Booren, Editor.

MONTEVIDEO

MONTEVIDEO AMERICAN-NEWS. 223 S First St, Montevideo, MN 56265. Telephone: 320-269-2156. FAX: 320-269-2159. E-MAIL: adrep@montnews.com. URL: http://www.montenews.com. Mailing Address: PO Box 99, Montevideo, MN 56265-0099. Year Established: 1911. Pub. Frequency: w. (Thu.) Page Size: broadsheet. Subscrip. Rate: $1 newsstand/cover; $45/yr local; $54/yr out of area; $60/yr out of state. Circulation: 48,000 per issue (paid). **Owner(s):** GateHouse Media, Inc, 350 WillowBrook Office Park, Fairport, NY 14450. Telephone: 585-598-0030. FAX: 585-248-2631. **Management:** Kurt Dahl, Publisher. Stacey Hoidal, Classified Adv. Mgr.. **Editorial:** John Givan, Editor. Bruce Olson, Sports.

STAR ADVISOR, THE. 223 S First St, Montevideo, MN 56265. Mailing Address: PO Box 99, Montevideo, MN 56265-0099. Pub. Frequency: w. (Mon.) Page Size: standard Circulation: 11,933 per issue (free). **Owner(s):** GateHouse Media, Inc, 350 WillowBrook Office Park, Fairport, NY 14450. **Management:** Kurt Dahl, Publisher. Dale Mooney, Advertising. Stacey Hoidal, Classified Adv. Mgr..

MONTGOMERY

MONTGOMERY MESSENGER. 310 S. First St., Montgomery, MN 56069-0049. Telephone: 507-364-8601. FAX: 507-364-8602. E-MAIL: mpaper@frontiernet.net. Mailing Address: PO Box 49, Montgomery, MN 56069-0049. Pub. Frequency: w. (Thu.) Page Size: broadsheet. Subscrip. Rate: $27/yr tri-county area; $34/yr mailed in state; $40/yr mailed out of state. Circulation: 2,120 per issue (paid). **Owner(s):** Suel Printing Co., PO Box 25, New Prague, MN 56071-0025. Telephone: 952-758-4435. **Management:** E. Charles Wann, Publisher. Mark Slavik, Advertising Manager. **Editorial:** Wade Young, Editor.

MOOSE LAKE

MOOSE LAKE STAR-GAZETTE. ISSN 0746-2980
PO Box 449, Moose Lake, MN 55767. Telephone: 218-485-4406. FAX: 218-485-0357. E-MAIL: evergreen@pinenet.com. Year Established: 1885. Pub. Frequency: w. (Wed.) Page Size: broadsheet. Subscrip. Rate: $.50 newsstand/cover; $24/yr local. Circulation: 2,800 per issue (paid). **Owner(s):** Jerry DeRungs, See address and contact information above. **Management:** Jerry DeRungs, President. **Editorial:** Jerry DeRungs, Editor.

MORA

KANABEC COUNTY TIMES. 107 S. Park St., Mora, MN 55051. Telephone: 320-679-2661. E-MAIL: wweber@ncis.com. URL: http://www.moraminn.com. Year Established: 1884. Pub. Frequency: w. (Thu.) Page Size: broadsheet. Subscrip. Rate: $.75 newsstand/cover; $30/yr mailed in county; $36.50/yr mailed out of county. Circulation: 3,000 per issue (paid). **Owner(s):** Eugene Johnson, See address and contact information above. **Management:** Wade Weber, Publisher. Annette Krist, Advertising Manager. Nancy Osterman, Classified Adv. Mgr.. **Editorial:** Andy Cummings, Editor.

MOUND

LAKER (MOUND), THE. P.O. Box 82, Mound, MN 55364. Telephone: 952-472-1140. FAX: 952-472-0516. URL: http://www.mnsun.com. Pub. Frequency: w. (Sat.) Page Size: broadsheet. Subscrip. Rate: $31/yr out of county; $36/yr in state; $37/yr out of state. Adv. Rate: B&W page $608 Circulation: 9,300 per issue (paid and free). **Owner(s):** American Community Newspapers LLC, 10917 Valley View Rd, Eden Prairie, MN 55344. Telephone: 952-392-6800. **Management:** Keith Anderson, Co-Publisher. Bill Holme, General Manager. Jeff Coolman, President.

PIONEER (MOUND), THE. P.O. Box 82, Mound, MN 55364. Telephone: 952-472-1140. FAX: 952-472-0516. URL: http://www.mnsun.com. Pub. Frequency: w. (Sat.) Page Size: broadsheet. Subscrip. Rate: $31/yr mailed out of county; $36/yr mailed in state; $37/yr mailed out of state. Adv. Rate: B&W page $544 Circulation: 6,500 per issue (paid and free). **Owner(s):** American Community Newspapers LLC, 10917 Valley View Rd., Eden Prairie, MN 55344. **Management:** Eric Serrano, General Manager. Gene Carr, President. Keith Anderson, Publisher. **Editorial:** Erin Pinegar, Editor.

MOUNTAIN LAKE

MOUNTAIN LAKE OBSERVER/BUTTERFIELD ADVOCATE. 237 N 11th St, Mountain Lake, MN 56159. Telephone: 507-427-2725. FAX: 507-427-2724. E-MAIL: observer@mtlakenews.com. URL: http://www.mtlakenews.com. Mailing Address: PO Box 429, Mountain Lake, MN 56159-0429. Pub. Frequency: w. (Wed.) Page Size: broadsheet. Subscrip. Rate: $1 newsstand/cover; $35.95/yr mailed in county & adj. cys.; $45.95/yr mailed out of area. Adv. Rate: col. inch $6 Circulation: 1,725 per issue (paid). **Owner(s):** Citizen Publishing Co., See address and contact information above. **Management:** Kim Anderson, Publisher. Sue Frederidkson, Advertising Manager. **Editorial:** Kurt Hildebrandt, Managing Editor.

NEW BRIGHTON

NEW BRIGHTON-MOUNDS VIEW BULLETIN. 909 Seventh Ave., N.W., New Brighton, MN 55112. Telephone: 651-633-2777. FAX: 651-633-3846. Mailing Address: PO Box 120608, New Brighton, MN 55112-2700. Year Established: 1938. Pub. Frequency: w. (Wed.) Page Size: broadsheet. Subscrip. Rate: $.50 newsstand/cover; $33.95/yr out of area. Circulation: 27,000 per issue (paid and free). **Owner(s):** Lillie Suburban Newspapers, Inc., 2515 E. Seventh Ave., St. Paul, MN 55109-3098. Telephone: 651-777-8800. FAX: 651-777-8288. **Management:** Jeff Enright, Publisher. Tony Fragnita, Advertising Manager. Virginia Flaherty, Classified Adv. Mgr.. **Editorial:** Mary Lee Hagert, Managing Editor.

SHOREVIEW-ARDEN HILLS BULLETIN. 909 Seventh Ave., New Brighton, MN 55112-3098. Telephone: 651-633-2777. FAX: 651-633-3846. Mailing Address: PO Box 120608, New Brighton, MN 55112-2700. Year Established: 1938. Pub. Frequency: w. (Wed.) Page Size: broadsheet. Subscrip. Rate: $.50 newsstand/cover; $29.95/yr out of area. Circulation: 12,000 per issue (paid and free). **Owner(s):** Lillie Suburban Newspapers, Inc., 2515 E. Seventh Ave., St. Paul, MN 55109-3098. Telephone: 651-777-8800. FAX: 651-777-8288. **Management:** Jeff Enright, Publisher. Tony Fragnita, Advertising Manager. Virginia Flaherty, Classified Adv. Mgr.. **Editorial:** Mary Lee Hagert, Managing Editor.

ST. ANTHONY BULLETIN. 909 Seventh Ave., N.W., New Brighton, MN 55112. Telephone: 651-633-2777. FAX: 651-633-3846. E-MAIL: bulletinnews@qwest.net. Mailing Address: PO Box 120608, New Brighton, MN 55112-2700. Year Established: 1938. Pub. Frequency: w. (Wed.) Page Size: broadsheet. Subscrip. Rate: $.50 newsstand/cover; $33.95/yr out of area. Circulation: 27,000 per issue (paid and free). **Owner(s):** Lillie Suburban Newspapers, Inc., 2515 E. Seventh Ave., St. Paul, MN 55109-3098. Telephone: 651-777-8800. FAX: 651-777-8288. **Management:** Jeff Enright, Publisher. Tony Fragnita, Advertising Manager. Virginia Flaherty, Classified Adv. Mgr.. **Editorial:** Mary Lee Hagert, Managing Editor.

NEW PRAGUE

NEW PRAGUE TIMES. PO Box 25, New Prague, MN 56071. E-MAIL: suelprat@means.net. URL: http://www.newpraguetimes.com. Year Established: 1889. Pub. Frequency: w. (Thu.) Page Size: broadsheet. Subscrip. Rate: $.75 newsstand/cover; $26/yr mailed in county; $32/yr mailed in state; $38/yr mailed out of state. Adv. Rate: col. inch $6.50 Circulation: 4,500 per issue (paid). **Owner(s):** Suel Printing Co., See address and contact information above. **Management:** Arthur S. Wann, General Manager. E. Charles Wann, President. Mark Slavik, Advertising Manager. Ann Slavik, Classified Adv. Mgr.. **Editorial:** Lois Suel Wann, Editor. Chuck Kajer, Managing Editor.

NEW YORK MILLS

NEW YORK MILLS HERALD. 108 S. Main Ave., New York Mills, MN 56567-0158. Telephone: 218-385-2275. FAX: 218-385-3626. E-MAIL: herald@eot.com. URL: http://www.newyorkmills.com. Mailing Address: PO Box 288, New York Mills, MN 56567. Pub. Frequency: w. (Thu.) Page Size: broadsheet. Subscrip. Rate: $1 newsstand/cover; $32/yr in county; $34/yr mailed out of county; $39/yr mailed out of state. Adv. Rate: col. inch $9.25 Circulation: 2,000 per issue (paid). **Owner(s):** Jeff Meyer, 101 Fifth St., N., Fargo, ND 58102. Telephone: 701-235-7311. **Management:** Lou Hoglund, Publisher. Becky Becker, Sales Manager. **Editorial:** Kevin Cederstrom, Editor.

NORTH BRANCH

E C M POST REVIEW. ISSN 0891-0731
6448 Main St., North Branch, MN 55056-0366. Telephone: 651-674-7025. FAX: 651-674-7026. E-MAIL: editor.postreview@ecm-inc.com. URL: http://www.ecm-inc.com. Mailing Address: PO Box 366, North Branch, MN 55056-0366. Year Established: 1875. Pub. Frequency: w. (Wed.) Page Size: tabloid. Subscrip. Rate: $.75 newsstand/cover; $34/yr mailed in county; $37/yr mailed out of county. Circulation: 2,500 per issue (paid). **Owner(s):** ECM Publishers, Inc., 4095 Coon Rapids Blvd., Coon Rapids, MN 55433. Telephone: 763-712-2400. FAX: 763-712-1480. **Management:** Julian L. Andersen, Publisher. Mary Eslinger, Advertising Manager. Corinne Kruse, Circulation Manager. **Editorial:** Mary Helen Swanson, Editor.

NORTHFIELD

NORTHFIELD NEWS (NORTHFIELD, MN). ISSN 1053-542X
115 W. Fifth St., Northfield, MN 55057. Telephone: 507-645-5615. E-MAIL: editor@northfield.org. URL: http://www.northfield.org. Year Established: 1876. Pub. Frequency: s-w. (Wed. & Sat.) Page Size: broadsheet. Subscrip. Rate: $1 newsstand/cover; $56/yr home delivery local; $60/yr mailed in state; $68/yr mailed elsewhere. Circulation: 6,200 per issue (paid). **Owner(s):** Huckle Publishing, Inc., See address and contact information above. **Management:** Renee Huckle, Publisher.

NORTHOME

NORTHOME RECORD & MIZPAH MESSAGE. 12061 Main St., Northome, MN 56661-0025. Telephone: 218-897-5278. Mailing Address: PO Box 25, Northome, MN 56661-0025. Year Established: 1901. Pub. Frequency: w. (Tue.) Page Size: tabloid. Subscrip. Rate: $.40 newsstand/cover; $18/yr in county; $21.50/yr in state; $24/yr out of state. Adv. Rate: col. inch $4.50 Circulation: 1,100 per issue (paid). **Owner(s):** Northome Record Inc., PO Box 25, Northome, MN 56661. Telephone: 218-897-5278. **Management:** J. Reed Anderson, Publisher. Karla Anderson, Advertising Manager. **Editorial:** J. Reed Anderson, Editor.

NORWOOD

NORWOOD YOUNG AMERICA TIMES. 510 Faxon Rd., Norwood, MN 55368. Telephone: 952-467-2271. FAX: 952-467-2294. E-MAIL: tmoen@acnpapers.com. URL: http://www.mnsun.com. Mailing Address: PO Box 10, Norwood, MN 55368. Pub. Frequency: w. (Thu.) Page Size: broadsheet. Subscrip. Rate: $1 newsstand/cover; $30/yr in county; $32/yr in state; $34/yr out of state. Adv. Rate: B&W page $315 Circulation: 2,450 per issue (paid). **Owner(s):** American Community Newspapers LLC, 10917 Valley View Rd, Eden Prairie, MN 55344. Telephone: 952-392-6800. **Management:** Keith Anderson, Publisher. **Editorial:** Todd Moen, Editor.

OKLEE

OKLEE HERALD, THE. Main St., Oklee, MN 56742. Telephone: 218-796-5181. FAX: 218-487-5251. E-MAIL: richards@gvtel.net. Mailing Address: PO Box 9, Oklee, MN 56742. Year Established: 1917. Pub. Frequency: w. (Thu.) Page Size: tabloid. Subscrip. Rate: $.75 newsstand/cover; $20/yr in county; $25/yr out of county. Circulation: 1,000 per issue (paid). **Owner(s):** Richards Publishing Co., Inc., Second & Main, PO Box 159, Gonvick, MN 56644. Telephone: 218-487-5225. **Management:** Dick Richards, Publisher. **Editorial:** Suzan Gunderson, Editor.

OLIVIA

OLIVIA TIMES JOURNAL. 816 E. Lincoln Ave., Olivia, MN 56277. Telephone: 320-523-2032. FAX: 320-523-2033. E-MAIL: otj@rencopub.com. Pub. Frequency: w. (Thu.) Page Size: broadsheet. Subscrip. Rate: $1 newsstand/cover; $30/yr in county; $36/yr out of county. Circulation: 1,650 per issue (controlled and free). **Owner(s):** Renco Publishing, Inc., 816 E. Lincoln Ave., Olivia, MN. Telephone: 320-523-2032. FAX: 320-523-2033. **Management:** Rose Hettig, Owner. **Editorial:** Sandy Grussing, Editor.

RENVILLE COUNTY SHOPPER. 816 E. Lincoln Ave., Olivia, MN 56277. Year Established: 1967. Pub. Frequency: w. (Mon.) Page Size: broadsheet Circulation: 5,100 per issue (free). **Owner(s):** Renco Publishing, Inc., See address and contact information above. **Management:** Rose Hettig, Publisher.

ORTONVILLE

ORTONVILLE INDEPENDENT. PO Box 336, Ortonville, MN 56278. Telephone: 320-839-6163. E-MAIL: mail@ortonvilleindependent.com. Year Established: 1920. Pub. Frequency: w. (Tue.) Page Size: broadsheet. Subscrip. Rate: $.75 newsstand/cover; $30/yr mailed in county; $34/yr mailed out of county; $38/yr mailed out of state. Adv. Rate: col. inch $6 Circulation: 3,700 per issue (paid). **Owner(s):** James D. & Jeannette Kaercher, Sue Kaercher-Blake, See address and contact information above. **Management:** James D. Kaercher, President. Suzette Kaercher-Blake, Publisher. Arlene Wiese, Office Manager. Suzette Kaercher-Blake, Sales Manager. **Editorial:** James D. Kaercher, Editor-in-Chief. Suzette Kaercher-Blake, Associate Editor.

OSAKIS

OSAKIS REVIEW, THE. ISSN 1040-6069
26 E. Main St., Osakis, MN 56360-0220. Telephone: 320-859-2143. FAX: 320-859-2054. Mailing Address: PO Box 220, Osakis, MN 56360-0220. Year Established: 1890. Pub. Frequency: w. (Tue.) Page Size: tabloid. Subscrip. Rate: $.75 newsstand/cover; $24.50/yr in county; $28/yr in state; $31.50/yr out of state. Circulation: 1,496 per issue (paid). **Owner(s):** Jeff Meyer, PO Box 2020, Fargo, ND 58107. Telephone: 701-235-7311. **Management:** Jody Hanson, Publisher. **Editorial:** Greta Petrich, Managing Editor.

OSSEO

CHAMPLIN/DAYTON PRESS. 33 Second St., N.E., Osseo, MN 55369-0280. Telephone: 763-425-3323. FAX: 763-425-2945. E-MAIL: mail@pressnews.com. URL: http://www.pressnews.com. Year Established: 1974. Pub. Frequency: w. (Tue.) Page Size: broadsheet. Subscrip. Rate: $1 newsstand/cover; $34/yr; $49 for 2 yrs.. Adv. Rate: B&W page $982 Circulation: 1,864 per issue (paid); 4,598 per issue (free). **Owner(s):** American Community Newspapers LLC, 10917 Valley View Rd., Eden Prairie, MN 55344. Telephone: 952-392-6801. **Management:** Jeff Coolman, President. Bruce Treichler, Publisher. Bruce Pierce, Circulation Manager. **Editorial:** Peggy Bakken, Executive Editor.

NORTH CROW RIVER NEWS. 33 Second St., N.E., Osseo, MN 55369. Telephone: 763-425-3323. FAX: 763-425-2945. E-MAIL: mail@pressnews.com. URL: http://www.mnsun.com. Mailing Address: PO Box 280, Osseo, MN 55369. Year Established: 1963. Pub. Frequency: w. (Mon.) Page Size: broadsheet. Subscrip. Rate: $1 newsstand/cover; $38/yr; $54 for 2 yrs.. Adv. Rate: B&W page $982.80 Circulation: 2,874 per issue (paid); 6,614 per issue (free). **Owner(s):** American Community Newspapers LLC, 10917 Valley View Rd., Eden Prairie, MN 55344. Telephone: 952-392-6801. **Management:** Jeff Coolman, President. Bruce Treichler, Publisher. Bruce Pierce, Circulation Manager. **Editorial:** Jeff Borowicz, Managing Editor.

OSSEO/MAPLE GROVE PRESS. 33 Second St., N.E., Osseo, MN 55369. Telephone: 763-425-3323. FAX: 763-425-4299. E-MAIL: sunpressmail@acnpapers.com. URL: http://www.pressnews.com. Mailing Address: PO Box 280, Osseo, MN 55369. Year Established: 1922. Pub. Frequency: w. (Wed.) Page Size: broadsheet. Subscrip. Rate: $1 newsstand/cover; $38/yr; $54 for 2 yrs.. Adv. Rate: B&W page $1,197 Circulation: 4,354 per issue (paid); 9,616 per issue (free). **Owner(s):** American Community Newspapers LLC, 10917 Valley View Rd., Eden Prairie, MN 55344. **Management:** Stacie Cormier, Publisher. **Editorial:** Peggy Bakken, Executive Editor. Jeff Borowicz, Managing Editor.

ROCKFORD AREA NEWS LEADER. 33 Second St., N.E., Osseo, MN 55369. Telephone: 763-425-3323. FAX: 763-425-2945. E-MAIL: sunpressmail@acnpapers.com. URL: http://www.pressnews.com. Mailing Address: PO Box 280, Osseo, MN 55369. Year Established: 1963. Pub. Frequency: w. (Mon.) Page Size: broadsheet. Subscrip. Rate: $1 newsstand/cover; $34/yr; $49 for 2 yrs.. Adv. Rate: B&W page $831.60 Circulation: 1,066 per issue (paid); 2,963 per issue (free). **Owner(s):** American Community Newspapers LLC, 10917 Valley View Rd., Eden Prairie, MN 55344. **Management:** Bruce Treichler, Publisher. Bruce Pierce, Circulation Manager. **Editorial:** Peggy Bakken, Executive Editor.

SOUTH CROW RIVER NEWS. 33 Second St., N.E., Osseo, MN 55369. Telephone: 763-425-3323. FAX: 763-425-2945. E-MAIL: sunpressmail@acnpapers.com. URL: http://www.pressnews.com. Mailing Address: PO Box 280, Osseo, MN 55369. Year Established: 1963. Pub. Frequency: w. (Mon.) Page Size: broadsheet. Subscrip. Rate: $1 newsstand/cover; $34/yr; $49 for 2 yrs.. Adv. Rate: B&W page $794 Circulation: 1,227 per issue (paid); 2,848 per issue (free). **Owner(s):** American Community Newspapers LLC, 10917 Valley View Rd., Eden Prairie, MN 55344. Telephone: 952-392-6801. **Management:** Stacie Cormier, Publisher. Bruce Treichler, Advertising Manager. Bruce Pierce, Circulation Manager. **Editorial:** Peggy Bakken, Executive Editor.

OWATONNA

OWATONNA AREA SHOPPER. 135 W. Pearl, Owatonna, MN 55060. Telephone: 507-451-2840. FAX: 507-444-2382. URL: http://www.owatonna.com. Pub. Frequency: w. (Sun.) Page Size: broadsheet Circulation: 13,480 per issue (free). **Owner(s):** Huckle Publishing, Inc., See address and contact information above. **Management:** Ron Ensley, Publisher. Debbie Ensley, Advertising Manager. Carol Harvey, Circulation Manager.

PARKERS PRAIRIE

PARKERS PRAIRIE INDEPENDENT (PARKERS PRAIRIE), THE. 114 N Otter Ave, Parkers Prairie, MN 56361. Telephone: 218-338-2741. FAX: 218-338-2745. E-MAIL: ppinews@me.com. URL: http://www.ppindependent.net. Year Established: 1902. Pub. Frequency: w. (Thu.) Page Size: broadsheet. Subscrip. Rate: $.75 newsstand/cover; $28/yr in county; $31/yr mailed out of county; $35/yr mailed out of state. Adv. Rate: col. inch $6.50 Circulation: 1,200 per issue (paid). **Owner(s):** Jennifer Marquandt, See address and contact information above. Jacquelyn Wehking, 117 N. Otter Ave., Parkers Prairie, MN 56361-0042. PO Box 42, Parkers Prairie, MN 56361. 117 N. Otter Ave., Parkers Prairie, MN 56361. Telephone: 218-338-2741. FAX: 218-338-2745. **Management:** Jacquelyn Wehking, Co-Publisher. Jennifer Marquadt, Manager. **Editorial:** Jacquelyn Wehking, Editor.

PAYNESVILLE

PAYNESVILLE PRESS, THE. 211 Washburne Ave., Paynesville, MN 56362-0054. Telephone: 320-243-3772. FAX: 320-243-4492. E-MAIL: paypress@paynesvillepress.com. URL: http://www.paynesvillearea.com. Year Established: 1887. Pub. Frequency: w. (Wed.) Page Size: broadsheet. Subscrip. Rate: $.75 newsstand/cover; $27/yr in county & adj. cys.; $33/yr in state; $40/yr elsewhere. Circulation: 2,700 per issue (paid). **Owner(s):** Paynesville Press, The, See address and contact information above. **Management:** Lynne Jacobson, Publisher. Betty Orbeck, Circulation Director. Carol Ambrose, Classified Adv. Mgr.. **Editorial:** Michael Jacobson, Editor.

PELICAN RAPIDS

PARK RAPIDS ENTERPRISE. 29 W. Mill, Pelican Rapids, MN 56572. Telephone: 218-863-1421. FAX: 218-863-1423. E-MAIL: enterprise@unitele.com. URL: http://www.parkrapidsenterprise.com. Mailing Address: PO Box 632, Pelican Rapids, MN 56572. Year Established: 1882. Pub. Frequency: s-w. (Wed. & Sat.) Page Size: broadsheet. Subscrip. Rate: $1 newsstand/cover; $39.50/yr in county; $47.50/yr mailed out of county; $54.50/yr mailed out of state. Adv. Rate: col. inch $9.65 Circulation: 6,000 per issue (paid). **Owner(s):** Jeff Meyer, PO Box 2020, Fargo, ND 58107. Telephone: 701-241-5400. **Management:** Michael Gravdahl, General Manager. Candy Parks, Advertising Manager. Joanne Roisum, Circulation Manager. Karen Holtan, Classified Adv. Mgr.. **Editorial:** LuAnn Hurd-Lof, Editor.

PEQUOT LAKES

ECHOLAND SHOPPER. PO Box 240, Pequot Lakes, MN 56472. Telephone: 218-568-8521. FAX: 218-568-5407. URL: http://www.pineandlakes.com. Year Established: 1975. Pub. Frequency: w. (Mon.) Page Size: broadsheet Circulation: 23,500 per issue (free). **Owner(s):** Echo Publishing, See address and contact information above. **Management:** Pete Mohs, Publisher. Ron Foss, Advertising Manager. **Editorial:** Bryan Clapper, Editor.

LAKE COUNTRY ECHO. PO Box 240, Pequot Lakes, MN 56472-0240. Telephone: 218-568-8521. FAX: 218-568-5407. URL: http://www.pineandlakes.com. Year Established: 1972. Pub. Frequency: w. (Thu.) Page Size: broadsheet. Subscrip. Rate: $.75 newsstand/cover; $29/yr in county; $32/yr mailed out of county. Circulation: 4,625 per issue (paid). **Owner(s):** Echo Publishing, See address and contact information above. **Management:** Pete Mohs, Publisher. Ron Foss, Advertising Manager. **Editorial:** Bryan Clapper, Editor.

PERHAM

PERHAM ENTERPRISE-BULLETIN. 222 S.E. Second St., Perham, MN 56573. Telephone: 218-346-5900. FAX: 218-346-5901. E-MAIL: perhameb@eot.com. URL: http://www.lakesurfer.com. Mailing Address: PO Box 288, Perham, MN 56573. Year Established: 1882. Pub. Frequency: w. (Thu.) Page Size: broadsheet. Subscrip. Rate: $1 newsstand/cover; $33/yr in county; $35/yr out of county; $40/yr out of state. Circulation: 3,175 per issue (paid). **Owner(s):** Jeff Meyer, PO Box 2020, Fargo, ND 58107. **Management:** Dennis Winskowski, Publisher. **Editorial:** Louis Hoglund, Editor. John George, Sports Editor.

PINE CITY

PINE CITY PIONEER. ISSN 0892-2012
405 Second Ave. S.E., Pine City, MN 55063. Telephone: 320-629-6771. FAX: 320-629-6772. E-MAIL: editor@pinecitynm.com. URL: http://www.pinecitymn.com. Pub. Frequency: w. (Thu.) Page Size: standard. Subscrip. Rate: $.75 newsstand/cover; $28/yr in county; $36/yr mailed in state. Circulation: 3,300 per issue (paid). **Owner(s):** Gene Johnson, See address and contact information above. **Management:** Wade Weber, Publisher. Annette Krist, Advertising Manager. Kim Fedder, Classified Adv. Mgr.. **Editorial:** Cindy Rolain, Editor.

PINE RIVER

PINE RIVER JOURNAL. 215 Norway Ave., Pine River, MN 56474-0370. Telephone: 218-587-2360. FAX: 218-587-2331. E-MAIL: journal@pineriverjournal.com. URL: http://www.pineandlakes.com. Mailing Address: PO Box 370, Pine River, MN 56474-0370. Pub. Frequency: w. (Thu.) Page Size: tabloid. Subscrip. Rate: $.75 newsstand/cover; $29/yr in county; $32/yr mailed out of county; $35/yr mailed out of state. Circulation: 1,925 per issue (paid). **Owner(s):** Echo Publishing, PO Box 240, Pequot Lakes, MN 56472. Telephone: 218-568-8521. **Management:** Pete Mohs, Publisher. Ron Foss, Advertising Manager. **Editorial:** Kelly Virden, Editor.

PIPER SHOPPER. 215 Norway Ave., Pine River, MN 56474-0370. Telephone: 218-587-2360. FAX: 218-587-2331. URL: http://www.pineandlakes.com. Mailing Address: PO Box 370, Pine River, MN 56474-0370. Pub. Frequency: w. (Mon.) Page Size: broadsheet Circulation: 13,036 per issue (paid). **Owner(s):** Echo Publishing, PO Box 240, Pequot Lakes, MN 56472-0240. Telephone: 218-568-8521. FAX: 218-568-5407. **Management:** Pete Mohs, Publisher. Ron Foss, Advertising Manager.

PIPESTONE

FREE STAR, THE. 101 Second St. NE, Pipestone, MN 56164. Telephone: 507-825-3333. FAX: 507-825-2168. E-MAIL: pipepub@pipstonestar.com. URL: http://www.pipestonestar.com. Mailing Address: PO Box 277, Pipestone, MN 56164-0277. Pub. Frequency: w. (Mon.) Page Size: broadsheet. Subscrip. Rate: $38/yr mailed. Adv. Rate: col. inch $8.60 Circulation: 11,010 per issue (free). **Owner(s):** Pipestone Publishing Co., See address and contact information above. **Management:** John Draper, Publisher. Paul Lorang, Advertising Manager. Glenda Otter, Circulation Manager. **Editorial:** Duane Winn, Editor. Matt Gilmore, Sports.

PIPESTONE COUNTY STAR. 101 Second St. NE, Pipestone, MN 56164. E-MAIL: pipepub@pipestonestar.com. URL: http://www.pipestonestar.com. Mailing Address: PO Box 277, Pipestone, MN 56164-0277. Year Established: 1879. Pub. Frequency: w. (Thu.) Page Size: broadsheet. Subscrip. Rate: $1 newsstand/cover; $37/yr home delivery in county; $44/yr mailed out of county. Adv. Rate: col. inch $9.05 Circulation: 3,375 per issue (paid). **Owner(s):** Pipestone Publishing Co., See address and contact information above. **Management:** John Draper, Publisher. Paul Lorang, Advertising Manager. Glenda Otter, Circulation Manager. **Editorial:** Duane Winn, Editor. Matt Gilmore, Sports.

PLAINVIEW

PLAINVIEW NEWS (PLAINVIEW, MN). 409 W. Broadway, Plainview, MN 55964. Telephone: 507-534-3121. FAX: 507-534-3920. Mailing Address: PO Box 457, Plainview, MN 55964. Pub. Frequency: w. (Thu.) Page Size: broadsheet. Subscrip. Rate: $.75 newsstand/cover; $29/yr in county & adj cys; $34/yr mailed in state; $42/yr mailed out of state. Circulation: 2,800 per issue (paid). **Owner(s):** Stumpf Publishing Co., 924 Whitewater Ave., St. Charles, MN 55972. Telephone: 507-932-3663. **Management:** Gary Stumpf, Publisher. Dan Stumpf, Advertising Manager. Mike Stumpf, Circulation Manager. **Editorial:** Brian Kilen, Editor.

PRESTON

FILLMORE COUNTY JOURNAL. 136 St. Anthony St., Preston, MN 55965. Telephone: 507-765-2151. FAX: 507-765-2468. E-MAIL: news@fillmorecountyjournal.com. URL: http://www.fillmorecountyjournal.com. Year Established: 1985. Pub. Frequency: w. (Mon.) Page Size: tabloid. Subscrip. Rate: $35/yr. Adv. Rate: col. inch $9.35 Circulation: 11,269 per issue (paid and free). **Owner(s):** John Torgrimson, See address and contact information above. **Management:** John Torgrimson, Publisher.

REPUBLICAN LEADER. 119 Filmore St., Preston, MN 55965-0027. Telephone: 507-765-2752. FAX: 507-765-2752. E-MAIL: leader@clear.lakes.com. URL: http://www.hometown-pages.com. Mailing Address: PO Box 27, Preston, MN 55965. Pub. Frequency: w. (Thu.) Page Size: broadsheet. Subscrip. Rate: $.75 newsstand/cover; $22/yr in county; $26/yr elsewhere. Circulation: 1,181 per issue (paid). **Owner(s):** Phillips Publishing, PO Box 112, Spring Valley, MN 55975. Telephone: 507-346-7365. **Management:** David Phillips, Publisher. **Editorial:** David Phillips, Editor.

PRINCETON

PRINCETON UNION-EAGLE. 208 N. Rum River Dr., Princeton, MN 55371. Telephone: 763-389-1222. FAX: 763-389-1728. URL: http://www.unioneagle.com. Mailing Address: PO Box 278, Princeton, MN 55371. Year Established: 1876. Pub. Frequency: w. (Thu.) Page Size: broadsheet. Subscrip. Rate: $.75 newsstand/cover; $25/yr in county; $34/yr out of county. Circulation: 4,000 per issue (paid). **Owner(s):** ECM Publishers, Inc., 4095 Coon Rapids Blvd., Coon Rapids, MN 55433. Telephone: 763-712-2400. FAX: 763-712-2480. **Management:** Jeff Athmann, President. Timothy J. Enger, Publisher. **Editorial:** Chris Schafer, Editor.

PRIOR LAKE

PRIOR LAKE AMERICAN. 14093 Commerce Ave., Prior Lake, MN 55372. Telephone: 952-447-6669. FAX: 952-447-6671. E-MAIL: editor@plamerican.com. URL: http://www.plamerican.com. Year Established: 1960. Pub. Frequency: w. (Sat.) Page Size: tabloid. Subscrip. Rate: $1 newsstand/cover; $25/yr local; $30/yr in county; $43/yr in state; $47/yr out of state. Circulation: 7,684 per issue (free). **Owner(s):** Laurie Hartmann, See address and contact information above. **Management:** Laurie Hartmann, Publisher. **Editorial:** Lori Carlson, Editor.

PROCTOR

PROCTOR JOURNAL. 215 Fifth St., Proctor, MN 55810-1686. Telephone: 218-624-3344. FAX: 218-624-7037. E-MAIL: journal@proctormn.com. URL: http://www.proctormn.com. Year Established: 1906. Pub. Frequency: w. (Thu.) Page Size: tabloid. Subscrip. Rate: $1 newsstand/cover; $26/yr in county; $30/yr mailed out of county. Adv. Rate: col. inch $7.35 Circulation: 2,000 per issue (paid). **Owner(s):** Jake Benson, See address and contact information above. **Management:** Jake Benson, Publisher. Diane Giuliani, Office Manager. **Editorial:** Jake Benson, Editor.

RAYMOND

RAYMOND/PRINSBURG NEWS,THE. 204 Spicer Ave, Raymond, MN 56282-0157. E-MAIL: rpnews@wecnet.com. Year Established: 1900. Pub. Frequency: w. (Wed) Page Size: standard. Subscrip. Rate: $.75 newsstand/cover; $24/mo. local; $28/mo. in state; $30/mo. out of state. Adv. Rate: col. inch $4 Circulation: 900 per issue (paid). **Owner(s):** TJ Almen, PO Box 157, Raymond, MN 56282-0157. Telephone: 320-967-4244. **Management:** TJ Almen, Publisher. **Editorial:** Diane Macht, Editor.

RED LAKE FALLS

RED LAKE FALLS GAZETTE, THE. PO Box 370, Red Lake Falls, MN 56750-0370. E-MAIL: rlfgaz@gvtel.com. Year Established: 1882. Pub. Frequency: w. (Wed.) Page Size: standard. Subscrip. Rate: $1 newsstand/cover; $29/yr local; $35/yr mailed in state; $39/yr mailed out of state. Adv. Rate: col. inch $4.90 Circulation: 1,500 per issue (paid). **Owner(s):** Times Publishing Co., 105 Main Ave S, Red Lake Falls, MN 56750. **Management:** Rod Thoreson, Publisher.

REDWOOD FALLS

REDWOOD FALLS LIVEWIRE. 219 S. Washington St., Redwood Falls, MN 56283. Telephone: 507-637-2929. FAX: 507-637-3175. URL: http://www.gatehousemedia.com. Mailing Address: PO Box 299, Redwood Falls, MN 56283. Pub. Frequency: w. (Thu.) Page Size: standard Circulation: 5,435 per issue (free). **Owner(s):** GateHouse Media, Inc, 350 WillowBrook Office Park, Fairport, NY 14450. Telephone: 585-598-0030. FAX: 585-248-2631. **Management:** Pat Schmidt, Publisher. Sue Rima, Advertising Manager.

REDWOOD GAZETTE, THE. 219 S. Washington St., Redwood Falls, MN 56283. Telephone: 507-637-2929. FAX: 507-637-3175. E-MAIL: redgazet@rconnect.com. URL: http://www.redwoodgazette.com. Mailing Address: PO Box 299, Redwood Falls, MN 56283. Year Established: 1869. Pub. Frequency: s-w. (Mon. & Thu.) Page Size: broadsheet. Subscrip. Rate: $1 newsstand/cover; $66/yr in county; $78/yr in adj. cys.; $85/yr out of area. Adv. Rate: col. inch $9.30 Circulation: 3,554 per issue (paid). **Owner(s):** GateHouse Media, Inc, 350 WillowBrook Office Park, Fairport, NY 14450. Telephone: 585-598-0030. FAX: 585-248-2631. **Management:** Pat Schmidt, Publisher. Sue Rima, Advertising Manager. **Editorial:** Troy Krause, Editor. Ben Stoterau, Sports Editor.

ROBBINSDALE

CRYSTAL/ROBBINSDALE SUN-POST. 4080 W. Broadway, Ste. 113, Robbinsdale, MN 55422. Telephone: 763-536-7500. FAX: 763-536-7519. E-MAIL: pmiller@mnsun.com. URL: http://www.mnsun.com. Pub. Frequency: w. (Thu.) Page Size: tabloid. Subscrip. Rate: $.75 newsstand/cover; $84/yr mailed. Adv. Rate: B&W page $1,685 Circulation: 26,410 per issue (paid and free). **Owner(s):** American Community Newspapers LLC, 10917 Valley View Rd., Eden Prairie, MN 55344. Telephone: 952-392-6801. **Management:** Jeffrey Coolman, Group Publisher. Pam Miller, Advertising Manager. Bruce Pierce, Circulation Manager. **Editorial:** Peggy Bakken, Executive Editor. Dave Patersen, Sports.

NEW HOPE/GOLDEN VALLEY SUN-POST. 4080 W. Broadway, Ste. 113, Robbinsdale, MN 55422. Telephone: 763-536-7500. FAX: 763-536-7519. E-MAIL: sunpost@mnsun.com. URL: http://www.mnsun.com. Year Established: 1974. Pub. Frequency: w. (Thu.) Page Size: tabloid. Subscrip. Rate: $.75 newsstand/cover; $84/yr mailed. Adv. Rate: B&W page $1,685 Circulation: 21,690 per issue (paid and free). **Owner(s):** American Community Newspapers LLC, 10917 Valley View Rd., Eden Prairie, MN 55344. Telephone: 952-392-6801. **Management:** Jeffrey Coolman, Group Publisher. Pam Miller, Advertising Manager. Herb Hesse, Circulation Manager. **Editorial:** Sue Webber, Editor. Peggy Bakken, Executive Editor. Dave Patersen, Sports.

ROSEAU

ROSEAU TIMES-REGION. 106 W. Center St., Roseau, MN 56751. Telephone: 218-463-1521. FAX: 218-463-1530. E-MAIL: rtr@mncable.net. Year Established: 1889. Pub. Frequency: w. (Sat.) Page Size: broadsheet. Subscrip. Rate: $1 newsstand/cover; $28/yr in county; $35/yr out of county. Adv. Rate: col. inch $5.25 Freelance Pay: $0.50/column-inch. Circulation: 4,150 per issue (paid). **Owner(s):** Jodi Driscoll, See address and contact information above. **Management:** Jodi Driscoll, Publisher.

RUSHFORD

TRI-COUNTY RECORD (RUSHFORD). 300 S. Mill St., Rushford, MN 55971. Telephone: 507-864-7700. FAX: 507-864-2356. E-MAIL: tricopub@rushford.net. URL: http://www.rushford.net. Mailing Address: PO Box 429, Rushford, MN 55971-0429. Year Established: 1915. Pub. Frequency: w. (Thu.) Page Size: broadsheet. Subscrip. Rate: $1 newsstand/cover; $28/yr; $32/yr out of county. Circulation: 1,650 per issue (paid). **Owner(s):** Tri-County Publishing, Inc., See address and contact information above. **Management:** Darlene J. Schober, Publisher. **Editorial:** Darlene J. Schober, Editor. Ron Witt, Reporter.

RUTHTON

BUFFALO RIDGE GAZETTE, THE. 320 Aetna St., Ruthton, MN 56170-0070. Telephone: 507-658-3919. FAX: 507-658-3404. E-MAIL: brgazette@woodstocktel.net. URL: http://www.buffaloridgegazette.com. Mailing Address: PO Box 70, Ruthton, MN 56170-0070. Year Established: 1974. Pub. Frequency: w. (Wed.) Page Size: broadsheet. Subscrip. Rate: $.50 newsstand/cover; $22/yr mailed in county; $27/yr mailed elsewhere. Adv. Rate: col. inch $4.20 Freelance Pay: $0.30/column-inch. Circulation: 500 per issue (paid). **Owner(s):** Hunt & Hunt Newspapers, 151 N. Tyler St., Tyler, MN 56178. Telephone: 507-247-5502. FAX: 507-247-5502. **Management:** Charles Hunt, Publisher. **Editorial:** Karen Minett, Managing Editor.

SAUK CENTRE

DAIRYLAND PEACH. 601 Sinclair Lewis Ave., Sauk Centre, MN 56378. Telephone: 320-352-6569. FAX: 320-352-6181. E-MAIL: print.saulkcentre@ecm-inc.com. Mailing Address: PO Box 285, Sauk Centre, MN 56378. Pub. Frequency: w. (Mon.) Page Size: standard. Subscrip. Rate: $32/yr out of area. Circulation: 29,400 per issue. **Owner(s):** ECM Publishers, Inc., 4095 Coon Rapids Blvd., Coon Rapids, MN 55433. Telephone: 763-712-2400. **Management:** Brian McCoy, General Manager.

SAUK CENTRE HERALD. 522 Sinclair Lewis Ave., Sauk Centre, MN 56378. Telephone: 320-352-6577. E-MAIL: jweyer@saukherald.com. URL: http://www.saukherald.com. Year Established: 1867. Pub. Frequency: w. (Tue.) Page Size: broadsheet. Subscrip. Rate: $1 newsstand/cover; $26/yr in area; $30/yr in state; $32/yr out of state. Adv. Rate: col. inch $4.42 Circulation: 3,550 per issue (paid). **Owner(s):** Dave Simpkins, See address and contact information above. **Management:** Dave Simpkins, Publisher. Pat Turner, Advertising. Lois Meyer, Business Manager. **Editorial:** Carol Moorman, Editor.

SEBEKA

SEBEKA-MENAHGA REVIEW MESSENGER. 112 Minnesota Ave., W., Sebeka, MN 56477-0309. Telephone: 218-837-5558. FAX: 218-837-5560. E-MAIL: remess@wcta.net. URL: http://www.reviewmessenger.com. Mailing Address: PO Box 309, Sebeka, MN 56477-0309. Year Established: 1898. Pub. Frequency: w. (Wed.) Page Size: broadsheet. Subscrip. Rate: $.75 newsstand/cover; $26/yr trade area; $32/yr in state; $36/yr out of state. Adv. Rate: col. inch $8.25 Circulation: 3,500 per issue (paid). **Owner(s):** Marjon Printers, Inc., PO Box 309, Sebeka, MN 56477. Telephone: 218-837-5558. FAX: 218-837-5560. **Management:** T.M. Bloomquist, President. Bernice Eckenrode, Advertising Manager. **Editorial:** T.M. Bloomquist, Editor.

SHAKOPEE

SHAKOPEE VALLEY NEWS. PO Box 8, Shakopee, MN 55379. Telephone: 952-445-3333. Year Established: 1900. Pub. Frequency: w. (Thu.) Page Size: broadsheet. Subscrip. Rate: $1 newsstand/cover; $27/yr in county; $40/yr out of county. Circulation: 5,425 per issue (paid). **Owner(s):** Southwest Suburban Publishing Co., See address and contact information above. **Management:** Stan Rolfdrud, Publisher. **Editorial:** Pat Minelli, Editor.

SHERBURN

MARTIN COUNTY STAR. ISSN 1542-927X
30 N Main St, Sherburn, MN 56171. E-MAIL: mcstar@frontiernet.net. Year Established: 1888. Pub. Frequency: w. (Wed.) Page Size: broadsheet. Subscrip. Rate: $1 newsstand/cover; $29/yr in county; $33/yr mailed in state; $38/yr mailed out of state. Adv. Rate: col. inch $5 Circulation: 1,200 per issue (paid). **Owner(s):** Al Klein, PO Box 820, Sherburn, MN 56171. Telephone: 507-764-6681. FAX: 507-764-2756. **Management:** Al Klein, Publisher. **Editorial:** Al Klein, Editor.

SLAYTON

MURRAY COUNTY WHEEL HERALD. 2734 Broadway Ave., Slayton, MN 56172. Telephone: 507-836-8726. FAX: 507-836-8942. E-MAIL: thewheel@rconnect.com. Mailing Address: PO Box 263, Slayton, MN 56172. Pub. Frequency: w. (Mon.) Page Size: broadsheet.Subscrip. Rate: $24/yr in county Circulation: 7,300 per issue (paid). **Owner(s):** Will Beers, PO Box 263, Slayton, MN 36172. Telephone: 507-386-8726. **Management:** Will Beers, Publisher. Randy Beers, Advertising Manager. Sherri Halbur, Circulation Manager. **Editorial:** Will Beers, Editor.

SLEEPY EYE

BROWN COUNTY REMINDER. 115 Second Ave, NE, Sleepy Eye, MN 56085. Telephone: 507-794-3511. FAX: 507-794-5031. Mailing Address: PO Box 499, Sleepy Eye, MN 56085. Pub. Frequency: w. (Mon.) Page Size: standard Circulation: 8,351 per issue (free). **Owner(s):** GateHouse Media, Inc, 350 WillowBrook Office Park, Fairport, NY 14450. Telephone: 585-598-0030. **Management:** Jenny Boettger, Publisher. Lida Rolloff, Circulation Manager.

SLEEPY EYE HERALD DISPATCH. 115 Second Ave, NE, Sleepy Eye, MN 56085. Telephone: 507-794-3511. FAX: 507-794-5031. URL: http://www.sleepyeyenews.com. Mailing Address: PO Box 499, Sleepy Eye, MN 56085. Year Established: 1880. Pub. Frequency: w. (Thu.) Page Size: broadsheet. Subscrip. Rate: $.75 newsstand/cover; $44/yr in county & adj. cys.; $52/yr in state; $59/yr out of state. Circulation: 2,800 per issue (paid). **Owner(s):** GateHouse Media, Inc, 350 WillowBrook Office Park, Fairport, NY 14450. Telephone: 585-598-0030. FAX: 585-248-2631. **Management:** Jenny Boettger, Publisher. Lida Rolloff, Circulation Manager. **Editorial:** Joshua Dixon, Managing Editor.

SPRING GROVE

SPRING GROVE HERALD. 115 W. Main St., Spring Grove, MN 55974. Telephone: 507-498-3868. FAX: 507-498-6397. E-MAIL: sgherald@springgrove.coop. URL: http://www.springgroveherald.com. Mailing Address: PO Box 68, Spring Grove, MN 55974. Year Established: 1890. Pub. Frequency: w. (Wed.) Page Size: broadsheet. Subscrip. Rate: $1 newsstand/cover; $30/yr in county; $34/yr out of county. Adv. Rate: col. inch $6.50 Freelance Pay: $25/story. Circulation: 1,375 per issue (paid). **Owner(s):** Phillips Publishing, PO Box 112, Spring Valley, MN 55975. Telephone: 507-346-7365. FAX: 507-346-7366. **Management:** David Phillips, Publisher. **Editorial:** Heather Gray, Managing Editor.Readers: Spring Grove area

ST. CHARLES

LEWISTON JOURNAL. 924 Whitewater Ave., St. Charles, MN 55972. Telephone: 507-932-3663. E-MAIL: ljournal@lakes.com. Year Established: 1929. Pub. Frequency: w. (Thu.) Page Size: broadsheet. Subscrip. Rate: $.75 newsstand/cover; $28/yr in county; $33/yr out of county. Circulation: 1,700 per issue (paid). **Owner(s):** Stumpf Publishing Co., See address and contact information above. **Management:** Daniel Stumpf, Publisher. **Editorial:** Nick Koverman, Editor.

ST. CHARLES PRESS. 924 Whitewater Ave., St. Charles, MN 55972. Telephone: 507-932-3663. E-MAIL: scpress@lakes.com. Year Established: 1877. Pub. Frequency: w. (Thu.) Page Size: broadsheet. Subscrip. Rate: $.75 newsstand/cover; $28/yr in county; $33/yr out of county. Freelance Pay: $0.75/column-inch. Circulation: 2,700 per issue (paid). **Owner(s):** Stumpf Publishing Co., See address and contact information above. **Management:** Dan Stumpf, Publisher. **Editorial:** Nick Koverman, Editor.

ST. JAMES

ST. JAMES PLAINDEALER. 604 First Ave, S, St. James, MN 56081-0067. Telephone: 507-375-3161. FAX: 507-375-3221. URL: http://www.stjamesnews.com. Mailing Address: PO Box 67, St. James, MN 56081. Year Established: 1891. Pub. Frequency: w. (Thu.) Page Size: broadsheet. Subscrip. Rate: $1 newsstand/cover; $44/yr in county & adj. cys.; $52/yr in state; $59/yr out of state. Adv. Rate: col. inch $8.60 Circulation: 3,000 per issue (paid). **Owner(s):** GateHouse Media, Inc, 350 WillowBrook Office Park, Fairport, NY 14450. Telephone: 585-598-0030. FAX: 585-248-2631. **Management:** Duane "Doc" Durheim, Publisher. Deb Melheim, Circulation Manager.

TOWN AND COUNTRY SHOPPER. 604 First Ave, S, St. James, MN 56081-0067. Telephone: 507-375-3161. FAX: 507-375-3221. Pub. Frequency: w. (Mon.) Page Size: tabloid Circulation: 10,485 per issue (free). **Owner(s):** GateHouse Media, Inc, 125 W. Springfield St., St. James, MO 65559. 350 WillowBrook Office Park, Fairport, NY 14450. Telephone: 585-598-0030. FAX: 585-248-2631. **Management:** Duane "Doc" Durheim, Publisher. Deb Melheim, Circulation Manager.

ST. PAUL

EAST SIDE REVIEW. 2515 E. Seventh Ave., St. Paul, MN 55109-3098. Telephone: 651-777-8800. FAX: 651-777-8288. Year Established: 1938. Pub. Frequency: w. (Mon.) Page Size: broadsheet Circulation: 21,000 per issue (free). **Owner(s):** Lillie Suburban Newspapers, Inc., See address and contact information above. **Management:** Jeff Enright, Publisher. Valerie Neisus, Advertising Manager. Virginia Flaherty, Classified Adv. Mgr.. **Editorial:** Scott Nichols, Editor. Mary Lee Hagert, Managing Editor.

LILLIE PERSPECTIVES. 2515 E. Seventh Ave., St. Paul, MN 55109-3098. Telephone: 651-777-8800. FAX: 651-777-8288. Year Established: 1938. Pub. Frequency: w. (Mon.) Page Size: broadsheet.Adv. Rate: col. inch $64.30 Circulation: 29,000 per issue (free). **Owner(s):** Lillie Suburban Newspapers, Inc., See address and contact information above. **Management:** Jeff Enright, Publisher. Valerie Niesuis, Advertising Manager. Pat Colburn, Circulation Manager. Virginia Flaherty, Classified Adv. Mgr.. **Editorial:** Mary Lee Hagert, Managing Editor.

MAPLEWOOD REVIEW. 2515 E. Seventh Ave., St. Paul, MN 55109-3098. Telephone: 651-777-8800. FAX: 651-777-8288. Year Established: 1938. Pub. Frequency: w. (Wed.) Page Size: broadsheet. Subscrip. Rate: $.50 newsstand/cover; $19.95/yr local area; $23.95/yr out of area. Circulation: 2,000 per issue (paid and free). **Owner(s):** Lillie Suburban Newspapers, Inc., 2515 E. Seventh Ave., St. Paul, MN 55109. Telephone: 651-777-8800. FAX: 651-777-8288. **Management:** Jeff Enright, Publisher. Tony Fragnita, Advertising Manager. Virginia Flaherty, Classified Adv. Mgr.. **Editorial:** Holly Wenzel, Editor. Mary Lee Hagert, Managing Editor.

OAKDALE-LAKE ELMO REVIEW. 2515 E. Seventh Ave., St. Paul, MN 55109. Telephone: 651-777-8800. FAX: 651-777-8288. Year Established: 1938. Pub. Frequency: w. (Wed.) Page Size: broadsheet. Subscrip. Rate: $50 newsstand/cover; $19.95/yr local area; $23.95/yr out of area. Circulation: 2,500 per issue (paid and free). **Owner(s):** Lillie Suburban Newspapers, Inc., See address and contact information above. **Management:** Jeff Enright, Publisher. Tony Fragnita, Advertising Manager. Virginia Flaherty, Classified Adv. Mgr.. **Editorial:** Holly Wenzel, Editor. Mary Lee Hagert, Managing Editor.

RAMSEY COUNTY REVIEW. 2515 E. Seventh Ave., St. Paul, MN 55109-3098. Telephone: 651-777-8800. FAX: 651-777-8288. Year Established: 1938. Pub. Frequency: w. (Wed.) Page Size: broadsheet. Subscrip. Rate: $.50 newsstand/cover; $19.95/yr area. Circulation: 2,000 per issue (paid). **Owner(s):** Lillie Suburban Newspapers, Inc., 2515 E. Seventh Ave., St. Paul, MN 55109. Telephone: 651-777-8800. FAX: 651-777-8288. **Management:** Jeff Enright, Publisher. Tony Fragnita, Advertising Manager. Virginia Flaherty, Classified Adv. Mgr.. **Editorial:** Holly Wenzel, Editor. Mary Lee Hagert, Managing Editor.

ROSEVILLE REVIEW. 2515 E. Seventh Ave., St. Paul, MN 55109-3098. Telephone: 651-777-8800. FAX: 651-777-8288. E-MAIL: lillienews@aol.com. Year Established: 1938. Pub. Frequency: w. (Tue.) Page Size: broadsheet. Subscrip. Rate: $.50 newsstand/cover; $19.95/yr in county; $23.95/yr out of county. Circulation: 18,000 per issue (free). **Owner(s):** Lillie Suburban Newspapers, Inc., 2515 E. Seventh Ave., St. Paul, MN 55109. Telephone: 651-777-8800. FAX: 651-777-8288. **Management:** Jeff Enright, Publisher. Tony Fragnita, Advertising Manager. Laurie Young, Circulation Manager. Virginia Flaherty, Classified Adv. Mgr.. **Editorial:** Katie Derdoski, Editor. Mary Lee Hagert, Managing Editor.

SOUTH-WEST REVIEW. 2515 E. Seventh Ave., St. Paul, MN 55109-3098. Telephone: 651-777-8800. FAX: 651-777-8288. Year Established: 1938. Pub. Frequency: w. (Sun.) Page Size: broadsheet Circulation: 26,000 per issue (free). **Owner(s):** Lillie Suburban Newspapers, Inc., See address and contact information above. **Management:** Jeff Enright, Publisher. Tony Fragnita, Advertising Manager. Lori Young, Circulation Manager. Virginia Flaherty, Classified Adv. Mgr.. **Editorial:** Seth Loy, Editor. Mary Lee Hagert, Managing Editor.

VILLAGER. 757 Snelling Ave., S., St. Paul, MN 55116-2250. Telephone: 651-699-1462. FAX: 651-699-6501. E-MAIL: displayads@myvillager.com. URL: http://www.myvillager.com. Year Established: 1953. Pub. Frequency: bi-w. (Wed.) Page Size: tabloid. Subscrip. Rate: $35/yr mailed out of area. Freelance Pay: $60-$200/article. Circulation: 60,000 per issue (free). **Owner(s):** Michael Mischke, See address and contact information above. **Management:** Michael Mischke, Publisher. **Editorial:** Dale Mischke, Editor.Readers: 100% of neighborhoods

WOODBURY-SOUTH MAPLEWOOD REVIEW. 2515 E. Seventh Ave., St. Paul, MN 55109-3098. Telephone: 651-777-8800. FAX: 651-777-8288. Year Established: 1938. Pub. Frequency: w. (Mon.) Page Size: broadsheet. Subscrip. Rate: $52/yr mailed. Circulation: 11,750 per issue (paid and free). **Owner(s):** Lillie Suburban Newspapers, Inc., See address and contact information above. **Management:** Jeff Enright, Publisher. Tony Fragnita, Advertising Manager. Laurie Young, Circulation Manager. Virginia Flaherty, Classified Adv. Mgr.. **Editorial:** Mary Lee Hagert, Managing Editor.

ST. PETER

ST. PETER HERALD. 311 S. Minnesota Ave., St. Peter, MN 56082. Telephone: 507-931-4520. Mailing Address: PO Box 446, St. Peter, MN 56082-0446. Year Established: 1884. Pub. Frequency: w. (Thu.) Page Size: broadsheet. Subscrip. Rate: $1 newsstand/cover; $40/yr in county; $47/yr out of county; $52/yr mailed out of state. Circulation: 2,900 per issue (paid). **Owner(s):** Mainstream Publications, LLC, See address and contact information above. **Management:** Peggy Carlson, Publisher. **Editorial:** Ed Lee, Managing Editor.

STAPLES

STAPLES WORLD. 224 Fourth St., N.E., Staples, MN 56479. Telephone: 218-894-1112. FAX: 218-894-3570. E-MAIL: info@staples world.com. Mailing Address: P.O. Box 100, Staples, MN 56479-0100. Year Established: 1890. Pub. Frequency: w. (Thu.) Page Size: broadsheet. Subscrip. Rate: $.75 newsstand/cover; $31/yr in county & adj. counties; $35/yr out of area; $39/yr out of state. Adv. Rate: col. inch $10.50 Circulation: 2,728 per issue (paid). **Owner(s):** Devlin Newspapers, Inc., See address and contact information above. **Management:** Brenda Halvorson, General Manager. Russ Devlin, Publisher. Gary Mueller, Advertising Manager. **Editorial:** Tom Crawford, Editor.

THIEF RIVER FALLS

NORTHERN WATCH. PO Box 100, Thief River Falls, MN 56701-0100. E-MAIL: trftimes@trftimes.com. URL: http://www.trftimes.com. Year Established: 1991. Pub. Frequency: w. (Sat.) Page Size: broadsheet.Adv. Rate: col. inch $8.85 Circulation: 23,000 per issue (free). **Owner(s):** Thief River Falls Times, Inc., 324 Main Ave., N., Thief River Falls, MN 56701-0100. Telephone: 218-681-4450. FAX: 218-681-4455. **Management:** John Mattson, Publisher. Dede Coltom, Advertising Manager. **Editorial:** Dave Hill, Editor.

THIEF RIVER FALLS TIMES (2007). ISSN 1936-2250
PO Box 100, Thief River Falls, MN 56701-0100. E-MAIL: trftimes@trftimes.com. URL: http://www.trftimes.com. Year Established: 1910. Pub. Frequency: w. (Wed.) Page Size: broadsheet. Subscrip. Rate: $1 newsstand/cover; $32/yr area; $42/yr mailed out of area; $59/yr mailed out of state. Adv. Rate: col. inch $6.50 Circulation: 5,100 per issue (paid). **Owner(s):** Thief River Falls Times, Inc., 324 Main Ave., N., Thief River Falls, MN 56701-0100. Telephone: 218-681-4450. FAX: 218-681-4455. **Management:** John P. Mattson, Publisher. Dede Coltom, Advertising Manager. Sue Philipp, Circulation Manager. **Editorial:** David Hill, Editor.

TOWER

TIMBERJAY, THE. 414 Main St., Tower, MN 55790-0636. Telephone: 218-753-2950. FAX: 218-753-2916. E-MAIL: editor@timberjay.com. URL: http://www.timberjay.com. Mailing Address: PO Box 636, Tower, MN 55790. Pub. Frequency: w. (Sat.) Page Size: standard. Subscrip. Rate: $1 newsstand/cover; $19/yr local; $34/yr out of area; $62/yr mailed 1st class. Circulation: 2,913 per issue (paid). **Owner(s):** Marshall Helmberger & Jodi Summit, 414 Main St., Tower, MN 55790-2950. Telephone: 218-753-2950. FAX: 218-753-2916. **Management:** Marshall Helmberger, Co-Publisher. **Editorial:** Jodi Summit, Editor. Marshall Helmberger, Editor-in-Chief.

TRACY

TRACY HEADLIGHT-HERALD. 207 Fourth St., Tracy, MN 56175. Telephone: 507-629-4300. FAX: 507-629-4301. E-MAIL: tracypub@rconnect.com. URL: http://www.headlightherald.com. Year Established: 1879. Pub. Frequency: w. (Wed.) Page Size: broadsheet. Subscrip. Rate: $1 newsstand/cover; $37/yr in county; $39/yr out of county; $46/yr mailed out of state. Adv. Rate: col. inch $6.20 Circulation: 2,100 per issue (paid). **Owner(s):** Tracy Publishing Co., Inc., See address and contact information above. **Management:** James Keul, President. Seth Schmidt, Publisher. Lisa Sell, Advertising Manager. Chris Schons, Circulation Manager. **Editorial:** Seth Schmidt, Editor.

Weeklies

TWO HARBORS

LAKE COUNTY NEWS-CHRONICLE. 109 Waterfront Dr., Two Harbors, MN 55616. Telephone: 218-834-2141. FAX: 218-834-2144. E-MAIL: chronicle@lcnewschronicle.com. Mailing Address: PO Box 158, Two Harbors, MN 55616. Year Established: 1895. Pub. Frequency: w. (Fri.) Page Size: broadsheet. Subscrip. Rate: $.75 newsstand/cover; $31/yr in county; $36/yr out of county; $41/yr out of state. Circulation: 3,600 per issue (paid). **Owner(s):** Superior Publishing Corp., 1105 Tower Ave, Superior, WI 54880. Telephone: 715-395-5725. FAX: 715-395-5729. **Management:** Jay T. Roesler, Publisher. Deb Shold, Advertising. **Editorial:** Forrest Johnson, Editor.

TYLER

TYLER TRIBUTE. 151 N. Tyler St., Tyler, MN 56178-0466. Telephone: 507-247-5502. FAX: 507-247-5502. E-MAIL: tribute@tylertribute.com. URL: http://www.tylertribute.com. Mailing Address: PO Box Q, Tyler, MN 56178-0466. Year Established: 1972. Pub. Frequency: w. (Thu.) Page Size: broadsheet. Subscrip. Rate: $.75 newsstand/cover; $29/yr home delivery in county; $40/yr mailed in state. Adv. Rate: col. inch $4.95 Circulation: 1,680 per issue (paid). **Owner(s):** Hunt & Hunt Newspapers, 151 N. Tyler St., Tyler, MN 56178. Telephone: 507-247-5502. FAX: 507-247-5502. **Management:** Charles R. Hunt, Publisher. **Editorial:** Charles R. Hunt, Managing Editor.

VERNDALE

VERNDALE SUN. 21 First Ave., S.W., Verndale, MN 56481-0254. Telephone: 218-445-5779. FAX: 218-445-5779. E-MAIL: vsunnews@wcta.net. Mailing Address: PO Box E, Verndale, MN 56481-0254. Pub. Frequency: w. (Thu.) Page Size: tabloid. Subscrip. Rate: $22.50/yr in state; $27.50/yr out of state. Circulation: 741 per issue (controlled). **Owner(s):** Peter Quirt, 21 First Ave., P.O. Box E, Verndale, MN 56481. Telephone: 218-445-5779. **Management:** Peter Quirt, Publisher. Marlane Wenzel, Office Manager. **Editorial:** Peter Quirt, Editor.

WABASHA

WABASHA COUNTY HERALD. 200 Industrial Ct., Wabasha, MN 55981-0109. Telephone: 651-565-3368. FAX: 651-565-4736. E-MAIL: wherald@mywdo.com. Year Established: 1858. Pub. Frequency: w. (Wed.) Page Size: broadsheet. Subscrip. Rate: $.75 newsstand/cover. Circulation: 3,283 per issue (controlled). **Owner(s):** Stumpf Publishing Co., See address and contact information above. **Management:** Daniel Stumpf, Publisher. Laura Timm, Advertising Manager. **Editorial:** Michael Smith, Editor.

WABASSO

WABASSO STANDARD. 715 W. Main St., Wabasso, MN 56293-0070. Telephone: 507-342-5143. FAX: 507-342-5144. E-MAIL: standard@rconnect.com. Mailing Address: PO Box 70, Wabasso, MN 56293-0070. Pub. Frequency: w. (Wed.) Page Size: broadsheet. Subscrip. Rate: $1 newsstand/cover; $32/yr mailed. Circulation: 1,166 per issue (controlled). **Owner(s):** GateHouse Media, Inc, 350 WillowBrook Office Park, Fairport, NY 14450. Telephone: 585-598-0030. FAX: 585-248-2631. **Management:** Rick Peterson, Publisher.

WACONIA

WACONIA PATRIOT, THE. 8 S. Elm St., Waconia, MN 55387. Telephone: 952-442-4414. FAX: 952-442-4428. E-MAIL: patriotgeneral@acnpapers.com. URL: http://www.waconiapatriot.com. Mailing Address: PO Box 5, Waconia, MN 55387-0005. Year Established: 1895. Pub. Frequency: w. (Thu.) Page Size: broadsheet. Subscrip. Rate: $1 newsstand/cover; $31/yr mailed in county & adj. cys.; $37/yr mailed out of state. Adv. Rate: B&W page $413 Circulation: 4,100 per issue (paid). **Owner(s):** American Community Newspapers LLC, 10917 Valley View Rd., Eden Prairie, MN 55344. Telephone: 952-392-6801. FAX: 952-829-0797. **Management:** Keith Anderson, Publisher. Pam Miller, Advertising Manager. **Editorial:** Peggy Bakken, Executive Editor.

WADENA

WADENA PIONEER JOURNAL. 314 S. Jefferson St., Wadena, MN 56482. Telephone: 218-631-2561. FAX: 218-631-1621. E-MAIL: editorial@wadenapj.com. URL: http://www.wadenapj.com. Mailing Address: PO Box 31, Wadena, MN 56482. Year Established: 1878. Pub. Frequency: w. (Thu.) Page Size: broadsheet. Subscrip. Rate: $1 newsstand/cover; $32/yr in area; $36/yr mailed in state; $43/yr mailed out of state. Circulation: 3,500 per issue (paid). **Owner(s):** Fargo Forum Communications, 101 Fifth St., N., Fargo, ND 58102. Telephone: 701-241-5404. **Management:** Randy Mohs, General Manager. **Editorial:** Anita Meyer, Editor.

WALKER

PILOT-INDEPENDENT, THE. 408 Minnesota Ave., W., Walker, MN 56484. Telephone: 218-547-1000. FAX: 218-547-3000. E-MAIL: pilot@walkermn.com. URL: http://www.walkermn.com. Mailing Address: PO Box 190, Walker, MN 56484-0190. Year Established: 1900. Pub. Frequency: w. (Wed.) Page Size: tabloid. Subscrip. Rate: $1 newsstand/cover; $31/yr home delivery in county; $38/yr mailed elsewhere. Circulation: 3,177 per issue (paid). **Owner(s):** Superior Publishing Corp., 1105 Tower Ave, Superior, WI 54880. Telephone: 715-395-5725. FAX: 715-395-5729. **Management:** Joe Sherman, Publisher. **Editorial:** Dean Morrill, Editor.

WARREN

WARREN SHEAF. PO Box 45, Warren, MN 56762. Telephone: 218-745-5174. FAX: 218-745-5175. Year Established: 1880. Pub. Frequency: w. (Wed.) Page Size: broadsheet. Subscrip. Rate: $.75 newsstand/cover; $27/yr in county; $35/yr mailed out of county. Circulation: 2,400 per issue (paid). **Owner(s):** Warren Sheaf Publishing Co., See address and contact information above. **Management:** Eric Mattson, Publisher. **Editorial:** Dave Jameson, Editor.

WARROAD

WARROAD PIONEER. 109 E. Lake St., Warroad, MN 56763. Telephone: 218-386-1594. FAX: 218-386-1072. E-MAIL: wpioneer@wiktel.com. Mailing Address: PO Box E, Warroad, MN 56763. Year Established: 1902. Pub. Frequency: w. (Thu.) Page Size: broadsheet. Subscrip. Rate: $1 newsstand/cover; $28/yr in county; $35/yr out of county. Circulation: 2,100 per issue (paid). **Owner(s):** Page 1 Publications, PO Box F, Greenbush, MN 56726. Telephone: 218-782-2275. FAX: 218-782-2277. **Management:** Julie Nordine, Publisher. **Editorial:** Bonnie Nordvall, Editor.

WASECA

WASECA COUNTY NEWS. ISSN 0745-8177
213 Second St., N.W., Waseca, MN 56093-0465. Telephone: 507-835-3380. FAX: 507-835-3435. E-MAIL: wcn@clear.lakes.com. URL: http://www.wasecacountynews.com. Mailing Address: PO Box 465, Waseca, MN 56093-065. Year Established: 1981. Pub. Frequency: s-w. (Tue. & Thu.) Page Size: broadsheet. Subscrip. Rate: $1 newsstand/cover; $56/yr carrier delivery; $60/yr mailed in state; $68/yr out of state. **Wire Service(s):** AP. Circulation: 3,263 per issue (paid). **Owner(s):** Mainstream Publications, LLC, See address and contact information above. **Management:** Julie Frazier, Publisher. Shari Borglum, Circulation Manager. **Editorial:** Julie Frazier, Editor. Ruth Anne Hager, Business Editor. Dale Kugath, Sports.

WATERTOWN

WATERTOWN/CARVER COUNTY NEWS. 130 Lewis Ave., S., Watertown, MN 55388. Telephone: 952-955-1111. FAX: 952-955-2241. URL: http://www.mnsun.com. Pub. Frequency: w. (Thu.) Page Size: broadsheet. Subscrip. Rate: $31/yr in county; $36/yr mailed in state; $37/yr mailed out of state. Adv. Rate: B&W page $315 Circulation: 2,250 per issue (paid). **Owner(s):** American Community Newspapers LLC, 10917 Valley View Rd., Eden Prairie, MN 55344. Telephone: 952-392-6801. **Management:** Jim Bart, Publisher. **Editorial:** Jim Bart, Editor.

WATERVILLE

LAKE REGION LIFE. 115 S. Third St., Waterville, MN 56096-1401. E-MAIL: lrlife@frontiernet.net. Pub. Frequency: w. (Wed.) Page Size: tabloid Circulation: 1,500 per issue (free). **Owner(s):** E. Charles Wann, See address and contact information above. **Management:** E. Charles Wann, Publisher.

WAYZATA

LAKESHORE WEEKLY NEWS. 1001 Twelve Oaks Center Dr., Wayzata, MN 55391. Telephone: 952-473-0890. FAX: 952-473-0895. E-MAIL: production@weeklynews.com. URL: http://www.weeklynews.com. Year Established: 1982. Pub. Frequency: w. (Tue.) Page Size: tabloid. Subscrip. Rate: $35/yr mailed. Adv. Rate: col. inch $25.50 Circulation: 25,000 per issue (paid and free). **Owner(s):** Lakeshore Communications, 1001 Twelve Oaks Center Dr., Wayzata, MN 55391. Telephone: 952-473-0890. FAX: 952-473-0895. **Management:** Mark Beckstrom, Publisher. Lorna Lynch, Office Manager. Mark Beckstrom, Sales Manager. **Editorial:** Jason King, Editor.

WELLS

WELLS MIRROR, THE. 40 W. Franklin, Wells, MN 56097. Telephone: 507-553-3131. FAX: 507-553-3132. E-MAIL: wellsmir@bevcomm.net. Year Established: 1913. Pub. Frequency: w. (Thu.) Page Size: standard. Subscrip. Rate: $.75 newsstand/cover; $26/yr in county; $28/yr out of county snowbirds; $30/yr out of state snowbirds. Circulation: 1,850 per issue (paid). **Owner(s):** Wells Mirror Co., See address and contact information above. **Management:** Dave Bonsack, Publisher. Heather Ronsack, Advertising Manager. **Editorial:** Laurie Bonsack, Editor.

WHEATON

WHEATON (MN) GAZETTE. 1114 Broadway, Wheaton, MN 56296-1308. Telephone: 320-563-8146. FAX: 320-563-8147. Pub. Frequency: w. (Tue.) Page Size: standard. Subscrip. Rate: $1 newsstand/cover; $30/yr in county. Circulation: 2,147 per issue (paid). **Owner(s):** William Kremer, See address and contact information above. **Management:** William Kremer, Publisher. Mike Kremer, Advertising Manager. **Editorial:** Mike Kremer, Managing Editor. Jim Smoger, News Editor.

WHITE BEAR LAKE

FOREST LAKE PRESS. 4779 Bloom Ave., White Bear Lake, MN 55110. Telephone: 651-407-1200. FAX: 651-429-1242. E-MAIL: ppadvertising@1zoom.net. URL: http://www.press-publications.com. Pub. Frequency: w. (Wed.) Page Size: broadsheet. Subscrip. Rate: $.75 newsstand/cover; $32/yr in county. Circulation: 13,433 per issue (paid and free). **Owner(s):** Press Publications, Inc., See address and contact information above. **Management:** Eugene D. Johnson, Publisher. Angela Homic, Advertising Manager. Mary Berg, Circulation Manager. Pat Daul, Associate Publisher. **Editorial:** Brenda Cornelius, Managing Editor. Paul Dols, Photographer.

QUAD COMMUNITY PRESS. ISSN 0892-1806
4779 Bloom Ave., White Bear Lake, MN 55110. Telephone: 651-407-1200. FAX: 651-429-1242. E-MAIL: pressadvertising@presspubs.com. URL: http://www.presspubs.com. Year Established: 1983. Pub. Frequency: w. (Tue.) Page Size: broadsheet. Subscrip. Rate: $.75 newsstand/cover; $32/yr in county. Circulation: 8,746 per issue (paid and free). **Owner(s):** Press Publications, Inc., See address and contact information above. **Management:** Eugene D. Johnson, Publisher. Angela Homic, Advertising Manager. Mary Berg, Circulation Manager. Pat Daul, Associate Publisher. **Editorial:** Brenda Cornelius, Managing Editor. Paul Dols, Photographer.

SHOREVIEW PRESS. 4779 Bloom Ave., White Bear Lake, MN 55110. Telephone: 651-407-1200. FAX: 651-429-1242. E-MAIL: pressadvertising@presspubs.com. URL: http://www.presspubs.com. Year Established: 1993. Pub. Frequency: w. (Tue.) Page Size: broadsheet. Subscrip. Rate: $.75 newsstand/cover; $32/yr. Adv. Rate: col. inch $11.54 Circulation: 10,495 per issue (paid and free). **Owner(s):** Press Publications, Inc., See address and contact information above. **Management:** Eugene D. Johnson, Publisher. Angela Homic, Advertising Manager. Mary Berg, Circulation Manager. Pat Daul, Associate Publisher. **Editorial:** Brenda Cornelius, Managing Editor. Paul Dols, Photographer.

ST. CROIX VALLEY PRESS. 4779 Bloom Ave., White Bear Lake, MN 55110. Telephone: 651-407-1200. FAX: 651-429-1242. E-MAIL: pressadvertising@presspubs.com. URL: http://www.presspubs.com. Year Established: 1978. Pub. Frequency: w. (Thu.) Page Size: tabloid. Subscrip. Rate: $.75 newsstand/cover; $32/yr in county. Circulation: 10,021 per issue (paid and free). **Owner(s):** Press Publications, Inc., See address and contact information above. **Management:** Eugene D. Johnson, Publisher. Angela Homic, Advertising Manager. Mary Berg, Circulation Manager. Pat Daul, Associate Publisher. **Editorial:** Brenda Cornelius, Managing Editor. Paul Dols, Photographer.

VADNAIS HEIGHTS PRESS. 4779 Bloom Ave., White Bear Lake, MN 55110. Telephone: 651-407-1200. FAX: 651-429-1242. E-MAIL: pressadvertising@presspubs.com. URL: http://www.presspubs.com. Pub. Frequency: w. (Wed.) Page Size: broadsheet. Subscrip. Rate: $.75 newsstand/cover; $32/yr home delivery in county. Circulation: 3,978 per issue (paid and free). **Owner(s):** Press Publications, Inc., See address and contact information above. **Management:** Eugene D. Johnson, Publisher. Angela Homic, Advertising Manager. Mary Berg, Circulation Manager. Pat Daul, Associate Publisher. **Editorial:** Brenda Cornelius, Managing Editor. Paul Dols, Photographer.

WHITE BEAR PRESS. 4779 Bloom Ave., White Bear Lake, MN 55110. Telephone: 651-407-1200. FAX: 651-429-1242. E-MAIL: pressadvertising@presspubs.com. URL: http://www.presspubs.com. Pub. Frequency: w. (Wed.) Page Size: broadsheet. Subscrip. Rate: $.75 newsstand/cover; $32/yr in county. Circulation: 19,321 per issue (paid and free). **Owner(s):** Press Publications, Inc., See address and contact information above. **Management:** Eugene D. Johnson, Publisher. Angela Homic, Advertising Manager. Mary Berg, Circulation Manager. Pat Daul, Associate Publisher. **Editorial:** Brenda Cornelius, Managing Editor. Paul Dols, Photographer.

WINDOM

COTTONWOOD COUNTY CITIZEN. 260 Tenth St., Windom, MN 56101. Telephone: 507-831-3740. FAX: 507-831-3740. E-MAIL: citizen@windomnews.com. URL: http://www.windomnews.com. Mailing Address: P.O. Box 309, Windom, MN 56101. Pub. Frequency: w. (Wed.) Page Size: broadsheet. Subscrip. Rate: $1 newsstand/cover; $38.95/yr in county & adj. cys.; $50.95/yr out of area. Adv. Rate: col. inch $7.60 Circulation: 3,300 per issue (paid). **Owner(s):** Citizen Publishing Co., See address and contact information above. **Management:** Trevor Slette, General Manager. Kim Anderson, Publisher. Linda Bramstadt, Advertising Manager. Cheryl Duerksen, Classified Editor. **Editorial:** Rahn Larson, Editor. Joel Alvstad, Sports Editor.

WINONA

WINONA POST. PO Box 27, Winona, MN 55987-0027. Telephone: 507-452-1262. FAX: 507-454-6409. URL: http://www.winonapost.com. Pub. Frequency: s-w. (Wed. & Sun.) Page Size: broadsheet.Subscrip. Rate: $60/yr mailed Circulation: 20,400 Sunday (free); 24,250 per issue (free). **Owner(s):** John & Frances Edstrom, See address and contact information above. **Management:** John Edstrom, Publisher. Patrick Marek, VP Mktg. & Sales. Mary Veraguth, Circulation Manager. **Editorial:** Frances Edstrom, Editor-in-Chief.

WINTHROP

WINTHROP NEWS. 110 N. Carver, Winthrop, MN 55396-0478. Telephone: 507-647-5357. FAX: 507-647-5358. E-MAIL: winnews@prairie.lakes.com. Pub. Frequency: w. (Wed.) Page Size: standard. Subscrip. Rate: $.75 newsstand/cover; $29/yr in state; $34/yr out of state. Circulation: 1,250 per issue (paid). **Owner(s):** Doug Hanson, See address and contact information above. **Management:** Doug Hanson, Publisher. **Editorial:** Michael Mattison, Editor.

WOODBURY

WOODBURY BULLETIN. 8420 City Center Dr., Woodbury, MN 55125-5308. Telephone: 651-730-4007. FAX: 651-702-0977. E-MAIL: editor@woodburybulletin.com. URL: http://www.woodburybulletin.com. Year Established: 1958. Pub. Frequency: w. (Wed.) Page Size: broadsheet. Subscrip. Rate: $1 newsstand/cover; $30/yr in county; $40/yr out of county. Circulation: 10,000 per issue (paid). **Owner(s):** Jeff Meyer, 101 Fifth St., N., Fargo, ND 58102. Telephone: 701-235-7311. **Management:** Jeff Patterson, General Manager. Steve Messick, Publisher. **Editorial:** Dave Andrewson, Editor.

ZUMBROTA

NEWS RECORD. 225 Main St, Zumbrota, MN 55992. E-MAIL: news@zumbrota.com. URL: http://www.zumbrota.com. Mailing Address: PO Box 97, Zumbrota, MN 55992-0097. Pub. Frequency: w. (Wed.) Page Size: broadsheet. Subscrip. Rate: $1 newsstand/cover; $27/yr in county; $32/yr out of area; $37/yr out of state. Adv. Rate: col. inch $7.50 Circulation: 3,761 per issue (paid). **Owner(s):** Grimsrud Publishing, Inc., See address and contact information above. **Management:** Peter Grimsrud, Publisher. **Editorial:** Matt Grimsrud, Editor.

MISSISSIPPI

ABERDEEN

ABERDEEN EXAMINER. 209 E. Commerce St., Aberdeen, MS 39730. Telephone: 662-369-4507. FAX: 662-369-4508. E-MAIL: examiner@intop.net. URL: http://www.djournal.com/pages/examiner. Mailing Address: PO Box 909, Tupelo, MS 39902-0909. Year Established: 1866. Pub. Frequency: w. (Wed.) Page Size: broadsheet. Subscrip. Rate: $.50 newsstand/cover; $25/yr in county; $32/yr out of county; $37/yr mailed out of state. Circulation: 2,678 per issue (paid). **Owner(s):** Journal Publishing Co., Inc., 1241 S Green St, Tupelo, MS 39902. Telephone: 662-842-2611. FAX: 662-842-2233. **Management:** Beth Bunch, General Manager. Jimmy Willis, Advertising Manager. Stacie Bell, Classified Adv. Mgr.. **Editorial:** Beth Bunch, Editor.

ACKERMAN

CHOCTAW PLAINDEALER, THE. 139 E. Main St., Ackerman, MS 39735. Telephone: 662-773-6241. FAX: 662-285-6695. E-MAIL: newsroom@winstoncountyjournal.com. URL: http://www.choctawplaindealer.com. Mailing Address: PO Box 4919, Ackerman, MS 39735. Pub. Frequency: w. (Thu.) Page Size: standard. Subscrip. Rate: $.50 newsstand/cover; $15/yr in state; $18/yr mailed out of state. Circulation: 1,618 per issue (paid). **Owner(s):** Boone Newspapers, Inc., 15222 Freewmen's Bend Rd., Northport, AL 35475. Telephone: 205-330-4100. **Management:** Joseph McCain, Publisher. Lisa Shanell, Advertising Manager. Susan Adcock, Classified Adv. Mgr.. **Editorial:** Joseph McCain, Editor.

AMORY

MONROE JOURNAL, THE. 115 S. Main St., Amory, MS 38821. Telephone: 662-256-5647. FAX: 662-256-5701. E-MAIL: news@monrow360.com. URL: http://www.monrow360.com. Mailing Address: PO Box 519, Amory, MS 38821. Year Established: 1917. Pub. Frequency: w. (Wed.) Page Size: broadsheet. Subscrip. Rate: $.50 newsstand/cover; $25/yr carrier delivery in county; $32/yr out of county; $37/yr mailed out of state. Circulation: 7,300 per issue (paid). **Owner(s):** Journal Publishing Co., Inc., 1241 S Green St, Tupelo, MS 39902. Telephone: 662-842-2611. FAX: 662-842-2233. **Management:** Beth Bunch, General Manager. Bonnie Parham, Advertising Manager. Batty Hubbard, Classified Adv. Mgr.. **Editorial:** Beth Bunch, Editor. Chris Wilson, Managing Editor.

ASHLAND

SOUTHERN ADVOCATE. 114 Church St., Ashland, MS 38603. Telephone: 662-224-6681. FAX: 662-224-6886. E-MAIL: sentinel@daydispatchh.com. Pub. Frequency: w. (Thu.) Page Size: standard. Subscrip. Rate: $.50 newsstand/cover; $35/yr out of state. Circulation: 1,331 per issue (paid). **Owner(s):** Albert Thompson, See address and contact information above. **Management:** Tim Watson, Advertising Director. **Editorial:** Gene Ladnier, Editor.

BALDWYN

BALDWYN NEWS, THE. 102 W. Main St., Baldwyn, MS 38824-1814. Telephone: 662-365-3232. FAX: 662-365-7989. E-MAIL: thebaldwynnews@dixie-net.com. Mailing Address: PO Box 130, Baldwyn, MS 38824. Pub. Frequency: w. (Wed.) Page Size: standard. Subscrip. Rate: $.50 newsstand/cover; $27/yr out of county; $34/yr out of state. Circulation: 2,500 per issue (paid). **Owner(s):** Kim Haynes, See address and contact information above. **Management:** Tammy Bullock, General Manager. **Editorial:** Tammy Bullock, Managing Editor.

BATESVILLE

PANOLIAN, THE. 363 Hwy 51 N, Batesville, MS 38606. Telephone: 662-563-4591. FAX: 662-563-5610. E-MAIL: thepanolian@panola.com. URL: http://www.thepanolian.com. Year Established: 1882. Pub. Frequency: s-w. (Tue. & Fri.) Page Size: standard. Subscrip. Rate: $.75 newsstand/cover; $39.95/yr in state; $54.95/yr mailed out of state. Adv. Rate: col. inch $7.35 Circulation: 5,700 per issue (paid). **Owner(s):** The Panolian, Inc., See address and contact information above. **Management:** John Howell, Publisher. Bob Boggan, Advertising Manager. Cassie White, Classified Adv. Mgr.. **Editorial:** Rupert Howell, Editor.

PANOLIAN ADVANTAGE, THE. 363 Hwy 51 N, Batesville, MS 38606. Telephone: 662-563-4591. FAX: 662-563-5610. E-MAIL: publisher@panolian.com. URL: http://www.panolian.com. Year Established: 1996. Pub. Frequency: w. (Wed.) Page Size: standard.Adv. Rate: col. inch $7.35 Circulation: 6,000 per issue (free). **Owner(s):** The Panolian, Inc., See address and contact information above. **Management:** Bob Boggan, Advertising Manager. Cassie White, Classified Adv. Mgr..Readers: Serves rural Panola County

BAY SPRINGS

IMPACT MAIL OF MERIDIAN. PO Box 449, Bay Springs, MS 39422. Telephone: 601-764-3104. FAX: 601-764-3106. Pub. Frequency: w. (Wed.) Page Size: tabloid. Circulation: 51,628 per issue (paid and controlled). **Owner(s):** Buckley Newspapers Inc., See address and contact information above. **Management:** Ronnie L. Buckley, Publisher. Kevin Williams, Advertising Manager.

JASPER COUNTY NEWS, THE. 3362 Hwy. 15, Bay Springs, MS 39422. Telephone: 601-764-3104. FAX: 601-764-3106. Mailing Address: PO Box 449, Bay Springs, MS 39422-0449. Year Established: 1920. Pub. Frequency: w. (Wed.) Page Size: standard. Subscrip. Rate: $.50 newsstand/cover; $25/yr in county; $35/yr out of county; $40/yr mailed out of state. Adv. Rate: col. inch $6 Circulation: 3,000 per issue (paid). **Owner(s):** Buckley Newspapers Inc., See address and contact information above. **Management:** Ronnie L. Buckley, Publisher. **Editorial:** Anna King, Editor. Kristi Scott, Advertising Editor.

BAY ST. LOUIS

BAY ST. LOUIS SEA COAST ECHO. 124 Court St., Bay St. Louis, MS 39520-2009. Telephone: 228-467-5474. FAX: 228-467-0333. E-MAIL: rponder@seacoastecho.com. URL: http://www.seacoastecho.com. Mailing Address: PO Box 2009, Bay St. Louis, MS 39521. Year Established: 1892. Pub. Frequency: s-w. (Thu. & Sun.) Page Size: broadsheet. Subscrip. Rate: $.75 newsstand/cover; $45/yr in county; $70/yr out of county; $70/yr out of state. Adv. Rate: col. inch $16 **Wire Service(s):** AP. Circulation: 7,500 Sunday (paid); 7,300 per issue (paid). **Owner(s):** Bay St. Louis Newspapers, Inc., See address and contact information above. **Management:** James R. Ponder, Publisher. **Editorial:** James R. Ponder, Editor. Geoff Belcher, Entertainment Editor.

BELMONT

BELMONT AND TISHOMINGO JOURNAL. 430 N. Second St., Belmont, MS 38827-0070. Telephone: 662-454-7196. FAX: 662-454-0055. Mailing Address: PO Box 70, Belmont, MS 38827. Year Established: 1971. Pub. Frequency: w. (Wed.) Page Size: broadsheet. Subscrip. Rate: $.50 newsstand/cover; $20/yr in state; $22/yr out of state. Adv. Rate: col. inch $5.50 Circulation: 1,784 per issue (paid). **Owner(s):** Belmont/Tishomingo Journal, Inc., See address and contact information above. **Management:** M. Wayne Mitchell, Publisher. **Editorial:** Catherine Mitchell, Editor.

BELZONI

BELZONI BANNER, THE. 115 E. Jackson St., Belzoni, MS 39038. Telephone: 662-247-3373. FAX: 662-247-3372. E-MAIL: banner@belzonicable.com. URL: http://www.thebelzonibanner.com. Mailing Address: PO Box 610, Belzoni, MS 39038. Year Established: 1923. Pub. Frequency: w. (Wed.) Page Size: broadsheet. Subscrip. Rate: $20/yr local area; $24/yr out of area. Circulation: 1,800 per issue (paid). **Owner(s):** Julian Toney, III, See address and contact information above. **Management:** Julian Toney III, Publisher. Mary McMillian, Advertising Manager. **Editorial:** Julian Toney III, Editor.

BILOXI

BILOXI D'IBERVILLE PRESS (2007). ISSN 1941-3068
819 Jackson St., Biloxi, MS 39530-4235. Telephone: 228-435-0720. FAX: 228-436-7737. E-MAIL: news@getthepress.com. URL: www.getthepress.com. Year Established: 1973. Pub. Frequency: w. (Fri.) Page Size: broadsheet. Subscrip. Rate: $24/yr in county; $48/yr out of county; $20/yr to senior citizens. Circulation: 5,000 per issue (paid and free). **Owner(s):** Family Media, Inc., See address and contact information above. **Management:** Patti Guide, Publisher. **Editorial:** Gene Coleman, Editor.

BOONEVILLE

BANNER-INDEPENDENT, THE. 208 N. Main St., Booneville, MS 38829. Telephone: 662-728-6214. FAX: 662-728-1636. Mailing Address: PO Box 10, Booneville, MS 38829. Year Established: 1898. Pub. Frequency: w. (Thu.) Page Size: broadsheet. Subscrip. Rate: $.50 newsstand/cover; $27.50/yr local; $37.50/yr mailed elsewhere. Adv. Rate: col. inch $7.35 Circulation: 5,000 per issue (paid). **Owner(s):** Paxton Media Group Llc, 201 S. Fourth St., Paducah, KY 42003. Telephone: 270-575-8600. FAX: 270-442-8188. **Management:** Reece Terry, Publisher. Christine Anderle, Office Manager. Renee Johnson, Advertising Manager. Cindy Leatherwood, Circulation Manager. **Editorial:** Kenny Goode, Editor.

BRANDON

RANKIN COUNTY NEWS, THE. Town Sq., 207 E. Government St., Brandon, MS 39042. Telephone: 601-825-8333. FAX: 601-825-8334. E-MAIL: rankincn@aol.com. Mailing Address: PO Box 107, Brandon, MS 39043-0107. Year Established: 1848. Pub. Frequency: w. (Wed.) Page Size: broadsheet. Subscrip. Rate: $.50 newsstand/cover; $18/yr in county; $21/yr mailed out of county; $24/yr mailed out of state. Adv. Rate: col. inch $6.50 Circulation: 8,000 per issue (paid). **Owner(s):** RCN Corp., See address and contact information above. **Management:** Marcus Bowers Jr., Publisher. Mary Carole Bowers, Business Manager. **Editorial:** Marcus Bowers Jr., Editor.

BROOKFIELD

LINN COUNTY LEADER. 107 N Main, Brookfield, MS 064628. Mailing Address: PO Box 40, Brookfield, MO 64628. Pub. Frequency: 3/w. (Mon., Wed., Fri.) Page Size: broadsheet. Subscrip. Rate: $.75 newsstand/cover; $75/yr in county. Circulation: 3,500 per issue (paid). **Owner(s):** GateHouse Media, Inc, 350 WillowBrook Office Park, Fairport, NY 14450. Telephone: 585-598-0030. FAX: 585-248-2631. **Management:** Rod Dixon, Publisher. **Editorial:** Stephanie Patterson, Editor.

BRUCE

CALHOUN COUNTY JOURNAL. PO Box 278, Bruce, MS 38915. E-MAIL: ccj@tycom.net. URL: http://www.calhouncountyjournal.com. Year Established: 1953. Pub. Frequency: w. (Thu.) Page Size: broadsheet. Subscrip. Rate: $.50 newsstand/cover; $22/yr in county; $32/yr mailed out of county out of town. Adv. Rate: col. inch $5.51 **Wire Service(s):** AP. Circulation: 4,700 per issue (paid). **Owner(s):** S. Gale Denley, See address and contact information above. **Management:** S. Gale Denley, Publisher. **Editorial:** Celia Denley-Hillhouse, Managing Editor. Lisa McNeece, Associate Editor.

CALHOUN CITY

MONITOR-HERALD, THE. 135 Public Square, Calhoun City, MS 38916. Telephone: 662-628-5241. FAX: 662-628-4651. E-MAIL: monitorherald@yahoo.com. URL: http://www.monitorherald.com. Year Established: 1899. Pub. Frequency: w. (Thu.) Page Size: broadsheet. Subscrip. Rate: $.25 newsstand/cover; $20/yr mailed in county & adj. counties; $27/yr in state; $32/yr out of state. Adv. Rate: col. inch $5 Circulation: 11,700 per issue (paid and free). **Owner(s):** Journal Publishing Co., Inc., P.O. Box 69, Calhoun city, MS 38916-0069. 1241 S Green St, Tupelo, MS 39902. Telephone: 662-842-2611. FAX: 662-842-2233. **Management:** Lisa Voyles, General Manager. Lori Marion, Advertising Manager. **Editorial:** Lisa Voyles, Managing Editor.Readers: Calhoun County, Miss.

CARTHAGE

CARTHAGINIAN, THE. 122 Franklin St., Carthage, MS 39051. Telephone: 601-267-4501. FAX: 601-267-5290. E-MAIL: thenews@netdoor.com. URL: http://www.thecarthaginian.com. Year Established: 1872. Pub. Frequency: w. (Thu.) Page Size: broadsheet. Subscrip. Rate: $.75 newsstand/cover; $28/yr in county; $32/yr out of county; $36/yr mailed out of state. Circulation: 5,700 per issue (paid). **Owner(s):** John H. Keith, See address and contact information above. **Management:** John H. Keith, Publisher. Wade Prather, Associate Publisher. **Editorial:** Mildred Dearman, Executive Editor.

CHARLESTON

SUN-SENTINEL. South Court Sq., Charleston, MS 38921. Telephone: 662-647-8462. FAX: 662-647-3830. E-MAIL: clay@charlestonsun.net. Mailing Address: PO Box 250, Charleston, MS 38921-0250. Pub. Frequency: w. (Thu.) Page Size: broadsheet. Subscrip. Rate: $.50 newsstand/cover; $18/yr in county; $21/yr out of county; $25/yr out of state. Adv. Rate: col. inch $5.50 Circulation: 2,591 per issue (paid). **Owner(s):** Emmerich Newspapers, Inc., 246 Briarwood Dr., Jackson, MS 39236. Telephone: 601-957-1122. **Management:** Wyatt Emmerich, Owner. Clay McFerrin, Publisher. Krista McFerrin, Advertising Director. **Editorial:** Clay McFerrin, Editor.

COLUMBIA

COLUMBIAN-PROGRESS. 318 Second St., Columbia, MS 39429. Telephone: 601-736-2611. FAX: 601-736-4507. E-MAIL: cp@pearlriver.net. URL: http://www.columbianprogress.com. Mailing Address: PO Box 1171, Columbia, MS 39429. Year Established: 1882. Pub. Frequency: s-w. (Thu. & Sat.) Page Size: standard. Subscrip. Rate: $.50 newsstand/cover; $30/yr mailed in county; $35/yr mailed in state; $40/yr mailed out of state. Circulation: 12,900 per issue (paid). **Owner(s):** Emmerich Newspapers, Inc., PO Box 16709, Jackson, MS 39236. Telephone: 601-957-1122. **Management:** Jeffrey M. Peyton, Publisher. Kim Gingell, Advertising. Julie Johnson, Advertising Director. **Editorial:** Jeffrey M. Peyton, Editor-in-Chief.

COLUMBUS

E-ZONE. 516 Main St., Columbus, MS 39701. Telephone: 662-328-2424. FAX: 662-329-8937. E-MAIL: artist@cdispatch.com. Mailing Address: PO Box 511, Columbus, MS 39703. Pub. Frequency: w. (Tue.) Page Size: standard. **Wire Service(s):** AP. Circulation: 13,000 per issue (free). **Owner(s):** Commercial Dispatch, Inc., See address and contact information above. **Management:** Birney Imes, General Manager. Diane Medley, Advertising Director. Bobby Tingle, Circulation Manager.

DE KALB

KEMPER COUNTY MESSENGER. PO Box 546, De Kalb, MS 39328. Telephone: 601-743-5760. FAX: 601-743-4430. E-MAIL: messenger@neshobademocrat.com. Year Established: 1940. Pub. Frequency: w. (Thu.) Page Size: broadsheet. Subscrip. Rate: $.50 newsstand/cover; $18/yr in county; $21/yr out of county; $24/yr out of state. Circulation: 2,500 per issue (paid). **Owner(s):** Jim Prince, See address and contact information above. **Management:** Austin Bishop III, Publisher. Elaine Tisdale, Office Manager. **Editorial:** Chris Baker, Editor.

FOREST

SCOTT COUNTY TIMES. 311 Smith St., Forest, MS 39407. Telephone: 601-469-2561. FAX: 601-469-2004. E-MAIL: shall@sctonline.net. URL: http://www.sctonline.net. Mailing Address: PO Box 89, Forest, MS 39074. Year Established: 1939. Pub. Frequency: w. (Wed.) Page Size: broadsheet. Subscrip. Rate: $.50 newsstand/cover; $25/yr mailed in county; $28/yr in state; $35/yr mailed out of state. Freelance Pay: $5-$25/article. Circulation: 5,700 per issue (paid). **Owner(s):** Emmerich Newspapers, Inc., PO Box 16709, Jackson, MS 39236. Telephone: 601-957-1122. **Management:** Sam R Hall, Publisher. Fran Pitts, Advertising Manager. Denese Jones, Classified Adv. Mgr.. **Editorial:** Sam R Hall, Editor.

FULTON

ITAWAMBA COUNTY TIMES, THE. 106 W. Main St., Fulton, MS 38843. Telephone: 662-862-3141. FAX: 662-862-7804. E-MAIL: itimes@intop.net. URL: http://www.djournal.com. Mailing Address: PO Box 909, Tupelo, MS 39902-0909. Year Established: 1945. Pub. Frequency: w. (Wed.) Page Size: broadsheet. Subscrip. Rate: $.50 newsstand/cover; $25/yr in county; $32/yr in state; $37/yr out of state. Circulation: 5,000 per issue (paid). **Owner(s):** Journal Publishing Co., Inc., 1241 S Green St, Tupelo, MS 39902. Telephone: 662-842-2611. FAX: 662-842-2233. **Management:** Alisha Holder, General Manager. Shilley Ausbiren, Advertising. Sandra Newton, Classified Adv. Mgr.. **Editorial:** Alisha Holder, Managing Editor.

HATTIESBURG

IMPACT OF HATTIESBURG. 110 S. 41st Ave., Hattiesburg, MS 39402. Telephone: 601-264-8181. FAX: 601-264-8398. E-MAIL: impacth@networth.tl.net. Mailing Address: PO Box 16958, Hattiesburg, MS 39404. Pub. Frequency: s-w. (Wed. & Fri.) Page Size: tabloid. Subscrip. Rate: $35/yr. Circulation: 60,779 per issue (paid and controlled). **Owner(s):** Buckley Newspapers Inc., PO Box 449, Bay Springs, MS 39422. Telephone: 601-764-3104. FAX: 601-764-3106. **Management:** Bob Barger, General Manager. Ronnie L. Buckley, Publisher. Bob Barger, Marketing Manager.

HAZLEHURST

COPIAH COUNTY COURIER. 103 S. Ragsdale Ave., Hazlehurst, MS 39083-0351. Mailing Address: PO Box 351, Hazlehurst, MS 39083-0315. Year Established: 1884. Pub. Frequency: w. (Wed.) Page Size: standard. Subscrip. Rate: $.50 newsstand/cover; $18/yr in county; $20/yr out of county; $24/yr mailed out of state. **Wire Service(s):** AP, PR. Circulation: 6,210 per issue (paid and free). **Owner(s):** James S. Lambert, See address and contact information above. **Management:** Joe Coats, Publisher. **Editorial:** Joe Coats, Editor.

HERNANDO

WEEKENDER (HERNANDO). 315 Losher St., Hernando, MS 38632. Telephone: 662-429-6397. FAX: 662-429-5229. E-MAIL: destimes@aol.com. URL: http://www.desototimes.com. Year Established: 1839. Pub. Frequency: w. (Sat.) Page Size: standard. Subscrip. Rate: $.50 newsstand/cover per issue; $108/yr mailed. Adv. Rate: col. inch $8.05 **Wire Service(s):** AP. Circulation: 24,400 per issue (free). **Owner(s):** PH Publications LLC, See address and contact information above. **Management:** Ron Tate, Publisher. Mandy Jones, Advertising Manager. Sherry Ray, Circulation Manager. Diane Smith, Classified Adv. Mgr.. **Editorial:** Chris Sheffield, Editor. Ron Caldwell, Sports Editor.

HOLLY SPRINGS

SOUTH REPORTER, THE. 157 S. Center St., Holly Springs, MS 38635. Telephone: 662-252-4261. FAX: 662-252-3388. E-MAIL: south@dixie-net.com. URL: htpp://www.southreporter.com. Year Established: 1865. Pub. Frequency: w. (Thu.) Page Size: broadsheet. Subscrip. Rate: $.50 newsstand/cover; $20/yr in county; $25/yr out of county. Circulation: 5,200 per issue (paid). **Owner(s):** South Reporter, See address and contact information above. **Management:** Barry Burleson, Publisher. **Editorial:** Barry Burleson, Editor.

HOUSTON

CHICKASAW JOURNAL & TIMES-POST. 225 E Madison St, Houston, MS 38851. Telephone: 662-456-3771. FAX: 662-456-5202. URL: http://www.chicasawjournal.com. Mailing Address: PO Box 629, Houston, MS 38851-0629. Year Established: 1906. Pub. Frequency: w. (Wed.) Page Size: broadsheet. Subscrip. Rate: $.75 newsstand/cover; $34/yr in county & adj. counties; $39/yr in state; $50/yr mailed out of state. Circulation: 15,000 per issue (paid). **Owner(s):** Journal Publishing Co., Inc., 1241 S Green St, Tupelo, MS 39902. Telephone: 662-842-2611. FAX: 662-842-2233. **Management:** Lisa Voyles, General Manager. Lori Marion, Advertising Manager. **Editorial:** Lisa Voyles, Managing Editor.

IUKA

TISHOMINGO COUNTY NEWS. 120 W. Front St, Iuka, MS 38852. Telephone: 662-423-2211. Year Established: 1885. Pub. Frequency: w. (Thu.) Page Size: standard. Subscrip. Rate: $.35 newsstand/cover; $18/yr local; $25/yr out of area. Circulation: 4,000 per issue (paid). **Owner(s):** John H. Biggs, See address and contact information above. **Management:** Charlotte McVay, Publisher. **Editorial:** Charlotte McVay, Editor.

JACKSON

JACKSON FREE PRESS. 2727 Old Canton Rd, Ste 224, Jackson, MS 39296. E-MAIL: publisher@jacksonfreepress.com. URL: http://www.jacksonfreepress.com. Year Established: 2002. Pub. Frequency: w. (Thu.) Page Size: tabloid. Subscrip. Rate: $100/yr home delivery. Adv. Rate: page $1,120 Circulation: 17,000 per issue (free). **Owner(s):** Jackson Free Press, PO Box 2067, Jackson, MS 39296. Telephone: 601-362-6121. FAX: 601-510-9019. **Management:** Todd Stauffer, Publisher. **Editorial:** Donna Ladd, Editor-in-Chief.

NORTHSIDE SUN, THE. 246 Briarwood Dr., Jackson, MS 39236. Telephone: 601-957-1122. FAX: 601-957-1533. E-MAIL: sun@northsidesun.com. Mailing Address: PO Box 16709, Jackson, MS 39236. Year Established: 1967. Pub. Frequency: w. (Thu.) Page Size: broadsheet. Subscrip. Rate: $.50 newsstand/cover; $18/yr mailed in county; $20/yr mailed out of county. Circulation: 9,301 per issue (paid). **Owner(s):** Emmerich Newspapers, Inc., See address and contact information above. **Management:** J. Wyatt Emmerich, Publisher. Tessy Sanli, Advertising Manager. Sharmeisha Jordon, Circulation Manager. **Editorial:** Jimmye Sweat, Editor.

WEBSTER PROGRESS-TIMES, THE. 246 Briarwood Dr., Jackson, MS 39236. E-MAIL: news@websterprogresstimes.com. URL: http://www.websterprogresstimes.com. Year Established: 1879. Pub. Frequency: w. (Thu.) Page Size: broadsheet. Subscrip. Rate: $.75 newsstand/cover; $23/yr in county; $28/yr out of county. Adv. Rate: col. inch $6.35 Circulation: 2,800 per issue (paid). **Owner(s):** Emmerich Newspapers, Inc., See address and contact information above. **Management:** Charlotte Newman, Advertising Director. **Editorial:** Russell Hood, News Editor.

KOSCIUSKO

STAR-HERALD (KOSCIUSKO), THE. ISSN 1048-4116
207 N. Madison St, Kosciusko, MS 39090-3626. Telephone: 662-289-2251. FAX: 662-289-2254. E-MAIL: news@starherald.net. URL: http://www.starherald.net. Year Established: 1866. Pub. Frequency: w. (Thu.) Page Size: broadsheet. Subscrip. Rate: $.75 newsstand/cover; $35/yr mailed in county area; $39/yr mailed in state; $42/yr mailed out of state. Circulation: 6,000 per issue (paid). **Owner(s):** Community Newspaper Holdings, Inc., 3500 Colonnade Pkwy., Ste. 600, Birmingham, AL 35243. Telephone: 205-298-7100. FAX: 205-298-7101. **Management:** Robert Robertson, Publisher. Cindi Compton, Advertising. **Editorial:** Robert Robertson, Editor. Nancy Green, Local News Editor.

LAUREL

IMPACT / LAUREL. 1010 N. 16th Ave., Laurel, MS 39441. Telephone: 601-649-1129. FAX: 601-649-0424. E-MAIL: impact/@networktel.net. Mailing Address: PO Box 4406, Laurel, MS 39440. Year Established: 1976. Pub. Frequency: s-w. (Wed. & Sun.) Page Size: tabloid Circulation: 28,200 Sunday (free); 35,000 per issue (free). **Owner(s):** Buckley Newspapers Inc., 3362 Hwy. 15, Bay Springs, MS 39422. Telephone: 601-764-3104. FAX: 601-764-3106. **Management:** Ronnie L. Buckley, Publisher. Bob Barger, Advertising Manager. **Editorial:** Ronnie L. Buckley, Editor.

LEXINGTON

HOLMES COUNTY HERALD. 308 Court Sq., Lexington, MS 39095-0060. Telephone: 662-834-1151. FAX: 662-834-1074. E-MAIL: hcherald@bellsouth.net. URL: http://www.holmescountyherald.com. Mailing Address: PO Box 60, Lexington, MS 39095-0060. Year Established: 1959. Pub. Frequency: w. (Thu.) Page Size: broadsheet. Subscrip. Rate: $25/yr mailed in county; $27/yr mailed out of county; $32/yr mailed out of state. Adv. Rate: col. inch $5.50 Circulation: 2,500 per issue (paid). **Owner(s):** East Holmes Publishing Enterprises, Inc., See address and contact information above. **Management:** Bruce Hill, Publisher. Julie Ellison, Circulation Manager.

LIBERTY

SOUTHERN HERALD, THE. ISSN 0893-3790
PO Box 674, Liberty, MS 39645. Telephone: 601-657-4818. FAX: 601-657-4818. Year Established: 1825. Pub. Frequency: w. (Thu.) Page Size: standard. Subscrip. Rate: $.50 newsstand/cover; $17/yr mailed in county; $22/yr mailed elsewhere. Circulation: 1,100 per issue (paid and free). **Owner(s):** Richard H. Stratton, See address and contact information above. **Management:** Richard H. Stratton, Publisher. **Editorial:** Richard H. Stratton, Editor.

LOUISVILLE

RED HILLS SHOPPERS GUIDE, THE. 119 N. Court Ave., Louisville, MS 39339. Telephone: 662-773-6241. FAX: 662-773-6242. Mailing Address: PO Box 469, Louisville, MS 39339. Year Established: 1892. Pub. Frequency: w. (Wed.) Page Size: broadsheet Circulation: 7,200 per issue (free). **Owner(s):** Boone Newspapers, Inc., 15222 Freemen's Bend Rd., Northport, AL 35475. Telephone: 205-330-4100. **Management:** Joseph McCain, Publisher. Brenda Perry, Circulation Manager. **Editorial:** Joseph McCain, Editor. Heather Jackson, Managing Editor.

WINSTON COUNTY JOURNAL. 119 N. Court Ave., Louisville, MS 39339. Telephone: 662-773-6241. FAX: 662-773-6242. E-MAIL: newsroom@winstoncountyjournal.com. URL: http://www.winstoncountyjournal.com. Mailing Address: PO Box 469, Louisville, MS 39339. Year Established: 1892. Pub. Frequency: w. (Wed.) Page Size: broadsheet. Subscrip. Rate: $.75 newsstand/cover; $25/yr mailed in county; $42/yr mailed out of county. Adv. Rate: col. inch $8.80 Circulation: 3,500 per issue (paid). **Owner(s):** Boone Newspapers, Inc., 15222 Freemen's Bend Rd., Northport, AL 35475. Telephone: 205-330-4100. **Management:** Joseph McCain, Publisher. Brenda Perry, Circulation Manager. Susan Adcock, Classified Adv. Mgr.. **Editorial:** Joseph McCain, Editor. Heather Jackson, Managing Editor.

LUCEDALE

GEORGE COUNTY TIMES. PO Box 238, Lucedale, MS 39452. Telephone: 601-947-2967. E-MAIL: gct@datasync.com. Pub. Frequency: w. (Thu.) Page Size: standard. Subscrip. Rate: $.25 newsstand/cover; $11/yr mailed in county; $15/yr mailed in adj. counties; $18/yr mailed elsewhere. Circulation: 5,300 per issue (paid). **Owner(s):** O.G. Sellers, See address and contact information above. **Management:** O.G. Sellers, Publisher. **Editorial:** O.G. Sellers, Editor.

MACON

MACON BEACON, THE. 403 S. Jefferson, Macon, MS 39341. Telephone: 662-726-4747. FAX: 662-726-4742. E-MAIL: beacon@ebicom.net. Mailing Address: PO Box 32, Macon, MS 39341. Year Established: 1849. Pub. Frequency: w. (Thu.) Page Size: broadsheet. Subscrip. Rate: $.50 newsstand/cover; $18/yr mailed in county; $23/yr mailed out of county; $26/yr mailed out of state. Circulation: 3,100 per issue (paid). **Owner(s):** R. Scott Boyd, See address and contact information above. **Management:** R. Scott Boyd, Publisher. **Editorial:** R. Scott Boyd, Editor.

MAGEE

MAGEE COURIER, THE. PO Box 338, Magee, MS 39111. Telephone: 601-849-3434. FAX: 601-849-6828. E-MAIL: courier@bellsouth.net. Year Established: 1899. Pub. Frequency: w. (Thu.) Page Size: broadsheet. Subscrip. Rate: $.50 newsstand/cover; $20/yr in county; $22/yr out of county. Circulation: 3,500 per issue (paid). **Owner(s):** Simpson Publishing Co., Inc., See address and contact information above. **Management:** Pat Brown, Publisher. Nancy Brown, Advertising Manager. Marsha Bratcher, Circulation Manager. **Editorial:** Pat Brown, Editor.

MAGNOLIA

MAGNOLIA GAZETTE, THE. PO Box 152, Magnolia, MS 39652. Telephone: 601-783-2441. Year Established: 1874. Pub. Frequency: w. (Thu.) Page Size: broadsheet. Subscrip. Rate: $.50 newsstand/cover; $20/yr in county; $35/yr out of state. Circulation: 1,200 per issue (paid). **Owner(s):** Magnolia Publishing Corp., See address and contact information above. **Management:** Dr. Lucius Lampton, Publisher. Ben Reese, Advertising Manager. **Editorial:** Dr. Lucius Lampton, Editor. Donna Dee Lee, Managing Editor.

NEW ALBANY

NEW ALBANY GAZETTE. 713 Carter Ave., New Albany, MS 38652. Telephone: 662-534-6321. FAX: 662-534-6355. E-MAIL: newalbanygazette@dixie-net.com. URL: http://www.newalbanygazette.com. Mailing Address: PO Box 300, New Albany, MS 38652. Year Established: 1887. Pub. Frequency: s-w. (Wed. & Fri.) Page Size: broadsheet. Subscrip. Rate: $.50 newsstand/cover; $37/yr mailed in county; $55/yr mailed in state. Circulation: 16,000 per issue (paid). **Owner(s):** Landmark Community Newspapers, Inc., PO Box 549, Shelbyville, KY 40065. Telephone: 502-633-2526. FAX: 502-633-2618. **Management:** Ed Trainor, General Manager. Ryan Bramlett, Advertising Manager. Chris Knox, Circulation Manager. **Editorial:** Lynn West, Managing Editor.

NEWTON

NEWTON RECORD, THE. 120 S. Main St., Newton, MS 39345. Telephone: 601-683-2001. FAX: 601-683-2360. E-MAIL: publisher@thenewtonrecord.com. URL: http://www.thenewtonrecord.com. Mailing Address: PO Box 60, Newton, MS 39345. Year Established: 1901. Pub. Frequency: w. (Wed.) Page Size: broadsheet. Subscrip. Rate: $.50 newsstand/cover (effective 2006); $100/yr carrier delivery in county; $116/yr mailed out of county; $152/yr mailed out of state. Freelance Pay: $25/article. Circulation: 3,000 per issue (paid). **Owner(s):** Community Newspaper Holdings, Inc., 3500 Colonnade Pkwy., Ste. 600, Birmingham, AL 35243. Telephone: 205-298-7100. FAX: 205-298-7101. **Management:** Robert Robertson, Publisher. Lisa Jay, Advertising. Betty Vance, Classified Adv. Mgr.. **Editorial:** Cheryl McLain, News Editor.

SHOPPING NEWS, THE. 120 S. Main St., Newton, MS 39345. Telephone: 601-683-2001. FAX: 601-683-2360. E-MAIL: advertising@thenewstonrecord.com. URL: http://www.thenewtonrecord.com. Mailing Address: PO Box 60, Newton, MS 39345. Year Established: 1980. Pub. Frequency: w. (Wed.) Page Size: broadsheet Circulation: 9,574 per issue (free). **Owner(s):** Community Newspaper Holdings, Inc., 3500 Colonnade Pkwy., Ste. 600, Birmingham, AL 35243. Telephone: 205-298-7100. FAX: 205-298-7101. **Management:** Robert Robertson, Publisher. Lisa Jay, Advertising. Betty Vance, Classified Adv. Mgr.. **Editorial:** Cheryl McLain, News Editor.

PHILADELPHIA

NESHOBA DEMOCRAT, THE. PO Box 30, Philadelphia, MS 39350. Telephone: 601-656-4000. E-MAIL: neshoba@cybertron.com. Year Established: 1881. Pub. Frequency: w. (Wed.) Page Size: standard. Subscrip. Rate: $.75 newsstand/cover; $24/yr mailed in county; $27/yr mailed out of county; $30/yr mailed out of state. Circulation: 7,500 per issue (paid). **Owner(s):** Neshoba Democrat Publishing Co., See address and contact information above. **Management:** James E. Prince III, Publisher. Annette Watkins, Advertising. Elsie Bishop, Circulation Manager. **Editorial:** James E. Prince III, Editor. Debbie Myers, Managing Editor.

PONTOTOC

PONTOTOC PROGRESS. 13 Jefferson St, Pontotoc, MS 38863. Telephone: 662-489-3511. FAX: 662-489-1369. E-MAIL: pontprog@pontotoc360.com. URL: http://www.pontotoc360.com. Mailing Address: PO Box 210, Pontotoc, MS 38863-0210. Year Established: 1929. Pub. Frequency: w. (Wed.) Page Size: broadsheet. Subscrip. Rate: $.75 newsstand/cover; $28/yr mailed in county; $35/yr mailed in state; $40/yr mailed out of state. Adv. Rate: col. inch $7.40 Freelance Pay: $1/column-inch. Circulation: 6,325 per issue (paid). **Owner(s):** Journal Publishing Co., Inc., 1241 S Green St, Tupelo, MS 39902. Telephone: 662-842-2611. FAX: 662-842-2233. **Management:** Joyce Jolly, Office Manager. Michele Williams, Advertising Manager. **Editorial:** Brenda Owen, Managing Editor.

POPLARVILLE

POPLARVILLE DEMOCRAT, THE. 109 W Pearl St, Poplarville, MS 39470. Telephone: 601-795-2247. FAX: 601-795-2248. URL: http://www.cnhi.com. Mailing Address: PO Box 549, Poplarville, MS 39470. Pub. Frequency: w. (Thu.) Page Size: broadsheet. Subscrip. Rate: $.50 newsstand/cover; $10/yr in county; $18/yr out of county. Circulation: 2,200 per issue (paid). **Owner(s):** Community Newspaper Holdings, Inc., 3500 Colonnade Pkwy., Ste. 600, Birmingham, AL 35243-7017. **Management:** Tom Andrews, Publisher. Julie Bounds, Advertising. **Editorial:** Kenneth Weir, Editor.

PORT GIBSON

MARKET. 708 Main St., Port Gibson, MS 39150-1002. Telephone: 601-437-5103. FAX: 601-437-4410. E-MAIL: pgreveille@aol.com. Mailing Address: PO Box 1002, Port Gibson, MS 39150-1002. Year Established: 1851. Pub. Frequency: w. (Thu.) Page Size: standard. Subscrip. Rate: $.50 newsstand/cover; $18/yr in state; $23/yr out of state. Circulation: 2,296 per issue (paid). **Owner(s):** Emma F. Crisler, PO Box 1002, Port Gibson, MS 39150. Telephone: 601-437-5103. FAX: 601-437-4410. **Management:** Emma F. Crisler, Publisher. Gerald Bufkin, Advertising. Janice Bufkin, Advertising Manager. **Editorial:** Emma F. Crisler, Managing Editor.

QUITMAN

CLARKE COUNTY TRIBUNE. 101 Main St., Quitman, MS 39355. Telephone: 601-776-3726. FAX: 601-776-5793. E-MAIL: cct@netpathway.com. Mailing Address: PO Box 900, Quitman, MS 39355. Year Established: 1908. Pub. Frequency: w. (Thu.) Page Size: standard. Subscrip. Rate: $.50 newsstand/cover; $18/yr mailed in county; $20/yr mailed out of county; $22/yr mailed out of state. Circulation: 3,339 per issue (paid). **Owner(s):** Emmerich Newspapers, Inc., PO Box 16709, Jackson, MS 39236. Telephone: 662-647-8462. **Management:** Janet Andrews, Publisher. Cindy Baxley, Advertising Manager. **Editorial:** Janet Andrews, Editor.

RALEIGH

SMITH COUNTY REFORMER. 153 Main St., Raleigh, MS 39153. Telephone: 601-782-4358. FAX: 601-782-9020. E-MAIL: nbi@teleclipse.net. Mailing Address: PO Box 187, Raleigh, MS 39153. Year Established: 1889. Pub. Frequency: w. (Wed.) Page Size: broadsheet. Subscrip. Rate: $.50 newsstand/cover; $18/yr mailed in county; $23/yr mailed out of county; $28/yr mailed out of state. Circulation: 2,570 per issue (paid). **Owner(s):** Buckley Newspapers Inc., 3362 Hwy. 15, Bay Springs, MS 39422. Telephone: 601-764-3104. **Management:** Ronnie L. Buckley, Publisher. Brenda Ingram, Advertising Manager. **Editorial:** Blenda Singleton, Editor.

RICHTON

RICHTON DISPATCH, THE. PO Box 429, Richton, MS 39476-0429. Telephone: 601-788-6031. FAX: 601-788-6031. E-MAIL: richtondispatch@c-gate.net. Year Established: 1905. Pub. Frequency: w. (Thu.) Page Size: standard. Subscrip. Rate: $.35 newsstand/cover; $18/yr in county; $19/yr in state; $23/yr elsewhere. Circulation: 1,800 per issue (paid). **Owner(s):** Dean Wilson, See address and contact information above. **Management:** Larry A Wilson, Publisher. **Editorial:** Larry A Wilson, Editor.

RIDGELAND

MADISON COUNTY HERALD. 670 Hwy. 51, Ste.C, Ridgeland, MS 39157. Telephone: 601-853-2899. FAX: 601-853-8720. URL: http://www.mcherald.com. Year Established: 1906. Pub. Frequency: 3/w. (Tues., Thu., & Sat.) Page Size: broadsheet. Subscrip. Rate: $.50 newsstand/cover; $16/yr in county; $20/yr out of county. Circulation: 4,500 per issue (paid). **Owner(s):** Gannett Company, Inc., 7950 Jones Branch Dr., McLean, VA 22107-0001. Telephone: 703-854-6000. **Management:** Tracy Roberts, Advertising Manager. **Editorial:** Leilani Pope, Editor. Annie Oeth, Managing Editor.

RIPLEY

SOUTHERN SENTINEL. PO Box 558, Ripley, MS 38663. Telephone: 662-837-8111. E-MAIL: sentinel@theonlinedispatch.com. Year Established: 1879. Pub. Frequency: s-w. (Wed. & Fri.) Page Size: broadsheet. Subscrip. Rate: $.75 newsstand/cover; $47.50/yr mailed in county; $53.75/yr mailed out of county; $56/yr mailed elsewhere. Circulation: 4,654 per issue (paid). **Owner(s):** Southern Sentinel, Inc., See address and contact information above. **Management:** Tim Watson, General Manager. **Editorial:** Hank Wiesner, Editor.

SENATOBIA

DEMOCRAT, THE. 219 E. Main St., Senatobia, MS 38668-0369. Telephone: 662-562-4414. FAX: 662-562-8866. E-MAIL: jlee@thedemocrat.com. URL: http://www.thedemocrat.com. Mailing Address: PO Box 369, Senatobia, MS 38668-0369. Year Established: 1881. Pub. Frequency: w. (Tue.) Page Size: broadsheet. Subscrip. Rate: $.50 newsstand/cover; $20/yr local; $25/yr in state; $30/yr out of state. Adv. Rate: col. inch $6.95 Circulation: 5,200 per issue (paid). **Owner(s):** North Mississippi Newspapers, Inc., See address and contact information above. **Management:** Joe Lee III, Publisher. Shirley Trimm, Advertising. Travis Ashcraft, Classified Adv. Mgr.. **Editorial:** Jay Lee, Editor. Melissa Turner, News Editor.

TYLERTOWN

TYLERTOWN TIMES, THE. 727 Beulah Ave., Tylertown, MS 39667. E-MAIL: ttimes@telepak.net. Year Established: 1907. Pub. Frequency: w. (Thu.) Page Size: broadsheet. Subscrip. Rate: $.50 newsstand/cover; $15/yr mailed in county; $35/yr elsewhere. Adv. Rate: col. inch $5.50 Circulation: 2,990 per issue (paid). **Owner(s):** Carolyn Dillon, See address and contact information above. **Management:** Carolyn Dillon, Publisher. **Editorial:** Carolyn Dillon, Editor.

WAYNESBORO

WAYNE COUNTY (MS) NEWS. 713 Lomax Dr., Waynesboro, MS 39367. Telephone: 601-735-4341. FAX: 601-735-1111. E-MAIL: publisher@thewayneconuthnews.com. URL: http://www.wayneconews.com. Mailing Address: PO Box 509, Waynesboro, MS 39367. Year Established: 1891. Pub. Frequency: w. (Wed.) Page Size: broadsheet. Subscrip. Rate: $.75 newsstand/cover; $26/yr in county; $39.50/yr mailed out of area. Circulation: 4,500 per issue (paid). **Owner(s):** Bolton Newspapers, Inc., 49 Hines St., Monroeville, AL 36460. Telephone: 251-575-3282. FAX: 251-575-3284. **Management:** Relda Freeman, Advertising. **Editorial:** Paul Keane, Editor.

WIGGINS

STONE COUNTY ENTERPRISE, THE. 143 S. First St., PO Box 157, Wiggins, MS 39577. Telephone: 601-928-4802. FAX: 601-928-2191. E-MAIL: heather@stonecountyenterprise.com. URL: http://www.stonecountyenterprise.com. Mailing Address: PO Box 157, Wiggins, MS 39577. Year Established: 1916. Pub. Frequency: w. (Wed.) Page Size: broadsheet. Subscrip. Rate: $.50 newsstand/cover; $25/yr mailed in county; $37/yr mailed out of county; $42/yr mailed out of state. Circulation: 3,600 per issue (paid). **Owner(s):** Stone County Enterprise, See address and contact information above. **Management:** Heather Freret, Publisher. Hope Wade, Advertising Manager. Charlotte Wippler, Circulation Manager. **Editorial:** Heather Freret, Editor.

YAZOO CITY

YAZOO HERALD. 1035 Grand Ave, Yazoo City, MS 39194. E-MAIL: lazyrey2@bellsouth.net. Year Established: 1872. Pub. Frequency: s-w. (Wed. & Sat.) Page Size: broadsheet. Subscrip. Rate: $.75 newsstand/cover; $39/yr in state; $55/yr out of state. Adv. Rate: col. inch $8.20 Circulation: 3,900 per issue (paid). **Owner(s):** Yazoo Newspaper, Inc., PO Box 720, Yazoo City, MS 39194. Telephone: 662-746-4911. FAX: 662-746-4915. **Management:** Gary Andrews, Publisher. Heather Spiars, Advertising Manager. Sue White, Circulation Manager. **Editorial:** Jason Patterson, Managing Editor.

MISSOURI

ALBANY

ALBANY LEDGER, THE. 213 W Clay St, Albany, MO 64402. Telephone: 660-726-3998. FAX: 660-726-3997. E-MAIL: news@aledger.net. URL: http://www.aledger.net. Mailing Address: PO Box 247, Albany, MO 64402. Year Established: 1868. Pub. Frequency: w. (Wed.) Page Size: broadsheet. Subscrip. Rate: $.75 newsstand/cover; $24/yr in county & adj. counties; $28/yr in state; $32/yr out of state. Circulation: 1,300 per issue (paid). **Owner(s):** Gentry County Publishing, LLC, See address and contact information above. **Management:** Christy Groves, Publisher. **Editorial:** Don Groves, Managing Editor.

ASHLAND

BOONE COUNTY JOURNAL. 104 W. Broadway, Ashland, MO 65010. Telephone: 573-657-2334. FAX: 573-657-2002. E-MAIL: bocojo@aol.com. Mailing Address: PO Box 197, Ashland, MO 65010-0197. Year Established: 1969. Pub. Frequency: w. (Wed.) Page Size: broadsheet. Subscrip. Rate: $21/yr in state; $32/yr out of state. Adv. Rate: col. inch $4 Circulation: 1,850 per issue (paid). **Owner(s):** Bruce Wallace, See address and contact information above. **Management:** Bruce Wallace, Publisher. **Editorial:** Bruce Wallace, Editor.

AURORA

AURORA ADVERTISER. ISSN 1041-1275
226 W. Church St., Aurora, MO 65605-0509. Telephone: 417-678-2115. E-MAIL: advert@dialnet.net. Mailing Address: PO Box 509, Aurora, MO 65605-0509. Pub. Frequency: s-w. (Tue. & Fri.) Page Size: standard. Subscrip. Rate: $.50 newsstand/cover per issue; $32.11/yr home delivery in city. Adv. Rate: color page $90 Circulation: 5,600. **Owner(s):** Lawrence County Newspapers, Inc., See address and contact information above. **Management:** Darren D. Sumner, President. Jewell Bagby, Advertising Manager. **Editorial:** Judy Dingman, Editor.

BELLE

BELLE BANNER. 217 Alvarado Ave., Belle, MO 65013-0711. Telephone: 573-859-3328. FAX: 573-859-6274. E-MAIL: kjl@sockets.net. Year Established: 1907. Pub. Frequency: w. (Wed.) Page Size: broadsheet. Subscrip. Rate: $.50 newsstand/cover; $21.55/yr local; $24.77/yr mailed in state; $25/yr mailed out of state. Circulation: 2,750 per issue (paid). **Owner(s):** Tri-County Newspapers LLC, See address and contact information above. **Management:** Kurt J. Lewis, Publisher. **Editorial:** Ron Lewis, Editor.

BLAND COURIER. 217 Alvarado, Belle, MO 65013. Telephone: 573-646-3312. FAX: 573-859-6274. E-MAIL: kjl@sockets.net. Mailing Address: PO Box 39, Bland, MO 65014. Year Established: 1901. Pub. Frequency: w. (Wed.) Page Size: broadsheet. Subscrip. Rate: $.50 newsstand/cover; $21.55/yr local; $24.77/yr in state; $25/yr out of state. Circulation: 900 per issue (paid). **Owner(s):** Tri-County Newspapers LLC, 217 Alvarado Ave., Belle, MO 65013-0711. Telephone: 573-859-3328. FAX: 573-859-6274. **Management:** Ron Lewis, General Manager. Kurt J. Lewis, Publisher.

BELTON

STAR-HERALD (BELTON), THE. 419 Main St, Belton, MO 64012. Telephone: 816-3311-5353. FAX: 816-322-2943. E-MAIL: editor@thestar-herald.com. URL: http://www.thestar-herald.com. Mailing Address: PO Box 379, Belton, MO 64012. Year Established: 1892. Pub. Frequency: w. (Thu.) Page Size: broadsheet. Subscrip. Rate: $.50 newsstand/cover; $26/yr in county; $33/yr in state; $38/yr out of state. Circulation: 4,500 per issue (paid). **Owner(s):** The/McClatchy Company, 2100 Q St, Sacramento, CA 95816. Telephone: 916-321-1936. FAX: 916-321-1869. **Management:** Sandy Nelson, Publisher. Vicki Daniel, Advertising Manager. Kim Ford, Circulation Manager. **Editorial:** Linda Thompson, Managing Editor. Brad Seiner, Sports Editor.

BETHANY

BETHANY REPUBLICAN-CLIPPER. 202 N. 16th St., Bethany, MO 64424. Telephone: 660-425-6325. FAX: 660-425-3441. E-MAIL: rclipper@grm.net. Mailing Address: PO Box 351, Bethany, MO 64424-0351. Year Established: 1873. Pub. Frequency: w. (Wed.) Page Size: broadsheet. Subscrip. Rate: $.50 newsstand/cover; $23/yr in county; $38/yr out of county; $44/yr out of state. Circulation: 3,500 per issue (paid). **Owner(s):** Bethany Printing Co., See address and contact information above. **Management:** Philip Conger, Publisher. Kathy Conger, Advertising Manager. **Editorial:** Philip Conger, Editor.

HARRISON COUNTY AD-VISOR. PO Box 106, Bethany, MO 64424. Telephone: 660-425-3433. FAX: 660-425-6984. E-MAIL: ad-visor@grm.net. Year Established: 1967. Pub. Frequency: w. (Tue.) Page Size: tabloid. Circulation: 7,000 per issue (controlled). **Owner(s):** Mona Selby, Ron Scott & Sherri Hippler, See address and contact information above. **Management:** Debra McChesney, Manager.

BOLIVAR

BOLIVAR HERALD-FREE PRESS. 335 Springfield Ave, Bolivar, MO 65613. Telephone: 417-326-7636. FAX: 417-326-7643. E-MAIL: daveb@cpimo.com. URL: http://www.bolivarmonews.com. Mailing Address: PO Box 330, Bolivar, AR 65613. Year Established: 1868. Pub. Frequency: s-w. (Wed. & Fri.) Page Size: broadsheet. Subscrip. Rate: $.75 newsstand/cover; $42/yr in county & adj. counties; $60/yr mailed out of area; $72/yr mailed out of state. Circulation: 7,400 per issue (paid). **Owner(s):** Community Publishers, Inc., 125 W Central Ave, Ste 318, Bentonville, AR 72712. Telephone: 479-271-3700. **Management:** David Berry, Publisher. Deanna Moore, Advertising Manager. Peggy Skopec, Classified Adv. Mgr.. **Editorial:** Katie Duncan, Associate Editor. Rebecca Baker, Editorial Assistant. Jess Hamlet, Reporter.

BOONVILLE

RECORD (BOONVILLE), THE. 412 E High St., Boonville, MO 65233. Telephone: 660-882-5335. FAX: 660-882-2256. Mailing Address: PO Box 47, Boonville, MO 65233. Pub. Frequency: w. (Tue.) Subscrip. Rate: $.50 newsstand/cover per issue; $35/yr. Circulation: 10,000 per issue (paid and free). **Owner(s):** GateHouse Media, Inc, 3000 Dundee Rd., Ste. 203, Northbrook, IL 60062. **Management:** Scott J. Jackson, Publisher. Jeff Glandon, Advertising Manager. Lisa Glasscock, Circulation Manager. **Editorial:** Karen Green, Editor.

BOWLING GREEN

BOWLING GREEN TIMES. ISSN 0162-6701
106 W. Main, Bowling Green, MO 63334-1642. Telephone: 573-324-2222. FAX: 573-324-3991. E-MAIL: bgtimes@nemonet.com. URL: http://www.bowlinggreentimes.com. Mailing Address: PO Box 110, Bowling Green, MO 63334. Year Established: 1874. Pub. Frequency: w. (Wed.) Page Size: broadsheet. Subscrip. Rate: $.50 newsstand/cover; $25/yr mailed in county; $34/yr mailed out of county. Circulation: 3,000 per issue (paid). **Owner(s):** Lakeway Publishers, Inc., 1609 W First N St., Morristown, TN 37814. Telephone: 423-581-5630. **Management:** Linda Luebrecht, General Manager. Walt Gilbert, Publisher. Laura Smith, Advertising Manager. **Editorial:** Nathan Lilley, Editor.

BRANSON

TANEY COUNTY TIMES. 519 W. Pacific, Branson, MO 65616. Telephone: 417-334-2285. FAX: 417-334-4789. E-MAIL: tctads@inter-linc.net. Mailing Address: PO Box 6670, Branson, MO 65615-6670. Year Established: 1995. Pub. Frequency: w. (Wed.) Page Size: broadsheet. Subscrip. Rate: $.50 newsstand/cover; $21.55/yr in county; $28/yr out of county. Adv. Rate: col. inch $5 Circulation: 3,979 per issue (paid). **Owner(s):** Kurt Lewis, PO Box 6670, Branson, MO 65615. Telephone: 417-334-2285. **Management:** Kurt Lewis, Publisher. Kim Green, Advertising. Kurt Lewis, Advertising Manager. **Editorial:** Criag Donze, Editor-in-Chief.

BROOKFIELD

SHO ME SHOPPER. 107-109 N. Main St., Brookfield, MO 64628. Telephone: 660-258-7237. FAX: 660-258-7238. URL: http://www.gatehousemedia.com. Mailing Address: PO Box 40, Brookfield, MO 64628. Pub. Frequency: w. (Mon.) Page Size: standard Circulation: 13,547 per issue (free). **Owner(s):** GateHouse Media, Inc, 350 WillowBrook Office Park, Fairport, NY 14450. Telephone: 585-598-0030. FAX: 585-248-2631. **Management:** Rod Dixon, Publisher. Stacey Jackson, Advertising Manager. Larry Bradley, Circulation Manager.

BUFFALO

BUFFALO REFLEX. 114 E. Lincoln St., Buffalo, MO 65622. Telephone: 417-345-2224. FAX: 417-345-2235. E-MAIL: buffaloreflex@cpimo.com. URL: http://www.buffaloreflex.com. Mailing Address: PO Box 770, Buffalo, MO 65622. Year Established: 1869. Pub. Frequency: w. (Wed.) Page Size: broadsheet. Subscrip. Rate: $.75 newsstand/cover; $28/yr in county & adj. cys.; $36/yr in state; $45/yr out of state .. Circulation: 5,000 per issue (paid). **Owner(s):** Community Publishers, Inc., PO Box 1049, Bentonville, AR 72712. Telephone: 501-271-3731. FAX: 501-273-7777. **Management:** Regina Blair, Advertising. **Editorial:** Paul Campbell, Editor.

BUTLER

NEWS-X PRESS. 5 N. Main St., Butler, MO 64730-0210. Telephone: 660-679-6126. FAX: 660-679-4905. E-MAIL: newsxpress@yourxgroup.com. URL: http://www.yourxgroup.com. Mailing Address: PO Box 210, Butler, MO 64730-0210. Year Established: 1984. Pub. Frequency: w. (Fri.) Page Size: standard. Subscrip. Rate: $1 newsstand/cover; $34.91/yr in county; $38.93/yr out of county (effective 2009); $30.56/yr out of state. Circulation: 3,300 per issue (paid). **Owner(s):** Jim & Carol Peters, 5 N. Main St., Butler, MO 64730. Telephone: 660-679-6126. FAX: 660-679-4905. **Management:** P. Schowengerdt, Advertising Manager. **Editorial:** C.A. Moore, Editor.

CALIFORNIA

CALIFORNIA DEMOCRAT. 319 S. High St., California, MO 65018. Telephone: 573-796-2135. FAX: 573-796-4220. E-MAIL: caldem1@yahoo.com. Mailing Address: PO Box 126, California, MO 65018. Year Established: 1858. Pub. Frequency: w. (Wed.) Page Size: broadsheet. Subscrip. Rate: $.50 newsstand/cover; $26/yr mailed in county; $32/yr mailed in state; $35/yr mailed out of state. Circulation: 4,000 per issue (paid). **Owner(s):** News Tribune Co., 210 Monroe St., Jefferson City, MO. **Management:** Ray Grimes, General Manager. Paula Kelsay, Circulation Manager. **Editorial:** Paula Earls, Editor. David Wilson, Reporter.

CAMDENTON

LAKE SUN LEADER - PENNYSAVER. 918 N State Hwy 5, Camdenton, MO 65020. Telephone: 573-346-2132. FAX: 573-346-4508. URL: http://www.gatehousemeadia.com. Pub. Frequency: w. (Wed.) Page Size: standard Circulation: 3,800 per issue (free). **Owner(s):** GateHouse Media, Inc, 350 WillowBrook Office Park, Fairport, NY 14450. Telephone: 585-598-0030. FAX: 585-248-2631. **Management:** Jules Molenda, Publisher. Lisa Miller, Advertising Manager.

CAMERON

CAMERON CITIZEN OBSERVER. PO Box 498, Cameron, MO 64429. Telephone: 816-632-7281. FAX: 816-632-4508. E-MAIL: news@cameron.net. Pub. Frequency: w. (Thu.) Page Size: broadsheet. Subscrip. Rate: $.75 newsstand/cover; $30/yr mailed in county; $34/yr mailed out of county; $49/yr mailed out of state. Circulation: 2,800 per issue (paid). **Owner(s):** Cameron Newspapers, Inc., See address and contact information above. **Management:** Jamey Honeycutt, Publisher. Tina Svoboda, Advertising Manager. **Editorial:** Andrew Bottrell, Editor.

ELDON ADVERTISER. 415 S Maple ST, Eldon, MO 65026. Telephone: 573-392-5659. FAX: 573-392-7755. E-MAIL: advertiser@vernonpublishing.com. URL: http://www.vpi-newspapers.com. Mailing Address: PO Box 315, Eldon, MO 65026-0315. Year Established: 1894. Pub. Frequency: w. (Thu..) Page Size: broadsheet. Subscrip. Rate: $.75 newsstand/cover; $39/yr in county; $44.50/yr out of county; $52.50/yr out of state. Adv. Rate: col. inch $4.60 Circulation: 4,300 per issue (paid). **Owner(s):** Vernon Publishing, Inc., 104 W Jasper St, Versailles, MO 65084. Telephone: 573-378-5441. **Management:** Dane Vernon, Publisher. **Editorial:** Tim Flora, Editor.

ELLINGTON

REYNOLDS COUNTY COURIER. 370 S Main St, Ellington, MO 63638. Telephone: 573-663-2243. FAX: 573-663-2763. E-MAIL: rcc@semo.net. Mailing Address: PO Box 130, Ellington, MO 63638. Year Established: 1876. Pub. Frequency: w. (Thu.) Page Size: broadsheet. Subscrip. Rate: $.75 newsstand/cover; $29/yr in county & adj. counties; $42/yr elsewhere. **Wire Service(s):** AP. Circulation: 2,300 per issue (paid). **Owner(s):** Ellinghouse Publishing Co., Inc, 101 W. Elm, Piedmont, MO 63957. Telephone: 573-223-7122. FAX: 573-223-7871. **Management:** Harold Ellinghouse, Publisher. Tanya Burress, Advertising Manager. Monica Stewart, Circulation Manager. **Editorial:** Harold Ellinghouse, Editor. Carol Groves, Reporter.

EXCELSIOR SPRINGS

EXCELSIOR SPRINGS STANDARD. 417 Thompson, Excelsior Springs, MO 64024. Telephone: 816-637-3147. FAX: 816-637-8411. E-MAIL: excelpub@epsi.net/leaderpress.com. Mailing Address: PO Box 70, Excelsior Springs, MO 64024. Year Established: 1889. Pub. Frequency: s-w. (Tue. & Fri.) Page Size: broadsheet. Subscrip. Rate: $.50 newsstand/cover; $9 carrier delivery local for 4 wks.. Circulation: 3,000 per issue (paid). **Owner(s):** Fackelman Newspaper Group, 1556-C Union Rd., Gastonia, NC 28054. **Management:** James Bouldin, Publisher. Wanda Rowe, Advertising Manager. Dane Copeland, Circulation Manager. Nancy Elmore, Business Manager. **Editorial:** Eric Copeland, Editor.

FARMINGTON

FARMINGTON PRESS. 218 N. Washington St., Farmington, MO 63640. Telephone: 573-756-8927. FAX: 573-756-9160. Mailing Address: PO Box 70, Farmington, MO 63640. Year Established: 1928. Pub. Frequency: w. (Thu.) Page Size: broadsheet. Subscrip. Rate: $.50 newsstand/cover; $40/yr home delivery. Circulation: 4,100 per issue (paid). **Owner(s):** Lee Enterprises, Inc., 900 N. Tucker Blvd., St. Louis, MO 63101. Telephone: 314-340-8000. **Management:** Doug Smith, General Manager. Mark Cedeck, Circulation Manager.

FAYETTE

DEMOCRAT-LEADER. ISSN 0746-9934
203 N. Main St., Fayette, MO 65248-0032. Telephone: 660-248-2235. FAX: 660-248-1200. E-MAIL: newspaper@mcmsys.com. URL: Htpp://www.fayettenewspapers.com. Mailing Address: PO Box 32, Fayette, MO 65248-0032. Year Established: 1874. Pub. Frequency: w. (Sat.) Page Size: standard. Subscrip. Rate: $.50 newsstand/cover; $29/yr in county; $36/yr in state; $48/yr out of state. Adv. Rate: col. inch $3.26 Circulation: 2,512 per issue (paid). **Owner(s):** Wood Creek Media, See address and contact information above. **Management:** James H. Steele, Publisher. **Editorial:** James H. Steele, Editor. Scott Skinner, Sports.

FAYETTE ADVERTISER, THE. ISSN 0746-9942
203 N. Main St., Fayette, MO 65248-0032. Telephone: 660-248-2235. FAX: 660-248-1200. E-MAIL: newspapr@mcmsys.com. URL: http://www.fayettenewspapers.com. Mailing Address: PO Box 32, Fayette, MO 65248-0032. Year Established: 1840. Pub. Frequency: w. (Wed.) Page Size: standard. Subscrip. Rate: $.50 newsstand/cover; $29/yr in county; $42/yr out of county; $48/yr mailed out of state. Adv. Rate: col. inch $3.50 Circulation: 2,512 per issue (paid). **Owner(s):** Wood Creek Media, See address and contact information above. **Management:** James H. Steele, Publisher. **Editorial:** James H. Steele, Editor.

FESTUS

JEFFERSON COUNTY JOURNAL (FESTUS). 1405 N. Truman Blvd., Festus, MO 63028. Telephone: 636-931-6636. FAX: 636-931-2638. E-MAIL: bdonnelly@yourjournal.com. URL: http://www.yourjournal.com. Pub. Frequency: 3/w. (Wed., Fri., Sun.) Page Size: broadsheet Circulation: 19,000 per issue (free). **Owner(s):** Suburban Journals, 14522 S Outer 40 Rd, 3rd Fl, Chesterfield, MO 63017. Telephone: 314-821-1110. **Management:** Bob Donnelly Jr., Publisher. Mike Berry, Circulation Manager. **Editorial:** Bill Phelan, Managing Editor.

MERAMEC JOURNAL, THE. 1405 N. Truman Blvd., Festus, MO 63028. Telephone: 636-931-6636. FAX: 636-931-2638. E-MAIL: bdonnelly@yourjournal.com. URL: http://www.yourjournal.com. Mailing Address: 1405 N. Truman Blvd., Festus, MO 63028-1177. Pub. Frequency: 3/w. (Wed., Fri., Sun.) Page Size: broadsheet. Circulation: 63,000 per issue (paid and free). **Owner(s):** Suburban Journals, 14522 S Outer 40 Rd, 3rd Fl, Chesterfield, MO 63017. Telephone: 314-821-1110. FAX: 314-972-1111. **Management:** Bob Donnelly Jr., Publisher. Mike Berry, Circulation Manager. **Editorial:** Bill Phelan, Managing Editor.

NEWS-DEMOCRAT JOURNAL. 1405 N. Truman Blvd., Festus, MO 63028-0309. Telephone: 636-931-6636. FAX: 636-931-2638. E-MAIL: bdonnelly@yourjournal.com. URL: http://www.yourjournal.com. Mailing Address: 1405 N. Truman Blvd., Festus, MO 63028-1177. Year Established: 1865. Pub. Frequency: 3/w. (Wed., Fri., Sun.) Page Size: broadsheet. Subscrip. Rate: $.50 newsstand/cover. Circulation: 61,800 per issue (paid and free). **Owner(s):** Suburban Journals, 14522 S Outer 40 Rd, 3rd Fl, Chesterfield, MO 63017. Telephone: 314-821-1110. **Management:** Bob Donnelly Jr., Publisher. Mike Berry, Circulation Manager. **Editorial:** Bill Phelan, Managing Editor.

FREDERICKTOWN

DEMOCRAT NEWS. 131 S. Main St., Fredericktown, MO 63645. Telephone: 573-783-3366. FAX: 573-783-6890. E-MAIL: democratnews@hotmail.com. URL: http://www.mydjconnection.com. Mailing Address: PO Box 471, Fredericktown, MO 63645. Year Established: 1870. Pub. Frequency: w. (Wed.) Page Size: broadsheet. Subscrip. Rate: $.50 newsstand/cover; $28/yr mailed in state; $34/yr mailed out of state. Circulation: 3,200 per issue (paid). **Owner(s):** Lee Enterprises, Inc., 900 N. Tucker Blvd., St. Louis, MO 63101. Telephone: 314-340-8000. **Management:** Alan Kopitsky, General Manager. Jim York, Publisher. Bob Mooney, Advertising. **Editorial:** Alan Kopitsky, Editor.

GAINESVILLE

OZARK COUNTY TIMES. 36 Court Sq., Gainesville, MO 65655. Telephone: 417-679-4641. FAX: 417-679-3423. E-MAIL: oct@ozarkcountytimes.com. URL: http://www.ozarkcountytimes.com. Mailing Address: PO Box 188, Gainesville, MO 65655. Year Established: 1883. Pub. Frequency: w. (Wed.) Page Size: broadsheet. Subscrip. Rate: $.50 newsstand/cover; $25/yr in county & adj. counties; $33/yr elsewhere. Adv. Rate: col. inch $6.25 Circulation: 3,800 per issue (paid). **Owner(s):** Dalton Wright, PO Box 192, Lebanon, MO 65536. Telephone: 417-532-9131. **Management:** Norene Prososki, Publisher. Steve Hutchings, Advertising Manager. **Editorial:** Betty Stanley, Editor.

GALLATIN

NORTH MISSOURIAN. 203 N. Main, Gallatin, MO 64640. Telephone: 660-663-2154. FAX: 660-663-2498. E-MAIL: gpc@northwestmissouri.com. URL: http://www.northwestmissouri.com. Mailing Address: P.O. Box 37, Gallatin, MO 64640-0037. Year Established: 1864. Pub. Frequency: w. (Wed.) Page Size: tabloid. Subscrip. Rate: $.50 newsstand/cover; $27/yr in state; $36/yr elsewhere. Circulation: 2,200 per issue (paid). **Owner(s):** Gallatin Publishing Co., See address and contact information above. **Management:** Darryl Wilkinson, Publisher. **Editorial:** Darryl Wilkinson, Editor.

GREENFIELD

VEDETTE, THE. 7 N Main St, Greenfield, MO 65661. Telephone: 417-637-2712. FAX: 417-637-2232. E-MAIL: greenfieldbedettegraphics@mchsi.com. Mailing Address: PO Box 216, Greenfield, MO 65661-0216. Year Established: 1866. Pub. Frequency: w. (Thu.) Page Size: standard. Subscrip. Rate: $.75 newsstand/cover; $33/yr in county. Circulation: 1,900 per issue (paid). **Owner(s):** GateHouse Media, Inc, 350 WillowBrook Office Park, Fairport, NY 14450. Telephone: 585-598-0030. FAX: 585-248-2631. **Management:** Marlene DeClue, Publisher. **Editorial:** Marlene DeClue, Editor.

HARRISONVILLE

CASS COUNTY DEMOCRAT MISSOURIAN. 301 S Lexington St, Harrisonville, MO 64701. Telephone: 816-380-3228. FAX: 816-380-7650. URL: http://www.democratmissourian.com. Year Established: 1881. Pub. Frequency: w. (Fri.) Page Size: broadsheet. Subscrip. Rate: $.50 newsstand/cover; $32/yr mailed in county; $43/yr mailed in MO & KS; $52/yr mailed elsewhere. Circulation: 6,450 per issue (paid). **Owner(s):** The/McClatchy Company, 2100 Q St., Sacramento, CA 95816-6816. **Management:** Sandy Nelson, Publisher. Pat Larson, Advertising Manager. Kim Ford, Circulation Manager. **Editorial:** Linda Thompson, Managing Editor. Stephanie Yeagle, Sports Editor.

HAZELWOOD

BELLEFONTAINE NEIGHBORS-JENNINGS JOURNAL. 7751 N. Lindbergh Blvd., Hazelwood, MO 63042. Telephone: 314-972-1111. FAX: 314-831-7643. E-MAIL: cmarty@yourjournal.com. URL: http://www.stltoday.com. Year Established: 1960. Pub. Frequency: s-w. (Wed. & Sun.) Page Size: broadsheet. Subscrip. Rate: $27/yr mailed for 3 mos.. Adv. Rate: col. inch $16.39 Circulation: 25,520 per issue (paid and free). **Owner(s):** Suburban Journals, 1714 Deer Tracks Trail, St. Louis, MO 63131. Telephone: 314-821-1110. **Management:** Carolyn Marty, Publisher. Tammy Mortensen, Advertising Manager.

FLORISSANT-BLACK JACK JOURNAL. 7751 N. Lindbergh Blvd., Hazelwood, MO 63042. Telephone: 314-972-1111. FAX: 314-831-7643. E-MAIL: tmortensen@yourjournal.com. URL: http://www.yourjournal.com. Pub. Frequency: s-w. (Wed. & Sun.) Page Size: broadsheet. Subscrip. Rate: $35/yr. Circulation: 34,755 per issue (paid and free). **Owner(s):** Suburban Journals, 1714 Deer Tracks Trail, St. Louis, MO 63131. Telephone: 314-821-1110. **Management:** Carolyn Marty, Publisher. Tammy Mortensen, Advertising Manager. Tim Felch, Circulation Manager. **Editorial:** Cathy Regazzi, Managing Editor.

HAZELWOOD-BRIDGETON JOURNAL. 7751 N. Lindbergh Blvd., Hazelwood, MO 63042. Telephone: 314-972-1111. FAX: 314-831-7643. E-MAIL: cmarty@yourjournal.com. URL: http://www.stltoday.com. Pub. Frequency: s-w. (Wed. & Sun.) Page Size: broadsheet Circulation: 12,180 per issue (free). **Owner(s):** Suburban Journals, 14522 S Outer 40 Rd, 3rd Fl, Chesterfield, MO 63017. Telephone: 314-821-1110. FAX: 314-972-1111. **Management:** Carolyn Marty, Publisher. Tammy Mortensen, Advertising Manager.

NORTH COUNTRY JOURNAL. 7751 N. Lindbergh Blvd., Hazelwood, MO 63042. Telephone: 314-972-1111. FAX: 314-831-7643. E-MAIL: cmarty@yourjournal.com. URL: http://www.stltoday.com. Pub. Frequency: s-w. (Wed. & Sun.) Page Size: broadsheet Circulation: 31,075 per issue (free). **Owner(s):** Suburban Journals, 1714 Deer Tracks Trail, St. Louis, MO 63131. Telephone: 314-821-1110. **Management:** Carolyn Marty, Publisher. Tammy Mortensen, Advertising Manager.

NORTH COUNTY JOURNAL. 7751 N. Lindbergh Blvd., Hazelwood, MO 63042-2126. Telephone: 314-972-1111. FAX: 314-831-7643. E-MAIL: newsroom@yourjournal.com. URL: http://www.yourjournal.com. Year Established: 1993. Pub. Frequency: s-w. (Sun. & Wed.) Page Size: broadsheet. Subscrip. Rate: $27 mailed. Adv. Rate: col. inch $20.06 Circulation: 47,017 Sunday (paid and free); 48,506 per issue (paid and free). **Owner(s):** Suburban Journals, 1714 Deer Tracks Trail, St. Louis, MO 63131. Telephone: 314-821-1110. **Management:** Carolyn Marty, Publisher. Kristie Baumgartner, Advertising Manager. Dan Crockwell, Circulation Manager. **Editorial:** Dan Barger, Editorial Director.

NORTH SIDE JOURNAL. 7751 N. Lindbergh Blvd., Hazelwood, MO 63042-2126. Telephone: 314-972-1111. FAX: 314-831-7643. E-MAIL: tmortensen@yourjournal.com. URL: http://www.yourjournal.com. Year Established: 1993. Pub. Frequency: w. (Wed.) Page Size: broadsheet. Subscrip. Rate: $27/yr mailed. Adv. Rate: col. inch $17.60 Circulation: 31,075 per issue (paid and free). **Owner(s):** Suburban Journals, 1714 Deer Tracks Trail, St. Louis, MO 63131. Telephone: 314-821-1110. **Management:** Carolyn Marty, Publisher. Tammy Mortensen, Advertising Manager. Rich Sisak, Circulation Manager. **Editorial:** Cathy Regazzi, Managing Editor.

OVERLAND-ST. ANN JOURNAL. 7751 N. Lindbergh Blvd., Hazelwood, MO 63042. Telephone: 314-972-1111. FAX: 314-831-7643. E-MAIL: cmarty@yourjournal.com. URL: http://www.stltoday.com. Pub. Frequency: w. (Wed.) Page Size: broadsheet Circulation: 24,040 per issue (free). **Owner(s):** Suburban Journals, 1714 Deer Tracks Trail, St. Louis, MO 63131. Telephone: 413-821-0843. **Management:** Carolyn Marty, Publisher.

HERMANN

HERMANN ADVERTISER-COURIER. 136 E. Fourth St., Hermann, MO 65041-0350. Telephone: 573-486-5418. FAX: 573-486-5524. E-MAIL: donac@ktis.net. Year Established: 1854. Pub. Frequency: w. (Wed.) Page Size: broadsheet. Subscrip. Rate: $.75 newsstand/cover; $28/yr mailed in county; $34/yr mailed out of county; $45/yr mailed out of state. Circulation: 4,000 per issue (paid). **Owner(s):** Lakeway Publishers of Missouri Inc., 136 E. Fourth St., Hermann, MO 65041. Telephone: 573-486-5418. **Management:** Jack Fishman, President. Walt Gilbert, Publisher. Cindy Kuhn, Office Manager. Glenda Scheele, Advertising Manager. **Editorial:** Don Kruse, Editor.

CAPE GIRARDEAU

CASSVILLE DEMOCRAT. 301 Broadway, Cape Girardeau, MO 63701. Telephone: 573-335-6611, 800-879-1210. FAX: 573-335-5018. E-MAIL: democrat@mo-net.com. Year Established: 1872. Pub. Frequency: w. (Wed.) Page Size: broadsheet. Subscrip. Rate: $.50 newsstand/cover; $22/yr in county; $31/yr out of county. Circulation: 5,100 per issue (paid). **Owner(s):** Rust Communications, Inc., See address and contact information above. **Management:** Lisa Blackwell, Advertising Manager. Darlene Wierman, Classified Adv. Mgr.. **Editorial:** Lisa Schlichtman, Editor. Susan Eschbach, Assistant Editor.

CARROLLTON

CARROLLTON DEMOCRAT. 102 E. Benton St., Carrollton, MO 64633. Telephone: 660-542-0881. FAX: 660-542-2580. E-MAIL: democrat@carolnet.com. Year Established: 1881. Pub. Frequency: s-w. (Tue. & Fri.) Page Size: broadsheet. Subscrip. Rate: $.50 newsstand/cover; $38/yr in county; $48/yr out of county. Circulation: 2,466 per issue (paid). **Owner(s):** Standard Herald, Inc., See address and contact information above. **Management:** Frank Mercer, Publisher. Judy Stroud, Advertising Manager. Tara Cooper, Circulation Manager. **Editorial:** Elaine Mercer, Editor. Colby Gordon, Sports.

WINDSOR REVIEW, THE. 102 E. Benton St., Carrollton, MO 64633. Telephone: 660-542-0881. FAX: 660-542-2580. Year Established: 1870. Pub. Frequency: w. (Thu.) Page Size: broadsheet. Subscrip. Rate: $.60 newsstand/cover; $24.95/yr in county; $33.95/yr out of county. Circulation: 1,850 per issue (paid). **Owner(s):** Standard Herald, Inc., See address and contact information above. **Management:** Frank Mercer, Publisher. **Editorial:** Colby Gordon, Editor.

CARTHAGE

CARTHAGE PRESS SCOPE, THE. 800 W Central, Carthage, MO 64836. Telephone: 417-358-2191. FAX: 417-358-7428. URL: http://www.carthagepress.com. Mailing Address: PO Box 678, Carthage, MO 64836. Pub. Frequency: w. (Wed.) Page Size: tabloid Circulation: 5,000 per issue (free). **Owner(s):** GateHouse Media, Inc, 350 WillowBrook Office Park, Fairport, NY 14450. Telephone: 585-598-0030. **Management:** Buzz Ball, General Manager. Tammy Collins, Advertising. Amy Willis, Circulation Manager. Amber Carter, Classified Adv. Mgr..

CARUTHERSVILLE

DEMOCRAT-ARGUS, THE. 403 Ward Ave, Caruthersville, MO 63830. URL: http://www.democratargus.com. Mailing Address: PO Box 1059, Caruthersville, MO 63830. Year Established: 1868. Pub. Frequency: w. (Thu.) Page Size: broadsheet. Subscrip. Rate: $.75 newsstand/cover; $30/yr in county; $60/yr elsewhere. Adv. Rate: col. inch $5.25 Circulation: 13,000 per issue (paid and free). **Owner(s):** Tennyson Publishing, 900 N. Broadway, Blytheville, AR 72316. Telephone: 870-763-4461. FAX: 870-763-6874. **Management:** Lisa Bryant, General Manager. **Editorial:** Herb Smith, Editor. Karol Wilcox, Assistant Editor.

CASSVILLE

BARRY COUNTY ADVERTISER. ISSN 0194-1542 904 West St., Cassville, MO 65625. Telephone: 417-847-3155. FAX: 417-847-4523. E-MAIL: litho@mo-net.com. Mailing Address: PO Box 488, Cassville, MO 65625. Year Established: 1966. Pub. Frequency: w. (Wed.) Page Size: tabloid. Subscrip. Rate: $.25 newsstand/cover; $32.02/yr. Adv. Rate: col. inch $8.40 Circulation: 12,000 per issue (paid). **Owner(s):** Jean Melton, PO Box 488, Cassville, MO 65625-0488. Telephone: 417-847-4475. FAX: 417-847-4523. **Management:** Jean Melton, Publisher. Johnnie Edie, Advertising Manager. Hazel Gripka, Circulation Manager. **Editorial:** Leatrice Strothers, Editor.

CENTRALIA

CENTRALIA FIRESIDE GUARD. 118 W. Sneed, Centralia, MO 65240. Year Established: 1868. Pub. Frequency: w. (Wed.) Page Size: broadsheet. Subscrip. Rate: $.50 newsstand/cover; $22.50/yr local; $25.50/yr mailed in state; $29.50/yr mailed out of state. Circulation: 4,300 per issue (paid). **Owner(s):** Charles & Janann Hedberg, See address and contact information above. **Management:** Charles Hedberg, Publisher. **Editorial:** Janann Hedberg, Editor.

CHARLESTON

CHARLESTON ENTERPRISE-COURIER. PO Box 69, Charleston, MO 63834. Year Established: 1874. Pub. Frequency: w. (Thu.) Page Size: broadsheet. Subscrip. Rate: $.40 newsstand/cover; $15/yr mailed in county; $23.50/yr mailed in state; $25/yr mailed out of state. Circulation: 3,500 per issue (paid). **Owner(s):** Enterprise-Courier, Inc., See address and contact information above. **Management:** Liz Anderson, President. Mildred Wallhausen, Publisher. Sabrina Harris, Advertising Manager. **Editorial:** Liz Anderson, Editor.

CHESTERFIELD

CHESTERFIELD JOURNAL. 14522 S Outer 40 Rd, 3rd Fl, Chesterfield, MO 63017. Telephone: 314-821-1110. FAX: 314-972-1111. E-MAIL: aowens@yourjournal.com. URL: http://www.yourjournal.com. Year Established: 1990. Pub. Frequency: s-w. (Wed. & Sun.) Page Size: broadsheet. Freelance Pay: $30/article. Circulation: 16,300 per issue (free). **Owner(s):** Suburban Journals, See address and contact information above. **Management:** Tom Rees, Publisher. Amy Owens, Advertising Manager. Dan Crockwell, Circulation Director. Gary Ratcliffe, Circulation Manager. Andrea Raines, Classified Adv. Mgr.. Amy Wolff, Admin. Assistant. **Editorial:** Monika Kleban, Managing Editor.

CITIZEN JOURNAL. 14522 S Outer 40 Rd, 3rd Fl, Chesterfield, MO 63017. Telephone: 314-821-1110. FAX: 314-972-1111. E-MAIL: aowens@yourjournal.com. URL: http://www.yourjournal.com. Year Established: 1968. Pub. Frequency: s-w. (Wed. & Sun.) Page Size: broadsheet. Subscrip. Rate: $84/yr in county; $110/yr mailed elsewhere. Circulation: 20,994 per issue (paid and free). **Owner(s):** Suburban Journals, See address and contact information above. **Management:** Tom Rees, Publisher. Amy Owens, Advertising Manager. Dan Crockwell, Circulation Director. Gary Ratcliffe, Circulation Manager. Andrea Raines, Classified Adv. Mgr.. Amy Wolff, Admin. Assistant. **Editorial:** Monika Kleban, Managing Editor.

MID-COUNTY JOURNAL. 14522 S Outer 40 Rd, 3rd Fl, Chesterfield, MO 63017. Telephone: 314-821-1110. FAX: 314-972-1111. E-MAIL: aowens@yourjournal.com. URL: http://www.yourjournal.com. Pub. Frequency: s-w. (Wed. & Sun.) Page Size: broadsheet. Subscrip. Rate: $84/yr; $110/yr mailed. Circulation: 13,400 per issue (paid and free). **Owner(s):** Suburban Journals, See address and contact information above. **Management:** Scott Wright, Publisher. Amy Owens, Advertising Manager. Dan Crockwell, Circulation Director. Gary Ratcliffe, Circulation Manager. Andrea Raines, Classified Adv. Mgr.. Amy Wolff, Admin. Assistant. **Editorial:** Monika Kleban, Managing Editor.

PRESS JOURNAL (CHESTERFIELD). 14522 S Outer 40 Rd, 3rd Fl, Chesterfield, MO 63017. Telephone: 314-821-1110. FAX: 314-972-1111. E-MAIL: aowens@yourjournal.com. URL: http://www.yourjournal.com. Pub. Frequency: s-w. (Wed. & Sun) Page Size: broadsheet. Subscrip. Rate: $84/yr mailed for Sun.; $110/yr mailed for Wed.. Circulation: 35,200 per issue (paid and free). **Owner(s):** Suburban Journals, See address and contact information above. **Management:** Tom Rees, Publisher. Amy Owens, Advertising Manager. Dan Crockwell, Circulation Director. Andrea Raines, Classified Adv. Mgr.. **Editorial:** Monika Kleban, Managing Editor.

WEBSTER-KIRKWOOD JOURNAL. 14522 S Outer 40 Rd, 3rd Fl, Chesterfield, MO 63017. Telephone: 314-821-1110. FAX: 314-972-1111. E-MAIL: aowens@yourjournal.com. URL: http://www.yourjournal.com. Pub. Frequency: s-w. (Wed. & Sun) Page Size: broadsheet. Subscrip. Rate: $84/yr; $110/yr mailed. Circulation: 23,475 Sunday (paid and free); 24,046 per issue (paid and free). **Owner(s):** Suburban Journals, See address and contact information above. **Management:** Tom Rees, Publisher. Amy Owens, Advertising Manager. Dan Crockwell, Circulation Director. Gary Ratcliffe, Circulation Manager. Andrea Raines, Classified Adv. Mgr.. Amy Wolff, Admin. Assistant. **Editorial:** Monika Kleban, Managing Editor.

WEST COUNTY JOURNAL. 14522 S Outer 40 Rd, 3rd Fl, Chesterfield, MO 63017. Telephone: 314-821-1110. FAX: 314-972-1111. E-MAIL: aowens@yourjournal.com. URL: http://www.stltoday.com. Pub. Frequency: s-w. (Wed. & Sun.) Page Size: broadsheet. Subscrip. Rate: $110/yr mailed Wed. or Sun.; $220/yr mailed Wed. & Sun.. Freelance Pay: $15-$100/article. Circulation: 28,850 per issue (paid and free). **Owner(s):** Suburban Journals, See address and contact information above. **Management:** Tom Rees, Publisher. Amy Owens, Advertising Manager. Dan Crockwell, Circulation Manager. Andrea Raines, Classified Adv. Mgr.. **Editorial:** Monica Kleban, Managing Editor.

CHILLICOTHE

CONSTITUTION TRIBUNE EXTRA. 818 Washington St., Chillicothe, MO 64601. Telephone: 660-646-2411. FAX: 660-646-2028. URL: http://www.gatehousemedia.com. Mailing Address: PO Box 707, Chillicothe, MO 64601. Pub. Frequency: w. (Wed.) Page Size: tabloid Circulation: 15,519 per issue (free). **Owner(s):** GateHouse Media, Inc, 350 WillowBrook Office Park, Fairport, NY 14450. Telephone: 585-598-0030. **Management:** Andrea Graves, Advertising Director. Connie Jones, Classified Adv. Mgr..

CLINTON

CLINTON EYE, THE. 212 S. Washington St., Clinton, MO 64735. Telephone: 660-885-2281. FAX: 660-885-2265. Mailing Address: PO Box 586, Clinton, MO 64735-0586. Pub. Frequency: w. (Thu.) Page Size: broadsheet. Subscrip. Rate: $.30 newsstand/cover; $16/yr in county; $25.50/yr out of county. Circulation: 700 per issue (paid). **Owner(s):** Democrat Publishing Co., See address and contact information above. **Management:** Kathleen Miles, Publisher. Katherine Miles, Advertising Manager. Mary Jo Witherspoon, Circulation Manager. Mike Gregory, Classified Adv. Mgr.. **Editorial:** Kathleen Miles, Editor. Daniel B. Miles Jr., Managing Editor.

KAYO, THE. 212 S. Washington St., Clinton, MO 64735. Telephone: 660-885-2281. FAX: 660-885-2265. Mailing Address: PO Box 586, Clinton, MO 64735-0586. Pub. Frequency: w. (Wed.) Page Size: broadsheet Circulation: 15,000 per issue (free). **Owner(s):** Democrat Publishing Co., See address and contact information above. **Management:** Kathleen Miles, Publisher. Katherine Miles, Advertising Manager. Mary Jo Witherspoon, Circulation Manager. Mike Gregory, Classified Adv. Mgr.. **Editorial:** Kathleen Miles, Editor. Daniel B. Miles Jr., Managing Editor.

COLUMBIA

WHEELS 'N DEALS. 1203 Wilks Blvd., Columbia, MO 65201. Telephone: 573-443-6014. URL: http://www.wheels-n-deals.com. Pub. Frequency: w. (Fri.) Page Size: broadsheet Circulation: 17,000 per issue (free). **Owner(s):** Tom Ridge, PO Box 256, Columbia, MO 65205. Telephone: 573-443-6014. FAX: 573-875-8988. **Management:** Anthony Holmes, Publisher. **Editorial:** Anthony Holmes, Editor.

CUBA

CUBA FREE PRESS. 501 E Washington Blvd, Cuba, MO 65453. Telephone: 573-885-7460. FAX: 573-885-3803. E-MAIL: news@cubafreepress.com. URL: http://www.cubafreepress.com. Mailing Address: P.O. Box 568, Cuba, MO 65453-0568. Year Established: 1960. Pub. Frequency: w. (Thu.) Page Size: broadsheet. Subscrip. Rate: $.75 newsstand/cover; $24.18/yr in county; $32.24/yr mailed out of county; $37.50/yr mailed out of state. Circulation: 4,300 per issue (paid). **Owner(s):** Three Rivers Publishing, Inc., See address and contact information above. **Management:** Rob Viehman, Publisher. Sandy Morice, Advertising. Janice Ransom, Circulation Manager. **Editorial:** Chris Case, Editor.

EXTRA (CUBA), THE. 501 E Washington Blvd, Cuba, MO 65453. Telephone: 573-885-7460. FAX: 573-885-3803. Mailing Address: P.O. Box 568, Cuba, MO 65453-0568. Pub. Frequency: w. (Thu.) Page Size: tabloid Circulation: 7,500 per issue (free). **Owner(s):** Three Rivers Publishing, Inc., See address and contact information above. **Management:** Rob Viehman, Publisher. Sandy Morice, Advertising. Janice Ransom, Circulation Manager.

DIXON

DIXON PILOT. 302 Locust St., Dixon, MO 65459. Telephone: 573-759-2127. FAX: 573-759-6226. E-MAIL: dixonpilotnews@yahoo.com. URL: http://www.dixonpilot.com. Mailing Address: PO Drawer V, Dixon, MO 65459-0450. Year Established: 1910. Pub. Frequency: w. (Wed.) Page Size: broadsheet. Subscrip. Rate: $.53 newsstand/cover; $30.35/yr in county & adj. cys.; $32.47/yr in state; $32/yr out of state. Circulation: 2,200 per issue (paid). **Owner(s):** Rick & Connie Blackburn, See address and contact information above. **Management:** Connie Blackburn, Publisher.

DONIPHAN

PROSPECT-NEWS, THE. 110 Washington St., Doniphan, MO 63935. Telephone: 573-996-2103. FAX: 573-996-2217. E-MAIL: pnpaper@semo.net. Mailing Address: PO Box 367, Doniphan, MO 63935. Year Established: 1874. Pub. Frequency: w. (Wed.) Page Size: broadsheet. Subscrip. Rate: $.75 newsstand/cover; $20/yr mailed in county; $35/yr mailed out of state. Circulation: 5,300 per issue (paid). **Owner(s):** Rust Communications, Inc., 301 Broadway, Cape Girardeau, MO 63701. Telephone: 314-335-6611. **Management:** Don Schrieber, Publisher. Tracy Holden, Advertising. **Editorial:** Barbie Rogers, Editor.

ELDON

AUTOGRAM-SENTINEL. 415 S Maple ST, Eldon, MO 65026. Telephone: 573-392-5659. FAX: 573-392-7755. E-MAIL: autogram-sentinel@vernonpublishing.com. URL: http://www.vpi-newspaper.com. Mailing Address: PO Box 315, Eldon, MO 65026-0315. Pub. Frequency: w. (Thu.) Page Size: broadsheet. Subscrip. Rate: $26.50/yr in county; $33.50/yr out of county; $38.50/yr mailed out of state. Adv. Rate: col. inch $3.35 Circulation: 1,950 per issue (paid). **Owner(s):** Vernon Publishing, Inc., 104 W Jasper St, Versailles, MO 65084. Telephone: 573-378-5441. **Management:** Dane Vernon, Publisher. **Editorial:** Tim Flora, Editor.

Weeklies

LOUISIANA PRESS-JOURNAL. 136 E. Fourth St., Hermann, MO 65401. Telephone: 574-486-5418. E-MAIL: valpj@big-river.net. Mailing Address: PO Box 466, Louisiana, MO 63353. Year Established: 1855. Pub. Frequency: w. (Wed.) Page Size: broadsheet. Subscrip. Rate: $.50 newsstand/cover; $24/yr local. Circulation: 3,500 per issue (paid). **Owner(s):** Lakeway Publishers of Missouri Inc., See address and contact information above. **Management:** Walt Gilbert, Publisher. **Editorial:** Walt Gilbert, Editor.

HERMITAGE

INDEX, THE. 109 Polk St., Hermitage, MO 65668. Telephone: 417-745-6404. FAX: 417-745-2222. E-MAIL: theindex@positech.net. Mailing Address: PO Box 127, Hermitage, MO 65668. Year Established: 1885. Pub. Frequency: w. (Wed.) Page Size: broadsheet. Subscrip. Rate: $.50 newsstand/cover; $24.50/yr mailed in county; $30.75/yr mailed out of county; $34/yr mailed out of state. Adv. Rate: col. inch $3.36 Circulation: 4,500 per issue (paid). **Owner(s):** Don & Kathy Ginnings, See address and contact information above. **Management:** Don Ginnings, Publisher. Kathy Ginnings, Advertising Manager. Pam Hutton, Circulation Manager. **Editorial:** Don Ginnings, Editor.

HOLDEN

HOLDEN IMAGE, THE. 117 E. Second St., Holden, MO 64040. Telephone: 816-732-5552. FAX: 816-732-4696. E-MAIL: holdenimage@earthlink.net. URL: http://www.holdenimage.com. Year Established: 1904. Pub. Frequency: w. (Wed.) Page Size: standard. Subscrip. Rate: $.50 newsstand/cover; $23/yr local; $34/yr out of state. Adv. Rate: col. inch $7 Circulation: 7,700 per issue (paid and free). **Owner(s):** Rusty & Cindy Hartwell, See address and contact information above. **Management:** Sheila Pemberton, Advertising Manager. Pat Zrachek, Business Manager. **Editorial:** Denise Brooks, Managing Editor. Christi Stowe, News Editor.

HOPKINS

HOPKINS JOURNAL, THE. 411 E. Bernard St., Hopkins, MO 64461-0170. Telephone: 660-778-3205. FAX: 660-778-3205. E-MAIL: hopkinsjournal@hotmail.com. Mailing Address: P.O. Box 170, Hopkins, MO 64461. Year Established: 1874. Pub. Frequency: w. (Thu.) Page Size: standard. Subscrip. Rate: $.45 newsstand/cover; $18.39/yr local. Adv. Rate: col. inch $4 Circulation: 925 per issue (paid). **Owner(s):** Steve & Darla Thompson, See address and contact information above. **Management:** Darla Thompson, Publisher. Steve Thompson, Advertising Manager. **Editorial:** Darla Thompson, Editor-in-Chief.

HOUSTON

HOUSTON HERALD. 113 N. Grand, Houston, MO 65483. Telephone: 417-967-2000. FAX: 417-967-2096. E-MAIL: editor@houstonherald.com. URL: http://www.houstonherald.com. Mailing Address: PO Box 170, Houston, MO 65483. Year Established: 1878. Pub. Frequency: w. (Thu.) Page Size: broadsheet. Subscrip. Rate: $.75 newsstand/cover; $29.95/yr in county; $31.50/yr adj. cys.; $45.55/yr elsewhere. Adv. Rate: col. inch $7.10 Circulation: 10,300 per issue (paid and free). **Owner(s):** Houston Newspapers, Inc., See address and contact information above. **Management:** Bradley G Gentry, Publisher. **Editorial:** Jeffrey McNiell, Managing Editor.

JACKSON

CASH-BOOK JOURNAL. 210 W. Main St., Jackson, MO 63755. Telephone: 573-243-3515. FAX: 573-243-3517. E-MAIL: cashbook@jacksonmo.com. URL: http://www.jacksonmo.com/cashbook.html. Mailing Address: PO Box 369, Jackson, MO 63755. Year Established: 1870. Pub. Frequency: w. (Wed.) Page Size: broadsheet. Subscrip. Rate: $.50 newsstand/cover; $21/yr in county; $23/yr mailed in adj. cys.; $27/yr mailed in state; $36/yr mailed out of state. Circulation: 11,500 per issue (paid). **Owner(s):** Jackson Publishing Co., See address and contact information above. **Management:** David Bloom, General Manager. Gerald Jones Sr., President. Gina Bader, Publisher. Jim Salzman, Advertising Manager. Elaine Hale, Circulation Manager. **Editorial:** David Bloom, Editor. Greg Dullum, Production Manager. Elane Moonier, Feature Editor.

JOPLIN

BIG NICKEL. 2916 E 20th St, Joplin, MO 64802. Telephone: 417-624-4100. FAX: 417-624-8503. URL: http://www.bignickel.com. Mailing Address: PO Box 1567, Joplin, MO 64801. Year Established: 1975. Pub. Frequency: w. (Thu.) Page Size: tabloid.Adv. Rate: col. inch $13.95 Circulation: 50,000 per issue (free). **Owner(s):** GateHouse Media, Inc, 350 WillowBrook Office Park, Fairport, NY 14450. Telephone: 585-598-0030. **Management:** Richard Watson, Publisher. Chuck Elliott, Advertising Manager. Jerry Snider, Circulation Manager.

KANSAS CITY

PITCH, THE. 1701 Main St., Kansas City, MO 64108. Telephone: 816-561-6061. FAX: 816-756-0502. E-MAIL: pitch@pitch.com. URL: http://www.pitch.com. Year Established: 1980. Pub. Frequency: w. (Thu.) Page Size: tabloid. Subscrip. Rate: $25 mailed for 6 mos.; $50/yr mailed. Freelance Pay: $25-$300/article. Circulation: 80,000 per issue (paid and controlled). **Owner(s):** Village Voice Media, Inc., 1201 E Jefferson St, Phoenix, AZ 85034. Telephone: 415-541-0700. FAX: 415-541-9096. **Management:** Ramon Larkin, Publisher. Andy Vihstadt, Circulation Director. Jeromey Bell, Classified Adv. Mgr.. Dennis Cashman, Sales Manager. **Editorial:** C.J. Janovy, Editor. Eric Barton, Managing Editor. Jason Harper, Music Editor.

KIRKSVILLE

KIRKSVILLE CRIER. 110 E. McPherson St., Kirksville, MO 63501. Telephone: 660-665-2808. FAX: 660-665-2608. Mailing Address: PO Box 809, Kirksville, MO 63501. Pub. Frequency: w. (Wed.) Page Size: standard Circulation: 18,500 per issue (free). **Owner(s):** GateHouse Media, Inc, 350 WillowBrook Office Park, Fairport, NY 14450. Telephone: 585-598-0030. **Management:** Larry W. Freels, Publisher. George Wriedt, Advertising Manager. Carole Murphy, Classified Adv. Mgr..

LAMAR

LAMAR DEMOCRAT. ISSN 0745-9300
900 N. Gulf St., Lamar, MO 64759-0458. Telephone: 417-682-5529. FAX: 417-682-5595. E-MAIL: lamardemocrat@tiadon.com. URL: http://www.lamardemocrat.com. Mailing Address: PO Box 458, Lamar, MO 64759-0458. Year Established: 1870. Pub. Frequency: s-w. (Wed. & Sat.) Page Size: broadsheet. Subscrip. Rate: $.50 newsstand/cover; $53.37/yr. Adv. Rate: col. inch $6.30 Circulation: 4,000 per issue (paid and free). **Owner(s):** Lamar Democrat, Inc., 900 N. Gulf St., Lamar, MO 64759. Telephone: 417-682-5529. **Management:** Douglas D. Davis, Publisher. Melody Metzger, Circulation Manager. **Editorial:** Rayma B. Davis, Editor. Chris Morrow, Sports.

LAURIE

WESTSIDE STAR. 165 Missouri Blvd, Ste 4, Laurie, MO 65038. Telephone: 573-374-3100. FAX: 573-374-0565. URL: http://www.westsidestar.net. Pub. Frequency: w. (Wed.) Page Size: standard Circulation: 9,400 per issue (free). **Owner(s):** GateHouse Media, Inc, 350 WillowBrook Office Park, Fairport, NY 14450. Telephone: 585-598-0030. FAX: 585-248-2631. **Management:** Gary Young, General Manager. Jules Molenda, Publisher. Jan Turner, Advertising Manager. **Editorial:** Gary Young, Editor. Wayne Kasper, Sports Editor.

LEE'S SUMMIT

LEE'S SUMMIT JOURNAL. ISSN 1059-650X
415 SE Douglas, Lee's Summit, MO 64063. Telephone: 816-524-2345. FAX: 816-524-5136. E-MAIL: editor@lsjournal.com. URL: http://www.lsjournal.com. Mailing Address: PO Box 387, Lee's Summit, MO 64063-0387. Year Established: 1881. Pub. Frequency: s-w. (Wed. & Fri.) Page Size: broadsheet. Subscrip. Rate: $55/yr home delivery local; $.50 newsstand/cover. **Wire Service(s):** AP. Circulation: 32,150 per issue (paid). **Owner(s):** The/McClatchy Company, 2100 Q St, Sacramento, CA 95816. Telephone: 916-321-1936. FAX: 916-321-1869. **Management:** Brent Miller, Publisher. John McCall, Circulation Manager. Ronda Moore, Classified Adv. Mgr.. Peter Gregg, Sales Manager. **Editorial:** Ann Sheer, Editor.

LEXINGTON

LEXINGTON NEWS, THE. 925 Main St., Lexington, MO 64067. Telephone: 660-259-2266. FAX: 660-259-4870. E-MAIL: ingtonnews@earthlink.net. Mailing Address: PO Box 279, Lexington, MO 64067. Year Established: 1800. Pub. Frequency: s-w. (Wed. & Fri.) Page Size: standard. Subscrip. Rate: $.50 newsstand/cover; $30.71/yr local; $43/yr mailed out of state. Circulation: 2,200 per issue (paid). **Owner(s):** Jack Krier, PO Box 69, Carrollton, MO 64633. Telephone: 816-542-0881. **Management:** Nancy Wisdom, General Manager. Frank Mercer, Publisher. Nancy Wisdom, Circulation Manager. **Editorial:** Mark Lamoree, Editor.

LIBERTY

GLADSTONE SUN NEWS. 963 W Liberty Dr, Liberty, MO 64068. Telephone: 816-781-1044. FAX: 816-781-1755. URL: http://www.sunpublications.com. Pub. Frequency: w. (Wed.) Page Size: broadsheet.Subscrip. Rate: $.50 newsstand/cover; $15/yr Circulation: 16,020 per issue (paid). **Owner(s):** News-Press & Gazette Co., PO Box 29, St. Joseph, MO 64502. Telephone: 816-271-8500. **Management:** Roy Biondi, Publisher. Jeff Martin, Advertising Manager. Carl Comstock, Circulation Manager. **Editorial:** Jan Havin, Editor. Joe Cook, Sports.

LIBERTY SUN NEWS. 963 W Liberty Dr, Liberty, MO 64068. Telephone: 816-781-1044. FAX: 816-781-1755. URL: http://www.sunpublications.com. Pub. Frequency: w. (Wed.) Page Size: broadsheet.Subscrip. Rate: $.50 newsstand/cover; $15/yr Circulation: 1,302 per issue (paid). **Owner(s):** News-Press & Gazette Co., PO Box 29, St. Joseph, MO 64502. Telephone: 816-271-8500. **Management:** Roy Biondi, Publisher. Jeff Martin, Advertising Manager. Carl Comstock, Circulation Manager. **Editorial:** Jan Havin, Editor. Joe Cook, Sports.

LIBERTY TRIBUNE. 104 N. Main St., Liberty, MO 64068. Telephone: 816-781-4941. FAX: 816-781-0909. Pub. Frequency: w. (Sat.) Page Size: broadsheet. Subscrip. Rate: $.50 newsstand/cover; $40/yr in county. Circulation: 12,048 per issue (paid). **Owner(s):** N P G Newspapers, Inc., 7007 N.E. Parvin Rd., Kansas City, MO 64117. Telephone: 816-454-9660. **Management:** H. Guyon Townsend III, Publisher. Ken Carpenter, Circulation Director. Linda Ladd, Classified Adv. Mgr.. **Editorial:** David Knopf, Managing Editor. Angie Borgedalen, Associate Editor. Kevin Goodwin, Sports Editor.

NORTHLAND SUN NEWS. 963 W Liberty Dr, Liberty, MO 64068. Telephone: 816-781-1044. FAX: 816-781-1755. URL: http://www.sunpublications.com. Pub. Frequency: w. (Thu.) Page Size: broadsheet.Subscrip. Rate: $.50 newsstand/cover; $15/yr Circulation: 5,300 per issue (paid). **Owner(s):** News-Press & Gazette Co., PO Box 29, St. Joseph, MO 64502. Telephone: 816-271-8500. **Management:** Roy Biondi, Publisher. Jeff Martin, Advertising Manager. Carl Comstock, Circulation Manager. **Editorial:** Jan Havin, Editor. Joe Cook, Sports.

PLATTE COUNTY SUN NEWS. ISSN 0899-5737
963 W Liberty Dr, Liberty, MO 64068. Telephone: 816-781-1044. FAX: 816-781-1755. E-MAIL: jhavin@sunpublications.com. URL: http://www.sunpublications.com. Year Established: 1885. Pub. Frequency: w. (Thu.) Page Size: standard. Subscrip. Rate: $.50 newsstand/cover; $15/yr. Circulation: 20,000 per issue (paid and free). **Owner(s):** News-Press & Gazette Co., PO Box 29, St. Joseph, MO 64502. Telephone: 816-271-8500. **Management:** Roy Biondi, Publisher. Jeff Martin, Advertising Manager. Carl Comstock, Circulation Manager. **Editorial:** Jan Havin, Editor. Joe Cook, Sports.

Weeklies

LINN

LINN UNTERRIFIED DEMOCRAT. 300 E. Main St., Linn, MO 65051. Telephone: 573-897-3150. FAX: 573-897-0076. E-MAIL: ud@osagecon.missouri.org. Year Established: 1866. Pub. Frequency: w. (Wed.) Page Size: broadsheet. Subscrip. Rate: $.75 newsstand/cover; $30/yr mailed in county; $94/yr mailed out of county; $50/yr mailed out of state. Circulation: 4,800 per issue (paid). **Owner(s):** Jerrilynn Voss, See address and contact information above. **Management:** Jerrilynn Voss, Publisher.

MACON

MACON JOURNAL. 204 W. Bourke St., Macon, MO 63552. Telephone: 660-385-3121. FAX: 660-385-3082. Mailing Address: PO Box 7, Macon, MO 63552. Pub. Frequency: w. (Mon.) Page Size: standard Circulation: 11,332 per issue (free). **Owner(s):** GateHouse Media, Inc, 350 WillowBrook Office Park, Fairport, NY 14450. Telephone: 585-598-0030. **Management:** Pat Quinly, Publisher. Chuck Kindle, Advertising Manager. Clinton House, Circulation Manager. Chandrea Growe, Classified Adv. Mgr..

MANSFIELD

MANSFIELD MIRROR, THE. PO Box 197, Mansfield, MO 65704. URL: http://www.mansfieldmirror.com. Pub. Frequency: w. Page Size: tabloid. Subscrip. Rate: $18/yr mailed in county & adj. counties; $20/yr mailed in state; $24/yr mailed out of state. Circulation: 4,500 per issue (paid). **Owner(s):** Lebanon Publishing Co., See address and contact information above. **Management:** Larry Dennis, Publisher. Sondra Gray, Advertising.

MARBLE HILL

BANNER-PRESS (MARBLE HILL). 103 Walnut St., Marble Hill, MO 63764. Telephone: 573-238-2821. FAX: 573-238-0020. E-MAIL: banpress@hotmail.com. Mailing Address: PO Box 109, Marble Hill, MO 63764. Year Established: 1881. Pub. Frequency: w. (Wed.) Page Size: broadsheet. Subscrip. Rate: $.75 newsstand/cover; $20/yr local; $27/yr mailed in MO & IL; $38/yr mailed elsewhere other states. Adv. Rate: col. inch $4.25 Circulation: 4,200 per issue (paid). **Owner(s):** Rust Communications, Inc., 301 Broadway, Cape Girardeau, MO 63701. Telephone: 573-335-6611. **Management:** Brad Holloway, General Manager. Jon Rust, Publisher. Sarah Gowen, Advertising Manager. Paula Ceabaugh, Circulation Manager. **Editorial:** Brad Holloway, Editor.

MARSHFIELD

MARSHFIELD MAIL, THE. 225 N. Clay St., Marshfield, MO 65706-1652. Telephone: 417-468-2013. FAX: 417-859-7930. E-MAIL: mikec@cpimo.com. URL: http://www.marshfieldmail.com. Mailing Address: P.O. Drawer A, Marshfield, MO 65706-0920. Year Established: 1892. Pub. Frequency: w. (Wed.) Page Size: standard. Subscrip. Rate: $.50 newsstand/cover; $28/yr in county & adj. cys.; $39/yr mailed out of area; $49.50/yr mailed out of state. Circulation: 5,500 per issue (paid and free). **Owner(s):** Community Publishers, Inc., 125 W Central Ave, Ste 318, Bentonville, AR 72712. Telephone: 479-271-3700. **Management:** Debbie Chapman, General Manager. **Editorial:** Chad Hunter, Editor. Mike Cullinan, Associate Editor.

MARTHASVILLE

MARTHASVILLE RECORD, THE. 303-B Depot St., Marthasville, MO 63357-0077. Telephone: 636-433-2223. FAX: 636-433-5955. E-MAIL: recnews@centurytel.net. Mailing Address: PO Box 77, Marthasville, MO 63357-0077. Year Established: 1896. Pub. Frequency: w. (Thu.) Page Size: broadsheet. Subscrip. Rate: $.35 newsstand/cover; $18.50/yr local; $20.65/yr in state; $20.50/yr out of state. Adv. Rate: col. inch $5.04 Circulation: 2,200 per issue (paid). **Owner(s):** Missourian Publishing Co., 14 W. Main St., Washington, MO 63090. Telephone: 636-239-7701. **Management:** Bill Miller Jr., Publisher. **Editorial:** Skip Cilley, Editor.

MARYVILLE

PENNY PRESS 2. 111 E. Jenkins St., Maryville, MO 64468. Telephone: 660-562-2424. FAX: 660-562-2823. URL: http://www.gatehousemedia.com. Mailing Address: PO Box 188, Maryville, MO 64468. Pub. Frequency: w. (Tue.) Page Size: tabloid Circulation: 16,150 per issue (free). **Owner(s):** GateHouse Media, Inc, 350 WillowBrook Office Park, Fairport, NY 14450. Telephone: 585-598-0030. FAX: 585-248-2631. **Management:** Mike Herring, Publisher. Phil Cobb, Advertising Manager. Rita Piveral, Classified Adv. Mgr..

MOBERLY

SHOPPER (MOBERLY), THE. 218 N. Williams St., Moberly, MO 65270. Telephone: 660-263-4123. FAX: 660-263-3626. Mailing Address: PO Box 697, Moberly, MO 65270. Pub. Frequency: w. (Wed.) Page Size: standard Circulation: 2,500 per issue (free). **Owner(s):** GateHouse Media, Inc, 350 WillowBrook Office Park, Fairport, NY 14450. Telephone: 585-598-0030. **Management:** Bob Cunningham, Publisher. Judy Orton, Advertising Director. Tammy Bradds, Circulation Manager. Nancy Bartolacci, Classified Adv. Mgr..

MONTGOMERY CITY

MONTGOMERY STANDARD. 115 W. Second St., Montgomery City, MO 63361-0190. Telephone: 573-564-2339. FAX: 573-564-2313. E-MAIL: standard@socket.com. Year Established: 1868. Pub. Frequency: w. (Wed.) Page Size: broadsheet. Subscrip. Rate: $.50 newsstand/cover; $18/yr in county; $25/yr out of county; $25/yr out of county to alumni. Adv. Rate: col. inch $4 Circulation: 3,800 per issue (paid). **Owner(s):** Montgomery Standard, Inc., 115 W. Second St., Montgomery City, MO 63361. Telephone: 573-564-2339. **Management:** John Fisher, Publisher. **Editorial:** John Fisher, Editor.

MOUND CITY

MOUND CITY NEWS. 511 State St., Mound City, MO 64470-0175. Telephone: 660-442-5423. FAX: 660-442-5423. E-MAIL: moundcitynews@socket.net. URL: http://www.northwestmissouri.com. Mailing Address: P.O. Box 175, Mound City, MO 64470-0175. Year Established: 1879. Pub. Frequency: w. (Thu.) Page Size: broadsheet. Subscrip. Rate: $.75 newsstand/cover; $26/yr in county; $28/yr in state; $31/yr elsewhere. Circulation: 2,409 per issue (paid). **Owner(s):** Mound City News, Inc., See address and contact information above. **Management:** Chris Boultinghouse, President. Linda Boultinghouse, Publisher.

MOUNTAIN GROVE

MOUNTAIN GROVE NEWS-JOURNAL, THE. 150 E. First St., Mountain Grove, MO 65711. Telephone: 417-926-5148. FAX: 417-926-6648. URL: http://www.news-journal.net. Mailing Address: PO Box 530, Mountain Grove, MO 65711. Year Established: 1890. Pub. Frequency: w. (Wed.) Page Size: broadsheet. Subscrip. Rate: $.75 newsstand/cover; $25.12/yr in county & adj. cys.; $32.14/yr mailed in state; $40/yr mailed out of state. Adv. Rate: col. inch $5 Circulation: 13,175 per issue (paid). **Owner(s):** Dalton Wright, PO Box 192, Lebanon, MO 65536. Telephone: 417-537-9131. **Management:** Dalton Wright, Publisher. Sandy Anderson, Advertising Manager. Jan Wood, Circulation Manager. **Editorial:** Doug Berger, Editor.

MT. VERNON

LAWRENCE COUNTY RECORD. PO Box 348, Mt. Vernon, MO 65712. Telephone: 417-466-2185. FAX: 417-466-7865. E-MAIL: lcrecord@centurytel.net. Mailing Address: PO Box 348, Mt. Vernon, MO 65712-0348. Year Established: 1876. Pub. Frequency: w. (Wed.) Page Size: broadsheet. Subscrip. Rate: $.50 newsstand/cover; $19.50/yr local; $32/yr out of state. Adv. Rate: col. inch $5.30 Circulation: 7,525 per issue (paid and free). **Owner(s):** Stephen C. & Kathy S. Fairchild, See address and contact information above. **Management:** Stephen C. Fairchild, General Manager. Kathy S. Fairchild, President. Stephen C. Fairchild, Publisher. Cheryl Reynolds, Advertising Manager. **Editorial:** Kathy S. Fairchild, Editor.

NEOSHO

POST (NEOSHO), THE. 1006 W. Harmony St., Neosho, MO 64850. Telephone: 417-451-1520. FAX: 417-451-6408. Mailing Address: PO Box 848, Neosho, MO 64850. Pub. Frequency: w. (Thu.) Page Size: standard. Subscrip. Rate: $.50 newsstand/cover; $21/yr in county. Circulation: 400 per issue (paid). **Owner(s):** GateHouse Media, Inc, 350 WillowBrook Office Park, Fairport, NY 14450. Telephone: 585-598-0030. FAX: 585-248-2631. **Management:** Rick Rogers, Publisher.

NIXA

NIXAXPRESS. 605 E Kathryn, Nixa, MO 65714. Mailing Address: PO Box 594, Nixa, MO 65714-0594. Pub. Frequency: w. (Fri.) Page Size: tabloid Circulation: 5,000 per issue (free). **Owner(s):** Community Publishers, Inc., PO Box 1049, Bentonville, AR 72712.

OCEAN SPRING

OCEAN SPRING RECORD. 715 Cox Ave., Ocean Spring, MO 39564. Telephone: 228-875-2791. FAX: 228-875-9569. Year Established: 1965. Pub. Frequency: w. (Thu.) Page Size: standard. Subscrip. Rate: $.50 newsstand/cover; $19.75/yr mailed in county; $27.75/yr mailed out of county. Circulation: 3,200 per issue (paid). **Owner(s):** J C Publishing, See address and contact information above. **Management:** James Ricketts, Publisher. Cindy Ricketts, Advertising. **Editorial:** James Ricketts, Editor.

OWENSVILLE

GASCONADE COUNTY REPUBLICAN. 106 E Washington Ave, Owensville, MO 65066. E-MAIL: wardpub@fidnet.com. URL: http://www.gasconadecountyrepublican.com. Mailing Address: PO Box 540, Owensville, MO 65066. Year Established: 1904. Pub. Frequency: w. (Wed.) Page Size: broadsheet. Subscrip. Rate: $.75 newsstand/cover; $30/yr local; $35/yr out of area. Adv. Rate: col. inch $4 Circulation: 9,800 per issue (paid and free). **Owner(s):** Warden Publishing Co., Inc., See address and contact information above. **Management:** Dennis Warden, Publisher. **Editorial:** Will Johnson, Sports Editor.

OZARK

CHRISTIAN COUNTY HEADLINER NEWS. 116 N. Second Ave., Ozark, MO 65721. Telephone: 417-581-3541. FAX: 417-581-3577. E-MAIL: chuckb@cpimo.com. Mailing Address: PO Box 490, Ozark, MO 65721. Year Established: 1967. Pub. Frequency: w. (Wed.) Page Size: broadsheet. Subscrip. Rate: $.50 newsstand/cover; $24/yr mailed in county & adj. cys.; $35/yr mailed in state; $43/yr mailed out of state. Circulation: 4,500 per issue (paid). **Owner(s):** Community Publishers, Inc., PO Box 1049, Bentonville, AR 72172. Telephone: 501-271-3700. FAX: 501-271-3744. **Management:** Chuck Branch, General Manager. Ralph Jensen, Advertising. **Editorial:** Donna Osborne, Managing Editor. Jason Michael, Sports Editor.

PALMYRA

PALMYRA SPECTATOR. PO Box 391, Palmyra, MO 63461. Telephone: 573-769-3111. E-MAIL: palspec@nemonet.com. Year Established: 1839. Pub. Frequency: w. (Wed.) Page Size: standard. Subscrip. Rate: $.50 newsstand/cover (effective 2005); $25.50/yr. Adv. Rate: col. inch $4.25 Circulation: 2,800 per issue (paid). **Owner(s):** Mark & Patricia Cheffey, See address and contact information above. **Management:** Mark Cheffey, Publisher. **Editorial:** Mark Cheffey, Editor.

PARIS

MONROE COUNTY CLARION. PO Box 207, Paris, MO 65275. Telephone: 660-327-4192. FAX: 660-327-4847. E-MAIL: appeal@parismo.net. URL: http//www.monroecountyappeal.com. Year Established: 1865. Pub. Frequency: w. (Thu.) Page Size: broadsheet. Subscrip. Rate: $.50 newsstand/cover; $21/yr area; $23/yr mailed in state; $24/yr mailed out of state. Circulation: 2,300 per issue (paid). **Owner(s):** Richard Fredrick, See address and contact information above. **Management:** Michael Daugherty, General Manager. Richard Fredrick, Publisher. **Editorial:** Michael Daugherty, Editor.

PERRYVILLE

PERRY COUNTY REPUBLIC-MONITOR, THE. 10 W. St. Maries St., Perryville, MO 63775. Telephone: 573-547-4567. FAX: 573-547-1643. E-MAIL: rpribble@perryvillenews.com. URL: http://www.perryvillenews.com. Mailing Address: PO Box 367, Perryville, MO 63775. Year Established: 1889. Pub. Frequency: s-w. (Tue. & Thu.) Page Size: broadsheet. Subscrip. Rate: $.75 newsstand/cover; $42.15/yr mailed in county & adj. cys.; $66.25/yr mailed elsewhere. Adv. Rate: col. inch $6.95 Circulation: 14,241 per issue (paid and free). **Owner(s):** PTS Inc., 221A 35th St., N.E., Fort Payne, AL 35967. Telephone: 256-845-4590. **Management:** Kate Martin, Publisher. Sandy Schnurbusch, Advertising. Beverly Fritsche, Classified Adv. Mgr.. **Editorial:** Kate Martin, Editor. Stacie Sargent, Sports Editor.

PIEDMONT

WAYNE COUNTY JOURNAL-BANNER. 101 W. Elm St., Piedmont, MO 63957. Telephone: 573-223-7122. FAX: 573-223-7871. E-MAIL: harold@waynecojournalbanner.com. URL: http://www.waynecojournalbanner.com. Mailing Address: PO Box 97, Piedmont, MO 63957-0097. Year Established: 1876. Pub. Frequency: w. (Thu.) Page Size: broadsheet. Subscrip. Rate: $.50 newsstand/cover; $30/yr local area; $43/yr out of area. **Wire Service(s):** AP. Circulation: 5,200 per issue (paid). **Owner(s):** Ellinghouse Publishing Co., Inc, See address and contact information above. **Management:** Harold T. Ellinghouse, President. Tonya Burress, Circulation Manager. Brenda Ellinghouse, Business Manager. **Editorial:** Brenda Ellinghouse, Editor. Karen Arledge, Composing Room Manager.

POTOSI

INDEPENDENT-JOURNAL, THE. 119 E. High St., Potosi, MO 63664-0340. Telephone: 573-438-5141. FAX: 573-438-4472. E-MAIL: theij@misn.com. Mailing Address: PO Box 340, Potosi, MO 63664-0340. Year Established: 1872. Pub. Frequency: w. (Thu.) Page Size: broadsheet. Subscrip. Rate: $.75 newsstand/cover; $30/yr. Adv. Rate: col. inch $5 Circulation: 5,350 per issue (paid and free). **Owner(s):** Independent-Journal, Inc., PO Box 340, Potosi, MO 63664. Telephone: 573-438-5141. FAX: 573-438-4472. **Editorial:** Neil Richards, Editor.

REPUBLIC

REPUBLIC MONITOR, THE. 249 Hwy 60 W, Republic, MO 65738. Telephone: 417-732-2525. FAX: 417-732-2980. E-MAIL: editor@republic-monitor.com. URL: http://www.republic-monitor.com. Year Established: 1893. Pub. Frequency: w. (Wed.) Page Size: broadsheet. Subscrip. Rate: $.50 newsstand/cover; $24/yr in county & adj. cys.; $35/yr in state; $43/yr out of state. Circulation: 4,000 per issue (paid and free). **Owner(s):** Community Publishers, Inc., PO Box 1049, Bentonville, AR 72172. Telephone: 501-271-3700. **Management:** Jennifer Reynolds, Advertising. **Editorial:** Amy Brant, News Editor. Jeff Kessinger, Sports Editor.

RICHLAND

PULASKI COUNTY DEMOCRAT, THE. 115 S. Chestnut, Richland, MO 65556. Telephone: 573-765-3391. FAX: 573-765-3235. E-MAIL: publisher@pulaskicountydemocrat.com. URL: http://www.pulaskicountydemocrat.com. Mailing Address: P.O. Box 757, Richland, MO 65557-0757. Pub. Frequency: w. (Fri.) Page Size: broadsheet. Subscrip. Rate: $.75 newsstand/cover; $26.74/yr mailed in county; $32.02/yr mailed in county incl. Richmond Mirror; $45/yr mailed out of state. Circulation: 4,200 per issue (paid). **Owner(s):** Dalton Wright, PO Box 192, Lebanon, MO 65536. Telephone: 417-537-9131. **Management:** Gail Wright, Publisher. **Editorial:** Steve Smith, Editor.

RICHLAND MIRROR, THE. 115 S. Chestnut, Richland, MO 65556. Telephone: 573-765-3391. FAX: 573-765-3235. URL: http://www.richlandmirror.com. Mailing Address: P.O. Box 757, Richland, MO 65557-0757. Pub. Frequency: w. (Wed.) Page Size: broadsheet. Subscrip. Rate: $.75 newsstand/cover; $26.74/yr in county; $32.09/yr in county incl. Pulaski County Democrat; $35/yr out of state. Circulation: 3,400 per issue (paid). **Owner(s):** Dalton Wright, PO Box 192, Lebanon, MO 65536. Telephone: 416-532-9131. **Management:** Gail Wright, Publisher. **Editorial:** Randy Scruggs, Managing Editor.

ROCK PORT

ATCHISON COUNTY MAIL, THE. 300 S. Main St., Rock Port, MO 64482. Telephone: 660-744-6245. FAX: 660-744-2645. E-MAIL: amail@rpt.coop. Mailing Address: PO Box 40, Rock Port, MO 64482. Year Established: 1878. Pub. Frequency: w. (Thu.) Page Size: broadsheet. Subscrip. Rate: $.75 newsstand/cover; $32/yr in county; $45/yr elsewhere. Adv. Rate: col. inch $6 Circulation: 2,200 per issue (paid). **Owner(s):** W C Farmer & Mike Farmer, See address and contact information above. **Management:** W C Farmer, Publisher. **Editorial:** Mike Farmer, Managing Editor.

ROGERSVILLE

SOUTH COUNTY MAIL. 111 Johnstown, Rogersville, MO 65742. Telephone: 417-753-2800. FAX: 417-753-2792. URL: http://www.southcountymail.com. Mailing Address: PO Box 677, Rogersville, MO 65742-0677. Pub. Frequency: w. (Wed.) Page Size: standard. Subscrip. Rate: $.75 newsstand/cover; $24/yr in area; $35/yr in state; $43/yr out of state. Circulation: 1,800 per issue (paid). **Owner(s):** Community Publishers, Inc., PO Box 1049, Bentonville, AR 72172. **Management:** Michael Hargrove, Advertising. **Editorial:** Alyssa Spradin, Editor.

SALEM

SALEM (MO) NEWS. 500 N. Washington St., Salem, MO 65560-0798. Telephone: 573-729-4126. FAX: 573-729-4920. E-MAIL: salemnews@earthlink.net. URL: http://www.salemnewsonline.com. Mailing Address: PO Box 798, Salem, MO 65560-0798. Year Established: 1923. Pub. Frequency: s-w. (Tue. & Thu.) Page Size: broadsheet. Subscrip. Rate: $.53 newsstand/cover; $38/yr local; $52/yr out of state. Adv. Rate: col. inch $5.25 Circulation: 12,250 per issue (paid and free). **Owner(s):** Salem Publishing Co., PO Box 798, Salem, MO 65560. Telephone: 573-729-4126. **Management:** Donald Dodd, Publisher. Karen Barred, Advertising Manager. Sheree Dodd, Circulation Manager. **Editorial:** Donald Dodd, Managing Editor.

SARCOXIE

PIERCE CITY LEADER-JOURNAL. 101 N. Sixth St., Sarcoxie, MO 64862. Telephone: 417-548-3311. FAX: 417-548-3312. E-MAIL: fstop@centurytel.net. Mailing Address: PO Box 400, Sarcoxie, MO 64862-0400. Year Established: 1905. Pub. Frequency: w. (Wed.) Page Size: standard. Subscrip. Rate: $.50 newsstand/cover; $18.76/yr in county; $21.44/yr out of county. Circulation: 1,000 per issue (paid). **Owner(s):** fstop Publications, LLC, See address and contact information above. **Management:** Katrina Keys, General Manager. Paul E. Donely, Publisher. Marlene Gish, Advertising Manager. **Editorial:** Paul E. Donely, Editor.

SARCOXIE RECORD, THE. 101 N. Sixth St., Sarcoxie, MO 64862. Telephone: 417-548-3311. FAX: 417-548-3312. E-MAIL: fstop@centurytel.net. Mailing Address: PO Box 400, Sarcoxie, MO 64862-0400. Year Established: 1901. Pub. Frequency: w. (Wed.) Page Size: standard. Subscrip. Rate: $.50 newsstand/cover; $18.76/yr in county; $21.44/yr out of county. Circulation: 1,400 per issue (paid). **Owner(s):** fstop Publications, LLC, See address and contact information above. **Management:** Katrina Keys, General Manager. Paul E. Donely, Publisher. Marlene Gish, Advertising Manager. **Editorial:** Paul E. Donely, Editor.

SAVANNAH

SAVANNAH REPORTER & ANDREW COUNTY DEMOCRAT. 115 S. Fourth St., Savannah, MO 64485. Telephone: 816-324-3149. E-MAIL: caslonbld@aol.com. URL: http://www.savannahreporter.com. Year Established: 1876. Pub. Frequency: w. (Thu.) Page Size: broadsheet. Subscrip. Rate: $.50 newsstand/cover; $20/yr local; $24/yr mailed in state; $26/yr mailed out of state. Circulation: 4,050 per issue (paid). **Owner(s):** Touchdown Publication, See address and contact information above. **Management:** Guy Spickman, Publisher. **Editorial:** Leslie Spickman, Managing Editor.

SEDALIA

PLAINSMAN WEEKLY NEWS. 700 S. Massachusetts St., Sedalia, MO 65301-1566. Telephone: 660-826-1000. FAX: 660-826-3913. E-MAIL: democrat@ozarks.net. Mailing Address: PO Box 848, Sedalia, MO 65302-0848. Year Established: 1980. Pub. Frequency: w. (Wed.) Page Size: tabloid Subscrip. Rate: $50/yr Circulation: 20,228 morning (free); 65,800 per issue (free). **Owner(s):** Freedom Communications, Inc., 17666 Fitch, Irvine, CA 92614. Telephone: 949-253-2300. FAX: 949-474-7675. **Management:** Charles Fischer, Publisher. Ray Amaguer, Advertising Director.

SEDALIA NEWS JOURNAL. 404 S. Ohio Ave., Sedalia, MO 65301. Telephone: 660-827-2425. FAX: 660-827-2427. E-MAIL: paperboy@sedalianewsjournal.com. Year Established: 1985. Pub. Frequency: w. (Thu.) Page Size: broadsheet. Subscrip. Rate: $.50 newsstand/cover; $28/yr in county; $36/yr out of county; $44/yr out of state. Circulation: 6,000 per issue (paid). **Owner(s):** Melton Publishing Co., See address and contact information above. **Management:** Greg Melton, Publisher. **Editorial:** Randy Kirby, Editor.

SEYMOUR

WEBSTER COUNTY CITIZEN. 221 S. Commercial St., Seymour, MO 65746-0190. Telephone: 417-935-2257. FAX: 417-935-2487. E-MAIL: citizen@webstercountycitizen.com. URL: http://www.webstercountycitizen.com. Mailing Address: PO Box 190, Seymour, MO 65746-0190. Year Established: 1907. Pub. Frequency: w. (Wed.) Page Size: broadsheet. Subscrip. Rate: $.50 newsstand/cover; $25/yr in county; $30/yr in state; $35/yr out of state. Adv. Rate: col. inch $4 **Wire Service(s):** AP. Circulation: 5,450 per issue (paid and free). **Owner(s):** Webster County Publishing Co., Inc., See address and contact information above. **Management:** Dan Wehmer, Publisher. Beverly Hannum, Advertising Manager. **Editorial:** Dan Wehmer, Editor. Fred Spriggs, News Editor.

SHELBYVILLE

SHELBY COUNTY HERALD. 109 E. Main St., Shelbyville, MO 63469-0225. Telephone: 573-633-2261. FAX: 573-633-2133. E-MAIL: herald@centurytell.net. Mailing Address: PO Box 225, Shelbyville, MO 63469-0225. Year Established: 1870. Pub. Frequency: w. (Wed.) Page Size: broadsheet. Subscrip. Rate: $.50 newsstand/cover; $25/yr local; $30/yr elsewhere. Adv. Rate: col. inch $3.80 Circulation: 2,000 per issue (paid). **Owner(s):** Dennis Williams, PO Box 10, Clarence, MO 63437-0010. Telephone: 573-633-2261. FAX: 573-633-2133. **Management:** Johnna Pantaleo, Advertising Manager. Martha East, Circulation Manager. **Editorial:** Martha East, Editor.

SHERIDAN

QUAD RIVER NEWS. ISSN 0747-0444
12634 Noble Rd., Sheridan, MO 64486. Telephone: 660-799-2699. FAX: 206-339-6720. E-MAIL: qdrvrnws@grm.net. Pub. Frequency: w. (Wed.) Page Size: broadsheet. Subscrip. Rate: $.50 newsstand/cover; $16/yr in county; $24/yr out of county. Adv. Rate: col. inch $2 Circulation: 750 per issue (paid). **Owner(s):** Joe & Viveka Stark, See address and contact information above. **Management:** Jesse Stark, Publisher. **Editorial:** Jesse Stark, Editor.

SMITHVILLE

SMITHVILLE HERALD, THE. 1001 S Commerical Ave, Smithville, MO 64089. Telephone: 816-532-4444. FAX: 816-532-4918. URL: http://www.smithvilleherald.com. Mailing Address: P.O. Box 1076, Smithville, MO 64089. Year Established: 1888. Pub. Frequency: w. (Wed.) Page Size: broadsheet. Subscrip. Rate: $.75 newsstand/cover; $28/yr mailed in county. Adv. Rate: col. inch $7.32 Circulation: 2,500 per issue (paid). **Owner(s):** N P G Newspapers, Inc., See address and contact information above. **Management:** Matt Daugherty, Publisher. Jim Card, Advertising Director. David Mapel, Circulation Manager. **Editorial:** Nancy Hull, Editor. Amy Neal, Managing Editor. Scott Trittrington, Sports Editor.

SPRINGFIELD

NEWS-LEADER. ISSN 1074-2743
651 Boonville, Springfield, MO 65806. Telephone: 417-836-1100. URL: http://www.news-leader.com/apps/pbcs.dll/frontpage. Year Established: 1989. Pub. Frequency: w. **Owner(s):** The Springfield News-Leader, See address and contact information above.

ST. CLAIR

ST. CLAIR MISSOURIAN, THE. 515 S. Main St., St. Clair, MO 63077. Telephone: 636-629-1027. FAX: 636-629-2810. URL: http://www.emissourian.com. Year Established: 1924. Pub. Frequency: s-w. (Wed. & Sat.) Page Size: broadsheet. Subscrip. Rate: $.75 newsstand/cover; $34.50/yr in county; $39/yr out of county; $68/yr out of state. **Wire Service(s):** AP. Circulation: 20,725 evening (paid). **Owner(s):** Missourian Publishing Co., 14 W. Main St., Washington, MO 63090. Telephone: 636-239-7701. **Management:** William Miller Sr., Publisher. Patti Smith, Advertising Manager. Shirley Holdmeier, Classified Adv. Mgr.. **Editorial:** William Miller Sr., Editor. Gregg Jones, Managing Editor.

ST. JAMES

ST. JAMES LEADER-JOURNAL. 125 W. Springfield St., St. James, MO 65559. Telephone: 573-265-3321. FAX: 573-265-3197. E-MAIL: leaderjournal@charter.net. Year Established: 1896. Pub. Frequency: w. (Wed.) Page Size: broadsheet. Subscrip. Rate: $.75 newsstand/cover; $29/yr in cy. & adjoining cys.; $35/yr out of area; $26/yr to senior citizens; $37/yr out of state. Circulation: 2,000 per issue (paid). **Owner(s):** GateHouse Media, Inc, 350 WillowBrook Office Park, Fairport, NY 14450. FAX: 585-248-2631. **Management:** Joel Goodridge, Publisher. Amy Crews, Advertising Manager. **Editorial:** Kristin Whitaker, Editor.

ST. JOSEPH

ST. JOSEPH TELEGRAPH, THE. 3715 Beck Rd., St. Joseph, MO 64506. Telephone: 816-364-1323. FAX: 816-364-3083. Mailing Address: PO Box 299, Savannah, MO 64485-0299. Year Established: 1989. Pub. Frequency: w. (Thu.) Page Size: tabloid. Subscrip. Rate: $32.38/yr mailed. Adv. Rate: col. inch $6 Circulation: 674 per issue (paid). **Owner(s):** Touchdown Publications, Inc., See address and contact information above. **Management:** Leslie Scott Speckman, Publisher. **Editorial:** Leslie Scott Speckman, Editor.

SUN TRIBUNE. 825 Edmond St., St. Joseph, MO 64501. E-MAIL: newsclerk@npgco.com. URL: http://www.suntrib.com. Mailing Address: PO Box 28100, Gladstone, MO 64188. Year Established: 1914. Pub. Frequency: w. (Thu.) Page Size: broadsheet. Subscrip. Rate: $.75 newsstand/cover. **Owner(s):** N P G Newspapers, Inc., 310 N.W. Englewood Rd., Gladstone, MO 64188. Telephone: 816-454-9660. FAX: 816-414-3331. **Management:** Tony Luke, General Manager. Jim Card, Advertising Manager. David Mapel, Circulation Director. **Editorial:** Amy Neal, Managing Editor.

ST. LOUIS

COMMUNITY NEWS (ST. LOUIS). 5748 Helen Ave., St. Louis, MO 63136. Telephone: 314-261-5555. FAX: 314-261-2776. E-MAIL: commnews@sbcglobal.net. Year Established: 1921. Pub. Frequency: w. (Wed.) Page Size: tabloid.Adv. Rate: col. inch $48 Circulation: 45,000 per issue (free). **Owner(s):** Huneke Publications, Inc., See address and contact information above. **Management:** Robert J. Huneke Jr., Publisher. Megan Weissenstein, Classified Adv. Mgr.. **Editorial:** C.R. Bockskopf, Editor.

LADUE NEWS. 8811 Ladue Rd., Ste. D, St. Louis, MO 63124. Telephone: 314-863-3737. FAX: 314-863-4445. E-MAIL: jacqueedwards@laduenews.com. URL: http://www.laduenews.com. Pub. Frequency: w. (Fri.) Page Size: broadsheet. Subscrip. Rate: $45/yr mailed. Circulation: 7,000 per issue (controlled and free). **Owner(s):** Suburban Journals, 1714 Deer Tracks Trail, St. Louis, MO 63131. Telephone: 314-821-1110. **Management:** Lauren Rechan, Publisher. Jacque Edwards, Advertising Manager. **Editorial:** Dorothy Weiner, Editor. Meredith Saner, Managing Editor. Michele Treacy, Creative Director.

OAKVILLE-MEHLVILLE JOURNAL. 4210 Chippewa, St. Louis, MO 63116. Telephone: 314-664-2700. FAX: 314-664-8533. E-MAIL: bcollier@yourjournal.com. URL: http://www.stltoday.com. Pub. Frequency: w. (Wed.) Page Size: broadsheet.Subscrip. Rate: $110/yr mailed Circulation: 18,975 per issue (free). **Owner(s):** Suburban Journals, 1714 Deer Tracks Trail, St. Louis, MO 63131. Telephone: 314-821-1110. **Management:** Jeff Parra, Publisher. Ed Rohrbach, Circulation Manager. **Editorial:** James "Buck" Collier, Managing Editor.

RIVERFRONT TIMES, THE. 6358 Delmar Blvd., Ste. 200, St. Louis, MO 63130. Telephone: 314-754-5966. FAX: 314-754-5955. URL: http://www.riverfronttimes.com. Year Established: 1977. Pub. Frequency: w. (Wed.) Page Size: tabloid.Subscrip. Rate: $50/yr mailed Circulation: 100,000 per issue (free). **Owner(s):** Village Voice Media, Inc., 1201 E Jefferson St, Phoenix, AZ 85034. Telephone: 415-541-0700. FAX: 415-541-9096. **Management:** Michael J. Wagner, Publisher. Kyle Ingram, Advertising Director. Brady Rehm, Classified Adv. Mgr.. **Editorial:** Tom Finkel, Editor. Ellis Conklin, Managing Editor. Annie Zaleski, Music Editor.

SOUTH CITY JOURNAL. 4210 Chippewa, St. Louis, MO 63116. Telephone: 314-664-2700. FAX: 314-664-8533. E-MAIL: bcollier@yourjournal.com. URL: http://www.stltoday.com. Pub. Frequency: w. (Wed.) Page Size: broadsheet.Subscrip. Rate: $110/yr mailed Circulation: 14,750 per issue (free). **Owner(s):** Suburban Journals, 1714 Deer Tracks Trail, St. Louis, MO 63131. Telephone: 314-821-1110. **Management:** Jeff Parra, Publisher. Ed Rohrbach, Circulation Manager. **Editorial:** James "Buck" Collier, Managing Editor.

SOUTH COUNTY JOURNAL. 4210 Chippewa, St. Louis, MO 63116. Telephone: 314-664-2700. FAX: 314-664-8533. E-MAIL: bcollier@yourjournal.com. URL: http://www.stltoday.com. Year Established: 1965. Pub. Frequency: s-w. (Wed. & Sun.) Page Size: broadsheet. Subscrip. Rate: $110/yr mailed. Freelance Pay: $15-$100/article. Circulation: 20,565 per issue (free). **Owner(s):** Suburban Journals, 1714 Deer Tracks Trail, St. Louis, MO 63131. Telephone: 314-821-1110. **Management:** Jeff Parra, Publisher. Ed Rohrbach, Circulation Manager. **Editorial:** James "Buck" Collier, Managing Editor.

SOUTH COUNTY TIMES. 122 W. Lockwood Ave., 2nd Fl., St. Louis, MO 63119. Telephone: 314-968-2699. FAX: 314-968-2961. E-MAIL: info@timesnewspapers.com. URL: http://www.timewsnewspaper.com. Year Established: 1947. Pub. Frequency: w. (Fri.) Page Size: tabloid. Subscrip. Rate: $30/yr mailed out of area. Adv. Rate: B&W page $1,195, color page $1,590 Circulation: 32,645 per issue (free). **Owner(s):** Webster-Kirkwood Times, Inc., See address and contact information above. **Management:** Mary Chambers, General Manager. Dwight Bitikofer, Publisher. **Editorial:** Don Corrigan, Editor-in-Chief. Kevin Murphy, Managing Editor. Marty Harris, Associate Editor. Diana Linsley, Photographer.

SOUTH SIDE JOURNAL. 4210 Chippewa, St. Louis, MO 63116. Telephone: 314-664-2700. FAX: 314-664-8533. E-MAIL: bcollier@yourjournal.com. URL: http://www.stltoday.com. Pub. Frequency: w. (Wed.) Page Size: broadsheet.Subscrip. Rate: $110/yr mailed Circulation: 27,500 per issue (free). **Owner(s):** Suburban Journals, 1714 Deer Tracks Trail, St. Louis, MO 63131. Telephone: 314-821-1110. **Management:** Jeff Parra, Publisher. Ed Rohrback, Classified Adv. Mgr.. **Editorial:** James "Buck" Collier, Managing Editor.

SOUTHWEST CITY JOURNAL. 4210 Chippewa, St. Louis, MO 63119. Telephone: 314-664-2700. E-MAIL: cmatonis@yourjournal.com. URL: http://www.stltoday.com. Year Established: 1921. Pub. Frequency: s-w. (Wed. & Sun..) Page Size: broadsheet. Subscrip. Rate: $110/yr mailed. Freelance Pay: $15-$100/article. Circulation: 23,210 per issue (free). **Owner(s):** Suburban Journals, 1714 Deer Tracks Trail, St. Louis, MO 63131. Telephone: 314-821-1110. **Management:** Jeff Parra, Publisher. Ed Rohrbach, Circulation Manager. **Editorial:** James "Buck" Collier, Managing Editor.

SOUTHWEST COUNTY JOURNAL. 4210 Chippewa, St. Louis, MO 63116. FAX: 314-664-8533. E-MAIL: cmatonis@yourjournal.com. URL: http://www.yourjournal.com. Year Established: 1990. Pub. Frequency: s-w. (Wed. & Sun.) Page Size: broadsheet. Subscrip. Rate: $110/yr mailed. Freelance Pay: $15-$100/article. Circulation: 28,705 per issue (free). **Owner(s):** Suburban Journals, 1714 Deer Tracks Trail, St. Louis, MO 63131. Telephone: 314-821-1110. **Management:** Jeff Parra, Publisher. Ed Rohrbach, Circulation Manager. **Editorial:** James "Buck" Collier, Managing Editor.

ST. LOUIS AMERICAN NEWSPAPER. 4242 Lindell Blvd., Ste. B-5, St. Louis, MO 63108. Telephone: 314-533-8000. FAX: 314-533-0038. E-MAIL: news@stlamerican.com. URL: http://www.stlamerican.com. Year Established: 1928. Pub. Frequency: w. (Thu.) Page Size: broadsheet. Subscrip. Rate: $40/yr mailed in county. **Wire Service(s):** AP. Circulation: 70,000 per issue (paid). **Owner(s):** Dr. Donald M. Suggs, See address and contact information above. **Management:** Donald M. Suggs, Publisher. Barbara Pettiford, Advertising Manager. Paul Reiter, Circulation Manager. Vida Taylor, Classified Adv. Mgr.. **Editorial:** Alvin Reid, City Editor. Earl Austin, Sports Editor.

WEBSTER-KIRKWOOD TIMES. 122 W. Lockwood Ave., 2nd Fl., St. Louis, MO 63119. Telephone: 314-968-2699. E-MAIL: info@timesnewspapers.com. URL: http://www.timesnewspapers.com. Year Established: 1978. Pub. Frequency: w. (Fri.) Page Size: tabloid. Subscrip. Rate: $30/yr mailed out of area. Adv. Rate: B&W page $1,195, color page $1,590 Circulation: 30,925 per issue (free). **Owner(s):** Webster-Kirkwood Times, Inc., See address and contact information above. **Management:** Mary Chambers, General Manager. Dwight Bitikofer, Publisher. **Editorial:** Don Corrigan, Editor-in-Chief. Kevin Murphy, Managing Editor. Marty Harris, Associate Editor. Diana Linsley, Photographer.

ST. PETERS

O'FALLON JOURNAL. 4212 N Service Rd, St. Peters, MO 63376. Telephone: 636-946-6111. FAX: 636-946-0086. E-MAIL: aburnham@yourjournal.com. URL: http://www.yourjournal.com. Year Established: 1963. Pub. Frequency: 3/w. (Wed., Fri., Sun.) Page Size: broadsheet Circulation: 17,000 per issue (free). **Owner(s):** Suburban Journals, 1714 Deer Tracks Trail, St. Louis, MO 63131. Telephone: 314-821-1110. **Management:** Amie Stein, Publisher. Adam Burnham, Advertising Director. John Nixon, Circulation Manager. **Editorial:** Brad Mudd, Managing Editor.

ST. CHARLES JOURNAL. 4212 N Service Rd, St. Peters, MO 63376. Telephone: 636-946-6111. FAX: 636-946-0086. E-MAIL: aburnham@yourjournal.com. URL: http://www.yourjournal.com. Year Established: 1957. Pub. Frequency: 3/w. (Wed., Fri., Sun.) Page Size: broadsheet. Circulation: 85,000 per issue (controlled). **Owner(s):** Suburban Journals, 1417 Deer Tracks Trail, St. Louis, MO 63113. Telephone: 314-821-1110. **Management:** Amie Stein, Publisher. Adam Burnham, Advertising Manager. John Nixon, Circulation Manager. **Editorial:** Brad Mudd, Managing Editor.

ST. PETERS JOURNAL. 4212 N Service Rd, St. Peters, MO 63303. Telephone: 636-946-6111. FAX: 636-946-0086. E-MAIL: aburnham@yourjournal.com. URL: http://www.yourjournal.com. Pub. Frequency: 3/w. (Wed., Fri., Sun.) Page Size: broadsheet. Subscrip. Rate: $45/yr mailed. Circulation: 13,000 per issue (paid and free). **Owner(s):** Suburban Journals, 1714 Deer Tracks Trail, St. Louis, MO 63131. Telephone: 314-821-1110. **Management:** Amie Stein, Publisher. Adam Burnham, Advertising Manager. John Nixon, Circulation Manager. **Editorial:** Brad Mudd, Managing Editor.

ST. ROBERT

FORT LEONARD WOOD GUIDE. 108 Holly Dr., St. Robert, MO 65584. Telephone: 573-336-3711. FAX: 573-336-4640. Mailing Address: PO Box 578, Waynesville, MO 65583. Pub. Frequency: w. (Thu.) Page Size: standard Circulation: 4,900 per issue (free). **Owner(s):** GateHouse Media, Inc, 350 WillowBrook Office Park, Fairport, NY 14450. Telephone: 585-598-0030. FAX: 585-248-2631. **Management:** Bill Mills, Publisher. Karen Hood, Advertising Manager. Linda Campbell, Circulation Manager.

PULASKI COUNTY WEEKLY. 108 Holly Dr., St. Robert, MO 65584. Telephone: 573-336-3711. FAX: 573-336-4640. URL: http://www.waynesvilledailyguide.com. Mailing Address: PO Box 578, Waynesville, MO 65583. Pub. Frequency: w. (Wed.) Page Size: broadsheet Circulation: 8,690 per issue (free). **Owner(s):** GateHouse Media, Inc, 350 WillowBrook Office Park, Fairport, NY 14450. Telephone: 585-598-0030. **Management:** Bill Mills, Publisher. Karen Hood, Advertising Manager. Linda Campbell, Circulation Manager.

STE. GENEVIEVE

STE. GENEVIEVE HERALD. 330 Market St., Ste. Genevieve, MO 63670-1638. Telephone: 573-883-2222. FAX: 573-883-2833. E-MAIL: bburr@stegenherald.com. URL: http//www.stegenherald.com. Mailing Address: PO Box 447, Ste. Genevieve, MO 63670-0447. Year Established: 1882. Pub. Frequency: w. (Wed.) Page Size: standard. Subscrip. Rate: $.50 newsstand/cover; $24/yr in county; $32/yr out of area. Adv. Rate: col. inch $8 Circulation: 4,700 per issue (paid). **Owner(s):** Ste. Genevieve Newspapers, Inc., See address and contact information above. **Management:** Janet Mace, General Manager. Robert J. Burr, Publisher. Jill Gettlinger, Advertising Manager. **Editorial:** Jean Rissover, Managing Editor. Margaret Jorgensen, Feature Editor. Michael Boyd Jr., Sports Editor.

STEELE

STEELE ENTERPRISE. 227 W. Main St., Steele, MO 63877. Telephone: 573-695-3415. FAX: 573-695-2114. E-MAIL: homenews@sheltonbbs.com. Mailing Address: PO Box 60, Steele, MO 63877. Year Established: 1921. Pub. Frequency: w. (Thu.) Page Size: standard. Subscrip. Rate: $.50 newsstand/cover; $18/yr in county; $36/yr mailed out of county. Circulation: 2,000 per issue (paid). **Owner(s):** Village News, Inc., PO Box 1108, Blytheville, AR 72316. Telephone: 870-763-4461. **Management:** David Tennyson, Publisher. **Editorial:** Tiffany Pritchard, Editor.

STEELVILLE

STEELVILLE STAR-CRAWFORD MIRROR. 106 S First St, Steelville, MO 65565. Telephone: 573-775-5454. FAX: 573-775-2668. E-MAIL: stvlstar@misn.com. URL: http://www.steelvillestar.com. Mailing Address: PO Box BG, Steelville, MO 65565. Year Established: 1872. Pub. Frequency: w. (Wed.) Page Size: tabloid. Subscrip. Rate: $.50 newsstand/cover; $22.78/yr mailed in county; $30.92/yr mailed out of county; $36/yr mailed out of state. Circulation: 2,850 per issue (paid). **Owner(s):** Three Rivers Publishing, Inc., 501 E Washington Blvd, Cuba, MO 65453. Telephone: 573-885-7460. **Management:** Roberta Shields, Advertising. Janice Ransom, Circulation Manager. **Editorial:** Ava Viehman, Editor.

STOCKTON

CEDAR COUNTY REPUBLICAN. 26 Public Sq, Stockton, MO 65785. Telephone: 417-276-3211. FAX: 417-276-5760. E-MAIL: marilyne@cedarrepublican.com. URL: http://www.cedarcountyrepublican.com. Mailing Address: PO Box 1018, Stockton, MO 65785. Year Established: 1888. Pub. Frequency: w. (Wed.) Page Size: broadsheet. Subscrip. Rate: $.75 newsstand/cover; $28/yr home delivery in county; $40/yr out of county; $52/yr mailed out of state. Adv. Rate: col. inch $6.75 Circulation: 3,249 per issue (paid). **Owner(s):** Community Publishers, Inc., PO Box 1049, Bentonville, AR 72712. Telephone: 479-271-3700. **Management:** Marilyn S. Ellis, General Manager. **Editorial:** Becky Groff, Reporter.

STOVER

MORGAN COUNTY PRESS. 201 N. Maple St., Stover, MO 65078. Telephone: 573-377-4616. FAX: 573-377-4515. URL: http://www.vip-newspapers.com/. Mailing Address: P.O. Box 130, Stover, MO 65078. Pub. Frequency: w. (Wed.) Subscrip. Rate: $26.50/yr in county; $33.50/yr in state; $38.50/yr out of state. Adv. Rate: col. inch $3.10 Circulation: 1,500 per issue (paid). **Owner(s):** Vernon Publishing, Inc., See address and contact information above. **Management:** Dane Vernon, Publisher. **Editorial:** Tim Flora, Editor.

SULLIVAN

SULLIVAN INDEPENDENT NEWS, THE. PO Box 268, Sullivan, MO 63080. Telephone: 573-468-6511. FAX: 573-468-4046. E-MAIL: nuz4u@fidnet.com. URL: http://www.mysullivannews.com. Year Established: 1962. Pub. Frequency: w. (Wed.) Page Size: tabloid. Subscrip. Rate: $.75 newsstand/cover; $34/yr mailed in county; $40/yr mailed out of county; $49/yr mailed out of state. Adv. Rate: col. inch $6 Circulation: 7,000 per issue (paid). **Owner(s):** Kathleen Manion, See address and contact information above. **Management:** Kathleen Manion, Publisher. Mark Hilse, Advertising Manager. **Editorial:** Kathleen Manion, Editor. Jim Bartle, Assistant Editor.

TARKIO

TARKIO AVALANCHE. 521 Main St., Tarkio, MO 64491. Telephone: 660-736-4111. FAX: 660-736-5700. E-MAIL: avalanche@msc.net. URL: http://www.northwestmissouri.com. Year Established: 1884. Pub. Frequency: w. (Thu.) Page Size: broadsheet. Subscrip. Rate: $.50 newsstand/cover; $22/yr mailed in county & adj. counties; $27.50/yr mailed elsewhere. **Wire Service(s):** AP. Circulation: 1,850 per issue (paid). **Owner(s):** Will Johnson, See address and contact information above. **Management:** Will Johnson, Publisher. **Editorial:** Will Johnson, Editor.

THAYER

SOUTH MISSOURIAN NEWS. 109 Chestnut St., Thayer, MO 65791. Telephone: 417-264-3085. FAX: 417-264-3814. E-MAIL: news@areawidenews.com. URL: http://www.areawidenews.com. Year Established: 1991. Pub. Frequency: w. (Thu.) Page Size: broadsheet. Subscrip. Rate: $.75 newsstand/cover; $33/yr home delivery in county; $40/yr mailed out of county. Adv. Rate: col. inch $6.75 Freelance Pay: $0.50/column-inch. Circulation: 1,532 per issue (paid). **Owner(s):** Rust Communications, Inc., 301 Broadway, Cape Girardeau, MO 63701. Telephone: 573-335-6611. **Management:** Erma Harris, General Manager. Rex Rust, President. Erma Harris, Publisher. Joyce Minor, Advertising Manager. Debra Perryman, Circulation Manager. **Editorial:** Erma Harris, Editor.

TIPTON

TIPTON TIMES. 123 W. Moniteau St., Tipton, MO 65081. URL: http://www.vpi-newspapers.com/Times/times.jsp. Pub. Frequency: w. (Thu.) Page Size: broadsheet. Subscrip. Rate: $27.50/yr in county; $34.50/yr in state; $39.50/yr out of state. Adv. Rate: col. inch $4.10 **Owner(s):** Vernon Publishing, Inc., 104 W Jasper St, Versailles, MO 65084. Telephone: 573-378-5441. **Management:** Dane Vernon, Publisher.

TROY

LINCOLN COUNTY JOURNAL (TROY). 20 Business Park Dr., Troy, MO 63379. Telephone: 636-528-9550. FAX: 636-528-6694. E-MAIL: lcjeditor@alwayson-line.net. URL: http://www.lincolncountyjournal.com. Pub. Frequency: w. (Mon) Page Size: broadsheet. Subscrip. Rate: $.50 newsstand/cover; $55/yr elsewhere. Circulation: 18,575 per issue (paid). **Owner(s):** Lakeway Publishing, See address and contact information above. **Management:** Pat Whiteside, Publisher. Sandy Turner, Advertising Manager. **Editorial:** Bob Simmons, Editor.

TROY FREE PRESS & SILEX INDEX. 20 Business Park Dr., Troy, MO 63379. Telephone: 636-528-9550. FAX: 636-528-6694. Pub. Frequency: w. (Wed.) Page Size: broadsheet. Subscrip. Rate: $.50 newsstand/cover; $23/yr in county; $35/yr out of county; $18/yr in county to senior citizens; $30/yr out of county to senior citizens. Circulation: 1,000 per issue (paid). **Owner(s):** Lakeway Publishing, See address and contact information above. **Management:** Pat Whiteside, Publisher. Sandy Turner, Advertising Manager. **Editorial:** Bob Simmons, Editor.

UNIONVILLE

UNIONVILLE REPUBLICAN, THE. 111 S. 16th St., Unionville, MO 63565-0365. Telephone: 660-947-2222. FAX: 660-947-2223. E-MAIL: urep@nemr.net. Mailing Address: PO Box 365, Unionville, MO 63565-0365. Year Established: 1865. Pub. Frequency: w. (Wed.) Page Size: standard. Subscrip. Rate: $.50 newsstand/cover; $20/yr in county; $24/yr out of county. Circulation: 2,300 per issue (paid). **Owner(s):** Ron & Teresa Kinzler, 111 S. 16th St., Unionville, MO 63565. Telephone: 816-947-2222. **Management:** Ron Kinzler, General Manager. **Editorial:** Teresa Kinzler, Editor.

VERSAILLES

HIGHWAY FIVE BEACON. 104 W. Jasper St., Versailles, MO 65084. Telephone: 573-378-5441. FAX: 573-378-4292. E-MAIL: beacon@vernonpublishing.com. URL: http://www.vpi-newspapers.com. Mailing Address: PO Box 348, Versailles, MO 65084-0348. Pub. Frequency: w. (Wed.) Page Size: broadsheet.Adv. Rate: col. inch $3.10 Circulation: 8,100 per issue (free). **Owner(s):** Vernon Publishing, Inc., See address and contact information above. **Management:** Dane Vernon, Publisher. Loren Muyer, Advertising. **Editorial:** Bryan Jones, Editor. Contact: Dane Vernon, Publisher; Loren Muyer, Advertising; Bryan Jones, Editor.

VERSAILLES LEADER-STATESMAN. 104 W. Jasper St., Versailles, MO 65084. Telephone: 573-378-5441. FAX: 573-378-4292. E-MAIL: leaderstatesman@vernonpublishing.com. URL: http://www.vpi-newspapers.com. Mailing Address: PO Box 348, Versailles, MO 65084-0348. Year Established: 1887. Pub. Frequency: w. (Thu.) Page Size: broadsheet. Subscrip. Rate: $.50 newsstand/cover; $29.50/yr in county; $36.50/yr in state; $41.50/yr out of state. Adv. Rate: col. inch $4.35 Circulation: 3,750 per issue (paid). **Owner(s):** Vernon Publishing, Inc., See address and contact information above. **Management:** Dane Vernon, Publisher. Loren Muyer, Advertising. **Editorial:** Bryan Jones, Editor. Contact: Dane Vernon, Publisher; Loren Muyer, Advertising; Bryan Jones, Editor.

VIENNA

MARIES COUNTY GAZETTE. Courthouse Sq., Vienna, MO 65582-0202. Telephone: 573-422-3441. FAX: 573-859-6274. Mailing Address: PO Box 202, Vienna, MO 65582. Year Established: 1876. Pub. Frequency: w. (Wed.) Page Size: broadsheet. Subscrip. Rate: $.50 newsstand/cover; $21.45/yr local; $24.66/yr in state. Circulation: 2,300 per issue (paid). **Owner(s):** Tri-County Newspapers LLC, 217 Alvarado, Belle, MO 65013. Telephone: 573-859-3328. FAX: 573-859-6274. **Management:** Kurt J. Lewis, Publisher. **Editorial:** Nichoel Snodgrass, Editor.

WARRENTON

WARRENTON JOURNAL. 111 W. Main, Warrenton, MO 63383. Telephone: 636-456-3481. FAX: 636-456-3020. E-MAIL: rcoleman@yourjournal.com. URL: http://www.yourjournal.com. Year Established: 1973. Pub. Frequency: w. (Wed.) Page Size: broadsheet Circulation: 14,100 per issue (free). **Owner(s):** Suburban Journals, 1714 Deer Tracks Trail, St. Louis, MO 63131. Telephone: 314-821-1110. **Management:** Richard Coleman, Publisher. Gary Ratcliffe, Circulation Manager.

WENTZVILLE JOURNAL. ISSN 0192-6896
220 E. Main St., Warrenton, MO 63383. Telephone: 636-456-3481. FAX: 636-456-3020. E-MAIL: rcoleman@yourjournal.com. URL: http://www.yourjournal.com. Year Established: 1966. Pub. Frequency: s-w. (Wed. & Sun.) Page Size: broadsheet. Circulation: 10,000 per issue (paid and free). **Owner(s):** Suburban Journals, 1714 Deer Tracks Trail, St. Louis, MO 63131. Telephone: 314-821-1110. **Management:** Richard Coleman, Publisher. Tim Muldoon, Circulation Manager. **Editorial:** Gina Parsons, Managing Editor.

WARSAW

BENTON COUNTY ENTERPRISE. 107 Main St., Warsaw, MO 65355. Telephone: 660-438-6312. Year Established: 1879. Pub. Frequency: w. (Thu.) Page Size: standard. Subscrip. Rate: $.50 newsstand/cover; $24/yr in county; $29/yr elsewhere. Circulation: 5,700 per issue (paid). **Owner(s):** M.K. White, See address and contact information above. **Management:** James White, Publisher. Heidi Tolliver, Business Manager. **Editorial:** James White, Editor. Venecia Simons, Production Manager.

WASHINGTON

WASHINGTON MISSOURIAN. 14 W. Main St., Washington, MO 63090. Telephone: 636-239-7701. FAX: 636-239-0915. E-MAIL: washnews@usmo.com. URL: http://www.emissourian.com. Year Established: 1860. Pub. Frequency: s-w. (Wed. & Sat.) Page Size: broadsheet. Subscrip. Rate: $.75 newsstand/cover; $34.50/yr in county; $39/yr adj counties.; $52/yr in state; $68/yr out of state. Adv. Rate: col. inch $9.70 **Wire Service(s):** AP. Circulation: 28,965 per issue (paid). **Owner(s):** Missourian Publishing Co., See address and contact information above. **Management:** William L. Miller, Publisher. Jane Haberberger, Advertising Director. Doug Warden, Circulation Manager. **Editorial:** William L. Miller, Editor. Bill Battle, Sports.

MONTANA

ANACONDA

ANACONDA LEADER, THE. 121 Main St., Anaconda, MT 59711. Telephone: 406-563-5283. FAX: 406-563-5284. Year Established: 1969. Pub. Frequency: s-w. (Wed. & Fri.) Page Size: broadsheet. Subscrip. Rate: $.50 newsstand/cover; $36/yr in county; $37.50/yr out of county; $48/yr out of state. Adv. Rate: col. inch $7.50 Circulation: 3,811 per issue (paid and free). **Owner(s):** Leader Printing & Supply, Inc., See address and contact information above. **Management:** Dean A. Neitz, Publisher. Micky Gee, Advertising Manager.

BIG SANDY

MOUNTAINEER, THE. 223 Johannes, Big Sandy, MT 59520. Telephone: 406-378-2176. FAX: 406-378-2176. E-MAIL: retigpub@ttck-cmc.net. Mailing Address: PO Box 529, Big Sandy, MT 59520. Year Established: 1911. Pub. Frequency: w. (Wed.) Page Size: broadsheet. Subscrip. Rate: $.50 newsstand/cover; $25/yr in county; $25/yr mailed in state; $28/yr mailed out of state. Circulation: 1,200 per issue (paid). **Owner(s):** Rettig Publishing, Inc., See address and contact information above. **Management:** James L. Rettig, Publisher. **Editorial:** James L. Rettig, Editor.

BIGFORK

BIGFORK EAGLE. 8293 Hwy. 35, Bigfork, MT 59911. Telephone: 406-837-5131. FAX: 406-837-1132. E-MAIL: newsdesk@bigforkeagle.com. URL: http://www.bigforkeagle.com. Mailing Address: PO Box 406, Bigfork, MT 59911. Year Established: 1979. Pub. Frequency: w. (Wed.) Page Size: broadsheet. Subscrip. Rate: $.50 newsstand/cover; $30/yr in county; $39/yr out of county; $49/yr mailed out of state. Circulation: 1,600 per issue (paid and free). **Owner(s):** Hagadone Corp., 111 S. First St., Coeur d'Alene, ID 83814-1937. Telephone: 208-667-3431. **Management:** Tom Kurdy, Publisher. Janet Kennedy, Office Manager. Noreen Hanson, Advertising Manager. **Editorial:** Mike Richeson, Managing Editor.

BROWNING

GLACIER REPORTER. 208 N Piegan, Browning, MT 59417. Telephone: 406-338-2090. FAX: 406-338-2410. E-MAIL: glacrptr@3rivers.net. URL: http://www.glacierreporter.com. Mailing Address: P O Box 349, Browning, MT 59417. Pub. Frequency: w. (Thu) Subscrip. Rate: $.75 newsstand/cover per issue; $30/yr in county; $35/yr mailed in state; $40/yr mailed out of state. Circulation: 1,800 per issue (paid and controlled). **Owner(s):** Brian & LeAnne Kavanagh, PO Box 1253, Cut Bank, MT 59427-1253. Telephone: 406-873-4128. FAX: 406-873-4129. 19 S Central, Cut Bank, MT 59427. **Management:** Brian Kavanagh, Owner. LeAnne Kavanagh, Publisher. Kathy Nevins, Office Manager. Marlene Augare, Advertising. **Editorial:** John McGill, Editor.

COLUMBIA FALLS

HUNGRY HORSE NEWS. 926 Nucleus Ave., Columbia Falls, MT 59912-0189. Telephone: 406-892-2151. FAX: 406-892-5600. E-MAIL: info@hungryhorsenews.com. URL: http://www.hungryhorsenews.com. Mailing Address: PO Box 189, Columbia Falls, MT 59912-0189. Year Established: 1946. Pub. Frequency: w. (Thu.) Page Size: broadsheet. Subscrip. Rate: $.75 newsstand/cover; $33/yr in county area; $43/yr mailed in state; $49/yr mailed out of state. Adv. Rate: col. inch $9.30 Circulation: 5,000 per issue (paid). **Owner(s):** Hagadone Corp., 111 S. First St., Coeur d'Alene, ID 83814-1937. Telephone: 208-667-3431. **Management:** Noreen Hanson, Advertising Manager. **Editorial:** Chris Peterson, Editor. Matt Epperson, Production Manager. Heidi Desch, Reporter.

CUT BANK

CUT BANK PIONEER PRESS. P O Box 847, Cut Bank, MT 59427. E-MAIL: cbpress@bresnan.net. URL: http://www.cutbankpioneerpress.com. Pub. Frequency: w. (Wed.) Subscrip. Rate: $.75 newsstand/cover per issue; $30/yr in county; $35/yr in state; $40/yr mailed out of state. Circulation: 1,600 per issue (paid and controlled). **Owner(s):** Brian & LeAnne Kavanagh, 19 S Central, Cut Bank, MT 59427. Telephone: 406-873-2201. FAX: 406-873-2443. **Management:** Brian Kavanagh, Owner. LeAnne Kavanagh, Publisher. Dawn Texidor, Office Manager. Jonna Tafelmeyer, Advertising.

FORT BENTON

RIVER PRESS, THE. 1114 Front St., Fort Benton, MT 59442-0069. Telephone: 406-622-3311. FAX: 406-622-5446. E-MAIL: riverpress@mtintouch.net. Mailing Address: PO Box 69, Fort Benton, MT 59442-0069. Year Established: 1880. Pub. Frequency: w. (Wed.) Page Size: standard. Subscrip. Rate: $.75 newsstand/cover; $25/yr in county; $30/yr out of county. Circulation: 2,100 per issue (paid). **Owner(s):** Mike Tichenor, PO Box 69, Fort Benton, MT 59442. Telephone: 406-622-3311. FAX: 406-622-5446. **Management:** Mike Tichenor, Publisher. **Editorial:** Mike Tichenor, Editor.

GLASGOW

GLASGOW COURIER, THE. 341 Third Ave., S, Glasgow, MT 59230. Telephone: 406-228-9301. E-MAIL: courier@nemontel.net. Year Established: 1913. Pub. Frequency: w. (Wed.) Page Size: standard. Subscrip. Rate: $.75 newsstand/cover; $33/yr in county; $37/yr out of county; $47/yr out of state. Circulation: 3,700 per issue (paid). **Owner(s):** Glasgow Courier, See address and contact information above. **Management:** Toy Olson, Advertising Manager. **Editorial:** Samar Fay, Editor.

GLENDIVE

GLENDIVE RANGER-REVIEW. 119 W. Bell St., Glendive, MT 59330. Telephone: 406-365-3303. FAX: 406-365-5435. E-MAIL: mtgranger@mcn.net. URL: http://www.rangerreview.com. Mailing Address: PO Box 61, Glendive, MT 59330. Year Established: 1881. Pub. Frequency: s-w. (Thu. & Sun.) Page Size: broadsheet. Subscrip. Rate: $.75 newsstand/cover; $39/yr carrier delivery; $56/yr mailed in state; $59/yr mailed out of state. Adv. Rate: col. inch $6 Circulation: 3,224 per issue (paid). **Owner(s):** Yellowstone Newspapers, 401 S. Main, Livingston, MT 59047. Telephone: 406-222-2000. **Management:** Gerry Zander, Publisher. Pat Boese, Advertising Manager. Janette Legato, Circulation Manager. **Editorial:** Jamie Crisafulli, Managing Editor. Codi Newton, Sports.

HARLOWTON

TIMES-CLARION, THE. ISSN 0889-5627
111 S. Central, Harlowton, MT 59036-0307. Telephone: 406-632-5633. FAX: 406-632-5644. E-MAIL: harlotms@mtintouch.net. Mailing Address: PO Box 307, Harlowton, MT 59036-0307. Year Established: 1917. Pub. Frequency: w. (Thu.) Page Size: standard. Subscrip. Rate: $.75 newsstand/cover; $26/yr in county; $32/yr in state. **Wire Service(s):** AP. Circulation: 1,600 per issue (paid). **Owner(s):** Shelli Randles, See address and contact information above. **Management:** Shelli Randles, Advertising Manager. **Editorial:** Shirley Wagner, Editor.

LEWISTOWN

LEWISTOWN NEWS-ARGUS. 521 W Main St, Lewistown, MT 59457. Telephone: 406-535-3401. FAX: 406-538-3405. E-MAIL: newsargus@lewistownnews.com. URL: http://www.lewistownnews.com. Year Established: 1883. Pub. Frequency: s-w. (Wed. & Sat.) Page Size: broadsheet. Subscrip. Rate: $.75 newsstand/cover; $52.50/yr mailed central montana. **Wire Service(s):** AP. Circulation: 4,200 per issue (paid). **Owner(s):** Central Montana Publishing Co., See address and contact information above. **Management:** John Sullivan, President. Oron L. Jacobs, Publisher. Dearlene Hodik, Advertising Manager. Shirley Shepard, Circulation Manager. Suzy Benzing, Classified Adv. Mgr.. **Editorial:** Jacques Ruttan, Editor.

LIBBY

WESTERN NEWS, THE. 311 California Ave., Libby, MT 59923. Telephone: 406-293-4124. FAX: 406-293-7187. E-MAIL: westnews@libby.org. URL: http://www.thewesternnews.com. Mailing Address: PO Box 1377, Libby, MT 59923. Year Established: 1902. Pub. Frequency: s-w. (Wed. & Fri.) Page Size: broadsheet. Subscrip. Rate: $.75 newsstand/cover; $23 for 6 mos. in county; $43/yr in county; $26 mailed for 6 mos. out of county; $47/yr mailed out of state. Freelance Pay: $0.50/column-inch. Circulation: 4,200 per issue (paid). **Owner(s):** Hagadone Corp., 111 S. First St., Coeur d'Alene, ID 83814-1937. Telephone: 208-667-3431. **Management:** Barbara Swenson, Publisher. **Editorial:** Erica Kirsch, Editor.

Weeklies

MISSOULA

MISSOULA INDEPENDENT. 115 S. Fourth St. W., Missoula, MT 59801. Telephone: 406-543-6609. URL: http://www.missoulanews.com. Year Established: 1991. Pub. Frequency: w. (Thu.) Page Size: tabloid Circulation: 20,000 per issue (free); 22,541 per issue (controlled and free). **Owner(s):** Matt Gibson, See address and contact information above. **Management:** Matt Gibson, Publisher. Rod Harsell, Sales Manager. **Editorial:** Brad Tyer, Editor.

PHILIPSBURG

PHILIPSBURG MAIL, THE. 123 E Broadway, Philipsburg, MT 59858. Telephone: 406-859-3223. FAX: 406-858-3640. E-MAIL: philipsburgmail@blackfoot.net. URL: http://www.philipsburgmail.com. Mailing Address: PO Box 160, Philipsburg, MT 59858. Year Established: 1886. Pub. Frequency: w. (Thu.) Page Size: broadsheet. Subscrip. Rate: $.75 newsstand/cover; $29/yr in state; $35/yr out of state. Circulation: 1,350 per issue (paid). **Owner(s):** Stevenson Newspapers Inc, PO Box 7306, Sheridan, WY 82801. Telephone: 307-673-6566. **Management:** Tom Mullen, Publisher. **Editorial:** Jolynn McClain, Editor.

POLSON

ADVERTISER (POLSON), THE. 3 Second Ave., Polson, MT 59864. Telephone: 406-883-4343. FAX: 406-883-4349. E-MAIL: editor@leaderadvertiser.com. URL: http://www.leaderadvertiser.com. Mailing Address: PO Box 1090, Polson, MT 59860. Pub. Frequency: w. (Wed.) Page Size: broadsheet Circulation: 26,000 per issue (free). **Owner(s):** Hagadone Corp., 111 S. First St., Coeur d'Alene, ID 83814-1937. Telephone: 208-667-3431. **Management:** Laurie Ramos, General Manager. Dan Drewry, Publisher. **Editorial:** Ethan Smith, Editor.

LAKE COUNTY LEADER. 3 Second Ave., Polson, MT 59860. Telephone: 406-883-4343. FAX: 406-883-4349. E-MAIL: editor@leaderadvertiser.com. URL: http://www.leaderadvertiser.com. Mailing Address: PO Box 1090, Polson, MT 59860. Year Established: 1910. Pub. Frequency: w. (Thu.) Page Size: broadsheet. Subscrip. Rate: $.50 newsstand/cover; $29/yr in county; $34/yr out of county; $38/yr out of state. Circulation: 5,700 per issue (paid). **Owner(s):** Hagadone Corp., 111 S. First St., Coeur d'Alene, ID 83814. Telephone: 208-667-3431. **Management:** Laurie Ramos, General Manager. Dan Drewry, Publisher. Andrea Downing, Advertising Manager. **Editorial:** Ethan Smith, Editor. Paul Feigleberg, Copy Editor.

SHELBY

SHELBY PROMOTER. 225 Main St, Shelby, MT 59474. Telephone: 406-434-5171. FAX: 406-434-5955. E-MAIL: promoter@3rivers.net. URL: http://www.shelbypromoter.com. Mailing Address: P O Box 610, Shelby, MT 59474. Pub. Frequency: w. (Thu.) Subscrip. Rate: $.75 newsstand/cover per issue; $30/yr in county; $35/yr mailed in state; $40/yr mailed out of state. Circulation: 2,100 per issue (paid and controlled). **Owner(s):** Brian & LeAnne Kavanagh, PO Box 1253, Cut Bank, MT 59427-1253. Telephone: 406-873-4128. FAX: 406-873-4129. 19 S Central, Cut Bank, MT 59427. **Management:** Brian Kavanagh, Owner. LeAnne Kavanagh, Publisher. Patti Warburton, Advertising. **Editorial:** Barbara Simonette, Editor.

SIDNEY

SIDNEY HERALD. 310 Second Ave., N.E., Sidney, MT 59270. Telephone: 406-433-2403. FAX: 406-433-7802. E-MAIL: publisher@sidneyherald.com. URL: http://sidneyherald.com. Year Established: 1908. Pub. Frequency: s-w. (Wed. & Sun.) Page Size: broadsheet. Subscrip. Rate: $.75 newsstand/cover; $49/yr carrier delivery; $56/yr motor route; $49/yr mailed in county; $56/yr mailed out of county in trade; $64/yr mailed out of county out of trade. Adv. Rate: col. inch $8.70 Freelance Pay: $0.50/column-inch. Circulation: 3,200 per issue (paid). **Owner(s):** Wick Communications, Inc., 333 W. Wilcox Dr., Ste. 302, Sierra Vista, AZ 85635. Telephone: 520-458-0200. FAX: 520-458-6166. **Management:** Libby Berndt, Publisher. Bev Forthun, Office Manager. Dawn Steinbeisser, Circulation Manager. **Editorial:** Bill Vander Weele, Editor.

VALIER

VALIERIAN, THE. 507 Teton Ave, Ste 2, Valier, MT 59486. Telephone: 406-279-340. FAX: 406-279-3435. E-MAIL: valierian@bresnan.net. URL: http://www.thevalierian.com. Mailing Address: P O Box 308, Valier, MT 59486. Pub. Frequency: w. (Thu.) Subscrip. Rate: $.50 newsstand/cover per issue; $20/yr in county; $25/yr mailed in state; $30/yr mailed out of state. Circulation: 500 per issue (paid and controlled). **Owner(s):** Brian & LeAnne Kavanagh, PO Box 1253, Cut Bank, MT 59427-1253. FAX: 406-873-4129. 19 S Central, Cut Bank, MT 59427. Telephone: 406-873-2201. **Management:** Brian Kavanagh, Owner. LeAnne Kavanagh, Publisher. Trina Jo Bradley, Advertising.

WHITEFISH

WHITEFISH PILOT. 312 Second St. E, Whitefish, MT 59937. Telephone: 406-862-3505. FAX: 406-862-3636. URL: http://www.whitefishpilot.com. Mailing Address: PO Box 488, Whitefish, MT 59937. Year Established: 1902. Pub. Frequency: w. (Thu.) Page Size: broadsheet. Subscrip. Rate: $.75 newsstand/cover; $35/yr mailed in county; $45/yr mailed out of county; $52/yr mailed out of state. Circulation: 4,400 per issue (paid). **Owner(s):** Hagadone Corp., 111 S. First St., Coeur d'Alene, ID 83814-1937. Telephone: 208-667-3431. **Management:** Rena Tintinger, General Manager. David Coombs, Publisher. Shauna Hess, Advertising Manager. Phil Holmes, Circulation Manager. **Editorial:** Rick Hanners, Editor.

WOLF POINT

HERALD-NEWS (WOLF POINT), THE. 408 Main St., Wolf Point, MT 59201. Telephone: 406-405-2222. FAX: 406-653-2221. E-MAIL: herald@midrivers.com. URL: http://www.wolfpointherald.com. Mailing Address: PO Box 639, Wolf Point, MT 59201. Year Established: 1913. Pub. Frequency: w. (Thu.) Page Size: broadsheet. Subscrip. Rate: $.85 newsstand/cover; $31/yr in county; $37/yr in state; $47/yr out of state. Circulation: 2,600 per issue (paid). **Owner(s):** Herald-News, Inc., See address and contact information above. **Management:** Darla Shumway, Publisher. **Editorial:** Darla Shumway, Editor.

NEBRASKA

ALBION

ADVISOR (ALBION). 1112 W. State St., Albion, NE 68620. Telephone: 402-395-9965. FAX: 402-395-9969. Pub. Frequency: w. (Tue.) Page Size: tabloid Circulation: 24,000 per issue (free). **Owner(s):** Huse Publishing Co., PO Box 977, Norfolk, NE 68702. Telephone: 402-371-1020. **Management:** Deb Condreny, General Manager. Jerry Huse, Publisher.

ALBION NEWS. PO Box 431, Albion, NE 68620. Telephone: 402-395-2115. FAX: 402-395-2772. Year Established: 1879. Pub. Frequency: w. (Wed.) Page Size: broadsheet. Subscrip. Rate: $.50 newsstand/cover; $20/yr local; $25/yr out of state. Circulation: 3,200 per issue (paid). **Owner(s):** Albion News, See address and contact information above. **Management:** Jean Kaup, Publisher. **Editorial:** Jean Kaup, Editor.

ALMA

HARLAN COUNTY JOURNAL. PO Box 9, Alma, NE 68920-0009. Telephone: 308-928-2143. FAX: 308-928-9914. E-MAIL: journal@frontiernet.net. Year Established: 1896. Pub. Frequency: w. (Thu.) Page Size: broadsheet. Subscrip. Rate: $.75 newsstand/cover; $29/yr mailed local; $33/yr mailed in Nebraska; $42/yr mailed out of state. Adv. Rate: col. inch $4.50 Circulation: 1,500 per issue (paid). **Owner(s):** Jack Krier, See address and contact information above. **Management:** Brandie Nissen, Office Manager. **Editorial:** Michelle Janicek, Editor.

ARAPAHOE

ARAPAHOE PUBLIC MIRROR. 420 Nebraska Ave, Arapahoe, NE 68922. Telephone: 308-962-7261. FAX: 308-962-7262. E-MAIL: arapmir@atcjit.net. Year Established: 1880. Pub. Frequency: w. (Wed) Page Size: broadsheet. Subscrip. Rate: $.75 newsstand/cover; $21.50/yr in state; $26/yr out of state. Circulation: 1,200 per issue (paid). **Owner(s):** Brada Gayle Schutz, Ted M. & Cheri Gill, See address and contact information above. **Management:** Gayle Gill Schutz, Publisher.

ARLINGTON

ARLINGTON CITIZEN. PO Box 460, Arlington, NE 68008. URL: http://www.enterprisepub.com. Mailing Address: PO Box 328, Blair, NE 68008-0328. Year Established: 1954. Pub. Frequency: w. (Thu.) Page Size: broadsheet. Subscrip. Rate: $.50 newsstand/cover; $21/yr in county. Circulation: 800 per issue (paid). **Owner(s):** Blair Enterprise Co., Inc., See address and contact information above. **Management:** Mark Rhoades, Publisher. Lynette Hansen, Advertising Manager. Sarah Babbitt, Circulation Manager. **Editorial:** Melissa Rice, Editor. Scott Kerber, Sports Editor.

ARTHUR

ARTHUR ENTERPRISE, THE. PO Box 165, Arthur, NE 69121. Telephone: 308-764-2402. E-MAIL: artent@neb-sandhills.net. URL: http://www.nebnet.net/arthur/. Year Established: 1911. Pub. Frequency: w. (Thu.) Page Size: tabloid. Subscrip. Rate: $.40 newsstand/cover; $16/yr mailed in county; $18/yr mailed out of state. Circulation: 400 per issue (paid and free). **Owner(s):** Robert J. Crouse, See address and contact information above. **Management:** Robert J. Crouse, Publisher. Karen A. Sizer, Advertising. **Editorial:** Robert J. Crouse, Editor.

ASHLAND

ASHLAND GAZETTE. 1518 Silver St, Ashland, NE 68003. Telephone: 402-944-3397. FAX: 402-944-3398. URL: http://www.ashlandgazette.com. Mailing Address: P.O. Box 127, Ashland, NE 68003. Pub. Frequency: w. (Thu.) Page Size: tabloid. Subscrip. Rate: $24/yr in state; $28/yr mailed out of state. **Owner(s):** Suburban Newspapers, Inc., 1413 S Washington St., Ste 300, Papillion, NE 68045. Telephone: 402-339-3331. FAX: 402-537-2997. **Management:** Dan Collin, Advertising. **Editorial:** Joe Evans, Editor.

ATKINSON

ATKINSON GRAPHIC, THE. 207 E. State St., Atkinson, NE 68713. Telephone: 402-925-5411. Mailing Address: PO Box 159, Atkinson, NE 68713. Year Established: 1882. Pub. Frequency: w. (Wed.) Page Size: broadsheet. Subscrip. Rate: $.50 newsstand/cover; $20.50/yr in state; $26/yr out of state. Circulation: 18,000 morning (paid); 2,100 per issue (paid). **Owner(s):** Gerald Z. & Roxanne Hollingsworth, See address and contact information above. **Management:** Gerald Z. Hollingsworth, Publisher. **Editorial:** Gerald Z. Hollingsworth, Editor.

AUBURN

AUBURN PRESS TRIBUNE. 830 Central Ave., Auburn, NE 68305. Telephone: 402-274-3185. FAX: 402-274-3273. E-MAIL: dwellman@anewspaper.net. URL: http://www.anewspaper.net. Year Established: 1882. Pub. Frequency: w. (Tue.) Page Size: broadsheet. Subscrip. Rate: $.50 newsstand/cover; $42/yr in county; $48/yr out of county; $52/yr mailed out of state. Circulation: 3,000 per issue (paid). **Owner(s):** Auburn Newspapers, See address and contact information above. **Management:** Kendall Neiman, Publisher. **Editorial:** Dennis Morgan, Editor. Darrell Wellman, Managing Editor.

NEMAHA COUNTY HERALD. 830 Central Ave., Auburn, NE 68305. Telephone: 402-274-3185. FAX: 402-274-3273. E-MAIL: dwellman@anewspaper.net. URL: http://www.anewspaper.net. Year Established: 1888. Pub. Frequency: w. (Fri.) Page Size: broadsheet. Subscrip. Rate: $.50 newsstand/cover; $42/yr local; $48/yr mailed out of area; $52/yr mailed out of state. Circulation: 3,000 per issue (paid). **Owner(s):** Auburn Newspapers, See address and contact information above. **Management:** Kendall Neiman, Publisher. **Editorial:** Darrell Wellman, Editor.

AURORA

AURORA NEWS-REGISTER. 1320 K St., Aurora, NE 68818. Telephone: 402-694-2131. E-MAIL: newsregister@hamilton.net. URL: http://www.auroranewsregister.com. Mailing Address: PO Box 70, Aurora, NE 68818-0070. Year Established: 1929. Pub. Frequency: w. (Wed.) Page Size: standard. Subscrip. Rate: $.75 newsstand/cover; $27/yr in county; $31/yr out of county; $37.50/yr out of state. Adv. Rate: col. inch $6.50 Circulation: 4,000 per issue (paid). **Owner(s):** Porchlight Publishing,Inc., See address and contact information above. **Management:** Kurt Johnson, Publisher. Dave Bradley, Advertising Manager. **Editorial:** Kurt Johnson, Editor. Laurie Pfeifer, Managing Editor.

BELLEVUE

BELLEVUE LEADER. ISSN 0193-0389
604 Fort Crook Rd N, Bellevue, NE 68005. Telephone: 402-733-7300. FAX: 402-733-9116. E-MAIL: news@bellevueleader.com. URL: http://www.bellevueleader.com. Year Established: 1973. Pub. Frequency: w. (Wed.) Page Size: broadsheet. Subscrip. Rate: $.50 newsstand/cover; $30/yr in county; $40/yr mailed out of county. Circulation: 5,000 per issue (paid). **Owner(s):** Suburban Newspapers, Inc., 1413 S Washington St., Ste 300, Papillion, NE 68045. Telephone: 402-339-3331. FAX: 402-537-2997. **Management:** Shon Barenklau, Publisher. **Editorial:** Ron Petak, Editor.

BLAIR

WASHINGTON COUNTY ENTERPRISE. PO Box 328, Blair, NE 68008. E-MAIL: mrhoades@enterprisepub.com. URL: http://www.enterprisepub.com. Year Established: 1892. Pub. Frequency: s-w. (Tue. & Fri.) Page Size: broadsheet. Subscrip. Rate: $.75 newsstand/cover; $33/yr in county; $45/yr out of county; $50/yr out of state. Circulation: 4,400 per issue (paid). **Owner(s):** Blair Enterprise Publishing Co., Inc., 138 N. 16th St., Blair, NE 68008. Telephone: 402-426-2221. **Management:** Kenneth H. Rhoades, Co-Publisher. Mark Rhoades, Publisher. Lynette Hanson, Advertising Manager. Sarah Babbitt, Circulation Manager. **Editorial:** Doug Barber, Editor.

WASHINGTON COUNTY PILOT-TRIBUNE. 138 N. 16th St., Blair, NE 68008-0328. Telephone: 402-426-2121. FAX: 402-426-2227. E-MAIL: news@blairnebraska.com. URL: http://www.enterprisepub.com. Mailing Address: PO Box 328, Blair, NE 68008-0328. Year Established: 1905. Pub. Frequency: s-w. (Tue. & Fri.) Page Size: broadsheet. Subscrip. Rate: $.75 newsstand/cover; $36/yr mailed in county; $48/yr mailed out of county; $54/yr mailed out of state. Adv. Rate: col. inch $7.75 Circulation: 3,825 per issue (paid). Owner(s): Blair Enterprise Co., Inc., See address and contact information above. Management: Mark Rhoades, Publisher. Lynette Hansen, Advertising Manager. Sarah Babbitt, Circulation Manager. Editorial: Doug Barber, Editor.

BROKEN ARROW

CUSTER COUNTY CHIEF. 305 S Tenth Ave, Broken Arrow, NE 68822. Telephone: 308-872-2471. FAX: 308-872-2415. E-MAIL: chiefads@custercountychief.com. URL: http://www.custercountychief.com. Mailing Address: PO Box 190, Broken Arrow, NE 68822-0190. Year Established: 1892. Pub. Frequency: s-w. (Mon. & Thu.) Page Size: broadsheet. Subscrip. Rate: $.75 newsstand/cover; $32/yr in area; $42/yr out of area. Adv. Rate: col. inch $5.50 Circulation: 3,800 per issue (paid); 8,400 per issue (free). Owner(s): Horizon Publications, Inc., 1120 N. Carbon St, Ste 100, Marion, IL 62959. Management: Deborah McCaslin, Publisher. Mary Coffman, Advertising. Racheal Chandler, Circulation Manager. Editorial: Kerri Rempp, Managing Editor.

BURWELL

BURWELL TRIBUNE, THE. PO Box 547, Burwell, NE 68823. Telephone: 308-346-4504. FAX: 308-346-4018. Year Established: 1892. Pub. Frequency: w. (Wed.) Page Size: broadsheet. Subscrip. Rate: $.75 newsstand/cover; $27/yr in county; $29/yr out of county; $32/yr mailed out of state. Circulation: 2,000 per issue (paid). Owner(s): Stephen DeLashmutt, See address and contact information above. Management: Stephen DeLashmutt, Publisher. Editorial: Misty S. DeLashmutt, Editor.

SARGENT LEADER. PO Box 547, Burwell, NE 68823. Telephone: 308-346-4504. FAX: 308-346-4018. Pub. Frequency: w. (Wed.) Page Size: broadsheet. Subscrip. Rate: $.75 newsstand/cover; $27/yr in county; $29/yr out of county; $32/yr mailed out of state. Circulation: 2,900 per issue (paid). Owner(s): Stephen DeLashmutt, See address and contact information above. Management: Steve DeLashmutt, General Manager. Johanna Holt, Advertising Manager. Editorial: Misty S. DeLashmutt, Editor.

CENTRAL CITY

CENTRAL CITY REPUBLICAN NONPAREIL. 802 C Ave., Central City, NE 68826. Telephone: 308-946-3081. Year Established: 1883. Pub. Frequency: w. (Thu.) Page Size: tabloid. Subscrip. Rate: $.75 newsstand/cover; $25/yr local; $27.50/yr in state; $32/yr out of state. Adv. Rate: col. inch $4.95 Circulation: 2,300 per issue (paid). Owner(s): Jensen Publishing Co., See address and contact information above. Management: Robert M. Jensen, Publisher. Penny Jensen, Office Manager. Tim Nicholas, Advertising Manager. Editorial: Robert M. Jensen, Editor. Tim Nicholas, Sports.

COLUMBUS

COLUMBUS AREA CHOICE. 1367 33rd Ave., Columbus, NE 68601. Telephone: 402-564-1025. FAX: 402-564-1403. Pub. Frequency: w. (Tue.) Page Size: tabloid Circulation: 25,000 per issue (free). Owner(s): Lee Enterprises, Inc., 201 N. Harrison St., Davenport, IA 52801. Management: Dan Thomas, General Manager.

COZAD

TRI-CITY TRIB. 320 W. Eighth St., Cozad, NE 69130. Telephone: 308-784-3644. FAX: 308-784-3647. E-MAIL: trib@ns.nque.com. Year Established: 1965. Pub. Frequency: w. (Thu.) Page Size: tabloid. Subscrip. Rate: $.50 newsstand/cover; $28/yr in county; $37/yr elsewhere. Circulation: 3,300 per issue (paid). Owner(s): Tri-City Trib, See address and contact information above. Management: Dean Dorsey, Publisher. Toby Roenfeldt, Advertising Manager. Editorial: Dean Dorsey, Editor.

CRETE

CRETE NEWS, THE. PO Box 40, Crete, NE 68333. Telephone: 402-826-2147. E-MAIL: bjfictum@navix.net. Year Established: 1871. Pub. Frequency: w. (Wed.) Page Size: broadsheet. Subscrip. Rate: $.75 newsstand/cover; $26.75/yr in county; $36/yr out of county. Circulation: 4,400 per issue (paid). Owner(s): Crete News, Inc., See address and contact information above. Management: Lloyd Reeves, Publisher. Pat Hier, Advertising Manager. John Reeves, Manager. Editorial: Josh Wolfe, News Editor.

DAVID CITY

BANNER-PRESS (DAVID CITY), THE. 339 E St., David City, NE 68632. Telephone: 402-367-3054. FAX: 402-367-3055. Mailing Address: PO Box 407, David City, NE 68632. Year Established: 1873. Pub. Frequency: w. (Thu.) Page Size: broadsheet. Subscrip. Rate: $.75 newsstand/cover; $30/yr local; $31/yr in state; $35/yr out of state. Circulation: 3,500 per issue (paid). Owner(s): Lee Enterprises, Inc., 201 N. Harrison St., Davenport, IA 52801-1924. Management: Larry Peirce, Publisher. Kim Cummings, Advertising Manager. Editorial: Larry Peirce, Editor.

DESHLER

DESHLER RUSTLER, THE. 307 Alice St., Deshler, NE 68340. Telephone: 402-365-7575. FAX: 402-365-4439. Year Established: 1986. Pub. Frequency: w. (Wed.) Page Size: standard. Subscrip. Rate: $.50 newsstand/cover; $21/yr in state; $25/yr out of state. Circulation: 1,600 per issue (paid). Owner(s): Lois Struve, See address and contact information above. Management: Lois Struve, Publisher. Dawn Schleif, Advertising. Editorial: Lois Struve, Editor-in-Chief. Paulette Hynek, News Editor.

ELKHORN

DOUGLAS COUNTY POST GAZETTE.   ISSN 0746-1437
117 Hillrise Center, Elkhorn, NE 68022. Telephone: 402-289-2329. FAX: 402-289-0861. E-MAIL: dcpostgazette@dcpostgazette.com. URL: http://www.dcpostgazette.com. Mailing Address: PO Box 677, Elkhorn, NE 68022. Year Established: 1895. Pub. Frequency: w. (Tue.) Page Size: broadsheet. Subscrip. Rate: $.50 newsstand/cover; $23/yr in county; $32/yr out of county; $37/yr out of state. Adv. Rate: col. inch $12.39 Circulation: 9,000 per issue (paid and free). Owner(s): Penny Overmann, See address and contact information above. Management: Mike Overmann, General Manager. Penny Overmann, Publisher. Mike Overmann, Advertising Manager. Editorial: Mary Lou Rodgers, Managing Editor.

FAIRBURY

FAIRBURY JOURNAL-NEWS, THE. 516 Fifth St., Fairbury, NE 68352. Telephone: 402-729-6141. E-MAIL: FJN@navix.net. URL: http://www.fairjnews.com. Year Established: 1892. Pub. Frequency: s-w. (Tue. & Fri.) Page Size: standard. Subscrip. Rate: $.50 newsstand/cover; $33/yr in county adj. counties; $50/yr in state & adj. states; $43/yr elsewhere. Circulation: 4,500 per issue (paid). Owner(s): McBattas Publishing Co., See address and contact information above. Management: Fred A. Arnold Jr., Publisher. Elaine Garrett, Office Manager. Susan Bartels, Advertising Manager. Diane Kujath, Circulation Manager.

FALLS CITY

FALLS CITY JOURNAL. 1810 Harlan St, Falls City, NE 68355. Telephone: 402-245-2431. FAX: 402-245-4404. Mailing Address: PO Box 128, Falls City, NE 68355-0128. Year Established: 1857. Pub. Frequency: s-w. (Tue. & Fri.) Page Size: broadsheet.Subscrip. Rate: $.50 newsstand/cover; $38/yr Circulation: 4,100 per issue (paid). Owner(s): Journal Publishing Co., See address and contact information above. Management: Scott Schock, Publisher. Diane Wing, Circulation Manager. Editorial: Scott Schock, Editor. Jason Schock, Sports.

GENEVA

NEBRASKA SIGNAL. 131 N. Ninth St., Geneva, NE 68361. Telephone: 402-759-3117. FAX: 402-759-4214. Year Established: 1874. Pub. Frequency: w. (Wed.) Page Size: broadsheet. Subscrip. Rate: $.75 newsstand/cover; $24.50/yr area; $28.50/yr out of area. Circulation: 3,707 per issue (paid). Owner(s): John Edgecombe, Jr., See address and contact information above. Management: John F. Edgecombe Jr., Publisher. Carol Strothkamp, Circulation Manager. Editorial: Greg Scellin, Editor.

GERING

GERING COURIER. 1428 Tenth St., Gering, NE 69341-2817. Telephone: 308-436-2222. FAX: 308-436-7127. URL: http://www.geringcourier.com. Mailing Address: PO Box 70, Gering, NE 69341-0070. Year Established: 1887. Pub. Frequency: w. (Thu.) Page Size: broadsheet. Subscrip. Rate: $.50 newsstand/cover; $19/yr in county; $21/yr out of county. Circulation: 2,000 per issue (paid). Owner(s): World Newspapers, Inc., Landmark Ctr., 1299 Farnam St., 15th Fl., Omaha, NE 68102-1841. Telephone: 402-444-1000. FAX: 402-345-9115. Management: Brad Staman, Publisher. Carole Steele, Advertising Manager. Editorial: Brad Staman, Editor. Jerry Purvis, Reporter.

LEXINGTON

LEXINGTON CLIPPER-HERALD. 114 W. Fifth St., Lexington, NE 68850-0599. Telephone: 308-324-5511. FAX: 308-324-5240. E-MAIL: terriebaker@lxch.com. Mailing Address: PO Box 599, Lexington, NE 68850-0599. Year Established: 1891. Pub. Frequency: s-w. (Wed. & Sat.) Page Size: broadsheet. Subscrip. Rate: $.50 newsstand/cover; $40/yr mailed in county; $49/yr mailed elsewhere. Circulation: 4,100 per issue (paid). Owner(s): World Newspapers, Inc., Landmark Ctr., 1299 Farnam St., 15th Fl., Omaha, NE 68102-1841. Telephone: 402-444-1000. FAX: 402-345-9115. Management: Terrie Baker, Publisher. Ann Johnson, Advertising Manager. Milette Ramm, Circulation Manager. Leona Buhlman, Business Manager. Editorial: Laurie Cicotello, Editor.

LINCOLN

LINCOLN JOURNAL STAR. 926 P St., Lincoln, NE 68508. Telephone: 402-475-4200. FAX: 402-473-7466. E-MAIL: mvtrio@safelink. URL: http://www.journalstar.com. Year Established: 1884. Pub. Frequency: w. (Wed.) Page Size: tabloid. Subscrip. Rate: $24/yr mailed in county. Adv. Rate: col. inch $6 Freelance Pay: $0.80/column-inch. Circulation: 30,000 per issue (free). Owner(s): Lee Enterprises, Inc., 201 N. Harrison St, Ste 600, Davenport, IA 52801-1924. Management: Juanita Rarick, Advertising. Tom Hiskey, Advertising Manager. Brady Svendgard, Circulation Manager. Editorial: Kathy Rutledge, Editor.

WOOD RIVER JOURNAL, THE. 926 P. St., Lincoln, NE 68508. Telephone: 402-475-4200. FAX: 402-473-7414. E-MAIL: wrjidaho@micron.net. URL: http://www.wrjournal.com. Year Established: 1881. Pub. Frequency: w. (Wed.) Page Size: tabloid. Subscrip. Rate: $25/yr in county $59/yr out of cy. Wire Service(s): AP. Circulation: 13,500 per issue (paid and free). Owner(s): Lee Enterprises, Inc., See address and contact information above. Management: Kim Patterson, Publisher. Editorial: Kristian Kennedy, Editor.

LYONS

LYONS MIRROR-SUN. 205 N. Second St., Lyons, NE 68038. Telephone: 402-687-2616. FAX: 402-687-2617. Mailing Address: PO Box 59, Lyons, NE 68038-0059. Year Established: 1883. Pub. Frequency: w. (Thu.) Page Size: broadsheet. Subscrip. Rate: $.65 newsstand/cover; $32/yr local; $38/yr elsewhere. Adv. Rate: col. inch $4.25 Circulation: 1,500 per issue (paid). Owner(s): Bobbie & Dewaine Gahan, 215 N. Engdahl Ave., Oakland, NE 68045. Telephone: 402-685-6229. Management: Bobbie Gahan, Publisher. Editorial: Jodie Jordan, Editor.

MINDEN

MINDEN COURIER, THE. 429 N. Colorado Ave., Minden, NE 68959-0379. Telephone: 308-832-2220. FAX: 308-832-2221. E-MAIL: courier@alltel.net. Year Established: 1890. Pub. Frequency: w. (Wed.) Page Size: broadsheet. Subscrip. Rate: $.75 newsstand/cover; $23/yr mailed in state; $25/yr mailed out of state. Adv. Rate: col. inch $5.50 Circulation: 2,800 per issue (paid). Owner(s): John & JoAnn Edgecombe, See address and contact information above. Management: JoAnn Edgecombe, Publisher. Editorial: Mike Gokie, Editor.

NORFOLK

NORFOLK AREA SHOPPER, THE. 404 Norfolk Ave., Norfolk, NE 68701. Telephone: 402-379-4100. FAX: 402-379-1289. E-MAIL: ads@norfolkareashopper.com. Pub. Frequency: w. (Wed.) Page Size: tabloid Circulation: 31,645 per issue (free). Owner(s): Northeast Shoppers LLC, PO Box 977, Norfolk, NE 68702. Telephone: 402-371-1020. FAX: 402-371-5802. Management: Julie Hermsen, General Manager. Debbie Windedahl, Business Manager.

O'NEILL

HOLT COUNTY INDEPENDENT. 114 N Fourth St, O'Neill, NE 68763. Telephone: 402-336-1220. FAX: 402-336-1222. E-MAIL: hci@inetnebr.com. Mailing Address: P O Box 360, O'Neill, NE 68763. Pub. Frequency: w. (Thu.) Page Size: broadsheet. Subscrip. Rate: $.65 newsstand/cover; $30/yr in county; $35/yr out of county; $40/yr out of state. Circulation: 3,800 per issue (paid). Owner(s): Holt County Independent, See address and contact information above. Management: James T Miles, General Manager. George T Miles, Advertising Manager. Editorial: George T Miles, Editor.

OAKLAND

OAKLAND INDEPENDENT. 217 N. Oakland Ave., Oakland, NE 68045-0085. Telephone: 402-685-5624. FAX: 402-685-5625. Mailing Address: PO Box 85, Oakland, NE 68045-0085. Year Established: 1880. Pub. Frequency: w. (Thu.) Page Size: standard. Subscrip. Rate: $.75 newsstand/cover; $35/yr local; $42/yr elsewhere. Circulation: 2,000 per issue (paid). **Owner(s):** Bobbie & Dewaine Gahan, 215 N. Engdahl Ave., Oakland, NE 68045. Telephone: 402-685-6229. **Management:** Dewaine Gahan, President. Bobbie Gahan, Publisher. **Editorial:** Bobbie Gahan, Editor.

OGALLALA

KEITH COUNTY NEWS. 116 W. A St., Ogallala, NE 69153. Telephone: 308-284-4046. FAX: 308-284-4048. Mailing Address: P.O. Box 359, Ogallala, NE 69153. Year Established: 1885. Pub. Frequency: s-w. (Mon. & Wed.) Page Size: broadsheet.Subscrip. Rate: $.50 newsstand/cover; $37/yr Circulation: 4,300 per issue (paid). **Owner(s):** Jeff Headley, Judy Curtis, Marilee Perlinger, See address and contact information above. **Management:** Jeff Headley, Publisher. Marilee Perlinger, Advertising Manager. Larry Strasburg, Circulation Manager. **Editorial:** Jeff Headley, Editor. Mary Pierce, News Editor. Herb Teter, Sports Editor.

OMAHA

NUECES COUNTY RECORD STAR. 7405 Irvington Rd, Omaha, NE 68122. Telephone: 402-331-3727. FAX: 402-331-4834. E-MAIL: recordstar@isl.com. URL: http://www.recordstar.com. Mailing Address: PO Box 1192, Robstown, TX 78380. Year Established: 1919. Pub. Frequency: w. (Thu.) Page Size: broadsheet. Subscrip. Rate: $.75 newsstand/cover; $23/yr in county. Circulation: 7,000 per issue (paid). **Owner(s):** American Consolidated Media, Inc., See address and contact information above. **Management:** Tony Morris, General Manager. **Editorial:** Jeff Tucker, Managing Editor. Tim Olmeda, News Editor.

OMAHA STAR. 2216 N. 24th St., Omaha, NE 68110. Telephone: 402-346-4041. FAX: 402-346-4064. E-MAIL: marguerita@omahastarinc.com. URL: http://www.omahastarinc.com. Mailing Address: PO Box 11128, Omaha, NE 68111. Year Established: 1938. Pub. Frequency: w. (Thu.) Page Size: standard. Subscrip. Rate: $.50 newsstand/cover; $30/yr local; $35/yr mailed out of area. Circulation: 30,000 per issue (paid). **Owner(s):** Marguerita L. Washington, See address and contact information above. **Management:** Dr. Marguerita L Washington, Publisher. Charlene Spencer, Office Manager. Phyllis Hicks, Advertising. Charlene Spencer, Advertising Director. Eleanor Riggs, Circulation Manager. Phyllis Hicks, Marketing Director. **Editorial:** Dr. Marguerita L Washington, Editor.

ORD

ORD QUIZ. 305 S. 16th St., Ord, NE 68862-1752. Telephone: 308-728-3262. FAX: 308-728-5715. E-MAIL: quiz@frontiernet.net. URL: http://www.ordquiz.com. Year Established: 1882. Pub. Frequency: w. (Wed.) Page Size: broadsheet. Subscrip. Rate: $.75 newsstand/cover; $36/yr. Adv. Rate: col. inch $6.30 Circulation: 2,200 per issue (paid). **Owner(s):** Quiz Graphic Arts, Inc., See address and contact information above. **Management:** Lynn Griffith, Publisher. **Editorial:** Lacy Griffith, Editor. Bonnie Griffith, Society Editor.

OVERTON

BEACON OBSERVER, THE. PO Box 330, Overton, NE 68863. Telephone: 308-987-2451. FAX: 308-987-2452. Year Established: 1898. Pub. Frequency: w. (Thu.) Page Size: broadsheet. Subscrip. Rate: $.75 newsstand/cover; $20/yr home delivery in county; $27/yr mailed out of county; $36/yr mailed out of state. Circulation: 1,700 per issue (controlled and free). **Owner(s):** Norman Taylor, See address and contact information above. **Management:** Norman Taylor, Publisher. **Editorial:** Norman Taylor, Editor.

PAPILLION

GRETNA BREEZE. 1413 S Washington St., Ste 300, Papillion, NE 68045. Telephone: 402-339-3331. FAX: 402-537-2997. E-MAIL: advertising@papilliontimes.com. URL: http://www.gretnabreeze.com. Pub. Frequency: w. (Thu.) Page Size: tabloid. Subscrip. Rate: $20/yr in county; $27/yr in adj. cys.; $32/yr mailed out of county. **Owner(s):** Suburban Newspapers, Inc., See address and contact information above. **Management:** Shon Barenklau, Publisher. Shon Baren Klau, Advertising. Melissa Vanek, Circulation Director. **Editorial:** Ron Petak, Editor. Mitch Beaumont, Managing Editor.

LAVISTA SUN. 1413 S Washington St., Ste 300, Papillion, NE 68045. Telephone: 402-339-3331. FAX: 402-537-2997. E-MAIL: advertising@lavistasun.com. URL: http://www.lavistasun.com. Pub. Frequency: w. (Thu.) Page Size: tabloid. Subscrip. Rate: $35/yr in county; $48/yr mailed adj.cys; $56/yr mailed out of county. Circulation: 20,000 per issue (paid and controlled). **Owner(s):** Suburban Newspapers, Inc., See address and contact information above. **Management:** Shon Barenklau, Publisher. Shon Baren Klau, Advertising. Melissa Vanek, Circulation Director. **Editorial:** Ron Petak, Editor. Mitch Beaumont, Managing Editor.

PAPILLION TIMES. ISSN 0883-1394
1413 S Washington St., Ste 300, Papillion, NE 68045. Telephone: 402-339-3331. FAX: 402-537-2997. E-MAIL: advertising@papilliontimes.com. URL: http://www.papilliontimes.com. Year Established: 1874. Pub. Frequency: w. (Thu.) Page Size: broadsheet. Subscrip. Rate: $.50 newsstand/cover; $35/yr home delivery in county; $48/yr mailed adj. cys; $56/yr mailed elsewhere. Adv. Rate: col. inch $15.75 Freelance Pay: $25/story. Circulation: 20,000 per issue (paid and free). **Owner(s):** Suburban Newspapers, Inc., See address and contact information above. **Management:** Shon Barenklau, Publisher. Shon Baren Klau, Advertising. Melissa Vanek, Circulation Director. Ann Oatman, Business Manager. **Editorial:** Mitch Beaumont, Managing Editor.

RALSTON RECORDER. 1413 S Washington St., Ste 300, Papillion, NE 68045. Telephone: 402-339-3331. FAX: 402-537-2997. E-MAIL: news@papilliontimes.com. URL: http://www.ralstonrecorder.com. Pub. Frequency: w. (Thu.) Page Size: tabloid. Subscrip. Rate: $18/yr in county; $27/yr in adj. cys.; $30/yr mailed out of county. **Owner(s):** Suburban Newspapers, Inc., See address and contact information above. **Management:** Shon Barenklau, Publisher. Shon Baren Klau, Advertising. Melissa Vanek, Circulation Director. **Editorial:** Ron Petak, Editor. Mitch Beaumont, Managing Editor.

PLAINVIEW

PLAINVIEW NEWS (PLAINVIEW, NE), THE. PO Box 9, Plainview, NE 68769-0009. Telephone: 402-582-4921. FAX: 402-582-4922. E-MAIL: plvwnews@plvwtelco.net. URL: http://www.plvwtelco.net/plvwnews. Year Established: 1892. Pub. Frequency: w. (Wed.) Page Size: broadsheet. Subscrip. Rate: $.50 newsstand/cover; $19/yr in county; $25/yr out of county; $28/yr out of state. Adv. Rate: col. inch $3.80 Circulation: 1,751 per issue (paid). **Owner(s):** Plainviews News, Inc., The, See address and contact information above. **Management:** Brook D Curtis, General Manager. **Editorial:** Brook D Curtis, Editor.

PLATTSMOUTH

PLATTSMOUTH JOURNAL, THE. 410 Main St., Plattsmouth, NE 68048. Telephone: 402-296-2141. FAX: 402-296-3401. E-MAIL: plattsmouth.advertising3@lee.net. URL: http://www.cass-news.com. Mailing Address: PO Box 250, Plattsmouth, NE 68048. Year Established: 1882. Pub. Frequency: w. (Thu.) Page Size: broadsheet. Subscrip. Rate: $.75 newsstand/cover; $39.50/yr home delivery in county. Adv. Rate: col. inch $6 Circulation: 5,400 per issue (paid). **Owner(s):** Lee Corp., See address and contact information above. **Management:** Jim Ristow, Publisher. Kevin Turner, Advertising Manager. Bryan Mowrer, Circulation Manager. **Editorial:** Patti Jo Petersen, Managing Editor. Brent Hardin, Sports Editor.

SCHUYLER

SCHUYLER SUN, THE. 1112 C St., Schuyler, NE 68661. Telephone: 402-352-2424. FAX: 402-352-3332. Mailing Address: PO Box 506, Schuyler, NE 68661-0506. Year Established: 1871. Pub. Frequency: w. (Thu.) Page Size: broadsheet. Subscrip. Rate: $.75 newsstand/cover; $28/yr mailed in state; $30/yr mailed out of state. Circulation: 2,784 per issue (paid). **Owner(s):** Lee Enterprises, Inc., 201 N. Harrison St., Davenport, IA 52801-1924. **Management:** Michael Rea, Publisher. Curt Mentzer, Advertising Manager. **Editorial:** Michael Rea, Editor.

SEWARD

SEWARD COUNTY INDEPENDENT. 129 S. Sixth St., Seward, NE 68434. Telephone: 402-643-3676. FAX: 402-643-6774. URL: http://www.sewardindependent.com. Mailing Address: PO Box 449, Seward, NE 68434-0449. Year Established: 1897. Pub. Frequency: w. (Wed.) Page Size: broadsheet. Subscrip. Rate: $.75 newsstand/cover; $34/yr in county; $36/yr out of adj. cy.; $48/yr in state; $51/yr out of state. Circulation: 3,900 per issue (paid). **Owner(s):** Blair Enterprise Co., Inc., 138 N. 16th St., Blair, NE 68008-0328. Telephone: 402-426-2121. **Management:** Kevin L Zading, Publisher. Lynn Dance, Advertising Manager. Tammy Leff, Circulation Manager. **Editorial:** Marcia Goff, Managing Editor. Stephanie Crofton, Sports Editor.

SOUTH SIOUX CITY

DAKOTA COUNTY STAR, THE. 1000 W. 29th, Ste 116, South Sioux City, NE 68776-0157. Telephone: 402-494-4264. FAX: 402-494-2414. E-MAIL: news@dakotacountystar.com. Mailing Address: PO Box 159, South Sioux City, NE 68776-0159. Year Established: 1909. Pub. Frequency: w. (Thu.) Page Size: broadsheet. Subscrip. Rate: $.75 newsstand/cover; $35/yr in county; $45/yr in state; $55/yr out of state. Adv. Rate: col. inch $11 Circulation: 3,000 per issue (paid); 11,000 per issue (free). **Owner(s):** Enterprise Publishing, Inc., PO Box 328, Blair, NE 68008-0328. Telephone: 402-426-2121. **Management:** Mark Rhoades, Publisher. Pat Rooney, Advertising Manager.

SPRINGVIEW

SPRINGVIEW HERALD. 102 S. Main St., Springview, NE 68778-0369. Telephone: 402-497-3651. FAX: 402-497-2651. E-MAIL: herald91@threeriver.net. Mailing Address: P.O. Box 369, Springview, NE 68778-0369. Year Established: 1886. Pub. Frequency: w. (Wed.) Page Size: tabloid. Subscrip. Rate: $.50 newsstand/cover; $22/yr local; $26/yr in state; $26/yr out of state. Adv. Rate: col. inch $4.25 Circulation: 800 per issue (paid and free). **Owner(s):** Keya Paha Publishing, LLC, See address and contact information above. **Management:** Aleta Newtson, Advertising Manager. Donna Ludemann, Circulation Manager.

SUPERIOR

SUPERIOR EXPRESS, THE. ISSN 0740-0969
148 E. Third St., Superior, NE 68978. Telephone: 402-879-3291. FAX: 402-879-3463. E-MAIL: tse@superiorne.com. URL: http://www.superiorne.com. Mailing Address: PO Box 408, Superior, NE 88978-0408. Year Established: 1900. Pub. Frequency: w. (Thu.) Page Size: broadsheet. Subscrip. Rate: $.50 newsstand/cover; $23/yr in state; $24.50/yr in KS; $34/yr elsewhere. Adv. Rate: col. inch $4 Circulation: 3,500 per issue (paid). **Owner(s):** Superior Publishing Co., See address and contact information above. **Management:** Bill Blauvelt, Publisher. Rita Blauvelt, Advertising Manager. **Editorial:** Chuck Mittan, Feature Editor.

SUTHERLAND

COURIER-TIMES. 824 First St., Sutherland, NE 69165. Telephone: 308-386-4617. FAX: 308-386-2437. E-MAIL: suthcourier@gpcom.net. Mailing Address: PO Box 367, Sutherland, NE 69165-0367. Year Established: 1895. Pub. Frequency: w. (Wed.) Page Size: tabloid. Subscrip. Rate: $.50 newsstand/cover; $20/yr in state; $25/yr out of state. Adv. Rate: col. inch $5 Circulation: 1,400 per issue (paid). **Owner(s):** Courier-Times, Inc., See address and contact information above. **Management:** Trenda Seifer, Publisher. **Editorial:** Ray Seifer, Sports Editor.

SYRACUSE

SYRACUSE JOURNAL-DEMOCRAT. 123 W 17th St, Syracuse, NE 68446. Telephone: 402-269-2135. FAX: 402-269-2392. Mailing Address: PO Box 0, Syracuse, NE 68446. Year Established: 1878. Pub. Frequency: w. (Thu.) Page Size: tabloid. Subscrip. Rate: $.75 newsstand/cover; $50/yr in county & Fremont, IA cy; $60/yr mailed out of area in NE & IA; $94/yr mailed elsewhere. Circulation: 3,415 per issue (paid). **Owner(s):** GateHouse Media, Inc, 350 WillowBrook Office Park, Fairport, NY 14450. Telephone: 585-598-0030. FAX: 585-248-2631. **Management:** Tim Larson, Publisher. Kathleen Kaufman, Advertising Manager. Janet Entler, Circulation Manager. **Editorial:** Tammy Pearson, Executive Editor.

TEKAMAH

PLAINDEALER, THE. PO Box 239, Tekamah, NE 68061. E-MAIL: support@midwestmessenger.com. URL: http://www.midwestmessenger.com. Pub. Frequency: w. Page Size: tabloid. Subscrip. Rate: $32/yr mailed in county; $40/yr mailed out of county. Circulation: 1,800 per issue (paid). **Owner(s):** Lee Agri-Media, Inc., 4023 State St, Bismark, ND 58803. Telephone: 701-255-4905. FAX: 800-594-8433. **Management:** Joe Zink, General Manager. Susan McAllister, Operations Manager. Amber Smith, Advertising Manager. Jodie Jordan, Circulation Manager. **Editorial:** Mark Jackson, Editor.

WAHOO

WAHOO NEWSPAPER. 564 N Broadway, Wahoo, NE 68066. Telephone: 402-443-4162. FAX: 402-443-4459. E-MAIL: wn55758@navix.net. URL: http://www.wahoonews.com. Year Established: 1885. Pub. Frequency: w. (Thu.) Page Size: broadsheet. Subscrip. Rate: $.75 newsstand/cover; $33/yr mailed in state; $38/yr mailed out of state. Circulation: 4,500 per issue (paid). **Owner(s):** Suburban Newspapers, Inc., 1413 S Washington St., Ste 300, Papillion, NE 68045. **Management:** Dan Collin, Advertising. Sue Lucas, Classified Adv. Mgr.. **Editorial:** Joe Evans, Editor. Jason Unger, Sports Editor.

WAVERLY

WAVERLY NEWS. 14210 Kenilworth, Waverly, NE 68462-0100. Telephone: 402-786-2344. FAX: 402-786-2343. E-MAIL: news@newswaverly.com. URL: http://www.newswaverly.com. Mailing Address: P.O. Box 100, Waverly, NE 68462. Pub. Frequency: w. (Thu.) Page Size: tabloid. Subscrip. Rate: $24/yr in county; $54/yr out of county. **Owner(s):** Suburban Newspapers, Inc., 1413 S Washington St., Ste 300, Papillion, NE 68045. Telephone: 402-339-3331. FAX: 402-537-2997. **Management:** Shon Baren Klau, Advertising. Melissa Vanek, Circulation Director. **Editorial:** Joe Evans, Editor.

WAYNE

WAYNE HERALD. 114 Main St., Wayne, NE 68787-0070. Telephone: 402-375-2600. FAX: 402-375-1888. E-MAIL: whclass@midlands.net. Mailing Address: PO Box 70, Wayne, NE 68787. Year Established: 1876. Pub. Frequency: w. (Thu.) Page Size: broadsheet. Subscrip. Rate: $.75 newsstand/cover; $33/yr area; $35/yr mailed in state; $48/yr mailed out of state. Adv. Rate: col. inch $7.13 Circulation: 2,000 per issue (paid). **Owner(s):** Smith Newspapers, Inc., PO Box 27, Fort Payne, AL 35967. Telephone: 205-845-5510. FAX: 205-845-5509. **Management:** Kevin Peterson, Publisher. Melissa Urbance, Advertising. **Editorial:** Clara Osten, Managing Editor.

WEST POINT

WEST POINT NEWS. PO Box 40, West Point, NE 68788. Telephone: 402-372-2461. FAX: 402-372-3530. E-MAIL: wpnews@cableone.net. URL: http://www.wpnews.com. Year Established: 1870. Pub. Frequency: w. (Wed.) Page Size: broadsheet. Subscrip. Rate: $.85 newsstand/cover; $34.75/yr mailed in county & adj. counties; $44.75/yr mailed in state; $54/yr mailed out of state. Circulation: 3,500 per issue (paid). **Owner(s):** Tom Kelly, See address and contact information above. **Management:** Tom Kelly, Publisher. Dawn Gall, Advertising. Colleen Ernesti, Circulation Manager. **Editorial:** Willis Mahannah, Editor.

YORK

TRADE & TRANSACTIONS. 400 Lincoln Ave., York, NE 68467. Telephone: 402-362-5561. FAX: 402-362-3697. Pub. Frequency: w. (Tue.) Page Size: broadsheet Circulation: 24,000 per issue (free). **Owner(s):** Morris Multimedia, Inc., PO Box 936, Augusta, GA 30903. Telephone: 706-724-0851. FAX: 706-722-7128. **Management:** Tom Schultz, General Manager. Brad Bolzki, Circulation Manager.

NEVADA

BOULDER CITY

BOULDER CITY NEWS. 508 Nevada Hwy., Ste.1, Boulder City, NV 89005. Telephone: 702-293-2302. FAX: 702-294-0977. E-MAIL: editor@hbctub.com. Mailing Address: PO Box 60065, Boulder City, NV 89006. Year Established: 1937. Pub. Frequency: w. (Thu.) Page Size: broadsheet. Subscrip. Rate: $.50 newsstand/cover; $20/yr home delivery; $30/yr mailed. Circulation: 5,500 per issue (paid). **Owner(s):** HBC Publications, 2290 Corporate Cir., Ste 250, Henderson, NV 89074. Telephone: 702-435-7700. **Management:** Coleen O'Callaghan, Co-Publisher. Nelson Oshita, Sales Manager. **Editorial:** Jean Norman, Managing Editor.

GARDNERVILLE

RECORD-COURIER (GARDNERVILLE), THE. 1503 Highway 395 N., Ste. G, Gardnerville, NV 89410. Telephone: 775-782-5121. FAX: 775-782-6152. E-MAIL: rc@tahoe.com. URL: http://www.recordcourier.com. Year Established: 1880. Pub. Frequency: 3/w. (Wed., Fri & Sun.) Page Size: standard. Subscrip. Rate: $.50 newsstand/cover; $46/yr local; $56/yr mailed. Circulation: 7,500 per issue (paid). **Owner(s):** Swift Newspapers, Inc., 500 Double Eagle Ct., Reno, NV 89511. Telephone: 775-850-7676. FAX: 775-850-7677. **Management:** Janet Geary, Publisher. Joanna Reeves, Advertising Director. Tony King, Circulation Manager. **Editorial:** Kurt J Hildebrand, Editor. Joey Crandall, Sports.

HAWTHORNE

MINERAL COUNTY INDEPENDENT-NEWS. 501 D St., Hawthorne, NV 89415-1270. Telephone: 775-945-2414. FAX: 775-945-1270. Mailing Address: PO Box 1270, Hawthorne, NV 89415-1270. Year Established: 1928. Pub. Frequency: w. (Thu.) Page Size: broadsheet. Subscrip. Rate: $.50 newsstand/cover; $30/yr in county; $35 mailed for 2 yrs. out of county. Circulation: 2,600 per issue (paid). **Owner(s):** Frank E., Tony, Ted Hughes, 501 D St., Hawthorne, NV 89415. Telephone: 775-945-2414. **Management:** Frank E. Hughes, Publisher. **Editorial:** Frank Hughes, Editor. Ted Hughes, Managing Editor.

HENDERSON

HENDERSON HOME NEWS. 2290 Corporate Cir., Ste. 250, Henderson, NV 89074-7713. E-MAIL: homenewsnv@aol.com. Pub. Frequency: s-w. (Tue. & Fri.) Page Size: broadsheet. Subscrip. Rate: $.50 newsstand/cover; $30/yr carrier delivery local; $50/yr mailed local. Adv. Rate: col. inch $15.50 Circulation: 7,600 per issue (paid). **Owner(s):** HBC Publications, Inc., See address and contact information above. **Management:** Colleeen O'Callaghan, Co-Publisher. Nelson Oshita, Sales Manager. **Editorial:** Jean Norman, Managing Editor.

INCLINE VILLAGE

NORTH LAKE TAHOE BONANZA. ISSN 0192-3129
925 Tahoe Blvd., Ste. 206, Incline Village, NV 89451. Telephone: 775-831-4666. FAX: 775-831-4222. E-MAIL: editor@tahoebonanza.com. URL: http://www.tahoebonanza.com. Mailing Address: PO Box 7820, Incline Village, NV 89452. Year Established: 1964. Pub. Frequency: w. (Wed., Fri. & Sun.) Page Size: standard. Subscrip. Rate: $48.25/yr home delivery in county; $90/yr mailed out of county. Circulation: 6,500 per issue (paid and free). **Owner(s):** Swift Newspapers, Inc., 500 Double Eagle Ct., Reno, NV 89511. Telephone: 775-850-7676. FAX: 775-850-7677. **Management:** Mary Jurkonis, Publisher. Cherie Hackelberg, Circulation Manager. Linda Carey, Business Manager. **Editorial:** Erin Roth, Editor. Travis Ambrose, Production Manager. Emma Garrard, Photographer.

LAS VEGAS

EUREKA SENTINEL. PO Box 70, Las Vegas, NV 89125-0070. Telephone: 702-477-3846. FAX: 702-251-0736. Year Established: 1870. Pub. Frequency: w. (Thu.) Page Size: tabloid. Subscrip. Rate: $.35 newsstand/cover; $26/yr in county $26/yr out of cy. Circulation: 550 per issue (paid). **Owner(s):** Stephens Media LLC, See address and contact information above. **Management:** Ken Kliewer, Publisher. **Editorial:** Kent Harper, Editor.

LAS VEGAS TODAY. PO Box 370250, Las Vegas, NV 89137. Telephone: 702-221-5056. Year Established: 1975. Pub. Frequency: w. (Wed.) Page Size: broadsheet Circulation: 100,000 per issue (free). **Owner(s):** Desert Media Group, See address and contact information above. **Management:** Mark Clark, General Manager. James Westmoreland, Advertising Manager. **Editorial:** Mark Clark, Editor.

TONOPAH TIMES-BONANZA & GOLDFIELD NEWS. PO Box 70, Las Vegas, NV 89125-0070. Telephone: 702-477-3846. FAX: 702-251-0736. Pub. Frequency: w. (Thu.) Page Size: tabloid. Subscrip. Rate: $.35 newsstand/cover; $29/yr in county. Circulation: 2,600 per issue (paid). **Owner(s):** Stephens Media LLC, See address and contact information above. **Management:** Marie Wujek, Publisher. Bobby Jean Roberts, Advertising Manager. **Editorial:** Doug McMurdo, Managing Editor.

LAUGHLIN

COLORADO RIVER WEEKENDER. 3100 S Needles Hwy, Ste 700, Laughlin, NV 89028. Telephone: 702-298-6090. FAX: 702-298-3626. URL: http://www.crweekender.com. Year Established: 1986. Pub. Frequency: w. (Fri.) Page Size: tabloid Circulation: 10,000 per issue (free). **Owner(s):** Brehm Communications, Inc., 16644 W. Bernardo Dr., Ste. 300, San Diego, CA 92127. Telephone: 619-451-6200. **Management:** Paul Stubler, General Manager. Chuck Rathbun, Publisher. Dave Horchak, Circulation Manager. Kathy Jones, Classified Adv. Mgr.. Sue Anderson, Business Manager.

LAUGHLIN NEVADA TIMES, THE. 3100 S Needles Hwy, Ste 700, Laughlin, NV 89028. Telephone: 702-298-6090. FAX: 702-298-3626. URL: http://www.laughlintimes.com. Year Established: 1990. Pub. Frequency: w. (Wed.) Page Size: tabloid Circulation: 10,000 per issue (free). **Owner(s):** Brehm Communications, Inc., 16644 W. Bernardo Dr., Ste. 300, San Diego, CA 92127. Telephone: 619-451-6200. **Management:** Paul Stubler, General Manager. Chuck Rathbun, Publisher. Dave Horchak, Circulation Manager. Kathy Jones, Classified Adv. Mgr.. **Editorial:** Robin Richards, Editor.

LOVELOCK

LOVELOCK REVIEW-MINER. 1475 Cornell Ave., Ste. 500, Lovelock, NV 89419. Telephone: 775-273-7245. FAX: 775-273-0500. E-MAIL: wendy@r-miner.lovelock.nv.us. URL: http://www.nevadarancher.com. Year Established: 1903. Pub. Frequency: w. (Thu.) Page Size: broadsheet. Subscrip. Rate: $.50 newsstand/cover; $26/yr in state; $36/yr mailed out of state; $43/yr mailed foreign. Circulation: 1,700 per issue (paid). **Owner(s):** Gwendolyn Bogh Carter, See address and contact information above. **Management:** Gwendolyn Carter, Publisher. Wendy Butler, Advertising. **Editorial:** Michelle Willms, Editor.

PAHRUMP

PAHRUMP VALLEY TIMES. 2160 E Calvada Blvd, Ste A, Pahrump, NV 89048. Telephone: 775-727-5102. FAX: 775-727-5309. E-MAIL: info@pvtimes.com. URL: http://www.pahrumpvalleytimes.com/. Year Established: 1981. Pub. Frequency: s-w. (Wed. & Fri.; w. until 1996) **Owner(s):** Pahrump Valley Times, See address and contact information above. **Management:** Marie Wujek, Publisher. **Editorial:** Mark Smith, Editor. Chuck King, Production Manager.

RENO

RENO NEWS & REVIEW. 708 N. Center St., Reno, NV 89501. Telephone: 775-324-4440. FAX: 775-324-4572. URL: http://www.newsreview.com/reno. Year Established: 1995. Pub. Frequency: w. (Thu.) Page Size: tabloid.Subscrip. Rate: $65/yr mailed Circulation: 27,000 per issue (free). **Owner(s):** Chico Community Publishing, Inc., 1015 20th St., Sacramento, CA 95814. Telephone: 916-498-1234. **Management:** John Murphy, General Manager. Jeff von Kaenel, President. Karen Brooke, Business Manager. **Editorial:** D. Brian Burghart, Editor. Anne Lesemann, Production Manager. Kat Kerlin, Art Editor. Dennis Myers, News Editor.Readers: Adults 21-54

WINNEMUCCA

HUMBOLDT SUN. ISSN 1082-2976
1022 S. Grass Valley Rd., Winnemucca, NV 89445. Telephone: 775-623-5011. FAX: 775-623-5243. E-MAIL: editorial@humboldtsun.com. URL: http://www.humboldtsun.com. Mailing Address: PO Box 3000, Winnemucca, NV 89446. Year Established: 1870. Pub. Frequency: s-w. (Tues. & Fri.) Page Size: broadsheet. Subscrip. Rate: $.50 newsstand/cover; $53/yr in county. **Wire Service(s):** AP. Circulation: 4,000 evening (paid). **Owner(s):** Diversified Suburban Newspapers (DSN Corp.), See address and contact information above. **Management:** Holly Rudy James, General Manager. Peter Bernhard, Publisher. **Editorial:** David Gouger, Editor. Tony Erquiga, Sports Writer.

YERINGTON

FERNLEY LEADER-DAYTON COURIER. 207 W. Goldfield Ave., Yerington, NV 89447. Telephone: 775-463-4242. FAX: 775-463-5547. E-MAIL: mvn@tele-net.net. Year Established: 1983. Pub. Frequency: w. (Wed.) Page Size: broadsheet. Subscrip. Rate: $.50 newsstand/cover; $21.50/yr. Adv. Rate: col. inch $4.90 Circulation: 3,500 per issue (controlled and free). **Owner(s):** Mason Valley News, Inc., See address and contact information above. **Management:** Dave Sanford, Publisher. Debra Hogarth, Advertising Manager. **Editorial:** Ami Ridling, Editor. Robert Perea, Sports.

MASON VALLEY NEWS. 207 W. Goldfield St., Yerington, NV 89447. Telephone: 775-463-4242. FAX: 775-463-5547. URL: http://www.masonvalleynews.com. Mailing Address: PO Box 841, Yerington, NV 89447. Year Established: 1917. Pub. Frequency: w. (Fri.) Page Size: broadsheet. Subscrip. Rate: $.50 newsstand/cover; $25/yr. Adv. Rate: col. inch $5.70 Circulation: 4,000 per issue (controlled and free). **Owner(s):** Gannett Company, Inc., 7950 Jones Branch Dr., McLean, VA 22107-0001. Telephone: 703-854-6000. **Management:** David Sanford, Publisher. Debra Hogarth, Advertising. **Editorial:** David Sanford, Editor. Robert Perea, Sports.

NEW HAMPSHIRE

BERLIN

BERLIN REPORTER, THE. 151 Main St., Berlin, NH 03570. Telephone: 603-752-1200. FAX: 603-752-2339. E-MAIL: berlinreporter@salmonpress.com. URL: http://www.breporter.com. Mailing Address: PO Box 38, Berlin, NH 03570. Year Established: 1897. Pub. Frequency: w. (Wed.) Page Size: tabloid. Subscrip. Rate: $.50 newsstand/cover; $21 home delivery for 6 mos.; $34/yr home delivery. Circulation: 5,000 morning (paid). **Owner(s):** Salmon Press, Inc., 5 Water St., Meredith, NH 03253. Telephone: 603-279-4516. **Management:** Rich Piatt, Publisher. Lucille Jalbert, Advertising. **Editorial:** Sara Young-Knox, Editor.

CLAREMONT

ARGUS-CHAMPION, THE. 401 River Rd, Claremont, NH 03743. Telephone: 603-543-3100. FAX: 603-542-9705. E-MAIL: argus@cyberportal.net.. Year Established: 1825. Pub. Frequency: w. (Wed.) Page Size: broadsheet. Subscrip. Rate: $.50 newsstand/cover; $25/yr in state. Circulation: 5,100 per issue (paid). **Owner(s):** Eagle Publications, Inc., See address and contact information above. **Management:** Harvey Hill, Publisher. Clyde Pinson, Advertising Director. Randy Yanick, Circulation Manager. **Editorial:** Mark Smith, Editor. Charlie Hentz, Sports Editor.

COLEBROOK

NEWS & SENTINEL, THE. 6 Bridge St., Colebrook, NH 03576. Telephone: 603-237-5001. FAX: 603-237-5060. E-MAIL: karenhladd@newsandsentinel.net. URL: http://www.colebrooknewsandsentinel.com. Mailing Address: P.O. Box 39, Colebrook, NH 03576. Year Established: 1870. Pub. Frequency: w. (Wed.) Page Size: tabloid. Subscrip. Rate: $.75 newsstand/cover; $30/yr in state; $32/yr out of state. Adv. Rate: col. inch $6 Circulation: 5,500 per issue (paid). **Owner(s):** Karen H. Harrigan Ladd, See address and contact information above. **Management:** Karen H. Ladd, Publisher. Butch Ladd, Advertising Manager. **Editorial:** Karen H. Ladd, Managing Editor.

CONWAY

CARROLL COUNTY INDEPENDENT, THE. 290 East Side Rd., Conway, NH 03818. Telephone: 603-539-4111. FAX: 603-539-5564. E-MAIL: cci@salmonpress.com. URL: http://www.carrollcountyindependent.com. Mailing Address: 530, Conway, NH 03818-0530. Year Established: 1881. Pub. Frequency: w. (Thu.) Page Size: broadsheet. Subscrip. Rate: $.75 newsstand/cover; $34/yr mailed in county; $47/yr mailed out of county. Circulation: 5,500 per issue (paid). **Owner(s):** Salmon Press, Inc., 5 Water St., Meredith, NH 03253. Telephone: 603-279-4516. FAX: 603-279-5331. **Management:** Rich Piatt, Publisher. Nancy Turner, Circulation Manager. Ann Hedison, Classified Adv. Mgr.. **Editorial:** Terry Leavitt, Editor.

MOUNT WASHINGTON VALLEY MOUNTAIN EAR. 290 East Side Rd., Conway, NH 03818. Telephone: 630-447-6336. FAX: 630-447-5474. E-MAIL: mtnear@landmarket.net. URL: http://www.mtear.com. Mailing Address: PO Box 530, Conway, NH 03818. Year Established: 1976. Pub. Frequency: w. (Thu.) Page Size: tabloid. Subscrip. Rate: $35/yr. Circulation: 15,000. **Owner(s):** Mount Washington Valley Mountain Ear, Inc., See address and contact information above. **Management:** Richard Stephen Piatt, Publisher. **Editorial:** Nina Perry, Managing Editor.

DERRY

DERRY NEWS. 46 W Broadway, Rte 102, Derry, NH 03038. Telephone: 603-437-7000. FAX: 603-437-0303. E-MAIL: editor@derrynews.com. URL: http://www.derrynews.com. Mailing Address: PO Box 307, Derry, NH 03038-0307. Year Established: 1880. Pub. Frequency: s-w. (Thu.) Page Size: broadsheet. Subscrip. Rate: $.75 newsstand/cover; $25/yr mailed in county. Adv. Rate: col. inch $18.28 Freelance Pay: $20-$30/article. Circulation: 6,538 per issue (paid). **Owner(s):** Community Newspaper Holdings, Inc., 3500 Colonnade Pkwy., Ste. 600, Birmingham, AL 35242. **Management:** Ellen Zappala, Publisher. Mark Miller, Advertising Director. Bruce Slichko, Circulation Manager. **Editorial:** Bill Gilman, Editor.

WEEKENDER (DERRY). 46 W Broadway, Rte 102, Derry, NH 03038. E-MAIL: editor@derrynews.com. URL: http://www.derrynews.com. Mailing Address: PO Box 307, Derry, NH 03038-0307. Pub. Frequency: w. (Fri.) Page Size: broadsheet Circulation: 222,910 per issue (free). **Owner(s):** Community Newspaper Holdings, Inc., 3500 Colonnade Pkwy., Ste. 600, Birmingham, AL 35242. **Management:** Ellen Zappala, Publisher. Mark Miller, Advertising Director. Bruce Slichko, Circulation Manager. **Editorial:** Marc Fortier, Editor.

HAMPTON

HAMPTON UNION. 32 Depot Sq., Hampton, NH 03842. Telephone: 603-926-4511. FAX: 603-772-3880. E-MAIL: edit@rcnewspapers.com. URL: http://www.seacoastonline.com. Mailing Address: PO Box 1104, Hampton, NH 03842. Year Established: 1901. Pub. Frequency: s-w. (Tue. & Fri.) Page Size: broadsheet. Subscrip. Rate: $.75 newsstand/cover; $142.48/yr mailed. Freelance Pay: $30-$50/story. Circulation: 4,852 per issue (paid). **Owner(s):** Ottaway Newspapers, Inc., PO Box 401, Campbell Hall, NY 10916. Telephone: 914-294-8181. **Management:** John Tabor, Publisher. Kymberlee Lauton, Advertising Director. Kelvin Parker, Circulation Director. Maribeth Girard, Marketing Director. **Editorial:** Carl Killeen, Editor.

HANOVER

QUECHEE TIMES. 35 S. Main St., Hanover, NH 03755. Telephone: 603-643-1441. FAX: 603-643-4644. Year Established: 1972. Pub. Frequency: q. Page Size: tabloid. Subscrip. Rate: $10/yr local. Circulation: 2,400 (paid and free). **Owner(s):** River Road Holdings, Inc, See address and contact information above. **Management:** Chris Blau, Publisher. **Editorial:** Kirsten Gehlbach, Editor.

HILLSBORO

MESSENGER (HILLSBORO), THE. 246 W. Main St., Hillsboro, NH 03244-1190. Telephone: 603-464-5588. FAX: 603-464-4106. E-MAIL: granitequill@mcttelecom.com. Mailing Address: PO Box 1190, Hillsboro, NH 03244-1190. Year Established: 1868. Pub. Frequency: w. (Fri.) Page Size: tabloid Circulation: 10,000 per issue (free). **Owner(s):** Granite Quill Publishers, PO Box 1190, Hillsborough, NH 03244. Telephone: 603-464-5588. **Management:** Leigh Bosse, Publisher. **Editorial:** Joyce Bosse, Editor.

HUDSON

HUDSON LITCHFIELD NEWS. 17 Executive Dr, Ste 1, Hudson, NH 03051. Telephone: 603-880-1516. FAX: 603-879-9707. E-MAIL: writehln@yahoo.com. URL: http://www.areanewsgroup.com. Year Established: 1990. Pub. Frequency: w. (Fri.) Page Size: tabloid Circulation: 11,500 per issue (free). **Owner(s):** Len Lathrop, See address and contact information above. **Editorial:** Len Lathrop, Editor.

KEENE

MONADNOCK HOME COMPANION. 60 West St., Keene, NH 03431. Telephone: 603-352-1234. FAX: 603-352-0437. URL: http://www.localnewsconnection.com. Mailing Address: PO Box 546, Keene, NH 03431. Pub. Frequency: w. (Fri.) Page Size: broadsheet. **Owner(s):** Keene Publishing Corp., See address and contact information above. **Management:** James A. Rousmaniere Jr., President. Thomas M. Ewing, Publisher. Colin R. Lyle, Advertising Manager. Patrick J. Trubiano, Circulation Manager. Lorraine Ellis, Classified Adv. Mgr.. **Editorial:** James A. Rousmaniere Jr., Editor. Tom Kearney, Executive Editor.

RIVER RECORD, THE. 60 West St., Keene, NH 03431. Telephone: 603-352-1234. FAX: 603-352-0437. URL: http://www.localnewsconnection.com. Mailing Address: PO Box 546, Keene, NH 03431. Pub. Frequency: w. (Fri.) Page Size: broadsheet. **Owner(s):** Keene Publishing Corp., See address and contact information above. **Management:** James A. Rousmaniere Jr., President. Thomas M. Ewing, Publisher. Colin R. Lyle, Advertising Manager. Patrick J. Trubiano, Circulation Manager. Lorraine Ellis, Classified Adv. Mgr.. **Editorial:** James A. Rousmaniere Jr., Editor. Tom Kearney, Executive Editor.

STAR SPANGLED BANNER. 60 West St., Keene, NH 03431. Telephone: 603-352-1234. FAX: 603-352-0437. URL: http://www.localnewsconnection.com. Mailing Address: PO Box 546, Keene, NH 03431. Pub. Frequency: w. (Fri.) Page Size: broadsheet. **Owner(s):** Keene Publishing Corp., See address and contact information above. **Management:** James A. Rousmaniere Jr., President. Thomas M. Ewing, Publisher. Colin R. Lyle, Advertising Manager. Patrick J. Trubiano, Circulation Manager. Lorraine Ellis, Classified Adv. Mgr.. **Editorial:** James A. Rousmaniere Jr., Editor. Tom Kearney, Executive Editor.

LANCASTER

COOS COUNTY DEMOCRAT. 79 Main St., Lancaster, NH 03584. Telephone: 603-788-4939. FAX: 603-788-3022. URL: http://www.cooscountydemocrat.com/. Mailing Address: PO Box 29, Lancaster, NH 03584. Year Established: 1838. Pub. Frequency: w. (Wed.) Page Size: broadsheet. Subscrip. Rate: $.75 newsstand/cover; $36/yr mailed in county; $49/yr mailed elsewhere. Adv. Rate: col. inch $7 Circulation: 6,500 per issue (paid). **Owner(s):** Salmon Press, Inc., 5 Water St., Meredith, NH 03253. Telephone: 603-279-4516. **Management:** Rich Piatt, Publisher. Nancy Turner, Circulation Manager. Ann Hedison, Classified Adv. Mgr.. **Editorial:** Eileen Alexander, Editor.

NORTHERN BEACON, THE. 79 Main St., Lancaster, NH 03584. Telephone: 603-788-4939. FAX: 603-788-3022. E-MAIL: democrat@salmonpress.com. URL: http://www.cooscountydemocrat.com. Mailing Address: PO Box 29, Lancaster, NH 03584. Year Established: 1971. Pub. Frequency: w. (Fri.) Page Size: tabloid.Adv. Rate: col. inch $8.50 Circulation: 14,000 per issue (free). **Owner(s):** Salmon Press, Inc., 5 Water St., Meredith, NH 03253. Telephone: 603-279-4516. **Management:** Rich Piatt, Publisher. Mary Keddy, Advertising. **Editorial:** Eileen Alexander, Editor. Lyndall Demers, Production Manager.

LITTLETON

COURIER (LITTLETON), THE. 33 Main St., Littleton, NH 03561. Telephone: 603-444-3927. FAX: 603-444-3920. E-MAIL: couriernews@salmonpress.com. URL: http://www.courier-littletonnh.com. Mailing Address: PO Box 230, Littleton, NH 03561. Year Established: 1889. Pub. Frequency: w. (Wed.) Page Size: broadsheet. Subscrip. Rate: $.75 newsstand/cover; $36/yr mailed in county; $49/yr mailed out of county. Circulation: 6,000 per issue (paid). **Owner(s):** Salmon Press, Inc., 5 Water St., Meredith, NH 03253. Telephone: 603-279-4516. **Management:** Rich Piatt, Publisher. Trisha Ilacqua, Advertising Manager. Nancy Turner, Circulation Manager. **Editorial:** Gina Hamilton, Editor. Krystin St George, Sports Editor.

MANCHESTER

SALEM OBSERVER. 1662 Elm St. Ste.100, Manchester, NH 03101-1243. Telephone: 603-314-0447. FAX: 603-314-0932. E-MAIL: editor@salemobserver.com. URL: http://www.yourneighborhood.news.com. Year Established: 1966. Pub. Frequency: w. (Thu.) Page Size: broadsheet.Adv. Rate: col. inch $11.90 Circulation: 10,000 per issue (paid). **Owner(s):** Union Leader Corp., 100 William Loeb Dr, Manchester, NH 03103. Telephone: 603-668-4321. FAX: 603-668-0040. **Management:** Amy Vellucci, Publisher. Therese Potvin, Marketing. Pam Young, Production Director. **Editorial:** Christine Heiser, Editor. Jerry Liptak, Sports Editor.

MEREDITH

MEREDITH NEWS, THE. 5 Water St., Meredith, NH 03253. Telephone: 603-279-4516. FAX: 603-279-3331. E-MAIL: mnews@meredithnhnews.com. URL: http://www.meredithnhnews.com. Year Established: 1880. Pub. Frequency: w. (Thu.) Page Size: broadsheet. Subscrip. Rate: $.75 newsstand/cover; $36/yr in county; $49/yr out of county. Circulation: 5,300 per issue (paid). **Owner(s):** Salmon Press, Inc., See address and contact information above. **Management:** Rich Piatt, Publisher. Nancy Turner, Circulation Manager. Ann Hedison, Classified Adv. Mgr.. **Editorial:** Keith Rogers, Editor.

WINNISQUAM ECHO. 5 Water St., Meredith, NH 03253. Telephone: 603-279-4516. FAX: 603-279-3331. Pub. Frequency: w. (Thu.) Page Size: broadsheet. Subscrip. Rate: $.50 newsstand/cover; $35/yr mailed. Circulation: 8,900 per issue (paid). **Owner(s):** Salmon Press, Inc., See address and contact information above. **Management:** Rich Piatt, Publisher. Mike Mackin, Advertising. Jean Foote, Classified Adv. Mgr.. **Editorial:** Susan Richards, Editor.

MILFORD

BEDFORD JOURNAL. 54 School St., Milford, NH 03055. Telephone: 603-673-3100. FAX: 603-673-8250. E-MAIL: news@bedfordjournal.com. URL: http://www.bedfordjournal.com. Mailing Address: PO Box 180, Milford, NH 03055-0180. Year Established: 1999. Pub. Frequency: w. (Thu.) Page Size: broadsheet. Subscrip. Rate: $50/yr mailed elsewhere. Circulation: 7,800 per issue (paid and free). **Owner(s):** Cabinet Press, Inc., See address and contact information above. **Management:** David Solomon, Publisher. **Editorial:** David Cummings, Editor.

CABINET, THE. 54 School St., Milford, NH 03055-0180. Telephone: 603-673-3100. FAX: 603-673-8250. E-MAIL: cabnews@cabinet.com. URL: http://www.cabinet.com. Mailing Address: PO Box 180, Milford, NH 03055-0180. Year Established: 1802. Pub. Frequency: w. (Thu.) Page Size: broadsheet. Subscrip. Rate: $.75 newsstand/cover; $26/yr in state; $38/yr out of state. Circulation: 8,000 per issue (paid). **Owner(s):** Cabinet Press, Inc., 54 School St., Milford, NH 03055. Telephone: 603-673-3100. FAX: 603-673-8250. **Management:** Frank Manley, Publisher. **Editorial:** Mike Cleveland, Editor.

HOLLIS BROOKLINE JOURNAL. 54 School St., Milford, NH 03055. Telephone: 603-673-3100. FAX: 603-673-8250. E-MAIL: cabinet@cabinet.com. URL: http://www.cabinet.com. Mailing Address: PO Box 180, Milford, NH 03055-0180. Year Established: 1994. Pub. Frequency: w. (Fri.) Page Size: broadsheet. Subscrip. Rate: $50/yr mailed out of area. Circulation: 5,000 per issue (paid and free). **Owner(s):** Cabinet Press, Inc., See address and contact information above. **Management:** David Solomon, Publisher. **Editorial:** David Cummings, Editor.

MERRIMACK JOURNAL. 54 School St., Milford, NH 03055. Telephone: 603-673-3100. FAX: 603-673-8250. E-MAIL: cabinet@cabinet.com. URL: http://www.cabinet.com. Mailing Address: PO Box 180, Milford, NH 03055-0180. Year Established: 1997. Pub. Frequency: w. (Fri.) Page Size: broadsheet. Subscrip. Rate: $50/yr mailed out of state. Circulation: 10,000 per issue (paid and free). **Owner(s):** Cabinet Press, Inc., See address and contact information above. **Management:** David Solomon, Publisher. **Editorial:** David Cummings, Editor.

PETERBOROUGH

MONADNOCK LEDGER. 20 Grove St., Peterborough, NH 03458. Telephone: 603-924-7172. FAX: 603-924-3681. URL: http://www.monadnockledger.com. Mailing Address: PO Box 36, Peterborough, NH 03458. Year Established: 1956. Pub. Frequency: w. (Thu.) Page Size: broadsheet. Subscrip. Rate: $.50 newsstand/cover; $24/yr in state; $32/yr out of state. Adv. Rate: col. inch $9.05 Circulation: 8,500 per issue (paid). **Owner(s):** Newspapers of New England, Inc., PO Box 1177, Concord, NH 03302-1177. Telephone: 603-224-5301. **Management:** Heather McKernan, Publisher. Charlie Paskus, Advertising. Mandy Sliver, Circulation Manager. **Editorial:** Dave Anderson, Editor. Joe Bills, Sports Editor.

PETERBOROUGH TRANSCRIPT, THE. 244 Sand Hill Rd., Peterborough, NH 03458. Telephone: 603-924-3333. FAX: 603-924-7946. E-MAIL: ptrans@monad.net. URL: http://www.peterboroughtranscript.com. Year Established: 1849. Pub. Frequency: w. (Thu.) Page Size: broadsheet. Subscrip. Rate: $.50 newsstand/cover; $24/yr in state; $30/yr out of state. Circulation: 5,900 per issue (paid). **Owner(s):** Joseph D. Cummings, See address and contact information above. **Management:** Joseph D. Cummings, Publisher. Elaine Cummings, Circulation Manager. **Editorial:** Joseph D. Cummings, Managing Editor. Dara Jernier, News Editor. Contact: Joseph D. Cummings, Publisher.

PLYMOUTH

RECORD ENTERPRISE, THE. Rte. 3, Fairgrounds Rd., Plymouth, NH 03264. Telephone: 603-536-1311. FAX: 603-536-8940. E-MAIL: record@coopresources.net. Mailing Address: PO Box 148, Plymouth, NH 03264. Pub. Frequency: w. (Thu.) Page Size: tabloid. Subscrip. Rate: $.75 newsstand/cover; $36/yr mailed in county; $47/yr mailed out of county. Adv. Rate: col. inch $5.15 Circulation: 6,500 per issue (paid). **Owner(s):** Salmon Press, Inc., 5 Water St., Meredith, NH 03253. Telephone: 603-279-4516. **Management:** Rich Piatt, Publisher. Mike McGrail, Circulation Manager. **Editorial:** Leith Sharps, Editor.

PORTSMOUTH

EXETER NEWS-LETTER. 111 Maplewood Ave., Portsmouth, NH 03801. Telephone: 603-772-6000. FAX: 603-772-3830. E-MAIL: exeternewsletter@seacoastonline.com. URL: http://www.seacoastonline.com. Mailing Address: PO Box 1104, Hampton, NH 03842. Year Established: 1831. Pub. Frequency: s-w. (Tue. & Fri.) Page Size: broadsheet. Subscrip. Rate: $.75 newsstand/cover; $126.30/yr mailed in county. **Wire Service(s):** AP. Circulation: 6,850 per issue (paid). **Owner(s):** Ottaway Newspapers, Inc., PO Box 401, Campbell Hall, NY 10916. Telephone: 914-294-8181. **Management:** John Tabor, Publisher. Kymberlee Lauton, Advertising Director. Kelvin Parker, Circulation Director. Maribeth Girard, Marketing Director. **Editorial:** Deborah McDermott, Editor. Howard Altschiller, Executive Editor.

YORK WEEKLY, THE. 111 Maplewood Ave., Portsmouth, NH 03801. Telephone: 603-436-1800. FAX: 603-427-0550. E-MAIL: yorkweekly@seacoastalonline.com. URL: http://www.seacoastonline.com. Pub. Frequency: w. (Wed.) Page Size: tabloid. Subscrip. Rate: $.75 newsstand/cover; $28.50/yr in state; $36.75/yr out of state. Adv. Rate: col. inch $11.45 Circulation: 3,702 per issue (paid). **Owner(s):** Ottaway Newspapers, Inc., PO Box 401, Campbell Hall, NY 10916. Telephone: 914-294-8181. **Management:** Marci Hait, General Manager. John Tabor, Publisher. Tannye Wold, Advertising Manager.

ROCHESTER

ROCHESTER TIMES (ROCHESTER), THE. 90 N. Main St., Rochester, NH 03867. Telephone: 603-332-2300. FAX: 603-330-0718. E-MAIL: thetimes@worldpath.net. Year Established: 1993. Pub. Frequency: w. (Thu.) Page Size: tabloid. Subscrip. Rate: $28/yr mailed. Freelance Pay: $20/story. Circulation: 34,000 per issue (paid and free). **Owner(s):** George J. Foster Co., 333 Central Ave., Dover, NH 03820. Telephone: 603-742-4455. **Management:** George J. Foster, Publisher. Donna Matthews, Advertising. **Editorial:** John Nolan, Editor-in-Chief.

STRATHAM

ROCKINGHAM NEWS. ISSN 1559-050X
7 Portsmouth Ave., Stratham, NH 03835. Telephone: 603-772-6000. FAX: 603-772-3830. E-MAIL: rockinghamnews@seacoastonline.com. URL: http://www.seacoastonline.com. Mailing Address: PO Box 1104, Hampton, NH 03842. Pub. Frequency: w. (Fri.) Page Size: broadsheet. Subscrip. Rate: $.75 newsstand/cover; $99/yr mailed. Adv. Rate: col. inch $11.25 Circulation: 5,963 per issue (paid). **Owner(s):** Ottaway Newspapers, Inc., PO Box 401, Campbell Hall, NY 10916. Telephone: 845-294-8181. **Management:** John Tabor, Publisher. Kymberlee Lauton, Advertising Director. Kelvin Parker, Circulation Director. **Editorial:** Barbara Polletta, Editor.

WOLFEBORO

GRANITE STATE NEWS, THE. ISSN 1060-0590
35 Center St., Wolfeboro, NH 03894. Telephone: 603-569-3126. FAX: 603-569-4743. E-MAIL: grunter@salmonpress.com. URL: http://www.granitestatenews.com. Mailing Address: PO Box 250, Wolfeboro Falls, NH 03896. Year Established: 1859. Pub. Frequency: w. (Thu.) Page Size: broadsheet. Subscrip. Rate: $.75 newsstand/cover; $36/yr mailed in county; $60/yr mailed out of county. Adv. Rate: col. inch $14 Circulation: 6,000 per issue (paid). **Owner(s):** Salmon Press, Inc., 5 Water St., Meredith, NH 03253. Telephone: 603-279-4516. **Management:** Richard Piatt, Publisher. Nancy Turner, Circulation Manager. Maureen Aselton, Classified Adv. Mgr. **Editorial:** Thomas Beeler, Editor.

NEW JERSEY

ALLENTOWN

REGISTER-NEWS, THE. 34 S. Main St., Allentown, NJ 08501. Telephone: 609-259-3584. FAX: 609-259-1182. E-MAIL: ads@pacpub.com. URL: http://www.registernews.com. Mailing Address: PO Box 446, Allentown, NJ 08501. Year Established: 1845. Pub. Frequency: w. (Thu.) Page Size: tabloid. Subscrip. Rate: $.60 newsstand/cover; $24.96/yr in county. Adv. Rate: col. inch $10.50 Freelance Pay: $25/article. Circulation: 4,190 per issue (paid). **Owner(s):** Princeton Packet, Inc., 300 Witherspoon St., Princeton, NJ 08540. Telephone: 609-924-3244. **Management:** James B. Kilgore, Publisher. Mark Mucelli, Advertising Manager. **Editorial:** Vanessa Sarada Holt, Managing Editor. Phil McAuliffe, Photographer. Kyle Moylan, Sports Editor.

BAYONNE

BAYONNE COMMUNITY NEWS. 13 East 21 St, Bayonne, NJ 07002. Telephone: 201-437-2460. FAX: 201-437-7127. E-MAIL: bcneditorial@hudsonreporter.com. URL: http://www.bayonnecommunitynews.com. Year Established: 1978. Pub. Frequency: w. (Wed.) Page Size: tabloid.Adv. Rate: col. inch $10.22 Circulation: 28,525 per issue (paid and controlled). **Owner(s):** Bayonne Community News, See address and contact information above. **Management:** David S Unger, Publisher. **Editorial:** Jenna King, Editor. Al Sullivan, Reporter.

BERNARDSVILLE

BERNARDSVILLE NEWS. 17-19 Morristown Rd., Bernardsville, NJ 07924. Telephone: 908-766-3900. FAX: 608-766-6365. E-MAIL: bernardsvillenews@recordernewspapers.com. URL: http://www.bernardsvillenews.com. Year Established: 1896. Pub. Frequency: w. (Thu.) Page Size: broadsheet. Subscrip. Rate: $.75 newsstand/cover; $32/yr in county; $35/yr out of county; $41/yr out of state. Circulation: 8,619 per issue (paid). **Owner(s):** Recorder Publishing Co., See address and contact information above. **Management:** Douglas McBride, Advertising Director. David W. Nelson, Circulation Director. Nancy Knowles Parker, Associate Publisher. **Editorial:** Charles Zavalick, Editor. Elizabeth K. Parker, Executive Editor. Phillip J. Nardone, Assistant Editor.

ECHOES-SENTINEL. PO Box 687, Bernardsville, NJ 07924. E-MAIL: echoes@recordernewspapers.com. URL: http://www.echoes-sentinel.com. Year Established: 1955. Pub. Frequency: w. (Wed.) Page Size: broadsheet. Subscrip. Rate: $1 newsstand/cover; $30/yr mailed in county; $38/yr mailed out of county; $45/yr mailed out of state. Circulation: 3,500 per issue (paid). **Owner(s):** Recorder Publishing Co., 17-19 Morristown Rd., Bernardsville, NJ 07924. Telephone: 908-766-3900. FAX: 908-766-6365. **Management:** Sherwood Spitz, Vice President. Douglas McBride, Advertising Director. David W. Nelson, Circulation Director. Stephen W. Parker, Business Manager. **Editorial:** Elizabeth K. Parker, Executive Editor.

BLACKWOOD

NEWS REPORT (BLACKWOOD). 201 Rte. 168 S., Black Horse Pike, Blackwood, NJ 08012. Telephone: 856-228-7300. FAX: 856-227-1207. URL: http://www.southjerseylocalnews.com. Mailing Address: PO Box 1609, Blackwood, NJ 08012. Year Established: 1960. Pub. Frequency: w. (Thu.) Page Size: tabloid. Subscrip. Rate: $.50 newsstand/cover; $19/yr mailed in county; $26.50/yr mailed out of county. Freelance Pay: $25/article. Circulation: 3,500 per issue (paid). **Owner(s):** Journal Register Co., 50 W State St, 12th Fl, Trenton, NJ 08608. Telephone: 609-396-2200. **Management:** Stephanie Leicht, Publisher. Pat Haughey, Advertising Director. Ed Krywucki, Circulation Manager. **Editorial:** Jordan Fenster, Editor.

PLAIN DEALER. 201 Rte. 168 S., Black Horse Pike, Blackwood, NJ 08012. E-MAIL: ingnews@aol.com. URL: http://www.southjerseylocalnews.com. Mailing Address: PO Box 1609, Blackwood, NJ 08012. Year Established: 1926. Pub. Frequency: w. (Thu.) Page Size: tabloid. Subscrip. Rate: $.50 newsstand/cover; $19/yr in county; $26.50/yr out of county. Circulation: 6,200 per issue (paid). **Owner(s):** Journal Register Co., 50 W State St, 12th Fl, Trenton, NJ 08608. Telephone: 609-396-2200. **Management:** Stephanie Leicht, Publisher. Pat Haughey, Advertising Director. Ed Krywucki, Circulation Manager. **Editorial:** Christina Paciolla, Executive Editor.

RECORD-BREEZE. 201 Rte. 168 S., Black Horse Pike, Blackwood, NJ 08012. Telephone: 856-228-7300. FAX: 856-227-1207. E-MAIL: recordbreeze@ingnews.com. URL: http://www.southjerseylocalnews.com. Mailing Address: PO Box 1609, Blackwood, NJ 08012. Year Established: 1919. Pub. Frequency: w. (Thu.) Page Size: tabloid. Subscrip. Rate: $.50 newsstand/cover; $19/yr mailed in county; $26.50/yr mailed out of county. Circulation: 3,500 per issue (paid). **Owner(s):** Journal Register Co., 50 W State St, 12th Fl, Trenton, NJ 08608. Telephone: 609-396-2200. **Management:** Stephanie Leicht, Publisher. Pat Haughey, Advertising Director. Ed Krywucki, Circulation Manager. **Editorial:** Christina Paciolla, Executive Editor.

BLOOMFIELD

BELLEVILLE POST. 266 Liberty St., Bloomfield, NJ 07003. Telephone: 973-743-4040. FAX: 973-680-8848. E-MAIL: editorial@localsource.com. URL: http://www.localsource.com. Mailing Address: PO Box 110, Bloomfield, NJ 07003. Year Established: 1982. Pub. Frequency: w. (Thu.) Page Size: broadsheet. Subscrip. Rate: $.75 newsstand/cover; $26/yr mailed in county; $36/yr mailed out of county. Adv. Rate: col. inch $15.75 Circulation: 12,000 per issue (paid). **Owner(s):** Worrall Community Newspapers, Inc., 1291 Stuyvesant Ave., Union, NJ 07083. Telephone: 908-686-7700. **Management:** David Worrall, Publisher. Ray Worrall, Advertising Director. **Editorial:** Tom Canavan, Editor-in-Chief. Chris Lang, Managing Editor.

GLEN RIDGE PAPER, THE. 266 Liberty St., Bloomfield, NJ 07003. Telephone: 973-743-4040. FAX: 973-680-8848. E-MAIL: wcn22@localsource.com. URL: http://localsource.com. Mailing Address: PO Box 110, Bloomfield, NJ 07003. Year Established: 1935. Pub. Frequency: w. (Thu.) Page Size: broadsheet. Subscrip. Rate: $.75 newsstand/cover; $26/yr mailed in county; $36/yr mailed out of county. Adv. Rate: col. inch $18.50 Circulation: 5,000 per issue (paid). **Owner(s):** Worrall Community Newspapers, Inc., 1291 Stuyvesant Ave., Union, NJ 07083. Telephone: 908-686-7700. **Management:** David Worrall, Publisher. Joseph Ornegri, Advertising Director. John D'Achino, Circulation Manager. Tom Yauch, Classified Adv. Mgr. **Editorial:** Steve Proctor, Editor. Tom Canavan, Editor-in-Chief. Nick Loffredo, Managing Editor.

INDEPENDENT PRESS OF BLOOMFIELD, THE. 266 Liberty St., Bloomfield, NJ 07003. Telephone: 973-743-4040. FAX: 973-680-8848. E-MAIL: wcn22@localservice.com. URL: http://www.localsource.com. Mailing Address: PO Box 110, Bloomfield, NJ 07003. Year Established: 1883. Pub. Frequency: w. (Thu.) Page Size: broadsheet. Subscrip. Rate: $.75 newsstand/cover; $26/yr mailed in county; $36/yr mailed out of county. Adv. Rate: col. inch $18.50 Circulation: 3,976 per issue (paid). **Owner(s):** Worrall Community Newspapers, Inc., 1291 Stuyvesant Ave., Union, NJ 07083. Telephone: 908-686-7700. **Management:** David Worrall, Publisher. Joseph Ornegri, Advertising Director. John D'Achino, Circulation Manager. Tom Yauch, Classified Adv. Mgr. **Editorial:** Steve Proctor, Editor. Raymond Worrall, Executive Editor. Nick Loffredo, Managing Editor.

NUTLEY JOURNAL. 266 Liberty St., Bloomfield, NJ 07003. Telephone: 973-743-4040. FAX: 973-680-8848. E-MAIL: news@thelocalsource.com. URL: http://www.localsource.com. Mailing Address: PO Box 110, Bloomfield, NJ 07003. Year Established: 1982. Pub. Frequency: w. (Thu.) Page Size: broadsheet. Subscrip. Rate: $.75 newsstand/cover; $26/yr in county; $36/yr mailed out of county. Adv. Rate: col. inch $16.50 Circulation: 10,400 per issue (paid). **Owner(s):** Worrall Community Newspapers, Inc., 1291 Stuyvesant Ave., Union, NJ 07083. Telephone: 908-686-7700. **Management:** David Worrall, Publisher. Joseph Ornegri, Advertising Director. John D'Achino, Circulation Manager. Tom Yauch, Classified Adv. Mgr. **Editorial:** Steve Proctor, Editor. Tom Canavan, Editor-in-Chief. Raymond Worrall, Executive Editor. Chris Lang, Managing Editor.

CALDWELL

PROGRESS (CALDWELL), THE. 6 Brookside Ave., Caldwell, NJ 07006-0072. Telephone: 973-226-8900. FAX: 973-226-0553. E-MAIL: editor@recordernewspapers.com. URL: http://www.theprogressnj.com. Mailing Address: PO Box 72, Caldwell, NJ 07006-0072. Year Established: 1911. Pub. Frequency: w. (Thu.) Page Size: broadsheet. Subscrip. Rate: $.50/yr newsstand/cover; $20/yr mailed in county; $25/yr mailed out of county; $28/yr mailed out of state. Circulation: 9,300 per issue (paid). **Owner(s):** Recorder Publishing Co., 6 Brookside Ave., Caldwell, NJ 07006. Telephone: 973-226-8900. **Management:** Elizabeth K Parker, Publisher. Douglas McBride, Advertising Director. Dan Witt, Advertising Manager. Kathy McDonough, Classified Adv. Mgr. **Editorial:** Rita Annan-Brady, Editor. Jaclyn Stolfi, Lifestyle Editor.

CAPE MAY

CAPE MAY STAR & WAVE. 600 Park Blvd. #5 W., Cape May, NJ 08204. E-MAIL: cmstarwave@aol.com. URL: http://www.starandwave.com. Year Established: 1854. Pub. Frequency: w. (Thu.) Page Size: standard. Subscrip. Rate: $.50 newsstand/cover; $22/yr in county; $25/yr out of county; $29/yr out of state. Circulation: 7,800 per issue (paid). **Owner(s):** Sample Media, Inc., See address and contact information above. **Management:** David Nahan, Publisher. Margaret Peterson, Circulation Manager. Mary Rudloff, Business Manager. **Editorial:** Susan Krysiak Avedissian, Editor.

CHATHAM

CHATHAM COURIER. 27 Bowers Lane, Chatham, NJ 07928. Telephone: 973-377-2000. FAX: 973-377-7721. E-MAIL: editor@chathamcourier.com. URL: http://www.chathamcourier.com. Mailing Address: PO Box 160, Madison, NJ 07940. Year Established: 1930. Pub. Frequency: w. (Thu.) Page Size: standard. Subscrip. Rate: $.50 newsstand/cover; $25/yr mailed in county; $32/yr mailed out of county; $38/yr mailed out of state. Circulation: 3,468 per issue (paid). **Owner(s):** Recorder Publishing Co., See address and contact information above. **Management:** Elizabeth Parker, Co-Publisher. Doug McBride, Advertising Director. David Nelson, Circulation Manager. **Editorial:** Max Pizarro, Editor. Elizabeth Parker, Executive Editor. Garry Herzog, Managing Editor.

CHESTER

MT. OLIVE CHRONICLE. 540 E. Main St., Chester, NJ 07930. Telephone: 908-879-4100. FAX: 908-879-0799. E-MAIL: mtolive@recordernewspapers.com. URL: http://www.recordernewspapers.com. Mailing Address: PO Box 600, Chester, NJ 07930-0600. Pub. Frequency: w. (Thu.) Page Size: standard. Subscrip. Rate: $.50 newsstand/cover; $20/yr mailed in county; $32/yr mailed out of county; $38/yr mailed out of state. Circulation: 5,000 per issue (paid). **Owner(s):** Recorder Publishing Co., 17-19 Morristown Rd., Bernardsville, NJ 07924. Telephone: 908-766-3900. **Management:** Steven Parker, Co-Publisher. Allison Spinella, Advertising Director. David Nelson, Circulation Manager. Nancy K. Parker, Associate Publisher. Stephen W. Parker, Business Manager. **Editorial:** Elizabeth K. Parker, Executive Editor. Philip Garber, Managing Editor.

OBSERVER-TRIBUNE. 540 E. Main St., Chester, NJ 07930. Telephone: 908-879-4100. FAX: 908-879-6141. E-MAIL: pgarber@recordernewspapers.com. URL: http://www.observer-tribune.com. Mailing Address: PO Box 600, Chester, NJ 07930. Year Established: 1936. Pub. Frequency: w. (Thu.) Page Size: broadsheet. Subscrip. Rate: $.75 newsstand/cover; $32/yr in county; $35/yr mailed out of county; $41/yr mailed out of state. Circulation: 12,000 per issue (paid). **Owner(s):** Recorder Publishing Co., 17-19 Morristown Rd., Bernardsville, NJ 07924. Telephone: 908-766-3900. **Management:** Stephen W. Parker, Co-Publisher. Alison Spinella, Advertising Director. Nancy Knowles Parker, Associate Publisher. **Editorial:** Elizabeth K. Parker, Executive Editor. Phil Garber, Managing Editor.

RANDOLPH REPORTER. 540 E. Main St., Chester, NJ 07930. Telephone: 908-879-4100. FAX: 908-879-0799. E-MAIL: mtolive@recordernewspapers.com. URL: http://www.recordernewspapers.com. Mailing Address: PO Box 600, Chester, NJ 07930-0600. Pub. Frequency: w. (Thu.) Page Size: standard. Subscrip. Rate: $.50 newsstand/cover; $23/yr mailed in county; $32/yr out of county; $38/yr out of state. Circulation: 4,043 per issue (paid). **Owner(s):** Recorder Publishing Co., 17-19 Morristown Rd., Bernardsville, NJ 07924. Telephone: 908-766-3900. **Management:** Steven Parker, Co-Publisher. Allison Spinella, Advertising Director. David Nelson, Circulation Manager. Nancy K. Parker, Associate Publisher. Stephen W. Parker, Business Manager. **Editorial:** Elizabeth K. Parker, Executive Editor. Phil Garber, Managing Editor. Phillip J. Nardone, Assistant Editor.

ROXBURY REGISTER, THE. 540 E. Main St., Chester, NJ 07930. Telephone: 908-879-4100. FAX: 908-879-0799. E-MAIL: pgarber@recordernewspapers.com. URL: http://www.recordernewspapers.com. Mailing Address: PO Box 600, Chester, NJ 07930-0600. Pub. Frequency: w. (Thu.) Page Size: broadsheet. Subscrip. Rate: $.50 newsstand/cover; $20/yr mailed in county; $32/yr mailed out of county; $38/yr mailed elsewhere. Circulation: 4,000 per issue (paid). **Owner(s):** Recorder Publishing Co., 17-19 Morristown Rd., Bernardsville, NJ 07924. Telephone: 908-766-3900. **Management:** Allison Spinella, Advertising Director. David Nelson, Circulation Manager. Nancy K. Parker, Associate Publisher. Stephen W. Parker, Business Manager. **Editorial:** Mike Condon, Editor. Elizabeth K. Parker, Executive Editor. Phil Garber, Managing Editor.

CINNAMINSON

ALL AROUND PENNSAUKEN. 104 Shenandoah Rd., Cinnaminson, NJ 08077. Telephone: 856-665-1000. FAX: 856-665-2749. Year Established: 2003. Pub. Frequency: w. (Thu.) Page Size: standard Circulation: 20,000 per issue (free). **Owner(s):** C N P Publications, See address and contact information above. **Management:** Karen Kennedy-Hall, General Manager.

PULSE OF CHERRY HILL, THE. 104 Shenandoah Rd, Cinnaminson, NJ 08077. Telephone: 856-786-4715. FAX: 856-786-3208. Mailing Address: P.O. Box 609, Waupaca, WI 54891. Year Established: 2003. Pub. Frequency: w. (Thu.) Page Size: standard Circulation: 28,000 per issue (free). **Owner(s):** Journal Community Publishing Group, 600 Industrial Dr., Waupaca, WI 54891. **Editorial:** James Kilrain, Editor.

TOWN NEWS/THE. 104 Shenandoah Rd., Cinnaminson, NJ 08077. Telephone: 856-665-1000. FAX: 856-665-2749. Year Established: 1970. Pub. Frequency: w. (Fri.) Page Size: tabloid.Adv. Rate: col. inch $10 Circulation: 8,000 per issue (paid and free). **Owner(s):** C N P Publications, See address and contact information above. **Management:** Gerard McConnell, Publisher. **Editorial:** Patti McConnell, Managing Editor.

CLARK

CRANFORD CHRONICLE. 301 Central Ave, Clark, NJ 07066. Telephone: 732-396-4223. FAX: 732-381-0098. E-MAIL: njnews@compuell.com. URL: http://www.cranford.com. Year Established: 1893. Pub. Frequency: w. (Wed.) Page Size: broadsheet. Subscrip. Rate: $.50 newsstand/cover; $25/yr in county. Circulation: 9,000 per issue (paid). **Owner(s):** Advance Publications, Inc., 950 Fingerboard Rd., Staten Island, NY 10305. Telephone: 718-981-1234. **Management:** David Tomasini, Publisher. Ted Wnoroski, Circulation Manager. John Bodnar, Sales Manager. **Editorial:** Greg Marx, Editor. Gregory Zeller, News Editor.

CLIFTON

CLIFTON JOURNAL. 1187 Main Ave., Ste. 2-D, Clifton, NJ 07011-2252. Telephone: 973-478-7958. FAX: 973-478-9754. E-MAIL: cliftonjournal@northjersey.com. URL: http://www.northjersey.com. Year Established: 1917. Pub. Frequency: w. (Thu.) Page Size: broadsheet.Adv. Rate: col. inch $13.90 Circulation: 30,630 per issue (free). **Owner(s):** North Jersey Media Group, 150 River St, Hackensack, NJ 07061-7172. Telephone: 201-646-4000. **Management:** Michael Lawson, Publisher. Garry DeYoung, Advertising Manager. Rose O'Riordan, Classified Adv. Mgr.. **Editorial:** Albina Sportelli, Editor.

NORTH JERSEY PROSPECTOR. ISSN 0745-8908 85 Crooks Ave., Clifton, NJ 07011-1011. Telephone: 973-773-8300. Year Established: 1933. Pub. Frequency: w. (Thu.) Page Size: tabloid. Subscrip. Rate: $.35 newsstand/cover; $30/yr. Circulation: 109,023 per issue (controlled and free). **Owner(s):** North Jersey Prospector, Inc., See address and contact information above. **Management:** Blanche Kubat, Publisher. A. Razumov, Advertising. Rich Grudzinski, Advertising Manager. Alfred Benkendorf, Circulation Manager. **Editorial:** Alexy Bidnik Jr., Editor. Marsha Razumov, Managing Editor. Sal Passarella, Assistant Editor. Gary Stevens, Entertainment Editor.

COLLINGSWOOD

RETROSPECT, THE. 732 Haddon Ave, Collingswood, NJ 08108. Telephone: 856-854-1400. FAX: 856-854-8790. URL: http://www.theretrospect.com. Year Established: 1902. Pub. Frequency: w. (Fri.) Page Size: tabloid. Subscrip. Rate: $.50 newsstand/cover; $20/yr in county; $28/yr out of county. Adv. Rate: col. inch $12.13 Freelance Pay: $35/story. Circulation: 5,500 per issue (paid). **Owner(s):** Ainsworth Media, Inc., See address and contact information above. **Management:** Brett T Ainsworth, Publisher. Coleen Glen, Circulation Manager. **Editorial:** Mark Swanson, Editor.

CRESSKILL

NORTHERN VALLEY SUBURBANITE. 300 Knickerbocker Rd., Ste. 1200, Cresskill, NJ 07626-1343. Telephone: 201-568-6090. FAX: 201-569-7308. E-MAIL: suburbanite@northjersey.com. URL: http://www.northjersey.com. Year Established: 1958. Pub. Frequency: w. (Wed.) Page Size: tabloid.Adv. Rate: col. inch $20.20 Circulation: 26,776 per issue (free). **Owner(s):** North Jersey Media Group, 150 River St, Hackensack, NJ 07601-7172. Telephone: 201-646-4000. **Management:** Stephen Borg, President. Janice Friedman, Publisher. Vinny Carnevale, Advertising Manager. **Editorial:** Carolyn Molyneaux, Editor.

TEANECK SUBURBANITE, THE. 300 Knickerbocker Rd., Ste. 1200, Cresskill, NJ 07626-1343. Telephone: 201-568-6090. FAX: 201-569-7308. E-MAIL: suburbanite@northjersey.com. URL: http://www.northjersey.com. Pub. Frequency: w. (Wed.) Page Size: tabloid. Subscrip. Rate: $65/yr. Adv. Rate: col. inch $17.70 Circulation: 11,665 per issue (free). **Owner(s):** North Jersey Media Group, 150 River St, Hackensack, NJ 07601-7172. Telephone: 201-646-4000. **Management:** Stephen Borg, President. Janice Friedman, Publisher. Vinny Carnevale, Advertising Manager. Kerry Rubin, Classified Adv. Mgr.. **Editorial:** Carolyn Molyneaux, Editor.

TWIN-BORO NEWS. 300 Knickerbocker Rd., Ste. 1200, Cresskill, NJ 07626-1343. Telephone: 201-568-6272. FAX: 201-568-6209. E-MAIL: twinboro@northjersey.com. URL: http://www.njmg.com. Year Established: 1947. Pub. Frequency: w. (Wed.) Page Size: tabloid.Adv. Rate: col. inch $15.10 Circulation: 20,706 per issue (free). **Owner(s):** North Jersey Media Group, 150 River St, Hackensack, NJ 07601-7172. Telephone: 201-646-4000. **Management:** Stephen Borg, President. Janice Friedman, Publisher. Vinny Carnevale, Advertising Manager. **Editorial:** William Slossar, Editor.

DAYTON

SOUTH BRUNSWICK POST. 401 Ridge Rd, Dayton, NJ 08810. Telephone: 732-329-9214. FAX: 732-329-8291. E-MAIL: ads@pacpub.com. URL: http://www.southbrunswickpost.com. Mailing Address: PO Box 309, Dayton, NJ 08810. Year Established: 1958. Pub. Frequency: w. (Thu.) Page Size: broadsheet. Subscrip. Rate: $.75 newsstand/cover; $39/yr in county. Adv. Rate: col. inch $25.80 Circulation: 3,850 per issue (paid). **Owner(s):** Princeton Packet, Inc., 300 Witherspoon St., Princeton, NJ 08540. Telephone: 609-924-3244. **Management:** James B. Kilgore, Publisher. **Editorial:** Hank Kalet, Editor.

DENVILLE

CITIZEN OF MORRIS COUNTY, THE. 24 E. Main St., Denville, NJ 07834. Telephone: 973-627-0400. FAX: 973-627-0403. Mailing Address: PO Box 7, Denville, NJ 07834. Pub. Frequency: w. (Wed.) Page Size: broadsheet. Subscrip. Rate: $.35 newsstand/cover; $17/yr mailed in county; $23/yr mailed out of county; $25/yr mailed out of state. Circulation: 7,000 per issue (paid). **Owner(s):** Recorder Publishing Co., 17-19 Morristown Rd., Bernardsville, NJ 07924. Telephone: 908-766-3900. **Management:** Steven Parker, Publisher. Lisa Notoli, Advertising Manager. **Editorial:** Audrey Davie, Editor.

EAST HADDONFIELD

HADDON HERALD/HADDON LIFE. 132 Kings Highway, East Haddonfield, NJ 08033. Telephone: 856-795-4920. FAX: 856-795-4923. E-MAIL: haddon@ingnews.com. URL: http://www.southjerseylocalnews.com. Pub. Frequency: w. Page Size: standard. Subscrip. Rate: $.50 newsstand/cover; $19/yr home delivery in county; $26.50/yr home delivery out of county. **Owner(s):** Journal Register Co., 50 W. State St., 12th Fl., Trenton, NJ 06808. **Management:** Stephanie Leicht, Publisher. Pat Haughey, Advertising Director. Ed Krywucki, Circulation Manager. Monica Carpenter, Classified Adv. Mgr.. **Editorial:** Christina Paciolla, Executive Editor.

EGG HARBOR TOWNSHIP

CURRENT OF ABSECON, PLEASANTVILLE, THE. 3129 Fire Rd, Ste 2, Egg Harbor Township, NJ 08234. Telephone: 609-383-8994. FAX: 609-383-0056. E-MAIL: sales@catamaranmedia.com. URL: http://www.shorenewstoday.com. Year Established: 1997. Pub. Frequency: w. (Fri.) Page Size: tabloid.Adv. Rate: col. inch $12.75 Circulation: 15,000 per issue (controlled and free). **Owner(s):** Catamaran Media LLC, 2087 S Shore Rd. 2nd Fl, Seaville, NJ 08230. **Management:** Richard Travers, Publisher. Lenore Brady, Advertising Director. Carl Price, Circulation Manager. Christopher Beausang, Classified Adv. Mgr.. **Editorial:** James Fitzpatrick, Editor. Stephanie Loder, Associate Editor. RJ Liberatore Jr., Sports Editor.

CURRENT OF EGG HARBOR TOWNSHIP, THE. ISSN 1520-6009 3129 Fire Rd, Ste 2, Egg Harbor Township, NJ 08234. Telephone: 609-383-8994. FAX: 609-383-0056. E-MAIL: sales@catamaranmedia.com. URL: http://www.shorenewstoday,com. Year Established: 1997. Pub. Frequency: w. (Thu.) Page Size: tabloid.Adv. Rate: col. inch $12.75 Circulation: 10,000 per issue (paid and controlled). **Owner(s):** Catamaran Media LLC, 2087 S Shore Rd. 2nd Fl, Seaville, NJ 08230. **Management:** Richard Travers, Publisher. Lenore Brady, Advertising Director. Carl Price, Circulation Manager. Christopher Beausang, Classified Adv. Mgr.. **Editorial:** James Fitzpatrick, Editor. Stephanie Loder, Associate Editor. RJ Liberatore Jr., Sports Editor.

CURRENT OF GALLOWAY, PORT REPUBLIC, THE. 3129 Fire Rd, Ste 2, Egg Harbor Township, NJ 08234. Telephone: 609-383-8994. FAX: 609-383-0056. E-MAIL: sales@catamaranmedia.com. URL: http://www.shorenewstoday.com. Year Established: 1997. Pub. Frequency: w. (Wed.) Page Size: tabloid.Adv. Rate: col. inch $12.75 Circulation: 10,000 per issue (controlled and free). **Owner(s):** Catamaran Media LLC, 2087 S Shore Rd. 2nd Fl, Seaville, NJ 08230. **Management:** Richard Travers, Publisher. Lenore Brady, Advertising Director. Carl Price, Circulation Manager. Christopher Beausang, Classified Adv. Mgr.. **Editorial:** James Fitzpatrick, Editor. Stephanie Loder, Associate Editor. RJ Liberatore Jr., Sports Editor.

CURRENT OF NORTHFIELD, LINWOOD, SOMERS POINT, THE. ISSN 1520-5983
3129 Fire Rd, Ste 2, Egg Harbor Township, NJ 08234. Telephone: 609-383-8994. FAX: 609-383-0056. E-MAIL: sales@catamaranmedia.com. URL: http://www.shorenewstoday.com. Year Established: 1997. Pub. Frequency: w. (Wed.) Page Size: tabloid.Adv. Rate: col. inch $12.75 Circulation: 12,500 per issue (controlled and free). **Owner(s):** Catamaran Media LLC, 2087 S Shore Rd. 2nd Fl, Seaville, NJ 08230. **Management:** Richard Travers, Publisher. Lenore Brady, Advertising Director. Carl Price, Circulation Manager. Christopher Beausang, Classified Adv. Mgr.. **Editorial:** James Fitzpatrick, Editor. Stephanie Loder, Associate Editor. RJ Liberatore Jr., Sports Editor.

DOWNBEACH CURRENT, THE. ISSN 1520-5967
3129 Fire Rd, Ste 2, Egg Harbor Township, NJ 08234. Telephone: 609-383-8994. FAX: 609-383-0056. E-MAIL: sales@catamaranmedia.com. URL: http://www.shorenewstoday.com. Year Established: 1997. Pub. Frequency: w. (Thu.) Page Size: tabloid.Adv. Rate: col. inch $12.75 Circulation: 6,500 per issue (controlled and free). **Owner(s):** Catamaran Media LLC, 2087 S Shore Rd. 2nd Fl, Seaville, NJ 08230. **Management:** Richard Travers, Publisher. Lenore Brady, Advertising Director. Carl Price, Circulation Manager. Christopher Beausang, Classified Adv. Mgr.. **Editorial:** James Fitzpatrick, Editor. Stephanie Loder, Associate Editor. RJ Liberatore Jr., Sports Editor.

FAIR LAWN

COMMUNITY NEWS (FAIR LAWN). 12-38 River Rd., Fair Lawn, NJ 07410-1802. Telephone: 201-791-8400. E-MAIL: communitynews@northjersey.com. URL: http://www.northjersey.com. Year Established: 1948. Pub. Frequency: w. (Wed.) Page Size: tabloid.Adv. Rate: col. inch $50.15 Circulation: 40,530 per issue (free). **Owner(s):** North Jersey Media Group, 150 River St, Hackensack, NJ 07601-7172. Telephone: 201-646-4000. **Management:** Stephen Borg, President. Sharon Puser, Publisher. Amy Weinhofer, Advertising Manager. Kerry Rubin, Classified Adv. Mgr.. **Editorial:** Richard Mardekian, Editor.

FLEMINGTON

HUNTERDON COUNTY DEMOCRAT. PO Box 32, Flemington, NJ 08822-0032. Telephone: 908-782-4747. FAX: 908-782-4706. E-MAIL: news@hedemocrat.com. URL: http://www.hunterdon-online.com. Year Established: 1825. Pub. Frequency: w. (Thu.) Page Size: standard. Subscrip. Rate: $.75 newsstand/cover; $16 for 6 mos. in county; $29/yr in county; $35/yr out of county. Circulation: 25,000 per issue (paid). **Owner(s):** NJN Publishing, See address and contact information above. **Management:** David Guidt, Publisher. Judy Morgan, Circulation Manager. Hank Soulen, Sales Manager. **Editorial:** Jay Langley, Executive Editor. Rick Epstein, Managing Editor.

FRANKLINVILLE

FRANKLIN TOWNSHIP SENTINEL. ISSN 0016-0040
PO Box 367, Franklinville, NJ 08322. Telephone: 856-694-1600. FAX: 856-694-0469. E-MAIL: ftsentinel@aol.com. Year Established: 1942. Pub. Frequency: w. Page Size: broadsheet. Subscrip. Rate: $13.50/yr. Adv. Rate: col. inch $8.25 Circulation: 4,475. **Owner(s):** James R. Kinkade, See address and contact information above. **Management:** James R. Kinkade, Publisher. Carol Kinkade, Office Manager. Cindy Marcs, Advertising Manager. **Editorial:** James R. Kinkade, Editor.

FREEHOLD

NEWS TRANSCRIPT. 3499 Rte 9 N, Ste 1B, Freehold, NJ 07728. E-MAIL: gmnews@gmnews.com. URL: http://www.gmnews.com. Mailing Address: PO Box 5001, Freehold, NJ 07728-5001. Year Established: 1888. Pub. Frequency: w. (Wed.) Page Size: tabloid.Subscrip. Rate: $25/yr mailed Circulation: 40,000 per issue (free). **Owner(s):** Greater Media Newspapers, See address and contact information above. **Management:** Kevin Wittman, Publisher. Jonathan Theophilakos, Advertising Director. Sandy Theo, Advertising Manager. Michele Nesbihal, Circulation Manager. Robert Waitt, Classified Adv. Mgr.. **Editorial:** Mark Rosman, Editor. Gregory Bean, Executive Editor. Doug McKenzie, Sports Editor.

TRI-TOWN NEWS (FREEHOLD). 3499 Rte 9 N, Ste 1B, Freehold, NJ 07728. Telephone: 732-358-5200. FAX: 732-780-4257. E-MAIL: gmntownews@gmnews.com. URL: http://www.gmnews.com. Mailing Address: PO Box 5001, Freehold, NJ 07728-5001. Pub. Frequency: w. (Thu) Subscrip. Rate: $25/yr mailed. Freelance Pay: $1/column-inch. **Owner(s):** Greater Media Newspapers, See address and contact information above. **Management:** Kevin Wittman, Publisher. Jonathan Theophilakos, Advertising Director. Michele Nesbihal, Circulation Manager. Robert Waitt, Classified Adv. Mgr.. **Editorial:** Mark Rosman, Editor. Gregory Bean, Executive Editor. Doug McKenzie, Sports Editor.

FRENCHTOWN

DELAWARE VALLEY NEWS. 207 Harrison St., Frenchtown, NJ 08825-0244. Telephone: 908-996-4047. FAX: 908-996-2238. E-MAIL: news@hcd.com. URL: http://www.nj.com. Mailing Address: PO Box 244, Frenchtown, NJ 08825-0244. Year Established: 1879. Pub. Frequency: w. (Thu.) Page Size: broadsheet.Subscrip. Rate: $.50 newsstand/cover; $18/yr Circulation: 4,800 per issue (paid). **Owner(s):** Hunterdon County Democrat, PO Box 32, Flemington, NJ 08822. Telephone: 908-782-4747. **Management:** David Gwidt, Publisher. Joli Weber, Advertising. Judy Morgan, Circulation Manager. **Editorial:** Nick DiGiovanni, Editor.

GARFIELD

MESSENGER (GARFIELD), THE. 48 Harrison Ave., Garfield, NJ 07026. Telephone: 973-473-1927. FAX: 973-546-4233. E-MAIL: majorpress@aol.com. Year Established: 1938. Pub. Frequency: w. (Thu.) Page Size: tabloid. Subscrip. Rate: $12/yr mailed. Adv. Rate: col. inch $7 Circulation: 1,500 per issue (paid). **Owner(s):** James & Nancy Huffman, 629 Victoria Ave., Paramus, NJ 07652. Telephone: 201-652-6155. FAX: 201-652-7126. **Management:** Nancy C Huffman, President. **Editorial:** Nancy C Huffman, Editor. James A Huffman, Managing Editor.

GLOUCESTER CITY

GLOUCESTER CITY NEWS. PO Box 151, Gloucester City, NJ 08030. Telephone: 856-456-1199. FAX: 856-456-1330. E-MAIL: gcneditor@netzero.com. URL: http://www.gloucestercitynews.com/. Year Established: 1927. Pub. Frequency: w. (Thu.) Page Size: tabloid. Subscrip. Rate: $.50 newsstand/cover; $19/yr in county. Freelance Pay: $25/article. Circulation: 5,000 per issue (paid and free). **Owner(s):** Albert Countryman, Jr., See address and contact information above. **Management:** Albert Countryman Jr., Publisher. Cynthia Marden, Office Manager. **Editorial:** Albert Countryman Jr., Editor.

HACKETTSTOWN

BLAIRSTOWN PRESS. 106 E. Moore St., Hackettstown, NJ 07840. Telephone: 908-852-1212. FAX: 908-852-9320. Mailing Address: PO Box 425, Blairstown, NJ 07825. Year Established: 1877. Pub. Frequency: w. (Thu.) Page Size: broadsheet. Subscrip. Rate: $.50 newsstand/cover; $21/yr in county. Circulation: 4,000 per issue (paid). **Owner(s):** Advance Publications, Inc., See address and contact information above. **Management:** Enid Logan, Publisher. Brian Hodge, Advertising. Ted Wnoroski, Circulation Manager. **Editorial:** Enid Logan, Editor.

COMMUNITY FORUM. 106 E. Moore St., Hackettstown, NJ 07840. Telephone: 908-852-1212. FAX: 908-852-9320. Mailing Address: PO Box 500, Hackettstown, NJ 07840. Year Established: 1972. Pub. Frequency: w. (Fri.) Page Size: broadsheet. Circulation: 53,511 per issue (paid and free). **Owner(s):** Advance Publications, Inc., 950 Fingerboard Rd., Staten Island, NY 10305. Telephone: 718-981-1234. **Management:** Steve Jankowski, Advertising. Ted Wnoroski, Circulation Manager. **Editorial:** Andy Loigus, Sports Editor.

NEWS (HACKETTSTOWN), THE. 106 E. Morris St., Hackettstown, NJ 07840. Telephone: 908-852-1212. FAX: 908-852-9320. E-MAIL: elogan@njnpublishing.com. Mailing Address: PO Box 500, Hackettstown, NJ 07840. Year Established: 1962. Pub. Frequency: w. (Wed.) Page Size: broadsheet. Subscrip. Rate: $.35 newsstand/cover; $21/yr in county; $25/yr out of county. Circulation: 1,300 per issue (paid). **Owner(s):** Advance Publications, Inc., 950 Fingerboard Rd., Staten Island, NY 10305. Telephone: 718-981-1234. **Management:** Enid Logan, Publisher. Robin Von Ohlsen, Advertising Manager. **Editorial:** Enid Logan, Editor-in-Chief.

STAR-GAZETTE, THE. 106 E. Moore St., Hackettstown, NJ 07840. Telephone: 908-852-1212. FAX: 908-852-9320. E-MAIL: elogan@njnpublishing.com. Mailing Address: PO Box 500, Hackettstown, NJ 07840. Pub. Frequency: w. (Wed. & Thu.) Page Size: broadsheet. Subscrip. Rate: $.50 newsstand/cover; $24/yr in county; $26/yr out of county. Circulation: 4,300 per issue (paid). **Owner(s):** Advance Publications, Inc., 950 Fingerboard Rd., Staten Island, NY 10305. Telephone: 718-981-1234. **Management:** Enid Logan, Publisher. Robin Von Ohlsen, Advertising Manager. Ted Wnoroski, Circulation Manager. **Editorial:** Enid Logan, Managing Editor. Linda Zetterberg, Production Manager.

WARREN REPORTER, THE. 106 E. Moore St., Hackettstown, NJ 07840. Telephone: 908-852-1212. FAX: 908-852-9320. Mailing Address: PO Box 500, Hackettstown, NJ 07840. Year Established: 1962. Pub. Frequency: w. (Thu.) Page Size: broadsheet. Freelance Pay: $25/article. Circulation: 53,000 per issue (free). **Owner(s):** Advance Publications, Inc., 950 Fingerboard Rd., Staten Island, NY 10305. Telephone: 718-981-1234. **Management:** Enid Logan, Publisher. Steve Jankowski, Advertising. Rich Salerno, Circulation Manager. **Editorial:** Enid Logan, Editor. Andy Loigus, Sports Editor.

HAMMONTON

ATLANTIC COUNTY RECORD. 115 12th St., Hammonton, NJ 08037. Mailing Address: PO Box 596, Hammonton, NJ 08037. Pub. Frequency: w. (Wed.) Page Size: broadsheet. Subscrip. Rate: $.50 newsstand/cover; $24/yr in county. Freelance Pay: $20/article. Circulation: 3,500 per issue (paid). **Owner(s):** Gannett Company, Inc., 7950 Jones Branch Dr, McLean, VA 22107. Telephone: 703-854-6000. **Management:** Nancy Monaghan, Publisher. Helme Kandle, Office Manager. Ray Breitwieser, Advertising Manager. **Editorial:** Norlynne Lubrano, Editor. Tom Ryan, Sports.

EGG HARBOR NEWS. ISSN 0746-7036
115 12th St., Hammonton, NJ 08037. Telephone: 609-561-2300. FAX: 866-692-6385. Mailing Address: PO Box 596, Hammonton, NJ 08037. Year Established: 1911. Pub. Frequency: w. (Wed.) Page Size: broadsheet. Subscrip. Rate: $.50 newsstand/cover; $24/yr in county. Circulation: 2,000 per issue (paid). **Owner(s):** Gannett Company, Inc., 7950 Jones Branch Dr., McLean, VA 22107-0001. Telephone: 703-854-6000. **Management:** Nancy Monaghan, Publisher. Helme Kandle, Office Manager. Ray Breitwieser, Advertising Manager. **Editorial:** Norlynne Lubrano, Executive Editor.

HAMMONTON NEWS. 12th St. & West End Ave., Hammonton, NJ 08037. Telephone: 609-561-2300. FAX: 609-567-2249. Mailing Address: PO Box 596, Hammonton, NJ 08037. Year Established: 1858. Pub. Frequency: w. (Wed.) Page Size: broadsheet. Subscrip. Rate: $.50 newsstand/cover; $24/yr in county. Freelance Pay: $30/article. Circulation: 6,500 per issue (paid). **Owner(s):** Gannett Company, Inc., 7950 Jones Branch Dr, McLean, VA 22107. Telephone: 703-854-6000. **Management:** Nancy Monaghan, Publisher. Helme Kandle, Office Manager. Ray Breitwieser, Advertising Manager. **Editorial:** Norlynne Lubrano, Editor. Tom Ryan, Sports.

MAINLAND JOURNAL. 115 12th St., Hammonton, NJ 08037. Mailing Address: PO Box 596, Hammonton, NJ 08037. Year Established: 1894. Pub. Frequency: w. (Wed.) Page Size: broadsheet. Subscrip. Rate: $.50 newsstand/cover; $21/yr in county. Freelance Pay: $20/article. Circulation: 5,000 per issue (paid). **Owner(s):** Gannett Company, Inc., 7950 Jones Branch Dr., McLean, VA 22107-0001. Telephone: 703-854-6000. **Management:** Nancy Monaghan, Publisher. Helme Kandle, Office Manager. Ray Breitwieser, Advertising Manager. **Editorial:** Norlynne Lubrano, Executive Editor. Tom Ryan, Sports Editor.

HAWTHORNE

HAWTHORNE PRESS. PO Box 1, Hawthorne, NJ 07507-0001. Telephone: 973-427-3330. E-MAIL: hawpress@bellatlantic.net. Year Established: 1924. Pub. Frequency: w. (Thu.) Page Size: tabloid. Subscrip. Rate: $.50 newsstand/cover; $20/yr local; $23/yr in state; $27/yr out of state. Circulation: 10,000 per issue (paid). **Owner(s):** William R. Missonellie, See address and contact information above. **Management:** William R. Missonellie, Publisher. Barbara Zakur, Advertising Manager. **Editorial:** Linda Missonellie, Editor.

HIGHTSTOWN

MESSENGER-PRESS, THE. Royal Plaza Center Rte 130 S, Hightstown, NJ 08520. Telephone: 609-924-3244. FAX: 608-259-1182. URL: http://www.packetonline.com. Mailing Address: PO Box 1449, Hightstown, NJ 08520. Year Established: 1903. Pub. Frequency: w. (Thu.) Page Size: broadsheet. Subscrip. Rate: $.60 newsstand/cover; $26.50/yr in county. Adv. Rate: col. inch $15.30 Circulation: 3,376 per issue (paid). **Owner(s):** Princeton Packet, Inc., See address and contact information above. **Management:** James B. Kilgore, Publisher. Joe McCarron, Advertising. Dan Trexler, Classified Adv. Mgr.. **Editorial:** Robert Heyman, Editor. Erica Hammond, Lifestyle Editor.

PRINCETON PACKET, THE. ISSN 0746-178X
Royal Plaza Center Rte 130 S, Hightstown, NJ 08520. Telephone: 609-924-3244. FAX: 609-924-3842. E-MAIL: webmaster@pacpub.com. URL: http://www.princetonpacket.com. Year Established: 1786. Pub. Frequency: s-w. (Tue. & Fri.) Page Size: broadsheet. Subscrip. Rate: $.75 newsstand/cover; $60.32/yr in county. Adv. Rate: col. inch $37.20 Circulation: 13,050 per issue (paid). **Owner(s):** Princeton Packet, Inc., See address and contact information above. **Management:** James B. Kilgore, Publisher. Carol Baumel, Advertising. **Editorial:** Rick Sinding, Managing Editor. Thomas Lederer, City Editor. Erica Hammond, Lifestyle Editor. Bob Muse, Sports Editor.

TEMPO/MIDDLESEX. Royal Plaza Center Rte 130 S, Hightstown, NJ 08520. Telephone: 609-924-5412. FAX: 609-924-3842. E-MAIL: ads@pacpub.com. URL: http://www.packpub.com. Pub. Frequency: w. (Thu.) Page Size: tabloid.Adv. Rate: col. inch $25.29 Circulation: 47,339 per issue (free). **Owner(s):** Princeton Packet, Inc., See address and contact information above. **Management:** James B. Kilgore, Publisher. Joe McCarron, Advertising. Steve Urbish, Circulation Director. **Editorial:** Rick Sinding, Managing Editor.

WINDSOR-HIGHTS HERALD. Royal Plaza Center Rte 130 S, Hightstown, NJ 08520. E-MAIL: ads@pacpub.com. URL: http://www.windsorhightsherald.com. Mailing Address: PO Box 1449, Hightstown, NJ 08520. Year Established: 1965. Pub. Frequency: w. (Fri.) Page Size: broadsheet. Subscrip. Rate: $.75 newsstand/cover; $39/yr in county. Adv. Rate: col. inch $23.60 Circulation: 3,925 per issue (paid). **Owner(s):** Princeton Packet, Inc., 300 Witherspoon St., Princeton, NJ 08540. Telephone: 609-924-3244, 609-924-5412. **Management:** James B. Kilgore, Publisher. Laurie L Smith, Advertising Director. **Editorial:** Mark Moffa, Editor. Erica Hammond, Lifestyle Editor.

HILLSBOROUGH

HILLSBOROUGH BEACON. 307 Omni Dr., Hillsborough, NJ 08844. Telephone: 908-359-0850. FAX: 908-359-3930. E-MAIL: ads@pacpub.com. URL: http://www.princetonpacket.com. Year Established: 1956. Pub. Frequency: w. (Thu.) Page Size: broadsheet. Subscrip. Rate: $.75 newsstand/cover; $37.80/yr mailed. Adv. Rate: col. inch $28.20 Freelance Pay: $20/article. Circulation: 4,411 per issue (paid). **Owner(s):** Princeton Packet, Inc., 300 Witherspoon St., Princeton, NJ 08540. Telephone: 609-924-3244. **Management:** James B. Kilgore, Publisher. Joe McCarron, Advertising. Dawn Apisa, Classified Adv. Mgr.. **Editorial:** John Patten, Managing Editor.

MANVILLE NEWS, THE. ISSN 1058-6857
307 Omni Dr., Hillsborough, NJ 08844. Telephone: 908-359-0850. FAX: 908-359-3930. E-MAIL: ads@pacpub.com. URL: http://www.manvillenews.com. Year Established: 1945. Pub. Frequency: w. (Thu.) Page Size: broadsheet. Subscrip. Rate: $.75 newsstand/cover; $39/yr mailed in county. Adv. Rate: col. inch $28.20 Freelance Pay: $15-$40/article. Circulation: 1,163 per issue (paid). **Owner(s):** Princeton Packet, Inc., 300 Witherspoon St., Princeton, NJ 08540. **Management:** James B. Kilgore, Publisher. Bernadette Angeline, Advertising. Dawn Apisa, Classified Adv. Mgr.. **Editorial:** John Patten, Managing Editor.

HOBOKEN

HOBOKEN REPORTER. 1400 Washington St., Hoboken, NJ 07030. Telephone: 201-798-7800. FAX: 201-798-0018. E-MAIL: lmalato@hudsonreporter.com; dunger@hudsonreporter.com. URL: http://www.hobokenreporter.com. Year Established: 1983. Pub. Frequency: w. (Sun.) Page Size: tabloid. Subscrip. Rate: $50/yr. Freelance Pay: $20-$50/article. Circulation: 17,600 Sunday (paid and free). **Owner(s):** Lucha Malato & David Unger, See address and contact information above. **Management:** David Unger, Publisher. Robert Lopez, Circulation Manager. **Editorial:** Caren Lissner, Editor.

HUDSON CURRENT. 1400 Washington St., Hoboken, NJ 07030. Telephone: 201-798-7800. FAX: 201-798-0018. E-MAIL: lmalato@hudsonreporter.com; dunger@hudsonreporter.com. URL: http://www.hudsonreporter.com. Year Established: 1990. Pub. Frequency: w. (Thu.) Page Size: tabloid. Subscrip. Rate: $25 for 6 mos.; $50/yr. Circulation: 10,000 per issue (paid and free). **Owner(s):** Lucha Malato & David Unger, See address and contact information above. **Management:** David S. Unger, Publisher. **Editorial:** Caren Lissner, Editor.

JERSEY CITY REPORTER. 1400 Washington St., Hoboken, NJ 07030. Telephone: 201-798-7800. FAX: 201-798-0018. E-MAIL: lmalata@hudsonreporter.com; dunger@hudsonreporter.com. URL: http://www.hudsonreporter.com. Pub. Frequency: w. (Sun.) Page Size: tabloid. Subscrip. Rate: $50/yr. Adv. Rate: col. inch $15.15 Circulation: 20,100 Sunday (paid and free); 9,000 per issue (paid and free). **Owner(s):** Lucha Malato & David Unger, See address and contact information above. **Management:** David Unger, Publisher. Robert Lopez, Circulation Manager. **Editorial:** Caren Lissner, Editor.

NORTH BERGEN REPORTER. 1400 Washington St., Hoboken, NJ 07030. Telephone: 201-798-7800. FAX: 201-798-0018. E-MAIL: lmalato@hudsonreporter.com; dunger@hudsonreporter.com. URL: http://www.hudsonreporter.com. Year Established: 1983. Pub. Frequency: w. (Sun.) Page Size: tabloid. Subscrip. Rate: $50/yr. Adv. Rate: col. inch $15.15 Circulation: 19,150 Sunday (paid and free). **Owner(s):** Lucha Malato & David Unger, See address and contact information above. **Management:** David Unger, Publisher. **Editorial:** Caren Lissner, Editor.

SECAUCUS REPORTER. 1400 Washington St., Hoboken, NJ 07030. Telephone: 201-798-7800. FAX: 201-798-0018. E-MAIL: lmalato@hudsonreporter.com. URL: http://www.hudsonreporter.com. Pub. Frequency: w. (Sun) Page Size: tabloid. Subscrip. Rate: $50/yr. Adv. Rate: col. inch $15.15 Circulation: 6,050 per issue (paid and free). **Owner(s):** Lucha Malato & David Unger, See address and contact information above. **Management:** David Unger, Publisher. Robert Lopez, Circulation Manager. **Editorial:** Caren Lissner, Editor.

UNION CITY REPORTER. 1400 Washington St., Hoboken, NJ 07030. Telephone: 201-798-7800. FAX: 201-798-0018. E-MAIL: lmalato@hudsonreporter.com; dunger@hudson reporter.com. URL: http://www.unioncityreporter.com. Year Established: 1997. Pub. Frequency: w. (Sun) Page Size: tabloid. Subscrip. Rate: $50/yr. Adv. Rate: col. inch $15.15 Circulation: 12,800 per issue (paid and free). **Owner(s):** Lucha Malato & David Unger, See address and contact information above. **Management:** David Unger, Publisher. Robert Lopez, Circulation Manager. **Editorial:** Caren Lissner, Editor.

WEEHAWKEN REPORTER. 1400 Washington St., Hoboken, NJ 07030. Telephone: 201-798-7800. FAX: 201-798-0018. E-MAIL: lmalato@hudsonreporter.com; dunger@hudsonreporter.com. URL: http://www.hudsonreporter.com. Year Established: 1986. Pub. Frequency: w. (Sun) Page Size: tabloid. Subscrip. Rate: $50/yr. Adv. Rate: col. inch $15.15 Circulation: 5,050 Sunday (paid and free). **Owner(s):** Lucha Malato & David Unger, See address and contact information above. **Management:** David Unger, Publisher. Robert Lopez, Circulation Manager. **Editorial:** Caren Lissner, Editor.

WEST NEW YORK REPORTER. 1400 Washington St., Hoboken, NJ 07030. Telephone: 201-798-7800. FAX: 201-798-0018. E-MAIL: Lmalato@hudsonreporter.com; dunger@hudsonreporter.com. URL: http://www.westnewyorkreporter.com. Year Established: 1997. Pub. Frequency: w. (Sun.) Page Size: tabloid. Subscrip. Rate: $50/yr. Adv. Rate: col. inch $15.15 Circulation: 9,200 Sunday (paid and free). **Owner(s):** Lucha Malato & David Unger, See address and contact information above. **Management:** David Unger, Publisher. **Editorial:** Caren Lissner, Editor.

HOPEWELL

BEACON (LAMBERTVILLE), THE. 10 Hopewell Village Sq., 52 E. Broad St., Hopewell, NJ 08525. Telephone: 609-466-1190. FAX: 609-466-2123. E-MAIL: packnews@pack.com. URL: http://www.princetonpacket.com. Mailing Address: PO Box 8, Hopewell, NJ 08534. Pub. Frequency: w. (Thu.) Page Size: broadsheet. Subscrip. Rate: $.75 newsstand/cover; $39/yr in county. Adv. Rate: col. inch $10.40 Circulation: 3,109 per issue (paid). **Owner(s):** Princeton Packet, Inc., See address and contact information above. **Management:** James Kilgore, Publisher. Joe McCarron, Advertising. Michele Plante, Advertising Director. **Editorial:** Mae Rhine, Managing Editor. Linda Seida, Writer.

HOPEWELL VALLEY NEWS. 10 Hopewell Village Sq., 52 E. Broad St., Hopewell, NJ 08525. Telephone: 609-466-1190. FAX: 609-466-2123. URL: http://www.packetonline.com. Mailing Address: PO Box 8, Hopewell, NJ 08525. Year Established: 1956. Pub. Frequency: w. (Thu.) Page Size: broadsheet. Subscrip. Rate: $.75 newsstand/cover; $34.84/yr in town. Adv. Rate: col. inch $15.30 Circulation: 4,395 per issue (paid). **Owner(s):** Princeton Packet, Inc., 300 Witherspoon St., Princeton, NJ 08540. Telephone: 609-924-3244, 609-924-5412. **Management:** Roxanne Kleinkauf, Advertising. **Editorial:** Ruth Peterson Luse, Managing Editor. Jim Green, Sports Editor.

LAWRENCE LEDGER, THE. ISSN 0746-1771
10 Hopewell Village Sq., 52 E. Broad St., Hopewell, NJ 08525. Telephone: 609-466-1190. FAX: 609-466-2123. E-MAIL: ads@pacpub.com. URL: http://www.lawrenceledger.com. Mailing Address: PO Box 8, Hopewell, NJ 08525. Year Established: 1968. Pub. Frequency: w. (Thu.) Page Size: broadsheet. Subscrip. Rate: $.75 newsstand/cover; $39/yr. Adv. Rate: col. inch $15.30 Freelance Pay: $15-$40/article. Circulation: 3,220 per issue (paid). **Owner(s):** Princeton Packet, Inc., Royal Plaza Center Rte 130 S, Hightstown, NJ 08520. Telephone: 609-924-3244. FAX: 609-921-2714. **Management:** James B. Kilgore, Publisher. Michele Plante, Advertising Director. **Editorial:** Erica Hammond, Lifestyle Editor. Jim Green, Sports Editor.

ISLAND HEIGHTS

GREENWICH VILLAGE GAZETTE. PO Box 1023, Island Heights, NJ 08732-1023. Telephone: 201-681-4698. URL: http://www.nycny.com. Year Established: 1996. Pub. Frequency: w. **Owner(s):** Greenwich Village Gazette, See address and contact information above. **Management:** Bob Gilford, Publisher. Howard Flysher, Advertising. **Editorial:** Richard Schiff, Editor.

KEARNY

OBSERVER (KEARNY), THE. 531 Kearny Ave., Kearny, NJ 07032. Telephone: 201-991-1600. FAX: 201-991-8941. URL: http://www.theobserver.com. Year Established: 1887. Pub. Frequency: w. (Wed.) Page Size: tabloid. Subscrip. Rate: $90/yr mailed 1st class. Adv. Rate: B&W page $1,326, color page $1,426 Circulation: 33,000 per issue (paid). **Owner(s):** Mary Tortoreti, Pres., See address and contact information above. **Management:** Robert Pezzolla, General Manager. Mary Tortoreti, President. Lisa Tortoreti Pezzolla, Publisher.

KINNELON

SUBURBAN TRENDS. 300 Kakeout Rd., Kinnelon, NJ 07405-2548. Telephone: 973-283-5600. FAX: 973-283-5623. E-MAIL: suburbantrends@northjersey.com. URL: http://www.northjersey.com. Year Established: 1958. Pub. Frequency: s-w. (Wed. & Sun.) Page Size: broadsheet. Subscrip. Rate: $.50 newsstand/cover; $.60 newsstand/cover Sun.; $39/yr in county. Adv. Rate: col. inch $13.60 Circulation: 10,565 Sunday (paid); 9,683 per issue (paid). **Owner(s):** North Jersey Media Goup, One River St, Hackensack, NJ 07601-7172. Telephone: 201-646-4000. FAX: 201-646-4310. **Management:** Stephen Borg, President. Michael Lawson, Publisher. Garry DeYoung, Advertising Manager. Rose O'Riordan, Classified Adv. Mgr.. **Editorial:** Matthew Fagen, Editor.

LEBANON

HUNTERDON REVIEW. 1128 Rte. 31 N., Lebanon, NJ 08833. Telephone: 908-735-4081. FAX: 908-735-2945. E-MAIL: cortparker@recordernewspapers.com. URL: http://www.hunterdonreview.com. Mailing Address: PO Box 5308, Clinton, NJ 08809. Year Established: 1868. Pub. Frequency: w. (Wed.) Page Size: broadsheet. Subscrip. Rate: $.50 newsstand/cover; $23/yr in county; $32/yr out of county; $38/yr out of state. Circulation: 4,900 per issue (paid). **Owner(s):** Recorder Publishing Co., 17-19 Morristown Rd., Bernardsville, NJ 07924. Telephone: 908-766-3900. **Management:** Lance Osborne, Advertising Manager. David W. Nelson, Circulation Director. Elizabeth K. Parker, Business Manager. **Editorial:** Elizabeth K. Parker, Executive Editor. Philip Nordone, Assistant Editor.

LIVINGSTON

WEST ESSEX TRIBUNE. 495 S. Livingston Ave., Livingston, NJ 07039-0065. Telephone: 973-992-1771. FAX: 973-992-7015. E-MAIL: livpaper@aol.com. URL: http://www.westessextribune.org. Mailing Address: PO Box 65, Livingston, NJ 07039-0065. Year Established: 1929. Pub. Frequency: w. (Thu.) Page Size: broadsheet. Subscrip. Rate: $.50 newsstand/cover; $20/yr in county; $25/yr out of county; $27/yr out of state. Adv. Rate: col. inch $10.95 Circulation: 7,500 per issue (paid). **Owner(s):** Jennifer Chciuk, See address and contact information above. **Management:** Jennifer Chciuk, President. Nancy B. Dinar, Vice President. Donna Cota, Advertising. Jennifer Chciuk, Advertising Manager. Lori Fine, Classified Adv. Mgr.. **Editorial:** Nancy B. Dinar, Editor. Christine Sablynski, Managing Editor.

MADISON

FLORHAM PARK EAGLE. 155 Main St., Madison, NJ 07940. Telephone: 973-377-2000. FAX: 973-377-7721. E-MAIL: editor@recordernewspapers.com. URL: http://www.florhamparkeagle.com. Mailing Address: PO Box 160, Madison, NJ 07940. Year Established: 1882. Pub. Frequency: w. (Thu.) Page Size: broadsheet. Subscrip. Rate: $.50 newsstand/cover; $25/yr mailed in county; $32/yr mailed out of county; $38/yr mailed out of state. Circulation: 3,000 per issue (paid). **Owner(s):** Recorder Publishing Co., 17-19 Morristown Rd., Bernardsville, NJ 07924. Telephone: 908-766-3900. FAX: 908-766-6365. **Management:** Elizabeth Parker, Co-Publisher. Doug McBride, Advertising Director. Allison Spinella, Advertising Manager. David Nelson, Circulation Manager. **Editorial:** George Danco, Editor. Elizabeth Parker, Executive Editor.

HANOVER EAGLE & REGIONAL WEEKLY NEWS. 155 Main St., Madison, NJ 07940. Telephone: 800-624-3684. FAX: 973-377-7721. E-MAIL: editor@recordernewspapers.com. URL: http://www.recordernewspapers.com/hanover_eagle/. Mailing Address: PO Box 160, Madison, NJ 07940. Year Established: 1956. Pub. Frequency: w. (Thu.) Page Size: standard. Subscrip. Rate: $.50 newsstand/cover; $23/yr in county; $32/yr out of county; $38/yr out of state. Adv. Rate: col. inch $10.60 Freelance Pay: $25-$50/article. Circulation: 3,088 per issue (paid). **Owner(s):** Recorder Publishing Co., 17-19 Morristown Rd., Bernardsville, NJ 07924. Telephone: 908-766-3900. FAX: 908-766-6365. **Management:** Elizabeth Parker, Co-Publisher. Doug McBride, Advertising Director. David Nelson, Circulation Manager. **Editorial:** Jim Lent, Editor. Elizabeth Parker, Executive Editor. Gary Hertzog, Managing Editor.

MADISON EAGLE. 155 Main St., Madison, NJ 07940. Telephone: 973-377-2000. FAX: 973-377-7721. E-MAIL: editor@recordernewspapers.com. URL: http://www.madisoneagle.com. Mailing Address: PO Box 160, Madison, NJ 07940. Year Established: 1880. Pub. Frequency: w. (Thu.) Page Size: broadsheet. Subscrip. Rate: $.50 newsstand/cover; $25/yr mailed in county; $32/yr mailed out of county; $38/yr mailed out of state. Adv. Rate: col. inch $9 Circulation: 3,343 per issue (paid). **Owner(s):** Recorder Publishing Co., 17-19 Morristown Rd., Bernardsville, NJ 07924. Telephone: 908-766-3900. FAX: 908-766-6365. **Management:** Elizabeth Parker, Co-Publisher. Allison Spinella, Advertising Director. Dave Nelson, Circulation Manager. **Editorial:** Elizabeth Parker, Executive Editor. Gary Herzog, Managing Editor.

MORRIS NEWS BEE. 155 Main St., Madison, NJ 07940. Telephone: 973-377-2000. FAX: 973-377-7721. E-MAIL: editor@recordernewspaper.com. URL: http://www.morrisnewsbee.com. Mailing Address: PO Box 160, Madison, NJ 07940. Year Established: 1946. Pub. Frequency: w. (Thu.) Page Size: broadsheet. Subscrip. Rate: $.50 newsstand/cover; $23/yr mailed in county; $32/yr mailed out of county; $38/yr mailed out of state. Circulation: 3,033 per issue (paid). **Owner(s):** Recorder Publishing Co., 17-19 Morristown Rd., Bernardsville, NJ 07924. Telephone: 908-766-3900. FAX: 908-766-6365. **Management:** Elizabeth Parker, Co-Publisher. Doug McBride, Advertising Director. David Nelson, Circulation Manager. **Editorial:** Jim Lent, Editor. Elizabeth Parker, Executive Editor. Phillip J. Nardone, Assistant Editor.

MANAHAWKIN

BEACH HAVEN TIMES. 345 E. Bay Ave., Manahawkin, NJ 08050. Telephone: 609-597-3211. FAX: 609-978-4592. E-MAIL: tbeacon@bellatlantic.net. URL: http://www.southernocean.com. Year Established: 1923. Pub. Frequency: w. (Wed.) Page Size: broadsheet. Subscrip. Rate: $.50 newsstand/cover; $24/yr mailed in county; $32/yr mailed out of county. Freelance Pay: $1/column-inch. Circulation: 7,196 per issue (paid). **Owner(s):** Gannett Company, Inc., 7950 Jones Branch Dr., McLean, VA 22107-0001. Telephone: 703-854-6000. **Management:** Robert Collins, Publisher. Marie Touhy, Advertising Manager. **Editorial:** John Hudzinski, Editor. Keith Newman, News Editor.

MANCHESTER

ADVANCE NEWS. 2048 Rte. 37, Manchester, NJ 08759. Telephone: 732-657-8936. FAX: 732-657-2970. Year Established: 1968. Pub. Frequency: w. (Wed.) Page Size: tabloid. Subscrip. Rate: $.25 newsstand/cover; $7.50/yr; $15 for 2 yrs.. Freelance Pay: $20/article. Circulation: 25,000 per issue (paid). **Owner(s):** Ciampi Publications LLC, 2048 Rte. 37, Lakehurst, NJ 08733. Telephone: 732-657-8936. **Management:** Stephen Crosson, Publisher. Rocco Varelli, Circulation Manager. **Editorial:** Rocco Varelli, Editor.

MAPLEWOOD

EAST ORANGE RECORD. 463 Valley St., Maplewood, NJ 07040. Telephone: 973-763-0700. FAX: 973-763-2557. E-MAIL: webmaster@localsource.com. URL: http://www.localsource.com. Year Established: 1899. Pub. Frequency: w. (Thu.) Page Size: broadsheet. Subscrip. Rate: $.75 newsstand/cover; $26/yr mailed in county; $36/yr mailed out of county. Adv. Rate: col. inch $15 Circulation: 3,500 per issue (paid). **Owner(s):** Worrall Community Newspapers, Inc., 1291 Stuyvesant Ave., Union, NJ 07083. Telephone: 908-686-7700. **Management:** David Worrall, Publisher. Joseph Ornegri, Advertising Director. John D'Achino, Circulation Manager. Tom Yauch, Classified Adv. Mgr.. **Editorial:** Steve Proctor, Editor. Tom Canavan, Editor-in-Chief. John Zucal, Managing Editor.

NEWS-RECORD OF MAPLEWOOD & SOUTH ORANGE. 463 Valley St., Maplewood, NJ 07040. Telephone: 973-763-0700. FAX: 973-763-2557. E-MAIL: editoral@localsource.com. URL: http://www.localsource.com. Mailing Address: PO Box 158, Maplewood, NJ 07040. Year Established: 1886. Pub. Frequency: w. (Thu.) Page Size: broadsheet. Subscrip. Rate: $.75 newsstand/cover; $26/yr mailed in county; $36/yr mailed out of county. Adv. Rate: col. inch $18.50 Circulation: 6,745 per issue (paid). **Owner(s):** Worrall Community Newspapers, Inc., 1291 Stuyvesant Ave., Union, NJ 07083. Telephone: 908-686-7700. **Management:** David Worrall, Publisher. Joseph Ornegri, Advertising Director. John D'Achino, Circulation Manager. Tom Yauch, Classified Adv. Mgr.. **Editorial:** Tara Hayden, Editor. Tom Caravan, Editor-in-Chief. Jim Sturdivant, Managing Editor.

ORANGE TRANSCRIPT. 463 Valley St., Maplewood, NJ 07040. Telephone: 973-763-0700. FAX: 973-763-2557. E-MAIL: essexcty@thelocalsource.com. URL: http://www.localsource.com. Year Established: 1898. Pub. Frequency: w. (Thu.) Page Size: broadsheet. Subscrip. Rate: $.75 newsstand/cover; $26/yr mailed in county; $36/yr mailed out of county. Adv. Rate: col. inch $15 Circulation: 2,150 per issue (paid). **Owner(s):** Worrall Community Newspapers, Inc., 1291 Stuyvesant Ave., Union, NJ 07083. Telephone: 908-686-7700. **Management:** David Worrall, Publisher. Joseph Ornegri, Advertising Director. John D'Achino, Circulation Manager. Tom Yauch, Classified Adv. Mgr.. **Editorial:** Steve Proctor, Editor. Tom Canavan, Editor-in-Chief. Raymond Worrall, Executive Editor.

VAILSBURG LEADER. 463 Valley St., Maplewood, NJ 07040. Telephone: 973-763-0700. FAX: 973-763-2557. URL: http://www.localsource.com. Mailing Address: PO Box 158, Maplewood, NJ 07040. Year Established: 1949. Pub. Frequency: w. (Thu.) Page Size: broadsheet. Subscrip. Rate: $.75 newsstand/cover; $26/yr in county; $36/yr out of county. Adv. Rate: col. inch $15 Circulation: 271 per issue (paid). **Owner(s):** Worrall Community Newspapers, Inc., 1291 Stuyvesant Ave., Union, NJ 07083. Telephone: 973-686-7700. **Management:** David Worrall, Publisher. Joseph Ornegri, Advertising Director. John D'Achino, Circulation Manager. Tom Yauch, Classified Adv. Mgr.. **Editorial:** David Jablonsky, Editor. Tom Canavan, Editor-in-Chief.

WEST ORANGE CHRONICLE. 463 Valley St., Maplewood, NJ 07040. Telephone: 973-763-0700. FAX: 973-763-2557. E-MAIL: wochronicle@yahoo.com. URL: http://www.localsource.com. Year Established: 1931. Pub. Frequency: w. (Thu.) Page Size: broadsheet. Subscrip. Rate: $.75 newsstand/cover; $26/yr mailed in county; $36/yr mailed out of county. Adv. Rate: col. inch $18.50 Circulation: 6,500 per issue (paid). **Owner(s):** Worrall Community Newspapers, Inc., 1291 Stuyvesant Ave., Union, NJ 07083. Telephone: 908-686-7700. **Management:** David Worrall, Publisher. Joseph Ornegri, Advertising Director. John D'Achino, Circulation Manager. Tom Yauch, Classified Adv. Mgr.. **Editorial:** Steve Proctor, Editor. Tom Caravan, Editor-in-Chief. Steve Gugliociello, Managing Editor.

MEDFORD

AD-LINES. 176 Rte. 70 at Jones Rd., Medford, NJ 08055. Telephone: 609-654-5000. FAX: 609-654-8237. Mailing Address: PO Box 1027, Medford, NJ 08055. Year Established: 1980. Pub. Frequency: w. (Wed.) Page Size: broadsheet Circulation: 43,000 per issue (free). **Owner(s):** Journal Register Co., 50 W State St, 12th Fl, Trenton, NJ 08608. Telephone: 609-396-2200. **Management:** Stephanie Leicht, Publisher. **Editorial:** Steve Doland, Editor.

CENTRAL RECORD. 176 Rte. 70 at Jones Rd., Medford, NJ 08055. Telephone: 609-654-5000. FAX: 609-654-8237. Mailing Address: PO Box 1027, Medford, NJ 08055. Year Established: 1896. Pub. Frequency: w. (Thu.) Page Size: broadsheet. Subscrip. Rate: $.50 newsstand/cover; $16/yr mailed. Circulation: 15,000 per issue (paid). **Owner(s):** Journal Register Co., 50 W State St, 12th Fl, Trenton, NJ 08608. Telephone: 609-396-2200. **Management:** Chris Henry, Publisher. **Editorial:** Steve Doland, Editor.

MAPLE SHADE PROGRESS. 176 Rte. 70 at Jones Rd., Medford, NJ 08055. Telephone: 856-779-7788. FAX: 856-654-8237. E-MAIL: msp@ingnews.com. Mailing Address: PO Box 1027, Medford, NJ 08055. Year Established: 1918. Pub. Frequency: w. (Fri.) Page Size: broadsheet. Subscrip. Rate: $.50 newsstand/cover; $16/yr local. Circulation: 3,000 per issue (paid and free). **Owner(s):** Journal Register Co., 50 W State St, 12th Fl, Trenton, NJ 08608. Telephone: 609-396-2200. **Management:** Chris Henry, Publisher. **Editorial:** Steve Doland, Editor.

MIDDLETOWN

COURIER (MIDDLETOWN), THE. 320 Kings Hwy. E, Middletown, NJ 07748. Telephone: 732-957-0070. FAX: 732-957-0143. Mailing Address: PO Box 399, Middletown, NJ 07748-0399. Year Established: 1955. Pub. Frequency: w. (Thu.) Page Size: tabloid. Subscrip. Rate: $.40 newsstand/cover; $18/yr in state; $22/yr out of state. Adv. Rate: col. inch $12.05 Freelance Pay: $25-$35/article. Circulation: 7,200 per issue (paid). **Owner(s):** Bayshore Press, Inc., See address and contact information above. **Management:** James J. Purcell, Publisher. Darlene Franklin, Advertising.

MILLBURN

ITEM OF MILLBURN & SHORT HILLS, THE. 343 Millburn Ave., Ste. 100, Millburn, NJ 07041-1940. Telephone: 973-376-1200. FAX: 973-376-8556. E-MAIL: theitem@northjersey.com. URL: http://www.northjersey.com. Year Established: 1888. Pub. Frequency: w. (Thu.) Page Size: broadsheet. Subscrip. Rate: $.75 newsstand/cover; $31/yr in county. Adv. Rate: col. inch $11.75 Circulation: 4,311 per issue (paid). **Owner(s):** North Jersey Media Group, 150 River St, Hackensack, NJ 07601-7172. Telephone: 201-646-4000. FAX: 201-646-4310. **Management:** Stephen Borg, President. Kathleen Hivish, Publisher. Nancy Connolly, Advertising Manager. Kerry Rubin, Classified Adv. Mgr.. **Editorial:** Carol De Graaf, Editor.

MONTCLAIR

MONTCLAIR TIMES, THE. 114 Valley Rd., Montclair, NJ 07042-2321. Telephone: 973-233-5000. FAX: 973-233-5032. E-MAIL: contactus@montclairtimes.com. URL: http://www.montclairtimes.com. Year Established: 1877. Pub. Frequency: w. (Thu.) Page Size: broadsheet. Subscrip. Rate: $.75 newsstand/cover; $26/yr in county; $31/yr in state. Adv. Rate: col. inch $15.10 Circulation: 10,222 per issue (paid). **Owner(s):** North Jersey Media Group, 150 River St, Hackensack, NJ 07601-7172. Telephone: 201-646-4000. **Management:** Stephen Borg, President. Kathleen Hivish, Publisher. Brian Winterberg, Advertising Manager. Kerry Rubin, Classified Adv. Mgr.. **Editorial:** Mark S. Porter, Editor.

MOORESTOWN

NEWSWEEKLY (MOORESTOWN). 301 Mill St, Moorestown, NJ 08057. Telephone: 856-231-7600. FAX: 856-231-4333. E-MAIL: newsweekly@ingnews.com. URL: http://www.moorestownnewsweekly.com. Year Established: 1966. Pub. Frequency: w. (Thu.) Page Size: tabloid. Subscrip. Rate: $.50 newsstand/cover; $19/yr mailed in county; $26.50/yr mailed out of county. Circulation: 8,600 per issue (paid). **Owner(s):** Journal Register Co., Lower Makefield Corporate Center, 790 Township Line Rd, 3rd. flr, Yardley, PA 19067. **Management:** Stephanie Leicht, Publisher. Pat Haughey, Advertising Director. Ed Krywucki, Circulation Manager. **Editorial:** Christina Paciolla, Executive Editor.

NEW EGYPT

NEW EGYPT PRESS. 4 Main St, New Egypt, NJ 08533. E-MAIL: ekrywucki@ingnews.com. URL: http://www.southjerseylocalnews.com/WebApp/appmanager/JRC/Weekly. Pub. Frequency: w. Subscrip. Rate: $21/yr home delivery in county; $28.50/yr home delivery out of county; $19/yr home delivery to senior citizens. **Owner(s):** Journal Register Co., See address and contact information above. **Management:** J. Wesley Rowe, Publisher. Pat Haughey, Advertising Director. Ed Krywucki, Circulation Manager. Monica Carpenter, Classified Adv. Mgr.. **Editorial:** Tony Regina, Executive Editor. Eric Colvin, Managing Editor.

NEW PROVIDENCE

INDEPENDENT PRESS. 80 South St., New Providence, NJ 07974. Telephone: 908-464-1025. FAX: 908-464-9085. Year Established: 1965. Pub. Frequency: w. (Wed.) Page Size: broadsheet. Subscrip. Rate: $.50 newsstand/cover; $75/yr mailed. Adv. Rate: col. inch $20.50 Freelance Pay: $30/article. Circulation: 35,200 per issue (paid and free). **Owner(s):** Advance Publications, Inc., 950 Fingerboard Rd., Staten Island, NY 10305. Telephone: 718-981-1234. **Management:** Michael J. Kelly, Publisher. Lew King, Circulation Manager. **Editorial:** Patricia Meola, Editor.

NUTLEY

BELLEVILLE TIMES. 90 Centre St., Nutley, NJ 07110. Telephone: 973-667-2100. FAX: 973-667-3904. E-MAIL: bellevilletimes@northjersey.com. URL: http://www.njmg.com. Year Established: 1909. Pub. Frequency: w. (Thu.) Page Size: broadsheet. Subscrip. Rate: $.50 newsstand/cover; $21.95/yr in county. Adv. Rate: col. inch $12.15 Circulation: 2,638 per issue (paid). **Owner(s):** North Jersey Media Group, 150 River St, Hackensack, NJ 07601-7172. Telephone: 201-646-4000. **Management:** Stephen Borg, President. Kathleen Hivish, Publisher. Nancy Connolly, Advertising Manager. Kerry Rubin, Classified Adv. Mgr.. **Editorial:** Paul Milo, Editor.

BLOOMFIELD LIFE. 90 Centre St., Nutley, NJ 07110. Telephone: 973-667-2100. FAX: 973-667-3904. E-MAIL: bloomfieldlife@northjersey.com. URL: http://www.njmg.com. Year Established: 1983. Pub. Frequency: w. (Thu.) Page Size: broadsheet. Subscrip. Rate: $.50 newsstand/cover; $21.95/yr in county; $31/yr mailed out of county. Adv. Rate: col. inch $11.80 Circulation: 3,120 per issue (paid). **Owner(s):** North Jersey Media Group, 150 River St, Hackensack, NJ 07601-7172. Telephone: 201-646-4000. **Management:** Stephen Borg, President. Kathleen Hivish, Publisher. Cynthia Werner, VP Circulation. Nancy Connolly, Advertising Manager. Kerry Rubin, Classified Adv. Mgr.. **Editorial:** Jonathan Sachs, Editor.

GLEN RIDGE VOICE. ISSN 1556-2514
90 Centre St., Nutley, NJ 07110. Telephone: 973-667-2100. FAX: 973-667-3904. E-MAIL: glenridge@northjersey.com. URL: http://www.njmg.com. Year Established: 1995. Pub. Frequency: w. (Thu.) Page Size: broadsheet. Subscrip. Rate: $.50 newsstand/cover; $24/yr in county. Adv. Rate: col. inch $10.95 Circulation: 646 per issue (paid). **Owner(s):** North Jersey Media Group, 150 River St, Hackensack, NJ 07601-7172. Telephone: 201-646-4000. **Management:** Stephen Borg, President. Kathleen Hivish, Publisher. Nancy Connolly, Advertising Manager. Kerry Rubin, Classified Adv. Mgr. **Editorial:** Jonathan Sachs, Editor.

NUTLEY SUN, THE. 90 Centre St., Nutley, NJ 07110. Telephone: 973-667-2100. FAX: 973-667-3904. E-MAIL: nutleysun@northjersey.com. URL: http://www.northjersey.com. Year Established: 1895. Pub. Frequency: w. (Thu.) Page Size: broadsheet. Subscrip. Rate: $.50 newsstand/cover; $21.95/yr in county. Adv. Rate: col. inch $16.50 Circulation: 4,662 per issue (paid). **Owner(s):** North Jersey Media Group, 150 River St, Hackensack, NJ 07601-7172. Telephone: 201-646-4000. FAX: 201-646-4310. **Management:** Stephen Borg, President. Kathleen Hivish, Publisher. Nancy Connolly, Advertising Manager. Kerry Rubin, Classified Adv. Mgr.. **Editorial:** Paul Milo, Editor.

OCEAN CITY

OCEAN CITY SENTINEL, THE. 112 E. Eighth St., Ocean City, NJ 08226-0238. Telephone: 609-399-5411. FAX: 609-399-0416. E-MAIL: oceancitysentinel@comcast.net. Mailing Address: PO Box 238, Ocean City, NJ 08226-0238. Year Established: 1881. Pub. Frequency: w. (Thu.) Page Size: broadsheet. Subscrip. Rate: $.50 newsstand/cover; $25/yr in county; $29/yr out of county. Adv. Rate: col. inch $13.25 Freelance Pay: $25-$75/story. Circulation: 9,500 per issue (paid). **Owner(s):** Sample Media, Inc., 112 E. Eighth St., Ocean City, NJ 08226. Telephone: 609-399-5411. **Management:** David Nahan, Publisher. Lee Polidori, Advertising Director. Mary Jane Weissenberg, Classified Adv. Mgr.. **Editorial:** David Nahan, Editor. Charles Wood, Sports.

PALISADES PARK

BERGEN NEWS/SUN BULLETIN, THE. 111 Grand Ave., Palisades Park, NJ 07650. Telephone: 201-947-5000. FAX: 201-947-6968. Year Established: 1950. Pub. Frequency: w. (Wed.) Page Size: tabloid. Subscrip. Rate: $.50 newsstand/cover; $32/yr in state; $42/yr out of state. Circulation: 38,000 per issue (controlled). **Owner(s):** News Publishing Co., See address and contact information above. **Management:** Jill Cohen, Publisher. Robert Bober, Advertising Director. **Editorial:** Douglas E Hall, Editor.

PRESS JOURNAL (PALISADES PARK), THE. 111 Grand Ave., Palisades Park, NJ 07650. Telephone: 201-947-5000. FAX: 201-947-6968. E-MAIL: dhall@bergennews.com. Year Established: 1874. Pub. Frequency: w. (Thu.) Page Size: tabloid. Subscrip. Rate: $.50 newsstand/cover; $32/yr in county; $42/yr out of county. Circulation: 10,160 per issue (controlled and free). **Owner(s):** News Publishing Co., See address and contact information above. **Management:** Phylis Cohen, President. Robert Bober, Advertising Director. Patricia Vozzo, Circulation Director. **Editorial:** Douglas E Hall, Editor. Sue Perkins, Food Editor.

PENNINGTON

BEACON (PENNINGTON), THE. 53 Pennington Hopewell Rd., Pennington, NJ 08534. Telephone: 609-466-1190. FAX: 609-466-2123. E-MAIL: advir@pacpub.com. URL: http://www.beaconnews.com. Mailing Address: PO Box 8, Hopewell, NJ 08525. Year Established: 1845. Pub. Frequency: w. (Thu.) Page Size: broadsheet. Subscrip. Rate: $.75 newsstand/cover; $36.30/yr in county. Adv. Rate: col. inch $11.50 Freelance Pay: $1/column-inch. Circulation: 7,900 per issue (controlled). **Owner(s):** Princeton Packet, Inc., The, 300 Witherspoon St., Princeton, NJ 08542. Telephone: 609-924-3244. FAX: 609-921-2714. **Management:** Gerri Guld, General Manager. James B. Kilgore, Publisher. Gerri Guld, Advertising Director. **Editorial:** Mae Rhein, Editor.

PHILLIPSBURG

PHILLIPSBURG FREE PRESS. 198 Chamber St., Phillipsburg, NJ 08865. Telephone: 908-859-4444. FAX: 908-859-3084. Mailing Address: PO Box 827, Phillipsburg, NJ 08865. Year Established: 1961. Pub. Frequency: w. (Thu.) Page Size: broadsheet. Subscrip. Rate: $.50 newsstand/cover; $18/yr mailed in NJ & PA; $23/yr mailed elsewhere. Circulation: 2,300 per issue (paid). **Owner(s):** Advance Publications, Inc., 950 Fingerboard Rd., Staten Island, NY 10305. Telephone: 718-981-1234. **Management:** Enid Logan, Publisher.

PRINCETON

CRANBURY PRESS, THE. 300 Witherspoon St., Princeton, NJ 08540. Telephone: 609-924-5412. E-MAIL: ads@pacpub.com. URL: http://www.cranburypress.com. Mailing Address: PO Box 309, Dayton, NJ 08810. Year Established: 1885. Pub. Frequency: w. (Fri.) Page Size: broadsheet. Subscrip. Rate: $.75 newsstand/cover; $39/yr in county. Adv. Rate: page $15.30 Circulation: 3,088 per issue (paid). **Owner(s):** Princeton Packet, Inc., See address and contact information above. **Management:** James B. Kilgore, Publisher. **Editorial:** Hank Kalet, Editor.

TOWN TOPICS. ISSN 0191-7056
4 Mercer St., Princeton, NJ 08540. Telephone: 609-924-2200. FAX: 609-924-8818. URL: http://www.towntopics.com. Mailing Address: PO Box 664, Princeton, NJ 08542. Year Established: 1946. Pub. Frequency: w. (Wed.) Page Size: tabloid. Subscrip. Rate: $.50 newsstand/cover; $35/yr local; $38/yr in NJ, NY, PA; $41/yr mailed elsewhere. Circulation: 14,435 per issue (paid and free). **Owner(s):** Lynn & Ken Smith, See address and contact information above. **Management:** Lynn Adams-Smith III, Publisher. Robin Broomer, Advertising Director. Irene Lee, Advertising Manager. **Editorial:** Lynn Adams-Smith III, Editor. Matthew Hersh, Assistant Editor. Bill Alden, Sports Editor.

RAHWAY

CLARK PATRIOT. PO Box 1061, Rahway, NJ 07065. Telephone: 732-574-1200. FAX: 732-388-4143. E-MAIL: cmdeditor@gmail.com. URL: http://www.new-jersey.ws. Year Established: 1965. Pub. Frequency: w. (Thu.) Page Size: tabloid. Subscrip. Rate: $.50 newsstand/cover; $15/yr in county; $50/yr out of county. Adv. Rate: col. inch $20 Wire Service(s): PR. Circulation: 2,000 per issue (paid and free). **Owner(s):** C M D Media, See address and contact information above. **Management:** Lisa McCormick, Publisher. **Editorial:** Paul Hadsall, Editor. Francene Kopas, Managing Editor. Readers: Homeowners, families, local retailers

NEWS-RECORD (ELIZABETH). PO Box 1061, Rahway, NJ 07065. Telephone: 732-574-1200. FAX: 732-388-4143. E-MAIL: cmdeditor@gmail.com. URL: http://www.new-jersey.ws. Year Established: 1822. Pub. Frequency: w. (Thu.) Page Size: tabloid. Subscrip. Rate: $.50 newsstand/cover; $15/yr in county; $50/yr out of county. Adv. Rate: col. inch $20 Wire Service(s): AP, PR. Circulation: 9,200 per issue (paid). **Owner(s):** C M D Media, See address and contact information above. **Management:** Lisa McCormick, Publisher. Francene Sciortino-Koaps, Advertising Director. **Editorial:** Paul Hadsall, Editor. Readers: Homeowners, families, local retailers

RAMSEY

HOME & STORE NEWS. PO Box 329, Ramsey, NJ 07446-0329. Telephone: 201-327-1212. FAX: 201-327-3684. E-MAIL: news@ourtown.com. Year Established: 1960. Pub. Frequency: w. (Wed.) Page Size: tabloid Circulation: 30,000 per issue (free). **Owner(s):** Arthur Aldrich, See address and contact information above. **Management:** Arthur Aldrich, Publisher. **Editorial:** Eleanor Harman, Editor.

OUR TOWN. 6 Main St., Ramsey, NJ 07446. Telephone: 201-327-1212. FAX: 201-322-3864. E-MAIL: news@ourtownnews.com. Year Established: 1973. Pub. Frequency: w. (Wed.) Page Size: tabloid. Freelance Pay: $35/article. Circulation: 23,000 per issue (free). **Owner(s):** Orangetown Telegram, See address and contact information above. **Management:** Arthur R. Aldrich Jr., Publisher. **Editorial:** Eleanor Harman, Editor. Arthur R. Aldrich Jr., Editor-in-Chief.

RIDGEWOOD

FRANKLIN LAKES/OAKLAND SUBURBAN NEWS. 41 Oak St., Ridgewood, NJ 07450-3805. Telephone: 201-612-5415. FAX: 201-612-5421. E-MAIL: suburbannews@northjersey.com. URL: http://www.northjersey.com. Year Established: 2001. Pub. Frequency: w. (Wed.) Page Size: tabloid. Subscrip. Rate: $18/yr mailed. Adv. Rate: col. inch $10.40 Circulation: 7,724 per issue (paid). **Owner(s):** North Jersey Media Group, 150 River St, Hackensack, NJ 07601-7172. Telephone: 201-646-4000. **Management:** Stephen Borg, President. Sharon Puser, Publisher. Amy Weinhofer, Advertising Manager. Kerry Rubin, Classified Adv. Mgr.. **Editorial:** Trudy Walz, Editor.

GLEN ROCK GAZETTE, THE. 41 Oak St., Ridgewood, NJ 07450-3805. Telephone: 201-612-5432. FAX: 201-612-5436. E-MAIL: glenrock@northjersey.com. URL: http://www.northjersey.com. Year Established: 1994. Pub. Frequency: w. (Fri.) Page Size: tabloid. Adv. Rate: col. inch $6.88 Circulation: 5,328 per issue (paid). **Owner(s):** North Jersey Media Group, 150 River St, Hackensack, NJ 07601-7172. Telephone: 201-646-4000. **Management:** Stephen Borg, President. Sharon Puser, Publisher. Amy Weinhofer, Advertising Manager. **Editorial:** Mike Daley, Editor.

MAHWAH SUBURBAN NEWS. 41 Oak St., Ridgewood, NJ 07450-3805. Telephone: 201-612-5415. FAX: 201-612-5421. E-MAIL: suburbannews@northjersey.com. URL: http://www.northjersey.com. Pub. Frequency: w. (Fri.) Page Size: tabloid. Subscrip. Rate: $18/yr mailed. Adv. Rate: col. inch $8.37 Circulation: 5,027 per issue (paid). **Owner(s):** North Jersey Media Group, 150 River St, Hackensack, NJ 07601-7172. Telephone: 201-646-4000. **Management:** Stephen Borg, President. Sharon Puser, Publisher. Amy Weinhofer, Advertising Manager. Kerry Rubin, Classified Adv. Mgr. **Editorial:** Trudy Walz, Editor. Nancy Rubenstein, Executive Editor.

MIDLAND PARK SUBURBAN NEWS. 41 Oak St., Ridgewood, NJ 07450-3805. Telephone: 201-612-5415. FAX: 201-612-5421. E-MAIL: suburbannews@northjersey.com. URL: http://www.northjersey.com. Pub. Frequency: w. (Wed.) Page Size: tabloid. Subscrip. Rate: $65/yr mailed. Adv. Rate: col. inch $5.18 Circulation: 2,653 per issue (free). **Owner(s):** North Jersey Media Group, 150 River St, Hackensack, NJ 07601-7172. Telephone: 201-646-4000. FAX: 201-646-4310. **Management:** Stephen Borg, President. Sharon Puser, Publisher. Amy Weinhofer, Advertising Manager. Kerry Rubin, Classified Adv. Mgr. **Editorial:** Trudy Walz, Editor.

RAMSEY SUBURBAN NEWS. 41 Oak St., Ridgewood, NJ 07450-3805. Telephone: 201-612-5432. FAX: 201-612-5436. E-MAIL: ramseysuburbannews@northjersey.com. URL: http://www.northjersey.com. Pub. Frequency: w. (Fri.) Page Size: tabloid. Subscrip. Rate: $18/yr mailed. Adv. Rate: col. inch $7.51 Circulation: 4,452 per issue (paid). **Owner(s):** North Jersey Media Group, 150 River St, Hackensack, NJ 07601-7172. Telephone: 201-646-4000. **Management:** Stephen Borg, President. Sharon Puser, Publisher. Amy Weinhofer, Advertising Manager. Kerry Rubin, Classified Adv. Mgr. **Editorial:** Trudy Walz, Editor.

RIDGEWOOD NEWS, THE. 41 Oak St., Ridgewood, NJ 07451. Telephone: 201-612-5400. FAX: 201-612-5410. E-MAIL: ridgewoodnews@northjersey.com. URL: http://www.northjersey.com. Year Established: 1889. Pub. Frequency: w. (Fri.) Page Size: broadsheet. Subscrip. Rate: $.50 newsstand/cover; $19.50/yr. Adv. Rate: col. inch $19.10 Circulation: 7,115 Sunday (paid); 6,873 per issue (paid). **Owner(s):** North Jersey Media Group, 150 River St, Hackensack, NJ 07601-7172. Telephone: 201-646-4000. **Management:** Stephen Borg, President. Sharon Puser, Publisher. Kerry Rubin, Classified Adv. Mgr. **Editorial:** Susan Sherrill, Editor.

SUBURBAN NEWS/VILLAGE GAZETTE. 41 Oak St., Ridgewood, NJ 07650-3805. Telephone: 201-612-5431. FAX: 201-612-5436. E-MAIL: suburbannews@northjersey.com. URL: http://www.northjersey.com. Year Established: 1957. Pub. Frequency: w. (Wed.) Page Size: tabloid. Adv. Rate: col. inch $14.65 Circulation: 7,770 per issue (free). **Owner(s):** North Jersey Media Group, 150 River St, Hackensack, NJ 07601-7172. Telephone: 201-646-4000. **Management:** Sharon Puser, Publisher. Amy Weinhofer, Advertising Manager. **Editorial:** Susan Sherrill, Editor.

TOWN JOURNAL, THE. 41 Oak St., Ridgewood, NJ 07450-3805. Telephone: 201-612-5400. FAX: 201-612-5436. E-MAIL: townjournal@northjersey.com. URL: http://www.northjersey.com. Year Established: 1974. Pub. Frequency: w. (Thu.) Page Size: tabloid. Subscrip. Rate: $18/yr. Adv. Rate: col. inch $12.50 Circulation: 7,386 per issue (paid). **Owner(s):** North Jersey Media Group, 150 River St, Hackensack, NJ 07601-7172. Telephone: 201-646-4000. **Management:** Stephen Borg, President. Sharon Puser, Publisher. Amy Weinhofer, Advertising Manager. Kerry Rubin, Classified Adv. Mgr. **Editorial:** Debie Wilkey, Editor.

TOWN NEWS. 41 Oak St., Ridgewood, NJ 07450-3805. Telephone: 201-612-5400. FAX: 201-612-5421. E-MAIL: townnews@northjersey.com. URL: http://www.northjersey.com. Year Established: 1952. Pub. Frequency: w. (Wed.) Page Size: tabloid. Adv. Rate: col. inch $19.48 Circulation: 14,497 per issue (free). **Owner(s):** North Jersey Media Group, 150 River St, Hackensack, NJ 07601-7172. Telephone: 201-646-4000. **Management:** Stephen Borg, President. Amy Weinhofer, Advertising Manager. Kerry Rubin, Classified Adv. Mgr. **Editorial:** Kelly Nicolaides, Editor.

WALDWICK SUBURBAN NEWS. 41 Oak St., Ridgewood, NJ 07450-3805. Telephone: 201-612-5415. FAX: 201-612-5421. E-MAIL: suburbannews@northjersey.com. URL: http://www.northjersey.com. Pub. Frequency: w. (Wed.) Page Size: tabloid. Subscrip. Rate: $65/yr mailed. Adv. Rate: col. inch $5.64 Circulation: 3,339 per issue (free). **Owner(s):** North Jersey Media Group, 150 River St, Hackensack, NJ 07061-7172. Telephone: 201-646-4000. **Management:** Sharon Puser, Publisher. Amy Weinhofer, Advertising Manager. Rose O'Riordan, Classified Adv. Mgr. **Editorial:** Trudy Walz, Editor.

WYCKOFF SUBURBAN NEWS. 41 Oak St., Ridgewood, NJ 07450-3805. Telephone: 201-612-5415. FAX: 201-612-5421. E-MAIL: suburbannews@newjersey.com. URL: http://www.northjersey.com. Pub. Frequency: w. (Wed.) Page Size: tabloid. Subscrip. Rate: $18/yr. Adv. Rate: col. inch $8.54 Circulation: 5,668 per issue (paid). **Owner(s):** North Jersey Media Group, PO Box 471, West Paterson, NJ 07424-0471. Telephone: 973-569-7000. FAX: 973-569-7310. **Management:** Sharon Puser, Publisher. Amy Weinhofer, Advertising Manager. Rose O'Riordan, Classified Adv. Mgr.. **Editorial:** Trudy Walz, Editor. Nancy Rubenstein, Executive Editor.

RIO GRANDE

CAPE MAY COUNTY HERALD. PO Box 400, Rio Grande, NJ 08242. Telephone: 609-886-8600. FAX: 609-886-1879. E-MAIL: bhuber@cmcherald.com. URL: http://www.capemaycountyherald.com. Year Established: 1965. Pub. Frequency: w. (Wed.) Page Size: tabloid. Subscrip. Rate: $38/yr home delivery. Circulation: 30,409 per issue (paid and free). **Owner(s):** Seawave Corp., See address and contact information above. **Management:** Art Hall, Publisher. Beth Huber, Advertising. Richard Plucker, Classified Adv. Mgr.. Preston Gibson, Development Manager. **Editorial:** Joseph R. Zelnik, Editor. Contact: James Vanore, Editor.

ROCKAWAY

PARSIPPANY LIFE. 100 Commons Way, Rockaway, NJ 07866. Telephone: 973-586-8190. FAX: 973-586-8199. URL: http://www.njmg.com. Year Established: 1983. Pub. Frequency: w. (Thu.) Page Size: broadsheet. Subscrip. Rate: $31/yr. Adv. Rate: col. inch $12.85 Circulation: 16,415 per issue (paid). **Owner(s):** North Jersey Media Group, 150 River St, Hackensack, NJ 07061-7172. Telephone: 201-646-4000. **Management:** Rose O'Riordan, Classified Adv. Mgr..

RUTHERFORD

SOUTH BERGENITE. 33 Lincoln Ave., Rutherford, NJ 07070-2112. Telephone: 201-933-1166. FAX: 201-933-5496. E-MAIL: southbergenite@northjersey.com. URL: http://www.njmg.com. Year Established: 1970. Pub. Frequency: w. (Wed.) Page Size: tabloid.Adv. Rate: col. inch $19.21 Freelance Pay: $15-$30/article. Circulation: 26,467 per issue (free). **Owner(s):** North Jersey Media Group, 150 River St, Hackensack, NJ 07601-7172. Telephone: 201-646-4000. FAX: 201-646-4310. **Management:** Stephen Borg, President. Janice Friedman, Publisher. Lorette Peloquine, Advertising Manager. Kerry Rubin, Classified Adv. Mgr.. **Editorial:** Jaimie Winters, Editor.

SEAVILLE

CAPE MAY GAZETTE, THE. 2087 S. Shore Rd., 2nd Fl., Seaville, NJ 08230. Telephone: 609-624-8900. FAX: 609-624-3470. E-MAIL: LBrady@oceancitygazette.com. URL: http://www.shorenewstoday.com. Pub. Frequency: w. (Thu.) Page Size: tabloid.Adv. Rate: col. inch $12.75 Circulation: 15,000 per issue (controlled and free). **Owner(s):** Catamaran Media LLC, See address and contact information above. **Management:** Richard Travers, Publisher. Lenore Brady, Advertising Director. Carl Price, Circulation Manager. Christopher Beausang, Classified Adv. Mgr.. **Editorial:** Rob Seitzinger, Managing Editor. Brian Cunniff, Sports Editor.

FREE TIME. 2087 S. Shore Rd., 2nd Fl., Seaville, NJ 08230. Telephone: 609-624-8900. FAX: 609-624-3470. URL: http://www.thewildwoodleader.com/ft/. Pub. Frequency: w. (Thu.) Page Size: standard.Adv. Rate: col. inch $7.20 Circulation: 25,000 per issue (free). **Owner(s):** Catamaran Media LLC, See address and contact information above. **Management:** Richard Travers, Publisher. Lenore Brady, Advertising Director. Carl Price, Circulation Manager. Christopher Beausang, Classified Adv. Mgr.. **Editorial:** Heather Holtzapfel James, Editor. Rob Seitzinger, Managing Editor.

MIDDLE TOWNSHIP GAZETTE. 2087 S. Shore Rd., 2nd Fl., Seaville, NJ 08230. Telephone: 609-624-8900. FAX: 609-624-3470. E-MAIL: sales@catamaranmedia.com. URL: http://www.shorenewstoday.com. Year Established: 1976. Pub. Frequency: w. (Thu.) Page Size: tabloid. Subscrip. Rate: $.50 newsstand/cover per issue. Adv. Rate: col. inch $11.75 Circulation: 13,000 per issue (paid). **Owner(s):** Catamaran Media LLC, See address and contact information above. **Management:** Lenore Brady, Advertising Director. Carl Price, Circulation Manager. Christopher Beausang, Classified Adv. Mgr.. **Editorial:** Rob Seitzinger, Editor. Bill Barlow, Associate Editor. Brian Cunniff, Sports Editor.

OCEAN CITY GAZETTE, THE. 2087 S. Shore Rd., 2nd Fl., Seaville, NJ 08230. Telephone: 609-624-8900. FAX: 609-624-3470. E-MAIL: LBrady@oceancitygazette.com. URL: http://www.shorenewstoday.com. Pub. Frequency: w. (Wed.) Page Size: tabloid.Adv. Rate: col. inch $12.75 Circulation: 9,000 per issue (controlled and free). **Owner(s):** Catamaran Media LLC, See address and contact information above. **Management:** Richard Travers, Publisher. Lenore Brady, Advertising Director. Carl Price, Circulation Manager. Christopher Beausang, Classified Adv. Mgr.. **Editorial:** Rob Seitzinger, Managing Editor. Bill Barlow, Associate Editor. Brian Cunniff, Sports Editor.

UPPER TOWNSHIP GAZETTE. 2087 S. Shore Rd., 2nd Fl., Seaville, NJ 08230. Telephone: 609-624-8900. FAX: 609-624-3470. E-MAIL: LBrady@oceancitygazette.com. URL: http://www.shorenewstoday.com. Pub. Frequency: w. (Thu.) Page Size: tabloid.Adv. Rate: col. inch $12.75 Circulation: 9,000 per issue (free). **Owner(s):** Catamaran Media LLC, See address and contact information above. **Management:** Richard Travers, Publisher. Lenore Brady, Advertising Director. Carl Price, Circulation Manager. Christopher Beausang, Classified Adv. Mgr.. **Editorial:** Rob Seitzinger, Editor. Brian Cunniff, Sports Editor.

WILDWOOD LEADER, THE. 2087 S. Shore Rd., 2nd Fl., Seaville, NJ 08230. Telephone: 609-624-8900. FAX: 609-624-3470. E-MAIL: sales@catamaranmedia.com. URL: http://www.shorenewstoday.com. Pub. Frequency: w. (Wed.) Page Size: tabloid.Adv. Rate: col. inch $6 Circulation: 4,000 per issue (free). **Owner(s):** Catamaran Media LLC, See address and contact information above. **Management:** Richard Travers, Publisher. Lenore Brady, Advertising Director. Christopher Beausang, Classified Adv. Mgr.. **Editorial:** Rob Seitzinger, Managing Editor. Bill Barlow, Associate Editor. RJ Liberatore Jr., Sports Editor.

SECAUCUS

SECAUCUS HOME NEWS. 766 Irving Pl., Secaucus, NJ 07094. Telephone: 201-867-2071. FAX: 201-865-3806. E-MAIL: shn1910@aol.com. Mailing Address: PO Box 1100, Secaucus, NJ 07096. Year Established: 1910. Pub. Frequency: w. (Thu.) Page Size: tabloid. Subscrip. Rate: $.50 newsstand/cover; $17/yr in county; $19/yr in state; $21/yr out of state. Circulation: 5,500 per issue (paid). **Owner(s):** Gretchen Henkel, See address and contact information above. **Management:** Gretchen Henkel, Publisher. Eileen Losurdo, Advertising. **Editorial:** Gretchen Henkel, Editor.

SOMERVILLE

BOUND BROOK CHRONICLE. 44 Veterans Memorial Dr., E., Somerville, NJ 08876. Telephone: 908-575-6660. FAX: 908-575-6683. Mailing Address: PO Box 699, Somerville, NJ 08876. Year Established: 1866. Pub. Frequency: w. (Thu.) Page Size: broadsheet. Subscrip. Rate: $.50 newsstand/cover; $25/yr in county; $28/yr out of county; $30/yr out of state. Circulation: 6,124 per issue (paid). **Owner(s):** Advance Publications, Inc., 950 Fingerboard Rd., Staten Island, NY 10305. Telephone: 718-981-1234. **Management:** Pete Leddy, Chief Executive Ofc. . David Tomasini, Publisher. Robin Chandler, Advertising Manager. Ted Wnoroski, Circulation Manager. **Editorial:** Michael Deak, Editor.

MIDDLESEX-DUNELLEN CHRONICLE. 44 Veterans Memorial Dr., E., Somerville, NJ 08876. Telephone: 908-575-6660. FAX: 908-575-6683. E-MAIL: njnnews@compuvell.com. Mailing Address: PO Box 699, Somerville, NJ 08876. Year Established: 1956. Pub. Frequency: w. (Sat.) Page Size: broadsheet.Subscrip. Rate: $.50 newsstand/cover; $28/yr Circulation: 4,300 per issue (paid). **Owner(s):** Advance Publications, Inc., 950 Fingerboard Rd., Staten Island, NY 10305. Telephone: 718-981-1234. **Management:** David Tomasini, Publisher. Carol Hladum, Advertising Director. Ted Wnoroski, Circulation Manager. **Editorial:** Rod Hirsch, Executive Editor. Craig Turpin, Managing Editor.

REPORTER (SOMERVILLE), THE. 44 Veterans Memorial Dr. E., Somerville, NJ 08876. Telephone: 908-575-6660. FAX: 908-575-6683. Mailing Address: PO Box 699, Somerville, NJ 08865. Pub. Frequency: w. (Thu.) Page Size: standard Circulation: 48,000 per issue (free). **Owner(s):** NJN Publishing, See address and contact information above. **Management:** Thomas H. Krekel, President. David Tomasini, Publisher. Robin Von Ohlsen, Advertising Director. Ted Wnoroski, Circulation Manager. **Editorial:** Craig Turpin, Editor. Rod Hirsch, Executive Editor. Linda Zetterberg, Production Manager. Allan Conover, Sports Editor.

SOMERSET MESSENGER GAZETTE. 44 Veterans Memorial Dr., E., Somerville, NJ 08876. E-MAIL: dlewars@njnpublishing.com. Mailing Address: PO Box 699, Somerville, NJ 08876. Year Established: 1825. Pub. Frequency: w. (Sat.) Page Size: broadsheet.Subscrip. Rate: $.50 newsstand/cover; $28/yr Circulation: 38,065 per issue (paid). **Owner(s):** Advance Publications, Inc., 950 Fingerboard Rd., Staten Island, NY 10305. Telephone: 718-981-1234. **Management:** David Tomasini, Publisher. Don Lewars, Advertising Director. Robin Von Ohlsen, Advertising Manager. **Editorial:** Rod Hirsch, Editor.

SPARTA

SPARTA INDEPENDENT. 33 Wilson Dr., Sparta, NJ 07871. Telephone: 973-300-0890. FAX: 973-300-0418. E-MAIL: njoffice@strausnews.com. URL: http://www.strausnews.com. Year Established: 1985. Pub. Frequency: w. (Thu.) Page Size: tabloid. Subscrip. Rate: $35/yr mailed. **Wire Service(s):** AP. Circulation: 8,600 per issue (free). **Owner(s):** Straus Media of Northern New Jersey, Inc., See address and contact information above. **Management:** Jean H. Straus, President. R. Peter Straus, Publisher. Rick Sophia, Advertising. Jed Hauck, Circulation Manager. Betty Allen, Sales Manager. **Editorial:** Mario Palomo, Editor.

SUCCASUNNA

50 PLUS. 309, Succasunna, NJ 07876-0309. Pub. Frequency: m. Page Size: tabloid. Subscrip. Rate: $10/yr local. Circulation: 40,000 per issue (paid and free). **Owner(s):** Lorraine Cintron, See address and contact information above. **Management:** Lorraine Cintron, Publisher. **Editorial:** Candee Cintron, Editor. Lorraine Cintron, Managing Editor.

SURF CITY

BEACHCOMBER. ISSN 0194-6307
1816 Long Beach Blvd., Surf City, NJ 08008. Telephone: 609-494-5900. FAX: 609-494-1437. E-MAIL: beachcomber@sandpaper.net. Pub. Frequency: w. (May 20-Sep. 2) Page Size: tabloid Circulation: 25,000 per issue (free). **Owner(s):** Jersey Shore News Magazines, Inc., See address and contact information above. **Management:** Curt Travers, Publisher. Cindy Linkaus, Advertising Director. Lee Little, Classified Adv. Mgr.. **Editorial:** Neil Roberts, Managing Editor. Jay Mann, Environmental Editor.

Weeklies

TOMS RIVER

OCEAN COUNTY REPORTER. 8 Robbins St., Toms River, NJ 08753. Telephone: 732-349-3000. FAX: 732-557-5758. Mailing Address: PO Box CN2449, Toms River, NJ 08754. Year Established: 1956. Pub. Frequency: w. (Thu.) Page Size: tabloid. Freelance Pay: $1/column-inch. **Wire Service(s):** CNS. Circulation: 100,107 per issue (free). **Owner(s):** Gannett Company, Inc., 7950 Jones Branch Dr., McLean, VA 22107-0001. Telephone: 703-854-6000. **Management:** Bonnie Russell, General Manager. Robert T. Collins, Publisher. Bonnie Russell, Advertising Director. Paul Haney, Advertising Manager. Gary Desanto, Circulation Manager. **Editorial:** Lisa Kruse, News Editor.

TRENTON

MILLBROOK ROUND TABLE. 50 W State St, 12th Fl, Trenton, NJ 08608. Telephone: 845-677-8241. FAX: 845-677-6337. E-MAIL: roundtable@midhudsoncentral.com. URL: http://www.millbrookroundtable.com. Year Established: 1888. Pub. Frequency: w. (Thu.) Page Size: broadsheet. Subscrip. Rate: $.75 newsstand/cover; $37/yr mailed in state; $42/yr mailed out of state. Circulation: 2,500 per issue (paid). **Owner(s):** Journal Register Co., See address and contact information above. **Management:** Ira Fusfeld, Publisher. Jeff Ohlbaum, Advertising Director. Larry Priest, Circulation Director. **Editorial:** Angela Batchelor, Editor. Ann Gibbons, Executive Editor.

UNION

EAGLE (UNION), THE. 1291 Stuyvesant Ave., Union, NJ 07083. Telephone: 908-686-7700. FAX: 908-688-6681. E-MAIL: editorial@localsource.com. URL: http://www.localsource.com. Year Established: 2006. Pub. Frequency: w. (Thu.) Page Size: broadsheet. Subscrip. Rate: $.75 newsstand/cover; $21/yr mailed in county; $31/yr mailed out of county. Adv. Rate: col. inch $16.50 Circulation: 1,500 per issue (paid). **Owner(s):** Worrall Community Newspapers, Inc., See address and contact information above. **Management:** David Worrall, Publisher. Joseph Ornegri, Advertising Director. John D'Achino, Circulation Manager. Tom Yauch, Classified Adv. Mgr.. **Editorial:** Steve Proctor, Editor. Tom Canavan, Editor-in-Chief. Raymond Worrall, Executive Editor.

IRVINGTON HERALD. 1291 Stuyvesant Ave., Union, NJ 07083. Telephone: 908-686-7700. FAX: 908-688-6681. E-MAIL: editorial@localsource.com. URL: http://www.localsource.com. Pub. Frequency: w. (Thu.) Page Size: broadsheet. Subscrip. Rate: $.75 newsstand/cover; $26/yr in county; $36/yr out of county. Adv. Rate: col. inch $15 Circulation: 1,800 per issue (paid). **Owner(s):** Worrall Community Newspapers, Inc., See address and contact information above. **Management:** David Worrall, Publisher. Joseph Ornegri, Advertising Director. John D'Achino, Circulation Manager. Tom Yauch, Classified Adv. Mgr.. **Editorial:** Tom Canavan, Editor-in-Chief. Raymond Worrall, Executive Editor.

OBSERVER (UNION), THE. 1291 Stuyvesant Ave., Union, NJ 07083. Telephone: 908-686-7700. FAX: 908-688-6681. E-MAIL: editorial@localsource.com. URL: http://www.localsource.com. Year Established: 1994. Pub. Frequency: w. (Thu.) Page Size: broadsheet. Subscrip. Rate: $.75 newsstand/cover; $26/yr mailed in county; $36/yr mailed out of county. Adv. Rate: col. inch $16.50 Circulation: 2,000 per issue (paid). **Owner(s):** Worrall Community Newspapers, Inc., See address and contact information above. **Management:** David Worrall, Publisher. Joseph Ornegri, Advertising Director. John D'Achino, Circulation Manager. Tom Yauch, Classified Adv. Mgr.. **Editorial:** Steve Proctor, Editor. Thomas Canavan, Editor-in-Chief. Raymond Worrall, Executive Editor.

PROGRESS (UNION), THE. 1291 Stuyvesant Ave., Union, NJ 07083. Telephone: 908-686-7700. FAX: 908-688-6681. E-MAIL: wcn22@local source.com. URL: http://www.localsource.com. Year Established: 2006. Pub. Frequency: w. (Thu.) Page Size: broadsheet. Subscrip. Rate: $.75 newsstand/cover; $21/yr in county; $31/yr mailed out of county. Adv. Rate: col. inch $16.50 Circulation: 4,000 per issue (paid). **Owner(s):** Worrall Community Newspapers, Inc., See address and contact information above. **Management:** David Worrall, Publisher. Joseph Ornegri, Advertising Director. John D'Achino, Circulation Manager. Tom Yauch, Classified Adv. Mgr.. **Editorial:** Thomas Canavan, Editor-in-Chief. Raymond Worrall, Executive Editor.

UNION LEADER. 1291 Stuyvesant Ave., Union, NJ 07083. Telephone: 908-686-7700. FAX: 908-688-6681. E-MAIL: editorial@localsource.com. URL: http://www.localsource.com. Year Established: 1925. Pub. Frequency: w. (Thu.) Page Size: broadsheet. Subscrip. Rate: $.75 newsstand/cover; $26/yr in county; $36/yr out of county. Adv. Rate: col. inch $18.50 Circulation: 6,927 per issue (paid). **Owner(s):** Worrall Community Newspapers, Inc., See address and contact information above. **Management:** David Worrall, Publisher. Joseph Ornegri, Advertising Director. John D'Achino, Circulation Manager. Tom Yauch, Classified Adv. Mgr.. **Editorial:** Steve Proctor, Editor. Tom Canavan, Editor-in-Chief. Raymond Worrall, Executive Editor.

WEST CALDWELL

FAIRFIELD CHRONICLE, THE. PO Box 6123, West Caldwell, NJ 07007-6123. Telephone: 973-227-4433. Pub. Frequency: w. (Thu.) Page Size: standard. Subscrip. Rate: $.20 newsstand/cover; $6/yr home delivery in county; $12/yr mailed in state; $36/yr mailed out of state. Adv. Rate: col. inch $15 Circulation: 10,700 per issue (paid). **Owner(s):** Reboli Publishing Co., See address and contact information above. **Management:** John A. Reboli, Publisher. Joan C. Beechey, Advertising Manager. Scott Meyer, Circulation Manager. **Editorial:** Kelly J. Kilborn, Editor-in-Chief. Susan Rothchild, Managing Editor.

MORRISTOWN NEWS, THE. PO Box 6123, West Caldwell, NJ 07007-6123. Telephone: 973-227-4433. FAX: 973-882-8553. Pub. Frequency: w. (Fri.) Page Size: standard. Subscrip. Rate: $.20 newsstand/cover in area; $6/yr. Adv. Rate: col. inch $10 Circulation: 9,200 per issue (paid). **Owner(s):** Reboli Publishing Co., See address and contact information above. **Management:** Scott Meyer, Circulation Manager. Rebecca Stein, Sales Manager. **Editorial:** Susan Rothchild, Managing Editor. Samuel Miller, News Editor.

PARSIPPANY NEWS, THE. PO Box 6123, West Caldwell, NJ 07007-6123. Telephone: 973-227-4433. Pub. Frequency: w. (Thu.) Page Size: standard. Subscrip. Rate: $.20 newsstand/cover in area; $6/yr local. Circulation: 12,100 per issue (paid). **Owner(s):** Reboli Publishing Co., See address and contact information above. **Management:** John A. Reboli, Publisher. Joan C. Beechey, Advertising Manager. Scott Meyer, Circulation Manager. Rebecca Stein, Sales Manager. **Editorial:** Kelly J. Kilborn, Editor-in-Chief. Susan Rothchild, Managing Editor. Samuel Miller, News Editor.

WEST PATERSON

VERONA-CEDAR GROVE TIMES. One Garret Mtn. Plz, 6th Fl, West Paterson, NJ 07424-0471. Telephone: 973-569-7000. FAX: 973-569-7310. E-MAIL: vcgtimes@northjersey.com. URL: http://www.vcgtimes.com. Mailing Address: PO Box 471, West Paterson, NJ 07424-0471. Year Established: 1948. Pub. Frequency: w. (Thu.) Page Size: broadsheet. Subscrip. Rate: $.75 newsstand/cover; $26/yr in county; $31/yr in state. Adv. Rate: col. inch $10.60 Circulation: 5,049 per issue (paid). **Owner(s):** North Jersey Media Group, 150 River St, Hackensack, NJ 07601-7172. Telephone: 201-646-4000. **Management:** Kathleen Hivish, Publisher. Kerry Rubin, Classified Adv. Mgr.. **Editorial:** Owen Proctor, Editor.

WAYNE TODAY & PASSAIC VALLEY TODAY. One Garret Mtn. Plz, 6th Fl, West Paterson, NJ 07424-0471. Telephone: 973-569-7000. FAX: 973-569-7310. E-MAIL: today@northjersey.com. URL: http://www.northjersey.com. Mailing Address: PO Box 471, West Paterson, NJ 07424-0471. Year Established: 1961. Pub. Frequency: w. (Thu.) Page Size: broadsheet.Adv. Rate: col. inch $14.05 Freelance Pay: $35/story. Circulation: 42,057 per issue (paid and free). **Owner(s):** North Jersey Media Group, 150 River St, Hackensack, NJ 07601-7172. Telephone: 201-646-4000. **Management:** Stephen Borg, President. Michael Lawson, Publisher. Garry DeYoung, Advertising Manager. Kerry Rubin, Classified Adv. Mgr.. **Editorial:** Christa Limone, Editor. Nancy Rubenstein, Executive Editor.

WESTFIELD

TIMES OF SCOTCH PLAINS & FANWOOD, THE. 50 Elm St., Westfield, NJ 07090. Telephone: 908-232-4407. FAX: 908-232-0473. E-MAIL: sales@goleader.com. URL: http://www.goleader.com/presskit. Mailing Address: PO Box 250, Scotch Plains, NJ 07091. Year Established: 1958. Pub. Frequency: w. (Thu.) Page Size: broadsheet. Subscrip. Rate: $.50 newsstand/cover; $24/yr mailed; $46 for 2 yrs.. Freelance Pay: $25-$40/article. Circulation: 1,600 per issue (paid). **Owner(s):** Horace R. & Gail S. Corbin, See address and contact information above. **Management:** Horace R. Corbin, Publisher. **Editorial:** David Corbin, Editor.

WESTFIELD LEADER. 50 Elm St., Westfield, NJ 07090. Telephone: 908-232-4407. FAX: 908-232-0473. E-MAIL: editor@goleader.com. URL: http://www.goleader.com/presskit. Year Established: 1890. Pub. Frequency: w. (Thu.) Page Size: standard.Subscrip. Rate: $.50 newsstand/cover; $24/yr Circulation: 7,500 per issue (paid). **Owner(s):** Horace R. & Gail S. Corbin, See address and contact information above. **Management:** Horace R. Corbin, Publisher. Fred Lecomte, Advertising. **Editorial:** David Corbin, Editor.

WESTWOOD

PASCACK VALLEY COMMUNITY LIFE. 345 Kinderkamack Rd., Westwood, NJ 07675. Telephone: 201-664-2501. FAX: 201-664-1332. E-MAIL: pvcommunitylife@northjersey.com. URL: http://www.northjersey.com. Year Established: 1950. Pub. Frequency: w. (Wed.) Page Size: tabloid. Subscrip. Rate: $45/yr local. Adv. Rate: col. inch $18.85 Circulation: 25,708 per issue (free). **Owner(s):** North Jersey Media Group, 150 River St, Hackensack, NJ 07601-7172. Telephone: 201-646-4000. **Management:** Stephen Borg, President. Amy Weinhofer, Advertising Manager. Kerry Rubin, Classified Adv. Mgr.. **Editorial:** Kevin Glynn, Editor.

NEW MEXICO

BELEN

VALENCIA COUNTY NEWS-BULLETIN. 1837 Calmino del Llano, Belen, NM 87002. Telephone: 505-864-4472. FAX: 505-864-3549. E-MAIL: newsbltn@aol.com. URL: http://www.news-bulletin.com. Mailing Address: PO Box 25, Belen, NM 87002. Year Established: 1911. Pub. Frequency: s-w. (Wed. & Sat.) Page Size: broadsheet. Subscrip. Rate: $.50 newsstand/cover; $36/yr in county; $44/yr elsewhere. Freelance Pay: $30-$40/story. **Wire Service(s):** AP. Circulation: 23,000 per issue (controlled and free). **Owner(s):** Albuquerque Publishing Co., 7777 Jefferson St. N.E., Albuquerque, NM 87109. Telephone: 505-823-3800. **Management:** Dave Puddu, Publisher. Rita Garcia, Advertising Director. Ronald Jones, Circulation Director. Melissa Montoya, Business Manager. **Editorial:** Sandy Battin, Editor.

ESPANOLA

RIO GRANDE SUN. 123 Railroad Ave., Espanola, NM 87532. Telephone: 505-753-2126. FAX: 505-753-2140. E-MAIL: rgsun@cybermesa.com. URL: http://www.riograndesun.com. Mailing Address: P.O. Box 790, Espanola, NM 87532. Year Established: 1956. Pub. Frequency: w. (Thu.) Page Size: broadsheet. Subscrip. Rate: $.50 newsstand/cover; $30/yr. Adv. Rate: col. inch $9.50 Circulation: 11,089 per issue (paid). **Owner(s):** Sun Co., Inc., See address and contact information above. **Management:** Robert E. Trapp, Publisher. Maria Garcia, Advertising Manager. **Editorial:** Robert E. Trapp, Editor. Robert B. Trapp, Managing Editor. Kevin Bensett, News Editor.

GRANTS

CIBOLA COUNTY BEACON. 523 N Santa Fe Ave, Grants, NM 87020. Telephone: 505-287-4411. FAX: 505-287-7822. E-MAIL: editor@cibolabeacon.com. URL: http://www.cibolabeacon.com. Mailing Address: PO Box 579, Grants, NM 87020. Year Established: 1941. Pub. Frequency: s-w. (Tue. & Fri.) Page Size: broadsheet. Subscrip. Rate: $.50 newsstand/cover; $18/yr home delivery; $48/yr motor route in county. Circulation: 3,500 per issue (paid). **Owner(s):** Wick Communications, Inc., 333 W. Wilcox Dr., Ste. 302, Sierra Vista, AZ 85635. **Management:** Donald Jaramillo, Publisher. **Editorial:** Joan Behar, Editor.

RATON

RATON RANGE, THE. ISSN 0896-1093
208 S. Third St., Raton, NM 87740. Telephone: 505-445-2721. FAX: 505-445-2723. E-MAIL: paulamurphyAratonrange.com. URL: http://www.ratonrange.com. Mailing Address: PO Box 1068, Raton, NM 87740. Year Established: 1881. Pub. Frequency: s-w. (Tue. & Fri.) Page Size: broadsheet. Subscrip. Rate: $.75 newsstand/cover; $45/yr in county; $50/yr out of county. Circulation: 3,000 per issue (paid). **Owner(s):** Peak Publications, Inc., See address and contact information above. **Management:** Paula Murphy, Publisher. **Editorial:** Todd Wildermuth, Editor. Bob Morris, Sports Editor.

RIO RANCHO

OBSERVER (RIO RANCHO), THE. ISSN 1049-7374
1594 Sara Rd., Rio Rancho, NM 87124. Telephone: 505-892-8080. FAX: 505-892-5719. E-MAIL: theobserve@aol.com. URL: http://www.observer-online.com. Year Established: 1973. Pub. Frequency: s-w. (Thu. & Sun.) Page Size: broadsheet. Subscrip. Rate: $.50 newsstand/cover; $15/yr local; $50/yr mailed. Freelance Pay: $1/column-inch. Circulation: 14,974 per issue (controlled and free). **Owner(s):** Wick Communications, Inc., 333 Wilcox Dr., Ste. 302, Sierra Vista, AZ 85635-1756. Telephone: 520-458-0200. FAX: 520-458-6166. **Management:** Shane Maddox, Publisher. Bob Lambert, Advertising Manager. Gregory Keirst, Circulation Manager. **Editorial:** Betta Ferrendelli, Managing Editor.

RUIDOSO

RUIDOSO NEWS, THE. ISSN 0745-5402
104 Park Ave, Ruidoso, NM 88345. Telephone: 505-257-4001. FAX: 505-257-7053. E-MAIL: editorial@ruidosonews.com. URL: http://www.ruidosonews.com. Mailing Address: PO Box 128, Ruidoso, NM 88345-0128. Year Established: 1946. Pub. Frequency: s-w. (Wed. & Fri.) Page Size: broadsheet. Subscrip. Rate: $.50 newsstand/cover; $38/yr mailed; $45/yr out of county. Circulation: 6,555 per issue (paid). **Owner(s):** MediaNews Group, Inc., 101 W Colfax Ave, Ste 1100, Denver, CO 80202. FAX: 303-954-6320. **Management:** Terry Fitzwater, Publisher. Dianne Gremillion, Advertising Director. Chris Gonzales, Circulation Manager. **Editorial:** Marty Racine, Editor.

SANTA FE

SANTA FE REPORTER, THE. 132 E. Marcy St., Santa Fe, NM 87501. Telephone: 505-988-5541. FAX: 505-988-5348. E-MAIL: advertising@sfreporter.com. URL: http://www.sfreporter.com. Mailing Address: PO Box 2306, Santa Fe, NM 87504-2306. Year Established: 1974. Pub. Frequency: w. (Wed.) Page Size: tabloid. Subscrip. Rate: $60/yr mailed local. Adv. Rate: col. inch $24 Circulation: 23,000 per issue (paid and free). **Owner(s):** Reporter Acquisition Co., PO Box 2306, Santa Fe, NM 87504. **Management:** Andy Dudzik, Publisher. Marcia Beverly, Advertising Manager. Andrew Buckley, Circulation Director. **Editorial:** Julia Goldberg, Editor.

SOCORRO

DEFENSOR-CHIEFTAIN. ISSN 0011-7633
200 Winkler, S.W., Socorro, NM 87801. Telephone: 505-835-0520. FAX: 505-835-1837. E-MAIL: editorial@dchieftain.com. URL: http://www.dchieftain.com. Year Established: 1970. Pub. Frequency: s-w. Page Size: broadsheet. Subscrip. Rate: $.50 newsstand/cover per issue; $28/yr home delivery in Socorro & Catron Cys.; $38/yr home delivery elsewhere; $23/yr home delivery to senior citizens. Circulation: 2,907. **Owner(s):** Number Nine Media, P.O. Drawer J, Albuquerque, NM 87103. **Management:** Dana Bowley, General Manager. Dave Puddu, Vice President. Doshia Lozano, Advertising. Norma Cevantes, Classified Adv. Mgr.. **Editorial:** Mary Baca, Circulation Editor. Jason Brooks, Sports.

TAOS

TAOS NEWS. PO Box U, Taos, NM 87571. Telephone: 505-758-2241. FAX: 505-758-9647. URL: http://www.taosnews.com. Year Established: 1893. Pub. Frequency: w. (Thu.) Page Size: broadsheet. Subscrip. Rate: $.75 newsstand/cover; $26/yr in county; $30/yr out of county; $35/yr out of state; $50/yr elsewhere. Freelance Pay: $1/column-inch. Circulation: 10,500 per issue (paid). **Owner(s):** Robin McKinney Martin, See address and contact information above. **Management:** Chris Baker, Publisher. Joanne Crass, Advertising Manager. Renee Romero, Circulation Director. **Editorial:** Eric Hedlund, Editor.

TRUTH OR CONSEQUENCES

HERALD (TRUTH OR CONSEQUENCES), THE. 1204 N. Date St., PO Box 752, Truth or Consequences, NM 87901-0752. Telephone: 505-894-2143. FAX: 505-894-7824. E-MAIL: herald@riolink.com. URL: http://www.heraldpub.com. Year Established: 1916. Pub. Frequency: w. (Wed.) Page Size: broadsheet. Subscrip. Rate: $.50 newsstand/cover; $25/yr in county; $35/yr out of county. Circulation: 4,500 per issue (paid). **Owner(s):** Herald Publishing Co., Inc., P O Drawer B Court-Sq Sta, Dublin, GA 31040. Telephone: 478-272-5522. **Management:** Mike Tooley, Publisher. Maureen Tooley, Advertising Manager. Contact: Carlos Padilla, Editor.

SIERRA COUNTY SENTINEL. 1747 E Third, PO Box 351, Truth or Consequences, NM 87901. Telephone: 505-894-3088. FAX: 505-894-3998. E-MAIL: gpkohs@zianet.com. URL: http://www.gpkmedia.com. Mailing Address: PO Box 351, Truth or Consequences, NM 87901-0351. Year Established: 1967. Pub. Frequency: w. (Wed.) Page Size: standard. Subscrip. Rate: $.50 newsstand/cover; $39/yr in county; $45/yr out of county. Circulation: 4,500 per issue (paid). **Owner(s):** Myrna Kohs, See address and contact information above. **Management:** Myrna Kohs, Publisher. **Editorial:** G. Patrick Kohs, Editor.

TUCUMCARI

QUAY COUNTY SUN. 902 S. First St., Tucumcari, NM 88401-1408. Telephone: 505-461-1952. FAX: 505-461-1965. Mailing Address: P.O. Drawer 1408, Tucumcari, NM 88401-1408. Year Established: 1975. Pub. Frequency: s-w. (Wed. & Sat.) Page Size: broadsheet. Subscrip. Rate: $.50 newsstand/cover; $.75 newsstand/cover Sat.; $39/yr. Circulation: 3,200 per issue (paid). **Owner(s):** Freedom Communications, Inc., 17666 Fitch, Irvine, CA 92614. Telephone: 949-253-2300. FAX: 949-474-7675. **Management:** T V Hagenah, Publisher. Courtney Cramer, Advertising. Jim Foster, Circulation Manager. **Editorial:** T V Hagenah, Editor.

NEW YORK

ADAMS

JEFFERSON COUNTY JOURNAL (ADAMS). 7 Main St, Adams, NY 13605. Telephone: 315-232-2141. FAX: 315-232-4586. E-MAIL: jcjesfucn@citlink.net. Mailing Address: PO Box 68, Adams, NY 13605-0068. Year Established: 1844. Pub. Frequency: w. (Wed.) Page Size: broadsheet. Subscrip. Rate: $.50 newsstand/cover; $22/yr in county; $27/yr out of county; $28/yr out of state. Circulation: 3,000 per issue (controlled). **Owner(s):** Journal Publishing Co., Inc., See address and contact information above. **Management:** Karl Fowler, Publisher. Allen Maitland, Advertising Manager. Kelly Wiggins, Circulation Manager. **Editorial:** Karl Fowler, Editor.

ALBANY

METROLAND. 419 Madison Ave., Albany, NY 12210. Telephone: 518-463-2500. FAX: 518-463-3712. URL: http://www.metroland.net. Year Established: 1978. Pub. Frequency: w. (Thu.) Page Size: tabloid Subscrip. Rate: $60/yr Circulation: 40,000 per issue (free). **Owner(s):** Stephen Leon, See address and contact information above. **Management:** Lisa Whalen, General Manager. Stephen Leon, Publisher. Marshall C. Lucier, Advertising Director. Shannon Dowen, Classified Adv. Mgr.. John Bracchi, Art Director. **Editorial:** Stephen Leon, Editor. Miriam Axel-Lute, News Editor.

ALDEN

ALDEN ADVERTISER. 13200 Broadway, Alden, NY 14004. Telephone: 716-937-9226. FAX: 716-937-9291. Year Established: 1914. Pub. Frequency: w. (Thu.) Page Size: tabloid. Subscrip. Rate: $.75 newsstand/cover; $24/yr mailed. Circulation: 3,650 per issue (paid). **Owner(s):** Weisbeck Publishing & Printing, Inc., See address and contact information above. **Management:** Leonard A. Weisbeck, President. Leonard A. Weisbeck Jr., Publisher. **Editorial:** Leonard A. Weisbeck Sr., Editor.

ALEXANDRIA BAY

THOUSAND ISLANDS SUN. 45501 NY State Rte. 12, Alexandria Bay, NY 13607-0277. Telephone: 315-482-2581. FAX: 315-482-6315. E-MAIL: tisun@gisco.net. Mailing Address: PO Box 277, Alexandria Bay, NY 13607-0277. Year Established: 1901. Pub. Frequency: w. (Wed.) Page Size: standard. Subscrip. Rate: $.60 newsstand/cover; $28/yr in county; $32/yr domestic out of cy; $40/yr in Canada. Adv. Rate: col. inch $6.12 Circulation: 7,000 per issue (paid). **Owner(s):** Thousand Islands Printing Co., Inc., PO Box 277, Alexandria Bay, NY 13607. Telephone: 315-482-2581. FAX: 315-482-6315. **Management:** Jeanne Snow, Publisher. Craig Snow, Advertising Manager. **Editorial:** Jeanne Snow, Editor.

ALTAMONT

ALTAMONT ENTERPRISE, THE. ISSN 0890-6025
123 Maple Ave., Altamont, NY 12009. Telephone: 518-861-6641. FAX: 518-861-5105. E-MAIL: altamontenterprise@csdsl.net. Mailing Address: PO Box 654, Altamont, NY 12009. Year Established: 1884. Pub. Frequency: w. (Thu.) Page Size: tabloid. Subscrip. Rate: $1 newsstand/cover; $28/yr in county; $30/yr out of county. Adv. Rate: col. inch $10.15 Circulation: 6,400 per issue (paid). **Owner(s):** James E. Gardner, See address and contact information above. **Management:** James E. Gardner, President. Cherie Lussier, Advertising Director. **Editorial:** Melissa Hale-Spencer, Editor.

AMENIA

HARLEM VALLEY TIMES. P.O. Box H, Amenia, NY 12501. Telephone: 845-373-8084. FAX: 845-373-8908. E-MAIL: hvtimes@midhudsoncentral.com. URL: http://www.midhudsoncentral.com. Year Established: 1852. Pub. Frequency: w. (Thu.) Page Size: broadsheet. Subscrip. Rate: $.75 newsstand/cover; $37/yr mailed in state; $43/yr mailed out of state. Circulation: 3,800 per issue (paid). **Owner(s):** Journal Register Co., 50 W State St, 12th Fl, Trenton, NJ 08608. Telephone: 609-396-2200. FAX: 609-396-2292. **Management:** Ira Fusfeld, Publisher. Jeff Ohlbaum, Advertising Director. Larry Priest, Circulation Director. **Editorial:** Darryl Gangloff, Editor. Ann Gibbons, Executive Editor.

AMITYVILLE

AMITYVILLE RECORD. ISSN 1554-0413
85 Broadway, Amityville, NY 11701. Telephone: 631-264-0077. FAX: 631-264-5310. E-MAIL: ACJnews@rcn.com. URL: http://www.amityvillerecord.com. Year Established: 1904. Pub. Frequency: w. (Wed.) Page Size: tabloid. Subscrip. Rate: $.50 newsstand/cover; $25/yr; $40 for 2 yrs.; $35/yr out of state. Adv. Rate: col. inch $9.50 Circulation: 2,500 per issue (paid). **Owner(s):** ACJ Communications, Inc., See address and contact information above. **Management:** Alfred James, President. Carolyn James, Publisher. Doris Giles, Circulation Manager. **Editorial:** Carolyn James, Executive Editor.

ARCADE

ARCADE PENNYSAVER. 277 Main St., Arcade, NY 14009-1212. URL: http://www.wnywired.net/pennysaver. Pub. Frequency: w. (Sun.) Page Size: tabloid Circulation: 11,380 per issue (free). **Owner(s):** H & K Publications, Inc., 50 Buffalo St., Hamburg, NY 14075. Telephone: 716-649-4413. **Management:** Tom Kluckhohn, Publisher. Sue Dildine, Office Manager. Steven Kluckhohn, Advertising Manager. Teri Scott, Circulation Manager.

BABYLON

BABYLON BEACON, THE. 65 Deer Park Ave., Babylon, NY 11702. Telephone: 631-587-5612. FAX: 631-587-0198. E-MAIL: acjnews@rcn.com. URL: http://www.babylonbeacon.com. Mailing Address: PO Box 670, Babylon, NY 11702. Year Established: 1966. Pub. Frequency: w. (Thu.) Page Size: tabloid. Subscrip. Rate: $.50 newsstand/cover; $25/yr; $40 for 2 yrs.; $52 for 3 yrs.; $35/yr out of state. Adv. Rate: col. inch $9.50 Freelance Pay: $10-$20/article. Circulation: 9,200 per issue (paid and free). **Owner(s):** ACJ Communications, Inc., 85 Broadway, Amityville, NY 11701. Telephone: 631-264-0077. **Management:** Alfred James, President. Carolyn James, Publisher. Maryann Heins, Advertising. Doris Giles, Circulation Manager. **Editorial:** Carolyn James, Editor.

BALLSTON SPA

BALLSTON JOURNAL. 35 Milton Ave., Ballston Spa, NY 12020. Telephone: 518-885-5238. FAX: 518-885-3752. Mailing Address: PO Box 1450, Clifton Park, NY 12065. Year Established: 1798. Pub. Frequency: w. (Thu.) Page Size: broadsheet. Subscrip. Rate: $.50 newsstand/cover; $20/yr in county; $22/yr out of county; $24/yr out of state. Freelance Pay: $0.50/column-inch. Circulation: 2,500 per issue (paid). **Owner(s):** Capital Region Weekly Newspaper Group, 2037 Rte. 9, Round Lake, NY 12151. Telephone: 518-877-7160. **Management:** Patrick Smith, Publisher. **Editorial:** Charles Hogan, Managing Editor.

BATH

STEUBEN COURIER-ADVOCATE, THE. 10 W. Steuben St., Bath, NY 14810. Telephone: 607-776-2121. FAX: 607-776-3967. E-MAIL: sacnews@linkny.com. Year Established: 1815. Pub. Frequency: w. (Sun.) Page Size: broadsheet. Subscrip. Rate: $2 mailed/wk.. Adv. Rate: col. inch $6 Circulation: 11,000 per issue (free). **Owner(s):** GateHouse Media, Inc, 350 WillowBrook Office Park, Fairport, NY 14450. Telephone: 585-598-0030. FAX: 585-248-2631. **Management:** Colleen Neeley, Publisher. Bonnie Covell, Circulation Manager. **Editorial:** Rob Price, Editor.

BAYSIDE

ASTORIA TIMES. 41-02 Bell Blvd., 2nd Fl., Bayside, NY 11361. Telephone: 718-229-0300. FAX: 718-274-2934. E-MAIL: sblank@timesledger.com. URL: http://www.timesledger.com. Year Established: 1998. Pub. Frequency: w. (Thu.) Page Size: tabloid. Subscrip. Rate: $.50 newsstand/cover; $21/yr in county; $37 for 2 yrs.. Adv. Rate: col. inch $6.16 Circulation: 2,210 per issue (paid). **Owner(s):** Queens Publishing Corp., See address and contact information above. **Management:** Steven Blank, Publisher. Howard Lavenda, Advertising Manager. Larry Clemens, Circulation Manager. Bonnie Reunis, Classified Adv. Mgr.. Jewell Davis, Art Director. **Editorial:** Roz Liston, Managing Editor.

BAYSIDE TIMES, THE. 41-02 Bell Blvd., 2nd Fl., Bayside, NY 11361. Telephone: 718-229-0300. FAX: 718-274-2934. E-MAIL: sblank@timesledger.com. URL: http://www.timesledger.com. Year Established: 1935. Pub. Frequency: w. (Thu.) Page Size: tabloid. Subscrip. Rate: $.50 newsstand/cover; $21/yr in county; $25/yr out of county. Adv. Rate: col. inch $11.80 Circulation: 11,061 per issue (paid). **Owner(s):** Queens Publishing Corp., See address and contact information above. **Management:** Steven Blank, Publisher. Howard Lavenda, Advertising Manager. Larry Clemens, Circulation Manager. Bonnie Reunis, Classified Adv. Mgr.. Jewell Davis, Art Director. **Editorial:** Roz Liston, Managing Editor. Rachel Schiffman, Production Manager.

FLUSHING TIMES, THE. 41-02 Bell Blvd., 2nd Fl., Bayside, NY 11361. Telephone: 718-229-0300. FAX: 718-274-2934. E-MAIL: sblank@timesledger.com. URL: http://www.timesledger.com. Year Established: 1992. Pub. Frequency: w. (Thu.) Page Size: tabloid. Subscrip. Rate: $.50 newsstand/cover; $21/yr in county; $37 for 2 yrs.. Adv. Rate: col. inch $6.16 Circulation: 4,959 per issue (paid). **Owner(s):** Queens Publishing Corp., See address and contact information above. **Management:** Steven Blank, Publisher. Howard Lavenda, Advertising Manager. Jay Feldman, Circulation Manager. Bonnie Reunis, Classified Adv. Mgr.. Jewell Davis, Art Director. **Editorial:** Steven Blank, Editor. Roz Liston, Managing Editor. Rachel Schiffman, Production Manager.

FOREST HILLS LEDGER. 41-02 Bell Blvd., 2nd Fl., Bayside, NY 11361. Telephone: 718-229-0300. FAX: 718-274-2934. E-MAIL: sblank@timesledger.com. URL: http://www.timesledger.com. Year Established: 1997. Pub. Frequency: w. (Thu.) Page Size: tabloid. Subscrip. Rate: $.50 newsstand/cover; $21/yr in county; $37 for 2 yrs.. Adv. Rate: col. inch $6.16 Circulation: 2,659 per issue (paid). **Owner(s):** Queens Publishing Corp., See address and contact information above. **Management:** Steven Blank, Publisher. Howard Lavenda, Advertising Manager. Beverly Townes, Circulation Manager. Bonnie Reunis, Classified Adv. Mgr.. Jewell Davis, Art Director. **Editorial:** Steven Blank, Editor. Roz Liston, Managing Editor. Rachel Schiffman, Production Manager.

FRESH MEADOWS TIMES, THE. 41-02 Bell Blvd., 2nd Fl., Bayside, NY 11361. Telephone: 718-229-0300. FAX: 718-274-2934. E-MAIL: sblank@timesledger.com. URL: http://www.timesledger.com. Year Established: 1993. Pub. Frequency: w. (Thu.) Page Size: tabloid. Subscrip. Rate: $.50 newsstand/cover; $21/yr in county; $37 for 2 yrs.. Adv. Rate: col. inch $6.16 Circulation: 1,758 per issue (paid). **Owner(s):** Queens Publishing Corp., See address and contact information above. **Management:** Steven Blank, Publisher. Howard Lavenda, Advertising Manager. Larry Clemens, Circulation Manager. Bonnie Reunis, Classified Adv. Mgr.. Jewell Davis, Art Director. **Editorial:** Roz Liston, Managing Editor. Rachel Schiffman, Production Manager.

GLEN OAKS LEDGER, THE. 41-02 Bell Blvd., 2nd Fl., Bayside, NY 11361. Telephone: 718-229-0300. FAX: 718-274-2934. E-MAIL: sblank@timesledger.com. URL: http://www.timesledger.com. Year Established: 1993. Pub. Frequency: w. (Thu.) Page Size: tabloid. Subscrip. Rate: $.50 newsstand/cover; $21/yr in county. Adv. Rate: col. inch $6.16 Circulation: 1,640 per issue (paid). **Owner(s):** Queens Publishing Corp., See address and contact information above. **Management:** Steven Blank, Publisher. William Shore, Advertising Manager. Beverly Townes, Circulation Manager. Bonnie Reunis, Classified Adv. Mgr.. Jewell Davis, Art Director. **Editorial:** Steven Blank, Editor. Roz Liston, Managing Editor. Rachel Schiffman, Production Manager.

JAMAICA TIMES, THE. 41-02 Bell Blvd., 2nd Fl., Bayside, NY 11361. Telephone: 718-229-0300. FAX: 718-274-2934. E-MAIL: sblank@timesledger.com. URL: http://www.timesledger.com. Year Established: 1994. Pub. Frequency: w. (Thu.) Page Size: tabloid. Subscrip. Rate: $.50 newsstand/cover; $21/yr in county; $37 for 2 yrs.. Adv. Rate: col. inch $6.16 Circulation: 3,174 per issue (paid). **Owner(s):** Queens Publishing Corp., See address and contact information above. **Management:** Steven Blank, Publisher. Beverly Townes, Circulation Manager. Bonnie Reunis, Classified Adv. Mgr.. Jewell Davis, Art Director. **Editorial:** Steven Blank, Editor. Roz Liston, Managing Editor. Rachel Schiffman, Production Manager.

LAURELTON TIMES. 41-02 Bell Blvd., 2nd Fl., Bayside, NY 11361. Telephone: 718-229-0300. FAX: 718-274-2934. E-MAIL: sblank@timesledger.com. URL: http://www.timesledger.com. Year Established: 1995. Pub. Frequency: w. (Thu.) Page Size: tabloid. Subscrip. Rate: $.50 newsstand/cover; $21/yr in county; $37 for 2 yrs.. Adv. Rate: col. inch $6.16 Circulation: 1,808 per issue (paid). **Owner(s):** Queens Publishing Corp., See address and contact information above. **Management:** Steven Blank, Publisher. Howard Lavenda, Advertising Manager. Larry Clemens, Circulation Manager. Bonnie Reunis, Classified Adv. Mgr.. Jewell Davis, Art Director. **Editorial:** Roz Liston, Managing Editor. Rachel Schiffman, Production Manager. Brian Rafferty, Editorial Advisor.

LITTLE NECK LEDGER, THE. 41-02 Bell Blvd., 2nd Fl., Bayside, NY 11361. Telephone: 718-229-0300. FAX: 718-274-2934. E-MAIL: sblank@timesledger.com. URL: http://www.timesledger.com. Year Established: 1918. Pub. Frequency: w. (Thu.) Page Size: tabloid. Subscrip. Rate: $.50 newsstand/cover; $21/yr in county. Adv. Rate: col. inch $6.16 Circulation: 3,113 per issue (paid). **Owner(s):** Queens Publishing Corp., See address and contact information above. **Management:** Steven Blank, Publisher. Jay Feldman, Circulation Manager. Bonnie Reunis, Classified Adv. Mgr.. Jewell Davis, Art Director. **Editorial:** Steven Blank, Editor. Roz Liston, Managing Editor. Rachel Schiffman, Production Manager.

QUEENS VILLAGE TIMES, THE. 41-02 Bell Blvd., 2nd Fl., Bayside, NY 11361. Telephone: 718-229-0300. FAX: 718-274-2934. E-MAIL: sblank@timesledger.com. URL: http://www.timesledger.com. Year Established: 1994. Pub. Frequency: w. (Thu.) Page Size: tabloid. Subscrip. Rate: $.50 newsstand/cover; $21/yr in county; $37 for 2 yrs.. Adv. Rate: col. inch $6.16 Circulation: 2,211 per issue (paid). **Owner(s):** Queens Publishing Corp., See address and contact information above. **Management:** Steven Blank, Publisher. Jay Feldman, Circulation Manager. Bonnie Reunis, Classified Adv. Mgr.. Jewell Davis, Art Director. **Editorial:** Steven Blank, Editor. Roz Liston, Managing Editor. Rachel Schiffman, Production Manager.

RICHMOND HILL TIMES. 41-02 Bell Blvd., 2nd Fl., Bayside, NY 11361. Telephone: 718-229-0300. FAX: 718-274-2934. E-MAIL: sblank@timesledger.com. URL: http://www.timesledger.com. Year Established: 1998. Pub. Frequency: w. (Thu.) Page Size: tabloid. Subscrip. Rate: $.50 newsstand/cover; $21/yr in county. Adv. Rate: col. inch $6.10 Circulation: 1,792 per issue (paid). **Owner(s):** Queens Publishing Corp., See address and contact information above. **Management:** Steven Blank, Publisher. Howard Lavenda, Advertising Manager. Jay Feldman, Circulation Manager. Bonnie Reunis, Classified Adv. Mgr.. Jewell Davis, Art Director. **Editorial:** Steven Blank, Editor. Roz Liston, Managing Editor. Rachel Schiffman, Production Manager.

RIDGEWOOD LEDGER. 41-02 Bell Blvd., 2nd Fl., Bayside, NY 11361. Telephone: 718-229-0300. FAX: 718-274-2934. E-MAIL: sblank@timesledger.com. URL: http://www.timesledger.com. Year Established: 1999. Pub. Frequency: w. (Thu.) Page Size: tabloid. Subscrip. Rate: $.50 newsstand/cover; $21/yr in county; $37 for 2 yrs.. Adv. Rate: col. inch $6.16 Circulation: 2,725 per issue (paid). **Owner(s):** Queens Publishing Corp., See address and contact information above. **Management:** Steven Blank, Publisher. Howard Lavenda, Advertising Manager. Jay Feldman, Circulation Manager. Bonnie Reunis, Classified Adv. Mgr.. Jewell Davis, Art Director. **Editorial:** Steven Blank, Editor. Roz Liston, Managing Editor. Rachel Schiffman, Production Manager.

WHITESTONE TIMES, THE. 41-02 Bell Blvd., 2nd Fl., Bayside, NY 11361. Telephone: 718-229-0300. FAX: 718-274-2934. E-MAIL: sblank@timesledger.com. URL: http://www.timesledger.com. Year Established: 1991. Pub. Frequency: w. (Thu.) Page Size: tabloid. Subscrip. Rate: $.50 newsstand/cover; $21/yr in county; $37 for 2 yrs. in county. Adv. Rate: col. inch $6.16 Circulation: 3,908 per issue (paid). **Owner(s):** Queens Publishing Corp., See address and contact information above. **Management:** Steven Blank, Publisher. Howard Lavenda, Advertising Manager. Larry Clemens, Circulation Manager. Bonnie Reunis, Classified Adv. Mgr.. Jewell Davis, Art Director. **Editorial:** Roz Liston, Managing Editor.

BOONVILLE

BOONVILLE HERALD & ADIRONDACK TOURIST. 105 E. Schuyler St., Boonville, NY 13309. E-MAIL: BOONHERALD@aol.com. URL: http://www.boonvilleherald.com. Mailing Address: PO Box 372, Boonville, NY 13309. Year Established: 1852. Pub. Frequency: w. Page Size: tabloid. Subscrip. Rate: $.50 newsstand/cover per issue; $18/yr in county. **Owner(s):** Black River Publishing Co., Inc., See address and contact information above. **Management:** Joe Kelly, Publisher. Sharon Belyea, Circulation Manager. **Editorial:** Sandra Hrim, Assistant Editor.

BRIDGEHAMPTON

DAN'S PAPERS. 2221 Montauk Hwy., Bridgehampton, NY 11932. Telephone: 631-537-0500. FAX: 631-537-3330. E-MAIL: editorial@danspapers.com. URL: http://www.danspapers.com. Mailing Address: PO Box 630, Bridgehampton, NY 11932-0630. Year Established: 1960. Pub. Frequency: w. (Thu.) Page Size: tabloid. Subscrip. Rate: $100/yr. Freelance Pay: $15-$75/story. Circulation: 71,000 per issue (free). **Owner(s):** News Communications, Inc., 174-15 Horace Harding Expy., Fresh Meadows, NY 11365. Telephone: 718-357-7400. FAX: 718-357-9417. **Management:** Jimmy Finklestein, President. Dan Rattiner, Publisher. Leslie Ernst, Advertising Manager. **Editorial:** Dan Rattiner, Editor-in-Chief.

MONTAUK PIONEER. 2221 Montauk Hwy., Bridgehampton, NY 11932. Telephone: 631-537-0500. FAX: 631-537-3330. E-MAIL: editorial@danspapers.com. URL: http://www.montaukpioneer.com. Mailing Address: PO Box 630, Bridgehampton, NY 11932-0630. Year Established: 1960. Pub. Frequency: w. (Fri.) Page Size: broadsheet. Subscrip. Rate: $38/yr mailed. Circulation: 13,000 per issue (paid and free). **Owner(s):** News Communications, Inc., 501 Madison Ave, 23rd Fl, New York, NY 10022-5608. Telephone: 212-689-2500. FAX: 212-689-1998. **Management:** Dan Rattiner, Publisher. Kathy Rae, Advertising Director. Carol Collinge, Classified Adv. Mgr.. **Editorial:** Dan Rattiner, Editor-in-Chief. David Rattiner, Managing Editor.

BROCKPORT

TRI-COUNTY ADVERTISER (BROCKPORT). 15 Main St., Brockport, NY 14420. Telephone: 585-637-5100. FAX: 585-637-0111. E-MAIL: tcady@rochester.rr.com. URL: http://www.tricountyadvertiser.org. Mailing Address: PO Box 378, Brockport, NY 14420. Year Established: 1957. Pub. Frequency: w. (Mon.) Page Size: tabloid.Adv. Rate: col. inch $8.12 Freelance Pay: $0.35/column-inch. Circulation: 16,000 per issue (free). **Owner(s):** Sally A. Cottrell, Ed. & Pub., See address and contact information above. **Management:** Sally A Cottrell, Publisher. Jennifer Schuler, Office Manager. Sally A Cottrell, Advertising Manager. Robert Cottrell, Circulation Manager. **Editorial:** Sally A Cottrell, Editor.

BRONX

BRONX NEWS. 135 Dreiser Loop, Bronx, NY 10475. Telephone: 718-671-1234. FAX: 914-636-8503. Mailing Address: PO Box 680, New Rochelle, NY 10801. Year Established: 1982. Pub. Frequency: w. (Thu.) Page Size: tabloid.Subscrip. Rate: $.35 newsstand/cover; $10/yr Circulation: 8,000 per issue (paid). **Owner(s):** Hersom Acorn Newspapers, LLC, See address and contact information above. **Management:** Christopher G Hagedorn, Publisher. **Editorial:** Christopher G Hagedorn, Editor. Danny Gesslein, Associate Editor.

BRONX PRESS-REVIEW. 6050 Riverdale Ave., Bronx, NY 10471-1604. Telephone: 718-543-5200. FAX: 718-543-4206. E-MAIL: bxny@aol.com. Year Established: 1940. Pub. Frequency: w. (Thu.) Page Size: tabloid. Subscrip. Rate: $.50 newsstand/cover (effective 2006); $15/yr in area (effective 2005); $35/yr out of area. Adv. Rate: col. inch $15 Circulation: 15,000 per issue (paid). **Owner(s):** Metro North Media Inc., See address and contact information above. **Management:** Andrew Wolf, Publisher. **Editorial:** John Desio, Editor.

CITY NEWS. 135 Dreiser Loop, Bronx, NY 10475. Telephone: 718-671-1234. FAX: 914-636-8503. Mailing Address: PO Box 680, New Rochelle, NY 10801. Year Established: 1969. Pub. Frequency: w. (Sat.) Page Size: tabloid Circulation: 16,000 per issue (free). **Owner(s):** Hersom Acorn Newspapers, LLC, See address and contact information above. **Management:** Christopher G Hagedorn, Publisher. **Editorial:** Christopher G Hagedorn, Editor. Danny Gesslein, Associate Editor.

PARKCHESTER NEWS. 135 Dreiser Loop, Bronx, NY 10475. Telephone: 718-671-1234. FAX: 914-636-8503. Mailing Address: PO Box 680, New Rochelle, NY 10801. Year Established: 1974. Pub. Frequency: w. (Fri.) Page Size: tabloid Circulation: 12,500 per issue (free). **Owner(s):** Hersom Acorn Newspapers, LLC, See address and contact information above. **Management:** Christopher G Hagedorn, Publisher. **Editorial:** Christopher G Hagedorn, Editor. Dan Gesslein, Associate Editor.

RIVERDALE PRESS. 6155 Broadway, Bronx, NY 10471. Telephone: 718-543-6065. FAX: 718-548-4038. E-MAIL: newsroom@riverdalepress.com. Year Established: 1950. Pub. Frequency: w. (Thu.) Page Size: broadsheet. Subscrip. Rate: $.75 newsstand/cover; $20/yr mailed in area; $39/yr mailed out of area. Adv. Rate: col. inch $23.50 Circulation: 14,500 per issue (paid). **Owner(s):** Dale Press, Inc., See address and contact information above. **Management:** Richard Stein, Publisher. Phyllis Steele, Advertising Manager. **Editorial:** Richard Stein, Editor.

RIVERDALE REVIEW. 6050 Riverdale Ave., Bronx, NY 10471-1604. Telephone: 718-543-5200. FAX: 718-543-4206. E-MAIL: bxny@aol.com. URL: http://www.riverdalereview.com. Year Established: 1993. Pub. Frequency: w. (Thu.) Page Size: tabloid Circulation: 20,000 per issue (free). **Owner(s):** Metro North Media Inc., See address and contact information above. **Management:** Andrew Wolf, Publisher. **Editorial:** Andrew Wolf, Editor.

BROOKLYN

BAY NEWS. 1733 Sheepshead Bay Rd., Brooklyn, NY 11235-3606. Telephone: 718-615-2500. FAX: 718-615-3828. URL: http://www.brooklynny.com. Year Established: 1945. Pub. Frequency: w. (Mon.) Page Size: tabloid. Subscrip. Rate: $.50 newsstand/cover; $20/yr. Circulation: 21,420 per issue (controlled and free). **Owner(s):** Courier-Life, Inc., See address and contact information above. **Management:** Clifford Luster, Co-Publisher. Steve Fine, Advertising Manager. Jennifer Stern, Circulation Manager. Glen Kosik, Classified Adv. Mgr.. **Editorial:** Ken Brown, Editor-in-Chief.

BAY RIDGE COURIER. 1733 Sheepshead Bay Rd., Brooklyn, NY 11235-3606. Telephone: 718-615-2500. FAX: 718-615-3835. E-MAIL: editorial@courierlife.com. URL: http://www.brooklynny.com. Year Established: 1978. Pub. Frequency: w. (Mon.) Page Size: tabloid. Subscrip. Rate: $.50 newsstand/cover; $20/yr mailed. Circulation: 10,225 per issue (controlled and free). **Owner(s):** Courier-Life, Inc., See address and contact information above. **Management:** Clifford Luster, Publisher. Steve Fine, Advertising Manager. Jennifer Stern, Circulation Manager. Glen Kosik, Classified Adv. Mgr.. **Editorial:** Kenneth Brown, Editor-in-Chief.

BROOKLYN EAGLE. 30 Henry St., Brooklyn, NY 11201. Telephone: 718-422-7400. FAX: 718-858-4483. Pub. Frequency: w. (Fri.) Page Size: tabloid. Subscrip. Rate: $.50 newsstand/cover; $35/yr; $50 for 2 yrs.; $60 for 3 yrs.. Circulation: 7,700 per issue (paid). **Owner(s):** Brooklyn Eagle Publications, Inc., See address and contact information above. **Management:** Dozier Hasty, Publisher. Patricia Higgins, Advertising Manager. Katherina Ramus, Circulation Manager. **Editorial:** Raanan Geberer, Editor.

BROOKLYN GRAPHIC. 1733 Sheepshead Bay Rd., Brooklyn, NY 11235-3606. Telephone: 718-615-2500. FAX: 718-615-3835. URL: http://www.brooklynny.com. Year Established: 1953. Pub. Frequency: w. (Mon.) Page Size: tabloid. Subscrip. Rate: $.50 newsstand/cover; $20/yr. Circulation: 9,370 per issue (paid and free). **Owner(s):** Courier-Life, Inc., See address and contact information above. **Management:** Clifford Luster, Co-Publisher. Steve Fine, Advertising Manager. Jennifer Stern, Circulation Manager. **Editorial:** Kenneth Brown, Editor-in-Chief.

BROOKLYN HEIGHTS COURIER. 1733 Sheepshead Bay Rd., Brooklyn, NY 11235-3606. Telephone: 718-615-2500. FAX: 718-615-3828. URL: http://www.brooklynny.com. Year Established: 1990. Pub. Frequency: w. (Mon.) Page Size: tabloid Subscrip. Rate: $50/yr Circulation: 72,000 per issue (free). **Owner(s):** Courier-Life, Inc., See address and contact information above. **Management:** Clifford Luster, Publisher. Steve Fine, Advertising Manager. Jennifer Stern, Circulation Manager. Glen Kosik, Classified Adv. Mgr.. **Editorial:** Kenneth Brown, Editor-in-Chief.

BROOKLYN HEIGHTS PRESS. 30 Henry St., Brooklyn, NY 11201. Telephone: 718-422-7400. FAX: 718-858-4483. E-MAIL: bdeagle@idt.net. Year Established: 1937. Pub. Frequency: w. (Thu.) Page Size: tabloid.Subscrip. Rate: $.50 newsstand/cover; $25/yr Circulation: 12,500 per issue (paid). **Owner(s):** Brooklyn Eagle Publications, Inc., See address and contact information above. **Management:** Dozier Hasty, Publisher. Patricia Higgins, Advertising Manager. **Editorial:** Henrik Krogius, Editor. Raanan Geberer, Managing Editor.

BROOKLYN HOME REPORTER & SUNSET NEWS. 8723 Third Ave., Brooklyn, NY 11209. Telephone: 718-238-6600. FAX: 718-238-6630. E-MAIL: homereporter@aol.com. URL: http://www.homereporter.net. Year Established: 1953. Pub. Frequency: w. (Fri.) Page Size: tabloid.Subscrip. Rate: $.50 newsstand/cover; $35/yr Circulation: 18,000 per issue (paid). **Owner(s):** Modern Media, Inc., See address and contact information above. **Management:** J. Frank Griffin, Owner. Bernard Sherman, Business Manager. **Editorial:** J. Frank Griffin, Editor.

BROOKLYN JOURNAL OF ARTS & URBAN AFFAIRS. 30 Henry St., Brooklyn, NY 11201. Telephone: 718-422-7400. FAX: 718-858-4483. Pub. Frequency: w. (Fri.) Page Size: broadsheet Circulation: 50,000 per issue (free). **Owner(s):** Brooklyn Eagle Publications, Inc., See address and contact information above. **Management:** Dozier Hasty, Publisher. Patricia Higgins, Advertising Manager. Katherina Ramus, Circulation Manager. **Editorial:** Raanan Geberer, Managing Editor.

BROOKLYN RECORD OF REAL ESTATE. ISSN 1553-7676 30 Henry St., Brooklyn, NY 11201. Telephone: 718-422-7400. FAX: 718-858-4483. E-MAIL: bdeagle@idt.net. Year Established: 1938. Pub. Frequency: w. (Fri.) Page Size: tabloid. Subscrip. Rate: $.25 newsstand/cover; $125/yr mailed. Circulation: 7,700 per issue (paid). **Owner(s):** Brooklyn Eagle Publications, Inc., See address and contact information above. **Management:** Dozier Hasty, Publisher. Patricia Higgins, Advertising Manager. Katherina Ramus, Circulation Manager. **Editorial:** Raanan Geberer, Managing Editor.

BROOKLYN SPECTATOR. 8723 Third Ave., Brooklyn, NY 11209. Telephone: 718-238-6600. FAX: 718-238-6630. E-MAIL: homereporter@aol.com. URL: http://www.homereporter.net. Year Established: 1933. Pub. Frequency: w. (Wed.) Page Size: tabloid.Subscrip. Rate: $.50 newsstand/cover; $35/yr Circulation: 18,000 per issue (paid). **Owner(s):** Modern Media, Inc., See address and contact information above. **Management:** J. Frank Griffin, Owner. Bernard Sherman, Business Manager. **Editorial:** J. Frank Griffin, Editor.

CANARSIE COURIER. 1142 E 92nd St., Brooklyn, NY 11236-3624. Telephone: 718-257-0600. FAX: 718-272-0870. E-MAIL: canarsiec@aol.com. URL: http://www.canarsiecourier.com. Year Established: 1921. Pub. Frequency: w. (Thu.) Page Size: tabloid. Subscrip. Rate: $.50 newsstand/cover; $20/yr mailed in county; $40/yr mailed elsewhere. **Wire Service(s):** AP. Circulation: 10,000 per issue (paid). **Owner(s):** Sandra Greco & Donna M. Marra, See address and contact information above. **Management:** Donna M. Marra, Publisher. Catherine Rosa, Business Manager. **Editorial:** Charles Rogers, Managing Editor. Neil S. Friedman, Feature Editor.

CANARSIE DIGEST. 1733 Sheepshead Bay Rd., Brooklyn, NY 11235-3606. Telephone: 718-615-2500. FAX: 718-615-3828. URL: http://www.brooklynny.com. Year Established: 1959. Pub. Frequency: w. (Mon.) Page Size: tabloid.Subscrip. Rate: $.50 newsstand/cover; $20/yr Circulation: 10,150 per issue (paid). **Owner(s):** Courier-Life, Inc., See address and contact information above. **Management:** Clifford Luster, Co-Publisher. Steve Fine, Advertising Manager. Jennifer Stern, Circulation Manager. Glen Kosik, Classified Adv. Mgr.. **Editorial:** Ken Brown, Editor-in-Chief.

CARIBBEAN LIFE. 1733 Sheepshead Bay Rd., Brooklyn, NY 11235-3606. Telephone: 718-615-2500. FAX: 718-615-3839. Pub. Frequency: w. (Tue.) Page Size: tabloid Circulation: 125,000 per issue (free). **Owner(s):** Courier-Life, Inc., See address and contact information above. **Management:** Clifford Luster, Co-Publisher. Don Holt, General Manager. Arnold Thibou, Publisher. Jennifer Stern, Circulation Manager. **Editorial:** Kenton Kirby, Editor-in-Chief.

CARROLL GARDENS/COBBLE HILL COURIER. 1733 Sheepshead Bay Rd., Brooklyn, NY 11235-3606. Telephone: 718-615-2500. FAX: 718-615-3828. Year Established: 1990. Pub. Frequency: w. (Mon.) Page Size: tabloid Subscrip. Rate: $50/yr Circulation: 81,000 per issue (free). **Owner(s):** Courier-Life, Inc., See address and contact information above. **Management:** Clifford Luster, Publisher. Jennifer Stern, Circulation Manager. Glen Kosik, Classified Adv. Mgr.. **Editorial:** Kenneth Brown, Editor. Elaine Zimmerman, Entertainment Editor.

FLATBUSH LIFE. 1733 Sheepshead Bay Rd., Brooklyn, NY 11235-3606. Telephone: 718-615-2500. FAX: 718-615-3835. URL: http://www.brooklynny.com. Year Established: 1956. Pub. Frequency: w. (Mon.) Page Size: tabloid.Subscrip. Rate: $.50 newsstand/cover; $20/yr Circulation: 12,360 per issue (paid). **Owner(s):** Courier-Life, Inc., See address and contact information above. **Management:** Clifford Luster, Co-Publisher. Steve Fine, Advertising Manager. Jennifer Stern, Circulation Manager. **Editorial:** Kenneth Brown, Editor-in-Chief.

GREENPOINT GAZETTE & ADVERTISER. 597 Manhattan Ave., Brooklyn, NY 11222-3919. Telephone: 718-389-6067. FAX: 718-349-3471. E-MAIL: gptgazette@aol.com. Year Established: 1973. Pub. Frequency: w. (Thu.) Page Size: tabloid. Subscrip. Rate: $.25 newsstand/cover; $20/yr in city; $25/yr out of city. **Wire Service(s):** CNS. Circulation: 5,010 per issue (paid and free). **Owner(s):** Community Gazette, Inc., See address and contact information above. **Management:** Virginia Bednarek, Co-Publisher. **Editorial:** Ralph Carrano, Editor.

KINGS COUNTY NEWS. 2446 E. 65th St., Brooklyn, NY 11234. Telephone: 718-763-7034. FAX: 718-763-7035. E-MAIL: editman1000@yahoo.com. Year Established: 1976. Pub. Frequency: w. (Mon.) Page Size: tabloid. Subscrip. Rate: $.50 newsstand/cover; $26/yr. Circulation: 92,000 per issue (controlled and free). **Owner(s):** E W A Publications, See address and contact information above. **Management:** Kenneth Brown, Publisher. Susan Berger, Advertising Manager. Phil Tarrington, Circulation Manager. **Editorial:** Kevin Browne, Editor.

KINGS COURIER. 1733 Sheepshead Bay Rd., Brooklyn, NY 11235-3606. Telephone: 718-615-3830. FAX: 718-615-3835. Year Established: 1951. Pub. Frequency: w. (Mon.) Page Size: tabloid. Subscrip. Rate: $.50 newsstand/cover; $20/yr. Circulation: 19,500 per issue (controlled and free). **Owner(s):** Courier-Life, Inc., See address and contact information above. **Management:** Clifford Luster, Co-Publisher. Steve Fine, Advertising Manager. Jennifer Stern, Circulation Manager. **Editorial:** Ken Brown, Editor-in-Chief.

NEW YORK METROPOLITAN NEWS. 2446 E. 65th St., Brooklyn, NY 11234. Telephone: 718-763-7034. FAX: 718-763-7035. Year Established: 1962. Pub. Frequency: w. (Mon.) Page Size: tabloid. Subscrip. Rate: $.50 newsstand/cover; $26/yr. Circulation: 283,000 per issue (controlled and free). **Owner(s):** E W A Publications, See address and contact information above. **Management:** Kenneth Brown, Publisher. Susan Berger, Advertising Manager. Phil Tarrington, Circulation Manager. **Editorial:** Kevin Browne, Editor.

PARK SLOPE COURIER. 1733 Sheepshead Bay Rd., Brooklyn, NY 11235-3606. Telephone: 718-615-2500. FAX: 718-615-3835. Year Established: 1990. Pub. Frequency: w. (Mon.) Page Size: tabloid.Subscrip. Rate: $50/yr Circulation: 101,000 per issue (free). **Owner(s):** Courier-Life, Inc., See address and contact information above. **Management:** Dan Holt, Co-Publisher. Clifford Luster, Publisher. Steve Fine, Advertising Manager. Jennifer Stern, Circulation Manager. **Editorial:** Kenneth Brown, Editor. Elaine Zimmerman, Entertainment Editor.

PHOENIX NEWSPAPER, THE. 30 Henry St., Brooklyn, NY 11201. Telephone: 718-422-7400. FAX: 718-858-4483. Year Established: 1972. Pub. Frequency: w. (Thu.) Page Size: tabloid. Subscrip. Rate: $.25 newsstand/cover; $125/yr mailed. Circulation: 13,000 per issue (paid). **Owner(s):** Brooklyn Eagle Publications, Inc., See address and contact information above. **Management:** Dozier Hasty, Publisher. Patricia Higgins, Advertising Manager. Katherina Ramus, Circulation Manager. **Editorial:** Raanan Geberer, Managing Editor.

STATEN ISLAND STAR REPORTER. 1733 Sheepshead Bay Rd., Brooklyn, NY 11235-3606. Telephone: 718-615-2500. FAX: 718-615-3828. E-MAIL: courierlife@spacelab.net. URL: http://www.brooklynny.com.Pub. Frequency: s-m. Page Size: tabloid Circulation: 34,000 per issue (free). **Owner(s):** Courier-Life, Inc., See address and contact information above. **Management:** Clifford Luster, Publisher. Howard Swingler, Advertising Manager. Jennifer Stern, Circulation Manager. Glen Kosik, Classified Adv. Mgr.. **Editorial:** Kenneth Brown, Editor.

BUFFALO

BUFFALO ROCKET. 2507 Delaware Ave., Buffalo, NY 14216. Telephone: 716-873-2594. FAX: 716-873-0809. E-MAIL: brocket@localnet.com. URL: http://www.gallagherprinting.com. Year Established: 1969. Pub. Frequency: w. (Fri.) Page Size: tabloid.Subscrip. Rate: $45/yr mailed local Circulation: 15,000 per issue (paid). **Owner(s):** Rocket Communications, Inc., See address and contact information above. **Management:** David H. Gallagher, Publisher. Mollie Hughes, Advertising Director. **Editorial:** Dennis Gallagher, Editor.

RIVERSIDE REVIEW. 215 Military Rd., Buffalo, NY 14207. Telephone: 716-877-8400. FAX: 716-877-8742. E-MAIL: rich@buffaloreview.com. Year Established: 1923. Pub. Frequency: w. (Wed.) Page Size: tabloid. Subscrip. Rate: $45/yr mailed. Circulation: 14,300 per issue (paid and free). **Owner(s):** Richard Mack, See address and contact information above. **Management:** Richard Mack, Publisher. Steve Liberatore, Advertising. **Editorial:** Richard Mack, Editor.

CAMBRIDGE

EAGLE (CAMBRIDGE), THE. ISSN 0745-9831 1 E Main St, Cambridge, NY 12816. Telephone: 518-677-5158. FAX: 518-677-8323. E-MAIL: eaglenews@gmail.com. Mailing Address: P.O. Box 493, Cambridge, NY 12816-0036. Year Established: 1981. Pub. Frequency: w. (Thu.) Page Size: tabloid. Subscrip. Rate: $36/yr mailed in state; $38/yr out of state. Adv. Rate: col. inch $9 Circulation: 4,250 per issue (paid and free). **Owner(s):** Eagle, The, See address and contact information above. **Management:** Eric Wilkins, Publisher. Meaghan Wilkins, Advertising Manager. **Editorial:** Eric Wilkins, Editor.

CANANDAIGUA

BRIGHTON-PITTSFORD POST. 73 Buffalo St, Canandaigua, NY 14424. Telephone: 585-394-0770. FAX: 585-394-1675. E-MAIL: post@mpnewspapers.com. URL: http://www.mpnewspapers.com. Year Established: 1932. Pub. Frequency: w. (Wed.) Page Size: broadsheet.Subscrip. Rate: $29.95/yr Circulation: 13,500 per issue (free). **Owner(s):** GateHouse Media, Inc, 350 WillowBrook Office Park, Fairport, NY 14450. Telephone: 585-598-0030. FAX: 585-248-2631. **Management:** Carl Helbig, Publisher. Jerry Grundman, Advertising Director. **Editorial:** Robert Matson, Executive Editor.

BROCKPORT-SPENCERPORT POST. 73 Buffalo St, Canandaigua, NY 14424. Telephone: 585-394-0770. FAX: 585-394-1675. E-MAIL: post@mpnewspapers.com. URL: http://www.mpnewspapers.com. Year Established: 1968. Pub. Frequency: w. (Thu.) Page Size: broadsheet.Subscrip. Rate: $33/yr mailed Circulation: 1,800 per issue (free). **Owner(s):** GateHouse Media, Inc, 350 WillowBrook Office Park, Fairport, NY 14450. Telephone: 585-598-0030. FAX: 585-248-2631. **Management:** Carl Helbig, Publisher. Jerry Grundman, Advertising Director. **Editorial:** Robert Matson, Executive Editor.

EAST ROCHESTER POST. ISSN 1531-0140 73 Buffalo St, Canandaigua, NY 14424. Telephone: 585-394-0770. FAX: 585-394-1675. E-MAIL: circulation@mpnewspapers.com. URL: http://www.mpnewspapers.com. Year Established: 1989. Pub. Frequency: w. (Wed.) Page Size: broadsheet.Subscrip. Rate: $29.95/yr mailed Circulation: 1,100 per issue (free). **Owner(s):** GateHouse Media, Inc, 350 WillowBrook Office Park, Fairport, NY 14450. Telephone: 585-598-0030. FAX: 585-248-2631. **Management:** Carl Helbig, Publisher. Jerry Grundman, Advertising Director. **Editorial:** Robert Matson, Executive Editor.

GATES-CHILI POST. ISSN 1553-2291 73 Buffalo St, Canandaigua, NY 14424. Telephone: 585-394-0770. FAX: 585-394-1675. E-MAIL: post@mpnewspapers.com. URL: http://www.mpnnow.com. Year Established: 1958. Pub. Frequency: w. (Wed.) Page Size: tabloid.Subscrip. Rate: $22.95/yr Circulation: 9,800 per issue (free). **Owner(s):** GateHouse Media, Inc, 350 WillowBrook Office Park, Fairport, NY 14450. Telephone: 585-598-0030. FAX: 585-248-2631. **Management:** Carl Helbig, Publisher. Jerry Grundman, Advertising Director. **Editorial:** Robert Matson, Executive Editor.

GREECE POST, THE. 73 Buffalo St, Canandaigua, NY 14424. Telephone: 585-394-0770. FAX: 585-394-1675. E-MAIL: post@mpsnewspapers.com. URL: http://www.mpnewspapers.com. Year Established: 1960. Pub. Frequency: w. (Thu.) Page Size: broadsheet. Subscrip. Rate: $29.95/yr mailed. Adv. Rate: col. inch $12.50 Circulation: 9,500 per issue (free). **Owner(s):** GateHouse Media, Inc, 350 WillowBrook Office Park, Fairport, NY 14450. Telephone: 585-598-0030. FAX: 585-248-2631. **Management:** Carl Helbig, Publisher. Jerry Grundman, Advertising Director. **Editorial:** Robert Matson, Executive Editor.

HENRIETTA POST. 73 Buffalo St, Canandaigua, NY 14424. Telephone: 585-394-0770. FAX: 585-394-1675. E-MAIL: post@mpnewspapers.com. URL: http://www.henriettapost.com. Year Established: 1964. Pub. Frequency: w. (Wed.) Page Size: broadsheet.Subscrip. Rate: $29.95/yr mailed Circulation: 3,000 per issue (free). **Owner(s):** GateHouse Media, Inc, 350 WillowBrook Office Park, Fairport, NY 14450. Telephone: 585-598-0030. FAX: 585-248-2631. **Management:** Carl Helbig, Publisher. Jerry Grundman, Advertising Director. **Editorial:** Robert Matson, Executive Editor.

IRONDEQUOIT POST-PRESS. 73 Buffalo St, Canandaigua, NY 14424. Telephone: 585-394-0770. FAX: 585-394-1675. E-MAIL: post@mpnewspapers.com. URL: http://www.mpnnow.com. Year Established: 1932. Pub. Frequency: w. (Thu.) Page Size: broadsheet.Subscrip. Rate: $29.95/yr local Circulation: 7,800 per issue (free). **Owner(s):** GateHouse Media, Inc, 350 WillowBrook Office Park, Fairport, NY 14450. Telephone: 585-598-0030. FAX: 585-248-2631. **Management:** Carl Helbig, Publisher. Jerry Grundman, Advertising Director. **Editorial:** Robert Matson, Executive Editor.

PENFIELD POST. 73 Buffalo St, Canandaigua, NY 14424. Telephone: 585-394-0770. FAX: 585-394-1675. E-MAIL: advertising@mpnnewspapers.com. URL: http://www.mpnnow.com. Year Established: 1950. Pub. Frequency: w. (Thu.) Page Size: broadsheet.Subscrip. Rate: $29.95/yr Circulation: 3,800 per issue (free). **Owner(s):** GateHouse Media, Inc, 350 WillowBrook Office Park, Fairport, NY 14450. Telephone: 585-598-0030. FAX: 585-248-2631. **Management:** Carl Helbig, Publisher. Jerry Grundman, Advertising Director. **Editorial:** Robert Matson, Executive Editor.

PERINTON-FAIRPORT POST. 73 Buffalo St, Canandaigua, NY 14424. Telephone: 585-394-0770. FAX: 585-394-1675. E-MAIL: post@mpnewspapers.com. URL: http://www.mpnewspapers.com. Year Established: 1932. Pub. Frequency: w. (Thu.) Page Size: broadsheet. Subscrip. Rate: $29.95/yr in county. Adv. Rate: col. inch $7.70 Circulation: 4,500 per issue (free). **Owner(s):** GateHouse Media, Inc, 350 WillowBrook Office Park, Fairport, NY 14450. Telephone: 585-598-0030. FAX: 585-248-2631. **Management:** Carl Helbig, Publisher. Jerry Grundman, Advertising Director. **Editorial:** Robert Matson, Executive Editor.

WEBSTER POST. ISSN 0745-3663
73 Buffalo St, Canandaigua, NY 14424. Telephone: 585-394-0770. FAX: 585-394-1675. URL: http://www.mpnnow.com. Year Established: 1992. Pub. Frequency: w. (Thu.) Page Size: broadsheet.Subscrip. Rate: $24.95/yr Circulation: 4,450 per issue (free). **Owner(s):** GateHouse Media, Inc, 350 WillowBrook Office Park, Fairport, NY 14450. Telephone: 585-598-0030. FAX: 585-248-2631. **Management:** Carl Helbig, Publisher. Jerry Grundman, Advertising Director. **Editorial:** Robert Matson, Executive Editor.

CANASTOTA

CANASTOTA BEE-JOURNAL. 114 Canal St, Canastota, NY 13032. Telephone: 314-697-7142. FAX: 314-697-6283. URL: http://www.cnylink.com. Mailing Address: PO Box 228, Canastota, NY 13032. Pub. Frequency: w. (Wed.) Page Size: broadsheet. Subscrip. Rate: $.50 newsstand/cover; $28/yr local. Adv. Rate: col. inch $23 Circulation: 2,050 per issue (paid). **Owner(s):** Eagle Newspapers LP, 5910 Firestone Dr., Syracuse, NY 13152. Telephone: 315-434-8889. FAX: 315-434-8883. **Management:** David Tyler, General Manager. Tami Grashof, Advertising Director. Laurie Newcomb, Circulation Manager. Julie Galvin, Classified Adv. Mgr.. **Editorial:** Martha Rush Conway, Editor. Tom Wanamker, Managing Editor.

ONEIDA PRESS. 114 Canal St, Canastota, NY 13032. Telephone: 314-697-7142. FAX: 314-697-6283. E-MAIL: newsroom@cnylink.com. URL: http://cnylink.com/aboutcny/. Mailing Address: PO Box 228, Canastota, NY 13032. Pub. Frequency: w. (Wed.) Page Size: tabloid.Adv. Rate: col. inch $6.30 Circulation: 5,000 per issue (controlled). **Owner(s):** Eagle Newspapers LP, 5910 Firestone Dr., Syracuse, NY 13152. Telephone: 315-434-8889. FAX: 315-434-8883. **Management:** David Tyler, General Manager. Tami Grashof, Advertising Director. Laurie Newcomb, Circulation Manager. Julie Galvin, Classified Adv. Mgr.. **Editorial:** Martha Rush Conway, Editor. Tom Wanamker, Managing Editor.

CANTON

ST. LAWRENCE PLAINDEALER. 75 Main St., Canton, NY 13617. Telephone: 315-386-8521. FAX: 315-386-8887. E-MAIL: pdealer@logd.com. Pub. Frequency: w. (Tue.) Page Size: broadsheet. Subscrip. Rate: $.50 newsstand/cover; $15.50/yr carrier delivery; $20.25/yr mailed in county; $23/yr mailed out of county. Circulation: 3,500 per issue (paid). **Owner(s):** Johnson Newspaper Corp., 260 Washington St., Watertown, NY 13601. Telephone: 315-782-1000. **Management:** Sean McNamara, Advertising Manager. John Wilson, Circulation Manager. **Editorial:** Paul Mitchell, Editor.

CARMEL

PUTNAM COUNTY COURIER, THE. ISSN 0890-1147
73 Gleneida Ave., Carmel, NY 10512. Telephone: 845-225-3633. FAX: 845-225-1914. E-MAIL: tacnews@aol.com. URL: http://www.midhudsoncentral.com. Mailing Address: PO Box 220, Carmel, NY 10512. Year Established: 1841. Pub. Frequency: w. (Thu.) Page Size: broadsheet. Subscrip. Rate: $.75 newsstand/cover; $37/yr mailed in state; $39/yr mailed out of state. Circulation: 6,200 per issue (paid). **Owner(s):** Journal Register Co., 50 W State St, 12th Fl, Trenton, NJ 08608. Telephone: 609-396-2200. FAX: 609-396-2292. **Management:** Ira Fusfeld, Publisher. Jeff Ohlbaum, Advertising Director. Larry Priest, Circulation Director. Mary Bradford, Classified Adv. Mgr.. **Editorial:** Helen Grosso, Editor. Ann Gibbons, Executive Editor.

CARTHAGE

CARTHAGE REPUBLICAN TRIBUNE. 237 State St, Carthage, NY 13619. Telephone: 315-493-1270. FAX: 315-493-1271. Mailing Address: PO Box 549, Carthage, NY 13619. Year Established: 1860. Pub. Frequency: w. (Thu.) Page Size: broadsheet. Subscrip. Rate: $1 newsstand/cover; $43/yr home delivery; $49.50/yr mailed. Adv. Rate: col. inch $4.85 Circulation: 3,000 per issue (paid). **Owner(s):** Johnson Newspaper Corp., 260 Washington St., Watertown, NY 13601. Telephone: 315-782-1000. **Management:** Cindy Aucter, General Manager. Shaw Connie, Advertising Manager. **Editorial:** Adam Atkinson, Editor.

CAZENOVIA

CAZENOVIA REPUBLICAN. 72 Albany St, Cazenovia, NY 13035. Telephone: 315-655-3415. FAX: 315-655-3813. URL: http://www.cnylink.com. Year Established: 1794. Pub. Frequency: w. (Wed.) Page Size: broadsheet. Subscrip. Rate: $.75 newsstand/cover; $28/yr in county; $30/yr out of county. Adv. Rate: col. inch $7.90 Circulation: 2,810 per issue (paid). **Owner(s):** Eagle Newspapers LP, 5910 Firestone Dr., Syracuse, NY 13152. Telephone: 315-434-8889. FAX: 315-434-8883. **Management:** David Tyler, General Manager. Tami Grashof, Advertising Director. Laurie Newcomb, Circulation Manager. Julie Galvin, Classified Adv. Mgr.. **Editorial:** Willie Kiernan, Editor. Tom Wanamker, Managing Editor.

CHITTENANGO-BRIDGEPORT TIMES. 72 Albany St, Cazenovia, NY 13035. Telephone: 315-655-3415. FAX: 315-655-3813. E-MAIL: madison@cnylink.com. URL: http://cnylink.com/aboutcny/. Mailing Address: PO Box 228, Canastota, NY 13032. Year Established: 1910. Pub. Frequency: w. (Wed.) Page Size: tabloid. Subscrip. Rate: $.75 newsstand/cover; $28/yr mailed in county; $31/yr mailed out of county; $33/yr mailed out of state. Adv. Rate: col. inch $5.70 Circulation: 1,600 per issue (paid). **Owner(s):** Eagle Newspapers LP, 5910 Firestone Dr., Syracuse, NY 13152. Telephone: 315-434-8889. **Management:** David Tyler, General Manager. Tami Grashof, Advertising Director. Laurie Newcomb, Circulation Manager. Julie Galvin, Classified Adv. Mgr.. **Editorial:** Martha Rush Conway, Editor. Tom Wanamker, Managing Editor.

HAMILTON-MORRISVILLE TRIBUNE. 72 Albany St, Cazenovia, NY 13035. Telephone: 315-655-3415. FAX: 315-655-3813. E-MAIL: kdam@cnylink.com. URL: http://www.cnylink.com. Pub. Frequency: w. (Wed.) Page Size: tabloid. Subscrip. Rate: $.50 newsstand/cover; $21/yr mailed in county. Adv. Rate: col. inch $7.50 Freelance Pay: $20-$25/article. Circulation: 950 per issue (paid). **Owner(s):** Eagle Newspapers LP, 5910 Firestone Dr., Syracuse, NY 13152. Telephone: 315-434-8889. FAX: 315-434-8883. **Management:** David Tyler, General Manager. Tami Grashof, Advertising Director. Laurie Newcomb, Circulation Manager. Julie Galvin, Classified Adv. Mgr.. **Editorial:** Willie Kiernan, Editor. Tom Wanamker, Managing Editor.

CENTRAL SQUARE

CITIZEN OUTLET. 3019 East Ave., Central Square, NY 13036. Telephone: 315-963-7813. FAX: 315-963-4087. E-MAIL: ocweeklies@caymail.com. Pub. Frequency: w. (Fri.) Page Size: tabloid.Subscrip. Rate: $.50 newsstand/cover; $15/yr Circulation: 4,050 per issue (paid). **Owner(s):** Mark Backus, 80 N Jefferson St, Mexico, NY 13114. Telephone: 315-963-7813. **Management:** Mark Backus, Publisher. **Editorial:** Roseann Parsons, Managing Editor.

CHATHAM

CHATHAM COURIER & ROUGHNOTES. ISSN 1064-4644
24 Park Row, Chatham, NY 12037. Telephone: 518-392-4141. FAX: 518-392-7322. Mailing Address: PO Box 355, Chatham, NY 12037. Year Established: 1825. Pub. Frequency: w. (Thu.) Page Size: tabloid. Subscrip. Rate: $1 newsstand/cover; $31/yr home delivery local; $34/yr mailed in county; $37/yr mailed out of county. **Wire Service(s):** AP. Circulation: 4,500 per issue (paid). **Owner(s):** Johnson Newspaper Corp., 260 Washington St., Watertown, NY 13601. Telephone: 315-782-1000. **Management:** Roger Coleman, General Manager. Brenda Nickles, Circulation Director. **Editorial:** Babette Ryder, Editor.

CHEEKTOWAGA

CHEEKTOWAGA TIMES. 343 Maryvale Dr., Cheektowaga, NY 14225. Telephone: 716-892-5323. FAX: 716-892-4925. E-MAIL: mail@cheektowagatimes.com. URL: http://www.cheektowagatimes.com. Year Established: 1946. Pub. Frequency: w. (Thu.) Page Size: tabloid.Subscrip. Rate: $.75 newsstand/cover; $25/yr Circulation: 4,000 per issue (paid). **Owner(s):** Elizabeth A. Gruber, 2416 E. Loyola Dr., Tempe, AZ 85202. Telephone: 716-892-5323. **Management:** James A. Gruber, General Manager. Elizabeth A. Gruber, Publisher. Colleen Bellere, Circulation Manager.

SPRINGVILLE JOURNAL. 78 Boxwood, Cheektowaga, NY 14225. Telephone: 716-668-5223. FAX: 716-592-4663. E-MAIL: info@springvillejournal.net. URL: http://www.springvillejournal.net. Year Established: 1867. Pub. Frequency: w. (Thu.) Page Size: tabloid. Subscrip. Rate: $1 newsstand/cover; $31/yr in state; $28/yr to military senior citizens. Circulation: 4,368 per issue (paid). **Owner(s):** Metro Group. Inc., See address and contact information above. H & K Publications, Inc., 41 E. Main St., Springville, NY 14141. **Management:** Tom Kluckhohn, Publisher. Teri Scott, Circulation Manager. Rick Manzone, Sales Manager. **Editorial:** Paul Chapman, Editor.

CLINTON

CLINTON COURIER. 4 Meadow St., Clinton, NY 13323-0294. Telephone: 315-853-3490. FAX: 315-853-3522. E-MAIL: clintoncourier@verizon.net. URL: http://www.clintoncourier.com. Mailing Address: PO Box 294, Clinton, NY 13323. Year Established: 1846. Pub. Frequency: w. (Wed.) Page Size: tabloid. Subscrip. Rate: $1 newsstand/cover; $31/yr home delivery in county; $46/yr mailed out of county. Adv. Rate: col. inch $15.61 Circulation: 2,170 per issue (paid). **Owner(s):** Charles & Cynthia Kershner, See address and contact information above. **Management:** Cynthia Kershner, Publisher. **Editorial:** Charles J. Kershner, Editor-in-Chief.

COBLESKILL

TIMES JOURNAL. PO Box 339, Cobleskill, NY 12043. Telephone: 518-234-2515. FAX: 518-234-7898. E-MAIL: tjournal@midtel.net. Year Established: 1876. Pub. Frequency: w. (Wed.) Page Size: broadsheet. Subscrip. Rate: $.75 newsstand/cover; $32/yr in county; $48/yr out of county. Adv. Rate: col. inch $6.50 Circulation: 7,300 per issue (paid). **Owner(s):** Jim Poole, See address and contact information above. **Management:** Jim Poole, Publisher. Kathy Rivenburg, Advertising Manager. **Editorial:** Patsy Nicosia, Editor.

CONKLIN

COUNTRY COURIER, THE. ISSN 1065-5891
1035 Conklin Rd, Conklin, NY 13748. Telephone: 607-775-0472. FAX: 607-775-5863. E-MAIL: mpinews@spectra.net. Mailing Address: PO Box 208, Conklin, NY 13748. Year Established: 1976. Pub. Frequency: w. (Wed.) Page Size: tabloid. Subscrip. Rate: $.75 newsstand/cover; $25/yr mailed in county; $27/yr out of county. Adv. Rate: col. inch $2.20 Circulation: 1,600 per issue (paid). **Owner(s):** Newspaper Publishers, Llc., See address and contact information above. **Management:** Don Einstein, President. **Editorial:** Elizabeth Einstein, Editor.

VESTAL TOWN CRIER. ISSN 1051-3574
1035 Conklin Rd, Conklin, NY 13748. Telephone: 607-775-0472. FAX: 607-775-5863. E-MAIL: mpinews@spectra.net. Mailing Address: PO Box 208, Conklin, NY 13748. Year Established: 1989. Pub. Frequency: w. (Wed.) Page Size: tabloid. Subscrip. Rate: $.75 newsstand/cover; $25/yr mailed in county; $27/yr mailed out of county. Adv. Rate: col. inch $2.20 Circulation: 1,400 per issue (paid). **Owner(s):** Newspaper Publishers, Llc., See address and contact information above. **Management:** Don Einstein, President. **Editorial:** Elizabeth Einstein, Editor.

WINDSOR STANDARD. ISSN 1059-5449
1035 Conklin Rd, Conklin, NY 13748. Telephone: 607-775-0472. FAX: 607-775-5863. Mailing Address: PO Box 208, Conklin, NY 13748. Year Established: 1879. Pub. Frequency: w. (Wed.) Page Size: tabloid. Subscrip. Rate: $.75 newsstand/cover; $25/yr in county; $27/yr mailed out of county. Adv. Rate: col. inch $2.20 Circulation: 1,500 per issue (paid). **Owner(s):** Newspaper Publishers, Llc., See address and contact information above. **Management:** Don Einstein, President. **Editorial:** Elizabeth Einstein, Editor.

COOPERSTOWN

COOPERSTOWN CRIER. 21 Railroad Ave, Cooperstown, NY 13326. Telephone: 607-547-9493. FAX: 607-547-1109. URL: http://www.coopercrier.com. Mailing Address: PO Box 1046, Cooperstown, NY 13326-1046. Pub. Frequency: w. (Thu.) Page Size: standard.Subscrip. Rate: $.75 newsstand/cover Circulation: 2,500 per issue (paid). **Owner(s):** Community Newspaper Holdings, Inc., 3500 Colonnade Pkwy., Ste. 600, Birmingham, AL 25243. **Management:** Rebecca Fogarty, Advertising. **Editorial:** James Austin, Editor. Michelle Miller, Writer.

CORTLAND

CORTLAND SUNDAY. 165 S. Main St., Cortland, NY 13045. Telephone: 607-753-3413. FAX: 607-753-8490. URL: http://scotsmanonline.com. Year Established: 1864. Pub. Frequency: w. (Sun.) Page Size: tabloid Circulation: 11,000 per issue (free). **Owner(s):** Scotsman Press, Inc., 750 W. Genesee St., Syracuse, NY 13321. Telephone: 315-472-7825. **Management:** Shawn Raymond, Advertising Manager. David Spering, Circulation Manager. **Editorial:** Debra Lun, Editor.

CUBA

PATRIOT & FREE PRESS. ISSN 0746-9969
34 Water St., Cuba, NY 14727-1490. Telephone: 585-968-2580. FAX: 585-968-2622. E-MAIL: patriot@eznet.net. URL: http://www.cubapatriot.com. Year Established: 1862. Pub. Frequency: w. (Wed.) Page Size: broadsheet. Subscrip. Rate: $.75 newsstand/cover; $23/yr mailed in county; $29/yr mailed out of state. Freelance Pay: $10/article. Circulation: 4,300 per issue (paid). **Owner(s):** Empire Phoenix Corp., 97 Pennsylvania Ave., Friendship, NY 14739. Telephone: 716-973-2025. **Management:** John Arden-Hopkins, Publisher. Nathan Daugherty, Advertising Manager. **Editorial:** John Arden-Hopkins, Editor.

DANSVILLE

GENESEE COUNTRY EXPRESS. 113 Main St., Dansville, NY 14437. Telephone: 585-335-2272. FAX: 585-335-6957. E-MAIL: gcexp@wynt.com. Year Established: 1851. Pub. Frequency: w. (Thu.) Page Size: broadsheet. Subscrip. Rate: $1 newsstand/cover; $37/yr in county. Circulation: 14,542 per issue (paid and free). **Owner(s):** GateHouse Media, Inc, 350 WillowBrook Office Park, Fairport, NY 14450. Telephone: 585-598-0030. FAX: 585-248-2631. **Management:** Frederick W. Kurtz, Publisher. **Editorial:** Peter Vogt, Editor.

GENESEEWAY SHOPPER. 113 Main St., Dansville, NY 14437. Telephone: 585-335-2272. FAX: 585-335-6957. Pub. Frequency: w. (Sun.) Page Size: tabloid Circulation: 11,642 per issue (free). **Owner(s):** GateHouse Media, Inc, 350 WillowBrook Office Park, Fairport, NY 14450. Telephone: 585-598-0030. FAX: 585-248-2631. **Management:** Frederick W. Kurtz, Publisher.

DELHI

DELAWARE COUNTY TIMES. ISSN 0745-0206 56 Main St., Delhi, NY 13753. Telephone: 607-746-2176. FAX: 607-746-3135. E-MAIL: info@kaatslife.com. Year Established: 1978. Pub. Frequency: w. (Fri.) Page Size: broadsheet. Subscrip. Rate: $.50 newsstand/cover; $24/yr in county; $26.50/yr mailed out of county. Adv. Rate: col. inch $3.50 Freelance Pay: $1/column-inch. Circulation: 1,500 per issue (paid). **Owner(s):** Donald F. Bishop, II, See address and contact information above. **Management:** Donald F. Bishop, President. Karen Naden, Advertising Manager.

DELMAR

BURNT HILLS SPOTLIGHT. 125 Adams St., Delmar, NY 12054. Telephone: 518-439-4949. FAX: 518-439-0608. Pub. Frequency: w. (Thu.) Page Size: tabloid. Subscrip. Rate: $.75 newsstand/cover; $26/yr local. Adv. Rate: col. inch $7.95 Circulation: 2,000 per issue (paid). **Owner(s):** Eagle Newspapers LP, 5910 Firestone Dr., Syracuse, NY 13152. Telephone: 315-434-8889. FAX: 315-434-8883. **Management:** John McIntyre, Publisher. William Kellert, Advertising Director. Brittany Worgan, Classified Adv. Mgr.. **Editorial:** Katherine McCarthy, Editor-in-Chief. Tim Mulligan, Managing Editor.

CLIFTON PARK/HALFMOON SPOTLIGHT. 125 Adams St., Delmar, NY 12054. Telephone: 518-439-4949. FAX: 518-439-0608. URL: http://www.cnylink.com. Pub. Frequency: w. (Thu.) Page Size: tabloid.Adv. Rate: col. inch $9.10 Circulation: 3,000 per issue (free). **Owner(s):** Eagle Newspapers LP, 5910 Firestone Dr., Syracuse, NY 13152. Telephone: 315-434-8889. FAX: 315-434-8883. **Management:** John McIntyre, Publisher. William Kellert, Advertising Director. Brittany Worgan, Classified Adv. Mgr.. **Editorial:** Katherine McCarthy, Editor-in-Chief. Tim Mulligan, Managing Editor.

COLONIE SPOTLIGHT. 125 Adams St., Delmar, NY 12054. Telephone: 518-439-4949. FAX: 518-439-0608. E-MAIL: spotlight@albany.net. Pub. Frequency: w. (Wed.) Page Size: tabloid. Subscrip. Rate: $.75 newsstand/cover; $26/yr in county. Adv. Rate: col. inch $9.95 Circulation: 2,500 per issue (paid). **Owner(s):** Eagle Newspapers LP, 5910 Firestone Dr., Syracuse, NY 13152. Telephone: 315-434-8889. FAX: 315-434-8883. **Management:** John McIntyre, Publisher. William Kellert, Advertising Director. Brittany Worgan, Classified Adv. Mgr.. **Editorial:** Katherine McCarthy, Editor-in-Chief. Tim Mulligan, Managing Editor.

GUILDERLAND SPOTLIGHT. 125 Adams St., Delmar, NY 12054. Telephone: 518-439-4949. FAX: 518-439-0608. URL: http://www.cnylink.com. Pub. Frequency: w. (Thu.) Page Size: tabloid. Subscrip. Rate: $.75 newsstand/cover; $15/yr local. Adv. Rate: col. inch $7.90 Circulation: 2,000 per issue (paid). **Owner(s):** Eagle Newspapers LP, 5910 Firestone Dr., Syracuse, NY 13152. Telephone: 315-434-8889. FAX: 315-434-8883. **Management:** John McIntyre, Publisher. William Kellert, Advertising Director. Brittany Worgan, Classified Adv. Mgr.. **Editorial:** Katherine McCarthy, Editor-in-Chief. Tim Mulligan, Managing Editor.

LOUDENVILLE SPOTLIGHT. 125 Adams St., Delmar, NY 12054. Telephone: 518-439-4949. FAX: 518-439-0608. E-MAIL: spotnews@albany.net. URL: http://www.cnylink.com. Pub. Frequency: w. (Wed.) Page Size: tabloid. Subscrip. Rate: $.75 newsstand/cover; $26/yr in county. Adv. Rate: col. inch $8.75 Circulation: 5,500 per issue (paid). **Owner(s):** Eagle Newspapers LP, 5910 Firestone Dr., Syracuse, NY 13152. Telephone: 315-434-8889. FAX: 315-434-8883. **Management:** John McIntyre, Publisher. William Kellert, Advertising Director. Brittany Worgan, Classified Adv. Mgr.. **Editorial:** Katherine McCarthy, Editor-in-Chief. Tim Mulligan, Managing Editor.

MALTA SPOTLIGHT. 125 Adams St., Delmar, NY 12054. Telephone: 518-439-4949. FAX: 518-439-0608. URL: http://www.cnylink.com. Pub. Frequency: w. (Thu.) Page Size: tabloid. Subscrip. Rate: $.75 newsstand/cover; $26/yr local. Adv. Rate: col. inch $7.95 Circulation: 2,000 per issue (paid). **Owner(s):** Eagle Newspapers LP, 5910 Firestone Dr., Syracuse, NY 13152. Telephone: 315-434-8889. FAX: 315-434-8883. **Management:** John McIntyre, Publisher. William Kellert, Advertising Director. Brittany Worgan, Classified Adv. Mgr.. **Editorial:** Katherine McCarthy, Editor-in-Chief. Tim Mulligan, Managing Editor.

MILTON SPOTLIGHT. 125 Adams St., Delmar, NY 12054. Telephone: 518-439-4949. FAX: 518-439-0608. Pub. Frequency: w. (Thu.) Page Size: tabloid. Subscrip. Rate: $.75 newsstand/cover; $26/yr local. Adv. Rate: col. inch $7.95 Circulation: 2,000 per issue (paid). **Owner(s):** Eagle Newspapers LP, 5910 Firestone Dr., Syracuse, NY 13152. Telephone: 315-434-8889. FAX: 315-434-8883. **Management:** John McIntyre, Publisher. William Kellert, Advertising Director. Brittany Worgan, Classified Adv. Mgr.. **Editorial:** Katherine McCarthy, Editor-in-Chief. Tim Mulligan, Managing Editor.

NISKAYUNA JOURNAL. 125 Adams St., Delmar, NY 12054. Telephone: 518-439-4949. FAX: 518-439-0608. URL: http://www.cnylink.com. Pub. Frequency: w. (Thu.) Page Size: tabloid. Subscrip. Rate: $.75 newsstand/cover; $26/yr local. Adv. Rate: col. inch $14.50 Circulation: 4,800 per issue (paid). **Owner(s):** Eagle Newspapers LP, 5910 Firestone Dr., Syracuse, NY 13152. Telephone: 315-434-8889. FAX: 315-434-8883. **Management:** John McIntyre, Publisher. William Kellert, Advertising Director. Brittany Worgan, Classified Adv. Mgr.. **Editorial:** Katherine McCarthy, Editor-in-Chief. Tim Mulligan, Managing Editor.

ROTTERDAM JOURNAL. 125 Adams St., Delmar, NY 12054. Telephone: 518-439-4949. FAX: 518-439-0608. URL: http://www.cnylink.com. Pub. Frequency: w. (Thu.) Page Size: tabloid.Adv. Rate: col. inch $14.50 Circulation: 4,800 per issue (free). **Owner(s):** Eagle Newspapers LP, 5910 Firestone Dr., Syracuse, NY 13152. Telephone: 315-434-8889. FAX: 315-434-8883. **Management:** John McIntyre, Publisher. William Kellert, Advertising Director. Brittany Worgan, Classified Adv. Mgr.. **Editorial:** Katherine McCarthy, Editor-in-Chief. Tim Mulligan, Managing Editor.

SARATOGA SPOTLIGHT. 125 Adams St., Delmar, NY 12054. Telephone: 518-439-4949. FAX: 518-439-0608. URL: http://www.cnylink.com. Pub. Frequency: w. (Thu.) Page Size: tabloid. Subscrip. Rate: $.75 newsstand/cover; $26/yr. Adv. Rate: col. inch $7.95 Circulation: 4,000 per issue (paid). **Owner(s):** Eagle Newspapers LP, 5910 Firestone Dr., Syracuse, NY 13152. Telephone: 315-434-8889. FAX: 315-434-8883. **Management:** John McIntyre, Publisher. William Kellert, Advertising Director. Brittany Worgan, Classified Adv. Mgr.. **Editorial:** Katherine McCarthy, Editor-in-Chief. Tim Mulligan, Managing Editor.

SCOTIA-GLENVILLE JOURNAL. 125 Adams St., Delmar, NY 12054. Telephone: 518-439-4949. FAX: 518-439-0608. URL: http://www.cnylink.com. Pub. Frequency: w. (Thu.) Page Size: tabloid.Adv. Rate: col. inch $14.50 Circulation: 5,000 per issue (free). **Owner(s):** Eagle Newspapers LP, 5910 Firestone Dr., Syracuse, NY 13152. Telephone: 315-434-8889. FAX: 315-434-8883. **Management:** John McIntyre, Publisher. William Kellert, Advertising Director. Brittany Worgan, Classified Adv. Mgr.. **Editorial:** Katherine McCarthy, Editor-in-Chief. Tim Mulligan, Managing Editor.

SPOTLIGHT (DELMAR), THE. 125 Adams St., Delmar, NY 12054. Telephone: 518-439-4949. FAX: 518-439-0608. E-MAIL: spotnews@albany.net. URL: http://www.cnylink.com. Year Established: 1955. Pub. Frequency: w. (Wed.) Page Size: tabloid. Subscrip. Rate: $.75 newsstand/cover; $26/yr in county; $32/yr out of county. Circulation: 7,000 per issue (paid). **Owner(s):** Eagle Newspapers LP, 5910 Firestone Dr., Syracuse, NY 13152. Telephone: 315-434-8889. FAX: 315-434-8883. **Management:** John McIntyre, Publisher. William Kellert, Advertising Director. Brittany Worgan, Classified Adv. Mgr.. **Editorial:** Katherine McCarthy, Editor-in-Chief. Tim Mulligan, Managing Editor.

DEPOSIT

DEPOSIT COURIER. 24 Laurel Bank Ave., Deposit, NY 13754-1251. Telephone: 607-467-3600. FAX: 607-467-5330. E-MAIL: cprint@ny.tds.net. Year Established: 1848. Pub. Frequency: w. (Wed.) Page Size: broadsheet. Subscrip. Rate: $.75 newsstand/cover; $26/yr in county; $30/yr out of county. Adv. Rate: col. inch $2.95 Freelance Pay: $0.15/column-inch. Circulation: 2,200 per issue (paid). **Owner(s):** Hilton A. Evans, See address and contact information above. **Management:** Hilton A. Evans, Publisher. **Editorial:** Hilton A. Evans, Editor.

DOBBS FERRY

RIVERTOWNS ENTERPRISE, THE. ISSN 0745-3477 PO Box 330, Dobbs Ferry, NY 10522-0330. Telephone: 914-478-2787. FAX: 914-478-2863. E-MAIL: rivertowns@optonline.net. Year Established: 1975. Pub. Frequency: w. (Fri.) Page Size: tabloid. Subscrip. Rate: $.75 newsstand/cover; $29/yr in county; $44/yr out of county. Circulation: 6,100 per issue (paid). **Owner(s):** W.H. White Publications, Inc., See address and contact information above. **Management:** Deborah White, Owner. Andrea Haggerty, Circulation Manager. **Editorial:** Timothy Lamorte, Editor.

DUNDEE

OBSERVER (DUNDEE), THE. 45 Water St., Dundee, NY 14837. Telephone: 607-243-7600. FAX: 607-243-5833. URL: http://www.fingerlakesmedia.com. Year Established: 1878. Pub. Frequency: w. (Wed.) Page Size: tabloid. Subscrip. Rate: $28/yr in state; $40/yr out of state; $.60 newsstand/cover. Adv. Rate: col. inch $4.50 Circulation: 3,200 per issue (paid and free). **Owner(s):** George Lawson, See address and contact information above. **Management:** Debbie Lawson, General Manager.

EAST AURORA

EAST AURORA ADVERTISER. 710 Main St., East Aurora, NY 14052. Telephone: 716-652-0320. FAX: 716-652-8383. URL: http://www.eastaurorany.com. Mailing Address: PO Box 118, Elma, NY 14059. Year Established: 1872. Pub. Frequency: w. (Thu.) Page Size: tabloid. Subscrip. Rate: $1 newsstand/cover; $29/yr mailed in county; $36/yr mailed out of county. Adv. Rate: col. inch $10.60 Circulation: 1,200 per issue (paid). **Owner(s):** Grant M. Hamilton, See address and contact information above. **Management:** Grant M Hamilton, Publisher. **Editorial:** Grant M Hamilton, Editor-in-Chief.

EAST HAMPTON

EAST HAMPTON STAR, THE. 153 Main St., East Hampton, NY 11937-2716. Telephone: 631-324-0002. FAX: 631-324-7943. E-MAIL: editor@easthamptonstar.com. URL: http://www.easthamptonstar.com. Mailing Address: PO Box 5002, East Hampton, NY 11937-0002. Year Established: 1885. Pub. Frequency: w. (Thu.) Page Size: broadsheet. Subscrip. Rate: $1 newsstand/cover; $35/yr in county; $45/yr out of county. Circulation: 16,000 per issue (paid). **Owner(s):** Helen S. Rattray, See address and contact information above. **Management:** Helen S. Rattray, President. Min Spear-Hefner, Advertising Manager. **Editorial:** David Rattray, Editor. Sheridan Sansegundo, Art Editor. Jack Y. Graves, Sports Editor.

INDEPENDENT TRAVELER-WATCHMAN, THE. 74 Montauk Hwy, Ste. 19, East Hampton, NY 11937. Telephone: 631-324-2500. FAX: 631-324-2351. E-MAIL: news@indyeastend.com. URL: http://www.indyeastend.com. Year Established: 1826. Pub. Frequency: w. (Wed.) Page Size: tabloid. Subscrip. Rate: $30/yr mailed in county; $39/yr mailed out of county. Circulation: 20,000 per issue (paid). **Owner(s):** The East Hampton Independent News Company, Inc., See address and contact information above. **Management:** James Mackin, Publisher. D N Moore, Advertising Director. Carolyn Phillips, Classified Adv. Mgr.. **Editorial:** Rich Murphy, Editor-in-Chief. Kitty Merrill, News Editor. Rich Smidt, Sports Editor.

EAST SETAUKET

PORT TIMES-RECORD, THE. 185 Rte 25A, East Setauket, NY 11733. Telephone: 631-751-7744. FAX: 631-751-4165. E-MAIL: jdiamant@tbrnewspapers.com. URL: http://www.tbrnewspapers.com. Mailing Address: PO Box 707, Setauket, NY 11733-0769. Year Established: 1989. Pub. Frequency: w. (Thu.) Page Size: tabloid. Subscrip. Rate: $.75 newsstand/cover; $35/yr home delivery in county; $50/yr mailed out of county. Circulation: 9,449 per issue (paid). **Owner(s):** Leah S. Dunaief, See address and contact information above. **Management:** Johness Kuisel, General Manager. Leah S. Dunaief, Publisher. Kathryn Mandracchia, Advertising Manager. Ellen Segal, Classified Adv. Mgr.. **Editorial:** Josh Diamant, Editor. Marie Murtagh, Executive Editor.

TIMES OF MIDDLE COUNTRY, THE. 185 Rte 25A, East Setauket, NY 11733. Telephone: 631-751-7744. FAX: 631-751-4165. Mailing Address: PO Box 707, Setauket, NY 11733-0769. Pub. Frequency: w. (Thu.) Page Size: tabloid. Subscrip. Rate: $.75 newsstand/cover; $35/yr home delivery in county; $50/yr home delivery out of county. Circulation: 8,000 per issue (paid). **Owner(s):** Leah S. Dunaief, See address and contact information above. **Management:** Johness Kuisel, General Manager. Leah S. Dunaief, Publisher. Kathryn Mandracchia, Advertising Manager. Ellen Segal, Classified Adv. Mgr.. **Editorial:** Alex Gillam, Editor. Marie Murtagh, Executive Editor.

TIMES OF NORTHPORT & EAST NORTHPORT, THE. 185 Rte 25A, East Setauket, NY 11733. Telephone: 631-751-7744. FAX: 631-751-4165. Mailing Address: PO Box 707, Setauket, NY 11733-0769. Pub. Frequency: w. (Thu.) Page Size: tabloid. Subscrip. Rate: $.75 newsstand/cover; $35/yr home delivery in county; $50/yr mailed out of county. Circulation: 8,000 per issue (paid). **Owner(s):** Leah S. Dunaief, See address and contact information above. **Management:** Johness Kuisel, General Manager. Leah S. Dunaief, Publisher. Kathryn Mandracchia, Advertising Manager. Ellen Segal, Classified Adv. Mgr.. **Editorial:** Patricia Proven, Editor. Marie Murtagh, Executive Editor.

TIMES OF SMITHTOWN TOWNSHIP, THE. 185 Rte 25A, East Setauket, NY 11733. Telephone: 631-751-7744. FAX: 631-751-4165. E-MAIL: joedarrow@tbrnewspapers.com. URL: http://www.tbrnewspapers.com. Mailing Address: PO Box 707, Setauket, NY 11733-0769. Year Established: 1989. Pub. Frequency: w. (Thu.) Page Size: tabloid. Subscrip. Rate: $.75 newsstand/cover; $35/yr home delivery in county; $50/yr out of county. Circulation: 7,000 per issue (paid). **Owner(s):** Leah S. Dunaief, See address and contact information above. **Management:** Johness Kuisel, General Manager. Leah S. Dunaief, Publisher. Kathryn Mandracchia, Advertising Manager. Ellen Segal, Classified Adv. Mgr.. **Editorial:** Joe Darrow, Editor. Marie Murtagh, Executive Editor.

VILLAGE BEACON-RECORD, THE. 185 Rte 25A, East Setauket, NY 11733. Telephone: 631-751-7744. FAX: 631-751-4165. E-MAIL: petermastro@tbrnewspapers.com. URL: http://www.tbrnewspapers.com. Mailing Address: PO Box 707, Setauket, NY 11733-0769. Year Established: 1986. Pub. Frequency: w. (Thu.) Page Size: tabloid. Subscrip. Rate: $.75 newsstand/cover; $35/yr home delivery in county; $50/yr mailed out of county. Circulation: 7,064 per issue (paid). **Owner(s):** Leah S. Dunaief, See address and contact information above. **Management:** Johness Kuisel, General Manager. Leah S. Dunaief, Publisher. Kathryn Mandracchia, Advertising Manager. Ellen Segal, Classified Adv. Mgr.. **Editorial:** Peter Mastrosimone, Editor. Marie Murtagh, Executive Editor.

VILLAGE TIMES HERALD, THE. ISSN 0889-8677
185 Rte 25A, East Setauket, NY 11733. Telephone: 631-751-7744. FAX: 631-751-4165. E-MAIL: leelutz@tbrnewspapers.com. URL: http://www.tbrnewspapers.com. Mailing Address: PO Box 707, Setauket, NY 11733-0769. Year Established: 1976. Pub. Frequency: w. (Thu.) Page Size: tabloid. Subscrip. Rate: $.75 newsstand/cover; $35/yr home delivery in county; $50/yr mailed out of county. Circulation: 12,637 per issue (paid). **Owner(s):** Leah S. Dunaief, See address and contact information above. **Management:** Johness Kuisel, General Manager. Leah S. Dunaief, Publisher. Kathryn Mandracchia, Advertising Manager. Ellen Segal, Classified Adv. Mgr.. **Editorial:** Lee Lutz, Editor. Marie Murtagh, Executive Editor.

ELIZABETHTOWN

ADIRONDACK JOURNAL. 14 Hand Ave., Elizabethtown, NY 12932. Telephone: 518-873-6368. FAX: 518-873-6360. E-MAIL: denpubs@willex.com. URL: http://www.denpubs.com. Mailing Address: PO Box 338, Elizabethtown, NY 12932-0338. Year Established: 1868. Pub. Frequency: w. (Sat.) Page Size: tabloid. Subscrip. Rate: $25/yr in county; $30/yr out of county. Adv. Rate: col. inch $15.50 Circulation: 10,734 per issue (free). **Owner(s):** Denton Publications, Inc., See address and contact information above. **Management:** Dan Alexander, Publisher. Cyndi Tucker, Advertising Manager. **Editorial:** Nancy O'Brien, Editor. John Gereau, Managing Editor.

CLINTON COUNTY FREE TRADER TODAY. 14 Hand Ave., Elizabethtown, NY 12932. Telephone: 518-873-6368. FAX: 518-873-6360. URL: http://www.denpubs.com. Mailing Address: PO Box 338, Elizabethtown, NY 12932-0338. Pub. Frequency: w. (Sat.) Page Size: tabloid.Adv. Rate: col. inch $15.50 Circulation: 13,000 per issue (free). **Owner(s):** Denton Publications, Inc., See address and contact information above. **Management:** Dan Alexander, Publisher. Cyndi Tucker, Advertising Manager. **Editorial:** Jennifer Meschinelli, Editor. John Gereau, Managing Editor.

NORTH COUNTRYMAN, THE. 14 Hand Ave., Elizabethtown, NY 12932. Telephone: 518-873-6368. FAX: 518-873-6360. E-MAIL: denpubs@willex.com. URL: http://www.denpubs.com. Mailing Address: PO Box 338, Elizabethtown, NY 12932-0338. Year Established: 1928. Pub. Frequency: w. (Sat.) Page Size: tabloid. Subscrip. Rate: $25/yr in county. Adv. Rate: col. inch $15.50 Circulation: 8,922 per issue (free). **Owner(s):** Denton Publications, Inc., See address and contact information above. **Management:** Cyndi Tucker, General Manager. Dan Alexander, Publisher. **Editorial:** John Gereau, Managing Editor.

NORTH CREEK NEWS ENTERPRISE. 14 Hand Ave., Elizabethtown, NY 12932. Telephone: 518-873-6368. FAX: 518-873-6360. Mailing Address: PO Box 338, Elizabethtown, NY 12932-0338. Pub. Frequency: w. (Sat.) Page Size: tabloid Circulation: 5,500 per issue (free). **Owner(s):** Denton Publications, Inc., See address and contact information above. **Management:** Dan Alexander, Publisher. Cyndi Tucker, Advertising Manager. **Editorial:** John Gereau, Managing Editor.

TIMES OF TI. 14 Hand Ave., Elizabethtown, NY 12932. Telephone: 518-873-6368. FAX: 518-873-6360. URL: http://www.denpubs.com. Mailing Address: PO Box 338, Elizabethtown, NY 12932-0338. Pub. Frequency: w. (Sat.) Page Size: tabloid. Subscrip. Rate: $28/yr. Adv. Rate: col. inch $15.50 Circulation: 9,041 per issue (free). **Owner(s):** Denton Publications, Inc., See address and contact information above. **Management:** Dan Alexander, Publisher. Cyndi Tucker, Advertising Manager. **Editorial:** Fred Herbst, Editor. John Gereau, Managing Editor.

TRI LAKES FREE TRADER. 14 Hand Ave., Elizabethtown, NY 12932. Telephone: 518-873-6368. FAX: 518-873-6360. URL: http://www.denpubs.com. Mailing Address: PO Box 338, Elizabethtown, NY 12932-0338. Pub. Frequency: w. (Sat.) Page Size: tabloid.Adv. Rate: col. inch $15.50 Circulation: 11,039 per issue (free). **Owner(s):** Denton Publications, Inc., See address and contact information above. **Management:** Dan Alexander, Publisher. Cyndi Tucker, Advertising Manager. **Editorial:** Jennifer Meschinelli, Editor. John Gereau, Managing Editor.

VALLEY NEWS (ELIZABETHTOWN). 14 Hand Ave., Elizabethtown, NY 12932. Telephone: 518-873-6368. FAX: 518-873-6360. E-MAIL: denpubs@willex.com. URL: http://www.denpubs.com. Mailing Address: PO Box 338, Elizabethtown, NY 12932-0338. Year Established: 1948. Pub. Frequency: w. (Sat.) Page Size: tabloid Circulation: 10,146 per issue (free). **Owner(s):** Denton Publications, Inc., See address and contact information above. **Management:** Dan Alexander, Publisher. Cyndi Tucker, Advertising Manager. **Editorial:** John Gereau, Managing Editor.

ELLENVILLE

PRESS (ELLENVILLE), THE. ISSN 1077-6133
1087 Ulster Heights Rd., Ellenville, NY 12428. Telephone: 845-647-7222. FAX: 845-647-7443. Year Established: 1873. Pub. Frequency: w. (Thu.) Page Size: tabloid. Subscrip. Rate: $.50 newsstand/cover; $27/yr mailed in county; $28/yr mailed out of county. Adv. Rate: col. inch $4.75 Circulation: 2,200 per issue (paid). **Owner(s):** Walkerwicz Communications, Inc., See address and contact information above. **Management:** Michael Walkerwicz, Publisher. **Editorial:** Michael Walkerwicz, Editor.

FLORAL PARK

FLORAL PARK BULLETIN. PO Box 227, Floral Park, NY 11002. Telephone: 516-775-2700. Year Established: 1941. Pub. Frequency: w. (Thu.) Page Size: tabloid.Subscrip. Rate: $.50 newsstand/cover; $18/yr Circulation: 8,500 per issue (paid). **Owner(s):** Carla Cohen, See address and contact information above. **Management:** Carla Cohen, President. Anna McCarthy, Advertising Manager. Emily Walsh, Circulation Manager. **Editorial:** Carla Cohen, Editor-in-Chief.

FRANKLIN SQUARE BULLETIN. 139 Tulip Ave., Floral Park, NY 11001. Telephone: 516-775-7700. FAX: 516-775-7605. Mailing Address: PO Box 155, Franklin Square, NY 11010. Year Established: 1938. Pub. Frequency: w. (Thu.) Page Size: tabloid.Subscrip. Rate: $.35 newsstand/cover; $15/yr Circulation: 8,700 per issue (paid). **Owner(s):** Nassau Border Papers, See address and contact information above. **Management:** Carla Cohen, Publisher. Anna V. McCarthy, Sales Manager. **Editorial:** Carla Cohen, Editor.

GATEWAY (FLORAL PARK), THE. PO Box 227, Floral Park, NY 11002. Telephone: 516-775-2700. Year Established: 1926. Pub. Frequency: w. (Wed.) Page Size: tabloid.Subscrip. Rate: $.50 newsstand/cover; $18/yr Circulation: 12,000 per issue (paid). **Owner(s):** Carla Cohen, See address and contact information above. **Management:** Carla Cohen, Publisher. Anna McCarthy, Advertising. **Editorial:** Carla Cohen, Editor.

FORT PLAIN

COURIER-STANDARD-ENTERPRISE. 81 Canal St., Fort Plain, NY 13339. Telephone: 518-993-2321. FAX: 518-993-4919. E-MAIL: cse@email2me.net. Mailing Address: PO Box 351, Fort Plain, NY 13339. Year Established: 1876. Pub. Frequency: w. (Wed.) Page Size: broadsheet. Subscrip. Rate: $.75 newsstand/cover; $22/yr in state; $26/yr out of state. Freelance Pay: $5/column-inch. Circulation: 4,000 per issue (paid). **Owner(s):** Tri-Village Publishers, Inc., One Venner Rd., Amsterdam, NY 12010. Telephone: 518-843-1100. **Management:** Kevin McClary, General Manager. Richard A. Barker, Publisher. Erica Arduini, Advertising Manager. **Editorial:** Bob Lindsay, Editor.

FRESH MEADOWS

QUEENS TRIBUNE. 174-15 Horace Harding Expy., Fresh Meadows, NY 11365. Telephone: 718-357-7400. FAX: 718-357-9417. E-MAIL: editor@queenstribune.com. URL: http://www.queenstribune.com. Year Established: 1970. Pub. Frequency: w. (Thu.) Page Size: tabloid. Subscrip. Rate: $12/yr. Circulation: 146,000 per issue (paid and free). **Owner(s):** News Communications, Inc., See address and contact information above. **Management:** Michael Schenkler, Publisher. Ted Olczak, Advertising Manager. Michael Nussbaum, Associate Publisher. **Editorial:** Angela Montefibese, Editor.

FULTON

FULTON PATRIOT. 1709 Oneida St., Fulton, NY 13069. Telephone: 315-592-2459. FAX: 315-598-6618. Year Established: 1823. Pub. Frequency: w. (Sat.) Page Size: standard. Subscrip. Rate: $7/yr in county; $14/yr out of county. Circulation: 5,500 per issue (paid). **Owner(s):** Fulton Newspapers, Inc., See address and contact information above. **Management:** Leroy N. Hodge, Publisher. **Editorial:** Leroy N. Hodge, Editor.

VALLEY NEWS (FULTON), THE. ISSN 1067-7755
1709 Oneida St., Fulton, NY 13069. Telephone: 315-592-2459. FAX: 315-598-6618. E-MAIL: valnews@dreamscape.com. URL: http://www.valleynewsonline.com. Mailing Address: PO Box 805, Fulton, NY 13069. Year Established: 1947. Pub. Frequency: s-w. (Wed. & Sat.) Page Size: tabloid. Subscrip. Rate: $.50 newsstand/cover; $21/yr mailed in county; $31/yr mailed out of county. Circulation: 7,900 per issue (paid). **Owner(s):** Fulton Newspapers, Inc., See address and contact information above. **Management:** Vincent Caravan, Publisher. **Editorial:** Andrew Henderson, Managing Editor.

GARDEN CITY

BALDWIN HERALD. 2 Endo Blvd, Garden City, NY 11530. Telephone: 516-569-4000. FAX: 516-569-4942. E-MAIL: baldwineditor@liherald.com. Year Established: 1925. Pub. Frequency: w. (Thu.) Page Size: tabloid. Subscrip. Rate: $.75 newsstand/cover; $29/yr mailed in county. Adv. Rate: B&W page $476 Circulation: 5,500 per issue (paid). **Owner(s):** Richner Communications, Inc., See address and contact information above. **Management:** Clifford Richner, Publisher. Michael Bologna, Vice President. Rhonda Glickman, VP Mktg. & Sales. Peggy Rogers, Circulation Manager. Ellen Reynolds, Classified Adv. Mgr.. **Editorial:** Michael Russo, Editor. John O'Connell, Executive Editor.

EAST MEADOW HERALD. 2 Endo Blvd, Garden City, NY 11530. Telephone: 516-569-4000. FAX: 516-569-4942. E-MAIL: emeadoweditor@liherald.com. URL: http://www.liherald.com. Year Established: 1964. Pub. Frequency: w. (Thu.) Page Size: tabloid. Subscrip. Rate: $.75 newsstand/cover; $29/yr in county; $42/yr out of county. Circulation: 3,000 per issue (paid). **Owner(s):** Richner Communications, Inc., See address and contact information above. **Management:** Clifford Richner, Publisher. Michael Bologna, Vice President. Rhonda Glickman, VP Mktg. & Sales. Peggy Rogers, Circulation Manager. Ellen Reynolds, Classified Adv. Mgr.. **Editorial:** Scott Brinton, Editor. John O'Connell, Executive Editor.

OCEANSIDE/ISLAND PARK HERALD. 2 Endo Blvd, Garden City, NY 11530. Telephone: 516-569-4000. FAX: 516-569-4942. E-MAIL: oceaneditors@liherald.com. Year Established: 1935. Pub. Frequency: w. (Thu.) Page Size: tabloid. Subscrip. Rate: $.75 newsstand/cover; $29/yr mailed in county. Adv. Rate: B&W page $476 Circulation: 6,000 per issue (paid). **Owner(s):** Richner Communications, Inc., See address and contact information above. **Management:** Clifford Richner, Publisher. Michael Bologna, Vice President. Rhonda Glickman, VP Mktg. & Sales. Peggy Rogers, Circulation Manager. Ellen Reynolds, Classified Adv. Mgr.. **Editorial:** Joe Kellard, Editor. John O'Connell, Executive Editor.

ROCKAWAY JOURNAL. 2 Endo Blvd, Garden City, NY 11530. Telephone: 516-569-4000. FAX: 516-569-4942. E-MAIL: joconnell@liherald.com. Year Established: 1883. Pub. Frequency: w. (Thu.) Page Size: tabloid. Subscrip. Rate: $.25 newsstand/cover; $29/yr mailed in county; $42/yr mailed out of county. Circulation: 1,917 per issue (paid). **Owner(s):** Richner Communications, Inc., See address and contact information above. **Management:** Clifford Richner, Publisher. Michael Bologna, Vice President. Rhonda Glickman, VP Mktg. & Sales. Peggy Rogers, Circulation Manager. Ellen Reynolds, Classified Adv. Mgr.. **Editorial:** John O'Connell, Executive Editor.

ROCKVILLE CENTRE HERALD. 2 Endo Blvd, Garden City, NY 11530. Telephone: 516-569-4000. FAX: 516-569-4942. Year Established: 1908. Pub. Frequency: w. (Thu.) Page Size: tabloid. Subscrip. Rate: $.75 newsstand/cover; $22/yr. Adv. Rate: B&W page $476 Circulation: 6,600 per issue (paid). **Owner(s):** Richner Communications, Inc., See address and contact information above. **Management:** Clifford Richner, Publisher. Michael Bologna, Vice President. Rhonda Glickman, VP Mktg. & Sales. Peggy Rogers, Circulation Manager. Ellen Reynolds, Classified Adv. Mgr.. **Editorial:** Judy Rattner, Editor. John O'Connell, Executive Editor.

GLENS FALLS

CHRONICLE (GLENS FALLS), THE. 15 Ridge St, Glens Falls, NY 12801-0153. Telephone: 518-792-1126. Mailing Address: P O Box 153, Glens Falls, NY 12801. Year Established: 1980. Pub. Frequency: w. (Thu.) Page Size: tabloid. Subscrip. Rate: $45/yr home delivery. Circulation: 26,500 per issue (paid and free). **Owner(s):** Lone Oak Publishing, Co., See address and contact information above. **Management:** Mark Frost, Owner. Patricia Maddock, Publisher. **Editorial:** Mark Frost, Editor-in-Chief. Contact: Sandra Hutchinson, Editor. Contact: Mark Frost, Editor-in-Chief. Contact: Patricia Maddock, Publisher. Contact: Patricia Maddock, Publisher. Contact: Patricia Maddock, Publisher. Contact: Patricia Maddock, Publisher.

GOSHEN

GOSHEN INDEPENDENT. 132 W. Main St., Goshen, NY 10924-0628. Telephone: 845-294-6111. FAX: 845-294-0532. E-MAIL: indynews@frontiernet.net. Mailing Address: PO Drawer A, Goshen, NY 10924. Year Established: 1812. Pub. Frequency: w. (Wed.) Page Size: tabloid. Subscrip. Rate: $.50 newsstand/cover; $25/yr in county; $30/yr out of county. Adv. Rate: col. inch $5 Circulation: 3,800 per issue (paid). **Owner(s):** Eugene Wright, Jr., See address and contact information above. **Management:** Eugene Wright Jr., Publisher. Theresa Paci, Office Manager.

GOUVERNEUR

GOUVERNEUR TRIBUNE PRESS. 74 Trinity Ave., Gouverneur, NY 13642. Telephone: 315-287-2100. FAX: 315-287-2397. Year Established: 1886. Pub. Frequency: w. (Thu.) Page Size: standard. Subscrip. Rate: $.75 newsstand/cover; $33/yr. Adv. Rate: col. inch $5.20 Freelance Pay: $0.10/column-inch. Circulation: 4,200 per issue (paid). **Owner(s):** Gouverneur Tribune Press, Inc., See address and contact information above. **Management:** Dick Sterling, General Manager. M. Dan McClelland, Publisher. Lisa LaVancha, Advertising. Bobbi Jenne, Circulation Manager. **Editorial:** Dick Sterling, Editor.

GOWANDA

GOWANDA PENNYSAVER NEWS. 62 W. Main St., Gowanda, NY 14070. Telephone: 716-532-2288. FAX: 716-532-3056. E-MAIL: maryp@pennysavers.com. URL: http://www.hkpublications.com. Year Established: 1939. Pub. Frequency: w. (Sun.) Page Size: tabloid Circulation: 11,150 per issue (free). **Owner(s):** H & K Publications, Inc., 50 Buffalo St., Hamburg, NY 14075. Telephone: 716-649-4413. FAX: 716-649-6374. **Management:** Tom Kluckhohn, Publisher. Steven Kluckhohn, Advertising Manager. **Editorial:** Mary Pankow, Editor.

GRAND ISLAND

GRAND ISLAND PENNYSAVER. 1859 Whitehaven Rd., Grand Island, NY 14072-0130. Telephone: 716-773-7676. FAX: 716-773-7190. E-MAIL: nfpnews@clmail.com. URL: http://www.wnypapers.com. Mailing Address: PO Box 130, Grand Island, NY 14072-0130. Year Established: 1949. Pub. Frequency: w. (Tue.) Page Size: tabloid. Subscrip. Rate: $44.95/yr outside area; $64.95 2/yrs. outside area. Adv. Rate: col. inch $9.91 Freelance Pay: $15-$30/word. Circulation: 7,300 per issue (paid and free). **Owner(s):** Niagara Frontier Publications, Inc., See address and contact information above. **Management:** A. Skip Mazenauer, Publisher. Francine Hirtreiter, Circulation Manager. **Editorial:** Karen Keefe, Editor. Terry Duffy, Managing Editor. Ralph Schwarz, Sports Editor.

ISLAND DISPATCH. 1859 Whitehaven Rd., Grand Island, NY 14072-0130. Telephone: 716-773-7676. FAX: 716-773-7190. E-MAIL: dispatch@wnypapers.com. URL: http://www.wnypapers.com. Mailing Address: PO Box 130, Grand Island, NY 14072-0130. Year Established: 1944. Pub. Frequency: w. (Fri.) Page Size: tabloid. Subscrip. Rate: $44.95 for 2 yrs. in county; $29.95/yr in county; $44.95/yr out of county. Adv. Rate: col. inch $13.20 Freelance Pay: $15-$30/article. Circulation: 2,100 per issue (paid). **Owner(s):** Niagara Frontier Publications, Inc., See address and contact information above. **Management:** A. Skip Mazenauer, Publisher. Francine Hirtreiter, Circulation Manager. **Editorial:** Karen Keefe, Editor. Terry Duffy, Managing Editor. Ralph Schwarz, Sports Editor.

LEWISTON-PORTER SENTINEL. 1859 Whitehaven Rd., Grand Island, NY 14072-0130. Telephone: 716-773-7676. FAX: 716-773-7190. E-MAIL: sentinel@wnypapers.com. URL: http://www.wnypapers.com. Mailing Address: PO Box 130, Grand Island, NY 14072-0130. Year Established: 1987. Pub. Frequency: w. (Sat.) Page Size: tabloid. Subscrip. Rate: $52/yr out of area; $104 for 2 yrs. out of area. Adv. Rate: col. inch $16.22 Freelance Pay: $15-$30/article. **Wire Service(s):** AP. Circulation: 10,650 per issue (paid and free). **Owner(s):** Niagara Frontier Publications, Inc., See address and contact information above. **Management:** A. Skip Mazenauer, Publisher. Francine Hirtreiter, Circulation Manager. **Editorial:** Terry Duffy, Managing Editor. Ralph Schwarz, Sports Editor.

NIAGARA/WHEATFIELD TRIBUNE. 1859 Whitehaven Rd., Grand Island, NY 14072-0130. Telephone: 716-773-7676. FAX: 716-773-7190. E-MAIL: tribune@wnypapers.com. URL: http://www.wnypapers.com. Mailing Address: PO Box 130, Grand Island, NY 14072-0130. Year Established: 1985. Pub. Frequency: w. (Thu.) Page Size: tabloid. Subscrip. Rate: $52/yr mailed out of area. Adv. Rate: col. inch $16.87 Freelance Pay: $15-$30/word. Circulation: 10,300 per issue (paid and controlled). **Owner(s):** Niagara Frontier Publications, Inc., See address and contact information above. **Management:** A. Skip Mazenauer, Publisher. Francine Hirtreiter, Circulation Manager. **Editorial:** Ralph Schwarz, Editor. Terry Duffy, Managing Editor.

GRANVILLE

GRANVILLE SENTINEL. 14 E. Main St., Granville, NY 12832. Telephone: 518-642-1234. FAX: 518-642-1344. E-MAIL: thesentinel@adelphia.net. URL: http://www.manchesternewspapers.com. Year Established: 1875. Pub. Frequency: w. (Wed.) Page Size: broadsheet. Subscrip. Rate: $.75 newsstand/cover; $29/yr in county; $39/yr elsewhere. Adv. Rate: col. inch $9.74 Freelance Pay: $0.25/column-inch. Circulation: 3,200 per issue (paid). **Owner(s):** Manchester Newspapers, Inc., See address and contact information above. **Management:** John N. Manchester, Publisher. Patty Alexander, Advertising Manager. Judy Cook, Circulation Manager. Allison Fabian, Classified Adv. Mgr.. **Editorial:** Bern Zovistoski, Editor. John N. Manchester, Editor-in-Chief.

LAKES REGION FREEPRESS, THE. 14 E. Main St., Granville, NY 12832. Telephone: 518-642-1234. FAX: 518-642-1344. URL: http://www.manchesternewspapers.com. Pub. Frequency: w. (Fri.) Page Size: tabloid.Adv. Rate: col. inch $10.22 Circulation: 7,400 per issue (free). **Owner(s):** Manchester Newspapers, Inc., See address and contact information above. **Management:** John N. Manchester, Publisher. Lisa Carter, Advertising Manager. Judy Cook, Circulation Manager. Allison Fabian, Classified Adv. Mgr.. **Editorial:** Bern Zovistoski, Editor. John N. Manchester, Editor-in-Chief.

NORTH COUNTRY FREEPRESS. 14 E. Main St., Granville, NY 12832. Telephone: 518-642-1234. FAX: 518-642-1344. E-MAIL: mannews@sover.net. URL: http://www.manchesternewspapers.com. Year Established: 1985. Pub. Frequency: w. (Fri.) Page Size: tabloid.Adv. Rate: col. inch $12.30 Freelance Pay: $0.25/column-inch. Circulation: 23,000 per issue (free). **Owner(s):** Manchester Newspapers, Inc., See address and contact information above. **Management:** John N. Manchester, Publisher. Lisa Carter, Advertising Manager. Judy Cook, Circulation Manager. Allison Fabian, Classified Adv. Mgr.. **Editorial:** Bern Zovistoski, Editor. John N. Manchester, Editor-in-Chief.

NORTHSHIRE FREEPRESS, THE. 14 E. Main St., Granville, NY 12832. Telephone: 518-642-1234. FAX: 518-642-1344. URL: http://www.manchesternewspapers.com. Pub. Frequency: w. (Fri.) Page Size: tabloid.Adv. Rate: col. inch $9.56 Circulation: 7,200 per issue (free). **Owner(s):** Manchester Newspapers, Inc., See address and contact information above. **Management:** John N. Manchester, Publisher. **Editorial:** Darrell Beebe, Editor. John N. Manchester, Editor-in-Chief.

WEEKENDER (GRANVILLE), THE. 14 E. Main St., Granville, NY 12832. Telephone: 518-642-1234. FAX: 518-642-1344. E-MAIL: thesentinel@adelphia.net. URL: http://www.manchesternewspapers.com. Pub. Frequency: w. (Fri.) Page Size: tabloid.Adv. Rate: col. inch $9.56 Circulation: 5,650 per issue (free). **Owner(s):** Manchester Newspapers, Inc., See address and contact information above. **Management:** John N. Manchester, Publisher. Judy Cook, Circulation Manager. Clara Clark, Classified Adv. Mgr.. **Editorial:** John N. Manchester, Editor-in-Chief.

GREAT NECK

NEW YORK TREND. ISSN 1083-5822
14 Bond St., Ste. 176, Great Neck, NY 10021. Telephone: 516-466-0028. FAX: 516-466-0062. E-MAIL: nytrend@aol.com. URL: http://www.nytrend.com. Year Established: 1989. Pub. Frequency: bi-w. Page Size: tabloid. Subscrip. Rate: $1.25 newsstand/cover per issue. Circulation: 70,000 per issue (paid and free). **Owner(s):** TTW Associates, See address and contact information above. **Management:** Teresa Williams, Publisher. Ken Harris, Advertising Manager. **Editorial:** Ken Harris, Editor.

GREENE

CHENANGO AMERICAN. 3 Foundry St., Greene, NY 13778-0566. Telephone: 607-656-4511. FAX: 607-656-8544. E-MAIL: hometownnews@frontiernet.net. Mailing Address: PO Box 566, Greene, NY 13778-0566. Year Established: 1855. Pub. Frequency: w. (Thu.) Page Size: tabloid. Subscrip. Rate: $.65 newsstand/cover; $23/yr home delivery Chenango & Broome cys; $28/yr mailed elsewhere. Circulation: 2,700 per issue (paid). **Owner(s):** Paul Hamilton, Sr., 5 Winkler Rd., Sidney, NY 13838-0570. Telephone: 607-561-3526. **Management:** Kenneth Paden, Publisher. **Editorial:** Pete Mansheffer, Editor.

OXFORD REVIEW-TIMES. 3 Foundry St., Greene, NY 13778-0566. Telephone: 607-656-4511. FAX: 607-656-8544. Mailing Address: PO Box 566, Greene, NY 13778-0566. Year Established: 1960. Pub. Frequency: w. (Thu.) Page Size: tabloid. Subscrip. Rate: $.65 newsstand/cover; $23/yr in county; $28/yr elsewhere. Adv. Rate: col. inch $3.25 Circulation: 3,500 per issue (paid). **Owner(s):** Paul Hamilton, Sr., 5 Winkler Rd., Sidney, NY 13138. Telephone: 607-561-3526. FAX: 607-563-7118. **Management:** Kenneth Paden, Publisher. **Editorial:** Pete Mansheffer, Editor.

WHITNEY POINT REPORTER. 3 Foundry St., Greene, NY 13778-0566. Telephone: 607-656-4511. FAX: 607-656-8544. Mailing Address: PO Box 566, Greene, NY 13778-0566. Year Established: 1850. Pub. Frequency: w. (Thu.) Page Size: tabloid. Subscrip. Rate: $.65 newsstand/cover; $23/yr in county; $28/yr out of area. Adv. Rate: col. inch $3.25 Circulation: 3,500 per issue (paid). **Owner(s):** Paul Hamilton, Sr., 5 Winkler Rd., Sidney, NY 13138-0570. Telephone: 607-561-3526. FAX: 607-563-7118. **Management:** Kenneth Paden, Publisher. **Editorial:** Peter Mansheffer, Editor.

GREENWICH

GREENWICH JOURNAL & SALEM PRESS. 35 Salem St., Greenwich, NY 12834. Telephone: 518-692-2266. FAX: 518-692-2589. Mailing Address: PO Box 185, Greenwich, NY 12834. Year Established: 1842. Pub. Frequency: w. (Thu.) Page Size: broadsheet. Subscrip. Rate: $.60 newsstand/cover; $26/yr in county; $29/yr mailed elsewhere. Circulation: 2,816 per issue (paid). **Owner(s):** Sally B. Tefft, See address and contact information above. **Management:** Sally . Tefft, President.

GREENWOOD LAKE

GREENWOOD LAKE & WEST MILFORD NEWS. ISSN 1065-1144
PO Box 1117, Greenwood Lake, NY 10925. Telephone: 845-477-2575. FAX: 845-477-2577. E-MAIL: glnews@greenwoodlakenews.com. URL: http://www.greenwoodlakenews.com. Year Established: 1964. Pub. Frequency: w. (Wed.) Page Size: tabloid. Subscrip. Rate: $.75 newsstand/cover; $26/yr in county; $29.50/yr out of county. Circulation: 4,000 per issue (paid). **Owner(s):** Greenwood Lake News, Inc., See address and contact information above. **Management:** Ann Chaimowitz, Publisher. **Editorial:** Ron Nowak, Editor.

HAMBURG

BLASDELL/LACKAWANNA PENNYSAVER. 50 Buffalo St., Hamburg, NY 14075. Telephone: 716-649-4413. FAX: 716-649-5940. E-MAIL: theresam@pennysavers.com. URL: http://www.pennysavers.com. Year Established: 1960. Pub. Frequency: w. (Sun.) Page Size: tabloid.Adv. Rate: col. inch $8.15 Circulation: 13,800 per issue (free). **Owner(s):** H & K Publications, Inc., See address and contact information above. **Management:** Tom Kluckhohn, Publisher. Steve Kluckhohn, Advertising Manager. Teri Scott, Circulation Manager.

HAMBURG PENNYSAVER. 50 Buffalo St., Hamburg, NY 14075. Telephone: 716-649-4413. FAX: 716-649-6374. E-MAIL: sek@HKPublications.com. URL: http://www.hkpublications.com. Year Established: 1939. Pub. Frequency: w. (Sun.) Page Size: tabloid Circulation: 25,400 per issue (free). **Owner(s):** H & K Publications, Inc., See address and contact information above. **Management:** Tom Kluckhohn, Publisher. Steve Kluckhohn, Advertising Manager. Teri Scott, Circulation Manager.

SUN (HAMBURG), THE. 50 Buffalo St., Hamburg, NY 14075. Telephone: 716-649-4040. FAX: 716-649-6374. E-MAIL: meyerdan@thesunnews.net. URL: http://www.thesunnews.net. Year Established: 1875. Pub. Frequency: w. (Thu.) Page Size: tabloid. Subscrip. Rate: $.75 newsstand/cover; $27/yr in state; $30.50/yr out of state. Freelance Pay: $22/article. Circulation: 10,000 per issue (paid). **Owner(s):** H & K Publications, Inc., See address and contact information above. **Management:** Tom Kluckhohn, Publisher. Steve Kluckhohn, Advertising Manager. Teri Scott, Circulation Manager. **Editorial:** Dan Meyer, Editor.

HAMILTON

MID-YORK WEEKLY. 14 Utica St., Hamilton, NY 13346. Telephone: 315-824-2150. FAX: 315-824-4220. E-MAIL: midyrk@dreamscape.com. URL: http://www.psaver.com. Year Established: 1828. Pub. Frequency: w. (Thu.) Page Size: broadsheet. Subscrip. Rate: $20/yr mailed out of area. Adv. Rate: col. inch $7.50 Circulation: 9,000 per issue (paid and free). **Owner(s):** Oneida Madison Pennysaver, See address and contact information above. **Management:** Donna Donovan, Publisher. **Editorial:** Carolyn Godfrey, Editor.

HEMPSTEAD

EAST MEADOW BEACON. 5 Centre St., Hempstead, NY 11550. Telephone: 516-481-5400. FAX: 516-481-8773. Year Established: 1950. Pub. Frequency: w. (Thu.) Page Size: tabloid. Subscrip. Rate: $.50 newsstand/cover; $12.50/yr in city; $15.50/yr out of city. Circulation: 5,800 per issue (paid). **Owner(s):** Kathleen Hoegl, See address and contact information above. **Editorial:** Barbara Yohe, Managing Editor.

HEMPSTEAD BEACON. 5 Centre St., Hempstead, NY 11550. Telephone: 516-481-5400. FAX: 516-481-8773. Year Established: 1951. Pub. Frequency: w. (Fri.) Page Size: tabloid. Subscrip. Rate: $.35 newsstand/cover; $12.50/yr in town; $15.50/yr out of town. Circulation: 5,100 per issue (paid). **Owner(s):** Kathleen Hoegl, See address and contact information above. **Editorial:** Sheila Noeth, Managing Editor.

MERRICK BEACON. 5 Centre St., Hempstead, NY 11550. Telephone: 516-481-5400. FAX: 516-481-8773. Year Established: 1950. Pub. Frequency: w. (Fri.) Page Size: tabloid. Subscrip. Rate: $.35 newsstand/cover; $12.50/yr in town; $15.50/yr out of town. Circulation: 4,000 per issue (paid). **Owner(s):** Kathleen Hoegl, See address and contact information above. **Editorial:** Sheila Noeth, Managing Editor.

UNIONDALE BEACON. 5 Centre St., Hempstead, NY 11550. Telephone: 516-481-5400. FAX: 516-481-8773. Year Established: 1951. Pub. Frequency: w. (Fri.) Page Size: tabloid. Subscrip. Rate: $.50 newsstand/cover; $12.50/yr in town; $15.50/yr out of town. Circulation: 5,300 per issue (paid). **Owner(s):** Kathleen Hoegl, See address and contact information above. **Management:** Peter Hoegl, Publisher. **Editorial:** Barbara Yohe, Managing Editor.

WEST HEMPSTEAD BEACON. 5 Centre St., Hempstead, NY 11550. Telephone: 516-481-5400. FAX: 516-481-8773. Year Established: 1951. Pub. Frequency: w. (Fri.) Page Size: tabloid. Subscrip. Rate: $.50 newsstand/cover; $12.50/yr in town; $15.50/yr out of town. Circulation: 5,200 per issue (paid). **Owner(s):** Kathleen Hoegl, See address and contact information above. **Editorial:** Sheila Noeth, Managing Editor.

HERKIMER

IMAGES. 111 Green St., Herkimer, NY 13350. Telephone: 315-866-2220. FAX: 315-866-5913. Mailing Address: PO Box 551, Herkimer, NY 13350. Pub. Frequency: w. (Sat.) Page Size: tabloid Circulation: 8,500 per issue (free). **Owner(s):** GateHouse Media, Inc, 350 WillowBrook Office Park, Fairport, NY 14450. Telephone: 585-598-0030. FAX: 585-248-2631. **Management:** Beth Brewer, Publisher. Pam Grande, Advertising Manager. Beth Brewer, Circulation Manager.

HICKSVILLE

BETHPAGE NEWSGRAM. 81 E. Barclay St., Hicksville, NY 11801. Telephone: 516-931-0012. FAX: 516-931-0027. Pub. Frequency: w. (Fri.) Page Size: tabloid. Subscrip. Rate: $.50 newsstand/cover; $14.50/yr mailed. Adv. Rate: page $350 Circulation: 2,980 per issue (paid). **Owner(s):** Litmor Publishing Corp., PO Box 398, Great Neck, NY 11021. Telephone: 516-487-1100. **Management:** Edward Norris, General Manager. Margaret M. Norris, Publisher. Edward Norris, Advertising Director. Carol Liptak, Circulation Manager. **Editorial:** Margaret M. Norris, Editor.

GARDEN CITY NEWS. 81 E. Barclay St., Hicksville, NY 11801. Telephone: 516-294-8900. FAX: 516-931-0027. Pub. Frequency: w. (Fri.) Page Size: tabloid. Subscrip. Rate: $.50 newsstand/cover; $21.50/yr mailed. Adv. Rate: page $550 Circulation: 8,140 per issue (paid). **Owner(s):** Litmor Publishing Corp., PO Box 398, Great Neck, NY 11021. Telephone: 516-487-1100. **Management:** Edward Norris, General Manager. Margaret M. Norris, Publisher. Edward Norris, Advertising Director. Carol Lipstak, Circulation Manager. **Editorial:** Karen Rubin, Editor.

GREAT NECK NEWS. 81 E. Barclay St., Hicksville, NY 11801. Telephone: 516-931-0012. FAX: 516-931-0027. Mailing Address: PO Box 398, Great Neck, NY 11021. Year Established: 1925. Pub. Frequency: w. (Fri.) Page Size: tabloid. Subscrip. Rate: $.50 newsstand/cover; $14.50/yr mailed. Adv. Rate: page $550 Circulation: 5,500 per issue (paid). **Owner(s):** Litmor Publishing Corp., PO Box 398, Great Neck, NY 11022. **Management:** Edward Norris, General Manager. Margaret M. Norris, Publisher. Edward Norris, Advertising Director. Carol Liptak, Circulation Manager. **Editorial:** Margaret M. Norris, Editor.

HICKSVILLE MID ISLAND TIMES. 81 E. Barclay St., Hicksville, NY 11801. Telephone: 516-294-8900. FAX: 516-931-0027. Pub. Frequency: w. (Fri.) Page Size: tabloid. Subscrip. Rate: $.35 newsstand/cover; $14.50/yr mailed. Adv. Rate: page $350 Circulation: 5,685 per issue (paid). **Owner(s):** Litmor Publishing Corp., PO Box 398, Great Neck, NY 11021. Telephone: 516-487-1100. **Management:** Edward Norris, General Manager. Margaret M. Norris, Publisher.

JERICHO-SYOSSET NEWS JOURNAL. 81 E. Barclay St., Hicksville, NY 11801. Telephone: 516-931-0012. FAX: 516-931-0027. Mailing Address: PO Box 398, Great Neck, NY 11021. Pub. Frequency: w. (Fri.) Page Size: tabloid. Subscrip. Rate: $.50 newsstand/cover; $14.50/yr mailed. Adv. Rate: page $450 Circulation: 1,278 per issue (paid). **Owner(s):** Litmor Publishing Corp., See address and contact information above. **Management:** Edward Norris, General Manager. Margaret M. Norris, Publisher. Edward Norris, Advertising Director. Carol Liptak, Circulation Manager. **Editorial:** Margaret M. Norris, Editor.

MID-ISLAND TIMES. ISSN 0747-4741
81 E. Barclay St., Hicksville, NY 11801. Telephone: 516-294-8900. Pub. Frequency: w. (Fri.) Page Size: tabloid. Subscrip. Rate: $.50 newsstand/cover; $14.50/yr mailed. Circulation: 5,685 per issue (paid). **Owner(s):** Litmor Publishing Corp., See address and contact information above. **Management:** Margaret M. Norris, Publisher. Edward Norris, Advertising. Carol Liptak, Circulation Manager. **Editorial:** Margaret M. Norris, Editor.

NEW HYDE PARK HERALD COURIER. 81 E. Barclay St., Hicksville, NY 11801. Telephone: 516-294-8900. FAX: 516-931-0027. Pub. Frequency: w. (Fri.) Page Size: tabloid. Subscrip. Rate: $.35 newsstand/cover; $10.50/yr mailed. Adv. Rate: page $450 Circulation: 2,875 per issue (paid). **Owner(s):** Litmor Publishing Corp., PO Box 398, Great Neck, NY 11021. Telephone: 516-487-1100. **Management:** Edward Norris, General Manager. Margaret M. Norris, Publisher. Edward Norris, Advertising Director. Carol Liptak, Circulation Manager. **Editorial:** Ann Cadigan, Editor.

SYOSSET ADVANCE. 81 E. Barclay St., Hicksville, NY 11801. Telephone: 516-931-0012. FAX: 516-931-0027. Mailing Address: PO Box 398, Great Neck, NY 11021. Pub. Frequency: w. (Fri.) Page Size: tabloid. Subscrip. Rate: $.50 newsstand/cover; $14.50/yr mailed. Adv. Rate: page $350 Circulation: 5,365 per issue (paid). **Owner(s):** Litmor Publishing Corp., See address and contact information above. **Management:** Edward Norris, General Manager. Margaret M. Norris, Publisher. Edward Norris, Advertising Director. Carol Liptak, Circulation Manager. **Editorial:** Margaret M. Norris, Editor.

WILLISTON TIMES. 81 E. Barclay St., Hicksville, NY 11801. Telephone: 516-931-0012. FAX: 516-931-0027. Mailing Address: PO Box 398, Great Neck, NY 11021. Pub. Frequency: w. (Fri.) Page Size: tabloid. Subscrip. Rate: $.50 newsstand/cover; $14.50/yr mailed. Adv. Rate: page $450 Circulation: 3,950 per issue (paid). **Owner(s):** Litmor Publishing Corp., See address and contact information above. **Management:** Edward Norris, General Manager. Margaret M. Norris, Publisher. Edward Norris, Advertising Director. Carol Liptak, Circulation Manager. **Editorial:** Ann Cadigan, Editor.

HIGHLAND FALLS

NEWS OF THE HIGHLANDS. PO Box 278, Highland Falls, NY 10928. Telephone: 845-446-4519. FAX: 845-446-0532. Year Established: 1891. Pub. Frequency: w. (Fri..) Page Size: broadsheet. Subscrip. Rate: $.60 newsstand/cover; $25/yr local. Circulation: 3,000 per issue (paid). **Owner(s):** News of the Highlands, Inc., See address and contact information above. **Management:** Joseph V. Gill, General Manager. Carol Vigillo, Advertising Director. **Editorial:** Frederick Brennan, Editor.

HONEOYE

HONEOYE HERALD, THE. P. O. Box 648, Honeoye, NY 14471-0648. Telephone: 585-374-5260. FAX: 585-374-8590. E-MAIL: news@honeoyeherald.com. Year Established: 2000. Pub. Frequency: w. (Wed.) Page Size: standard. Subscrip. Rate: $.50 newsstand/cover; $30/yr in state; $36/yr out of state. Adv. Rate: col. inch $7.50 Circulation: 1,400 per issue (paid). **Owner(s):** Michael C. Fowler, PO Box 370, Naples, NY 14512. **Management:** Mike Fowler, Publisher. **Editorial:** Mike Fowler, Editor. Margaret Peisher, Production Manager.

HOWARD BEACH

FORUM OF QUEENS. 102-05 159th Ave, Howard Beach, NY 11411. Telephone: 718-845-3221. FAX: 718-738-7645. Year Established: 1977. Pub. Frequency: w. (Thu.) Page Size: tabloid. Subscrip. Rate: $30/yr mailed. Circulation: 6,000 per issue (paid and free). **Owner(s):** Forum South Newspapers, See address and contact information above. **Management:** Patricia Adams, Publisher. **Editorial:** Patricia Adams, Editor-in-Chief.

HUNTINGTON

HALF HOLLOW HILLS. 322 Main St., Huntington, NY 11743. Telephone: 631-427-7000. FAX: 631-427-5820. E-MAIL: longisler@aol.com. URL: http://www.longislandernews.com. Pub. Frequency: w. (Thu.) Page Size: tabloid. Subscrip. Rate: $21/yr in county; $31/yr mailed out of county; $17.50/yr in county to senior citizens. Circulation: 15,000 per issue (free). **Owner(s):** Long Islander Newspapers, Inc., See address and contact information above. **Management:** James Koutsis, Publisher. John Stokes, Advertising. **Editorial:** Peter Sloggatt, Editor.

LONG ISLANDER. ISSN 0886-8328
322 Main St., Huntington, NY 11743. Telephone: 631-427-7000. FAX: 631-427-5820. E-MAIL: info@longislandernews.com. URL: http://www.longislandernews.com. Pub. Frequency: w. (Thu.) Page Size: tabloid. Subscrip. Rate: $.75 newsstand/cover; $21/yr in county; $31/yr mailed out of county; $17.50/yr in county to senior citizens. Circulation: 10,500 per issue (paid). **Owner(s):** Long Islander Newspapers, Inc., See address and contact information above. **Management:** James Koutsis, Publisher. John Stokes, Advertising. **Editorial:** Peter Sloggatt, Editor.

NORTHPORT JOURNAL. 322 Main St., Huntington, NY 11743. Telephone: 631-427-7000. FAX: 631-427-5820. E-MAIL: info2longislandernews.com. URL: http://www.longislandernews.com. Pub. Frequency: w. (Thu.) Page Size: tabloid. Subscrip. Rate: $.75 newsstand/cover; $21/yr in county; $31/yr mailed out of county; $17.50/yr in county to senior citizens. Circulation: 1,393 per issue (paid). **Owner(s):** Long Islander Newspapers, Inc., See address and contact information above. **Management:** James Koutsis, Publisher. John Stokes, Advertising. **Editorial:** Peter Sloggatt, Editor.

RECORD (HUNTINGTON), THE. 322 Main St., Huntington, NY 11743. Telephone: 516-427-7000. FAX: 516-427-5820. E-MAIL: info@longislandernews.com. URL: http://www.longislandernews.com. Year Established: 1932. Pub. Frequency: w. (Thu.) Page Size: tabloid. Subscrip. Rate: $.75 newsstand/cover; $21/yr in county; $31/yr mailed out of county; $17.50/yr in county to senior citizens. Freelance Pay: $25/article. Circulation: 10,000 per issue (paid). **Owner(s):** Long Islander Newspapers, Inc., See address and contact information above. **Management:** James Koutsis, Publisher. John Stokes, Advertising Manager. **Editorial:** Peter Sloggatt, Editor.

ITHACA

ITHACA TIMES. 109 N. Cayuga St., Ithaca, NY 14850-0027. Telephone: 607-277-7000. FAX: 607-277-1012. URL: http://www.ithacatimes.com. Year Established: 1972. Pub. Frequency: w. (Wed.) Page Size: tabloid. Subscrip. Rate: $26.95/yr out of county. Circulation: 28,600 per issue (controlled). **Owner(s):** Finger Lakes Community Newspapers, Inc., PO Box 6475, Ithaca, NY 14851. Telephone: 607-277-7000. **Management:** James Bilinski, Publisher. **Editorial:** Jill Raygor, Editor.

LACKAWANNA

FRONT PAGE (LACKAWANNA). 2703 S. Park Ave., Lackawanna, NY 14218-1511. Telephone: 716-823-8222. FAX: 716-821-0550. E-MAIL: newsroomfpg@wny.twcbc.com. Year Established: 1959. Pub. Frequency: w. (Wed.) Page Size: tabloid. Subscrip. Rate: $.50 newsstand/cover; $18/yr mailed in county; $27/yr mailed out of county. Adv. Rate: col. inch $8.78 Circulation: 7,500 per issue (paid). **Owner(s):** Front Page Group, Inc., See address and contact information above. **Management:** William Delmont, Publisher. **Editorial:** William Delmont, Editor.

SOUTH BUFFALO NEWS. 2703 S. Park Ave., Lackawanna, NY 14218-1511. Telephone: 716-823-8222. FAX: 716-821-0550. E-MAIL: newsroomfpg@wny.twbc.com. Year Established: 1919. Pub. Frequency: w. (Wed.) Page Size: tabloid. Subscrip. Rate: $.50 newsstand/cover; $18/yr in county; $27/yr out of county. Adv. Rate: col. inch $8.78 Circulation: 5,000 per issue (paid). **Owner(s):** Front Page Group, Inc., See address and contact information above. **Management:** William Delmont, Publisher. Beverly Ann Mazur, Office Manager. **Editorial:** William Delmont, Editor.

LAKE PLACID

LAKE PLACID NEWS. 6179 Sentinel Rd., Lake Placid, NY 12946. Telephone: 518-523-4401. FAX: 518-523-1351. E-MAIL: lpnews@northnet.org. Year Established: 1905. Pub. Frequency: w. (Thu.) Page Size: broadsheet. Subscrip. Rate: $1 newsstand/cover; $42/yr in area; $60/yr out of area. Circulation: 3,500 per issue (paid). **Owner(s):** Ogden Newspapers of Minnesota, Inc., 1500 Main St., Wheeling, WV 26003. Telephone: 304-233-0100. **Management:** Catherine Moore, Publisher. Edgaritta Norris, Advertising Manager. **Editorial:** Ed Forbes, Editor.

LAWRENCE

FRANKLIN SQUARE LIFE HERALD. PO Box 9001, Lawrence, NY 11559. Telephone: 516-569-4000. FAX: 516-569-4942. Pub. Frequency: w. (Thu.) Page Size: tabloid. Subscrip. Rate: $.75 newsstand/cover; $25/yr. Adv. Rate: B&W page $476 Circulation: 6,500 per issue (paid). **Owner(s):** Richner Communications, Inc., See address and contact information above. **Management:** Clifford Richner, Publisher. Rhonda Glickman, Advertising Director. **Editorial:** Jerry Burke, Editor.

LONG BEACH HERALD. PO Box 9001, Lawrence, NY 11559. Telephone: 516-569-4000. FAX: 516-569-4942. E-MAIL: feedback@liherald.com. Year Established: 1990. Pub. Frequency: w. (Thu.) Page Size: tabloid. Subscrip. Rate: $.75 newsstand/cover; $22/yr town; $30/yr mailed elsewhere. Circulation: 7,000 per issue (paid). **Owner(s):** Richner Communications, Inc., See address and contact information above. **Management:** Clifford Richner, Publisher. Rhonda Glickman, Advertising Director. Stephanie Hearn, Classified Adv. Mgr.. **Editorial:** Doug Miller, Editor.

LONG ISLAND GRAPHIC-ROOSEVELT PRESS. PO Box 9001, Lawrence, NY 11559. Telephone: 516-569-4000. FAX: 516-569-4942. Pub. Frequency: w. (Wed.) Page Size: tabloid.Subscrip. Rate: $.75 newsstand/cover; $25/yr Circulation: 1,200 per issue (paid). **Owner(s):** Richner Communications, Inc., See address and contact information above. **Management:** Clifford Richner, Publisher. Rhonda Glickman, Advertising Director. **Editorial:** John O'Connell, Editor.

NASSAU HERALD. PO Box 9001, Lawrence, NY 11559. Telephone: 516-569-4000. FAX: 516-569-4942. E-MAIL: nassaueditor@liherald.com. URL: http://www.liherald.com. Year Established: 1924. Pub. Frequency: w. (Thu.) Page Size: tabloid. Subscrip. Rate: $.75 newsstand/cover; $22/yr mailed in county; $30/yr mailed out of county. Circulation: 10,500 per issue (paid). **Owner(s):** Richner Communications, Inc., See address and contact information above. **Management:** Clifford Richner, Publisher. Rhonda Glickman, Advertising Director. Lori Berger, Classified Adv. Mgr.. **Editorial:** Jeff Lipton, Editor.

PRIMETIME. PO Box 9001, Lawrence, NY 11559. Telephone: 516-569-4000. FAX: 516-569-4942. Year Established: 1987. Pub. Frequency: w. (Fri.) Page Size: tabloid Circulation: 108,240 per issue (free). **Owner(s):** Richner Communications, Inc., See address and contact information above. **Management:** Clifford Richner, Publisher. Rhonda Glickman, Advertising Director. Stephanie Hearn, Classified Adv. Mgr..

SOUTH SHORE RECORD. ISSN 0038-352X
PO Box 9001, Lawrence, NY 11559. Telephone: 516-569-4000. URL: http://www.liherald.com. Year Established: 1953. Pub. Frequency: w. (Thu.) Page Size: tabloid. Subscrip. Rate: $25/yr. Adv. Rate: B&W page $476 Circulation: 21,000. **Owner(s):** Richner Communications, Inc., See address and contact information above. **Management:** Stuart Richner, Publisher.

VALLEY STREAM HERALD. PO Box 9001, Lawrence, NY 11559. Telephone: 516-569-4000. FAX: 516-569-4942. E-MAIL: feedback@liherald.com. Year Established: 1990. Pub. Frequency: w. (Thu.) Page Size: tabloid. Subscrip. Rate: $.75 newsstand/cover; $25/yr mailed in county; $30/yr mailed out of county. Circulation: 9,121 per issue (paid). **Owner(s):** Richner Communications, Inc., See address and contact information above. **Management:** Clifford Richner, Publisher. Rhonda Glickman, Advertising Director. Stephanie Hearn, Classified Adv. Mgr.. **Editorial:** Nichole Falco, Editor.

VILLAGE HERALD. PO Box 9001, Lawrence, NY 11559. Telephone: 516-569-4000. FAX: 516-569-4942. E-MAIL: villeditor@liherald.com. URL: http://www.liherald.com. Year Established: 1964. Pub. Frequency: w. (Thu.) Page Size: tabloid. Subscrip. Rate: $.75 newsstand/cover; $22/yr mailed in county (effective 2005); $30/yr mailed out of county. Adv. Rate: page $476 Circulation: 5,500 per issue (paid). **Owner(s):** Richner Communications, Inc., See address and contact information above. **Management:** Clifford Richner, Publisher. Rhonda Glickman, Advertising Director. Lori Berger, Classified Adv. Mgr.. **Editorial:** Cindy Roth, Editor.

LINDENHURST

SOUTH BAY'S NEWSPAPER. 150 W. Hoffman Ave., Lindenhurst, NY 11757-4043. Telephone: 631-226-2636. E-MAIL: editorsb@southbaynews.com. URL: http://www.southbaynews.com. Year Established: 1953. Pub. Frequency: w. (Wed.) Page Size: tabloid Circulation: 114,385 per issue (free). **Owner(s):** Excel Promotions Corp., See address and contact information above. **Management:** Richard Freedman, General Manager. **Editorial:** J.M. Freedman, Editor.

LOCUST VALLEY

LEADER (LOCUST VALLEY), THE. 160 Birch Hill Rd., Locust Valley, NY 11560. Telephone: 516-671-7442. FAX: 516-671-7442. E-MAIL: leader@optonline.net. Year Established: 1946. Pub. Frequency: w. (Wed.) Page Size: tabloid. Subscrip. Rate: $.50 newsstand/cover; $22/yr; $40 for 2 yrs.. Freelance Pay: $1.50/column-inch. Circulation: 3,800 per issue (paid). **Owner(s):** Lally Communications, Inc., See address and contact information above. **Management:** Sally Bandow, Sales Manager. **Editorial:** Philip Szulc, Editor.

LONG ISLAND CITY

QUEENS GAZETTE, THE. ISSN 1547-3538
42-16 34th Ave, Long Island City, NY 11101. Telephone: 718-361-6161. FAX: 718-784-7552. E-MAIL: qgazette@aol.com. URL: http://www.qgazette.com/. Pub. Frequency: w. Page Size: tabloid. Subscrip. Rate: $26/yr. **Owner(s):** Service Advertising Group Inc., See address and contact information above. **Management:** Vinny DuPre, General Manager. Tony Barsamian, Publisher. Julie Wager, Advertising Director. Ed Husser, Art Director. **Editorial:** Linda Wilson, Editor. Denise Gallo, Production Manager.

WOODSIDE HERALD. 1305 44th Ave, Long Island City, NY 11101-6919. Telephone: 718-729-3772. FAX: 718-729-8614. E-MAIL: woodsideherald@aol.com. Year Established: 1935. Pub. Frequency: w. (Fri.) Page Size: tabloid. Subscrip. Rate: $26/yr mailed. Freelance Pay: $75/article. Circulation: 15,000 per issue (paid and free). **Owner(s):** Buster Sabba, See address and contact information above. **Management:** Erin Cabezas, Director. Buster Sabba, Publisher. **Editorial:** Buster Sabba, Editor.

LOWVILLE

JOURNAL & REPUBLICAN. ISSN 1551-9201
7567 State St., Lowville, NY 13367. Telephone: 315-376-3525. FAX: 315-376-4136. E-MAIL: caucter@lowville.com. URL: http://www.lowville.com. Year Established: 1830. Pub. Frequency: w. (Fri.) Page Size: broadsheet. Subscrip. Rate: $1 newsstand/cover; $43/yr mailed in state; $49.50/yr mailed out of state. Circulation: 5,000 per issue (paid). **Owner(s):** Lowville Newspapers Corp., See address and contact information above. **Management:** John B. Johnson Sr., President. Cindy Aucter, Publisher. **Editorial:** Adam Atkinson, Editor.

MAHOPAC

BEACON LIGHT. 928 S. Lake Blvd., Mahopac, NY 10541. Telephone: 845-628-8400. FAX: 845-628-8400. Pub. Frequency: w. (Wed.) Page Size: tabloid. Subscrip. Rate: $.25 newsstand/cover; $10/yr mailed in county; $20/yr mailed out of county. Circulation: 2,700 per issue (paid). **Owner(s):** Gateway Papers, Inc., See address and contact information above. **Management:** Don Hall, Publisher. **Editorial:** Karen Placek, Editor.

BREWSTER TIMES. 928 S. Lake Blvd., Mahopac, NY 10541. Telephone: 845-628-8400. FAX: 845-628-8400. E-MAIL: putnampress@aol.com. Pub. Frequency: w. (Wed.) Page Size: tabloid. Subscrip. Rate: $.25 newsstand/cover; $10/yr mailed in county; $20/yr mailed out of county. Circulation: 8,200 per issue (paid). **Owner(s):** Gateway Papers, Inc., See address and contact information above. **Management:** Don Hall, Publisher. **Editorial:** Karen Placek, Editor.

CARMEL TIMES. 928 S. Lake Blvd., Mahopac, NY 10541. Telephone: 845-628-8400. FAX: 845-628-8400. Pub. Frequency: w. (Wed.) Page Size: tabloid. Subscrip. Rate: $.25 newsstand/cover; $10/yr in county; $20/yr out of county. Circulation: 11,800 per issue (paid). **Owner(s):** Gateway Papers, Inc., See address and contact information above. **Management:** Don Hall, Publisher. **Editorial:** Karen Placek, Editor.

EAST FISHKILL RECORD. 928 S. Lake Blvd., Mahopac, NY 10541. Telephone: 845-628-8400. FAX: 845-628-8400. Mailing Address: PO Box 608, Mahopac, NY 10541. Year Established: 1858. Pub. Frequency: w. (Wed.) Page Size: tabloid. Subscrip. Rate: $.25 newsstand/cover; $10/yr mailed in county; $20/yr mailed out of county. Circulation: 3,100 per issue (paid). **Owner(s):** Gateway Papers, Inc., See address and contact information above. **Management:** Don Hall, Publisher. **Editorial:** Karen Placek, Editor.

FISHKILL STANDARD. 928 S. Lake Blvd., Mahopac, NY 10541. Telephone: 845-628-8400. FAX: 845-628-8400. Mailing Address: PO Box 608, Mahopac, NY 10541. Pub. Frequency: w. (Wed.) Page Size: tabloid. Subscrip. Rate: $.25 newsstand/cover; $10/yr mailed in county; $20/yr mailed out of county. Circulation: 6,200 per issue (paid). **Owner(s):** Gateway Papers, Inc., See address and contact information above. **Management:** Don Hall, Publisher. **Editorial:** Karen Placek, Editor.

GRANGE INDEPENDENT, LA. 928 S. Lake Blvd., Mahopac, NY 10541. Telephone: 845-628-8400. FAX: 845-628-8400. Mailing Address: PO Box 608, Mahopac, NY 10541. Pub. Frequency: w. (Wed.) Page Size: tabloid. Subscrip. Rate: $.25 newsstand/cover; $10/yr in county; $20/yr out of county. Circulation: 2,600 per issue (paid). **Owner(s):** Putman County Press, See address and contact information above. **Management:** Don Hall, Publisher. **Editorial:** Karen Placek, Editor.

MAHOPAC PRESS. 928 S. Lake Blvd., Mahopac, NY 10541. Telephone: 845-628-8400. FAX: 845-628-8400. Pub. Frequency: w. (Wed.) Page Size: tabloid. Subscrip. Rate: $.25 newsstand/cover; $10/yr in county; $20/yr out of county. Circulation: 3,200 per issue (paid). **Owner(s):** Gateway Papers, Inc., See address and contact information above. **Management:** Don Hall, Publisher. **Editorial:** Karen Placek, Editor.

MASPETH

FOREST HILLS/REGO PARK TIMES. 69-60 Grand Ave., Maspeth, NY 11378. Telephone: 718-639-7000. FAX: 718-429-1234. E-MAIL: news@queensledger.com. URL: http://www.queensledger.com. Mailing Address: PO Box 376, Maspeth, NY 11378. Year Established: 1995. Pub. Frequency: w. (Thu.) Page Size: tabloid. Subscrip. Rate: $.35 newsstand/cover; $15/yr; $20/yr mailed out of area. Adv. Rate: col. inch $17.06 Circulation: 18,000 per issue (paid). **Owner(s):** Walter H. Sanchez, II, See address and contact information above. **Management:** Tammy Sanchez, General Manager. Walter H. Sanchez II, Publisher. Lora Sanchez, Advertising Manager. Jessie Almonte, Circulation Manager. **Editorial:** Walter H. Sanchez II, Editor. Shane Miller, Managing Editor. Nick D'Arienzo, Sports Editor.

GLENDALE REGISTER. 69-60 Grand Ave., Maspeth, NY 11378. Telephone: 718-639-7000. FAX: 718-429-1234. E-MAIL: news@queensledger.com. URL: http://www.queensledger.com. Mailing Address: PO Box 376, Maspeth, NY 11378. Year Established: 1935. Pub. Frequency: w. (Thu.) Page Size: tabloid. Subscrip. Rate: $.35 newsstand/cover; $15/yr area; $20/yr mailed out of area. Adv. Rate: col. inch $17.06 Circulation: 8,000 per issue (paid). **Owner(s):** Walter H. Sanchez, II, See address and contact information above. **Management:** Tammy Sanchez, General Manager. Walter H. Sanchez II, Publisher. Lora Sanchez, Advertising Manager. Jessie Almonte, Circulation Manager. **Editorial:** Walter H. Sanchez II, Editor. Shane Miller, Managing Editor. Nick D'Arienzo, Sports Editor.

LEADER/OBSERVER OF WOODHAVEN, RICHMOND HILLS, HOWARD BEACH. 69-60 Grand Ave., Maspeth, NY 11378. Telephone: 718-639-7000. FAX: 718-429-1234. E-MAIL: news@queensledger.com. URL: http://www.queensledger.com. Mailing Address: PO Box 376, Maspeth, NY 11378. Year Established: 1909. Pub. Frequency: w. (Thu.) Page Size: tabloid. Subscrip. Rate: $.35 newsstand/cover; $15/yr mailed in county; $20/yr mailed out of county. Adv. Rate: col. inch $17.06 Circulation: 25,000 per issue (paid). **Owner(s):** Walter H. Sanchez, II, See address and contact information above. **Management:** Tammy Sanchez, General Manager. Walter H. Sanchez II, Publisher. Lora Sanchez, Advertising Manager. Jessie Almonte, Circulation Manager. **Editorial:** Walter H. Sanchez II, Editor. Shane Miller, Managing Editor. Nick D'Arienzo, Sports Editor.

LONG ISLAND CITY/ASTORIA, JACKSON HEIGHTS JOURNAL. 69-60 Grand Ave., Maspeth, NY 11378. Telephone: 718-639-7000. FAX: 718-429-1234. E-MAIL: news@queensledger.com. URL: http://www.queensledger.com. Mailing Address: PO Box 376, Maspeth, NY 11378. Year Established: 1986. Pub. Frequency: w. (Thu.) Page Size: tabloid. Subscrip. Rate: $.35 newsstand/cover; $15/yr in county; $18/yr out of county. Adv. Rate: col. inch $17.06 Freelance Pay: $25/story. Circulation: 23,000 per issue (paid). **Owner(s):** Walter H. Sanchez, II, See address and contact information above. **Management:** Tammy Sanchez, General Manager. Walter H. Sanchez II, Publisher. Lora Sanchez, Advertising Manager. Jessie Almonte, Circulation Manager. **Editorial:** Walter H. Sanchez II, Editor. Shane Miller, Managing Editor. Nick D'Arienzo, Sports Editor.

QUEENS EXAMINER, THE. 69-60 Grand Ave., Maspeth, NY 11378. Telephone: 718-639-7000. FAX: 718-429-1234. E-MAIL: news@queensledger.com. URL: http://www.queensledger.com. Mailing Address: PO Box 376, Maspeth, NY 11378. Year Established: 1999. Pub. Frequency: w. (Thu.) Page Size: tabloid. Subscrip. Rate: $.35 newsstand/cover; $15/yr; $20/yr mailed out of area. Adv. Rate: col. inch $17.06 Circulation: 16,000 per issue (paid). **Owner(s):** Walter H. Sanchez, II, See address and contact information above. **Management:** Tammy Sanchez, General Manager. Walter H. Sanchez II, Publisher. Lora Sanchez, Advertising Manager. Jessie Almonte, Circulation Manager. **Editorial:** Walter H. Sanchez II, Editor. Shane Miller, Managing Editor. Nick D'Arienzo, Sports Editor.

QUEENS LEDGER. 69-60 Grand Ave., Maspeth, NY 11378. Telephone: 718-639-7000. FAX: 718-429-1234. E-MAIL: queensledger@inyc.com. URL: http://www.queensledger.com. Mailing Address: PO Box 376, Maspeth, NY 11378. Year Established: 1873. Pub. Frequency: w. (Thu.) Page Size: tabloid. Subscrip. Rate: $.35 newsstand/cover; $15/yr mailed in county; $20/yr mailed out of county. Adv. Rate: col. inch $17.06 Freelance Pay: $20/article. Circulation: 30,000 per issue (paid). **Owner(s):** Walter H. Sanchez, II, See address and contact information above. **Management:** Tammy Sanchez, General Manager. Walter H. Sanchez II, Publisher. Lora Sanchez, Advertising Manager. Jessie Almonte, Circulation Manager. **Editorial:** Walter H. Sanchez II, Editor. Shane Miller, Managing Editor. Nick D'Arienzo, Sports Editor.

Weeklies

MASSAPEQUA PARK

MASSAPEQUA POST. ISSN 1553-2569
1045-B Park Blvd., Massapequa Park, NY 11762. Telephone: 516-798-5100. FAX: 516-798-5296. E-MAIL: acjnews@rcn.com. URL: http://www.massapequapost.com. Year Established: 1954. Pub. Frequency: w. (Wed.) Page Size: tabloid. Subscrip. Rate: $.50 newsstand/cover; $25/yr mailed in state; $40 mailed for 2 yrs. in state; $35/yr mailed out of state. Adv. Rate: col. inch $9.50 Circulation: 8,000 per issue (paid). **Owner(s):** ACJ Communications, Inc., 85 Broadway, Amityville, NY 11701. FAX: 631-264-5310. **Management:** Alfred James, President. Carolyn James, Publisher. Maryann Heins, Advertising. Doris Giles, Circulation Manager. **Editorial:** Carolyn James, Executive Editor.

MASSENA

FREE TRADER. W. Hatfield St., Massena, NY 13662. Telephone: 315-769-7149. FAX: 315-764-7440. E-MAIL: freetrad@twcny.rr.com. Year Established: 1981. Pub. Frequency: w. (Thu.) Page Size: tabloid Circulation: 16,000 per issue (free). **Owner(s):** Bob Noreault, See address and contact information above. **Management:** Mame Noreault, Publisher. **Editorial:** Mame Noreault, Editor.

MATTITUCK

NEWS-REVIEW (MATTITUCK), THE. 7785 Main Rd., Mattituck, NY 11952. Telephone: 631-298-3200. FAX: 631-298-3287. E-MAIL: mail@timesreview.com. URL: http://www.timesreview.com. Mailing Address: PO Box 1500, Matituck, NY 11952. Year Established: 1950. Pub. Frequency: w. (Thu.) Page Size: tabloid. Subscrip. Rate: $1 newsstand/cover; $35/yr in county; $44/yr out of county. Freelance Pay: $30/story. Circulation: 5,000 per issue (paid). **Owner(s):** Times/Review Newspapers Corp., See address and contact information above. **Management:** Andrew Olsen, Co-Publisher. Troy Gustavson, President. Janice Robinson, Advertising. Tina Volinski, Circulation Manager. Meg Marcus, Classified Adv. Mgr.. **Editorial:** John Stefans, Editor. Mike Gasparino, Associate Editor. Bob Liepa, Sports Editor.

SUFFOLK TIMES. ISSN 1543-7736
7785 Main Rd., Mattituck, NY 11952. Telephone: 631-298-3200. FAX: 631-298-3287. E-MAIL: mail@timesreview.com. URL: http://www.suffolktimes.com. Mailing Address: PO Box 1500, Matituck, NY 11952. Year Established: 1857. Pub. Frequency: w. (Thu.) Page Size: tabloid. Subscrip. Rate: $1 newsstand/cover; $35/yr in county; $44/yr out of county. Freelance Pay: $30/article. Circulation: 11,000 per issue (paid and free). **Owner(s):** Times/Review Newspapers Corp., See address and contact information above. **Management:** Andrew Olsen, Co-Publisher. Troy Gustavson, President. Janice Robinson, Advertising. Tina Volinski, Circulation Manager. Meg Marcus, Classified Adv. Mgr.. **Editorial:** Denise Civiletti, Executive Editor. Eileen Duff, Associate Editor. Bob Liepa, Sports Editor.

MERRICK

BELLMORE LIFE. 1840 Merrick Ave, Merrick, NY 11566. Telephone: 516-378-5320. FAX: 516-378-0287. E-MAIL: lmpub@optonline.net. URL: http://www.bellmorelife.com. Year Established: 1964. Pub. Frequency: w. (Wed.) Page Size: tabloid. Subscrip. Rate: $20/yr; $.75 newsstand/cover. Adv. Rate: col. inch $16.10 Circulation: 3,009 (paid). **Owner(s):** L & M Publications, Inc., See address and contact information above. **Management:** Linda Toscano, Publisher. **Editorial:** Paul Laursen, Editor.

FREEPORT BALDWIN LEADER, THE. 1840 Merrick Ave, Merrick, NY 11566. Telephone: 516-378-5320. FAX: 516-378-0287. E-MAIL: lmpub@optonline.net. URL: http://www.freeportbaldwinleader.com. Year Established: 1935. Pub. Frequency: w. (Thu.) Page Size: tabloid. Subscrip. Rate: $75 newsstand/cover; $17/yr. Adv. Rate: col. inch $9.38 Circulation: 1,287 per issue (paid and free). **Owner(s):** L & M Publications, Inc., See address and contact information above. **Management:** Linda Toscano, President. Joyce MacMonigle, Circulation Manager. **Editorial:** Paul Laursen, Editor.

MERRICK LIFE. 1840 Merrick Ave, Merrick, NY 11566. Telephone: 516-378-5320. FAX: 516-378-0287. E-MAIL: lmpub@optonline.net. URL: http://www.merricklife.com. Year Established: 1938. Pub. Frequency: w. (Thu.) Page Size: tabloid. Subscrip. Rate: $.75 newsstand/cover; $25/yr; $39 for 2 yrs.. Adv. Rate: col. inch $17.22 Circulation: 4,641 per issue (paid). **Owner(s):** L & M Publications, Inc., See address and contact information above. **Management:** Linda Toscano, President. **Editorial:** Paul Laursen, Editor.

WANTAGH - SEAFORD CITIZEN. 1840 Merrick Ave, Merrick, NY 11566. Telephone: 516-378-5320. FAX: 516-378-0287. E-MAIL: lmpub@optonline.net. URL: http://www.wantaghseafordcitizen.com. Year Established: 1953. Pub. Frequency: w. (Wed.) Page Size: tabloid. Subscrip. Rate: $18/yr; $.75 newsstand/cover. Adv. Rate: col. inch $15.12 Circulation: 3,337 (paid). **Owner(s):** L & M Publications, Inc., See address and contact information above. **Management:** Linda Toscano, Publisher. Paul Roberts, Advertising Manager. **Editorial:** Paul Laursen, Editor.

MEXICO

INDEPENDENT MIRROR. 80 N Jefferson St, Mexico, NY 13114. Telephone: 315-963-7813. FAX: 315-963-4087. E-MAIL: ocweeklies@caymail.com. Mailing Address: PO Box 129, Mexico, NY 13114. Year Established: 1861. Pub. Frequency: w. (Sat.) Page Size: tabloid. Subscrip. Rate: $.50 newsstand/cover; $15/yr in area. Circulation: 3,100 per issue (paid). **Owner(s):** Mark Backus, See address and contact information above. **Management:** Mark Backus, Publisher. **Editorial:** Roseann Parsons, Managing Editor.

PHOENIX REGISTER. 80 N. Jefferson St, Mexico, NY 13114. Telephone: 315-963-7813. E-MAIL: ocweeklies@aol.com. URL: http://www.members.ocweeklies.com. Mailing Address: PO Box 129, Mexico, NY 13114. Year Established: 1912. Pub. Frequency: w. (Wed.) Page Size: tabloid. Subscrip. Rate: $.50 newsstand/cover; $15/yr in area; $25/yr out of area. Circulation: 3,400 per issue (paid). **Owner(s):** Oswego County Weeklies, See address and contact information above. **Management:** Mark Backus, Publisher. **Editorial:** Rose Ann Parsons, Managing Editor.

MILLBROOK

VOICE LEDGER, THE. 52 Front St, Millbrook, NY 12545. Telephone: 845-677-8241. E-MAIL: tacnews@aol.com. URL: http://www.midhudsoncentral.com. Year Established: 1969. Pub. Frequency: w. (Thu.) Page Size: broadsheet. Subscrip. Rate: $.75 newsstand/cover; $36/yr in state; $42/yr out of state. Circulation: 2,500 per issue (paid). **Owner(s):** Taconic Newspapers, See address and contact information above. **Management:** Ira Fusfeld, Publisher. Larry Priest, Circulation Director. **Editorial:** Jason Miller, Editor. Ann Gibbons, Executive Editor.

MILLERTON

MILLERTON NEWS, THE. Main St., Millerton, NY 12546. Telephone: 518-789-4401. FAX: 518-789-9247. E-MAIL: mnews@taconic.net. URL: http://www.millertonnews.com. Mailing Address: PO Box AD, Millerton, NY 12546. Year Established: 1934. Pub. Frequency: w. (Thu.) Page Size: broadsheet. Subscrip. Rate: $1.25 newsstand/cover; $45/yr in county; $55/yr out of county. Circulation: 1,290 per issue (paid). **Owner(s):** Lakeville Journal LLC, PO Box 1688, Lakeville, CT 06039-1688. **Management:** Janet Manko, Publisher. Anna Mae Kupferer, Advertising Manager. **Editorial:** Whitney Joseph, Executive Editor.

MINEOLA

FARMINGDALE OBSERVER. 132 E. Second St., Mineola, NY 11501-3522. Telephone: 516-747-8282. FAX: 516-742-5867. URL: http://www.antonnews.com. Year Established: 1965. Pub. Frequency: w. (Fri.) Page Size: tabloid. Subscrip. Rate: $.75 newsstand/cover; $20/yr in county; $40/yr out of county. Adv. Rate: page $290 Circulation: 4,001 per issue (paid). **Owner(s):** Anton Community Newspapers, See address and contact information above. **Management:** Cary Seaman, General Manager. Angela Anton, Publisher. Harriet Heffernan, Advertising Director. Tom McGee, Advertising Manager. Peter Nyquist, Circulation Director. Paul Scheuer, Art Director. **Editorial:** Jaime Tomeo, Editor. Contact: Dan Rossett, Editor.

FLORAL PARK DISPATCH. 132 E. Second St., Mineola, NY 11501-3522. Telephone: 516-747-8282. FAX: 516-742-5867. E-MAIL: floralparkdispatch@antonnews.com. URL: Http://www.antonnews.com. Year Established: 1927. Pub. Frequency: w. (Fri.) Page Size: tabloid. Subscrip. Rate: $.75 newsstand/cover; $20/yr in county; $40/yr out of county; $35 for 2 yrs.; $48 for 3 yrs.. Circulation: 1,428 per issue (paid). **Owner(s):** Anton Community Newspapers, See address and contact information above. **Management:** Cary Seaman, General Manager. Angela V. Anton, Publisher. Harriet Heffernan, Advertising Manager. Peter Nyquist, Circulation Director. Paul Scheuer, Art Director. **Editorial:** Carisa Keane, Editor.

GARDEN CITY LIFE. ISSN 1040-0745
132 E. Second St., Mineola, NY 11501-3522. Telephone: 516-747-8282. FAX: 516-742-5867. E-MAIL: gardencitylife@antonnews.com. URL: http://www.antonnews.com. Year Established: 1985. Pub. Frequency: w. (Thu.) Page Size: tabloid. Subscrip. Rate: $.75 newsstand/cover; $15/yr in county; $35/yr out of county. Circulation: 3,251 per issue (paid). **Owner(s):** Anton Community Newspapers, See address and contact information above. **Management:** Cary Seaman, General Manager. Angela Anton, Publisher. Harriet Heffernan, Advertising Director. Peter Nyquist, Circulation Manager. Paul Scheuer, Art Director. **Editorial:** Carisa Keane, Editor. Mary O"Brien, Sports.

GLEN COVE RECORD PILOT. 132 E. Second St., Mineola, NY 11501-3522. Telephone: 516-747-8282. FAX: 516-742-5867. E-MAIL: glencoverecordpilot@anton.com. URL: http://www.antonnews.com. Year Established: 1875. Pub. Frequency: w. (Thu.) Page Size: tabloid. Subscrip. Rate: $.75 newsstand/cover; $23/yr in county; $43/yr out of county. Adv. Rate: page $525 Freelance Pay: $20-$30/story. Circulation: 7,256 per issue (paid). **Owner(s):** Anton Community Newspapers, See address and contact information above. **Management:** Billy Delventhal, General Manager. Angela S. Anton, Publisher. Harriet Heffernan, Advertising Manager. Peter Nyquist, Circulation Director. Paul Scheuer, Art Director. **Editorial:** Carla Sentella, Editor. Jana Miller North, Writer.

GREAT NECK RECORD. 132 E. Second St., Mineola, NY 11501-3522. Telephone: 516-747-8282. FAX: 516-742-5867. E-MAIL: greatneckrecord@anton.com. URL: http://www.antonnews.com. Year Established: 1907. Pub. Frequency: w. (Thu.) Page Size: tabloid. Subscrip. Rate: $.75 newsstand/cover; $23/yr in county; $43/yr out of county. Adv. Rate: page $525 Circulation: 6,277 per issue (paid). **Owner(s):** Anton Community Newspapers, See address and contact information above. **Management:** Cary Seaman, General Manager. Angela S. Anton, Publisher. Valerie Link, Advertising. Harriet Heffernan, Advertising Manager. Peter Nyquist, Circulation Manager. Paul Scheuer, Art Director. **Editorial:** Wendy Kreitzman, Editor. Carol Frank, Editorial Assistant.

HICKSVILLE ILLUSTRATED NEWS. 132 E. Second St., Mineola, NY 11501-3522. Telephone: 516-747-8282. FAX: 516-742-5867. E-MAIL: hicksvilleillustratednews@anton.com. URL: http://www.antonnews.com. Year Established: 1949. Pub. Frequency: w. (Fri.) Page Size: tabloid. Subscrip. Rate: $.75 newsstand/cover; $20/yr in county; $40/yr out of county. Adv. Rate: page $525 Freelance Pay: $20-$30/article. Circulation: 5,299 per issue (paid). **Owner(s):** Anton Community Newspapers, See address and contact information above. **Management:** Cary Seaman, General Manager. Angela S. Anton, Publisher. Roseann Peritore, Advertising. Harriet Heffernan, Advertising Director. Tom McGee, Advertising Manager. Peter Nyquist, Circulation Director. **Editorial:** Victoria Caruso, Editor. Cathy Greenfield, Photographer.

ILLUSTRATED NEWS, THE. 132 E. Second St., Mineola, NY 11501-3522. Telephone: 516-747-8282. FAX: 516-742-5867. E-MAIL: illustratednews@anton.com. URL: http://www.antonnews.com. Year Established: 1927. Pub. Frequency: w. (Fri.) Page Size: tabloid. Subscrip. Rate: $.75 newsstand/cover; $15/yr in county; $35/yr out of county. Adv. Rate: page $440 Freelance Pay: $20-$30/article. Circulation: 3,971 per issue (paid). **Owner(s):** Anton Community Newspapers, See address and contact information above. **Management:** Cary Seaman, General Manager. Angela S. Anton, Publisher. Lou Sanders, Advertising. Harriet Heffernan, Advertising Manager. Peter Nyquist, Circulation Director. Paul Scheuer, Art Director. **Editorial:** Maggie Whitely, Editor.

LEVITTOWN TRIBUNE. ISSN 0586-0660
132 E. Second St., Mineola, NY 11501-3522. FAX: 516-746-5867. E-MAIL: levittowntribune@antonnews.com. URL: http://www.antonnews.com. Year Established: 1947. Pub. Frequency: w. (Fri.) Page Size: tabloid. Subscrip. Rate: $.75 newsstand/cover; $20/yr in county; $40/yr out of county. Adv. Rate: page $290 Circulation: 4,924 per issue (paid). **Owner(s):** Anton Community Newspapers, See address and contact information above. **Management:** Cary Seaman, General Manager. Angela S. Anton, Publisher. Harriet Heffernan, Advertising Director. Thomas McGee, Advertising Manager. Peter Nyquist, Circulation Director. **Editorial:** Jaime Tomeo, Editor.

MANHASSET PRESS. 132 E. Second St., Mineola, NY 11501-3522. Telephone: 516-747-8282. FAX: 516-742-5867. E-MAIL: manhassetpress@antonnews.com. URL: http://www.antonnews.com. Year Established: 1958. Pub. Frequency: w. (Thu.) Page Size: tabloid. Subscrip. Rate: $.75 newsstand/cover; $23/yr in county; $43/yr out of county. Adv. Rate: page $440 Circulation: 4,840 per issue (paid). **Owner(s):** Anton Community Newspapers, 132 E. Second St., Mineola, NY 11501. Telephone: 516-747-8282. FAX: 516-742-5867. **Management:** Cary Seaman, General Manager. Angela S. Anton, Publisher. Andrea Bernstein, Advertising. Harriet Heffernan, Advertising Manager. Peter Nyquist, Circulation Director. Paul Scheuer, Art Director. **Editorial:** Pat Grace, Editor. Eileen Brennan, Executive Editor.

MASSAPEQUAN OBSERVER. 132 E. Second St., Mineola, NY 11501-3522. FAX: 516-742-5867. E-MAIL: massapeqan@antonnews.com. URL: http://www.antonnews.com. Year Established: 1957. Pub. Frequency: w. (Fri..) Page Size: tabloid. Subscrip. Rate: $.75 newsstand/cover; $15/yr in county; $35/yr out of county. Adv. Rate: page $290 Freelance Pay: $20-$30/article. Circulation: 2,223 per issue (paid). **Owner(s):** Anton Community Newspapers, See address and contact information above. **Management:** Cary Seaman, General Manager. Angela S. Anton, Publisher. Harriet Heffernan, Advertising Manager. Peter Nyquist, Circulation Director. Paul Scheuer, Art Director. Thomas McGee, Public Rel. Mgr.. **Editorial:** Joe Scotchie, Editor.

MINEOLA AMERICAN. 132 E. Second St., Mineola, NY 11501-3522. Telephone: 516-747-8282. FAX: 516-742-5867. E-MAIL: mineolaamerican@anton.com. URL: http://www.antonnews.com. Year Established: 1952. Pub. Frequency: w. (Wed.) Page Size: tabloid. Subscrip. Rate: $.75 newsstand/cover; $20/yr in county; $40/yr out of county. Adv. Rate: page $440 Circulation: 4,498 per issue (paid). **Owner(s):** Anton Community Newspapers, See address and contact information above. **Management:** Cary Seaman, General Manager. Angela S. Anton, Publisher. Roseann Peritore, Advertising. Harriet Heffernan, Advertising Director. Peter Nyquist, Circulation Director. Paul Scheuer, Art Director. **Editorial:** Joseph Rizza, Editor.

OYSTER BAY ENTERPRISE PILOT. 132 E. Second St., Mineola, NY 11501. Telephone: 516-747-8282. FAX: 516-742-5867. E-MAIL: oysterbayenterprisepilot@anton.com. URL: http://www.antonnews.com. Year Established: 1885. Pub. Frequency: w. (Thu.) Page Size: tabloid. Subscrip. Rate: $.75 newsstand/cover; $15/yr home delivery in county; $32/yr mailed out of county. Adv. Rate: page $290 Circulation: 3,084 per issue (paid). **Owner(s):** Anton Community Newspapers, 132 E. Second St., Mineola, NY 11501-3522. **Management:** Cary Seaman, General Manager. Angela Anton, Publisher. Tom McGee, Advertising Manager. Peter Nyquist, Circulation Director. **Editorial:** Dagmar Fors Karppi, Editor.

PLAINVIEW HERALD. 132 E. Second St., Mineola, NY 11501. Telephone: 516-747-8282. FAX: 516-742-5867. E-MAIL: plainviewherald@anton.com. URL: http://www.antonnews.com. Pub. Frequency: w. (Fri.) Page Size: tabloid. Subscrip. Rate: $.75 newsstand/cover; $20/yr in county; $40/yr out of county. Circulation: 908 per issue (paid). **Owner(s):** Anton Community Newspapers, See address and contact information above. **Management:** William Delventhal Jr., General Manager. Angela S. Anton, Publisher. Harriet Heffernan, Advertising Director. Thomas McGee, Advertising Manager. Peter Nyquist, Circulation Director. Paul Scheuer, Art Director. **Editorial:** Denise Nash, Editor. Contact: Dan Rosett, Editor.

PORT WASHINGTON NEWS. ISSN 0438-0940
132 E. Second St., Mineola, NY 11501-3522. Telephone: 516-747-8282. FAX: 516-742-5867. E-MAIL: portwashingtonnews@anton.com. URL: http://www.antonnews.com. Year Established: 1903. Pub. Frequency: w. (Thu.) Page Size: tabloid. Subscrip. Rate: $.75 newsstand/cover; $23/yr in county; $43/yr out of county. Adv. Rate: page $525 Freelance Pay: $20-$30/story. Circulation: 7,785 per issue (paid). **Owner(s):** Anton Community Newspapers, See address and contact information above. **Management:** Cary Seaman, General Manager. Angela Anton, Publisher. Mari Gaudet, Advertising. Harriet Heffernan, Advertising Manager. Peter Nyquist, Circulation Director. **Editorial:** Jackie Pierangelo, Editor.

ROSLYN NEWS, THE. 132 E. Second St., Mineola, NY 11501-3522. Telephone: 516-747-8282. E-MAIL: roslynnews@anton.com. URL: http://www.antonnews.com. Year Established: 1877. Pub. Frequency: w. (Thu.) Page Size: tabloid. Subscrip. Rate: $.75 newsstand/cover; $23/yr in county; $43/yr out of county. Adv. Rate: page $440 Circulation: 4,710 per issue (paid). **Owner(s):** Anton Community Newspapers, See address and contact information above. **Management:** Cary Seaman, General Manager. Angela S.Anton, Publisher. Andrea Bernstein, Advertising. Harriet Heffernan, Advertising Manager. Peter Nyquist, Circulation Director. Paul Scheuer, Art Director. **Editorial:** Joe Scotchie, Editor.

SYOSSET JERICHO TRIBUNE. 132 E. Second St., Mineola, NY 11501-3522. Telephone: 516-747-8282. FAX: 516-742-5867. E-MAIL: syosserjerichotribune@anton.com. URL: http://www.antonnews.com. Pub. Frequency: w. (Fri.) Page Size: tabloid. Subscrip. Rate: $.75 newsstand/cover; $20/yr in county; $40/yr out of county. Adv. Rate: page $440 Circulation: 4,224 per issue (paid). **Owner(s):** Anton Community Newspapers, See address and contact information above. **Management:** Cary Seaman, General Manager. Angela S. Anton, Publisher. Peter Nyquist, Circulation Director. Paul Scheuer, Art Director. **Editorial:** Denise Nash, Editor.

THREE VILLAGE TIMES. 132 E. Second St., Mineola, NY 11501-3522. Telephone: 516-747-8282. FAX: 516-742-5867. E-MAIL: threevillagetimes@anton.com. URL: http://www.antonnews.com. Year Established: 1927. Pub. Frequency: w. (Fri.) Page Size: tabloid. Subscrip. Rate: $.75 newsstand/cover; $20/yr in county; $40/yr out of county. Circulation: 1,830 per issue (paid). **Owner(s):** Anton Community Newspapers, 132 E. Second St., Mineola, NY 11501. Telephone: 516-747-8282. FAX: 516-742-5861. **Management:** Cary Seaman, General Manager. Angela S. Anton, Publisher. Harriet Heffernan, Advertising Manager. Peter Nyquist, Circulation Director. Paul Scheuer, Art Director. **Editorial:** Joe Rizza, Executive Editor.

WESTBURY TIMES. 132 E. Second St., Mineola, NY 11501-3522. Telephone: 516-747-8282. FAX: 516-742-5867. E-MAIL: westburytimes@anton.com. URL: http://www.antonnews.com. Mailing Address: PO Box 1578, Mineola, NY 11501. Year Established: 1907. Pub. Frequency: w. (Thu.) Page Size: tabloid. Subscrip. Rate: $.75 newsstand/cover; $20/yr in county; $40/yr out of county. Adv. Rate: page $290 Freelance Pay: $20-$30/article. Circulation: 3,370 per issue (paid). **Owner(s):** Anton Community Newspapers, See address and contact information above. **Management:** Cary Seaman, General Manager. Angela S. Anton, Publisher. Harriet Heffernan, Advertising Director. Thomas McGee, Advertising Manager. Peter Nyquist, Circulation Director. Paul Scheuer, Art Director. **Editorial:** Victoria Caruso, Editor.

MONROE

PHOTO NEWS. 45 Gilbert St., Monroe, NY 10950. Telephone: 845-782-4000. FAX: 845-782-1711. E-MAIL: editor.pn@strausnews.com. Year Established: 1967. Pub. Frequency: w. (Fri.) Page Size: tabloid.Subscrip. Rate: $35/yr; $65 for 2 yrs. Circulation: 9,900 per issue (paid). **Owner(s):** Straus Communications, See address and contact information above. **Management:** Jeanne Straus, President. Bob Quinn, Publisher. R. Peter Straus, Chairman of the Board. **Editorial:** Bob Quinn, Editor-in-Chief.

WARWICK ADVERTISER, THE. 45 Gilbert St., Monroe, NY 10950. Telephone: 845-782-4000. FAX: 845-782-1711. Mailing Address: PO Box 190, Warwick, NY 10990. Year Established: 1866. Pub. Frequency: w. (Fri.) Page Size: tabloid. Subscrip. Rate: $35/yr. Circulation: 8,200 per issue (paid and free). **Owner(s):** Straus Communications, See address and contact information above. **Management:** Jeanne Straus, President. Bob Quinn, Publisher. R. Peter Straus, Chairman of the Board. **Editorial:** Bob Quinn, Editor-in-Chief. R. Peter Straus, Editorial Advisor.

MORAVIA

MORAVIA REPUBLICAN REGISTER. 6 Central St., Moravia, NY 13118-0591. Telephone: 315-497-1551. Year Established: 1863. Pub. Frequency: w. (Wed.) Page Size: tabloid. Subscrip. Rate: $.75 newsstand/cover; $23.50/yr in county. Adv. Rate: col. inch $5.25 Circulation: 2,500 per issue (paid). **Owner(s):** Community Newspapers, See address and contact information above. **Management:** Bernard McGuerty III, Publisher. **Editorial:** Bernard McGuerty III, Editor.

SOUTHERN CAYUGA TRIBUNE. 6 Central St., Moravia, NY 13118-0591. Telephone: 315-497-1551. Pub. Frequency: w. (Wed.) Page Size: tabloid. Subscrip. Rate: $.75 newsstand/cover; $23.50/yr in county. Adv. Rate: col. inch $5.25 Circulation: 2,500 per issue (paid). **Owner(s):** Community Newspapers, See address and contact information above. **Management:** Bernard McGuerty III, Publisher. **Editorial:** Bernard McGuerty III, Editor.

MT. KISCO

PATENT TRADER. ISSN 0746-1836
185 Kisco Ave., Mt. Kisco, NY 10549. Telephone: 914-666-6924. FAX: 914-666-6018. Year Established: 1956. Pub. Frequency: w. (Thur.) Page Size: broadsheet. Subscrip. Rate: $.75 newsstand/cover; $45.24/yr. **Wire Service(s):** AP. Circulation: 16,000 per issue (paid). **Owner(s):** Gannett Suburban Newspapers, One Gannett Dr., White Plains, NY 10604. Telephone: 914-694-5000. **Editorial:** Tracy Trinciotta, Editor. Joe Lombardi, Sports.

NANUET

ROCKLAND COUNTY TIMES. 119 Main St., 2nd Fl., Nanuet, NY 10954-2882. Telephone: 845-627-1414. FAX: 845-627-1411. E-MAIL: letters@rocklandcountytimes.com. URL: http://www.rocklandtimes.com. Year Established: 1888. Pub. Frequency: w. (Thu.) Page Size: broadsheet. Subscrip. Rate: $.50 newsstand/cover; $25/yr in county. Adv. Rate: col. inch $14.71 Circulation: 18,000 per issue (paid). **Owner(s):** Citizen Publishing Corp., See address and contact information above. **Management:** Armand Miele, Publisher. Marge Formato, Circulation Manager. **Editorial:** Dan Stack, Managing Editor. Robert P. Knight, City Editor.

NAPLES

NAPLES RECORD, THE. 188 S. Main St., Naples, NY 14512-0370. Telephone: 585-374-5260. FAX: 585-374-8590. E-MAIL: news@Naplesrecord.com. Mailing Address: PO Box 370, Naples, NY 14512-0370. Year Established: 1870. Pub. Frequency: w. (Wed.) Page Size: standard. Subscrip. Rate: $.75 newsstand/cover; $30/yr in state; $36/yr out of state. Adv. Rate: col. inch $7.50 Circulation: 1,800 per issue (paid). **Owner(s):** Michael C. Fowler, PO Box 370, Naples, NY 14512. **Management:** Mike Fowler, Publisher. **Editorial:** Mike Fowler, Editor. Margaret Fowler, Production Manager.

NARROWSBURG

RIVER REPORTER, THE. PO Box 150, Narrowsburg, NY 12764. Telephone: 845-252-7414. FAX: 845-252-3298. E-MAIL: editor@riverreporter.com. URL: http://www.riverreporter.com. Year Established: 1975. Pub. Frequency: w. (Thu.) Page Size: tabloid. Subscrip. Rate: $.75 newsstand/cover; $21 for 6 mos.; $30/yr. Adv. Rate: col. inch $7 Freelance Pay: $10-$30/article. Circulation: 4,300 per issue (paid). **Owner(s):** Stuart Communications, Inc., See address and contact information above. **Management:** Laurie Stuart, General Manager. Danielle Gaebel, Sales Manager. **Editorial:** Connie Kern, Production Manager. Dave Hulse, News Editor.

NESCONSET

BROOKHAVEN REVIEW. 120 Lake Ave S. Ste.22, Nesconset, NY 11767. Telephone: 631-265-3500. FAX: 631-265-3504. E-MAIL: messenger127e@aol.com. Mailing Address: PO Box 925, Smithtown, NY 11787. Year Established: 1888. Pub. Frequency: w. (Thu.) Page Size: tabloid. Subscrip. Rate: $.75 newsstand/cover; $21.50/yr mailed in county; $27/yr mailed out of county. Circulation: 3,500 per issue (paid). **Owner(s):** Sal DiPeri & Phillip L. Sciarillo, See address and contact information above. **Management:** Philip Sciarillo, Publisher. **Editorial:** Philip Sciarillo, Managing Editor.

MEDFORD NEWS. 120 Lake Ave S. Ste.22, Nesconset, NY 11767. Telephone: 631-265-3500. FAX: 631-265-3504. Mailing Address: PO Box 925, Smithtown, NY 11787. Year Established: 1912. Pub. Frequency: w. (Thu.) Page Size: tabloid. Subscrip. Rate: $.75 newsstand/cover; $21.50/yr in county; $27/yr out of county. Circulation: 10,000 per issue (paid). **Owner(s):** Sal DiPeri & Phillip L. Sciarillo, See address and contact information above. **Management:** Philip Sciarillo, Publisher. **Editorial:** Philip Sciarillo, Editor-in-Chief.

RONKONKOMA REVIEW. 120 Lake Ave S. Ste.22, Nesconset, NY 11767. Telephone: 631-265-3500. FAX: 631-265-3504. E-MAIL: messenger127e@aol.com. Mailing Address: PO Box 925, Smithtown, NY 11787. Year Established: 1959. Pub. Frequency: w. (Thu.) Page Size: tabloid. Subscrip. Rate: $.75 newsstand/cover; $21.50/yr in county; $27/yr out of county. Circulation: 3,500 per issue (paid). **Owner(s):** Sal DiPeri & Phillip L. Sciarillo, See address and contact information above. **Management:** Sal DiPeri, President. Philip Sciarillo, Publisher. **Editorial:** Philip Sciarillo, Editor.

SMITHTOWN MESSENGER. 120 Lake Ave S. Ste.22, Nesconset, NY 11767. Telephone: 631-265-3500. FAX: 631-265-3504. E-MAIL: messenger127e@aol.com. Mailing Address: PO Box 925, Smithtown, NY 11787. Year Established: 1887. Pub. Frequency: w. (Thu.) Page Size: tabloid. Subscrip. Rate: $.75 newsstand/cover; $21.50/yr in county; $27/yr out of county. Freelance Pay: $15-$20/article. Circulation: 10,000 per issue (paid). **Owner(s):** Sal DiPeri & Phillip L. Sciarillo, See address and contact information above. **Management:** Philip Sciarillo, Publisher. **Editorial:** Philip Sciarillo, Editor-in-Chief.

NEW ROCHELLE

REVIEW PRESS. 92 North Ave., New Rochelle, NY 10801-7413. Telephone: 914-637-2203. FAX: 914-637-2210. Year Established: 1902. Pub. Frequency: w. (Thu.) Page Size: broadsheet. Subscrip. Rate: $.25 newsstand/cover; $26/yr mailed. Circulation: 2,200 per issue (paid). **Owner(s):** Gannett Company, Inc., 7950 Jones Branch Dr., McLean, VA 22107-0001. Telephone: 703-854-6000. **Management:** Gary Shurlock, President. **Editorial:** Gerald McKinstry, Editor.

NEW YORK

BANNER (NEW YORK), THE. 620 8th Ave, New York, NY 10018. Telephone: 212-556-1234. FAX: 212-556-7614. URL: http://www.coulterpress.com. Mailing Address: PO Box 306, West Boylston, MA 01583-0306. Pub. Frequency: w. (Thu.) Page Size: tabloid. Subscrip. Rate: $.75 newsstand/cover; $25/yr. Adv. Rate: col. inch $7.65 Circulation: 2,100 per issue (paid). **Owner(s):** New York Times Company, See address and contact information above. **Management:** Gary Hutner, Publisher. Ron Chapdelaine, Advertising Manager. Donna Traylor, Classified Adv. Mgr.. **Editorial:** Jan Gottesman, Managing Editor.

CHELSEA CLINTON NEWS. 63 W 38th St, Ste 206, New York, NY 10018. Telephone: 212-268-8600. FAX: 212-268-9049. URL: http://www.manhattanmedia.com/chelsea_westsider.php. Year Established: 1939. Pub. Frequency: w. (Wed.) Page Size: tabloid Subscrip. Rate: $24/yr Circulation: 5,000 per issue (paid). **Owner(s):** Manhattan Media, LLC, See address and contact information above.

DOWNTOWN EXPRESS. 145 6th Ave, New York, NY 10013. Telephone: 646-452-2496. FAX: 212-229-2790. E-MAIL: francescoregini@gmail.com. URL: http://www.downtownexpress.com. Year Established: 1986. Pub. Frequency: w. (Thu.) Page Size: tabloid Circulation: 40,000 per issue (free). Owner(s): Community Media LLC, See address and contact information above. Management: John Sutter, Publisher. Francesco Regini, Advertising Director. Editorial: John Sutter, Editor. Josh Rogers, Associate Editor.

ITEM (NORTHBORO), THE. 620 8th Ave, New York, NY 10018. Telephone: 212-556-1234. FAX: 212-556-7614. E-MAIL: clintonitem@yahoo.com. URL: http://www.coulterpress.com. Year Established: 1893. Pub. Frequency: s-w. (Tue. & Fri.) Page Size: broadsheet. Subscrip. Rate: $.75 newsstand/cover; $27/yr. Adv. Rate: col. inch $10.40 Circulation: 5,700 per issue (paid). Owner(s): New York Times Company, See address and contact information above. Management: Gary Hutner, Publisher. Ron Chapdelaine, Advertising. Editorial: Jan Gottesman, Managing Editor.

NEW YORK GOOD NEWS. 101 St Marks Pl, New York, NY 10009. Year Established: 1966. Pub. Frequency: irreg. Page Size: standard. Subscrip. Rate: $10/yr. Owner(s): Planet Capital, See address and contact information above. Management: Steve Kraus, Publisher. Editorial: Steve Kraus, Editor.

NEW YORK OBSERVER.   ISSN 1052-2948
915 Broadway, New York, NY 10021. FAX: 212-980-2087. E-MAIL: comments@observer.com. URL: http://www.observer.com. Year Established: 1987. Pub. Frequency: w. (49 issues) Page Size: broadsheet. Subscrip. Rate: $32/yr. Circulation: 51,000. Owner(s): New York Observer Co., Inc., See address and contact information above. Management: Brian Kempner, President. Arthur L Carter, Publisher. Barry Lewis, Vice President. Betty Shaw Lederman, Associate Publisher. Editorial: Peter Kaplan, Editor. Peter Stevenson, Executive Editor. Tom McGeveran, Managing Editor. Terry Golway, City Editor.

NEW YORK PRESS.   ISSN 1538-1412
63 W 38th St, Ste 206, New York, NY 10018. Telephone: 212-268-8600. FAX: 212-268-9049. URL: http://nypress.com. Year Established: 1988. Pub. Frequency: w. (Wed.) Page Size: tabloid. Subscrip. Rate: $105/yr. Circulation: 115,000 per issue (paid and free). Owner(s): Manhattan Media, LLC, See address and contact information above.

NEW YORK TIMES LARGE PRINT WEEKLY. 620 8th Ave, New York, NY 10018. Telephone: 212-556-1234. FAX: 212-556-7614. URL: http://www.nytimes.com. Year Established: 1967. Pub. Frequency: w. (Mon.) Page Size: tabloid. Subscrip. Rate: $85.80/yr domestic; $161.20/yr in Canada; $1.65/wk.. Circulation: 8,000 per issue. Owner(s): New York Times Company, See address and contact information above. Management: Dan Barber, Advertising. Editorial: Tom Brady, Editor.

OUR TOWN EAST SIDE. 63 W 38th St, Ste 206, New York, NY 10018. Telephone: 212-268-8600. FAX: 212-268-9049. URL: http://ourtownny.com Year Established: 1970. Pub. Frequency: w. (Thu.) Page Size: tabloid Subscrip. Rate: $75/yr Circulation: 55,000 per issue (free). Owner(s): Manhattan Media, LLC, See address and contact information above.

PETALUMA ARGUS-COURIER. 620 8th Ave, New York, NY 10018. Telephone: 212-556-1234. FAX: 212-556-7614. E-MAIL: argus@arguscourier.com. URL: http://www.arguscourier.com. Mailing Address: PO Box 1091, Petaluma, CA 94953. Year Established: 1855. Pub. Frequency: w. (Wed.) Page Size: broadsheet. Subscrip. Rate: $.50 newsstand/cover; $29.50/yr mailed in county; $37.50/yr out of county. Wire Service(s): AP. Circulation: 10,000 per issue (paid). Owner(s): New York Times Company, See address and contact information above. Management: John Burns, Publisher. Kathleen Crayne, Advertising. Editorial: Chris Samson, Managing Editor.

RECORD (NORTHBORO), THE. 620 8th Ave, New York, NY 10018. Telephone: 212-556-1234. FAX: 212-556-7614. URL: http://www.coulterpress.com. Pub. Frequency: w. (Thu.) Page Size: tabloid Circulation: 27,400 per issue (free). Owner(s): New York Times Company, See address and contact information above. Management: Gary Hutner, Publisher. Ron Chapdelaine, Advertising Manager. Teresa Tierney, Circulation Manager. Rose Demers, Classified Adv. Mgr.. Editorial: Amy Renczkowski, Editor.

VILLAGE VOICE, THE.   ISSN 0042-6180
36 Cooper Sq, New York, NY 10003. E-MAIL: editor@villagevoice.com. URL: http://www.villagevoice.com/. Year Established: 1955. Pub. Frequency: w. Page Size: tabloid. Subscrip. Rate: $99/yr mailed domestic; $142/yr mailed foreign; $2.50 newsstand/cover outside New York City. Wire Service(s): AP. Circulation: 253,000. Owner(s): Village Voice Media, Inc., See address and contact information above. Management: Martin Jorgensen, General Manager. Arthur Howe, President. Judy Miszner, Publisher. George Troyano, Advertising. Robert Kasner, Circulation Director. Randolph Schmidt, Classified Adv. Mgr.. Minh Uong, Art Director. Editorial: Donald Forst, Editor-in-Chief. Laura Conway, Executive Editor. Doug Simmons, Managing Editor. Ted Keller, Creative Director. Alex Press, Copy Chief. Staci Schwartz, Photo Editor.

VILLAGER (NEW YORK).   ISSN 0042-6202
145 6th Ave, New York, NY 10013. Telephone: 646-452-2496. FAX: 212-229-2790. URL: http://www.thevillager.com. Year Established: 1933. Pub. Frequency: w. (Wed.) Page Size: tabloid. Subscrip. Rate: $29/yr. Freelance Pay: $0.50/word. Circulation: 15,000. Owner(s): Community Media LLC, See address and contact information above. Management: John Sutter, Publisher. Francesco Regini, Advertising Director. David Jaffe, Circulation Manager. Editorial: John Sutter, Editor. Lincoln Anderson, Associate Editor.10016 see NATIONAL NEWSPAPERS

WEST SIDE SPIRIT.   ISSN 0886-0785
63 W 38th St, Ste 206, New York, NY 10018. Telephone: 212-268-8600. FAX: 212-268-9049. URL: http://westsidespirit.com. Year Established: 1989. Pub. Frequency: w. Page Size: standard. Subscrip. Rate: $75/yr. Circulation: 60,000. Owner(s): Manhattan Media, LLC, See address and contact information above.

WESTSIDER, THE. 63 W 38th St, Ste 206, New York, NY 10018. Telephone: 212-268-8600. FAX: 212-268-9049. URL: http://www.manhattanmedia.com/chelsea_westsider.php. Year Established: 1973. Pub. Frequency: w. (Thu.) Page Size: tabloid. Subscrip. Rate: $24/yr. Freelance Pay: $0.77/column-inch. Circulation: 15,000 per issue (paid and free). Owner(s): Manhattan Media, LLC, See address and contact information above.

NEWARK

LYONS CLYDE SAVANNAH SHOPPING. 613 S. Main St., Newark, NY 14513. Telephone: 315-331-6956. FAX: 315-331-1053. E-MAIL: editor@cgazette.com. URL: http://www.cgazette.com. Pub. Frequency: w. (Wed.) Page Size: broadsheet Circulation: 6,700 per issue (free). Owner(s): Ad Group, Inc., See address and contact information above. Management: John H. VanDusen, Publisher. Jim O'Connell, Advertising. Editorial: Sandra Marcano, Editor.

NEWARK PENNYSAVER. 613 S. Main St., Newark, NY 14513. Telephone: 315-331-6956. FAX: 315-331-1053. E-MAIL: editor@cgazette.com. URL: http://www.cgazette.com. Pub. Frequency: w. (Tue) Page Size: broadsheet Circulation: 7,200 per issue (free). Owner(s): Ad Group, Inc., See address and contact information above. Management: John H. VanDusen, Publisher. Jim O'Connell, Advertising. Editorial: Sandra Marcano, Editor.

NORTH MASSAPEQUA

BELLMORE-MERRICK OBSERVER. 508 Atlanta Ave., North Massapequa, NY 11758. Telephone: 516-679-9888. FAX: 516-731-0338. Year Established: 1949. Pub. Frequency: w. (Thu.) Page Size: tabloid. Subscrip. Rate: $10/yr home delivery in county; $12/yr mailed out of county. Circulation: 5,000 per issue (paid). Owner(s): Observer Newspapers, Inc., See address and contact information above. Management: Jackson B. Pokress, Publisher. Editorial: Jackson B. Pokress, Editor.

NORTH TONAWANDA

KENMORE RECORD-ADVERTISER. 435 River Rd., North Tonawanda, NY 14120. Telephone: 716-693-1000. FAX: 716-693-8573. URL: http://www.tonawanda-news.com. Mailing Address: PO Box 668, North Tonawanda, NY 14120-0668. Year Established: 1914. Pub. Frequency: w. (Fri.) Page Size: broadsheet. Wire Service(s): AP, GNS. Circulation: 33,400 per issue (free). Owner(s): Community Newspaper Holdings, Inc., 3500 Colonnade Pkwy., Ste. 600, Birmingham, AL 35243. Telephone: 205-298-7100. FAX: 205-298-7101. Management: Steve Hall, Publisher. Matt Green, Advertising Manager. AndreeRenee Simpson, Classified Adv. Mgr.. Editorial: Carlene Peterson, Managing Editor.

NORTHPORT

OBSERVER (NORTHPORT), THE. 179 Main St., Northport, NY 11768. Telephone: 631-261-6124. FAX: 631-265-6237. Mailing Address: PO Box 60, Northport, NY 11768. Year Established: 1922. Pub. Frequency: w. (Thu.) Page Size: tabloid.Subscrip. Rate: $.75 newsstand/cover; $23/yr Circulation: 10,000 per issue (paid). Owner(s): North Shore News Group, One Brookside Dr., Smithtown, NY 11787. Telephone: 631-265-2100. Management: Bernard Paley, Publisher. Jennifer Paley, Associate Publisher. Editorial: David Ambro, Editor.

ORCHARD PARK

SOUTHTOWNS CITIZEN. 6519 E. Quaker St., Orchard Park, NY 14127. Telephone: 716-662-0001. FAX: 716-667-3001. E-MAIL: stcitizen@aol.com. Year Established: 1932. Pub. Frequency: w. (Sat.) Page Size: tabloid. Subscrip. Rate: $1 newsstand/cover; $33/yr local; $28/yr local to senior citizens. Adv. Rate: col. inch $12.95 Circulation: 6,500 per issue (paid). Owner(s): Coleman Communications Corp., See address and contact information above. Management: Christopher Coleman, Publisher. Raymond M. Huss, Advertising Director. Editorial: John Hakes, Editor.

OSWEGO

PALLADIUM PENNYSAVER. 140 W. First St., Oswego, NY 13126. Telephone: 315-343-3800. FAX: 315-343-0273. Pub. Frequency: w. (Sat.) Page Size: tabloid Circulation: 6,300 per issue (free). Owner(s): GateHouse Media, Inc, 350 WillowBrook Office Park, Fairport, NY 14450. Telephone: 585-598-0030. FAX: 585-248-2631. Management: Paul Scott, Publisher. Michael Russo, Advertising Manager. Toby Clawson, Circulation Manager.

OVID

REVEILLE/BETWEEN THE LAKES. 6946 Rte. 96A, Ovid, NY 14521. Telephone: 607-869-5344. FAX: 607-869-9208. E-MAIL: revblt@rochester.rr.com. Mailing Address: PO Box 557, Seneca Falls, NY 13148-0557. Year Established: 1855. Pub. Frequency: w. (Thu.) Page Size: tabloid. Subscrip. Rate: $.50 newsstand/cover; $24.95/yr in county; $26.95/yr out of county. Circulation: 2,313 per issue (paid). Owner(s): Reveille Publishing Co., Inc., PO Box 557, Seneca Falls, NY 13148. Telephone: 607-869-5344. FAX: 607-869-9208. Management: Joe Siccardi, Publisher.

OWEGO

OWEGO PENNYSAVER. 181 Front St., Owego, NY 13827. Telephone: 607-687-2434. FAX: 607-687-2931. E-MAIL: opennysaver@stny.rr.com. URL: http://www.owegopennysaver.com. Mailing Address: PO Box 149, Owego, NY 13827-0149. Pub. Frequency: w. (Sun.) Page Size: standard Circulation: 22,000 per issue (free). Owner(s): Times-Shamrock Communications, 149 Penn Ave., Scranton, PA 18503. Management: James E. Towner, Publisher. Gail Williams, Advertising Director. Ken Chaffee, Circulation Director. Editorial: Wendy Post, Editor.

OYSTER BAY

OYSTER BAY GUARDIAN. PO Box 28, Oyster Bay, NY 11771. Telephone: 516-922-4215. FAX: 516-922-4227. Year Established: 1899. Pub. Frequency: w. (Fri.) Page Size: broadsheet. Subscrip. Rate: $.60 newsstand/cover; $22/yr local; $40 for 2 yrs. local; $27/yr mailed out of state; $18/yr local to senior citizens. Circulation: 30,000 per issue (paid). Owner(s): Helen Dolan, See address and contact information above. Management: Susanna Petersen, Advertising Manager. Editorial: David Criblez, Editor.

PALMYRA

COURIER-JOURNAL. 612 E. Main St., Palmyra, NY 14522. Telephone: 315-597-6655. FAX: 315-597-6947. E-MAIL: courierjournal@adnetcommunitynews.com. Year Established: 1838. Pub. Frequency: w. (Wed.) Page Size: tabloid. Subscrip. Rate: $.50 newsstand/cover; $18.50/yr local area. Circulation: 2,700 per issue (paid). Owner(s): AdNet Community News, 2495 Brickyard Rd., Canandaigua, NY 14424. Telephone: 716-394-4510. Management: Lawrence Lucieer, Publisher. Justin Williams, Circulation Manager. Thomas L. Klemann, Sales Manager. Editorial: Tracy Curry, Editor.

PATCHOGUE

LONG ISLAND ADVANCE. 20 Medford Ave., Patchogue, NY 11772-0780. Telephone: 631-475-1000. FAX: 631-475-1565. E-MAIL: advletters@optonline.net. URL: http://www.longislandadvance.com. Mailing Address: PO Box 780, Patchogue, NY 11772-0780. Year Established: 1871. Pub. Frequency: w. (Thu.) Page Size: tabloid.Subscrip. Rate: $1 newsstand/cover; $30/yr Circulation: 13,000 per issue (paid). Owner(s): John T. Tuthill, III, See address and contact information above. Management: Joanne La Barca, General Manager. John T. Tuthill III, Publisher. Terry Tuthill, Advertising Manager. Editorial: Mark Nolan, Editor.

PAWLING

PAWLING NEWS CHRONICLE.   ISSN 0747-2188
3 Memorial Ave., Pawling, NY 12564. Telephone: 845-677-8241. FAX: 845-677-6337. URL: http://www.midhudsoncentral.com. Year Established: 1870. Pub. Frequency: w. (Thu.) Page Size: tabloid. Subscrip. Rate: $.75 newsstand/cover; $37/yr mailed in state; $42/yr mailed out of state. Circulation: 2,357 per issue (paid). Owner(s): Journal Register Co., 50 W State St, 12th Fl, Trenton, NJ 08608. Telephone: 609-396-2200. FAX: 609-396-2292. Management: Ira Fusfeld, Publisher. Jeff Ohlbaum, Advertising Director. Larry Priest, Circulation Director. Mary Bradford, Classified Adv. Mgr.. Editorial: Matt Rohr, Editor. Ann Gibbons, Executive Editor.

PELHAM

TRI-STATE MEDIA GROUP. 510 5th Ave, Pelham, NY 10803. E-MAIL: fregini@tsmediagroup.com. URL: http://www.tristatemediagroup.com. Mailing Address: PO Box 589, Pelham, NY 10803-0589. Year Established: 1985. Pub. Frequency: w. (Wed.) Page Size: tabloid. Circulation: 388,210 per issue (controlled and free). **Owner(s):** Pennysaver Group, Inc., See address and contact information above. **Management:** Herb Solomon, Publisher. Frank Regini, Advertising Director. Fred Libowitz, Circulation Manager. Cheryl Russo, Classified Adv. Mgr..

PENN YAN

CHRONICLE AD-VISER. 138 Main St., Penn Yan, NY 14527-1299. Telephone: 315-536-4422. FAX: 315-536-0682. Year Established: 1935. Pub. Frequency: w. (Sun.) Page Size: standard.Adv. Rate: col. inch $12.97 Circulation: 5,500 per issue (free). **Owner(s):** GateHouse Media, Inc, 350 WillowBrook Office Park, Fairport, NY 14450. Telephone: 585-598-0030. FAX: 585-248-2631. **Management:** Karen Morris, Publisher. Laurie Nichiporuk, Advertising. Candy Scutt, Advertising Manager. **Editorial:** Gwen Chamberlain, Editor.

CHRONICLE-EXPRESS, THE. 138 Main St., Penn Yan, NY 14527-1299. Telephone: 315-536-4422. FAX: 315-536-0682. E-MAIL: ChronicleKaren@rochester.rr.com. Year Established: 1824. Pub. Frequency: w. (Wed.) Page Size: broadsheet. Subscrip. Rate: $.75 newsstand/cover; $33/yr in county. Adv. Rate: col. inch $10 Circulation: 4,550 per issue (paid). **Owner(s):** GateHouse Media, Inc, 350 WillowBrook Office Park, Fairport, NY 14450. Telephone: 585-598-0030. FAX: 585-248-2631. **Management:** Karen Morris, Publisher. Candy Scutt, Advertising Manager. **Editorial:** Gwen Chamberlain, Editor.

PORT CHESTER

WESTMORE NEWS. 38 Broad St., Port Chester, NY 10573-4197. Telephone: 914-939-6864. FAX: 914-939-6877. E-MAIL: editor@westmorenews.com. URL: http://www.westmorenews.com. Year Established: 1964. Pub. Frequency: w. (Fri.) Page Size: tabloid. Subscrip. Rate: $.75 newsstand/cover; $37/yr. Adv. Rate: col. inch $13 Circulation: 3,500 per issue (paid). **Owner(s):** Westmore News, Inc., 38 Broad St., Port Chester, NY 10573. Telephone: 914-939-6864. FAX: 914-939-6877. **Management:** Richard Abel, Publisher. **Editorial:** Jananne Abel, Editor.

PORT JEFFERSON STATION

YANKEE TRADER. 4747 Nesconset Hwy., Unit 7, Port Jefferson Station, NY 11776-2866. Telephone: 631-331-3300. FAX: 631-207-4907. Year Established: 1966. Pub. Frequency: w. (Wed.) Page Size: tabloid Circulation: 280,000 per issue (free). **Owner(s):** Tribune Company, 435 N Michigan Ave, Chicago, IL 60601. Telephone: 312.222.9100. **Management:** Louis Sito, Advertising Director. Bill Pratt, Circulation Manager. **Editorial:** Barbara Fisher, Editor.

PORT JERVIS

GAZETTE (PORT JERVIS), THE. 158 Pike St., Port Jervis, NY 12771. Telephone: 845-858-2123. FAX: 845-858-8484. URL: http://www.recordonline.com. Year Established: 1850. Pub. Frequency: w. (Fri.) Page Size: tabloid. Subscrip. Rate: $.25 newsstand/cover; $18.50/yr. Circulation: 9,500 per issue (paid and free). **Owner(s):** Ottaway Newspapers, Inc., PO Box 401, Campbell Hall, NY 10916. Telephone: 914-294-8181. **Management:** Joe A. Vanderhoof, Publisher. Phil Hudson, Circulation Manager. **Editorial:** Tom Reek, Editor.

POUND RIDGE

COUNTRY SHOPPER. 40 Westchester Ave., Pound Ridge, NY 10576. Telephone: 914-764-4678. FAX: 914-764-4662. Mailing Address: PO Box 190, Pound Ridge, NY 10576. Pub. Frequency: w. (Thu.) Page Size: tabloid Circulation: 30,000 per issue (free). **Owner(s):** Journal Community Publishing Group, 600 Industrial Dr., PO Box 609, Waupaca, WI 54981. Telephone: 715-258-4896. **Management:** Ezra Karp, General Manager. **Editorial:** Lillian Petruccione, Editor.

PULASKI

SALMON RIVER NEWS. One Broad St., Pulaski, NY 13142. Telephone: 315-298-6517. FAX: 315-963-4087. E-MAIL: ocweeklies@claymail. Year Established: 1973. Pub. Frequency: w. (Fri..) Page Size: tabloid.Subscrip. Rate: $.50 newsstand/cover; $15/yr Circulation: 8,000 per issue (paid). **Owner(s):** Mark Backus, 80 N Jefferson St, Mexico, NY 13114. Telephone: 315-963-7813. FAX: 315-963-4087. **Management:** Mark Backus, Publisher. **Editorial:** Mary Coon, Editor. Roseann Parsons, Managing Editor.

RAVENA

GREENVILLE LOCAL. 164 Main St., Ravena, NY 12143-0370. Telephone: 518-756-2030. E-MAIL: nherald@brickrow.net. Year Established: 1932. Pub. Frequency: w. (Thu.) Page Size: tabloid. Subscrip. Rate: $.75 newsstand/cover; $27/yr local; $31/yr out of area. Freelance Pay: $45/story. Circulation: 1,150 per issue (paid). **Owner(s):** Bleezarde Publishing, Inc., See address and contact information above. **Management:** Richard G. Bleezarde, Publisher. **Editorial:** Richard G. Bleezarde, Editor.

RAVENA NEWS HERALD. 164 Main St., Ravena, NY 12143-0370. Telephone: 518-756-2030. FAX: 518-756-8555. E-MAIL: nherald@brickrow.net. Mailing Address: PO Box 370, Ravena, NY 12143-0370. Year Established: 1874. Pub. Frequency: w. (Thu.) Page Size: tabloid. Subscrip. Rate: $.75 newsstand/cover; $34/yr in Greene & Albany cys.; $38/yr mailed elsewhere. Freelance Pay: $50/story. Circulation: 3,200 per issue (paid). **Owner(s):** Bleezarde Publishing, Inc., 164 Main St., Ravena, NY 12143-0307. Telephone: 518-756-2030. FAX: 518-756-8555. **Management:** Richard G. Bleezarde, Publisher. **Editorial:** Richard G. Bleezarde, Editor.

RED CREEK

POST-HERALD. ISSN 1081-8405
6784 Main St., Red Creek, NY 13143. Telephone: 315-754-6229. FAX: 315-754-6431. E-MAIL: editor@wayuga.com. URL: http://www.wayuga.com. Mailing Address: PO Box 199, Red Creek, NY 13143-0199. Year Established: 1894. Pub. Frequency: w. (Wed.) Page Size: tabloid. Subscrip. Rate: $1 newsstand/cover; $20/yr mailed local; $30/yr mailed out of state. Adv. Rate: col. inch $4.63 Circulation: 2,900 per issue (paid). **Owner(s):** Angelo G. Palermo, See address and contact information above. **Management:** Christopher Palermo, President. Chuck Palermo, Advertising Manager. **Editorial:** Louise Hoffman-Broach, Editor.

REGO PARK

QUEENS CHRONICLE. 62-33 Woodhaven Blvd., Rego Park, NY 11374. Telephone: 718-205-8000. FAX: 718-205-0150. E-MAIL: mailbox@qchron.com. URL: http://www.queenschronicle.com. Mailing Address: PO Box 74-7769, Rego Park, NY 11374-7769. Year Established: 1979. Pub. Frequency: w. (Thu.) Page Size: tabloid. Subscrip. Rate: $25/yr. Adv. Rate: page $20.50 Freelance Pay: $35/article. Circulation: 160,000 per issue (paid and free). **Owner(s):** Mark I Publications, Inc., 66-22 Fleet St., Forest Hills, NY 11375. Telephone: 718-261-4341. **Management:** Ray Sito, General Manager. Mark Weidler, President. Lester Cordero, Circulation Manager. Jan Schulman, Art Director. **Editorial:** Liz Rhoades, Managing Editor.

RHINEBECK

GAZETTE ADVERTISER, THE. 7 Livingston St., Rhinebeck, NY 12572-1505. Telephone: 845-876-3033. FAX: 845-876-2361. URL: http://www.gazetteadvertiser.com. Year Established: 1846. Pub. Frequency: w. (Thu.) Page Size: broadsheet. Subscrip. Rate: $.75 newsstand/cover; $36/yr mailed in state; $42/yr mailed out of state; $32/yr mailed in state to senior citizens; $38/yr mailed out of state to senior citizens. Circulation: 5,500 per issue (paid). **Owner(s):** Journal Register Co., 50 W State St, 12th Fl, Trenton, NJ 08608. Telephone: 609-396-2200. FAX: 609-396-2292. **Management:** Ira Fusfeld, Publisher. Jeff Ohlbaum, Advertising Director. Larry Priest, Circulation Director. Mary Bradford, Classified Adv. Mgr.. **Editorial:** Christopher Lennon, Editor. Ann Gibbons, Executive Editor.

HYDE PARK TOWNSMAN. 7 Livingston St., Rhinebeck, NY 12572-1505. Telephone: 845-876-3033. FAX: 845-876-2361. E-MAIL: tacnews@aol.com. URL: http://www.midhudsoncentral.com. Mailing Address: PO Box 316, Millbrook, NY 12545. Year Established: 1959. Pub. Frequency: w. (Thu.) Page Size: broadsheet. Subscrip. Rate: $.75 newsstand/cover; $37/yr mailed in state; $42/yr mailed out of state. Circulation: 2,000 per issue (paid). **Owner(s):** Journal Register Co., 50 W. State St., 12th Fl., Trenton, NJ 08608-1298. **Management:** Ira Fusfeld, Publisher. Jeff Ohlbaum, Advertising Director. Larry Priest, Circulation Director. Mary Bradford, Classified Adv. Mgr.. **Editorial:** Christopher Lennon, Editor. Ann Gibbons, Executive Editor.

REGISTER-HERALD (PINE PLAINS), THE. 7 Livingston St., Rhinebeck, NY 12572-1505. Telephone: 845-876-3033. FAX: 845-876-2361. E-MAIL: registerherald@midhutsoncenter.com. URL: http://www.theregisterherald.com. Year Established: 1859. Pub. Frequency: w. (Thu.) Page Size: broadsheet. Subscrip. Rate: $.75 newsstand/cover; $37/yr mailed in state; $42/yr mailed out of state. Circulation: 2,300 per issue (paid). **Owner(s):** Journal Register Co., 50 W State St, 12th Fl, Trenton, NJ 08608. Telephone: 609-396-2200. FAX: 609-396-2292. **Management:** Ira Fusfeld, Publisher. Jeff Ohlbaum, Advertising Director. Larry Priest, Circulation Director. Mary Bradford, Classified Adv. Mgr.. **Editorial:** Darryl Gangloff, Editor. Ann Gibbons, Executive Editor.

RIDGEWOOD

TIMES NEWSWEEKLY & RIDGEWOOD TIMES. 6658 Fresh Pond Rd., Ridgewood, NY 11385-3245. Telephone: 718-821-7500. FAX: 718-456-0120. E-MAIL: info@timesnewsweekly.com. URL: http://www.timesnewsweekly.com. Year Established: 1908. Pub. Frequency: w. (Thu.) Page Size: tabloid. Subscrip. Rate: $.40 newsstand/cover; $20/yr local; $25/yr out of area. Circulation: 30,000 per issue (paid). **Owner(s):** Ridgewood Times Printing & Publishing Co., PO Box 860299, Ridgewood, NY 11386. **Management:** Maureen E. Walthers, Publisher. Liz Collegio, Business Manager. **Editorial:** Maureen E. Walthers, Editor. Bill Mitchell, Managing Editor.

ROCHESTER

FAIRPORT COMMUNITY NEWS. 2808 Dewey Ave., Rochester, NY 14616. Telephone: 585-663-0068. FAX: 585-663-0146. E-MAIL: greece@adnetdirect.net. Year Established: 1948. Pub. Frequency: s-w. (Mon. & Tue.) Page Size: tabloid. Circulation: 164,900 per issue (paid and free). **Owner(s):** Suburban Circle Publications, 2808 Dewey Ave., Rochester, NY 14612. Telephone: 716-394-4510. **Management:** Larry M. Lucieer, President. **Editorial:** Carol Harvey, Editor.

ROUND LAKE

MALTA PENNYSAVER. 2037 Rte. 9, Round Lake, NY 12151. Telephone: 518-877-7160. FAX: 518-877-7824. Mailing Address: PO Box 1450, Clifton Park, NY 12065. Year Established: 1997. Pub. Frequency: w. (Sat.) Page Size: tabloid.Subscrip. Rate: $1.50/wk. elsewhere Circulation: 96,000 per issue (free). **Owner(s):** Capital Region Weekly Newspaper Group, See address and contact information above. **Management:** Patrick Smith, Publisher. **Editorial:** Patrick Smith, Editor.

MONEYSAVER, THE SPA CITY JOURNAL. 2037 Rte. 9, Round Lake, NY 12151. Telephone: 518-877-7160. FAX: 518-877-7824. Year Established: 1969. Pub. Frequency: w. (Sat) Page Size: tabloid Circulation: 26,075 per issue (free). **Owner(s):** Capital Region Weekly Newspaper Group, See address and contact information above. **Management:** Patrick Smith, Publisher. **Editorial:** Patrick Smith, Editor.

SARATOGA SPRINGS

COMMUNITY NEWS (SARATOGA SPRINGS). 20 Lake Ave., Saratoga Springs, NY 12866-2356. FAX: 518-587-7750. E-MAIL: cnews@saratogian.com. URL: http://www.cnweekly.com. Year Established: 1969. Pub. Frequency: w. (Fri.) Page Size: broadsheet. **Wire Service(s):** AP. Circulation: 27,361 per issue (free). **Owner(s):** Journal Register Co., Lower Makefield Corporate Center, 790 Township Line Rd, 3rd. flr, Yardley, PA 19067. Telephone: 215-504-4200. 50 W State St, 12th Fl, Trenton, NJ 08608. **Management:** Frank McGivern, Publisher. Linda Bibeault, Advertising Director. Nerlin Toth, Circulation Director. Carolyn Killion, Classified Adv. Mgr.. **Editorial:** Donna Bell, Editor. Barbara Lombardo, Managing Editor.

SAUGERTIES

MOUNTAIN PENNYSAVER. 858 Rte. 212, Saugerties, NY 12477. Telephone: 845-246-4985. FAX: 845-246-5108. Pub. Frequency: w. (Sun.) Page Size: tabloid Circulation: 22,000 per issue (free). **Owner(s):** GateHouse Media, Inc, 350 WillowBrook Office Park, Fairport, NY 14450. Telephone: 585-598-0030. FAX: 585-248-2631. **Management:** Ryan Hallam, Publisher. Jeremiah Henderson, Advertising Manager. **Editorial:** Ryan Hallam, Editor.

SAUGERTIES PENNYSAVER. 858 Rte. 212, Saugerties, NY 12477. Telephone: 845-246-4985. FAX: 845-246-5108. Pub. Frequency: w. (Sat.) Page Size: tabloid Circulation: 9,000 per issue (free). **Owner(s):** GateHouse Media, Inc, 350 WillowBrook Office Park, Fairport, NY 14450. Telephone: 585-598-0030. FAX: 585-248-2631. **Management:** Ryan Hallam, Publisher. Jeremiah Henderson, Advertising Manager. **Editorial:** Ryan Hallam, Editor.

SAUGERTIES POST STAR. 858 Rte. 212, Saugerties, NY 12477. Telephone: 845-246-4985. FAX: 845-246-5108. Year Established: 1877. Pub. Frequency: w. (Thu.) Page Size: tabloid. Subscrip. Rate: $.75 newsstand/cover; $35/yr in county; $40/yr mailed out of county. Circulation: 2,000 per issue (paid). **Owner(s):** GateHouse Media, Inc, 350 WillowBrook Office Park, Fairport, NY 14450. Telephone: 585-598-0030. FAX: 585-248-2631. **Management:** Ryan Hallam, Publisher. Jeremiah Henderson, Advertising Manager. **Editorial:** Heather Polanchak, Editor.

SAYVILLE

FIRE ISLAND TIDE. 40 Main St., Sayville, NY 11782. Telephone: 631-567-7470. FAX: 631-563-1352. E-MAIL: fireislandtide@aol.com. Year Established: 1976. Pub. Frequency: bi-w. (May-Sep.) Page Size: tabloid.Subscrip. Rate: $1 newsstand/cover; $28/yr Circulation: 35,000 per issue (paid). **Owner(s):** Fire Island Tide, Inc., PO Box 8, Patchogue, NY 11772. Telephone: 631-567-7470. **Management:** Warren C. McDowell, Publisher.

ISLIP BULLETIN. 23 Candee Ave., Sayville, NY 11782-0367. Telephone: 631-589-6200. FAX: 631-589-3246. E-MAIL: scnletters@aol.com. Mailing Address: PO Box 367, Sayville, NY 11782-0367. Year Established: 1946. Pub. Frequency: w. (Thu.) Page Size: tabloid. Subscrip. Rate: $.75 newsstand/cover; $26/yr mailed in county; $33/yr mailed out of county. Circulation: 6,000 per issue (paid). Owner(s): Johnlor Publications, Ltd., PO Box 780, Patchogue, NY 11772. Telephone: 631-475-1000. FAX: 631-475-1565. Management: Joann Labarca, General Manager. John T. Tuthill III, Publisher. Vicki Ann Morales, Circulation Manager. Terry Tuthill, Assistant Publisher. Editorial: Jeffrey Bessen, Editor.

SUFFOLK COUNTY NEWS.   ISSN 1065-1470
23 Candee Ave., Sayville, NY 11782. Telephone: 631-589-6200. FAX: 631-589-3246. E-MAIL: scnletters@aol.com. Mailing Address: PO Box 367, Sayville, NY 11782. Year Established: 1884. Pub. Frequency: w. (Thu.) Page Size: tabloid. Subscrip. Rate: $1 newsstand/cover; $30/yr in county; $41/yr out of county. Circulation: 10,000 per issue (paid). Owner(s): Johnlor Publications, Ltd., PO Box 780, Patchogue, NY 11772. Telephone: 516-475-1000. Management: Joann Labarca, General Manager. John Tuthill III, Publisher. Terry Tuthill, Advertising Manager. Vicki Ann Morales, Circulation Manager. Editorial: Jeffrey Bessen, Editor.

SCARSDALE

SCARSDALE INQUIRER, THE. PO Box 418, Scarsdale, NY 10583. Telephone: 914-725-2500. FAX: 914-725-1552. E-MAIL: lleavitt@scarsdalenews.com. Year Established: 1901. Pub. Frequency: w. (Fri.) Page Size: broadsheet. Subscrip. Rate: $1 newsstand/cover; $39/yr in county; $60/yr out of county. Circulation: 6,800 per issue (paid and free). Owner(s): S.I. Communications, Inc., See address and contact information above. Management: Deborah White, Publisher. Barbara Yeaker, Advertising Manager. Editorial: Linda Leavitt, Editor.

SHELTER ISLAND

SHELTER ISLAND REPORTER. 50 N. Ferry Rd., Shelter Island, NY 11964-0756. Telephone: 631-749-1000. FAX: 631-749-0144. Mailing Address: PO Box 756, Shelter Island, NY 11964-0756. Year Established: 1959. Pub. Frequency: w. (Thu.) Page Size: tabloid. Subscrip. Rate: $1 newsstand/cover; $25/yr in county; $35/yr out of county. Circulation: 3,300 per issue (paid). Owner(s): Times/Review Newspapers, Inc., PO Box 1500, Mattituck, NY 11952. Telephone: 631-298-3200. Management: Andrew Olsen, Co-Publisher. Troy Gustavson, President. Keith Schultz, Advertising. Ethel Michalak, Circulation Manager. Meg Marcus, Classified Adv. Mgr.. Editorial: Peter Boody, Editor. Archer Brown, Community Editor.

SIDNEY

TRI-TOWN NEWS (SIDNEY). PO Box 570, Sidney, NY 13838. Telephone: 607-563-3526. FAX: 607-563-8999. Pub. Frequency: w. (Wed.) Page Size: standard. Subscrip. Rate: $.75 newsstand/cover; $26/yr home delivery local; $30/yr mailed out of area. Circulation: 6,000 per issue (paid). Owner(s): Paul Hamilton, Sr. & Wiley L. Vincent, See address and contact information above. Management: Anna Ritchey, Advertising Manager. Cathy Palladino, Circulation Manager. Editorial: Nancy Burns, Editor. Peter Mansheffer, Sports.

SKANEATELES

MARCELLUS OBSERVER.   ISSN 1066-1352
2 Fennell St, Skaneateles, NY 13152. Telephone: 315-685-8338. FAX: 315-685-8338. E-MAIL: news@eagle-news.com. URL: http://www.cnylink.com. Year Established: 1879. Pub. Frequency: w. (Wed.) Page Size: tabloid. Subscrip. Rate: $.75 newsstand/cover; $25/yr. Adv. Rate: col. inch $9.50 Circulation: 1,425 per issue (paid). Owner(s): Eagle Newspapers LP, 5910 Firestone Dr., Syracuse, NY 13152. Telephone: 315-434-8889. Management: David Tyler, General Manager. Richard Keene, President. Tami Grashof, Advertising Director. Julie Galvin, Classified Adv. Mgr.. Editorial: Tom Wanamker, Managing Editor.

SKANEATELES PRESS. 2 Fennell St, Skaneateles, NY 13152. E-MAIL: press-observer@cnylink.com. URL: http://www.cnylink.com. Year Established: 1939. Pub. Frequency: w. (Wed.) Page Size: broadsheet. Subscrip. Rate: $.75 newsstand/cover; $25/yr mailed in county; $30/yr mailed out of state. Adv. Rate: col. inch $9.05 Circulation: 2,900 per issue (paid). Owner(s): Eagle Newspapers LP, 5910 Firestone Dr., Syracuse, NY 13152. Management: David Tyler, General Manager. Tami Grashof, Advertising Director. Julie Galvin, Classified Adv. Mgr.. Editorial: Ellen Leahey, Editor. Tom Wanamker, Managing Editor.

SMITHTOWN

COMMACK NEWS. One Brookside Dr., Smithtown, NY 11787. Telephone: 631-265-2100. FAX: 631-265-6237. Mailing Address: PO Box 805, Smithtown, NY 11787-0805. Year Established: 1964. Pub. Frequency: w. (Thu.) Page Size: tabloid. Subscrip. Rate: $.75 newsstand/cover; $28/yr Circulation: 10,000 per issue (paid). Owner(s): North Shore News Group, See address and contact information above. Management: Bernard Paley, Publisher. Jennifer Paley, Associate Publisher. Editorial: David Ambro, Editor.

ISLIP NEWS. One Brookside Dr., Smithtown, NY 11787. Telephone: 631-265-2100. FAX: 631-265-6237. Mailing Address: PO Box 805, Smithtown, NY 11787-0805. Year Established: 1950. Pub. Frequency: w. (Thu.) Page Size: tabloid. Subscrip. Rate: $.75 newsstand/cover; $28/yr Circulation: 3,500 per issue (paid). Owner(s): North Shore News Group, See address and contact information above. Management: Bernard Paley, Publisher. Jennifer Paley, Associate Publisher. Editorial: David Ambro, Editor.

SMITHTOWN NEWS, THE. One Brookside Dr., Smithtown, NY 11787. Telephone: 631-265-2100. FAX: 631-265-6237. E-MAIL: smithnews@specdata.com. Mailing Address: PO Box 805, Smithtown, NY 11787-0805. Year Established: 1945. Pub. Frequency: w. (Thu.) Page Size: tabloid. Subscrip. Rate: $.75 newsstand/cover; $28/yr Circulation: 11,500 per issue (paid). Owner(s): North Shore News Group, See address and contact information above. Management: Bernard Paley, Publisher. Jennifer Paley, Associate Publisher. Editorial: David Ambro, Editor.

SODUS

SODUS WILLIAMSON PENNYSAVER. 6890 Ridge Rd., East, Sodus, NY 14551. Telephone: 315-483-6331. FAX: 315-483-2280. E-MAIL: editor@cgazette.com. URL: http://www.cgazette.com. Pub. Frequency: w. (Tue.) Page Size: broadsheet Circulation: 7,900 per issue (free). Owner(s): Ad Group, Inc., 613 S. Main St., Newark, NY 14513. Telephone: 315-331-6956. FAX: 315-331-1053. Management: John H. VanDusen, Publisher. Jim O'Connell, Advertising. Editorial: Sandra Marcano, Editor.

SOUTHAMPTON

SOUTHAMPTON PRESS.   ISSN 0745-6484
135 Windmill Ln., Southampton, NY 11968. Telephone: 631-283-4100. FAX: 631-283-4927. E-MAIL: mailbag@southamptonpress.com. URL: http://www.southamptonpress.com. Mailing Address: P.O. Drawer 1207, Southampton, NY 11969. Year Established: 1897. Pub. Frequency: w. (Thu.) Page Size: broadsheet. Subscrip. Rate: $1 newsstand/cover; $35/yr in county; $45/yr mailed out of county. Freelance Pay: $50-$100/article. Circulation: 20,000 per issue (controlled and free). Owner(s): Joseph P. Louchheim, See address and contact information above. Management: Joseph P. Louchheim, Publisher. Paul Conroy, Advertising Manager. Courtney Ratcliffe., Circulation Manager. Editorial: Joseph Shaw, Editor.

SPECULATOR

HAMILTON COUNTY NEWS. Rte. 30, Speculator, NY 12164-0166. Telephone: 518-548-6898. FAX: 518-548-5305. E-MAIL: hcnews@frontiernet.net. URL: http://www.hamconews.com. Mailing Address: PO Box 166, Speculator, NY 12164-0166. Year Established: 1947. Pub. Frequency: w. (Tue.) Page Size: tabloid. Subscrip. Rate: $.50 newsstand/cover; $21/yr in county; $25/yr out of county; $30/yr out of state. Adv. Rate: col. inch $10.75 Freelance Pay: $30/article. Circulation: 4,500 per issue (paid). Owner(s): William J. Kline & Son, Inc., One Venner Rd., Amsterdam, NY 12010-0166. Telephone: 518-548-6898. FAX: 518-548-5305. Management: Cristine Meixner, General Manager. Kevin McCary, Publisher. Arthur Simmons, Advertising Manager. Lisa Guadagno, Circulation Manager.

SPENCERPORT

HAMLIN-CLARKSON HERALD. 1835 N Union St, Spencerport, NY 14559-0106. Telephone: 585-352-3411. FAX: 585-352-4811. E-MAIL: westside@netacc.net. URL: http://www.westsidenewsonline.com. Mailing Address: PO Box 106, Spencerport, NY 14559-0106. Year Established: 1988. Pub. Frequency: w. (Sun.) Page Size: tabloid. Subscrip. Rate: $35/yr elsewhere. Adv. Rate: col. inch $8.55 Freelance Pay: $2/column-inch. Circulation: 6,150 per issue (paid and free). Owner(s): Westside News Inc., See address and contact information above. Management: Keith Ryan, Publisher. Karen Fien, Advertising. Don Griffin, Circulation Manager. Editorial: Evelyn Dow, Editor.

SUBURBAN NEWS SOUTH EDITION. 1835 N Union St, Spencerport, NY 14559-0106. Telephone: 585-352-3411. FAX: 585-352-4811. E-MAIL: westside@netacc.net. URL: http://www.westsidenewsonline.com. Mailing Address: PO Box 106, Spencerport, NY 14559-0106. Year Established: 1953. Pub. Frequency: w. (Sun.) Page Size: tabloid. Subscrip. Rate: $35/yr mailed. Adv. Rate: col. inch $26.78 Freelance Pay: $2/column-inch. Circulation: 32,000 per issue (paid and free). Owner(s): Westside News Inc., See address and contact information above. Management: Keith Ryan, Publisher. Karen Fien, Advertising. Don Griffin, Circulation Manager. Editorial: Evelyn Dow, Editor.

SUBURBAN NEWS WEST EDITION. 1835 N Union St, Spencerport, NY 14559-0106. Telephone: 585-352-3411. FAX: 585-352-4811. E-MAIL: westside@netacc.net. URL: http://www.westsidenewsonline.com. Mailing Address: PO Box 106, Spencerport, NY 14559-0106. Year Established: 1989. Pub. Frequency: w. (Sun.) Page Size: tabloid. Subscrip. Rate: $35/yr mailed elsewhere. Adv. Rate: col. inch $8.55 Freelance Pay: $2/column-inch. Circulation: 8,650 per issue (paid and free). Owner(s): Westside News Inc., See address and contact information above. Management: Keith Ryan, Publisher. Karen Fien, Advertising. Don Griffin, Circulation Manager. Editorial: Evelyn Dow, News Editor.

SPRINGVILLE

SPRINGVILLE PENNYSAVER. 49 E. Main St., Springville, NY 14141. Telephone: 716-592-2818. FAX: 716-592-2538. E-MAIL: ads@pennysaver.com. URL: http://www.pennysaver.com. Year Established: 1964. Pub. Frequency: w. (Sun.) Page Size: tabloid. Adv. Rate: col. inch $9.94 Circulation: 10,200 per issue (free). Owner(s): H & K Publications, Inc., 50 Buffalo St., Hamburg, NY 14075. Telephone: 716-649-4413. FAX: 716-649-5940. Management: Tom Kluckhohn, Publisher. Steve Kluckhohn, Advertising Manager. Teri Scott, Circulation Manager.

SYRACUSE

BALDWINSVILLE MESSENGER. 5910 Firestone Dr., Syracuse, NY 13152. Telephone: 315-434-8889. FAX: 315-434-8883. E-MAIL: messenger@cnylink.com. URL: http://cnylink.com/aboutcny/. Year Established: 1846. Pub. Frequency: w. (Wed.) Page Size: broadsheet. Subscrip. Rate: $.75 newsstand/cover; $25/yr in county; $28/yr mailed out of county. Adv. Rate: col. inch $10.10 Circulation: 7,200 per issue (paid). Owner(s): Eagle Newspapers LP, See address and contact information above. Management: David Tyler, General Manager. Tami Grashof, Advertising Director. Laurie Newcomb, Circulation Manager. Julie Galvin, Classified Adv. Mgr.. Editorial: Erin Smith, Editor. Tom Wanamker, Managing Editor.

CAMILLUS ADVOCATE. 5910 Firestone Dr., Syracuse, NY 13152. Telephone: 315-434-8889. FAX: 315-434-8883. URL: http://www.cnylink.com. Year Established: 1926. Pub. Frequency: w. (Wed.) Page Size: broadsheet. Subscrip. Rate: $.75 newsstand/cover; $25/yr mailed. Adv. Rate: col. inch $10.10 Freelance Pay: $20/article. Circulation: 2,215 per issue (paid). Owner(s): Eagle Newspapers LP, See address and contact information above. Management: David Tyler, General Manager. Tami Grashof, Advertising Director. Laurie Newcomb, Circulation Manager. Julie Galvin, Classified Adv. Mgr.. Editorial: Matt Craver, Editor. Tom Wanamker, Managing Editor.

DEWITT TIMES. 5910 Firestone Dr., Syracuse, NY 13152. Telephone: 315-434-8889. FAX: 315-434-8883. URL: http://www.cnylink.com. Year Established: 1970. Pub. Frequency: w. (Wed.) Page Size: tabloid. Subscrip. Rate: $.75 newsstand/cover; $28/yr in county. Adv. Rate: col. inch $23 Freelance Pay: $0.25/word. Circulation: 1,375 per issue (paid). Owner(s): Eagle Newspapers LP, See address and contact information above. Management: David Tyler, General Manager. Tami Grashof, Advertising Director. Laurie Newcomb, Circulation Manager. Julie Galvin, Classified Adv. Mgr.. Editorial: Tammy Zimmerman, Editor. Tom Wanamker, Managing Editor.

EAGLE BULLETIN. 5910 Firestone Dr., Syracuse, NY 13152. Telephone: 315-434-8889. FAX: 315-434-8883. E-MAIL: newsroom@cnylink.com. URL: http://www.cnylink.com. Year Established: 1850. Pub. Frequency: w. (Wed.) Page Size: tabloid. Subscrip. Rate: $.75 newsstand/cover; $28/yr in county. Adv. Rate: col. inch $11.85 Freelance Pay: $10/article. Circulation: 7,032 per issue (paid). Owner(s): Eagle Newspapers LP, See address and contact information above. Management: David Tyler, General Manager. Tami Grashof, Advertising Director. Laurie Newcomb, Circulation Manager. Julie Galvin, Classified Adv. Mgr.. Editorial: Tammy Zimmerman, Editor. Tom Wanamker, Managing Editor.

LIVERPOOL REVIEW. 5910 Firestone Dr., Syracuse, NY 13152. Telephone: 315-434-8889. FAX: 315-434-8883. Year Established: 1926. Pub. Frequency: w. (Wed.) Page Size: tabloid. Subscrip. Rate: $.75 newsstand/cover; $28/yr in county. Adv. Rate: col. inch $23 Circulation: 4,005 per issue (paid). **Owner(s):** Eagle Newspapers LP, See address and contact information above. **Management:** David Tyler, General Manager. Tami Grashof, Advertising Director. Laurie Newcomb, Circulation Manager. Julie Galvin, Classified Adv. Mgr.. **Editorial:** Sarah Hall, Editor. Tom Wanamker, Managing Editor.

NORTH SYRACUSE STAR-NEWS. 5910 Firestone Dr., Syracuse, NY 13152. Telephone: 315-434-8889. FAX: 315-434-8883. URL: http://www.cnylink. com. Year Established: 1924. Pub. Frequency: w. (Wed.) Page Size: broadsheet. Subscrip. Rate: $.75 newsstand/cover; $28/yr in county. Adv. Rate: col. inch $23 Circulation: 3,725 per issue (paid). **Owner(s):** Eagle Newspapers LP, See address and contact information above. **Management:** David Tyler, General Manager. Tami Grashof, Advertising Director. Laurie Newcomb, Circulation Manager. Julie Galvin, Classified Adv. Mgr.. **Editorial:** Brett Findlay, Editor. Tom Wanamker, Managing Editor.

ONONDAGA VALLEY NEWS. 750 W. Genesee St., Syracuse, NY 13204-2306. Telephone: 315-472-7825. FAX: 315-478-1434. E-MAIL: pennyserver@scotsmanpress.com. URL: http://www.scotsmanonline.com. Mailing Address: PO Box 4970, Syracuse, NY 13221-4970. Year Established: 1956. Pub. Frequency: w. (Mon.) Page Size: tabloid. Subscrip. Rate: $.25 newsstand/cover; $15/yr mailed. Adv. Rate: col. inch $9,013 Circulation: 6,861 per issue (paid and free). **Owner(s):** Scotsman Press, Inc., 750 W. Genesee St., Syracuse, NY 13221-2306. Telephone: 315-472-7825. **Management:** A. Loren Colburn, Publisher. Greg Borowski, Advertising Manager. David Spearing, Circulation Manager. Patricia Puzzo, Classified Adv. Mgr.. **Editorial:** Debra Lun, Editor.

PENNYWISE VILLAGER. 750 W. Genesee St., Syracuse, NY 13204. Telephone: 315-472-7825. FAX: 315-478-1434. E-MAIL: pennysaver@scotsmanpress.com. URL: http://www.scotsmanonline.com. Mailing Address: PO Box 4970, Syracuse, NY 13221. Pub. Frequency: w. (Mon.) Page Size: tabloid. Subscrip. Rate: $.25 newsstand/cover; $15/yr mailed local. Adv. Rate: col. inch $7.58 Circulation: 9,732 per issue (paid and free). **Owner(s):** Scotsman Press, Inc., See address and contact information above. **Management:** A. Loren Colburn, Publisher. David Spearing, Circulation Manager. Thomas C. Cuskey, Associate Publisher. **Editorial:** Debra Lun, Editor.

SCOTSMAN COMMUNITY PUBLICATIONS. 750 W. Genesee St., Syracuse, NY 13321-2306. Telephone: 315-472-7825. FAX: 315-478-1434. E-MAIL: pennysaver@scotsmanpress.com. URL: http://www.scotsmanonline.com. Year Established: 1954. Pub. Frequency: w. (Mon.) Page Size: tabloid. Subscrip. Rate: $.30 newsstand/cover; $15/yr mailed. Circulation: 284,972 per issue (paid and free). **Owner(s):** Scotsman Press, Inc., PO Box 4970, Syracuse, NY 13221-4970. Telephone: 315-472-7825. FAX: 315-478-1434. **Management:** John Badoud Jr., President. A. Loren Colburn, Publisher. David Spearing, Circulation Manager. Thomas C. Cuskey, Associate Publisher. **Editorial:** Michael Farnsworth, Editor.

SOLVAY GEDDES PRESS. 5910 Firestone Dr., Syracuse, NY 13152. Telephone: 315-434-8889. FAX: 315-434-8883. URL: http://www.cnylink.com. Pub. Frequency: w. (Wed.) Page Size: tabloid. Subscrip. Rate: $.75 newsstand/cover; $28/yr in county. Adv. Rate: col. inch $11.10 Circulation: 4,200 per issue (paid). **Owner(s):** Eagle Newspapers LP, See address and contact information above. **Management:** David Tyler, General Manager. Tami Grashof, Advertising Director. Laurie Newcomb, Circulation Manager. Julie Galvin, Classified Adv. Mgr.. **Editorial:** Tom Wanamker, Managing Editor.

SYRACUSE CITY EAGLE. 5910 Firestone Dr., Syracuse, NY 13152. Telephone: 315-434-8889. FAX: 315-434-8883. URL: http://www.cnylink.com. Pub. Frequency: w. (Thu.) Page Size: tabloid. Subscrip. Rate: $.75 newsstand/cover; $28/yr in county; $29/yr out of county. Adv. Rate: col. inch $10.80 Circulation: 5,500 per issue (paid). **Owner(s):** Eagle Newspapers LP, See address and contact information above. **Management:** David Tyler, General Manager. Tami Grashof, Advertising Director. Laurie Newcomb, Circulation Manager. Julie Galvin, Classified Adv. Mgr.. **Editorial:** Tom Wanamker, Managing Editor.

SYRACUSE NEW TIMES. ISSN 0893-844X
1415 W Genesee St, Syracuse, NY 13204. E-MAIL: snt@syracusenewtimes.com. URL: http://www.syracusenewtimes.com. Year Established: 1969. Pub. Frequency: w. (Wed.) Page Size: tabloid. Subscrip. Rate: $24.95/yr. Freelance Pay: $25-$150/article. Circulation: 40,000 (controlled). **Owner(s):** A. Zimmer Ltd., See address and contact information above. **Editorial:** Molly English-Bowers, Editor-in-Chief.

TRUMANSBURG

CANDOR CHRONICLE. 51 N. Main St., Trumansburg, NY 14886. Telephone: 607-387-3181. FAX: 607-387-9421. E-MAIL: flcn@lightlink.com. Mailing Address: PO Box 714, Trumansburg, NY 14886. Pub. Frequency: w. (Wed.) Page Size: tabloid. Subscrip. Rate: $.50 newsstand/cover; $21/yr in county; $25/yr out of county. Circulation: 5,000 per issue (paid). **Owner(s):** Finger Lakes Community Newspapers, Inc., PO Box 6475, Ithaca, NY 14851. Telephone: 607-277-7000. **Management:** James Bilinski, Publisher. Tom Olson, Advertising Manager. **Editorial:** Steven Ferarri, Managing Editor.

INTERLAKEN REVIEW. 51 N. Main St., Trumansburg, NY 14886. Telephone: 607-387-3181. FAX: 607-387-9421. E-MAIL: flcn@lightlink.com. Mailing Address: PO Box 714, Trumansburg, NY 14886. Pub. Frequency: w. (Wed.) Page Size: tabloid. Subscrip. Rate: $.50 newsstand/cover; $21/yr in county; $25/yr out of county; $20/yr in county to senior citizens. Circulation: 6,000 per issue (paid). **Owner(s):** Finger Lakes Community Newspapers, Inc., PO Box 6475, Ithaca, NY 14851. Telephone: 607-277-7000. **Management:** James Bilinski, Publisher. **Editorial:** Steven Ferarri, Managing Editor.

NEWFIELD NEWS. 51 N. Main St., Trumansburg, NY 14886. Telephone: 607-387-3181. FAX: 607-387-9421. Mailing Address: PO Box 714, Trumansburg, NY 14886. Pub. Frequency: w. (Wed.) Page Size: tabloid. Subscrip. Rate: $.75 newsstand/cover; $24/yr in county; $23/yr out of county. Circulation: 5,000 per issue (paid). **Owner(s):** Finger Lakes Community Newspapers, Inc., PO Box 6475, Ithaca, NY 14850. Telephone: 607-277-7000. **Management:** James Bilinski, Publisher. Tom Olson, Advertising Manager. **Editorial:** Steven Ferarri, Managing Editor.

OVID GAZETTE. 51 N. Main St., Trumansburg, NY 14886. Telephone: 607-387-3181. FAX: 607-387-9421. E-MAIL: flcn@lightlink.com. Mailing Address: PO Box 714, Trumansburg, NY 14886. Pub. Frequency: w. (Wed.) Page Size: tabloid. Subscrip. Rate: $.50 newsstand/cover; $21/yr in county; $25/yr out of county. Circulation: 7,000 per issue (paid). **Owner(s):** Finger Lakes Community Newspapers, Inc., PO Box 6475, Ithaca, NY 14851. Telephone: 607-277-7000. **Management:** James Bilinski, Publisher. **Editorial:** Terra Chapek, Managing Editor.

SPENCER RANDOM HARVEST WEEKLY. 51 N. Main St., Trumansburg, NY 14886. Telephone: 607-387-3181. FAX: 607-387-9421. E-MAIL: flcn@lightlink.com. Mailing Address: PO Box 714, Trumansburg, NY 14886. Pub. Frequency: w. (Wed.) Page Size: tabloid. Subscrip. Rate: $.50 newsstand/cover; $21/yr in county; $25/yr out of county. Circulation: 7,000 per issue (paid). **Owner(s):** Finger Lakes Community Newspapers, Inc., PO Box 6475, Ithaca, NY 14851. Telephone: 607-277-7000. **Management:** James Bilinski, Publisher. Tom Olson, Advertising Manager. **Editorial:** Steven Ferarri, Managing Editor.

TRUMANSBURG FREE PRESS. 51 N. Main St., Trumansburg, NY 14886. Telephone: 607-387-3181. FAX: 607-387-9421. E-MAIL: flcn@lightlink.com. Mailing Address: PO Box 714, Trumansburg, NY 14886. Pub. Frequency: w. (Wed.) Page Size: tabloid. Subscrip. Rate: $.50 newsstand/cover; $21/yr in county; $25/yr out of county. Circulation: 10,000 per issue (paid). **Owner(s):** Finger Lakes Community Newspapers, Inc., PO Box 6475, Ithaca, NY 14851. Telephone: 607-277-7000. **Management:** James Bilinski, Publisher. Tom Olson, Advertising Manager. **Editorial:** Steven Ferarri, Managing Editor.

TUPPER LAKE

TUPPER LAKE FREE PRESS & HERALD. 136 Park St., Tupper Lake, NY 12986. Telephone: 518-359-2166. FAX: 518-359-2295. Year Established: 1895. Pub. Frequency: w. (Wed.) Page Size: broadsheet. Subscrip. Rate: $.60 newsstand/cover; $32/yr mailed in county; $39/yr mailed out of county. Adv. Rate: col. inch $5.46 Circulation: 3,700 per issue (paid and free). **Owner(s):** M. Dan McClelland, See address and contact information above. **Management:** Judy McClelland, Advertising Manager. **Editorial:** Sue Mitchell, Editor.

WADING RIVER

COMMUNITY JOURNAL. Rte. 25A & Dogwood Dr., Wading River, NY 11792. Telephone: 631-929-8882. FAX: 631-929-4560. Mailing Address: PO Box 619, Wading River, NY 11792-0619. Year Established: 1978. Pub. Frequency: w. (Thu.) Page Size: tabloid. Subscrip. Rate: $.25 newsstand/cover; $50/yr mailed. Circulation: 7,000 per issue (paid). **Owner(s):** Bernadette Smith Budd, See address and contact information above. **Management:** Bernadette Smith Budd, Publisher. **Editorial:** Bernadette Smith Budd, Editor-in-Chief.

NORTH SHORE SUN. ISSN 1541-9320
6298 Rte 25A, Wading River, NY 11792. Telephone: 631-929-6166. FAX: 631-929-6735. E-MAIL: mail@timesreview.com. URL: http://www.timesreview.com. Mailing Address: P.O. Box 547, Wading River, NY 11792. Pub. Frequency: w. (Fri.) Page Size: broadsheet. Subscrip. Rate: $.75 newsstand/cover; $25/yr in county; $35/yr out of county. Circulation: 3,000 per issue (paid). **Owner(s):** Times/Review Newspapers Corp., PO Box 1500, Mattituck, NY 11952. Telephone: 631-298-3200. **Management:** Andrew Olsen, Co-Publisher. Janice Robinson, Advertising. Tina Volinski, Circulation Manager. Meg Marcus, Classified Adv. Mgr.. **Editorial:** Drew Crouthamel, Editor. Grant Parpan, Sports Editor.

WALDEN

MID HUDSON TIMES. 23 E. Main St., Walden, NY 12586. Telephone: 845-778-2181. FAX: 845-778-1196. E-MAIL: wwtimes@aol.com. Year Established: 1989. Pub. Frequency: w. (Wed.) Page Size: tabloid. Subscrip. Rate: $.75 newsstand/cover; $28/yr mailed in county; $31/yr mailed out of county. Adv. Rate: col. inch $8.30 Freelance Pay: $25-$35/story. Circulation: 3,000 per issue (paid). **Owner(s):** Wallkill Valley Publications, Inc., PO Box 10234, Newburgh, NY 12552-0234. Telephone: 914-561-0170. **Management:** Carl J. Aiello, Publisher. **Editorial:** Carl J. Aiello, Editor.

WALLKILL VALLEY TIMES, THE. 23 E. Main St., Walden, NY 12586. Telephone: 845-778-2181. FAX: 845-778-1196. E-MAIL: WVTimes@aol.com. Year Established: 1983. Pub. Frequency: w. (Wed.) Page Size: tabloid. Subscrip. Rate: $.75 newsstand/cover; $28/yr mailed in county; $31/yr out of county. Circulation: 5,000 per issue (paid). **Owner(s):** Wallkill Valley Publications, Inc., See address and contact information above. **Management:** Carl J. Aiello, Publisher. Mary Cronan, Circulation Manager. **Editorial:** Carl J. Aiello, Editor.

WALTON

WALTON REPORTER, THE. 181 Delaware St., Walton, NY 13856. Telephone: 607-865-4131. E-MAIL: news@reporterco.com. URL: http://www.reporterco.com/newspaperhome.html. Year Established: 1881. Pub. Frequency: w. (Wed.) Page Size: tabloid. Subscrip. Rate: $.75 newsstand/cover; $28/yr in county; $35/yr out of county. Freelance Pay: $0.50/column-inch. Circulation: 7,200 per issue (paid). **Owner(s):** Leonard & Amy Govern, See address and contact information above. **Management:** Len Govern, President. Judy Bowker, Office Manager. Amy Govern, Advertising Manager. **Editorial:** Glenn S. Graves, Editor.

WAPPINGERS FALLS

BEACON FREE PRESS. 84 E. Main St., Wappingers Falls, NY 12590-2599. Telephone: 845-297-3723. FAX: 845-297-6810. E-MAIL: newsplace@aol.com. Year Established: 1962. Pub. Frequency: w. (Wed.) Page Size: broadsheet. Subscrip. Rate: $25/yr. Adv. Rate: col. inch $12.06 **Wire Service(s):** AP. Circulation: 8,000 per issue (paid and free). **Owner(s):** Wappingers Falls Shopper, Inc., See address and contact information above. **Management:** Albert Osten, President. Ronald K. Hill, Advertising. John Instone, Marketing Director. **Editorial:** John Darcy, Managing Editor.

SOUTHERN DUTCHESS NEWS. ISSN 0192-9631
84 E. Main St., Wappingers Falls, NY 12590-2599. Telephone: 914-297-3723. FAX: 914-297-6810. E-MAIL: newsplace@aol.com. Year Established: 1953. Pub. Frequency: w. Page Size: broadsheet. Subscrip. Rate: $25/yr. Adv. Rate: col. inch $12.95 **Wire Service(s):** AP. Circulation: 27,000 (paid). **Owner(s):** Wappingers Falls Shopper, Inc., See address and contact information above. **Management:** Albert Osten, Publisher. Ronald K. Hill, Advertising. John Instone, Marketing Director. **Editorial:** John Darcy, Managing Editor.

WARWICK

WARWICK VALLEY DISPATCH. 2 Oakland Ave., Warwick, NY 10990. Telephone: 845-986-2216. FAX: 845-987-1180. Year Established: 1885. Pub. Frequency: w. (Wed.) Page Size: tabloid. Subscrip. Rate: $.50 newsstand/cover; $24/yr in county; $26/yr out of county. Circulation: 2,700 per issue (paid). **Owner(s):** Eugene Wright, See address and contact information above. **Management:** Min Joe Hong, Publisher. Lon Tytell, Advertising. **Editorial:** Jennifer O'Connor, Editor.

WASHINGTONVILLE

ORANGE COUNTY POST. 17 Goshen Ave., PO Box 500, Washingtonville, NY 10992. Telephone: 845-496-3611. FAX: 845-496-1715. E-MAIL: ocpnews@frontiernet.net. Pub. Frequency: w. (Tue.) Page Size: tabloid. Subscrip. Rate: $.50 newsstand/cover; $22/yr in county; $26/yr out of county. Circulation: 2,600 per issue (paid). **Owner(s):** Spear Printing Co., Inc., See address and contact information above. **Management:** Cathy Schwartz, Office Manager. Pam Lewis, Advertising Manager. Howard Spear, Circulation Manager. **Editorial:** John Spear, Editor.

WATKINS GLEN

WATKINS REVIEW & EXPRESS. ISSN 1041-6250
210 N. Franklin St., Watkins Glen, NY 14891. Telephone: 607-535-1500. FAX: 607-535-2500. Year Established: 1854. Pub. Frequency: w. (Wed.) Page Size: tabloid. Subscrip. Rate: $.60 newsstand/cover; $24/yr in county; $34/yr mailed in state. Circulation: 3,200 per issue (paid). **Owner(s):** Finger Lakes Media, PO Box 127, Dundee, NY 14387. Telephone: 607-535-2711. **Management:** George Lawson, Publisher. Donna Wilber, Advertising. **Editorial:** Gwen Chamberlain, Editor.

WEBSTER

WAYNE COUNTY MAIL. ISSN 0745-7685
2010 Empire Blvd., Webster, NY 14580. E-MAIL: wcmail@empirestateweeklies.com. Year Established: 1901. Pub. Frequency: w. (Thu.) Page Size: tabloid.Subscrip. Rate: $.75 newsstand/cover; $20/yr Circulation: 1,750 per issue (paid). **Owner(s):** Empire State Weeklies, See address and contact information above. **Management:** W David Young, President. Beth Ficarro, Advertising Manager. **Editorial:** Mike Sorenson, Editor.

WEBSTER HERALD. ISSN 0745-1377
2010 Empire Blvd., Webster, NY 14580. E-MAIL: websterherald@empirestateweeklies.com. Year Established: 1899. Pub. Frequency: w. (Wed.) Page Size: tabloid. Subscrip. Rate: $.75 newsstand/cover; $24/yr. Adv. Rate: col. inch $8.33 Circulation: 4,897 per issue (paid). **Owner(s):** Empire State Weeklies, See address and contact information above. **Management:** W David Young, President. Beth Ficarro, Advertising Manager. **Editorial:** Mike Sorenson, Managing Editor.

WESTFIELD

SENTINEL NEWS, THE. 41 E. Main St., Westfield, NY 14787. Telephone: 716-326-3163. FAX: 716-326-3165. Mailing Address: PO Box 38, Westfield, NY 14787. Year Established: 1834. Pub. Frequency: w. (Thu.) Page Size: broadsheet. Subscrip. Rate: $.50 newsstand/cover; $24/yr in county; $26/yr out of county. Circulation: 1,100 per issue (paid). **Owner(s):** Ogden Newspapers of Minnesota, Inc., 1500 Main St., Wheeling, WV 26003. Telephone: 304-233-0100. **Management:** Melissa Bramer, Publisher. **Editorial:** Jim Rush, Editor.

WESTFIELD REPUBLICAN. ISSN 1071-1074
41 E. Main St., Westfield, NY 14787. Telephone: 716-326-3163. FAX: 716-326-3165. Mailing Address: PO Box 38, Westfield, NY 14787. Year Established: 1855. Pub. Frequency: w. (Thu.) Page Size: broadsheet. Subscrip. Rate: $.50 newsstand/cover; $24/yr in county; $26/yr out of county. Circulation: 2,000 per issue (paid). **Owner(s):** Ogden Newspapers of Minnesota, Inc., 1500 Main St., Wheeling, WV 26003. Telephone: 304-233-0100. **Management:** Joyce Koawon, Publisher. **Editorial:** Jim Rush, Editor.

WESTHAMPTON BEACH

SOUTHAMPTON PRESS (THE WESTERN EDITION). PO Box 1071, Westhampton Beach, NY 11978. E-MAIL: west@southamptonpress.com. URL: http://www.southamptonpress.com. Year Established: 1907. Pub. Frequency: w. (Thu.) Page Size: broadsheet. Subscrip. Rate: $1 newsstand/cover; $35/yr in county; $45/yr out of county. Circulation: 8,000 per issue (paid). **Owner(s):** Joseph P. Louchheim, 135 Windmill Ln., Southampton, NY 11968. Telephone: 631-283-4100. FAX: 631-283-4927. **Management:** Joseph P. Louchheim, President. Paul Conroy, Advertising Manager. Courtney Ratcliffe., Circulation Manager. Neil Salvaggio, Classified Adv. Mgr.. **Editorial:** Frank Cosanza, Editor-in-Chief.

WHITE PLAINS

SUBURBAN STREET NEWS. 170 Hamilton Ave., Ste. 21, White Plains, NY 10601-1729. Telephone: 914-428-0930. FAX: 914-428-9077. E-MAIL: jcb@oped.com. URL: http://www.suburbanstreet.com.Year Established: 1976 Pub. Frequency: m. Circulation: 25,000 per issue (free). **Owner(s):** Suburban Street News, Inc., See address and contact information above. **Management:** James Benerofe, Publisher. **Editorial:** James Benerofe, Editor. Steve Morton, Creative Director.

WHITEHALL

WHITEHALL (NY) TIMES. 126 Main St., Whitehall, NY 12887. Telephone: 518-642-1234. FAX: 518-642-1344. E-MAIL: thetimes@adelphia.net. URL: http://www.manchesternewspapers.com. Mailing Address: PO Box 119, Whitehall, NY 12887. Year Established: 1815. Pub. Frequency: w. (Thu.) Page Size: tabloid. Subscrip. Rate: $.75 newsstand/cover; $29/yr in area; $39/yr out of area. Adv. Rate: col. inch $9.74 Circulation: 2,000 per issue (paid). **Owner(s):** Manchester Newspapers, Inc., 14 E. Main St., Granville, NY 12832. Telephone: 518-642-1234. FAX: 518-642-1344. **Management:** John N. Manchester, Publisher. Lisa Carter, Advertising Manager. Judy Cook, Circulation Manager. Allison Fabian, Classified Adv. Mgr.. **Editorial:** Bern Zovistoski, Editor. John N. Manchester, Editor-in-Chief.

WILLIAMSVILLE

AMHERST BEE. ISSN 1095-9432
5564 Main St., Williamsville, NY 14221. Telephone: 716-632-4700. FAX: 716-633-8601. E-MAIL: read@beenews.com. URL: http://www.beenews.com. Mailing Address: PO Box 150, Buffalo, NY 14231-0150. Year Established: 1879. Pub. Frequency: w. (Wed.) Page Size: tabloid. Subscrip. Rate: $1 newsstand/cover; $39/yr in county; $36/yr to senior citizens; $55/yr out of county. Circulation: 14,214 per issue (paid). **Owner(s):** Bee Publications, Inc., See address and contact information above. **Management:** Trey Measer, Publisher. Mary Anne Cappon, Advertising Director. Michael Measer, Circulation Manager. Holly Smith, Classified Adv. Mgr.. **Editorial:** David Sherman, Managing Editor. Jessica Finch, Associate Editor. Bob Kupczyk, Feature Editor. Jill Schmelzer, Lifestyle Editor.

CHEEKTOWAGA BEE. ISSN 1094-9852
5564 Main St., Williamsville, NY 14221. Telephone: 716-632-4700. FAX: 716-633-8601. E-MAIL: read@beenews.com. URL: http://www.beenews.com. Mailing Address: PO Box 150, Buffalo, NY 14231-0150. Year Established: 1977. Pub. Frequency: w. (Thu.) Page Size: tabloid. Subscrip. Rate: $1 newsstand/cover; $35/yr in county; $32/yr in county to senior citizens; $50/yr out of county. Circulation: 1,900 per issue (paid). **Owner(s):** Bee Publications, Inc., See address and contact information above. **Management:** Trey Measer, Publisher. Dean Hutter, Advertising Manager. Michael Measer, Circulation Manager. Holly Smith, Classified Adv. Mgr.. **Editorial:** Keaton DePriest, Editor. David Sherman, Managing Editor. Bob Kupczyk, Feature Editor.

CLARENCE BEE. ISSN 1094-852X
5564 Main St., Williamsville, NY 14221. Telephone: 716-632-4700. FAX: 716-633-8601. URL: http://www.beenews.com. Mailing Address: PO Box 150, Buffalo, NY 14231-0150. Year Established: 1937. Pub. Frequency: w. (Wed.) Page Size: tabloid. Subscrip. Rate: $1 newsstand/cover; $35/yr mailed in county; $32/yr mailed to senior citizens; $50/yr mailed out of county. Circulation: 4,700 per issue (paid). **Owner(s):** Bee Publications, Inc., See address and contact information above. **Management:** Trey Measer, Publisher. Mary Anne Cappon, Advertising Director. Dean Hutter, Advertising Manager. Michael Measer, Circulation Manager. Holly Smith, Classified Adv. Mgr.. **Editorial:** Kimberly Karcher, Editor. David Sherman, Managing Editor. Bob Kupczyk, Feature Editor.

DEPEW BEE. ISSN 0746-4460
5564 Main St., Williamsville, NY 14221. Telephone: 716-632-4700. FAX: 716-633-8601. E-MAIL: read@beenews.com. URL: http://www.beenews.com. Mailing Address: PO Box 150, Buffalo, NY 14231-0150. Year Established: 1893. Pub. Frequency: w. (Thu.) Page Size: tabloid. Subscrip. Rate: $1 newsstand/cover; $35/yr in county; $32/yr to senior citizens; $50/yr out of county. Circulation: 1,390 per issue (paid). **Owner(s):** Bee Publications, Inc., See address and contact information above. **Management:** Trey Measer, Publisher. Dean Hutter, Advertising Manager. Michael Measer, Circulation Manager. Holly Smith, Classified Adv. Mgr.. **Editorial:** Hank Huber, Editor. Bob Kupczyk, Feature Editor. Jill Schmelzer, Lifestyle Editor.

EAST AURORA BEE. ISSN 0898-2945
5564 Main St., Williamsville, NY 14221. Telephone: 716-632-4700. FAX: 716-633-8601. E-MAIL: read@beenews.com. URL: http://www.beenews.com. Mailing Address: PO Box 150, Buffalo, NY 14231-0150. Year Established: 1987. Pub. Frequency: w. (Thu.) Page Size: tabloid. Subscrip. Rate: $1 newsstand/cover; $35/yr mailed in county; $32/yr mailed in county to senior citizens; $50/yr mailed out of county. Circulation: 1,900 per issue (paid). **Owner(s):** Bee Publications, Inc., See address and contact information above. **Management:** Trey Measer, Publisher. Mary Anne Cappon, Advertising Director. Dean Hutter, Advertising Manager. Michael Measer, Circulation Manager. Holly Smith, Classified Adv. Mgr.. **Editorial:** Terri Medina, Editor. David Sherman, Managing Editor. Bob Kupczyk, Feature Editor.

KEN-TON BEE. ISSN 0745-6875
5564 Main St., Williamsville, NY 14221. Telephone: 716-632-4700. FAX: 716-633-8601. E-MAIL: read@beenews.com. URL: http://www.beenews.com. Mailing Address: PO Box 150, Buffalo, NY 14231-0150. Year Established: 1892. Pub. Frequency: w. (Wed.) Page Size: tabloid. Subscrip. Rate: $1 newsstand/cover; $35/yr in county; $32/yr to senior citizens; $50/yr out of county. Circulation: 2,431 per issue (paid). **Owner(s):** Bee Publications, Inc., See address and contact information above. **Management:** Trey Measer, Publisher. Dean Hutter, Advertising Manager. Michael Measer, Circulation Manager. Holly Smith, Classified Adv. Mgr.. **Editorial:** Nick Primerano, Editor. David Sherman, Managing Editor. Jill Schmelzer, Lifestyle Editor.

LANCASTER BEE. ISSN 0746-4487
5564 Main St., Williamsville, NY 14221. Telephone: 716-632-4700. FAX: 716-633-8601. E-MAIL: read@beenews.com. URL: http://www.beenews.com. Mailing Address: PO Box 150, Buffalo, NY 14231-0150. Year Established: 1877. Pub. Frequency: w. (Thu.) Page Size: tabloid. Subscrip. Rate: $1 newsstand/cover; $35/yr in county; $32/yr to senior citizens; $50/yr out of county. Circulation: 3,540 per issue (paid). **Owner(s):** Bee Publications, Inc., See address and contact information above. **Management:** Trey Measer, Publisher. Dean Hutter, Advertising Manager. Michael Measer, Circulation Manager. Holly Smith, Classified Adv. Mgr.. **Editorial:** Hank Huber, Editor. David Sherman, Managing Editor. Bob Kupczyk, Feature Editor.

ORCHARD PARK BEE. ISSN 0896-9876
5564 Main St., Williamsville, NY 14221. Telephone: 716-632-4700. FAX: 716-633-8601. URL: http://www.beenews.com. Mailing Address: PO Box 150, Buffalo, NY 14231-0150. Year Established: 1986. Pub. Frequency: w. (Thu.) Page Size: tabloid. Subscrip. Rate: $1 newsstand/cover; $35/yr in county; $32/yr to senior citizens; $50/yr out of county. Circulation: 11,000 per issue (paid). **Owner(s):** Bee Publications, Inc., See address and contact information above. **Management:** Trey Measer, Publisher. Dean Hutter, Advertising Manager. Michael Measer, Circulation Manager. Holly Smith, Classified Adv. Mgr.. **Editorial:** Christopher Gordon, Editor. David Sherman, Managing Editor. Bob Kupczyk, Feature Editor. Jill Schmelzer, Lifestyle Editor.

WEST SENECA BEE. ISSN 1095-7952
5564 Main St., Williamsville, NY 14221. Telephone: 716-632-4700. FAX: 716-633-8601. E-MAIL: read@beenews.com. URL: http://www.beenews.com. Mailing Address: PO Box 150, Buffalo, NY 14231-0150. Year Established: 1980. Pub. Frequency: w. (Thu.) Page Size: tabloid. Subscrip. Rate: $1 newsstand/cover (effective 2005); $35/yr in county; $32/yr in county to senior citizens; $50/yr out of county. Circulation: 5,962 per issue (paid). **Owner(s):** Bee Publications, Inc., See address and contact information above. **Management:** Trey Measer, Publisher. Dean Hutter, Advertising Manager. Michael Measer, Circulation Manager. Holly Smith, Classified Adv. Mgr.. **Editorial:** Breann Howell, Editor. David Sherman, Managing Editor. Bob Kupczyk, Feature Editor. Jill Schmelzer, Lifestyle Editor.

WINDHAM

WINDHAM JOURNAL. Main St., Windham, NY 12496. Telephone: 518-734-4400. FAX: 518-734-5179. E-MAIL: windhamj@localnet.com. Mailing Address: PO Box 128, Windham, NY 12496. Year Established: 1857. Pub. Frequency: w. (Thu.) Page Size: broadsheet. Subscrip. Rate: $1 newsstand/cover; $31/yr home delivery. Circulation: 2,000 per issue (paid). **Owner(s):** Johnson Newspaper Corp., 260 Washington St., Watertown, NY 13601. Telephone: 315-782-1000. **Management:** Roger Coleman, General Manager. Pamela Geskie, Advertising Director. Brenda Nickles, Circulation Director. **Editorial:** Lori Anander, Editor.

WOLCOTT

WAYNE COUNTY STAR. ISSN 1064-7619
12039 Main St., Wolcott, NY 14590. Telephone: 315-594-2506. FAX: 315-594-6331. E-MAIL: star@wayuga.com. Year Established: 1821. Pub. Frequency: w. (Wed.) Page Size: broadsheet. Subscrip. Rate: $1 newsstand/cover; $16/yr mailed in county; $21/yr mailed out of county. Freelance Pay: $25/article. Circulation: 5,200 per issue (paid). **Owner(s):** Wayuga Community Newspapers, Inc., 6784 Main St., Red Creek, NY 13143. Telephone: 315-754-6229. **Management:** Christopher M. Palermo, Publisher. Chuck Palermo, Advertising. **Editorial:** Louise Hoffman-Broach, Managing Editor.

WOODSTOCK

ULSTER COUNTY TOWNSMAN, THE. PO Box 308, Woodstock, NY 12498-0308. Telephone: 845-679-2145. FAX: 845-679-4304. E-MAIL: blake@lookseek.com. Year Established: 1953. Pub. Frequency: w. (Thu.) Page Size: broadsheet. Subscrip. Rate: $.40 newsstand/cover; $26/yr in county; $30/yr out of county. Adv. Rate: col. inch $6 Freelance Pay: $1.50/column-inch. Circulation: 2,500 per issue (paid). **Owner(s):** J. Blake Killin, See address and contact information above. **Management:** J. Blake Killin, President. **Editorial:** J. Blake Killin, Editor.

YONKERS

EASTCHESTER RECORD. 40 Larkin Plz., Yonkers, NY 10701. Telephone: 914-965-4000. FAX: 914-965-2892. Year Established: 1891. Pub. Frequency: w. (Thu.) Page Size: broadsheet. Subscrip. Rate: $1 newsstand/cover; $25/yr. Freelance Pay: $50/article. Circulation: 3,949 per issue (paid). **Owner(s):** Martinelli Publications, See address and contact information above. **Management:** Francesca Martinelli, Publisher. John Alfieri, Advertising Manager. **Editorial:** Louise Montclare, Editor.

HARRISON INDEPENDENT. 40 Larkin Plz., Yonkers, NY 10701. Telephone: 914-965-4000. FAX: 914-965-2892. E-MAIL: kmrmone@aol.com. Year Established: 1962. Pub. Frequency: w. (Thu.) Page Size: broadsheet. Subscrip. Rate: $1 newsstand/cover; $25/yr. Freelance Pay: $50/article. Circulation: 3,200 per issue (paid). **Owner(s):** Martinelli Publications, See address and contact information above. **Management:** Francesca Martinelli, Publisher. John Alfieri, Advertising Manager. **Editorial:** Louise Montclare, Editor.

HOME NEWS & TIMES. 40 Larkin Plz., Yonkers, NY 10701. Telephone: 914-965-4000. FAX: 914-965-2892. E-MAIL: rmrmone@aol.com. Year Established: 1905. Pub. Frequency: w. (Thu.) Page Size: broadsheet. Subscrip. Rate: $1 newsstand/cover; $25/yr. Freelance Pay: $50/article. Circulation: 12,479 per issue (paid). **Owner(s):** Martinelli Publications, See address and contact information above. **Management:** Francesca Martinelli, Publisher. John Alfieri, Advertising Manager. **Editorial:** Louise Montclare, Editor.

MT. VERNON INDEPENDENT. 40 Larkin Plz., Yonkers, NY 10701. Telephone: 914-965-4000. FAX: 914-965-2892. E-MAIL: rmrmone@aol.com. Year Established: 1990. Pub. Frequency: w. (Thu.) Page Size: broadsheet. Subscrip. Rate: $1 newsstand/cover; $25/yr. Freelance Pay: $50/article. Circulation: 4,000 per issue (paid). **Owner(s):** Martinelli Publications, See address and contact information above. **Management:** Francesca Martinelli, Publisher. John Alfieri, Advertising Manager. **Editorial:** Louise Montclare, Editor.

NORTHCASTLE NEWS. 40 Larkin Plz., Yonkers, NY 10701. Telephone: 914-965-4000. FAX: 914-965-2892. E-MAIL: rmrmone@aol.com. Year Established: 1963. Pub. Frequency: w. (Thu.) Page Size: broadsheet. Subscrip. Rate: $1 newsstand/cover; $25/yr. Freelance Pay: $50/article. Circulation: 3,516 per issue (paid). **Owner(s):** Martinelli Publications, See address and contact information above. **Management:** Francesca Martinelli, Publisher. John Alfieri, Advertising. **Editorial:** Louise Montclare, Editor.

PELHAM SUN, THE. 40 Larkin Plz., Yonkers, NY 10701. Telephone: 914-965-4000. FAX: 914-965-2892. E-MAIL: rmmone@aol.com. Year Established: 1910. Pub. Frequency: w. (Thu.) Page Size: broadsheet. Subscrip. Rate: $1 newsstand/cover; $25/yr. Freelance Pay: $50/article. Circulation: 2,750 per issue (paid). **Owner(s):** Martinelli Publications, See address and contact information above. **Management:** Francesca Martinelli, Publisher. John Alfieri, Advertising Manager. **Editorial:** Louise Montclare, Editor.

RYE CHRONICLE, THE. 40 Larkin Plz., Yonkers, NY 10701. Telephone: 914-965-4000. FAX: 914-965-2892. E-MAIL: rmrmone@aol.com. Year Established: 1903. Pub. Frequency: w. (Thu.) Page Size: broadsheet. Subscrip. Rate: $1 newsstand/cover; $25/yr. Freelance Pay: $50/article. Circulation: 3,200 per issue (paid). **Owner(s):** Martinelli Publications, See address and contact information above. **Management:** Francesca Martinelli, Publisher. Stephen Jannetti, Advertising Manager. **Editorial:** Louise Montclare, Editor.

SOUND VIEW NEWS, THE. 40 Larkin Plz., Yonkers, NY 10701. Telephone: 914-965-4000. FAX: 914-965-2892. Year Established: 1980. Pub. Frequency: w. (Thu.) Page Size: broadsheet. Subscrip. Rate: $1 newsstand/cover; $25/yr. Freelance Pay: $50/article. Circulation: 4,000 per issue (paid). **Owner(s):** Martinelli Publications, See address and contact information above. **Management:** Francesca Martinelli, Publisher. Millie Gutierrez, Advertising Manager. **Editorial:** Louise Montclare, Editor.

YORKTOWN HEIGHTS

NORTH COUNTY NEWS (YORKTOWN HEIGHTS). 1520 Front St., Yorktown Heights, NY 10598. Telephone: 914-962-4748. FAX: 914-962-6753. E-MAIL: editor@northcountynews.com. URL: http://www.nypennysaver.com. Year Established: 1966. Pub. Frequency: w. (Wed.) Page Size: tabloid. Subscrip. Rate: $.75 newsstand/cover; $35/yr local; $40/yr elsewhere. Adv. Rate: col. inch $7.75 Circulation: 9,200 per issue (paid). **Owner(s):** Northern Tier Publishing Corp., See address and contact information above. **Management:** Jean Secor, President. Paul Cardi, Advertising Manager. Gary Olsen, Circulation Manager. **Editorial:** Rick Pezzullo, Managing Editor. Martin Wilbur, Assistant Editor. Lisa Trapasso, Lifestyle Editor. Ray Gallagher, Sports Editor.

PENNYSAVER (YORKTOWN HEIGHTS). 1520 Front St., Yorktown Heights, NY 10598. Telephone: 914-962-3871. FAX: 914-962-4820. URL: http://www.nypennysaver.com. Year Established: 1958. Pub. Frequency: w. (Wed.) Page Size: tabloid Circulation: 351,885 per issue (free). **Owner(s):** Yorktown Pennysaver Corp., See address and contact information above. **Management:** John W. Chase, Publisher. Gary Olson, Circulation Manager. Susan Berliner, Promotion Manager.

NORTH CAROLINA

ALBEMARLE

STANLY NEWS & PRESS. 237 W. North St., Albemarle, NC 28002. Telephone: 704-982-2121. FAX: 704-983-7999. URL: http://www.thesnaponline.com. Mailing Address: PO Box 488, Albemarle, NC 28002. Year Established: 1880. Pub. Frequency: 3/w. (Tue., Thu., Sun.) Page Size: broadsheet. Subscrip. Rate: $.75 newsstand/cover; $1 newsstand/cover Sun.; $48/yr carrier delivery in county; $63/yr mailed out of county; $70/yr mailed out of state. Adv. Rate: col. inch $7.61 Circulation: 10,300 per issue (paid); 10,600 Sunday (paid). **Owner(s):** Community Newspaper Holdings, Inc., 3500 Colonnade Pkwy., Ste. 600, Birmingham, AL 35243. Telephone: 205-298-7100. FAX: 205-298-7101. **Management:** Sandy Selvy, Publisher. Tammy Buck, Advertising Manager. Rick Curlee, Circulation Manager. Daniell Ingold, Classified Adv. Mgr.. **Editorial:** Matt Irwin, Managing Editor. Jo Anne Efird, Lifestyle Editor.

ANDREWS

ANDREWS JOURNAL, THE. 116 Chestnut St, Andrews, NC 28901. Telephone: 828-321-4271. E-MAIL: theandrewsjoural@verizon.net. URL: http://www.theandrewsjournal.com. Pub. Frequency: w. (Thu.) Subscrip. Rate: $16/yr in Cherokee,C.ay & Graham counties; $25/yr out of county; $25/yr mailed out of state. **Owner(s):** Community Newspapers (Athens), Inc., PO Box 792, Athens, GA 30603. Telephone: 706-548-0010. FAX: 706-548-0808. **Management:** David Brown, Publisher. Beth Stewart, Advertising. Linda Simpson, Circulation Manager. Glenn Harbison, Associate Publisher. **Editorial:** Cindy Gibson, Editor.

ANGIER

ANGIER INDEPENDENT. PO Box 878, Angier, NC 27501. Telephone: 919-639-4913. Year Established: 1972. Pub. Frequency: w. (Tue.) Page Size: broadsheet. Subscrip. Rate: $.75 newsstand/cover; $20/yr in state; $30/yr out of state. Circulation: 5,000 per issue (paid). **Owner(s):** Angier Independent, Inc., See address and contact information above. **Management:** Bart Adams, Publisher. Melissa Lee, Advertising. **Editorial:** Jamie Peterson, Editor.

APEX

APEX HERALD, THE. 616 W Chatham St, Apex, NC 27502. Telephone: 919-362-6356. FAX: 919-362-1369. URL: http://www.theapexherald.com. Mailing Address: PO Box 1539, Apex, NC 27502-1539. Year Established: 1956. Pub. Frequency: w. (Thu.) Page Size: broadsheet. Subscrip. Rate: $.50 newsstand/cover; $22/yr in county; $32/yr out of county. Freelance Pay: $20/story. Circulation: 4,000 per issue (paid). **Owner(s):** Heartland Publications, LLC, 20 Research Pkwy, Ste G, Old Saybrook, CT 06475. Telephone: 860-388-3470. FAX: 860-388-3490. **Management:** D. Gaither Perry, Publisher. Helen Hairr, Advertising Director. Jackie Perry, Circulation Manager. **Editorial:** Shawn Daley, Editor.

ASHEBORO

RANDOLPH GUIDE, THE. 431 S. Fayetteville St., Asheboro, NC 27203. Telephone: 336-625-5576. FAX: 336-625-1128. E-MAIL: guide@asheboro.com. Mailing Address: PO Box 1044, Asheboro, NC 27204-1044. Year Established: 1954. Pub. Frequency: w. (Wed.) Page Size: broadsheet. Subscrip. Rate: $.50 newsstand/cover; $18/yr in county; $25/yr elsewhere. Circulation: 4,700 evening (paid and free). **Owner(s):** Community Newspaper Holdings, Inc., 3500 Colonnade Pkwy., Ste. 600, Birmingham, AL 35243. Telephone: 205-298-7100. FAX: 205-298-7101. **Management:** Patricia Edwards, General Manager. Brenda West, Advertising. **Editorial:** Patricia Edwards, Editor.

ASHEVILLE

ASHEVILLE GLOBAL REPORT. ISSN 1536-1071
PO Box 1504, Asheville, NC 28802. E-MAIL: editors@agrnews.org. URL: http://www.agrnews.org.Pub. Frequency: w. Circulation: 2,600 per issue (free). **Owner(s):** Asheville Global Report, See address and contact information above. **Editorial:** Eamon Martin, Editor.

MOUNTAIN XPRESS. 2 Wall St., Asheville, NC 28801. Telephone: 828-251-1333. FAX: 828-251-1311. E-MAIL: xpress@mountainx.com. URL: http://www.mountainx.com. Mailing Address: PO Box 144, Asheville, NC 28802. Year Established: 1994. Pub. Frequency: w. (Wed.) Page Size: tabloid. Subscrip. Rate: $34/yr mailed 3rd class. Freelance Pay: $0.05-$0.10/word. Circulation: 27,000 per issue (controlled and free). **Owner(s):** Green Lined Media, Inc., See address and contact information above. **Management:** Jeff Fobes, Publisher. Breah Parker, Advertising Director. Sammy Cox, Circulation Manager. **Editorial:** Melanie McGee, Art Editor.

BELHAVEN

BEAUFORT-HYDE NEWS, THE. 283 Waters St., Belhaven, NC 27810. Telephone: 252-943-2688. FAX: 252-953-3299. E-MAIL: bhnews@beaufortco.com. Pub. Frequency: w. (Wed.) Page Size: broadsheet. Subscrip. Rate: $.50 newsstand/cover; $24/yr mailed. Circulation: 2,000 per issue (paid). **Owner(s):** Cox Newspapers, Inc., 6205 Peachtree Dunwoody Rd, Atlanta, GA 30328. **Management:** Carole McKay, Publisher. Virginia Bright, Advertising Manager. **Editorial:** Carole McKay, Editor.

BELMONT

BANNER NEWS, THE. 132 N. Main St., Belmont, NC 28012. Telephone: 704-825-0104. FAX: 704-825-0894. E-MAIL: news@thebanner.com. Mailing Address: PO Box 589, Belmont, NC 28012. Year Established: 1929. Pub. Frequency: w. (Wed.) Page Size: broadsheet. Subscrip. Rate: $.50 newsstand/cover; $27/yr in county; $28.50/yr out of county; $33.50/yr mailed out of state. Circulation: 2,500 per issue (paid). **Owner(s):** Republic Newspapers, Inc., PO Box 769, Kings Mountain, NC 28086. Telephone: 704-739-0611. FAX: 704-739-7496. **Management:** Doug Horne, President. Bill Parson, Publisher. Stacy Cobb, Advertising Manager. **Editorial:** Diane Terby, Editor. Rich Hallman, Sports.

BENSON

FOUR OAKS-BENSON NEWS IN REVIEW. PO Box 9, Benson, NC 27504. Telephone: 919-894-3331. FAX: 919-894-1069. E-MAIL: fobnews@aol.com. Year Established: 1910. Pub. Frequency: w. (Wed.) Page Size: broadsheet. Subscrip. Rate: $.50 newsstand/cover; $14/yr in county; $16/yr out of county. Circulation: 4,500 per issue (paid). **Owner(s):** Ralph E. Delano, See address and contact information above. **Management:** Norman Delano, General Manager. Lynn Hales, Advertising Manager. **Editorial:** Mike Dart, Editor.

BLACK MOUNTAIN

BLACK MOUNTAIN NEWS. 118 Cherry St., Ste. 201, Black Mountain, NC 28711. Telephone: 828-669-8727. FAX: 828-669-8619. E-MAIL: jennifer@blackmountainnews.com. URL: http://www.blackmountainnews.com. Mailing Address: PO Box 9, Black Mountain, NC 28711. Year Established: 1945. Pub. Frequency: w. (Thu.) Page Size: broadsheet. Subscrip. Rate: $.50 newsstand/cover; $23/yr in county; $30/yr mailed out of county; $35/yr mailed out of state. Adv. Rate: col. inch $7.50 Freelance Pay: $30/story. Circulation: 4,000 per issue (paid and free). **Owner(s):** Gannett Company, Inc., 7950 Jones Branch Dr., McLean, VA 22107-0001. **Management:** Jennifer Fitzgerald, General Manager. **Editorial:** Jennifer Fitzgerald, Editor.

BLOWING ROCK

BLOWING ROCKET, THE. ISSN 1071-0574
452 Sunset Dr., Ste. 1, Blowing Rock, NC 28605. Telephone: 828-295-7522. FAX: 828-295-7507. E-MAIL: blowingrocket@wataugademocrat.com. URL: Http://www.blowingrocket.com. Mailing Address: PO Box 1630, Greenville, TN 37743. Year Established: 1932. Pub. Frequency: w. (Thu.) Page Size: tabloid. Subscrip. Rate: $.50 newsstand/cover; $22/yr in county; $34/yr in state; $47/yr out of state. Adv. Rate: col. inch $4.40 Circulation: 4,500 per issue (paid). **Owner(s):** Jones Media Group, 121 W Summer St, Greenville, TN 37745. Telephone: 423-581-0088. FAX: 423-235-7012. **Management:** Thomas Wilson, Publisher. Carley Klein, Advertising. Crystal Owens, Circulation Manager. Brenda Minton, Classified Adv. Mgr.. **Editorial:** Jerry W. Burns, Editor.

BOONE

MOUNTAIN TIMES (BOONE). 474 Industrial Park Dr, Boone, NC 28607. Telephone: 828-264-6397. FAX: 828-262-0282. URL: http://www.mountaintimes.com. Mailing Address: PO Box1815, Boone, NC 28607. Year Established: 1978. Pub. Frequency: w. (Thu.) Page Size: tabloid. Subscrip. Rate: $.50 newsstand/cover; $18/yr. Circulation: 18,000. **Owner(s):** Jones Media Group, PO Box 1630, Greenville, TN 37744. 121 W Summer St, Greenville, TN 37745. Telephone: 423-581-0088. FAX: 423-235-7012. **Management:** Jason Reagan, Group Publisher. Charlie Price, Advertising Manager. Randy Feimster, Circulation Manager. Brenda Minton, Classified Adv. Mgr.. **Editorial:** Jason Reagan, Editor. Kim Johnson, Managing Editor.

WATAUGA DEMOCRAT. 474 Industrial Park Dr, Boone, NC 28607. Telephone: 828-264-6397. FAX: 828-262-0282. E-MAIL: newspaper@wataugademocrat.com. URL: http://www.wataugademocrat.com. Mailing Address: PO Box1815, Boone, NC 28607. Year Established: 1888. Pub. Frequency: 3/w. (Mon., Wed., Fri.) Page Size: broadsheet. Subscrip. Rate: $.50 newsstand/cover; $50/yr mailed in county; $93/yr mailed out of county; $142/yr mailed out of state. Adv. Rate: col. inch $7.95 **Wire Service(s):** AP. Circulation: 8,000 per issue (paid). **Owner(s):** Jones Media Group, 121 W Summer St, Greenville, TN 37745. Telephone: 423-581-0088. FAX: 423-235-7012. **Management:** Jason Reagan, Group Publisher. Charlie Price, Advertising Manager. Randy Feimster, Circulation Manager. Brenda Minton, Classified Adv. Mgr.. **Editorial:** Jason Reagan, Editor.

BREVARD

TRANSYLVANIA TIMES, THE. 100 N. Broad St., Brevard, NC 28712. Telephone: 828-833-8156. FAX: 828-883-8158. E-MAIL: ttimes@infoave.net. URL: http://www.transylvaniatimes.com/. Mailing Address: P.O. Box 32, Brevard, NC 28712. Year Established: 1900. Pub. Frequency: s-w. (Mon. & Thu.) Page Size: broadsheet. Subscrip. Rate: $.50 newsstand/cover; $23/yr in county; $26/yr out of county. Adv. Rate: page $5.60 Circulation: 8,500 per issue (paid). **Owner(s):** Stella A. Trapp, See address and contact information above. **Management:** Stella A. Trapp, Publisher. Karen Anthony, Advertising Manager. **Editorial:** John Lanier, Editor. Derek Mckissock, News Editor.

BRYSON CITY

SMOKEY MOUNTAIN TIMES. 114 Everett St., Bryson City, NC 28713. Telephone: 828-488-2189. FAX: 828-488-0315. E-MAIL: news@thesmokeymountaintimes.com. URL: http://www.thesmokeymountaintimes.com. Mailing Address: P. O . Box 730, Bryson City, NC 28713. Year Established: 1883. Pub. Frequency: w. (Thu.) Subscrip. Rate: $15.97/yr in county; $22.36/yr out of county; $24/yr mailed out of state. **Owner(s):** Community Newspapers (Athens), Inc., PO Box 792, Athens, GA 30603. **Management:** Clay Wilson, Publisher. Brandy Baudrand, Advertising. **Editorial:** Dawn Duplak, Production Manager. Pete Lawson, Senior Editor.

BURGAW

PENDER CHRONICLE. 108 Courthouse Ave., Burgaw, NC 28425-0726. Telephone: 910-259-2504. FAX: 910-259-6277. E-MAIL: nbradshaw@hloprint.com. Mailing Address: PO Box 726, Burgaw, NC 28425. Year Established: 1896. Pub. Frequency: w. (Wed.) Page Size: broadsheet. Subscrip. Rate: $.50 newsstand/cover; $20/yr in county; $30/yr out of county; $40/yr out of state. Circulation: 5,418 per issue (paid). **Owner(s):** H.L. Oswald Enterprises, Inc., 107 N College, Wallace, NC 28466. Telephone: 910-285-2178. **Management:** Gary Weaver, General Manager. H.L. Oswald III, Publisher. Mary Hart Oswald, Advertising. **Editorial:** Sammie Carter, Editor.

PENDER POST. 201A W. Fremont St., Burgaw, NC 28425. Telephone: 910-259-9111. FAX: 910-259-9112. E-MAIL: postnews@bizec.rr.com. Mailing Address: PO Box 955, Burgaw, NC 28425-0955. Year Established: 1971. Pub. Frequency: w. (Wed.) Page Size: broadsheet. Subscrip. Rate: $.50 newsstand/cover; $20/yr in county; $26/yr out of county. Adv. Rate: col. inch $6.50 Circulation: 5,000 per issue (paid). **Owner(s):** Pender Publishing, PO Box 955, Burgaw, NC 28425. Telephone: 910-259-9111. **Management:** Cindy Ramsey, Publisher. Ann Beach, Office Manager. **Editorial:** Cindy H. Ramsey, Editor.

BURNSVILLE

YANCEY COMMON TIMES JOURNAL. 22 N. Main St., Burnsville, NC 28714. Telephone: 828-682-2120. FAX: 828-682-3701. E-MAIL: timesjournalnews@trccomputing.com. Mailing Address: P.O. Drawer 280, Burnsville, NC 28714. Year Established: 1993. Pub. Frequency: w. (Wed.) Page Size: broadsheet. Subscrip. Rate: $.50 newsstand/cover; $20.50/yr in county; $28.50/yr in state; $35/yr out of state. Adv. Rate: col. inch $7.25 Freelance Pay: $2/column-inch. Circulation: 7,000 per issue (paid). **Owner(s):** Trib Publications, Inc., PO Box 648, Manchester, GA 31816. Telephone: 706-846-4336. **Management:** Pat Randolph, General Manager. Jody Higgins, Publisher. Pat Randolph, Advertising Manager. Audria Briggs, Circulation Manager. **Editorial:** Jody Higgins, Editor.

CARY

CARY NEWS, THE. 212 E. Chatham St., Cary, NC 27511. Telephone: 919-460-2600. FAX: 919-460-6034. E-MAIL: jandrews@nando.com. Mailing Address: PO Box 4949, Cary, NC 27519. Year Established: 1963. Pub. Frequency: w. (Thu.) Page Size: standard. Subscrip. Rate: $.50 newsstand/cover; $18/yr. **Wire Service(s):** AP. Circulation: 15,000 per issue (paid). **Owner(s):** The/McClatchy Company, PO Box 15779, Sacramento, CA 95852. Telephone: 916-321-1000. **Management:** Carol Allen, Publisher. **Editorial:** Keith King, Editor.

CHAPEL HILL

CHAPEL HILL NEWS, THE. ISSN 1070-2741 505 W. Franklin St., Chapel Hill, NC 27516. Telephone: 919-932-2000. FAX: 919-968-4953. URL: http://www.chapelhillnews.com. Mailing Address: PO Box 870, Chapel Hill, NC 27514. Year Established: 1923. Pub. Frequency: s-w. (Wed. & Sun.) Page Size: broadsheet. Subscrip. Rate: $.50 newsstand/cover; $104/yr mailed. **Wire Service(s):** AP, NYT. Circulation: 24,000 per issue (free). **Owner(s):** The/McClatchy Company, 2100 Q St, Sacramento, CA 95816. **Management:** Brenda Larson, Publisher. Peter Tompkins, Advertising Manager. Sean O'Rourke, Circulation Manager. **Editorial:** Mark Schultz, Editor. Don Evans, News Editor. Elliott Warnock, Sports Editor.

CHERRYVILLE

CHERRYVILLE EAGLE. 107 1/2 E. Main St., Cherryville, NC 28021. Telephone: 704-435-6752. FAX: 704-435-8293. E-MAIL: kmhnews@aol.com. Mailing Address: PO Box 699, Cherryville, SC 28021. Year Established: 1905. Pub. Frequency: w. (Wed.) Page Size: broadsheet. Subscrip. Rate: $.50 newsstand/cover; $27/yr gaston & cleveland cys; $28.50/yr mailed out of area; $33.50/yr mailed out of state. Circulation: 3,000 per issue (paid). **Owner(s):** Republic Newspapers, Inc., PO Box 769, Kings Mountain, NC 28086. Telephone: 704-739-0611. FAX: 704-739-7496. **Management:** Doug Horne, Owner. Bill Fulton, Office Manager. Dean Lutz, Advertising. **Editorial:** Todd Hagans, Editor.

CLAYTON

CLAYTON NEWS-STAR. PO Box 157, Clayton, NC 27520. Telephone: 919-553-7234. FAX: 919-553-5858. E-MAIL: editor@claytonnew-star.com. URL: http://www.claytonnews-star.com. Year Established: 1911. Pub. Frequency: w. (Tue.) Page Size: broadsheet. Subscrip. Rate: $.50 newsstand/cover; $20/yr home delivery in county; $26.50/yr mailed out of county; $38/yr mailed out of state; $15.90/yr in county to senior citizens. Circulation: 10,600 per issue (paid). **Owner(s):** Stewart McLeod, See address and contact information above. **Management:** Stewart McLeod, Publisher. Shirley Johnson, Advertising Manager. **Editorial:** Margaret Richie, Executive Editor. Cathy Marraccini, News Editor.

CLEMMONS

CLEMMONS COURIER, THE. 3600 Clemmons Rd., Clemmons, NC 27012. Telephone: 336-766-4126. FAX: 336-766-7350. E-MAIL: courier9@bellsouth.net. URL: http://www.clemmonscourier.com. Mailing Address: PO Box 765, Clemmons, NC 27012. Year Established: 1960. Pub. Frequency: w. (Thu.) Page Size: standard. Subscrip. Rate: $.50 newsstand/cover; $15/yr in state; $20/yr out of state. Circulation: 3,200 per issue (paid). **Owner(s):** Evening Post Publishing Co., 134 Columbus St., Charleston, SC 29403. Telephone: 803-577-7111. **Management:** Dwight Sparks, Publisher. Christy Clark, Advertising. Kay Henderson, Circulation Manager. **Editorial:** Dwight Sparks, Editor. Chris Mackie, Sports Editor.

CREEDMOOR

BUTNER-CREEDMOOR NEWS, THE. 418 N Main St, Creedmoor, NC 27522. Telephone: 919-528-2393. FAX: 919-528-0288. E-MAIL: bcnews@mindspring.com. URL: http://www.butnercreedmoornews.org. Mailing Address: PO Box 726, Creedmoor, NC 27522. Year Established: 1965. Pub. Frequency: w. (Thu.) Page Size: standard. Subscrip. Rate: $.50 newsstand/cover; $32.10/yr in state; $36/yr out of state; $80/yr foreign. Adv. Rate: col. inch $8.50 Circulation: 5,300 per issue (paid). **Owner(s):** Harry R. Coleman, See address and contact information above. **Management:** Harry R. Coleman, Publisher. Penny Carpenter, Office Manager. Gail Locklear, Circulation Manager. **Editorial:** Harry R. Coleman, Editor.

DURHAM

CAROLINA TIMES, THE. 923 Old Fayetteville St., Durham, NC 27701. Telephone: 919-682-2913. FAX: 919-688-8434. E-MAIL: ctimes@compuserve.com. Mailing Address: PO Box 3825, Durham, NC 27702. Year Established: 1926. Pub. Frequency: w. (Thu.) Page Size: broadsheet. Subscrip. Rate: $.30 newsstand/cover; $19.25/yr mailed in county; $23.43/yr mailed out of county. Freelance Pay: $25-$150/article. **Wire Service(s):** AP. Circulation: 5,800 per issue (paid). **Owner(s):** United Publishers, Inc., See address and contact information above. **Management:** Kenneth Edmonds, Publisher.

INDEPENDENT (DURHAM), THE. 302 E Pettigrew St, 3rd fl., Durham, NC 27701. Telephone: 919-286-1972. FAX: 919-286-4274. E-MAIL: editors@indyweek.com. URL: http://www.indyweek.com. Mailing Address: PO Box 2690, Durham, NC 27715. Year Established: 1983. Pub. Frequency: w. (Wed.) Page Size: tabloid. Subscrip. Rate: $45/yr mailed indiv.; $55/yr inst.. Circulation: 50,000 per issue (paid and free). **Owner(s):** Carolina Independent Publications, See address and contact information above. **Management:** Susan Harper, General Manager. Susan Watson, Publisher. Gloria Mock, Advertising Manager. **Editorial:** Lisa Sorg, Editor. Jennifer Strom, Managing Editor.

EDENTON

CHOWAN HERALD, THE. 421 S. Broad St., Edenton, NC 27932-1935. Telephone: 252-482-4418. FAX: 252-482-4410. E-MAIL: chowanherald@earthlink.net. Mailing Address: PO Box 207, Edenton, NC 27932-0207. Year Established: 1934. Pub. Frequency: w. (Wed.) Page Size: standard. Subscrip. Rate: $.50 newsstand/cover; $25.64/yr in county; $41.70/yr mailed out of county; $43.84/yr mailed out of state. Circulation: 5,000 evening (paid). **Owner(s):** Cox Newspapers, Inc., 6205 Peachtree Dunwoody Rd., Atlanta, GA 30328. Telephone: 678-645-0000. **Management:** Robert S Piazza, Publisher. Ashley Missiri, Advertising Manager. **Editorial:** Rebecca Bunch, Editor.

ELIZABETHTOWN

BLADEN EXTRA. 228 W Broad St, Elizabethtown, NC 28337. Telephone: 910-862-4163. FAX: 910-862-6602. E-MAIL: ads@bladenjournal.com. URL: http://www.bladenjournal.com. Mailing Address: PO Box 70, Elizabethtown, NC 28337-0070.Pub. Frequency: w. (Tue.) Page Size: standard Circulation: 4,500 evening (free). **Owner(s):** Heartland Publications, LLC, 20 Research Pkwy, Ste G, Old Saybrook, CT 06475. Telephone: 860-388-3470. FAX: 860-388-3490. **Management:** Tim Wilkins, General Manager. Amanda Pait, Advertising Manager. Joval Royal, Classified Adv. Mgr..

BLADEN JOURNAL. 228 W Broad St, Elizabethtown, NC 28337. Telephone: 910-862-4163. FAX: 910-862-6602. E-MAIL: ads@bladenjournal.com. URL: http://www.bladenjournal.com. Mailing Address: PO Box 70, Elizabethtown, NC 28337-0070. Year Established: 1899. Pub. Frequency: s-w. (Tue. & Fri.) Page Size: broadsheet. Subscrip. Rate: $.50 newsstand/cover; $37.45/yr in county; $49.22/yr out of county; $57/yr out of state. Adv. Rate: col. inch $9.05 **Wire Service(s):** AP. Circulation: 4,400 morning (paid). **Owner(s):** Heartland Publications, LLC, 20 Research Pkwy, Ste G, Old Saybrook, CT 06475. Telephone: 860-388-3470. FAX: 860-388-3490. **Management:** Tim Wilkins, General Manager. Lynn McLamb, Publisher. Amanda Pait, Advertising Manager. Gladys Edwards, Circulation Manager. Joval Royal, Classified Adv. Mgr.. **Editorial:** Tim Wilkins, Editor.

FARMVILLE

FARMVILLE ENTERPRISE, THE. 121 S. Main St., Farmville, NC 27828. Telephone: 252-753-4126. FAX: 252-753-4127. E-MAIL: farmvilleenterprise@earthlink.net. Year Established: 1910. Pub. Frequency: w. (Wed.) Page Size: broadsheet. Subscrip. Rate: $.50 newsstand/cover; $24.95/yr in county; $28/yr mailed out of county; $33/yr mailed out of state. Circulation: 2,500 per issue (paid). **Owner(s):** Cox Newspapers, Inc., 6205 Peachtree Dunwoody Rd, Atlanta, GA 30328. **Management:** Donna Kemp, Publisher. **Editorial:** Michael Barrett, Editor.

FOREST CITY

COUNTY COURIER (FOREST CITY). 601 Oak St., Forest City, NC 28043. Telephone: 828-245-8355. FAX: 828-248-2790. URL: http://www.thedigitalcourier.com. Mailing Address: PO Box 1149, Forest City, NC 28043. Year Established: 1926. Pub. Frequency: w. (Wed.) Page Size: broadsheet.Subscrip. Rate: $.50 newsstand/cover; $9.50/yr Circulation: 12,000 per issue (free). **Owner(s):** Paxton Media Group Llc, 201 S. Fourth St., Paducah, KY 42003. Telephone: 270-575-8600. FAX: 270-442-8188. **Management:** Jim Brown, Publisher. Lori Falkner, Advertising Director. Heather Rhodes, Classified Adv. Mgr.. Joyce Ferguson, Business Manager. **Editorial:** Mike Gavin, Managing Editor. Alex Podlogar, Sports Editor.

FRANKLIN

FRANKLIN (NC) PRESS. 40 Depot St., Franklin, NC 28734. Telephone: 828-524-2010. FAX: 828-524-8821. E-MAIL: news@thefranklinpress.com. URL: http://www.thefranklinpress.com. Mailing Address: PO Box 350, Franklin, NC 28744. Year Established: 1886. Pub. Frequency: s-w. (Wed. & Fri.) Page Size: broadsheet. Subscrip. Rate: $.50 newsstand/cover; $22.50/yr home delivery in county; $39/yr home delivery out of county. Circulation: 9,200 per issue (paid). **Owner(s):** Community Newspapers (Athens), Inc., PO Box 792, Athens, GA 30603. Telephone: 706-548-0010. FAX: 706-548-0808. **Management:** Rachel Hoskins, Publisher. Deb Reeves, Advertising Manager. Dorothy Haplin, Classified Adv. Mgr.. **Editorial:** Barbara McRea, Editor. Andy Scheidler, Sports Editor.

FREMONT

WAYNE WILSON NEWS LEADER. ISSN 0746-6803
113 N. Wilson St., Fremont, NC 27830. Telephone: 919-242-6301. FAX: 919-936-2065. E-MAIL: newsbar@esn.net. Mailing Address: PO Box 158, Fremont, NC 27830. Pub. Frequency: w. (Thu.) Page Size: standard. Subscrip. Rate: $.75 newsstand/cover; $20/yr mailed local; $26/yr mailed out of area; $31/yr mailed out of state. Circulation: 2,000 per issue (paid). **Owner(s):** Barry Merrill, PO Box 597, Princeton, NC 27569-0597. Telephone: 919-936-9891. FAX: 919-936-2065. **Management:** Barry Merrill, Publisher. **Editorial:** Barry Merrill, Editor.

FUQUAY-VARINA

FUQUAY-VARINA INDEPENDENT. 209 E Vance St, Fuquay-Varina, NC 27526. Telephone: 919-552-5675. FAX: 919-552-7564. URL: http://www.fuquay-varinaindependent.com. Mailing Address: PO Box 669, Fuquay-Varina, NC 27526. Pub. Frequency: w. (Thu.) Page Size: broadsheet. Subscrip. Rate: $.50 newsstand/cover; $22/yr in county; $32/yr out of county. Circulation: 4,000 per issue (paid). **Owner(s):** Heartland Publications, LLC, 20 Research Pkwy, Ste G, Old Saybrook, CT 06475. Telephone: 860-388-3470. FAX: 860-388-3490. **Management:** D. Gaither Perry, Publisher. Helen Hairr, Advertising Director. Jackie Perry, Circulation Manager. Jason Kubota, Classified Adv. Mgr.. **Editorial:** Janet Kangas, Editor.

HOLLY SPRINGS POST. 209 E Vance St, Fuquay-Varina, NC 27526. Telephone: 919-552-5675. FAX: 919-552-7564. URL: http://www.hollyspringssun.com. Mailing Address: PO Box 669, Fuquay-Varina, NC 27526. Pub. Frequency: w. (Thu.) Page Size: broadsheet. Subscrip. Rate: $.50 newsstand/cover; $22/yr in county; $32/yr out of county. Circulation: 3,500 per issue (paid). **Owner(s):** Heartland Publications, LLC, 20 Research Pkwy, Ste G, Old Saybrook, CT 06475. Telephone: 860-388-3470. FAX: 860-388-3490. **Management:** D. Gaither Perry, Publisher. Helen Hairr, Advertising Director. Jackie Perry, Circulation Manager. Jason Kubota, Classified Adv. Mgr.. **Editorial:** Janet Kangas, Editor.

GARNER

CLEVELAND POST. Hwy 70-E, Ste 503-L, Garner, NC 27529. Telephone: 919-772-1166. FAX: 919-779-7824. URL: http://www.clevelandpost.com. Mailing Address: PO Box 466, Garner, NC 27529. Year Established: 1975. Pub. Frequency: w. (Wed.) Page Size: tabloid. Subscrip. Rate: $.50 newsstand/cover; $22/yr in county; $32/yr out of county. Circulation: 3,500 per issue (paid). **Owner(s):** Heartland Publications, LLC, 20 Research Pkwy, Ste G, Old Saybrook, CT 06475. Telephone: 860-388-3470. FAX: 860-388-3490. **Management:** D. Gaither Perry, Publisher. Helen Hairr, Advertising Director. Jackie Perry, Circulation Manager. **Editorial:** John Cate, Editor. Wilotha Davis III, Associate Editor.

GARNER NEWS. Hwy 70-E, Ste 503-L, Garner, NC 27529. Telephone: 919-772-1166. FAX: 919-779-7824. E-MAIL: garnernews@mindspring.com. URL: Http://www.garnernews.net. Mailing Address: PO Box 466, Garner, NC 27529. Year Established: 1962. Pub. Frequency: w. (Wed.) Page Size: broadsheet. Subscrip. Rate: $.50 newsstand/cover; $22/yr in county; $32/yr out of county. Circulation: 5,200 per issue (paid). **Owner(s):** Heartland Publications, LLC, 20 Research Pkwy, Ste G, Old Saybrook, CT 06475. Telephone: 860-388-3470. FAX: 860-388-3490. **Management:** D. Gaither Perry, Publisher. Helen Hairr, Advertising Director. Jackie Perry, Circulation Manager. Jason Kubota, Classified Adv. Mgr.. **Editorial:** John Cate, Editor. Wilotha Davis III, Associate Editor.

GATESVILLE

GATES COUNTY INDEX. 715 N. Main St., Gatesville, NC 27938. Telephone: 252-357-0960. FAX: 252-332-3940. Mailing Address: PO Box 146, Gatesville, NC 27938. Year Established: 1942. Pub. Frequency: w. (Wed.) Page Size: broadsheet. Subscrip. Rate: $.50 newsstand/cover; $22.50/yr in county; $31.25/yr out of county; $35/yr mailed out of state. Circulation: 2,400 per issue (paid). **Owner(s):** Boone Newspapers, Inc., 15222 Freemen's Bend Rd., Northport, AL 35475. Telephone: 205-330-4100. **Management:** Jeff Findley, Publisher. Sidney Joyner, Advertising Manager. David Friedman, Circulation Manager. Donna Jenkins, Business Manager. **Editorial:** Cal Bryant, Editor.

GRAHAM

ALAMANCE NEWS, THE. PO Box 431, Graham, NC 27253-0431. Telephone: 336-228-7851. FAX: 336-229-9602. Year Established: 1875. Pub. Frequency: w. (Thu.) Page Size: standard. Subscrip. Rate: $.50 newsstand/cover; $20/yr in county; $29/yr out of county. Circulation: 7,100 per issue (paid). **Owner(s):** Boney Publishers, Inc., See address and contact information above. **Management:** Tom Boney Jr., Publisher. **Editorial:** Tom Boney Jr., Editor.

GREENVILLE

DUPLIN TIMES - PROGRESS SENTINEL. PO Box 1967, Greenville, NC 27835. Telephone: 252-329-9500. E-MAIL: duplintimespub@earthlink.net. Year Established: 1935. Pub. Frequency: w. (Thu.) Page Size: standard. Subscrip. Rate: $.50 newsstand/cover; $18/yr local; $25.50/yr in state; $35/yr out of state. Adv. Rate: col. inch $7.70 Circulation: 10,000 per issue (paid). **Owner(s):** Cooke Communications North Carolina LLC, See address and contact information above.

GRIFTON

TIMES-LEADER, THE. 209 S. Highland Ave., Grifton, NC 28530-9467. Telephone: 252-524-4376. FAX: 252-524-3312. E-MAIL: thetimesleaderudv@earthlink.net. Mailing Address: PO Box 369, Grifton, NC 28530-0369. Year Established: 1912. Pub. Frequency: w. (Wed.) Page Size: standard. Subscrip. Rate: $.50 newsstand/cover in county; $19.95/yr home delivery in county; $27.50/yr mailed out of county; $35.95/yr mailed out of state. Adv. Rate: col. inch $6.40 Circulation: 2,550 per issue (paid). **Owner(s):** Cox Newspapers, Inc., 6205 Peachtree Dunwoody Rd., Atlanta, GA 30328. **Management:** Mitchell Oakley, Publisher. Kyle Stephens, Advertising. **Editorial:** Amanda Manning, Managing Editor.

HAVELOCK

HAVELOCK NEWS, THE. 230 Stonebridge Sq., Havelock, NC 28532-9505. Telephone: 252-444-1999. FAX: 252-444-1057. URL: http://havenews.com. Mailing Address: PO Box 777, Havelock, NC 28532-0777. Year Established: 1986. Pub. Frequency: w. (Wed.) Page Size: standard. Subscrip. Rate: $.50 newsstand/cover; $20/yr in state; $40/yr out of state. Circulation: 2,500 per issue (paid). **Owner(s):** Freedom Communications, Inc., 17666 Fitch, Irvine, CA 92614. Telephone: 949-253-2300. **Management:** Jim Bretzius, Publisher. Judy Avery, Advertising Director. Jeff White, Circulation Manager. **Editorial:** Hunter Bretzius, Editor.

HAYESVILLE

CLAY COUNTY PROGRESS. 43 Main St., Hayesville, NC 28904. Telephone: 828-389-8431. FAX: 828-389-9997. E-MAIL: claycoprog@webworkz.com. URL: http://www.claycountyprogress.com. Mailing Address: PO Box 483, Hayesville, NC 28904-0483. Pub. Frequency: w. (Thu.) Page Size: standard. Subscrip. Rate: $.50 newsstand/cover; $17/yr home delivery in county; $25/yr mailed out of county; $25/yr mailed out of state. Adv. Rate: col. inch $6.30 Circulation: 3,850 per issue (controlled). **Owner(s):** Community Newspapers (Athens), Inc., PO Box 792, Athens, GA 30603. Telephone: 706-548-0010. **Management:** Becky Long, Publisher. Tracey Sprinkles, Marketing Director.

HERTFORD

PERQUIMANS WEEKLY. 119 W. Grubb St., Hertford, NC 27944. Telephone: 252-426-5728. FAX: 252-426-4625. E-MAIL: perquimansweekly@nccox.com. Mailing Address: PO Box 277, Hertford, NC 27944. Year Established: 1932. Pub. Frequency: w. (Wed.) Page Size: broadsheet. Subscrip. Rate: $.35 newsstand/cover; $24.20/yr mailed in state; $26.40/yr mailed out of state. Adv. Rate: col. inch $6 Circulation: 2,000 per issue (paid). **Owner(s):** Cox Newspapers, Inc., 6205 Peachtree Dunwoody Rd, Atlanta, GA 30328. Telephone: 404-843-5000. **Management:** Susan Harris, Publisher. Beverly Alexander, Advertising. **Editorial:** Susan Harris, Editor.

HICKORY

HICKORY NEWS, THE. 270 Union Sq. Common, Hickory, NC 28601. Telephone: 828-328-6164. FAX: 828-322-6398. E-MAIL: editorial@hickorynews.net. URL: http://www.hickorynews.net. Mailing Address: PO Box 2650, Hickory, NC 28603. Year Established: 1970. Pub. Frequency: w. (Thu.) Page Size: broadsheet.Adv. Rate: col. inch $5.95 Circulation: 5,500 per issue (paid). **Owner(s):** Freedom Communications, Inc., 17666 Fitch, Irvine, CA 92614. Telephone: 949-253-2300. FAX: 949-474-7675. **Management:** Skip Foster, General Manager. Maragrita Venegas, Publisher. Mickey Price, Advertising Director. Jeff Isenhouer, Circulation Manager. **Editorial:** Maragrita Venegas, Editor.

HICKORY NEWS EXTRA. 270 Union Sq. Common, Hickory, NC 28601. Telephone: 828-328-6164. FAX: 828-322-6398. URL: http://www.hickorynews.net. Mailing Address: PO Box 2650, Hickory, NC 28603. Year Established: 1970. Pub. Frequency: w. (Thu.) Page Size: tabloid Circulation: 10,000 per issue (free). **Owner(s):** Freedom Communications, Inc., 17666 Fitch, Irvine, CA 92614. Telephone: 949-253-2300. FAX: 949-474-7675. **Management:** Skip Foster, General Manager. Jeff Isenhouer, Operations Manager. Don Elmore, Advertising Director. **Editorial:** Margarita Venegas, Editor.

HIGHLANDS

HIGHLANDER (HIGHLANDS), THE. 134 N Fifth St, Highlands, NC 28741-0249. Telephone: 828-526-4114. FAX: 828-526-3658. E-MAIL: hilands@aol.com. URL: http://www.highlandsnews.com. Mailing Address: P.O. Box 249, Highlands, NC 28741-0249. Year Established: 1958. Pub. Frequency: s-w. (Tue. & Fri.) Page Size: standard. Subscrip. Rate: $.50 newsstand/cover; $23/yr home delivery in county in Macon & Jackson ctys.; $31/yr mailed out of county. Adv. Rate: col. inch $8.11 Circulation: 4,100 per issue (paid). **Owner(s):** Community Newspapers (Athens), Inc., PO Box 792, Athens, GA 30603. Telephone: 706-548-0010. **Management:** Eric NeSmith, Publisher. **Editorial:** Eric NeSmith, Editor.

HILLSBOROUGH

NEWS OF ORANGE COUNTY, THE. ISSN 1071-1716
109 E. King St., Hillsborough, NC 27278. Telephone: 919-732-2171. FAX: 919-732-4852. E-MAIL: editorial@newsoforange.com. URL: http://www.newsoforange.com. Mailing Address: PO Box 580, Hillsborough, NC 27278. Year Established: 1893. Pub. Frequency: w. (Wed.) Page Size: broadsheet. Subscrip. Rate: $.50 newsstand/cover; $23/yr in county; $31/yr elsewhere. Adv. Rate: col. inch $7.55 Circulation: 8,000 per issue (paid and free). **Owner(s):** Womack Publishing Co., Inc., PO Box 111, Chatham, VA 24531. Telephone: 434-432-1654. **Management:** Charles A. Womack Jr., President. Tom Spargur, Publisher. Kyle Butler, Advertising Director. **Editorial:** Jonathan Coleman, Editor.

KENANSVILLE

DUPLIN TODAY. 102 Front St., Kenansville, NC 28349-0069. Telephone: 910-296-0239. FAX: 910-296-0239. E-MAIL: duplintimespub@earthlink.net. Mailing Address: PO Box 69, Kenansville, NC 28349-0069. Pub. Frequency: w. (Thu.) Page Size: standard Circulation: 12,600 per issue (free). **Owner(s):** Cox Newspapers, Inc., 6205 Peachtree Dunwoody Rd., Atlanta, GA 30328. Telephone: 678-645-0000. **Management:** Gary Scott, Publisher. **Editorial:** Gary Scott, Editor.

Weeklies

KENLY

KENLY NEWS. PO Box 39, Kenly, NC 27542. Telephone: 919-284-2295. FAX: 919-284-6397. E-MAIL: rstewart@kenlynews.com. Year Established: 1973. Pub. Frequency: w. (Wed.) Page Size: broadsheet. Subscrip. Rate: $.75 newsstand/cover; $21/yr local; $28/yr mailed out of area; $33/yr mailed out of state. Circulation: 3,200 per issue (paid). **Owner(s):** Richard D. Stewart, See address and contact information above. **Management:** Richard D. Stewart, Publisher. Virginia Lee, Advertising Manager. **Editorial:** Richard D. Stewart, Editor.

KERNERSVILLE

KERNERSVILLE NEWS. 300 E. Mountain St., Kernersville, NC 27284. Telephone: 336-993-2161. FAX: 336-993-0931. URL: http://www.kernersvillenews.com. Mailing Address: PO Box 337, Kernersville, NC 27285. Year Established: 1938. Pub. Frequency: 3/w. (Tue., Thu., Sat.) Page Size: standard. Subscrip. Rate: $.50 newsstand/cover; $34.50/yr local. Circulation: 21,000 per issue (paid and free). **Owner(s):** Carter Publishing Co., See address and contact information above. **Management:** John Owensby, Publisher. Connie Owensby, Vice President. Tracy Cardwell, Advertising Manager. **Editorial:** John Owensby, Editor.

LA GRANGE

WEEKLY GAZETTE, THE. 108 S. Caswell St., La Grange, NC 28551-1708. Telephone: 252-566-3028. FAX: 252-566-5318. E-MAIL: theweeklygazette@embarqmail.com. Year Established: 1972. Pub. Frequency: w. (Wed.) Page Size: standard.Subscrip. Rate: $.50 newsstand/cover; $24/yr Circulation: 1,500 per issue (paid). **Owner(s):** PAB Publishing Co., Inc., See address and contact information above. **Management:** Glenn Penuel, Publisher. **Editorial:** Glenn Penuel, Editor.

LINCOLNTON

LINCOLN TIMES-NEWS. 119 W. Water St., Lincolnton, NC 28092. Telephone: 704-735-3031. FAX: 704-735-3037. E-MAIL: lincolntimesnews@ltnews.com. URL: http://www.lincolntimesnews.com. Mailing Address: PO Box 40, Lincolnton, NC 28092-0040. Year Established: 1903. Pub. Frequency: 3/w. (Mon., Wed., Fri.) Page Size: standard. Subscrip. Rate: $.50 newsstand/cover; $54.60/yr home delivery in county; $54.60/yr mailed in state; $64/yr mailed out of state. **Wire Service(s):** AP. Circulation: 10,005 evening (paid). **Owner(s):** Western Carolina Publishing Co., See address and contact information above. **Management:** Jerry G. Leedy, Publisher. Robert Parker, Advertising Manager. Robin Ledford, Circulation Manager. **Editorial:** Steve Steiner, Managing Editor. Sarah Gano, Lifestyle Editor. John Mark Brooks, Sports.

LITTLETON

LITTLETON OBSERVER, THE. 454 Timberlane Dr., Littleton, NC 27850-0417. Telephone: 252-586-6397. FAX: 252-586-6875. Mailing Address: PO Box 100, Littleton, NC 27850-0100. Year Established: 1955. Pub. Frequency: w. (Thu.) Page Size: broadsheet. Subscrip. Rate: $.75 newsstand/cover; $21/yr mailed in county; $23/yr mailed out of county; $25/yr mailed out of state. Freelance Pay: $6/column-inch. Circulation: 3,000 per issue (paid). **Owner(s):** Maurice Emery, See address and contact information above. **Management:** Maurice Emery, Publisher. Anita Alston, Office Manager. **Editorial:** Maurice Emery, Editor.

LOUISBURG

FRANKLIN TIMES. 109 S Bickett Blvd., Louisburg, NC 27549. Telephone: 919-496-6503. FAX: 919-496-1689. E-MAIL: ad@thefranklintimes.com. URL: http://www.thefranklintimes.com. Mailing Address: PO Box 119, Louisburg, NC 27549-0119. Year Established: 1870. Pub. Frequency: s-w. (Wed. & Sat.) Page Size: broadsheet. Subscrip. Rate: $.75 newsstand/cover; $29/yr home delivery in county; $46/yr in state; $58/yr out of state. Adv. Rate: col. inch $9.50 Freelance Pay: $0.50/column-inch. Circulation: 8,700 per issue (paid). **Owner(s):** Gary Cunard, See address and contact information above. **Management:** Gary Cunard, Publisher. Donna Cunard, Advertising Manager. Gill Kearney, Circulation Director. **Editorial:** Kathy Harrelson, Managing Editor.

LUMBERTON

RED SPRINGS CITIZEN, THE. 2175 N Roberts Ave, Lumberton, NC 28359. Telephone: 910-739-4322. FAX: 910-739-6553. Mailing Address: PO Box 1028, Lumberton, NC 28359. Pub. Frequency: w. (Thu.) Page Size: tabloid. Subscrip. Rate: $.50 newsstand/cover; $15.90/yr in county; $21.20/yr out of county; $30/yr out of state. Circulation: 2,650 per issue (paid). **Owner(s):** Heartland Publications, LLC, 20 Research Pkwy, Ste G, Old Saybrook, CT 06475. Telephone: 860-388-3470. FAX: 860-388-3490. **Management:** Trip Hatley, Advertising Director. Ed Knight, Circulation Manager. **Editorial:** Donnie Douglas, Editor.

ST. PAULS REVIEW. 2175 N Roberts Ave, Lumberton, NC 28359. Telephone: 910-739-4322. FAX: 910-739-6553. Mailing Address: PO Box 1028, Lumberton, NC 28359. Pub. Frequency: w. (Thu.) Page Size: broadsheet. Subscrip. Rate: $.50 newsstand/cover; $15.90/yr in county; $21.20/yr out of county; $30/yr out of state. Circulation: 2,800 per issue (paid). **Owner(s):** Heartland Publications, LLC, 20 Research Pkwy, Ste G, Old Saybrook, CT 06475. Telephone: 860-388-3470. FAX: 860-388-3490. **Management:** Trip Hatley, Advertising Director. Ed Knight, Circulation Manager. **Editorial:** Donnie Douglas, Editor.

MADISON

MADISON MESSENGER, THE. ISSN 0892-1814
208 W. Murphy St., Madison, NC 27025. Telephone: 336-548-6047. FAX: 336-548-2853. E-MAIL: slawson@reidsvillereview.com. URL: http://www.madison-messenger.com. Mailing Address: PO Box 508, Madison, NC 27025. Year Established: 1915. Pub. Frequency: s-w. (Wed. & Fri.) Page Size: broadsheet. Subscrip. Rate: $.50 newsstand/cover; $25/yr in state; $55/yr out of state. Freelance Pay: $5/column-inch. Circulation: 7,000 per issue (paid). **Owner(s):** Media General, Inc., 333 E. Franklin St., Richmond, VA 23219. Telephone: 804-649-6000. FAX: 804-775-8090. **Management:** Ellen Ishmael, Publisher. Jodi Vasquez, Advertising Director. Jessica Byerly, Advertising Manager. Paul Richman, Circulation Manager. **Editorial:** Steve Lawson, Editor.

MANTEO

COASTLAND TIMES. ISSN 1069-4722
501 Budleigh St., Manteo, NC 27954. Telephone: 252-473-2105. FAX: 252-473-1515. Year Established: 1935. Pub. Frequency: 3/w. (Tue., Thu., Sun.) Page Size: broadsheet. Subscrip. Rate: $.50 newsstand/cover; $39.66/yr in county. Adv. Rate: col. inch $6.72 **Wire Service(s):** AP. Circulation: 8,000 per issue (paid). **Owner(s):** Times Printing Co., Inc., See address and contact information above. **Management:** F.W. Meekins, Publisher. **Editorial:** F.W. Meekins, Editor.

MARION

MCDOWELL EXPRESS. 136 Logan St., Marion, NC 28752. Telephone: 828-652-3313. FAX: 828-652-4769. URL: http://www.mcdowellnews.com. Mailing Address: PO Box 610, Marion, NC 28752-0610. Pub. Frequency: w. (Thu.) Page Size: standard Circulation: 8,550 per issue (free). **Owner(s):** Media General, Inc., 333 E. Franklin St., Richmond, VA 23219. Telephone: 434-649-6000. **Management:** David Setzer, Publisher. Keith Austin, Advertising Manager. **Editorial:** Scott Hollifield, Editor.

MARSHVILLE

HOME NEWS, THE. PO Box 100, Marshville, NC 28103. Telephone: 704-624-5068. FAX: 704-624-2371. Year Established: 1892. Pub. Frequency: w. (Thu.) Page Size: broadsheet. Subscrip. Rate: $.50 newsstand/cover; $21/yr in county; $26/yr elsewhere. Circulation: 3,000 per issue (paid). **Owner(s):** John Edmondson, See address and contact information above. **Management:** John Edmondson, Advertising Manager. **Editorial:** John Edmondson, Editor.

MEBANE

MEBANE ENTERPRISE. ISSN 1067-0858
106 N. Fourth St., Mebane, NC 27302. Telephone: 919-563-3555. FAX: 919-563-9242. E-MAIL: mebenter@mebtel.net. Year Established: 1908. Pub. Frequency: w. (Wed.) Page Size: broadsheet. Subscrip. Rate: $.50 newsstand/cover; $22/yr. Adv. Rate: col. inch $6.65 Circulation: 6,900 per issue (paid and free). **Owner(s):** Womack Publishing Co., Inc., PO Box 111, Chatham, VA 24531. Telephone: 434-432-1654. **Management:** Natalie Isley, General Manager. Tammy Davis, Advertising. **Editorial:** Algernon Primm, Editor.

MOCKSVILLE

DAVIE COUNTY ENTERPRISE-RECORD. 171 S. Main St., Mocksville, NC 27028. Telephone: 336-751-2120. FAX: 336-751-9760. URL: http://www.enterprise-record.com/. Mailing Address: PO Box 99, Mocksville, NC 27028-0099. Year Established: 1916. Pub. Frequency: w. (Thu.) Page Size: broadsheet. Subscrip. Rate: $.50 newsstand/cover; $20/yr mailed in state; $25/yr mailed out of state. Circulation: 8,100 per issue (paid). **Owner(s):** Davie County Publishing Co., Inc., See address and contact information above. **Management:** Robin Fergusson, General Manager. Dwight Sparks, Publisher. Ray Tutterow, Advertising Manager. **Editorial:** Dwight Sparks, Editor. Mike Barnhardt, Managing Editor.

MOORESVILLE

MOORESVILLE TRIBUNE. 147 E. Center Ave., Mooresville, NC 28115. Telephone: 704-664-5554. FAX: 704-664-3614. E-MAIL: news@mooresvilletribune.com. URL: http://www.mooresvilletribune.com. Mailing Address: PO Box 300, Mooresville, NC 28115. Year Established: 1932. Pub. Frequency: s-w. (Wed. & Fri.) Page Size: broadsheet.Subscrip. Rate: $.50 newsstand/cover; $52/yr Circulation: 6,000 per issue (paid). **Owner(s):** Media General, Inc., 333 E. Franklin St., Richmond, VA 23219. **Management:** Tim Dearman, Publisher. Sherry Montero, Advertising Manager. Bud Welch, Circulation Manager. **Editorial:** Dale Gowing, Editor. Larry Sullivan, Sports Editor.

MOREHEAD CITY

CARTERET COUNTY NEWS-TIMES. 4034 Arendell St., Morehead City, NC 28557. Telephone: 252-726-7081. FAX: 252-726-6016. E-MAIL: newstimes@aol.com:. URL: http://www.carteretnewstimes.com. Mailing Address: P.O. Box 1679, Morehead City, NC 28557. Year Established: 1912. Pub. Frequency: 3/w. (Sun., Wed., Fri.) Page Size: broadsheet. Subscrip. Rate: $.50 newsstand/cover; $62.40/yr home delivery; $63.29/yr mailed in county; $99.77/yr mailed in state. **Wire Service(s):** AP. Circulation: 12,200 Sunday (paid); 12,200 per issue (paid). **Owner(s):** Carteret Publishing, Inc., See address and contact information above. **Management:** Lockwood B. Phillips, Publisher. Patti Kittrell, Advertising Manager. Joyce Ferrell, Circulation Director. Rosa Garner, Circulation Manager. Renee Fuller, Classified Adv. Mgr.. **Editorial:** Walter D. Phillips, Editor. Beth Blake, Managing Editor. Brad Rich, Asst. Managing Ed.. Mark Hibbs, Business Editor. Dennis Thomason, Sports Editor.

TOPSAIL VOICE. 4034 Arendell St., Morehead City, NC 28557. Telephone: 252-726-7081. FAX: 252-726-6016. Mailing Address: P.O. Box 1679, Morehead City, NC 28557. Pub. Frequency: w. **Owner(s):** Carteret Publishing, Inc., See address and contact information above.

MORGANTON

BURKE MARKETPLACE. 301 Collett St., Morganton, NC 28655. Telephone: 828-437-2161. FAX: 828-437-5372. E-MAIL: newsherald@hci.net. URL: http://www.morganton.com. Mailing Address: PO Box 280, Morganton, NC 28680-0280. Pub. Frequency: w. (Wed.) Page Size: broadsheet Circulation: 8,000 per issue (free). **Owner(s):** Media General, Inc., 333 E. Franklin St., Richmond, VA 23219. Telephone: 804-649-6000. FAX: 804-649-6898. **Management:** David Crawley, Publisher. Randy Hart, Advertising Director. Kimberly Mahle, Circulation Director. **Editorial:** Duke Conover, Editor. Kevin Lumpkin, Sports Editor.

MT. OLIVE

MOUNT OLIVE TRIBUNE. 301 Hwy. 55, W., Mt. Olive, NC 28365. Telephone: 919-658-9456. FAX: 919-658-9559. E-MAIL: publisher@mountolivetribune.com. URL: http://www.mountolivetribune.com. Mailing Address: PO Box 1039, Mt. Olive, NC 28365. Year Established: 1904. Pub. Frequency: s-w. (Tue. & Fri.) Page Size: broadsheet. Subscrip. Rate: $.50 newsstand/cover; $24.48/yr mailed in county; $36.67/yr mailed out of county. Adv. Rate: col. inch $7.85 Circulation: 5,000 per issue (paid). **Owner(s):** Benmot Publishing Co., PO Box 6159, Raleigh, NC 27628. Telephone: 919-788-0950. **Management:** Becky Cole, Advertising Manager. **Editorial:** Steve Herring, Editor.

MURPHY

CHEROKEE SCOUT. ISSN 0746-3987
89 Sycamore St, Murphy, NC 28906. Telephone: 828-837-5122. FAX: 828-837-5832. E-MAIL: dbrown@cherokeescout.com. URL: http://www.cherokeescout.com. Mailing Address: PO Box 190, Murphy, NC 28906. Year Established: 1889. Pub. Frequency: w. (Wed.) Page Size: broadsheet. Subscrip. Rate: $.75 newsstand/cover; $22/yr in county; $35/yr out of county. Adv. Rate: col. inch $12.75 Circulation: 9,500 per issue (paid). **Owner(s):** Community Newspapers (Athens), Inc., PO Box 792, Athens, GA 30603. Telephone: 706-548-0010. FAX: 706-548-0808. **Management:** David Brown, Publisher. Donna Brown, Circulation Manager. Donna Cook, Sales Manager. **Editorial:** Robert Horne, Editor.

NASHVILLE

NASHVILLE GRAPHIC. 203 W. Washington St., Nashville, NC 27856. Telephone: 252-459-7101. FAX: 252-459-3052. Year Established: 1895. Pub. Frequency: w. (Wed.) Page Size: broadsheet. Subscrip. Rate: $.75 newsstand/cover; $22.50/yr in county; $25.29/yr out of county. Circulation: 4,500 per issue (controlled and free). **Owner(s):** Nash County Newspapers, Inc., See address and contact information above. **Management:** JoAnne Cooper, Publisher. Cindy Hale, Circulation Manager. JoAnne Cooper, Business Manager.

NEWLAND

AVERY JOURNAL-TIMES, THE. 335 Linville St, Newland, NC 28657. Telephone: 828-733-2448. FAX: 828-733-0639. URL: http://www.averyjournal.com. Mailing Address: PO Box 1330, Newland, NC 28657. Year Established: 1870. Pub. Frequency: w. (Thu..) Page Size: broadsheet. Subscrip. Rate: $.50 newsstand/cover; $22.50/yr in county. Adv. Rate: col. inch $6.95 Circulation: 4,000 per issue (paid). **Owner(s):** Jones Media Group, 121 W Summer St, Greenville, TN 37745. Telephone: 423-581-0088. FAX: 423-235-7012. **Management:** Nancy Morrison, Publisher. **Editorial:** Nancy Morrison, Editor.

NORTH WILKESBORO

JOURNAL-PATRIOT. ISSN 1090-6290
711 Main St., North Wilkesboro, NC 28659. Telephone: 336-838-4117. FAX: 336-838-9864. E-MAIL: wilkesjp@wilkes.net. Year Established: 1906. Pub. Frequency: 3/w. (Mon., Wed., Fri.) Page Size: broadsheet. Subscrip. Rate: $.35 newsstand/cover; $37.50/yr mailed in county; $46.66/yr mailed out of county; $40/yr mailed out of state. Circulation: 16,000 per issue (paid). **Owner(s):** Carter-Hubbard Publishing Co., Inc., See address and contact information above. **Management:** John Hubbard, Co-Publisher. Nellie Archibald, Advertising Manager. Debbie Church, Circulation Manager. **Editorial:** Charles Williams, Editor. Justin Griffin, Sports.

WILKES JOURNAL-PATRIOT. 711 Main St., North Wilkesboro, NC 28659-4211. Telephone: 336-838-4117. FAX: 336-838-9864. Year Established: 1906. Pub. Frequency: 3/w. (Mon., Wed., & Fri.) Page Size: broadsheet. Subscrip. Rate: $.35 newsstand/cover; $34.08/yr in county; $36.21/yr out of county; $35/yr out of state. Adv. Rate: col. inch $5.95 Circulation: 15,000 per issue (paid). **Owner(s):** Carter-Hubbard Publishing Co., Inc., 711 Main St., North Wilkesboro, NC 28659. Telephone: 336-838-4117. FAX: 336-838-9864. **Management:** John W. Hubbard, Publisher. Nellie Archibald, Advertising Manager. **Editorial:** Charles Williams, Editor.

OLD FORT

NEWS BULLETIN OF MCDOWELL COUNTY, THE. PO Box 638, Old Fort, NC 28762-0638. Telephone: 828-668-4783. FAX: 828-668-4722. Year Established: 1973. Pub. Frequency: w. (Wed.) Page Size: broadsheet. Subscrip. Rate: $.25 newsstand/cover; $15/yr in county; $20/yr mailed out of county. Circulation: 2,000 per issue (controlled and free). **Owner(s):** Eleanor White & Thurman Padgham, See address and contact information above. **Management:** Thurman Padgham, General Manager. **Editorial:** Eleanor White, Editor.

ORIENTAL

PAMLICO NEWS. 406 Broad St., Oriental, NC 28571-9772. Telephone: 252-249-1555. FAX: 252-249-0857. E-MAIL: cn1106@coastal.net.com. URL: http://www.pamliconews.com. Pub. Frequency: w. (Wed.) Page Size: standard. Subscrip. Rate: $.50 newsstand/cover; $20/yr in county; $35/yr mailed out of county; $45/yr mailed out of state. Circulation: 4,800 per issue (paid). **Owner(s):** Nancy Winfrey, See address and contact information above. **Management:** Frieda Hudson, Publisher. **Editorial:** Tory Thorp, Editor.

OXFORD

OXFORD PUBLIC LEDGER. 200 W. Spring St., Oxford, NC 27565. Telephone: 919-693-2646. FAX: 919-693-3704. E-MAIL: opl@earthlink.net. Year Established: 1881. Pub. Frequency: s-w. (Mon. & Thu.) Page Size: broadsheet. Subscrip. Rate: $.50 newsstand/cover; $29.43/yr mailed in county; $32.64/yr mailed in state. Circulation: 6,500 per issue (paid). **Owner(s):** Royster Critcher, See address and contact information above. **Management:** Ronald N. Critcher, President. Charles S. Critcher, Publisher. Ronald N. Critcher, Advertising Manager. Charles S. Critcher, Circulation Manager. **Editorial:** Al Carson, Editor.

PITTSBORO

CHATHAM RECORD, THE. 19 Hillsboro St., Pittsboro, NC 27312-5891. Telephone: 919-542-3013. FAX: 919-542-2590. URL: http://www.thechathamnews.com. Mailing Address: PO Box 459, Pittsboro, NC 27312-0459. Pub. Frequency: w. (Thu.) Page Size: standard. Subscrip. Rate: $.50 newsstand/cover; $20/yr local; $25/yr out of county. Circulation: 3,100 per issue (paid). **Owner(s):** Chatham News Publishing Co., See address and contact information above. **Management:** Alan D. Resch, Publisher. **Editorial:** Alan D. Resch, Editor. Randall Rigsbee, Managing Editor. Don Beane, Sports Editor.

PLYMOUTH

ROANOKE BEACON. PO Box 726, Plymouth, NC 27962. Telephone: 252-793-2123. FAX: 252-793-5365. E-MAIL: roanokebeacon@mchsi.com. Year Established: 1889. Pub. Frequency: w. (Wed.) Page Size: broadsheet. Subscrip. Rate: $.75 newsstand/cover; $24.50/yr home delivery local. Circulation: 4,700 per issue (paid). **Owner(s):** Washington County Newspapers, Inc., See address and contact information above. **Management:** Gary Cunard, Publisher. Lois Perez, Advertising. Gloria Cox, Classified Adv. Mgr.. **Editorial:** Gary Cunard, Editor.

PRINCETON

PRINCETON NEWS LEADER. 119 W. Edwards St., Princeton, NC 27569. Telephone: 919-936-9891. FAX: 919-936-2065. E-MAIL: newsbar@esn.net. Mailing Address: PO Box 597, Princeton, NC 27569-0587. Pub. Frequency: w. (Wed.) Page Size: standard. Subscrip. Rate: $.75 newsstand/cover; $20/yr mailed local; $26/yr mailed in state; $31/yr mailed out of state. Circulation: 2,000 per issue (paid). **Owner(s):** Barry Merrill, PO Box 597, Princeton, NC 27569. Telephone: 919-936-9891. FAX: 919-936-2065. **Management:** Barry Merrill, Publisher. **Editorial:** Barry Merrill, Editor.

RAEFORD

NEWS-JOURNAL (RAEFORD), THE. 119 W. Elwood Ave., Raeford, NC 28376. Telephone: 910-875-2121. FAX: 910-875-7256. URL: http://www.thenews-journal.com. Mailing Address: PO Box 550, Raeford, NC 28376. Year Established: 1905. Pub. Frequency: w. (Wed.) Subscrip. Rate: $.75 newsstand/cover; $26/yr in county; $38/yr out of county. Adv. Rate: col. inch $7.50 Circulation: 4,500 per issue (paid). **Owner(s):** Dickson Press, Inc., See address and contact information above. **Management:** Robert Dickson, Publisher. **Editorial:** Patricia Wilson, Editor.

RICHLANDS

RICHLANDS-BEULAVILLE ADVERTISER-NEWS. 9100 Richlands Hwy, Richlands, NC 28574. Telephone: 910-324-5062. FAX: 910-324-6267. Mailing Address: PO Box 487, Richlands, NC 28574. Year Established: 1975. Pub. Frequency: w. (Wed.) Page Size: broadsheet. Subscrip. Rate: $.50 newsstand/cover; $20/yr in Duplin & Onslow cys.; $30/yr out of county; $40/yr out of state. Circulation: 4,200 per issue (paid). **Owner(s):** H.L. Oswald Enterprises, Inc., 107 N College, Wallace, NC 28466. Telephone: 910-285-2178. FAX: 910-285-3179. **Management:** Gary Weaver, General Manager. H.L. Oswald III, Publisher. Mike Sears, Advertising. Karen Hudson, Advertising Manager. **Editorial:** Sammie Carter, Editor.

ROBBINSVILLE

GRAHAM STAR, THE. 774 Tallulch Rd., Robbinsville, NC 28771. Telephone: 828-479-3383. FAX: 828-479-1044. E-MAIL: news@grahamstar.com. URL: http://www.grahamstar.com. Mailing Address: PO Box 69, Robbinsville, NC 28771-0068. Year Established: 1950. Pub. Frequency: w. (Thu.) Page Size: broadsheet. Subscrip. Rate: $.50 newsstand/cover; $14.50/yr in county; $22/yr out of county. Adv. Rate: col. inch $8.95 Circulation: 3,400 per issue (paid). **Owner(s):** Community Newspapers (Athens), Inc., PO Box 792, Athens, GA 30603. Telephone: 706-548-0010. **Management:** Matthew Osborne, Publisher. Melanie Oswalt, Advertising Manager. **Editorial:** Matthew Osborne, Editor.

SCOTLAND NECK

COMMONWEALTH PROGRESS. 613 Main St, Scotland Neck, NC 27874. Telephone: 252-826-2111. FAX: 252-826-2110. E-MAIL: cprogress@embarqmail.com. Pub. Frequency: w. (Wed.) Page Size: broadsheet. Subscrip. Rate: $.50 newsstand/cover; $21/yr area; $18.90/yr to senior citizens. Adv. Rate: col. inch $7 Circulation: 3,000 per issue (paid). **Owner(s):** Shearin Publishing, See address and contact information above. **Management:** Marvin Shearin, Publisher. Shirley Arthur, Advertising Manager. **Editorial:** Joe Holliday, Managing Editor.

SHELBY

SHELBY SHOPPER & INFO. 503 N. Lafayette St., Shelby, NC 28150-4426. Telephone: 704-484-1047. FAX: 704-484-1067. E-MAIL: advertising@shelbyinfo.com. URL: http://www.shelbyinfo.com. Year Established: 1984. Pub. Frequency: w. (w Thu.) Page Size: tabloid.Adv. Rate: col. inch $9.50 Circulation: 29,000 per issue (free). **Owner(s):** Greg Ledford, See address and contact information above. **Management:** Greg Ledford, Publisher. Mike Marlow, Circulation Director. **Editorial:** Milton Andrews, Editor.

SILER CITY

CHATHAM NEWS, THE. 303 W. Raleigh St., Siler City, NC 27344-3725. Telephone: 919-663-3232. FAX: 919-663-4042. URL: http://www.thechathamnews.com. Mailing Address: PO Box 290, Siler City, NC 27344-0290. Pub. Frequency: w. (Thu.) Page Size: broadsheet. Subscrip. Rate: $.50 newsstand/cover; $20/yr in county; $25/yr out of county. Circulation: 6,100 per issue (paid). **Owner(s):** Chatham News Publishing Co., See address and contact information above. **Management:** Alan D. Resch, Publisher. Deidre Brown, Advertising. Jeanne Pierce, Circulation Manager. **Editorial:** Alan D. Resch, Editor. Randall Rigsbee, Managing Editor. Don Beane, Sports Editor.

SMITHFIELD

SMITHFIELD HERALD. 125 S. Fourth St., Smithfield, NC 27577. Telephone: 919-934-2176. FAX: 919-989-7093. E-MAIL: sbolejac@nando.com. URL: http://www.smithfieldherald.com. Mailing Address: PO Box 1417, Smithfield, NC 27577. Year Established: 1882. Pub. Frequency: s-w. (Tue. & Fri.) Page Size: broadsheet. Subscrip. Rate: $.50 newsstand/cover; $53/yr mailed out of state. Adv. Rate: col. inch $22.42 Circulation: 15,103 per issue (paid). **Owner(s):** The/McClatchy Company, PO Box 15779, Sacramento, CA 95852. Telephone: 916-321-1936. **Management:** S.E. Thorndyke Jr., Publisher. Kim Young-Taylor, Advertising Manager. Gina Rogers, Circulation Director. **Editorial:** Scott Bolejack, Managing Editor. Traci Ashley, News Editor. Clay Best, Sports Editor.

SNOW HILL

STANDARD LACONIC, THE. 756 S. E. Third St., Snow Hill, NC 28580. Telephone: 252-747-3882. FAX: 252-747-7656. E-MAIL: standardlaconic@nccox.com. Mailing Address: PO Box 128, Snow Hill, NC 25850. Pub. Frequency: w. (Wed.) Page Size: broadsheet. Subscrip. Rate: $.50 newsstand/cover; $22/yr local; $28/yr elsewhere. Circulation: 3,300 per issue (paid). **Owner(s):** Cox Newspapers, Inc., 6205 Peachtree Dunwoody Rd, Atlanta, GA 30328. **Management:** Mitchell Oakley, Publisher.

SOUTHERN PINES

SOUTHERN PINES PILOT. 145 W. Pennsylvania Ave., Southern Pines, NC 28387. Telephone: 910-692-7271. FAX: 910-692-9382. URL: http://www.thepilot.com. Mailing Address: PO Box 58, Southern Pines, NC 28388. Year Established: 1920. Pub. Frequency: 3/w. (Mon. ,Wed., Fri.) Page Size: broadsheet. Subscrip. Rate: $.50 newsstand/cover; $47.95/yr home delivery local; $54.25/yr mailed in county; $60.50/yr mailed out of county; $69.50/yr mailed out of state. Circulation: 17,000 per issue (paid). **Owner(s):** David Woronoff, See address and contact information above. **Management:** David Woronoff, Publisher. Pat Taylor, Advertising Director. Darlene Stark, Circulation Director. Jennifer Bowles, Classified Adv. Mgr.. **Editorial:** Steve Bouser, Editor. David Sinclair, Managing Editor. Faye Dasen, Feature Editor. Glenn M. Sides, Photographer. Hunter Chase, Sports Editor.

SOUTHPORT

STATE PORT PILOT, THE. 114 E. Moore St., Southport, NC 28461-0548. Telephone: 910-457-4568. FAX: 910-457-9427. E-MAIL: pilot@stateportpilot.com. URL: http://www.stateportpilot.com. Mailing Address: PO Box 10548, Southport, NC 28461-0548. Year Established: 1928. Pub. Frequency: w. (Wed.) Page Size: broadsheet. Subscrip. Rate: $.50 newsstand/cover; $18/yr in county; $26/yr out of county; $32/yr out of state. Adv. Rate: col. inch $7.50 Circulation: 9,917 per issue (paid). **Owner(s):** The State Port Pilot, Inc., See address and contact information above. **Management:** Ed Harper, Publisher. Beth Powell, Advertising Manager. Brenda Fiedler, Classified Adv. Mgr.. **Editorial:** Ed Harper, Editor. Suzi Drake, Feature Editor. Lee Hinnant, Government Affrs. Ed..

SPRING HOPE

SPRING HOPE ENTERPRISE. 113 Ash St., Spring Hope, NC 27882. Telephone: 252-478-3651. FAX: 252-478-3075. E-MAIL: shenterprise@earthlink.net. URL: http://www.springhopeenterprise.com. Mailing Address: PO Box 399, Spring Hope, NC 27882-0399. Year Established: 1947. Pub. Frequency: w. (Thu.) Page Size: standard. Subscrip. Rate: $.75 newsstand/cover; $25/yr mailed in county; $35/yr mailed out of county. Adv. Rate: col. inch $7 Circulation: 3,000 per issue (paid and free). **Owner(s):** Ken Ripley, See address and contact information above. **Management:** Ken Ripley, Publisher. Michelle Shearin, Advertising Manager. **Editorial:** Ken Ripley, Editor.

SPRUCE PINE

MITCHELL NEWS JOURNAL. 261 Locust St., Spruce Pine, NC 28777. Telephone: 828-765-2071. FAX: 828-765-1616. E-MAIL: editor@mitchellnews.com. URL: http://www.mitchellnews.com. Mailing Address: PO Box 339, Spruce Pine, NC 28777. Year Established: 1927. Pub. Frequency: w. (Wed.) Page Size: broadsheet. Subscrip. Rate: $.50 newsstand/cover; $20/yr home delivery in county; $30/yr mailed out of county; $35/yr mailed out of state. Freelance Pay: $50/story. Circulation: 6,200 per issue (paid). **Owner(s):** Community Newspapers (Athens), Inc., PO Box 792, Athens, GA 30603. **Management:** Andy Ashurst, Publisher. Elaine Priesmeyer, Office Manager. Cindy Lindsey, Advertising. **Editorial:** Andy Ashurst, Editor.

ST. PAULS

SAINT PAULS REVIEW, THE. 218 W Broad St, St. Pauls, NC 28384. Telephone: 910-865-4179. FAX: 910-865-4995. Mailing Address: PO Box 265, St. Pauls, NC 28384. Pub. Frequency: w. (Thu.) Page Size: tabloid. Subscrip. Rate: $.50 newsstand/cover; $15.90/yr in county; $30/yr mailed out of state. Adv. Rate: col. inch $3 Circulation: 2,750 per issue (paid). **Owner(s):** Heartland Publications, LLC, 20 Research Pkwy, Ste G, Old Saybrook, CT 06475. Telephone: 860-388-3470. FAX: 860-388-3490. **Management:** Lynn McLamb, Publisher. **Editorial:** L. Paul Terry, Editor.

SWANSBORO

TIDELAND NEWS. 774 W Corbett Ave, Swansboro, NC 28584. Telephone: 910-326-5066. FAX: 910-326-1165. URL: http://www.tidelandnews.com. Mailing Address: PO Box 1000, Swansboro, NC 28584-1000. Year Established: 1979. Pub. Frequency: w. (Wed.) Page Size: broadsheet. Subscrip. Rate: $.50 newsstand/cover; $19/yr home delivery local. Adv. Rate: col. inch $6.20 Freelance Pay: $35/article. Circulation: 3,200 per issue (paid). **Owner(s):** Carteret Publishing, Inc., 4034 Arendell St., Morehead City, NC 28557. Telephone: 252-726-7081. FAX: 252-726-6016. **Management:** Lockwood B. Phillips, Publisher. Jennifer Pearce, Advertising Manager. Dan Parker, Circulation Manager. **Editorial:** Jimmy Willimas, Editor.

SYLVA

SYLVA HERALD & RURALITE. 539 W Main St, Sylva, NC 28779-0307. Telephone: 828-586-2611. FAX: 828-586-2637. E-MAIL: news@thesylvaherald.com. URL: http://www.thesylvaherald.com. Mailing Address: P. O. Box 307, Sylva, NC 28779-0307. Year Established: 1926. Pub. Frequency: w. (Thu.) Page Size: broadsheet. Subscrip. Rate: $.50 newsstand/cover; $20.20/yr mailed in county; $34.24/yr mailed out of county; $32/yr mailed out of state. Circulation: 7,200 per issue (paid). **Owner(s):** Community Newspapers (Athens), Inc., PO Box 792, Athens, GA 30603. **Management:** Steve Gray, General Manager. Margo Gray, Advertising Manager. Carolyn Hoyle, Circulation Director. **Editorial:** Lynn Hotaling, Editor. Rose Hopper, Feature Editor. Carey Phillips, Sports Editor.

Weeklies

TABOR CITY

TABOR-LORIS TRIBUNE. PO Box 67, Tabor City, NC 28463. Telephone: 910-653-3153. FAX: 910-653-9440. Year Established: 1946. Pub. Frequency: w. (Wed.) Page Size: broadsheet. Subscrip. Rate: $.25 newsstand/cover; $14.95/yr local; $18.95/yr mailed elsewhere. Freelance Pay: $0.25/column-inch. Circulation: 3,800 per issue (paid). **Owner(s):** W. Horace Carter, See address and contact information above. **Management:** David Snipes, General Manager. W. Horace Carter, President. Deuce Niven, Publisher. Joyce Sammons, Advertising. **Editorial:** Deuce Niven, Editor. Penny Holmes, Production Manager.

TAYLORSVILLE

TAYLORSVILLE TIMES, THE. 24 E Main Ave, Taylorsville, NC 28681. Telephone: 828-632-2532. FAX: 828-632-8233. E-MAIL: taylorsvilletimes@taylorsvilletimes.com. URL: http://www.taylorsvilletimes.com/. Year Established: 1886. Pub. Frequency: w. (Wed.) Page Size: broadsheet. Subscrip. Rate: $.50 newsstand/cover; $25.62/yr mailed in county; $35.23/yr mailed out of county. Adv. Rate: col. inch $6 Circulation: 7,000 per issue (paid). **Owner(s):** Walter L. Sharpe, See address and contact information above. **Management:** Walter L. Sharpe, Publisher. Wesley Sharpe, Advertising. **Editorial:** Walter L. Sharpe, Editor. Micah Henry, Managing Editor. Donny Pennell, Sports.

THOMASVILLE

THOMASVILLE TIMES. 512 Turner St., Thomasville, NC 27360. Telephone: 336-472-9500. FAX: 336-476-7272. E-MAIL: hyde@tville.times. URL: http://www.thomasvilletimes.net. Mailing Address: PO Box 549, Thomasville, NC 27361. Year Established: 1890. Pub. Frequency: 3/w. (Tue., Thu., Sat.) Page Size: broadsheet. Subscrip. Rate: $.50 newsstand/cover; $46/yr home delivery; $56/yr mailed. **Wire Service(s):** AP. Circulation: 5,500 per issue (paid). **Owner(s):** High Point Enterprises, Inc., 210 Church St., High Point, NC 27262. Telephone: 910-888-3500. **Management:** Sarah Smith, General Manager. John Walker, Publisher. Elizabeth Hyde, Advertising Manager. Carolyn Bennett, Circulation Manager. **Editorial:** Lisa Wall, Editor. R,J, Beatty, Sports.

TROY

MONTGOMERY HERALD (TROY). 139 Bruton St., Troy, NC 27371. Telephone: 910-576-6051. FAX: 910-576-1050. E-MAIL: herald@mc-online.net. URL: http://www.montgomeryherald.com. Mailing Address: PO Box 466, Troy, NC 27371. Year Established: 1884. Pub. Frequency: w. (Wed.) Page Size: broadsheet. Subscrip. Rate: $.75 newsstand/cover; $23/yr in county; $32/yr out of county. Circulation: 6,700 per issue (paid). **Owner(s):** Womack Publishing Co., Inc., PO Box 111, Chatham, VA 24531. Telephone: 434-432-1654. **Management:** Tammy Haywood, Advertising Manager. **Editorial:** Tammy Dunn, Editor. J.W. Houston, Sports.

WADESBORO

ANSON RECORD, THE. 115 W Martin St, Wadesboro, NC 28170. Telephone: 704-694-2161. FAX: 704-694-7060. E-MAIL: ansonrecord@alltel.net. URL: http://www.ansonrecord.com. Mailing Address: PO Box 959, Wadesboro, NC 28170. Year Established: 1881. Pub. Frequency: w. (Wed.) Page Size: broadsheet. Subscrip. Rate: $.50 newsstand/cover; $19.50/yr in county; $25/yr out of county zones 1 & 2; $30/yr mailed out of state zones 3-10. Circulation: 7,500 per issue (paid). **Owner(s):** Heartland Publications, LLC, 20 Research Pkwy, Ste G, Old Saybrook, CT 06475. Telephone: 860-388-3470. FAX: 860-388-3490. **Management:** David Deese, Publisher. Amanda Henry, Advertising. Gwen Tyson, Circulation Manager. **Editorial:** Thomas Thacker, Editor.

WAKE FOREST

WAKE WEEKLY, THE. 229 E. Owen Ave., Wake Forest, NC 27587. Telephone: 919-556-3182. FAX: 919-556-2233. E-MAIL: email@wakeweekly.com. URL: http://www.wakeweekly.com. Mailing Address: PO Box 1919, Wake Forest, NC 27588. Year Established: 1947. Pub. Frequency: w. (Thu.) Page Size: broadsheet. Subscrip. Rate: $.75 newsstand/cover; $26.50/yr in county & adj cys; $34.45/yr out of area; $36/yr out of state. Circulation: 8,900 per issue (paid). **Owner(s):** Greg Allen, See address and contact information above. **Management:** Greg Allen, Publisher. Janet C. Rose, Advertising. Bridget Mickschutz, Circulation Director. **Editorial:** Suzanne Rook, Editor. John Whitfield, Associate Editor.

WALLACE

WALLACE ENTERPRISE, THE. 107 N College, Wallace, NC 28466. Telephone: 910-285-2178. FAX: 910-285-3179. E-MAIL: enterprise@duplinnet.com. Mailing Address: PO Box 699, Wallace, NC 28466-0699. Year Established: 1923. Pub. Frequency: s-w. (Mon. & Thu.) Page Size: broadsheet. Subscrip. Rate: $.50 newsstand/cover; $25/yr in county; $40/yr out of county; $50/yr out of state. Circulation: 7,500 per issue (paid). **Owner(s):** H.L. Oswald Enterprises, Inc., See address and contact information above. **Management:** Gary Weaver, General Manager. H.L. Oswald III, Publisher. Mary Hart Oswald, Advertising. **Editorial:** Sammie Carter, Editor.

WARSAW-FAISON NEWS. 107 N College, Wallace, NC 28466. Telephone: 910-285-2178. Mailing Address: PO Box 427, Warsaw, NC 28398. Year Established: 1955. Pub. Frequency: w. (Thu.) Page Size: broadsheet. Subscrip. Rate: $.50 newsstand/cover; $20/yr in county; $30/yr out of county; $40/yr out of state. Circulation: 4,000 per issue (paid). **Owner(s):** H.L. Oswald Enterprises, Inc., See address and contact information above. **Management:** Gary Weaver, General Manager. H.L. Oswald III, Publisher. Mary Hart Oswald, Advertising. **Editorial:** Sammie Carter, Editor.

WALNUT COVE

STOKES NEWS. 1072 N. Main St., Ste. 102, Walnut Cove, NC 27052. Telephone: 336-591-8191. Year Established: 1872. Pub. Frequency: w. (Thu.) Page Size: broadsheet. Subscrip. Rate: $.50 newsstand/cover; $25/yr mailed in county; $31.40/yr mailed out of county; $31.85/yr mailed out of state. Circulation: 9,000 per issue (paid). **Owner(s):** Mid-South Management Inc., See address and contact information above. **Management:** Michael Milligan, Publisher. Shannon Fenner, Advertising Manager. **Editorial:** Ben McNeely, News Editor.

WARRENTON

WARREN RECORD, THE. 112 N. Main St., Warrenton, NC 27589. Telephone: 252-257-3341. FAX: 252-257-1413. E-MAIL: warrenrecord@vance.net. URL: http://www.warrenrecord.com. Mailing Address: PO Box 70, Warrenton, NC 27589. Year Established: 1896. Pub. Frequency: w. (Wed.) Page Size: broadsheet. Subscrip. Rate: $.75 newsstand/cover; $24/yr in county; $34/yr mailed out of county. Adv. Rate: col. inch $6.15 Circulation: 5,600 per issue (paid). **Owner(s):** Womack Publishing Co., Inc., 30 Main St., Chatham, VA 24531. Telephone: 434-432-1654. FAX: 434-432-4050. **Management:** Barry Fogg, Advertising. **Editorial:** Jennifer Bollinger, Editor.

WAYNESVILLE

ENTERPRISE MOUNTAINEER, THE. 220 N. Main St., Waynesville, NC 28786. Telephone: 828-452-0661. FAX: 828-452-0665. E-MAIL: jeff@themountaineer.com. URL: http://www.themountaineer.com. Mailing Address: P.O. Drawer 129, Waynesville, NC 28786. Year Established: 1884. Pub. Frequency: 3/w. (Mon., Wed., Fri.) Page Size: broadsheet. Subscrip. Rate: $.50 newsstand/cover; $67/yr carrier delivery in county; $108.60/yr mailed in state; $104/yr mailed out of state. Circulation: 12,500 per issue (paid). **Owner(s):** Mountaineer Publishing Co., Inc., See address and contact information above. **Management:** Jeff Schumacher, General Manager. Jonathan Key, President. Wanda Long, Circulation Manager. **Editorial:** Vicki Hyatt, Editor. Chuck Fiebernitz, Sports Editor.

WEST JEFFERSON

JEFFERSON POST, THE. 203 S. Second Ave., West Jefferson, NC 28694. Telephone: 336-246-7164. FAX: 336-246-7165. E-MAIL: cabothamilton@jeffersonpost.com. URL: http://www.jeffersonpost.com. Mailing Address: PO Box 808, West Jefferson, NC 28694. Year Established: 1925. Pub. Frequency: s-w. (Tue. & Fri.) Page Size: broadsheet. Subscrip. Rate: $.50 newsstand/cover; $33.50/yr in county; $44/yr out of county. Freelance Pay: $0.75/column-inch. Circulation: 11,700 per issue (paid and free). **Owner(s):** Mid-South Management Co., Inc., PO Box 1634, Spartensburg, SC 29304. Telephone: 864-583-2907. **Management:** Cabot Hamilton, General Manager. Jo Evelyn Roop, Circulation Manager. **Editorial:** Jim Thompson, Editor.

WHITEVILLE

NEWS REPORTER, THE. 127 W Columbus St., Whiteville, NC 28472. Telephone: 910-642-4104. FAX: 910-642-1856. E-MAIL: leshigh@newsreporter.biz. URL: http://www.whiteville.com. Year Established: 1896. Pub. Frequency: s-w. (Mon. & Thu.) Page Size: broadsheet. Subscrip. Rate: $.50 newsstand/cover per issue; $30/yr in county; $55/yr out of state. Adv. Rate: col. inch $9.79 **Wire Service(s):** AP. Circulation: 10,334 per issue (paid and free). **Owner(s):** News Reporter, Inc., See address and contact information above. **Management:** Jim High, Publisher. Mickey Greer, Advertising Manager. J.C. Hefner, Business Manager. **Editorial:** Les High, Editor. Clara Cartrette, News Editor. Dan Biser, Sports Editor.

NEWS/TIMES. 127 W Columbus St., Whiteville, NC 28472. Telephone: 910-642-4104. FAX: 910-642-1856. E-MAIL: editor@thenewstimes.com. Year Established: 1928. Pub. Frequency: w. (Wed.) Page Size: standard. Subscrip. Rate: $25/yr mailed out of town. Adv. Rate: col. inch $5.40 Circulation: 7,530 per issue (paid). **Owner(s):** News Reporter, Inc., See address and contact information above. **Management:** Bob Morgan, Advertising Manager. Ginny Haley, Circulation Manager. **Editorial:** Bob Morgan, Editor.

WILLIAMSTON

ENTERPRISE (WILLIAMSTON), THE. 106 W. Main St., Williamston, NC 27892. Telephone: 252-792-1181. FAX: 252-792-1921. E-MAIL: theenterprisepub@earthlink.net. Mailing Address: PO Box 387, Williamston, NC 27892. Year Established: 1899. Pub. Frequency: s-w. (Tue. & Thu.) Page Size: broadsheet. Subscrip. Rate: $.50 newsstand/cover; $39.95/yr; $43.95/yr mailed out of county; $55.95/yr mailed elsewhere. Adv. Rate: col. inch $6.95 Circulation: 5,100 per issue (paid). **Owner(s):** Cox Newspapers, Inc., 6205 Peachtree Dunwoody Rd, Atlanta, GA 30328. Telephone: 404-843-5000. **Management:** Dallas F. Coltrain, Publisher. Elaine Davidson, Circulation Manager. **Editorial:** Nita Smith, Editor. Earl Bailey, Production Manager.

WEEKLY HERALD, THE. 106 W. Main St., Williamston, NC 27892. Mailing Address: PO Box 179, Robersonville, NC 27871. Year Established: 1914. Pub. Frequency: w. (Fri.) Page Size: broadsheet. Subscrip. Rate: $.50 newsstand/cover; $14.50, $19.50/yr home delivery local. Adv. Rate: col. inch $4.65 Circulation: 1,000 per issue (paid and free). **Owner(s):** Cox Newspapers, Inc., 6205 Peachtree Dunwoody Rd., Atlanta, GA 30328. Telephone: 678-645-0000. **Management:** Dallas F. Coltrain, Publisher. Elaine Davidson, Circulation Manager. **Editorial:** Nita H Smith, Managing Editor. Earl Bailey, Production Manager.

WILMINGTON

AD-PAK, THE. 210 Old Dairy Rd, Wilmington, NC 28405. Telephone: 910-791-0688. FAX: 910-791-9534. E-MAIL: jeff@adpakweekly.com. URL: http://www.adpakweekly.com. Mailing Address: PO Box 12430, Wilmington, NC 28405. Year Established: 1976. Pub. Frequency: w. (Wed.) Page Size: tabloid.Adv. Rate: col. inch $10 Circulation: 22,800 per issue (controlled). **Owner(s):** Morris Multimedia, Inc., 27 Abercorn St., Savannah, GA 31401. Telephone: 912-233-1281. **Management:** Jeff Phenicie, Publisher. John McKinney, Circulation Director. **Editorial:** Susie Riddle, Production Manager.Readers: General

WINDSOR

BERTIE LEDGER-ADVANCE. 105 E. Granville St., Windsor, NC 27983-0069. Telephone: 252-794-3185. FAX: 252-794-2835. E-MAIL: ledger-advance@coastalnet.com. Mailing Address: P.O. Drawer 69, Windsor, NC 27983-0069. Year Established: 1928. Pub. Frequency: w. (Wed.) Page Size: standard. Subscrip. Rate: $.50 newsstand/cover; $22/yr in county; $29.98/yr mailed in state; $33.60/yr mailed out of state. Adv. Rate: col. inch $4.50 Circulation: 4,000 per issue (paid). **Owner(s):** Cox Newspapers, Inc., 6205 Peachtree Dunwoody Rd, Atlanta, GA 30328. **Management:** Jay Jenkins, Publisher. Robert Taylor, Advertising Manager. **Editorial:** Jay Jenkins, Editor. Charles Harris, News Editor.

YADKINVILLE

YADKIN RIPPLE, THE. 115 Jackson St., PO Box 7, Yadkinville, NC 27055. Telephone: 336-679-4900. FAX: 336-679-2340. Year Established: 1892. Pub. Frequency: w. (Thu.) Page Size: standard. Subscrip. Rate: $.50 newsstand/cover; $25.50/yr in county; $27/yr out of county; $31.50/yr out of state. Adv. Rate: col. inch $5.75 Circulation: 5,700 per issue (paid). **Owner(s):** Mid-South Management Co., PO Box 1634, Spartenburg, SC 29304. Telephone: 864-583-2907. **Management:** Rabel Good, Publisher. Sara Byrd, Advertising Manager. **Editorial:** Judy Combs, Editor. Andy Matthews, Assistant Editor.

YANCEYVILLE

CASWELL MESSENGER. 137 Main St., Yanceyville, NC 27379. Telephone: 336-694-4145. FAX: 336-694-5637. URL: http://www.aconews.com. Mailing Address: PO Box 100, Yanceyville, NC 27379. Year Established: 1926. Pub. Frequency: w. (Wed.) Page Size: broadsheet. Subscrip. Rate: $.75 newsstand/cover; $24/yr in county; $32/yr out of county. Circulation: 4,800 per issue (paid). **Owner(s):** Womack Publishing Co., Inc., PO Box 111, Chatham, VA 24531. Telephone: 434-432-1654. **Management:** Linda Sikes, General Manager. Charles A. Womack Jr., President. Sheri Hughes, Advertising Manager. **Editorial:** Gordon Bendall, Editor.

ZEBULON

EASTERN WAKE NEWS. 110 N. Arendell Ave., Zebulon, NC 27597. Telephone: 919-269-6101. FAX: 919-269-8383. E-MAIL: goldleafads@nawdo.com. URL: http://www.easternwakenews.com. Mailing Address: PO Box 1167, Zebulon, NC 27597. Pub. Frequency: w. (Thu.) Page Size: tabloid. Subscrip. Rate: $.50 newsstand/cover; $20/yr in county; $24/yr out of county; $31/yr out of state. Circulation: 7,000 per issue (paid). **Owner(s):** The/McClatchy Company, 2100 Q St, Sacramento, CA 95816. **Management:** Eddie Thorndyke, Publisher. Mark Alston, Advertising Director. **Editorial:** Johnny Whitfield, Managing Editor.

NORTH DAKOTA

ASHLEY

ASHLEY TRIBUNE, THE. 119 W. Main St., Ashley, ND 58413-7003. Telephone: 701-288-3531. FAX: 701-288-3532. Mailing Address: P.O. Box 178, Ashley, ND 58413-0178. Pub. Frequency: w. (Wed.) Page Size: standard. Subscrip. Rate: $.75 newsstand/cover; $28/yr in county; $33/yr in state; $38/yr out of state. Circulation: 1,450 per issue (paid). **Owner(s):** Ashley Tribune, The, See address and contact information above. **Management:** Tony Bender, Owner. **Editorial:** Tony Bender, Editor.

BEULAH

BEULAH BEACON. 324 Second Ave., N.E., Beulah, ND 58523-0609. Telephone: 701-873-4381. FAX: 701-873-2383. E-MAIL: coalnews@westriv.com. Year Established: 1970. Pub. Frequency: w. (Thu.) Page Size: broadsheet. Subscrip. Rate: $.75 newsstand/cover; $28/yr in state; $40/yr out of state. Circulation: 2,500 per issue (paid). **Owner(s):** BHG, Inc., PO Box 309, Garrison, ND 58540. Telephone: 701-463-2201. **Management:** Mike Gackle, Publisher. Ken Beauchamp, Advertising Manager. **Editorial:** Casey Thompson, Editor.

BISMARCK

BISMARCK/MANDAN FINDER. 707 E. Front Ave., Bismarck, ND 58504. Telephone: 701-258-6900. FAX: 701-223-0195. E-MAIL: finder@nbonline.com. URL: http://www.finderads.com. Mailing Address: PO Box 908, Mandan, ND 58554. Year Established: 1974. Pub. Frequency: w. (Wed.) Page Size: tabloid. Circulation: 39,000 per issue (paid and free). **Owner(s):** Lee Enterprises, Inc., 201 N. Harrison St., Davenport, IA 52801-1924. **Management:** Rebecca Albers, General Manager. Julie Bechtel, Publisher. Rebecca Albers, Advertising Manager.

BOTTINEAU

COURANT, THE. PO Box 29, Bottineau, ND 58318. Telephone: 701-228-2605. FAX: 701-228-5864. Year Established: 1885. Pub. Frequency: w. (Tue.) Page Size: standard. Subscrip. Rate: $.75 newsstand/cover; $28/yr in county; $30/yr out of county; $38/yr out of state. Circulation: 3,500 per issue (paid). **Owner(s):** Hills & Plains Free Press, Inc., See address and contact information above. **Management:** Mike Manston, General Manager. Twilla Glinz, President. Mike Manston, Publisher. Jackie Bullinger, Advertising Manager. Wanda Gravseth, Circulation Manager. **Editorial:** Scott Wagar, Editor.

BOWMAN

FINDER, THE. 18 S. Main St., Bowman, ND 58623. Telephone: 701-523-5623. FAX: 701-523-3441. E-MAIL: finder@ndsupernet.com. URL: http://www.bowmanfinder.com. Mailing Address: PO Box F, Bowman, ND 58623. Year Established: 1962. Pub. Frequency: w. (Wed.) Page Size: broadsheet. Subscrip. Rate: $31/yr mailed in county; $36/yr mailed out of county; $43/yr mailed out of state. Adv. Rate: col. inch $6.35 Circulation: 17,000 per issue (paid and free). **Owner(s):** Country Media, Inc., 1615 First Ave., Scotts Bluff, NE 69361. Telephone: 308-635-1892. **Management:** Karen Paulson, Publisher. Cindy Domagala, Circulation Manager. **Editorial:** Amy Getz, Reporter.

CASSELTON

CASS COUNTY REPORTER. ISSN 1074-1801
122 Sixth Ave., N., Casselton, ND 58012-0190. Telephone: 701-347-4493. FAX: 701-347-4495. E-MAIL: cassreporter@casscounty.net. Mailing Address: PO Box 190, Casselton, ND 58012-0190. Year Established: 1881. Pub. Frequency: w. (Wed.) Page Size: broadsheet. Subscrip. Rate: $.75 newsstand/cover; $33/yr local; $39/yr elsewhere. Circulation: 2,500 per issue (controlled and free). **Owner(s):** Sean & Cheryl Kelly, 122 Sixth Ave., N., Casselton, ND 58012. **Management:** Cheryl Kelly, Publisher. Tom Monialaws, Advertising Manager. **Editorial:** Tim Morrissey, Editor.

CROSBY

JOURNAL (CROSBY), THE. ISSN 0886-6007
217 N. Main, Crosby, ND 58730. Telephone: 701-965-6088. FAX: 701-965-6089. E-MAIL: journal@crosbynd.com. Mailing Address: PO Box E, Crosby, ND 58730. Year Established: 1902. Pub. Frequency: w. (Wed.) Subscrip. Rate: $.75 newsstand/cover; $27/yr local; $40/yr out of area. Circulation: 2,600 per issue (paid). **Owner(s):** Steve Andrist, See address and contact information above. **Management:** Steve Andrist, Publisher. Bonnie Anderson, Circulation Manager. **Editorial:** Steve Andrist, Editor.

ELGIN

CARSON PRESS. ISSN 0899-7624
606 East St N., Elgin, ND 58533-7104. E-MAIL: gcn@westriv.com. URL: http://www.wrtc.com/gcn/. Year Established: 1908. Pub. Frequency: w. (Wed.) Page Size: broadsheet. Subscrip. Rate: $.75 newsstand/cover; $24/yr mailed in county; $30/yr mailed in state; $35/yr mailed out of state. Circulation: 1,200 per issue (paid). **Owner(s):** Duane & Gail Schatz, See address and contact information above.

GRANT COUNTY NEWS (ELGIN). 606 East St N., Elgin, ND 58533-7104. E-MAIL: GCN@Westriv.com. Year Established: 1910. Pub. Frequency: w. (Wed.) Page Size: broadsheet. Subscrip. Rate: $.75 newsstand/cover; $24/yr in county; $30/yr in state; $35/yr out of state. Circulation: 2,312 per issue (paid and free). **Owner(s):** Duane & Gail Schatz, See address and contact information above. **Management:** Jill Friesz, Publisher. **Editorial:** Jill Friesz, Managing Editor.

ENDERLIN

MOURE CHRONICLE, LA. 209 Fourth Ave, Enderlin, ND 58027. Telephone: 701-883-5393. FAX: 701-883-5076. E-MAIL: enderlinindependent@mlgc. Pub. Frequency: w. (Wed.) Page Size: broadsheet. Subscrip. Rate: $.50 newsstand/cover; $23/yr in county; $26/yr in state; $30/yr out of state. Adv. Rate: col. inch $5.50 Circulation: 1,100 per issue (paid). **Owner(s):** Enderlin Independent, See address and contact information above. **Management:** Ruth E McCleerey, Publisher. **Editorial:** Ruth E McCleerey, Editor-in-Chief.

FARGO

MORRIS SUN TRIBUNE. 101 5th St N, Fargo, ND 58102. Telephone: 701-235-7311. FAX: 701-241-5406. E-MAIL: morrtrib@info-link.net. URL: http://www.morrissuntribune.com. Year Established: 1878. Pub. Frequency: s-w. (Wed. & Sat.) Page Size: broadsheet. Subscrip. Rate: $1 newsstand/cover; $46/yr mailed in county & adj. counties; $52/yr mailed out of area. Adv. Rate: col. inch $8.25 Circulation: 3,000 per issue (paid). **Owner(s):** Forum Communications Company, See address and contact information above.Readers: Stevens County Minnesota

GARRISON

MCLEAN COUNTY INDEPENDENT. 91 N. Main St., Garrison, ND 58540-0309. Telephone: 701-463-2201. FAX: 701-463-7487. E-MAIL: independ@restel.net. URL: http://www.nd-bhginc.com. Year Established: 1905. Pub. Frequency: w. (Thu.) Page Size: tabloid. Subscrip. Rate: $.75 newsstand/cover; $28/yr in state; $40/yr out of state. Freelance Pay: $5-$50/article. Circulation: 3,875 per issue (paid). **Owner(s):** BHG, Inc., PO Box 309, Garrison, ND 58540. Telephone: 701-463-2201. **Management:** Mike Gackle, President. Don Gackle, Publisher. Angela Kolden, Advertising Manager. Deb Hanson, Circulation Manager. Fran Beierle, Classified Adv. Mgr.. **Editorial:** Stu Merry, Editor.

GRAFTON

WALSH COUNTY RECORD, THE. ISSN 1067-5922
420 Hill Ave., Grafton, ND 58237. Telephone: 701-352-0640. FAX: 701-352-1502. E-MAIL: jackie@wcrecord.com. URL: http://www.wcrecord.com. Year Established: 1889. Pub. Frequency: w. (Wed.) Page Size: broadsheet. Subscrip. Rate: $1 newsstand/cover; $34/yr local walsh pembina & ramsey cys; $38/yr in state; $42/yr out of state. Circulation: 3,600 per issue (paid). **Owner(s):** Morgan Printing, Inc., See address and contact information above. **Management:** John Morgan, General Manager. Jackie Thompson, Publisher. Tim Martin, Advertising Director. Debbie Bender, Circulation Manager. **Editorial:** Todd Morgan, Editor.

HARVEY

HERALD-PRESS (HARVEY). 913 Lincoln Ave., Harvey, ND 58341. Telephone: 701-324-4646. FAX: 701-324-4647. E-MAIL: heraldpress@gondtc.com. URL: http://www.harveyheraldpress.com. Year Established: 1897. Pub. Frequency: w. (Sat.) Page Size: broadsheet. Subscrip. Rate: $.75 newsstand/cover; $28/yr in county; $33/yr in state; $39/yr out of state. Adv. Rate: col. inch $5.15 Circulation: 2,200 per issue (paid). **Owner(s):** Eldredge Publishing Co., Inc., See address and contact information above. **Management:** Janine Schmitz, General Manager. Charles Eldredge, Publisher. Edie Schell, Advertising Manager. Patti Phillips, Circulation Manager. **Editorial:** Janine Schmitz, Editor.

HAZEN

HAZEN STAR. 26 E. Main St., Hazen, ND 58545. Telephone: 701-748-2255. FAX: 701-748-5768. E-MAIL: star@westriv.com. URL: http://www.nd-bhginc.com. Mailing Address: P O Box 508, Hazen, ND 58545. Year Established: 1914. Pub. Frequency: w. (Thu.) Page Size: broadsheet. Subscrip. Rate: $.75 newsstand/cover; $28/yr in state; $40/yr out of state. Circulation: 2,300 per issue (paid). **Owner(s):** BHG, Inc., PO Box 309, Garrison, ND 58540. Telephone: 701-463-2201. **Management:** Mike Gackle, Publisher. President. Doreen Ost, Advertising Manager. **Editorial:** Brian Gehring, Editor.

JAMESTOWN

PRAIRIE POST. ISSN 1073-0699
120 Second St., N.W., Jamestown, ND 58402-1268. Telephone: 701-252-2796. FAX: 701-252-5751. Mailing Address: PO Box 1760, Jamestown, ND 58402-1268. Year Established: 1972. Pub. Frequency: w. (Tue.) Page Size: tabloid Circulation: 17,889 per issue (free). **Owner(s):** Jeff Meyer, 101 Fifth St., N., Fargo, ND 58102. Telephone: 701-235-7311. **Management:** I. Bruce Henke, Publisher. Zenith Mayer, Advertising Manager. Brenda Kinkade, Circulation Manager.

LANGDON

CAVALIER COUNTY REPUBLICAN. 618 Third St., Langdon, ND 58249. Telephone: 701-256-5311. FAX: 701-256-5841. E-MAIL: ccr@utma.com. Year Established: 1888. Pub. Frequency: w. (Mon.) Page Size: broadsheet. Subscrip. Rate: $.75 newsstand/cover; $36/yr domestic area; $41/yr in state; $51/yr out of state. Circulation: 2,100 per issue (paid). **Owner(s):** Country Media, Inc., PO Box 444, Tillamook, OR 97141. **Management:** Lori Peterson, Publisher. **Editorial:** Amy Freier, Editor.

LINTON

LINTON EMMONS COUNTY RECORD. 201 N Broadway, P O Box 38, Linton, ND 58552-0038. Telephone: 701-254-4537. FAX: 701-254-4909. E-MAIL: info@lintonnd.com. URL: http://www.ecrecord.com. Year Established: 1884. Pub. Frequency: w. (Thu.) Page Size: tabloid. Subscrip. Rate: $.75 newsstand/cover; $35/yr local; $40/yr mailed in state; $45/yr mailed out of state. Adv. Rate: col. inch $6.50 Circulation: 3,000 per issue (paid). **Owner(s):** Allan Burke, See address and contact information above. **Management:** Allan C Burke, Publisher. Bob Tschritter, Advertising. **Editorial:** Allan C Burke, Editor. Mark Weber, Sports.

LISBON

RANSOM COUNTY GAZETTE & ENTERPRISE. 310 Main St., Lisbon, ND 58054. Telephone: 701-683-4128. FAX: 701-683-4129. E-MAIL: info@rcgazette.com. URL: http://www.rcgazette.com. Year Established: 1882. Pub. Frequency: w. (Mon.) Page Size: broadsheet. Subscrip. Rate: $.75 newsstand/cover; $29/yr in state; $33/yr out of state. Circulation: 3,600 per issue (paid). **Owner(s):** Sean W. Kelly, See address and contact information above. **Management:** Sean W. Kelly, Publisher. Denise Seelig, Office Manager. Cheryl A. Kelly, Advertising Manager. **Editorial:** Terri Barta, Managing Editor. Joe Howell, Sports.

MANDAN

MANDAN NEWS. 100 Second Ave NW, Mandan, ND 58554. E-MAIL: editor@mandan-news.com. URL: http://www.mandan-news.com. Year Established: 1975. Pub. Frequency: w. (Fri.) Page Size: tabloid. Subscrip. Rate: $.50 newsstand/cover; $33/yr out of city; $37/yr out of state. Adv. Rate: col. inch $6.50 Circulation: 1,800 per issue (paid). **Owner(s):** Lee Enterprises, Inc., 201 N. Harrison St., Davenport, IA 52801-1924. **Management:** Ken Rogers, General Manager. **Editorial:** Brian L Gray, Editor.

Weeklies

MINNEWAUKAN

BENSON COUNTY FARMERS PRESS. 120 B Ave. North, Minnewaukan, ND 58351-0098. Telephone: 701-473-5436. FAX: 701-473-5736. E-MAIL: farmerspress@stellarnet.com. URL: http://www.bensoncountynews.com. Mailing Address: PO Box 98, Minnewaukan, ND 58351-0098. Year Established: 1884. Pub. Frequency: w. (Wed.) Page Size: broadsheet. Subscrip. Rate: $.85 newsstand/cover; $42/yr in state; $48/yr out of state; $100/yr foreign. Adv. Rate: col. inch $6.02 Circulation: 2,403 per issue (paid and free). **Owner(s):** Consolidated Newspapers, Inc., See address and contact information above. **Management:** Richard M. Peterson, President. **Editorial:** Richard M. Peterson, Editor.Readers: Benson County residents

NEWELL

VALLEY IRRIGATOR, THE. 209 Dartmouth, Newell, ND 57760. Telephone: 605-456-2585. FAX: 605-456-2587. E-MAIL: irrig@sdplains.com. URL: http://www.newell.bhen.com. Mailing Address: PO Box 167, Newell, SD 57760. Year Established: 1907. Pub. Frequency: w. (Wed.) Page Size: broadsheet. Subscrip. Rate: $1 newsstand/cover; $36/yr in county; $52.50/yr out of county; $59.25/yr mailed out of state. Adv. Rate: col. inch $8.10 Circulation: 1,000 per issue (paid). **Owner(s):** Lee Enterprises, Inc., 201 N. Harrison St., Davenport, IA 52801. **Management:** Karen Wallace, Office Manager. **Editorial:** Karen Wallace, Editor.

NORWOOD

NORWOOD GLEANER, THE. 22 N Main St, Norwood, ND 58267. Telephone: 701-587-6126. Mailing Address: PO Box C, Northwood, ND 58267. Year Established: 1890. Pub. Frequency: w. (Mon.) Page Size: tabloid. Subscrip. Rate: $.75 newsstand/cover; $30/yr in state; $37/yr out of state. Circulation: 1,000 per issue (paid). **Owner(s):** Beth Johnson, See address and contact information above. **Management:** Beth Johnson, Publisher. **Editorial:** Beth Johnson, Editor. Karen Bilden, Reporter.

ROLLA

TURTLE MOUNTAIN STAR, THE. PO Box 849, Rolla, ND 58367. Telephone: 701-477-6495. FAX: 701-477-3182. E-MAIL: tmstar@utma.com. Year Established: 1888. Pub. Frequency: w. (Mon.) Page Size: broadsheet. Subscrip. Rate: $.75 newsstand/cover; $28/yr local; $30/yr in state; $36/yr out of state. Adv. Rate: col. inch $5 Circulation: 4,000 per issue (paid). **Owner(s):** Jason Nordmark, See address and contact information above. **Management:** Jason Nordmark, Publisher. **Editorial:** Jason Nordmark, Editor.

RUGBY

PIERCE COUNTY TRIBUNE. 219 S. Main Ave., Rugby, ND 58368. Telephone: 701-776-5252. FAX: 701-776-2159. E-MAIL: pctrugby@gondtc.com. Mailing Address: PO Box 385, Rugby, ND 58368. Year Established: 1887. Pub. Frequency: w. (Sat.) Page Size: broadsheet. Subscrip. Rate: $.75 newsstand/cover; $30/yr in state; $36/yr out of state. Adv. Rate: col. inch $7 Circulation: 2,700 per issue (paid). **Owner(s):** Ogden Newspapers of Minnesota, Inc., 1500 Main St., Wheeling, WV 26003. Telephone: 304-233-0100. **Management:** Phyllis Wiggins, Office Manager. Sonia Mullally, Advertising Manager. **Editorial:** Matt Mullally, Editor.

TURTLE LAKE

MCLEAN COUNTY JOURNAL. 210 Main St., Turtle Lake, ND 58575-0220. Telephone: 701-448-2649. FAX: 701-448-2666. E-MAIL: turtle@westriv.com. URL: http://www.nd-bhginc.com. Mailing Address: PO Box 220, Turtle Lake, ND 58575-0220. Year Established: 1902. Pub. Frequency: w. (Thu.) Page Size: tabloid. Subscrip. Rate: $.75 newsstand/cover; $28/yr in state; $40/yr mailed out of state. Adv. Rate: col. inch $5.25 Circulation: 925 per issue (paid and controlled). **Owner(s):** BHG, Inc., PO Box 309, Garrison, ND 58540. Telephone: 701-463-2201. **Management:** Jill Denning-Gackle, Publisher. **Editorial:** Ellen Tinker, Editor.

UNDERWOOD

UNDERWOOD NEWS. P.O. Box 179, Underwood, ND 58576. Telephone: 701-442-5535. FAX: 701-462-8128. E-MAIL: bhgnews@westriv.com. URL: http://www.nd-bhginc.com. Pub. Frequency: w. (Thu.) Page Size: broadsheet. Subscrip. Rate: $.50 newsstand/cover; $28/yr in state; $40/yr out of state. Circulation: 900 per issue (paid). **Owner(s):** BHG, Inc., PO Box 309, Garrison, ND 58540. Telephone: 701-463-2201. **Management:** Mike Gackle, Publisher. **Editorial:** Julie Arbach, Editor.

WASHBURN

CENTER REPUBLICAN. 607 Main Ave., Washburn, ND 58577. Telephone: 701-462-8126. FAX: 701-748-5768. E-MAIL: star@westriu.com. URL: http://www.nd-bhginc.com. Mailing Address: PO Box 340, Washburn, ND 58577-0340. Year Established: 1906. Pub. Frequency: w. (Thu.) Page Size: standard. Subscrip. Rate: $.75 newsstand/cover; $28/yr mailed in county; $40/yr mailed out of county. Circulation: 700 per issue (paid). **Owner(s):** BHG, Inc., PO Box 309, Garrison, ND 58540. Telephone: 701-463-2201. **Management:** Mike Gackle, Publisher. **Editorial:** Karlene Gehring, Editor.

LEADER-NEWS (WASHBURN). ISSN 0888-0220
607 Main Ave., Washburn, ND 58577. Telephone: 701-462-8126. FAX: 701-748-5768. E-MAIL: bhgnews@westriv.com. URL: http://www.nd-bhginc.com. Mailing Address: PO Box 340, Washburn, ND 58577-0340. Pub. Frequency: w. Page Size: tabloid. Subscrip. Rate: $.75 newsstand/cover; $28/yr in state; $40/yr out of state. Circulation: 1,900 per issue (paid). **Owner(s):** BHG, Inc., PO Box 309, Garrison, ND 58540. Telephone: 701-463-2201. **Editorial:** Deb Torkelson, Editor.

WEST FARGO

MIDWEEK (WEST FARGO). 322 Sheyenne St., West Fargo, ND 58078-0457. Telephone: 701-282-2443. FAX: 701-282-9248. E-MAIL: gary@midweek-pioneer.com. URL: http://www.wfpioneer.com. Mailing Address: P.O. Box 457, West Fargo, ND 58078-0457. Year Established: 1969. Pub. Frequency: w. (Tue.) Page Size: tabloid. Circulation: 56,000 per issue (paid and free). **Owner(s):** Donovan C. Witham, See address and contact information above. **Management:** Roz Randorf, Publisher. Ilene Munter, Circulation Manager. **Editorial:** Mike Schoomer, Editor.

WEST FARGO PIONEER. 322 Sheyenne St., West Fargo, ND 58078-0457. Telephone: 701-282-2443. FAX: 701-282-9248. Mailing Address: P.O. Box 457, West Fargo, ND 58078-0457. Year Established: 1967. Pub. Frequency: w. (Wed.) Page Size: tabloid. Subscrip. Rate: $.75 newsstand/cover; $30/yr mailed in county; $33/yr mailed out of county. Circulation: 2,900 per issue (paid). **Owner(s):** Pioneer Enterprises, Inc., See address and contact information above. **Management:** Roz Randorff, Publisher. Eileen Munter, Circulation Manager. **Editorial:** Mike Schoomer, Editor.

WILLISTON

WILLISTON PLAINS REPORTER. 14 W. Fourth St., Williston, ND 58801. Telephone: 701-572-6311. FAX: 701-572-1965. Mailing Address: PO Box 1447, Williston, ND 58802. Pub. Frequency: w. (Wed.) Page Size: broadsheet. **Wire Service(s):** AP. Circulation: 12,500 per issue (free). **Owner(s):** Wick Communications, Inc., 333 W. Wilcox Dr., Ste. 302, Sierra Vista, AZ 85635. **Management:** Donald J. Mrachek, Publisher. **Editorial:** Donald J. Mrachek, Editor.

OHIO

AKRON

SUBURBANITE, THE. 3577 S Arlington Rd, Ste B, Akron, OH 44312. Telephone: 330-899-2872. FAX: 330-896-7633. E-MAIL: suburbanite@cantonrep.com. Year Established: 1965. Pub. Frequency: w. (Mon.) Page Size: tabloid. Subscrip. Rate: $.50 newsstand/cover; $22.50/yr local. Circulation: 33,000 per issue (paid and free). **Owner(s):** GateHouse Media, Inc, 350 WillowBrook Office Park, Fairport, NY 14450. Telephone: 585-598-0030. FAX: 585-248-2631. **Management:** Sandra Mills, Advertising. **Editorial:** Tamara Proctor, Managing Editor.

ANTWERP

ANTWERP BEE-ARGUS. ISSN 0003-617X
113 N Main St, Antwerp, OH 45813. Telephone: 419-258-8161. FAX: 419-258-9365. Mailing Address: PO Box 1065, Antwerp, OH 45813-1065. Year Established: 1883. Pub. Frequency: w. Page Size: broadsheet. Subscrip. Rate: $21/yr in IN, MI, OH (effective 2006); $22/yr out of state. Circulation: 1,300 (paid). **Owner(s):** Antwerp Bee-Argus, See address and contact information above. **Management:** June L Temple, Publisher. Sandra Kay Temple, Advertising. **Editorial:** Sandra Kay Temple, Editor.

ARCHBOLD

ARCHBOLD BUCKEYE. 207 N. Defiance St., Archbold, OH 43502-1160. Telephone: 419-445-4466. URL: http://www.archboldbuckeye.com. Year Established: 1905. Pub. Frequency: w. (Wed.) Page Size: broadsheet. Subscrip. Rate: $1 newsstand/cover; $39/yr Fulton, Henry, Williams, Defiance counties; $46/yr mailed elsewhere. Adv. Rate: col. inch $8.40 Circulation: 3,000 per issue (paid). **Owner(s):** Archbold Buckeye, Inc., See address and contact information above. **Management:** Sharon S. Taylor, General Manager. Ross W. Taylor, Publisher. Mary Huber, Advertising. Brent Taylor, Circulation Manager. **Editorial:** David A. Pugh, News Editor.

FARMLAND NEWS. ISSN 0093-5832
104 Depot St., Archbold, OH 43502. Telephone: 419-445-9456. FAX: 419-445-4444. E-MAIL: ads@farmlandnews.com. URL: http://www.FarmlandNews.com. Mailing Address: P.O.Box 240, Archbold, OH 43502-0240. Year Established: 1959. Pub. Frequency: w. (Tue.) Page Size: tabloid. Subscrip. Rate: $39/yr. Adv. Rate: col. inch $9 Circulation: 3,546 per issue (paid). **Owner(s):** Jed W. Grisez, See address and contact information above. **Management:** Jed W. Grisez, Publisher. Dianne Lantz, Production Director. **Editorial:** Jeremy J. Rohrs, Editor.Readers: Northwest Ohio

ATHENS

ATHENS NEWS. ISSN 0882-8695
14 N. Court St., Athens, OH 45701. Telephone: 740-594-8219. FAX: 740-592-5695. URL: http://www.athensnews.com. Year Established: 1977. Pub. Frequency: s-w. (Mon. & Thu.) Page Size: tabloid Circulation: 18,000 per issue (free). **Owner(s):** Athens News Inc., The, See address and contact information above. **Management:** Bruce Mitchell, Publisher. Marcey Williams, Classified Adv. Mgr.. **Editorial:** Terry Smith, Editor. Nick Claussen, Associate Editor. Ed Venrick, Photo Editor.

ATTICA

BLOOMVILLE GAZETTE. 26 N. Main St., Attica, OH 44807-0516. Telephone: 419-426-3491. FAX: 419-426-2003. E-MAIL: copy@atticahub.com. URL: http://www.atticahub.com. Mailing Address: PO Box 516, Attica, OH 44807-0516. Year Established: 1901. Pub. Frequency: w. (Thu.) Page Size: broadsheet. Subscrip. Rate: $.55 newsstand/cover; $24/yr. Adv. Rate: col. inch $3.90 Circulation: 4,000 per issue (paid). **Owner(s):** Seneca Publishing, Inc., 26 N. Main St., Attica, OH 44807. Telephone: 419-426-3491. **Management:** Jeffrey Cook, Publisher. **Editorial:** Donna Phillip, Editor.

AVON LAKE

NORTH RIDGEVILLE PRESS. 158 Lear Road, Avon Lake, OH 44012. Telephone: 866-732-1240. FAX: 440-930-5923. E-MAIL: thepress@bright.net. Mailing Address: PO Box 39089, North Ridgeville, OH 44039. Year Established: 1983. Pub. Frequency: w. (Wed.) Page Size: tabloid. Subscrip. Rate: $.50 newsstand/cover; $24/yr local; $25.50/yr elsewhere. Adv. Rate: col. inch $8.75 Circulation: 3,800 per issue (paid). **Owner(s):** Douthit Communications, Inc., PO Box 760, Sandusky, OH 44871. Telephone: 419-625-5825. **Management:** H. Kenneth Douthit III, Publisher. Janet Sanner, Advertising Manager. **Editorial:** Lori Switaj, Managing Editor.

PRESS (AVON LAKE), THE. 158 Lear Rd., Avon Lake, OH 44012-0300. Telephone: 440-933-5100. FAX: 440-933-7904. E-MAIL: news@2presspapers.com. Mailing Address: PO Box 300, Avon Lake, OH 44012-0300. Year Established: 1950. Pub. Frequency: w. (Wed.) Page Size: tabloid. Subscrip. Rate: $.60 newsstand/cover; $27.50/yr mailed in area; $32.50/yr mailed out of area. Adv. Rate: col. inch $13.75 Circulation: 9,000 per issue (paid and free). **Owner(s):** Douthit Communications, Inc., 620 Warren St., Sandusky, OH 44870. Telephone: 419-625-5825. FAX: 419-625-2834. **Management:** Janet Sanner, General Manager. **Editorial:** Lori Switaj, News Editor.

BARBERTON

BARBERTON HERALD. ISSN 0890-8591
70 Fourth St., N.W., Barberton, OH 44203. Telephone: 330-753-1068. FAX: 330-753-1021. E-MAIL: barbherald@aol.com. Year Established: 1927. Pub. Frequency: w. (Thu.) Page Size: broadsheet. Subscrip. Rate: $.50 newsstand/cover; $18/yr mailed in county & adj. cys.; $29/yr mailed out of area. Circulation: 7,900 per issue (paid). **Owner(s):** Richardson Publishing Co., See address and contact information above. **Management:** Cathy Robertson, Publisher. Jim Colombo, Advertising. Jennifer Shaffer, Circulation Manager. **Editorial:** Bob Morehead, Managing Editor. Randy Broadwater, Sports.

BARNESVILLE

BARNESVILLE ENTERPRISE. 166 E Main St, Barnesville, OH 43713. Telephone: 740-425-1912. FAX: 740-425-2545. E-MAIL: enterprise@1st.net. Mailing Address: P O Box 30, Barnesville, OH 43713. Year Established: 1866. Pub. Frequency: w. (Wed.) Page Size: oversize. Subscrip. Rate: $.60 newsstand/cover; $23/yr in state; $30/yr out of state. Circulation: 4,825 per issue (paid). **Owner(s):** Dix Communications Group, 212 E. Liberty St., Wooster, OH 44691. Telephone: 330-264-1125. FAX: 330-264-3756. **Management:** Robert C. Dix, Publisher. Scott Fisher, Advertising. Jennifer Laity, Classified Adv. Mgr.. **Editorial:** Erin Donnelly, Editor.

BATAVIA

CLERMONT SUN, THE. 465 E. Main St., Batavia, OH 45103. Telephone: 513-732-2511. FAX: 513-732-6344. URL: http://www.clermontsun.com. Mailing Address: PO Box 366, Batavia, OH 45103. Year Established: 1828. Pub. Frequency: w. (Thu.) Page Size: broadsheet. Subscrip. Rate: $.50 newsstand/cover; $15/yr in county; $30/yr out of county. Circulation: 3,300 per issue (paid). **Owner(s):** The Sun Group Newspapers, See address and contact information above. **Management:** Mary Patrick Latham, Publisher. Tony Adams, Advertising Manager. Virginia Burns, Circulation Manager. **Editorial:** Art Hunter, Editor.

BEACHWOOD

BEDFORD SUN BANNER. ISSN 0746-262X 3355 Richmond Rd., Ste. 171, Beachwood, OH 44122-4171. Telephone: 216-464-6397. FAX: 216-986-5891. E-MAIL: sun@sunnews.com. URL: http://www.sunnews.com. Year Established: 1970. Pub. Frequency: w. (Thu.) Page Size: broadsheet. Subscrip. Rate: $.65 newsstand/cover; $32.50/yr carrier delivery; $39/yr mailed. Adv. Rate: col. inch $12.45 Circulation: 4,072 per issue (paid). **Owner(s):** Sun Media, Inc., 5510 Cloverleaf Pkwy., Cleveland, OH 44125-4887. Telephone: 216-986-2600. FAX: 216-986-2380. **Management:** John Urbancich, President. Dwight Schulz, Operations Manager. Dennis Mudry, Advertising Manager. Jim Reynolds, Circulation Director. Emil DeSanto, Classified Adv. Mgr.. **Editorial:** Mary Jane Skala, Editor. Linda Kinsey, Executive Editor. Linda Hoy Socha, Assistant Editor. Stan Urankar, Entertainment Editor.

CHAGRIN HERALD SUN. 3355 Richmond Rd., Ste. 171, Beachwood, OH 44122-4171. Telephone: 216-464-6397. FAX: 216-986-5891. E-MAIL: sun@sunnews.com. URL: http://www.sunnews.com. Year Established: 1948. Pub. Frequency: w. (Thu.) Page Size: broadsheet. Subscrip. Rate: $.65 newsstand/cover; $32.50/yr; $39/yr mailed. Adv. Rate: col. inch $27.20 Circulation: 19,817 per issue (paid). **Owner(s):** Sun Media, Inc., 5510 Cloverleaf Pkwy., Cleveland, OH 44125-4887. Telephone: 216-986-2600. FAX: 216-986-2380. **Management:** John Urbancich, General Manager. Dennis Mudry, Advertising Manager. Jim Reynolds, Circulation Director. Emil DeSanto, Classified Adv. Mgr.. **Editorial:** Mary Jane Skala, Editor. Linda Kinsey, Executive Editor. Stan Urankar, Entertainment Editor.

EUCLID SUN JOURNAL. 3355 Richmond Rd., Ste. 171, Beachwood, OH 44122-4171. Telephone: 216-464-6397. FAX: 216-986-5891. E-MAIL: sun@sunnews.com. URL: http://www.sunnews.com. Year Established: 1945. Pub. Frequency: w. (Thu.) Page Size: broadsheet. Subscrip. Rate: $.65 newsstand/cover; $32.50/yr carrier delivery; $39/yr mailed. Adv. Rate: col. inch $30.70 Circulation: 10,958 per issue (paid). **Owner(s):** Sun Media, Inc., 5510 Cloverleaf Pkwy., Cleveland, OH 44125-4887. Telephone: 216-986-2600. FAX: 216-986-2380. **Management:** Gerald H. Gordon, General Manager. John Urbancich, President. Dwight Schulz, Operations Manager. Dennis Mudry, Advertising Manager. Jim Reynolds, Circulation Director. Emil DeSanto, Classified Adv. Mgr.. **Editorial:** Mary Jane Skala, Editor. Stan Urankar, Entertainment Editor. Barbara Collier, Food Editor.

SOLON HERALD SUN. 3355 Richmond Rd., Ste. 171, Beachwood, OH 44122-4171. Telephone: 216-464-6397. FAX: 216-986-5891. E-MAIL: sun@sunnews.com. URL: http://www.sunnews.com. Year Established: 1948. Pub. Frequency: w. (Thu.) Page Size: broadsheet. Subscrip. Rate: $.65 newsstand/cover; $32.50/yr carrier delivery; $39/yr mailed. Adv. Rate: col. inch $27.20 Freelance Pay: $25/article. Circulation: 19,817 per issue (paid). **Owner(s):** Sun Media, Inc., 5510 Cloverleaf Pkwy., Cleveland, OH 44125-4887. Telephone: 216-986-2600. FAX: 216-986-2380. **Management:** John Urbancich, General Manager. Dennis Mudry, Advertising Manager. Emil DeSanto, Classified Adv. Mgr.. **Editorial:** Mary Jane Skala, Editor. Linda Kinsey, Executive Editor.

SUN MESSENGER, THE. 3355 Richmond Rd., Ste. 171, Beachwood, OH 44122-4171. Telephone: 216-464-6397. FAX: 216-986-5891. E-MAIL: sun@sunnews.com. URL: http://www.sunnews.com. Year Established: 1952. Pub. Frequency: w. (Thu.) Page Size: broadsheet. Subscrip. Rate: $.65 newsstand/cover; $32.50/yr carrier delivery; $39/yr mailed. Adv. Rate: col. inch $29.70 Circulation: 11,801 per issue (paid). **Owner(s):** Sun Media, Inc., 5510 Cloverleaf Pkwy., Cleveland, OH 44125-4887. Telephone: 216-986-2600. FAX: 216-986-2380. **Management:** John Urbancich, President. Dwight Schulz, Operations Manager. Dennis Mudry, Advertising Manager. Jim Reynolds, Circulation Manager. Emil DeSanto, Classified Adv. Mgr.. **Editorial:** Mary Jane Skala, Editor. Linda Kinsey, Executive Editor. Stan Urankar, Entertainment Editor.

SUN PRESS, THE. 3355 Richmond Rd., Ste. 171, Beachwood, OH 44122-4171. Telephone: 216-464-6397. FAX: 216-986-5891. E-MAIL: sun@sunnews.com. URL: http://www.sunnews.com. Year Established: 1946. Pub. Frequency: w. (Thu.) Page Size: broadsheet. Subscrip. Rate: $.65 newsstand/cover; $16.25 carrier delivery for 6 mos.; $32.50/yr; $39/yr mailed. Adv. Rate: col. inch $35.40 Circulation: 16,559 per issue (paid). **Owner(s):** Sun Media, Inc., 5510 Cloverleaf Pkwy., Cleveland, OH 44125-4887. Telephone: 216-986-2600. FAX: 216-986-2380. **Management:** John Urbancich, President. Dwight Schulz, Operations Manager. Dennis Mudry, Advertising Manager. Jim Reynolds, Circulation Director. Emil DeSanto, Classified Adv. Mgr.. **Editorial:** Mary Jane Skala, Editor. Stan Urankar, Entertainment Editor. Barbara Collier, Food Editor.

SUN SCOOP JOURNAL. 3355 Richmond Rd., Ste. 171, Beachwood, OH 44122-4171. Telephone: 216-464-6397. FAX: 216-986-5891. E-MAIL: sun@sunnews.com. URL: http://www.sunnews.com.. Year Established: 1919. Pub. Frequency: w. (Thu.) Page Size: broadsheet. Subscrip. Rate: $.65 newsstand/cover; $32.50/yr mailed in county; $33.80/yr mailed out of county. Adv. Rate: col. inch $29.75 Circulation: 16,664 per issue (paid). **Owner(s):** Sun Media, Inc., 5510 Cloverleaf Pkwy., Cleveland, OH 44125-4887. Telephone: 216-986-2600. FAX: 216-986-2380. **Management:** John Urbancich, President. Dennis Mudry, Advertising Manager. Jim Reynolds, Circulation Manager. Emil DeSanto, Classified Adv. Mgr.. **Editorial:** Mark Morilak, Editor. Linda Kinsey, Executive Editor.

WEST GEAUGA SUN. 3355 Richmond Rd., Ste. 171, Beachwood, OH 44122-4171. Telephone: 216-464-6397. FAX: 216-986-5891. E-MAIL: sun@sunnews.com. URL: http://www.sunnews.com. Year Established: 1994. Pub. Frequency: w. (Thu.) Page Size: broadsheet. Subscrip. Rate: $.60 newsstand/cover; $16.25 carrier delivery for 6 mos.; $32.50/yr home delivery; $16.90 mailed for 6 mos.; $39/yr mailed. Adv. Rate: col. inch $27.20 Circulation: 19,817 per issue (paid). **Owner(s):** Sun Media, Inc., 5510 Cloverleaf Pkwy., Cleveland, OH 44125-4887. Telephone: 216-986-2600. FAX: 216-986-2380. **Management:** John Urbancich, President. Dwight Schulz, Operations Manager. Dennis Mudly, Advertising Manager. Emil DeSanto, Classified Adv. Mgr.. **Editorial:** Mary Jane Skala, Editor. Linda Kinsey, Executive Editor. Stan Urankar, Entertainment Editor.

BELLEVUE

RFD NEWS, THE. 131 E. Main St., Bellevue, OH 44811. Telephone: 419-483-7410. FAX: 419-483-3617. E-MAIL: rfdnews@bizwoh.rr.com. Mailing Address: PO Box 367, Bellevue, OH 48811. Year Established: 1958. Pub. Frequency: s-m. (2nd & 4th Mon.) Page Size: tabloid. Subscrip. Rate: $18.50/yr mailed. Circulation: 70,000 per issue (controlled and free). **Owner(s):** Gazette Publishing Co., 107 N. Sandusky St., Bellevue, OH 44811. Telephone: 419-483-4190. FAX: 419-483-3737. **Management:** Mark Clark, General Manager. **Editorial:** Mark Clark, Editor.

BELLVILLE

BELLVILLE STAR, THE. 107 Main St, Bellville, OH 44813. Telephone: 419-886-2291. FAX: 419-886-2704. Pub. Frequency: w. (Thu.) Page Size: broadsheet. Subscrip. Rate: $.05 newsstand/cover; $28/yr in county. Circulation: 2,200 per issue (paid). **Owner(s):** Brown Publishing Co., 10222 Alliance Rd, Cincinnati, OH 45040. Telephone: 513-794-5040. FAX: 513-794-5480. **Management:** Vicki Taylor, Publisher. Cole Kolikohn, Advertising. **Editorial:** Peggy Mershon, Editor.

BEREA

NEWS SUN (BEREA), THE. 32 Park St., Berea, OH 44017-1516. Telephone: 216-986-7550. FAX: 216-986-7551. E-MAIL: sun@sunnews.com. URL: http://www.sunnews.com. Year Established: 1924. Pub. Frequency: w. (Thu.) Page Size: broadsheet. Subscrip. Rate: $.60 newsstand/cover; $32.50/yr carrier delivery; $39/yr mailed. Adv. Rate: col. inch $28.60 Circulation: 16,255 per issue (paid). **Owner(s):** Sun Media, Inc., 5510 Cloverleaf Pkwy., Cleveland, OH 44125-4887. Telephone: 216-524-0830. FAX: 216-642-5547. **Management:** John Urbancich, President. Dwight Schulz, Operations Manager. Laurie Toth, Advertising Manager. Jim Reynolds, Circulation Director. Emil DeSanto, Classified Adv. Mgr.. **Editorial:** Linda Kramer, Editor. Linda M. Kinsey, Executive Editor.

PARMA SUN POST. 32 Park St., Berea, OH 44017-1516. Telephone: 216-986-7550. FAX: 216-986-7551. E-MAIL: sun@sunnews.com. URL: http://www.sunnews.com. Year Established: 1936. Pub. Frequency: w. (Thu.) Page Size: broadsheet. Subscrip. Rate: $.65 newsstand/cover; $32.50/yr carrier delivery; $39/yr mailed. Adv. Rate: col. inch $39.20 Circulation: 21,685 per issue (paid). **Owner(s):** Sun Media, Inc., 5510 Cloverleaf Pkwy., Cleveland, OH 44125-4887. Telephone: 216-986-2600. FAX: 216-986-2380. **Management:** John Urbancich, President. Dwight Schulz, Operations Manager. Geoff Short, Advertising Manager. Jim Reynolds, Circulation Director. **Editorial:** Linda Kramer, Editor. Linda M. Kinsey, Executive Editor. Debbie Palmer, Assistant Editor.

SUN STAR, THE. 32 Park St., Berea, OH 44071. Telephone: 216-986-7550. FAX: 216-986-7551. E-MAIL: sun@sunnews.com. URL: http://www.sunnews.com. Year Established: 1958. Pub. Frequency: w. (Thu.) Page Size: broadsheet. Subscrip. Rate: $.60 newsstand/cover; $32.50/yr carrier delivery; $39/yr mailed. Adv. Rate: col. inch $19.25 Circulation: 12,022 per issue (paid). **Owner(s):** Sun Media, Inc., 5510 Cloverleaf Pkwy., Cleveland, OH 44125-4887. Telephone: 216-986-2600. FAX: 216-986-2380. **Management:** John Urbancich, President. Dwight Schulz, Operations Manager. Laurie Toth, Advertising Manager. Jim Reynolds, Circulation Director. Emil DeSanto, Classified Adv. Mgr.. **Editorial:** Linda Kramer, Editor. Linda Kinsey, Executive Editor. Debbie Palmer, Assistant Editor. Stan Urankar, Entertainment Editor.

Weeklies

BLUFFTON

BLUFFTON NEWS, THE. 101 N. Main St., Bluffton, OH 45817. Telephone: 419-358-8010. FAX: 419-358-5027. E-MAIL: editor@blufftonnews.com. Year Established: 1875. Pub. Frequency: w. (Thu.) Page Size: standard. Subscrip. Rate: $1.50 newsstand/cover; $45/yr in state; $55/yr out of state. Circulation: 2,900 per issue (paid). **Owner(s):** Bluffton News Printing & Publishing Co., See address and contact information above. **Management:** Tom Edwards, Publisher. **Editorial:** Fred Steiner, Editor.

BRYAN

COUNTYLINE, THE. 127 S. Walnut St., Bryan, OH 43506. Telephone: 419-636-1111. FAX: 419-636-8937. Year Established: 1953. Pub. Frequency: w. (Sun.) Page Size: tabloid. Subscrip. Rate: $30/yr mailed. Circulation: 23,871 Sunday (paid and free). **Owner(s):** Bryan Publishing Co., The, See address and contact information above. **Management:** Dean Howard, Manager.

BYESVILLE

BYESVILLE VILLAGE REPORTER. 185 S Second St, Byesville, OH 43723-1303. Telephone: 740-685-2073. FAX: 740-432-6219. Pub. Frequency: w. (Thu.) Page Size: standard. Subscrip. Rate: $.50 newsstand/cover; $18/yr. Adv. Rate: col. inch $3 Circulation: 800 per issue (paid). **Owner(s):** Dix Communications Group, 212 E. Liberty St., Wooster, OH 44691. Telephone: 330-264-1125. FAX: 216-264-3756. **Management:** Ed Archibald, Advertising Director. Chris Cryder, Circulation Manager. Lynn Berger, Classified Adv. Mgr.. Carol Ringer, Manager.

CADIZ

HARRISON NEWS-HERALD, THE. 130 N. Main St., Cadiz, OH 43907. Telephone: 740-942-2796. FAX: 740-942-4667. E-MAIL: newsroom@harrisonnewsherald.com. URL: http://www.harrisonnewsherald.com. Mailing Address: PO Box 127, Cadiz, OH 43907. Year Established: 1968. Pub. Frequency: w. (Mon.) Page Size: broadsheet. Subscrip. Rate: $.75 newsstand/cover; $19.50/yr local; $39.50/yr in state; $50/yr out of state. Circulation: 6,000 per issue (paid). **Owner(s):** David & Emily Schloss, See address and contact information above. **Management:** David Schloss, Publisher. Susan Petrisko, Advertising. David DeTorio, Advertising Manager. Maurine Huntsman, Circulation Manager. **Editorial:** Kay Keyser-Sedgmer, Managing Editor.

CALDWELL

JOURNAL-LEADER, THE. 309 Main St., Caldwell, OH 43724. Telephone: 740-732-2341. FAX: 740-732-7288. Year Established: 1859. Pub. Frequency: w. (Mon.) Page Size: broadsheet. Subscrip. Rate: $.75 newsstand/cover; $33/yr in county; $35/yr out of county. Circulation: 5,000 per issue (controlled and free). **Owner(s):** Southeast Publications, Inc., See address and contact information above. **Management:** David Evans, General Manager. **Editorial:** Sara Delancey, Associate Editor.

CAMBRIDGE

ADVANTAGE (CAMBRIDGE), THE. 831 Wheeling Ave., Cambridge, OH 43725. Telephone: 740-439-3531. FAX: 740-432-6219. Mailing Address: PO Box 10, Cambridge, OH 43725. Pub. Frequency: s-w. (Thu. & Sun.) Page Size: standard.Adv. Rate: col. inch $3 Circulation: 12,800 per issue (free). **Owner(s):** Dix Communications Group, 212 E. Liberty St., Wooster, OH 44691. Telephone: 330-264-1125. FAX: 216-264-3756. **Management:** Ed Archibald, Advertising Director. Chris Cryder, Circulation Manager. Lynn Berger, Classified Adv. Mgr.. **Editorial:** Ray Booth, Executive Editor.

NEW CONCORD LEADER. 831 Wheeling Ave., Cambridge, OH 43725. Telephone: 740-439-3531. FAX: 740-432-6219. Mailing Address: PO Box 10, Cambridge, OH 43725. Pub. Frequency: w. (Sun.) Page Size: broadsheet. Subscrip. Rate: $.50 newsstand/cover; $21/yr in county. Circulation: 1,200 per issue (paid). **Owner(s):** Dix Communications Group, 212 E. Liberty St., Wooster, OH 44691. Telephone: 330-264-1125. FAX: 216-264-3756. **Management:** Robert C. Dix, Publisher. Fred McBride, Advertising. **Editorial:** Niki Wolfe, Editor.

CAREY

PROGRESSOR-TIMES, THE. 1198 E. Findlay St., P.O. Box 37, Carey, OH 43316-0037. Telephone: 419-396-7567. FAX: 419-396-7527. Year Established: 1873. Pub. Frequency: w. (Wed.) Page Size: standard. Subscrip. Rate: $.50 newsstand/cover; $25/yr mailed in state. Circulation: 4,200 per issue (paid). **Owner(s):** Stephen C. Zender, See address and contact information above. **Management:** Stephen C. Zender, Publisher. Amy Zender Yeater, Advertising Manager. Jenny Freeman, Circulation Manager. **Editorial:** Stephen C. Zender, Editor-in-Chief.

CARROLLTON

FREE PRESS STANDARD. 43 E. Main St., Carrollton, OH 44615-9983. Telephone: 330-627-5591. FAX: 330-627-3195. E-MAIL: adfps44615@yahoo.com. URL: http://www.freepressstandard.com. Mailing Address: PO Box 37, Carrollton, OH 44615-9983. Year Established: 1831. Pub. Frequency: w. (Thu.) Page Size: broadsheet. Subscrip. Rate: $.50 newsstand/cover; $22.50/yr local; $45/yr in state; $55/yr out of state. Adv. Rate: col. inch $9.95 Circulation: 7,500 per issue (paid and free). **Owner(s):** Maynard A. Buck, Jr., 135 Poplar Ln., Cadiz, OH 43907. Telephone: 740-942-2796. **Management:** William Peterson, General Manager. Maynard A. Buck Jr., Publisher. Connie Trushel, Advertising Manager. Melissa Burgess, Classified Adv. Mgr.. **Editorial:** Carol McIntire, Editor. Donald E. Rutledge, Associate Editor.

CHESTERLAND

CHESTERLAND NEWS. 8389 Mayfield Rd., B4, Chesterland, OH 44026-2534. Telephone: 440-729-7667. FAX: 440-729-8240. E-MAIL: chestrnews@aol.com. Year Established: 1967. Pub. Frequency: w. (Wed.) Page Size: tabloid.Subscrip. Rate: $23/yr out of area Circulation: 7,000 per issue (free). **Owner(s):** Pamela Gable, See address and contact information above. **Management:** Pamela Gable, Publisher.

CHILLICOTHE

ROSS COUNTY ADVERTISER. 147 W Water St, Chillicothe, OH 45601. Telephone: 740-773-5010. FAX: 740-773-5021. E-MAIL: cclark@jcpgroup.com. URL: http://www.jcpgroup.com. Year Established: 1978. Pub. Frequency: w. (Sun.) Page Size: tabloid Circulation: 26,500 per issue (free). **Owner(s):** Hersam Acorn Newspapers LLC, 16 Bailey Ave., Ridgefield, CT 06877. Telephone: 203-438-6544. FAX: 203-861-0023. **Management:** Chris Clark, Advertising Manager. **Editorial:** Gary Schreck, Production Manager.

CINCINNATI

CINCINNATI DOWNTOWNER. ISSN 1051-8606
128 E. Sixth St., Ste 806, Cincinnati, OH 45202. Telephone: 513-241-9906. FAX: 513-241-7235. Year Established: 1979. Pub. Frequency: w. Page Size: tabloid.Adv. Rate: page $142,450; trim 11.25 x 15 Circulation: 18,000 (controlled). **Owner(s):** Taylor Communications, See address and contact information above. **Management:** Doug M Taylor, Publisher. Sheri Brendle, Advertising. **Editorial:** Doug M Taylor, Editor.

DELHI PRESS. 5556 Cheviot Rd., Cincinnati, OH 45247. Telephone: 513-923-3111. FAX: 513-923-1806. URL: http://www.communitypress.com. Year Established: 1924. Pub. Frequency: w. (Wed.) Page Size: broadsheet. Subscrip. Rate: $.50 newsstand/cover; $2.50/mo. voluntary pay; $105/yr mailed. Circulation: 10,503 per issue (paid and free). **Owner(s):** Community Press Newspapers, 7950 Jones Branch Dr, McLean, VA 22107. Telephone: 703-854-6000. **Management:** Susan McHugh, General Manager. Doug Hubbuch, Advertising Manager. Sharon Schachleiter, Circulation Manager. **Editorial:** Susan McHugh, Editor. Marc Emral, Senior Editor. Jennie Key, Community Editor.

HILLTOP PRESS. 5556 Cheviot Rd., Cincinnati, OH 45247. Telephone: 513-923-3111. FAX: 513-923-1806. E-MAIL: dhubbuch@communitypress.com. URL: http://www.communitypress.com. Year Established: 1918. Pub. Frequency: w. (Wed.) Page Size: broadsheet. Subscrip. Rate: $.50 newsstand/cover; $2.50/mo. voluntary pay; $105/yr mailed. Circulation: 20,000 per issue (controlled and free). **Owner(s):** Community Press Newspapers, 7950 Jones Branch Dr, McLean, VA 22107. Telephone: 703-854-6000. **Management:** Susan McHugh, General Manager. Doug Hubbuch, Advertising Manager. Sharon Schachleiter, Circulation Manager. **Editorial:** Susan McHugh, Editor. Marc Emral, Senior Editor. Jennie Key, Community Editor.

NORTHWEST PRESS. 5556 Cheviot Rd., Cincinnati, OH 45247. Telephone: 513-923-3111. FAX: 513-923-1806. E-MAIL: dhubbuch@communitypress.com. URL: http://www.communitypress.com. Year Established: 1918. Pub. Frequency: w. (Wed.) Page Size: broadsheet. Subscrip. Rate: $.50 newsstand/cover; $2.50/mo. voluntary pay; $105/yr mailed. Circulation: 16,610 per issue (paid). **Owner(s):** Community Press Newspapers, 7950 Jones Branch Dr, McLean, VA 22107. Telephone: 703-854-6000. **Management:** Susan McHugh, General Manager. Doug Hubbuch, Advertising Manager. Sharon Schachleiter, Circulation Manager. **Editorial:** Susan McHugh, Editor. Marc Emral, Senior Editor. Jennie Key, Community Editor.

PRICE HILL PRESS. 5556 Cheviot Rd., Cincinnati, OH 45247. Telephone: 513-923-3111. FAX: 513-923-1806. E-MAIL: dhubbuch@communitypress.com. URL: http://www.communitypress.com. Year Established: 1924. Pub. Frequency: w. (Wed.) Page Size: broadsheet. Subscrip. Rate: $.50 newsstand/cover; $2.50/mo. voluntary pay; $105/yr mailed. Circulation: 6,942 per issue (controlled and free). **Owner(s):** Community Press Newspapers, 7950 Jones Branch Dr, McLean, VA 22107. Telephone: 703-854-6000. **Management:** Susan McHugh, General Manager. Doug Hubbuch, Advertising Manager. Sharon Schachleiter, Circulation Manager. **Editorial:** Susan McHugh, Editor. Marc Emral, Senior Editor. Jennie Key, Community Editor.

SPRINGBORO SUN. 10222 Alliance Rd, Cincinnati, OH 45040. Telephone: 513-794-5040. FAX: 513-794-5480. URL: http://www.sndnews.com. Pub. Frequency: w. (Thu.) Page Size: broadsheet Circulation: 5,500 per issue (free). **Owner(s):** Brown Publishing Co., See address and contact information above. **Management:** Frank Beeson, Publisher. **Editorial:** Cindy Eisen, Editor. Terry Baver, Managing Editor.

WESTERN HILLS PRESS. 5556 Cheviot Rd., Cincinnati, OH 45247. Telephone: 513-923-3111. FAX: 513-923-1806. E-MAIL: dhubbuch@communitypress.com. URL: http://www.communitypress.com. Year Established: 1924. Pub. Frequency: w. (Wed.) Page Size: broadsheet. Subscrip. Rate: $.50 newsstand/cover; $2.50/mo. voluntary pay; $105/yr mailed. Circulation: 18,000 per issue (paid and free). **Owner(s):** Community Press Newspapers, 7950 Jones Branch Dr, McLean, VA 22107. Telephone: 703-854-6000. **Management:** Susan McHugh, General Manager. Doug Hubbuch, Advertising Manager. Sharon Schachleiter, Circulation Manager. **Editorial:** Susan McHugh, Editor. Marc Emral, Senior Editor. Jennie Key, Community Editor.

CIRCLEVILLE

PICKAWAY COUNTY ADVERTISER. 123 W. Main St, Circleville, OH 43113. Telephone: 740-477-3386. FAX: 740-474-9750. E-MAIL: jparker@jcpgroup.com. URL: http://www.pickaway.theadvertiser.net. Pub. Frequency: w. (Sun.) Page Size: broadsheet Circulation: 20,285 per issue (free). **Owner(s):** Journal Community Publishing Group, 600 Industrial Dr., Waupaca, WI 54891. **Management:** Jim Parker, General Manager. Lisa Stocklin, Advertising.

CLEVELAND

BRECKSVILLE GAZETTE. 7014 Mill Rd., Cleveland, OH 44141. Telephone: 440-526-7977. FAX: 440-526-7114. E-MAIL: production@gazette-news.com. Mailing Address: PO Box 166, Jefferson, OH 44047-0166. Year Established: 1975. Pub. Frequency: s-m. (Wed.) Page Size: tabloid. Subscrip. Rate: $.50 newsstand/cover; $10/yr mailed; $19 mailed for 2 yrs.. Circulation: 10,000 per issue (paid). **Owner(s):** Gazette Newspapers, See address and contact information above. **Management:** Joyce McFadden, Publisher. **Editorial:** Joyce McFadden, Editor.

BROOKLYN SUN JOURNAL. 5510 Cloverleaf Pkwy., Cleveland, OH 44125-4887. Telephone: 216-986-2600. FAX: 216-986-2380. E-MAIL: sun@sunnews.com. URL: http://www.sunnews.com. Year Established: 1918. Pub. Frequency: w. (Thu.) Page Size: broadsheet. Subscrip. Rate: $.65 newsstand/cover; $32.50/yr carrier delivery; $33.80/yr mailed. Adv. Rate: col. inch $18.80 Circulation: 6,889 per issue (paid). **Owner(s):** Sun Media, Inc., See address and contact information above. **Management:** John Urbancich, President. Dwight Schulz, Operations Manager. Jim Reynolds, Circulation Director. Emil DeSanto, Classified Adv. Mgr.. Robert C. Palmer, Sales Manager. **Editorial:** Carol Kovach, Editor. Linda Kinsey, Executive Editor.

CLEVELAND SCENE. 1468 W. Ninth St., Ste. 805, Cleveland, OH 44113. Telephone: 216-241-7550. FAX: 216-802-7212. E-MAIL: scene@clevescene.com. URL: http://www.clevescene.com. Mailing Address: PO Box 15029, Cleveland, OH 44115-0029. Year Established: 1970. Pub. Frequency: w. (Wed.) Page Size: tabloid Circulation: 65,000 per issue (free). **Owner(s):** New Times Inc., 1201 E. Jefferson, Phoenix, AZ 85034. Telephone: 602-271-0040. FAX: 602-238-4800. **Management:** Ramon Larkin, Publisher. Joe Strailey, Classified Adv. Mgr.. Chris Hutchins, Sales Manager. **Editorial:** Pete Kotz, Editor.

GARFIELD MAPLE-SUN. ISSN 1086-1254
5510 Cloverleaf Pkwy., Cleveland, OH 44125-4887. Telephone: 216-986-2600. FAX: 216-986-2380. E-MAIL: sun@sunnews.com. URL: http://www.sunnews.com. Year Established: 1918. Pub. Frequency: w. (Thu.) Page Size: broadsheet. Subscrip. Rate: $.60 newsstand/cover; $32.50/yr carrier delivery; $39/yr mailed. Adv. Rate: col. inch $23.95 Circulation: 7,829 per issue (paid). **Owner(s):** Sun Media, Inc., See address and contact information above. **Management:** John Urbancich, President. Dwight Schulz, Operations Manager. Jim Reynolds, Circulation Director. Emil DeSanto, Classified Adv. Mgr.. **Editorial:** Carol Kovach, Editor. Linda Kinsey, Executive Editor. Stan Urankar, Entertainment Editor.

NORDONIA HILLS SUN. 5510 Cloverleaf Pkwy., Cleveland, OH 44125-4887. Telephone: 216-986-2600. FAX: 216-986-2380. E-MAIL: sun@sunnews.com. URL: http://www.sunnews.com. Year Established: 1994. Pub. Frequency: w. (Thu.) Page Size: broadsheet. Subscrip. Rate: $.60 newsstand/cover; $32.50/yr carrier delivery; $39/yr mailed. Adv. Rate: col. inch $15 Circulation: 19,167 per issue (paid). **Owner(s):** Sun Media, Inc., See address and contact information above. **Management:** John Urbancich, President. Dwight Schulz, Operations Manager. Jim Reynolds, Circulation Director. Emil DeSanto, Classified Adv. Mgr.. Robert C. Palmer, Sales Manager. **Editorial:** Carol Kovach, Editor. Linda Kinsey, Executive Editor. Stan Urankar, Entertainment Editor. Barbara Collier, Food Editor.

SUN COURIER, THE. 5510 Cloverleaf Pkwy., Cleveland, OH 44125-4887. Telephone: 216-524-0830. FAX: 216-642-5547. E-MAIL: sun@sunnews.com. URL: http://www.sunnews.com. Year Established: 1969. Pub. Frequency: w. (Thu.) Page Size: broadsheet. Subscrip. Rate: $.65 newsstand/cover; $32.50/yr carrier delivery; $39/yr mailed. Adv. Rate: col. inch $18.65 Circulation: 6,789 per issue (paid). **Owner(s):** Sun Media, Inc., See address and contact information above. **Management:** John Urbancich, President. Dwight Schulz, Operations Manager. Jim Reynolds, Circulation Director. Emil DeSanto, Classified Adv. Mgr.. **Editorial:** Carol Kovach, Editor. Linda Kinsey, Executive Editor. Stan Ukrankar, Entertainment Editor.

TWINSBURG SUN, THE. 5510 Cloverleaf Pkwy., Cleveland, OH 44125-4887. Telephone: 216-986-2600. FAX: 216-986-2380. E-MAIL: sun@sunnews.com. URL: http://www.sunnews.com. Year Established: 1994. Pub. Frequency: w. (Thu.) Page Size: broadsheet. Subscrip. Rate: $.60 newsstand/cover; $32.50/yr carrier delivery; $39/yr mailed. Adv. Rate: col. inch $15 Circulation: 19,167 per issue (paid). **Owner(s):** Sun Media, Inc., See address and contact information above. **Management:** John Urbancich, President. Dwight Schulz, Operations Manager. Dennis Mudry, Advertising Manager. Jim Reynolds, Circulation Director. **Editorial:** Carol Kovach, Editor. Linda Kinsey, Executive Editor. Rodger Vozat, Assistant Editor.

CLYDE

CLYDE ENTERPRISE. 109 N Main St, Clyde, OH 43410. Telephone: 419-547-9194. E-MAIL: clydenews@bizwoh.r.r.com. Mailing Address: PO Box 29, Clyde, OH 43410. Year Established: 1878. Pub. Frequency: w. (Wed.) Page Size: broadsheet. Subscrip. Rate: $.75 newsstand/cover; $38.50/yr in state. Circulation: 2,200 per issue (paid). **Owner(s):** Gazette Publishing Co., 107 N. Sandusky St., Bellevue, OH. Telephone: 419-483-4190. **Management:** Jack Trainor, General Manager. Thomas Smith, President. Jack Trainor, Advertising. **Editorial:** Rebecca Brooks, Editor.

COLDWATER

MERCER COUNTY CHRONICLE. 116 W Main St, Coldwater, OH 45828. Telephone: 419-678-2324. FAX: 419-678-4659. E-MAIL: mercercountychronicle@bright.net. URL: http://www.mercercountychronicle.com. Mailing Address: P O Box 105, Coldwater, OH 45828-0105. Year Established: 1902. Pub. Frequency: w. (Thu.) Page Size: broadsheet. Subscrip. Rate: $.75 newsstand/cover; $32/yr in county; $40/yr in adjacent cys. Adv. Rate: col. inch $6.25 Freelance Pay: $20/article. Circulation: 2,400 per issue (paid). **Owner(s):** Delphos Newspapers, 405 N. Main St., Delphos, OH 45833. Telephone: 419-692-5050. FAX: 419-692-7704. **Management:** Robin Link, Publisher. **Editorial:** Robin Link, Editor.

COLUMBIA STATION

RURAL - URBAN RECORD. ISSN 0192-9771 PO Box 966, Columbia Station, OH 44028. Telephone: 440-236-8982. FAX: 440-236-9198. E-MAIL: news@rural-urbanrecord.com. Year Established: 1955. Pub. Frequency: w. (Mon.) Page Size: tabloid. Subscrip. Rate: $33/yr out of area. Adv. Rate: col. inch $10 Circulation: 19,500 per issue (paid and free). **Owner(s):** Leonard & Lee Boise, See address and contact information above. **Management:** Leonard Boise, Publisher. Lee Boise, Business Manager. **Editorial:** Leonard Boise, Editor.

COLUMBUS

BEXLEY NEWS. 5257 Sinclair Rd., Columbus, OH 43229. Telephone: 614-785-1212. E-MAIL: snpnews@acncolumbus.com. URL: http://www.ColumbusLocalNews.com. Year Established: 1964. Pub. Frequency: w. (Wed.) Page Size: tabloid. Subscrip. Rate: $.50 newsstand/cover; $30/yr mailed in county; $35/yr mailed out of county. Circulation: 9,588 per issue (paid). **Owner(s):** Suburban News Publications, See address and contact information above. **Management:** James Toms, Publisher. Laura Hammett, Advertising Manager. Tom Banik, Circulation Manager. Karen Reitz, Classified Adv. Mgr.. **Editorial:** Joe Meyer, Editor.

BIG WALNUT NEWS. 5257 Sinclair Rd., Columbus, OH 43229. Telephone: 614-785-1212. E-MAIL: snpnews@acncolumbus.com. URL: http://www.ColumbusLocalNews.com. Mailing Address: PO Box 29912, Columbus, OH 43229. Pub. Frequency: w. (Wed.) Page Size: tabloid. Subscrip. Rate: $.50 newsstand/cover; $30/yr in county; $40/yr out of county. Circulation: 6,414 per issue (paid). **Owner(s):** Suburban News Publications, See address and contact information above. **Management:** James Toms, Publisher. Laura Hammett, Advertising Manager. Tom Banik, Circulation Manager. **Editorial:** Joe Meyer, Editor.

BOOSTER, THE. 5257 Sinclair Rd., Columbus, OH 43229. Telephone: 614-785-1212. E-MAIL: SNPnews@acncolumbus.com. URL: http://www.ColumbusLocalNews.com. Year Established: 1933. Pub. Frequency: w. (Wed.) Page Size: tabloid. Subscrip. Rate: $.50 newsstand/cover; $30/yr in county; $35/yr out of county. Circulation: 17,221 per issue (paid). **Owner(s):** Suburban News Publications, See address and contact information above. **Management:** James Toms, Publisher. Laura Hammett, Advertising Manager. Tom Banik, Circulation Manager. **Editorial:** Joe Meyer, Editor.

COLUMBUS ALIVE. 62 E Broad St, Columbus, OH 43215. Telephone: 614-221-2449. FAX: 614-221-2456. E-MAIL: mail@columbusalive.com. URL: http://www.columbusalive.com. Year Established: 1984. Pub. Frequency: w. (Thu.) Page Size: tabloid. Subscrip. Rate: $50/yr mailed. Adv. Rate: B&W page $1,820 Freelance Pay: $25-$300/article. Circulation: 45,000 per issue (paid and free). **Owner(s):** Columbus Alive, Inc., See address and contact information above. **Management:** Katie Wolfe Lloyd, Publisher. Amy Bishop, Advertising Director. Bob Hite, Circulation Manager. **Editorial:** Brian Lindamood, Managing Editor. Melissa Starker, Assistant Editor.

COLUMBUS MESSENGER. 3500 Sullivant Ave., Columbus, OH 43204. Telephone: 614-272-5422. FAX: 614-272-0684. E-MAIL: phildaubel@columbusmessenger.com. URL: http://www.columbusmessenger.com. Year Established: 1974. Pub. Frequency: w. (Mon.) Page Size: tabloid. Subscrip. Rate: $65/yr mailed. Circulation: 115,349 per issue (paid and controlled). **Owner(s):** Columbus Messenger, See address and contact information above. **Management:** Phil Daubel, Publisher. Douglas Henry, Advertising Director. Carolyn Sapp, Classified Adv. Mgr.. **Editorial:** Rick Palsgrove, Managing Editor.

DUBLIN NEWS. 5257 Sinclair Rd., Columbus, OH 43229. Telephone: 614-785-1212. E-MAIL: snpnews@acncolumbus.com. URL: http://www.ColumbusLocalNews.com. Mailing Address: PO Box 29912, Columbus, OH 43229. Year Established: 1978. Pub. Frequency: w. (Wed.) Page Size: tabloid. Subscrip. Rate: $.50 newsstand/cover; $30/yr in county; $40/yr out of county. Circulation: 19,845 per issue (paid). **Owner(s):** Suburban News Publications, See address and contact information above. **Management:** James Toms, Publisher. Laura Hammett, Advertising Manager. Tom Banik, Circulation Manager. Karen Reitz, Classified Adv. Mgr.. **Editorial:** Joe Meyer, Managing Editor. John Hulkenberg, Sports Editor.

GAHANA NEWS. 5257 Sinclair Rd., Columbus, OH 43229. Telephone: 614-785-1212. E-MAIL: snpnews@acncolumbus.com. URL: http://www.ColumbusLocalNews.com. Mailing Address: PO Box 29912, Columbus, OH 43229. Pub. Frequency: w. (Wed.) Page Size: tabloid. Subscrip. Rate: $.50 newsstand/cover; $30/yr in county; $40/yr mailed out of county. Circulation: 13,984 per issue (paid). **Owner(s):** Suburban News Publications, See address and contact information above. **Management:** James Toms, Publisher. Laura Hammett, Advertising Manager. Tom Banik, Circulation Manager. Karen Reitz, Classified Adv. Mgr.. **Editorial:** Joe Meyer, Editor.

GERMAN VILLAGE GAZETTE. 5257 Sinclair Rd., Columbus, OH 43229. Telephone: 614-785-1212. E-MAIL: snpnews@acncolumbus.com. URL: http://www.ColumbusLocalNews.com. Mailing Address: PO Box 29912, Columbus, OH 43229. Pub. Frequency: w. (Thu.) Page Size: tabloid. Subscrip. Rate: $.50 newsstand/cover; $30/yr in county; $40/yr mailed out of county 3rd class mail. Circulation: 4,770 per issue (paid). **Owner(s):** Suburban News Publications, See address and contact information above. **Management:** James Toms, Publisher. Laura Hammett, Advertising Manager. Tom Banik, Circulation Manager. **Editorial:** Joe Meyer, Editor.

GROVE CITY NEWS. 5257 Sinclair Rd., Columbus, OH 43229. Telephone: 614-785-1212. FAX: 614-842-4760. URL: http://www.snponline.com. Mailing Address: PO Box 29912, Columbus, OH 43229. Pub. Frequency: w. (Thu.) Page Size: tabloid. Subscrip. Rate: $.50 newsstand/cover; $30/yr in county; $40/yr out of county. Circulation: 10,600 per issue (paid). **Owner(s):** Suburban News Publications, See address and contact information above. **Management:** James Toms, Publisher. Sonshine Parrett, Advertising Manager. Tom Banik, Circulation Manager. **Editorial:** Joe Meyer, Editor.

HILLIARD NORTHWEST NEWS. 5257 Sinclair Rd., Columbus, OH 43229. URL: http://www.snponline.com. Pub. Frequency: w. (Wed.) Page Size: tabloid. Subscrip. Rate: $.50 newsstand/cover; $30/yr in county; $35/yr out of county. Circulation: 20,000 per issue (paid and free). **Owner(s):** Suburban News Publications, See address and contact information above. **Management:** Jim Toms, Publisher. Sonshine Parrett, Advertising Manager. Tom Banik, Circulation Manager. Ron Boyd, Classified Adv. Mgr.. **Editorial:** Joe Meyer, Managing Editor. Richard Ades, Copy Chief.

NEW ALBANY NEWS. 5257 Sinclair Rd., Columbus, OH 43229. Telephone: 614-785-1212. E-MAIL: snpnews@acncolumbus.com. URL: http://www.ColumbusLocalNews.com. Mailing Address: PO Box 29912, Columbus, OH 43229. Pub. Frequency: w. (Wed.) Page Size: tabloid. Subscrip. Rate: $.50 newsstand/cover; $30/yr in county; $40/yr out of county. Circulation: 6,900 per issue (paid). **Owner(s):** Suburban News Publications, See address and contact information above. **Management:** James Toms, Publisher. Laura Hammett, Advertising Manager. Tom Banik, Circulation Manager. **Editorial:** Joe Meyer, Editor.

NORTHLAND NEWS. 5257 Sinclair Rd., Columbus, OH 43229. Telephone: 614-785-1212. FAX: 614-785-1881. E-MAIL: snpnews@acncolumbus.com. URL: http://www.ColumbusLocalNews.com. Mailing Address: PO Box 29912, Columbus, OH 43229. Pub. Frequency: w. (Wed.) Page Size: tabloid. Subscrip. Rate: $.50 newsstand/cover; $30/yr in county; $35/yr out of county. Circulation: 20,305 per issue (paid). **Owner(s):** Suburban News Publications, See address and contact information above. **Management:** James Toms, Publisher. Laura Hammett, Advertising Manager. Tom Banik, Circulation Manager. Karen Reitz, Classified Adv. Mgr.. **Editorial:** Joe Meyer, Editor. Clif Wiltshire, Managing Editor.

NORTHWEST COLUMBUS NEWS. 5257 Sinclair Rd., Columbus, OH 43229. Telephone: 614-451-1212. E-MAIL: snpnews@acncolumbus.com. URL: http://www.ColumbusLocalNews.com. Year Established: 1980. Pub. Frequency: w. (Wed.) Page Size: tabloid. Subscrip. Rate: $.50 newsstand/cover; $30/yr in county; $35/yr out of county. Circulation: 7,735 per issue (paid). **Owner(s):** Suburban News Publications, See address and contact information above. **Management:** James Toms, Publisher. Laura Hammett, Advertising Manager. Tom Banik, Circulation Manager. Karen Reitz, Classified Adv. Mgr.. **Editorial:** Joe Meyer, Managing Editor. John Hulkenberg, Sports Editor.

OLENTANGY VALLEY NEWS. 5257 Sinclair Rd., Columbus, OH 43229. Telephone: 614-785-1212. E-MAIL: snpnews@acncolumbus.com. URL: http://www.ColumbusLocalNews.com. Mailing Address: PO Box 29912, Columbus, OH 43229. Pub. Frequency: w. (Wed.) Page Size: tabloid. Subscrip. Rate: $.50 newsstand/cover; $30/yr in county; $40/yr mailed out of county. Circulation: 19,495 per issue (paid). **Owner(s):** Suburban News Publications, See address and contact information above. **Management:** James Toms, Publisher. Laura Hammett, Advertising Manager. Tom Banik, Circulation Manager. Karen Reitz, Classified Adv. Mgr.. **Editorial:** Joe Meyer, Editor.

OTHER PAPER (COLUMBUS), THE. PO Box 29913, Columbus, OH 43229. Telephone: 614-847-3800. FAX: 614-848-3838. URL: http://www.theotherpaper.com. Pub. Frequency: w. (Thu.) Page Size: broadsheet.Subscrip. Rate: $40/yr mailed out of state Circulation: 53,000 per issue (free). **Owner(s):** Max S. Brown, See address and contact information above. **Management:** Max S. Brown, Publisher. Rheta Gallgher, Advertising Manager. Clete Boyr, Circulation Manager. **Editorial:** Danny Russell, Editor.

PICKERINGTON TIMES-SUN. 5257 Sinclair Rd., Columbus, OH 43229. Telephone: 614-451-1212. FAX: 614-785-1881. E-MAIL: snpnews@acncolumbus.com. URL: http://www.columbuslocalnews.com. Pub. Frequency: w. (Wed.) Page Size: tabloid. Subscrip. Rate: $.50 newsstand/cover; $40/yr mailed in county. Circulation: 13,450 per issue (paid). **Owner(s):** Suburban News Publications, See address and contact information above. **Management:** James Toms, Publisher. Laura Hammett, Advertising Manager. Karen Reitz, Classified Adv. Mgr.. **Editorial:** Joe Meyer, Editor.

REYNOLDSBURG NEWS. 5257 Sinclair Rd., Columbus, OH 43229. Telephone: 614-785-1212. FAX: 614-785-1881. E-MAIL: snpnews@acncolumbus.com. URL: http://www.ColumbusLocalNews.com. Pub. Frequency: w. (Wed.) Page Size: tabloid. Subscrip. Rate: $.50 newsstand/cover; $30/yr local; $35/yr out of area. Circulation: 14,450 per issue (paid). **Owner(s):** Suburban News Publications, See address and contact information above. **Management:** James Toms, Publisher. Laura Hammett, Advertising Manager. Tom Banik, Circulation Manager. **Editorial:** Joe Meyer, Editor.

TIMES (COLUMBUS), THE. 5257 Sinclair Rd., Columbus, OH 43229. Telephone: 614-785-1212. E-MAIL: snpnews@acncolumbus.com. URL: http://www.ColumbusLocalNews.com. Mailing Address: PO Box 29912, Columbus, OH 43229. Year Established: 1871. Pub. Frequency: w. (Wed.) Page Size: tabloid. Subscrip. Rate: $.50 newsstand/cover; $30/yr in county; $35/yr out of county. Circulation: 10,835 per issue (paid). **Owner(s):** Suburban News Publications, See address and contact information above. **Management:** James Toms, Publisher. Laura Hammett, Advertising Manager. Tom Banik, Circulation Manager. Karen Reitz, Classified Adv. Mgr.. **Editorial:** Joe Meyer, Editor. Clif Wiltshire, Managing Editor.

TRI-VILLAGE NEWS. 5257 Sinclair Rd., Columbus, OH 43229. Telephone: 614-785-1212. FAX: 614-785-1881. E-MAIL: snpnews@acncolumbus.com. URL: http://www.ColumbusLocalNews.com. Mailing Address: PO Box 29912, Columbus, OH 43229. Year Established: 1931. Pub. Frequency: w. (Wed.) Page Size: tabloid. Subscrip. Rate: $.50 newsstand/cover; $30/yr in county; $35/yr out of county. Circulation: 5,674 per issue (paid). **Owner(s):** Suburban News Publications, See address and contact information above. **Management:** James Toms, Publisher. Laura Hammett, Advertising Manager. Tom Banik, Circulation Manager. Karen Reitz, Classified Adv. Mgr.. **Editorial:** Joe Meyer, Editor.

UPPER ARLINGTON NEWS. 5257 Sinclair Rd., Columbus, OH 43229. Telephone: 614-785-1212. E-MAIL: snpnews@acncolumbus.con. URL: http://www.ColumbusLocalNews.com. Year Established: 1933. Pub. Frequency: w. (Wed.) Page Size: tabloid. Subscrip. Rate: $.50 newsstand/cover; $30/yr mailed in county; $35/yr mailed out of county. Freelance Pay: $10-$25/story. Circulation: 16,151 per issue (paid). **Owner(s):** Suburban News Publications, See address and contact information above. **Management:** James Toms, Publisher. Laura Hammett, Advertising Manager. Tom Banik, Circulation Manager. Karen Reitz, Classified Adv. Mgr.. **Editorial:** Joe Meyer, Editor. Clif Wiltshire, Managing Editor.

WESTERVILLE NEWS & PUBLIC OPINION. 5257 Sinclair Rd., Columbus, OH 43229. E-MAIL: snpews@acncolumbus.com. URL: http://www.ColumbusLocalNews.com. Year Established: 1867. Pub. Frequency: w. (Wed.) Page Size: tabloid. Subscrip. Rate: $.50 newsstand/cover; $30/yr mailed in county; $35/yr mailed out of state. Circulation: 26,000 per issue (paid and free). **Owner(s):** Suburban News Publications, See address and contact information above. **Management:** James A. Toms, Publisher. Laura Hammett, Advertising Manager. Tom Banik, Circulation Manager. Karen Reitz, Classified Adv. Mgr.. **Editorial:** Joe Meyer, Managing Editor.

WESTLAND NEWS. 5257 Sinclair Rd., Columbus, OH 43229. Telephone: 614-785-1212. FAX: 614-785-1881. E-MAIL: snpnews@acncolumbus.com. URL: http://www.ColumbusLocalNews.com. Pub. Frequency: w. (Thu.) Page Size: tabloid. Subscrip. Rate: $.50 newsstand/cover; $30/yr local; $35/yr out of area. Circulation: 9,055 per issue (paid). **Owner(s):** Suburban News Publications, See address and contact information above. **Management:** James Toms, Publisher. Laura Hammett, Advertising Manager. Tom Banik, Circulation Manager. Karen Reitz, Classified Adv. Mgr.. **Editorial:** Joe Meyer, Editor. Clif Wiltshire, Managing Editor.

WHITEHALL NEWS. 5257 Sinclair Rd., Columbus, OH 43229. Telephone: 614-785-1212. E-MAIL: snpnews@acncolumbus.com. URL: http://www.ColumbusLocalNews.com. Mailing Address: PO Box 29912, Columbus, OH 43229. Year Established: 1986. Pub. Frequency: w. (Wed.) Page Size: tabloid. Subscrip. Rate: $.50 newsstand/cover; $30/yr mailed in county; $35/yr mailed out of county. Circulation: 9,301 per issue (paid). **Owner(s):** Suburban News Publications, See address and contact information above. **Management:** James Toms, Publisher. Laura Hammett, Advertising Manager. Tom Banik, Circulation Manager. Karen Reitz, Classified Adv. Mgr.. **Editorial:** Joe Meyer, Editor.

WORTHINGTON NEWS. 5257 Sinclair Rd., Columbus, OH 43229. Telephone: 614-785-1212. E-MAIL: snpnews@acncolumbus.com. URL: http://www.ColumbusLocalNews.com. Mailing Address: PO Box 29912, Columbus, OH 43229. Year Established: 1926. Pub. Frequency: w. (Wed.) Page Size: tabloid. Subscrip. Rate: $.50 newsstand/cover; $30/yr in county; $35/yr out of county. Circulation: 19,036 per issue (paid). **Owner(s):** Suburban News Publications, See address and contact information above. **Management:** James Toms, Publisher. Laura Hammett, Advertising Manager. Tom Banik, Circulation Manager. Karen Reitz, Classified Adv. Mgr.. **Editorial:** Joe Meyer, Managing Editor.

COLUMBUS GROVE

PUTNAM COUNTY VIDETTE. 109 W Sycamore St, Columbus Grove, OH 45830. Telephone: 419-659-2173. FAX: 419-659-2760. URL: http://www.brownpublishing.com. Mailing Address: PO Box 127, Columbus Grove, OH 45830-0127. Year Established: 1873. Pub. Frequency: w. (Wed.) Page Size: broadsheet. Subscrip. Rate: $.50 newsstand/cover; $29/yr in county; $31/yr mailed in state; $33/yr mailed out of state. Circulation: 1,150 per issue (paid). **Owner(s):** Brown Publishing Co., 10222 Alliance Rd, Cincinnati, OH 45040. **Management:** Mark Constance, Publisher. **Editorial:** Mike Hohenbrink, Editor.

COSHOCTON

COSHOCTON COUNTY ADVERTISER. 1100 Fairy Falls Dr Ste 1, Coshocton, OH 43812. Telephone: 740-622-4122. FAX: 740-623-0618. E-MAIL: mfortune@jcpgroup.com. URL: http://www.jcpgroup.com. Pub. Frequency: w. (Sun) Page Size: broadsheet. **Owner(s):** Journal Community Publishing Group, 600 Industrial Dr., Waupaca, WI 54891. Telephone: 715-258-8450. **Management:** Mark Fortune, General Manager.

COVINGTON

PENNY SAVER (COVINGTON). 395 S. High St., Covington, OH 45318-0069. Telephone: 937-473-2028. FAX: 937-473-2500. E-MAIL: production@arenspub.com. URL: http://www.arenspub.com. Mailing Address: PO Box 69, Covington, OH 45318-0069. Pub. Frequency: w. (Mon.) Page Size: tabloid. Subscrip. Rate: $.25 newsstand/cover; $19/yr mailed. Adv. Rate: col. inch $9.28 Circulation: 10,700 per issue (paid). **Owner(s):** Covington Arens Corp., See address and contact information above. **Management:** Gary L. Godfrey, Publisher. Don Selanders, Advertising Manager. Connie Didier, Circulation Manager. **Editorial:** Jean Devlin, Editor.

STILLWATER VALLEY ADVERTISER. 395 S. High St., Covington, OH 45318-0069. Telephone: 937-473-2028. FAX: 937-473-2500. E-MAIL: garyg@arenspub.com. URL: http://www.arenspub.com. Mailing Address: PO Box 69, Covington, OH 45318-0069. Year Established: 1954. Pub. Frequency: w. (Wed.) Page Size: tabloid. Subscrip. Rate: $.25 newsstand/cover; $19/yr mailed. Circulation: 10,500 per issue (paid). **Owner(s):** Covington Arens Corp., See address and contact information above. **Management:** Gary L. Godfrey, Publisher. Don Selanders, Advertising Manager. Connie Didier, Circulation Manager. **Editorial:** Jean Devlin, Editor.

CRESTLINE

CRESTLINE ADVOCATE. 312 N. Seltzer St., Crestline, OH 44827. Telephone: 419-683-3355. FAX: 419-683-0175. E-MAIL: crestlineadvocate@midohio.twcbc.com. Mailing Address: PO Box 226, Crestline, OH 44827-0226. Year Established: 1869. Pub. Frequency: w. (Wed.) Page Size: standard. Subscrip. Rate: $.50 newsstand/cover; $27/yr mailed; $50 home delivery for 2 yrs.. Adv. Rate: col. inch $6 Circulation: 2,300 per issue (paid). **Owner(s):** Crestline Advocate, Inc., See address and contact information above. **Management:** Joseph Polito, President. Kim Ross-Polito, Publisher. **Editorial:** Kim Ross-Polito, Editor.Readers: Community

DALTON

DALTON GAZETTE & KIDRON NEWS. PO Box 495, Dalton, OH 44618-0495. Telephone: 330-828-8401. FAX: 330-828-8401. Year Established: 1875. Pub. Frequency: w. Page Size: tabloid. Subscrip. Rate: $.45 newsstand/cover; $24.50/yr in county; $25/yr in state; $25.50/yr out of state. Circulation: 1,489 per issue (paid). **Owner(s):** Francis Woodruff, See address and contact information above. **Management:** Francis Woodruff, Publisher.

DEFIANCE

HENRY COUNTY AD-PAK, THE. 624 W Second St, Defiance, OH 43512. Telephone: 419-784-5441. FAX: 419-784-1492. Pub. Frequency: w. (Mon.) Page Size: tabloid Circulation: 12,614 per issue (free). **Owner(s):** Dix Communications Group, 212 E. Liberty St., Wooster, OH 44691. Telephone: 330-264-1125. FAX: 216-264-3756. **Management:** Steve VanDemark, General Manager. Mark Ryan, Advertising Manager. Betty Lentz, Circulation Manager. Gina Beatty, Classified Adv. Mgr..

DELTA

DELTA ATLAS. 212 Main St., Delta, OH 43515. Telephone: 419-822-3231. FAX: 419-822-3289. Year Established: 1882. Pub. Frequency: w. (Tue.) Page Size: broadsheet. Subscrip. Rate: $.50 newsstand/cover; $15/yr local; $14/yr local to senior citizens. Circulation: 2,000 per issue (paid). **Owner(s):** Thomas W. Mack, See address and contact information above. **Management:** Thomas W. Mack, Advertising Manager. **Editorial:** Thomas W. Mack, Editor.

EATON

REGISTER-HERALD. 1332 N. Barron St., Eaton, OH 45320-1016. Telephone: 937-456-5553. FAX: 937-456-3558. E-MAIL: info@registerherald.com. URL: http://www.registerherald.com. Year Established: 1820. Pub. Frequency: s-w. (Wed. & Sat.) Page Size: broadsheet. Subscrip. Rate: $.75 newsstand/cover; $30/yr in county; $40/yr out of county; $46/yr out of state. Circulation: 14,000 Saturday (free); 6,800 per issue (paid). **Owner(s):** Brown Publishing Co., 10222 Alliance Rd, Cincinnati, OH 45040. **Management:** Deron Newman, Publisher. **Editorial:** Leslie Collins, Editor. Deron Newman, Managing Editor. Ryan Peverly, Sports.

ENGLEWOOD

ENGLEWOOD INDEPENDENT. 5 N. Walnut St., Englewood, OH 45322. Telephone: 937-836-2619. FAX: 937-836-1940. E-MAIL: englewood@tcnewsnet.com. URL: http://www.tcnewsnet.com. Mailing Address: PO Box 100, Englewood, OH 45420. Pub. Frequency: w. (Wed.) Page Size: broadsheet. Subscrip. Rate: $.50 newsstand/cover; $27/yr in town; $31/yr in county; $35/yr out of county. Circulation: 7,600 per issue (paid). **Owner(s):** Brown Publishing Co., 10222 Alliance Rd, Cincinnati, OH 45040. Telephone: 513-794-5040. FAX: 513-794-5480. **Management:** Frank Beeson, Publisher. Mike Savage, Advertising Manager. **Editorial:** Ron Nunnari, Editor. Terry Baver, Managing Editor.

ENON

ENON MESSENGER. P. O. Box 335, Enon, OH 45323. Telephone: 937-864-1136. FAX: 937-845-3577. E-MAIL: messenger@tcnewsnet.com. URL: http://www.sndnews.com. Pub. Frequency: w. (Tue.) Page Size: broadsheet. Subscrip. Rate: $.50 newsstand/cover; $27/yr carrier delivery local; $35/yr mailed in county; $39/yr mailed out of county. Circulation: 2,900 per issue (paid). **Owner(s):** Brown Publishing Co., 10222 Alliance Rd, Cincinnati, OH 45040. Telephone: 513-794-5040. FAX: 513-794-5480. **Management:** Frank Beeson, Publisher. **Editorial:** Merrilee Embs, Editor. Terry Baver, Managing Editor.

FRANKLIN

FRANKLIN CHRONICLE, THE. 129 S. Main St., Franklin, OH 45005. Telephone: 937-746-3691. FAX: 937-746-6013. E-MAIL: franklinchronicle@millerpublishing.com. Year Established: 1875. Pub. Frequency: w. (Wed.) Page Size: standard. Subscrip. Rate: $.75 newsstand/cover; $29/yr in county. Adv. Rate: col. inch $8 Freelance Pay: $0.50/column-inch. Circulation: 2,500 per issue (paid). **Owner(s):** Miller Publishing Co., 230 S. Second St., Miamisburg, OH 45342. Telephone: 937-866-3331. **Management:** Donald Miller, Publisher. D.J. Miller, Circulation Manager. **Editorial:** Dan Darragh, Editor.

SPRINGBORO STAR PRESS. 129 S. Main St., Franklin, OH 45005. Telephone: 937-746-3691. FAX: 937-746-6013. Year Established: 1976. Pub. Frequency: w. (Wed.) Page Size: broadsheet. Subscrip. Rate: $.75 newsstand/cover; $29/yr in state. Circulation: 1,500 per issue (paid). **Owner(s):** Miller Publishing Co., 230 S. Second St., Miamisburg, OH 45342. Telephone: 937-866-3331. FAX: 937-866-6011. **Management:** Donald Miller, Publisher. D.J. Miller, Circulation Manager. **Editorial:** Dan Darragh, Editor.

GERMANTOWN

GERMANTOWN PRESS. 21 E Center St., Germantown, OH 45327. Telephone: 937-855-2300. FAX: 937-855-3860. E-MAIL: Pcox@coxohio.com. URL: http://www.germantownpress.com. Pub. Frequency: w. (Thu.) Page Size: broadsheet.Subscrip. Rate: $.75 newsstand/cover; $26/yr Circulation: 2,300 per issue (paid). **Owner(s):** Cox Newspapers, Inc., 6205 Peachtree Dunwoody Rd, Atlanta, GA 30328. **Management:** Don Miller, Publisher. **Editorial:** Dawn Beigel, Editor.

GRANVILLE

COMMUNITY BOOSTER, THE. 110 E. Elm St., Granville, OH 43023. Telephone: 740-587-3397. FAX: 740-587-3398. Mailing Address: PO Box 357, Granville, OH 43023. Year Established: 1949. Pub. Frequency: w. (Fri.) Page Size: tabloid. **Wire Service(s):** GNS. Circulation: 94,000 per issue (free). **Owner(s):** Gannett Company, Inc., 7950 Jones Branch Dr., McLean, VA 22107-0001. Telephone: 703-854-6000. **Management:** Bob Robbins, Publisher. Mike Forrer, Advertising. **Editorial:** Chuck Peterson, Editor.

GRANVILLE SENTINEL, THE. 110 E. Elm St., Granville, OH 43023. E-MAIL: chuck.petersen@thomnews.com. Mailing Address: PO Box 357, Granville, OH 43023. Year Established: 1970. Pub. Frequency: w. (Thu.) Page Size: tabloid. Subscrip. Rate: $.50 newsstand/cover; $23/yr in county; $28/yr out of county. Freelance Pay: $1.25/column-inch. Circulation: 2,500 per issue (paid). **Owner(s):** Gannett Company, Inc., 7950 Jones Branch Dr., McLean, VA 22102. **Management:** Bob Robbins, Publisher. Jeff Gold, Advertising Manager. Jeff Simmons, Circulation Director. **Editorial:** Chuck Peterson, Editor.

GREENVILLE

EARLY BIRD, THE. 5312 Sebring-Warner Rd., Greenville, OH 45331. Telephone: 937-548-3330. FAX: 937-548-3376. E-MAIL: publisher@earlybirdpaper.com. URL: http://www.earlybirdpaper.com. Year Established: 1968. Pub. Frequency: w. (Sun.) Page Size: broadsheet. Subscrip. Rate: $50/yr. Adv. Rate: col. inch $20 Circulation: 27,800 per issue (paid and free). **Owner(s):** Carol L. Ball, See address and contact information above. **Management:** Carol L. Ball, Publisher. Louanna Gwinn, Advertising Manager. Don Ballard, Circulation Manager. **Editorial:** Ryan Berry, Editor. Shannie Foreman, Production Manager. Joy Roseberry, Assistant Editor.Readers: For the general population

HARTVILLE

HARTVILLE NEWS. 316 E. Maple St., Hartville, OH 44632. E-MAIL: knowlespress@sbcglobal.net. Mailing Address: P.O. Box 428, Hartville, OH 44632-0428. Year Established: 1930. Pub. Frequency: w. (Wed.) Page Size: tabloid. Subscrip. Rate: $.60 newsstand/cover; $30/yr inarea; $36/yr mailed elsewhere. Adv. Rate: col. inch $6.90 Circulation: 3,000 per issue (paid). **Owner(s):** Knowles Press, Inc., See address and contact information above. **Management:** Rosalee Haines, President. **Editorial:** Rosalee Haines, Editor.

HEATH

HEATH NEWS. 619 Industrial Pkwy., Heath, OH 43056. Telephone: 740-522-8566. FAX: 740-522-8578. Year Established: 1963. Pub. Frequency: w. (Thu.) Page Size: tabloid. Subscrip. Rate: $.30 newsstand/cover; $14/yr in county; $16/yr out of county; $20/yr elsewhere. Circulation: 5,000 per issue (paid). **Owner(s):** Heartland Communications, See address and contact information above. **Management:** Randal Almendinger, Owner. Randal Aldmeninger, Publisher. Randal Almendinger, Advertising Manager. **Editorial:** Kym Harmon, Editor.

HILLSBORO

TIMES-GAZETTE COUNTY SHOPPER. 209 S High St, Hillsboro, OH 45133. Telephone: 937-393-3456. FAX: 937-393-2059. URL: http://www.timesgazette.com. Pub. Frequency: w. (Thu.) Page Size: standard Circulation: 20,000 per issue (free). **Owner(s):** Dix Communications Group, 212 E. Liberty St., Wooster, OH 44691. Telephone: 330-264-1125. FAX: 216-264-3756. **Management:** Rory Ryan, Publisher. Sharon Kersey, Advertising Manager. Brenda Earley, Circulation Director.

HUBER HEIGHTS

HUBER HEIGHTS COURIER. 7089 Taylorsville Rd., Huber Heights, OH 45424. Telephone: 937-236-4990. FAX: 937-236-4176. E-MAIL: GSmart@tcnewsnet.com. URL: http://www.sndnews.com. Pub. Frequency: w. (Wed.) Page Size: broadsheet. Subscrip. Rate: $.50 newsstand/cover; $27/yr mailed in county; $35/yr mailed out of county. Circulation: 9,000 per issue (paid and free). **Owner(s):** Brown Publishing Co., 10222 Alliance Rd, Cincinnati, OH 45040. Telephone: 513-794-5040. FAX: 513-794-5480. **Management:** Frank Beeson, Publisher. **Editorial:** Greg Smart, Editor. Terry Baver, Managing Editor.

JEFFERSON

COURIER (CONNEAUT), THE. 46 W Jefferson St, Jefferson, OH 44047. Telephone: 440-576-9115. FAX: 440-576-2735. URL: http://www.gazettenewspapers.com. Mailing Address: PO Box 166, Jefferson, OH 44047-0166. Year Established: 1992. Pub. Frequency: w. (Wed.) Page Size: broadsheet. Subscrip. Rate: $.50 newsstand/cover; $26/yr in county; $42/yr out of county. Adv. Rate: col. inch $8 Circulation: 2,800 per issue (paid). **Owner(s):** Gazette Newspapers, See address and contact information above. **Management:** Bill Creed, General Manager. John Lampson, Publisher. Cheryl Copeland, Circulation Manager. **Editorial:** Patrick Williams, Editor.

GAZETTE (JEFFERSON), THE. 46 W Jefferson St, Jefferson, OH 44047. Telephone: 440-576-9115. FAX: 440-576-2735. URL: http://www.gazettenewspapers.com. Mailing Address: PO Box 166, Jefferson, OH 44047-0166. Year Established: 1876. Pub. Frequency: w. (Wed.) Subscrip. Rate: $.50 newsstand/cover; $26/yr in county; $42/yr out of county. Circulation: 2,500 per issue (paid). **Owner(s):** Gazette Newspapers, See address and contact information above. **Management:** Bill Creed, General Manager. John Lampson, Publisher. Cheryl Copeland, Circulation Manager. **Editorial:** Brian Ewig, Editor.

PYMATUNING AREA NEWS. 46 W Jefferson St, Jefferson, OH 44047. Telephone: 440-576-9115. FAX: 440-576-2735. URL: http://www.gazettenewspapers.com. Mailing Address: PO Box 166, Jefferson, OH 44047-0166. Year Established: 1876. Pub. Frequency: w. (Wed.) Page Size: broadsheet. Subscrip. Rate: $.50 newsstand/cover; $26/yr in county; $42/yr out of county. Adv. Rate: col. inch $8 Circulation: 1,962 per issue (paid). **Owner(s):** Gazette Newspapers, See address and contact information above. **Management:** Bill Creed, General Manager. John Lampson, Publisher. Cheryl Copeland, Circulation Manager.

SHORES NEWS, THE. 46 W Jefferson St, Jefferson, OH 44047. Telephone: 440-576-9115. FAX: 440-576-2735. URL: http://www.gazettenewspapers.com. Mailing Address: PO Box 166, Jefferson, OH 44047-0166. Pub. Frequency: m. Page Size: tabloid.Subscrip. Rate: $.50 newsstand/cover Circulation: 1,250 per issue (paid). **Owner(s):** Gazette Newspapers, See address and contact information above. **Management:** Bill Creed, General Manager. John Lampson, Publisher. Cheryl Copeland, Circulation Manager.

VALLEY NEWS (JEFFERSON), THE. 46 W Jefferson St, Jefferson, OH 44047. Telephone: 440-576-9115. FAX: 440-576-2735. URL: http://www.gazettenewspapers.com. Mailing Address: PO Box 166, Jefferson, OH 44047-0166. Year Established: 1895. Pub. Frequency: w. (Wed.) Page Size: tabloid. Subscrip. Rate: $.50 newsstand/cover; $23/yr in area; $35/yr elsewhere. Adv. Rate: col. inch $8 Circulation: 1,300 per issue (paid). **Owner(s):** Gazette Newspapers, See address and contact information above. **Management:** Bill Creed, General Manager. John Lampson, Publisher. Cheryl Copeland, Circulation Manager.

KETTERING

CENTERVILLE-BELLBROOK TIMES. ISSN 1049-8117
3085 Woodman Dr., Ste. 170, Kettering, OH 45420. Telephone: 937-294-7000. FAX: 937-294-2981. E-MAIL: timesnews@erinet.com. URL: http://www.sndnews.com. Year Established: 1984. Pub. Frequency: w. (Wed.) Page Size: broadsheet. Subscrip. Rate: $.50 newsstand/cover; $27/yr. Circulation: 20,000 per issue (paid and free). **Owner(s):** Brown Publishing Co., 10222 Alliance Rd, Cincinnati, OH 45040. Telephone: 513-794-5040. FAX: 513-794-5480. **Management:** Frank Beeson, Publisher. Lane Moon, Advertising Manager. **Editorial:** Terry Baver, Managing Editor. Jodi Brock, Assistant Editor.

KETTERING-OAKWOOD TIMES. ISSN 8750-8141
3085 Woodman Dr., Ste. 170, Kettering, OH 45420. Telephone: 937-294-7000. FAX: 937-294-2981. E-MAIL: timesnews@erinet.com. URL: http://www.sndnews.com. Year Established: 1956. Pub. Frequency: w. (Sat.) Page Size: broadsheet. Subscrip. Rate: $.50 newsstand/cover; $27/yr mailed. Circulation: 26,000 per issue (paid). **Owner(s):** Brown Publishing Co., 10222 Alliance Rd, Cincinnati, OH 45040. **Management:** Frank Beeson, Publisher. **Editorial:** Bill Duffield, Editor. Terry Baver, Managing Editor.

TIMES WEEKEND. 3085 Woodman Dr., Kettering, OH 45420. Telephone: 937-294-7000. FAX: 937-294-2981. URL: http://www.tcnewsnet.com. Pub. Frequency: w. (Sat.) Page Size: broadsheet. Subscrip. Rate: $.50 newsstand/cover; $26/yr mailed. Circulation: 26,000 per issue (paid). **Owner(s):** Brown Publishing Co., 10222 Alliance Rd, Cincinnati, OH 45040. Telephone: 513-794-5040. FAX: 513-794-5480. **Management:** Frank Beeson, Group Publisher. Mike Savage, Publisher. Karen Weller, Circulation Manager. **Editorial:** Bill Duffield, Editor. Terry Baver, Managing Editor.

LEBANON

WESTERN STAR (LEBANON). 200 Harmon Ave., Lebanon, OH 45036. Telephone: 513-932-3010. FAX: 513-932-6056. E-MAIL: tbarr@coxohio.com. URL: http://www.western-star.com. Year Established: 1807. Pub. Frequency: w. (Thu.) Page Size: broadsheet. Subscrip. Rate: $1 newsstand/cover; $65/yr motor route in area; $104/yr mailed in state. Circulation: 25,000 per issue (paid). **Owner(s):** Cox Newspapers, Inc., 6205 Peachtree Dunwoody Rd., Atlanta, GA 30328. Telephone: 678-645-0000. **Management:** Thomas Barr, Publisher. Kathy Lane, Advertising Manager. Vickie Grubb, Circulation Manager. **Editorial:** Thomas Barr, Editor. Linda Weisenborn, Photographer. Scott Hayes, Sports.

LIBERTY CORNER

LIBERTY PRESS, THE. 107-1 East St., Liberty Corner, OH 43532-0006. Telephone: 419-533-2401. FAX: 419-533-2401. Year Established: 1882. Pub. Frequency: w. (Thu.) Page Size: broadsheet. Subscrip. Rate: $.50 newsstand/cover; $22/yr in county; $24/yr out of county; $26/yr out of state. Circulation: 1,300 per issue (paid). **Owner(s):** Donald & Susan Mickens, See address and contact information above. **Management:** Donald Mickens, President. Susan Mickens, Sales Manager. **Editorial:** Kaye Lingruen, News Editor.

LIBERTY TOWNSHIP

FAIRFIELD ECHO. 7378 Liberty One Dr., Liberty Township, OH 45044. Telephone: 513-829-7900. FAX: 513-863-6777. E-MAIL: echo@one.net. URL: http://www.fairfield-echo.com. Year Established: 1956. Pub. Frequency: w. (Wed.) Page Size: broadsheet. Subscrip. Rate: $1 newsstand/cover. Freelance Pay: $25/article. Circulation: 19,000 per issue (free). **Owner(s):** Cox Newspapers, Inc., 6205 Peachtree Dunwoody Rd, Atlanta, GA 30328. Telephone: 404-843-5000. **Management:** Bill Lubbers, Advertising Manager. Rita Bowman, Classified Adv. Mgr.. **Editorial:** Sarah Buehrle, Editor.

PULSE-JOURNAL. 7368 Liberty One Dr., Liberty Township, OH 45044. Telephone: 513-755-5060. FAX: 513-755-5077. E-MAIL: rgillette@coxohio.com. URL: http://www.pulsejournal.com. Year Established: 1976. Pub. Frequency: w. (Thu.) Page Size: broadsheet. Subscrip. Rate: $1 newsstand/cover. Circulation: 47,000 per issue (paid and free). **Owner(s):** Cox Newspapers, Inc., 6205 Peachtree Dunwoody Rd, Atlanta, GA 30328. Telephone: 404-843-5000. **Management:** Ann Hoffman, Publisher. Kathy Lane, Advertising Manager. Vicky Hoekstra, Circulation Manager. **Editorial:** Sarah Buehrle, Editor. John Boyle, Sports.

LOGAN

HOCKING VALLEY ADVERTISER. 51 S. Spring St., Logan, OH 43138. Telephone: 740-385-1969. FAX: 740-385-8458. E-MAIL: hvadvertiser@ohiohills.com. URL: http://www.jcpgroup.com. Mailing Address: PO Box 247, Logan, OH 43138. Year Established: 1984.Pub. Frequency: w. (Sun.) Page Size: tabloid Circulation: 9,816 Sunday (free). **Owner(s):** Journal Community Publishing Group, 600 Industrial Dr., PO Box 609, Waupaca, WI 54981. Telephone: 715-258-8450. **Management:** Linda McMandaway, General Manager. Karen Henderson, Office Manager.

LONDON

WEEKLY REVIEW. 30 S Oak St, London, OH 43140. Telephone: 740-852-1616. FAX: 740-852-1620. Mailing Address: PO Box 390, London, OH 43140-0390. Year Established: 1882. Pub. Frequency: w. (Mon.) Page Size: broadsheet Circulation: 14,000 per issue (free). **Owner(s):** Central Ohio Printing Corporation, See address and contact information above. **Management:** Gregg Rettig, Publisher. Kim Boyd, Advertising Manager. **Editorial:** Mac Cordell, Managing Editor.

LOUDONVILLE

HOLMES COUNTY HUB. 255 W Main St, Loudonville, OH 44842. E-MAIL: hub@the-daily-record.com. Mailing Address: PO Box 151, Millersburg, OH 44654. Year Established: 1825. Pub. Frequency: w. (Thu.) Page Size: broadsheet. Subscrip. Rate: $.75 newsstand/cover; $31.50/yr local; $36.50/yr out of area. Circulation: 4,500 per issue (paid). **Owner(s):** Dix Communications Group, 212 E. Liberty St., Wooster, OH 44691. Telephone: 330-264-1125. **Management:** William McKinney, General Manager. Rhonda Geer, Advertising Director. **Editorial:** Lance White, Managing Editor.

LOUDONVILLE TIMES, THE. 255 W Main St, Loudonville, OH 44842. Telephone: 419-994-5600. FAX: 419-994-5826. E-MAIL: jimb@bright.net. Year Established: 1873. Pub. Frequency: w. (Tue.) Page Size: broadsheet. Subscrip. Rate: $.50 newsstand/cover; $26/yr in county; $27/yr mailed in state; $31/yr mailed out of state. Adv. Rate: col. inch $6.40 Circulation: 2,300 per issue (paid). **Owner(s):** Dix Communications Group, 212 E. Liberty St., Wooster, OH 44691. Telephone: 330-264-1125. FAX: 216-264-3756. **Management:** Troy Dix, Publisher. Jason Gwinnup, Advertising Director. Deb Boreman, Circulation Manager. **Editorial:** Jim Brewer, Editor.Readers: Loudonville-Perryville area

MOHICAN AREA SHOPPER. 255 W Main St, Loudonville, OH 44842. Telephone: 419-994-5600. FAX: 419-994-5826. E-MAIL: tkline@times-gazette.com. Year Established: 1966. Pub. Frequency: w. (Mon.) Page Size: standard.Adv. Rate: col. inch $6.65 Circulation: 12,500 per issue (free). **Owner(s):** Dix Communications Group, 212 E. Liberty St., Wooster, OH 44691. Telephone: 330-264-1125. FAX: 216-264-3756. **Management:** Troy Dix, Publisher. Jason Gwinnup, Advertising Director. Deb Boreman, Circulation Manager. **Editorial:** Jim Brewer, Editor.Readers: Greater Loudonville area

LOUISVILLE

LOUISVILLE HERALD, THE. 308 S. Mills St, Louisville, OH 44641-0170. Telephone: 330-875-5610. FAX: 330-875-4475. E-MAIL: theherald@mac.com. URL: www.louisvilleherald.com. Mailing Address: PO Box 170, Louisville, OH 44641-0170. Year Established: 1887. Pub. Frequency: w. (Thu.) Page Size: broadsheet. Subscrip. Rate: $.70 newsstand/cover; $26/yr in county. Adv. Rate: col. inch $5.50 Circulation: 2,952 per issue (paid). **Owner(s):** Frank & Jackie Clapper, See address and contact information above. **Management:** Paul M. Clapper, Publisher. Jackie Clapper, Advertising Manager. Doris Guarnieri, Circulation Manager. **Editorial:** Frank H. Clapper, Editor.

LOVELAND

BETHEL JOURNAL, THE. ISSN 1066-7458
394 Wards Corner Rd., Ste. 170, Loveland, OH 45140. Telephone: 513-248-8600. FAX: 513-248-1938. E-MAIL: therron@communitypress.com. URL: http://www.communitypress.com. Year Established: 1898. Pub. Frequency: w. (Thu.) Page Size: broadsheet. Subscrip. Rate: $.50 newsstand/cover; $18/yr in county; $20/yr out of county. Circulation: 2,228 per issue (paid). **Owner(s):** Community Press Newspapers, 7950 Jones Branch Dr, McLean, VA 22107. Telephone: 703-854-6000. **Management:** Susan McHugh, General Manager. Tom Braig, Advertising Manager. Steve Barraco, Circulation Manager. **Editorial:** Susan McHugh, Editor. Melanie Laughman, Senior Editor.

CLERMONT COMMUNITY JOURNAL. 394 Wards Corner Rd., Ste. 170, Loveland, OH 45140-8300. Telephone: 513-248-8600. FAX: 513-248-1938. E-MAIL: therron@communitypress.com. URL: http://www.communitypress.com. Year Established: 1970. Pub. Frequency: w. (Wed.) Page Size: broadsheet. Subscrip. Rate: $.50 newsstand/cover; $2.50/mo. voluntary pay; $105/yr mailed. Circulation: 23,814 per issue (paid and free). **Owner(s):** Community Press Newspapers, 7950 Jones Branch Dr, McLean, VA 22107. Telephone: 703-854-6000. **Management:** Susan McHugh, General Manager. Rhonda Ford, Advertising Director. Tom Braig, Advertising Manager. Steve Barraco, Circulation Manager. **Editorial:** Susan McHugh, Editor. Melanie Laughman, Senior Editor.

EASTERN HILLS JOURNAL. 394 Wards Corner Rd., Ste. 170, Loveland, OH 45140. Telephone: 513-248-8600. FAX: 513-248-1938. E-MAIL: mlaughman@communitypress.com. URL: http://www.communitypress.com. Year Established: 1935. Pub. Frequency: w. (Wed.) Page Size: broadsheet. Subscrip. Rate: $.50 newsstand/cover; $2.50/mo. voluntary pay; $105/yr mailed. Circulation: 13,128 per issue (paid and free). **Owner(s):** Community Press Newspapers, 7950 Jones Branch Dr, McLean, VA 22107. Telephone: 703-854-6000. **Management:** Susan McHugh, Executive Director. Tom Braig, Advertising Manager. **Editorial:** Susan McHugh, Editor. Melanie Laughman, Senior Editor.

FOREST HILLS JOURNAL. 394 Wards Corner Rd., Ste. 170, Loveland, OH 45140-8300. Telephone: 513-248-8600. FAX: 513-248-1938. E-MAIL: foresthills@communitypress.com. URL: http://www.communitypress.com. Year Established: 1961. Pub. Frequency: w. (Wed.) Page Size: broadsheet. Subscrip. Rate: $.50 newsstand/cover; $2.50/mo. voluntary pay; $105/yr mailed. Circulation: 14,072 per issue (paid and free). **Owner(s):** Community Press Newspapers, 7950 Jones Branch Dr, McLean, VA 22107. Telephone: 703-854-6000. **Management:** Susan McHugh, General Manager. Tom Braig, Advertising Manager. Steve Barraco, Circulation Manager. **Editorial:** Susan McHugh, Editor. Melanie Laughman, Senior Editor.

INDIAN HILL JOURNAL. 394 Wards Corner Rd., Ste. 170, Loveland, OH 45140-8300. Telephone: 513-248-8600. FAX: 513-248-1938. E-MAIL: rmaloney@communitypress.com. URL: http://www.communitypress.com. Year Established: 1988. Pub. Frequency: w. (Wed.) Page Size: broadsheet. Subscrip. Rate: $.50 newsstand/cover; $2.50/mo. voluntary pay; $105/yr mailed. Circulation: 12,000 per issue (paid and free). **Owner(s):** Community Press Newspapers, 7950 Jones Branch Dr, McLean, VA 22107. Telephone: 703-854-6000. **Management:** Susan McHugh, General Manager. Tom Braig, Advertising Manager. Steve Barraco, Circulation Manager. **Editorial:** Susan McHugh, Editor. Melanie Laughman, Senior Editor.

Weeklies

LOVELAND HERALD. 394 Wards Corner Rd., Ste. 170, Loveland, OH 45140-8300. Telephone: 513-248-8600. FAX: 513-248-1938. E-MAIL: rmaloney@communitypress.com. URL: http://www.communitypress.com. Year Established: 1916. Pub. Frequency: w. (Wed.) Page Size: broadsheet. Subscrip. Rate: $.50 newsstand/cover; $2.50/mo. voluntary pay; $105/yr mailed. Circulation: 6,014 per issue (paid and free). **Owner(s):** Community Press Newspapers, 7950 Jones Branch Dr, McLean, VA 22107. Telephone: 703-854-6000. **Management:** Susan McHugh, General Manager. Tom Braig, Advertising Manager. Steve Barraco, Circulation Manager. **Editorial:** Dick Maloney, Editor. Melanie Laughman, Senior Editor.

MILFORD-MIAMI ADVERTISER. ISSN 0745-2764
394 Wards Corner Rd., Ste. 170, Loveland, OH 45140-8300. Telephone: 513-248-8600. FAX: 513-248-1938. E-MAIL: therron@communitypress.com. URL: http://www.communitypress.com. Year Established: 1951. Pub. Frequency: w. (Wed.) Page Size: broadsheet. Subscrip. Rate: $.50 newsstand/cover; $2.50/mo. voluntary pay; $105/yr mailed. Circulation: 8,150 per issue (free). **Owner(s):** Community Press Newspapers, 7950 Jones Branch Dr, McLean, VA 22107. Telephone: 703-854-6000. **Management:** Susan McHugh, General Manager. Tom Braig, Advertising Manager. Steve Barraco, Circulation Manager. **Editorial:** Susan McHugh, Editor.

NORTH CLERMONT COMMUNITY JOURNAL. 394 Wards Corner Rd., Ste. 170, Loveland, OH 45140-8300. Telephone: 513-248-8600. FAX: 513-248-1938. E-MAIL: clermont@communitypress.com. URL: http://www.communitypress.com. Pub. Frequency: w. (Wed.) Page Size: broadsheet. Subscrip. Rate: $.50 newsstand/cover; $2.50/mo. voluntary pay; $105/yr mailed. Circulation: 16,000 per issue (paid and free). **Owner(s):** Community Press Newspapers, 7950 Jones Branch Dr, McLean, VA 22107. Telephone: 703-854-6000. **Management:** Susan McHugh, General Manager. Tom Braig, Advertising Manager. Steve Barraco, Circulation Manager. **Editorial:** Susan McHugh, Editor.

NORTHEAST SUBURBAN LIFE PRESS. 394 Wards Corner Rd., Ste. 170, Loveland, OH 45140. Telephone: 513-248-8600. FAX: 513-248-1938. E-MAIL: rmaloney@communitypress.com. URL: http://www.communitypress.com. Year Established: 1963. Pub. Frequency: w. (Wed.) Page Size: broadsheet. Subscrip. Rate: $.50 newsstand/cover; $2.50/mo. voluntary pay; $105/yr mailed. Circulation: 8,906 per issue (paid and free). **Owner(s):** Community Press Newspapers, 7950 Jones Branch Dr, McLean, VA 22107. Telephone: 703-854-6000. **Management:** Susan McHugh, General Manager. Tom Braig, Advertising Manager. Steve Barraco, Circulation Manager. **Editorial:** Dick Maloney, Editor. Melanie Laughman, Senior Editor.

SUBURBAN LIFE (LOVELAND). 394 Wards Corner Rd., Ste. 170, Loveland, OH 45140-8300. Telephone: 513-248-8600. FAX: 513-248-1938. E-MAIL: rmaloney@communitypress.com. URL: http://www.communitypress.com. Year Established: 1961. Pub. Frequency: w. (Wed.) Page Size: broadsheet. Subscrip. Rate: $.50 newsstand/cover; $2.50/mo. voluntary pay; $105/yr mailed. Circulation: 8,161 per issue (paid and free). **Owner(s):** Community Press Newspapers, 7950 Jones Branch Dr, McLean, VA 22107. Telephone: 703-854-6000. **Management:** Susan McHugh, General Manager. Tom Braig, Advertising Manager. Steve Barraco, Circulation Manager. **Editorial:** Eric Spangler, Editor. Melanie Laughman, Senior Editor.

TRI-COUNTY PRESS (LOVELAND). 394 Wards Corner Rd., Ste. 170, Loveland, OH 45140. Telephone: 513-923-3111. FAX: 513-923-1806. E-MAIL: tmonjaras@communitypress.com. URL: http://www.communitypress.com. Pub. Frequency: w. (Wed.) Page Size: broadsheet. Subscrip. Rate: $.50 newsstand/cover; $2.50/mo. voluntary pay; $105/yr mailed. Circulation: 7,744 per issue (paid and free). **Owner(s):** Community Press Newspapers, 7950 Jones Branch Dr, McLean, VA 22107. Telephone: 703-854-6000. **Management:** Susan McHugh, General Manager. Tammy Monjaras, Advertising Manager. Steve Barraco, Circulation Manager. **Editorial:** Eric Spangler, Editor. Melanie Laughman, Senior Editor.

MADISON

LAKE COUNTY GAZETTE, THE. 2899 Hubbard Rd, Madison, OH 44057. Telephone: 440-428-0790. FAX: 440-428-0786. URL: http://www.gazettenewspapers.com. Mailing Address: PO Box 166, Jefferson, OH 44047-0166. Pub. Frequency: w. (Mon.) Page Size: broadsheet. Subscrip. Rate: $.50 newsstand/cover; $23/yr in county; $35/yr out of county. Adv. Rate: col. inch $10.94 Circulation: 8,000 per issue (paid). **Owner(s):** Gazette Newspapers, 46 W Jefferson St, Jefferson, OH 44047. Telephone: 440-576-9115. FAX: 440-576-2735. **Management:** Bill Creed, General Manager. John Lampson, Publisher. Cheryl Copeland, Circulation Manager. **Editorial:** Barb Vanveville, Editor.

LAKE COUNTY TRIBUNE, THE. 2899 Hubbard Rd, Madison, OH 44057. Telephone: 440-428-0790. FAX: 440-428-0786. URL: http://www.gazettenewspapers.com. Mailing Address: PO Box 166, Jefferson, OH 44047-0166. Pub. Frequency: w. (Thu.) Page Size: broadsheet. Subscrip. Rate: $.50 newsstand/cover; $23/yr in county; $35/yr out of county. Adv. Rate: col. inch $8 Circulation: 4,500 per issue (paid). **Owner(s):** Gazette Newspapers, 46 W Jefferson St, Jefferson, OH 44047. Telephone: 440-576-9115. FAX: 440-576-2735. **Management:** Bill Creed, General Manager. John Lampson, Publisher. **Editorial:** Stacy Puzzo, Editor.

MANCHESTER

SIGNAL (MANCHESTER), THE. 414 E. Seventh St., Manchester, OH 45144-1402. Telephone: 937-549-2800. FAX: 937-549-3611. E-MAIL: masigna@dragonbbs.com. Year Established: 1883. Pub. Frequency: w. (Thu.) Page Size: broadsheet. Subscrip. Rate: $.50 newsstand/cover; $20/yr in state; $25/yr out of state. Adv. Rate: col. inch $5.90 Circulation: 3,500 per issue (paid). **Owner(s):** William G. Woolard, Jr., 414 E. Seventh St., Manchester, OH 45144. Telephone: 937-549-2800. FAX: 937-549-3611. **Management:** William G. Woolard Jr., Publisher. Nicolle Politt-Melissa, Advertising Manager. Sherry Woolard, Circulation Manager. **Editorial:** William G. Woolard Jr., Editor.

MCARTHUR

VINTON COUNTY COURIER. 116 W. Main St., McArthur, OH 45651. Telephone: 740-596-5393. FAX: 740-596-4226. URL: http://www.tcnewsnet.com. Mailing Address: PO Box 468, McArthur, OH 45651. Year Established: 1971. Pub. Frequency: w. (Wed.) Page Size: broadsheet. Subscrip. Rate: $.50 newsstand/cover; $36.50/yr in county; $48.50/yr elsewhere. Adv. Rate: col. inch $5.75 Circulation: 3,400 per issue (paid). **Owner(s):** Brown Publishing Co., 10222 Alliance Rd, Cincinnati, OH 45040. Telephone: 513-794-5040. FAX: 513-794-5480. **Management:** Gary Merrill, Publisher. Sherrie Bossart, Advertising Manager. **Editorial:** Wendy VanSickle, Editor.

MCCONNELSVILLE

MORGAN COUNTY HERALD. 89 W. Main St., McConnelsville, OH 43756-0268. Telephone: 740-962-3377. FAX: 740-962-6861. URL: http://www.mchnews.com. Mailing Address: P.O. Box 268, McConnelsville, OH 43756-0268. Year Established: 1844. Pub. Frequency: w. (Wed.) Page Size: broadsheet. Subscrip. Rate: $.85 newsstand/cover; $34/yr in adjoining cys; $38/yr out of area. Adv. Rate: col. inch $8.40 Circulation: 4,592 per issue (paid and free). **Owner(s):** Morgan County Publishing Co., See address and contact information above. **Management:** Jack Barnes, Publisher. Gabe Hartl, Advertising Director. Darlene Haines, Circulation Manager. **Editorial:** Don Keller, Editor.

MEDINA

BRUNSWICK SUN TIMES. ISSN 0894-1645
2795 Medina Rd., Rte. 18, Medina, OH 44256-8163. Telephone: 330-725-2314. FAX: 330-725-2314. E-MAIL: sun@sunnews.com. URL: http://www.sunnews.com. Year Established: 1972. Pub. Frequency: w. (Thu.) Page Size: broadsheet. Subscrip. Rate: $.65 newsstand/cover; $32.50/yr carrier delivery; $39/yr mailed. Adv. Rate: col. inch $15.60 Circulation: 6,418 per issue (paid). **Owner(s):** Sun Media, Inc., 5510 Cloverleaf Pkwy., Cleveland, OH 44125-4887. Telephone: 216-986-2600. FAX: 216-986-2380. **Management:** John Urbancich, President. Dwight Schulz, Operations Manager. Tim Schmidt, Circulation Director. **Editorial:** Glenn Wojciak, Editor. Linda M. Kinsey, Executive Editor. Stan Urankar, Entertainment Editor.

MEDINA SUN, THE. 2795 Medina Rd., Rte. 18, Medina, OH 44256-8163. Telephone: 330-725-1147. FAX: 330-725-2314. E-MAIL: sun@sunnews.com. URL: http://www.sunnews.com. Year Established: 1995. Pub. Frequency: w. (Thu.) Page Size: broadsheet. Subscrip. Rate: $.65 newsstand/cover; $32.50/yr carrier delivery; $39/yr mailed. Adv. Rate: col. inch $14.20 Circulation: 11,503 per issue (paid). **Owner(s):** Sun Media, Inc., 5510 Cloverleaf Pkwy., Cleveland, OH 44125. Telephone: 216-986-2600. FAX: 216-986-2380. **Management:** John Urbancich, President. Dwight Schulz, Operations Manager. Phil Grom, Advertising Manager. Jim Reynolds, Circulation Director. Emil DeSanto, Classified Adv. Mgr.. **Editorial:** Glenn Wojciak, Editor. Linda Kinsey, Executive Editor. Clifford Anthony, Business Editor.

MONTROSE SUN, THE. 2795 Medina Rd., Rte. 18, Medina, OH 44256-8163. Telephone: 330-725-1147. FAX: 330-725-2314. E-MAIL: sun@sunnews.com. URL: http://www.sunnews.com. Year Established: 2000. Pub. Frequency: w. (Thu.) Page Size: broadsheet. Subscrip. Rate: $.65 newsstand/cover; $32.50/yr carrier delivery; $39/yr mailed. Adv. Rate: col. inch $21.70 Circulation: 23,121 per issue (paid). **Owner(s):** Sun Media, Inc., 5510 Cloverleaf Pkwy., Cleveland, OH 44125-4887. Telephone: 216-524-0830. FAX: 215-642-5547. **Management:** John Urbancich, President. Jim Reynolds, Circulation Director. Emil DeSanto, Classified Adv. Mgr.. **Editorial:** Charles Aukeman, Editor. Linda Kinsey, Executive Editor. Barbara Collier, Food Editor.

SUN BANNER PRIDE. 2795 Medina Rd., Rte. 18, Medina, OH 44256-8163. Telephone: 330-725-1147. FAX: 330-725-2314. E-MAIL: sun@sunnews.com. URL: http://www.sunnews.com. Year Established: 1865. Pub. Frequency: w. (Thu.) Page Size: broadsheet. Subscrip. Rate: $.65 newsstand/cover; $32.50/yr carrier delivery; $39/yr mailed. Adv. Rate: col. inch $14.55 Circulation: 2,625 per issue (paid). **Owner(s):** Sun Media, Inc., 5510 Cloverleaf Pkwy., Cleveland, OH 44125-4887. Telephone: 216-986-2600. FAX: 216-986-2380. **Management:** John Urbancich, President. Dwight Schulz, Operations Manager. Tim Schmidt, Circulation Manager. Emil DeSanto, Classified Adv. Mgr.. **Editorial:** Charles Aukerman, Editor. Stan Urankar, Entertainment Editor. Barbara Collier, Food Editor.

MIAMISBURG

MIAMISBURG WEST CARROLTON NEWS. 230 S. Second St., Miamisburg, OH 45342. Telephone: 937-866-3331. FAX: 937-866-6011. URL: http://www.mwcnews.com. Mailing Address: PO Box 108, Miamisburg, OH 45343. Year Established: 1880. Pub. Frequency: w. (Wed.) Page Size: broadsheet. Subscrip. Rate: $.50 newsstand/cover; $39/yr in county. Freelance Pay: $25-$30/article. **Wire Service(s):** CNS. Circulation: 6,000 per issue (paid). **Owner(s):** Miller Publishing Co., See address and contact information above. **Management:** Don Miller, Owner. **Editorial:** Steve Sandlin, Managing Editor. John Cummings, Sports Editor.

MILLBURY

METRO PRESS, THE. 1550 Woodville Rd., Millbury, OH 43447. Telephone: 419-836-2221. FAX: 419-836-1319. E-MAIL: zoz@presspublications.com. URL: http://www.presspublications.com. Mailing Address: PO Box 169, Millbury, OH 43447. Year Established: 1971. Pub. Frequency: w. (Mon.) Page Size: tabloid. Subscrip. Rate: $.50 newsstand/cover; $24/yr mailed. Adv. Rate: col. inch $14.42 Freelance Pay: $25-$100/article. Circulation: 20,564 per issue (paid and free). **Owner(s):** Douthit Communications, Inc., 620 Warren St., Sandusky, OH 44870. Telephone: 419-625-5825. **Management:** John Szozda, General Manager. Jordan Szozda, Circulation Manager. **Editorial:** John Szozda, Editor. Larry Limpf, News Editor.

PRESS (MILLBURY), THE. 1550 Woodville Rd., Millbury, OH 43447. Telephone: 419-836-2221. FAX: 419-836-1319. E-MAIL: news@presspublications.com. URL: http://www.presspublications.com. Mailing Address: PO Box 169, Millbury, OH 43447. Year Established: 1972. Pub. Frequency: w. (Mon.) Page Size: tabloid. Subscrip. Rate: $.50 newsstand/cover; $24/yr mailed. Adv. Rate: col. inch $23.70 Freelance Pay: $25-$100/article. Circulation: 38,240 per issue (paid and free). **Owner(s):** Douthit Communications, Inc., 620 Warren St., Sandusky, OH 44870. Telephone: 419-625-5825. **Management:** John Szozda, Advertising Manager. Jordan Szozda, Circulation Manager. **Editorial:** John Szozda, Managing Editor.

MILLERSBURG

HOLMES COUNTY SHOPPER. 25 N Clay St, Millersburg, OH 44654. Telephone: 330-674-5676. FAX: 330-674-3780. Mailing Address: PO Box 151, Millersburg, OH 44654. Pub. Frequency: w. (Thu.) Page Size: tabloid Circulation: 25,000 per issue (free). **Owner(s):** Dix Communications Group, 212 E. Liberty St., Wooster, OH 44691. Telephone: 330-264-1125. **Management:** William McKinney, General Manager. Rhonda Geer, Advertising Director. **Editorial:** Lance White, Managing Editor.

MINERVA

NEWS LEADER (MINERVA), THE. ISSN 1078-0858
177 Curry St., Minerva, OH 44657-0030. Telephone: 330-868-5222. FAX: 330-868-3273. E-MAIL: newsleader@alliancelink.com. Mailing Address: PO Box 30, Minerva, OH 44657-0030. Year Established: 1937. Pub. Frequency: w. (Thu.) Page Size: broadsheet. Subscrip. Rate: $.50 newsstand/cover; $26/yr in state; $39/yr out of state. Circulation: 4,000 per issue (paid). **Owner(s):** Dix Communications Group, 212 E. Liberty St., Wooster, OH 44691. Telephone: 330-264-1125. FAX: 330-264-3756. **Management:** G. Charles Dix II, Publisher. Jeff Kaplan, Advertising Director. Carol Carle, Classified Adv. Mgr.. **Editorial:** Kimberly Lewis, Editor.

PRESS-NEWS, THE. 177 Curry St., Minerva, OH 44657. Telephone: 330-868-3505. FAX: 330-868-3273. E-MAIL: pressnews@alliancelink.com. Mailing Address: PO Box 777, Waynesburg, OH 44688. Year Established: 1897. Pub. Frequency: w. (Thu.) Page Size: broadsheet. Subscrip. Rate: $.50 newsstand/cover; $24/yr in state; $36/yr out of state. Circulation: 3,000 per issue (paid). **Owner(s):** Dix Communications Group, 212 E. Liberty St., Wooster, OH 44691. Telephone: 330-264-1125. FAX: 330-264-3756. **Management:** G. Charles Dix II, Publisher. Linda Stark, Advertising Manager. Carol Carle, Classified Adv. Mgr.. **Editorial:** Karen Mundy, Editor.

MINSTER

COMMUNITY POST, THE. 326 N Main St, Ste 200, Minster, OH 45865. Telephone: 419-628-2369. FAX: 419-628-4712. URL: http://www.minstercommunitypost.com. Mailing Address: PO Box 155, Minster, OH 45865-0155. Year Established: 1896. Pub. Frequency: w. (Thu.) Page Size: broadsheet. Subscrip. Rate: $.50 newsstand/cover; $26/yr in county & adj. cys.; $29/yr elsewhere. Owner(s): Horizon Publications, Inc., 1120 N. Carbon St, Ste 100, Marion, IL 62959. Management: Deb Zwez, Publisher. Carol Kohen, Advertising. Editorial: Eric Maki, Editor.

MONTPELIER

LEADER ENTERPRISE. 319 W. Main St., Montpelier, OH 43543. Telephone: 419-485-3113. FAX: 419-485-3114. Year Established: 1880. Pub. Frequency: w. (Wed.) Page Size: broadsheet. Subscrip. Rate: $.50 newsstand/cover; $23/yr in county; $26/yr out of county. Circulation: 1,200 per issue (paid). Owner(s): Bryan Publishing Co., The, 127 S. Walnut St., Bryan, OH 43506. Telephone: 419-636-1111. Management: Carol Goebel, Advertising Manager. Editorial: J.L. Schmucker, Managing Editor.

MT. GILEAD

MORROW COUNTY ADVERTISER. 245 Neal Ave, Ste A, Mt. Gilead, OH 43338. Telephone: 419-946-3010. FAX: 419-947-7241. URL: http://www.brownpublishing.com. Mailing Address: PO Box 149, Mt. Gilead, OH 43338. Pub. Frequency: w. (Sun.) Page Size: tabloid Circulation: 17,831 per issue (free). Owner(s): Brown Publishing Co., 10222 Alliance Rd, Cincinnati, OH 45040. Telephone: 513-794-5040. FAX: 513-794-5480. Editorial: Tim Picard, Editor.

MORROW COUNTY INDEPENDENT. 245 Neal Ave, Ste A, Mt. Gilead, OH 43338. Telephone: 419-946-3010. FAX: 419-947-7241. URL: http://www.brownpublishing.com. Mailing Address: PO Box 149, Mt. Gilead, OH 43338. Year Established: 1848. Pub. Frequency: w. (Wed.) Page Size: broadsheet. Subscrip. Rate: $1 newsstand/cover; $28/yr in county; $30/yr out of county; $32/yr out of state. Circulation: 1,100 per issue (paid and free). Owner(s): Brown Publishing Co., 10222 Alliance Rd, Cincinnati, OH 45040. Telephone: 513-794-5040. FAX: 513-794-5480. Management: Vicki Taylor, Publisher. Editorial: Tim Picard, Editor.

MORROW COUNTY SENTINEL. 245 Neal Ave, Ste A, Mt. Gilead, OH 43338. Telephone: 419-946-3010. FAX: 419-947-7241. E-MAIL: ncp@bright.net. Mailing Address: PO Box 149, Mt. Gilead, OH 43338. Year Established: 1848. Pub. Frequency: w. (Wed.) Page Size: broadsheet. Subscrip. Rate: $1 newsstand/cover; $37/yr in county; $39/yr out of county. Adv. Rate: col. inch $7.14 Circulation: 4,100 per issue (paid). Owner(s): Brown Publishing Co., 10222 Alliance Rd, Cincinnati, OH 45040. Management: Vicki Taylor, Publisher. Editorial: Tim Picard, Editor.

MT. ORAB

BROWN COUNTY PRESS. 219 S. High St., Mt. Orab, OH 45154. Telephone: 937-444-3441. FAX: 937-444-2652. E-MAIL: bcpress@frognet.net. Mailing Address: PO Box 453, Mt. Orab, OH 45154. Year Established: 1973. Pub. Frequency: w. (Sun.) Page Size: broadsheet. Subscrip. Rate: $.25 newsstand/cover. Circulation: 16,300 per issue (paid and free). Owner(s): The Sun Group Newspapers, 465 E. Main St., Batavia, OH 45103. Telephone: 513-732-2511. FAX: 513-732-6344. Management: Mary Patrick Latham, Publisher. Tony Adams, Advertising Manager. Editorial: Wayne Boblitt, Managing Editor.

NEW CARLISLE

NEW CARLISLE SUN. 225 S. Main St., New Carlisle, OH 45344. Telephone: 937-845-3861. FAX: 937-845-3577. E-MAIL: membs@tcnewsnet.com. URL: http://www.tcnewsnet.com. Year Established: 1878. Pub. Frequency: w. (Wed.) Page Size: broadsheet. Subscrip. Rate: $.50 newsstand/cover; $26/yr home delivery; $35/yr mailed in county; $39/yr mailed out of county. Freelance Pay: $20/story. Circulation: 3,100 per issue (paid). Owner(s): Brown Publishing Co., 10222 Alliance Rd, Cincinnati, OH 45040. Telephone: 513-794-5040. FAX: 513-794-5480. Management: Frank Beeson, Publisher. Peggy Reeder, Circulation Manager. Editorial: Merrilee Embs, Editor. Terry Baver, Managing Editor.

NEW LEXINGTON

PERRY COUNTY TRIBUNE. 399 Lincoln Park Dr, Ste A, New Lexington, OH 43764. Telephone: 740-342-4121. FAX: 740-342-4131. URL: http://www.brownpublishing.com. Mailing Address: PO Box 312, New Lexington, OH 43764. Year Established: 1940. Pub. Frequency: w. (Wed.) Page Size: broadsheet. Subscrip. Rate: $1 newsstand/cover; $38/yr in county; $42/yr mailed out of county. Circulation: 4,400 per issue (paid). Owner(s): Brown Publishing Co., 10222 Alliance Rd, Cincinnati, OH 45040. Telephone: 513-794-5040. FAX: 513-794-5480. Management: Deb Hutmire, Publisher. Dave Shubert, Advertising. Editorial: Anthony Shipley, Editor.

PERRY COUNTY TRIBUNE SHOPPER. 399 Lincoln Park Dr, Ste A, New Lexington, OH 43764. Telephone: 740-342-4121. FAX: 740-342-4131. Mailing Address: PO Box 312, New Lexington, OH 43764.Pub. Frequency: w. (Sun.) Circulation: 15,200 per issue (free). Owner(s): Brown Publishing Co., 10222 Alliance Rd, Cincinnati, OH 45040. Telephone: 513-794-5040. FAX: 513-794-5480. Management: Deb Hutmire, Publisher. Dave Shubert, Advertising. Editorial: Cindy Shroyer, Editor.

PERRY-MORGAN ADVERTISER. 116 S Main St., New Lexington, OH 43764. Telephone: 740-342-5483. FAX: 740-342-5305. E-MAIL: twhite@jcpgroup.com. URL: http://perry.theadvertiser.net/. Pub. Frequency: w. (Sun.) Page Size: broadsheet Circulation: 13,418 per issue (free). Owner(s): Journal Community Publishing Group, 600 Industrial Dr., Waupaca, WI 54891, Telephone: 715-258-8450. Management: Thomas White, General Manager.

NEWARK

NEWARK/LICKING ADVERTISER. 195 Union St., Newark, OH 43055. Telephone: 740-522-2502. FAX: 740-522-2498. URL: http://www.theadvertiser.net. Mailing Address: PO Box 686, Newark, OH 43058. Year Established: 1978. Pub. Frequency: w. (Sat.) Page Size: tabloid Circulation: 37,000 per issue (free). Owner(s): Journal Community Publishing Group, 600 Industrial Dr., PO Box 609, Waupaca, WI 54981. Telephone: 715-258-8450. Management: Thomas White, General Manager.

NEWCOMERSTOWN

NEWCOMERSTOWN NEWS. 140 W Main St, Newcomerstown, OH 43832. Telephone: 740-498-7117. FAX: 740-498-5624. E-MAIL: nctnews@sbcglobal.net. Mailing Address: PO Box 30, Newcomerstown, OH 43832-0030. Year Established: 1898. Pub. Frequency: w. (Wed.) Page Size: broadsheet. Subscrip. Rate: $.50 newsstand/cover; $23/yr in state; $30/yr out of state. Circulation: 3,400 per issue (paid). Owner(s): Dix Communications Group, 212 E. Liberty St., Wooster, OH 44691. Telephone: 330-264-1125. FAX: 216-264-3756. Management: Robert C. Dix, Publisher. Shirley Johnson, Advertising. Editorial: Niki Wolfe, Editor.

NORTH OLMSTED

LAKEWOOD SUN POST. 28895 Lorain Rd., North Olmsted, OH 44070-4042. Telephone: 440-777-3800. FAX: 440-777-8423. E-MAIL: sun@sunnews.com. URL: http://www.sunnews.com. Year Established: 1917. Pub. Frequency: w. (Thu.) Page Size: broadsheet. Subscrip. Rate: $.65 newsstand/cover; $32.50/yr carrier delivery; $39/yr mailed. Adv. Rate: col. inch $26.30 Circulation: 7,816 per issue (paid). Owner(s): Sun Media, Inc., 5510 Cloverleaf Pkwy., Cleveland, OH 44125-4887. Telephone: 216-986-2600. FAX: 216-986-2380. Management: John Urbancich, President. Dwight Schulz, Operations Manager. Laurie Toth, Advertising Manager. Jim Reynolds, Circulation Director. Emil DeSanto, Classified Adv. Mgr.. Editorial: Kevin Burns, Editor. Linda M. Kinsey, Executive Editor. Ken Wood, Assistant Editor.

SUN (NORTH OLMSTED), THE. 28895 Lorain Rd., North Olmsted, OH 44070. Telephone: 440-777-3800. FAX: 216-986-6071. E-MAIL: sun@sunnews.com. URL: http://www.sunnews.com. Year Established: 1990. Pub. Frequency: w. (Thu.) Page Size: broadsheet. Subscrip. Rate: $.60 newsstand/cover; $32.50/yr carrier delivery; $33.80/yr mailed. Adv. Rate: col. inch $10.60 Circulation: 2,999 per issue (paid). Owner(s): Sun Media, Inc., 5510 Cloverleaf Pkwy., Cleveland, OH 44125-4887. Telephone: 216-986-2600. FAX: 216-986-2380. Management: John Urbancich, President. Dwight Schulz, Operations Manager. Dennis Mundry, Advertising Manager. Tim Schmidt, Circulation Director. Emil DeSanto, Classified Adv. Mgr.. Editorial: Kevin Burns, Editor. John Urbancich, Executive Editor. Bob Eisenbarth, Assistant Editor. Clifford Anthony, Business Editor. Stan Urankar, Entertainment Editor.

SUN HERALD (NORTH OLMSTAD), THE. 28895 Lorain Rd., North Olmsted, OH 44070. Telephone: 440-777-3800. FAX: 216-986-6071. E-MAIL: sun@sunnews.com. URL: http://www.sunnews.com. Year Established: 1965. Pub. Frequency: w. (Thu.) Page Size: broadsheet. Subscrip. Rate: $.65 newsstand/cover; $32.50/yr carrier delivery; $39/yr mailed. Adv. Rate: col. inch $31.25 Circulation: 13,493 evening (paid). Owner(s): Sun Media, Inc., 5510 Cloverleaf Pkwy., Cleveland, OH 44125-4887. Telephone: 216-986-2600. FAX: 216-986-2380. Management: John Urbancich, President. Laurie Toth, Advertising Manager. Tim Schmidt, Circulation Director. Editorial: Kevin Burns, Editor. Linda Kinsey, Executive Editor. Ken Wood, Assistant Editor. Stan Urankar, Entertainment Editor. Barbara Collier, Food Editor.

WEST SIDE SUN NEWS. 28895 Lorain Rd., North Olmsted, OH 44070-4042. Telephone: 440-777-3800. FAX: 440-777-8423. E-MAIL: sun@sunnews.com. URL: http://www.sunnews.com. Year Established: 1918. Pub. Frequency: w. (Thu.) Page Size: broadsheet. Subscrip. Rate: $.65 newsstand/cover; $32.50/yr carrier delivery; $39/yr mailed. Adv. Rate: col. inch $26.70 Circulation: 10,628 per issue (paid). Owner(s): Sun Media, Inc., 5510 Cloverleaf Pkwy., Cleveland, OH 44125-4887. Telephone: 216-986-2600. FAX: 216-986-2380. Management: John Urbancich, President. Dwight Schulz, Operations Manager. Laurie Toth, Advertising Manager. Jim Reynolds, Circulation Director. Emil DeSanto, Classified Adv. Mgr.. Editorial: Kevin Burns, Editor. Linda M. Kinsey, Executive Editor. Ken Wood, Assistant Editor. Clifford Anthony, Business Editor.

OAK HARBOR

OTTAWA COUNTY EXPONENT, THE. ISSN 1059-9045 PO Box 70, Oak Harbor, OH 43449. Telephone: 419-898-5361. FAX: 419-848-0501. E-MAIL: julielyn@dcache.net. Mailing Address: PO Box 70, Oak Harbor, OH 43449-0070. Year Established: 1871. Pub. Frequency: w. (Fri.) Page Size: broadsheet. Subscrip. Rate: $.50 newsstand/cover; $26/yr town; $35/yr in state; $35/yr out of state. Adv. Rate: col. inch $6.50 Circulation: 2,700 per issue (paid). Owner(s): Gazette Publishing, See address and contact information above. Management: Tom Smith, Publisher. Editorial: Rick Miller, Editor.

OBERLIN

NEWS TIMES. 10 Oberlin, Oberlin, OH 44074. Telephone: 440-988-2801. FAX: 440-988-2802. Mailing Address: PO Box 67, Amherst, OH 44001. Year Established: 1874. Pub. Frequency: w. (Wed.) Page Size: standard.Subscrip. Rate: $.75 newsstand/cover; $32/yr Circulation: 2,500 per issue (paid). Owner(s): Gazette Publishing Co., 107 N. Sandusky St., Bellevue, OH 44811. Telephone: 419-483-4190. Management: Ken Carpenter, General Manager. Tom Smith, Publisher. Editorial: Kathleen Willbond, Editor.

OBERLIN NEWS-TRIBUNE. 42 S. Main St., Oberlin, OH 44074. Telephone: 440-7751611. FAX: 440-774-2167. E-MAIL: carpenter@theoberlinnews.com. Mailing Address: PO Box 29, Oberlin, OH 44074. Year Established: 1901. Pub. Frequency: w. (Tue.) Page Size: standard. Subscrip. Rate: $.75 newsstand/cover; $32/yr. Adv. Rate: col. inch $8.75 Freelance Pay: $8/story. Circulation: 2,000 per issue (paid). Owner(s): Gazette Publishing Co., 107 N. Sandusky St., Bellevue, OH 44811. Telephone: 419-483-4190. Management: Tom Smith, Publisher. Ken Carpenter, Advertising Manager. Editorial: Kathleen Willbond, Editor.

ONTARIO

TRIBUNE-COURIER (ONTARIO). 347 Allen Dr., Ontario, OH 44862-0127. E-MAIL: tribune@neo.rr.com. URL: http://www.tribune-courier.com. Mailing Address: PO Box 127, Ontario, OH 44862-0127. Year Established: 1961. Pub. Frequency: w. (Thu.) Page Size: broadsheet. Subscrip. Rate: $.50 newsstand/cover; $25/yr in state; $46/yr out of state. Adv. Rate: col. inch $6.50 Circulation: 2,225 per issue (paid). Owner(s): Frank & Betty Stumbo, See address and contact information above. Management: Frank A. Stumbo, Publisher. Kim Knapp, Advertising Manager. Betty E Stumbo, Secretary.

OTTAWA

PUTNAM COUNTY ADVERTISER. 232 E Main St, Ottawa, OH 45875. Telephone: 419-523-5709. FAX: 419-523-3512. URL: http://www.brownpublishing.com. Mailing Address: PO Box 149, Ottawa, OH 45875. Year Established: 1918. Pub. Frequency: w. (Wed.) Page Size: broadsheet Circulation: 12,000 per issue (free). Owner(s): Brown Publishing Co., 10222 Alliance Rd, Cincinnati, OH 45040. Telephone: 513-794-5040. FAX: 513-794-5480. Management: Mark Constance, Publisher. Mary Burt, Advertising.

PUTNAM COUNTY SENTINEL. 232 E Main St, Ottawa, OH 45875. Telephone: 419-523-5709. FAX: 419-523-3512. URL: http://www.putnamsentinel.com. Mailing Address: PO Box 149, Ottawa, OH 45875. Year Established: 1855. Pub. Frequency: w. (Wed.) Page Size: broadsheet. Subscrip. Rate: $1 newsstand/cover; $42.50/yr in county; $51.50/yr mailed out of county. Circulation: 7,700 per issue (paid). Owner(s): Brown Publishing Co., 10222 Alliance Rd, Cincinnati, OH 45040. Telephone: 513-794-5040. FAX: 513-794-5480. Management: Mark Constance, Publisher. Mary Burt, Advertising. Editorial: Mike Hohenbrink, Editor. Charlie Warnimont, Sports Editor.

OXFORD

OXFORD PRESS. 15 S. Beech St., Oxford, OH 45056. Telephone: 513-523-4139. FAX: 513-523-1935. E-MAIL: pub@oxfordpress.com. URL: http://www.oxfordpress.com. Year Established: 1932. Pub. Frequency: w. (Fri.) Page Size: broadsheet. Subscrip. Rate: $.50 newsstand/cover; $20/yr home delivery local; $30/yr mailed local. Adv. Rate: col. inch $6.81 Circulation: 4,500 per issue (paid). **Owner(s):** Cox Newspapers, Inc., 6205 Peachtree Dunwoody Rd, Atlanta, GA 30328. **Management:** Ann Hoffman, Publisher. **Editorial:** Robert A. Ratterman, Editor.

PATASKALA

PATASKALA STANDARD, THE. 350 S. Main St., Pataskala, OH 43062-0007. Telephone: 740-927-2991. FAX: 740-927-2930. Mailing Address: PO Box 7, Pataskala, OH 43062-0007. Year Established: 1886. Pub. Frequency: w. (Thu.) Page Size: standard. Subscrip. Rate: $.50 newsstand/cover; $22/yr in county; $24/yr out of county. Circulation: 4,800 per issue (paid). **Owner(s):** Gannett Company, Inc., 7950 Jones Branch Dr., McLean, VA 22107-0001. Telephone: 703-854-6000. **Management:** Bob Robbins, Publisher. Jeff Gold, Advertising Manager. **Editorial:** Bill Evenson, Editor.

POST (PATASKALA), THE. 190 E. Broad St., Pataskala, OH 43062. Telephone: 740-593-4010. URL: http://www.ohio.edu. Year Established: 1997. Pub. Frequency: w. (Sat.) Page Size: standard Circulation: 8,500 per issue (free). **Owner(s):** Randal Aldinger, See address and contact information above. **Management:** James Rodgers, General Manager.

PAULDING

PAULDING COUNTY PROGRESS, THE. 113 S. Williams St., Paulding, OH 45879. Telephone: 419-399-4015. FAX: 419-399-4030. E-MAIL: progress@progressnewspaper.org. URL: http://www.progressnewspaper.org. Mailing Address: PO Box 180, Paulding, OH 45879. Year Established: 1945. Pub. Frequency: w. (Wed.) Page Size: broadsheet. Subscrip. Rate: $.70 newsstand/cover; $34/yr in county & adj. cys.; $44/yr elsewhere. Circulation: 4,300 per issue (paid). **Owner(s):** Delphos Newspapers, 405 N. Main St., Delphos, OH 45833. Telephone: 419-695-0015. **Management:** Doug Nutter, Publisher. Claudia Nutter, Advertising Manager. **Editorial:** Melinda Krick, Editor.

WEEKLY REMINDER. 113 S. Williams St., Paulding, OH 45879. Telephone: 419-399-4015. FAX: 419-399-4030. E-MAIL: progress@progresnewspaper.org. URL: http://www.progressnewspaper.org. Mailing Address: PO Box 180, Paulding, OH 45879. Year Established: 1972. Pub. Frequency: w. (Mon.) Page Size: broadsheet Circulation: 10,000 per issue (free). **Owner(s):** Delphos Newspapers, 405 N. Main St., Delphos, OH 45833. Telephone: 419-695-0015. **Management:** Doug Nutter, Publisher. Claudia Nutter, Advertising Manager. Ruth Snodgrass, Circulation Manager. **Editorial:** Melinda Krick, Editor.

PERRYSBURG

PERRYSBURG MESSENGER-JOURNAL. ISSN 1064-2021 117 E. Second St., Perrysburg, OH 43551. Telephone: 419-874-2528. E-MAIL: welch@glasscity.net. URL: http://www.perrysburg.com. Mailing Address: PO Box 267, Perrysburg, OH 43552. Year Established: 1853. Pub. Frequency: w. (Wed.) Page Size: broadsheet. Subscrip. Rate: $.50 newsstand/cover; $25/yr in county. Adv. Rate: col. inch $7.80 Circulation: 14,000 per issue (paid and free). **Owner(s):** Welch Publishing Co., See address and contact information above. **Management:** Robert C. Welch, President. John B. Welch, Publisher. Matthew H. Welch, Advertising Manager. Sharon Terdoest, Circulation Manager. **Editorial:** Deb Buker, Managing Editor.

PORT CLINTON

BEACON (PORT CLINTON), THE. 205 S.E. Catawba Rd., Port Clinton, OH 43452. Telephone: 419-732-2154. FAX: 419-734-5382. Year Established: 1983. Pub. Frequency: w. (Thu.) Page Size: tabloid. Subscrip. Rate: $35/yr mailed out of county. Circulation: 17,000 per issue (paid and free). **Owner(s):** John R. Schaffner, See address and contact information above. **Management:** John R. Schaffner, Publisher. **Editorial:** John R. Schaffner, Editor.

RAVENNA

MR. THRIFTY #1. 126 N Chestnut St, Ravenna, OH 44266. Telephone: 330-296-9657. FAX: 330-296-2698. Pub. Frequency: w. (Sat.) Page Size: tabloid.Adv. Rate: col. inch $6.24 Circulation: 10,556 per issue (free). **Owner(s):** Dix Communications Group, 212 E. Liberty St., Wooster, OH 44691. Telephone: 330-264-1125. **Management:** David Dix, Publisher. Charlotte Doherty, Classified Adv. Mgr..

MR. THRIFTY #7. 126 N Chestnut St, Ravenna, OH 44266. Telephone: 330-296-9657. FAX: 330-296-2698. Pub. Frequency: w. (Mon.) Page Size: tabloid Circulation: 21,828 per issue (free). **Owner(s):** Dix Communications Group, 212 E. Liberty St., Wooster, OH 44691. Telephone: 330-264-1125. **Management:** David Dix, Publisher. Charlotte Doherty, Classified Adv. Mgr..

RIPLEY

RIPLEY BEE, THE. 134 N Front St, Ripley, OH 45167. Telephone: 937-392-4321. FAX: 937-392-4124. Pub. Frequency: w. (Thu.) Page Size: standard. Subscrip. Rate: $.50 newsstand/cover; $18/yr in county. Circulation: 2,500 per issue (paid). **Owner(s):** Brown Publishing Co., 10222 Alliance Rd, Cincinnati, OH 45040. Telephone: 513-794-5040. FAX: 513-794-5480. **Management:** Steven Triplett, Publisher. Bill Cornette, Advertising. **Editorial:** Marsha Mundy, Editor.

ROCKY RIVER

LAKEWOOD NEWS TIMES, THE. 21190 Center Ridge Rd.., #1, Rocky River, OH 44116. Telephone: 440-356-3027. FAX: 440-356-0515. E-MAIL: thetimes@cavtel.net. Mailing Address: PO Box 40216, Bay Village, OH 44140-0216. Year Established: 1996. Pub. Frequency: w. (Thu.) Page Size: broadsheet. Subscrip. Rate: $.35 newsstand/cover; $29.50/yr. Adv. Rate: col. inch $33.91 Freelance Pay: $7/story. Circulation: 1,000 per issue (paid and free). **Owner(s):** Gottschalk Publishing Co., Inc., See address and contact information above. **Management:** Eleanor J. Gottschalk, Publisher. **Editorial:** Eleanor J. Gottschalk, Editor. Aharon Bucholtz, Managing Editor. William J. Wahl, Production Manager.

OLMSTED-FAIRVIEW TIMES, THE. 21190 Center Ridge Rd.., #1, Rocky River, OH 44116. Telephone: 440-356-3027. FAX: 440-356-0515. E-MAIL: thetimes@cavtel.net. Mailing Address: PO Box 40216, Bay Village, OH 44140-0216. Year Established: 1998. Pub. Frequency: w. (Thu.) Page Size: broadsheet. Subscrip. Rate: $.35 newsstand/cover; $29.50/yr. Adv. Rate: col. inch $33.91 Freelance Pay: $7/story. Circulation: 1,000 per issue (paid and free). **Owner(s):** Gottschalk Publishing Co., Inc., See address and contact information above. **Management:** Eleanor Gottschalk, Publisher. **Editorial:** Eleanor Gottschalk, Editor. Aharon Bucholtz, Managing Editor. William J. Wahl, Production Manager.

WESTLAKER TIMES, THE. ISSN 0746-9802 21190 Center Ridge Rd.., #1, Rocky River, OH 44116. Telephone: 440-356-3027. FAX: 440-356-0515. E-MAIL: thetimes@cavtel.net. Mailing Address: PO Box 40216, Bay Village, OH 44140-0216. Year Established: 1983. Pub. Frequency: w. (Thu.) Page Size: broadsheet. Subscrip. Rate: $.35 newsstand/cover; $29.50/yr. Adv. Rate: col. inch $33.91 Freelance Pay: $7/story. Circulation: 4,500 per issue (paid and free). **Owner(s):** Gottschalk Publishing Co., Inc., See address and contact information above. **Management:** Eleanor J. Gottschalk, Publisher. Eleanor Gottschalk, Advertising Manager. **Editorial:** Eleanor J. Gottschalk, Editor. Aharon Bucholtz, Managing Editor. William J. Wahl, Production Manager.

ROSSFORD

ROSSFORD RECORD-JOURNAL. 215 Osborne St., Rossford, OH 43460. Telephone: 419-874-4491. Mailing Address: PO Box 145, Rossford, OH 43460. Year Established: 1939. Pub. Frequency: w. (Thu.) Page Size: broadsheet. Subscrip. Rate: $.50 newsstand/cover; $20/yr in county; $23/yr out of county. Circulation: 1,700 per issue (paid). **Owner(s):** Welch Publishing Co., PO Box 267, Perrysburg, OH 43552. Telephone: 419-874-2528. **Management:** Robert C. Welch, President. John B. Welch, Publisher. Matthew H. Welch, Advertising Manager. **Editorial:** Diana Hersch, Editor.

SABINA

SABINA ADVERTISER. 58 N. Howard, St., Sabina, OH 45169. Telephone: 937-584-2122. FAX: 937-584-2122. Year Established: 1948. Pub. Frequency: w. (Fri.) Page Size: tabloid Circulation: 5,400 per issue (free). **Owner(s):** Gaskins Printing, Inc., See address and contact information above. **Management:** Brenda Gaskins May, Publisher. **Editorial:** Brenda Gaskins May, Editor.

SANDUSKY

CHAGRIN VALLEY TIMES. ISSN 0194-3685 520 Warren St, Sandusky, OH 44870. Telephone: 419-625-5825. FAX: 419-621-2149. E-MAIL: editor@chagrinvalleytimes.com. URL: http://www.chagrinvalleytimes.com. Mailing Address: PO Box 150, Chagrin Falls, OH 44022-0150. Year Established: 1971. Pub. Frequency: w. (Thu.) Page Size: tabloid. Subscrip. Rate: $.75 newsstand/cover; $30/yr in Cuyahoga & Geauga cys.; $33/yr mailed out of county. Adv. Rate: col. inch $24.40 Freelance Pay: $35/story. Circulation: 14,000 per issue (paid). **Owner(s):** Chagrin Valley Publishing Co., See address and contact information above. **Management:** Carole Vigliotti, General Manager. H. Kenneth Douthit, Publisher. **Editorial:** David C. Lange, Editor.Readers: Residents

SOLON TIMES, THE. ISSN 0194-3677 520 Warren St, Sandusky, OH 44870. E-MAIL: cvt@chagrinvalleytimes.com. URL: http://www.chagrinvalleytimes.com. Mailing Address: PO Box 150, Chagrin Falls, OH 44022-0150. Year Established: 1977. Pub. Frequency: w. (Thu.) Page Size: tabloid. Subscrip. Rate: $.75 newsstand/cover; $30/yr in Cuyahoga & Geauga cys.; $33/yr in state. Adv. Rate: col. inch $20.75 Freelance Pay: $35/story. Circulation: 5,600 per issue (paid). **Owner(s):** Chagrin Valley Publishing Co., See address and contact information above. **Management:** Carole Vigliotti, General Manager. H. Kenneth Douthit, Publisher. **Editorial:** David C. Lange, Editor.Readers: Residents

SPENCERVILLE

JOURNAL NEWS (SPENCERVILLE). 126 N. Broadway, Spencerville, OH 45887-1265. Telephone: 419-647-4981. FAX: 419-647-4778. Mailing Address: PO Box 8, Spencerville, OH 45887-1265. Year Established: 1879. Pub. Frequency: w. (Thu.) Page Size: broadsheet. Subscrip. Rate: $.60 newsstand/cover; $29/yr mailed in county; $32/yr mailed out of county; $36/yr mailed out of state. **Owner(s):** Journal News, The, See address and contact information above. **Management:** Doris Beebe, Publisher. **Editorial:** Richard Beebe, Editor.

ST. MARYS

EXTRA MERCHANDISER. 102 E Spring St, St. Marys, OH 45885. Telephone: 419-394-7414. FAX: 419-394-7202. Year Established: 1982. Pub. Frequency: w. (Wed.) Page Size: broadsheet Circulation: 13,369 per issue (free). **Owner(s):** Horizon Publications, Inc., 1120 N. Carbon St, Ste 100, Marion, IL 62959. **Management:** Deb Zwez, Publisher. Karen Brown, Advertising Director. Quinn Gilbert, Circulation Manager. **Editorial:** Tom Wehrhahn, Managing Editor.

STOW

AURORA ADVOCATE. 1619 Commerce Dr, Stow, OH 44224-1759. Telephone: 330-688-0088. FAX: 330-688-1588. E-MAIL: rsekella@recordpub.net. URL: www.auroraadvocate.com. Year Established: 1972. Pub. Frequency: w. (Wed.) Page Size: tabloid. Subscrip. Rate: $.50 newsstand/cover; $18/yr carrier delivery in county; $40/yr mailed. Adv. Rate: col. inch $10.80 Circulation: 6,263 per issue (paid and free). **Owner(s):** Dix Communications Group, 212 E. Liberty St., Wooster, OH 44691. Telephone: 330-264-1125. FAX: 216-264-3756. **Management:** David Dix, Publisher. Sam Lane, Advertising. **Editorial:** Ken Lahmers, Editor.

BEDFORD TIMES-REGISTER. 1619 Commerce Dr, Stow, OH 44224-1759. Telephone: 330-688-0088. FAX: 330-688-1588. E-MAIL: brenner@recordpub.net. URL: http://www.bedfordtimesregister.com. Year Established: 1891. Pub. Frequency: w. (Thu.) Page Size: tabloid. Subscrip. Rate: $.50 newsstand/cover; $16/yr in county; $42/yr mailed. Circulation: 2,541 per issue (paid). **Owner(s):** Dix Communications Group, 212 E. Liberty St., Wooster, OH 44691. Telephone: 330-264-1125. FAX: 216-264-3756. **Management:** David Dix, Publisher. Angela Zivny, Advertising. Margaret Gotschall, Circulation Director. **Editorial:** Mike Lesko, Editor.

CUYAHOGA FALLS NEWS-PRESS. 1619 Commerce Dr, Stow, OH 44224-1759. Telephone: 330-688-0088. FAX: 330-688-1588. E-MAIL: pkeren@recordpub.com. URL: http://www.fallsnewspress.com. Year Established: 1929. Pub. Frequency: w. (Thu.) Page Size: tabloid. Subscrip. Rate: $.50 newsstand/cover; $18/yr in county; $42/yr mailed. Circulation: 23,500 per issue (paid and free). **Owner(s):** Dix Communications Group, 212 E. Liberty St., Wooster, OH 44691. Telephone: 330-264-1125. FAX: 216-264-3756. **Management:** David Dix, Publisher. Jannie Jordan, Advertising. Margaret Gotschall, Circulation Director. **Editorial:** Phil Keren, Editor. Erica Peterson, Executive Editor.

GATEWAY NEWS, THE. 1619 Commerce Dr, Stow, OH 44224-1759. Telephone: 330-688-0088. FAX: 330-688-1588. URL: http://www.thegatewaynews.com. Year Established: 1918. Pub. Frequency: w. (Wed.) Page Size: tabloid. Subscrip. Rate: $.50 newsstand/cover; $18/yr home delivery; $42/yr mailed. Adv. Rate: col. inch $10.68 Circulation: 5,759 per issue (paid and free). **Owner(s):** Dix Communications Group, 212 E. Liberty St., Wooster, OH 44691. Telephone: 330-264-1125. FAX: 216-264-3756. **Management:** David Dix, Publisher. Diane Kozloski, Advertising. Margaret Gotschall, Circulation Director. **Editorial:** Bob Gaetjens, Editor.

HUDSON HUB-TIMES. 1619 Commerce Dr, Stow, OH 44224-1759. Telephone: 330-688-0088. FAX: 330-688-1588. E-MAIL: rsekella@recordpub.net. URL: http://www.hudsonhubtimes.com. Pub. Frequency: s-w. (Sun. & Wed.) Page Size: tabloid. Subscrip. Rate: $.50 newsstand/cover; $20/yr carrier delivery; $60/yr mailed. Adv. Rate: col. inch $11.04 Circulation: 10,242 per issue (paid and free). **Owner(s):** Dix Communications Group, 212 E. Liberty St., Wooster, OH 44691. Telephone: 330-264-1125. FAX: 216-264-3756. **Management:** David Dix, Publisher. LeeAnn Shupe, Advertising. Margaret Gotschall, Circulation Director. **Editorial:** Bill Hammerstrom, Editor.

MAPLE HEIGHTS PRESS. 1619 Commerce Dr, Stow, OH 44224-1759. Telephone: 330-688-0088. FAX: 330-688-1588. E-MAIL: rrecker@recordpub.net. URL: http://www.mapleheightspress.com. Year Established: 1948. Pub. Frequency: w. (Thu.) Page Size: tabloid. Subscrip. Rate: $.50 newsstand/cover; $16/yr in county; $42/yr mailed out of county. Circulation: 5,100 per issue (paid). **Owner(s):** Dix Communications Group, 212 E. Liberty St., Wooster, OH 44691. Telephone: 330-264-1125. FAX: 216-264-3756. **Management:** David Dix, Publisher. Angela Zivny, Advertising. Margaret Gotschall, Circulation Director. **Editorial:** Mike Lesko, Editor.

NEWS LEADER (STOW). 1619 Commerce Dr., Stow, OH 44224. Telephone: 330-688-0088. FAX: 330-688-1588. E-MAIL: rsekella@recordpub.net. URL: http.//www.recordpub.com. Mailing Address: PO Box 46059, Bedford, OH 44146. Pub. Frequency: w. (Wed.) Page Size: tabloid. Subscrip. Rate: $.50 newsstand/cover; $14/yr carrier delivery; $20/yr mailed. Circulation: 11,106 per issue (paid and free). **Owner(s):** Record Publishing Co. LLC, 126 N. Chestnut St., Ravenna, OH 44266. Telephone: 216-296-9657. **Management:** Richard Sekella, General Manager. David E. Dix, Publisher. Sandy Boyle, Sales Manager. Harry Newman, Asst. General Mgr.. **Editorial:** Eric Marotta, Editor. Erica Peterson, Executive Editor.

STOW SENTRY. ISSN 0192-9410
1619 Commerce Dr, Stow, OH 44224-1759. Telephone: 330-688-0088. FAX: 330-688-1588. URL: http://www.stowsentry.com. Year Established: 1969. Pub. Frequency: w. (Sun.) Page Size: tabloid. Subscrip. Rate: $.50 newsstand/cover; $18/yr home delivery; $84/yr mailed. Adv. Rate: col. inch $11.64 Freelance Pay: $15/story. Circulation: 16,297 per issue (paid). **Owner(s):** Dix Communications Group, 212 E. Liberty St., Wooster, OH 44691. Telephone: 330-264-1125. FAX: 216-264-3756, 330-264-3756. **Management:** David Dix, Publisher. Jan Michalec, Advertising. Margaret Gotschall, Circulation Director. **Editorial:** Sean Gerski, Editor. Andrea Cole, Associate Editor.

TALLMADGE EXPRESS. 1619 Commerce Dr, Stow, OH 44224-1759. Telephone: 330-688-0088. FAX: 330-688-1588. E-MAIL: rskella@recordpub.net. URL: http://www.tallmadgeexpress.com. Pub. Frequency: w. (Sun.) Page Size: tabloid. Subscrip. Rate: $.50 newsstand/cover; $18/yr carrier delivery; $42/yr mailed. Adv. Rate: col. inch $10.80 Circulation: 7,661 per issue (paid). **Owner(s):** Dix Communications Group, 212 E. Liberty St., Wooster, OH 44691. Telephone: 330-264-1125. FAX: 216-264-3756. **Management:** David Dix, Publisher. Tracey Braziel, Advertising. Margaret Gotschall, Circulation Director. **Editorial:** Jaime Gerard, Editor.

TWINSBURG BULLETIN, THE. 1619 Commerce Dr, Stow, OH 44224-1759. Telephone: 330-688-0088. FAX: 330-688-1588. E-MAIL: twinsburgbulletin@recordpub.net. URL: http://www.twinsburgbulletin.com. Pub. Frequency: w. (Thu.) Page Size: tabloid. Subscrip. Rate: $.50 newsstand/cover; $18/yr home delivery in county; $42/yr mailed out of county. Adv. Rate: col. inch $10.80 Circulation: 9,374 per issue (paid). **Owner(s):** Dix Communications Group, 212 E. Liberty St., Wooster, OH 44691. Telephone: 330-264-1125. FAX: 216-264-3756. **Management:** David Dix, Publisher. Mick Marano, Advertising. Margaret Gotschall, Circulation Director. **Editorial:** Erica Peterson, Executive Editor. Robert Recker, Senior Editor.

STRUTHERS

HOMETOWN JOURNAL. 32 State St, Ste 204, Struthers, OH 44471-1952. Telephone: 330-755-2155. FAX: 330-755-0320. E-MAIL: news@hometownjournal.biz. URL: http://www.hometownjournal.biz/. Year Established: 1928. Pub. Frequency: w. (Thu.) Page Size: standard. Subscrip. Rate: $.35 newsstand/cover; $20/yr domestic town; $25/yr domestic out of town. Adv. Rate: col. inch $8 Circulation: 6,000 per issue (paid and free). **Owner(s):** Nancy Johngrass, See address and contact information above. **Management:** Nancy Johngrass, Publisher. **Editorial:** Nancy Johngrass, Editor. John Cutlip, Editorial Assistant.

SUNBURY

SUNBURY NEWS. 40 S. Vernon St., PO Box 59, Sunbury, OH 43074. URL: http://www.sunburynews.com. Mailing Address: PO Box 59, Sunbury, OH 43074. Year Established: 1873. Pub. Frequency: w. (Thu.) Page Size: broadsheet. Subscrip. Rate: $.50 newsstand/cover; $20/yr local. Circulation: 3,200 per issue (paid). **Owner(s):** Gary Atkinson, 18 E. William St., Delaware, OH 43015. Telephone: 740-965-3891. FAX: 740-965-3992. **Management:** Gary Adkisson, Publisher. Bud Burke, Advertising Manager. Suzanne Bigbie, Circulation Manager. Diane Sorrell, Classified Adv. Mgr.. **Editorial:** Gary Henery, Editor. Adam King, Sports Editor.

SWANTON

SWANTON ENTERPRISE. 97 N. Main St., Swanton, OH 43558. Telephone: 419-826-3580. FAX: 419-826-3590. Year Established: 1886. Pub. Frequency: w. (Tue.) Page Size: broadsheet. Subscrip. Rate: $.75 newsstand/cover; $34/yr. Adv. Rate: col. inch $7.90 Circulation: 2,000 per issue (paid). **Owner(s):** Gazette Publishing Co., 107 N. Sandusky St., Bellevue, OH 44811. Telephone: 419-483-4190. **Management:** Robert Krumm, General Manager. Thomas Smith, President. Tamra Torres, Advertising. **Editorial:** Marcus Bowling, Executive Editor. B.J. Lord, News Editor. Drew Stambaugh, Sports Editor.

SYLVANIA

SYLVANIA HERALD. 5700 Monroe St., Ste. 406, Sylvania, OH 43560. Telephone: 419-885-9222. FAX: 419-885-0764. Mailing Address: PO Box 8830, Toledo, OH 43623. Year Established: 1910. Pub. Frequency: w. (Wed.) Page Size: broadsheet. Subscrip. Rate: $.50 newsstand/cover; $25/yr in county; $35/yr out of county. Freelance Pay: $15/story. Circulation: 10,000 per issue (paid). **Owner(s):** Delphos Newspapers, 405 N. Main St., Delphos, OH 45833. Telephone: 419-692-5050. FAX: 419-692-7704. **Management:** Don Hemple, Publisher. Tonia Saunders, Advertising. **Editorial:** Mark Griffin, Editor.

WEST TOLEDO HERALD. 5700 Monroe St., Ste. 406, Sylvania, OH 43560. Telephone: 419-885-9222. FAX: 419-885-0764. URL: http://www.delphosherald.com. Mailing Address: PO Box 8830, Toledo, OH 43623. Year Established: 1970. Pub. Frequency: w. (Wed.) Page Size: broadsheet. Subscrip. Rate: $.50 newsstand/cover; $22/yr mailed in county; $32/yr out of county. Circulation: 25,000 per issue (paid). **Owner(s):** Delphos Newspapers, 405 N. Main St., Delphos, OH 45833. Telephone: 419-695-0015. FAX: 419-692-7704. **Management:** Don Hemple, Publisher. Tonia Saunders, Advertising. **Editorial:** Mark Griffin, Editor.

TIPP CITY

TIPP CITY HERALD. 1455 W. Main St., Tipp City, OH 45371. Telephone: 937-667-8512. FAX: 937-667-8987. E-MAIL: mkelly@tcnewsnet.com. URL: http://www.newsnet.com. Year Established: 1859. Pub. Frequency: w. (Wed.) Page Size: broadsheet. Subscrip. Rate: $.50 newsstand/cover; $35/yr mailed in county; $39/yr out of county. Circulation: 3,000 per issue (paid). **Owner(s):** Brown Publishing Co., 10222 Alliance Rd, Cincinnati, OH 45040. Telephone: 513-794-5040. FAX: 513-794-5480. **Management:** Frank Beeson, Publisher. Duane McCloud, Advertising Manager. Brandie Ertel, Circulation Manager. **Editorial:** Mike Kelly, Editor. Terry Baver, Managing Editor.

WEST MILTON RECORD. 1455 W. Main St., Tipp City, OH 45371. Telephone: 937-667-8512. FAX: 937-667-8987. E-MAIL: msavage@brownpublishing.com. URL: http://www.tcnewsnet.com. Pub. Frequency: w. (Wed.) Page Size: broadsheet. Subscrip. Rate: $.50 newsstand/cover; $31/yr mailed in county; $35/yr mailed out of county. Circulation: 1,500 per issue (paid). **Owner(s):** Brown Publishing Co., 10222 Alliance Rd, Cincinnati, OH 45040. Telephone: 513-794-5040. FAX: 513-794-5480. **Management:** Frank Beeson, Publisher. **Editorial:** Mike Kelly, Editor. Terry Baver, Managing Editor.

TOLEDO

POINT & SHORELAND JOURNAL. 5198 N. Summit St., Toledo, OH 43611. Telephone: 419-729-2855. FAX: 419-874-7311. E-MAIL: editor@pointandshoreland.com. Mailing Address: PO Box 5166, Toledo, OH 43611. Year Established: 1978. Pub. Frequency: w. (Tue.) Page Size: broadsheet. Subscrip. Rate: $.50 newsstand/cover; $20/yr mailed. Adv. Rate: col. inch $7.80 Circulation: 9,000 per issue (paid and free). **Owner(s):** Welch Publishing Co., PO Box 267, Perrysburg, OH 43552. Telephone: 419-874-2528. **Management:** John B. Welch, Publisher. **Editorial:** James Welch, Editor.

TOLEDO CITY PAPER. 1120 Adams St, Toledo, OH 43624. Telephone: 419-244-9859. FAX: 419-244-9871. E-MAIL: sales@toledocitypaper.com. URL: http://www.toledocitypaper.com. Pub. Frequency: w. (Wed.) Page Size: tabloid. Subscrip. Rate: $75/yr. Circulation: 32,000 per issue (paid and controlled). **Owner(s):** Adams Street Publishing Co, See address and contact information above. **Management:** Collette Jacobs, Publisher. **Editorial:** Jason Webber, Editor.

UTICA

UTICA HERALD. 120 S. Main St., Utica, OH 43080. Telephone: 740-892-2771. FAX: 740-892-2771. Mailing Address: PO Box 515, Utica, OH 43080-0515. Year Established: 1878. Pub. Frequency: w. (Thu.) Page Size: broadsheet. Subscrip. Rate: $.25 newsstand/cover; $14/yr in county; $16/yr out of county; $18/yr out of state. Adv. Rate: col. inch $5 Circulation: 2,100 per issue (paid). **Owner(s):** Randall Almendinger, 190 E. Broad St., Pataskala, OH 43062. Telephone: 614-964-6226. **Management:** Randall Almendinger, Publisher. **Editorial:** Alan Reed, Editor.

VAN WERT

SIGN OF THE TIMES. 700 Fox Rd., Van Wert, OH 45891. Telephone: 419-238-2285. FAX: 419-238-0447. URL: http://www.timesbulletin.com. Mailing Address: PO Box 271, Van Wert, OH 45891. Year Established: 1990. Pub. Frequency: w. (Mon.) Page Size: broadsheet Circulation: 9,000 per issue (free). **Owner(s):** Brown Publishing Co., 10222 Alliance Rd, Cincinnati, OH 45040. Telephone: 513-794-5040. FAX: 513-794-5480. **Management:** Robb Krecklow, Publisher. Tracy Bishop, Advertising Manager. **Editorial:** Cindy Wood, Editor.

VANDALIA

VANDALIA DRUMMER NEWS. 320 James E. Bohanan Dr., Vandalia, OH 45377. Telephone: 937-890-6030. FAX: 937-890-9153. E-MAIL: rjohnson@tcnewsnet.com. URL: http://www.tcnewsnet.com. Pub. Frequency: w. (Wed.) Page Size: broadsheet. Subscrip. Rate: $.50 newsstand/cover; $38/yr in county; $42/yr out of county. Circulation: 5,100 per issue (paid). **Owner(s):** Brown Publishing Co., 10222 Alliance Rd, Cincinnati, OH 45040. Telephone: 513-794-5040. FAX: 513-794-5480. **Management:** Mike Savage, Publisher. **Editorial:** Rachel Johnson, Editor. Terry Baver, Managing Editor.

VERMILION

VERMILION PHOTOJOURNAL. 630 N. Main St., Vermilion, OH 44089. Telephone: 440-967-5268. FAX: 440-967-2535. E-MAIL: info@vermilion-news.com. Mailing Address: PO Box 23, Vermilion, OH 44089. Year Established: 1959. Pub. Frequency: w. (Thu.) Page Size: tabloid. Subscrip. Rate: $.60 newsstand/cover; $25/yr local; $20/yr to senior citizens. Circulation: 4,000 per issue (paid and free). **Owner(s):** Douthit Communications, Inc., PO Box 760, Sandusky, OH 44871. Telephone: 419-625-5825. **Management:** Karen Cornelius, General Manager. Susan Borso, Advertising.

VERSAILLES

VERSAILLES POLICY, THE. 1080 Aubert Dr., Versailles, OH 45380. Telephone: 937-526-9131. FAX: 937-526-9891. E-MAIL: vpolicy@earthlink.net. Mailing Address: PO Box 74, Versailles, OH 45380-0074. Year Established: 1875. Pub. Frequency: w. (Wed.) Page Size: standard. Subscrip. Rate: $.75 newsstand/cover; $25/yr in state; $30/yr out of state. Adv. Rate: col. inch $6 Circulation: 2,450 per issue (paid). **Owner(s):** Scott Langston, See address and contact information above. **Management:** Scott Langston, Publisher. **Editorial:** Scott Langston, Editor-in-Chief.

WAPAKONETA

SHELBY REVIEW. 520 Industrial Dr., Wapakoneta, OH 45895. Telephone: 419-738-2128. FAX: 419-738-5352. URL: http://www.wapakdailynews.com. Mailing Address: PO Box 389, Wapakoneta, OH 45895. Year Established: 1978. Pub. Frequency: w. (Tue.) Page Size: broadsheet.Subscrip. Rate: $20/yr mailed Circulation: 4,685 per issue (paid). **Owner(s):** Horizon Publications, Inc., See address and contact information above. **Management:** Dianna Epperly, Publisher. Karen Brown, Advertising Director. Beverly Putman, Circulation Manager. **Editorial:** William Laney, Editor.

WAUSEON

FULTON COUNTY EXPOSITOR. ISSN 1546-3532
201 N Fulton, Wauseon, OH 43567. Telephone: 419-335-2010. FAX: 419-335-2030. Mailing Address: PO Box 376, Wauseon, OH 43567-0376. Year Established: 1854. Pub. Frequency: s-w. (Tue. & Thu.) Page Size: broadsheet. Subscrip. Rate: $1 newsstand/cover; $46/yr mailed in county; $58.50/yr mailed out of county; $62.50/yr mailed out of state. Adv. Rate: col. inch $9 Circulation: 5,000 per issue (paid). **Owner(s):** Brown Media Holdings, See address and contact information above. **Management:** Robert Krumm, Publisher. Denise Drenning, Advertising Manager. **Editorial:** Steve Colon, Editor.

WAVERLY

PIKE COUNTY NEWS WATCHMAN, THE. 219 W. Emmitt Ave., Waverly, OH 45690. Telephone: 740-947-2149. FAX: 740-947-1344. Mailing Address: PO Box 151, Waverly, OH 45690. Year Established: 1975. Pub. Frequency: s-w. (Sun. & Wed.) Page Size: broadsheet. Subscrip. Rate: $.50 newsstand/cover; $45/yr in county; $53.90/yr out of county. Circulation: 4,600 per issue (paid). **Owner(s):** Brown Publishing Co., 10222 Alliance Rd, Cincinnati, OH 45040. Telephone: 513-794-5040. FAX: 513-794-5480. **Management:** Kerry Lawson, Publisher. Ken Crisp, Circulation Manager. Angie Ross, Classified Adv. Mgr.. **Editorial:** Brian Perkins, Editor.

WELLSTON

TELEGRAM (WELLSTON), THE. 12 S Ohio Ave, Wellston, OH 45692. Telephone: 740-384-6102. FAX: 740-384-3063. E-MAIL: telegram@zoomnet.net. Year Established: 1896. Pub. Frequency: w. (Thu.) Page Size: broadsheet. Subscrip. Rate: $.25 newsstand/cover; $25/yr in county; $30/yr out of county. Circulation: 6,200 per issue (controlled and free). **Owner(s):** Steven P. Keller, See address and contact information above. **Management:** Steven P Keller, Publisher. **Editorial:** Steven P Keller, Editor-in-Chief.

WEST UNION

PEOPLE'S DEFENDER, THE. 229 N. Cross St., West Union, OH 45693. Telephone: 937-544-2391. FAX: 937-544-2298. URL: http://www.peoplesdefender.com. Mailing Address: PO Box 308, West Union, OH 45693. Year Established: 1866. Pub. Frequency: w. (Wed.) Page Size: broadsheet. Subscrip. Rate: $.50 newsstand/cover; $22/yr in county; $25/yr out of county. Circulation: 8,500 per issue (paid). **Owner(s):** Brown Publishing Co., 10222 Alliance Rd, Cincinnati, OH 45040. Telephone: 513-794-5040. FAX: 513-794-5480. **Management:** Bill Lange, Publisher. Troy Jolly, Advertising Manager. Perla Uhl, Circulation Manager. Rachael Hazelbaker, Classified Adv. Mgr.. **Editorial:** Bill Lange, Editor.

WESTLAKE

WEST LIFE. 26933 Westwood Rd. Ste 200, Westlake, OH 44145. Telephone: 440-871-5797. FAX: 440-871-3824. E-MAIL: info@westlifenews.com. URL: http://www.westlifenews.com. Mailing Address: PO Box 45014, Westlake, OH 44145. Year Established: 1958. Pub. Frequency: w. (Wed.) Page Size: tabloid. Subscrip. Rate: $.75 newsstand/cover; $30/yr mailed in county; $33/yr mailed out of county. Circulation: 15,000 per issue (paid). **Owner(s):** Douthit Communications, Inc., 620 Warren St., Sandusky, OH 44870. Telephone: 419-625-5825. **Management:** Peter Deverall, General Manager. H. Kenneth Douthit III, President. Peter Deverall, Advertising. **Editorial:** Brad Miklosovic, Editor-in-Chief.

WHEELERSBURG

SCIOTO VOICE, THE. 8593 Ohio River Rd., Wheelersburg, OH 45694-0400. Telephone: 740-574-8494. FAX: 740-574-2329. E-MAIL: info@thesciotovoice.com. URL: http://www.thesciotovoice.com. Mailing Address: PO Box 400, Wheelersburg, OH 45694-0400. Year Established: 1973. Pub. Frequency: w. (Thu.) Page Size: broadsheet. Subscrip. Rate: $.50 newsstand/cover; $20/yr mailed in county; $25/yr mailed out of county. Adv. Rate: col. inch $5.60 Circulation: 4,000 per issue (paid). **Owner(s):** Voice Newspapers, Inc., PO Box 400, Wheelersburg, OH 45694. Telephone: 740-574-8494. **Management:** Debbie Allard, Publisher. Charmion Ruggles, Office Manager. Sargina Royal, Circulation Manager. **Editorial:** Debbie Allard, Editor.

WILLARD

WILLARD TIMES-JUNCTION. 211 Myrtle Ave., Willard, OH 44890. Telephone: 419-935-0184. FAX: 419-933-2031. E-MAIL: willardtj@willardohio.net. URL: http://www.sdgnewsgroup.com. Mailing Address: PO Box 368, Willard, OH 44890. Year Established: 1883. Pub. Frequency: s-w. (Mon. & Thu.) Page Size: broadsheet. Subscrip. Rate: $.35 newsstand/cover; $34/yr mailed in county; $41.50/yr mailed out of county. Circulation: 4,200 per issue (paid). **Owner(s):** Shelby Daily Globe, Inc., 37 W. Main St., Shelby, OH 44875. Telephone: 419-342-4276. **Management:** Karla Souslin, General Manager. Ken Gove, Publisher. **Editorial:** Jim Fairchild, News Editor.

WILLSHIRE

PHOTO STAR. ISSN 0191-7935
307 State St, Box B, Willshire, OH 45898. E-MAIL: photonews@verizon.net. Year Established: 1895. Pub. Frequency: w. Page Size: tabloid. Subscrip. Rate: $32/yr mailed. Circulation: 11,500. **Owner(s):** Photo Star, See address and contact information above. **Management:** John Bunner, Advertising. **Editorial:** Judith E Bunner, Editor.

WILMINGTON

STAR REPUBLICAN. 47 S. South St., Wilmington, OH 45177. Telephone: 937-382-7796. FAX: 937-382-4392. URL: http://www.wnewsj.com. Year Established: 1870. Pub. Frequency: w. (Sun.) Page Size: broadsheet. Subscrip. Rate: $26/yr mailed. Circulation: 22,000 per issue (paid and free). **Owner(s):** Brown Publishing Co., 10222 Alliance Rd, Cincinnati, OH 45040. Telephone: 513-794-5040. FAX: 513-794-5480. **Management:** Pamela Stricker, Publisher. Sharon Kersey, Advertising Manager. Michelle Kline, Classified Adv. Mgr.. **Editorial:** Rachel Colliver, Editor.

WOODSFIELD

MONROE COUNTY BEACON. 103 E. Court St., Woodsfield, OH 43793-0070. Telephone: 740-472-0734. FAX: 740-472-0735. E-MAIL: monroecountybeacon@sbcglobal.net. URL: http://www.monroecountybeacononline.com. Mailing Address: PO Box 70, Woodsfield, OH 43793-0070. Year Established: 1937. Pub. Frequency: w. (Thu.) Page Size: broadsheet. Subscrip. Rate: $.95 newsstand/cover; $36/yr school district; $32/yr to senior citizens; $42/yr mailed elsewhere; $37/yr mailed elsewhere to senior citizens. Adv. Rate: col. inch $8.40 Circulation: 4,950 per issue (paid). **Owner(s):** Delphos Newspapers, 405 N. Main St., Delphos, OH 45833. Telephone: 419-695-0015. FAX: 419-695-7602. **Management:** Arlean Selvy, Publisher. **Editorial:** Arlean Selvy, Editor.

WORTHINGTON

DUBLIN VILLAGER. 670 Lakeview Plz. Blvd., Ste. F, Worthington, OH 43085. Telephone: 614-438-8100. FAX: 614-438-8110. E-MAIL: thisweek@infinet.com. URL: http://www.thisweeknews.com. Year Established: 1990. Pub. Frequency: w. (Thu.) Page Size: broadsheet. Subscrip. Rate: $21 mailed for 3 mos.; $84/yr mailed. Adv. Rate: col. inch $11.35 Circulation: 23,546 per issue (free). **Owner(s):** This Week Community Newspapers, PO Box 341890, Columbus, OH 43234-1890. Telephone: 614-438-8100. FAX: 614-438-8110. **Editorial:** Ben Cason, Executive Editor. Craig McDonald, Managing Editor. Stella Scharf, Assignment Editor. Sandy Wallace, News Editor.

GROVE CITY RECORD. 670 Lakeview Plz. Blvd., Worthington, OH 43085-1890. Telephone: 614-438-8100. FAX: 614-438-8110. E-MAIL: thisweek@infinet.com. URL: http://www.thisweeknews.com. Year Established: 1927. Pub. Frequency: w. (Thu.) Page Size: broadsheet. Subscrip. Rate: $.50 newsstand/cover; $24/yr mailed in county; $27/yr out of county. Adv. Rate: col. inch $10.70 Circulation: 3,587 per issue (paid). **Owner(s):** This Week Community Newspapers, PO Box 341890, Columbus, OH 43234-1890. Telephone: 614-438-8100. FAX: 614-438-8110. **Management:** Traci Hogue, Advertising Manager. Jerry Wilson, Circulation Manager. Carla Daniel, Classified Adv. Mgr.. **Editorial:** Jeff Donahue, Editor. Ben Cason, Executive Editor. Craig McDonald, Managing Editor. Stella Scharf, Assignment Editor. Paul Comstock, Community Editor. Lee Cochran, Sports Editor.

JOHNSTOWN INDEPENDENT. 670 Lakeview Plz. Blvd., Ste. F, Worthington, OH 43085-1890. Telephone: 614-438-8100. FAX: 614-438-8110. E-MAIL: thisweek@infinet.com. URL: http://thisweeknews.com. Mailing Address: PO Box 341890, Columbus, OH 43234-1890. Year Established: 1884. Pub. Frequency: w. (Thu.) Page Size: broadsheet. Subscrip. Rate: $.50 newsstand/cover; $23/yr mailed in county; $44 mailed for 2 yrs. in county; $26/yr mailed out of county Sat.. Adv. Rate: col. inch $9.10 Circulation: 2,138 per issue (paid). **Owner(s):** This Week Community Newspapers, PO Box 341890, Columbus, OH 43232-1890. Telephone: 614-438-8100. FAX: 614-438-8110. **Management:** Traci Hogue, Advertising Manager. Jerry Wilson, Circulation Manager. Carla Daniel, Classified Adv. Mgr.. **Editorial:** Ben Cason, Executive Editor. Craig McDonald, Managing Editor. Stella Scharf, Assignment Editor. Lee Cochran, Sports Editor.

LICKING COUNTY SUN. 670 Lakeview Plz. Blvd., Ste. F, Worthington, OH 43085. Telephone: 614-438-8100. FAX: 614-438-8110. URL: http://www.thisweeknews.com. Pub. Frequency: w. (Sun.) Page Size: broadsheet. Subscrip. Rate: $23/yr mailed. Adv. Rate: col. inch $6.30 Circulation: 7,203 per issue (free). **Owner(s):** This Week Community Newspapers, PO Box 341890, Columbus, OH 43234. Telephone: 614-438-8100. FAX: 614-438-8110. **Management:** Traci Hogue, Advertising Manager. Steven Finch, Circulation Manager. **Editorial:** Ben Cason, Executive Editor. Craig McDonald, Managing Editor. Paul Comstock, Community Editor. Sandy Wallace, News Editor. Lee Cochran, Sports Editor.

ROCKY FORK ENTERPRISE. 670 Lakeview Plaza Blvd., Suite F, Worthington, OH 43085. E-MAIL: editorial@thisweeknews.com. URL: http://www.thisweeknews.com. Year Established: 1931. Pub. Frequency: w. (Thu.) Page Size: broadsheet. Subscrip. Rate: $21 mailed for 3 mos.; $84/yr mailed. Adv. Rate: col. inch $10.25 Circulation: 16,180 per issue (free). **Owner(s):** This Week Community Newspapers, PO Box 341890, Columbus, OH 43234. Telephone: 614-438-8100. FAX: 614-438-8110. **Management:** Traci Hogue, Advertising Manager. Jerry Wilson, Circulation Manager. Carla Daniel, Classified Adv. Mgr.. **Editorial:** Ben Cason, Executive Editor. Craig McDonald, Managing Editor. Stella Scharf, Assignment Editor. Paul Comstock, Community Editor. Lee Cochran, Sports.

THIS WEEK IN BEXLEY. 670 Lakeview Plz. Blvd., Ste. F, Worthington, OH 43085. Telephone: 614-438-8100. FAX: 614-438-8110. E-MAIL: thisweek@infinet.com. URL: http://www.thisweeknews.com. Year Established: 1990. Pub. Frequency: w. (Thu.) Page Size: broadsheet. Subscrip. Rate: $84/yr mailed. Adv. Rate: col. inch $9.15 Circulation: 9,952 per issue (free). **Owner(s):** This Week Community Newspapers, PO Box 341890, Columbus, OH 43234-1890. Telephone: 614-438-8100. FAX: 614-438-8110. **Management:** Traci Hogue, Advertising Manager. Jerry Wilson, Circulation Manager. Carla Daniel, Classified Adv. Mgr.. **Editorial:** Ben Cason, Executive Editor. Craig McDonald, Managing Editor. Stella Scharf, Assignment Editor. Paul Comstock, Community Editor. Sandy Wallace, News Editor. Lee Cochran, Sports Editor.

THIS WEEK IN BIG WALNUT. 670 Lakeview Plz. Blvd., Ste. F, Worthington, OH 43085. Telephone: 614-438-8100. FAX: 614-438-8110. E-MAIL: thisweek@infinet.com. URL: http://www.thisweeknews.com. Mailing Address: PO Box 341890, Columbus, OH 43234-1890. Pub. Frequency: w. (Sun.) Page Size: broadsheet. Subscrip. Rate: $84/yr mailed. Adv. Rate: col. inch $8 Circulation: 6,274 per issue (free). **Owner(s):** This Week Community Newspapers, PO Box 341890, Columbus, OH 43240-1890. Telephone: 614-438-8100. FAX: 614-438-8110. **Management:** Traci Hogue, Advertising Manager. Steven Finch, Circulation Manager. **Editorial:** Ben Cason, Executive Editor. Craig McDonald, Managing Editor. Stella Scharf, Assignment Editor. Paul Comstock, Community Editor. Sandy Wallace, News Editor. Lee Cochran, Sports Editor.

THIS WEEK IN CLINTONVILLE. 670 Lakeview Plz. Blvd., Ste. F, Worthington, OH 43085. Telephone: 614-438-8100. FAX: 614-438-8110. E-MAIL: thisweek@infinet.com. URL: http://www.thisweeknews.com. Year Established: 1990. Pub. Frequency: w. (Thu.) Page Size: broadsheet. Subscrip. Rate: $84/yr mailed. Adv. Rate: col. inch $9.95 Circulation: 14,622 per issue (free). **Owner(s):** This Week Community Newspapers, PO Box 341890, Columbus, OH 43234-1890. Telephone: 614-438-8100. FAX: 614-438-8110. **Management:** Traci Hogue, Advertising Manager. Steven Finch, Circulation Manager. Carla Daniel, Classified Adv. Mgr.. **Editorial:** Ben Cason, Executive Editor. Craig McDonald, Managing Editor. Stella Scharf, Assignment Editor. Paul Comstock, Community Editor. Sandy Wallace, News Editor. Lee Cochran, Sports Editor.

THIS WEEK IN DELAWARE. 670 Lakeview Plz. Blvd., Ste. F, Worthington, OH 43085-1890. Telephone: 614-438-8100. FAX: 614-438-8110. E-MAIL: thisweek@infinet.com. URL: http://www.thisweeknews.com. Year Established: 1990. Pub. Frequency: w. (Sun.) Page Size: broadsheet.Subscrip. Rate: $84/yr mailed Circulation: 18,003 per issue (free). **Owner(s):** This Week Community Newspapers, PO Box 341890, Columbus, OH 43234-1890. Telephone: 614-438-8100. FAX: 614-438-8110. **Management:** Traci Hogue, Advertising Manager. Steven Finch, Circulation Manager. Carla Daniel, Classified Adv. Mgr.. **Editorial:** Ben Cason, Executive Editor. Craig McDonald, Managing Editor. Stella Scharf, Assignment Editor. Paul Comstock, Community Editor. Sandy Wallace, News Editor. Lee Cochran, Sports Editor.

THIS WEEK IN GRANDVIEW. 670 Lakeview Plz. Blvd., Ste. F, Worthington, OH 43085. Telephone: 614-438-8100. FAX: 614-438-8110. E-MAIL: thisweek@infinet.com. URL: http://www.thisweeknews.com. Year Established: 1990. Pub. Frequency: w. (Thu.) Page Size: broadsheet. Subscrip. Rate: $84/yr mailed. Adv. Rate: col. inch $9 Circulation: 6,094 per issue (free). **Owner(s):** This Week Community Newspapers, PO Box 341890, Columbus, OH 43234-1890. Telephone: 614-438-8100. FAX: 614-438-8110. **Management:** Traci Hogue, Advertising Manager. Steven Finch, Circulation Manager. Carla Daniel, Classified Adv. Mgr.. **Editorial:** Ben Cason, Executive Editor. Craig McDonald, Managing Editor. Stella Scharf, Assignment Editor. Paul Comstock, Community Editor. Sandy Wallace, News Editor. Lee Cochran, Sports Editor.

THIS WEEK IN HILLIARD. 670 Lakeview Plz. Blvd., Ste. F, Worthington, OH 43085. Telephone: 614-438-8100. FAX: 614-438-8110. E-MAIL: thisweek@infinet.com. URL: http://www.thisweeknews.com. Year Established: 1990. Pub. Frequency: w. (Thu.) Page Size: broadsheet. Subscrip. Rate: $84/yr mailed. Adv. Rate: col. inch $10.30 Circulation: 23,682 per issue (free). **Owner(s):** This Week Community Newspapers, PO Box 341890, Columbus, OH 43234-1890. Telephone: 614-438-8100. FAX: 614-438-8110. **Management:** Traci Hogue, Advertising Manager. Steven Finch, Circulation Manager. Carla Daniel, Classified Adv. Mgr.. **Editorial:** Ben Cason, Executive Editor. Craig McDonald, Managing Editor. Stella Scharf, Assignment Editor. Paul Comstock, Community Editor. Sandy Wallace, News Editor. Lee Cochran, Sports Editor.

THIS WEEK IN NEW ALBANY. 670 Lakeview Plz. Blvd., Ste. F, Worthington, OH 43085. Telephone: 614-438-8100. FAX: 614-438-8110. E-MAIL: thisweek@infinet.com. URL: http://www.thisweeknews.com. Year Established: 1993. Pub. Frequency: w. (Thu.) Page Size: broadsheet. Subscrip. Rate: $84/yr mailed. Adv. Rate: col. inch $7.20 Circulation: 5,678 per issue (free). **Owner(s):** This Week Community Newspapers, PO Box 341890, Columbus, OH 43234-1890. Telephone: 614-438-8100. FAX: 614-438-8110. **Management:** Traci Hogue, Advertising Manager. Jerry Wilson, Circulation Manager. Carla Daniel, Classified Adv. Mgr.. **Editorial:** Ben Cason, Executive Editor. Craig McDonald, Managing Editor. Stella Scharf, Assignment Editor. Paul Comstock, Community Editor. Sandy Wallace, News Editor. Lee Cochran, Sports Editor.

THIS WEEK IN NORTHLAND. 670 Lakeview Plz. Blvd., Ste. F, Worthington, OH 43085. Telephone: 614-438-8100. FAX: 614-438-8110. E-MAIL: thisweek@infinet.com. URL: http://www.thisweeknews.com. Year Established: 1990. Pub. Frequency: w. (Thu.) Page Size: broadsheet. Subscrip. Rate: $84/yr mailed. Adv. Rate: col. inch $11.05 Circulation: 19,419 per issue (free). **Owner(s):** This Week Community Newspapers, PO Box 341890, Columbus, OH 43234-1890. Telephone: 614-438-8100. FAX: 614-438-8110. **Management:** Traci Hogue, Advertising Manager. Steven Finch, Circulation Manager. Carla Daniel, Classified Adv. Mgr.. **Editorial:** Ben Cason, Executive Editor. Craig McDonald, Managing Editor. Stella Scharf, Assignment Editor. Lee Cochran, Sports Editor.

THIS WEEK IN OLENTANGY/POWELL. 670 Lakeview Plz. Blvd., Ste. F, Worthington, OH 43085-1890. Telephone: 614-438-8100. FAX: 614-438-8110. E-MAIL: thisweek@infinet.com. URL: http://www.thisweeknews.com. Year Established: 1990. Pub. Frequency: w. (Thu.) Page Size: broadsheet. Subscrip. Rate: $84/yr mailed. Adv. Rate: col. inch $9.90 Circulation: 16,487 per issue (free). **Owner(s):** This Week Community Newspapers, PO Box 341890, Columbus, OH 43234-1890. Telephone: 614-438-8100. FAX: 614-438-8110. **Management:** Traci Hogue, Advertising Manager. Steven Finch, Circulation Manager. Carla Daniel, Classified Adv. Mgr.. **Editorial:** Ben Cason, Executive Editor. Craig McDonald, Managing Editor. Stella Scharf, Assignment Editor. Paul Comstock, Community Editor. Sandy Wallace, News Editor. Lee Cochran, Sports Editor.

THIS WEEK IN PICKERINGTON. 670 Lakeview Plz. Blvd., Ste. F, Worthington, OH 43085. Telephone: 614-438-8100. FAX: 614-438-8110. E-MAIL: adservices@thisweeknews.com. URL: http://www.thisweeknews.com. Year Established: 1990. Pub. Frequency: w. (Thu.) Page Size: broadsheet. Subscrip. Rate: $84/yr mailed. Adv. Rate: col. inch $9.70 Circulation: 14,188 per issue (free). **Owner(s):** This Week Community Newspapers, PO Box 341890, Columbus, OH 43234-1890. Telephone: 614-438-8100. FAX: 614-438-8110. **Management:** Traci Hogue, Advertising Manager. Steven Finch, Circulation Manager. Carla Daniel, Classified Adv. Mgr.. **Editorial:** Ben Cason, Executive Editor. Craig McDonald, Managing Editor. Stella Scharf, Assignment Editor. Lee Cochran, Sports Editor.

THIS WEEK IN REYNOLDSBURG. 670 Lakeview Plz. Blvd., Ste. F, Worthington, OH 43085. Telephone: 614-438-8100. FAX: 614-438-8110. E-MAIL: thisweek@infinet.com. URL: http://www.thisweeknews.com. Year Established: 1990. Pub. Frequency: w. (Thu.) Page Size: broadsheet. Subscrip. Rate: $84/yr mailed. Adv. Rate: col. inch $9.90 Circulation: 15,287 per issue (free). **Owner(s):** This Week Community Newspapers, PO Box 341890, Columbus, OH 43234-1890. Telephone: 614-438-8100. FAX: 614-438-8110. **Management:** Traci Hogue, Advertising Manager. Steven Finch, Circulation Manager. Carla Daniel, Classified Adv. Mgr.. **Editorial:** Ben Cason, Executive Editor. Craig McDonald, Managing Editor. Stella Scharf, Assignment Editor. Paul Comstock, Community Editor. Sandy Wallace, News Editor. Lee Cochran, Sports Editor.

THIS WEEK IN SOUTHSIDE. 670 Lakeview Plz. Blvd., Ste. F, Worthington, OH 43085. Telephone: 614-438-8100. FAX: 614-438-8110. E-MAIL: thisweek@infinet.com. URL: http://www.thisweeknews.com. Year Established: 1990. Pub. Frequency: w. (Sun.) Page Size: broadsheet. Subscrip. Rate: $84/yr mailed. Adv. Rate: col. inch $11.60 Circulation: 21,616 per issue (free). **Owner(s):** This Week Community Newspapers, PO Box 341890, Columbus, OH 43234-1890. Telephone: 614-438-8100. FAX: 614-438-8110. **Management:** Traci Hogue, Advertising Manager. Steven Finch, Circulation Manager. Carla Daniel, Classified Adv. Mgr.. **Editorial:** Ben Cason, Executive Editor. Craig McDonald, Managing Editor. Stella Scharf, Assignment Editor. Paul Comstock, Community Editor. Sandy Wallace, News Editor. Lee Cochran, Sports Editor.

THIS WEEK IN UPPER ARLINGTON. 670 Lakeview Plz. Blvd., Ste. F, Worthington, OH 43085. Telephone: 614-438-8100. FAX: 614-438-8110. E-MAIL: thisweek@infinet.com. URL: http://www.thisweeknews.com. Year Established: 1990. Pub. Frequency: w. (Thu.) Page Size: broadsheet. Subscrip. Rate: $84/yr mailed. Adv. Rate: col. inch $10.55 Circulation: 22,167 per issue (free). **Owner(s):** This Week Community Newspapers, PO Box 341890, Columbus, OH 43234-1890. Telephone: 614-438-8100. FAX: 614-438-8110. **Management:** Traci Hogue, Advertising Manager. Steven Finch, Circulation Manager. Carla Daniel, Classified Adv. Mgr.. **Editorial:** Ben Cason, Executive Editor. Craig McDonald, Managing Editor. Stella Scharf, Assignment Editor. Paul Comstock, Community Editor. Sandy Wallace, News Editor. Lee Cochran, Sports Editor.

THIS WEEK IN WESTERVILLE. 670 Lakeview Plz. Blvd., Ste. F, Worthington, OH 43085. Telephone: 614-438-8100. FAX: 614-438-8110. E-MAIL: thisweek@infinet.com. URL: http://www.thisweeknews.com. Year Established: 1990. Pub. Frequency: w. (Thu.) Page Size: broadsheet. Subscrip. Rate: $84/yr mailed. Adv. Rate: col. inch $11.65 Circulation: 26,526 per issue (free). **Owner(s):** This Week Community Newspapers, PO Box 341890, Columbus, OH 43234-1890. Telephone: 614-438-8100. FAX: 614-438-8110. **Management:** Traci Hogue, Advertising Manager. Steven Finch, Circulation Manager. Carla Daniel, Classified Adv. Mgr.. **Editorial:** Ben Cason, Executive Editor. Craig McDonald, Managing Editor. Stella Scharf, Assignment Editor. Lee Cochran, Sports Editor.

THIS WEEK IN WESTSIDE. 670 Lakeview Plz. Blvd., Ste. F, Worthington, OH 43085. Telephone: 614-438-8100. FAX: 614-438-8110. E-MAIL: thisweek@infinet.com. URL: http://www.thisweeknews.com. Year Established: 1990. Pub. Frequency: w. (Thu.) Page Size: broadsheet. Subscrip. Rate: $84/yr mailed. Adv. Rate: col. inch $11.60 Circulation: 22,788 per issue (free). **Owner(s):** This Week Community Newspapers, PO Box 341890, Columbus, OH 43234-1890. Telephone: 614-438-8100. FAX: 614-438-8110. **Management:** Traci Hogue, Advertising Manager. Steven Finch, Circulation Manager. **Editorial:** Ben Cason, Executive Editor. Craig McDonald, Managing Editor. Stella Scharf, Assignment Editor. Paul Comstock, Community Editor. Sandy Wallace, News Editor. Lee Cochran, Sports Editor.

THIS WEEK IN WORTHINGTON. 670 Lakeview Plz. Blvd., Ste. F, Worthington, OH 43085-1890. Telephone: 614-438-8100. FAX: 614-438-8110. E-MAIL: thisweek@infinet.com. URL: http://www.thisweeknews.com. Year Established: 1990. Pub. Frequency: w. (Thu.) Page Size: broadsheet. Subscrip. Rate: $84/yr mailed. Adv. Rate: col. inch $11.60 Circulation: 21,496 per issue (free). **Owner(s):** This Week Community Newspapers, PO Box 341890, Columbus, OH 43234-1890. Telephone: 614-438-8100. FAX: 614-438-8110. **Management:** Traci Hogue, Advertising Manager. Steven Finch, Circulation Manager. Shelly Donovan, Classified Adv. Mgr.. **Editorial:** Ben Cason, Executive Editor. Craig McDonald, Managing Editor. Stella Scharf, Assignment Editor. Paul Comstock, Community Editor. Sandy Wallace, News Editor. Lee Cochran, Sports Editor.

XENIA

GREENE COUNTY SUNDAY SHOPPER. 30 S. Detroit St., Xenia, OH 45385. Pub. Frequency: w. (Sun.) Page Size: broadsheet Circulation: 22,000 per issue (free). **Owner(s):** Brown Publishing Co., 10222 Alliance Rd, Cincinnati, OH 45040. Telephone: 513-794-5040. FAX: 513-794-5480. **Management:** Jon Noel, Publisher. Barbara Van De Venter, Advertising Director. Gina Riefstahl, Circulation Director.

YOUNGSTOWN

BOARDMAN NEWS. 6221 Market St., Youngstown, OH 44512. Telephone: 330-758-6397. FAX: 330-758-2658. Year Established: 1947. Pub. Frequency: w. (Thu.) Page Size: broadsheet. Subscrip. Rate: $.35 newsstand/cover; $20/yr renewals; $25/yr new subscriptions. Adv. Rate: col. inch $6 Freelance Pay: $5/article. Circulation: 9,000 per issue (paid). **Owner(s):** John A. Darnell, Sr. & John A. Darnell, Jr., See address and contact information above. **Management:** John A. Darnell Sr., Publisher. Charles Reigrut, Advertising Manager. **Editorial:** John A. Darnell Jr., Editor-in-Chief.

ZANESVILLE

ZANESVILLE MUSKINGUM ADVERTISER. 760 Linden Ave., Zanesville, OH 43701-2353. Telephone: 740-453-0615. FAX: 740-453-9504. E-MAIL: ebruns@jcpgroup.com. URL: http://www.zanesville.theadvertiser.net. Mailing Address: PO Box 2353, Zanesville, OH 43701-2353. Year Established: 1976. Pub. Frequency: w. (Sun.) Page Size: tabloid Circulation: 35,457 per issue (free). **Owner(s):** Journal Community Publishing Group, 600 Industrial Dr., PO Box 609, Waupaca, WI 54981. Telephone: 715-258-8450. **Management:** Ernie Bruns, General Manager.

OKLAHOMA

ALTUS

FREDERICK LEADER. 218 W Commerce, Altus, OK 73521. Telephone: 580-482-1221. FAX: 580-482-5709. URL: http://www.altustimes.com. Mailing Address: PO Box 578, Altus, OK 73521-0578. Year Established: 1904. Pub. Frequency: s-w. (Wed & Sun.) Page Size: broadsheet. Subscrip. Rate: $.50 newsstand/cover; $30/yr carrier delivery; $42/yr mailed in state; $52/yr mailed out of state. Circulation: 1,200 Sunday (paid); 1,100 per issue (paid). **Owner(s):** Heartland Publications, LLC, 20 Research Pkwy, Ste G, Old Saybrook, CT 06475. Telephone: 860-388-3470. FAX: 860-388-3490. **Management:** Bill Murphy, Publisher. Sandy Graham, Circulation Manager. **Editorial:** Michael Bush, Editor.

ANTLERS

ANTLERS AMERICAN, THE. 110 E Main St, Antlers, OK 74534. Telephone: 580-298-3314. FAX: 580-298-3316. URL: http://www.theantlersamerican.com. Mailing Address: PO Box 578, Antlers, OK 74534. Pub. Frequency: w. (Thu.) Page Size: broadsheet. Subscrip. Rate: $.50 newsstand/cover; $21/yr in county & adj. cys.; $28.50/yr in state; $36.50/yr out of state. Circulation: 3,100 per issue (paid). **Owner(s):** Horizon Publications, Inc., 1120 N. Carbon St, Ste 100, Marion, IL 62959. **Management:** Brad House, Publisher. Shelly Baskin, Advertising. Linda Winters, Classified Adv. Mgr.. **Editorial:** Gwen Tucker-Smith, Reporter.

Weeklies

ATOKA

ATOKA COUNTY TIMES. 1004 W. 13th, Atoka, OK 74525. Telephone: 580-889-3319. FAX: 580-889-2300. E-MAIL: acatoka@atoka.net. Pub. Frequency: w. (Wed.) Page Size: broadsheet. Subscrip. Rate: $.75 newsstand/cover; $26/yr mailed in county; $30/yr mailed out of county; $40/yr mailed out of state. Adv. Rate: col. inch $4.60 Circulation: 4,200 per issue (paid). **Owner(s):** Foster & Louise Cain, See address and contact information above. **Management:** Louise Cain, Publisher. Ron Linscott, Advertising Manager. **Editorial:** Kevin Hilley, Editor.

BETHANY

TRIBUNE (BETHANY), THE. PO Box 40, Bethany, OK 73008. Telephone: 405-789-1962. FAX: 405-789-4253. E-MAIL: tribune@mmcable.com. Year Established: 1923. Pub. Frequency: w. (Thu.) Page Size: broadsheet. Subscrip. Rate: $.50 newsstand/cover; $20/yr in county; $23/yr mailed out of county; $28/yr mailed out of state; $16/yr to senior citizens. Circulation: 3,500 per issue (paid). **Owner(s):** Quaid Publishing, See address and contact information above. **Management:** Gloria Quaid, Publisher. **Editorial:** Gloria Quaid, Editor.

BIXBY

BIXBY BULLETIN. 103 N Cabanis, Bixby, OK 74008. Telephone: 918-366-4655. FAX: 918-366-4642. URL: http://www.bixbybulletin.com. Year Established: 1905. Pub. Frequency: w. (Thu.) Page Size: broadsheet. Subscrip. Rate: $.50 newsstand/cover; $19.95/yr mailed in county; $33.45/yr mailed out of county; $40.45/yr mailed out of state. Adv. Rate: col. inch $6.25 Circulation: 1,800 per issue (paid). **Owner(s):** Community Publishers, Inc., PO Box 1049, Bentonville, AR 72172. Telephone: 501-271-3700. **Management:** Allison Jay, Advertising. Kevin Hook, Advertising Director. **Editorial:** Jo-Ann Jennings, Editor.

BLACKWELL

BLACKWELL JOURNAL-TRIBUNE. 113 E Blackwell Ave, Blackwell, OK 74631. Telephone: 580-363-3370. FAX: 580-363-4415. E-MAIL: news@blackwelljournaltribune.net. Year Established: 1893. Pub. Frequency: 3/w. (Tue., Thu., Sat.) Page Size: broadsheet. Subscrip. Rate: $.75 newsstand/cover; $6 carrier delivery/mo.; $11.10 mailed/mo. in state. **Wire Service(s):** AP. Circulation: 2,515 evening (paid); 2,670 Sunday (paid). **Owner(s):** American Hometown Publishing, Inc., See address and contact information above. **Management:** Bruce Jones, Publisher. Tiaunna Wiedman, Advertising Manager. Jennifer Lambert, Circulation Manager. **Editorial:** Bruce Jones, Managing Editor.

BOISE CITY

BOISE CITY NEWS, THE. 105 W. Main St., Boise City, OK 73933. Telephone: 580-544-2222. FAX: 580-544-3281. E-MAIL: bcnews@ptsi.net. URL: http://www.boisecitynews.org. Mailing Address: PO Box 278, Boise City, OK 73933-0278. Year Established: 1898. Pub. Frequency: w. (Wed.) Page Size: broadsheet. Subscrip. Rate: $.60 newsstand/cover; $29.50/yr local; $32.50/yr out of area. Adv. Rate: col. inch $4.40 Circulation: 1,700 per issue (paid). **Owner(s):** Gene Cawley, See address and contact information above. **Management:** Cawley Steve, Publisher. Linda David, Advertising Manager. **Editorial:** C.F. David, Editor.

BRISTOW

BRISTOW NEWS. 112 W. Sixth Ave., Bristow, OK 74010. Telephone: 918-367-2282. FAX: 918-367-2724. Mailing Address: PO Box 840, Bristow, OK 74010. Year Established: 1948. Pub. Frequency: w. (Wed.) Page Size: oversize. Subscrip. Rate: $.50 newsstand/cover; $33/yr mailed in county; $38/yr mailed out of county incl record-citizen. Circulation: 3,300 per issue (paid and free). **Owner(s):** Sumner Media Group, 114 E. Seventh St., Okmulgee, OK 74447. Telephone: 918-756-3600. **Management:** Carolyn Ashford, General Manager. Sharon Reagan, Advertising Manager. **Editorial:** Carolyn Ashford, Editor.

RECORD-CITIZEN, THE. 112 W. Sixth Ave., Bristow, OK 74010. Telephone: 918-367-2282. FAX: 918-367-2724. E-MAIL: bristownews@sbcglobal.net. Mailing Address: PO Box 840, Bristow, OK 74010-0840. Year Established: 1898. Pub. Frequency: s-w. (Fri. & Wed.) Page Size: broadsheet. Subscrip. Rate: $.50 newsstand/cover; $33/yr mailed in county; $39/yr mailed out of county incl bristow news; $48/yr mailed out of state incl bristow news. Circulation: 2,700 per issue (paid). **Owner(s):** Carolyn Ashford, See address and contact information above. **Management:** Carolyn Ashford, Publisher. Sharon Reagan, Advertising Manager. **Editorial:** Carolyn Ashford, Editor.

BROKEN ARROW

BROKEN ARROW LEDGER. 524 W Main St, Broken Arrow, OK 74012. Telephone: 918-258-7171. FAX: 918-258-9908. E-MAIL: banews@neighbor-newspapers.com. URL: http://www.neighbor-newspapers.com. Year Established: 1903. Pub. Frequency: w. (Wed. & Sat.) Page Size: standard Adv. Rate: col. inch $8 Circulation: 4,000 (paid). **Owner(s):** Community Publishers, Inc., PO Box 1049, Bentonville, AR 72172. **Management:** Scheryl Reynolds, Advertising. **Editorial:** Bob Lewis, Managing Editor. Bob Bothell, Business Editor. Judy Collis, News Editor. Doug Quinn, Sports Editor.

CHANDLER

LINCOLN COUNTY NEWS (CHANDLER). PO Box 248, Chandler, OK 74834. Telephone: 405-258-1818. FAX: 405-258-1824. E-MAIL: lcn@brightok.net. Year Established: 1891. Pub. Frequency: w. (Thu.) Page Size: broadsheet. Subscrip. Rate: $.50 newsstand/cover; $19/yr in county; $23/yr out of county; $27/yr out of state. Freelance Pay: $0.30/column-inch. Circulation: 4,100 per issue (paid). **Owner(s):** Stephen E. Mathis, See address and contact information above. **Management:** Stephen E. Mathis, Publisher. P. Dawn Mathis, Advertising Manager. **Editorial:** Stephen E. Mathis, Managing Editor.

CHEROKEE

CHEROKEE MESSENGER & REPUBLICAN. PO Box 245, Cherokee, OK 73728. Telephone: 580-596-3344. FAX: 580-596-2959. Year Established: 1900. Pub. Frequency: w. (Thu.) Page Size: broadsheet. Subscrip. Rate: $.50 newsstand/cover; $23/yr mailed in county; $31/yr mailed out of county; $39/yr mailed out of state. Adv. Rate: col. inch $6 Circulation: 2,500 per issue (paid). **Owner(s):** Jo Hammer, See address and contact information above. **Management:** Steve Booher, Publisher. **Editorial:** Carol Angle, Editor.

COLLINSVILLE

COLLINSVILLE NEWS. ISSN 0890-9040
1113 W Main, Collinsville, OK 74021. Telephone: 918-371-9666. FAX: 918-371-9668. URL: http://www.neighbor-newspapers.com. Year Established: 1899. Pub. Frequency: w. (Wed.) Page Size: broadsheet. Subscrip. Rate: $.50 newsstand/cover; $22.95/yr in county; $35.50/yr out of county. Adv. Rate: col. inch $7.85 Circulation: 1,704 per issue (paid). **Owner(s):** Community Publishers, Inc., PO Box 1049, Bentonville, AR 72172. Telephone: 501-271-3700. **Management:** Kelly Stowe, Advertising. Connie Collins, Classified Adv. Mgr.. **Editorial:** Randy Cowling, Managing Editor. Bill Johnston, News Editor.

CORDELL

CORDELL BEACON, THE. 115 E. Main St., Cordell, OK 73632. Telephone: 405-832-3333. FAX: 405-832-3335. E-MAIL: thebeacon@cordellbeacon.com. URL: http://www.cordellbeacon.com. Year Established: 1897. Pub. Frequency: w. (Wed.) Page Size: broadsheet. Subscrip. Rate: $.50 newsstand/cover; $19.75/yr mailed in county; $26/yr mailed out of county; $34/yr mailed out of state. Adv. Rate: col. inch $6 Circulation: 3,700 per issue (paid). **Owner(s):** Cordell Beacon Co., Inc., See address and contact information above. **Management:** K. Brett Wesner, Publisher. Keri Wiggs, Advertising. **Editorial:** Zonelle Rainbolt, Editor.

COWETA

COWETA AMERICAN. 109 S Broadway, Coweta, OK 74429. Telephone: 918-486-4444. FAX: 918-486-3827. Year Established: 1893. Pub. Frequency: w. (Wed) Page Size: broadsheet. Subscrip. Rate: $.50 newsstand/cover; $22.95/yr in county; $36.10/yr mailed out of county; $43.65/yr mailed out of state. Adv. Rate: col. inch $7.75 Circulation: 3,300 per issue (paid). **Owner(s):** Community Publishers, Inc., PO Box 1049, Bentonville, AR 72172. **Management:** Donna Ramsey, Advertising Manager. Kathey Childers, Classified Adv. Mgr.. **Editorial:** Bob Lewis, Managing Editor. Christy Wheeland, News Editor.

DURANT

BRYAN COUNTY STAR, THE. 301 W. Arkansas St., Durant, OK 74701. Telephone: 580-924-6499. FAX: 580-924-7685. E-MAIL: bcstar@plylerpublishing.com. Year Established: 1962. Pub. Frequency: w. (Thu.) Page Size: standard. Subscrip. Rate: $.30 newsstand/cover; $14/yr in Bryan Co.; $18/yr in state Oklohama; $22/yr out of state. Circulation: 300 per issue (paid). **Owner(s):** Linda Plyler, PO Box 1427, Durant, OK 74702. Telephone: 580-924-6499. FAX: 580-924-6664. **Management:** Linda Plyler, Publisher. **Editorial:** Linda Plyler, Managing Editor.

EAKLY

COUNTRY CONNECTION NEWS, THE. ISSN 0746-4789
315 Main St., Eakly, OK 73033. Telephone: 405-797-3648. FAX: 405-797-3663. E-MAIL: bblock@prodigy.com. Year Established: 1982. Pub. Frequency: w. (Tue.) Page Size: broadsheet. Subscrip. Rate: $.50 newsstand/cover; $25/yr in state; $28/yr out of state. Circulation: 2,000 per issue (paid). **Owner(s):** Joyce Carney, See address and contact information above. **Management:** Joyce Carney, Publisher. Amanda Carney, Office Manager. Carrie Carney, Advertising. Rusty Carney, Circulation Manager. **Editorial:** Joyce Carney, Managing Editor.

EL RENO

HARTFORD ADVOCATE. ISSN 0192-8503
PO Box 9, El Reno, OK 73036. Telephone: 405-262-5180. FAX: 405-262-3541. E-MAIL: feedback@newmassmedia.com. URL: http://www.hartfordadvocate.com. Year Established: 1975. Pub. Frequency: w. Page Size: tabloid. Subscrip. Rate: $160/yr mailed in county. Adv. Rate: page $2,190 Circulation: 45,000 per issue (paid and controlled). **Owner(s):** Tribune Corp., See address and contact information above. **Management:** Joshua Mamis, Publisher. Emily Lukasiewicz, Operations Manager. Sean Hitchcock, Advertising Manager. **Editorial:** John Adamian, Managing Editor. Peter Morlock, Production Manager.

FAIRVIEW

FAIRVIEW REPUBLICAN. 112 N. Main St., Fairview, OK 73737. Telephone: 580-227-4439. FAX: 580-227-4430. E-MAIL: news@fairviewrepublican.com. URL: http://www.fairviewrepublican.com. Mailing Address: PO Box 497, Fairview, OK 73737-0497. Year Established: 1900. Pub. Frequency: w. (Thu.) Page Size: broadsheet. Subscrip. Rate: $.50 newsstand/cover; $23/yr mailed in county; $31/yr mailed out of county; $39/yr mailed out of state. Circulation: 3,000 per issue (controlled and free). **Owner(s):** Jo Hammer, PO Box 245, Cherokee, OK 73728. Telephone: 580-596-3344. **Management:** Jo Hammer, General Manager. Hoby Hammer, Publisher.

GROVE

DELAWARE COUNTY JOURNAL. 27 W. Third St., Ste A, Grove, OK 74344. Telephone: 918-786-2228. FAX: 918-253-4380. Mailing Address: PO Box 450969, Grove, OK 74345. Pub. Frequency: w. (Wed.) Subscrip. Rate: $.50 newsstand/cover; $18/yr in county. Circulation: 3,200 per issue (paid). **Owner(s):** Grove Sun Newspaper Co., See address and contact information above. **Management:** Peter M. Crow, Publisher. Tom Gray, Advertising Manager. Billie Organ, Circulation Manager.

HARTSHORNE

HARTSHORNE SUN. 1005 Penn Ave, Hartshorne, OK 74547. Telephone: 918-297-2577. FAX: 918-297-2577. URL: http://www.cnhi.com. Mailing Address: PO Box 330, Hartshorne, OK 74547-0330. Pub. Frequency: w. (Thu.) Page Size: broadsheet. Subscrip. Rate: $.50 newsstand/cover; $19.75/yr in county; $24/yr in state; $29.10/yr out of state. Circulation: 1,700 per issue (paid). **Owner(s):** Community Newspaper Holdings, Inc., 3500 Colonnade Pkwy., Ste. 600, Birmingham, AL 35243-1031. **Management:** John Tucker, Publisher. Lois Eddington, Advertising. **Editorial:** Jim Nicholson, Editor.

HENRYETTA

HENRYETTA FREE-LANCE. 812 W. Main St., Henryetta, OK 74437. Telephone: 918-652-3311. FAX: 918-652-7347. E-MAIL: newseditor2@mindspring.com. Mailing Address: PO Box 848, Henryetta, OK 74437. Year Established: 1901. Pub. Frequency: 3/w. (Tue., Fri. & Sun.) Page Size: broadsheet. Subscrip. Rate: $.50 newsstand/cover; $1 Sun.; $39/yr carrier delivery; $45/yr mailed in county; $45/yr out of county; $50/yr out of state. Adv. Rate: col. inch $6.30 Freelance Pay: $5-$15/article. **Wire Service(s):** AP. Circulation: 2,200 evening (paid); 2,400 Sunday (paid). **Owner(s):** Sumner Media Group, 114 E. Seventh St., Okmulgee, OK 74447. Telephone: 918-756-3600. **Management:** Renee Browning, Publisher. Summer Thomas-Noah, Advertising Manager. Carri Stanton, Circulation Manager. **Editorial:** Nancy Miller, Managing Editor.

HOBART

HOBART DEMOCRAT-CHIEF. PO Box 432, Hobart, OK 73651. Year Established: 1901. Pub. Frequency: w. (Thu.) Page Size: broadsheet. Subscrip. Rate: $.75 newsstand/cover; $27/yr carrier delivery in county; $40/yr mailed in state. Adv. Rate: col. inch $7 Circulation: 3,200 per issue (paid). **Owner(s):** Democrat-Chief Publishing Co. Inc., 407 S. Main St., Hobart, OK 73651. Telephone: 580-726-3333. FAX: 580-726-3431. **Management:** Neville Hancock, Co-Publisher. Joe Hancock, Publisher. Molly Nagel, Advertising Manager. Pauletta Hayworth, Circulation Manager. **Editorial:** Todd Hancock, News Editor.

HOLDENVILLE

HOLDENVILLE NEWS. 112 S. Creek, Holdenville, OK 74848. Telephone: 405-379-5411. FAX: 405-379-5413. E-MAIL: holdenvillenews@itlnet.net. Mailing Address: PO Box 751, Holdenville, OK 74848. Year Established: 1927. Pub. Frequency: s-w. (Wed. & Sun.) Page Size: tabloid. Subscrip. Rate: $.50 newsstand/cover; $5 carrier delivery/mo.; $13 carrier delivery for 3 mos.. Circulation: 2,000 per issue (paid). **Owner(s):** Francis Stipe, PO Box 751, Holdenville, OK 74838. Telephone: 405-379-5411. **Management:** Francis Stipe, Publisher. Tammy White, Office Manager. **Editorial:** Bill Crawford, Editor.

HOMINY

HOMINY NEWS-PROGRESS. 115 W. Main St., Hominy, OK 74035. Telephone: 918-885-2101. FAX: 918-885-4596. Mailing Address: PO Box 38, Hominy, OK 74035. Year Established: 1973. Pub. Frequency: w. (Wed.) Page Size: standard. Subscrip. Rate: $.50 newsstand/cover; $17.50/yr local; $20/yr mailed out of area; $30/yr mailed out of state. Circulation: 1,650 per issue (paid). **Owner(s):** Ferguson & Ferguson, S. Broadway, Cleveland, OK 74020. **Management:** Ramona Brown, General Manager. D. Jo Ferguson, Publisher. **Editorial:** Ramona Brown, Editor.

KINGFISHER

KINGFISHER TIMES & FREE PRESS. 323 N. Main St., Kingfisher, OK 73750. Telephone: 405-375-3220. FAX: 405-375-3222. E-MAIL: kingfishertimes@pldi.net. URL: http://www.kingfisherpress.net. Mailing Address: P.O. Box 209, Kingfisher, OK 73750. Year Established: 1889. Pub. Frequency: s-w. (Wed. & Sun.) Page Size: broadsheet. Subscrip. Rate: $.50 newsstand/cover; $27.50/yr in county; $36/yr out of county; $46.50/yr out of state. Freelance Pay: $0.25/column-inch. Circulation: 3,800 per issue (paid). **Owner(s):** Kingfisher Newspapers Inc., See address and contact information above. **Management:** Gary Reid, Publisher. Robin Johnston, Advertising Manager. **Editorial:** Barry Reid, Editor.

KONAWA

KONAWA LEADER. 102 N Broadway St, Konawa, OK 74849. Telephone: 580-925-3187. FAX: 580-925-3729. Mailing Address: PO Box 157, Konawa, OK 74849. Year Established: 1893. Pub. Frequency: w. (Thu.) Page Size: broadsheet. Subscrip. Rate: $.50 newsstand/cover; $20/yr in area. Circulation: 2,000 per issue (paid). **Owner(s):** Ed Gallagher, See address and contact information above. **Management:** Ed Gallagher, Publisher. **Editorial:** Ed Gallagher, Editor.

MADILL

MADILL RECORD. P O Box 529, Madill, OK 73446. Telephone: 580-795-3355. FAX: 580-795-3530. E-MAIL: madillrecord@okpress.com. Year Established: 1895. Pub. Frequency: w. (Thu) Page Size: broadsheet. Subscrip. Rate: $.50 newsstand/cover; $20/yr in county; $27/yr mailed in state (effective 2005); $32/yr mailed out of state. Circulation: 4,450 per issue (paid). **Owner(s):** John D. Montgomery, See address and contact information above. **Management:** Mark Codner, Publisher. Lori Trent, Advertising Manager. **Editorial:** Mark Codner, Editor.

MANNFORD

MANNFORD EAGLE. 103-B Cimarron St, Mannford, OK 74044. Telephone: 918-865-3030. FAX: 918-865-3026. URL: http://www.commpub.com. Pub. Frequency: w. (Wed.) Page Size: broadsheet. Subscrip. Rate: $.50 newsstand/cover; $19.95/yr in county; $34.45/yr out of county; $42.75/yr out of state. Circulation: 2,000 per issue (paid). **Owner(s):** Community Publishers, Inc., PO Box 1049, Bentonville, AR 72172. Telephone: 501-271-3700. **Management:** Mike Brown, Publisher. Chris Kain, Advertising Manager. **Editorial:** Tim Farley, Managing Editor. Jasmine Patrick, News Editor.

MIDWEST CITY

SUN (MIDWEST CITY), THE. 351 N Air Depot Blvd., Midwest City, OK 73110. Telephone: 405-737-3050. FAX: 405-733-2068. URL: http://www.mwcsun.com. Mailing Address: PO Box 50067, Midwest City, OK 73140. Pub. Frequency: s-w (Wed. & Sun.) Page Size: broadsheet. Subscrip. Rate: $.50 newsstand/cover; $36/yr in county; $40/yr out of county. Circulation: 7,000 per issue (paid). **Owner(s):** Community Newspaper Holdings, Inc., 3500 Colonnade Pkwy., Ste. 600, Birmingham, AL 25243. **Management:** Jeremy Stillwell, Publisher. Michelle Wright, Advertising. Robin Handy, Circulation Manager.

MUSKOGEE

FORT GIBSON TIMES. 214 Wall St, Muskogee, OK 74402. Telephone: 918-684-2828. FAX: 918-687-6270. URL: http://www.muskogeephoenix.com. Mailing Address: PO Box 1968, Muskogee, OK 74402. Pub. Frequency: w. (Wed.) Page Size: broadsheet. Subscrip. Rate: $.50 newsstand/cover; $18.95/yr local. Circulation: 1,200 per issue (paid). **Owner(s):** Community Newspaper Holdings, Inc., 3500 Colonnade Pkwy., Ste. 600, Birmingham, AL 35242. **Management:** Larry Corvi, Publisher. Jermaine Mondaine, Advertising Manager. Tina Frost, Classified Adv. Mgr. **Editorial:** Vicky Holland, Executive Editor.

NEWCASTLE

NEWCASTLE PACER, THE. PO Box 429, Newcastle, OK 73065. Telephone: 405-387-5277. FAX: 405-387-9863. Year Established: 1978. Pub. Frequency: w. (Thu.) Page Size: broadsheet. Subscrip. Rate: $.50 newsstand/cover; $18/yr local; $20/yr elsewhere. Circulation: 1,700 per issue (controlled and free). **Owner(s):** Newcastle Pacer, Inc., See address and contact information above. **Management:** Tom Bolitho, Publisher. **Editorial:** Kelly Wray, Editor.

NORMAN

MOORE AMERICAN, THE. 215 E. Comanche St., Norman, OK 73069. Telephone: 405-321-1800. FAX: 405-366-3516. E-MAIL: smeditor@southwestbell.net. URL: http://www.themooreamerican.com. Mailing Address: P.O. Drawer 1058, Norman, OK 73070. Year Established: 1935. Pub. Frequency: w. (Tue.) Page Size: broadsheet. Subscrip. Rate: $.50 newsstand/cover; $24.95/yr mailed in county. **Wire Service(s):** AP. Circulation: 1,800 per issue (paid and free). **Owner(s):** Community Newspaper Holdings, Inc., 3500 Colonnade Pkwy., Ste. 600, Birmingham, AL 35243-2304. Telephone: 205-298-7100. FAX: 205-298-7108. **Management:** David Stringer, Publisher. Saundra Morris, Advertising Manager. Maurice Barcomb, Circulation Manager. Nicole Losoya, Classified Adv. Mgr.. **Editorial:** Linda Henley, City Editor. Michael Kinney, Sports.

NOWATA

NOWATA STAR. 126 E. Cherokee St., Nowata, OK 74048. Telephone: 918-273-2446. FAX: 918-273-0537. Mailing Address: PO Box 429, Nowata, OK 74048. Year Established: 1904. Pub. Frequency: w. (Wed.) Page Size: broadsheet. Subscrip. Rate: $.50 newsstand/cover; $23/yr in county. Adv. Rate: col. inch $5 Freelance Pay: $0.50/column-inch. Circulation: 2,700 per issue (paid and free). **Owner(s):** Vinita Printing Co., Inc., 138 S Wilson, Vinita, OK 74301. Telephone: 918-256-6422. FAX: 918-256-7100. **Management:** John Link, General Manager. Phillip Reid, Publisher. Janet Link, Advertising. John Link, Circulation Manager.

OKLAHOMA CITY

CAPITOL HILL BEACON. 124 W. Commerce, Oklahoma City, OK 73109. Telephone: 405-232-4151. FAX: 405-235-0818. E-MAIL: capitol_hill_beacon@okpress.com. Year Established: 1905. Pub. Frequency: w. (Thu.) Page Size: standard. Subscrip. Rate: $.50 newsstand/cover; $25/yr mailed. Circulation: 1,200 per issue (paid). **Owner(s):** Beacon Publishing Co., See address and contact information above. **Management:** David Sellers, Publisher. **Editorial:** David Sellers, Editor.

OKLAHOMA CITY FRIDAY. 10801 N. Quail Plaza Dr., Oklahoma City, OK 73120. Telephone: 405-755-3311. FAX: 405-755-3315. URL: http://www.okcfriday.com. Mailing Address: PO Box 20340, Oklahoma City, OK 73156. Year Established: 1974. Pub. Frequency: w. (Fri.) Page Size: broadsheet. Subscrip. Rate: $1 newsstand/cover (effective 2006); $25, $35/yr in county. Adv. Rate: col. inch $20 **Wire Service(s):** AP. Circulation: 8,240 per issue (paid). **Owner(s):** Nichols Hills Publishing Co., See address and contact information above. **Management:** Rose Lane, General Manager. J. Leland Gourley, Publisher. **Editorial:** Vicki Gourley, Executive Editor. Peter Gill, Managing Editor.

OOLOGAH

OOLOGAH LAKE LEADER. 109 S. Maple, Oologah, OK 74053. Telephone: 918-443-2428. FAX: 918-443-2429. E-MAIL: oologahinfo@sbcglobal.net. URL: http://www.oologah.net. Mailing Address: PO Box 1175, Oologah, OK 74053-1175. Year Established: 1982. Pub. Frequency: w. (Thu.) Page Size: broadsheet. Subscrip. Rate: $.75 newsstand/cover; $24/yr home delivery in county; $26/yr mailed in state; $55/yr mailed out of state. Adv. Rate: col. inch $5.80 Circulation: 5,500 per issue (paid and free). **Owner(s):** Oologah Lake Leader LCC, See address and contact information above. **Management:** Faith L Wylie, General Manager. John M. Wylie II, Publisher. Carolyn Estes, Marketing Director. **Editorial:** John M. Wylie II, Editor-in-Chief. Chris Edens, City Editor.Readers: Northwest Rogers County OK

OWASSO

CATOOSA TIMES HERALD. 202 E Second Ave, Ste 101, Owasso, OK 74055. URL: http://www.neighbor-newspapers.com. Year Established: 1965. Pub. Frequency: w. (Wed.) Page Size: broadsheet. Subscrip. Rate: $.50 newsstand/cover; $19.95/yr in county; $33.45/yr mailed out of county; $40.45/yr mailed out of state. Circulation: 1,500 per issue (paid). **Owner(s):** Community Publishers, Inc., PO Box 1049, Bentonville, AR 72172. **Management:** Cyndi Knoten, Advertising. **Editorial:** Vicki Albright, Editor. Randy Cowling, Managing Editor.

OWASSO REPORTER. 202 E Second Ave, Ste 101, Owasso, OK 74055. E-MAIL: owassoreporter@intcom.net. URL: http://www.neighbor-newspapers.com. Year Established: 1970. Pub. Frequency: w. (Tue. & Wed.) Page Size: broadsheet. Subscrip. Rate: $.50 newsstand/cover; $40/yr in county; $54.95/yr mailed out of county; $73.65/yr mailed out of state. Circulation: 7,000 per issue (paid). **Owner(s):** Community Publishers, Inc., PO Box 1049, Bentonville, AR 72172. Telephone: 501-271-3700. **Management:** Cyndi Knoten, Advertising. Glenna Todd, Advertising Manager. **Editorial:** Randy Cowling, Managing Editor. Rick Heaton, Associate Editor.

PAWHUSKA

PAWHUSKA JOURNAL-CAPITAL. 700 Kihekah St., Pawhuska, OK 74056. Telephone: 918-287-1590. FAX: 918-287-1804. Mailing Address: PO Box 238, Pawhuska, OK 74056. Year Established: 1904. Pub. Frequency: w. (Wed.) Page Size: broadsheet. Subscrip. Rate: $1 newsstand/cover; $72/yr in county; $90/yr mailed out of county $78yr. Adv. Rate: col. inch $5.71 Circulation: 2,400 per issue (paid). **Owner(s):** Stephens Media LLC, 1111 W. Bonanza Rd., Las Vegas, NV 89106. Telephone: 702-383-0211. **Management:** Sherry Gann, Publisher. Leona Jones, Advertising Manager. Summer Trent, Classified Adv. Mgr. **Editorial:** Sherry Gann, Editor. Misty Brinkman, Production Manager. Dena Alexander, Photographer.

PERRY

TRI-COUNTY JOURNAL. 714 Delaware St., Perry, OK 73077. Telephone: 580-336-2222. FAX: 580-336-3222. Mailing Address: PO Box 311, Perry, OK 73077-0311. Year Established: 1916. Pub. Frequency: w. (Wed.) Page Size: broadsheet. Subscrip. Rate: $.50 newsstand/cover per issue; $20/yr home delivery in city. Circulation: 14,893 per issue (paid). **Owner(s):** Perry Daily Journal, Inc., See address and contact information above. **Management:** Phillip Reid, Publisher. Maria Lemons, Advertising. Mickey Anson, Circulation Manager. **Editorial:** Sue Scholz, Editor.

PURCELL

PURCELL REGISTER. 225 W. Main St., Purcell, OK 73080. E-MAIL: info@purcellregister.com. URL: http://www.purcellregister.com. Mailing Address: PO Box 191, Purcell, OK 73080. Year Established: 1887. Pub. Frequency: w. (Thu.) Page Size: broadsheet. Subscrip. Rate: $.50 newsstand/cover; $20/yr in adj. cys.; $25/yr mailed in state; $35/yr mailed out of state. Circulation: 6,200 per issue (paid). **Owner(s):** McClain County Publishing Co., Inc., See address and contact information above. **Management:** Gracie Montgomery, General Manager. Vickie Foraker, Advertising Manager. **Editorial:** Susie Williams, Managing Editor.

SALLISAW

SEQUOYAH COUNTY TIMES. 111 N. Oak St., Sallisaw, OK 74955-4637. Telephone: 918-775-4433. FAX: 918-775-3023. E-MAIL: info@seqcotimes.com. URL: http://www.sequoyahcountytimes.com. Year Established: 1932. Pub. Frequency: s-w. (Thu. & Sun.) Page Size: broadsheet. Subscrip. Rate: $.75 newsstand/cover; $25.50/yr local trade area; $55/yr elsewhere. Adv. Rate: col. inch $6.40 Circulation: 6,610 per issue (paid and free). **Owner(s):** Cookson Hills Publishers, Inc., 111 N. Oak St., Sallisaw, OK 74955. Telephone: 918-775-4433. FAX: 918-775-3023. **Management:** Jim Mayo, President. Delanna Nutter, Advertising Manager. **Editorial:** Jim Mayo, Editor. Sally Maxwell, Managing Editor. Mike Erwin, Sports.

SAND SPRINGS

SAND SPRINGS LEADER. 303 N McKinley, Sand Springs, OK 74063. Telephone: 918-245-6634. FAX: 918-241-3610. E-MAIL: dhughes@neighbor-newspapers.com. URL: http://www.neighbor-newspapers.com. Year Established: 1912. Pub. Frequency: s-w. (Wed. & Sun.) Page Size: broadsheet. Subscrip. Rate: $.50 newsstand/cover; $35/yr in county; $61.70/yr mailed out of county; $73.65/yr mailed out of state. Circulation: 5,228 per issue (paid). **Owner(s):** Community Publishers, Inc., PO Box 1049, Bentonville, AR 72172. Telephone: 501-271-3700. **Management:** Chris Kain, Advertising Manager. **Editorial:** Dustin Hughes, Managing Editor. Rodney Echohawk, Sports Editor.Deadline: Features-Tue., 12:00 pm for Wed.; Fri., 12:00 pm for Sun.; News-Tue., 12:00 pm for Wed.; Fri., 12:00 pm for Sun.; Other-Tue., Thu., Fri., 12:00 pm.; Photo-Tue., 12:00 pm for Wed.; Fri., 12:00 pm for Sun.

TULSA COUNTY NEWS. 303 N McKinley, Sand Springs, OK 74063. Telephone: 918-245-6634. FAX: 918-241-3610. URL: http://www.neighbor-newspapers.com. Pub. Frequency: w. (Thu.) Page Size: tabloid. Subscrip. Rate: $.50 newsstand/cover; $19.65/yr in county; $26.05/yr mailed out of county; $31.05/yr out of state. Adv. Rate: col. inch $7.20 Circulation: 1,200 per issue (paid and free). **Owner(s):** Community Publishers, Inc., PO Box 1049, Bentonville, AR 72172. Telephone: 501-271-3700. **Management:** Chris Kain, Advertising Manager. **Editorial:** Anna Brown, Editor. Dustin Hughes, Managing Editor.

SKIATOOK

SKIATOOK JOURNAL. 500 W Rogers, Skiatook, OK 74070. Telephone: 918-396-1616. FAX: 918-396-1618. URL: http://www.commpub.com/publications.html. Year Established: 1985. Pub. Frequency: w. (Wed.) Page Size: broadsheet. Subscrip. Rate: $.50 newsstand/cover; $22.95/yr in county; $35.50/yr mailed out of county; $42.50/yr mailed out of state. Adv. Rate: col. inch $6.85 Circulation: 3,000 per issue (paid). **Owner(s):** Community Publishers, Inc., PO Box 1049, Bentonville, AR 72172. **Management:** Kelly Stowe, Advertising. **Editorial:** Randy Cowling, Managing Editor.

STIGLER

COUNTRY STAR. 204 S. Broadway, Stigler, OK 74462. Telephone: 918-967-4655. FAX: 918-967-4289. E-MAIL: sns@swis.net. Pub. Frequency: w. (Thu.) Page Size: broadsheet.Subscrip. Rate: $33/yr Circulation: 4,000 per issue (free). **Owner(s):** Linus G. Williams, See address and contact information above. **Management:** Linus G. Williams, President. Linus Williams Jr., Advertising Manager. Georgia Speegle, Circulation Manager. **Editorial:** Sharon Johnson, Editor.

STIGLER NEWS-SENTINEL. 204 S. Broadway, Stigler, OK 74462. Telephone: 918-967-4655. FAX: 918-967-4289. E-MAIL: sns@swis.net. Year Established: 1930. Pub. Frequency: w. (Thu.) Page Size: broadsheet. Subscrip. Rate: $.50 newsstand/cover; $28/yr mailed in county; $35/yr mailed out of county; $38/yr mailed out of state. Circulation: 4,100 per issue (paid). **Owner(s):** Linus G. Williams, See address and contact information above. **Management:** Linus G. Williams, President. Linus Williams Jr., Advertising Manager. Georgia Speegle, Circulation Manager. **Editorial:** Sharon Johnson, Editor.

STILWELL

STILWELL DEMOCRAT-JOURNAL. 118 N. Second St., Stilwell, OK 74960. Telephone: 918-696-2228. FAX: 918-696-7066. Mailing Address: PO Box 508, Stilwell, OK 74960. Year Established: 1897. Pub. Frequency: w. (Wed.) Page Size: standard. Subscrip. Rate: $.50 newsstand/cover; $21/yr mailed in county; $27/yr mailed out of county; $31/yr mailed out of state. Circulation: 6,300 per issue (paid). **Owner(s):** Community Newspaper Holdings, Inc., 3500 Colonnade Pkwy., Ste. 600, Birmingham, AL 35243. Telephone: 205-298-7100. FAX: 205-298-7101. **Management:** Gary Jackson, Publisher. Alice Rankin, Advertising Manager. **Editorial:** Keith Neale, Editor.

STRATFORD

STRATFORD (OK) STAR. 130 E. Main St., Stratford, OK 74872. Telephone: 580-759-2282. FAX: 405-867-5115. Mailing Address: PO Box 210, Stratford, OK 74872. Pub. Frequency: w. (Thu.) Page Size: standard. Subscrip. Rate: $.50 newsstand/cover; $18/yr mailed in county; $25/yr mailed out of county. Circulation: 1,500 per issue (paid). **Owner(s):** Kenneth R. Wood, See address and contact information above. **Management:** Kenneth R. Wood, Publisher. **Editorial:** Kenneth R. Wood, Editor.

TISHOMINGO

JOHNSTON COUNTY CAPITAL-DEMOCRAT. PO Box 520, Tishomingo, OK 73460. Telephone: 580-371-2356. FAX: 580-371-9648. E-MAIL: capital_democrat@yahoo.com. Year Established: 1900. Pub. Frequency: w. (Thu.) Page Size: broadsheet. Subscrip. Rate: $.50 newsstand/cover; $22/yr mailed in county; $29/yr mailed out of county; $35/yr mailed out of state. Circulation: 3,250 per issue (paid). **Owner(s):** Ray Lokey, See address and contact information above. **Management:** Ray Lokey, Publisher. **Editorial:** Ray Lokey, Editor. John Small, News Editor.

TONKAWA

TONKAWA NEWS, THE. 108 N. Seventh St., Tonkawa, OK 74653-0250. Telephone: 580-628-2532. FAX: 580-628-4044. Year Established: 1894. Pub. Frequency: w. (Thu.) Page Size: broadsheet. Subscrip. Rate: $.50 newsstand/cover; $21/yr home delivery local. Circulation: 1,800 per issue (paid). **Owner(s):** H. Lyle Becker, See address and contact information above. **Management:** H. Lyle Becker, President. Kelli Hacker, Circulation Manager. **Editorial:** H. Lyle Becker, Editor-in-Chief.

TULSA

GLENPOOL POST. 8545 E 41st St, Tulsa, OK 74145. Telephone: 918-663-1414. FAX: 918-610-6130. URL: http://www.neighbor-newspapers.com. Pub. Frequency: w. (Thu.) Page Size: broadsheet. Subscrip. Rate: $.50 newsstand/cover; $19.95/yr in county; $24.95/yr out of county. Circulation: 1,000 per issue (paid). **Owner(s):** Community Publishers, Inc., PO Box 1049, Bentonville, AR 72172. Telephone: 501-271-3700. **Management:** Kevin Hook, Advertising Director. **Editorial:** Dee A. Duren, Editor.

JENKS JOURNAL. 8545 E 41st St, Tulsa, OK 74145. Telephone: 918-663-1414. FAX: 918-610-6130. URL: http://www.neighbor-newspapers.com. Year Established: 1957. Pub. Frequency: w. (Thu.) Page Size: broadsheet. Subscrip. Rate: $.50 newsstand/cover; $19.95/yr in county; $33.45/yr out of county. Adv. Rate: col. inch $7.85 Circulation: 2,000 per issue (paid). **Owner(s):** Community Publishers, Inc., PO Box 1049, Bentonville, AR 72172. Telephone: 501-271-3700. **Management:** Allison Jay, Advertising. Kevin Hook, Advertising Director. **Editorial:** Don Diehl, Editor.

OKLAHOMA EAGLE. 624 E. Archer St., Tulsa, OK 74120. Telephone: 918-582-7124. FAX: 918-582-8905. E-MAIL: okeagle@wiltel.net. Mailing Address: P O Box 3267, Tulsa, OK 74101. Year Established: 1921. Pub. Frequency: w. (Thu.) Page Size: standard.Subscrip. Rate: $.50 newsstand/cover; $28/yr Circulation: 14,000 per issue (paid). **Owner(s):** James O. Goodwin, See address and contact information above. **Management:** Goodwin O. James, Publisher. Joe Goodwin, Advertising Manager. **Editorial:** Joe Goodwin, Editor.

WAGONER

WAGONER TRIBUNE, THE. 221 E Cherokee, Wagoner, OK 74467. Telephone: 918-485-5505. FAX: 918-485-8442. URL: http://www.neighbor-newspapers.com. Year Established: 1894. Pub. Frequency: w. (Thu.) Page Size: broadsheet. Subscrip. Rate: $.50 newsstand/cover; $27.65/yr in county; $43.65/yr mailed out of county; $51.20/yr mailed out of state. Adv. Rate: col. inch $8 Circulation: 3,094 per issue (paid). **Owner(s):** Community Publishers, Inc., PO Box 1049, Bentonville, AR 72172. Telephone: 501-271-3700. **Management:** Katherine Pritchett, Advertising. **Editorial:** Bob Lewis, Managing Editor. Jeff Riggs, News Editor. Zane Thomas, Sports Editor.

WATONGA

WATONGA REPUBLICAN, THE. 104 E. Main St., Watonga, OK 73772-0030. Telephone: 580-623-4922. FAX: 580-623-4925. E-MAIL: new@wrnew.net. Mailing Address: PO Box 30, Watonga, OK 73772-0030. Year Established: 1892. Pub. Frequency: w. (Wed.) Page Size: broadsheet. Subscrip. Rate: $.50 newsstand/cover; $34/yr in state; $39/yr out of state. Adv. Rate: col. inch $4.40 Circulation: 3,200 per issue (paid). **Owner(s):** Tim Curtin, PO Box 30, Watonga, OK 73772. Telephone: 405-623-4922. **Management:** Tim Curtin, Publisher. **Editorial:** Darrell Rice, News Director.

WAURIKA

WAURIKA NEWS-DEMOCRAT. 111 E Broadway, Waurika, OK 73573. Telephone: 580-228-2316. FAX: 580-228-3647. URL: http://www.waurikademocrat.com. Pub. Frequency: w. (Thu.) Page Size: broadsheet. Subscrip. Rate: $.50 newsstand/cover; $22.25/yr mailed in county; $29.50/yr mailed out of county; $37.35/yr mailed out of state. Circulation: 2,000 per issue (paid). **Owner(s):** Community Newspaper Holdings, Inc., 3500 Colonnade Pkwy., Ste. 600, Birmingham, AL 25243. Telephone: 205-298-7101. **Management:** Floyd Jernigan, Advertising Director. **Editorial:** Floyd Jernigan, Editor.

WESTVILLE

WESTVILLE REPORTER, THE. 122 S Williams, Westville, OK 74965. Telephone: 918-723-5445. FAX: 918-723-5511. URL: http://www.journalexpress.net. Mailing Address: PO Box 550, Westville, OK 74965-0550. Year Established: 1855. Pub. Frequency: w. (Thu.) Page Size: standard.Subscrip. Rate: $.50 newsstand/cover Circulation: 2,700 per issue (paid). **Owner(s):** Community Newspaper Holdings, Inc., 3500 Colonnade Pkwy., Ste. 600, Birmingham, AL 25243. **Management:** Gary Jackson, Publisher. Alice Rankin, Advertising Manager. **Editorial:** Romona Brown, Editor.

WETUMKA

HUGHES COUNTY TIMES. 120 S. Main St., Wetumka, OK 74883. Telephone: 405-452-3294. FAX: 405-452-3329. Year Established: 1930. Pub. Frequency: w. (Thu.) Page Size: broadsheet. Subscrip. Rate: $.50 newsstand/cover; $17.50/yr in county; $22.50/yr mailed out of county; $7.50/yr mailed out of state. Circulation: 2,500 per issue (paid). **Owner(s):** William C. Morgan, See address and contact information above. **Management:** William C. Morgan, Publisher. Peggy Smith, Office Manager. **Editorial:** William C. Morgan, Editor.

WEWOKA

WEWOKA TIMES. 210 S. Wewoka Ave., Wewoka, OK 74884. Telephone: 405-257-3341. FAX: 405-257-3313. Mailing Address: PO Box 61, Wewoka, OK 74884. Year Established: 1926. Pub. Frequency: w. (Wed.) Page Size: broadsheet. Subscrip. Rate: $.50 newsstand/cover; $24/yr mailed. **Wire Service(s):** AP. Circulation: 1,200 per issue (paid). **Owner(s):** Seminole Producer, See address and contact information above. **Management:** Stu Phillips, Publisher. Levina Morgan, Advertising.

YUKON

YUKON REVIEW. 110 S. Fifth St., Yukon, OK 73099. Telephone: 405-354-5264. FAX: 405-350-3044. E-MAIL: revieweditor@sbcglobal.net. Mailing Address: PO Box 851400, Yukon, OK 73085. Year Established: 1963. Pub. Frequency: s-w. (Wed. & Sat.) Page Size: broadsheet.Subscrip. Rate: $.50 newsstand/cover; $30/yr Circulation: 9,500 per issue (paid). **Owner(s):** Randel & Karen Grigsby, See address and contact information above. **Management:** Bart Nicholson, General Manager. Randel Grigsby, Publisher. Bart Nicholson, Advertising Manager. Heyle Durbin, Classified Adv. Mgr.. **Editorial:** Conrad Dudderar, Managing Editor. Chuck Richerman, Sports Editor.

OREGON

BAKER CITY

RECORD-COURIER (BAKER CITY), THE. 1718 Main, Baker City, OR 97814. E-MAIL: news@therconline.com. URL: http://www.therconline.com. Mailing Address: PO Box 70, Baker City, OR 97814-0070. Year Established: 1901. Pub. Frequency: w. (Thu.) Page Size: oversize. Subscrip. Rate: $30/yr local; $34/yr out of area. Adv. Rate: col. inch $5.50 Circulation: 2,500 per issue (paid). **Owner(s):** Brinton Estate, 2525 Court St., Baker City, OR 97814. Telephone: 541-523-5353. **Management:** Greg Brinton, Publisher. Bow L. McEwen, Office Manager. Dave Conn, Advertising Manager. **Editorial:** Debby Schoeningh, Editor.Readers: Baker County

BANDON

BANDON WESTERN WORLD. 1185 Baltimore St., Bandon, OR 97411-0248. Telephone: 541-347-2423. FAX: 541-347-2424. Mailing Address: PO Box 248, Bandon, OR 97411-0248. Year Established: 1912. Pub. Frequency: w. (Thu.) Page Size: broadsheet. Subscrip. Rate: $.50 newsstand/cover; $26/yr in state; $40/yr mailed out of state. Freelance Pay: $25/article. Circulation: 3,100 per issue (paid). **Owner(s):** Lee Enterprises, Inc., 201 N Harrison St, Davenport, IA 52801-1939. Telephone: 563-383-2100. **Management:** Greg Stevens, Publisher. Claudia Slosser, Advertising Manager. Mary Franson, Circulation Manager. **Editorial:** Elise Hamner, Editor.

BROOKINGS

CURRY COASTAL PILOT. 507 Chetco Ave., Brookings, OR 97415. Telephone: 541-469-3123. FAX: 541-469-4679. E-MAIL: mail@currypilot.com. URL: http://www.currypilot.com. Mailing Address: PO Box 700, Brookings, OR 97415. Year Established: 1946. Pub. Frequency: s-w. (Wed. & Sat.) Page Size: broadsheet. Subscrip. Rate: $.50 newsstand/cover; $38/yr home delivery local; $48/yr mailed elsewhere. Adv. Rate: col. inch $10.75 Freelance Pay: $1/column-inch. Circulation: 7,000 per issue (paid and free). **Owner(s):** Western Communication, Inc., 1777 S.W. Chandler Ave., Bend, OR 97702. Telephone: 541-382-1811. **Management:** Charles Kocher, Publisher. Cindy Vosburg, Advertising Director. **Editorial:** Scott Graves, Editor.Readers: For Zip codes 97415 & 97444

BURNS

BURNS TIMES-HERALD. 355 N. Broadway, Burns, OR 97720-1704. Telephone: 541-573-2022. FAX: 541-573-3915. E-MAIL: btherald@burnstimes.com. URL: http://www.burnstimesherald.com. Year Established: 1887. Pub. Frequency: w. (Wed.) Page Size: broadsheet. Subscrip. Rate: $.50 newsstand/cover; $25/yr home delivery; $27/yr mailed in county; $36/yr mailed out of county. Adv. Rate: col. inch $6.75 Circulation: 3,200 per issue (paid). **Owner(s):** Western Communication, Inc., 1777 S.W. Chandler Ave., Bend, OR 97702. Telephone: 541-382-1811. **Management:** Sue Pedersen, General Manager. Scott j Olson, Publisher. Sue Pedersen, Advertising. **Editorial:** Debbie Raney, Editor.

CANBY

CANBY HERALD. 241 N. Grant St., Canby, OR 97013. Telephone: 503-266-6831. FAX: 503-266-6836. URL: http://www.canbyherald.com. Mailing Address: PO Box 1108, Canby, OR 97013. Year Established: 1906. Pub. Frequency: s-w. (Wed. & Sat.) Page Size: standard. Subscrip. Rate: $.50 newsstand/cover; $36/yr mailed in county; $42/yr mailed out of county. Adv. Rate: col. inch $10.50 Circulation: 5,400 per issue (paid). **Owner(s):** Eagle Newspapers, Inc., 4901 Indian School Rd., N.E., Salem, OR 97305. Telephone: 503-393-1774. **Management:** William D Cassel, Publisher.

CONDON

TIMES-JOURNAL (CONDON), THE. P.O. Box 746, Condon, OR 97823. E-MAIL: times-journal@jncable.com. Year Established: 1886. Pub. Frequency: w. (Thu.) Page Size: standard. Subscrip. Rate: $.50 newsstand/cover; $28/yr in county; $38/yr out of county. Circulation: 1,500 per issue (paid). **Owner(s):** McLaren & Janet Stinchfield, 319 S. Main St., Condon, OR 97823-0746. Telephone: 541-384-2421. FAX: 541-384-2411. **Management:** Janet Stinchfield, Publisher. McLaren Stinchfield, Advertising Manager. **Editorial:** McLaren Stinchfield, Editor-in-Chief.

COQUILLE

SENTINEL (COQUILLE), THE. PO Box 400, Coquille, OR 97423. Telephone: 541-396-3191. FAX: 541-396-3624. Year Established: 1882. Pub. Frequency: w. (Wed.) Page Size: standard. Subscrip. Rate: $.50 newsstand/cover; $24/yr in county. Circulation: 3,500 per issue (paid). **Owner(s):** Bear Media Inc, See address and contact information above. **Management:** Mikel Chavez, Publisher. **Editorial:** Anna Chavez, Editor.

COTTAGE GROVE

COTTAGE GROVE SENTINEL. 116 N. Sixth St., Cottage Grove, OR 97424. Telephone: 541-942-3325. FAX: 541-942-3328. E-MAIL: news@cgsentinel.com. URL: http://www.cgsentinel.com. Mailing Address: PO Box 35, Cottage Grove, OR 97424. Year Established: 1889. Pub. Frequency: w. (Wed.) Page Size: standard. Subscrip. Rate: $.50 newsstand/cover; $22/yr domestic area; $29/yr out of area. Circulation: 4,750 per issue (paid). **Owner(s):** Lee Enterprises, Inc., 215 N. Main St., Davenport, IA 52801. Telephone: 563-383-2100. **Management:** Rosie Lilja, Office Manager. Amy Callahan, Advertising Manager. **Editorial:** Jonni Gratton, Editor.

CRESWELL

CHRONICLE (CRESWELL), THE. PO Box 428, Creswell, OR 97426. Telephone: 541-895-2197. FAX: 541-895-2361. E-MAIL: the chronicle@earthlink.net. Pub. Frequency: w. Subscrip. Rate: $.50 newsstand/cover; $22/yr. **Owner(s):** Helen Hollyer, Publ., See address and contact information above. **Management:** Helen Hollyer, Publisher. Danyelle Glendenning, Advertising Director.

DALLAS

POLK COUNTY ITEMIZER-OBSERVER. 147 S. E. Court St., Dallas, OR 97338. Telephone: 503-623-2373. FAX: 503-623-2395. URL: http://www.itemizerobserver.com. Mailing Address: PO Box 108, Dallas, OR 97338-0108. Year Established: 1875. Pub. Frequency: w. (Wed.) Page Size: tabloid. Subscrip. Rate: $.50 newsstand/cover; $24/yr in county; $30/yr out of county; $35/yr mailed out of state. Circulation: 6,800 per issue (paid and free). **Owner(s):** Eagle Newspapers, Inc., 4901 Indian School Rd., N.E., Salem, OR 97305. Telephone: 503-393-1774. **Management:** Dave Weston, Publisher. Heidi Mowery, Advertising. Nancy Adams, Circulation Manager. Dawn Ohren, Classified Adv. Mgr.. **Editorial:** Dave Weston, Editor. Marc Faulconer, Managing Editor.

DAYTON

DAYTON TRIBUNE. PO Box 69, Dayton, OR 97114-0069. Telephone: 503-864-2310. FAX: 503-864-2310. E-MAIL: tribune@onlinemac.com. Year Established: 1912. Pub. Frequency: w. (Thu.) Page Size: tabloid. Subscrip. Rate: $.10 newsstand/cover; $7.50/yr mailed. Circulation: 428 per issue (paid). **Owner(s):** George & Edwina Meitzen, See address and contact information above. **Editorial:** George Meitzen, Editor.

DRAIN

DRAIN ENTERPRISE. 309 First St., Drain, OR 97435-0026. Telephone: 541-836-2241. FAX: 541-836-2243. E-MAIL: drainenterprise@earthlink.net. Mailing Address: PO Box 26, Drain, OR 97435-0026. Year Established: 1950. Pub. Frequency: w. (Thu.) Page Size: tabloid. Subscrip. Rate: $.40 newsstand/cover; $15.50/yr in county. Circulation: 1,200 per issue (paid). **Owner(s):** Betty Anderson, PO Box 26, Drain, OR 97435. Telephone: 541-836-2241. **Management:** Betty Anderson, Publisher. **Editorial:** Sue Anderson, Editor.

EAGLE POINT

UPPER ROGUE INDEPENDENT. 11136 Hwy. 62, Eagle Point, OR 97524. Telephone: 541-826-7700. FAX: 541-826-1340. E-MAIL: urindependent@wave.net. URL: http://www.urindependent.com. Mailing Address: PO Box 900, Eagle Point, OR 97524. Year Established: 1976. Pub. Frequency: w. (Tue.) Page Size: tabloid. Subscrip. Rate: $15.60 newsstand/cover; $15/yr in county; $23/yr out of county; $9.75/yr to senior citizens in area. Adv. Rate: col. inch $7.75 Circulation: 16,000 per issue (paid and free). **Owner(s):** Nancy Leonard, See address and contact information above. **Management:** Nancy Leonard, Publisher. **Editorial:** Nancy Leonard, Editor-in-Chief. Ralph McKechnie, Sports Editor.

ENTERPRISE

WALLOWA COUNTY CHIEFTAIN. 106 N W First St, Enterprise, OR 97828. Telephone: 541-426-4567, 541-426-4568. FAX: 541-426-3921. URL: http://www.wallowa.com. Mailing Address: P. O. Box 338, Enterprise, OR 97828. Pub. Frequency: w. (Wed.) Page Size: broadsheet. Subscrip. Rate: $33/yr home delivery in county & online; $48/yr mailed out of county & online. **Owner(s):** East Oregonian Publishing Co., P.O. Box 1089, Pendleton, OR 97801. Telephone: 541-966-0800. **Management:** Cheryl Jenkins, General Manager. Betty Settergren, Advertising Manager. **Editorial:** Billy Jo Jannen, Editor. Elane Dickenson, Community Editor.

ESTACADO

ESTACADA NEWS. 313 S W Hwy 224, Estacado, OR 97222. Telephone: 503-630-3241. FAX: 503-630-5840. URL: http://www.estacadanews.com. Pub. Frequency: w. (Wed.) Subscrip. Rate: $26/yr; $.50/yr newsstand/cover. Circulation: 3,000 per issue (controlled and free). **Owner(s):** Pamplin Media Group, 6605 S E Lake Rd, Portland, OR 97222. Telephone: 503-684-0360. **Management:** Steve Clark, President. Paula Nelson, Advertising. **Editorial:** Clinton Vining, Editor.

FLORENCE

SIUSLAW NEWS, THE. 148 Maple St., Florence, OR 97439. Telephone: 541-997-3441. FAX: 541-997-7979. E-MAIL: paperads@oregonfast.net. Mailing Address: PO Box 10, Florence, OR 97439. Year Established: 1890. Pub. Frequency: s-w. (Wed. & Sat.) Page Size: broadsheet. Subscrip. Rate: $.50 newsstand/cover; $45/yr in county; $70/yr mailed out of county; $120/yr mailed out of state. Circulation: 6,200 per issue (paid). **Owner(s):** News Media Corp., 211 Hwy. 38 E., Rochelle, IL 61608. Telephone: 815-562-2061. **Management:** John Bartlett, Publisher. Pam Girard, Advertising Manager. Mike Capps, Circulation Manager. **Editorial:** Bob Serra, Editor. Ned Hickson, Sports.

FOREST GROVE

NEWS-TIMES (FOREST GROVE). ISSN 1042-8518
2038 Pacific Ave, Forest Grove, OR 97116-0408. Telephone: 503-357-3181. FAX: 503-359-8456. E-MAIL: news@forestgrovenewstime.com. URL: http://www.forestgrovenewstimes.com. Year Established: 1887. Pub. Frequency: w. (Wed.) Page Size: standard. Subscrip. Rate: $.50 newsstand/cover; $24/yr in county; $37/yr out of county. Circulation: 6,000 per issue (paid). **Owner(s):** Pamplin Media Group, 6605 S E Lake Rd, Portland, OR 97222. Telephone: 503-684-0360. FAX: 503-620-3433. **Management:** Steve Clark, President. John Schrag, Publisher. Whitney Johnson, Advertising. Vicki Gideon, Circulation Manager. **Editorial:** Nancy Townsley, Associate Editor. Zack Palmer, Sports.

GOLD BEACH

CURRY COUNTY REPORTER. PO Box 766, Gold Beach, OR 97444. Telephone: 541-247-6643. FAX: 541-247-6644. E-MAIL: molly@currycountyreporter.com. URL: http://www.currycountyreporter.com. Year Established: 1914. Pub. Frequency: w. (Wed.) Page Size: broadsheet. Subscrip. Rate: $.50 newsstand/cover; $22/yr in county; $29/yr out of county. Circulation: 2,786 per issue (paid). **Owner(s):** Curry County Reporter, Inc., See address and contact information above. **Management:** Molly Walker, General Manager. Jim & Molly Walker, Publisher. **Editorial:** Jim Walker, Editor.

GRANTS PASS

COUNTRY WEEKLY. 409 SE Seventh St, Grants Pass, OR 97526. Telephone: 541-474-3700. FAX: 541-474-3824. URL: http://www.thedailycourier.com. Mailing Address: PO Box 1468, Grants Pass, OR 97528. Pub. Frequency: w. (Wed.) Page Size: broadsheet. Adv. Rate: col. inch $5.76 Circulation: 17,000 per issue (free). **Owner(s):** Courier Publishing Co., See address and contact information above. **Management:** Dennis Mack, Publisher. Gene Napler, Advertising Manager. Dean Rich, Circulation Director. Debbie Thomas, Classified Adv. Mgr.. **Editorial:** Barbara Hahn, Editor.

GRESHAM

EAST COUNTY NEWS. 1190 N E Division St, Gresham, OR 97030. Telephone: 503-665-2181. FAX: 503-669-2760. E-MAIL: editor@eastcountynews.com. URL: http://www.eastcountynews.com. Year Established: 1911. Pub. Frequency: m. Page Size: broadsheet. Subscrip. Rate: $12/yr home delivery in county; $24/yr home delivery out of county; $24/yr mailed out of state. Circulation: 26,000 per issue (paid). **Owner(s):** Pamplin Media Group, 6605 S E Lake Rd, Portland, OR 97222. Telephone: 503-684-0360. FAX: 503-620-3433. **Management:** Steve Clark, President. Mark Garber, Publisher. Kevin Hohnbaum, Circulation Director. Ryan McVicker, Circulation Manager. **Editorial:** Eric Hendricksen, Editor.

GRESHAM OUTLOOK, THE. 1190 N E Division, Gresham, OR 97030. Telephone: 503-665-2181. FAX: 503-669-2760. E-MAIL: news@theoutlookonline.com. URL: http://www.theoutlookonline.com. Mailing Address: P O Box 747, Gresham, OR 97030. Pub. Frequency: s-w. (Wed. & Sat.) Subscrip. Rate: $.50 newsstand/cover; $35/yr in county & adj. cys.; $66/yr out of area; $78/yr out of state. **Owner(s):** Pamplin Media Group, 6605 S E Lake Rd, Portland, OR 97222. Telephone: 503-684-0360. FAX: 503-620-3433. **Management:** Steve Clark, President. Mark Garber, Publisher. Jennifer Groza, Advertising. Kevin Hohnbaum, Circulation Director. **Editorial:** Tiffany O'Dell, Managing Editor. Kari Hastings, News Editor. David Ball, Sports.

HILLSBORO

HILLSBORO ARGUS. ISSN 8750-5479
150 S.E. Third Ave., Hillsboro, OR 97123-0588. Telephone: 503-648-1131. FAX: 503-648-9191. E-MAIL: clark.gallagher@hillsboroargus.com. URL: http://www.hillsboroargus.com/. Year Established: 1873. Pub. Frequency: s-w. (Tue. & Fir.) Page Size: broadsheet. Subscrip. Rate: $.50 newsstand/cover; $39.95/yr. Adv. Rate: col. inch $17 Circulation: 11,576 per issue (paid). **Owner(s):** The Hillsboro Argus, Inc., See address and contact information above. **Management:** Clark Gallagher, Publisher. Tom Bumstead, Advertising Director. Sandy Grounds, Circulation Manager. **Editorial:** Gary Stutzman, Managing Editor.

WEST VALLEY COURIER. 150 S.E. Third Ave., Hillsboro, OR 97123. Telephone: 503-648-1131. E-MAIL: billriggs@hillsboroargus.com. Year Established: 1965. Pub. Frequency: w. (Wed.) Page Size: broadsheet.Adv. Rate: col. inch $6.25 Circulation: 29,358 per issue (free). **Owner(s):** The Hillsboro Argus, Inc., See address and contact information above. **Management:** Clark Gallagher, General Manager. John Naughton, Advertising Manager. Sandy Grounds, Circulation Manager. **Editorial:** Gary Stutzman, Managing Editor.

HOOD RIVER

HOOD RIVER NEWS. 419 State Ave., Hood River, OR 97031. Telephone: 541-386-1234. FAX: 541-386-6796. E-MAIL: hrnews@hoodrivernews.com. URL: http://www.hoodrivernews.com. Mailing Address: PO Box 390, Hood River, OR 97031. Year Established: 1905. Pub. Frequency: s-w. (Wed. & Sat.) Page Size: broadsheet. Subscrip. Rate: $.75 newsstand/cover; $42/yr in area; $68/yr elsewhere. Circulation: 5,500 per issue (paid). **Owner(s):** Eagle Newspapers, Inc., 4901 Indian School Rd, NE, Salem, OR 97309. Telephone: 503-393-1774. **Management:** Joseph Petshow, Publisher. Joe Deckard, Advertising Manager. Steve Annala, Circulation Manager. **Editorial:** Kirby Neumann-Rea, Editor.

JOHN DAY

BLUE MOUNTAIN EAGLE. 195 N Canyon Blvd, John Day, OR 97845. Telephone: 541-575-0710. FAX: 541-575-1244. E-MAIL: editor@bluemountaineagle.com. URL: http://www.bluemountaineagle.com. Mailing Address: P.O. Box 1089, Pendleton, OR 97801-1089. Year Established: 1898. Pub. Frequency: w. (Wed.) Page Size: broadsheet. Subscrip. Rate: $29/yr home delivery in county; $35/yr mailed in state; $42/yr mailed out of state. Circulation: 2,872 per issue (paid). **Owner(s):** East Oregonian Publishing Co., See address and contact information above. **Management:** Marissa Allen, General Manager. Linda Boyer, Advertising. Brenda Bagett, Classified Editor. **Editorial:** Scotta Callister, Editor. Brenda Bagett, Circulation Editor.

KING CITY

REGAL COURIER. 11735 S W Queen Elizabeth Ave,Ste 106, King City, OR 97224. Telephone: 503-639-5414. FAX: 503-968-7397. Pub. Frequency: m. Subscrip. Rate: $.35 newsstand/cover per issue Circulation: 4,000 per issue (free). **Owner(s):** Pamplin Media Group, 6605 S E Lake Rd, Portland, OR 97222. Telephone: 503-684-0360. FAX: 503-620-3433. **Management:** Steve Clark, President. Deanie Bush, Advertising. Kevin Hohnbaum, Circulation Director. **Editorial:** Bob Schoenberg, Editor. Bill Hunter, Garden Editor.

LAKE OSWEGO

LAKE OSWEGO REVIEW. ISSN 0889-2369
400 Second St, Lake Oswego, OR 97034. Telephone: 503-635-8811. FAX: 503-635-8817. E-MAIL: email@lakeoswegoreview.com. URL: http://www.lakeoswegoreview.com. Year Established: 1936. Pub. Frequency: w. (Thu.) Page Size: standard. Subscrip. Rate: $.75 newsstand/cover; $30/yr in county; $56/yr out of county; $66/yr mailed out of state. Adv. Rate: col. inch $11.95 Circulation: 8,200 per issue (paid). **Owner(s):** Pamplin Media Group, 6605 S E Lake Rd, Portland, OR 97222. Telephone: 503-684-0360. FAX: 503-620-3433. **Management:** J Brian Monihan, Publisher. Christine Moore, Advertising. Kevin Hohnbaum, Circulation Director. Gini Kraemer, Circulation Manager. **Editorial:** Martin Forbes, Editor.

WEST LINN TIDINGS. 400 Second St, Lake Oswego, OR 97034. Telephone: 503-635-8811. FAX: 503-635-8817. E-MAIL: bmonihan@lakeoswegoreview.com. URL: http://www.westlinntidings.com. Year Established: 1981. Pub. Frequency: w. (Thu.) Page Size: broadsheet. Subscrip. Rate: $.75 newsstand/cover; $28/yr mailed local; $48/yr mailed out of area; $60/yr mailed out of state. Adv. Rate: col. inch $10.95 Circulation: 4,300 per issue (paid). **Owner(s):** Pamplin Media Group, 6605 S E Lake Rd, Portland, OR 97222. Telephone: 503-684-0360. FAX: 503-620-3433. **Management:** Steve Clark, President. J Brian Monihan, Publisher. Christine Moore, Advertising. Kevin Hohnbaum, Circulation Director. Gini Kraemer, Circulation Manager. **Editorial:** Bill Stewart, Sports Editor.

LAKEVIEW

LAKE COUNTY EXAMINER. ISSN 1062-5313
739 N. Second St., Lakeview, OR 97630. Telephone: 541-947-3378. FAX: 541-947-4359. E-MAIL: news@lakecountyexam.com. URL: http://www.lakecountyexam.com. Mailing Address: PO Box 271, Lakeview, OR 97630. Year Established: 1880. Pub. Frequency: w. (Wed.) Page Size: broadsheet. Subscrip. Rate: $.50 newsstand/cover; $23/yr mailed in county; $29/yr out of county. Circulation: 2,545 per issue (paid). **Owner(s):** Pioneer Newspapers, See address and contact information above. **Management:** Tillie Flynn, General Manager. **Editorial:** Vickie Clemens, Circulation Editor.

LEBANON

LEBANON EXPRESS. 90 E. Grant St., Lebanon, OR 97355. Telephone: 541-258-3151. FAX: 541-259-3569. E-MAIL: lebanonexpress@lee.net. URL: http://www.lebanonexpress.com. Mailing Address: PO Box 459, Lebanon, OR 97355. Year Established: 1887. Pub. Frequency: w. (Wed.) Page Size: broadsheet. Subscrip. Rate: $.50 newsstand/cover; $24/yr local. Circulation: 3,500 per issue (paid). **Owner(s):** Lee Enterprises, Inc., 215 N. Main St., Davenport, IA 52801. Telephone: 563-383-2100. FAX: 563-323-9608. **Management:** Martha Wells, Publisher. Lise Grato, Advertising Manager. **Editorial:** A. K. Dugan, Editor.

LINCOLN CITY

NEWS GUARD, THE. 930 SE Hwy 101, Lincoln City, OR 97367. Telephone: 541-994-2178. FAX: 541-994-7613. E-MAIL: knewton@orcoastnews.com. URL: http://www.thenewsguard.com. Mailing Address: PO Box 848, Lincoln City, OR 97367-0848. Year Established: 1927. Pub. Frequency: w. (Wed.) Page Size: broadsheet. Subscrip. Rate: $.50 newsstand/cover; $24/yr in county; $36/yr out of county. Adv. Rate: col. inch $10 Circulation: 5,500 per issue (paid). **Owner(s):** Oregon Coast Newspapers, LLC, See address and contact information above. **Management:** Georgia Newton, General Manager. Kathleen Newton, Publisher. Heather Hatton, Advertising Manager. **Editorial:** Joe Happ, Editor. Karen Vittek, Managing Editor. Gary Thain, Sports Editor.

MADRAS

MADRAS PIONEER, THE. 341 SE Fifth St, Madras, OR 97741. Telephone: 541-475-2275. FAX: 541-475-3710. URL: http://www.madraspioneer.com. Year Established: 1904. Pub. Frequency: w. (Wed.) Page Size: standard. Subscrip. Rate: $.50 newsstand/cover; $25/yr in county; $35/yr out of county. Circulation: 4,020 per issue (paid and free). **Owner(s):** Eagle Newspapers, Inc., 4901 Indian School Rd., N.E., Salem, OR 97305. Telephone: 503-393-1774. **Management:** Joy DeHaan, Advertising Manager. Bev Schonneker, Circulation Manager. **Editorial:** Susan Matheny, Editor. Holly Gill, News Editor.

MCMINNVILLE

NEWS-REGISTER. 611 E 3rd St, McMinnville, OR 97128-4518. Telephone: 503-472-5114. FAX: 503-472-9151. E-MAIL: jbladine@newsregister.com. Year Established: 1866. Pub. Frequency: 3/w. (Tue., Thu., Sat.) Page Size: broadsheet. Subscrip. Rate: $.75 newsstand/cover; $18 for 3 mos.; $60/yr. **Wire Service(s):** AP. Circulation: 10,200 per issue (paid). **Owner(s):** Bladine Family, See address and contact information above. **Management:** Guy Everingham, General Manager. Jeb Bladine, Publisher. Christy Nielsen, Advertising Director. **Editorial:** Jeb Bladine, Editor. Steve Bagwell, Managing Editor.

MOLALLA

MOLALLA PIONEER. 217 Main St, Molalla, OR 97033. Telephone: 503-829-2301. FAX: 503-829-2317. URL: http://www.molallapioneer.com. Mailing Address: PO Box 168, Molalla, OR 97033-0168. Year Established: 1913. Pub. Frequency: s-w. (Wed. & Sat.) Page Size: broadsheet. Subscrip. Rate: $.50 newsstand/cover; $36/yr home delivery; $42/yr mailed. **Owner(s):** Eagle Newspapers, Inc., 4901 Indian School Rd, NE, Salem, OR 97309. **Management:** William D Cassel, Publisher. Sandy Storey, Advertising Manager. Bob LaPlace, Circulation Manager. Patsy Lusted, Classified Adv. Mgr.. **Editorial:** Joe Wilson, Editor.

MYRTLE CREEK

DOUGLAS COUNTY MAIL. PO Box 729, Myrtle Creek, OR 97457. Telephone: 541-863-5233. FAX: 541-863-5234. E-MAIL: dcmail@pioneer-net.com. Year Established: 1902. Pub. Frequency: w. (Thu.) Page Size: tabloid. Subscrip. Rate: $.50 newsstand/cover; $20/yr in county; $26/yr out of county. Adv. Rate: col. inch $5.20 Circulation: 3,000 per issue (paid). **Owner(s):** Umpqua Free Press, Inc., See address and contact information above. **Management:** Robert Cheney Sr., Publisher. Angela Caldwell, Advertising. **Editorial:** Steve Wicker, Editor.

NEWBERG

NEWBERG GRAPHIC, THE. 500 E Hancock St, Newberg, OR 97132. Telephone: 503-538-2181. FAX: 503-538-1632. E-MAIL: jpetshow@eaglenewspapers.com. URL: http://www.newberggraphic.com. Mailing Address: PO Box 700, Newberg, OR 97132-0700. Year Established: 1888. Pub. Frequency: s-w. (Wed. & Sat.) Page Size: broadsheet. Subscrip. Rate: $.50 newsstand/cover; $36/yr in county. Adv. Rate: col. inch $10 Circulation: 11,500 per issue (paid and free). **Owner(s):** Eagle Newspapers, Inc., 4901 Indian School Rd., N.E., Salem, OR 97305. Telephone: 503-393-1774. FAX: 503-463-9898. **Management:** Allen Herriges, Publisher. Monty Gant, Advertising Director. Richard Nistler, Circulation Director. Gisele Forrest, Classified Adv. Mgr.. **Editorial:** Allen Herriges, Editor. Gary Allen, News Editor.

NEWPORT

NEWS-TIMES (NEWPORT). 831 N.E. Avery St., Newport, OR 97365. Telephone: 541-265-8571. FAX: 541-265-3103. URL: http://www.newportnewstimes.com. Mailing Address: PO Box 965, Newport, OR 97365. Year Established: 1892. Pub. Frequency: s-w. (Wed. & Fri.) Page Size: standard. Subscrip. Rate: $.50 newsstand/cover; $49/yr mailed in county; $85/yr mailed out of county. Circulation: 10,500 per issue (controlled and free). **Owner(s):** Lee Enterprises, Inc., 201 N. Harrison St., Davenport, IA 52801-1924. **Management:** Mark Bryan, Publisher. Barb Fry, Advertising Manager. **Editorial:** Gail Kimberling, Editor.

PENDLETON

PENDLETON RECORD, THE. 811 S E Court, Pendleton, OR 97801. Telephone: 541-276-2853. FAX: 541-278-2916. E-MAIL: penrecor@uci.net. Mailing Address: PO Box 69, Pendleton, OR 97801-0069. Year Established: 1911. Pub. Frequency: w. (Thu.) Page Size: tabloid. Subscrip. Rate: $.50 newsstand/cover; $25/yr local. Circulation: 1,000 per issue (paid). **Owner(s):** Marguerite Maznaritz, See address and contact information above. **Management:** Marguerite Maznaritz, Publisher. **Editorial:** Marguerite Maznaritz, Editor.

PORTLAND

BEAVERTON VALLEY TIMES. 6605 S E Lake Rd, Portland, OR 97222. Telephone: 503-684-0360. FAX: 503-620-3433. URL: http://www.beavertonvalleytimes.com. Year Established: 1920. Pub. Frequency: w. (Thu.) Page Size: broadsheet. Subscrip. Rate: $.75 newsstand/cover; $30/yr in county; $56/yr out of county; $66/yr out of state. Circulation: 6,600 per issue (paid). **Owner(s):** Pamplin Media Group, See address and contact information above. **Management:** Steve Clark, President. Christine Moore, Advertising. Kevin Hohnbaum, Circulation Director. **Editorial:** Miles Vance, Sports.

BEE (PORTLAND), THE. 1837 S E Harold St., Portland, OR 97202-4932. Telephone: 503-232-2326. FAX: 503-232-9787. E-MAIL: readthebee@myexcel.com. URL: http://www.readthebee.com. Year Established: 1906. Pub. Frequency: m. Page Size: tabloid. Subscrip. Rate: $14/yr mailed in county; $24/yr mailed elsewhere. Adv. Rate: col. inch $23 Circulation: 19,500 per issue (paid and free). **Owner(s):** Pamplin Media Group, 6605 S E Lake Rd, Portland, OR 97222. Telephone: 503-684-0360. FAX: 503-620-3433. **Management:** Eric Norberg, General Manager. Steve Clark, President. J Brian Monihan, Publisher. Kevin Hohnbaum, Circulation Director. **Editorial:** Eric Norberg, Editor.Readers: Everyone in Inner Southeast Portland, Oregon

CLACKAMAS REVIEW. 6605 S E Lake Rd, Portland, OR 97222. Telephone: 503-684-0360. FAX: 503-620-3433. E-MAIL: editor@clackamasrevier.com. URL: http://www.clackamasreview.com. Year Established: 1922. Pub. Frequency: w. (Wed.) Page Size: tabloid. Subscrip. Rate: $.50 newsstand/cover; $24/yr in county. Circulation: 80,000 per issue (paid and free). **Owner(s):** Pamplin Media Group, See address and contact information above. **Management:** Steve Clark, President. Angela Fox, Publisher. Gini Kraemer, Circulation Manager. **Editorial:** Anthony Roberts, Editor. Matthew Graham, Associate Editor. John Denny, Sports Editor.

OREGON CITY NEWS. 6605 S E Lake Rd, Portland, OR 97222. Telephone: 503-684-0360. FAX: 503-620-3433. E-MAIL: editor@clackamasreview.com. URL: http://www.oregoncitynewsonline.com. Pub. Frequency: w. (Wed.) Page Size: tabloid. Subscrip. Rate: $.50 newsstand/cover; $24/yr in county; $44/yr out of county; $56/yr mailed out of state. Adv. Rate: page $20 Circulation: 8,000 per issue (paid and free). **Owner(s):** Pamplin Media Group, See address and contact information above. **Management:** Steve Clark, President. Angela Fox, Publisher. Kathy Schaub, Advertising. Kevin Hohnbaum, Circulation Director. Gini Kraemer, Circulation Manager. **Editorial:** Anthony Roberts, Editor. Matthew Graham, Associate Editor. John Denny, Sports Editor.

PORTLAND TRIBUNE. 6605 S E Lake Rd, Portland, OR 97222. Telephone: 503-684-0360. FAX: 503-620-3433. URL: http://www.portlandtribune.com. Pub. Frequency: w. (Thu.) Page Size: standard.Subscrip. Rate: $40/yr mailed Circulation: 80,000 per issue (paid). **Owner(s):** Pamplin Media Group, See address and contact information above. **Management:** Steve Clark, President. Jill Weisensee, Advertising Director. Kevin Hohnbaum, Circulation Director. **Editorial:** Steve Brandon, Sports.

SHERWOOD GAZETTE. 6605 S E Lake Rd, Portland, OR 97222. Telephone: 503-684-0360. FAX: 503-620-3433. E-MAIL: email@sherwoodgazette.com. URL: http://www.sherwoodgazette.com.Pub. Frequency: m. Page Size: broadsheet Circulation: 6,000 per issue (free). **Owner(s):** Pamplin Media Group, See address and contact information above. **Management:** Steve Clark, President. Christine Moore, Advertising. Kim Stephens, Circulation Manager. **Editorial:** Kelly Moyer, Editor. Nick Peterson, Managing Editor.

SOUTHWEST COMMUNITY CONNECTION. 6605 S E Lake Rd, Portland, OR 97222. Telephone: 503-684-0360. FAX: 503-620-3433. URL: http://www.swcommconnection.com. Pub. Frequency: m. (1st. of mo.) Page Size: tabloid Circulation: 11,000 per issue (free). **Owner(s):** Pamplin Media Group, See address and contact information above. **Management:** Steve Clark, President. J Brian Monihan, Publisher. Shelley Casley, Advertising. Kevin Hohnbaum, Circulation Director. **Editorial:** Jessie Kirk, Editor.

ST. JOHNS REVIEW. 2209 N. Schofield, Portland, OR 97217-8195. Telephone: 503-283-5086. FAX: 503-735-1446. E-MAIL: Reviewnewspaper@comcast.net. Year Established: 1904. Pub. Frequency: bi-w. (Fri.) Page Size: tabloid Subscrip. Rate: $12/yr Circulation: 3,500 per issue (paid). **Owner(s):** Gayla Patton, 2209 N. Schofield, Portland, OR 97172-8195. Telephone: 503-283-5086. FAX: 503-735-1446. **Management:** Gayla Patton, Publisher.

TIMES, THE. 6605 S E Lake Rd, Portland, OR 97222. Telephone: 503-684-0360. FAX: 503-620-3433. URL: http://www.tigardtimes.com. Pub. Frequency: w. (Thu.) Page Size: broadsheet. Subscrip. Rate: $.75 newsstand/cover; $30/yr in county; $56/yr out of county; $66/yr mailed out of state. Circulation: 4,800 per issue (paid). **Owner(s):** Pamplin Media Group, See address and contact information above. **Management:** Steve Clark, President. Kevin Hohnbaum, Circulation Director. **Editorial:** Dan Brood, Sports.

TUALATIN TIMES. 6605 S E Lake Rd, Portland, OR 97222. Telephone: 503-684-0360. FAX: 503-620-3433. E-MAIL: mkelly@commnewspapers.com. URL: http://www.tualatintimes.com. Year Established: 1956. Pub. Frequency: w. (Thu.) Page Size: broadsheet. Subscrip. Rate: $.75 newsstand/cover; $30/yr in county; $56/yr out of county; $66/yr mailed out of state. Circulation: 3,300 per issue (paid). **Owner(s):** Pamplin Media Group, See address and contact information above. **Management:** Steve Clark, President. Christine Moore, Advertising. Kevin Hohnbaum, Circulation Director. **Editorial:** Dan Brood, Sports.

WILLAMETTE WEEK. 2220 N.W. Quimby St., Portland, OR 97210-2624. Telephone: 503-243-2122. FAX: 503-243-1115. E-MAIL: rmeeker@wweek.com. URL: http://www.wweek.com. Year Established: 1974. Pub. Frequency: w. (Wed.) Page Size: tabloid. Subscrip. Rate: $90/yr mailed 3rd class; $180/yr mailed 1st class. Circulation: 90,000 per issue (paid and free). **Owner(s):** City of Roses Newspaper Co., See address and contact information above. **Management:** Richard H. Meeker, Publisher. Jane Smith-McClaskey, Advertising Manager. Robert Lehrkind, Circulation Director. Maria Perry, Classified Adv. Mgr.. **Editorial:** Mark L Zusman, Editor. Henry Stern, News Editor.

PRINEVILLE

CENTRAL OREGONIAN, THE. 558 N. Main St., Prineville, OR 97754-1199. Telephone: 541-447-6205. FAX: 503-447-1754. E-MAIL: wschaffer@eaglenewspapers.com. URL: http://www.centraloregonian.com. Year Established: 1882. Pub. Frequency: s-w. (Tue. & Fri.) Page Size: broadsheet. Subscrip. Rate: $.50 newsstand/cover; $33/yr carrier delivery; $41/yr mailed in Crook & Wheeler cys.. Adv. Rate: col. inch $8 Freelance Pay: $0.25/column-inch. Circulation: 4,650 per issue (paid). **Owner(s):** Eagle Newspapers, Inc., 4901 Indian School Rd., N.E., Salem, OR 97305. Telephone: 503-393-1774. **Management:** Vance Tong, Publisher. Teresa Tooley, Advertising Manager. Patricia McManus, Classified Adv. Mgr.. **Editorial:** Vance Tong, Editor. Shelby Case, Associate Editor.

REDMOND

REDMOND SPOKESMAN. 226 N. Sixth St., Redmond, OR 97756. Telephone: 541-548-2184. FAX: 541-548-3203. E-MAIL: news@redmondspokesman.com, classified@redmondspokesman.com. Mailing Address: PO Box 788, Redmond, OR 97756. Year Established: 1910. Pub. Frequency: w. (Wed.) Page Size: broadsheet. Subscrip. Rate: $.35 newsstand/cover; $20/yr mailed in state; $36/yr mailed out of state. Freelance Pay: $1.50/column-inch. Circulation: 5,100 per issue (paid). **Owner(s):** Western Communication, Inc., 1777 S.W. Chandler Ave., Bend, OR 97702. Telephone: 541-382-1811. FAX: 541-383-0372. **Management:** Gary Husman, Publisher. Denise Duval, Advertising Manager. Nancy Povey, Circulation Manager. **Editorial:** Leslie Hole, Editor.

REEDSPORT

UMPQUA POST, THE. 495 Fir Ave., Reedsport, OR 97467. Telephone: 541-271-7474. FAX: 541-271-6855. Pub. Frequency: w. (Wed.) Page Size: standard. Subscrip. Rate: $.50 newsstand/cover; $22/yr in county; $35/yr mailed out of county. Circulation: 1,900 per issue (paid). **Owner(s):** Lee Enterprises, Inc., 201 N Harrison St, Davenport, IA 52801-1939. Telephone: 563-383-2100. **Management:** Greg Stevens, Publisher. Julie Cummings, Advertising Manager. Peggy Roberson, Classified Adv. Mgr.. **Editorial:** Kathy Erickson, Executive Editor. Rick Osborn, Managing Editor.

ROGUE RIVER

ROGUE RIVER PRESS. 211 Pine St., Rogue River, OR 97537. Telephone: 541-582-1707. FAX: 541-582-0201. E-MAIL: rrpress@rogueriverpress.com. URL: http://www.rogueriverpress.com. Year Established: 1962. Pub. Frequency: w. (Wed.) Page Size: tabloid. Subscrip. Rate: $.50 newsstand/cover; $19/yr in county; $29/yr out of county. Adv. Rate: col. inch $5.50 Circulation: 2,000 per issue (paid and free). **Owner(s):** River Press Publishing, Inc., See address and contact information above. **Management:** Dave Ehrhardt, Publisher. **Editorial:** Dave Ehrhardt, Editor-in-Chief.

SALEM

HERMISTON HERALD, THE. PO Box 2048, Salem, OR 97308. Telephone: 503-364-4431. URL: http://www.hermistonherald.com. Year Established: 1906. Pub. Frequency: s-w. (Wed. & Fri.) Page Size: broadsheet. Subscrip. Rate: $.50 newsstand/cover; $31.25/yr mailed in county; $42.50/yr out of county. **Wire Service(s):** AP. Circulation: 3,100 per issue (paid). **Owner(s):** East Oregonian Publishing Co., See address and contact information above. Western Communication, Inc., 333 E. Main St., Hermiston, OR 97838. **Management:** Jeanne Hoffman, General Manager. Deb Sampson, Circulation Manager. **Editorial:** Dean Brickey, Editor. Daniel Wattenburger, Sports Editor.

SANDY

SANDY POST. 39110 Proctor Blvd, Ste B, Sandy, OR 97055. Telephone: 503-668-5548. FAX: 503-668-0748. E-MAIL: postnews@aol.com. URL: http://www.sandypost.com. Pub. Frequency: w. (Wed.) Page Size: standard. Subscrip. Rate: $.50 newsstand/cover; $22/yr mailed in county; $40/yr mailed out of county; $52/yr mailed out of state. Circulation: 3,000 per issue (paid). **Owner(s):** Pamplin Media Group, 6605 S E Lake Rd, Portland, OR 97222. Telephone: 503-684-0360. FAX: 503-620-3433. **Management:** Steve Clark, President. Mark Garber, Publisher. Jennifer Groza, Advertising. Kevin Hohnbaum, Circulation Director. Ryan McVicker, Circulation Manager. **Editorial:** Marcus Hathcock, Editor. Michael Cade, Sports.

SEASIDE

SEASIDE SIGNAL. 1555 Roosevelt, Seaside, OR 97138. Telephone: 503-738-5561. FAX: 503-738-5672. E-MAIL: signaleditor@seasidesignal.com. URL: http://www.seasidesignal.com. Year Established: 1905. Pub. Frequency: w. (Thu.) Page Size: tabloid. Subscrip. Rate: $.50 newsstand/cover; $26/yr in county. Freelance Pay: $1/column-inch. Circulation: 3,200 per issue (paid). **Owner(s):** Pacific Coast Newspapers, Inc., See address and contact information above. **Management:** Jesse J. Mullen, Publisher. Ane McIntyre, Advertising. **Editorial:** Katherine Head, Editor.

SILVERTON

APPEAL TRIBUNE. 399 S Water St., Silverton, OR 97381. Telephone: 503-873-8385. FAX: 503-873-8064. E-MAIL: sanews@sales.gannett.com. URL: http://www.silvertonappeal.com. Mailing Address: PO Box 35, Silverton, OR 97381. Year Established: 1880. Pub. Frequency: w. (Wed.) Page Size: standard. Subscrip. Rate: $.50 newsstand/cover; $21/yr carrier delivery in county; $27/yr mailed in county; $30/yr mailed out of county. Freelance Pay: $1-$1.50/column-inch. Circulation: 7,800 per issue (paid and free). **Owner(s):** Gannett Company, Inc., 7950 Jones Branch Dr., McLean, VA 22107-0001. Telephone: 703-854-6000. **Management:** Steve Silberman, Publisher. Patrick McKenzie, Advertising. Jennine Perkinson, Advertising Director. Art Hyson, Circulation Manager. Valerie Thorne, Classified Adv. Mgr..

SPRINGFIELD

▼**SPRINGFIELD TIMES.** 741 Main St, Springfield, OR 97477. Telephone: 541-741-7368. FAX: 541-741-7380. URL: http://www.springfieldtimes.net/. Year Established: 2009. Pub. Frequency: w. Subscrip. Rate: $24/yr mailed; $28/yr mailed out of county; $32/yr mailed out of state. **Owner(s):** S J Olson Publishing, Inc., See address and contact information above. **Management:** Scott Olson, Publisher. **Editorial:** Craig Murphy, Editor.

ST. HELENS

CHRONICLE AND SENTINEL -MIST. 195 S.15th St., St. Helens, OR 97051. E-MAIL: news@thechronicleonline.com. Mailing Address: P.O. Box 1153, ST. Helens, OR 97051. Year Established: 1881. Pub. Frequency: s-w. (Wed. & Sat.) Page Size: standard. Subscrip. Rate: $.50 newsstand/cover; $24/yr in county; $31/yr mailed out of county; $35/yr mailed out of state. Circulation: 17,900 per issue (paid and free). **Owner(s):** Parsons Associates, Inc., See address and contact information above. **Management:** Pamela Petersen, Publisher. **Editorial:** Brian Stimson, Editor.

STAYTON

STAYTON MAIL, THE. P.O. Box 400, Stayton, OR 97383. Telephone: 503-769-6338. FAX: 503-769-6207. URL: http://www.staytonmail.com. Year Established: 1892. Pub. Frequency: w. (Wed.) Page Size: broadsheet. Subscrip. Rate: $.50 newsstand/cover; $21/yr carrier delivery; $27/yr mailed in county; $30/yr mailed out of county. Freelance Pay: $1-$1.50/column-inch. Circulation: 3,250 per issue (paid). **Owner(s):** Statesman Journal, 280 N. Church St., Salem, OR 22234. Telephone: 503-399-6611. **Management:** Patrick McKenzie, Advertising. Jennine Perkonson, Advertising Director. Art Hyson, Circulation Manager. **Editorial:** Don Currie, Editor. Pete Martini, Sports Editor.

SWEET HOME

NEW ERA, THE. 1313 Main St., Sweet Home, OR 97386. Telephone: 541-367-2135. FAX: 541-367-2137. E-MAIL: scott@sweethomenews.com. URL: http://www.sweethomenews.com. Mailing Address: PO Box 39, Sweet Home, OR 97386. Year Established: 1929. Pub. Frequency: w. (Wed.) Page Size: broadsheet. Subscrip. Rate: $.50 newsstand/cover; $25/yr mailed in county; $31/yr mailed out of county. Circulation: 8,000 per issue (paid). **Owner(s):** Scott & Miriam Swanson, See address and contact information above. **Management:** Scott Swanson, Publisher. Miriam Swanson, Advertising Director. Friel Severns, Classified Adv. Mgr.. **Editorial:** Scott Swanson, Editor-in-Chief.

TILLAMOOK

HEADLIGHT HERALD. 1908 Second, Tillamook, OR 97141. Telephone: 503-842-7535. FAX: 503-842-8842. E-MAIL: headlightherald@orcoastnews.com. URL: http://www.tillamookheadlightherald.com. Year Established: 1888. Pub. Frequency: w. (Wed.) Page Size: broadsheet. Subscrip. Rate: $.50 newsstand/cover; $28/yr mailed in county; $36/yr mailed out of county. Freelance Pay: $0.25/column-inch. Circulation: 9,000 per issue (paid). **Owner(s):** Oregon Coast Newspapers, LLC, See address and contact information above. **Management:** Kathleen Newton, Publisher. Letha Blair, Advertising. Judy Pullen, Circulation Manager. **Editorial:** Joe Happ, Editor. Ken O'Toole, Managing Editor. Linda Ediger, Community Editor. Michael O'Brien, Sports Editor.

VALE

MALHEUR ENTERPRISE. PO Box 310, Vale, OR 97918. Telephone: 541-473-3377. FAX: 541-473-3268. E-MAIL: malent@micron.net. Mailing Address: PO Box 310, Vale, OR 97918-0310. Year Established: 1909. Pub. Frequency: w. (Wed.) Page Size: broadsheet. Subscrip. Rate: $.60 newsstand/cover; $23/yr in county; $33/yr out of county. Circulation: 2,350 per issue (paid). **Owner(s):** Julie Schaffeld, See address and contact information above. **Management:** Julie Schaffeld, Publisher. **Editorial:** Rachel Haueter, Editor.

WILSONVILLE

WILSONVILLE SPOKESMAN. 30250 SW Pkwy Ave., Wilsonville, OR 97070. Telephone: 503-682-3935. FAX: 503-682-6265. URL: http://www.canbyherald.com. Pub. Frequency: w. (Wed.) Page Size: standard. Subscrip. Rate: $.50 newsstand/cover; $24/yr mailed. Adv. Rate: col. inch $5.75 Circulation: 4,300 per issue (paid). **Owner(s):** Eagle Newspapers, Inc., 4901 Indian School Rd., N.E., Salem, OR 97305. Telephone: 503-393-1774. FAX: 503-463-9898. **Management:** William D Cassel, Publisher. Kim Mahar, Advertising. **Editorial:** Kurt Kipp, Editor.

WOODBURN

WOODBURN INDEPENDENT. 650 N First, Woodburn, OR 97071. Telephone: 503-981-3441. FAX: 503-981-1253. URL: http://www.woodburnindependent.com. Mailing Address: PO Box 97, Woodburn, OR 97071. Year Established: 1888. Pub. Frequency: s-w. (Wed. & Sat.) Page Size: standard. Subscrip. Rate: $.50 newsstand/cover; $36/yr home delivery in area; $42/yr mailed out of area. Circulation: 4,200 per issue (paid). **Owner(s):** Eagle Newspapers, Inc., 4901 Indian School Rd., N.E., Salem, OR 97305. Telephone: 503-393-1774. FAX: 503-463-9898. **Management:** Les Reitan, Publisher. Nikki DeBuse, Advertising Manager. Gerry Adams, Circulation Manager. Susie Singletary, Classified Adv. Mgr.. **Editorial:** John Baker, News Editor.

PENNSYLVANIA

ALBION

ALBION NEWS, THE. 16 Market St., Albion, PA 16401. Telephone: 814-756-4133. FAX: 814-756-5643. E-MAIL: news@albionnews.com. URL: http://www.gazettenewspapers.com. Mailing Address: PO Box 166, Jefferson, OH 44047-0166. Year Established: 1901. Pub. Frequency: w. (Wed.) Page Size: tabloid. Subscrip. Rate: $.50 newsstand/cover; $26/yr in area; $42/yr out of area. Circulation: 3,500 per issue (paid). **Owner(s):** Gazette Newspapers, 46 W Jefferson St, Jefferson, OH 44047. Telephone: 440-576-9115. FAX: 440-576-2735. **Management:** Bill Creed, General Manager. John Lampson, Publisher. **Editorial:** Sean Ratican, Editor.

EDINBORO NEWS, THE. 16 Market St., Albion, PA 16401. Telephone: 814-756-4133. FAX: 814-756-5643. URL: http://www.gazettenewspapers.com. Mailing Address: PO Box 166, Jefferson, OH 44047-0166. Pub. Frequency: w. (Wed.) Subscrip. Rate: $.50 newsstand/cover (effective 2007); $26/yr in county. Adv. Rate: col. inch $12.94 Circulation: 3,100 per issue (paid). **Owner(s):** Gazette Newspapers, 46 W Jefferson St, Jefferson, OH 44047. Telephone: 440-576-9115. FAX: 440-576-2735. **Management:** Bill Creed, General Manager. John Lampson, Publisher. Cheryl Copeland, Circulation Manager.

ALLENTOWN

EAST PENN PRESS. 1633 N. 26th St., Allentown, PA 18104. Telephone: 610-740-0944. FAX: 610-740-0947. E-MAIL: eppubl@ptd.net. URL: http://www.tnonline.com. Year Established: 1959. Pub. Frequency: w. (Wed.) Page Size: broadsheet. Subscrip. Rate: $.50 newsstand/cover per issue; $23.40/yr mailed in county; $31.20/yr mailed out of county. Adv. Rate: col. inch $5.10 Circulation: 7,000 per issue (paid and free). **Owner(s):** Pencor Co., 613 Third St., Palmerton, PA 18071. Telephone: 215-826-2115. FAX: 215-826-7626. **Management:** Fred Masenheimer, Publisher. Donald Reese, Advertising Director. Peg Stocking, Advertising Manager. Kathy Carpenter, Circulation Manager. Kim Silliman, Classified Adv. Mgr.. **Editorial:** Corrine Durdock, Editor. Robert Urban, Managing Editor.

NORTHAMPTON PRESS. 1633 N. 26th St., Allentown, PA 18104. Telephone: 610-740-0944. FAX: 610-740-0947. E-MAIL: eppubl@ptd.net. URL: http://www.tnonline.com. Year Established: 1998. Pub. Frequency: w. (Thu.) Page Size: broadsheet. Subscrip. Rate: $.50 newsstand/cover; $23.40/yr in county; $31.20/yr out of county. Adv. Rate: col. inch $5.10 Circulation: 4,400 per issue (controlled and free). **Owner(s):** Pencor Co., 613 Third St., Palmerton, PA 18071. Telephone: 610-826-2115. FAX: 610-826-7626. **Management:** Scott Masenheimer, General Manager. Fred Masenheimer, Publisher. Donald Reese, Advertising Director. Peg Stocking, Advertising Manager. Kim Silliman, Classified Adv. Mgr.. **Editorial:** Kelly Lutterschmidt, Editor. Robert Urban, Managing Editor.

Weeklies

NORTHWESTERN PRESS. 1633 N. 26th St., Allentown, PA 18104. Telephone: 610-740-0944. FAX: 610-740-0947. E-MAIL: eppubl@ptd.net. URL: http://www.tnonline.com. Year Established: 1994. Pub. Frequency: w. (Thu.) Page Size: broadsheet. Subscrip. Rate: $.50 newsstand/cover; $23.40/yr in county; $31.20/yr mailed out of county. Adv. Rate: col. inch $5.10 Circulation: 72,000 per issue (controlled and free). **Owner(s):** Pencor Co., 613 Third St., Palmerton, PA 18071. Telephone: 610-826-2115. FAX: 215-826-7626. **Management:** Scott Masenheimer, General Manager. Fred Masenheimer, Publisher. Donald Reese, Advertising Director. Peg Stocking, Advertising Manager. Kim Silliman, Classified Adv. Mgr.. **Editorial:** Debbie Palmeri, Editor. Robert Urban, Managing Editor.

PARKLAND PRESS. 1633 N. 26th St., Allentown, PA 18104. Telephone: 610-740-0944. FAX: 610-740-0947. E-MAIL: eppubl@ptd.net. URL: http://www.tnonline.com. Year Established: 1989. Pub. Frequency: w. (Thu.) Page Size: broadsheet. Subscrip. Rate: $.50 newsstand/cover; $23.40/yr in county; $31.20/yr out of county. Adv. Rate: col. inch $5.10 Circulation: 7,200 per issue (controlled and free). **Owner(s):** Pencor Co., 613 Third St., Palmerton, PA 18071. Telephone: 610-826-2115. FAX: 610-826-7626. **Management:** Fred Masenheimer, Publisher. Donald Reese, Advertising Director. Peg Stocking, Advertising Manager. Kim Silliman, Classified Adv. Mgr.. **Editorial:** Debbie Palmeri, Editor. Robert Urban, Managing Editor.

SALISBURY PRESS. 1633 N. 26th St., Allentown, PA 18104. Telephone: 610-740-0944. FAX: 610-740-0947. URL: http://www.tnonline.com. Pub. Frequency: w. (Wed.) Page Size: broadsheet. Subscrip. Rate: $.50 newsstand/cover; $23.40/yr in county; $31.20/yr mailed out of county. Adv. Rate: col. inch $9.25 Circulation: 4,000 per issue (paid). **Owner(s):** Pencor Co., 613 Third St., Palmerton, PA 18071. Telephone: 610-826-2115. FAX: 610-826-7626. **Management:** Fred Masenheimer, Publisher. Donald Reese, Advertising Director. Peg Stocking, Advertising Manager. Kim Silliman, Classified Adv. Mgr.. **Editorial:** Corrine Durdock, Editor. Robert Urban, Managing Editor.

WHITEHALL-COPLAY PRESS. 1633 N. 26th St., Allentown, PA 18104. E-MAIL: eppubl@ptd.net. URL: http://www.tnonline.com. Year Established: 1992. Pub. Frequency: w. (Wed.) Page Size: broadsheet. Subscrip. Rate: $.50 newsstand/cover; $23.40/yr in county; $31.20/yr mailed out of county. Adv. Rate: col. inch $5.10 Circulation: 4,400 per issue (controlled and free). **Owner(s):** Pencor Co., 613 Third St., Palmerton, PA 18071. Telephone: 610-826-2115. FAX: 610-826-7626. **Management:** Scott Masenheimer, General Manager. Fred Masenheimer, Publisher. Peg Stocking, Advertising Manager. Kim Silliman, Classified Adv. Mgr.. **Editorial:** Kelly Lutterschmidt, Editor.

ARDMORE

MAIN LINE TIMES. 311 E Lancaster Ave, Ardmore, PA 19003. Telephone: 610-642-4300. FAX: 610-449-0419. E-MAIL: advertising@mainlinetimes.com. URL: http://www.mainlinetimes.com. Year Established: 1930. Pub. Frequency: w. (Thu.) Page Size: broadsheet. Subscrip. Rate: $.50 newsstand/cover (effective 2007); $37.40/yr carrier delivery (effective 2006); $45.20/yr mailed in state; $50/yr mailed out of state. Circulation: 16,800 per issue (controlled and free). **Owner(s):** Journal Register Co., 50 W State St, 12th Fl, Trenton, NJ 08608. Telephone: 609-396-2200. FAX: 609-396-2292. **Management:** Dianne Ryan-Paschall, Publisher. Adam Chylinski, Circulation Manager. Pat Collins, Classified Adv. Mgr.. **Editorial:** Susan Greenspon, Managing Editor.

BOYERTOWN

BOYERTOWN AREA TIMES. 124 N. Chestnut St., Boyertown, PA 19512. Telephone: 610-367-6041. FAX: 610-369-0233. URL: http://www.berksmontnews.com. Year Established: 1857. Pub. Frequency: w. (Thu.) Page Size: broadsheet. Subscrip. Rate: $.50 newsstand/cover; $26/yr. Circulation: 6,482 per issue (paid and free). **Owner(s):** Berks-Mont Newspapers, Inc., See address and contact information above. **Management:** James C Webb, Publisher. John Varady, Advertising Manager. **Editorial:** Rebecca Erdman, Editor. Eric Webb, Sports Editor.

SOUTHERN BERKS NEWS, THE. 124 N. Chestnut St., Boyertown, PA 19512. Telephone: 610-367-6041. FAX: 610-369-0233. E-MAIL: editor@berksmostnews.com. URL: http://www.berksmontnews.com. Mailing Address: P.O. Box 565, Boyertown, PA 19512. Year Established: 1885. Pub. Frequency: w. (Wed.) Page Size: broadsheet. Subscrip. Rate: $25/yr home delivery. Circulation: 5,500 per issue (paid and free). **Owner(s):** Berks-Mont Newspapers, Inc., See address and contact information above. **Management:** James Davidheiser, General Manager. James C Webb, Publisher. John Varady, Advertising Manager. **Editorial:** Rebecca Erdman, Editor.

BRADFORD

BRADFORD JOURNAL/MINER. PO Box 17, Bradford, PA 16701-0017. Telephone: 814-362-6563. FAX: 814-465-3468. E-MAIL: bradfordjournal@gmail.com. URL: http://www.bradfordjournal.com. Year Established: 1832. Pub. Frequency: w. (Thu.) Page Size: tabloid. Subscrip. Rate: $1 newsstand/cover; $36.50/yr local (effective 2008); $49.50/yr out of county. Adv. Rate: col. inch $8.32 Circulation: 5,500 per issue (paid). **Owner(s):** Grant & Debra Nichols, 265 South Ave, Bradford, PA 16701. 69 Garlock Hollow, Bradford, PA 16701. **Editorial:** Debra Nichols, Editor.

BRISTOL

BRISTOL PILOT. 220 Radcliffe St., Bristol, PA 19007. Telephone: 215-788-1682. FAX: 215-788-6328. E-MAIL: pilot@ingnews.com. URL: http://www.bristolpilot.com. Mailing Address: PO Box 232, Bristol, PA 19007. Year Established: 1986. Pub. Frequency: w. (Thu.) Page Size: tabloid. Subscrip. Rate: $.50 newsstand/cover; $16/yr mailed; $13/yr mailed to senior citizens. Circulation: 7,200 per issue (paid). **Owner(s):** Journal Register Co., 50 W State St, 12th Fl, Trenton, NJ 08608. Telephone: 609-396-2200. FAX: 609-396-2292. **Management:** Stephanie Leicht, Publisher. Bob McCarron, Advertising Manager. Ed Krywucki, Circulation Manager. **Editorial:** Tim Chicirda, Editor.

BROOKVILLE

JEFFERSONIAN DEMOCRAT. 301 Main St., Brookville, PA 15825. Telephone: 814-849-5339. FAX: 814-849-4333g. E-MAIL: jeffdem@alltell.net. Year Established: 1839. Pub. Frequency: w. (Thu.) Page Size: broadsheet. Subscrip. Rate: $.60 newsstand/cover; $32.95/yr mailed in state; $39.95/yr mailed out of state. Circulation: 4,000 per issue (paid). **Owner(s):** Independent Publications, Inc., See address and contact information above. **Management:** Bill McClean, President. Dennis Bonavita, Publisher. Ann Speer, Advertising. Jim Nestlerode, Circulation Manager. Denise Foelkrod, Classified Adv. Mgr.. **Editorial:** Randy Bartley, Editor. Patty Slaughter, Lifestyle Editor. Mike Carnhonan, Sports.

CANTON

CANTON INDEPENDENT-SENTINEL. 4 W. Main St., Canton, PA 17724. Telephone: 570-673-5151. FAX: 570-673-5152. E-MAIL: cisnews@frontiernet.net. URL: http://www.thecantonsentinel.com. Mailing Address: PO Box 128, Canton, PA 17724-0128. Year Established: 1871. Pub. Frequency: w. (Thu.) Page Size: broadsheet. Subscrip. Rate: $.75 newsstand/cover; $30/yr area; $33/yr mailed in state; $38/yr mailed out of state. Adv. Rate: col. inch $4 Circulation: 2,700 per issue (paid and free). **Owner(s):** John Shaffer, 62 W. Union St., Canton, PA 17724. Telephone: 570-673-4296. **Management:** John Shaffer, Publisher. Jane Riggs, Advertising Manager. Lois Shaffer, Business Manager. **Editorial:** John Shaffer, Editor-in-Chief. Andrea Sutton, News Editor.

CARBONDALE

CARBONDALE NEWS, THE. ISSN 0746-3510
41 N. Church St., Carbondale, PA 18407. Telephone: 570-282-3300. FAX: 570-282-3950. E-MAIL: cdaleads@echoes.net. Year Established: 1872. Pub. Frequency: w. (Wed.) Page Size: broadsheet. Subscrip. Rate: $.75 newsstand/cover; $30/yr. Adv. Rate: col. inch $7.28 Circulation: 4,400 per issue (paid). **Owner(s):** GateHouse Media, Inc, 350 WillowBrook Office Park, Fairport, NY 14450. Telephone: 585-598-0030. FAX: 585-248-2631. **Management:** Michelle Hessling, Publisher. Stacey Tierney, Office Manager. Crystal Chiricos, Advertising. Jeri Hancock, Circulation Manager. **Editorial:** Tom Fontana, Editor.

CARLISLE

SENTINEL (CARLISLE), THE. 457 E. North St., Carlisle, PA 17013. Telephone: 717-243-2611. FAX: 717-243-3121. URL: http://www.cumberlink.com. Mailing Address: PO Box 130, Carlisle, PA 17013. Pub. Frequency: d. Page Size: standard. Subscrip. Rate: $.50 newsstand/cover; $1 newsstand/cover Sun.; $13 home delivery/mo.. Circulation: 13,500 morning (paid); 15,448 Sunday (paid); 15,536 per issue (paid). **Owner(s):** Lee Enterprises, Inc., 201 N. Harrison St., Davenport, IA 52801-1924. **Management:** Carol Talley, Publisher. Sean Spielvogel, Circulation Manager. Scott Barlup, Sales Manager. **Editorial:** Hope Stephan, Executive Editor.

CLARION

CLARION (PA) NEWS. 645 Main St., Clarion, PA 16214-0647. Telephone: 814-226-7000. FAX: 814-226-7518. E-MAIL: mllogue@theclarionnews.com. URL: http://www.theclarionnews.com. Year Established: 1841. Pub. Frequency: s-w. (Tue. & Thu.) Page Size: broadsheet. Subscrip. Rate: $.50 newsstand/cover; $34.32/yr home delivery. Adv. Rate: col. inch $11.16 Circulation: 6,924 per issue (paid). **Owner(s):** Western Penn Newspapers, 645 Main St., Clarion, PA 16214. Telephone: 814-226-7000. **Management:** Patrick C. Boyle, Publisher. Mary Louise Logue, Advertising Manager. Jeff McLaughlin, Circulation Manager. **Editorial:** Rodney Sherman, Editor. Jeff Say, Sports Editor.

CLARKS SUMMIT

JOURNAL (ABINGTON), THE. ISSN 1931-8871
211 S. State St., Clarks Summit, PA 18411. Telephone: 570-587-1148. FAX: 570-586-3980. Year Established: 1929. Pub. Frequency: w. (Wed.) Page Size: broadsheet.Subscrip. Rate: $.50 newsstand/cover; $20/yr Circulation: 3,800 per issue (paid). **Owner(s):** Knight Ridder, Inc., 50 W. San Fernando St., Ste. 1200, San Jose, CA 95113. Telephone: 408-938-7700, 831-938-7777. **Management:** Julie Imel, General Manager.

CLAYSVILLE

WEEKLY RECORDER, THE. PO Box F, Claysville, PA 15323-0506. Telephone: 724-663-7742. FAX: 724-663-3698. E-MAIL: recorder@pulsenet.com. Year Established: 1888. Pub. Frequency: w. (Fri.) Page Size: tabloid. Subscrip. Rate: $.75 newsstand/cover; $30/yr mailed in state; $32/yr mailed elsewhere. Freelance Pay: $15/story. Circulation: 3,200 per issue (paid). **Owner(s):** Weekly Recorder, See address and contact information above. **Management:** Cody Knotts, Publisher. Joanne Knotts, Advertising Manager. **Editorial:** Cody Knotts, Editor.

COCHRANTON

AREA SHOPPER. 1477 Rt. 19, Cochranton, PA 16314. Telephone: 814-425-7272. FAX: 814-425-7311. Year Established: 1953. Pub. Frequency: w. (Sat.) Page Size: standard Circulation: 75,000 per issue (paid). **Owner(s):** Miller Printing & Publishing Co., Inc., See address and contact information above. **Management:** Brian Miller, Publisher. **Editorial:** Brian Miller, Editor.

COLUMBIA

COLUMBIA LEDGER. 243 Locust St., Columbia, PA 17512. Telephone: 717-684-0687. FAX: 717-684-4121. URL: http://www.chronicleledgernewsgroup.com. Year Established: 1991. Pub. Frequency: w. (Thu.) Page Size: broadsheet.Subscrip. Rate: $.50 newsstand/cover; $20.95/yr Circulation: 3,500 per issue (paid). **Owner(s):** Journal Register Co., 50 W State St, 12th Fl, Trenton, NJ 08608. Telephone: 609-396-2200. **Management:** Edward S. Condra, Publisher. Dick Carrigan, Advertising Director. Teresa Pennington, Classified Adv. Mgr.. **Editorial:** Fran Maye, Senior Editor.

CONSHOHOCKEN

RECORDER (CONSHOHOCKEN), THE. 700 Fayette St., Conshohocken, PA 19428. Telephone: 610-828-4600. FAX: 610-941-0547. E-MAIL: recorder@ingnews.com. Year Established: 1869. Pub. Frequency: w. (Thu.) Page Size: tabloid. Subscrip. Rate: $.50 newsstand/cover; $17/yr in county; $24.50/yr out of county. Circulation: 3,500 per issue (paid). **Owner(s):** Journal Register Co., 50 W State St, 12th Fl, Trenton, NJ 08608. Telephone: 609-396-2200. FAX: 609-396-2292. **Management:** Stephanie Leicht, Publisher. Mary Kay Cavanaugh, Advertising Manager. Ed Krywucki, Circulation Manager.

COUDERSPORT

POTTER LEADER-ENTERPRISE. 6 W Second St, Coudersport, PA 16915. Telephone: 814-274-8044. FAX: 814-274-8120. URL: http://www.potterleaderenterprise.com. Mailing Address: PO Box 29, Coudersport, PA 16915-0029. Year Established: 1874. Pub. Frequency: w. (Wed.) Page Size: broadsheet. Subscrip. Rate: $1 newsstand/cover; $44/yr mailed in county; $46/yr mailed in state; $49/yr mailed out of state. Freelance Pay: $15/article. Circulation: 12,000 per issue (paid). **Owner(s):** Community Media Group, Inc, PO Box 10, West Frankfort, IL 62896. Telephone: 618-937-6412. **Management:** James Monks, Publisher. **Editorial:** Donald Gilliland, Managing Editor. Teri McDowell, News Editor. Neil Linderman, Sports.

CRANBERRY TOWNSHIP

CRANBERRY EAGLE. 83 Dutilh Rd., Cranberry Township, PA 16066. Telephone: 724-282-8000. FAX: 724-282-1280. URL: http://www.butlereagle.com. Pub. Frequency: w. (Wed.) Page Size: standard Circulation: 20,262 per issue (free). **Owner(s):** Eagle Printing Co., 114 W. Diamond St., Butler, PA 16001. Telephone: 724-282-8000. **Management:** Vernon L. Wise Jr., Publisher. Lisa McIntyre, Advertising. Al Frederick, Circulation Manager. **Editorial:** Bob Schultz, Editor.

NEWS WEEKLY (CRANBERRY TOWNSHIP). 83 Dutilh Rd., Cranberry Township, PA 16066. Telephone: 724-776-4270. E-MAIL: news@butlereagle.com. URL: http://www.butlereagle.com. Pub. Frequency: w. (Wed.) Page Size: broadsheet Circulation: 20,262 per issue (free). **Owner(s):** Eagle Printing Co., 114 W. Diamond St., Butler, PA 16001. Telephone: 724-282-8000. **Management:** Vernon L. Wise Jr., Publisher. Lisa McIntyre, Advertising. Al Frederick, Circulation Manager. **Editorial:** Bob Schultz, Editor.

DOWNINGTOWN

PARKESBURG POST. 36 W. Lancaster Ave., Ste. 2, Downingtown, PA 19335. E-MAIL: ledger@allaroundphilly.com. URL: http://www.coatesvilleledger.com. Year Established: 1990. Pub. Frequency: w. (Thu.) Page Size: broadsheet. Subscrip. Rate: $.50 newsstand/cover; $24/yr home delivery in county; $32/yr mailed out of county; $37/yr mailed out of state. Circulation: 3,500 per issue (paid and free). **Owner(s):** Journal Register Co., 50 W State St, 12th Fl, Trenton, NJ 08608. Telephone: 609-396-2200. **Management:** Edward Condra, Publisher. Velma Warren, Advertising. Brian Collins, Advertising Manager. Teresa Pennington, Classified Adv. Mgr.. **Editorial:** Bryan Robinson, Editor. Fran Maye, News Editor.

DOYLESTOWN

DOYLESTOWN PATRIOT. ISSN 1047-9155
350 S Main St, Doylestown, PA 18901. Telephone: 215-340-9811. E-MAIL: doyles@ingnews.com. URL: http://www.buckslocalnews.com/. Year Established: 1988. Pub. Frequency: w. Subscrip. Rate: $19/yr motor route in county; $26.50/yr mailed out of county. **Owner(s):** Journal Register Co., See address and contact information above. **Management:** Stephanie Leicht, Publisher. Bob McCarron, Advertising Director. Monica Carpenter, Classified Editor. Andy Rozek, Controller. **Editorial:** Gina V Stevens, Editor. Steve Sherman, Sports.

DREXEL HILL

MARCUS HOOK PRESS. 3245 Garrett Rd., Drexel Hill, PA 19026. Telephone: 610-259-4141. FAX: 610-626-0693. E-MAIL: mail@presspublishing.org. Year Established: 1916. Pub. Frequency: w. (Thu.) Page Size: tabloid. Subscrip. Rate: $10/yr mailed. Adv. Rate: col. inch $6 Circulation: 3,500 per issue (paid). **Owner(s):** Press Publishing Co., See address and contact information above. **Editorial:** M M Girard, Editor.

RIDLEY PRESS. 3245 Garrett Rd., Drexel Hill, PA 19026. Telephone: 610-259-4141. FAX: 610-626-0693. E-MAIL: mail@presspublishing.org. Year Established: 1964. Pub. Frequency: w. (Thu.) Page Size: tabloid. Subscrip. Rate: $7/yr. Adv. Rate: col. inch $6 Circulation: 4,000 per issue (paid). **Owner(s):** Press Publishing Co., See address and contact information above. **Editorial:** P A Girard, Editor.

UPPER DARBY PRESS. 3245 Garrett Rd., Drexel Hill, PA 19026. Telephone: 610-259-4141. FAX: 610-626-0693. E-MAIL: mail@presspublishing.org. Year Established: 1926. Pub. Frequency: w. (Thu.) Page Size: tabloid. Subscrip. Rate: $10/yr mailed. Adv. Rate: col. inch $6 Circulation: 4,000 per issue (paid). **Owner(s):** Press Publishing Co., See address and contact information above. **Editorial:** P A Girard, Editor.

YEADON TIMES. 3245 Garrett Rd., Drexel Hill, PA 19026. Telephone: 610-259-4141. FAX: 610-626-0693. E-MAIL: mail@presspublishing.org. Year Established: 1929. Pub. Frequency: w. (Thu.) Page Size: tabloid. Subscrip. Rate: $10/yr mailed. Adv. Rate: col. inch $6 Circulation: 3,000 per issue (paid). **Owner(s):** Press Publishing Co., See address and contact information above. **Editorial:** M M Girard, Editor.

DUDLEY

BROAD TOP BULLETIN. PO Box 215, Dudley, PA 16634. E-MAIL: btbulletin@verizon.net. Mailing Address: PO Box 188, Saxton, PA 16678-0188. Year Established: 1947. Pub. Frequency: w. (Tue.) Page Size: broadsheet. Subscrip. Rate: $.50 newsstand/cover; $28/yr in state; $35/yr out of state. Adv. Rate: col. inch $4.50 Circulation: 3,250 per issue (paid). **Owner(s):** Jon Baughman, See address and contact information above. **Management:** Jon Baughman, Publisher. Davena Brechbiel, Advertising Director. Shari McElwee, Circulation Manager. Peggy Whited, Business Manager. **Editorial:** Jon Baughman, Editor.

DUSHORE

SULLIVAN REVIEW. P O Box 305, Dushore, PA 18614. Telephone: 570-928-8403. FAX: 570-928-8006. E-MAIL: sully@epix.net. Year Established: 1878. Pub. Frequency: w. (Thu.) Page Size: broadsheet. Subscrip. Rate: $.75 newsstand/cover; $31/yr in county; $40/yr in state; $45/yr out of state. Adv. Rate: col. inch $7.80 Circulation: 7,000 per issue (paid). **Owner(s):** John A. Showmaker, See address and contact information above. **Management:** Stefana Shoemaker, Publisher. Tammy Bird, Advertising Manager. Rose Gumble, Circulation Manager. **Editorial:** T.W. Showmaker, Editor.

EAST STROUDSBURG

POCONO SHOPPER. 96 S. Courtland St., East Stroudsburg, PA 18301. Telephone: 570-421-4800. FAX: 570-421-4255. E-MAIL: pshopper@ptid.net. Mailing Address: PO Box 424, East Stroudsburg, PA 18301. Year Established: 1975. Pub. Frequency: w. (Wed.) Page Size: tabloid. Circulation: 29,000 per issue (paid and controlled). **Owner(s):** Times-Shamrock Communications, 149 Penn Ave., Scranton, PA 18503. Telephone: 570-348-9100. **Management:** David Barry, General Manager. Janice Kosman, Advertising. Joe Polinski, Circulation Manager. **Editorial:** Susan Gesford, Editor.

EBENSBERG

MAINLINER, THE. 975 Rowena Dr., Ebensberg, PA 15931. Telephone: 814-472-4110. FAX: 814-472-2275. E-MAIL: mainlinenews@verizon.net. URL: http://www.mainlinenewspapers.com. Mailing Address: PO Box 777, Ebensberg, PA 15931. Pub. Frequency: w. (Wed.) Page Size: broadsheet. Subscrip. Rate: $.50 newsstand/cover; $26/yr in county; $32/yr mailed in state; $42/yr mailed out of state. Freelance Pay: $20/article. Circulation: 3,642 per issue (paid). **Owner(s):** Latrobe Printing & Publishing, See address and contact information above. **Management:** William Anderson, Publisher. Melissa Shirk, Advertising. ClareAnn Lasinsky, Circulation Manager. **Editorial:** Paula Varner, Managing Editor. Justin Eger, Bureau Chief.

MOUNTAINEER-HERALD, THE. 975 Rowena Dr., Ebensberg, PA 15931. Telephone: 814-472-4110. FAX: 814-472-2275. E-MAIL: mtnherald@aol.com. URL: http://www.mainlinenewspapers.com. Mailing Address: PO Box 777, Ebensberg, PA 15931. Year Established: 1853. Pub. Frequency: w. (Wed.) Page Size: broadsheet. Subscrip. Rate: $.50 newsstand/cover; $26/yr mailed in county; $32/yr mailed out of county; $42/yr mailed out of state. Circulation: 3,200 per issue (paid). **Owner(s):** Latrobe Printing & Publishing, 1211 Ligonier St., Latrobe, PA 15650. **Management:** William Anderson, Publisher. Barbara Cordoro, Advertising. Beth Murphy, Classified Adv. Mgr.. **Editorial:** Paula Varner, Managing Editor.

ELIZABETHTOWN

ELIZABETHTOWN CHRONICLE. ISSN 1526-2510
25 Center Sq., Elizabethtown, PA 17022-2014. Telephone: 717-367-7152. FAX: 717-367-3655. E-MAIL: etchron@igateway.com. URL: http://www.elizabethtownchronicle.com. Year Established: 1869. Pub. Frequency: w. (Thu.) Page Size: broadsheet. Subscrip. Rate: $.50 newsstand/cover; $24/yr mailed in county; $25/yr mailed out of county; $35/yr mailed out of state. Circulation: 4,000 per issue (paid and free). **Owner(s):** Journal Register Co., 50 W State St, 12th Fl, Trenton, NJ 08608. Telephone: 609-396-2200. **Management:** Edward S. Condra, Publisher. Kerry Myers, Advertising Director. Mary Swartzell, Circulation Manager. **Editorial:** Andrea Thatcher, Editor. Larry White, Sports Editor.

EMPORIUM

CAMERON COUNTY ECHO. PO Box 308, Emporium, PA 15834-0308. Telephone: 814-486-3711. FAX: 814-486-0990. E-MAIL: echo308@penn.com. Year Established: 1963. Pub. Frequency: w. (Wed.) Page Size: broadsheet. Subscrip. Rate: $.75 newsstand/cover; $24/yr mailed in county; $28/yr mailed out of county. Circulation: 4,000 per issue (paid). **Owner(s):** Cameron County Echo, See address and contact information above. **Management:** David Brown, Publisher. Nancy A. Fragale, Advertising Manager. **Editorial:** Nancy A. Fragale, Editor.

EPHRATA

EPHRATA REVIEW. One E. Main St., Ephrata, PA 17522. Telephone: 717-733-6397. FAX: 717-733-6058. Mailing Address: PO Box 527, Ephrata, PA 17522. Year Established: 1878. Pub. Frequency: w. (Wed.) Page Size: standard. Subscrip. Rate: $.35 newsstand/cover; $13.50/yr in county; $19/yr out of county; $23/yr out of state. Circulation: 11,000 per issue (paid). **Owner(s):** Lancaster Newspapers, Inc., 8 W. King St., Lancaster, PA 17603. Telephone: 717-733-6397. **Management:** William Burgess, General Manager. Dave Colton, Advertising Manager. Lisa Vallery, Circulation Manager. **Editorial:** Andy Fasnacht, Editor.

FORT WASHINGTON

AMBLER GAZETTE. 290 Commerce Dr., Fort Washington, PA 19034. Telephone: 215-542-0200. FAX: 215-643-9475. URL: http://www.montgomerynews.com. Mailing Address: PO Box 1628, Fort Washington, PA 19034. Year Established: 1882. Pub. Frequency: w. (Wed.) Page Size: broadsheet. Subscrip. Rate: $.50 newsstand/cover; $34.95/yr home delivery; $40.95/yr mailed in county; $45.95/yr out of county. Adv. Rate: col. inch $27 Circulation: 10,511 per issue (paid). **Owner(s):** Journal Register Co., 50 W State St, 12th Fl, Trenton, NJ 08608. Telephone: 609-396-2200. **Management:** Betsy Wilson, Publisher. Stephanie Leicht, Advertising Manager. Lynne McGarbey, Classified Adv. Mgr.. **Editorial:** Mike Morsch, Managing Editor.

CENTRAL BUCKS LIFE. 290 Commerce Dr., Fort Washington, PA 19034. Telephone: 215-542-0200. FAX: 215-643-9475. URL: http://www.centralbuckslife.com. Mailing Address: PO Box 1628, Fort Washington, PA 19034. Pub. Frequency: w. (Thu.) Page Size: broadsheet. Subscrip. Rate: $.50 newsstand/cover; $12.95/yr mailed in county; $28.95/yr out of county. Circulation: 3,276 per issue (paid). **Owner(s):** Journal Register Co., 50 W State St, 12th Fl, Trenton, NJ 08608. Telephone: 609-396-2200. **Management:** Betsy Wilson, Publisher. Allan Ash, Advertising Director. John Mcquire, Circulation Manager. **Editorial:** Melissa Mattison, Editor. Mike Morsch, Executive Editor.

COLONIAL, THE. 290 Commerce Dr., Fort Washington, PA 19034. Telephone: 215-542-0200. FAX: 215-643-9475. URL: http://www.montgomerynews.com. Mailing Address: PO Box 1628, Fort Washington, PA 19034. Year Established: 1961. Pub. Frequency: w. (Thu.) Page Size: broadsheet. Subscrip. Rate: $.50 newsstand/cover; $20.95/yr carrier delivery; $30.95/yr out of county. Adv. Rate: col. inch $9.59 Circulation: 3,499 per issue (paid). **Owner(s):** Journal Register Co., 50 W. State St., 12th Fl., Trenton, NJ 06808. Telephone: 609-396-2200. **Management:** Betsy Wilson, Publisher. Allan Ash, Advertising Director. Maureen Schmid, Classified Adv. Mgr.. **Editorial:** Mike Morsch, Managing Editor.

GLENSIDE NEWS. 290 Commerce Dr., Fort Washington, PA 19034. Telephone: 215-542-0200. FAX: 215-643-9475. E-MAIL: ssmith@montgomerynews.com. URL: http://www.montgomerynews.com. Mailing Address: PO Box 1628, Fort Washington, PA 19034. Year Established: 1923. Pub. Frequency: w. (Wed.) Page Size: broadsheet. Subscrip. Rate: $.50 newsstand/cover; $40.95/yr home delivery in county; $45.95/yr mailed out of county. Adv. Rate: col. inch $23.24 Circulation: 3,048 per issue (paid). **Owner(s):** Journal Register Co., 50 W State St, 12th Fl, Trenton, NJ 08608. Telephone: 609-396-2200. **Management:** Betsy Wilson, Publisher. Allan Ash, Advertising Director. Maureen Schmid, Classified Adv. Mgr.. **Editorial:** Sean Smith, Editor. Mike Morsch, Executive Editor. Dave Holloway, Sports.

GLOBE, THE. 290 Commerce Dr., Fort Washington, PA 19034. Telephone: 215-542-0200. FAX: 215-643-9275. URL: http://www.montgomerynews.com. Mailing Address: PO Box 1628, Fort Washington, PA 19034. Year Established: 1927. Pub. Frequency: w. (Thu.) Page Size: broadsheet. Subscrip. Rate: $.50 newsstand/cover; $24.95/yr carrier delivery; $30.95/yr mailed out of county. Adv. Rate: col. inch $12.40 Circulation: 2,485 per issue (paid). **Owner(s):** Journal Register Co., 50 W State St, 12th Fl, Trenton, NJ 08608. Telephone: 609-396-2292. **Management:** Betsy Wilson, Publisher. Allan Ash, Advertising Director. Maureen Schmid, Classified Adv. Mgr.. **Editorial:** Mike Morsch, Executive Editor.

MONTGOMERY LIFE. 290 Commerce Dr., Fort Washington, PA 19034. Telephone: 215-542-0200. FAX: 215-643-9475. URL: http://www.montgomerynews.com. Mailing Address: PO Box 1628, Fort Washington, PA 19034. Year Established: 1961. Pub. Frequency: w. (Fri.) Page Size: broadsheet. Subscrip. Rate: $.50 newsstand/cover; $12.95/yr mailed in county; $30.95/yr mailed out of county. Adv. Rate: col. inch $10.48 Circulation: 22,600 per issue (paid). **Owner(s):** Journal Register Co., 50 W State St, 12th Fl, Trenton, NJ 08608. **Management:** Betsy Wilson, Publisher. Allan Ash, Advertising Director. Joe Carter, Circulation Manager. Maureen Schmid, Classified Adv. Mgr.. **Editorial:** Mike Morsch, Executive Editor.

NORTH PENN LIFE. ISSN 1554-429X
290 Commerce Dr., Fort Washington, PA 19034. Telephone: 215-542-0200. FAX: 215-643-9457. URL: http://www.montgomerynews.com. Mailing Address: PO Box 1628, Fort Washington, PA 19034. Year Established: 1974. Pub. Frequency: w. (Fri.) Page Size: broadsheet. Subscrip. Rate: $.50 newsstand/cover; $17.95/yr carrier delivery; $33.95/yr out of county. Adv. Rate: col. inch $10.92 Circulation: 21,681 per issue (controlled and free). **Owner(s):** Journal Register Co., 50 W State St, 12th Fl, Trenton, NJ 08608. Telephone: 609-396-2292. **Management:** Betsy Wilson, Publisher. Allan Ash, Advertising Director. Maureen Schmid, Classified Adv. Mgr.. **Editorial:** Mike Morsch, Executive Editor. Neree Aron Sando, News Editor.

PUBLIC SPIRIT. 290 Commerce Dr., Fort Washington, PA 19034. Telephone: 215-542-0200. FAX: 215-643-9475. URL: http://www.montgomerynews.com/site/ Mailing Address: PO Box 1628, Fort Washington, PA 19034. Pub. Frequency: w. (Wed.) Page Size: broadsheet. Subscrip. Rate: $.50 newsstand/cover; $34/yr carrier delivery; $34/yr mailed in county; $45/yr mailed out of county. Circulation: 10,717 per issue (paid). **Owner(s):** Journal Register Co., 50 W State St, 12th Fl, Trenton, NJ 08608. Telephone: 609-396-2200. **Management:** Betsy Wilson, Publisher. Allan Ash, Advertising Director. John Mcquire, Circulation Manager. Maureen Schmid, Classified Adv. Mgr.. **Editorial:** Scott Roman, Editor. Mike Morsch, Executive Editor.

SPRING-FORD REPORTER. 290 Commerce Dr., Fort Washington, PA 19034. Telephone: 215-542-0200. FAX: 215-643-9475. E-MAIL: bwilson@journalregister.com. URL: http://www.montgomerynews.com. Mailing Address: PO Box 1628, Fort Washington, PA 19034. Pub. Frequency: w. (Wed.) Page Size: broadsheet. Subscrip. Rate: $.50 newsstand/cover; $28.95/yr carrier delivery; $28.95/yr mailed in county; $34.95/yr out of state. Adv. Rate: col. inch $14.46 Circulation: 3,912 per issue (paid). **Owner(s):** Journal Register Co., 50 W State St, 12th Fl, Trenton, NJ 08608. Telephone: 609-396-2200. **Management:** Betsy Wilson, Publisher. Allan Ash, Advertising Director. John Maguire, Circulation Manager.

SPRINGFIELD SUN (FORT WASHINGTON). 290 Commerce Dr., Fort Washington, PA 19034. URL: http://www.springfieldsun.com. Year Established: 1946. Pub. Frequency: w. (Thu.) Page Size: broadsheet. Subscrip. Rate: $.50 newsstand/cover; $40.95/yr carrier delivery; $40.95/yr mailed in county; $45.95/yr mailed out of county. Adv. Rate: col. inch $23.58 Circulation: 2,768 per issue (paid). **Owner(s):** Journal Register Co., 50 W. State St., 12th Fl., Trenton, NJ 08608. Telephone: 609-369-2200. **Management:** Betsy Wilson, Publisher. Allan Ash, Advertising Director. **Editorial:** Adam Greenberg, Editor. Mike Morsch, Executive Editor. Sarah Sando, Managing Editor. Dave Holloway, Sports Editor.

TIMES CHRONICLE. 290 Commerce Dr., Fort Washington, PA 19034. Telephone: 215-542-0200. FAX: 215-643-9475. URL: http://www.montgomerynews.com. Mailing Address: PO Box 1628, Fort Washington, PA 19034. Year Established: 1894. Pub. Frequency: w. (Wed.) Page Size: broadsheet. Subscrip. Rate: $.50 newsstand/cover; $40.95/yr carrier delivery; $40.95/yr mailed in developing nations; $45.95/yr mailed out of state. Adv. Rate: col. inch $23.24 Circulation: 7,275 per issue (paid). **Owner(s):** Journal Register Co., 50 W State St, 12th Fl, Trenton, NJ 08608. Telephone: 609-396-2292. **Management:** Allan Ash, Advertising Director. Maureen Schmid, Classified Adv. Mgr.. **Editorial:** Sean Smith, Editor. Mike Morsch, Executive Editor.

WILLOW GROVE GUIDE. 290 Commerce Dr., Fort Washington, PA 19034. Telephone: 215-542-0200. FAX: 215-643-9475. URL: http://www.montgomerynews.com. Mailing Address: PO Box 1628, Fort Washington, PA 19034. Year Established: 1925. Pub. Frequency: w. (Wed.) Page Size: broadsheet. Subscrip. Rate: $.50 newsstand/cover; $34.95/yr carrier delivery; $34.95/yr mailed in county; $45.95/yr mailed out of state. Adv. Rate: col. inch $21.83 Circulation: 1,457 per issue (paid). **Owner(s):** Journal Register Co., 50 W State St, 12th Fl, Trenton, NJ 08608. Telephone: 609-396-2200. **Management:** Betsy Wilson, Publisher. Allan Ash, Advertising Director. **Editorial:** Scott Roman, Editor. Mike Morsch, Executive Editor.

GREENCASTLE

ECHO-PILOT. 29 Center Sq., Greencastle, PA 17225. Telephone: 717-597-2164. FAX: 717-597-3754. E-MAIL: advertising@echo-pilot.com. URL: http://www.echo-pilot.com. Mailing Address: PO Box 159, Greencastle, PA 17225-0159. Pub. Frequency: w. (Wed.) Page Size: broadsheet. Subscrip. Rate: $.75 newsstand/cover; $20/yr in county; $25/yr out of county. Circulation: 2,383 per issue (paid). **Owner(s):** GateHouse Media, Inc, 350 WillowBrook Office Park, Fairport, NY 14450. Telephone: 585-598-0030. FAX: 585-248-2631. **Management:** Mary Menard, Advertising. **Editorial:** Joyce Nowell, Editor.

GROVE CITY

ALLIED NEWS. 201 Erie St., Grove City, PA 16127. Telephone: 724-458-5010. FAX: 724-458-1609. E-MAIL: news@alliednews.com. URL: http://www.alliednews.com. Mailing Address: PO Box 190, Grove City, PA 16127. Year Established: 1879. Pub. Frequency: s-w. (Wed. & Sat) Page Size: broadsheet. Subscrip. Rate: $.50 newsstand/cover; $26/yr carrier delivery & motor rte; $55/yr mailed. Circulation: 5,000 per issue (paid). **Owner(s):** Community Newspaper Holdings, Inc., 3500 Colonnade Pkwy., Ste. 600, Birmingham, AL 35243. Telephone: 205-298-7100. **Management:** John L. Lima, Publisher. Denise Gabany, Advertising. Kim Barnes, Classified Adv. Mgr.. **Editorial:** Tina Horner, Editor. Corey Corbin, Sports.

HAMBURG

HAMBURG ITEM. 302 State St., Hamburg, PA 19526. Telephone: 610-562-7515. FAX: 610-562-4644. E-MAIL: item@berksmontnews.com. URL: http://www.berksmontnews.com/item.html. Year Established: 1875. Pub. Frequency: w. (Wed.) Page Size: standard. Subscrip. Rate: $25/yr in county; $29/yr out of county; $34/yr out of state. Adv. Rate: col. inch $5.20 Circulation: 3,980 per issue (paid). **Owner(s):** Berks-Mont Newspapers, Inc., 124 N. Chestnut St., Boyertown, PA 19512. Telephone: 610-367-6041. FAX: 610-369-0233. **Management:** James C Webb, Publisher. Denise Schaeffer, Advertising Manager. **Editorial:** Nikki Murry, Editor.

PATRIOT (HAMBURG), THE. ISSN 1041-4029
302 State St., Hamburg, PA 19526. Telephone: 610-683-7343. FAX: 610-562-4644. E-MAIL: thepatriotnews@hotmail.com. URL: http://www.berksmontnews.com. Year Established: 1874. Pub. Frequency: w. (Thu.) Page Size: standard. Subscrip. Rate: $.50 newsstand/cover; $22/yr in county; $34/yr mailed out of county; $39/yr mailed out of state. Circulation: 6,100 per issue (paid). **Owner(s):** Berks-Mont Newspapers, Inc., 124 N. Chestnut St., Boyertown, PA 19512. Telephone: 610-367-6041. FAX: 610-369-0233. **Management:** Jim Davidheiser, General Manager. James C Webb, Publisher. John Varady, Advertising Director.

HAVERTOWN

NEWS OF DELAWARE COUNTY. Manoa Shopping Ctr., 1305 West Chester Pike, Havertown, PA 19083. Telephone: 610-446-8700. FAX: 610-449-0419. E-MAIL: bredavid@newsofdelawarecounty.com. URL: http://www.newsofdelawarecounty.com. Year Established: 1930. Pub. Frequency: w. (Wed.) Page Size: broadsheet. Subscrip. Rate: $.50 newsstand/cover; $32.20/yr home delivery in area; $42.60/yr mailed in Philadelphia region; $45.20/yr mailed out of state. Circulation: 32,000 per issue (paid and free). **Owner(s):** Journal Register Co., 50 W State St, 12th Fl, Trenton, NJ 08608. Telephone: 609-396-2200. **Management:** Dianne Ryan-Paschall, Publisher. Mary DeStafney, Advertising Director. Adam Chylinski, Circulation Manager. **Editorial:** Brigette ReDavid, Managing Editor. Len Rosen, Sports Editor.

HAWLEY

NEWS EAGLE, THE. ISSN 1052-4460
307 Main Ave, Hawley, PA 18428. Telephone: 570-226-4547. FAX: 570-226-4448. E-MAIL: news@neagle.com. URL: http://www.neagle.com. Mailing Address: PO Box E, Hawley, PA 18428. Year Established: 1957. Pub. Frequency: s-w. (Wed. & Sat.) Page Size: broadsheet. Subscrip. Rate: $.75 newsstand/cover; $55/yr mailed in Wayne & Pike cys.; $90/yr mailed out of area. Circulation: 6,500 per issue (paid). **Owner(s):** GateHouse Media, Inc, 350 WillowBrook Office Park, Fairport, NY 14450. Telephone: 585-598-0030. FAX: 585-248-2631. **Management:** Steve Mountain, Publisher. Glen Khoury, Advertising Manager. **Editorial:** Thomas Renn, Managing Editor.

HERSHEY

HERSHEY CHRONICLE, THE. ISSN 8750-8753
513 W. Chocolate Ave., Hershey, PA 17033. Telephone: 717-533-2900. FAX: 717-531-2561. E-MAIL: editor@hersheychron.com. URL: http://www.hersheychronicle.com. Year Established: 1984. Pub. Frequency: w. (Thu.) Page Size: broadsheet. Subscrip. Rate: $.50 newsstand/cover; $24/yr in area; $35/yr mailed out of state. Adv. Rate: col. inch $6.10 Freelance Pay: $30/story. **Wire Service(s):** AP. Circulation: 5,000 per issue (paid). **Owner(s):** Journal Register Co., 50 W State St, 12th Fl, Trenton, NJ 08608. Telephone: 609-396-2200. **Management:** Edward S. Condra, Publisher. Mary Swartzell, Circulation Manager. **Editorial:** Matt Solovey, Editor.

HOLMES

SPRINGFIELD PRESS. 1914 Parker Ave., Holmes, PA 19143. Telephone: 610-522-9350. FAX: 610-522-9355. E-MAIL: springfield-news@allaroundphilly.com. Mailing Address: PO Box 291, Springfield, PA 19064. Year Established: 1931. Pub. Frequency: w. (Wed.) Page Size: tabloid. Subscrip. Rate: $.50 newsstand/cover; $22/yr area. Circulation: 5,650 per issue (paid and free). **Owner(s):** Journal Register Co., 50 W State St, 12th Fl, Trenton, NJ 08608. Telephone: 609-396-2200. **Management:** Rich Crowe, Publisher. **Editorial:** Donna McCole, Editor.

HONESDALE

WEEKLY ALMANAC, THE. ISSN 1063-2794
3202 Lake Ariel Hwy., Honesdale, PA 18431. Telephone: 570-253-9270. FAX: 570-2538937. URL: http://www.weeklyalmanac.com. Year Established: 1990. Pub. Frequency: w. (Thu.) Page Size: tabloid. Subscrip. Rate: $.75 newsstand/cover; $37/yr mailed in city. Circulation: 4,800 per issue (paid). **Owner(s):** Princeton Packet, Inc., The, 300 Witherspoon St, Princeton, NJ 08542. Telephone: 609-924-3244. **Management:** Jim Kilgore, Publisher. **Editorial:** Mary Baldwin, Editor-in-Chief.

HORSHAM

BUCKS COUNTY TRIBUNE. 390 Easton Rd., Horsham, PA 19044-2592. Telephone: 215-675-6600. FAX: 215-675-8251. E-MAIL: progressnews@comcast.net. URL: http://www.progressnews.biz. Year Established: 1961. Pub. Frequency: w. (Wed.) Page Size: tabloid. Subscrip. Rate: $79/yr mailed out of area. Adv. Rate: col. inch $21 Circulation: 15,000 per issue (controlled and free). **Owner(s):** Progress Newspapers, Inc., 390 Easton Rd., Horsham, PA 19044. Telephone: 215-675-6600. **Management:** Matthew Petersohn, Publisher. **Editorial:** Sandra Petersohn, Editor.

MONTGOMERY COUNTY PROGRESS. 390 Easton Rd., Horsham, PA 19044. Telephone: 215-675-6600. FAX: 215-675-8251. E-MAIL: progressnews@comcast.net. URL: http://www.progressnews.biz. Year Established: 1953. Pub. Frequency: w. (Wed.) Page Size: tabloid. Subscrip. Rate: $79/yr mailed. Adv. Rate: col. inch $21 Circulation: 15,000 per issue (paid and free). **Owner(s):** Progress Newspapers, Inc., See address and contact information above. **Management:** Matthew Petersohn, Publisher. **Editorial:** Sandra L. Petersohn, Editor-in-Chief.

SUNDAY BUCKS COUNTY TELEGRAPH. 390 Easton Rd., Horsham, PA 19044. Telephone: 215-675-6600. FAX: 215-675-8251. E-MAIL: progressnews@comcast.net. URL: http://www.progressnews.biz. Year Established: 2006. Pub. Frequency: m. Page Size: tabloid. Subscrip. Rate: $79/yr mailed. Adv. Rate: col. inch $21 Circulation: 8,700 per issue (paid and free). **Owner(s):** Progress Newspapers, Inc., See address and contact information above. **Management:** Matthew Petersohn, Publisher. **Editorial:** Sandra L. Petersohn, Editor-in-Chief.

HUMMELSTOWN

SUN (HUMMELSTOWN), THE. ISSN 1942-4442
40 W Main St, Hummelstown, PA 17036. Telephone: 717-566-3251. FAX: 717-566-6196. E-MAIL: news@thesunontheweb.com. URL: http://www.thesunontheweb.com. Year Established: 1871. Pub. Frequency: w. (Wed.) Page Size: broadsheet. Subscrip. Rate: $.50 newsstand/cover; $24/yr in state; $28/yr out of state. Adv. Rate: col. inch $8 Circulation: 7,400 per issue (paid). **Owner(s):** Debra & David Buffington, See address and contact information above. **Management:** Debra Buffington, Publisher. **Editorial:** David Buffington, Editor.

JOHNSONBURG

JOHNSONBURG PRESS, INC., THE. 517 Market St., Johnsonburg, PA 15845. Telephone: 814-965-2503. FAX: 814-965-2504. E-MAIL: jbgpress@mcentral.com. Year Established: 1892. Pub. Frequency: w. (Wed.) Page Size: standard. Subscrip. Rate: $.60 newsstand/cover; $25/yr home delivery in town. Circulation: 2,500 per issue (paid). **Owner(s):** Johnsonburg Press, Inc., The, See address and contact information above. **Management:** Frances Fowler, President. John E. Fowler, Vice President. **Editorial:** Frances Fowler, Editor. John E. Fowler, Managing Editor.

KENNETT SQUARE

AVON GROVE SUN. ISSN 1532-0308
112 E. State St., Kennett Square, PA 19348. E-MAIL: agsun@comcast.net. Year Established: 1999. Pub. Frequency: w. (Thu.) Page Size: broadsheet. Subscrip. Rate: $.50 newsstand/cover; $26/yr home delivery in county; $32/yr mailed out of county; $37/yr mailed out of state. Circulation: 10,000 per issue (paid). **Owner(s):** Journal Register Co., 50 W State St, 12th Fl, Trenton, NJ 08608. Telephone: 609-396-2200. **Management:** Edward S. Condra, Publisher. Mike Doyle, Advertising Director. Teresa Pennington, Classified Adv. Mgr.. **Editorial:** Maria J S Bednarz, Editor. Sandra Rumanek, Executive Editor.

CHADDS FORD POST. 112 E State St, Kennett Square, PA 19348. E-MAIL: cfp@mailkennettpaper.com. URL: http://www.kennettpaper.com. Pub. Frequency: w. (Thu.) Subscrip. Rate: $25/yr in county; $32/yr out of county; $35/yr out of state. **Owner(s):** Journal Register Co., 50 W. State St., 12th Fl., Trenton, NJ 08608. **Management:** Edward S. Condra, Publisher. Mike Doyle, Advertising Director. Teresa Pennington, Classified Adv. Mgr.. **Editorial:** Richard Schwartzman, Editor.

KENNETT PAPER, THE. ISSN 0894-0274
112 E. State St., Kennett Square, PA 19348. Telephone: 610-444-6590. FAX: 610-444-4931. E-MAIL: editor@mailkennettpaper.com.com. URL: http://www.kennettpaper.com. Year Established: 1986. Pub. Frequency: w. (Thu.) Page Size: broadsheet. Subscrip. Rate: $.50 newsstand/cover; $24/yr home delivery in county; $30/yr mailed out of county; $35/yr mailed in state. Circulation: 6,000 per issue (paid). **Owner(s):** Journal Register Co., 50 W State St, 12th Fl, Trenton, NJ 08608. Telephone: 609-396-2200. **Management:** Edward S. Condra, Publisher. Teresa Pennington, Classified Adv. Mgr.. **Editorial:** Christine Barber, Editor.

SIGNAL ITEM. ISSN 1047-0662
610 Beatty Rd., Monroeville, PA 15146. Telephone: 412-856-7400. FAX: 412-856-7954. E-MAIL: newsitem@gatewaynewspapers.com. URL: http://www.signalitemstar.com. Year Established: 1873. Pub. Frequency: w. (Wed.) Page Size: tabloid. Subscrip. Rate: $.50 newsstand/cover; $25/yr in county; $40/yr out of county. Circulation: 4,537 per issue (paid). **Owner(s):** Gateway Newspapers, See address and contact information above. **Management:** Scott Patterson, President. Kathleen Brieck, Advertising Manager. Kris Ranker, Classified Adv. Mgr.. **Editorial:** Edith Hughes, Executive Editor. Bob Pastin, Managing Editor. Chris Scarnati, Sports Editor.

TIMES EXPRESS. 610 Beatty Rd., Monroeville, PA 15146. Telephone: 412-856-7400. FAX: 412-856-7954. E-MAIL: timesexpress@trinity-pgh.com. URL: http://www.timesexpressstar.com. Year Established: 1893. Pub. Frequency: w. (Wed.) Page Size: broadsheet. Subscrip. Rate: $.50 newsstand/cover; $25/yr home delivery. Circulation: 5,847 per issue (paid). **Owner(s):** Gateway Newspapers, See address and contact information above. **Management:** Ralph Martin, General Manager. Gary Siegel, Advertising Manager. Kris Ranker, Classified Adv. Mgr.. **Editorial:** Alan Wallace, Editor. Edith Hughes, Executive Editor. Micheal Love, Sports Editor.

WOODLAND PROGRESS. 610 Beatty Rd., Monroeville, PA 15146. Telephone: 412-856-7400. FAX: 412-856-7954. E-MAIL: progress@trinity-pgh.com. URL: http://www.woodlandhillsstar.com. Pub. Frequency: w. (Wed.) Page Size: tabloid. Subscrip. Rate: $.50 newsstand/cover; $25/yr. **Owner(s):** Gateway Newspapers, See address and contact information above. **Management:** Gary Siegel, Advertising Director. Jon Kennell, Circulation Director. Kris Ranker, Classified Adv. Mgr.. **Editorial:** Alan Wallace, Editor. Edith Hughes, Executive Editor. Micheal Love, Sports Editor.

MONTROSE

SUSQUEHANNA COUNTY INDEPENDENT. 24 S. Main St., Montrose, PA 18801. Telephone: 570-278-6397. FAX: 570-278-4305. E-MAIL: mtrose@epix.net. URL: http://www.independentweekender.com. Year Established: 1816. Pub. Frequency: w. (Wed.) Page Size: tabloid.Subscrip. Rate: $.55 newsstand/cover; $26/yr Circulation: 3,500 per issue (paid). **Owner(s):** Times-Shamrock Communications, 149 Penn Ave,, Scranton, PA 18503. **Management:** David Barry, Publisher. Gail Williams, Advertising Director. Ken Chaffee, Circulation Manager. **Editorial:** Susan Gesford, Editor.

SUSQUEHANNA COUNTY WEEKENDER. 24 S. Main St., Montrose, PA 18801. E-MAIL: mtrose@epix.net. URL: http://www.independentweekender.com. Year Established: 1816. Pub. Frequency: w. (Fri.) Page Size: tabloid Circulation: 16,500 per issue (free). **Owner(s):** Times-Shamrock Communications, 149 Penn Ave., Scranton, PA 18503. **Management:** David Barry, Publisher. Gail Williams, Advertising Director. Ken Chaffee, Circulation Manager. **Editorial:** Susan Gesford, Editor.

MOSCOW

VILLAGER (MOSCOW), THE. PO Box 655, Moscow, PA 18444. E-MAIL: moscowvillager@verizon.net. Year Established: 1961. Pub. Frequency: w. (Wed.) Page Size: broadsheet. Subscrip. Rate: $.50 newsstand/cover; $25/yr in state; $29/yr out of state. Circulation: 4,300 per issue (paid). **Owner(s):** GateHouse Media, Inc, 232 N. Main St., Moscow, PA 18444. **Management:** Michelle Hessling, General Manager. Karen Newbon, Advertising. **Editorial:** Ryan O'Malley, Editor.

MOUNTAIN TOP

MOUNTAINTOP EAGLE. 85 S. Main Rd., Mountain Top, PA 18707. Telephone: 570-474-6397. FAX: 570-474-9272. E-MAIL: mteagle@ptd.net. URL: http://www.mteagle.com. Mailing Address: P.O. Box 10, Mountain Top, PA 18707. Year Established: 1969. Pub. Frequency: w. (Wed.) Page Size: broadsheet. Subscrip. Rate: $.50 newsstand/cover; $28/yr; $32/yr out of county; $40/yr out of state. Adv. Rate: col. inch $9.25 Circulation: 3,000 per issue (paid). **Owner(s):** Stephanie & Charles Grubert, See address and contact information above. **Management:** Stephanie Grubert, Publisher. **Editorial:** Stephanie Grubert, Editor. Kathleen Flower, Managing Editor.

MT JOY

ELIZABETHTOWN MOUNT JOY MERCHANDISER. 1425 W Main St, Mt Joy, PA 17552. Telephone: 717-653-1833. FAX: 717-492-2577, 717-653-6065. Mailing Address: 1425 W Main St, PO Box 500, Mt. Joy, PA 17552. Year Established: 1959. Pub. Frequency: w. (Wed.) Page Size: tabloid. Subscrip. Rate: $36/yr mailed 3rd class; $70/yr mailed 1st class. Circulation: 18,882 per issue (paid and free). **Owner(s):** Engle Printing & Publishing Co., Inc., See address and contact information above. **Management:** Charles Engle, President. John Hemperly, Sales Manager. **Editorial:** Greg Schneider, Sports Editor.

MT. PLEASANT

MOUNT PLEASANT JOURNAL, THE. 23 S. Church St., Mt. Pleasant, PA 15666. Telephone: 724-547-5722. FAX: 724-887-5115. Mailing Address: PO Box 222, Scottdale, PA 15683-0222. Year Established: 1873. Pub. Frequency: w. (Thu.) Page Size: broadsheet. Subscrip. Rate: $1.50 newsstand/cover; $26/yr in county; $38/yr out of county; $40/yr out of state. Adv. Rate: col. inch $9.25 Freelance Pay: $0.20/column-inch. Circulation: 5,492 per issue (paid). **Owner(s):** Laurel Group Press, 229 Pittsburgh St., Scottdale, PA 15683. Telephone: 724-887-7400. **Management:** Joseph F. Soforic, General Manager. Charles D. Hixson, Advertising Manager. Marcella Kohuth, Circulation Manager. **Editorial:** Diana R. Lasko, Editor.

MUNHALL

VALLEY MIRROR, THE. 3910 Main St., Munhall, PA 15120-3299. Telephone: 412-462-0626. FAX: 412-462-1847. E-MAIL: valleymirror@comcast.net. URL: http://www.valleymirror.com. Year Established: 1913. Pub. Frequency: w. (Thu.) Page Size: tabloid. Subscrip. Rate: $.50 newsstand/cover; $35/yr. Adv. Rate: col. inch $7 Circulation: 6,000 per issue (paid). **Owner(s):** Woodland Publishing Co., See address and contact information above. **Management:** Anthony Munson, President. **Editorial:** Marilyn L. Schiavoni, News Editor.

NANTY GLO

NANTY GLO JOURNAL, THE. ISSN 0746-4037
975 Roberts St., Nanty Glo, PA 15943. Telephone: 814-472-4110. FAX: 814-472-2275. E-MAIL: mainlinenews@verizon.net. URL: http://www.mainlinenewspapers.com. Pub. Frequency: w. (Wed.) Page Size: broadsheet. Subscrip. Rate: $.50 newsstand/cover; $26/yr in county; $32/yr mailed out of county; $42/yr mailed out of state. Freelance Pay: $20/article. Circulation: 3,088 per issue (paid). **Owner(s):** Latrobe Printing & Publishing, PO Box 111, Latrobe, PA 15650. Telephone: 724-537-3351. **Management:** Barbara Cordoro, Advertising. Beth Murphy, Classified Adv. Mgr.. **Editorial:** Paula Varner, Managing Editor. William L. Martin, Bureau Chief.

NEW BETHLEHEM

LEADER-VINDICATOR, THE. 435 Broad St., New Bethlehem, PA 16242. Telephone: 814-275-3131. FAX: 814-275-3531. E-MAIL: leadervindicator@alltel.net. Year Established: 1885. Pub. Frequency: w. (Wed.) Page Size: standard. Subscrip. Rate: $.50 newsstand/cover; $24.95/yr in state; $45/yr out of state. Adv. Rate: col. inch $6.35 Circulation: 5,400 per issue (paid). **Owner(s):** McClean Publishing Co., Inc., See address and contact information above. **Management:** Ryan T. Wells, General Manager. **Editorial:** Josh Walzak, Editor. Ronald Willison, Sports Editor.

NEW BLOOMFIELD

DUNCANNON RECORD. 51 N. Church St., New Bloomfield, PA 17068. Telephone: 717-582-4305. FAX: 717-582-7933. E-MAIL: editor@perrycountytimes.com. URL: http://www.perrycountytimes.com. Mailing Address: PO Box 130, New Bloomfield, PA 17068. Year Established: 1886. Pub. Frequency: w. (Thu.) Page Size: broadsheet. Subscrip. Rate: $.50 newsstand/cover; $27/yr in county; $40/yr out of county; $50/yr out of state. Circulation: 2,289 per issue (paid). **Owner(s):** Advance Publications, Inc., 950 Fingerboard Rd., Staten Island, NY 10305. Telephone: 718-981-1234. **Management:** Rick White, Publisher. Pam Wilson, Circulation Manager. **Editorial:** Wade Fowler, Editor. Gary Thomas, Managing Editor. John Alvanitakis, Sports Editor.

NEWS-SUN (NEW BLOOMFIELD), THE. ISSN 0889-3810
51 N. Church St., New Bloomfield, PA 17068. Telephone: 717-582-4305. FAX: 717-582-7933. E-MAIL: editor@perrycountytimes.com. URL: http://www.perrycountytimes.com. Mailing Address: PO Box 130, New Bloomfield, PA 17068. Year Established: 1868. Pub. Frequency: w. (Wed.) Page Size: broadsheet. Subscrip. Rate: $.50 newsstand/cover; $27/yr in county; $40/yr out of county; $50/yr mailed out of state. Freelance Pay: $0.25/column-inch. Circulation: 3,020 per issue (paid). **Owner(s):** Advance Publications, Inc., 950 Fingerboard Rd., Staten Island, NY 10305. Telephone: 718-981-1234. **Management:** Rick White, Publisher. Pam Wilson, Circulation Manager. **Editorial:** Wade Fowler, Editor. Gary Thomas, Managing Editor. John Alvanitakis, Sports Editor.

PERRY COUNTY TIMES. 51 N. Church St., New Bloomfield, PA 17068. Telephone: 717-582-4305. FAX: 717-582-7933. E-MAIL: editor@perrycountytimes.com. URL: http://www.perrycountytimes.com. Mailing Address: PO Box 130, New Bloomfield, PA 17068. Year Established: 1886. Pub. Frequency: w. (Thu.) Page Size: broadsheet. Subscrip. Rate: $.50 newsstand/cover; $27/yr in county; $40/yr mailed out of county; $50/yr mailed out of state. Circulation: 5,066 per issue (paid). **Owner(s):** Advance Publications, Inc., 950 Fingerboard Rd., Staten Island, NY 10305. Telephone: 718-981-1234. **Management:** Rick White, Publisher. Pam Wilson, Circulation Manager. **Editorial:** Wade Fowler, Editor. Gary Thomas, Managing Editor. John Alvanitakis, Sports Editor.

NEW CASTLE

POPNATION. 27 N. Mercer St., New Castle, PA 16101. Telephone: 724-654-6651. FAX: 724-654-9593. Mailing Address: PO Box 60, New Castle, PA 16103. Pub. Frequency: w. (Fri.) Page Size: standard Circulation: 10,013 per issue (free). **Owner(s):** Community Newspaper Holdings, Inc., 3500 Colonnade Pkwy., Ste. 600, Birmingham, AL 35242. **Management:** Max Thomson, Publisher. Ed Gaydos, Advertising Manager. DuWayne Nelson, Circulation Manager. Bryan Zeigler, Classified Adv. Mgr.. **Editorial:** Mitchell Olszak, Managing Editor.

SOUTH COUNTY NEWS. 27 N. Mercer St., New Castle, PA 16101. Telephone: 724-654-6651. FAX: 724-654-9593. Mailing Address: PO Box 60, New Castle, PA 16103. Pub. Frequency: w. (Wed.) Page Size: standard.Adv. Rate: col. inch $5.50 Circulation: 8,700 per issue (free). **Owner(s):** Community Newspaper Holdings, Inc., 3500 Colonnade Pkwy., Ste. 600, Birmingham, AL 35243-2304. Telephone: 205-298-7100. **Management:** Max Thomson, Publisher. Ed Gaydos, Advertising Manager. DuWayne Nelson, Circulation Manager. Bryan Zeigler, Classified Adv. Mgr.. **Editorial:** Mitchell Olszak, Managing Editor.

NEW HOPE

NEW HOPE GAZETTE. 142 S. Main St., New Hope, PA 18938-0180. Telephone: 215-862-9435. FAX: 215-862-2160. E-MAIL: newhope@ingnews.com. URL: http://www.newhopegazette.com. Mailing Address: PO Box 180, New Hope, PA 18938-0180. Year Established: 1948. Pub. Frequency: w. (Thu.) Page Size: tabloid. Subscrip. Rate: $.50 newsstand/cover; $23.50/yr mailed in county; $29.50/yr mailed out of county. Circulation: 4,500 per issue (paid). **Owner(s):** Journal Register Co., 50 W State St, 12th Fl, Trenton, NJ 08608. Telephone: 609-396-2200. FAX: 609-396-2292. **Management:** Stephanie Leicht, Publisher. Bob McCarron, Advertising Manager. **Editorial:** Scott Edwards, Editor. Steve Sherman, Sports.

NEWTOWN

ADVANCE OF BUCKS COUNTY. 203 South State St, Newtown, PA 18940. Telephone: 215-968-2244. FAX: 215-968-3501. E-MAIL: advance@ingnews.com. URL: http://www.advanceofbucks.com. Mailing Address: PO Box 910, Newtown, PA 18940-2150. Year Established: 1877. Pub. Frequency: w. (Thu.) Page Size: tabloid. Subscrip. Rate: $.50 newsstand/cover; $23.50/yr mailed in county; $29.50/yr mailed out of county. Circulation: 6,000 per issue (paid). **Owner(s):** Journal Register Co., 50 W State St, 12th Fl, Trenton, NJ 08608. Telephone: 609-396-2200. FAX: 609-396-2292. **Management:** Stephanie Leicht, Publisher. Paula Reynolds, Advertising Manager. Monica Carpenter, Classified Adv. Mgr.. **Editorial:** Nancy Pickering, Editor. Steve Sherman, Sports Editor.

NEWTOWN SQUARE

COUNTY PRESS (NEWTOWN SQUARE). 3732 West Chester Pike, Newtown Square, PA 19073-0249. Telephone: 610-356-6664. FAX: 610-353-5321. Mailing Address: PO Box 249, Newtown Square, PA 19073-0249. Year Established: 1931. Pub. Frequency: w. (Wed.) Page Size: tabloid. Subscrip. Rate: $18/yr; $30 for 2 yrs.; $42 for 3 yrs.. Adv. Rate: col. inch $10.47 Circulation: 5,153 per issue (paid and free). **Owner(s):** Journal Register Co., 50 W State St, 12th Fl, Trenton, NJ 08608. Telephone: 609-396-2200. **Management:** Richard Crowe, Publisher. **Editorial:** William Lawrence, Editor.

HAVERFORD PRESS. 3732 West Chester Pike, Newtown Square, PA 19073-0249. Telephone: 610-356-3820. FAX: 610-353-5321. E-MAIL: ads@allaroundphilly.com. URL: http://www.countypressonline.com. Mailing Address: PO Box 249, Newtown Square, PA 19073-0249. Year Established: 1985. Pub. Frequency: w. (Wed.) Page Size: tabloid. Subscrip. Rate: $.50 newsstand/cover; $20/yr. Adv. Rate: col. inch $10.47 Circulation: 2,715 per issue (paid and free). **Owner(s):** Journal Register Co., 50 W State St, 12th Fl, Trenton, NJ 08608. Telephone: 609-396-2200. **Management:** Richard Crowe, Publisher. **Editorial:** William Lawrence, Editor.

LANCASTER

SUNDAY NEWS. ISSN 0749-7067
8 W. King St., Lancaster, PA 17608-1328. FAX: 717-291-4950. E-MAIL: sunnews@lancnews.com. URL: http://www.lancasteronline.com. Mailing Address: PO Box 1328, Lancaster, PA 17608. Year Established: 1923. Pub. Frequency: w. (Sun.) Page Size: broadsheet. Subscrip. Rate: $1.75 newsstand/cover. **Wire Service(s):** AP, NYT, MCT. Circulation: 102,688 Sunday (paid). **Owner(s):** Lancaster Newspapers, Inc., See address and contact information above. **Management:** Harold Miller, Advertising Director. Keith Kirthner, Circulation Manager. Russell Gillespie, Classified Adv. Mgr.. **Editorial:** David Hennigan, Editor. Marv Adams, News Editor.

LIGONIER

LIGONIER ECHO, THE. 112 W. Main St., Ligonier, PA 15658-1290. Telephone: 724-238-2111. FAX: 724-887-5115. E-MAIL: echo@ligonier.com. URL: http://www.laurelgrouponline.com. Year Established: 1888. Pub. Frequency: w. (Thu.) Page Size: broadsheet. Subscrip. Rate: $.50 newsstand/cover; $26/yr in county; $38/yr out of county; $40/yr out of state. Adv. Rate: col. inch $7.75 Freelance Pay: $0.25/column-inch. Circulation: 4,528 per issue (paid). **Owner(s):** Laurel Group Press, 229 Pittsburgh St., Scottdale, PA 15683-0222. Telephone: 724-887-7400. FAX: 724-887-5115. **Management:** Joseph F. Soforic, General Manager. Waide Miller, Advertising Manager. Marcella Kohuth, Circulation Manager. **Editorial:** Richard Schwab, Editor.

LIGONIER FREE GAZETTE, THE. PO Box G, Ligonier, PA 15658-1607. Telephone: 724-238-5749. FAX: 724-238-5190. E-MAIL: ekaymyers@hughes.net. Year Established: 1990. Pub. Frequency: q. Page Size: tabloid Adv. Rate: page $850 Circulation: 28,000 per issue (free). **Owner(s):** E. Kay Myers, See address and contact information above. **Management:** E. Kay Myers, Publisher. **Editorial:** Gertrude Myers, Editor.

LITITZ

LITITZ RECORD EXPRESS, THE. 22 E. Main St., Lititz, PA 17543. Telephone: 717-626-2191. FAX: 717-626-1210. Mailing Address: PO Box 366, Lititz, PA 17543. Year Established: 1877. Pub. Frequency: w. (Thu.) Page Size: broadsheet. Subscrip. Rate: $.35 newsstand/cover; $13.50/yr mailed in county; $20.50/yr mailed out of county. Adv. Rate: col. inch $10.50 Circulation: 8,250 per issue (paid and free). **Owner(s):** Lancaster Newspapers, Inc., 8 W. King St., Lancaster, PA 17603. Telephone: 717-291-8811. FAX: 717-399-6506. **Management:** William Burgess, General Manager. Beverly Ken, Advertising Manager. Lisa Vallery, Circulation Manager. **Editorial:** Steve Seeber, News Editor.

MARTINSBURG

MORRISONS COVE HERALD. 113 N. Market St., Martinsburg, PA 16662-0165. Telephone: 814-793-2144. FAX: 814-793-4882. E-MAIL: mcherald@pa.net. Year Established: 1885. Pub. Frequency: w. (Thu.) Page Size: broadsheet. Subscrip. Rate: $.75 newsstand/cover; $27/yr mailed in county; $30/yr mailed in state; $32/yr mailed out of state. Circulation: 7,000 per issue (paid). **Owner(s):** Morrisons Cove Herald, Inc., See address and contact information above. **Management:** David Snyder, Publisher. Kathy Arnold, Advertising Manager. David Snyder, Business Manager. **Editorial:** David Snyder, Editor.

MCCONNELLSBURG

FULTON COUNTY NEWS. 417 E. Market St., McConnellsburg, PA 17233. Telephone: 717-977-8063. FAX: 717-485-5187. E-MAIL: fultoncountynews@comcast.net. URL: http://www.fultoncountynews.com. Mailing Address: PO Box 297, McConnellsburg, PA 17233. Year Established: 1899. Pub. Frequency: w. (Thu.) Page Size: standard. Subscrip. Rate: $.75 newsstand/cover; $25/yr in county; $30/yr out of county; $35/yr out of state. Adv. Rate: col. inch $7.15 **Wire Service(s):** AP. Circulation: 6,400 per issue (paid). **Owner(s):** Jamie S. Greathead, See address and contact information above. **Management:** Jamie Greathead, Owner. **Editorial:** Chanin Rotz, Editor. Lindsay Mellott, Copy Editor.

MCKEES ROCKS

SUBURBAN GAZETTE. 421 Locust St., McKees Rocks, PA 15136-3599. Telephone: 412-331-2645. E-MAIL: gazette@stargate.net. Year Established: 1892. Pub. Frequency: w. (Wed.) Page Size: tabloid. Subscrip. Rate: $.40 newsstand/cover; $25/yr in county; $32/yr out of county. Circulation: 8,300 per issue (paid). **Owner(s):** Virginia A. Schramm, 421 Locust St., McKees Rocks, PA 15136. Telephone: 412-331-2645. **Management:** James C. DiNardo, General Manager. Virginia A. Schramm, President. **Editorial:** James C. DiNardo, Editor.

MCMURRAY

ALMANAC (MCMURRAY), THE. ISSN 0193-581X
395 Valley Brook Rd., Ste 2, McMurray, PA 15317. Telephone: 724-941-7725. FAX: 724-941-8685. E-MAIL: lbeale@thealmanac.net. URL: http://www.thealmanac.net. Year Established: 1968. Pub. Frequency: w. (Wed.) Page Size: broadsheet. Subscrip. Rate: $.50 newsstand/cover. Circulation: 55,000 per issue (paid and free). **Owner(s):** Observer Publishing Co., 122 S. Main St., Washington, PA 15301. Telephone: 724-222-2200. **Management:** Liza N Beale, General Manager. Judi Smith, Circulation Director. Rob Anders, Sales Manager. **Editorial:** Patty Van Horn, Editor.

MEDIA

TOWN TALK NEWSPAPERS. 24 W. Baltimore Ave., Media, PA 19063. Telephone: 610-566-6755. FAX: 610-566-1261. E-MAIL: towntalknp@aol.com. URL: http://www.towntalknews.com. Mailing Address: PO Box 110, Media, PA 19063. Year Established: 1963. Pub. Frequency: w. (Wed.) Page Size: tabloid.Adv. Rate: col. inch $11.20 Circulation: 85,000 per issue (free). **Owner(s):** Journal Register Co., 50 W State St, 12th Fl, Trenton, NJ 08608. Telephone: 609-396-2200. FAX: 609-396-2292. **Management:** Rich Crowe, Publisher. **Editorial:** Christina Parker, Editor.

MIDDLEBURG

SNYDER COUNTY TIMES. 405 E. Main St., Middleburg, PA 17842. Telephone: 570-837-6065. FAX: 570-837-0776. E-MAIL: displayad@snydercountytimes.com. URL: http://www.snydercountytimes.com. Mailing Address: PO Box 356, Middleburg, PA 17842. Year Established: 1997. Pub. Frequency: w. (Sat.) Page Size: broadsheet. Subscrip. Rate: $.45 newsstand/cover; $18/yr in county; $28/yr mailed out of county; $37/yr mailed out of state. Adv. Rate: col. inch $7.25 Freelance Pay: $0.25/column-inch. Circulation: 15,989 per issue (paid and free). **Owner(s):** Snyder County Times, Inc., See address and contact information above. **Management:** Susan Weaver, Publisher. **Editorial:** Susan Weaver, Editor.

UNION COUNTY TIMES (MIDDLEBURG). 405 E. Main St., Middleburg, PA 17842. Telephone: 570-837-6065. FAX: 570-837-0776. E-MAIL: displayad@snydercountytimes.com. URL: http://www.snydercountytimes.com. Mailing Address: PO Box 356, Middleburg, PA 17842. Pub. Frequency: w. (Sat.) Page Size: broadsheet. Subscrip. Rate: $.45 newsstand/cover; $23/yr in county; $28/yr out of county; $37/yr out of state. Adv. Rate: col. inch $7,025 Circulation: 9,400 per issue (paid). **Owner(s):** Snyder County Times, Inc., See address and contact information above. **Management:** Susan Weaver, Publisher. **Editorial:** Susan Weaver, Editor.

MIFFLINBURG

MIFFLINBURG TELEGRAPH, THE. 358 Walnut St., Mifflinburg, PA 17844. Telephone: 570-966-2255. FAX: 570-966-0062. E-MAIL: heidi@mifflinburgtelegraph.com. URL: http://www.mifflinburgtelegraph.com. Year Established: 1862. Pub. Frequency: w. (Thu.) Page Size: tabloid. Subscrip. Rate: $.25 newsstand/cover; $14/yr in county; $14/yr out of county. Adv. Rate: col. inch $5 Circulation: 550 per issue (paid). **Owner(s):** John Stamm, See address and contact information above. **Management:** John Stamm, Publisher. **Editorial:** Heidi Criswell, Editor.

MIFFLINTOWN

JUNIATA SENTINEL. Old Rte. 22 W., Mifflintown, PA 17059. Telephone: 717-436-8206. FAX: 717-436-5174. Mailing Address: PO Box 127, Mifflintown, PA 17059. Year Established: 1846. Pub. Frequency: w. (Wed.) Page Size: standard. Subscrip. Rate: $.50 newsstand/cover; $18/yr mailed in county; $26/yr mailed out of county; $30/yr mailed out of state. Circulation: 8,000 per issue (paid). **Owner(s):** Advance Publications, Inc., 950 Fingerboard Rd., Staten Island, NY 10305. Telephone: 718-981-1234. **Management:** Rick White, Publisher. **Editorial:** Carol Smith, Editor.

MILFORD

PIKE COUNTY DISPATCH. ISSN 1059-2377
PO Box 186, Milford, PA 18337. Telephone: 570-296-6641. FAX: 570-296-2610. E-MAIL: suedl@ptd.net. Year Established: 1826. Pub. Frequency: w. (Thu.) Page Size: broadsheet. Subscrip. Rate: $.75 newsstand/cover; $38/yr in state; $44/yr out of state. Freelance Pay: $30/story. Circulation: 6,000 per issue (paid). **Owner(s):** Sue Doty-Lloyd, See address and contact information above. **Management:** Sue Doty-Lloyd, Publisher. Caren Delukey, Advertising. **Editorial:** Christopher Jones, Editor.

MILLERSBURG

UPPER DAUPHIN SENTINEL. PO Box 250, Millersburg, PA 17061. Telephone: 717-692-4737. FAX: 717-692-2420. E-MAIL: uds@epix.net. URL: http://www.sentinelnow.com. Year Established: 1972. Pub. Frequency: w. (Tue.) Page Size: broadsheet. Subscrip. Rate: $.50 newsstand/cover; $26/yr in state; $30/yr mailed out of state; $34/yr mailed elsewhere. Adv. Rate: col. inch $6.95 Circulation: 9,500 per issue (paid). **Owner(s):** Kocher Enterprises, Inc., See address and contact information above. **Management:** Ben L. Kocher, Publisher. Dale Hoy, Advertising Manager. **Editorial:** Duane Good, Editor.

MONACA

BEAVER VALLEY STAR (ONLINE EDITION). 1016 Bechtel St., Monaca, PA 15061. Telephone: 724-774-4380. FAX: 724-774-2197. E-MAIL: beavervalley.star@trinity-pgh.com. URL: http://www.beavervalleystar.com. Pub. Frequency: w. (Wed.) Page Size: tabloid. Circulation: 10,000 per issue (paid and free). **Owner(s):** Gateway Newspapers, 610 Beatty Rd., Monroeville, PA 15146. Telephone: 412-856-7400. **Management:** Lee Mooty, Publisher. Kathleen Brieck, Advertising Manager. Kris Ranker, Classified Adv. Mgr.. **Editorial:** Vince Townley, Editor.

MONROEVILLE

ADVANCE LEADER, THE. 610 Beatty Rd., Monroeville, PA 15146. Telephone: 412-856-7400. FAX: 412-856-7954. E-MAIL: advance.leader@gatewaynewspapers.xom. URL: http://www.plumborostar.com. Year Established: 1901. Pub. Frequency: w. (Wed.) Page Size: broadsheet.Subscrip. Rate: $.50 newsstand/cover; $25/yr Circulation: 5,879 per issue (paid). **Owner(s):** Gateway Newspapers, See address and contact information above. **Management:** Gary Siegel, Advertising Manager. Jon Kennell, Circulation Director. **Editorial:** Dave Titinus, Editor. Micheal Love, Sports Editor.

MURRYSVILLE STAR. 610 Beatty Rd., Monroeville, PA 15146. Telephone: 412-856-7400. FAX: 412-856-7954. E-MAIL: gateway@gatewaynewspapers.com. URL: http://www.murrysvillestar.com. Year Established: 1972. Pub. Frequency: w. (Wed.) Page Size: broadsheet. Subscrip. Rate: $.50 newsstand/cover; $25/yr in county; $40/yr out of county. Circulation: 5,721 per issue (paid and free). **Owner(s):** Gateway Newspapers, See address and contact information above. **Management:** Lee Mooty, Publisher. Gary Siegel, Advertising Manager. Jon Kennell, Circulation Director. Kris Ranker, Classified Adv. Mgr.. **Editorial:** Kevin Ritchart, Editor. Edith Hughes, Executive Editor. Jim McNamara, Sports.

NORWIN STAR. 610 Beatty Rd., Monroeville, PA 15146. Telephone: 412-856-7400. FAX: 412-856-7954. E-MAIL: norwin.star@gatewaynewspapers.com. URL: http://www.norwinstar.com. Pub. Frequency: w. (Wed.) Page Size: tabloid. Subscrip. Rate: $.50 newsstand/cover; $25/yr in county; $40/yr out of county. **Owner(s):** Gateway Newspapers, See address and contact information above. **Management:** Gary Siegel, Advertising Manager. Kris Ranker, Classified Adv. Mgr.. **Editorial:** Jim McNamara, Sports.

PENN HILLS PROGRESS. 610 Beatty Rd., Monroeville, PA 15146. Telephone: 412-856-7400. FAX: 412-856-7954. E-MAIL: progress@gatewaynewspapers.com. URL: http://www.pennhillsstar.com. Year Established: 1963. Pub. Frequency: w. (Wed.) Page Size: broadsheet. Subscrip. Rate: $.50 newsstand/cover (effective 2005); $25/yr. **Owner(s):** Gateway Newspapers, See address and contact information above. **Management:** Gary Siegel, Advertising Manager. Jon Kennell, Circulation Director. **Editorial:** Alan Wallace, Editor. Micheal Love, Sports Editor.

PLUM ADVANCE LEADER. 610 Beatty Rd., Monroeville, PA 15146. Telephone: 412-856-7400. FAX: 412-856-7954. E-MAIL: gateway-editorial@gatewaynewspaper.com. URL: http://www.plumborostar.com. Year Established: 1964. Pub. Frequency: w. (Wed.) Page Size: standard. Subscrip. Rate: $.50 newsstand/cover; $25/yr mailed. **Owner(s):** Gateway Newspapers, See address and contact information above. **Management:** Gary Siegel, Advertising Director. Jon Kennell, Circulation Director. Kris Ranker, Classified Adv. Mgr.. **Editorial:** Dave Titinus, Editor. Michael Love, Sports.

PROGRESS (MONROEVILLE), THE. 610 Beatty Rd., Monroeville, PA 15146. Telephone: 412-856-7400. FAX: 412-856-7954. E-MAIL: gateway@ghplus.infl.net. URL: http://www.ghplus.com. Year Established: 1948. Pub. Frequency: w. (Wed.) Page Size: broadsheet.Subscrip. Rate: $.50 newsstand/cover; $25/yr Circulation: 7,004 per issue (paid). **Owner(s):** Gateway Newspapers, See address and contact information above. **Management:** Scott Patterson, President. Lee Mooty, Publisher. Harry Kelly, Advertising Manager. **Editorial:** Edith Hughes, Executive Editor.

Weeklies

PITTSBURGH CITY PAPER. ISSN 1066-0062
650 Smithfield St., Ste. 2200, Pittsburgh, PA 15222. Telephone: 412-316-3342. FAX: 412-316-3388. E-MAIL: bdoering@steelcitymedia.com. URL: http://www.pghcitypaper.com. Year Established: 1991. Pub. Frequency: w. (Wed.) Page Size: tabloid. Subscrip. Rate: $60 for 6 mos.; $110/yr. Adv. Rate: page $2,500 Circulation: 77,500 per issue (paid and free). **Owner(s):** Saul Frischling, See address and contact information above. **Management:** Robert J Doering, Advertising Director. Jim Lavrinc, Circulation Manager. Chris Kohan, Sales Manager. Lisa Cunningham, Production Director. **Editorial:** Chris Potter, Editor. Bill O'Driscoll, Entertainment Editor.

SEWICKLEY HERALD STAR. 1964 Greentree Rd, Pittsburgh, PA 15220. Telephone: 412-388-5800. FAX: 412-388-0900. E-MAIL: sewickley.herald@gatewaynewspapers.com. URL: http://www.sewickleystar.com. Pub. Frequency: w. (Wed.) Page Size: tabloid. Subscrip. Rate: $.50 newsstand/cover; $25/yr in county; $40/yr out of county. **Owner(s):** Gateway Newspapers, 610 Beatty Rd., Monroeville, PA 15146. Telephone: 412-856-7400. FAX: 412-856-7954. **Management:** Kathleen Brieck, Advertising Manager. Kris Ranker, Classified Adv. Mgr.. **Editorial:** Dona Dreeland, Editor. Jon Paul Creese, Sports Editor.

SOUTH HILLS RECORD. 1964 Greentree Rd., Pittsburgh, PA 15220. Telephone: 412-388-5800. FAX: 412-884-3106. E-MAIL: shillsl@ghplusinfi.net. URL: http://www.ghplus.com. Year Established: 1903. Pub. Frequency: w. (Thu.) Page Size: tabloid. Subscrip. Rate: $.50 newsstand/cover; $20.80/yr carrier delivery; $25/yr mailed in county; $40/yr mailed out of county. Circulation: 7,000 per issue (paid). **Owner(s):** Gateway Newspapers, 610 Beatty Rd., Monroeville, PA 15146. Telephone: 412-856-7400. FAX: 412-856-7954. **Management:** Larry Dorschner, Publisher. Kathleen Brieck, Advertising Manager. **Editorial:** Kevin R Ritchart, Editor. Edith Hughes, Executive Editor. Ray Fisher, Sports Editor.

SOUTH PITTSBURGH REPORTER. 813 E. Warrington Ave., Pittsburgh, PA 15210. Telephone: 412-481-0266. FAX: 412-488-8011. E-MAIL: news@sopghreporter.com. Year Established: 1939. Pub. Frequency: w. (Tue.) Page Size: tabloid. Subscrip. Rate: $55/yr mailed. Adv. Rate: col. inch $8.10 Circulation: 12,000 per issue (paid and controlled). **Owner(s):** William T. Smith Jr., See address and contact information above. **Management:** William T. Smith Jr., Publisher. **Editorial:** Thomas Smith, Managing Editor.

PITTSTON

SUNDAY DISPATCH. 109 New St., Pittston, PA 18640. Telephone: 570-655-1418. FAX: 570-883-1266. Year Established: 1948. Pub. Frequency: w. (Sun) Page Size: tabloid.Subscrip. Rate: $1 newsstand/cover; $52/yr Circulation: 10,000 per issue (paid). **Owner(s):** Knight Ridder, Inc., 50 W. San Fernando St., Ste. 1200, San Jose, CA 95113. Telephone: 831-938-7700. FAX: 831-938-7755. **Management:** Steven Morris, Advertising Manager. **Editorial:** Eddie Ackerman, Editor. Ed Philin, Managing Editor. Tom Bubul, Production Manager. Jack Smiles, Sports.

PORT ROYAL

TIMES (PORT ROYAL), THE. 111 W. Fourth St., Port Royal, PA 17082. Telephone: 717-527-2213. FAX: 717-527-2787. E-MAIL: thetimes@nmax.net. Year Established: 1876. Pub. Frequency: w. (Wed.) Page Size: standard. Subscrip. Rate: $.50 newsstand/cover; $14/yr in county; $20/yr out of county. Circulation: 2,500 per issue (paid). **Owner(s):** Donna K. Swartz, See address and contact information above. **Management:** Donna K. Swartz, Publisher. Ruthann Benner, Classified Adv. Mgr.. **Editorial:** Donna K. Swartz, Editor.

PORTAGE

PORTAGE DISPATCH, THE. 808 Caldwell Ave., Ste. 103, Portage, PA 15946. Telephone: 814-736-8905. FAX: 814-736-8908. E-MAIL: mainlinenews@verizon.com. URL: http://www.mainlinenewspapers.com. Year Established: 1904. Pub. Frequency: w. (Wed.) Page Size: broadsheet. Subscrip. Rate: $.50 newsstand/cover; $26/yr in county; $30/yr mailed in state; $39/yr mailed out of state. Freelance Pay: $20/article. Circulation: 5,303 per issue (paid). **Owner(s):** Latrobe Printing & Publishing, PO Box 111, Latrobe, PA 15650. Telephone: 724-537-3351. **Management:** William Anderson, Publisher. Melissa Shirk, Advertising. Dave Thompson, Circulation Manager. Beth Murphy, Classified Adv. Mgr.. **Editorial:** Paula Varner, Managing Editor. Emily Stewart, Reporter.

PUNXUTAWNEY

JEFFERSON COUNTY NEIGHBORS, THE. ISSN 1065-268X
510 Pine St, Punxutawney, PA 15767. Telephone: 814-938-8740. FAX: 814-938-3794. E-MAIL: publisher@punxsutawneyspirit.com. URL: http://www.punxsutawneyspirit.com. Mailing Address: PO Box 444, Punxutawney, PA 15767. Year Established: 1991. Pub. Frequency: w. (Sat.) Page Size: standard.Adv. Rate: col. inch $6.60 **Wire Service(s):** AP. Circulation: 7,525 per issue (free). **Owner(s):** Horizon Publications, Inc., 1120 N. Carbon St., Ste.100, Marion, IL 62959. Telephone: 618-993-1693. FAX: 618-997-4018. **Management:** Mary Jude Troupe, Publisher. Helen Long, Circulation Manager. **Editorial:** Tom Chapin, Editor.

QUAKERTOWN

FREE PRESS (QUAKERTOWN), THE. 312 W. Broad St., Quakertown, PA 18951. Telephone: 215-536-6820. FAX: 215-536-7201. Year Established: 1881. Pub. Frequency: w. (Wed.) Page Size: broadsheet.Subscrip. Rate: $35/yr mailed Circulation: 10,200 per issue (paid). **Owner(s):** Berks-Mont Newspapers, Inc., See address and contact information above. **Management:** Chris Barnes, Publisher. Lanita Lum, Manager. **Editorial:** Chris Barnes, Editor.

QUARRYVILLE

SOLANCO SUN LEDGER. 22 E. State St., Quarryville, PA 17566. Telephone: 717-786-2992. FAX: 717-786-8679. E-MAIL: ledger@allaroundphilly.com. URL: http://www.solancosunledger.com. Year Established: 1882. Pub. Frequency: w. (Thu.) Page Size: broadsheet. Subscrip. Rate: $.50 newsstand/cover; $24/yr in county; $32/yr mailed out of county; $37/yr mailed out of state. Circulation: 4,600 per issue (free). **Owner(s):** Journal Register Co., 50 W State St, 12th Fl, Trenton, NJ 08608. Telephone: 609-396-2200. **Management:** Edward S. Condra, Publisher. Dick Carrigan, Advertising Director. Teresa Pennington, Classified Adv. Mgr.. **Editorial:** Fran Maye, Editor.

RED HILL

TOWN & COUNTRY. P.O. Box 462, Red Hill, PA 18076-0462. E-MAIL: townandcountry@upvnews.com. URL: http://www.upvnews.com. Year Established: 1899. Pub. Frequency: w. (Thu.) Page Size: tabloid. Subscrip. Rate: $.50 newsstand/cover; $26/yr in county & adj ones (effective 2008); $35/yr mailed in state; $50/yr mailed out of state. Adv. Rate: col. inch $7.50 Circulation: 6,000 per issue (paid). **Owner(s):** L J R Publishing, LLC, 2508 Kutztown Rd, Pennsburg, PA 19073. Telephone: 215-679-5060. **Management:** Larry J Roeder, Publisher. **Editorial:** Larry J Roeder, Editor.Readers: Regional

ROBINSON TWP.

BRIDGEVILLE STAR NEWS. ISSN 1047-0670
5500 Steubenville Pike, Montour Plz., Ste. 1-A, Robinson Twp., PA 15136-1401. E-MAIL: newsitem@ghplus.infi.net. URL: http://www.bridgevillestar.com. Year Established: 1926. Pub. Frequency: w. (Wed.) Page Size: tabloid.Subscrip. Rate: $.50 newsstand/cover; $25/yr Circulation: 2,519 per issue (paid). **Owner(s):** Gateway Newspapers, 610 Beatty Rd., Monroeville, PA 15146. FAX: 412-856-7954, 412-388-5801. **Management:** Larry Dorschner, Publisher. Kathleen Brieck, Advertising Manager. Kris Ranker, Classified Adv. Mgr.. **Editorial:** Bob Pastin, Managing Editor. Chris Scarnati, Sports Editor.

CORAOPOLIS RECORD, THE. ISSN 1047-0689
5500 Stubenville Pike, Mountour Plz., Ste. 1-A, Robinson Twp., PA 15136. Telephone: 412-388-5800. FAX: 412-856-7954. E-MAIL: gateway@ghplus.infi.net. URL: http://www.ghplus.com. Year Established: 1903. Pub. Frequency: w. (Wed.) Page Size: tabloid. Subscrip. Rate: $.50 newsstand/cover; $.40 home delivery/wk.; $25/yr. Circulation: 4,862 per issue (paid). **Owner(s):** Gateway Newspapers, 610 Beatty Rd., Monroeville, PA 15146. Telephone: 412-856-7400. FAX: 412-856-7954. **Management:** Kathleen Brieck, Advertising Manager. Jon Kennell, Circulation Director. Kris Ranker, Classified Adv. Mgr.. **Editorial:** Edith Hughes, Executive Editor. Bob Pastin, Managing Editor. Chris Scarnati, Sports Editor.

ROYERSFORD

REPORTER OF THE SPRING-FORD AREA. 265 Main St., Royersford, PA 19468. Telephone: 610-948-4850. FAX: 610-948-5914. Year Established: 1872. Pub. Frequency: w. (Thu.) Page Size: broadsheet. Subscrip. Rate: $.50 newsstand/cover; $28.95/yr carrier delivery in county; $28.95/yr mailed in county; $34.95/yr mailed elsewhere. Circulation: 5,008 per issue (paid and free). **Owner(s):** Journal Register Co., 50 W State St, 12th Fl, Trenton, NJ 08608. Telephone: 609-396-2200. **Management:** Betsy Wilson, Publisher. Michele Meckler, Advertising Manager. John Maguire, Circulation Manager. **Editorial:** Sarah Sando, Managing Editor. Dave Holloway, Sports.

VALLEY ITEM. 265 Main St., Royersford, PA 19468. Telephone: 610-948-4850. FAX: 610-948-5914. E-MAIL: bwilson@montgomerynews.com. URL: http://www.valleyitem.com. Pub. Frequency: w. (Wed.) Page Size: broadsheet. Subscrip. Rate: $.50 newsstand/cover; $24.95/yr home delivery in county; $24.95/yr mailed out of county; $34.95/yr mailed out of state. Adv. Rate: col. inch $14.46 Circulation: 3,148 per issue (paid). **Owner(s):** Journal Register Co., 50 W State St, 12th Fl, Trenton, NJ 08608. Telephone: 609-396-2200. **Management:** Betsy Wilson, Publisher. Michele Meckler, Advertising Director. John Maguire, Circulation Manager. **Editorial:** Sarah Sando, Editor. Fred Behringer, Executive Editor. Sarah Sando, Managing Editor. Dave Holloway, Sports.

SAYRE

SAYRE TIMES EXTRA, THE. 201 N. Lehigh Ave., Sayre, PA 18840. Telephone: 570-888-9643. FAX: 570-888-6463. URL: http://www.gatehousemedia.com.Pub. Frequency: Sat.) Page Size: standard Circulation: 8,300 per issue (free). **Owner(s):** GateHouse Media, Inc, 350 WillowBrook Office Park, Fairport, NY 14450. Telephone: 585-598-0030. FAX: 585-248-2631. **Management:** Ted Mike Jr., Publisher. Vickee Mike, Advertising Director.

SCHUYLKILL HAVEN

CALL (SCHUYLKILL HAVEN), THE. PO Box 178, Schuylkill Haven, PA 17972. Telephone: 570-385-3120. FAX: 570-385-0725. Year Established: 1891. Pub. Frequency: w. (Thu.) Page Size: standard. Subscrip. Rate: $.75 newsstand/cover; $30/yr in county; $35/yr mailed out of county; $40/yr mailed out of state. Adv. Rate: col. inch $9.70 Circulation: 4,445 per issue (paid). **Owner(s):** Call Newspapers, Inc., See address and contact information above. **Management:** Fred V. Knecht, Publisher. William Knecht, Advertising Manager. **Editorial:** LaJeune Steidle, Editor.

SCOTTDALE

ADVISOR (SCOTTDALE), THE. 229 Pittsburgh St., Scottdale, PA 15683. Telephone: 724-887-7400. FAX: 724-887-5115. E-MAIL: igp@scottdale.com. Mailing Address: PO Box 222, Scottdale, PA 15683. Year Established: 1978. Pub. Frequency: w. (Thu.) Page Size: broadsheet. Subscrip. Rate: $.35 newsstand/cover; $18.60/yr in county; $28.60/yr in state; $31.60/yr out of state. Freelance Pay: $0.20/column-inch. Circulation: 3,426 per issue (paid). **Owner(s):** Laurel Group Press, 229 Pittsburgh St., Scottdale, PA 15683-0222. Telephone: 724-887-7400. **Management:** Joseph F. Soforic, Publisher. Arthur Myers, Advertising Manager. Marcella Kohuth, Circulation Manager. **Editorial:** Paul S. Brittain, Editor.

INDEPENDENT-OBSERVER, THE. 229 Pittsburgh St., Scottdale, PA 15683-0222. Telephone: 724-887-6101. FAX: 724-887-5115. E-MAIL: lgpa@scottdale.com. Mailing Address: PO Box 222, Scottdale, PA 15683-0222. Year Established: 1879. Pub. Frequency: w. (Thu.) Page Size: broadsheet. Subscrip. Rate: $.50 newsstand/cover; $26/yr in county; $38/yr out of county; $40/yr out of state. Adv. Rate: col. inch $7.75 Circulation: 3,470 per issue (paid). **Owner(s):** Laurel Group Press, 229 Pittsburgh St., Scottdale, PA 15683. Telephone: 412-887-7400. **Management:** Joseph F. Soforic, General Manager. Charles Hixson, Advertising Manager. Marcella Kohuth, Circulation Manager. **Editorial:** Marlena C. Soloman, Editor.

JEANNETTE SPIRIT, THE. ISSN 0746-5971
229 Pittsburgh St., Scottdale, PA 15683. Telephone: 412-887-7400. Mailing Address: PO Box 530, Jeannette, PA 15644. Year Established: 1983. Pub. Frequency: w. (Thu.) Page Size: standard. Subscrip. Rate: $.45 newsstand/cover; $23/yr in county; $31/yr mailed out of county; $33/yr mailed out of state. Adv. Rate: col. inch $7.75 Freelance Pay: $0.25/column-inch. Circulation: 2,086 per issue (paid). **Owner(s):** Laurel Group Press, See address and contact information above. **Management:** Joseph F. Soforic, General Manager. Arthur Meyers, Advertising Manager. Marcella Kohuth, Circulation Manager. **Editorial:** Gregory L. Stock, Editor.

SHARON

HUBBARD PRESS. 52 S Dock St, Sharon, PA 16146. Telephone: 724-981-6100. FAX: 724-981-7844. Mailing Address: PO Box 51, Sharon, PA 16146-0051. Year Established: 1997. Pub. Frequency: w. (Sat.) Page Size: standard Circulation: 4,000 per issue (free). **Owner(s):** Community Newspaper Holdings, Inc., 3500 Colonnade Pkwy., Ste. 600, Birmingham, AL 35243-2304. Telephone: 205-298-7100. FAX: 205-298-7108. **Management:** John L. Lima, Publisher. Sharon Sorg, Advertising Director. **Editorial:** John Zavinski, Editor.

NORTHERN CAMBRIA

STAR COURIER, THE. 520 Philadelphia Ave., Northern Cambria, PA 15714. Telephone: 814-472-4110. FAX: 814-948-7563. E-MAIL: mainlinenews@verizon.net. URL: http://www.mainlinenewspapers.com. Mailing Address: PO Box 1158, Northern Cambria, PA 15714. Year Established: 1902. Pub. Frequency: w. (Wed.) Page Size: broadsheet. Subscrip. Rate: $.50 newsstand/cover; $26/yr mailed in county; $32/yr mailed out of county; $42/yr mailed out of state. Freelance Pay: $10/article. Circulation: 4,700 per issue (paid). **Owner(s):** Latrobe Printing & Publishing, PO Box 111, Latrobe, PA 15650. Telephone: 724-537-3351. **Management:** William Anderson, Publisher. Jane Murphy, Advertising. **Editorial:** Paula Varner, Managing Editor. Kasey Miller, Bureau Chief.

ORBISONIA

VALLEY LOG, THE. 111 S. Ridgley St., Orbisonia, PA 17243-0219. Telephone: 814-447-5506. FAX: 814-447-3050. E-MAIL: vallog@penn.com. URL: http://www.valleylog.com. Mailing Address: PO Box 219, Orbisonia, PA 17243-0219. Year Established: 1980. Pub. Frequency: w. (Wed.) Page Size: broadsheet. Subscrip. Rate: $.50 newsstand/cover; $12.50 for 6 mos. in county; $25/yr in county; $35/yr mailed out of county. Adv. Rate: col. inch $4 Circulation: 3,700 per issue (paid). **Owner(s):** C. Arnold McClure, See address and contact information above. **Management:** C. Arnold McClure, President. Linda McClure, Business Manager. **Editorial:** Tammy E. Foor, Editor.

OXFORD

CHESTER COUNTY PRESS. c/o Randy Lieberman, 309 Limestone Rd, PO Box 520, Oxford, PA 19363-0520. Telephone: 610-932-2444. FAX: 610-932-2246. E-MAIL: mfmm182@prodigy.com. URL: http://www.chestercounty.com/press. Year Established: 1866. Pub. Frequency: w. (Wed.) Page Size: broadsheet. Subscrip. Rate: $.60 newsstand/cover; $28/yr in county; $35/yr out of county; $24/yr to senior citizens. **Wire Service(s):** AP. Circulation: 17,000 per issue (paid). **Owner(s):** AdPro, Inc., 5000 Limestone Rd., Oxford, PA 19363. Telephone: 610-932-2444. **Management:** Andrew H. Lieberman, Publisher. Malisa Maurits, Office Manager. Alan E. Turns, Advertising Manager. **Editorial:** Carla Lucas, News Editor.

OXFORD TRIBUNE. 407 Market St, Oxford, PA 19363. Telephone: 610-932-8530. FAX: 610-932-2808. E-MAIL: oxfordtribune@zoominternet.net. Year Established: 1986. Pub. Frequency: w. (Thu.) Page Size: broadsheet. Subscrip. Rate: $.50 newsstand/cover; $24/yr home delivery in county; $32/yr mailed out of county; $37/yr mailed out of state. Circulation: 3,000 per issue (paid and free). **Owner(s):** Journal Register Co., 50 W State St, 12th Fl, Trenton, NJ 08608. Telephone: 609-396-2200. **Management:** Edward S. Condra, Publisher. Dick Carrigan, Advertising Director. Teresa Pennington, Classified Adv. Mgr.. **Editorial:** Michelle Sensenig, Editor. Fran Maye, Senior Editor.

PHILADELPHIA

BREEZE, THE. 9999 Gantry Rd., Philadelphia, PA 19115. Telephone: 215-969-5100. FAX: 215-969-5400. E-MAIL: dfoster@newsgleaner.com. Year Established: 1927. Pub. Frequency: w. (Thu.) Page Size: tabloid. Subscrip. Rate: $.35 newsstand/cover; $75/yr mailed. Circulation: 21,750 per issue (paid and free). **Owner(s):** News Gleaner Publications, Inc., See address and contact information above. **Management:** Stephine Leicht, Publisher. John Steinruck, Advertising Manager. Pat McNally, Circulation Manager. **Editorial:** David J. Foster, Editor.

CHESTNUT HILL LOCAL.   ISSN 0009-3394
8434 Germantown Ave, Philadelphia, PA 19118. Telephone: 215-248-8800. E-MAIL: lea@chestnuthilllocal.com. URL: http://www.chestnuthilllocal.com. Year Established: 1958. Pub. Frequency: w. Page Size: tabloid. Subscrip. Rate: $20/yr; $38 for 2 yrs.. Freelance Pay: $25-$35/story. Circulation: 10,000. **Owner(s):** Chestnut Hill Community Association, See address and contact information above. **Management:** Frank Moeschlin, Advertising. Karl-Eric Strandberg, Advertising Manager. Cheryl Massaro, Circulation Manager. Mary Flannery, Classified Adv. Mgr.. **Editorial:** Lea Citton Stanley, Editor. Pete Mazzaccaro, Associate Editor. Len Lear, Entertainment Editor.

GERMANTOWN COURIER. 6220 Ridge Ave, Philadelphia, PA 19119. Telephone: 215-848-8792. FAX: 215-848-0474. E-MAIL: editor@germantown.com. URL: http://www.germantowncourier.com.. Mailing Address: PO Box 18971, Philadelphia, PA 19119. Year Established: 1936. Pub. Frequency: w. (Wed.) Page Size: tabloid. Subscrip. Rate: $20/yr mailed. Circulation: 20,000 per issue (controlled and free). **Owner(s):** Journal Register Co., 50 W State St, 12th Fl, Trenton, NJ 08608. Telephone: 609-396-2200. FAX: 609-396-2292. **Management:** Dianne Ryan-Paschall, Publisher. James Clarke, Circulation Manager. Bob Canner, Classified Adv. Mgr.. **Editorial:** Karl Biemuller, Managing Editor.

JUNIATA NEWS. 2241 N. Fifth St., Philadelphia, PA 19133-2599. Telephone: 215-739-8197. FAX: 215-739-9290. E-MAIL: juniatanews@comcast.net. Mailing Address: PO Box 15336, Philadelphia, PA 19111-5336. Year Established: 1934. Pub. Frequency: w. (Tue.) Page Size: tabloid. Subscrip. Rate: $.25 newsstand/cover; $75/yr mailed. Circulation: 10,000 per issue (paid and free). **Owner(s):** Gerard R. Lineman, See address and contact information above.

LEADER (PHILADELPHIA), THE. 2385 W. Cheltenham Ave., Ste. 182, Philadelphia, PA 19150-1506. Telephone: 215-885-4111. FAX: 215-885-0226. E-MAIL: leader@ingnews.com. URL: http://www.wolLeader.com. Year Established: 1962. Pub. Frequency: w. (Wed.) Page Size: tabloid. Subscrip. Rate: $78/yr mailed. Adv. Rate: col. inch $14.50 Circulation: 29,000 per issue (controlled and free). **Owner(s):** Journal Register Co., 50 W State St, 12th Fl, Trenton, NJ 08608. Telephone: 609-396-2200. FAX: 609-396-2292. **Management:** Richard Plyler, General Manager. Stephanie Leicht, Publisher. **Editorial:** Gene Szostak, Editor.

MT. AIRY TIMES EXPRESS. 6220 Ridge Ave, Philadelphia, PA 19119. Telephone: 215-848-8792. FAX: 215-848-0474. E-MAIL: editor@germantowncourier.com. URL: http://www.germantown.com. Year Established: 1991. Pub. Frequency: w. (Wed.) Page Size: tabloid. Subscrip. Rate: $35/yr mailed. Freelance Pay: $25/story. Circulation: 14,000 per issue (paid and free). **Owner(s):** Journal Register Co., PO Box 18971, Philadelphia, PA 19119. 50 W State St, 12th Fl, Trenton, NJ 08608. Telephone: 609-396-2200. FAX: 609-396-2292. **Management:** Dianne Ryan-Paschall, Publisher. James Clarke, Circulation Manager. Bob Canner, Classified Adv. Mgr.. **Editorial:** Karl Biemuller, Managing Editor.

NEWS GLEANER. 9999 Gantry Rd., Philadelphia, PA 19115. Telephone: 215-969-5100. FAX: 215-969-5400. URL: http://www.newsgleaner.com. Year Established: 1882. Pub. Frequency: w. (Wed.) Page Size: broadsheet. Subscrip. Rate: $25 newsstand/cover; $90/yr mailed. **Wire Service(s):** AP. Circulation: 147,177 per issue (paid and free). **Owner(s):** Journal Register Co., 50 W State St, 12th Fl, Trenton, NJ 08608. Telephone: 609-396-2292. **Management:** Stephanie Leicht, Publisher. Monica Carpenter, Advertising Director. John Steinruck, Advertising Manager. John Mcquire, Circulation Manager. **Editorial:** Patrick McNally, News Editor. Stuart London, Sports Editor.

NEWSGLEANER - BUSTLETON - SOMERTON EDITION. 9999 Gantry Rd., Philadelphia, PA 19115. Telephone: 215-969-5100. FAX: 215-969-5400. URL: http://newsgleaner.com. Year Established: 1882.Pub. Frequency: w. (Wed.) Subscrip. Rate: $154/yr Circulation: 120,000 (paid). **Owner(s):** News Gleaner Publications, Inc., See address and contact information above. **Management:** Stephine Leicht, Publisher.

NEWSGLEANER - FAR NORTHEAST EDITION. 9999 Gautry Rd., Philadelphia, PA 19115. URL: http://www.newsgleaner.com. Year Established: 1979. Pub. Frequency: w. (Wed.) Subscrip. Rate: $154/yr Circulation: 120,000 per issue (paid). **Owner(s):** News Gleaner Publications, Inc., See address and contact information above. **Management:** Stephine Leicht, Publisher.

NEWSGLEANER - FRANKFORD - OXFORD CIRCLE EDITION. 9999 Gautry Rd., Philadelphia, PA 19115. URL: http://www.newsgleaner.com. Year Established: 1882.Pub. Frequency: w. (Wed.) Subscrip. Rate: $154/yr Circulation: 120,000 (paid). **Owner(s):** News Gleaner Publications, Inc., See address and contact information above. **Management:** Stephine Leicht, Publisher.

NEWSGLEANER - MAYFAIR - NORTHEAST EDITION. 9999 Gautry Rd., Philadelphia, PA 19115. URL: http://www.newsgleaner.com. Year Established: 1939.Pub. Frequency: w. (Wed.) Subscrip. Rate: $154/yr Circulation: 120,000 (paid). **Owner(s):** News Gleaner Publications, Inc., See address and contact information above. **Management:** Stephine Leicht, Publisher.

OLNEY TIMES. 6001 N. Fifth St., Philadelphia, PA 19120. Telephone: 215-424-0700. FAX: 215-424-4082. URL: http://www.olneytimes.com. Year Established: 1909. Pub. Frequency: w. (Thu.) Page Size: broadsheet. Subscrip. Rate: $75/yr mailed. Adv. Rate: col. inch $10 Circulation: 22,000 per issue (free). **Owner(s):** Journal Register Co., 50 W State St, 12th Fl, Trenton, NJ 08608. Telephone: 609-396-2200. **Management:** Jean Pleis, General Manager. Stephanie Leicht, Publisher. John Steinruck, Advertising Manager. **Editorial:** David Henry, Executive Editor.

PHILADELPHIA CITY PAPER.   ISSN 0733-6349
123 Chestnut St, 3rd Fl, Philadelphia, PA 19106. Telephone: 215-735-8444. FAX: 215-599-0634. E-MAIL: adinfo@citypaper.net. URL: http://citypaper.net. Year Established: 1981. Pub. Frequency: w. (Thu.) Page Size: tabloid. Subscrip. Rate: $1 newsstand/cover; $52/yr mailed. Circulation: 94,000 (controlled and free). **Owner(s):** Metro Week Corp., See address and contact information above. **Management:** Bruce Schimmel, Founder. Paul Curci, Publisher. Amy Stoller, Advertising Director. Danny Coniglio, Classified Adv. Mgr.. **Editorial:** Diane Swierczynski, Editor-in-Chief. Brian Hickey, Managing Editor. Ashlea Halpern, Associate Editor. Patrick Rapa, Entertainment Editor.

PHILADELPHIA WEEKLY. 1500 Walnut St., 3rd Fl., Philadelphia, PA 19102. Telephone: 215-563-7400. FAX: 215-563-6799. URL: http://www.philadelphiaweekly.com. Year Established: 1971. Pub. Frequency: w. (Wed.) Page Size: tabloid. Subscrip. Rate: $30 for 6 mos.; $55/yr. Adv. Rate: col. inch $56 Circulation: 105,500 per issue (paid and free). **Owner(s):** Review Publishing, Ltd., See address and contact information above. **Management:** Anthony Clifton, Chief Executive Ofc. . Nancy Stuski, Publisher. Stephanie Kaplan, Advertising Director. Stephen P. Brown, Circulation Manager. Beth Douglas, Classified Adv. Mgr. **Editorial:** Tim Whitaker, Editor. Sara Kelly, Executive Editor. Liz Spikol, Managing Editor. Steve Volk, Senior Editor. Jeffrey Barg, Associate Editor. Jessica Griffin, Photographer.

REVIEW (PHILADELPHIA), THE. 6220 Ridge Ave., Philadelphia, PA 19128-3306. Telephone: 215-483-7300. FAX: 215-483-2073. E-MAIL: review@ingnews.com. URL: http://www.roxreview.com. Year Established: 1902. Pub. Frequency: w. (Wed.) Page Size: broadsheet. Subscrip. Rate: $.50 newsstand/cover; $49/yr. Adv. Rate: col. inch $18.90 Circulation: 23,500 per issue (paid). **Owner(s):** Journal Register Co., 50 W. State St., 12th Fl., Trenton, NJ 08608-1298. Telephone: 609-396-2200. FAX: 609-396-2292. **Management:** Stephanie Leicht, Publisher. Monica Carpenter, Advertising Director. Ed Krywucki, Circulation Manager. **Editorial:** George Beetham, Editor.

SOUTH PHILLY REVIEW. 1500 Sansom St, Philadelphia, PA 19102. Telephone: 215-336-2500. FAX: 215-336-1112. E-MAIL: cmarone@southphillyreview.com. URL: http://www.southphillyreview.com. Year Established: 1996. Pub. Frequency: w. (Thu.) Page Size: tabloid Circulation: 62,000 per issue (free). **Owner(s):** Review Publishing, Ltd., See address and contact information above. **Management:** Anthony Clifton, Chief Executive Ofc. . George Troyano, President. John Gallo, Publisher. Anthony Clifton, Chairman. George Troyano, COO. John Gallo, Vice President. Daniel Tangi, Advertising Manager. Mark Romano, Marketing. **Editorial:** Cynthia Marone, Editor. Bill Gelman, Managing Editor.Readers: South Phila. residents and former residents

PHOENIXVILLE

TOWNSHIP VOICE, THE. 225 Bridge St., Phoenixville, PA 19460. Telephone: 610-933-8926. FAX: 610-933-1187. URL: http://www.phoenixnews.com. Pub. Frequency: w. (Thu.) Page Size: broadsheet Circulation: 20,000 per issue (free). **Owner(s):** Journal Register Co., 50 W. State St., 12th Fl., Trenton, NJ 08608. Telephone: 609-396-2200. **Management:** Alexander N Gould, General Manager. Mike Doyk, Advertising Manager. Chuck Hirsch, Classified Adv. Mgr.. **Editorial:** Patricia Matson, Editor.

PINE GROVE

PRESS HERALD. 181 S. Tulpehocken, Pine Grove, PA 17963. Telephone: 570-385-3120. FAX: 570-385-0725. Mailing Address: PO Box 7, Pine Grove, PA 17963. Year Established: 1877. Pub. Frequency: w. (Thu.) Page Size: standard. Subscrip. Rate: $.75 newsstand/cover; $30/yr in county; $35/yr out of county; $40/yr out of state. Circulation: 3,157 per issue (paid). **Owner(s):** Call Newspapers, Inc., PO Box 178, Schuylkill Haven, PA 17972. Telephone: 717-385-3120. **Management:** William Knecht, Publisher.

PITTSBURGH

CARNEGIE SIGNAL ITEM STAR. 1964 Greentree Rd, Pittsburgh, PA 15220. Telephone: 412-388-5800. FAX: 412-388-0900. E-MAIL: signal.item@gatewaynewspapers.com. URL: http://www.signalitemstar.com. Pub. Frequency: w. (Wed.) Page Size: tabloid. Subscrip. Rate: $.50 newsstand/cover; $25/yr in county; $40/yr out of county. **Owner(s):** Gateway Newspapers, 610 Beatty Rd., Monroeville, PA 15146. Telephone: 412-856-7400. FAX: 412-856-7954. **Management:** Kathleen Brieck, Advertising Manager. Kris Ranker, Classified Adv. Mgr.. **Editorial:** Bob Pastin, Managing Editor. Chris Scarnati, Sports Editor.

CORAOPOLIS-MOON RECORD. 1964 Greentree Rd, Pittsburgh, PA 15220. Telephone: 412-388-5800. FAX: 412-388-0900. E-MAIL: therecords@gatewaynewspapers.com. URL: http://www.moonrecordstar.com. Pub. Frequency: w. (Wed.) Page Size: standard. Subscrip. Rate: $.50 newsstand/cover; $25/yr in county; $40/yr out of county. **Owner(s):** Gateway Newspapers, 610 Beatty Rd., Monroeville, PA 15146. Telephone: 412-856-7400. FAX: 412-856-7954. **Management:** Vince Townley, Publisher. Kathleen Brieck, Advertising Manager. Jon Kennell, Circulation Director. Kris Ranker, Classified Adv. Mgr.. **Editorial:** Vince Townley, Editor. Chris Scarnati, Sports Editor.

HERALD (PITTSBURGH), THE. 101 Emerson Ave, Pittsburgh, PA 15215. Telephone: 412-782-2121. FAX: 412-782-1195. Pub. Frequency: w. (Thu.) Page Size: broadsheet. Subscrip. Rate: $.50 newsstand/cover; $30/yr in county; $35/yr out of county. Circulation: 5,000 per issue (paid) **Owner(s):** Westminster Holdings, Inc, 610 Beatty Rd, Monroeville, PA 15146. Telephone: 412-856-7400. **Management:** Richard M Schaise, Publisher. Karen Carter, Advertising Manager. **Editorial:** Edith Hughes, Managing Editor.

SHIPPENSBURG

NEWS-CHRONICLE, THE. 1011 Ritner Hwy., Shippensburg, PA 17257-0100. Telephone: 717-532-4101. FAX: 717-532-3020. E-MAIL: nceditor@earthlink.net. Mailing Address: PO Box 100, Shippensburg, PA 17257-0100. Year Established: 1875. Pub. Frequency: s-w. (Tue. & Fri.) Page Size: broadsheet. Subscrip. Rate: $.40 newsstand/cover; $36.40/yr in county; $47.80/yr zones 1-5; $52/yr zones 6-8. **Wire Service(s):** AP, CNS. Circulation: 6,400 per issue (paid and free). **Owner(s):** Latrobe Printing & Publishing, PO Box 111, Latrobe, PA 15650. Telephone: 724-537-3351. FAX: 814-472-2275. **Management:** Chris P. Miles, Publisher. **Editorial:** Leslie Berrier, Production Manager.

VALLEY TIMES-STAR. 1011 Ritner Hwy., Shippensburg, PA 17257. FAX: 717-532-3020. E-MAIL: nceditor@earthlink.net. Mailing Address: PO Box 100, Shippensburg, PA 17257. Year Established: 1858. Pub. Frequency: w. (Wed.) Page Size: broadsheet. Subscrip. Rate: $.40 newsstand/cover; $20.30/yr area. Circulation: 3,100 per issue (paid). **Owner(s):** Latrobe Printing & Publishing, PO Box 111, Latrobe, PA 15650. Telephone: 724-537-3351. FAX: 814-472-2275. **Management:** Chris P. Miles, Publisher. **Editorial:** Leslie Berrier, Production Manager.

SLIPPERY ROCK

SLIPPERY ROCK/GROVE CITY EAGLE. 120 Franklin St., Ste. 1-B, Slippery Rock, PA 16057. Telephone: 724-794-6797. FAX: 724-794-5694. URL: http://www.butlereagle.com. Pub. Frequency: w. (Fri.) Page Size: broadsheet Circulation: 12,325 per issue (free). **Owner(s):** Eagle Printing Co, 114 W. Diamond St., Butler, PA 16001. Telephone: 724-282-8000. FAX: 724-282-1280. **Management:** Vernon L. Wise Jr., Publisher. Nedra Schetch, Advertising. Richard Brest, Circulation Manager. **Editorial:** Chris Miller, Editor.

SOUDERTON

PERKASIE NEWS-HERALD. 673 E. Broad St., Souderton, PA 18964. Telephone: 215-257-6839. FAX: 215-723-8779. E-MAIL: bmcclennen@montgomerynews.com. URL: http://www.montgomerynews.com. Mailing Address: PO Box 64459, Souderton, PA 18964. Year Established: 1881. Pub. Frequency: w. (Wed.) Page Size: broadsheet. Subscrip. Rate: $.50 newsstand/cover; $29.95/yr mailed in state; $36.95/yr mailed out of state. Circulation: 6,850 per issue (paid and free). **Owner(s):** Journal Register Co., Lower Makefield Corporate Center, 790 Township Line Rd, 3rd. flr, Yardley, PA 19067. Telephone: 215-504-4200. **Management:** Betsy Wilson, President. Michele Meckler, Advertising Manager. Joe Flenders, Circulation Manager. **Editorial:** Barbara McClennen, Editor.

SOUDERTON INDEPENDENT. 673 E. Broad St., Souderton, PA 18964. Telephone: 215-723-4801. FAX: 215-723-8779. E-MAIL: bmcclennen@montgomerynews.com. URL: http://www.montgomerynews.com. Mailing Address: PO Box 64459, Souderton, PA 18964. Year Established: 1878. Pub. Frequency: w. (Wed.) Page Size: broadsheet. Subscrip. Rate: $.50 newsstand/cover; $28.95/yr carrier delivery; $28.95/yr mailed in county; $34.95/yr mailed elsewhere. Adv. Rate: col. inch $9.74 Circulation: 5,812 per issue (paid). **Owner(s):** Journal Register Co., 50 W State St, 12th Fl, Trenton, NJ 08608. Telephone: 609-396-2200. **Management:** Betsy Wilson, President. Joe Flenders, Circulation Manager. **Editorial:** Barbara McClennen, Editor.

TIONESTA

FOREST PRESS. 165 Elm St., Tionesta, PA 16353-0366. Telephone: 814-755-4900. FAX: 814-755-4429. E-MAIL: forestpress1@yahoo.com. Mailing Address: PO Box 366, Tionesta, PA 16353-0366. Year Established: 1867. Pub. Frequency: w. (Wed.) Page Size: tabloid. Subscrip. Rate: $.50 newsstand/cover; $21/yr in county $24/yr out of cy. Circulation: 4,500 per issue (paid). **Owner(s):** Edwin R. Patrick, PO Box 366, Tionesta, PA 16353. Telephone: 814-755-4900. **Management:** Edwin R. Patrick, Publisher. Gordon Nygren, Advertising Manager. Kathy Culver, Circulation Manager.

TREVOSE

BRIDESBURG STAR. 2512 Metropolitan Dr., Trevose, PA 19053. Telephone: 215-355-9009. FAX: 215-355-4857. E-MAIL: starsads@aol.com. Year Established: 1997. Pub. Frequency: w. (Wed.) Page Size: tabloid. Subscrip. Rate: $130/yr mailed. Circulation: 4,000 per issue (paid and controlled). **Owner(s):** Philadelphia Media Holding, Inc., See address and contact information above. **Management:** George Troyano, Publisher. Pat Buzine, Advertising Manager. **Editorial:** Ryan Smith, Editor.

FISHTOWN STAR. 2512 Metropolitan Dr., Trevose, PA 19053. Telephone: 215-925-7827. FAX: 215-355-4857. E-MAIL: starads@phillynews.com. Year Established: 1975. Pub. Frequency: w. (Wed.) Page Size: tabloid. Subscrip. Rate: $90/yr mailed. Circulation: 12,000 per issue (controlled and free). **Owner(s):** Star Publications, Inc., See address and contact information above. **Management:** George Troyano, Publisher. John Lehman, Advertising Manager. **Editorial:** Ryan Smith, Editor.

GIRARD HOME NEWS. 2512 Metropolitan Dr., Trevose, PA 19053. Telephone: 215-925-7827. FAX: 215-355-4857. E-MAIL: starsads@phillynews.com. Year Established: 1937. Pub. Frequency: w. (Thu.) Page Size: tabloid.Subscrip. Rate: $90/yr mailed Circulation: 8,000 per issue (free). **Owner(s):** Star Publications, Inc., See address and contact information above. **Management:** George Troyano, Publisher. John Lehman, Advertising Manager. **Editorial:** Matt Petaccio, Editor.

NORTH STAR (PHILADELPHIA). 2512 Metropolitan Dr., Trevose, PA 19053. Telephone: 215-355-9009. FAX: 215-355-4857. E-MAIL: starads@aol.com. Year Established: 1975. Pub. Frequency: w. (Wed.) Page Size: tabloid. Subscrip. Rate: $130/yr mailed. Circulation: 6,000 per issue (paid and controlled). **Owner(s):** Philadelphia Media Holding, Inc., See address and contact information above. **Management:** George Troyano, Publisher. Pat Buzine, Advertising Manager. **Editorial:** Ryan Smith, Editor.

NORTHEAST TIMES. 2512 Metropolitan Dr., Trevose, PA 19053. Telephone: 215-332-3300. FAX: 215-355-4812. E-MAIL: pronews@phillynews.com. URL: http://www.northeasttimes.com. Year Established: 1934. Pub. Frequency: w. (Wed.) Page Size: tabloid. Subscrip. Rate: $42/yr mailed. Freelance Pay: $15-$25/story. Circulation: 116,000 per issue (paid and free). **Owner(s):** Broad Street Community Newspapers, See address and contact information above. **Management:** Darwin Woordt, Publisher. Chuck McKane, Advertising Manager. Mary Silverstein, Circulation Manager. Ellen Pursley, Classified Adv. Mgr.. **Editorial:** John J. Scanlon, Editor. Fred Gussoff, Managing Editor. Joe Mason, Sports Editor.

PORT RICHMOND STAR. 2512 Metropolitan Dr., Trevose, PA 19053. Telephone: 215-355-9009. FAX: 215-355-4857. E-MAIL: starsads@aol.com. Year Established: 1978. Pub. Frequency: w. (Wed.) Page Size: tabloid. Subscrip. Rate: $130/yr mailed. Circulation: 12,000 per issue (paid and controlled). **Owner(s):** Philadelphia Media Holding, Inc., See address and contact information above. **Management:** George Troyano, Publisher. Pat Buzine, Advertising Manager. **Editorial:** Ryan Smith, Editor.

THREE STAR EDITION. 2512 Metropolitan Dr., Trevose, PA 19053. Telephone: 215-355-9009. FAX: 215-355-4857. E-MAIL: star@phillynews.com. Year Established: 1975. Pub. Frequency: w. (Wed.) Page Size: tabloid. Subscrip. Rate: $130/yr mailed. Circulation: 6,000 per issue (controlled and free). **Owner(s):** Philadelphia Media Holding, Inc., See address and contact information above. **Management:** George Troyano, Publisher. Steve Engel, Advertising Manager. **Editorial:** Ryan Smith, Editor.

TREND MIDWEEK. 2512 Metropolitan Dr., Trevose, PA 19053. Telephone: 215-332-3300. FAX: 215-355-4812. Pub. Frequency: w. (Wed.) Page Size: tabloid Circulation: 10,000 per issue (free). **Owner(s):** Broad Street Community Newspapers, See address and contact information above. **Management:** Darwin Woordt, Publisher. Mary Silverstein, Circulation Manager. Ellen Pursley, Classified Adv. Mgr..

TUNKHANNOCK

WYOMING COUNTY ADVANCE. 16 E. Tioga St., Tunkhannock, PA 18657. Telephone: 570-836-2123. FAX: 570-836-3378. Mailing Address: PO Box 59, Tunkhannock, PA 18657-0059. Year Established: 1999. Pub. Frequency: w. (Fri.) Page Size: tabloid Circulation: 15,400 per issue (free). **Owner(s):** Times-Shamrock Communications, PO Box 3311, Scranton, PA 18505. Telephone: 717-348-9100.

WYOMING COUNTY PRESS EXAMINER, THE. 16 E. Tioga St., Tunkhannock, PA 18657. Telephone: 570-836-2123. FAX: 570-836-3378. URL: http://www.newage-examiner.com. Mailing Address: PO Box 59, Tunkhannock, PA 18657. Year Established: 1870. Pub. Frequency: w. (Wed.) Page Size: broadsheet. Subscrip. Rate: $.80 newsstand/cover; $34/yr in state; $39/yr mailed out of state. Freelance Pay: $15/article. Circulation: 5,600 per issue (paid). **Owner(s):** Times-Shamrock Communications, 149 Penn Ave., Scranton, PA 18503. Telephone: 570-348-9100. **Management:** James E. Towner, Publisher. Gail Williams, Advertising Manager. **Editorial:** Robert L Baker, Editor. Nathan Milner, Sports.

VALLEY VIEW

CITIZEN-STANDARD, THE. 104 W. Main St., Valley View, PA 17983. Telephone: 570-682-9081. FAX: 570-682-8734. E-MAIL: csnews@adelphia.net. URL: http://www.citizenstandard.com. Mailing Address: PO Box 147, Valley View, PA 17983. Year Established: 1932. Pub. Frequency: w. (Wed.) Page Size: broadsheet. Subscrip. Rate: $.50 newsstand/cover; $27/yr local; $29/yr out of area. Circulation: 4,460 per issue (paid and free). **Owner(s):** Times-Shamrock Communications, PO Box 3311, Scranton, PA 18505. Telephone: 717-398-9100. **Management:** Linda Schylaske, Publisher. Stacy Hoover, Advertising Manager. **Editorial:** Linda Schylaske, Editor. Rebecca Zemencik, Assistant Editor.

VANDERGRIFT

ALLEGHENY-HYDE PARK EXPRESS. 143 Washington Ave., Vandergrift, PA 15690. Telephone: 724-567-5656. FAX: 724-568-3818. E-MAIL: buttermilkfalls@comcast.net. Year Established: 2004. Pub. Frequency: w. (Sat.) Page Size: tabloid. Subscrip. Rate: $38.61/yr mailed. Adv. Rate: col. inch $16 Circulation: 4,254 per issue (paid and free). **Owner(s):** Buttermilk Falls Co., See address and contact information above. **Management:** Donald Cole, Publisher. Nathan Cole, Advertising Manager. **Editorial:** Cheryl Carrico, Editor.

APOLLO NEWS-RECORD. 143 Washington Ave., Vandergrift, PA 15690. Telephone: 724-567-5656. FAX: 724-568-3818. E-MAIL: buttermilkfalls@comcast.net. Year Established: 1897. Pub. Frequency: w. (Sat.) Page Size: tabloid. Subscrip. Rate: $.55 newsstand/cover; $38.61/yr mailed. Adv. Rate: col. inch $16 Circulation: 4,947 per issue (paid and free). **Owner(s):** Buttermilk Falls Co., See address and contact information above. **Management:** Donald Cole, Publisher. Nathan Cole, Advertising Manager. **Editorial:** Cheryl Carrico, Editor.

LEECHBURG ADVANCE. 143 Washington Ave., Vandergrift, PA 15690. Telephone: 724-567-5656. FAX: 724-568-3818. Year Established: 1887. Pub. Frequency: w. (Sat.) Page Size: tabloid. Subscrip. Rate: $.55 newsstand/cover; $38.61/yr mailed. Adv. Rate: col. inch $16 Circulation: 3,502 per issue (paid and free). **Owner(s):** Buttermilk Falls Co., See address and contact information above. **Management:** Donald Cole, Publisher. Nathan Cole, Advertising Manager. **Editorial:** Cheryl Carrico, Editor.

VANDERGRIFT NEWS. 143 Washington Ave., Vandergrift, PA 15690. Telephone: 724-567-5656. FAX: 724-568-3818. E-MAIL: buttermilkfalls@comcast.net. Year Established: 1905. Pub. Frequency: s-w. (Sat.) Page Size: tabloid. Subscrip. Rate: $.55 newsstand/cover; $38.61/yr mailed. Circulation: 9,414 per issue (paid and free). **Owner(s):** Buttermilk Falls Co., See address and contact information above. **Management:** Donald Cole, Publisher. Nathan Cole, Advertising Manager. **Editorial:** Cheryl Carrico, Editor.

Weeklies

WAYNE

KING OF PRUSSIA COURIER. 134 N. Wayne Ave., Wayne, PA 19087. Telephone: 610-688-3000. E-MAIL: editor@waynesuburban.com. URL: http://www.kingofprussiacourier.com. Mailing Address: PO Box 409, Wayne, PA 19087. Year Established: 1964. Pub. Frequency: w. (Wed.) Page Size: broadsheet Circulation: 7,000 per issue (free). **Owner(s):** Journal Register Co., 50 W State St, 12th Fl, Trenton, NJ 08608. Telephone: 609-396-2200. **Management:** Dianne Ryan-Paschall, Publisher. Andrea Corum, Advertising Director. James Clarke, Circulation Manager. **Editorial:** James D Myers Jr., Managing Editor. Michael Beirne, Sports Editor.

SUBURBAN ADVERTISER, THE. 134 N. Wayne Ave., Wayne, PA 19087. Telephone: 610-688-3000. FAX: 610-524-1997. E-MAIL: editor@waynesuburban.com. URL: http://www.waynesuburban.com. Mailing Address: PO Box 409, Wayne, PA 19087. Year Established: 1961. Pub. Frequency: w. (Thu.) Page Size: broadsheet Circulation: 18,000 per issue (free). **Owner(s):** Journal Register Co., 50 W State St, 12th Fl, Trenton, NJ 08608. Telephone: 609-396-2200. **Management:** Dianne Ryan-Paschall, Publisher. Andrea Corum, Advertising Director. Sue Smith, Advertising Manager. **Editorial:** Dennis Daylor, Editor. Erin DeStefano, Managing Editor.

SUBURBAN & WAYNE TIMES, THE. 134 N. Wayne Ave., Wayne, PA 19087. Telephone: 610-688-3000. FAX: 610-964-1346. URL: http://www.waynesuburban.com. Mailing Address: PO Box 409, Wayne, PA 19087. Year Established: 1885. Pub. Frequency: w. (Thu.) Page Size: broadsheet. Subscrip. Rate: $.50 newsstand/cover; $38.50/yr carrier delivery local; $42.95/yr mailed in state. Circulation: 11,583 per issue (paid). **Owner(s):** Journal Register Co., 50 W State St, 12th Fl, Trenton, NJ 08608. Telephone: 609-396-2200. **Management:** Dianne Ryan-Paschall, Publisher. Andrea Corum, Advertising Director. **Editorial:** Erin DeStefano, Managing Editor. Ryan Richards, News Editor. Michael Beirne, Sports Editor.

WAYNESBURG

GREENE COUNTY MESSENGER. 95 E High St, Ste 107, Waynesburg, PA 15370. Telephone: 724-852-2251. FAX: 724-852-2271. E-MAIL: ad@greeneburgmessenger.com. URL: http://www.greenemessenger.com. Pub. Frequency: w. (Fri.) Page Size: broadsheet. Subscrip. Rate: $.75 newsstand/cover; $3.50 carrier delivery/wk.; $3.75 motor route/wk.. Circulation: 3,500 per issue (paid). **Owner(s):** Calkins Media Inc., 8400 Rte. 13, Levittown, PA 19057. **Management:** Miriam Ofsanik, General Manager. Jennifer Bates, Advertising Manager. **Editorial:** Steve Barrett, Editor. Bobby Fox, Sports.

WEEDVILLE

BENNETTS VALLEY NEWS. PO Box 158, Weedville, PA 15868. Telephone: 814-787-4454. Year Established: 1953. Pub. Frequency: w. (Thu.) Page Size: broadsheet. Subscrip. Rate: $.40 newsstand/cover; $17/yr in state; $20/yr out of state. Circulation: 700 per issue (paid). **Owner(s):** Jim Leonard, See address and contact information above. **Management:** Jim Leonard, Publisher. **Editorial:** Jim Leonard, Editor.

WELLSBORO

MANSFIELD GAZETTE. 25 East Ave, Wellsboro, PA 16901. Telephone: 570-724-2287. FAX: 570-724-2278. Mailing Address: PO Box 118, Wellsboro, PA 16901. Pub. Frequency: w. (Wed.) Page Size: broadsheet. Subscrip. Rate: $1 newsstand/cover; $50/yr in county; $53/yr out of county. Circulation: 2,500 per issue (paid). **Owner(s):** Community Media Group, Inc, PO Box 10, West Frankfort, IL 62896. Telephone: 618-937-6412. **Management:** James Monks, General Manager. Karen Oberholtzer, Circulation Manager. **Editorial:** Gayle Morrow, Editor.

WELLSBORO GAZETTE, THE. 25 East Ave, Wellsboro, PA 16901. Telephone: 570-724-2287. FAX: 570-724-2278. E-MAIL: wellgaz@epix.net. URL: http://www.tiogapublishing.com. Mailing Address: PO Box 118, Wellsboro, PA 16901. Year Established: 1874. Pub. Frequency: w. (Wed.) Page Size: broadsheet. Subscrip. Rate: $1 newsstand/cover; $50/yr in county; $53/yr out of county. Circulation: 7,500 per issue (paid). **Owner(s):** Community Media Group, Inc, PO Box 10, West Frankfort, IL 62896. Telephone: 618-937-6412. **Management:** James Monks, General Manager. Karen Oberholtzer, Circulation Manager. **Editorial:** Gayle Morrow, Editor.

WEST NEWTON

TIMES-SUN, THE. 205 E. Main St., West Newton, PA 15089-1153. Telephone: 724-872-6800. FAX: 724-887-5115. E-MAIL: igp@scottdale.com. URL: http://www.laurelgrouponline.com. Year Established: 1878. Pub. Frequency: w. (Thu.) Page Size: broadsheet. Subscrip. Rate: $.45 newsstand/cover; $23.60/yr in county; $35.60/yr out of county; $37.60/yr out of state. Adv. Rate: col. inch $7.75 Freelance Pay: $0.20/column-inch. Circulation: 3,177 per issue (paid). **Owner(s):** Laurel Group Press, 229 Pittsburgh St., Scottsdale, PA 15683-0222. Telephone: 724-887-7400. FAX: 724-887-5115. **Management:** Joseph F. Soforic, General Manager. Arthue Myers, Advertising Manager. Marcella Kohuth, Circulation Manager. **Editorial:** Gretchen Pletcher, Editor. Rich Zahrobsky, Production Manager.

WESTCHESTER

COATESVILLE LEDGER. 250 N. Bradford Ave, Westchester, PA 19382. Telephone: 610-518-1363. FAX: 610-518-1358. E-MAIL: downingtown@kennett.net. URL: http://www.coatesvilleledger.com. Year Established: 1994. Pub. Frequency: w. (Thu.) Page Size: broadsheet. Subscrip. Rate: $.50 newsstand/cover; $24/yr home delivery in county; $32/yr mailed out of county; $37/yr mailed out of state. Circulation: 6,000 per issue (free). **Owner(s):** Journal Register Co., 50 W State St, 12th Fl, Trenton, NJ 08608. Telephone: 609-396-2200. **Management:** Edward S. Condra, Publisher. Velma Warren, Advertising. Teresa Pennington, Classified Adv. Mgr.. **Editorial:** Nick Browne, Editor.

DOWNINGTOWN LEDGER. ISSN 1532-0324 250 N. Bradford Ave, Westchester, PA 19382. E-MAIL: downingtown@kennett.net. URL: http://www.downingtownledger.com. Year Established: 1996. Pub. Frequency: w. (Thu.) Page Size: broadsheet. Subscrip. Rate: $.50 newsstand/cover; $24/yr home delivery in county; $32/yr mailed out of county; $37/yr mailed out of state. Circulation: 2,900 per issue (paid). **Owner(s):** Journal Register Co., 50 W State St, 12th Fl, Trenton, NJ 08608. Telephone: 609-396-2200. **Management:** Edward S. Condra, Publisher. Velma Warren, Advertising. Mike Doyle, Advertising Manager. Teresa Pennington, Classified Adv. Mgr.. **Editorial:** Nick Browne, Editor.

WESTFIELD

FREE PRESS-COURIER. 202 E Main St, Westfield, PA 16950-0515. Telephone: 814-367-2230. FAX: 814-367-5092. E-MAIL: freepress@penn.com. Year Established: 1878. Pub. Frequency: w. (Wed.) Page Size: standard. Subscrip. Rate: $.75 newsstand/cover; $33/yr mailed Potter & Tioga cys.; $35/yr mailed elsewhere. Circulation: 2,500 per issue (paid). **Owner(s):** Community Media Group, Inc, PO Box 10, West Frankfort, IL 62896. Telephone: 618-937-6412. **Management:** Beverly Trowbridge, General Manager. **Editorial:** Sharon Corderman, Editor.

WEXFORD

CRANBERRY JOURNAL. 11565 Perry Hwy. Ste. 9, Wexford, PA 15090. E-MAIL: cranberry.journal@gatewaynewspapers.com. URL: http://www.cranberrystar.com. Pub. Frequency: w. (Wed.) Page Size: tabloid. Subscrip. Rate: $.50 newsstand/cover; $25/yr. **Owner(s):** Gateway Newspapers, See address and contact information above. **Management:** Karen Strickland, Advertising Manager. Kris Ranker, Classified Adv. Mgr.. **Editorial:** Dave McElhinny, Editor. Edith Hughes, Executive Editor.

NORTH JOURNAL. 11565 Perry Hwy. Ste. 9, Wexford, PA 15090. Telephone: 724-940-5042. FAX: 724-940-5055. E-MAIL: north.journal@trinity-pgh.com. URL: http://www.northjournalstar.com. Pub. Frequency: w. (Wed.) Page Size: tabloid. Subscrip. Rate: $.25 newsstand/cover; $8/yr. **Owner(s):** Gateway Newspapers, 11565 Perry Hwy., Ste. 9., Wexford, PA 15090. Telephone: 724-940-5043. **Management:** Karen Strickland, Advertising Manager. Kris Ranker, Classified Adv. Mgr.. **Editorial:** Josh Schwoebel, Editor. Jerry Clark, Sports Editor.

WHITE HAVEN

JOURNAL-HERALD (WHITE HAVEN), THE. 211 Main St., White Haven, PA 18661. Telephone: 570-443-8321. Year Established: 1879. Pub. Frequency: w. (Thu.) Page Size: broadsheet. Subscrip. Rate: $.50 newsstand/cover; $25/yr in county; $30/yr out of county. Adv. Rate: col. inch $4 Circulation: 1,250 per issue (paid). **Owner(s):** Journal Newspapers of Pennsylvania, Inc., See address and contact information above. **Management:** Clara Holder, President. Seth Isenberg, Advertising Manager. **Editorial:** Ruth Isenberg, Editor-in-Chief. Seth Isenberg, Business Editor. Steve Stallone, Sports Editor.

JOURNAL MOUNTAIN TOP. 211 Main St., White Haven, PA 18661. Telephone: 570-443-8321. E-MAIL: journalnews@catvexpress.net. Year Established: 1996. Pub. Frequency: m. Page Size: broadsheet.Subscrip. Rate: $25/yr mailed Circulation: 3,500 per issue (free). **Owner(s):** Journal Newspapers of Pennsylvania, Inc., 211 Main St., White Haven, PA 08661. Telephone: 570-443-8321. **Management:** Clara Holder, President. Seth Isenberg, Publisher. **Editorial:** Maryellen Aton, Editor. Steve Stallone, Sports Editor.

JOURNAL OF POCONO PLATEAU. 211 Main St., White Haven, PA 18661. Telephone: 570-443-8321. E-MAIL: journalnews@catvexpress.net. Year Established: 1995. Pub. Frequency: w. (Thu.) Page Size: tabloid. Subscrip. Rate: $30/yr mailed in state; $37/yr mailed out of state. Circulation: 14,000 per issue (controlled). **Owner(s):** Journal Newspapers of Pennsylvania, Inc., See address and contact information above. **Management:** Clara Holder, President. Seth Isenberg, Publisher. **Editorial:** Ruth Isenberg, Editor-in-Chief. Steve Stallone, Sports Editor.

JOURNAL-VALLEY VIEWS. 211 Main St., White Haven, PA 18661. Telephone: 570-443-9131. E-MAIL: journalnews@catvexpress.net. Year Established: 1994. Pub. Frequency: m. Page Size: tabloid. Subscrip. Rate: $22/yr. Adv. Rate: col. inch $7 Circulation: 6,500 per issue (paid and controlled). **Owner(s):** Journal Newspapers of Pennsylvania, Inc., See address and contact information above. **Management:** Seth Isenberg, Advertising Manager. **Editorial:** Ruth Isenberg, Editor-in-Chief. Donnell Stump, Assistant Editor.

NEWS OF THE POCONOS. 211 Main St., White Haven, PA 18661. Telephone: 570-443-8321. E-MAIL: newsofpoconos@catvexpress.net. Year Established: 1976. Pub. Frequency: m. (Thu.) Page Size: tabloid. Subscrip. Rate: $16/yr. Adv. Rate: col. inch $16 Circulation: 25,000 per issue (paid and controlled). **Owner(s):** Journal Newspapers of Pennsylvania, Inc., See address and contact information above. **Management:** Clara Holder, President. Seth Isenberg, Publisher. **Editorial:** Mary Perez, Editor. Ruth Isenberg, Editor-in-Chief. Steve Stalline, Sports Editor.

WYNNEWOOD

MAIN LINE LIFE. 311 E Lancaster Ave, Wynnewood, PA 19096. Telephone: 610-896-9555. FAX: 610-896-9560. URL: http://www.mainlinelife.com. Year Established: 1995. Pub. Frequency: w. (Wed.) Page Size: broadsheet. Subscrip. Rate: $.50 newsstand/cover; $31.95/yr home delivery local; $38.95/yr mailed out of county; $28.75/yr mailed in county to senior citizens. Adv. Rate: col. inch $22.34 Circulation: 4,600 per issue (paid). **Owner(s):** Journal Register Co., 50 W State St, 12th Fl, Trenton, NJ 08608. Telephone: 609-396-2292. **Management:** Dianne Ryan-Paschall, Publisher. Erika Spielman, Advertising Director. **Editorial:** Tom Murray, Managing Editor. Jeff Cobb, News Editor.

YARDLEY

YARDLEY NEWS. 76 S. Main St., Yardley, PA 19067. Telephone: 215-493-2794. FAX: 215-321-0527. E-MAIL: yardley@ingnews.com. URL: http://www.yardleynews.com. Mailing Address: PO Box 334, Yardley, PA 19067. Year Established: 1946. Pub. Frequency: w. (Thu.) Page Size: tabloid. Subscrip. Rate: $.50 newsstand/cover; $23.50/yr mailed. Circulation: 6,000 per issue (controlled and free). **Owner(s):** Journal Register Co., 50 W State St, 12th Fl, Trenton, NJ 08608. Telephone: 609-396-2200. FAX: 609-396-2292. **Management:** Stephanie Leicht, Publisher. Bob McCarron, Advertising Manager. **Editorial:** Matthew Fleeshman, Editor. Steve Sherman, Sports Editor.

YEAGERTOWN

COUNTY OBSERVER. 310 S. Main St., Yeagertown Plz., Ste. A-1, Yeagertown, PA 17099. Telephone: 717-248-9366. FAX: 717-248-9377. Mailing Address: PO Box 470, Yeagertown, PA 17099. Year Established: 1975. Pub. Frequency: w. (Wed.) Page Size: broadsheet. Subscrip. Rate: $.50 newsstand/cover; $21/yr mailed in county; $28/yr mailed out of county. Adv. Rate: col. inch $5.84 Freelance Pay: $20/story. Circulation: 5,000 per issue (paid). **Owner(s):** Ogden Newspapers of Minnesota, Inc., 1500 Main St., Wheeling, WV 26003. Telephone: 304-233-0100. **Management:** Pat Fultz, Advertising Manager. **Editorial:** Joe Cannon, Editor.

RHODE ISLAND

BRISTOL

BRISTOL PHOENIX. One Bradford St., Bristol, RI 02809. Telephone: 401-253-6000. FAX: 401-253-6055. E-MAIL: briancomfort@eastbaynewspapers.com. URL: http://www.eastbayri.com. Year Established: 1837. Pub. Frequency: w. (Thu.) Page Size: tabloid. Subscrip. Rate: $.75 newsstand/cover; $27.50/yr in county; $41/yr mailed in New England; $46/yr mailed elsewhere. Circulation: 6,100 per issue (paid). **Owner(s):** Phoenix-Times Publishing Co., One Bradford St., Bristol, RI 02809-0090. Telephone: 401-253-6000. **Management:** Matthew Hayes, Publisher. Jane McHenry, Advertising Director. **Editorial:** Josh Bickford, Editor. Steve Rogers, Sports.

EAST PROVIDENCE

EAST PROVIDENCE POST. 1027 Waterman Ave., East Providence, RI 02914-1314. Telephone: 401-434-7210. FAX: 401-434-9469. Mailing Address: 99 Webster St., Pawtucket, RI 02861-1017. Year Established: 1955. Pub. Frequency: w. (Thu.) Page Size: tabloid. Subscrip. Rate: $.50 newsstand/cover; $20/yr in county. Adv. Rate: col. inch $5.74 Circulation: 12,000 per issue (paid). **Owner(s):** New Herald Press, 99 Webster St., Pawtucket, RI 72644. Telephone: 401-434-7210. **Management:** Jen Memerova, Advertising Manager. **Editorial:** Victor Alvarez, Editor.

SEEKONK STAR. 1027 Waterman Ave., East Providence, RI 02914-1314. Telephone: 401-434-7210. FAX: 401-434-9469. URL: http:www.eastbayri.com. Year Established: 1972. Pub. Frequency: w. (Thu.) Page Size: tabloid. Subscrip. Rate: $.50 newsstand/cover; $24/yr in county; $25/yr out of state; $17.50/yr in county for senior citizens. Adv. Rate: col. inch $3.90 Circulation: 4,000 per issue (paid). **Owner(s):** New Herald Press, 99 Webster St., Pawtucket, RI 02861. Telephone: 401-434-7210. **Management:** Jen Memerova, Advertising Manager. **Editorial:** Victor Alvarez, Editor.

GREENVILLE

NORTH PROVIDENCE BREEZE, THE. 592 Putnam Pike, Greenville, RI 02828. Telephone: 401-949-2700. FAX: 401-949-2420. E-MAIL: news@breezeobserver.com. URL: http://www.breezeobserver.com.Pub. Frequency: w. (Thu.) Circulation: 2,000 per issue (paid). **Owner(s):** Observer Publishing Co., See address and contact information above. **Management:** Tom Ward, Publisher. Paul Sciaraffa, Advertising Director. **Editorial:** Marcia Green, Editor. Lucille Benoit, Managing Editor.

VALLEY BREEZE-OBSERVER. 592 Putnam Pike, Greenville, RI 02828. Telephone: 401-949-2700. FAX: 401-949-2420. E-MAIL: news@breezeobserver.com. URL: http://www.breezeobserver.com. Year Established: 1956. Pub. Frequency: w. (Thu.) Page Size: tabloid Circulation: 10,500 per issue (paid). **Owner(s):** Observer Publishing Co., See address and contact information above. **Management:** Jamie Quinn, Publisher. Paul Sciaraffa, Advertising Manager. **Editorial:** Marcia Green, Editor. Lucille Benoit, Managing Editor.

JAMESTOWN

JAMESTOWN PRESS, THE. 42 Narragansett Ave., Jamestown, RI 02835. Telephone: 401-423-3200. FAX: 401-423-1661. E-MAIL: jtownpress@aol.com. URL: http://www.jamestownpress.com. Year Established: 1989. Pub. Frequency: w. (Thu.) Page Size: tabloid. Subscrip. Rate: $35/yr mailed. Circulation: 6,100 per issue (paid and controlled). **Owner(s):** Jeff McDonough, See address and contact information above. **Management:** Alice Dunn, General Manager. Jeff McDonough, Publisher. Pat Holtzman, Advertising. **Editorial:** Jeff McDonough, Editor-in-Chief. Chris Irby, Managing Editor.

NEWPORT

NEWPORT MERCURY. ISSN 1083-7728
101 Malbone Rd., Newport, RI 02840. Telephone: 401-849-3300. FAX: 401-849-3300. E-MAIL: news@newportri.com. URL: http://www.newportdailynews.com. Mailing Address: PO Box 420, Newport, RI 02840-0420. Year Established: 1758. Pub. Frequency: w. (Fri.) Page Size: broadsheet. Subscrip. Rate: $.50 newsstand/cover; $45/yr in area. Circulation: 1,275 per issue (paid). **Owner(s):** E.A. Sherman Publishing Co., See address and contact information above. **Management:** Albert K. Sherman Jr., Publisher. Bob Cross, Advertising Manager. Robert Bidlack, Circulation Manager. **Editorial:** Janine Weisman, Managing Editor. Scott Barrett, Sports Editor.

NEWPORT THIS WEEK. 33 Marlborough St., Newport, RI 02840. Telephone: 401-847-7766. FAX: 401-846-4974. E-MAIL: info@newportthisweek.com. URL: http://www.newportthisweek.com. Year Established: 1973. Pub. Frequency: w. (Wed.) Page Size: tabloid. Freelance Pay: $25/story. Circulation: 14,000 per issue (free). **Owner(s):** Eastbay Newspapers, PO Box 90, Bristol, RI 02809-0090. Telephone: 401-253-6000. **Management:** Mathew Hayes, Publisher. Melinda Gross, Advertising Manager. **Editorial:** Beth Bottis, Editor.

PROVIDENCE

PROVIDENCE PHOENIX. 150 Chestnut St., Providence, RI 02903. Telephone: 401-273-6397. FAX: 401-273-0920. E-MAIL: submit@phx.com. URL: http://www.thephoenix.com. Year Established: 1978. Pub. Frequency: w. (Thu.) Page Size: tabloid. Subscrip. Rate: $80/yr mailed 3rd class; $200/yr mailed 1st class. Adv. Rate: B&W page $11,550 Circulation: 64,000 per issue (free). **Owner(s):** Phoenix Media Communications Group, 126 Brookline Ave., Boston, MA 02215. Telephone: 617-536-5390. **Management:** Stephen M. Mindich, Publisher. A. William Risteen, Advertising Director. Maureen Roberts, Circulation Director. Terry Ryan, Classified Adv. Mgr.. Steve Brown, Associate Publisher. **Editorial:** Peter Kadzis, Editor. Lou Papineau, Managing Editor. Ian Dennis, News Editor.

TIVERTON

SAKONNET TIMES. East Side Crossings, 1701 Stafford Rd, Unit 1, Tiverton, RI 02878. Telephone: 401-683-1000. FAX: 401-537-9155. E-MAIL: sakonnet@eastbaynewspapers.com. URL: http://www.eastbayri.com. Year Established: 1966. Pub. Frequency: w. (Thu.) Page Size: tabloid. Subscrip. Rate: $.75 newsstand/cover; $27.50/yr in county; $46/yr elsewhere. Circulation: 6,378 per issue (paid). **Owner(s):** Phoenix-Times Publishing Co., One Bradford St., Bristol, RI 02809-0090. Telephone: 401-253-6000. **Management:** Matthew Hayes, Publisher. Jane McHenry, Advertising Director. **Editorial:** Bruce Burdett, Editor. Matthew Hayes, Managing Editor. Steve Rogers, Sports.

WAKEFIELD

COVENTRY COURIER, THE. 187 Main St., Wakefield, RI 02879. Telephone: 401-789-9744. FAX: 401-789-1550. E-MAIL: jswanson@ricentral.com. URL: http://www.coventrycourier.com. Pub. Frequency: w. (Fri.) Page Size: broadsheet. Subscrip. Rate: $.75 newsstand/cover; $32/yr in state; $45/yr out of state; $24/yr to students. Circulation: 1,000 per issue (paid). **Owner(s):** Journal Register Co., 50 W State St, 12th Fl, Trenton, NJ 08608. Telephone: 609-396-2200. FAX: 609-396-2292. **Management:** David Dear Jr., Publisher. Jody Boucher, Advertising Director. Ann Gallagher, Circulation Manager. **Editorial:** Jennifer Swanson, Editor.

EAST GREENWICH PENDULUM, THE. 187 Main St., Wakefield, RI 02879. Telephone: 401-789-9744. FAX: 401-828-5073. URL: http://www.eastgreenwichpendulum.com. Mailing Address: PO Box 232, Wakefield, RI 02880. Year Established: 1854. Pub. Frequency: w. (Thu.) Page Size: broadsheet. Subscrip. Rate: $.50 newsstand/cover; $32/yr home delivery in state; $45/yr home delivery out of state. Circulation: 3,000 per issue (paid). **Owner(s):** Journal Register Co., 50 W State St, 12th Fl, Trenton, NJ 08608. Telephone: 609-396-2200. **Management:** David Dear Jr., Publisher. Jody Boucher, Advertising Director. Anne Gallagher, Circulation Manager. **Editorial:** Jonathan Gibbs, Editor. Eric Rueb, Sports.

NARRAGANSETT TIMES, THE. ISSN 1040-1938
187 Main St., Wakefield, RI 02879. Telephone: 401-789-9744. FAX: 401-789-1550. E-MAIL: jbarrett@ricentral.com. URL: http://www.narragansetttimes.com. Mailing Address: PO Box 232, Wakefield, RI 02880. Year Established: 1855. Pub. Frequency: s-w. (Wed. & Fri.) Page Size: broadsheet. Subscrip. Rate: $.50 newsstand/cover; $50/yr mailed in state; $83/yr mailed out of state. Circulation: 19,000 per issue (paid). **Owner(s):** Journal Register Co., 50 W State St, 12th Fl, Trenton, NJ 08608. Telephone: 609-396-2200. **Management:** David Dear Jr., Publisher. Jody Boucher, Advertising Director. Anne Gallagher, Circulation Manager. **Editorial:** Joel D Barrett, Executive Editor.

STANDARD-TIMES (NORTH KINGSTOWN), THE. ISSN 1040-3337
187 Main St., Wakefield, RI 02879. Telephone: 401-789-9744. FAX: 401-789-1550. E-MAIL: nkstandardtimes@aol.com. URL: http://www.ricentral.com. Year Established: 1888. Pub. Frequency: w. (Thu.) Page Size: broadsheet. Subscrip. Rate: $.50 newsstand/cover; $36/yr home delivery in county; $60/yr mailed out of state. Circulation: 5,091 per issue (paid). **Owner(s):** Journal Register Co., 50 W State St, 12th Fl, Trenton, NJ 08608. Telephone: 609-396-2200. **Management:** David Dear Jr., Publisher. Jody Boucher, Advertising Director. Ann Gallagher, Circulation Manager. **Editorial:** Joel D Barrett, Executive Editor.

WARREN

BARRINGTON TIMES. 139 Main St., Warren, RI 02885. Telephone: 401-245-6000. FAX: 401-537-9154. E-MAIL: tedhayes@eastbaynewspapers.com. URL: http://www.eastbayri.com. Mailing Address: PO Box 227, Barrington, RI 02806. Year Established: 1958. Pub. Frequency: w. (Wed.) Page Size: tabloid. Subscrip. Rate: $.75 newsstand/cover; $27.50/yr in county; $41/yr mailed in New England; $46/yr elsewhere. Circulation: 5,300 per issue (paid). **Owner(s):** Phoenix-Times Publishing Co., One Bradford St., Bristol, RI 02809. Telephone: 401-253-6000. **Management:** Matthew Hayes, Publisher. Jane McHenry, Advertising Director. **Editorial:** Josh Bickford, Editor. Scott Pickering, Managing Editor. Lynda Rego, Copy Chief. Steve Rogers, Sports.

WARREN TIMES-GAZETTE. 139 Main St., Warren, RI 02885. Telephone: 401-245-6000. FAX: 401-245-3640. E-MAIL: warren@eastbaynewspapers.com. URL: http://www.eastbayri.com. Mailing Address: PO Box 50, Warren, RI 02885. Year Established: 1866. Pub. Frequency: w. (Wed.) Page Size: tabloid. Subscrip. Rate: $27.50/yr in county; $41/yr in New England; $46/yr elsewhere; $.75 newsstand/cover. Circulation: 3,094 per issue (paid). **Owner(s):** Phoenix-Time Publishing Co., One Bradford St., Bristol, RI 02809-0090. Telephone: 401-253-6000. **Management:** Matthew Hayes, Publisher. Jane McHenry, Advertising Manager. **Editorial:** Denise Kinney, Editor. Scott Pickering, Managing Editor. Steve Rogers, Sports.

WARWICK

CRANSTON HERALD. 1944 Warwick Ave., Warwick, RI 02889. Telephone: 401-732-3100. URL: http://www.warwickonline.com. Year Established: 1921. Pub. Frequency: w. (Thu.) Page Size: standard. Subscrip. Rate: $.50 newsstand/cover; $23/yr. Adv. Rate: col. inch $8 Freelance Pay: $10-$30/article. Circulation: 3,800 per issue (paid). **Owner(s):** Beacon Communications Corp., See address and contact information above. **Management:** Richard Fleischer, General Manager. John I. Howell, Publisher. **Editorial:** John I. Howell, Managing Editor. Bill Koch, Sports Editor.

JOHNSTON SUN RISE. 1944 Warwick Ave., Ste 4, Warwick, RI 02889. Telephone: 401-732-3100. FAX: 401-732-3110. E-MAIL: johns@johnstonsunrise.net. URL: http://www.johnstonsunrise.net. Year Established: 1998. Pub. Frequency: w. (Thu.) Page Size: tabloid Circulation: 6,500 per issue (free). **Owner(s):** Observer Publishing Co., See address and contact information above. **Management:** Richard G. Fleischer, General Manager. John I Howell Jr., Publisher. Gina Fugere, Advertising. Donna Carbone, Circulation Manager. Sue Howarth, Classified Editor. **Editorial:** John Serpa, Editor.

WARWICK BEACON. 1944 Warwick Ave., Warwick, RI 02889. Telephone: 401-732-3100. FAX: 401-732-3100. URL: http://www.warwickonline.com. Year Established: 1953. Pub. Frequency: s-w. (Tue. & Thu.) Page Size: broadsheet. Subscrip. Rate: $.50 newsstand/cover; $39/yr; $46/yr mailed out of state. Adv. Rate: col. inch $11 Freelance Pay: $15-$30/article. Circulation: 10,000 per issue (paid). **Owner(s):** Beacon Communications Corp., See address and contact information above. **Management:** Richard Fleischer, General Manager. John I Howell, Publisher. Suzanne Wendoloski, Advertising. **Editorial:** Donna Carbove, Circulation Editor. Chris Koch, Sports Editor.

WYOMING

CHARIHO TIMES. 1171 Main St., Wyoming, RI 02898. Telephone: 401-539-0100. FAX: 401-539-2330. E-MAIL: Gmcgovern@ricentral.com. URL: http://www.ricentral.com. Mailing Address: PO Box 620, Wyoming, RI 02898. Year Established: 1993. Pub. Frequency: w. (Thu.) Page Size: broadsheet. Subscrip. Rate: $.75 newsstand/cover; $32/yr in state; $39/yr out of state; $20 to students for 9 mos.. Circulation: 3,000 per issue (paid). **Owner(s):** Southern Rhode Island Newspapers, 187 Main St., Wakefield, RI 02880. Telephone: 401-789-9744. FAX: 401-789-1550. **Management:** Terri Lei Feste, Publisher. Jody Boucher, Advertising Director. Phil Rowell, Circulation Manager. **Editorial:** Galen McGovern, Editor.

SOUTH CAROLINA

ABBEVILLE

PRESS & BANNER, THE. 107-109 W. Pickens St., Abbeville, SC 29620-2426. Telephone: 864-366-5461. FAX: 864-366-5463. E-MAIL: bannercorp@chorter.net. Mailing Address: PO Box 769, Abbeville, SC 29620. Year Established: 1844. Pub. Frequency: w. (Wed.) Page Size: standard. Subscrip. Rate: $.75 newsstand/cover; $25/yr local; $40/yr mailed elsewhere. Adv. Rate: col. inch $7.50 Circulation: 7,000 per issue (paid). **Owner(s):** Banner Corp., 107-109 W. Pickens St., Abbeyville, SC 29620. Telephone: 864-366-5461. **Management:** John Riley West, Publisher. **Editorial:** John Riley West, Editor.

BAMBERG

ADVERTIZER-HERALD, THE. 369 McGee St., Bamberg, SC 29003. Telephone: 803-245-5204. FAX: 803-245-3900. E-MAIL: editor@kilguspublishing.com. URL: http://www.advertizerherald.com. Mailing Address: PO Box 929, Bamberg, SC 29003. Year Established: 1967. Pub. Frequency: w. (Wed.) Page Size: broadsheet. Subscrip. Rate: $.50 newsstand/cover; $20/yr in county; $28/yr mailed out of county; $35/yr mailed out of state. Circulation: 4,350 per issue (paid). **Owner(s):** Upstate Newspapers, Inc., PO Box 648, Manchester, GA 31816. Telephone: 706-846-4336. FAX: 703-846-4418. **Management:** Gary West, General Manager. Bob Tribble, President. Gary West, Publisher.

HOLLY HILL OBSERVER, THE. 369 McGee St, Bamberg, SC 29003. Telephone: 803-245-5204. FAX: 803-245-3900. Mailing Address: PO Box 929, Bamberg, SC 29003. Year Established: 1972. Pub. Frequency: w. (Wed.) Page Size: broadsheet. Subscrip. Rate: $.50 newsstand/cover per issue; $17.50/yr in county; $27.50/yr out of county; $35/yr out of state. Circulation: 2,000 per issue (paid). **Owner(s):** Trib Publications Inc., PO Box 648, Manchester, GA 31816. Telephone: 706-846-4336. **Management:** Joyce M. Searson, General Manager. Robert E Tribble, President. **Editorial:** Joyce M. Searson, Editor.

NORTH TRADE JOURNAL. 369 McGee St., Bamberg, SC 29003-0929. Telephone: 803-245-5204. FAX: 803-245-3900. E-MAIL: kilguspub@Oburg.net. Mailing Address: PO Box 929, Bamberg, SC 29003-0929. Pub. Frequency: w. (Wed.) Page Size: standard. Subscrip. Rate: $.50 newsstand/cover; $20/yr in county; $28/yr mailed out of county; $35/yr mailed out of state. Circulation: 2,000 per issue (paid). **Owner(s):** Upstate Newspapers, Inc., PO Box 648, Manchester, GA 31816. Telephone: 706-846-4336. FAX: 706-846-4418. **Management:** Gary West, General Manager. Bob Tribble, President. Gary West, Publisher.

BARNWELL

PEOPLE-SENTINEL, THE. 9988 Dunbarton Blvd, Barnwell, SC 29812. Telephone: 803-259-3501. FAX: 803-259-2703. E-MAIL: psentinel@aol.com. URL: http://www.thepeoplesentinel.com. Year Established: 1877. Pub. Frequency: w. (Wed.) Page Size: broadsheet. Subscrip. Rate: $.50 newsstand/cover; $22/yr in county; $28/yr mailed out of county; $35/yr mailed out of state. Adv. Rate: col. inch $10.56 Circulation: 6,574 per issue (paid). **Owner(s):** Morris Multimedia, Inc., P.O. Box 1255, Barnwell, SC 29812. PO Box 936, Augusta, GA. **Management:** Laura McKenzie, Publisher. Chris McDado, Circulation Manager. **Editorial:** Tim Hicks, Managing Editor. Lisa Still, News Editor. Michael Young, Sports Editor.

BATESBURG

TWIN-CITY NEWS (BATESBURG), THE. 114 E. Columbia Ave., Batesburg, SC 29006. Telephone: 803-532-6203. FAX: 803-532-6204. Year Established: 1925. Pub. Frequency: w. (Thu.) Page Size: standard. Subscrip. Rate: $.50 newsstand/cover; $15/yr local; $25/yr mailed out of state. Circulation: 4,800 per issue (paid). **Owner(s):** Bruner Press, PO Box 2529, Leesville, SC 29070. Telephone: 803-532-6203. FAX: 803-532-6204. **Management:** Sara F. Bruner, Publisher. **Editorial:** Sara F. Bruner, Editor.

Weeklies

BEAUFORT

LOWCOUNTRY SHOPPER. 1556 Salem Rd., Beaufort, SC 29902. FAX: 843-524-8728. Mailing Address: PO Box 399, Beaufort, SC 29901-0399. Year Established: 1972. Pub. Frequency: w. (Wed.) Page Size: tabloid Circulation: 18,500 per issue (free). **Owner(s):** The/McClatchy Company, 2100 Q St, Sacramento, CA 95816. Telephone: 916-321-1936. FAX: 916-321-1869. **Management:** Sara Borton, General Manager. Bryan Osborn, Advertising Manager. **Editorial:** Chris Passante, Managing Editor.

BELTON

NEWS-CHRONICLE. 310 Public Sq., Belton, SC 29627. Telephone: 864-338-6124. FAX: 864-338-1109. E-MAIL: newschronicle@aol.com. URL: http://www.newschronicle.com. Mailing Address: PO Box 606, Belton, SC 29627. Year Established: 1990. Pub. Frequency: w. (Wed.) Page Size: standard. Subscrip. Rate: $.50 newsstand/cover; $18/yr local; $20.50/yr mailed in state; $25/yr mailed out of state. Circulation: 4,300 per issue (controlled and free). **Owner(s):** News-Chronicle Inc., See address and contact information above. **Management:** Christy Minor, Advertising. Lynn Robinson, Sales Manager. **Editorial:** Elaine Ellison-Rider, Editor-in-Chief. Debbie Rogers, Sports.

BENNETTSVILLE

MARLBORO HERALD-ADVOCATE. 100 Fayetteville Ave., Bennettsville, SC 29512. Telephone: 843-479-3815. FAX: 843-479-7671. E-MAIL: ads@heraldadvocate.com. Year Established: 1874. Pub. Frequency: s-w. (Mon. & Thu.) Page Size: broadsheet. Subscrip. Rate: $.50 newsstand/cover; $35/yr local; $40/yr out of county. Adv. Rate: col. inch $6 Circulation: 6,800 per issue (paid). **Owner(s):** Marlboro Publishing Co., Inc., See address and contact information above. **Management:** Dan McNiel, General Manager. William L. Kinney Jr., Publisher. Linda Wilson, Advertising Manager. Dan McNiel, Circulation Manager. **Editorial:** William L. Kinney Jr., Editor-in-Chief.

MARLBORO SHOPPER. 100 Fayetteville Ave., Bennettsville, SC 29512. Telephone: 843-479-3815. FAX: 843-479-7671. E-MAIL: ads@heraldadvocate.com. Year Established: 1984. Pub. Frequency: w. (Tue.) Page Size: standard.Adv. Rate: col. inch $2.50 Circulation: 13,500 per issue (free). **Owner(s):** Marlboro Publishing Co., Inc., See address and contact information above. **Management:** Dan McNiel, General Manager. William L. Kinney Jr., President. Linda Wilson, Advertising Manager. Dan McNeil, Circulation Manager. **Editorial:** William L. Kinney Jr., Editor.

BISHOPVILLE

LEE COUNTY OBSERVER. 218 N Main St, Bishopville, SC 29010. Telephone: 803-484-9431. FAX: 803-484-5055. E-MAIL: editor@sc.rr.com. Year Established: 1902. Pub. Frequency: w. (Wed.) Page Size: broadsheet. Subscrip. Rate: $.50 newsstand/cover; $30/yr in county; $35/yr out of county; $37/yr out of state. Adv. Rate: col. inch $6.75 Circulation: 4,000 per issue (paid and free). **Owner(s):** Morris Newspaper Corporation, 27 Abercorn St., Savannah, GA 31401. Telephone: 912-233-1281. FAX: 912-232-4639. **Management:** Michael Mischner, Publisher. Millie Scott, Advertising. **Editorial:** Gee Atkinson, Editor.

BLYTHEWOOD

COUNTRY CHRONICLE (BLYTHEWOOD). PO Box 904, Blythewood, SC 29016. Telephone: 803-786-5681. FAX: 803-591-1544. E-MAIL: editor@countrychronicle.com. URL: http://www.countrychronicle.com. Year Established: 1998. Pub. Frequency: w. **Owner(s):** Morris Newspaper Corporation, 27 Abercorn St., Savannah, GA 31401. Telephone: 912-233-1281. FAX: 912-232-4639.

CAMDEN

CHRONICLE-INDEPENDENT. 909 W DeKalb St, Camden, SC 29020. Telephone: 803-432-6157. FAX: 803-432-7609. E-MAIL: editor@ci-camden.com. URL: http://www.chronicle-independent.com. Year Established: 1889. Pub. Frequency: 3/w. (Mon., Wed., Fri.) Page Size: broadsheet. Subscrip. Rate: $.50 newsstand/cover; $64/yr mailed in area. Circulation: 8,000 per issue (paid). **Owner(s):** Morris Newspaper Corporation, 27 Abercorn St., Savannah, GA 31401. Telephone: 912-233-1281. FAX: 912-232-4639. **Management:** Michael Mischner, Publisher. Betsy Greenway, Advertising Manager. B.G. Mays, Circulation Manager. **Editorial:** Martin Cahn, Managing Editor. Shiela McKinney, Lifestyle Editor. Tom Didato, Sports.

LAKE WATEREE NEWS. 909 W DeKalb St, Camden, SC 29020. Telephone: 803-432-6157. FAX: 803-432-7609. Year Established: 2001. Pub. Frequency: q. **Owner(s):** Morris Newspaper Corporation, 27 Abercorn St., Savannah, GA 31401. Telephone: 912-233-1281. FAX: 912-232-4639.

CHERAW

CHERAW CHRONICLE, THE. ISSN 0889-0617
114 Front St., Cheraw, SC 29520. Telephone: 843-537-5261. FAX: 843-537-4518. E-MAIL: news@thecherawchronicle.com. URL: http://www.thecherawchronicle.com. Mailing Address: PO Box 1389, Cheraw, SC 29520. Year Established: 1885. Pub. Frequency: w. (Thu.) Page Size: standard. Subscrip. Rate: $.50 newsstand/cover; $22/yr home delivery in county; $35/yr home delivery out of county. Circulation: 8,050 per issue (paid and free). **Owner(s):** Community Newspapers (Athens), Inc., PO Box 792, Athens, GA 30603. Telephone: 706-548-0010. **Management:** Rick Bacon, Publisher. Sandra Deese, Advertising. Rhoda Locklear, Circulation Manager. **Editorial:** Bob Sloan, Editor.

CHESNEE

CHESNEE TRIBUNE. PO Box 158, Chesnee, SC 29323. Telephone: 864-461-2815. FAX: 864-839-2621. E-MAIL: htn@aol.com. URL: http://www.hometown-news.com. Pub. Frequency: w. (Wed.) Page Size: standard. Subscrip. Rate: $.50 newsstand/cover; $25/yr in county; $27.50/yr out of county; $35/yr elsewhere. Adv. Rate: col. inch $4.50 Circulation: 1,500 per issue (paid). **Owner(s):** Home Town News Inc., See address and contact information above. **Management:** Steve Blackwell, Publisher. Mike Minnix, Advertising. Phil Buchheit, Advertising Director. **Editorial:** Angela Mallette, Editor.

CHESTER

NEWS & REPORTER, THE. 104 York St., Chester, SC 29706. Telephone: 803-385-3177. FAX: 803-581-2518. E-MAIL: newsdepartment@onlinechester.com. URL: http://www.onlinechester.com. Mailing Address: PO Box 250, Chester, SC 29706. Year Established: 1869. Pub. Frequency: s-w. (Wed. & Fri.) Page Size: broadsheet. Subscrip. Rate: $.50 newsstand/cover; $36/yr in county; $51/yr in NC & SC; $59/yr elsewhere. Circulation: 7,500 per issue (paid). **Owner(s):** Landmark Community Newspapers, Inc., PO Box 549, Shelbyville, KY 40065. Telephone: 502-633-2526. **Management:** William J. Aultman, General Manager. Fran T Dodds, Advertising. David Minors, Circulation Manager. **Editorial:** Don Dibley, Editor. Travis Jenkins, Sports Editor.

CLINTON

CLINTON CHRONICLE, THE. 513 N. Broad St., Clinton, SC 29325. Telephone: 864-833-1900. FAX: 864-833-1902. E-MAIL: chronicle@charterinternet.com. Mailing Address: PO Box 180, Clinton, SC 29325. Year Established: 1900. Pub. Frequency: w. (Wed.) Page Size: broadsheet. Subscrip. Rate: $.75 newsstand/cover (effective 2006); $35/yr mailed in county; $50/yr mailed out of county. Adv. Rate: col. inch $8.25 Circulation: 5,000 per issue (controlled and free). **Owner(s):** Laurens County Newspapers, Inc., See address and contact information above. **Management:** Larry B. Franklin, Publisher. Shirley Pace, Advertising. **Editorial:** Jennifer Brown, Editor.

COLUMBIA

CAROLINA PANORAMA. 2346 Two Notch Rd., Ste. B, Columbia, SC 29204. Telephone: 803-256-4015. FAX: 803-256-6732. E-MAIL: cpanorama@aol.com. Mailing Address: P.O. Box 11205, Columbia, SC 29211-1205. Year Established: 1985. Pub. Frequency: w. (Thu.) Page Size: standard.Subscrip. Rate: $25/yr Circulation: 12,000 per issue (paid). **Owner(s):** T M Publishing, See address and contact information above. **Management:** Nat Abraham Sr., Publisher. Natalie McKinnie, Advertising Manager. **Editorial:** Nate Abraham Jr., Editor.

CONWAY

HORRY INDEPENDENT. 2510 Main St., Conway, SC 29526. Telephone: 843-248-6882. FAX: 843-248-6024. E-MAIL: hinews@sccoast.net. Year Established: 1980. Pub. Frequency: w. (Thu.) Page Size: broadsheet. Subscrip. Rate: $.50 newsstand/cover; $25/yr. Freelance Pay: $5-$50/article. Circulation: 6,000 per issue (paid and free). **Owner(s):** Waccamaw Publishers, PO Box 740, Conway, SC 29528. Telephone: 803-248-6671. **Management:** Steve Robertson, Publisher. Tom Browr, Advertising Manager. Nichole Gore, Circulation Manager. **Editorial:** Kathy Ropp, Editor.

DARLINGTON

NEWS & PRESS, THE. 117 S. Main St., Darlington, SC 29532. Telephone: 843-393-3811. FAX: 843-393-6811. E-MAIL: athomas@newandpress.com. URL: http://www.newsandpress.com. Mailing Address: PO Box 513, Darlington, SC 29540. Year Established: 1874. Pub. Frequency: w. (Thu.) Page Size: standard. Subscrip. Rate: $.50 newsstand/cover; $20/yr mailed in state; $30/yr mailed out of state. Circulation: 6,200 per issue (paid). **Owner(s):** Morrell L. Thomas, Jr., See address and contact information above. **Management:** Ann Thomas, General Manager. Morrell L. Thomas Jr., President. April Asaro, Advertising. Genise Calcutt, Advertising Manager. **Editorial:** Neil Hopwood, Editor. David Levin, Sports Editor.

DILLON

DILLON HERALD, THE. 505 Hwy. 301 N., Dillon, SC 29536. Telephone: 843-774-3311. FAX: 843-841-1930. E-MAIL: jd@thedillonherald.com. URL: http://www.thedillonherald.com. Year Established: 1894. Pub. Frequency: s-w. (Tue. & Thu.) Page Size: broadsheet. Subscrip. Rate: $.50 newsstand/cover; $38.75/yr local; $52.90/yr elsewhere. Adv. Rate: col. inch $7.14 **Wire Service(s):** AP. Circulation: 7,450 per issue (paid and free). **Owner(s):** Herald Publishing Co., Inc., PO Drawer 1288, Dillon, SC 29536-1288. **Management:** Johnnie Daniels, General Manager. A B Jordan III, Publisher. Jodi Hayes, Circulation Manager. James R Usher Jr., Business Manager. **Editorial:** Betsy Finklea, Editor.

EASLEY

EASLEY PROGRESS, THE. 205 Russell St., Easley, SC 29640. Telephone: 864-855-0355. FAX: 864-855-6825. E-MAIL: easleyprogress@worldnet.att.net. URL: http://www.easleypublications.com. Mailing Address: PO Box 709, Easley, SC 29641-0709. Year Established: 1902. Pub. Frequency: s-w. (Wed. & Fri.) Page Size: broadsheet. Subscrip. Rate: $.50 newsstand/cover; $18/yr mailed in county. Adv. Rate: col. inch $7.15 Circulation: 10,500 per issue (controlled and free). **Owner(s):** Easley Publications, See address and contact information above. **Management:** Benjie Milligan, Publisher. Bree Youngblood, Office Manager. Bonnie Lesley, Advertising Manager. **Editorial:** Ben Robinson, Editor. Amanda Foster, Lifestyle Editor.

EDGEFIELD

CITIZEN NEWS, THE. 201 Main St., Edgefield, SC 29824. Telephone: 803-637-5306. FAX: 803-637-5661. Mailing Address: PO Box 448, Edgefield, SC 29824. Pub. Frequency: w. (Wed.) Page Size: standard. Subscrip. Rate: $.50 newsstand/cover; $18/yr in county; $22/yr out of county; $36/yr out of state. Circulation: 4,257 per issue (paid). **Owner(s):** Community Communications LLC, See address and contact information above. **Management:** Christopher Cole, General Manager. **Editorial:** Christopher Cole, Editor.

FLORENCE

NEWS JOURNAL, THE. 1810 Second Loop Rd, Ste 12, Florence, SC 29501. Telephone: 843-667-9656. FAX: 843-661-7102. E-MAIL: flonewsjournal@aol.com. Year Established: 1982. Pub. Frequency: w. (Wed.) Page Size: broadsheet. Subscrip. Rate: $75/yr elsewhere. Circulation: 36,800 per issue (controlled and free). **Owner(s):** Morris Newspaper Corporation, 27 Abercorn St., Savannah, GA 31401. Telephone: 912-233-1281. FAX: 912-232-4639. **Management:** Don Swartz, Publisher. Jay Harris, Circulation Manager. **Editorial:** Brenda Harrison, Editor.

FORT MILL

FORT MILL TIMES. 124 Main St., Fort Mill, SC 29715. Telephone: 803-547-2353. FAX: 803-547-2321. E-MAIL: news@fortmilltimes.com. URL: http://www.fortmilltimes.com. Mailing Address: PO Box 250, Fort Mill, SC 29716. Year Established: 1892. Pub. Frequency: w. (Thu.) Page Size: broadsheet. Subscrip. Rate: $21/yr mailed in county; $40/yr mailed out of state. Circulation: 6,800 per issue (paid). **Owner(s):** The/McClatchy Company, 2100 Q St., Sacramento, CA 95816-6816. **Management:** Patricia Larson, Publisher. Misty Hall, Advertising. Sherry Avant, Advertising Manager. **Editorial:** Mike Harrison, Editor.

FOUNTAIN INN

TRIBUNE-TIMES. ISSN 0747-1165
1314 N. Main St., Fountain Inn, SC 29644. Telephone: 864-967-9580. FAX: 864-967-9585. URL: http://www.tribunetimes.com. Mailing Address: PO Box 1179, Simpsonville, SC 29681. Year Established: 1911. Pub. Frequency: w. (Wed.) Page Size: broadsheet. Subscrip. Rate: $.25 newsstand/cover; $26/yr in county $34/yr out of state; $34/yr mailed out of area $34/yr out of state. Circulation: 34,000 per issue (paid). **Owner(s):** Gannett Company, Inc., 7950 Jones Branch Dr., McLean, VA 22107-0001. Telephone: 703-854-6000. **Management:** Sudie Gambrell, General Manager. Steve Brandt, Publisher. Wanda Edney, Advertising Manager. **Editorial:** Ron DeKett, Senior Editor. Mike Burns, Sports Editor.

TRIBUNE TIMES. 1314 N. Main St., Fountain Inn, SC 29644. Telephone: 864-967-9580. FAX: 864-967-9585. URL: http://www.tribunetimes.com. Mailing Address: PO Box 1179, Simpsonville, SC 29681. Pub. Frequency: w. (Wed.) Page Size: standard. Subscrip. Rate: $.25 newsstand/cover; $26/yr in county; $34/yr elsewhere. Circulation: 37,000 per issue (paid). **Owner(s):** Gannett Company, Inc., 7950 Jones Branch Dr., McLean, VA 22107-0001. Telephone: 703-854-6000. **Management:** Sudie Gambrell, General Manager. Steve Brandt, Publisher. Jay Stafford, Office Manager. **Editorial:** Ron DeKett, Senior Editor. Mike Burns, Sports Editor.

GAFFNEY

GAFFNEY LEDGER, THE. ISSN 0748-934X
1604 Floyd Baker Blvd., Gaffney, SC 29340. Telephone: 864-489-1131. FAX: 864-487-7667. E-MAIL: cody@gaffneyledger.com. URL: http://www.gaffneyledger.com. Mailing Address: PO Box 670, Gaffney, SC 29342. Year Established: 1894. Pub. Frequency: 3/w. (Mon., Wed., Fri.) Page Size: broadsheet. Subscrip. Rate: $.50 newsstand/cover; $67.50/yr in county; $75/yr out of county. **Wire Service(s):** AP. Circulation: 8,500 per issue (paid). **Owner(s):** Cody Sossamon, See address and contact information above. **Management:** Cody Sossamon, Publisher. Robert Martin, Advertising Manager. Phyllis Wilson, Classified Adv. Mgr.. **Editorial:** Konie Jordan, Editor-in-Chief. Cody Sossamon, Book Review Editor. Laura Parker, Family Editor.

GEORGETOWN

GEORGETOWN TIMES, THE. 615 Front St., Georgetown, SC 29440. Telephone: 843-546-4148. FAX: 843-546-2395. E-MAIL: advetising@gtowntimes.com. URL: http://www.gtowntimes.com. Mailing Address: PO Box 2778, Georgetown, SC 29442. Year Established: 1797. Pub. Frequency: 3/w. (Mon., Wed., Fri.) Page Size: broadsheet. Subscrip. Rate: $.25 newsstand/cover; $30/yr mailed in county; $40/yr mailed out of state. Adv. Rate: col. inch $6.30 Freelance Pay: $30/article. **Wire Service(s):** AP. Circulation: 9,100 per issue (paid). **Owner(s):** Evening Post Publishing Co., 134 Columbus St., Charleston, SC 29403. Telephone: 843-577-7111. **Management:** John Carr, Publisher. April Todd, Classified Adv. Mgr.. **Editorial:** Jason Lesley, Editor. Roger Green, Sports Editor.

GOOSE CREEK

GOOSE CREEK GAZETTE, THE. 205 Goose Creek Blvd., Ste. 11-A, Goose Creek, SC 29445. Telephone: 843-572-0511. FAX: 843-572-0312. E-MAIL: gcgazette@innova.net. URL: http://www.goosecreekgazette.com. Mailing Address: PO Box 304, Goose Creek, SC 29445. Year Established: 1978. Pub. Frequency: w. (Thu.) Page Size: broadsheet. Circulation: 11,200 per issue (controlled and free). **Owner(s):** Evening Post Publishing Co., 134 Columbus St., Charleston, SC 29403. Telephone: 843-577-7111. FAX: 843-937-5545. **Management:** Ellen Priest, Publisher. Melinda Mazzone, Advertising. **Editorial:** Michael Truslow, Editor.

GREENVILLE

METROBEAT. 250 Executive Center Dr., #107 B-70, Greenville, SC 29615. Telephone: 864-232-479. FAX: 864-370-0500. URL: http://www.metrobeat.net. Pub. Frequency: w. (Tue.) Page Size: tabloid Subscrip. Rate: $60/yr Circulation: 20,000 per issue (free). **Owner(s):** Debra Eason, See address and contact information above. **Management:** Clinton Carmichael, Publisher. Scott Williams, Business Manager. **Editorial:** James Shannon, Editor. Lynn Armonaitis, Creative Director.

GREER

GREER CITIZEN, THE. 105 Victoria St, Greer, SC 29651. Telephone: 864-877-8076. E-MAIL: ads@greercitizen.com. URL: http://greercitizen.com/. Year Established: 1918. Pub. Frequency: w. (Wed.) Page Size: standard. Subscrip. Rate: $.50 newsstand/cover. Adv. Rate: col. inch $7.85 Circulation: 10,500 per issue (paid). **Owner(s):** The Greer Citizen, See address and contact information above. **Management:** Don Wilder, Publisher.

HAMPTON

HAMPTON COUNTY GUARDIAN. 200 Lee Ave., Hampton, SC 29924. Telephone: 803-943-4645. FAX: 803-943-9365. URL: Http://www.hamptoncountyguardian.com. Mailing Address: PO Box 625, Hampton, SC 29924. Year Established: 1879. Pub. Frequency: w. (Thu.) Page Size: standard. Subscrip. Rate: $.50 newsstand/cover; $22/yr mailed in county; $28/yr mailed out of county; $35/yr mailed out of state. Circulation: 4,550 per issue (paid). **Owner(s):** Community Newspapers (Athens), Inc., PO Box 792, Athens, GA 30603. Telephone: 706-548-0010. **Management:** Wayne Knuckles, Publisher. **Editorial:** Shellie Murdaugh, Editor.

HANAHAN

HANAHAN, GOOSE CREEK & NORTH CHARLESTON NEWS. 1231 Yeamans Hall Rd., Hanahan, SC 29410 . Telephone: 843-747-5773. FAX: 843-744-5505. E-MAIL: hanahancom@aol.com. Year Established: 1959. Pub. Frequency: w. (Wed.) Page Size: tabloid.Subscrip. Rate: $22/yr mailed Circulation: 11,000 per issue (paid). **Owner(s):** Rod Shealy, PO Box 60580, Charleston, SC 29419. Telephone: 803-747-5773. **Management:** Kirk Luther, Publisher. **Editorial:** Kirk Luther, Editor.

HARTSVILLE

DARCO NEWS & BUYERS GUIDE. 416 W. Carolina Ave., Hartsville, SC 29550-4524. Telephone: 843-332-0858. FAX: 843-332-7368. Pub. Frequency: w. (Wed.) Page Size: broadsheet Circulation: 16,141 per issue (free). **Owner(s):** Morris Multimedia, Inc., PO Box 210, Cumming, GA 30028. Telephone: 770-887-3126. **Management:** Robert Thompson, Publisher. Crystal Gibson, Advertising Manager. Russell Truett, Circulation Manager.

MESSENGER (HARTSVILLE), THE. 207 E. Carolina St., Hartsville, SC 29550. Telephone: 843-332-6545. FAX: 843-332-1341. E-MAIL: themessenger@hartsvillemessenger.com. URL: http://www.hartsvillemessenger.com. Mailing Address: PO Box 1865, Hartsville, SC 29551. Year Established: 1893. Pub. Frequency: s-w. (Wed. & Fri.) Page Size: broadsheet. Subscrip. Rate: $.50 newsstand/cover; $35/yr in county; $50/yr in state; $60/yr mailed out of state. Freelance Pay: $0.25/column-inch. Circulation: 5,500 per issue (paid). **Owner(s):** Graham Osteen, Jr., See address and contact information above. **Management:** Graham Osteen II, Publisher. Mike Bowen, Advertising Director. Tiffany Tumage, Classified Editor. **Editorial:** Graham Osteen II, Editor. Jim Faile, Managing Editor. Ardie Arvidson, Lifestyle Editor. Eddie Newman, Sports Editor.

HEMINGWAY

WEEKLY OBSERVER, THE. 108 N. Main St., Hemingway, SC 29554. Telephone: 843-558-3323. E-MAIL: dgreen@florencenews.com. URL: http://www.scnow.com/scp/community/observer. Mailing Address: PO Box 309, Hemingway, SC 29554. Year Established: 1973. Pub. Frequency: w. (Wed.) Page Size: broadsheet. Subscrip. Rate: $.25 newsstand/cover; $12/yr mailed in county; $25/yr mailed out of county; $10/yr mailed in county to senior citizens. Adv. Rate: col. inch $5.25 Circulation: 2,100 per issue (paid and free). **Owner(s):** Media General, Inc., 333 E. Franklin St., Richmond, VA 23219. Telephone: 804-649-6898. **Management:** Mark Laskowski, Publisher. Katina Pope, Office Manager. Kay Byrd, Advertising. **Editorial:** David Green, Editor.Readers: Eastern Williamsburg County, Northern Georgetown County, Southern Florence County, Southern Marion County

HOLLY HILL

SANTEE STRIPER. 8513 Old State Rd., Holly Hill, SC 29059. Telephone: 803-496-3242. FAX: 803-496-3051. E-MAIL: kilgus@news@tri-countyelectric.net. Mailing Address: PO Box 700, Holly Hill, SC 29059. Pub. Frequency: w. (Wed.) Page Size: broadsheet. Subscrip. Rate: $.50 newsstand/cover; $17.50/yr mailed in county; $25/yr mailed out of county; $35/yr mailed out of state. Circulation: 1,500 per issue (paid). **Owner(s):** Upstate Newspapers, Inc., PO Box 648, Manchester, GA 31816. Telephone: 706-846-4336. FAX: 706-846-4418. **Management:** Gary West, General Manager. Bob Tribble, President. Gary West, Publisher. **Editorial:** Linda Asselle, Managing Editor.

INMAN

INMAN TIMES. PO Box 7, Inman, SC 29349. Telephone: 864-472-9548. FAX: 864-472-5398. Pub. Frequency: w. (Wed.) Page Size: standard. Subscrip. Rate: $.50 newsstand/cover; $25/yr in county; $30/yr mailed out of county; $35/yr mailed out of state. Circulation: 3,800 per issue (paid). **Owner(s):** Home Town News Inc., See address and contact information above. **Management:** Stephen Blackwell, Publisher. **Editorial:** Jed Blackwell, Editor.

IRMO

LAKE MURRAY NEWS. PO Box 175, Irmo, SC 29063-0175. Telephone: 803-772-7506. FAX: 803-772-7795. E-MAIL: lakemurraynews@aol.com. Pub. Frequency: w. (Thu.) Page Size: tabloid. Subscrip. Rate: $.40 newsstand/cover; $22/yr in county. Circulation: 6,800 per issue (paid). **Owner(s):** Rod Shealy, See address and contact information above. **Management:** Rod Shealy, Publisher. **Editorial:** Rod Shealy, Editor.

NEW IRMO NEWS. PO Box 175, Irmo, SC 29063-0175. Telephone: 803-772-7506. FAX: 803-772-7795. E-MAIL: irmonews@aol.com. Pub. Frequency: w. (Thu.) Page Size: tabloid. Subscrip. Rate: $.40 newsstand/cover; $22/yr domestic. Circulation: 9,000 per issue (paid). **Owner(s):** Rod Shealy, See address and contact information above. **Management:** Rod Shealy, Publisher. **Editorial:** Rod Shealy, Editor.

NORTHEAST NEWS. PO Box 175, Irmo, SC 29063-0175. Telephone: 803-772-7506. FAX: 803-772-7795. Pub. Frequency: w. (Thu.) Page Size: tabloid. Subscrip. Rate: $.40 newsstand/cover; $22/yr mailed in county. Circulation: 4,500 per issue (paid). **Owner(s):** Rod Shealy, See address and contact information above. **Management:** Rod Shealy, Publisher. **Editorial:** Ollie Moye, Editor.

KINGSTREE

NEWS (KINGSTREE), THE. 511 N Longstreet St, Kingstree, SC 29556-0574. Telephone: 843-355-6397. FAX: 843-355-6530. URL: http://www.kingstreenews.com. Mailing Address: PO Box 574, Kingstree, SC 29556-0574. Year Established: 1972. Pub. Frequency: w. (Wed.) Page Size: standard. Subscrip. Rate: $.50 newsstand/cover; $19/yr in county; $25/yr out of county; $32/yr mailed out of state. Adv. Rate: col. inch $6.85 Circulation: 4,800 per issue (paid). **Owner(s):** Evening Post Publishing Co., 134 Columbus St., Charleston, SC 29403. Telephone: 843-577-7111. **Management:** Tami Rodgers, Publisher. Beth Ward, Advertising. Patricia McCrea, Circulation Manager.

LAKE CITY

LAKE CITY NEWS & POST. 107 N. Aclaine St., Lake City, SC 29560-2425. Telephone: 843-394-3571. FAX: 843-394-5057. E-MAIL: news@lakecitynews.com. Mailing Address: PO Box 429, Lake City, SC 29560-2425. Pub. Frequency: w. (Wed.) Page Size: broadsheet. Subscrip. Rate: $.50 newsstand/cover; $17/yr local; $28/yr out of county. Circulation: 2,500 per issue (paid). **Owner(s):** Media General, Inc., 333 E. Franklin St., Richmond, VA 23219. Telephone: 804-649-6000. **Editorial:** Adrel Melangley, Editor.

LAKE WYLIE

LAKE WYLIE PILOT. 8 Executive Ct, Lake Wylie, SC 29710. Telephone: 803-831-8166. FAX: 803-831-0660. URL: http://www.lakewyliepilot.com. Pub. Frequency: w. (Tue.) Page Size: broadsheet.Subscrip. Rate: $21/yr mailed Circulation: 10,769 per issue (free). **Owner(s):** The/McClatchy Company, 2100 Q St., Sacramento, CA 95816-6816. **Management:** Mary Pettus, Publisher. Lisa Pinckney, Advertising. **Editorial:** Catherine Sweisberger, Editor.

LANCASTER

LANCASTER NEWS. ISSN 0745-7421
701 N. White St., Lancaster, SC 29720. Telephone: 803-283-1133. FAX: 803-283-8969. URL: http://www.lancasternews.com. Mailing Address: PO Box 640, Lancaster, SC 29721. Year Established: 1852. Pub. Frequency: 3/w. (Wed., Fri., Sun.) Page Size: standard. Subscrip. Rate: $.50 newsstand/cover; $49.95/yr in county. **Wire Service(s):** AP. Circulation: 13,000 per issue (paid). **Owner(s):** Landmark Communications, Inc., PO Box 549., Shelbyville, KY 40066. Telephone: 502-633-4334. **Management:** Susan Rowell, Publisher. Leigh Irrington, Advertising Manager. Angie Vincent, Circulation Manager. **Editorial:** Barbara Howell, Editor. Robert Howey, Sports Editor.

LANDRUM

NEWS LEADER (LANDRUM), THE. 146 N. Trade Ave., Landrum, SC 29356. Telephone: 864-457-3337. FAX: 864-457-5231. Mailing Address: PO Box 9, Landrum, SC 29356. Year Established: 1955. Pub. Frequency: w. (Wed.) Page Size: broadsheet. Subscrip. Rate: $.50 newsstand/cover; $18.50/yr in county; $28.50/yr out of county; $35/yr out of state. Circulation: 2,500 per issue (paid). **Owner(s):** Trib Publications, Inc., PO Box 648, Manchester, GA 31816. Telephone: 706-846-4336. **Management:** Jody McPherson, General Manager.

LAURENS

ADVERTISER EXTRA, THE. 226 W. Laurens St., Laurens, SC 29360-2960. Telephone: 864-984-2586. FAX: 864-984-4039. E-MAIL: advertiser@charter.net. Mailing Address: PO Box 490, Laurens, SC 29360-0490. Pub. Frequency: w. (Sat.) Page Size: standard Circulation: 8,500 per issue (free). **Owner(s):** James D., Chris C., Mark Brown, See address and contact information above. **Management:** James D Brown, Publisher. **Editorial:** John Clayton, Editor.

LAURENS COUNTY ADVERTISER. PO Box 490, Laurens, SC 29360. Telephone: 864-984-2586. FAX: 864-984-4039. E-MAIL: advertiser@charter.net. Year Established: 1885. Pub. Frequency: w. (Wed.) Page Size: broadsheet. Subscrip. Rate: $.75 newsstand/cover; $30/yr mailed in county; $45/yr mailed in state; $55/yr mailed out of state. Circulation: 18,465 per issue (paid). **Owner(s):** James D.; Chris C.; Mark Brown, See address and contact information above. **Management:** Chris C. Brown, Publisher. James D. Brown, Advertising. Pam Neighbors, Circulation Manager. **Editorial:** John Clayton, Editor. Roslyn Martin, Society Editor. John Clayton, Sports Editor.

Weeklies

LEXINGTON

LEXINGTON COUNTY CHRONICLE & THE DISPATCH-NEWS. 131 Swartz Rd, Lexington, SC 29072. Telephone: 803-359-7633. FAX: 803-359-2936. E-MAIL: lexchron@alltel.net. URL: http://www.lexingtonchronicle.com. Mailing Address: PO Box 9, Lexington, SC 29071-0009. Year Established: 1992. Pub. Frequency: w. (Thu.) Page Size: broadsheet. Subscrip. Rate: $.75 newsstand/cover; $28/yr in county; $40/yr out of county; $26/yr to senior citizens. Adv. Rate: col. inch $10.25 Circulation: 7,600 per issue (paid). **Owner(s):** Jerry & MacLeod Bellune, See address and contact information above. **Management:** MacLeod Bellune, Publisher. **Editorial:** Jerry Bellune, Editor. Vicki Shealy, Metro Editor. Brian Sullivan, Sports Editor.

LORIS

LORIS SCENE, THE. 4103 Main St., Loris, SC 29569. Telephone: 843-756-1447. FAX: 843-756-7800. E-MAIL: llsnews@sccoast.net. Year Established: 1992. Pub. Frequency: w. (Wed.) Page Size: tabloid. Subscrip. Rate: $.50 newsstand/cover; $19/yr in county; $29/yr out of county. Circulation: 2,000 per issue (free). **Owner(s):** Steve Robertson, See address and contact information above. **Management:** Steve Robertson, President. Annette Norris, Advertising Manager. **Editorial:** Michael Smith, Editor.

LORIS TIMES. 4107 Walnut St., Loris, SC 29569-0796. Telephone: 843-756-7224. FAX: 843-756-7812. E-MAIL: nmbtimes@gte.net. Mailing Address: PO Box 796, Loris, SC 29569. Year Established: 1991. Pub. Frequency: w. (Thu.) Page Size: broadsheet. Subscrip. Rate: $.25 newsstand/cover; $13/yr in county; $18/yr out of county; $25/yr out of state. Adv. Rate: col. inch $4 Circulation: 4,500 per issue (paid). **Owner(s):** Pauline L. Lowman, PO Box 725, North Myrtle Beach, SC 29597-0725. Telephone: 843-249-3525. FAX: 843-249-7012. **Management:** Mike Lowman, General Manager. Pauline L Lowman, Publisher. **Editorial:** Pauline L Lowman, Managing Editor.

MANNING

MANNING TIMES, THE. 4 S. Brooks St., Manning, SC 29102. Telephone: 803-435-8422. FAX: 803-435-4189. Mailing Address: PO Box 576, Manning, SC 29102. Year Established: 1882. Pub. Frequency: w. (Thu.) Page Size: broadsheet. Subscrip. Rate: $.75 newsstand/cover; $30/yr local; $40/yr elsewhere. Adv. Rate: col. inch $4 Circulation: 4,000 per issue (paid). **Owner(s):** Smith Newspapers Inc., PO Box 27, Fort Payne, AL 35967. Telephone: 205-845-5510. **Management:** Cleve Dowell, Publisher. Carol Dowell, Circulation Manager. Joanne Taylor, Sales Manager. **Editorial:** Cathy Gilbert, Editor.

MARION

MARION STAR & MULLINS ENTERPRISE. 211 Bobby Gerald Pkwy., Marion, SC 29571. Telephone: 843-423-2050. FAX: 843-423-2542. E-MAIL: starandenterprise@scnow.com. Mailing Address: PO Box 880, Marion, SC 29571-0880. Pub. Frequency: w. (Wed.) Page Size: broadsheet. Subscrip. Rate: $.50 newsstand/cover; $18/yr mailed in county; $28/yr mailed out of county. Circulation: 12,000 per issue (paid). **Owner(s):** Media General, Inc., 333 E. Franklin St., Richmond, VA 23219. Telephone: 804-649-6000. **Management:** Mike Miller, Publisher. Kathy Sawyer, Advertising Manager. David Johnson, Circulation Manager. **Editorial:** Dianne P. Owens, Editor. Kevin Tindall, Reporter.

MCCORMICK

MCCORMICK MESSENGER. 120 Main St., McCormick, SC 29835-9518. Telephone: 864-852-3311. FAX: 864-852-3528. E-MAIL: mccmess@wctel.net. Mailing Address: PO Box 1807, McCormick, SC 29835-1807. Year Established: 1902. Pub. Frequency: w. (Thu.) Page Size: standard. Subscrip. Rate: $.50 newsstand/cover; $25/yr in county; $30/yr out of county. Adv. Rate: col. inch $4.75 Circulation: 2,700 per issue (paid). **Owner(s):** McCormick Media Inc., See address and contact information above. **Management:** Vicki Dorn, General Manager. Ashley Creswell, Advertising Manager. **Editorial:** Vicki Dorn, Editor.

MONCKS CORNER

BERKELEY INDEPENDENT, THE. 320 E. Main St., Moncks Corner, SC 29461. Telephone: 843-761-6397. FAX: 843-899-6996. E-MAIL: berkeleyind@infoave.net. URL: http://www.berkeleyind.com. Mailing Address: PO Box 427, Moncks Corner, SC 29461-0427. Year Established: 1987. Pub. Frequency: w. (Wed.) Page Size: broadsheet. Subscrip. Rate: $.50 newsstand/cover; $22/yr. Adv. Rate: col. inch $6.45 Circulation: 9,000 per issue (paid). **Owner(s):** Evening Post Publishing Co., 134 Columbus St., Charleston, SC 29403. Telephone: 843-577-7111. **Management:** Ellen Priest, Publisher. Frances Wright, Advertising Manager. Jackie Edgeworth, Circulation Manager. **Editorial:** Doug Dickerson, Editor.

MT PLEASANT

JOURNAL (JAMES ISLAND), THE. 1558 Ben Sawyer Blvd, Ste B, Mt Pleasant, SC 29464. Telephone: 843-849-1778. FAX: 843-849-0214. E-MAIL: editor@islandpapers.com. URL: http://www.moultrienews.com. Mailing Address: PO Box 279, Sullivan's Island, SC 29482. Year Established: 1968. Pub. Frequency: w. (Thu.) Page Size: broadsheet. Subscrip. Rate: $17/yr mailed. Adv. Rate: col. inch $7.16 Circulation: 8,573 per issue (free). **Owner(s):** Island Publications, Inc., See address and contact information above. **Management:** Vickey Boyd, Publisher. **Editorial:** Bill Walker, Editor.

MOULTRIE NEWS, THE. 1558 Ben Sawyer Blvd, Ste B, Mt Pleasant, SC 29464. Telephone: 843-849-1778. FAX: 843-849-0214. E-MAIL: editor@islandpapers.com. URL: http://www.islandpapers.com. Mailing Address: PO Box 279, Sullivan's Island, SC 29482. Year Established: 1964. Pub. Frequency: w. (Wed.) Page Size: broadsheet. Subscrip. Rate: $40/yr mailed. Adv. Rate: col. inch $11 Circulation: 26,500 per issue (paid and free). **Owner(s):** Island Publications, Inc., See address and contact information above. **Management:** Vickey Boyd, Publisher. **Editorial:** Bill Walker, Editor.

NEWBERRY

HERALD & NEWS, THE. 1716 Main St., Newberry, SC 29108. Telephone: 803-276-0625. FAX: 803-276-1517. Mailing Address: PO Box 558, Newberry, SC 29108-0558. Pub. Frequency: 3/w. (Mon., Wed., Fri.) Page Size: standard Circulation: 16,000 per issue (free). **Owner(s):** Crescent Media Group, PO Box 1634, Spartanburg, SC 29304. Telephone: 864-583-2907. **Management:** Rex Goss, Publisher. Cassandra Moneymaker, Advertising Manager. Sherry Rowe, Classified Adv. Mgr.. **Editorial:** Holly Astwood, Editor. Paul Gable, Sports Editor.

NEWBERRY OBSERVER, THE. 1716 Main St., Newberry, SC 29108. Telephone: 803-276-0625. FAX: 803-276-1517. URL: http://www.newberryobserver.com. Mailing Address: PO Box 558, Newberry, SC 29108. Year Established: 1865. Pub. Frequency: 3/w. (Mon., Wed., Fri.) Page Size: broadsheet. Subscrip. Rate: $.50 newsstand/cover; $52/yr in county; $63/yr out of county. Adv. Rate: col. inch $7.46 Circulation: 16,900 per issue (paid). **Owner(s):** Crescent Media Group, PO Box 1634, Spartanburg, SC 29304. Telephone: 864-583-2907. **Management:** Rex Goss, Publisher. Mary Watson, Circulation Manager. **Editorial:** Holly Astwood, Editor. Sherry Rowe, Production Manager.

NINETY SIX

STAR & BEACON, THE. 111 E Main St., Ninety Six, SC 29666-1003. Telephone: 864-543-3444. FAX: 864-543-3440. Pub. Frequency: w. (Tue.) Page Size: standard. Subscrip. Rate: $.50 newsstand/cover; $18/yr home delivery in county; $20.50/yr mailed out of county; $15/yr home delivery in county; $17.50/yr mailed out of county. Circulation: 9,000 per issue (paid). **Owner(s):** Judith M. Burns, 610 Phoenix St., Greenwood, SC 29646. Telephone: 864-223-1411. FAX: 864-223-7331. **Management:** Judith M. Burns, Publisher. Joan Butler, Advertising Manager. **Editorial:** David Morgan, Editor.

NORTH MYRTLE BEACH

NORTH MYRTLE BEACH TIMES. 203 N. Kings Hwy., North Myrtle Beach, SC 29582-0725. Telephone: 843-249-3525. FAX: 843-249-7012. E-MAIL: nmbtimes@gte.net. URL: http://www.northmyrtlebeach.net. Year Established: 1971. Pub. Frequency: w. (Thu.) Page Size: standard. Subscrip. Rate: $.50 newsstand/cover; $30/yr mailed local; $35/yr mailed out of county; $45/yr mailed out of state. Adv. Rate: col. inch $7.50 Circulation: 20,000 per issue (paid). **Owner(s):** Pauline L. Lowman, PO Box 725, North Myrtle Beach, SC 29597-0725. Telephone: 843-249-3525. FAX: 843-249-7012. **Management:** Pauline L Lowman, Publisher. **Editorial:** Pauline L Lowman, Managing Editor.

PAGELAND

PAGELAND PROGRESSIVE-JOURNAL, THE. ISSN 1063-8415 28825 Hwy. 9, Pageland, SC 29728. Telephone: 843-672-2358. FAX: 843-672-5593. E-MAIL: ppj@shtc.net. Mailing Address: PO Box 218, Pageland, GA 29728. Year Established: 1910. Pub. Frequency: w. (Tue.) Page Size: broadsheet. Subscrip. Rate: $.50 newsstand/cover; $15/yr in county; $20/yr out of county. Adv. Rate: col. inch $4 Circulation: 4,400 per issue (paid). **Owner(s):** Brian Hough, See address and contact information above. **Management:** Brian Hough, Publisher. Jane Hough, Advertising Manager. **Editorial:** Brian Hough, Editor-in-Chief.

PAWLEYS ISLAND

COASTAL OBSERVER (PAWLEYS ISLAND). ISSN 8750-3425 PO Box 1170, Pawleys Island, SC 29585-1170. Telephone: 843-237-8438. FAX: 843-235-0084. E-MAIL: coastalobserverpub@sc.rr.com. URL: http://www.coastalobserver.com. Year Established: 1982. Pub. Frequency: w. (Thu.) Page Size: broadsheet. Subscrip. Rate: $.25 newsstand/cover; $14/yr Georgetown & Horry cys; $17/yr mailed in state; $23/yr mailed out of state. Adv. Rate: col. inch $8 Circulation: 5,400 per issue (paid). **Owner(s):** Southeastern Publishing, See address and contact information above. **Management:** M.P. Swenson, Publisher. **Editorial:** Charles Swenson, Editor.

PICKENS

PICKENS SENTINEL. 109 Garvin St., Pickens, SC 29671. Telephone: 864-878-2453. FAX: 864-878-2454. Mailing Address: PO Box 95, Pickens, SC 29671. Year Established: 1872. Pub. Frequency: w. (Wed.) Page Size: broadsheet. Subscrip. Rate: $.50 newsstand/cover; $20/yr mailed in county; $26/yr mailed out of county. Circulation: 8,000 per issue (paid). **Owner(s):** Crescent Media Group, PO Box 1634, Spartanburg, SC 29304. Telephone: 864-583-2907. **Management:** Rocky Nimmons, General Manager. Pat Revis, Advertising. **Editorial:** Sandy Foster, Editor.

RIDGELAND

HARDEEVILLE TIMES. 104 S. Railroad St., Ridgeland, SC 29936. Telephone: 843-726-6161. FAX: 843-726-8661. Mailing Address: PO Box 1030, Ridgeland, SC 29936. Pub. Frequency: w. (Wed.) Page Size: broadsheet. Subscrip. Rate: $.35 newsstand/cover; $17/yr in county; $31/yr out of county. Circulation: 2,500 per issue (paid). **Owner(s):** Morris Multimedia, Inc., PO Box 936, Augusta, GA 30903-0936. Telephone: 706-724-0851. FAX: 706-722-7125. **Management:** Larry Miller, Publisher. Annmarie Baldwin, Advertising Manager. **Editorial:** Jessica Dailey, Editor.

JASPER COUNTY SUN. ISSN 1072-3986 104 S. Railroad St., Ridgeland, SC 29936. Telephone: 843-726-6161. FAX: 843-726-8661. URL: http://www.jaspercountysun.com. Mailing Address: PO Box 1030, Ridgeland, SC 29936. Year Established: 1993. Pub. Frequency: w. (Wed.) Page Size: broadsheet. Subscrip. Rate: $.50 newsstand/cover; $23/yr in county; $35/yr out of county; $40/yr out of state. Adv. Rate: col. inch $9 Circulation: 2,700 per issue (paid). **Owner(s):** Morris Multimedia, Inc., PO Box 936, Augusta, GA 30903-0936. Telephone: 706-724-0851. FAX: 706-722-7125. **Management:** Ann Kennedy, Publisher. Catina Gadson, Advertising Manager. **Editorial:** Anthony Garzilla, Editor.

SALUDA

SALUDA STANDARD SENTINEL. 302 N. Main St., Saluda, SC 29138. Telephone: 864-445-2527. FAX: 864-445-8679. E-MAIL: sentinel@saludasc.com. URL: http://www.saludastandard-sentinel.com. Mailing Address: PO Box 668, Saluda, SC 29138. Year Established: 1946. Pub. Frequency: w. (Thu.) Page Size: broadsheet. Subscrip. Rate: $.50 newsstand/cover; $18/yr mailed in county; $23/yr mailed out of county. Adv. Rate: col. inch $5.40 Circulation: 4,500 per issue (paid). **Owner(s):** Ralph Shealy, See address and contact information above. **Management:** Ralph Shealy, Publisher. Freda Glover, Advertising Manager. **Editorial:** Ralph Shealy, Editor.

SENECA

GOLDEN CORNER SHOPPERS GUIDE. 210 W N. First St, Seneca, SC 29678. Telephone: 864-882-2375. FAX: 864-882-2381. Mailing Address: PO Box 547, Seneca, SC 29679-0547. Pub. Frequency: w. (Mon.) Page Size: broadsheet Circulation: 32,000 per issue (free). **Owner(s):** Edwards Group Inc, 125 Eagles Nest, Seneca, SC 29678. Telephone: 864-882-3272. **Management:** Jerry Edward, General Manager. Jay Brooks, Advertising Director. Scott Nickles, Circulation Director. Diane Winstead, Classified Adv. Mgr..

SPARTANBURG

SPARTANBURG COUNTY NEWS. PO Box 5211, Spartanburg, SC 29302. Telephone: 864-476-3513. FAX: 864-476-3511. E-MAIL: hmtn@aol.com. URL: http://www.hometownnews.com. Pub. Frequency: w. (Wed.) Page Size: standard. Subscrip. Rate: $.50 newsstand/cover; $25/yr in county; $27.50/yr out of county; $35/yr elsewhere. Circulation: 1,000 per issue (paid). **Owner(s):** Home Town News Inc., See address and contact information above. **Management:** Steve Blackwell, Publisher. Mike Minnix, Advertising Manager. **Editorial:** Ernie Lambert, Editor.

SPARTENBURY

CITIZEN NEWS. 314 S Pine St, Spartenbury, SC 29304. Telephone: 864-583-2907. E-MAIL: mike@phenixcitizen.com. Pub. Frequency: w. (Thu.) Page Size: broadsheet. Subscrip. Rate: $.50 newsstand/cover; $20/yr in state; $25/yr out of state. Circulation: 16,500 per issue (paid). **Owner(s):** Mid South Management Co., See address and contact information above. **Management:** Amy Overton, Publisher. **Editorial:** Amy Overton, Executive Editor.

ST. GEORGE

EAGLE-RECORD, THE. 5549 Memorial Blvd., St. George, SC 29477-2473. Telephone: 843-563-3121. FAX: 843-563-5355. E-MAIL: eagleundascorerecord@bellsouth.net. Mailing Address: PO Box 278, St. George, SC 29477-0278. Year Established: 1899. Pub. Frequency: w. (Thu.) Page Size: broadsheet. Subscrip. Rate: $.50 newsstand/cover; $18/yr mailed in county; $21.50/yr mailed out of county; $24/yr mailed out of state. Adv. Rate: col. inch $3.50 Circulation: 3,100 per issue (paid). **Owner(s):** William M. Owens, See address and contact information above. **Management:** William M. Owens, Publisher. Vicky M. Owens, Advertising Manager. Julie O. McAlhany, Circulation Manager. **Editorial:** William M. Owens, Editor. Martha Rose Brown, Reporter.

ST.MATTHEWS

CALHOUN TIMES (ST. MATTHEWS). 1632 Bridge St., St.Matthews, SC 29135-1353. Telephone: 803-874-3137. FAX: 803-874-1588. E-MAIL: calhountimesscar@aol.com. Mailing Address: PO Box 176, St. Matthews, SC 29135-0176. Year Established: 1892. Pub. Frequency: w. (Thu.) Page Size: standard. Subscrip. Rate: $.35 newsstand/cover; $15/yr mailed in state; $20/yr mailed out of state. Circulation: 2,200 per issue (paid). **Owner(s):** Edwin C. Morris, Sr., See address and contact information above. **Management:** Edwin C. Morris, Jr. Jr., Publisher. **Editorial:** Edwin Morris, Sr. Sr., Editor.

SUMMERVILLE

SUMMERVILLE JOURNAL SCENE, THE. 104 E. Doty Ave., Summerville, SC 29483. Telephone: 843-873-9424. FAX: 843-873-9432. URL: http://www.summervillejournalscene.com. Mailing Address: PO Box 715, Summerville, SC 29484. Year Established: 1972. Pub. Frequency: s-w. (Wed. & Fri.) Page Size: broadsheet. Subscrip. Rate: $.50 newsstand/cover; $28/yr mailed in state; $43/yr mailed out of state. Circulation: 9,000 per issue (paid). **Owner(s):** Evening Post Publishing Co., 134 Columbus St., Charleston, SC 29403. Telephone: 843-577-7111. FAX: 843-937-5545. **Management:** Ellen Priest, Publisher. Angela Vest, Advertising Manager. Marilyn Erwin, Classified Adv. Mgr. **Editorial:** Ellen Priest, Editor.

TRAVELERS REST

TRAVELERS REST MONITOR. PO Box 247, Travelers Rest, SC 29690-0247. Telephone: 864-836-6820. FAX: 864-836-8048. Pub. Frequency: w. (Wed.) Page Size: broadsheet. Subscrip. Rate: $.50 newsstand/cover; $22/yr in county. Circulation: 6,000 per issue (paid). **Owner(s):** Larry R. & Virginia C. Atkins, See address and contact information above. **Management:** Larry R. Atkins, Publisher. Virginia C. Atkins, Circulation Manager. **Editorial:** Rachel Branch, Editor. Roger Jewell, Sports Editor.

UNION

TIMES ADVERTISER, THE. 100 Times Blvd., Union, SC 29379-7705. Telephone: 864-427-1234. FAX: 864-427-1237. Pub. Frequency: w. (Mon.) Page Size: broadsheet Circulation: 6,800 per issue (free). **Owner(s):** Mid South Management Co., See address and contact information above. **Management:** Anthony Summerlin, Publisher. Debbie Woodard, Advertising. Don Cody, Circulation Director. Brenda Gallo, Classified Adv. Mgr. **Editorial:** Graham Williams, Editor.

WALTERBORO

PRESS & STANDARD, THE. 113 E. Washington St., Walterboro, SC 29488-3915. Telephone: 843-549-2586. FAX: 843-549-2446. E-MAIL: pressads@lowcountry.com. Year Established: 1877. Pub. Frequency: s-w. (Tue. & Fri.) Page Size: broadsheet. Subscrip. Rate: $.75 newsstand/cover; $44/yr in county; $55/yr out of county. Adv. Rate: col. inch $7.25 Circulation: 6,500 per issue (paid). **Owner(s):** Smith Newspapers, Inc., PO Box 27, Fort Payne, AL 35967. Telephone: 205-845-5510. **Management:** Taylor M Smith, President. Anne Padget, Advertising Director. Rhonda Sauls, Circulation Manager. **Editorial:** Taylor M Smith, Editor-in-Chief. Bryan Linder, Sports Editor.

SHOPPER (WALTERBORO), THE. 113 Washington St, Walterboro, SC 29488. Telephone: 843-549-2586. FAX: 843-549-2446. E-MAIL: annpadgett@lowcountry.com. Pub. Frequency: w. (Wed.) Page Size: tabloid. Circulation: 18,000 per issue (paid and free). **Owner(s):** Smith Newspapers Inc., See address and contact information above. **Management:** Anne Padgett, General Manager. Taylor M Smith, Publisher. Rhonda Sauls, Circulation Manager.

WESTMINSTER

KEOWEE COURIER. 100 Main St., Westminster, SC 29693. Telephone: 864-647-5404. FAX: 864-647-5405. Mailing Address: PO Box 278, Westminster, SC 29393. Year Established: 1849. Pub. Frequency: w. (Wed.) Page Size: standard. Subscrip. Rate: $.50 newsstand/cover; $17.50/yr mailed in county; $27.50/yr mailed in state; $35/yr mailed out of state. Adv. Rate: col. inch $5.15 Circulation: 2,858 per issue (paid). **Owner(s):** Trib Publications Inc., PO Box 648, Manchester, GA 31816. Telephone: 706-846-4336. **Management:** Robert E Tribble, Publisher. **Editorial:** Ashton Hester, Editor. Mary Beth King, Managing Editor.

WESTMINSTER NEWS, THE. 100 Main St., Westminster, SC 29693. Telephone: 864-647-5404. FAX: 864-647-5405. Mailing Address: PO Box 278, Westminster, SC 29393. Year Established: 1954. Pub. Frequency: w. (Wed.) Page Size: standard. Subscrip. Rate: $.50 newsstand/cover; $17.50/yr mailed in county; $27.50/yr in state; $36/yr out of state. Circulation: 3,500 per issue (paid). **Owner(s):** Trib Publications Inc., PO Box 648, Manchester, GA 31816. Telephone: 706-846-4336. **Editorial:** Rolann Lee, Editor. Mary Beth King, Managing Editor.

WILLIAMSTON

JOURNAL (WILLIAMSTON), THE. 106 W. Main St., Williamston, SC 29697. Telephone: 864-847-7361. FAX: 864-847-9879. E-MAIL: editor@thejournalonline.com. URL: http://www.thejournalonline.com. Mailing Address: PO Box 369, Williamston, SC 29697. Year Established: 1955. Pub. Frequency: w. (Wed.) Page Size: broadsheet. Subscrip. Rate: $.75 newsstand/cover; $26/yr in county. Adv. Rate: col. inch $7.25 Circulation: 5,100 per issue (paid). **Owner(s):** William C. Meade, See address and contact information above. **Management:** Richard Meade, General Manager. William C. Meade, Publisher. **Editorial:** David C. Meade, Editor.

WILLIAMSTON JOURNAL. 106 W Main St, Williamston, SC 29697. E-MAIL: editor@thejournalonline.com. URL: http://www.journalonline.com. Mailing Address: P O Box 369, Williamston, SC 29697. Pub. Frequency: w. (Wed.) Page Size: broadsheet.Subscrip. Rate: $26/yr in county Circulation: 5,100 per issue (paid). **Owner(s):** David Meade, See address and contact information above. **Management:** David Meade, Publisher. **Editorial:** William Meade, Editor.

WINNSBORO

HERALD INDEPENDENT, THE. 127 N. Congress St., Winnsboro, SC 29180. Telephone: 803-635-4016. FAX: 803-635-2948. E-MAIL: herald_ind@infoave.net. URL: http://www.heraldindependent.com. Mailing Address: PO Box 90, Winnsboro, SC 29180-0090. Year Established: 1844. Pub. Frequency: s-w. (Tue. & Fri.) Page Size: broadsheet. Subscrip. Rate: $.50 newsstand/cover; $32/yr mailed in state; $34/yr mailed out of state. Wire Service(s): AP. Circulation: 5,000 per issue (paid and free). **Owner(s):** Crescent Media Group, PO Box 1634, Spartanburg, SC 29304. Telephone: 864-583-2907. **Management:** Todd Rainwater, Publisher. Heather Hamacher, Advertising Manager. Nell Turner, Classified Adv. Mgr. **Editorial:** Brian Garner, Editor.

YORK

ENQUIRER-HERALD. 30 N Congress St, Ste 100, York, SC 29745. E-MAIL: news@enquirerherald.com. URL: http://www.enquirerherald.com. Pub. Frequency: w. (Thu.) Page Size: broadsheet. Subscrip. Rate: $.50 newsstand/cover; $14/yr in county; $18/yr out of county. Circulation: 6,500 per issue (paid). **Owner(s):** The/McClatchy Company, PO Box 15779, Sacramento, CA 95852. Telephone: 916-321-1936. **Management:** Patricia Larson, Publisher. April Wynn, Advertising. Kristin Alley, Advertising Manager. **Editorial:** Jonathan Allen, Editor. Elizabeth Foster, Executive Editor.

SOUTH DAKOTA

ALCESTER

ALCESTER UNION & HUDSONITE, THE. 110 E. First St., Alcester, SD 57001-0227. Telephone: 605-934-2640. FAX: 605-934-2096. E-MAIL: parapub@iw.net. URL: http://www.ahenews.com. Mailing Address: PO Box 227, Alcester, SD 57001-0227. Year Established: 1889. Pub. Frequency: w. (Thu.) Page Size: tabloid. Subscrip. Rate: $.75 newsstand/cover; $25/yr in county; $29/yr out of county. Adv. Rate: col. inch $4.20 Freelance Pay: $0.35/column-inch. Circulation: 1,057 per issue (paid). **Owner(s):** Paul Buum, PO Box 227, Alcester, SD 57001, Telephone: 605-934-2640. FAX: 605-934-2096. **Management:** Paul Buum, Publisher. Michele Buum, Circulation Manager. **Editorial:** Paul Buum, Editor-in-Chief.

ARLINGTON

ARLINGTON SUN, THE. 208 S. Main St., Arlington, SD 57212. Telephone: 605-983-5491. FAX: 605-983-5715. E-MAIL: asn@mchsi.com. URL: http://www.rfdnewsgroup.com/arlington/arlington_home.htm. Mailing Address: PO Box 387, Arlington, SD 57212. Year Established: 1885. Pub. Frequency: w. (Thu.) Page Size: tabloid. Subscrip. Rate: $.65 newsstand/cover; $34.98/yr in area; $36.55/yr out of area. Adv. Rate: col. inch $4.25 Circulation: 950 per issue (paid). **Owner(s):** R F D News Group Inc., 222 Kasan Ave., Volga, SD 57071. Telephone: 605-627-9471. FAX: 605-627-9310. **Management:** Chris Schumacher, Publisher. **Editorial:** Frank Crisler, Editor. Wendy Royston, Assistant Editor.

BELLE FOURCHE

BELLE FOURCHE POST/BEE. 1004 Fifth Ave., Belle Fourche, SD 57717. Telephone: 605-892-2528. FAX: 605-892-2529. E-MAIL: bfpost@mato.com. URL: http://www.bhcn.com. Mailing Address: PO Box 400, Belle Fourche, SD 57717. Year Established: 1902. Pub. Frequency: s-w. (Wed. & Sat.) Page Size: broadsheet. Subscrip. Rate: $.75 newsstand/cover; $48/yr in county; $90.99 for 2 yrs. in county; $48/yr trade area; $53/yr out of trade area; $63/yr out of state. Adv. Rate: col. inch $5 Circulation: 2,000 per issue (paid). **Owner(s):** Country Media, Inc., 1615 First Ave., Scotts Bluff, NE 69361. Telephone: 308-635-1892. **Management:** Chrisann Mateer, Publisher. **Editorial:** Milo Dailey, Editor.

BRANDON

BRANDON VALLEY CHALLENGER. 1300 E. Rushmore Dr., Brandon, SD 57005. Telephone: 605-582-6025. FAX: 605-582-7184. E-MAIL: challenger@prairiepubs.com. Mailing Address: PO Box 257, Brandon, SD 57005. Year Established: 1985. Pub. Frequency: w. (Wed.) Page Size: broadsheet. Subscrip. Rate: $.60 newsstand/cover; $27/yr in county; $33/yr out of county. Adv. Rate: col. inch $4.75 Circulation: 950 per issue (paid). **Owner(s):** Gannett Company, Inc., 7950 Jones Branch Dr, McLean, VA 22107. Telephone: 703-854-6000. **Management:** Jim Wilber, General Manager. Mary Thompson, Circulation Manager. Carolyn Lamberty, Classified Adv. Mgr.. **Editorial:** Ken Curley, Editor.

BUFFALO

NATION'S CENTER NEWS. 604 W. Fourth St., Buffalo, SD 57720. Telephone: 605-375-3228. FAX: 605-375-3615. E-MAIL: ncn@sdplains.com. URL: http://www.bhpioneer.com. Mailing Address: PO Box 107, Buffalo, SD 57720. Year Established: 1979. Pub. Frequency: w. (Wed.) Page Size: tabloid. Subscrip. Rate: $.75 newsstand/cover; $30/yr. Circulation: 1,250 per issue (controlled and free). **Owner(s):** Seaton Publishing, PO Box 7, Spearfish, SD 57783. Telephone: 605-642-2761. **Management:** Stewart Huntington, Publisher. Wendy Beck, Sales Manager. **Editorial:** Linda Stephens, Editor-in-Chief. Wally Stephens, Sports Editor.

CANISTOTA

CANISTOTA CLIPPER. 210 W. Main St., Canistota, SD 57012. Telephone: 605-396-3181. FAX: 605-396-3289. E-MAIL: andersonpubl@unitelsd.com. Mailing Address: PO Box 128, Canistota, SD 57012. Year Established: 1902. Pub. Frequency: w. (Thu.) Page Size: broadsheet. Subscrip. Rate: $.55 newsstand/cover; $25/yr mailed in area; $30/yr mailed out of area. Circulation: 600 per issue (paid). **Owner(s):** Matt Anderson, See address and contact information above. **Management:** Matt Anderson, Publisher. Jenny McCoy, Advertising. **Editorial:** Matt Anderson, Editor.

CANOVA HERALD. 210 W. Main St., Canistota, SD 57012. Telephone: 605-396-3181. FAX: 605-396-3289. E-MAIL: andersonpubl@unitelsd.com. Mailing Address: PO Box 128, Canistota, SD 57012. Pub. Frequency: w. (Thu.) Page Size: broadsheet. Subscrip. Rate: $.55 newsstand/cover; $21.20/yr mailed in area; $25/yr mailed out of area. Circulation: 2,000 per issue (paid). **Owner(s):** Matt Anderson, See address and contact information above. **Management:** Matt Anderson, Publisher. Jenny McCoy, Advertising. **Editorial:** Matt Anderson, Editor.

HARTFORD AREA NEWS. 210 W. Main St., Canistota, SD 57012. Telephone: 605-396-3181. FAX: 605-396-3289. E-MAIL: andersonpubl@unitelsd.com. Mailing Address: PO Box 128, Canistota, SD 57012. Year Established: 1902. Pub. Frequency: w. (Thu.) Page Size: broadsheet. Subscrip. Rate: $.55 newsstand/cover; $25/yr mailed in area; $30/yr mailed out of area. Circulation: 640 per issue (paid). **Owner(s):** Matt Anderson, See address and contact information above. **Management:** Matt Anderson, Publisher. Jenny McCoy, Advertising. **Editorial:** Matt Anderson, Editor.

HUMBOLT JOURNAL. 210 W. Main St., Canistota, SD 57012. Telephone: 605-396-3181. FAX: 605-396-3289. E-MAIL: andersonpubl@unitelsd.com. Mailing Address: PO Box 128, Canistota, SD 57012. Year Established: 1902. Pub. Frequency: w. (Thu.) Page Size: broadsheet. Subscrip. Rate: $.55 newsstand/cover; $26.50/yr mailed in state; $30/yr mailed out of state. Circulation: 600 per issue (paid). **Owner(s):** Matt Anderson, See address and contact information above. **Management:** Matt Anderson, Publisher. Jenny McCoy, Advertising. **Editorial:** Matt Anderson, Editor.

MARION RECORD. 210 W. Main St., Canistota, SD 57012. Telephone: 605-396-3181. FAX: 605-396-3289. E-MAIL: andersonpubl@unitelsd.com. Mailing Address: PO Box 128, Canistota, SD 57012. Pub. Frequency: w. (Thu.) Page Size: standard. Subscrip. Rate: $.55 newsstand/cover; $26.50/yr mailed in state; $30/yr mailed out of state. Circulation: 6,000 per issue (free). **Owner(s):** Matt Anderson, See address and contact information above. **Management:** Matt Anderson, Publisher. Jenny McCoy, Advertising. **Editorial:** Matt Anderson, Editor.

MONTROSE HERALD. 210 W. Main St., Canistota, SD 57012. Telephone: 605-396-3181. FAX: 605-396-3289. E-MAIL: andersonpubl@unitelsd.com. Mailing Address: PO Box 128, Canistota, SD 57012. Pub. Frequency: w. (Thu.) Page Size: broadsheet. Subscrip. Rate: $.55 newsstand/cover; $25/yr mailed in county; $30/yr mailed out of county. Circulation: 500 per issue (paid). **Owner(s):** Matt Anderson, See address and contact information above. **Management:** Matt Anderson, Publisher. Jenny McCoy, Advertising. **Editorial:** Matt Anderson, Editor.

CUSTER

CUSTER COUNTY CHRONICLE. PO Box 551, Custer, SD 57730. Telephone: 605-673-2217. E-MAIL: custerchronicle@gwtc.net. Year Established: 1880. Pub. Frequency: w. (Wed.) Page Size: broadsheet. Subscrip. Rate: $.75 newsstand/cover; $32/yr local; $37/yr out of area. Circulation: 2,150 per issue (paid). **Owner(s):** Southern Hills Publishing Inc., See address and contact information above. **Management:** Charles Najacht, Publisher. **Editorial:** Norma Najacht, Editor.

DEADWOOD

LAWRENCE COUNTY JOURNAL. ISSN 1556-0244
376 Main St., Ste. A, Deadwood, SD 57732-0512. Telephone: 605-578-3305. FAX: 605-578-2023. E-MAIL: lawcent@deadwood.net. URL: http://www.lawrencecountyjournal.com. Year Established: 1973. Pub. Frequency: s-w. (Wed. & Sat.) Page Size: broadsheet. Subscrip. Rate: $.75 newsstand/cover; $48/yr in county; $54/yr in state; $63/yr mailed out of state. Adv. Rate: col. inch $5.50 Freelance Pay: $1/column-inch. **Wire Service(s):** AP. Circulation: 1,200 per issue (paid). **Owner(s):** Country Media, Inc., 1615 First Ave., Scotts Bluff, NE 69361. Telephone: 308-635-1892. **Management:** Hollie Stalder, Publisher. Kim Westland, Advertising. **Editorial:** Tim Velder, Editor. Mike Besso, Sports.

DELL RAPIDS

BALTIC BEACON. 414 E. Fourth St., Dell Rapids, SD 57022. Telephone: 605-428-5441. FAX: 605-428-5992. E-MAIL: Tribune@dellrapids.net. Year Established: 1889. Pub. Frequency: w. (Wed.) Page Size: tabloid. Subscrip. Rate: $.60 newsstand/cover; $18/yr mailed in county; $23/yr mailed out of county. Circulation: 315 per issue (paid). **Owner(s):** Gannett Company, Inc., 7950 Jones Branch Dr., McLean, VA 22107-0001. Telephone: 703-854-6000. **Management:** Suzie Bullion, General Manager. Carolyn Lamberty, Classified Adv. Mgr.. **Editorial:** Suzie Bullion, Editor.

DELL RAPIDS TRIBUNE. 414 E. Fourth St., Dell Rapids, SD 57022. Telephone: 605-428-5441. FAX: 605-428-5992. E-MAIL: tribune@dellrapids.net. URL: http://www.dellrapidstribune.com. Year Established: 1985. Pub. Frequency: w. (Wed.) Page Size: tabloid. Subscrip. Rate: $.60 newsstand/cover; $27/yr in county; $33/yr mailed out of county. Circulation: 1,400 per issue (paid). **Owner(s):** Gannett Company, Inc., 7950 Jones Branch Dr, McLean, VA 22107. Telephone: 703-854-6000. **Management:** Suzie Bullion, General Manager. Mary Thompson, Circulation Manager. Carolyn Lamberty, Classified Adv. Mgr.. **Editorial:** Suzie Bullion, Editor.

ELKTON

ELKTON RECORD, THE. 205 Elk St., Elkton, SD 57026. Telephone: 605-542-4831. FAX: 605-542-1306. E-MAIL: ern@mchsi.com. URL: http://www.rfdnewsgroup.com/elkton/about.htm. Mailing Address: PO Box K, Elkton, SD 57026. Year Established: 1883. Pub. Frequency: w. (Thu.) Page Size: tabloid. Subscrip. Rate: $.65 newsstand/cover; $34.98/yr in area; $36.55/yr out of state. Adv. Rate: col. inch $4.25 Circulation: 489 (paid). **Owner(s):** R F D News Group Inc., 222 Kasan Ave., Volga, SD 57071. Telephone: 605-627-9471. FAX: 605-627-9310. **Management:** Chris Schumacher, Publisher. **Editorial:** Holly Wydeck, Editor.

EUREKA

NORTHWEST BLADE, THE. PO Box 797, Eureka, SD 57437-0797. Telephone: 605-284-2631. FAX: 605-284-2632. E-MAIL: acmehl@valleytel.net. Year Established: 1884. Pub. Frequency: w. (Wed.) Page Size: broadsheet. Subscrip. Rate: $.50 newsstand/cover; $25/yr local; $28/yr mailed in state; $30/yr mailed out of state. Circulation: 1,650 per issue (paid). **Owner(s):** Arlo & Bonnie Mehlhaff, See address and contact information above. **Management:** Arlo Mehlhaff, Publisher. **Editorial:** Bonnie Mehlhaff, Editor.

FLANDREAU

MOODY COUNTY ENTERPRISE. 107 Second St., W., Flandreau, SD 57028. Telephone: 605-997-3725. FAX: 605-997-3194. URL: http://www.moodycountyenterprise.com. Mailing Address: PO Box 71, Flandreau, SD 57028. Year Established: 1885. Pub. Frequency: w. (Wed.) Page Size: broadsheet. Subscrip. Rate: $.50 newsstand/cover; $29/yr mailed in county; $35/yr mailed out of county; $50/yr mailed elsewhere. Freelance Pay: $0.15/column-inch. Circulation: 3,600 per issue (paid). **Owner(s):** News Media Corp., PO Box 46, Rochelle, IL 61068. Telephone: 815-562-2061. **Management:** Roger Janssen, General Manager. **Editorial:** Cynthia Sheppard, Editor.

HILL CITY

HILL CITY PREVAILER-NEWS. 114 Main St., Ste. 1, Hill City, SD 57745-0266. Telephone: 605-574-2538. FAX: 605-574-2538. E-MAIL: prevail@gwtc.net. Mailing Address: PO Box 266, Hill City, SD 57745-0266. Year Established: 1972. Pub. Frequency: w. (Wed.) Page Size: standard. Subscrip. Rate: $.75 newsstand/cover; $30/yr in state; $40/yr mailed out of state. Adv. Rate: col. inch $4.50 Circulation: 1,600 per issue (paid and free). **Owner(s):** Southern Hills Publishing Inc., PO Box 551, Custer, SD 57730. Telephone: 605-673-2217. FAX: 605-673-3321. **Management:** Charles Najacht, Publisher. Ann Fuchs, Advertising. **Editorial:** Jason Ferguson, Editor.

HOT SPRINGS

HOT SPRINGS STAR. 107 N. Chicago St., Hot Springs, SD 57747-1631. Telephone: 605-745-4170. FAX: 605-745-3161. E-MAIL: hsstar@gwtc.net. URL: http://www.hotspringsstar.com. Mailing Address: PO Box 1000, Hot Springs, SD 57747-1631. Year Established: 1886. Pub. Frequency: w. (Tue.) Page Size: tabloid. Subscrip. Rate: $.75 newsstand/cover; $36/yr mailed in county; $48/yr mailed out of state. Adv. Rate: col. inch $6.10 Circulation: 2,500 per issue (paid). **Owner(s):** Country Media, Inc., 1615 First Ave., Scotts Bluff, NE 69361. Telephone: 308-635-1892. **Management:** Brett Nachtigall, Publisher. Sheryl Grimes, Advertising Manager. **Editorial:** Cathy Nelson, Editor.

IPSWICH

IPSWICH TRIBUNE. 103 Main St., Ipswich, SD 57451-0007. Telephone: 605-426-6471. FAX: 605-426-6202. E-MAIL: iptribune@midconetwork.com. Pub. Frequency: w. (Wed.) Page Size: broadsheet. Subscrip. Rate: $.57 newsstand/cover; $25/yr in county; $28/yr out of county; $30/yr out of state. Circulation: 1,105 per issue (paid). **Owner(s):** Gibson Publishing Co., See address and contact information above. **Management:** Dwain Gibson, Publisher. **Editorial:** Tena Gibson, Editor.

ROSCOE HOSMER INDEPENDENT. 103 Main St., Ipswich, SD 57451-0007. Telephone: 605-426-6471. FAX: 605-426-6202. E-MAIL: iptribune@midconetwork.com. Pub. Frequency: w. (Wed.) Page Size: broadsheet. Subscrip. Rate: $.57 newsstand/cover; $25/yr in county; $28/yr out of county; $30/yr out of state. Circulation: 700 per issue (paid). **Owner(s):** Gibson Publishing Co., See address and contact information above. **Management:** Dwain Gibson, Publisher. **Editorial:** Tena Gibson, Editor.

MENNO

HUTCHINSON HERALD, THE. 203 S. Fifth St., Menno, SD 57045-0506. Telephone: 605-387-5158. FAX: 605-387-5148. E-MAIL: hherald@gwtc.net. Mailing Address: PO Box 506, Menno, SD 57045-0506. Year Established: 1882. Pub. Frequency: w. (Wed.) Page Size: standard. Subscrip. Rate: $.75 newsstand/cover; $30/yr mailed in state; $32/yr mailed out of state. Circulation: 1,058 per issue (paid and free). **Owner(s):** Tim L. Waltner, PO Box 537, Menno, SD 57045. Telephone: 605-387-5158. **Management:** Tim L. Waltner, Publisher. Jason Scharberg, Advertising Manager. **Editorial:** Erik Kaufman, Editor.

MILBANK

GRANT COUNTY REVIEW. 225 S. Main St., Milbank, SD 57252-0390. Telephone: 605-432-4516. FAX: 605-432-4516. E-MAIL: gcreview@tnic.com. Mailing Address: PO Box 390, Milbank, SD 57252-0390. Year Established: 1880. Pub. Frequency: w. (Wed.) Page Size: broadsheet. Subscrip. Rate: $.75 newsstand/cover; $30.50/yr in county; $35/yr out of county. Adv. Rate: col. inch $6.50 Circulation: 4,100 per issue (paid). **Owner(s):** Phyllis Justice, PO Box 390, Milbank, SD 57252. Telephone: 605-432-4516. FAX: 605-432-4516. **Management:** Phyllis Justice, Publisher. **Editorial:** Phyllis Justice, Editor. Clarence Justice, Associate Editor.

PARK RIVER

WALSH COUNTY PRESS. 404 Briggs Ave., S., Park River, SD 58270. Telephone: 701-284-6333. FAX: 701-284-6091. Year Established: 1881. Pub. Frequency: w. (Sat.) Page Size: broadsheet. Subscrip. Rate: $1 newsstand/cover; $34/yr in county; $42/yr elsewhere. Circulation: 1,500 per issue (paid). **Owner(s):** Walsh County Press, Inc., See address and contact information above. **Management:** Michael Ahneman, President. Dennis Olson, Publisher. Mark Jensen, Advertising Manager. **Editorial:** Mark Jensen, Editor.

REDFIELD

REDFIELD PRESS. 16 E. Seventh Ave., Redfield, SD 57469. Telephone: 605-472-0822. FAX: 605-472-3634. Mailing Address: PO Box 440, Redfield, SD 57469. Year Established: 1898. Pub. Frequency: w. (Wed.) Page Size: broadsheet. Subscrip. Rate: $.75 newsstand/cover; $35/yr local trade area; $45/yr mailed out of area. Circulation: 3,000 per issue (paid). **Owner(s):** News Media Corp., PO Box 46, Rochelle, IL 61068. Telephone: 815-562-2061. **Management:** Mark Davis, Publisher. Erin Schroeder, Advertising.

SELBY

SELBY RECORD. 4411 Main St., Selby, SD 57472. Telephone: 605-649-7866. FAX: 605-649-7866. Mailing Address: PO Box 421, Selby, SD 57472. Year Established: 1888. Pub. Frequency: w. (Thu.) Page Size: tabloid. Subscrip. Rate: $.75 newsstand/cover; $24/yr mailed local; $29/yr mailed in state; $32/yr mailed out of state. Circulation: 1,100 per issue (paid). **Owner(s):** Sharon Wolff, See address and contact information above. **Management:** Sharon Wolff, Publisher. **Editorial:** Sharon Wolff, Managing Editor.

SISSETON

SISSETON COURIER. 117 E. Oak, Sisseton, SD 57262-0169. Telephone: 605-698-7642. FAX: 605-698-3641. E-MAIL: news@sissetoncourier.com. URL: http://sissetoncourier.com. Mailing Address: PO Box 169, Sisseton, SD 57262-0169. Year Established: 1892. Pub. Frequency: w. (Tue.) Page Size: broadsheet. Subscrip. Rate: $1 newsstand/cover; $45/yr mailed local; $50/yr mailed elsewhere. Circulation: 3,941 per issue (paid). **Owner(s):** Harley Deutsch, See address and contact information above. **Management:** Harley Deutsch, Publisher. **Editorial:** Harley Deutsch, Editor.

STURGIS

BLACK HILLS PRESS. 1022 Main St., Sturgis, SD 57785. Telephone: 605-347-2503. FAX: 605-347-2321. E-MAIL: mctt@countrymedia.net. URL: http://www.meadecountytimes.com. Mailing Address: PO Box 69, Sturgis, SD 57785. Year Established: 1900. Pub. Frequency: w. (Sat.) Page Size: tabloid. Subscrip. Rate: $.75 newsstand/cover; $48/yr mailed local; $53/yr mailed out of area; $63/yr mailed out of state. Adv. Rate: col. inch $6.15 Circulation: 2,700 per issue (paid). **Owner(s):** Country Media, Inc., 1615 First Ave., Scotts Bluff, NE 69361. Telephone: 308-635-1892. **Management:** Heath Owens, Publisher. Jennifer Harris, Advertising. Heath Owens, Advertising Manager. Pam Buhler, Classified Adv. Mgr.. **Editorial:** Bill Cissell, Editor. Jason Gross, Sports.

MEADE COUNTY TIMES-TRIBUNE. 1022 Main St., Sturgis, SD 57785. Telephone: 605-347-2503. FAX: 605-347-2321. E-MAIL: baiblock@countrymedia.net. URL: http://www.meadecountytimes.com. Mailing Address: PO Box 69, Sturgis, SD 57785. Year Established: 1930. Pub. Frequency: w. (Wed.) Page Size: tabloid. Subscrip. Rate: $.75 newsstand/cover; $48/yr mailed local; $53/yr mailed out of area; $63/yr mailed out of state. Adv. Rate: col. inch $6.15 Circulation: 3,000 per issue (paid and free). **Owner(s):** Country Media, Inc., 1615 First Ave., Scotts Bluff, NE 69361. Telephone: 308-635-1892. **Management:** Heath Owens, Publisher. Jennifer Harris, Advertising. Pam Buhler, Classified Adv. Mgr.. **Editorial:** Bill Cissell, Editor.

VERMILLION

BROADCASTER PRESS. 201 W. Cherry St., Vermillion, SD 57069-0256. Telephone: 605-624-2695. FAX: 605-624-2696. URL: http://www.plaintalk.com. Mailing Address: PO Box 256, Vermillion, SD 57069-0256. Pub. Frequency: w. (Tue.) Page Size: standard Circulation: 10,500 per issue (free). **Owner(s):** Morris Multimedia, Inc., PO Box 936, Augusta, GA 30903-0936. Telephone: 706-724-0851. FAX: 706-722-7125. **Management:** Gary Wood, General Manager. Sheila Prosser, Advertising Manager. **Editorial:** David Lias, Editor.

PLAIN TALK, THE. ISSN 1054-3449
201 W. Cherry St., Vermillion, SD 57069. Telephone: 605-624-2695. FAX: 605-624-2696. E-MAIL: whwpress@btgnet.com. URL: http://www.plaintalk.net. Mailing Address: PO Box 256, Vermillion, SD 57069. Year Established: 1884. Pub. Frequency: w. (Fri.) Page Size: standard.Subscrip. Rate: $.75 newsstand/cover; $24.38/yr Circulation: 2,000 per issue (paid). **Owner(s):** Morris Multimedia, Inc., PO Box 936, Augusta, GA. Telephone: 706-724-0856. **Management:** Gary Wood, General Manager. Sheila Prosser, Advertising Manager. **Editorial:** David Lias, Editor.

WAKONDA TIMES. 201 W. Cherry St., Vermillion, SD 57069-0256. Telephone: 605-624-2695. FAX: 605-624-2696. URL: http://www.plaintalk.net. Mailing Address: PO Box 256, Vermillion, SD 57069-0256. Pub. Frequency: w. (Fri.) Page Size: broadsheet. Subscrip. Rate: $.75 newsstand/cover; $24.38/yr local. Adv. Rate: col. inch $3.50 Circulation: 1,000 per issue (paid). **Owner(s):** Morris Multimedia, Inc., PO Box 936, Augusta, GA 30903-0936. Telephone: 706-724-0851. FAX: 706-722-7125. **Management:** Gary Wood, General Manager. Sheila Prosser, Advertising Manager. **Editorial:** David Lias, Editor.

VOLGA

TRI-CITY STAR, THE. 222 Kasan Ave., Volga, SD 57071. Telephone: 605-627-9471. FAX: 605-627-9310. E-MAIL: t.s.a@mchsi.com. URL: http://www.rfdnewsgroup.com/tri-city-star/contact.htm. Mailing Address: PO Box 326, Toronto, SD 57268-0326. Pub. Frequency: w. (Thu.) Page Size: tabloid. Subscrip. Rate: $.65 newsstand/cover; $34.98/yr in area; $36.55/yr out of state. Adv. Rate: col. inch $4.25 Circulation: 576 per issue (paid). **Owner(s):** R F D News Group Inc., See address and contact information above. **Management:** Chris Schumacher, Publisher. **Editorial:** Paul Ekren, Editor.

VOLGA TRIBUNE, THE. 222 Kasan Ave., Volga, SD 57071. Telephone: 605-627-9471. FAX: 605-627-9310. E-MAIL: rfdnews@mchsi.com. URL: http://www.rfdnewsgroup.com/volga/about.htm. Mailing Address: PO Box 18, Volga, SD 57071-0018. Year Established: 1882. Pub. Frequency: w. (Thu.) Page Size: tabloid. Subscrip. Rate: $.65 newsstand/cover; $34.65/yr in area; $36.55/yr out of state. Adv. Rate: col. inch $4.25 Circulation: 676 per issue (paid). **Owner(s):** R F D News Group Inc., See address and contact information above. **Management:** Chris Schumacher, Publisher. Marge Hoff, Classified Adv. Mgr.. **Editorial:** Jane Utecht, Editor.

WEBSTER

WEBSTER REPORTER & FARMER. 624 S. Main St., Webster, SD 57274-0030. Telephone: 605-345-3356. FAX: 605-345-3739. E-MAIL: suhrs@reporterandfarmer.com. URL: http://www.reporterandfarmer.com. Mailing Address: PO Box 30, Webster, SD 57274-0030. Year Established: 1881. Pub. Frequency: w. (Mon.) Page Size: broadsheet. Subscrip. Rate: $1 newsstand/cover; $33.50/yr mailed in county & adj. counties; $40/yr mailed in state; $43.50/yr mailed out of state. Circulation: 3,500 per issue (paid). **Owner(s):** John & Le Ann Suhr, 624 S. Main St., Webster, SD 57274. Telephone: 605-345-3356. FAX: 605-345-3739. **Management:** John Suhr, Publisher. **Editorial:** John Suhr, Editor.

WINNER

WINNER ADVOCATE. 125 W. Third St., Winner, SD 57580-0071. Telephone: 605-842-1481. FAX: 605-842-1979. E-MAIL: winner@gwtc.net. Year Established: 1910. Pub. Frequency: w. (Wed.) Page Size: broadsheet. Subscrip. Rate: $1 newsstand/cover; $36.68/yr mailed in county & adj. counties; $44.47/yr mailed elsewhere. Adv. Rate: col. inch $7.25 Circulation: 3,500 per issue (paid). **Owner(s):** Bill Sniffin, 28 Boulder Loop, Lander, WY 82520. **Management:** Bill Sniffin, Publisher. Cheryl Schroeder, Advertising Manager. Trish Arvin, Business Manager. **Editorial:** Dan Bechtold, Editor.

YANKTON

MISSOURI VALLEY SHOPPER. 216 W. Fourth St., Yankton, SD 57078. Telephone: 605-665-5884. FAX: 605-665-5882. Pub. Frequency: w. (Tue.) Page Size: tabloid Circulation: 9,800 per issue (free). **Owner(s):** Morris Multimedia, Inc., PO Box 936, Augusta, GA 30903-0936. Telephone: 706-724-0851. FAX: 706-722-7125. **Management:** Heather Heimes, Advertising Director.

TENNESSEE

ALAMO

CROCKETT TIMES, THE. 46 W. Main St., Alamo, TN 38001. Telephone: 731-696-4558. FAX: 731-696-4650. Mailing Address: PO Box 160, Alamo, TN 38001. Year Established: 1873. Pub. Frequency: w. (Thu.) Page Size: broadsheet. Subscrip. Rate: $.50 newsstand/cover; $20/yr mailed in county; $30/yr mailed out of county. Circulation: 4,200 per issue (paid). **Owner(s):** Robert B. & Patricia Sims, See address and contact information above. **Management:** Robert B Sims, Publisher. William Sims, Associate Publisher. **Editorial:** Patricia Sims, Managing Editor.

ARLINGTON

EAST SHELBY REVIEW. 11975 Hwy 70, Arlington, TN 38002. Telephone: 901-867-2306. E-MAIL: sereview@bellsouth.net. Mailing Address: PO Box 280, Arlington, TN 38002-0280. Year Established: 1989. Pub. Frequency: w. (Wed.) Page Size: broadsheet.Subscrip. Rate: $.50 newsstand/cover Circulation: 5,400 per issue (free). **Owner(s):** Don Dowdle, Ed. & Publisher, PO Box 423, Somerville, TN 38068. Telephone: 901-465-4042. FAX: 901-465-5493. **Management:** Don Dowdle, Publisher. **Editorial:** Bob Koenig, Editor-in-Chief.

ASHLAND CITY

ASHLAND CITY TIMES. 202A N. Main, Ashland City, TN 37015-1318. Telephone: 615-792-4230. FAX: 615-792-3671. URL: http://www.ashlandcitytimes.com. Pub. Frequency: w. (Wed) Page Size: standard. Subscrip. Rate: $.50 newsstand/cover; $18/yr in county; $24/yr out of county; $30/yr mailed out of state. Freelance Pay: $25/article. Circulation: 6,500 per issue (paid). **Owner(s):** Gannett Company, Inc., PO Box 158, Ashland City, TN 37015-1318. 7950 Jones Branch Dr., McLean, VA 22102. Telephone: 703-854-6000. **Management:** Shirley Bradley, Advertising Manager. **Editorial:** Gary Burton, Editor.

BARTLETT

BARTLETT EXPRESS, THE. 6187 Stage Rd., Bartlett, TN 38134. Telephone: 901-388-1500. FAX: 901-386-3157. E-MAIL: express@bartlettexpress.com. URL: http://www.bartlettexpress.com. Mailing Address: PO Box 34967, Bartlett, TN 38134. Year Established: 1978. Pub. Frequency: w. (Thu.) Page Size: broadsheet. Subscrip. Rate: $.50 newsstand/cover; $22/yr in county; $30/yr mailed out of county. Adv. Rate: col. inch $11.05 Circulation: 7,000 per issue (paid). **Owner(s):** Bartlett Newspapers Inc., See address and contact information above. **Management:** Chip Turner, Publisher. Sheilah Hill, Advertising. **Editorial:** John Fee, Editor. Mike O'Kelly, Sports.

CORDOVA BEACON, THE. 6187 Stage Rd., Bartlett, TN 38134. Telephone: 901-388-1500. FAX: 901-386-3157. Mailing Address: PO Box 34967, Bartlett, TN 38134. Pub. Frequency: w. (Thu.) Page Size: broadsheet.Subscrip. Rate: $.50 newsstand/cover; $22/yr Circulation: 10,000 per issue (free). **Owner(s):** Bartlett Newspapers Inc., See address and contact information above. **Management:** Chip Turner, Publisher. **Editorial:** John Fee, Editor.

BENTON

POLK COUNTY NEWS/CITIZEN ADVANCE. ISSN 0883-881X
3 Main St, PO Box 129, Benton, TN 37307. Telephone: 423-338-2818. FAX: 423-338-4574. E-MAIL: polknews@aol.com. Pub. Frequency: w. (Wed.) Page Size: standard. Subscrip. Rate: $.50 newsstand/cover; $15/yr in area. Circulation: 3,600 per issue (paid). **Owner(s):** Ingrid Buehler, See address and contact information above. **Management:** Randolph Buehler, Publisher. **Editorial:** Ingrid Buehler, Editor.

BOLIVAR

BULLETIN-TIMES. 410 W. Market St., Bolivar, TN 38008. Telephone: 731-658-3691. FAX: 731-658-7222. E-MAIL: bulletin@aeneas.net. URL: http://www.bulletintimes.com. Mailing Address: PO Box 152, Bolivar, TN 38008. Year Established: 1865. Pub. Frequency: w. (Wed.) Page Size: broadsheet. Subscrip. Rate: $.75 newsstand/cover; $28/yr mailed in county; $35/yr mailed in state; $50/yr mailed out of state. Adv. Rate: col. inch $8.25 Circulation: 5,200 per issue (paid). **Owner(s):** Delphos Newspapers, 405 N. Main St., Delphos, OH 45833. Telephone: 419-695-0015. **Management:** Cheryl McGraw, Publisher. **Editorial:** Sherri Osteen, Editor.

HARDEMAN COUNTY SHOPPER. 410 W. Market, Bolivar, TN 38008. E-MAIL: btpublisher@bellsouth.net. URL: http://www.bulletintimes.com. Mailing Address: PO Box 152, Bolivar, TN 38008. Pub. Frequency: w. (Wed.) Page Size: standard Circulation: 15,000 per issue (free). **Owner(s):** Delphos Newspapers, 405 N. Main St., Delphos, OH 45833. Telephone: 419-695-0015. **Management:** Cheryl McGraw, Publisher. Robin Trout, Circulation Manager. **Editorial:** Sherri Osteen, Editor.

BROWNSVILLE

BROWNSVILLE STATES-GRAPHIC. ISSN 0893-3839
42 S. Washington, Brownsville, TN 38012. Telephone: 731-772-1172. FAX: 731-772-5451. E-MAIL: graphik1@bellsouth.net. Mailing Address: PO Box 59, Brownsville, TN 38012-0059. Year Established: 1867. Pub. Frequency: w. (Thu.) Page Size: standard. Subscrip. Rate: $.75 newsstand/cover; $23/yr in county; $30/yr mailed in state; $37/yr mailed out of state. Circulation: 5,400 per issue (paid). **Owner(s):** Hayword County Newspapers LLC, See address and contact information above. **Management:** Belinda Ramsey, Publisher. **Editorial:** Belinda Ramsey, Editor.

BYRDSTOWN

PICKETT COUNTY PRESS. PO Box 268, Byrdstown, TN 38549. Telephone: 931-864-3675. E-MAIL: picketpress@twlakes.net. URL: http://www.pickettcountypress.com. Year Established: 1974. Pub. Frequency: w. (Thu.) Page Size: broadsheet. Subscrip. Rate: $.50 newsstand/cover; $20/yr in state; $25/yr out of state. Circulation: 2,000 per issue (paid). **Owner(s):** Amanda Bond, See address and contact information above. **Management:** James E. Hill, Publisher. **Editorial:** James E. Hill, Editor.

CAMDEN

CAMDEN CHRONICLE, THE. 144 W. Main St., Camden, TN 38320. Telephone: 731-584-7200. E-MAIL: bentonco@usit.net. URL: http://www.camden-chronicle.com. Year Established: 1889. Pub. Frequency: w. (Wed.) Page Size: broadsheet. Subscrip. Rate: $.75 newsstand/cover; $28/yr in county area; $39/yr in state; $49/yr mailed out of state; $26/yr to senior citizens. Circulation: 6,700 per issue (paid). **Owner(s):** Magic Valley Publishing, See address and contact information above. **Management:** Dennis Richardson, Publisher. Vanessa Witt, Advertising Manager. **Editorial:** Lisa Richardson, Editor.

MAGIC VALLEY SHOPPER'S NEWS. 144 W. Main St., Camden, TN 38320. Mailing Address: PO Box 899, Camden, TN 38320. Year Established: 1979. Pub. Frequency: w. (Tue.) Page Size: broadsheet. Circulation: 9,200 per issue (paid and free). **Owner(s):** Magic Valley Publishing, See address and contact information above. **Management:** Dennis Richardson, Publisher. Vanessa Witt, Advertising Manager. **Editorial:** Dennis Richardson, Editor.

Weeklies

CARTHAGE

CARTHAGE COURIER. 509 Main St., Carthage, TN 37030-0239. Telephone: 615-735-1110. FAX: 615-735-0635. Mailing Address: PO Box 239, Carthage, TN 37030-0239. Year Established: 1807. Pub. Frequency: w. (Thu.) Page Size: broadsheet. Subscrip. Rate: $.50 newsstand/cover; $15/yr in county; $17/yr mailed out of county; $20/yr mailed out of state. Circulation: 5,700 per issue (paid). **Owner(s):** Hershel Lake, PO Box 239, Carthage, TN 37030. Telephone: 615-735-1110. **Management:** Hershel Lake, Owner. Scott Winfree, Publisher. Allison Tisdale, Circulation Manager. Vicki Bennett, Art Director. **Editorial:** Eddie West, Editor. Scott Winfree, Sports.

CELINA

CITIZEN-STATESMAN. 801 E. Lake Ave., Celina, TN 38551-0230. Telephone: 931-243-2235. FAX: 931-243-2232. E-MAIL: citizen@multipro.com. Mailing Address: PO Box 670, Celina, TN 8551-0670. Pub. Frequency: w. (Wed.) Page Size: broadsheet. Subscrip. Rate: $.50 newsstand/cover; $15/yr in county; $21/yr in state; $23/yr out of state. Circulation: 2,600 per issue (paid). **Owner(s):** Patsy Judd, See address and contact information above. **Management:** Patsy Judd, Publisher. Michelle Cahill, Advertising Manager. **Editorial:** Ed Cahill, Editor.

CENTERVILLE

HICKMAN COUNTY TIMES. 104 N. Central Ave., Centerville, TN 37033. Telephone: 931-729-4282. FAX: 931-729-4282. E-MAIL: hctimes@centerville.net. Mailing Address: PO Box 100, Centerville, TN 37033. Pub. Frequency: w. (Mon.) Subscrip. Rate: $.50 newsstand/cover; $18/yr in county; $24/yr in state; $29/yr out of state. Circulation: 5,700 per issue (paid). **Owner(s):** Jim Crawford, Jr., 106 W. Fifth St., Tuscumbia, AL 35674. Telephone: 256-383-8471. **Management:** Jim Crawford Jr., Publisher. Cathleen Clark, Advertising Manager. **Editorial:** Brad Martin, Editor.

CLINTON

COURIER-NEWS, THE. 233 N. Hicks St., Clinton, TN 37716. Telephone: 865-457-2515. FAX: 865-457-1586. E-MAIL: ron@hometownclinton.com. URL: http://www.hometownclinton.com. Mailing Address: PO Box 270, Clinton, TN 37717. Year Established: 1887. Pub. Frequency: s-w. (Wed. & Sun.) Page Size: standard. Subscrip. Rate: $.50 newsstand/cover; $38/yr in county; $40/yr mailed adj. counties; $52/yr mailed out of area. Circulation: 7,300 Sunday (paid); 6,500 per issue (paid). **Owner(s):** Republic Newspapers, Inc., 11863 Kingston Pike, Knoxville, TN 37922. Telephone: 865-675-6397. **Management:** Nick Drewry, President. Ron Bridgman, Publisher. Brenda Foster, Classified Adv. Mgr.. Liz Suddath, Marketing Director. **Editorial:** Ron Bridgman, Editor. Bobbie Marcom, Circulation Editor. Elaine Barber, Composing Room Manager.

COLLIERVILLE

INDEPENDENT (COLLIERVILLE). 1085 Halle Park Cir., Ste. 103, Collierville, TN 38017. Telephone: 901-853-7060. FAX: 901-854-0727. E-MAIL: collind@bellsouth.net. URL: http://www.thecolliervilleindependent.com. Year Established: 1982. Pub. Frequency: w. (Wed.) Page Size: broadsheet. Subscrip. Rate: $.50 newsstand/cover; $18/yr local; $23/yr out of area. Circulation: 12,000 per issue (paid and free). **Owner(s):** Southern Media, Inc., See address and contact information above. **Management:** Fred Eason, Owner. Kathy Garett, Advertising Manager. **Editorial:** Joan Crowe, Assistant Editor.

COVINGTON

COVINGTON LEADER. 2001 Hwy. 51 S., Covington, TN 38019. Telephone: 901-476-7116. FAX: 901-476-0373. E-MAIL: publisher@covingtonleader.com. URL: http://www.covingtonleader.com. Mailing Address: PO Box 529, Covington, TN 38019-0529. Year Established: 1886. Pub. Frequency: s-w. (Tue. & Fri.) Page Size: broadsheet. Subscrip. Rate: $.75 newsstand/cover; $32/yr home delivery in county; $43/yr home delivery out of county; $70/yr mailed out of state. Adv. Rate: col. inch $6.50 Circulation: 6,000 per issue (paid). **Owner(s):** Albrecht Newspapers, Inc., 410 E. Spring St., Ste. G, Cookeville, TN 38501. Telephone: 931-372-8015. **Management:** Jay Albrecht, General Manager. **Editorial:** Gwen Matheny, Lifestyle Editor. Greg Little, News Editor. Jeff Ireland, Sports.

CROSSVILLE

CROSSVILLE CHRONICLE. 125 West Ave., Crossville, TN 38555-4694. Telephone: 931-484-5145. FAX: 931-456-7683. E-MAIL: chronicle@volfirst.net. URL: http://www.crossville-chronicle.com. Mailing Address: PO Box 449, Crossville, TN 38557-4694. Year Established: 1886. Pub. Frequency: 3/w. (Tue., Wed., Fri.) Page Size: broadsheet. Subscrip. Rate: $.50 newsstand/cover; $51/yr mailed in county; $53/yr mailed out of county; $70/yr mailed out of state. **Wire Service(s):** AP. Circulation: 34,000 per issue (paid). **Owner(s):** Community Newspaper Holdings, Inc., 3500 Colonnade Pkwy., Ste. 600, Birmingham, AL 35243. Telephone: 205-298-7100. FAX: 205-298-7101. **Management:** Pauline Sherrer, Publisher. Becky Gillag, Advertising. **Editorial:** Mike Moser, Editor.

FAIRFIELD GLADE SUN. 125 West Ave., Crossville, TN 38555-4694. Telephone: 931-484-5145. FAX: 931-456-7683. Mailing Address: PO Box 449, Crossville, TN 38557-4694. Pub. Frequency: w. (Wed.) Page Size: broadsheet. Subscrip. Rate: $37/yr mailed in county 3rd class; $65/yr mailed in county 1st class; $40/yr mailed out of county 3rd class. Circulation: 4,000 per issue (paid). **Owner(s):** Community Newspaper Holdings, Inc., 3500 Colonnade Pkwy., Ste. 600, Birmingham, AL 35243. **Management:** Pauline Sherrer, Publisher. Becky Gillag, Advertising.

DAYTON

HERALD-NEWS (DAYTON), THE. 3687 Rhea County Hwy., Dayton, TN 37321. Telephone: 423-775-6111. FAX: 423-775-8259. URL: http://www.rhea.xtn.net. Mailing Address: PO Box 286, Dayton, TN 37321. Year Established: 1898. Pub. Frequency: s-w. (Wed. & Sun.) Page Size: broadsheet. Subscrip. Rate: $.50 newsstand/cover; $1 Sun.; $54/yr in county; $56/yr adj. cys.; $66/yr elsewhere. Adv. Rate: col. inch $19.50 Circulation: 13,700 Sunday (paid); 5,700 per issue (paid). **Owner(s):** Jones Media Group, PO Box 1630, Greenville, TN 37744. **Management:** Keith Locke, Advertising Manager. Belinda Dillard, Classified Adv. Mgr.. **Editorial:** John Carpenter, Editor.

DICKSON

DICKSON HERALD, THE. ISSN 0747-041X
104 Church St., Dickson, TN 37055. Telephone: 615-446-2811. FAX: 615-446-5560. E-MAIL: dxn@us.inter.net. URL: http://www.dicksonherald.com. Mailing Address: PO Box 587, Dickson, TN 37056-0587. Year Established: 1907. Pub. Frequency: s-w. (Wed. & Fri.) Page Size: broadsheet. Subscrip. Rate: $.50 newsstand/cover; $24/yr mailed in county; $18/yr mailed in county to senior citizens; $36/yr mailed adj. counties; $48/yr mailed out of area. Circulation: 19,500 per issue (paid and free). **Owner(s):** Gannett Company, Inc., 7950 Jones Branch Dr., McLean, VA 22107-0001. Telephone: 703-854-6000. **Management:** Chris Beyer, General Manager.

DOVER

STEWART HOUSTON TIMES, THE. 314 Spring St., Dover, TN 37058. Telephone: 931-232-5421. FAX: 931-232-8224. Pub. Frequency: w. (Tue.) Page Size: broadsheet. Subscrip. Rate: $.50 newsstand/cover; $19/yr in county; $17/yr in county to senior citizens; $36/yr elsewhere. Circulation: 6,000 per issue (paid). **Owner(s):** Gannett Company, Inc., 7950 Jones Branch Dr, McLean, VA 22107. Telephone: 703-854-6000.

DRESDEN

DRESDEN ENTERPRISE. 113 Wilson St, Box 139, Dresden, TN 38225-0139. E-MAIL: enterprise@dresdenenterprises.com. URL: http://www.dresdenenterprise.com. Mailing Address: P.O. Box 139, Dresden, TN 38225. Year Established: 1883. Pub. Frequency: w. (Wed.) Page Size: broadsheet. Subscrip. Rate: $18/yr in county; $20/yr in adj. cys.; $28/yr elsewhere. Adv. Rate: col. inch $5.75 Circulation: 5,200 (paid). **Owner(s):** Tri-County Publishing, Inc., See address and contact information above. **Management:** Ramona Washburn, Publisher. **Editorial:** Jeff Washburn, Editor. David Fisher, Associate Editor.

WEST TENNESSEE ADVERTISER. 113 Wilson St, Box 139, Dresden, TN 38225-0139. Mailing Address: P.O. Box 139, Dresden, TN 38225.Pub. Frequency: w. (Tue.) Circulation: 14,100 per issue (free). **Owner(s):** Tri-County Publishing, Inc., See address and contact information above.

DUNLAP

DUNLAP TRIBUNE, THE. PO Box 487, Dunlap, TN 37327. Telephone: 423-949-2505. FAX: 423-949-5297. Pub. Frequency: w. (Thu.) Page Size: standard. Subscrip. Rate: $.50 newsstand/cover; $20/yr in county; $25/yr mailed out of county. Circulation: 3,150 per issue (paid and free). **Owner(s):** Valley Publishing Co., Inc., See address and contact information above. **Management:** Robert Hale, Publisher. **Editorial:** Sandy Dodson, Editor.

DYER

TRI-CITY REPORTER, THE. 121 S. Main St, Dyer, TN 38330. Telephone: 731-692-3506. FAX: 731-692-4844. E-MAIL: news@tricityreporter.net. URL: http://www.tricityreporter.net. Mailing Address: PO Box 266, Dyer, TN 38330. Year Established: 1892. Pub. Frequency: w. (Thu.) Page Size: broadsheet. Subscrip. Rate: $.39 newsstand/cover; $33/yr mailed in county; $45/yr mailed in state; $45/yr mailed out of state. Adv. Rate: col. inch $5.60 Circulation: 3,500 per issue (paid). **Owner(s):** American Hometown Publishing, Inc., PO Box 408, Humboldt, TN 38343. Telephone: 731-784-2531. **Editorial:** Cindy East, Managing Editor.

DYERSBURG

DYERSBURG NEWS. 294 Hwy. 51 N., Dyersburg, TN 38025-0040. Telephone: 731-285-4091. FAX: 731-286-6183. Mailing Address: PO Box 808, Dyersburg, TN 38025-0040. Pub. Frequency: w. (Wed.) Page Size: broadsheet Circulation: 7,500 per issue (paid). **Owner(s):** Rust Communications, Inc., 301 Broadway, Cape Girardeau, MO 63701. Telephone: 573-335-6611. **Management:** Shelia Rouse Kelly, Publisher. Terry Brock, Circulation Director.

ERWIN

ERWIN RECORD, THE. 218 Gay St., Erwin, TN 37650. Telephone: 423-743-4112. FAX: 423-743-6125. Mailing Address: P.O. Box 700, Erwin, TN 37650. Year Established: 1927. Pub. Frequency: w. (Tue) Page Size: standard. Subscrip. Rate: $.50 newsstand/cover; $24/yr mailed in county; $30/yr mailed out of county. Adv. Rate: col. inch $4.17 Circulation: 4,550 per issue (paid). **Owner(s):** Press Holding Corp., See address and contact information above. **Management:** Mark A. Stevens, Publisher. Betty Davis, Advertising Director. Brenda Sparks, Circulation Manager. **Editorial:** Jerry Hilliard, Assistant Editor. Keith Whitson, Lifestyle Editor.

FAYETTEVILLE

ELK VALLEY TIMES, THE. 418 N. Elk Ave., Fayetteville, TN 37334. Telephone: 931-433-6151. FAX: 931-433-6040. E-MAIL: evtpub@lcs.net. URL: http://www.elkvalleytimes.com. Mailing Address: PO Box 9, Fayetteville, TN 37334-0009. Year Established: 1850. Pub. Frequency: w. (Wed.) Page Size: broadsheet. Subscrip. Rate: $.75 newsstand/cover; $25/yr in area; $32/yr mailed out of area. Circulation: 8,600 per issue (paid). **Owner(s):** Lakeway Publishers, Inc., 1609 W First N St., Morristown, TN 37814. Telephone: 615-581-5630. **Management:** Lucy A. Carter, Publisher. **Editorial:** Lucy A. Carter, Editor.

GAINESBORO

JACKSON COUNTY SENTINAL. 211 S. Main St., Gainesboro, TN 38562-0037. Telephone: 931-823-1274. FAX: 931-268-4339. Pub. Frequency: w. (Wed.) Page Size: tabloid. Subscrip. Rate: $.50 newsstand/cover; $16/yr local; $36/yr elsewhere. Circulation: 3,300 per issue (paid). **Owner(s):** Andy Mitchell, See address and contact information above. **Management:** Andy Mitchell, Publisher. **Editorial:** Andy Mitchell, Editor.

GALLATIN

COUNTRY TRADER. 322 W. Main St., Gallatin, TN 37066. Telephone: 615-230-7636. FAX: 615-452-9772. E-MAIL: countrytraderads@aol.com. Year Established: 1989. Pub. Frequency: w. (Thu.) Page Size: tabloid Circulation: 14,000 per issue (free). **Owner(s):** Ken Bartlett & Steve Fann, See address and contact information above. **Management:** Ken Bartlett, Publisher. **Editorial:** Ken Bartlett, Editor.

NEWS-EXAMINER (GALLATIN). One Examiner Ct., Gallatin, TN 37066. Telephone: 615-452-2561. FAX: 615-452-9110. URL: http://www.galantinnewsexaminer.com. Mailing Address: PO Box 1387, Gallatin, TN 37066. Year Established: 1840. Pub. Frequency: 3/w. (Mon., Wed., Fri.) Page Size: broadsheet. Subscrip. Rate: $.50 newsstand/cover; $42/yr in county. Circulation: 11,400 per issue (paid). **Owner(s):** Gannett Company, Inc., 7950 Jones Branch Dr., McLean, VA 22107-0001. Telephone: 703-854-6000. **Management:** Roger Watson, General Manager. **Editorial:** Debra Highland, Editor. Kitty Kulakowski, Feature Editor. Glenn Castleberry, News Editor. Cecil Joyce, Sports Editor.

GERMANTOWN

GERMANTOWN NEWS, THE. 7545 North St., Germantown, TN 38138. Telephone: 901-754-0337. FAX: 901-754-2961. E-MAIL: gtnews@midsouth.rr.com. URL: http://www.germantownnews.com. Year Established: 1974. Pub. Frequency: w. (Wed.) Page Size: broadsheet. Subscrip. Rate: $.50 newsstand/cover; $25/yr in county. Circulation: 7,000 per issue (paid). **Owner(s):** Germantown News Inc., See address and contact information above. **Management:** Gail F Dorband, General Manager. Whitney Williams, Advertising. **Editorial:** Gail F Dorband, Editor.

SHELBY SUN TIMES. 7508 Capital Dr., Ste. 2, Germantown, TN 38138-0801. Telephone: 901-755-7386. FAX: 901-755-0827. E-MAIL: suntimes@midsouth.rr.com. Year Established: 1987. Pub. Frequency: w. (Thu.) Page Size: tabloid. Subscrip. Rate: $.25 newsstand/cover; $20/yr mailed. Adv. Rate: col. inch $20 Circulation: 35,500 per issue (free). **Owner(s):** Lynn H. Sanders, 7508 Capital Dr., Germantown, TN 38138. Telephone: 901-755-7386. FAX: 901-755-0827. **Management:** Lynn H. Sanders, General Manager. **Editorial:** Walter Wellman, Editor.

HARTSVILLE

HARTSVILLE VIDETTE, THE. ISSN 0891-169X
111 Marlene St., Hartsville, TN 37074. Telephone: 615-374-3556. FAX: 615-374-4002. E-MAIL: thevidette@bellsouth.net. URL: http://www.hartsvillevidette.com. Mailing Address: PO Box 47, Hartsville, TN 37074-0047. Year Established: 1862. Pub. Frequency: w. (Thu.) Page Size: standard. Subscrip. Rate: $.50 newsstand/cover; $16/yr in county; $30/yr surrounding cys; $40/yr out of state. Circulation: 2,300 per issue (paid). **Owner(s):** Sandusky Newspapers, Inc., 314 W. Market St., Sandusky, OH 44870. Telephone: 419-625-5500. **Management:** Marie Allmon, Office Manager.

HENDERSON

CHESTER COUNTY INDEPENDENT. 218 S. Church Ave., Henderson, TN 38340-2638. Telephone: 731-989-4624. FAX: 731-989-5008. URL: http://www.chestercountyindependent.com. Mailing Address: PO Box 306, Henderson, TN 38340-0306. Pub. Frequency: w. (Thu.) Page Size: tabloid. Subscrip. Rate: $.55 newsstand/cover; $23/yr in county; $30/yr in state; $37/yr mailed out of state. Circulation: 10,000 per issue (paid). **Owner(s):** Walter S. Whaley, See address and contact information above. **Management:** Scott Whaley, Publisher. Jeff Clark Jr., Advertising Manager. **Editorial:** Scott Whaley, Editor. James Webb, Sports Editor.

HENDERSONVILLE

HENDERSONVILLE STAR NEWS. ISSN 0193-5143
105 Maple Row Blvd., Hendersonville, TN 37077. Telephone: 615-824-8480. FAX: 615-824-3126. E-MAIL: cpuryear@mkcngroup.com. URL: http://www.hendersonvillestarnews.com. Mailing Address: PO Box 68, Hendersonville, TN 37077. Year Established: 1951. Pub. Frequency: s-w. (Wed. & Fri.) Page Size: broadsheet. **Wire Service(s):** AP. Circulation: 16,500 per issue (paid). **Owner(s):** Gannett Company, Inc., 7950 Jones Branch Dr., McLean, VA 22107-0001. Telephone: 703-854-6000. **Management:** Roger Watson, General Manager. Sheryl Puryear, Business Manager. **Editorial:** Cheryl Tatum, Editor.

HOHENWALD

LEWIS COUNTY HERALD (HOHENWALD). 31 E. Linden, Hohenwald, TN 38462-0069. Telephone: 931-796-3191. FAX: 931-796-2153. Pub. Frequency: w. (Thu.) Page Size: tabloid. Subscrip. Rate: $.50 newsstand/cover; $10/yr local. Circulation: 3,500 per issue (controlled). **Owner(s):** Byrne K. Dunn, See address and contact information above. **Management:** Byrne K. Dunn, Publisher. **Editorial:** Byrne K. Dunn, Editor.

HUMBOLDT

COLLIERVILLE HERALD, THE. ISSN 0746-5939
PO Box 408, Humboldt, TN 38343. Telephone: 731-784-2531. E-MAIL: editor@colliervilleherald.net. URL: http://www.colliervilleherald.net. Year Established: 1870. Pub. Frequency: w. (Thu.) Page Size: broadsheet. Subscrip. Rate: $.75 newsstand/cover; $24/yr mailed in county; $29/yr mailed out of county. Adv. Rate: col. inch $10.45 Circulation: 6,500 per issue (paid). **Owner(s):** American Hometown Publishing, Inc., See address and contact information above. Van Pritchartt, 148 N. Main St., Collierville, TN 38017. Telephone: 901-853-2241. FAX: 901-853-8507. **Management:** Lee Ann Krueger, Publisher. **Editorial:** Joan Crowe, Editor. Cindy East, Managing Editor. Michael Ward, Sports.

HUMBOLDT CHRONICLE, THE. 2606 East End Dr., Humboldt, TN 38343. Telephone: 731-784-2531. FAX: 731-784-2533. URL: http://www.humboldtchronicle.com. Mailing Address: PO Box 448, Humboldt, TN 38343. Year Established: 1887. Pub. Frequency: w. (Wed.) Page Size: broadsheet. Subscrip. Rate: $.50 newsstand/cover; $25/yr in county; $40/yr elsewhere. Circulation: 4,700 per issue (paid). **Owner(s):** Infostructure Print Division, See address and contact information above. **Management:** Frank Warmath, Owner. April Jackson, Publisher. Beverly Ward, Advertising Manager. **Editorial:** Danny Wade, Associate Editor.

HUNTINGTON

CARROLL COUNTY NEWS-LEADER. PO Box 888, Huntington, TN 38344. Telephone: 731-986-2253. FAX: 731-986-3585. URL: http://www.newsleaderonline.com. Year Established: 1868. Pub. Frequency: s-w. (Tue. & Thu.) Page Size: broadsheet. Subscrip. Rate: $.50 newsstand/cover; $29/yr mailed in county; $41/yr mailed out of county; $54/yr mailed out of state. Circulation: 6,700 per issue (paid). **Owner(s):** Magic Valley Publishing, See address and contact information above. **Management:** Dennis Richardson, Publisher. Faye Lockhart, Sales Manager. **Editorial:** Shirley Nanney, Editor.

JAMESTOWN

FENTRESS COURIER. 114 White Oak St., Jamestown, TN 38556-1198. Telephone: 931-879-4040. FAX: 931-879-7716. E-MAIL: fencourier@dwadkes.net. Mailing Address: PO Box 1198, Jamestown, TN 38556-1198. Pub. Frequency: w. (Wed.) Page Size: tabloid. Subscrip. Rate: $.50 newsstand/cover; $20/yr local. Circulation: 5,000 per issue (paid). **Owner(s):** Bill Bowden, See address and contact information above. **Management:** Bill Bowden, Publisher. **Editorial:** Bill Bowden, Editor.

JEFFERSON

STANDARD BANNER, THE. PO Box 310, Jefferson, TN 37760-0310. Telephone: 423-475-2081. FAX: 423-475-8539. E-MAIL: news@standardbanner.com. URL: http://www.standardbanner.com. Year Established: 1927. Pub. Frequency: s-w. (Tue. & Thu.) Page Size: broadsheet. Subscrip. Rate: $.50 newsstand/cover; $29.50/yr in county; $44/yr out of county; $50/yr out of state. Circulation: 6,400 per issue (paid). **Owner(s):** Jefferson County Standard Publishing Co., Inc., See address and contact information above. **Management:** Tom Gentry, Publisher. Shane Cook, Advertising Manager. Leanne Jenkins, Classified Adv. Mgr.. **Editorial:** Dale Gentry, Editor.

JONESBOROUGH

HERALD & TRIBUNE. 702 W. Jackson Blvd., Jonesborough, TN 37659. Telephone: 423-753-3136. FAX: 423-753-6528. URL: http://www.heraldandtribune.com. Mailing Address: PO Box 277, Jonesborough, TN 37659-0227. Year Established: 1869. Pub. Frequency: w. (Wed.) Page Size: broadsheet. Subscrip. Rate: $.50 newsstand/cover; $20/yr mailed local area; $30/yr mailed out of area. Circulation: 4,500 per issue (paid). **Owner(s):** Sandusky Newspapers, Inc., 314 W. Market St., Sandusky, OH 44870. Telephone: 419-625-5500. **Management:** Lynn Richardson, General Manager. Bea Casey, Advertising. Lynn Richardson, Advertising Director. Kathy Grindstaff, Classified Adv. Mgr.. **Editorial:** Byran Stevens, Managing Editor.

KINGSTON

ROANE COUNTY NEWS, THE. 204 Franklin St., Kingston, TN 37763. Telephone: 865-376-3481. FAX: 865-376-1945. E-MAIL: rcnews@bellsouth.net. URL: http://www.roanecounty.com. Mailing Address: PO Box 610, Kingston, TN 37763. Year Established: 1957. Pub. Frequency: 3/w. (Mon., Wed., Fri.) Page Size: broadsheet. Subscrip. Rate: $.50 newsstand/cover; $45/yr home delivery in county; $67/yr mailed in state; $90/yr mailed out of state. Adv. Rate: col. inch $10.454 Circulation: 9,500 per issue (paid). **Owner(s):** Landmark Community Newspapers, Inc., PO Box 549, Shelbyville, KY 40065. Telephone: 502-633-2526. **Management:** John Teglas, General Manager. Robin Phelan, Advertising Manager. Jennifer Irish, Classified Adv. Mgr.. **Editorial:** Terri Likens, Editor.

ROCKWOOD TIMES. 204 Franklin St., Kingston, TN 37763. Telephone: 865-376-3481. FAX: 865-376-1945. E-MAIL: rcnews@bellsouth.net. URL: http://www.roanecounty.com. Mailing Address: PO Box 610, Kingston, TN 37763. Pub. Frequency: w. (Mon.) Page Size: broadsheet. Subscrip. Rate: $.35 newsstand/cover; $5.95/yr. Adv. Rate: col. inch $4.08 Circulation: 400 per issue (controlled and free). **Owner(s):** Landmark Community Newspapers, Inc., PO Box 549, Shelbyville, KY 40065. Telephone: 502-633-2526. **Management:** John Teglas, General Manager. Robin Phelan, Advertising Manager. **Editorial:** Terri Likens, Editor. Goose Lindsey, Sports Editor.

KNOXVILLE

FARRAGUT PRESS. 11863 Kingston Pike, Knoxville, TN 37934. Telephone: 865-675-6397. E-MAIL: editor@farragutpress.com. URL: http://www.farragutpress.com. Pub. Frequency: w. (Thu.) Page Size: tabloid. Subscrip. Rate: $.25 newsstand/cover; $26/yr local; $26/yr in state; $35/yr out of state. Circulation: 15,665 per issue (paid). **Owner(s):** Republic Newspapers, Inc., See address and contact information above. **Management:** Dan Barile, Publisher. Linda Gildner, Circulation Manager. **Editorial:** Dan Barile, Editor.

TRI-COUNTY NEWS (KNOXVILLE). 9010 Chapman Hwy., Knoxville, TN 37920. Telephone: 865-577-5935. FAX: 865-577-9896. E-MAIL: tricnews@Planetc.com. Mailing Address: PO Box 130, Seymour, TN 37865-0130. Year Established: 1955. Pub. Frequency: w. (Tue.) Page Size: tabloid. Subscrip. Rate: $.35 newsstand/cover; $22/yr local. Circulation: 2,600 per issue (paid and free). **Owner(s):** Paul Hamilton, See address and contact information above. **Management:** Paul L. Hamilton, General Manager. Gladys E. Hamilton, Publisher. **Editorial:** Marty L. Hamilton, Editor.

LA FOLLETTE

JELLICO ADVANCE SENTINEL. 225 N. First St., La Follette, TN 37766. Telephone: 423-562-8468. FAX: 423-566-7060. Mailing Address: PO Box 1261, La Follette, TN 37766. Year Established: 1880. Pub. Frequency: w. (Tue.) Page Size: tabloid. Subscrip. Rate: $.25 newsstand/cover; $8.50/yr in county; $10.50/yr mailed elsewhere. Circulation: 850 per issue (paid). **Owner(s):** Landmark Community Newspapers, Inc., PO Box 549, Shelbyville, KY 40065. Telephone: 502-633-2526. **Management:** Linn Hudson, Publisher. **Editorial:** Linn Hudson, Editor.

LA FOLLETTE PRESS. 225 N. First St., La Follette, TN 37766. Telephone: 423-562-8468. FAX: 423-566-7060. E-MAIL: ads@lafollettepress.com. URL: http://www.lafollettepress.com. Mailing Address: PO Box 1261, La Follette, TN 37766. Year Established: 1910. Pub. Frequency: w. (Thu.) Page Size: broadsheet. Subscrip. Rate: $18/yr in county; $32/yr out of county; $.50 newsstand/cover. Circulation: 10,300 per issue (paid). **Owner(s):** Landmark Community Newspapers, Inc., PO Box 549, Shelbyville, KY 40065. **Management:** Linn Hudson, Publisher. **Editorial:** Linn Hudson, Editor. Michell Stults, Circulation Editor. Dwane Wilder, Sports Editor.

LAFAYETTE

MACON COUNTY TIMES. ISSN 0745-5976
200 Times Ave, Lafayette, TN 37083. Telephone: 615-666-2440. FAX: 615-666-4909. URL: http://www.maconcountytimes.com. Mailing Address: PO Box 129, Lafayette, TN 37083. Year Established: 1919. Pub. Frequency: w. (Thu.) Page Size: broadsheet. Subscrip. Rate: $.50 newsstand/cover; $16.50/yr mailed in county & adj. counties; $24/yr mailed in state; $30/yr mailed elsewhere. Circulation: 6,000 per issue (paid). **Owner(s):** Heartland Publications, LLC, 20 Research Pkwy, Ste G, Old Saybrook, CT 06475. Telephone: 860-388-3470. FAX: 860-388-3490. **Management:** Gerry Greenway, Publisher. Hope Green, Advertising. Cindy Patterson, Business Manager. **Editorial:** Gerry Greenway, Editor.

LAWRENCEBURG

DEMOCRAT-UNION. 238 Hughes, Lawrenceburg, TN 38464. Telephone: 931-762-2222. FAX: 931-762-4191. Mailing Address: PO Box 685, Lawrenceburg, TN 38464. Year Established: 1884. Pub. Frequency: s-w. (Tue. & Fri.) Page Size: broadsheet. Subscrip. Rate: $.50 newsstand/cover; $19.50/yr mailed local. Circulation: 12,700 per issue (paid). **Owner(s):** Jim Crawford , Jr., See address and contact information above. **Management:** Jim Crawford Jr., Publisher. Charlie Crawford, Advertising. **Editorial:** Jim Crawford Jr., Editor. Bobby Crawford, Associate Editor.

LEBANON

WILSON POST LLC. 216 Hartmann Dr, Lebanon, TN 37087. Telephone: 615-444-6008. FAX: 615-444-6018. E-MAIL: wwnews@wilsonpost.com. URL: http://www.wilsonpost.com. Year Established: 1978. Pub. Frequency: 2/w. (Wed. & Fri.) Page Size: tabloid. Subscrip. Rate: $.50 newsstand/cover; $28/yr local. Adv. Rate: col. inch $12 Circulation: 2,600 per issue (controlled); 7,000 per issue (paid). **Owner(s):** Wilson Post, Llc., See address and contact information above. **Management:** Sam Hutcher, President. John B Bryan, Publisher. Charma Hawkins, Advertising Manager. Diann Gibson, Circulation Manager. **Editorial:** Jennifer Horton, Editor-in-Chief.

LENOIR CITY

NEWS HERALD (LENOIR CITY). 201 Simpson Rd., Lenoir City, TN 37771. Telephone: 865-986-6581. FAX: 865-988-3261. Mailing Address: PO Box 310, Lenoir City, TN 37771. Year Established: 1885. Pub. Frequency: s-w. (Mon. & Thu.) Page Size: broadsheet. Subscrip. Rate: $.75 newsstand/cover; $51/yr in county; $55/yr adj. cys.. Circulation: 21,215 per issue (paid and free). **Owner(s):** Jones Media Group, 121 W Summer St, Greenville, TN 37745. Telephone: 423-581-0088. FAX: 423-235-7012. **Management:** Kevin Burcham, Publisher. Ray Trachan, Advertising Manager. **Editorial:** Linda Brewer, Editor. Dewey Morgan, Sports Editor.

LEWISBURG

LEWISBURG TRIBUNE. 121 First Ave., Lewisburg, TN 37091. Telephone: 931-359-1188. FAX: 931-359-1847. E-MAIL: news@ltrib-gaz.com. URL: http://www.ltrib-gaz.com. Mailing Address: PO Box 2667, Lewisburg, TN 37091. Pub. Frequency: w. (Thu.) Page Size: standard. Subscrip. Rate: $.50 newsstand/cover; $24 mailed for 6 mos. in county; $30/yr; $36/yr out of county includes marshall gazette. Circulation: 7,800 per issue (paid). **Owner(s):** Lewisburg Tribune, Inc., See address and contact information above. **Management:** T. H. Hawkins III, Publisher. Leeanne Robison, Advertising Manager. Carmen Truitt, Classified Adv. Mgr.. **Editorial:** Greg Lowe, Editor. Lewis Scheuchenzuber, Sports.

MARSHALL GAZETTE. 121 First Ave., Lewisburg, TN 37091. Telephone: 931-359-1188. FAX: 931-359-1847. URL: http://www.ltrib-gaz.com. Mailing Address: PO Box 2667, Lewisburg, TN 37091. Pub. Frequency: w. (Tue.) Page Size: standard. Subscrip. Rate: $.50 newsstand/cover; $30/yr mailed in county; $36/yr mailed out of county incl. Lewisburg Tribune. Circulation: 7,800 per issue (paid). **Owner(s):** Lewisburg Tribune, Inc., See address and contact information above. **Management:** T. H. Hawkins III, Publisher. Carmen Truitt, Circulation Manager. **Editorial:** Greg Lowe, Editor. Lewis Scheuchenzuber, Sports.

LEXINGTON

LEXINGTON PROGRESS. 508 S. Broad St., Lexington, TN 38351. Telephone: 731-968-6397. FAX: 731-968-9560. E-MAIL: lexprogressnews@bellsouth.net. Pub. Frequency: w. (Wed.) Page Size: broadsheet. Subscrip. Rate: $.75 newsstand/cover; $18/yr in county; $26/yr mailed in state; $32/yr mailed out of state. Circulation: 8,700 per issue (paid). **Owner(s):** Lexington Progress Inc., See address and contact information above. **Management:** Tom Franklin, Publisher. Susan Small, Advertising Manager. Heather Greenway, Circulation Manager. **Editorial:** Mike Reed, Editor.

LINDEN

BUFFALO RIVER REVIEW. 115 S. Mill St., Linden, TN 37096. Telephone: 931-589-2169. FAX: 931-589-3858. Mailing Address: PO Box 914, Linden, TN 37096. Year Established: 1976. Pub. Frequency: w. (Wed.) Page Size: broadsheet. Subscrip. Rate: $.50 newsstand/cover; $20/yr local; $26/yr in state; $32/yr out of state. Adv. Rate: col. inch $3.20 Circulation: 3,000 per issue (paid). **Owner(s):** Buffalo Review, Inc., See address and contact information above. **Management:** Sherri Groom, General Manager. Sam Kennedy, Publisher. **Editorial:** Randy Mackin, Editor-in-Chief.

LIVINGSTON

LIVINGSTON (TN) ENTERPRISE. 203 S. Church St., Livingston, TN 38570. Telephone: 931-823-1274. FAX: 931-268-9125. E-MAIL: editor@twlakes.net. Mailing Address: PO Box 129, Livingston, TN 38570. Year Established: 1892. Pub. Frequency: w. (Tue.) Page Size: broadsheet. Subscrip. Rate: $16/yr local; $30/yr out of area; $.50 newsstand/cover. Circulation: 5,500 per issue (paid). **Owner(s):** Andy Mitchell, See address and contact information above. **Management:** Andy Mitchell, Publisher. **Editorial:** Andy Mitchell, Editor.

OVERTON COUNTY NEWS. 415 W. Main St., Livingston, TN 38570-1846. Telephone: 931-823-6485. FAX: 931-823-6486. E-MAIL: news@overtoncountynews.com. Mailing Address: PO Box 479, Livingston, TN 38570-1846. Year Established: 1967. Pub. Frequency: w. (Tue.) Page Size: broadsheet. Subscrip. Rate: $.50 newsstand/cover; $21/yr local; $34/yr in state; $38/yr elsewhere. Circulation: 5,550 per issue (controlled). **Owner(s):** Carson & Vicki Oliver, 415 W. Main St., Livingston, TN. Telephone: 931-823-6485. FAX: 931-823-6486. **Management:** Carson Oliver, Publisher. **Editorial:** Dewain Peek, Editor.

LYNCHBURG

MOORE COUNTY NEWS. 30 Hiles St., Lynchburg, TN 37352. Telephone: 931-759-7302. Mailing Address: PO Drawer 500, Public Square, Lynchburg, TN 37352-0500. Pub. Frequency: w. (Thu.) Page Size: standard. Subscrip. Rate: $.50 newsstand/cover; $13/yr in county; $20/yr out of state. Circulation: 1,500 per issue (paid). **Owner(s):** Marilyn Craig, See address and contact information above. **Management:** Bonnie Lewis, Advertising Manager. **Editorial:** Bonnie Lewis, Editor.

MANCHESTER

MANCHESTER TIMES. 300 N. Spring St., Manchester, TN 37355. Telephone: 931-728-7577. FAX: 931-728-7614. E-MAIL: nettimes@les.net. URL: http://www.manchestertimes.com. Mailing Address: PO Box 760, Tullahoma, TN 37388. Year Established: 1881. Pub. Frequency: w. (Wed.) Page Size: broadsheet. Subscrip. Rate: $.50 newsstand/cover; $22/yr local; $33/yr out of area. Circulation: 6,500 per issue (paid). **Owner(s):** Lakeway Publishers, Inc., 1609 W First N St., Morristown, TN 37814. Telephone: 423-581-5630. **Management:** Chuck Cunningham, Advertising Manager. Janice Frazier, Circulation Manager. **Editorial:** Linda Barr, Editor.

MAYNARDVILLE

UNION NEWS LEADER. 3755 Maynardville Hwy., Maynardville, TN 37807. Telephone: 865-992-3392. FAX: 865-992-6861. E-MAIL: enewspaper@aol.com. URL: http://www.unionnewsleader.com. Pub. Frequency: w. (Tue.) Page Size: standard. Subscrip. Rate: $.50 newsstand/cover; $15/yr in county; $20/yr out of county; $23/yr out of state. Adv. Rate: B&W page $693, col. inch $5.50 Circulation: 3,300 per issue (paid). **Owner(s):** Chris Upton & Elbra Davis, **Management:** Chris Upton, Publisher. **Editorial:** Elbra Davis, Editor.

MCKENZIE

MCKENZIE BANNER. 3 Banner Row, McKenzie, TN 38201. Telephone: 731-352-3323. FAX: 731-352-3322. E-MAIL: washburn@mckenziebanner.com. URL: http://www.mckenziebanner.com. Year Established: 1870. Pub. Frequency: w. (Wed.) Page Size: broadsheet. Subscrip. Rate: $.50 newsstand/cover; $22/yr in state; $36/yr mailed elsewhere. Adv. Rate: col. inch $5.75 Circulation: 6,000 per issue (paid). **Owner(s):** Tri-County Publishing, Inc., See address and contact information above. **Management:** Ramona Washburn, Publisher. **Editorial:** Jeff Washburn, Editor.

MCMINNVILLE

SOUTHERN STANDARD. 105 College St, PO Box 150, McMinnville, TN 37111. Telephone: 931-473-2191. URL: http://www.southernstandard.com. Year Established: 1879. Pub. Frequency: 3/w. (Sun., Wed., Fri.) Page Size: broadsheet. Subscrip. Rate: $.50 newsstand/cover; $.75 newsstand/cover Sun.; $19 carrier delivery/quarter; $20.50 mailed/quarter; $34 home delivery for 6 mos.. Circulation: 8,400 per issue (paid). **Owner(s):** Morris Newspaper Corporation, 27 Abercorn St., Savannah, GA 31401. Telephone: 912-233-1281. FAX: 912-232-4639. **Management:** Sharon Patrick, General Manager. Patricia Zechman, Publisher. Steve Warner, Circulation Manager. **Editorial:** James Clark, Editor.

MEMPHIS

EAST MEMPHIS SHOPPERS NEWS. 622 S. Highland, Memphis, TN 38111-4356. Telephone: 901-458-8030. FAX: 901-458-3104. E-MAIL: hpress@shoppers-news.net. URL: http://www.memphisshoppernews.com. Pub. Frequency: w. (Wed.) Page Size: standard Circulation: 193,000 per issue (free). **Owner(s):** Shoppers Press of Memphis, Inc., See address and contact information above. **Management:** Kathy Garrett, Advertising Manager.

MEMPHIS FLYER. 460 Tennessee St., Ste. 200, Memphis, TN 38103. Telephone: 901-521-9000. FAX: 901-521-0129. E-MAIL: letters@memphisflyer.com. URL: http://www.memphisflyer.com. Mailing Address: PO Box 1738, Memphis, TN 38101. Pub. Frequency: w. (Wed.) Page Size: tabloid. Subscrip. Rate: $50/yr. Circulation: 55,000 per issue (paid and free). **Owner(s):** Contemporary Media, See address and contact information above. **Management:** Kenneth Neill, Publisher. Jeffrey Goldberg, Advertising Director. Robbie French, Circulation Manager. Deshaune Barnes McGhee, Classified Adv. Mgr.. **Editorial:** Bruce VanWyngarden, Editor. Susan Ellis, Managing Editor.

MEMPHIS SILVER STAR NEWS. 3019 Park Ave., Memphis, TN 38114-3003. Telephone: 901-452-8828. FAX: 901-452-1656. E-MAIL: silverstarnews@bellsouth.net. Year Established: 1986. Pub. Frequency: w. (Wed.) Page Size: standard.Subscrip. Rate: $.50 newsstand/cover; $27.50/yr Circulation: 28,000 per issue (paid). **Owner(s):** Jimmy Delnoah Williams, See address and contact information above. **Management:** Jimmy Delnoah Williams, Publisher. **Editorial:** Jimmy Delnoah Williams, Editor.

MILAN

MIRROR-EXCHANGE. 1104 S. Main St., Milan, TN 38358. Telephone: 731-686-1632. FAX: 731-686-9005. E-MAIL: bob@milanmirrorexchange.com. URL: http://www.milanmirrorexchange.com. Mailing Address: PO Box 549, Milan, TN 38358. Year Established: 1965. Pub. Frequency: w. (Tue.) Page Size: broadsheet. Subscrip. Rate: $.50 newsstand/cover; $25/yr mailed in county; $30/yr mailed out of county; $35/yr mailed out of state. Freelance Pay: $40/article. Circulation: 5,500 per issue (paid). **Owner(s):** Mirror-Exchange, Inc., See address and contact information above. **Management:** Bob Parkins, Publisher. Melanie Day, Advertising Manager. Scarlet Parkins, Circulation Manager. Melissa West, Classified Adv. Mgr.. **Editorial:** Bob Parkins, Editor. Victor Parkins, Sports.

MILLINGTON

MILLINGTON STAR, THE. 5107 Easley Ave., Millington, TN 38053-0305. Telephone: 901-872-2286. FAX: 901-872-2965. E-MAIL: mstar@bigriver.net. URL: http://www.millingtonstar.com. Year Established: 1952. Pub. Frequency: w. (Wed.) Page Size: broadsheet. Subscrip. Rate: $.50 newsstand/cover; $22/yr in county; $28/yr out of county. Adv. Rate: col. inch $10 Circulation: 3,500 per issue (paid). **Owner(s):** B.N.I., PO Box 305, Millington, TN 38083-0305. Telephone: 901-872-2286. **Management:** Walter Einhart, Publisher. Sue Moore, Advertising. Allyson Duncan, Circulation Manager.

MOUNTAIN CITY

TOMAHAWK, THE. 118 S. Church St., Mountain City, TN 37683. Telephone: 423-727-6121. FAX: 423-727-4833. URL: http://www.thetomahawk.com. Mailing Address: PO Box 90, Mountain City, TN 37683. Year Established: 1874. Pub. Frequency: w. (Wed.) Page Size: standard. Subscrip. Rate: $.50 newsstand/cover; $26/yr in county; $36/yr out of county; $22/yr in county to senior citizens; $32/yr out of county; $30/yr to students. Circulation: 5,700 per issue (paid). **Owner(s):** Sandusky Newspapers, Inc., 314 W. Market St., Sandusky, OH 44870. Telephone: 419-625-5500. **Management:** Bill Thomas, General Manager. Rita A. Cornett, Advertising Manager. **Editorial:** Bill Thomas, Editor.

MT. JULIET

MESSENGER (MT. JULIET), THE. 11509 Lebonon Rd, Mt. Juliet, TN 37122. FAX: 615-860-2797. Year Established: 1982. Pub. Frequency: w. (Wed.) **Owner(s):** Messenger Messenger Corp., PO Box 626, Madison, TN 37115. **Management:** Michael Robinson, General Manager. Bill C Robinson, President. **Editorial:** Michael Robinson, Editor.

NASHVILLE

BELLE MEADE NEWS. 2323 Crestmoor Rd., Nashville, TN 37215-2722. Telephone: 615-298-1500. FAX: 615-298-1015. Pub. Frequency: w. (Thu.) Page Size: standard. Subscrip. Rate: $10/yr local; $25/yr in state. Circulation: 23,500 per issue (controlled and free). **Owner(s):** GCA Publishing Co., See address and contact information above. **Management:** Gary W. Cunningham, Publisher. **Editorial:** Sandy Campbell, Editor.

BRENTWOOD JOURNAL, THE. 1100 Broadway, Nashville, TN 37203. Telephone: 615-259-8000. E-MAIL: wam@tennessean.com. URL: http://www.tennessean.com. Mailing Address: PO Box 681988, Franklin, TN 37068-1988. Pub. Frequency: w. (Thu.) Page Size: broadsheet. Subscrip. Rate: $.50 newsstand/cover; $24/yr carrier delivery; $36/yr mailed in state. **Wire Service(s):** AP. Circulation: 11,000 per issue (paid and free). **Owner(s):** Tennessean, See address and contact information above. **Management:** Mike Giangreco, General Manager. Ellen Leifeld, President. Stephanie Ezzel, Advertising, Nikki Hay, Advertising Director. Leila Trussler, Circulation Director. Nancy Slattery, Classified Adv. Mgr.. **Editorial:** Will Jordan, Associate Editor.

GREEN HILLS NEWS. 2323 Crestmoor Rd., Nashville, TN 37215-2722. Telephone: 615-298-1500. FAX: 615-298-1015. E-MAIL: gcanews@aol.com. Pub. Frequency: w. (Thu.) Page Size: tabloid Circulation: 23,487 per issue (free). **Owner(s):** GCA Publishing Co., See address and contact information above. **Management:** Gary W. Cunningham, Publisher. **Editorial:** Sandy Campbell, Editor.

NASHVILLE SCENE, THE. 2120 Eighth Ave. S., Nashville, TN 37204-2204. Telephone: 615-244-7989. FAX: 615-244-8578. URL: http://www.nashvillescene.com. Pub. Frequency: w. (Thu.) Page Size: standard. Subscrip. Rate: $69/yr mailed. Circulation: 55,000 per issue (paid and free). **Owner(s):** Village Voice Media, Inc., 36 Cooper Sq., New York, NY 10003. Telephone: 212-260-0232. **Management:** Chris Ferrell, Publisher. Ginny Staggs, Advertising Director. Julie Rutter, Associate Publisher. Gracey Davis, Controller. **Editorial:** Liz Garrigan, Editor.

WESTVIEW. 8120 Sawyer-Brown Rd., Ste. 107, Nashville, TN 37221-1410. Telephone: 615-646-6131. FAX: 615-662-0946. E-MAIL: westview78@aol.com. URL: http://www.westviewonline.com. Mailing Address: PO Box 210183, Nashville, TN 37221. Year Established: 1978. Pub. Frequency: w. (Wed.) Page Size: tabloid. Subscrip. Rate: $25/yr local. Adv. Rate: col. inch $12.95 Circulation: 10,000 per issue (paid and free). **Owner(s):** Evelyn Underwood, See address and contact information above. **Management:** Evelyn Underwood, Publisher. Melissa Evans, Circulation Director. **Editorial:** Paula Winters, Editor.

ONEIDA

INDEPENDENT HERALD (ONEIDA). 19391 N. Alberta St., Oneida, TN 37841. Telephone: 423-569-6343. FAX: 423-569-9566. E-MAIL: proy@highland.net. URL: http://www.ihoneida.com. Pub. Frequency: w. (Thu.) Page Size: broadsheet. Subscrip. Rate: $.50 newsstand/cover; $16/yr in state; $20/yr out of state. Adv. Rate: col. inch $3.90 Circulation: 5,000 per issue (paid). **Owner(s):** Liberty Press, See address and contact information above. **Management:** Paul Roy, Publisher. **Editorial:** Ben Garrett, Editor.

SCOTT COUNTY NEWS. ISSN 8750-5940 PO Box 4399, Oneida, TN 37841. Telephone: 423-569-8351. FAX: 423-569-4500. E-MAIL: scn@highland.net. Year Established: 1916. Pub. Frequency: w. (Thu.) Page Size: broadsheet. Subscrip. Rate: $.50 newsstand/cover; $17/yr in county; $20/yr in state; $26/yr out of county. Circulation: 7,000 per issue (controlled and free). **Owner(s):** James Bell, See address and contact information above. **Management:** Shelia K. Erwin, Publisher. Gary Hollis, Advertising Manager. **Editorial:** Richard Magyar Jr., Editor.

PARSONS

NEWS LEADER (PARSONS), THE. 46 S. Tennessee Ave., Parsons, TN 38363-0340. Telephone: 731-847-6354. FAX: 731-847-9120. Year Established: 1926. Pub. Frequency: w. (Wed.) Subscrip. Rate: $.50 newsstand/cover; $17/yr in county; $23/yr out of county; $27/yr out of state. **Owner(s):** Sam Kennedy (Parsons), PO Box 340, Parsons, TN 38363. **Management:** Melissa Scott, General Manager. Joyce Duke, Advertising Manager. **Editorial:** Jason Scott, Production Manager. Melissa Scott, News Editor.

PIGEON FORGE

TENNESSEE STAR JOURNAL. 2713 Parkway, Pigeon Forge, TN 37868. Telephone: 865-453-0626. FAX: 865-453-4888. E-MAIL: editor@kmsfia.com. URL: http://www.tennesseestarjournal.com. Mailing Address: PO Box 898, Pigeon Forge, TN 37868. Pub. Frequency: w. (Thu.) Page Size: broadsheet. Subscrip. Rate: $.50 newsstand/cover; $20/yr in state; $24/yr out of state. Circulation: 10,000 per issue (paid). **Owner(s):** Gatlinburg Gazette, See address and contact information above. **Management:** Becky Dodgen, Advertising. **Editorial:** Jim Callicott, Managing Editor.

PIKEVILLE

BLEDSONIAN-BANNER, THE. PO Box 370, Pikeville, TN 37367. Telephone: 423-447-2996. FAX: 423-447-2997. Pub. Frequency: w. (Thu.) Page Size: broadsheet. Subscrip. Rate: $.50 newsstand/cover; $20/yr in county; $25/yr out of county. Circulation: 3,300 per issue (paid). **Owner(s):** Robert W. Hale & Amy Hale, See address and contact information above. **Management:** Amy S. Hale, Publisher. **Editorial:** Sandy Dodsen, Editor.

PORTLAND

PORTLAND LEADER, THE. 109 S. Broadway, Portland, TN 37148-1303. Telephone: 615-325-9241. FAX: 615-325-9243. E-MAIL: pleader@bellsouth.net. Pub. Frequency: w. (Wed.) Page Size: broadsheet.Subscrip. Rate: $.50 newsstand/cover; $24/yr Circulation: 3,000 per issue (paid). **Owner(s):** Paxton Media Group Llc, 201 S. Fourth St., Paducah, KY 42003. Telephone: 270-575-8600. FAX: 270-442-8188. **Management:** Wanda Rogers, Advertising Manager. Frieda Scott, Circulation Director. **Editorial:** Jan Witherspoon, Editor.

PULASKI

PRESS PLUS. 308 W. College St., Pulaski, TN 38478. Telephone: 931-363-3544. FAX: 931-363-4319. E-MAIL: citifzen@igiles.net. Year Established: 1982. Pub. Frequency: w. (Wed.) Page Size: broadsheet Circulation: 5,400 per issue (free). **Owner(s):** S. Hershel Lake, See address and contact information above. **Management:** Steven C. Lake, Publisher. **Editorial:** Scott Stewart, Editor.

PULASKI CITIZEN. 308 W. College St., Pulaski, TN 38478. Telephone: 931-363-3544. FAX: 931-363-4319. E-MAIL: citizenW@igiles.net. Year Established: 1854. Pub. Frequency: w. (Tue.) Page Size: broadsheet. Subscrip. Rate: $.50 newsstand/cover; $30/yr in county; $36/yr out of county. Adv. Rate: col. inch $6.30 Circulation: 8,400 per issue (paid). **Owner(s):** S. Hershel Lake, See address and contact information above. **Management:** S. Hershel Lake, President. Steven C. Lake, Publisher. Martha Horn, Advertising Manager. **Editorial:** Scott Stewart, Editor.

PULASKI CITIZEN/GILES FREE PRESS. 308 W. College St., Pulaski, TN 38478. Telephone: 931-363-4548. FAX: 931-363-4319. E-MAIL: citizen@igiles.net. Year Established: 1961. Pub. Frequency: w. (Thu.) Page Size: broadsheet. Subscrip. Rate: $.50 newsstand/cover; $30/yr in county; $36/yr out of county. Adv. Rate: col. inch $7.84 Circulation: 8,400 per issue (paid). **Owner(s):** S. Hershel Lake, See address and contact information above. **Management:** S. Hershel Lake, President. Steven C. Lake, Publisher. Martha Horn, Advertising Manager. **Editorial:** Scott Stewart, Editor.

RIPLEY

LAUDERDALE COUNTY ENTERPRISE. 145 E. Jackson Ave., Ripley, TN 38063-0289. Telephone: 731-635-1771. FAX: 731-635-2111. E-MAIL: enterprisenewspaper@hotmail.com. Mailing Address: PO Box 289, Ripley, TN 38063-0289. Year Established: 1885. Pub. Frequency: w. (Thu.) Page Size: standard. Subscrip. Rate: $.50 newsstand/cover; $18/yr in county; $24/yr out of county; $30/yr out of state. Adv. Rate: col. inch $4.85 Circulation: 4,956 per issue (paid). **Owner(s):** William A. Klutts, See address and contact information above. **Management:** Terry Ford, Advertising Manager.

LAUDERDALE VOICE, THE. 127 N. Main St., Ripley, TN 38063. Telephone: 731-635-1238. FAX: 731-635-3394. Mailing Address: PO Box 249, Ripley, TN 38063. Pub. Frequency: w. (Wed.) Page Size: standard. Subscrip. Rate: $.50 newsstand/cover; $18/yr local. Circulation: 4,050 per issue (paid). **Owner(s):** Jay Heath, 127 N. Main St., Ripley, TN. Telephone: 731-635-1238. **Editorial:** Jay Heath, Editor.

ROGERSVILLE

ROGERSVILLE REVIEW. 316 E Main St, Rogersville, TN 37857. Telephone: 423-272-7422. FAX: 423-272-7889. E-MAIL: review@xtn.net. URL: http://www.hawkins.xtn.net. Mailing Address: PO Box 100, Rogersville, TN 37857. Year Established: 1885. Pub. Frequency: s-w. (Wed. & Sat.) Page Size: standard. Subscrip. Rate: $.50 newsstand/cover; $38/yr in county; $42/yr mailed out of county; $48/yr mailed out of state. Adv. Rate: col. inch $9.10 Circulation: 6,000 per issue (paid). **Owner(s):** Jones Media Group, 121 W Summer St, Greenville, TN 37745. Telephone: 423-638-4181, 423-581-0088. **Management:** Ellen Myatt, Publisher. Melissa Jones, Advertising Director. Pat Smith, Circulation Manager. Windy Tinta, Classified Adv. Mgr.. **Editorial:** Ellen Myatt, Editor.

RUTLEDGE

GRAINGER COUNTY NEWS. PO Box 218, Rutledge, TN 37861-0218. Telephone: 423-828-5254. E-MAIL: ruttn@aol.com. Year Established: 1928. Pub. Frequency: w. (Fri.) Page Size: broadsheet. Subscrip. Rate: $.50 newsstand/cover; $15/yr in county. Adv. Rate: col. inch $3.75 Circulation: 4,600 per issue (paid). **Owner(s):** Linda Witt, See address and contact information above. **Management:** Linda Witt, Publisher. Laura Macka, Advertising Manager. **Editorial:** Linda Witt, Editor.

SAVANNAH

COURIER (SAVANNAH), THE. 801 Main St., Savannah, TN 38372. Telephone: 731-925-6397. FAX: 731-925-6310. Mailing Address: PO Box 340, Savannah, TN 38372. Year Established: 1884. Pub. Frequency: w. (Thu.) Page Size: standard. Subscrip. Rate: $.50 newsstand/cover; $18/yr local; $24/yr out of area; $28/yr out of state. Circulation: 9,200 per issue (paid and controlled). **Owner(s):** Savannah Publishing Co., Inc., See address and contact information above. **Management:** Kathryn Craddock, President. **Editorial:** Jim Thompson, Editor.

SELMER

INDEPENDENT APPEAL. 111 N. Second St., Selmer, TN 38375. Telephone: 731-645-5346. FAX: 731-645-3591. E-MAIL: newspaper@independentappeal.com. URL: http://www.independentappeal.com. Mailing Address: PO Box 220, Selmer, TN 39385. Year Established: 1902. Pub. Frequency: w. (Wed.) Page Size: broadsheet. Subscrip. Rate: $.50 newsstand/cover; $16/yr in county; $24/yr mailed out of county; $30/yr mailed out of state. Circulation: 7,400 per issue (paid). **Owner(s):** Janet Rail, See address and contact information above. **Management:** Janet Rail, Publisher. Melba Higgins, Advertising. **Editorial:** Janet Rail, Editor.

SEVIERVILLE

MOUNTAIN PRESS EXTRA. 119 Riverbend Dr., PO Box 4810, Sevierville, TN 37864. Telephone: 865-428-0746. FAX: 865-453-4913. URL: http://www.themountainpress.com. Pub. Frequency: w. (Mon.) Page Size: tabloid Circulation: 17,000 per issue (free). **Owner(s):** Paxton Media Group, LLC, 201 S. Fourth St., Paducah, KY 93923. Telephone: 831-624-1536. FAX: 831-624-3225. **Management:** Jana Thomasson, Publisher. Robert McCarty, Circulation Manager. Lynn Perells, Marketing Director. **Editorial:** Edward Fulford, Editor.

SEYMOUR

TRI-COUNTY NEWS (SEYMOUR). PO Box 130, Seymour, TN 37865-0130. Telephone: 865-577-5935. FAX: 865-577-9896. E-MAIL: news@comcast.net. Pub. Frequency: w. (Tue.) Page Size: broadsheet. Subscrip. Rate: $.35 newsstand/cover; $22/yr in county; $25/yr out of county. Circulation: 3,500 per issue (paid). **Owner(s):** Marty Hamilton, See address and contact information above. **Management:** Paul Hamilton, General Manager. Marty Hamilton, Publisher. **Editorial:** Marty Hamilton, Editor.

SMITHVILLE

SMITHVILLE REVIEW. 106 S First St, Smithville, TN 37166. E-MAIL: sreview@dekalb.net. URL: http://www.smithvillereview.net. Year Established: 1892. Pub. Frequency: w. (Wed.) Page Size: broadsheet. Subscrip. Rate: $.75 newsstand/cover; $29/yr in county; $34/yr mailed elsewhere. Circulation: 4,500 per issue (paid). **Owner(s):** Morris Newspaper Corporation, 27 Abercorn St., Savannah, GA 31401. **Management:** Dennis Stanley, General Manager. Patricia Zechman, Publisher. **Editorial:** Dennis Stanley, Editor.

SMYRNA

RUTHERFORD COURIER, THE. 103 Front St., Smyrna, TN 37167. Telephone: 615-459-3868. FAX: 615-459-3878. E-MAIL: rutherfordcourier@nashville.com. URL: http://www.rutherfordcourier.com. Mailing Address: PO Box 127, Smyrna, TN 37167. Year Established: 1931. Pub. Frequency: w. (Thu.) Page Size: broadsheet Circulation: 23,000 per issue (free). **Owner(s):** Morris Multimedia, Inc., PO Box 210, Cumming, GA 30028. Telephone: 770-887-3126. **Management:** Judi Terzotis, Publisher. **Editorial:** Mary Reedes, Editor.

SOMERVILLE

FAYETTE COUNTY REVIEW. PO Box 423, Somerville, TN 38068. Telephone: 901-465-4042. FAX: 901-465-5493. E-MAIL: fcreview@bellsouth.net. URL: http://www.fayettecountyreview.com. Year Established: 1982. Pub. Frequency: w. (Wed.) Page Size: broadsheet. Subscrip. Rate: $.35 newsstand/cover; $10/yr in county; $24/yr mailed elsewhere. Adv. Rate: col. inch $5.50 Circulation: 8,900 per issue (free). **Owner(s):** Don Dowdle, Ed. & Publisher, See address and contact information above. **Management:** Melissa Ferge, Office Manager. **Editorial:** Don Dowdle, Editor. Michael Osburn, Sports.

FAYETTE FALCON, THE. 101 W. Court Sq., Somerville, TN 38068. Telephone: 901-465-3587. FAX: 901-465-3568. URL: http://www.fayettefalcon.com. Mailing Address: PO Box 39, Somerville, TN 38068. Year Established: 1837. Pub. Frequency: w. (Wed.) Page Size: standard. Subscrip. Rate: $.25 newsstand/cover; $10/yr in county; $17/yr mailed out of state. Freelance Pay: $0.50/column-inch. **Wire Service(s):** AP. Circulation: 4,000 per issue (paid and free). **Owner(s):** Butch Rhea, See address and contact information above. **Management:** Butch Rhea, Publisher. P.J. Bartholomew, Advertising Manager. Karula Nolan, Circulation Manager. **Editorial:** Butch Rhea, Editor.

SOUTH PITTSBURG

JASPER JOURNAL (SOUTH PITTSBURG). PO Box 765, South Pittsburg, TN 37347. E-MAIL: mcnews@marioncountynews.net. URL: http://www.marioncountynews.net. Year Established: 1938. Pub. Frequency: w. (Tue.) Page Size: broadsheet. Subscrip. Rate: $.75 newsstand/cover; $25/yr in county; $32/yr out of county. Circulation: 3,600 per issue (paid). **Owner(s):** Marion County Newspapers, Inc., 307 Elm Ave., South Pittsburg, TN 37380. Telephone: 423-827-6312. FAX: 423-837-8715. **Management:** Ralph Bush, Publisher. Allen Kirk, Advertising Manager. Debbie Keahey, Circulation Manager. **Editorial:** Brett King, Managing Editor.

SEQUATCHIE VALLEY PURCHASE. 307 Elm Ave., South Pittsburg, TN 37380. Telephone: 423-837-6312. FAX: 423-837-8715. E-MAIL: mcnews@marioncountynew.net. Pub. Frequency: w. (Wed.) Page Size: standard Circulation: 9,000 per issue (free). **Owner(s):** Marion County Newspapers, Inc., See address and contact information above. **Management:** Ralph Bush, Publisher. Allen Kirk, Advertising Manager.

SOUTH PITTSBURG HUSTLER, THE. PO Box 765, South Pittsburg, TN 37347. E-MAIL: mcnews@marioncountynews.net. URL: http://www.marioncountynews.net. Year Established: 1899. Pub. Frequency: w. (Thu.) Page Size: broadsheet. Subscrip. Rate: $.75 newsstand/cover; $25/yr in county; $32/yr out of county. Circulation: 2,400 per issue (paid). **Owner(s):** Marion County Newspapers, Inc., 307 Elm Ave., South Pittsburg, TN 37380. Telephone: 423-837-6312. **Management:** Ralph Bush, Publisher. Allen Kirk, Advertising Manager. Debbie Keahey, Circulation Manager. **Editorial:** Brett King, Managing Editor.

SPARTA

EXPOSITOR, THE. ISSN 0745-6026
34 W. Bockman Way, Sparta, TN 38583. Telephone: 931-836-3284. FAX: 931-836-6273. E-MAIL: editor@blomand.net. URL: http://www.spartaexpositor.net. Mailing Address: PO Box 179, Sparta, TN 38583. Year Established: 1876. Pub. Frequency: s-w. (Mon. & Thu.) Page Size: broadsheet. Subscrip. Rate: $.50 newsstand/cover; $40/yr local; $58/yr mailed out of area; $58/yr mailed out of state. Circulation: 11,200 per issue (paid and free). **Owner(s):** Smith Newspapers, Inc., PO Box 27, Fort Payne, AL 35967. Telephone: 205-845-5510. **Management:** Suzanne Dickerson, Publisher. Christie Hatmaker, Advertising Manager. Linda Bussell, Circulation Manager. **Editorial:** Kim Wood, Editor.

SPRINGFIELD

ROBERTSON COUNTY TIMES. 505 W. Court Sq., Springfield, TN 37172. Telephone: 615-384-3567. FAX: 615-384-1221. E-MAIL: rctgenmgr@mtcngroup.com. URL: http://www.rctimes.com. Mailing Address: PO Box 637, Springfield, TN 37172. Year Established: 1922. Pub. Frequency: w. (Wed.) Page Size: broadsheet. Subscrip. Rate: $.50 newsstand/cover; $18/yr in county; $24/yr out of county; $30/yr mailed out of state. Circulation: 10,000 per issue (paid). **Owner(s):** Gannett Company, Inc., 7950 Jones Branch Dr., McLean, VA 22107-0001. Telephone: 703-854-6000. **Management:** Janice Suter, Publisher. Lana Osborne, Office Manager. Janice Suter, Advertising Manager. **Editorial:** Cindy Kelly, Editor. Joshua Wilkins, Sports Editor.

SWEETWATER

ADVOCATE & DEMOCRAT. 609 E. North St., Sweetwater, TN 37874. Telephone: 423-337-7101. URL: http://www.advocatedemocrat.com. Mailing Address: PO Box 1630, Greenville, TN 37743. Pub. Frequency: 3/w. (Sun., Wed., Fri.) Page Size: broadsheet. Subscrip. Rate: $.50 newsstand/cover; $1 newsstand/cover Sun.; $59/yr in county; $78/yr out of county; $93/yr elsewhere. Adv. Rate: col. inch $9.75 Circulation: 4,000 per issue (paid); 15,000 Sunday (free). **Owner(s):** Jones Media Group, 121 W Summer St, Greenville, TN 37745. Telephone: 423-581-0088. FAX: 423-235-7012. **Management:** Tom Overton, Publisher. David Smith, Circulation Manager. Sharon Livingston, Classified Adv. Mgr.. **Editorial:** Mia Rhodarmer, Editor.

ADVOCATE PENNY SAVER. 609 E. North St., Sweetwater, TN 37874. Telephone: 423-337-7101. FAX: 423-337-5932. URL: http://wwwadvocateanddemocrat.com. Mailing Address: PO Box 1630, Greenville, TN 37743. Year Established: 1927. Pub. Frequency: w. (Sun.) Page Size: broadsheet Circulation: 15,000 Sunday (free). **Owner(s):** Jones Media Group, 121 W Summer St, Greenville, TN 37745. Telephone: 423-581-0088. FAX: 423-235-7012. **Management:** Thomas J. Overton III, Publisher. David Smith, Circulation Manager. Sharon Livingston, Classified Adv. Mgr.. **Editorial:** Mia Rhodarmer, Editor.

TAZEWELL

CLAIBORNE PROGRESS. 1705 Main St, Tazewell, TN 37879. Telephone: 423-626-3222. FAX: 423-626-6868. E-MAIL: claibprogress@centuryinter.net. URL: http://wwwmiddlesborodailynews.com/claiborne_progress. Mailing Address: PO Box 40, Tazewell, TN 37879. Year Established: 1887. Pub. Frequency: w. (Wed.) Page Size: broadsheet. Subscrip. Rate: $.50 newsstand/cover; $25/yr in county; $27.25/yr mailed out of county; $31/yr mailed out of state. Adv. Rate: col. inch $6.30 Circulation: 6,941 per issue (paid). **Owner(s):** Heartland Publications, LLC, 20 Research Pkwy, Ste G, Old Saybrook, CT 06475. Telephone: 860-388-3470. FAX: 860-388-3490. **Management:** Tom Spargur, Publisher. Patricia Cheek, Advertising Director. Lisa Gray, Circulation Manager. Mary Gordon, Classified Adv. Mgr.. **Editorial:** Richard Evans, Editor.

TIPTONVILLE

LAKE COUNTY BANNER, THE. 315 Church St., Tiptonville, TN 38079-0047. Telephone: 731-253-6666. FAX: 731-253-6667. URL: htttp://www/lakecountybanner.com. Pub. Frequency: w. (Wed.) Page Size: broadsheet. Subscrip. Rate: $.75 newsstand/cover; $26/yr in county; $30/yr out of county; $36/yr elsewhere. Circulation: 3,300 per issue (paid). **Owner(s):** Banner Printing Co., See address and contact information above. **Management:** Lori Long, General Manager. Evan Jones, Publisher. **Editorial:** Evan Jones, Editor.

TRACY CITY

GRUNDY COUNTY HERALD. 1234 Oak St., Tracy City, TN 37387. Telephone: 931-592-2781. FAX: 931-598-5812. E-MAIL: gcherald@blomand.net. URL: http://www.grundycountyherald.com. Mailing Address: PO Box 189, Tracy City, TN 37387. Year Established: 1932. Pub. Frequency: w. (Thu.) Page Size: broadsheet. Subscrip. Rate: $.50 newsstand/cover; $23/yr in county; $30/yr out of county; $21/yr to senior citizens. Adv. Rate: col. inch $6.51 Circulation: 5,000 per issue (paid). **Owner(s):** Lakeway Publishers, Inc., 1609 W First N St., Morristown, TN 37814. Telephone: 423-581-5630. **Management:** Joyle Caldwell, General Manager. Jeff Fishman, Publisher. Renee Campbell, Advertising Manager. **Editorial:** David Lowrie, Sports Editor.

TRENTON

HERALD GAZETTE (TRENTON), THE. 111 E. First St., Trenton, TN 38392. Telephone: 731-855-1711. FAX: 731-855-9587. E-MAIL: danny@trentongazette.com. URL: http://www.trentongazette.com. Mailing Address: PO Box 7, Trenton, TN 38382-0007. Year Established: 1968. Pub. Frequency: w. (Wed.) Page Size: broadsheet. Subscrip. Rate: $.50 newsstand/cover; $25/yr mailed in county; $30/yr mailed in state; $35/yr mailed out of state. Adv. Rate: col. inch $5.26 Circulation: 3,100 per issue (paid). **Owner(s):** Herald Gazette, Inc., The, See address and contact information above. **Management:** Danny Jones, Publisher. Brandy Howard, Circulation Manager. **Editorial:** Danny Jones, Editor. Gary Smith, Sports Editor.

TULLAHOMA

TULLAHOMA NEWS AND GUARDIAN, THE. 505 Lakeway Place, Tullahoma, TN 37388. URL: http://www.tullahomanews.com. Mailing Address: PO Box 400, Tullahoma, TN 37388. Year Established: 1946. Pub. Frequency: 3/w. (Wed., Fri., Sun.) Page Size: standard. Subscrip. Rate: $.50 newsstand/cover; $1 newsstand/cover Sun.; $53/yr local; $65/yr mailed elsewhere. **Wire Service(s):** AP. Circulation: 12,600 Sunday (paid); 8,500 per issue (paid). **Owner(s):** Lakeway Publishers, Inc., 1609 W First N St., Morristown, TN 37814. Telephone: 423-581-5630. **Management:** Jeff Fishman, Publisher. Harry Hill, Advertising Manager. James Bowden, Circulation Manager. Harry Hill, Assistant Publisher. **Editorial:** Bob Kyer, Editor. Betty Dement, Associate Editor.

UNION CITY

OBION COUNTY WEEKLY. 613 E Jackson St, Union City, TN 38281. Telephone: 731-885-0744. FAX: 731-885-0782. Mailing Address: PO Box 430, Union City, TN 38281. Pub. Frequency: w. (Wed.) Page Size: broadsheet.Adv. Rate: col. inch $2 Circulation: 5,600 per issue (free). **Owner(s):** Critchlow/David Sr., David, Jr. & Scott, See address and contact information above. **Management:** David Critchlow, Sr., Publisher. Gloria Chesteen, Advertising Manager. Glenda Langford, Classified Adv. Mgr.. **Editorial:** David Critchlow, Jr., Managing Editor.

WEAKLEY COUNTY PRESS. PO Box 430, Union City, TN 38281. E-MAIL: wcpnews@frontiernet.net. URL: http://www.wcpnews.com. Year Established: 1885. Pub. Frequency: s-w. (Tue. & Thu.) Page Size: broadsheet. Subscrip. Rate: $.50 newsstand/cover; $33/yr mailed. Adv. Rate: col. inch $6 Circulation: 4,500 per issue (paid). **Owner(s):** Critchlow/David Sr., David, Jr. & Scott, See address and contact information above. **Management:** David Critchlow, Sr., Publisher. Linda Stockton, Circulation Manager. **Editorial:** Tracy Sharp, Editor.

WARTBURG

MORGAN COUNTY NEWS. 224 Maiden St., Wartburg, TN 37887. Telephone: 423-346-6225. FAX: 423-346-5788. Mailing Address: PO Box 346, Wartburg, TN 37887. Year Established: 1917. Pub. Frequency: w. (Wed.) Page Size: broadsheet. Subscrip. Rate: $.50 newsstand/cover; $23/yr local; $32/yr in state; $42.50/yr out of state. Circulation: 4,600 per issue (paid). **Owner(s):** Landmark Community Newspapers, Inc., PO Box 549, Shelbyville, KY 40065. Telephone: 502-633-2526. **Management:** Johnny Kegles, Publisher. Faye Williams, Circulation Manager. **Editorial:** Judy Underwood, Editor.

WAVERLY

NEWS-DEMOCRAT (WAVERLY), THE. 302-A W. Main St., Waverly, TN 37185. Telephone: 931-296-2426. E-MAIL: newsdemocrat@bellsouth.net. URL: http://www.thenews-democrat.com. Mailing Address: PO Box 626, Waverly, TN 37185. Year Established: 1954. Pub. Frequency: w. (Fri.) Page Size: broadsheet. Subscrip. Rate: $.50 newsstand/cover; $25/yr in county; $40/yr out of county. Adv. Rate: col. inch $5 Circulation: 4,000 per issue (paid). **Owner(s):** Sam Kennedy (Waverly), See address and contact information above. **Management:** Bill Ridings, Publisher. **Editorial:** Win Anderson, Editor.

WAYNESBORO

WAYNE COUNTY NEWS (WAYNESBORO). 119 E.Hollis St., Waynesboro, TN 38485. Telephone: 931-722-5429. FAX: 931-722-5429. E-MAIL: waynecountynews@tds.net. Mailing Address: P.O. Box 156, Waynesboro, TN 38485-0156. Year Established: 1857. Pub. Frequency: w. (Wed.) Page Size: broadsheet. Subscrip. Rate: $.40 newsstand/cover; $12/yr in county; $15/yr out of county. Adv. Rate: col. inch $2.85 Circulation: 6,900 per issue (paid). **Owner(s):** Wayne County News, Inc., See address and contact information above. **Management:** Dan Cole, Publisher. Kathy Brison, Advertising Manager. **Editorial:** Kathy Brison, Managing Editor.

WINCHESTER

HERALD-CHRONICLE, THE. ISSN 0893-3707
904 Dinah Shore Blvd., Winchester, TN 37398. Telephone: 931-967-2298. E-MAIL: whcnews@lcs.net. URL: http://www.heraldchronicle.com. Year Established: 1845. Pub. Frequency: s-w. (Tue. & Fri.) Page Size: broadsheet. Subscrip. Rate: $36/yr in county; $43/yr out of county; $.50 newsstand/cover. Freelance Pay: $10-$25/article. Circulation: 10,000 per issue (paid). **Owner(s):** Franklin County Publishing Co., Inc., See address and contact information above. **Management:** Barry Lamb, General Manager. Davis Sons, Publisher. Rebecca Cowan, Advertising Manager. **Editorial:** Davis Sans, Editor. Bob Salmon, Sports Editor.

WOODBURY

CANNON COURIER. 210 W. Water St., Woodbury, TN 37190-1117. Telephone: 615-563-2512. FAX: 615-563-2519. URL: http://www.canoncourier.com. Pub. Frequency: w. (Tue.) Page Size: broadsheet. Subscrip. Rate: $.50 newsstand/cover; $18/yr mailed in county; $22/yr mailed out of county; $24/yr mailed out of state. Circulation: 4,400 per issue (paid). **Owner(s):** Cannon Courier Inc., See address and contact information above. **Management:** Ron Fryar, Publisher. Teresa Stoetzel, Advertising Manager. **Editorial:** Kevin Halpern, Editor.

TEXAS

ABERNATHY

ABERNATHY WEEKLY REVIEW. ISSN 0895-4291
916 Ave D, Abernathy, TX 79311. Telephone: 806-298-2033. E-MAIL: abernathyreview@yahoo.com. Mailing Address: PO Box 160, Abernathy, TX 79311-0160. Year Established: 1921. Pub. Frequency: w. (Fri.) Page Size: broadsheet. Subscrip. Rate: $.50 newsstand/cover; $21/yr mailed in county; $25/yr mailed out of county. Adv. Rate: col. inch $3.95 Circulation: 850 per issue (paid). **Owner(s):** Ken Magness, See address and contact information above. **Management:** Ken Magness, Publisher. **Editorial:** Ken Magness, Editor. Contact: Scott Luce, Advertising Manager.

ADDISON

CARROLLTON LEADER. 14875 Landmark Blvd, Ste 110, Addison, TX 75254. Telephone: 972-628-4061. FAX: 971-436-7432. URL: http://www.scntx.com. Pub. Frequency: w. (Thu.) Page Size: broadsheet. Subscrip. Rate: $.50 newsstand/cover; $25/yr home delivery local; $39.95/yr mailed in county; $59.95/yr mailed out of county. Circulation: 4,000 per issue (paid). **Owner(s):** Star Community Newspapers, See address and contact information above. **Management:** Jack Bick, Publisher. Patty Linkford, Advertising Manager. Ken McEwen, Circulation Manager. **Editorial:** Crystal Forester, Editor.

COLONY COURIER LEADER, THE. 14875 Landmark Blvd, Ste 110, Addison, TX 75254. Telephone: 972-628-4061. FAX: 971-436-7432. Year Established: 1988. Pub. Frequency: w. (Wed..) Page Size: tabloid. Subscrip. Rate: $.50/yr newsstand/cover; $25/yr home delivery in county; $39.95/yr mailed in county. Circulation: 4,000 per issue (paid). **Owner(s):** Star Community Newspapers, See address and contact information above. **Management:** Jack Bick, Publisher. Patty Linkford, Advertising Manager. **Editorial:** Blaine Crimmins, Managing Editor.

COPPELL GAZETTE. 14875 Landmark Blvd, Ste 110, Addison, TX 75254. Telephone: 972-628-4061. FAX: 971-436-7432. URL: http://www.scntx.com. Pub. Frequency: w. (Thu.) Page Size: broadsheet. Subscrip. Rate: $.50 newsstand/cover (effective 2006); $25/yr home delivery local; $39.95/yr mailed in county; $59.95/yr mailed out of county. Circulation: 6,000 per issue (paid). **Owner(s):** Star Community Newspapers, See address and contact information above. **Management:** Jack Bick, Publisher. Patty Linkford, Advertising Manager. Ken McEwen, Circulation Manager. **Editorial:** Crystal Forester, Editor. Mike Norris, Editorial Page Editor.

FLOWER MOUND LEADER. 14875 Landmark Blvd, Ste 110, Addison, TX 75254. Telephone: 972-628-4061. FAX: 971-436-7432. URL: http://www.scntx.com. Pub. Frequency: s-w. (Wed. & Sat.) Page Size: broadsheet. Subscrip. Rate: $.50/yr newsstand/cover; $35/yr home delivery local; $75.95/yr mailed in county; $108.95/yr mailed out of county. Circulation: 6,500 per issue (paid). **Owner(s):** Star Community Newspapers, See address and contact information above. **Management:** Jack Bick, Publisher. Patty Linkford, Advertising Manager. Ken McEwen, Circulation Manager. **Editorial:** Crystal Forester, Editor.

LEWISVILLE LEADER. ISSN 0745-6174
14875 Landmark Blvd, Ste 110, Addison, TX 75254. Telephone: 972-628-4061. FAX: 971-436-7432. URL: http://www.lewisvilleleader.com. Year Established: 1895. Pub. Frequency: s-w. (Wed. & Sat.) Page Size: broadsheet. Subscrip. Rate: $.50 newsstand/cover; $1 newsstand/cover Sat.; $35/yr home delivery local; $75.95/yr mailed in county; $108.95/yr mailed out of county. **Wire Service(s):** UPI. Circulation: 33,000 per issue (paid and free). **Owner(s):** Star Community Newspapers, See address and contact information above. **Management:** Patty Linkford, Advertising Manager. Ken McEwen, Circulation Manager. **Editorial:** Crystal Forester, Editor. Rick Mann, Managing Editor.

SOUTHLAKE TIMES. 14875 Landmark Blvd, Ste 110, Addison, TX 75254. Telephone: 972-628-4061. FAX: 971-436-7432. URL: http://www.scntx.com. Pub. Frequency: w. (Wed.) Page Size: broadsheet. Subscrip. Rate: $.50 newsstand/cover; $25/yr home delivery local; $59.95/yr mailed out of county. **Owner(s):** Star Community Newspapers, See address and contact information above. **Management:** Jack Bick, Publisher. Patty Linkford, Advertising Manager. Ken McEwen, Circulation Manager. **Editorial:** Crystal Forester, Editor.

ALPINE

ALPINE AVALANCHE. 118 N. Fifth St., Alpine, TX 79830. Telephone: 432-837-3334. FAX: 432-837-7181. E-MAIL: editor@alpineavalanche.com. URL: http://www.alpineavalanche.com. Mailing Address: PO Box 719, Alpine, TX 79831. Year Established: 1891. Pub. Frequency: w. (Thu.) Page Size: broadsheet. Subscrip. Rate: $.75 newsstand/cover; $32/yr in county; $38/yr in state; $43/yr out of state. Adv. Rate: col. inch $6.50 Circulation: 4,000 per issue (paid). **Owner(s):** Granite Publications, PO Box 1010, Taylor, TX 75674. Telephone: 512-352-1009. **Management:** Mike Perry, Publisher. Roxann Chavez, Advertising. Valerie Richard, Classified Adv. Mgr.. Valeri Stair, Subscription . **Editorial:** Cindy Perry, Production Manager.

ALVIN

ALVIN ADVERTISER. 570 Dula St., Alvin, TX 77511. Telephone: 281-331-4421. FAX: 281-331-4424. E-MAIL: alvinsun@argohouston.com. Year Established: 1890. Pub. Frequency: w. (; Wed.) Page Size: standard. Subscrip. Rate: $.50 newsstand/cover per issue; $28/yr. Adv. Rate: col. inch $9.30 Circulation: 17,000 per issue (free). **Owner(s):** Henderson Newspapers, Inc., PO Box 1390, Rosenberg, TX 77471-1390. Telephone: 281-342-8691. **Management:** Jim Schwind, Publisher. Dolores Schaeffer, Circulation Manager. Betty Crawford, Classified Adv. Mgr.. **Editorial:** Ed Looby, Managing Editor.

ALVIN SUN-ADVERTISER. 570 Dula St., Alvin, TX 77511. Telephone: 281-331-4421. FAX: 281-331-4424. E-MAIL: alvinsun@swbell.net. URL: http://www.alvinsun.net. Pub. Frequency: w. (Sun.) Page Size: broadsheet. Subscrip. Rate: $.50 newsstand/cover; $20/yr home delivery in area; $32/yr mailed in county. Circulation: 10,000 Sunday (paid and controlled). **Owner(s):** Henderson Newspapers, Inc., PO Box 1390, Rosenberg, TX 77471-1390. Telephone: 281-342-8691. **Management:** Jim Schwind, Publisher. Randall Gill, Advertising Director. Melissa Garcia, Circulation Manager. Betty Crawford, Classified Adv. Mgr.. **Editorial:** Jim Schwind, Editor. Tony Floyd, Managing Editor.

ALVIN SUN & ADVERTISER. 570 Dula St., Alvin, TX 77511. Telephone: 281-331-4421. FAX: 281-331-4424. E-MAIL: alvinsun@swbell.net. Year Established: 1890. Pub. Frequency: 3/w. (Mon., Wed., Sun.) Page Size: broadsheet. Subscrip. Rate: $.50 newsstand/cover Sat.-Sun.; $32/yr. Adv. Rate: col. inch $5.57 Circulation: 18,000 (free); 4,000 per issue (paid). **Owner(s):** Hartman Publishing, Inc., PO Box 1390, Rosenberg, TX 77471-1390. Telephone: 281-342-8691. **Management:** Jim Schwind, Publisher. Sue Whitley, Office Manager. **Editorial:** Jim Schwind, Editor. Jane Faulkner, Managing Editor. Stephen Collins, Sports.

ANAHUAC

PROGRESS (ANAHUAC), THE. 209 Willcox St, Anahuac, TX 77514. Telephone: 409-267-6131. FAX: 409-267-4157. Mailing Address: PO Box 100, Anahuac, TX 77514-0100. Year Established: 1908. Pub. Frequency: w. (Wed.) Page Size: broadsheet. Subscrip. Rate: $.50 newsstand/cover; $17.50/yr in county. Circulation: 2,200 per issue (paid). **Owner(s):** Granite Publications, PO Box 1010, Taylor, TX 75674. Telephone: 512-352-1009. **Management:** Emmett McKinley, Publisher. **Editorial:** Sue Hawthorne, Editor.

ANDREWS

ANDREWS COUNTY NEWS, THE. 210 E. Broadway, Andrews, TX 79714. Telephone: 432-523-2085. FAX: 432-523-9492. URL: http://www.andrewscountynews.com. Year Established: 1934. Pub. Frequency: s-w. (Thu. & Sun.) Page Size: standard. Subscrip. Rate: $.75 newsstand/cover; $35/yr mailed in county; $60/yr mailed adj. counties; $60/yr mailed out of area. Adv. Rate: col. inch $7 Circulation: 3,249 per issue (paid and controlled). **Owner(s):** Roberts Publishing, Inc., See address and contact information above. **Management:** Don Ingram, Publisher. Priscilla Rider, Advertising Director. William C Gonzales, Circulation Manager. Monica Martinez, Classified Adv. Mgr.. Brooke Lopez, Classified Editor. **Editorial:** Jennifer Shoe, Lifestyle Editor. Sam Kaufman, News Editor. Rudy Diaz, Sports Editor.

ARANSAS PASS

ARANSAS PASS PROGRESS, THE. 346 S. Houston, Aransas Pass, TX 78335-2100. URL: http://www.aransaspassprogress.com. Mailing Address: P.O. Drawer 2100, Aransas Pass, TX 73336-2100. Pub. Frequency: w. (Wed.) Page Size: broadsheet. Subscrip. Rate: $.75 newsstand/cover; $29/yr in county; $39/yr mailed out of county; $48/yr mailed out of state. Circulation: 3,000 per issue (paid). **Owner(s):** Richards Publishing Co., Inc., See address and contact information above. **Management:** Clay Morgan, Publisher. Patsy Dicken, Business Manager. Josie Torres, Classified Editor. **Editorial:** Kurt Mogonye, Editor.

ATLANTA

ATLANTA CITIZENS JOURNAL. 306 W. Main St., Atlanta, TX 75551. Telephone: 903-796-7133. FAX: 903-796-3294. Mailing Address: PO Box 1188, Atlanta, TX 75551. Year Established: 1879. Pub. Frequency: s-w. (Wed. & Sun.) Page Size: broadsheet. Subscrip. Rate: $.50 newsstand/cover; $42/yr local; $47/yr in state. Circulation: 4,300 per issue (paid). **Owner(s):** Westward Communications LLC, 907B E. Main St., Humble, TX 77338. Telephone: 281-446-5929. **Management:** Debbie Milton, Publisher. Kim Holcombe, Advertising Manager. Patricia Buster, Classified Adv. Mgr.. **Editorial:** Tom Burkdine, Editor. Steve Williams, Sports Editor. Contact: Pat Wellenkamp, Publisher; Bill Beard, Editor.

AUSTIN

AUSTIN CHRONICLE. ISSN 1074-0740
PO Box 49066, Austin, TX 78765. Telephone: 512-454-5766. FAX: 512-458-6910. E-MAIL: mail@austinchronicle.com. URL: http://www.austinchronicle.com/. Year Established: 1981. Pub. Frequency: w. Page Size: tabloid. Subscrip. Rate: $35 for 6 mos.; $60/yr. Circulation: 90,000 (controlled). **Owner(s):** Austin Chronicle Corp., See address and contact information above. **Management:** Nick Barbaro, Publisher. Carol Flagg, Advertising Director. Dan Hardick, Circulation Manager. Cassidy Frazier, Classified Adv. Mgr.. Erin Collier, Marketing Director. **Editorial:** Louis Black, Editor. Cindy Widner, Managing Editor. Robert Faires, Art Editor. Shawn Badgley, Book Review Editor. Virginia Wood, Food Editor. John Anderson, Photographer.

LAKE TRAVIS VIEW. 1213 Ranch Rd. 6203, Austin, TX 78734-6206. Telephone: 512-263-1101. FAX: 512-263-3583. E-MAIL: news@ltview.com. URL: http://www.laketravisview.com. Mailing Address: PO Box 107 Ranch Rd., PMB5F, Austin, TX 78716. Pub. Frequency: w. (Thu.) Page Size: standard. Subscrip. Rate: $.50 newsstand/cover; $32.34/yr in county; $40.56/yr out of county. Circulation: 3,000 per issue (paid). **Owner(s):** Cox Newspapers, Inc., 6205 Peachtree Dunwoody Rd, Atlanta, GA 30328. Telephone: 404-843-5000. **Management:** Jay Plotkin, Publisher. Danny Esposito, Advertising. **Editorial:** Gary Dinges, Editor. Dan Kleiner, Sports Editor.

TEXAS OBSERVER. ISSN 0040-4519
307 W. Seventh St., Austin, TX 78701-2917. Telephone: 800-939-6620. FAX: 512-477-0746. E-MAIL: observer@texasobserver.org. URL: http://www.texasobserver.org. Year Established: 1954. Pub. Frequency: bi-w. Page Size: standard. Subscrip. Rate: $2.25 newsstand/cover per issue; $32/yr local; $59 for 2 yrs. local. Adv. Rate: B&W page $300, color page $400; trim 10 x 8 Freelance Pay: $25-$100/article. Circulation: 10,000 (paid). **Owner(s):** Texas Democracy Foundation, See address and contact information above. **Management:** Charlotte McCann, Publisher. Lara George, Advertising. **Editorial:** Barbara Belejack, Editor.

WESTLAKE PICAYUNE. 3103 Bee Caves Rd., Austin, TX 78746. Telephone: 512-327-2990. FAX: 512-328-6470. E-MAIL: news@westlake-picayune.com. URL: http://www.westlakepicayune.com. Mailing Address: PO Box 160790, Austin, TX 78716. Year Established: 1977. Pub. Frequency: w. (Thu.) Page Size: tabloid. Subscrip. Rate: $.50 newsstand/cover; $36/yr in county; $41/yr out of county outside of cy. Freelance Pay: $15/story. Circulation: 3,500 per issue (paid). **Owner(s):** Cox Newspapers, Inc., 6205 Peachtree Dunwoody Rd., Atlanta, GA 30328. Telephone: 678-645-0000. **Management:** Jason Jarrett, Publisher. Kristi Johnson, Advertising Director. **Editorial:** Ed Allen, Editor. Thomas Jones, Sports.

AZLE

AZLE NEWS. 321 W. Main St., Azle, TX 76020. Telephone: 817-270-3340. FAX: 817-270-5300. E-MAIL: bobbuckel@azlenews.net. URL: http://www.azlenews.net. Year Established: 1953. Pub. Frequency: w. (Thu.) Page Size: broadsheet. Subscrip. Rate: $.75 newsstand/cover; $28.50/yr in county; $34.50/yr out of county; $24.50/yr in county to senior citizens. Adv. Rate: col. inch $5 Circulation: 4,914 per issue (paid). **Owner(s):** Azle Tri-County Advertiser, Inc., See address and contact information above. **Management:** Bob Buckel, President. Kim Ware, Advertising Director. **Editorial:** Edwin Newton, Editor. Mark Campbell, Sports Editor.

BASTROP

BASTROP ADVERTISER, THE. 908 Water St., Bastrop, TX 78602-3834. Telephone: 512-321-2557. FAX: 512-321-1680. E-MAIL: news@bastropadvertiser.com. Mailing Address: PO Box 459, Bastrop, TX 78602. Year Established: 1853. Pub. Frequency: s-w. (Thu. & Sat.) Page Size: standard. Subscrip. Rate: $.50 newsstand/cover; $48.88/yr in county; $57.20/yr in state; $74.88/yr out of county. Adv. Rate: col. inch $6.45 Circulation: 5,100 per issue (controlled). **Owner(s):** Cox Newspapers, Inc., 6205 Peachtree Dunwoody Rd., Atlanta, GA 30328. Telephone: 678-645-0000. **Management:** Janice Butler, Publisher. **Editorial:** Davis McAuley, Editor.

BEEVILLE

BEEVILLE BEE-PICAYUNE. 111 N. Washington St., Beeville, TX 78104. Telephone: 361-358-2550. FAX: 361-358-5323. E-MAIL: beepic@sbcglobal.net. URL: http://www.bee-picayune.com. Mailing Address: P O Box 10, Beeville, TX 78104. Pub. Frequency: 2/w. Circulation: 6,500. **Owner(s):** Beeville Publishing Co., See address and contact information above. **Management:** Karl Arnst, Advertising. **Editorial:** Chip Latcham, Copy Editor.

BELLVILLE

BELLVILLE TIMES. 106 E. Palm St., Bellville, TX 77418. Telephone: 979-865-3131. FAX: 979-865-3132. Year Established: 1879. Pub. Frequency: w. (Thu.) Page Size: broadsheet. Subscrip. Rate: $.75 newsstand/cover; $30/yr mailed in county; $35/yr mailed out of county; $41.50/yr mailed out of state. Circulation: 3,683 per issue (paid). **Owner(s):** Austin County Publishing Co., Inc., See address and contact information above. **Management:** Bruce White, Publisher. Jim Maler, Advertising Manager. **Editorial:** Jim Maler, Editor.

BLANCO

BLANCO COUNTY NEWS. ISSN 1049-2216
PO Box 429, Blanco, TX 78606. Telephone: 830-833-4812. FAX: 830-833-4246. E-MAIL: bcnews@moment.net. URL: http://www.blancocountynews.com. Year Established: 1883. Pub. Frequency: w. (Wed.) Page Size: broadsheet. Subscrip. Rate: $.75 newsstand/cover; $33/yr in county; $39/yr mailed in state; $50/yr mailed out of state. Adv. Rate: col. inch $4.75 **Wire Service(s):** AP. Circulation: 3,700 per issue (controlled and free). **Owner(s):** Brett Wesner, See address and contact information above. **Management:** Brett Wesner, Publisher. Bill Hunter, Advertising. **Editorial:** Charles Willgren, Editor.

BOOKER

BOOKER NEWS, THE. 204 S. Main, Booker, TX 79005. Telephone: 806-658-4732. FAX: 806-658-4424. Year Established: 1921. Pub. Frequency: w. (Thu.) Page Size: standard. Subscrip. Rate: $.50 newsstand/cover; $20/yr in county; $25/yr elsewhere. Circulation: 1,100 per issue (paid and free). **Owner(s):** Kayla & Jerry Parvin, See address and contact information above. **Management:** Jerry Parvin, Publisher. **Editorial:** Kayla Parvin, Editor-in-Chief.

BOWIE

BOWIE NEWS. 218 W. Tarrant St., Bowie, TX 76230. Telephone: 940-872-2247. FAX: 940-872-4812. E-MAIL: bnews@sbcglobal.net. URL: http://www.bowienewsinc.com. Mailing Address: PO Box 831, Bowie, TX 76230. Year Established: 1920. Pub. Frequency: s-w. (Thu. & Sun.) Page Size: broadsheet. Subscrip. Rate: $.50 newsstand/cover; $25/yr in county; $30/yr mailed out of county; $35/yr mailed out of state. Circulation: 5,000 per issue (paid). **Owner(s):** Connie Winter, See address and contact information above. **Management:** Barbara Green, General Manager. Connie Winter, Publisher. Melody Hamilton, Advertising Manager. Donna Fallis, Business Manager. **Editorial:** Barbara Green, Editor.

MONTAGUE COUNTY SHOPPER, THE. 1300 E. Wise St., Bowie, TX 76230. Telephone: 940-872-6186. FAX: 940-872-3559. E-MAIL: shopper@morgan.net. URL: http://www.shopper.morgan.net. Year Established: 1980. Pub. Frequency: w. (Thu.) Page Size: tabloid. Subscrip. Rate: $25/yr mailed out of county. Circulation: 11,900 per issue (paid and free). Owner(s): Montague County Shopper, See address and contact information above. Management: Cindy Croxton, Advertising. Editorial: Sharon McKinley, Production Manager.

BRACKETTVILLE

BRACKETT NEWS, THE. 507 S. Ann St., Brackettville, TX 78832-1039. Telephone: 830-563-2852. FAX: 830-563-9538. E-MAIL: tbnews@sbcglobal.net. Mailing Address: PO Box 1039, Brackettville, TX 78832. Year Established: 1989. Pub. Frequency: w. (Thu.) Page Size: standard. Subscrip. Rate: $.50 newsstand/cover; $20/yr in county; $25/yr out of county; $27.50/yr out of state. Circulation: 1,000 per issue (paid and free). Owner(s): Jewel F. Robinson, See address and contact information above. Management: Jewel F. Robinson, Publisher. Dimple Henry, Advertising Manager. Editorial: Gus Garcia, Editor.

BRADY

BRADY STANDARD-HERALD. 201 S. Bridge St., Brady, TX 76825. Telephone: 325-597-2959. FAX: 325-597-1434. E-MAIL: bsh@centex.net. URL: http://www.heartotexasnews.com. Year Established: 1909. Pub. Frequency: s-w. (Tue. & Fri.) Page Size: broadsheet. Subscrip. Rate: $.50 newsstand/cover; $30/yr mailed in county; $37/yr mailed in state; $50/yr mailed out of state. Circulation: 3,100 per issue (paid). Owner(s): Brady Standard-Herald, Inc., See address and contact information above. Management: Larry Smith, Publisher. Tina Willis, Advertising Director. Editorial: James Stewart, Editor. James Steward, Sports.

BRIDGEPORT

BRIDGEPORT INDEX. 916 Halsell, Bridgeport, TX 76426-1150. Telephone: 940-683-4021. E-MAIL: bridgeportindex@wccs.net. Year Established: 1898. Pub. Frequency: w. (Thu.) Page Size: broadsheet. Subscrip. Rate: $.50 newsstand/cover; $25/yr in county; $30/yr out of county. Circulation: 3,000 per issue (paid). Owner(s): Bridwell Publishing Co., See address and contact information above. Management: Keith Bridwell, Publisher. Editorial: Keith Bridwell, Editor.

CHICO TEXAN. 916 Halsell, Bridgeport, TX 76426-1150. Telephone: 940-683-4021. Mailing Address: PO Box 1150, Bridgeport, TX 76426-1150. Pub. Frequency: w. (Thu.) Page Size: broadsheet. Subscrip. Rate: $.25 newsstand/cover; $25/yr in county (effective 2005); $30/yr out of county. Circulation: 900 per issue (paid). Owner(s): Bridwell Publishing Co., See address and contact information above. Management: Keith Bridwell, Publisher. Editorial: Keith Bridwell, Editor.

BROWNFIELD

BROWNFIELD NEWS. 409 W. Hill St., Brownfield, TX 79316. Telephone: 806-637-4535. FAX: 806-637-3795. E-MAIL: bnews@door.net. URL: http://www.brownfieldonline.com. Mailing Address: P.O. Drawer 1272, Brownfield, TX 79316. Year Established: 1904. Pub. Frequency: s-w. (Wed. & Sun.) Page Size: broadsheet. Subscrip. Rate: $.75 newsstand/cover; $32.95/yr carrier delivery in county; $39.95/yr mailed in state; $46.95/yr mailed out of state. Adv. Rate: col. inch $5 Circulation: 6,000 per issue (paid). Owner(s): Lynn Brisendine, See address and contact information above. Management: Lynn Brisendine, Publisher. Russ McKee, Advertising Manager. Lynna Cunningham, Classified Adv. Mgr.. Editorial: Lynn Brisendine, Editor. Mitch Word, Sports Editor. Gary Peebles, Writer.

BRYAN

PRESS (BRYAN), THE. 1729 Briarcrest Dr, Bryan, TX 77802. Telephone: 979-823-0088. FAX: 979-774-0053. URL: http://www.theeagle.com. Mailing Address: PO Box 3000, Bryan, TX 77805. Year Established: 1966. Pub. Frequency: w. (Thu.) Circulation: 5,000 per issue (free). Owner(s): Evening Post Publishing Co., 134 Columbus St., Charleston, SC 29403. Telephone: 843-577-7111. Management: Chris Zoller, Advertising Manager. Wayne Nedbalek, Circulation Manager. Joy Warren, Classified Adv. Mgr.. Editorial: Donnis Baggett, Editor.

BURLESON

ALVARADO STAR. 319 N. Burleson Blvd., Burleson, TX 76028. Telephone: 817-295-0486. FAX: 817-295-5278. E-MAIL: alvaradostar@thestargroup.com. URL: http://thestargroup.com. Mailing Address: PO Box 909, Burleson, TX 76097-0909. Pub. Frequency: w. (Thu.) Page Size: broadsheet. Subscrip. Rate: $.50 newsstand/cover; $18/yr in county. Circulation: 2,000 per issue (paid). Owner(s): The Star Group, See address and contact information above. Management: James Moody, Publisher. Amy Johnson, Advertising. Cathy Smith, Advertising Director. Editorial: Lisa Urban, Editor.

CROWLEY STAR. 319 N. Burleson Blvd., Burleson, TX 76028. Telephone: 817-295-0486. FAX: 817-295-5278. E-MAIL: Joycresslar@thestargroup.com. URL: http://www.thestargroup.com. Mailing Address: PO Box 909, Burleson, TX 76097-0909. Year Established: 1979. Pub. Frequency: bi-m. Page Size: broadsheet. Subscrip. Rate: $.50 newsstand/cover; $18/yr. Circulation: 2,540. Owner(s): The Star Group, See address and contact information above. Management: James Moody, Publisher. Amy Johnson, Advertising. Cathy Smith, Advertising Director. Editorial: Joy Cressler, Editor.

JOSHUA STAR. 319 N. Burleson Blvd., Burleson, TX 76028. Telephone: 817-295-0486. FAX: 817-295-5278. E-MAIL: joshuastar@thestargroup.com. URL: http://www.thestargroup.com. Mailing Address: PO Box 909, Burleson, TX 76097-0909. Pub. Frequency: w. (Thu.) Page Size: broadsheet. Subscrip. Rate: $.50 newsstand/cover; $18/yr in county. Circulation: 2,000 per issue (paid). Owner(s): The Star Group, See address and contact information above. Management: James Moody, Publisher. Amy Johnson, Advertising. Cathy Smith, Advertising Director. Editorial: Leslie Stewart, Editor.

KEENE STAR. 319 N. Burleson Blvd., Burleson, TX 76028. Telephone: 817-295-0486. FAX: 817-295-5278. E-MAIL: keenestar@thestargroup.com. URL: www.thestargroup.com. Mailing Address: PO Box 909, Burleson, TX 76097-0909. Year Established: 1993. Pub. Frequency: w. (Thu.) Page Size: broadsheet. Subscrip. Rate: $.50 newsstand/cover; $18/yr in county. Circulation: 1,500 per issue (paid). Owner(s): The Star Group, See address and contact information above. Management: James Moody, Publisher. Amy Johnson, Advertising. Cathy Smith, Advertising Director. Editorial: Paul Gnadt, Editor.

SOUTH TARRANT STAR. 319 N. Burleson Blvd., Burleson, TX 76028. Telephone: 817-295-0486. FAX: 817-295-5278. E-MAIL: ads@thestargroup.com. URL: http://www.thestargroup.com. Mailing Address: PO Box 909, Burleson, TX 76097-0909. Pub. Frequency: w. (Mon.) Page Size: broadsheet. Subscrip. Rate: $.50 newsstand/cover; $18/yr in county. Circulation: 1,000 per issue (paid). Owner(s): The Star Group, See address and contact information above. Management: James Moody, Publisher. Cathy Smith, Advertising Director. Editorial: Lisa Urban, Editor.

BURNET

BURNET BULLETIN. 1001 Buchanan Dr., Ste. 2, Burnet, TX 78611. Telephone: 512-756-6136. FAX: 512-756-8911. E-MAIL: burnetbulletin@281.com. Mailing Address: PO Box 160, Burnet, TX 78611. Year Established: 1873. Pub. Frequency: w. (Wed.) Page Size: broadsheet. Subscrip. Rate: $.50 newsstand/cover; $26/yr mailed in county; $36/yr mailed out of county. Circulation: 3,000 per issue (paid). Owner(s): American Consolidated Media, Inc., 1420 N. Mockingbird Ln, Ste 100, Dallas, TX 75247. Telephone: 214-691-1066. FAX: 214-691-4086. Management: Stan Woody, Publisher. Editorial: Chris Crews, Editor.

CALDWELL

BURLESON COUNTY TRIBUNE. 306 W. Hwy. 21, Caldwell, TX 77836-1122. Telephone: 979-567-3286. FAX: 979-567-7898. E-MAIL: news@bctribune.com. URL: http://www.bctribune.com. Year Established: 1884. Pub. Frequency: w. (Thu.) Page Size: broadsheet. Subscrip. Rate: $1 newsstand/cover; $32/yr mailed in county; $37/yr mailed in state; $43/yr mailed out of state. Adv. Rate: col. inch $7.85 Circulation: 4,300 per issue (paid). Owner(s): Burleson County Publishing Co., See address and contact information above. Management: Sam Preuss, Publisher. Editorial: Roy Sanders, Managing Editor.

CAMERON

CAMERON HERALD, THE. 108 E. First St., Cameron, TX 76520. Telephone: 254-697-6671. FAX: 254-697-4902. E-MAIL: herald@cameronherald.com. URL: http://www.cameronherald.com. Mailing Address: PO Box 1230, Cameron, TX 76520. Year Established: 1860. Pub. Frequency: w. (Thu.) Page Size: broadsheet. Subscrip. Rate: $.75 newsstand/cover; $29/yr mailed in county; $34/yr mailed out of county; $40/yr mailed out of state. Circulation: 4,000 per issue (paid). Owner(s): Granite Publications, PO Box 1010, Taylor, TX 75674. Telephone: 830-693-3334. Management: Richard Stone, Publisher. Marie Bakken, Classified Adv. Mgr.. Editorial: Richard Stone, Editor. Mike Peck, Managing Editor.

CANYON

CANYON NEWS. 1500 Fifth Ave., Canyon, TX 79015. Telephone: 806-655-7121. FAX: 806-655-0823. E-MAIL: cnews@canyonnews.com. URL: http://www.canyonnews.com. Year Established: 1896. Pub. Frequency: s-w. (Thu. & Sun) Page Size: broadsheet. Subscrip. Rate: $.75 newsstand/cover; $36/yr home delivery local (effective 2005); $42/yr elsewhere. Adv. Rate: col. inch $5.85 Circulation: 4,100 per issue (paid and free). Owner(s): Randall County Publishing Co., See address and contact information above. Management: Brad Tooley, President. Debbie Aylesworth, Advertising Manager. David Baum, Circulation Manager. Katy Ely, Classified Adv. Mgr.. Editorial: Greg Jaklewicz, Editor. Tim Ritter, Sports.

CARTHAGE

PANOLA WATCHMAN. 109 W. Panola St., Carthage, TX 75633. Telephone: 903-693-7888. FAX: 903-693-5857. E-MAIL: pwatchman@dctexas.net. Year Established: 1873. Pub. Frequency: s-w. (Wed. & Sun.) Page Size: standard. Subscrip. Rate: $.50 newsstand/cover; $35/yr in county; $47/yr out of county. Circulation: 4,028 per issue (paid). Owner(s): Westward Communications LLC, 907B E. Main St., Humble, TX 77338. Telephone: 281-446-5929. Management: Bill Holder, Publisher. Lynnette Jeans, Advertising Manager. Kay Sapaugh, Circulation Manager. Editorial: Ted Leach, Sports.

CEDAR PARK

HILL COUNTRY NEWS. 103 Woods Ln., Cedar Park, TX 78613. Telephone: 512-259-4449. FAX: 512-259-8889. URL: http://www.hillcountry.com. Mailing Address: PO Box 1777, Cedar Park, TX 78630. Year Established: 1967. Pub. Frequency: s-w. (Wed. & Fri.) Page Size: standard. Subscrip. Rate: $.50 newsstand/cover; $30/yr in county; $60/yr mailed out of county. Circulation: 33,000 per issue (paid and free). Owner(s): Sweat Equity Newspapers, Inc., See address and contact information above. Management: Don Moore, Publisher. Deborah Mathison, Advertising Manager. Shelley Mulligan, Classified Adv. Mgr.. Editorial: Tamra Spence, Editor. Robert Thomas, Sports Editor.

CENTER

LIGHT & CHAMPION. 137 San Augustine St., Center, TX 75935. Telephone: 936-598-3377. FAX: 936-598-6394. E-MAIL: cvelvin@qzip.net. Mailing Address: PO Box 1989, Center, TX 75935. Year Established: 1877. Pub. Frequency: s-w. (Tue. & Fri.) Page Size: broadsheet. Subscrip. Rate: $.75 newsstand/cover; $40/yr in county; $59/yr mailed elsewhere. Circulation: 4,000 per issue (paid). Owner(s): PTS Inc., 221A 35th St., N.E., Fort Payne, AL 35967. Management: JoAnna Martin, Publisher. Lee Jenkins, Circulation Manager. Editorial: John Krueger, Editor.

CHILDRESS

CHILDRESS INDEX. 226 Main St., Childress, TX 79201. Telephone: 940-937-2525. FAX: 940-937-2239. E-MAIL: index@chipshot.net. Year Established: 1888. Pub. Frequency: 3/w. (Tue., Thu., Sun.) Page Size: standard. Subscrip. Rate: $.50 newsstand/cover; $42/yr carrier delivery; $46/yr mailed out of county. Wire Service(s): AP. Circulation: 2,900 Sunday (paid); 2,900 per issue (paid). Owner(s): Childress Index, Inc., See address and contact information above. Management: Clemi Higley Blackburn, Publisher. Anna Burchell, Advertising Manager. Ryan Mills, Circulation Manager. Callie Decker, Classified Adv. Mgr..

CISCO

CISCO PRESS. 700 Conrad Hilton Ave., Cisco, TX 76437. Telephone: 254-442-2244. FAX: 254-629-2092. Mailing Address: PO Box 29, Eastland, TX 76448-0029. Year Established: 1870. Pub. Frequency: s-w. (Thu. & Sun.) Page Size: broadsheet. Subscrip. Rate: $.50 newsstand/cover; $23/yr mailed in county; $28/yr mailed in state; $40/yr mailed out of state. Freelance Pay: $5/article. Circulation: 2,000 per issue (paid). Owner(s): Eastland County Newspapers, Inc., 215 S. Seaman St, Eastland, TX 76448. Telephone: 254-629-1707. Management: Gaynell O'Brien, Co-Publisher. Gary Grady, Advertising Manager. Margaret Hallmark, Circulation Manager. Editorial: Ladonna Latham, Editor.

CLARKSVILLE

CLARKSVILLE TIMES, THE. ISSN 1040-2489 106 E. Main St., Clarksville, TX 75426. Telephone: 903-427-5616. FAX: 903-427-3068. E-MAIL: ctimes@classicnet.net. URL: http://www.clarksvillenews.net. Mailing Address: PO Box 1018, Clarksville, TX 75426. Year Established: 1875. Pub. Frequency: w. (Thu.) Page Size: broadsheet. Subscrip. Rate: $.50 newsstand/cover; $20/yr in county; $28/yr out of county. Freelance Pay: $50/story. Circulation: 3,250 per issue (paid). Owner(s): Red River Media, See address and contact information above. Editorial: Bryan Giguree, Managing Editor. Bruce Williams, Sports.

CLEVELAND

CLEVELAND ADVOCATE. 106 W Hanson St, Cleveland, TX 77328. Telephone: 281-592-2626. FAX: 281-592-2629. E-MAIL: charris@hcnonline.com. URL: http://www.clevelandadvocate.com. Year Established: 1917. Pub. Frequency: w. (Wed.) Page Size: broadsheet. Subscrip. Rate: $.50 newsstand/cover; $24.50/yr home delivery in county; $27.50/yr home delivery out of county. Circulation: 4,524 per issue (paid). **Owner(s):** ASP Westward LP, 523 N Sam Houston Pkwy E.Ste 600, Houston, TX 77060-4011. Telephone: 281-668-1100. **Management:** Dianne Brady, General Manager. Clayton Harris, Publisher. **Editorial:** Vanesa Bradhier, Editor.

DAYTON NEWS. 106 W Hanson St, Cleveland, TX 77328. Telephone: 281-592-2626. FAX: 281-592-2629. E-MAIL: dnewseditor@hcnonline.com. URL: http://www.hcnonline.com/site/news.asp?brd=1574&nav_sec=72138. Pub. Frequency: w. (Wed.) Page Size: broadsheet. **Owner(s):** ASP Westward LP, 523 N Sam Houston Pkwy E.Ste 600, Houston, TX 77060-4011. Telephone: 281-668-1100. **Management:** Dianne Brady, General Manager. Clayton Harris, Publisher. **Editorial:** Mike George, Editor.

EASTEX ADVOCATE. 106 W Hanson St, Cleveland, TX 77328. Telephone: 281-592-2626. E-MAIL: charris@hcnonline.com. URL: http://www.hcnonline.com. Pub. Frequency: w. (Wed.) Page Size: broadsheet. **Owner(s):** ASP Westward LP, 523 N Sam Houston Pkwy Ste, 600, Houston, TX 77060-4011. **Management:** Dianne Brady, General Manager. Clayton Harris, Publisher. **Editorial:** Vanesa Bradhier, Editor.

COLEMAN

COLEMAN CHRONICLE & DEMOCRAT VOICE. 208 W. Pecan, Coleman, TX 76834. Telephone: 325-625-4128. FAX: 325-625-4129. E-MAIL: dvoice@web-access.net. URL: http://www.colemanpaper.com. Mailing Address: PO Box 840, Coleman, TX 76834. Year Established: 1881. Pub. Frequency: s-w. (Tue. & Thu.) Page Size: broadsheet. Subscrip. Rate: $.50 newsstand/cover; $29.95/yr mailed in county; $32.95/yr mailed out of county; $41.95/yr mailed elsewhere. Circulation: 3,100 per issue (paid). **Owner(s):** Brett and Evan Autry, See address and contact information above. **Management:** Ken Autry, Co-Publisher. Brett Autry, Publisher. **Editorial:** Ken Autry, Managing Editor.

COLUMBUS

BANNER PRESS NEWSPAPER, THE. ISSN 0891-1118
1217 Bowie St., Columbus, TX 78934. Telephone: 979-732-6243. FAX: 979-732-6245. E-MAIL: banner@industryinet.com. Year Established: 1985. Pub. Frequency: w. (Thu.) Page Size: broadsheet. Subscrip. Rate: $.75 newsstand/cover; $30/yr in county; $35/yr mailed in state; $40/yr mailed out of state. Adv. Rate: col. inch $4.50 Circulation: 4,500 per issue (paid). **Owner(s):** McFerg Industries, PO Box 490, Columbus, TX 78934-0490. Telephone: 979-732-6243. **Management:** Chad Ferguson, Owner. **Editorial:** Chad Ferguson, Editor.

COMANCHE

COMANCHE CHIEF, THE. 205 W. Grand St., Comanche, TX 76442. Telephone: 325-356-2636. FAX: 325-356-5380. Year Established: 1873. Pub. Frequency: w. (Thu.) Page Size: broadsheet. Subscrip. Rate: $.50 newsstand/cover; $20/yr mailed in county; $22.50/yr mailed out of county; $25/yr mailed out of state. Circulation: 4,300 per issue (paid). **Owner(s):** James C. & Mary Wilkerson, See address and contact information above. **Management:** James C. Wilkerson, Publisher. **Editorial:** James C. Wilkerson, Editor. Lance Wilkerson, Associate Editor.

COPPELL

CITIZENS' ADVOCATE. 446 W. Bethel Rd., Coppell, TX 75019-4416. Telephone: 972-462-8192. FAX: 972-304-0203. Mailing Address: PO Box 557, Coppell, TX 75019-0557. Year Established: 1984. Pub. Frequency: w. (Fri.) Page Size: standard.Subscrip. Rate: $.35 newsstand/cover; $20/yr Circulation: 5,500 per issue (paid). **Owner(s):** Dan Mara Inc., See address and contact information above. **Management:** Jean Murph, Publisher. **Editorial:** Jean Murph, Editor.

COPPERAS COVE

COPPERAS COVE LEADER-PRESS. PO Box 370, Copperas Cove, TX 76522. Telephone: 254-547-4207. FAX: 254-542-3299. E-MAIL: news@coveleaderpress.com. URL: http://www.coveleaderpress.com. Mailing Address: PO Box 370, Copperas Cove, TX 76522-0370. Year Established: 1894. Pub. Frequency: s-w. (Tue. & Fri.) Page Size: broadsheet. Subscrip. Rate: $.50 newsstand/cover; $36/yr local; $75/yr in state; $85/yr out of state. Adv. Rate: col. inch $6.75 Freelance Pay: $25/story. Circulation: 3,100 per issue (paid). **Owner(s):** Larry Hauk, See address and contact information above. **Management:** Larry Hauk, Publisher. Joyce Hauk, Advertising Manager. **Editorial:** Crystal McCoy, News Editor. John Eubanks, Sports Editor.Readers: For the residents of Copperas Cove.

CORRIGAN

CORRIGAN TIMES, THE. 202 E. Front St., Corrigan, TX 75939. Telephone: 936-398-2535. FAX: 936-398-2536. URL: http://www.easttexasnews.com. Mailing Address: PO Box 1115, Corrigan, TX 75939. Year Established: 1954. Pub. Frequency: w. (Thu.) Page Size: broadsheet. Subscrip. Rate: $.50 newsstand/cover; $14/yr in county; $17/yr in state; $21/yr out of state. Adv. Rate: col. inch $4.34 Circulation: 1,450 per issue (paid). **Owner(s):** Polk County Publishing Co., PO Box 1276, Livingston, TX 77351. Telephone: 936-327-4357. **Management:** Alvin Holley, Publisher. Pam Smith, Advertising. **Editorial:** Kim Popham, Editor.

CRANE

CRANE NEWS. 401 S. Gaston, Crane, TX 79731. Telephone: 432-558-3541. FAX: 432-558-2676. E-MAIL: cranenews@apex2000.net. Year Established: 1947. Pub. Frequency: w. (Thu.) Page Size: broadsheet. Subscrip. Rate: $.50 newsstand/cover; $18/yr in county; $21/yr mailed in state; $24/yr mailed out of state. Adv. Rate: col. inch $6 Circulation: 1,500 per issue (paid). **Owner(s):** News Publishing Co., See address and contact information above. **Management:** Clara Greer, Publisher. **Editorial:** Clara Greer, Editor.

CROCKETT

HOUSTON COUNTY COURIER. ISSN 1090-9990
102 S. Seventh St, Crockett, TX 75835. Telephone: 936-544-2238. FAX: 936-544-4088. E-MAIL: hccnews@lcc.net. URL: http://www.houstoncountycourier.com/. Mailing Address: PO Box 551, Crockett, TX 75835. Year Established: 1890. Pub. Frequency: s-w. (Thu. & Sun.) Page Size: broadsheet. Subscrip. Rate: $.50 newsstand/cover; $25/yr mailed in county; $28/yr mailed out of county; $32/yr mailed out of state. Circulation: 5,500 per issue (paid). **Owner(s):** Polk County Publishing Co., PO Box 1276, Livingston, TX 77351. **Management:** Jeannine Rhone, General Manager. Alvin Holley, Publisher. James Kerby, Advertising Manager. **Editorial:** Larry Lamb, Sports.

CUERO

CUERO RECORD. 119 E. Main St., Cuero, TX 77954. Telephone: 361-275-3464. FAX: 361-275-3131. E-MAIL: crecord@tisd.net. URL: http://www.cuerorecord.com. Mailing Address: PO Box 351, Cuero, TX 77954. Year Established: 1894. Pub. Frequency: w. (Wed.) Page Size: broadsheet. Subscrip. Rate: $.50 newsstand/cover; $24/yr mailed in county; $29/yr mailed out of county. Circulation: 3,600 per issue (paid). **Owner(s):** Hartman Newspapers, Inc., See address and contact information above. **Management:** Glenn Rea, Publisher. Pam Pritchett, Advertising Manager. Kerry Lott, Circulation Manager. **Editorial:** Glenn Rea, Editor.

DALHART

DALHART TEXAN. 410 Denrock Ave., Dalhart, TX 79022. Telephone: 806-244-4511. FAX: 806-244-2395. E-MAIL: daltexan@xit.net. Year Established: 1901. Pub. Frequency: w. (Mon., Wed., Fri.) Page Size: broadsheet. Subscrip. Rate: $.50 newsstand/cover; $60/yr carrier delivery; $75/yr mailed. Circulation: 2,500 evening (paid). **Owner(s):** Susan J. Clay, See address and contact information above. **Management:** Susan J. Clay, Publisher. Tammy Cruze, Advertising Manager. **Editorial:** Jean McDaniel, Editor.

DALLAS

DALLAS OBSERVER. ISSN 0732-0299
2501 Oak Lawn Ave, Dallas, TX 75201. Telephone: 214-757-9000. FAX: 214-757-8590. E-MAIL: letters@dallasobserver.com. URL: http://www.dallasobserver.com. Mailing Address: PO Box 190289, Dallas, TX 75219-0289. Pub. Frequency: w. (Thu.) Page Size: standard Circulation: 110,000 per issue (free). **Owner(s):** Village Voice Media, Inc., 1201 E Jefferson St, Phoenix, AZ 85034. Telephone: 415-541-0700. FAX: 415-541-9096. **Management:** Stuart Folb, Publisher. Carlos Garcia, Circulation Director. Randy Frasier, Circulation Manager. Dan Hyer, Classified Adv. Mgr.. Amy Hite, Sales Manager. **Editorial:** Julie Lyons, Editor. Patrick Williams, Managing Editor.

DALLAS WHITE ROCKER NEWS. ISSN 1049-3387
10809 Garland Rd., Dallas, TX 75218-0698. Telephone: 214-327-9335. FAX: 214-327-9374. Year Established: 1945. Pub. Frequency: w. (Thu.) Page Size: broadsheet. Subscrip. Rate: $.50 newsstand/cover; $25/yr in county; $44 for 2 yrs.; $25/yr out of county; $19/yr local to senior citizens. Freelance Pay: $1.25/column-inch. Circulation: 4,008 per issue (paid). **Owner(s):** Retta Hanie, See address and contact information above. **Management:** Retta Hanie, Publisher. Frances Gunter, Advertising Manager. **Editorial:** Retta Hanie, Editor. Bob Hanie, Photographer. Anthony Jones, Writer.

JACKSON COUNTRY TIMES-JOURNAL, THE. 1420 W Mockingbird Ln, Ste 100, Dallas, TX 75247-4932. Telephone: 214-540-6312. FAX: 214-751-3930. E-MAIL: info@timesjournal.com. URL: http://www.timesjournal.com. Year Established: 1847. Pub. Frequency: 3/w. (Sun., Tue., Thu.) Page Size: broadsheet. Subscrip. Rate: $.50 newsstand/cover; $.75 newsstand/cover Sun.; $57.50/yr home delivery in county; $94/yr mailed out of county. Adv. Rate: col. inch $10.95 Circulation: 5,500 per issue (paid). **Owner(s):** A C M dba A C M Ohio LLC, See address and contact information above. **Management:** Norman Gilliland, Publisher. Teresa Maynard, Advertising Manager. Kristina Sexton, Circulation Manager. Sandra Leonard, Classified Adv. Mgr.. Tracy Royster, Business Manager. **Editorial:** Phillip Buffington, Assistant Editor. James Leonard, Graphics Editor. Paul Boggs, Sports Editor.Readers: Community

OAK CLIFF TRIBUNE. PO Box 4650, Dallas, TX 75208. E-MAIL: octrib@sbcglobal.net. Year Established: 1903. Pub. Frequency: w. (Thu.) Page Size: tabloid. Subscrip. Rate: $.50 newsstand/cover; $30/yr in county. Adv. Rate: col. inch $14.75 Circulation: 4,100 per issue (paid). **Owner(s):** Oak Cliff Tribune Ltd., 1005 W. Jefferson Blvd., Ste. 103, Dallas, TX 75208. Telephone: 214-943-7755. FAX: 214-943-7775. **Management:** Mark Housewright, Publisher. **Editorial:** Allison Pless, Managing Editor.

PARK CITIES NEWS. 8115 Preston Rd., Ste 120, Dallas, TX 75225. Telephone: 214-3697570. FAX: 214-369-7736. E-MAIL: pcn@parkcitiesnews.com. URL: http://www.parkcitiesnews.com. Year Established: 1938. Pub. Frequency: w. (Thu.) Page Size: broadsheet. Subscrip. Rate: $.50 newsstand/cover; $29/yr in county; $34/yr in state; $48/yr mailed out of state. Adv. Rate: col. inch $35 Circulation: 25,000 per issue (paid). **Owner(s):** Marjorie B. Waters, See address and contact information above. **Management:** Marjorie B. Waters, Publisher. **Editorial:** Thomas R. Waters, Editor. Peter Waters, Managing Editor.

DECATUR

WISE COUNTY MESSENGER. ISSN 0746-8679
115 S. Trinity, Decatur, TX 76234-0149. Telephone: 940-627-5987. FAX: 940-627-1004. E-MAIL: news@wcmessenger.com. URL: http://www.wcmessenger.com. Year Established: 1880. Pub. Frequency: s-w. (Thu. & Sun.) Page Size: broadsheet. Subscrip. Rate: $.50 newsstand/cover; $30/yr in county; $35/yr out of county; $40/yr out of state. Adv. Rate: col. inch $6 Circulation: 7,000 per issue (paid). **Owner(s):** Wise County Messenger, Inc., PO Box 149, Decatur, TX 76234. Telephone: 940-627-5987. FAX: 940-627-1004. **Management:** Mark Jordan, General Manager. Roy Eaton, President. Lisa Davis, Advertising Manager. Jeannine Eaton, Business Manager. **Editorial:** Skip Nichols, Editor. Robert Morgan, Sports.

DENISON

BRYAN SHOPPER. 331 W. Woodard St., Denison, TX 75021. Telephone: 903-465-7171. FAX: 903-465-1453. Year Established: 1976. Pub. Frequency: w. (Wed.) Page Size: tabloid Circulation: 17,000 per issue (free). **Owner(s):** Stephens Media LLC, 1111 W. Bonanza Rd., Las Vegas, NV 89106. Telephone: 702-383-0211. FAX: 702-383-4676. **Management:** Richard White, Publisher. Ken Langford, Classified Adv. Mgr..

GRAYSON COUNTY SHOPPER. 331 W. Woodard St., Denison, TX 75020. Telephone: 903-465-1400. FAX: 903-465-1453. E-MAIL: rwhite@graysoncountyshopper.com. Mailing Address: PO Box 329, Denison, TX 75021. Year Established: 1970. Pub. Frequency: w. (Wed.) Page Size: tabloid Circulation: 52,600 per issue (free). **Owner(s):** Stephens Media LLC, 111 W. Bonanza Rd., Las Vegas, NV 89103. Telephone: 702-383-0211. **Management:** Richard White, Publisher.

SHOPPER (DENISON), THE. 331 Westwoodard, Denison, TX 75020. Telephone: 903-465-1400. FAX: 903-465-1453. Mailing Address: PO Box 1249, Denison, TX 75020. Year Established: 1986. Pub. Frequency: w. (Wed.) Page Size: tabloid Circulation: 50,600 per issue (free). **Owner(s):** Stevens Media Group, 1111 W Bonanza Rd, Las Vegas, NV 89106. Telephone: 702-383-0211. **Management:** Richard White, Publisher. **Editorial:** Richard White, Editor.

DESOTO

CEDAR HILL TODAY. 1701 N. Hampton, Ste. C, Desoto, TX 75115. Telephone: 972-298-4211. FAX: 972-298-6369. E-MAIL: addirector@todaynewspaper.net. URL: http://www.todaynewspapers.net. Year Established: 1965. Pub. Frequency: w. (Thu.) Page Size: standard. Subscrip. Rate: $.50 newsstand/cover; $25/yr in city; $33/yr out of city. Circulation: 3,000 per issue (paid and free). **Owner(s):** Richard Collins, PO Box 381029, Duncanville, TX 75138. Telephone: 972-298-4211. FAX: 972-298-6369. **Management:** Richard Collins, Publisher. Kim Petty, Advertising Manager. Ron Midkiff, Circulation Manager. **Editorial:** Kirk Dickey, Editor. Robin Gooch, Managing Editor. Loyd Brumfield, News Editor.

DESOTO TODAY. 1701 N. Hampton, Ste. C, Desoto, TX 75115. Telephone: 972-298-4211. FAX: 972-298-6369. E-MAIL: addirector@todaynewspapers.net. URL: http://www.todaynewspapers.net. Year Established: 1977. Pub. Frequency: w. (Thu.) Page Size: broadsheet. Subscrip. Rate: $.50 newsstand/cover; $25/yr in county; $33/yr out of county. Freelance Pay: $25/story. Circulation: 8,200 per issue (paid and free). **Owner(s):** Richard Collins, See address and contact information above. **Management:** Richard Collins, Publisher. Kim Petty, Advertising Director. Ron Midkiff, Circulation Manager. **Editorial:** Daphne Brown, Editor.

DUNCANVILLE TODAY. ISSN 0888-1960
1701 N. Hampton, Ste. C, Desoto, TX 75115. Telephone: 972-298-4211. FAX: 972-298-6369. E-MAIL: addirector@todaynewspapers.net. URL: http://www.todaynewspapers.net. Mailing Address: PO Box 381029, Duncanville, TX 75138-1029. Year Established: 1960. Pub. Frequency: w. (Thu.) Page Size: broadsheet. Subscrip. Rate: $.50 newsstand/cover; $25/yr in county; $33/yr out of county. Circulation: 10,179 per issue (paid and free). **Owner(s):** Richard Collins, See address and contact information above. **Management:** Richard Collins, Publisher. Kim Petty, Advertising Director. Ron Midkiff, Circulation Manager. **Editorial:** Mark Robinson, Editor. Angel Morris, News Editor.

LANCASTER TODAY. ISSN 1065-0644
1701 N. Hampton, Ste. C, Desoto, TX 75115. Telephone: 972-298-4211. FAX: 972-298-6369. E-MAIL: addirector@todaynewspaper.net. URL: http://www.todaynews.net. Mailing Address: PO Box 381029, Duncanville, TX 75138. Year Established: 1975. Pub. Frequency: w. (Thu.) Page Size: standard. Subscrip. Rate: $.50 newsstand/cover; $25/yr in city; $33/yr out of city. Circulation: 4,500 per issue (paid and free). **Owner(s):** Richard Collins, See address and contact information above. **Management:** Richard Collins, Publisher. Kim Petty, Advertising Manager. Ron Midkiff, Circulation Manager. **Editorial:** Steve Snyder, Editor. Robin Gooch, Editorial Advisor.

DIBOLL

FREE PRESS (DIBOLL), THE. 207 N. Temple Dr., Diboll, TX 75941. Telephone: 936-829-1801. FAX: 936-829-1811. E-MAIL: croach@freepress.com. Year Established: 1952. Pub. Frequency: w. (Thu.) Page Size: broadsheet. Subscrip. Rate: $.50 newsstand/cover; $20/yr in county; $26/yr mailed out of county. Circulation: 3,561 per issue (paid). **Owner(s):** Temple-Inland, Inc., See address and contact information above. **Management:** Candace Velvin, Publisher. Rebecca Herchman, Advertising Manager. Christy Roach, Circulation Manager. **Editorial:** Candace Velvin, Editor.

DRIFTWOOD

NEWS-DISPATCH, THE. ISSN 0746-603X
1000 Rolling Oaks, Driftwood, TX 78619. Telephone: 512-842-1117. FAX: 512-847-1590. E-MAIL: redrob37@aol.com. Mailing Address: PO Box 227, Driftwood, TX 78619. Year Established: 1982. Pub. Frequency: w. (Thu.) Page Size: broadsheet. Subscrip. Rate: $.50 newsstand/cover; $25/yr in county; $30/yr in state; $35/yr out of state. Adv. Rate: col. inch $6.77 Circulation: 2,000 per issue (paid). **Owner(s):** Dale Roberson, See address and contact information above. **Management:** Dale Roberson, Publisher. Joyce Roberson, Circulation Manager. **Editorial:** Dale Roberson, Editor-in-Chief.

DUMAS

MOORE COUNTY NEWS-PRESS. 702 S Meredith St, Dumas, TX 79029. Telephone: 806-935-4111. FAX: 806-935-2348. E-MAIL: lreynolds@moorenews.com. URL: http://www.moorenews.com. Mailing Address: PO Box 757, Dumas, TX 79029. Year Established: 1927. Pub. Frequency: s-w. (Thu. & Sun.) Page Size: broadsheet. Subscrip. Rate: $.75 newsstand/cover; $47.25/yr carrier delivery in county; $63/yr mailed out of county. Freelance Pay: $0.30/column-inch. Circulation: 4,100 per issue (paid and free). **Owner(s):** Lancaster Management, Inc., 645 Walnut St., Gadsden, AL 35901. Telephone: 256-543-3417. **Management:** Wanda Brooks, Publisher. Robin Brooks, Advertising. **Editorial:** Michael Wright, Managing Editor. Jim Merriott, Sports Editor.

DUNCANVILLE

GRAND PRAIRIE. PO Box 381029, Duncanville, TX 75138. E-MAIL: addirector@todaynewspapers.net. URL: http://www.todaynewspapers.net. Year Established: 1968. Pub. Frequency: w. (Thu.) Page Size: broadsheet. Subscrip. Rate: $.50 newsstand/cover; $25/yr in city; $33/yr out of city. Circulation: 2,000 per issue (paid). **Owner(s):** Richard Collins, 1701 N. Hampton, Ste. C, Desoto, TX 75115. Telephone: 972-298-4211. FAX: 972-298-6369. **Management:** Kim Petty, Advertising Manager. Ron Midkiff, Circulation Manager. **Editorial:** Samuel Smith, Editor. Robin Gooch, Managing Editor.

EAGLE LAKE

EAGLE LAKE HEADLIGHT. PO Box 67, Eagle Lake, TX 77434. Telephone: 979-234-5521. FAX: 979-234-5522. E-MAIL: eaglelakeheadlight@bcglobal.net. Year Established: 1903. Pub. Frequency: w. (Thu.) Page Size: broadsheet. Subscrip. Rate: $.50 newsstand/cover; $15.50/yr in county; $17/yr out of county; $20/yr out of state. Adv. Rate: col. inch $3.60 Circulation: 2,200 per issue (paid). **Owner(s):** Bruce Beal, See address and contact information above. **Management:** James Sweet, Publisher. **Editorial:** Douglas Beal, Editor.

EAGLE PASS

EAGLE PASS NEWS GUIDE. 1342 Main St, Eagle Pass, TX 78852. Telephone: 830-773-2309. FAX: 830-773-3398. URL: epnewsguide@sbcglobal.net. Mailing Address: PO Box 764, Eagle Pass, TX 78853. Year Established: 1886. Pub. Frequency: s-w. (Thu. & Sun.) Page Size: standard. Subscrip. Rate: $.50 newsstand/cover; $19.50/yr mailed in county; $34.50/yr mailed in state; $38.50/yr mailed out of state. Adv. Rate: col. inch $4.41 Circulation: 5,000 per issue (paid). **Owner(s):** Guide Publishing Co., See address and contact information above. **Management:** Cathleen McBeath, Publisher. Blake McBeath, Advertising Manager.

EASTLAND

EASTLAND TELEGRAM. 215 S. Seaman St, Eastland, TX 76448. Telephone: 254-629-1707. FAX: 254-629-2092. E-MAIL: telegram@texascountry.net. Mailing Address: PO Box 29, Eastland, TX 76448-0029. Year Established: 1968. Pub. Frequency: s-w. (Thu. & Sun.) Page Size: broadsheet. Subscrip. Rate: $.50 newsstand/cover; $23/yr mailed in county; $28/yr mailed out of county. Adv. Rate: col. inch $6 Circulation: 2,200 per issue (paid). **Owner(s):** Eastland County Newspapers, Inc., See address and contact information above. **Management:** Gaynell O'Brien, Co-Publisher. Gary Grady, Advertising Manager. **Editorial:** H.V. O'Brien, Editor.

RANGER TIMES. 215 S. Seaman St, Eastland, TX 76448. Telephone: 254-629-1707. FAX: 254-629-2092. Mailing Address: PO Box 29, Eastland, TX 76448-0029. Year Established: 1919. Pub. Frequency: s-w. (Thu. & Sun.) Page Size: broadsheet. Subscrip. Rate: $.50 newsstand/cover; $23/yr mailed in county; $29/yr mailed out of county; $41/yr mailed out of state. Circulation: 1,000 per issue (paid). **Owner(s):** Eastland County Newspapers, Inc., See address and contact information above. **Management:** Gaynell O'Brien, Co-Publisher. Gary Grady, Advertising Manager. **Editorial:** Margaret Hentrick, Editor.

RISING STAR, THE. 215 S. Seaman St, Eastland, TX 76448. Telephone: 254-629-1707. FAX: 254-629-2092. Year Established: 1892. Pub. Frequency: w. (Thu.) Page Size: standard. Subscrip. Rate: $.50 newsstand/cover; $16/yr mailed in county; $22/yr mailed in state; $23/yr mailed out of state. Circulation: 865 per issue (paid and free). **Owner(s):** Eastland County Newspapers, Inc., See address and contact information above. **Management:** Gaynell O'Brien, Co-Publisher. Gary Grady, Advertising Manager. **Editorial:** Paula Carpenter, Managing Editor.

EDGEWOOD

EDGEWOOD ENTERPRISE. 101 E Houston St., Edgewood, TX 75117. Telephone: 903-962-4275. FAX: 903-962-3660. E-MAIL: vweaver@etcnonline.com. Mailing Address: PO Box 7, Edgewood, TX 75117. Pub. Frequency: w. (Thu.) Page Size: broadsheet. Subscrip. Rate: $.40 newsstand/cover; $19/yr in county; $24.50/yr out of county. Circulation: 700 per issue (paid). **Owner(s):** ASP Westward LP, 523 N Sam Houston Pkwy Ste, 600, Houston, TX 77060-4011. Telephone: 281-446-5979. **Management:** Veta Weaver, General Manager.

EDINBURG

EDINBURG REVIEW. 215 E. University Dr., Edinburg, TX 78539. Telephone: 956-383-2705. FAX: 956-383-3172. E-MAIL: edinrev@aol.com. Mailing Address: PO Box 148, Edinburg, TX 78540-0148. Year Established: 1914. Pub. Frequency: w. (Wed. & Sun.) Page Size: standard. Subscrip. Rate: $5 mailed/mo.. **Wire Service(s):** AP. Circulation: 4,772 evening (paid); 5,000 Sunday (paid). **Owner(s):** Hidalgo Publishing Co., Inc., See address and contact information above. **Management:** Pearl A. Mathis, President. Mari Davis, Classified Adv. Mgr.. **Editorial:** Charlene Rodriguez, Managing Editor.

EDNA

JACKSON COUNTY HERALD-TRIBUNE. 306 N. Wells, Edna, TX 77957. Telephone: 361-782-3547. FAX: 361-782-6002. E-MAIL: jmoser@jacksonconews.com. Mailing Address: PO Box 1099, Edna, TX 77957. Year Established: 1906. Pub. Frequency: w. (Wed.) Page Size: standard. Subscrip. Rate: $.75 newsstand/cover; $25.50/yr in county; $35.50/yr mailed out of county. Circulation: 3,500 per issue (paid). **Owner(s):** Jim Moser, See address and contact information above. **Management:** Jim Moser, Publisher. Pam Harvey, Advertising Manager. **Editorial:** Jim Moser, Editor. Anita Cavazos, Writer.

EL CAMPO

EL CAMPO LEADER-NEWS. 203 E. Jackson, El Campo, TX 77437. Telephone: 979-543-3363. FAX: 979-543-0097. E-MAIL: chris_barbee@leader-news.com. URL: http://www.leader-news.com. Mailing Address: PO Box 1180, El Campo, TX 77437-1180. Year Established: 1885. Pub. Frequency: s-w. (Wed. & Sat.) Page Size: broadsheet. Subscrip. Rate: $.75 newsstand/cover; $34/yr in county; $46/yr out of county. Freelance Pay: $5-$6/article. Circulation: 5,700 per issue (paid). **Owner(s):** El Campo Newspapers, Inc., See address and contact information above. **Management:** Fred V. Barbee Jr., President. Penny Janak, Circulation Manager. Diane David, Classified Adv. Mgr.. **Editorial:** Chris F. Barbee, Editor-in-Chief. Shannonn Crabtree, News Editor. Shawn Price, Sports Editor.

ELDORADO

ELDORADO SUCCESS, THE. 204 S.W. Main St., Eldorado, TX 76936. Telephone: 325-853-3125. FAX: 325-853-3378. E-MAIL: success@myeldorado.net. URL: http://www.myeldorado.net. Mailing Address: PO Box 1115, Eldorado, TX 76936-1115. Pub. Frequency: w. (Thu.) Page Size: broadsheet. Subscrip. Rate: $.75 newsstand/cover; $21.83/yr in county; $27.43/yr mailed out of county. Adv. Rate: col. inch $5 Circulation: 1,100 per issue (paid). **Owner(s):** Masked Rider Publishing, Inc., See address and contact information above. **Management:** Randy Mankin, Publisher. Kathy Mankin, Office Manager. Staci Cortez, Advertising. **Editorial:** Randy Mankin, Editor.

FALFURRIAS

FALFURRIAS FACTS. 219 E. Rice St., Falfurrias, TX 78355. Telephone: 361-325-2200. FAX: 361-325-2200. Year Established: 1906. Pub. Frequency: w. (Thu.) Page Size: broadsheet. Subscrip. Rate: $.50 newsstand/cover; $26/yr home delivery local; $30/yr mailed out of area. Adv. Rate: col. inch $4 Circulation: 2,247 per issue (paid). **Owner(s):** Falfurrias Publishing Co., Inc., See address and contact information above. **Management:** Marcelo Silva, Publisher. SanJuanita Olivarez, Advertising Manager. **Editorial:** Marcelo Silva, Editor.

FLORESVILLE

FLORESVILLE CHRONICLE-JOURNAL. 1433 Third St., Floresville, TX 78114-0820. Telephone: 830-393-2111. FAX: 830-393-9012. E-MAIL: journal@felpsis.net. Mailing Address: PO Box 820, Floresville, TX 78114-0820. Year Established: 1877. Pub. Frequency: w. (Thu.) Page Size: broadsheet. Subscrip. Rate: $.50 newsstand/cover; $24/yr mailed in county; $26/yr mailed out of county; $30/yr mailed out of state. Circulation: 4,320 per issue (paid). **Owner(s):** Thomas Brossat, See address and contact information above. **Management:** Thomas Brossat, Publisher. **Editorial:** Thomas Brossat, Editor.

FLOWER MOUND

ARGYLE MESSENGER, THE. 3121 Cross Timbers Rd, Ste 105, Flower Mound, TX 75028. Telephone: 817-439-3022. FAX: 972-724-2420. URL: http://www.argylemessenger.com. Pub. Frequency: w. (Fri.) Page Size: standard.Subscrip. Rate: $31/yr mailed Circulation: 10,000 per issue (free). **Owner(s):** The/McClatchy Company, 2100 Q St, Sacramento, CA 95816. Telephone: 916-321-1936. FAX: 916-321-1869. **Management:** Bill Lewis, Group Publisher. Carol Odum, Advertising. Jessicca Foster, Classified Adv. Mgr.. **Editorial:** Lyn Pry, Editor. Zach Warner, Sports.

FLOWER MOUND MESSENGER, THE. 3121 Cross Timbers Rd, Ste 105, Flower Mound, TX 75028. Telephone: 817-439-3022. FAX: 972-724-2420. URL: http://www.flowermoundmessenger.com. Pub. Frequency: w. (Fri.) Page Size: standard.Subscrip. Rate: $31/yr mailed Circulation: 7,000 per issue (free). **Owner(s):** The/McClatchy Company, 2100 Q St., Sacramento, CA 95816-6816. **Management:** Bill Lewis, Group Publisher. Carol Odum, Advertising. Jessicca Foster, Classified Adv. Mgr.. **Editorial:** Lyn Pry, Editor. Zach Warner, Sports.

FLOYDADA

FLOYD COUNTY HESPERIAN-BEACON. 111 E. Missouri St., Floydada, TX 79235. Telephone: 806-983-3737. FAX: 806-983-3141. E-MAIL: floydada@amaonline.com. URL: http://www.hesperianbeacon.com. Year Established: 1896. Pub. Frequency: w. (Thu.) Page Size: broadsheet. Subscrip. Rate: $.50 newsstand/cover; $23/yr carrier delivery in county; $25/yr mailed out of county. Circulation: 2,600 per issue (paid). **Owner(s):** Caprock Sentinel Corp., 706 Barton Blvd., Austin, TX 78704. Telephone: 512-443-7918. **Management:** Alice Towery Gilroy, Publisher. Barbara Anderson, Circulation Manager. **Editorial:** Alice Towery Gilroy, Editor.

FORT STOCKTON

FORT STOCKTON PIONEER. ISSN 1077-8659
PO Box 1528, Fort Stockton, TX 79735. Telephone: 432-336-2281. FAX: 432-336-6432. E-MAIL: pioneer@fspioneer.com. URL: http://www.fortstocktonpioneer.com. Year Established: 1908. Pub. Frequency: w. (Thu.) Page Size: broadsheet. Subscrip. Rate: $.75 newsstand/cover; $29/yr mailed local; $36/yr mailed in county; $41/yr mailed in state. Circulation: 3,500 per issue (paid). **Owner(s):** Big Bend Communications, Inc., See address and contact information above. **Management:** Richard Nelson, Publisher. **Editorial:** Richard Nelson, Editor. Kathy Sarabia, Managing Editor.

FORT WORTH

BENBROOK NEWS. 7820 Wyatt Dr., Fort Worth, TX 76108-2533. Telephone: 817-246-2473. FAX: 817-246-2474. Year Established: 1939. Pub. Frequency: w. (Thu.) Page Size: tabloid. Subscrip. Rate: $50/yr. Adv. Rate: B&W page $702 Circulation: 9,500 per issue (paid and free). **Owner(s):** Suburban Newspapers, Inc., 7820 Wyatt Dr., Fort Worth, TX 76108. Telephone: 817-246-2473. **Management:** Robert Underwood, Publisher. **Editorial:** Charlsea Littlefield, Managing Editor.

RIVER OAKS NEWS. 7820 Wyatt Dr., Fort Worth, TX 76108-2533. Telephone: 817-246-2473. FAX: 817-246-2474. Year Established: 1940. Pub. Frequency: w. (Thu.) Page Size: tabloid. Subscrip. Rate: $50/yr mailed out of county. Adv. Rate: col. inch $11 Circulation: 7,500 per issue (free). **Owner(s):** Suburban Newspapers, Inc., 7820 Wyatt Dr., Fort Worth, TX 76108. Telephone: 817-247-2474. **Management:** Robert Underwood III, Owner. **Editorial:** Charlsea Littlefield, Managing Editor.

WHITE SETTLEMENT BOMBER NEWS. 7820 Wyatt Dr., Fort Worth, TX 76108-2533. Telephone: 817-246-2473. FAX: 817-246-2474. Year Established: 1940. Pub. Frequency: w. (Thu.) Page Size: tabloid. Subscrip. Rate: $50/yr mailed out of county. Adv. Rate: page $702 Circulation: 13,000 per issue (paid and free). **Owner(s):** Suburban Newspapers, Inc., 7820 Wyatt Dr., Fort Worth, TX 76108. Telephone: 817-246-2473. **Management:** Robert Underwood, Owner. **Editorial:** Charlsea Littlefield, Managing Editor.

FORTH WORTH

FORT WORTH WEEKLY. 1204-B W. Seventh St., Ste. 20 1, Forth Worth, TX 76102. Telephone: 817-321-9700. FAX: 817-335-9575. URL: http://www.fwweekly.com. Pub. Frequency: w. (Thu.) Page Size: standard Circulation: 65,000 per issue (free). **Owner(s):** Lee Newquist, See address and contact information above. **Management:** Lee Newquist, Publisher. Michael Newquist, Advertising Director. Blair Pearce, Classified Adv. Mgr.. **Editorial:** Gayle Reaves, Editor. Anthony Mariani, Associate Editor.

FREDERICKSBURG

FREDERICKSBURG STANDARD/RADIO POST. ISSN 0747-0061
712 W. Main St., Fredericksburg, TX 78624-0473. Telephone: 830-997-2155. FAX: 830-990-0036. E-MAIL: fbgnews@fredericksburgstandard.com. URL: http://www.fredericksburgstandard.com/. Mailing Address: PO Box 1639, Fredericksburg, TX 78624-0473. Year Established: 1888. Pub. Frequency: w. (Wed.) Page Size: broadsheet. Subscrip. Rate: $.75 newsstand/cover; $31/yr mailed in county & adj. counties; $35/yr mailed in state; $36/yr mailed out of state. Adv. Rate: col. inch $9.65 Circulation: 9,700 per issue (paid). **Owner(s):** Fredericksburg Publishing Co, Inc., PO Box 1639, Fredericksbrg, TX 78624. Telephone: 830-997-2155. FAX: 830-990-0036. **Management:** Terrill D. Collier, President. Kim Jung, Advertising Manager. Sherrie Geistweidt, Circulation Manager. **Editorial:** Cathy Collier, Editor. Yvonne Hartmann, Society Editor.

FREER

FREER PRESS, THE. 309 E. Hahl St., Freer, TX 78357. Telephone: 361-394-7402. FAX: 361-394-5386. E-MAIL: lataine@vsta.com. Year Established: 1981. Pub. Frequency: w. (Wed.) Page Size: broadsheet. Subscrip. Rate: $.50 newsstand/cover; $15/yr in county; $20/yr mailed out of county; $13/yr in county to senior citizens. Adv. Rate: col. inch $3 Circulation: 1,129 per issue (paid and free). **Owner(s):** Tony Morris, See address and contact information above. **Management:** Tony Morris, Publisher. Linda Drennan, Advertising Manager. **Editorial:** Sue Fleming, Editor.

FRISCO

CELINA RECORD. 8820 W Main St, Ste 2000, Frisco, TX 75034. Telephone: 469-633-7777. FAX: 469-633-7779. URL: http://www.ssntx.com. Pub. Frequency: w. (Thu.) Page Size: broadsheet. Subscrip. Rate: $.50 newsstand/cover; $25/yr home delivery local; $39.95/yr mailed in county; $59.95/yr mailed out of county. Circulation: 2,800 per issue (paid). **Owner(s):** Star Community Newspapers, 14875 Landmark Blvd, Ste 110, Addison, TX 75254. Telephone: 972-628-4061. **Management:** Bill Weaver, Publisher. Donna Zarnbiosi, Advertising Manager. **Editorial:** Blaine Crimmins, Managing Editor.

FRISCO ENTERPRISE. 8820 W Main St, Ste 2000, Frisco, TX 75034. Telephone: 469-633-7777. FAX: 469-633-7779. URL: http://www.scntx.com. Pub. Frequency: w. (Fri.) Page Size: broadsheet. Subscrip. Rate: $.50 newsstand/cover; $25/yr home delivery local; $39.95/yr mailed out of county; $59.95/yr mailed out of state. Circulation: 3,500 per issue (paid). **Owner(s):** Star Community Newspapers, 14875 Landmark Blvd, Ste 110, Addison, TX 75254. Telephone: 972-628-4061. **Management:** Bill Weaver, Publisher. Donna Zarnbiosi, Advertising Manager. **Editorial:** Blaine Crimmins, Managing Editor.

GAIL

BORDEN STAR, THE. PO Box 137, Gail, TX 79738. Telephone: 806-756-4313. FAX: 806-756-4310. E-MAIL: kdean@bcisd.net. Year Established: 1972. Pub. Frequency: w. (Wed.) Page Size: tabloid. Subscrip. Rate: $.25 newsstand/cover; $12/yr. Adv. Rate: col. inch $2 Circulation: 450 per issue (paid and free). **Owner(s):** Borden Star, The, See address and contact information above. **Editorial:** Kerri Dean, Managing Editor.

GARLAND

GARLAND MORNING NEWS. ISSN 1045-3997
613 State St., Garland, TX 75040. Telephone: 214-977-8222. FAX: 214-977-7586. E-MAIL: rleszcynski@dallasnews.com. URL: http://www.garlandmorningnews.com. Year Established: 1887. Pub. Frequency: s-w. (Thu. & Sun.) Page Size: standard. Subscrip. Rate: $.50 newsstand/cover; $1.50 Sun.; $31 mailed/mo.. **Owner(s):** Belo Corp., P.O. Box 655237, Dallas, TX 75265-5237. **Management:** Glenn Smith, Advertising Manager. John Halsh, Circulation Manager. **Editorial:** Ray Leszcynski, Editor.

GATESVILLE

GATESVILLE MESSENGER/STAR FORUM, THE. ISSN 0894-4954
116 S. Sixth St., Gatesville, TX 76528. Telephone: 254-865-5212. FAX: 254-865-2361. E-MAIL: editor@gatesvillemessinger.com. URL: http://www.gatesvillemessenger.com. Mailing Address: P.O. Box 799, Gatesville, TX 76528. Year Established: 1881. Pub. Frequency: s-w. (Wed. & Sat.) Page Size: broadsheet. Subscrip. Rate: $.75 newsstand/cover; $30.47/yr mailed in county; $40.63/yr mailed out of county; $49.06/yr mailed out of state. Adv. Rate: col. inch $7.20 Circulation: 4,400 per issue (paid). **Owner(s):** Messenger Publishing Co., See address and contact information above. **Management:** Marshall Day, President. Debbie Day, Office Manager. Danielle Backstrom, Advertising. Chelsi Hall, Advertising Manager. Ashley Pruitt, Circulation Director. Janice Holden, Classified Adv. Mgr.. Larry Kennedy, Assistant Publisher. **Editorial:** Larry Kennedy, Editor. Danielle Backstrom, Composing Room Manager. Ashley Pruitt, Lifestyle Editor. Robert Kent, Sports.

GEORGETOWN

WILLIAMSON COUNTY SUN, THE. 707 Main St., Georgetown, TX 78627-0039. Telephone: 512-930-4824. FAX: 512-863-2474. Mailing Address: PO Box 39, Georgetown, TX 78626. Year Established: 1974. Pub. Frequency: w. (Wed. & Sat.) Page Size: broadsheet. Subscrip. Rate: $.50 newsstand/cover; $32/yr mailed in county; $49/yr mailed out of county. Circulation: 19,300 per issue (paid). **Owner(s):** Linda Scarbrough & Clark Thurmond, See address and contact information above. **Management:** Linda Scarbrough, President. Clark Thurmond, Publisher. **Editorial:** Jane Lane, Editor-in-Chief.

GIDDINGS

GIDDINGS TIMES & NEWS. 170 N. Knox Ave., Giddings, TX 78942. Telephone: 979-542-2222. FAX: 979-542-9410. Mailing Address: PO Box 947, Giddings, TX 78942. Year Established: 1888. Pub. Frequency: w. (Thu.) Page Size: broadsheet. Subscrip. Rate: $1 newsstand/cover; $32/yr in county; $37/yr mailed out of county; $43/yr mailed out of state. Circulation: 6,200 per issue (paid). **Owner(s):** Preuss Printing Co., See address and contact information above. **Management:** David True, General Manager. Buddy Preuss, Publisher. **Editorial:** David True, Editor.

GILMER

GILMER MIRROR. ISSN 8750-0884
214 E. Marshall St., Gilmer, TX 75644-0250. Telephone: 903-843-2503. FAX: 903-843-5123. E-MAIL: info@gilmermirror.com. URL: http://www.gilmermirror.com. Mailing Address: PO Box 250, Gilmer, TX 75644-0250. Year Established: 1877. Pub. Frequency: s-w. (Wed. & Sat.) Page Size: broadsheet. Subscrip. Rate: $.50 newsstand/cover; $27/yr in county; $31/yr in state; $35/yr out of state. Freelance Pay: $0.20/column-inch. Circulation: 4,300 per issue (paid). **Owner(s):** Greeneway Enterprises, PO Box 250, Gilmer, TX 75644. Telephone: 903-843-2503. **Management:** William R. Greene, Publisher. Suzanne Patterson, Advertising Manager. Sandee Gipson, Circulation Manager. Kathy Davidson, Classified Adv. Mgr.. **Editorial:** Mac Overton, News Editor. Russ Greene, Sports. Betty Cook, Womens Interest Editor.

GLADEWATER

GLADEWATER MIRROR. 201 S. Dean St., Gladewater, TX 75647. Telephone: 903-845-2235. FAX: 903-845-2237. E-MAIL: gladewatermirror@aol.com. Mailing Address: PO Box 1549, Gladewater, TX 75647. Year Established: 1949. Pub. Frequency: w. (Wed.) Page Size: broadsheet. Subscrip. Rate: $.50 newsstand/cover; $30/yr in county; $35/yr out of county; $39/yr out of state. Freelance Pay: $0.75/column-inch. Circulation: 1,900 per issue (paid). **Owner(s):** ASP Westward LP, 523 N Sam Houston Pkwy Ste, 600, Houston, TX 77060-4011. **Management:** Jim Bardwell, Publisher. Seria Dassing, Advertising Manager. Tiffany Hobbs, Circulation Manager. **Editorial:** Bob Runyon, Editor.

GLEN ROSE

GLEN ROSE REPORTER. PO Box 2009, Glen Rose, TX 76043. Telephone: 254-897-2282. FAX: 254-897-9423. Year Established: 1887. Pub. Frequency: w. (Thu.) Page Size: broadsheet. Subscrip. Rate: $.50 newsstand/cover; $15/yr mailed local; $20/yr mailed in state; $35/yr mailed out of state. Circulation: 2,900 per issue (paid). **Owner(s):** Glen Rose Publishing Co., See address and contact information above. **Management:** Dan McCarty, Publisher. Barbara Woodward, Advertising Manager. Dan McCarty, Circulation Manager. **Editorial:** Dan McCarty, Editor.

GONZALES

GONZALES INQUIRER. 622 St. Paul St., Gonzales, TX 78629. Telephone: 830-672-2861. FAX: 830-672-7029. E-MAIL: news@gonzalesinquirer.com. URL: http://www.gonzalesinquirer.com. Mailing Address: PO Box 616, Gonzales, TX 78629. Year Established: 1853. Pub. Frequency: s-w. (Tue. & Fri.) Page Size: broadsheet. Subscrip. Rate: $.75 newsstand/cover; $39/yr in county; $44/yr out of county; $64/yr out of state. Circulation: 4,000 per issue (paid). **Owner(s):** Granite Publications, PO Box 1010, Taylor, TX 75674. Telephone: 512-352-1009. **Management:** Jim Cunningham, Publisher. Debbie Toliver, Advertising Manager. Sue Grauke, Circulation Manager. Dorothy Voigt, Classified Editor. **Editorial:** Bob Thaxton, Editor. Mike McCracken, Sports Editor.

Weeklies

GORMAN

GORMAN PROGRESS, THE. PO Box 68, Gorman, TX 76454. Telephone: 254-734-2410. FAX: 254-734-2799. E-MAIL: gprogress@txbusiness.com. Year Established: 1900. Pub. Frequency: w. (Wed.) Page Size: broadsheet. Subscrip. Rate: $.40 newsstand/cover; $15/yr in county; $20/yr mailed in state; $22/yr mailed out of state. Circulation: 1,000 per issue (paid). **Owner(s):** Lonnie Bennett, See address and contact information above. **Management:** Lonnie Bennett, Publisher. **Editorial:** Lonnie Bennett, Editor.

GRAFORD

LAKE COUNTRY SUN. 617 N FM2353 Ste 4, Graford, TX 76449-3106. Telephone: 940-779-3040. FAX: 940-779-3064. E-MAIL: gnipub@brazosnet.com. URL: http://www.lakecountrysun.com. Year Established: 1987. Pub. Frequency: w. (Fri.) Page Size: broadsheet. Subscrip. Rate: $.75 newsstand/cover; $24.99/yr in county; $30.99/yr in state; $36.99/yr out of state. Adv. Rate: col. inch $4.80 Circulation: 1,900 per issue (paid). **Owner(s):** MediaNews Group, Inc., 101 W Colfax Ave, Ste 1100, Denver, CO 80202. FAX: 303-954-6320. **Management:** Roy Robinson, Publisher. **Editorial:** Beth Watson, Managing Editor.

GRAHAM

BRECKENRIDGE AMERICAN. PO Box 600, Graham, TX 76450-0608. Telephone: 940-549-7800. FAX: 940-549-4364. URL: http://www.breckenridgeamerican.com. Year Established: 1920. Pub. Frequency: s-w. (Wed. & Sat.) Page Size: standard. Subscrip. Rate: $.75 newsstand/cover; $30.99/yr in county; $43.99/yr in state. **Owner(s):** Graham Newspapers, Inc., See address and contact information above. MediaNews Group, Inc., 114 E Elm St, Breckenridge, TX 76424. 101 W Colfax Ave, Ste 1100, Denver, CO 80202. FAX: 303-954-6320. **Management:** Roy Robinson, Publisher. Lynna Lobstein, Classified Adv. Mgr.. **Editorial:** Don Treul, Editor.

GRAHAM LEADER. 620 Oak St, Graham, TX 76450. Telephone: 940-549-7800. FAX: 940-549-4364. E-MAIL: editor@grahamleader.com. URL: http://www.grahamleader.com. Year Established: 1876. Pub. Frequency: s-w. (Wed. & Sun.) Page Size: broadsheet. Subscrip. Rate: $.75 newsstand/cover; $29.99/yr in county; $42.99/yr out of county; $61.99/yr out of state. Adv. Rate: col. inch $8.40 Circulation: 4,863 per issue (paid). **Owner(s):** Graham Newspapers, Inc., See address and contact information above. MediaNews Group, Inc., 620 Oak St., Graham, TX 76450-0600. 101 W Colfax Ave, Ste 1100, Denver, CO 80202. FAX: 303-954-6320. **Management:** Roy Robinson, Publisher. Dan Taylor, Advertising Director. Patty Pardue, Circulation Manager. **Editorial:** David Rupkalvis, Editor. Clay Stewart, Sports Editor.

GRANBURY

HOOD COUNTY NEWS. 1501 S. Morgan St., Granbury, TX 76048. Telephone: 800-588-7066. FAX: 817-279-8371. E-MAIL: jtidwell@hcnews.com. URL: http://www.hcnews.com. Mailing Address: P.O. Box 879, Granbury, TX 76048. Year Established: 1886. Pub. Frequency: 3/w. (Tue., Thu., Sat.) Page Size: broadsheet. Subscrip. Rate: $.50 newsstand/cover; $39/yr in county; $59/yr out of county; $79/yr out of state. Circulation: 11,400 per issue (paid). **Owner(s):** Jerry Tidwell, See address and contact information above. **Management:** Jerry Tidwell, Publisher. Mary Jo Whitehead, Advertising Director. **Editorial:** Roger Enlow, Editor. Jerry Tidwell, Editor-in-Chief. Rick Mauch, Sports.

GRAND SALINE

GRAND SALINE SUN. 116 N. Main St., Grand Saline, TX 75140. Telephone: 903-962-4275. FAX: 903-962-3660. E-MAIL: sun@grandsaline.com. URL: http://www.hcnonline.com. Mailing Address: PO Box 608, Grand Saline, TX 75140. Year Established: 1894. Pub. Frequency: w. (Thu.) Page Size: broadsheet. Subscrip. Rate: $.50 newsstand/cover; $21/yr in county; $30/yr out of county; $34/yr out of state. Adv. Rate: col. inch $4.25 Circulation: 2,500 per issue (paid). **Owner(s):** ASP Westward LP, 523 N Sam Houston Pkwy Ste, 600, Houston, TX 77060-4011. **Management:** Veta Weaver, General Manager.

GREENVILLE

COMMERCE JOURNAL. 2305 King St., Greenville, TX 75401. Telephone: 903-886-3196. FAX: 903-455-6281. URL: http://www.heraldbanner.com. Mailing Address: PO Box 6000, Greenville, TX 75403-6000. Year Established: 1889. Pub. Frequency: w. (Wed.) Page Size: broadsheet. Subscrip. Rate: $.50 newsstand/cover; $28.40/yr deliv. Freelance Pay: $0.25/column-inch. Circulation: 1,500 per issue (paid). **Owner(s):** Community Newspaper Holdings, Inc., 3500 Colonnade Pkwy., Ste. 600, Birmingham, AL 35243. Telephone: 205-298-7100. FAX: 205-298-7101. **Management:** Lisa Chappell, Publisher. Deb Gentry, Advertising Director. Robert Spillers, Circulation Director. Shelley Morgan, Classified Adv. Mgr. **Editorial:** Derek Price, Editor. Warren Morrison, Managing Editor.

HUNT COUNTY SHOPPER. 3617 Wesley, Greenville, TX 75401. Telephone: 903-455-5254. FAX: 903-455-3297. E-MAIL: huntcountyshopper@swbell.net. URL: http://www.hcshopper.com. Mailing Address: PO Box 906, Greenville, TX 75403. Year Established: 1965. Pub. Frequency: w. (Thu.) Page Size: tabloid.Adv. Rate: col. inch $5.75 Circulation: 25,000 per issue (free). **Owner(s):** Warren Hope, See address and contact information above. **Management:** Warren Hope, Publisher. **Editorial:** Warren Hope, Editor.

GROESBECK

GROESBECK JOURNAL. PO Box 440, Groesbeck, TX 76642. Telephone: 254-729-5103. FAX: 254-729-8310. E-MAIL: groesbeckjournal@glade.net. URL: http://www.groesbeckjournal.com. Year Established: 1892. Pub. Frequency: w. (Thu.) Page Size: broadsheet. Subscrip. Rate: $.50 newsstand/cover; $16/yr in county; $19/yr in state; $21/yr out of state; $24/yr foreign. Adv. Rate: col. inch $5 Circulation: 4,600 per issue (paid). **Owner(s):** Groesbeck Journal, Inc., See address and contact information above. **Management:** Thomas E. Hawkins, Publisher. **Editorial:** Thomas E. Hawkins, Editor.

GROVETON

GROVETON NEWS. 134 E First St, Groveton, TX 75845. Telephone: 936-642-1891. FAX: 936-642-1196. Pub. Frequency: w. (Thu.) Page Size: broadsheet. Subscrip. Rate: $.50 newsstand/cover; $13.75/yr in county; $17/yr out of county. Circulation: 2,000 per issue (paid). **Owner(s):** Polk County Publishing Co., PO Box 1276, Livingston, TX 77351. Telephone: 936-327-4357. FAX: 936-327-7156. **Management:** Alvin Holley, Publisher. **Editorial:** Lee Smith, Editor.

GUN BARREL CITY

CEDAR CREEK PILOT.   ISSN 1046-8633
1012 W. Main St., Ste. 105, Gun Barrel City, TX 75147. Telephone: 903-887-8051. FAX: 903-887-8225. E-MAIL: sales@cedarcreekpilot.com. URL: http://www.cedarcreekpilot.com. Year Established: 1970. Pub. Frequency: w. (Thu.) Page Size: broadsheet. Subscrip. Rate: $.50 newsstand/cover; $17.50/yr mailed local; $30/yr mailed in state; $32/yr mailed out of state. Circulation: 4,800 per issue (paid). **Owner(s):** Community Newspaper Holdings, Inc., 3500 Colonnade Pkwy., Ste. 600, Birmingham, AL 35243. Telephone: 205-298-7100. FAX: 205-298-7101. **Management:** Kathi Nailing, General Manager. David Sullens, Publisher. Linda Fernald, Advertising. **Editorial:** Janice Arnsdorff, Editor.

HALLETTSVILLE

HALLETTSVILLE TRIBUNE-HERALD. 108 S. Texana St., Hallettsville, TX 77964. Telephone: 361-798-2481. FAX: 361-798-9902. E-MAIL: tribune@stisp.com. Mailing Address: PO Box 427, Hallettsville, TX 77964-0427. Year Established: 1931. Pub. Frequency: w. (Wed.) Page Size: standard. Subscrip. Rate: $.75 newsstand/cover; $32/yr in county; $37/yr out of county; $44/yr out of state. Circulation: 4,000 per issue (paid). **Owner(s):** Preuss Printing Co., 170 N. Knox Ave., Giddings, TX 78942. Telephone: 979-542-2222. FAX: 979-542-9410. **Management:** L.M. Preuss III, President. Sam Preuss, Publisher.

HAMILTON

HAMILTON HERALD-NEWS. 112 E. Main, Hamilton, TX 76531. Telephone: 254-386-3145. FAX: 254-386-3001. URL: http://www.herald-news.com. Mailing Address: PO Box 833, Hamilton, TX 76531. Year Established: 1875. Pub. Frequency: w. (Thu.) Page Size: broadsheet. Subscrip. Rate: $.50 newsstand/cover; $20/yr mailed in county & adj. cys.; $25/yr mailed elsewhere. Circulation: 3,700 per issue (paid). **Owner(s):** Hamilton Publishing Co., Inc., See address and contact information above. **Management:** Kenneth Miller, Publisher. Darla Cole, Circulation Manager. **Editorial:** Kenneth Miller, Editor.

HASKELL

HASKELL FREE PRESS. 420 N. First St., Haskell, TX 79521. Telephone: 940-864-2686. FAX: 940-864-2687. E-MAIL: hfp@valornet.com. Mailing Address: PO Box 555, Haskell, TX 79521-0555. Year Established: 1886. Pub. Frequency: w. (Thu.) Page Size: broadsheet. Subscrip. Rate: $.75 newsstand/cover; $25/yr mailed in county; $34/yr mailed elsewhere. Adv. Rate: col. inch $4.25 Circulation: 2,000 per issue (paid). **Owner(s):** John McDougal, See address and contact information above. **Management:** John McDougal, Publisher. Lisa Shaw, Circulation Manager.

HEMPHILL

SABINE COUNTY REPORTER-RAMBLER. 250 Worth St., Hemphill, TX 75948. Telephone: 409-787-2172. FAX: 409-787-4300. Year Established: 1883. Pub. Frequency: w. (Wed.) Page Size: standard. Subscrip. Rate: $.75 newsstand/cover; $22/yr in county; $33/yr out of county. Circulation: 3,600 per issue (paid). **Owner(s):** Stephanie Corley, See address and contact information above. **Management:** Stephanie Corley, Publisher. **Editorial:** Tracy Lane, Editor.

HEMPSTEAD

WALLER COUNTY NEWS-CITIZEN.   ISSN 0164-4203
705 12th St., Hempstead, TX 77445. Telephone: 979-826-3361. FAX: 979-826-3360. E-MAIL: wcnewscitizen@hcnonline.com. URL: http://www.wallerconewscitizen.com. Mailing Address: PO Box 556, Hempstead, TX 77445. Year Established: 1890. Pub. Frequency: w. (Thu.) Page Size: broadsheet. Subscrip. Rate: $.50 newsstand/cover; $24/yr in county; $28/yr out of county. Adv. Rate: col. inch $7.61 Circulation: 1,850 per issue (paid). **Owner(s):** ASP Westward LP, 523-N Sam Houston Pkwy, Ste 600, Houston, TX 77060. Telephone: 281-668-1100. **Management:** Jed Young, Publisher. Buckie Wimberly, Advertising Manager. Bea Wimberly, Sales Manager. Linda K. Payne, Business Manager. **Editorial:** Billy Dragoo, Editor-in-Chief.

HONDO

HONDO ANVIL HERALD. 1601 Ave. K, Hondo, TX 78861. Telephone: 830-426-3346. FAX: 830-426-3348. URL: http://www.hondoanvilherald.com. Mailing Address: PO Box 400, Hondo, TX 78861-0400. Year Established: 1886. Pub. Frequency: w. (Thu.) Page Size: broadsheet. Subscrip. Rate: $.75 newsstand/cover; $20/yr local; $25/yr out of county; $35/yr out of state. Adv. Rate: col. inch $6 Circulation: 4,848 per issue (paid). **Owner(s):** W.E. Berger, See address and contact information above. **Management:** Jeff Berger, Co-Publisher. Lois Davis, Advertising Manager. Cathy Walton, Circulation Manager. Theresa House, Classified Adv. Mgr. **Editorial:** Frances Guinn, Editor.

SABINAL SAMPLER. 1601 Ave. K, Hondo, TX 78861. Telephone: 830-426-3346. FAX: 830-426-3348. Mailing Address: PO Box 400, Hondo, TX 78861-0400. Year Established: 1950. Pub. Frequency: w. (Wed.) Page Size: broadsheet.Adv. Rate: col. inch $6 Circulation: 600 per issue (free). **Owner(s):** W.E. Berger, See address and contact information above. **Management:** W.E. Berger, President. **Editorial:** Frances Guinn, Editor.

HOUSTON

BELLAIRE EXAMINER. 2444 Times Blvd Ste 200, Houston, TX 77005. Telephone: 713-520-1226. FAX: 713-520-1193. E-MAIL: bellaireeditor@hcnonline.com. URL: http://www.examinernews.com.Pub. Frequency: w. (Wed.) Circulation: 18,000 per issue (free). **Owner(s):** ASP Westward LP, 523 N Sam Houston Pkwy Ste, 600, Houston, TX 77060-4011. **Management:** Ernest Stevenson, Advertising Director. **Editorial:** Charlotte Aguilar, Editor.

CITIZEN (HUMBLE), THE. 17511 El Camino Real, Ste 131, Houston, TX 77058. Telephone: 281-488-1108. FAX: 281-286-0750. URL: http://www.thecitizen-online.com. Mailing Address: PO Box 57907, Webster, TX 77598. Year Established: 1960. Pub. Frequency: w. (Wed.) Subscrip. Rate: $.50 newsstand/cover; $36/yr home delivery in county. Freelance Pay: $0.50/column-inch. Circulation: 40,000 per issue (paid). **Owner(s):** ASP Westward LP, 523 N Sam Houston Pkwy, Ste 600, Houston, TX 77060. **Management:** Sharon Rickel, Publisher. Jan Shinkle, Circulation Manager. **Editorial:** Mary Alys Cherry, Managing Editor. Chuck Hlava, Sports Editor.

COPPERFIELD SUN. 3730 FM 1960 W., Ste. 108, Houston, TX 77068. Telephone: 281-440-1470. FAX: 281-392-2331. E-MAIL: 1960editorial@hcnonline.com. URL: http://www.the1960sun.com. Pub. Frequency: w. (Thu.) Page Size: broadsheet. Subscrip. Rate: $.35 newsstand/cover. Adv. Rate: col. inch $18.69 Freelance Pay: $35-$50/article. Circulation: 11,500 per issue (paid and free). **Owner(s):** ASP Westward LP, 523 N Sam Houston Pkwy, Ste 600, Houston, TX 77060. **Management:** Clayton Harris, Publisher. **Editorial:** Steve Love, Editor.

GREATER HOUSTON WEEKLY. 2444 Times Blvd Ste 200, Houston, TX 77005. Telephone: 713-520-1226. FAX: 713-520-1193. E-MAIL: mwilliams@hcnonline.com. URL: http://www.hcnonline.com. Pub. Frequency: w. (Thu.) Page Size: broadsheet. **Owner(s):** ASP Westward LP, 523 N Sam Houston Pkwy, Ste 600, Houston, TX 77060-4011. **Management:** James Pollard, Advertising Director. **Editorial:** Michael Williams, Editor.

HOUSTON FORWARD TIMES. 4411 Almesa Rd., Houston, TX 77004. Telephone: 713-526-4727. FAX: 713-526-3170. URL: http://www.forwardtimes.com. Mailing Address: PO Box 8346, Houston, TX 77288-8346. Year Established: 1960. Pub. Frequency: w. (Wed.) Page Size: broadsheet. Subscrip. Rate: $.50 newsstand/cover; $18.50 for 6 mos.; $30/yr; $50 for 2 yrs.. Adv. Rate: col. inch $28.60 Circulation: 63,000 per issue (paid). **Owner(s):** Lenora Carter, See address and contact information above. **Management:** Lenora Carter, President. Henrietta Smith, Advertising Manager. **Editorial:** Lenora Carter, Managing Editor.

HOUSTON INFORMER. 5445 Almeda Rd, Ste 415, Houston, TX 77004. Telephone: 713-528-4442. FAX: 713-528-4448. E-MAIL: houstoninformer@yahoo.com. Year Established: 1893. Pub. Frequency: w. (Fri.) Page Size: broadsheet.Subscrip. Rate: $55/yr mailed in county Circulation: 30,000 per issue (paid). **Owner(s):** Pluria Marshall, Jr., 3906 Daphne St., Houston, TX 77021. Telephone: 713-527-8261. **Management:** Hexer Holliday, General Manager. Pluria Marshall Jr., Publisher.

HOUSTON PRESS. 1621 Milam, Ste 100, Houston, TX 77002. Telephone: 713-280-2400. FAX: 713-280-2444. URL: http://www.houstonpress.com. Year Established: 1989. Pub. Frequency: w. Page Size: tabloid. Subscrip. Rate: $60/yr. Circulation: 250,000. **Owner(s):** Village Voice Media, Inc., 1201 E Jefferson St, Phoenix, AZ 85034. Telephone: 415-541-0700. FAX: 415-541-9096. **Management:** Stuart Folb, Publisher. Dana Donovan, Advertising Director. Michael Serwatka, Circulation Director. Jose Lopez, Circulation Manager. Todd Crenshaw, Classified Adv. Mgr.. Amy Jones, Sales Manager. **Editorial:** Margaret Downing, Editor. Cathy Matusow, Associate Editor. John Nova Lomax, Music Editor.

HOUSTON TRIBUNE. 373 1/2 W 19th St, Ste A, Houston, TX 7708. Telephone: 713-862-9603. E-MAIL: tribune@ev1.net. URL: http://www.houstontribune.com. Year Established: 1986. Pub. Frequency: m. Page Size: standard. Subscrip. Rate: $35/yr. Adv. Rate: col. inch $49.25; trim 12.25 x 10 Circulation: 22,500. **Owner(s):** Tribune Publishing Company, Inc., See address and contact information above. **Editorial:** Amy Stevens, Editor. Marty Ehlert, Managing Editor.

MEMORIAL EXAMINER. 2444 Times Blvd Ste 200, Houston, TX 77005. Telephone: 713-520-1226. FAX: 713-520-1193. E-MAIL: asutton@hcnonline.com. URL: http://www.examinernews.com. Year Established: 2004. Pub. Frequency: w. (Fri.) Page Size: broadsheet. Subscrip. Rate: $.35 newsstand/cover. Adv. Rate: col. inch $18.69 Circulation: 15,000 per issue (paid and free). **Owner(s):** ASP Westward LP, 523 N Sam Houston Pkwy Ste, 600, Houston, TX 77060-4011. **Editorial:** Andrea Sutton, Editor.

MOUNTAIN SUN, THE. 5701 Woodway Dr., Ste. 131, Houston, TX 77057-1589. E-MAIL: mmtnsun@ktc.com. Year Established: 1881. Pub. Frequency: w. (Wed.) Page Size: broadsheet Circulation: 6,400 per issue (free). **Owner(s):** Southern Newspapers, Inc., See address and contact information above. **Management:** Greg Shrader, Publisher. Marie Schwartzkopf, Advertising Manager. Judy Rodgers, Circulation Manager. **Editorial:** Greg Shrader, Editor.

RIVER OAKS EXAMINER. 2444 Times Blvd Ste 200, Houston, TX 77005. Telephone: 713-520-1226. FAX: 713-520-1193. E-MAIL: mhorton@hcnonline.com. URL: http://www.examinernews.com. Year Established: 2002.Pub. Frequency: w. (Thu.) Circulation: 11,300 per issue (free). **Owner(s):** ASP Westward LP, 523 N Sam Houston Pkwy Ste, 600, Houston, TX 77060-4011. **Management:** Ernest Stevenson, Advertising Director. **Editorial:** Michael Reed, Editor. Marianne Horton, Managing Editor.

WEST UNIVERSITY EXAMINER. 2444 Times Blvd Ste 200, Houston, TX 77005. Telephone: 713-520-1226. FAX: 713-520-1193. E-MAIL: westueditor@hcnonline.com. URL: http://www.examinernews.com/west_university/. Year Established: 2001.Pub. Frequency: w. (Wed.) Circulation: 13,875 per issue (free). **Owner(s):** ASP Westward LP, 523 N Sam Houston Pkwy Ste, 600, Houston, TX 77060-4011. **Editorial:** Michael Reed, Editor.

1960 SUN. 3730 FM 1960 W., Ste. 108, Houston, TX 77068. Telephone: 281-440-1470. FAX: 281-537-7528. E-MAIL: 1960editorial@hcnonline.com. URL: http://www.the1960sun.com. Pub. Frequency: w. (Wed.) Page Size: broadsheet. Subscrip. Rate: $.35 newsstand/cover. Adv. Rate: col. inch $23.25 Circulation: 91,000 per issue (paid and free). **Owner(s):** ASP Westward LP, 523 N Sam Houston Pkwy, Ste 600, Houston, TX 77060. **Management:** Clayton Harris, Publisher. **Editorial:** Steve Love, Editor.

HOWE

TEXOMA ENTERPRISE. 805 N. Hughes, Howe, TX 75459. Telephone: 903-532-6012. FAX: 903-532-6012. E-MAIL: howeenterprise@texoma.net. URL: http://www.texomaenterprise.com. Year Established: 1963. Pub. Frequency: w. (Thu.) Page Size: standard. Subscrip. Rate: $.75 newsstand/cover; $19.50/yr in county; $24.50/yr out of county. Adv. Rate: col. inch $5 Circulation: 638 per issue (paid and free). **Owner(s):** Dale Rideout, See address and contact information above. **Management:** Dale Rideout, Publisher. Lana Rideout, Circulation Manager. **Editorial:** Lana Rideout, Editor-in-Chief. Contact: Lana Rideout, Editor-in-Chief.

HUMBLE

EAST MONTGOMERY COUNTY OBSERVER. 301 Main St., Humble, TX 77338. Telephone: 281-446-1071. FAX: 281-446-6901. E-MAIL: ccalvert@hcnonline.com. URL: http://www.theeastmontgomerycountyobserver.com. Year Established: 1942. Pub. Frequency: w. (Wed.) Page Size: broadsheet. Subscrip. Rate: $.50 newsstand/cover. Adv. Rate: col. inch $15.77 Circulation: 12,928 per issue (controlled and free). **Owner(s):** Houston Community Newspapers, Inc., 907-B E. Main St., Humble, TX 77338-4662. Telephone: 281-446-5969. **Management:** Tom Cook, Publisher. Carolyn Hardcastle, Office Manager. Linda Mickelson, Classified Adv. Mgr.. **Editorial:** Cynthia Calvert, Editor.

IDALOU

IDALOU BEACON. 201 W. First St., Idalou, TX 79329-0887. E-MAIL: jbeacon@dtspeel.net. Year Established: 1957. Pub. Frequency: w. (Fri.) Page Size: broadsheet. Subscrip. Rate: $.75 newsstand/cover; $22/yr local; $28/yr out of county; $35/yr out of state. Circulation: 1,000 per issue (paid and free). **Owner(s):** Jona Janet, PO Box 887, Idalou, TX 79329-0887. Telephone: 806-892-2233. **Management:** Jona Janet, Publisher.

IOWA PARK

IOWA PARK LEADER. 112 W. Cash St., Iowa Park, TX 76367-2824. Telephone: 940-592-4431. FAX: 940-592-4431. Mailing Address: PO Box 430, Iowa Park, TX 76367-0430. Year Established: 1969. Pub. Frequency: w. (Thu.) Page Size: standard. Subscrip. Rate: $.50 newsstand/cover; $17/yr in county; $20/yr mailed out of county; $23/yr mailed out of state. Adv. Rate: col. inch $2.88 Circulation: 2,500 per issue (paid). **Owner(s):** Bob & Dolores Hamilton, See address and contact information above. **Management:** Dolores Hamilton, Publisher. Kari Collins, Advertising Manager. **Editorial:** Dolores Hamilton, Editor.

JACKSBORO

JACK COUNTY HERALD, THE. 212 N. Church St., Jacksboro, TX 76458-0070. Telephone: 940-567-2616. FAX: 940-567-2071. E-MAIL: jnnews@digitalpassage.com. URL: http://www.jacksboronewspapers.com. Mailing Address: P.O. Drawer 70, Jacksboro, TX 76458. Pub. Frequency: w. (Fri.) Page Size: broadsheet. Subscrip. Rate: $.50 newsstand/cover; $25.99/yr in county in cy. & adj. cys.. Circulation: 2,500 per issue (paid). **Owner(s):** MediaNews Group, Inc., 101 W Colfax Ave, Ste 1100, Denver, CO 80202. FAX: 303-954-6320. **Management:** Roy Robinson, Publisher. Sharyn Ellis, Advertising Manager. **Editorial:** Amy Riley, Managing Editor.

JACKSBORO GAZETTE - NEWS. 212 N. Church St., Jacksboro, TX 76458-0070. Telephone: 940-567-2616. FAX: 940-567-2071. E-MAIL: jnnews@digitalpassage.com. URL: http://www.jacksboronewspapers.com. Mailing Address: P.O. Drawer 70, Jacksboro, TX 76458-0070. Pub. Frequency: w. (Tue.) Page Size: broadsheet. Subscrip. Rate: $.50 newsstand/cover; $26.99/yr in county & adj. cys.. Circulation: 2,500 per issue (paid). **Owner(s):** MediaNews Group, Inc., 101 W Colfax Ave, Ste 1100, Denver, CO 80202. FAX: 303-954-6320. **Management:** Roy Robinson, Publisher. Sharyn Ellis, Advertising Manager. **Editorial:** Amy Riley, Managing Editor.

JASPER

JASPER NEWSBOY, THE. 302 N. Wheeler, Jasper, TX 75951. Telephone: 409-384-3441. FAX: 409-384-8803. E-MAIL: newsboy@inu.net. URL: htttp://www.home.southeasttexasalive.com. Mailing Address: PO Box 1419, Jasper, TX 75951-1419. Year Established: 1865. Pub. Frequency: w. (Wed.) Page Size: broadsheet. Subscrip. Rate: $.50 newsstand/cover; $24/yr in county; $30/yr out of county; $35/yr out of state. Circulation: 21,000 per issue (paid). **Owner(s):** Hearst Corp., 959 Eighth Ave, New York, NY 10019. **Management:** Willis Webb, Publisher. **Editorial:** Willis Webb, Editor.

JEFFERSON

JEFFERSON JIMPLECUTE. ISSN 1060-3476 205 W. Austin, Jefferson, TX 75657. Telephone: 903-665-2462. E-MAIL: jjimp@internetwork.net. Year Established: 1848. Pub. Frequency: w. (Thu.) Page Size: broadsheet. Subscrip. Rate: $.50 newsstand/cover; $20/yr in county; $23/yr mailed in state; $26/yr mailed out of state. Circulation: 2,500 per issue (paid). **Owner(s):** Vic Parker, See address and contact information above. **Management:** Vic Parker, Publisher. **Editorial:** Vic Parker, Editor.

JONESTOWN

NORTH LAKE TRAVIS LOG. 19621 RM 1431, Jonestown, TX 78645. Telephone: 512-267-4449. FAX: 512-267-4464. E-MAIL: news@nltlog.com. Mailing Address: PO Box 4910, Lago Vista, TX 78645. Year Established: 1981. Pub. Frequency: w. (Thu.) Page Size: tabloid. Subscrip. Rate: $35/yr mailed 3rd class; $80/yr mailed 1st class. Adv. Rate: col. inch $10.60 Circulation: 5,900 per issue (paid and free). **Owner(s):** Cox Newspapers, Inc., 6205 Peachtree Dunwoody Rd, Atlanta, GA 30328. **Management:** Bob Freer, Publisher. **Editorial:** Mike Parker, Editor.

JUNCTION

JUNCTION EAGLE, THE. 215 N. Sixth St., Junction, TX 76849. Telephone: 325-446-2610. FAX: 325-446-4025. Year Established: 1882. Pub. Frequency: w. (Wed.) Page Size: standard. Subscrip. Rate: $.50 newsstand/cover; $20/yr in county; $23/yr out of county; $25/yr mailed out of state. Circulation: 2,450 per issue (paid). **Owner(s):** Debbie Cooper Kistler, See address and contact information above. **Management:** Debbie Cooper Kistler, Publisher. **Editorial:** Debbie Cooper Kistler, Managing Editor.

KARNES CITY

COUNTYWIDE, THE. 110 S. Market St., Karnes City, TX 78118-0129. Telephone: 830-780-3924. FAX: 830-780-3711. E-MAIL: editor@fcountywide.com. URL: http://www.thecountywide.com. Mailing Address: PO Box 129, Karnes City, TX 78118-0129. Year Established: 1891. Pub. Frequency: w. (Wed.) Page Size: broadsheet. Subscrip. Rate: $.50 newsstand/cover; $25/yr home delivery in county; $32/yr home delivery out of county. Adv. Rate: col. inch $6 Freelance Pay: $0.05/word. Circulation: 3,016 per issue (paid). **Owner(s):** Karnes Multimedia, Inc., 110 S. Market St., Karnes City, TX 78118. Telephone: 830-780-3924. **Management:** Joe Baker, Publisher. Sharon Menn, Advertising Manager. Joe Baker, Circulation Manager.

KATY

KATY SUN. 2501 S Mason Rd #240, Katy, TX 77450. Telephone: 281-674-1390. FAX: 281-392-2331. E-MAIL: katyeditor@hcnonline.com. URL: http://www.katysun.com. Pub. Frequency: w. (Wed.) Page Size: standard. **Owner(s):** ASP Westward LP, 523 N Sam Houston Pkwy Ste, 600, Houston, TX 77060-4011. Telephone: 281-446-5979. FAX: 281-668-1100. **Management:** Barbara McNeil, Publisher. Ernest Stevenson, Advertising Director. **Editorial:** Dustin Wenzel, Editor.

KAUFMAN

KAUFMAN HERALD, THE. 300 N. Washington, Kaufman, TX 75142. Telephone: 972-932-2171. FAX: 972-932-2172. E-MAIL: leskh@tvec.net. URL: http://www.kaufmanherald.com. Mailing Address: PO Box 460, Kaufman, TX 75142. Year Established: 1886. Pub. Frequency: w. (Thu.) Page Size: broadsheet. Subscrip. Rate: $.50 newsstand/cover; $22/yr in county; $28/yr out of county; $35/yr out of state. Circulation: 4,200 per issue (paid). **Owner(s):** Hartman Newspapers, Inc., PO Box 1390, Rosenberg, TX 77471. Telephone: 281-342-8691. **Management:** Michael Gresham, Publisher. Monica Lewis, Advertising. Becky Dickerson, Classified Adv. Mgr.. **Editorial:** Michael Gresham, Editor. Jeanie Davis, Managing Editor.

KELLER

KELLER CITIZEN, THE. 1103 Keller Pkwy, Ste 101, Keller, TX 76248. Telephone: 817-431-2231. FAX: 817-431-5534. E-MAIL: toverman@Kellercitizen.com. URL: http://www.kellercitizen.com. Mailing Address: PO Box 615, Keller, TX 76244. Year Established: 1980. Pub. Frequency: w. (Fri..) Page Size: broadsheet. Subscrip. Rate: $.50 newsstand/cover; $50/yr. Adv. Rate: col. inch $12 Circulation: 36,000 per issue (free). **Owner(s):** The/McClatchy Company, 2100 Q St., Sacramento, CA 95816-6816. **Management:** William C Lewis, Publisher. Pam Nolte, Circulation Manager. **Editorial:** Todd Overman, News Editor.

KERMIT

WINKLER COUNTY NEWS. 109 S. Poplar, Kermit, TX 79745. Telephone: 432-586-2561. FAX: 432-586-2562. Year Established: 1936. Pub. Frequency: w. (Thu.) Page Size: standard. Subscrip. Rate: $.50 newsstand/cover; $19/yr carrier delivery in county; $29/yr mailed out of county. Circulation: 3,700 per issue (paid). **Owner(s):** Golden West Free Press Co., See address and contact information above. **Management:** Richard E. McLaughlin, Publisher. Phyllis Thomas, Advertising Manager. **Editorial:** Richard E. McLaughlin, Editor. Bert Brewer, Managing Editor.

KINGSVILLE

KINGSVILLE RECORD, THE. 105 S. Fifth St., Kingsville, TX 78363. Telephone: 361-592-4304. FAX: 361-592-1015. E-MAIL: bobodom@kingsvillerecord.net. URL: http://www.kingsvillerecord.net. Mailing Address: PO Box 951, Kingsville, TX 78364. Year Established: 1906. Pub. Frequency: s-w. (Wed. & Sun) Page Size: broadsheet. Subscrip. Rate: $.50 newsstand/cover; $1 newsstand/cover Sun.; $39/yr home delivery in county; $42/yr mailed in county; $47/yr out of county. Circulation: 7,000 per issue (paid). **Owner(s):** Kingsville Publishing Co., See address and contact information above. **Management:** Bob Odom, Publisher. **Editorial:** Bob Odom, Editor.

KINGWOOD

OBSERVER (KINGWOOD, HUMBLE, ATASCOCITA, EAST MONTGOMERY, SPRING), THE. 1117 Kingwood Dr., Kingwood, TX 77339. Telephone: 281-359-2799. FAX: 281-359-0017. E-MAIL: observereditor@hcnonline.com. URL: http://www.hcnonline.com. Year Established: 1942. Pub. Frequency: w. (Wed.) Page Size: broadsheet. Subscrip. Rate: $.50 newsstand/cover. Circulation: 80,000 per issue (controlled and free). **Owner(s):** ASP Westward LP, 523 N Sam Houston Pkwy, Ste 600, Houston, TX 77060. Telephone: 281-668-1100. **Management:** Trish Oliva, General Manager. Clayton Harris, Publisher. **Editorial:** Cory Turner, Sports Editor.

OBSERVER (KINGWOOD), THE. 1129 Kingwood Dr., Kingwood, TX 77339. Telephone: 281-359-2799. FAX: 281-359-0017. Year Established: 1942. Pub. Frequency: w. (Wed.) Page Size: broadsheet. Circulation: 21,375 per issue (paid and controlled). **Owner(s):** Houston Community Newspapers, Inc., 301 Main St., Humble, TX 77338. Telephone: 866-446-5979. FAX: 281-446-0742. **Management:** Tom Cook, Publisher. **Editorial:** Cynthia Calvert, Editor.

LA GRANGE

FAYETTE COUNTY RECORD, THE. 127 S Washington, La Grange, TX 78945. Telephone: 409-968-3155. FAX: 409-968-6767. E-MAIL: fcrecord@cmaassess.com. URL: http://www.fayettecountyrecord.com. Mailing Address: PO Box 400, La Grange, TX 78945. Year Established: 1922. Pub. Frequency: s-w. (Tue. & Fri.) Page Size: broadsheet. Subscrip. Rate: $.75 newsstand/cover; $37/yr in county; $40/yr in state. Adv. Rate: col. inch $7 Circulation: 5,912 per issue (paid). **Owner(s):** Fayette County Record, Inc., See address and contact information above. **Management:** Larry C. Jackson, Publisher. Aileen Loehr, Advertising. Thereisa Koopmann, Circulation Manager. **Editorial:** Larry C. Jackson, Editor.

LA PORTE

BAYSHORE SUN. 820 S. Eighth St., La Porte, TX 77571. Telephone: 281-471-1234. FAX: 281-471-5763. E-MAIL: john@bayshoresun.com. Year Established: 1947. Pub. Frequency: s-w. (Wed. & Sun.) Page Size: broadsheet. Subscrip. Rate: $.50 newsstand/cover; $30/yr in county; $33/yr mailed out of county. Circulation: 13,000 per issue (paid). **Owner(s):** Hartman Newspapers, Inc., PO Box 1390, Rosenberg, TX 77471. **Management:** John Black, Publisher. Karolyn Kellogg, Classified Adv. Mgr.. **Editorial:** John Black, Editor.

LAMESA

LAMESA PRESS-REPORTER. 523 N. First St., Lamesa, TX 79331. Telephone: 806-872-2623. FAX: 806-872-2177. E-MAIL: editor@pressreporter.com. Year Established: 1905. Pub. Frequency: s-w. (Wed. & Sun.) Page Size: broadsheet. Subscrip. Rate: $.75 newsstand/cover; $33/yr mailed in county; $39/yr mailed in state; $44/yr mailed out of state. Adv. Rate: col. inch $4.50 Freelance Pay: $0.50/column-inch. Circulation: 3,600 per issue (paid and free). **Owner(s):** Roberts Publishing Co., 210 E. Broadway, Andrews, TX 79714. Telephone: 915-523-3232. FAX: 915-523-9492. **Management:** Russel Skiles, Publisher. Gay Shafner, Circulation Manager. Gloria Shaw, Classified Adv. Mgr.. **Editorial:** Herrel Halmark, Editor.

LEVELLAND

LEVELLAND HOCKLEY COUNTY NEWS-PRESS. 711 Auston St., Levelland, TX 79336. Telephone: 806-894-3121. FAX: 806-894-7957. E-MAIL: levellandnews@valornet.com. Mailing Address: P.O. Drawer 1628, Levelland, TX 79336-1628. Year Established: 1925. Pub. Frequency: s-w. (Wed. & Sun.) Page Size: standard. Subscrip. Rate: $.50 newsstand/cover; $30/yr in county; $40/yr out of county; $48/yr out of state. Circulation: 4,950 Sunday (paid and free); 4,490 per issue (paid and free). **Owner(s):** Stephen & Pat Enterprises, See address and contact information above. **Management:** Pat Henry, Publisher. Michelle Davis, Classified Adv. Mgr.. Paul Pinkert, Sales Manager. **Editorial:** John Rigg, News Editor. Mitch Word, Sports Editor.

LIBERTY

LIBERTY GAZETTE. 314 Main St., Liberty, TX 77575-4806. Telephone: 936-336-6416. FAX: 936-336-9400. E-MAIL: mail@libertygazette.com. Mailing Address: PO Box 1908, Liberty, TX 77575. Year Established: 1960. Pub. Frequency: w. (Tue.) Page Size: broadsheet.Adv. Rate: col. inch $5.25 Circulation: 9,100 per issue (free). **Owner(s):** Cynthia Smith, See address and contact information above. **Management:** Cynthia Smith, Publisher. **Editorial:** Edith Smith, Editor.

PONY EXPRESS MAIL. 314 Main St., Liberty, TX 77575-4806. Telephone: 936-336-6416. FAX: 936-336-9400. E-MAIL: mail@thelibertygazette.com. Mailing Address: PO Box 1908, Liberty, TX 77575. Year Established: 1981. Pub. Frequency: w. (Tue.) Page Size: broadsheet.Adv. Rate: col. inch $4.83 Circulation: 4,806 per issue (free). **Owner(s):** Cynthia Smith, See address and contact information above. **Management:** Cynthia Smith, Publisher. **Editorial:** Edith Smith, Editor.

VINDICATOR, THE.   ISSN 0746-6838
301 Vera Ln, Liberty, TX 77575. Telephone: 936-336-3611. FAX: 936-336-3345. Mailing Address: PO Box 9189, Liberty, TX 77575. Year Established: 1887. Pub. Frequency: s-w. (Wed. & Sun.) Page Size: broadsheet. Subscrip. Rate: $.50 newsstand/cover; $30/yr in county; $35/yr out of county; $40/yr out of state. Circulation: 5,300 per issue (paid and free). **Owner(s):** Granite Publications, PO Box 1010, Taylor, TX 75674. Telephone: 512-352-1009. **Management:** Emmett McKinley, Publisher. Carol Cubeczka, Advertising Manager. **Editorial:** Jerry Jaulding, Managing Editor.

LITTLEFIELD

LAMB COUNTY LEADER-NEWS. 313 W. Fourth St., Littlefield, TX 79339. Telephone: 806-385-4481. FAX: 806-385-4640. E-MAIL: leadernews@valornet.com. Mailing Address: PO Box 310, Littlefield, TX 79339. Year Established: 1923. Pub. Frequency: s-w. (Wed. & Sun.) Page Size: standard. Subscrip. Rate: $.50 newsstand/cover; $26/yr in county; $36/yr out of county; $42/yr out of state. Circulation: 2,800 per issue (paid and free). **Owner(s):** Stephen & Pat Enterprises, 711 Auston St., Levelland, TX 79336. Telephone: 806-385-4481. **Management:** Pat Henry, Publisher. Greta Raber, Advertising Manager. **Editorial:** Joella Lovvorn, Editor. Joe Gonzales, Sports Editor.

LIVINGSTON

BIG THICKET MESSENGER. PO Box 1276, Livingston, TX 77351. Telephone: 936-327-4357. FAX: 936-327-7156. Mailing Address: PO Box 1111, Rye, TX 77369. Pub. Frequency: w. (Thu.) Page Size: broadsheet Circulation: 4,800 per issue (free). **Owner(s):** Polk County Publishing Co., See address and contact information above. **Management:** Cheryl Goodwin, General Manager. Alvin Holley, Publisher.

LAKE LIVINGSTON PROGRESS. 100 Calhoun St, Livingston, TX 77351. Telephone: 936-324-4357. FAX: 936-327-7156. E-MAIL: polknews@livingston.net. URL: http://www.easttexasnews.com. Pub. Frequency: w. (Thu.) Page Size: broadsheet Circulation: 6,000 per issue (free). **Owner(s):** Polk County Publishing Co., PO Box 1276, Livingston, TX 77351. Telephone: 936-327-4357. **Management:** Alvin Holley, Publisher. **Editorial:** Barbara White, Editor.

POLK COUNTY ENTERPRISE. 100 Calhoun St, Livingston, TX 77351. Telephone: 936-324-4357. FAX: 936-327-7156. E-MAIL: polknews@livingston.net. URL: http://www.easttexasnews.com. Mailing Address: PO Box 1276, Livingston, TX 77351-1276. Year Established: 1882. Pub. Frequency: s-w. (Thu. & Sun.) Page Size: broadsheet. Subscrip. Rate: $.50 newsstand/cover; $20/yr in county; $22/yr out of county; $24/yr out of state. Circulation: 8,300 per issue (paid). **Owner(s):** Polk County Publishing Co., PO Box 1276, Livingston, TX 77351. Telephone: 936-327-4357. **Management:** Alvin Holley, Publisher. Linda Holley, Advertising Manager. Georgia Bailey, Business Manager. **Editorial:** Barbara White, Editor.

LLANO

LLANO NEWS. 813 Berry St., Llano, TX 78643. Telephone: 325-247-4433. FAX: 325-247-3338. E-MAIL: thenews@tstar.net. URL: http://www.llanonews.com. Mailing Address: PO Box 187, Llano, TX 78643. Year Established: 1889. Pub. Frequency: w. (Wed.) Page Size: standard. Subscrip. Rate: $.50 newsstand/cover; $19/yr in county; $26/yr mailed out of county; $40/yr mailed out of state. Circulation: 4,400 per issue (paid). **Owner(s):** Sandra Wesner, See address and contact information above. **Management:** Ken Wesner, Publisher. Sandra Wesner, Circulation Manager. **Editorial:** Jimmy Stephenson, Editor.

LOCKHART

LOCKHART POST REGISTER. 111 S. Church St., Lockhart, TX 78644. Telephone: 512-398-4886. FAX: 512-398-6144. Year Established: 1872. Pub. Frequency: w. (Thu.) Page Size: broadsheet. Subscrip. Rate: $.75 newsstand/cover; $25/yr in county; $35/yr mailed out of county. Adv. Rate: col. inch $7.70 Circulation: 4,000 per issue (paid). **Owner(s):** Dana Garrett, See address and contact information above. **Management:** Dana Garrett, Publisher. Tracy Cannon, Advertising Manager. P. Rodriguez, Classified Adv. Mgr.. **Editorial:** Kathi Bliss, News Editor.

LULING

LULING NEWSBOY & SIGNAL. 415 E. Davis St, Luling, TX 78648-2316. Telephone: 830-875-2116. FAX: 830-875-2124. E-MAIL: slulingnewsboy@austin.rr.com. Year Established: 1940. Pub. Frequency: w. (Thu.) Page Size: broadsheet. Subscrip. Rate: $.75 newsstand/cover; $29/yr in county; $33/yr mailed out of county; $39/yr mailed out of state. Adv. Rate: col. inch $5.35 Circulation: 2,500 per issue (paid). **Owner(s):** Luling Publishing Co., Inc., See address and contact information above. **Management:** Karen McCrary-Plunque, General Manager. Josephine White, Office Manager. **Editorial:** Karen McCrary-Plunque, Editor.

MABANK

LAKE AREA LEADER. 1316 S Third St, Ste 108, Mabank, TX 75147-7680. Telephone: 903-887-4511. FAX: 903-887-4510. E-MAIL: advertising@themonitor.net. URL: http://www.themonitor.net. Mailing Address: PO Box 48, Mabank, TX 75147. Year Established: 1990. Pub. Frequency: w. (Wed.) Page Size: broadsheet.Adv. Rate: col. inch $8.50 Circulation: 25,000 per issue (free). **Owner(s):** John Buzzetta, See address and contact information above. **Management:** Susan Harrison, General Manager. John Buzzetta, Publisher. Ronda Pennington, Advertising Manager.

MONITOR (MABANK), THE.   ISSN 1049-3409

1316 S Third St, Ste 108, Mabank, TX 75147-7680. Telephone: 903-887-4511. FAX: 903-887-4510. E-MAIL: publisher@themonitor.net. URL: http://www.themonitor.net. Mailing Address: PO Box 48, Mabank, TX 75147. Year Established: 1972. Pub. Frequency: s-w. (Thu. & Sun.) Page Size: broadsheet. Subscrip. Rate: $.50 newsstand/cover; $22.50/yr in county; $30/yr out of county. Circulation: 5,000 per issue (paid). **Owner(s):** John Buzzetta, See address and contact information above. **Management:** Susan Harrison, General Manager. John Buzzetta, Publisher. Ronda Pennington, Advertising Manager. **Editorial:** Pearl Cantrell, Editor.

MAINSFIELD

MANSFIELD NEWS-MIRROR.   ISSN 0746-3847
119 N Main St, Mainsfield, TX 76063. Telephone: 817-423-4451. FAX: 817-423-0730. E-MAIL: lwinter@star-telegram.com. URL: http://www.mansfieldnewsmirror.com. Mailing Address: P O Box 337, Mainsfield, TX 706068. Year Established: 1883. Pub. Frequency: w. (Fri.) Page Size: broadsheet. Subscrip. Rate: $.50 newsstand/cover; $38.95/yr mailed in county. Circulation: 4,500 per issue (paid). **Owner(s):** The/McClatchy Company, 2100 Q St, Sacramento, CA 95816. **Management:** Lance Winter, Publisher. Michael Eddleman, Advertising Manager. **Editorial:** Bridgette Cummings, Editor.

MARBLE FALLS

MARBLE FALLS HIGHLANDER. PO Box 1000, Marble Falls, TX 78654. Telephone: 830-693-4367. FAX: 830-693-3650. URL: http://www.highlandernews.com. Year Established: 1956. Pub. Frequency: s-w. (Tue. & Fri.) Page Size: broadsheet. Subscrip. Rate: $.50 newsstand/cover; $52/yr in county; $90/yr mailed out of county; $90/yr mailed out of state. Adv. Rate: col. inch $9 Circulation: 6,500 per issue (paid). **Owner(s):** Bar 30 Media, See address and contact information above. **Management:** Roy Bode, Publisher. Ellen Bode, Advertising. Linda Burton, Business Manager. **Editorial:** Phil Schoch, Managing Editor. Stephen Colwell, Sports Editor.Readers: For Southern Burnet County, Texas

MASON

MASON COUNTY NEWS. P.O. Box 1729, Mason, TX 76856. Telephone: 325-347-5757. FAX: 325-347-5668. E-MAIL: masonnew@hctc.net. URL: http://www.hillcountrytexas.com. Year Established: 1877. Pub. Frequency: w. (Wed.) Page Size: broadsheet. Subscrip. Rate: $.50 newsstand/cover; $23/yr in county; $26/yr out of county; $35/yr out of state. Circulation: 2,850 per issue (paid). **Owner(s):** Scott Wesner, See address and contact information above. **Management:** Scott Wesner, Publisher. Heather Hudson, Advertising. **Editorial:** Gerry Gamel, Editor. Scott Wesner, Editor-in-Chief.

MATADOR

MOTLEY COUNTY TRIBUNE.   ISSN 0897-4322
724 Dundee, Matador, TX 79244-0490. Telephone: 806-347-2400. FAX: 806-347-2774. Mailing Address: PO Box 490, Matador, TX 79244-0490. Year Established: 1891. Pub. Frequency: w. (Thu.) Page Size: standard. Subscrip. Rate: $.50 newsstand/cover; $24/yr in county; $25/yr out of county. Adv. Rate: col. inch $3.75 Circulation: 1,175 per issue (paid). **Owner(s):** Carla M. Meador, 724 Dundee, Matador, TX 79244. Telephone: 806-347-2400. **Management:** Carla M. Meador, Owner. **Editorial:** Carla M. Meador, Editor.

MATHIS

MATHIS NEWS. 620 E. San Patricio Ave., Mathis, TX 78368. Telephone: 361-547-3274. FAX: 361-547-3275. E-MAIL: mathisnews@sbcglobal.net. Year Established: 1914. Pub. Frequency: w. (Wed.) Page Size: broadsheet. Subscrip. Rate: $.75 newsstand/cover; $27.50/yr in county; $34.50/yr out of county. Circulation: 2,200 per issue (paid). **Owner(s):** San Patricio Publishing Co., Inc., 117 S. Rachal, Sinton, TX 78387. Telephone: 512-364-1270. **Management:** James F Tracy Jr., Co-Publisher. John H Tracy, Advertising. **Editorial:** Charles Sullivan, Managing Editor.

MAXIA

HUBBARD CITY NEWS.   ISSN 1067-7305
214 N. Railroad, Maxia, TX 76667. FAX: 254-562-3121. E-MAIL: news@mexiadailynews.com. URL: http://www.cnhi.com/newspapers. Mailing Address: PO Box 431, Mexia, TX 76667. Year Established: 1881. Pub. Frequency: w. (Thu.) Page Size: broadsheet. Subscrip. Rate: $.50 newsstand/cover; $14/yr mailed in county; $16/yr mailed out of county; $18/yr mailed out of state. Circulation: 1,100 per issue (paid). **Owner(s):** Community Newspaper Holdings, Inc., 3500 Colonnade Pkwy., Ste. 600, Birmingham, AL 35243. Telephone: 205-298-7100. FAX: 205-298-7101. **Management:** Lynette Copley, Publisher. **Editorial:** Barbara Minze, Editor.

MCALLEN

VALLEY TOWN CRIER. 1811 N. 23rd St., McAllen, TX 78501. Telephone: 956-682-2423. FAX: 956-630-6371. E-MAIL: info@valleytowncrier.com. Year Established: 1964. Pub. Frequency: w. (Wed.) Page Size: broadsheet Circulation: 90,000 per issue (free). **Owner(s):** Valley Newspapers Holding, See address and contact information above. **Management:** Jack Wilson, General Manager. Rafael Rodriguez, Advertising Manager. Beto Rodriguez, Circulation Manager. **Editorial:** Brad Nibert, Editor.

MENARD

MENARD NEWS & MESSENGER, THE. 220 Gay St., Menard, TX 76859. Telephone: 325-396-2243. FAX: 325-386-2739. E-MAIL: menard1@airmail.net. Mailing Address: PO Box 248, Menard, TX 76859-0248. Year Established: 1893. Pub. Frequency: w. (Thu.) Page Size: standard. Subscrip. Rate: $.50 newsstand/cover; $25/yr in county; $30/yr in state; $35/yr out of state. Adv. Rate: col. inch $4 Circulation: 1,200 per issue (paid). **Owner(s):** Dan Feather, Jr., See address and contact information above. **Management:** Dan Feather Jr., Publisher. **Editorial:** Dorothy Kerns, Managing Editor.

MERIDIAN

BOSQUE COUNTY NEWS. 114 N. Main St., Meridian, TX 76665. Telephone: 254-435-6333. FAX: 254-435-6335. E-MAIL: bosque@htcomp.net. Mailing Address: PO Box 343, Meridian, TX 76665. Year Established: 1990. Pub. Frequency: w. (Wed.) Page Size: broadsheet. Subscrip. Rate: $.50 newsstand/cover; $24/yr in county; $27/yr out of county; $30/yr out of state. Circulation: 2,000 per issue (controlled and free). **Owner(s):** Robby James, See address and contact information above. **Management:** Evan Moore, Publisher. La Dawn Garland, Advertising. **Editorial:** La Dawn Garland, Managing Editor.

MESQUITE

MESQUITE NEWS. ISSN 0746-4126
303 N. Galloway Ave., Mesquite, TX 75149-4325. Telephone: 972-285-6301. FAX: 972-288-9383. E-MAIL: morrisons@scripps.com. URL: http://www.mesquitenews.com. Mailing Address: PO Box 850136, Mesquite, TX 75185-0136. Year Established: 1882. Pub. Frequency: w. (Thu.) Page Size: broadsheet. Subscrip. Rate: $.50 newsstand/cover; $25/yr home delivery; $39.95/yr mailed in county; $59.95/yr mailed out of county. Circulation: 33,000 per issue (paid and free). **Owner(s):** Star Community Newspapers, 14875 Landmark Blvd, Ste 110, Addison, TX 75254. Telephone: 972-628-4061. FAX: 971-436-7432. **Management:** Bill Weaver, Publisher. Carolyn Perry, Advertising. Ken McEwen, Circulation Manager. **Editorial:** Brian Porter, Managing Editor.

ROWLETT LAKESHORE TIMES, THE. 303 N. Galloway Ave., Mesquite, TX 75149-4325. Telephone: 972-285-6301. FAX: 972-288-9383. URL: http://www.scntx.com. Pub. Frequency: w. (Fri.) Page Size: standard. Subscrip. Rate: $.50 newsstand/cover; $25/yr home delivery local; $39.95/yr mailed in county; $59.95/yr mailed out of county. Circulation: 5,500 per issue (paid). **Owner(s):** Star Community Newspapers, 14875 Landmark Blvd, Ste 110, Addison, TX 75254. Telephone: 972-628-4061. FAX: 971-436-7432. **Management:** Bill Weaver, Publisher. Carolyn Perry, Advertising. Ken McEwen, Circulation Manager. **Editorial:** Brian Porter, Managing Editor.

MIAMI

MIAMI CHIEF, THE. ISSN 0746-0082
207 E. Commercial St., Miami, TX 79059. Telephone: 806-868-2521. FAX: 806-868-6051. E-MAIL: mchief@yft.net. Mailing Address: PO Box 396, Miami, TX 79059-0396. Year Established: 1899. Pub. Frequency: w. (Thu.) Page Size: tabloid. Subscrip. Rate: $.50 newsstand/cover; $20/yr local; $26/yr mailed elsewhere. Circulation: 650 per issue (paid). **Owner(s):** Sandy Black, See address and contact information above. **Management:** Sandy Black, Publisher. **Editorial:** Sandy Black, Editor-in-Chief.

MIDLOTHIAN

MIDLOTHIAN MIRROR, INC., THE. 111 Back Alley, Midlothian, TX 76065. Telephone: 972-775-3322. FAX: 972-775-4669. E-MAIL: themidlothianmirror@juno.com. URL: http://www.midlothianmirror.com. Mailing Address: PO Box 70, Midlothian, TX 76065-0070. Year Established: 1882. Pub. Frequency: w. (Wed.) Page Size: standard. Subscrip. Rate: $.50 newsstand/cover; $18/yr in county; $20/yr in state; $22/yr out of state; $40/yr elsewhere out of country. Adv. Rate: col. inch $5 **Owner(s):** American Consolidated Media, Inc., 1420 N. Mockingbird Ln, Ste 100, Dallas, TX 75247. Telephone: 214-691-4066. FAX: 214-691-4086. **Management:** Floyd Ingram, Publisher. Jennifer Kesterson, Advertising Manager. Dianna Glenn, Business Manager. **Editorial:** Neal White, Editor.

MINERAL WELLS

PALO PINTO COUNTY SHOPPER. 300 S.E. First St., Mineral Wells, TX 76067. Telephone: 940-325-4466. FAX: 940-325-2020. Mailing Address: PO Box 370, Mineral Wells, TX 76068. Pub. Frequency: w. (Wed.) Page Size: broadsheet Circulation: 14,200 per issue (free). **Owner(s):** Community Newspaper Holdings, Inc., 3500 Colonnade Pkwy., Ste. 600, Birmingham, AL 35243. Telephone: 205-298-7100. FAX: 205-298-7101. **Management:** Mel Rhodes, Publisher. Stacy Choate, Circulation Director. Glenna Barham, Classified Adv. Mgr.. **Editorial:** David May, Managing Editor.

MONAHANS

MONAHANS NEWS. 107 W. Second St., Monahans, TX 79756. Telephone: 432-943-4313. FAX: 432-943-4314. E-MAIL: monnews@planetlink.net. Mailing Address: PO Box 767, Monahans, TX 79756-0767. Year Established: 1931. Pub. Frequency: s-w. (Tue. & Fri.) Page Size: broadsheet. Subscrip. Rate: $1 newsstand/cover; $41.50/yr in county; $44.50/yr mailed in state; $79.50/yr mailed elsewhere. Circulation: 3,200 per issue (paid). **Owner(s):** Smoky Briggs, See address and contact information above. **Management:** Smoky Briggs, Publisher. Johanna Gray, Advertising. Jerry Caldwell, Circulation Manager. **Editorial:** Paula Bard, Editor.

MUNDAY

MUNDAY COURIER, THE. ISSN 8750-6750
111 E. B St., Munday, TX 76371-0130. Telephone: 940-422-4314. FAX: 940-422-4333. E-MAIL: mcourier@westex.net. Year Established: 1971. Pub. Frequency: w. (Wed.) Page Size: broadsheet. Subscrip. Rate: $.50 newsstand/cover; $18/yr in county; $23/yr in state. Circulation: 1,300 per issue (paid and free). **Owner(s):** The Munday Courier, Inc., See address and contact information above. **Management:** Jay White, Publisher. **Editorial:** Cynthia White, Editor.

NAVASOTA

NAVASOTA EXAMINER. 115 Railroad St, Navasota, TX 77868. Telephone: 936-825-6484. FAX: 936-825-2230. E-MAIL: publisher@navasotaexaminer.com. URL: http://www.navasotaexaminer.com. Mailing Address: PO Box 751, Navasota, TX 77868. Year Established: 1894. Pub. Frequency: w. (Wed.) Page Size: broadsheet. Subscrip. Rate: $.50 newsstand/cover; $29/yr in county; $32/yr in state; $50/yr out of state. Adv. Rate: col. inch $7 Circulation: 5,500 per issue (paid and free). **Owner(s):** Granite Publishing, See address and contact information above. **Management:** Dave Kucifer, Publisher. Tiffany Lara, Advertising. John Williams, Circulation Manager. **Editorial:** Dave Kucifer, Editor. Dave Lewis, Managing Editor.

NEDERLAND

MIDCOUNTY CHRONICLE. 808 B Hwy 69 N, Nederland, TX 77627. Telephone: 409-722-0479. FAX: 409-729-7626. E-MAIL: mcc@hearstnp.com. URL: http://www.midcountychronicle.com. Mailing Address: PO Box 2140, Nederland, TX 77627. Year Established: 1931. Pub. Frequency: s-w. (Wed.) Page Size: standard. Subscrip. Rate: $27/yr mailed. Adv. Rate: col. inch $12 Circulation: 25,000 per issue (paid and free). **Owner(s):** Hearst Corp., 959 Eighth Ave, New York, NY 10019. **Management:** Craig Stark, General Manager. **Editorial:** Monique Quibodeaux, Managing Editor. Dennis Kutac, Writer.

NEW ULM

NEW ULM ENTERPRISE. 910 FM 109, New Ulm, TX 78950. Telephone: 979-992-3351. Mailing Address: PO Box 128, New Ulm, TX 78950. Year Established: 1910. Pub. Frequency: w. (Thu.) Page Size: standard. Subscrip. Rate: $.50 newsstand/cover; $22/yr mailed in state; $26/yr mailed out of state. Adv. Rate: col. inch $3.53 Circulation: 1,475 per issue (paid). **Owner(s):** Maridel Dungen, See address and contact information above. **Management:** Maridel Dunger, Publisher. **Editorial:** Maridel Dungen, Editor.

OLNEY

OLNEY ENTERPRISE, THE. 213 E Main St, Olney, TX 76374. Telephone: 940-564-5558. FAX: 940-564-3992. E-MAIL: editor@olneyenterprise.com. URL: http://www.olneyenterprise.com. Mailing Address: P O Box 577, Olney, TX 76374. Year Established: 1910. Pub. Frequency: w. (Thu.) Page Size: broadsheet. Subscrip. Rate: $.75 newsstand/cover; $23.99/yr in county; $27.99/yr mailed out of county; $33.99/yr mailed out of state. Adv. Rate: col. inch $6.60 Circulation: 1,400 per issue (paid). **Owner(s):** MediaNews Group, Inc., 101 W Colfax Ave, Ste 1100, Denver, CO 80202. FAX: 303-954-6320. **Management:** Tommye Leemann, General Manager. Roy Robinson, Publisher. Karen Harris, Advertising Manager. Tommye Leemann, Classified Adv. Mgr.. **Editorial:** Mindi Kimbro, Editor.

PALACIOS

PALACIOS BEACON. 453 Commerce St., Palacios, TX 77465. Telephone: 361-972-3009. FAX: 361-972-2610. E-MAIL: editor@palaciosbeacon.com. URL: http://www.palaciosbeacon.com. Mailing Address: PO Box 817, Palacios, TX 77465. Year Established: 1907. Pub. Frequency: w. (Wed.) Page Size: standard. Subscrip. Rate: $.50 newsstand/cover; $22/yr in county; $28/yr out of county. Circulation: 2,200 per issue (paid). **Owner(s):** David Toney, PO Box 488, West Columbia, TX 77461. Telephone: 409-345-3128. **Management:** Nick West, Publisher. Rachel Barker, Advertising Manager. **Editorial:** Nick West, Editor.

PASADENA

DEER PARK BROADCASTER, THE. 102 S Shaver St, Pasadena, TX 7753506. Telephone: 713—477-0221. E-MAIL: jmjscribe@aol.com. URL: http://www.deerparkprogress.com. Pub. Frequency: w. (Wed.) Page Size: broadsheet Circulation: 11,750 per issue (free). **Owner(s):** ASP Westward LP, 523 N Sam Houston Pkwy Ste, 600, Houston, TX 77060-4011. **Management:** Tom Hartwell, Publisher. Carolynn Ellis, Advertising Manager. Maria Arizpe, Circulation Director. **Editorial:** Rob Vanya, Editor. Jennifer Akers, Sports.

DEER PARK PROGRESS, THE. 102 S Shaver St, Pasadena, TX 7753506. E-MAIL: jmjscribe@aol.com. URL: Http://www.HCNonline.com. Year Established: 1957. Pub. Frequency: w. (Sun.) Page Size: tabloid. Subscrip. Rate: $.50 newsstand/cover; $19.50/yr mailed in county; $23/yr mailed out of county. Circulation: 13,000 per issue (paid). **Owner(s):** ASP Westward LP, 523 N Sam Houston Pkwy Ste, 600, Houston, TX 77060-4011. **Management:** Gordon Gallatin, Publisher. **Editorial:** Rob Vanya, Editor.

NORTH CHANNEL SENTINEL. 102 S Shaver St, Pasadena, TX 77506. Telephone: 713-477-0221. FAX: 713-477-9090. E-MAIL: sentinelsun@hcnonline.com. URL: http://www.northchannelsentinel.com. Pub. Frequency: w. (Thu.) Page Size: broadsheet. Subscrip. Rate: $.35 newsstand/cover. Adv. Rate: col. inch $14.36 Circulation: 33,714 per issue (controlled and free). **Owner(s):** ASP Westward LP, 523 N Sam Houston Pkwy Ste, 600, Houston, TX 77060-4011. **Management:** Gordon Gallatin, Publisher. Jim Wadzinski, Advertising Director. **Editorial:** David Taylor, Editor.

PEARLAND

FRIENDSWOOD & PEARLAND REPORTER NEWS. 2404 S. Park, Pearland, TX 77581. Telephone: 281-485-7501. FAX: 281-485-6397. E-MAIL: tpp-@swbell.net. URL: htpp://www.thereporternews.com. Year Established: 1970. Pub. Frequency: w. (Wed.) Page Size: broadsheet. Subscrip. Rate: $.50 newsstand/cover; $25/yr in state; $30/yr out of state. Freelance Pay: $1/column-inch. Circulation: 11,000 per issue (paid and free). **Owner(s):** Randy & Laura Emmons, See address and contact information above. **Management:** Laura Emmons, Publisher. Randy Emmons, Circulation Manager. **Editorial:** Twila Lindblade, Editor.

FRIENDSWOOD JOURNAL. 2206 E Broadway St, Pearland, TX 77588. Telephone: 281-485-2785. FAX: 281-485-4464. E-MAIL: fjournald@hcnonline.com. URL: http://www.hcnonline.com. Pub. Frequency: w. (Thu.) Page Size: broadsheet. Subscrip. Rate: $.50 newsstand/cover per issue; $26/yr home delivery. **Owner(s):** ASP Westward LP, 523 N Sam Houston Pkwy E.Ste 600, Houston, TX 77060-4011. Telephone: 281-668-1100. **Management:** Margarette Chasteen, General Manager. **Editorial:** Tom Jacobs, Editor.

PEARLAND JOURNAL. 2206 E Broadway St, Pearland, TX 77588. Telephone: 281-485-2785. FAX: 281-485-4464. E-MAIL: mchasteen@hcnonline.com. URL: http://www.hcnonline.com. Pub. Frequency: w. (Thu.) Page Size: broadsheet. Subscrip. Rate: $.50 newsstand/cover per issue; $26/yr home delivery. **Owner(s):** ASP Westward LP, 523 N Sam Houston Pkwy E.Ste 600, Houston, TX 77060-4011. Telephone: 281-668-1100. **Management:** Margarette Chasteen, General Manager. **Editorial:** Tom Jacobs, Editor.

PECOS

PECOS ENTERPRISE. ISSN 0746-4231
324 S. Cedar St., Pecos, TX 79772-2057. Telephone: 432-445-5475. FAX: 432-445-4321. E-MAIL: news@pecos.net. URL: http://www.pecos.net/news. Mailing Address: PO Box 2057, Pecos, TX 79772. Year Established: 1887. Pub. Frequency: 3/w. (Tue., Fri., Sun.) Page Size: broadsheet. Subscrip. Rate: $.50 newsstand/cover; $9 mailed/mo. in county; $102/yr mailed in county; $120/yr mailed out of county. Adv. Rate: col. inch $8.63 **Wire Service(s):** AP. Circulation: 2,500 evening (paid and free); 4,600 Sunday (paid and free). **Owner(s):** Buckner News Alliance, 2101 4th Ave., Ste. 1870, Seattle, WA 98121-2345. **Management:** Philip F. Buckner, President. York Briggs, Publisher. Christine Bitolas, Advertising. Peggy McCracken, Business Manager. **Editorial:** Jon Fulbright, Managing Editor. Rosie Flores, Lifestyle Editor. Jon Fulbright, Sports.

PFLUGERVILLE

PFLUGERVILLE PFLAG. 200 W. Main St., Ste., 200A, Pflugerville, TX 78660. Telephone: 512-251-2220. FAX: 512-251-6221. E-MAIL: news@pflugervillepflag.com. Mailing Address: PO Box 447, Pflugerville, TX 78691-0447. Pub. Frequency: w. (Thu.) Page Size: standard. Subscrip. Rate: $.50 newsstand/cover; $33.28/yr. Adv. Rate: col. inch $8.35 **Owner(s):** Cox Newspapers, Inc., 6205 Peachtree Dunwoody Rd., Atlanta, GA 30328. Telephone: 678-645-0000. **Management:** Sandy Flora, Publisher. Peter Corpus, Advertising Director. **Editorial:** Sandy Flora, Editor. Tiffany Young, Assistant Editor. Chris Grant, Sports Editor.

PITTSBURG

PITTSBURG GAZETTE. 112 Quitman St., Pittsburg, TX 75686. Telephone: 903-856-6629. FAX: 903-856-0510. E-MAIL: pittsgazette@aol.com. URL: http://www.thepittsburggazette.com. Year Established: 1884. Pub. Frequency: w. (Thu.) Page Size: standard. Subscrip. Rate: $.50 newsstand/cover; $27.50/yr in county; $38/yr out of county; $46/yr out of state. Circulation: 3,150 per issue (paid). **Owner(s):** ASP Westward LP, 523 N Sam Houston Pkwy Ste, 600, Houston, TX 77060-4011. **Management:** Debbie Knox, Publisher. Todd Gentry, Advertising Manager. Shannon Dean, Circulation Manager. **Editorial:** Susan Taft, Editor.

PLANO

ALLEN AMERICAN, THE. 624 Krona Dr, Ste 170, Plano, TX 75074. Telephone: 972-398-4200. FAX: 972-398-4470. URL: http://www.scntx.com. Pub. Frequency: w. (Thu.) Page Size: broadsheet. Subscrip. Rate: $.50 newsstand/cover; $25/yr carrier delivery; $39.95/yr mailed in county; $59.95/yr mailed out of county. Circulation: 3,000 per issue (free). **Owner(s):** Star Community Newspapers, 14875 Landmark Blvd, Ste 110, Addison, TX 75254. Telephone: 972-628-4061. FAX: 971-436-7432. **Management:** Bill Weaver, Publisher. Scott Carr, Advertising Manager. Ken McEwen, Circulation Manager. **Editorial:** Rick Mann, Managing Editor.

PLANO INSIDER. 624 Krona Dr, Ste 170, Plano, TX 75074. Telephone: 972-398-4200. FAX: 972-398-4470. E-MAIL: scott.carr@scntx.com. URL: http://www.scntx.com. Pub. Frequency: w. (Sun.) Page Size: standard Circulation: 50,000 per issue (free). **Owner(s):** Star Community Newspapers, 14875 Landmark Blvd, Ste 110, Addison, TX 75254. Telephone: 972-628-4061. FAX: 971-436-7432. **Management:** Scott Wright, Publisher. Scott Carr, Advertising Manager. Ken McEwen, Circulation Manager. Sharon Marrow, Classified Adv. Mgr.. **Editorial:** Jeannie Millendu, Managing Editor. Mike Norris, Editorial Page Editor.

PLEASANTON

PLEASANTON EXPRESS. 89 Pulliam, Pleasanton, TX 78064. Telephone: 860-569-6130. FAX: 860-569-6100. E-MAIL: gblack@pleasantonexpress.com. URL: http://www.pleasantonexpress.com. Mailing Address: P.O. Box 880, Pleasanton, TX 78064. Year Established: 1909. Pub. Frequency: w. (Wed.) Page Size: broadsheet. Subscrip. Rate: $.50 newsstand/cover; $25/yr home delivery in county; $30/yr out of area; $35/yr out of state; $20/yr local to senior citizens. Circulation: 8,450 per issue (paid). **Owner(s):** Wilkerson Publishing Co., See address and contact information above. **Management:** Judy Wilkerson, Co-Publisher. Mary Gallegos, Advertising Manager. Rhonda Chancellor, Circulation Manager. **Editorial:** Sue B Elizondo, Editor. Gerald Black, News Editor. Daniel Elizonda, Sports Editor.

PORT ISABEL

PORT ISABEL-SOUTH PADRE ITEM PRESS. 413 E. Railroad St., Port Isabel, TX 78578. Telephone: 956-943-5545. FAX: 956-943-4782. E-MAIL: hhpub1@aol.com. Mailing Address: PO Box 308, Port Isabel, TX 78578. Year Established: 1950. Pub. Frequency: s-w. (Mon. & Thu.) Page Size: broadsheet. Subscrip. Rate: $.50 newsstand/cover; $22/yr in county; $36/yr out of county. Circulation: 4,500 per issue (paid and free). **Owner(s):** New Horizon Publishers, Inc., 356 N Sam Houston Blvd, San Benito, TX 78586. Telephone: 956-399-2436. **Management:** Matt Thornton, Advertising Director. **Editorial:** Danno Wise, Managing Editor.

PORT LAVACA

PORT LAVACA WAVE. 107 E. Austin, Port Lavaca, TX 77979. Telephone: 361-552-9788. FAX: 361-552-3108. E-MAIL: tfrench@plwave.com. URL: http://www.portlavacawave.com. Mailing Address: PO Box 88, Port Lavaca, TX 77979-0088. Year Established: 1890. Pub. Frequency: s-w. (Wed. & Sat.) Page Size: broadsheet. Subscrip. Rate: $.50 newsstand/cover; $31.50/yr in county; $46.50/yr mailed out of county; $57.50/yr mailed out of state. Adv. Rate: col. inch $7.50 Circulation: 8,000 per issue (paid and free). **Owner(s):** Port Lavaca Wave, Inc., See address and contact information above. **Management:** Tania French, Publisher. Cathy Buehring, Advertising Manager. Rita Boudreaux, Circulation Manager. **Editorial:** Tania French, Managing Editor.

PORTLAND

PORTLAND NEWS. 1105 Railroad Ste. B, Portland, TX 78374. Telephone: 361-643-1566. FAX: 361-643-1400. E-MAIL: dhamilton@sanpatpublishing.com. Pub. Frequency: w. (Thu.) Page Size: broadsheet. Subscrip. Rate: $.75 newsstand/cover; $39/yr mailed in county; $48.75/yr mailed out of county; $50/yr mailed out of state. Circulation: 4,000 per issue (paid). **Owner(s):** San Patricio Publishing Co., Inc., 117 S. Rachal, Sinton, TX 78387. Telephone: 512-364-1270. **Management:** James F Tracy Jr., Co-Publisher. John H Tracy, Advertising Manager. **Editorial:** Dianna Hamilton, Editor.

POTTSBORO

DENISON PRESS. 706 N.FM, Pottsboro, TX 75076-0817. Telephone: 903-786-4051. FAX: 903-786-2250. Mailing Address: P.O. Box 817, Pottsboro, TX 75076-0817. Pub. Frequency: w. **Owner(s):** Texoma Press LLC, See address and contact information above. **Management:** Frank Alvarez Sr., Publisher. **Editorial:** Frank Alvarez Sr., Editor.

POTTSBORO PRESS. 706 N.FM, Pottsboro, TX 75076-0817. Telephone: 903-786-4051. FAX: 903-786-2250. E-MAIL: potts-denpress@cablerocket. Mailing Address: P.O. Box 817, Pottsboro, TX 75076-0817. Year Established: 1984. Pub. Frequency: w. (Thu.) Page Size: standard. Subscrip. Rate: $.50 newsstand/cover; $24/yr in county; $33/yr mailed in state; $39/yr mailed out of state. Circulation: 2,500 per issue (paid). **Owner(s):** Texoma Press LLC, See address and contact information above. **Management:** Frank Alvarez Sr., Publisher. **Editorial:** Frank Alvarez Sr., Editor.

QUITMAN

WOOD COUNTY DEMOCRAT. 111 W. Lipscomb, Quitman, TX 75783. Telephone: 903-763-4522. FAX: 903-763-2313. E-MAIL: democrat@etcnonline.com. URL: http://www.hcnonline.com. Mailing Address: PO Box 308, Quitman, TX 75783. Year Established: 1893. Pub. Frequency: w. (Wed.) Page Size: broadsheet. Subscrip. Rate: $.50 newsstand/cover; $27.50/yr in county; $42/yr in state. Adv. Rate: col. inch $7.90 Circulation: 3,500 per issue (paid). **Owner(s):** ASP Westward LP, 523 N Sam Houston Pkwy, Ste 600, Houston, TX 77060. **Management:** Joyce Hathcock, Publisher. Toni Cole, Circulation Manager. **Editorial:** Wilbur Callaway, Sports.

RICHARDSON

RICHARDSON MORNING NEWS. ISSN 1045-4004
1202 Richardson Dr., Ste. 210, Richardson, TX 75080. Telephone: 214-977-8222. FAX: 214-977-7586. E-MAIL: richnews@airmail.net. URL: htp://www.dallasnews.com. Year Established: 1958. Pub. Frequency: s-w. (Thu. & Sun.) Page Size: broadsheet. Subscrip. Rate: $.50 newsstand/cover; $36/yr carrier delivery. Circulation: 10,000 Sunday (paid); 10,000 per issue (paid). **Owner(s):** Belo Corp., P.O. Box 655237, Dallas, TX 75265-5237. **Management:** James Maroney III, Publisher. Pat Westrech, Advertising Manager. **Editorial:** Bob Bersano, Editor.

ROCKDALE

ROCKDALE REPORTER. 221-225 E. Cameron, Rockdale, TX 76567-2972. Telephone: 512-446-5838. FAX: 512-446-5317. E-MAIL: staff@rockdalereporter.com. URL: http://www.rockdalereporter.com. Year Established: 1893. Pub. Frequency: w. (Thu.) Page Size: broadsheet. Subscrip. Rate: $.75 newsstand/cover; $26/yr local; $30/yr in state; $37/yr out of state. Adv. Rate: col. inch $9 Circulation: 4,499 per issue (paid). **Owner(s):** J.W. Cooke, PO Box 552, Rockdale, TX 76567-0552. Telephone: 512-446-5838. FAX: 512-446-5317. **Management:** Ken Esten Cooke, General Manager. J.W. Cooke, Publisher. Kathy Cooke, Advertising Manager. Kelley Zapata, Circulation Manager. Linda Whorton, Classified Adv. Mgr.. **Editorial:** Mike Brown, Editor.

ROUND ROCK

ROUND ROCK LEADER. ISSN 0164-9124
105 S. Blair St., Round Rock, TX 78664. Telephone: 512-255-5827. FAX: 512-255-3733. E-MAIL: mj@rrleader.com. URL: http://www.rrleader.com. Mailing Address: PO Box 459, Round Rock, TX 78680-0459. Year Established: 1877. Pub. Frequency: 3/w. (Tue., Thu., Sat.) Page Size: broadsheet. Subscrip. Rate: $.50 newsstand/cover; $35/yr in Williamson & Travis cys.; $50/yr mailed elsewhere. Circulation: 5,400 per issue (paid); 2,100 per issue (free). **Owner(s):** Todd Publications, Inc., 4620 Lake View, Austin, TX 78731. Telephone: 512-255-5827. FAX: 512-255-3733. **Management:** Steve Laukhuf, General Manager. Jennifer Heddlesten, Advertising Manager. John Wallace, Circulation Manager. Tajah Liddy, Classified Adv. Mgr.. **Editorial:** Brad Stutzman, Managing Editor. Marcial Guajardo, Associate Editor. Jeff Caspersen, Sports.

SAN ANTONIO

METROCOM HERALD, THE. 7137 Military Dr., W., San Antonio, TX 78227. Telephone: 210-453-3300. FAX: 210-675-4577. E-MAIL: jflinn@primetimenewspapers.com. Pub. Frequency: w. (Thu.) Page Size: tabloid.Adv. Rate: col. inch $13.54 Circulation: 33,600 per issue (free). **Owner(s):** Prime Time Newspapers, 17400 Judson Rd, San Antonio, TX 78247. Telephone: 210-675-4500. FAX: 210-675-4577. **Management:** Kim Sipper, Publisher. Sylvia Chapman Black, Sales Manager. **Editorial:** Jeff Flinn, Editor-in-Chief.

NORTH SAN ANTONIO TIMES. 17400 Judson Rd, San Antonio, TX 78247. Telephone: 210-736-4450. FAX: 210-736-5506. URL: http://www.primetimenewspapers.com. Year Established: 1952. Pub. Frequency: w. (Thu.) Page Size: tabloid. Subscrip. Rate: $.75 newsstand/cover per issue; $45/yr home delivery. Circulation: 90,000 per issue (paid and free). **Owner(s):** Prime Time Newspapers, See address and contact information above. **Management:** Nancy Lipton, Publisher. Linda Hardin, Advertising Manager. Veronica Geisel, Circulation Manager. **Editorial:** Philip Billnitzer, Managing Editor.

SAN ANTONIO CURRENT. 1500 N. St. Mary's St., San Antonio, TX 78215. Telephone: 210-227-0044. FAX: 210-227-6611. URL: http://www.sacurrent.com. Pub. Frequency: w. (Wed.) Page Size: tabloid. Subscrip. Rate: $45 for 6 mos.; $85/yr. Circulation: 50,000 per issue (paid and free). **Owner(s):** Times-Shamrock Communications, 149 Penn Ave., Scranton, PA 18503. **Management:** Dan Farley, Group Publisher. Chris Sexson, Publisher. Nancy Lagleder, Advertising Manager. Dorinda Reyna, Circulation Manager. Jennifer Sanders, Classified Adv. Mgr.. **Editorial:** Elaine Wolff, Editor. Brian Villalobos, Associate Editor.

SOUTHSIDE REPORTER. 2203 S. Hackberry, San Antonio, TX 78210. Telephone: 210-534-8848. FAX: 210-534-7134. E-MAIL: ssr2@primetimenewspapers.com. Year Established: 1935. Pub. Frequency: w. (Thu.) Page Size: tabloid. Subscrip. Rate: $50 newsstand/cover. Adv. Rate: col. inch $19.55 Freelance Pay: $30/story. Circulation: 79,900 per issue (paid and controlled). **Owner(s):** Prime Time Newspapers, Inc., 17400 Judson Rd., San Antonio, TX 78247. Telephone: 210-453-3300. FAX: 210-534-7134. **Management:** William Johnson, President. Paul Davis, Publisher. Veronica Geisel, Circulation Manager. **Editorial:** Paul Davis, Editor. Jay Foraker, Managing Editor.

SAN AUGUSTINE

SAN AUGUSTINE TRIBUNE. 807 E Columbia St, San Augustine, TX 75972. Telephone: 936-275-2181. FAX: 936-275-0572. E-MAIL: SATribune@Sabinenet.com. Mailing Address: P.O. Box 539, San Augustine, TX 75972. Year Established: 1909. Pub. Frequency: w. (Thu.) Page Size: standard. Subscrip. Rate: $.75 newsstand/cover; $20/yr in county; $25/yr local; $28/yr elsewhere. Adv. Rate: col. inch $5 Circulation: 5,000 per issue (paid). **Owner(s):** Stephen Hays, See address and contact information above. **Management:** Stephen Hays, Publisher. **Editorial:** Stephen Hays, Editor.

SAN BENITO

SAN BENITO NEWS. 356 N Sam Houston Blvd, San Benito, TX 78586. Telephone: 956-399-2436. FAX: 956-399-2430. Mailing Address: P.O. Box 1791, San Benito, TX 78586. Year Established: 1946. Pub. Frequency: s-w. (Wed. & Sat.) Page Size: broadsheet. Subscrip. Rate: $.50 newsstand/cover; $30/yr carrier delivery; $32/yr mailed in county; $38/yr mailed out of county. Adv. Rate: col. inch $5 Circulation: 5,100 per issue (paid). **Owner(s):** New Horizon Publishers, Inc., See address and contact information above. **Management:** Leroy Gomez, Advertising. Armando Trevino, Circulation Manager. **Editorial:** Michael Rodriguez, Managing Editor.

SEALY

SEALY NEWS. 193 Schmidt Rd., Sealy, TX 77474-2390. Telephone: 979-885-3562. FAX: 979-885-3564. E-MAIL: sealynews@phoenix.net. URL: http://www.sealynews.com. Mailing Address: PO Box 480, Sealy, TX 77474-0480. Year Established: 1887. Pub. Frequency: s-w. (Tue. & Fri.) Page Size: broadsheet. Subscrip. Rate: $.75 newsstand/cover; $39/yr in county; $50/yr mailed out of county; $70/yr mailed out of state. Circulation: 4,000 per issue (paid). **Owner(s):** Sealy Publications, Inc., PO Box 480, Sealy, TX 77474. Telephone: 979-885-3562. **Management:** Mike Eddleman, Publisher. Patty Minter, Office Manager. Kristin Ybarra, Classified Adv. Mgr.. **Editorial:** Mike Eddleman, Editor. Lindsey Vaculin, Reporter. Dylan Pearcy, Sports Writer.

SEYMOUR

BAYLOR COUNTY BANNER. 109 E. Morris St., Seymour, TX 76380-0912. Telephone: 940-889-2616. FAX: 940-889-3610. Mailing Address: P.O. Box 912, Seymour, TX 76380-0912. Year Established: 1895. Pub. Frequency: w. (Thu.) Page Size: standard. Subscrip. Rate: $.50 newsstand/cover; $20/yr in county; $25/yr out of county; $28/yr out of state. Adv. Rate: col. inch $5 Circulation: 2,500 per issue (paid). **Owner(s):** Matt Gwinn, See address and contact information above. **Management:** Matt Gwinn, Publisher. Ann Myers, Circulation Manager. **Editorial:** Matt Gwinn, Editor-in-Chief.

SILSBEE

SILSBEE BEE. PO Box 547, Silsbee, TX 77656. Telephone: 409-385-5278. E-MAIL: news@sillsbee.com. URL: http://www.silsbeebee.com. Year Established: 1919. Pub. Frequency: w. (Wed.) Page Size: broadsheet. Subscrip. Rate: $.50 newsstand/cover; $20/yr local; $24/yr elsewhere. Circulation: 6,500 per issue (paid). **Owner(s):** Danny Reneau, See address and contact information above. **Management:** Danny Reneau, Publisher. Jan Reneau, Advertising Manager. **Editorial:** Danny Reneau, Editor.

SINTON

ODEM-EDROY TIMES. P O Drawer B, Sinton, TX 78387. Telephone: 361-364-1270. FAX: 361-364-4358. E-MAIL: editor@sanpatpublishing.com. URL: http://www.sanpatpublishing.com. Year Established: 1948. Pub. Frequency: w. (Thu.) Page Size: broadsheet. Subscrip. Rate: $.50 newsstand/cover; $35/yr mailed in county; $43/yr mailed out of county; $45.50/yr mailed out of state. Adv. Rate: col. inch $5.50 Circulation: 600 per issue (paid). **Owner(s):** San Patricio Publishing Co., Inc., 117 S. Rachal, Sinton, TX 78387. **Management:** James F Tracy Jr., Co-Publisher. John H Tracy, Advertising. **Editorial:** Kurt Mogonye, Editor.

SAN PATRICIO COUNTY NEWS. P O Drawer B, Sinton, TX 78387. Telephone: 361-364-1270. FAX: 361-364-4358. E-MAIL: editor@sanpatpublishing.com. Year Established: 1908. Pub. Frequency: w. (Wed.) Page Size: broadsheet. Subscrip. Rate: $.75 newsstand/cover; $39/yr mailed in county; $48.75/yr mailed out of county; $50/yr mailed out of state. Adv. Rate: col. inch $7.55 Circulation: 2,500 per issue (paid). **Owner(s):** San Patricio Publishing Co., Inc., 117 S. Rachal, Sinton, TX 78387. **Management:** James F Tracy Jr., Co-Publisher. **Editorial:** James F Tracy Jr., Editor.

SMITHVILLE

SMITHVILLE TIMES, THE. 303 Main St., Smithville, TX 78957-1426. Telephone: 512-237-4655. FAX: 512-237-5443. E-MAIL: news@smithvilletimes.com. Mailing Address: PO Box 659, Smithville, TX 79857-0659. Year Established: 1892. Pub. Frequency: w. (Thu.) Page Size: broadsheet.Subscrip. Rate: $.50 newsstand/cover Circulation: 3,100 per issue (paid). **Owner(s):** Cox Newspapers, Inc., 6205 Peachtree Dunwoody Rd., Atlanta, GA 30328. Telephone: 678-645-0000. **Management:** Mark Gwin, Publisher. Fran Hunter, Advertising Director. Kathy Lynch, Classified Editor. **Editorial:** Mark Gwin, Managing Editor. Erin Boyd, Reporter.

SOUTH PADRE ISLAND

COASTAL CURRENT WEEKLY, THE. 2600 Padre Blvd, Ste L, South Padre Island, TX 78598. Telephone: 956-761-9341. FAX: 956-761-1436. URL: http://www.spislandbreez.com. Mailing Address: PO Box 2429, South Padre Island, TX 78597. Year Established: 1991. Pub. Frequency: w. (Fri.) Page Size: tabloid. Freelance Pay: $25/article. Circulation: 25,000 per issue (paid and controlled). **Owner(s):** Freedom Communications, Inc., 17666 Fitch, Irvine, CA 92714. Telephone: 714-253-9292. FAX: 714-474-7675. **Management:** George Cox, Publisher. Darren Goller, Advertising Manager. **Editorial:** Ryan Henry, Managing Editor.

ISLAND BREEZE. 2600 Padre Blvd, Ste L, South Padre Island, TX 78598. Telephone: 956-761-9341. FAX: 956-761-1436. Mailing Address: PO Box 2429, South Padre Island, TX 78597. Year Established: 1824. Pub. Frequency: 3/w. (Fri., Sat., Sun.) Page Size: tabloid. Subscrip. Rate: $.50 newsstand/cover; $27/yr in county; $34/yr out of county. Circulation: 12,000 per issue (free). **Owner(s):** Freedom Communications, Inc., 17666 Fitch, Irvine, CA 92714. Telephone: 949-253-2300. FAX: 714-474-7675. **Management:** George Cox, Publisher. Darren Goller, Advertising Manager. **Editorial:** Ryan Henry, Managing Editor.

SOUTHLAKE

COLLEYVILLE COURIER, THE. 1721 E Southlake Blvd, Ste 100, Southlake, TX 76092. Telephone: 817-439-3022. FAX: 817-439-3140. URL: http://www.colleyvilletexascourier.com. Pub. Frequency: w. (Fri.) Page Size: standard.Subscrip. Rate: $31/yr mailed Circulation: 24,000 per issue (free). **Owner(s):** The/McClatchy Company, 2100 Q St, Sacramento, CA 95816. Telephone: 916-321-1936. FAX: 916-321-1869. **Management:** Bill Lewis, Group Publisher. Gary Hardee, Publisher. Debbie Roach, Advertising. Jessicca Foster, Classified Adv. Mgr.. **Editorial:** Alice Murray, Editor. Zach Warner, Sports.

SOUTHLAKE JOURNAL, THE. 1721 E Southlake Blvd, Ste 100, Southlake, TX 76092. Telephone: 817-439-3022. FAX: 817-439-3140. URL: http://www.southlakejournal.com/. Year Established: 1989. Pub. Frequency: w. (Fri.) Page Size: standard.Subscrip. Rate: $31/yr mailed Circulation: 9,000 per issue (free). **Owner(s):** The/McClatchy Company, 2100 Q St., Sacramento, CA 95816-6816. **Management:** Angela Paris, Advertising. Debbie Rauen, Advertising Manager. Jessicca Foster, Classified Adv. Mgr.. **Editorial:** Alice Murray, Editor. Charles Young, Executive Editor. Zach Warner, Sports.

WESTLAKE FIRST NEWS. 1721 E Southlake Blvd, Ste 100, Southlake, TX 76092. Telephone: 817-439-3022. FAX: 817-439-3140. URL: http://www.colleyvilletexascourier.com. Pub. Frequency: w. (Fri.) Page Size: standard.Subscrip. Rate: $31/yr mailed Circulation: 30,000 per issue (free). **Owner(s):** The/McClatchy Company, 2100 Q St, Sacramento, CA 95816. **Management:** Bill Lewis, Group Publisher. Debbie Rauen, Advertising Manager. Jessicca Foster, Classified Adv. Mgr.. **Editorial:** Alice Murray, Editor. Zach Warner, Sports.

SPEARMAN

HANSFORD COUNTY REPORTER-STATESMAN. 213 Main St., Spearman, TX 79081. Telephone: 806-659-3434. Year Established: 1907. Pub. Frequency: w. (Thu.) Page Size: standard. Subscrip. Rate: $.75 newsstand/cover; $25/yr mailed in county; $30/yr mailed out of county. Circulation: 1,700 per issue (paid). **Owner(s):** Gary Smith, See address and contact information above. **Management:** Gary Smith, Publisher. Catherine Smith, Advertising Manager. **Editorial:** Carolyn Cummings, Editor. Catherine Smith, Managing Editor.

SPRINGTOWN

SPRINGTOWN EPIGRAPH, THE. 109 E. First St., Springtown, TX 76082. Telephone: 817-220-7217. FAX: 817-523-4457. E-MAIL: bobbuckel@azlenews.net. URL: http://www.azlenews.net. Mailing Address: PO Box 557, Springtown, TX 76082-0557. Year Established: 1976. Pub. Frequency: w. (Thu.) Page Size: broadsheet. Subscrip. Rate: $.75 newsstand/cover; $28.50/yr in county; $34.50/yr out of county. Adv. Rate: col. inch $6.65 Circulation: 2,600 per issue (paid and free). **Owner(s):** Azle Tri-County Advertiser, Inc., 321 W. Main St., Azle, TX 76020. Telephone: 817-270-3340. **Management:** Bob Buckel, Publisher. Kim Ware, Advertising Director. **Editorial:** Edwin Newton, Editor. Mark Campbell, Sports Editor.

STAMFORD

STAMFORD AMERICAN. 113 E. Mcharg, Stamford, TX 79553. Telephone: 325-773-3621. FAX: 325-773-3622. E-MAIL: news@ashnewspapers.com. URL: http://www.stamfordamerican.com. Year Established: 1922. Pub. Frequency: w. (Thu.) Page Size: standard. Subscrip. Rate: $.50 newsstand/cover; $20/yr in county; $23/yr in state; $25/yr out of state. Circulation: 1,800 per issue (paid). **Owner(s):** Becky Alambar, See address and contact information above. **Management:** Becky Alambar, Publisher.

SUGAR LAND

FORT BEND/SOUTHWEST SUN. 13815 Southwest Fwy., Sugar Land, TX 77478. Telephone: 281-242-1812. FAX: 281-242-1891. E-MAIL: fbeditor@hcnonline.com. URL: http://www.fortbendsouthwestsun.com. Year Established: 1967. Pub. Frequency: w. (Wed.) Page Size: broadsheet. Subscrip. Rate: $20/yr mailed. Adv. Rate: col. inch $21.52 Circulation: 64,000 per issue (free). **Owner(s):** ASP Westward LP, 523 N Sam Houston Pkwy Ste, 600, Houston, TX 77060-4011. **Management:** Darlene Hall, General Manager. Jim Ellis, Circulation Manager. **Editorial:** John Pape, Editor.

SULPHUR SPRINGS

COUNTRY WORLD. 401 Church St., Sulphur Springs, TX 75482. Telephone: 903-885-8663. FAX: 903-885-8768. Mailing Address: PO Box 598, Sulphur Springs, TX 75483. Pub. Frequency: w. (Thu.) Page Size: tabloid.Subscrip. Rate: $.50 newsstand/cover; $24/yr Circulation: 3,000 per issue (paid). **Owner(s):** Echo Publishing Co., See address and contact information above. **Management:** Scott Keys, Publisher. Jimmy Horton, Advertising Manager. Kristie Hayes, Circulation Manager. **Editorial:** Lori Cope, Managing Editor.

TAFT

TAFT TRIBUNE. 120 Green Ave., Taft, TX 78390. Telephone: 361-528-2515. FAX: 361-528-2516. E-MAIL: BTRACY@sanpatpublishing.com. URL: http://www.sanpatpublishing.com. Year Established: 1922. Pub. Frequency: w. (Wed.) Page Size: broadsheet. Subscrip. Rate: $.75 newsstand/cover; $39/yr mailed in county; $47.75/yr mailed out of county; $50/yr mailed out of state. Adv. Rate: col. inch $7.20 Circulation: 1,100 per issue (paid). **Owner(s):** San Patricio Publishing Co., Inc., 117 S. Rachal, Sinton, TX 78387. Telephone: 361-364-1270. **Management:** James F Tracy Jr., Co-Publisher. Belinda Tracy, Advertising Manager. **Editorial:** Belinda Tracy, Editor.

THE WOODLANDS

(WOODLANDS) VILLAGER, THE. 1600 Lake Front Cir., Ste. 190, The Woodlands, TX 77380. Telephone: 281-367-5309. FAX: 281-363-3299. E-MAIL: villagereditor@hcnonline.com. URL: http://www.thewoodlandsvillager.com. Mailing Address: PO Box 7089, The Woodlands, TX 77387. Year Established: 1977. Pub. Frequency: w. (Thu.) Page Size: broadsheet. Subscrip. Rate: $.50 newsstand/cover. Adv. Rate: col. inch $13.36 Circulation: 38,000 per issue (controlled and free). **Owner(s):** ASP Westward LP, 523 N Sam Houston Pkwy Ste, 600, Houston, TX 77060-4011. **Management:** Ray Biggerstaff, Publisher. **Editorial:** Charlie Bier, Editor.

TOMBALL

MAGNOLIA POTPOURRI. 825 Village Square, Tomball, TX 77375. Telephone: 281-357-0882. FAX: 281-357-8935. E-MAIL: ajones@henonline.com. URL: http://www.thetomballpotpourri.com. Pub. Frequency: w. (Wed.) Page Size: broadsheet Circulation: 46,000 per issue (free). **Owner(s):** ASP Westward LP, 523 N Sam Houston Pkwy Ste, 600, Houston, TX 77060-4011. **Management:** Jed Young, Publisher. Lisa Osterhaus, Advertising Manager. **Editorial:** Allan Jones, Editor.

TOMBALL POTPOURRI, THE. 825 Village Square, Tomball, TX 77375. Telephone: 281-357-0882. FAX: 281-357-8935. E-MAIL: ajones@henonline.com. URL: http://www.thetomballpotpourri.com. Pub. Frequency: w. (Wed.) Page Size: broadsheet.Adv. Rate: col. inch $10.88 Circulation: 46,000 per issue (controlled and free). **Owner(s):** ASP Westward LP, 523 N Sam Houston Pkwy Ste, 600, Houston, TX 77060-4011. **Management:** Jed Young, Publisher. Lisa Osterhaus, Advertising Manager. **Editorial:** Allan Jones, Editor.

TRENTON

TRENTON TRIBUNE. 115 Hamilton, Trenton, TX 75490-0043. Telephone: 903-989-2325. E-MAIL: trentontribune@texoma.net. Year Established: 1909. Pub. Frequency: w. (Thu.) Page Size: standard. Subscrip. Rate: $.50 newsstand/cover; $20/yr in county; $33/yr out of county. Circulation: 1,100 per issue (paid). **Owner(s):** Tom M. Holmes, See address and contact information above. **Management:** Tom M. Holmes, President.

TRINITY

TRINITY STANDARD. 116 W. Main, Trinity, TX 75862. Telephone: 936-594-2126. FAX: 936-594-7547. URL: http://www.easttexasnews.com. Mailing Address: PO Box 712, Trinity, TX 75862-0714. Pub. Frequency: w. (Thu.) Page Size: broadsheet. Subscrip. Rate: $.50 newsstand/cover; $13.75/yr in county; $17/yr in state; $19.50/yr out of state. Circulation: 2,500 per issue (paid). **Owner(s):** Polk County Publishing Co., PO Box 1276, Livingston, TX 77351. Telephone: 936-327-4357. FAX: 936-327-7156. **Management:** Alvin Holley, Publisher. Mary McClure, Advertising. **Editorial:** Greg Peak, Editor.

UVALDE

UVALDE LEADER-NEWS. 110 N. East St., Uvalde, TX 78801. Telephone: 830-278-3335. FAX: 830-278-9191. URL: http://www.uvaldeleadernews.com. Year Established: 1879. Pub. Frequency: s-w. (Thu. & Sun.) Page Size: broadsheet. Subscrip. Rate: $.75 newsstand/cover; $34.50/yr in county; $37.50/yr mailed out of county; $49/yr mailed out of state. Circulation: 6,000 per issue (paid). **Owner(s):** Craig K. Garnett, 110 N. East St., Uvalde, TX 78802-0740. Telephone: 830-278-3335. **Management:** Craig K. Garnett, Publisher. Steve Balke, Advertising Manager. Betty Dearing, Circulation Manager. Norma Ybarra, Classified Adv. Mgr.. **Editorial:** Adam Yanelli, Managing Editor. James Bolz, Sports Editor.

VAN HORN

VAN HORN ADVOCATE, THE. 100 Broadway, Van Horn, TX 79855. Telephone: 432-283-2003. FAX: 432-283-7334. E-MAIL: lsimpson@vanhornadvocate.com. URL: http://www.vanhornadvocate.com. Mailing Address: PO Box 8, Van Horn, TX 79855-0008. Year Established: 1910. Pub. Frequency: w. (Thu.) Page Size: standard. Subscrip. Rate: $.50 newsstand/cover; $25/yr local. Adv. Rate: col. inch $4.50 Circulation: 1,000 per issue (paid). **Owner(s):** Larry Simpson, See address and contact information above. **Management:** Larry Simpson, Publisher. Dawn Simpson, Assistant Publisher.

VEGA

VEGA ENTERPRISE, THE. 116 S. Main St., Vega, TX 79092. Telephone: 806-267-2230. FAX: 806-267-2889. E-MAIL: vegaent@arn.net. Mailing Address: PO Box 130, Vega, TX 79092. Pub. Frequency: w. (Thu.) Page Size: standard. Subscrip. Rate: $.75 newsstand/cover; $17.50/yr in county; $20/yr mailed out of county. Circulation: 900 per issue (paid). **Owner(s):** Quincy Taylor, See address and contact information above. **Management:** Quincy Taylor, Publisher. **Editorial:** Quincy Taylor, Editor.

VIDOR

VIDORIAN, THE. 450 W. Bolivar, Vidor, TX 77662. Telephone: 409-769-5428. FAX: 409-769-2600. Mailing Address: PO Box 1236, Vidor, TX 77670. Year Established: 1955. Pub. Frequency: s-w. (Wed. & Fri.) Page Size: broadsheet. Subscrip. Rate: $.25 newsstand/cover; $15/yr. Circulation: 12,700 per issue (paid and free). **Owner(s):** A. Randall Luker, See address and contact information above. **Management:** A. Randall Luker, President. A. Merle Luker, Publisher. Renee Luker, Advertising Manager. **Editorial:** A. Randall Luker, Editor-in-Chief.

WACO

SUBURBAN COURIER, THE. 1020 N. 25th St., Waco, TX 76707. Telephone: 254-754-3511. FAX: 254-754-3541. E-MAIL: news@wacocitizen.com. URL: http://www.wacocitizen.com. Year Established: 1890. Pub. Frequency: w. (Thu.) Page Size: broadsheet. Subscrip. Rate: $.35 newsstand/cover; $20/yr in county; $24/yr out of county; $24/yr out of state. Adv. Rate: col. inch $3.50 Circulation: 900 per issue (paid). **Owner(s):** Citizen Newspapers, Inc., See address and contact information above. **Management:** Bill Foster, Publisher. **Editorial:** Bill Foster, Managing Editor.

WACO CITIZEN, THE. 1020 N. 25th St., Waco, TX 76707. Telephone: 254-754-3511. FAX: 254-754-3541. E-MAIL: news@wacocitizen.com. URL: http://www.wacocitizen.com. Year Established: 1946. Pub. Frequency: w. (Thu.) Page Size: broadsheet. Subscrip. Rate: $.35 newsstand/cover; $24/yr in county; $34.50/yr out of county. Adv. Rate: page $516.60; 6 x 21 Freelance Pay: $0.40/column-inch. Circulation: 2,200 per issue (paid). **Owner(s):** Citizen Newspapers, Inc., See address and contact information above. **Management:** Bill Foster, Publisher. **Editorial:** Bill Foster, Editor.

WALLIS

WALLIS NEWS-REVIEW. 6705 Commerce St., Wallis, TX 77485-0668. Telephone: 979-478-6412. FAX: 409-478-6412. Mailing Address: PO Box 668, Wallis, TX 77485-0668. Year Established: 1974. Pub. Frequency: w. (Thu.) Page Size: broadsheet. Subscrip. Rate: $.50 newsstand/cover; $18/yr mailed in state; $22/yr mailed out of state. Adv. Rate: col. inch $3.53 Circulation: 1,250 per issue (paid). **Owner(s):** Maridel Dungen, 910 FM 109, New Ulm, TX 78950. Telephone: 979-992-3351. **Management:** Maridel Dunger, Publisher. **Editorial:** Lucille Jemela, Editor.

WAXAHACHIE

ALVARADO POST. 200 W Marwin, Waxahachie, TX 75165. Telephone: 972-937-3310. FAX: 972-937-1139. E-MAIL: alvpost@swbell.net. Mailing Address: PO Box 877, Waxahachie, TX 75165. Pub. Frequency: w. (Thu.) Page Size: broadsheet. Subscrip. Rate: $.50 newsstand/cover; $18/yr mailed. Adv. Rate: col. inch $4 Circulation: 3,000 per issue (paid). **Owner(s):** Waxahachie Newspapers, Inc., See address and contact information above. **Management:** Neal White, Publisher. **Editorial:** Debra Wesson, Editor.

WEATHERFORD

WEATHERFORD TELEGRAM. 112 S Main, Weatherford, TX 98372. Telephone: 817-594-9902. Pub. Frequency: w. (Wed.) Page Size: standard Circulation: 32,203 per issue (free). **Owner(s):** The/McClatchy Company, 2100 Q St, Sacramento, CA 95816. **Management:** Lance Winter, Publisher. Julie Gartner, Advertising. **Editorial:** Terry Evans, Editor.

WEBSTER

BAY AREA CITIZEN. 100 E NASA Pkwy, Webster, TX 77598. Telephone: 281-488-1108. FAX: 281-332-6901. E-MAIL: citizen@hcnonline.com. URL: http://www.thecitizen-online.com. Pub. Frequency: w. (Thu.) Page Size: broadsheet. Subscrip. Rate: $.50 newsstand/cover per issue; $36/yr home delivery. **Owner(s):** ASP Westward LP, 523 N Sam Houston Pkwy E.Ste 600, Houston, TX 77060-4011. Telephone: 281-668-1100. **Management:** Margarette Chasteen, General Manager. **Editorial:** Mary Alys Cherry, Managing Editor.

WEIMER

WEIMAR MERCURY. ISSN 1071-0329
200 W. Main St., Weimer, TX 78962. Telephone: 979-725-9595. FAX: 979-725-9051. E-MAIL: mercury@weimarmercury.comercury@cvtv.net. Mailing Address: P.O.Box 277, Weimer, TX 78962. Year Established: 1888. Pub. Frequency: w. (Thu.) Page Size: broadsheet. Subscrip. Rate: $.50 newsstand/cover; $19.50/yr in county; $22/yr out of county; $21/yr out of state. Circulation: 3,500 per issue (paid). **Owner(s):** Bruce Beal, See address and contact information above. **Management:** Bruce Beal, Publisher. **Editorial:** Bruce Beal, Editor.

WESLACO

MID VALLEY TOWN CRIER. 401 S. Iowa, Weslaco, TX 78596. Telephone: 956-969-2543. FAX: 956-968-0855. E-MAIL: ads@midvalleytowncrier.com. Mailing Address: PO Box 8308, Weslaco, TX 78596. Year Established: 1967. Pub. Frequency: w. (Wed., Fri. & Sun.) Page Size: broadsheet.Adv. Rate: col. inch $13 Freelance Pay: $15/story. Circulation: 23,500 per issue (free). **Owner(s):** Freedom Communications, Inc., 17666 Fitch, Irvine, CA 92614. **Management:** Steve Paterson, Publisher. Adam Rodriguiz, Circulation Manager. **Editorial:** Lupe Garcia, Editorial Assistant.

WEST

WEST NEWS. 214 N Oak, West, TX 76691. Year Established: 1890. Pub. Frequency: w. (Thu.) Page Size: broadsheet. Subscrip. Rate: $.50 newsstand/cover; $21/yr. Adv. Rate: col. inch $4 Circulation: 3,100 per issue (paid). **Owner(s):** Cechoslovak Publishing Co., PO Box 38, West, TX 76691. Telephone: 254-826-3718. FAX: 254-826-3719. **Management:** Linn Pescaia, Publisher. Sue Pescaia, Advertising Manager. **Editorial:** Larry Knapek, Editor.

WEST COLUMBIA

BRAZORIA COUNTY NEWS, THE. PO Box 488, West Columbia, TX 77461. Telephone: 979-793-6560. FAX: 979-345-5308. URL: http://www.brazoriacountynews.org. Year Established: 1962. Pub. Frequency: w. (Thu.) Page Size: broadsheet. Subscrip. Rate: $.35 newsstand/cover; $80/yr mailed. Adv. Rate: col. inch $6 Circulation: 11,000 per issue (paid and free). **Owner(s):** David Toney, See address and contact information above. **Management:** Rebecca Hutchinson, General Manager. **Editorial:** Teena Maenza, Editor.

GULF COAST TRIBUNE, THE. PO Box 488, West Columbia, TX 77461. Telephone: 979-793-6560. FAX: 979-345-5308. Year Established: 1962. Pub. Frequency: w. (Thu.) Page Size: broadsheet. Subscrip. Rate: $.35 newsstand/cover; $17.50/yr in county; $30/yr out of county. Circulation: 1,400 per issue (paid). **Owner(s):** David Toney, See address and contact information above. **Management:** David Toney, Publisher. Jeri Mager, Advertising Manager. **Editorial:** Rebecca Hutchinson, Managing Editor.

WHARTON

WHARTON JOURNAL-SPECTATOR. ISSN 1076-7266
PO Box 111, Wharton, TX 77488-0111. Telephone: 979-532-8840. FAX: 979-532-8845. URL: http://www.journal-spectator.com. Year Established: 1888. Pub. Frequency: s-w. (Wed. & Sat.) Page Size: broadsheet. Subscrip. Rate: $.75 newsstand/cover; $39/yr in county; $54/yr in state; $62/yr out of state. Adv. Rate: col. inch $7.14 Circulation: 4,550 per issue (paid). **Owner(s):** River Publishers, Inc., See address and contact information above. **Management:** Larry C. Jackson, General Manager. Dick Elam, President. Sasie Jackson, Advertising Manager. Emily Clark, Circulation Manager. Helen Sevier, Classified Adv. Mgr.. **Editorial:** Larry C. Jackson, Editor. Burlon Parsons, Lifestyle Editor. Ron Sanders, News Editor. Mike Konvicka, Sports Editor.

WHITE OAK

WHITE OAK INDEPENDENT. ISSN 1053-1513
100 N. White Oak Rd., White Oak, TX 75693. Telephone: 903-845-5349. FAX: 903-845-5349. E-MAIL: newman@longview.net. Mailing Address: PO Box 445, White Oak, TX 75693-0445. Year Established: 1990. Pub. Frequency: w. (Thu.) Page Size: broadsheet. Subscrip. Rate: $.50 newsstand/cover; $20/yr. Freelance Pay: $0.50/column-inch. Circulation: 1,200 per issue (paid). **Owner(s):** Jeff & Winnie Newman, See address and contact information above. **Management:** Jeff Newman, Publisher. **Editorial:** Winnie Newman, Editor-in-Chief.

WINNSBORO

WINNSBORO NEWS. 105 E. Locuat, Winnsboro, TX 75494. Telephone: 903-342-5247. FAX: 903-342-3266. E-MAIL: winnsboronews@cox-internet.com. Mailing Address: PO Box 87, Winnsboro, TN 75494. Year Established: 1907. Pub. Frequency: w. (Thu.) Page Size: standard. Subscrip. Rate: $.50 newsstand/cover; $25/yr mailed in county; $35/yr mailed out of county. Circulation: 4,650 per issue (paid). **Owner(s):** Pen-Wheel Press, See address and contact information above. **Management:** Thomas F. Pendergast, Publisher. Karen W. Pendergast, Circulation Manager. **Editorial:** Karen W. Pendergast, Managing Editor. Marc Hall, Sports.

WOODVILLE

TYLER COUNTY BOOSTER. ISSN 1043-0350
205 W. Bluff St, Woodville, TX 75979. Telephone: 409-283-2516. FAX: 409-283-2560. E-MAIL: polknews@livingston.net. Mailing Address: PO Box 339, Woodville, TX 75979-0339. Year Established: 1930. Pub. Frequency: w. (Wed.) Page Size: broadsheet. Subscrip. Rate: $.50 newsstand/cover; $14/yr in county; $17/yr out of county; $21/yr out of state. Circulation: 4,500 per issue (paid and free). **Owner(s):** Polk County Publishing Co., PO Box 1276, Livingston, TX 77351. Telephone: 936-327-4357. FAX: 936-327-7156. **Management:** John Morrison, General Manager. Alvin Holley, Publisher. Becky Byley, Advertising. **Editorial:** John Morrison, Editor.

WYLIE

WYLIE NEWS, THE. 110 N. Ballard St, Wylie, TX 75098. Telephone: 972-422-5515. FAX: 972-442-4318. E-MAIL: publisher@wylienews.com. URL: http://www.wylienews.com. Mailing Address: PO Box 369, Wylie, TX 75098. Year Established: 1947. Pub. Frequency: w. (Wed.) Page Size: broadsheet. Subscrip. Rate: $.50 newsstand/cover; $23/yr local; $28/yr in state; $35/yr out of state. Adv. Rate: col. inch $13.15 Circulation: 4,106 per issue (paid). **Owner(s):** C & S Media, Inc., See address and contact information above. **Management:** Chad B. Engbrock, Publisher. Janice Martz, Advertising. **Editorial:** Chad B. Engbrock, Editor-in-Chief. Donnita Nesbit Fisher, Managing Editor.

YOAKUM

YOAKUM HERALD-TIMES. 312 Lott, Yoakum, TX 77995. Telephone: 361-293-5266. Mailing Address: PO Box 798, Yoakum, TX 77995. Year Established: 1892. Pub. Frequency: w. (Wed.) Page Size: broadsheet. Subscrip. Rate: $.75 newsstand/cover; $31/yr in county; $37/yr out of county; $42/yr out of state. Circulation: 3,000 per issue (paid). **Owner(s):** Preuss Printing Co., 170 N. Knox Ave., Giddings, TX 78942. Telephone: 979-542-2222. **Management:** David True, General Manager. Nadine Rex, Advertising Director. **Editorial:** David True, Editor.

UTAH

AMERICAN FORK

AMERICAN FORK CITIZEN. 59 W. Main St., American Fork, UT 84003-0007. Telephone: 801-756-7669. FAX: 801-756-5274. E-MAIL: nueditor@heraldextra.com. URL: http://www.newutah.com. Mailing Address: PO Box 7, American Fork, UT 84003. Year Established: 1903. Pub. Frequency: w. (Thu.) Page Size: broadsheet. Subscrip. Rate: $.50 newsstand/cover; $36.40/yr in county; $45.40/yr out of county. Circulation: 30,000 per issue (paid). **Owner(s):** Lee Enterprises, Inc., 201 N Harrison St, Davenport, IA 52801-1939. **Management:** Lane Dubois, Advertising Manager. Jennette Esplain, Circulation Manager. **Editorial:** Barbara Christiansen, Managing Editor.

LONE PEAK PRESS. 59 W. Main St., American Fork, UT 84003. Telephone: 801-756-7669. FAX: 801-756-5274. E-MAIL: nveditor@heralextra.com. Mailing Address: PO Box 7, American Fork, UT 84003. Pub. Frequency: w. (Thu.) Page Size: broadsheet. Subscrip. Rate: $.50 newsstand/cover; $36.40/yr in county; $45.40/yr out of county. Adv. Rate: col. inch $15 Circulation: 12,000 per issue (paid). **Owner(s):** Lee Enterprises, Inc., 201 N Harrison St, Davenport, IA 52801-1939. **Management:** Lane Dubois, Advertising Manager. **Editorial:** Mark Haddock, Managing Editor.

PLEASANT GROVE REVIEW. 59 W. Main St., American Fork, UT 84003. Telephone: 801-756-7669. FAX: 801-756-5274. E-MAIL: nueditor@heraldextra.com. Mailing Address: PO Box 7, American Fork, UT 84003-0007. Year Established: 1905. Pub. Frequency: w. (Thu.) Page Size: broadsheet. Subscrip. Rate: $.50 newsstand/cover; $36.40/yr mailed in county; $45.40/yr mailed out of county. Adv. Rate: col. inch $15 Circulation: 2,000 per issue (paid). **Owner(s):** Lee Enterprises, Inc., 201 N Harrison St, Davenport, IA 52801-1939. **Management:** Kirk Parkinson, Publisher. Lane Dubois, Advertising Manager. **Editorial:** Cathy Allred, Managing Editor.

BOUNTIFUL

DAVIS COUNTY CLIPPER. ISSN 1061-1223
1370 S. 500 W., Bountiful, UT 84011-0267. Telephone: 801-296-6500. FAX: 801-295-3044. E-MAIL: news@davisclipper.com. URL: http://www.davisclipper.com. Mailing Address: PO Box 267, Bountiful, UT 84011-0267. Year Established: 1891. Pub. Frequency: s-w. (Tue. & Thu.) Page Size: standard. Subscrip. Rate: $.50 newsstand/cover; $35/yr mailed in county; $55/yr mailed out of county. Circulation: 46,000 per issue (paid and free). **Owner(s):** Gail Stahle, Pub., See address and contact information above. **Management:** R. Gail Stahle, Publisher. Gene Milne, Advertising Manager. **Editorial:** Rolf Koecher, Editor.

BRIGHAM CITY

BOX ELDER NEWS JOURNAL. 55 South 100 W., Brigham City, UT 84302. E-MAIL: newsjournal@benewsjournal.com. URL: http://www.benewsjournal.com. Mailing Address: PO Box 370, Brigham City, UT 84302. Year Established: 1896. Pub. Frequency: w. (Wed.) Page Size: broadsheet. Subscrip. Rate: $.75 newsstand/cover; $30/yr in county; $40/yr out of county. Adv. Rate: col. inch $10 Circulation: 11,300 per issue (paid and free). **Owner(s):** Box Elder News & Journal, Inc., See address and contact information above. **Management:** Charles C. Claybaugh, Publisher. Sharon Stephens, Advertising. Lynn Elliott, Classified Adv. Mgr.. **Editorial:** Lori Hunsaker, Editor.

CASTLE DALE

EMERY COUNTY PROGRESS. ISSN 0747-2129
410 E. Main St, Ste B, Castle Dale, UT 84513. Telephone: 435-381-2431. FAX: 435-381-5431. E-MAIL: editor@ecprogress.com. URL: http://www.ecprogress.com. Mailing Address: PO Box 589, Castle Dale, UT 84513. Year Established: 1900. Pub. Frequency: w. (Tue.) Page Size: broadsheet. Subscrip. Rate: $.50 newsstand/cover; $25/yr in county; $30/yr out of county; $35/yr out of state. Circulation: 2,500 per issue (paid). **Owner(s):** Brehm Communications, Inc., 16644 W. Bernardo Dr., Ste. 300, San Diego, CA 92127. Telephone: 858-451-6200. FAX: 858-451-3814. **Management:** Richard Shaw, Publisher. Jenni Fasselin, Advertising Manager. **Editorial:** Patsy Stoddard, Editor.

DELTA

MILLARD COUNTY GAZETTE. PO Box 609, Delta, UT 84624. Telephone: 435-864-4050. FAX: 435-864-4050. E-MAIL: gazette@xmission.com. Mailing Address: PO Box 609, Delta, UT 84624-0609. Year Established: 1978. Pub. Frequency: w. (Tue.) Page Size: tabloid.Adv. Rate: col. inch $6.85 Circulation: 5,000 per issue (paid and free). **Owner(s):** Dale Whipple, See address and contact information above. **Management:** Shirley Westenskow, General Manager. **Editorial:** Shirley Westenskow, Editor.

KANAB

SOUTHERN UTAH NEWS. ISSN 0049-1659
26 N. Main, Kanab, UT 84741. Telephone: 435-644-2900. FAX: 435-644-2926. Year Established: 1930. Pub. Frequency: w. (Wed.) Page Size: standard. Subscrip. Rate: $.35 newsstand/cover per issue; $25/yr local; $35/yr out of area. Circulation: 1,900. **Owner(s):** Southern Utah Publishing Co., See address and contact information above. **Management:** Dennis Brunner, Publisher. **Editorial:** Dixie Brunner, Editor.

MAGNA

KEARNS POST. 8980 W. 2700 S., Magna, UT 84044. Telephone: 801-250-5656. FAX: 801-250-5685.Pub. Frequency: bi-w. Page Size: broadsheet Circulation: 2,000 per issue (free). **Owner(s):** J. Howard & Bonnie Stahle, See address and contact information above. **Management:** J. Howard Stahle, Publisher. Bonnie Stahle, Advertising Manager. **Editorial:** Andrew Weeks, Editor. D. Packer, Production Manager.

MAGNA TIMES. 8980 W. 2700 S., Magna, UT 84044. Telephone: 801-250-5656. FAX: 801-250-5685. Pub. Frequency: w. (Thu.) Page Size: tabloid.Subscrip. Rate: $.50 newsstand/cover; $20/yr Circulation: 8,000 per issue (paid). **Owner(s):** J. Howard & Bonnie Stahle, See address and contact information above. **Management:** J. Howard Stahle, Publisher. Bonnie Stahle, Advertising Manager. **Editorial:** Andrew Weeks, Editor. D. Packer, Production Manager.

WEST VALLEY NEWS. 8980 W. 2700 S., Magna, UT 84044. Telephone: 801-250-5656. FAX: 801-250-5685. E-MAIL: magwest@xmission.com. Pub. Frequency: w. (Thu.) Page Size: standard.Subscrip. Rate: $.50 newsstand/cover; $20/yr Circulation: 5,500 per issue (paid). **Owner(s):** J. Howard & Bonnie Stahle, See address and contact information above. **Management:** J. Howard Stahle, Publisher. Bonnie Stahle, Advertising Manager. **Editorial:** Andrew Weeks, Editor. D. Packer, Production Manager.

OREM

OREM GENEVA TIMES. 538 S. State St., Orem, UT 84058. Telephone: 801-225-1340. FAX: 801-225-1341. E-MAIL: oremtimes@networld.com. URL: http://www.harktheherald.com/orem. Mailing Address: PO Box 65, Orem, UT 84059. Year Established: 1937. Pub. Frequency: w. (Thu.) Page Size: standard. Subscrip. Rate: $.50 newsstand/cover; $26/yr in area. Adv. Rate: col. inch $5.95 Circulation: 5,900 per issue (controlled and free). **Owner(s):** Lee Enterprises, Inc., 201 N Harrison St, Davenport, IA 52801-1939. Telephone: 563-383-2100. **Management:** Kirk Parkinson, Publisher. **Editorial:** Marc Haddock, City Editor. Landon Olson, Sports Editor.

PRICE

SUN ADVOCATE. 845 E. Main St., Price, UT 84501. Telephone: 435-637-0732. FAX: 435-637-2716. E-MAIL: gm@sunad.com. URL: http://www.sunad.com. Year Established: 1892. Pub. Frequency: s-w. (Tue. & Thu.) Page Size: broadsheet. Subscrip. Rate: $.50 newsstand/cover; $37/yr in county; $40/yr mailed out of county; $54/yr mailed out of state. Circulation: 4,700 per issue (paid). **Owner(s):** Brehm Communications, Inc., 16644 W. Bernardo Dr., Ste. 300, San Diego, CA 92128. Telephone: 858-451-6200. **Management:** Ken Larson, Publisher. Darla Lee, Circulation Director. **Editorial:** Lynnda Johnson, Editor. Rick Shaw, Sports Editor.

PROVO

LEHI FREE PRESS. 1555 N. Freedom Blvd., Provo, UT 84604. Telephone: 801-344-2935. FAX: 801-373-5489. E-MAIL: dhnews@heraldextra.com. URL: http://www.heraldextra.comnorthcounty.com. Mailing Address: P.O. Box 717, Provo, UT 84603. Year Established: 1903. Pub. Frequency: w. (Thu.) Page Size: broadsheet. Subscrip. Rate: $.50 newsstand/cover; $36.40/yr in county; $45.40/yr out of county. Adv. Rate: col. inch $11 Circulation: 37,025 per issue (paid). **Owner(s):** Lee Enterprises, Inc., See address and contact information above. **Management:** Jenette Esplin, Circulation Manager. **Editorial:** Barbara Christiansen, Managing Editor.

PYRAMID, THE. 1555 N. Freedom Blvd., Provo, UT 84604. Telephone: 810-344-2935. FAX: 810-373-5489. E-MAIL: cbnews@heraldextra.com. URL: http://www.heraldextra.com/northcounty.com. Mailing Address: P.O. Box 717, Provo, UT 84603. Year Established: 1892. Pub. Frequency: w. (Thu.) Page Size: broadsheet. Subscrip. Rate: $.50 newsstand/cover; $20/yr in county; $23/yr out of county. Adv. Rate: col. inch $8.50 Circulation: 985 per issue (paid). **Owner(s):** Lee Enterprises, Inc., See address and contact information above. **Management:** Kirk Parkinson, Publisher. **Editorial:** Cheryl Brewer, Managing Editor.

RICHFIELD

REAPER EXTRA, THE. 65 W. Center, Richfield, UT 84701. Telephone: 435-896-5476. FAX: 435-896-8123. URL: http://www.richfieldreaper.com. Mailing Address: PO Box 730, Richfield, UT 84701. Year Established: 1964. Pub. Frequency: w. (Thu.) Page Size: tabloid Circulation: 5,000 per issue (free). **Owner(s):** Brehm Communications, Inc., 16644 W. Bernardo Dr., Ste. 300, San Diego, CA 92127. Telephone: 858-451-6200. **Management:** Mark Fuellenbach, Publisher. Charles Hawley, Advertising Manager. Marge Fuellenbach, Circulation Manager.

RICHFIELD REAPER. 65 W. Center, Richfield, UT 84701. Telephone: 435-896-5476. FAX: 435-896-8123. E-MAIL: reapered@richfieldreaper.com. URL: http://www.richfieldreaper.com. Mailing Address: PO Box 730, Richfield, UT 84701. Year Established: 1964. Pub. Frequency: w. (Wed.) Page Size: broadsheet. Subscrip. Rate: $.75 newsstand/cover; $32/yr in area; $45/yr out of area. Circulation: 6,600 per issue (free). **Owner(s):** Brehm Communications, Inc., 16644 W. Bernardo Dr., Ste. 300, San Diego, CA 92127. Telephone: 858-451-6200. **Management:** Charles Hawley, General Manager. Mark Fuellenbach, Publisher. Charles Hawley, Advertising Manager. Marge Fuellenbach, Circulation Manager. **Editorial:** Sandy Phillips, Editor. David Anderson, Associate Editor.

ROOSEVELT

UINTAH BASIN STANDARD. 268 S 200 E, Roosevelt, UT 84066-3109. Telephone: 435-722-5131. FAX: 435-722-4140. E-MAIL: ubsnews@ubtanet.com. URL: http://www.ubstandard.com. Year Established: 1913. Pub. Frequency: w. (Tue.) Page Size: broadsheet. Subscrip. Rate: $.50 newsstand/cover; $26/yr local in area; $38/yr out of area. Circulation: 4,310 per issue (paid). **Owner(s):** Brehm Communications, Inc., 16644 W. Bernardo Dr., Ste. 300, San Diego, CA 92128. **Management:** Craig Ashby, Publisher. Bonnie Parish, Advertising. **Editorial:** Lezlee Whiting, Managing Editor.

SALT LAKE CITY

SALT LAKE CITY WEEKLY. 248 S. Main, Salt Lake City, UT 84101. Telephone: 801-575-7003. FAX: 801-575-6106. E-MAIL: comments@slweekly.com. URL: http://www.slweekly.com. Year Established: 1984. Pub. Frequency: w. (Thu.) Page Size: tabloid. Subscrip. Rate: $40/yr mailed. Adv. Rate: page $2,944 Freelance Pay: $0.16/word. Circulation: 60,000 per issue (controlled and free). **Owner(s):** John Saltas, See address and contact information above. **Management:** Jim Rizzi, Publisher. Doug Kruithof, Advertising. Larry Carter, Circulation Manager. **Editorial:** John Yewell, Editor.

TOOELE

TOOELE TRANSCRIPT-BULLETIN. 58 N. Main St., Tooele, UT 84074. Telephone: 435-882-0050. E-MAIL: tbp@tooeletranscript.com. URL: http://www.tooeletranscript.com. Mailing Address: PO Box 390, Tooele, UT 84074-0390. Year Established: 1894. Pub. Frequency: s-w. (Tue. & Thu.) Page Size: broadsheet. Subscrip. Rate: $.50 newsstand/cover; $35/yr carrier delivery; $40/yr mailed in county; $46/yr mailed out of county. Adv. Rate: col. inch $6 Circulation: 7,850 per issue (paid). **Owner(s):** Scott, Perry, Clayton, Curtis, Bruce Dunn, See address and contact information above. **Management:** Clayton Dunn, Publisher. Kathleen Dunn, Office Manager. Clayton Dunn, Advertising Manager. Bruce Dunn, Business Manager. **Editorial:** Mike Call, Managing Editor.

TREMONTON

LEADER (TREMONTON), THE. ISSN 0747-1416
119 E. Main St., Tremonton, UT 84337. Telephone: 435-257-5182. FAX: 435-257-6175. E-MAIL: theleader@citlink.net. Year Established: 1914. Pub. Frequency: w. (Wed.) Page Size: standard. Subscrip. Rate: $.75 newsstand/cover; $23/yr in county; $30/yr out of county. Adv. Rate: col. inch $9.70 Freelance Pay: $1.25/column-inch. Circulation: 7,100 per issue (paid and free). **Owner(s):** Robert Mashall, See address and contact information above. **Management:** Greg Madson, General Manager. Barrie Petty, Office Manager. Emily Cutler, Advertising. **Editorial:** Arianne Cope, Editor.

VERNAL

VERNAL EXPRESS. ISSN 0892-1091
54 N Vernal Ave, Vernal, UT 84078. Telephone: 435-789-3511. FAX: 435-789-8690. E-MAIL: editor@vernal.com. URL: http://www.vernal.com. Year Established: 1891. Pub. Frequency: w. (Wed.) Page Size: broadsheet. Subscrip. Rate: $.50 newsstand/cover; $26/yr in county & adj. cys.; $36/yr in state; $39/yr out of state. Freelance Pay: $1/column-inch. Circulation: 4,883 per issue (paid). **Owner(s):** Brehm Communications, Inc., 16644 W. Bernardo Dr., Ste. 300, San Diego, CA 92128. Telephone: 858-451-6200. **Management:** Kevin Ashby, Publisher. **Editorial:** Kevin Ashby, Editor.

VERMONT

BELLOWS FALLS

BELLOWS FALLS TOWN CRIER. 24 Rockingham St, Bellows Falls, VT 05101-0459. Telephone: 802-463-9591. FAX: 802-4639818. E-MAIL: news @vermontobserver. URL: http://www.thetowncriers.com. Mailing Address: P O Box 459, Bellow Falls, VT 05101-0459. Year Established: 1984. Pub. Frequency: w. (Fri.) Page Size: tabloid. Subscrip. Rate: $35/yr mailed. Adv. Rate: col. inch $11.10 Circulation: 12,000 per issue (paid and controlled). Owner(s): MediaNews Group, Inc., 101 W Colfax Ave, Ste 1100, Denver, CO 80202. FAX: 303-954-6320. Management: Bob Larson, Publisher. Editorial: Cicely Eastman, Managing Editor.

BRADFORD

IT'S CLASSIFIED. PO Box 886, Bradford, VT 05033-0886. Telephone: 802-222-5152. FAX: 802-222-4942. E-MAIL: mail@itsclassidied.com. URL: http://www.itsclassified.com. Year Established: 1989. Pub. Frequency: w. (Fri.) Page Size: tabloid.Adv. Rate: col. inch $5 Circulation: 18,000 per issue (free). Owner(s): It's Classfied, Inc., See address and contact information above. Management: Peter Mallary, Publisher. Frances Mallery, Advertising Manager. Editorial: Frances Mallary, Editor.

JOURNAL OPINION.   ISSN 0746-1674
48 Main St, Bradford, VT 05033. Telephone: 802-222-5281. FAX: 802-222-5438. E-MAIL: jonews@together.net. URL: http://jonews.com. Mailing Address: PO Box 378, Bradford, VT 05033. Year Established: 1866. Pub. Frequency: w. (Wed.) Page Size: broadsheet. Subscrip. Rate: $.60 newsstand/cover; $18/yr mailed in VT & NH; $25/yr mailed elsewhere. Circulation: 4,500 per issue (paid). Owner(s): Connie Sanville, See address and contact information above. Management: Connie Sanville, General Manager. Editorial: Alex Nuti-deBiasi, Editor.

BRATTLEBORO

BRATTLEBORO TOWN CRIER. 62 Black Mountain Rd., Brattleboro, VT 05302. Telephone: 802-257-7771. FAX: 802-257-2211. Mailing Address: PO Box 802, Brattleboro, VT 05301. Year Established: 1961. Pub. Frequency: w. (Fri.) Page Size: tabloid.Subscrip. Rate: $26/yr mailed Circulation: 12,000 per issue (paid). Owner(s): Roger Miller, See address and contact information above. Management: Bob LaPierre, General Manager. Jim Wells, Publisher. Tim Gorts, Circulation Manager.

CHESTER

MESSAGE FOR THE WEEK. 197 Elm St., Chester, VT 05143. Telephone: 802-875-4790. FAX: 802-875-4792. E-MAIL: message@vermontel.com. Mailing Address: PO Box 759, Chester, VT 05143. Year Established: 1972. Pub. Frequency: w. (Wed.) Page Size: tabloid. Circulation: 26,000 per issue (paid and controlled). Owner(s): Wes & Teresa Johnson, See address and contact information above. Management: Harvey Hill, Publisher. Clyde Pinson, Advertising Manager. Editorial: Paul Larochelle, Editor. Robert Smith, Co-Editor.

ENOSBURG FALLS

COUNTY COURIER (ENOSBURG FALLS). 342 Main St., Enosburg Falls, VT 05450-0398. Telephone: 802-933-4375. FAX: 802-933-4907. E-MAIL: countycourier@vgmail.com. URL: http://www.countycourieronline.com. Year Established: 1878. Pub. Frequency: w. (Thu.) Page Size: tabloid. Subscrip. Rate: $.75 newsstand/cover; $25/yr mailed in county; $29.50/yr mailed out of county. Adv. Rate: col. inch $6.90 Circulation: 4,100 per issue (paid). Owner(s): Franklin Press, Inc., See address and contact information above. Management: Alison Dubilier, Publisher. Editorial: Ethan Dezotelle, Editor.

FAIRFAX

BUYERS DIGEST. 57 Yankee Park Rd., Fairfax, VT 05454. Telephone: 802-893-4214. FAX: 802-891-1112. URL: http://www.buyersdigest.com. Year Established: 1972. Pub. Frequency: w. (Tue) Page Size: tabloid Circulation: 68,000 per issue (free). Owner(s): Gannett Company, Inc., 7950 Jones Branch Dr., McLean, VA 22107-0001. Telephone: 703-854-6000. Management: James Carey, Publisher. Annette Crawford, Advertising.

HARDWICK

HARDWICK GAZETTE.   ISSN 0744-5512
Main St., Hardwick, VT 05843. Telephone: 802-472-6521. FAX: 802-472-6522. E-MAIL: news@thehardwickgazette.com. Mailing Address: PO Box 367, Hardwick, VT 05843-0367. Year Established: 1889. Pub. Frequency: w. (Wed.) Page Size: broadsheet. Subscrip. Rate: $.75 newsstand/cover; $33/yr in state; $36/yr out of state. Circulation: 2,800 per issue (paid). Owner(s): Hardwick Publishing Co., Inc., See address and contact information above. Management: Ross Connelly, Co-Publisher. Susan Jarzyna, Advertising Manager. Editorial: Ross Connelly, Editor. Dave Morse, Sports.

KILLINGTON

MOUNTAIN TIMES (KILLINGTON), THE. 5465 US Rte 4, Killington, VT 05751. Telephone: 802-422-2399. FAX: 802-422-2395. E-MAIL: mtntimes@vermontel.com. URL: http://www.mountaintimes.info. Mailing Address: PO Box 183, Killington, VT 05751. Year Established: 1971. Pub. Frequency: w. (Thu.) Page Size: tabloid. Subscrip. Rate: $85/yr mailed. Adv. Rate: col. inch $9.90 Circulation: 14,000 per issue (paid and free). Owner(s): BRD Corp., See address and contact information above. Management: Royal Barnard, Publisher. Zip Barnard, Advertising Manager. Editorial: Royal Barnard, Managing Editor.

LUDLOW

BLACK RIVER TRIBUNE. 110-A Main St., Ludlow, VT 05149-1010. Telephone: 802-228-8178. FAX: 802-228-8000. E-MAIL: janupton@ludl.tds.net. Mailing Address: PO Box 156, Ludlow, VT 05149-0156. Pub. Frequency: w. (Wed.) Page Size: broadsheet.Subscrip. Rate: $25/yr Circulation: 3,500 per issue (paid). Owner(s): Home Town Press Inc., 509 Greenwood St., Barnesville, GA 30204. Telephone: 770-358-0754. Management: Leo F. Graham, Publisher. Janet A. Upton, Advertising Manager. Editorial: Leo F. Graham, Editor. Janet A. Upton, Assistant Editor.

MANCHESTER CENTER

MANCHESTER JOURNAL, THE.   ISSN 1062-5070
51 Memorial Ave, Manchester Center, VT 05255. Telephone: 802-362-2222. FAX: 802-362-5327. E-MAIL: news@manchesterjournal.com. URL: http://www.manchesterjournal.com. Year Established: 1861. Pub. Frequency: w. (Fri.) Page Size: broadsheet. Subscrip. Rate: $40/yr mailed out of area. Adv. Rate: col. inch $8.25 Circulation: 12,000 per issue (paid and free). Owner(s): MediaNews Group, Inc., 101 W Colfax Ave, Ste 1100, Denver, CO 80202. FAX: 303-954-6320. Management: Edward L Wood, Publisher. Susan Plaisance, Advertising. Editorial: Andrew McKeever, Managing Editor.

MIDDLEBURY

ADDISON INDEPENDENT/ADDISON COUNTY INDEPENDENT. PO Box 31, Middlebury, VT 05753. E-MAIL: news@addisonindependent.com. URL: http://www.addisonindependent.com. Year Established: 1946. Pub. Frequency: s-w. (Mon. & Thu.) Page Size: tabloid. Subscrip. Rate: $.50 newsstand/cover; $33/yr in state; $44/yr out of state. Adv. Rate: col. inch $10 Wire Service(s): AP. Circulation: 16,000 per issue (controlled and free). Owner(s): The Champlain Valley Newspaper Group, See address and contact information above.

COLCHESTER SUN, THE. PO Box 31, Middlebury, VT 05753. E-MAIL: advertising@colchester.com. URL: Colchester Sun. Pub. Frequency: w. Page Size: standard.Adv. Rate: col. inch $9 Circulation: 7,500 per issue (free). Owner(s): The Champlain Valley Newspaper Group, See address and contact information above.

ESSEX REPORTER. PO Box 31, Middlebury, VT 05753. E-MAIL: angelo@essexreporter.com. URL: http://www.essexreporter.com. Pub. Frequency: w. (Thu.) Page Size: standard Circulation: 8,500 per issue (free). Owner(s): The Champlain Valley Newspaper Group, See address and contact information above.

MILTON INDEPENDENT. PO Box 31, Middlebury, VT 05753. E-MAIL: indy@together.net. URL: http://www.miltonindy.com. Pub. Frequency: w. (Thu.) Page Size: broadsheet. Subscrip. Rate: $70/yr mailed. Adv. Rate: col. inch $9 Circulation: 6,000 per issue (paid and free). Owner(s): The Champlain Valley Newspaper Group, See address and contact information above.

VALLEY VOICE, THE. 656 Exchange St., Middlebury, VT 05753. Telephone: 802-388-6366. FAX: 802-388-6368. E-MAIL: vvoice@together.net. Pub. Frequency: w. (Wed.) Page Size: broadsheet Circulation: 11,000 per issue (free). Owner(s): Cheryl White, See address and contact information above. Management: Cheryl White, Publisher. Editorial: Tammy White, Managing Editor.

MORRISVILLE

NEWS & CITIZEN. 417 Brooklyn St, Morrisville, VT 05661. Telephone: 802-888-2212. FAX: 802-888-2173. E-MAIL: edit@newsandcitizen.com. URL: http://www.newsandcitizen.com. Mailing Address: PO Box 369, Morrisville, VT 05661. Year Established: 1881. Pub. Frequency: w. (Thu.) Page Size: standard. Subscrip. Rate: $.50 newsstand/cover; $23/yr mailed in state; $28/yr mailed elsewhere. Circulation: 3,500 per issue (paid). Owner(s): Bradley Limoge Publishers, Inc., See address and contact information above. Management: Bradley A. Limoge, Publisher. Rick White, Advertising. Linda Rushford, Circulation Manager. Teena Bullard, Classified Adv. Mgr.. Editorial: J.B. McKinley, Editor.

TRANSCRIPT, THE. 417 Brooklyn St, Morrisville, VT 05661. Telephone: 802-888-2212. FAX: 802-888-2173. E-MAIL: news@newandcitizen.com. URL: http://www.newsandcitizen.com. Mailing Address: PO Box 369, Morrisville, VT 05661. Year Established: 1973. Pub. Frequency: w. (Mon.) Page Size: tabloid Circulation: 13,000 per issue (free). Owner(s): Bradley Limoge Publishers, Inc., See address and contact information above. Management: Bradley A. Limoge, Publisher. Rick White, Advertising. Linda Rushford, Circulation Manager. Teena Bullard, Classified Adv. Mgr.. Editorial: J.B. McKinley, Editor.

NORTHFIELD

NORTHFIELD NEWS (NORTHFIELD, VT). Old Village Hall, 40 Central St., Northfield, VT 05756. Telephone: 802-485-6329. FAX: 802-485-7909. E-MAIL: nnews@trans-video.net. Year Established: 1878. Pub. Frequency: w. (Thu.) Page Size: tabloid. Subscrip. Rate: $.65 newsstand/cover; $28/yr mailed in state; $32/yr mailed elsewhere. Circulation: 1,450 per issue (paid). Owner(s): Northfield News, See address and contact information above. Management: Celia Barnes Barnes, Publisher. Editorial: Celia Barnes Barnes, Editor.

RANDOLPH

HERALD OF RANDOLPH, THE. 30 Peasant St, Randolph, VT 05060. Telephone: 802-728-3232. FAX: 802-728-9275. E-MAIL: editor@ourherald.com. URL: http://www.ourherald.com. Mailing Address: PO Box 309, Randolph, VT 05060-0309. Year Established: 1874. Pub. Frequency: w. (Thu.) Page Size: broadsheet. Subscrip. Rate: $.75 newsstand/cover; $29/yr local; $34/yr out of area. Adv. Rate: col. inch $9.29 Freelance Pay: $1.50/column-inch. Circulation: 6,000 per issue (paid). Owner(s): M.D. Drysdale, See address and contact information above. Management: M. Dickey Drysdale, Publisher. Jill Montgomery, Advertising Manager. Editorial: Martha Slater, Editor.

RICHMOND

TIMES INK!. PO Box 532, Richmond, VT 05477. Telephone: 802-434-2690. E-MAIL: thetimrsink@aol.com.Pub. Frequency: m. Page Size: broadsheet Circulation: 5,000 per issue (free). Owner(s): Vermont Publications, See address and contact information above. Management: Carol Maider, Business Manager. Editorial: Heidi Racht, Editor.

RUTLAND

ADDISON EAGLE. 48 Evelyn St., Rutland, VT 05701. Mailing Address: PO Box 940, Shelbourne, VT 05482-0940. Pub. Frequency: w. (Sat.) Page Size: tabloid.Adv. Rate: col. inch $15.50 Circulation: 14,000 per issue (free). Owner(s): New Market Press, Inc., See address and contact information above. Management: Thomas Jackson, General Manager. Edward Coats, Publisher. Thomas Jackson, Advertising Manager. Editorial: Katy Demong, Editor.

RUTLAND TRIBUNE. 48 Evelyn St., Rutland, VT 05701. Telephone: 802-985-2400. FAX: 802-985-2490. Mailing Address: PO Box 940, Shelbourne, VT 05482-0940. Year Established: 1966. Pub. Frequency: w. (Wed.) Page Size: tabloid. Subscrip. Rate: $35/yr mailed 3rd class. Adv. Rate: col. inch $15.50 Circulation: 8,500 per issue (free). Owner(s): New Market Press, Inc., See address and contact information above. Management: Thomas Jackson, General Manager. Edward Coats, Publisher. Thomas Jackson, Advertising Manager. Editorial: Katy Demong, Editor.

SOUTH COUNTY SENTINEL. 48 Evelyn St., Rutland, VT 05701. Telephone: 802-985-2400. FAX: 802-985-2490. Mailing Address: PO Box 940, Shelbourne, VT 05482-0940. Pub. Frequency: w. (Sat.) Page Size: tabloid.Adv. Rate: col. inch $15.50 Circulation: 8,000 per issue (free). Owner(s): New Market Press, Inc., See address and contact information above. Management: Thomas Jackson, General Manager. Edward Coats, Publisher. Thomas Jackson, Advertising Manager. Editorial: Katy Demong, Editor.

VERMONT TIMES. 48 Evelyn St., Rutland, VT 05701. Telephone: 802-985-2400. FAX: 802-985-2490. E-MAIL: vttimes@together.net. Mailing Address: PO Box 940, Shelbourne, VT 05482-0940. Year Established: 1990. Pub. Frequency: w. (Wed.) Page Size: tabloid. Subscrip. Rate: $35/yr mailed for 3rd class; $90/yr mailed for 1st class. Adv. Rate: color page $15.50 Circulation: 36,000 per issue (free). **Owner(s):** New Market Press, Inc., See address and contact information above. **Management:** Thomas Jackson, General Manager. Edward Coats, Publisher. Thomas Jackson, Advertising Manager. **Editorial:** Katy Demong, Editor.

SHELBURNE

SHELBURNE NEWS. 5138 Shelburne Rd., Shelburne, VT 05482-0752. Telephone: 802-985-3091. E-MAIL: advertising@shelburnenews.com. URL: http://www.shelburnenews.com. Mailing Address: PO Box 752, Shelburne, VT 05482-0752. Pub. Frequency: w. (Thu.) Page Size: broadsheet Circulation: 30,000 per issue (free). **Owner(s):** Wind Ridge Publishing, See address and contact information above. **Management:** Holly Bartlett, Publisher. Susan Davis, Advertising Director. **Editorial:** Margp Callahan, Editor.

SOUTH BURLINGTON

OTHER PAPER (SOUTH BURLINGTON), THE. PO Box 2032, South Burlington, VT 05407-2032. Telephone: 802-864-6670. FAX: 802-864-3379. E-MAIL: otherpaper@aol.com. Pub. Frequency: s-m. (1st & 3rd Thu.) Page Size: standard Circulation: 7,500 per issue (free). **Owner(s):** George Chamberland, See address and contact information above. **Management:** George Chamberland, Publisher. **Editorial:** George Chamberland, Editor.

SOUTH HERO

ISLANDER (SOUTH HERO), THE. 21 Sunset View Rd., South Hero, VT 05486. E-MAIL: islander@vermontislander.com. URL: http://www.champlainislander.com. Mailing Address: PO Box 212, South Hero, VT 05486. Year Established: 1974. Pub. Frequency: w. (Tue.) Page Size: tabloid. Subscrip. Rate: $1.25 mailed/wk. out of area. Circulation: 6,000 per issue (paid and free). **Owner(s):** Northern Champlain Islander, Inc., See address and contact information above. **Editorial:** George D Fowler, Editor.

SPRINGFIELD

SPRINGFIELD REPORTER, THE. 151 Summer St., Springfield, VT 05156-3503. Telephone: 802-885-2246. FAX: 802-885-9821. E-MAIL: reporter@vermontel.net. Year Established: 1976. Pub. Frequency: w. (Wed.) Page Size: tabloid. Subscrip. Rate: $.50 newsstand/cover; $28/yr mailed in area. Adv. Rate: col. inch $4.50 Freelance Pay: $45/article. Circulation: 2,000 per issue (paid and free). **Owner(s):** Rodney W. Arnold, See address and contact information above. **Management:** Rodney W. Arnold, Publisher. **Editorial:** Rodney W. Arnold, Editor-in-Chief.

STOWE

STOWE REPORTER, THE. 49 School St., Stowe, VT 05672. Telephone: 802-253-2101. URL: http://www.stowereporter.com. Mailing Address: PO Box 489, Stowe, VT 05672-0489. Year Established: 1958. Pub. Frequency: w. (Thu.) Page Size: tabloid. Subscrip. Rate: $.50 newsstand/cover; $23/yr mailed in state; $33/yr mailed out of state; $42/yr mailed elsewhere. Adv. Rate: col. inch $6.16 **Wire Service(s):** AP. Circulation: 5,600 per issue (paid). **Owner(s):** Reporter Press, Inc., See address and contact information above. **Management:** A. Biddle Duke, Publisher. Joan Joslin, Advertising Manager. **Editorial:** Peter Hartt, Managing Editor.

VERMONT JOURNAL. 65 S Main St, Rte 100, Stowe, VT 05672. Telephone: 802-253-4623. FAX: 802-253-9569. E-MAIL: editor@vermontjournal.com. URL: http://www.vermontjournal.com. Mailing Address: PO Box 1535, Stowe, VT 05672. Pub. Frequency: w. (Thu.) Subscrip. Rate: $52/yr mailed. Adv. Rate: col. inch $14.50 Circulation: 7,000 per issue (free). **Owner(s):** Vermont Publishing Co., 281 N. Main St., St. Albans, VT 05478. Telephone: 802-524-9771. **Management:** Bob Miller, Publisher. Rick McMann, Advertising. **Editorial:** John Bauer, Editor.

WAITSFIELD

VALLEY REPORTER, THE. Mad River Green, Waitsfield, VT 05673-0119. Telephone: 802-496-3928. FAX: 802-496-4703. E-MAIL: vreporter@madriver.com. Mailing Address: PO Box 119, Waitsfield, VT 05673-0119. Year Established: 1971. Pub. Frequency: w. (Thu.) Page Size: tabloid. Subscrip. Rate: $.50 newsstand/cover; $15/yr mailed in state; $25/yr mailed out of state. Circulation: 3,500 per issue (controlled and free). **Owner(s):** Valley Reporter, Inc., The, See address and contact information above. **Management:** Al Benjamin, President. Pat Clark, Publisher. **Editorial:** Lisa Loomis, Editor.

WEST DOVER

DEERFIELD VALLEY NEWS. PO Box 310, West Dover, VT 05356. Telephone: 802-464-3388. FAX: 802-464-7255. E-MAIL: sales@vermontmedia.com. URL: http://www.dvalnews.com. Year Established: 1966. Pub. Frequency: w. (Thu.) Page Size: tabloid.Subscrip. Rate: $.75 newsstand/cover; $35/yr Circulation: 5,000 per issue (paid). **Owner(s):** Vermont Media Publishing Company Ltd., See address and contact information above. **Management:** Victoria Capital, General Manager. Randy L. Capitani, Publisher. **Editorial:** Mike Eldred, News Editor.

WILLISTON

WILLISTON OBSERVER. PO Box 1158, Williston, VT 05495-1158. Telephone: 802-879-4839. FAX: 802-872-0151. URL: http://www.willistonobserver.com. Pub. Frequency: w. (Thu.) Page Size: standard.Adv. Rate: B&W page $835 Circulation: 7,000 per issue (free). **Owner(s):** Paul Apfelbaum & Marianne Apfelbaum, See address and contact information above. **Management:** Paul Apfelbaum, Publisher. Wendy Ewing, Advertising. **Editorial:** Greg Elias, Editor.

WINDSOR

WINDSOR AREA OBSERVER. 13 Maple St, Windsor, VT 05089. Telephone: 802-674-6630. FAX: 802-674-6834. E-MAIL: vstand@sover.net. Pub. Frequency: w. (Mon.) Page Size: standard. Subscrip. Rate: $.75 newsstand/cover; $45/yr local. Circulation: 1,000 per issue (paid). **Owner(s):** Matthew & Shelly Jervis, See address and contact information above.

WOODSTOCK

VERMONT STANDARD. 466 Rte. 4 W., Woodstock, VT 05091. Telephone: 802-457-1313. FAX: 802-457-3639. E-MAIL: vstand@sover.net. Mailing Address: PO Box 88, Woodstock, VT 05091. Year Established: 1853. Pub. Frequency: w. (Thu.) Page Size: standard. Subscrip. Rate: $.75 newsstand/cover; $35/yr mailed; $60 mailed for 2 yrs.. Adv. Rate: col. inch $8.25 **Wire Service(s):** AP. Circulation: 5,200 per issue (paid). **Owner(s):** Vermont Standard, Inc., See address and contact information above. **Management:** Jon Estey, General Manager. Henry Nachman, Owner. Phillip C. Camp, Publisher. Pattie Webster, Circulation Manager. **Editorial:** Kevin Forrest, Editor.

VIRGIN ISLANDS

ST. JOHN

TRADEWINDS. ISSN 0895-0970
PO Box 1500,CRUZBAY, St. John, VI 00831. Telephone: 340-776-6496. E-MAIL: info@tradewinds.vi. URL: http://stjohntradewindsnews.com. Year Established: 1972. Pub. Frequency: bi-w. (Mon.) Page Size: standard. Subscrip. Rate: $.75 newsstand/cover; $40/yr; $75 for 2 yrs.. Circulation: 3,000 per issue (paid). **Owner(s):** St. John Tradewinds, Inc., See address and contact information above. **Management:** Malinda Nelson, Advertising. **Editorial:** Tom Oat, Editor. Jamie Elliott, Writer.

VIRGINIA

ABINGDON

ABINGDON VIRGINIAN. 170 E. Main St., Abingdon, VA 24210-2839. Telephone: 276-628-2962. FAX: 276-676-6220. E-MAIL: editor@abvnews.com. URL: http://www.abvanews.com. Year Established: 1841. Pub. Frequency: w. (Wed.) Page Size: tabloid. Subscrip. Rate: $25/yr in county; $30/yr out of county. Adv. Rate: col. inch $7 Circulation: 4,500 per issue (paid). **Owner(s):** Martha M. Weisfeld, See address and contact information above. **Management:** Martha M. Weisfeld, President. **Editorial:** Robert Weisfeld, Editor.

WASHINGTON COUNTY NEWS (ABINGDON). 143 W. Main St., Abingdon, VA 24210. Telephone: 276-628-7101. FAX: 276-628-1195. URL: http://www.washconews.com. Mailing Address: PO Box 399, Abingdon, VA 24212. Year Established: 1948. Pub. Frequency: w. (Wed.) Page Size: standard. Subscrip. Rate: $.50 newsstand/cover; $24/yr local; $28/yr out of area. Freelance Pay: $20/article. Circulation: 5,000 per issue (paid). **Owner(s):** Media General, Inc., 333 E. Franklin St., Richmond, VA 23219. Telephone: 804-649-6000. **Management:** Dan Kegley, General Manager. Jill Rust, Advertising. **Editorial:** Dan Kegley, Editor.

ALEXANDRIA

SUN GAZETTE, THE. ISSN 1065-1632
6408 Edsell Rd., Alexandria, VA 22312. Telephone: 703-738-2520. FAX: 703-738-2531. E-MAIL: sunedit@erols.com. URL: http://www.sungazette.net. Year Established: 1937. Pub. Frequency: w. (Thu.) Page Size: tabloid Circulation: 32,000 per issue (paid). **Owner(s):** Suburban Sun Gazette, See address and contact information above. **Editorial:** Scott McCaffrey, Editor. Dave Facinoli, Sports Editor.

ALTAVISTA

ALTAVISTA JOURNAL. 600 Main St., Altavista, VA 24517. Telephone: 434-369-6688. FAX: 434-369-6689. E-MAIL: aljournal@adelphia.net. URL: http://www.wpcva.com/altavista. Mailing Address: PO Box 630, Altavista, VA 24517. Year Established: 1909. Pub. Frequency: w. (Wed.) Page Size: broadsheet. Subscrip. Rate: $.75 newsstand/cover; $24/yr in county; $34/yr out of county. Circulation: 11,000 per issue (paid). **Owner(s):** Womack Publishing Co., Inc., PO Box 111, Chatham, VA 24531. Telephone: 434-432-1654. **Management:** Chad Harrison, Publisher. Kathy Keesee, Advertising Manager. Bonnie Davis, Classified Adv. Mgr.. **Editorial:** Jonathan Parker, Editor.

AMELIA COURT HOUSE

AMELIA BULLETIN MONITOR, THE. ISSN 0746-1798
16311 Goodes Bridge Rd., Amelia Court House, VA 23002-0123. Telephone: 804-561-3655. FAX: 804-561-2065. E-MAIL: contacts@ameliamonitor.com. URL: http://www.ameliamonitor.com. Mailing Address: PO Box 123, Amelia Court House, VA 23002-0003. Year Established: 1973. Pub. Frequency: w. (Thu.) Page Size: tabloid. Subscrip. Rate: $.50 newsstand/cover; $13/yr in county; $22/yr mailed in state; $28/yr mailed out of state. Circulation: 10,000 per issue (paid and free). **Owner(s):** Ann B. Salster, See address and contact information above. **Management:** Ann B. Salster, Publisher. B. Thompson, Advertising Manager. **Editorial:** Wayne Russell, Editor-in-Chief.

AMHERST

AMHERST NEW ERA-PROGRESS. 134 Second St., Amherst, VA 24521. Telephone: 434-946-7195. FAX: 434-946-2684. E-MAIL: cmarsh@neweraprogress.com. URL: http://www.neweraprogress.com. Mailing Address: PO Box 90, Amherst, VA 24521. Year Established: 1879. Pub. Frequency: w. (Thu.) Page Size: broadsheet. Subscrip. Rate: $.50 newsstand/cover; $18/yr in county; $24/yr out of county. Circulation: 5,000 per issue (paid). **Owner(s):** Media General, Inc., 333 E. Franklin St., Richmond, VA 23219. Telephone: 434-649-6000. **Management:** Dean Smith, General Manager. Terry H. Jamerson, Publisher. Sarah Tyler, Advertising. Cathy Marsh, Classified Editor. **Editorial:** David Hylton, Managing Editor.

NELSON COUNTY TIMES. 134 Second St., Amherst, VA 24521. Telephone: 434-946-7195. FAX: 434-946-2684. E-MAIL: editor@nelsoncountytimes.com. URL: http://www.nelsoncountytimes.com. Mailing Address: PO Box 90, Amherst, VA 24521. Pub. Frequency: w. (Thu.) Page Size: broadsheet. Subscrip. Rate: $.50 newsstand/cover; $18/yr mailed in county; $24/yr mailed out of county. Circulation: 4,700 per issue (paid). **Owner(s):** Media General, Inc., 333 E. Franklin St., Richmond, VA 23219. Telephone: 434-649-6000. **Management:** Dean Smith, General Manager. Terry H. Jamerson, Publisher. Sarah Magyari, Advertising. Cathy Marsh, Classified Editor. **Editorial:** David Hylton, Managing Editor.

APPOMATTOX

APPOMATTOX TIMES-VIRGINIAN. 507 Court St., Appomattox, VA 24522. Telephone: 434-352-8215. FAX: 434-352-2216. E-MAIL: timesva@nesbeonline.com. URL: timesvirginian.com. Mailing Address: PO Box 2097, Appomattox, VA 24522. Year Established: 1892. Pub. Frequency: w. (Wed.) Page Size: broadsheet. Subscrip. Rate: $.75 newsstand/cover; $24/yr local; $34/yr out of county. Circulation: 4,000 per issue (paid). **Owner(s):** Womack Publishing Co., Inc., PO Box 111, Chatham, VA 24531. Telephone: 434-432-1654. **Management:** Marvin Hamlatt, General Manager. Charles Womack, Publisher.

ASHLAND

HERALD-PROGRESS. 11293 Air Park Rd., Ashland, VA 23005-3436. Telephone: 804-798-9031. FAX: 804-798-9036. E-MAIL: hpnews@herald-progress.com. URL: http://www.hanoverva.com. Year Established: 1881. Pub. Frequency: w. (Thu.) Page Size: broadsheet. Subscrip. Rate: $.50 newsstand/cover; $20/yr in county; $31/yr out of county; $34/yr mailed out of state. Freelance Pay: $0.60/column-inch. **Wire Service(s):** AP. Circulation: 7,200 per issue (paid and free). **Owner(s):** Herald-Progress, Inc., See address and contact information above. **Management:** William B. Trimble, President. Cathy Collins, Publisher. Brenda Gregory, Advertising Manager. **Editorial:** Gregory K. Glasser, Editor.

Weeklies

BEDFORD

BEDFORD BULLETIN. 402 E. Main St., Bedford, VA 24523. Telephone: 540-586-8612. FAX: 540-586-0834. E-MAIL: busmgr@bedfordbulletin.com. URL: http://www.bedfordbulletin.com. Mailing Address: PO Box 331, Bedford, VA 24523. Year Established: 1857. Pub. Frequency: w. (Wed.) Page Size: broadsheet. Subscrip. Rate: $.75 newsstand/cover; $32/yr in county; $40/yr out of county; $50/yr out of state. Circulation: 8,100 per issue (paid). **Owner(s):** Landmark Community Newspapers, Inc., PO Box 549, Shelbyville, KY 40065. Telephone: 502-633-4390. **Management:** Jay Bondurant, Publisher. Lynn Hurst, Advertising Manager. Debra Dooley, Circulation Manager. Gale Wasson, Business Manager. **Editorial:** Tom Wilmouth, Editor. John Barnhart, Associate Editor. Mike Forster, Sports Editor.

BERRYVILLE

CLARKE TIMES-COURIER. 16 W. Main St., Berryville, VA 22611. Telephone: 540-955-1111. FAX: 540-955-1334. E-MAIL: plettie@timespapers.com. URL: http://www.timescommunity.com. Mailing Address: PO Box 32, Berryville, VA 22611-1341. Year Established: 1869. Pub. Frequency: w. (Thu.) Page Size: broadsheet. Subscrip. Rate: $.50 newsstand/cover; $49.95/yr mailed in county; $49.95/yr mailed out of county. Circulation: 3,160 per issue (paid and free). **Owner(s):** Arcom Publications, Inc., 13873 Park Center Rd., Ste. 301, Herndon, VA 20171. **Management:** Peter W Arundel, Vice President. Connie Fields, Advertising Manager. Ron Sauer, Circulation Manager. **Editorial:** Pam Lettie, Editor.

BIG STONE GAP

POST (BIG STONE GAP), THE. 215 Wood Ave., E., Big Stone Gap, VA 24219. Telephone: 276-523-1141. FAX: 276-523-1175. E-MAIL: scook@coalfield.com. URL: http://www.coalfield.com. Mailing Address: PO Box 250, Big Stone Gap, VA 24219. Year Established: 1890. Pub. Frequency: w. (Wed.) Page Size: broadsheet. Subscrip. Rate: $.75 newsstand/cover; $30/yr in county; $56/yr mailed out of county. Circulation: 4,176 per issue (paid and free). **Owner(s):** Wise Printing Co., See address and contact information above. **Management:** Ida Holyfield, Publisher. Beverly Mullins, Advertising. Geneva Thomas, Circulation Manager. **Editorial:** Ida Holyfield, Editor.

BLACKSTONE

COURIER-RECORD. 111 W. Maple St., Blackstone, VA 23824. Telephone: 434-292-3019. FAX: 434-292-5966. E-MAIL: adl@courier-record.com. URL: http://www.courier-record.com. Mailing Address: P.O. Box 460, Blackstone, VA 23824. Year Established: 1890. Pub. Frequency: w. (Wed.) Page Size: broadsheet. Subscrip. Rate: $.75 newsstand/cover; $20/yr in county; $30/yr mailed out of county; $40/yr mailed out of state. Circulation: 7,100 per issue (paid and free). **Owner(s):** Nottoway Publishing Co., Inc., See address and contact information above. **Management:** William D. Coleburn, General Manager. **Editorial:** William D. Coleburn, Editor.

BOWLING GREEN

CAROLINE PROGRESS, THE. 115 N. Main St., Bowling Green, VA 22427. Telephone: 804-633-5005. URL: http://www.carolineprogress.com. Year Established: 1919. Pub. Frequency: w. (Wed.) Page Size: broadsheet. Subscrip. Rate: $.50 newsstand/cover; $23/yr in county; $38/yr out of county. Circulation: 10,000 per issue (paid). **Owner(s):** Northern Neck Newspaper Group, See address and contact information above. **Editorial:** Tabitha LaRue, Editor.

BROOKNEAL

UNION STAR, THE. 241 Main St., Brookneal, VA 24528. Telephone: 434-376-2795. FAX: 434-376-2676. E-MAIL: news@theunionstar.com. URL: http://www.theunionstar.com. Pub. Frequency: w. (Wed.) Page Size: broadsheet. Subscrip. Rate: $.75 newsstand/cover; $24/yr in county; $34/yr out of county. Adv. Rate: col. inch $6.85 Circulation: 3,000 per issue (paid). **Owner(s):** Womack Publishing Co., Inc., 30 N. Main St., Chatham, VA 24531. **Management:** Donna Guthrie, General Manager. Charles A. Womack Jr., Publisher. Pat Kent, Advertising. **Editorial:** Paula Bryant, Editor.

CHARLOTTESVILLE

CHARLOTTESVILLE-ALBEMARLE TRIBUNE. 250 W. Main St., Charlottesville, VA 22902. Telephone: 434-979-0373. FAX: 434-971-5821. Mailing Address: PO Box 3428, Charlottesville, VA 22903. Year Established: 1954. Pub. Frequency: w. (Thu.) Page Size: tabloid. Subscrip. Rate: $.50 newsstand/cover; $30/yr. Circulation: 12,000 per issue (paid and free). **Owner(s):** Agnes White, See address and contact information above. **Management:** David White, Publisher. **Editorial:** Agnes White, Editor.

RURAL VIRGINIAN. 685 W. Rio Rd., Charlottesville, VA 22906. Telephone: 434-978-7200. FAX: 434-978-7204. E-MAIL: rv@dailyprogress.com. Mailing Address: PO Box 9030, Charlottesville, VA 22906. Pub. Frequency: w. (Wed.) Page Size: tabloid Circulation: 10,700 per issue (paid). **Owner(s):** Media General, Inc., 333 E. Franklin St., Richmond, VA 23219. Telephone: 804-649-6000. **Management:** Lawrence McConnell, Publisher. John Kimbel, Advertising Manager. Alan West, Circulation Manager. **Editorial:** Lou Hatter, Editor.

CHASE CITY

NEWS-PROGRESS, THE. PO Box 337, Chase City, VA 23924. Telephone: 434-374-0103. FAX: 434-372-3911. E-MAIL: newsprogress@kerrlake.com. Year Established: 1888. Pub. Frequency: s-w. (Mon. & Wed.) Page Size: broadsheet. Subscrip. Rate: $.50 newsstand/cover; $16/yr mailed in county; $20/yr mailed out of county; $30/yr mailed out of state. Circulation: 7,675 per issue (paid). **Owner(s):** Mecklenburg News, Inc., See address and contact information above. **Management:** Keith A. Shelton, Publisher. **Editorial:** Robert Benning, Editor.

CHATHAM

STAR-TRIBUNE (CHATHAM). ISSN 1074-5114
PO Box 111, Chatham, VA 24531. Telephone: 434-432-1654. Year Established: 1869. Pub. Frequency: w. (Wed.) Page Size: broadsheet. Subscrip. Rate: $.75 newsstand/cover; $24/yr in county; $29/yr out of county. Adv. Rate: col. inch $7.40 Circulation: 9,000 per issue (paid). **Owner(s):** Womack Publishing Co., Inc., See address and contact information above. **Management:** Tim Davis, General Manager. Charles Womack Jr., Publisher. Marjie Dawson, Advertising Manager. Shirley Adkins, Circulation Manager. Dianne Meadows, Classified Adv. Mgr.. **Editorial:** Tim Davis, Editor.

CHRISTIANSBURG

NEWS MESSENGER, THE. 20 N Main St, Christiansburg, VA 24073. Telephone: 540-382-6171. FAX: 540-382-3009. E-MAIL: ads@newsmessenger.net. URL: mainstreetnewspapers.com. Mailing Address: PO Box 419, Christiansburg, VA 24068. Year Established: 1869. Pub. Frequency: s-w. (Wed. & Sat.) Page Size: broadsheet. Subscrip. Rate: $.50 newsstand/cover; $29.99/yr in county; $37/yr out of county. Circulation: 10,505 per issue (controlled and free). **Owner(s):** Main Street Newspapers, Inc., See address and contact information above. **Management:** Lawson Koeppel, Publisher. Lynn Hurst, Advertising Manager. **Editorial:** Amanda Bolen, Managing Editor. David Grimes, Sports Editor.

RADFORD NEWS JOURNAL. 20 N Main St, Christiansburg, VA 24073. Telephone: 540-382-6171. FAX: 540-382-3009. E-MAIL: news@newsmessenger.net. URL: http://www.mainstreetnewspapers.com. Mailing Address: PO Box 419, Christiansburg, VA 24068. Year Established: 1884. Pub. Frequency: s-w. (Wed. & Sat.) Page Size: broadsheet. Subscrip. Rate: $.50 newsstand/cover; $29.99/yr in county; $33/yr out of county; $37/yr out of state. Circulation: 10,800 per issue (controlled and free). **Owner(s):** Main Street Newspapers, Inc., 1633 W. Main St., Salem, VA 24153. Telephone: 540-389-9355. FAX: 540-389-2930. **Management:** Jeffery Stumb, Owner. Lawson Koeppel, Publisher. Lynn Hurst, Advertising Manager. **Editorial:** Amanda Bolen, Managing Editor.

CLARKSVILLE

MECKLENBURG SUN. 602 Virginia Ave., Clarksville, VA 23927. Telephone: 434-374-8152. FAX: 434-374-8153. E-MAIL: news@themecklenburgsun.com. URL: http://www.themecklenburgsun.com. Mailing Address: PO Box 997, Clarksville, VA 23927. Year Established: 1976. Pub. Frequency: w. (Wed.) Page Size: broadsheet. Subscrip. Rate: $.25 newsstand/cover; $9/yr in county; $22/yr out of county. Adv. Rate: col. inch $5.50 Circulation: 16,085 per issue (paid). **Owner(s):** Tom McLaughlin, P.O. Drawer 100, South Boston, VA 24592. Telephone: 434-572-2928. **Management:** Tom McLaughlin, Publisher. Shannon Martinette, Advertising Manager. **Editorial:** Tom McLaughlin, Editor.

CLINTWOOD

DICKENSON STAR, THE. ISSN 0746-584X
Main St., Clintwood, VA 24228. Telephone: 276-926-8816. FAX: 276-926-8827. E-MAIL: thestar@mountnet.com. Mailing Address: PO Box 707, Clintwood, VA 24228. Year Established: 1966. Pub. Frequency: w. (Wed.) Page Size: broadsheet. Subscrip. Rate: $.75 newsstand/cover; $44/yr mailed in county; $46/yr mailed out of county. Freelance Pay: $25/article. **Wire Service(s):** AP. Circulation: 6,500 per issue (paid). **Owner(s):** Michael N. & Jenay Tate, See address and contact information above. **Management:** Jenay Tate, President. Michael N Tate, Publisher. Shell Childress, Advertising Manager. Pam Charles, Circulation Manager. **Editorial:** Paula Tate, Editor. Jenay Tate, Executive Editor.

CREWE

CREWE - BURKEVILLE JOURNAL. ISSN 8755-9463
107 W Carolina Ave, Crewe, VA 23930. Telephone: 434-645-7534. FAX: 434-645-1848. Year Established: 1959. Pub. Frequency: w. (Thu.) Page Size: standard. Subscrip. Rate: $17/yr in county; $22/yr in state; $27/yr out of state. Circulation: 6,000 (paid). **Owner(s):** M & S Publishing Co., Inc., See address and contact information above. **Editorial:** Rick R Gunter, Editor.

CULPEPER

COMMUNITY CLASSIFIED. 122 W. Spencer St., Culpeper, VA 22701. Telephone: 540-825-0771. URL: http://www.starexponent.com. Mailing Address: PO Box 111, Culpeper, VA 22701. Pub. Frequency: w. (Wed.) Page Size: standard. Subscrip. Rate: $25.35 mailed for 13 wks.; $50.70 mailed for 26 wks.; $101.40/yr mailed. Circulation: 13,000 per issue (paid and controlled). **Owner(s):** Media General, Inc., 333 E. Franklin St., Richmond, VA 23219. Telephone: 434-649-6000. **Management:** C. Kirk Read, Publisher. Gloria Williams, Advertising Manager. Patricia Graham, Circulation Manager. **Editorial:** Robert Humphries, Editor.

DRAKES BRANCH

CHARLOTTE GAZETTE. PO Box 214, Drakes Branch, VA 23937. Telephone: 434-568-3341. FAX: 434-568-3731. Year Established: 1873. Pub. Frequency: w. (Wed.) Page Size: broadsheet. Subscrip. Rate: $.50 newsstand/cover; $18/yr mailed in county; $20/yr mailed out of county; $22/yr mailed out of state. Circulation: 3,600 per issue (paid). **Owner(s):** Charlotte Publishing, Inc., See address and contact information above. **Management:** Dorothy C. Tucker, Publisher. **Editorial:** Otis Tucker III, Managing Editor.

ELKTON

VALLEY BANNER, THE. 157 W. Spotswood Ave., Elkton, VA 22827-0126. Telephone: 540-298-9444. FAX: 540-298-2560. E-MAIL: vbnews@comcast.net. Mailing Address: PO Box 126, Elkton, VA 22827-0126. Year Established: 1966. Pub. Frequency: w. (Thu.) Page Size: standard. Subscrip. Rate: $.25 newsstand/cover; $17/yr local; $22/yr elsewhere. Adv. Rate: col. inch $9.40 Circulation: 4,475 per issue (paid and free). **Owner(s):** Byrd Newspaper Group, 231 S. Liberty St., Harrisonburg, VA 22801. Telephone: 540-574-6200. **Management:** Peter Yates, Publisher. Carol Helmintoller, Advertising Manager. Tommy Bridges, Circulation Manager. **Editorial:** Travis Long, Editor. Ted Hayes, Feature Editor.

EMPORIA

INDEPENDENT MESSENGER. 111 Baker St, Emporia, VA 23847. Telephone: 434-634-4153. FAX: 434-634-0783. E-MAIL: news@imnews.com. URL: http://www.independentmessenger.com. Mailing Address: PO Box 786, Emporia, VA 23847. Year Established: 1896. Pub. Frequency: s-w. (Wed. & Sun.) Page Size: broadsheet. Subscrip. Rate: $.50 newsstand/cover; $26/yr in county; $32/yr local VA & NC; $40/yr elsewhere. Adv. Rate: col. inch $9.25 Circulation: 6,800 per issue (paid). **Owner(s):** Womack Publishing Co., Inc., PO Box 111, Chatham, VA 24531. Telephone: 804-432-1654. **Management:** Becky Hinkle, Advertising Manager. **Editorial:** Don Koralewski, Editor.

FALLS CHURCH

FALLS CHURCH NEWS-PRESS. 929 W. Broad St., Ste. 200, Falls Church, VA 22046. Telephone: 703-532-3267. FAX: 703-532-3396. E-MAIL: letters@fcnp.com. URL: http://www.fcnp.com. Year Established: 1991. Pub. Frequency: w. (Thur.) Page Size: tabloid. Subscrip. Rate: $75/yr mailed 1st class. Adv. Rate: col. inch $23.50 Circulation: 30,100 per issue (free). **Owner(s):** Benton Communications, Inc., See address and contact information above. **Management:** Nicholas Benton, Publisher. Hawthorne Blackwell, Advertising Director. **Editorial:** Nicholas Benton, Editor-in-Chief. Jody Fellows, Managing Editor.

FARMVILLE

FARMVILLE HERALD, THE. 114 North St., Farmville, VA 23901. Telephone: 434-392-4151. FAX: 434-392-3366. E-MAIL: farmher@moonstar.com. URL: http://www.farmvilleherald.com. Mailing Address: P.O. Box 307, Farmville, VA 23901. Year Established: 1890. Pub. Frequency: s-w. (Wed. & Fri.) Page Size: broadsheet. Subscrip. Rate: $.50 newsstand/cover; $28/yr in county; $38/yr out of county. Adv. Rate: col. inch $8.15 Circulation: 8,775 per issue (paid). **Owner(s):** William B. Wall, See address and contact information above. **Management:** James Kendrick, President. Steven E. Wall, Publisher. **Editorial:** Ken Woodley III, Editor.

FREE NEWS, THE. 114 North St., Farmville, VA 23901. Telephone: 434-392-4151. FAX: 434-392-3366. E-MAIL: farmher@moonstar.com. URL: http://www.farmvilleherald.com. Year Established: 1980. Pub. Frequency: w. (Mon.) Page Size: broadsheet Circulation: 15,000 per issue (free). **Owner(s):** William B. Wall, See address and contact information above. **Management:** Steven E. Wall, Publisher. Jacqueline T. Newman, Advertising Manager. **Editorial:** Ken Woodley III, Editor.

FINCASTLE

FINCASTLE HERALD, THE. 276 Botetourt Rd., Fincastle, VA 24090. Telephone: 540-473-2741. FAX: 540-473-2742. E-MAIL: herald@rbnet.com. URL: http://www.mainstreetnewspapers.com. Mailing Address: PO Box 127, Fincastle, VA 24090. Year Established: 1866. Pub. Frequency: w. (Wed.) Page Size: broadsheet. Subscrip. Rate: $.50 newsstand/cover; $24/yr in county; $32/yr out of county. Freelance Pay: $25/article. Circulation: 7,400 per issue (paid). **Owner(s):** Blue Ridge Newspapers, 1633 W. Main St., Salem, VA 24153. Telephone: 540-389-9355. FAX: 540-389-2930. **Management:** Lawson Koeppel, Publisher. Debbi Starr, Advertising. Vickie Henderson, Advertising Manager. Rhonda Fleming, Classified Adv. Mgr.. **Editorial:** Edwin L. McCoy, Executive Editor.

FLOYD

FLOYD PRESS. 710 E. Main St., Floyd, VA 24091. Telephone: 540-745-2127. FAX: 540-745-2123. E-MAIL: news@floydpress.com. URL: http://www.floydpress.com. Mailing Address: PO Box 155, Floyd, VA 24091. Year Established: 1891. Pub. Frequency: w. (Thu.) Page Size: standard. Subscrip. Rate: $.50 newsstand/cover; $21/yr in county; $29/yr out of county. Circulation: 5,200 per issue (paid). **Owner(s):** Media General, Inc., 333 E. Franklin St., Richmond, VA 23219-0001. Telephone: 804-649-6000. **Management:** Sam Cooper, Publisher. Candace Gibbs, Circulation Manager. Sarah Snead, Classified Editor. **Editorial:** Wanda Combs, Editor.

FRANKLIN

TIDEWATER NEWS, THE. 1000 Armory Dr., Franklin, VA 23851. Telephone: 757-562-3187. FAX: 757-562-6795. E-MAIL: betty.ramsey@tidewaternews.com. URL: http://www.tidewaternews.com. Year Established: 1905. Pub. Frequency: s-w. (Thu. & Sun.) Page Size: standard. Subscrip. Rate: $.50 newsstand/cover; $45/yr in county. Adv. Rate: col. inch $9.75 Circulation: 8,500 per issue (paid and controlled). **Owner(s):** Boone Newspapers, Inc., P.O. Box 497, Franklin, VA 23851. 15222 Freemen's Bend Rd., Northport, AL 35475. Telephone: 205-330-4100. **Management:** Steve Stewart, President. Yvette Brozzo, Office Manager. Betty Ramsey, Advertising Director.

FRONT ROYAL

WARREN SENTINEL (FRONT ROYAL), THE. 429 N Royal, Front Royal, VA 22630. Telephone: 540-635-4174. FAX: 540-635-7478. E-MAIL: sentinel@rma.edu. Mailing Address: PO Box 1297, Front Royal, VA 22630. Pub. Frequency: w. (Thu.) Page Size: broadsheet. Subscrip. Rate: $.50 newsstand/cover; $12/yr in county; $20/yr out of county. Circulation: 5,600 per issue (paid). **Owner(s):** Thomas T. Byrd, See address and contact information above. **Management:** Tammy Batcha, General Manager. Thomas T. Byrd, Publisher. Debra Henry, Advertising. **Editorial:** Joe Farruggia, Editor.

GALAX

GAZETTE (GALAX), THE. 108 W. Stuart Dr., Galax, VA 24333. Telephone: 276-236-5178. FAX: 276-236-0756. URL: http://www.galaxgazette.com. Mailing Address: PO Box 68, Galax, VA 24333. Year Established: 1876. Pub. Frequency: 3/w. (Mon., Wed., Fri.) Page Size: broadsheet. Subscrip. Rate: $.50 newsstand/cover; $41/yr local; $66/yr out of area; $89/yr out of state. Circulation: 8,600 per issue (paid). **Owner(s):** Landmark Community Newspapers, Inc., PO Box 549, Shelbyville, KY 40065. Telephone: 502-633-2526. **Management:** Chuck Burress, Publisher. Randy Kegley, Advertising Manager. Vicki Ayers, Circulation Manager. **Editorial:** Amy Hauslohner, Editor.

GLOUCESTER

GLOUCESTER-MATHEWS GAZETTE JOURNAL. PO Box 2060, Gloucester, VA 23061. Telephone: 804-693-3101. E-MAIL: info@gazettejournal.net. URL: http://www.gazettejournal.net. Year Established: 1904. Pub. Frequency: w. (Thu.) Page Size: broadsheet. Subscrip. Rate: $.50 newsstand/cover; $20/yr in county; $24/yr out of county. **Wire Service(s):** AP. Circulation: 11,000 per issue (paid). **Owner(s):** Tidewater Newspapers, Inc., See address and contact information above. **Management:** John W. Cooke, President. A. Lynch, Advertising Manager. Patty Strigle, Circulation Manager. **Editorial:** Elsa Cooke-Verbyla, Editor. Charlie Koenig, Sports.

GOOCHLAND

GOOCHLAND GAZETTE. 3052 River Rd., W., Goochland, VA 23063. Telephone: 804-556-3135. FAX: 804-556-4237. E-MAIL: sales@cvagazette.com. URL: http://www.cvagazette.com. Mailing Address: PO Box 139, Goochland, VA 23063. Year Established: 1955. Pub. Frequency: w. (Thu.) Page Size: tabloid. Subscrip. Rate: $.50 newsstand/cover; $30/yr in county; $40/yr out of county. Adv. Rate: col. inch $9.90 Circulation: 10,200 per issue (free). **Owner(s):** JGF Media, Inc., PO Box 5146, Charlottesville, VA 22905. Telephone: 804-977-2002. **Management:** Debbie Knotts, Advertising. **Editorial:** Wesley Hester, Editor. Ken Oder, Managing Editor.

GRUNDY

VIRGINIA MOUNTAINEER. PO Box 2040, Grundy, VA 24614-2040. Telephone: 276-935-2123. FAX: 276-935-2125. E-MAIL: virginiamountaineer@yahoo.com. Year Established: 1922. Pub. Frequency: w. (Thu.) Page Size: broadsheet. Subscrip. Rate: $.50 newsstand/cover; $24.50/yr in county; $36/yr out of county. Adv. Rate: col. inch $7 Circulation: 8,600 per issue (paid). **Owner(s):** Mountaineer Publishing Co., Inc., See address and contact information above. **Management:** Sam Bartley, Advertising Manager. Ernestine Looney, Circulation Manager. **Editorial:** Cathy St. Clair, News Editor.

HEATHSVILLE

NORTHUMBERLAND ECHO. PO Box 180, Heathsville, VA 22473. Telephone: 804-580-3444. FAX: 804-580-6826. E-MAIL: news@nortumberlandecho.com. URL: http://www.northumberlandecho.com. Year Established: 1902. Pub. Frequency: w. (Wed.) Page Size: broadsheet. Subscrip. Rate: $.50 newsstand/cover; $23/yr in county; $38/yr out of area; $40/yr out of state. Circulation: 5,000 per issue (paid). **Owner(s):** Michael Diederich, See address and contact information above. **Management:** Michael Diederich, Publisher. **Editorial:** Colston Newton, Editor.

HERNDON

ANNANDALE TIMES. 13873 Park Center Rd., Ste. 301, Herndon, VA 20171. Telephone: 703-478-6666. FAX: 703-435-9754. E-MAIL: nvtimes@aol.com. URL: http://www.timespapers.com. Year Established: 2000. Pub. Frequency: w. (Thu.) Page Size: broadsheet. Subscrip. Rate: $29.95/yr mailed. Circulation: 18,000 per issue (paid and free). **Owner(s):** Arcom Publications, Inc., See address and contact information above. **Management:** Peter Arundel, Publisher. Peter W Arundel, Vice President. Rose Mary Felton, Advertising Manager. Ron Sauer, Circulation Manager. Hugo Lembert, Classified Adv. Mgr.. **Editorial:** Marcia McAllister, Editor. Steve Cahill, Executive Editor. Kali Schumitz, Managing Editor.

BURKE TIMES, THE. 13873 Park Center Rd., Ste. 301, Herndon, VA 20171. Telephone: 703-478-6666. FAX: 703-435-9754. E-MAIL: nvtimes@aol.com. URL: http://www.timespapers.com. Pub. Frequency: w. (Thu.) Page Size: broadsheet. Subscrip. Rate: $.25 newsstand/cover; $29.95/yr in county; $39.95/yr mailed out of county. Adv. Rate: col. inch $22.30 Circulation: 39,323 per issue (paid and free). **Owner(s):** Arcom Publications, Inc., See address and contact information above. **Management:** Peter Arundel, Publisher. Peter W Arundel, Vice President. Rose Mary Felton, Advertising Manager. Ron Sauer, Circulation Manager. **Editorial:** Marcia McAllister, Executive Editor. Kali Schumitz, Managing Editor. Briteny Boyd, Lifestyle Editor.

CENTREVILLE TIMES. 13873 Park Center Rd., Ste. 301, Herndon, VA 20171. Telephone: 703-478-6666. FAX: 703-435-9754. E-MAIL: nvtimes@aol.com. URL: http://www.timespapers.com. Pub. Frequency: w. (Thu.) Page Size: broadsheet. Subscrip. Rate: $29.95/yr mailed. Circulation: 15,000 per issue (paid and free). **Owner(s):** Arcom Publications, Inc., See address and contact information above. **Management:** Peter Arundel, Publisher. Peter W Arundel, Vice President. Rose Mary Felton, Advertising Manager. Ron Sauer, Circulation Manager. **Editorial:** Kali Schumitz, Managing Editor. Phillip Creel, Sports.

CHANTILLY TIMES. 13873 Park Center Rd., Ste. 301, Herndon, VA 20171. Telephone: 703-478-6666. FAX: 703-435-9754. E-MAIL: nvtimes@aol.com. URL: http://www.timespapers.com. Pub. Frequency: w. (Thu.) Page Size: broadsheet. Subscrip. Rate: $29.95/yr mailed. Circulation: 6,980 per issue (paid and free). **Owner(s):** Arcom Publications, Inc., See address and contact information above. **Management:** Peter Arundel, Publisher. Peter W Arundel, Vice President. Rose Mary Felton, Advertising Manager. Ron Sauer, Circulation Manager. **Editorial:** Kali Schumitz, Managing Editor. Phillip Creel, Sports.

FAIRFAX STATION TIMES. 13873 Park Center Rd., Ste. 301, Herndon, VA 20171. Telephone: 703-478-6666. FAX: 703-435-9754. E-MAIL: nvtimes@aol.com. URL: http://www.timespapers.com. Pub. Frequency: w. (Thu.) Page Size: broadsheet. Subscrip. Rate: $29.95/yr mailed. Circulation: 5,250 per issue (paid and free). **Owner(s):** Arcom Publications, Inc., See address and contact information above. **Management:** Peter Arundel, Publisher. Peter W Arundel, Vice President. Rose Mary Felton, Advertising Manager. Ron Sauer, Circulation Manager. **Editorial:** Steve Cahill, Executive Editor. Kali Schumitz, Managing Editor. Briteny Boyd, Lifestyle Editor.

FAIRFAX TIMES. 13873 Park Center Rd., Ste. 301, Herndon, VA 20171. Telephone: 703-478-6666. FAX: 703-435-9754. URL: http://www.fairfaxtimes.com/. Pub. Frequency: w. (Thu.) Page Size: broadsheet. Subscrip. Rate: $29.95/yr mailed. Circulation: 19,150 per issue (paid and free). **Owner(s):** Arcom Publications, Inc., See address and contact information above. **Management:** Peter Arundel, Publisher. Peter W Arundel, Vice President. Rose Mary Felton, Advertising Manager. Ron Sauer, Circulation Manager. Hugo Lembert, Classified Adv. Mgr.. **Editorial:** Steve Cahill, Executive Editor. Kali Schumitz, Managing Editor. Briteny Boyd, Lifestyle Editor.

GREAT FALLS TIMES. 13873 Park Center Rd., Ste. 301, Herndon, VA 20171. Telephone: 703-478-6666. FAX: 703-435-9754. E-MAIL: nvtimes@aol.com. URL: http://www.timespapers.com. Year Established: 1986. Pub. Frequency: w. (Wed.) Page Size: tabloid. Subscrip. Rate: $.50 newsstand/cover; $29.95/yr mailed in county; $29.95/yr mailed out of county. Circulation: 4,000 per issue (paid and free). **Owner(s):** Arcom Publications, Inc., See address and contact information above. **Management:** Peter Arundel, Publisher. Peter W Arundel, Vice President. Rose Mary Felton, Advertising Manager. Ron Sauer, Circulation Manager. Hugo Lembert, Classified Adv. Mgr.. **Editorial:** Marcia McAllister, Executive Editor. Kali Schumitz, Managing Editor. Briteny Boyd, Lifestyle Editor.

HERNDON TIMES. 13873 Park Center Rd., Ste. 301, Herndon, VA 20171. Telephone: 703-478-6666. FAX: 703-435-9754. E-MAIL: nvtimes@aol.com. URL: http://www.timespapers.com. Pub. Frequency: w. (Wed.) Page Size: broadsheet. Subscrip. Rate: $.50 newsstand/cover; $29.95/yr mailed in county; $29.95/yr mailed out of county. Circulation: 12,041 per issue (paid and free). **Owner(s):** Arcom Publications, Inc., See address and contact information above. **Management:** Peter Arundel, Publisher. Peter W Arundel, Vice President. Rose Mary Felton, Advertising Manager. Ron Sauer, Circulation Manager. Angie Howard, Classified Adv. Mgr.. **Editorial:** Kali Schumitz, Managing Editor.

RESTON TIMES. 13873 Park Center Rd., Ste. 301, Herndon, VA 20171. Telephone: 703-478-6666. FAX: 703-435-9754. E-MAIL: nvtimes@aol.com. URL: http://www.timespapers.com. Year Established: 1965. Pub. Frequency: w. (Wed.) Page Size: broadsheet. Subscrip. Rate: $.50 newsstand/cover; $29.95/yr in county; $29.95/yr out of county. Circulation: 16,527 per issue (paid and free). **Owner(s):** Arcom Publications, Inc., See address and contact information above. **Management:** Peter Arundel, Publisher. Peter W Arundel, Vice President. Rose Mary Felton, Advertising Manager. Ron Sauer, Circulation Manager. Lance Lewis, Classified Adv. Mgr.. **Editorial:** Kali Schumitz, Managing Editor. Phillip Creel, Sports.

SPRINGFIELD TIMES COURIER. 13873 Park Center Rd., Ste. 301, Herndon, VA 20171. Telephone: 703-478-6666. FAX: 703-435-9754. E-MAIL: nvtimes@aol.com. URL: http://www.timespapers.com. Pub. Frequency: w. (Thu.) Page Size: broadsheet. Subscrip. Rate: $.50 newsstand/cover; $29.95/yr in county; $29.95/yr mailed out of county. Circulation: 23,500 per issue (paid and free). **Owner(s):** Arcom Publications, Inc., See address and contact information above. **Management:** Peter Arundel, Publisher. Peter W Arundel, Vice President. Rose Mary Felton, Advertising Manager. Ron Sauer, Circulation Manager. Lance Lewis, Classified Adv. Mgr.. **Editorial:** Steve Cahill, Executive Editor. Kali Schumitz, Managing Editor. Briteny Boyd, Lifestyle Editor.

VIENNA TIMES. 13873 Park Center Rd., Ste. 301, Herndon, VA 20171. Telephone: 703-478-6666. FAX: 703-435-9754. E-MAIL: nvtimes@aol.com. URL: http://www.timespapers.com. Year Established: 1985. Pub. Frequency: w. (Thu.) Page Size: broadsheet. Subscrip. Rate: $.50 newsstand/cover; $29.95/yr mailed in county; $29.95/yr mailed out of county. Circulation: 13,787 per issue (paid and free). **Owner(s):** Arcom Publications, Inc., See address and contact information above. **Management:** Peter Arundel, Publisher. Peter W Arundel, Vice President. Rose Mary Felton, Advertising Manager. Ron Sauer, Circulation Manager. Lance Lewis, Classified Adv. Mgr.. **Editorial:** Kali Schumitz, Managing Editor.

HILLSVILLE

CARROLL NEWS, THE. 1192 W. Stuart Dr., PO Box 487, Hillsville, VA 24343. Telephone: 276-728-7311. FAX: 276-728-4119. E-MAIL: sdotton@carrollnews.com. URL: http://www.thecarrollnews.com. Year Established: 1920. Pub. Frequency: w. (Wed.) Page Size: broadsheet. Subscrip. Rate: $.50 newsstand/cover; $20/yr in county. Circulation: 6,700 per issue (paid). **Owner(s):** Mid-South Management Co., Inc., 314 S. Pine St., Spartanburg, SC 29304. Telephone: 864-583-2907. **Management:** Mark Davis, General Manager. Mike Milligan, Publisher. **Editorial:** Dee Ann Lindsey, Editor.

INDEPENDENCE

DECLARATION, THE. 578-D Guynn Shopping Ctr., Independence, VA 24348-0070. Telephone: 276-773-2222. FAX: 276-773-2287. E-MAIL: declaration@adelphia.net. Mailing Address: PO Box 70, Independence, VA 24348-0070. Year Established: 1980. Pub. Frequency: w. (Wed.) Page Size: broadsheet. Subscrip. Rate: $.50 newsstand/cover; $24/yr in area; $37/yr mailed out of area. Circulation: 3,000 per issue (paid and free). **Owner(s):** Landmark Community Newspapers, Inc., See address and contact information above. **Management:** Larry Chambers, Publisher. Linda Litz, Advertising Manager. Amy Adkins, Circulation Manager. **Editorial:** Larry Chambers, Editor.

KILMARNOCK

RAPPAHANNOCK RECORD. 27 Main St., Kilmarnock, VA 22482. Telephone: 804-435-1701. FAX: 804-435-2632. E-MAIL: mail@rrecord.com. URL: http://www.rrecord.com. Mailing Address: P.O. Box 400, Kilmarnock, VA 22482. Year Established: 1916. Pub. Frequency: w. (Thu.) Page Size: broadsheet. Subscrip. Rate: $.75 newsstand/cover; $25/yr in county; $36/yr out of county. Adv. Rate: col. inch $9 Circulation: 8,031 per issue (paid and free). **Owner(s):** Rappahannock Record, Inc., See address and contact information above. **Management:** Fred A. Gaskins, Publisher. Sara Amiss, Advertising Manager. Anna Harrison, Circulation Manager. **Editorial:** Robert Mason Jr., Editor-in-Chief.

KING GEORGE

JOURNAL (KING GEORGE), THE. 10250 Kings Hwy., King George, VA 22485. Telephone: 540-775-2024. FAX: 540-775-4099. E-MAIL: news@journalpress.com. URL: http://www.journalpress.com. Mailing Address: PO Box 409, King George, VA 22485. Pub. Frequency: w. (Wed.) Page Size: broadsheet. Subscrip. Rate: $.50 newsstand/cover; $22.50/yr in county. Circulation: 7,500 per issue (paid). **Owner(s):** Jessica Herrink, See address and contact information above. **Management:** Jessica Herrink, President. Ruth Herrink, Publisher. Steve Detwiler, Advertising. Charlene Franks, Circulation Manager. **Editorial:** Ruth Herrink, Editor.

LAWRENCEVILLE

BRUNSWICK TIMES-GAZETTE. 213 Main St., Lawrenceville, VA 23868. Telephone: 434-848-2114. FAX: 434-848-2115. E-MAIL: editor@btg.com. Mailing Address: PO Box 250, Lawrenceville, VA 23868. Year Established: 1887. Pub. Frequency: w. (Wed.) Page Size: broadsheet. Subscrip. Rate: $.50 newsstand/cover; $14.75/yr in county. Adv. Rate: col. inch $6.95 Circulation: 3,900 per issue (paid). **Owner(s):** Byerly Publications, Inc., 1000 Armory Dr., Franklin, VA 23851. Telephone: 757-562-3187. **Management:** Hanes Byerly, President. Tom Childrey, Advertising Manager. Gary Hamilton, Circulation Manager. **Editorial:** Susan Kenney, Editor.

LEESBURG

ASHBURN STERLING. 9 E. Market St., Leesburg, VA 20176-3013. Telephone: 703-777-1111. FAX: 703-771-0036. URL: http://www.loudountimes.com/. Pub. Frequency: w. (Wed.) Page Size: standard.Adv. Rate: col. inch $20.50 Circulation: 26,292 (paid and free). **Owner(s):** Arcom Publications, Inc., 13873 Park Center Rd, Ste 301, Herndon, VA 20171. Telephone: 703-435-9754. FAX: 703-478-6666. **Management:** Jules Molenda, General Manager. Peter Arundel, Publisher. Peter W Arundel, Vice President. Ron Sauer, Circulation Manager. Angie Howard, Classified Adv. Mgr.. **Editorial:** Paul K. Smith, Editor. Carl Lukat, Sports Editor.

LEESBURG TODAY. One E. Market St., Leesburg, VA 20176-3014. Telephone: 703-771-8800. FAX: 703-771-8833. URL: http://www.leesburg2day.com. Year Established: 1988. Pub. Frequency: w. (Fri.) Page Size: tabloid. Subscrip. Rate: $80/yr mailed 1st class. Circulation: 43,000 per issue (paid and controlled). **Owner(s):** Amendment I, Inc., See address and contact information above. **Management:** Jean Carr, General Manager. Libby Pinner, Advertising Manager. Valarie Phillips, Business Manager. **Editorial:** Norman Styer, Editor.

LOUDOUN TIMES-MIRROR. 9 E. Market St., Leesburg, VA 20176-0036. Telephone: 703-777-1111. FAX: 703-771-0036. E-MAIL: ltmeditor@timespapers.com. URL: http://www.timespapers.com. Mailing Address: PO Box 359, Leesburg, VA 20178. Year Established: 1798. Pub. Frequency: w. (Wed.) Page Size: broadsheet. Subscrip. Rate: $.50 newsstand/cover; $23.95/yr in county; $29.95/yr mailed in county; $39.95/yr mailed out of county. Circulation: 18,000 per issue (paid). **Owner(s):** Arcom Publications, Inc., 13873 Park Center Rd, Ste 301, Herndon, VA 20171. Telephone: 703-435-9754. FAX: 703-478-6666. **Management:** Jules Molenda, General Manager. Peter Arundel, Publisher. Peter W Arundel, Vice President. Ron Sauer, Circulation Manager. Angie Howard, Classified Adv. Mgr.. **Editorial:** Paul K. Smith, Editor. Martin Casey, Executive Editor. Eileen Carlton, Lifestyle Editor. Carl Lukat, Sports Editor.

LEXINGTON

NEWS-GAZETTE (LEXINGTON). PO Box 1153, Lexington, VA 24450. E-MAIL: publisher@thenews-gazette.com. URL: http://www.thenews-gazette.com. Mailing Address: PO Box 1153, Lexington, VA 24450. Year Established: 1801. Pub. Frequency: w. (Wed.) Page Size: broadsheet. Subscrip. Rate: $.75 newsstand/cover; $25.95/yr mailed in county; $35.95/yr mailed out of county; $40.95/yr mailed out of state. Adv. Rate: col. inch $12.15 Circulation: 8,125 per issue (paid). **Owner(s):** News-Gazette Corp., See address and contact information above. **Management:** M.W. Paxton IV, Publisher. Shannon Tinsley, Advertising Manager. Connie Montgomery, Circulation Manager. Tonia Watterson, Classified Adv. Mgr.. **Editorial:** Darryl Woodson, Editor. Doug Chase, Sports Editor.Readers: Rockbridge, County, Virginia

ROCKBRIDGE WEEKLY. ISSN 1064-7759
107 E. Washington St., Lexington, VA 24450. Telephone: 540-464-6600. FAX: 540-464-6603. E-MAIL: publisher2rockbridgeweekly.com. URL: http://www.rockbridgeweekly.com. Mailing Address: PO Box 1331, Lexington, VA 24450. Year Established: 1981. Pub. Frequency: w. (Wed.) Page Size: broadsheet. Subscrip. Rate: $.50 newsstand/cover; $17/yr in county; $30/yr out of area. Circulation: 5,600 per issue (paid). **Owner(s):** Jerry Clark, PO Box 791, Buena Vista, VA 24416. **Management:** Jerry Clark, Publisher. Tammy Paitsel, Circulation Manager. Jerry Clark, Marketing Director. **Editorial:** Jerry Clark, Editor. Tammy Lipscomb, Production Manager. David Grimes, Sports.

WEEKENDER (LEXINGTON), THE. 20 W. Nelson St., Lexington, VA 24450. Telephone: 540-463-3113. FAX: 540-464-6397. E-MAIL: editor@thenews-gazette.com. URL: http://www.thenews-gazette.com. Mailing Address: PO Box 1153, Lexington, VA 24450. Year Established: 1989. Pub. Frequency: w. (Sat.) Page Size: broadsheet.Adv. Rate: col. inch $12.15 Circulation: 15,500 per issue (controlled). **Owner(s):** News-Gazette Corp., See address and contact information above. **Management:** M.W. Paxton IV, President. Shannon Tinsley, Advertising Manager. Connie Montgomery, Circulation Manager. Tonia Watterson, Classified Adv. Mgr.. **Editorial:** Darryl Woodson, Editor.Readers: Rockbridge County, Virginia

LOUISA

CENTRAL VIRGINIAN, THE. 29 Rescue Ln, Louisa Cy Industrial Air Park, Louisa, VA 23093. Telephone: 540-967-0368. FAX: 540-967-3847. E-MAIL: cvads@firstva.com. URL: http://www.thecentralvirginian.com. Mailing Address: PO Box 464, Louisa, VA 23093. Year Established: 1912. Pub. Frequency: w. (Thu.) Page Size: broadsheet. Subscrip. Rate: $.50 newsstand/cover; $25/yr in Louisa & Fluvanna cys.; $31/yr in state; $34/yr out of state. Adv. Rate: col. inch $9 Circulation: 8,000 per issue (paid). **Owner(s):** C V Corporation of Virginia, See address and contact information above. **Management:** Cathy Collins, Publisher. Kelly Seay, Advertising Manager. Ashley Tarry, Circulation Manager. **Editorial:** Deana D Meredith, Managing Editor. Contact: Kelly Seay, Advertising Manager. Contact: Kelly Seay, Advertising Manager. Contact: Kelly Seay, Advertising Manager. Contact: Kelly Seay, Advertising Manager.

LURAY

PAGE NEWS & COURIER. 17 S. Broad St., Luray, VA 22835. Telephone: 540-743-5123. FAX: 540-743-4779. E-MAIL: pagenews@shentel.net. Mailing Address: PO Box 707, Luray, VA 22835. Year Established: 1867. Pub. Frequency: w. (Thu.) Page Size: standard. Subscrip. Rate: $.50 newsstand/cover; $20/yr in county; $25/yr out of county. Circulation: 7,500 per issue (paid). **Owner(s):** Page-Shenandoah News Corp., 231 S. Liberty St., Harrisonburg, VA 22801. Telephone: 540-574-6200. **Management:** Richard Morin, President. Cindi Banach, Advertising. Patti Burner, Circulation Manager. **Editorial:** James Caudill, Editor.

MADISON

MADISON COUNTY EAGLE, THE. 201 N. Main St., Madison, VA 22727. Telephone: 540-948-5121. FAX: 540-948-3045. E-MAIL: news @ madison-news.com. URL: http://www.madison-news.com. Mailing Address: PO Box 325, Madison, VA 22727. Year Established: 1911. Pub. Frequency: w. (Thu.) Page Size: broadsheet. Subscrip. Rate: $.50 newsstand/cover; $25/yr in county; $27/yr out of county. Circulation: 4,300 per issue (paid). **Owner(s):** Media General, Inc., 333 E. Franklin St., Richmond, VA 23219. Telephone: 804-649-6000. **Management:** Tina Smith, Office Manager. Patrick Newell, Advertising Manager. **Editorial:** Don Richeson, Editor. Greg K. Glassner, Managing Editor.

MARION

SMYTH COUNTY MARKET PLACE. 119 S. Sheffey St., Marion, VA 24354. Telephone: 276-783-5121. FAX: 276-783-9713. E-MAIL: wnews@naxs.com. URL: http://www.swvatoday.com. Mailing Address: PO Box 640, Marion, VA 24354. Pub. Frequency: w. (Fri.) Page Size: tabloid Circulation: 9,800 per issue (free). **Owner(s):** Media General, Inc., 333 E. Franklin St., Richmond, VA 23219. Telephone: 804-649-6000. **Management:** Sam Cooper, Publisher. Robin Lowery, Advertising. Louis Corpus, Circulation Manager. Deanna Allen, Classified Adv. Mgr.. **Editorial:** Stephanie Porter-Nichols, Managing Editor.

SMYTH COUNTY NEWS & MESSENGER. ISSN 0744-0766
119 S. Sheffey St., Marion, VA 24354. Telephone: 276-783-5121. FAX: 276-783-9713. E-MAIL: mkeen@wythenews.com. URL: http://www.swvatoday.com. Mailing Address: PO Box 640, Marion, VA 24354. Year Established: 1884. Pub. Frequency: s-w. (Wed. & Sat.) Page Size: broadsheet. Subscrip. Rate: $.75 newsstand/cover; $36/yr in county; $50/yr mailed out of county; $59/yr mailed out of state. Circulation: 6,000 per issue (paid). **Owner(s):** Media General, Inc., 333 E. Franklin St., Richmond, VA 23219. Telephone: 804-649-6000. **Management:** Sam Cooper, Publisher. Robin Lowery, Advertising. Louis Corpus, Circulation Manager. Deanna Allen, Classified Adv. Mgr.. **Editorial:** Stephanie Porter-Nichols, Managing Editor.

MCLEAN

ALEXANDRIA GAZETTE PACKET. 7913 Westpark Dr., McLean, VA 22102. Telephone: 703-821-5050. FAX: 703-917-0997. E-MAIL: connect@erols.com. URL: http://www.connectionnewspapers.com. Year Established: 1784. Pub. Frequency: w. (Thu.) Page Size: tabloid. Subscrip. Rate: $25/yr mailed. Freelance Pay: $15-$25/story. Circulation: 15,500 per issue (controlled and free). **Owner(s):** Connection Newspapers, LLC, See address and contact information above. **Management:** Mary Kimm, Publisher. Helen Walutes, Advertising Manager. Ann Oliver, Circulation Manager. Andrea Smith, Classified Adv. Mgr.. **Editorial:** Mary Anne Weber, Editor. Rich Sanders, Sports Editor.

ARLINGTON CONNECTION, THE. 7913 Westpark Dr., McLean, VA 22102. Telephone: 703-821-5050. FAX: 703-917-0997. E-MAIL: arlington@connectionnewspapers.com. URL: http://www.connectionnewspapers.com. Year Established: 1988. Pub. Frequency: w. (Wed.) Page Size: tabloid. Subscrip. Rate: $17/yr local; $30/yr elsewhere. Circulation: 7,550 per issue (controlled and free). **Owner(s):** Connection Newspapers, LLC, See address and contact information above. **Management:** Mary Kimm, Publisher. Lou Emery, Advertising Manager. Linda Pecquex, Circulation Manager. Andrea Smith, Classified Adv. Mgr.. **Editorial:** Steve Hibbard, Editor. Greg Wyshynski, Sports Editor.

BIRGMINGHAM-BLOOMFIELD ECCENTRIC, THE. 7950 Jones Branch Dr, McLean, VA 22107. Telephone: 703-854-5000. URL: http://www.observer-eccentric.com. Pub. Frequency: s-w. (Thu. & Sun.) Page Size: broadsheet. Subscrip. Rate: $.75 newsstand/cover; $51/yr home delivery in county; $72.95/yr mailed in county; $108.95/yr mailed out of county. Circulation: 85,000 per issue (paid). **Owner(s):** Observer, Eccentric & Mirror Newspapers, Inc., See address and contact information above. **Management:** Peter Neill, Publisher. Marty Carry, Advertising Director. Frank Cibor, Classified Adv. Mgr.. **Editorial:** Susan Rosiek, Executive Editor. Joe Bauman, Managing Editor. Mike Rosenbaum, Sports Editor.

BURKE CONNECTION. 7913 Westpark Dr., McLean, VA 22102. Telephone: 703-821-5050. FAX: 703-917-0997. E-MAIL: burke@connectionnewspapers.com. URL: http://www.connectionnewspapers.com. Pub. Frequency: w. (Thu.) Page Size: tabloid. Subscrip. Rate: $.25 newsstand/cover; $17/yr local; $30/yr elsewhere. Circulation: 14,600 per issue (free). **Owner(s):** Connection Newspapers, LLC, See address and contact information above. **Management:** Mary Kimm, Publisher. Steve Hogan, Advertising Manager. Ann Oliver, Circulation Manager. Andrea Smith, Classified Adv. Mgr.. **Editorial:** Mike O'Connell, Editor. Greg Wyshynski, Sports Editor.

CENTRE VIEW. 7913 Westpark Dr., McLean, VA 22102. Telephone: 703-821-5050. FAX: 703-917-0997. E-MAIL: centreview@connectionnewspapers.com. URL: http://www.connectionnewspapers.com. Pub. Frequency: w. (Thu.) Page Size: tabloid. Subscrip. Rate: $.25 newsstand/cover; $50/yr elsewhere. Circulation: 20,000 per issue (free). **Owner(s):** Connection Newspapers, LLC, See address and contact information above. **Management:** Mary Kimm, Publisher. Karen Washburn, Advertising Manager. Linda Pecquex, Circulation Manager. Andrea Smith, Classified Adv. Mgr.. **Editorial:** Steve Hibbard, Editor. Paul Frommelt, Sports Editor.

FAIRFAX CONNECTION. 7913 Westpark Dr., McLean, VA 22102. Telephone: 703-821-5050. FAX: 703-917-0991. E-MAIL: fairfax@connectionnewspapers.com. URL: http://www.connectionnewspapers.com. Year Established: 1987. Pub. Frequency: w. (Thu.) Page Size: tabloid Circulation: 8,300 per issue (free). **Owner(s):** Connection Newspapers, LLC, See address and contact information above. **Management:** Mary Kimm, Publisher. Steve Hogan, Advertising Manager. Ann Oliver, Circulation Manager. Andrea Smith, Classified Adv. Mgr.. **Editorial:** Mike O'Connell, Editor. Greg Wyshynski, Sports Editor.

FAIRFAX STATION/LAUREL HILL/CLIFTON CONNECTION. 7913 Westpark Dr., McLean, VA 22102. Telephone: 703-821-5050. FAX: 703-917-0997. E-MAIL: fairfax@connectionnewspapers.com. URL: http://www.connectionnewspapers.com. Pub. Frequency: w. (Thu.) Page Size: tabloid. Subscrip. Rate: $.25 newsstand/cover; $50/yr elsewhere. Circulation: 4,500 per issue (paid and controlled). **Owner(s):** Connection Newspapers, LLC, See address and contact information above. **Management:** Mary Kimm, Publisher. Michael Sontag, Advertising Manager. Ann Oliver, Circulation Manager. Andrea Smith, Classified Adv. Mgr.. **Editorial:** Mike O'Connell, Editor. Lea Mae Rice, Assistant Editor. Greg Wyshynski, Sports Editor.

GREAT FALLS CONNECTION. 7913 Westpark Dr., McLean, VA 22102. Telephone: 703-821-5050. FAX: 703-917-0997. E-MAIL: mclean@connectionnewspapers.com. Pub. Frequency: w. (Wed.) Page Size: tabloid.Subscrip. Rate: $17/yr local; $35/yr elsewhere Circulation: 5,960 per issue (free). **Owner(s):** Connection Newspapers, LLC, See address and contact information above. **Management:** Mary Kimm, Publisher. Salome Howard-Gaibler, Advertising Manager. Linda Pecquex, Circulation Manager. Andrea Smith, Classified Adv. Mgr.. **Editorial:** Kamilla Gary, Editor. BJ Koubaroulis, Sports Editor.

HERNDON CONNECTION. 7913 Westpark Dr., McLean, VA 22102. Telephone: 703-821-5050. FAX: 703-917-0991. E-MAIL: herndon@connectionnewspapers.com. URL: http://www.connectionnewspapers.com. Pub. Frequency: w. (Wed.) Page Size: tabloid. Subscrip. Rate: $.25 newsstand/cover; $17/yr carrier delivery local; $25/yr carrier delivery elsewhere. Circulation: 10,000 per issue (free). **Owner(s):** Connection Newspapers, LLC, See address and contact information above. **Management:** Mary Kimm, Publisher. Ceci Ferrin, Advertising. Linda Pecquex, Circulation Manager. Andrea Smith, Classified Adv. Mgr.. **Editorial:** Steve Mauren, Editor. BJ Koubaroulis, Sports Editor.

LANCASTER-FAIRFIELD ADVERTISER. 7950 Jones Branch Dr, McLean, VA 22107. URL: http://www.lancaster.theadvertiser.net. Year Established: 1974. Pub. Frequency: w. (Sun.) Page Size: tabloid Circulation: 35,231 per issue (free). **Owner(s):** Gannett Company, Inc., See address and contact information above. Journal Community Publishing Group, 3675 Dolson Ct., Carroll, OH 43112. 600 Industrial Dr., PO Box 609, Waupaca, WI 54981. Telephone: 715-258-8450. **Management:** Rick Szabrak, Publisher.

LOUDOUN CONNECTION. 7913 Westpark Dr., McLean, VA 22102. Telephone: 703-821-5050. FAX: 703-917-0997. E-MAIL: loudoun@connectionnewspapers.com. URL: http://www.connectionnewspapers.com. Pub. Frequency: w. (Wed.) Page Size: tabloid. Subscrip. Rate: $.25 newsstand/cover; $50/yr elsewhere. Circulation: 11,800 per issue (paid). **Owner(s):** Connection Newspapers, LLC, See address and contact information above. **Management:** Mary Kimm, Publisher. Don Park, Advertising. Linda Pecquex, Circulation Manager. Andrea Smith, Classified Adv. Mgr.. **Editorial:** Jennifer Lesinski, Editor. Paul Frommelt, Sports Editor.

MCLEAN CONNECTION. 7913 Westpark Dr., McLean, VA 22102. Telephone: 703-821-5050. FAX: 703-917-0991. E-MAIL: mclean@connectionnewspapers.com. URL: http://www.connectionnewspapers.com. Pub. Frequency: w. (Wed.) Page Size: tabloid. Subscrip. Rate: $.25 newsstand/cover; $17/yr mailed; $30/yr mailed elsewhere. Circulation: 8,400 per issue (paid and free). **Owner(s):** Connection Newspapers, LLC, See address and contact information above. **Management:** Mary Kimm, Publisher. Trisha Hamilton, Advertising Manager. Linda Pecquex, Circulation Manager. Andrea Smith, Classified Adv. Mgr.. **Editorial:** Kamilla Gary, Editor. BJ Koubaroulis, Sports Editor.

MOUNT VERNON GAZETTE. 7913 Westpark Dr., McLean, VA 22102. Telephone: 703-821-5050. FAX: 703-917-0997. E-MAIL: gazettepacket@erols.com. URL: http://www.connectionnewspapers.com. Pub. Frequency: w. (Thu.) Page Size: tabloid. Subscrip. Rate: $.25 newsstand/cover residents of Mount Vernon (effective 2006); $25/yr carrier delivery. Circulation: 13,500 per issue (paid). **Owner(s):** Connection Newspapers, LLC, See address and contact information above. **Management:** Mary Kimm, Publisher. Ginger Krup, Advertising. Ann Oliver, Circulation Manager. Andrea Smith, Classified Adv. Mgr.. **Editorial:** Mary Anne Weber, Editor. Rich Sanders, Sports Editor.

POTOMAC ALMANAC. 7913 Westpark Dr., McLean, VA 22102. Telephone: 703-821-5050. FAX: 703-917-0997. URL: http://www.connectionnewspapers.com. Year Established: 1957. Pub. Frequency: w. (Wed.) Page Size: tabloid. Subscrip. Rate: $25/yr mailed in county; $50/yr mailed out of area. Circulation: 12,500 per issue (paid and free). **Owner(s):** Connection Newspapers, LLC, See address and contact information above. **Management:** Mary Kimm, Publisher. Kenny Lourie, Advertising Manager. Andrea Smith, Classified Adv. Mgr.. **Editorial:** Alex Scofield, Editor.

RESTON CONNECTION. 7913 Westpark Dr., McLean, VA 22102. Telephone: 703-821-5050. FAX: 703-917-0991. E-MAIL: reston@connectionnewspapers.com. URL: http://www.connectionnewspapers.com. Year Established: 1988. Pub. Frequency: w. (Wed.) Page Size: tabloid. Subscrip. Rate: $.25 newsstand/cover; $17/yr local; $30/yr elsewhere. Circulation: 9,700 per issue (paid and controlled). **Owner(s):** Connection Newspapers, LLC, See address and contact information above. **Management:** Mary Kimm, Publisher. Winslow Wacker, Advertising Manager. Linda Pecquex, Circulation Manager. Andrea Smith, Classified Adv. Mgr.. **Editorial:** Steve Mauren, Editor. BJ Koubaroulis, Sports Editor.

SPRINGFIELD CONNECTION. 7913 Westpark Dr., McLean, VA 22102. Telephone: 703-821-5050. FAX: 703-917-0991. E-MAIL: springfield@connectionnewspapers.com. URL: http://www.connectionnewspapers.com. Pub. Frequency: w. (Thu.) Page Size: tabloid Circulation: 11,000 per issue (free). **Owner(s):** Connection Newspapers, LLC, See address and contact information above. **Management:** Mary Kimm, Publisher. Steve Hogan, Advertising Manager. Ann Oliver, Circulation Manager. Andrea Smith, Classified Adv. Mgr.. **Editorial:** Mike O'Connell, Editor. Lea Mae Rice, Assistant Editor. Greg Wyshynski, Sports Editor.

VIENNA/OAKTON CONNECTION. 7913 Westpark Dr., McLean, VA 22102. Telephone: 703-821-5050. FAX: 703-917-0997. E-MAIL: connect@erols.com. URL: http://www.connectionnewspapers.com. Pub. Frequency: w. (Wed.) Page Size: tabloid.Subscrip. Rate: $50/yr elsewhere Circulation: 12,900 per issue (paid). **Owner(s):** Connection Newspapers, LLC, See address and contact information above. **Management:** Mary Kimm, Publisher. Linda Pecquex, Circulation Manager. Andrea Smith, Classified Adv. Mgr.. **Editorial:** Steve Mauren, Editor. BJ Koubaroulis, Sports Editor.

MECHANICSVILLE

MECHANICSVILLE LOCAL. 6400 Mechanicsville Tpke, Mechanicsville, VA 23111. Telephone: 804-746-1235. FAX: 804-730-0476. E-MAIL: mechlocal@aol.com. URL: http://www.mechlocal.com. Year Established: 1984. Pub. Frequency: w. (Wed.) Page Size; tabloid. Subscrip. Rate: $35/yr mailed in county; $35/yr mailed out of county. Circulation: 25,500 per issue (paid and free). **Owner(s):** Richmond Suburban Newspapers, See address and contact information above. **Management:** Joe Dobson, General Manager. Joy Monopoli, Publisher. Tom Haynie, Advertising Manager. Sandra Talley, Circulation Manager. **Editorial:** Ken Odor, Editor.

MONETA

SMITH MOUNTAIN EAGLE. 14245 Moneta Rd., Moneta, VA 24121. Telephone: 540-297-1222. FAX: 540-297-1944. E-MAIL: eaglenews@direcway.com. Mailing Address: PO Box 231, Moneta, VA 24121. Pub. Frequency: w. (Wed.) Page Size: broadsheet. Subscrip. Rate: $.75 newsstand/cover; $24/yr in area; $34/yr out of area. Circulation: 4,000 per issue (paid). **Owner(s):** Womack Publishing Co., Inc., PO Box 111, Chatham, VA 24531. Telephone: 434-432-1654. FAX: 434-432-1005. **Management:** Rob Lyon, General Manager. Charles Womack, Publisher. Beth Meador, Advertising Manager. **Editorial:** Rob Lyon, Editor.

MONTEREY

RECORDER (MONTEREY), THE. 10 Water St., Monterey, VA 24465. Telephone: 540-468-2147. FAX: 540-468-2048. Mailing Address: PO Box 10, Monterey, VA 24465. Pub. Frequency: w. (Fri.) Page Size: tabloid. Subscrip. Rate: $1 newsstand/cover; $29.95/yr in county; $34.95/yr out of county; $38.95/yr out of state. **Owner(s):** Recorder Publishing of Virginia, See address and contact information above. **Management:** Ann Adams, General Manager. P. Lea Campbell, Publisher. **Editorial:** P. Lea Campbell, Editor.

MONTROSS

WESTMORELAND NEWS. 105 Court Sq., Montross, VA 22520. Telephone: 804-493-8096. FAX: 804-493-8009. E-MAIL: wnews@sylvaninfo.net. Mailing Address: PO Box 699, Montross, VA 22520. Year Established: 1947. Pub. Frequency: w. (Wed.) Page Size: broadsheet. Subscrip. Rate: $.50 newsstand/cover; $23/yr in county; $34/yr out of county. Circulation: 8,200 per issue (paid and free). **Owner(s):** Northern Neck Newspaper Group LLC, See address and contact information above. **Management:** Steve Weddle, General Manager. Kate Boylan, Advertising. **Editorial:** Steve Weddle, Editor.

NEW CASTLE

NEW CASTLE RECORD. 318 Court St., New Castle, VA 24127. E-MAIL: newcastle@rbnet.com. URL: http://www.newcastlerecord.com. Mailing Address: PO Box 116, New Castle, VA 24127. Year Established: 1885. Pub. Frequency: w. (Wed.) Page Size: broadsheet. Subscrip. Rate: $.50 newsstand/cover; $30/yr local; $26/yr in county; $34/yr out of state. Circulation: 2,000 per issue (paid). **Owner(s):** Main Street Newspapers, Inc., See address and contact information above. **Management:** Wilson Koeppel, Publisher. Vickie Henderson, Advertising Manager. **Editorial:** Lawson Koeppel, Editor. Meg Hibbert, News Editor. Brian Hoffman, Sports.

NORTON

COALFIELD PROGRESS, THE. ISSN 0889-3330
725 Park Ave., Norton, VA 24273-0380. Telephone: 276-679-1101. FAX: 276-679-5922. E-MAIL: npimedia@mounet.com. URL: http://www.coalfield.com. Mailing Address: PO Box 380, Norton, VA 24273-0380. Year Established: 1911. Pub. Frequency: s-w. (Tue. & Thu.) Page Size: broadsheet. Subscrip. Rate: $.75 newsstand/cover; $44/yr mailed in county; $76/yr mailed out of county. **Wire Service(s):** AP. Circulation: 8,885 per issue (paid and free). **Owner(s):** Norton Press, Inc., PO Box 380, Norton, VA 24273. Telephone: 276-679-1101. **Management:** Michael Tate, President. Jenay Tate, Publisher. Bill Endean, Advertising Director. Becky McElroy, Circulation Manager. **Editorial:** Jenay Tate, Editor.

ORANGE

ORANGE COUNTY REVIEW. 110 Berry Hill Rd., Orange, VA 22960. Telephone: 540-672-1266. FAX: 540-672-3719. E-MAIL: news@orangenews.com. URL: http://www.orangenews.com. Mailing Address: PO Box 589, Orange, VA 22960. Year Established: 1931. Pub. Frequency: w. (Thu.) Page Size: broadsheet. Subscrip. Rate: $.50 newsstand/cover; $25/yr in county; $27/yr out of county. Circulation: 7,450 per issue (paid). **Owner(s):** Media General, Inc., 333 E. Franklin St., Richmond, VA 23219. Telephone: 804-649-6000. **Management:** John Hall, Publisher. Nancy Embree, Advertising Director. Patricia Aitken, Business Manager. **Editorial:** Jeff Poole, Editor. Steve Evans, Managing Editor.

PEARISBURG

VIRGINIAN-LEADER. 511 Mountain Lake Ave., Pearisburg, VA 24134-1629. Telephone: 540-921-3434. FAX: 540-921-2563. E-MAIL: krakes@virginianleader.com. URL: http://www.virginianleader.com. Year Established: 1857. Pub. Frequency: w. (Wed.) Page Size: standard. Subscrip. Rate: $.50 newsstand/cover; $25/yr mailed in Giles & Monroe cys.; $35/yr mailed elsewhere. Adv. Rate: col. inch $5.70 Circulation: 5,865 per issue (paid). **Owner(s):** Virginian Leader Corp., See address and contact information above. **Management:** Kenneth Rakes, Publisher. Angie Palmer, Advertising Manager. **Editorial:** Roger Mullins, Editor. Amy Gilmer, Managing Editor.

PENNINGTON GAP

POWELL VALLEY NEWS. 125 E. Morgan Ave., Pennington Gap, VA 24277. Telephone: 276-546-1210. FAX: 276-546-5468. Mailing Address: PO Box 459, Pennington Gap, VA 24277-0459. Year Established: 1920. Pub. Frequency: w. (Wed.) Page Size: broadsheet. Subscrip. Rate: $.50 newsstand/cover; $25/yr mailed in county & adj. cys.; $30/yr mailed out of area. Adv. Rate: col. inch $5.50 Circulation: 7,537 per issue (paid). **Owner(s):** Shirley A. Watson, See address and contact information above. **Management:** Rick L. Watson, Publisher. Jim Ewing, Circulation Manager. Shirley Watson, Marketing Director. **Editorial:** Rick L. Watson, Editor. Louise Carver, Managing Editor.

PURCELLVILLE

BLUE RIDGE LEADER, THE. 128 S. 20th St., Purcellville, VA 20132. Telephone: 540-338-6200. FAX: 540-338-2647. E-MAIL: blueridgeleader@aol.com. Year Established: 1984. Pub. Frequency: w. (Fri.) Page Size: tabloid. Subscrip. Rate: $.35 newsstand/cover; $20/yr local. Circulation: 30,000 per issue (controlled and free). **Owner(s):** Jane Ann Simpson, See address and contact information above. **Management:** Jane Ann Simpson, Publisher. Pam Morris, Advertising. **Editorial:** Mark Dewey, Editor.

RESTON

MCLEAN TIMES. 1760 Reston Pkwy., Ste. 411, Reston, VA 20190-3316. Telephone: 703-437-5400. FAX: 703-437-6019. E-MAIL: nvtimes.aol.com. URL: http://www.timespapers.com. Pub. Frequency: w. (Wed.) Page Size: tabloid. Subscrip. Rate: $29.95/yr mailed. Circulation: 14,000 per issue (paid and free). **Owner(s):** Arcom Publications, Inc., 13873 Park Center Rd, Ste 301, Herndon, VA 20171. FAX: 703-478-6666. **Management:** Peter Arundel, Publisher. Peter W Arundel, Vice President. Rose Mary Felton, Advertising Manager. Ron Sauer, Circulation Manager. **Editorial:** Steve Cahill, Editor. Kali Schumitz, Managing Editor. Briteny Boyd, Lifestyle Editor.

RICHLANDS

MOUNTAIN ADVISOR. 1206 Second St., Richlands, VA 24641. Telephone: 276-963-1081. FAX: 276-963-0123. E-MAIL: aleffel@richlands-news-press.com. URL: http://www.richlands-news-press.com. Mailing Address: PO Box 818, Richlands, VA 24641. Pub. Frequency: w. (Sat.) Page Size: broadsheet Circulation: 14,000 per issue (free). **Owner(s):** Media General, Inc., 333 E. Franklin St., Richmond, VA 23126. Telephone: 804-649-6000. **Management:** Opel Bandy, General Manager. Samuel F. Cooper, Publisher. Audria Leffel, Advertising Director. **Editorial:** Mike Still, Executive Editor.

RICHLANDS NEWS PRESS. 1206 Second St., Richlands, VA 24641. Telephone: 276-963-1081. FAX: 276-963-0123. E-MAIL: aleffel@richlands-news-press.com. URL: http://www.richlands-news-press.com. Mailing Address: PO Box 818, Richlands, VA 24641. Year Established: 1933. Pub. Frequency: w. (Wed.) Page Size: broadsheet. Subscrip. Rate: $.50 newsstand/cover; $27/yr in county. Circulation: 6,400 per issue (paid). **Owner(s):** Media General, Inc., 333 E. Franklin St., Richmond, VA 23219. Telephone: 804-649-6000. FAX: 804-775-8090. **Management:** Opel Bandy, General Manager. Samuel F. Cooper, Publisher. Audria Leffel, Advertising Director. **Editorial:** Mike Still, Executive Editor. Bill Patton, Photographer. Dave Cox, Sports.

TAZEWELL COUNTY FREE PRESS. 1249 Front St., Richlands, VA 24641. Telephone: 276-963-0127. FAX: 276-963-0127. E-MAIL: freepres@netscope.net. Mailing Address: PO Box 1205, Richlands, VA 24641. Year Established: 1976. Pub. Frequency: w. (Wed.) Page Size: broadsheet. Subscrip. Rate: $20 mailed for 6 mos.. Adv. Rate: col. inch $8 **Wire Service(s):** AP. Circulation: 13,500 per issue (paid and free). **Owner(s):** Lynna Mitchell, 406 Buchanan St., Richlands, VA 24641. Telephone: 276-963-2308. **Management:** Lynna Mitchell, General Manager.

ROCKY MOUNT

FRANKLIN NEWS-POST, THE. PO Box 250, Rocky Mount, VA 24151-0250. Telephone: 540-483-5113. FAX: 540-483-8013. E-MAIL: fnpevents@cherterinkmet.com. Year Established: 1905. Pub. Frequency: 3/w. (Mon., Wed., Fri.) Page Size: broadsheet. Subscrip. Rate: $.50 newsstand/cover; $40/yr in county; $45/yr out of county. Circulation: 8,300 per issue (paid). **Owner(s):** Franklin County Newspapers, Inc., See address and contact information above. **Management:** R.B. Hundley, Publisher. Stephanie Bradley, Advertising Manager. Tammy Bowles, Circulation Director. **Editorial:** R.B. Hundley, Editor. Ken Bradley, News Editor.

SALEM

SALEM TIMES-REGISTER. 1633 W. Main St., Salem, VA 24153. Telephone: 540-389-9355. FAX: 540-389-2930. E-MAIL: salemtimes@rbnet.com. URL: http://www.mainnewspapers.com. Year Established: 1854. Pub. Frequency: w. (Thu.) Page Size: broadsheet. Subscrip. Rate: $.50 newsstand/cover; $26/yr in county; $30/yr home delivery local; $34/yr out of county; $34/yr mailed out of state. Circulation: 5,000 per issue (paid). **Owner(s):** Main Street Newspapers, Inc., See address and contact information above. **Management:** Wilson Koeppel, Publisher. Lynn Hurst, Advertising Manager. Ken Bowen, Circulation Manager. **Editorial:** Billy Powell, Production Manager. Meg Hibbert, News Editor. Brian Hoffman, Sports.

SOUTH BOSTON

SOUTH BOSTON GAZETTE-VIRGINIAN. 3201-3209 Halifax Rd., South Boston, VA 24592. Telephone: 434-572-3945. FAX: 434-572-1173. E-MAIL: gazette@gazettevirginian.com. URL: http://www.gazettevirginian.com. Mailing Address: P.O. Box 524, South Boston, VA 24592. Year Established: 1903. Pub. Frequency: 3/w. (Mon., Wed., Fri.) Page Size: broadsheet. Subscrip. Rate: $.50 newsstand/cover; $24/yr in county; $40/yr out of county; $50/yr mailed elsewhere. Adv. Rate: col. inch $5.25 **Wire Service(s):** AP. Circulation: 15,774 per issue (paid and free). **Owner(s):** Keith A. Shelton, See address and contact information above. **Management:** Keith A. Shelton, President. Patricia C. Seat, Advertising Manager. Dolores Cole, Circulation Manager. Lisa Gravitt, Classified Adv. Mgr.. **Editorial:** Beth Robertson, Editor. Joe Chandler, Sports Editor.

SOUTH HILL

SOUTH HILL ENTERPRISE. 914 W. Danville St., South Hill, VA 23970. Telephone: 434-447-3178. FAX: 434-447-5931. E-MAIL: shenews@msinets.com. URL: http://www.southhillenterprise.com. Mailing Address: PO Box 60, South Hill, VA 23970. Year Established: 1905. Pub. Frequency: s-w. (Wed. & Sun.) Page Size: broadsheet. Subscrip. Rate: $.50 newsstand/cover; $25/yr mailed in county & adj. counties; $37/yr mailed out of area. Circulation: 8,500 per issue (paid and free). **Owner(s):** Womack Publishing Co., Inc., PO Box 111, Chatham, VA 24531. Telephone: 434-432-1654. **Management:** John Peters, General Manager. Baretta Taylor, Advertising Manager. **Editorial:** Brad Johnson, Editor. Dennis Smith, Sports.

STAFFORD

STAFFORD COUNTY SUN. ISSN 1538-3903
PO Box 1400, Stafford, VA 22554. Telephone: 540-659-4466. FAX: 540-659-0039. URL: http://www.staffordcountysun.com. Year Established: 19??. Pub. Frequency: w. **Owner(s):** Media General, Inc., See address and contact information above. **Management:** Mary Rose, Advertising. **Editorial:** Tracy Bell, Managing Editor.

STANARDSVILLE

GREENE COUNTY RECORD. 113 Main St., Stanardsville, VA 22973. Telephone: 434-985-2315. FAX: 434-985-8356. E-MAIL: subscriptions@greene-news.com. URL: http://www.greene-news.com. Mailing Address: PO Box 66, Stanardsville, VA 22973. Year Established: 1914. Pub. Frequency: w. (Thu.) Page Size: broadsheet. Subscrip. Rate: $.50 newsstand/cover; $25/yr in county; $27/yr out of county. Freelance Pay: $10-$20/story. Circulation: 3,200 per issue (paid). **Owner(s):** Media General, Inc., 333 E. Franklin St., Richmond, VA 23219. Telephone: 804-649-6000. **Management:** John Hall, Publisher. Donna Dunivan, Advertising. **Editorial:** Jay Crawford, Editor.

STUART

ENTERPRISE (STUART), THE. 129 N. Main St., Stuart, VA 24171. Telephone: 276-694-3101. FAX: 276-694-5110. E-MAIL: mail@theenterprise.net. URL: http://www.theenterprise.net. Mailing Address: PO Box 348, Stuart, VA 24171-0348. Year Established: 1876. Pub. Frequency: w. (Wed.) Page Size: standard. Subscrip. Rate: $.35 newsstand/cover; $15/yr local; $20/yr elsewhere. Circulation: 5,900 per issue (paid). **Owner(s):** Gail M. Harding, See address and contact information above. **Management:** Gail M. Harding, Publisher. Pam Hall, Advertising Manager. Gail M. Harding, Circulation Manager. **Editorial:** Nancy M. Lindsey, Editor. Stephen Henderson, Sports.

SUTHERLAND

DINWIDDIE MONITOR. 20121 Cox Rd, Sutherland, VA 23885. Telephone: 804-733-8636. FAX: 804-732-6322. E-MAIL: dmmonitor@earthlink.net. Mailing Address: PO Box 399, Sutherland, VA 23885. Pub. Frequency: w. (Wed.) Page Size: standard. Subscrip. Rate: $.50 newsstand/cover; $20/yr. Adv. Rate: col. inch $9.25 Circulation: 4,500 per issue (paid). **Owner(s):** Tom Page, See address and contact information above. **Management:** Tom Page, Publisher. **Editorial:** Tom Page, Editor.

TAZEWELL

CLINCH VALLEY NEWS. 119 Fincastle Tpke., Tazewell, VA 24651. Telephone: 276-988-4770. FAX: 276-988-3815. E-MAIL: aleffel@richlands-news-press.com. URL: http://www.richlands-news-press.com. Mailing Address: PO Box 977, Tazewell, VA 24651. Year Established: 1845. Pub. Frequency: w. (Wed.) Page Size: broadsheet. Subscrip. Rate: $.50 newsstand/cover (effective 2006); $27/yr in county. Circulation: 3,400 per issue (paid). **Owner(s):** Media General, Inc., 333 E. Franklin St., Richmond, VA 23219. Telephone: 804-649-6000. FAX: 804-775-8090. **Management:** Samuel S. Cooper, Publisher. Audria Leffel, Advertising Manager. Mary Childress, Circulation Manager. **Editorial:** Mike Still, Executive Editor.

URBANNA

SOUTHSIDE SENTINEL. 276 Virginia St., Urbanna, VA 23175-0549. Telephone: 804-758-2328. FAX: 804-758-5896. E-MAIL: editor@ssentinel.com. URL: http://www.ssentinel.com. Mailing Address: PO Box 549, Urbanna, VA 23175-0549. Year Established: 1896. Pub. Frequency: w. (Thu.) Page Size: broadsheet. Subscrip. Rate: $.50 newsstand/cover; $24/yr in county; $30/yr out of county. Adv. Rate: col. inch $9.75 Circulation: 5,531 per issue (paid and free). **Owner(s):** Frederick A. & Elizabeth Lee Gaskins, See address and contact information above. **Management:** Frederick A. Gaskins, Publisher. Deborah Haynes, Advertising Manager. Peggy Baughan, Circulation Manager. **Editorial:** John T. Hardin, Managing Editor.

VICTORIA

KENBRIDGE-VICTORIA DISPATCH. PO Box 40, Victoria, VA 23974. Telephone: 434-696-5550. FAX: 434-696-2958. E-MAIL: kvdispatch@earthlink.net. Year Established: 1970. Pub. Frequency: w. (Wed.) Page Size: broadsheet. Subscrip. Rate: $.50 newsstand/cover; $16/yr in county; $18/yr out of county; $20/yr out of state. Circulation: 2,902 per issue (paid). **Owner(s):** Charlotte Publishing, Inc., See address and contact information above. **Management:** Dorothy C. Tucker, Publisher. Wanda Fix, Circulation Director. **Editorial:** Mark Hamlet, Editor.

VINTON

VINTON MESSENGER. ISSN 8750-7919
118 Lee Ave., Vinton, VA 24179. Telephone: 540-343-2648. FAX: 540-389-2930. E-MAIL: vmnews@intelos.net. URL: http://www.mainstreetnewspapers.com. Mailing Address: PO Box 508, Vinton, VA 24179. Year Established: 1960. Pub. Frequency: w. (Thu.) Page Size: broadsheet. Subscrip. Rate: $.50 newsstand/cover; $26/yr in county; $30/yr out of county; $40/yr mailed out of state. Adv. Rate: col. inch $7.28 Freelance Pay: $15/story. Circulation: 3,500 per issue (paid). **Owner(s):** Main Street Newspapers, Inc., 1633 W. Main St., Salem, VA 24153. Telephone: 540-389-9355. FAX: 540-389-2930. **Management:** Gene Marrano, General Manager. Lawson Koeppel, Publisher. Lynn Hurst, Advertising Manager. **Editorial:** Gene Marrano, Editor.

WARRENTON

FAUQUIER CITIZEN. 39 Culpepper St., Warrenton, VA 20188. Telephone: 540-347-5522. FAX: 540-349-8676. E-MAIL: lemerson@citizenet.com. URL: http://www.citizenet.com. Mailing Address: PO Box 631, Warrenton, VA 20188. Year Established: 1989. Pub. Frequency: w. (Fri.) Page Size: tabloid. Subscrip. Rate: $.50 newsstand/cover; $23/yr in county; $35/yr out of county. **Wire Service(s):** AP. Circulation: 8,500 per issue (paid). **Owner(s):** Ellen F. & Lawrence K. Emerson, 13873 Park Center Rd, Ste 301, Herndon, VA 20171. Telephone: 703-478-6666. **Management:** Authur Arundel, Publisher. Pam Lymington, Advertising. **Editorial:** John Toler, Executive Editor. Peter Brewington, Sports Editor.

FAUQUIER TIMES-DEMOCRAT. 39 Culpepper St., Warrenton, VA 20186. Telephone: 540-347-4222. FAX: 540-349-8676. E-MAIL: ftdeditor@crosslink.net. URL: http://www.timespapers.com. Mailing Address: PO Box 631, Warrenton, VA 20188-0631. Year Established: 1817. Pub. Frequency: w. (Wed.) Page Size: broadsheet. Subscrip. Rate: $.50 newsstand/cover; $21/yr in county; $27/yr mailed out of county. Adv. Rate: col. inch $13.80 Freelance Pay: $15-$50/article. Circulation: 16,000 per issue (paid). **Owner(s):** Arcom Publications, Inc., 13873 Park Center Rd., Ste. 301, Herndon, VA 20171. **Management:** Peter Arundel, Publisher. Peter W Arundel, Vice President. Pam Lymington, Advertising. **Editorial:** John T. Toler, Executive Editor. Bill Walsh, Managing Editor. Peter Brewington, Sports Editor.

WARSAW

NORTHERN NECK NEWS. 132 Court St., Warsaw, VA 22572. Telephone: 804-333-6397. FAX: 804-333-0033. E-MAIL: news@northernnecknews.com. URL: http://www.northernnecknews.com. Mailing Address: PO Box 8, Warsaw, VA 22572. Year Established: 1879. Pub. Frequency: w. (Wed.) Page Size: tabloid. Subscrip. Rate: $.50 newsstand/cover; $23/yr in county; $34/yr out of county. Circulation: 6,500 per issue (paid). **Owner(s):** Northern Neck Newspaper Group LLC, See address and contact information above. **Management:** Steve Weddle, General Manager. Mike Diedrich, Publisher. Janice Bryant, Advertising Manager. **Editorial:** Steve Weddle, Editor.

WASHINGTON

RAPPAHANNOCK NEWS. 249 Main St., Washington, VA 22747. Telephone: 540-675-3349. FAX: 540-675-3088. URL: http://www.timescommunity.com. Mailing Address: PO Box 59, Washington, VA 22747. Pub. Frequency: w. (Thu.) Page Size: broadsheet. Subscrip. Rate: $.50 newsstand/cover; $21/yr mailed in county; $27/yr mailed out of county. Circulation: 3,000 per issue (paid). **Owner(s):** Arcom Publications, Inc., 13873 Park Center Rd., Ste. 301, Herndon, VA 20171. Telephone: 703-478-6666. FAX: 703-435-9754. **Management:** Anita Sherman, General Manager. Peter Arundel, Publisher. Peter W Arundel, Vice President. Stefanie Hilflin, Advertising. Joe Whistler, Circulation Manager. Angie Howard, Classified Adv. Mgr.. **Editorial:** Anita Sherman, Executive Editor.

WEST POINT

TIDEWATER REVIEW. 425 12th St, West Point, VA 23181. Telephone: 804-843-2282. FAX: 804-843-4404. E-MAIL: mail@tidewaterreview.com. Mailing Address: PO Box 271, West Point, VA 23181. Year Established: 1889. Pub. Frequency: w. (Wed.) Page Size: broadsheet. Subscrip. Rate: $.50 newsstand/cover; $23/yr in county; $38/yr out of county. Circulation: 5,000 per issue (paid). **Owner(s):** Tribune Publishing Company, Inc., 435 N. Michigan Ave, Chicago, IL 60601. Telephone: 312-222-3232. **Management:** William C. O'Donovan, Publisher. Shari French, Advertising. Jennifer Hayes, Advertising Manager. **Editorial:** Robin Lawson, Editor. Joe Gedro, Sports Editor.

WOODSTOCK

SHENANDOAH VALLEY-HERALD, THE. ISSN 0746-6846
207 N. Main St., Woodstock, VA 22664. Telephone: 540-459-4078. FAX: 540-459-4077. E-MAIL: svh@shentel.net. Mailing Address: PO Box 507, Woodstock, VA 22664. Year Established: 1806. Pub. Frequency: w. (Wed.) Page Size: broadsheet. Subscrip. Rate: $.50 newsstand/cover; $20/yr in county; $25/yr out of county. Circulation: 6,400 per issue (paid). **Owner(s):** Page-Shenandoah News Corp., 231 S. Liberty St., Harrisonburg, VA 22801. Telephone: 540-574-6200. **Management:** Richard Morin, President. Tracy Rittenour, Classified Adv. Mgr.. **Editorial:** Gary Pinnell, Managing Editor. Jeff Brammer, Sports Editor.

WYTHEVILLE

BLAND COUNTY MESSENGER. 460 W. Main St., Wytheville, VA 24382. Telephone: 276-228-6611. FAX: 276-228-7260. E-MAIL: wnews@naxs.com. URL: http://www.blandcountynews.com. Year Established: 1922. Pub. Frequency: w. (Wed.) Page Size: broadsheet. Subscrip. Rate: $.50 newsstand/cover; $20.50/yr in county; $24.62/yr out of county; $28.60/yr out of state; $18.45/yr in county to senior citizens; $22.62/yr out of county to senior citizens. Circulation: 2,500 per issue (paid). **Owner(s):** Media General, Inc., 333 E. Franklin St., Richmond, VA 23219. Telephone: 804-649-6000. **Management:** Sam Cooper, Publisher. Debbie Maxwell, Operations Manager. Sarah Snead, Advertising Manager. Tim Booth, Circulation Manager. **Editorial:** Stephanie Porter-Nichols, Executive Editor. Jeff Simmons, Managing Editor.

ENTERPRISE BUYERS' CATALOGUE. 460 W. Main St., Wytheville, VA 24382. Telephone: 276-228-6611. FAX: 276-228-7260. Year Established: 1986. Pub. Frequency: w. (Fri.) Page Size: tabloid Circulation: 7,350 per issue (free). **Owner(s):** Media General, Inc., 333 E. Franklin St., Richmond, VA 23219. Telephone: 804-649-6000. **Management:** Sam Cooper, Publisher. Lena Dean, Circulation Director. Sarah Snead, Classified Editor. **Editorial:** Lori Blevins, Editor. Stephanie Porter-Nichols, Executive Editor. Jeff Simmons, News Editor.

WYTHEVILLE ENTERPRISE. 460 W. Main St., Wytheville, VA 24382. Telephone: 276-228-6611. FAX: 276-228-7260. E-MAIL: dshallar@wythenews.com. URL: http://www.wythenews.com. Year Established: 1870. Pub. Frequency: 3/w. (Tue, Thu., Sat.) Page Size: broadsheet. Subscrip. Rate: $.50 newsstand/cover; $39/yr in county; $56/yr out of county; $60.25/yr out of state. Circulation: 8,000 per issue (paid). **Owner(s):** Media General, Inc., 333 E. Franklin St., Richmond, VA 23219. Telephone: 804-649-6000. **Management:** Sam Cooper, Publisher. Linda Crigger, Advertising Director. Lena Dean, Circulation Director. Donna Shallar, Circulation Manager. **Editorial:** Mark Sage, Editor. Stephanie Porter-Nichols, Executive Editor. Jeff Simmons, Managing Editor.

YORKTOWN

YORKTOWN CRIER & POQUOSON POST. 4824 George Washington Hwy., Yorktown, VA 23692. Telephone: 757-898-7225. FAX: 757-890-0119. E-MAIL: crier@yorktowncrier.com. URL: http://www.yorktowncrier.com/. Mailing Address: PO Box 978, Yorktown, VA 23692. Year Established: 1978. Pub. Frequency: w. (Thu.) Page Size: broadsheet. Subscrip. Rate: $.50 newsstand/cover; $20/yr in state; $25/yr out of state. Adv. Rate: col. inch $9.50 Circulation: 5,000 per issue (paid and free). **Owner(s):** Spectrum Publishing, Inc., 4824 George Washington Hwy., P.O. Box 978, Richmond, VA 23219. Telephone: 757-848-7225. FAX: 757-890-0119. **Management:** Wayne Meisner, Publisher. Louise Black, Advertising Manager. Jean Woodworth, Classified Adv. Mgr.. **Editorial:** Beth Meisner, Editor. Lois Chesley, News Editor.

WASHINGTON

ANACORTES

ANACORTES AMERICAN. 901 Sixth St., Anacortes, WA 98221. Telephone: 360-293-3122. FAX: 360-293-5000. E-MAIL: feedback@goanacortes.com. URL: http://www.goanacortes.com. Mailing Address: PO Box 39, Anacortes, WA 98221. Year Established: 1890. Pub. Frequency: w. (Wed.) Page Size: broadsheet. Subscrip. Rate: $.75 newsstand/cover; $32/yr on island; $47/yr out of county. Circulation: 4,800 per issue (paid). **Owner(s):** Skagit Valley Publishing Co., PO Box 578, Mt. Vernon, WA 98273. Telephone: 360-424-3251. **Management:** Jack Darnton, Publisher. Shirley Chikami, Office Manager. Gregg McConnell, Advertising Manager. Larry Bryant, Circulation Manager. **Editorial:** Jack Darnton, Editor. Elaine Walker, Art Editor. Gordon Weeks, News Editor. Kerry Hoover, Sports Editor.

BAINBRIDGE ISLAND

BAINBRIDGE ISLAND REVIEW. ISSN 0745-7391
403 N. Madison Ave., Bainbridge Island, WA 98110. E-MAIL: marketing@soundpublishing.com. URL: http://www.bainbridgereview.com. Mailing Address: PO Box 10817, Bainbridge Island, WA 98110. Year Established: 1923. Pub. Frequency: s-w. (Wed. & Sat.) Page Size: broadsheet. Subscrip. Rate: $.75 newsstand/cover; $38/yr carrier delivery in city; $55/yr mailed in state; $87/yr mailed out of state. Adv. Rate: col. inch $19.60 Circulation: 12,901 per issue (paid and free). **Owner(s):** Sound Publishing, Inc., See address and contact information above. **Management:** Chritiana Allen-Hoch, Publisher. Lori Maxim, Vice President. Stephanie McGuiness, Circulation Manager. **Editorial:** Doug Crist, Editor.

BATTLE GROUND

REFLECTOR, THE. 20 N.W. 20th Ave., Battle Ground, WA 98604-2020. Telephone: 360-687-5151. FAX: 360-687-5162. URL: http://www.thereflector.com. Mailing Address: PO Box 2020, Battle Ground, WA 98604-2020. Year Established: 1909. Pub. Frequency: w. (Wed.) Page Size: broadsheet. Subscrip. Rate: $40/yr mailed in county; $45/yr mailed out of county. Adv. Rate: col. inch $14 Freelance Pay: $2.75/column-inch. Circulation: 26,160 per issue (paid and free). **Owner(s):** Case Publishing Co., Inc., 20 N.W. 20th Ave., Battle Ground, WA 98604. Telephone: 360-687-5151. FAX: 360-687-5162. **Management:** Marvin F. Case, Publisher. Darlene Carr, Advertising Director. Heidi Wetzler, Circulation Manager. **Editorial:** Marvin F. Case, Editor.

BELLINGHAM

CASCADIA WEEKLY. ISSN 1931-3292
PO Box 2833, Bellingham, WA 98227-2833. URL: http://www.cascadiaweekly.com. Pub. Frequency: w. (Wed.) Page Size: tabloid Subscrip. Rate: $70/yr Circulation: 7,500 per issue (free). **Owner(s):** Cascadia Newspaper Co., LLC, See address and contact information above. **Management:** Tim Johnson, Publisher. Marcus McCoy, Advertising Director. **Editorial:** Tim Johnson, Editor. Amy Kepferle, Community Editor. Carey Ross, Music Editor.

BOTHELL

NORTHSHORE CITIZEN. ISSN 0739-9286
18120 Bothell Way, N.E., Ste. A1, Bothell, WA 98011. Telephone: 425-486-1231. FAX: 425-452-3022. E-MAIL: news@northshorecitizen.com. URL: http://www.northshorecitizen.com. Mailing Address: P.O. Box 647, Bothell, WA 98011. Year Established: 1903. Pub. Frequency: w. (Thu.) Page Size: broadsheet. Subscrip. Rate: $.50 newsstand/cover; $2.50/mo.; $30/yr. Circulation: 5,000 per issue (paid). **Owner(s):** Horvitz Newspapers, Inc., 500 180th Ave N E, #1750, Bellevue, WA 98004. Telephone: 425-274-4780. FAX: 425-274-4781. **Management:** Jeffrey Andrews, General Manager. Dennis Law, Publisher. Molly Cimball-Malloy, Advertising. **Editorial:** Barry Rochford, Editor. David Nelson, Photo. Andrew Nystrom, Sports Editor.

BREMERTON

BREMERTON PATRIOT, THE. 520 Burwell St., Bremerton, WA 98110. E-MAIL: marketing@soundpublishing.com. URL: http://www.bremertonpatriot.com. Year Established: 1999. Pub. Frequency: w. (Sat.) Page Size: broadsheet. Subscrip. Rate: $.50 newsstand/cover; $19/yr carrier delivery local; $39/yr mailed in state; $45/yr mailed out of state. Adv. Rate: col. inch $19.05 Circulation: 12,901 per issue (paid and free). **Owner(s):** Sound Publishing, Inc., 7689 N.E. Day Rd., Bainbridge Island, WA 98110. Telephone: 206-842-8305. FAX: 206-780-9562. **Management:** Lori Maxim, Vice President. Myra Campbell, Circulation Manager. **Editorial:** Aaron Manahan, Sports Writer.

BURIEN

FEDERAL WAY NEWS. 14006 1st Ave, Ste. B, Burien, WA 98168. Telephone: 253-838-7622. FAX: 253-838-7443. Year Established: 1954. Pub. Frequency: s-w. (Wed. & Sat.) Page Size: broadsheet. Subscrip. Rate: $.50 newsstand/cover; $26/yr home delivery in area; $42/yr mailed out of area. Freelance Pay: $15/article. Circulation: 42,000 per issue (paid and free). **Owner(s):** Robinson Newspapers, See address and contact information above. **Management:** Jerry Robinson, Publisher. Rose Ehl, Advertising Director. Bob Tornow, Circulation Manager. **Editorial:** Ken Robinson, Editor. Tim Clinton, Sports.

HIGHLINE TIMES/DES MOINES NEWS. 14006 1st Ave, Ste. B, Burien, WA 98168. Telephone: 206-444-4873. FAX: 206-444-4877. E-MAIL: hteditor@robinsonnews.com. URL: http://www.robinsonnews.com. Year Established: 1945. Pub. Frequency: w. (Wed.) Page Size: tabloid. Subscrip. Rate: $.50 newsstand/cover; $26/yr home delivery; $42/yr mailed. Circulation: 16,000 per issue (paid and free). **Owner(s):** Robinson Newspapers, See address and contact information above. **Management:** Jerry Robinson, Publisher. Janet Grella, Advertising Manager. Tim Robinson, Associate Publisher. **Editorial:** Eric Mathison, Editor. Ralph Nichols, Associate Editor. Tim Clinton, Sports.

CAMAS

CAMAS/WASHOUGAL POST RECORD. 425 N.E. Fourth Ave., Camas, WA 98607. Telephone: 360-834-2141. FAX: 360-834-3423. E-MAIL: hkibbee@eaglenewspapers.com. URL: http://www.camaspostrecord.com. Mailing Address: PO Box 1013, Camas, WA 98607. Year Established: 1908. Pub. Frequency: w. (Tue.) Page Size: broadsheet. Subscrip. Rate: $.50 newsstand/cover; $21/yr carrier delivery local; $34/yr mailed in Clark & Skamania cys.; $41/yr mailed out of area. Adv. Rate: col. inch $10 Circulation: 4,600 per issue (paid). **Owner(s):** Eagle Newspapers, Inc., 4901 Indian School Rd, NE, Salem, OR 97309. Telephone: 503-393-1774. **Management:** Michael Gallagher, Publisher. Florence Hutson, Advertising Manager. Shelly Atwell, Circulation Manager. **Editorial:** Heather Kibbee, Editor.

CASHMERE

CASHMERE VALLEY RECORD. 201 Cottage Ave, Cashmere, WA 98815. Telephone: 509-782-3781. FAX: 509-782-9074. E-MAIL: echo@leavenworthecho.com. URL: http://www.leavenworthecho.com. Mailing Address: PO Box N, Cashmere, WA 98815. Pub. Frequency: w. (Wed.) Page Size: broadsheet. Subscrip. Rate: $.75 newsstand/cover; $27/yr mailed in county; $28/yr mailed out of county; $31/yr mailed out of state. Circulation: 1,800 per issue (paid). **Owner(s):** Prairie Media, Inc., 215 14th St., Leavenworth, WA 98826. Telephone: 509-548-5286. **Management:** Bill Forhan, Publisher. Carol Forhan, Advertising. **Editorial:** Bill Forhan, Editor.

CATHLAMET

WAHKIAKUM COUNTY EAGLE, THE. 77 Main St., Cathlamet, WA 98612-0368. Telephone: 360-795-3391. FAX: 360-795-3983. Mailing Address: PO Box 368, Cathlamet, WA 98612. Year Established: 1891. Pub. Frequency: w. (Thu.) Page Size: broadsheet. Subscrip. Rate: $.60 newsstand/cover. Adv. Rate: col. inch $2.20 Circulation: 1,611 per issue (paid). **Owner(s):** Eric R. Nelson, See address and contact information above. **Management:** Eric R. Nelson, Publisher. **Editorial:** Eric R. Nelson, Editor-in-Chief.

CHELAN

LAKE CHELAN MIRROR. 315 Woodin Ave, Chelan, WA 98816. Telephone: 509-682-2213. FAX: 509-682-4209. E-MAIL: mirror@lakechelanmirror.com. URL: http://www.lakechelanmirror.com. Mailing Address: PO Box 249, Chelan, WA 98816. Year Established: 2002. Pub. Frequency: w. (Wed.) Page Size: broadsheet. Subscrip. Rate: $.75 newsstand/cover; $29/yr in Chelan & Douglas cys.; $33/yr in state; $43/yr out of state. Circulation: 5,000 per issue (paid). **Owner(s):** Prairie Media, Inc., 215 14th St., Leavenworth, WA 98826. Telephone: 548-548-5286. **Management:** David Forhan, General Manager. Bill Forhan, Publisher. Carol Forhan, Advertising. **Editorial:** Ralph Schwartz, Editor.

CHENEY

CHENEY FREE PRESS. 1616 W. First St., Cheney, WA 99004. Telephone: 509-235-6184. FAX: 509-235-2887. E-MAIL: cfp@cheneyfreepress.com. URL: http://www.cheneyfreepress.com. Mailing Address: P.O. Box 218, Cheney, WA 99004. Year Established: 1896. Pub. Frequency: w. (Thu.) Page Size: broadsheet. Subscrip. Rate: $.75 newsstand/cover; $24/yr in county; $36/yr mailed out of county. Circulation: 11,900 per issue (paid). **Owner(s):** Free Press Publishing, See address and contact information above. **Management:** Bill Ifft, President. Harlan Shellabarger, Publisher. Rubi Geary, Circulation Manager. **Editorial:** John McCallum, Editor.

Weeklies

COLFAX

WHITMAN COUNTY GAZETTE. PO Box 770, Colfax, WA 99111. Telephone: 509-397-4333. E-MAIL: gazette@colfax.com. Year Established: 1877. Pub. Frequency: w. (Thu.) Page Size: broadsheet. Subscrip. Rate: $.50 newsstand/cover; $21/yr mailed in county; $30/yr mailed out of county. Circulation: 4,450 per issue (paid). **Owner(s):** Gazette Publishing LLC, See address and contact information above. **Management:** Gordon Forgey, Publisher. Chris Olsrud, Advertising Manager. Gordon Forgey, Circulation Manager. **Editorial:** Jerry Jones, Editor.

COLVILLE

STATESMAN-EXAMINER, THE. 220 S Main St, Colville, WA 99114. Telephone: 509-684-4567. FAX: 509-684-3849. E-MAIL: publisher@statesmanexaminer.com. URL: http://www.statesmanexaminer.com. Mailing Address: PO Box 271, Colville, WA 99114. Year Established: 1948. Pub. Frequency: w. (Wed.) Page Size: broadsheet. Subscrip. Rate: $.75 newsstand/cover; $29/yr in county & adj. cys.; $37/yr out of county. Adv. Rate: col. inch $11.50 Circulation: 23,757 per issue (paid and free). **Owner(s):** Horizon Publications, Inc., 1120 N. Carbon St, Ste 100, Marion, IL 62959. **Management:** Chris Cowbrough, Publisher. Nadia Willey, Advertising. Teresa Skeen, Circulation Manager. **Editorial:** Chris Cowbrough, Editor.

CONNELL

FRANKLIN COUNTY GRAPHIC. 346 S. Columbia, Connell, WA 99326-0160. Telephone: 509-234-3181. FAX: 509-234-3182. Mailing Address: PO Box 160, Connell, WA 99326-0160. Pub. Frequency: w. (Thu.) Page Size: broadsheet. Subscrip. Rate: $.40 newsstand/cover; $25/yr in county; $30/yr out of county. Circulation: 3,000 per issue (paid and free). **Owner(s):** Kathy Valdez, 346 S. Columbia, Connell, WA 99326. Telephone: 509-234-3181. FAX: 509-234-3182. **Management:** Kathy Valdez, Publisher. **Editorial:** Kathy Valdez, News Editor.

DAYTON

DAYTON CHRONICLE. 358 E. Main St., Dayton, WA 99328. Telephone: 509-382-2221. E-MAIL: daychron@bmi.net. Year Established: 1878. Pub. Frequency: w. (Wed.) Page Size: standard. Subscrip. Rate: $.50 newsstand/cover; $23/yr mailed in county; $29/yr mailed in state; $33/yr mailed out of state. Adv. Rate: col. inch $5.88 Circulation: 1,700 per issue (controlled and free). **Owner(s):** Jack Williams, See address and contact information above. **Management:** Jack Williams, Publisher. **Editorial:** Jack Williams, Editor.

DEER PARK

DEER PARK TRIBUNE. 104 N. Main St., Deer Park, WA 99006-5086. Telephone: 509-276-5043. FAX: 509-276-2041. E-MAIL: cathie@dptribune.biz. URL: http://www.dptribune.biz. Year Established: 1906. Pub. Frequency: w. (Wed.) Page Size: broadsheet. Subscrip. Rate: $.50 newsstand/cover; $23/yr local; $33/yr out of area. Adv. Rate: col. inch $8 Freelance Pay: $1/column-inch. Circulation: 12,000 per issue (paid). **Owner(s):** Horizon Publications, Inc., 1120 N. Carbon St., Ste.100, Marion, IL 62959. FAX: 618-997-4018. **Management:** Cathie Babbick, Publisher. **Editorial:** Tom Costigan, Editor.

EASTSOUND

ISLANDS' SOUNDER, THE. 41 N. Beach Rd., Eastsound, WA 98245. E-MAIL: marketing@soundpublishing.com. URL: http://www.islandssounder.com. Mailing Address: PO Box 758, Eastsound, WA 98245. Year Established: 1953. Pub. Frequency: w. (Wed.) Page Size: broadsheet. Subscrip. Rate: $.75 newsstand/cover; $26/yr home delivery in county; $50/yr mailed out of county. Adv. Rate: col. inch $12.05 Circulation: 2,881 per issue (paid). **Owner(s):** Sound Publishing, Inc., See address and contact information above. **Management:** Elyse Van Den Bosch, Publisher. Lori Maxim, Vice President. Ellen Schones, Circulation Manager. **Editorial:** Ted Grossman, Editor.

ENUMCLAW

ENUMCLAW COURIER-HERALD. 1627 Cole St., Enumclaw, WA 98022. Telephone: 360-825-2555. FAX: 360-825-1092. E-MAIL: bmarcum@courierherald.com. URL: http://www.courierherald.com. Mailing Address: PO Box 157, Enumclaw, WA 98022. Year Established: 1901. Pub. Frequency: w. (Wed.) Page Size: broadsheet. Subscrip. Rate: $.75 newsstand/cover; $32/yr mailed in King & Pierce cys.; $37/yr mailed elsewhere. Freelance Pay: $25/article. Circulation: 6,500 per issue (paid). **Owner(s):** Enumclaw Courier-Herald LLC, See address and contact information above. **Management:** William Marcum, Publisher. Martha Boston, Advertising Manager. Linda Bondhus, Circulation Manager. Jessica Hughes, Classified Adv. Mgr.. **Editorial:** Kevin Hanson, Editor. Brenda Sexton, Reporter.

EPHRATA

GRANT COUNTY JOURNAL. 29 Alder SW, Ephrata, WA 98823. E-MAIL: moser@gcjournal.net. Year Established: 1907. Pub. Frequency: s-w. (Mon. & Thu.) Page Size: broadsheet. Subscrip. Rate: $.75 newsstand/cover; $40/yr carrier delivery in county or mailed; $50/yr mailed out of county; $65/yr mailed out of state. Adv. Rate: col. inch $8.15 **Wire Service(s):** AP. Circulation: 3,100 per issue (controlled and free). **Owner(s):** Jeffrey G. Fletcher, PO Box 998, Ephrata, WA 98823. Telephone: 509-754-4636. FAX: 509-754-0996. **Management:** Jeffrey G. Fletcher, Publisher. Bob Richardson, Advertising Manager. **Editorial:** Randy Bracht, Managing Editor. Kerry C Moser, Production Manager. Kim Jorgensen, Community Editor. Joe Dennis, Editorial Page Editor. Steven Smith, Sports Editor.

FEDERAL WAY

FEDERAL WAY MIRROR. 1414 S. 324th St., Ste. B-210, Federal Way, WA 98003. E-MAIL: marketing@soundpublishing.com. URL: http://www.fedwaymirror.com. Year Established: 1998. Pub. Frequency: s-w. (Wed. & Sat.) Page Size: broadsheet. Subscrip. Rate: $.50 newsstand/cover; $29/yr home delivery; $64/yr mailed in state; $89/yr mailed out of state. Adv. Rate: col. inch $23.55 Circulation: 30,237 per issue (paid). **Owner(s):** Sound Publishing, Inc., See address and contact information above. **Management:** Debbie Kaufman, Publisher. Lori Maxim, Vice President. Konnie McConnell, Circulation Manager. **Editorial:** Pat Jenkins, Editor.

FERNDALE

RECORD - JOURNAL (FERNDALE). 2008 Main St., Ferndale, WA 98248-0038. Telephone: 360-384-1411. FAX: 360-384-1417. E-MAIL: recjourn@nas.com. Year Established: 1885. Pub. Frequency: w. (Wed.) Page Size: broadsheet. Subscrip. Rate: $.75 newsstand/cover; $27/yr in county. Adv. Rate: col. inch $14.65 Freelance Pay: $0.45/column-inch. Circulation: 6,850 per issue (paid and free). **Owner(s):** Ferndale Record, Inc., PO Box 38, Ferndale, WA 98248. **Management:** Michael D Lewis, Publisher. Kim Winjum, Advertising Director. Roni Hall, Circulation Manager. **Editorial:** Hollie Brown, Editor.

FRIDAY HARBOR

JOURNAL OF THE SAN JUAN ISLANDS. ISSN 0734-3809 640 Mullis St., Friday Harbor, WA 98250-0519. Telephone: 360-378-5696. E-MAIL: rwalker@sanjanjournal.com. URL: http://www.sanjuanjournal.com. Mailing Address: PO Box 519, Friday Harbor, WA 98250-0519. Year Established: 1906. Pub. Frequency: w. (Wed.) Page Size: tabloid. Subscrip. Rate: $.75 newsstand/cover; $35/yr carrier delivery on island; $55/yr mailed in county; $125/yr mailed out of county. Adv. Rate: col. inch $12.05 Circulation: 3,946 per issue (paid). **Owner(s):** Sound Publishing, Inc., See address and contact information above. **Management:** Elyse Van den Bosch, Publisher. Lori Maxim, Vice President. Ron Bates, Advertising. **Editorial:** Richard Walker, Editor.

GIG HARBOR

PENINSULA GATEWAY. ISSN 1066-2065 3555 Erickson St., Gig Harbor, WA 98335. Telephone: 253-851-9921. FAX: 253-851-3939. E-MAIL: richallock@gateline.com. URL: http://www.gateline.com. Mailing Address: PO Box 407, Gig Harbor, WA 98335. Year Established: 1917. Pub. Frequency: w. (Wed.) Page Size: broadsheet. Subscrip. Rate: $.50 newsstand/cover; $25/yr mailed in Pierce & Kitsap cys.; $49/yr out of area; $60/yr out of state. Adv. Rate: col. inch $17 Circulation: 28,000 per issue (paid and free). **Owner(s):** The/McClatchy Company, 2100 Q St., Sacramento, CA 95816-6816. Telephone: 916-321-1936. **Management:** George LeMasurier, Publisher. Mike Leonard, Advertising Manager. **Editorial:** Brian McLean, News Editor. Jacob Adams, Sports.

GOLDENDALE

GOLDENDALE SENTINEL. 117 W. Main St., Goldendale, WA 98620-9526. Telephone: 509-773-3777. FAX: 509-773-4737. E-MAIL: sentinel@gorge.net. URL: http://www.goldendale.com. Year Established: 1879. Pub. Frequency: w. (Thu.) Page Size: standard. Subscrip. Rate: $.75 newsstand/cover; $32/yr mailed in county; $42/yr mailed out of county. Circulation: 3,200 per issue (paid). **Owner(s):** Andrew J. McNab, 117 W. Main St., Goldendale, WA 98620. Telephone: 509-773-3777. **Management:** Andrew J. McNab, President. Eva France, Circulation Manager. **Editorial:** Russ Miller, Editor.

GRANDVIEW

GRANDVIEW HERALD. 107 Division St., Grandview, WA 98930. Telephone: 509-882-3712. FAX: 509-882-2833. E-MAIL: gherald@bentonrea.com. URL: http://www.grandviewherald.com. Year Established: 1922. Pub. Frequency: w. (Wed.) Page Size: standard. Subscrip. Rate: $.50 newsstand/cover; $37/yr local; $45/yr out of area. Circulation: 2,550 per issue (paid). **Owner(s):** Fournier Media Services, See address and contact information above. **Management:** John L. Fournier Jr., Publisher. Judy Marie, Advertising Manager. **Editorial:** Debra Richards, Editor.

ISSAQUAH

ISSAQUAH PRESS, THE. 45 Front St., S., Issaquah, WA 98027-1328. Telephone: 425-392-6434. FAX: 425-391-1541. E-MAIL: isspress@isspress.com. URL: http://www.issaquahpress.com. Mailing Address: PO Box 1328, Issaquah, WA 98027-1328. Year Established: 1900. Pub. Frequency: w. (Wed.) Page Size: broadsheet. Subscrip. Rate: $.75 newsstand/cover; $26/yr mailed in county; $38/yr mailed in state; $41/yr mailed out of state. Adv. Rate: col. inch $21 Freelance Pay: $60-$100/article. Circulation: 15,000 per issue (paid). **Owner(s):** Seattle Times Co., PO Box 70, Seattle, WA 98111. Telephone: 206-464-2111. **Management:** Carolyn Kelly, President. Deborah L. Berto, Publisher. Jill Green, Advertising Manager. **Editorial:** Kathleen Merrill, Editor. Bob Taylor, Sports.Readers: Residents of Issaquah

LANGLEY

SOUTH WHIDBEY RECORD. 5603 Bayview Rd., Langley, WA 98620. E-MAIL: marketing@soundpublishing.com. URL: http://www.southwhidbeyrecord.com. Mailing Address: PO Box 387, Langley, WA 98260. Year Established: 1913. Pub. Frequency: s-w. (Wed. & Sat.) Page Size: broadsheet. Subscrip. Rate: $.50 newsstand/cover; $38/yr carrier delivery in county; $48/yr mailed in state; $66/yr mailed out of state. Adv. Rate: col. inch $14.10 Circulation: 5,346 per issue (paid). **Owner(s):** Sound Publishing, Inc., 7689 N.E. Day Rd., Bainbridge Island, WA 98110. Telephone: 206-842-8305. FAX: 206-780-9562. **Management:** Melissa Richardson, Publisher. Lori Maxim, Vice President. Elayne Watts, Circulation Manager. Lorinda Kay, Sales Manager.

LEAVENWORTH

LEAVENWORTH ECHO. 215 14th St., Leavenworth, WA 98826. Telephone: 509-548-5286. FAX: 509-548-4789. E-MAIL: echo@leavenworthecho.com. URL: http://www.leavenworthecho.com. Mailing Address: PO Box 39, Leavenworth, WA 98826. Year Established: 1906. Pub. Frequency: w. (Wed.) Page Size: broadsheet. Subscrip. Rate: $.75 newsstand/cover; $27/yr mailed in county; $28/yr mailed out of county; $31/yr mailed out of state. Circulation: 2,400 per issue (paid). **Owner(s):** Prairie Media, Inc., See address and contact information above. **Management:** Bill Forhan, Publisher. Carol Forhan, Advertising. **Editorial:** Bill Forhan, Editor.

LONG BEACH

CHINOOK OBSERVER. ISSN 0739-9200 205 Bolstad Ave., E., Ste. 2, Long Beach, WA 98631. Telephone: 360-642-8181. FAX: 360-642-8105. E-MAIL: chinook@aone.com. URL: http://www.chinookobserver.com. Mailing Address: PO Box 427, Long Beach, WA 98631. Year Established: 1900. Pub. Frequency: w. (Wed.) Page Size: broadsheet. Subscrip. Rate: $.75 newsstand/cover; $30/yr mailed in county; $40/yr mailed out of county. Circulation: 7,200 per issue (paid). **Owner(s):** East Oregonian Publishing Co., P.O. Box 1089, Pendleton, OR 97801. Telephone: 541-966-0800. **Management:** Matt Winters, Publisher. Sheryl Schisler, Advertising Manager. **Editorial:** Matt Winters, Editor.

LOPEZ ISLAND

ISLANDS' WEEKLY. 131 Weeks Rd., Lopez Island, WA 982661. E-MAIL: marketing@soundpublishing.com. URL: http://www.islandsweekly.net. Year Established: 1953. Pub. Frequency: w. (Tue.) Page Size: broadsheet.Adv. Rate: col. inch $12.05 Circulation: 8,191 per issue (free). **Owner(s):** Sound Publishing, Inc., See address and contact information above. **Management:** Elyse Van Den Bosch, Publisher. Lori Maxim, Vice President. **Editorial:** Ted Grossman, Editor.

LYNDEN

LYNDEN TRIBUNE. 113 Sixth St, Box 153, Lynden, WA 98264. E-MAIL: editor@lyndentribune.com. URL: http://www.lyndentribune.com. Mailing Address: PO Box 153, Lynden, WA 98264-0153. Year Established: 1888. Pub. Frequency: w. (Wed.) Page Size: broadsheet. Subscrip. Rate: $.75 newsstand/cover; $32/yr in county; $42/yr mailed out of county; $47/yr mailed out of state. Adv. Rate: col. inch $20.50 Circulation: 13,500 per issue (paid and free). Owner(s): Lewis Publishing Co., See address and contact information above. **Management:** Michael D. Lewis, Publisher. Mary Jo Lewis, Advertising Manager. Karina DeLange, Circulation Manager. **Editorial:** Calvin Bratt, Editor. Timothy Newcomb, Assistant Editor. Mark Reimer, Reporter. Caleb Breakey, Sports Editor.

LYNNWOOD

EDMONDS ENTERPRISE. 4303 198th St., S.W., Lynnwood, WA 98036. Telephone: 425-673-6500. FAX: 425-774-8622. E-MAIL: edmonds@heraldnet.com. URL: http://www.enterprisenewspapers.com. Mailing Address: PO Box 977, Lynnwood, WA 98046. Year Established: 1958. Pub. Frequency: w. (Wed.) Page Size: tabloid.Subscrip. Rate: $30/yr mailed out of county Circulation: 16,000 per issue (free). Owner(s): Washington Post Co., 1150 15th St, N W, Washington, DC 20071. Telephone: 202-334-7100. **Management:** John Souza, Advertising Director. Monica Moyer, Circulation Director. **Editorial:** Chris Fyall, Editor. Sarah Koenig, Education Editor. Andrea Miller, Feature Editor. David Pan, Sports Editor.

LYNNWOOD/MOUNTLAKE TERRACE ENTERPRISE. 4303 198th St., S.W., Lynnwood, WA 98036. Telephone: 425-673-6500. FAX: 425-774-8622. E-MAIL: lynnwood@heraldnet.com. URL: http://www.enterprisenewspapers.com. Mailing Address: PO Box 977, Lynnwood, WA 98046. Year Established: 1958. Pub. Frequency: w. (Wed.) Page Size: tabloid.Subscrip. Rate: $30/yr mailed Circulation: 24,000 per issue (free). Owner(s): Washington Post Co., 1150 15th St, N W, Washington, DC 20071. Telephone: 202-334-7100. **Management:** John Souza, Advertising Director. Monica Moyer, Circulation Director. **Editorial:** Oscar Halpert, Editor. Sarah Koenig, Education Editor. Andrea Miller, Feature Editor. David Pan, Sports.

MILL CREEK ENTERPRISE. 4303 198th St., S.W., Lynnwood, WA 98036. Telephone: 425-673-6500. FAX: 425-774-8622. E-MAIL: millcreek@heraldnet.com. URL: http://www.entprisenewspapers.com. Pub. Frequency: w. (Wed.) Page Size: tabloid.Subscrip. Rate: $30/yr mailed Circulation: 10,000 per issue (free). Owner(s): Washington Post Co., 1150 15th St, N W, Washington, DC 20071. Telephone: 202-334-7100. **Management:** John Souza, Advertising Director. Monica Moyer, Circulation Director. **Editorial:** Alexis Bacharach, Editor. Sarah Koenig, Education Editor. Andrea Miller, Feature Editor. Chris Goodenow, Photographer. David Pan, Sports.

MAPLE VALLEY

VOICE OF THE VALLEY. PO Box 307, Maple Valley, WA 98038-0307. Telephone: 425-432-9696. FAX: 425-432-0701. E-MAIL: voicd9696@comcast.net. Year Established: 1968. Pub. Frequency: w. (Tue.) Page Size: tabloid. Subscrip. Rate: $40/yr. Circulation: 16,600 per issue (paid and free). Owner(s): S. Hipple, See address and contact information above. **Management:** Saundra Hipple, Publisher. Sherry Johnson, Advertising. Donna Hayes, Associate Publisher. **Editorial:** Saundra Hipple, Editor.

MARYSVILLE

MARYSVILLE GLOBE, THE. PO Box 145, Marysville, WA 98270. Telephone: 360-659-1300. FAX: 360-658-0350. E-MAIL: mglobe@premier1.net. Year Established: 1891. Pub. Frequency: w. (Wed.) Page Size: broadsheet. Subscrip. Rate: $.75 newsstand/cover; $34/yr in county; $72/yr mailed out of county. Circulation: 7,500 per issue (paid and free). Owner(s): Sun News, Inc., See address and contact information above. **Management:** Kris Passey, Publisher. Sue Stevensen, Advertising Manager. **Editorial:** Scott Frank, Managing Editor. Sara Arney, Feature Editor.

MORTON

EAST COUNTY JOURNAL, THE. 278 W. Main Ave., Morton, WA 98356. Telephone: 360-496-5993. FAX: 360-496-5110. E-MAIL: jdevaul@myhome.net. URL: http://www.devaulpublishing.com. Mailing Address: PO Box M, Morton, WA 98356. Year Established: 1942. Pub. Frequency: w. (Wed.) Page Size: broadsheet. Subscrip. Rate: $.50 newsstand/cover; $19/yr mailed in county to alumni; $26/yr mailed out of county; $34/yr mailed out of state. Adv. Rate: col. inch $13.10 Circulation: 7,000 per issue (paid). Owner(s): DeVaul Publishing, Inc., 459 N.E. Washington Ave., Chehalis, WA 98532. Telephone: 360-748-6848. FAX: 360-748-6841. **Management:** Frank DeVaul, Publisher. Judy DeVaul, Advertising Manager. **Editorial:** Dan Fisher, Managing Editor.

NEWPORT

GEM STATE MINER. 421 S. Spokane, Newport, WA 99156. Telephone: 509-447-2433. FAX: 509-447-9222. E-MAIL: theminer@povn.com. URL: http://www.pendoreillerivervalley.com. Mailing Address: PO Box 349, Newport, WA 99156. Year Established: 1901. Pub. Frequency: w. (Wed.) Page Size: broadsheet. Subscrip. Rate: $.75 newsstand/cover; $21.50/yr in county; $30.50/yr out of county. Circulation: 3,000 per issue (paid). Owner(s): Willenbrock Publications, Inc., See address and contact information above. **Management:** Fred J. Willenbrock II, Publisher. J. Lindsay Guscott, Advertising. Susan Willenbrock, Business Manager. **Editorial:** Michelle Nedved, News Editor. William Love, Sports Editor.

NEWPORT MINER. 421 S. Spokane, Newport, WA 99156. Telephone: 509-447-2433. FAX: 509-447-9222. E-MAIL: theminer@povn.com. URL: http://www.pendoreillerivervalley.com. Mailing Address: PO Box 349, Newport, WA 99156. Year Established: 1901. Pub. Frequency: w. (Wed.) Page Size: broadsheet. Subscrip. Rate: $.75 newsstand/cover; $21.50/yr mailed in county; $30.50/yr mailed out of county. Circulation: 3,200 per issue (paid). Owner(s): Willenbrock Publications, Inc., See address and contact information above. **Management:** Fred J. Willenbrock II, Publisher. J. Lindsay Guscott, Advertising Manager. Susan Willenbrock, Business Manager. **Editorial:** Fred J. Willenbrock II, Editor. William Love, Sports Editor.

OAK HARBOR

NORTHWEST NAVIGATOR-WHIDBEY. 800 S.E. Barrington, Oak Harbor, WA 98277. Telephone: 360-675-6611. FAX: 360-679-2695. E-MAIL: marketing@soundpublishing.com. URL: http://www.nsawi.navy.mil/crosswin. Mailing Address: PO Box 10, Oak Harbor, WA 98277. Year Established: 1958. Pub. Frequency: w. (Fri.) Page Size: broadsheet.Adv. Rate: col. inch $16.75 Circulation: 8,607 per issue (free). Owner(s): Sound Publishing, Inc., 7689 N.E. Day Rd., Bainbridge Island, WA 98110. Telephone: 206-842-8302. FAX: 206-780-9562. **Management:** Lisa Hutchings, Publisher. Lori Maxim, Vice President. **Editorial:** Fred Watson, Editor.

WHIDBEY NEWS-TIMES. 800 S.E. Barrington, Oak Harbor, WA 98277. Telephone: 360-675-6611. FAX: 360-679-2695. E-MAIL: marketing@soundpublishing.com. URL: http://www.whidbeynewstimes.com. Mailing Address: PO Box 10, Oak Harbor, WA 98277. Year Established: 1898. Pub. Frequency: s-w. (Wed. & Sat.) Page Size: broadsheet. Subscrip. Rate: $.50 newsstand/cover; $38/yr carrier delivery local; $38/yr mailed in state. Adv. Rate: col. inch $16.75 Circulation: 7,900 per issue (paid). Owner(s): Sound Publishing, Inc., 7689 N.E. Day Rd., Bainbridge Island, WA 98110. Telephone: 206-842-8305. FAX: 206-842-8030. **Management:** Marcia Van Dyke, Publisher. Lori Maxim, Vice President. Marcia Van Dyke, Advertising Manager. **Editorial:** Jim Larsen, Editor.

OMAK

CHRONICLE (OMAK), THE. 618 Okoma Dr, Omak, WA 98841. Telephone: 509-826-1110. FAX: 509-826-5819. E-MAIL: chronicle@omakchronicle.com. URL: http://www.omakchronicle.com. Mailing Address: PO Box 553, Omak, WA 98841. Year Established: 1910. Pub. Frequency: w. (Wed.) Subscrip. Rate: $.75 newsstand/cover per issue; $28/yr home delivery in county; $40/yr in state; $55/yr out of state. Adv. Rate: col. inch $11.25 Circulation: 7,000 per issue (paid). Owner(s): Eagle Newspapers, Inc., 4901 Indian School Rd, NE, Salem, OR 97309. **Management:** Alex Paul, Publisher. Kris Vigoren, Circulation Manager. **Editorial:** Dee Camp, Managing Editor.

ORTING

GAZETTE (ORTING), THE. 208 Corrin Ave SW, PO Box 1231, Orting, WA 98360. Telephone: 360-893-5103. FAX: 360-893-6501. E-MAIL: gazettenews@comcast.net. URL: www.countrygazette.com. Year Established: 1991. Pub. Frequency: w. (Wed.) Page Size: standard. Subscrip. Rate: $15/yr in county; $30/yr out of county. Adv. Rate: B&W page $400; 16.25 x 10 Circulation: 7,100 (paid and free). Owner(s): Lafromboise Newspapers, Inc., 321 N. Pearl St., Centralia, WA 98531. Telephone: 360-736-3311. FAX: 360-736-4796. **Editorial:** Chris Thomas, Editor.

OTHELLO

OTHELLO OUTLOOK, THE.   ISSN 1056-8328
125 S. First St., Othello, WA 99344. Telephone: 509-488-3342. FAX: 509-488-3345. URL: http://www.othellooutlook.com. Mailing Address: PO Box O, Othello, WA 99344. Year Established: 1947. Pub. Frequency: w. (Thu.) Page Size: standard. Subscrip. Rate: $.75 newsstand/cover; $25/yr in county; $35/yr out of county. Circulation: 2,000 per issue (paid). Owner(s): Zaser-Longston, 1802-136th Pl., N.E., Seattle, WA 98005. Telephone: 206-562-7997. FAX: 206-562-4785. **Management:** Eric LaFontaine, Publisher. Joe Rosales, Advertising Manager. **Editorial:** Bob Kirkpatrick, Editor.

PORT ORCHARD

PORT ORCHARD INDEPENDENT. 2950 SE Mill Hill Dr., Port Orchard, WA 98366. E-MAIL: marketing@soundpublishing.com. URL: http://www.portorchardindependent.com. Mailing Address: PO Box 27, Port Orchard, WA 98366. Year Established: 1890. Pub. Frequency: w. (Wed. & Sat.) Page Size: broadsheet. Subscrip. Rate: $.50 newsstand/cover; $30/yr carrier delivery; $60/yr mailed in state; $90/yr mailed out of state. Adv. Rate: col. inch $19.05 Circulation: 18,369 per issue (paid and free). Owner(s): Sound Publishing, Inc., 7689 N.E. Day Rd., Bainbridge Island, WA 98110. Telephone: 206-842-8305. FAX: 206-842-8030. **Management:** Rich Peterson, Publisher. Lori Maxim, Vice President. **Editorial:** Jeff Rhodes, Editor.

PORT TOWNSEND

PORT TOWNSEND & JEFFERSON COUNTY LEADER.   ISSN 1050-1460
226 Adams St., Port Townsend, WA 98368. Telephone: 360-385-2900. E-MAIL: newss@ptleader.com. URL: http://www.ptleader.com. Year Established: 1889. Pub. Frequency: w. (Wed.) Page Size: broadsheet. Subscrip. Rate: $.75 newsstand/cover; $32/yr mailed in county; $50/yr mailed out of county. Adv. Rate: col. inch $13.50 Circulation: 9,300 per issue (paid). Owner(s): Port Townsend Publishing Co., Inc., See address and contact information above. **Management:** Scott Wilson, Publisher. Patti Walden, Advertising Manager. Virginia Smith, Circulation Manager. **Editorial:** Scott Wilson, Editorial Page Editor. Patrick J. Sullivan, News Editor.

POULSBO

KIRKLAND REPOTER. 19351 8th Ave. NE, Ste. 106, Poulsbo, WA 98370. Telephone: 360-394-5800. URL: http://www.KirklandReporter.com. Year Established: 1978. Pub. Frequency: w. (Wed.) Page Size: tabloid.Adv. Rate: col. inch $24.85 Circulation: 26,400 per issue (paid). Owner(s): Sound Publishing, Inc., See address and contact information above. Pacific Publishing Co., 720 Market St, Kirkland, WA 98033. **Management:** Mike Walter, Publisher.

NORTH KITSAP HERALD. 18887 Hwy. 305 Ste. 700, Poulsbo, WA 98370. E-MAIL: marketing@soundpublications.com. URL: http://www.northkitsapherald.com. Year Established: 1901. Pub. Frequency: s-w. (Wed. & Sat.) Page Size: broadsheet. Subscrip. Rate: $.50 newsstand/cover; $30/yr carrier delivery in county; $58/yr mailed in state; $89/yr mailed out of state. Adv. Rate: col. inch $19.05 Circulation: 12,808 per issue (paid and free). Owner(s): Sound Publishing, Inc., 7689 N.E. Day Rd., Bainbridge Island, WA 98110. Telephone: 206-842-8305. FAX: 206-842-8030. **Management:** Lori Maxim, Publisher.

PUYALLUP

HERALD (PUYALLUP), THE.   ISSN 1526-5846
822 E Main Ave, Puyallup, WA 98372. Telephone: 253-841-2481. FAX: 253-840-8249. E-MAIL: editor@puyallupherald.com. URL: http://www.puyallup-herald.com. Mailing Address: PO Box 517, Puyallup, WA 98372. Pub. Frequency: w. (Thu.) Page Size: standard. Subscrip. Rate: $.50 newsstand/cover; $23/yr in Pierce & King cys; $45/yr in state. Circulation: 22,000 per issue (paid). Owner(s): The/McClatchy Company, 2100 Q St, Sacramento, CA 95816. **Management:** George LeMasurier, Publisher. Bob Danielle, Advertising Manager. Mary Morgan, Circulation Manager. **Editorial:** Heather Meier, Editor.

RAYMOND

WILLAPA HARBOR HERALD.   ISSN 1065-3805
209-1/2 Duryea, Raymond, WA 98577. Telephone: 360-942-3466. FAX: 360-942-3487. E-MAIL: whhgm@aol.com. Mailing Address: PO Box 706, Raymond, WA 98577. Year Established: 1906. Pub. Frequency: w. (Wed.) Page Size: broadsheet. Subscrip. Rate: $.75 newsstand/cover; $22/yr mailed in county; $35/yr mailed out of county. Circulation: 7,000 per issue (paid and free). Owner(s): Flannery Publications, See address and contact information above. **Management:** Pat Myers, Publisher. Gina Lanaville, Advertising. **Editorial:** George Kunke, Editor.

ROYAL CITY

SOUTH COUNTY SUN, THE.   ISSN 1547-2310
138 Camelin St, Ste B, Royal City, WA 99357. Telephone: 509-346-9723. FAX: 509-346-1469. E-MAIL: info@southcountysun.com. URL: http://www.southcountysun.com. Mailing Address: PO Box 267, Royal City, WA 99357-0219. Year Established: 1985. Pub. Frequency: w. (Wed.) Subscrip. Rate: $.75 newsstand/cover; $35/yr. Circulation: 1,000 per issue (controlled and free). Owner(s): Genuine Media, 41 S 6th Ave, Othello, WA 99349. Telephone: 509-346-9723. FAX: 509-346-1469. **Management:** Phillip Leitz, Publisher. **Editorial:** Lisa Leitz, Editor.

Weeklies

SEATTLE

BALLARD NEWS TRIBUNE. 2208 N.W. Market St., Ste. 202, Seattle, WA 98107. Telephone: 206-783-1244. FAX: 206-789-2455. E-MAIL: bnteditor@robinsonnews.com. URL: http://www.robinsonnews.com. Pub. Frequency: w. (Wed.) Page Size: standard. Subscrip. Rate: $.50 newsstand/cover; $26/yr home delivery; $42/yr mailed. Circulation: 8,500 per issue (paid). **Owner(s):** Robinson Newspapers, 14006 1st Ave, Ste. B, Burien, WA 98168. Telephone: 206-444-4873. **Management:** Tim Robinson, General Manager. Jerry Robinson, Publisher. Jamie McCormick, Advertising Manager. Margaret Seefeld, Classified Adv. Mgr.. **Editorial:** Adam Richter, Editor.

BEACON HILL NEWS, THE. 4000 Aurora Ave., N Ste 100, Seattle, WA 98101. Telephone: 206-461-1300. E-MAIL: mdillon@nwlink.com. URL: http://www.pacificpublishingcompany.com. Year Established: 1924. Pub. Frequency: w. (Wed.) Page Size: tabloid. Subscrip. Rate: $.50 newsstand/cover; $30/yr mailed. Adv. Rate: col. inch $25 Circulation: 9,000 per issue (controlled and free). **Owner(s):** Pacific Publishing Co., See address and contact information above. **Management:** Mike Dillon, Publisher. LaNece Green, Advertising Manager. Jim Christenson, Circulation Manager. Barbara Blair, Classified Adv. Mgr.. **Editorial:** Richard Jameson, Editor.

CAPITOL HILL TIMES. 4000 Aurora Ave., N Ste 100, Seattle, WA 98101. Telephone: 206-461-1300. E-MAIL: mdillon@nwlink.com. URL: http://www.pacificpublishingcompany.com. Year Established: 1926. Pub. Frequency: w. (Wed.) Page Size: tabloid. Subscrip. Rate: $.50 newsstand/cover; $30/yr. Adv. Rate: col. inch $25 Circulation: 13,000 per issue (paid). **Owner(s):** Pacific Publishing Co., See address and contact information above. **Management:** Mike Dillon, Publisher. Sherri Maxwell, Advertising Manager. Rachel Leloo, Circulation Manager. **Editorial:** Doug Schwartz, Editor.

MADISON PARK TIMES. 4000 Aurora Ave., N Ste 100, Seattle, WA 98101. Telephone: 206-461-1300. FAX: 206-461-1292. E-MAIL: mptimes@nwlink.com. Year Established: 1983. Pub. Frequency: m. (Wed.) Page Size: tabloid. Subscrip. Rate: $.25 newsstand/cover; $12/yr. Adv. Rate: col. inch $28 Circulation: 8,100 per issue (paid). **Owner(s):** Pacific Publishing Co., See address and contact information above. **Management:** Mike Dillon, Publisher. Jim Christenson, Circulation Manager. Barbara Blair, Classified Adv. Mgr.. Lucinda Germer, Art Director. **Editorial:** Vera Chan-Pool, Editor.

NORTH SEATTLE HERALD-OUTLOOK. 4000 Aurora Ave., N Ste 100, Seattle, WA 98101. Telephone: 206-461-1300. E-MAIL: mdillon@nwlink.com. URL: http://www.pacificpublishingcompany.com. Year Established: 1917. Pub. Frequency: w. (Wed.) Page Size: tabloid. Subscrip. Rate: $.50 newsstand/cover; $30/yr. Adv. Rate: col. inch $25 Circulation: 1,000 per issue (controlled and free). **Owner(s):** Pacific Publishing Co., See address and contact information above. **Management:** Mike Dillon, Publisher. Melanie Hendricks, Advertising Manager. Jim Christenson, Circulation Manager. Barbara Blair, Classified Adv. Mgr.. **Editorial:** Vera Chan-Pool, Editor. Bradley Enghaus, Photographer.

QUEEN ANNE-MAGNOLIA NEWS. 4000 Aurora Ave., N Ste 100, Seattle, WA 98101. Telephone: 206-461-1300. FAX: 206-461-1292. Mailing Address: P.O. Box 80156, Seattle, WA 98101. Year Established: 1919. Pub. Frequency: w. (Wed.) Page Size: tabloid. Subscrip. Rate: $.75 newsstand/cover; $1.50 home delivery/mo.; $35/yr mailed. Circulation: 20,800 per issue (controlled and free). **Owner(s):** Pacific Publishing Co., See address and contact information above. **Management:** Brenda L French, Publisher. Sandy Hood, Advertising Manager. Jim Christenson, Circulation Manager. **Editorial:** Richard Jameson, Editor. Maggie Larrick, Managing Editor.

SEATTLE WEEKLY. 1008 Western Ave., Ste. 300, Seattle, WA 98104. Telephone: 206-623-0500. FAX: 206-467-4338. E-MAIL: info@seattleweekly.com. URL: http://www.seattleweekly.com. Year Established: 1976. Pub. Frequency: w. (Wed.) Page Size: tabloid. Subscrip. Rate: $150/yr mailed. Adv. Rate: B&W page $3,875 Circulation: 110,000 per issue (paid and free). **Owner(s):** Village Voice Media, Inc., 36 Cooper Sq, New York, NY 10003. **Management:** Ken Stocker, Publisher. Jay Kraus, Circulation Manager. Kent O Winkler, Classified Adv. Mgr.. **Editorial:** Mark Fefer, Editor-in-Chief. Mike Seely, Managing Editor. Claudia Johns, Production Manager. Nina Shapiro, Senior Editor. Jane Sherman, Art Editor.

SOUTH DISTRICT JOURNAL. 4000 Aurora Ave., N Ste 100, Seattle, WA 98101. Telephone: 206-461-1300. FAX: 206-461-1292. Year Established: 1924. Pub. Frequency: w. (Wed.) Page Size: tabloid. Subscrip. Rate: $.50 newsstand/cover (effective 2005); $30/yr. Adv. Rate: col. inch $25 Circulation: 9,200 per issue (controlled and free). **Owner(s):** Pacific Publishing Co., See address and contact information above. **Management:** Mike Dillon, Publisher. LaNece Green, Advertising Manager. Jim Christenson, Circulation Manager. Barbara Blair, Classified Adv. Mgr.. **Editorial:** Richard Jameson, Editor.

WASHINGTON FREE PRESS. PMB #178, 1463 E. Republican St., Seattle, WA 98112. E-MAIL: editor@wafreepress.org. URL: http://www.washingtonfreepress.org. Pub. Frequency: bi-m. Page Size: tabloid. Subscrip. Rate: $16/yr. **Owner(s):** Washington Free Press, See address and contact information above. **Editorial:** Doug Collins, Editor. Renee Kjartan, Co-Editor.

WEST SEATTLE HERALD. 2604 California Ave, SW, Seattle, WA 98116. Telephone: 206-932-0300. FAX: 206-937-1223. E-MAIL: wseditor@robinsonnews.com. URL: http://www.robinsonnews.com. Year Established: 1923. Pub. Frequency: w. (Wed.) Page Size: tabloid. Subscrip. Rate: $.50 newsstand/cover; $29/yr home delivery local; $52/yr mailed. Adv. Rate: col. inch $30 Freelance Pay: $25/story. Circulation: 10,500 per issue (paid). **Owner(s):** Robinson Newspapers, 14006 1st Ave, Ste. B, Burien, WA 98168. **Management:** Tim Robinson, General Manager. Jerry Robinson, Publisher. Matt Lewis, Advertising Manager. Betty Serpa, Classified Adv. Mgr.. **Editorial:** Jack Mayne, Editor.

WHITE CENTER NEWS. 2604 California Ave, SW, Seattle, WA 98116. Telephone: 206-932-0300. FAX: 206-937-1223. E-MAIL: wseditor@robinsonnews.com. URL: http://www.robinsonnews.com. Mailing Address: PO Box 16069, Seattle, WA 98116. Pub. Frequency: w. (Wed.) Page Size: standard. Subscrip. Rate: $.50 newsstand/cover; $29/yr home delivery; $52/yr mailed. Circulation: 4,000 per issue (paid). **Owner(s):** Robinson Newspapers, 14006 1st Ave, Ste. B, Burien, WA 98168. **Management:** Tim Robinson, General Manager. Jerry Robinson, Publisher. Matt Lewis, Advertising Manager. Betty Serpa, Classified Adv. Mgr.. **Editorial:** Jack Mayne, Editor.

SEQUIM

SEQUIM GAZETTE. 147 W. Washington St., Sequim, WA 98382. URL: http://www.sequimgazette.com. Mailing Address: PO Box 1750, Sequim, WA 98382. Year Established: 1974. Pub. Frequency: w. (Wed.) Page Size: tabloid. Subscrip. Rate: $.75 newsstand/cover; $24/yr area; $40/yr mailed elsewhere. Circulation: 8,325 per issue (paid). **Owner(s):** Olympic View Publishing LLC, See address and contact information above. **Management:** Sue Ellen Riesau, Publisher. **Editorial:** Dan Ross, Editor.

SHELTON

SHELTON-MASON COUNTY JOURNAL. 227 W Cota St, Shelton, WA 98584. Telephone: 360-426-4412. FAX: 360-426-9399. E-MAIL: journal@masoncounty.com. URL: http://www.masoncounty.com. Mailing Address: PO Box 430, Shelton, WA 98584. Year Established: 1886. Pub. Frequency: w. (Thu.) Page Size: broadsheet. Subscrip. Rate: $.75 newsstand/cover; $32/yr in county; $46/yr out of county; $56/yr out of state. Adv. Rate: col. inch $12.75 Circulation: 9,600 per issue (paid). **Owner(s):** Tom and Annie Mullen, See address and contact information above. **Management:** Daniel Mancuso, Publisher.Readers: Mason County residents and visitors

SILVERDALE

CENTRAL KITSAP REPORTER. 9989 Silverdale Way NW, Ste. 109, Silverdale, WA 98383. E-MAIL: marketing@soundpublishing.com. URL: http://www.centralkitsapreporter.com. Year Established: 1983. Pub. Frequency: s-w. (Wed. & Sat.) Page Size: broadsheet. Subscrip. Rate: $.50 newsstand/cover; $29/yr home delivery local; $59/yr mailed in state; $78/yr mailed out of state. Adv. Rate: col. inch $19.60 Circulation: 19,031 per issue (paid and free). **Owner(s):** Sound Publishing, Inc., See address and contact information above. **Management:** Lisa Hutchings, Publisher. Lori Maxim, Vice President. Myra Campbell, Circulation Manager. **Editorial:** Sean Lamphere, Editor. Aaron Manahan, Sports Writer.

NORTHWEST NAVIGATOR-KITSAP. 9989 Silverdale Way NW, Ste. 109, Silverdale, WA 98383. E-MAIL: marketing@soundpublishing.com. URL: http://www.northwestnavigator. Year Established: 2000. Pub. Frequency: w. (Fri.) Page Size: broadsheet. Subscrip. Rate: $39/yr mailed. Adv. Rate: col. inch $19.60 Circulation: 8,607 per issue (free). **Owner(s):** Sound Publishing, Inc., 7689 N.E. Day Rd., Bainbridge Island, WA 98110. Telephone: 206-842-8305. FAX: 206-780-9562. **Management:** Lisa Hutchings, Publisher. Lori Maxim, Vice President. **Editorial:** Fred Watson, Editor.

SNOHOMISH

EVERETT NEWS TRIBUNE. 127 Ave. C, Ste. B, Snohomish, WA 98290. Telephone: 360-568-4121. FAX: 360-568-1484. E-MAIL: ads@snoho.com. URL: http://www.snoho.com. Mailing Address: PO Box 499, Snohomish, WA 98291-0499. Pub. Frequency: w. (Wed.) Page Size: tabloid. Subscrip. Rate: $.50 newsstand/cover; $28/yr mailed in county; $34/yr out of county. Circulation: 36,000 per issue (paid). **Owner(s):** Mach Publishing Inc., PO Box 499, Snohomish, WA 98291-0499. Telephone: 360-568-4121. FAX: 360-568-1484. **Management:** Dave Mach, Publisher. Becky Reed, Advertising Manager. Joanne Cole, Circulation Manager. **Editorial:** Tina Potterf, Editor.

MUKILTEO TRIBUNE. 127 Ave. C, Ste. B, Snohomish, WA 98290. Telephone: 360-568-4121. FAX: 360-568-1484. E-MAIL: ads@snoho.com. URL: http://www.snoho.com. Mailing Address: PO Box 499, Snohomish, WA 98291-0499. Pub. Frequency: w. (Wed.) Page Size: tabloid. Subscrip. Rate: $.50 newsstand/cover; $28/yr mailed in county; $34/yr out of county. Circulation: 36,000 per issue (paid). **Owner(s):** Mach Publishing Inc., PO Box 499, Snohomish, WA. Telephone: 360-568-4121. FAX: 360-568-1484. **Management:** Dave Mach, Publisher. Becky Reed, Advertising Manager. Joanne Cole, Circulation Manager. **Editorial:** Tina Potterf, Editor.

SNOHOMISH COUNTY TRIBUNE. 127 Ave. C, Ste. B, Snohomish, WA 98290. Telephone: 360-568-4121. FAX: 360-568-1484. URL: http://www.snoho.com. Mailing Address: PO Box 499, Snohomish, WA 98291-0499. Year Established: 1891. Pub. Frequency: w. (Wed.) Page Size: tabloid. Subscrip. Rate: $.50 newsstand/cover; $28/yr mailed in county; $34/yr mailed out of county. Adv. Rate: col. inch $22.67 Circulation: 36,000 per issue (paid). **Owner(s):** Mach Publishing Inc., PO Box 499, Snohomish, WA 98291. Telephone: 360-568-4121. FAX: 360-568-1484. **Management:** Dave Mach, Publisher. Becky Reed, Advertising Manager. Joanne Cole, Circulation Manager. **Editorial:** Bill Reinert, Editor.

SPOKANE

VALLEY NEWS HERALD. 523 N. Pines Rd., Spokane, WA 99206. Telephone: 509-924-2440. FAX: 509-927-1154. E-MAIL: vnh@onemain.com. Mailing Address: PO Box 142020, Spokane, WA 99214. Year Established: 1920. Pub. Frequency: w. (Fri.) Page Size: broadsheet. Subscrip. Rate: $.50 newsstand/cover; $20/yr in county; $30/yr out of county. Circulation: 8,070 per issue (paid). **Owner(s):** Free Press Publishing, See address and contact information above. **Management:** Mike Huffman, General Manager. Bill Ifft, President. **Editorial:** Mike Huffman, Editor.

STANWOOD

STANWOOD-CAMANO NEWS. 9005 271st St., N.W., Stanwood, WA 98292. Telephone: 360-629-2155. E-MAIL: phonebook@scnews.com. URL: http://www.scnews.com. Pub. Frequency: w. (Tue.) Page Size: standard. Subscrip. Rate: $30/wk.; $54 12 wks.. Adv. Rate: col. inch $11.20 Circulation: 15,200 per issue (free). **Owner(s):** Stanwood/Camano Net, See address and contact information above. **Management:** Dave Pinkham, Publisher. Brian Bretland, Advertising Manager. **Editorial:** John Dean, Editor. Scott Rutledge, Production Manager. Sharon Bartlett, Circulation Editor.

TENINO

TENINO INDEPENDENT, THE. 297 W. Sussex Ave., Tenino, WA 98589-4004. Telephone: 360-264-2500. FAX: 360-264-2955. E-MAIL: fdevaul@myhome.net. URL: http://www.devaulpublishing.com. Mailing Address: PO Box 4004, Tenino, WA 98589. Year Established: 1922. Pub. Frequency: w. (Wed.) Page Size: broadsheet. Subscrip. Rate: $.50 newsstand/cover; $19/yr mailed in county; $26/yr mailed in state; $34/yr mailed out of state. Circulation: 1,800 per issue (paid). **Owner(s):** DeVaul Publishing, Inc., 429 N. Market Blvd., Chehalis, WA 98531. Telephone: 360-748-3335. FAX: 360-748-3336. **Management:** Frank DeVaul, Publisher. Judy DeVaul, Advertising Manager. **Editorial:** Dan Fisher, Managing Editor.

TOPPENISH

REVIEW INDEPENDENT, THE. 11 E. Toppenish Ave., Toppenish, WA 98948. Telephone: 509-865-4055. FAX: 509-862-2655. E-MAIL: flintpub@yahoo.com. Mailing Address: PO Box 511, Toppenish, WA 98948. Year Established: 1904. Pub. Frequency: w. (Wed.) Page Size: tabloid. Subscrip. Rate: $.50 newsstand/cover; $24/yr mailed in county; $36/yr mailed out of county; $21/yr mailed in county to senior citizens. Adv. Rate: col. inch $9.50 Circulation: 3,700 per issue (paid). **Owner(s):** James A. Flint, See address and contact information above. **Management:** James A. Flint, Publisher. **Editorial:** James A. Flint, Editor.

VASHON ISLAND

VASHON ISLAND BEACHCOMBER. 17502 S.W. Vashon Hwy., Vashon Island, WA 98070. E-MAIL: marketing@soundpublication.com. URL: http://www.vashonbeachcomber.com. Mailing Address: PO Box 447, Vashon Island, WA 98070. Year Established: 1957. Pub. Frequency: w. (Wed.) Page Size: broadsheet. Subscrip. Rate: $.75 newsstand/cover; $25/yr carrier delivery; $45/yr mailed in state; $55/yr mailed out of state. Adv. Rate: col. inch $11.05 Circulation: 3,821 per issue (paid). **Owner(s):** Sound Publishing, Inc., 7689 N.E. Day Rd., Bainbridge Island, WA 98110. Telephone: 206-842-8305. FAX: 206-780-9562. **Management:** Lee Ockinga, Publisher. Lori Maxim, Vice President. **Editorial:** Allison Arthur, Editor.

WAITSBURG

TIMES (WAITSBURG), THE. 139 Main St., Waitsburg, WA 99361-0097. Telephone: 509-337-6631. FAX: 509-337-6045. E-MAIL: loyalbaker@juno.com. Mailing Address: PO Box 97, Waitsburg, WA 99361-0097. Year Established: 1878. Pub. Frequency: w. (Thu.) Page Size: standard. Subscrip. Rate: $.75 newsstand/cover; $29/yr Walla Walla & Columbia cys.; $31/yr in state; $34/yr out of state. Circulation: 1,400 per issue (paid). **Owner(s):** Loyal & Kathy Baker, See address and contact information above. **Management:** Kathy Baker, Publisher. Loyal Baker, Advertising Manager. **Editorial:** Loyal Baker, Editor.

WHITE SALMON

ENTERPRISE (WHITE SALMON), THE. 220 Jewett Ave, White Salmon, WA 98672. Telephone: 509-493-2112. FAX: 509-493-2399. E-MAIL: ebakke@whitesalmonenterprise.com. URL: http://www.whitesalmonenterprise.com. Mailing Address: PO Box 218, White Salmon, WA 98672. Year Established: 1903. Pub. Frequency: w. (Thu.) Page Size: tabloid. Subscrip. Rate: $.50 newsstand/cover; $25/yr in county; $40/yr out of county. Circulation: 2,700 (paid). **Owner(s):** Eagle Newspapers, Inc., 4901 Indian School Rd, NE, Salem, OR 97309. **Management:** Lyn Lamson, Classified Adv. Mgr.. Elaine Bakke, Associate Publisher. **Editorial:** Jesse Burkhardt, Editor.

WOODINVILLE

NORTHLAKE NEWS. 13342 N.E. 175th St., Woodinville, WA 98072. Telephone: 425-483-0606. FAX: 425-486-7593. E-MAIL: editor@woodville.com. URL: http://www.nwnews.com. Mailing Address: PO Box 587, Woodinville, WA 98072-0587. Year Established: 1976. Pub. Frequency: w. (Mon.) Page Size: tabloid.Adv. Rate: col. inch $16 Circulation: 37,100 per issue (free). **Owner(s):** Northwest News, See address and contact information above. **Management:** Julie Unruh, Publisher. **Editorial:** Karen Diefendorf, Editor.

VALLEY VIEW (WOODINVILLE). 13342 N.E. 175th St., Woodinville, WA 98072. Telephone: 425-483-0606. FAX: 425-486-7593. URL: http://www.nwnews.com. Mailing Address: PO Box 587, Woodinville, WA 98072-0587. Year Established: 1976. Pub. Frequency: w. (Mon.) Page Size: tabloid.Adv. Rate: col. inch $16 Circulation: 37,100 per issue (free). **Owner(s):** Northwest News, See address and contact information above. **Management:** Julie Unruh, Publisher. **Editorial:** Lisa Allen, Editor.

WOODINVILLE WEEKLY. 13342 N.E. 175th St., Woodinville, WA 98072. Telephone: 425-483-0606. FAX: 425-486-7593. URL: http://www.nwnews.com. Mailing Address: PO Box 587, Woodinville, WA 98072-0587. Year Established: 1976. Pub. Frequency: w. (Mon.) Page Size: tabloid.Adv. Rate: col. inch $16 Circulation: 31,700 per issue (free). **Owner(s):** Northwest News, See address and contact information above. **Management:** Julie Unruh, Publisher. **Editorial:** Karen Diefendorf, Editor.

YELM

NISQUALLY VALLEY NEWS. 118 Prairie Park St., Yelm, WA 98597. Telephone: 360-458-2681. FAX: 360-458-5741. E-MAIL: velmnews@velmonline.com. URL: http://www.nisquallyvalleyonline.com. Mailing Address: PO Box 597, Yelm, WA 98597. Year Established: 1921. Pub. Frequency: w. (Fri.) Page Size: standard. Subscrip. Rate: $.50 newsstand/cover; $23/yr mailed in county; $30/yr mailed out of county. Adv. Rate: col. inch $10.75 Circulation: 3,600 per issue (paid). **Owner(s):** Lafromboise Newspapers, Inc., 321 N. Pearl St., Centralia, WA 98531. Telephone: 360-736-3311. **Management:** Keven Graves, General Manager. J.R. Lafromboise, President. Dennis R. Waller, Publisher. **Editorial:** Keven Graves, Editor-in-Chief.

WEST VIRGINIA

BERKELEY SPRINGS

MORGAN MESSENGER, THE. ISSN 0895-1594
16 N. Mercer St., Berkeley Springs, WV 25411. Telephone: 304-258-1800. FAX: 304-258-8441. E-MAIL: news@morganmessenger.comepid.net. URL: http://www.morganmessenger.com. Mailing Address: PO Box 567, Berkeley Springs, WV 25411. Year Established: 1893. Pub. Frequency: w. (Wed.) Page Size: standard. Subscrip. Rate: $.70 newsstand/cover; $25.44/yr mailed in town. Circulation: 5,700 per issue (paid). **Owner(s):** Morgan Messenger, Inc., See address and contact information above. **Management:** Jim Buzzerd, Publisher. Sandy Buzzerd, Advertising Manager. **Editorial:** John Douglas, Editor.

BRIDGEPORT

BRIDGEPORT (WV) NEWS. The Blake Ctr, 1400 Johnson Ave, Bridgeport, WV 26330. Telephone: 304-842-8840. FAX: 304-842-8842. E-MAIL: news@bridgeportwvnew.com. URL: http://www.cpubco.com. Pub. Frequency: w. (Thu.) Page Size: broadsheet. Subscrip. Rate: $.50 newsstand/cover; $15/yr local; $22/yr mailed. Adv. Rate: col. inch $6.95 Circulation: 3,200 per issue (paid). **Owner(s):** Clarksburg Publishing Co., 324 Hewes Ave, Clarksburg, WV 26301. Telephone: 304-624-1400. FAX: 304-622-3629. **Management:** J. Cecil Jarvis, Publisher. Deborah Veltri, Advertising Manager. **Editorial:** Jeff Toquinto, Editor.

BUCKHANNON

RECORD-DELTA, THE. 2-B Clarksburg Rd., Buckhannon, WV 26201. Telephone: 304-472-2800. FAX: 304-472-0537. E-MAIL: deltaeditorial@wvdsl.net. URL: http://www.therecorddelta.com. Year Established: 1976. Pub. Frequency: 3/w. (Mon., Wed., Fri.) Page Size: broadsheet. Subscrip. Rate: $.50 newsstand/cover; $86.89/yr mailed in county; $95.70/yr mailed out of county; $81/yr mailed in county to senior citizens. Circulation: 5,000 per issue (paid). **Owner(s):** Mountaineer Newspapers, See address and contact information above. **Management:** Tammy Lyons, Publisher. Caron Atkins, Advertising. **Editorial:** Brian Bergstrom, Editor.

CHARLES TOWN

SPIRIT OF JEFFERSON-ADVOCATE. 210 N. George St., Charles Town, WV 25414-1504. Telephone: 304-725-2046. FAX: 304-728-6856. E-MAIL: pat@spiritofjefferson.com. Mailing Address: PO Box 966, Charles Town, WV 25414-0966. Year Established: 1844. Pub. Frequency: w. (Thu.) Page Size: broadsheet. Subscrip. Rate: $.50 newsstand/cover; $25/yr mailed in county; $27/yr mailed in state; $28/yr mailed out of state. Adv. Rate: col. inch $6.90 Circulation: 5,000 per issue (paid and free). **Owner(s):** Jefferson Publishing Co., Inc., See address and contact information above. **Management:** Edward W Dockeney Jr., Publisher. Cara Young, Office Manager. Edward W Dockeney Jr., Advertising Manager. **Editorial:** Edward W Dockeney Jr., Editor.

CLAY

CLAY COUNTY FREE PRESS. 291 Main St., Clay, WV 25043-0180. Telephone: 304-587-4250. FAX: 304-587-7300. E-MAIL: news@claycountyfreepress.com. URL: http://www.claycountyfreepress.com. Mailing Address: PO Box 180, Clay, WV 25043-0180. Year Established: 1888. Pub. Frequency: w. (Wed.) Page Size: tabloid. Subscrip. Rate: $.50 newsstand/cover; $20/yr in county; $25/yr mailed out of county; $30/yr mailed out of state. Circulation: 4,480 per issue (paid). **Owner(s):** Clinton Nichols, PO Box 180, Clay, WV 02503-0180. Telephone: 304-587-4250. FAX: 304-587-7329. **Management:** Jacob Nichols, Publisher. **Editorial:** Rene Moore, Editor.

CULLODEN

CABELL STANDARD, THE. 2085 US Rte. 60, Culloden, WV 25510. Telephone: 304-743-1222. FAX: 304-562-6214. E-MAIL: admin@cabellstandard.com. URL: http://www.cabellstandard.com. Mailing Address: PO Box 186, Culloden, WV 25510. Year Established: 1898. Pub. Frequency: w. (Tue.) Page Size: tabloid. Subscrip. Rate: $.50 newsstand/cover; $22/yr in county; $38/yr in state; $48/yr out of state. Adv. Rate: col. inch $7.50 Circulation: 1,500 per issue (paid). **Owner(s):** West Virginia Standard Co., See address and contact information above. **Management:** Jack Bailey, President. Dan Butcher, Publisher. Jeff Gandee, Advertising Manager. Alvie Watts, Circulation Manager. **Editorial:** Lee Arnold, Editor.

PUTNAM STANDARD, THE. 2085 US Rte. 60, Culloden, WV 25510. Telephone: 304-743-1222. FAX: 304-562-6214. E-MAIL: admin@cabellstandard.com. URL: http//www.putnamstandard.com. Mailing Address: PO Box 186, Culloden, WV 25510. Year Established: 1955. Pub. Frequency: w. (Tue.) Page Size: tabloid. Subscrip. Rate: $22/yr in county; $38/yr in state; $48/yr out of state. Adv. Rate: col. inch $7.50 Circulation: 1,500 per issue (free). **Owner(s):** West Virginia Standard Co., See address and contact information above. **Management:** Jack Bailey, President. Dan Butcher, Publisher. Jeff Gandee, Advertising Manager. Alvie Watts, Circulation Manager. **Editorial:** Lee Arnold, Editor.

FRANKLIN

PENDLETON TIMES, THE. 205 N. Main St., Franklin, WV 26807-0906. Telephone: 304-358-2304. FAX: 304-358-2304. Mailing Address: PO Box 906, Franklin, WV 26807-0906. Year Established: 1913. Pub. Frequency: w. (Thu.) Page Size: tabloid. Subscrip. Rate: $.50 newsstand/cover; $24/yr mailed in state; $25/yr out of state. Circulation: 5,300 per issue (paid). **Owner(s):** William McCoy, Jr., PO Box 906, Franklin, WV 26807. Telephone: 304-358-2304. **Management:** John McCoy, General Manager. William McCoy Jr., Publisher. Pam Hartman, Circulation Manager. **Editorial:** Ed Tallman, Editor.

GLENVILLE

GLENVILLE DEMOCRAT, THE. P.O. Box 458, Glenville, WV 26351. Telephone: 304-462-7309. FAX: 304-462-7300. E-MAIL: glenvillenewsad@rtol.net. Year Established: 1904. Pub. Frequency: w. (Thu.) Page Size: broadsheet. Subscrip. Rate: $.50 newsstand/cover; $21.20/yr mailed in county; $26.50/yr mailed out of county; $28/yr mailed out of state. Circulation: 2,000 per issue (paid). **Owner(s):** David Corcoran, See address and contact information above. **Management:** David Corcoran Sr., President. Shamae Wiant, Circulation Manager.

GLENVILLE PATHFINDER. P.O. Box 458, Glenville, WV 26351. Telephone: 304-462-7309. FAX: 304-462-7300. E-MAIL: glenvillenewsad@rtol.net. Year Established: 1892. Pub. Frequency: w. (Thu.) Page Size: broadsheet. Subscrip. Rate: $.50 newsstand/cover; $21.20/yr mailed in county; $26.50/yr mailed in state; $28/yr mailed out of state. Circulation: 1,530 per issue (paid). **Owner(s):** David Corcoran, See address and contact information above. **Management:** David Corcoran Sr., President. Shamae Wiant, Circulation Manager.

GRAFTON

MOUNTAIN STATESMAN. ISSN 0745-1334
914 W. Main St., Grafton, WV 26354. Telephone: 304-265-3333. FAX: 304-265-3342. E-MAIL: gftemail@aol.com. URL: http://www.mountainstatesman.com. Mailing Address: PO Box 218, Grafton, WV 26354. Pub. Frequency: 3/w. (Mon., Wed., Fri.) Page Size: broadsheet. Subscrip. Rate: $.35 newsstand/cover; $73.62/yr home delivery in county; $79.08/yr mailed out of county. Circulation: 3,300 per issue (paid). **Owner(s):** News Media Corp., PO Box 46, Rochelle, IL 61068. Telephone: 815-562-2061. **Management:** Jean Ellerman, Publisher. Linda Hess, Advertising. Carolyn Flesher, Circulation Manager. Donna Moore, Classified Adv. Mgr.. **Editorial:** Beth Clawges, Editor. Brian Moore, Sports Editor.

GRANTSVILLE

CALHOUN CHRONICLE. ISSN 1040-399X
353 Main St., Grantsville, WV 26147. Telephone: 304-354-6917. FAX: 304-354-6917. E-MAIL: contact@calhounchronicle.com. URL: http://www.calhounchronicle.com. Mailing Address: PO Box 400, Grantsville, WV 26147. Year Established: 1883. Pub. Frequency: w. (Thu.) Page Size: standard. Subscrip. Rate: $.50 newsstand/cover; $20.67/yr mailed in county; $26.82/yr mailed out of county; $29.90/yr mailed out of state. Circulation: 3,500 per issue (paid). **Owner(s):** Helen Morris, See address and contact information above. **Management:** Helen Morris, Publisher. **Editorial:** Newton Nichols, Editor.

HAMLIN

LINCOLN JOURNAL, THE. 308, Hamlin, WV 25523-0308. E-MAIL: lincolnjournal@zoominternet.net. URL: http://www.lincolnjournal.com. Mailing Address: PO Box 308, Hamlin, WV 25523-0308. Year Established: 1903. Pub. Frequency: w. (Wed.) Page Size: broadsheet. Subscrip. Rate: $.75 newsstand/cover; $23.95/yr mailed in county; $32.50/yr mailed out of county; $39.50/yr mailed out of state. Adv. Rate: col. inch $9.45 Freelance Pay: $15-$30/story. Circulation: 5,285 per issue (paid and free). **Owner(s):** Lincoln Journal, Inc., The, See address and contact information above. **Management:** Patty Robinson, General Manager. Thomas A. Robinson, President. Barbara Cummings, Advertising Manager.

LINCOLN TIMES, THE. 308, Hamlin, WV 25523-0308. E-MAIL: lincolnjournal@zoominternet.net. URL: http://www.lincolnjournal.com. Mailing Address: PO Box 308, Hamlin, WV 25523-0308. Year Established: 1990. Pub. Frequency: w. (Fri.) Page Size: broadsheet Circulation: 12,650 per issue (free). **Owner(s):** Lincoln Journal, Inc., The, See address and contact information above. **Management:** Thomas A. Robinson, President. Barbara Cummings, Advertising Manager. **Editorial:** Patty Robinson, Managing Editor. Ron Gregory, Sports Editor.

LINCOLN WEEKLY NEWS SENTINEL. 308, Hamlin, WV 25523-0308. E-MAIL: lincolnjournal@zoominternet.net. URL: http://www.lincolnjournal.com. Mailing Address: PO Box 308, Hamlin, WV 25523-0308. Year Established: 1910. Pub. Frequency: w. (Wed.) Page Size: broadsheet. Subscrip. Rate: $.75 newsstand/cover; $23.95/yr in county; $32.50/yr out of county. Circulation: 1,800 per issue (paid). **Owner(s):** Lincoln Journal, Inc., The, See address and contact information above. **Management:** Patty Robinson, General Manager. Thomas A. Robinson, President. Barbara Cummings, Advertising Manager. **Editorial:** Thomas A. Robinson, Editor. Ron Gregory, Sports Editor.

HARRISVILLE

PENNSBORO NEWS, THE. 103 N. Spring St., Harrisville, WV 26362. Telephone: 304-643-4947. FAX: 304-643-4717. E-MAIL: news@ritchiecountynews.com. Mailing Address: P O Box 241, Harrisville, WV 26362. Year Established: 1892. Pub. Frequency: w. (Wed.) Page Size: broadsheet. Subscrip. Rate: $.50 newsstand/cover; $21.20/yr in county; $28.40/yr out of county; $34/yr out of state. Adv. Rate: col. inch $3.75 Circulation: 4,800 per issue (paid). **Owner(s):** James McGoldrick, See address and contact information above. **Management:** James McGoldrick, Publisher. **Editorial:** Jennifer S Gregg, News Editor.

RITCHIE GAZETTE. PO Box 215, Harrisville, WV 26362. Telephone: 304-643-2221. FAX: 304-643-2156. E-MAIL: gazette@zoominternet.net. Mailing Address: PO Box 215, Harrisville, WV 26362-0215. Year Established: 1873. Pub. Frequency: w. (Wed.) Page Size: standard. Subscrip. Rate: $25/yr in county; $30/yr in state; $35/yr out of state. Circulation: 3,820 per issue (paid). **Owner(s):** Ritchie Gazette Publishing LLC, See address and contact information above. **Management:** Debbie Frederick, Advertising Manager. Denise Shiflet, Circulation Manager. **Editorial:** Denise J. Shiflet, Editor.

HINTON

HINTON NEWS. 210 Second Ave., Hinton, WV 25951. Telephone: 304-466-0005. E-MAIL: hinton1000@aol.com. URL: http://www.hinton.com. Year Established: 1901. Pub. Frequency: w. (Tue.) Page Size: broadsheet. Subscrip. Rate: $.53 newsstand/cover; $22.26/yr in county; $26.50/yr in state; $30/yr out of state. Freelance Pay: $0.15/word. Circulation: 4,200 per issue (paid). **Owner(s):** Hinton Publishing Co., Inc., See address and contact information above. **Management:** Fred Long, Publisher. Nellie Robertson, Circulation Manager. **Editorial:** Fred Long, Managing Editor.

HURRICANE

HURRICANE BREEZE. 488 Hurricane Creek Rd., Hurricane, WV 25526. Telephone: 304-562-9881. Mailing Address: P.O. Box 310, Hurricane, WV 25526. Year Established: 1900. Pub. Frequency: w. (Thu.) Page Size: broadsheet. Subscrip. Rate: $.35 newsstand/cover; $14.84/yr in county; $19.61/yr in state; $21.73/yr out of state. Circulation: 1,200 per issue (paid). **Owner(s):** Ron Allen, See address and contact information above. **Management:** Elizabeth Allen, Publisher. Ron Allen, Advertising Manager. **Editorial:** Ron Allen, Editor.

KEYSER

TODAY'S SHOPPER. 24 Armstrong St., Keyser, WV 26726. Telephone: 304-788-3333. FAX: 304-788-3398. Mailing Address: PO Box 879, Keyser, WV 26726. Pub. Frequency: w. (Sat.) Page Size: standard Circulation: 14,800 per issue (free). **Owner(s):** GateHouse Media, Inc, 350 WillowBrook Office Park, Fairport, NY 14450. Telephone: 585-598-0030. **Management:** Randy Lewis, Publisher. Christy Jamison, Circulation Manager. Kathy Murphy, Classified Adv. Mgr..

KINGWOOD

PRESTON COUNTY JOURNAL. ISSN 1072-0057
110 W. Main St., Kingwood, WV 26537. Telephone: 304-329-0090. FAX: 304-329-2450. E-MAIL: ppitina@atlanticbb.net. Year Established: 1866. Pub. Frequency: w. (Wed.) Page Size: broadsheet. Subscrip. Rate: $.50 newsstand/cover; $23/yr in county; $29/yr out of county. Circulation: 5,700 per issue (paid). **Owner(s):** Preston County Journal, See address and contact information above. **Management:** Gary Bolyard, Publisher. Carol Peters, Advertising Manager. Dennis Peters, Business Manager. **Editorial:** Tina Bolyard, Editor.

LEWISBURG

GREENBRIER VALLEY RANGER. 200 S. Court St., Lewisburg, WV 24901-0471. Telephone: 304-645-1206. FAX: 304-645-7104. E-MAIL: dailynewsad@charter.net. Mailing Address: PO Box 471, Lewisburg, WV 24901-0471. Year Established: 1981. Pub. Frequency: s-w. (Wed. & Sun.) Page Size: broadsheet.Adv. Rate: col. inch $10 Circulation: 26,976 per issue (free). **Owner(s):** Moffitt Newspapers, Inc., PO Box 8565, Roanoke, VA 24014. Telephone: 540-344-2489. **Management:** Frank Spicer, Publisher. Judy Steele, Advertising Manager. Crystal McNeely, Circulation Manager. **Editorial:** Joyce Arbaugh, Editor.

MOUNTAIN MESSENGER (LEWISBURG). 122 N. Court St., Lewisburg, WV 24901. Telephone: 304-647-5724. FAX: 304-647-5767. E-MAIL: ads@mountainmessenger.com. URL: http://www.mountainmessenger.com. Mailing Address: PO Box 429, Lewisburgh, WV 24901. Year Established: 1985. Pub. Frequency: w. (Sat.) Page Size: broadsheet. Subscrip. Rate: $15/yr carrier delivery local; $19.08/yr mailed in county & adj. cys.; $24/yr mailed in state; $28/yr mailed out of state. Adv. Rate: col. inch $9 **Wire Service(s):** AP. Circulation: 10,500 per issue (paid and free). **Owner(s):** Michael Showell, See address and contact information above. **Management:** Michael Showell, Publisher. Rebecca Hanson, Advertising Manager. **Editorial:** Carol Hall, Editor.

MADISON

COAL VALLEY NEWS. 350 Main St, Madison, WV 25130. Telephone: 304-369-1165. FAX: 304-369-1166. E-MAIL: aalexander@coalvalleynews.com. URL: http://www.coalvalleynews.com. Mailing Address: PO Box 508, Madison, WV 25130. Year Established: 1925. Pub. Frequency: w. (Wed.) Page Size: broadsheet. Subscrip. Rate: $.75 newsstand/cover; $30/yr mailed in state. Circulation: 5,200 per issue (paid). **Owner(s):** Heartland Publications, LLC, 1 W Main St, Clinton, CT 06413. Telephone: 860-664-1075. FAX: 860-664-1085. **Management:** Angela Alexander, General Manager. Debbie Schultz, Advertising. **Editorial:** Joanie Newman, Editor. Jay Fankhauser, Sports.

MARLINTON

POCAHONTAS TIMES. ISSN 0738-8373
810 Second Ave., Marlinton, WV 24954. Telephone: 304-799-4973. FAX: 304-799-6466. E-MAIL: pepritt@pocahontastimes.com. URL: http://www.pocahontastimes.com. Year Established: 1883. Pub. Frequency: w. (Thu.) Page Size: standard. Subscrip. Rate: $.40 newsstand/cover; $15.90/yr mailed in county; $23.32/yr mailed in state; $25/yr mailed out of state. Adv. Rate: col. inch $4.75 Circulation: 5,850. **Owner(s):** Pocahontas Times, See address and contact information above. **Management:** Carol Moore, Classified Editor. **Editorial:** Pamela E Pritt, Editor. Cynthia Johnson, Managing Editor. Drew Tanner, Reporter.

MONTGOMERY

MONTGOMERY (WV) HERALD. 406 Lee St, Montgomery, WV 25136. Telephone: 304-442-4156. FAX: 304-442-8753. E-MAIL: news@montgomery-herald.com. URL: http://www.montgomery-herald.com. Mailing Address: PO Box 240, Montgomery, WV 25136-0240. Year Established: 1940. Pub. Frequency: w. (Wed.) Page Size: broadsheet. Subscrip. Rate: $.50 newsstand/cover; $25.80/yr mailed in state. Circulation: 1,500 per issue (paid). **Owner(s):** Community Newspaper Holdings, Inc., 3500 Colonnade Pkwy., Ste. 600, Birmingham, AL 35243-7017. **Management:** Frank Wood, Publisher. Chuck Jessup, Advertising Director. **Editorial:** Cheryl Keenan, Managing Editor.

MOOREFIELD

MOOREFIELD EXAMINER. 132 S. Main St., Moorefield, WV 26836-0380. Telephone: 304-530-6397. FAX: 304-530-6400. E-MAIL: examiner@hardynet.com. URL: www.moorefieldexaminer.com. Mailing Address: PO Box 380, Moorefield, WV 26836. Year Established: 1845. Pub. Frequency: w. (Wed.) Page Size: broadsheet. Subscrip. Rate: $.50 newsstand/cover; $25.50/yr mailed in county; $29/yr mailed out of county; $33.15/yr mailed out of state. **Wire Service(s):** AP. Circulation: 4,600 per issue (paid). **Owner(s):** R.E. Fisher Co., Inc., See address and contact information above. **Management:** David O. Heishman, General Manager. Phoebe F. Heishman, Publisher. **Editorial:** Phoebe F. Heishman, Editor. Diane Hypes, News Editor.

MOUNDSVILLE

GREEN TAB. 518 Seventh St., Moundsville, WV 26041. Telephone: 304-845-4050. FAX: 304-845-4312. Mailing Address: PO Box 126, Glendale, WV 26038. Year Established: 1926. Pub. Frequency: w. (Sun.) Page Size: tabloid Circulation: 16,300 per issue (free). **Owner(s):** Robert W. Munn, Sr., See address and contact information above. **Management:** Robert W. Munn Jr., Publisher. Cindy Fetty, Circulation Manager. **Editorial:** Robert W. Munn Jr., Editor.

MULLENS

MULLENS ADVOCATE. 217 Moran Ave., Mullens, WV 25882. Telephone: 304-294-4144. FAX: 304-294-4144. E-MAIL: mullinsadvocate@hotmail.com. Year Established: 1913. Pub. Frequency: w. (Tue.) Page Size: broadsheet. Subscrip. Rate: $.30 newsstand/cover; $14.84/yr in county; $24.38/yr out of county. Circulation: 3,500 per issue (paid). **Owner(s):** Jack Moffitt, See address and contact information above. **Management:** Greg Spinella, Publisher. **Editorial:** Charlene Cook, Managing Editor.

NEW MARTINSVILLE

WETZEL CHRONICLE. 1100 Third St., New Martinsville, WV 26155. Telephone: 304-455-3300. FAX: 304-455-1275. E-MAIL: mgalluzzo@wetzelchronicle.com. URL: http://www.wetzelchronicle.com. Mailing Address: PO Box 289, New Martinsville, WV 26155. Year Established: 1888. Pub. Frequency: w. (Wed.) Page Size: standard. Subscrip. Rate: $.50 newsstand/cover; $25/yr mailed in state; $28/yr mailed out of state. Adv. Rate: col. inch $8 Circulation: 7,000 per issue (paid). **Owner(s):** Ogden Newspapers of Minnesota, Inc., 1500 Main St., Wheeling, WV 26003. Telephone: 304-233-0100. **Management:** Bob Munn, Publisher. **Editorial:** Amy Witschey, Editor. Bruce Crawford, Sports.

OAK HILL

FAYETTE TRIBUNE. 417 Main St, W., Oak Hill, WV 25901. Telephone: 304-469-3373. FAX: 304-469-4105. E-MAIL: ckeenan@fayettetribune.com. URL: http://www.fayettetribune.com. Mailing Address: PO Box 139, Oak Hill, WV 25901-0139. Year Established: 1897. Pub. Frequency: s-w. (Mon. & Thu.) Page Size: broadsheet. Subscrip. Rate: $.50 newsstand/cover; $42/yr carrier delivery in county; $46/yr mailed elsewhere. Circulation: 6,000 per issue (paid). **Owner(s):** Community Newspaper Holdings, Inc., 3500 Colonnade Pkwy., Ste. 600, Birmingham, AL 35242. **Management:** Frank Wood, Publisher. Chuck Jessup, Advertising Director. Debbie Maxwell, Advertising Manager. Mark Campbell, Circulation Director. **Editorial:** Cheryl Keenan, Managing Editor.

PARSONS

PARSONS ADVOCATE. ISSN 0747-3303
412 Second St., Parsons, WV 26287. E-MAIL: admin@personsadvocate.com. URL: http://www.parsonsadvocate.com. Mailing Address: PO Box 345, Parsons, WV 26287. Year Established: 1896. Pub. Frequency: w. (Wed.) Page Size: standard. Subscrip. Rate: $.50 newsstand/cover; $25/yr in state; $30/yr out of state. Adv. Rate: col. inch $5 Circulation: 4,000 per issue (paid). **Owner(s):** Stadelman Publishing LLC, See address and contact information above. **Management:** Chris Stadelman, Publisher. Mikie Dunmire, Advertising Manager. **Editorial:** Chris Stadelman, Editor.

PETERSBURG

GRANT COUNTY PRESS. 47 S. Main St., Petersburg, WV 26847. Telephone: 304-257-1844. FAX: 304-257-1691. E-MAIL: news@grantcountypress.com. URL: http://www.grantcountypress.com. Mailing Address: PO Box 39, Petersburg, WV 26847. Year Established: 1896. Pub. Frequency: w. (Tue.) Page Size: broadsheet. Subscrip. Rate: $.75 newsstand/cover; $24.50/yr in county; $26.50/yr in state; $30/yr out of state. Adv. Rate: col. inch $6.50 Circulation: 5,100 per issue (paid). **Owner(s):** Potomac Valley Press, Inc., See address and contact information above. **Management:** James Tetrick, President. Stacy Champ, Advertising. Jodi Fouch, Advertising Manager. **Editorial:** Bill Fouch, Editor. Tom Hencke, News Editor.

PHILIPPI

BARBOUR DEMOCRAT, THE. 113 Church St., Philippi, WV 26416. Telephone: 304-457-2222. FAX: 304-457-2235. E-MAIL: thebarbourdemocratLLC@yahoo.com. Mailing Address: PO Box 459, Philippi, WV 26416. Year Established: 1893. Pub. Frequency: w. (Wed.) Page Size: standard. Subscrip. Rate: $.40 newsstand/cover; $27.18/yr mailed in state; $32.15/yr mailed out of state. Adv. Rate: col. inch $4.25 Circulation: 5,100 per issue (paid). **Owner(s):** The Barbour Democrat LLC, 113 Church St., Philippi, WV 24616. **Management:** J Eric Cutright, Owner. **Editorial:** Lars O Byrne, Editor.

PIEDMONT

PIEDMONT HERALD. PO Box 68, Piedmont, WV 26750. Telephone: 304-355-2381. FAX: 304-355-2383. Year Established: 1879. Pub. Frequency: w. (Tue.) Page Size: standard. Subscrip. Rate: $.38 newsstand/cover; $25/yr mailed in county; $26/yr mailed out of county. Adv. Rate: col. inch $2.30 Circulation: 1,200 per issue (paid). **Owner(s):** William T. Hood, See address and contact information above. **Management:** William T. Hood, Publisher. **Editorial:** William T. Hood, Editor.

PRINCETON

PRINCETON TIMES. 109 Thorn St., Princeton, WV 24740. Telephone: 304-425-8191. FAX: 304-487-1632. E-MAIL: ttoler@ptonline.net. Mailing Address: PO Box 1199, Princeton, WV 24740-1199. Year Established: 1961. Pub. Frequency: w. (Fri.) Page Size: broadsheet. Subscrip. Rate: $.50 newsstand/cover; $30/yr in state. Circulation: 6,200 per issue (paid). **Owner(s):** Community Newspaper Holdings, Inc., 3500 Colonnade Pkwy., Ste. 600, Birmingham, AL 35243. Telephone: 205-298-7100. **Management:** Randy Deason, Publisher. Terri Hale, Advertising Manager. **Editorial:** Tammie Toler, Editor.

RAVENSWOOD

JACKSON STAR NEWS, THE. 410 Race St., Ravenswood, WV 26164. Telephone: 304-273-9333. FAX: 304-372-5544. E-MAIL: editor@jacksonnewspapers.com. URL: http://www.jacksonnewspapers.com. Year Established: 1955. Pub. Frequency: w. (Thu.) Page Size: broadsheet. Subscrip. Rate: $.75 newsstand/cover; $41/yr in county; $53/yr out of county. Circulation: 20,500 per issue (paid). **Owner(s):** GateHouse Media, Inc, 350 WillowBrook Office Park, Fairport, NY 14450. Telephone: 585-598-0030. FAX: 585-248-2631. **Management:** Mike Ruben, Publisher. **Editorial:** Greg Matics, Managing Editor.

RIPLEY

JACKSON HERALD (RIPLEY). 305 N Church St, Ripley, WV 25271. Telephone: 304-372-4222. FAX: 304-372-5544. E-MAIL: ads@jacksonnewspapers.com. URL: http://www.jacksonnewspapers.com. Year Established: 1876. Pub. Frequency: w. (Thu.) Subscrip. Rate: $.75 newsstand/cover per issue; $41/yr mailed in county; $53/yr mailed out of county; $56/yr mailed out of state. Circulation: 9,200. **Owner(s):** GateHouse Media, Inc, 350 WillowBrook Office Park, Fairport, NY 14450. Telephone: 585-598-0030. FAX: 585-248-2631. **Management:** Mike Ruben, Publisher. **Editorial:** Greg Matics, Managing Editor.

STAR HERALD WEEKENDER. 305 N Church St, Ripley, WV 25271. Telephone: 304-372-4222. FAX: 304-372-5544. Pub. Frequency: w. (Sat.) Page Size: broadsheet Circulation: 13,500 per issue (free). **Owner(s):** GateHouse Media, Inc, 350 WillowBrook Office Park, Fairport, NY 14450. Telephone: 585-598-0030. **Management:** Mike Ruben, Publisher. **Editorial:** Greg Matics, Managing Editor.

ROMNEY

HAMPSHIRE REVIEW. 25 S. Grafton St., Romney, WV 26757. Telephone: 304-822-3871. FAX: 304-822-4487. E-MAIL: internet@hampshirereview.com. URL: http://www.hampshirereview.com. Mailing Address: P.O. Box 1036, Romney, WV 26757. Year Established: 1829. Pub. Frequency: w. (Wed.) Page Size: broadsheet. Subscrip. Rate: $.75 newsstand/cover; $34.13/yr mailed in county; $34.13/yr out of state. Circulation: 6,950 per issue (paid). **Owner(s):** Cornwell & Ailes, Inc., See address and contact information above. **Management:** Lana Bean, Advertising Manager. Patty Grates, Classified Adv. Mgr.. Karen Moreland, Business Manager. **Editorial:** Elli Goyette, Editor.

SHEPHERDSTOWN

SHEPHERDSTOWN CHRONICLE. 123-C S. Duke St., Shepherdstown, WV 25443. Telephone: 304-876-3380. FAX: 304-876-1957. E-MAIL: edit@shepherdstownchronicle.com. URL: http://www.shepherdstownchronicle.com. Mailing Address: PO Box 2088, Shepherdstown, WV 25443. Year Established: 1991. Pub. Frequency: w. (Fri.) Page Size: tabloid. Subscrip. Rate: $.50 newsstand/cover; $15/yr mailed in county; $20/yr mailed in state; $25/yr mailed out of state. Adv. Rate: col. inch $6.97 Circulation: 2,000 per issue (paid). **Owner(s):** Ogden Newspapers of Minnesota, Inc., 1500 Main St., Wheeling, WV 26003. Telephone: 304-233-0100. **Management:** Tami Ruschell, Advertising. **Editorial:** Daniel Friend, Editor.

SISTERSVILLE

TYLER STAR NEWS. 727 Wells St., Sistersville, WV 26175. Telephone: 304-652-4141. FAX: 304-652-1454. E-MAIL: editor@tylerstarnews.com. URL: http://www.tylerstarnews.com. Mailing Address: PO Box 191, Sistersville, WV 26175. Year Established: 1878. Pub. Frequency: w. (Wed.) Page Size: standard. Subscrip. Rate: $.50 newsstand/cover; $25/yr mailed in state; $28/yr mailed out of state. Adv. Rate: col. inch $8 Circulation: 4,800 per issue (paid). **Owner(s):** Ogden Newspapers of Minnesota, Inc., 1500 Main St., Wheeling, WV 26003. Telephone: 304-233-0100. **Management:** Brian Clutter, Publisher. Lisa Northcraft, Advertising. **Editorial:** Jonay Corley, Editor.

SPENCER

ROANE COUNTY REPORTER. 210 E. Main St., Spencer, WV 25276-1602. E-MAIL: spennews@wirefire.com. URL: http://www.thetimesrecord.net. Mailing Address: 210 E. Main St., Spencer, WV 25276-1602. Year Established: 1915. Pub. Frequency: w. (Thu.) Page Size: broadsheet. Subscrip. Rate: $.60 newsstand/cover; $28/yr in county; $31/yr in state (effective 2005); $36/yr out of state. Circulation: 3,179 per issue (paid). **Owner(s):** Spencer Newspapers, Inc., See address and contact information above. **Management:** David J. Hedges, Publisher. Danny Jarvis, Advertising Manager. Eleanor J. Reber, Circulation Manager. **Editorial:** Jim Cooper, Editor.

TIMES RECORD (SPENCER), THE. 210 E. Main St., Spencer, WV 25276-1602. E-MAIL: dhedges@thetimesrecord.net. URL: http://www.thetimesrecord.net. Mailing Address: 210 E. Main St., Spencer, WV 25276-1602. Year Established: 1914. Pub. Frequency: w. (Thu.) Page Size: broadsheet. Subscrip. Rate: $.50 newsstand/cover; $26/yr in state; $30/yr out of state. Circulation: 3,246 per issue (paid). **Owner(s):** Spencer Newspapers, Inc., See address and contact information above. **Management:** David J. Hedges, Publisher. Danny Jarvis, Advertising Manager. Deborah Nicoles, Business Manager. **Editorial:** Jim Cooper, Editor.

SUMMERSVILLE

NICHOLAS CHRONICLE. 718 Broad St., Summersville, WV 26651. Telephone: 304-872-2251. FAX: 304-872-2254. Mailing Address: PO Box 503, Summersville, WV 26651. Year Established: 1880. Pub. Frequency: w. (Thu.) Page Size: broadsheet. Subscrip. Rate: $.50 newsstand/cover; $25/yr mailed in state; $30/yr mailed out of state. Wire Service(s): AP. Circulation: 7,190 per issue (paid). **Owner(s):** Nicholas County Publishing Co., Inc., See address and contact information above. **Management:** Matthew R. Yeager, Publisher. Steve Beal, Advertising Manager. Brenda Shafer, Circulation Manager. **Editorial:** Ray Corbin, Editor. Matthew R. Yeager, Managing Editor.

SUTTON

BRAXTON CITIZEN'S NEWS. 501 Main St., Sutton, WV 26601. Telephone: 304-765-5193. FAX: 304-765-2754. E-MAIL: quality@rtol.net. URL: http://www.bcn-news.com. Year Established: 1976. Pub. Frequency: w. (Tue.) Page Size: broadsheet. Subscrip. Rate: $.27 newsstand/cover; $15/yr mailed in county; $21/yr mailed in state; $29.75/yr mailed out of state. Circulation: 6,500 per issue (paid). **Owner(s):** Ed Given, See address and contact information above. **Management:** Ed Given, Publisher. Allison Given, Advertising Manager. Tara Helmick, Circulation Manager. **Editorial:** Ed Given, Editor.

BRAXTON DEMOCRAT-CENTRAL. 201 Second St, Sutton, WV 26601. Telephone: 304-765-5555. FAX: 304-765-5555. Year Established: 1883. Pub. Frequency: w. (Fri.) Page Size: broadsheet. Subscrip. Rate: $.25 newsstand/cover; $11.49/yr in county; $16/yr out of county; $22.50/yr out of state. Circulation: 4,200 per issue (paid). **Owner(s):** Craig A. Smith, See address and contact information above. **Management:** Craig A. Smith, Publisher. Joan Bias, Advertising Manager. **Editorial:** Craig A. Smith, Managing Editor.

UNION

MONROE WATCHMAN. 400 Main St., Union, WV 24983. Telephone: 304-772-3016. Mailing Address: PO Box 179, Union, WV 24983. Year Established: 1872. Pub. Frequency: w. (Thu.) Page Size: broadsheet. Subscrip. Rate: $.50 newsstand/cover; $20.67/yr mailed in state; $22/yr mailed out of state. Circulation: 4,200 per issue (paid). **Owner(s):** Dale Mohler, See address and contact information above. **Management:** Dale Mohler, Publisher. John Honaker, Advertising. **Editorial:** Dr. H. Craig Mohler, Editor.

WEBSTER SPRINGS

WEBSTER ECHO. 219 Back Fork St., Webster Springs, WV 26288. Telephone: 304-847-5828. FAX: 304-847-5991. E-MAIL: websterecho@citlink.net. Year Established: 1882. Pub. Frequency: w. (Wed.) Page Size: broadsheet. Subscrip. Rate: $.50 newsstand/cover; $25.97/yr mailed in county; $29.75/yr mailed out of state. Circulation: 3,000 per issue (paid). **Owner(s):** Thomas C. Clark, See address and contact information above. **Management:** Thomas C. Clark, Publisher. **Editorial:** Thomas C. Clark, Editor.

WEBSTER REPUBLICAN. 219 Back Fork St., Webster Springs, WV 26288. Telephone: 304-847-5828. FAX: 304-847-5991. E-MAIL: websterecho@citlink.net. Year Established: 1882. Pub. Frequency: w. (Wed.) Page Size: broadsheet. Subscrip. Rate: $.50 newsstand/cover; $24.91/yr mailed in county; $29.75/yr mailed out of state. Circulation: 1,800 per issue (paid). **Owner(s):** Thomas C. Clark, See address and contact information above. **Management:** Thomas C. Clark, Publisher. **Editorial:** Jean Nulter, Editor.

WELLSBURG

BROOKE COUNTY REVIEW. 319 Charles St., Wellsburg, WV 26070-1714. Telephone: 304-737-0946. FAX: 304-737-0297. E-MAIL: brookereviewnews@comcast.net. Mailing Address: PO Box 591, Wellsburg, WV 26070-0591. Year Established: 1937. Pub. Frequency: w. (Fri.) Page Size: broadsheet. Subscrip. Rate: $.55 newsstand/cover; $26/yr mailed. Adv. Rate: col. inch $4 Circulation: 2,000 per issue (paid). **Owner(s):** Brooke Publishing Inc., See address and contact information above. **Management:** J.W. George Wallace, Publisher. **Editorial:** Sandra Loar, Editor.

WEST UNION

HERALD RECORD, THE. 202 E. Main St., West Union, WV 26456. Pub. Frequency: w. (Tue.) Page Size: broadsheet. Subscrip. Rate: $.42 newsstand/cover; $18.02/yr mailed local; $19.08/yr mailed out of county; $21/yr mailed out of state. Adv. Rate: col. inch $2 Circulation: 2,900 per issue (paid). **Owner(s):** Virginia Nicholson, See address and contact information above. **Editorial:** Virginia Nicholson, Editor.

WESTON

WESTON DEMOCRAT, THE. 306 Main Ave, Weston, WV 26452. Telephone: 304-269-1600. FAX: 304-269-4035. E-MAIL: news@westondemocrat.com. URL: http://www.westondemocrat.com. Mailing Address: PO Box 968, Weston, WV 26452. Year Established: 1867. Pub. Frequency: w. (Wed.) Page Size: broadsheet. Subscrip. Rate: $.50 newsstand/cover; $18/yr in county; $23/yr out of county; $23/yr out of state. Adv. Rate: col. inch $3.90 Circulation: 8,000 per issue (paid). **Owner(s):** Robert Billeter, See address and contact information above. **Management:** Robert Billeter, Publisher. Connie Sharpe, Advertising Manager. **Editorial:** Robert Billeter, Editor.

WILLIAMSON

GILBERT TIMES, THE. 100 Block E Third Ave, Williamson, WV 25661. Telephone: 304-235-4242. FAX: 304-235-0730. Mailing Address: PO Box 1660, Williamson, WV 25661. Year Established: 1910. Pub. Frequency: w. (Wed.) Page Size: broadsheet. Subscrip. Rate: $.50 newsstand/cover; $25/yr home delivery in county; $32/yr mailed elsewhere. Circulation: 2,700 per issue (paid). **Owner(s):** Heartland Publications, LLC, 20 Research Pkwy, Ste G, Old Saybrook, CT 06475. Telephone: 860-388-3470. FAX: 860-388-3490. **Management:** D. Gaither Perry, Publisher. Renee Kessler, Advertising Manager. Chad Whitt, Circulation Manager. Kasey Baldwin, Classified Adv. Mgr.. **Editorial:** Teddy Paynter, Editor.

INDEPENDENT HERALD (WILLIAMSON), THE. 100 Block E Third Ave, Williamson, WV 25661. Telephone: 304-235-4242. FAX: 304-235-0730. URL: http://www.williamsondailynews.com. Mailing Address: PO Box 1660, Williamson, WV 25661. Year Established: 1910. Pub. Frequency: w. (Wed.) Page Size: standard. Subscrip. Rate: $.50 newsstand/cover; $25/yr home delivery in county; $32/yr mailed out of county. Circulation: 3,000 per issue (paid). **Owner(s):** Heartland Publications, LLC, 20 Research Pkwy, Ste G, Old Saybrook, CT 06475. Telephone: 860-388-3470. FAX: 860-388-3490. **Management:** D. Gaither Perry, Publisher. Renee Kessler, Advertising Manager. Chad Whitt, Circulation Manager. Kasey Baldwin, Classified Adv. Mgr.. **Editorial:** Teddy Paynter, Editor.

WISCONSIN

ABBOTSFORD

RECORD-REVIEW, THE. 103 W. Spruce St., Abbotsford, WI 54405-0677. Telephone: 715-223-2342. E-MAIL: rr@tpprinting.com. URL: http://www.centralwinews.com/recordreview. Mailing Address: P.O. Box 677, Abbotsford, WI 54405-0677. Year Established: 1964. Pub. Frequency: w. (Wed.) Page Size: tabloid. Subscrip. Rate: $1 newsstand/cover; $32/yr in state; $38/yr in WI, IA, MI, MN; $43/yr elsewhere. Adv. Rate: col. inch $9 Circulation: 2,700 per issue (paid). **Owner(s):** Carol O'Leary, See address and contact information above. **Management:** Carol O'Leary, Publisher. Jane Kroeplin, Circulation Manager. **Editorial:** Peter Weinschenk, Editor-in-Chief.

TRIBUNE-PHONOGRAPH. 103 W. Spruce St., Abbotsford, WI 54405. Telephone: 715-223-3505. FAX: 715-223-2342. E-MAIL: tp@tpprinting.com. URL: http://www.centralwinews.com/tribune. Mailing Address: P.O. Box 677, Abbotsford, WI 54405-0677. Year Established: 1964. Pub. Frequency: w. (Wed.) Page Size: tabloid. Subscrip. Rate: $1 newsstand/cover; $32/yr in state; $38/yr mailed in IL, IA, MI, MN; $43/yr elsewhere. Adv. Rate: col. inch $9 Circulation: 2,550 per issue (paid). **Owner(s):** Carol O'Leary, See address and contact information above. **Management:** Carol O'Leary, Publisher. Jane Kroeplin, Circulation Manager. **Editorial:** Todd Schmidt, Editor.

ADAMS

ADAMS COUNTY TIMES. PO Box 99, Adams, WI 53910. Telephone: 608-339-7844. FAX: 608-339-3903. E-MAIL: media@afnewspaper.com. Year Established: 1940. Pub. Frequency: w. (Wed.) Page Size: broadsheet. Subscrip. Rate: $1.50 newsstand/cover; $40/yr in county; $45/yr out of county; $53/yr mailed out of state. Circulation: 4,600 per issue (paid). **Owner(s):** News Publishing Inc., See address and contact information above. **Management:** Nancy Sorenson, General Manager. Richard A. Hannagan, Publisher. Nancy Sorenson, Business Manager.

Weeklies

AMERY

AMERY FREE PRESS. 215 S. Keller, Amery, WI 54001. Telephone: 715-268-8101. FAX: 715-268-5300. Year Established: 1889. Pub. Frequency: w. (Tue.) Page Size: broadsheet. Subscrip. Rate: $1 newsstand/cover; $30/yr in county; $35/yr out of county; $40/yr out of state. **Wire Service(s):** UPI. Circulation: 5,000 per issue (paid). **Owner(s):** Sondreal Enterprises, Inc., See address and contact information above. **Management:** Palmer Sondreal, Publisher. Pamela Humpal, Advertising Manager. **Editorial:** Palmer Sondreal, Editor. Steven R. Sondreal, Sports Editor.

ANTIGO

ANTIGO AREA SHOPPERS GUIDE. 809 Fifth Ave., Antigo, WI 54409-1938. Telephone: 715-623-5024. FAX: 715-623-5389. E-MAIL: theguide@antigoshopper.com. URL: http://www.antigoshopper.com. Year Established: 1954. Pub. Frequency: w. (Tue.) Page Size: tabloid.Adv. Rate: col. inch $7.25 Circulation: 12,969 per issue (free). **Owner(s):** Antigo Area Shoppers Guide, Inc., See address and contact information above. **Management:** Robyn Seis, General Manager. Jeanne Tatro, Advertising. Lisa Wiltse, Circulation Manager. Agnes Wiedemeier, Classified Adv. Mgr..

ARCADIA

ARCADIA NEWS-LEADER. 625 Dettloff Dr., Arcadia, WI 54612-0220. Telephone: 608-323-3366. FAX: 608-323-2185. E-MAIL: editor@arcadianewsleader.com. Mailing Address: PO Box 220, Arcadia, WI 54612-0220. Year Established: 1875. Pub. Frequency: w. (Thu.) Page Size: standard. Subscrip. Rate: $1 newsstand/cover; $30/yr in county; $34/yr in state; $43/yr out of state. Circulation: 2,500 per issue (paid). **Owner(s):** Blaschko Enterprises, See address and contact information above. **Management:** Chuck Blaschko, Publisher. **Editorial:** Jessica Shawley, Editor.

ARGYLE

PECATONICA VALLEY LEADER. 101 N. State St., Argyle, WI 53504. Telephone: 608-523-4284. FAX: 608-543-9011. Mailing Address: PO Box 116, Argyle, WI 53504. Year Established: 1888. Pub. Frequency: w. (Thu.) Page Size: tabloid. Subscrip. Rate: $.75 newsstand/cover; $25/yr mailed in state; $35/yr mailed out of state. Circulation: 1,700 per issue (paid). **Owner(s):** John P. & Thomas M. Reilly, 106 W. Merrimac St., Dodgeville, WI 53533. Telephone: 608-935-2331. **Management:** Gary McKenzie, Advertising Manager. Paula Fredrickson, Circulation Manager. **Editorial:** Gary McKenzie, Editor.

BALDWIN

BALDWIN BULLETIN. 805 Main St, P O Box 76, Baldwin, WI 54002. Telephone: 715-684-2484. E-MAIL: pehew@baldwin-telecom.net. URL: /bulletin. Year Established: 1872. Pub. Frequency: w. (Tue.) Page Size: broadsheet. Subscrip. Rate: $.75 newsstand/cover; $22/yr in county; $30/yr out of county; $36/yr out of state. Circulation: 3,000 per issue (paid). **Owner(s):** Thomas A., Peter C. & Muriel Hawley, See address and contact information above. **Management:** Peter C Hawley, President. Thomas A Hawley, Publisher. **Editorial:** Thomas A Hawley, Editor.

BALSAM LAKE

COUNTY LEDGER PRESS. 105 Main St., Balsam Lake, WI 54810. Telephone: 715-485-3121. E-MAIL: pcledger@lakeland,com. Year Established: 1898. Pub. Frequency: w. (Thu.) Page Size: broadsheet. Subscrip. Rate: $.75 newsstand/cover; $24/yr in county; $29/yr out of county. Circulation: 5,500 per issue (paid). **Owner(s):** Ledger Publications, Inc., See address and contact information above. **Management:** Thomas C. Miller, Publisher. **Editorial:** Thomas C. Miller, Editor.

BARRON

BARRON NEWS SHIELD. ISSN 0896-5560
1021 E Woodland, Barron, WI 54812. E-MAIL: newsshield@chibardun.net. URL: http://www.news-shield.com. Mailing Address: PO Box 100, Barron, WI 54812. Year Established: 1876. Pub. Frequency: w. (Wed.) Page Size: broadsheet. Subscrip. Rate: $1 newsstand/cover; $33/yr mailed in county; $34.50/yr mailed out of county; $38/yr mailed out of state. Adv. Rate: col. inch $5.75 Circulation: 4,300 per issue (paid). **Owner(s):** James Bell, See address and contact information above. **Management:** James Bell, Publisher. **Editorial:** Eric Quade, Editor.Readers: Southern Barron County

BEAVER DAM

TRI COUNTY. 805 Park Ave., Beaver Dam, WI 53916. Telephone: 920-887-0321. FAX: 920-887-8790. Mailing Address: PO Box 558, Beaver Dam, WI 53916.Pub. Frequency: w. (Wed.) Circulation: 29,000 (free). **Owner(s):** Capital Newspapers, Inc., 1901 Fish Hatchery Rd., Madison, WI 53713. **Management:** Jim Kelsh, Publisher. Scott Zeinemann, Advertising Manager. Teresa Klinger, Circulation Manager.

BELDENVILLE

HIAWATHA VALLEY SHOPPER. N6042 790th St, Beldenville, WI 54003. Telephone: 715-273-4601. FAX: 715-273-4769. E-MAIL: info@helmerprinting.com. Mailing Address: PO Box 40, Beldenville, WI 54003-0040. Year Established: 1955.Pub. Frequency: w. (Sun.) Page Size: tabloid Circulation: 60,000 Sunday (paid). **Owner(s):** Helmer Printing Co., Inc., See address and contact information above. **Management:** Milton Helmer, Publisher. Mark Helmer, Sales Manager. **Editorial:** Milton Helmer, Editor.

BELLEVILLE

BELLEVILLE RECORDER. PO Box 50, Belleville, WI 53508. Telephone: 608-424-3232. Year Established: 1866. Pub. Frequency: w. (Wed.) Page Size: tabloid. Subscrip. Rate: $.75 newsstand/cover; $30/yr in state; $38/yr mailed out of state. Circulation: 1,550 per issue (paid). **Owner(s):** Stuart M. Shapiro, See address and contact information above. **Management:** Stuart M. Shapiro, Publisher.

BERLIN

BERLIN JOURNAL. ISSN 8755-4003
301 June St., Berlin, WI 54923. Telephone: 920-361-1515. FAX: 920-361-1518. Mailing Address: PO Box 10, Berlin, WI 54923. Year Established: 1870. Pub. Frequency: w. (Thu.) Page Size: tabloid. Subscrip. Rate: $.75 newsstand/cover; $28/yr in county; $50/yr out of county; $57/yr out of state. Circulation: 3,300 per issue (paid). **Owner(s):** Ty Gonyo, See address and contact information above. **Management:** Ty Gonyo, Publisher. Kristian Troudt, Advertising Manager. **Editorial:** Jason Fox, Editor.

BILLBOARD, THE. 301 June St., Berlin, WI 54923. Telephone: 920-361-1515. FAX: 920-361-1518. Mailing Address: PO Box 10, Berlin, WI 54923. Pub. Frequency: w. (Tue.) Page Size: tabloid Circulation: 25,000 per issue (free). **Owner(s):** Ty Gonyo, See address and contact information above. **Management:** Ty Gonyo, Publisher. Kristian Troudt, Advertising Manager.

FOX LAKE REPRESENTATIVE. 301 June St., Berlin, WI 54923. Telephone: 920-361-1515. FAX: 920-361-1518. Mailing Address: PO Box 10, Berlin, WI 54923. Year Established: 1868. Pub. Frequency: w. (Thu.) Page Size: tabloid. Subscrip. Rate: $.75 newsstand/cover; $18/yr local; $34/yr in state; $47/yr out of state. Circulation: 400 per issue (paid). **Owner(s):** Ty Gonyo, See address and contact information above. **Management:** Ty Gonyo, Publisher. Kristian Troudt, Advertising Manager. **Editorial:** Jason Fox, Editor.

GREEN LAKE COUNTY REPORTER. ISSN 8755-3988
301 June St., Berlin, WI 54923. Telephone: 920-361-1515. FAX: 920-361-1518. Mailing Address: PO Box 10, Berlin, WI 54923. Year Established: 1900. Pub. Frequency: w. (Thu.) Page Size: broadsheet. Subscrip. Rate: $.75 newsstand/cover; $28/yr local; $50/yr in state; $57/yr out of state. Circulation: 1,350 per issue (paid). **Owner(s):** Ty Gonyo, See address and contact information above. **Management:** Ty Gonyo, Publisher. Kristian Troudt, Advertising Manager. **Editorial:** Jason Fox, Editor.

MARKESAN REGIONAL REPORTER. 301 June St., Berlin, WI 54923. Telephone: 920-361-1515. FAX: 920-361-1518. Mailing Address: PO Box 10, Berlin, WI 54923. Pub. Frequency: w. (Thu.) Page Size: tabloid. Subscrip. Rate: $.75 newsstand/cover; $28/yr local; $44/yr in state; $57/yr out of state. Circulation: 1,300 per issue (paid). **Owner(s):** Ty Gonyo, See address and contact information above. **Management:** Ty Gonyo, Publisher. Kristian Troudt, Advertising Manager. **Editorial:** Jason Fox, Editor.

PRINCETON TIMES-REPUBLIC. ISSN 8755-397X
301 June St., Berlin, WI 54923. Telephone: 920-361-1515. FAX: 920-361-1518. Mailing Address: PO Box 10, Berlin, WI 54923. Pub. Frequency: w. (Thu.) Page Size: tabloid. Subscrip. Rate: $.75 newsstand/cover; $28/yr in county; $50/yr in state; $57/yr out of state. Circulation: 1,475 per issue (paid). **Owner(s):** Ty Gonyo, See address and contact information above. **Management:** Ty Gonyo, Publisher. Kristian Troudt, Advertising Manager. **Editorial:** Jason Fox, Editor.

BLACK EARTH

NEWS-SICKLE ARROW. 1126 Mills St., Black Earth, WI 53515. Telephone: 608-767-3655. FAX: 608-767-2222. URL: http://www.newspubinc.com/main.asp?SectionID=6. Mailing Address: PO Box 286, Black Earth, WI 53515. Pub. Frequency: w. (Thu.) Page Size: broadsheet. Circulation: 2,800 per issue (paid and free). **Owner(s):** News Publishing Co., See address and contact information above. **Management:** Dan Witte, Publisher. Marc Mickelson, Advertising. Louise Ellis, Classified Adv. Mgr.. **Editorial:** John Donaldson, Managing Editor.

BLACK RIVER FALLS

BANNER JOURNAL. 409 E. Main St., Black River Falls, WI 54615. Telephone: 715-284-4304. FAX: 715-284-4634. URL: http://www.newspubinc.com. Year Established: 1856. Pub. Frequency: w. (Wed.) Page Size: tabloid. Subscrip. Rate: $1 newsstand/cover; $35/yr mailed in state; $48/yr mailed out of state. Freelance Pay: $0.25/column-inch. Circulation: 4,600 per issue (paid). **Owner(s):** News Publishing Co., 1126 Mills St., Black Earth, WI 53515. Telephone: 608-767-3655. FAX: 608-767-2222. **Management:** Kathy Potter, General Manager. Dan Witte, Publisher. **Editorial:** Jeanette Ruxton, Editor.

JACKSON COUNTY CHRONICLE. 35 S. First St., Black River Falls, WI 54615. Telephone: 715-284-0085. FAX: 715-284-0087. E-MAIL: news@jacksoncountychronicle.com. URL: http://www.jacksoncountychronicle.com. Year Established: 1895. Pub. Frequency: w. (Wed.) Page Size: tabloid. Subscrip. Rate: $1 newsstand/cover; $32/yr mailed in state; $43.50/yr mailed out of state. Circulation: 4,000 per issue (paid). **Owner(s):** Lee Enterprises, Inc., 215 N. Main St., Davenport, IA 52801. Telephone: 563-383-2100. **Management:** Chris Hardie, Publisher. Barb Formanek, Advertising Manager. **Editorial:** Matthew Perenchio, Editor.

BLAIR

BLAIR PRESS. 109 N. Gilbert St., Blair, WI 54616-0187. Telephone: 608-989-2531. FAX: 608-989-9615. E-MAIL: blairprs@triwest.net. Mailing Address: PO Box 187, Blair, WI 54616. Year Established: 1893. Pub. Frequency: w. (Thu.) Page Size: broadsheet. Subscrip. Rate: $.75 newsstand/cover; $26/yr in county; $31/yr out of county; $35/yr out of state. Adv. Rate: col. inch $6.53 Circulation: 1,400 per issue (paid). **Owner(s):** Lee Henschel, See address and contact information above. **Management:** Lee Henschel, Publisher.

BLOOMER

BLOOMER ADVANCE. 1210 15th Ave., Bloomer, WI 54724. Telephone: 715-568-3100. FAX: 715-568-3111. E-MAIL: badvance@bloomer.net. URL: http://www.badvance.com. Mailing Address: P.O. Box 25, Bloomer, WI 54724. Year Established: 1888. Pub. Frequency: w. (Wed.) Page Size: broadsheet. Subscrip. Rate: $.75 newsstand/cover; $24/yr in county; $26/yr out of county; $28/yr out of state. Adv. Rate: col. inch $4.76 Circulation: 3,300 per issue (paid). **Owner(s):** Mary Ann Sarno, See address and contact information above. **Management:** Mary Sarno, Publisher.

BOSCOBEL

BOSCOBEL DIAL. 901 Wisconsin Ave, Boscobel, WI 53805. Telephone: 608-375-4458. FAX: 608-375-2369. E-MAIL: dialnews@mwt.net. Year Established: 1872. Pub. Frequency: w. (Thu.) Page Size: broadsheet. Subscrip. Rate: $1 newsstand/cover; $33/yr mailed in state; $41/yr mailed out of state. Circulation: 5,800 per issue (paid). **Owner(s):** Morris Newspaper Corporation, 27 Abercorn St., Savannah, GA 31401. Telephone: 912-233-1281. FAX: 912-232-4639. **Management:** John D. Ingebritsen, Publisher. Jean Roth, Advertising Manager. **Editorial:** Charley Preusser, Editor.

BRILLION

BRILLION NEWS. ISSN 0749-7210
425 W. Ryan St., Brillion, WI 54110. Telephone: 920-756-2222. FAX: 920-756-2701. E-MAIL: kris@zanderpressinc.com. URL: http://www.thebrillionnews.com. Year Established: 1894. Pub. Frequency: w. (Wed.) Page Size: tabloid. Subscrip. Rate: $.75 newsstand/cover; $28/yr in county; $35/yr out of county. Adv. Rate: col. inch $6.73 Circulation: 2,000 per issue (paid). **Owner(s):** Zander Press, Inc., See address and contact information above. **Management:** Kris Bastian, Publisher.

BRODHEAD

INDEPENDENT-REGISTER, THE. 922 W. Exchange St., Brodhead, WI 53520. Telephone: 608-897-2193. FAX: 608-897-4137. E-MAIL: paper@indreg.com. URL: http://www.indreg.com. Mailing Address: PO Box 255, Brodhead, WI 53520. Year Established: 1861. Pub. Frequency: w. (Wed.) Page Size: tabloid. Subscrip. Rate: $.85 newsstand/cover; $28/yr in county; $30/yr in state; $37/yr out of state. Adv. Rate: col. inch $7.91 Circulation: 2,000 per issue (paid); 7,500 per issue (free). **Owner(s):** Kim Markham, See address and contact information above. **Management:** Kim Markham, Publisher. Deb Fitzgerald, Circulation Manager. Shirley Sauer, Sales Manager. **Editorial:** Gary Rosendahl, Editor.

BURLINGTON

BURLINGTON STANDARD PRESS. 700 N Pine St, Burlington, WI 53105. Telephone: 262-763-3511. FAX: 262-763-2238. E-MAIL: news@standardpress.com. URL: http://www.standardpress.com. Year Established: 1863. Pub. Frequency: w. (Thu.) Page Size: broadsheet. Subscrip. Rate: $1 newsstand/cover; $32.95/yr mailed local; $36.50/yr mailed in county; $52.50/yr mailed out of state. Circulation: 4,800 per issue (paid). **Owner(s):** Southern Lakes Newspapers LLC, 700 N Pine St, Burlington, WI 35105. Telephone: 262-763-3511. FAX: 262-763-2238. **Management:** Jack Cruger, Publisher. Karen Dubinsky, Advertising. Dee Fladwood, Advertising Director. **Editorial:** Ed Nadolski, Editor-in-Chief.

HI-LITER. 700 N Pine St, Burlington, WI 53105. FAX: 262-767-2683. Year Established: 1954. Pub. Frequency: w. (Wed.) Page Size: tabloid Circulation: 33,500 per issue (free). **Owner(s):** Southern Lakes Newspapers LLC, See address and contact information above. **Management:** Jack Cruger, Publisher. Dave Roegner, Advertising Manager.

WESTINE REPORT. ISSN 0749-6990
700 N Pine St, Burlington, WI 53105. Telephone: 262-763-2572, 262-763-3511. E-MAIL: news@waterfordpost.com. URL: http://www.westinereport.com. Year Established: 1869. Pub. Frequency: w. (Fri.) Page Size: broadsheet. Subscrip. Rate: $1 newsstand/cover; $29.50/yr mailed in county; $56 mailed for 2 yrs. in county. Adv. Rate: col. inch $9.25 Circulation: 1,750 per issue (paid). **Owner(s):** Southern Lakes Newspapers LLC, See address and contact information above. **Management:** Jack Cruger, Publisher. Dee Fladwood, Advertising Manager. **Editorial:** Christine Lupella, Editor.

CADOTT

CADOTT SENTINEL. ISSN 0885-0798
PO Box 70, Cadott, WI 54727. Telephone: 715-289-4978. Year Established: 1917. Pub. Frequency: w. (Thu.) Page Size: broadsheet. Subscrip. Rate: $1 newsstand/cover; $25/yr mailed in county; $27/yr mailed in state; $35/yr mailed out of state. Circulation: 3,200 per issue (paid). **Owner(s):** Trygg J. Hansen, See address and contact information above. **Management:** Trygg Hansen, Publisher. **Editorial:** Trygg Hansen, Editor.

CAMBRIDGE

CAMBRIDGE NEWS. ISSN 0749-7202
201 W. North St., Cambridge, WI 53523-0008. Telephone: 608-423-3213. FAX: 608-423-7802. Mailing Address: PO Box 8, Cambridge, WI 53523. Year Established: 1892. Pub. Frequency: w. (Thu.) Page Size: tabloid. Subscrip. Rate: $.75 newsstand/cover; $31/yr in county; $39/yr mailed out of county. Adv. Rate: col. inch $6.45 Circulation: 2,000 per issue (paid). **Owner(s):** Hometown News Group, PO Box 801, Fort Atkinson, WI 53538. Telephone: 920-563-5553. **Management:** Brian Knox, Publisher. Chris Klauk, Advertising Manager. Luann Niebling, Circulation Manager. **Editorial:** Amy Alder, Editor.

CAMPBELLSPORT

CAMPBELLSPORT NEWS. 101 N. Fond du Lac Ave., Campbellsport, WI 53010-0138. Telephone: 920-533-8338. FAX: 920-533-5579. E-MAIL: cnnews@charterandnet.com. Mailing Address: PO Box 138, Campbellsport, WI 53010-0138. Year Established: 1899. Pub. Frequency: w. (Thu.) Page Size: tabloid. Subscrip. Rate: $.75 newsstand/cover; $32/yr in county; $34/yr mailed out of county; $38/yr mailed out of state. Circulation: 2,300 per issue (paid). **Owner(s):** Andrew Johnson, PO Box 138, Campbellsport, WI 53010. Telephone: 920-533-8338. **Management:** Andrew Johnson, Publisher. **Editorial:** Andrea Hanson Abler, Managing Editor.

CASHTON

CASHTON RECORD. 713 Broadway, Cashton, WI 54619-0100. Telephone: 608-654-7330. FAX: 608-654-7324. E-MAIL: cashtonrecord@centurytel.net. Year Established: 1896. Pub. Frequency: w. (Wed.) Page Size: tabloid. Subscrip. Rate: $.75 newsstand/cover; $23/yr local; $35/yr mailed out of state. Circulation: 1,600 per issue (paid and free). **Owner(s):** Paul Fanning, PO Box 100, Cashton, WI 54619. Telephone: 608-654-7330. FAX: 608-654-7324. **Management:** Paul Fanning, President. Kay Fossum, Advertising Manager. **Editorial:** Kim Fanning, Editor.

CEDARBURG

NEWS GRAPHIC (CEDARBURG). N19 W6733 Commerce Ct, Cedarburg, WI 53012. Telephone: 262-375-5100. FAX: 262-375-5107. E-MAIL: mschroeder@conleynet.com. URL: http://www.gmtoday.com. Mailing Address: PO Box 47, Cedarburg, WI 53012-0047. Year Established: 1883. Pub. Frequency: s-w. (Mon. & Thu.) Page Size: broadsheet. Subscrip. Rate: $.75 newsstand/cover; $36.99/yr mailed in county; $48/yr mailed out of county; $58/yr mailed out of state. Circulation: 10,000 per issue (paid). **Owner(s):** Conley Publishing Group, Ltd., 119 Monroe St., Beaver Dam, WI 53916. Telephone: 920-885-7800. **Management:** Phil Paige, Publisher. Heather Rogge, Advertising Manager. **Editorial:** Jan Rockley, Managing Editor. Mark Eldridge, Sports Editor.

OZAUKEE GUIDE. N19 W6733 Commerce Ct, Cedarburg, WI 53012. Telephone: 262-375-5100. FAX: 262-375-5107. Mailing Address: PO Box 47, Cedarburg, WI 53012-0047. Pub. Frequency: w. (Wed.) Page Size: tabloid Circulation: 29,000 per issue (free). **Owner(s):** Conley Publishing Group, Ltd., 119 Monroe St., Beaver Dam, WI 53916. Telephone: 920-885-7800. **Management:** Phil Paige, Publisher. Heather Rogge, Advertising Manager. **Editorial:** Kollin Kawinski, Managing Editor.

CHETEK

CHETEK ALERT, THE. 312 Knapp St., Chetek, WI 54728. Telephone: 715-924-4118. FAX: 715-924-4122. E-MAIL: chetekalert@citypapers.com. URL: http://www.chetekalert.com. Mailing Address: PO Box 5, Chetek, WI 54728. Year Established: 1882. Pub. Frequency: w. (Wed.) Page Size: broadsheet. Subscrip. Rate: $.75 newsstand/cover; $27/yr in county; $30/yr out of county; $36/yr out of state. Circulation: 3,600 per issue (paid). **Owner(s):** Melodee A. Eckerman, See address and contact information above. **Management:** Melodee A. Eckerman, Publisher. **Editorial:** Shane Samuels, Editor.

CHILTON

CHILTON TIMES-JOURNAL. 19 E. Main St., Chilton, WI 53014. Telephone: 920-849-7036. FAX: 920-849-4651. E-MAIL: calumetadvertiser@charter.net. URL: http://www.chiltontimesjournal.com. Year Established: 1857. Pub. Frequency: w. (Thu.) Page Size: tabloid. Subscrip. Rate: $.75 newsstand/cover; $36.40/yr in county; $49.40/yr out of county. Freelance Pay: $0.35/column-inch. Circulation: 5,000 per issue (paid). **Owner(s):** James Moran, See address and contact information above. **Management:** James Moran, Publisher. Amanda VanGompel, Circulation Manager. **Editorial:** James Lawrence, Editor.

CLINTON

CLINTON TOPPER, THE. 407 Church St., Clinton, WI 53525-0443. Telephone: 608-676-4111. FAX: 608-676-4664. E-MAIL: clintontopper1@aol.com. Mailing Address: PO Box 443, Clinton, WI 53525-0443. Year Established: 1938. Pub. Frequency: w. (Thu.) Page Size: tabloid. Subscrip. Rate: $.60 newsstand/cover; $26.95/yr local; $33.25/yr elsewhere. Adv. Rate: col. inch $7.30 Circulation: 1,500 per issue (paid). **Owner(s):** Rock Valley Publishing LLC, 11512 N. Second St., Machesney Park, IL 61115. Telephone: 815-877-4044. FAX: 815-654-4857. **Management:** Randy Johnson, General Manager. Jack Cruger, Publisher. Celeste Thompson, Advertising. Lindy Sweet, Circulation Manager.

SHARON REPORTER, THE. 407 Church St., Clinton, WI 53525-0443. Telephone: 608-676-4111. FAX: 608-676-4664. Mailing Address: PO Box 443, Clinton, WI 53525-0443. Year Established: 1878. Pub. Frequency: w. (Wed.) Page Size: broadsheet. Subscrip. Rate: $.60 newsstand/cover; $27/yr mailed in county; $30/yr mailed out of county. Circulation: 850 per issue (paid). **Owner(s):** Rock Valley Publishing LLC, 11512 N. Second St., Machesney Park, IL 61115. Telephone: 815-877-4044. **Management:** Randy Johnson, General Manager. Jack Cruger, Publisher. Celeste Thompson, Advertising. Lindi Sweet, Circulation Manager.

CLINTONVILLE

CLINTONVILLE TRIBUNE-GAZETTE. ISSN 0749-7024
13 11th St, Clintonville, WI 54929. Telephone: 715-823-3151. FAX: 715-823-7479. Mailing Address: PO Box 270, Clintonville, WI 54929-0270. Year Established: 1881. Pub. Frequency: w. (Thu.) Page Size: broadsheet. Subscrip. Rate: $1 newsstand/cover; $35/yr mailed in county; $41/yr mailed out of county. Adv. Rate: col. inch $5.75 Circulation: 3,450 per issue (paid). **Owner(s):** GateHouse Media, Inc, 350 WillowBrook Office Park, Fairport, NY 14450. Telephone: 585-598-0030. FAX: 585-248-2631. **Management:** Jeff Hoffman, Publisher. **Editorial:** Nancy Weineke, Editor.

COCHRANE

BUFFALO COUNTY JOURNAL. 104 E. Fifth St., Cochrane, WI 54622. Telephone: 608-248-2451. FAX: 608-248-2422. Mailing Address: PO Box 40, Cochrane, WI 54622-0040. Year Established: 1861. Pub. Frequency: w. (Thu.) Page Size: tabloid. Subscrip. Rate: $.75 newsstand/cover; $29/yr in county & adj. cys.; $34/yr out of area; $42/yr mailed out of state. Adv. Rate: col. inch $4.60 Circulation: 875 per issue (paid). **Owner(s):** Valley Publications, PO Box 109, Wabasha, MN 55981. Telephone: 612-565-3368. **Management:** Gary Stumpf, Publisher. Faith McFarlin, Advertising Manager. **Editorial:** Faith McFarlin, Managing Editor.

COCHRANE-FOUNTAIN CITY RECORDER. 104 E. Fifth St., Cochrane, WI 54622. Telephone: 608-248-2451. FAX: 608-248-2422. Mailing Address: PO Box 40, Cochrane, WI 54622-0040. Pub. Frequency: w. (Thu.) Page Size: broadsheet. Subscrip. Rate: $.75 newsstand/cover; $28/yr in county & adj. cys.; $32/yr out of area; $41/yr out of state. Adv. Rate: col. inch $4.60 Circulation: 2,000 per issue (paid). **Owner(s):** Valley Publications, PO Box 109, Wabasha, MN 55981. Telephone: 612-565-3368. **Management:** Gary Stumpf, Publisher. Faith McFarlin, Advertising Manager. **Editorial:** Faith McFarlin, Managing Editor.

COLFAX

COLFAX MESSENGER. PO Box 517, Colfax, WI 54730-0517. Telephone: 715-962-3535. FAX: 715-962-3413. Year Established: 1897. Pub. Frequency: w. (Wed.) Page Size: broadsheet. Subscrip. Rate: $.75 newsstand/cover; $25/yr mailed in county; $30/yr out of county. Circulation: 1,250 per issue (paid). **Owner(s):** Carlton DeWitt, See address and contact information above. **Management:** Carlton DeWitt, Publisher. **Editorial:** Marlin Raveling, Editor.

COLUMBUS

COLUMBUS JOURNAL. 101 S. Ludington St., Columbus, WI 53925. Telephone: 920-623-3160. FAX: 920-623-9383. Mailing Address: PO Box 188, Columbus, WI 53925. Year Established: 1861. Pub. Frequency: w. (Sat.) Page Size: tabloid. Subscrip. Rate: $1/yr newsstand/cover; $46.80/yr mailed in state & elsewhere. **Wire Service(s):** AP. Circulation: 2,000 per issue (paid). **Owner(s):** Capital Newspapers, Inc., 1901 Fish Hatchery Rd, Madison, WI 53713. Telephone: 608-252-6200. **Management:** Jim Kelsh, Publisher. **Editorial:** Paul Scharf, Editor.

CORNELL

CORNELL & LAKE HOLCOMBE COURIER. ISSN 0885-078X
121 Main St., Cornell, WI 54732. Telephone: 715-239-6688. FAX: 715-239-6200. E-MAIL: cornellcourier@centurytel.net. Mailing Address: PO Box 546, Cornell, WI 54732. Year Established: 1915. Pub. Frequency: w. (Thu.) Page Size: broadsheet. Subscrip. Rate: $1 newsstand/cover; $30/yr local; $33/yr in state; $40/yr out of state. Circulation: 3,200 per issue (paid). **Owner(s):** Trygg J. Hansen, PO Box 546, Cornell, WI 54732-0546. Telephone: 715-239-6688. FAX: 715-239-6200. **Management:** Trygg J. Hansen, Publisher. **Editorial:** Trygg Hansen, Editor.

COTTAGE GROVE

HERALD-INDEPENDENT, THE. ISSN 0745-6646
202 W. Cottage Grove Rd., Ste. D, Cottage Grove, WI 53527. Telephone: 608-839-1544. FAX: 608-839-8750. E-MAIL: herald-independent@hometownnewsgroup.com. Year Established: 1968. Pub. Frequency: w. (Thu.) Page Size: tabloid.Subscrip. Rate: $.75 newsstand/cover; $32/yr Circulation: 2,200 per issue (paid). **Owner(s):** Hometown News Group, 207 E. Main St., Sun Prairie, WI 53590. Telephone: 608-837-2521. **Management:** Brian Knox, Publisher. Mike Wilson, Advertising Manager. Luann Niebling, Circulation Manager. **Editorial:** Adam Mella, Editor.

CRANDON

FOREST REPUBLICAN, THE. PO Box 367, Crandon, WI 54520. Telephone: 715-478-3315. E-MAIL: frnews@charter.net. URL: http://www.forestrepublican.com. Year Established: 1885. Pub. Frequency: w. (Wed.) Page Size: broadsheet. Subscrip. Rate: $.75 newsstand/cover; $22.50/yr in county; $24.50/yr mailed out of county; $27.50/yr mailed out of state. Circulation: 3,900 per issue (paid). **Owner(s):** Lee Enterprises, Inc., 201 N. Harrison St, Ste 600, Davenport, IA 52801-1924. **Management:** Jay Anderle, Publisher. **Editorial:** Dean Acheson, Managing Editor.

CUBA CITY

TRI-COUNTY PRESS (CUBA CITY). 223 S Main St, Cuba City, WI 53807. E-MAIL: tcpnews@yousq.net. Year Established: 1894. Pub. Frequency: w. (Thu.) Page Size: tabloid. Subscrip. Rate: $1 newsstand/cover; $29/yr mailed in state; $34/yr mailed out of state Ia.& IL.; $42/yr mailed elsewhere. Circulation: 2,600 per issue (paid). **Owner(s):** Morris Newspaper Corporation, 27 Abercorn St., Savannah, GA 31401. **Management:** John D. Ingebritsen, Publisher. Jamie Ruehle, Office Manager. Brian Muldoon, Advertising Manager. **Editorial:** Stephanie Schroeder, Editor.

CUMBERLAND

CUMBERLAND ADVOCATE. 1375 Second Ave., Cumberland, WI 54829. Telephone: 715-822-4469. FAX: 715-822-4451. E-MAIL: news@cumberland-advocate.com. URL: http://www.cumberland-advocate.com. Mailing Address: PO Box 637, Cumberland, WI 54829. Year Established: 1881. Pub. Frequency: w. (Wed.) Page Size: broadsheet. Subscrip. Rate: $.75 newsstand/cover; $30/yr local; $33/yr elsewhere. Adv. Rate: col. inch $5.25 Circulation: 3,000 per issue (paid). **Owner(s):** Jackson County Publications, Inc., See address and contact information above. **Management:** Paul Bucher, Publisher. **Editorial:** Paul Bucher, Editor.

DARLINGTON

REPUBLICAN JOURNAL (DARLINGTON). 316 Main St, Darlington, WI 53530. Telephone: 608-776-4425. FAX: 608-776-4301. E-MAIL: repjournal@yahoo.com. URL: http://www.rjnews.com. Year Established: 1862. Pub. Frequency: w. (Thu.) Page Size: tabloid. Subscrip. Rate: $1 newsstand/cover; $37/yr in county & adj. cys.; $44/yr out of area. Adv. Rate: col. inch $5.30 Circulation: 3,600 per issue (paid). **Owner(s):** Morris Newspaper Corporation, 27 Abercorn St., Savannah, GA 31401. Telephone: 912-233-1281. FAX: 912-232-4639. **Management:** Brian Lund, Publisher. Marilyn Johns, Advertising. Emily Massingill, Circulation Manager. **Editorial:** Hillary Dickerson, Managing Editor.

DE PERE

DE PERE JOURNAL. ISSN 0748-6219
126 S. Broadway, De Pere, WI 54115-5066. Telephone: 920-336-4221. E-MAIL: info@deperejournal.com. URL: http://www.deperejournal.com. Mailing Address: P.O. Box 5066, De Pere, WI 54115-5066. Year Established: 1871. Pub. Frequency: w. (Thu.) Page Size: broadsheet. Subscrip. Rate: $.50 newsstand/cover; $22/yr mailed. Adv. Rate: col. inch $7.90 Circulation: 3,700 per issue (paid). **Owner(s):** Metropolitan Newspaper Corp., PO Box 2467, Green Bay, WI 54306. Telephone: 920-432-2941. **Management:** Jeanette Gerke, General Manager. Frank Wood Jr., Publisher. **Editorial:** Patti Zarling, Editor.

DEERFIELD

INDEPENDENT (DEERFIELD). 23 N. Main St., Deerfield, WI 53531. Telephone: 608-764-5515. FAX: 608-764-8214. Mailing Address: P.O. Box 27, Deerfield, WI 53531. Year Established: 1885. Pub. Frequency: w. (Thu.) Page Size: broadsheet. Subscrip. Rate: $.75 newsstand/cover; $31/yr in county; $41/yr out of county. Freelance Pay: $0.20/column-inch. Circulation: 1,850 per issue (paid). **Owner(s):** Hometown News Group, 28 Milwaukee Ave., W., Fort Atkinson, WI 53538. Telephone: 920-563-5551. **Management:** Brian Knox, Publisher. Mike Wilson, Advertising Manager. Luann Niebling, Circulation Manager. **Editorial:** Amy Alder, Editor.

DEFOREST

DEFOREST TIMES-TRIBUNE. 406 N. Main St., DeForest, WI 53532. Telephone: 608-846-5576. FAX: 608-846-5757. E-MAIL: news@deforestimes.com. Year Established: 1895. Pub. Frequency: w. (Thu.) Page Size: broadsheet. Subscrip. Rate: $1 newsstand/cover; $26/yr mailed in county; $29.50/yr mailed in state. Circulation: 2,300 per issue (paid). **Owner(s):** Arthur M. Drake, See address and contact information above. **Management:** Arthur Drake, Publisher. Richard Emerson, Advertising Manager.

DELAVAN

DELAVAN ENTERPRISE, THE. 621 E Geneva St, Delavan, WI 53115. Telephone: 262-728-6316. FAX: 262-728-0449. URL: http://www.delavanenterprise.com. Year Established: 1979. Pub. Frequency: w. (Thu.) Page Size: broadsheet. Subscrip. Rate: $1 newsstand/cover; $32.95/yr mailed in county; $36/yr mailed out of county; $42/yr mailed out of state. Circulation: 4,000 per issue (paid). **Owner(s):** Southern Lakes Newspapers LLC, 700 N Pine St, Burlington, WI 530105. Telephone: 262-763-3511. **Management:** Ed Nadolski, Publisher. **Editorial:** Tom Aiello, Editor. Ed Nadolski, Editor-in-Chief.

WEEK, THE. 1436 Mound Rd., Delavan, WI 53115. Telephone: 262-728-5505. FAX: 262-728-5706. E-MAIL: theweek@theweekextra.com. Mailing Address: PO Box 366, Delavan, WI 53115-0366. Year Established: 1979. Pub. Frequency: s-w. (Sun & Thu.) Page Size: broadsheet.Adv. Rate: col. inch $24 Circulation: 33,500 Sunday (free); 15,000 per issue (free). **Owner(s):** Bliss Communications, One S. Parker Dr., Janesville, WI 53545. Telephone: 800-236-0852. **Management:** John Halverson, Publisher. Phil Bonyata, Circulation Manager. Patricia Bladow, Marketing Director.

DENMARK

DENMARK PRESS. 138 Main St., Denmark, WI 54208. Telephone: 920-863-2154. FAX: 920-863-6102. Mailing Address: PO Box 610, Denmark, WI 54208. Year Established: 1883. Pub. Frequency: w. (Thu.) Page Size: broadsheet. Subscrip. Rate: $.50 newsstand/cover; $25/yr in adj. cys.; $29/yr in state; $33/yr out of state. Circulation: 2,700 per issue (paid). **Owner(s):** Frank Wood, See address and contact information above. **Management:** Patti Rasmussen, General Manager. Cat Mueller, Advertising. **Editorial:** Patti Rasmussen, Editor.

DODGEVILLE

DODGEVILLE CHRONICLE, THE. 106 W. Merrimac St., Dodgeville, WI 53533. Telephone: 608-935-2331. FAX: 608-935-9531. Year Established: 1862. Pub. Frequency: w. (Thu.) Page Size: broadsheet. Subscrip. Rate: $1 newsstand/cover per issue; $35/yr mailed in state. Adv. Rate: col. inch $8.05 Circulation: 5,600 evening (paid). **Owner(s):** Dodgeville Chronicle Inc., See address and contact information above. **Management:** Pat Reilly, Publisher. Todd Novak, Advertising Manager. **Editorial:** Pat Reilly, Editor. Mike Reilly, News.

DURAND

COURIER-WEDGE. 103 W. Main St., Durand, WI 54736. Telephone: 715-672-4252. FAX: 715-672-4254. Year Established: 1861. Pub. Frequency: w. (Thu.) Page Size: broadsheet. Subscrip. Rate: $.75 newsstand/cover; $28/yr in county; $33/yr out of county. Circulation: 4,300 per issue (paid). **Owner(s):** Gary, Michael & Dan Stumpf, 200 Industrial Ct., Wabasha, MN 55981. **Management:** Michael Stumpf, President. Gary Stumpf, Publisher. **Editorial:** Deb Claxton, Editor.

EAGLE RIVER

VILAS COUNTY NEWS-REVIEW. 425 W Mill St, Eagle River, WI 54521. E-MAIL: erpub@nnex.net. URL: http://www.vilascountynewsreview.com. Mailing Address: PO Box 1929, Eagle River, WI 54521-1929. Year Established: 1886. Pub. Frequency: w. (Wed.) Page Size: broadsheet. Subscrip. Rate: $1.25 newsstand/cover; $50/yr local; $57/yr in state; $68/yr out of state. Adv. Rate: col. inch $11 Circulation: 10,250 per issue (paid). **Owner(s):** Delphos Newspapers, 405 N. Main St., Delphos, OH 45833. Telephone: 419-692-5050. **Management:** Byron McNutt, Publisher. **Editorial:** Kurt Krueger, Editor.

EAST TROY

EAST TROY NEWS. ISSN 0749-5943
2100 Church St., East Troy, WI 53120. Telephone: 262-642-7451. FAX: 262-642-5934. E-MAIL: ed@easttroynews.com. URL: http://www.easttroynews.com/. Year Established: 1893. Pub. Frequency: w. (Thu.) Page Size: broadsheet. Subscrip. Rate: $.75 newsstand/cover; $29.50/yr. Adv. Rate: col. inch $9.25 Circulation: 2,600. **Owner(s):** Southern Lakes Newspapers LLC, 700 N Pine St, Burlington, WI 53105. **Management:** Jack Cruger, Publisher. Dee Fladwood, Advertising Manager. **Editorial:** Kurt Killberg, Editor. Steve Kilpin, Sports.

EDGERTON

EDGERTON REPORTER. 21 N. Henry St., Edgerton, WI 53534. Telephone: 608-884-3367. FAX: 608-884-8187. E-MAIL: deverson@directionspub.com. Year Established: 1878. Pub. Frequency: w. (Wed.) Page Size: broadsheet. Subscrip. Rate: $.80 newsstand/cover; $30/yr in city; $32/yr in state; $34/yr out of state. Adv. Rate: col. inch $8.56 Circulation: 3,812 per issue (paid). **Owner(s):** Reporter Co., Inc., The, See address and contact information above. **Management:** Diane Everson, Publisher. Dave Fitzgerald, Marketing Director. **Editorial:** Helen Everson, Editor.

ELKHORN

ELKHORN INDEPENDENT. ISSN 1076-4569
11 W. Walworth St., Elkhorn, WI 53121. Telephone: 262-723-2250. FAX: 262-723-7424. E-MAIL: elkinde@elkhornindependent.com. URL: http://www.elkhornindependent.com. Year Established: 1853. Pub. Frequency: w. (Thu.) Page Size: broadsheet. Subscrip. Rate: $1 newsstand/cover; $29.50/yr mailed in county. Freelance Pay: $25/article. Circulation: 2,500 per issue (controlled and free). **Owner(s):** Southern Lakes Newspapers LLC, 700 N Pine St, Burlington, WI 53105. **Management:** Jack Cruger, Publisher. Dee Fladwood, Advertising Manager. **Editorial:** Lucas Lauderback, Editor. Ed Nadolski, Editor-in-Chief.

ELLSWORTH

PIERCE COUNTY HERALD. 126 S. Chestnut St., Ellsworth, WI 54011. Telephone: 715-273-4334. FAX: 715-273-4335. E-MAIL: pch@rivertowns.net. URL: http://www.rivertowns.net. Year Established: 1867. Pub. Frequency: w. (Wed.) Page Size: standard. Subscrip. Rate: $1.25 newsstand/cover; $35/yr home delivery in county; $50/yr mailed out of county. Adv. Rate: col. inch $7.15 Circulation: 4,700 per issue (paid). **Owner(s):** Jeff Meyer, 101 Fifth St., N., Fargo, ND 58102. Telephone: 701-235-7311. **Management:** Al Schmid, General Manager. Steve Dzubay, Publisher. Robin Kruse, Advertising Manager. Maggie Hall, Circulation Manager. **Editorial:** Bill Kirk, Editor. Sean Scallon, Sports Editor.

FENNIMORE

FENNIMORE TIMES. 1150 Lincoln Ave, PO Box 177, Fennimore, WI 53809. Telephone: 608-822-3912. FAX: 608-822-3916. E-MAIL: fennimoretimes@mail.tds.net. Year Established: 1889. Pub. Frequency: w. (Thu.) Page Size: broadsheet. Subscrip. Rate: $1 newsstand/cover; $26/yr in county; $32/yr mailed out of county; $41/yr mailed out of state. Circulation: 1,800 per issue (paid). **Owner(s):** Morris Newspaper Corporation, 27 Abercorn St., Savannah, GA 31401. Telephone: 912-233-1281. FAX: 912-232-4639. **Management:** John D. Ingebritsen, Publisher. Judi Nelson, Circulation Manager. **Editorial:** Correne Morgan, Editor.

FLORENCE

FLORENCE MINING NEWS. PO Box 79, Florence, WI 54121. Telephone: 715-528-3276. FAX: 715-528-5676. E-MAIL: upnorth2@borderlandnet.net. URL: http://www.wildriversnews.com. Year Established: 1881. Pub. Frequency: w. (Wed.) Page Size: tabloid. Subscrip. Rate: $1 newsstand/cover; $30/yr mailed in county; $35/yr mailed & adj. counties; $41/yr mailed elsewhere. Adv. Rate: col. inch $4.35 Circulation: 1,808 per issue (paid). **Owner(s):** Borderland Publishing, Inc., 640 Central Ave., Florence, WI 54121. **Management:** Hank Murphy, Publisher. **Editorial:** Hank Murphy, Editor.

FOND DU LAC

ACTION PUBLICATIONS. N6637 Rolling Meadows Dr., Fond Du Lac, WI 54936. Telephone: 920-922-8640. FAX: 920-922-0125. E-MAIL: classified@actionadvertiser.com. URL: http://www.actiononline.net. Year Established: 1970. Pub. Frequency: s-w. (Wed. & Sun.) Page Size: tabloid.Subscrip. Rate: $168/yr mailed out of area Circulation: 46,725 Sunday (free); 34,435 per issue (free). **Owner(s):** Gannett Company, Inc., 7950 Jones Branch Dr, McLean, VA 22107. **Management:** Bill Hackney, Publisher. Joe Bembnister, Advertising Manager. Gail Blavat, Circulation Manager. **Editorial:** Scott Witchow, Editor.

FREDERIC

INDIANHEAD ADVERTISER. 303 N. Wisconsin Ave., Frederic, WI 54837. E-MAIL: addept@centurytel.net. Mailing Address: P.O. Box 490, Frederic, WI 54837. Year Established: 1970. Pub. Frequency: w. (Mon.) Page Size: tabloid.Adv. Rate: col. inch $5.60 Circulation: 19,420 per issue (free). **Owner(s):** Inter-County Cooperative Publishing Association, See address and contact information above. **Management:** Doug Panek, General Manager. Carolyn Foltz, Circulation Manager.

INTER-COUNTY LEADER. 303 N. Wisconsin Ave., Frederic, WI 54837. Telephone: 715-327-4236. FAX: 715-327-4870. E-MAIL: the-leader@centurytel.net. URL: http://www.the-leader.net. Mailing Address: P.O. Box 490, Frederic, WI 54837. Year Established: 1933. Pub. Frequency: w. (Wed.) Page Size: tabloid. Subscrip. Rate: $1 newsstand/cover; $29/yr in Polk & Burnett cys.; $33/yr in adj. cys.; $36/yr elsewhere. Circulation: 7,500 per issue (paid). **Owner(s):** Inter-County Cooperative Publishing Association, See address and contact information above. **Management:** Doug Panek, General Manager. **Editorial:** Gary King, Editor.

GALESVILLE

GALESVILLE REPUBLICAN. 19852 Court Ave., Galesville, WI 54630-0695. Telephone: 608-582-2330. E-MAIL: news@galerep.com. URL: http://www.galerep.com. Year Established: 1874. Pub. Frequency: w. (Wed.) Page Size: tabloid. Subscrip. Rate: $.50 newsstand/cover; $26/yr in county; $31/yr out of county; $41/yr out of state. Circulation: 1,875 per issue (paid). **Owner(s):** John Graf, See address and contact information above. **Management:** John Graf, Publisher. **Editorial:** Rose Eddy, Editor.

GAYS MILLS

CRAWFORD COUNTY INDEPENDENT-KICKAPOO SCOUT. 320 Main St., Gays Mills, WI 54631. Telephone: 608-735-4413. FAX: 608-735-4419. E-MAIL: dialnews@mwt.net. Mailing Address: P.O. Box 188, Gays Mills, WI 54631. Year Established: 1970. Pub. Frequency: w. (Thu.) Page Size: broadsheet. Subscrip. Rate: $.75 newsstand/cover; $28/yr mailed in state; $33/yr mailed out of state. Circulation: 2,000 per issue (paid). **Owner(s):** Morris Newspaper Corporation, 27 Abercorn St., Savannah, GA 31401. Telephone: 912-233-1281. FAX: 912-232-4639. **Management:** Jean Roth, General Manager. Bonnie Olson, Advertising Manager. **Editorial:** Charley Preusser, Editor.

GERMANTOWN

EXPRESS NEWS. W130 N 10437 Washington Dr, Germantown, WI 53022. Telephone: 262-238-6397. FAX: 262-242-9450. E-MAIL: advertising@discoverhometown.com. URL: http://www.discoverhometown.com. Year Established: 1994. Pub. Frequency: w. (Tue.) Page Size: tabloid Circulation: 200,000 per issue (free). **Owner(s):** Hometown Publications, See address and contact information above. **Management:** Ken Ubert, Publisher. Rob Ubert, Advertising Manager. **Editorial:** Jeff Jones, Editor.

GLENWOOD CITY

TRIBUNE PRESS REPORTER. 105 Misty Ct., Glenwood City, WI 54013-0038. Telephone: 715-265-4646. FAX: 715-265-7496. E-MAIL: tribune@dewittmedia.com. Mailing Address: PO Box 38, Glenwood City, WI 54013. Year Established: 1889. Pub. Frequency: w. (Wed.) Page Size: broadsheet. Subscrip. Rate: $1 newsstand/cover; $30/yr local; $35/yr mailed in state; $40/yr mailed out of state. Circulation: 2,800 per issue (paid). **Owner(s):** Carlton DeWitt, See address and contact information above. **Management:** Carlton DeWitt, Publisher. Shawn DeWitt, Advertising Manager.

GLIDDEN

GLIDDEN ENTERPRISE. 342 Grant St, Glidden, WI 54527. Telephone: 715-264-3481. Mailing Address: PO Box 128, Glidden, WI 54527. Year Established: 1906. Pub. Frequency: w. (Wed.) Page Size: broadsheet. Subscrip. Rate: $.50 newsstand/cover; $24/yr mailed in county; $26/yr mailed out of county. Circulation: 1,450 per issue (paid). **Owner(s):** Glidden Enterprises, Inc., See address and contact information above. **Management:** Robert Hart, Publisher. **Editorial:** Robert Hart, Editor.

GRANTSBURG

BURNETT COUNTY SENTINEL. 114 Madison Ave., Grantsburg, WI 54840-0397. Telephone: 715-463-2341. FAX: 715-463-5138. E-MAIL: byron@burnettcountysentel.com. URL: http://www.burnettcountysentinel.com. Mailing Address: PO Box 397, Grantsburg, WI 54840-0397. Year Established: 1962. Pub. Frequency: w. (Wed.) Page Size: broadsheet. Subscrip. Rate: $1 newsstand/cover; $34/yr local; $40/yr mailed out of area. Adv. Rate: col. inch $6.30 **Wire Service(s):** AP. Circulation: 4,000 per issue (paid). **Owner(s):** Sentinel Publications, Inc., 114 Madison Ave., Grantsburg, WI 54840. Telephone: 715-463-2341. **Management:** Eugene Johnson, President. Byron Higgin, Publisher. Delene Berger, Office Manager. Sandy Eng, Advertising Manager. **Editorial:** Byron Higgin, Editor.

HAMMOND

CENTRAL SAINT CROIX NEWS. 815 Davis St., Hammond, WI 54015. Telephone: 715-796-2356. FAX: 715-796-2355. E-MAIL: cscnaog@win.bright.net. Mailing Address: PO Box 208, Hammond, WI 54015. Year Established: 1873. Pub. Frequency: w. (Thu.) Page Size: broadsheet. Subscrip. Rate: $.75 newsstand/cover; $20/yr in county; $23/yr out of county. Freelance Pay: $15/story. Circulation: 1,215 per issue (paid). **Owner(s):** Michelle Calcagno, See address and contact information above. **Management:** Michelle Calcagno, Publisher. **Editorial:** Michelle Calcagno, Editor.

HARTFORD

TIMES PRESS. 55 E. Sumner, Hartford, WI 53027. Telephone: 262-670-1500. FAX: 262-670-6689. E-MAIL: timespress@conleynet.com. URL: http://www.gmtoday.com. Year Established: 1876. Pub. Frequency: w. (Thu.) Page Size: tabloid. Subscrip. Rate: $.50 newsstand/cover; $20/yr home delivery in county; $27/yr mailed out of county; $31/yr mailed out of state. Circulation: 5,300 per issue (paid). **Owner(s):** Conley Publishing Group, Ltd., 119 Monroe St., Beaver Dam, WI 53916. Telephone: 920-885-7800. **Management:** Steve Ciccantelli, Publisher. Mary Meyer, Advertising Manager. Kim Dietrick, Circulation Manager. Kristi Wolf, Classified Adv. Mgr.. **Editorial:** Phil Hermann, Editor.

HARTLAND

KETTLE MORAINE INDEX. 440 Cardinal Ln., Hartland, WI 53029. Telephone: 262-367-3272. FAX: 262-367-7414. E-MAIL: kmindex@jcpgroup.com. URL: http://www.kmindex.com. Mailing Address: PO Box 200, Hartland, WI 53029. Year Established: 1942. Pub. Frequency: w. (Thu.) Page Size: tabloid. Subscrip. Rate: $.50 newsstand/cover; $23.70/yr in county; $29/yr out of county; $46.45/yr out of state. Circulation: 2,228 per issue (paid). **Owner(s):** Journal Community Publishing Group, 600 Industrial Dr., PO Box 609, Waupaca, WI 54981. Telephone: 715-258-8450. **Management:** Gary J. Jasiek, Publisher. Lori Marchek, Advertising Manager. **Editorial:** Erin Mellone, Editor.

LAKE COUNTRY REPORTER. 440 Cardinal Ln., Hartland, WI 53029. Telephone: 262-367-3272. FAX: 262-367-7414. E-MAIL: lakenews@jcpgroup.com. URL: http://www.thelakecountryreporter.com. Mailing Address: PO Box 200, Hartland, WI 53029. Year Established: 1954. Pub. Frequency: s-w. (Tue. & Thu.) Page Size: tabloid. Subscrip. Rate: $.50 newsstand/cover; $35/yr in county; $43.95/yr out of county; $82.85/yr out of state. Adv. Rate: col. inch $17.49 Circulation: 8,949 per issue (paid). **Owner(s):** Journal Community Publishing Group, 600 Industrial Dr., PO Box 609, Waupaca, WI 54981. Telephone: 715-258-8450. **Management:** Gary J. Jasiek, General Manager. Alan Chang, Circulation Manager. Lori Marchek, Sales Manager. **Editorial:** Scott Peterson, Editor. Erin Mellone, Reporter.

SUSSEX SUN. ISSN 1064-2102
440 Cardinal Ln., Hartland, WI 53029. Telephone: 414-367-3272. FAX: 414-367-7414. E-MAIL: lakenews@add-inc.com. URL: http://www.sussexsun.com. Mailing Address: PO Box 200, Hartland, WI 53029. Year Established: 1963. Pub. Frequency: w. (Tue.) Page Size: tabloid. Subscrip. Rate: $.50 newsstand/cover; $23.70/yr in county; $29/yr out of county; $46.45/yr out of state. Circulation: 2,949 per issue (paid). **Owner(s):** Journal Community Publishing Group, 600 Industrial Dr., PO Box 609, Waupaca, WI 54981. Telephone: 715-258-8450. **Management:** Gary J. Jasiek, Publisher. Lori Marchek, Advertising Manager. **Editorial:** Scott Peterson, Managing Editor.

HAYWARD

SAWYER COUNTY RECORD. 15617-B Hwy. 63 N., Hayward, WI 54843. Telephone: 715-634-4881. FAX: 715-634-8191. E-MAIL: scrnews@win.bright.net. Mailing Address: PO Box 191, Hayward, WI 54843. Year Established: 1893. Pub. Frequency: w. (Wed.) Page Size: broadsheet. Subscrip. Rate: $1 newsstand/cover; $33/yr mailed local; $50/yr out of area. Circulation: 7,000 per issue (paid). **Owner(s):** Superior Publishing Corp., 1105 Tower Ave, Superior, WI 54880. Telephone: 715-395-5725. FAX: 715-395-5729. **Management:** Andy Pennington, Publisher. Sue Johnston, Advertising Manager. Laura Fosterling, Circulation Manager. **Editorial:** Paul Mitchell, Editor.

HILLSBORO

HILLSBORO SENTRY-ENTERPRISE. ISSN 0749-7016
PO Box 469, Hillsboro, WI 54634. Telephone: 608-489-2264. FAX: 608-489-2348. E-MAIL: sentry@mwt.net. Year Established: 1885. Pub. Frequency: w. (Thu.) Page Size: tabloid. Subscrip. Rate: $.75 newsstand/cover; $29/yr local; $33/yr mailed in state; $39/yr mailed out of state. Freelance Pay: $0.50/column-inch. Circulation: 1,800 per issue (paid). **Owner(s):** Morris Newspaper Corporation, 27 Abercorn St., Savannah, GA 31401. Telephone: 912-233-1281. FAX: 912-232-4639. **Management:** John D. Ingebritsen, Publisher. Mary Sterba, Advertising Manager. **Editorial:** Ryan Billingham, Editor.

NEIGHBORS (HILLSBORO). 839 Water Ave., Hillsboro, WI 54634. Telephone: 608-489-2264. FAX: 608-489-2348. E-MAIL: sentry@mwt.net. Mailing Address: P.O. Box 469, Hillsboro, WI 54634. Pub. Frequency: m. (1st & 3rd Thu.) Page Size: standard Circulation: 5,000 per issue (free). **Owner(s):** Jack Knowles, See address and contact information above. **Management:** John Ingelbritsen, Publisher. Mary Sterba, Advertising Manager. **Editorial:** Jack Knowles, Editor.

HORICON

HORICON REPORTER. ISSN 1053-9972
411 E. Lake St., Horicon, WI 53032. Telephone: 920-485-2016. FAX: 920-485-4820. E-MAIL: horiconreporter@shcglobal.net. Mailing Address: PO Box 164, Horicon, WI 53032. Year Established: 1883. Pub. Frequency: w. (Thu.) Page Size: broadsheet. Subscrip. Rate: $.75 newsstand/cover; $30/yr mailed in county; $34/yr mailed out of county; $38/yr mailed out of state. Circulation: 2,100 per issue (paid). **Owner(s):** Wisconsin Free Press, Inc., 126 Bridge St., Mayville, WI 53050. Telephone: 902-387-2211. **Management:** Andrew Johnson, Publisher. Lana Louden, Advertising Manager.

HUDSON

HUDSON STAR-OBSERVER. ISSN 0749-7008
226 Locust St., Hudson, WI 54016-0147. Telephone: 715-386-9333. FAX: 715-386-9891. E-MAIL: hsoeditor@rivertowns.net. URL: http://www.rivertowns.com. Year Established: 1854. Pub. Frequency: w. (Thu.) Page Size: broadsheet. Subscrip. Rate: $1.25 newsstand/cover; $44/yr in county; $62/yr mailed out of county. **Wire Service(s):** AP. Circulation: 7,500 per issue (paid). **Owner(s):** Jeff Meyer, PO Box 2020, Fargo, ND 58107. Telephone: 701-235-7311. **Management:** Steve Dzubay, Publisher. Mary Beth Kremer, Advertising Manager. **Editorial:** Douglas W. Stohlberg, Executive Editor. Randy Hanson, Associate Editor.

HURLEY

IRON COUNTY MINER. 216 Copper St, Hurley, WI 54534. Telephone: 715-561-3405. FAX: 715-561-3799. Year Established: 1885. Pub. Frequency: w. (Thu.) Page Size: broadsheet. Subscrip. Rate: $.50 newsstand/cover; $29/yr mailed in county; $34/yr mailed out of county. Circulation: 3,000 per issue (paid). **Owner(s):** Iron County Miner, See address and contact information above. **Management:** Ernest Moore, Owner. **Editorial:** Ernest Moore, Editor.

IOLA

IOLA HERALD. ISSN 0886-8360
105 Pinecrest Ln., Ste. D, Iola, WI 54945-0235. Telephone: 715-445-3415. FAX: 715-445-3988. E-MAIL: waupacanews@gglbbs.com. Mailing Address: PO Box 235, Iola, WI 54945-0235. Year Established: 1891. Pub. Frequency: w. (Thu.) Page Size: tabloid. Subscrip. Rate: $.85 newsstand/cover; $29/yr in county; $36/yr mailed in state; $41/yr mailed out of state. Circulation: 2,000 per issue (paid). **Owner(s):** Trey & Mary Foerster, See address and contact information above. **Management:** Trey Foerster, Publisher. Mary Foerster, Advertising. Tamara Mortensen, Circulation Manager. **Editorial:** Jane Myhra, Editor.

MANAWA ADVOCATE. 105 Pinecrest Ln., Ste. D, Iola, WI 54945-0235. Telephone: 715-445-3415. FAX: 715-445-3988. E-MAIL: iolaherald@yahoo.com. Mailing Address: PO Box 235, Iola, WI 54945-0235. Year Established: 1890. Pub. Frequency: w. (Thu.) Page Size: tabloid. Subscrip. Rate: $.85 newsstand/cover; $29/yr in county; $36/yr in state; $41/yr out of state. Circulation: 2,000 per issue (paid). **Owner(s):** Trey & Mary Foerster, See address and contact information above. **Management:** Trey Foerster, Publisher. Mary Foerster, Advertising. Tamara Mortensen, Circulation Manager. **Editorial:** Jane Myhra, Editor.

JUNEAU

DODGE COUNTY INDEPENDENT-NEWS. 122 S. Main St., Juneau, WI 53039. Telephone: 920-386-2421. FAX: 920-386-2422. URL: http://www.wdtimes.com. Mailing Address: PO Box 167, Juneau, WI 53039. Year Established: 1893. Pub. Frequency: w. (Thu.) Page Size: broadsheet. Subscrip. Rate: $.50 newsstand/cover; $18/yr in county; $26/yr out of county. Freelance Pay: $0.25/column-inch. Circulation: 1,200 per issue (paid). **Owner(s):** Times Publishing Co., 113-115 W. Main St., Watertown, WI 53094. Telephone: 920-261-5161. FAX: 920-261-5102. **Management:** Kevin C. Clifford, General Manager. James M. Clifford, Publisher. Rhonda Boyd, Advertising Manager. Jodi Rydstrom, Classified Adv. Mgr.. **Editorial:** Thomas Schultz, Managing Editor.

KAUKAUNA

TIMES-VILLAGER. 1900 Crooks Ave., Kaukauna, WI 54130-0229. Telephone: 920-759-2000. FAX: 920-759-7344. E-MAIL: editor@timesvillager.com. URL: http://www.timesvillager.com. Mailing Address: P.O. Box 229, Kaukauna, WI 54130-0229. Year Established: 1880. Pub. Frequency: s-w. (Wed. & Sat.) Page Size: tabloid. Subscrip. Rate: $.50 newsstand/cover; $40/yr mailed in county; $43/yr mailed in state; $44/yr out of state. Adv. Rate: col. inch $9 Circulation: 6,800 per issue (paid and free). **Owner(s):** Kaukauna Times Publishing, See address and contact information above. **Management:** Bart Landsverk, General Manager. Glenn Hansen, Publisher. **Editorial:** Brian Roebke, Editor.

KENOSHA

KENOSHA BULLETIN. 5800 Seventh Ave., Kenosha, WI 53140. Telephone: 262-656-1000. FAX: 262-656-1255. Year Established: 1981. Pub. Frequency: w. (Mon.) Page Size: broadsheet. Freelance Pay: $1.15/column-inch. Circulation: 60,000 per issue (free). **Owner(s):** United Communications Corp., See address and contact information above. **Management:** Kenneth L. Dowdell, Publisher. Kenneth McElroy, Advertising Manager. James DeMarco, Circulation Manager. **Editorial:** Dave Marren, Sports Editor.

LAKE GENEVA REGIONAL NEWS. 5800 Seventh Ave., Kenosha, WI 53141. URL: http://www.lakegenevanews.net. Year Established: 1873. Pub. Frequency: w. (Thu.) Page Size: standard. Subscrip. Rate: $1 newsstand/cover; $32.50/yr mailed in county; $37.50/yr mailed in state; $42.50/yr mailed out of state. Adv. Rate: col. inch $10.05 Circulation: 6,000 per issue (paid). **Owner(s):** United Communications Corp., See address and contact information above.

WESTERN KENOSHA COUNTY BULLETIN. 5800 Seventh Ave., Kenosha, WI 53410. Pub. Frequency: w. (Mon.) Page Size: broadsheet. Freelance Pay: $1/column-inch. Circulation: 16,000 per issue (free). **Owner(s):** United Communications Corp., See address and contact information above. **Management:** Kenneth L. Dowdell, Publisher. Kenneth McElroy, Advertising Manager. James DeMarco, Circulation Manager. **Editorial:** Dave Marren, Sports Editor.

KEWASKUM

KEWASKUM STATESMAN. 355 Main St., Kewaskum, WI 53040-0098. Telephone: 262-626-2626. FAX: 262-626-1382. E-MAIL: akuehl@@kewaskumstatesman.com. URL: http://www.kewaskumstatesman.com. Mailing Address: PO Box 98, Kewaskum, WI 53040-0098. Year Established: 1895. Pub. Frequency: w. (Thu.) Page Size: tabloid. Subscrip. Rate: $.55 newsstand/cover; $25/yr in state; $30/yr out of state. Circulation: 3,500 per issue (paid). **Owner(s):** Lana Kuehl, 355 Main St., Kewaskum, WI 53040. Telephone: 262-626-2626. FAX: 262-626-1382. **Management:** Cheryl Kuehl, Office Manager. Sheri Baldi, Advertising Director. Nicole Rawley, Classified Adv. Mgr.. Andrew R. Kuehl, Business Manager. **Editorial:** Lana Kuehl, Editor.

KEWAUNEE

KEWAUNEE ENTERPRISE. 203 Ellis St, Kewaunee, WI 54216. Telephone: 930-388-3175. FAX: 930-388-0609. E-MAIL: email@gokewauneecounty.com. URL: http://www.kewauneeenterprise.com. Mailing Address: PO Box 86, Kewaunee, WI 54216. Year Established: 1859. Pub. Frequency: w. (Thu.) Page Size: broadsheet. Subscrip. Rate: $.50 newsstand/cover; $25/yr carrier delivery local or motor rte; $29/yr mailed in state; $33/yr mailed out of state. Adv. Rate: col. inch $8.80 Circulation: 1,800 per issue (paid). **Owner(s):** Gannett Company, Inc., 7950 Jones Branch Dr., McLean, VA 22102. **Management:** Bill Nusbaum, Publisher. Dave Wood, Advertising Manager. Scott Daily, Circulation Director.

KIEL

TEMPO (KIEL). 606 Fremont St., Kiel, WI 53042. Telephone: 920-894-2828. FAX: 920-894-2161. E-MAIL: graphics@deltapublications.com. URL: http://www.deltapublications.com. Mailing Address: PO Box 237, Kiel, WI 53042. Pub. Frequency: w. (Tue.) Page Size: tabloid Circulation: 20,500 per issue (free). **Owner(s):** Delta Publications Co., Inc., See address and contact information above. **Management:** Mike Mathes, Publisher. Joe Mathes, Advertising Manager. Janet Wesley, Circulation Manager. Sharon Meyer, Classified Adv. Mgr..

TRI-COUNTY NEWS (KIEL). 606 Fremont St., Kiel, WI 53042. Telephone: 920-894-2828. FAX: 920-894-2161. E-MAIL: graphics@deltapublications.com. URL: http://www.deltapublications.com/. Mailing Address: PO Box 237, Kiel, WI 53042. Year Established: 1893. Pub. Frequency: w. (Thu.) Page Size: tabloid. Subscrip. Rate: $.75 newsstand/cover; $25/yr mailed tri-cy. area; $35/yr mailed out of area; $45/yr mailed out of state. Adv. Rate: col. inch $5.40 Circulation: 4,500 per issue (paid and free). **Owner(s):** Delta Publications Co., Inc., See address and contact information above. **Management:** Mike Mathes, Publisher. Joe Mathes, Advertising Manager. Janet Wesley, Circulation Manager. Sharon Meyer, Classified Adv. Mgr.. **Editorial:** Mark Sherry, Editor. Craig Hoffman, Sports Editor.

LA CROSSE

FOXXY SHOPPER. 401 N. Third St., La Crosse, WI 54601-3281. URL: http://www.tricountyfoxxy.com. Year Established: 1975. Pub. Frequency: w. (Mon.) Page Size: broadsheet.Subscrip. Rate: $130/yr mailed 1st class Circulation: 90,000 per issue (free). **Owner(s):** Lee Enterprises, Inc., 215 N. Main St., Davenport, IA 52801. Telephone: 563-383-2100. **Management:** Chris Hardie, General Manager. Barb Formanek, Advertising Manager.

LADYSMITH

LADYSMITH NEWS. ISSN 0749-7059
120 W. Third St., Ladysmith, WI 54848. Telephone: 715-532-5591. FAX: 715-532-6644. E-MAIL: ladynews@centurytel.net. URL: http://www.ladysmithnews.com. Mailing Address: PO Box 189, Ladysmith, WI 54848. Year Established: 1895. Pub. Frequency: w. (Thu.) Page Size: broadsheet. Subscrip. Rate: $1 newsstand/cover; $35.50/yr in county & adj. cys.; $43/yr out of area; $48.50/yr out of state. Adv. Rate: col. inch $6.95 Circulation: 5,700 per issue (paid). **Owner(s):** Bell Press Inc., See address and contact information above. **Management:** Leslie Harmon, General Manager. James C. Bell, Publisher. Christine Bell, Advertising Manager. **Editorial:** John M. Terrill, Editor. Bob Veness, Sports Editor.

LAKE MILLS

LAKE MILLS LEADER. 320 N. Main St., Lake Mills, WI 53551-0060. Telephone: 920-648-2334. FAX: 920-648-8187. E-MAIL: lakemillsleader@hometownnewsgroup.com. URL: http://www.hometownnewsgroup.com. Mailing Address: PO Box 310, Lake Mills, WI 53551-0310. Year Established: 1878. Pub. Frequency: w. (Thu.) Page Size: broadsheet. Subscrip. Rate: $.75 newsstand/cover; $31/yr in county; $41/yr out of county. Adv. Rate: col. inch $7.25 Circulation: 3,000 per issue (paid). **Owner(s):** Hometown News Group, 28 Milwaukee Ave., W., Fort Atkinson, WI 53538. Telephone: 920-563-5551. **Management:** Wayne Toske, General Manager. Brian Knox, Publisher. Mike Wilson, Advertising Manager. Luann Niebling, Circulation Manager. **Editorial:** Randy Radtke, Editor.

LANCASTER

GRANT COUNTY HERALD INDEPENDENT. 208 W. Cherry St., Lancaster, WI 53813-0310. Telephone: 608-723-2151. FAX: 608-723-7272. E-MAIL: lannews@tds.net. Mailing Address: PO Box 310, Lancaster, WI 53813-0310. Year Established: 1843. Pub. Frequency: w. (Thu.) Page Size: broadsheet. Subscrip. Rate: $1 newsstand/cover; $36/yr mailed in county; $39/yr mailed out of county; $51/yr mailed out of state. Circulation: 3,800 per issue (paid). **Owner(s):** Morris Newspaper Corporation, 27 Abercorn St., Savannah, GA 31401. Telephone: 912-233-1281. FAX: 912-232-4639. **Management:** John D. Ingebritsen, Publisher. Kevin Kelly, Advertising Manager. **Editorial:** David Timmerman, Editor.

LODI

LODI ENTERPRISE. 146 S. Main St., Lodi, WI 53555. Telephone: 608-592-3261. FAX: 608-592-3866. E-MAIL: lodient@chorus.net. Mailing Address: PO Box 16, Lodi, WI 53555. Year Established: 1894. Pub. Frequency: w. (Thu.) Page Size: broadsheet. Subscrip. Rate: $.75 newsstand/cover; $34/yr in area; $41/yr mailed out of area. Circulation: 2,500 per issue (paid). **Owner(s):** Hometown News Group, PO Box 801, Fort Atkinson, WI 53538. Telephone: 920-563-5551. **Management:** Brian Knox, Publisher. Mike Wilson, Advertising Manager. Luann Niebling, Circulation Manager. **Editorial:** Peg Zaemisch, Editor.

LOYAL

LOYAL TRIBUNE RECORD GLEANER. 318 N. Main St., Loyal, WI 54446-. Telephone: 715-255-8531. FAX: 715-255-8357. Year Established: 1894. Pub. Frequency: w. (Wed.) Page Size: broadsheet. Subscrip. Rate: $1 newsstand/cover; $29/yr mailed in state. Circulation: 3,600 per issue (paid). **Owner(s):** TRG, Inc., See address and contact information above. **Management:** Dean Lesar, Publisher. **Editorial:** Dean Lesar, Editor.

MADISON

ISTHMUS. ISSN 1081-4043
101 King St., Madison, WI 53703. Telephone: 608-251-5627. FAX: 608-251-2165. E-MAIL: edit@isthmus.com. URL: http://www.thedailypage.com. Year Established: 1976. Pub. Frequency: w. Page Size: tabloid. Subscrip. Rate: $50/yr domestic; $100/yr foreign. Circulation: 58,000. **Owner(s):** Vincent O'Hern, See address and contact information above. **Management:** Vincent O'Hern, Publisher. Bob Ausheles, Advertising. Tom Dehlinger, Circulation Manager. **Editorial:** Marc Eisen, Editor.

MARKETPLACE (MADISON). 1901 Fish Hatchery Rd., Madison, WI 53713. E-MAIL: jschroeter@capitalnewspapers.com. URL: http://www.madison.com/cls/. Mailing Address: PO Box 8056, Madison, WI 53708. Pub. Frequency: w. (Wed.) Page Size: tabloid Circulation: 10,000 per issue (free). **Owner(s):** Capital Newspapers, Inc., See address and contact information above. **Management:** Jeff Schroeter, Advertising Director. Kim Wustrack, Circulation Manager. Matt Meyers, Manager. Contact: Andrea Rhoades, Advertising Director; Victoria Gilpin, Advertising Manager; Jean Suckow, Circulation Director; Matt Forsyth, Classified Adv. Mgr.; Jim Lewers, Managing Editor; Greg Smith, Assignment Editor; Tricia Newall, Lifestyle Editor; Teresa Thorpe, News Editor; Jason Cook, Photo Editor; Ryan Suchomel, Sports Editor.

SHOPPER STOPPER EXTRA. 1901 Fish Hatchery Rd, Madison, WI 53713. Telephone: 608-252-6200. FAX: 608-250-4155. Mailing Address: PO Box 8457, Madison, WI 53708-8457. Pub. Frequency: w. (Sun.) Page Size: tabloid Circulation: 8,000 per issue (free). **Owner(s):** Capital Newspapers, Inc., See address and contact information above. **Management:** Jeff Schroeter, Advertising Director. Phil Stoddard, Circulation Director. Matt Meyers, Classified Adv. Mgr..

MANITOWOC

LAKESHORE CHRONICLE. 902 Franklin St., Manitowoc, WI 54220-0790. Telephone: 920-684-4433. FAX: 920-684-4416. E-MAIL: htrnews@htrnews.com. URL: http://www.htrnews.com. Mailing Address: PO Box 790, Manitowoc, WI 54221-0790. Year Established: 1972. Pub. Frequency: s-w. (Wed. & Sun.) Page Size: broadsheet. Subscrip. Rate: $10/yr voluntary subscription. **Wire Service(s):** AP. Circulation: 31,400 per issue (free). **Owner(s):** Gannett Company, Inc., 7950 Jones Branch Dr., McLean, VA 22107-0001. Telephone: 703-854-6000. **Management:** Bill Hackney, General Manager. Bill Nusbaum, Publisher. Lowell Johnson, Advertising Director. **Editorial:** Russ Budzisz, Managing Editor.

MARION

MARION ADVERTISER. 109 N. Main, Marion, WI 54950. Telephone: 715-754-5444. Mailing Address: PO Box 268, Marion, WI 54950. Year Established: 1895. Pub. Frequency: w. (Thu.) Page Size: broadsheet. Subscrip. Rate: $.75 newsstand/cover; $25/yr mailed in county & adj. cys.; $28/yr mailed out of area; $32/yr mailed out of state. Circulation: 3,000 per issue (paid). **Owner(s):** Daniel S. Brandenburg, See address and contact information above. **Management:** Daniel S. Brandenburg, Publisher. Patsy Brandenburg, Circulation Manager. **Editorial:** Daniel S. Brandenburg, Editor. Patsy Brandenburg, Managing Editor.

MARKESAN

NEIGHBORS. 51 E. John St., Markesan, WI 53946. Telephone: 920-398-2334. FAX: 920-398-3835. URL: http://www.wiscnews.com. Mailing Address: PO Box 397, Markesan, WI 53946. Year Established: 1881. Pub. Frequency: w. (Sat.) Page Size: tabloid. Subscrip. Rate: $1 newsstand/cover; $46.80 in state & out of state. Adv. Rate: col. inch $6.60 **Wire Service(s):** AP. Circulation: 8,300 per issue (paid). **Owner(s):** Capital Newspapers, Inc., 1901 Fish Hatchery Rd., Madison, WI 53713. **Management:** Jim Kelsh, Publisher. Francine Weatherwax, Advertising Manager. Lisa Alvarado, Circulation Manager. **Editorial:** Hank Snyder, Associate Editor.

MAUSTON

BUYER'S GUIDE CENT SAVER. 115 Oak St., Mauston, WI 53948. Telephone: 608-847-6224. FAX: 608-847-5457. Mailing Address: PO Box 220, Mauston, WI 53948. Pub. Frequency: w. (Sat.) Page Size: tabloid Circulation: 15,155 per issue (free). **Owner(s):** Lee Enterprises, Inc., 201 N. Harrison St., Davenport, IA 52801-1924. **Management:** David Gentry, Publisher. Linda Goldbeck, Advertising Manager. Debbie Sprague, Circulation Manager. Carrie Champlin, Classified Adv. Mgr..

JUNEAU COUNTY STAR-TIMES. 201 E. State St., Mauston, WI 53948. Telephone: 608-847-7341. FAX: 608-847-4867. URL: http://www.jcs.wiscnews.com. Mailing Address: PO Box 220, Mauston, WI 53948-0220. Pub. Frequency: s-w. (Wed. & Sat.) Page Size: broadsheet. Subscrip. Rate: $.75 newsstand/cover; $14 home delivery in county for 13 wks.; $40/yr home delivery in county. Circulation: 3,800 per issue (paid). **Owner(s):** Capital Newspapers, Inc., 1901 Fish Hatchery Rd, Madison, WI 53713. Telephone: 608-252-6200. **Management:** George Althoff, Publisher. Julie Brown, Advertising Manager. Teresa Klinger, Circulation Manager. Carrie Champlin, Classified Adv. Mgr.. **Editorial:** Rhonda Siebecker Rothe, Editor. David Vantress, Sports.

MAYVILLE

MAYVILLE NEWS, THE. 126 Bridge St., Mayville, WI 53050-0271. Telephone: 920-387-2211. FAX: 920-387-5515. E-MAIL: editorAmayvillenews.com. Mailing Address: PO Box 271, Mayville, WI 53050-0271. Year Established: 1892. Pub. Frequency: w. (Thu.) Page Size: broadsheet. Subscrip. Rate: $.75 newsstand/cover; $32/yr mailed in county; $34/yr mailed out of county; $38/yr mailed out of state. Circulation: 4,090 per issue (paid). **Owner(s):** Andrew Johnson, PO Box 271, Mayville, WI 53050. Telephone: 920-387-2211. FAX: 920-387-5515. **Management:** Andrew Johnson, Publisher. **Editorial:** Sally Kahlhamer, Editor.

MCFARLAND

MCFARLAND THISTLE. 5124 Farwell St., McFarland, WI 53558. Telephone: 608-838-6435. FAX: 608-838-4927. E-MAIL: mcfthistle@mailbag.com. Year Established: 1966. Pub. Frequency: w. (Wed.) Page Size: tabloid. Subscrip. Rate: $.75 newsstand/cover; $32/yr in county. Circulation: 1,250 per issue (paid). **Owner(s):** Hometown News Group, 28 Milwaukee Ave., W., Fort Atkinson, WI 53538. Telephone: 920-563-5551. **Management:** Brian Knox, Publisher. Mike Wilson, Advertising Manager. Luann Niebling, Circulation Manager. **Editorial:** Kathleen Osten, Editor.

MEDFORD

STAR NEWS (MEDFORD), THE. 116 S. Wisconsin Ave., Medford, WI 54451. Telephone: 715-748-2626. FAX: 715-748-2699. E-MAIL: starnews@centralwinews.com. URL: http://www.centralwinews.com. Mailing Address: PO Box 180, Medford, WI 54451-0180. Year Established: 1875. Pub. Frequency: w. (Thu.) Page Size: tabloid. Subscrip. Rate: $1 newsstand/cover; $35/yr in county; $37/yr in state; $45/yr out of state. Adv. Rate: col. inch $7 Circulation: 6,500 per issue (paid). **Owner(s):** Central Wisconsin Publications, Inc., See address and contact information above. **Management:** Kristine O'Leary, General Manager. Carol O'Leary, Publisher. Kelly Schmidt, Advertising Manager. Sam Ingorsoll, Classified Adv. Mgr.. **Editorial:** Carol O'Leary, Editor. Brian Wilson, News Editor. Matt Frey, Sports Editor.

MENOMONIE

DUNN COUNTY NEWS, THE. 710 Main St., Menomonie, WI 54751. Telephone: 715-235-3411. FAX: 715-235-0936. E-MAIL: editor@dunnconnect.com. URL: http://www.dunnconnect.com. Mailing Address: PO Box 40, Menomonie, WI 54751. Year Established: 1860. Pub. Frequency: s-w. (Wed. & Sun.) Page Size: broadsheet. Subscrip. Rate: $.75 newsstand/cover; $57.75/yr carrier delivery; $57.75/yr motor route; $65/yr mailed elsewhere. Adv. Rate: col. inch $10.87 Circulation: 4,500 per issue (paid). **Owner(s):** Lee Enterprises, Inc., 215 N. Main St., Davenport, IA 52801. Telephone: 563-383-2100. FAX: 563-383-9608. **Management:** Steve Jahn, Publisher. Denny Bodoh, Advertising Manager. Kim Spaeth, Circulation Director. Jada Nowling, Circulation Manager. **Editorial:** Barb Lyon, Editor.

MERRILL

FOTO NEWS. ISSN 0191-8958
807 E. First St., Merrill, WI 54452. Telephone: 715-536-7121. FAX: 715-539-3686. E-MAIL: fotonews@jcpgroup.com. URL: http://www.merrillfotonews.com. Year Established: 1969. Pub. Frequency: w. (Wed.) Page Size: tabloid. Subscrip. Rate: $38/yr mailed. Adv. Rate: col. inch $15.50 Circulation: 16,400 per issue (controlled and free). **Owner(s):** Journal Community Publishing Group, 600 Industrial Dr., PO Box 609, Waupaca, WI 54981. Telephone: 715-258-8450. FAX: 715-258-4896. **Management:** Tim Schreiber, General Manager. **Editorial:** Collin Lueck, Editor.

MIDDLETON

MIDDLETON TIMES-TRIBUNE. 7611 Elmwood Ave., Ste 102, Middleton, WI 53562. Telephone: 608-836-1601. FAX: 608-836-3759. E-MAIL: newsmtt@newspubline.com. URL: http://www.newspubinc.com. Mailing Address: PO Box 620006, Middleton, WI 53562. Year Established: 1893. Pub. Frequency: w. (Thu.) Page Size: tabloid. Subscrip. Rate: $1 newsstand/cover; $32/yr mailed in state; $44/yr mailed out of state. Adv. Rate: col. inch $11.78 Circulation: 4,000 per issue (paid). **Owner(s):** News Publishing Co., 1126 Mills St., Black Earth, WI 53515. Telephone: 608-767-3655. FAX: 608-767-2222. **Management:** Dan Witte, Publisher. Gail Johnson, Advertising. **Editorial:** John Donaldson, Managing Editor. Matt Geiger, News Editor. Rob Reischel, Sports Editor.

MILTON

MILTON COURIER. 513 Vernal Ave, Milton, WI 53563. Telephone: 608-868-2442. FAX: 608-868-4664. E-MAIL: mcourier@charter.net. URL: http://www.hometownnewsgroup.com. Mailing Address: PO Box 69, Milton, WI 53563. Year Established: 1879. Pub. Frequency: w. (Thu.) Page Size: tabloid. Subscrip. Rate: $.75 newsstand/cover; $22/yr in state; $24/yr out of state. Circulation: 3,300 per issue (paid). **Owner(s):** Hometown News Group, 28 Milwaukee Ave., W., Fort Atkinson, WI 53538. Telephone: 920-563-5551. **Management:** Brian Knox, Publisher. Susan Angell, Advertising Manager. Judy Lippincott, Circulation Manager. **Editorial:** Doug Welch, Managing Editor. Rick Miller, Associate Editor.

MILWAUKEE

MILWAUKEE POST. 3397 S. Howell Ave, Milwaukee, WI 53027. Telephone: 414-744-6370. FAX: 414-744-6884. Year Established: 1883.Pub. Frequency: w. (Wed.) Page Size: broadsheet Circulation: 26,000 (free). **Owner(s):** Conley Publishing Group, Ltd., 119 Monroe St., Beaver Dam, WI 53916. Telephone: 920-885-7800. **Management:** Daryl Skaradzinski, General Manager. Lynn Talaska, Office Manager. Daryl Skaradzinski, Advertising Manager. **Editorial:** Christian Williams, Editor.

SHEPHERD EXPRESS. ISSN 1071-5185
207 E. Buffalo St., Ste. 410, Milwaukee, WI 53202. E-MAIL: mastbury@shepex.com. URL: http://www.expressmilwaukee.com. Year Established: 1982. Pub. Frequency: w. (Thu.) Page Size: tabloid. Freelance Pay: $10-$450/article. Circulation: 59,750 per issue (free). **Owner(s):** Alternative Publications Inc., 207 E. Buffalo St., Ste. 410, Milwaukee, WI 53202. Telephone: 414-276-2222. FAX: 414-276-3312. **Management:** Louis Fortis, President. Matt Astbury, Finance Director. Mark Krueger, Advertising. Valerie Vos, Marketing.

SOUTHEASTERN STAR. PO Box 6279, Milwaukee, WI 53206. Telephone: 414-449-4870. E-MAIL: milwaukeecourier@aol.com. URL: http://www.milwaukeecourier.org. Year Established: 1960. Pub. Frequency: w. (Thu.) Page Size: tabloid. Subscrip. Rate: $25/yr mailed. Freelance Pay: $15/article. Circulation: 5,000 per issue (free). **Owner(s):** Jerrel Jones, See address and contact information above. **Management:** Jerrel Jones, President. Faithe Colas, Advertising Manager. **Editorial:** Faithe Colas, Editor.

MINERAL POINT

DEMOCRAT TRIBUNE, THE. 334 High St., Mineral Point, WI 53565. Telephone: 608-987-2141. FAX: 608-935-9531. Year Established: 1847. Pub. Frequency: w. (Thu.) Page Size: tabloid. Subscrip. Rate: $.75 newsstand/cover; $25/yr in state; $35/yr out of state. Circulation: 1,172 per issue (paid). **Owner(s):** T. Michael Reilly & J. Patrick Reilly, See address and contact information above. **Management:** T. Michael Reilly, President. J. Patrick Reilly, Publisher. T. Michael Reilly, Advertising Manager. Todd D. Novak, Circulation Manager. **Editorial:** Jeanie Lewis, Editor.

MINOCQUA

LAKELAND TIMES. ISSN 0746-4274
PO Box 790, Minocqua, WI 54548. Telephone: 715-356-5236. URL: http://www.lakelandtimes.com. Year Established: 1891. Pub. Frequency: s-w. (Tue. & Fri.) Page Size: tabloid. Subscrip. Rate: $.75 newsstand/cover; $48/yr local; $58/yr mailed out of area. Adv. Rate: col. inch $5.20 Circulation: 10,500 per issue (paid). **Owner(s):** Don Walker, See address and contact information above. **Management:** Greg Walker, General Manager. Don Walker, Publisher. Heather Holmes, Sales Manager.

MONDOVI

MONDOVI HERALD-NEWS. 123 W. Main St., Mondovi, WI 54755. Telephone: 715-926-4970. FAX: 715-926-4928. E-MAIL: mhnews@mhnews.biz. Mailing Address: P.O. Box 67, Mondovi, WI 54755. Year Established: 1876. Pub. Frequency: w. (Thu.) Page Size: standard. Subscrip. Rate: $.75 newsstand/cover; $30/yr home delivery in county; $35/yr mailed out of county; $43/yr mailed out of state. Adv. Rate: col. inch $6.82 Circulation: 3,500 per issue (paid). **Owner(s):** Perry Nyseth, See address and contact information above. **Management:** Perry Nyseth, Publisher. **Editorial:** Cynthia Gibson, Editor.

MONTELLO

MARQUETTE COUNTY TRIBUNE. 120 Underwood Ave., Montello, WI 53949. Telephone: 608-297-2424. FAX: 608-297-9293. E-MAIL: marquettetribune@maqs.net. URL: http://www.marquettecountytribune.com. Mailing Address: PO Box 188, Montello, WI 53949. Year Established: 1859. Pub. Frequency: w. (Thu.) Page Size: tabloid. Subscrip. Rate: $1 newsstand/cover; $28/yr in state; $35/yr out of state. Adv. Rate: col. inch $7.40 Circulation: 4,500 per issue (paid and free). **Owner(s):** News Publishing Co., 1126 Mills St., Black Earth, WI 53515. Telephone: 608-767-3655. FAX: 608-767-2222. **Management:** Mary Faltz, General Manager. **Editorial:** Mary Faltz, Editor. Rob Fullmer, Reporter.

MOSINEE

MOSINEE TIMES, THE. ISSN 0748-8297
407 Third St., Mosinee, WI 54455-1495. Telephone: 715-693-2300. FAX: 715-693-1574. E-MAIL: motimes@mtc.net. Year Established: 1895. Pub. Frequency: w. (Thu.) Page Size: broadsheet. Subscrip. Rate: $.50 newsstand/cover; $24/yr in county; $30/yr in state; $34/yr out of state. Adv. Rate: col. inch $5.25 Circulation: 2,560 per issue (paid and free). **Owner(s):** Mosinee Times Publishing, Inc., See address and contact information above. **Management:** Jim Kress, Publisher.

MT. HOREB

MOUNT HOREB MAIL. 114 E Main St, Mt. Horeb, WI 53572. Telephone: 608-437-5553. FAX: 608-437-3443. E-MAIL: newspubl@tds.net. URL: http://www.newspubinc.com. Year Established: 1900. Pub. Frequency: w. (Thu.) Page Size: tabloid. Subscrip. Rate: $1 newsstand/cover; $35/yr in state; $47/yr out of state. Circulation: 2,400 per issue (paid). **Owner(s):** News Publishing Co., 1126 Mills St., Black Earth, WI 53515. Telephone: 608-767-3655. FAX: 608-767-2222. **Management:** Dan Witte, Publisher. Timothy Sweeney, Advertising Manager. **Editorial:** Gary Schuetz, Editor. John Donaldson, Managing Editor.

MUKWONAGO

MUKWONAGO CHIEF. 555 Bay View Rd., Ste. 1, Mukwonago, WI 53149-0204. Telephone: 262-363-4045. FAX: 262-363-8573. E-MAIL: mukpubs@jcpgroup.com. URL: http://www.jcpgroup.com. Mailing Address: PO Box 204, Mukwonago, WI 53149-0204. Year Established: 1889. Pub. Frequency: w. (Wed.) Page Size: tabloid. Subscrip. Rate: $.50 newsstand/cover; $26/yr in county; $36/yr out of county. Circulation: 5,200 per issue (controlled and free). **Owner(s):** Journal Community Publishing Group, 600 Industrial Dr., Waupaca, WI 54891. Telephone: 715-258-8450. **Management:** James Flaherty, Publisher. Carol Golden, Circulation Manager. **Editorial:** James Flaherty, Editor.

NEILLSVILLE

CLARK COUNTY PRESS. 614 Hewitt St., Neillsville, WI 54456. Telephone: 715-743-2600. FAX: 715-743-5460. Mailing Address: PO Box 149, Neillsville, WI 54456. Year Established: 1989. Pub. Frequency: w. (Wed.) Page Size: tabloid. Subscrip. Rate: $1 newsstand/cover; $28/yr in county; $33/yr mailed out of county; $43/yr mailed elsewhere. Circulation: 3,600 per issue (paid). **Owner(s):** News Publishing Co., PO Box 286, Black Earth, WI 53515. Telephone: 608-767-3655. **Management:** Kathy Potter, General Manager. Dan Witte, President. Kathy Potter, Advertising Manager.

NEW BERLIN

BAY VIEWER, THE. ISSN 0895-2817
15700 W Cleveland Ave., New Berlin, WI 53151. Telephone: 262-938-5000. FAX: 262-938-5001. E-MAIL: communitynews@cninewsonline.com. URL: http://www.cninewsonline.com. Year Established: 1976. Pub. Frequency: w. (Thu.) Page Size: tabloid. Subscrip. Rate: $.75 newsstand/cover; $28.25/yr local; $59.25/yr in state & surrounding states; $86.45/yr elsewhere. Circulation: 1,529 per issue (paid). **Owner(s):** CNI Community Newspapers, Inc., See address and contact information above. **Management:** Cristy Garcia-Thomas, Publisher. Steve Lyles, Advertising Director. Dave Rice, Circulation Manager. Kate House, Classified Adv. Mgr.. **Editorial:** Amy Muehlbauer, Editor. Sue Gronemus, Managing Editor. Mark Hutchinson, Sports Editor.

BROOKFIELD NEWS. 15700 W Cleveland Ave., New Berlin, WI 53151. Telephone: 262-938-5000. E-MAIL: communitynews@cninewsonline.com. URL: http://www.brookfieldnow.com. Year Established: 1955. Pub. Frequency: w. (Thu.) Page Size: tabloid. Subscrip. Rate: $.75 newsstand/cover; $28.25/yr local; $59.25/yr in state incl. MI, MN, IL, IA; $86.45/yr mailed elsewhere. Circulation: 6,330 per issue (paid). **Owner(s):** CNI Community Newspapers, Inc., See address and contact information above. **Management:** Cristy Garcia-Thomas, Publisher. Steve Lyles, Advertising Manager. Kate House, Classified Adv. Mgr.. **Editorial:** Michael Zahn, Editor. Sue Gronemus, Managing Editor.

BROWN DEER HERALD. 15700 W Cleveland Ave., New Berlin, WI 53151. Telephone: 262-938-5000. E-MAIL: communitynews@cninewsonline.com. URL: http://www.cninewsonline.com. Year Established: 1928. Pub. Frequency: w. (Thu.) Page Size: tabloid. Subscrip. Rate: $.75 newsstand/cover; $26.50/yr local; $56.25/yr out of area; $83.45/yr elsewhere. Circulation: 1,596 per issue (paid). **Owner(s):** CNI Community Newspapers, Inc., See address and contact information above. **Management:** Cristy Garcia-Thomas, Publisher. Steve Lyles, Advertising Director. **Editorial:** Sue Gronemus, Managing Editor. Sue Nord, Local News Editor.

CUDAHY REMINDER-ENTERPRISE. 15700 W Cleveland Ave., New Berlin, WI 53151. Telephone: 262-938-5000. FAX: 262-938-5001. E-MAIL: communitynews@cninewsonline.com. URL: http://www.cninewsonline.com. Year Established: 1909. Pub. Frequency: w. (Thu.) Page Size: tabloid. Subscrip. Rate: $.75 newsstand/cover; $28.25/yr local; $59.25/yr in state incl. MI, MN, IL, IA; $86.45/yr elsewhere. Circulation: 3,434 per issue (paid). **Owner(s):** CNI Community Newspapers, Inc., See address and contact information above. **Management:** Cristy Garcia-Thomas, Publisher. Steve Lyles, Advertising Director. Kate House, Classified Adv. Mgr.. **Editorial:** Amy Muehlbauer, Editor. Sue Gronemus, Managing Editor. Mark Hutchinson, Sports Editor.

Weeklies

ELM GROVE ELM LEAVES. 15700 W Cleveland Ave., New Berlin, WI 53151. Telephone: 262-938-5000. FAX: 262-938-5001. E-MAIL: communitynews@cninewsonline.com. URL: http://www.cninewsonline.com. Pub. Frequency: w. (Thu.) Page Size: tabloid. Subscrip. Rate: $.75 newsstand/cover; $28.25/yr local; $59.25/yr in state incl. MI, MN, IL, IA; $86.45/yr elsewhere. Circulation: 1,581 per issue (paid). **Owner(s):** CNI Community Newspapers, Inc., See address and contact information above. **Management:** Cristy Garcia-Thomas, Publisher. Steve Lyles, Advertising Director. Dave Rice, Circulation Manager. Kate House, Classified Adv. Mgr.. **Editorial:** Michael Zahn, Editor. Sue Gronemus, Managing Editor.

FOX POINT-BAYSIDE-RIVER HILLS HERALD. 15700 W Cleveland Ave., New Berlin, WI 53151. Telephone: 262-938-5000. E-MAIL: communitynews@cnionline.com. URL: http://www.cninewsonline.com. Year Established: 1928. Pub. Frequency: w. (Thu.) Page Size: tabloid. Subscrip. Rate: $.75 newsstand/cover; $26.50/yr local; $56.50/yr out of area; $83.45/yr elsewhere. Circulation: 1,966 per issue (paid). **Owner(s):** CNI Community Newspapers, Inc., See address and contact information above. **Management:** Cristy Garcia-Thomas, Publisher. Steve Lyles, Advertising Director. **Editorial:** Roger Bartel, Editor-in-Chief. Sue Nord, Local News Editor.

FRANKLIN HUB. 15700 W Cleveland Ave., New Berlin, WI 53151. Telephone: 262-938-5000. FAX: 262-938-5001. E-MAIL: communitynewsl@add-inc.com. URL: http://www.cninewsonline.com. Year Established: 1927. Pub. Frequency: w. (Thu.) Page Size: tabloid. Subscrip. Rate: $.75 newsstand/cover; $28.25/yr local; $59.25/yr mailed in state incl. MN, MI, IL, IA; $86.45/yr mailed elsewhere. Circulation: 3,588 per issue (paid). **Owner(s):** CNI Community Newspapers, Inc., See address and contact information above. **Management:** Cristy Garcia-Thomas, Publisher. Steve Lyles, Advertising Manager. Dave Rice, Circulation Manager. Kate House, Classified Adv. Mgr.. **Editorial:** Jennifer Pfaff, Editor. Roger Bartel, Editor-in-Chief. Sue Gronemus, Managing Editor.

GERMANTOWN BANNER-PRESS. 15700 W Cleveland Ave, New Berlin, WI 53151. Telephone: 262-938-5000. FAX: 262-938-5001. E-MAIL: communitynews@jcninewsonline.com. URL: http://www.cninewsonline.com. Year Established: 1955. Pub. Frequency: w. (Thu.) Page Size: tabloid. Subscrip. Rate: $.75 newsstand/cover; $28.25/yr local; $59.25/yr mailed in state & MI, MN, IL, IA; $86.45/yr mailed elsewhere. Circulation: 8,204 per issue (paid). **Owner(s):** Journal Community Publishing Group, 600 Industrial Dr., PO Box 609, Waupaca, WI 54981. Telephone: 715-258-8450. FAX: 715-258-4896. **Management:** Cristy Garcia-Thomas, Publisher. Steve Lyles, Advertising Director. Dave Rice, Circulation Manager. Kate House, Classified Adv. Mgr.. **Editorial:** Katie Klein, Editor. Sue Gronemus, Managing Editor. Tom Skibosh, Sports Editor.

GLENDALE HERALD. 15700 W Cleveland Ave., New Berlin, WI 53151. Telephone: 262-938-5000. E-MAIL: communitynews@cninewsonline.com. URL: http://www.cninewsonline.com. Year Established: 1928. Pub. Frequency: w. (Thu.) Page Size: tabloid. Subscrip. Rate: $.75 newsstand/cover; $26.50/yr local; $56.25/yr out of area; $83.45/yr elsewhere. Circulation: 1,840 per issue (paid). **Owner(s):** CNI Community Newspapers, Inc., See address and contact information above. **Management:** Cristy Garcia-Thomas, Publisher. Steve Lyles, Advertising Director. Kate House, Classified Adv. Mgr.. **Editorial:** Sue Nord, Local News Editor.

GREENDALE VILLAGE LIFE. 15770 W. Cleveland Ave., New Berlin, WI 53151. E-MAIL: communitynews@cninewsonline.com. URL: http://www.cninewsonline.com. Year Established: 1960. Pub. Frequency: w. (Thu.) Page Size: tabloid. Subscrip. Rate: $.75 newsstand/cover; $28.25/yr local; $59.25/yr in state incl. MN, MI, IL, IA; $86.45/yr elsewhere. Circulation: 2,947 per issue (paid). **Owner(s):** CNI Community Newspapers, Inc., See address and contact information above. **Management:** Cristy Garcia-Thomas, Publisher. Steve Lyles, Advertising Director. Dave Rice, Circulation Manager. Kate House, Classified Adv. Mgr.. **Editorial:** Jennifer Pfaff, Editor. Sue Gronemus, Managing Editor.

GREENFIELD OBSERVER. ISSN 1050-1185
15700 W Cleveland Ave., New Berlin, WI 53151. Telephone: 262-938-5000. E-MAIL: communitynews@cninewsonline.com. URL: http://www.cninewsonline.com. Year Established: 1962. Pub. Frequency: w. (Thu.) Page Size: tabloid. Subscrip. Rate: $.75 newsstand/cover; $28.25/yr local; $59.25/yr in state & MI, MN, IL, IA; $86.45/yr elsewhere. Circulation: 3,469 per issue (controlled and free). **Owner(s):** CNI Community Newspapers, Inc., See address and contact information above. **Management:** Cristy Garcia-Thomas, Publisher. Steve Lyles, Advertising Director. Dave Rice, Circulation Manager. Kate House, Classified Adv. Mgr.. **Editorial:** Jennifer Pfaff, Editor. Sue Gronemus, Managing Editor.

HALES CORNER VILLAGE HUB. 15700 W Cleveland Ave., New Berlin, WI 53151. Telephone: 262-938-5000. FAX: 262-938-5001. E-MAIL: communitynews@add-inc.com. URL: http://www.cninewsonline.com. Pub. Frequency: w. (Thu.) Page Size: tabloid. Subscrip. Rate: $.75 newsstand/cover; $28.25/yr local; $59.25/yr in state & MN, MI, IL, IA; $86.45/yr elsewhere. Circulation: 2,000 per issue (paid). **Owner(s):** CNI Community Newspapers, Inc., See address and contact information above. **Management:** Cristy Garcia-Thomas, Publisher. Steve Lyles, Advertising Director. Kate House, Classified Adv. Mgr.. **Editorial:** Roger Bartel, Editor-in-Chief. Sue Gronemus, Managing Editor.

MENOMONEE FALLS NEWS. 15700 W Cleveland Ave, New Berlin, WI 53151. Telephone: 262-938-5000. FAX: 262-938-5001. E-MAIL: communitynews@cninewsonline.com. URL: http://www.cninewsonline.com. Year Established: 1894. Pub. Frequency: w. (Thu.) Page Size: tabloid. Subscrip. Rate: $.75 newsstand/cover; $28.25/yr local; $59.25/yr mailed in state & surrounding states; $86.45/yr mailed elsewhere. Circulation: 4,075 per issue (paid). **Owner(s):** Journal Community Publishing Group, 600 Industrial Dr., PO Box 609, Waupaca, WI 54981. Telephone: 715-258-8450. FAX: 715-258-4896. **Management:** Cristy Garcia-Thomas, Publisher. Steve Lyles, Advertising Director. Kate House, Classified Adv. Mgr.. **Editorial:** Katie Klein, Editor. Tom Skibosh, Sports Editor.

MEQUON-THIENSVILLE COURANT. ISSN 1089-4225
15700 W Cleveland Ave., New Berlin, WI 53151. Telephone: 262-938-5000. FAX: 262-938-5001. E-MAIL: communitynews@cninewsonline.com. URL: http://www.cninewsonline.com. Year Established: 1992. Pub. Frequency: w. (Thu.) Page Size: tabloid. Subscrip. Rate: $.75 newsstand/cover; $28.25/yr local; $59.25/yr mailed in state incl. MN, MI, IL, IA (effective 2006); $89.25/yr mailed elsewhere. Circulation: 1,468 per issue (paid). **Owner(s):** CNI Community Newspapers, Inc., See address and contact information above. **Management:** Cristy Garcia-Thomas, Publisher. Steve Lyles, Advertising Manager. Kate House, Classified Adv. Mgr.. **Editorial:** Sue Gronemus, Managing Editor. Katie Klein, Local News Editor. Matt Newman, Sports Editor.

MUSKEGO SUN. 15700 W Cleveland Ave., New Berlin, WI 53151. Telephone: 262-938-5000. E-MAIL: communitynews@cninewsonline.com. URL: http://www.cninewsonline.com. Year Established: 1927. Pub. Frequency: w. (Thu.) Page Size: tabloid. Subscrip. Rate: $.75 newsstand/cover; $28.25/yr local; $59.25/yr in state & surrounding states; $86.45/yr mailed elsewhere. Circulation: 3,574 per issue (paid). **Owner(s):** CNI Community Newspapers, Inc., See address and contact information above. **Management:** Cristy Garcia-Thomas, Publisher. Steve Lyles, Advertising Director. Kate House, Classified Adv. Mgr.. **Editorial:** Roger Bartel, Editor-in-Chief. Sue Gronemus, Managing Editor.

NEW BERLIN CITIZEN. 15700 W Cleveland Ave., New Berlin, WI 53151. Telephone: 262-938-5000. E-MAIL: communitynews@cninewsonline.com. URL: http://www.cninewsonline.com. Pub. Frequency: w. (Thu.) Page Size: tabloid. Subscrip. Rate: $.75 newsstand/cover; $28.25/yr local; $59.25/yr out of area incl. MI, MN, IL, IA; $86/yr elsewhere. Circulation: 4,500 per issue (paid). **Owner(s):** CNI Community Newspapers, Inc., See address and contact information above. **Management:** Cristy Garcia-Thomas, Publisher. Steve Lyles, Advertising Director. Kate House, Classified Adv. Mgr.. **Editorial:** Michael Zahn, Editor. Sue Gronemus, Managing Editor.

NORTH SHORE HERALD. 15700 W Cleveland Ave., New Berlin, WI 53151. Telephone: 262-938-5000. FAX: 262-938-5001. E-MAIL: communitynews@cninewsonline.com. URL: http://www.cninewsonline.com. Mailing Address: PO Box 510210, New Berlin, WI 53151. Year Established: 1928. Pub. Frequency: w. (Thu.) Page Size: tabloid. Subscrip. Rate: $.75 newsstand/cover; $28.25/yr local; $59.25/yr mailed in state incl. MI, MN, IL, IA; $86.45/yr mailed out of area. Circulation: 12,000 per issue (paid). **Owner(s):** CNI Community Newspapers, Inc., See address and contact information above. **Management:** Cristy Garcia-Thomas, Publisher. Steve Lyles, Advertising Director. Dave Rice, Circulation Manager. Kate House, Classified Adv. Mgr.. **Editorial:** Sue Gronemus, Managing Editor. Sue Nord, Local News Editor. Matt Newman, Sports Editor.

OAK CREEK PICTORIAL. 15700 W Cleveland Ave., New Berlin, WI 53151. Telephone: 262-938-5000. FAX: 262-938-5001. E-MAIL: communitynews@cninewsonline.com. URL: http://www.cninewsonline.com. Pub. Frequency: w. (Thu.) Page Size: tabloid. Subscrip. Rate: $.75 newsstand/cover; $28.25/yr local; $59.25/yr in state incl. MN, MI, IL, IA; $86.45/yr elsewhere. Circulation: 4,566 per issue (paid). **Owner(s):** CNI Community Newspapers, Inc., See address and contact information above. **Management:** Cristy Garcia-Thomas, Publisher. Steve Lyles, Advertising Director. Kate House, Classified Adv. Mgr.. **Editorial:** Jennifer Pfaff, Editor. Sue Gronemus, Managing Editor.

SHOREWOOD HERALD. 15700 W Cleveland Ave., New Berlin, WI 53151. Telephone: 262-938-5000. E-MAIL: communnitynews@cninewsonline.com. URL: http://www.cninewsonline.com. Year Established: 1927. Pub. Frequency: w. (Thu.) Page Size: tabloid. Subscrip. Rate: $.75 newsstand/cover; $28.25/yr local; $59.25/yr in state incl. MI, MN, IL, IA; $86.45/yr elsewhere. Circulation: 1,811 per issue (paid). **Owner(s):** CNI Community Newspapers, Inc., See address and contact information above. **Management:** Cristy Garcia-Thomas, Publisher. Steve Lyles, Advertising Director. Kate House, Classified Adv. Mgr.. **Editorial:** Sue Nord, Local News Editor.

SOUTH MILWAUKEE VOICE GRAPHIC. 15700 W Cleveland Ave., New Berlin, WI 53151. Telephone: 262-938-5000. E-MAIL: communitynews@cninewsonline.com. URL: http://www.cninewsonline.com. Year Established: 1892. Pub. Frequency: w. (Thu.) Page Size: tabloid. Subscrip. Rate: $.75 newsstand/cover; $28.25/yr mailed local; $59.25/yr mailed in state incl. MN, MI, IL, IA; $86.45/yr mailed elsewhere. Circulation: 3,645 per issue (paid). **Owner(s):** CNI Community Newspapers, Inc., See address and contact information above. **Management:** Cristy Garcia-Thomas, Publisher. Steve Lyles, Advertising Director. Dave Rice, Circulation Manager. Kate House, Classified Adv. Mgr.. **Editorial:** Amy Muehlbauer, Editor. Sue Gronemus, Managing Editor.

ST. FRANCIS REMINDER - ENTERPRISE. 15700 W Cleveland Ave., New Berlin, WI 53151. Telephone: 262-938-5000. FAX: 262-938-5001. URL: http://www.cninewsonline.com. Year Established: 1909. Pub. Frequency: w. (Thu.) Page Size: tabloid. Subscrip. Rate: $.75 newsstand/cover; $28.25/yr local; $59.25/yr mailed in state incl. MN, MI, IL, IA; $86.45/yr mailed elsewhere. Circulation: 1,312 per issue (paid). **Owner(s):** CNI Community Newspapers, Inc., See address and contact information above. **Management:** Cristy Garcia-Thomas, Publisher. Steve Lyles, Advertising Director. Kate House, Classified Adv. Mgr.. **Editorial:** Amy Muehlbauer, Editor. Sue Gronemus, Managing Editor.

WAUWATOSA NEWS-TIMES. 15700 W Cleveland Ave., New Berlin, WI 53151. Telephone: 262-938-5000. FAX: 262-938-5001. E-MAIL: communitynews@cninewsonline.com. URL: http://www.wauwatosanow.com. Year Established: 1898. Pub. Frequency: w. (Thu.) Page Size: tabloid. Subscrip. Rate: $.75 newsstand/cover; $28.25/yr local (effective 2006); $59.25/yr in state incl. MN, MI, IL, IA (effective 2005); $86.45/yr elsewhere. Circulation: 6,286 per issue (paid). **Owner(s):** CNI Community Newspapers, Inc., See address and contact information above. **Management:** Cristy Garcia-Thomas, Publisher. Steve Lyles, Advertising Director. Kate House, Classified Adv. Mgr.. **Editorial:** Jeanne Wieland, Editor. Sue Gronemus, Managing Editor.

WEST ALLIS STAR. 15700 W Cleveland Ave., New Berlin, WI 53151. Telephone: 262-938-5000. FAX: 262-938-5001. E-MAIL: communitynews@cninewsonline.com. URL: http://www.cninewsonline.com. Year Established: 1916. Pub. Frequency: w. (Thu.) Page Size: tabloid. Subscrip. Rate: $.75 newsstand/cover; $28.25/yr local; $59.25/yr in state incl. MN, MI, IL, IA; $86.45/yr elsewhere. Circulation: 4,926 per issue (paid). **Owner(s):** CNI Community Newspapers, Inc., See address and contact information above. **Management:** Steve Lyles, General Manager. Cristy Garcia-Thomas, Publisher. Dave Rice, Circulation Manager. Kate House, Classified Adv. Mgr.. **Editorial:** Roger Bartel, Editor-in-Chief. Sue Gronemus, Managing Editor.

NEW GLARUS

POST MESSENGER RECORDER. 109 5th Ave, Ste A, New Glarus, WI 53574. Telephone: 608-527-5252. FAX: 608-527-5285. E-MAIL: postmess@tds.net. URL: http://www.newspubinc.com/main.asp?SectionID=9. Mailing Address: P O Box 65, New Glarus, WI 53576. Year Established: 1897. Pub. Frequency: w. (Wed.) Page Size: tabloid. Circulation: 2,643 per issue (paid and free). **Owner(s):** News Publishing Co., 1126 Mills St., Black Earth, WI 53515. Telephone: 608-767-3655. FAX: 608-767-2222. **Management:** Dan Witte, Publisher. Marc Mickelson, Advertising. Louise Ellis, Classified Adv. Mgr.. **Editorial:** John Donaldson, Managing Editor.Readers: Bellevill, Monticello, and New Glarus areas

NEW LONDON

PRESS-STAR. 416 N. Water St., New London, WI 54961-0283. Telephone: 920-982-4321. FAX: 920-982-7672. Mailing Address: PO Box 264, New London, WI 54961-0283. Year Established: 1891. Pub. Frequency: w. (Thu.) Page Size: tabloid. Subscrip. Rate: $.75 newsstand/cover; $24/yr in county; $30/yr mailed out of county; $36/yr mailed out of state. Circulation: 4,500 per issue (paid and free). **Owner(s):** Journal Community Publishing Group, 600 Industrial Dr., PO Box 609, Waupaca, WI 54981. Telephone: 715-258-8450. **Management:** William Melendes, Publisher. Bill Jahnke, Circulation Manager. **Editorial:** John Faucher, Editor.

NEW RICHMOND

NEW RICHMOND NEWS. 127 S. Knowles Ave., New Richmond, WI 54017. Telephone: 715-246-6881. FAX: 715-246-7117. URL: http://www.rivertowns.net. Mailing Address: PO Box 338, New Richmond, WI 54017. Year Established: 1869. Pub. Frequency: w. (Thu.) Page Size: broadsheet. Subscrip. Rate: $1.25 newsstand/cover; $42/yr mailed in county; $55/yr out of county. Circulation: 5,000 per issue (paid). **Owner(s):** Jeff Meyer, 101 Fifth St., N., Fargo, ND 58102. Telephone: 701-235-7311. **Management:** Michael Burke, General Manager. Steve Dzubay, Publisher. Rene Findlay, Advertising Manager. **Editorial:** Jeff Holmquist, Editor.

OCONOMOWOC

OCONOMOWOC ENTERPRISE. 212 E Wisconsin Ave, Oconomowoc, WI 53066. Telephone: 262-567-5511. FAX: 262-567-1723. Mailing Address: PO Box B, Oconomowoc, WI 53066. Year Established: 1888. Pub. Frequency: w. (Thu.) Page Size: broadsheet. Subscrip. Rate: $.50 newsstand/cover; $20.80/yr home delivery local; $28.60/yr mailed within 50 mi.; $36.40/yr mailed elsewhere. Adv. Rate: col. inch $7.95 Circulation: 6,000 per issue (paid). **Owner(s):** Conley Publishing Group, Ltd., 119 Monroe St., Beaver Dam, WI 53916. Telephone: 920-885-7800. **Management:** Kevin Passon, Publisher. Jim Ramseyer, Advertising Manager. Jan Luebke, Circulation Manager. **Editorial:** Kevin Passon, Editor.

OCONTO FALLS

OCONTO COUNTY TIMES-HERALD. 107 S. Main St., Oconto Falls, WI 54154-0128. Telephone: 920-848-3427. FAX: 920-848-3430. E-MAIL: timesherald@ez-net.com. Year Established: 1897. Pub. Frequency: s-w. (Sun & Wed.) Page Size: broadsheet. Subscrip. Rate: $.75 newsstand/cover; $23/yr in county; $33/yr out of county. Adv. Rate: col. inch $9.65 Circulation: 4,950 per issue (controlled and free). **Owner(s):** Roger F. Shellman, See address and contact information above. **Management:** Roger F Shellman, Publisher. Sandy Leisch, Advertising Manager. Dayle Smoot, Circulation Manager. **Editorial:** Roger F Shellman, Editor.

OMRO

OMRO HERALD, THE. 127 W. Main St., Omro, WI 54963. Telephone: 920-685-2707. FAX: 920-361-1518. Year Established: 1895. Pub. Frequency: w. (Thu.) Page Size: tabloid. Subscrip. Rate: $.75 newsstand/cover; $28/yr local; $50/yr in state; $57/yr out of state. Circulation: 1,125 per issue (paid). **Owner(s):** Ty Gonyo, 301 June St., Berlin, WI 54923. Telephone: 920-361-1515. **Management:** Ty Gonyo, Publisher. Kristian Troudt, Advertising Manager. **Editorial:** Jason Fox, Editor.

OREGON

FITCHBURG STAR. 845 Market St., Oregon, WI 53575. Telephone: 608-835-6677. FAX: 608-835-0130. Year Established: 1974. Pub. Frequency: bi-w. (Thu.) Page Size: tabloid.Adv. Rate: col. inch $9.95 Circulation: 6,600 per issue (free). **Owner(s):** Woodward Communications Inc., PO Box 688, Dubuque, IA 52004-0668. Telephone: 563-588-5611. FAX: 563-588-5739. **Management:** Aaron Lawry, Advertising. **Editorial:** Bill Livick, Editor.

OREGON OBSERVER. 845 Market St., Oregon, WI 53575. E-MAIL: oregonobserver@wcinet.com. URL: http://www.oregonobserver.com. Year Established: 1844. Pub. Frequency: w. (Thu.) Page Size: tabloid. Subscrip. Rate: $1 newsstand/cover; $32/yr in county; $40/yr mailed out of county. Adv. Rate: col. inch $7.25 Circulation: 3,050 per issue (paid). **Owner(s):** Woodward Communications Inc., PO Box 688, Dubuque, IA 52004-0688. Telephone: 563-588-5611. FAX: 563-588-5739. **Management:** Aaron Lawry, Advertising. **Editorial:** Bill Livick, Editor. Seth Javag, Reporter. Jeremy Jones, Sports Editor.

ORFORDVILLE

ORFORDVILLE JOURNAL & FOOTVILLE NEWS. 124 E. Spring St., Orfordville, WI 53576-0248. Telephone: 608-879-2211. FAX: 608-879-2211. Year Established: 1909. Pub. Frequency: w. (Wed.) Page Size: tabloid. Subscrip. Rate: $.40 newsstand/cover; $18/yr in county; $21/yr out of county. Circulation: 1,250 per issue (paid). **Owner(s):** George E. Stewart, See address and contact information above. **Management:** George E. Stewart, Publisher. **Editorial:** George E. Stewart, Editor.

OSCEOLA

OSCEOLA SUN. 108 Cascade St., Osceola, WI 54020-0248. Telephone: 715-294-2314. E-MAIL: sun@centurytel.net. Year Established: 1897. Pub. Frequency: w. (Wed.) Page Size: broadsheet. Subscrip. Rate: $.75 newsstand/cover; $24/yr in Polk & St Croix cys.; $32/yr in state. Freelance Pay: $25/story. Circulation: 2,000 per issue (paid). **Owner(s):** Gene Johnson, See address and contact information above. **Management:** Carter Johnson, Publisher. Sue VanBuskirk, Advertising Manager. Carrie Larson, Circulation Manager. **Editorial:** Kyle Weaver, Editor.

OSHKOSH

OSHKOSH BUYERS GUIDE. 314 N. Koeller St., Oshkosh, WI 54902. Telephone: 920-235-1790. FAX: 920-235-1833. E-MAIL: info@jcpgroup.com. URL: http://www.oshkoshinfo.com. Year Established: 1937. Pub. Frequency: w. (Wed.) Page Size: tabloid.Adv. Rate: col. inch $12 Freelance Pay: $15-$20/article. Circulation: 26,000 per issue (free). **Owner(s):** Journal Community Publishing Group, 600 Industrial Dr., PO Box 609, Waupaca, WI 54981. Telephone: 715-258-8450. **Management:** Larry Antony, General Manager.

OSSEO

TRI-COUNTY NEWS (OSSEO). 51119 Omaha St., Osseo, WI 54758-0460. Telephone: 715-597-3313. FAX: 715-597-2705. E-MAIL: jenpbinc@triwest.net. Mailing Address: PO Box 460, Osseo, WI 54758-0460. Year Established: 1900. Pub. Frequency: w. (Thu.) Page Size: standard. Subscrip. Rate: $.75 newsstand/cover; $21/yr in county. Circulation: 3,500 per issue (paid). **Owner(s):** Ted Nyseth, See address and contact information above. **Management:** Ted Nyseth, Publisher. **Editorial:** Michelle Jensen, Managing Editor.

OSSTO

AUGUSTA AREA TIMES. ISSN 0749-7083
PO Box 460, Ossto, WI 54758. Telephone: 715-597-3313. FAX: 715-597-2705. Year Established: 1900. Pub. Frequency: w. (Wed.) Page Size: standard. Subscrip. Rate: $.75 newsstand/cover; $20/yr mailed local; $24/yr mailed out of area (effective 2005); $28/yr mailed out of state. Circulation: 1,500 per issue (paid). **Owner(s):** Triad Publication, Llc., See address and contact information above. **Management:** Chad P Nysteth, Publisher.

OWEN

O-W ENTERPRISE. ISSN 1047-8361
325 Central Ave, Owen, WI 54460. Telephone: 715-229-2103. FAX: 715-229-2104. E-MAIL: owenterprise@charter.net. Year Established: 1906. Pub. Frequency: w. (Wed.) Page Size: tabloid. Subscrip. Rate: $.75 newsstand/cover; $30/yr in county; $35/yr in state; $40/yr mailed elsewhere. Adv. Rate: col. inch $6 Circulation: 1,100 per issue (paid). **Owner(s):** Mark T. Renderman, See address and contact information above. **Management:** Mark T. Renderman, Publisher. **Editorial:** Nathan J. LePage, Editor.

PARK FALLS

PARK FALLS HERALD. 259 Second Ave., N., Park Falls, WI 54552. Telephone: 715-762-4940. FAX: 715-762-2757. E-MAIL: herald@parkfallswi.com. URL: http://www.parkfallswi.com. Mailing Address: PO Box 410, Park Falls, WI 54552. Year Established: 1900. Pub. Frequency: w. (Thu.) Page Size: tabloid. Subscrip. Rate: $.75 newsstand/cover; $31/yr in county; $36/yr mailed in state; $41/yr mailed out of state. Freelance Pay: $5-$50/article. Circulation: 3,500 per issue (paid). **Owner(s):** Superior Publishing Corp., 1105 Tower Ave., Superior, WI 54880-1502. **Management:** Kenneth Dischler, Publisher. **Editorial:** Kenneth Dischler, Editor.

PESHTIGO

PESHTIGO TIMES. PO Box 187, Peshtigo, WI 54157. Telephone: 715-582-4541. FAX: 715-582-4662. Year Established: 1929. Pub. Frequency: w. (Wed.) Page Size: broadsheet. Subscrip. Rate: $.60 newsstand/cover; $23/yr in county; $35/yr in state; $38/yr out of state. Circulation: 12,000 per issue (paid). **Owner(s):** Pesch Publishing Co., Inc., See address and contact information above. **Management:** Mary Ann Gardon, Publisher. Chuck Gardon, Advertising Manager. **Editorial:** Mike Gardon, Sports.

PHILLIPS

BEE (PHILLIPS), THE. 115 N. Lake Ave., Phillips, WI 54555-0170. Telephone: 715-339-3036. FAX: 715-339-4300. E-MAIL: bee@mx3.com. URL: http://www.phillipswi.com. Mailing Address: PO Box 170, Phillips, WI 54555-0170. Year Established: 1884. Pub. Frequency: w. (Thu.) Page Size: tabloid. Subscrip. Rate: $1 newsstand/cover; $36/yr mailed in county; $41/yr mailed out of county; $41/yr mailed out of state. Adv. Rate: col. inch $7 Circulation: 4,500 per issue (paid). **Owner(s):** Superior Publishing Corp., 1105 Tower Ave, Superior, WI 54880. Telephone: 715-395-5725. FAX: 715-395-5729. **Management:** Trisha Kempkes, Publisher. Sue Mergen, Advertising Manager. Linda Haskins, Classified Adv. Mgr.. **Editorial:** Trisha Kempkes, Editor.

PLATTEVILLE

GRANT, IOWA, LAFAYETTE SHOPPING NEWS, THE. 41 Means Dr., Platteville, WI 53818. Telephone: 608-348-3388. FAX: 608-348-2374. E-MAIL: kneumeister@wcinet.com. URL: http://www.wcinet.com. Mailing Address: PO Box 500, Platteville, WI 53818-0500. Pub. Frequency: w. (Tue.) Page Size: standard. Subscrip. Rate: $35/yr mailed 3rd class; $120/yr mailed 1st class. Adv. Rate: col. inch $11.33 Circulation: 21,071 per issue (free). **Owner(s):** Woodward Communications Inc., PO Box 688, Dubuque, IA 52004-0668. Telephone: 563-588-5687. **Management:** Kathy Neumeister, Publisher. Jacque Engling, Business Manager.

PLATTEVILLE JOURNAL. 25 E. Main St, Platteville, WI 53818. Telephone: 608-348-3006. FAX: 608-348-7979. Year Established: 1899. Pub. Frequency: w. (Wed.) Page Size: broadsheet. Subscrip. Rate: $1 newsstand/cover; $26/yr in county; $32/yr mailed out of county. Circulation: 7,000 per issue (paid). **Owner(s):** Morris Newspaper Corporation, 27 Abercorn St., Savannah, GA 31401. Telephone: 912-233-1281. FAX: 912-232-4639. **Management:** John D. Ingebritsen, Publisher. Ann Rupp, Advertising Manager. **Editorial:** Dean Wackerfshaufer, Editor.

SHOPPING NEWS. PO Box 500, Platteville, WI 53818-0500. Telephone: 608-348-2374. FAX: 608-348-3388. E-MAIL: kneumeister@wcinet.com. URL: http://www.shoppingnewspapers.com. Year Established: 1950. Pub. Frequency: w. (Tue.) Page Size: tabloid. Subscrip. Rate: $35/yr mailed 3rd class. Adv. Rate: col. inch $1,225 Circulation: 37,100 per issue (free). **Owner(s):** Woodward Communications Inc., PO Box 688, Dubuque, IA 52004. Telephone: 563-588-5611. FAX: 563-588-5739. **Management:** Kathy Neumeister, Publisher. Lori Droessler, Advertising Manager. Shelley Brown, Circulation Manager. Jacque Engling, Business Manager. **Editorial:** Kathy Neumeister, Editor.

PLYMOUTH

PLYMOUTH-REVIEW, THE. 113 E. Mill St., Plymouth, WI 53073-1776. Telephone: 920-893-6411. FAX: 920-893-5505. E-MAIL: reply@plymouthreview.com. URL: http://www.plymouth-review.com. Mailing Address: P.O. Box 317, Plymouth, WI 53073. Pub. Frequency: s-w. (Tue. & Thu.) Page Size: tabloid. Subscrip. Rate: $.75 newsstand/cover; $36/yr in county; $54/yr out of county. Circulation: 17,600 per issue (paid). **Owner(s):** Wisconsin News Press, Inc., See address and contact information above. **Management:** Barry S. Johanson, Publisher. Debbie Mueller, Circulation Manager. Mary Blanke, Classified Adv. Mgr.. Ian Johanson, Associate Publisher. **Editorial:** Sue Mroz, Feature Editor. Emmitt Feldner, News Editor.

SHEBOYGAN FALLS NEWS. ISSN 0897-4543
113 E. Mill St., Plymouth, WI 53073. E-MAIL: reply@plymouth-review.com. URL: http://www.plymouth-review.com. Mailing Address: P.O. Box 317, Plymouth, WI 53073. Year Established: 1980. Pub. Frequency: w. (Wed.) Page Size: broadsheet. Subscrip. Rate: $.75 newsstand/cover; $39/yr in county; $44/yr out of county. Circulation: 2,200 per issue (paid). **Owner(s):** Wisconsin News Press, Inc., See address and contact information above. **Management:** Barry S. Johanson, Publisher. Debbie Mueller, Circulation Manager. Ian Johanson, Associate Publisher. **Editorial:** Sue Mroz, Feature Editor. Jed Buelow, News Editor.

PORT WASHINGTON

OZAUKEE PRESS. ISSN 0749-7164
125 E. Main St., Port Washington, WI 53074. Telephone: 262-284-3494. FAX: 262-284-0067. E-MAIL: news@ozaukeepress.com. URL: http://www.ozaukeepress.com. Mailing Address: P.O. Box 249, Port Washington, WI 53047-0249. Year Established: 1939. Pub. Frequency: w. (Thu.) Page Size: tabloid. Subscrip. Rate: $1.25 newsstand/cover; $35/yr in state; $49/yr out of state. Circulation: 15,500 per issue (paid). **Owner(s):** Port Publications, See address and contact information above. **Management:** William Schanen, III III, Publisher. Holly Ostermann, Advertising Manager. Doris Stuht, Circulation Manager. **Editorial:** William Schanen, IV IV, Managing Editor.

PORTAGE

SHOPPER STOPPER. 1640 LaDawn Dr., Portage, WI 53901-0470. Telephone: 608-745-3500. FAX: 608-745-3530. URL: http://www.scwn.com. Mailing Address: PO Box 470, Portage, WI 53901-0470. Year Established: 1970. Pub. Frequency: s-w. (Wed. & Sun.) Page Size: tabloid. Subscrip. Rate: $25/yr mailed 3rd class. Adv. Rate: col. inch $6.82 Circulation: 127,000 per issue (free). **Owner(s):** Capital Newspapers, Inc., 1901 Fish Hatchery Rd., Madison, WI 53713. **Management:** George Althoff, Publisher. Julie Brown, Advertising Manager. Debbie Sprague, Circulation Manager.

Weeklies

WISCONSIN DELLS EVENTS. 1640 LaDawn Dr., Portage, WI 53901-0470. Telephone: 608-254-8327. FAX: 608-355-8328. E-MAIL: wde-news@capitalnewspapers.com. URL: http://www.wiscnews.com/wde/. Mailing Address: PO Box 116, Wisconsin Dells, WI 53965. Year Established: 1905. Pub. Frequency: s-w. (Wed. & Sat.) Page Size: broadsheet. Subscrip. Rate: $.75 newsstand/cover; $40/yr mailed in county; $42/yr mailed out of county; $53/yr mailed out of state. Circulation: 2,100 per issue (paid). **Owner(s):** Capital Newspapers, Inc., 1901 Fish Hatchery Rd., Madison, WI 53713. **Management:** George Althoff, Publisher. Julie Brown, Advertising Manager. **Editorial:** Kay Lapp James, Editor. Jim denHollander, Sports.

WISCONSIN REMINDER. 1640 LaDawn Dr., Portage, WI 53901-0470. Mailing Address: PO Box 470, Portage, WI 53901-0470. Pub. Frequency: s-w. (Wed. & Sun.) Page Size: standard Circulation: 15,000 per issue (free). **Owner(s):** Capital Newspapers, Inc., 1901 Fish Hatchery Rd., Madison, WI 53713. **Management:** George Althoff, Publisher. Julie Brown, Advertising Manager.

POYNETTE

POYNETTE PRESS. 125 N. Main St., Poynette, WI 53955-0037. Telephone: 608-635-2565. FAX: 608-635-4542. Mailing Address: PO Box 37, Poynette, WI 53955-0037. Year Established: 1884. Pub. Frequency: w. (Wed.) Page Size: broadsheet. Subscrip. Rate: $.75 newsstand/cover; $23/yr home delivery in county; $26.50/yr mailed out of county. Circulation: 1,300 per issue (paid). **Owner(s):** Art Drake, See address and contact information above. **Management:** Art Drake, Publisher. Lynn Auclar, Advertising. **Editorial:** Art Drake, Editor.

PRAIRIE DU CHIEN

COURIER PRESS, THE. 132 S. Beaumont Rd., Prairie Du Chien, WI 53821. Telephone: 608-326-2441. FAX: 608-326-2443. Mailing Address: PO Box 149, Prairie Du Chien, WI 53821. Year Established: 1848. Pub. Frequency: s-w. (Mon. & Wed.) Page Size: tabloid. Subscrip. Rate: $.75 newsstand/cover; $39.50/yr in area; $49.50/yr out of area. Circulation: 16,000 per issue (controlled and free). **Owner(s):** Howe Printing Co., PO Box 149, Prairie du Chien, WI 53821. **Management:** Gary J. Howe, Publisher. **Editorial:** Kelli Pattee, Editor.

WISCONSIN-IOWA SHOPPING NEWS. 405 N. Marquatte, Prairie Du Chien, WI 53821-0097. Telephone: 608-326-2457. FAX: 608-326-6621. E-MAIL: prairieshopnews@wcinet.com. URL: http://www.wcinet.com. Mailing Address: PO Box 97, Prairie Du Chien, WI 53821-0097. Pub. Frequency: w. (Tue.) Page Size: standard. Subscrip. Rate: $28/yr mailed 3rd class. Adv. Rate: col. inch $6.65 Circulation: 19,000 per issue (free). **Owner(s):** Woodward Communications Inc., PO Box 688, Dubuque, IA 52004-0688. Telephone: 563-588-5687. **Management:** Jesse Aspenson, General Manager. Greg Tangeman, Advertising Manager.

PRESCOTT

PRESCOTT JOURNAL. 311 Dakota St., Prescott, WI 54021. Telephone: 715-262-5454. FAX: 715-262-5474. E-MAIL: presjour@pressenter.com. URL: http://www.prescott-journal.pressenter.com. Year Established: 1855. Pub. Frequency: w. (Thu.) Page Size: broadsheet. Subscrip. Rate: $.75 newsstand/cover; $29/yr in county & adj. cys.; $38/yr out of area; $45/yr out of state. Circulation: 4,500 (paid). **Owner(s):** Weekly Newspapers, Inc., See address and contact information above. **Management:** Gary B. Rawn, Publisher. Jenny Kusch, Advertising Manager. **Editorial:** Matthew Perenchio, Editor. Gary B. Rawn, Managing Editor.

RANDOM LAKE

SOUNDER, THE. 405 Second St, Random Lake, WI 53075-0346. Telephone: 920-994-9244. FAX: 920-994-4817. E-MAIL: sounder@execpc.com. URL: http://www.thesounder.com. Mailing Address: PO Box 346, Random Lake, WI 53075-0346. Year Established: 1918. Pub. Frequency: w. (Thu.) Page Size: tabloid. Subscrip. Rate: $.50 newsstand/cover; $19/yr in Sheyboygan & Ozaukee cys.; $21.50/yr out of area; $24/yr out of state. Adv. Rate: col. inch $3.63 Circulation: 2,922 per issue (paid). **Owner(s):** Times Printing Co., Inc., 100 Industrial Dr., Random Lake, WI 53075-1636. Telephone: 920-994-4396. FAX: 920-994-2088. **Management:** Gary J. Feider, Advertising Manager. **Editorial:** Gary J. Feider, Editor-in-Chief.

REEDSBURG

REEDSBURG TIMES-PRESS. 126 S. Walnut St., Reedsburg, WI 53959. Telephone: 608-524-4336. FAX: 608-524-4337. E-MAIL: rtp@ads.jvlnet.com. URL: http://www.wiscnews.com. Mailing Address: PO Box 269, Reedsburg, WI 53959. Year Established: 1860. Pub. Frequency: s-w. (Wed. & Sat.) Page Size: broadsheet. Subscrip. Rate: $.60 newsstand/cover; $26/yr mailed in state; $42/yr mailed out of state. Circulation: 1,500 per issue (paid). **Owner(s):** Capital Newspapers, Inc., 1640 LaDawn Dr., Portage, WI 53901-0470. Telephone: 800-236-2110. **Management:** George Althoff, Publisher. Teresa Klinger, Circulation Manager. **Editorial:** Emily Bialkowski, Editor. Brady Ambrose, Sports.

RICE LAKE

CHRONOTYPE, THE. 28 S. Main St., Rice Lake, WI 54868. Telephone: 715-234-2121. FAX: 715-234-5232. E-MAIL: newsroom@chronotype.com. URL: http://www.ricelakeonline.com. Mailing Address: PO Box 30, Rice Lake, WI 54868. Year Established: 1874. Pub. Frequency: w. (Wed.) Page Size: broadsheet. Subscrip. Rate: $1 newsstand/cover (effective 2006); $37/yr within 50 mi. radius; $48/yr mailed out of area. Adv. Rate: col. inch $9.15 **Wire Service(s):** AP. Circulation: 9,300 per issue (paid). **Owner(s):** Chronotype Publishing, Inc., See address and contact information above. **Management:** Warren Dorrance, Publisher. Robert V. Dorrance, Advertising Director. James Stravan, Circulation Manager. **Editorial:** Sam Finazzo, Editor. David Greschner, Sports Editor.

RICHLAND CENTER

RICHLAND OBSERVER. 172 E. Court St., Richland Center, WI 53581. Telephone: 608-647-6141. Year Established: 1854. Pub. Frequency: w. (Thu.) Page Size: tabloid. Subscrip. Rate: $.75 newsstand/cover; $25/yr mailed in state; $39/yr mailed out of state. Circulation: 4,000 per issue (paid). **Owner(s):** Erik R. Olson, See address and contact information above. **Management:** Erik R. Olson, Publisher. **Editorial:** Erik R. Olson, Editor.

RICHLAND SHOPPING NEWS. 174 N. Main St., Richland Center, WI 53581. Telephone: 608-647-2911. FAX: 608-647-7238. E-MAIL: rcentershopnews@wcinet.com. URL: http://www.wcinet.com. Mailing Address: PO Box 272, Richland Center, WI 53581-0272. Year Established: 1932. Pub. Frequency: w. Page Size: standard. Subscrip. Rate: $30/yr mailed local 3rd class. Adv. Rate: col. inch $5.77 Circulation: 13,500 per issue (free). **Owner(s):** Woodward Communications Inc., PO Box 688, Dubuque, IA 52004-0688. Telephone: 563-588-5687. **Management:** Deb Mullarkey, General Manager. Nancy Noble-Culver, Advertising Manager.

RIPON

BERLIN BUYERS' GUIDE. 321 Watson St., Ripon, WI 54971. Telephone: 920-748-2750. FAX: 920-748-2750. URL: http://www.5countybuyersguide.com. Mailing Address: PO Box 301, Ripon, WI 54971. Year Established: 1945. Pub. Frequency: w. (Sat.) Page Size: tabloid. Circulation: 22,400 per issue (paid and free). **Owner(s):** Schroeder Media LLC, See address and contact information above. **Management:** John McClure, General Manager. Sarah Sine, Advertising Manager.

FIVE COUNTY BUYER'S GUIDE. 321 Watson St., Ripon, WI 54971. Telephone: 920-748-2750. FAX: 920-748-2750. URL: http://www.5countybuyersguide.com. Mailing Address: PO Box 301, Ripon, WI 54971. Pub. Frequency: w. (Sat.) Page Size: standard Circulation: 21,500 per issue (free). **Owner(s):** Schroeder Media LLC, See address and contact information above. **Management:** John McClure, General Manager. Sarah Sine, Advertising Manager.

RIPON COMMONWEALTH PRESS. ISSN 0748-6863
656 Douglas St., P.O. Box 344, Ripon, WI 54971. Telephone: 920-748-3017. FAX: 920-748-3028. Mailing Address: PO Box 344, Ripon, WI 54971-0344. Year Established: 1864. Pub. Frequency: w. (Thu.) Page Size: broadsheet. Subscrip. Rate: $.75 newsstand/cover; $28/yr mailed in county; $34/yr mailed out of county; $41/yr mailed out of state. Circulation: 3,600 per issue (paid). **Owner(s):** Ripon Community Publications, See address and contact information above. **Management:** Tim Lyke, Publisher. Bob Chikowski, Advertising Manager. Cathy Eason, Circulation Manager. **Editorial:** Ian Stepleton, Editor. Bryan Rose, Sports Editor.

RIVER FALLS

RIVER FALLS JOURNAL. 2815 Prairie Dr., River Falls, WI 54022-0025. Telephone: 715-425-1561. FAX: 715-425-5666. E-MAIL: rfj@rivertowns.net. URL: http://www.rivertowns.net. Mailing Address: PO Box 25, River Falls, WI 54022-0025. Year Established: 1854. Pub. Frequency: w. (Thu.) Page Size: broadsheet. Subscrip. Rate: $1.25 newsstand/cover; $45/yr in county; $66/yr out of county. Adv. Rate: col. inch $9.50 Freelance Pay: $20-$50/story. Circulation: 4,400 per issue (paid). **Owner(s):** Jeff Meyer, PO Box 2020, Fargo, ND 58107. Telephone: 701-235-7311. **Management:** Steve Dzubay, Publisher. Mary Beth Kremer, Advertising Manager. Kate Cook, Classified Adv. Mgr.. **Editorial:** Phil Pfuehler, Editor. Bob Burrows, Sports Editor.Readers: 54022 & surrounds

SAUK CITY

SAUK PRAIRIE EAGLE. 725 Water St., Sauk City, WI 53583. Telephone: 608-643-0118. FAX: 608-643-0120. E-MAIL: spe-editorial@capitalnewspapers.com. URL: http://www.wiscnews.com/spe. Mailing Address: PO Box 670, Sauk City, WI 53583. Pub. Frequency: w. (Wed.) Page Size: broadsheet. Subscrip. Rate: $.75 newsstand/cover; $26/yr mailed in state; $42/yr mailed out of state. Circulation: 1,800 per issue (paid). **Owner(s):** Capital Newspapers, Inc., 1901 Fish Hatchery Rd, Madison, WI 53713. Telephone: 608-252-6200. **Management:** George Althoff, Publisher. Eric Hilton, Advertising. **Editorial:** Donna Stehling, Editor.

SAUK-PRAIRIE STAR. 801 Water St., Sauk City, WI 53583. Telephone: 608-643-3444. FAX: 608-643-4988. E-MAIL: saukstar@charterinternet.com. URL: http://www.newspubinc.com. Mailing Address: PO Box 606, Sauk City, WI 53583. Year Established: 1844. Pub. Frequency: w. (Thu.) Page Size: tabloid. Subscrip. Rate: $.75 newsstand/cover; $31/yr in state; $47/yr out of state. Circulation: 3,200 per issue (paid). **Owner(s):** News Publishing Co., 1126 Mills St., Black Earth, WI 53515. PO Box 286, Black Earth, WI 53515. Telephone: 608-767-3655. **Management:** Dan Witte, Publisher. Laura Gordon, Advertising Manager. **Editorial:** Mike Carrignan, Editor.

SEYMOUR

TIMES-PRESS (SEYMOUR). 205 N. Main St., Seymour, WI 54165-0128. Telephone: 920-833-2517. FAX: 920-833-2454. E-MAIL: cohlerr@add-inc.com. Mailing Address: PO Box 128, Seymour, WI 54165. Year Established: 1886. Pub. Frequency: w. (Thu.) Page Size: tabloid. Subscrip. Rate: $.60 newsstand/cover; $26/yr mailed in county; $30/yr out of county; $35/yr out of state. Circulation: 2,400 per issue (paid). **Owner(s):** Journal-Sentinel, PO Box 661, Milwaukee, WI 53201. Telephone: 920-224-2115. **Management:** Rick Cohler, Publisher. **Editorial:** Rick Cohler, Editor-in-Chief.

SHEBOYGAN

SHORELINE CHRONICLE. 632 Center Ave., Sheboygan, WI 53081. Telephone: 920-459-8820. FAX: 920-459-7449. E-MAIL: shoremac@excel.net. URL: http://www.sheboygan-press.com. Mailing Address: PO Box 358, Sheboygan, WI 53082-0358. Year Established: 1976. Pub. Frequency: w. (Tue.) Page Size: tabloid Circulation: 40,200 per issue (free). **Owner(s):** Gannett Company, Inc., 7950 Jones Branch Dr., McLean, VA 22107-0001. Telephone: 703-854-6000. **Management:** Don Therp, Advertising Manager. Manny Nevarez, Circulation Director.

SHELL LAKE

WASHBURN COUNTY REGISTER. ISSN 8755-0520
11 W. Fifth Ave., Shell Lake, WI 54871-0455. Telephone: 715-468-2314. FAX: 715-468-4900. E-MAIL: wcregister@centurytel.net. URL: http://www.wcregister.net. Mailing Address: PO Box 455, Shell Lake, WI 54871-0455. Year Established: 1889. Pub. Frequency: w. (Thu.) Page Size: tabloid. Subscrip. Rate: $.75 newsstand/cover; $25/yr local; $32/yr in WI & MN; $37/yr elsewhere. Circulation: 1,580 per issue (paid). **Owner(s):** Inter County Cooperative Publishing Association, 303 N. Wisconsin Ave., Frederic, WI 54837. Telephone: 715-327-4236. **Management:** Jackie Moody, Advertising. Doug Panek, Manager. **Editorial:** Gary King, Editor.

SPARTA

MONROE COUNTY DEMOCRAT. 1302 River Rd., Sparta, WI 54656-0252. URL: http://www.spartanewspapers.com. Mailing Address: PO Box 252, Sparta, WI 54656-0252. Year Established: 1859. Pub. Frequency: w. (Thu.) Page Size: broadsheet. Subscrip. Rate: $.75 newsstand/cover; $35/yr in county; $38/yr out of county; $47/yr mailed out of state. Adv. Rate: col. inch $7.75 Circulation: 4,900 per issue (paid). **Owner(s):** Monroe County Publishers, Inc., See address and contact information above. **Management:** Theodore C. Radde, General Manager. Zel S. Rice, President. William Gleiss, Publisher. Mark Hayes, Advertising Manager. **Editorial:** William Gleiss, Editor. J.P. Schaller, Sports Editor.

SPARTA HERALD. 1302 River Rd., Sparta, WI 54656-0252. Telephone: 608-269-3186. FAX: 608-269-6876. URL: http://www.spartanewspapers.com. Mailing Address: PO Box 252, Sparta, WI 54656-0252. Year Established: 1858. Pub. Frequency: w. (Mon.) Page Size: broadsheet. Subscrip. Rate: $.75 newsstand/cover; $36/yr mailed local; $39/yr mailed in state; $48/yr mailed out of state. Adv. Rate: col. inch $8.05 Circulation: 4,850 per issue (paid). **Owner(s):** Monroe County Publishers, Inc., PO Box 252, Sparta, WI 54656. Telephone: 608-269-3186. **Management:** Theodore C. Radde, General Manager. Zel S. Rice, President. Patrick Mulvaney, Publisher. Mark Hayes, Advertising Manager. **Editorial:** J.P. Schaller, Sports Editor.

SPOONER

EVERGREEN SHOPPING GUIDE. 509 Front St., Spooner, WI 54801. Telephone: 715-635-2181. FAX: 715-635-2186. E-MAIL: advocate@spacestar.net. URL: http://www.spooneradvocate.com. Mailing Address: PO Box 338, Spooner, WI 54801. Year Established: 1985. Pub. Frequency: w. (Mon.) Page Size: tabloid.Adv. Rate: col. inch $5.25 Circulation: 18,116 per issue (paid and free). **Owner(s):** Superior Publishing Corp., 1105 Tower Ave., Superior, WI 54880-1502. **Management:** Janet Krokson, Publisher. Michelle Carlson, Advertising. Mary Zehm, Circulation Manager. **Editorial:** Bill Thornley, Editor.

SPOONER ADVOCATE. ISSN 8755-6995
509 Front St., Spooner, WI 54801. Telephone: 715-635-2181. FAX: 715-635-2186. E-MAIL: advocate@spacestar.net. URL: http://www.spooneronline.com. Mailing Address: PO Box 338, Spooner, WI 54801. Year Established: 1901. Pub. Frequency: w. (Thu.) Page Size: broadsheet. Subscrip. Rate: $1 newsstand/cover; $34/yr local; $55/yr out of area. Adv. Rate: col. inch $5.25 Circulation: 4,775 per issue (paid). **Owner(s):** Superior Publishing Corp., 1105 Tower Ave., Superior, WI 54880-1502. **Management:** Janet Krokson, Publisher. Michelle Carlson, Advertising Manager. Mary Zehm, Circulation Manager. **Editorial:** William Thornley, Editor.

SPRING VALLEY

SPRING VALLEY SUN/ELMWOOD ARGUS. 216 S. McKay Ave., Spring Valley, WI 54767. Telephone: 715-778-4395. FAX: 715-778-4695. E-MAIL: editor@baldwin-telecom.net. Mailing Address: P.O. Box 69, Spring Valley, WI 54767. Year Established: 1896. Pub. Frequency: w. (Wed.) Page Size: tabloid. Subscrip. Rate: $.75 newsstand/cover; $25/yr mailed in county; $30/yr mailed in WI & MN; $35/yr mailed elsewhere. Adv. Rate: col. inch $4.50 Circulation: 1,200 per issue (paid). **Owner(s):** Paul Seeling, See address and contact information above. **Management:** Paul Seeling, Publisher. **Editorial:** Paul Seeling, Editor.

STANLEY

STANLEY REPUBLICAN. 131 E First Ave, Stanley, WI 54768. Telephone: 715-644-3319. FAX: 715-644-5452. Mailing Address: P.O. Box 185, Stanley, WI 54768-0185. Year Established: 1896. Pub. Frequency: w. (Thu.) Page Size: standard. Subscrip. Rate: $.75 newsstand/cover; $23/yr local; $27/yr in state; $32/yr out of state. Circulation: 2,500 per issue (paid). **Owner(s):** B.J. Fazendin, See address and contact information above. **Management:** B.J. Fazendin, Publisher.

STOUGHTON

STOUGHTON COURIER HUB. ISSN 1049-0655
135 W. Main, Ste. 102, Stoughton, WI 53589-2135. Telephone: 608-873-6671. FAX: 608-873-3473. E-MAIL: stoughtoneditor@wcinet.com. URL: http://www.stoughtonnews.com. Year Established: 1867. Pub. Frequency: w. (Thu.) Page Size: tabloid. Subscrip. Rate: $1 newsstand/cover; $33/yr in county; $41/yr out of county. Adv. Rate: col. inch $7.50 Circulation: 4,500 per issue (paid). **Owner(s):** Woodward Communications Inc., PO Box 688, Dubuque, IA 52004-0688. Telephone: 563-588-5687. FAX: 563-588-5739. **Management:** Judy Shingler, General Manager. **Editorial:** Rick Hummell, Managing Editor. Jeremy Jones, Sports Editor.

STURGEON BAY

DOOR COUNTY ADVOCATE. 235 N Third Ave, Sturgeon Bay, WI 54235. Telephone: 920-743-3321. FAX: 920-743-5817. Mailing Address: PO Box 130, Sturgeon Bay, WI 54235-0130. Year Established: 1862. Pub. Frequency: s-w. (Wed. & Sat.) Page Size: broadsheet. Subscrip. Rate: $.50 newsstand/cover; $45/yr mailed in county; $50/yr mailed in state; $66/yr mailed out of state. Circulation: 12,806. **Owner(s):** Gannett Company, Inc., 7950 Jones Branch Dr., McLean, VA 22102. Telephone: 703-854-6000. **Management:** Gina Ward-Schmelzer, General Manager. Matt Luders, Advertising Manager. Tom Anschutz, Circulation Manager. **Editorial:** Chuck Carlson, Editor.

SUN PRAIRIE

STAR (SUN PRAIRIE), THE. 207 E. Main St., Sun Prairie, WI 53590-0645. Telephone: 608-837-2521. FAX: 608-825-4460. E-MAIL: spdesign@hometownnewsgroup.com. URL: http://www.hometownnewsgroup.com. Mailing Address: PO Box 645, Sun Prairie, WI 53531. Year Established: 1877. Pub. Frequency: w. (Thu.) Page Size: broadsheet. Subscrip. Rate: $.75 newsstand/cover; $31/yr in county; $41/yr out of county. Adv. Rate: col. inch $10.10 Freelance Pay: $0.25/column-inch. Circulation: 5,340 per issue (paid). **Owner(s):** Hometown News Group, 28 Milwaukee Ave., W., Fort Atkinson, WI 53538. **Management:** Wayne Toske, General Manager. Mike Wilson, Advertising Manager. Amy Ross, Classified Adv. Mgr.. **Editorial:** Chris Mertes, Editor.

SUPERIOR

BUDGETEER NEWS. 1105 Tower Ave, Superior, WI 54880. Telephone: 715-395-5725. FAX: 715-395-5729. E-MAIL: budgeteer@mx3.com. URL: http://www.duluth.com. Year Established: 1930. Pub. Frequency: s-w. (Wed. & Sun.) Page Size: broadsheet. Subscrip. Rate: $55/yr mailed. Circulation: 47,553 Sunday (controlled and free); 6,439 per issue (controlled and free). **Owner(s):** Superior Publishing Corp., 222 W. Superior St, Ste 100, Duluth, MN 55802. Telephone: 218-732-1207. FAX: 218-727-7348. **Management:** Jeff Swor, General Manager. Tom West, Publisher. Aaron Becher, Advertising Manager. **Editorial:** Tom West, Editor.

THORP

THORP COURIER. ISSN 0885-2375
403 N. Washington, Thorp, WI 54771. Telephone: 715-669-5525. FAX: 715-667-5596. Mailing Address: PO Box 487, Thorp, WI 54771-0487. Year Established: 1883. Pub. Frequency: w. (Wed.) Page Size: broadsheet. Subscrip. Rate: $.75 newsstand/cover; $22/yr mailed in county; $27/yr mailed out of county; $30/yr mailed elsewhere. Circulation: 2,300 per issue (paid). **Owner(s):** Thorp Courier Printing Publications, Inc., See address and contact information above. **Management:** Mark J. LaGasse, Publisher. **Editorial:** Mark J. LaGasse, Editor.

TOMAH

TOMAH JOURNAL. 903 Superior Ave., Tomah, WI 54660. Telephone: 608-372-4123. FAX: 608-372-2791. URL: http://tomahjournal.com. Mailing Address: PO Box 190, Tomah, WI 54660. Year Established: 1867. Pub. Frequency: w. (Thu.) Page Size: broadsheet. Subscrip. Rate: $.75 newsstand/cover; $34/yr mailed in county; $39/yr mailed out of county; $48/yr mailed out of state. **Wire Service(s):** AP. Circulation: 5,300 per issue (paid). **Owner(s):** Lee Enterprises, Inc., 201 N. Harrison St., Davenport, IA 52801-1924. **Management:** Chris Hardie, Publisher. Tom Kelley, Advertising Manager. **Editorial:** John Froelich, Editor-in-Chief. Steve Rundio, Sports Editor.

TOMAH MONITOR-HERALD. 903 Superior Ave., Tomah, WI 54660. Telephone: 608-372-4123. FAX: 608-372-2791. URL: http://www.tomahjournal.com. Mailing Address: PO Box 190, Tomah, WI 54660. Year Established: 1881. Pub. Frequency: w. (Mon.) Page Size: broadsheet. Subscrip. Rate: $.75 newsstand/cover; $34/yr mailed in county incl. Tomah Journal; $39/yr mailed out of county incl. Tomah Journal; $48/yr mailed elsewhere incl. Tomah Journal. **Wire Service(s):** AP. Circulation: 5,500 per issue (paid). **Owner(s):** Lee Enterprises, Inc., 201 N. Harrison St., Davenport, IA 52801-1924. **Management:** Chris Hardie, Publisher. Tom Kelley, Advertising Manager. **Editorial:** John Froelich, Editor-in-Chief.

TOMAHAWK

TOMAHAWK LEADER. 315 W Wisconsin Ave, Tomahawk, WI 544487. Telephone: 715-453-2151. E-MAIL: news@tomahawkleader.com. URL: http://www.tomahawkleader.com. Mailing Address: PO Box 345, Tomahawk, WI 54487. Year Established: 1886. Pub. Frequency: w. (Tue.) Page Size: broadsheet. Subscrip. Rate: $1 newsstand/cover; $34/yr home delivery in Lincoln, Oneida & Price cys.; $45/yr mailed out of area; $54/yr mailed elsewhere. Adv. Rate: col. inch $11.25 Circulation: 9,200 per issue (paid and free). **Owner(s):** Larry & Kathy Tobin, See address and contact information above. **Management:** Kathy Tobin, Co-Publisher. Larry M Tobin, Advertising Manager. Alice Gray, Circulation Manager. **Editorial:** Kathy Tobin, Editor. Tom Colstad, Sports.

TURTLE LAKE

TURTLE LAKE TIMES, THE. 419 S. Maple, Turtle Lake, WI 54889-0088. Telephone: 715-986-4675. URL: http://www.turtlelakewi.com. Mailing Address: PO Box 88, Turtle Lake, WI 54889-0088. Year Established: 1900. Pub. Frequency: w. (Thu.) Page Size: standard. Subscrip. Rate: $.60 newsstand/cover; $16/yr mailed in county; $20/yr mailed in adj. counties. Circulation: 1,000 per issue (paid). **Owner(s):** David J. Slack, PO Box 88, Turtle Lake, WI 54889. Telephone: 715-986-4675. **Management:** David J. Slack, Publisher. Denise Slack, Advertising Manager. **Editorial:** David J. Slack, Editor.

TWIN LAKES

RICHMOND SPRINGS GROVE REPORT. 147 E. Main St., Twin Lakes, WI 53181. Telephone: 262-877-2813. FAX: 262-877-3619. E-MAIL: annette@westoshareport.com. URL: http://www.westoshareport.com. Mailing Address: PO Box 992, Twin Lakes, WI 53181. Pub. Frequency: w. (Sat.) Page Size: broadsheet. Subscrip. Rate: $.50 newsstand/cover; $17.95/yr in area; $29.50/yr out of area. Circulation: 1,200 per issue (paid). **Owner(s):** Southern Lakes Newspapers LLC, 700 N Pine St, Burlington, WI 53105. **Management:** Peter Cruger, Publisher. Dee Fladwood, Advertising Manager. **Editorial:** Annette Newcomb, Editor. Ed Nadolski, Editor-in-Chief.

TWIN LAKES REPORT. 147 E. Main St., Twin Lakes, WI 53181. Telephone: 262-877-2813. FAX: 262-877-3619. E-MAIL: annette@westoshareport.com. URL: http://www.westoshareport.com. Mailing Address: PO Box 992, Twin Lakes, WI 53181. Pub. Frequency: w. (Fri.) Page Size: broadsheet. Subscrip. Rate: $.50 newsstand/cover; $19.95/yr local; $29.50/yr out of area. Circulation: 10,000 per issue (paid). **Owner(s):** Southern Lakes Newspapers LLC, 700 N Pine St, Burlington, WI 53105. **Management:** Jack Cruger, Publisher. Dee Fladwood, Advertising Manager. **Editorial:** Annette Newcomb, Editor. Ed Nadolski, Editor-in-Chief.

WESTOSHA REPORT. 147 E. Main St., Twin Lakes, WI 53181. Telephone: 262-877-2813. FAX: 262-877-3619. E-MAIL: annette@westoshareport.com. URL: http://www.westoshareport.com. Mailing Address: PO Box 992, Twin Lakes, WI 53181. Year Established: 1956. Pub. Frequency: w. (Sat.) Page Size: broadsheet.Adv. Rate: col. inch $12.75 Circulation: 12,300 per issue (free). **Owner(s):** Southern Lakes Newspapers LLC, 700 N Pine St, Burlington, WI 53105. Telephone: 262-763-2575. FAX: 262-767-2683. **Management:** Ed Nadolski, Publisher. Dee Fladwood, Advertising Manager. **Editorial:** Annette Newcomb, Editor.

VALDERS

VALDERS JOURNAL. 204 N. Liberty St., Valders, WI 54245. Telephone: 920-775-4331. FAX: 920-775-4474. E-MAIL: vjournal@lakefield.net. Mailing Address: PO Box 400, Valders, WI 54245. Year Established: 1940. Pub. Frequency: w. (Thu.) Page Size: tabloid. Subscrip. Rate: $.75 newsstand/cover; $22/yr mailed in county; $32/yr mailed out of county. Adv. Rate: col. inch $7.50 **Wire Service(s):** AP. Circulation: 2,400 per issue (paid). **Owner(s):** Brian & Mary Thomsen, See address and contact information above. **Management:** Brian Thomsen, Publisher. **Editorial:** Mary Thomsen, Editor.

VERONA

VERONA PRESS. 120 W. Vernon Ave., Verona, WI 53593-0006. Telephone: 608-845-9559. FAX: 608-845-9550. E-MAIL: veronapress@wcinet.com. URL: http://www.veronapresswi.com. Year Established: 1965. Pub. Frequency: w. (Thu.) Page Size: tabloid. Subscrip. Rate: $1 newsstand/cover; $32/yr home delivery in Rock & Dane cyrs.; $40/yr mailed elsewhere. Adv. Rate: col. inch $7.25 Circulation: 2,500 per issue (paid and free). **Owner(s):** Woodward Communications Inc., PO Box 688, Dubuque, IA 52004-0688. Telephone: 563-588-5611. FAX: 563-588-5739. **Management:** Lisa Speropulos, Advertising. **Editorial:** Bill Livick, Editor. Jeremy Jones, Sports Editor.

VIROQUA

VERNON COUNTY BROADCASTER. 124 W. Court St., Viroqua, WI 54665. Telephone: 608-637-3137. FAX: 608-637-8557. E-MAIL: vcbnews@frontiernet.net. URL: http://www.vernonbroadcaster.com. Mailing Address: PO Box 472, Viroqua, WI 54665. Year Established: 1856. Pub. Frequency: w. (Thu.) Page Size: broadsheet. Subscrip. Rate: $.75 newsstand/cover; $32/yr local; $41.40/yr mailed in state; $47/yr mailed out of state. Adv. Rate: col. inch $8 Circulation: 6,180 per issue (paid). **Owner(s):** Lee Enterprises, Inc., 201 N. Harrison St., Davenport, IA 52801-1924. **Management:** Chris Hardie, Publisher. Barb Formanek, Advertising Manager. Linda Fortney, Circulation Manager. **Editorial:** Matt Johnson, Editor. Angela Cina, News Editor.

WALWORTH

BAY TIMES, THE. 202 N. Main St., Walworth, WI 53184. Telephone: 262-763-3511. FAX: 262-275-5259. Mailing Address: PO Box 129, Walworth, WI 53184-0129. Pub. Frequency: w. (Thu.) Page Size: broadsheet. Subscrip. Rate: $1 newsstand/cover; $29.50/yr mailed in county; $32.50/yr mailed out of county; $49/yr mailed out of state. Circulation: 500 per issue (paid). **Owner(s):** Southern Lakes Newspapers LLC, 700 N Pine St, Burlington, WI 53105. **Management:** Jack Cruger, Publisher. Dee Fladwood, Advertising Manager. **Editorial:** Carrie Dampier, Editor. Ed Nadolski, Editor-in-Chief.

WALWORTH TIMES, THE. 202 N. Main St., Walworth, WI 53184. Telephone: 262-763-3511. FAX: 262-275-5259. E-MAIL: lgilmore@walworthtimes.com. URL: http://walworthtimes.com. Mailing Address: PO Box 129, Walworth, WI 53184-0129. Year Established: 1904. Pub. Frequency: w. (Thu.) Page Size: broadsheet. Subscrip. Rate: $.75 newsstand/cover; $29.50/yr mailed in county; $32.50/yr mailed in WI & IL; $49/yr mailed elsewhere. Freelance Pay: $0.50/column-inch. Circulation: 4,000 per issue (paid). **Owner(s):** Southern Lakes Newspapers LLC, 700 N Pine St, Burlington, WI 53105. **Management:** Jack Cruger, Publisher. Dee Fladwood, Advertising Manager. **Editorial:** Linda Gilmore, Editor. Ed Nadolski, Editor-in-Chief.

WASHBURN

COUNTY JOURNAL (WASHBURN), THE. ISSN 1041-9942 324 W Bayfield St, Washburn, WI 54891. Telephone: 715-373-5500. FAX: 715-373-5546. E-MAIL: ctyjournal@baysat.net. URL: http://www.washburnwi.com. Mailing Address: PO Box 637, Washburn, WI 54891-0637. Year Established: 1984. Pub. Frequency: w. (Thu.) Page Size: broadsheet. Subscrip. Rate: $.75 newsstand/cover; $29/yr mailed in area; $39/yr mailed out of area. Adv. Rate: col. inch $4.90 Circulation: 3,700 per issue (paid and free). **Owner(s):** County Journal, Inc., See address and contact information above. **Management:** Dennis Meske, General Manager. **Editorial:** Eric Sharp, Editor.

WATERFORD

WATERFORD POST. 300 E. Main St., Ste. 3, Waterford, WI 53185. Telephone: 262-514-2510. FAX: 262-514-2514. E-MAIL: news@waterfordpost.com. URL: http://www.waterfordpost.com. Year Established: 1877. Pub. Frequency: w. (Fri.) Page Size: broadsheet. Subscrip. Rate: $1 newsstand/cover; $29.50/yr mailed local; $32.50/yr mailed out of county; $49/yr mailed out of state. Adv. Rate: col. inch $9.25 Circulation: 2,250 per issue (paid). **Owner(s):** Southern Lakes Newspapers LLC, 700 N Pine St, Burlington, WI 53105. Telephone: 262-763-2575. **Management:** Jack Cruger, Publisher. Dee Fladwood, Advertising Manager. **Editorial:** Christine Lupella, Editor. Ed Nadolski, Editor-in-Chief.

WATERLOO

COURIER (WATERLOO, 1870), THE. 114 N. Monroe, Waterloo, WI 53594. Telephone: 920-478-2188. FAX: 920-478-3618. Mailing Address: PO Box 6, Waterloo, WI 53594. Year Established: 1870. Pub. Frequency: w. (Thu.) Page Size: broadsheet. Subscrip. Rate: $.75 newsstand/cover; $25/yr in county; $35/yr out of county. Freelance Pay: $0.25/column-inch. Circulation: 2,500 per issue (paid). **Owner(s):** Hometown News Group, 207 E. Main St., Sun Prairie, WI 53590-0645. Telephone: 608-837-2521. FAX: 608-825-4460. **Management:** Brian Knox, Publisher. Mike Wilson, Advertising Manager. Luann Niebling, Circulation Manager. **Editorial:** Jake Jacobsen, Editor.

WAUNAKEE

WAUNAKEE TRIBUNE. 105 South St., Waunakee, WI 53597. Telephone: 608-849-5227. E-MAIL: news@waunakeetribune.com. URL: http://www.waunakeetribune.com. Year Established: 1920. Pub. Frequency: w. (Thu.) Page Size: broadsheet. Subscrip. Rate: $.60 newsstand/cover; $32.50/yr in state; $40/yr out of state. Adv. Rate: col. inch $9 Circulation: 3,500 per issue (paid). **Owner(s):** Arthur M. Drake, See address and contact information above. **Management:** Arthur M. Drake, Publisher. Betty Teetzen, Advertising. Kim Reed, Advertising Manager. **Editorial:** Arthur M. Drake, Editor.

WAUPACA

CHRONICLE (WAUPACA), THE. 717 Tenth St, Waupaca, WI 54981. Telephone: 715-258-5546. FAX: 715-258-8162. Mailing Address: PO Box 152, Waupaca, WI 54981-0152. Pub. Frequency: w. (Thu.) Page Size: broadsheet.Subscrip. Rate: $.75 newsstand/cover; $25/yr Circulation: 4,500 per issue (paid). **Owner(s):** Waupaca Publishing Co., See address and contact information above. **Management:** Mike Sievwright, Advertising. **Editorial:** Sharon Vanryzes, Editor.

TRI-COUNTY ADVERTISER (WAUPACA). 717 Tenth St, Waupaca, WI 54981. Telephone: 715-258-5546. FAX: 715-258-8162. Mailing Address: PO Box 152, Waupaca, WI 54981-0152. Pub. Frequency: w. (Tue) Page Size: broadsheet Circulation: 9,000 per issue (free). **Owner(s):** Waupaca Publishing Co., See address and contact information above. **Management:** Scott Turner, Publisher. Mike Sievwright, Advertising Manager.

WAUPACA POST. 717 Tenth St, Waupaca, WI 54981. Telephone: 715-258-5546. FAX: 715-258-8162. Mailing Address: PO Box 152, Waupaca, WI 54981-0152. Pub. Frequency: w. (Wed.) Page Size: tabloid. Subscrip. Rate: $.75 newsstand/cover; $25/yr. Wire Service(s): AP. Circulation: 8,000 per issue (paid). **Owner(s):** Waupaca Publishing Co., See address and contact information above. **Management:** Scott Turner, Publisher. Mike Sievwright, Advertising. **Editorial:** Bob Cloud, Editor.

WISCONSIN STATE FARMER. 717 Tenth St, Waupaca, WI 54981. Telephone: 715-258-5546. FAX: 715-258-8162. E-MAIL: sales@wisfarmer.com. URL: http://www.wisfarmer.com. Mailing Address: PO Box 152, Waupaca, WI 54981-0152. Year Established: 1956. Pub. Frequency: w. (Fri.) Page Size: broadsheet. Subscrip. Rate: $.50 newsstand/cover; $25/yr mailed. Adv. Rate: col. inch $10.70 Freelance Pay: $30-$50/article. Wire Service(s): AP. Circulation: 30,100 per issue (paid and free). **Owner(s):** Waupaca Publishing Co., See address and contact information above. **Management:** Cal Krisher, Advertising Manager. **Editorial:** Carla Gunst, Editor.

WAUTOMA

WAUSHARA ARGUS. Hwy. 21 & 73 E., Wautoma, WI 54982. Telephone: 920-787-3334. FAX: 920-787-2883. E-MAIL: argus@wausharaargus.com. URL: http://www.wausharaargus.com. Mailing Address: PO Box 838, Wautoma, WI 54982. Year Established: 1859. Pub. Frequency: w. (Wed.) Page Size: broadsheet. Subscrip. Rate: $.75 newsstand/cover; $30/yr mailed in county & adj. cys.; $28/yr to senior citizens; $40/yr elsewhere. Circulation: 6,200 per issue (paid). **Owner(s):** Delphos Newspapers, 405 N. Main St., Delphos, OH 45833. Telephone: 419-695-0015. **Management:** Murray Cohen, President. Mary Kunasch, Publisher. Ron Felten, Advertising Manager. **Editorial:** Mary Kunasch, Editor. Wes Lungwitz, News Editor. Marge Williams, Production Editor.

WEST BEND

SUNDAY POST (WEST BEND). 100 S. Sixth Ave., West Bend, WI 53095. Telephone: 262-306-5000. FAX: 262-338-1984. Mailing Address: PO Box 478, West Bend, WI 53095. Pub. Frequency: w. (Sun.) Page Size: standard Circulation: 8,000 per issue (free). **Owner(s):** Conley Publishing Group, Ltd., 119 Monroe St., Beaver Dam, WI 53916. Telephone: 920-885-7800. **Management:** Steve Ciccantelli, Publisher. Lois Evans, Advertising Manager. Kim Dietrick, Circulation Manager. Kristi Wolf, Classified Adv. Mgr.. **Editorial:** Jill Badzinski, Managing Editor.

WEST SALEM

HOLMEN COURIER. 103 S Leonard St, West Salem, WI 54669. Telephone: 608-786-1950. FAX: 608-786-1670. URL: http://www.holmencourier.com. Mailing Address: PO Box 140, West Salem, WI 54669-0140. Pub. Frequency: w. (Fri.) Page Size: broadsheet. Subscrip. Rate: $.75 newsstand/cover; $26.50/yr in county; $37.25/yr out of county. Circulation: 1,500 per issue (paid). **Owner(s):** Lee Enterprises, Inc., 201 N. Harrison St., Ste. 600, Davenport, IA 52801-1924. **Management:** Chris Hardie, Publisher. Ben Baker, Advertising Manager. **Editorial:** Randy Erickson, Editor.

ONALASKA COMMUNITY LIFE. 153 S. Leonard St., West Salem, WI 54669. Telephone: 608-786-1950. Mailing Address: PO Box 140, West Salem, WI 54669-0140. Pub. Frequency: w. (Fri.) Page Size: broadsheet. **Owner(s):** Lee Enterprises, Inc., 201 N. Harrison St., Ste. 600, Davenport, IA 52801-1924. **Management:** Chris Hardie, Publisher. Ben Baker, Advertising Manager. **Editorial:** Randy Erickson, Editor.

WEST SALEM COULEE NEWS. 103 S Leonard St, West Salem, WI 54669. URL: http://www.couleenews.com. Mailing Address: PO Box 140, West Salem, WI 54669-0140. Year Established: 1879. Pub. Frequency: w. (Thu.) Page Size: broadsheet. Subscrip. Rate: $.75 newsstand/cover; $32.90/yr in county; $35/yr in state; $48.80/yr out of state. Freelance Pay: $25/story. Circulation: 2,350 per issue (paid). **Owner(s):** Lee Enterprises, Inc., 201 N. Harrison St., Davenport, IA 52801-1924. **Management:** Chris Hardie, Publisher. Ben Baker, Advertising Manager. **Editorial:** Randy Erickson, Editor.

WHITEHALL

WHITEHALL (WI) TIMES. 36435 Main St., Whitehall, WI 54773-0095. Telephone: 715-538-4765. FAX: 715-538-4540. Year Established: 1860. Pub. Frequency: w. (Thu.) Page Size: standard. Subscrip. Rate: $.75 newsstand/cover; $24/yr mailed in county; $31/yr mailed out of state. Adv. Rate col. inch $4.83 Circulation: 2,450 per issue (paid). **Owner(s):** Charles Gauger, PO Box 95, Whitehall, WI 54773. Telephone: 715-538-4765. **Management:** Charles Gauger, Publisher. **Editorial:** Scott Thomson, Editor.

WHITEWATER

PALMYRA ENTERPRISE, THE. 162 W. Main St., Whitewater, WI 53190. Telephone: 262-763-3363. FAX: 262-473-5635. E-MAIL: jackley@southernlakesnewspapers.com. Mailing Address: PO Box M, Palmyra, WI 53156. Pub. Frequency: w. (Fri.) Page Size: broadsheet. Subscrip. Rate: $.35/yr newsstand/cover; $19.95/yr mailed in county. Circulation: 3,500 per issue (paid). **Owner(s):** Southern Lakes Newspapers LLC, 700 N Pine St, Burlington, WI 53105. **Management:** Jack Cruger, Publisher. Dee Fladwood, Advertising Manager. **Editorial:** Carrie Dampier, Editor. Ed Nadolski, Editor-in-Chief.

WINNECONNE

WINNECONNE NEWS. 908 E. Main St., Winneconne, WI 54986. Telephone: 920-582-4541. FAX: 920-582-4417. E-MAIL: winneconnenews@rogerspublishing.com. Mailing Address: PO Box 370, Winneconne, WI 54986-370. Year Established: 1930. Pub. Frequency: w. (Wed.) Page Size: tabloid. Subscrip. Rate: $.60 newsstand/cover; $25/yr mailed in county; $45/yr mailed out of county. Circulation: 1,650 per issue (paid). **Owner(s):** John Rogers, See address and contact information above. **Management:** John Rogers, Publisher. **Editorial:** Becky LaDue, Editor.

WINTER

SAWYER COUNTY GAZETTE. 5133 N. Main St., Winter, WI 54896-0099. Telephone: 715-266-2511. FAX: 715-266-2511. E-MAIL: sawyercountygazette@pctcnet.com. Mailing Address: PO Box 99, Winter, WI 54896-0099. Year Established: 1908. Pub. Frequency: w. (Wed.) Page Size: standard. Subscrip. Rate: $.50 newsstand/cover; $20/yr mailed in county; $24/yr mailed out of county. Adv. Rate: col. inch $3 Circulation: 2,250 per issue (paid and free). **Owner(s):** Meredith Rickert, See address and contact information above. **Management:** Meredith Rickert, Publisher.

WITTENBERG

WITTENBERG ENTERPRISE-NEWS. 110 W Vinal St, Wittenberg, WI 54499. Telephone: 715-253-2737. FAX: 715-253-2700. E-MAIL: press@wittenbergnet.net. Mailing Address: P.O. Box 190, Wittenberg, WI 54499. Year Established: 1893. Pub. Frequency: w. (Thu.) Page Size: broadsheet. Subscrip. Rate: $.45 newsstand/cover; $16.50/yr in county; $18.75/yr out of county; $20.25/yr out of state. Circulation: 16,000 per issue (paid). **Owner(s):** Sally Boldig, Gordon C. Boldig, Steve Block & Darlene Block, See address and contact information above. **Editorial:** Gordon C Boldig, Editor.

WYOMING

BUFFALO

BUFFALO BULLETIN. PO Box 730, Buffalo, WY 82834. Telephone: 307-684-2223. E-MAIL: publisher@buffalobulletin.com. URL: http://www.buffalobulletin.com. Year Established: 1894. Pub. Frequency: w. (Thu.) Page Size: broadsheet. Subscrip. Rate: $.75 newsstand/cover; $37/yr in state; $49/yr out of state. Adv. Rate: col. inch $11.50 Circulation: 4,250 per issue (paid). **Owner(s):** Buffalo Bulletin, See address and contact information above. **Management:** Robert H. Hicks, Owner. Susan Carr, Publisher. **Editorial:** Martin Reed, News Editor.

CHEYENNE

WARREN SENTINEL (CHEYENNE), THE. 202 E. 18th St., Cheyenne, WY 82001. Telephone: 307-632-5666. FAX: 307-632-1554. E-MAIL: jwlemail@aol.com. URL: http://www.wkyominghq.com. Pub. Frequency: w. (Fri.) Page Size: tabloid. Subscrip. Rate: $48/yr mailed. Adv. Rate: col. inch $7.14 Circulation: 5,200 per issue (paid and free). **Owner(s):** News Media Corp., 211 Hwy. 38 E., Rochelle, IL 61608. Telephone: 815-562-2061. FAX: 815-562-2060. **Management:** Jim Wood, Publisher. Amy Bennet, Advertising.

CODY

CODY ENTERPRISE.   ISSN 0747-2498
1301 Big Horn Ave., Cody, WY 82414. Telephone: 307-587-2231.
FAX: 307-587-5208. E-MAIL: office@codyenterprise.com. URL:
http://www.codyenterprise.com. Mailing Address: PO Box 1090,
Cody, WY 82414-1090. Year Established: 1899. Pub. Frequency:
s-w. (Mon. & Wed.) Page Size: broadsheet. Subscrip. Rate: $.75
newsstand/cover; $36/yr. Adv. Rate: col. inch $11 Circulation:
7,100 per issue (controlled and free). **Owner(s):** Sage Publishing
Co., Inc., See address and contact information above.
Management: Bruce McCormack, Publisher. John Malmberg,
Advertising Manager. **Editorial:** Bruce McCormack, Editor. Darian
Dudrick, Managing Editor. John Sides, Production Manager.

EVANSTON

UINTA COUNTY HERALD. 1565 S. Hwy. 150, Ste. D, Evanston, WY
82930-0210. Telephone: 307-789-6560. FAX: 307-789-2700.
Mailing Address: PO Box 210, Evanston, WY 82930-0210. Year
Established: 1938. Pub. Frequency: s-w. (Tue. & Fri.) Page Size:
broadsheet. Subscrip. Rate: $.75 newsstand/cover (effective
2005); $58.50/yr mailed in county (effective 2004); $62/yr out of
county. Adv. Rate: col. inch $13.13 **Wire Service(s):** AP.
Circulation: 7,700 per issue (paid and free). **Owner(s):** Wyoming
Newspapers, Inc., 1565 S. Hwy. 150, Ste. D, Evanston, WY
82930. Telephone: 307-789-6560. **Management:** Mike Jensen,
Publisher. Melissa Bowman, Circulation Manager. **Editorial:** Matt
Ottinger, Editor. Jim Higgins, Sports Editor.

GUERNSEY

GUERNSEY GAZETTE, THE. 40 S. Wyoming St., Guernsey, WY
82214. Telephone: 307-836-2021. FAX: 307-836-2021. E-MAIL:
ggeditor@guernseygazette.com. URL:
http://www.guernseygazette.com. Mailing Address: PO Box 370,
Guernsey, WY 82214. Pub. Frequency: w. (Tue.) Page Size:
tabloid. Subscrip. Rate: $.50 newsstand/cover; $22.25/yr in
county; $26.55/yr out of county. Adv. Rate: col. inch $9.60
Circulation: 1,000 per issue (paid). **Owner(s):** Wyoming
Newspapers, Inc., 1007 Eighth St., Wheatland, WY 82201.
Telephone: 307-322-2627. FAX: 307-322-9612. **Management:** Jeff
Robertson, Publisher. Ken Barnes, Advertising Manager. **Editorial:**
Vicky Hood, Editor.

JACKSON

JACKSON HOLE NEWS & GUIDE. 1225 Maple Way, Jackson, WY
83001. Telephone: 307-733-2047. FAX: 307-733-2138. E-MAIL:
editor@jhnewsandguide.com. URL:
http://www.jhnewsandguide.com. Mailing Address: PO Box 7445,
Jackson, WY 83002. Year Established: 1952. Pub. Frequency: w.
(Wed.) Page Size: tabloid. Subscrip. Rate: $.50 newsstand/cover;
$32/yr in county; $39/yr out of county. Adv. Rate: col. inch $16.50
Wire Service(s): AP. Circulation: 11,500 per issue (paid).
Owner(s): Jackson Hole News Inc., See address and contact
information above. **Management:** Michael Sellett, Publisher. Kevin
Olson, Advertising Director. Curtis Coffman, Circulation Manager.
Editorial: Angus M. Thuemer Jr., Co-Editor.

KEMMERER

KEMMERER GAZETTE. 708 J.C. Penney Dr., Kemmerer, WY
83101-0030. Telephone: 307-877-3347. FAX: 307-877-3736.
E-MAIL: editor@kemmerergazette.com. URL:
http://www.kemmerergazette.com. Mailing Address: PO Box 30,
Kemmerer, WY 83101-0030. Year Established: 1901. Pub.
Frequency: w. (Thu.) Page Size: standard. Subscrip. Rate: $.50
newsstand/cover; $32/yr in county; $34/yr out of county.
Circulation: 2,000 per issue (paid). **Owner(s):** News Media Corp.,
211 Hwy. 38 E., Rochelle, IL 61608. Telephone: 815-562-2061.
FAX: 815-526-2060. **Management:** Mike Jensen, Publisher. Roger
Capellen, Circulation Manager. **Editorial:** Sara Millhouse, Editor.

LANDER

LANDER JOURNAL. 332 Main St., Lander, WY 82520. Telephone:
307-332-2323. FAX: 307-635-3912. E-MAIL:
newsdept@wyoming.com. URL: http://www.landerjournal.net. Year
Established: 1886. Pub. Frequency: s-w. (Wed. & Sun.) Page
Size: broadsheet. Subscrip. Rate: $.75 newsstand/cover; $39.95/yr
mailed in county; $49.95/yr mailed out of county. Freelance Pay:
$0.05/word. Circulation: 11,000 Sunday (paid); 3,400 per issue
(paid). **Owner(s):** Steve Peck, PO Box 993, Riverton, WY 82501.
Telephone: 307-856-2244. **Management:** Steve Peck, Publisher.
Ann McGowan, Advertising Manager. Jan Meeks, Circulation
Manager. **Editorial:** Steve Peck, Editor. Alicia Giuffrida, Managing
Editor. Bruce Tippet, Sports Editor.

WIND RIVER NEWS. 332 Main St., Lander, WY 82520. Telephone:
307-332-2323. FAX: 307-635-3912. E-MAIL: wpress@trib.com.
URL: http://www.wyopress.org. Year Established: 1978. Pub.
Frequency: w. (Thu.) Page Size: broadsheet. Subscrip. Rate: $.50
newsstand/cover; $18.75/yr in county; $21.75/yr out of county.
Circulation: 1,350 per issue (paid). **Owner(s):** Steve Peck, See
address and contact information above. **Management:** Steve
Peck, Publisher. Anne McGowan, Advertising Manager. Jan
Meeks, Circulation Manager. **Editorial:** Ernie Over, Editor.

LINGLE

LINGLE GUIDE.   ISSN 1061-1789
228 Main St, Lingle, WY 82223. Telephone: 307-532-2184. FAX:
307-532-2283. E-MAIL: jaremail@aol.com. URL:
http://www.lingleguide.com. Mailing Address: PO Box 278, Lingle,
WY 82223. Year Established: 1917. Pub. Frequency: w. (Tue.)
Page Size: tabloid. Subscrip. Rate: $.50 newsstand/cover;
$23.50/yr in county; $30.95/yr mailed out of county. Circulation:
400 per issue (paid). **Owner(s):** News Media Corp., 211 Hwy. 38
E., Rochelle, IL 61608. Telephone: 815-562-2961. **Management:**
Jeff Robertson, Publisher. **Editorial:** Jeff Robertson, Editor. Kim
Notebottom, Writer.

LOVELL

LOVELL CHRONICLE, THE. PO Box 787, Lovell, WY 82431.
Telephone: 307-548-2217. E-MAIL: info@lovellchronicle.com. URL:
http://www.lovellchronicle.com. Year Established: 1906. Pub.
Frequency: w. (Thu.) Page Size: broadsheet. Subscrip. Rate: $.50
newsstand/cover; $22/yr in county; $30/yr in state; $34/yr out of
state; $20 to students for 9 mos.. Circulation: 2,142 per issue
(paid and free). **Owner(s):** David & Susan Peck, See address
and contact information above. **Management:** David H. Peck,
Publisher. Gladys McNeil, Circulation Manager. **Editorial:** Pat
Parmer, Composing Room Manager. Karla Pomeroy, News Editor.

LUSK

LUSK HERALD. 227 S. Main St., Lusk, WY 82225. Telephone:
307-334-2867. FAX: 307-334-2514. URL:
http://www.newsmediacorporation.com. Mailing Address: PO Box
30, Lusk, WY 82225. Year Established: 1886. Pub. Frequency: w.
(Wed.) Page Size: tabloid. Subscrip. Rate: $.75 newsstand/cover;
$35.25/yr mailed in county; $40.45/yr mailed out of county. Adv.
Rate: col. inch $7.39 Circulation: 1,450 per issue (paid).
Owner(s): News Media Corp., 211 Hwy. 38 E., Rochelle, IL
61608. Telephone: 815-562-2061. FAX: 815-562-2060.
Management: Jeff Robertson, Publisher. Dolores Halstead, Office
Manager.

LYMAN

BRIDGER VALLEY PIONEER.   ISSN 1088-100X
225 W. Owen St., Lyman, WY 82937. Telephone: 307-787-3229.
FAX: 307-787-6795. E-MAIL: bvpioneer@bves.net. URL:
http://www.bridgevalleypioneer.com. Mailing Address: PO Box 538,
Lyman, WY 82937. Year Established: 1976. Pub. Frequency: w.
(Fri.) Page Size: broadsheet. Subscrip. Rate: $.50
newsstand/cover; $24.25/yr in county; $26.25/yr out of county.
Adv. Rate: col. inch $6.29 Circulation: 1,800 per issue (controlled
and free). **Owner(s):** News Media Corp., 211 Hwy. 38 E.,
Rochelle, IL 61608. Telephone: 815-562-2061. FAX:
815-562-2060. **Management:** Mike Jensen, Publisher. Amy Ferrin,
Classified Adv. Mgr..

MOORCROFT

MOORCROFT LEADER. 304 Riley, Moorcroft, WY 82721. Telephone:
307-756-3371. FAX: 307-756-9827. E-MAIL:
mleader@collinscom.com. Mailing Address: PO Box 67, Moorcroft,
WY 82721-0067. Year Established: 1912. Pub. Frequency: w.
(Thu.) Page Size: tabloid. Subscrip. Rate: $.75 newsstand/cover;
$21/yr in county; $23/yr out of county. Adv. Rate: col. inch $6.25
Circulation: 1,000 per issue. **Owner(s):** Margaret Bauer, 17 Big
Buck Dr., Pine Haven, WY 82721. **Management:** Margaret Bauer,
Publisher. Dianna Neugebauer, Office Manager. **Editorial:**
Margaret Bauer, Editor-in-Chief.

NEWCASTLE

NEWS LETTER JOURNAL. PO Box 40, Newcastle, WY 82701.
Telephone: 307-746-2777. FAX: 307-746-2660. E-MAIL:
editor@newlj.com. URL: http://www.newsletterjournal.com. Year
Established: 1889. Pub. Frequency: w. (Wed.) Page Size:
standard. Subscrip. Rate: $.75 newsstand/cover; $37.50/yr in
county; $49/yr out of county. Adv. Rate: col. inch $6 Circulation:
2,500 per issue (paid). **Owner(s):** Tom Mullen, See address and
contact information above. **Management:** Tom Mullen, Publisher.
Colleen Green, Advertising. Becky Nagle, Classified Editor.

RIVERTON

ADVERTISER (RIVERTON), THE. 608 E Pershing, Riverton, WY
82501. Telephone: 307-857-6114. FAX: 307-856-4356. Pub.
Frequency: w. (Wed.) Page Size: standard Circulation: 19,000 per
issue (free). **Owner(s):** Edwards Group Inc, 125 Eagles Nest,
Seneca, SC 29678. Telephone: 864-882-3272. **Management:**
Jerry Edwards, Publisher.

SARATOGA

SARATOGA SUN. 116 E. Bridge St., Saratoga, WY 82331.
Telephone: 307-326-8311. FAX: 307-326-5108. E-MAIL:
saratogasun@unetcommandor.com. Year Established: 1888. Pub.
Frequency: w. (Wed.) Page Size: tabloid. Subscrip. Rate: $.75
newsstand/cover; $30/yr mailed in county; $37/yr mailed in state;
$40/yr mailed out of state. Adv. Rate: col. inch $6.10 Circulation:
1,900 per issue (paid). **Owner(s):** Saratoga Sun, Inc., See
address and contact information above. **Management:** Gary
Stevenson, Publisher. Sue Stevenson, Business Manager.
Editorial: Coy Hobbs, Editor.

TORRINGTON

PLATTE COUNTY RECORD-TIMES. 2025 Main St., Torrington, WY
82240. E-MAIL: wyrt@aol.com. URL:
http://www.pcrecordtimes.com. Year Established: 1900. Pub.
Frequency: w. (Wed.) Page Size: broadsheet. Subscrip. Rate:
$.75 newsstand/cover; $36.95/yr in county; $43.95/yr in
mailed out of county. Adv. Rate: col. inch $10.50 **Wire Service(s):**
AP, PR. Circulation: 2,800 per issue (paid). **Owner(s):** News
Media Corp., 1007 Eighth St, Wheatland, WY 82201.
Management: Jeff Robertson, Publisher. Ken Barnes, Advertising.
Editorial: Amber Ningen, Editor. Contact: Ken Barnes,
Advertising.

TORRINGTON TELEGRAM. 2025 Main St., Torrington, WY 82240.
Telephone: 307-532-2184. FAX: 307-532-2283. E-MAIL:
torr.news@torringtontelegrm.com. URL:
http://www.torringtontelegram.com. Mailing Address: PO Box 1058,
Torrington, WY 82240. Year Established: 1911. Pub. Frequency:
s-w. (Wed. & Fri.) Page Size: broadsheet. Subscrip. Rate: $.75
newsstand/cover; $54.95/yr mailed in county; $62.45/yr mailed out
of county. Adv. Rate: col. inch $9.29 **Wire Service(s):** AP.
Circulation: 2,500 per issue (paid). **Owner(s):** News Media Corp.,
211 Hwy. 38 E., Rochelle, IL 61608. Telephone: 815-562-2061.
FAX: 815-562-2060. **Management:** Jeff Robertson, Publisher.

Weeklies

ALTOONA HERALD, THE (Altoona, IA) 11489
ALTOONA MIRROR (Altoona, PA) 11388
ALTOONA/PLEASANT HILL PRESS CITIZEN (Des Moines, IA) 11491
ALTUS TIMES (Altus, OK) 11384
ALVA REVIEW-COURIER (Alva, OK) 11384
ALVARADO POST (Waxahachie, TX) 11642
ALVARADO STAR (Burleson, TX) 11632
ALVIN ADVERTISER (Alvin, TX) 11631
ALVIN SUN & ADVERTISER (Alvin, TX) 11631
ALVIN SUN-ADVERTISER (Alvin, TX) 11631
AMADOR LEDGER-DISPATCH (Jackson, CA) 11430
AMARILLO GLOBE-NEWS (Amarillo, TX) 11397
AMBLER GAZETTE (Fort Washington, PA) 11611
AMBOY NEWS, THE (Amboy, IL) 11466
AMELIA BULLETIN MONITOR, THE (Amelia Court House, VA) 11645
AMERICAN CLASSIFIEDS (Champaign, IL) 11468
AMERICAN CLASSIFIEDS (Pelham, AL) 11415
AMERICAN (FARGO), THE (Blackduck, MN) 11534
AMERICAN FORK CITIZEN (American Fork, UT) 11642
AMERICAN JOURNAL (WESTBROOK) (Westbrook, ME) 11511
AMERICAN MONDAY (Murphysboro, IL) 11476
AMERICAN NEWS (Aberdeen, SD) 11394
AMERICAN PRESS (LAKE CHARLES) (Lake Charles, LA) 11353
AMERICUS TIMES-RECORDER (Americus, GA) 11334
AMERY FREE PRESS (Amery, WI) 11658
AMESBURY NEWS (Beverly, MA) 11515
AMHERST BEE (Williamsville, NY) 11584
AMHERST BULLETIN (Amherst, MA) 11515
AMHERST NEW ERA-PROGRESS (Amherst, VA) 11645
AMITE TANGI DIGEST (Amite, LA) 11506
AMITY OBSERVER (Shelton, CT) 11446
AMITYVILLE RECORD (Amityville, NY) 11569
ANACONDA LEADER, THE (Anaconda, MT) 11555
ANACORTES AMERICAN (Anacortes, WA) 11651
ANADARKO DAILY NEWS (Anadarko, OK) 11384
ANAHEIM BULLETIN (Anaheim, CA) 11425
ANAHEIM HILLS NEWS (Anaheim, CA) 11425
ANAMOSA JOURNAL-EUREKA (Anamosa, IA) 11489
ANCHORAGE DAILY NEWS (Anchorage, AK) 11320
ANDALUSIA STAR NEWS (Andalusia, AL) 11319
ANDERSON INDEPENDENT-MAIL (Anderson, SC) 11393
ANDERSON NEWS, THE (Lawrenceburg, KY) 11503
ANDOVER TOWNSMAN (Andover, MA) 11515
ANDREWS COUNTY NEWS, THE (Andrews, TX) 11631
ANDREWS JOURNAL, THE (Andrews, NC) 11585
ANGIER INDEPENDENT (Angier, NC) 11585
ANKENY PRESS CITIZEN (Ankeny, IA) 11490
ANNANDALE ADVOCATE (Annandale, MN) 11534
ANNANDALE TIMES (Herndon, VA) 11647
ANNARBORCOM (Ann Arbor, MI) 11357
ANNISTON STAR (Anniston, AL) 11319
ANOKA COUNTY SHOPPER (Coon Rapids, MN) 11536
ANOKA COUNTY UNION (Coon Rapids, MN) 11536
ANSON RECORD, THE (Wadesboro, NC) 11590
ANTELOPE VALLEY PRESS (Palmdale, CA) 11326
ANTHONY REPUBLICAN, THE (Anthony, KS) 11496
ANTIGO AREA SHOPPERS GUIDE (Antigo, WI) 11658
ANTIGO DAILY JOURNAL (Antigo, WI) 11407
ANTIOCH NEWS (Grayslake, IL) 11473
ANTIOCH REVIEW (Waukegan, IL) 11483
ANTLERS AMERICAN, THE (Antlers, OK) 11603
ANTRIM COUNTY NEWS (Bellaire, MI) 11525
ANTWERP BEE-ARGUS (Antwerp, OH) 11592
APACHE JUNCTION - GOLD CANYON INDEPENDENT (Apache Junction, AZ) 11417
APALACHICOLA TIMES, THE (Apalachicola, FL) 11448

APEX HERALD, THE (Apex, NC) 11585
APOLLO NEWS-RECORD (Vandergrift, PA) 11617
APOPKA CHIEF, THE (Apopka, FL) 11448
APPALACHIAN NEWS-EXPRESS (Pikeville, KY) 11505
APPEAL TRIBUNE (Silverton, OR) 11609
APPEAL-DEMOCRAT (Marysville, CA) 11325
APPLE VALLEY NEWS (Apple Valley, CA) 11426
APPLE VALLEY THISWEEK (Burnsville, MN) 11535
APPLE VALLEY/ROSEMOUNT/EAGAN SUN-CURRENT (Eden Prairie, MN) 11537
APPLETON PRESS (Appleton, MN) 11534
APPOMATTOX TIMES-VIRGINIAN (Appomattox, VA) 11645
ARAB TRIBUNE (Arab, AL) 11411
ARANSAS PASS PROGRESS, THE (Aransas Pass, TX) 11631
ARAPAHOE PUBLIC MIRROR (Arapahoe, NE) 11556
ARBUTUS TIMES (Baltimore, MD) 11511
ARCADE PENNYSAVER (Arcade, NY) 11569
ARCADIA NEWS-LEADER (Arcadia, WI) 11658
ARCHBOLD BUCKEYE (Archbold, OH) 11592
ARCO ADVERTISER (Arco, ID) 11464
ARCOLA RECORD HERALD (Arcola, IL) 11466
ARCTIC SOUNDER, THE (Barrow, AK) 11416
ARDEN HILLS/FALCON HEIGHTS/ROSEVILLE FOCUS NEWS (Columbia Heights, MN) 11536
AREA SHOPPER (Cochranton, PA) 11610
ARENAC COUNTY INDEPENDENT (Standish, MI) 11532
ARGONAUT, THE (Los Angeles, CA) 11431
ARGUS LEADER (Sioux Falls, SD) 11395
ARGUS OBSERVER (Ontario, OR) 11387
ARGUS, THE (Fremont, CA) 11324
ARGUS-CHAMPION, THE (Claremont, NH) 11559
ARGUS-PRESS, THE (Owosso, MI) 11359
ARGYLE MESSENGER, THE (Flower Mound, TX) 11634
ARIZONA CITY INDEPENDENT EDITION (Arizona City, AZ) 11417
ARIZONA DAILY STAR (Tucson, AZ) 11322
ARIZONA DAILY SUN (Flagstaff, AZ) 11321
ARIZONA REPUBLIC (Phoenix, AZ) 11321
ARIZONA SILVER BELT (Globe, AZ) 11418
ARK (TIBURON), THE (Tiburon, CA) 11438
ARK (TIBURON), THE (Tiburon, CA) 11438
ARKADELPHIA DAILY SIFTINGS HERALD (Arkadelphia, AR) 11322
ARKADELPHIA EXTRA (Arkadelphia, AR) 11420
ARKANSAS CITY TRAVELER (Arkansas City, KS) 11348
ARKANSAS DEMOCRAT-GAZETTE (Little Rock, AR) 11323
ARKANSAS TIMES (Little Rock, AR) 11422
ARLINGTON ADVOCATE (Lexington, MA) 11519
ARLINGTON CITIZEN (Arlington, NE) 11556
ARLINGTON CONNECTION, THE (McLean, VA) 11648
ARLINGTON ENTERPRISE (Arlington, MN) 11534
ARLINGTON HEIGHTS JOURNAL & TOPICS (Des Plaines, IL) 11469
ARLINGTON HEIGHTS POST (Arlington Heights, IL) 11466
ARLINGTON STAR-TELEGRAM (Arlington, TX) 11397
ARLINGTON SUN, THE (Arlington, SD) 11623
ARMADA TIMES (Armada, MI) 11525
AROOSTOOK REPUBLICAN & NEWS (Caribou, ME) 11509
ARTESIA DAILY PRESS (Artesia, NM) 11370
ARTHUR ENTERPRISE, THE (Arthur, NE) 11556
ARTHUR GRAPHIC CLARION (Arthur, IL) 11466
ARVADA SENTINEL (Arvada, CO) 11439
ASBURY PARK PRESS (Neptune, NJ) 11369
ASHBURN STERLING (Leesburg, VA) 11648
ASHEVILLE CITIZEN-TIMES (Asheville, NC) 11375
ASHEVILLE GLOBAL REPORT (Asheville, NC) 11585
ASHFORD POWER (Dothan, AL) 11412
ASHLAND CITY TIMES (Ashland City, TN) 11625

ASHLAND DAILY TIDINGS (Ashland, OR) 11386
ASHLAND GAZETTE (Ashland, NE) 11556
ASHLAND TAB (Framingham, MA) 11518
ASHLAND TIMES-GAZETTE (Ashland, OH) 11379
ASHLEY COUNTY LEDGER (Hamburg, AR) 11422
ASHLEY COUNTY SHOPPERS GUIDE (Crossett, AR) 11421
ASHLEY NEWS (Du Quoin, IL) 11471
ASHLEY NEWS OBSERVER, THE (Crossett, AR) 11421
ASHLEY TRIBUNE, THE (Ashley, ND) 11591
ASHTON GAZETTE (Ashton, IL) 11466
ASKOV AMERICAN (Askov, MN) 11534
ASPEN DAILY NEWS (Aspen, CO) 11329
ASPEN HILL GAZETTE (Gaithersburg, MD) 11513
ASPEN TIMES, THE (Aspen, CO) 11329
ASTORIA SOUTH FULTON ARGUS (Astoria, IL) 11467
ASTORIA TIMES (Bayside, NY) 11569
ATASCADERO NEWS (Rochelle, IL) 11480
ATCHISON COUNTY MAIL, THE (Rock Port, MO) 11552
ATCHISON DAILY GLOBE (Atchison, KS) 11348
ATHENS BANNER HERALD (Athens, GA) 11334
ATHENS DAILY REVIEW (Athens, TX) 11397
ATHENS MESSENGER, THE (Athens, OH) 11379
ATHENS NEWS (Athens, OH) 11592
ATHOL DAILY NEWS (Athol, MA) 11355
ATKINS CHRONICLE, THE (Atkins, AR) 11420
ATKINSON COUNTY CITIZEN (Pearson, GA) 11462
ATKINSON GRAPHIC, THE (Atkinson, NE) 11556
ATLANTA CITIZENS JOURNAL (Atlanta, TX) 11631
ATLANTA DAILY WORLD (Atlanta, GA) 11456
ATLANTA JOURNAL - CONSTITUTION, THE (Atlanta, GA) 11335
ATLANTIC COUNTY RECORD (Hammonton, NJ) 11563
ATLANTIC NEWS-TELEGRAPH (Atlantic, IA) 11346
ATMORE ADVANCE (Atmore, AL) 11411
ATOKA COUNTY TIMES (Atoka, OK) 11603
ATWATER SIGNAL, THE (Merced, CA) 11432
ATWATER TIMES (Merced, CA) 11432
ATWOOD HERALD (Mt Zion, IL) 11476
AUBURN CITIZEN (Auburn, IL) 11467
AUBURN JOURNAL (Auburn, CA) 11323
AUBURN NEWS (Webster, MA) 11524
AUBURN PRESS TRIBUNE (Auburn, NE) 11556
AUBURN TRADER (Auburn, CA) 11426
AUCTIONEER, THE (Pekin, IN) 11488
AUDUBON COUNTY ADVOCATE JOURNAL (Audubon, IA) 11490
AUGUSTA AREA TIMES (Ossto, WI) 11665
AUGUSTA CHRONICLE, THE (Augusta, GA) 11335
AUGUSTA DAILY GAZETTE (Augusta, KS) 11349
AURORA ADVERTISER (Aurora, MO) 11548
AURORA ADVOCATE (Stow, OH) 11600
AURORA NEWS-REGISTER (Aurora, NE) 11556
AURORA SENTINEL (Aurora, CO) 11439
AUSTELL NEIGHBOR (Marietta, GA) 11461
AUSTIN AMERICAN-STATESMAN (Austin, TX) 11397
AUSTIN CHRONICLE (Austin, TX) 11631
AUSTIN DAILY HERALD (Austin, MN) 11360
AUSTIN WEEKLY NEWS (Oak Park, IL) 11477
AUTOGRAM-SENTINEL (Eldon, MO) 11549
AVALON BAY NEWS, THE (Avalon, CA) 11426
AVENAL PROGRESS (Avenal, CA) 11426
AVENTURA NEWS (South Miami, FL) 11455
AVENUE NEWS, THE (Baltimore, MD) 11511
AVERY JOURNAL-TIMES, THE (Newland, NC) 11588
AVON GROVE SUN (Kennett Square, PA) 11612
AVON MESSENGER (Rayham, MA) 11522
AVON SENTINEL (Abingdon, IL) 11466
AVOYELLES JOURNAL (Marksville, LA) 11507
AYER PUBLIC SPIRIT, THE (Devens, MA) 11517

Title Index

1590 BROADCASTER (Lowell, MA) **11519**

1960 SUN (Houston, TX) **11637**

50 PLUS (Succasunna, NJ) **11567**

A

A P G NEWS (APG, MD) **11511**

ABBEVILLE HERALD (Abbeville, AL) **11411**

ABBEVILLE MERIDIONAL (Abbeville, LA) **11352**

ABERDEEN EXAMINER (Aberdeen, MS) **11545**

ABERDEEN TIMES (Aberdeen, ID) **11464**

ABERNATHY WEEKLY REVIEW (Abernathy, TX) **11630**

ABILENE REFLECTOR-CHRONICLE (Abilene, KS) **11348**

ABILENE REPORTER-NEWS (Abilene, TX) **11396**

ABINGDON ARGUS (Abingdon, IL) **11466**

ABINGDON VIRGINIAN (Abingdon, VA) **11645**

ABINGTON MARINER (Marshfield, MA) **11520**

ACORN, THE (Agoura Hills, CA) **11425**

ACTION PUBLICATIONS (Fond Du Lac, WI) **11660**

ACWORTH NEIGHBOR (Marietta, GA) **11461**

AD EXPRESS (Centerville, IA) **11491**

ADA EVENING NEWS (Ada, OK) **11384**

ADAIR COUNTY FREE PRESS (Greenfield, IA) **11492**

ADAIR NEWS, THE (Adair, IA) **11489**

ADAIR PROGRESS, THE (Columbia, KY) **11501**

ADAIR RUSSELL SHOPPER, THE (Columbia, KY) **11501**

ADAMS COUNTY RECORD, THE (Council, ID) **11464**

ADAMS COUNTY TIMES (Adams, WI) **11657**

ADDISON EAGLE (Rutland, VT) **11644**

ADDISON INDEPENDENT/ADDISON COUNTY INDEPENDENT (Middlebury, VT) **11644**

ADDISON/BENSENVILLE PRESS (St Charles, IL) **11481**

ADEL NEWS TRIBUNE (Adel, GA) **11456**

ADIRONDACK DAILY ENTERPRISE (Saranac Lake, NY) **11375**

ADIRONDACK JOURNAL (Elizabethtown, NY) **11574**

AD-LINES (Medford, NJ) **11565**

AD-PAK, THE (Wilmington, NC) **11590**

ADRIAN ACCESS SHOPPER (Adrian, MI) **11525**

ADRIAN MEDLEY (Adrian, MI) **11525**

ADVANCE LEADER, THE (Monroeville, PA) **11613**

ADVANCE MONTICELLONIAN (Monticello, AR) **11423**

ADVANCE NEWS (Manchester, NJ) **11565**

ADVANCE NEWS OF ELKHART COUNTY (Nappanee, IN) **11487**

ADVANCE OF BUCKS COUNTY (Newtown, PA) **11614**

ADVANCE PROGRESS, THE (Vidalia, GA) **11463**

ADVANCE, THE (Blissfield, MI) **11525**

ADVANCE-YEOMAN (Paducah, KY) **11504**

ADVANTAGE (CAMBRIDGE), THE (Cambridge, OH) **11594**

ADVANTAGE (OLNEY) (Olney, IL) **11478**

ADVANTAGE (VIDALIA), THE (Vidalia, GA) **11463**

ADVERTISER (BUNKER HILL), THE (Bunker Hill, IL) **11468**

ADVERTISER EXTRA, THE (Laurens, SC) **11621**

ADVERTISER (IRON MOUNTAIN), THE (Iron Mountain, MI) **11528**

ADVERTISER (LOUISA), THE (Louisa, KY) **11503**

ADVERTISER (MAYSVILLE) (Maysville, KY) **11504**

ADVERTISER (MT STERLING), THE (Mt Sterling, KY) **11504**

ADVERTISER (PARIS), THE (Paris, KY) **11504**

ADVERTISER (POLSON), THE (Polson, MT) **11556**

ADVERTISER (RIVERTON), THE (Riverton, WY) **11669**

ADVERTISER-DEMOCRAT (Norway, ME) **11510**

ADVERTISER-GLEAM (Guntersville, AL) **11414**

ADVERTISER-TRIBUNE (Tiffin, OH) **11383**

ADVERTIZER-HERALD, THE (Bamberg, SC) **11619**

AD-VISOR (Honor, MI) **11528**

ADVISOR & SOURCE, THE (Shelby Township, MI) **11532**

ADVISOR (ALBION) (Albion, NE) **11556**

ADVISOR (ATTLEBORO) (Attleboro, MA) **11515**

ADVISOR (NORTH HAVEN), THE (North Haven, CT) **11446**

ADVISOR (SCOTTDALE), THE (Scottdale, PA) **11616**

ADVOCATE & DEMOCRAT (Sweetwater, TN) **11630**

ADVOCATE (BATON ROUGE) (Baton Rouge, LA) **11353**

ADVOCATE (CLIFTON), THE (Clifton, IL) **11469**

ADVOCATE DEMOCRAT, THE (Crawfordville, GA) **11458**

ADVOCATE (FAIRHAVEN), THE (Fairhaven, MA) **11518**

ADVOCATE (NEWARK), THE (Newark, OH) **11382**

ADVOCATE (NORTH ADAMS), THE (North Adams, MA) **11521**

ADVOCATE PENNY SAVER (Sweetwater, TN) **11630**

ADVOCATE (STAMFORD), THE (Stamford, CT) **11331**

ADVOCATE-MESSENGER (Danville, KY) **11351**

ADVOCATE-TRIBUNE (Granite Falls, MN) **11538**

AEGIS, THE (Bel Air, MD) **11512**

AFTON STAR-ENTERPRISE (Afton, IA) **11489**

AGAWAM ADVERTISER NEWS (Feeding Hills, MA) **11518**

AIKEN STANDARD (Aiken, SC) **11393**

AITKIN INDEPENDENT AGE (Aitkin, MN) **11533**

AJO COPPER NEWS (Ajo, AZ) **11417**

AKRON BEACON JOURNAL (Poulsbo, WA) **11405**

AKRON HOMETOWNER (Akron, IA) **11489**

AKRON NEWS REPORTER (Akron, CO) **11439**

ALABAMA MESSENGER (Birmingham, AL) **11411**

ALAMANCE NEWS, THE (Graham, NC) **11587**

ALAMEDA TIMES-STAR (Oakland, CA) **11325**

ALAMOGORDO DAILY NEWS (Alamogordo, NM) **11370**

ALASKA STAR (Eagle River, AK) **11416**

ALBANY AREA ADVERTISER (Albany, GA) **11456**

ALBANY DEMOCRAT-HERALD (Albany, OR) **11386**

ALBANY HERALD, THE (Albany, GA) **11334**

ALBANY JOURNAL (Albany, GA) **11456**

ALBANY LEDGER, THE (Albany, MO) **11548**

ALBERT LEA TRIBUNE (Albert Lea, MN) **11360**

ALBIA UNION-REPUBLICAN (Albia, IA) **11489**

ALBION NEWS (Albion, NE) **11556**

ALBION NEWS, THE (Albion, PA) **11609**

ALBION RECORDER (Albion, MI) **11525**

ALBUQUERQUE JOURNAL (Albuquerque, NM) **11370**

ALBUQUERQUE TRIBUNE, THE (Albuquerque, NM) **11370**

ALCESTER UNION & HUDSONITE, THE (Alcester, SD) **11623**

ALDEN ADVANCE (Alden, MN) **11534**

ALDEN ADVERTISER (Alden, NY) **11569**

ALEXANDRIA GAZETTE PACKET (McLean, VA) **11648**

ALEXANDRIA NEWS WEEKLY (Alexandria, LA) **11506**

ALGONA UPPER DES MOINES (Algona, IA) **11489**

ALGONQUIN COUNTRYSIDE (Algonquin, IL) **11466**

ALICE ECHO-NEWS JOURNAL (Alice, TX) **11397**

ALISO VIEJO NEWS (Lake Forest, CA) **11430**

ALL AROUND PENNSAUKEN (Cinnaminson, NJ) **11562**

ALLEGAN COUNTY NEWS (Allegan, MI) **11525**

ALLEGHENY-HYDE PARK EXPRESS (Vandergrift, PA) **11617**

ALLEN AMERICAN, THE (Plano, TX) **11640**

ALLEN COUNTY TIMES (New Haven, IN) **11487**

ALLIANCE REVIEW, THE (Alliance, OH) **11379**

ALLIANCE TIMES-HERALD (Alliance, NE) **11366**

ALLIED NEWS (Grove City, PA) **11612**

ALLSTON/BRIGHTON TAB (Needham, MA) **11521**

ALMA TIMES, THE (Blackshear, GA) **11457**

ALMANAC (MCMURRAY), THE (McMurray, PA) **11613**

ALMANAC (MENLO PARK), THE (Menlo Park, CA) **11432**

ALPENA NEWS, THE (Alpena, MI) **11357**

ALPENA STAR (Mt Pleasant, MI) **11530**

ALPINE AVALANCHE (Alpine, TX) **11631**

ALPINE SUN (Alpine, CA) **11425**

ALSIP EXPRESS (Midlothian, IL) **11476**

ALSIP-BLUE ISLAND STAR (Tinley Park, IL) **11482**

ALTAMONT ENTERPRISE, THE (Altamont, NY) **11569**

ALTAMONT NEWS, THE (Altamont, IL) **11466**

ALTAVISTA JOURNAL (Altavista, VA) **11645**

AZLE NEWS (Azle, TX) **11631**

AZUSA HERALD (West Covina, CA) **11438**

B

BABYLON BEACON, THE (Babylon, NY) **11569**

BAINBRIDGE ISLAND REVIEW (Bainbridge Island, WA) **11651**

BAINBRIDGE POST-SEARCHLIGHT (Bainbridge, GA) **11457**

BAKER CITY HERALD (Baker City, OR) **11387**

BAKER COUNTY PRESS, THE (MacClenny, FL) **11452**

BAKER OBSERVER (Baker, LA) **11506**

BAKERSFIELD CALIFORNIAN (Bakersfield, CA) **11324**

BALATON PRESS-TRIBUNE (Balaton, MN) **11534**

BALD KNOB BANNER (Bald Knob, AR) **11420**

BALDWIN BULLETIN (Baldwin, WI) **11658**

BALDWIN HERALD (Garden City, NY) **11574**

BALDWIN TIMES (Bay Minette, AL) **11411**

BALDWINSVILLE MESSENGER (Syracuse, NY) **11582**

BALDWYN NEWS, THE (Baldwyn, MS) **11545**

BALLARD NEWS TRIBUNE (Seattle, WA) **11654**

BALLSTON JOURNAL (Ballston Spa, NY) **11569**

BALTIC BEACON (Dell Rapids, SD) **11624**

BALTIMORE CITY PAPER (Baltimore, MD) **11511**

BALTIMORE GUIDE, THE (Baltimore, MD) **11511**

BALTIMORE MESSENGER (Towson, MD) **11515**

BALTIMORE TIMES (Baltimore, MD) **11511**

BANCROFT REGISTER, THE (Bancroft, IA) **11490**

BANDON WESTERN WORLD (Bandon, OR) **11606**

BANKS COUNTY NEWS (Homer, GA) **11460**

BANNER JOURNAL (Black River Falls, WI) **11658**

BANNER (NEW YORK), THE (New York, NY) **11579**

BANNER NEWS, THE (Belmont, NC) **11585**

BANNER PRESS NEWSPAPER, THE (Columbus, TX) **11633**

BANNER (WEST BOYLSTON & BOYLSTON), THE (Clinton, MA) **11516**

BANNER-GAZETTE (Pekin, IN) **11488**

BANNER-GRAPHIC (Greencastle, IN) **11343**

BANNER-INDEPENDENT, THE (Booneville, MS) **11545**

BANNER-NEWS (Magnolia, AR) **11323**

BANNER-PRESS (BRENHAM), THE (Brenham, TX) **11397**

BANNER-PRESS (DAVID CITY), THE (David City, NE) **11557**

BANNER-PRESS (MARBLE HILL) (Marble Hill, MO) **11551**

BAR HARBOR TIMES (Bar Harbor, ME) **11509**

BARABOO NEWS REPUBLIC (Baraboo, WI) **11407**

BARBER COUNTY INDEX (Medicine Lodge, KS) **11498**

BARBERTON HERALD (Barberton, OH) **11592**

BARBOUR DEMOCRAT, THE (Philippi, WV) **11656**

BARBOURVILLE MOUNTAIN ADVOCATE (Barbourville, KY) **11500**

BARGAIN BANNER, THE (Harlan, KY) **11502**

BARGAIN HUNTER (TAFT) (Taft, CA) **11438**

BARGAIN NEWS (Trumbull, CT) **11447**

BARGAINEER (Zion, IL) **11484**

BARGAINEER, THE (Aberdeen, MD) **11511**

BARNESVILLE ENTERPRISE (Barnesville, OH) **11593**

BARNESVILLE RECORD REVIEW (Barnesville, MN) **11534**

BARNSTABLE PATRIOT, THE (Hyannis, MA) **11519**

BARRE GAZETTE, THE (Barre, MA) **11515**

BARRINGTON COURIER-REVIEW (Algonquin, IL) **11466**

BARRINGTON TIMES (Warren, RI) **11619**

BARRON NEWS SHIELD (Barron, WI) **11658**

BARROW COUNTY NEWS, THE (Cumming, GA) **11458**

BARRY COUNTY ADVERTISER (Cassville, MO) **11549**

BARTLESVILLE EXAMINER-ENTERPRISE (Bartlesville, OK) **11384**

BARTLETT EXPRESS, THE (Bartlett, TN) **11625**

BARTLETT/HANOVER PARK/STREAM WOOD PRESS (Downers Grove, IL) **11470**

BARTOW NEIGHBOR, THE (Cartersville, GA) **11458**

BASTROP ADVERTISER, THE (Bastrop, TX) **11631**

BASTROP DAILY ENTERPRISE (Bastrop, LA) **11353**

BATAVIA DAILY NEWS (Batavia, NY) **11371**

BATAVIA REPUBLICAN, THE (St Charles, IL) **11481**

BATAVIA SUN (Aurora, IL) **11467**

BATESVILLE GUARD (Batesville, AR) **11322**

BATH COUNTY NEWS-OUTLOOK (Owingsville, KY) **11504**

BATON ROUGE SHOPPER (Baton Rouge, LA) **11506**

BATTLE CREEK ENQUIRER (Battle Creek, MI) **11357**

BATTLE CREEK SHOPPER NEWS (Battle Creek, MI) **11525**

BATTLE LAKE REVIEW (Battle Lake, MN) **11534**

BAUDETTE REGION, THE (Baudette, MN) **11534**

BAXLEY NEWS-BANNER, THE (Baxley, GA) **11457**

BAXTER BULLETIN (Mountain Home, AR) **11323**

BAY AREA CITIZEN (Webster, TX) **11642**

BAY BEACON, THE (Niceville, FL) **11453**

BAY BULLETIN, THE (Melbourne, FL) **11453**

BAY CITY TIMES, THE (Bay City, MI) **11357**

BAY CITY TRIBUNE (Bay City, TX) **11397**

BAY NEWS (Brooklyn, NY) **11570**

BAY RIDGE COURIER (Brooklyn, NY) **11570**

BAY ST LOUIS SEA COAST ECHO (Bay St Louis, MS) **11545**

BAY TIMES (Stevensville, MD) **11515**

BAY TIMES, THE (Walworth, WI) **11668**

BAY VIEWER, THE (New Berlin, WI) **11663**

BAY VOICE (New Baltimore, MI) **11530**

BAYLOR COUNTY BANNER (Seymour, TX) **11641**

BAYONNE COMMUNITY NEWS (Bayonne, NJ) **11561**

BAYSHORE SUN (La Porte, TX) **11638**

BAYSIDE TIMES, THE (Bayside, NY) **11569**

BAYTOWN SUN (Baytown, TX) **11397**

BEACH & BAY PRESS (San Diego, CA) **11436**

BEACH HAVEN TIMES (Manahawkin, NJ) **11565**

BEACH REPORTER, THE (Manhattan Beach, CA) **11432**

BEACHCOMBER (Surf City, NJ) **11567**

BEACHCOMBER (LONG BEACH) (Long Beach, CA) **11431**

BEACHES LEADER, THE (Jacksonville Beach, FL) **11451**

BEACON (CONCORD), THE (Concord, MA) **11516**

BEACON FREE PRESS (Wappingers Falls, NY) **11583**

BEACON HILL NEWS, THE (Seattle, WA) **11654**

BEACON (LAMBERTVILLE), THE (Hopewell, NJ) **11564**

BEACON LIGHT (Mahopac, NY) **11577**

BEACON NEWS, THE (Aurora, IL) **11338**

BEACON OBSERVER, THE (Overton, NE) **11558**

BEACON (PENNINGTON), THE (Pennington, NJ) **11566**

BEACON (PORT CLINTON), THE (Port Clinton, OH) **11600**

BEACON-VILLAGER, THE (Concord, MA) **11516**

BEAR FACTS OF MAINE, INC, THE (South Waterford, ME) **11511**

BEATRICE DAILY SUN (Beatrice, NE) **11366**

BEATTYVILLE ENTERPRISE (Beattyville, KY) **11500**

BEAUFORT GAZETTE (Beaufort, SC) **11393**

BEAUFORT-HYDE NEWS, THE (Belhaven, NC) **11585**

BEAUMONT ENTERPRISE (Beaumont, TX) **11397**

BEAUREGARD DAILY NEWS (De Ridder, LA) **11353**

BEAVER COUNTY TIMES (Beaver, PA) **11388**

BEAVER VALLEY STAR (ONLINE EDITION) (Monaca, PA) **11613**

BEAVERCREEK NEWS-CURRENT (Kettering, OH) **11381**

BEAVERTON VALLEY TIMES (Portland, OR) **11608**

BECKER COUNTY RECORD (Detroit Lakes, MN) **11536**

BEDFORD BULLETIN (Bedford, VA) **11646**

BEDFORD GAZETTE/GAZETTE SUNDAY (Bedford, PA) **11388**

BEDFORD JOURNAL (Milford, NH) **11560**

BEDFORD MINUTEMAN (Concord, MA) **11516**

BEDFORD SUN BANNER (Beachwood, OH) **11593**

BEDFORD TIMES-PRESS, THE (Bedford, IA) **11490**

BEDFORD TIMES-REGISTER (Stow, OH) **11600**

BEE (PHILLIPS), THE (Phillips, WI) **11665**

BEE (PORTLAND), THE (Portland, OR) **11608**

BEEBE NEWS (Beebe, AR) **11420**

BEECHER CITY JOURNAL (Beecher City, IL) **11467**

BEEVILLE BEE-PICAYUNE (Beeville, TX) **11631**

BELLAIR BEE (Seminole, FL) **11455**

BELLAIRE EXAMINER (Houston, TX) **11636**

BELLE BANNER (Belle, MO) **11548**

BELLE FOURCHE POST/BEE (Belle Fourche, SD) **11623**

BELLE MEADE NEWS (Nashville, TN) **11628**

BELLE PLAINE HERALD (Belle Plaine, MN) **11534**

BELLE PLAINE NEWS, THE (Belle Plaine, KS) **11496**

BELLE PLAINS UNION (Belle Plaine, IA) **11490**

BELLEFONTAINE EXAMINER (Bellefontaine, OH) **11379**

BELLEFONTAINE NEIGHBORS-JENNINGS JOURNAL (Hazelwood, MO) **11550**

BELLEVILLE ENTERPRISE (Wayne, MI) **11533**

BELLEVILLE JOURNAL (Swansea, IL) **11482**

BELLEVILLE NEWS-DEMOCRAT (Belleville, IL) **11338**

BELLEVILLE POST (Bloomfield, NJ) **11561**

BELLEVILLE RECORDER (Belleville, WI) **11658**

BELLEVILLE TELESCOPE (Belleville, KS) **11496**

BELLEVILLE TIMES (Nutley, NJ) **11565**

BELLEVUE GAZETTE, THE (Bellevue, OH) **11379**

BELLEVUE HERALD-LEADER (Bellevue, IA) **11490**

BELLEVUE LEADER (Bellevue, NE) **11556**

BELLINGHAM HERALD (Bellingham, WA) **11404**

BELLMORE LIFE (Merrick, NY) **11578**

BELLMORE-MERRICK OBSERVER (North Massapequa, NY) **11580**

BELLOWS FALLS TOWN CRIER (Bellows Falls, VT) **11644**

BELLVILLE STAR, THE (Bellville, OH) **11593**

BELLVILLE TIMES (Bellville, TX) **11631**

BELMOND INDEPENDENT (Belmond, IA) **11490**

BELMONT AND TISHOMINGO JOURNAL (Belmont, MS) **11545**

BELMONT CITIZEN-HERALD (Lexington, MA) **11519**

BELOIT CALL (Beloit, KS) **11496**

BELOIT DAILY NEWS (Beloit, WI) **11407**

BELVIDERE REPUBLICAN (Belvidere, IL) **11467**

BELZONI BANNER, THE (Belzoni, MS) **11545**

BENBROOK NEWS (Fort Worth, TX) **11635**

BENICIA HERALD (Benicia, CA) **11324**

BENNETTS VALLEY NEWS (Weedville, PA) **11618**

BENNINGTON BANNER (Bennington, VT) **11402**

BENSENVILLE/WOOD DALE PRESS (Oak Brook, IL) **11477**

BENSON COUNTY FARMERS PRESS (Minnewaukan, ND) **11592**

BENT COUNTY DEMOCRAT (Las Animas, CO) **11441**

BENTON COUNTY DAILY RECORD (Bentonville, AR) **11322**

BENTON COUNTY ENTERPRISE (Warsaw, MO) **11555**

BENTON COURIER (Benton, AR) **11322**

BENTON REVIEW, THE (Fowler, IN) **11485**

BENZIE COUNTY RECORD PATRIOT (Frankfort, MI) **11527**

BEREA CITIZEN, THE (Berea, KY) **11500**

BERGEN NEWS/SUN BULLETIN, THE (Palisades Park, NJ) **11566**

BERKELEY INDEPENDENT, THE (Moncks Corner, SC) **11622**

BERKSHIRE EAGLE (Pittsfield, MA) **11356**

BERKSHIRE PENNY SAVER (Lee, MA) **11519**

BERKSHIRE RECORD (Great Barrington, MA) **11518**

BERLIN BUYERS' GUIDE (Ripon, WI) **11666**

BERLIN DAILY SUN (Berlin, NH) **11368**

BERLIN JOURNAL (Berlin, WI) **11658**

BERLIN REPORTER, THE (Berlin, NH) **11559**

BERNARDSVILLE NEWS (Bernardsville, NJ) **11561**

BERNE TRI-WEEKLY NEWS (Berne, IN) **11484**

BERRIEN COUNTY RECORD (Buchanan, MI) **11525**

BERRIEN PRESS (Nashville, GA) **11462**

BERRYESSA SUN (Milipitas, CA) **11433**

Title

BERTIE LEDGER-ADVANCE (Windsor, NC) **11590**
BERWYN/CICERO LIFE (North Riverside, IL) **11477**
BETHANY REPUBLICAN-CLIPPER (Bethany, MO) **11548**
BETHEL BEACON (New Milford, CT) **11445**
BETHEL CITIZEN, THE (Bethel, ME) **11509**
BETHEL JOURNAL, THE (Loveland, OH) **11597**
BETHESDA GAZETTE (Gaithersburg, MD) **11513**
BETHPAGE NEWSGRAM (Hicksville, NY) **11576**
BETTENDORF NEWS (Bettendorf, IA) **11490**
BEULAH BEACON (Beulah, ND) **11591**
BEVERLY CITIZEN (Beverly, MA) **11515**
BEVERLY HILLS COURIER (Beverly Hills, CA) **11426**
BEVERLY HILLS TODAY & PALM SPRINGS TODAY (Rancho
    Mirage, CA) **11326**
BEVERLY HILLS WEEKLY (Beverly Hills, CA) **11426**
BEVERLY NEWS (Midlothian, IL) **11476**
BEVERLY REVIEW, THE (Chicago, IL) **11468**
BEXLEY NEWS (Columbus, OH) **11595**
BIDDEFORD-SACO-OLD ORCHARD BEACH COURIER
    (Biddeford, ME) **11509**
BIENVILLE DEMOCRAT & RINGGOLD RECORD (Arcadia, LA)
    11506
BIG BEAR GRIZZLY (Big Bear Lake, CA) **11426**
BIG BEAR SHOPPER (Big Bear Lake, CA) **11426**
BIG NICKEL (Joplin, MO) **11551**
BIG SANDY NEWS, THE (Louisa, KY) **11503**
BIG SPRING HERALD (Big Spring, TX) **11397**
BIG THICKET MESSENGER (Livingston, TX) **11638**
BIG WALNUT NEWS (Columbus, OH) **11595**
BIGFORK EAGLE (Bigfork, MT) **11555**
BILLBOARD, THE (Berlin, WI) **11658**
BILLERICA MINUTEMAN (Concord, MA) **11516**
BILLINGS GAZETTE (Billings, MT) **11366**
BILOXI D'IBERVILLE PRESS (2007) (Biloxi, MS) **11545**
BIRD CITY TIMES (Bird City, KS) **11496**
BIRD ISLAND UNION (Bird Island, MN) **11534**
BIRGMINGHAM-BLOOMFIELD ECCENTRIC, THE (McLean, VA)
    11648
BIRMINGHAM NEWS (Birmingham, AL) **11319**
BIRMINGHAM WEEKLY (Birmingham, AL) **11411**
BISBEE DAILY REVIEW (Bisbee, AZ) **11321**
BISBEE OBSERVER, THE (Bisbee, AZ) **11417**
BISCAYNE BAY TRIBUNE (South Miami, FL) **11455**
BISMARCK TRIBUNE (Bismarck, ND) **11378**
BISMARCK/MANDAN FINDER (Bismarck, ND) **11591**
BIXBY BULLETIN (Bixby, OK) **11603**
BLACK FOREST NEWS & PALMER DIVIDE PIONEER (Colorado
    Springs, CO) **11440**
BLACK HILLS PIONEER (Spearfish, SD) **11395**
BLACK HILLS PRESS (Sturgis, SD) **11625**
BLACK MOUNTAIN NEWS (Black Mountain, NC) **11585**
BLACK RIVER TRIBUNE (Ludlow, VT) **11644**
BLACKBELT GAZETTE (Demopolis, AL) **11412**
BLACKDUCK SHOPPER, THE (Blackduck, MN) **11534**
BLACKSHEAR TIMES, THE (Blackshear, GA) **11457**
BLACKSTONE VALLEY TRIBUNE (Whitinsville, MA) **11524**
BLACKWELL JOURNAL-TRIBUNE (Blackwell, OK) **11603**
BLADE (FAIRBURY), THE (Fairbury, IL) **11471**
BLADE (TOLEDO), THE (Sylvania, OH) **11383**
BLADEN EXTRA (Elizabethtown, NC) **11586**
BLADEN JOURNAL (Elizabethtown, NC) **11586**
BLAINE BANNER (Blaine, MN) **11534**
BLAINE-SPRING LAKE PARK LIFE (Coon Rapids, MN) **11536**
BLAIR PRESS (Blair, WI) **11658**
BLAIRSTOWN PRESS (Hackettstown, NJ) **11563**
BLANCO COUNTY NEWS (Blanco, TX) **11631**
BLAND COUNTY MESSENGER (Wytheville, VA) **11651**
BLAND COURIER (Belle, MO) **11548**

BLASDELL/LACKAWANNA PENNYSAVER (Hamburg, NY)
    11575
BLEDSONIAN-BANNER, THE (Pikeville, TN) **11629**
BLOOMER ADVANCE (Bloomer, WI) **11658**
BLOOMFIELD DEMOCRAT, THE (Bloomfield, IA) **11490**
BLOOMFIELD JOURNAL (Bristol, CT) **11443**
BLOOMFIELD LIFE (Nutley, NJ) **11565**
BLOOMINGTON SUN-CURRENT (Eden Prairie, MN) **11537**
BLOOMVILLE GAZETTE (Attica, OH) **11592**
BLOUNT COUNTIAN, THE (Oneonta, AL) **11415**
BLOWING ROCKET, THE (Blowing Rock, NC) **11585**
BLUE MOUND LEADER (Blue Mound, IL) **11467**
BLUE MOUNTAIN EAGLE (John Day, OR) **11607**
BLUE RIDGE LEADER, THE (Purcellville, VA) **11649**
BLUE SPRINGS EXAMINER (Blue Springs, MO) **11363**
BLUE WATER VOICE, THE (New Baltimore, MI) **11530**
BLUEFIELD DAILY TELEGRAPH (Bluefield, WV) **11406**
BLUFFTON NEWS, THE (Bluffton, OH) **11593**
BLUFFTON NEWS-BANNER (Bluffton, IN) **11342**
BLUFFTON TODAY (Bluffton, SC) **11393**
BLYTHEVILLE COURIER NEWS (Blytheville, AR) **11322**
BOARDMAN NEWS (Youngstown, OH) **11603**
BOCA BEACON (Boca Grande, FL) **11449**
BOCA RATON NEWS (Boca Raton, FL) **11332**
BOCA TIMES, THE (Pompano Beach, FL) **11454**
BODEGA BAY NAVIGATOR (Bodega Bay, CA) **11426**
BOISE CITY NEWS, THE (Boise City, OK) **11604**
BOISE WEEKLY (Boise, ID) **11464**
BOLINGBROOK SUN, THE (Plainfield, IL) **11480**
BOLINGBROOK/WOODRIDGE/LISLE REPORTER (Downers
    Grove, IL) **11470**
BOLIVAR COMMERCIAL, THE (Cleveland, MS) **11362**
BOLIVAR HERALD-FREE PRESS (Bolivar, MO) **11548**
BOLTON COMMON, THE (Harvard, MA) **11518**
BONANZA VALLEY VOICE (Brooten, MN) **11535**
BONITA BANNER (Bonita Springs, FL) **11449**
BONNER COUNTY DAILY BEE (Sandpoint, ID) **11338**
BONNER SPRINGS-EDWARDSVILLE CHIEFTAIN, THE (Bonner
    Springs, KS) **11496**
BONNERS FERRY HERALD (Bonners Ferry, ID) **11464**
BONNY BUYER (West Point, IA) **11496**
BOOKER NEWS, THE (Booker, TX) **11631**
BOONE COUNTY JOURNAL (Ashland, MO) **11548**
BOONE COUNTY RECORDER (Fort Mitchell, KY) **11501**
BOONE COUNTY SHOPPING NEWS (Boone, IA) **11490**
BOONE NEWS-REPUBLICAN (Boone, IA) **11346**
BOONEVILLE DEMOCRAT (Booneville, AR) **11420**
BOONVILLE DAILY NEWS (Boonville, MO) **11363**
BOONVILLE HERALD & ADIRONDACK TOURIST (Boonville, NY)
    11570
BOONVILLE STANDARD, THE (Boonville, IN) **11484**
BOOSTER LAKE VIEW EDITION (Oak Park, IL) **11477**
BOOSTER, THE (Columbus, OH) **11595**
BOOSTER WICKER EDITION (Oak Park, IL) **11478**
BOOTHBAY REGISTER (Boothbay Harbor, ME) **11509**
BORDEN STAR, THE (Gail, TX) **11635**
BORGER NEWS-HERALD (Borger, TX) **11397**
BOSCOBEL DIAL (Boscobel, WI) **11658**
BOSQUE COUNTY NEWS (Meridian, TX) **11639**
BOSSIER BANNER-PROGRESS (Bossier City, LA) **11506**
BOSSIER PRESS-TRIBUNE (Bossier City, LA) **11506**
BOSTON GLOBE, THE (Boston, MA) **11355**
BOSTON HERALD (Boston, MA) **11355**
BOULDER CITY NEWS (Boulder City, NV) **11559**
BOUND BROOK CHRONICLE (Somerville, NJ) **11567**
BOURBON COUNTY CITIZEN (Paris, KY) **11504**
BOURBON NEWS-MIRROR (Bourbon, IN) **11484**
BOURNE ENTERPRISE (Falmouth, MA) **11518**
BOUTIQUE & VILLAGER (Burlingame, CA) **11426**

BOWDON BULLETIN (Carrollton, GA) **11457**
BOWIE BLADE-NEWS (Bowie, MD) **11512**
BOWIE NEWS (Bowie, TX) **11631**
BOWIE STAR (Landover, MD) **11513**
BOWLING GREEN TIMES (Bowling Green, MO) **11548**
BOX ELDER NEWS JOURNAL (Brigham City, UT) **11643**
BOYERTOWN AREA TIMES (Boyertown, PA) **11610**
BOYNTON TIMES, THE (Pompano Beach, FL) **11454**
BOZEMAN DAILY CHRONICLE (Bozeman, MT) **11366**
BRACKEN COUNTY NEWS, THE (Brooksville, KY) **11500**
BRACKETT NEWS, THE (Brackettville, TX) **11632**
BRADENTON HERALD (Bradenton, FL) **11332**
BRADFORD COUNTY TELEGRAPH (Starke, FL) **11455**
BRADFORD ERA, THE (Bradford, PA) **11388**
BRADFORD JOURNAL/MINER (Bradford, PA) **11610**
BRADY STANDARD-HERALD (Brady, TX) **11632**
BRAIDWOOD JOURNAL, THE (Wilmington, IL) **11483**
BRAINERD DAILY DISPATCH, THE (Brainerd, MN) **11360**
BRAINTREE FORUM (Weymouth, MA) **11524**
BRANDON NEWS & SHOPPER, THE (Brandon, FL) **11449**
BRANDON VALLEY CHALLENGER (Brandon, SD) **11623**
BRANDYWINE COMMUNITY NEWS (Yorklyn, DE) **11448**
BRANFORD NEWS (Branford, FL) **11449**
BRANFORD REVIEW, THE (Guilford, CT) **11444**
BRANSON DAILY NEWS (Hollister, MO) **11364**
BRANTLEY ENTERPRISE, THE (Nahunta, GA) **11462**
BRATTLEBORO REFORMER (Brattleboro, VT) **11402**
BRATTLEBORO TOWN CRIER (Brattleboro, VT) **11644**
BRAXTON CITIZEN'S NEWS (Sutton, WV) **11657**
BRAXTON DEMOCRAT-CENTRAL (Sutton, WV) **11657**
BRAZIL TIMES (Brazil, IN) **11342**
BRAZORIA COUNTY NEWS, THE (West Columbia, TX) **11642**
BREA PROGRESS (Anaheim, CA) **11425**
BRECKENRIDGE AMERICAN (Graham, TX) **11635**
BRECKINRIDGE HERALD-NEWS (Hardinsburg, KY) **11502**
BRECKSVILLE GAZETTE (Cleveland, OH) **11594**
BREDA NEWS (Breda, IA) **11490**
BREESE JOURNAL (Breese, IL) **11467**
BREEZE, THE (Philadelphia, PA) **11615**
BREMEN ENQUIRER, THE (Bremen, IN) **11484**
BREMER COUNTY INDEPENDENT (Waverly, IA) **11496**
BREMERTON PATRIOT, THE (Bremerton, WA) **11651**
BRENTWOOD JOURNAL, THE (Nashville, TN) **11628**
BREWSTER TIMES (Mahopac, NY) **11577**
BREWTON STANDARD, THE (Brewton, AL) **11411**
BRIDESBURG STAR (Trevose, PA) **11617**
BRIDGEPORT INDEX (Bridgeport, TX) **11632**
BRIDGEPORT LEADER (Bridgeport, IL) **11467**
BRIDGEPORT NEWS (CHICAGO) (Chicago, IL) **11468**
BRIDGEPORT NEWS (SHELTON), THE (Shelton, CT) **11446**
BRIDGEPORT (WV) NEWS (Bridgeport, WV) **11655**
BRIDGER VALLEY PIONEER (Lyman, WY) **11669**
BRIDGETON NEWS (Bridgeton, NJ) **11369**
BRIDGEVIEW INDEPENDENT (Midlothian, IL) **11476**
BRIDGEVILLE STAR NEWS (Robinson Twp, PA) **11616**
BRIDGEWATER INDEPENDENT (Rayham, MA) **11522**
BRIDGTON NEWS, THE (Bridgton, ME) **11509**
BRIGHTON PARK LIFE (Chicago, IL) **11468**
BRIGHTON STANDARD BLADE (Brighton, CO) **11439**
BRIGHTON-PITTSFORD POST (Canandaigua, NY) **11571**
BRILLION NEWS (Brillion, WI) **11658**
BRINKLEY ARGUS (Brinkley, AR) **11420**
BRISTOL BAY TIMES, THE (Dillingham, AK) **11416**
BRISTOL HERALD COURIER (Bristol, VA) **11403**
BRISTOL PHOENIX (Bristol, RI) **11618**
BRISTOL PILOT (Bristol, PA) **11610**
BRISTOL PRESS, THE (Bristol, CT) **11331**
BRISTOW NEWS (Bristow, OK) **11604**
BRITT NEWS-TRIBUNE (Britt, IA) **11490**

BROAD TOP BULLETIN (Dudley, PA) **11611**

BROADCASTER PRESS (Vermillion, SD) **11625**

BROCKPORT-SPENCERPORT POST (Canandaigua, NY) **11571**

BROKEN ARROW LEDGER (Broken Arrow, OK) **11604**

BRONSON JOURNAL, THE (Coldwater, MI) **11526**

BRONX NEWS (Bronx, NY) **11570**

BRONX PRESS-REVIEW (Bronx, NY) **11570**

BROOK REPORTER, THE (Kentland, IN) **11486**

BROOKE COUNTY REVIEW (Wellsburg, WV) **11657**

BROOKFIELD JOURNAL (New Milford, CT) **11445**

BROOKFIELD NEWS (New Berlin, WI) **11663**

BROOKFIELD SUBURBAN LIFE (North Riverside, IL) **11477**

BROOKFIELD/LYONS/MCCOOK SUBURBAN LIFE (Oak Brook, IL) **11477**

BROOKHAVEN REVIEW (Nesconset, NY) **11579**

BROOKINGS REGISTER (Brookings, SD) **11394**

BROOKLINE TAB (Needham, MA) **11521**

BROOKLYN CENTER/BROOKLYN PARK SUN POST (Eden Prairie, MN) **11537**

BROOKLYN CHRONICLE (Brooklyn, IA) **11490**

BROOKLYN DAILY EAGLE & DAILY BULLETIN (Brooklyn, NY) **11371**

BROOKLYN EAGLE (Brooklyn, NY) **11570**

BROOKLYN GRAPHIC (Brooklyn, NY) **11570**

BROOKLYN HEIGHTS COURIER (Brooklyn, NY) **11570**

BROOKLYN HEIGHTS PRESS (Brooklyn, NY) **11570**

BROOKLYN HOME REPORTER & SUNSET NEWS (Brooklyn, NY) **11570**

BROOKLYN JOURNAL OF ARTS & URBAN AFFAIRS (Brooklyn, NY) **11571**

BROOKLYN PARK SUN POST (Eden Prairie, MN) **11537**

BROOKLYN RECORD OF REAL ESTATE (Brooklyn, NY) **11571**

BROOKLYN SPECTATOR (Brooklyn, NY) **11571**

BROOKLYN SUN JOURNAL (Cleveland, OH) **11594**

BROOKVILLE AMERICAN (Brookville, IN) **11484**

BROOKVILLE DEMOCRAT (Brookville, IN) **11485**

BROOMFIELD ENTERPRISE (Broomfield, CO) **11439**

BROWARD TIMES (Fort Lauderdale, FL) **11451**

BROWN COUNTY DEMOCRAT (Nashville, IN) **11487**

BROWN COUNTY PRESS (Mt Orab, OH) **11599**

BROWN COUNTY REMINDER (Sleepy Eye, MN) **11543**

BROWN DEER HERALD (New Berlin, WI) **11663**

BROWNFIELD NEWS (Brownfield, TX) **11632**

BROWNSVILLE HERALD, THE (Brownsville, TX) **11397**

BROWNSVILLE STATES-GRAPHIC (Brownsville, TN) **11625**

BROWNWOOD BULLETIN, THE (Brownwood, TX) **11397**

BRUNSWICK CITIZEN (Brunswick, MD) **11512**

BRUNSWICK NEWS, THE (Brunswick, GA) **11335**

BRUNSWICK SUN TIMES (Medina, OH) **11598**

BRUNSWICK TIMES-GAZETTE (Lawrenceville, VA) **11648**

BRUSH NEWS-TRIBUNE (Brush, CO) **11439**

BRYAN COUNTY NEWS (Richmond Hill, GA) **11462**

BRYAN COUNTY STAR, THE (Durant, OK) **11604**

BRYAN SHOPPER (Denison, TX) **11633**

BRYAN TIMES, THE (Bryan, OH) **11379**

BRYAN-COLLEGE STATION EAGLE (Bryan, TX) **11397**

BUCKEYE SUN, THE (Buckeye, AZ) **11417**

BUCKEYE VALLEY NEWS (Buckeye, AZ) **11417**

BUCKS COUNTY COURIER TIMES (Levittown, PA) **11390**

BUCKS COUNTY TRIBUNE (Horsham, PA) **11612**

BUCKSPORT ENTERPRISE, THE (Bucksport, ME) **11509**

BUDGETEER NEWS (Superior, WI) **11667**

BUFFALO BULLETIN (Buffalo, WY) **11668**

BUFFALO CENTER TRIBUNE (Buffalo Center, IA) **11490**

BUFFALO COUNTY JOURNAL (Cochrane, WI) **11659**

BUFFALO GROVE COUNTRYSIDE (Arlington Heights, IL) **11466**

BUFFALO GROVE JOURNAL & TOPICS (Des Plaines, IL) **11470**

BUFFALO NEWS (Buffalo, NY) **11371**

BUFFALO REFLEX (Buffalo, MO) **11548**

BUFFALO RIDGE GAZETTE, THE (Ruthton, MN) **11542**

BUFFALO RIVER REVIEW (Linden, TN) **11628**

BUFFALO ROCKET (Buffalo, NY) **11571**

BUGLE, THE (Bolinbrook, IL) **11467**

BUHL HERALD (Buhl, ID) **11464**

BULLETIN (BEND), THE (Bend, OR) **11387**

BULLETIN (CRESTVIEW), THE (Crestview, FL) **11450**

BULLETIN (MILFORD), THE (Milford, CT) **11445**

BULLETIN-TIMES (Bolivar, TN) **11625**

BULLHEAD CITY BEE (Bullhead City, AZ) **11417**

BUNKER HILL GAZETTE NEWS (Hillsboro, IL) **11474**

BURBANK-STICKNEY INDEPENDENT (Midlothian, IL) **11476**

BUREAU COUNTY REPUBLICAN (Princeton, IL) **11480**

BURKE CONNECTION (McLean, VA) **11648**

BURKE MARKETPLACE (Morganton, NC) **11588**

BURKE TIMES, THE (Herndon, VA) **11647**

BURLESON COUNTY TRIBUNE (Caldwell, TX) **11632**

BURLINGTON COUNTY TIMES (Willingboro, NJ) **11370**

BURLINGTON FREE PRESS (Burlington, VT) **11402**

BURLINGTON STANDARD PRESS (Burlington, WI) **11659**

BURLINGTON UNION (Concord, MA) **11517**

BURNET BULLETIN (Burnet, TX) **11632**

BURNETT COUNTY SENTINEL (Grantsburg, WI) **11661**

BURNS TIMES-HERALD (Burns, OR) **11606**

BURNSVILLE THISWEEK (Burnsville, MN) **11535**

BURNSVILLE/SAVAGE/LAKEVILLE SUN-CURRENT (Eden Prairie, MN) **11537**

BURNT HILLS SPOTLIGHT (Delmar, NY) **11573**

BURR RIDGE/DARIEN/WILLOWBROOK SUBURBAN LIFE (Oak Brook, IL) **11477**

BURTON NEWS, THE (Flint, MI) **11527**

BURTONSVILLE GAZETTE (Silver Spring, MD) **11514**

BURWELL TRIBUNE, THE (Burwell, NE) **11557**

BUTLER COUNTY BANNER, THE (Morgantown, KY) **11504**

BUTLER COUNTY NEWS (Greenville, AL) **11413**

BUTLER COUNTY TRIBUNE JOURNAL (Allison, IA) **11489**

BUTLER EAGLE (Butler, PA) **11388**

BUTLER EXPRESS, THE (Greenville, AL) **11413**

BUTNER-CREEDMOOR NEWS, THE (Creedmoor, NC) **11586**

BUY LINE, THE (Ware, MA) **11524**

BUYERS DIGEST (Fairfax, VT) **11644**

BUYER'S GUIDE CENT SAVER (Mauston, WI) **11662**

BYESVILLE VILLAGE REPORTER (Byesville, OH) **11593**

BYRON REVIEW (Byron, MN) **11535**

C

C V N, THE (New Bedford, MA) **11356**

CABELL STANDARD, THE (Culloden, WV) **11655**

CABINET, THE (Milford, NH) **11560**

CABOT STAR HERALD/WEEKEND (Cabot, AR) **11420**

CABOT STAR-HERALD (Cabot, AR) **11420**

CADDO CITIZEN (Vivian, LA) **11508**

CADILLAC EVENING NEWS (Cadillac, MI) **11357**

CADIZ RECORD, THE (Cadiz, KY) **11500**

CADOTT SENTINEL (Cadott, WI) **11659**

CAHOKIA-DUPO JOURNAL (Swansee, IL) **11482**

CAIRO CITIZEN (Cairo, IL) **11468**

CAIRO MESSENGER (Cairo, GA) **11457**

CAJUN GAZETTE, THE (Pierre Part, LA) **11508**

CALAIS ADVERTISER (Calais, ME) **11509**

CALEDONIA ARGUS, THE (Caledonia, MN) **11535**

CALEDONIAN-RECORD, THE (St Johnsbury, VT) **11403**

CALHOUN CHRONICLE (Grantsville, WV) **11655**

CALHOUN COUNTY JOURNAL (Bruce, MS) **11546**

CALHOUN (GA) TIMES (Calhoun, GA) **11457**

CALHOUN NEWS-HERALD (Hardin, IL) **11473**

CALHOUN TIMES (ST MATTHEWS) (StMatthews, SC) **11623**

CALHOUN-LIBERTY JOURNAL, THE (Bristol, FL) **11449**

CALIFORNIA DEMOCRAT (California, MO) **11548**

CALIFORNIAN, THE (Temecula, CA) **11328**

CALL NEWS, THE (Citronelle, AL) **11412**

CALL (SCHUYLKILL HAVEN), THE (Schuylkill Haven, PA) **11616**

CALL, THE (Woonsocket, RI) **11393**

CALL-LEADER (Elwood, IN) **11343**

CALMAR COURIER (Calmar, IA) **11490**

CALOOSA BELLE (La Belle, FL) **11452**

CALUMET PRESS, THE (Hammond, IN) **11486**

CALVERT INDEPENDENT (Prince Frederick, MD) **11514**

CAMAS/WASHOUGAL POST RECORD (Camas, WA) **11651**

CAMBRIDGE CHRONICLE (Somerville, MA) **11523**

CAMBRIDGE CHRONICLE (GENESEO) (Geneseo, IL) **11472**

CAMBRIDGE NEWS (Cambridge, WI) **11659**

CAMBRIDGE TAB (Needham, MA) **11521**

CAMDEN CHRONICLE, THE (Camden, TN) **11625**

CAMDEN HERALD, THE (Camden, ME) **11509**

CAMDEN NEWS (Camden, AR) **11322**

CAMERON CITIZEN OBSERVER (Cameron, MO) **11548**

CAMERON COUNTY ECHO (Emporium, PA) **11611**

CAMERON HERALD, THE (Cameron, TX) **11632**

CAMILLA ENTERPRISE (Camilla, GA) **11457**

CAMILLUS ADVOCATE (Syracuse, NY) **11582**

CAMP VERDE JOURNAL, THE (Camp Verde, AZ) **11417**

CAMPBELL COMMUNITY RECORDER (Fort Mitchell, KY) **11502**

CAMPBELL COUNTY RECORDER (Fort Mitchell, KY) **11502**

CAMPBELL REPORTER, THE (San Jose, CA) **11436**

CAMPBELLSPORT NEWS (Campbellsport, WI) **11659**

CANARSIE COURIER (Brooklyn, NY) **11571**

CANARSIE DIGEST (Brooklyn, NY) **11571**

CANASTOTA BEE-JOURNAL (Canastota, NY) **11572**

CANBY HERALD (Canby, OR) **11606**

CANBY NEWS (Canby, MN) **11535**

CANDOR CHRONICLE (Trumansburg, NY) **11583**

CANISTOTA CLIPPER (Canistota, SD) **11623**

CANNON COURIER (Woodbury, TN) **11630**

CANNON FALLS BEACON (Cannon Falls, MN) **11535**

CANON CITY DAILY RECORD (Canon City, CO) **11329**

CANOVA HERALD (Canistota, SD) **11624**

CANTON CITIZEN (Canton, MA) **11516**

CANTON EAGLE (Wayne, MI) **11533**

CANTON INDEPENDENT-SENTINEL (Canton, PA) **11610**

CANTON JOURNAL (Rayham, MA) **11522**

CANTON OBSERVER (Livonia, MI) **11529**

CANYON COURIER (Evergreen, CO) **11440**

CANYON NEWS (Canyon, TX) **11632**

CAPE COD CHRONICLE (Chatham, MA) **11516**

CAPE COD TIMES (Hyannis, MA) **11356**

CAPE CODDER, THE (Orleans, MA) **11522**

CAPE CORAL DAILY BREEZE (Cape Coral, FL) **11332**

CAPE COURIER, THE (Cape Elizabeth, ME) **11509**

CAPE GAZETTE (Lewes, DE) **11448**

CAPE MAY COUNTY HERALD (Rio Grande, NJ) **11567**

CAPE MAY GAZETTE, THE (Seaville, NJ) **11567**

CAPE MAY STAR & WAVE (Cape May, NJ) **11562**

CAPISTRANO VALLEY NEWS (Lake Forest, CA) **11430**

CAPITAL (ANNAPOLIS), THE (Annapolis, MD) **11354**

CAPITAL CITY WEEKLY (Juneau, AK) **11416**

CAPITAL JOURNAL (Pierre, SD) **11394**

CAPITAL TIMES, THE (Madison, WI) **11408**

CAPITAL WEEKLY (Augusta, ME) **11509**

CAPITOL HILL BEACON (Oklahoma City, OK) **11605**

CAPITOL HILL TIMES (Seattle, WA) **11654**

CAPTIVA CURRENT (Sanibel, FL) **11455**

CARBONDALE NEWS, THE (Carbondale, PA) **11610**

CARIBBEAN LIFE (Brooklyn, NY) **11571**

CARIBOU COUNTY SUN (Soda Springs, ID) **11465**

CARLISLE CITIZEN, THE (Carlisle, IA) **11490**

CARLISLE COUNTY NEWS, THE (Bardwell, KY) **11500**

CARLISLE INDEPENDENT (Carlisle, AR) **11421**

CARLISLE MOSQUITO (Carlisle, MA) **11516**

CARLISLE SENTINEL (Carlisle, PA) **11388**

CARLSBAD CURRENT-ARGUS (Carlsbad, NM) **11370**

CARLYLE UNION BANNER (Carlyle, IL) **11468**

CARMEL PINE CONE (Pacific Grove, CA) **11434**

CARMEL TIMES (Mahopac, NY) **11577**

CARMI TIMES (Carmi, IL) **11338**

CARMICHAEL TIMES (Carmichael, CA) **11427**

CARNEGIE SIGNAL ITEM STAR (Pittsburgh, PA) **11615**

CAROL STREAM PRESS (Glen Ellyn, IL) **11472**

CAROLINA PANORAMA (Columbia, SC) **11620**

CAROLINA TIMES, THE (Durham, NC) **11586**

CAROLINE PROGRESS, THE (Bowling Green, VA) **11646**

CARRABELLE TIMES, THE (Apalachicola, FL) **11448**

CARROLL COUNTY COMET (Flora, IN) **11485**

CARROLL COUNTY INDEPENDENT, THE (Conway, NH) **11560**

CARROLL COUNTY NEWS-LEADER (Huntington, TN) **11627**

CARROLL COUNTY REVIEW (Thomson, IL) **11482**

CARROLL COUNTY TIMES (Westminster, MD) **11355**

CARROLL GARDENS/COBBLE HILL COURIER (Brooklyn, NY) **11571**

CARROLL NEWS, THE (Hillsville, VA) **11648**

CARROLLTON DEMOCRAT (Carrollton, MO) **11549**

CARROLLTON GAZETTE PATRIOT (Carrollton, IL) **11468**

CARROLLTON LEADER (Addison, TX) **11630**

CARROLLWOOD NEWS (Tampa, FL) **11455**

CARSON BULLETIN (Compton, CA) **11427**

CARSON PRESS (Elgin, ND) **11591**

CARTERET COUNTY NEWS-TIMES (Morehead City, NC) **11588**

CARTHAGE COURIER (Carthage, TN) **11626**

CARTHAGE PRESS (Carthage, MO) **11363**

CARTHAGE PRESS SCOPE, THE (Carthage, MO) **11549**

CARTHAGE REPUBLICAN TRIBUNE (Carthage, NY) **11572**

CARTHAGINIAN, THE (Carthage, MS) **11546**

CARVER REPORTER (Marshfield, MA) **11520**

CARY NEWS, THE (Cary, NC) **11586**

CARY-GROVE COUNTRYSIDE (Algonquin, IL) **11466**

CASA GRANDE DISPATCH (Casa Grande, AZ) **11321**

CASCADIA WEEKLY (Bellingham, WA) **11651**

CASEY COUNTY NEWS (Liberty, KY) **11503**

CASEY COUNTY SHOPPER, THE (Columbia, KY) **11501**

CASEY REPORTER, THE (Casey, IL) **11468**

CASH-BOOK JOURNAL (Jackson, MO) **11551**

CASHMERE VALLEY RECORD (Cashmere, WA) **11651**

CASHTON RECORD (Cashton, WI) **11659**

CASPER STAR TRIBUNE (Casper, WY) **11409**

CASS CITY CHRONICLE (Cass City, MI) **11526**

CASS COUNTY DEMOCRAT MISSOURIAN (Harrisonville, MO) **11550**

CASS COUNTY REPORTER (Casselton, ND) **11591**

CASS COUNTY STAR-GAZETTE (Beardstown, IL) **11467**

CASSOPOLIS VIGILANT (Niles, MI) **11530**

CASSVILLE DEMOCRAT (Cape Girardeau, MO) **11549**

CASTINE PATRIOT (Castine, ME) **11510**

CASTLE ROCK NEWS-PRESS (Castle Rock, CO) **11440**

CASWELL MESSENGER (Yanceyville, NC) **11590**

CATALINA ISLANDER, THE (Avalon, CA) **11426**

CATONSVILLE TIMES (Baltimore, MD) **11512**

CATOOSA COUNTY NEWS, THE (Ringgold, GA) **11462**

CATOOSA TIMES HERALD (Owasso, OK) **11605**

CAVALIER COUNTY REPUBLICAN (Langdon, ND) **11591**

CAZENOVIA REPUBLICAN (Cazenovia, NY) **11572**

CECIL WHIG (Elkton, MD) **11355**

CEDAR COUNTY REPUBLICAN (Stockton, MO) **11554**

CEDAR CREEK PILOT (Gun Barrel City, TX) **11636**

CEDAR HILL TODAY (Desoto, TX) **11633**

CEDAR KEY BEACON (Cedar Key, FL) **11449**

CEDAR LAKE JOURNAL (Lowell, IN) **11487**

CEDAR VALLEY DAILY TIMES (Vinton, IA) **11348**

CEDARTOWN STANDARD (Cedartown, GA) **11458**

CELINA RECORD (Frisco, TX) **11635**

CENTER POST DISPATCH (Monte Vista, CO) **11441**

CENTER REPUBLICAN (Washburn, ND) **11592**

CENTERVILLE-BELLBROOK TIMES (Kettering, OH) **11597**

CENTRAL BUCKS LIFE (Fort Washington, PA) **11611**

CENTRAL CITY REPUBLICAN NONPAREIL (Central City, NE) **11557**

CENTRAL COAST SUN BULLETIN (Morro Bay, CA) **11433**

CENTRAL KENTUCKY NEWS-JOURNAL (Campbellsville, KY) **11500**

CENTRAL KITSAP REPORTER (Silverdale, WA) **11654**

CENTRAL OREGONIAN, THE (Prineville, OR) **11608**

CENTRAL RECORD (Medford, NJ) **11565**

CENTRAL SAINT CROIX NEWS (Hammond, WI) **11661**

CENTRAL VIRGINIAN, THE (Louisa, VA) **11648**

CENTRALIA FIRESIDE GUARD (Centralia, MO) **11549**

CENTRE DAILY TIMES (State College, PA) **11392**

CENTRE VIEW (McLean, VA) **11649**

CENTREVILLE PRESS (Centreville, AL) **11412**

CENTREVILLE TIMES (Herndon, VA) **11647**

CERES COURIER (Ceres, CA) **11427**

CHADDS FORD POST (Kennett Square, PA) **11612**

CHADRON RECORD, THE (Davenport, IA) **11491**

CHAFFEE COUNTY TIMES, THE (Buena Vista, CO) **11440**

CHAGRIN HERALD SUN (Beachwood, OH) **11593**

CHAGRIN VALLEY TIMES (Sandusky, OH) **11600**

CHALLIS MESSENGER (Challis, ID) **11464**

CHAMPLIN/DAYTON PRESS (Osseo, MN) **11541**

CHANHASSEN VILLAGER (Chanhassen, MN) **11535**

CHANTILLY TIMES (Herndon, VA) **11647**

CHANUTE TRIBUNE (Miami, OK) **11385**

CHAPEL HILL HERALD (Chapel Hill, NC) **11375**

CHAPEL HILL NEWS, THE (Chapel Hill, NC) **11586**

CHARIHO TIMES (Wyoming, RI) **11619**

CHARITON HERALD-PATRIOT (Chariton, IA) **11491**

CHARITON LEADER, THE (Chariton, IA) **11491**

CHARLES CITY PRESS (Charles City, IA) **11346**

CHARLESTON DAILY MAIL (Charleston, WV) **11406**

CHARLESTON ENTERPRISE-COURIER (Charleston, MO) **11549**

CHARLESTON EXPRESS (Charleston, AR) **11421**

CHARLESTON GAZETTE, THE (Charleston, WV) **11406**

CHARLESTOWN PATRIOT & SOMERVILLE CHRONICLE (Charlestown, MA) **11516**

CHARLEVOIX COURIER (Charlevoix, MI) **11526**

CHARLOTTE GAZETTE (Drakes Branch, VA) **11646**

CHARLOTTE OBSERVER (Charlotte, NC) **11376**

CHARLOTTE SHOPPING GUIDE (Charlotte, MI) **11526**

CHARLOTTE SUN HERALD (Charlotte Harbor, FL) **11332**

CHARLOTTESVILLE-ALBEMARLE TRIBUNE (Charlottesville, VA) **11646**

CHARLTON COUNTY HERALD (Folkston, GA) **11460**

CHASE COUNTY LEADER-NEWS (Cottonwood Falls, KS) **11497**

CHASKA HERALD (Chaska, MN) **11535**

CHATFIELD NEWS (Chatfield, MN) **11536**

CHATHAM CLARION (Auburn, IL) **11467**

CHATHAM COURIER (Chatham, NJ) **11562**

CHATHAM COURIER & ROUGHNOTES (Chatham, NY) **11572**

CHATHAM NEWS, THE (Siler City, NC) **11589**

CHATHAM RECORD, THE (Pittsboro, NC) **11589**

CHATSWORTH TIMES, THE (Chatsworth, GA) **11458**

CHATTANOOGA TIMES FREE PRESS (Chattanooga, TN) **11395**

CHATTOOGA PRESS (Rome, GA) **11462**

CHEBOYGAN DAILY TRIBUNE (Cheboygan, MI) **11357**

CHEEKTOWAGA BEE (Williamsville, NY) **11584**

CHEEKTOWAGA TIMES (Cheektowaga, NY) **11572**

CHELMSFORD INDEPENDENT (Concord, MA) **11517**

CHELSEA CLINTON NEWS (New York, NY) **11579**

CHELSEA RECORD (Revere, MA) **11523**

CHELSEA STANDARD, THE (Chelsea, MI) **11526**

CHENANGO AMERICAN (Greene, NY) **11575**

CHENEY FREE PRESS (Cheney, WA) **11651**

CHERAW CHRONICLE, THE (Cheraw, SC) **11620**

CHEROKEE COUNTY HERALD (Centre, AL) **11412**

CHEROKEE LEDGER-NEWS (Woodstock, GA) **11463**

CHEROKEE MESSENGER & REPUBLICAN (Cherokee, OK) **11604**

CHEROKEE SCOUT (Murphy, NC) **11588**

CHEROKEE TRIBUNE, THE (Canton, GA) **11335**

CHERRYVILLE EAGLE (Cherryville, NC) **11586**

CHESHIRE HERALD (Cheshire, CT) **11443**

CHESNEE TRIBUNE (Chesnee, SC) **11620**

CHESTER COUNTY INDEPENDENT (Henderson, TN) **11627**

CHESTER COUNTY PRESS (Oxford, PA) **11615**

CHESTERFIELD JOURNAL (Chesterfield, MO) **11549**

CHESTERLAND NEWS (Chesterland, OH) **11594**

CHESTERTON TRIBUNE (Chesterton, IN) **11342**

CHESTNUT HILL LOCAL (Philadelphia, PA) **11615**

CHETEK ALERT, THE (Chetek, WI) **11659**

CHEVY CHASE GAZETTE (Gaithersburg, MD) **11513**

CHICAGO DEFENDER (Chicago, IL) **11338**

CHICAGO GAZETTE (Chicago, IL) **11468**

CHICAGO JOURNAL (Oak Park, IL) **11478**

CHICAGO LAWNDALE NEWS (Cicero, IL) **11469**

CHICAGO RIDGE CITIZEN (Midlothian, IL) **11476**

CHICAGO SUN-TIMES (Chicago, IL) **11338**

CHICAGO WEST SIDE TIMES (Cicero, IL) **11469**

CHICKASAW JOURNAL & TIMES-POST (Houston, MS) **11546**

CHICO ENTERPRISE-RECORD (Chico, CA) **11324**

CHICO NEWS & REVIEW (Chico, CA) **11427**

CHICO TEXAN (Bridgeport, TX) **11632**

CHICOPEE HERALD, THE (East Longmeadow, MA) **11517**

CHICOPEE REGISTER, THE (Chicopee, MA) **11516**

CHICOT COUNTY SPECTATOR (Lake Village, AR) **11422**

CHIEFLAND CITIZEN (Chiefland, FL) **11449**

CHILDRESS INDEX (Childress, TX) **11632**

CHILKAT VALLEY NEWS (Haines, AK) **11416**

CHILLICOTHE GAZETTE (Chillicothe, OH) **11380**

CHILLICOTHE TIMES-BULLETIN (Peoria, IL) **11479**

CHILTON TIMES-JOURNAL (Chilton, WI) **11659**

CHINO VALLEY REVIEW (Chino Valley, AZ) **11418**

CHINOOK OBSERVER (Long Beach, WA) **11652**

CHIPPEWA HERALD,THE (Chippewa Falls, WI) **11407**

CHISAGO COUNTY PRESS (Lindstrom, MN) **11539**

CHISHOLM TRIBUNE PRESS, THE (Chisholm, MN) **11536**

CHITTENANGO-BRIDGEPORT TIMES (Cazenovia, NY) **11572**

CHOCTAW ADVOCATE (Butler, AL) **11411**

CHOCTAW PLAINDEALER, THE (Ackerman, MS) **11545**

CHOWAN HERALD, THE (Edenton, NC) **11586**

CHRISMAN LEADER, THE (Chrisman, IL) **11469**

CHRISTIAN COUNTY HEADLINER NEWS (Ozark, MO) **11552**

CHRISTIAN SCIENCE MONITOR (TREELESS EDITION) (DAILY ONLINE), THE (Boston, MA) **11355**

CHRONICLE AD-VISER (Penn Yan, NY) **11581**

CHRONICLE AND SENTINEL -MIST (St Helens, OR) **11609**

CHRONICLE (CENTRALIA), THE (Centralia, WA) **11404**

CHRONICLE (CRESWELL), THE (Creswell, OR) **11607**

CHRONICLE (GLENS FALLS), THE (Glens Falls, NY) **11575**
CHRONICLE (HOOPESTON), THE (Hoopeston, IL) **11474**
CHRONICLE NEWS, THE (Trinidad, CO) **11330**
CHRONICLE (NORTH DARTMOUTH), THE (North Dartmouth, MA) **11521**
CHRONICLE (OMAK), THE (Omak, WA) **11653**
CHRONICLE SHOPPER (Leavenworth, KS) **11498**
CHRONICLE TELEGRAM, THE (Elyria, OH) **11380**
CHRONICLE TIMES (Cherokee, IA) **11346**
CHRONICLE (WAUPACA), THE (Waupaca, WI) **11668**
CHRONICLE (WILLIMANTIC), THE (Willimantic, CT) **11332**
CHRONICLE-EXPRESS, THE (Penn Yan, NY) **11581**
CHRONICLE-INDEPENDENT (Camden, SC) **11620**
CHRONICLE-TRIBUNE (Marion, IN) **11344**
CHRONOTYPE, THE (Rice Lake, WI) **11666**
CHURCH POINT NEWS (Church Point, LA) **11506**
CIBOLA COUNTY BEACON (Grants, NM) **11568**
CINCINNATI DOWNTOWNER (Cincinnati, OH) **11594**
CINCINNATI ENQUIRER, THE (Cincinnati, OH) **11380**
CINCINNATI POST (Cincinnati, OH) **11380**
CIRCLEVILLE HERALD (Dallas, TX) **11398**
CISCO PRESS (Cisco, TX) **11632**
CISSNA PARK NEWS (Cissna Park, IL) **11469**
CITIZEN & GEORGIAN (Montezuma, GA) **11462**
CITIZEN (AUBURN), THE (Auburn, NY) **11371**
CITIZEN (DOVER), THE (Laconia, NH) **11368**
CITIZEN (FAYETTEVILLE), THE (Fayetteville, GA) **11459**
CITIZEN (HAMTRAMCK), THE (Hamtramck, MI) **11528**
CITIZEN (HUMBLE), THE (Houston, TX) **11636**
CITIZEN JOURNAL (Chesterfield, MO) **11549**
CITIZEN (MANSFIELD), THE (Waldron, AR) **11425**
CITIZEN NEWS (Spartenbury, SC) **11623**
CITIZEN NEWS, THE (Edgefield, SC) **11620**
CITIZEN OF MORRIS COUNTY, THE (Denville, NJ) **11562**
CITIZEN OUTLET (Central Square, NY) **11572**
CITIZEN TELEGRAM, THE (Rifle, CO) **11442**
CITIZEN TRIBUNE (Morristown, TN) **11396**
CITIZEN VOICE & TIMES (Irvine, KY) **11503**
CITIZEN-JOURNAL, THE (Boyne City, MI) **11525**
CITIZENS' ADVOCATE (Coppell, TX) **11633**
CITIZEN'S NEWS (Naugatuck, CT) **11445**
CITIZEN'S VOICE, THE (Wilkes Barre, PA) **11392**
CITIZEN-STANDARD, THE (Valley View, PA) **11617**
CITIZEN-STATESMAN (Celina, TN) **11626**
CITRUS COUNTY CHRONICLE (Crystal River, FL) **11332**
CITY NEWS (Bronx, NY) **11570**
CITY PAGES (Minneapolis, MN) **11540**
CLACKAMAS REVIEW (Portland, OR) **11608**
CLAIBORNE PROGRESS (Tazewell, TN) **11630**
CLANTON ADVERTISER (Clanton, AL) **11319**
CLARA CITY HERALD (Clara City, MN) **11536**
CLARE SENTINEL (Clare, MI) **11526**
CLAREMONT COURIER (Claremont, CA) **11427**
CLAREMORE DAILY PROGRESS (Claremore, OK) **11384**
CLARENCE BEE (Williamsville, NY) **11584**
CLARENDON HILLS DOINGS, THE (Hinsdale, IL) **11474**
CLARENDON HILLS/DARIEN SUBURBAN LIFE (Downers Grove, IL) **11470**
CLARINDA HERALD JOURNAL (Clarinda, IA) **11491**
CLARION JOURNAL, THE (Columbia, IL) **11469**
CLARION NEWS (CORYDON) (Corydon, IN) **11485**
CLARION (PA) NEWS (Clarion, PA) **11610**
CLARION-LEDGER, THE (Jackson, MS) **11362**
CLARK COUNTY PRESS (Neillsville, WI) **11663**
CLARK PATRIOT (Rahway, NJ) **11566**
CLARKE COUNTY DEMOCRAT, THE (Grove Hill, AL) **11413**
CLARKE COUNTY SHOPPERS GUIDE (Demopolis, AL) **11412**
CLARKE COUNTY TRIBUNE (Quitman, MS) **11547**
CLARKE TIMES-COURIER (Berryville, VA) **11646**

CLARKSBURG EXPONENT TELEGRAM (Clarksburg, WV) **11406**
CLARKSDALE PRESS REGISTER (Clarksdale, MS) **11362**
CLARKSTON ECCENTRIC (Rochester, MI) **11531**
CLARKSTON NEWS (Clarkston, MI) **11526**
CLARKSVILLE TIMES, THE (Clarksville, TX) **11632**
CLASSIFIED GAZETTE (San Rafael, CA) **11437**
CLAXTON ENTERPRISE (Claxton, GA) **11458**
CLAY CENTER DISPATCH (Clay Center, KS) **11349**
CLAY CITY, THE (Clay City, IN) **11485**
CLAY CITY TIMES, THE (Stanton, KY) **11505**
CLAY COUNTY COURIER (Corning, AR) **11421**
CLAY COUNTY DEMOCRAT (Rector, AR) **11424**
CLAY COUNTY FREE PRESS (Clay, WV) **11655**
CLAY COUNTY PROGRESS (Hayesville, NC) **11587**
CLAY TIMES JOURNAL (Lineville, AL) **11414**
CLAY TODAY (Orange Park, FL) **11453**
CLAYTON COUNTY REGISTER, THE (Elkader, IA) **11492**
CLAYTON NEIGHBOR (Forest Park, GA) **11460**
CLAYTON NEWS DAILY (Jonesboro, GA) **11336**
CLAYTON NEWS-STAR (Clayton, NC) **11586**
CLAYTON RECORD (Clayton, AL) **11412**
CLAYTON TRIBUNE, THE (Clayton, GA) **11458**
CLEAR CREEK COURANT (Shelbyville, KY) **11505**
CLEAR LAKE OBSERVER-AMERICAN (Clearlake, CA) **11427**
CLEAR-RIDGE REPORTER (Chicago, IL) **11468**
CLEARWATER CITIZEN (Seminole, FL) **11455**
CLEARWATER GAZETTE & BEACH VIEWS (Clearwater, FL) **11449**
CLEARWATER PROGRESS, THE (Kamiah, ID) **11465**
CLEARWATER TRIBUNE (Orofino, ID) **11465**
CLEBURNE NEWS, THE (Heflin, AL) **11414**
CLEBURNE TIMES-REVIEW (Cleburne, TX) **11397**
CLEMMONS COURIER, THE (Clemmons, NC) **11586**
CLERMONT COMMUNITY JOURNAL (Loveland, OH) **11597**
CLERMONT SUN, THE (Batavia, OH) **11593**
CLEVELAND ADVOCATE (Cleveland, TX) **11633**
CLEVELAND COUNTY HERALD (Rison, AR) **11424**
CLEVELAND DAILY BANNER (Cleveland, TN) **11395**
CLEVELAND POST (Garner, NC) **11587**
CLEVELAND SCENE (Cleveland, OH) **11594**
CLEWISTON NEWS (Clewiston, FL) **11450**
CLIFTON JOURNAL (Clifton, NJ) **11562**
CLIFTON PARK/HALFMOON SPOTLIGHT (Delmar, NY) **11573**
CLINCH COUNTY NEWS, THE (Homerville, GA) **11460**
CLINCH VALLEY NEWS (Tazewell, VA) **11650**
CLINTON CHRONICLE, THE (Clinton, SC) **11620**
CLINTON COUNTY FREE TRADER TODAY (Elizabethtown, NY) **11574**
CLINTON COUNTY NEWS (ALBANY) (Albany, KY) **11500**
CLINTON COUNTY NEWS (GRAND LEDGE) (Grand Ledge, MI) **11527**
CLINTON COUNTY NEWS (MASCOUTAH) (Mascoutah, IL) **11475**
CLINTON COURIER (Clinton, NY) **11572**
CLINTON DAILY DEMOCRAT (Clinton, MO) **11363**
CLINTON DAILY JOURNAL (Clinton, IL) **11339**
CLINTON DAILY NEWS (Clinton, OK) **11384**
CLINTON EYE, THE (Clinton, MO) **11549**
CLINTON HERALD (Clinton, IA) **11347**
CLINTON RECORDER (Guilford, CT) **11444**
CLINTON TOPPER, THE (Clinton, WI) **11659**
CLINTONVILLE TRIBUNE-GAZETTE (Clintonville, WI) **11659**
CLIO MESSENGER, THE (Flint, MI) **11527**
CLIPPIN' THE RIVER (Bullhead City, AZ) **11417**
CLIVE/WINDSOR HEIGHTS PRESS CITIZEN (Des Moines, IA) **11491**
CLOVERDALE REVEILLE (Cloverdale, CA) **11427**
CLOVIS INDEPENDENT (Clovis, CA) **11427**

CLOVIS NEWS JOURNAL (Clovis, NM) **11370**
CLYDE ENTERPRISE (Clyde, OH) **11594**
COACHELLA VALLEY WHITE SHEET (Palm Desert, CA) **11434**
COAL CITY COURANT (Wilmington, IL) **11483**
COAL VALLEY NEWS (Madison, WV) **11656**
COALFIELD PROGRESS, THE (Norton, VA) **11649**
COALINGA RECORD (Coalinga, CA) **11427**
COASTAL COURIER (Hinesville, GA) **11460**
COASTAL CURRENT WEEKLY, THE (South Padre Island, TX) **11641**
COASTAL JOURNAL (Bath, ME) **11509**
COASTAL OBSERVER (LAKE WORTH) (Lake Worth, FL) **11452**
COASTAL OBSERVER (PAWLEYS ISLAND) (Pawleys Island, SC) **11622**
COASTAL POST (Bolinas, CA) **11426**
COASTAL VIEW NEWS (Carpinteria, CA) **11427**
COASTLAND TIMES (Manteo, NC) **11588**
COATESVILLE LEDGER (Westchester, PA) **11618**
COCHRAN JOURNAL (Cochran, GA) **11458**
COCHRANE-FOUNTAIN CITY RECORDER (Cochrane, WI) **11659**
CODY ENTERPRISE (Cody, WY) **11669**
COEUR D'ALENE PRESS, THE (Coeur d'Alene, ID) **11337**
COFFEY COUNTY REPUBLICAN, THE (Burlington, KS) **11497**
COFFEYVILLE JOURNAL, THE (Coffeyville, KS) **11349**
COHASSET MARINER (Hingham, MA) **11519**
COLBERT COUNTY REPORTER (Tuscumbia, AL) **11415**
COLBY FREE PRESS (Colby, KS) **11349**
COLCHESTER SUN, THE (Middlebury, VT) **11644**
COLD SPRING RECORD (Cold Spring, MN) **11536**
COLDWATER SHOPPER GUIDE (Coldwater, MI) **11526**
COLEMAN CHRONICLE & DEMOCRAT VOICE (Coleman, TX) **11633**
COLFAX JASPER CO TRIBUNE (Colfax, IA) **11491**
COLFAX MESSENGER (Colfax, WI) **11659**
COLFAX RECORD (Colfax, CA) **11427**
COLLEGE PARK GAZETTE (Landover, MD) **11513**
COLLEYVILLE COURIER, THE (Southlake, TX) **11641**
COLLIERVILLE HERALD, THE (Humboldt, TN) **11627**
COLLINSVILLE HERALD JOURNAL (Collinsville, IL) **11469**
COLLINSVILLE NEWS (Collinsville, OK) **11604**
COLONIAL, THE (Fort Washington, PA) **11611**
COLONIE SPOTLIGHT (Delmar, NY) **11573**
COLONY COURIER LEADER, THE (Addison, TX) **11630**
COLORADO RIVER WEEKENDER (Laughlin, NV) **11559**
COLTON COURIER, THE (San Bernardino, CA) **11435**
COLUMBIA BASIN HERALD (Moses Lake, WA) **11405**
COLUMBIA COUNTY NEWS TIMES, THE (Evans, GA) **11459**
COLUMBIA DAILY TRIBUNE (Columbia, MO) **11364**
COLUMBIA FLIER (Columbia, MD) **11512**
COLUMBIA HEIGHTS/FRIDLEY FOCUS NEWS (Columbia Heights, MN) **11536**
COLUMBIA LEDGER (Columbia, PA) **11610**
COLUMBIA MISSOURIAN (Columbia, MO) **11364**
COLUMBIAN-PROGRESS (Columbia, MS) **11546**
COLUMBUS ALIVE (Columbus, OH) **11595**
COLUMBUS AREA CHOICE (Columbus, NE) **11557**
COLUMBUS DAILY ADVOCATE (Columbus, KS) **11349**
COLUMBUS DISPATCH (Columbus, OH) **11380**
COLUMBUS JOURNAL (Columbus, WI) **11659**
COLUMBUS LEDGER-ENQUIRER (Columbus, GA) **11335**
COLUMBUS MESSENGER (Columbus, OH) **11595**
COLUMBUS TELEGRAM (Columbus, NE) **11366**
COLUSA COUNTY SUN-HERALD (Colusa, CA) **11427**
COMANCHE CHIEF, THE (Comanche, TX) **11633**
COMER NEWS, THE (Comer, GA) **11458**
COMMACK NEWS (Smithtown, NY) **11582**

COMMERCE JOURNAL (Greenville, TX) **11636**

COMMERCE NEWS (Commerce, GA) **11458**

COMMERCIAL APPEAL, THE (Memphis, TN) **11396**

COMMERCIAL DISPATCH, THE (Columbus, MS) **11362**

COMMERCIAL RECORD (ALLEGAN) (Saugatuck, MI) **11532**

COMMERCIAL-EXPRESS (Vicksburg, MI) **11533**

COMMERCIAL-NEWS (Danville, IL) **11339**

COMMONWEALTH JOURNAL (Somerset, KY) **11352**

COMMONWEALTH PROGRESS (Scotland Neck, NC) **11589**

COMMUNITY ADVERTISER (Farmingdale, ME) **11510**

COMMUNITY ADVOCATE, THE (Westborough, MA) **11524**

COMMUNITY BOOSTER, THE (Granville, OH) **11596**

COMMUNITY CLASSIFIED (Culpeper, VA) **11646**

COMMUNITY FORUM (Hackettstown, NJ) **11563**

COMMUNITY JOURNAL (Wading River, NY) **11583**

COMMUNITY MIRROR (Gonzales, LA) **11507**

COMMUNITY NEWS (FAIR LAWN) (Fair Lawn, NJ) **11563**

COMMUNITY NEWS (SARATOGA SPRINGS) (Saratoga Springs, NY) **11581**

COMMUNITY NEWS (ST LOUIS) (St Louis, MO) **11553**

COMMUNITY NEWSPAPER, THE (South Miami, FL) **11455**

COMMUNITY POST, THE (Minster, OH) **11599**

COMMUNITY RECORDER OF NORTHERN KENTUCKY (Fort Mitchell, KY) **11502**

COMMUNITY SHOPPER (SEARCY) (Searcy, AR) **11424**

COMMUNITY TIMES (Westminster, MD) **11515**

COMPTON BULLETIN (Compton, CA) **11427**

CONCORD JOURNAL, THE (Concord, MA) **11517**

CONCORD MONITOR (Concord, NH) **11368**

CONCORDIA BLADE-EMPIRE (Concordia, KS) **11349**

CONCORDIA SENTINEL (Ferriday, LA) **11507**

CONEJOS COUNTY CITIZEN, THE (Monte Vista, CO) **11442**

CONNECT SAVANNAH (Savannah, GA) **11463**

CONNECTICUT POST (Bridgeport, CT) **11331**

CONNERSVILLE NEWS-EXAMINER (Connersville, IN) **11343**

CONSTITUTION TRIBUNE EXTRA (Chillicothe, MO) **11549**

CONSTITUTION-TRIBUNE (Chillicothe, MO) **11363**

CONSUMERS' EDGE (Baton Rouge, LA) **11506**

CONTRA COSTA SUN (Walnut Creek, CA) **11438**

CONTRA COSTA TIMES (Walnut Creek, CA) **11328**

CONWAY COUNTY PETIT JEAN COUNTRY HEADLIGHT (Morrilton, AR) **11423**

CONWAY DAILY SUN, THE (North Conway, NH) **11368**

COOK COUNTY NEWS-HERALD (Grand Marais, MN) **11538**

COOLIDGE EXAMINER (Coolidge, AZ) **11418**

COON RAPIDS HERALD (Coon Rapids, MN) **11536**

COOPERSTOWN CRIER (Cooperstown, NY) **11572**

COOS COUNTY DEMOCRAT (Lancaster, NH) **11560**

COPIAH COUNTY COURIER (Hazlehurst, MS) **11546**

COPPELL GAZETTE (Addison, TX) **11630**

COPPER BASIN NEWS (Kearny, AZ) **11418**

COPPER COUNTRY NEWS (Globe, AZ) **11418**

COPPER ERA, THE (Safford, AZ) **11419**

COPPERAS COVE LEADER-PRESS (Copperas Cove, TX) **11633**

COPPERFIELD SUN (Houston, TX) **11636**

COPPEROPOLIS HERALD (Copperopolis, CA) **11428**

CORAL GABLES NEWS (South Miami, FL) **11455**

CORAL SPRINGS FORUM (Coconut Creek, FL) **11450**

CORAOPOLIS RECORD, THE (Robinson Twp, PA) **11616**

CORAOPOLIS-MOON RECORD (Pittsburgh, PA) **11615**

CORBIN WHITLEY NEWS JOURNAL (Williamsburg, KY) **11506**

CORDELE DISPATCH (Cordele, GA) **11335**

CORDELL BEACON, THE (Cordell, OK) **11604**

CORDOVA BEACON, THE (Bartlett, TN) **11625**

CORDOVA TIMES (Cordova, AK) **11416**

CORNELL & LAKE HOLCOMBE COURIER (Cornell, WI) **11659**

CORNER NEWS, THE (Auburn, AL) **11411**

CORNING OBSERVER (Corning, CA) **11428**

CORONADO EAGLE & JOURNAL (Coronado, CA) **11428**

CORONA-NORCO INDEPENDENT (Riverside, CA) **11435**

CORPUS CHRISTI CALLER-TIMES (Corpus Christi, TX) **11398**

CORRIDOR NEWS (Poway, CA) **11434**

CORRIGAN TIMES, THE (Corrigan, TX) **11633**

CORRY JOURNAL (Corry, PA) **11388**

CORSICANA DAILY SUN (Corsicana, TX) **11398**

CORTEZ JOURNAL, THE (Cortez, CO) **11440**

CORTLAND STANDARD (Cortland, NY) **11372**

CORTLAND SUNDAY (Cortland, NY) **11572**

CORVALLIS GAZETTE-TIMES (Corvallis, OR) **11387**

CORYDON DEMOCRAT (Corydon, IN) **11485**

COSHOCTON COUNTY ADVERTISER (Coshocton, OH) **11596**

COSHOCTON TRIBUNE (Coshocton, OH) **11380**

COTTAGE GROVE SENTINEL (Cottage Grove, OR) **11606**

COTTONWOOD CHRONICLE (Cottonwood, ID) **11464**

COTTONWOOD COUNTY CITIZEN (Windom, MN) **11545**

COTTONWOOD JOURNAL EXTRA (Cottonwood, AZ) **11418**

COUNCIL GROVE REPUBLICAN (Council Grove, KS) **11349**

COUNTRY CHRONICLE (BLYTHEWOOD) (Blythewood, SC) **11620**

COUNTRY CLUB HILLS-HAZEL CREST STAR (Tinley Park, IL) **11482**

COUNTRY CONNECTION NEWS, THE (Eakly, OK) **11604**

COUNTRY COURIER, THE (Conklin, NY) **11572**

COUNTRY GAZETTE, THE (Milford, MA) **11520**

COUNTRY JOURNAL (Huntington, MA) **11519**

COUNTRY PEDDLER (Bowling Green, KY) **11500**

COUNTRY SHOPPER (Pound Ridge, NY) **11581**

COUNTRY STAR (Stigler, OK) **11605**

COUNTRY TRADER (Gallatin, TN) **11626**

COUNTRY WEEKLY (Grants Pass, OR) **11607**

COUNTRY WORLD (Sulphur Springs, TX) **11641**

COUNTRYSIDE SUBURBAN LIFE (Downers Grove, IL) **11470**

COUNTRYSIDE/INDIAN HEAD PK/HODGKINS/WILLOW SPR/PLEASANTDALE SUBURBAN LIFE (Oak Brook, IL) **11477**

COUNTY COURIER (ENOSBURG FALLS) (Enosburg Falls, VT) **11644**

COUNTY COURIER (FOREST CITY) (Forest City, NC) **11586**

COUNTY GLOBE, THE (Frederick, MD) **11512**

COUNTY JOURNAL (PERCY) (Percy, IL) **11480**

COUNTY JOURNAL (WASHBURN), THE (Washburn, WI) **11668**

COUNTY LEDGER PRESS (Balsam Lake, WI) **11658**

COUNTY LINE REMINDER (Ortonville, MI) **11531**

COUNTY MESSENGER, THE (Brandenburg, KY) **11500**

COUNTY OBSERVER (Yeagertown, PA) **11618**

COUNTY PRESS (LAPEER), THE (Lapeer, MI) **11529**

COUNTY PRESS (NEWTOWN SQUARE) (Newtown Square, PA) **11614**

COUNTY PRESS (PARMA) (Parma, MI) **11531**

COUNTY WIDE (Machias, ME) **11510**

COUNTYLINE, THE (Bryan, OH) **11593**

COUNTYWIDE, THE (Karnes City, TX) **11637**

COURANT, THE (Bottineau, ND) **11591**

COURIER (CONNEAUT), THE (Jefferson, OH) **11597**

COURIER (CONROE), THE (Conroe, TX) **11398**

COURIER (FINDLAY), THE (Findlay, OH) **11380**

COURIER GAZETTE (Rockland, ME) **11511**

COURIER (HOUMA), THE (New York, NY) **11373**

COURIER JOURNAL (CRESCENT CITY), THE (Crescent City, FL) **11450**

COURIER JOURNAL (FLORENCE) (Florence, AL) **11413**

COURIER (LINCOLN), THE (Lincoln, IL) **11340**

COURIER (LITTLETON), THE (Littleton, NH) **11560**

COURIER (MIDDLETOWN), THE (Middletown, NJ) **11565**

COURIER NEWS (BRIDGEWATER), THE (Bridgewater, NJ) **11369**

COURIER NEWS (ELGIN), THE (Elgin, IL) **11339**

COURIER (PLANT CITY), THE (Plant City, FL) **11454**

COURIER PRESS, THE (Prairie Du Chien, WI) **11666**

COURIER (RENSSELAER), THE (Rensselaer, IN) **11488**

COURIER (RUSSELLVILLE), THE (Russellville, AR) **11323**

COURIER (SAVANNAH), THE (Savannah, TN) **11629**

COURIER (WATERLOO, 1859) (Waterloo, IA) **11348**

COURIER (WATERLOO, 1870), THE (Waterloo, WI) **11668**

COURIER-EXPRESS/TRI-COUNTY SUNDAY (Du Bois, PA) **11388**

COURIER-GAZETTE, THE (Rockland, ME) **11511**

COURIER-HERALD, THE (Dublin, GA) **11335**

COURIER-JOURNAL (Palmyra, NY) **11580**

COURIER-JOURNAL, THE (Louisville, KY) **11352**

COURIER-NEWS, THE (Clinton, TN) **11626**

COURIER-OBSERVER (Potsdam, NY) **11374**

COURIER-POST, THE (Cherry Hill, NJ) **11369**

COURIER-RECORD (Blackstone, VA) **11646**

COURIER-STANDARD-ENTERPRISE (Fort Plain, NY) **11574**

COURIER-TIMES (Sutherland, NE) **11558**

COURIER-TIMES (NEW CASTLE), THE (New Castle, IN) **11345**

COURIER-TRIBUNE, THE (Asheboro, NC) **11375**

COURIER-WEDGE (Durand, WI) **11660**

COURTLAND JOURNAL-EMPIRE (Courtland, KS) **11497**

COUSHATTA CITIZEN (Coushatta, LA) **11506**

COVENTRY COURIER, THE (Wakefield, RI) **11619**

COVINGTON LEADER (Covington, TN) **11626**

COVINGTON NEWS (Covington, GA) **11458**

COWETA AMERICAN (Coweta, OK) **11604**

COWETA CITIZEN REVIEW, THE (Fayetteville, GA) **11459**

CRAIG DAILY PRESS (Craig, CO) **11329**

CRANBERRY EAGLE (Cranberry Township, PA) **11611**

CRANBERRY JOURNAL (Wexford, PA) **11618**

CRANBURY PRESS, THE (Princeton, NJ) **11566**

CRANE NEWS (Crane, TX) **11633**

CRANFORD CHRONICLE (Clark, NJ) **11562**

CRANSTON HERALD (Warwick, RI) **11619**

CRAWFORD COUNTY INDEPENDENT-KICKAPOO SCOUT (Gays Mills, WI) **11661**

CRAWFORDSVILLE JOURNAL REVIEW (Crawfordsville, IN) **11343**

CRESCENT-NEWS (Defiance, OH) **11380**

CRESTLINE ADVOCATE (Crestline, OH) **11596**

CRESTLINE COURIER-NEWS (Lake Arrowhead, CA) **11430**

CRESTON NEWS ADVERTISER (Creston, IA) **11347**

CRESTVIEW NEWS BULLETIN (Crestview, FL) **11450**

CRETE NEWS, THE (Crete, NE) **11557**

CRETE-UNIVERSITY PARK-BEECHER STAR (Tinley Park, IL) **11482**

CREWE - BURKEVILLE JOURNAL (Crewe, VA) **11646**

CRISFIELD TIMES, THE (Crisfield, MD) **11512**

CRITTENDEN PRESS, THE (Marion, KY) **11504**

CROCKETT TIMES, THE (Alamo, TN) **11625**

CROFTON NEWS-CRIER (Bowie, MD) **11512**

CROOKSTON DAILY TIMES (Crookston, MN) **11360**

CROOKSTON VALLEY SHOPPER (Crookston, MN) **11536**

CROSBY-IRONTON COURIER (Crosby, MN) **11536**

CROSSVILLE CHRONICLE (Crossville, TN) **11626**

CROTHERSVILLE TIMES (Crothersville, IN) **11485**

CROWLEY POST-SIGNAL (Lafayette, LA) **11353**

CROWLEY STAR (Burleson, TX) **11632**

CROWN POINT STAR (Crown Point, IN) **11485**

CRYSTAL/ROBBINSDALE SUN-POST (Robbinsdale, MN) **11542**

CUBA FREE PRESS (Cuba, MO) **11549**

CUDAHY REMINDER-ENTERPRISE (New Berlin, WI) **11663**

CUERO RECORD (Cuero, TX) **11633**

CULLMAN TIMES (Cullman, AL) **11319**

CULLMAN TRIBUNE (Cullman, AL) **11412**

CULPEPER STAR EXPONENT (Culpeper, VA) **11403**

CULVER CITIZEN (Culver, IN) **11485**
CUMBERLAND ADVOCATE (Cumberland, WI) **11660**
CUMBERLAND COUNTY NEWS (Burkesville, KY) **11500**
CUMBERLAND TIMES-NEWS (Cumberland, MD) **11354**
CUMBERLAND TRADING POST, THE (Middlesboro, KY) **11504**
CUPERTINO COURIER (San Jose, CA) **11436**
CURRENT OF ABSECON, PLEASANTVILLE, THE (Egg Harbor Township, NJ) **11562**
CURRENT OF EGG HARBOR TOWNSHIP, THE (Egg Harbor Township, NJ) **11562**
CURRENT OF GALLOWAY, PORT REPUBLIC, THE (Egg Harbor Township, NJ) **11563**
CURRENT OF NORTHFIELD, LINWOOD, SOMERS POINT, THE (Egg Harbor Township, NJ) **11563**
CURRY COASTAL PILOT (Brookings, OR) **11606**
CURRY COUNTY REPORTER (Gold Beach, OR) **11607**
CUSHING DAILY CITIZEN (Cushing, OK) **11384**
CUSTER COUNTY CHIEF (Broken Arrow, NE) **11557**
CUSTER COUNTY CHRONICLE (Custer, SD) **11624**
CUT BANK PIONEER PRESS (Cut Bank, MT) **11555**
CUYAHOGA FALLS NEWS-PRESS (Stow, OH) **11600**
CYNTHIANA DEMOCRAT, THE (Cynthiana, KY) **11501**

D

DADEVILLE RECORD (Alexander City, AL) **11411**
DAHLONEGA NUGGET, THE (Dahlonega, GA) **11458**
DAILY ADVANCE (Elizabeth City, NC) **11376**
DAILY ADVERTISER, THE (Lafayette, LA) **11353**
DAILY ADVOCATE (Greenville, OH) **11381**
DAILY AMERICAN (Somerset, PA) **11392**
DAILY AMERICAN REPUBLIC (POPLAR BLUFF) (Poplar Bluff, MO) **11365**
DAILY AMERICAN (WEST FRANKFORT) (West Frankfort, IL) **11342**
DAILY ARDMOREITE, THE (Ardmore, OK) **11384**
DAILY ASTORIAN, THE (Astoria, OR) **11387**
DAILY BANNER (Cambridge, MD) **11354**
DAILY BREEZE (Torrance, CA) **11328**
DAILY CAMERA, THE (Boulder, CO) **11329**
DAILY CHRONICLE (De Kalb, IL) **11339**
DAILY CITIZEN (Beaver Dam, WI) **11407**
DAILY CITIZEN NEWS (Dalton, GA) **11335**
DAILY CITIZEN, THE (Searcy, AR) **11323**
DAILY CLAY COUNTY ADVOCATE-PRESS (Flora, IL) **11339**
DAILY CLINTONIAN (Clinton, IN) **11342**
DAILY COMET (New York, NY) **11373**
DAILY COMMERCIAL (Leesburg, FL) **11333**
DAILY CORINTHIAN (Corinth, MS) **11362**
DAILY COURIER (CONNELLSVILLE) (Connellsville, PA) **11388**
DAILY COURIER (FOREST CITY) (Forest City, NC) **11376**
DAILY COURIER OBSERVER, THE (Massena, NY) **11373**
DAILY COURIER, THE (Yuma, AZ) **11322**
DAILY DEMOCRAT (Woodland, CA) **11329**
DAILY DISPATCH (DOUGLAS), THE (Douglas, AZ) **11321**
DAILY DISPATCH (HENDERSON), THE (Henderson, NC) **11376**
DAILY DUNKLIN DEMOCRAT (Kennett, MO) **11364**
DAILY FREEMAN (Kingston, NY) **11372**
DAILY FREEMAN JOURNAL (Webster City, IA) **11348**
DAILY GATE CITY (Keokuk, IA) **11347**
DAILY GAZETTE (Schenectady, NY) **11375**
DAILY GAZETTE (STERLING) (Sterling, IL) **11342**
DAILY GLOBE (Worthington, MN) **11362**
DAILY GUIDE (St Robert, MO) **11365**
DAILY HAMPSHIRE GAZETTE (Northampton, MA) **11356**
DAILY HERALD (ARLINGTON HEIGHTS) (Arlington Heights, IL) **11338**

DAILY HERALD (COLUMBIA) (Columbia, TN) **11395**
DAILY HERALD (PROVO), THE (Provo, UT) **11402**
DAILY HERALD (TYRONE), THE (Tyrone, PA) **11392**
DAILY HOME (Talladega, AL) **11320**
DAILY IBERIAN, THE (New Iberia, LA) **11353**
DAILY INDEPENDENT (ASHLAND), THE (Ashland, KY) **11351**
DAILY INDEPENDENT, THE (Ridgecrest, CA) **11326**
DAILY INTER LAKE, THE (Kalispell, MT) **11366**
DAILY IOWEGIAN (Centerville, IA) **11346**
DAILY ITEM (LYNN), THE (Lynn, MA) **11356**
DAILY ITEM (SUNBURY), THE (Sunbury, PA) **11392**
DAILY JEFFERSON COUNTY UNION (Fort Atkinson, WI) **11408**
DAILY JEFFERSONIAN, THE (Cambridge, OH) **11379**
DAILY JOURNAL (Park Hills, MO) **11365**
DAILY JOURNAL (FERGUS FALLS), THE (Fergus Falls, MN) **11360**
DAILY JOURNAL (FRANKLIN), THE (Franklin, IN) **11343**
DAILY JOURNAL (INTERNATIONAL FALLS), THE (International Falls, MN) **11361**
DAILY JOURNAL (KANKAKEE), THE (Kankakee, IL) **11340**
DAILY JOURNAL (SENECA), THE (Seneca, SC) **11394**
DAILY JOURNAL (VINELAND), THE (Vineland, NJ) **11370**
DAILY LEADER, THE (Brookhaven, MS) **11362**
DAILY LEDGER (CANTON) (Canton, IL) **11338**
DAILY LEDGER (FISHERS) (Fishers, IN) **11485**
DAILY LOCAL NEWS (Westchester, PA) **11392**
DAILY MAIL (Catskill, NY) **11371**
DAILY MAIL/HERALD MAIL (Nevada, MO) **11365**
DAILY MESSENGER (Canandaigua, NY) **11371**
DAILY MESSENGER, THE (Seneca, SC) **11394**
DAILY MINING GAZETTE (Houghton, MI) **11358**
DAILY MOUNTAIN EAGLE (Jasper, AL) **11320**
DAILY NEWS (BOGALUSA), THE (Bogalusa, LA) **11353**
DAILY NEWS (BOWLING GREEN) (Bowling Green, KY) **11351**
DAILY NEWS (GREENVILLE) (Greenville, MI) **11358**
DAILY NEWS (HUNTINGDON) (Huntingdon, PA) **11389**
DAILY NEWS (IRON MOUNTAIN) (Iron Mountain, MI) **11358**
DAILY NEWS (JACKSONVILLE) (Jacksonville, NC) **11376**
DAILY NEWS JOURNAL, THE (Murfreesboro, TN) **11396**
DAILY NEWS (LONG VIEW), THE (Longview, WA) **11405**
DAILY NEWS OF KINGSPORT (Kingsport, TN) **11396**
DAILY NEWS OF NEWBURYPORT, THE (Newburyport, MA) **11356**
DAILY NEWS (RHINELANDER), THE (Rhinelander, WI) **11409**
DAILY NEWS (RICHMOND) (Richmond, MO) **11365**
DAILY NEWS TRANSCRIPT (Needham, MA) **11356**
DAILY NEWS TRIBUNE, THE (Waltham, MA) **11357**
DAILY NEWS (WAHPETON) (Wahpeton, ND) **11379**
DAILY NEWS (WEST BEND) (West Bend, WI) **11409**
DAILY NEWS (WOODLAND HILLS), LA (Woodland Hills, CA) **11329**
DAILY NEWS-BULLETIN, THE (Brookfield, MO) **11363**
DAILY NEWS-RECORD (Harrisonburg, VA) **11403**
DAILY NEWS-SUN (Sun City, AZ) **11321**
DAILY NONPAREIL (Council Bluff, IA) **11347**
DAILY PILOT, THE (Costa Mesa, CA) **11324**
DAILY POST-ATHENIAN (Athens, TN) **11395**
DAILY PRESS (ASHLAND), THE (Ashland, WI) **11407**
DAILY PRESS (ESCANABA), THE (Escanaba, MI) **11358**
DAILY PRESS (NEWPORT NEWS), THE (Chicago, IL) **11338**
DAILY PRESS (ST MARYS), THE (St Marys, PA) **11392**
DAILY PRESS (VICTORVILLE) (Victorville, CA) **11328**
DAILY PROGRESS (Charlottesville, VA) **11403**
DAILY RECORD (Ellensburg, WA) **11404**
DAILY RECORD (DUNN), THE (Dunn, NC) **11376**
DAILY RECORD (LAWRENCEVILLE), THE (Lawrenceville, IL) **11340**

DAILY RECORD (PARSIPPANY) (Parsippany, NJ) **11369**
DAILY RECORD (WOOSTER), THE (Wooster, OH) **11383**
DAILY REFLECTOR (Greenville, NC) **11376**
DAILY REPORTER (COLDWATER), THE (Coldwater, MI) **11357**
DAILY REPORTER (GREENFIELD) (Greenfield, IN) **11343**
DAILY REPUBLIC (FAIRFIELD) (Fairfield, CA) **11324**
DAILY REPUBLIC (MITCHELL) (Mitchell, SD) **11394**
DAILY REPUBLICAN REGISTER (Mt Carmel, IL) **11340**
DAILY REVIEW ATLAS (Monmouth, IL) **11340**
DAILY REVIEW (HAYWOOD), THE (Haywood, CA) **11325**
DAILY REVIEW (MORGAN CITY), THE (Morgan City, LA) **11353**
DAILY REVIEW/SUNDAY REVIEW (Towanda, PA) **11392**
DAILY ROCKET-MINER (Rock Springs, WY) **11410**
DAILY SENTINEL & SUN SENTINEL (Rome, NY) **11374**
DAILY SENTINEL (GRAND JUNCTION), THE (Grand Junction, CO) **11330**
DAILY SENTINEL (NACOGDOCHES), THE (Nacogdoches, TX) **11400**
DAILY SENTINEL (POMEROY), THE (Pomeroy, OH) **11382**
DAILY SENTINEL (SCOTTSBORO), THE (Scottsboro, AL) **11320**
DAILY SITKA SENTINEL (Sitka, AK) **11321**
DAILY SOUTHERNER, THE (Tarboro, NC) **11378**
DAILY SPARKS TRIBUNE, THE (Sparks, NV) **11368**
DAILY STANDARD, THE (Celina, OH) **11380**
DAILY STAR (GRENADA), THE (Grenada, MS) **11362**
DAILY STAR (ONEONTA), THE (Oneonta, NY) **11374**
DAILY STAR-JOURNAL, THE (Warrensburg, MO) **11365**
DAILY STATESMAN (Dexter, MO) **11364**
DAILY SUN NEWS (Sunnyside, WA) **11405**
DAILY TELEGRAM (ADRIAN), THE (Adrian, MI) **11357**
DAILY TELEGRAM (SUPERIOR) (Superior, WI) **11409**
DAILY TIMES CHRONICLE (Woburn, MA) **11357**
DAILY TIMES (FARMINGTON), THE (Farmington, NM) **11370**
DAILY TIMES HERALD (Carroll, IA) **11346**
DAILY TIMES LEADER (West Point, MS) **11363**
DAILY TIMES (MARYVILLE) (Maryville, TN) **11396**
DAILY TIMES (OTTAWA) (Ottawa, IL) **11341**
DAILY TIMES (PRYOR), THE (Pryor, OK) **11386**
DAILY TIMES (SALISBURY), THE (Salisbury, MD) **11355**
DAILY TIMES-CALL (Longmont, CO) **11330**
DAILY TRIBUNE (Wisconsin Rapids, WI) **11409**
DAILY TRIBUNE (HIBBING), THE (Hibbing, MN) **11361**
DAILY TRIBUNE NEWS, THE (Cartersville, GA) **11335**
DAILY TRIBUNE (ROYAL OAK), THE (Royal Oak, MI) **11359**
DAILY TRIPLICATE, THE (Crescent City, CA) **11324**
DAILY WORLD (Opelousas, LA) **11354**
DAILY WORLD (ABERDEEN), THE (Aberdeen, WA) **11404**
DAILY WORLD T M C (Helena, AR) **11422**
DAILY WORLD, THE (Helena, AR) **11323**
DAIRYLAND PEACH (Sauk Centre, MN) **11542**
DAKOTA COUNTY STAR, THE (South Sioux City, NE) **11558**
DAKOTA COUNTY TRIBUNE (Burnsville, MN) **11535**
DALHART TEXAN (Dalhart, TX) **11633**
DALLAS MORNING NEWS, THE (Dallas, TX) **11398**
DALLAS NEW ERA (Dallas, GA) **11459**
DALLAS OBSERVER (Dallas, TX) **11633**
DALLAS WHITE ROCKER NEWS (Dallas, TX) **11633**
DALTON GAZETTE & KIDRON NEWS (Dalton, OH) **11596**
DAMASCUS GAZETTE (Gaithersburg, MD) **11513**
DANA POINT NEWS (Lake Forest, CA) **11430**
DANIELSVILLE MONITOR, THE (Comer, GA) **11458**
DAN'S PAPERS (Bridgehampton, NY) **11570**
DANVERS HERALD (Beverly, MA) **11515**
DANVILLE NEWS (Danville, PA) **11388**
DANVILLE REGISTER & BEE (Danville, VA) **11403**
DAPHNE BULLETIN (Daphne, AL) **11412**
DARCO NEWS & BUYERS GUIDE (Hartsville, SC) **11621**

Title

DARIEN NEWS (Darien, GA) **11459**
DARIEN NEWS-REVIEW (Darien, CT) **11443**
DARIEN TIMES, THE (Darien, CT) **11443**
DAVIE COUNTY ENTERPRISE-RECORD (Mocksville, NC) **11588**
DAVIS COUNTY CLIPPER (Bountiful, UT) **11643**
DAVIS ENTERPRISE (Davis, CA) **11324**
DAVISON FLAGSTAFF (Flint, MI) **11527**
DAVISON INDEX, THE (Davison, MI) **11526**
DAWSON COMMUNITY NEWS (Dawsonville, GA) **11459**
DAWSON NEWS & ADVERTISER (Dawsonville, GA) **11459**
DAWSON NEWS, INC, THE (Dawson, GA) **11459**
DAWSON SPRINGS PROGRESS (Dawson Springs, KY) **11501**
DAY (NEW LONDON), THE (New London, CT) **11331**
DAYTON CHRONICLE (Dayton, WA) **11652**
DAYTON DAILY NEWS (Dayton, OH) **11380**
DAYTON NEWS (Cleveland, TX) **11633**
DAYTON TRIBUNE (Dayton, OR) **11607**
DAYTONA PENNYSAVER (Ormond Beach, FL) **11453**
DE LAND-DELTONA BEACON, THE (De Land, FL) **11450**
DE PERE JOURNAL (De Pere, WI) **11660**
DE QUEEN DAILY CITIZEN, THE (DeQueen, AR) **11322**
DE QUINCY NEWS (DeQuincy, LA) **11507**
DE SOTO TIMES TODAY (Hernando, MS) **11362**
DE VALLS BLUFF TIMES (Hazen, AR) **11422**
DE WITT ERA ENTERPRISE (De Witt, AZ) **11418**
DEARBORN COUNTY REGISTER (Lawrenceburg, IN) **11486**
DEARBORN TIMES-HERALD (Dearborn, MI) **11526**
DECATUR DAILY DEMOCRAT, THE (Decatur, IN) **11343**
DECATUR DAILY, THE (Decatur, AL) **11319**
DECATUR HERALD (Gentry, AR) **11421**
DECATUR TRIBUNE (Decatur, IL) **11469**
DECLARATION, THE (Independence, VA) **11648**
DECORAH PUBLIC OPINION & DECORAH JOURNAL (Decorah, IA) **11491**
DEDHAM TIMES (Dedham, MA) **11517**
DEER PARK BROADCASTER, THE (Pasadena, TX) **11639**
DEER PARK PROGRESS, THE (Pasadena, TX) **11639**
DEER PARK TRIBUNE (Deer Park, WA) **11652**
DEERFIELD BEACH OBSERVER (Deerfield Beach, FL) **11450**
DEERFIELD REVIEW (Waukegan, IL) **11483**
DEERFIELD TIMES, THE (Pompano Beach, FL) **11454**
DEERFIELD VALLEY NEWS (West Dover, VT) **11645**
DEFENSOR-CHIEFTAIN (Socorro, NM) **11568**
DEFOREST TIMES-TRIBUNE (DeForest, WI) **11660**
DEFUNIAK SPRINGS HERALD-BREEZE (DeFuniak Springs, FL) **11450**
DEKALB NEIGHBOR, THE (Chamblee, GA) **11458**
DEL NORTE PROSPECTOR (Monte Vista, CO) **11442**
DEL RIO NEWS-HERALD (Del Rio, TX) **11398**
DELANO EAGLE (Delano, MN) **11536**
DELANO RECORD, THE (Delano, CA) **11428**
DELAVAN ENTERPRISE, THE (Delavan, WI) **11660**
DELAVAN TIMES, THE (Delavan, IL) **11469**
DELAWARE BEACHCOMBER (Rehoboth Beach, DE) **11448**
DELAWARE COAST PRESS (Rehoboth Beach, DE) **11448**
DELAWARE COUNTY DAILY/SUNDAY TIMES (Primos, PA) **11391**
DELAWARE COUNTY JOURNAL (Grove, OK) **11604**
DELAWARE COUNTY TIMES (Delhi, NY) **11573**
DELAWARE GAZETTE (Delaware, OH) **11380**
DELAWARE STATE NEWS (Dover, DE) **11332**
DELAWARE VALLEY NEWS (Frenchtown, NJ) **11563**
DELAWARE WAVE (Bethany Beach, DE) **11447**
DELHI EXPRESS (Winton, CA) **11439**
DELHI PRESS (Cincinnati, OH) **11594**

DELL RAPIDS TRIBUNE (Dell Rapids, SD) **11624**
DELPHOS DAILY HERALD (Delphos, OH) **11380**
DELRAY TIMES, THE (Pompano Beach, FL) **11454**
DELTA ATLAS (Delta, OH) **11596**
DELTA COUNTY INDEPENDENT (Delta, CO) **11440**
DELTA DEMOCRAT-TIMES (Greenville, MS) **11362**
DELTA WIND, THE (Delta Junction, AK) **11416**
DELTA/WAVERLY COMMUNITY NEWS (Grand Ledge, MI) **11527**
DEMING HEADLIGHT, THE (Deming, NM) **11370**
DEMOCRAT NEWS (Fredericktown, MO) **11550**
DEMOCRAT, THE (Senatobia, MS) **11547**
DEMOCRAT TRIBUNE, THE (Mineral Point, WI) **11663**
DEMOCRAT-ARGUS, THE (Caruthersville, MO) **11549**
DEMOCRAT-LEADER (Fayette, MO) **11550**
DEMOCRAT-MESSAGE (Mt Sterling, IL) **11476**
DEMOCRAT-REPORTER, THE (Linden, AL) **11414**
DEMOCRAT-UNION (Lawrenceburg, TN) **11627**
DEMOPOLIS TIMES, THE (Demopolis, AL) **11319**
DENAIR DISPATCH (Merced, CA) **11432**
DENISON BULLETIN & REVIEW (Denison, IA) **11491**
DENISON PRESS (Pottsboro, TX) **11640**
DENMARK PRESS (Denmark, WI) **11660**
DENTON RECORD-CHRONICLE (Denton, TX) **11398**
DENVER HERALD-DISPATCH (Denver, CO) **11440**
DENVER POST (Denver, CO) **11329**
DEPEW BEE (Williamsville, NY) **11584**
DEPOSIT COURIER (Deposit, NY) **11573**
DEQUEEN BEE (DeQueen, AR) **11421**
DERBY REPORTER, THE (Derby, KS) **11349**
DERRICK, THE (Oil City, PA) **11390**
DERRY NEWS (Derry, NH) **11560**
DES MOINES COUNTY NEWS, THE (West Burlington, IA) **11496**
DES MOINES PRESS CITIZEN (Des Moines, IA) **11491**
DES MOINES REGISTER (Des Moines, IA) **11347**
DES PLAINES JOURNAL (Des Plaines, IL) **11470**
DES PLAINES TIMES (Park Ridge, IL) **11479**
DESERET MORNING NEWS (Salt Lake City, UT) **11402**
DESERT DISPATCH (Barstow, CA) **11324**
DESERT MOBILE HOME NEWS (Palm Desert, CA) **11434**
DESERT POST WEEKLY (Cathedral City, CA) **11427**
DESERT SUN, THE (Palm Springs, CA) **11326**
DESERT TRAIL (Twentynine Palms, CA) **11438**
DESHLER RUSTLER, THE (Deshler, NE) **11557**
DESOTO SUN (Arcadia, FL) **11332**
DESOTO TODAY (Desoto, TX) **11634**
DESTIN LOG (Destin, FL) **11450**
DETROIT FREE PRESS (Detroit, MI) **11357**
DETROIT LAKES TRIBUNE (Detroit Lakes, MN) **11537**
DETROIT NEWS (Detroit, MI) **11358**
DEVIL'S LAKE JOURNAL (Devil's Lake, ND) **11378**
DEWITT TIMES (Syracuse, NY) **11582**
DEWITT-BATH REVIEW (St Johns, MI) **11532**
DEXTER LEADER, THE (Chelsea, MI) **11526**
DIAMOND TRAIL NEWS (Sully, IA) **11495**
DICKENSON STAR, THE (Clintwood, VA) **11646**
DICKINSON COUNTY NEWS, THE (Spirit Lake, IA) **11495**
DICKINSON PRESS, THE (Dickinson, ND) **11378**
DICKSON HERALD, THE (Dickson, TN) **11626**
DIGGER SHOPPER & NEWS, THE (Oroville, CA) **11434**
DILLON HERALD, THE (Dillon, SC) **11620**
DINWIDDIE MONITOR (Sutherland, VA) **11650**
DISPATCH (LEXINGTON), THE (New York, NY) **11373**
DISPATCH (MOLINE), THE (Moline, IL) **11340**
DIVERNON NEWS (Auburn, IL) **11467**
DIXIE NEWS (Florence, KY) **11501**

DIXON PILOT (Dixon, MO) **11549**
DIXON TRIBUNE (Dixon, CA) **11428**
DODGE CITY DAILY GLOBE (Dodge City, KS) **11349**
DODGE COUNTY INDEPENDENT-NEWS (Juneau, WI) **11661**
DODGE COUNTY NEWS, THE (Eastman, GA) **11459**
DODGEVILLE CHRONICLE, THE (Dodgeville, WI) **11660**
DOLORES STAR, THE (Dolores, CO) **11440**
DOMINION POST, THE (Morgantown, WV) **11406**
DONALDSONVILLE CHIEF (Donaldsonville, LA) **11507**
DONALSONVILLE NEWS (Donalsonville, GA) **11459**
DONNELSON STAR (West Point, IA) **11496**
DOON PRESS (Doon, IA) **11492**
DOOR COUNTY ADVOCATE (Sturgeon Bay, WI) **11667**
DORAL TRIBUNE, THE (South Miami, FL) **11455**
DORCHESTER ARGUS-CITIZEN (Hyde Park, MA) **11519**
DORCHESTER STAR (Cambridge, MD) **11512**
DOTHAN EAGLE (Dothan, AL) **11319**
DOTHAN PROGRESS (Dothan, AL) **11412**
DOUGLAS COUNTY MAIL (Myrtle Creek, OR) **11608**
DOUGLAS COUNTY NEWS PRESS (Castle Rock, CO) **11440**
DOUGLAS COUNTY POST GAZETTE (Elkhorn, NE) **11557**
DOUGLAS COUNTY SENTINEL (Douglasville, GA) **11335**
DOUGLAS ENTERPRISE (Douglas, GA) **11459**
DOUGLAS NEIGHBOR, THE (Douglasville, GA) **11459**
DOUGLAS SHOPPER (Douglas, GA) **11459**
DOVE CREEK PRESS (Dove Creek, CO) **11440**
DOVER POST, THE (Dover, DE) **11447**
DOVER TIMES, THE (Atkins, AR) **11420**
DOVER-SHERBORN PRESS, THE (Needham, MA) **11521**
DOWAGIAC DAILY NEWS (Niles, MI) **11359**
DOWNBEACH CURRENT, THE (Egg Harbor Township, NJ) **11563**
DOWNEAST COASTAL PRESS, THE (Cutler, ME) **11510**
DOWNERS GROVE SUN (Naperville, IL) **11476**
DOWNEY PATRIOT (Downey, CA) **11428**
DOWNINGTOWN LEDGER (Westchester, PA) **11618**
DOWNRIVER VOICE (New Baltimore, MI) **11530**
DOWNTOWN EXPRESS (New York, NY) **11580**
DOWNTOWN GAZETTE (Long Beach, CA) **11431**
DOWNTOWN NEWS (South Miami, FL) **11455**
DOWNTOWNER, THE (Washington, DC) **11448**
DOYLESTOWN PATRIOT (Doylestown, PA) **11611**
DRAIN ENTERPRISE (Drain, OR) **11607**
DRESDEN ENTERPRISE (Dresden, TN) **11626**
DRUMMER, THE (Buffalo, MN) **11535**
DU QUOIN EVENING CALL (Du Quoin, IL) **11339**
DU QUOIN NEWS, THE (Du Quoin, IL) **11471**
DUBLIN NEWS (Columbus, OH) **11595**
DUBLIN VILLAGER (Worthington, OH) **11602**
DULUTH NEWS TRIBUNE (Fargo, ND) **11378**
DUMAS CLARION (Dumas, AR) **11421**
DUNCAN BANNER, THE (Duncan, OK) **11384**
DUNCANNON RECORD (New Bloomfield, PA) **11614**
DUNCANVILLE TODAY (Desoto, TX) **11634**
DUNDALK EAGLE, THE (Baltimore, MD) **11512**
DUNLAP TRIBUNE, THE (Dunlap, TN) **11626**
DUNN COUNTY NEWS, THE (Menomonie, WI) **11663**
DUNSMUIR NEWS (Mt Shasta, CA) **11433**
DUNWOODY CRIER (Atlanta, GA) **11456**
DUPLIN TIMES - PROGRESS SENTINEL (Greenville, NC) **11587**
DUPLIN TODAY (Kenansville, NC) **11587**
DURANGO HERALD (Durango, CO) **11329**
DURANT DAILY DEMOCRAT (Durant, OK) **11384**
DUTCH HARBOR FISHERMAN, THE (Dutch Harbor, AK) **11416**
DUXBURY REPORTER (Marshfield, MA) **11520**

DYERSBURG NEWS (Dyersburg, TN) **11626**
DYERSVILLE COMMERCIAL (Dyersville, IA) **11492**

E

E C M POST REVIEW (North Branch, MN) **11540**
EAGAN SUN-CURRENT (Eden Prairie, MN) **11537**
EAGAN THISWEEK (Burnsville, MN) **11535**
EAGLE BULLETIN (Syracuse, NY) **11582**
EAGLE (CAMBRIDGE), THE (Cambridge, NY) **11571**
EAGLE GROVE EAGLE (Eagle Grove, IA) **11492**
EAGLE LAKE HEADLIGHT (Eagle Lake, TX) **11634**
EAGLE PASS NEWS GUIDE (Eagle Pass, TX) **11634**
EAGLE TIMES (Claremont, NH) **11368**
EAGLE TRIBUNE, THE (North Andover, MA) **11356**
EAGLE (UNION), THE (Union, NJ) **11567**
EAGLE VALLEY ENTERPRISE (Gypsum, CO) **11441**
EAGLE-HERALD (Marinette, WI) **11408**
EAGLE-RECORD, THE (St George, SC) **11623**
EARLY BIRD, THE (Greenville, OH) **11596**
EARLY COUNTY NEWS (Blakely, GA) **11457**
EASLEY PROGRESS, THE (Easley, SC) **11620**
EAST ARKANSAS NEWS LEADER, THE (Wynne, AR) **11425**
EAST AURORA ADVERTISER (East Aurora, NY) **11573**
EAST AURORA BEE (Williamsville, NY) **11584**
EAST BAY EXPRESS (Emeryville, CA) **11428**
EAST BOSTON SUN TRANSCRIPT (Revere, MA) **11523**
EAST BRIDGEWATER STAR (Rayham, MA) **11522**
EAST COBBER (Marietta, GA) **11461**
EAST COUNTY CALIFORNIAN (El Cajon, CA) **11428**
EAST COUNTY JOURNAL, THE (Morton, WA) **11653**
EAST COUNTY NEWS (Gresham, OR) **11607**
EAST DES MOINES PRESS CITIZEN (Des Moines, IA) **11491**
EAST FISHKILL RECORD (Mahopac, NY) **11577**
EAST GRAND RAPIDS CADENCE (Jenison, MI) **11528**
EAST GREENWICH PENDULUM, THE (Wakefield, RI) **11619**
EAST HAMPTON STAR, THE (East Hampton, NY) **11573**
EAST HARTFORD GAZETTE, THE (East Hartford, CT) **11443**
EAST HAVEN ADVERTISER (Guilford, CT) **11444**
EAST HAVEN COURIER (Madison, CT) **11444**
EAST LAUDERDALE NEWS (Rogersville, AL) **11415**
EAST MEADOW BEACON (Hempstead, NY) **11576**
EAST MEADOW HERALD (Garden City, NY) **11574**
EAST MEMPHIS SHOPPERS NEWS (Memphis, TN) **11628**
EAST MONTGOMERY COUNTY OBSERVER (Humble, TX) **11637**
EAST ORANGE RECORD (Maplewood, NJ) **11565**
EAST OREGONIAN, THE (Pendleton, OR) **11387**
EAST PENN PRESS (Allentown, PA) **11609**
EAST PEORIA TIMES-COURIER (Peoria, IL) **11479**
EAST PROVIDENCE POST (East Providence, RI) **11618**
EAST ROCHESTER POST (Canandaigua, NY) **11571**
EAST SHELBY REVIEW (Arlington, TN) **11625**
EAST SIDE HERALD (Indianapolis, IN) **11486**
EAST SIDE HERALD, THE (Indianapolis, IN) **11486**
EAST SIDE REVIEW (St Paul, MN) **11543**
EAST ST LOUIS JOURNAL (Swansee, IL) **11482**
EAST ST LOUIS MONITOR (East St Louis, IL) **11471**
EAST TROY NEWS (East Troy, WI) **11660**
EASTCHESTER RECORD (Yonkers, NY) **11584**
EASTERN ARIZONA COURIER (Safford, AZ) **11419**
EASTERN COLORADO PLAINSMAN (Hugo, CO) **11441**
EASTERN GAZETTE, THE (Dexter, ME) **11510**
EASTERN HILLS JOURNAL (Loveland, OH) **11597**
EASTERN KENTUCKY SHOPPER (Paintsville, KY) **11504**
EASTERN WAKE NEWS (Zebulon, NC) **11591**
EASTEX ADVOCATE (Cleveland, TX) **11633**
EASTLAND TELEGRAM (Eastland, TX) **11634**

EASTON BULLETIN (Rockland, MA) **11523**
EASTON COURIER (Shelton, CT) **11446**
EASTON JOURNAL (Milford, MA) **11521**
EASTSIDER (Pompano Beach, FL) **11454**
EASTWAVE (Los Angeles, CA) **11431**
EASY READER (Hermosa Beach, CA) **11429**
EATON RAPIDS COMMUNITY NEWS (Charlotte, MI) **11526**
EATONTON MESSENGER, THE (Eatonton, GA) **11459**
ECHO PRESS, THE (Alexandria, MN) **11534**
ECHOES-SENTINEL (Bernardsville, NJ) **11561**
ECHOLAND SHOPPER (Pequot Lakes, MN) **11541**
ECHO-PILOT (Greencastle, PA) **11612**
ECLECTIC OBSERVER, THE (Wetumpka, AL) **11416**
EDEN DAILY NEWS (Eden, NC) **11376**
EDEN PRAIRIE NEWS (Chanhassen, MN) **11535**
EDEN PRAIRIE SUN-CURRENT (Eden Prairie, MN) **11537**
EDGE, THE (NEW SMYRNA BEACH) (New Smyrna Beach, FL) **11453**
EDGEBROOK-SAUGANASH TIMES REVIEW (Park Ridge, IL) **11479**
EDGERTON ENTERPRISE, THE (Edgerton, MN) **11537**
EDGERTON REPORTER (Edgerton, WI) **11660**
EDGEWOOD ENTERPRISE (Edgewood, TX) **11634**
EDGEWOOD REMINDER (Edgewood, IA) **11492**
EDINA SUN-CURRENT (Eden Prairie, MN) **11537**
EDINBORO NEWS, THE (Albion, PA) **11609**
EDINBURG REVIEW (Edinburg, TX) **11634**
EDISON-NORWOOD TIMES REVIEW (Park Ridge, IL) **11479**
EDMOND SUN, THE (Edmond, OK) **11385**
EDMONDS ENTERPRISE (Lynnwood, WA) **11653**
EDMONSON NEWS (Brownsville, KY) **11500**
EDMONTON HERALD-NEWS (Edmonton, KY) **11501**
EDWARDSBURG ARGUS (Niles, MI) **11531**
EDWARDSVILLE INTELLIGENCER (Edwardsville, IL) **11339**
EDWARDSVILLE JOURNAL (Collinsville, IL) **11469**
EFFINGHAM DAILY NEWS (Effingham, IL) **11339**
EFFINGHAM HERALD, THE (Rincon, GA) **11462**
EGG HARBOR NEWS (Hammonton, NJ) **11563**
EL CAMPO LEADER-NEWS (El Campo, TX) **11634**
EL DORADO HILLS TELEGRAPH (Folsom, CA) **11428**
EL DORADO NEWS-TIMES (El Dorado, AR) **11322**
EL DORADO TIMES (El Dorado, KS) **11349**
EL PASO JOURNAL (El Paso, IL) **11471**
EL PASO TIMES (El Paso, TX) **11398**
EL SEGUNDO HERALD (El Segundo, CA) **11428**
ELBA CLIPPER, THE (Elba, AL) **11412**
ELBERT COUNTY NEWS (Castle Rock, CO) **11440**
ELBERTON STAR & EXAMINER, THE (Elberton, GA) **11459**
ELBURN HERALD (Elburn, IL) **11471**
ELDON ADVERTISER (Eldon, MO) **11550**
ELDORA HERALD-LEDGER (Eldora, IA) **11492**
ELDORADO DAILY JOURNAL (Eldorado, IL) **11339**
ELDORADO SUCCESS, THE (Eldorado, TX) **11634**
ELIZABETHTON STAR (Elizabethton, TN) **11395**
ELIZABETHTOWN CHRONICLE (Elizabethtown, PA) **11611**
ELIZABETHTOWN MOUNT JOY MERCHANDISER (Mt Joy, PA) **11614**
ELK CITY DAILY NEWS (Elk City, OK) **11385**
ELK GROVE CITIZEN (Elk Grove, CA) **11428**
ELK GROVE JOURNAL (Des Plaines, IL) **11470**
ELK GROVE VILLAGE TIMES (Arlington Heights, IL) **11466**
ELK VALLEY TIMES, THE (Fayetteville, TN) **11626**
ELKHORN INDEPENDENT (Elkhorn, WI) **11660**
ELKO DAILY FREE PRESS (Elko, NV) **11367**
ELKTON RECORD, THE (Elkton, SD) **11624**
ELLSWORTH AMERICAN, THE (Ellsworth, ME) **11510**
ELLSWORTH COUNTY INDEPENDENT REPORTER, THE (Ellsworth, KS) **11497**
ELLWOOD CITY LEDGER (Ellwood City, PA) **11389**

ELM GROVE ELM LEAVES (New Berlin, WI) **11664**
ELM LEAVES (Oak Park, IL) **11478**
ELMHURST DOINGS, THE (Hinsdale, IL) **11474**
ELMHURST PRESS (Glen Ellyn, IL) **11472**
ELOY ENTERPRISE (Eloy, AZ) **11418**
ELY ECHO (Ely, MN) **11538**
ELY TIMES (Ely, NV) **11367**
EMERY COUNTY PROGRESS (Castle Dale, UT) **11643**
EMMETSBURG DEMOCRAT (Emmetsburg, IA) **11492**
EMMETSBURG REPORTER (Emmetsburg, IA) **11492**
EMPORIA GAZETTE (Emporia, KS) **11349**
ENFIELD PRESS (Enfield, CT) **11444**
ENGLAND DEMOCRAT (England, AR) **11421**
ENGLEWOOD HERALD (Littleton, CO) **11441**
ENGLEWOOD INDEPENDENT (Englewood, OH) **11596**
ENGLEWOOD REVIEW, THE (Englewood, FL) **11450**
ENGLEWOOD SUN (Englewood, FL) **11332**
ENID NEWS & EAGLE (Enid, OK) **11385**
ENNIS DAILY NEWS (Ennis, TX) **11398**
ENON MESSENGER (Enon, OH) **11596**
ENQUIRER-BULLETIN (Burlingame, CA) **11427**
ENQUIRER-GAZETTE (Upper Marlboro, MD) **11515**
ENQUIRER-HERALD (York, SC) **11623**
ENQUIRER-JOURNAL, THE (Monroe, NC) **11377**
ENTERPRISE (BROCTON), THE (Brocton, MA) **11355**
ENTERPRISE BUYERS' CATALOGUE (Wytheville, VA) **11651**
ENTERPRISE DISPATCH (Cokato, MN) **11536**
ENTERPRISE JOURNAL (Columbia, IL) **11469**
ENTERPRISE (KENTLAND), THE (Kentland, IN) **11486**
ENTERPRISE LEDGER, THE (Enterprise, AL) **11320**
ENTERPRISE (LEXINGTON PARK), THE (California, MD) **11512**
ENTERPRISE MOUNTAINEER, THE (Waynesville, NC) **11590**
ENTERPRISE (PONCHATOULA), THE (Ponchatoula, LA) **11508**
ENTERPRISE (STUART), THE (Stuart, VA) **11650**
ENTERPRISE (WHITE SALMON), THE (White Salmon, WA) **11655**
ENTERPRISE (WILLIAMSTON), THE (Williamston, NC) **11590**
ENTERPRISE-JOURNAL (McComb, MS) **11362**
ENUMCLAW COURIER-HERALD (Enumclaw, WA) **11652**
EPHRATA REVIEW (Ephrata, PA) **11611**
ERIE TIMES-NEWS (Erie, PA) **11389**
ERLANGER RECORDER (Fort Mitchell, KY) **11502**
ERWIN RECORD, THE (Erwin, TN) **11626**
ESCALON TIMES, THE (Escalon, CA) **11428**
ESCAMBIA SUN PRESS (Pensacola, FL) **11454**
ESCONDIDO NEWS-REPORTER (Los Angeles, CA) **11431**
ESSEX INDEPENDENT, THE (Shenandoah, IA) **11495**
ESSEX REPORTER (Middlebury, VT) **11644**
ESSN'S INOY HERALD WEEKLY (Indianapolis, IN) **11486**
ESTACADA NEWS (Estacado, OR) **11607**
ESTES PARK TRAIL-GAZETTE (Denver, CO) **11440**
ESTHERVILLE DAILY NEWS (Estherville, IA) **11347**
ESTILL COUNTY TRIBUNE, THE (Irvine, KY) **11503**
EUCLID SUN JOURNAL (Beachwood, OH) **11593**
EUDORA ENTERPRISE (Lake Village, AR) **11422**
EUFAULA TRIBUNE (Eufaula, AL) **11412**
EUNICE NEWS (Eunice, LA) **11507**
EUREKA HERALD (Eureka, KS) **11497**
EUREKA SENTINEL (Las Vegas, NV) **11559**
EUREKA SPRINGS TIMES-ECHO (Eureka Springs, AR) **11421**
EUSTIS LAKE REGION NEWS (Mt Dora, FL) **11453**
EVANSTON REVIEW (Glenview, IL) **11472**
EVANSVILLE COURIER & PRESS (Evansville, IN) **11343**
EVENING LEADER, THE (St Marys, OH) **11383**
EVENING NEWS (Benton, IL) **11338**

EVENING NEWS (JEFFERSONVILLE), THE (Jeffersonville, IN) 11344

EVENING STAR, THE (Auburn, IN) 11342

EVENING SUN (Hanover, PA) 11389

EVENING SUN, THE (Norwich, NY) 11374

EVENING TELEGRAM, THE (Herkimer, NY) 11372

EVENING TIMES (LITTLE FALLS), THE (Little Falls, NY) 11372

EVENING TIMES (WEST MEMPHIS) (West Memphis, AR) 11323

EVENING WORLD, THE (Linton, IN) 11344

EVERETT INDEPENDENT (Revere, MA) 11523

EVERETT LEADER-HERALD & NEWS GAZETTE (Everett, MA) 11518

EVERETT NEWS TRIBUNE (Snohomish, WA) 11654

EVERGREEN COURANT, THE (Evergreen, AL) 11413

EVERGREEN PARK COURIER (Midlothian, IL) 11476

EVERGREEN SHOPPING GUIDE (Spooner, WI) 11667

EXCELSIOR SPRINGS STANDARD (Excelsior Springs, MO) 11550

EXCELSIOR/SHOREWOOD/CHANHASSEN SUN-SAILOR (Eden Prairie, MN) 11537

EXETER NEWS-LETTER (Portsmouth, NH) 11561

EXETER SUN, THE (Exeter, CA) 11428

EXPLORER NEWSPAPER (TUCSON), THE (Tucson, AZ) 11420

EXPONENT (BROOKLYN), THE (Brooklyn, MI) 11525

EXPONENT (EAST GRAND FORKS), THE (East Grand Forks, MN) 11537

EXPOSITOR, THE (Sparta, TN) 11630

EXPRESS (LOCK HAVEN), THE (Lock Haven, PA) 11390

EXPRESS NEWS (Germantown, WI) 11661

EXPRESSIONS (Coeur d'Alene, ID) 11464

EXPRESS-SOUTHERN EDITION, THE (Dover, DE) 11447

EXPRESS-STAR, THE (Chickasha, OK) 11384

EXPRESS-TIMES, THE (Easton, PA) 11389

EXTRA (CUBA), THE (Cuba, MO) 11549

EXTRA MERCHANDISER (St Marys, OH) 11600

EXTRA (STUTTGART), THE (Stuttgart, AR) 11425

E-ZONE (Columbus, MS) 11546

F

FACTS (CLUTE), THE (Clute, TX) 11397

FAIRBANKS DAILY NEWS-MINER (Fairbanks, AK) 11320

FAIRBORN DAILY HERALD (Xenia, OH) 11383

FAIRBURY JOURNAL-NEWS, THE (Fairbury, NE) 11557

FAIRFAX CONNECTION (McLean, VA) 11649

FAIRFAX STATION TIMES (Herndon, VA) 11647

FAIRFAX STATION/LAUREL HILL/CLIFTON CONNECTION (McLean, VA) 11649

FAIRFAX TIMES (Herndon, VA) 11647

FAIRFIELD CHRONICLE, THE (West Caldwell, NJ) 11568

FAIRFIELD CITIZEN NEWS, THE (Fairfield, CT) 11444

FAIRFIELD COUNTY WEEKLY, THE (Bridgeport, CT) 11443

FAIRFIELD ECHO (Liberty Township, OH) 11597

FAIRFIELD GLADE SUN (Crossville, TN) 11626

FAIRFIELD LEDGER (Fairfield, IA) 11347

FAIRHOPE COURIER, THE (Fairhope, AL) 11413

FAIRMONT SENTINEL (Fairmont, MN) 11360

FAIRPORT COMMUNITY NEWS (Rochester, NY) 11581

FAIRVIEW HEIGHTS JOURNAL (Swansee, IL) 11482

FAIRVIEW HEIGHTS TRIBUNE (Mascoutah, IL) 11475

FAIRVIEW REPUBLICAN (Fairview, OK) 11604

FALFURRIAS FACTS (Falfurrias, TX) 11634

FALLS CHURCH NEWS-PRESS (Falls Church, VA) 11646

FALLS CITY JOURNAL (Falls City, NE) 11557

FALMOUTH ENTERPRISE, THE (Falmouth, MA) 11518

FALMOUTH OUTLOOK, THE (Falmouth, KY) 11501

FARIBAULT COUNTY REGISTER (Blue Earth, MN) 11535

FARIBAULT DAILY NEWS (Faribault, MN) 11360

FARINA NEWS, THE (Farina, IL) 11471

FARMER & MINER (Brighton, CO) 11439

FARMER CITY JOURNAL (Farmer City, IL) 11471

FARMER'S WEEKLY REVIEW (Joliet, IL) 11474

FARMINGDALE OBSERVER (Mineola, NY) 11578

FARMINGTON INDEPENDENT (Farmington, MN) 11538

FARMINGTON OBSERVER (Livonia, MI) 11529

FARMINGTON PRESS (Farmington, MO) 11550

FARMINGTON THISWEEK (Burnsville, MN) 11535

FARMINGTON VALLEY POST, THE (Bristol, CT) 11443

FARMLAND NEWS (Archbold, OH) 11592

FARMSIDE OF HUNTLEY/MARENGO/UNION, THE (St Charles, IL) 11481

FARMVILLE ENTERPRISE, THE (Farmville, NC) 11586

FARMVILLE HERALD, THE (Farmville, VA) 11646

FARRAGUT PRESS (Knoxville, TN) 11627

FAUQUIER CITIZEN (Warrenton, VA) 11650

FAUQUIER TIMES-DEMOCRAT (Warrenton, VA) 11650

FAYETTE ADVERTISER, THE (Fayette, MO) 11550

FAYETTE COUNTY RECORD, THE (La Grange, TX) 11638

FAYETTE COUNTY REVIEW (Somerville, TN) 11629

FAYETTE COUNTY UNION (West Union, IA) 11496

FAYETTE DAILY NEWS (Fayetteville, GA) 11335

FAYETTE FALCON, THE (Somerville, TN) 11629

FAYETTE TRIBUNE (Oak Hill, WV) 11656

FAYETTEVILLE OBSERVER, THE (Fayetteville, NC) 11376

FEDERAL WAY MIRROR (Federal Way, WA) 11652

FEDERAL WAY NEWS (Burien, WA) 11651

FENNIMORE TIMES (Fennimore, WI) 11660

FENTON PRESS, THE (Flint, MI) 11527

FENTRESS COURIER (Jamestown, TN) 11627

FENWAY NEWS, THE (Boston, MA) 11516

FERDINAND NEWS, THE (Ferdinand, IN) 11485

FERNLEY LEADER-DAYTON COURIER (Yerington, NV) 11559

FILLMORE COUNTY JOURNAL (Preston, MN) 11542

FILLMORE HERALD (Fillmore, CA) 11428

FINCASTLE HERALD, THE (Fincastle, VA) 11647

FINDER, THE (Bowman, ND) 11591

FINGER LAKES TIMES, THE (Geneva, NY) 11372

FIRE ISLAND TIDE (Sayville, NY) 11581

FIREBAUGH/MENDOTA JOURNAL (Kerman, CA) 11430

FISHER REPORTER, THE (Fisher, IL) 11471

FISHKILL STANDARD (Mahopac, NY) 11577

FISHTOWN STAR (Trevose, PA) 11617

FITCHBURG STAR (Oregon, WI) 11665

FIVE CITIES TIMES PRESS-RECORDER (Arroyo Grande, CA) 11426

FIVE COUNTY BUYER'S GUIDE (Ripon, WI) 11666

FLAGLER/PALM COAST NEWS TRIBUNE, THE (Palm Coast, FL) 11454

FLANAGAN HOME TIMES (Pontiac, IL) 11480

FLASHES SHOPPING GUIDE (Allegan, MI) 11525

FLATBUSH LIFE (Brooklyn, NY) 11571

FLEMINGSBURG GAZETTE (Flemingsburg, KY) 11501

FLINT JOURNAL, THE (Flint, MI) 11358

FLINT TOWNSHIP NEWS, THE (Flint, MI) 11527

FLORAL PARK BULLETIN (Floral Park, NY) 11574

FLORAL PARK DISPATCH (Mineola, NY) 11578

FLORALA NEWS, THE (Florala, AL) 11413

FLORENCE CITIZEN (Florence, CO) 11441

FLORENCE MINING NEWS (Florence, WI) 11660

FLORENCE RECORDER (Fort Mitchell, KY) 11502

FLORENCE REMINDER & BLADE-TRIBUNE (Florence, AZ) 11418

FLORESVILLE CHRONICLE-JOURNAL (Floresville, TX) 11634

FLORHAM PARK EAGLE (Madison, NJ) 11564

FLORIDA KEYS KEYNOTER (Marathon, FL) 11452

FLORIDA TIMES-UNION, THE (Jacksonville, FL) 11333

FLORIDA TODAY (Melbourne, FL) 11333

FLORISSANT-BLACK JACK JOURNAL (Hazelwood, MO) 11550

FLOWER MOUND LEADER (Addison, TX) 11631

FLOWER MOUND MESSENGER, THE (Flower Mound, TX) 11634

FLOYD COUNTY HESPERIAN-BEACON (Floydada, TX) 11634

FLOYD COUNTY TIMES, THE (Prestonsburg, KY) 11505

FLOYD PRESS (Floyd, VA) 11647

FLUME, THE (Bailey, CO) 11439

FLUSHING OBSERVER, THE (Flint, MI) 11527

FLUSHING TIMES, THE (Bayside, NY) 11569

FOLSOM TELEGRAPH (Folsom, CA) 11429

FONTANA HERALD NEWS (Fontana, CA) 11429

FOOTHILLS TRADER (Torrington, CT) 11447

FORD COUNTY PRESS (Melvin, IL) 11475

FORDYCE NEWS-ADVOCATE (Fordyce, AR) 11421

FOREST CITY SUMMIT (Forest City, IA) 11492

FOREST HILLS ADVANCE (Jenison, MI) 11529

FOREST HILLS JOURNAL (Loveland, OH) 11597

FOREST HILLS LEDGER (Bayside, NY) 11569

FOREST HILLS/REGO PARK TIMES (Maspeth, NY) 11577

FOREST LAKE PRESS (White Bear Lake, MN) 11544

FOREST LAKE TIMES (Forest Lake, MN) 11538

FOREST LEAVES (Oak Park, IL) 11478

FOREST PARK REVIEW (Oak Park, IL) 11478

FOREST PRESS (Tionesta, PA) 11617

FOREST REPUBLICAN, THE (Crandon, WI) 11659

FOREST-BLADE, THE (Swainsboro, GA) 11463

FORRESTON JOURNAL (Oregon, IL) 11478

FORSYTH COUNTY NEWS (Cumming, GA) 11458

FORSYTH HERALD (Alpharetta, GA) 11456

FORT BEND/SOUTHWEST SUN (Sugar Land, TX) 11641

FORT BRAGG ADVOCATE-NEWS (Ft Bragg, CA) 11429

FORT COLLINS COLORADOAN (Fort Collins, CO) 11329

FORT DODGE MESSENGER (Fort Dodge, IA) 11347

FORT GIBSON TIMES (Muskogee, OK) 11605

FORT LEONARD WOOD GUIDE (St Robert, MO) 11554

FORT LUPTON PRESS (Brighton, CO) 11439

FORT MADISON DAILY DEMOCRAT (Fort Madison, IA) 11347

FORT MEADE LEADER, THE (Fort Meade, FL) 11451

FORT MILL TIMES (Fort Mill, SC) 11620

FORT MORGAN TIMES, THE (Fort Morgan, CO) 11329

FORT MYERS BEACH BULLETIN (Fort Myers, FL) 11451

FORT MYERS BEACH OBSERVER (Fort Myers Beach, FL) 11451

FORT SCOTT TRIBUNE, THE (Fort Scott, KS) 11349

FORT STOCKTON PIONEER (Fort Stockton, TX) 11635

FORT THOMAS RECORDER (Fort Mitchell, KY) 11502

FORT WASHINGTON GAZETTE (Gaithersburg, MD) 11513

FORT WAYNE NEWS-SENTINEL (Wheeling, WV) 11407

FORT WORTH STAR-TELEGRAM (Sacramento, CA) 11327

FORT WORTH WEEKLY (Forth Worth, TX) 11635

FORUM OF QUEENS (Howard Beach, NY) 11576

FORUM, THE (Fargo, ND) 11378

FOSSTON THIRTEEN TOWNS (Fosston, MN) 11538

FOSTER CITY PROGRESS (Burlingame, CA) 11427

FOSTER'S DAILY DEMOCRAT (Dover, NH) 11368

FOTO NEWS (Merrill, WI) 11663

FOUNTAIN HILLS TIMES, THE (Fountain Hills, AZ) 11418

FOUNTAIN VALLEY NEWS / EL PASO COUNTY NEWS (Fountain, CO) 11441

FOUR OAKS-BENSON NEWS IN REVIEW (Benson, NC) 11585

FOWLER ENSIGN (Sanger, CA) 11437

FOWLER TRIBUNE, THE (Fowler, CO) 11441

FOX LAKE PRESS (Grayslake, IL) 11473

FOX LAKE REPRESENTATIVE (Berlin, WI) 11658

FOX POINT-BAYSIDE-RIVER HILLS HERALD (New Berlin, WI) 11664

FOX VALLEY SHOPPING NEWS, THE (Yorkville, IL) 11484

FOX VALLEY VILLAGES SUN (Naperville, IL) **11477**
FOXBORO REPORTER, THE (Foxboro, MA) **11518**
FOXXY SHOPPER (La Crosse, WI) **11662**
FRAMINGHAM TAB (Framingham, MA) **11518**
FRANKENMUTH NEWS (Frankenmuth, MI) **11527**
FRANKFORT TIMES (Frankfort, IN) **11343**
FRANKFORT-MOKENA STAR (Tinley Park, IL) **11482**
FRANKLIN BANNER-TRIBUNE (Franklin, LA) **11353**
FRANKLIN CHALLENGER (Greenwood, IN) **11486**
FRANKLIN CHRONICLE, THE (Franklin, OH) **11596**
FRANKLIN COUNTY CITIZEN (Lavonia, GA) **11461**
FRANKLIN COUNTY GRAPHIC (Connell, WA) **11652**
FRANKLIN COUNTY PLUS (Russellville, AL) **11415**
FRANKLIN COUNTY TIMES (Russellville, AL) **11415**
FRANKLIN FAVORITE (Franklin, KY) **11502**
FRANKLIN HUB (New Berlin, WI) **11664**
FRANKLIN JOURNAL (Farmington, ME) **11510**
FRANKLIN LAKES/OAKLAND SUBURBAN NEWS (Ridgewood, NJ) **11566**
FRANKLIN (NC) PRESS (Franklin, NC) **11586**
FRANKLIN NEWS-POST, THE (Rocky Mount, VA) **11650**
FRANKLIN PARK HERALD-JOURNAL, THE (Oak Park, IL) **11478**
FRANKLIN PRESS (WEST FRANKFORT) (West Frankfort, IL) **11483**
FRANKLIN SQUARE BULLETIN (Floral Park, NY) **11574**
FRANKLIN SQUARE LIFE HERALD (Lawrence, NY) **11576**
FRANKLIN SUN, THE (Winnsboro, LA) **11508**
FRANKLIN TIMES (Louisburg, NC) **11588**
FRANKLIN TOWNSHIP SENTINEL (Franklinville, NJ) **11563**
FREDERICK CITY GAZETTE (Frederick, MD) **11513**
FREDERICK LEADER (Altus, OK) **11603**
FREDERICK NEWS-POST, THE (Frederick, MD) **11355**
FREDERICKSBURG STANDARD/RADIO POST (Fredericksburg, TX) **11635**
FREE LANCE-STAR, THE (Fredericksburg, VA) **11403**
FREE NEWS, THE (Farmville, VA) **11647**
FREE PRESS ADVOCATE (Wilmington, IL) **11483**
FREE PRESS (DIBOLL), THE (Diboll, TX) **11634**
FREE PRESS (MANKATO), THE (Mankato, MN) **11361**
FREE PRESS (NORTH ATTLEBORO), THE (North Attleboro, MA) **11521**
FREE PRESS (QUAKERTOWN), THE (Quakertown, PA) **11616**
FREE PRESS (ROCKLAND), THE (Rockland, ME) **11511**
FREE PRESS STANDARD (Carrollton, OH) **11594**
FREE PRESS (TAMPA), THE (Tampa, FL) **11455**
FREE PRESS-COURIER (Westfield, PA) **11618**
FREE STAR, THE (Pipestone, MN) **11542**
FREE TIME (Seaville, NJ) **11567**
FREE TRADER (Massena, NY) **11578**
FREEBORN COUNTY SHOPPER (Albert Lea, MN) **11533**
FREEPORT BALDWIN LEADER, THE (Merrick, NY) **11578**
FREEPORT SHOPPING NEWS (Freeport, IL) **11471**
FREER PRESS, THE (Freer, TX) **11635**
FREETIME (Herrin, IL) **11474**
FREMONT BULLETIN (Milpitas, CA) **11433**
FREMONT MILLS BEACON ENTERPRISE (Malvern, IA) **11493**
FREMONT TRIBUNE (Fremont, NE) **11367**
FRESH MEADOWS TIMES, THE (Bayside, NY) **11569**
FRESNO BEE, THE (Fresno, CA) **11324**
FRIENDSWOOD & PEARLAND REPORTER NEWS (Pearland, TX) **11639**
FRIENDSWOOD JOURNAL (Pearland, TX) **11639**
FRISCO ENTERPRISE (Frisco, TX) **11635**
FRONT PAGE (LACKAWANNA) (Lackawanna, NY) **11576**
FROSTPROOF NEWS, THE (Frostproof, FL) **11451**
FRUITA TIMES (Fruita, CO) **11441**
FT LAUDERDALE EASTSIDER, THE (Pompano Beach, FL) **11454**

FULTON COUNTY EXPOSITOR (Wauseon, OH) **11601**
FULTON COUNTY NEWS (McConnellsburg, PA) **11613**
FULTON COUNTY SHOPPER (Canton, IL) **11468**
FULTON DEMOCRAT (Lewistown, IL) **11475**
FULTON JOURNAL (Fulton, IL) **11471**
FULTON LEADER (Fulton, KY) **11502**
FULTON PATRIOT (Fulton, NY) **11574**
FULTON SHOPPER (Fulton, KY) **11502**
FULTON SUN, THE (Fulton, MO) **11364**
FUQUAY-VARINA INDEPENDENT (Fuquay-Varina, NC) **11587**

G

GADSDEN COUNTY TIMES (Quincy, FL) **11454**
GADSDEN TIMES (New York, NY) **11373**
GAFFNEY LEDGER, THE (Gaffney, SC) **11621**
GAHANA NEWS (Columbus, OH) **11595**
GAINESVILLE BUYERS GUIDE (Gainesville, FL) **11451**
GAINESVILLE DAILY REGISTER (Gainesville, TX) **11398**
GAINESVILLE SUN, THE (New York, NY) **11373**
GAITHERSBURG GAZETTE (Gaithersburg, MD) **11513**
GALENA GAZETTE (Galena, IL) **11471**
GALESVILLE REPUBLICAN (Galesville, WI) **11661**
GALION INQUIRER (Galion, OH) **11381**
GALLATIN DEMOCRAT (Shawneetown, IL) **11481**
GALLIPOLIS DAILY TRIBUNE (Gallipolis, OH) **11381**
GALT HERALD, THE (Galt, CA) **11429**
GALVA NEWS (Galva, IL) **11472**
GALVESTON COUNTY DAILY NEWS, THE (Galveston, TX) **11398**
GARDEN CITY LIFE (Mineola, NY) **11578**
GARDEN CITY NEWS (Hicksville, NY) **11576**
GARDEN CITY OBSERVER (Livonia, MI) **11529**
GARDEN CITY TELEGRAM (Garden City, KS) **11349**
GARDEN ISLAND NEWSPAPER (Lihue, HI) **11337**
GARDENA VALLEY NEWS (Gardena, CA) **11429**
GARDNER NEWS (Gardner, MA) **11355**
GARFIELD MAPLE-SUN (Cleveland, OH) **11594**
GARLAND MORNING NEWS (Garland, TX) **11635**
GARNER NEWS (Garner, NC) **11587**
GARRARD CENTRAL RECORD, THE (Lancaster, KY) **11503**
GARY CRUSADER (Gary, IN) **11486**
GASCONADE COUNTY REPUBLICAN (Owensville, MO) **11552**
GASPARILLA GAZETTE (Boca Grande, FL) **11449**
GASPARILLA GAZETTE (Boca Raton, FL) **11449**
GASTON GAZETTE (Gastonia, NC) **11376**
GATE CITY FREE PRESS (Keokuk, IA) **11493**
GATES COUNTY INDEX (Gatesville, NC) **11587**
GATES-CHILI POST (Canandaigua, NY) **11571**
GATESVILLE MESSENGER/STAR FORUM, THE (Gatesville, TX) **11635**
GATEWAY (FLORAL PARK), THE (Floral Park, NY) **11574**
GATEWAY NEWS, THE (Stow, OH) **11600**
GATEWAY SHOPPER (Sturgis, MI) **11532**
GAYLORD HERALD TIMES (Gaylord, MI) **11527**
GAYLORD HUB, THE (Gaylord, MN) **11538**
GAZETTE ADVERTISER, THE (Rhinebeck, NY) **11581**
GAZETTE (CEDAR RAPIDS), THE (Cedar Rapids, IA) **11346**
GAZETTE (COLORADO SPRINGS), THE (Colorado Springs, CO) **11329**
GAZETTE (GAITHERSBURG), THE (Gaithersburg, MD) **11513**
GAZETTE (GALAX), THE (Galax, VA) **11647**
GAZETTE (JEFFERSON), THE (Jefferson, OH) **11597**
GAZETTE (ORTING), THE (Orting, WA) **11653**
GAZETTE (PECATONICA), THE (Pecatonica, IL) **11479**
GAZETTE (PORT JERVIS), THE (Port Jervis, NY) **11581**
GAZETTE-DEMOCRAT (Anna, IL) **11466**
GAZETTE-ENTERPRISE (Seguin, TX) **11401**
GEIST TOPICS/NORTHEAST EDITION (Fishers, IN) **11485**

GEM STATE MINER (Newport, WA) **11653**
GENESEE COUNTRY EXPRESS (Dansville, NY) **11573**
GENESEEWAY SHOPPER (Dansville, NY) **11573**
GENESEO REPUBLIC (Geneseo, IL) **11472**
GENEVA COUNTY REAPER (Geneva, AL) **11413**
GENEVA COUNTY SHOPPER (Geneva, AL) **11413**
GENEVA REPUBLICAN, THE (Glen Ellyn, IL) **11472**
GENEVA SUN (Aurora, IL) **11467**
GENOA JOURNAL (Sycamore, IL) **11482**
GENTRY COURIER-JOURNAL (Gentry, AR) **11421**
GEORGE COUNTY TIMES (Lucedale, MS) **11547**
GEORGETOWN CURRENT, THE (Washington, DC) **11448**
GEORGETOWN CURRENT, THE (Washington, DC) **11448**
GEORGETOWN NEWS-GRAPHIC (Georgetown, KY) **11502**
GEORGETOWN RECORD (Beverly, MA) **11516**
GEORGETOWN TIMES, THE (Georgetown, SC) **11621**
GEORGIA POST, THE (Roberta, GA) **11462**
GEORGIA TIMES-UNION (Brunswick, GA) **11335**
GERING COURIER (Gering, NE) **11557**
GERMAN VILLAGE GAZETTE (Columbus, OH) **11595**
GERMANTOWN BANNER-PRESS (New Berlin, WI) **11664**
GERMANTOWN COURIER (Philadelphia, PA) **11615**
GERMANTOWN GAZETTE (Gaithersburg, MD) **11513**
GERMANTOWN NEWS, THE (Germantown, TN) **11626**
GERMANTOWN PRESS (Germantown, OH) **11596**
GETTYSBURG TIMES (Gettysburg, PA) **11389**
GIBSON CITY COURIER (Gibson City, IL) **11472**
GIBSON COUNTY TODAY (Princeton, IN) **11488**
GIDDINGS TIMES & NEWS (Giddings, TX) **11635**
GILA COUNTY ADVANTAGE (Globe, AZ) **11418**
GILBERT TIMES, THE (Williamson, WV) **11657**
GILLESPIE AREA NEWS (Gillespie, IL) **11472**
GILMAN STAR (Gilman, IL) **11472**
GILMER MIRROR (Gilmer, TX) **11635**
GILROY DISPATCH, THE (Gilroy, CA) **11324**
GIRARD HOME NEWS (Trevose, PA) **11617**
GIRARD PRESS (Augusta, GA) **11457**
GIVEAWAY, THE (Scottsburg, IN) **11488**
GLACIER REPORTER (Browning, MT) **11555**
GLADES COUNTY DEMOCRAT (Clewiston, FL) **11450**
GLADEWATER MIRROR (Gladewater, TX) **11635**
GLADSTONE SUN NEWS (Liberty, MO) **11551**
GLADWIN COUNTY RECORD & BEAVERTON CLARION (Gladwin, MI) **11527**
GLASFORD GAZETTE, THE (Glasford, IL) **11472**
GLASGOW COURIER, THE (Glasgow, MT) **11555**
GLASGOW DAILY TIMES (Glasgow, KY) **11351**
GLASTONBURY CITIZEN (Glastonbury, CT) **11444**
GLEANER, THE (Henderson, KY) **11351**
GLEN COVE RECORD PILOT (Mineola, NY) **11578**
GLEN ELLYN NEWS (Glen Ellyn, IL) **11472**
GLEN ELLYN PRESS (Elmhurst, IL) **11471**
GLEN ELLYN SUN (Naperville, IL) **11477**
GLEN OAKS LEDGER, THE (Bayside, NY) **11569**
GLEN RIDGE PAPER, THE (Bloomfield, NJ) **11561**
GLEN RIDGE VOICE (Nutley, NJ) **11566**
GLEN ROCK GAZETTE, THE (Ridgewood, NJ) **11566**
GLEN ROSE REPORTER (Glen Rose, TX) **11635**
GLENCOE ENTERPRISE (Glencoe, MN) **11538**
GLENCOE NEWS (Glenview, IL) **11472**
GLENDALE HEIGHTS/BLOOMINGDALE PRESS (St Charles, IL) **11481**
GLENDALE HERALD (New Berlin, WI) **11664**
GLENDALE NEWS-PRESS (Glendale, CA) **11324**
GLENDALE REGISTER (Maspeth, NY) **11577**
GLENDALE STAR, THE (Glendale, AZ) **11418**
GLENDIVE RANGER-REVIEW (Glendive, MT) **11555**
GLENDORA PRESS HIGHLANDER (West Covina, CA) **11438**
GLENNVILLE SENTINEL, THE (Glennville, GA) **11460**

GLENPOOL POST (Tulsa, OK) **11606**

GLENSIDE NEWS (Fort Washington, PA) **11611**

GLENVIEW ANNOUNCEMENTS (Glenview, IL) **11472**

GLENVILLE DEMOCRAT, THE (Glenville, WV) **11655**

GLENVILLE PATHFINDER (Glenville, WV) **11655**

GLENWOOD HERALD (Glenwood, AR) **11422**

GLENWOOD OPINION-TRIBUNE (Glenwood, IA) **11492**

GLENWOOD SPRINGS POST INDEPENDENT (Glenwood Springs, CO) **11330**

GLIDDEN ENTERPRISE (Glidden, WI) **11661**

GLOBE, THE (Fort Washington, PA) **11611**

GLOBE-GAZETTE (Mason City, IA) **11347**

GLOUCESTER CITY NEWS (Gloucester City, NJ) **11563**

GLOUCESTER COUNTY TIMES (Woodbury, NJ) **11370**

GLOUCESTER DAILY TIMES (Gloucester, MA) **11356**

GLOUCESTER-MATHEWS GAZETTE JOURNAL (Gloucester, VA) **11647**

GLYNCO OBSERVER, THE (Brunswick, GA) **11457**

GOLDEN CORNER SHOPPERS GUIDE (Seneca, SC) **11622**

GOLDEN PRAIRIE NEWS (Assumption, IL) **11467**

GOLDEN TRANSCRIPT (Golden, CO) **11441**

GOLDEN TRIANGLE NEWS (San Diego, CA) **11436**

GOLDENDALE SENTINEL (Goldendale, WA) **11652**

GOLDSBORO NEWS-ARGUS (Goldsboro, NC) **11376**

GOLF MILL JOURNAL (Des Plaines, IL) **11470**

GONZALES INQUIRER (Gonzales, TX) **11635**

GONZALES TRIBUNE (Soledad, CA) **11437**

GONZALES WEEKLY CITIZEN (Gonzales, LA) **11507**

GOOCHLAND GAZETTE (Goochland, VA) **11647**

GOOD TIMES (Santa Cruz, CA) **11437**

GOODING COUNTY LEADER (Gooding, ID) **11464**

GOODLAND STAR NEWS, THE (Goodland, KS) **11497**

GOOSE CREEK GAZETTE, THE (Goose Creek, SC) **11621**

GORMAN PROGRESS, THE (Gorman, TX) **11635**

GOSHEN INDEPENDENT (Goshen, NY) **11575**

GOSHEN NEWS, THE (Goshen, IN) **11343**

GOUVERNEUR TRIBUNE PRESS (Gouverneur, NY) **11575**

GOWANDA PENNYSAVER NEWS (Gowanda, NY) **11575**

GRAFTON NEWS, THE (North Grafton, MA) **11521**

GRAHAM LEADER (Graham, TX) **11635**

GRAHAM STAR, THE (Robbinsville, NC) **11589**

GRAINGER COUNTY NEWS (Rutledge, TN) **11629**

GRAND BLANC NEWS, THE (Flint, MI) **11527**

GRAND FORKS HERALD (Grand Forks, ND) **11378**

GRAND HAVEN TRIBUNE (Grand Haven, MI) **11358**

GRAND ISLAND INDEPENDENT (Grand Island, NE) **11367**

GRAND ISLAND PENNYSAVER (Grand Island, NY) **11575**

GRAND JUNCTION FREE PRESS (Grand Junction, CO) **11330**

GRAND LEDGE INDEPENDENT, THE (Grand Ledge, MI) **11527**

GRAND PRAIRIE (Duncanville, TX) **11634**

GRAND PRAIRIE HERALD (Hazen, AR) **11422**

GRAND RAPIDS PRESS, THE (Grand Rapids, MI) **11358**

GRAND RAPIDS/HERALD-REVIEW (Grand Rapids, MN) **11538**

GRAND SALINE SUN (Grand Saline, TX) **11636**

GRAND TRAVERSE HERALD (Traverse City, MI) **11532**

GRAND VALLEY EAST ADVANCE (Jenison, MI) **11529**

GRAND VALLEY WEST ADVANCE (Jenison, MI) **11529**

GRANDVIEW HERALD (Grandview, WA) **11652**

GRANGE INDEPENDENT, LA (Mahopac, NY) **11577**

GRANITE CITY PRESS RECORD JOURNAL (Collinsville, IL) **11469**

GRANITE STATE NEWS, THE (Wolfeboro, NH) **11561**

GRANT COUNTY HERALD INDEPENDENT (Lancaster, WI) **11662**

GRANT COUNTY JOURNAL (Ephrata, WA) **11652**

GRANT COUNTY NEWS (ELGIN) (Elgin, ND) **11591**

GRANT COUNTY NEWS (WILLIAMSTOWN) (Dry Ridge, KY) **11501**

GRANT COUNTY PRESS (Petersburg, WV) **11656**

GRANT COUNTY REVIEW (Milbank, SD) **11624**

GRANT, IOWA, LAFAYETTE SHOPPING NEWS, THE (Platteville, WI) **11665**

GRANTS PASS DAILY COURIER (Grants Pass, OR) **11387**

GRANVILLE SENTINEL (Granville, NY) **11575**

GRANVILLE SENTINEL, THE (Granville, OH) **11596**

GRASS VALLEY TRADER (Auburn, CA) **11426**

GRATIOT COUNTY HERALD (Ithaca, MI) **11528**

GRAVETTE NEWS HERALD (Gravette, AR) **11422**

GRAYSLAKE REVIEW (Waukegan, IL) **11483**

GRAYSLAKE TIMES (Grayslake, IL) **11473**

GRAYSON COUNTY NEWS-GAZETTE (Leitchfield, KY) **11503**

GRAYSON COUNTY SHOPPER (Denison, TX) **11633**

GRAYSON JOURNAL-ENQUIRER (Grayson, KY) **11502**

GREAT BEND TRIBUNE (Great Bend, KS) **11349**

GREAT FALLS CONNECTION (McLean, VA) **11649**

GREAT FALLS TIMES (Herndon, VA) **11647**

GREAT FALLS TRIBUNE (Great Falls, MT) **11366**

GREAT LAKES MARINERS (Grand Marais, MI) **11528**

GREAT LANDER BUSH MAILER (Anchorage, AK) **11416**

GREAT NECK NEWS (Hicksville, NY) **11576**

GREAT NECK RECORD (Mineola, NY) **11578**

GREATER HOUSTON WEEKLY (Houston, TX) **11636**

GREECE POST, THE (Canandaigua, NY) **11571**

GREELEY TRIBUNE (Greeley, CO) **11330**

GREEN BAY PRESS-GAZETTE (Green Bay, WI) **11408**

GREEN HILLS NEWS (Nashville, TN) **11628**

GREEN LAKE COUNTY REPORTER (Berlin, WI) **11658**

GREEN RIVER REPUBLICAN (Horse Cave, KY) **11503**

GREEN TAB (Moundsville, WV) **11656**

GREEN VALLEY NEWS & SUN (Green Valley, AZ) **11418**

GREENACRES OBSERVER (Lake Worth, FL) **11452**

GREENBELT GAZETTE (Landover, MD) **11513**

GREENBELT NEWS REVIEW (Greenbelt, MD) **11513**

GREENBRIER VALLEY RANGER (Lewisburg, WV) **11656**

GREENDALE VILLAGE LIFE (New Berlin, WI) **11664**

GREENE COUNTY INDEPENDENT (Eutaw, AL) **11412**

GREENE COUNTY MESSENGER (Waynesburg, PA) **11617**

GREENE COUNTY RECORD (Stanardsville, VA) **11650**

GREENE COUNTY SUNDAY SHOPPER (Xenia, OH) **11603**

GREENE RECORDER, THE (Greene, IA) **11492**

GREENFIELD ATHOL-ORANGE TOWN CRIER (Greenfield, MA) **11518**

GREENFIELD NEWS (Greenfield, CA) **11429**

GREENFIELD OBSERVER (New Berlin, WI) **11664**

GREEN/HALE SHOPPERS GUIDE (Demopolis, AL) **11412**

GREENPOINT GAZETTE & ADVERTISER (Brooklyn, NY) **11571**

GREENSBORO WATCHMAN, THE (Greensboro, AL) **11413**

GREENSBURG DAILY NEWS (Greensburg, IN) **11343**

GREENSBURG RECORD-HERALD (Greensburg, KY) **11502**

GREENUP COUNTY NEWS-TIMES (Greenup, KY) **11502**

GREENUP PRESS (Greenup, IL) **11473**

GREENVILLE (AL) ADVOCATE, THE (Greenville, AL) **11413**

GREENVILLE COMMUNITY NEWS (Hockessin, DE) **11447**

GREENVILLE (IL) ADVOCATE, THE (Greenville, IL) **11473**

GREENVILLE LOCAL (Ravena, NY) **11581**

GREENVILLE NEWS (Greenville, SC) **11394**

GREENVILLE RECORD-ARGUS (Greenville, PA) **11389**

GREENWICH CITIZEN (Greenwich, CT) **11444**

GREENWICH JOURNAL & SALEM PRESS (Greenwich, NY) **11575**

GREENWICH POST (Ridgefield, CT) **11446**

GREENWICH TIME (Greenwich, CT) **11331**

GREENWICH VILLAGE GAZETTE (Island Heights, NJ) **11564**

GREENWOOD & SOUTHSIDE CHALLENGER (Greenwood, IN) **11486**

GREENWOOD COMMONWEALTH (Greenwood, MS) **11362**

GREENWOOD DEMOCRAT (Greenwood, AR) **11422**

GREENWOOD LAKE & WEST MILFORD NEWS (Greenwood Lake, NY) **11575**

GREER CITIZEN, THE (Greer, SC) **11621**

GRESHAM OUTLOOK, THE (Gresham, OR) **11607**

GRETNA BREEZE (Papillion, NE) **11558**

GRIDLEY HERALD, THE (Gridley, CA) **11429**

GRIDLEY SHOPPING NEWS, THE (Gridley, CA) **11429**

GRIFFIN DAILY NEWS (Griffin, GA) **11335**

GRINNELL HERALD-REGISTER (Grinnell, IA) **11492**

GRIZZLY WEEKENDER (Big Bear Lake, CA) **11426**

GROESBECK JOURNAL (Groesbeck, TX) **11636**

GROSSE POINTE NEWS (Grosse Pointe Farms, MI) **11528**

GROTON HERALD, THE (Groton, MA) **11518**

GROTON LANDMARK (Devens, MA) **11517**

GROVE CITY NEWS (Columbus, OH) **11595**

GROVE CITY RECORD (Worthington, OH) **11602**

GROVE SUN, THE (Grove, OK) **11385**

GROVETON NEWS (Groveton, TX) **11636**

GRUNDY COUNTY HERALD (Tracy City, TN) **11630**

GRUNDY REGISTER (Grundy Center, IA) **11492**

GRUNION GAZETTE (Long Beach, CA) **11431**

GRYGLA EAGLE (Gonvick, MN) **11538**

GUAM VARIETY (Saipan, MP) **11360**

GUARDIAN, THE (Monroe, MI) **11530**

GUERNSEY GAZETTE, THE (Guernsey, WY) **11669**

GUILDERLAND SPOTLIGHT (Delmar, NY) **11573**

GUILFORD COURIER, THE (Madison, CT) **11444**

GULF COAST TRIBUNE, THE (West Columbia, TX) **11642**

GUNNISON COUNTRY TIMES (Gunnison, CO) **11441**

GURDON TIMES, THE (Gurdon, AR) **11422**

GURNEE JOURNAL (Grayslake, IL) **11473**

GURNEE REVIEW (Waukegan, IL) **11483**

GUTHRIE CENTER TIMES (Guthrie Center, IA) **11492**

GUTHRIE NEWS LEADER (Guthrie, OK) **11385**

GUTTENBERG PRESS, THE (Guttenberg, IA) **11492**

GUYMON DAILY HERALD (Guymon, OK) **11385**

GWINNETT DAILY POST (Lawrenceville, GA) **11336**

H

HADDON HERALD/HADDON LIFE (East Haddonfield, NJ) **11562**

HAGERSTOWN EXPONENT, THE (Hagerstown, IN) **11486**

HALES CORNER VILLAGE HUB (New Berlin, WI) **11664**

HALF HOLLOW HILLS (Huntington, NY) **11576**

HALF MOON BAY REVIEW (Half Moon Bay, CA) **11429**

HALIFAX/PLYMPTON REPORTER (Marshfield, MA) **11520**

HALLETTSVILLE TRIBUNE-HERALD (Hallettsville, TX) **11636**

HAMBURG ITEM (Hamburg, PA) **11612**

HAMBURG PENNYSAVER (Hamburg, NY) **11575**

HAMBURG REPORTER, THE (Hamburg, IA) **11493**

HAMDEN CHRONICLE, THE (Milford, CT) **11445**

HAMILTON COUNTY NEWS (Speculator, NY) **11582**

HAMILTON HERALD-NEWS (Hamilton, TX) **11636**

HAMILTON-MORRISVILLE TRIBUNE (Cazenovia, NY) **11572**

HAMILTON/WENHAM CHRONICLE (Beverly, MA) **11516**

HAMLIN-CLARKSON HERALD (Spencerport, NY) **11582**

HAMMOND DAILY STAR (Hammond, LA) **11353**

HAMMONTON NEWS (Hammonton, NJ) **11563**

HAMPSHIRE JOURNAL (Sycamore, IL) **11482**

HAMPSHIRE REVIEW (Romney, WV) **11657**

HAMPTON CHRONICLE (Hampton, IA) **11493**

HAMPTON COUNTY GUARDIAN (Hampton, SC) **11621**

HAMPTON UNION (Hampton, NH) **11560**

HANAHAN, GOOSE CREEK & NORTH CHARLESTON NEWS (Hanahan, SC) **11621**

HANCEVILLE HERALD (Hanceville, AL) **11414**

HANCOCK CLARION (Hawesville, KY) **11502**
HANCOCK COUNTY JOURNAL-PILOT (Carthage, IL) **11468**
HANCOCK COUNTY QUILL (Stronghurst, IL) **11481**
HANCOCK NEWS (Hancock, MD) **11513**
HANNIBAL COURIER-POST (Hannibal, MO) **11364**
HANOVER EAGLE & REGIONAL WEEKLY NEWS (Madison, NJ) **11564**
HANOVER MARINER (Marshfield, MA) **11520**
HANSFORD COUNTY REPORTER-STATESMAN (Spearman, TX) **11641**
HANSON TOWN CRIER (Rayham, MA) **11522**
HARALSON GATEWAY-BEACON, THE (Bremen, GA) **11457**
HARBOR BEACH TIMES (Harbor Beach, MI) **11528**
HARBOR NEWS, THE (Madison, CT) **11444**
HARBOR SOUND (Brunswick, GA) **11457**
HARDEEVILLE TIMES (Ridgeland, SC) **11622**
HARDEMAN COUNTY SHOPPER (Bolivar, TN) **11625**
HARDIN COUNTY (IL) INDEPENDENT (Elizabethtown, IL) **11471**
HARDIN COUNTY INDEX (Eldora, IA) **11492**
HARDIN COUNTY (KY) INDEPENDENT (Elizabethtown, KY) **11501**
HARDWICK GAZETTE (Hardwick, VT) **11644**
HARLAN COUNTY JOURNAL (Alma, NE) **11556**
HARLAN DAILY ENTERPRISE (Harlan, KY) **11351**
HARLAN NEWS-ADVERTISER (Harlan, IA) **11493**
HARLAN TRIBUNE (Harlan, IA) **11493**
HARLEM IRVING TIMES (Park Ridge, IL) **11479**
HARLEM VALLEY TIMES (Amenia, NY) **11569**
HARRINGTON JOURNAL, THE (Harrington, DE) **11447**
HARRIS COUNTY JOURNAL (Manchester, GA) **11461**
HARRISBURG DAILY REGISTER (Harrisburg, IL) **11340**
HARRISON COUNTY AD-VISOR (Bethany, MO) **11548**
HARRISON DAILY TIMES (Harrison, AR) **11322**
HARRISON INDEPENDENT (Yonkers, NY) **11585**
HARRISON NEWS-HERALD, THE (Cadiz, OH) **11593**
HARRODSBURG HERALD, THE (Harrodsburg, KY) **11502**
HART COUNTY NEWS-HERALD, THE (Horse Cave, KY) **11503**
HARTFORD ADVOCATE (El Reno, OK) **11604**
HARTFORD AREA NEWS (Canistota, SD) **11624**
HARTFORD COURANT, THE (Chicago, IL) **11339**
HARTFORD NEWS (Hartford, CT) **11444**
HARTFORD NEWS-HERALD (Geneva, AL) **11413**
HARTSELLE ENQUIRER (Hartselle, AL) **11414**
HARTSHORNE SUN (Hartshorne, OK) **11604**
HARTSVILLE VIDETTE, THE (Hartsville, TN) **11627**
HARTVILLE NEWS (Hartville, OH) **11596**
HARTWELL SUN, THE (Hartwell, GA) **11460**
HARVARD HILLSIDE (Devens, MA) **11517**
HARVARD POST, THE (Harvard, MA) **11518**
HARWICH ORACLE (Orleans, MA) **11522**
HASKELL FREE PRESS (Haskell, TX) **11636**
HASTINGS BANNER (Hastings, MI) **11528**
HASTINGS DAILY TRIBUNE (Hastings, NE) **11367**
HASTINGS REMINDER (Hastings, MI) **11528**
HASTINGS STAR GAZETTE (Hastings, MN) **11538**
HATTIESBURG AMERICAN (Hattiesburg, MS) **11362**
HAVELOCK NEWS, THE (Havelock, NC) **11587**
HAVERFORD PRESS (Newtown Square, PA) **11614**
HAVERHILL GAZETTE, THE (Haverhill, MA) **11519**
HAVRE DAILY NEWS, THE (Havre, MT) **11366**
HAWAII TRIBUNE-HERALD (Hilo, HI) **11337**
HAWK EYE, THE (Hutchinson, KS) **11349**
HAWKINSVILLE DISPATCH & NEWS (Hawkinsville, GA) **11460**
HAWLEY HERALD (Hawley, MN) **11538**
HAWTHORNE PRESS (Hawthorne, NJ) **11563**
HAXTUN-FLEMING HERALD, THE (Haxtun, CO) **11441**
HAYS DAILY NEWS (Hays, KS) **11349**

HAZARD HERALD (Hazard, KY) **11502**
HAZELWOOD-BRIDGETON JOURNAL (Hazelwood, MO) **11550**
HAZEN STAR (Hazen, ND) **11591**
HAZLETON STANDARD SPEAKER (Hazleton, PA) **11389**
H-DESERT SHOPPER (Yucca Valley, CA) **11439**
HEADLAND OBSERVER (Dothan, AL) **11412**
HEADLIGHT HERALD (Tillamook, OR) **11609**
HEALDSBURG TRIBUNE (Healdsburg, CA) **11429**
HEATH NEWS (Heath, OH) **11596**
HEMPSTEAD BEACON (Hempstead, NY) **11576**
HENDERSON COUNTY QUILL (Stronghurst, IL) **11481**
HENDERSON DAILY NEWS (Henderson, TX) **11398**
HENDERSON HOME NEWS (Henderson, NV) **11559**
HENDERSONVILLE STAR NEWS (Hendersonville, TN) **11627**
HENDERSONVILLE TIMES-NEWS (New York, NY) **11373**
HENDRICKS COUNTY FLYER (Avon, IN) **11484**
HENRIETTA POST (Canandaigua, NY) **11571**
HENRY COUNTY AD-PAK, THE (Defiance, OH) **11596**
HENRY COUNTY ADVERTIZER-SHOPPER (Geneseo, IL) **11472**
HENRY COUNTY LOCAL (Eminence, KY) **11501**
HENRY DAILY HERALD, THE (McDonough, GA) **11336**
HENRY NEWS REPUBLICAN (Henry, IL) **11473**
HENRYETTA FREE-LANCE (Henryetta, OK) **11604**
HERALD & NEWS (Klamath Falls, OR) **11387**
HERALD & NEWS, THE (Newberry, SC) **11622**
HERALD & REVIEW (Decatur, IL) **11339**
HERALD & TRIBUNE (Jonesborough, TN) **11627**
HERALD AMERICAN (Los Angeles, CA) **11431**
HERALD BANNER (Greenville, TX) **11398**
HERALD BULLETIN, THE (Anderson, IN) **11342**
HERALD (CAHOKIA), THE (Cahokia, IL) **11468**
HERALD COASTER, THE (Rosenberg, TX) **11400**
HERALD DEMOCRAT (Sherman, TX) **11401**
HERALD (EVERETTE), THE (Everett, WA) **11405**
HERALD GAZETTE (BARNESVILLE), THE (Barnesville, GA) **11457**
HERALD GAZETTE (TRENTON), THE (Trenton, TN) **11630**
HERALD INDEPENDENT, THE (Winnsboro, SC) **11623**
HERALD JOURNAL (LOGAN), THE (Logan, UT) **11402**
HERALD JOURNAL, THE (Greensboro, GA) **11460**
HERALD LEDGER (Eddyville, KY) **11501**
HERALD MAIL, THE (Hagerstown, MD) **11355**
HERALD (NEW BRITAIN), THE (New Britain, CT) **11331**
HERALD NEWS (FALL RIVER), THE (Fall River, MA) **11355**
HERALD NEWS (JOLIET), THE (Joliet, IL) **11340**
HERALD OF RANDOLPH, THE (Randolph, VT) **11644**
HERALD (PITTSBURGH), THE (Pittsburgh, PA) **11615**
HERALD (PUYALLUP), THE (Puyallup, WA) **11653**
HERALD RECORD, THE (West Union, WV) **11657**
HERALD (ROCK HILL), THE (Rock Hill, SC) **11394**
HERALD (ROCKTON), THE (Rockton, IL) **11480**
HERALD (SHARON), THE (Sharon, PA) **11391**
HERALD STANDARD (Uniontown, PA) **11392**
HERALD TIMES REPORTER (Manitowoc, WI) **11408**
HERALD (TRUTH OR CONSEQUENCES), THE (Truth or Consequences, NM) **11569**
HERALD (WASHBURN), THE (Washburn, IL) **11483**
HERALD-CHRONICLE, THE (Winchester, TN) **11630**
HERALD-CITIZEN (Cookeville, TN) **11395**
HERALD/COUNTRY MARKET, THE (Bourbonnais, IL) **11467**
HERALD-DEMOCRAT (LEADVILLE) (Leadville, CO) **11441**
HERALD-DISPATCH, THE (Huntington, WV) **11406**
HERALD-ENTERPRISE (Golconda, IL) **11473**
HERALD-INDEPENDENT, THE (Cottage Grove, WI) **11659**
HERALD-JOURNAL (New York, NY) **11373**
HERALD-JOURNAL, THE (Monticello, IN) **11344**
HERALD-LEADER (FITZGERALD), THE (Fitzgerald, GA) **11460**
HERALD-LEADER, THE (Siloam Springs, AR) **11424**

HERALD-NEWS (DAYTON), THE (Dayton, TN) **11626**
HERALD-NEWS (WOLF POINT), THE (Wolf Point, MT) **11556**
HERALD-PALLADIUM, THE (St Joseph, MI) **11360**
HERALD-PRESS (HARVEY) (Harvey, ND) **11591**
HERALD-PRESS (HUNTINGTON) (Huntington, IN) **11343**
HERALD-PROGRESS (Ashland, VA) **11645**
HERALD-REPUBLICAN (Angola, IN) **11342**
HERALD-STAR & WEIRTON DAILY TIMES (Steubenville, OH) **11383**
HERALD-STAR, THE (Edinburg, IL) **11471**
HERALD-SUN, THE (Durham, NC) **11376**
HERALD-TIMES (Bloomington, IN) **11342**
HERALD-TRIBUNE (Batesville, IN) **11484**
HERALD-TRIBUNE, THE (Cartersville, GA) **11458**
HERALD-ZEITUNG (New Braunfels, TX) **11400**
HEREFORD BRAND (Hereford, TX) **11398**
HERINGTON TIMES (Herington, KS) **11497**
HERITAGE VILLAGER (Southbury, CT) **11446**
HERMANN ADVERTISER-COURIER (Hermann, MO) **11550**
HERMISTON HERALD, THE (Salem, OR) **11609**
HERNANDO TODAY (Brooksville, FL) **11332**
HERNDON CONNECTION (McLean, VA) **11649**
HERNDON TIMES (Herndon, VA) **11647**
HERRIN SPOKESMAN (Herrin, IL) **11474**
HERSCHER PILOT (Herscher, IL) **11474**
HERSHEY CHRONICLE, THE (Hershey, PA) **11612**
HESPERIA RESORTER (Hesperia, CA) **11429**
HESPERIA STAR (Hesperia, CA) **11429**
HIAWATHA VALLEY SHOPPER (Beldenville, WI) **11658**
HIAWATHA WORLD (Hiawatha, KS) **11497**
HICKMAN COUNTY GAZETTE (Clinton, KY) **11501**
HICKMAN COUNTY TIMES (Centerville, TN) **11626**
HICKMAN COURIER (Hickman, KY) **11503**
HICKORY DAILY RECORD (Hickory, NC) **11376**
HICKORY HILLS CITIZEN (Midlothian, IL) **11476**
HICKORY NEWS EXTRA (Hickory, NC) **11587**
HICKORY NEWS, THE (Hickory, NC) **11587**
HICKSVILLE ILLUSTRATED NEWS (Mineola, NY) **11578**
HICKSVILLE MID ISLAND TIMES (Hicksville, NY) **11576**
HIDDEN VALLEY PRESS (Steamboat Springs, CO) **11442**
HI-DESERT STAR (Yucca Valley, CA) **11439**
HIGH POINT ENTERPRISE (High Point, NC) **11376**
HIGH SPRINGS HERALD, THE (High Springs, FL) **11451**
HIGH TIMBER TIMES (Evergreen, CO) **11440**
HIGHLAND NEWS LEADER (Highland, IL) **11474**
HIGHLAND PARK NEWS (Waukegan, IL) **11483**
HIGHLANDER (HIGHLANDS), THE (Highlands, NC) **11587**
HIGHLANDER (West Covina, CA) **11438**
HIGHLANDS RANCH HERALD (Littleton, CO) **11441**
HIGHLINE TIMES/DES MOINES NEWS (Burien, WA) **11651**
HIGHWAY FIVE BEACON (Versailles, MO) **11555**
HI-LITER (Burlington, WI) **11659**
HILL CITY PREVAILER-NEWS (Hill City, SD) **11624**
HILL COUNTRY NEWS (Cedar Park, TX) **11632**
HILLIARD NORTHWEST NEWS (Columbus, OH) **11595**
HILLSBORO ARGUS (Hillsboro, OR) **11607**
HILLSBORO JOURNAL (Hillsboro, IL) **11474**
HILLSBORO SENTRY-ENTERPRISE (Hillsboro, WI) **11661**
HILLSBORO STAR-JOURNAL (Hillsboro, KS) **11497**
HILLSBOROUGH BEACON (Hillsborough, NJ) **11564**
HILLSDALE DAILY NEWS (Hillsdale, MI) **11358**
HILLTOP PRESS (Cincinnati, OH) **11594**
HILMAR TIMES (Merced, CA) **11433**
HINGHAM JOURNAL, THE (Hingham, MA) **11519**
HINSDALE DOINGS, THE (Hinsdale, IL) **11474**
HINSDALE/OAKBROOK/WILLOWBROOK SUBURBAN LIFE (Downers Grove, IL) **11470**
HINTON NEWS (Hinton, WV) **11656**
HI-RISER (Pompano Beach, FL) **11454**

Title

HOBART CHRONICLE (Valparaiso, IN) **11488**
HOBART DEMOCRAT-CHIEF (Hobart, OK) **11604**
HOBBS NEWS-SUN (Hobbs, NM) **11370**
HOBOKEN REPORTER (Hoboken, NJ) **11564**
HOCKESSIN COMMUNITY NEWS (Hockessin, DE) **11447**
HOCKING VALLEY ADVERTISER (Logan, OH) **11597**
HOFFMAN ESTATES REVIEW (Arlington Heights, IL) **11466**
HOGANSVILLE HERALD (Manchester, GA) **11461**
HOISINGTON DISPATCH (Hoisington, KS) **11497**
HOLBROOK SUN (Weymouth, MA) **11524**
HOLBROOK TIMES (Rockland, MA) **11523**
HOLBROOK TRIBUNE NEWS (Holbrook, AZ) **11418**
HOLDEN IMAGE, THE (Holden, MO) **11551**
HOLDENVILLE NEWS (Holdenville, OK) **11604**
HOLDREGE DAILY CITIZEN (Holdrege, NE) **11367**
HOLLAND SENTINEL, THE (Holland, MI) **11358**
HOLLIS BROOKLINE JOURNAL (Milford, NH) **11560**
HOLLISTER FREE LANCE (Gilroy, CA) **11324**
HOLLISTON TAB (Framingham, MA) **11518**
HOLLY HILL OBSERVER, THE (Bamberg, SC) **11619**
HOLLY SPRINGS POST (Fuquay-Varina, NC) **11587**
HOLLYWOOD INDEPENDENT (Los Angeles, CA) **11431**
HOLMEN COURIER (West Salem, WI) **11668**
HOLMES COUNTY HERALD (Lexington, MS) **11546**
HOLMES COUNTY HUB (Loudonville, OH) **11597**
HOLMES COUNTY SHOPPER (Millersburg, OH) **11598**
HOLMES COUNTY TIMES ADVERTISER (Bonifay, FL) **11449**
HOLMES COUNTY TIMES-ADVERTISER (Bonifay, FL) **11449**
HOLT COMMUNITY NEWS (Grand Ledge, MI) **11527**
HOLT COUNTY INDEPENDENT (O'Neill, NE) **11557**
HOLTON RECORDER (Holton, KS) **11497**
HOLTVILLE TRIBUNE (Holtville, CA) **11429**
HOLYOKE SUN, THE (Chicopee, MA) **11516**
HOME & STORE NEWS (Ramsey, NJ) **11566**
HOME NEWS & TIMES (Yonkers, NY) **11585**
HOME NEWS, THE (Marshville, NC) **11588**
HOME NEWS TRIBUNE, THE (East Brunswick, NJ) **11369**
HOMER GLEN-LOCKPORT-LEMON STAR (Tinley Park, IL) **11482**
HOMER NEWS (Homer, AK) **11416**
HOMER SUN (Plainfield, IL) **11480**
HOMESTEAD NEWS (South Miami, FL) **11455**
HOMETOWN JOURNAL (Struthers, OH) **11601**
HOMETOWN SHOPPER (Willimantic, CT) **11447**
HOMEWOOD-FLOSSMOORE-GLENWOOD-OLYMPIA FIELDS STAR (Tinley Park, IL) **11482**
HOMINY NEWS-PROGRESS (Hominy, OK) **11604**
HONDO ANVIL HERALD (Hondo, TX) **11636**
HONEOYE HERALD, THE (Honeoye, NY) **11576**
HONOLULU ADVERTISER, THE (Honolulu, HI) **11337**
HONOLULU STAR-BULLETIN (Honolulu, HI) **11337**
HOOD COUNTY NEWS (Granbury, TX) **11636**
HOOD RIVER NEWS (Hood River, OR) **11607**
HOOPESTON CHRONICLE (Rensselaer, IN) **11488**
HOPE STAR, THE (Hope, AR) **11323**
HOPE STAR-JOURNAL (Hope, IN) **11486**
HOPEWELL NEWS (Hopewell, VA) **11403**
HOPEWELL VALLEY NEWS (Hopewell, NJ) **11564**
HOPKINS JOURNAL, THE (Hopkins, MO) **11551**
HOPKINS/EAST MINNETONKA SUN-SAILOR (Eden Prairie, MN) **11537**
HOPKINTON CRIER (Framingham, MA) **11518**
HORICON REPORTER (Horicon, WI) **11661**
HORNELL EVENING TRIBUNE/SUNDAY SPECTATOR (Hornell, NY) **11372**
HORRY INDEPENDENT (Conway, SC) **11620**
HOT SPRINGS STAR (Hot Springs, SD) **11624**
HOUGHTON LAKE RESORTER (Houghton Lake, MI) **11528**
HOULTON PIONEER TIMES (Houlton, ME) **11510**

HOUR, THE (Norwalk, CT) **11331**
HOUSATONIC LIVING (New Milford, CT) **11445**
HOUSTON CHRONICLE (Houston, TX) **11399**
HOUSTON COUNTY COURIER (Crockett, TX) **11633**
HOUSTON FORWARD TIMES (Houston, TX) **11636**
HOUSTON HERALD (Houston, MO) **11551**
HOUSTON HOME JOURNAL, THE (Perry, GA) **11336**
HOUSTON INFORMER (Houston, TX) **11636**
HOUSTON PRESS (Houston, TX) **11636**
HOUSTON TRIBUNE (Houston, TX) **11636**
HOWARD COUNTY TIMES (Columbia, MD) **11512**
HUBBARD CITY NEWS (Maxia, TX) **11638**
HUBBARD PRESS (Sharon, PA) **11616**
HUBER HEIGHTS COURIER (Huber Heights, OH) **11596**
HUDSON CURRENT (Hoboken, NJ) **11564**
HUDSON HERALD, THE (Hudson, IA) **11493**
HUDSON HUB-TIMES (Stow, OH) **11601**
HUDSON LITCHFIELD NEWS (Hudson, NH) **11560**
HUDSON STAR-OBSERVER (Hudson, WI) **11661**
HUDSON SUN (Marlborough, MA) **11519**
HUGHES COUNTY TIMES (Wetumka, OK) **11606**
HUGHSON CHRONICLE (Merced, CA) **11433**
HUGO DAILY NEWS (Hugo, OK) **11385**
HULL TIMES, THE (Hull, MA) **11519**
HUMBOLDT BEACON, THE (Fontuna, CA) **11429**
HUMBOLDT CHRONICLE, THE (Humboldt, TN) **11627**
HUMBOLDT INDEPENDENT (Humboldt, IA) **11493**
HUMBOLDT SUN (Winnemucca, NV) **11559**
HUMBOLT JOURNAL (Canistota, SD) **11624**
HUNGRY HORSE NEWS (Columbia Falls, MT) **11555**
HUNT COUNTY SHOPPER (Greenville, TX) **11636**
HUNTERDON COUNTY DEMOCRAT (Flemington, NJ) **11563**
HUNTERDON REVIEW (Lebanon, NJ) **11564**
HUNTINGTON BEACH/FOUNTAIN VALLEY INDEPENDENT (Costa Mesa, CA) **11428**
HUNTINGTON HERALD, THE (Shelton, CT) **11446**
HUNTSVILLE ITEM, THE (Huntsville, TX) **11399**
HUNTSVILLE TIMES, THE (Huntsville, AL) **11320**
HURON COUNTY PRESS (Bad Axe, MI) **11525**
HURON DAILY TRIBUNE (Bad Axe, MI) **11357**
HURRICANE BREEZE (Hurricane, WV) **11656**
HUTCHINSON HERALD, THE (Menno, SD) **11624**
HUTCHINSON LEADER (Hutchinson, MN) **11538**
HUTCHINSON NEWS (Hutchinson, KS) **11349**
HYATTSVILLE/RIVERDALE GAZETTE (Landover, MD) **11513**
HYDE PARK HERALD (Chicago, IL) **11468**
HYDE PARK TOWNSMAN (Rhinebeck, NY) **11581**
HYDE PARK/MATTAPAN TRIBUNE (Hyde Park, MA) **11519**

I

IDAHO COUNTY FREE PRESS (Grangeville, ID) **11464**
IDAHO ENTERPRISE (Malad City, ID) **11465**
IDAHO FALLS POST REGISTER (Idaho Falls, ID) **11337**
IDAHO MOUNTAIN EXPRESS (Ketchum, ID) **11465**
IDAHO PRESS-TRIBUNE (Nampa, ID) **11337**
IDAHO STATE JOURNAL (Seattle, WA) **11405**
IDAHO STATESMAN, THE (Boise, ID) **11337**
IDALOU BEACON (Idalou, TX) **11637**
IDYLLWILD TOWN CRIER (Idyllwild, CA) **11429**
ILE CAMERA, THE (Grosse Ile, MI) **11528**
ILLINOIS TIMES (Springfield, IL) **11481**
ILLINOIS TIMES, THE (Munster, IN) **11345**
ILLIOPOLIS SENTINEL (Illiopolis, IL) **11474**
ILLUSTRATED NEWS, THE (Mineola, NY) **11578**
IMAGE (GREENFIELD) (Greenfield, IN) **11486**
IMAGES (Herkimer, NY) **11576**
IMMOKALEE BULLETIN (La Belle, FL) **11452**

IMPACT / LAUREL (Laurel, MS) **11546**
IMPACT MAIL OF MERIDIAN (Bay Springs, MS) **11545**
IMPACT OF HATTIESBURG (Hattiesburg, MS) **11546**
IMPERIAL BEACH EAGLE & TIMESN (Imperial Beach, CA) **11430**
IMPERIAL VALLEY PRESS (El Centro, CA) **11324**
INDEPENDENCE BULLETIN-JOURNAL (Independence, IA) **11493**
INDEPENDENCE DAILY REPORTER (Independence, KS) **11349**
INDEPENDENCE EXAMINER, THE (Independence, MO) **11364**
INDEPENDENCE NEWS, THE (Independence, KS) **11497**
INDEPENDENT APPEAL (Selmer, TN) **11629**
INDEPENDENT (COLLIERVILLE) (Collierville, TN) **11626**
INDEPENDENT (DEERFIELD) (Deerfield, WI) **11660**
INDEPENDENT (DURHAM), THE (Durham, NC) **11586**
INDEPENDENT ENTERPRISE (Payette, ID) **11465**
INDEPENDENT (GALLUP) (Gallup, NM) **11370**
INDEPENDENT HERALD (ONEIDA) (Oneida, TN) **11629**
INDEPENDENT HERALD (WILLIAMSON), THE (Williamson, WV) **11657**
INDEPENDENT (LEROY), THE (Leroy, MN) **11539**
INDEPENDENT (LIVERMORE), THE (Livermore, CA) **11431**
INDEPENDENT (MASSILLON), THE (Massillon, OH) **11382**
INDEPENDENT MESSENGER (Emporia, VA) **11646**
INDEPENDENT MIRROR (Mexico, NY) **11578**
INDEPENDENT NEWS (Georgetown, IL) **11472**
INDEPENDENT NEWS HERALD (Clarissa, MN) **11536**
INDEPENDENT PRESS (New Providence, NJ) **11565**
INDEPENDENT PRESS OF BLOOMFIELD, THE (Bloomfield, NJ) **11561**
INDEPENDENT RECORD (Helena, MT) **11366**
INDEPENDENT (ROBERTSDALE), THE (Robertsdale, AL) **11415**
INDEPENDENT TRAVELER-WATCHMAN, THE (East Hampton, NY) **11573**
INDEPENDENT TRIBUNE (Kannapolis, NC) **11377**
INDEPENDENT (WINAMAC), THE (Winamac, IN) **11489**
INDEPENDENT-JOURNAL, THE (Potosi, MO) **11552**
INDEPENDENT-OBSERVER, THE (Scottdale, PA) **11616**
INDEPENDENT-REGISTER, THE (Brodhead, WI) **11658**
INDEX, THE (Hermitage, MO) **11551**
INDEX-JOURNAL (Greenwood, SC) **11394**
INDIAN HILL JOURNAL (Loveland, OH) **11597**
INDIANA GAZETTE, THE (Indiana, PA) **11389**
INDIANAPOLIS RECORDER (Indianapolis, IN) **11486**
INDIANAPOLIS STAR & NEWS (Indianapolis, IN) **11344**
INDIANHEAD ADVERTISER (Frederic, WI) **11660**
INFO (GARY) (Gary, IN) **11486**
INGHAM COUNTY COMMUNITY NEWS (Grand Ledge, MI) **11528**
INGLEWOOD TRIBUNE (Compton, CA) **11428**
INKSTER LEDGER-STAR (Wayne, MI) **11533**
INLAND VALLEY DAILY BULLETIN (Ontario, CA) **11326**
INMAN TIMES (Inman, SC) **11621**
INNER CITY (New Haven, CT) **11445**
INQUIRER & MIRROR, THE (Nantucket, MA) **11521**
INSIDE PUBLICATION (Chicago, IL) **11469**
INTELLIGENCER (DOYLESTOWN), THE (Doylestown, PA) **11388**
INTELLIGENCER JOURNAL (Lancaster, PA) **11389**
INTELLIGENCER, THE (Wheeling, WV) **11407**
INTELLIGENCER-RECORD, THE (Horsham, PA) **11389**
INTER-COUNTY LEADER (Frederic, WI) **11660**
INTERIOR JOURNAL, THE (Stanford, KY) **11505**
INTERLAKEN REVIEW (Trumansburg, NY) **11583**
INTERMOUNTAIN NEWS, THE (Burney, CA) **11427**
INTER-MOUNTAIN, THE (Elkins, WV) **11406**
INTOWNER, THE (Washington, DC) **11448**

Title

KENBRIDGE-VICTORIA DISPATCH (Victoria, VA) 11650

KENDALL COUNTY RECORD (Yorkville, IL) 11484

KENDALL GAZETTE (South Miami, FL) 11455

KENLY NEWS (Kenly, NC) 11587

KENMORE RECORD-ADVERTISER (North Tonawanda, NY) 11580

KENNEBEC JOURNAL (Augusta, ME) 11354

KENNESAW NEIGHBOR, THE (Marietta, GA) 11461

KENNETT PAPER, THE (Kennett Square, PA) 11612

KENOSHA BULLETIN (Kenosha, WI) 11662

KENOSHA NEWS (Kenosha, WI) 11408

KENSINGTON GAZETTE (Gaithersburg, MD) 11513

KENT COUNTY DAILY TIMES (West Warwick, RI) 11393

KENT COUNTY NEWS (Chestertown, MD) 11512

KEN-TON BEE (Williamsville, NY) 11584

KENTON COMMUNITY RECORDER (Fort Mitchell, KY) 11502

KENTON TIMES (Kenton, OH) 11381

KENTUCKY ENQUIRER (Cincinnati, OH) 11380

KENTUCKY GAZETTE, THE (Frankfort, KY) 11502

KENTUCKY NEW ERA (Hopkinsville, KY) 11351

KENTUCKY POST, THE (Covington, KY) 11351

KENTUCKY STANDARD (Bardstown, KY) 11500

KENTWOOD ADVANCE (Jenison, MI) 11529

KENTWOOD LEDGER (Kentwood, LA) 11507

KENYON LEADER (Kenyon, MN) 11539

KEOWEE COURIER (Westminster, SC) 11623

KERMAN NEWS (Kerman, CA) 11430

KERN VALLEY SUN (Lake Isabella, CA) 11431

KERNERSVILLE NEWS (Kernersville, NC) 11587

KERRVILLE DAILY TIMES (Kerrville, TX) 11399

KETCHIKAN DAILY NEWS (Ketchikan, AK) 11321

KETTERING-OAKWOOD TIMES (Kettering, OH) 11597

KETTLE MORAINE INDEX (Hartland, WI) 11661

KEWASKUM STATESMAN (Kewaskum, WI) 11662

KEWAUNEE ENTERPRISE (Kewaunee, WI) 11662

KEY LARGO FREE PRESS (Tavernier, FL) 11456

KEY WEST CITIZEN, THE (Key West, FL) 11333

KEY WEST KEYNOTER, THE (Key West, FL) 11451

KILGORE NEWS HERALD (Kilgore, TX) 11399

KILLEEN DAILY HERALD (Killeen, TX) 11399

KING CITY RUSTLER (King City, CA) 11430

KING OF PRUSSIA COURIER (Wayne, PA) 11617

KINGFISHER TIMES & FREE PRESS (Kingfisher, OK) 11604

KINGMAN DAILY MINER (Kingman, AZ) 11321

KINGMAN LEADER-COURIER, THE (Kingman, KS) 11497

KINGS COUNTY NEWS (Brooklyn, NY) 11571

KINGS COURIER (Brooklyn, NY) 11571

KINGSBURG RECORDER (Kingsburg, CA) 11430

KINGSPORT TIMES-NEWS (Kingsport, TN) 11396

KINGSTON MARINER (Marshfield, MA) 11520

KINGSTON REPORTER (Plymouth, MA) 11522

KINGSVILLE RECORD, THE (Kingsville, TX) 11637

KINMUNDY EXPRESS (Kinmundy, IL) 11474

KINSTON DAILY FREE PRESS (Kinston, NC) 11377

KIOWA COUNTY PRESS (Eads, CO) 11440

KIOWA COUNTY SIGNAL (Greenburg, KS) 11497

KIRKLAND REPOTER (Poulsbo, WA) 11653

KIRKSVILLE CRIER (Kirksville, MO) 11551

KIRKSVILLE DAILY EXPRESS (Kirksville, MO) 11364

KITSAP SUN (Bremerton, WA) 11404

KNOXVILLE JOURNAL EXPRESS, THE (Knoxville, IA) 11493

KODIAK DAILY MIRROR (Kodiak, AK) 11321

KOKOMO TRIBUNE (Kokomo, IN) 11344

KONAWA LEADER (Konawa, OK) 11604

L

L A WEEKLY (Los Angeles, CA) 11431

LA CANADA VALLEY SUN (La Canada, CA) 11430

LA CROSSE TRIBUNE (La Crosse, WI) 11408

LA FOLLETTE PRESS (La Follette, TN) 11627

LA GRANGE DAILY NEWS (La Grange, GA) 11336

LA GRANGE DOINGS, THE (Hinsdale, IL) 11474

LA GRANGE STANDARD NEWS (La Grange, IN) 11486

LA JOLLA LIGHT (La Jolla, CA) 11430

LA JOLLA VILLAGE NEWS (San Diego, CA) 11436

LA PORTE HERALD-ARGUS (La Porte, IN) 11344

LACON HOME JOURNAL (Lacon, IL) 11475

LADUE NEWS (St Louis, MO) 11553

LADYSMITH NEWS (Ladysmith, WI) 11662

LAFAYETTE COUNTY DEMOCRAT (Lewisville, AR) 11422

LAFAYETTE LEADER (Lafayette, IN) 11486

LAFAYETTE SUN, THE (Lafayette, LA) 11507

LAGRANGE/LAGRANGE PARK/WESTERN SPRINGS SUBURBAN LIFE (LaGrange Park, IL) 11475

LAGUAN NIGUEL NEWS (Lake Forest, CA) 11430

LAGUNA NEWS POST (Lake Forest, CA) 11431

LAHONTAN VALLEY NEWS & FALLON EAGLE STANDARD (Fallon, NV) 11368

LAJUNTA TRIBUNE-DEMOCRAT (La Junta, CO) 11330

LAKE AREA LEADER (Mabank, TX) 11638

LAKE CHELAN MIRROR (Chelan, WA) 11651

LAKE CITY NEWS & POST (Lake City, SC) 11621

LAKE CITY REPORTER (Lake City, FL) 11333

LAKE COUNTRY ECHO (Pequot Lakes, MN) 11541

LAKE COUNTRY REPORTER (Hartland, WI) 11661

LAKE COUNTRY SUN (Graford, TX) 11635

LAKE COUNTY BANNER, THE (Tiptonville, TN) 11630

LAKE COUNTY EXAMINER (Lakeview, OR) 11608

LAKE COUNTY GAZETTE, THE (Madison, OH) 11598

LAKE COUNTY LEADER (Polson, MT) 11556

LAKE COUNTY NEWS-CHRONICLE (Two Harbors, MN) 11544

LAKE COUNTY RECORD-BEE (Lakeport, CA) 11325

LAKE COUNTY STAR (Baldwin, MI) 11525

LAKE COUNTY TRIBUNE, THE (Madison, OH) 11598

LAKE ELSINORE VALLEY SUN-TRIBUNE (Riverside, CA) 11435

LAKE FORESTER (Waukegan, IL) 11483

LAKE GENEVA REGIONAL NEWS (Kenosha, WI) 11662

LAKE HAVASU CITY WHITE SHEET (Lake Havasu City, AZ) 11418

LAKE LIVINGSTON PROGRESS (Livingston, TX) 11638

LAKE LOS ANGELES NEWS (Lake Los Angeles, CA) 11431

LAKE MILLS LEADER (Lake Mills, WI) 11662

LAKE MURRAY NEWS (Irmo, SC) 11621

LAKE NEWS (CALVERT CITY), THE (Calvert City, KY) 11500

LAKE NEWS (FRUITLAND PARK) (Fruitland Park, FL) 11451

LAKE OCONEE BREEZE (Madison, GA) 11461

LAKE ORION ECCENTRIC (Rochester, MI) 11531

LAKE OSWEGO REVIEW (Lake Oswego, OR) 11607

LAKE PLACID JOURNAL (Lake Placid, FL) 11452

LAKE PLACID NEWS (Lake Placid, NY) 11576

LAKE POWELL CHRONICLE (Page, AZ) 11419

LAKE REGION LIFE (Waterville, MN) 11544

LAKE REGION MONITOR (Keystone Heights, FL) 11452

LAKE REGION TIMES (Madison Lake, MN) 11539

LAKE SUN LEADER (Camdenton, MO) 11363

LAKE SUN LEADER - PENNYSAVER (Camdenton, MO) 11548

LAKE TRAVIS VIEW (Austin, TX) 11631

LAKE VILLA RECORD (Grayslake, IL) 11473

LAKE VILLA/LINDENHURST REVIEW (Waukegan, IL) 11483

LAKE WALES NEWS (Lake Wales, FL) 11452

LAKE WATEREE NEWS (Camden, SC) 11620

LAKE WORTH FORUM (Wellington, FL) 11456

LAKE WORTH HERALD (Lake Worth, FL) 11452

LAKE WYLIE PILOT (Lake Wylie, SC) 11621

LAKE ZURICH COURIER (Algonquin, IL) 11466

LAKEFIELD STANDARD (Jackson, MN) 11539

LAKELAND SHOPPING GUIDE (Alexandria, MN) 11534

LAKELAND TIMES (Minocqua, WI) 11663

LAKER (LUTZ), THE (Lutz, FL) 11452

LAKER (MOUND), THE (Mound, MN) 11540

LAKES REGION FREEPRESS, THE (Granville, NY) 11575

LAKESHORE CHRONICLE (Manitowoc, WI) 11662

LAKESHORE WEEKLY NEWS (Wayzata, MN) 11544

LAKEVILLE CALL (Rayham, MA) 11522

LAKEVILLE JOURNAL, THE (Lakeville, CT) 11444

LAKEVILLE SUN-CURRENT (Eden Prairie, MN) 11537

LAKEVILLE THISWEEK (Burnsville, MN) 11535

LAKEWOOD NEWS TIMES, THE (Rocky River, OH) 11600

LAKEWOOD SENTINEL (Lakewood, CO) 11441

LAKEWOOD SUN POST (North Olmsted, OH) 11599

LAMAR DAILY NEWS (Lamar, CO) 11330

LAMAR DEMOCRAT (Lamar, MO) 11551

LAMAR DEMOCRAT (VERNON) (Vernon, AL) 11416

LAMAR LEADER (Sulligent, AL) 11415

LAMB COUNTY LEADER-NEWS (Littlefield, TX) 11638

LAMBERTON NEWS (Lamberton, MN) 11539

LAMESA PRESS-REPORTER (Lamesa, TX) 11638

LAMONT REPORTER (Lamont, CA) 11431

LANCASTER BEE (Williamsville, NY) 11584

LANCASTER EAGLE-GAZETTE (Lancaster, OH) 11381

LANCASTER NEW ERA (Lancaster, PA) 11390

LANCASTER NEWS (Lancaster, SC) 11621

LANCASTER TIMES & CLINTON COURIER (Clinton, MA) 11516

LANCASTER TODAY (Desoto, TX) 11634

LANCASTER-FAIRFIELD ADVERTISER (McLean, VA) 11649

LANDER JOURNAL (Lander, WY) 11669

LANDMARK, THE (Oak Park, IL) 11478

LANDOVER GAZETTE (Landover, MD) 11513

LANHAM GAZETTE (Landover, MD) 11514

LANIER COUNTY NEWS (Lakeland, GA) 11461

L'ANSE SENTINEL (L'Anse, MI) 11529

LANSING STATE JOURNAL (Lansing, MI) 11358

LANSING THIS WEEK WEEKLY (Leavenworth, KS) 11498

LARAMIE BOOMERANG (Laramie, WY) 11409

LARGO GAZETTE (Landover, MD) 11514

LARGO LEADER (Seminole, FL) 11455

LARUE COUNTY HERALD-NEWS (Hodgenville, KY) 11503

LAS CRUCES SUN-NEWS (Las Cruces, NM) 11370

LAS VEGAS DAILY OPTIC (Las Vegas, NM) 11371

LAS VEGAS REVIEW-JOURNAL (Las Vegas, NV) 11368

LAS VEGAS SUN (Henderson, NV) 11368

LAS VEGAS TODAY (Las Vegas, NV) 11559

LAS VIRGENES ENTERPRISE (Woodland Hills, CA) 11439

LATHROP BULLETIN (Manteca, CA) 11432

LATROBE BULLETIN (Latrobe, PA) 11390

LAUDERDALE COUNTY ENTERPRISE (Ripley, TN) 11629

LAUDERDALE VOICE, THE (Ripley, TN) 11629

LAUGHLIN NEVADA TIMES, THE (Laughlin, NV) 11559

LAUREL GAZETTE (Landover, MD) 11514

LAUREL LEADER (Laurel, MD) 11514

LAUREL LEADER-CALL (Laurel, MS) 11362

LAURELTON TIMES (Bayside, NY) 11570

LAURENS COUNTY ADVERTISER (Laurens, SC) 11621

LAURINBURG EXCHANGE (Laurinburg, NC) 11377

Title

LOWELL LEDGER (Lowell, MI) 11530
LOWELL SUN (Lowell, MA) 11356
LOWELL TRIBUNE (Lowell, IN) 11487
LOWNDES SIGNAL, THE (Greenville, AL) 11413
LOYAL TRIBUNE RECORD GLEANER (Loyal, WI) 11662
LUBBOCK AVALANCHE-JOURNAL (Lubbock, TX) 11399
LUBEC LIGHT, THE (Lubec, ME) 11510
LUDINGTON DAILY NEWS (Ludington, MI) 11358
LUFKIN DAILY NEWS, THE (Lufkin, TX) 11399
LULING NEWSBOY & SIGNAL (Luling, TX) 11638
LUSK HERALD (Lusk, WY) 11669
LUTZ COMMUNITY NEWS (Lutz, FL) 11452
LUVERNE JOURNAL, THE (Greenville, AL) 11413
LYNDEN TRIBUNE (Lynden, WA) 11653
LYNN JOURNAL (Revere, MA) 11523
LYNNFIELD VILLAGER (Lynnfield, MA) 11519
LYNNWOOD/MOUNTLAKE TERRACE ENTERPRISE (Lynnwood, WA) 11653
LYNWOOD JOURNAL (Compton, CA) 11428
LYNWOOD PRESS EDITION (Los Angeles, CA) 11431
LYONS CLYDE SAVANNAH SHOPPING (Newark, NY) 11580
LYONS DAILY NEWS (Lyons, KS) 11350
LYONS MIRROR-SUN (Lyons, NE) 11557
LYONS RECORDER, THE (Lyons, CO) 11441
LYON-SIOUX PRESS (Rock Rapids, IA) 11495

M

M & M JOURNAL (Hillsboro, IL) 11474
MABLETON NEIGHBOR, THE (Marietta, GA) 11461
MACHIAS VALLEY NEWS OBSERVER (Calous, ME) 11509
MACKINAW JOURNAL (Cheboygan, MI) 11526
MACOMB DAILY, THE (Mt Clemens, MI) 11359
MACOMB EAGLE (Macomb, IL) 11475
MACOMB JOURNAL (Macomb, IL) 11340
MACOMB TOWNSHIP VOICE, THE (New Baltimore, MI) 11530
MACON BEACON, THE (Macon, MS) 11547
MACON CHRONICLE-HERALD (Macon, MO) 11364
MACON COUNTY TIMES (Lafayette, TN) 11627
MACON JOURNAL (Macon, MO) 11551
MACOUPIN COUNTY ENQUIRER-DEMOCRAT (Carlinville, IL) 11468
MACOUPIN COUNTY SHOPPER (Hillsboro, IL) 11474
MADELIA TIMES-MESSENGER (Madelia, MN) 11539
MADERA TRIBUNE (Madera, CA) 11325
MADILL RECORD (Madill, OK) 11605
MADISON COUNTY (AL) RECORD (Madison, AL) 11414
MADISON COUNTY (AR) RECORD (Huntsville, AR) 11422
MADISON COUNTY CARRIER (Madison, FL) 11452
MADISON COUNTY CHRONICLE (Worden, IL) 11484
MADISON COUNTY EAGLE, THE (Madison, VA) 11648
MADISON COUNTY HERALD (Ridgeland, MS) 11547
MADISON COUNTY JOURNAL (Danielsville, GA) 11459
MADISON COURIER (Madison, IN) 11344
MADISON DAILY LEADER (Madison, SD) 11394
MADISON EAGLE (Madison, NJ) 11565
MADISON ENTERPRISE-RECORDER, THE (Madison, FL) 11452
MADISON JOURNAL (Tallulah, LA) 11508
MADISON MESSENGER, THE (Madison, NC) 11588
MADISON NEWS, THE (Madison, KS) 11498
MADISON PARK TIMES (Seattle, WA) 11654
MADISON PRESS, THE (London, OH) 11381
MADRAS PIONEER, THE (Madras, OR) 11608
MAGEE COURIER, THE (Magee, MS) 11547
MAGIC VALLEY SHOPPER'S NEWS (Camden, TN) 11625
MAGNA TIMES (Magna, UT) 11643
MAGNOLIA GAZETTE, THE (Magnolia, MS) 11547
MAGNOLIA POTPOURRI (Tomball, TX) 11641

MAHNOMEN PIONEER, THE (Mahnomen, MN) 11539
MAHOPAC PRESS (Mahopac, NY) 11577
MAHWAH SUBURBAN NEWS (Ridgewood, NJ) 11566
MAIL TRIBUNE (Medford, OR) 11387
MAIL-JOURNAL, THE (Milford, IN) 11487
MAIN LINE LIFE (Wynnewood, PA) 11618
MAIN LINE TIMES (Ardmore, PA) 11610
MAIN STREET NEWS (Essex, CT) 11444
MAINLAND JOURNAL (Hammonton, NJ) 11563
MAINLINER, THE (Ebensberg, PA) 11611
MALDEN EVENING NEWS (Malden, MA) 11356
MALDEN OBSERVER (Medford, MA) 11520
MALHEUR ENTERPRISE (Vale, OR) 11609
MALIBU SURFSIDE NEWS (Malibu, CA) 11432
MALIBU TIMES (Malibu, CA) 11432
MALONE TELEGRAM (Malone, NY) 11372
MALTA PENNYSAVER (Round Lake, NY) 11581
MALTA SPOTLIGHT (Delmar, NY) 11573
MALVERN DAILY RECORD (Malvern, AR) 11323
MALVERN LEADER, THE (Malvern, IA) 11493
MAMMOTH TIMES (Mammoth Lakes, CA) 11432
MAMOU ACADIAN PRESS (Ville Platte, LA) 11508
MANASSAS JOURNAL MESSENGER (Manassas, VA) 11403
MANAWA ADVOCATE (Iola, WI) 11661
MANCHESTER CRICKET, THE (Manchester, MA) 11519
MANCHESTER JOURNAL, THE (Manchester Center, VT) 11644
MANCHESTER (KY) ENTERPRISE, THE (Manchester, KY) 11504
MANCHESTER (MI) ENTERPRISE, THE (Manchester, MI) 11530
MANCHESTER PRESS (Manchester, IA) 11493
MANCHESTER STAR-MERCURY (Manchester, GA) 11461
MANCHESTER TIMES (Manchester, TN) 11628
MANCOS TIMES, THE (Cortez, CO) 11440
MANDAN NEWS (Mandan, ND) 11591
MANHASSET PRESS (Mineola, NY) 11578
MANHATTAN MERCURY (Manhattan, KS) 11350
MANISTEE NEWS ADVOCATE (Manistee, MI) 11359
MANISTIQUE PIONEER-TRIBUNE (Manistique, MI) 11530
MANNFORD EAGLE (Mannford, OK) 11605
MANNING TIMES, THE (Manning, SC) 11622
MANSFIELD ENTERPRISE (Mansfield, LA) 11507
MANSFIELD GAZETTE (Wellsboro, PA) 11618
MANSFIELD MIRROR, THE (Mansfield, MO) 11551
MANSFIELD NEWS, THE (Milford, MA) 11521
MANSFIELD NEWS-MIRROR (Mainsfield, TX) 11638
MANTECA BULLETIN (Manteca, CA) 11325
MANVILLE NEWS, THE (Hillsborough, NJ) 11564
MAPLE HEIGHTS PRESS (Stow, OH) 11601
MAPLE LAKE MESSENGER (Maple Lake, MN) 11539
MAPLE RIVER MESSENGER (Mapleton, MN) 11539
MAPLE SHADE PROGRESS (Medford, NJ) 11565
MAPLE VALLEY NEWS (Hastings, MI) 11528
MAPLEWOOD REVIEW (St Paul, MN) 11543
MAQUOKETA SENTINEL-PRESS (Maquoketa, IA) 11494
MARATHON/BIG PINE/LOWER KEYS FREE PRESS (Marathon, FL) 11452
MARBLE FALLS HIGHLANDER (Marble Falls, TX) 11638
MARBLEHEAD REPORTER (Marblehead, MA) 11519
MARCELLUS OBSERVER (Skaneateles, NY) 11582
MARCO ISLAND EAGLE (Marco Island, FL) 11452
MARCUS HOOK PRESS (Drexel Hill, PA) 11611
MARENGO COUNTY SHOPPERS GUIDE (Demopolis, AL) 11412
MARGATE FORUM (Coconut Creek, FL) 11450
MARIANAS VARIETY NEWS & VIEWS (Saipan, MP) 11360
MARIANNA COURIER INDEX (Marianna, AR) 11423
MARICOPA MONITOR (Maricopa, AZ) 11419

MARIES COUNTY GAZETTE (Vienna, MO) 11555
MARIETTA DAILY JOURNAL (Marietta, GA) 11336
MARIETTA TIMES (Marietta, OH) 11381
MARIN INDEPENDENT JOURNAL (Novato, CA) 11325
MARIN SCOPE (Sausalito, CA) 11437
MARION ADVERTISER (Marion, WI) 11662
MARION COUNTY RECORD (Marion, KS) 11498
MARION COUNTY REMINDER (Knoxville, IA) 11493
MARION DAILY EXTRA (Marion, IL) 11475
MARION DAILY REPUBLICAN (Marion, IL) 11340
MARION RECORD (Canistota, SD) 11624
MARION STAR & MULLINS ENTERPRISE (Marion, SC) 11622
MARION STAR, THE (Marion, OH) 11381
MARION TIMES-STANDARD (Marion, AL) 11414
MARIPOSA GAZETTE (Mariposa, CA) 11432
MARKESAN REGIONAL REPORTER (Berlin, WI) 11658
MARKET (Port Gibson, MS) 11547
MARKET SHOPPER, THE (Delano, CA) 11428
MARKETEER (GONZALES), THE (Gonzales, LA) 11507
MARKETPLACE (GAYLORD) (Gaylord, MI) 11527
MARKETPLACE (MADISON) (Madison, WI) 11662
MARLBORO HERALD-ADVOCATE (Bennettsville, SC) 11620
MARLBORO SHOPPER (Bennettsville, SC) 11620
MARLBOROUGH ENTERPRISE (Marlborough, MA) 11520
MARQUETTE COUNTY TRIBUNE (Montello, WI) 11663
MARQUETTE TRIBUNE (MARQUETTE) (Marquette, KS) 11498
MARSHALL CHRONICLE (Marshall, MI) 11530
MARSHALL COMMUNITY AD-VISOR (Marshall, MI) 11530
MARSHALL DEMOCRAT-NEWS (Marshall, MO) 11364
MARSHALL GAZETTE (Lewisburg, TN) 11628
MARSHALL INDEPENDENT (Marshall, MN) 11361
MARSHALL INDEPENDENT CHOICE, THE (Casey, IL) 11468
MARSHALL MOUNTAIN WAVE (Marshall, AR) 11423
MARSHALL NEWS MESSENGER, THE (Marshall, TX) 11399
MARSHFIELD MAIL, THE (Marshfield, MO) 11552
MARSHFIELD MARINER (Marshfield, MA) 11520
MARSHFIELD NEWS-HERALD (Marshfield, WI) 11408
MARSHFIELD REPORTER (Marshfield, MA) 11520
MARTHASVILLE RECORD, THE (Marthasville, MO) 11552
MARTIN COUNTY STAR (Sherburn, MN) 11543
MARTINEZ NEWS GAZETTE (Martinez, CA) 11432
MARTINSVILLE BULLETIN (Martinsville, VA) 11403
MARYLAND BEACHCOMBER, THE (Ocean City, MD) 11514
MARYLAND GAZETTE (Glen Burnie, MD) 11513
MARYLAND INDEPENDENT (Waldorf, MD) 11515
MARYLAND TIMES PRESS (Ocean City, MD) 11514
MARYSVILLE ADVOCATE, THE (Marysville, KS) 11498
MARYSVILLE GLOBE, THE (Marysville, WA) 11653
MARYSVILLE JOURNAL-TRIBUNE (Marysville, OH) 11382
MARYVILLE DAILY FORUM (Maryville, MO) 11364
MASCOUTAH HERALD (Mascoutah, IL) 11475
MASHPEE ENTERPRISE (Falmouth, MA) 11518
MASHPEE/COTUIT PENNYSAVER (Yarmouthport, MA) 11524
MASON COUNTY DEMOCRAT (Havana, IL) 11473
MASON COUNTY NEWS (Mason, TX) 11638
MASON VALLEY NEWS (Yerington, NV) 11559
MASSAPEQUA POST (Massapequa Park, NY) 11578
MASSAPEQUAN OBSERVER (Mineola, NY) 11578
MAT - SU VALLEY FRONTIERSMAN, THE (Wasilla, AK) 11417
MATHIS NEWS (Mathis, TX) 11638
MAUI NEWS, THE (Wailuku, HI) 11337
MAUI TIME WEEKLY (Lahaina, HI) 11464
MAUMELLE MONITOR (Maumelle, AR) 11423
MAYFIELD MESSENGER (Mayfield, KY) 11352
MAYO FREE PRESS (Branford, FL) 11449
MAYVILLE MONITOR (Mayville, MI) 11530
MAYVILLE NEWS, THE (Mayville, WI) 11662
MCCOOK DAILY GAZETTE (McCook, NE) 11367
MCCORMICK MESSENGER (McCormick, SC) 11622

MCCREARY COUNTY RECORD (Whitley City, KY) **11506**
MCCURTAIN DAILY GAZETTE (Idabel, OK) **11385**
MCDONOUGH DEMOCRAT (Bushnell, IL) **11468**
MCDOWELL EXPRESS (Marion, NC) **11588**
MCDOWELL NEWS, THE (Marion, NC) **11377**
MCDUFFIE PROGRESS, THE (Thomson, GA) **11463**
MCFARLAND THISTLE (McFarland, WI) **11663**
MCGEHEE-DERMOTT TIMES NEWS (McGehee, AR) **11423**
MCINTOSH TIMES (McIntosh, MN) **11539**
MCKEESPORT DAILY NEWS (McKeesport, PA) **11390**
MCKENZIE BANNER (McKenzie, TN) **11628**
MCKINNEY COURIER GAZETTE (McKinney, TX) **11399**
MCLEAN CONNECTION (McLean, VA) **11649**
MCLEAN COUNTY INDEPENDENT (Garrison, ND) **11591**
MCLEAN COUNTY JOURNAL (Turtle Lake, ND) **11592**
MCLEAN COUNTY NEWS (Calhoun, KY) **11500**
MCLEAN TIMES (Reston, VA) **11650**
MCLEANSBORO TIMES-LEADER (McLeansboro, IL) **11475**
MCLEOD COUNTY CHRONICLE, THE (Glencoe, MN) **11538**
MCPHERSON SENTINEL (McPherson, KS) **11350**
MEADE COUNTY TIMES-TRIBUNE (Sturgis, SD) **11625**
MEADVILLE TRIBUNE, THE (Meadville, PA) **11390**
MEBANE ENTERPRISE (Mebane, NC) **11588**
MECHANICSVILLE LOCAL (Mechanicsville, VA) **11649**
MECKLENBURG SUN (Clarksville, VA) **11646**
MEDFIELD PRESS (Needham, MA) **11521**
MEDFORD DAILY MERCURY (Malden, MA) **11356**
MEDFORD NEWS (Nesconset, NY) **11579**
MEDFORD TRANSCRIPT, THE (Medford, MA) **11520**
MEDINA COUNTY GAZETTE (Medina, OH) **11382**
MEDINA SUN, THE (Medina, OH) **11598**
MELBOURNE TIMES, THE (Melbourne, AR) **11423**
MELROSE BEACON (Melrose, MN) **11539**
MELROSE FREE PRESS (Danvers, MA) **11517**
MELROSE PARK HERALD (Oak Park, IL) **11478**
MEMORIAL EXAMINER (Houston, TX) **11636**
MEMPHIS FLYER (Memphis, TN) **11628**
MEMPHIS SILVER STAR NEWS (Memphis, TN) **11628**
MENA STAR (Mena, AR) **11423**
MENARD COUNTY REVIEW (Petersburg, IL) **11480**
MENARD NEWS & MESSENGER, THE (Menard, TX) **11639**
MENDOCINO BEACON, THE (Ft Bragg, CA) **11429**
MENDOTA REPORTER, THE (Mendota, IL) **11475**
MENOMONEE FALLS NEWS (New Berlin, WI) **11664**
MEQUON-THIENSVILLE COURANT (New Berlin, WI) **11664**
MERAMEC JOURNAL, THE (Festus, MO) **11550**
MERCED COUNTY TIMES (Merced, CA) **11433**
MERCED SUN-STAR (Merced, CA) **11325**
MERCER COUNTY CHRONICLE (Coldwater, OH) **11595**
MERCURY (POTTSTOWN), THE (Pottstown, PA) **11391**
MEREDITH NEWS, THE (Meredith, NH) **11560**
MERIDIAN STAR (Meridian, MS) **11362**
MERIWETHER VINDICATOR (Manchester, GA) **11461**
MERRICK BEACON (Hempstead, NY) **11576**
MERRICK LIFE (Merrick, NY) **11578**
MERRIMACK JOURNAL (Milford, NH) **11560**
MERRIMACK RIVER CURRENT (Danvers, MA) **11517**
MESA INDEPENDENT (Apache Junction, AZ) **11417**
MESABI DAILY NEWS (Virginia, MN) **11361**
MESQUITE NEWS (Mesquite, TX) **11639**
MESSAGE FOR THE WEEK (Chester, VT) **11644**
MESSENGER (ATTICA), THE (Attica, IN) **11484**
MESSENGER (GARFIELD), THE (Garfield, NJ) **11563**
MESSENGER (HARTSVILLE), THE (Hartsville, SC) **11621**
MESSENGER (HILLSBORO), THE (Hillsboro, NH) **11560**
MESSENGER INDEX (Emmett, ID) **11464**
MESSENGER (MADISONVILLE), THE (Madisonville, KY)
    11352
MESSENGER (MT JULIET), THE (Mt Juliet, TN) **11628**

MESSENGER-INQUIRER (Owensboro, KY) **11352**
MESSENGER-PRESS, THE (Hightstown, NJ) **11563**
METCALFE COUNTY LIGHT (Edmonton, KY) **11501**
METRO EAST WEEKENDER, THE (O'Fallon, IL) **11477**
METRO (PHILADELPHIA) (Philadelphia, PA) **11391**
METRO PRESS, THE (Millbury, OH) **11598**
METRO SANTA CRUZ (Santa Cruz, CA) **11437**
METRO SILICON VALLEY (San Jose, CA) **11436**
METRO TIMES (Detroit, MI) **11526**
METROBEAT (Greenville, SC) **11621**
METROCOM HERALD, THE (San Antonio, TX) **11640**
METROLAND (Albany, NY) **11569**
METROPOLIS PLANET (Metropolis, IL) **11475**
METROWEST DAILY NEWS (Framingham, MA) **11355**
METTER ADVERTISER, THE (Metter, GA) **11461**
MEXIA DAILY NEWS (Mexia, TX) **11399**
MEXICO LEDGER, THE (Mexico, MO) **11364**
MIAMI CHIEF, THE (Miami, TX) **11639**
MIAMI COUNTY REPUBLIC (Paola, KS) **11499**
MIAMI HERALD, THE (Miami, FL) **11333**
MIAMI LAKER (Miami Lakes, FL) **11453**
MIAMI NEW TIMES (Miami, FL) **11453**
MIAMI NEWS-RECORD (Miami, OK) **11385**
MIAMISBURG WEST CARROLTON NEWS (Miamisburg, OH)
    11598
MICHIGAN CITY NEWS-DISPATCH (Michigan City, IN) **11344**
MID HUDSON TIMES (Walden, NY) **11583**
MID VALLEY NEWS (El Monte, CA) **11428**
MID VALLEY TOWN CRIER (Weslaco, TX) **11642**
MIDCOUNTY CHRONICLE (Nederland, TX) **11639**
MID-COUNTY JOURNAL (Chesterfield, MO) **11549**
MIDDLE TOWNSHIP GAZETTE (Seaville, NJ) **11567**
MIDDLEBORO GAZETTE (Middleboro, MA) **11520**
MIDDLESBORO DAILY NEWS (Middlesboro, KY) **11352**
MIDDLESEX-DUNELLEN CHRONICLE (Somerville, NJ) **11567**
MIDDLETON GAZETTE (Middleton, ID) **11465**
MIDDLETON TIMES-TRIBUNE (Middleton, WI) **11663**
MIDDLETOWN JOURNAL, THE (Middletown, OH) **11382**
MIDDLETOWN NEWS, THE (Middletown, IN) **11487**
MIDDLETOWN PRESS (Middletown, CT) **11331**
MIDDLETOWN TRANSCRIPT (Middletown, DE) **11448**
MIDDLETOWN VALLEY CITIZEN (Brunswick, MD) **11512**
MIDDLETOWN/BRUNSWICK GAZETTE (Frederick, MD) **11513**
MID-IOWA ENTERPRISE (Clive, IA) **11491**
MID-ISLAND TIMES (Hicksville, NY) **11576**
MIDLAND DAILY NEWS (Midland, MI) **11359**
MIDLAND PARK SUBURBAN NEWS (Ridgewood, NJ) **11566**
MIDLAND REPORTER-TELEGRAM (Midland, TX) **11399**
MIDLOTHIAN MIRROR, INC, THE (Midlothian, TX) **11639**
MIDLOTHIAN-BREMEN MESSENGER (Midlothian, IL) **11476**
MIDWAY DRILLER (Taft, CA) **11438**
MIDWEEK (KANEOHE) (Kaneohe, HI) **11464**
MIDWEEK, THE (DeKalb, IL) **11469**
MIDWEEK (WEST FARGO) (West Fargo, ND) **11592**
MID-YORK WEEKLY (Hamilton, NY) **11575**
MIFFLINBURG TELEGRAPH, THE (Mifflinburg, PA) **11613**
MILAN NEWS-LEADER, THE (Saline, MI) **11532**
MILES CITY STAR (Miles City, MT) **11366**
MILFORD CHRONICLE (Milford, DE) **11448**
MILFORD DAILY NEWS, THE (Milford, MA) **11356**
MILFORD MIRROR (Shelton, CT) **11446**
MILFORD TIMES (South Lyon, MI) **11532**
MILFORD WEEKLY (Milford, CT) **11445**
MILFORD-MIAMI ADVERTISER (Loveland, OH) **11598**
MILL CREEK COMMUNITY NEWS (Hockessin, DE) **11447**
MILL CREEK ENTERPRISE (Lynnwood, WA) **11653**
MILL VALLEY HERALD (Sausalito, CA) **11437**
MILLARD COUNTY GAZETTE (Delta, UT) **11643**
MILLBROOK ROUND TABLE (Trenton, NJ) **11567**

MILLBURY-SUTTON CHRONICLE (Millbury, MA) **11521**
MILLE LACS COUNTY TIMES (Milaca, MN) **11540**
MILLEN NEWS, THE (Millen, GA) **11462**
MILLER COUNTY LIBERAL (Colquitt, GA) **11458**
MILLERTON NEWS, THE (Millerton, NY) **11578**
MILLINGTON STAR, THE (Millington, TN) **11628**
MILLVILLE NEWS (Bridgeton, NJ) **11369**
MILPITAS POST (Milipitas, CA) **11433**
MILTON COURIER (Milton, WI) **11663**
MILTON INDEPENDENT (Middlebury, VT) **11644**
MILTON RECORD TRANSCRIPT (Milton Village, MA) **11521**
MILTON SPOTLIGHT (Delmar, NY) **11573**
MILTONVALE RECORD (Miltonvale, KS) **11498**
MILWAUKEE JOURNAL SENTINEL (Milwaukee, WI) **11408**
MILWAUKEE POST (Milwaukee, WI) **11663**
MINDEN COURIER, THE (Minden, NE) **11557**
MINDEN PRESS-HERALD (Minden, LA) **11353**
MINEOLA AMERICAN (Mineola, NY) **11579**
MINERAL COUNTY INDEPENDENT-NEWS (Hawthorne, NV)
    11559
MINERAL COUNTY MINER (Monte Vista, CO) **11442**
MINERAL DAILY NEWS-TRIBUNE (Keyser, WV) **11406**
MINERAL WELLS INDEX (Mineral Wells, TX) **11399**
MINIDOKA COUNTY NEWS (Davenport, IA) **11491**
MINING JOURNAL, THE (Marquette, MI) **11359**
MINNEOTA MASCOT (Minneota, MN) **11540**
MINONK NEWS DISPATCH EDITION (Minonk, IL) **11476**
MINOT DAILY NEWS (Minot, ND) **11379**
MIRROR-EXCHANGE (Milan, TN) **11628**
MISHAWAKA ENTERPRISE (Mishawaka, IN) **11487**
MISSISSIPPI PRESS (Pascagoula, MS) **11363**
MISSOULA INDEPENDENT (Missoula, MT) **11556**
MISSOULIAN, THE (Missoula, MT) **11366**
MISSOURI VALLEY SHOPPER (Yankton, SD) **11625**
MISSOURI VALLEY TIMES-NEWS (Missouri Valley, IA) **11494**
MITCHELL COUNTY PRESS-NEWS (Osage, IA) **11494**
MITCHELL NEWS JOURNAL (Spruce Pine, NC) **11589**
MOBERLY MONITOR INDEX (Moberly, MO) **11365**
MODERN NEWS (Harrisburg, AR) **11422**
MODESTO BEE, THE (Modesto, CA) **11325**
MODOC COUNTY RECORD (Alturas, CA) **11425**
MOHAVE VALLEY DAILY NEWS (Bullhead City, AZ) **11321**
MOHICAN AREA SHOPPER (Loudonville, OH) **11597**
MOJAVE DESERT NEWS, THE (California City, CA) **11427**
MOLALLA PIONEER (Molalla, OR) **11608**
MONADNOCK HOME COMPANION (Keene, NH) **11560**
MONADNOCK LEDGER (Peterborough, NH) **11560**
MONAHANS NEWS (Monahans, TX) **11639**
MONDOVI HERALD-NEWS (Mondovi, WI) **11663**
MONETT TIMES (Monett, MO) **11365**
MONEY STRETCHER (Galatia, IL) **11471**
MONEYSAVER (Randolph, MA) **11522**
MONEYSAVER, THE SPA CITY JOURNAL (Round Lake, NY)
    11581
MONITOR (MABANK), THE (Mabank, TX) **11638**
MONITOR REVIEW, THE (Adams, MN) **11533**
MONITOR, THE (McAllen, TX) **11399**
MONITOR-HERALD, THE (Calhoun City, MS) **11546**
MONROE COUNTY BEACON (Woodsfield, OH) **11602**
MONROE COUNTY CITIZEN (Tompkinsville, KY) **11506**
MONROE COUNTY CLARION (Paris, MO) **11552**
MONROE COUNTY DEMOCRAT (Sparta, WI) **11666**
MONROE COUNTY REPORTER, THE (Forsyth, GA) **11460**
MONROE COUNTY SUN, THE (Clarendon, AR) **11421**
MONROE COURIER (Shelton, CT) **11446**
MONROE EVENING NEWS (Monroe, MI) **11359**
MONROE JOURNAL (Monroeville, AL) **11414**
MONROE JOURNAL, THE (Amory, MS) **11545**
MONROE LEGACY (Monroe, IA) **11494**

MONROE NEWS (Albia, IA) **11489**

MONROE TIMES, THE (Monroe, WI) **11408**

MONROE WATCHMAN (Union, WV) **11657**

MONTAGUE COUNTY SHOPPER, THE (Bowie, TX) **11632**

MONTANA STANDARD, THE (Butte, MT) **11366**

MONTAUK PIONEER (Bridgehampton, NY) **11570**

MONTCLAIR TIMES, THE (Montclair, NJ) **11565**

MONTCLARION (Alameda, CA) **11425**

MONTE VISTA JOURNAL (Monte Vista, CO) **11442**

MONTEREY COUNTY HERALD, THE (Monterey, CA) **11325**

MONTEREY COUNTY WEEKLY (Seaside, CA) **11437**

MONTEVIDEO AMERICAN-NEWS (Montevideo, MN) **11540**

MONTEZUMA REPUBLICAN, THE (Montezuma, IA) **11494**

MONTGOMERY ADVERTISER (Montgomery, AL) **11320**

MONTGOMERY COUNTY NEWS (Mt Ida, AR) **11423**

MONTGOMERY COUNTY NEWS, THE (Hillsboro, IL) **11474**

MONTGOMERY COUNTY PROGRESS (Horsham, PA) **11612**

MONTGOMERY COUNTY SENTINEL (Rockville, MD) **11514**

MONTGOMERY HERALD (TROY) (Troy, NC) **11590**

MONTGOMERY INDEPENDENT (Montgomery, AL) **11414**

MONTGOMERY LIFE (Fort Washington, PA) **11611**

MONTGOMERY MESSENGER (Montgomery, MN) **11540**

MONTGOMERY MONITOR (Soperton, GA) **11463**

MONTGOMERY STANDARD (Montgomery City, MO) **11552**

MONTGOMERY VILLAGE GAZETTE (Gaithersburg, MD) **11513**

MONTGOMERY VILLAGE NEWS (Montgomery Village, MD) **11514**

MONTGOMERY (WV) HERALD (Montgomery, WV) **11656**

MONTICELLO EXPRESS (Monticello, IA) **11494**

MONTICELLO NEWS (Monticello, FL) **11453**

MONTICELLO NEWS, THE (Monticello, GA) **11462**

MONTICELLO TIMES (Eden Prairie, MN) **11537**

MONTROSE DAILY PRESS (Montrose, CO) **11330**

MONTROSE HERALD (Canistota, SD) **11624**

MONTROSE SUN, THE (Medina, OH) **11598**

MOODY COUNTY ENTERPRISE (Flandreau, SD) **11624**

MOORCROFT LEADER (Moorcroft, WY) **11669**

MOORE AMERICAN, THE (Norman, OK) **11605**

MOORE COUNTY NEWS (Lynchburg, TN) **11628**

MOORE COUNTY NEWS-PRESS (Dumas, TX) **11634**

MOOREFIELD EXAMINER (Moorefield, WV) **11656**

MOORESVILLE DECATUR TIMES, THE (Mooresville, IN) **11487**

MOORESVILLE TRIBUNE (Mooresville, NC) **11588**

MOOSE LAKE STAR-GAZETTE (Moose Lake, MN) **11540**

MOOSEHEAD MESSENGER (Greenville, ME) **11510**

MORAVIA REPUBLICAN REGISTER (Moravia, NY) **11579**

MOREHEAD NEWS, THE (Morehead, KY) **11504**

MORENCI OBSERVER (Morenci, MI) **11530**

MORGAN COUNTY HERALD (McConnelsville, OH) **11598**

MORGAN COUNTY NEWS (Wartburg, TN) **11630**

MORGAN COUNTY PRESS (Stover, MO) **11554**

MORGAN HILL TIMES (Morgan Hill, CA) **11433**

MORGAN MESSENGER, THE (Berkeley Springs, WV) **11655**

MORNING CALL, THE (Allentown, PA) **11388**

MORNING JOURNAL (LISBON) (Lisbon, OH) **11381**

MORNING JOURNAL (LORAIN) (Lorain, OH) **11381**

MORNING NEWS (FLORENCE) (Florence, SC) **11394**

MORNING NEWS OF NORTHWEST ARKANSAS (Springdale, AR) **11323**

MORNING NEWS, THE (Blackfoot, ID) **11337**

MORNING SENTINEL (CENTRALIA) (Centralia, IL) **11338**

MORNING SENTINEL (WATERVILLE) (Waterville, ME) **11354**

MORNING SUN, THE (Mt Pleasant, MI) **11359**

MORNING TIMES (Sayre, PA) **11391**

MOROCCO COURIER, THE (Kentland, IN) **11486**

MORRIS DAILY HERALD (Morris, IL) **11340**

MORRIS NEWS BEE (Madison, NJ) **11565**

MORRIS SUN TRIBUNE (Fargo, ND) **11591**

MORRISON COUNTY RECORD (Little Falls, MN) **11539**

MORRISONS COVE HERALD (Martinsburg, PA) **11613**

MORRISONVILLE TIMES (Morrisonville, IL) **11476**

MORRISTOWN NEWS, THE (West Caldwell, NJ) **11568**

MORROW COUNTY ADVERTISER (Mt Gilead, OH) **11599**

MORROW COUNTY INDEPENDENT (Mt Gilead, OH) **11599**

MORROW COUNTY SENTINEL (Mt Gilead, OH) **11599**

MORTON COURIER (Morton, IL) **11476**

MORTON GROVE CHAMPION (Park Ridge, IL) **11479**

MORTON TIMES-NEWS (Peoria, IL) **11479**

MOSCOW-PULLMAN DAILY NEWS (Moscow, ID) **11337**

MOSINEE TIMES, THE (Mosinee, WI) **11663**

MOTLEY COUNTY TRIBUNE (Matador, TX) **11638**

MOULTON ADVERTISER, THE (Moulton, AL) **11414**

MOULTRIE NEWS, THE (Mt Pleasant, SC) **11622**

MOULTRIE OBSERVER, THE (Moultrie, GA) **11336**

MOUND CITY NEWS (Mound City, MO) **11552**

MOUNDSVILLE DAILY ECHO (Moundsville, WV) **11406**

MOUNDVILLE TIMES (Moundville, AL) **11414**

MOUNT AIRY GAZETTE (Mt Airy, MD) **11514**

MOUNT AIRY NEWS (Mt Airy, NC) **11377**

MOUNT AYR RECORD-NEWS (Mount Ayr, IA) **11494**

MOUNT GREENWOOD EXPRESS (Midlothian, IL) **11476**

MOUNT HOREB MAIL (Mt Horeb, WI) **11663**

MOUNT OLIVE TRIBUNE (Mt Olive, NC) **11588**

MOUNT PLEASANT DAILY TRIBUNE (Mt Pleasant, TX) **11400**

MOUNT PLEASANT JOURNAL, THE (Mt Pleasant, PA) **11614**

MOUNT PROSPECT JOURNAL (Des Plaines, IL) **11470**

MOUNT PROSPECT TIMES (Park Ridge, IL) **11479**

MOUNT SHASTA HERALD (Mt Shasta, CA) **11433**

MOUNT STERLING ADVOCATE (Mt Sterling, KY) **11504**

MOUNT VERNON DEMOCRAT (Mt Vernon, IN) **11487**

MOUNT VERNON GAZETTE (McLean, VA) **11649**

MOUNT VERNON NEWS (Mt Vernon, OH) **11382**

MOUNT WASHINGTON VALLEY MOUNTAIN EAR (Conway, NH) **11560**

MOUNTAIN ADVISOR (Richlands, VA) **11650**

MOUNTAIN CITIZEN, THE (Inez, KY) **11503**

MOUNTAIN DEMOCRAT (Placerville, CA) **11326**

MOUNTAIN EAGLE, THE (Whitesburg, KY) **11506**

MOUNTAIN ECHO, THE (Ft Payne, AL) **11413**

MOUNTAIN GROVE NEWS-JOURNAL, THE (Mountain Grove, MO) **11552**

MOUNTAIN HOME NEWS (Mountain Home, ID) **11465**

MOUNTAIN LAKE OBSERVER/BUTTERFIELD ADVOCATE (Mountain Lake, MN) **11540**

MOUNTAIN MAIL, THE (Salida, CO) **11330**

MOUNTAIN MESSENGER (Downieville, CA) **11428**

MOUNTAIN MESSENGER (LEWISBURG) (Lewisburg, WV) **11656**

MOUNTAIN NEWS, THE (Lake Arrowhead, CA) **11430**

MOUNTAIN PENNYSAVER (Saugerties, NY) **11581**

MOUNTAIN PRESS (Auberry, CA) **11426**

MOUNTAIN PRESS EXTRA (Sevierville, TN) **11629**

MOUNTAIN SHOPPER (Lake Arrowhead, CA) **11430**

MOUNTAIN STATESMAN (Grafton, WV) **11655**

MOUNTAIN SUN, THE (Houston, TX) **11637**

MOUNTAIN TIMES (BOONE) (Boone, NC) **11585**

MOUNTAIN TIMES (KILLINGTON), THE (Killington, VT) **11644**

MOUNTAIN VIEW VOICE (Mountain View, CA) **11433**

MOUNTAIN XPRESS (Asheville, NC) **11585**

MOUNTAINEER ECHO, THE (Flippin, AR) **11421**

MOUNTAINEER, THE (Big Sandy, MT) **11555**

MOUNTAINEER-HERALD, THE (Ebensberg, PA) **11611**

MOUNTAINTOP EAGLE (Mountain Top, PA) **11614**

MOURE CHRONICLE, LA (Enderlin, ND) **11591**

MOWER COUNTY SHOPPER (Austin, MN) **11534**

MOWER COUNTY SHOPPING NEWS (Austin, MN) **11534**

MR THRIFTY #1 (Ravenna, OH) **11600**

MR THRIFTY #7 (Ravenna, OH) **11600**

MT AIRY TIMES EXPRESS (Philadelphia, PA) **11615**

MT OLIVE CHRONICLE (Chester, NJ) **11562**

MT OLIVE HERALD, THE (Mt Olive, IL) **11476**

MT PLEASANT NEWS (Mt Pleasant, IA) **11348**

MT VERNON INDEPENDENT (Yonkers, NY) **11585**

MT ZION REGION NEWS (Mt Zion, IL) **11476**

MUKILTEO TRIBUNE (Snohomish, WA) **11654**

MUKWONAGO CHIEF (Mukwonago, WI) **11663**

MULLENS ADVOCATE (Mullens, WV) **11656**

MULLET WRAPPER (Pensacola, FL) **11454**

MUNDAY COURIER, THE (Munday, TX) **11639**

MUNDELEIN JOURNAL (Grayslake, IL) **11473**

MUNDELEIN REVIEW (Waukegan, IL) **11483**

MUNISING NEWS (Munising, MI) **11530**

MURFREESBORO DIAMOND (Murfreesboro, AR) **11423**

MURPHYSBORO AMERICAN (Murphysboro, IL) **11476**

MURRAY COUNTY WHEEL HERALD (Slayton, MN) **11543**

MURRAY LEDGER & TIMES (Murray, KY) **11352**

MURRYSVILLE STAR (Monroeville, PA) **11613**

MUSCATINE JOURNAL (Muscatine, IA) **11348**

MUSKEGO SUN (New Berlin, WI) **11664**

MUSKEGON CHRONICLE, THE (Muskegon, MI) **11359**

MUSKOGEE DAILY PHOENIX & TIMES-DEMOCRAT (Muskogee, OK) **11385**

MYSTIC RIVER PRESS (Mystic, CT) **11445**

N

NANTY GLO JOURNAL, THE (Nanty Glo, PA) **11614**

NAPA VALLEY REGISTER (Napa, CA) **11325**

NAPERVILLE SUN (Naperville, IL) **11341**

NAPLES DAILY NEWS (Naples, FL) **11333**

NAPLES RECORD, THE (Naples, NY) **11579**

NARRAGANSETT TIMES, THE (Wakefield, RI) **11619**

NASHUA REPORTER (Nashua, IA) **11494**

NASHVILLE GRAPHIC (Nashville, NC) **11588**

NASHVILLE NEWS (Nashville, AR) **11423**

NASHVILLE NEWS, THE (Nashville, IL) **11477**

NASHVILLE SCENE, THE (Nashville, TN) **11628**

NASSAU COUNTY RECORD (Callahan, FL) **11449**

NASSAU HERALD (Lawrence, NY) **11577**

NATCHEZ DEMOCRAT (Natchez, MS) **11363**

NATCHITOCHES TIMES (Natchitoches, LA) **11353**

NATICK BULLETIN & TAB (Framingham, MA) **11518**

NATIONAL TOMBSTONE EPITAPH, THE (Tombstone, AZ) **11419**

NATION'S CENTER NEWS (Buffalo, SD) **11623**

NAVASOTA EXAMINER (Navasota, TX) **11639**

NEBRASKA CITY NEWS-PRESS (Nebraska City, NE) **11367**

NEBRASKA SIGNAL (Geneva, NE) **11557**

NEEDHAM TIMES (Needham, MA) **11521**

NEEDLES DESERT STAR (Needles, CA) **11433**

NEIGHBOR, THE (Attica, IN) **11484**

NEIGHBORS (Markesan, WI) **11662**

NEIGHBORS (HILLSBORO) (Hillsboro, WI) **11661**

NELSON COUNTY TIMES (Amherst, VA) **11645**

NEMAHA COUNTY HERALD (Auburn, NE) **11556**

NEODESHA DERRICK, THE (Neodesha, KS) **11498**

NEOGA NEWS (Casey, IL) **11468**

NEOSHO DAILY NEWS, THE (Neosho, MO) **11365**

NESHOBA DEMOCRAT (Philadelphia, MS) **11547**

NESS COUNTY NEWS, THE (Ness City, KS) **11498**

NEVADA APPEAL (Carson City, NV) **11367**

NEVADA COUNTY PICAYUNE (Prescott, AR) **11424**

NEVADA JOURNAL (OMAHA) (Nevada, IA) **11494**

NEW ALBANY GAZETTE (New Albany, MS) **11547**

NEW ALBANY NEWS (Columbus, OH) **11595**

NEW BAY WEEKLY (Annapolis, MD) **11511**

NEW BERLIN BEE (Auburn, IL) **11467**

NEW BERLIN CITIZEN (New Berlin, WI) **11664**

NEW BRIGHTON-MOUNDS VIEW BULLETIN (New Brighton, MN) **11540**

NEW BUFFALO TIMES (New Buffalo, MI) **11530**

NEW CANAAN ADVERTISER (New Canaan, CT) **11445**

NEW CANAAN NEWS-REVIEW (New Canaan, CT) **11445**

NEW CARLISLE SUN (New Carlisle, OH) **11599**

NEW CARROLLTON GAZETTE (Landover, MD) **11514**

NEW CASTLE NEWS (New Castle, PA) **11390**

NEW CASTLE RECORD (New Castle, VA) **11649**

NEW CASTLE WEEKLY, THE (New Castle, DE) **11448**

NEW CITY (Chicago, IL) **11469**

NEW CONCORD LEADER (Cambridge, OH) **11594**

NEW EGYPT PRESS (New Egypt, NJ) **11565**

NEW ERA, THE (Sweet Home, OR) **11609**

NEW FAIRFIELD CITIZEN NEWS (New Fairfield, CT) **11445**

NEW GLOUCESTER NEWS (New Gloucester, ME) **11510**

NEW HAMPTON TRIBUNE (New Hampton, IA) **11494**

NEW HAVEN ADVOCATE (New Haven, CT) **11445**

NEW HAVEN REGISTER (New Haven, CT) **11331**

NEW HOPE GAZETTE (New Hope, PA) **11614**

NEW HOPE/GOLDEN VALLEY SUN-POST (Robbinsdale, MN) **11542**

NEW HYDE PARK HERALD COURIER (Hicksville, NY) **11576**

NEW IRMO NEWS (Irmo, SC) **11621**

NEW JERSEY HERALD (Newton, NJ) **11369**

NEW LONDON COUNTY PENNYSAVER (Old Saybrook, CT) **11446**

NEW MARKET/URBANA GAZETTE (Frederick, MD) **11513**

NEW MILFORD TIMES (New Milford, CT) **11446**

NEW PRAGUE TIMES (New Prague, MN) **11540**

NEW RICHMOND NEWS (New Richmond, WI) **11665**

NEW RIVER RECORD (Greenbush, MN) **11538**

NEW TIMES (San Luis Obispo, CA) **11436**

NEW TIMES (PHOENIX) (Phoenix, AZ) **11419**

NEW ULM ENTERPRISE (New Ulm, TX) **11639**

NEW YORK DAILY NEWS, THE (New York, NY) **11373**

NEW YORK GOOD NEWS (New York, NY) **11580**

NEW YORK METROPOLITAN NEWS (Brooklyn, NY) **11571**

NEW YORK MILLS HERALD (New York Mills, MN) **11540**

NEW YORK OBSERVER (New York, NY) **11580**

NEW YORK POST (New York, NY) **11373**

NEW YORK PRESS (New York, NY) **11580**

NEW YORK TIMES LARGE PRINT WEEKLY (New York, NY) **11580**

NEW YORK TIMES, THE (New York, NY) **11373**

NEW YORK TREND (Great Neck, NY) **11575**

NEWARK PENNYSAVER (Newark, NY) **11580**

NEWARK POST, THE (Newark, DE) **11448**

NEWARK/LICKING ADVERTISER (Newark, OH) **11599**

NEWBERG GRAPHIC, THE (Newberg, OR) **11608**

NEWBERRY OBSERVER, THE (Newberry, SC) **11622**

NEWBURGH-CHANDLER REGISTER (Newburgh, IN) **11487**

NEWCASTLE PACER, THE (Newcastle, OK) **11605**

NEWCOMERSTOWN NEWS (Newcomerstown, OH) **11599**

NEWFIELD NEWS (Trumansburg, NY) **11583**

NEWINGTON TOWN CRIER (Bristol, CT) **11443**

NEWPORT DAILY EXPRESS (Newport, VT) **11402**

NEWPORT DAILY NEWS, THE (Newport, RI) **11393**

NEWPORT INDEPENDENT (Newport, AR) **11423**

NEWPORT MERCURY (Newport, RI) **11619**

NEWPORT MINER (Newport, WA) **11653**

NEWPORT PLAIN TALK, THE (Newport, TN) **11396**

NEWPORT THIS WEEK (Newport, RI) **11619**

NEWS & ADVANCE (Lynchburg, VA) **11403**

NEWS & CITIZEN (Morrisville, VT) **11644**

NEWS & FARMER/JEFFERSON REPORTER (Louisville, GA) **11461**

NEWS & OBSERVER, THE (Raleigh, NC) **11377**

NEWS & PRESS, THE (Darlington, SC) **11620**

NEWS & RECORD, THE (Greensboro, NC) **11376**

NEWS & REPORTER, THE (Chester, SC) **11620**

NEWS & SENTINEL, THE (Colebrook, NH) **11560**

NEWS BULLETIN (Utulei, AS) **11321**

NEWS BULLETIN OF MCDOWELL COUNTY, THE (Old Fort, NC) **11588**

NEWS CHIEF, THE (Winter Haven, FL) **11334**

NEWS (DENHAM SPRINGS), THE (Denham Springs, LA) **11507**

NEWS EAGLE, THE (Hawley, PA) **11612**

NEWS ENTERPRISE, THE (Los Alamitos, CA) **11431**

NEWS EXAMINER, THE (Lutcher, LA) **11507**

NEWS GAZETTE, THE (Bayard, IA) **11490**

NEWS GLEANER (Philadelphia, PA) **11615**

NEWS GRAPHIC (CEDARBURG) (Cedarburg, WI) **11659**

NEWS GUARD, THE (Lincoln City, OR) **11608**

NEWS (HACKETTSTOWN), THE (Hackettstown, NJ) **11563**

NEWS HERALD (Panama City, FL) **11334**

NEWS HERALD (LENOIR CITY) (Lenoir City, TN) **11627**

NEWS HERALD (MORGANTON), THE (Morganton, NC) **11377**

NEWS JOURNAL (MANSFIELD) (Mansfield, OH) **11381**

NEWS JOURNAL (NEW CASTLE), THE (New Castle, DE) **11332**

NEWS JOURNAL, THE (Florence, SC) **11620**

NEWS (KINGSTREE), THE (Kingstree, SC) **11621**

NEWS LEADER (CLEMONT), THE (Clermont, FL) **11450**

NEWS LEADER (FERNANDINA) (Fernandina Beach, FL) **11451**

NEWS LEADER (LANDRUM), THE (Landrum, SC) **11621**

NEWS LEADER (MINERVA), THE (Minerva, OH) **11598**

NEWS LEADER (PARSONS), THE (Parsons, TN) **11629**

NEWS LEADER (STAUNTON), THE (Staunton, VA) **11404**

NEWS LEADER (STOW) (Stow, OH) **11601**

NEWS LETTER JOURNAL (Newcastle, WY) **11669**

NEWS MESSENGER, THE (Christiansburg, VA) **11646**

NEWS OBSERVER, THE (Blue Ridge, GA) **11457**

NEWS OF DELAWARE COUNTY (Havertown, PA) **11612**

NEWS OF ORANGE COUNTY, THE (Hillsborough, NC) **11587**

NEWS OF THE HIGHLANDS (Highland Falls, NY) **11576**

NEWS OF THE POCONOS (White Haven, PA) **11618**

NEWS RECORD (Zumbrota, MN) **11545**

NEWS REPORT (BLACKWOOD) (Blackwood, NJ) **11561**

NEWS REPORTER, THE (Whiteville, NC) **11590**

NEWS REVIEW (Ridgecrest, CA) **11435**

NEWS (SALEM), THE (Salem, AR) **11424**

NEWS SENTINEL (Knoxville, TN) **11396**

NEWS SUN (Sebring, FL) **11455**

NEWS SUN (BEREA), THE (Berea, OH) **11593**

NEWS SUN (WAUKEGAN), THE (Waukegan, IL) **11342**

NEWS TIMES (Oberlin, OH) **11599**

NEWS TRANSCRIPT (Freehold, NJ) **11563**

NEWS TRIBUNE (La Salle, IL) **11340**

NEWS TRIBUNE (JEFFERSON CITY) (Jefferson City, MO) **11364**

NEWS TRIBUNE, THE (Tacoma, WA) **11405**

NEWS VIRGINIAN, THE (Waynesboro, VA) **11404**

NEWS WEEKLY (CRANBERRY TOWNSHIP) (Cranberry Township, PA) **11611**

NEWS-BANNER, THE (Covington, LA) **11507**

NEWS-CAPITAL & DEMOCRAT (McAlester, OK) **11385**

NEWS-CHRONICLE (Belton, SC) **11620**

NEWS-CHRONICLE, THE (Shippensburg, PA) **11617**

NEWS-COURIER, THE (Athens, AL) **11319**

NEWSDAY (Melville, NY) **11373**

NEWS-DEMOCRAT & LEADER (Russellville, KY) **11505**

NEWS-DEMOCRAT JOURNAL (Festus, MO) **11550**

NEWS-DEMOCRAT, THE (Carrollton, KY) **11500**

NEWS-DEMOCRAT (WAVERLY), THE (Waverly, TN) **11630**

NEWS-DISPATCH, THE (Driftwood, TX) **11634**

NEWS-ENTERPRISE (Elizabethtown, KY) **11351**

NEWS-EXAMINER (GALLATIN) (Gallatin, TN) **11626**

NEWS-EXAMINER (MONTPELIER) (Montpelier, ID) **11465**

NEWS-GAZETTE (LEXINGTON) (Lexington, VA) **11648**

NEWS-GAZETTE, THE (Winchester, IN) **11346**

NEWSGLEANER - BUSTLETON - SOMERTON EDITION (Philadelphia, PA) **11615**

NEWSGLEANER - FAR NORTHEAST EDITION (Philadelphia, PA) **11615**

NEWSGLEANER - FRANKFORD - OXFORD CIRCLE EDITION (Philadelphia, PA) **11615**

NEWSGLEANER - MAYFAIR - NORTHEAST EDITION (Philadelphia, PA) **11615**

NEWS-HERALD (OIL CITY), THE (Oil City, PA) **11390**

NEWS-HERALD (PORT CLINTON) (Port Clinton, OH) **11382**

NEWS-HERALD (SOUTHGATE), THE (Southgate, MI) **11532**

NEWS-HERALD (WILLOUGHBY) (Willoughby, OH) **11383**

NEWS-ITEM (Shamokin, PA) **11391**

NEWS-JOURNAL (DAYTONA BEACH), THE (Daytona Beach, FL) **11332**

NEWS-JOURNAL (NORTH MANCHESTER), THE (North Manchester, IN) **11487**

NEWS-JOURNAL (RAEFORD), THE (Raeford, NC) **11589**

NEWS-LEADER (Springfield, MO) **11553**

NEWS-LEADER (FERNANDINA BEACH) (Fernandina Beach, FL) **11451**

NEWS-LEDGER, THE (West Sacramento, CA) **11438**

NEWS-MESSENGER (FREMONT), THE (Fremont, OH) **11381**

NEWS-PRESS, THE (Fort Myers, FL) **11333**

NEWS-PROGRESS (Sullivan, IL) **11481**

NEWS-PROGRESS, THE (Chase City, VA) **11646**

NEWS-RECORD (ELIZABETH) (Rahway, NJ) **11566**

NEWS-RECORD (MABEL) (Mabel, MN) **11539**

NEWS-RECORD OF MAPLEWOOD & SOUTH ORANGE (Maplewood, NJ) **11565**

NEWS-RECORD, THE (Cerro Gordo, IL) **11468**

NEWS-REGISTER (McMinnville, OR) **11608**

NEWS-REPORTER, THE (Washington, GA) **11463**

NEWS-REVIEW (MATTITUCK), THE (Mattituck, NY) **11578**

NEWS-REVIEW (ROSEBURG), THE (Roseburg, OR) **11387**

NEWS-SICKLE ARROW (Black Earth, WI) **11658**

NEWS-STAR (Oak Park, IL) **11478**

NEWS-STAR, THE (Monroe, LA) **11353**

NEWS-SUN (Fairmount, IN) **11485**

NEWS-SUN (KENDALLVILLE), THE (Kendallville, IN) **11344**

NEWS-SUN (NEW BLOOMFIELD), THE (New Bloomfield, PA) **11614**

NEWS/TIMES (Whiteville, NC) **11590**

NEWS-TIMES (FOREST GROVE) (Forest Grove, OR) **11607**

NEWS-TIMES (HARTFORD CITY) (Hartford City, IN) **11343**

NEWS-TIMES (NEWPORT) (Newport, OR) **11608**

NEWS-TIMES, THE (Danbury, CT) **11331**

NEWS-TOPIC (Lenoir, NC) **11377**

NEWSWEEKLY (MOORESTOWN) (Moorestown, NJ) **11565**

NEWSWEEKLY, THE (Sebewaing, MI) **11532**

NEWS-X PRESS (Butler, MO) **11548**

NEWTON CITIZEN (Covington, GA) **11335**

NEWTON COUNTY TIMES, THE (Jasper, AR) **11422**

NEWTON DAILY NEWS (Newton, IA) **11348**

NEWTON KANSAN, THE (Newton, KS) **11350**

NEWTON PRESS-MENTOR (Newton, IL) **11477**

NEWTON RECORD, THE (Newton, MS) **11547**

NEWTON TAB (Needham, MA) **11521**

NEWTOWN BEE, THE (Newtown, CT) **11446**

NIAGARA GAZETTE (Niagara Falls, NY) **11374**

NIAGARA/WHEATFIELD TRIBUNE (Grand Island, NY) **11575**

NICHOLAS CHRONICLE (Summersville, WV) **11657**

NICHOLAS COUNTIAN AND THE CARLISLE MERCURY, THE (Carlisle, KY) 11500

NILES DAILY STAR (Niles, MI) 11359

NILES HERALD-SPECTATOR (Park Ridge, IL) 11479

NILES JOURNAL (Des Plaines, IL) 11470

NISHNA VALLEY TRIBUNE (Audubon, IA) 11490

NISKAYUNA JOURNAL (Delmar, NY) 11573

NISQUALLY VALLEY NEWS (Yelm, WA) 11655

NIXAXPRESS (Nixa, MO) 11552

NOBLES COUNTY REVIEW (Adrian, MN) 11533

NOBLESVILLE LEDGER, THE (Fishers, IN) 11485

NOGALES INTERNATIONAL (Nogales, AZ) 11419

NOKOMIS FREE PRESS-PROGRESS (Nokomis, IL) 11477

NOME NUGGET (Nome, AK) 11416

NORDONIA HILLS SUN (Cleveland, OH) 11594

NORFOLK AREA SHOPPER, THE (Norfolk, NE) 11557

NORFOLK DAILY NEWS (Norfolk, NE) 11367

NORMAN COUNTY INDEX (Ada, MN) 11533

NORMAN TRANSCRIPT (Norman, OK) 11385

NORRIDGE/HARWOOD HEIGHTS NEWS (Park Ridge, IL) 11479

NORRIDGE-HARWOOD HEIGHTS NEWS (Park Ridge, IL) 11479

NORRIS CITY BANNER (Norris City, IL) 11477

NORTH ADAMS TRANSCRIPT (North Adams, MA) 11356

NORTH ANDOVER CITIZEN (Beverly, MA) 11516

NORTH BARTOW NEWS (Adairsville, GA) 11456

NORTH BAY BOHEMIAN (Santa Rosa, CA) 11437

NORTH BERGEN REPORTER (Hoboken, NJ) 11564

NORTH CHANNEL SENTINEL (Pasadena, TX) 11639

NORTH CLERMONT COMMUNITY JOURNAL (Loveland, OH) 11598

NORTH COAST JOURNAL OF POLITICS, PEOPLE & ART, THE (Arcata, CA) 11426

NORTH COUNTRY FREEPRESS (Granville, NY) 11575

NORTH COUNTRY JOURNAL (Hazelwood, MO) 11550

NORTH COUNTRY SUN (Ironwood, MI) 11528

NORTH COUNTRYMAN, THE (Elizabethtown, NY) 11574

NORTH COUNTY JOURNAL (Hazelwood, MO) 11550

NORTH COUNTY NEWS (RED BUD) (Red Bud, IL) 11480

NORTH COUNTY NEWS (TOWSON) (Towson, MD) 11515

NORTH COUNTY NEWS (YORKTOWN HEIGHTS) (Yorktown Heights, NY) 11585

NORTH COUNTY SHOPPING NEWS (Atascadero, CA) 11426

NORTH COUNTY TIMES (Escondido, CA) 11324

NORTH CREEK NEWS ENTERPRISE (Elizabethtown, NY) 11574

NORTH CROW RIVER NEWS (Osseo, MN) 11541

NORTH END AGENTS (Hartford, CT) 11444

NORTH GEORGIA NEWS (Blairsville, GA) 11457

NORTH HAVEN COURIER (Madison, CT) 11444

NORTH HAVEN POST, THE (Milford, CT) 11445

NORTH JEFFERSON NEWS (Gardendale, AL) 11413

NORTH JERSEY PROSPECTOR (Clifton, NJ) 11562

NORTH JOURNAL (Wexford, PA) 11618

NORTH KITSAP HERALD (Poulsbo, WA) 11653

NORTH LAKE TAHOE BONANZA (Incline Village, NV) 11559

NORTH LAKE TRAVIS LOG (Jonestown, TX) 11637

NORTH LIBERTY LEADER, THE (Solon, IA) 11495

NORTH MACOMB VOICE (New Baltimore, MI) 11530

NORTH MARIN NEWS (Novato, CA) 11433

NORTH MISSOURIAN (Gallatin, MO) 11550

NORTH MYRTLE BEACH TIMES (North Myrtle Beach, SC) 11622

NORTH PENN LIFE (Fort Washington, PA) 11611

NORTH PORT SUN (North Port, FL) 11333

NORTH POTOMAC GAZETTE (Gaithersburg, MD) 11513

NORTH PROVIDENCE BREEZE, THE (Greenville, RI) 11618

NORTH READING TRANSCRIPT (North Reading, MA) 11522

NORTH RIDGEVILLE PRESS (Avon Lake, OH) 11592

NORTH SAN ANTONIO TIMES (San Antonio, TX) 11640

NORTH SCOTT PRESS, THE (Eldridge, IA) 11492

NORTH SCOTTSDALE INDEPENDENT (Scottsdale, AZ) 11419

NORTH SEATTLE HERALD-OUTLOOK (Seattle, WA) 11654

NORTH SHORE HERALD (New Berlin, WI) 11664

NORTH SHORE SUN (Wading River, NY) 11583

NORTH SHORE SUNDAY (Beverly, MA) 11516

NORTH SIDE JOURNAL (Hazelwood, MO) 11550

NORTH SIDE NEWS (Gooding, ID) 11464

NORTH SIDE TOPICS (Fishers, IN) 11485

NORTH STAR NEWS (Karlstad, MN) 11539

NORTH STAR (PHILADELPHIA) (Trevose, PA) 11617

NORTH SYRACUSE STAR-NEWS (Syracuse, NY) 11583

NORTH TRADE JOURNAL (Bamberg, SC) 11619

NORTH VERNON PLAIN DEALER (North Vernon, IN) 11487

NORTH VERNON SUN (North Vernon, IN) 11487

NORTH WOODS CALL (Charlevoix, MI) 11526

NORTHAMPTON PRESS (Allentown, PA) 11609

NORTHBOROUGH-SOUTHBOROUGH VILLAGER, THE (Marlborough, MA) 11520

NORTHBROOK STAR (Glenview, IL) 11473

NORTHCASTLE NEWS (Yonkers, NY) 11585

NORTHEAST ARKANSAS MERCHANDISER (Corning, AR) 11421

NORTHEAST BOOSTER (Towson, MD) 11515

NORTHEAST EDITION (Los Angeles, CA) 11432

NORTHEAST GEORGIAN, THE (Cornelia, GA) 11458

NORTHEAST HERALD, THE (Indianapolis, IN) 11486

NORTHEAST IOWA SHOPPER, THE (New Hampton, IA) 11494

NORTHEAST JOHNSON COUNTY SUN (Overland Park, KS) 11499

NORTHEAST MISSISSIPPI DAILY JOURNAL (Tupelo, MS) 11363

NORTHEAST NEWS (Irmo, SC) 11621

NORTHEAST REPORTER (Towson, MD) 11515

NORTHEAST SUBURBAN LIFE PRESS (Loveland, OH) 11598

NORTHEAST TIMES (Trevose, PA) 11617

NORTHEASTER (Minneapolis, MN) 11540

NORTHERN BEACON, THE (Lancaster, NH) 11560

NORTHERN LIGHT, THE (Baudette, MN) 11534

NORTHERN MICHIGAN NEWS (Cadillac, MI) 11526

NORTHERN NECK NEWS (Warsaw, VA) 11650

NORTHERN STAR (Gaylord, MI) 11527

NORTHERN STAR, THE (Clinton, MN) 11536

NORTHERN VALLEY SUBURBANITE (Cresskill, NJ) 11562

NORTHERN VIRGINIA DAILY (Strasburg, VA) 11404

NORTHERN WATCH (Thief River Falls, MN) 11543

NORTHERN WYOMING DAILY NEWS (Worland, WY) 11410

NORTHFIELD ADVANCE (Jenison, MI) 11529

NORTHFIELD NEWS (NORTHFIELD, MN) (Northfield, MN) 11540

NORTHFIELD NEWS (NORTHFIELD, VT) (Northfield, VT) 11644

NORTHGLENN-THORNTON SENTINEL (Thornton, CO) 11442

NORTHLAKE NEWS (Woodinville, WA) 11655

NORTHLAND NEWS (Columbus, OH) 11595

NORTHLAND SUN NEWS (Liberty, MO) 11551

NORTHNEWS (Minneapolis, MN) 11540

NORTHOME RECORD & MIZPAH MESSAGE (Northome, MN) 11541

NORTHPORT GAZETTE, THE (Northport, AL) 11414

NORTHPORT JOURNAL (Huntington, NY) 11576

NORTHSHIRE FREEPRESS, THE (Granville, NY) 11575

NORTHSHORE CITIZEN (Bothell, WA) 11651

NORTHSIDE NEIGHBOR, THE (Atlanta, GA) 11457

NORTHSIDE SUN, THE (Jackson, MS) 11546

NORTHUMBERLAND ECHO (Heathsville, VA) 11647

NORTHVILLE RECORD (Northville, MI) 11531

NORTHWEST ALABAMIAN (Haleyville, AL) 11414

NORTHWEST ARKANSAS TIMES (Fayetteville, AR) 11322

NORTHWEST BLADE, THE (Eureka, SD) 11624

NORTHWEST COLUMBUS NEWS (Columbus, OH) 11595

NORTHWEST CURRENT, THE (Washington, DC) 11448

NORTHWEST FLORIDA DAILY NEWS (Fort Walton Beach, FL) 11333

NORTHWEST HERALD (Crystal Lake, IL) 11339

NORTHWEST IOWA SHOPPER (Spencer, IA) 11495

NORTHWEST JOURNAL (Des Plaines, IL) 11470

NORTHWEST NAVIGATOR-KITSAP (Silverdale, WA) 11654

NORTHWEST NAVIGATOR-WHIDBEY (Oak Harbor, WA) 11653

NORTHWEST PRESS (Cincinnati, OH) 11594

NORTHWEST SIDE PRESS (Chicago, IL) 11469

NORTHWEST SIGNAL (Napoleon, OH) 11382

NORTHWEST TOPICS (Fishers, IN) 11485

NORTHWEST VALLEY NEWS (Sun City, AZ) 11419

NORTHWESTERN ILLINOIS DISPATCH (Savanna, IL) 11481

NORTHWESTERN PRESS (Allentown, PA) 11610

NORTON COURIER (Rockland, MA) 11523

NORTON MIRROR (Milford, MA) 11521

NORTON TELEGRAM, THE (Norton, KS) 11498

NORTON-LAKESHORE EXAMINER (Muskegon, MI) 11530

NORWALK CITIZEN-NEWS (Greenwich, CT) 11444

NORWALK REFLECTOR (Norwalk, CT) 11331

NORWELL MARINER (Marshfield, MA) 11520

NORWICH BULLETIN (Norwich, CT) 11331

NORWIN STAR (Monroeville, PA) 11613

NORWOOD BULLETIN (Norwood, MA) 11522

NORWOOD GLEANER, THE (Norwood, ND) 11592

NORWOOD POST (Boulder, CO) 11439

NORWOOD YOUNG AMERICA TIMES (Norwood, MN) 11541

NOTES, THE (Yarmouth, ME) 11511

NOVATO ADVANCE (Novato, CA) 11433

NOVI NEWS (Northville, MI) 11531

NOWATA STAR (Nowata, OK) 11605

NUECES COUNTY RECORD STAR (Omaha, NE) 11558

NUTLEY JOURNAL (Bloomfield, NJ) 11561

NUTLEY SUN, THE (Nutley, NJ) 11566

NUVO (Indianapolis, IN) 11486

N'WEST IOWA REVIEW (Sheldon, IA) 11495

O

O C WEEKLY (Santa Ana, CA) 11437

OAK BROOK DOINGS, THE (Hinsdale, IL) 11474

OAK CLIFF TRIBUNE (Dallas, TX) 11633

OAK CREEK PICTORIAL (New Berlin, WI) 11664

OAK FOREST-CRESTWOOD-MIDLOTHIAN STAR (Tinley Park, IL) 11482

OAK LAWN INDEPENDENT (Midlothian, IL) 11476

OAK LAWN-PALOS-WORTH TOWNSHIPS (Tinley Park, IL) 11482

OAK LEAVES, THE (Oak Park, IL) 11478

OAK RIDGER, THE (Oak Ridge, TN) 11396

OAKDALE JOURNAL (Oakdale, LA) 11508

OAKDALE LEADER (Oakdale, CA) 11433

OAKDALE-LAKE ELMO REVIEW (St Paul, MN) 11543

OAKLAND CITY JOURNAL (Princeton, IN) 11488

OAKLAND HERALD, THE (Avoca, IA) 11490

OAKLAND INDEPENDENT (Oakland, NE) 11558

OAKLAND PRESS, THE (Pontiac, MI) 11359

OAKLAND TRIBUNE, THE (Oakland, CA) 11325

OAKLEY GRAPHIC (Oakley, KS) 11498

OAKVILLE-MEHLVILLE JOURNAL (St Louis, MO) 11553

OBERLIN HERALD, THE (Oberlin, KS) 11498

OBERLIN NEWS-TRIBUNE (Oberlin, OH) 11599

OBION COUNTY WEEKLY (Union City, TN) 11630

OBSERVATEUR, L' (La Place, LA) 11507

OBSERVER (BELGRADE), THE (Belgrade, MN) **11534**
OBSERVER (DEWITT), THE (DeWitt, IA) **11492**
OBSERVER (DUNDEE), THE (Dundee, NY) **11573**
OBSERVER (DUNKIRK) (Dunkirk, NY) **11372**
OBSERVER (KEARNY), THE (Kearny, NJ) **11564**
OBSERVER (KINGWOOD, HUMBLE, ATASCOCITA, EAST MONTGOMERY, SPRING), THE (Kingwood, TX) **11637**
OBSERVER (KINGWOOD), THE (Kingwood, TX) **11637**
OBSERVER (LA GRANDE), THE (La Grande, OR) **11387**
OBSERVER (NEW SMYRNA), THE (New Smyrna Beach, FL) **11333**
OBSERVER NEWS ENTERPRISE, THE (Newton, NC) **11377**
OBSERVER NEWS, THE (Ruskin, FL) **11454**
OBSERVER (NORTHPORT), THE (Northport, NY) **11580**
OBSERVER REPORTER (Toms River, NJ) **11369**
OBSERVER (RIO RANCHO), THE (Rio Rancho, NM) **11568**
OBSERVER (ROYAL PALM BEACH), THE (Royal Palm Beach, FL) **11454**
OBSERVER (UNION), THE (Union, NJ) **11568**
OBSERVER-DISPATCH (Utica, NY) **11375**
OBSERVER-REPORTER/GREEN COUNTY (Waynesburg, PA) **11392**
OBSERVER-REPORTER/WASHINGTON COUNTY (Washington, PA) **11392**
OBSERVER-TRIBUNE (Chester, NJ) **11562**
OCEAN CITY GAZETTE, THE (Seaville, NJ) **11567**
OCEAN CITY SENTINEL, THE (Ocean City, NJ) **11566**
OCEAN COUNTY REPORTER (Toms River, NJ) **11567**
OCEAN PINES INDEPENDENT (Ocean City, MD) **11514**
OCEAN REEF PRESS (Key Largo, FL) **11451**
OCEAN SPRING RECORD (Ocean Spring, MO) **11552**
OCEANA'S HERALD-JOURNAL (Hart, MI) **11528**
OCEANSIDE/ISLAND PARK HERALD (Garden City, NY) **11574**
OCONEE ENTERPRISE, THE (Watkinsville, GA) **11463**
OCONOMOWOC ENTERPRISE (Oconomowoc, WI) **11665**
OCONTO COUNTY TIMES-HERALD (Oconto Falls, WI) **11665**
ODEM-EDROY TIMES (Sinton, TX) **11641**
ODESSA AMERICAN (Odessa, TX) **11400**
OELWEIN DAILY REGISTER (Oelwein, IA) **11348**
O'FALLON JOURNAL (St Peters, MO) **11554**
O'FALLON PROGRESS (O'Fallon, IL) **11477**
OGEMAW COUNTY HERALD (West Branch, MI) **11533**
OGEMAW/OSCODA COUNTY STAR (Gaylord, MI) **11527**
OGLE COUNTY LIFE (Oregon, IL) **11478**
OGLETHORPE ECHO, THE (Lexington, GA) **11461**
OHIO COUNTY NEWS (Rising Sun, IN) **11488**
OHIO COUNTY TIMES NEWS (Hartford, KY) **11502**
OJAI VALLEY NEWS (Ojai, CA) **11434**
OKALOOSA NEWS EXTRA (Crestview, FL) **11450**
OKEECHOBEE NEWS (Okeechobee, FL) **11333**
OKLAHOMA CITY FRIDAY (Oklahoma City, OK) **11605**
OKLAHOMA EAGLE (Tulsa, OK) **11606**
OKLAHOMAN, THE (Oklahoma City, OK) **11385**
OKLEE HERALD, THE (Oklee, MN) **11541**
OKMULGEE DAILY TIMES (Okmulgee, OK) **11385**
OLATHE NEWS, THE (Olathe, KS) **11350**
OLATHE SUN (Overland Park, KS) **11499**
OLD COLONY MEMORIAL (Plymouth, MA) **11522**
OLDHAM ERA, THE (La Grange, KY) **11503**
OLENTANGY VALLEY NEWS (Columbus, OH) **11595**
OLIVE HILL TIMES (Morehead, KY) **11504**
OLIVIA TIMES JOURNAL (Olivia, MN) **11541**
OLMSTED-FAIRVIEW TIMES, THE (Rocky River, OH) **11600**
OLNEY DAILY MAIL (Olney, IL) **11341**
OLNEY ENTERPRISE, THE (Olney, TX) **11639**
OLNEY GAZETTE (Gaithersburg, MD) **11513**
OLNEY TIMES (Philadelphia, PA) **11615**
OLYMPIA REVIEW (Minier, IL) **11476**
OLYMPIAN, THE (Olympia, WA) **11405**

OMAHA STAR (Omaha, NE) **11558**
OMAHA WORLD-HERALD (Omaha, NE) **11367**
OMRO HERALD, THE (Omro, WI) **11665**
ONALASKA COMMUNITY LIFE (West Salem, WI) **11668**
ONAWA DEMOCRAT (Onawa, IA) **11494**
ONAWA SENTINEL (Onawa, IA) **11494**
ONAWAY OUTLOOK (Onaway, MI) **11531**
ONEIDA DAILY DISPATCH (Oneida, NY) **11374**
ONEIDA PRESS (Canastota, NY) **11572**
ONLOOKER, THE (Foley, AL) **11413**
ONONDAGA VALLEY NEWS (Syracuse, NY) **11583**
ONTONAGON HERALD, THE (Ontonagon, MI) **11531**
OOLOGAH LAKE LEADER (Oologah, OK) **11605**
OPELIKA-AUBURN NEWS (Opelika, AL) **11320**
OPP NEWS (Opp, AL) **11415**
OQUAWKA CURRENT (Oquawka, IL) **11478**
ORANGE COUNTIAN (Paoli, IN) **11487**
ORANGE COUNTY NEWS (Garden Grove, CA) **11429**
ORANGE COUNTY POST (Washingtonville, NY) **11583**
ORANGE COUNTY REGISTER, THE (Santa Ana, CA) **11327**
ORANGE COUNTY REVIEW (Orange, VA) **11649**
ORANGE COVE MOUNTAIN TIMES (Reedley, CA) **11435**
ORANGE LEADER (Orange, TX) **11400**
ORANGE TRANSCRIPT (Maplewood, NJ) **11565**
ORCHARD PARK BEE (Williamsville, NY) **11584**
ORD QUIZ (Ord, NE) **11558**
OREGON CITY NEWS (Portland, OR) **11608**
OREGON COUNTY RECORD (Salem, AR) **11424**
OREGON OBSERVER (Oregon, WI) **11665**
OREGONIAN, THE (Portland, OR) **11387**
OREM GENEVA TIMES (Orem, UT) **11643**
ORFORDVILLE JOURNAL & FOOTVILLE NEWS (Orfordville, WI) **11665**
ORION GAZETTE (Geneseo, IL) **11472**
ORLAND PARK-ORLAND HILLS (Tinley Park, IL) **11482**
ORLAND PRESS-REGISTER (Orland, CA) **11434**
ORLAND TOWNSHIP MESSENGER (Midlothian, IL) **11476**
ORLANDO SENTINEL (Chicago, IL) **11339**
ORLANDO WEEKLY, THE (Orlando, FL) **11453**
OROVILLE MERCURY-REGISTER (Oroville, CA) **11326**
ORTONVILLE INDEPENDENT (Ortonville, MN) **11541**
OSAGE COUNTY CHRONICLE (Burlingame, KS) **11497**
OSAKIS REVIEW, THE (Osakis, MN) **11541**
OSAWATOMIE GRAPHIC (Osawatomie, KS) **11498**
OSCEOLA COUNTY GAZETTE-TRIBUNE (Sibley, IA) **11495**
OSCEOLA NEWS-GAZETTE (Kissimmee, FL) **11452**
OSCEOLA PIONEER (Reed City, MI) **11531**
OSCEOLA SENTINEL-TRIBUNE (Osceola, IA) **11494**
OSCEOLA SUN (Osceola, WI) **11665**
OSCEOLA TIMES, THE (Osceola, AR) **11423**
OSCODA PRESS (Oscoda, MI) **11531**
OSGOOD JOURNAL (Versailles, IN) **11489**
OSHKOSH BUYERS GUIDE (Oshkosh, WI) **11665**
OSHKOSH NORTHWESTERN (Oshkosh, WI) **11408**
OSKALOOSA HERALD, THE (Oskaloosa, IA) **11348**
OSKALOOSA INDEPENDENT (Oskaloosa, KS) **11498**
OSSEO/MAPLE GROVE PRESS (Osseo, MN) **11541**
OSSIAN BEE, THE (Ossian, IA) **11494**
OSSIAN JOURNAL (Ossian, IN) **11487**
OTHELLO OUTLOOK, THE (Othello, WA) **11653**
OTHER PAPER (COLUMBUS), THE (Columbus, OH) **11595**
OTHER PAPER (SOUTH BURLINGTON), THE (South Burlington, VT) **11645**
OTIS NOTICE, THE (Cotuit, MA) **11517**
OTTAWA ADVANCE (Jenison, MI) **11529**
OTTAWA COUNTY EXPONENT, THE (Oak Harbor, OH) **11599**
OTTAWA HERALD (Ottawa, KS) **11350**
OTTAWA TIMES SHOPPER, THE (Ottawa, KS) **11498**
OTTUMWA COURIER (Ottumwa, IA) **11348**

OUR TOWN (Ramsey, NJ) **11566**
OUR TOWN EAST SIDE (New York, NY) **11580**
OUR TOWN NEWS (Coral Springs, FL) **11450**
OURAY COUNTY PLAINDEALER (Ouray, CO) **11442**
OUTLOOK (ALEXANDER CITY), THE (Alexander City, AL) **11319**
OVER THE MOUNTAIN JOURNAL (Birmingham, AL) **11411**
OVERLAND PARK SUN (Overland Park, KS) **11499**
OVERLAND-ST ANN JOURNAL (Hazelwood, MO) **11550**
OVERTON COUNTY NEWS (Livingston, TN) **11628**
OVID GAZETTE (Trumansburg, NY) **11583**
OVIEDO VOICE, THE (Oviedo, FL) **11453**
O-W ENTERPRISE (Owen, WI) **11665**
OWASSO REPORTER (Owasso, OK) **11605**
OWATONNA AREA SHOPPER (Owatonna, MN) **11541**
OWATONNA PEOPLE'S PRESS (Owatonna, MN) **11361**
OWEGO PENNYSAVER (Owego, NY) **11580**
OWINGS MILLS TIMES (Baltimore, MD) **11512**
OWYHEE AVALANCHE (Homedale, ID) **11464**
OXFORD ECCENTRIC, THE (Livonia, MI) **11529**
OXFORD PRESS (Oxford, OH) **11600**
OXFORD PUBLIC LEDGER (Oxford, NC) **11589**
OXFORD REGISTER, THE (Belle Plaine, KS) **11496**
OXFORD REVIEW-TIMES (Greene, NY) **11575**
OXFORD TRIBUNE (Oxford, PA) **11615**
OYSTER BAY ENTERPRISE PILOT (Mineola, NY) **11579**
OYSTER BAY GUARDIAN (Oyster Bay, NY) **11580**
OZARK COUNTY TIMES (Gainesville, MO) **11550**
OZARK JOURNAL, THE (Imboden, AR) **11422**
OZARK MOUNTAIN TRADER, THE (Berryville, AR) **11420**
OZAUKEE GUIDE (Cedarburg, WI) **11659**
OZAUKEE PRESS (Port Washington, WI) **11665**

P

PACIFIC SUN (Palo Alto, CA) **11434**
PACIFICA TRIBUNE (Pacifica, CA) **11434**
PADUCAH SUN, THE (Paducah, KY) **11352**
PAGE NEWS & COURIER (Luray, VA) **11648**
PAGELAND PROGRESSIVE-JOURNAL, THE (Pageland, SC) **11622**
PAGOSA SPRINGS SUN (Pagosa Springs, CO) **11442**
PAHRUMP VALLEY TIMES (Pahrump, NV) **11559**
PAINTSVILLE HERALD, THE (Paintsville, KY) **11504**
PALACIOS BEACON (Palacios, TX) **11639**
PALATINE COUNTRYSIDE (Arlington Heights, IL) **11466**
PALATINE JOURNAL/TOPICS (Des Plaines, IL) **11470**
PALATKA DAILY NEWS (Palatka, FL) **11333**
PALAU HORIZON (Saipan, MP) **11533**
PALESTINE HERALD-PRESS (Palestine, TX) **11400**
PALISADE TRIBUNE (Palisade, CO) **11442**
PALISADIAN-POST (Pacific Palisades, CA) **11434**
PALLADIUM PENNYSAVER (Oswego, NY) **11580**
PALLADIUM-ITEM (Richmond, IN) **11345**
PALLADIUM-TIMES, THE (Oswego, NY) **11374**
PALM BEACH DAILY NEWS (Palm Beach, FL) **11334**
PALM BEACH POST (West Palm Beach, FL) **11334**
PALMYRA ENTERPRISE, THE (Whitewater, WI) **11668**
PALMYRA SPECTATOR (Palmyra, MO) **11552**
PALO ALTO DAILY NEWS (Palo Alto, CA) **11326**
PALO ALTO WEEKLY (Palo Alto, CA) **11434**
PALO PINTO COUNTY SHOPPER (Mineral Wells, TX) **11639**
PALO VERDE VALLEY TIMES (Blythe, CA) **11426**
PALOS CITIZEN (Midlothian, IL) **11476**
PALOS VERDES PENINSULA NEWS (Rancho Palos Verdes, CA) **11435**
PALOUSE LIVING (Moscow, ID) **11465**
PAMLICO NEWS (Oriental, NC) **11589**
PAMPA NEWS (Pampa, TX) **11400**

PANA NEWS-PALLADIUM (Pana, IL) **11479**
PANOLA WATCHMAN (Carthage, TX) **11632**
PANOLIAN ADVANTAGE, THE (Batesville, MS) **11545**
PANOLIAN, THE (Batesville, MS) **11545**
PANTAGRAPH, THE (Bloomington, IL) **11338**
PAOLI NEWS (Paoli, IN) **11487**
PAOLI REPUBLICAN (Paoli, IN) **11488**
PAPER (BARRY), THE (Barry, IL) **11467**
PAPER (ELKHART COUNTY EDITION), THE (Goshen, IN) **11486**
PAPER (GALESBURG), THE (Galesburg, IL) **11472**
PAPER (KOSCIUSKO COUNTY EDITION), THE (Warsaw, IN) **11489**
PAPER OF WABASH COUNTY, THE (Wabash, IN) **11489**
PAPILLION TIMES (Papillion, NE) **11558**
PARADISE POST (Paradise, CA) **11434**
PARAGOULD DAILY PRESS (Paragould, AR) **11323**
PARIS BEACON NEWS (Paris, IL) **11341**
PARIS EXPRESS (Paris, AR) **11424**
PARIS NEWS, THE (Paris, TX) **11400**
PARIS POST-INTELLIGENCER (Paris, TN) **11396**
PARK CITIES NEWS (Dallas, TX) **11633**
PARK FALLS HERALD (Park Falls, WI) **11665**
PARK FOREST-MATTESON-RICHTON PARK STAR (Tinley Park, IL) **11482**
PARK LABREA NEWS/BEVERLY PRESS (Los Angeles, CA) **11432**
PARK RAPIDS ENTERPRISE (Pelican Rapids, MN) **11541**
PARK RECORD, THE (Denver, CO) **11440**
PARK RIDGE HERALD-ADVOCATE (Park Ridge, IL) **11479**
PARK RIDGE JOURNAL (Des Plaines, IL) **11470**
PARK SLOPE COURIER (Brooklyn, NY) **11571**
PARKCHESTER NEWS (Bronx, NY) **11570**
PARKE COUNTY SENTINEL (Rockville, IN) **11488**
PARKER CHRONICLE (Castle Rock, CO) **11440**
PARKER PIONEER (Parker, AZ) **11419**
PARKER-BLYTHE WHITE SHEET (Lake Havasu City, AZ) **11418**
PARKERS PRAIRIE INDEPENDENT (PARKERS PRAIRIE), THE (Parkers Prairie, MN) **11541**
▼PARKERSBURG NEWS AND SENTINEL (Parkersburg, WV) **11407**
PARKESBURG POST (Downingtown, PA) **11611**
PARKLAND GAZETTE (Coral Springs, FL) **11450**
PARKLAND PRESS (Allentown, PA) **11610**
PARLIER POST (Reedley, CA) **11435**
PARMA SUN POST (Berea, OH) **11593**
PARSIPPANY LIFE (Rockaway, NJ) **11567**
PARSIPPANY NEWS, THE (West Caldwell, NJ) **11568**
PARSONS ADVOCATE (Parsons, WV) **11656**
PARSONS SUN (Parsons, KS) **11350**
PASADENA CITIZEN (Pasadena, TX) **11400**
PASADENA STAR-NEWS, THE (Pasadena, CA) **11326**
PASADENA WEEKLY (Pasadena, CA) **11434**
PASCACK VALLEY COMMUNITY LIFE (Westwood, NJ) **11568**
PASCO NEWS (Mt Dora, FL) **11453**
PASO ROBLES PRESS, THE (Paso Robles, CA) **11434**
PATASKALA STANDARD, THE (Pataskala, OH) **11600**
PATENT TRADER (Mt Kisco, NY) **11579**
PATRIOT & FREE PRESS (Cuba, NY) **11572**
PATRIOT (HAMBURG), THE (Hamburg, PA) **11612**
PATRIOT LEDGER, THE (Quincy, MA) **11356**
PATRIOT (WEBSTER), THE (Webster, MA) **11524**
PATRIOT-NEWS (Harrisburg, PA) **11389**
PAULDING COUNTY PROGRESS, THE (Paulding, OH) **11600**
PAULDING COUNTY SENTINEL (Douglasville, GA) **11459**
PAULDING NEIGHBOR, THE (Dallas, GA) **11459**
PAULLINA TIMES (Paullina, IA) **11494**
PAULS VALLEY DAILY DEMOCRAT (Pauls Valley, OK) **11386**

PAW PAW COURIER-LEADER, THE (Paw Paw, MI) **11531**
PAWHUSKA JOURNAL-CAPITAL (Pawhuska, OK) **11605**
PAWLING NEWS CHRONICLE (Pawling, NY) **11580**
PAWNEE POST (Auburn, IL) **11467**
PAXTON DAILY RECORD (Paxton, IL) **11341**
PAYNESVILLE PRESS, THE (Paynesville, MN) **11541**
PAYSON ROUNDUP (Payson, AZ) **11419**
PEABODY GAZETTE BULLETIN (Peabody, KS) **11499**
PEABODY-LYNNFIELD WEEKLY NEWS (Peabody, MA) **11522**
PEACHTREE CITIZEN REVIEW, THE (Fayetteville, GA) **11459**
PEARLAND JOURNAL (Pearland, TX) **11639**
PECATONICA VALLEY LEADER (Argyle, WI) **11658**
PECOS ENTERPRISE (Pecos, TX) **11639**
PEKIN DAILY TIMES (Pekin, IL) **11341**
PELHAM JOURNAL (Pelham, GA) **11462**
PELHAM SUN, THE (Yonkers, NY) **11585**
PELICAN PRESS (Sarasota, FL) **11455**
PELICAN, THE (Pensacola, FL) **11454**
PELLA CHRONICLE (Pella, IA) **11494**
PEMBROKE MARINER (Marshfield, MA) **11520**
PEMBROKE MARINER/REPORTER (Marshfield, MA) **11520**
PENASEE GLOBE (Wayland, MI) **11533**
PENDER CHRONICLE (Burgaw, NC) **11586**
PENDER POST (Burgaw, NC) **11586**
PENDLETON RECORD, THE (Pendleton, OR) **11608**
PENDLETON TIMES, THE (Franklin, WV) **11655**
PENFIELD POST (Canandaigua, NY) **11571**
PENINSULA BEACON, THE (San Diego, CA) **11436**
PENINSULA CLARION (Kenai, AK) **11320**
PENINSULA DAILY NEWS (Port Angeles, WA) **11405**
PENINSULA GATEWAY (Gig Harbor, WA) **11652**
PENINSULA INDEPENDENT (Burlingame, CA) **11427**
PENN HILLS PROGRESS (Monroeville, PA) **11613**
PENNSBORO NEWS, THE (Harrisville, WV) **11656**
PENNY PINCHER (RIDGECREST) (Ridgecrest, CA) **11435**
PENNY PRESS 2 (Maryville, MO) **11552**
PENNY SAVER (COVINGTON) (Covington, OH) **11596**
PENNY SAVER (THREE RIVERS) (Three Rivers, MI) **11532**
PENNY SAVER (TINLEY PARK), THE (Tinley Park, IL) **11482**
PENNYSAVER (BREA) (Brea, CA) **11426**
PENNYSAVER (MONMOUTH) (Monmouth, IL) **11476**
PENNYSAVER (YORKTOWN HEIGHTS) (Yorktown Heights, NY) **11585**
PENNYWISE VILLAGER (Syracuse, NY) **11583**
PENOBSCOT TIMES (Old Town, ME) **11510**
PENSACOLA NEWS JOURNAL (Pensacola, FL) **11334**
PENSACOLA VOICE (Pensacola, FL) **11454**
PEOPLE'S DEFENDER, THE (West Union, OH) **11602**
PEOPLE-SENTINEL, THE (Barnwell, SC) **11619**
PEORIA INDEPENDENT (Sun City, AZ) **11419**
PEORIA JOURNAL STAR (Peoria, IL) **11341**
PEORIA TIMES (Glendale, AZ) **11418**
PEORIA TIMES OBSERVER (Peoria, IL) **11479**
PEPPERELL FREE PRESS (Devens, MA) **11517**
PERHAM ENTERPRISE-BULLETIN (Perham, MN) **11541**
PERINTON-FAIRPORT POST (Canandaigua, NY) **11572**
PERKASIE NEWS-HERALD (Souderton, PA) **11617**
PERQUIMANS WEEKLY (Hertford, NC) **11587**
PERRY CHIEF (Perry, IA) **11494**
PERRY COUNTY NEWS, THE (Tell City, IN) **11488**
PERRY COUNTY PETIT JEAN COUNTRY HEADLIGHT (Morrilton, AR) **11423**
PERRY COUNTY REPUBLIC-MONITOR, THE (Perryville, MO) **11552**
PERRY COUNTY TIMES (New Bloomfield, PA) **11614**
PERRY COUNTY TRIBUNE (New Lexington, OH) **11599**
PERRY COUNTY TRIBUNE SHOPPER (New Lexington, OH) **11599**
PERRY DAILY JOURNAL (Perry, OK) **11386**

PERRY NEWS-HERALD (Perry, FL) **11454**
PERRY TACO TIMES (Perry, FL) **11454**
PERRY-MORGAN ADVERTISER (New Lexington, OH) **11599**
PERRYSBURG MESSENGER-JOURNAL (Perrysburg, OH) **11600**
PERU TRIBUNE (Peru, IN) **11345**
PESHTIGO TIMES (Peshtigo, WI) **11665**
PETALUMA ARGUS-COURIER (New York, NY) **11580**
PETERBOROUGH TRANSCRIPT, THE (Peterborough, NH) **11561**
PETERSBURG OBSERVER (Petersburg, IL) **11480**
PETERSBURG PILOT (Petersburg, AK) **11416**
PETOSKEY NEWS-REVIEW (Petoskey, MI) **11359**
PETOSKEY/CHARLEVOIX STAR (Petoskey, MI) **11531**
PETROSKEY STAR (Gaylord, MI) **11527**
PFLUGERVILLE PFLAG (Pflugerville, TX) **11640**
PHAROS-TRIBUNE (Logansport, IN) **11344**
PHILADELPHIA CITY PAPER (Philadelphia, PA) **11615**
PHILADELPHIA DAILY NEWS (Philadelphia, PA) **11391**
PHILADELPHIA INQUIRER (Philadelphia, PA) **11391**
PHILADELPHIA WEEKLY (Philadelphia, PA) **11615**
PHILIPSBURG MAIL, THE (Philipsburg, MT) **11556**
PHILLIPS COUNTY REVIEW (Phillipsburg, KS) **11499**
PHILLIPSBURG FREE PRESS (Phillipsburg, NJ) **11566**
PHOENIX NEWSPAPER, THE (Brooklyn, NY) **11571**
PHOENIX (PHOENIXVILLE), THE (Phoenixville, PA) **11391**
PHOENIX PRESS WEEKLY (Phoenix, AZ) **11419**
PHOENIX REGISTER (Mexico, NY) **11578**
PHOTO NEWS (Monroe, NY) **11579**
PHOTO STAR (Willshire, OH) **11602**
PIATT COUNTY JOURNAL-REPUBLICAN (Champaign, IL) **11468**
PICAYUNE ITEM (Picayune, MS) **11363**
PICKAWAY COUNTY ADVERTISER (Circleville, OH) **11594**
PICKENS COUNTY HERALD (Carrollton, AL) **11412**
PICKENS COUNTY PROGRESS (Jasper, GA) **11460**
PICKENS SENTINEL (Pickens, SC) **11622**
PICKERINGTON TIMES-SUN (Columbus, OH) **11595**
PICKETT COUNTY PRESS (Byrdstown, TN) **11625**
PICTORIAL GAZETTE (Guilford, CT) **11444**
PIEDMONT HERALD (Piedmont, WV) **11656**
PIEDMONTER, THE (Alameda, CA) **11425**
PIERCE CITY LEADER-JOURNAL (Sarcoxie, MO) **11553**
PIERCE COUNTY HERALD (Ellsworth, WI) **11660**
PIERCE COUNTY TRIBUNE (Rugby, ND) **11592**
PIGGOTT TIMES, THE (Piggott, AR) **11424**
PIKE COUNTY DISPATCH (Milford, PA) **11613**
PIKE COUNTY EXPRESS (Pittsfield, IL) **11480**
PIKE COUNTY JOURNAL & REPORTER (Zebulon, GA) **11463**
PIKE COUNTY NEWS WATCHMAN, THE (Waverly, OH) **11602**
PIKES PEAK COURIER VIEW (Woodland Park, CO) **11443**
PILOT NEWS, THE (Plymouth, IN) **11345**
PILOT-INDEPENDENT, THE (Walker, MN) **11544**
PINAL COUNTY STAR WATCH (Casa Grande, AZ) **11417**
PINE BLUFF COMMERCIAL (Pine Bluff, AR) **11323**
PINE CITY PIONEER (Pine City, MN) **11541**
PINE ISLAND EAGLE (Fort Myers, FL) **11451**
PINE JOURNAL (Cloquet, MN) **11536**
PINE RIVER JOURNAL (Pine River, MN) **11541**
PINE RIVER TIMES (Bayfield, CO) **11439**
PINELAND PENNYSAVER, THE (Jesup, GA) **11461**
PINEVILLE SUN-CUMBERLAND COURIER (Pineville, KY) **11505**
PINNACLE, THE (Hollister, CA) **11429**
PIONEER (BALDWIN), THE (Baldwin, MI) **11357**
PIONEER (BEMIDJI), THE (Bemidji, MN) **11360**
PIONEER (MOUND), THE (Mound, MN) **11540**
PIONEER NEWS (Shepherdsville, KY) **11505**
PIONEER REPUBLICAN, THE (Marengo, IA) **11494**

PIONEER/OSCEOLA EDITION, THE (Reed City, MI) **11531**
PIPER SHOPPER (Pine River, MN) **11541**
PIPESTONE COUNTY STAR (Pipestone, MN) **11542**
PIQUA DAILY CALL (Piqua, OH) **11382**
PISCATAQUIS OBSERVER, THE (Dover-Foxcroft, ME) **11510**
PITCH, THE (Kansas City, MO) **11551**
PITTSBURG GAZETTE (Pittsburg, TX) **11640**
PITTSBURG MORNING SUN (Pittsburg, KS) **11350**
PITTSBURGH CITY PAPER (Pittsburgh, PA) **11616**
PITTSBURGH POST-GAZETTE (Pittsburgh, PA) **11391**
PITTSBURGH TRIBUNE-REVIEW (Pittsburgh, PA) **11391**
PITTSFIELD GAZETTE, THE (Pittsfield, MA) **11522**
PLACENTIA NEWS-TIMES (Anaheim, CA) **11425**
PLACER HERALD, THE (Rocklin, CA) **11435**
PLACER SENTINEL (AUBURN) (Auburn, CA) **11426**
PLAIN DEALER (Blackwood, NJ) **11561**
PLAIN DEALER, THE (Cleveland, OH) **11380**
PLAIN TALK, THE (Vermillion, SD) **11625**
PLAINDEALER, THE (Tekamah, NE) **11558**
PLAINFIELD SUN (Plainfield, IL) **11480**
PLAINSMAN, THE (Huron, SD) **11394**
PLAINSMAN WEEKLY NEWS (Sedalia, MO) **11553**
PLAINVIEW DAILY HERALD (Plainview, TX) **11400**
PLAINVIEW HERALD (Mineola, NY) **11579**
PLAINVIEW NEWS (PLAINVIEW, MN) (Plainview, MN) **11542**
PLAINVIEW NEWS (PLAINVIEW, NE), THE (Plainview, NE) **11558**
PLANO INSIDER (Plano, TX) **11640**
PLANO STAR COURIER (Plano, TX) **11400**
PLANT CITY SHOPPER (Plant City, FL) **11454**
PLANTATION FORUM (Davie, FL) **11450**
PLANTER, THE (Apopka, FL) **11449**
PLAQUEMINES GAZETTE (Belle Chasse, LA) **11506**
PLAQUEMINES WATCHMAN (Belle Chasse, LA) **11506**
PLATTE COUNTY RECORD-TIMES (Torrington, WY) **11669**
PLATTE COUNTY SUN NEWS (Liberty, MO) **11551**
PLATTEVILLE JOURNAL (Platteville, WI) **11665**
PLATTSMOUTH JOURNAL, THE (Plattsmouth, NE) **11558**
PLEASANT GROVE REVIEW (American Fork, UT) **11643**
PLEASANT PLAINS PRESS (Auburn, IL) **11467**
PLEASANTON EXPRESS (Pleasanton, TX) **11640**
PLEASANTON WEEKLY (Pleasanton, CA) **11434**
PLUM ADVANCE LEADER (Monroeville, PA) **11613**
PLYMOUTH OBSERVER (Livonia, MI) **11529**
PLYMOUTH SUN-SAILOR (Eden Prairie, MN) **11537**
PLYMOUTH-REVIEW, THE (Plymouth, WI) **11665**
POCAHONTAS RECORD-DEMOCRAT (Pocahontas, IA) **11494**
POCAHONTAS STAR HERALD (Pocahontas, AR) **11424**
POCAHONTAS TIMES (Marlinton, WV) **11656**
POCONO RECORD (Stroudsburg, PA) **11392**
POCONO SHOPPER (East Stroudsburg, PA) **11611**
POINT & SHORELAND JOURNAL (Toledo, OH) **11601**
POINT PLEASANT REGISTER (Point Pleasant, WA) **11405**
POINT REYES LIGHT (Point Reyes Station, CA) **11434**
POINTE COUPEE BANNER (New Roads, LA) **11508**
POLK COUNTY DEMOCRAT, THE (Charlotte Harbor, FL) **11449**
POLK COUNTY ENTERPRISE (Livingston, TX) **11638**
POLK COUNTY ITEMIZER-OBSERVER (Dallas, OR) **11607**
POLK COUNTY NEWS/CITIZEN ADVANCE (Benton, TN) **11625**
POLK COUNTY PRESS (Mulberry, FL) **11453**
POLK COUNTY PRESS CITIZEN (Des Moines, IA) **11491**
POLK SHOPPER (Winter Haven, FL) **11456**
POMPANO TIMES, THE (Pompano Beach, FL) **11454**
PONCA CITY NEWS (Ponca City, OK) **11386**
PONCHATOULA TIMES, THE (Ponchatoula, LA) **11508**
PONTIAC DAILY LEADER (Pontiac, IL) **11341**
PONTOTOC PROGRESS (Pontotoc, MS) **11547**
PONY EXPRESS MAIL (Liberty, TX) **11638**

POOLER NEWS (Pooler, GA) **11462**
POOLESVILLE GAZETTE (Gaithersburg, MD) **11513**
POPE COUNTY TRIBUNE (Glenwood, MN) **11538**
POPLARVILLE DEMOCRAT, THE (Poplarville, MS) **11547**
POPNATION (New Castle, PA) **11614**
PORT ARTHUR NEWS (Port Arthur, TX) **11400**
PORT ISABEL-SOUTH PADRE ITEM PRESS (Port Isabel, TX) **11640**
PORT LAVACA WAVE (Port Lavaca, TX) **11640**
PORT ORCHARD INDEPENDENT (Port Orchard, WA) **11653**
PORT RICHMOND STAR (Trevose, PA) **11617**
PORT ST LUCIE NEWS (Port St Lucie, FL) **11334**
PORT TIMES-RECORD, THE (East Setauket, NY) **11573**
PORT TOWNS GAZETTE (Landover, MD) **11514**
PORT TOWNSEND & JEFFERSON COUNTY LEADER (Port Townsend, WA) **11653**
PORT WASHINGTON NEWS (Mineola, NY) **11579**
PORTAGE CHRONICLE (Valparaiso, IN) **11489**
PORTAGE DAILY REGISTER, THE (Portage, WI) **11408**
PORTAGE DISPATCH, THE (Portage, PA) **11616**
PORTALES NEWS-TRIBUNE (Portales, NM) **11371**
PORTERVILLE RECORDER, THE (Porterville, CA) **11326**
PORTLAND LEADER, THE (Portland, TN) **11629**
PORTLAND NEWS (Portland, TX) **11640**
PORTLAND PHOENIX (Boston, MA) **11516**
PORTLAND PRESS HERALD (Portland, ME) **11354**
PORTLAND REVIEW & OBSERVER (Grand Ledge, MI) **11528**
PORTLAND TRIBUNE (Portland, OR) **11608**
PORTSMOUTH DAILY TIMES (Portsmouth, OH) **11382**
PORTSMOUTH HERALD (Portsmouth, NH) **11368**
POST & MAIL, THE (Columbia City, IN) **11342**
POST AND COURIER, THE (Charleston, SC) **11393**
POST (BIG STONE GAP), THE (Big Stone Gap, VA) **11646**
POST FALLS PRESS (Post Falls, ID) **11338**
POST FALLS TRIBUNE, THE (Post Falls, ID) **11465**
POST JOURNAL, THE (Machesney Park, IL) **11475**
POST MESSENGER RECORDER (New Glarus, WI) **11664**
POST (NEOSHO), THE (Neosho, MO) **11552**
POST (PATASKALA), THE (Pataskala, OH) **11600**
POST SHOPPER (Pacific Palisades, CA) **11434**
POST-BULLETIN (Rochester, MN) **11361**
POST-CRESCENT, THE (Appleton, WI) **11407**
POST-DISPATCH (Russellville, AR) **11424**
POST-HERALD (Red Creek, NY) **11581**
POST-JOURNAL, THE (Jamestown, NY) **11372**
POST/SOUTH (Plaquemine, LA) **11508**
POST-STANDARD (Syracuse, NY) **11375**
POST-STAR, THE (Glens Falls, NY) **11372**
POST-TRIBUNE (Merriville, IN) **11344**
POST-TRIBUNE (JEFFERSON CITY) (Jefferson City, MO) **11364**
POTEAU DAILY NEWS (Poteau, OK) **11386**
POTOMAC ALMANAC (McLean, VA) **11649**
POTOMAC GAZETTE (Gaithersburg, MD) **11513**
POTOMAC NEWS (Woodbridge, VA) **11404**
POTTER LEADER-ENTERPRISE (Coudersport, PA) **11610**
POTTSBORO PRESS (Pottsboro, TX) **11640**
POTTSVILLE REPUBLICAN - HERALD (Pottsville, PA) **11391**
POUGHKEEPSIE JOURNAL (Poughkeepsie, NY) **11374**
POWAY NEWS CHIEFTAIN (Poway, CA) **11434**
POWDER SPRINGS NEIGHBOR, THE (Marietta, GA) **11461**
POWELL VALLEY NEWS (Pennington Gap, VA) **11649**
POWER COUNTY PRESS, THE (American Falls, ID) **11464**
POYNETTE PRESS (Poynette, WI) **11666**
PRAIRIE CITY NEWS (Prairie City, IA) **11495**
PRAIRIE POST (Jamestown, ND) **11591**
PRAIRIE SHOPPER, THE (La Fayette, IL) **11474**
PRAIRIE SHOPPER (WILMINGTON), THE (Wilmington, IL) **11484**

PRAIRIE VILLAGE SUN (Overland Park, KS) **11499**
PRATT TRIBUNE (Pratt, KS) **11350**
PRATTVILLE PROGRESS (Prattville, AL) **11415**
PRESCOTT JOURNAL (Prescott, WI) **11666**
PRESCOTT VALLEY TRIBUNE, THE (Prescott Valley, AZ) **11419**
PRESQUE ISLE ADVANCE (Rogers City, MI) **11531**
PRESQUE ISLE STAR (Alpena, MI) **11525**
PRESS & BANNER, THE (Abbeville, SC) **11619**
PRESS & GUIDE (Dearborn, MI) **11526**
PRESS - REGISTER (Mobile, AL) **11320**
PRESS & STANDARD, THE (Walterboro, SC) **11623**
PRESS & SUN-BULLETIN (Vestal, NY) **11375**
PRESS ARGUS-COURIER (Van Buren, AR) **11425**
PRESS (AVON LAKE), THE (Avon Lake, OH) **11592**
PRESS (BRYAN), THE (Bryan, TX) **11632**
PRESS (ELLENVILLE), THE (Ellenville, NY) **11574**
PRESS ENTERPRISE (Bloomsburg, PA) **11388**
PRESS HERALD (Pine Grove, PA) **11615**
PRESS JOURNAL (CHESTERFIELD) (Chesterfield, MO) **11549**
PRESS JOURNAL (PALISADES PARK), THE (Palisades Park, NJ) **11566**
PRESS JOURNAL (STUART) (Stuart, FL) **11334**
PRESS (LOS ANGELES), THE (Los Angeles, CA) **11432**
PRESS (MILLBURY), THE (Millbury, OH) **11598**
PRESS OF ATLANTIC CITY, THE (Pleasantville, NJ) **11369**
PRESS PLUS (Pulaski, TN) **11629**
PRESS TRIBUNE, THE (Melbourne, FL) **11453**
PRESS-DISPATCH, THE (Petersburg, IN) **11488**
PRESS-ENTERPRISE, THE (Riverside, CA) **11326**
PRESS-NEWS, THE (Minerva, OH) **11598**
PRESS-REPUBLICAN (Plattsburgh, NY) **11374**
PRESS-SENTINEL, THE (Jesup, GA) **11461**
PRESS-STAR (New London, WI) **11664**
PRESS-TELEGRAM (LONG BEACH) (Long Beach, CA) **11325**
PRESS-TRIBUNE, THE (Roseville, CA) **11435**
PRESTON CITIZEN (Montpelier, ID) **11465**
PRESTON COUNTY JOURNAL (Kingwood, WV) **11656**
PREVIEW COMMUNITY WEEKLY (Traverse City, MI) **11532**
PRICE HILL PRESS (Cincinnati, OH) **11594**
PRIEST RIVER TIMES (Priest River, ID) **11465**
PRIMETIME (Lawrence, NY) **11577**
PRINCE GEORGES POST (Upper Marlboro, MD) **11515**
PRINCE GEORGE'S SENTINEL (Seabrook, MD) **11514**
PRINCETON DAILY CLARION (Princeton, IN) **11345**
PRINCETON NEWS LEADER (Princeton, NC) **11589**
PRINCETON PACKET, THE (Hightstown, NJ) **11563**
PRINCETON TIMES (Princeton, WV) **11656**
PRINCETON TIMES-REPUBLIC (Berlin, WI) **11658**
PRINCETON UNION-EAGLE (Princeton, MN) **11542**
PRIOR LAKE AMERICAN (Prior Lake, MN) **11542**
PROCTOR JOURNAL (Proctor, MN) **11542**
PROGRESS (ANAHUAC), THE (Anahuac, TX) **11631**
PROGRESS (CALDWELL), THE (Caldwell, NJ) **11561**
PROGRESS (CAVE CITY), THE (Cave City, KY) **11501**
PROGRESS (MONROEVILLE), THE (Monroeville, PA) **11613**
PROGRESS (UNION), THE (Union, NJ) **11568**
PROGRESS-INDEX (Petersburg, VA) **11404**
PROGRESSOR-TIMES, THE (Carey, OH) **11594**
PROMENADE (FORT LAUDERDALE) (Fort Lauderdale, FL) **11451**
PROSPECT HEIGHTS JOURNAL (Des Plaines, IL) **11470**
PROSPECT-NEWS, THE (Doniphan, MO) **11549**
PROVIDENCE JOURNAL (Providence, RI) **11393**
PROVIDENCE PHOENIX (Providence, RI) **11619**
PROVINCETOWN BANNER (Provincetown, MA) **11522**
PROVISO HERALD (Oak Park, IL) **11478**
PUBLIC OPINION, THE (Chambersburg, PA) **11388**
PUBLIC SPIRIT (Fort Washington, PA) **11612**

Title

PUEBLO CHIEFTAIN (Pueblo, CO) **11330**
PULASKI CITIZEN (Pulaski, TN) **11629**
PULASKI CITIZEN/GILES FREE PRESS (Pulaski, TN) **11629**
PULASKI COUNTY DEMOCRAT, THE (Richland, MO) **11552**
PULASKI COUNTY JOURNAL (Winamac, IN) **11489**
PULASKI COUNTY WEEKLY (St Robert, MO) **11554**
PULSE OF CHERRY HILL, THE (Cinnaminson, NJ) **11562**
PULSE-JOURNAL (Liberty Township, OH) **11597**
PUNXSUTAWNEY SPIRIT, THE (Punxutawney, PA) **11391**
PURCELL REGISTER (Purcell, OK) **11605**
PUTNAM COUNTY ADVERTISER (Ottawa, OH) **11599**
PUTNAM COUNTY COURIER, THE (Carmel, NY) **11572**
PUTNAM COUNTY RECORD (Granville, IL) **11473**
PUTNAM COUNTY SENTINEL (Ottawa, OH) **11599**
PUTNAM COUNTY VIDETTE (Columbus Grove, OH) **11596**
PUTNAM STANDARD, THE (Culloden, WV) **11655**
PYMATUNING AREA NEWS (Jefferson, OH) **11597**
PYRAMID, THE (Provo, UT) **11643**

Q

QUAD COMMUNITY PRESS (White Bear Lake, MN) **11544**
QUAD RIVER NEWS (Sheridan, MO) **11553**
QUAD-CITY TIMES (Davenport, IA) **11347**
QUAY COUNTY SUN (Tucumcari, NM) **11569**
QUECHEE TIMES (Hanover, NH) **11560**
QUEEN ANNE-MAGNOLIA NEWS (Seattle, WA) **11654**
QUEEN CREEK INDEPENDENT (Apache Junction, AZ) **11417**
QUEENS CHRONICLE (Rego Park, NY) **11581**
QUEENS EXAMINER, THE (Maspeth, NY) **11577**
QUEENS GAZETTE, THE (Long Island City, NY) **11577**
QUEENS LEDGER (Maspeth, NY) **11577**
QUEENS TRIBUNE (Fresh Meadows, NY) **11574**
QUEENS VILLAGE TIMES, THE (Bayside, NY) **11570**
QUINCY HERALD-WHIG (Quincy, IL) **11341**
QUINCY SUN (Quincy, MA) **11522**
QUITMAN FREE PRESS (Quitman, GA) **11462**

R

RADFORD NEWS JOURNAL (Christiansburg, VA) **11646**
RALSTON RECORDER (Papillion, NE) **11558**
RAMONA SENTINEL (Gilroy, CA) **11429**
RAMSEY COUNTY REVIEW (St Paul, MN) **11543**
RAMSEY SUBURBAN NEWS (Ridgewood, NJ) **11566**
RANCHO BERNARDO NEWS JOURNAL (Poway, CA) **11434**
RANCHO BERNARDO SUN (San Diego, CA) **11436**
RANCHO NEWS (Riverside, CA) **11435**
RANCHO SANTA MARGARITA NEWS (Lake Forest, CA) **11431**
RANDOLPH COUNTY HERALD TRIBUNE (Chester, IL) **11468**
RANDOLPH GUIDE, THE (Asheboro, NC) **11585**
RANDOLPH HERALD (Rayham, MA) **11522**
RANDOLPH LEADER (Roanoke, AL) **11415**
RANDOLPH REPORTER (Chester, NJ) **11562**
RANDOM LENGTHS NEWS (San Pedro, CA) **11437**
RANGE TIMES (Biwabik, MN) **11534**
RANGELEY HIGHLANDER (Rangeley, ME) **11511**
RANGER, THE (Riverton, WY) **11409**
RANGER TIMES (Eastland, TX) **11634**
RANKIN COUNTY NEWS, THE (Brandon, MS) **11545**
RANKIN INDEPENDENT (Cissna Park, IL) **11469**
RANSOM COUNTY GAZETTE & ENTERPRISE (Lisbon, ND) **11591**
RANTOUL PRESS (Rantoul, IL) **11480**
RAPID CITY JOURNAL (Rapid City, SD) **11395**
RAPPAHANNOCK NEWS (Washington, VA) **11650**
RAPPAHANNOCK RECORD (Kilmarnock, VA) **11648**

RARE REMINDER (Rocky Hill, CT) **11446**
RATON RANGE, THE (Raton, NM) **11568**
RAVALLI REPUBLIC (Hamilton, MT) **11366**
RAVENA NEWS HERALD (Ravena, NY) **11581**
RAWLINS DAILY TIMES, THE (Rawlins, WY) **11409**
RAYMOND/PRINSBURG NEWS,THE (Raymond, MN) **11542**
RAYNE ACADIAN-TRIBUNE, THE (Rayne, LA) **11508**
RAYNE INDEPENDENT (Rayne, LA) **11508**
RAYNHAM CALL (Rayham, MA) **11522**
RAYNHAM JOURNAL (Rockland, MA) **11523**
READING ADVOCATE, THE (Concord, MA) **11517**
READING EAGLE (Reading, PA) **11391**
REAPER EXTRA, THE (Richfield, UT) **11643**
RECORD - JOURNAL (FERNDALE) (Ferndale, WA) **11652**
RECORD (BOONVILLE), THE (Boonville, MO) **11548**
RECORD ENTERPRISE, THE (Plymouth, NH) **11561**
RECORD (GAINSVILLE), THE (Gainsville, FL) **11451**
RECORD GAZETTE (Banning, CA) **11426**
RECORD HERALD (CINCINNATI) (Washington Court House, OH) **11383**
RECORD HERALD (WAYNESBORO) (Waynesboro, PA) **11392**
RECORD (HUNTINGTON), THE (Huntington, NY) **11576**
RECORD (LEITCHFIELD), THE (Leitchfield, KY) **11503**
RECORD (NORTHBORO), THE (New York, NY) **11580**
RECORD (PAXTON), THE (Paxton, IL) **11479**
RECORD SEARCHLIGHT (Redding, CA) **11326**
RECORD (STOCKTON), THE (Stockton, CA) **11328**
RECORD, THE (Kansas City, KS) **11497**
RECORD (TROY), THE (Troy, NY) **11375**
RECORD (WEST PATERSON), THE (West Paterson, NJ) **11370**
RECORD-BREEZE (Blackwood, NJ) **11561**
RECORD-CITIZEN, THE (Bristow, OK) **11604**
RECORD-COURIER (Ravenna, OH) **11382**
RECORD-COURIER (BAKER CITY), THE (Baker City, OR) **11606**
RECORD-COURIER (GARDNERVILLE), THE (Gardnerville, NV) **11559**
RECORD-DELTA, THE (Buckhannon, WV) **11655**
RECORDER (AMSTERDAM), THE (Amsterdam, NY) **11371**
RECORDER (CONSHOHOCKEN), THE (Conshohocken, PA) **11610**
RECORDER (GREENFIELD), THE (Greenfield, MA) **11356**
RECORDER (MONTEREY), THE (Monterey, VA) **11649**
RECORDER (PRINCE FREDERICK), THE (Prince Frederick, MD) **11514**
RECORDER-HERALD (Salmon, ID) **11465**
RECORD-HERALD & INDIANOLA TRIBUNE (Indianola, IA) **11493**
RECORD-JOURNAL (Meriden, CT) **11331**
RECORD-OBSERVER (Centreville, MD) **11512**
RECORD-REVIEW, THE (Abbotsford, WI) **11657**
RED BAY NEWS (Red Bay, AL) **11415**
RED BLUFF DAILY NEWS (Red Bluff, CA) **11326**
RED HILLS SHOPPERS GUIDE, THE (Louisville, MS) **11547**
RED LAKE FALLS GAZETTE, THE (Red Lake Falls, MN) **11542**
RED OAK EXPRESS (Red Oak, IA) **11495**
RED SPRINGS CITIZEN, THE (Lumberton, NC) **11588**
RED WING REPUBLICAN EAGLE (Red Wing, MN) **11361**
REDDING PILOT, THE (Georgetown, CT) **11444**
REDFIELD PRESS (Redfield, SD) **11624**
REDFORD OBSERVER (Birmingham, MI) **11525**
REDLANDS DAILY FACTS (Redlands, CA) **11326**
REDLANDS GREEN SHEET (Redlands, CA) **11435**
REDMOND SPOKESMAN (Redmond, OR) **11609**
REDWOOD CITY TRIBUNE (Burlingame, CA) **11427**
REDWOOD FALLS LIVEWIRE (Redwood Falls, MN) **11542**
REDWOOD GAZETTE, THE (Redwood Falls, MN) **11542**

REDWOOD TIMES (Garberville, CA) **11429**
REEDLEY EXPONENT (Reedley, CA) **11435**
REEDSBURG TIMES-PRESS (Reedsburg, WI) **11666**
REFLECTOR, THE (Battle Ground, WA) **11651**
REGAL COURIER (King City, OR) **11607**
REGIONAL NEWS (Palos Heights, IL) **11478**
REGIONAL NEWS, THE (La Porte, IN) **11486**
REGIONAL STANDARD (Middletown, CT) **11445**
REGISTER CITIZEN (Torrington, CT) **11331**
REGISTER (PALMER), THE (Palmer, MA) **11522**
REGISTER STAR (Rockford, IL) **11341**
REGISTER (YARMOUTHPORT), THE (Yarmouthport, MA) **11524**
REGISTER-GUARD, THE (Eugene, OR) **11387**
REGISTER-HERALD (Eaton, OH) **11596**
REGISTER-HERALD (BECKLEY), THE (Beckley, WV) **11406**
REGISTER-HERALD (PINE PLAINS), THE (Rhinebeck, NY) **11581**
REGISTER-MAIL, THE (Galesburg, IL) **11339**
REGISTER-NEWS (MT VERNON), THE (Mt Vernon, IL) **11341**
REGISTER-NEWS, THE (Allentown, NJ) **11561**
REGISTER-PAJARONIAN (Watsonville, CA) **11328**
REGISTER-STAR (Hudson, NY) **11372**
REIDSVILLE REVIEW (Reidsville, NC) **11377**
REMINDER (EAST LONGMEADOW), THE (East Longmeadow, MA) **11517**
REMINDER/METRO WEST, THE (East Longmeadow, MA) **11517**
REMINGTON PRESS (Rensselaer, IN) **11488**
RENO GAZETTE-JOURNAL (Reno, NV) **11368**
RENO NEWS & REVIEW (Reno, NV) **11559**
RENSSELAER REPUBLICAN (Rensselaer, IN) **11345**
RENVILLE COUNTY SHOPPER (Olivia, MN) **11541**
REPORTER (CHICAGO), THE (Chicago, IL) **11469**
REPORTER (DOWNERS GROVE) (Downers Grove, IL) **11470**
REPORTER EXTRA, THE (Coldwater, MI) **11526**
REPORTER (FOND DU LAC), THE (Fond Du Lac, WI) **11407**
REPORTER (MELBOURNE), THE (Melbourne, FL) **11453**
REPORTER NEWSPAPER, THE (Palos Heights, IL) **11479**
REPORTER OF THE SPRING-FORD AREA (Royersford, PA) **11616**
REPORTER (PALOS HEIGHTS), THE (Palos Heights, IL) **11479**
REPORTER (SOMERVILLE), THE (Somerville, NJ) **11567**
REPORTER (TAVERNIER), THE (Tavernier, FL) **11456**
REPORTER, THE (Lansdale, PA) **11390**
REPORTER (VACAVILLE), THE (Vacaville, CA) **11328**
REPORTER-TIMES, THE (Martinsville, IN) **11344**
REPOSITORY, THE (Canton, OH) **11379**
REPUBLIC MONITOR, THE (Republic, MO) **11552**
REPUBLIC, THE (Columbus, IN) **11342**
REPUBLICAN (HENDRICKS), THE (Danville, IN) **11485**
REPUBLICAN JOURNAL (BELFAST) (Belfast, ME) **11509**
REPUBLICAN JOURNAL (DARLINGTON) (Darlington, WI) **11660**
REPUBLICAN LEADER (Preston, MN) **11542**
REPUBLICAN, THE (Oakland, MD) **11514**
REPUBLIC-TIMES (Waterloo, IL) **11483**
RESIDENT (STONINGTON), THE (Pawcatuck, CT) **11446**
RESTON CONNECTION (McLean, VA) **11649**
RESTON TIMES (Herndon, VA) **11647**
RETROSPECT, THE (Collingswood, NJ) **11562**
REVEILLE/BETWEEN THE LAKES (Ovid, NY) **11580**
REVERE JOURNAL, THE (Revere, MA) **11523**
REVIEW APPEAL (Franklin, TN) **11395**
REVIEW (EAST LIVERPOOL), THE (East Liverpool, OH) **11380**
REVIEW (ERIE), THE (Erie, IL) **11471**
REVIEW INDEPENDENT, THE (Toppenish, WA) **11654**

REVIEW (PHILADELPHIA), THE (Philadelphia, PA) **11615**
REVIEW PRESS (New Rochelle, NY) **11579**
REVIEW TIMES (Fostoria, OH) **11380**
REVIEW-REPUBLICAN, THE (Attica, IN) **11484**
REVUE & NEWS (Alpharetta, GA) **11456**
REYNOLDS COUNTY COURIER (Ellington, MO) **11550**
REYNOLDSBURG NEWS (Columbus, OH) **11595**
RFD NEWS, THE (Bellevue, OH) **11593**
RIALTO RECORD (San Bernardino, CA) **11436**
RICHARDSON MORNING NEWS (Richardson, TX) **11640**
RICHFIELD REAPER (Richfield, UT) **11643**
RICHFIELD SUN-CURRENT (Eden Prairie, MN) **11537**
RICHLAND BEACON-NEWS (Rayville, LA) **11508**
RICHLAND MIRROR, THE (Richland, MO) **11552**
RICHLAND OBSERVER (Richland Center, WI) **11666**
RICHLAND SHOPPING NEWS (Richland Center, WI) **11666**
RICHLANDS NEWS PRESS (Richlands, VA) **11650**
RICHLANDS-BEULAVILLE ADVERTISER-NEWS (Richlands, NC)
    11589
RICHMOND COUNTY DAILY JOURNAL (Rockingham, NC)
    11377
RICHMOND HILL TIMES (Bayside, NY) **11570**
RICHMOND REGISTER (Richmond, KY) **11352**
RICHMOND SPRINGS GROVE REPORT (Twin Lakes, WI)
    11667
RICHMOND TIMES-DISPATCH (Richmond, VA) **11404**
RICHTON DISPATCH, THE (Richton, MS) **11547**
RIDGEFIELD PRESS, THE (Ridgefield, CT) **11446**
RIDGEWAY NEWS (Shawneetown, IL) **11481**
RIDGEWOOD LEDGER (Bayside, NY) **11570**
RIDGEWOOD NEWS, THE (Ridgewood, NJ) **11566**
RIDGWAY RECORD (Ridgway, PA) **11391**
RIDGWAY SUN (Ridgway, CO) **11442**
RIDLEY PRESS (Drexel Hill, PA) **11611**
RIO BLANCO HERALD TIMES (Meeker, CO) **11441**
RIO GRANDE SUN (Espanola, NM) **11568**
RIPLEY BEE, THE (Ripley, OH) **11600**
RIPON BULLETIN (Manteca, CA) **11432**
RIPON COMMONWEALTH PRESS (Ripon, WI) **11666**
RISING STAR, THE (Eastland, TX) **11634**
RISING SUN RECORDER (Rising Sun, IN) **11488**
RITCHIE GAZETTE (Harrisville, WV) **11656**
RIVER EAST NEWS BULLETIN (Glastonbury, CT) **11444**
RIVER FALLS JOURNAL (River Falls, WI) **11666**
RIVER GROVE MESSENGER (Oak Park, IL) **11478**
RIVER OAKS EXAMINER (Houston, TX) **11637**
RIVER OAKS NEWS (Fort Worth, TX) **11635**
RIVER PRESS, THE (Fort Benton, MT) **11555**
RIVER RECORD, THE (Keene, NH) **11560**
RIVER REPORTER, THE (Narrowsburg, NY) **11579**
RIVER VALLEY ADVERTISER, THE (Van Buren, AR) **11425**
RIVERBANK NEWS, THE (Riverbank, CA) **11435**
RIVERDALE PRESS (Bronx, NY) **11570**
RIVERDALE REVIEW (Bronx, NY) **11570**
RIVERFRONT TIMES, THE (St Louis, MO) **11553**
RIVERLAND NEWS (Dunnellon, FL) **11450**
RIVERSIDE BULLETIN, THE (Los Angeles, CA) **11432**
RIVERSIDE GREEN SHEET (Redlands, CA) **11435**
RIVERSIDE REVIEW (Buffalo, NY) **11571**
RIVERSIDE SUBURBAN LIFE (North Riverside, IL) **11477**
RIVERTON REGISTER & TRI CITY REGISTER (Riverton, IL)
    11480
RIVERTOWNS ENTERPRISE, THE (Dobbs Ferry, NY) **11573**
ROANE COUNTY NEWS, THE (Kingston, TN) **11627**
ROANE COUNTY REPORTER (Spencer, WV) **11657**
ROANOKE BEACON (Plymouth, NC) **11589**
ROANOKE RAPIDS DAILY & SUNDAY HERALD (Roanoke
    Rapids, NC) **11377**
ROANOKE TIMES, THE (Roanoke, VA) **11404**

ROBERTSON COUNTY TIMES (Springfield, TN) **11630**
ROBESONIAN, THE (Lumberton, NC) **11377**
ROBINSON DAILY NEWS (Robinson, IL) **11341**
ROCHELLE NEWS LEADER (Rochelle, IL) **11480**
ROCHESTER DEMOCRAT & CHRONICLE (Rochester, NY)
    11374
ROCHESTER SENTINEL, THE (Rochester, IN) **11345**
ROCHESTER TIMES (AUBURN) (Auburn, IL) **11467**
ROCHESTER TIMES (ROCHESTER), THE (Rochester, NH)
    11561
ROCK COUNTY STAR HERALD (Luverne, MN) **11539**
ROCK ISLAND ARGUS, THE (Rock Island, IL) **11341**
ROCKAWAY JOURNAL (Garden City, NY) **11574**
ROCKBRIDGE WEEKLY (Lexington, VA) **11648**
ROCKDALE CITIZEN (Conyers, GA) **11335**
ROCKDALE NEIGHBOR, THE (Chamblee, GA) **11458**
ROCKDALE REPORTER (Rockdale, TX) **11640**
ROCKFORD AREA NEWS LEADER (Osseo, MN) **11541**
ROCKFORD JOURNAL, THE (Machesney Park, IL) **11475**
ROCKFORD SQUIRE, THE (Rockford, MI) **11531**
ROCKFORD/CEDAR SPRINGS ADVANCE (Jenison, MI) **11529**
ROCKINGHAM NEWS (Stratham, NH) **11561**
ROCKLAND COUNTY TIMES (Nanuet, NY) **11579**
ROCKLAND MARINER (Marshfield, MA) **11520**
ROCKMART JOURNAL (Rockmart, GA) **11462**
ROCKVILLE CENTRE HERALD (Garden City, NY) **11574**
ROCKVILLE GAZETTE (Gaithersburg, MD) **11513**
ROCKWOOD TIMES (Kingston, TN) **11627**
ROCKY FORD DAILY GAZETTE (Rocky Ford, CO) **11330**
ROCKY FORK ENTERPRISE (Worthington, OH) **11602**
ROCKY HILL POST (Bristol, CT) **11443**
ROCKY MOUNT TELEGRAM (Rocky Mount, NC) **11377**
ROGERS HOMETOWN NEWS (Rogers, AR) **11424**
ROGERSVILLE REVIEW (Rogersville, TN) **11629**
ROGUE RIVER PRESS (Rogue River, OR) **11609**
ROLLA DAILY NEWS (Rolla, MO) **11365**
ROLLING MEADOWS JOURNAL/TOPICS (Des Plaines, IL)
    11470
ROLLING MEADOWS REVIEW (Arlington Heights, IL) **11466**
ROME NEWS-TRIBUNE (Rome, GA) **11336**
ROMEO OBSERVER, THE (Romeo, MI) **11531**
ROMULUS ROMAN (Wayne, MI) **11533**
RONKONKOMA REVIEW (Nesconset, NY) **11579**
ROSAMOND WEEKLY NEWS (Rosamond, CA) **11435**
ROSCOE HOSMER INDEPENDENT (Ipswich, SD) **11624**
ROSCOMMON COUNTY HERALD-NEWS (Roscommon, MI)
    11531
ROSCOMMON COUNTY STAR (Gaylord, MI) **11527**
ROSEAU TIMES-REGION (Roseau, MN) **11542**
ROSELLE/ITASCA PRESS (St Charles, IL) **11481**
ROSEMONT JOURNAL (Des Plaines, IL) **11470**
ROSEMOUNT THISWEEK (Burnsville, MN) **11535**
ROSEVILLE INDEPENDENT (Macomb, IL) **11475**
ROSEVILLE REVIEW (St Paul, MN) **11543**
ROSLINDALE TRANSCRIPT (Needham, MA) **11521**
ROSLYN NEWS, THE (Mineola, NY) **11579**
ROSS COUNTY ADVERTISER (Chillicothe, OH) **11594**
ROSS VALLEY REPORTER (Sausalito, CA) **11437**
ROSSFORD RECORD-JOURNAL (Rossford, OH) **11600**
ROSWELL DAILY RECORD (Roswell, NM) **11371**
ROSWELL-ALPHARETTA NEIGHBOR (Roswell, GA) **11462**
ROTTERDAM JOURNAL (Delmar, NY) **11573**
ROUND LAKE NEWS (Grayslake, IL) **11473**
ROUND ROCK LEADER (Round Rock, TX) **11640**
ROUTE 40 FLIER, THE (Newark, DE) **11448**
ROWLETT LAKESHORE TIMES, THE (Mesquite, TX) **11639**
ROXBURY REGISTER, THE (Chester, NJ) **11562**
ROYSTON NEWS LEADER (Royston, GA) **11462**
RUIDOSO NEWS, THE (Ruidoso, NM) **11568**

RUMFORD FALLS TIMES (Rumford, ME) **11511**
RURAL - URBAN RECORD (Columbia Station, OH) **11595**
RURAL VIRGINIAN (Charlottesville, VA) **11646**
RUSH COUNTY NEWS (La Crosse, KS) **11498**
RUSHVILLE REPUBLICAN (Rushville, IN) **11345**
RUSHVILLE TIMES, THE (Rushville, IL) **11480**
RUSSELL COUNTY NEWS (Russell, KS) **11499**
RUSSELL COUNTY NEWS, THE (Russell Springs, KY) **11505**
RUSSELL REGISTER (Jamestown, KY) **11503**
RUSTON DAILY LEADER (Ruston, LA) **11354**
RUTHERFORD COURIER, THE (Smyrna, TN) **11629**
RUTLAND HERALD (Rutland, VT) **11403**
RUTLAND TRIBUNE (Rutland, VT) **11644**
RYE CHRONICLE, THE (Yonkers, NY) **11585**

S

S F WEEKLY (San Francisco, CA) **11436**
S I TRADER (West Frankfort, IL) **11483**
SABINA ADVERTISER (Sabina, OH) **11600**
SABINAL SAMPLER (Hondo, TX) **11636**
SABINE BANNER (Many, LA) **11507**
SABINE COUNTY REPORTER-RAMBLER (Hemphill, TX) **11636**
SABINE INDEX (Many, LA) **11507**
SACRAMENTO BEE (Sacramento, CA) **11327**
SACRAMENTO BULLETIN, THE (Sacramento, CA) **11435**
SACRAMENTO NEWS & REVIEW (Sacramento, CA) **11435**
SADDLEBACK VALLEY NEWS (Lake Forest, CA) **11431**
SAGINAW NEWS, THE (Saginaw, MI) **11359**
SAGINAW PRESS, THE (Saginaw, MI) **11532**
SAINT ELMO BANNER (St Elmo, IL) **11481**
SAINT FRANCIS HERALD, THE (St Francis, KS) **11499**
SAINT PAULS REVIEW, THE (St Pauls, NC) **11589**
SAKONNET TIMES (Tiverton, RI) **11619**
SALAMANCA PRESS (Salamanca, NY) **11374**
SALEM DEMOCRAT, THE (Salem, IN) **11488**
SALEM LEADER, THE (Salem, IN) **11488**
SALEM (MO) NEWS (Salem, MO) **11553**
SALEM NEWS (BEVERLY) (Beverly, MA) **11355**
SALEM OBSERVER (Manchester, NH) **11560**
SALEM (OH) NEWS (Salem, OH) **11382**
SALEM TIMES-COMMONER (Salem, IL) **11480**
SALEM TIMES-REGISTER (Salem, VA) **11650**
SALINA JOURNAL (Salina, KS) **11350**
SALINAS CALIFORNIAN, THE (Salinas, CA) **11327**
SALINE REPORTER, THE (Saline, MI) **11532**
SALISBURY POST (Salisbury, NC) **11378**
SALISBURY PRESS (Allentown, PA) **11610**
SALMON RIVER NEWS (Pulaski, NY) **11581**
SALT LAKE CITY WEEKLY (Salt Lake City, UT) **11643**
SALT LAKE TRIBUNE, THE (Salt Lake Cty, UT) **11402**
SALUDA STANDARD SENTINEL (Saluda, SC) **11622**
SALYERSVILLE INDEPENDENT, THE (Salyersville, KY) **11505**
SAMOA NEWS (Pago Pago, AS) **11321**
SAMOA NEWS (PAGO PAGO) (Pago Pago, AS) **11417**
SAMPSON INDEPENDENT, THE (Clinton, NC) **11376**
SAMSON LEDGER (Geneva, AL) **11413**
SAN ANGELO STANDARD-TIMES (San Angelo, TX) **11400**
SAN ANTONIO CURRENT (San Antonio, TX) **11640**
SAN ANTONIO EXPRESS-NEWS (San Antonio, TX) **11400**
SAN AUGUSTINE TRIBUNE (San Augustine, TX) **11640**
SAN BENITO NEWS (San Benito, TX) **11640**
SAN BERNARDINO BULLETIN, THE (Los Angeles, CA) **11432**
SAN BERNARDINO COUNTY SUN (San Bernardino, CA)
    11327
SAN BERNARDINO GREEN SHEET (Redlands, CA) **11435**
SAN CARLOS APACHE MOCCASIN (Globe, AZ) **11418**
SAN DIEGO DOWNTOWN NEWS (San Diego, CA) **11436**

Title

SAN DIEGO READER (San Diego, CA) **11436**
SAN DIEGO UNION-TRIBUNE (San Diego, CA) **11327**
SAN FERNANDO VALLEY SUN (San Fernando, CA) **11436**
SAN FRANCISCO CHRONICLE (San Francisco, CA) **11327**
SAN FRANCISCO EXAMINER (San Francisco, CA) **11327**
SAN FRANCISCO INDEPENDENT (San Francisco, CA) **11436**
SAN FRANCISCO METRO REPORTER (San Francisco, CA) **11436**
SAN FRANCISCO OBSERVER (San Francisco, CA) **11436**
SAN GABRIEL VALLEY TRIBUNE (West Covina, CA) **11328**
SAN JOSE MERCURY NEWS (San Jose, CA) **11327**
SAN MANUEL MINER, THE (San Manuel, AZ) **11419**
SAN MARCOS DAILY RECORD (San Marcos, TX) **11401**
SAN MARINO TRIBUNE (San Marino, CA) **11436**
SAN MATEO COUNTY TIMES (San Mateo, CA) **11327**
SAN MATEO WEEKLY (Burlingame, CA) **11427**
SAN PATRICIO COUNTY NEWS (Sinton, TX) **11641**
SAN PEDRO VALLEY NEWS-SUN (Benson, AZ) **11417**
SAN RAFAEL NEWS POINTER (Sausalito, CA) **11437**
SAN RAMON VALLEY TIMES, THE (Danville, CA) **11324**
SAND MOUNTAIN REPORTER, THE (Albertville, AL) **11411**
SAND SPRINGS LEADER (Sand Springs, OK) **11605**
SANDERSVILLE PROGRESS (Sandersville, GA) **11462**
SANDUSKY REGISTER (Sandusky, OH) **11382**
SANDWICH ENTERPRISE (Falmouth, MA) **11518**
SANDWICH/SAGAMORE PENNYSAVER (Yarmouthport, MA) **11525**
SANDY POST (Sandy, OR) **11609**
SANDY SPRINGS NEIGHBOR, THE (Atlanta, GA) **11457**
SANFORD (FL) HERALD, THE (Sanford, FL) **11455**
SANFORD (NC) HERALD, THE (Sanford, NC) **11378**
SANFORD NEWS (Sanford, ME) **11511**
SANGER HERALD (Sanger, CA) **11437**
SANIBEL-CAPTIVA ISLANDER (Sanibel, FL) **11455**
SANILAC COUNTY NEWS (Sandusky, MI) **11532**
SANTA BARBARA INDEPENDENT (Santa Barbara, CA) **11437**
SANTA BARBARA NEWS-PRESS (Santa Barbara, CA) **11327**
SANTA CRUZ COUNTY SENTINEL (Scotts Valley, CA) **11327**
SANTA FE REPORTER, THE (Santa Fe, NM) **11568**
SANTA MARIA TIMES (Santa Maria, CA) **11327**
SANTA PAULA TIMES (Santa Paula, CA) **11437**
SANTA ROSA FREE PRESS (Milton, FL) **11453**
SANTA ROSA PRESS DEMOCRAT (New York, NY) **11373**
SANTA YNEZ VALLEY EXTRA EDITION (Solvang, CA) **11438**
SANTA YNEZ VALLEY NEWS (Solvang, CA) **11438**
SANTAN SUN NEWS (Chandler, AZ) **11418**
SANTEE STRIPER (Holly Hill, SC) **11621**
SAPULPA DAILY HERALD, THE (Sapulpa, OK) **11386**
SARASOTA HERALD-TRIBUNE (New York, NY) **11373**
SARATOGA NEWS (Los Gatos, CA) **11432**
SARATOGA SPOTLIGHT (Delmar, NY) **11573**
SARATOGA SUN (Saratoga, WY) **11669**
SARATOGIAN, THE (Saratoga Springs, NY) **11375**
SARCOXIE RECORD, THE (Sarcoxie, MO) **11553**
SARGENT LEADER (Burwell, NE) **11557**
SATURDAY ADVANTAGE, THE (Monte Vista, CO) **11442**
SATURDAY MORNING PRESS (Craig, CO) **11440**
SAUGERTIES PENNYSAVER (Saugerties, NY) **11581**
SAUGERTIES POST STAR (Saugerties, NY) **11581**
SAUGUS ADVERTISER (Beverly, MA) **11516**
SAUK CENTRE HERALD (Sauk Centre, MN) **11542**
SAUK PRAIRIE EAGLE (Sauk City, WI) **11666**
SAUK-PRAIRIE STAR (Sauk City, WI) **11666**
SAULT STE MARIE EVENING NEWS (Sault Ste Marie, MI) **11360**
SAVANNA TIMES JOURNAL (Savanna, IL) **11481**
SAVANNAH MORNING NEWS (Savannah, GA) **11336**

SAVANNAH REPORTER & ANDREW COUNTY DEMOCRAT (Savannah, MO) **11553**
SAWYER COUNTY GAZETTE (Winter, WI) **11668**
SAWYER COUNTY RECORD (Hayward, WI) **11661**
SAYRE TIMES EXTRA, THE (Sayre, PA) **11616**
SCARBOROUGH LEADER (Biddeford, ME) **11509**
SCARSDALE INQUIRER, THE (Scarsdale, NY) **11582**
SCENE (FREEPORT), THE (Freeport, IL) **11471**
SCENIC RANGE NEWS (Bovey, MN) **11535**
SCHALLER HERALD (Schaller, IA) **11495**
SCHAUMBURG REVIEW (Arlington Heights, IL) **11466**
SCHUYLER SUN, THE (Schuyler, NE) **11558**
SCIOTO VOICE, THE (Wheelersburg, OH) **11602**
SCITUATE MARINER (Marshfield, MA) **11520**
SCOOP TODAY, THE (Lena, IL) **11475**
SCOTIA-GLENVILLE JOURNAL (Delmar, NY) **11573**
SCOTSMAN COMMUNITY PUBLICATIONS (Syracuse, NY) **11583**
SCOTSMAN (RUM RIVER AREA) (Cambridge, MN) **11535**
SCOTSMAN, THE (Cambridge, MN) **11535**
SCOTT COUNTY ADVERTISER (Waldron, AR) **11425**
SCOTT COUNTY JOURNAL (Pekin, IN) **11488**
SCOTT COUNTY NEWS (Oneida, TN) **11629**
SCOTT COUNTY TIMES (Forest, MS) **11546**
SCOTTSDALE-ASHBURN INDEPENDENT (Midlothian, IL) **11476**
SCOTTSVILLE CITIZEN-TIMES (Scottsville, KY) **11505**
SCRANTON TIMES TRIBUNE (Scranton, PA) **11391**
SEALY NEWS (Sealy, TX) **11640**
SEASIDE SIGNAL (Seaside, OR) **11609**
SEATTLE POST-INTELLIGENCER (ONLINE) (Seattle, WA) **11405**
SEATTLE WEEKLY (Seattle, WA) **11654**
SEBASTIAN SUN (Sebastian, FL) **11455**
SEBEKA-MENAHGA REVIEW MESSENGER (Sebeka, MN) **11542**
SECAUCUS HOME NEWS (Secaucus, NJ) **11567**
SECAUCUS REPORTER (Hoboken, NJ) **11564**
SEDALIA DEMOCRAT, THE (Sedalia, MO) **11365**
SEDALIA NEWS JOURNAL (Sedalia, MO) **11553**
SEDONA RED ROCK NEWS (Sedona, AZ) **11419**
SEEKONK STAR (East Providence, RI) **11618**
SELBY RECORD (Selby, SD) **11624**
SELMA ENTERPRISE (Selma, CA) **11437**
SELMA TIMES-JOURNAL (Selma, AL) **11320**
SEMINOLE BEACON (Seminole, FL) **11455**
SEMINOLE PRODUCER (Seminole, OK) **11386**
SENTINEL & ENTERPRISE (Fitchburg, MA) **11355**
SENTINEL (BELCHERTOWN), THE (Belchertown, MA) **11515**
SENTINEL (CARLISLE), THE (Carlisle, PA) **11610**
SENTINEL (COQUILLE), THE (Coquille, OR) **11606**
SENTINEL (HANFORD), THE (Hanford, CA) **11325**
SENTINEL (LEWISTOWN), THE (Lewistown, PA) **11390**
SENTINEL (MARSHFIELD), THE (Marshfield, MA) **11520**
SENTINEL NEWS, THE (Westfield, NY) **11584**
SENTINEL (RADCLIFF), THE (Radcliff, KY) **11505**
SENTINEL-ECHO, THE (London, KY) **11503**
SENTINEL-RECORD, THE (Hot Springs, AR) **11323**
SENTINEL-TRIBUNE (Bowling Green, OH) **11379**
SENTRY, THE (Pompano Beach, FL) **11454**
SEQUATCHIE VALLEY PURCHASE (South Pittsburg, TN) **11629**
SEQUIM GAZETTE (Sequim, WA) **11654**
SEQUOYAH COUNTY TIMES (Sallisaw, OK) **11605**
SEWARD COUNTY INDEPENDENT (Seward, NE) **11558**
SEWARD PHOENIX LOG, THE (Seward, AK) **11416**
SEWICKLEY HERALD STAR (Pittsburgh, PA) **11616**
SHAFTER PRESS (Shafter, CA) **11437**
SHAKOPEE VALLEY NEWS (Shakopee, MN) **11542**

SHARON ADVOCATE (Norwood, MA) **11522**
SHARON REPORTER, THE (Clinton, WI) **11659**
SHARP COUNTY RECORD (Salem, AR) **11424**
SHAWANO LEADER (Shawano, WI) **11409**
SHAWNEE NEWS-STAR, THE (Shawnee, OK) **11386**
SHAWNEE/MERRIAM SUN (Overland Park, KS) **11499**
SHEBOYGAN FALLS NEWS (Plymouth, WI) **11665**
SHEBOYGAN PRESS, THE (Sheboygan, WI) **11409**
SHELBURNE NEWS (Shelburne, VT) **11645**
SHELBY COUNTY HERALD (Shelbyville, MO) **11553**
SHELBY COUNTY REPORTER (Columbiana, AL) **11412**
SHELBY DAILY GLOBE (Shelby, OH) **11382**
SHELBY PROMOTER (Shelby, MT) **11556**
SHELBY REVIEW (Wapakoneta, OH) **11601**
SHELBY SHOPPER & INFO (Shelby, NC) **11589**
SHELBY STAR, THE (Shelby, NC) **11378**
SHELBY SUN TIMES (Germantown, TN) **11627**
SHELBYVILLE DAILY UNION (Shelbyville, IL) **11341**
SHELBYVILLE NEWS (Shelbyville, IN) **11345**
SHELBYVILLE SENTINEL-NEWS (Shelbyville, KY) **11505**
SHELBYVILLE TIMES-GAZETTE (Shelbyville, TN) **11396**
SHELDON MAIL-SUN (Sheldon, IA) **11495**
SHELLEY PIONEER (Shelley, ID) **11465**
SHELTER ISLAND REPORTER (Shelter Island, NY) **11582**
SHELTON-MASON COUNTY JOURNAL (Shelton, WA) **11654**
SHENANDOAH VALLEY-HERALD, THE (Woodstock, VA) **11651**
SHEPHERD EXPRESS (Milwaukee, WI) **11663**
SHEPHERDSTOWN CHRONICLE (Shepherdstown, WV) **11657**
SHERBURNE COUNTY CITIZEN, THE (Becker, MN) **11534**
SHERIDAN HEADLIGHT, THE (Sheridan, AR) **11424**
SHERIDAN PRESS (Sheridan, WY) **11410**
SHERWOOD GAZETTE (Portland, OR) **11608**
SHERWOOD VOICE (Sherwood, AR) **11424**
SHIRLEY ORACLE (Devens, MA) **11517**
SHO ME SHOPPER (Brookfield, MO) **11548**
SHOPPER (DENISON), THE (Denison, TX) **11633**
SHOPPER GUIDE (DERBY) (Derby, KS) **11497**
SHOPPER (HALSTAD), THE (Halstad, MN) **11538**
SHOPPER (MOBERLY), THE (Moberly, MO) **11552**
SHOPPER (PENSACOLA), THE (Pensacola, FL) **11454**
SHOPPER (SOUTH HOLLAND), THE (South Holland, IL) **11481**
SHOPPER SPREE (Burlington, IA) **11490**
SHOPPER STOPPER (Portage, WI) **11665**
SHOPPER STOPPER EXTRA (Madison, WI) **11662**
SHOPPER (WALTERBORO), THE (Walterboro, SC) **11623**
SHOPPER/PLUS (Shelbyville, KY) **11505**
SHOPPERS EXTRA (Blackfoot, ID) **11464**
SHOPPER'S GUIDE (Bardstown, KY) **11500**
SHOPPERS GUIDE, THE (Lena, IL) **11475**
SHOPPER'S WEEKLY, THE (Dodge City, KS) **11497**
SHOPPING GUIDE (Palmer, MA) **11522**
SHOPPING NEWS (Platteville, WI) **11665**
SHOPPING NEWS, THE (Newton, MS) **11547**
SHORE LINE TIMES (Guilford, CT) **11444**
SHORELINE CHRONICLE (Sheboygan, WI) **11666**
SHORELINE/LAKE FOREST PARK ENTERPRISE (Lynnwood, WA) **11405**
SHORES NEWS, THE (Jefferson, OH) **11597**
SHOREVIEW PRESS (White Bear Lake, MN) **11544**
SHOREVIEW-ARDEN HILLS BULLETIN (New Brighton, MN) **11540**
SHOREWOOD HERALD (New Berlin, WI) **11664**
SHOSHONE NEWS-PRESS (Kellogg, ID) **11337**
SHREWSBURY CHRONICLE (Marlborough, MA) **11520**
SIBLEY SHOPPER (Arlington, MN) **11534**
SIDNEY DAILY NEWS (Sidney, OH) **11383**
SIDNEY HERALD (Sidney, MT) **11556**

SIDNEY SUN-TELEGRAPH (Sidney, NE) **11367**

SIERRA COUNTY SENTINEL (Truth or Consequences, NM) **11569**

SIERRA STAR, THE (Oakhurst, CA) **11433**

SIERRA SUN (Truckee, CA) **11438**

SIERRA VISTA HERALD (Sierra Vista, AZ) **11321**

SIGN OF THE TIMES (Van Wert, OH) **11601**

SIGNAL ITEM (Monroeville, PA) **11614**

SIGNAL (MANCHESTER), THE (Manchester, OH) **11598**

SIGNAL MOUNTAIN POST (Fort Oglethorpe, GA) **11460**

SIGNAL (VALENCIA), THE (Valencia, CA) **11328**

SIGOURNEY NEWS-REVIEW (Hampton, IA) **11493**

SILSBEE BEE (Silsbee, TX) **11641**

SILVER CITY DAILY PRESS & INDEPENDENT (Silver City, NM) **11371**

SILVER CREEK HERALD (Snowflake, AZ) **11419**

SILVER SPRING GAZETTE (Silver Spring, MD) **11514**

SILVERTON STANDARD & THE MINER (Silverton, CO) **11442**

SIOUX CITY JOURNAL, THE (Sioux City, IA) **11348**

SISKIYOU DAILY NEWS (Yreka, CA) **11329**

SISSETON COURIER (Sisseton, SD) **11624**

SIUSLAW NEWS, THE (Florence, OR) **11607**

SKAGIT VALLEY HERALD (Mt Vernon, WA) **11405**

SKANEATELES PRESS (Skaneateles, NY) **11582**

SKIATOOK JOURNAL (Skiatook, OK) **11605**

SKOKIE REVIEW (Park Ridge, IL) **11479**

SKYLINE (Oak Park, IL) **11478**

SKYWAY NEWS (Minneapolis, MN) **11540**

SLEEPY EYE HERALD DISPATCH (Sleepy Eye, MN) **11543**

SLIDELL SENTRY-NEWS (Slidell, LA) **11354**

SLIPPERY ROCK/GROVE CITY EAGLE (Slippery Rock, PA) **11617**

SMACKOVER JOURNAL (Smackover, AR) **11424**

SMART SHOPPER (LIGONIER), THE (Ligonier, IN) **11487**

SMITH COUNTY PIONEER (Smith Center, KS) **11499**

SMITH COUNTY REFORMER (Raleigh, MS) **11547**

SMITH MOUNTAIN EAGLE (Moneta, VA) **11649**

SMITHFIELD HERALD (Smithfield, NC) **11589**

SMITHTOWN MESSENGER (Nesconset, NY) **11579**

SMITHTOWN NEWS, THE (Smithtown, NY) **11582**

SMITHVILLE HERALD, THE (Smithville, MO) **11553**

SMITHVILLE REVIEW (Smithville, TN) **11629**

SMITHVILLE TIMES, THE (Smithville, TX) **11641**

SMOKEY MOUNTAIN TIMES (Bryson City, NC) **11586**

SMYRNA BREEZE, THE (New Smyrna Beach, FL) **11453**

SMYRNA/CLAYTON SUN-TIMES (Smyrna, DE) **11448**

SMYTH COUNTY MARKET PLACE (Marion, VA) **11648**

SMYTH COUNTY NEWS & MESSENGER (Marion, VA) **11648**

SNOHOMISH COUNTY TRIBUNE (Snohomish, WA) **11654**

SNOWMASS VILLAGE SUN (Snowmass Village, CO) **11442**

SNYDER COUNTY TIMES (Middleburg, PA) **11613**

SNYDER DAILY NEWS (Snyder, TX) **11401**

SODUS WILLIAMSON PENNYSAVER (Sodus, NY) **11582**

SOLANCO SUN LEDGER (Quarryville, PA) **11616**

SOLARES HILL (Key West, FL) **11451**

SOLEDAD BEE (Soledad, CA) **11437**

SOLON HERALD SUN (Beachwood, OH) **11593**

SOLON TIMES, THE (Sandusky, OH) **11600**

SOLVAY GEDDES PRESS (Syracuse, NY) **11583**

SOMERSET HERALD (Princess Anne, MD) **11514**

SOMERSET MESSENGER GAZETTE (Somerville, NJ) **11567**

SOMERVILLE JOURNAL (Somerville, MA) **11523**

SOMERVILLE NEWS, THE (Somerville, MA) **11523**

SONOMA WEST/TIMES & NEWS (Sebastopol, CA) **11437**

SONORAN NEWS (Cave Creek, AZ) **11417**

SOPERTON NEWS, THE (Soperton, GA) **11463**

SORENTO NEWS (Hillsboro, IL) **11474**

SOUDERTON INDEPENDENT (Souderton, PA) **11617**

SOULVINE (Los Angeles, CA) **11432**

SOUND, THE (Madison, CT) **11445**

SOUND VIEW NEWS, THE (Yonkers, NY) **11585**

SOUNDER, THE (Random Lake, WI) **11666**

SOURCE (MADISON), THE (Madison, CT) **11445**

SOUTH ADVANCE (Jenison, MI) **11529**

SOUTH ALABAMIAN (Jackson, AL) **11414**

SOUTH ARKANSAS SUN (Hampton, AR) **11422**

SOUTH BALTIMORE GUIDE (Baltimore, MD) **11512**

SOUTH BAY'S NEWSPAPER (Lindenhurst, NY) **11577**

SOUTH BEND TRIBUNE (South Bend, IN) **11345**

SOUTH BENTON STAR-PRESS (Belle Plaine, IA) **11490**

SOUTH BERGENITE (Rutherford, NJ) **11567**

SOUTH BOSTON GAZETTE-VIRGINIAN (South Boston, VA) **11650**

SOUTH BOSTON TRIBUNE (Boston, MA) **11516**

SOUTH BRUNSWICK POST (Dayton, NJ) **11562**

SOUTH BUFFALO NEWS (Lackawanna, NY) **11576**

SOUTH CENTRAL SHOPPER (McPherson, KS) **11498**

SOUTH CITY JOURNAL (St Louis, MO) **11553**

SOUTH COUNTY GAZETTE (Annapolis, MD) **11511**

SOUTH COUNTY JOURNAL (St Louis, MO) **11553**

SOUTH COUNTY MAIL (Rogersville, MO) **11553**

SOUTH COUNTY NEWS (New Castle, PA) **11614**

SOUTH COUNTY SENTINEL (Rutland, VT) **11644**

SOUTH COUNTY SUN, THE (Royal City, WA) **11653**

SOUTH COUNTY TIMES (St Louis, MO) **11554**

SOUTH COUNTY WEEKENDER (Webster, MA) **11524**

SOUTH CROW RIVER NEWS (Osseo, MN) **11541**

SOUTH DADE NEWS LEADER (Homestead, FL) **11451**

SOUTH DES MOINES PRESS CITIZEN (Des Moines, IA) **11491**

SOUTH DISTRICT JOURNAL (Seattle, WA) **11654**

SOUTH END NEWS (Boston, MA) **11516**

SOUTH FLORIDA SUN-SENTINEL (Fort Lauderdale, FL) **11333**

SOUTH FORK TIMES, THE (Monte Vista, CO) **11442**

SOUTH FULTON CITIZEN (Fayetteville, GA) **11459**

SOUTH FULTON NEIGHBOR, THE (Forest Park, GA) **11460**

SOUTH HAVEN TRIBUNE (South Haven, MI) **11532**

SOUTH HILL ENTERPRISE (South Hill, VA) **11650**

SOUTH HILLS RECORD (Pittsburgh, PA) **11616**

SOUTH HOLLAND-THORTON TOWNSHIP STAR (Tinley Park, IL) **11482**

SOUTH IDAHO PRESS (Burley, ID) **11337**

SOUTH LAKE ADVERTISER (Lowell, IN) **11487**

SOUTH LAKE PRESS (Clermont, FL) **11450**

SOUTH LYON HERALD (South Lyon, MI) **11532**

SOUTH MILWAUKEE VOICE GRAPHIC (New Berlin, WI) **11664**

SOUTH MISSOURIAN NEWS (Thayer, MO) **11554**

▼SOUTH OAKLAND ECCENTRIC (McLean, VA) **11403**

SOUTH PASADENA REVIEW (South Pasadena, CA) **11438**

SOUTH PHILLY REVIEW (Philadelphia, PA) **11615**

SOUTH PITTSBURG HUSTLER, THE (South Pittsburg, TN) **11630**

SOUTH PITTSBURGH REPORTER (Pittsburgh, PA) **11616**

SOUTH PORTLAND SENTRY (Biddeford, ME) **11509**

SOUTH REPORTER, THE (Holly Springs, MS) **11546**

SOUTH SHORE NEWS (Ruskin, FL) **11454**

SOUTH SHORE NEWS (ROCKLAND) (Rockland, MA) **11523**

SOUTH SHORE RECORD (Lawrence, NY) **11577**

SOUTH SIDE JOURNAL (St Louis, MO) **11554**

SOUTH ST PAUL/INVER GROVE HEIGHTS SUN-CURRENT (Eden Prairie, MN) **11537**

SOUTH TAMPA NEWS (Tampa, FL) **11455**

SOUTH TARRANT STAR (Burleson, TX) **11632**

SOUTH WASHINGTON COUNTY BULLETIN (Cottage Grove, MN) **11536**

SOUTH WHIDBEY RECORD (Langley, WA) **11652**

SOUTHAMPTON PRESS (Southampton, NY) **11582**

SOUTHAMPTON PRESS (THE WESTERN EDITION) (Westhampton Beach, NY) **11584**

SOUTHBRIDGE EVENING NEWS (Southbridge, MA) **11356**

SOUTHEAST MISSOURIAN (Cape Girardeau, MO) **11363**

SOUTHEASTERN STAR (Milwaukee, WI) **11663**

SOUTHERN ADVOCATE (Ashland, MS) **11545**

SOUTHERN BERKS NEWS, THE (Boyertown, PA) **11610**

SOUTHERN CAYUGA TRIBUNE (Moravia, NY) **11579**

SOUTHERN COUNTY NEWS (Thornton, IA) **11495**

SOUTHERN DUTCHESS NEWS (Wappingers Falls, NY) **11583**

SOUTHERN HERALD, THE (Liberty, MS) **11546**

SOUTHERN ILLINOISAN, THE (Carbondale, IL) **11338**

SOUTHERN PINES PILOT (Southern Pines, NC) **11589**

SOUTHERN SCENE, THE (Metropolis, IL) **11475**

SOUTHERN SENTINEL (Ripley, MS) **11547**

SOUTHERN STANDARD (McMinnville, TN) **11628**

SOUTHERN STAR (Ozark, AL) **11415**

SOUTHERN UTAH NEWS (Kanab, UT) **11643**

SOUTHINGTON OBSERVER (Waterbury, CT) **11447**

SOUTHLAKE JOURNAL, THE (Southlake, TX) **11641**

SOUTHLAKE TIMES (Addison, TX) **11631**

SOUTHSIDE REPORTER (San Antonio, TX) **11640**

SOUTHSIDE SENTINEL (Urbanna, VA) **11650**

SOUTHSIDE TIMES (Beech Grove, IN) **11484**

SOUTHTOWN STAR (Tinley Park, IL) **11342**

SOUTHTOWNS CITIZEN (Orchard Park, NY) **11580**

SOUTHWEST CITY JOURNAL (St Louis, MO) **11554**

SOUTHWEST COMMUNITY CONNECTION (Portland, OR) **11608**

SOUTHWEST COUNTY JOURNAL (St Louis, MO) **11554**

SOUTHWEST DAILY NEWS (Sulphur, LA) **11354**

SOUTHWEST DAILY TIMES (Liberal, KS) **11350**

SOUTHWEST HERALD/ZONE B (Chicago, IL) **11469**

SOUTHWEST IOWA SHOPPER, THE (Atlantic, IA) **11490**

SOUTHWEST JOURNAL, THE (Minneapolis, MN) **11540**

SOUTHWEST NEWS HERALD/ZONE A (Chicago, IL) **11469**

SOUTHWEST NEWS-HERALD (Chicago, IL) **11469**

SOUTH-WEST REVIEW (St Paul, MN) **11543**

SOUTHWEST SHOPPER (Chicago, IL) **11469**

SOUTHWEST TIMES RECORD (Fort Smith, AR) **11322**

SOUTHWEST TIMES, THE (Pulaski, VA) **11404**

SOUTHWESTERN JOURNAL NEWS (Brighton, IL) **11468**

SOUTHWICK SUFFIELD NEWS (Feeding Hills, MA) **11518**

SPARTA HERALD (Sparta, WI) **11667**

SPARTA INDEPENDENT (Sparta, NJ) **11567**

SPARTA NEWS-PLAINDEALER (Sparta, IL) **11481**

SPARTA/KENT CITY ADVANCE (Jenison, MI) **11529**

SPARTANBURG COUNTY NEWS (Spartanburg, SC) **11622**

SPECTATOR (OZARK), THE (Ozark, AR) **11424**

SPECTATOR (SOMERSET), THE (Somerset, MA) **11523**

SPECTRUM (ST GEORGE), THE (St George, UT) **11402**

SPEEDWAY TOWN PRESS (Speedway, IN) **11488**

SPENCER COUNTY JOURNAL DEMOCRAT (Rockport, IN) **11488**

SPENCER COUNTY LEADER (Dale, IN) **11485**

SPENCER DAILY REPORTER (Spencer, IA) **11348**

SPENCER EVENING WORLD (Spencer, IN) **11345**

SPENCER MAGNET (Taylorsville, KY) **11505**

SPENCER NEW LEADER (Spencer, MA) **11523**

SPENCER RANDOM HARVEST WEEKLY (Trumansburg, NY) **11583**

SPINAL COLUMN NEWSWEEKLY (Waterford, MI) **11533**

SPIRIT OF JEFFERSON-ADVOCATE (Charles Town, WV) **11655**

SPOKESMAN-REVIEW, THE (Spokane, WA) **11405**

SPOONER ADVOCATE (Spooner, WI) **11667**

SPOTLIGHT (DELMAR), THE (Delmar, NY) **11573**

Title

SPOTLIGHT (INDIANAPOLIS), THE (Indianapolis, IN) 11486
SPRING GROVE HERALD (Spring Grove, MN) 11543
SPRING HOPE ENTERPRISE (Spring Hope, NC) 11589
SPRING VALLEY SUN/ELMWOOD ARGUS (Spring Valley, WI) 11667
SPRING VALLEY TRIBUNE (Washington, DC) 11448
SPRINGBORO STAR PRESS (Franklin, OH) 11596
SPRINGBORO SUN (Cincinnati, OH) 11594
SPRINGFIELD CONNECTION (McLean, VA) 11649
SPRINGFIELD (KY) SUN (Springfield, KY) 11505
SPRINGFIELD NEWS-LEADER, THE (Springfield, MO) 11365
SPRINGFIELD NEWS-SUN (Springfield, OH) 11383
SPRINGFIELD PRESS (Holmes, PA) 11612
SPRINGFIELD REPORTER, THE (Springfield, VT) 11645
SPRINGFIELD SHOPPER (Springfield, IL) 11481
SPRINGFIELD SUN (FORT WASHINGTON) (Fort Washington, PA) 11612
SPRINGFIELD TIMES COURIER (Herndon, VA) 11647
▼SPRINGFIELD TIMES (Springfield, OR) 11609
SPRING-FORD REPORTER (Fort Washington, PA) 11612
SPRINGHILL PRESS (Springhill, LA) 11508
SPRINGS VALLEY HERALD (French Lick, IN) 11485
SPRINGTOWN EPIGRAPH, THE (Springtown, TX) 11641
SPRINGVIEW HERALD (Springview, NE) 11558
SPRINGVILLE JOURNAL (Cheektowaga, NY) 11572
SPRINGVILLE PENNYSAVER (Springville, NY) 11582
ST ANTHONY BULLETIN (New Brighton, MN) 11540
ST AUGUSTINE RECORD, THE (St Augustine, FL) 11334
ST BERNARD VOICE, THE (Arabi, LA) 11506
ST CHARLES JOURNAL (St Peters, MO) 11554
ST CHARLES PRESS (St Charles, MN) 11543
ST CHARLES REPUBLICAN, THE (St Charles, IL) 11481
ST CHARLES SUN (Aurora, IL) 11467
ST CLAIR MISSOURIAN, THE (St Clair, MO) 11553
ST CLAIR NEWS-AEGIS (Pell City, AL) 11415
ST CLAIR TIMES (Pell City, AL) 11415
ST CLOUD TIMES (St Cloud, MN) 11361
ST CROIX AVIS (St Croix, VI) 11403
ST CROIX VALLEY PEACH (Forest Lake, MN) 11538
ST CROIX VALLEY PRESS (White Bear Lake, MN) 11544
ST FRANCIS REMINDER - ENTERPRISE (New Berlin, WI) 11664
ST HELENA STAR (St Helena, CA) 11438
ST IGNACE NEWS, THE (St Ignace, MI) 11532
ST JAMES LEADER-JOURNAL (St James, MO) 11553
ST JAMES PLAINDEALER (St James, MN) 11543
ST JOHN NEWS (St John, KS) 11499
ST JOHN VALLEY TIMES (Madawaska, ME) 11510
ST JOHNS REMINDER (St Johns, MI) 11532
ST JOHNS REVIEW (Portland, OR) 11608
ST JOSEPH NEWS-PRESS (St Joseph, MO) 11365
ST JOSEPH TELEGRAPH, THE (St Joseph, MO) 11553
ST LAWRENCE PLAINDEALER (Canton, NY) 11572
ST LOUIS AMERICAN NEWSPAPER (St Louis, MO) 11554
ST LOUIS PARK SUN-SAILOR (Eden Prairie, MN) 11537
ST LOUIS POST-DISPATCH (St Louis, MO) 11365
ST MARIES GAZETTE RECORD (St Maries, ID) 11465
ST MARTINVILLE TECHE NEWS (St Martinville, LA) 11508
ST MARY JOURNAL (Morgan City, LA) 11508
ST MARYS STAR (St Marys, KS) 11499
ST MARY'S TODAY (California, MD) 11512
ST PAUL PIONEER PRESS (St Paul, MN) 11361
ST PAULS REVIEW (Lumberton, NC) 11588
ST PETER HERALD (St Peter, MN) 11543
ST PETERS JOURNAL (St Peters, MO) 11554
ST PETERSBURG TIMES (St Petersburg, FL) 11334
ST TAMMANY FARMER (Covington, LA) 11507
STAFFORD COUNTY SUN (Stafford, VA) 11650
STAMFORD AMERICAN (Stamford, TX) 11641

STAMFORD LIFESTYLES (Norwalk, CT) 11446
STANDARD & TIMES (Tuscumbia, AL) 11415
STANDARD BANNER, THE (Jefferson, TN) 11627
STANDARD DEMOCRAT, THE (Sikeston, MO) 11365
STANDARD JOURNAL, THE (St Anthony, ID) 11465
STANDARD LACONIC, THE (Snow Hill, NC) 11589
STANDARD-EXAMINER (Ogden, UT) 11402
STANDARD-JOURNAL (Milton, PA) 11390
STANDARD-TIMES (NEW BEDFORD), THE (New Bedford, MA) 11356
STANDARD-TIMES (NORTH KINGSTOWN), THE (Wakefield, RI) 11619
STANLEY REPUBLICAN (Stanley, WI) 11667
STANLY NEWS & PRESS (Albemarle, NC) 11585
STANWOOD-CAMANO NEWS (Stanwood, WA) 11654
STAPLES WORLD (Staples, MN) 11543
STAR & BEACON, THE (Ninety Six, SC) 11622
STAR ADVISOR, THE (Montevideo, MN) 11540
STAR BANNER (New York, NY) 11373
STAR BEACON (Ashtabula, OH) 11379
STAR COURIER, THE (Northern Cambria, PA) 11615
STAR EXTRA (Hope, AR) 11422
STAR HERALD WEEKENDER (Ripley, WV) 11657
STAR NEWS (Elk River, MN) 11537
STAR NEWS (CHULA VISTA), THE (Chula Vista, CA) 11427
STAR NEWS (MEDFORD), THE (Medford, WI) 11663
STAR PRESS, THE (Muncie, IN) 11345
STAR PROGRESS (Anaheim, CA) 11426
STAR REPUBLICAN (Wilmington, OH) 11602
STAR SHOPPER (Elk River, MN) 11538
STAR SPANGLED BANNER (Keene, NH) 11560
STAR (SUN PRAIRIE), THE (Sun Prairie, WI) 11667
STAR TRADER (Beardstown, IL) 11467
STAR TRIBUNE (Minneapolis, MN) 11361
STAR-ADVOCATE, THE (Melbourne, FL) 11453
STAR-COURIER (Kewanee, IL) 11340
STAR-DEMOCRAT, THE (Easton, MD) 11355
STAR-GAZETTE (Elmira, NY) 11372
STAR-GAZETTE EXTRA (Beardstown, IL) 11467
STAR-GAZETTE, THE (Hackettstown, NJ) 11563
STAR-HERALD (Scottsbluff, NE) 11367
STAR-HERALD (BELTON), THE (Belton, MO) 11548
STAR-HERALD (KOSCIUSKO), THE (Kosciusko, MS) 11546
STAR-HERALD (PRESQUE ISLE), THE (Presque Isle, ME) 11511
STARKVILLE DAILY NEWS (Starkville, MS) 11363
STAR-LEDGER, THE (Newark, NJ) 11369
STAR-NEWS, THE (McCall, ID) 11465
STAR-PENNY STRETCHER (Mancelona, MI) 11530
STAR-TRIBUNE (BERRYVILLE) (Berryville, AR) 11420
STAR-TRIBUNE (CHATHAM) (Chatham, VA) 11646
STATE (COLUMBIA), THE (Columbia, SC) 11394
STATE GAZETTE (Dyersburg, TN) 11395
STATE JOURNAL (Frankfort, KY) 11351
STATE JOURNAL-REGISTER, THE (Springfield, IL) 11341
STATE PORT PILOT, THE (Southport, NC) 11589
STATEN ISLAND ADVANCE (Staten Island, NY) 11375
STATEN ISLAND STAR REPORTER (Brooklyn, NY) 11571
STATESBORO HERALD (Statesboro, GA) 11336
STATESMAN JOURNAL (Salem, OR) 11387
STATESMAN-EXAMINER, THE (Colville, WA) 11652
STATESVILLE RECORD & LANDMARK (Statesville, NC) 11378
STAUNTON STAR TIMES (Staunton, IL) 11481
STAYTON MAIL, THE (Stayton, OR) 11609
STE GENEVIEVE HERALD (Ste Genevieve, MO) 11554
STEAMBOAT PILOT (Steamboat Springs, CO) 11442
STEAMBOAT TODAY (Steamboat Springs, CO) 11330
STEARNS-MORRISON ENTERPRISE (Albany, MN) 11533
STEELE ENTERPRISE (Steele, MO) 11554

STEELVILLE LEDGER (Steeleville, IL) 11481
STEELVILLE STAR-CRAWFORD MIRROR (Steelville, MO) 11554
STEPHENVILLE EMPIRE-TRIBUNE (Stephenville, TX) 11401
STERLING JOURNAL-ADVOCATE (Sterling, CO) 11330
STEUBEN COURIER-ADVOCATE, THE (Bath, NY) 11569
STEVENS POINT JOURNAL, THE (Stevens Point, WI) 11409
STEWART HOUSTON TIMES, THE (Dover, TN) 11626
STEWART-WEBSTER-JOURNAL-PATRIOT (Richland, GA) 11462
STIGLER NEWS-SENTINEL (Stigler, OK) 11605
STILLWATER GAZETTE (Stillwater, MN) 11361
STILLWATER NEWSPRESS (Stillwater, OK) 11386
STILLWATER VALLEY ADVERTISER (Covington, OH) 11596
STILWELL DEMOCRAT-JOURNAL (Stilwell, OK) 11606
STOKES NEWS (Walnut Cove, NC) 11590
STONE COUNTY CITIZEN (Mountain View, AR) 11423
STONE COUNTY ENTERPRISE, THE (Wiggins, MS) 11548
STONE COUNTY LEADER (Mountain View, AR) 11423
STONEHAM INDEPENDENT, THE (Stoneham, MA) 11523
STONEHAM SUN (Beverly, MA) 11516
STORM LAKE PILOT TRIBUNE (Storm Lake, IA) 11495
STORM LAKE TIMES, THE (Storm Lake, IA) 11495
STORY CITY HERALD (Story City, IA) 11495
STOUGHTON CHRONICLE (Rockland, MA) 11523
STOUGHTON COURIER HUB (Stoughton, WI) 11667
STOUGHTON JOURNAL (Needham, MA) 11521
STOW SENTRY (Stow, OH) 11601
STOWE REPORTER, THE (Stowe, VT) 11645
STRAITS AREA STAR (Sheboygan, MI) 11532
STRATFORD BARD (Milford, CT) 11445
STRATFORD (OK) STAR (Stratford, OK) 11606
STRATFORD STAR (SHELTON) (Shelton, CT) 11446
STUART NEWS (Stuart, FL) 11334
STURGIS JOURNAL (Sturgis, MI) 11360
STURGIS NEWS (Sturgis, KY) 11505
STUTTGART DAILY LEADER (Stuttgart, AR) 11323
SUBURBAN & WAYNE TIMES, THE (Wayne, PA) 11617
SUBURBAN ADVERTISER, THE (Wayne, PA) 11617
SUBURBAN COURIER, THE (Waco, TX) 11642
SUBURBAN GAZETTE (McKees Rocks, PA) 11613
SUBURBAN JOURNAL (Des Plaines, IL) 11470
SUBURBAN LIFE (LOVELAND) (Loveland, OH) 11598
SUBURBAN LIFE (OAK BROOK) (Oak Brook, IL) 11477
SUBURBAN NEWS SOUTH EDITION (Spencerport, NY) 11582
SUBURBAN NEWS WEST EDITION (Spencerport, NY) 11582
SUBURBAN NEWS/VILLAGE GAZETTE (Ridgewood, NJ) 11566
SUBURBAN STREET NEWS (White Plains, NY) 11584
SUBURBAN TRENDS (Kinnelon, NJ) 11564
SUBURBANITE, THE (Akron, OH) 11592
SUDBURY TOWN CRIER, THE (Framingham, MA) 11518
SUFFOLK COUNTY NEWS (Sayville, NY) 11582
SUFFOLK NEWS-HERALD (Suffolk, VA) 11404
SUFFOLK TIMES (Mattituck, NY) 11578
SULLIVAN DAILY TIMES (Sullivan, IN) 11345
SULLIVAN INDEPENDENT NEWS, THE (Sullivan, MO) 11554
SULLIVAN REVIEW (Dushore, PA) 11611
SULPHUR SPRINGS NEWS-TELEGRAM (Sulphur Springs, TX) 11401
SUMMER BEACON (Biddeford, ME) 11509
SUMMERVILLE JOURNAL SCENE, THE (Summerville, SC) 11623
SUMMERVILLE NEWS, THE (Summerville, GA) 11463
SUMMIT COUNTY JOURNAL (Frisco, CO) 11441
SUMMIT DAILY NEWS (Frisco, CO) 11329
SUMNER GAZETTE (Sumner, IA) 11495
SUMNER PRESS (Sumner, IL) 11482

SUMTER COUNTY RECORD-JOURNAL, THE (Livingston, AL) **11414**

SUMTER COUNTY TIMES (Bushnell, FL) **11449**

SUMTER SHOPPER (Fruitland Park, FL) **11451**

SUN & NEWS, THE (Hastings, MI) **11528**

SUN ADVOCATE (Price, UT) **11643**

SUN (BALTIMORE), THE (Chicago, IL) **11339**

SUN BANNER PRIDE (Medina, OH) **11598**

SUN CHRONICLE, THE (Attleboro, MA) **11355**

SUN CITIES INDEPENDENT (Dover, DE) **11447**

SUN CITY NEWS (Riverside, CA) **11435**

SUN CITY WEST INDEPENDENT (Dover, DE) **11447**

SUN (CLEWISTON), THE (Clewiston, FL) **11450**

SUN COAST NEWS (New Port Richey, FL) **11453**

SUN COURIER, THE (Cleveland, OH) **11594**

SUN FOCUS NEWS (Columbia Heights, MN) **11536**

SUN FOCUS, THE (Columbia Heights, MN) **11536**

SUN GAZETTE, THE (Alexandria, VA) **11645**

SUN (HAMBURG), THE (Hamburg, NY) **11575**

SUN HERALD (GULFPORT), THE (Lexington, KY) **11352**

SUN HERALD (NORTH OLMSTAD), THE (North Olmsted, OH) **11599**

SUN (HUMMELSTOWN), THE (Hummelstown, PA) **11612**

SUN JOURNAL, THE (Lewiston, ME) **11354**

SUN MESSENGER, THE (Beachwood, OH) **11593**

SUN (MIDWEST CITY), THE (Midwest City, OK) **11605**

SUN (MT VERNON), THE (Mt Vernon, IA) **11494**

SUN NEWS, THE (Myrtle Beach, SC) **11394**

SUN NEWSPAPER, THE (Seal Beach, CA) **11437**

SUN NEWSPAPERS (SAN DIEGO) (San Bernardino, CA) **11436**

SUN (NORTH OLMSTED), THE (North Olmsted, OH) **11599**

SUN POST NEWS, THE (San Clemente, CA) **11436**

SUN POST, THE (Miami Beach, FL) **11453**

SUN PRESS, THE (Beachwood, OH) **11593**

SUN REPORTER (San Francisco, CA) **11436**

SUN (RUSKIN), THE (Ruskin, FL) **11454**

SUN SCOOP JOURNAL (Beachwood, OH) **11593**

SUN STAR, THE (Berea, OH) **11593**

SUN TIMES NEWS ONLINE (Ste Genevieve, MO) **11365**

SUN TIMES WEEKLY (Jacksonville Beach, FL) **11451**

SUN TRIBUNE (St Joseph, MO) **11553**

SUN (YUMA), THE (Yuma, AZ) **11322**

SUNBELT SHOPPER (Cordele, GA) **11458**

SUNBURY NEWS (Sunbury, OH) **11601**

SUNDAY BUCKS COUNTY TELEGRAPH (Horsham, PA) **11612**

SUNDAY DISPATCH (Pittston, PA) **11616**

SUNDAY INDEPENDENT, THE (Owosso, MI) **11531**

SUNDAY NEWS (Lancaster, PA) **11613**

SUNDAY POST (WEST BEND) (West Bend, WI) **11668**

SUNDAY TIMES, THE (Dearborn, MI) **11526**

SUNFLOWER SHOPPER (Pratt, KS) **11499**

SUN-JOURNAL (New Bern, NC) **11377**

SUNNY ISLES BEACH SUN (South Miami, FL) **11455**

SUNNYVALE SUN (San Jose, CA) **11436**

SUNRISE FORUM (Coconut Creek, FL) **11450**

SUNRISER NEWS (Ossian, IN) **11487**

SUN-SENTINEL (Charleston, MS) **11546**

SUN-TIMES, THE (Heber Springs, AR) **11422**

SUPER SHOPPER (Yuma, AZ) **11420**

SUPERIOR EXPRESS, THE (Superior, NE) **11558**

SURPRISE INDEPENDENT (Dover, DE) **11447**

SUSQUEHANNA COUNTY INDEPENDENT (Montrose, PA) **11614**

SUSQUEHANNA COUNTY WEEKENDER (Montrose, PA) **11614**

SUSSEX COUNTIAN (Georgetown, DE) **11447**

SUSSEX POST, THE (Seaford, DE) **11448**

SUSSEX SUN (Hartland, WI) **11661**

SUWANNEE DEMOCRAT (Live Oak, FL) **11452**

SWAMPSCOTT REPORTER (Marblehead, MA) **11519**

SWANTON ENTERPRISE (Swanton, OH) **11601**

SWAP SHEET (Ridgecrest, CA) **11435**

SWARTZ CREEK NEWS (Flint, MI) **11527**

SWEETWATER REPORTER (Sweetwater, TX) **11401**

SWIFT COUNTY MONITOR-NEWS (Benson, MN) **11534**

SWITZERLAND DEMOCRAT (Vevay, IN) **11489**

SYKESVILLE/ELDERSBURG GAZETTE (Mt Airy, MD) **11514**

SYLVA HERALD & RURALITE (Sylva, NC) **11589**

SYLVANIA HERALD (Sylvania, OH) **11601**

SYLVANIA TELEPHONE, THE (Sylvania, GA) **11463**

SYLVESTER LOCAL NEWS (Sylvester, GA) **11463**

SYOSSET ADVANCE (Hicksville, NY) **11576**

SYOSSET JERICHO TRIBUNE (Mineola, NY) **11579**

SYRACUSE CITY EAGLE (Syracuse, NY) **11583**

SYRACUSE JOURNAL-DEMOCRAT (Syracuse, NE) **11558**

SYRACUSE NEW TIMES (Syracuse, NY) **11583**

T

TABOR-LORIS TRIBUNE (Tabor City, NC) **11590**

TAFT TRIBUNE (Taft, TX) **11641**

TAHLEQUAH DAILY PRESS (Tahlequah, OK) **11386**

TAHOE DAILY TRIBUNE (South Lake Tahoe, CA) **11327**

TAHOE WORLD (Tahoe City, CA) **11438**

TAKOMA PARK GAZETTE (Silver Spring, MD) **11515**

TALBOTTON NEW ERA (Manchester, GA) **11461**

TALLAHASSEE DEMOCRAT (Tallahassee, FL) **11334**

TALLASSEE TRIBUNE (Tallassee, AL) **11415**

TALLMADGE EXPRESS (Stow, OH) **11601**

TAMA NEWS-HERALD, THE (Tama, IA) **11495**

TAMARAC FORUM (Coconut Creek, FL) **11450**

TAMPA TRIBUNE, THE (Tampa, FL) **11334**

TANEY COUNTY TIMES (Branson, MO) **11548**

TAOS NEWS (Taos, NM) **11569**

TARKIO AVALANCHE (Tarkio, MO) **11554**

TATTNALL JOURNAL (Reidsville, GA) **11462**

TAUNTON CALL (Rayham, MA) **11523**

TAUNTON DAILY GAZETTE (Taunton, MA) **11357**

TAVARES CITIZEN (Mt Dora, FL) **11453**

TAYLOR COUNTY NEWS (Butler, GA) **11457**

TAYLOR DAILY PRESS (Taylor, TX) **11401**

TAYLORSVILLE TIMES, THE (Taylorsville, NC) **11590**

TAYLORVILLE BREEZE-COURIER (Taylorville, IL) **11342**

TAZEWELL COUNTY FREE PRESS (Richlands, VA) **11650**

TAZEWELL COUNTY SHOPPER (Pekin, IL) **11479**

TEANECK SUBURBANITE, THE (Cresskill, NJ) **11562**

TECUMSEH HERALD (Tecumseh, MI) **11532**

TEHACHAPI NEWS (Tehachapi, CA) **11438**

TELEGRAM (WELLSTON), THE (Wellston, OH) **11602**

TELEGRAPH (ALTON), THE (Alton, IL) **11338**

TELEGRAPH (COUNTY EDITION), THE (Jerseyville, IL) **11340**

TELEGRAPH (DIXON), THE (Dixon, IL) **11339**

TELEGRAPH HERALD (Dubuque, IA) **11347**

TELEGRAPH (HUDSON), THE (Hudson, NH) **11368**

TELEGRAPH (MACON), THE (Macon, GA) **11336**

TELEGRAPH (NORTH PLATTE), THE (North Platte, NE) **11367**

TELEGRAPH (QUAD COUNTY EDITION), THE (Jerseyville, IL) **11474**

TELEGRAPH-FORUM (Bucyrus, OH) **11379**

TELFAIR ENTERPRISE, THE (McRae, GA) **11461**

TELLURIDE DAILY PLANET (Telluride, CO) **11330**

TEMPLE DAILY TELEGRAM (Temple, TX) **11401**

TEMPLE TERRACE BEACON (Lutz, FL) **11452**

TEMPLE TERRACE NEWS (Tampa, FL) **11456**

TEMPO (KIEL) (Kiel, WI) **11662**

TEMPO, THE (Byron, IL) **11468**

TEMPO/MIDDLESEX (Hightstown, NJ) **11564**

TENINO INDEPENDENT, THE (Tenino, WA) **11654**

TENNESSEAN, THE (Nashville, TN) **11396**

TENNESSEE STAR JOURNAL (Pigeon Forge, TN) **11629**

TERRAPIN TIMES, THE (Bel Air, MD) **11512**

TERRELL TRIBUNE, THE (Terrell, TX) **11401**

TETON VALLEY NEWS (Driggs, ID) **11464**

TEUTOPOLIS PRESS (Teutopolis, IL) **11482**

TEWKSBURY ADVOCATE (Concord, MA) **11517**

TEWKSBURY TOWN CRIER (Wilmington, MA) **11524**

TEXARKANA GAZETTE (Texarkana, TX) **11401**

TEXAS CITY SUN (Texas City, TX) **11401**

TEXAS OBSERVER (Austin, TX) **11631**

TEXOMA ENTERPRISE (Howe, TX) **11637**

THE DALLES CHRONICLE (The Dalles, OR) **11388**

THE/BOOSTER (BULLHEAD CITY) (Bullhead City, AZ) **11417**

THE/OGDENSBURG JOURNAL/ADVANCE NEWS (Ogdensburg, NY) **11374**

THE/WILLITS NEWS (Willits, CA) **11439**

THIEF RIVER FALLS TIMES (2007) (Thief River Falls, MN) **11543**

THIS WEEK IN BEXLEY (Worthington, OH) **11602**

THIS WEEK IN BIG WALNUT (Worthington, OH) **11602**

THIS WEEK IN CLINTONVILLE (Worthington, OH) **11602**

THIS WEEK IN DELAWARE (Worthington, OH) **11602**

THIS WEEK IN GRANDVIEW (Worthington, OH) **11602**

THIS WEEK IN HILLIARD (Worthington, OH) **11603**

THIS WEEK IN NEW ALBANY (Worthington, OH) **11603**

THIS WEEK IN NORTHLAND (Worthington, OH) **11603**

THIS WEEK IN OLENTANGY/POWELL (Worthington, OH) **11603**

THIS WEEK IN PICKERINGTON (Worthington, OH) **11603**

THIS WEEK IN REYNOLDSBURG (Worthington, OH) **11603**

THIS WEEK IN SOUTHSIDE (Worthington, OH) **11603**

THIS WEEK IN UPPER ARLINGTON (Worthington, OH) **11603**

THIS WEEK IN WESTERVILLE (Worthington, OH) **11603**

THIS WEEK IN WESTSIDE (Worthington, OH) **11603**

THIS WEEK IN WORTHINGTON (Worthington, OH) **11603**

THOMASTON EXPRESS, THE (Thomaston, CT) **11447**

THOMASTON TIMES, THE (Birmingham, AL) **11411**

THOMASVILLE TIMES (Thomasville, NC) **11590**

THOMASVILLE TIMES-ENTERPRISE (Thomasville, GA) **11336**

THOMPSON COURIER & RAKE REGISTER (Thompson, IA) **11495**

THORP COURIER (Thorp, WI) **11667**

THOUSAND ISLANDS SUN (Alexandria Bay, NY) **11569**

THOUSAND OAKS ACORN (Agoura Hills, CA) **11425**

THOUSANDSTICKS NEWS (Hyden, KY) **11503**

THREE RIVERS COMMERCIAL-NEWS (Three Rivers, MI) **11360**

THREE STAR EDITION (Trevose, PA) **11617**

THREE VILLAGE TIMES (Mineola, NY) **11579**

THRIF-T-NIKEL COMMUNITY SHOPPING GUIDE (Ottawa, IL) **11478**

THRIFTY NICKEL WANT ADS (Davenport, IA) **11491**

THUMB BLANKET (Bad Axe, MI) **11525**

TIDELAND NEWS (Swansboro, NC) **11589**

TIDEWATER NEWS, THE (Franklin, VA) **11647**

TIDEWATER REVIEW (West Point, VA) **11651**

TIDEWATER TRADER (Chestertown, MD) **11512**

TIFTAREA SHOPPER (Tifton, GA) **11463**

TIFTON GAZETTE, THE (Tifton, GA) **11336**

TILLER & TOILER (Larned, KS) **11350**

TIMBERJAY, THE (Tower, MN) **11543**

TIMES & DEMOCRAT, THE (Orangeburg, SC) **11394**

TIMES ADVERTISER, THE (Union, SC) **11623**

TIMES ARGUS (Barre, VT) **11402**

TIMES CHRONICLE (Fort Washington, PA) **11612**

TIMES CITIZEN (Iowa Falls, IA) **11493**

TIMES (COLUMBUS), THE (Columbus, OH) **11595**

Title

TIMES DAILY (New York, NY) 11374

TIMES DISPATCH (Walnut Ridge, AR) 11425

TIMES EXPRESS (Monroeville, PA) 11614

TIMES (GAINESVILLE), THE (Gainesville, GA) 11335

TIMES HERALD (NORRISTOWN), THE (Norristown, PA) 11390

TIMES HERALD (OLEAN), THE (Olean, NY) 11374

TIMES HERALD (PORT HURON), THE (Port Huron, MI) 11359

TIMES HERALD-RECORD (Middletown, NY) 11373

TIMES INK! (Richmond, VT) 11644

TIMES JOURNAL (Cobleskill, NY) 11572

TIMES JOURNAL, THE (Russell Springs, KY) 11505

TIMES LEADER (MARTINS FERRY) (Martins Ferry, OH) 11382

TIMES LEADER (PRINCETON), THE (Princeton, KY) 11505

TIMES LEADER (WILKES BARRE), THE (Wilkes Barre, PA) 11392

TIMES (MELBOURNE), THE (Melbourne, FL) 11453

TIMES (MUNSTER), THE (Munster, IN) 11487

TIMES NEWS, THE (Lehighton, PA) 11390

TIMES NEWSWEEKLY & RIDGEWOOD TIMES (Ridgewood, NY) 11581

TIMES (NORTH LITTLE ROCK), THE (North Little Rock, AR) 11423

TIMES OBSERVER (Warren, PA) 11392

TIMES OF ACADIANA, THE (Lafayette, LA) 11507

TIMES OF MIDDLE COUNTRY, THE (East Setauket, NY) 11573

TIMES OF NORTHEAST BENTON COUNTY (Pea Ridge, AR) 11424

TIMES OF NORTHPORT & EAST NORTHPORT, THE (East Setauket, NY) 11574

TIMES OF SCOTCH PLAINS & FANWOOD, THE (Westfield, NJ) 11568

TIMES OF SMITHTOWN TOWNSHIP, THE (East Setauket, NY) 11574

TIMES OF TI (Elizabethtown, NY) 11574

TIMES (OTTAWA), THE (Ottawa, IL) 11341

TIMES (PAWTUCKET), THE (Pawtucket, RI) 11393

TIMES (PORT ROYAL), THE (Port Royal, PA) 11616

TIMES PRESS (Hartford, WI) 11661

TIMES RECORD (Aledo, IL) 11466

TIMES RECORD (FAYETTE), THE (Fayette, AL) 11413

TIMES RECORD NEWS (Wichita Falls, TX) 11402

TIMES RECORD (SPENCER), THE (Spencer, WV) 11657

TIMES RECORDER, THE (Zanesville, OH) 11384

TIMES (SHREVEPORT), THE (Shreveport, LA) 11354

TIMES, THE (Portland, OR) 11608

TIMES (TRENTON), THE (Trenton, NJ) 11369

TIMES UNION (Albany, NY) 11371

TIMES (WAITSBURG), THE (Waitsburg, WA) 11655

TIMES WEEKEND (Kettering, OH) 11597

TIMES WEST VIRGINIAN (Fairmont, WV) 11406

TIMES-ARGUS (Central City, KY) 11501

TIMES-BULLETIN, THE (Van Wert, OH) 11383

TIMES-CLARION, THE (Harlowton, MT) 11555

TIMES-COURIER (CHARLESTON) (Charleston, IL) 11338

TIMES-COURIER (ELLIJAY) (Ellijay, GA) 11459

TIMES-GAZETTE COUNTY SHOPPER (Hillsboro, OH) 11596

TIMES-GAZETTE, THE (Hillsboro, OH) 11381

TIMES-GEORGIAN (Carrolton, GA) 11335

TIMES-HERALD (FORREST CITY) (Forrest City, AR) 11322

TIMES-HERALD (NOTTINGHAM) (Nottingham, MD) 11514

TIMES-HERALD, THE (Newnan, GA) 11336

TIMES-HERALD (VALLEJO) (Vallejo, CA) 11328

TIMES-INDICATOR (Fremont, MI) 11527

TIMES-JOURNAL (CONDON), THE (Condon, OR) 11606

TIMES-JOURNAL (FORT PAYNE), THE (Fort Payne, AL) 11320

TIMES-LEADER, THE (Grifton, NC) 11587

TIMES-MAIL (Bedford, IN) 11342

TIMES-NEWS, THE (Burlington, NC) 11375

TIMES-NEWS (TWIN FALLS), THE (Twin Falls, ID) 11338

TIMES-PICAYUNE (New Orleans, LA) 11354

TIMES-PLAIN DEALER (Cresco, IA) 11491

TIMES-PRESS (SEYMOUR) (Seymour, WI) 11666

TIMES-RECORD (BRUNSWICK), THE (Brunswick, ME) 11354

TIMES-RECORD (DENTON), THE (Denton, MD) 11512

TIMES-REPORTER, THE (New Philadelphia, OH) 11382

TIMES-REPUBLICAN (CORYDON) (Corydon, IA) 11491

TIMES-REPUBLICAN (MARSHALLTOWN) (Marshalltown, IA) 11347

TIMES-SENTINEL, THE (Goddard, KS) 11497

TIMES-STANDARD (Eureka, CA) 11324

TIMES-SUN, THE (West Newton, PA) 11618

TIMES-TRIBUNE (Corbin, KY) 11351

TIMES-UNION (Warsaw, IN) 11346

TIMES-VILLAGER (Kaukauna, WI) 11661

TINLEY PARK STAR (Tinley Park, IL) 11482

TIPP CITY HERALD (Tipp City, OH) 11601

TIPTON CONSERVATIVE & ADVERTISER (Tipton, IA) 11495

TIPTON TIMES (Tipton, MO) 11554

TISHOMINGO COUNTY NEWS (Iuka, MS) 11546

TITUSVILLE HERALD (Titusville, PA) 11392

TOCCOA RECORD (Toccoa, GA) 11463

TODAY IN PEACHTREE CITY (Fayetteville, GA) 11335

TODAY'S NEWS-HERALD (Lake Havasu City, AZ) 11321

TODAY'S SHOPPER (Keyser, WV) 11656

TODAY'S SUNBEAM (Salem, NJ) 11369

TODD COUNTY COUNTRY COURIER (Browerville, MN) 11535

TODD COUNTY STANDARD, THE (Elkton, KY) 11501

TOLEDO CHRONICLE (Tama, IA) 11495

TOLEDO CITY PAPER (Toledo, OH) 11601

TOMAH JOURNAL (Tomah, WI) 11667

TOMAH MONITOR-HERALD (Tomah, WI) 11667

TOMAHAWK LEADER (Tomahawk, WI) 11667

TOMAHAWK, THE (Mountain City, TN) 11628

TOMBALL POTPOURRI, THE (Tomball, TX) 11641

TOMPKINSVILLE NEWS (Tompkinsville, KY) 11506

TONAWANDA NEWS (North Tonawanda, NY) 11374

TONKAWA NEWS, THE (Tonkawa, OK) 11606

TONOPAH TIMES-BONANZA & GOLDFIELD NEWS (Las Vegas, NV) 11559

TOOELE TRANSCRIPT-BULLETIN (Tooele, UT) 11643

TOPEKA CAPITAL-JOURNAL (Topeka, KS) 11351

TOPSAIL VOICE (Morehead City, NC) 11588

TORRINGTON TELEGRAM (Torrington, WY) 11669

TOWN & COUNTRY (Red Hill, PA) 11616

TOWN & COUNTRY SHOPPER (Milaca, MN) 11540

TOWN & COUNTRY WEEKLY (Ottawa, IL) 11478

TOWN - CRIER (Wellington, FL) 11456

TOWN AND COUNTRY SHOPPER (St James, MN) 11543

TOWN CRIER (Stockbridge, MI) 11532

TOWN CRIER ADVERTISER (Aledo, IL) 11466

TOWN CROSSINGS (North Andover, MA) 11521

TOWN JOURNAL, THE (Ridgewood, NJ) 11566

TOWN MEETING, THE (Gaylord, MI) 11527

TOWN 'N COUNTRY NEWS (Tampa, FL) 11456

TOWN NEWS (Ridgewood, NJ) 11566

TOWN NEWS/THE (Cinnaminson, NJ) 11562

TOWN OF PARADISE VALLEY INDEPENDENT (Scottsdale, AZ) 11419

TOWN REMINDER (South Hadley, MA) 11523

TOWN TALK NEWSPAPERS (Media, PA) 11613

TOWN TALK, THE (Alexandria, LA) 11352

TOWN TIMES (MIDDLEFIELD) (Middlefield, CT) 11445

TOWN TIMES (WATERTOWN) (Watertown, CT) 11447

TOWN TOPICS (Princeton, NJ) 11566

TOWNE COURIER, THE (Grand Ledge, MI) 11528

TOWNS COUNTY HERALD (Hiawassee, GA) 11460

TOWNSEND TIMES (Devens, MA) 11517

TOWNSHIP TIMES (Saginaw, MI) 11532

TOWNSHIP VOICE, THE (Phoenixville, PA) 11615

TOWSON TIMES (Towson, MD) 11515

TRACY HEADLIGHT-HERALD (Tracy, MN) 11543

TRACY PRESS (Tracy, CA) 11328

TRADE & TRANSACTIONS (York, NE) 11559

TRADEWINDS (St John, VI) 11645

TRAER STAR-CLIPPER (Traer, IA) 11496

TRANSCRIPT, THE (Morrisville, VT) 11644

TRANSYLVANIA TIMES, THE (Brevard, NC) 11586

TRAVELERS REST MONITOR (Travelers Rest, SC) 11623

TRAVERSE CITY RECORD-EAGLE (Traverse City, MI) 11360

TREND MIDWEEK (Trevose, PA) 11617

TRENTON REPUBLICAN TIMES (Trenton, MO) 11365

TRENTON SUN (Trenton, IL) 11482

TRENTON TRIBUNE (Trenton, TX) 11641

TRENTONIAN, THE (Trenton, NJ) 11369

TRI - CITY REGISTER (Auburn, IL) 11467

TRI COUNTY (Beaver Dam, WI) 11658

TRI COUNTY BUYERS GUIDE (Sault Ste Marie, MI) 11532

TRI LAKES FREE TRADER (Elizabethtown, NY) 11574

TRI STATE WHITE SHEET (Lake Havasu City, AZ) 11419

TRIBUNE & GEORGIAN (St Marys, GA) 11463

TRIBUNE (AMES), THE (Ames, IA) 11346

TRIBUNE (BETHANY), THE (Bethany, OK) 11603

TRIBUNE CHRONICLE (Warren, OH) 11383

TRIBUNE (ELKIN), THE (Clinton, CT) 11443

TRIBUNE (FORT PIERCE), THE (Fort Pierce, FL) 11333

TRIBUNE (MESA), THE (Mesa, AZ) 11321

TRIBUNE (NEW ALBANY), THE (New Albany, IN) 11345

TRIBUNE PRESS REPORTER (Glenwood City, WI) 11661

TRIBUNE (SAN LUIS OBISPO), THE (San Luis Obispo, CA) 11327

TRIBUNE (SEYMOUR), THE (Seymour, IN) 11345

TRIBUNE TIMES (Fountain Inn, SC) 11620

TRIBUNE-COURIER (ONTARIO) (Ontario, OH) 11599

TRIBUNE-COURIER (PADUCAH) (Benton, KY) 11500

TRIBUNE-DEMOCRAT, THE (Johnstown, PA) 11389

TRIBUNE-PHONOGRAPH (Abbotsford, WI) 11657

TRIBUNE-REVIEW (Greensburg, PA) 11389

TRIBUNE-STAR, THE (Terre Haute, IN) 11346

TRIBUNE-TIMES (Fountain Inn, SC) 11620

TRI-CITY HERALD (Kennewick, WA) 11405

TRI-CITY LEDGER (Flomaton, AL) 11413

TRI-CITY NEWS (Cumberland, KY) 11501

TRI-CITY RECORD, THE (Watervliet, MI) 11533

TRI-CITY REGISTER (Riverton, IL) 11480

TRI-CITY REPORTER, THE (Dyer, TN) 11626

TRI-CITY STAR, THE (Volga, SD) 11625

TRI-CITY TIMES (Imlay City, MI) 11528

TRI-CITY TRIB (Cozad, NE) 11557

TRI-CITY TRIBUNE (Marked Tree, AR) 11423

TRI-COUNTY ADVERTISER (BROCKPORT) (Brockport, NY) 11570

TRI-COUNTY ADVERTISER (KEWANEE) (Kewanee, IL) 11474

TRI-COUNTY ADVERTISER (WAUPACA) (Waupaca, WI) 11668

TRI-COUNTY CITIZEN (Chesaning, MI) 11526

TRI-COUNTY JOURNAL (Perry, OK) 11605

TRI-COUNTY NEWS (COTTONWOOD) (Cottonwood, MN) 11536

TRI-COUNTY NEWS (ELMWOOD) (Elmwood, IL) 11471

TRI-COUNTY NEWS (KIEL) (Kiel, WI) 11662

TRI-COUNTY NEWS (KNOXVILLE) (Knoxville, TN) 11627

TRI-COUNTY NEWS (OSSEO) (Osseo, WI) 11665

TRI-COUNTY NEWS (SEYMOUR) (Seymour, TN) 11629

TRI-COUNTY NEWS (SOUTH BEND) (South Bend, IN) 11488

TRI-COUNTY PRESS (CUBA CITY) (Cuba City, WI) 11660

TRI-COUNTY PRESS (LOVELAND) (Loveland, OH) 11598

TRI-COUNTY RECORD (RUSHFORD) (Rushford, MN) **11542**

TRI-COUNTY RECORD (RUSSELLVILLE) (Russellville, AR) **11424**

TRI-COUNTY SPECIAL (Auburn, IA) **11490**

TRI-COUNTY TIMES (Beardstown, IL) **11467**

TRI-COUNTY TIMES, THE (Ames, IA) **11489**

TRI-LAKES TRIBUNE (Monument, CO) **11442**

TRIMBLE BANNER (Bedford, KY) **11500**

TRINITY JOURNAL, THE (Weaverville, CA) **11438**

TRINITY STANDARD (Trinity, TX) **11641**

TRI-PEAKS TRADER (Russellville, AR) **11424**

TRI-STATE MEDIA GROUP (Pelham, NY) **11581**

TRI-STATE PENNYSAVER PRESS (Ridgefield, CT) **11446**

TRI-TOWN NEWS (FREEHOLD) (Freehold, NJ) **11563**

TRI-TOWN NEWS (SIDNEY) (Sidney, NY) **11582**

TRI-TOWN TRANSCRIPT (Beverly, MA) **11516**

TRI-VALLEY HERALD (Pleasanton, CA) **11326**

TRI-VILLAGE NEWS (Columbus, OH) **11595**

TROUBLESOME CREEK TIMES (Hindman, KY) **11503**

TROY DAILY NEWS (Troy, OH) **11383**

TROY FREE PRESS & SILEX INDEX (Troy, MO) **11554**

TROY MESSENGER, THE (Troy, AL) **11415**

TROY-SOMERSET GAZETTE (Troy, MI) **11533**

TRUE CITIZEN, THE (Waynesboro, GA) **11463**

TRUMANN DEMOCRAT (Trumann, AR) **11425**

TRUMANSBURG FREE PRESS (Trumansburg, NY) **11583**

TRUMBULL TIMES (Shelton, CT) **11446**

TRUTH, THE (Elkhart, IN) **11343**

TRYON DAILY BULLETIN (Tryon, NC) **11378**

TUALATIN TIMES (Portland, OR) **11608**

TUCSON CITIZEN (ONLINE) (Tucson, AZ) **11322**

TUCSON WEEKLY (Tucson, AZ) **11420**

TULARE ADVANCE-REGISTER (Tulare, CA) **11328**

TULLAHOMA NEWS AND GUARDIAN, THE (Tullahoma, TN) **11630**

TULSA COUNTY NEWS (Sand Springs, OK) **11605**

TULSA WORLD (Tulsa, OK) **11386**

TUNDRA DRUMS, THE (Anchorage, AK) **11416**

TUPPER LAKE FREE PRESS & HERALD (Tupper Lake, NY) **11583**

TURLOCK JOURNAL (Turlock, CA) **11438**

TURTLE LAKE TIMES, THE (Turtle Lake, WI) **11667**

TURTLE MOUNTAIN STAR, THE (Rolla, ND) **11592**

TUSCALOOSA NEWS, THE (New York, NY) **11374**

TUSCOLA COUNTY ADVERTISER (Caro, MI) **11526**

TUSCOLA REVIEW (Tuscola, IL) **11482**

TUSKEGEE NEWS (Tuskegee, AL) **11415**

TUSTIN NEWS, THE (Irvine, CA) **11430**

TWIN CITIES TIMES (Sausalito, CA) **11437**

TWIN CITY NEWS (CHATTAHOOCHIE), THE (Chattahoochee, FL) **11449**

TWIN CITY TIMES/RIVERDALE FREE PRESS (Riverdale, CA) **11435**

TWIN LAKES REPORT (Twin Lakes, WI) **11667**

TWIN-BORO NEWS (Cresskill, NJ) **11562**

TWIN-CITY NEWS (BATESBURG), THE (Batesburg, SC) **11619**

TWINSBURG BULLETIN, THE (Stow, OH) **11601**

TWINSBURG SUN, THE (Cleveland, OH) **11594**

TYLER COUNTY BOOSTER (Woodville, TX) **11642**

TYLER MORNING TELEGRAPH (Tyler, TX) **11401**

TYLER STAR NEWS (Sistersville, WV) **11657**

TYLER TRIBUTE (Tyler, MN) **11544**

TYLERTOWN TIMES, THE (Tylertown, MS) **11547**

TYRONE CITIZEN, THE (Fayetteville, GA) **11460**

U

UINTA COUNTY HERALD (Evanston, WY) **11669**

UINTAH BASIN STANDARD (Roosevelt, UT) **11643**

UKIAH DAILY JOURNAL, THE (Ukiah, CA) **11328**

ULSTER COUNTY TOWNSMAN, THE (Woodstock, NY) **11584**

ULYSSES NEWS (Ulysses, KS) **11499**

UMPQUA POST, THE (Reedsport, OR) **11609**

UNDERWOOD NEWS (Underwood, ND) **11592**

UNION CITY DAILY MESSENGER (Union City, TN) **11396**

UNION CITY REGISTER TRIBUNE (Coldwater, MI) **11526**

UNION CITY REPORTER (Hoboken, NJ) **11564**

UNION COUNTY ADVOCATE, THE (Morganfield, KY) **11504**

UNION COUNTY TIMES (LAKE BUTLER) (Lake Butler, FL) **11452**

UNION COUNTY TIMES (MIDDLEBURG) (Middleburg, PA) **11613**

UNION DAILY TIMES (Union, SC) **11394**

UNION DEMOCRAT, THE (Sonora, CA) **11327**

UNION ENTERPRISE (Allegan, MI) **11525**

UNION (GRASS VALLEY), THE (Grass Valley, CA) **11324**

UNION LEADER (Union, NJ) **11568**

UNION LEADER/NEW HAMPSHIRE SUNDAY NEWS (Manchester, NH) **11368**

UNION NEWS LEADER (Maynardville, TN) **11628**

UNION SPRINGS HERALD (Union Springs, AL) **11416**

UNION STAR, THE (Brookneal, VA) **11646**

UNIONDALE BEACON (Hempstead, NY) **11576**

UNION-NEWS/SUNDAY REPUBLICAN (Springfield, MA) **11357**

UNION-RECORDER, THE (Milledgeville, GA) **11336**

UNIONVILLE REPUBLICAN, THE (Unionville, MO) **11555**

UPPER ARLINGTON NEWS (Columbus, OH) **11595**

UPPER CAPE CODDER, THE (Yarmouthport, MA) **11525**

UPPER COUNTRY NEWS-REPORTER (Cambridge, ID) **11464**

UPPER DARBY PRESS (Drexel Hill, PA) **11611**

UPPER DAUPHIN SENTINEL (Millersburg, PA) **11613**

UPPER MARLBORO STAR (Landover, MD) **11514**

UPPER ROGUE INDEPENDENT (Eagle Point, OR) **11607**

UPPER SANDUSKY DAILY CHIEF-UNION (Upper Sandusky, OH) **11383**

UPPER TOWNSHIP GAZETTE (Seaville, NJ) **11567**

URBANA DAILY CITIZEN (Urbana, OH) **11383**

URBANDALE PRESS CITIZEN (Des Moines, IA) **11491**

UTICA HERALD (Utica, OH) **11601**

UVALDE LEADER-NEWS (Uvalde, TX) **11641**

V

V C REPORTER (Pasadena, CA) **11434**

VADNAIS HEIGHTS PRESS (White Bear Lake, MN) **11544**

VAIL DAILY (Avon, CO) **11329**

VAIL TRAIL (Avon, CO) **11439**

VAILSBURG LEADER (Maplewood, NJ) **11565**

VALDERS JOURNAL (Valders, WI) **11667**

VALDEZ VANGUARD (Valdez, AK) **11416**

VALDOSTA DAILY TIMES, THE (Valdosta, GA) **11336**

VALENCIA COUNTY NEWS-BULLETIN (Belen, NM) **11568**

VALIERIAN, THE (Valier, MT) **11556**

VALLEY ADVOCATE (Easthampton, MA) **11518**

VALLEY BANNER, THE (Elkton, VA) **11646**

VALLEY BREEZE-OBSERVER (Greenville, RI) **11618**

VALLEY CITY TIMES-RECORD (Valley City, ND) **11379**

VALLEY COURIER (ALAMOSA) (Alamosa, CO) **11329**

VALLEY COURIER (MADISON) (Madison, CT) **11445**

VALLEY DISPATCH, THE (Lowell, MA) **11519**

VALLEY FALLS VINDICATOR (Valley Falls, KS) **11499**

VALLEY GAZETTE (Shelton, CT) **11446**

VALLEY INDEPENDENT, THE (Monessen, PA) **11390**

VALLEY IRRIGATOR, THE (Newell, ND) **11592**

VALLEY ITEM (Royersford, PA) **11616**

VALLEY JOURNAL (Carbondale, CO) **11440**

VALLEY JOURNAL (HALSTAD), THE (Halstad, MN) **11538**

VALLEY LOG, THE (Orbisonia, PA) **11615**

VALLEY MIRROR, THE (Munhall, PA) **11614**

VALLEY MORNING STAR (Harlingen, TX) **11398**

VALLEY NEWS DISPATCH (Tarentum, PA) **11392**

VALLEY NEWS (ELIZABETHTOWN) (Elizabethtown, NY) **11574**

VALLEY NEWS (FULTON), THE (Fulton, NY) **11574**

VALLEY NEWS HERALD (Spokane, WA) **11654**

VALLEY NEWS (JEFFERSON), THE (Jefferson, OH) **11597**

VALLEY NEWS TODAY (Shenandoah, IA) **11348**

VALLEY NEWS (WEST LEBANON) (West Lebanon, NH) **11369**

VALLEY REPORTER, THE (Waitsfield, VT) **11645**

VALLEY ROADRUNNER (Valley Center, CA) **11438**

VALLEY STREAM HERALD (Lawrence, NY) **11577**

VALLEY SUN (Wasilla, AK) **11417**

VALLEY SUN, THE (Scottsboro, AL) **11415**

VALLEY TIMES (Pleasanton, CA) **11326**

VALLEY TIMES (DERBY), THE (Derby, CT) **11443**

VALLEY TIMES (RIVERSIDE), THE (Riverside, CA) **11435**

VALLEY TIMES-NEWS, THE (Lanett, AL) **11320**

VALLEY TIMES-STAR (Shippensburg, PA) **11617**

VALLEY TOWN CRIER (McAllen, TX) **11639**

VALLEY VANTAGE (Woodland Hills, CA) **11439**

VALLEY VIEW (SAN FERNANDO) (San Fernando, CA) **11436**

VALLEY VIEW (WOODINVILLE) (Woodinville, WA) **11655**

VALLEY VISTA (Douglas, AZ) **11418**

VALLEY VOICE, THE (Middlebury, VT) **11644**

VALPARAISO NEWS (Valparaiso, IN) **11489**

VAN BUREN COUNTY ADVERTISER (Gobles, MI) **11527**

VAN BUREN COUNTY DEMOCRAT (Clinton, AR) **11421**

VAN HORN ADVOCATE, THE (Van Horn, TX) **11642**

VANDALIA DRUMMER NEWS (Vandalia, OH) **11601**

VANDERGRIFT NEWS (Vandergrift, PA) **11617**

VASHON ISLAND BEACHCOMBER (Vashon Island, WA) **11654**

VASSAR PIONEER TIMES (Vassar, MI) **11533**

VEDETTE, THE (Greenfield, MO) **11550**

VEGA ENTERPRISE, THE (Vega, TX) **11642**

VENICE GONDOLIER SUN (Venice, FL) **11456**

VENTURA COUNTY REPORTER (Ventura, CA) **11438**

VENTURA COUNTY STAR (Ventura, CA) **11328**

VERDE INDEPENDENT (Cottonwood, AZ) **11418**

VERMILION PHOTOJOURNAL (Vermilion, OH) **11601**

VERMONT JOURNAL (Stowe, VT) **11645**

VERMONT NEWS GUIDE (Ridgefield, CT) **11446**

VERMONT STANDARD (Woodstock, VT) **11645**

VERMONT TIMES (Rutland, VT) **11645**

VERNAL EXPRESS (Vernal, UT) **11643**

VERNDALE SUN (Verndale, MN) **11544**

VERNON COUNTY BROADCASTER (Viroqua, WI) **11667**

VERNON DAILY RECORD (Vernon, TX) **11401**

VERNON HILLS REVIEW (Waukegan, IL) **11483**

VERONA PRESS (Verona, WI) **11667**

VERONA-CEDAR GROVE TIMES (West Paterson, NJ) **11568**

VERSAILLES LEADER-STATESMAN (Versailles, MO) **11555**

VERSAILLES POLICY, THE (Versailles, OH) **11601**

VERSAILLES REPUBLICAN (Versailles, IN) **11489**

VESTAL TOWN CRIER (Conklin, NY) **11572**

VEVAY REVEILLE-ENTERPRISE (Vevay, IN) **11489**

VICKSBURG POST, THE (Vicksburg, MS) **11363**

VICTORIA ADVOCATE (Victoria, TX) **11401**

VIDETTE-TIMES (Valparaiso, IN) **11346**

VIDORIAN, THE (Vidor, TX) **11642**

VIENNA TIMES (Herndon, VA) **11647**

VIENNA TIMES, THE (Vienna, IL) **11483**

VIENNA/OAKTON CONNECTION (McLean, VA) **11649**

VIEW, THE (Belleville, MI) **11525**

VILAS COUNTY NEWS-REVIEW (Eagle River, WI) **11660**

VILLA PARK ARGUS (Glen Ellyn, IL) **11472**

ULRICH'S PERIODICALS DIRECTORY 2010

VILLA PARK REVIEW (Lombard, IL) **11475**
VILLA RICAN, THE (Carrolton, GA) **11457**
VILLAGE BEACON-RECORD, THE (East Setauket, NY) **11574**
VILLAGE HERALD (Lawrence, NY) **11577**
VILLAGE TIMES HERALD, THE (East Setauket, NY) **11574**
VILLAGE VINE (Fremont, IA) **11492**
VILLAGE VOICE, THE (New York, NY) **11580**
VILLAGER (St Paul, MN) **11543**
VILLAGER JOURNAL, THE (Salem, AR) **11424**
VILLAGER (MOSCOW), THE (Moscow, PA) **11614**
VILLAGER (NEW YORK) (New York, NY) **11580**
VILLAGER (NEW YORK) (New York, NY) **11580**
VILLAGES DAILY SUN, THE (Lady Lake, FL) **11333**
VILLE PLATTE GAZETTE (Ville Platte, LA) **11508**
VINCENNES SUN-COMMERCIAL (Vincennes, IN) **11346**
VINDICATOR, THE (Liberty, TX) **11638**
VINDICATOR (YOUNGSTOWN), THE (Youngstown, OH) **11384**
VINEYARD GAZETTE (Edgartown, MA) **11518**
VINITA DAILY JOURNAL (Vinita, OK) **11386**
VINTON COUNTY COURIER (McArthur, OH) **11598**
VINTON MESSENGER (Vinton, VA) **11650**
VINTON NEWS (Sulphur, LA) **11508**
VIRGIN ISLANDS DAILY NEWS, THE (Scranton, PA) **11391**
VIRGINIA MOUNTAINEER (Grundy, VA) **11647**
VIRGINIAN REVIEW (Covington, VA) **11403**
VIRGINIAN-LEADER (Pearisburg, VA) **11649**
VIRGINIAN-PILOT, THE (Norfolk, VA) **11403**
VISALIA TIMES-DELTA (Visalia, CA) **11328**
VISITOR (BEVERLY HILL), THE (Beverly Hill, FL) **11449**
VISTAS (King City, CA) **11430**
VIVA (Douglas, AZ) **11418**
VOICE LEDGER, THE (Millbrook, NY) **11578**
VOICE (NEW BALTIMORE), THE (New Baltimore, MI) **11530**
VOICE OF SOUTH MARION (Belleview, FL) **11449**
VOICE OF THE MOUNTAIN (Mt Shasta, CA) **11433**
VOICE OF THE VALLEY (Maple Valley, WA) **11653**
VOICE WEEKEND (New Baltimore, MI) **11530**
VOICES (Woodbury, CT) **11447**
VOICE-TRIBUNE, THE (Louisville, KY) **11504**
VOLGA TRIBUNE, THE (Volga, SD) **11625**
VOLUNTEER, THE (Durand, IL) **11471**
VOYAGEUR PRESS OF MCGREGOR, THE (McGregor, MN) **11539**

W

WABASH PLAIN DEALER (Wabash, IN) **11346**
WABASHA COUNTY HERALD (Wabasha, MN) **11544**
WABASSO STANDARD (Wabasso, MN) **11544**
WACO CITIZEN, THE (Waco, TX) **11642**
WACO TRIBUNE HERALD (Waco, TX) **11402**
WACONIA PATRIOT, THE (Waconia, MN) **11544**
WADENA PIONEER JOURNAL (Wadena, MN) **11544**
WADSWORTH JOURNAL (Grayslake, IL) **11473**
WAGONER TRIBUNE, THE (Wagoner, OK) **11606**
WAHKIAKUM COUNTY EAGLE, THE (Cathlamet, WA) **11651**
WAHOO NEWSPAPER (Wahoo, NE) **11558**
WAKE WEEKLY, THE (Wake Forest, NC) **11590**
WAKEFIELD DAILY ITEM, THE (Wakefield, MA) **11357**
WAKEFIELD OBSERVER (Beverly, MA) **11516**
WAKONDA TIMES (Vermillion, SD) **11625**
WAKULLA NEWS (Crawfordville, FL) **11450**
WALDO INDEPENDENT, THE (Belfast, ME) **11509**
WALDRON NEWS (Waldron, AR) **11425**
WALDWICK SUBURBAN NEWS (Ridgewood, NJ) **11566**
WALKER COUNTY MESSENGER (La Fayette, GA) **11461**
WALKERSVILLE/THURMONT GAZETTE (Frederick, MD) **11513**
WALKER/WESTSIDE ADVANCE (Jenison, MI) **11529**

WALLA WALLA UNION-BULLETIN (Walla Walla, WA) **11405**
WALLACE ENTERPRISE, THE (Wallace, NC) **11590**
WALLER COUNTY NEWS-CITIZEN (Hempstead, TX) **11636**
WALLIS NEWS-REVIEW (Wallis, TX) **11642**
WALLKILL VALLEY TIMES, THE (Walden, NY) **11583**
WALLOWA COUNTY CHIEFTAIN (Enterprise, OR) **11607**
WALPOLE TIMES, THE (Walpole, MA) **11523**
WALSH COUNTY PRESS (Park River, SD) **11624**
WALSH COUNTY RECORD, THE (Grafton, ND) **11591**
WALTON REPORTER, THE (Walton, NY) **11583**
WALTON TRIBUNE, THE (Monroe, GA) **11462**
WALWORTH TIMES, THE (Walworth, WI) **11668**
WAMPUM SAVER (Show Low, AZ) **11419**
WAMPUM SAVER (CASA GRANDE) (Casa Grande, AZ) **11417**
WANDERER, THE (Mattapoisett, MA) **11520**
WANTAGH - SEAFORD CITIZEN (Merrick, NY) **11578**
WAPAKONETA DAILY NEWS (Wapakoneta, OH) **11383**
WARE RIVER NEWS, THE (Ware, MA) **11524**
WAREHAM COURIER (Marshfield, MA) **11520**
WAREHAM PENNYSAVER (Marshfield, MA) **11520**
WARNER CENTER NEWS (Woodland Hills, CA) **11439**
WARREN EAGLE-DEMOCRAT (Warren, AR) **11425**
WARREN RECORD, THE (Warrenton, NC) **11590**
WARREN REPORTER, THE (Hackettstown, NJ) **11563**
WARREN SENTINEL (CHEYENNE), THE (Cheyenne, WY) **11668**
WARREN SENTINEL (FRONT ROYAL), THE (Front Royal, VA) **11647**
WARREN SHEAF (Warren, MN) **11544**
WARREN TIMES-GAZETTE (Warren, RI) **11619**
WARRENTON JOURNAL (Warrenton, MO) **11555**
WARRENVILLE POST, THE (Saint Charles, IL) **11480**
WARRICK EAST (Boonville, IN) **11484**
WARROAD PIONEER (Warroad, MN) **11544**
WARSAW-FAISON NEWS (Wallace, NC) **11590**
WARWICK ADVERTISER, THE (Monroe, NY) **11579**
WARWICK BEACON (Warwick, RI) **11619**
WARWICK VALLEY DISPATCH (Warwick, NY) **11583**
WASCO TRIBUNE (Wasco, CA) **11438**
WASECA COUNTY NEWS (Waseca, MN) **11544**
WASHBURN COUNTY REGISTER (Shell Lake, WI) **11666**
WASHBURN LEADER (Washburn, IL) **11483**
WASHINGTON CITY PAPER (Washington, DC) **11448**
WASHINGTON CITY PAPER (Washington, DC) **11448**
WASHINGTON COUNTY EDITION (Salem, IN) **11488**
WASHINGTON COUNTY ENTERPRISE (Blair, NE) **11556**
WASHINGTON COUNTY (KS) NEWS (Washington, KS) **11499**
WASHINGTON COUNTY NEWS (ABINGDON) (Abingdon, VA) **11645**
WASHINGTON COUNTY NEWS (CHATOM) (Chatom, AL) **11412**
WASHINGTON COUNTY NEWS (CHIPLEY) (Chipley, FL) **11449**
WASHINGTON COUNTY PILOT-TRIBUNE (Blair, NE) **11557**
WASHINGTON COURIER (Washington, IL) **11483**
WASHINGTON DAILY NEWS (Washington, NC) **11378**
WASHINGTON EVENING JOURNAL (Washington, IA) **11348**
WASHINGTON FREE PRESS (Seattle, WA) **11654**
WASHINGTON MISSOURIAN (Washington, MO) **11555**
WASHINGTON NEWS-REPORTER (Washington, GA) **11463**
WASHINGTON POST, THE (Washington, DC) **11332**
WASHINGTON TIMES REPORTER, THE (Peoria, IL) **11480**
WASHINGTON TIMES-HERALD (Washington, IN) **11346**
WASHINGTON'S HILL RAG (Washington, DC) **11448**
WATAUGA DEMOCRAT (Boone, NC) **11586**
WATCHMAN, THE (Clinton, LA) **11506**
WATERBURY REPUBLICAN-AMERICAN (Waterbury, CT) **11332**
WATERFORD NEWS (Merced, CA) **11433**
WATERFORD POST (Waterford, WI) **11668**
WATERTOWN (NY) DAILY TIMES (Watertown, NY) **11375**

WATERTOWN PUBLIC OPINION (Watertown, SD) **11395**
WATERTOWN TAB & PRESS (Needham, MA) **11521**
WATERTOWN (WI) DAILY TIMES (Watertown, WI) **11409**
WATERTOWN/CARVER COUNTY NEWS (Watertown, MN) **11544**
WATKINS REVIEW & EXPRESS (Watkins Glen, NY) **11584**
WATONGA REPUBLICAN, THE (Watonga, OK) **11606**
WAUCONDA COURIER (Algonquin, IL) **11466**
WAUCONDA LEADER (Grayslake, IL) **11473**
WAUKESHA FREEMAN (Waukesha, WI) **11409**
WAUKON STANDARD (Waukon, IA) **11496**
WAUNAKEE TRIBUNE (Waunakee, WI) **11668**
WAUPACA POST (Waupaca, WI) **11668**
WAURIKA NEWS-DEMOCRAT (Waurika, OK) **11606**
WAUSAU DAILY HERALD (Wausau, WI) **11409**
WAUSHARA ARGUS (Wautoma, WI) **11668**
WAUWATOSA NEWS-TIMES (New Berlin, WI) **11664**
WAVE, THE (Los Angeles, CA) **11432**
WAVERLY DEMOCRAT (Waverly, IA) **11496**
WAVERLY JOURNAL (Waverly, IL) **11483**
WAVERLY NEWS (Waverly, NE) **11559**
WAXAHACHIE DAILY LIGHT (Waxahachie, TX) **11402**
WAYCROSS JOURNAL HERALD (Waycross, GA) **11337**
WAYLAND TOWN CRIER (Framingham, MA) **11518**
WAYNE COUNTY JOURNAL-BANNER (Piedmont, MO) **11552**
WAYNE COUNTY MAIL (Webster, NY) **11584**
WAYNE COUNTY (MS) NEWS (Waynesboro, MS) **11548**
WAYNE COUNTY NEWS (WAYNESBORO) (Waynesboro, TN) **11630**
WAYNE COUNTY OUTLOOK (Monticello, KY) **11504**
WAYNE COUNTY PRESS (Fairfield, IL) **11471**
WAYNE COUNTY STAR (Wolcott, NY) **11584**
WAYNE COUNTY (WV) NEWS (Wayne, WV) **11407**
WAYNE EAGLE (Wayne, MI) **11533**
WAYNE HERALD (Wayne, NE) **11559**
WAYNE INDEPENDENT, THE (Honesdale, PA) **11389**
WAYNE TODAY & PASSAIC VALLEY TODAY (West Paterson, NJ) **11568**
WAYNE WILSON NEWS LEADER (Fremont, NC) **11587**
WAYZATA/ORONO/LONG LAKE SUN-SAILOR (Eden Prairie, MN) **11537**
WEAKLEY COUNTY PRESS (Union City, TN) **11630**
WEATHERFORD DAILY NEWS (Weatherford, OK) **11386**
WEATHERFORD DEMOCRAT (Weatherford, TX) **11402**
WEATHERFORD TELEGRAM (Weatherford, TX) **11642**
WEBSTER COUNTY CITIZEN (Seymour, MO) **11553**
WEBSTER ECHO (Webster Springs, WV) **11657**
WEBSTER HERALD (Webster, NY) **11584**
WEBSTER POST (Canandaigua, NY) **11572**
WEBSTER PROGRESS-TIMES, THE (Jackson, MS) **11546**
WEBSTER REPORTER & FARMER (Webster, SD) **11625**
WEBSTER REPUBLICAN (Webster Springs, WV) **11657**
WEBSTER TIMES, THE (Webster, MA) **11524**
WEBSTER-KIRKWOOD JOURNAL (Chesterfield, MO) **11549**
WEBSTER-KIRKWOOD TIMES (St Louis, MO) **11554**
WEDNESDAY JOURNAL OF OAK PARK & RIVER FOREST (Oak Park, IL) **11478**
WEDNESDAY MAGAZINE (Overland Park, KS) **11499**
WEED PRESS (Mt Shasta, CA) **11433**
WEEHAWKEN REPORTER (Hoboken, NJ) **11564**
WEEK, THE (Delavan, WI) **11660**
WEEKDAY (Lake Park, FL) **11452**
WEEKEND VOICE (Richmond, MI) **11531**
WEEKENDER (BEL AIR), THE (Bel Air, MD) **11512**
WEEKENDER (DERRY) (Derry, NH) **11560**
WEEKENDER (GRANVILLE), THE (Granville, NY) **11575**
WEEKENDER (HERNANDO) (Hernando, MS) **11546**
WEEKENDER (LEXINGTON), THE (Lexington, VA) **11648**
WEEKLY ALMANAC, THE (Honesdale, PA) **11612**

Title

WILLISTON PLAINS REPORTER (Williston, ND) **11592**
WILLISTON TIMES (Hicksville, NY) **11576**
WILLOW GLEN RESIDENT (San Jose, CA) **11436**
WILLOW GROVE GUIDE (Fort Washington, PA) **11612**
WILLOWS JOURNAL (Willows, CA) **11439**
WILMETTE LIFE (Glenview, IL) **11473**
WILMINGTON ADVOCATE (Concord, MA) **11517**
WILMINGTON BEACON (Compton, CA) **11428**
WILMINGTON NEWS-JOURNAL (Wilmington, OH) **11383**
WILMINGTON STAR NEWS (New York, NY) **11374**
WILMINGTON TOWN CRIER (Wilmington, MA) **11524**
WILSON COUNTY CITIZEN (Fredonia, KS) **11497**
WILSON DAILY TIMES (Wilson, NC) **11378**
WILSON POST LLC (Lebanon, TN) **11627**
WILSONVILLE SPOKESMAN (Wilsonville, OR) **11609**
WILTON BULLETIN (Wilton, CT) **11447**
WILTON LIFESTYLES (Norwalk, CT) **11446**
WINCHENDON COURIER (Winchendon, MA) **11524**
WINCHESTER STAR (Lexington, MA) **11519**
WINCHESTER STAR, THE (Winchester, VA) **11404**
WINCHESTER SUN (Winchester, KY) **11352**
WIND RIVER NEWS (Lander, WY) **11669**
WINDHAM JOURNAL (Windham, NY) **11584**
WINDSOR AREA OBSERVER (Windsor, VT) **11645**
WINDSOR BEACON (Windsor, CO) **11443**
WINDSOR JOURNAL (Bristol, CT) **11443**
WINDSOR LOCKS JOURNAL (Bristol, CT) **11443**
WINDSOR REVIEW, THE (Carrollton, MO) **11549**
WINDSOR STANDARD (Conklin, NY) **11572**
WINDSOR TIMES, THE (Windsor, CA) **11439**
WINDSOR TRIBUNE (Greeley, CO) **11330**
WINDSOR-HIGHTS HERALD (Hightstown, NJ) **11564**
WINFIELD DAILY COURIER (Winfield, KS) **11351**
WINKLER COUNTY NEWS (Kermit, TX) **11637**
WINN PARISH ENTERPRISE (Natchitoches, LA) **11508**
WINNEBAGO HANCOCK SHOPPER (Forest City, IA) **11492**
WINNECONNE NEWS (Winneconne, WI) **11668**
WINNER ADVOCATE (Winner, SD) **11625**
WINNETKA TALK (Glenview, IL) **11473**
WINNISQUAM ECHO (Meredith, NH) **11560**
WINNSBORO NEWS (Winnsboro, TX) **11642**
WINONA DAILY NEWS (Winona, MN) **11361**
WINONA POST (Winona, MN) **11545**
WINSLOW MAIL (Winslow, AZ) **11420**
WINSTED JOURNAL, THE (Winsted, CT) **11447**
WINSTON COUNTY JOURNAL (Louisville, MS) **11547**
WINSTON-SALEM JOURNAL (Winston-Salem, NC) **11378**
WINTER PARK MANIFEST (Winter Park, CO) **11443**
WINTER PARK-MAITLAND OBSERVER (Winter Park, FL) **11456**

WINTER SPRING VOICE (Oviedo, FL) **11453**
WINTERSET MADISONIAN (Winterset, IA) **11496**
WINTHROP NEWS (Winthrop, MN) **11545**
WINTHROP SUN TRANSCRIPT (Revere, MA) **11523**
WINTON TIMES (Merced, CA) **11433**
WIREGRASS FARMER, THE (Ashburn, GA) **11456**
WISCASSET NEWSPAPER (Wiscasset, ME) **11511**
WISCONSIN DELLS EVENTS (Portage, WI) **11666**
WISCONSIN REMINDER (Portage, WI) **11666**
WISCONSIN STATE FARMER (Waupaca, WI) **11668**
WISCONSIN STATE JOURNAL (Madison, WI) **11408**
WISCONSIN-IOWA SHOPPING NEWS (Prairie Du Chien, WI) **11666**
WISE COUNTY MESSENGER (Decatur, TX) **11633**
WISE GUIDE, THE (Westbrook, ME) **11511**
WITTENBERG ENTERPRISE-NEWS (Wittenberg, WI) **11668**
WOBURN ADVOCATE (Concord, MA) **11517**
WOLCOTT ENTERPRISE (Wolcott, IN) **11489**
WOLFE COUNTY NEWS, THE (Campton, KY) **11500**
WOOD COUNTY DEMOCRAT (Quitman, TX) **11640**
WOOD RIVER JOURNAL, THE (Lincoln, NE) **11557**
WOODBINE TWINER (Woodbine, IA) **11496**
WOODBURN INDEPENDENT (Woodburn, OR) **11609**
WOODBURY BULLETIN (Woodbury, MN) **11545**
WOODBURY-SOUTH MAPLEWOOD REVIEW (St Paul, MN) **11543**
WOODFORD COUNTY JOURNAL (Eureka, IL) **11471**
WOODFORD COUNTY JOURNAL/ROANOKE BENSON EDITION (Roanoke, IL) **11480**
WOODFORD COURIER (Washington, IL) **11483**
WOODFORD SUN (Versailles, KY) **11506**
WOODINVILLE WEEKLY (Woodinville, WA) **11655**
WOODLAND PROGRESS (Monroeville, PA) **11614**
(WOODLANDS) VILLAGER, THE (The Woodlands, TX) **11641**
WOODRUFF COUNTY MONITOR LEADER ADVOCATE (McCrory, AR) **11423**
WOODSIDE HERALD (Long Island City, NY) **11577**
WOODSTOCK INDEPENDENT, THE (Woodstock, IL) **11484**
WOODWARD NEWS (Woodward, OK) **11386**
WORCESTER COUNTY MESSENGER (Pocomoke City, MD) **11514**
WORLD (BARRE), THE (Orlando, FL) **11453**
WORLD (COOS BAY), THE (Coos Bay, OR) **11387**
WORTH CITIZEN (Midlothian, IL) **11476**
WORTHINGTON NEWS (Columbus, OH) **11596**
WRANGELL SENTINEL (Wrangell, AK) **11417**
WRAY GAZETTE (Wray, CO) **11443**
WRIGHT COUNTY JOURNAL-PRESS (Buffalo, MN) **11535**
WRIGHTSVILLE HEADLIGHT, THE (Wrightsville, GA) **11463**
WYCKOFF SUBURBAN NEWS (Ridgewood, NJ) **11567**

WYLIE NEWS, THE (Wylie, TX) **11642**
WYNNE PROGRESS (Wynne, AR) **11425**
WYOMING ADVANCE (Jenison, MI) **11529**
WYOMING COUNTY ADVANCE (Tunkhannock, PA) **11617**
WYOMING COUNTY PRESS EXAMINER, THE (Tunkhannock, PA) **11617**
WYOMING TRIBUNE-EAGLE (Cheyenne, WY) **11409**
WYTHEVILLE ENTERPRISE (Wytheville, VA) **11651**

X

XENIA DAILY GAZETTE (Xenia, OH) **11384**

Y

YADKIN RIPPLE, THE (Yadkinville, NC) **11590**
YAKIMA HERALD-REPUBLIC (Yakima, WA) **11406**
YANCEY COMMON TIMES JOURNAL (Burnsville, NC) **11586**
YANKEE SHOPPER (Webster, MA) **11524**
YANKEE TRADER (Port Jefferson Station, NY) **11581**
YANKTON DAILY PRESS & DAKOTAN (Yankton, SD) **11395**
YARDLEY NEWS (Yardley, PA) **11618**
YAZOO HERALD (Yazoo City, MS) **11548**
YEADON TIMES (Drexel Hill, PA) **11611**
YELL COUNTY RECORD (Danville, AR) **11421**
YOAKUM HERALD-TIMES (Yoakum, TX) **11642**
YORK COUNTY COAST STAR (Kennebunk, ME) **11510**
YORK DAILY RECORD - YORK SUNDAY NEWS (York, PA) **11393**
YORK DISPATCH/YORK SUNDAY NEWS (York, PA) **11393**
YORK NEWS-TIMES (York, NE) **11367**
YORK WEEKLY, THE (Portsmouth, NH) **11561**
YORKTOWN CRIER & POQUOSON POST (Yorktown, VA) **11651**
YPSILANTI COURIER (Belleville, MI) **11525**
YUCAIPA & CALIMESA NEWS MIRROR (Yucaipa, CA) **11439**
YUKON REVIEW (Yukon, OK) **11606**
YUMA PIONEER (Yuma, CO) **11443**
YUMA WHITE SHEET (Yuma, AZ) **11420**

Z

ZACHARY PLAINSMAN-NEWS (Zachary, LA) **11508**
ZANESVILLE MUSKINGUM ADVERTISER (Zanesville, OH) **11603**
ZEELAND RECORD (Zeeland, MI) **11533**
ZEPHYRHILLS NEWS (Zephyrhills, FL) **11456**
ZION-BENTON NEWS (Zion, IL) **11484**
ZIONSVILLE TIMES SENTINEL (Zionsville, IN) **11489**